T0390280

2025

Harris
Southern California
Business Directory and Buyers Guide

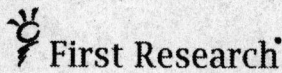

Published February 2025 next update February 2026

Publisher

Mergent Inc.
444 Madison Ave
New York, NY 10022

©Mergent Inc All Rights Reserved
2025 Mergent Business Press
ISSN 1080-2614
ISBN 978-1-63053-009-9

TABLE OF CONTENTS

SUMMARY OF CONTENTS

Number of Companies 18,401

Number of Decision Makers 32,044

Minimum Number of Employees (Services) 70

Minimum Number of Employees (Manufacturers) 23

EXPLANATORY NOTES

How to Cross-Reference in This Directory

Sequential Entry Numbers. Each establishment in the Geographic Section is numbered sequentially (G-0000). The number assigned to each establishment is referred to as its "entry number." To make cross-referencing easier, each listing in the Geographic, SIC, Alphabetic and Product Sections includes the establishment's entry number. To facilitate locating an entry in the Geographic Section, the entry numbers for the first listing on the left page and the last listing on the right page are printed at the top of the page next to the city name.

Source Suggestions Welcome

Although all known sources were used to compile this directory, it is possible that companies were inadvertently omitted. Your assistance in calling attention to such omissions would be greatly appreciated. A special form on the facing page will help you in the reporting process.

Analysis

Every effort has been made to contact all firms to verify their information. The one exception to this rule is the annual sales figure, which is considered by many companies to be confidential information. Therefore, estimated sales have been calculated by multiplying the nationwide average sales per employee for the firm's major SIC/NAICS code by the firm's number of employees. Nationwide averages for sales per employee by SIC/NAICS codes are provided by the U.S. Department of Commerce and are updated annually. All sales—sales (est)—have been estimated by this method. The exceptions are parent companies (PA), division headquarters (DH) and headquarter locations (HQ) which may include an actual corporate sales figure—sales (corporate-wide) if available.

Types of Companies

Descriptive and statistical data are included for companies in the entire state. These comprise manufacturers, machine shops, fabricators, assemblers and printers. Also identified are corporate offices in the state.

Employment Data

The employment figure shown in the Products & Services Section includes male and female employees and embraces all levels of the company. This directory includes manufacturing companies with 23 or more employees and service companies with 70 or more employees. This figure is for the facility listed and does not include other plants or offices. It should be recognized that these figures represent an approximate year-round average. These employment figures are broken into codes A through F and used in the Alphabetic and Geographic Sections to further help you in qualifying a company. Be sure to check the footnotes at the bottom of the page for the code breakdowns.

Standard Industrial Classification (SIC)

The Standard Industrial Classification (SIC) system used in this directory was developed by the federal government for use in classifying establishments by the type of activity they are engaged in. The SIC classifications used in this directory are from the 1987 edition published by the U.S. Government's Office of Management and Budget. The SIC system separates all activities into broad industrial divisions (e.g., manufacturing, mining, retail trade). It further subdivides each division. The range of manufacturing industry classes extends from two-digit codes (major industry group) to four-digit codes (product).

For example:

Industry Breakdown	Code	Industry, Product, etc.
*Major industry group	20	Food and kindred products
Industry group	203	Canned and frozen foods
*Industry	2033	Fruits and vegetables, etc.

*Classifications used in this directory

Only two-digit and four-digit codes are used in this directory.

Arrangement

1. The **Geographic Section** contains complete in-depth corporate data. This section is sorted by cities listed in alphabetical order and companies listed alphabetically within each city. A County/City Index for referencing cities within counties precedes this section.

IMPORTANT NOTICE: It is a violation of both federal and state law to transmit an unsolicited advertisement to a facsimile machine. Any user of this product that violates such laws may be subject to civil and criminal penalties, which may exceed $500 for each transmission of an unsolicited facsimile. Mergent Inc. provides fax numbers for lawful purposes only and expressly forbids the use of these numbers in any unlawful manner.

2. The **Standard Industrial Classification (SIC) Section** lists companies under approximately 500 four-digit SIC codes. An alphabetical and a numerical index precedes this section. A company can be listed under several codes. The codes are in numerical order with companies listed alphabetically under each code.

3. The **Alphabetic Section** lists all companies with their full physical or mailing addresses and telephone number.

4. The **Product & Services Section** lists companies under unique Harris categories. An index preceding this section lists all product categories in alphabetical order. Companies can be listed under several categories.

USER'S GUIDE TO LISTINGS

PRODUCT & SERVICES SECTION

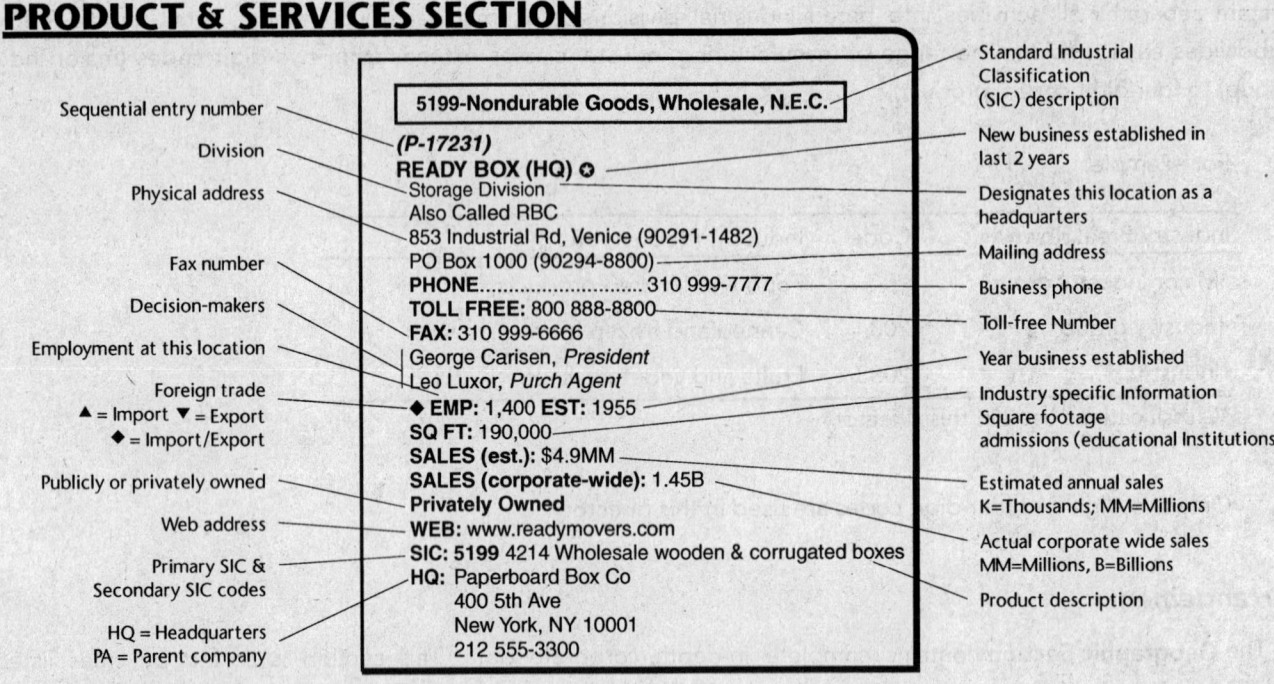

Sequential entry number

Division

Physical address

Fax number

Decision-makers

Employment at this location

Foreign trade
▲ = Import ▼ = Export
◆ = Import/Export

Publicly or privately owned

Web address

Primary SIC &
Secondary SIC codes

HQ = Headquarters
PA = Parent company

5199-Nondurable Goods, Wholesale, N.E.C.

(P-17231)
READY BOX (HQ) ✪
Storage Division
Also Called RBC
853 Industrial Rd, Venice (90291-1482)
PO Box 1000 (90294-8800)
PHONE..............................310 999-7777
TOLL FREE: 800 888-8800
FAX: 310 999-6666
George Carisen, *President*
Leo Luxor, *Purch Agent*
◆ **EMP:** 1,400 **EST:** 1955
SQ FT: 190,000
SALES (est.): $4.9MM
SALES (corporate-wide): 1.45B
Privately Owned
WEB: www.readymovers.com
SIC: 5199 4214 Wholesale wooden & corrugated boxes
HQ: Paperboard Box Co
400 5th Ave
New York, NY 10001
212 555-3300

Standard Industrial
Classification
(SIC) description

New business established in
last 2 years

Designates this location as a
headquarters

Mailing address

Business phone

Toll-free Number

Year business established

Industry specific Information
Square footage
admissions (educational Institutions)

Estimated annual sales
K=Thousands; MM=Millions

Actual corporate wide sales
MM=Millions, B=Billions

Product description

ALPHABETIC SECTION

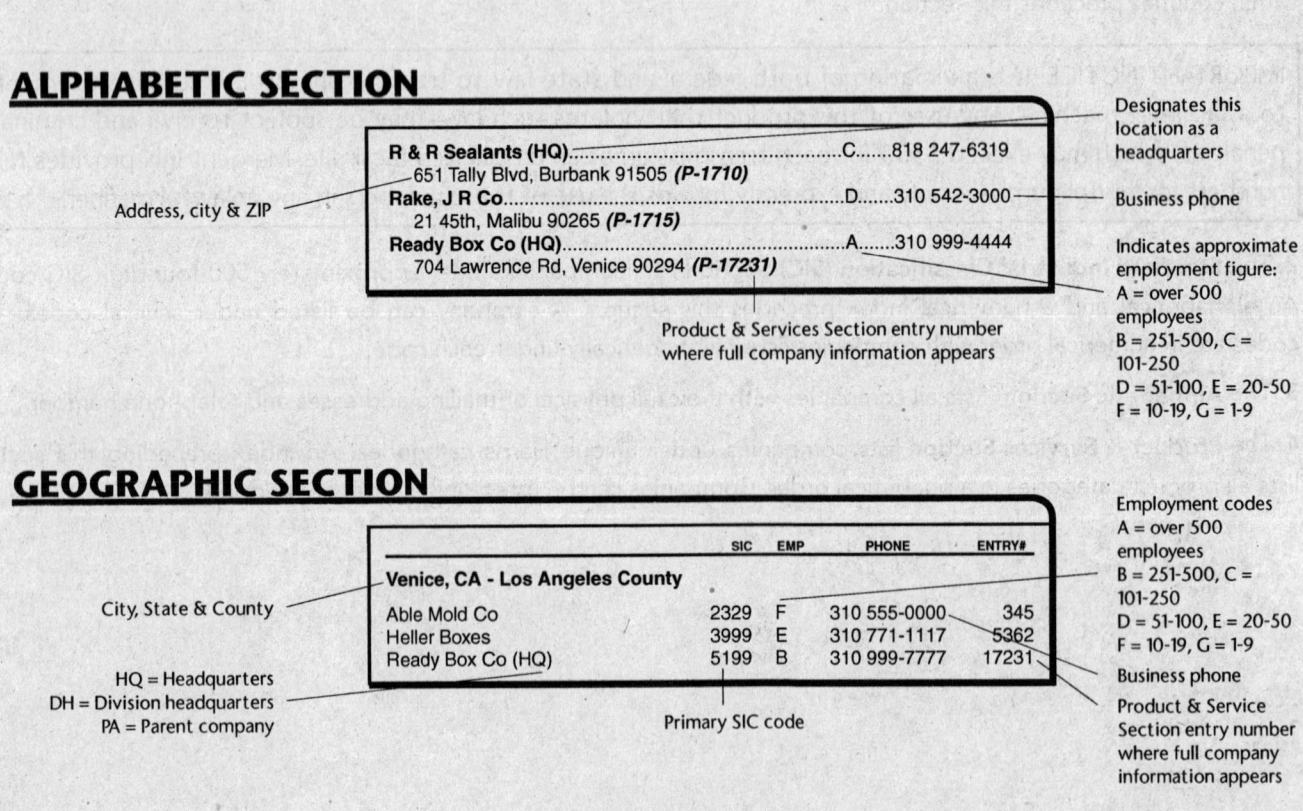

Address, city & ZIP

R & R Sealants (HQ)....................................C......818 247-6319
651 Tally Blvd, Burbank 91505 **(P-1710)**
Rake, J R Co.....................................D......310 542-3000
21 45th, Malibu 90265 **(P-1715)**
Ready Box Co (HQ)....................................A......310 999-4444
704 Lawrence Rd, Venice 90294 **(P-17231)**

Product & Services Section entry number
where full company information appears

Designates this
location as a
headquarters

Business phone

Indicates approximate
employment figure:
A = over 500
employees
B = 251-500, C =
101-250
D = 51-100, E = 20-50
F = 10-19, G = 1-9

GEOGRAPHIC SECTION

City, State & County

HQ = Headquarters
DH = Division headquarters
PA = Parent company

	SIC	EMP	PHONE	ENTRY#
Venice, CA - Los Angeles County				
Able Mold Co	2329	F	310 555-0000	345
Heller Boxes	3999	E	310 771-1117	5362
Ready Box Co (HQ)	5199	B	310 999-7777	17231

Primary SIC code

Employment codes
A = over 500
employees
B = 251-500, C =
101-250
D = 51-100, E = 20-50
F = 10-19, G = 1-9

Business phone

Product & Service
Section entry number
where full company
information appears

NUMERICAL INDEX of SIC DESCRIPTIONS
ALPHABETICAL INDEX of SIC DESCRIPTIONS

PRODUCTS & SERVICES SECTION

Companies listed alphabetically under their primary SIC
In-depth company data listed

ALPHABETIC SECTION

Company listings in alphabetical order

GEOGRAPHIC INDEX

Companies sorted by city in alphabetical order

SIC

PRDTS & SVCS

ALPHABETIC

GEOGRAPHIC

SIC INDEX

Standard Industrial Classification Numerical Index

S I C

SIC NO	PRODUCT

01 agricultural production - crops

0131 Cotton
0134 Irish potatoes
0139 Field crops, except cash grain
0161 Vegetables and melons
0171 Berry crops
0172 Grapes
0173 Tree nuts
0174 Citrus fruits
0175 Deciduous tree fruits
0179 Fruits and tree nuts, nec
0181 Ornamental nursery products
0182 Food crops grown under cover
0191 General farms, primarily crop

02 agricultural production - livestock and animal specialties

0241 Dairy farms
0252 Chicken eggs
0273 Animal aquaculture
0279 Animal specialties, nec
0291 General farms, primarily animals

07 agricultural services

0711 Soil preparation services
0721 Crop planting and protection
0722 Crop harvesting
0723 Crop preparation services for market
0742 Veterinary services, specialties
0751 Livestock services, except veterinary
0752 Animal specialty services
0761 Farm labor contractors
0762 Farm management services
0781 Landscape counseling and planning
0782 Lawn and garden services
0783 Ornamental shrub and tree services

08 forestry

0811 Timber tracts

10 metal mining

1021 Copper ores
1041 Gold ores
1081 Metal mining services
1099 Metal ores, nec

12 coal mining

1221 Bituminous coal and lignite-surface mining
1231 Anthracite mining
1241 Coal mining services

13 oil and gas extraction

1311 Crude petroleum and natural gas
1321 Natural gas liquids
1381 Drilling oil and gas wells
1382 Oil and gas exploration services
1389 Oil and gas field services, nec

14 mining and quarrying of nonmetallic minerals, except fuels

1422 Crushed and broken limestone
1429 Crushed and broken stone, nec
1442 Construction sand and gravel
1446 Industrial sand
1474 Potash, soda, and borate minerals
1479 Chemical and fertilizer mining
1481 Nonmetallic mineral services
1499 Miscellaneous nonmetallic mining

15 construction - general contractors & operative builders

1521 Single-family housing construction
1522 Residential construction, nec
1531 Operative builders
1541 Industrial buildings and warehouses

1542 Nonresidential construction, nec

16 heamy construction, except building construction, contractor

1611 Highway and street construction
1622 Bridge, tunnel, and elevated highway
1623 Water, sewer, and utility lines
1629 Heavy construction, nec

17 construction - special trade contractors

1711 Plumbing, heating, air-conditioning
1721 Painting and paper hanging
1731 Electrical work
1741 Masonry and other stonework
1742 Plastering, drywall, and insulation
1743 Terrazzo, tile, marble, mosaic work
1751 Carpentry work
1752 Floor laying and floor work, nec
1761 Roofing, siding, and sheetmetal work
1771 Concrete work
1781 Water well drilling
1791 Structural steel erection
1793 Glass and glazing work
1794 Excavation work
1795 Wrecking and demolition work
1796 Installing building equipment
1799 Special trade contractors, nec

20 food and kindred products

2011 Meat packing plants
2013 Sausages and other prepared meats
2015 Poultry slaughtering and processing
2021 Creamery butter
2022 Cheese; natural and processed
2023 Dry, condensed, evaporated products
2024 Ice cream and frozen deserts
2026 Fluid milk
2032 Canned specialties
2033 Canned fruits and specialties
2034 Dehydrated fruits, vegetables, soups
2035 Pickles, sauces, and salad dressings
2037 Frozen fruits and vegetables
2038 Frozen specialties, nec
2041 Flour and other grain mill products
2043 Cereal breakfast foods
2044 Rice milling
2045 Prepared flour mixes and doughs
2047 Dog and cat food
2048 Prepared feeds, nec
2051 Bread, cake, and related products
2052 Cookies and crackers
2053 Frozen bakery products, except bread
2061 Raw cane sugar
2063 Beet sugar
2064 Candy and other confectionery products
2066 Chocolate and cocoa products
2068 Salted and roasted nuts and seeds
2076 Vegetable oil mills, nec
2077 Animal and marine fats and oils
2079 Edible fats and oils
2082 Malt beverages
2083 Malt
2084 Wines, brandy, and brandy spirits
2085 Distilled and blended liquors
2086 Bottled and canned soft drinks
2087 Flavoring extracts and syrups, nec
2091 Canned and cured fish and seafoods
2092 Fresh or frozen packaged fish
2095 Roasted coffee
2096 Potato chips and similar snacks
2097 Manufactured ice
2098 Macaroni and spaghetti
2099 Food preparations, nec

21 tobacco products

2111 Cigarettes

22 textile mill products

2211 Broadwoven fabric mills, cotton
2221 Broadwoven fabric mills, manmade
2231 Broadwoven fabric mills, wool
2241 Narrow fabric mills
2252 Hosiery, nec
2253 Knit outerwear mills
2257 Weft knit fabric mills
2259 Knitting mills, nec
2261 Finishing plants, cotton
2262 Finishing plants, manmade
2269 Finishing plants, nec
2273 Carpets and rugs
2295 Coated fabrics, not rubberized
2297 Nonwoven fabrics
2298 Cordage and twine
2299 Textile goods, nec

23 apparel, finished products from fabrics & similar materials

2311 Men's and boy's suits and coats
2321 Men's and boy's furnishings
2323 Men's and boy's neckwear
2325 Men's and boy's trousers and slacks
2326 Men's and boy's work clothing
2329 Men's and boy's clothing, nec
2331 Women's and misses' blouses and shirts
2335 Women's, junior's, and misses' dresses
2337 Women's and misses' suits and coats
2339 Women's and misses' outerwear, nec
2341 Women's and children's underwear
2342 Bras, girdles, and allied garments
2353 Hats, caps, and millinery
2361 Girl's and children's dresses, blouses
2369 Girl's and children's outerwear, nec
2381 Fabric dress and work gloves
2384 Robes and dressing gowns
2386 Leather and sheep-lined clothing
2387 Apparel belts
2389 Apparel and accessories, nec
2391 Curtains and draperies
2392 Household furnishings, nec
2393 Textile bags
2394 Canvas and related products
2395 Pleating and stitching
2396 Automotive and apparel trimmings
2399 Fabricated textile products, nec

24 lumber and wood products, except furniture

2411 Logging
2421 Sawmills and planing mills, general
2426 Hardwood dimension and flooring mills
2431 Millwork
2434 Wood kitchen cabinets
2435 Hardwood veneer and plywood
2439 Structural wood members, nec
2441 Nailed wood boxes and shook
2448 Wood pallets and skids
2449 Wood containers, nec
2451 Mobile homes
2452 Prefabricated wood buildings
2491 Wood preserving
2499 Wood products, nec

25 furniture and fixtures

2511 Wood household furniture
2512 Upholstered household furniture
2514 Metal household furniture
2515 Mattresses and bedsprings
2517 Wood television and radio cabinets
2519 Household furniture, nec
2521 Wood office furniture
2522 Office furniture, except wood

SIC NO	PRODUCT

2531 Public building and related furniture
2541 Wood partitions and fixtures
2542 Partitions and fixtures, except wood
2591 Drapery hardware and blinds and shades
2599 Furniture and fixtures, nec

26 paper and allied products

2611 Pulp mills
2621 Paper mills
2631 Paperboard mills
2652 Setup paperboard boxes
2653 Corrugated and solid fiber boxes
2655 Fiber cans, drums, and similar products
2656 Sanitary food containers
2657 Folding paperboard boxes
2671 Paper; coated and laminated packaging
2672 Paper; coated and laminated, nec
2673 Bags: plastic, laminated, and coated
2674 Bags: uncoated paper and multiwall
2675 Die-cut paper and board
2676 Sanitary paper products
2677 Envelopes
2678 Stationery products
2679 Converted paper products, nec

27 printing, publishing and allied industries

2711 Newspapers
2721 Periodicals
2731 Book publishing
2741 Miscellaneous publishing
2752 Commercial printing, lithographic
2754 Commercial printing, gravure
2759 Commercial printing, nec
2761 Manifold business forms
2782 Blankbooks and looseleaf binders
2789 Bookbinding and related work
2791 Typesetting
2796 Platemaking services

28 chemicals and allied products

2812 Alkalies and chlorine
2813 Industrial gases
2816 Inorganic pigments
2819 Industrial inorganic chemicals, nec
2821 Plastics materials and resins
2822 Synthetic rubber
2824 Organic fibers, noncellulosic
2833 Medicinals and botanicals
2834 Pharmaceutical preparations
2835 Diagnostic substances
2836 Biological products, except diagnostic
2841 Soap and other detergents
2842 Polishes and sanitation goods
2843 Surface active agents
2844 Toilet preparations
2851 Paints and allied products
2865 Cyclic crudes and intermediates
2869 Industrial organic chemicals, nec
2873 Nitrogenous fertilizers
2875 Fertilizers, mixing only
2879 Agricultural chemicals, nec
2891 Adhesives and sealants
2892 Explosives
2893 Printing ink
2895 Carbon black
2899 Chemical preparations, nec

29 petroleum refining and related industries

2911 Petroleum refining
2951 Asphalt paving mixtures and blocks
2952 Asphalt felts and coatings
2992 Lubricating oils and greases
2999 Petroleum and coal products, nec

30 rubber and miscellaneous plastic products

3011 Tires and inner tubes
3021 Rubber and plastics footwear
3052 Rubber and plastics hose and beltings
3053 Gaskets; packing and sealing devices
3061 Mechanical rubber goods
3069 Fabricated rubber products, nec
3081 Unsupported plastics film and sheet

3082 Unsupported plastics profile shapes
3083 Laminated plastics plate and sheet
3084 Plastics pipe
3085 Plastics bottles
3086 Plastics foam products
3088 Plastics plumbing fixtures
3089 Plastics products, nec

31 leather and leather products

3111 Leather tanning and finishing
3131 Footwear cut stock
3143 Men's footwear, except athletic
3144 Women's footwear, except athletic
3149 Footwear, except rubber, nec
3161 Luggage
3171 Women's handbags and purses
3172 Personal leather goods, nec
3199 Leather goods, nec

32 stone, clay, glass, and concrete products

3211 Flat glass
3221 Glass containers
3229 Pressed and blown glass, nec
3231 Products of purchased glass
3241 Cement, hydraulic
3251 Brick and structural clay tile
3253 Ceramic wall and floor tile
3259 Structural clay products, nec
3261 Vitreous plumbing fixtures
3264 Porcelain electrical supplies
3269 Pottery products, nec
3271 Concrete block and brick
3272 Concrete products, nec
3273 Ready-mixed concrete
3275 Gypsum products
3281 Cut stone and stone products
3291 Abrasive products
3295 Minerals, ground or treated
3296 Mineral wool
3299 Nonmetallic mineral products,

33 primary metal industries

3312 Blast furnaces and steel mills
3313 Electrometallurgical products
3315 Steel wire and related products
3317 Steel pipe and tubes
3321 Gray and ductile iron foundries
3322 Malleable iron foundries
3324 Steel investment foundries
3325 Steel foundries, nec
3331 Primary copper
3334 Primary aluminum
3339 Primary nonferrous metals, nec
3341 Secondary nonferrous metals
3353 Aluminum sheet, plate, and foil
3354 Aluminum extruded products
3355 Aluminum rolling and drawing, nec
3356 Nonferrous rolling and drawing, nec
3357 Nonferrous wiredrawing and insulating
3363 Aluminum die-castings
3364 Nonferrous die-castings except aluminum
3365 Aluminum foundries
3366 Copper foundries
3369 Nonferrous foundries, nec
3398 Metal heat treating
3399 Primary metal products

34 fabricated metal products

3411 Metal cans
3412 Metal barrels, drums, and pails
3421 Cutlery
3423 Hand and edge tools, nec
3425 Saw blades and handsaws
3429 Hardware, nec
3431 Metal sanitary ware
3432 Plumbing fixture fittings and trim
3433 Heating equipment, except electric
3441 Fabricated structural metal
3442 Metal doors, sash, and trim
3443 Fabricated plate work (boiler shop)
3444 Sheet metalwork
3446 Architectural metalwork

3448 Prefabricated metal buildings
3449 Miscellaneous metalwork
3451 Screw machine products
3452 Bolts, nuts, rivets, and washers
3462 Iron and steel forgings
3463 Nonferrous forgings
3465 Automotive stampings
3469 Metal stampings, nec
3471 Plating and polishing
3479 Metal coating and allied services
3483 Ammunition, except for small arms, nec
3484 Small arms
3489 Ordnance and accessories, nec
3491 Industrial valves
3492 Fluid power valves and hose fittings
3493 Steel springs, except wire
3494 Valves and pipe fittings, nec
3495 Wire springs
3496 Miscellaneous fabricated wire products
3498 Fabricated pipe and fittings
3499 Fabricated metal products, nec

35 industrial and commercial machinery and computer equipment

3511 Turbines and turbine generator sets
3519 Internal combustion engines, nec
3523 Farm machinery and equipment
3524 Lawn and garden equipment
3531 Construction machinery
3532 Mining machinery
3533 Oil and gas field machinery
3534 Elevators and moving stairways
3535 Conveyors and conveying equipment
3536 Hoists, cranes, and monorails
3537 Industrial trucks and tractors
3541 Machine tools, metal cutting type
3542 Machine tools, metal forming type
3544 Special dies, tools, jigs, and fixtures
3545 Machine tool accessories
3546 Power-driven handtools
3547 Rolling mill machinery
3548 Welding apparatus
3549 Metalworking machinery, nec
3554 Paper industries machinery
3555 Printing trades machinery
3556 Food products machinery
3559 Special industry machinery, nec
3561 Pumps and pumping equipment
3562 Ball and roller bearings
3563 Air and gas compressors
3564 Blowers and fans
3565 Packaging machinery
3566 Speed changers, drives, and gears
3567 Industrial furnaces and ovens
3568 Power transmission equipment, nec
3569 General industrial machinery,
3571 Electronic computers
3572 Computer storage devices
3575 Computer terminals
3577 Computer peripheral equipment, nec
3578 Calculating and accounting equipment
3579 Office machines, nec
3581 Automatic vending machines
3582 Commercial laundry equipment
3585 Refrigeration and heating equipment
3589 Service industry machinery, nec
3592 Carburetors, pistons, rings, valves
3593 Fluid power cylinders and actuators
3594 Fluid power pumps and motors
3599 Industrial machinery, nec

36 electronic & other electrical equipment & components

3612 Transformers, except electric
3613 Switchgear and switchboard apparatus
3621 Motors and generators
3624 Carbon and graphite products
3625 Relays and industrial controls
3629 Electrical industrial apparatus
3631 Household cooking equipment
3632 Household refrigerators and freezers
3634 Electric housewares and fans
3639 Household appliances, nec

SIC NO	PRODUCT

3641 Electric lamps
3643 Current-carrying wiring devices
3644 Noncurrent-carrying wiring devices
3645 Residential lighting fixtures
3646 Commercial lighting fixtures
3647 Vehicular lighting equipment
3648 Lighting equipment, nec
3651 Household audio and video equipment
3652 Prerecorded records and tapes
3661 Telephone and telegraph apparatus
3663 Radio and t.v. communications equipment
3669 Communications equipment, nec
3671 Electron tubes
3672 Printed circuit boards
3674 Semiconductors and related devices
3675 Electronic capacitors
3676 Electronic resistors
3677 Electronic coils and transformers
3678 Electronic connectors
3679 Electronic components, nec
3691 Storage batteries
3692 Primary batteries, dry and wet
3694 Engine electrical equipment
3695 Magnetic and optical recording media
3699 Electrical equipment and supplies, nec

37 transportation equipment

3711 Motor vehicles and car bodies
3713 Truck and bus bodies
3714 Motor vehicle parts and accessories
3715 Truck trailers
3716 Motor homes
3721 Aircraft
3724 Aircraft engines and engine parts
3728 Aircraft parts and equipment, nec
3731 Shipbuilding and repairing
3732 Boatbuilding and repairing
3743 Railroad equipment
3751 Motorcycles, bicycles, and parts
3761 Guided missiles and space vehicles
3764 Space propulsion units and parts
3769 Space vehicle equipment, nec
3792 Travel trailers and campers
3795 Tanks and tank components
3799 Transportation equipment, nec

38 measuring, photographic, medical, & optical goods, & clocks

3812 Search and navigation equipment
3821 Laboratory apparatus and furniture
3822 Environmental controls
3823 Process control instruments
3824 Fluid meters and counting devices
3825 Instruments to measure electricity
3826 Analytical instruments
3827 Optical instruments and lenses
3829 Measuring and controlling devices, nec
3841 Surgical and medical instruments
3842 Surgical appliances and supplies
3843 Dental equipment and supplies
3844 X-ray apparatus and tubes
3845 Electromedical equipment
3851 Ophthalmic goods
3861 Photographic equipment and supplies
3873 Watches, clocks, watchcases, and parts

39 miscellaneous manufacturing industries

3911 Jewelry, precious metal
3914 Silverware and plated ware
3915 Jewelers' materials and lapidary work
3931 Musical instruments
3942 Dolls and stuffed toys
3944 Games, toys, and children's vehicles
3949 Sporting and athletic goods, nec
3952 Lead pencils and art goods
3955 Carbon paper and inked ribbons
3961 Costume jewelry
3965 Fasteners, buttons, needles, and pins
3991 Brooms and brushes
3993 Signs and advertising specialties
3996 Hard surface floor coverings, nec
3999 Manufacturing industries, nec

40 railroad transportation

4011 Railroads, line-haul operating

41 local & suburban transit & interurban highway transportation

4111 Local and suburban transit
4119 Local passenger transportation, nec
4121 Taxicabs
4131 Intercity and rural bus transportation
4141 Local bus charter service
4142 Bus charter service, except local
4151 School buses

42 motor freight transportation

4212 Local trucking, without storage
4213 Trucking, except local
4214 Local trucking with storage
4215 Courier services, except by air
4221 Farm product warehousing and storage
4222 Refrigerated warehousing and storage
4225 General warehousing and storage
4226 Special warehousing and storage, nec

44 water transportation

4424 Deep sea domestic transportation of freight
4481 Deep sea passenger transportation, except ferry
4489 Water passenger transportation
4491 Marine cargo handling
4492 Towing and tugboat service
4493 Marinas
4499 Water transportation services, nec

45 transportation by air

4512 Air transportation, scheduled
4513 Air courier services
4522 Air transportation, nonscheduled
4581 Airports, flying fields, and services

46 pipelines, except natural gas

4613 Refined petroleum pipelines
4619 Pipelines, nec

47 transportation services

4724 Travel agencies
4725 Tour operators
4729 Passenger transportation arrangement
4731 Freight transportation arrangement
4783 Packing and crating
4785 Inspection and fixed facilities
4789 Transportation services, nec

48 communications

4812 Radiotelephone communication
4813 Telephone communication, except radio
4832 Radio broadcasting stations
4833 Television broadcasting stations
4841 Cable and other pay television services
4899 Communication services, nec

49 electric, gas and sanitary services

4911 Electric services
4922 Natural gas transmission
4924 Natural gas distribution
4931 Electric and other services combined
4932 Gas and other services combined
4939 Combination utilities, nec
4941 Water supply
4952 Sewerage systems
4953 Refuse systems
4959 Sanitary services, nec
4971 Irrigation systems

50 wholesale trade - durable goods

5012 Automobiles and other motor vehicles
5013 Motor vehicle supplies and new parts
5014 Tires and tubes
5021 Furniture
5023 Homefurnishings
5031 Lumber, plywood, and millwork
5032 Brick, stone, and related material
5033 Roofing, siding, and insulation
5039 Construction materials, nec

5043 Photographic equipment and supplies
5044 Office equipment
5045 Computers, peripherals, and software
5046 Commercial equipment, nec
5047 Medical and hospital equipment
5049 Professional equipment, nec
5051 Metals service centers and offices
5063 Electrical apparatus and equipment
5064 Electrical appliances, television and radio
5065 Electronic parts and equipment, nec
5072 Hardware
5074 Plumbing and hydronic heating supplies
5075 Warm air heating and air conditioning
5078 Refrigeration equipment and supplies
5082 Construction and mining machinery
5083 Farm and garden machinery
5084 Industrial machinery and equipment
5085 Industrial supplies
5087 Service establishment equipment
5088 Transportation equipment and supplies
5091 Sporting and recreation goods
5092 Toys and hobby goods and supplies
5093 Scrap and waste materials
5094 Jewelry and precious stones
5099 Durable goods, nec

51 wholesale trade - nondurable goods

5111 Printing and writing paper
5112 Stationery and office supplies
5113 Industrial and personal service paper
5122 Drugs, proprietaries, and sundries
5131 Piece goods and notions
5136 Men's and boy's clothing
5137 Women's and children's clothing
5139 Footwear
5141 Groceries, general line
5142 Packaged frozen goods
5143 Dairy products, except dried or canned
5144 Poultry and poultry products
5145 Confectionery
5146 Fish and seafoods
5147 Meats and meat products
5148 Fresh fruits and vegetables
5149 Groceries and related products, nec
5159 Farm-product raw materials, nec
5162 Plastics materials and basic shapes
5169 Chemicals and allied products, nec
5171 Petroleum bulk stations and terminals
5172 Petroleum products, nec
5181 Beer and ale
5182 Wine and distilled beverages
5191 Farm supplies
5192 Books, periodicals, and newspapers
5193 Flowers and florists supplies
5194 Tobacco and tobacco products
5198 Paints, varnishes, and supplies
5199 Nondurable goods, nec

52 building materials, hardware, garden supplies & mobile homes

5211 Lumber and other building materials
5231 Paint, glass, and wallpaper stores
5251 Hardware stores
5261 Retail nurseries and garden stores

53 general merchandise stores

5311 Department stores
5331 Variety stores
5399 Miscellaneous general merchandise

54 food stores

5411 Grocery stores
5431 Fruit and vegetable markets
5441 Candy, nut, and confectionery stores
5461 Retail bakeries
5499 Miscellaneous food stores

55 automotive dealers and gasoline service stations

5511 New and used car dealers
5521 Used car dealers
5531 Auto and home supply stores
5541 Gasoline service stations

S
I
C

SIC NO	PRODUCT

5551 Boat dealers
5561 Recreational vehicle dealers
5571 Motorcycle dealers
5599 Automotive dealers, nec

56 apparel and accessory stores

5611 Men's and boys' clothing stores
5621 Women's clothing stores
5632 Women's accessory and specialty stores
5651 Family clothing stores
5661 Shoe stores
5699 Miscellaneous apparel and accessories

57 home furniture, furnishings and equipment stores

5712 Furniture stores
5713 Floor covering stores
5719 Miscellaneous homefurnishings
5722 Household appliance stores
5734 Computer and software stores
5736 Musical instrument stores

58 eating and drinking places

5812 Eating places
5813 Drinking places

59 miscellaneous retail

5912 Drug stores and proprietary stores
5921 Liquor stores
5932 Used merchandise stores
5941 Sporting goods and bicycle shops
5942 Book stores
5943 Stationery stores
5944 Jewelry stores
5945 Hobby, toy, and game shops
5946 Camera and photographic supply stores
5947 Gift, novelty, and souvenir shop
5949 Sewing, needlework, and piece goods
5961 Catalog and mail-order houses
5963 Direct selling establishments
5992 Florists
5994 News dealers and newsstands
5995 Optical goods stores
5999 Miscellaneous retail stores, nec

60 depository institutions

6011 Federal reserve banks
6021 National commercial banks
6022 State commercial banks
6029 Commercial banks, nec
6035 Federal savings institutions
6061 Federal credit unions
6062 State credit unions
6091 Nondeposit trust facilities
6099 Functions related to depository banking

61 nondepository credit institutions

6111 Federal and federally sponsored credit
6141 Personal credit institutions
6153 Short-term business credit
6159 Miscellaneous business credit
6162 Mortgage bankers and correspondents
6163 Loan brokers

62 security & commodity brokers, dealers, exchanges & services

6211 Security brokers and dealers
6221 Commodity contracts brokers, dealers
6282 Investment advice
6289 Security and commodity service

63 insurance carriers

6311 Life insurance
6321 Accident and health insurance
6324 Hospital and medical service plans
6331 Fire, marine, and casualty insurance
6351 Surety insurance
6361 Title insurance
6371 Pension, health, and welfare funds

64 insurance agents, brokers and service

6411 Insurance agents, brokers, and service

65 real estate

6512 Nonresidential building operators
6513 Apartment building operators
6514 Dwelling operators, except apartments
6515 Mobile home site operators
6519 Real property lessors, nec
6531 Real estate agents and managers
6541 Title abstract offices
6552 Subdividers and developers, nec
6553 Cemetery subdividers and developers

67 holding and other investment offices

6712 Bank holding companies
6719 Holding companies, nec
6722 Management investment, open-ended
6726 Investment offices, nec
6732 Trusts: educational, religious, etc.
6733 Trusts, nec
6794 Patent owners and lessors
6798 Real estate investment trusts
6799 Investors, nec

70 hotels, rooming houses, camps, and other lodging places

7011 Hotels and motels
7021 Rooming and boarding houses
7032 Sporting and recreational camps
7033 Trailer parks and campsites
7041 Membership-basis organization hotels

72 personal services

7211 Power laundries, family and commercial
7213 Linen supply
7215 Coin-operated laundries and cleaning
7216 Drycleaning plants, except rugs
7217 Carpet and upholstery cleaning
7218 Industrial launderers
7219 Laundry and garment services, nec
7221 Photographic studios, portrait
7231 Beauty shops
7261 Funeral service and crematories
7291 Tax return preparation services
7299 Miscellaneous personal services

73 business services

7311 Advertising agencies
7312 Outdoor advertising services
7313 Radio, television, publisher representatives
7319 Advertising, nec
7322 Adjustment and collection services
7323 Credit reporting services
7331 Direct mail advertising services
7334 Photocopying and duplicating services
7335 Commercial photography
7336 Commercial art and graphic design
7338 Secretarial and court reporting
7342 Disinfecting and pest control services
7349 Building maintenance services, nec
7352 Medical equipment rental
7353 Heavy construction equipment rental
7359 Equipment rental and leasing, nec
7361 Employment agencies
7363 Help supply services
7371 Custom computer programming services
7372 Prepackaged software
7373 Computer integrated systems design
7374 Data processing and preparation
7375 Information retrieval services
7376 Computer facilities management
7378 Computer maintenance and repair
7379 Computer related services, nec
7381 Detective and armored car services
7382 Security systems services
7383 News syndicates
7384 Photofinish laboratories
7389 Business services, nec

75 automotive repair, services and parking

7513 Truck rental and leasing, without drivers
7514 Passenger car rental
7515 Passenger car leasing
7519 Utility trailer rental

7521 Automobile parking
7532 Top and body repair and paint shops
7534 Tire retreading and repair shops
7537 Automotive transmission repair shops
7538 General automotive repair shops
7539 Automotive repair shops, nec
7542 Carwashes
7549 Automotive services, nec

76 miscellaneous repair services

7622 Radio and television repair
7623 Refrigeration service and repair
7629 Electrical repair shops
7641 Reupholstery and furniture repair
7692 Welding repair
7694 Armature rewinding shops
7699 Repair services, nec

78 motion pictures

7812 Motion picture and video production
7819 Services allied to motion pictures
7822 Motion picture and tape distribution
7829 Motion picture distribution services
7832 Motion picture theaters, except drive-in
7833 Drive-in motion picture theaters
7841 Video tape rental

79 amusement and recreation services

7922 Theatrical producers and services
7929 Entertainers and entertainment groups
7933 Bowling centers
7941 Sports clubs, managers, and promoters
7948 Racing, including track operation
7991 Physical fitness facilities
7992 Public golf courses
7993 Coin-operated amusement devices
7996 Amusement parks
7997 Membership sports and recreation clubs
7999 Amusement and recreation, nec

80 health services

8011 Offices and clinics of medical doctors
8021 Offices and clinics of dentists
8031 Offices and clinics of osteopathic physicians
8041 Offices and clinics of chiropractors
8042 Offices and clinics of optometrists
8049 Offices of health practitioner
8051 Skilled nursing care facilities
8052 Intermediate care facilities
8059 Nursing and personal care, nec
8062 General medical and surgical hospitals
8063 Psychiatric hospitals
8069 Specialty hospitals, except psychiatric
8071 Medical laboratories
8072 Dental laboratories
8082 Home health care services
8092 Kidney dialysis centers
8093 Specialty outpatient clinics, nec
8099 Health and allied services, nec

81 legal services

8111 Legal services

82 educational services

8211 Elementary and secondary schools
8221 Colleges and universities
8222 Junior colleges
8231 Libraries
8243 Data processing schools
8249 Vocational schools, nec
8299 Schools and educational services

83 social services

8322 Individual and family services
8331 Job training and related services
8351 Child day care services
8361 Residential care
8399 Social services, nec

84 museums, art galleries and botanical and zoological gardens

8412 Museums and art galleries

SIC

SIC INDEX

Standard Industrial Classification Alphabetical Index

SIC NO	PRODUCT

A

3291 Abrasive products
6321 Accident and health insurance
8721 Accounting, auditing, and bookkeeping
2891 Adhesives and sealants
7322 Adjustment and collection services
9431 Administration of public health programs
9441 Administration of social and manpower programs
7311 Advertising agencies
7319 Advertising, nec
2879 Agricultural chemicals, nec
3563 Air and gas compressors
4513 Air courier services
4522 Air transportation, nonscheduled
4512 Air transportation, scheduled
3721 Aircraft
3724 Aircraft engines and engine parts
3728 Aircraft parts and equipment, nec
4581 Airports, flying fields, and services
2812 Alkalies and chlorine
3363 Aluminum die-castings
3354 Aluminum extruded products
3365 Aluminum foundries
3355 Aluminum rolling and drawing, nec
3353 Aluminum sheet, plate, and foil
3483 Ammunition, except for small arms, nec
7999 Amusement and recreation, nec
7996 Amusement parks
3826 Analytical instruments
2077 Animal and marine fats and oils
0273 Animal aquaculture
0279 Animal specialties, nec
0752 Animal specialty services
1231 Anthracite mining
6513 Apartment building operators
2389 Apparel and accessories, nec
2387 Apparel belts
3446 Architectural metalwork
8712 Architectural services
7694 Armature rewinding shops
2952 Asphalt felts and coatings
2951 Asphalt paving mixtures and blocks
5531 Auto and home supply stores
3581 Automatic vending machines
7521 Automobile parking
5012 Automobiles and other motor vehicles
2396 Automotive and apparel trimmings
5599 Automotive dealers, nec
7539 Automotive repair shops, nec
7549 Automotive services, nec
3465 Automotive stampings
7537 Automotive transmission repair shops

B

2673 Bags: plastic, laminated, and coated
2674 Bags: uncoated paper and multiwall
3562 Ball and roller bearings
6712 Bank holding companies
7231 Beauty shops
5181 Beer and ale
2063 Beet sugar
0171 Berry crops
2836 Biological products, except diagnostic
1221 Bituminous coal and lignite-surface mining
2782 Blankbooks and looseleaf binders
3312 Blast furnaces and steel mills
3564 Blowers and fans
5551 Boat dealers
3732 Boatbuilding and repairing
3452 Bolts, nuts, rivets, and washers
2731 Book publishing
5942 Book stores
2789 Bookbinding and related work
5192 Books, periodicals, and newspapers
8422 Botanical and zoological gardens
2086 Bottled and canned soft drinks

7933 Bowling centers
2342 Bras, girdles, and allied garments
2051 Bread, cake, and related products
3251 Brick and structural clay tile
5032 Brick, stone, and related material
1622 Bridge, tunnel, and elevated highway
2211 Broadwoven fabric mills, cotton
2221 Broadwoven fabric mills, manmade
2231 Broadwoven fabric mills, wool
3991 Brooms and brushes
7349 Building maintenance services, nec
4142 Bus charter service, except local
8611 Business associations
8748 Business consulting, nec
7389 Business services, nec

C

4841 Cable and other pay television services
3578 Calculating and accounting equipment
5946 Camera and photographic supply stores
2064 Candy and other confectionery products
5441 Candy, nut, and confectionery stores
2091 Canned and cured fish and seafoods
2033 Canned fruits and specialties
2032 Canned specialties
2394 Canvas and related products
3624 Carbon and graphite products
2895 Carbon black
3955 Carbon paper and inked ribbons
3592 Carburetors, pistons, rings, valves
1751 Carpentry work
7217 Carpet and upholstery cleaning
2273 Carpets and rugs
7542 Carwashes
5961 Catalog and mail-order houses
3241 Cement, hydraulic
6553 Cemetery subdividers and developers
3253 Ceramic wall and floor tile
2043 Cereal breakfast foods
2022 Cheese; natural and processed
1479 Chemical and fertilizer mining
2899 Chemical preparations, nec
5169 Chemicals and allied products, nec
0252 Chicken eggs
8351 Child day care services
2066 Chocolate and cocoa products
2111 Cigarettes
0174 Citrus fruits
8641 Civic and social associations
1241 Coal mining services
2295 Coated fabrics, not rubberized
7993 Coin-operated amusement devices
7215 Coin-operated laundries and cleaning
8221 Colleges and universities
4939 Combination utilities, nec
7336 Commercial art and graphic design
6029 Commercial banks, nec
5046 Commercial equipment, nec
3582 Commercial laundry equipment
3646 Commercial lighting fixtures
8732 Commercial nonphysical research
7335 Commercial photography
8731 Commercial physical research
2754 Commercial printing, gravure
2752 Commercial printing, lithographic
2759 Commercial printing, nec
6221 Commodity contracts brokers, dealers
4899 Communication services, nec
3669 Communications equipment, nec
5734 Computer and software stores
7376 Computer facilities management
7373 Computer integrated systems design
7378 Computer maintenance and repair
3577 Computer peripheral equipment, nec
7379 Computer related services, nec
3572 Computer storage devices

3575 Computer terminals
5045 Computers, peripherals, and software
3271 Concrete block and brick
3272 Concrete products, nec
1771 Concrete work
5145 Confectionery
5082 Construction and mining machinery
3531 Construction machinery
5039 Construction materials, nec
1442 Construction sand and gravel
2679 Converted paper products, nec
3535 Conveyors and conveying equipment
2052 Cookies and crackers
3366 Copper foundries
1021 Copper ores
2298 Cordage and twine
2653 Corrugated and solid fiber boxes
3961 Costume jewelry
0131 Cotton
4215 Courier services, except by air
2021 Creamery butter
7323 Credit reporting services
0722 Crop harvesting
0721 Crop planting and protection
0723 Crop preparation services for market
1311 Crude petroleum and natural gas
1422 Crushed and broken limestone
1429 Crushed and broken stone, nec
3643 Current-carrying wiring devices
2391 Curtains and draperies
7371 Custom computer programming services
3281 Cut stone and stone products
3421 Cutlery
2865 Cyclic crudes and intermediates

D

0241 Dairy farms
5143 Dairy products, except dried or canned
7374 Data processing and preparation
8243 Data processing schools
0175 Deciduous tree fruits
4424 Deep sea domestic transportation of freight
4481 Deep sea passenger transportation, except ferry
2034 Dehydrated fruits, vegetables, soups
3843 Dental equipment and supplies
8072 Dental laboratories
5311 Department stores
7381 Detective and armored car services
2835 Diagnostic substances
2675 Die-cut paper and board
7331 Direct mail advertising services
5963 Direct selling establishments
7342 Disinfecting and pest control services
2085 Distilled and blended liquors
2047 Dog and cat food
3942 Dolls and stuffed toys
2591 Drapery hardware and blinds and shades
1381 Drilling oil and gas wells
5813 Drinking places
7833 Drive-in motion picture theaters
5912 Drug stores and proprietary stores
5122 Drugs, proprietaries, and sundries
2023 Dry, condensed, evaporated products
7216 Drycleaning plants, except rugs
5099 Durable goods, nec
6514 Dwelling operators, except apartments

E

5812 Eating places
2079 Edible fats and oils
4931 Electric and other services combined
3634 Electric housewares and fans
3641 Electric lamps
4911 Electric services
5063 Electrical apparatus and equipment
5064 Electrical appliances, television and radio

SIC NO	PRODUCT
3699	Electrical equipment and supplies, nec
3629	Electrical industrial apparatus
7629	Electrical repair shops
1731	Electrical work
3845	Electromedical equipment
3313	Electrometallurgical products
3671	Electron tubes
3675	Electronic capacitors
3677	Electronic coils and transformers
3679	Electronic components, nec
3571	Electronic computers
3678	Electronic connectors
5065	Electronic parts and equipment, nec
3676	Electronic resistors
8211	Elementary and secondary schools
3534	Elevators and moving stairways
7361	Employment agencies
3694	Engine electrical equipment
8711	Engineering services
7929	Entertainers and entertainment groups
2677	Envelopes
3822	Environmental controls
7359	Equipment rental and leasing, nec
1794	Excavation work
9131	Executive and legislative combined
9111	Executive offices
2892	Explosives

F

SIC NO	PRODUCT
2381	Fabric dress and work gloves
3499	Fabricated metal products, nec
3498	Fabricated pipe and fittings
3443	Fabricated plate work (boiler shop)
3069	Fabricated rubber products, nec
3441	Fabricated structural metal
2399	Fabricated textile products, nec
8744	Facilities support services
5651	Family clothing stores
5083	Farm and garden machinery
0761	Farm labor contractors
3523	Farm machinery and equipment
0762	Farm management services
4221	Farm product warehousing and storage
5191	Farm supplies
5159	Farm-product raw materials, nec
3965	Fasteners, buttons, needles, and pins
6111	Federal and federally sponsored credit
6061	Federal credit unions
6011	Federal reserve banks
6035	Federal savings institutions
2875	Fertilizers, mixing only
2655	Fiber cans, drums, and similar products
0139	Field crops, except cash grain
2261	Finishing plants, cotton
2262	Finishing plants, manmade
2269	Finishing plants, nec
6331	Fire, marine, and casualty insurance
5146	Fish and seafoods
3211	Flat glass
2087	Flavoring extracts and syrups, nec
5713	Floor covering stores
1752	Floor laying and floor work, nec
5992	Florists
2041	Flour and other grain mill products
5193	Flowers and florists supplies
3824	Fluid meters and counting devices
2026	Fluid milk
3593	Fluid power cylinders and actuators
3594	Fluid power pumps and motors
3492	Fluid power valves and hose fittings
2657	Folding paperboard boxes
0182	Food crops grown under cover
2099	Food preparations, nec
3556	Food products machinery
5139	Footwear
3131	Footwear cut stock
3149	Footwear, except rubber, nec
4731	Freight transportation arrangement
5148	Fresh fruits and vegetables
2092	Fresh or frozen packaged fish
2053	Frozen bakery products, except bread
2037	Frozen fruits and vegetables
2038	Frozen specialties, nec
5431	Fruit and vegetable markets
0179	Fruits and tree nuts, nec
6099	Functions related to depository banking
7261	Funeral service and crematories
5021	Furniture
2599	Furniture and fixtures, nec
5712	Furniture stores

G

SIC NO	PRODUCT
3944	Games, toys, and children's vehicles
4932	Gas and other services combined
3053	Gaskets; packing and sealing devices
5541	Gasoline service stations
7538	General automotive repair shops
0291	General farms, primarily animals
0191	General farms, primarily crop
9199	General government, nec
3569	General industrial machinery,
8062	General medical and surgical hospitals
4225	General warehousing and storage
5947	Gift, novelty, and souvenir shop
2361	Girl's and children's dresses, blouses
2369	Girl's and children's outerwear, nec
1793	Glass and glazing work
3221	Glass containers
1041	Gold ores
0172	Grapes
3321	Gray and ductile iron foundries
5149	Groceries and related products, nec
5141	Groceries, general line
5411	Grocery stores
3761	Guided missiles and space vehicles
3275	Gypsum products

H

SIC NO	PRODUCT
3423	Hand and edge tools, nec
3996	Hard surface floor coverings, nec
5072	Hardware
5251	Hardware stores
3429	Hardware, nec
2426	Hardwood dimension and flooring mills
2435	Hardwood veneer and plywood
2353	Hats, caps, and millinery
8099	Health and allied services, nec
3433	Heating equipment, except electric
7353	Heavy construction equipment rental
1629	Heavy construction, nec
7363	Help supply services
1611	Highway and street construction
5945	Hobby, toy, and game shops
3536	Hoists, cranes, and monorails
6719	Holding companies, nec
8082	Home health care services
5023	Homefurnishings
2252	Hosiery, nec
6324	Hospital and medical service plans
7011	Hotels and motels
5722	Household appliance stores
3639	Household appliances, nec
3651	Household audio and video equipment
3631	Household cooking equipment
2392	Household furnishings, nec
2519	Household furniture, nec
3632	Household refrigerators and freezers

I

SIC NO	PRODUCT
2024	Ice cream and frozen deserts
8322	Individual and family services
5113	Industrial and personal service paper
1541	Industrial buildings and warehouses
3567	Industrial furnaces and ovens
2813	Industrial gases
2819	Industrial inorganic chemicals, nec
7218	Industrial launderers
5084	Industrial machinery and equipment
3599	Industrial machinery, nec
2869	Industrial organic chemicals, nec
1446	Industrial sand
5085	Industrial supplies
3537	Industrial trucks and tractors
3491	Industrial valves

SIC NO	PRODUCT
7375	Information retrieval services
2816	Inorganic pigments
4785	Inspection and fixed facilities
1796	Installing building equipment
3825	Instruments to measure electricity
6411	Insurance agents, brokers, and service
4131	Intercity and rural bus transportation
8052	Intermediate care facilities
3519	Internal combustion engines, nec
6282	Investment advice
6726	Investment offices, nec
6799	Investors, nec
0134	Irish potatoes
3462	Iron and steel forgings
4971	Irrigation systems

J

SIC NO	PRODUCT
3915	Jewelers' materials and lapidary work
5094	Jewelry and precious stones
5944	Jewelry stores
3911	Jewelry, precious metal
8331	Job training and related services
8222	Junior colleges

K

SIC NO	PRODUCT
8092	Kidney dialysis centers
2253	Knit outerwear mills
2259	Knitting mills, nec

L

SIC NO	PRODUCT
8631	Labor organizations
3821	Laboratory apparatus and furniture
3083	Laminated plastics plate and sheet
9512	Land, mineral, and wildlife conservation
0781	Landscape counseling and planning
7219	Laundry and garment services, nec
3524	Lawn and garden equipment
0782	Lawn and garden services
3952	Lead pencils and art goods
2386	Leather and sheep-lined clothing
3199	Leather goods, nec
3111	Leather tanning and finishing
9222	Legal counsel and prosecution
8111	Legal services
8231	Libraries
6311	Life insurance
3648	Lighting equipment, nec
7213	Linen supply
5921	Liquor stores
0751	Livestock services, except veterinary
6163	Loan brokers
4111	Local and suburban transit
4141	Local bus charter service
4119	Local passenger transportation, nec
4214	Local trucking with storage
4212	Local trucking, without storage
2411	Logging
2992	Lubricating oils and greases
3161	Luggage
5211	Lumber and other building materials
5031	Lumber, plywood, and millwork

M

SIC NO	PRODUCT
2098	Macaroni and spaghetti
3545	Machine tool accessories
3541	Machine tools, metal cutting type
3542	Machine tools, metal forming type
3695	Magnetic and optical recording media
3322	Malleable iron foundries
2083	Malt
2082	Malt beverages
8742	Management consulting services
6722	Management investment, open-ended
8741	Management services
2761	Manifold business forms
2097	Manufactured ice
3999	Manufacturing industries, nec
4493	Marinas
4491	Marine cargo handling
1741	Masonry and other stonework
2515	Mattresses and bedsprings
3829	Measuring and controlling devices, nec

SIC NO	PRODUCT
2011	Meat packing plants
5147	Meats and meat products
3061	Mechanical rubber goods
5047	Medical and hospital equipment
7352	Medical equipment rental
8071	Medical laboratories
2833	Medicinals and botanicals
8699	Membership organizations, nec
7997	Membership sports and recreation clubs
7041	Membership-basis organization hotels
5136	Men's and boy's clothing
2329	Men's and boy's clothing, nec
2321	Men's and boy's furnishings
2323	Men's and boy's neckwear
2311	Men's and boy's suits and coats
2325	Men's and boy's trousers and slacks
2326	Men's and boy's work clothing
5611	Men's and boys' clothing stores
3143	Men's footwear, except athletic
3412	Metal barrels, drums, and pails
3411	Metal cans
3479	Metal coating and allied services
3442	Metal doors, sash, and trim
3398	Metal heat treating
2514	Metal household furniture
1081	Metal mining services
1099	Metal ores, nec
3431	Metal sanitary ware
3469	Metal stampings, nec
5051	Metals service centers and offices
3549	Metalworking machinery, nec
2431	Millwork
3296	Mineral wool
3295	Minerals, ground or treated
3532	Mining machinery
5699	Miscellaneous apparel and accessories
6159	Miscellaneous business credit
3496	Miscellaneous fabricated wire products
5499	Miscellaneous food stores
5399	Miscellaneous general merchandise
5719	Miscellaneous homefurnishings
3449	Miscellaneous metalwork
1499	Miscellaneous nonmetallic mining
7299	Miscellaneous personal services
2741	Miscellaneous publishing
5999	Miscellaneous retail stores, nec
6515	Mobile home site operators
2451	Mobile homes
6162	Mortgage bankers and correspondents
7822	Motion picture and tape distribution
7812	Motion picture and video production
7829	Motion picture distribution services
7832	Motion picture theaters, except drive-in
3716	Motor homes
3714	Motor vehicle parts and accessories
5013	Motor vehicle supplies and new parts
3711	Motor vehicles and car bodies
5571	Motorcycle dealers
3751	Motorcycles, bicycles, and parts
3621	Motors and generators
8412	Museums and art galleries
5736	Musical instrument stores
3931	Musical instruments

N

SIC NO	PRODUCT
2441	Nailed wood boxes and shook
2241	Narrow fabric mills
6021	National commercial banks
4924	Natural gas distribution
1321	Natural gas liquids
4922	Natural gas transmission
5511	New and used car dealers
5994	News dealers and newsstands
7383	News syndicates
2711	Newspapers
2873	Nitrogenous fertilizers
8733	Noncommercial research organizations
3644	Noncurrent-carrying wiring devices
6091	Nondeposit trust facilities
5199	Nondurable goods, nec
3364	Nonferrous die-castings except aluminum
3463	Nonferrous forgings

SIC NO	PRODUCT
3369	Nonferrous foundries, nec
3356	Nonferrous rolling and drawing, nec
3357	Nonferrous wiredrawing and insulating
3299	Nonmetallic mineral products,
1481	Nonmetallic mineral services
6512	Nonresidential building operators
1542	Nonresidential construction, nec
2297	Nonwoven fabrics
8059	Nursing and personal care, nec

O

SIC NO	PRODUCT
5044	Office equipment
2522	Office furniture, except wood
3579	Office machines, nec
8041	Offices and clinics of chiropractors
8021	Offices and clinics of dentists
8011	Offices and clinics of medical doctors
8042	Offices and clinics of optometrists
8031	Offices and clinics of osteopathic physicians
8049	Offices of health practitioner
1382	Oil and gas exploration services
3533	Oil and gas field machinery
1389	Oil and gas field services, nec
1531	Operative builders
3851	Ophthalmic goods
5995	Optical goods stores
3827	Optical instruments and lenses
3489	Ordnance and accessories, nec
2824	Organic fibers, noncellulosic
0181	Ornamental nursery products
0783	Ornamental shrub and tree services
7312	Outdoor advertising services

P

SIC NO	PRODUCT
5142	Packaged frozen goods
3565	Packaging machinery
4783	Packing and crating
5231	Paint, glass, and wallpaper stores
1721	Painting and paper hanging
2851	Paints and allied products
5198	Paints, varnishes, and supplies
3554	Paper industries machinery
2621	Paper mills
2671	Paper; coated and laminated packaging
2672	Paper; coated and laminated, nec
2631	Paperboard mills
2542	Partitions and fixtures, except wood
7515	Passenger car leasing
7514	Passenger car rental
4729	Passenger transportation arrangement
6794	Patent owners and lessors
6371	Pension, health, and welfare funds
2721	Periodicals
6141	Personal credit institutions
3172	Personal leather goods, nec
2999	Petroleum and coal products, nec
5171	Petroleum bulk stations and terminals
5172	Petroleum products, nec
2911	Petroleum refining
2834	Pharmaceutical preparations
7334	Photocopying and duplicating services
7384	Photofinish laboratories
3861	Photographic equipment and supplies
5043	Photographic equipment and supplies
7221	Photographic studios, portrait
7991	Physical fitness facilities
2035	Pickles, sauces, and salad dressings
5131	Piece goods and notions
4619	Pipelines, nec
1742	Plastering, drywall, and insulation
3085	Plastics bottles
3086	Plastics foam products
5162	Plastics materials and basic shapes
2821	Plastics materials and resins
3084	Plastics pipe
3088	Plastics plumbing fixtures
3089	Plastics products, nec
2796	Platemaking services
3471	Plating and polishing
2395	Pleating and stitching
5074	Plumbing and hydronic heating supplies
3432	Plumbing fixture fittings and trim

SIC NO	PRODUCT
1711	Plumbing, heating, air-conditioning
9221	Police protection
2842	Polishes and sanitation goods
3264	Porcelain electrical supplies
1474	Potash, soda, and borate minerals
2096	Potato chips and similar snacks
3269	Pottery products, nec
5144	Poultry and poultry products
2015	Poultry slaughtering and processing
7211	Power laundries, family and commercial
3568	Power transmission equipment, nec
3546	Power-driven handtools
3448	Prefabricated metal buildings
2452	Prefabricated wood buildings
7372	Prepackaged software
2048	Prepared feeds, nec
2045	Prepared flour mixes and doughs
3652	Prerecorded records and tapes
3229	Pressed and blown glass, nec
3334	Primary aluminum
3692	Primary batteries, dry and wet
3331	Primary copper
3399	Primary metal products
3339	Primary nonferrous metals, nec
3672	Printed circuit boards
5111	Printing and writing paper
2893	Printing ink
3555	Printing trades machinery
3823	Process control instruments
3231	Products of purchased glass
5049	Professional equipment, nec
8621	Professional organizations
8063	Psychiatric hospitals
2531	Public building and related furniture
7992	Public golf courses
8743	Public relations services
2611	Pulp mills
3561	Pumps and pumping equipment

R

SIC NO	PRODUCT
7948	Racing, including track operation
3663	Radio and t.v. communications equipment
7622	Radio and television repair
4832	Radio broadcasting stations
7313	Radio, television, publisher representatives
4812	Radiotelephone communication
3743	Railroad equipment
4011	Railroads, line-haul operating
2061	Raw cane sugar
3273	Ready-mixed concrete
6531	Real estate agents and managers
6798	Real estate investment trusts
6519	Real property lessors, nec
5561	Recreational vehicle dealers
4613	Refined petroleum pipelines
4222	Refrigerated warehousing and storage
3585	Refrigeration and heating equipment
5078	Refrigeration equipment and supplies
7623	Refrigeration service and repair
4953	Refuse systems
9641	Regulation of agricultural marketing
9621	Regulation, administration of transportation
3625	Relays and industrial controls
8661	Religious organizations
7699	Repair services, nec
8361	Residential care
1522	Residential construction, nec
3645	Residential lighting fixtures
5461	Retail bakeries
5261	Retail nurseries and garden stores
7641	Reupholstery and furniture repair
2044	Rice milling
2095	Roasted coffee
2384	Robes and dressing gowns
3547	Rolling mill machinery
5033	Roofing, siding, and insulation
1761	Roofing, siding, and sheetmetal work
7021	Rooming and boarding houses
3021	Rubber and plastics footwear
3052	Rubber and plastics hose and beltings

S

SIC NO	PRODUCT
2068	Salted and roasted nuts and seeds
2656	Sanitary food containers
2676	Sanitary paper products
4959	Sanitary services, nec
2013	Sausages and other prepared meats
3425	Saw blades and handsaws
2421	Sawmills and planing mills, general
4151	School buses
8299	Schools and educational services
5093	Scrap and waste materials
3451	Screw machine products
3812	Search and navigation equipment
3341	Secondary nonferrous metals
7338	Secretarial and court reporting
6289	Security and commodity service
6211	Security brokers and dealers
7382	Security systems services
3674	Semiconductors and related devices
5087	Service establishment equipment
3589	Service industry machinery, nec
7819	Services allied to motion pictures
8999	Services, nec
2652	Setup paperboard boxes
4952	Sewerage systems
5949	Sewing, needlework, and piece goods
3444	Sheet metalwork
3731	Shipbuilding and repairing
5661	Shoe stores
6153	Short-term business credit
3993	Signs and advertising specialties
3914	Silverware and plated ware
1521	Single-family housing construction
8051	Skilled nursing care facilities
3484	Small arms
2841	Soap and other detergents
8399	Social services, nec
0711	Soil preparation services
3764	Space propulsion units and parts
3769	Space vehicle equipment, nec
3544	Special dies, tools, jigs, and fixtures
3559	Special industry machinery, nec
1799	Special trade contractors, nec
4226	Special warehousing and storage, nec
8069	Specialty hospitals, except psychiatric
8093	Specialty outpatient clinics, nec
3566	Speed changers, drives, and gears
3949	Sporting and athletic goods, nec
5091	Sporting and recreation goods
7032	Sporting and recreational camps
5941	Sporting goods and bicycle shops
7941	Sports clubs, managers, and promoters
6022	State commercial banks
6062	State credit unions
5112	Stationery and office supplies
2678	Stationery products
5943	Stationery stores
3325	Steel foundries, nec

SIC NO	PRODUCT
3324	Steel investment foundries
3317	Steel pipe and tubes
3493	Steel springs, except wire
3315	Steel wire and related products
3691	Storage batteries
3259	Structural clay products, nec
1791	Structural steel erection
2439	Structural wood members, nec
6552	Subdividers and developers, nec
6351	Surety insurance
2843	Surface active agents
3841	Surgical and medical instruments
3842	Surgical appliances and supplies
8713	Surveying services
3613	Switchgear and switchboard apparatus
2822	Synthetic rubber

T

SIC NO	PRODUCT
3795	Tanks and tank components
7291	Tax return preparation services
4121	Taxicabs
3661	Telephone and telegraph apparatus
4813	Telephone communication, except radio
4833	Television broadcasting stations
1743	Terrazzo, tile, marble, mosaic work
8734	Testing laboratories
2393	Textile bags
2299	Textile goods, nec
7922	Theatrical producers and services
0811	Timber tracts
7534	Tire retreading and repair shops
3011	Tires and inner tubes
5014	Tires and tubes
6541	Title abstract offices
6361	Title insurance
5194	Tobacco and tobacco products
2844	Toilet preparations
7532	Top and body repair and paint shops
4725	Tour operators
4492	Towing and tugboat service
5092	Toys and hobby goods and supplies
7033	Trailer parks and campsites
3612	Transformers, except electric
5088	Transportation equipment and supplies
3799	Transportation equipment, nec
4789	Transportation services, nec
4724	Travel agencies
3792	Travel trailers and campers
0173	Tree nuts
3713	Truck and bus bodies
7513	Truck rental and leasing, without drivers
3715	Truck trailers
4213	Trucking, except local
6733	Trusts, nec
6732	Trusts: educational, religious, etc.
3511	Turbines and turbine generator sets
2791	Typesetting

SIC NO	PRODUCT

U

SIC NO	PRODUCT
3081	Unsupported plastics film and sheet
3082	Unsupported plastics profile shapes
2512	Upholstered household furniture
5521	Used car dealers
5932	Used merchandise stores
7519	Utility trailer rental

V

SIC NO	PRODUCT
3494	Valves and pipe fittings, nec
5331	Variety stores
2076	Vegetable oil mills, nec
0161	Vegetables and melons
3647	Vehicular lighting equipment
0742	Veterinary services, specialties
7841	Video tape rental
3261	Vitreous plumbing fixtures
8249	Vocational schools, nec

W

SIC NO	PRODUCT
5075	Warm air heating and air conditioning
3873	Watches, clocks, watchcases, and parts
4489	Water passenger transportation
4941	Water supply
4499	Water transportation services, nec
1781	Water well drilling
1623	Water, sewer, and utility lines
2257	Weft knit fabric mills
3548	Welding apparatus
7692	Welding repair
5182	Wine and distilled beverages
2084	Wines, brandy, and brandy spirits
3495	Wire springs
5632	Women's accessory and specialty stores
5137	Women's and children's clothing
2341	Women's and children's underwear
2331	Women's and misses' blouses and shirts
2339	Women's and misses' outerwear, nec
2337	Women's and misses' suits and coats
5621	Women's clothing stores
3144	Women's footwear, except athletic
3171	Women's handbags and purses
2335	Women's, junior's, and misses' dresses
2449	Wood containers, nec
2511	Wood household furniture
2434	Wood kitchen cabinets
2521	Wood office furniture
2448	Wood pallets and skids
2541	Wood partitions and fixtures
2491	Wood preserving
2499	Wood products, nec
2517	Wood television and radio cabinets
1795	Wrecking and demolition work

X

SIC NO	PRODUCT
3844	X-ray apparatus and tubes

PRODUCTS & SERVICES SECTION

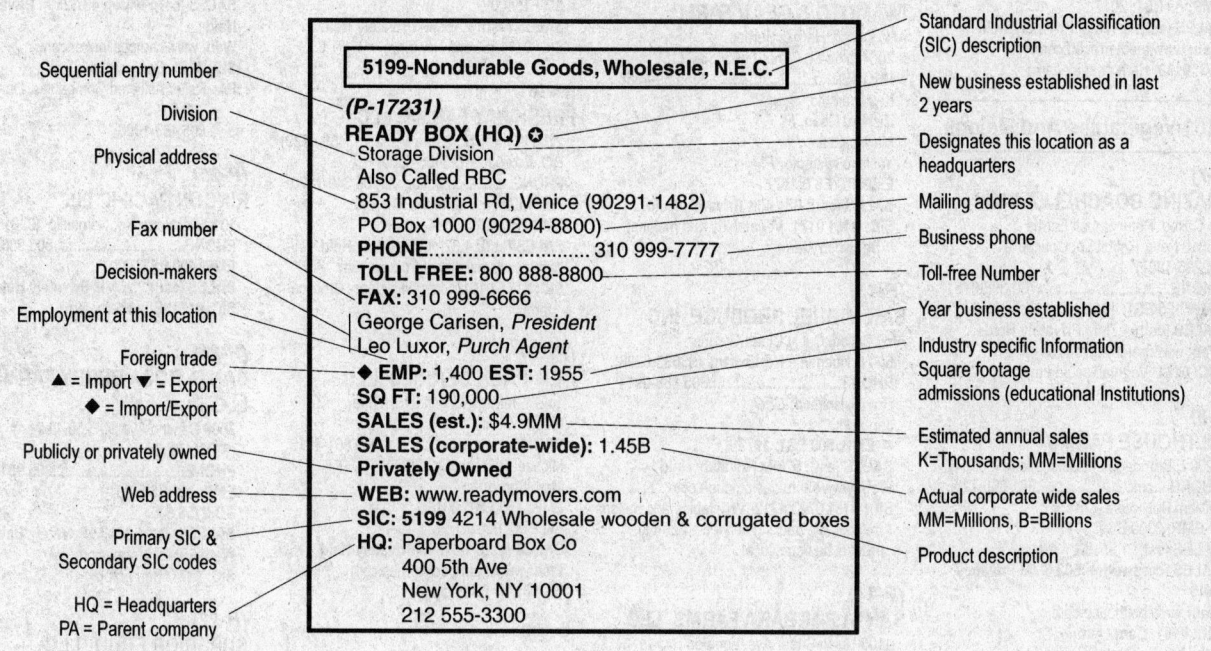

Diagram labels (left side, top to bottom):
- Sequential entry number
- Division
- Physical address
- Fax number
- Decision-makers
- Employment at this location
- Foreign trade
  ▲ = Import ▼ = Export
  ◆ = Import/Export
- Publicly or privately owned
- Web address
- Primary SIC & Secondary SIC codes
- HQ = Headquarters
  PA = Parent company

Central box:

5199-Nondurable Goods, Wholesale, N.E.C.

(P-17231)
READY BOX (HQ) ✪
Storage Division
Also Called RBC
853 Industrial Rd, Venice (90291-1482)
PO Box 1000 (90294-8800)
PHONE............................. 310 999-7777
TOLL FREE: 800 888-8800
FAX: 310 999-6666
George Carisen, *President*
Leo Luxor, *Purch Agent*
◆ **EMP:** 1,400 **EST:** 1955
SQ FT: 190,000
SALES (est.): $4.9MM
SALES (corporate-wide): 1.45B
Privately Owned
WEB: www.readymovers.com
SIC: 5199 4214 Wholesale wooden & corrugated boxes
HQ: Paperboard Box Co
       400 5th Ave
       New York, NY 10001
       212 555-3300

Diagram labels (right side, top to bottom):
- Standard Industrial Classification (SIC) description
- New business established in last 2 years
- Designates this location as a headquarters
- Mailing address
- Business phone
- Toll-free Number
- Year business established
- Industry specific Information Square footage admissions (educational Institutions)
- Estimated annual sales K=Thousands; MM=Millions
- Actual corporate wide sales MM=Millions, B=Billions
- Product description

- Companies in this section are listed numerically under their primary SIC Companies are in alphabetical order under each code.
- A numerical and alphabetical index precedes this section.
- **Sequential Entry Numbers.** Each establishment in this section is numbered sequentially. The number assigned to each establishment's Entry Number. To make cross-referencing easier, each listing in the Product's & Services, Alphabetic and Geographical Section includes the establishment's entry number. To facilitate locating an entry in this section, the entry numbers for the first listing on the left page and the last listing on the right page are printed at the top of the page next to the Standard Industrial Classification (SIC) description.
- Further information can be found in the Explanatory Notes starting on page 5.
- See the footnotes for symbols and abbreviations.

IMPORTANT NOTICE: It is a violation of both federal and state law to transmit an unsolicited advertisement to a facsimile machine. Any user of this product that violates such laws may be subject to civil and criminal penalties which may exceed $500 for each transmission of an unsolicited facsimile. Mergent Inc. provides fax numbers for lawful purposes only and expressly forbids the use of these numbers in any unlawful manner.

0131 Cotton

(P-1)
J G BOSWELL COMPANY
21101 Bear Mountain Blvd, Bakersfield
(93311-9412)
P.O. Box 9759 (93389-9759)
PHONE............................661 327-7721
Dave Cosyns, *Mgr*
EMP: 603
SALES (corp-wide): 370.2MM **Privately Held**
Web: www.eastlakeco.com
SIC: 0131 0111 0724 Cotton; Wheat; Cotton ginning
PA: J. G. Boswell Company
       101 W Walnut St
       626 583-3000

(P-2)
VIGNOLO FARMS INC
16456 Slater Ave, Bakersfield
(93308-9738)

PHONE............................661 746-2148
EMP: 97
SALES (corp-wide): 2.93MM **Privately Held**
Web: www.topbrassmarketing.com
SIC: 0131 0172 0134 Cotton; Grapes; Irish potatoes
PA: Vignolo Farms, Inc.
       33342 Dresser Ave
       661 746-2148

0134 Irish Potatoes

(P-3)
TASTEFUL SELECTIONS LLC
13003 Di Giorgio Rd, Arvin (93203-9529)
PHONE............................661 854-3998
EMP: 334 **EST:** 2010
SALES (est): 37.91MM **Privately Held**
Web: www.tastefulselections.com

SIC: 0134 5148 0723 Irish potatoes; Potatoes, fresh; Crop preparation services for market

0139 Field Crops, Except Cash Grain

(P-4)
GARLIC COMPANY (PA)
18602 Zerker Rd, Shafter (93263-9101)
PHONE............................661 393-4212
John Layous, *Mng Pt*
Joe Lane, *
◆ **EMP:** 80 **EST:** 1980
SQ FT: 150,000
SALES (est): 158.69MM
SALES (corp-wide): 158.69MM **Privately Held**
Web: www.thegarliccompany.com
SIC: 0139 2099 0191 Herb or spice farm; Food preparations, nec; General farms, primarily crop

(P-5)
HAYDAY FARMS INC
15500 S Commercial St, Blythe
(92225-2750)
P.O. Box 1226 (92226-1226)
PHONE............................760 922-4713
Atsuya Ichida, *Pr*
Dale Tyson, *
◆ **EMP:** 75 **EST:** 1986
SQ FT: 2,160
SALES (est): 2.34MM **Privately Held**
Web: www.haydayfarms.com
SIC: 0139 0722 0723 Hay farm; Hay, machine harvesting services; Field crops, except cash grains, market preparation services

(P-6)
MEDTERRA CBD LLC
18500 Von Karman Ave Ste 100, Irvine
(92612-0518)
PHONE............................800 971-1288
John Hartenbach, *CEO*

John Preston Larsen, *
EMP: 89 **EST:** 2017
SALES (est): 9.12MM **Privately Held**
Web: www.medterracbd.com
SIC: 0139 Herb or spice farm

0161 Vegetables And Melons

(P-7)
AMAZING COACHELLA INC
Also Called: Peter Rabbit Farms
85810 Peter Rabbit Ln, Coachella
(92236-1897)
PHONE....................760 398-0151
EMP: 100 **EST:** 1950
SALES (est): 4.7MM **Privately Held**
Web: www.peterrabbitfarms.com
SIC: 0161 Vegetables and melons

(P-8)
BOLTHOUSE FARMS
3200 E Brundage Ln, Bakersfield (93304)
PHONE....................661 366-7205
William Bolthouse, *Owner*
◆ **EMP:** 2300 **EST:** 1915
SALES (est): 1.55MM
SALES (corp-wide): 562.6MM **Privately
Held**
Web: www.bolthouse.com
SIC: 0161 Carrot farm
HQ: Wm. Bolthouse Farms, Inc.
7200 E Brundage Ln
Bakersfield CA 93307
800 467-4683

(P-9)
BOSKOVICH FARMS INC
4224 Pleasant Valley Rd, Camarillo
(93012-8533)
P.O. Box 1352 (93032-1352)
PHONE....................805 987-1443
Ken Mumford, *Mgr*
EMP: 108
SALES (corp-wide): 46.32MM **Privately
Held**
Web: www.boskovichfarms.com
SIC: 0161 0115 Vegetables and melons;
Corn
PA: Boskovich Farms, Inc.
711 Diaz Ave
805 487-2299

(P-10)
FRESH VENTURE FARMS LLC
1181 S Wolff Rd, Oxnard (93033-2105)
PHONE....................805 754-4449
EMP: 80 **EST:** 2012
SQ FT: 4,000
SALES (est): 2.15MM **Privately Held**
SIC: 0161 0191 Vegetables and melons;
General farms, primarily crop

(P-11)
GENERIS HOLDINGS LP (PA)
7200 E Brundage Ln, Bakersfield
(93307-3016)
PHONE....................661 366-7209
Jeffrey Dunn, *CEO*
EMP: 232 **EST:** 2019
SALES (est): 562.6MM
SALES (corp-wide): 562.6MM **Privately
Held**
Web: www.bolthouse.com
SIC: 0161 2037 2033 2099 Carrot farm; Fruit
juices; Vegetable juices: packaged in cans,
jars, etc.; Sauce, gravy, dressing, and dip
mixes

(P-12)
IWAMOTO & GEAN FARM
Also Called: Harry's Berries
2064 Olga St, Oxnard (93036-2715)
PHONE....................805 659-4568
Kaz Iwamoto, *Genl Pt*
Richard Gean, *Pt*
Mariko Gean, *Pt*
Yoshiko Iwamoto, *Pt*
EMP: 70 **EST:** 1977
SALES (est): 984.43K **Privately Held**
SIC: 0161 0171 Vegetables and melons;
Strawberry farm

(P-13)
SAN MIGUEL PRODUCE INC
Also Called: Cut N Clean Greens
600 E Hueneme Rd, Oxnard (93033-8298)
PHONE....................805 488-0981
Roy I Nishimori, *CEO*
Jan Berk, *
▲ **EMP:** 500 **EST:** 1979
SALES (est): 52MM **Privately Held**
Web: www.sanmiguelproduce.com
SIC: 0161 0723 4212 Vegetables and melons
; Vegetable packing services; Farm to
market haulage, local

(P-14)
SANTA BARBARA FARMS LLC
1105 Union Sugar Ave, Lompoc
(93436-9737)
PHONE....................805 736-5608
John Donati, *Pr*
EMP: 190
SALES (corp-wide): 24.23MM **Privately
Held**
SIC: 0161 0181 Vegetables and melons;
Florists' greens and flowers
PA: Santa Barbara Farms, Llc
1200 Union Sugar Ave
805 736-9776

0171 Berry Crops

(P-15)
DARENSBERRIES LLC
Also Called: D B Specialty Farms
714 S Blosser Rd, Santa Maria
(93458-4914)
P.O. Box 549 (93456-0549)
PHONE....................805 937-8000
EMP: 250 **EST:** 1994
SQ FT: 1,500
SALES (est): 2.52MM **Privately Held**
Web: www.darensberries.com
SIC: 0171 Strawberry farm

(P-16)
ECLIPSE BERRY FARMS LLC
11812 San Vicente Blvd Ste 250, Los
Angeles (90049-6632)
PHONE....................310 207-7879
Norman Gilfenbain, *Managing Member*
Robert Wiviott, *Managing Member**
Rudy Garza, *Managing Member**
Ventura Strawberry, *
▼ **EMP:** 100 **EST:** 1999
SQ FT: 2,500
SALES (est): 2.47MM **Privately Held**
SIC: 0171 5148 Berry crops; Fresh fruits and
vegetables

(P-17)
ETCHANDY FARMS LLC
4324 E Vineyard Ave, Oxnard
(93036-1056)
P.O. Box 5770 (93031-5770)
PHONE....................805 983-4700

EMP: 99 **EST:** 2014
SQ FT: 400
SALES (est): 2.16MM **Privately Held**
SIC: 0171 Strawberry farm

(P-18)
FRESHWAY FARMS LLC
2165 W Main St, Santa Maria (93458-9739)
P.O. Box 5369 (93456-5369)
PHONE....................805 349-7170
Paul M Allen, *Managing Member*
EMP: 150 **EST:** 2014
SALES (est): 4.32MM **Privately Held**
Web: www.mainstreetproduce.com
SIC: 0171 0161 Strawberry farm; Broccoli
farm

(P-19)
GEM-PACK BERRIES LLC
14271 Jeffrey Rd Unit 315, Irvine
(92620-3405)
PHONE....................949 861-4919
Michael D Etchandy, *CEO*
Marc Serrio, *
EMP: 150 **EST:** 2016
SQ FT: 2,000
SALES (est): 2.31MM **Privately Held**
Web: www.gem-packberries.com
SIC: 0171 Berry crops

(P-20)
J&G BERRY FARMS LLC
720 Rosemary Rd, Santa Maria
(93454-8007)
PHONE....................831 750-9408
Jose Luis Rocha, *Managing Member*
Guadalupe Rocha, *
EMP: 220 **EST:** 2016
SALES (est): 1.64MM **Privately Held**
SIC: 0171 7389 Strawberry farm; Business
Activities at Non-Commercial Site

(P-21)
LAS POSAS BERRY FARMS LLC
730 S A St, Oxnard (93030-7138)
PHONE....................805 483-1000
Manuel Magdaleno, *CEO*
EMP: 100 **EST:** 2013
SALES (est): 1.87MM **Privately Held**
SIC: 0171 Berry crops

(P-22)
ORANGE COUNTY PRODUCE LLC
210 W Walnut Ave, Fullerton (92832-2347)
PHONE....................949 451-0880
Matthew K Kawamura, *Managing Member*
EMP: 100 **EST:** 1998
SALES (est): 3.04MM **Privately Held**
Web: www.ocproduce.com
SIC: 0171 Strawberry farm

(P-23)
RED BLOSSOM SALES INC
865 Black Rd, Santa Maria (93458-9701)
PHONE....................805 349-9404
Ruben Trevino, *Mgr*
EMP: 572
Web: www.redblossom.com
SIC: 0171 Strawberry farm
PA: Red Blossom Sales, Inc.
400 W Ventura Blvd # 140

(P-24)
REITER AFFL COMPANIES LLC
124 Carmen Ln Ste A, Santa Maria
(93458-7768)
PHONE....................805 925-8577
Mario Pena, *Mgr*

EMP: 87
SALES (corp-wide): 43.32MM **Privately
Held**
Web: www.campbellrinker.com
SIC: 0171 Berry crops
PA: Reiter Affiliated Companies, Llc
730 S A St
805 483-1000

(P-25)
RINCON PACIFIC LLC
1312 Del Norte Rd, Camarillo (93010-8502)
PHONE....................805 986-8806
EMP: 100 **EST:** 2001
SALES (est): 2.15MM **Privately Held**
SIC: 0171 Strawberry farm

(P-26)
SANTA ROSA BERRY FARMS LLC
3500 Camino Ave Ste 250, Oxnard
(93030-7999)
PHONE....................805 981-3060
EMP: 300 **EST:** 2010
SQ FT: 3,500
SALES (est): 4.16MM **Privately Held**
Web: www.srbfarms.com
SIC: 0171 Berry crops

(P-27)
SUPERIOR FRUIT LLC
4324 E Vineyard Ave, Oxnard
(93036-1056)
PHONE....................805 485-2519
Richard Jones, *
EMP: 200 **EST:** 2017
SQ FT: 6,000
SALES (est): 1.32MM **Privately Held**
SIC: 0171 Strawberry farm

0172 Grapes

(P-28)
7TH STANDARD RANCH COMPANY
Also Called: Sun Pacific Farming
33374 Lerdo Hwy, Bakersfield
(93308-9782)
PHONE....................661 399-0416
Berne Evans, *Pt*
Robert Reniers, *Pt*
EMP: 500 **EST:** 1986
SQ FT: 140,000
SALES (est): 5.81MM **Privately Held**
Web: www.sunpacific.com
SIC: 0172 4222 Grapes; Refrigerated
warehousing and storage

(P-29)
ANTHONY VINEYARDS INC
52301 Enterprise Way, Coachella
(92236-2708)
PHONE....................760 391-5488
Roberto Bianco, *Mgr*
EMP: 100
SALES (corp-wide): 12.58MM **Privately
Held**
Web: www.anthonyvineyards.com
SIC: 0172 0174 Grapes; Grapefruit grove
PA: Anthony Vineyards, Inc.
5512 Valpredo Ave
661 858-6211

(P-30)
BABCOCK ENTERPRISES INC
Also Called: Babcock Vineyards
5175 E Highway 246, Lompoc
(93436-9613)

P.O. Box 637 (93438-0637)
PHONE..............................805 736-1455
Bryan Babcock, *Pr*
Walter Babcock, *
Bryan Babcock, *VP*
Mona Babcock, *
EMP: 25 **EST:** 1979
SALES (est): 2.42MM **Privately Held**
Web: www.babcockwinery.com
SIC: 0172 2084 8734 Grapes; Wines; Food
testing service

(P-31)
GIUMARRA VINEYARDS CORPORATION
Giumarra Winery
11220 Edison Hwy, Bakersfield
(93307-8431)
P.O. Box 1969 (93303-1969)
PHONE..............................661 395-7071
Barry Douglas, *Mgr*
EMP: 259
SALES (corp-wide): 72.36MM **Privately
Held**
Web: www.giumarravineyards.com
SIC: 0172 Grapes
PA: Giumarra Vineyards Corporation
11220 Edison Hwy
661 395-7000

(P-32)
GIUMARRA VINEYARDS CORPORATION (PA)
11220 Edison Hwy, Edison (93220)
P.O. Box 1969 (93303-1969)
PHONE..............................661 395-7000
Wayne Childress, *CEO*
Mimi Corsaro-dorsey, *Sec*
Jeffrey Giumarra, *
◆ **EMP:** 500 **EST:** 1946
SQ FT: 10,000
SALES (est): 72.36MM
SALES (corp-wide): 72.36MM **Privately
Held**
Web: www.giumarravineyards.com
SIC: 0172 2084 2086 Grapes; Wines; Fruit
drinks (less than 100% juice): packaged in
cans, etc.

(P-33)
J & L VINEYARDS
1850 Ramada Dr Ste 3, Paso Robles
(93446-3932)
PHONE..............................559 268-1627
Donald Laub, *Pt*
Raymond Jacobson, *Pt*
EMP: 100 **EST:** 1980
SALES (est): 689.08K **Privately Held**
SIC: 0172 Grapes

(P-34)
JAKOV DULCICH AND SONS LLC
31956 Peterson Rd, Mc Farland
(93250-9606)
PHONE..............................661 792-6360
Jakov Dulcich, *Prin*
▲ **EMP:** 250 **EST:** 1963
SALES (est): 14.69MM **Privately Held**
Web: www.dulcich.com
SIC: 0172 Grapes

(P-35)
M CARATAN DISC INC
Also Called: Caliente Farms
33787 Cecil Ave, Delano (93215-9597)
PHONE..............................661 725-2566
Martin Caratin, *CEO*
▼ **EMP:** 150 **EST:** 1946

SQ FT: 6,000
SALES (est): 4.84MM **Privately Held**
Web: www.mcaratan.com
SIC: 0172 0174 0723 Grapes; Orange grove
; Almond hulling and shelling services

(P-36)
RENZONI VINEYARDS INC
Also Called: Robert Rnzoni Vineyards Winery
37350 De Portola Rd, Temecula
(92592-9024)
PHONE..............................951 302-8466
Robert Renzoni, *Pr*
Fred Renzoni, *
▲ **EMP:** 37 **EST:** 2007
SALES (est): 2.32MM **Privately Held**
Web: www.robertrenzonivineyards.com
SIC: 0172 2084 Grapes; Wines

(P-37)
TREASURY WINE ESTATES AMERICAS
Also Called: Meridian Vineyards
7000 E Highway 46, Paso Robles
(93446-7390)
P.O. Box 3289 (93447-3289)
PHONE..............................805 237-6000
Jim Schaefer, *Mgr*
EMP: 27
Web: www.treasurywineestates.com
SIC: 0172 2084 Grapes; Wines, brandy, and
brandy spirits
HQ: Treasury Wine Estates Americas
Company
555 Gateway Dr
Napa CA 94558
707 259-4500

0173 Tree Nuts

(P-38)
AGRESERVES INC
15443 Beech Ave, Wasco (93280-7604)
PHONE..............................661 391-9000
Ren Fairbanks, *Brnch Mgr*
EMP: 135
SALES (corp-wide): 4.54B **Privately Held**
Web: www.southvalleyfarms.com
SIC: 0173 Almond grove
HQ: Agreserves, Inc.
60 E South Temple # 1600
Salt Lake City UT 84111

(P-39)
J G BOSWELL COMPANY
36889 Highway 58, Buttonwillow
(93206-9616)
PHONE..............................661 764-9000
EMP: 498
SALES (corp-wide): 370.2MM **Privately
Held**
Web: www.eastlakeco.com
SIC: 0173 0161 0131 Pistachio grove;
Tomato farm; Cotton
PA: J. G. Boswell Company
101 W Walnut St
626 583-3000

(P-40)
WONDERFUL ORCHARDS LLC
Also Called: Wonderfulpistachiosandalmonds
13646 Highway 33, Lost Hills (93249-9719)
P.O. Box 400 (93249-0400)
PHONE..............................661 797-6400
Dennis Elam, *Brnch Mgr*
EMP: 255
SALES (corp-wide): 2.04B **Privately Held**
Web: www.wonderfulorchards.com

SIC: 0173 0191 Almond grove; General
farms, primarily crop
HQ: Wonderful Orchards Llc
6801 E Lerdo Hwy
Shafter CA 93263
661 399-4456

(P-41)
WONDERFUL ORCHARDS LLC
21707 Lerdo Hwy, Mc Kittrick (93251-9758)
PHONE..............................661 797-2509
Robert Baker, *Mgr*
EMP: 102
SALES (corp-wide): 2.04B **Privately Held**
Web: www.wonderfulorchards.com
SIC: 0173 0191 Almond grove; General
farms, primarily crop
HQ: Wonderful Orchards Llc
6801 E Lerdo Hwy
Shafter CA 93263
661 399-4456

(P-42)
WONDERFUL ORCHARDS LLC (HQ)
6801 E Lerdo Hwy, Shafter (93263-9610)
PHONE..............................661 399-4456
◆ **EMP:** 150 **EST:** 1998
SQ FT: 10,000
SALES (est): 179.26MM
SALES (corp-wide): 2.04B **Privately Held**
Web: www.wonderfulorchards.com
SIC: 0173 0179 Almond grove; Olive grove
PA: The Wonderful Company Llc
11444 W Olympic Blvd Fl 1
310 966-5700

0174 Citrus Fruits

(P-43)
EXETER PACKERS INC
Also Called: Sun Pacific Shippers
1095 E Green St, Pasadena (91106-2503)
PHONE..............................626 993-6245
Bob Reniers, *Genl Mgr*
EMP: 119
SALES (corp-wide): 42.6MM **Privately
Held**
Web: www.sunpacific.com
SIC: 0174 0172 0161 0723 Orange grove;
Grapes; Tomato farm; Fruit (fresh) packing
services
PA: Exeter Packers, Inc.
1250 E Myer Ave
559 592-5168

(P-44)
SATICOY LEMON ASSOCIATION
Also Called: Saticoy Fruit Exchange
7560 Bristol Rd, Ventura (93003-7027)
P.O. Box 46 (93061-0046)
PHONE..............................805 654-6500
John Elliott, *Brnch Mgr*
EMP: 99
SALES (corp-wide): 21.99MM **Privately
Held**
Web: www.saticoylemon.com
SIC: 0174 Lemon grove
PA: Saticoy Lemon Association
103 N Peck Rd
805 654-6500

(P-45)
WONDERFUL COMPANY LLC
Also Called: Paramount Citrus
1901 S Lexington St, Delano (93215-9207)
PHONE..............................661 720-2400
Freddie Hernandez, *Mgr*
EMP: 273

SALES (corp-wide): 2.04B **Privately Held**
Web: www.wonderful.com
SIC: 0174 3911 Citrus fruits; Jewelry,
precious metal
PA: The Wonderful Company Llc
11444 W Olympic Blvd Fl 1
310 966-5700

0175 Deciduous Tree Fruits

(P-46)
NISSHO OF CALIFORNIA INC
89055 64th Ave, Thermal (92274-9607)
PHONE..............................760 727-9719
Abel Bustamante, *Mgr*
EMP: 309
SALES (corp-wide): 26.25MM **Privately
Held**
Web: www.nisshoca.com
SIC: 0175 Deciduous tree fruits
PA: Nissho Of California, Inc.
1902 S Santa Fe Ave
760 727-9719

0179 Fruits And Tree Nuts, Nec

(P-47)
DOLE HOLDING COMPANY LLC
1 Dole Dr, Westlake Village (91362-7300)
PHONE..............................818 879-6600
David H Murdock, *Ch Bd*
EMP: 74999 **EST:** 2004
SALES (est): 443.07K **Privately Held**
SIC: 0179 0174 0175 0161 Pineapple farm;
Citrus fruits; Deciduous tree fruits; Lettuce
farm
PA: Dhm Holding Company, Inc.
One Dole Drive

(P-48)
HADLEY DATE GARDENS INC
47382 Madison St, Indio (92201-6630)
PHONE..............................760 347-3044
EMP: 79
SALES (corp-wide): 2.63MM **Privately
Held**
Web: www.hadleys.com
SIC: 0179 Date orchard
PA: Hadley Date Gardens, Inc.
79220 Corp Ctr Dr Ste 102
760 399-5191

(P-49)
HENRY AVOCADO CORPORATION (HQ)
Also Called: Customripe Avocado Company
2208 Harmony Grove Rd, Escondido
(92029-2054)
P.O. Box 300867 (92030-0867)
PHONE..............................760 745-6632
Philip Henry, *Pr*
◆ **EMP:** 70 **EST:** 1924
SQ FT: 35,000
SALES (est): 20.04MM
SALES (corp-wide): 1.23B **Publicly Held**
Web: www.henryavocado.com
SIC: 0179 4213 Avocado orchard; Trucking,
except local
PA: Mission Produce, Inc.
2710 Camino Del Sol
805 981-3650

(P-50)
MUNGER BROS LLC
Also Called: Munger Farm
786 Road 188, Delano (93215-9508)
PHONE..............................661 721-0390

P R O D U C T S & S V C S

Kewel K Munger, *
▲ EMP: 600 EST: 1998
SQ FT: 50,000
SALES (est): 5.61MM **Privately Held**
SIC: 0179 2033 Avocado orchard; Canned
　fruits and specialties

0181 Ornamental Nursery Products

(P-51)
A-G SOD FARMS INC
Also Called: Addink Turf
2900 Adams St Ste C120, Riverside
(92504-8317)
PHONE..............................951 687-7581
Sonya Dawe, *Mgr*
EMP: 78
SALES (corp-wide): 16.87MM **Privately Held**
Web: www.agsod.com
SIC: 0181 Sod farms
PA: A-G Sod Farms, Inc.
　2900 Adams St Ste C120
　951 687-7581

(P-52)
DEVIL MOUNTAIN WHL NURS LLC
29001 Ortega Hwy, San Juan Capistrano
(92675)
PHONE..............................949 496-9356
EMP: 93
SALES (corp-wide): 4.3B **Publicly Held**
Web: www.devilmountainnursery.com
SIC: 0181 Nursery stock, growing of
HQ: Devil Mountain Wholesale Nursery, Llc
　9885 Alcosta Blvd
　San Ramon CA 94583

(P-53)
DRAMM AND ECHTER INC
Also Called: D&E Propogators
1150 Quail Gardens Dr, Encinitas
(92024-2365)
PHONE..............................760 436-0188
◆ EMP: 85 EST: 1972
SALES (est): 2.41MM **Privately Held**
Web: www.drammechter.com
SIC: 0181 5193 Flowers: grown under cover
　(e.g., greenhouse production); Flowers and
　nursery stock

(P-54)
EUROAMERICAN PROPAGATORS LLC
32149 Aquaduct Rd, Bonsall (92003-4807)
PHONE..............................760 731-6029
▲ EMP: 375
Web: www.euroamericanpropagators.com
SIC: 0181 Ornamental nursery products

(P-55)
FLORAL GIFT HM DECOR INTL INC
3200 Golf Course Dr Ste B, Ventura
(93003-7615)
P.O. Box 2673 (93011-2673)
PHONE..............................818 849-8832
Dolly Ives, *CEO*
Edwin M Ives, *
▲ EMP: 25 EST: 1973
SALES (est): 762.4K **Privately Held**
SIC: 0181 3999 Florists' greens, cultivated:
　growing of; Foliage, artificial and preserved

(P-56)
GLAD-A-WAY GARDENS INC
2669 E Clark Ave, Santa Maria
(93455-5815)
P.O. Box 2550 (93457-2550)
PHONE..............................805 938-0569
Brian Caird, *Pr*
Erin Caird, *
Lance Runels, *
▲ EMP: 172 EST: 1964
SQ FT: 15,000
SALES (est): 3.3MM **Privately Held**
Web: www.gladaway.com
SIC: 0181 Flowers: grown under cover (e.g.,
　greenhouse production)

(P-57)
HINES GROWERS INC
Also Called: Cshg Holdings
27368 Via Industria Ste 201, Temecula
(92590-4856)
PHONE..............................800 554-4065
▲ EMP: 527 EST: 2012
SALES (est): 396.48K
SALES (corp-wide): 115.34B **Publicly Held**
SIC: 0181 5261 Ornamental nursery products
　; Retail nurseries and garden stores
HQ: Csn Winddown, Inc.
　27368 Via Industria # 20
　Temecula CA 92590

(P-58)
HINES HORTICULTURE INC (PA)
Also Called: Hines Nurseries
12621 Jeffery Rd, Irvine (92620)
PHONE..............................949 559-4444
▲ EMP: 500 EST: 1920
SALES (est): 446.34MM **Privately Held**
SIC: 0181 5261 Ornamental nursery products
　; Retail nurseries and garden stores

(P-59)
LA VERNE NURSERY INC
3653 Center St, Piru (93040-8051)
PHONE..............................805 521-0111
EMP: 90
Web: www.everde.com
SIC: 0181 Nursery stock, growing of
PA: La Verne Nursery, Inc.
　1025 N Todd Ave

(P-60)
MARATHON LAND INC
2599 E Hueneme Rd, Oxnard (93033-8112)
P.O. Box 579 (93044-0579)
PHONE..............................805 488-3585
TOLL FREE: 800
Jurgen Gramckow, *Pr*
EMP: 130 EST: 1977
SQ FT: 3,000
SALES (est): 1.93MM **Privately Held**
Web: www.sod.com
SIC: 0181 Sod farms

(P-61)
MULROSES USA INC
741 S San Pedro St, Los Angeles
(90014-2417)
PHONE..............................213 489-1761
Patricio Nasser, *Mgr*
EMP: 100 EST: 2010
SALES (est): 1.55MM **Privately Held**
SIC: 0181 Roses, growing of

(P-62)
NORMANS NURSERY INC
Also Called: Norman's Nursery
5770 Casitas Pass Rd, Carpinteria
(93013-3061)

PHONE..............................805 684-1411
Martin Manzo, *Mgr*
EMP: 142
SALES (corp-wide): 41.58MM **Privately Held**
Web: www.normansnursery.com
SIC: 0181 Nursery stock, growing of
PA: Norman's Nursery, Inc.
　8665 Duarte Rd
　626 285-9795

(P-63)
OLIVE HILL GREENHOUSES INC
3508 Olive Hill Rd, Fallbrook (92028-8296)
P.O. Box 1510 (92088-1510)
PHONE..............................760 728-4596
George A Godfrey, *Owner*
▲ EMP: 100 EST: 1974
SQ FT: 2,000
SALES (est): 4.29MM **Privately Held**
Web: www.olivehill.net
SIC: 0181 Nursery stock, growing of

(P-64)
PACIFIC ERTH RSRCES LTD A CAL
Also Called: Pacific Sod
315 Hueneme Rd, Camarillo (93012-8522)
P.O. Box 240 (93011-0240)
PHONE..............................209 892-3000
Raymond Freitas, *Mgr*
EMP: 90
SALES (corp-wide): 3.07MM **Privately Held**
SIC: 0181 Sod farms
PA: Pacific Earth Resources, Ltd., A
　California Limited Partnership
　305 Hueneme Rd
　805 986-8277

(P-65)
PACIFIC ERTH RSRCES LTD A CAL (PA)
Also Called: Pacific Sd/Pcfic Arbor Nrsries
305 Hueneme Rd, Camarillo (93012-8522)
P.O. Box 240 (93011-0240)
PHONE..............................805 986-8277
Richard Rogers, *Mng Pt*
Elizabeth Rogers, *Pt*
EMP: 80 EST: 1958
SQ FT: 8,000
SALES (est): 3.07MM
SALES (corp-wide): 3.07MM **Privately Held**
SIC: 0181 Sod farms

(P-66)
PLANTEL NURSERIES INC
3990 Foxen Canyon Rd, Santa Maria
(93454-9666)
PHONE..............................805 934-4300
Gerald Tonascia, *Mgr*
EMP: 270
SALES (corp-wide): 19.39MM **Privately Held**
Web: www.plantelnurseries.com
SIC: 0181 5193 Seeds, vegetable: growing of
　; Nursery stock
PA: Plantel Nurseries, Inc.
　2775 E Clark Ave
　805 349-8952

(P-67)
PLUG CONNECTION INC
2627 Ramona Dr, Vista (92084-1634)
PHONE..............................760 631-0992
Tim Wada, *Pr*
Bradley Rhoads, *
▲ EMP: 80 EST: 1987
SQ FT: 350,000

SALES (est): 10.3MM **Privately Held**
Web: www.plugconnection.com
SIC: 0181 Nursery stock, growing of

(P-68)
RICHARD WILSON WELLINGTON
Also Called: Colorama Wholesale Nursery
1025 N Todd Ave, Azusa (91702-1602)
P.O. Box 1328 (91740-1328)
PHONE..............................626 812-7881
Richard Wilson, *Owner*
▲ EMP: 100 EST: 1984
SQ FT: 70,000
SALES (est): 1.92MM **Privately Held**
Web: www.coloramanursery.com
SIC: 0181 5193 Nursery stock, growing of;
　Nursery stock

(P-69)
RIVER RIDGE FARMS INC
3135 Los Angeles Ave, Oxnard
(93036-1010)
PHONE..............................805 647-6880
Rieuwert Jan Vis, *Pr*
▲ EMP: 95 EST: 1992
SQ FT: 440
SALES (est): 2.18MM **Privately Held**
Web: www.riverridgefarms.net
SIC: 0181 5193 Flowers, grown in field
　nurseries; Plants, potted

(P-70)
SUPERIOR SOD I LP
17821 17th St Ste 165, Tustin
(92780-2172)
P.O. Box 1911 (93581-5911)
PHONE..............................909 923-5068
Michael Considine, *Pt*
Richard H Considine, *Pt*
Peter Moore, *Pt*
Trudy Considine, *Pt*
EMP: 125 EST: 1988
SQ FT: 1,400
SALES (est): 1.72MM **Privately Held**
Web: www.superiorsod.com
SIC: 0181 0782 Sod farms; Lawn and
　garden services

(P-71)
WESTERLAY ORCHIDS LP
Also Called: Westerlay Orchids
3504 Via Real, Carpinteria (93013-3048)
PHONE..............................805 684-5411
Antoine Overgaag, *Pr*
▲ EMP: 117 EST: 2003
SALES (est): 4.68MM **Privately Held**
Web: www.westerlayorchids.com
SIC: 0181 Flowers: grown under cover (e.g.,
　greenhouse production)

0182 Food Crops Grown Under Cover

(P-72)
HOKTO KINOKO COMPANY
130 S Myers St, Los Angeles (90033-3212)
PHONE..............................323 526-1155
EMP: 94
Web: www.hokto-kinoko.com
SIC: 0182 Mushrooms, grown under cover
HQ: Hokto Kinoko Company
　2033 Marilyn Ln
　San Marcos CA 92069

(P-73)
HOUWELINGS CAMARILLO INC
645 Laguna Rd, Camarillo (93012-8523)
PHONE..............................805 250-1600

Cornelius Houweling, *CEO*
EMP: 338 **EST:** 2021
SQ FT: 3,000,000
SALES (est): 12.11MM **Privately Held**
Web: www.houwelings.com
SIC: 0182 Food crops grown under cover

(P-74)
MOUNTAIN MEADOW MUSHROOMS INC
Also Called: Laseta Organica
26948 N Broadway, Escondido
(92026-8315)
PHONE...........................760 749-1201
Bob Crouch, *Pr*
Elizabeth Crouch, *
Manuel Zuniga, *
Roberto Ramirez, *
EMP: 72 **EST:** 1982
SQ FT: 110,000
SALES (est): 2.89MM **Privately Held**
Web: www.mmmushroom.com
SIC: 0182 Mushrooms, grown under cover

0191 General Farms, Primarily Crop

(P-75)
BLACKJACK FRMS DE LA CSTA CNTL
Also Called: Black Jack Farms
2385 A St, Santa Maria (93455-1073)
PHONE...........................805 347-1333
Jose Garcia, *CEO*
EMP: 140 **EST:** 2017
SALES (est): 2.36MM **Privately Held**
SIC: 0191 General farms, primarily crop

(P-76)
BRAGA FRESH FAMILY FARMS INC
Also Called: Braga Fresh Imperial
817 W Hackleman Rd, El Centro
(92243-9508)
PHONE...........................760 353-1155
Asa Braga, *Owner*
EMP: 199
SALES (corp-wide): 150MM **Privately Held**
Web: www.bragafresh.com
SIC: 0191 General farms, primarily crop
PA: Braga Fresh Family Farms, Inc.
33750 Moranda Rd
831 675-2154

(P-77)
CENTRAL COAST AGRICULTURE INC (PA)
0701 Santa Rosa Rd, Buellton
(93427-8400)
PHONE...........................805 694-8594
Thomas Martin, *CEO*
EMP: 25 **EST:** 2015
SALES (est): 21.85MM **Privately Held**
Web: www.ccagriculture.com
SIC: 0191 2099 General farms, primarily crop
; Food preparations, nec

(P-78)
COLORADO FARMS LLC
400 Camarillo Ranch Rd Ste 107, Camarillo
(93012-5901)
PHONE...........................805 389-0401
Renato Martinez, *
EMP: 200 **EST:** 2005
SALES (est): 2.28MM **Privately Held**
SIC: 0191 General farms, primarily crop

(P-79)
CRYSTAL ORGANIC FARMS LLC
10000 Stockdale Hwy Ste 200, Bakersfield
(93311-3603)
PHONE...........................661 845-5200
Jeff Meger, *Pr*
EMP: 70 **EST:** 2003
SALES (est): 735.43K
SALES (corp-wide): 577.4MM **Privately Held**
SIC: 0191 General farms, primarily crop
PA: Grimmway Enterprises, Inc.
12064 Buena Vista Blvd
800 301-3101

(P-80)
DV CUSTOM FARMING LLC
2101 Mettler Frontage Rd E, Bakersfield
(93307-9649)
PHONE...........................661 858-2888
EMP: 80 **EST:** 2004
SALES (est): 2.49MM **Privately Held**
SIC: 0191 General farms, primarily crop

(P-81)
GREENHEART FARMS INC
Also Called: Greenheart
902 Zenon Way, Arroyo Grande
(93420-5807)
PHONE...........................805 481-2234
Hoy Buell, *CEO*
Henry Katzenstein, *
Leo Wolf, *
▲ **EMP:** 350 **EST:** 1979
SQ FT: 225,000
SALES (est): 18.19MM **Privately Held**
Web: www.greenheartfarms.com
SIC: 0191 General farms, primarily crop

(P-82)
GRIMMWAY ENTERPRISES INC
Also Called: Premiere Packing
6301 Zerker Rd, Shafter (93263-9628)
P.O. Box 81498 (93380-1498)
PHONE...........................661 399-0844
Randy Mower, *VP*
EMP: 112
SALES (corp-wide): 577.4MM **Privately Held**
Web: www.grimmway.com
SIC: 0191 0174 General farms, primarily crop
; Citrus fruits
PA: Grimmway Enterprises, Inc.
12064 Buena Vista Blvd
800 301-3101

(P-83)
JOE HEGER FARMS LLC
1625 Drew Rd, El Centro (92243-9584)
PHONE...........................760 353-5111
EMP: 150 **EST:** 1000
SALES (est): 4.43MM **Privately Held**
SIC: 0191 General farms, primarily crop

(P-84)
RANCHO LAGUNA FARMS LLC
2410 W Main St, Santa Maria (93458-9712)
P.O. Box 6617 (93456-6617)
PHONE...........................805 925-7805
Larry Ferini, *Managing Member*
Tracy Ferini, *
EMP: 100 **EST:** 1996
SALES (est): 4.99MM **Privately Held**
Web: www.lagunaproduce.com
SIC: 0191 General farms, primarily crop

(P-85)
REITER AFFL COMPANIES LLC
1755 E Stowell Rd, Santa Maria
(93454-8002)
PHONE...........................805 346-1073
Jesus Madrazo, *Mgr*
EMP: 87
SALES (corp-wide): 43.32MM **Privately Held**
Web: www.berry.net
SIC: 0191 General farms, primarily crop
PA: Reiter Affiliated Companies, Llc
730 S A St
805 483-1000

(P-86)
SAN DIEGO FARMS LLC
519 Cassou Rd, San Marcos (92069-9711)
PHONE...........................760 736-4072
EMP: 111
SALES (corp-wide): 17.43MM **Privately Held**
Web: www.freshorigins.com
SIC: 0191 General farms, primarily crop
PA: San Diego Farms Llc
570 Quarry Rd
760 736-4072

(P-87)
SCARBOROUGH FARMS INC
731 Pacific Ave, Oxnard (93030-7322)
P.O. Box 1267 (93032-1267)
PHONE...........................805 483-9113
Ann Stein, *Pr*
Wayne G Jansen, *
Ann Stein, *VP*
EMP: 150 **EST:** 1986
SALES (est): 9.21MM **Privately Held**
Web: www.scarboroughfarms.com
SIC: 0191 General farms, primarily crop

(P-88)
TREESAP FARMS LLC
Also Called: Everde Growers
2500 Rainbow Valley Blvd, Fallbrook
(92028-9778)
PHONE...........................760 990-7770
Jonathan Saperstein, *Brnch Mgr*
EMP: 166
SALES (corp-wide): 141.6MM **Privately Held**
Web: www.everde.com
SIC: 0191 General farms, primarily crop
PA: Treesap Farms, Llc
5151 Mtchlldale St Ste B2
713 613-5600

0241 Dairy Farms

(P-89)
ALTA-DENA CERTIFIED DAIRY LLC (DH)
17637 E Valley Blvd, City Of Industry
(91744-5731)
PHONE...........................626 964-6401
Jack Tewers, *
Steve Schaffer, *
Bob Pettigrew, *
EMP: 370 **EST:** 1945
SQ FT: 100,000
SALES (est): 10.81MM
SALES (corp-wide): 21.72B **Privately Held**
Web: www.altadenadairy.com
SIC: 0241 Dairy farms
HQ: Dean West Ii, Llc
2515 Mckinney Ave # 1100
Dallas TX 75201

(P-90)
DFA DAIRY BRANDS FLUID LLC
17851 Railroad St, City Of Industry
(91748-1118)
PHONE...........................800 395-7004
EMP: 326
SALES (corp-wide): 21.72B **Privately Held**
Web: www.dfamilk.com
SIC: 0241 Dairy farms
HQ: Dfa Dairy Brands Fluid, Llc
1405 N 98th St
Kansas City KS 66111
816 801-6455

(P-91)
HOLLANDIA DAIRY INC (PA)
622 E Mission Rd, San Marcos
(92069-1999)
PHONE...........................760 744-3222
TOLL FREE: 800
Peter De Jong, *CEO*
Patrick Schallberger, *
Arie H Dejong, *
EMP: 185 **EST:** 1950
SQ FT: 20,000
SALES (est): 44.68MM
SALES (corp-wide): 44.68MM **Privately Held**
Web: www.hollandiadairy.com
SIC: 0241 Milk production

(P-92)
MAPLE DAIRY LP
Also Called: Maple Dairy
15857 Bear Mountain Blvd, Bakersfield
(93311-9413)
PHONE...........................661 396-9600
John Bos, *Pt*
A J Bos, *Pt*
EMP: 75 **EST:** 1998
SALES (est): 8.4MM **Privately Held**
Web: www.makinmilk.com
SIC: 0241 Dairy farms

0252 Chicken Eggs

(P-93)
DEMLER BROTHERS LLC
25818 Highway 78, Ramona (92065-6309)
PHONE...........................760 789-2457
EMP: 99 **EST:** 2016
SALES (est): 4.81MM **Privately Held**
SIC: 0252 Chicken eggs

0273 Animal Aquaculture

(P-94)
RUNNING TIDE TECHNOLOGIES INC
1590 Rosecrans Ave, Manhattan Beach
(90266-3727)
P.O. Box 10304 (04104-0304)
PHONE...........................207 835-7010
Matthew Odlin, *CEO*
Justine Simon, *
EMP: 88 **EST:** 2017
SALES (est): 7.97MM **Privately Held**
Web: www.runningtide.com
SIC: 0273 Animal aquaculture

0279 Animal Specialties, Nec

(P-95)
HONEY ISABELLS INC
Also Called: Isabell's Honey Farm
539 N Glenoaks Blvd Ste 207b, Burbank
(91502-3208)
PHONE...........................800 708-8485
Oganes Kabakchuzyan, *CEO*
EMP: 46 **EST:** 2019
SALES (est): 2.16MM **Privately Held**
Web: www.isabellshoneyfarm.com

SIC: 0279 2099 Apiary (bee and honey farm) ; Honey, strained and bottled

0291 General Farms, Primarily Animals

(P-96)
BAJA FRESH SUPERMARKET
Also Called: Monrovia Ranch Market
14827 Seventh St, Victorville (92395-4023)
P.O. Box 661912 (91066-1912)
PHONE..........................760 843-7730
Franco Duenas, *Brnch Mgr*
EMP: 330
SIC: 0291 General farms, primarily animals
PA: E & T Foods, Inc.
　　328 W Huntington Dr

(P-97)
R RANCH MARKET
1112 Walnut Ave, Tustin (92780-5607)
PHONE..........................714 573-1182
Jubira Martinez, *Owner*
EMP: 290 EST: 2011
SALES (est): 1.02MM
SALES (corp-wide): 28.16MM **Privately Held**
Web: www.rranchmarkets.com
SIC: 0291 General farms, primarily animals
PA: R-Ranch Market, Incorporated
　　13985 Live Oak Ave
　　626 814-2900

(P-98)
SHARP HEALTHCARE
Also Called: Sharp Rees-Stealy Med Group
1400 E Palomar St, Chula Vista (91913-1800)
PHONE..........................619 397-3088
Donna Mills, *CEO*
EMP: 72
SALES (corp-wide): 1.9B **Privately Held**
Web: www.sharp.com
SIC: 0291 General farms, primarily animals
PA: Sharp Healthcare
　　8695 Spectrum Ctr Blvd
　　858 499-4000

(P-99)
TAWA SUPERMARKET INC
Also Called: 99 Ranch Market
4024 Grand Ave, Chino (91710-5436)
PHONE..........................909 760-8899
EMP: 112
SALES (corp-wide): 490.41MM **Privately Held**
Web: www.99ranch.com
SIC: 0291 General farms, primarily animals
PA: Tawa Supermarket, Inc.
　　6281 Regio Ave
　　714 521-8899

0711 Soil Preparation Services

(P-100)
AC IRRIGATION HOLDCO LLC
4700 Stockdale Hwy, Bakersfield (93309-2654)
PHONE..........................661 368-3550
Derek Yurosek, *Managing Member*
Jonathan Thomas, *
EMP: 163 EST: 2018
SALES (est): 1.63MM **Privately Held**
SIC: 0711 Soil preparation services

0721 Crop Planting And Protection

(P-101)
SUNRIDGE NURSERIES INC
441 Vineland Rd, Bakersfield (93307-9556)
PHONE..........................661 363-8463
Craig Stoller, *CEO*
Glen Stoller, *
Terrie Stoller, *
EMP: 70 EST: 1977
SQ FT: 60,000
SALES (est): 13.44MM **Privately Held**
Web: www.sunridgenurseries.com
SIC: 0721 Vines, cultivation of

0722 Crop Harvesting

(P-102)
BOSWELL PROPERTIES INC
101 W Walnut St, Pasadena (91103-3636)
PHONE..........................626 583-3000
EMP: 410 EST: 1982
SALES (est): 478.81K
SALES (corp-wide): 370.2MM **Privately Held**
Web: www.perfectdomain.com
SIC: 0722 6552 Cotton, machine harvesting services; Subdividers and developers, nec
PA: J. G. Boswell Company
　　101 W Walnut St
　　626 583-3000

0723 Crop Preparation Services For Market

(P-103)
APEEL TECHNOLOGY INC (PA)
Also Called: Apeel Sciences
71 S Los Carneros Rd, Goleta (93117-5506)
PHONE..........................805 203-0146
Luiz Beling, *CEO*
William Strong, *
EMP: 283 EST: 2012
SALES (est): 48.97MM
SALES (corp-wide): 48.97MM **Privately Held**
Web: www.apeel.com
SIC: 0723 2099 Crop preparation services for market; Almond pastes

(P-104)
BOSKOVICH FARMS INC (PA)
711 Diaz Ave, Oxnard (93030-7247)
P.O. Box 1352 (93032-1352)
PHONE..........................805 487-2299
George S Boskovich Junior, *CEO*
Philip J Boskovich Junior, *Pr*
▲ EMP: 205 EST: 1915
SQ FT: 7,000
SALES (est): 46.32MM
SALES (corp-wide): 46.32MM **Privately Held**
Web: www.boskovichfarms.com
SIC: 0723 5812 0161 Crop preparation services for market; Eating places; Rooted vegetable farms

(P-105)
CAL TREEHOUSE ALMONDS LLC
2115 Road 144, Delano (93215-9524)
P.O. Box 286 (93216-0286)
PHONE..........................661 725-6334
Robert Houston, *Pr*

EMP: 123
SQ FT: 68,803
SALES (corp-wide): 24.96MM **Privately Held**
Web: www.treehousealmonds.com
SIC: 0723 Crop preparation services for market
PA: Treehouse California Almonds Llc
　　6914 Road 160
　　559 757-5020

(P-106)
CORONA - CLLEGE HTS ORNGE LMON
8000 Lincoln Ave, Riverside (92504-4343)
PHONE..........................951 359-6451
John Demshki, *Pr*
▼ EMP: 300 EST: 1905
SQ FT: 180,000
SALES (est): 4.44MM **Privately Held**
Web: www.cchcitrus.com
SIC: 0723 Fruit (fresh) packing services

(P-107)
FISHER RANCH LLC
10610 Ice Plant Rd, Blythe (92225-2757)
PHONE..........................760 922-4151
EMP: 99 EST: 1998
SALES (est): 3.34MM **Privately Held**
Web: www.fisherranch.com
SIC: 0723 Field crops, except cash grains, market preparation services

(P-108)
GRIMMWAY ENTERPRISES INC
6101 Zerker Rd, Shafter (93263-9611)
P.O. Box 81498 (93380-1498)
PHONE..........................661 393-3320
Bob Grimm, *Prin*
EMP: 446
SALES (corp-wide): 577.4MM **Privately Held**
Web: www.grimmway.com
SIC: 0723 Vegetable packing services
PA: Grimmway Enterprises, Inc.
　　12064 Buena Vista Blvd
　　800 301-3101

(P-109)
GRIMMWAY ENTERPRISES INC
Also Called: Grimmway Frozen Foods
830 Sycamore Rd, Arvin (93203-2132)
P.O. Box 81498 (93380-1498)
PHONE..........................661 854-6250
Brandon Grimm, *Mgr*
EMP: 474
SALES (corp-wide): 577.4MM **Privately Held**
Web: www.grimmway.com
SIC: 0723 Vegetable packing services
PA: Grimmway Enterprises, Inc.
　　12064 Buena Vista Blvd
　　800 301-3101

(P-110)
GRIMMWAY ENTERPRISES INC
Also Called: Grimmway Farms
11412 Malaga Rd, Arvin (93203-9641)
P.O. Box 81498 (93380-1498)
PHONE..........................661 854-6200
EMP: 432
SALES (corp-wide): 577.4MM **Privately Held**
Web: www.grimmway.com
SIC: 0723 4783 Vegetable packing services; Containerization of goods for shipping
PA: Grimmway Enterprises, Inc.
　　12064 Buena Vista Blvd
　　800 301-3101

(P-111)
GRIMMWAY ENTERPRISES INC
Also Called: Grimmway Farms
6900 Mountain View Rd, Bakersfield (93307-9627)
P.O. Box 81498 (93380-1498)
PHONE..........................661 845-5200
Bob Grimm, *Owner*
EMP: 200
SALES (corp-wide): 1.86B **Privately Held**
Web: www.grimmway.com
SIC: 0723 Vegetable packing services
PA: Grimmway Enterprises, Inc.
　　12064 Buena Vista Blvd
　　800 301-3101

(P-112)
GUADALUPE COOLING COMPANY INC
2040 Guadalupe Rd, Guadalupe (93434)
PHONE..........................805 343-2331
TOLL FREE: 800
Dan Vincent, *Mgr*
EMP: 73
SALES (corp-wide): 7.25MM **Privately Held**
Web: www.westernprecooling.com
SIC: 0723 Vacuum cooling
PA: Guadalupe Cooling Company Inc
　　2040 Guadalupe Rd
　　805 249-3110

(P-113)
KERN RIDGE GROWERS LLC
25429 Barbara St, Arvin (93203-9748)
P.O. Box 455 (93203-0455)
PHONE..........................661 854-3141
▼ EMP: 500 EST: 1973
SQ FT: 53,000
SALES (est): 48.27MM **Privately Held**
Web: www.kernridge.com
SIC: 0723 5148 Vegetable packing services; Vegetables, fresh

(P-114)
LIMONEIRA COMPANY (PA)
Also Called: Limoneira
1141 Cummings Rd, Santa Paula (93060-9709)
PHONE..........................805 525-5541
Harold S Edwards, *Pr*
Scott S Slater, *
Mark Palamountain, *Corporate Secretary*
◆ EMP: 75 EST: 1893
SALES (est): 179.9MM
SALES (corp-wide): 179.9MM **Publicly Held**
Web: www.limoneira.com
SIC: 0723 0174 0179 6531 Fruit (fresh) packing services; Citrus fruits; Avocado orchard; Real estate agents and managers

(P-115)
MISSION PRODUCE INC (PA)
Also Called: MISSION
2710 Camino Del Sol, Oxnard (93030-7967)
P.O. Box 5267 (93031)
PHONE..........................805 981-3650
◆ EMP: 98 EST: 1983
SALES (est): 1.23B
SALES (corp-wide): 1.23B **Publicly Held**
Web: www.missionproduce.com
SIC: 0723 0179 5431 Fruit (fresh) packing services; Avocado orchard; Fruit stands or markets

(P-116)
MONARCH NUT COMPANY LLC
Also Called: Munger Farms
786 Road 188, Delano (93215-9508)
PHONE..................661 725-6458
Kamie Munger, *Managing Member*
David Munger, *
◆ **EMP:** 250 **EST:** 1986
SQ FT: 20,000
SALES (est): 19.2MM **Privately Held**
SIC: 0723 7389 Tree nuts (general) hulling and shelling services; Packaging and labeling services

(P-117)
RAMCO ENTERPRISES LP
Also Called: Ramco Employment Services
520 E 3rd St Ste B, Oxnard (93030-0182)
PHONE..................805 486-9328
Jesse Espinoza, *Brnch Mgr*
EMP: 446
SALES (corp-wide): 32.34MM **Privately Held**
Web: www.ramcoenterpriseslp.com
SIC: 0723 Crop preparation services for market
PA: Ramco Enterprises, L.P.
710 La Guardia St
831 758-5272

(P-118)
SATICOY LEMON ASSOCIATION (PA)
Also Called: Saticoy Fruit Exchange
103 N Peck Rd, Santa Paula (93060-3099)
P.O. Box 46 (93061-0046)
PHONE..................805 654-6500
Glenn A Miller, *Pr*
Jerry Pogorzelski, *
Jima Garrett, *
▲ **EMP:** 100 **EST:** 1933
SALES (est): 21.99MM
SALES (corp-wide): 21.99MM **Privately Held**
Web: www.saticoylemon.com
SIC: 0723 Fruit (fresh) packing services

(P-119)
SUN WORLD INTERNATIONAL INC (PA)
16351 Driver Rd, Bakersfield (93308-9733)
P.O. Box 80298 (93380-0298)
PHONE..................661 392-5000
Keith Brackpool, *Ch Bd*
Timothy J Shaheen, *
Bernardo Calvo, *
Gerardo Lugo, *Chief Commercial Officer*
◆ **EMP:** 1500 **EST:** 1976
SQ FT: 160,000
SALES (est): 44.92MM **Privately Held**
Web: www.sun-world.com
SIC: 0723 0172 0174 0175 Vegetable crops market preparation services; Grapes; Citrus fruits; Deciduous tree fruits

(P-120)
TALLEY FARMS
2900 Lopez Dr, Arroyo Grande (93420-4999)
P.O. Box 360 (93421-0360)
PHONE..................805 489-2508
Brian Talley, *Pr*
Rayn Talley, *
Todd Talley, *
Rosemary Talley, *
EMP: 175 **EST:** 1954
SQ FT: 2,000
SALES (est): 9.04MM **Privately Held**
Web: www.talleyfarmsfreshharvest.com

SIC: 0723 0161 Vegetable packing services; Vegetables and melons

(P-121)
TANIMURA ANTLE FRESH FOODS INC
Also Called: Salad Time Farms
4401 Foxdale St, Baldwin Park (91706-2161)
P.O. Box 4070 (93912-4070)
PHONE..................831 424-6100
Randy Sipled, *Mgr*
EMP: 561
SALES (corp-wide): 321.47MM **Privately Held**
Web: www.taproduce.com
SIC: 0723 Vegetable packing services
PA: Tanimura & Antle Fresh Foods, Inc.
1 Harris Rd
831 455-2950

(P-122)
WEST PAK AVOCADO INC (PA)
Also Called: Avocado Packer & Shipper
38655 Sky Canyon Dr, Murrieta (92563-2536)
PHONE..................951 296-5757
▲ **EMP:** 110 **EST:** 1982
SALES (est): 96.6MM
SALES (corp-wide): 96.6MM **Privately Held**
Web: www.westpakavocado.com
SIC: 0723 Crop preparation services for market

(P-123)
WONDERFUL CITRUS PACKING LLC (HQ)
Also Called: Paramount Citrus Packing Co
1901 S Lexington St, Delano (93215-9207)
PHONE..................661 720-2400
Craig B Cooper, *Managing Member*
◆ **EMP:** 273 **EST:** 1950
SQ FT: 400,000
SALES (est): 280.36MM
SALES (corp-wide): 2.04B **Privately Held**
Web: www.wonderfulcitrus.com
SIC: 0723 0174 2033 Fruit (fresh) packing services; Orange grove; Fruit juices: fresh
PA: The Wonderful Company Llc
11444 W Olympic Blvd Fl 1
310 966-5700

(P-124)
WONDERFUL COMPANY LLC
5001 California Ave, Bakersfield (93309-1671)
PHONE..................559 781-7438
EMP: 1013
SALES (corp-wide): 2.04B **Privately Held**
Web: www.wonderful.com
SIC: 0723 Fruit crops market preparation services
PA: The Wonderful Company Llc
11444 W Olympic Blvd Fl 1
310 966-5700

(P-125)
WONDERFUL COMPANY LLC
6801 E Lerdo Hwy, Shafter (93263-9610)
PHONE..................661 399-4456
EMP: 1583
SALES (corp-wide): 2.04B **Privately Held**
Web: www.wonderful.com
SIC: 0723 Fruit crops market preparation services
PA: The Wonderful Company Llc
11444 W Olympic Blvd Fl 1
310 966-5700

(P-126)
WONDERFUL COMPANY LLC
11444 W Olympic Blvd Ste 210, Los Angeles (90064-1559)
PHONE..................661 720-2609
Craig B Cooper, *Mgr*
EMP: 380
SALES (corp-wide): 2.04B **Privately Held**
Web: www.wonderful.com
SIC: 0723 Fruit (fresh) packing services
PA: The Wonderful Company Llc
11444 W Olympic Blvd Fl 1
310 966-5700

0742 Veterinary Services, Specialties

(P-127)
DELPHIC ENTERPRISES INC
Also Called: Pinnacle Veterinary Center
23026 Soledad Canyon Rd, Santa Clarita (91350-2634)
PHONE..................661 254-2000
Nirip Shokar, *Pr*
EMP: 72 **EST:** 2016
SALES (est): 1.98MM
SALES (corp-wide): 83.63MM **Privately Held**
Web: www.vetsantaclarita.com
SIC: 0742 Animal hospital services, pets and other animal specialties
HQ: People, Pets And Vets, Llc
141 Longwater Dr
Norwell MA 02061
360 866-7331

(P-128)
LM VETERINARY ENTERPRISES INC
8725 Santa Monica Blvd, West Hollywood (90069-4507)
PHONE..................310 659-5287
EMP: 71
SALES (corp-wide): 282.61K **Privately Held**
SIC: 0742 Veterinary services, specialties
PA: Lm Veterinary Enterprises, Inc.
1412 Huntington Dr

(P-129)
MERCY FOR ANIMALS INC
8033 W Sunset Blvd Ste 864, Los Angeles (90046-2401)
PHONE..................347 839-6464
Nathan Runkle, *CEO*
EMP: 136 **EST:** 2015
SALES (est): 29.24MM **Privately Held**
Web: www.mercyforanimals.org
SIC: 0742 Veterinary services, specialties

(P-130)
MOULTON ANIMAL HOSPITAL INC
27261 La Paz Rd Ste I, Laguna Beach (92677-3604)
PHONE..................949 831-7297
Stanley Creighton D.v.m., *Pr*
EMP: 75 **EST:** 1989
SALES (est): 865.27K
SALES (corp-wide): 595.04MM **Privately Held**
SIC: 0742 Animal hospital services, pets and other animal specialties
HQ: National Veterinary Associates, Inc.
1 Baxter Way
Westlake Village CA 91362
805 777-7722

(P-131)
PEOPLE PETS AND VETS LLC
Also Called: Prestige Animal Hospital South
10986 Sierra Ave Ste 400, Fontana (92337-7673)
PHONE..................909 453-4213
Sudeep Wahla, *Brnch Mgr*
EMP: 208
SALES (corp-wide): 83.63MM **Privately Held**
Web: www.prestigeanimalhospital.com
SIC: 0742 Animal hospital services, pets and other animal specialties
HQ: People, Pets And Vets, Llc
141 Longwater Dr
Norwell MA 02061
360 866-7331

(P-132)
PEOPLE PETS AND VETS LLC
Also Called: Prestige Animal Hospital North
16055 Sierra Lakes Pkwy Ste 100, Fontana (92336-4597)
PHONE..................909 329-2860
Sudeep S Wahla, *Brnch Mgr*
EMP: 244
SALES (corp-wide): 83.63MM **Privately Held**
Web: www.prestigeanimalhospital.com
SIC: 0742 Animal hospital services, pets and other animal specialties
HQ: People, Pets And Vets, Llc
141 Longwater Dr
Norwell MA 02061
360 866-7331

(P-133)
VALLEY ANIMAL MEDICAL CENTER
46920 Jefferson St, Indio (92201-7920)
PHONE..................760 342-4711
Gary Homec, *Pr*
EMP: 700 **EST:** 1979
SQ FT: 12,000
SALES (est): 737.89K **Privately Held**
Web: www.animalmedicalvets.com
SIC: 0742 Animal hospital services, pets and other animal specialties
PA: Pet Drx Veterinary Group, Inc.
560 South Winchester Blvd

(P-134)
VCA ANIMAL HOSPITALS INC
Also Called: VCA West Los Angles Anmal Hosp
1900 S Sepulveda Blvd, Los Angeles (90025-5620)
PHONE..................310 473-2951
David Bruyette, *Brnch Mgr*
EMP: 109
SALES (corp-wide): 42.84B **Privately Held**
Web: www.vca.com
SIC: 0742 Animal hospital services, pets and other animal specialties
HQ: Vca Animal Hospitals, Inc.
12401 W Olympic Blvd
Los Angeles CA 90064

(P-135)
VETERINARY PRACTICE ASSOC INC
Also Called: Veterinary Specialty Hospital
10435 Sorrento Valley Rd, San Diego (92121-1607)
PHONE..................949 833-9020
Keith P Richter, *CEO*
EMP: 150 **EST:** 2004
SQ FT: 26,280
SALES (est): 3.72MM **Privately Held**
Web: www.vshsd.com

SIC: 0742 Animal hospital services, pets and other animal specialties

(P-136)
VICAR OPERATING INC (DH)
Also Called: Veterinary Centers America VCA
12401 W Olympic Blvd, Los Angeles
(90064-1022)
PHONE....................310 571-6500
Robert Antin, *Pr*
EMP: 91 EST: 1985
SALES (est): 22.23MM
SALES (corp-wide): 42.84B **Privately Held**
Web: www.vcaantech.com
SIC: 0742 Animal hospital services, pets and other animal specialties
HQ: Vca Inc.
　　12401 W Olympic Blvd
　　Los Angeles CA 90064
　　310 571-6500

0751 Livestock Services, Except Veterinary

(P-137)
AMERICAN BEEF PACKERS INC
13677 Yorba Ave, Chino (91710-5059)
PHONE....................909 628-4888
Lawrence Miller, *Pr*
EMP: 250 EST: 2008
SALES (est): 20.7MM **Privately Held**
SIC: 0751 2011 5147 Slaughtering: custom livestock services; Beef products, from beef slaughtered on site; Meats and meat products

---

0752 Animal Specialty Services

(P-138)
OJAI RAPTOR CENTER
370 Baldwin Rd, Ojai (93023-9705)
P.O. Box 182 (93022-0182)
PHONE....................805 649-6884
Kimberly Stroud, *Dir*
EMP: 70 EST: 2000
SALES (est): 717.9K **Privately Held**
Web: www.ojairaptorcenter.org
SIC: 0752 Shelters, animal

0761 Farm Labor Contractors

(P-139)
JUAN CARLOS ALVARDO
Also Called: Alvardo Contracting
1301 Willow Pl, Wasco (93280-2557)
PHONE....................661 758-6128
Juan Alvarado, *Owner*
▲ EMP: 100 EST: 1993
SALES (est): 358.79K **Privately Held**
SIC: 0761 Crew leaders, farm labor: contracting services

0762 Farm Management Services

(P-140)
AG-WISE ENTERPRISES INC (PA)
5100 California Ave Ste 209, Bakersfield
(93309-0716)
P.O. Box 9729 (93389-9729)
PHONE....................661 325-1567
Bruce Berreta, *Pr*
Ed Ray, *

EMP: 150 EST: 1983
SQ FT: 4,400
SALES (est): 16.42MM **Privately Held**
Web: www.ag-wiseinc.com
SIC: 0762 Farm management services

(P-141)
ESPARZA ENTERPRISES INC
251 W Main St Ste G&F, Brawley
(92227-2201)
PHONE....................760 344-2031
Luis Esparza, *Brnch Mgr*
EMP: 792
SALES (corp-wide): 135MM **Privately Held**
Web: www.esparzainc.com
SIC: 0762 Farm management services
PA: Esparza Enterprises, Inc.
　　3851 Fruitvale Ave
　　661 831-0002

(P-142)
ILLUME AGRICULTURE LLC
9100 Ming Ave Ste 200, Bakersfield
(93311-1329)
P.O. Box 22020 (93390-2020)
PHONE....................661 587-5198
Jeffrey Fabbri, *Managing Member*
EMP: 120 EST: 1939
SALES (est): 4.7MM **Privately Held**
Web: www.illumeag.com
SIC: 0762 5963 2099 Farm management services; Food services, direct sales; Box lunches, for sale off premises

(P-143)
LARRY JACINTO FARMING INC
9555 N Wabash Ave, Redlands
(92374-2714)
P.O. Box 275 (92359-0275)
PHONE....................909 794-2276
Larry Jacinto, *Pr*
Dennis Drexler, *
EMP: 100 EST: 1992
SQ FT: 3,000
SALES (est): 2.05MM **Privately Held**
Web: www.jacintofarms.com
SIC: 0762 Farm management services

(P-144)
MESA VINEYARD MANAGEMENT INC (PA)
110 Gibson Rd, Templeton (93465-9510)
P.O. Box 789 (93465-0789)
PHONE....................805 434-4100
Dana Merrill, *Pr*
Matt Andrus, *
EMP: 75 EST: 1988
SQ FT: 3,200
SALES (est): 6.92MM **Privately Held**
Web: www.mesavineyard.com
SIC: 0762 Vineyard management and maintenance services

(P-145)
SUN PACIFIC FARMING COOP INC
Also Called: Sun Pacific Farms
33374 Lerdo Hwy, Bakersfield
(93308-9782)
PHONE....................661 399-0376
Ernie Larson, *Mgr*
EMP: 96
SALES (corp-wide): 6.36MM **Privately Held**
Web: www.sunpacific.com
SIC: 0762 5148 0174 Citrus grove management and maintenance services; Fresh fruits and vegetables; Citrus fruits
PA: Sun Pacific Farming Cooperative, Inc.
　　1250 E Myer Ave

559 592-7121

0781 Landscape Counseling And Planning

(P-146)
AMERICAN LANDSCAPE INC
Also Called: American Golf Construction
7013 Owensmouth Ave, Canoga Park
(91303-2006)
PHONE....................818 999-2041
Gary Peterson, *Pr*
Jamie Tsui, *
▲ EMP: 250 EST: 1973
SQ FT: 14,000
SALES (est): 892.58K **Privately Held**
Web: www.americanlandscape.com
SIC: 0781 Landscape services

(P-147)
AMERICAN LANDSCAPE MGT INC (PA)
Also Called: Custom Lawn Services
7013 Owensmouth Ave, Canoga Park
(91303-2006)
PHONE....................818 999-2041
Mickey Strauss, *Pr*
Gary Peterson, *
EMP: 125 EST: 1975
SQ FT: 14,000
SALES (est): 1.92MM **Privately Held**
Web: www.americanlandscape.com
SIC: 0781 Landscape services

(P-148)
AZTECA LANDSCAPE
4073 Mennes Ave, Riverside (92509-6722)
PHONE....................951 369-9210
EMP: 85
SIC: 0781 Landscape services
PA: Azteca Landscape
　　1180 Olympic Dr Ste 207

(P-149)
BENCHMARK LANDSCAPE SVCS INC
12575 Stowe Dr, Poway (92064-6805)
PHONE....................858 513-7190
John A Mohns, *Pr*
Sharon R Mohns, *
EMP: 220 EST: 1984
SQ FT: 18,000
SALES (est): 8.07MM **Privately Held**
Web: www.benchmarklandscape.com
SIC: 0781 Landscape services

(P-150)
BENNETT ENTPS A CAL LDSCP CNTG
Also Called: Bennett Landscape
25889 Belle Porte Ave, Harbor City
(90710-3393)
PHONE....................310 534-3543
Sean Bennett, *Pr*
EMP: 90 EST: 1977
SQ FT: 10,500
SALES (est): 6.93MM **Privately Held**
Web: www.bennett-landscape.com
SIC: 0781 Landscape services

(P-151)
BRIGHTVIEW COMPANIES LLC
11555 Coley River Cir, Fountain Valley
(92708-4224)
PHONE....................714 437-1586
EMP: 220
Web: www.brightview.com

SIC: 0781 Landscape services
PA: Brightview Companies, Llc
　　2275 Research Blvd

(P-152)
BRIGHTVIEW GOLF MAINT INC
405 Glen Annie Rd, Santa Barbara
(93117-1427)
PHONE....................805 968-6400
Richard Hasah, *Mgr*
EMP: 116
SALES (corp-wide): 2.77B **Publicly Held**
SIC: 0781 Landscape services
HQ: Brightview Golf Maintenance, Inc.
　　980 Jolly Rd Ste 300
　　Blue Bell PA 19422
　　818 223-8500

(P-153)
BRIGHTVIEW LANDSCAPE DEV INC
8450 Miramar Pl, San Diego (92121-2528)
PHONE....................858 458-9900
Vince Germann, *Mgr*
EMP: 300
SQ FT: 16,050
SALES (corp-wide): 2.77B **Publicly Held**
Web: www.brightview.com
SIC: 0781 Landscape services
HQ: Brightview Landscape Development, Inc.
　　27001 Agoura Rd Ste 350
　　Calabasas CA 91301
　　818 223-8500

(P-154)
BRIGHTVIEW LANDSCAPE SVCS INC
8500 Miramar Pl, San Diego (92121-2530)
PHONE....................858 458-1900
Patrick Ceatter, *Mgr*
EMP: 114
SALES (corp-wide): 2.77B **Publicly Held**
Web: www.brightview.com
SIC: 0781 Landscape services
HQ: Brightview Landscape Services, Inc.
　　27001 Agoura Rd Ste 350
　　Agoura Hills CA 91301
　　818 223-8500

(P-155)
BRIGHTVIEW LANDSCAPE SVCS INC
8726 Calabash Ave, Fontana (92335-3040)
PHONE....................909 946-3196
Leon Vitort, *Brnch Mgr*
EMP: 114
SALES (corp-wide): 2.77B **Publicly Held**
Web: www.brightview.com
SIC: 0781 Landscape services
HQ: Brightview Landscape Services, Inc.
　　27001 Agoura Rd Ste 350
　　Agoura Hills CA 91301
　　818 223-8500

(P-156)
BRIGHTVIEW LANDSCAPE SVCS INC
6464 Hollister Ave Ste 8, Goleta
(93117-3110)
PHONE....................805 642-9300
Frank Annino, *Mgr*
EMP: 123
SALES (corp-wide): 2.77B **Publicly Held**
Web: www.brightview.com
SIC: 0781 Landscape services
HQ: Brightview Landscape Services, Inc.
　　27001 Agoura Rd Ste 350
　　Agoura Hills CA 91301
　　818 223-8500

(P-157)

BRIGHTVIEW LANDSCAPE SVCS INC

1960 S Yale St, Santa Ana (92704-3929)
PHONE..............................714 546-7843
Dave Hanson, *Mgr*
EMP: 276
SALES (corp-wide): 2.77B **Publicly Held**
Web: www.brightview.com
SIC: 0781 0782 Landscape services; Lawn and garden services
HQ: Brightview Landscape Services, Inc.
   27001 Agoura Rd Ste 350
   Agoura Hills CA 91301
   818 223-8500

(P-158)

BRIGHTVIEW LANDSCAPE SVCS INC

32202 Paseo Adelanto, San Juan Capistrano (92675-3601)
PHONE..............................714 546-7843
EMP: 104
SALES (corp-wide): 2.77B **Publicly Held**
Web: www.brightview.com
SIC: 0781 Landscape services
HQ: Brightview Landscape Services, Inc.
   27001 Agoura Rd Ste 350
   Agoura Hills CA 91301
   818 223-8500

(P-159)

BRIGHTVIEW LANDSCAPE SVCS INC

17813 S Main St Ste 105, Gardena (90248-3542)
PHONE..............................310-327-8700
Andrea Musick, *Mgr*
EMP: 266
SQ FT: 1,530
SALES (corp-wide): 2.77B **Publicly Held**
Web: www.brightview.com
SIC: 0781 0782 Landscape services; Landscape contractors
HQ: Brightview Landscape Services, Inc.
   27001 Agoura Rd Ste 350
   Agoura Hills CA 91301
   818 223-8500

(P-160)

BRIGHTVIEW TREE COMPANY

P.O. Box 1611 (92307-0031)
PHONE..............................760 955-2560
EMP: 86
SALES (corp-wide): 4.3B **Publicly Held**
Web: www.devilmountainnursery.com
SIC: 0781 Landscape services
HQ: Brightview Tree Company
   24151 Ventura Blvd # 100
   Calabasas CA 91302
   818 223-0500

(P-161)

CALIFORNIA SKATEPARKS

285 N Benson Ave, Upland (91786-5614)
PHONE..............................909 949-1601
Joseph M Ciaglia Junior, *CEO*
Joseph M Ciaglia Junior, *Pr*
EMP: 150 **EST:** 1977
SALES (est): 3.42MM **Privately Held**
Web: www.californiaskateparks.com
SIC: 0781 Landscape services

(P-162)

CENTRESCAPES INC

165 Gentry St, Pomona (91767-2184)
PHONE..............................909 392-3303
Mark Marcus, *Pr*
Grace Loya, *

EMP: 88 **EST:** 1992
SQ FT: 7,000
SALES (est): 2.26MM **Privately Held**
Web: www.centrescapes.com
SIC: 0781 Landscape services

(P-163)

CONSERVE LANDCARE LLC

72265 Manufacturing Rd, Thousand Palms (92276-6615)
PHONE..............................760 343-1433
George Gonzalez, *CEO*
Jay Powell, *VP*
EMP: 78 **EST:** 2011
SALES (est): 972.38K **Privately Held**
Web: www.conservelandcare.com
SIC: 0781 Landscape services

(P-164)

CRESTVIEW LANDSCAPE INC

13949 Ventura Blvd, Sherman Oaks (91423-3584)
PHONE..............................818 962-7771
Harold Young, *CEO*
Augustine Bucio, *
EMP: 100 **EST:** 2020
SALES (est): 2.55MM **Privately Held**
Web: www.crestviewlandscape.com
SIC: 0781 Landscape services

(P-165)

DL LONG LANDSCAPING INC

5475 G St, Chino (91710-5233)
PHONE..............................909 628-5531
David L Long, *Pr*
EMP: 100 **EST:** 1974
SQ FT: 1,550
SALES (est): 3.1MM **Privately Held**
SIC: 0781 Landscape architects

(P-166)

EXECUTIVE LANDSCAPE INC

2131 Huffstatler St, Fallbrook (92028-8861)
P.O. Box P.O. Box 1075 (92088-1075)
PHONE..............................760 731-9036
Edwin Earle, *CEO*
Kathleen D Earle, *
Walter Earle, *
EMP: 230 **EST:** 1993
SQ FT: 1,800
SALES (est): 4.71MM **Privately Held**
Web: www.executivelandscapeinc.com
SIC: 0781 Landscape services

(P-167)

FENDERSCAPE INCORPORATED

Also Called: Proscape Landscape
1446 E Hill St, Signal Hill (00755-3527)
PHONE..............................562 988-2228
David Fender, *Pr*
Linda Fender, *
EMP: 127 **EST:** 1984
SQ FT: 1,893
SALES (est): 2.41MM **Privately Held**
Web: www.proscapelandscaping.com
SIC: 0781 Landscape services

(P-168)

FINLEYS TREE & LANDCARE INC

1209 W 228th St, Torrance (90502-2325)
PHONE..............................310 326-9818
Steve Finley, *Prin*
EMP: 150 **EST:** 2006
SALES (est): 2.78MM **Privately Held**
Web: www.finleystreeandlandcare.com
SIC: 0781 Landscape services

(P-169)

FS COMMERCIAL LANDSCAPE INC (PA)

5151 Pedley Rd, Riverside (92509-3937)
PHONE..............................951 360-7070
G John Wood, *Pr*
EMP: 75 **EST:** 1993
SQ FT: 1,500
SALES (est): 4.32MM **Privately Held**
Web: www.fscommerciallandscape.com
SIC: 0781 Landscape services

(P-170)

GOTHIC LANDSCAPING INC

Also Called: Gothic Grounds Mgmt
27413 Tourney Rd Ste 200, Valencia (91355-5606)
PHONE..............................661 257-5085
Ron Georgio, *Pr*
EMP: 121
SALES (corp-wide): 119.26MM **Privately Held**
Web: www.gothiclandscape.com
SIC: 0781 0782 Landscape services; Lawn and garden services
PA: Gothic Landscaping, Inc.
   27413 Tourney Rd
   661 678-1400

(P-171)

GREENSCREEN

Also Called: Atmospheric-Greenscreen
725 S Figueroa St Ste 1825, Los Angeles (90017-2827)
PHONE..............................310 837-0526
Ruth Katzenstein, *Pr*
John Souza, *CEO*
EMP: 34 **EST:** 1995
SQ FT: 1,200
SALES (est): 784.07K **Privately Held**
Web: www.tournesol.com
SIC: 0781 7363 3446 Landscape planning services; Help supply services; Architectural metalwork

(P-172)

HARVEST LANDSCAPE ENTPS INC (PA)

Also Called: Harvest Landscape Maintenance
8030 E Crystal Dr, Anaheim (92807-2524)
P.O. Box 3877 (92857-0877)
PHONE..............................714 693-8100
Stephen G Schinhofen, *CEO*
Robert Gavela, *CPO*
EMP: 156 **EST:** 2003
SALES (est): 22.52MM
SALES (corp-wide): 22.52MM **Privately Held**
Web: www.hlei.us
SIC: 0781 Landscape services

(P-173)

HEAVILAND ENTERPRISES INC

8710 Miramar Pl, San Diego (92121-2551)
PHONE..............................858 412-1576
EMP: 115
SALES (corp-wide): 8.26MM **Privately Held**
Web: www.brightview.com
SIC: 0781 Landscape services
PA: Heaviland Enterprises, Inc.
   2180 La Mirada Dr
   760 598-7065

(P-174)

HYDRO-DIG INC

700 E Sycamore St, Anaheim (92805-2831)
PHONE..............................714 772-9947
Martin C Rippens, *Pr*

Gary Tavan, *
EMP: 70 **EST:** 1964
SQ FT: 5,000
SALES (est): 308.3K **Privately Held**
SIC: 0781 Landscape architects

(P-175)

I PWLC INC

408 Olive Ave, Vista (92083-3438)
P.O. Box 3557 (92085-3557)
PHONE..............................760 630-0231
Richard Ruiz, *CEO*
EMP: 90 **EST:** 2004
SQ FT: 1,000
SALES (est): 2.37MM **Privately Held**
Web: www.pacwestlandcare.com
SIC: 0781 Landscape services

(P-176)

MARINA MAINTENANCE GROUP INC

Also Called: Marina Landscape Maint Inc
1900 S Lewis St, Anaheim (92805-6718)
PHONE..............................714 939-6600
Robert B Cowan, *CEO*
EMP: 450 **EST:** 2014
SALES (est): 2.64MM
SALES (corp-wide): 2.77B **Publicly Held**
Web: www.marinaco.com
SIC: 0781 Landscape services
HQ: Brightview Landscapes, Llc
   980 Jolly Rd Ste 300
   Blue Bell PA 19422
   484 567-7204

(P-177)

MERCHANTS LANDSCAPE SERVICES

8748 Industrial Ln # 1, Rancho Cucamonga (91730-4526)
PHONE..............................909 981-1022
Freddy Martinez, *Mgr*
EMP: 96
SALES (corp-wide): 54.62MM **Privately Held**
Web: www.merchantslandscape.com
SIC: 0781 Landscape planning services
HQ: Merchants Landscape Services, Inc
   1639 E Edinger Ave Ste C
   Santa Ana CA 92705
   714 972-8200

(P-178)

MISSION LDSCP COMPANIES INC

16672 Millikan Ave, Irvine (92606-5008)
P.O. Box 16069 (92623-6069)
PHONE..............................714 545-9962
David Dubois, *CEO*
Beth Du Boise, *
Cindy Clark, *
EMP: 200 **EST:** 1973
SQ FT: 11,000
SALES (est): 20.31MM **Privately Held**
Web: www.missionlandscape.com
SIC: 0781 Landscape services

(P-179)

NATURES IMAGE INC

20361 Hermana Cir, Lake Forest (92630-8701)
PHONE..............................949 680-4400
Michelle M Caruana, *CEO*
John Caruana, *
EMP: 95 **EST:** 1996
SQ FT: 13,800
SALES (est): 8.18MM **Privately Held**
Web: www.naturesimage.net

SIC: 0781 0782 Landscape services;
Landscape contractors

(P-180)
NIEVES LANDSCAPE INC
1629 E Edinger Ave, Santa Ana
(92705-5001)
PHONE....................714 835-7332
Gregorio Nieves, *Pr*
Patricia White, *
EMP: 150 **EST:** 1985
SALES (est): 5.98MM **Privately Held**
Web: www.nieveslandscape.com
SIC: 0781 Landscape services

(P-181)
NISSHO OF CALIFORNIA INC (PA)
1902 S Santa Fe Ave, Vista (92083-7721)
PHONE....................760 727-9719
Nobu J Kato, *CEO*
Ed Trotter, *
EMP: 111 **EST:** 1989
SQ FT: 10,000
SALES (est): 26.25MM
SALES (corp-wide): 26.25MM **Privately Held**
Web: www.nisshoca.com
SIC: 0781 0782 Landscape services; Turf installation services, except artificial

(P-182)
NN JAESCHKE INC
9610 Waples St, San Diego (92121-2992)
PHONE....................858 550-7900
Ned Heiskell, *Pr*
Kelley Brewster, *Ex VP*
EMP: 26 **EST:** 2004
SALES (est): 1.95MM **Privately Held**
Web: www.nnj.com
SIC: 0781 7349 1389 Landscape services; Janitorial service, contract basis; Construction, repair, and dismantling services

(P-183)
PAC WEST LAND CARE INC
Also Called: Pacific West Tree Service
408 Olive Ave, Vista (92083-3438)
P.O. Box 99 (92085-0099)
PHONE....................760 630-0231
Barry Blue, *Pr*
EMP: 130 **EST:** 1979
SQ FT: 3,000
SALES (est): 1.86MM **Privately Held**
Web: www.pacwestlandcare.com
SIC: 0781 Landscape services

(P-184)
PACIFIC GREEN LANDSCAPE INC (PA)
8834 Winter Gardens Blvd, Lakeside
(92040-5419)
PHONE....................619 390-1546
Michael C Regan, *Pr*
EMP: 109 **EST:** 1979
SQ FT: 1,450
SALES (est): 4.39MM
SALES (corp-wide): 4.39MM **Privately Held**
Web: www.pacificgreenlandscape.com
SIC: 0781 Landscape services

(P-185)
PIERRE LANDSCAPE INC
5455 2nd St, Irwindale (91706-2072)
PHONE....................626 587-2121
Harold Young, *CEO*
Joseph Lowden, *

Monty Khouri, *
EMP: 200 **EST:** 1980
SQ FT: 9,425
SALES (est): 42.06MM **Privately Held**
Web: www.pierrelandscape.com
SIC: 0781 Landscape architects

(P-186)
PLATINUM LANDSCAPE INC
42575 Melanie Pl Ste C, Palm Desert
(92211-5162)
PHONE....................760 200-3673
Christopher Johnson, *Pr*
Cherie Johnson, *
EMP: 150 **EST:** 2002
SQ FT: 3,000
SALES (est): 618.25K **Privately Held**
Web: www.platinumlandscapeinc.com
SIC: 0781 Landscape services

(P-187)
PRIORITY LANDSCAPE SVCS LLC
521 Mercury Ln, Brea (92821-4831)
PHONE....................714 255-2940
Michael Rocha, *
EMP: 80 **EST:** 2018
SALES (est): 491.67K **Privately Held**
SIC: 0781 Landscape services

(P-188)
RANCHO DEL ORO LDSCP MAINT INC
4167 Avenida De La Plata Ste 109,
Oceanside (92056-6029)
P.O. Box 4608 (92052-4608)
PHONE....................760 726-0215
Uriel Espinoza, *Pr*
Richard Kirk, *
Albertano Cardenas, *
EMP: 73 **EST:** 2001
SQ FT: 1,400
SALES (est): 2.26MM **Privately Held**
Web: www.rdolandscape.com
SIC: 0781 Landscape services

(P-189)
ROLLING GREEN INC
401 W 4th St, San Bernardino
(92401-1418)
P.O. Box 452 (91752-0452)
PHONE....................951 360-9294
Juan Vasquez Junior, *Pr*
Domingo Vasquez, *
Joane Ward, *
EMP: 252 **EST:** 2001
SALES (est): 2.8MM **Privately Held**
Web: www.rgtreecare.com
SIC: 0781 0783 Landscape services; Planting, pruning, and trimming services

(P-190)
SAN VAL CORP (PA)
Also Called: San Val Alarm System
72203 Adelaid St, Thousand Palms
(92276-2321)
P.O. Box 12860 (92255-2860)
PHONE....................760 346-3999
Robert L Sandifer, *Pr*
Sharon L Sandifer, *
EMP: 425 **EST:** 1975
SALES (est): 4.65MM
SALES (corp-wide): 4.65MM **Privately Held**
Web: www.sunshinelandscapecv.com
SIC: 0781 7381 Landscape services; Burglary protection service

(P-191)
SHASTA LANDSCAPING INC
1340 Descanso Ave, San Marcos
(92069-1306)
PHONE....................760 744-6551
Leonard R Hogan, *CEO*
Leonard R Hogan, *CEO*
Daniel Hogan, *
Debara Prescott, *
Susan Hogan, *
EMP: 75 **EST:** 1979
SQ FT: 6,000
SALES (est): 2.55MM **Privately Held**
Web: www.shastalandscaping.com
SIC: 0781 Landscape services

(P-192)
SOUTHWEST LANDSCAPE INC
2205 S Standard Ave, Santa Ana
(92707-3036)
P.O. Box 15611 (92735-0611)
PHONE....................714 545-1084
Dan Hansen, *Pr*
Robert Hansen, *
EMP: 80 **EST:** 1982
SQ FT: 7,800
SALES (est): 2.39MM **Privately Held**
Web: www.southwestlandscapeinc.com
SIC: 0781 Landscape services

(P-193)
SPECIALIZED LDSCP MGT SVCS INC
Also Called: SLM Services
4212 Peast Los Angeles Ave # 4211, Simi
Valley (93063)
PHONE....................805 520-7590
Rene Emeterio, *Pr*
Wendy Emeterio, *
EMP: 77 **EST:** 2006
SALES (est): 2.35MM **Privately Held**
Web: www.slmlandscape.net
SIC: 0781 Landscape services

(P-194)
SPERBER LDSCP COMPANIES LLC (PA)
Also Called: Conserve Construction
30700 Russell Ranch Rd Ste 120,
Westlake Village (91362-9503)
PHONE....................818 437-1029
Richard A Sperber, *CEO*
EMP: 240 **EST:** 2018
SALES (est): 5.87MM
SALES (corp-wide): 5.87MM **Privately Held**
SIC: 0781 Landscape services

(P-195)
TERRA PACIFIC LANDSCAPE (HQ)
12891 Nelson St, Garden Grove
(92840-5018)
PHONE....................714 567-0177
Rich Wingard, *Pr*
EMP: 89 **EST:** 1988
SALES (est): 3.18MM
SALES (corp-wide): 119.26MM **Privately Held**
Web: www.terrapac.com
SIC: 0781 Landscape services
PA: Gothic Landscaping, Inc.
27413 Tourney Rd
661 678-1400

(P-196)
TREEBEARD LANDSCAPE INC
9917 Campo Rd, Spring Valley
(91977-1609)

P.O. Box 2777 (91979-2777)
PHONE....................619 697-8302
Tim Hillman, *Pr*
Craig Des Lauriers, *
EMP: 100 **EST:** 1974
SQ FT: 2,500
SALES (est): 2.3MM **Privately Held**
Web: www.treebeardlandscape.com
SIC: 0781 Landscape services

0782 Lawn And Garden Services

(P-197)
AMERICAN LANDSCAPE MGT INC
Also Called: Custom Lawn Services
1607 Los Angeles Ave Ste I, Ventura
(93004-3237)
PHONE....................805 647-5077
Armondo Bello, *Mgr*
EMP: 75
Web: www.americanlandscape.com
SIC: 0782 0783 0781 Landscape contractors; Ornamental shrub and tree services; Landscape planning services
PA: American Landscape Management, Inc.
7013 Owensmouth Ave

(P-198)
AZTEC LANDSCAPING INC (PA)
7980 Lemon Grove Way, Lemon Grove
(91945-1820)
PHONE....................619 464-3303
Genaro Garcia, *Pr*
Ramon Aguilar, *
Rafael Aguilar, *
EMP: 180 **EST:** 1981
SQ FT: 30,000
SALES (est): 23.16MM
SALES (corp-wide): 23.16MM **Privately Held**
Web: www.azteclandscaping.com
SIC: 0782 0783 7349 Landscape contractors; Ornamental shrub and tree services; Janitorial service, contract basis

(P-199)
BRIGHTVIEW LANDSCAPES LLC
2180 La Mirada Dr, Vista (92081-8815)
PHONE....................760 598-7065
EMP: 150
SALES (corp-wide): 2.77B **Publicly Held**
Web: www.brightview.com
SIC: 0782 1542 Landscape contractors; Commercial and office buildings, renovation and repair
HQ: Brightview Landscapes, Llc
980 Jolly Rd Ste 300
Blue Bell PA 19422
484 567-7204

(P-200)
CAL-WEST NURSERIES INC
138 North Dr, Norco (92860-1637)
PHONE....................951 270-0667
Michael Whiting, *Pr*
EMP: 150 **EST:** 1968
SQ FT: 1,700
SALES (est): 4.02MM **Privately Held**
Web: www.calwestlandscape.com
SIC: 0782 0181 Landscape contractors; Nursery stock, growing of

▲ = Import ▼ = Export
◆ = Import/Export

(P-201)

CALIFORNIA LDSCP & DESIGN INC
Also Called: CA Landscape and Design
273 N Benson Ave, Upland (91786-5614)
PHONE....................909 949-1601
Joseph Ciaglia Junior, *CEO*
Margaret Mingura, *
EMP: 120 EST: 1988
SQ FT: 1,500
SALES (est): 5.31MM **Privately Held**
Web: www.calandscape.com
SIC: 0782 Landscape contractors

(P-202)

CAM PROPERTIES INC
Also Called: Emerald Landscape Services Inc
26415 Summit Cir, Santa Clarita
(91350-2991)
PHONE....................714 844-2200
John C Croul, *Pr*
EMP: 70 EST: 1986
SALES (est): 1.52MM
SALES (corp-wide): 21.9MM **Privately Held**
Web:
www.emeraldlandscapeservices.com
SIC: 0782 0781 Landscape contractors; Landscape planning services
PA: Stay Green Inc.
26415 Summit Cir
661 291-2800

(P-203)

DESERT HAVEN ENTERPRISES
43437 Copeland Cir, Lancaster
(93535-4672)
P.O. Box 2110 (93539-2110)
PHONE....................661 948-8402
Jenni C Moran, *CEO*
Roberta Terry, *
EMP: 543 EST: 1954
SQ FT: 15,000
SALES (est): 15.19MM **Privately Held**
Web: www.deserthaven.org
SIC: 0782 8331 Lawn and garden services; Work experience center

(P-204)

DIVERSCAPE INC
Also Called: Diversified Landscape Co
21730 Bundy Canyon Rd, Wildomar
(92595-8780)
PHONE....................951 245-1686
Vicki Moralez, *Pr*
Paul Moralez, *
EMP: 90 EST: 1989
SQ FT: 1,000
SALES (est): 4.87MM **Privately Held**
Web: www.diversifiedlandscape.com
SIC: 0782 1611 Garden maintenance services; General contractor, highway and street construction

(P-205)

DOOSE LANDSCAPE INCORPORATED
785 E Mission Rd, San Marcos
(92069-1903)
PHONE....................760 591-4500
Robert J Doose, *Pr*
Tom Doose, *
Susan Daugherty, *
Shelley Nolet, *
EMP: 85 EST: 1967
SQ FT: 11,300
SALES (est): 2.66MM **Privately Held**
Web: www.doose.com
SIC: 0782 Landscape contractors

(P-206)

EXCEL LANDSCAPE INC
710 Rimpau Ave Ste 108, Corona
(92879-5724)
P.O. Box 77995 (92877-0133)
PHONE....................951 735-9650
Jose Alfaro, *Pr*
▲ EMP: 120 EST: 1975
SQ FT: 1,200
SALES (est): 2.01MM **Privately Held**
Web: www.excellandscape.com
SIC: 0782 Lawn care services

(P-207)

GOTHIC LANDSCAPING INC (PA)
Also Called: Gothic Ground Management
27413 Tourney Rd, Santa Clarita
(91355-5602)
PHONE....................661 678-1400
Jon S Georgio, *Pr*
Mike Georgio, *Prin*
Roger Zino, *Vice Chairman*
Ronald Georgio, *VP*
EMP: 200 EST: 1984
SQ FT: 5,000
SALES (est): 119.26MM
SALES (corp-wide): 119.26MM **Privately Held**
Web: www.gothiclandscape.com
SIC: 0782 Landscape contractors

(P-208)

GS BROTHERS INC (PA)
20331 Main St, Carson (90745-1033)
PHONE....................310 833-1369
Alan M Gaudenti, *Pr*
Robert M Gaudenti, *
EMP: 190 EST: 1963
SALES (est): 2.45MM **Privately Held**
Web: www.gsbrothers.com
SIC: 0782 Landscape contractors

(P-209)

HEAVILAND ENTERPRISES INC (PA)
2180 La Mirada Dr, Vista (92081-8815)
PHONE....................760 598-7065
TOLL FREE: 800
EMP: 75 EST: 1978
SQ FT: 2,500
SALES (est): 8.26MM
SALES (corp-wide): 8.26MM **Privately Held**
Web: www.brightview.com
SIC: 0782 1542 Landscape contractors; Commercial and office buildings, renovation and repair

(P-210)

IRRISCAPE CONSTRUCTION INC
20182 Carancho Rd, Temecula
(92590-4348)
PHONE....................951 694-6936
Robert Smith, *Pr*
EMP: 100 EST: 1983
SQ FT: 1,500
SALES (est): 4.54MM **Privately Held**
Web: www.irriscapeconstruction.com
SIC: 0782 Landscape contractors

(P-211)

JAMES H COWAN & ASSOCIATES INC
5126 Clareton Dr Ste 200, Agoura Hills
(91301-4529)
P.O. Box 386 (91376)
PHONE....................310 457-2574
Clark J Cowan, *Pr*
Kendall Whitney, *
EMP: 95 EST: 1952
SQ FT: 3,500
SALES (est): 2.46MM **Privately Held**
SIC: 0782 Landscape contractors

(P-212)

JIMENEZ NURSERY INC
Also Called: Jimenez Nursery and Landscapes
3800 Via Real, Carpinteria (93013-3051)
P.O. Box 2460 (93120-2460)
PHONE....................805 684-7955
Manuel Jimenez, *CEO*
Alicia Jimenez, *
EMP: 100 EST: 1996
SALES (est): 4.45MM **Privately Held**
Web: www.jimeneznursery.com
SIC: 0782 Landscape contractors

(P-213)

KITSON LANDSCAPE MGT INC
5787 Thornwood Dr, Goleta (93117-3801)
PHONE....................805 681-9460
Sarah Kitson, *Pr*
Brent Kitson, *
Sally Kitson, *
David Fudurich, *
EMP: 80 EST: 1969
SQ FT: 52,272
SALES (est): 5.46MM **Privately Held**
Web: www.kitsonlandscape.com
SIC: 0782 Landscape contractors

(P-214)

LANDCARE USA LLC
Also Called: Trugreen
770 Metcalf St, Escondido (92025-1667)
PHONE....................760 747-1174
Brett Horan, *Brnch Mgr*
EMP: 79
SALES (corp-wide): 124.7MM **Privately Held**
Web: www.landcare.com
SIC: 0782 Lawn care services
PA: Landcare Usa L.L.C.
5295 Westview Dr Ste 100
301 874-3300

(P-215)

LANDCARE USA LLC
Also Called: Trugreen
5248 Governor Dr, San Diego
(92122-2800)
PHONE....................858 453-1755
Craig Gerber, *Mgr*
EMP: 92
SALES (corp-wide): 124.7MM **Privately Held**
Web: www.trugreen.com
SIC: 0782 Lawn care services
PA: Landcare Usa L.L.C.
5295 Westview Dr Ste 100
301 874-3300

(P-216)

LANDCARE USA LLC
Also Called: Trugreen
216 N Clara St, Santa Ana (92703-3518)
PHONE....................949 559-7771
Kenny Stites, *Brnch Mgr*
EMP: 92
SALES (corp-wide): 124.7MM **Privately Held**
Web: www.landcare.com
SIC: 0782 Landscape contractors
PA: Landcare Usa L.L.C.
5295 Westview Dr Ste 100
301 874-3300

(P-217)

LANDSCAPE DEVELOPMENT INC (PA)
28447 Witherspoon Pkwy, Valencia
(91355-4174)
PHONE....................661 295-1970
Mark J Crutcher, *CEO*
Gary Horton, *
Casper Correll, *
Tim Myers, *
Jenny Lunde, *
▲ EMP: 350 EST: 1983
SALES (est): 119.86MM
SALES (corp-wide): 119.86MM **Privately Held**
Web: www.landscapedevelopment.com
SIC: 0782 5039 Landscape contractors; Soil erosion control fabrics

(P-218)

LANDSCAPE DEVELOPMENT INC
1290 Carbide Dr, Corona (92881-7268)
PHONE....................951 371-9370
Tom Mcdaniel, *Pr*
EMP: 148
SALES (corp-wide): 119.86MM **Privately Held**
Web: www.landscapedevelopment.com
SIC: 0782 Landscape contractors
PA: Landscape Development, Inc.
28447 Witherspoon Pkwy
661 295-1970

(P-219)

LIBERTY LANDSCAPING INC (PA)
5212 El Rivino Rd, Riverside (92509-1807)
PHONE....................951 683-2999
Alejandro Casillas, *Pr*
EMP: 200 EST: 1997
SQ FT: 43,560
SALES (est): 8.72MM
SALES (corp-wide): 8.72MM **Privately Held**
Web: www.libertylandscaping.com
SIC: 0782 0783 Landscape contractors; Tree trimming services for public utility lines

(P-220)

MARINA LANDSCAPE INC
Also Called: Marina
3707 W Garden Grove Blvd, Orange
(92868-4803)
PHONE....................714 939-6600
EMP: 430 EST: 1982
SALES (est): 83.62MM **Privately Held**
Web: www.marinaco.com
SIC: 0782 Landscape contractors

(P-221)

MARIPOSA LANDSCAPES INC (PA)
Also Called: Mariposa Horticultural Entps
6232 Santos Diaz St, Irwindale
(91702-3267)
PHONE....................626 960-0196
Terry Noriega, *Pr*
Antonio Valenzuela, *
EMP: 98 EST: 1977
SQ FT: 2,000
SALES (est): 23.7MM
SALES (corp-wide): 23.7MM **Privately Held**
Web: www.mariposa-ca.com
SIC: 0782 Garden maintenance services

(P-222)

MERCHANTS LANDSCAPE SERVICES

2865 Main St Ste A, Chula Vista
(91911-4848)
PHONE.............................619 778-6239
Eric Anderson, *Mgr*
EMP: 97
SALES (corp-wide): 54.62MM **Privately Held**
Web: www.merchantslandscape.com
SIC: 0782 Landscape contractors
HQ: Merchants Landscape Services, Inc
1639 E Edinger Ave Ste C
Santa Ana CA 92705
714 972-8200

(P-223)

MONARCH LANDSCAPE HOLDINGS LLC (PA)

550 S Hope St Ste 1675, Los Angeles
(90071-2692)
PHONE.............................213 816-1750
Tony W Lee, *Managing Member*
EMP: 150 **EST:** 2015
SALES (est): 194.41MM
SALES (corp-wide): 194.41MM **Privately Held**
Web: www.monarchlandscape.com
SIC: 0782 Garden services

(P-224)

MPL ENTERPRISES INC

Also Called: Mike Parker Landscape
2302 S Susan St, Santa Ana (92704-4421)
PHONE.............................714 545-1717
Michael Parker, *Pr*
EMP: 90 **EST:** 1976
SQ FT: 2,000
SALES (est): 2.11MM **Privately Held**
Web: www.mikeparkerlandscape.com
SIC: 0782 Landscape contractors

(P-225)

NAMVARS INC

11815 Sorrento Valley Rd Ste A, San Diego
(92121-1047)
P.O. Box 400 (92003-0400)
PHONE.............................858 792-5461
Ali A Namvar, *Prin*
EMP: 80 **EST:** 1988
SALES (est): 852.77K **Privately Held**
Web: www.roya.com
SIC: 0782 Landscape contractors

(P-226)

NEW WAY LANDSCAPE & TREE SVCS

5752 Kearny Villa Rd, San Diego
(92123-1112)
PHONE.............................858 505-8300
Randy Newhard, *CEO*
Kathryn Dejong, *
Dan Suhovecky, *
Debra Newhard, *
EMP: 175 **EST:** 1980
SALES (est): 20.37MM **Privately Held**
Web: www.newwaypro.com
SIC: 0782 Landscape contractors

(P-227)

OCONNELL LANDSCAPE MAINT INC

Also Called: O'Connell Landscape Maint
860 E Watson Center Rd, Carson
(90745-4120)
PHONE.............................800 339-1106
Jack Rush, *Brnch Mgr*
EMP: 539

SALES (corp-wide): 37.33MM **Privately Held**
Web: www.oclm.com
SIC: 0782 Landscape contractors
PA: O'connell Landscape Maintenance Inc.
23091 Arroyo Vista
949 589-2007

(P-228)

PARK WEST LANDSCAPE INC

13105 Crenshaw Blvd, Hawthorne
(90250-5513)
PHONE.............................310 363-4100
Rose Vargas, *Brnch Mgr*
EMP: 91
SALES (corp-wide): 71.21MM **Privately Held**
Web: www.parkwestinc.com
SIC: 0782 Landscape contractors
HQ: Park West Landscape, Inc.
22421 Gilberto Ste A
Rcho Sta Marg CA 92688

(P-229)

PARK WEST LANDSCAPE MAINT INC (PA)

Also Called: Park Landscape Maint 1-2-3-4
22421 Gilberto Ste A, Rcho Sta Marg
(92688-2104)
PHONE.............................949 546-8300
Robert Morrison, *Pr*
Mike Tracy, *
Tom Tracy, *Stockholder*
Tom England, *
EMP: 300 **EST:** 1986
SQ FT: 10,000
SALES (est): 1.72MM
SALES (corp-wide): 1.72MM **Privately Held**
Web: www.parkwestinc.com
SIC: 0782 Lawn care services

(P-230)

PARKWOOD LANDSCAPE MAINT INC

16443 Hart St, Van Nuys (91406-4608)
PHONE.............................818 988-9677
David Melito, *Pr*
EMP: 95 **EST:** 1988
SQ FT: 1,500
SALES (est): 619.83K **Privately Held**
Web: www.parkwoodlandscape.com
SIC: 0782 Landscape contractors

(P-231)

PENNEY LAWN SERVICE INC

Also Called: Penny Lawn Service
4000 Allen Rd, Bakersfield (93314-9091)
PHONE.............................661 587-4788
Dan Penny, *Owner*
Sandy Penny, *
EMP: 100 **EST:** 1989
SQ FT: 1,275
SALES (est): 2.38MM **Privately Held**
Web: www.penneylawnservice.com
SIC: 0782 Landscape contractors

(P-232)

RESIDENT GROUP SERVICES INC (PA)

Also Called: Rgs Services
1156 N Grove St, Anaheim (92806-2109)
PHONE.............................714 630-5300
TOLL FREE: 800
James M Gilly, *Pr*
Michael K Hayde, *
EMP: 149 **EST:** 1983
SQ FT: 15,000
SALES (est): 4.85MM

SALES (corp-wide): 4.85MM **Privately Held**
Web: www.mysupportservicesgroup.com
SIC: 0782 Landscape contractors

(P-233)

RICHMOND ENGINEERING CO INC

Also Called: Lewis Lifetime Tools
15472 Markar Rd, Poway (92064-2313)
PHONE.............................800 589-7058
Daniel Wright, *Pr*
◆ **EMP:** 120 **EST:** 1954
SQ FT: 120,000
SALES (est): 1.85MM **Privately Held**
Web: www.yardbutler.com
SIC: 0782 Lawn and garden services

(P-234)

RMA LAND CONSTRUCTION INC

2707 Saturn St, Brea (92821-6705)
PHONE.............................714 985-2888
EMP: 79
Web: www.rmaland.com
SIC: 0782 1542 Landscape contractors;
Commercial and office building, new
construction

(P-235)

SOTO COMPANY INC

34275 Camino Capistrano Ste A,
Capistrano Beach (92624-1917)
PHONE.............................949 493-9403
Joe Soto, *Pr*
Carol Soto, *
EMP: 75 **EST:** 1975
SQ FT: 4,000
SALES (est): 2.26MM **Privately Held**
Web: www.sotocompany.com
SIC: 0782 Landscape contractors

(P-236)

SUNSET LANDSCAPE MAINTENANCE

27201 Burbank, El Toro (92610-2500)
P.O. Box 1333 (91702-1333)
PHONE.............................949 455-4636
James Roughan, *Pr*
Claudia Roughan, *
EMP: 100 **EST:** 1976
SQ FT: 6,300
SALES (est): 2.32MM **Privately Held**
Web: www.andrelandscape.com
SIC: 0782 Landscape contractors

(P-237)

TIERRA VERDE RESOURCES INC (PA)

1545 Lake Dr, Encinitas (92024-5224)
PHONE.............................857 777-6190
Matthew Carona, *CEO*
Matthew Carona, *Prin*
Louis Mann, *Pr*
Collin Howard, *CFO*
EMP: 110 **EST:** 1975
SALES (est): 1.07MM
SALES (corp-wide): 1.07MM **Privately Held**
SIC: 0782 Landscape contractors

(P-238)

TRACY RYDER LANDSCAPE INC

Also Called: Tracy Ryder Landscape Cnstr
22421 Gilberto Ste A, Rcho Sta Marg
(92688-2104)
PHONE.............................949 858-7017
Michael S Tracy, *Mgr*
EMP: 70
SALES (corp-wide): 71.21MM **Privately Held**

Web: www.tracytechnologies.com
SIC: 0782 Lawn and garden services
HQ: Tracy Ryder Landscape, Inc.
4550 Smiley Rd
Las Vegas NV 89115
702 248-6336

(P-239)

TROPICAL PLAZA NURSERY INC

9642 Santiago Blvd, Villa Park
(92867-2521)
PHONE.............................714 998-4100
Leslie T Fields, *Pr*
Mike Feilds, *
EMP: 100 **EST:** 1950
SQ FT: 5,000
SALES (est): 2.35MM **Privately Held**
Web: www.tropicalplaza.com
SIC: 0782 Landscape contractors

(P-240)

ULTIMATE LANDSCAPING MGT

700 E Sycamore St, Anaheim (92805-2831)
PHONE.............................714 502-9711
James Berne, *Pr*
EMP: 80 **EST:** 1984
SALES (est): 2.3MM **Privately Held**
SIC: 0782 Landscape contractors

(P-241)

VENCO WESTERN INC

2400 Eastman Ave, Oxnard (93030-5187)
PHONE.............................805 981-2400
TOLL FREE: 800
Linda Del Nagro Burr, *Pr*
William Burr Stcklder, *Prin*
EMP: 200 **EST:** 1977
SQ FT: 15,000
SALES (est): 9.55MM **Privately Held**
Web: www.vencowestern.com
SIC: 0782 Landscape contractors

(P-242)

VINTAGE ASSOCIATES INC

Also Called: Vintage Nursery
78755 Darby Rd, Bermuda Dunes
(92203-9621)
P.O. Box 5250 (92248-5250)
PHONE.............................760 772-3673
Gregory Gritters, *Pr*
EMP: 160 **EST:** 1989
SQ FT: 1,000
SALES (est): 8.68MM **Privately Held**
Web: www.vintagelandscape.com
SIC: 0782 5193 5261 Landscape contractors
; Nursery stock; Retail nurseries

(P-243)

WEST COAST ARBORISTS INC (PA)

2200 E Via Burton, Anaheim (92806-1221)
PHONE.............................714 991-1900
EMP: 100 **EST:** 1972
SALES (est): 47.18MM
SALES (corp-wide): 47.18MM **Privately Held**
Web: www.wcainc.com
SIC: 0782 Landscape contractors

0783 Ornamental Shrub And Tree Services

(P-244)

CLS LANDSCAPE MANAGEMENT INC

Also Called: Cls Landscape Management
4329 State St Ste B, Montclair
(91763-6082)

PHONE...................909 628-3005
Kevin L Davis, *Pr*
Kimberly Davis, *
EMP: 325 EST: 1983
SQ FT: 2,500
SALES (est): 21.09MM **Privately Held**
Web: www.clslandscape.com
SIC: 0783 0782 Ornamental shrub and tree services; Lawn and garden services

(P-245)

ORIGINAL MOWBRAYS TREE SVC INC

Also Called: Mowbray's Tree Service
686 E Mill St, San Bernardino (92408-1610)
EMP: 200 **EST:** 1972
SQ FT: 1,000
SALES (est): 41.1MM **Privately Held**
Web: www.mowbrays.com
SIC: 0783 Tree trimming services for public utility lines

(P-246)

PACIFIC COAST TREE EXPERTS

21525 Strathern St, Canoga Park (91304-4137)
PHONE...................805 506-1211
Nicolas Pinedo, *Prin*
Armando Valdez, *
Antonio Ramirez Bonilla, *
Nicolas Pinedo, *Pr*
EMP: 150 **EST:** 2010
SALES (est): 799.02K **Privately Held**
Web: www.pacificcoasttreeexperts.com
SIC: 0783 Planting, pruning, and trimming services

(P-247)

WEST COAST ARBORISTS INC

11405 Nardo St, Ventura (93004-3201)
PHONE...................805 671-5092
Lorenzo Perez, *Owner*
EMP: 116
SALES (corp-wide): 47.18MM **Privately Held**
Web: www.westcoastarborists.com
SIC: 0783 Planting, pruning, and trimming services
PA: West Coast Arborists, Inc.
2200 E Via Burton
714 991-1900

(P-248)

WEST COAST ARBORISTS INC

21718 Walnut Ave, Grand Terrace (92313-4437)
PHONE...................909 783-6544
Patrick Mahoney, *Pr*
EMP: 117
SALES (corp-wide): 47.18MM **Privately Held**
Web: www.westcoastarborists.com
SIC: 0783 Planting, pruning, and trimming services
PA: West Coast Arborists, Inc.
2200 E Via Burton
714 991-1900

0811 Timber Tracts

(P-249)

BRIGHTVIEW TREE COMPANY

Also Called: Specimen Contracting
9500 Foothill Blvd, Sunland (91040-1857)
PHONE...................818 951-5500
Tadd Russikoff, *Mgr*
EMP: 86
SALES (corp-wide): 4.3B **Publicly Held**
Web: www.brightview.com

SIC: 0811 Tree farm
HQ: Brightview Tree Company
24151 Ventura Blvd # 100
Calabasas CA 91302
818 223-8500

(P-250)

BRIGHTVIEW TREE COMPANY

Also Called: Environmental Industries
3200 W Telegraph Rd, Fillmore (93015-9623)
PHONE...................714 546-7975
Susan Flores, *Brnch Mgr*
EMP: 86
SALES (corp-wide): 4.3B **Publicly Held**
Web: www.brightview.com
SIC: 0811 0782 Tree farm; Lawn services
HQ: Brightview Tree Company
24151 Ventura Blvd # 100
Calabasas CA 91302
818 223-8500

(P-251)

HOLIDAY TREE FARMS INC

329 Van Norman Rd, Montebello (90640-5314)
P.O. Box 1688 (91793-1688)
PHONE...................323 276-1900
Greg Rondeau, *Prin*
EMP: 126
SALES (corp-wide): 19.4MM **Privately Held**
Web: www.holidaytreefarm.com
SIC: 0811 Tree farm
PA: Holiday Tree Farms, Inc.
800 Nw Cornell Ave
541 753-3236

1021 Copper Ores

(P-252)

LUSTROS INC

9025 Carlton Hills Blvd Ste A, Santee (92071-7905)
PHONE...................619 449-4800
William Farley, *Ch Bd*
EMP: 44 **EST:** 2012
SQ FT: 1,530
SALES (est): 896.23K **Privately Held**
Web: www.perfectdomain.com
SIC: 1021 Copper ore mining and preparation

1041 Gold Ores

(P-253)

GOLDEN QUEEN MINING CO LLC

2818 Silver Queen Rd, Mojave (93501-7021)
P.O. Box 1030 (93502-1030)
PHONE...................661 824-4300
Thomas Clay, *Ch Bd*
Robert Walish, *
Andree St-germain, *CFO*
EMP: 180 **EST:** 2014
SQ FT: 2,500
SALES (est): 27.73MM
SALES (corp-wide): 57.04MM **Privately Held**
Web: www.goldenqueenllc.com
SIC: 1041 Gold ores mining
PA: Golden Queen Mining Co. Ltd
880-580 Hornby St
604 417-7952

(P-254)

LOST DUTCHMANS MININGS ASSN (DH)

43445 Business Park Dr Ste 113, Temecula (92590-3671)
P.O. Box 891509 (92589-1509)
PHONE...................951 699-4749
Perry Massie, *Pr*
Tom Massie, *
▲ **EMP:** 30 **EST:** 1995
SQ FT: 3,200
SALES (est): 2.78MM
SALES (corp-wide): 50.77MM **Privately Held**
Web: www.goldprospectors.org
SIC: 1041 Gold ores
HQ: Outdoor Channel Holdings, Inc.
1000 Chopper Cir
Denver CO 80204

(P-255)

STAVATTI INDUSTRIES LTD

3670 El Camino Dr, San Bernardino (92404-2025)
P.O. Box 211258 (55121-2658)
PHONE...................651 238-5369
Christopher R Beskar, *Brnch Mgr*
EMP: 42
SALES (corp-wide): 887.61K **Privately Held**
Web: www.stavatti.com
SIC: 1041 1081 3511 3533 Gold ores mining ; Metal mining exploration and development services; Turbines and turbine generator set units, complete; Oil and gas field machinery
PA: Stavatti Industries Ltd
1061 Tiffany Dr
651 238-5369

1081 Metal Mining Services

(P-256)

PERERA CNSTR & DESIGN INC

2890 Inland Empire Blvd Ste 102, Ontario (91764-4649)
PHONE...................909 484-6350
Henry Perera Junior, *CEO*
Henry Perera, *CFO*
EMP: 35 **EST:** 1989
SQ FT: 20,000
SALES (est): 35.16MM **Privately Held**
Web: www.pererainc.com
SIC: 1081 Metal mining exploration and development services

1099 Metal Ores, Nec

(P-257)

MP MATERIALS CORP

67750 Bailey Rd, Mountain Pass (92366)
PHONE...................702 844-6111
EMP: 71
SALES (corp-wide): 253.44MM **Publicly Held**
Web: www.mpmaterials.com
SIC: 1099 Rare-earth ores mining
PA: Mp Materials Corp.
1700 S Pvlion Ctr Dr Ste
702 844-6111

1221 Bituminous Coal And Lignite-surface Mining

(P-258)

CHEVRON MINING INC

Moly

67750 Bailey Rd, Mountain Pass (92366)
PHONE...................760 856-7625
EMP: 245
SALES (corp-wide): 162.47B **Publicly Held**
SIC: 1221 Surface mining, bituminous, nec
HQ: Chevron Mining Inc.
116 Invrneco Dr E Ste 207
Englewood CO 80112
303 930-3600

1231 Anthracite Mining

(P-259)

GRUBB & NADLER INC

1719 Rainbow Valley Blvd, Fallbrook (92028-9774)
PHONE...................760 728-0040
Thomas Emery, *Mgr*
EMP: 30
Web: www.floragrubb.com
SIC: 1231 Preparation plants, anthracite
PA: Grubb & Nadler, Inc.
1634 Jerrold Ave

(P-260)

MIDSTREAM ENERGY PARTNERS USA

9224 Tupman Rd, Tupman (93276)
PHONE...................661 765-4087
EMP: 37 **EST:** 2012
SALES (est): 7.01MM **Privately Held**
Web: www.midstreamenergy.us
SIC: 1231 1382 1311 1321 Anthracite mining ; Oil and gas exploration services; Crude petroleum and natural gas; Natural gas liquids

1241 Coal Mining Services

(P-261)

RIO TINTO MINERALS INC

Also Called: Reno Tenco
14486 Borax Rd, Boron (93516-2017)
PHONE...................760 762-7121
Xiaoling Liu, *CEO*
Hugo Bague, *
Preston Chiaro, *
◆ **EMP:** 150 **EST:** 2006
SALES (est): 42.27MM
SALES (corp-wide): 54.04B **Privately Held**
Web: www.borax.com
SIC: 1241 Coal mining services
HQ: U.S. Borax Inc.
200 E Randolph St # 7100
Chicago IL 60601
773 270-6500

(P-262)

TAFT PRODUCTION COMPANY

950 Petroleum Club Rd, Taft (93268-9748)
P.O. Box 1277 (93268-1277)
PHONE...................661 765-7194
Daniel S Jaffee, *Pr*
EMP: 95 **EST:** 2002
SALES (est): 9.67MM
SALES (corp-wide): 437.59MM **Publicly Held**
Web: www.oildri.com
SIC: 1241 1081 Coal mining services; Metal mining services
PA: Oil-Dri Corporation Of America
410 N Mich Ave Ste 400
312 321-1515

PRODUCTS & SVCS

1311 Crude Petroleum And Natural Gas

(P-263)
AERA ENERGY LLC
Also Called: Kernridge Division
19590 7th Standard Rd, Mc Kittrick
(93251-9709)
PHONE..................................661 334-3100
Marie Crosby, *Prin*
EMP: 143
SALES (corp-wide): 316.62B **Privately Held**
Web: www.aeraenergy.com
SIC: 1311 Natural gas production
HQ: Aera Energy Services Company
10000 Ming Ave
Bakersfield CA 93311
661 665-5000

(P-264)
AERA ENERGY LLC
10000 Ming Ave, Bakersfield (93389)
Rural Route 11164 (93389)
PHONE..................................661 665-5000
Francisco J Leon, *Pr*
Jay A Bys, *CCO*
Sergio De Castro, *Sr VP*
Omar Hayat, *Operations*
Manuela Nelly Molina, *Ex VP*
EMP: 918 **EST:** 1994
SALES (est): 6.55MM
SALES (corp-wide): 2.8B **Publicly Held**
SIC: 1311 Crude petroleum production
PA: California Resources Corporation
1 World Trade Ctr Ste 150
888 848-4754

(P-265)
BERRY PETROLEUM COMPANY LLC
28700 Hovey Hills Rd, Taft (93268)
P.O. Box 925 (93268-0925)
PHONE..................................661 769-8820
Tom Cruise, *Mgr*
EMP: 51
SALES (corp-wide): 903.46MM **Publicly Held**
Web: www.berrypetroleum.com
SIC: 1311 Crude petroleum production
HQ: Berry Petroleum Company, Llc
11117 River Run Blvd
Bakersfield CA 93311
661 616-3900

(P-266)
BERRY PETROLEUM COMPANY LLC (HQ)
11117 River Run Blvd, Bakersfield
(93311-8957)
PHONE..................................661 616-3900
Trem Smith, *Pr*
EMP: 24 **EST:** 1985
SALES (est): 130.26MM
SALES (corp-wide): 903.46MM **Publicly Held**
Web: www.berrypetroleum.com
SIC: 1311 Crude petroleum production
PA: Berry Corporation (Bry)
16000 Dallas Pkwy Ste 500
661 616-3900

(P-267)
BERRY PETROLEUM COMPANY LLC
25121 Sierra Hwy, Newhall (91321-2007)
PHONE..................................661 255-6066
Eddie Azevedo, *Mgr*

EMP: 51
SALES (corp-wide): 903.46MM **Publicly Held**
Web: www.berrypetroleum.com
SIC: 1311 Crude petroleum production
HQ: Berry Petroleum Company, Llc
11117 River Run Blvd
Bakersfield CA 93311
661 616-3900

(P-268)
BETA OPERATING COMPANY LLC
Also Called: Beta Offshore
111 W Ocean Blvd, Long Beach
(90802-4622)
PHONE..................................562 628-1526
EMP: 54
SALES (corp-wide): 307.6MM **Publicly Held**
Web: www.betaoffshore.com
SIC: 1311 Crude petroleum production
HQ: Beta Operating Company, Llc
500 Dallas St Ste 1600
Houston TX 77002

(P-269)
BREITBURN ENERGY PARTNERS LP
707 Wilshire Blvd Ste 4600, Los Angeles
(90017-3612)
PHONE..................................213 225-5900
EMP: 671
SIC: 1311 Crude petroleum production

(P-270)
CALIFORNIA RESOURCES CORP (PA)
1 World Trade Ctr Ste 1500, Long Beach
(90831-1500)
PHONE..................................888 848-4754
Francisco J Leon, *Pr*
Tiffany Thom Cepak, *Ch Bd*
Manuela Molina, *Ex VP*
Michael L Preston, *Chief Strategy Officer*
Jay A Bys, *CCO*
EMP: 66 **EST:** 2014
SALES (est): 2.8B
SALES (corp-wide): 2.8B **Publicly Held**
Web: www.crc.com
SIC: 1311 Crude petroleum and natural gas

(P-271)
CALIFORNIA RESOURCES PROD CORP (HQ)
Also Called: Vintage Production California
27200 Tourney Rd Ste 200, Santa Clarita
(91355-4910)
PHONE..................................661 869-8000
EMP: 125 **EST:** 2005
SALES (est): 21.79MM
SALES (corp-wide): 2.8B **Publicly Held**
Web: www.crc.com
SIC: 1311 1382 Crude petroleum production;
Oil and gas exploration services
PA: California Resources Corporation
1 World Trade Ctr Ste 150
888 848-4754

(P-272)
CALIFORNIA RESOURCES PROD CORP
4900 W Lokern Rd, Mc Kittrick
(93251-9764)
PHONE..................................661 869-8000
EMP: 25
SALES (corp-wide): 2.8B **Publicly Held**
Web: www.crc.com

SIC: 1311 1382 Crude petroleum production;
Oil and gas exploration services
HQ: California Resources Production
Corporation
27200 Tourney Rd Ste 200
Santa Clarita CA 91355

(P-273)
CARBON CALIFORNIA COMPANY LLC
270 Quail Ct Ste 201, Santa Paula
(93060-9206)
PHONE..................................805 933-1901
Patrick R Mcdonald, *CEO*
Mark D Pierce, *Pr*
Kevin D Struzeski, *CFO*
EMP: 30 **EST:** 2016
SALES (est): 3.52MM
SALES (corp-wide): 116.63MM **Privately Held**
Web: www.carbonenergycorp.com
SIC: 1311 Crude petroleum and natural gas
PA: Carbon Energy Corporation
1700 Broadway Ste 1170
720 407-7043

(P-274)
HATHAWAY LLC
4205 Atlas Ct, Bakersfield (93308-4510)
P.O. Box 81385 (93380-1385)
PHONE..................................661 393-2004
Charles Hathaway, *
EMP: 38 **EST:** 2000
SQ FT: 4,500
SALES (est): 7.95MM **Privately Held**
Web: www.hathawayllc.com
SIC: 1311 Crude petroleum production

(P-275)
OCCIDENTAL PETROLEUM CORPORATION OF CALIFORNIA
Also Called: OXY
10889 Wilshire Blvd, Los Angeles
(90024-4201)
EMP: 3600
SIC: 1311 Crude petroleum production

(P-276)
THE STRAND ENERGY COMPANY
515 S Flower St Ste 4800, Los Angeles
(90071-2241)
PHONE..................................213 225-5900
EMP: 380
SIC: 1311 Crude petroleum and natural gas
production

(P-277)
THUMS LONG BEACH COMPANY
111 W Ocean Blvd Ste 800, Long Beach
(90802-7930)
PHONE..................................562 624-3400
EMP: 205
SIC: 1311 Crude petroleum production

(P-278)
TIDELANDS OIL PRODUCTION INC
Also Called: Partnrship Prmnt Ptro Chnse En
301 E Ocean Blvd St 300, Long Beach
(90802-4830)
PHONE..................................562 436-9918
EMP: 30
SIC: 1311 8748 4925 Crude petroleum
production; Business consulting, nec; Gas
production and/or distribution

(P-279)
TRI-VALLEY CORPORATION
4927 Calloway Dr Ste 101, Bakersfield
(93312-9719)
PHONE..................................661 864-0500
EMP: 25
Web: www.tri-valleycorp.com
SIC: 1311 1382 1041 Crude petroleum and
natural gas; Oil and gas exploration services
; Gold ores

(P-280)
UNIFIED FIELD SERVICES CORP
6906 Downing Ave, Bakersfield
(93308-5812)
PHONE..................................661 325-8962
Wesley R Furrh Junior, *Pr*
EMP: 39 **EST:** 2015
SALES (est): 7.57MM **Privately Held**
Web: www.unifiedfsc.com
SIC: 1311 Crude petroleum and natural gas

(P-281)
VAQUERO ENERGY INCORPORATED
15545 Hermosa Rd, Bakersfield
(93307-9477)
PHONE..................................661 363-7240
Ken Hunter, *Pr*
EMP: 50 **EST:** 2007
SALES (est): 9.9MM **Privately Held**
Web: www.vaqueroenergy.com
SIC: 1311 Crude petroleum production

(P-282)
WEST NEWPORT OIL COMPANY
5800 W Coast Hwy, Newport Beach
(92663-2002)
P.O. Box 1487 (92659-0487)
PHONE..................................949 631-1100
Robert A Armstrong, *Pr*
Jay Stair, *VP*
Margaret Armstrong, *Sec*
EMP: 24 **EST:** 1975
SALES (est): 4.91MM
SALES (corp-wide): 4.91MM **Privately Held**
SIC: 1311 Crude petroleum production
PA: Armstrong Petroleum Corporation
5800 W Coast Hwy
949 650-4000

(P-283)
WORLD OIL CORP
9302 Garfield Ave, South Gate
(90280-3896)
P.O. Box 1 (90280-0001)
PHONE..................................562 928-0100
Robert S Roth, *CEO*
EMP: 147 **EST:** 1973
SALES (est): 31.37MM **Privately Held**
Web: www.worldoilcorp.com
SIC: 1311 Crude petroleum and natural gas

1321 Natural Gas Liquids

(P-284)
HEXAGON AGILITY INC
3335 Susan St Ste 100, Costa Mesa
(92626-1647)
PHONE..................................949 236-5520
Hans Peter Havdal, *CEO*
Seung Baik, *Pr*
EMP: 46 **EST:** 2016
SALES (est): 20.16MM **Privately Held**
Web: www.hexagongroup.com
SIC: 1321 Natural gas liquids production
PA: Hexagon Composites Asa
Korsegata 4b

1381 Drilling Oil And Gas Wells

(P-285)
AERA ENERGY SERVICES COMPANY
Also Called: Security Front Desk
59231 Main Camp Rd, Mc Kittrick (93251-9740)
PHONE..........................661 665-4400
Mike Brown, *Prin*
EMP: 127
SALES (corp-wide): 316.62B **Privately Held**
Web: www.aeraenergy.com
SIC: 1381 Directional drilling oil and gas wells
HQ: Aera Energy Services Company
  10000 Ming Ave
  Bakersfield CA 93311
  661 665-5000

(P-286)
AERA ENERGY SERVICES COMPANY
Also Called: Aera Energy South Midway
29235 Highway 33, Maricopa (93252-9793)
PHONE..........................661 665-3200
Andy Anderson, *Mgr*
EMP: 78
SALES (corp-wide): 316.62B **Privately Held**
Web: www.aeraenergy.com
SIC: 1381 Directional drilling oil and gas wells
HQ: Aera Energy Services Company
  10000 Ming Ave
  Bakersfield CA 93311
  661 665-5000

(P-287)
AERA ENERGY SERVICES COMPANY (HQ)
10000 Ming Ave, Bakersfield (93311-1301)
P.O. Box 11164 (93389-1164)
PHONE..........................661 665-5000
Erik Bartsch, *Pr*
EMP: 800 **EST:** 1994
SALES (est): 490.16MM
SALES (corp-wide): 316.62B **Privately Held**
Web: www.aeraenergy.com
SIC: 1381 Directional drilling oil and gas wells
PA: Shell Plc
  Shell Centre
  207 934-3363

(P-288)
ELYSIUM JENNINGS LLC
1600 Norris Rd, Bakersfield (93308-2234)
PHONE..........................661 679-1700
EMP: 125 **EST:** 2003
SALES (est): 6.21MM **Privately Held**
SIC: 1381 Drilling oil and gas wells
PA: E & B Natural Resources Management Corporation
  1608 Norris Rd

(P-289)
EXCALIBUR WELL SERVICES CORP
22034 Rosedale Hwy, Bakersfield (93314-9704)
PHONE..........................661 589-5338
Stephen Layton, *Pr*
Stephen Layton, *CEO*
Frachsco Galesi, *

Gordon Isbel, *
EMP: 120 **EST:** 2006
SALES (est): 8.54MM **Privately Held**
Web: www.excaliburwellservices.com
SIC: 1381 1389 Drilling oil and gas wells; Fishing for tools, oil and gas field

(P-290)
GEO GUIDANCE DRILLING SVCS INC (PA)
200 Old Yard Dr, Bakersfield (93307-4268)
P.O. Box 42647 (93384-2647)
PHONE..........................661 833-9999
Joseph Williams, *CEO*
Matt Lemke, *
Charles B Peters, *
EMP: 25 **EST:** 2011
SQ FT: 3,000
SALES (est): 8.04MM **Privately Held**
Web: www.geoguidancedrilling.com
SIC: 1381 Drilling oil and gas wells

(P-291)
GOLDEN STATE DRILLING INC
3500 Fruitvale Ave, Bakersfield (93308-5106)
PHONE..........................661 589-0730
Philip F Phelps, *Pr*
Velma Phelps, *
James Phelps, *
EMP: 75 **EST:** 1977
SALES (est): 4.75MM **Privately Held**
Web: www.gsdrilling.com
SIC: 1381 Directional drilling oil and gas wells

(P-292)
LEON KROUS DRILLING INC
9300 Borden Ave, Sun Valley (91352-2006)
PHONE..........................818 833-4654
Leon Krus, *Pr*
EMP: 25 **EST:** 1981
SQ FT: 1,000
SALES (est): 11.47MM **Privately Held**
Web: leonkrousdrilling.thebluebook.com
SIC: 1381 Directional drilling oil and gas wells

(P-293)
PETRO-LUD INC
12625 Jomani Dr Ste 104, Bakersfield (93312-3445)
PHONE..........................661 747-4779
Clayton Ludington, *Prin*
EMP: 24 **EST:** 2012
SALES (est): 2.57MM **Privately Held**
Web: www.petro-lud.com
SIC: 1381 Drilling oil and gas wells

1382 Oil And Gas Exploration Services

(P-294)
ARGUELLO INC
17100 Calle Mariposa Reina, Goleta (93117-9737)
PHONE..........................805 567-1632
James C Flores, *Pr*
John F Wombwell, *
Doss Dourgeois, *
Winston Taldert, *
EMP: 30 **EST:** 1999
SALES (est): 6.38MM
SALES (corp-wide): 22.86B **Publicly Held**
SIC: 1382 Oil and gas exploration services
HQ: Freeport-Mcmoran Oil & Gas Llc
  21 Waterway Ave Ste 250
  Spring TX 77380
  713 579-6000

(P-295)
BNK PETROLEUM (US) INC
925 Broadbeck Dr Ste 220, Newbury Park (91320-1272)
PHONE..........................805 484-3613
Wolf E Regener, *Pr*
Gary W Johnson, *
Ray W Payne, *OF US Operations**
Steven M Warshauer, *Exploration Vice President**
EMP: 25 **EST:** 2006
SALES (est): 9.64MM **Privately Held**
Web: www.bnkpetroleum.com
SIC: 1382 Oil and gas exploration services

(P-296)
BREITBURN ENERGY HOLDINGS LLC
707 Wilshire Blvd Ste 4600, Los Angeles (90017-3612)
PHONE..........................213 225-5900
EMP: 35 **EST:** 2009
SALES (est): 2.92MM **Privately Held**
Web: www.breitburn.com
SIC: 1382 Oil and gas exploration services

(P-297)
CALIFRNIA RSRCES ELK HILLS LLC
27200 Tourney Rd Ste 200, Santa Clarita (91355-4910)
PHONE..........................661 412-0000
Michael L Preston, *
Marshall D Smith, *
EMP: 400 **EST:** 1997
SALES (est): 26.9MM
SALES (corp-wide): 2.8B **Publicly Held**
SIC: 1382 Oil and gas exploration services
PA: California Resources Corporation
  1 World Trade Ctr Ste 150
  888 848-4754

(P-298)
DCOR LLC (PA)
Also Called: Dcor
1000 Town Center Dr Fl 6, Oxnard (93036-1132)
P.O. Box 3401 (93006-3401)
PHONE..........................805 535-2000
Andrew Prestridge, *
Alan C Templeton, *
Jeff Warren, *
Bob Garcia, *
EMP: 100 **EST:** 2001
SALES (est): 44.53MM
SALES (corp-wide): 44.53MM **Privately Held**
Web: www.dcorllc.com
SIC: 1382 Oil and gas exploration services

(P-299)
DRILLMEC INC
8140 Rosecrans Ave, Paramount (90723-2754)
PHONE..........................281 885-0777
Paulo Brando Ballerini, *Pr*
Massimo Tartagni, *
◆ **EMP:** 74 **EST:** 1998
SALES (est): 4.65MM **Privately Held**
Web: www.drillmecinc.com
SIC: 1382 Oil and gas exploration services
HQ: Soilmec Spa
  Via Dismano 5819
  Cesena FC 47522
  054 731-9111

(P-300)
E & B NTRAL RESOURCES MGT CORP (PA)

1608 Norris Rd, Bakersfield (93308-2234)
PHONE..........................661 387-8500
Steve Layton, *Pr*
Zac Hale, *
Hany Francis, *
EMP: 65 **EST:** 1972
SALES (est): 40.75MM **Privately Held**
Web: www.ebresources.com
SIC: 1382 Oil and gas exploration services

(P-301)
E & B NTRAL RESOURCES MGT CORP
1848 Perkins Rd, New Cuyama (93254)
P.O. Box 179 (93254-0179)
PHONE..........................661 766-2501
Edward Fetterman, *Brnch Mgr*
EMP: 39
Web: www.ebresources.com
SIC: 1382 Oil and gas exploration services
PA: E & B Natural Resources Management Corporation
  1608 Norris Rd

(P-302)
EAGLE DOMINION ENERGY CORP
Also Called: Eagle Dominion Trust
3020 W Olive Ave, Burbank (91505-4537)
P.O. Box 7004 (93031-7004)
PHONE..........................270 366-4817
Roger H Shears, *Mgr*
Roger H Shears, *Pr*
Nancy Davis, *
Mary Pickford, *Prin*
EMP: 35 **EST:** 1997
SQ FT: 1,500
SALES (est): 474.13K **Privately Held**
SIC: 1382 Oil and gas exploration services

(P-303)
FREEPORT-MCMORAN OIL & GAS LLC
1200 Discovery Dr Ste 500, Bakersfield (93309-7038)
PHONE..........................661 322-7600
Kiran Leal, *Mgr*
EMP: 110
SALES (corp-wide): 22.86B **Publicly Held**
Web: www.fcx.com
SIC: 1382 Oil and gas exploration services
HQ: Freeport-Mcmoran Oil & Gas Llc
  21 Waterway Ave Ste 250
  Spring TX 77380
  713 579-6000

(P-304)
FREEPORT-MCMORAN OIL & GAS LLC
5640 S Fairfax Ave, Los Angeles (90056-1266)
PHONE..........................323 298-2200
Charlotte Hargett, *Dir*
EMP: 99
SALES (corp-wide): 22.86B **Publicly Held**
Web: www.fcx.com
SIC: 1382 Oil and gas exploration services
HQ: Freeport-Mcmoran Oil & Gas Llc
  21 Waterway Ave Ste 250
  Spring TX 77380
  713 579-6000

(P-305)
FREEPORT-MCMORAN OIL & GAS LLC
760 W Hueneme Rd, Oxnard (93033-9013)
PHONE..........................805 567-1601
Eric Vang, *Brnch Mgr*
EMP: 34

PRODUCTS & SVCS

SALES (corp-wide): 22.86B **Publicly Held**
Web: www.fcx.com
SIC: **1382** Oil and gas exploration services
HQ: Freeport-Mcmoran Oil & Gas Llc
21 Waterway Ave Ste 250
Spring TX 77380
713 579-6000

(P-306)
GREKA INTEGRATED INC
Also Called: Greka
1700 Sinton Rd, Santa Maria (93458-9708)
P.O. Box 5489 (93456-5489)
PHONE..................805 347-8700
Randeep S Grewal, *CEO*
Susan Whalen, *
Ken Miller, *
▲ EMP: 145 EST: 2000
SALES (est): 6.99MM **Privately Held**
Web: www.greka.com
SIC: **1382** Oil and gas exploration services

(P-307)
LINNCO LLC
5201 Truxtun Ave, Bakersfield
(93309-0421)
PHONE..................661 616-3900
EMP: 888
SALES (corp-wide): 12.05MM **Privately Held**
SIC: **1382** Oil and gas exploration services
PA: Linnco, Llc
600 Travis St Ste 5100
281 840-4000

(P-308)
NEWPORT ENERGY
19200 Von Karman Ave Ste 400, Irvine
(92612-8512)
PHONE..................408 230-7545
Nyle Khan, *CEO*
Gordon Burk, *COO*
EMP: 25 EST: 1984
SQ FT: 5,000
SALES (est): 1.64MM **Privately Held**
SIC: **1382** Oil and gas exploration services

(P-309)
OCCIDENTAL PETROLEUM INVESTMENT CO INC
10889 Wilshire Blvd Fl 10, Los Angeles
(90024-4213)
PHONE..................310 208-8800
EMP: 4000
SIC: **1382** 8744 Oil and gas exploration services; Facilities support services

(P-310)
PHOENIX CPITL GROUP HLDNGS LLC
18575 Jamboree Rd Ste 830, Irvine
(92612-2557)
PHONE..................303 749-0074
Dam Ferrari, *CEO*
Lindsey Wilson, *COO*
Curtis Allen, *CFO*
EMP: 50 EST: 2019
SALES (est): 9.33MM **Privately Held**
Web: www.phxcapitalgroup.com
SIC: **1382** Oil and gas exploration services

(P-311)
QRE OPERATING LLC
707 Wilshire Blvd Ste 4600, Los Angeles
(90017-3612)
PHONE..................213 225-5900
Alan L Smith, *Managing Member*
EMP: 129 EST: 2010
SALES (est): 1.47MM **Privately Held**

SIC: **1382** Oil and gas exploration services
PA: Qr Energy, Lp
707 Wlshire Blvd Ste 4600

(P-312)
SAMEDAN OIL CORPORATION
Also Called: Noble Energy
1360 Landing Ave, Seal Beach
(90740-6525)
PHONE..................661 319-5038
EMP: 449
SALES (corp-wide): 7.36MM **Privately Held**
Web: www.chevron.com
SIC: **1382** Oil and gas exploration services
PA: Samedan Oil Corporation
1001 Noble Energy Way
580 223-4110

(P-313)
SENTINEL PEAK RSOURCES CAL LLC
5640 S Fairfax Ave, Los Angeles
(90056-1266)
PHONE..................323 298-2200
EMP: 79
SALES (corp-wide): 83.66MM **Privately Held**
Web: www.sentinelpeakresources.com
SIC: **1382** Oil and gas exploration services
HQ: Sentinel Peak Resources California Llc
6501 E Belleview Ave # 400
Englewood CO 80111
720 749-1105

(P-314)
SENTINEL PEAK RSOURCES CAL LLC
1200 Discovery Dr Ste 100, Bakersfield
(93309-7033)
PHONE..................661 395-5214
EMP: 79
SALES (corp-wide): 83.66MM **Privately Held**
Web: www.sentinelpeakresources.com
SIC: **1382** Oil and gas exploration services
HQ: Sentinel Peak Resources California Llc
6501 E Belleview Ave # 400
Englewood CO 80111
720 749-1105

(P-315)
SIGNAL HILL PETROLEUM INC
2633 Cherry Ave, Signal Hill (90755-2008)
PHONE..................562 595-6440
Jerrel Barto, *Ch Bd*
Craig C Barto, *
EMP: 49 EST: 1984
SALES (est): 27.28MM **Privately Held**
Web: www.shpi.net
SIC: **1382** Geological exploration, oil and gas field

(P-316)
WARREN E&P INC
Also Called: Warren E & P
400 Oceangate Ste 200, Long Beach
(90802-4306)
PHONE..................214 393-9688
James A Watt, *CEO*
Romy Massey, *Contact Person*
EMP: 67 EST: 1973
SQ FT: 7,000
SALES (est): 22.04K **Privately Held**
Web: www.warrenresources.com
SIC: **1382** Oil and gas exploration services
PA: Warren Resources, Inc.
14131 Midway Rd Ste 500

1389 Oil And Gas Field Services, Nec

(P-317)
B & B PIPE AND TOOL CO (PA)
3035 Walnut Ave, Long Beach
(90807-5295)
PHONE..................562 424-0704
Craig Braly, *Pr*
Stephanie Braly, *
▲ EMP: 23 EST: 1951
SQ FT: 2,000
SALES (est): 7.08MM
SALES (corp-wide): 7.08MM **Privately Held**
Web: www.bbpipe.com
SIC: **1389** Oil field services, nec

(P-318)
BASIC ENERGY SERVICES INC
6710 Stewart Way, Bakersfield (93308)
PHONE..................661 588-3800
EMP: 34
SALES (corp-wide): 411.38MM **Privately Held**
Web: www.basicenergyservices.com
SIC: **1389** Oil field services, nec
PA: Basic Energy Services, Inc.
801 Cherry St Ste 2100
817 334-4100

(P-319)
C&J WELL SERVICES LLC
3752 Allen Rd, Bakersfield (93314-9242)
PHONE..................661 589-5220
Joana Lerma, *Managing Member*
Danielle Hunter, *
EMP: 900 EST: 2021
SALES (est): 12.43MM **Privately Held**
Web: www.cjwellservices.com
SIC: **1389** Servicing oil and gas wells

(P-320)
CAELUS CORPORATION
26226 Enterprise Ct, Lake Forest
(92630-8405)
P.O. Box 51865 (92619-1865)
PHONE..................949 877-7170
Andre Afshar, *CEO*
EMP: 25 EST: 2017
SALES (est): 3.08MM **Privately Held**
SIC: **1389** 1522 1542 8741 Construction, repair, and dismantling services; Residential construction, nec; Custom builders, non-residential; Construction management

(P-321)
CAPSULE MANUFACTURING INC
Also Called: Capsule Mfg
1399 N Miller St, Anaheim (92806-1412)
PHONE..................949 245-4151
Chad Bowker, *Pr*
EMP: 68 EST: 2015
SALES (est): 1.33MM **Privately Held**
Web: www.capsulemfg.com
SIC: **1389** Construction, repair, and dismantling services

(P-322)
CASING SPECIALTIES INC
12454 Snow Rd, Bakersfield (93314-8015)
PHONE..................661 399-5522
Russell C Davis, *Owner*
EMP: 25 EST: 2010
SALES (est): 4.98MM **Privately Held**
Web: www.casingspecialties.com

SIC: **1389** Cementing oil and gas well casings

(P-323)
CASTRO CONSTRUCTION LLC
18375 Ventura Blvd, Tarzana (91356-4218)
PHONE..................689 220-9145
Ghil Castro, *Pr*
EMP: 25 EST: 2020
SALES (est): 1.43MM **Privately Held**
SIC: **1389** Construction, repair, and dismantling services

(P-324)
CJ BERRY WELL SERVICES MGT LLC
3752 Allen Rd, Bakersfield (93314-9242)
PHONE..................661 589-5220
Joana Lerma, *Prin*
Danielle Hunter, *
Stacy Urbina, *
EMP: 900 EST: 2021
SALES (est): 7.6MM **Privately Held**
SIC: **1389** Servicing oil and gas wells

(P-325)
CJD CONSTRUCTION SVCS INC
503 E Route 66, Glendora (91740-3506)
PHONE..................626 335-1116
Diego A Debenedetto, *Pr*
Diego Dibenedetto, *
EMP: 40 EST: 2004
SALES (est): 1.2MM **Privately Held**
Web: www.canyonair.com
SIC: **1389** Construction, repair, and dismantling services

(P-326)
CL KNOX INC
Also Called: Advanced Industrial Services
34933 Imperial Ave, Bakersfield
(93308-9579)
PHONE..................661 837-0477
Leslie Knox, *Pr*
Chris Knox, *
EMP: 80 EST: 1992
SALES (est): 10MM **Privately Held**
Web: www.clknoxinc.com
SIC: **1389** 8742 Oil field services, nec; Industrial consultant

(P-327)
CUMMINGS VACUUM SERVICE INC
Also Called: Cummings Transportation
112 El Paso Rd, Bakersfield (93314-3718)
PHONE..................661 746-1786
Pam Cummings, *Pr*
Ted Cummings, *
EMP: 60 EST: 1980
SALES (est): 8.4MM **Privately Held**
Web: www.cummings2.com
SIC: **1389** Oil field services, nec

(P-328)
DE VRIES INTERNATIONAL INC (PA)
17671 Armstrong Ave, Irvine (92614-5727)
PHONE..................949 252-1212
Don Devries, *Pr*
◆ EMP: 27 EST: 1984
SALES (est): 9.93MM
SALES (corp-wide): 9.93MM **Privately Held**
Web: www.devriesintl.com
SIC: **1389** Lease tanks, oil field: erecting, cleaning, and repairing

▲ = Import ▼ = Export
◆ = Import/Export

(P-329)
ENGEL & GRAY INC
745 W Betteravia Rd Ste A, Santa Maria (93455-1298)
P.O. Box 5020 (93456-5020)
PHONE..............................805 925-2771
Carl W Engel Junior, *Pr*
Robert Engel, *
EMP: 35 **EST:** 1946
SQ FT: 3,000
SALES (est): 4.9MM **Privately Held**
Web: www.engelandgray.com
SIC: 1389 1623 7389 2875 Construction, repair, and dismantling services; Pipeline construction, nsk; Crane and aerial lift service; Compost

(P-330)
ETHOSENERGY FIELD SERVICES LLC (DH)
10455 Slusher Dr # 12, Santa Fe Springs (90670-3750)
PHONE..............................310 639-3523
Mark Jones, *Pr*
Patricia Lelito, *CFO*
Mike Fieldhouse, *VP Opers*
EMP: 45 **EST:** 1970
SALES (est): 20.2MM
SALES (corp-wide): 5.9B **Privately Held**
Web: www.ethosenergyfs.com
SIC: 1389 8711 3462 Oil consultants; Industrial engineers; Pump, compressor, and turbine forgings
HQ: Ethosenergy Gts Holdings (Us), Llc
3100 S Sam Houston Pkwy E
Houston TX 77047

(P-331)
GROUP H ENGINEERING
2030 Vista Ave, Sierra Madre (91024-1554)
PHONE..............................818 999-0999
Michael Karaiban, *Pt*
Anke Hamalian, *Pt*
EMP: 30 **EST:** 2001
SALES (est): 368.43K **Privately Held**
SIC: 1389 Construction, repair, and dismantling services

(P-332)
HALLIBURTON COMPANY
34722 7th Standard Rd, Bakersfield (93314-9435)
PHONE..............................661 393-8111
Dennis Lovett, *Brnch Mgr*
EMP: 52
Web: www.halliburton.com
SIC: 1389 Oil field services, nec
PA: Halliburton Company
3000 N Sam Houston Pkwy E

(P-333)
HAMO CONSTRACTION
3650 Altura Ave, La Crescenta (91214-2460)
PHONE..............................818 415-3334
Hamlet Karamyan, *Owner*
EMP: 47 **EST:** 2013
SALES (est): 525K **Privately Held**
SIC: 1389 Construction, repair, and dismantling services

(P-334)
HILLS WLDG & ENGRG CONTR INC
Also Called: Hwe Mechanical
22038 Stockdale Hwy, Bakersfield (93314-8889)
PHONE..............................661 746-5400
Debora M Hill, *VP*

Robert Hill, *Stockholder**
EMP: 92 **EST:** 1999
SALES (est): 4.03MM **Privately Held**
Web: www.hillswelding.com
SIC: 1389 Testing, measuring, surveying, and analysis services

(P-335)
HIRSH INC
Also Called: Better Mens Clothes
860 S Los Angeles St # 900, Los Angeles (90014-3311)
PHONE..............................213 622-9441
EMP: 50
SALES (est): 1.09MM **Privately Held**
SIC: 1389 Lease tanks, oil field: erecting, cleaning, and repairing

(P-336)
HORIZON WELL LOGGING INC
711 Saint Andrews Way, Lompoc (93436-1326)
PHONE..............................805 733-0972
Doug Milham, *Pr*
William Gilmore, *Dir*
James Eastes, *Dir*
▲ **EMP:** 30 **EST:** 1992
SALES (est): 6.08MM **Privately Held**
Web: www.horizon-well-logging.com
SIC: 1389 Oil field services, nec

(P-337)
INSTRUMENT CONTROL SERVICES
Also Called: I C S
6085 King Dr Unit 100, Ventura (93003-7178)
PHONE..............................805 642-1999
Michael Leblanc, *CEO*
Joseph Edward Locklear, *
Michael Leblanc, *VP*
EMP: 45 **EST:** 1995
SQ FT: 6,100
SALES (est): 11.33MM **Privately Held**
Web: www.instrumentcontrol.com
SIC: 1389 7699 7373 7299 Construction, repair, and dismantling services; Industrial equipment services; Systems integration services; Banquet hall facilities

(P-338)
JAGUAR ENERGY LLC (PA)
2404 Colony Plz, Newport Beach (92660-6357)
PHONE..............................949 706-7060
EMP: 27 **EST:** 2016
SALES (est): 925.83K
SALES (corp-wide): 925.83K **Privately Held**
SIC: 1389 Oil field services, nec

(P-339)
JERRY MELTON & SONS CNSTR INC
Also Called: Jerry Melton & Sons Cnstr
100 Jamison Ln, Taft (93268-4329)
PHONE..............................661 765-5546
Jerry W Melton, *Pr*
Judy Melton, *
Steven Melton, *
Karen Melton, *
EMP: 85 **EST:** 1971
SALES (est): 4.08MM **Privately Held**
SIC: 1389 Oil and gas wells: building, repairing and dismantling

(P-340)
JOHN M PHILLIPS LLC
Also Called: John M Phillips Oil Field Eqp

2800 Gibson St, Bakersfield (93308-6106)
PHONE..............................661 327-3118
Melody Shamaker, *Off Mgr*
EMP: 35
SALES (corp-wide): 4.47MM **Privately Held**
Web: www.johnmphillips.com
SIC: 1389 Oil field services, nec
PA: John M. Phillips, Llc
2755 Dawson Ave
562 595-7363

(P-341)
K C RESTORATION CO INC
1514 W 130th St, Gardena (90249-2104)
PHONE..............................310 280-0597
Carolyn Lehne Macleod, *Pr*
Steve Lehne, *
Katherine Cecilia Lehne, *
EMP: 35 **EST:** 1991
SALES (est): 5.04MM **Privately Held**
Web: www.kcrestorationinc.com
SIC: 1389 2431 1752 1741 Construction, repair, and dismantling services; Windows and window parts and trim, wood; Wood floor installation and refinishing; Masonry and other stonework

(P-342)
KUSTER CO OIL WELL SERVICES
Also Called: Kuster Company
2900 E 29th St, Long Beach (90806-2315)
PHONE..............................562 595-0661
John Davidson, *CEO*
▲ **EMP:** 23 **EST:** 1996
SALES (est): 1.58MM **Privately Held**
Web: www.probe1.com
SIC: 1389 Oil field services, nec
PA: Probe Holdings, Inc.
1132 Everman Pkwy Ste 100

(P-343)
M-I LLC
Also Called: M-I Swaco
4400 Fanucchi Way, Shafter (93263-9552)
PHONE..............................661 321-5400
Forest Purpiance, *Brnch Mgr*
EMP: 31
Web: www.slb.com
SIC: 1389 Mud service, oil field drilling
HQ: M-I L.L.C.
5950 N Course Dr
Houston TX 77072
281 561-1300

(P-344)
MDM SOLUTIONS LLC
575 Anton Blvd Ste 300, Costa Mesa (92626-7161)
PHONE..............................800 669-6361
Michael Flowor, *Managing Member*
Michael Bryant, *
Cynthia Williams, *
Doug Sipe, *
EMP: 310 **EST:** 2015
SALES (est): 4.14MM **Privately Held**
Web: www.mdmcorp.com
SIC: 1389 Oil and gas wells: building, repairing and dismantling

(P-345)
MMI SERVICES INC
4042 Patton Way, Bakersfield (93308-5030)
PHONE..............................661 589-9366
Steve Mcgowan, *CEO*
Steve Mcgowan, *Pr*
Mel Mcgowan, *CEO*
Eric Olson, *
EMP: 250 **EST:** 1985

SQ FT: 4,500
SALES (est): 24.14MM **Privately Held**
Web: www.mmi-services.com
SIC: 1389 Oil field services, nec

(P-346)
NABORS WELL SERVICES CO
1025 Earthmover Ct, Bakersfield (93314-9529)
PHONE..............................661 588-6140
Tom Jaquez, *Mgr*
EMP: 148
Web: www.nabors.com
SIC: 1389 Oil field services, nec
HQ: Nabors Well Services Co.
515 W Greens Rd Ste 1000
Houston TX 77067
281 874-0035

(P-347)
NABORS WELL SERVICES CO
7515 Rosedale Hwy, Bakersfield (93308-5727)
PHONE..............................661 589-3970
Alan Pounds, *Mgr*
EMP: 207
Web: www.nabors.com
SIC: 1389 1382 Servicing oil and gas wells; Oil and gas exploration services
HQ: Nabors Well Services Co.
515 W Greens Rd Ste 1000
Houston TX 77067
281 874-0035

(P-348)
NABORS WELL SERVICES CO
1954 James Rd, Bakersfield (93308-9749)
PHONE..............................661 392-7668
Dave Warner, *Dist Mgr*
EMP: 274
Web: www.nabors.com
SIC: 1389 Oil field services, nec
HQ: Nabors Well Services Co.
515 W Greens Rd Ste 1000
Houston TX 77067
281 874-0035

(P-349)
NABORS WELL SERVICES CO
19431 S Santa Fe Ave, Compton (90221-5912)
PHONE..............................310 639-7074
EMP: 74
Web: www.nabors.com
SIC: 1389 Oil field services, nec
HQ: Nabors Well Services Co.
515 W Greens Rd Ste 1000
Houston TX 77067
281 874-0035

(P-350)
NABORS WELL SERVICES CO
2567 N Ventura Ave # C, Ventura (93001-1201)
PHONE..............................805 648-2731
Paul Smith, *Mgr*
EMP: 74
Web: www.nabors.com
SIC: 1389 Oil field services, nec
HQ: Nabors Well Services Co.
515 W Greens Rd Ste 1000
Houston TX 77067
281 874-0035

(P-351)
OIL WELL SERVICE COMPANY
10255 Enos Ln, Shafter (93263-9572)
PHONE..............................661 746-4809
Rick Hobbs, *Off Mgr*
EMP: 60

P R O D U C T S

&

S V C S

SALES (corp-wide): 15.71MM **Privately Held**
Web: www.ows1.com
SIC: **1389** Swabbing wells
PA: Oil Well Service Company
1241 E Burnett St
562 612-0600

(P-352)
OIL WELL SERVICE COMPANY (PA)
1241 E Burnett St, Signal Hill (90755-3594)
PHONE.............................562 612-0600
Jack Frost, *Pr*
Matt Hensley, *
Connie Laws, *
Richard Laws, *
EMP: 105 EST: 1940
SALES (est): 15.71MM
SALES (corp-wide): 15.71MM **Privately Held**
Web: www.ows1.com
SIC: **1389** Oil field services, nec

(P-353)
OIL WELL SERVICE COMPANY
Also Called: Oil Well Service
1015 Mission Rock Rd, Santa Paula
(93060-9730)
PHONE.............................805 525-2103
Harvey Himinell, *Mgr*
EMP: 60
SALES (corp-wide): 35.06MM **Privately Held**
Web: www.ows1.com
SIC: **1389** Oil field services, nec
PA: Oil Well Service Company
1241 E Burnett St
562 612-0600

(P-354)
ONE STRUCTURAL INC
19326 Ventura Blvd Ste 200, Tarzana
(91356-3032)
PHONE.............................626 252-0778
David Tashroudian, *Pr*
EMP: 35 EST: 2015
SALES (est): 2.33MM **Privately Held**
SIC: **1389** Construction, repair, and dismantling services

(P-355)
OWEN OIL TOOLS LP
5001 Standard St, Bakersfield
(93308-4500)
PHONE.............................661 637-1380
Frank Isbell, *Mgr*
EMP: 62
SALES (corp-wide): 509.79MM **Privately Held**
Web: www.ocsresponds.com
SIC: **1389** Oil field services, nec
HQ: Owen Oil Tools Lp
12001 County Rd 1000
Godley TX 76044
817 551-0540

(P-356)
PACIFIC PETROLEUM CALIFORNIA INC
Also Called: Oil Field Services
1615 E Betteravia Rd Ste A, Santa Maria
(93454-9000)
P.O. Box 2646 (93457)
PHONE.............................805 925-1947
EMP: 285 EST: 2005
SALES (est): 16.78MM **Privately Held**
Web: www.ppcinc.biz

SIC: **1389** 7353 Lease tanks, oil field: erecting, cleaning, and repairing; Oil field equipment, rental or leasing

(P-357)
PACIFIC PROCESS SYSTEMS INC (PA)
7401 Rosedale Hwy, Bakersfield
(93308-5736)
PHONE.............................661 321-9681
Jerry Wise, *CEO*
Alan George, *
Robert Peterson, *
▼ EMP: 90 EST: 1995
SQ FT: 7,000
SALES (est): 24.93MM **Privately Held**
Web: www.pps-equipment.com
SIC: **1389** 7353 5082 Testing, measuring, surveying, and analysis services; Oil field equipment, rental or leasing; Oil field equipment

(P-358)
PC MECHANICAL INC
2803 Industrial Pkwy, Santa Maria
(93455-1811)
PHONE.............................805 925-2888
Lew Parker, *Pr*
Mitch Caron, *
Mary Parker, *
Brandon Burginger, *
EMP: 50 EST: 1991
SQ FT: 67,000
SALES (est): 10.07MM **Privately Held**
Web: www.pcmechanical.com
SIC: **1389** Oil field services, nec

(P-359)
PRODUCTION DATA INC
1210 33rd St, Bakersfield (93301-2124)
P.O. Box 3266 (93385-3266)
PHONE.............................661 327-4776
Gerald Tonnelli, *Pr*
EMP: 35 EST: 1972
SQ FT: 1,800
SALES (est): 6.36MM **Privately Held**
Web: www.productiondatainc.com
SIC: **1389** Oil field services, nec

(P-360)
PROS INCORPORATED
3400 Patton Way, Bakersfield (93308-5722)
P.O. Box 20996 (93390-0996)
PHONE.............................661 589-5400
Robert Lewis, *Pr*
EMP: 58 EST: 2007
SALES (est): 22.32MM **Privately Held**
Web: www.proswelltesting.com
SIC: **1389** Oil field services, nec

(P-361)
PSC INDUSTRIAL OUTSOURCING LP
Also Called: Hydrochempsc
200 Old Yard Dr, Bakersfield (93307-4268)
PHONE.............................661 833-9991
Peter Burger, *Prin*
EMP: 74
SALES (corp-wide): 5.41B **Publicly Held**
Web: www.hpc-industrial.com
SIC: **1389** Oil field services, nec
HQ: Psc Industrial Outsourcing, Lp
900 Georgia Ave
Deer Park TX 77536
713 393-5600

(P-362)
RPC INC
1100 N Magnolia Ave Ste H, El Cajon
(92020-1953)

PHONE.............................619 334-6244
Roger Ramos, *Prin*
EMP: 29 EST: 2008
SALES (est): 5.18MM **Privately Held**
Web: www.usrpc.com
SIC: **1389** Oil field services, nec

(P-363)
SCHLUMBERGER TECHNOLOGY CORP
Also Called: Dowell Schlumberger
6120 Snow Rd, Bakersfield (93308-9531)
P.O. Box 81437 (93380-1437)
PHONE.............................661 864-4721
Ron Melnyk, *Brnch Mgr*
EMP: 100
Web: www.slb.com
SIC: **1389** 1382 Oil field services, nec; Oil and gas exploration services
HQ: Schlumberger Technology Corp
300 Schlumberger Dr
Sugar Land TX 77478
281 285-8500

(P-364)
TITAN OILFIELD SERVICES INC
Also Called: Titan Oilfield Services
21535 Kratzmeyer Rd, Bakersfield
(93314-9482)
PHONE.............................661 861-1630
Terry Hibbitts, *CEO*
Terry Hibbitts, *Pr*
Tim Barman, *
Tony Palacpac, *
EMP: 68 EST: 2011
SALES (est): 9.95MM **Privately Held**
Web: www.vinemarketing.com
SIC: **1389** Oil field services, nec

(P-365)
TOTAL-WESTERN INC (HQ)
Also Called: Roberts Engineers
8049 Somerset Blvd, Paramount
(90723-4396)
PHONE.............................562 220-1450
Paul F Conrad, *CEO*
Earl Grebing, *
Mary A Pool, *
Jerry Balos, *
Payman Farrokhyar, *
EMP: 49 EST: 1972
SQ FT: 13,000
SALES (est): 44.04MM
SALES (corp-wide): 489.53MM **Privately Held**
Web: www.total-western.com
SIC: **1389** Oil field services, nec
PA: Bragg Investment Company, Inc.
6251 N Paramount Blvd
562 984-2400

(P-366)
TRUITT OILFIELD MAINT CORP
1051 James Rd, Bakersfield (93308-9753)
P.O. Box 5066 (93388-5066)
PHONE.............................661 871-4099
Kimberly Sue New, *Pr*
Steve New, *
EMP: 300 EST: 1978
SQ FT: 3,000
SALES (est): 23.72MM **Privately Held**
Web: www.truittcorp.com
SIC: **1389** Oil field services, nec

(P-367)
TRYAD SERVICE CORPORATION
5900 E Lerdo Hwy, Shafter (93263-4023)
PHONE.............................661 391-1524
James Varner, *Pr*
Danny Seely, *

▲ EMP: 90 EST: 1933
SALES (est): 9.18MM **Privately Held**
Web: www.jdrush.com
SIC: **1389** Oil and gas wells: building, repairing and dismantling

(P-368)
U S WEATHERFORD L P
2815 Fruitvale Ave, Bakersfield
(93308-5907)
PHONE.............................661 589-9483
Rick Benton, *Brnch Mgr*
EMP: 231
Web: www.weatherford.com
SIC: **1389** Oil field services, nec
HQ: U S Weatherford L P
1221 Evangeline Thruway
Broussard LA 70518
337 347-5300

(P-369)
VANDERRA RESOURCES LLC
1801 Century Park E Ste 2400, Los Angeles
(90067-2326)
PHONE.............................817 439-2220
EMP: 500
SIC: **1389** Oil field services, nec

(P-370)
WELBILT INC
3835 E Thousand Oaks Blvd Unit 315,
Westlake Village (91362-3637)
PHONE.............................310 339-1555
Ben Hunter, *CEO*
EMP: 25 EST: 2022
SALES (est): 1.64MM **Privately Held**
Web: www.welbiltsc.com
SIC: **1389** Construction, repair, and dismantling services

1422 Crushed And Broken Limestone

(P-371)
AZUSA ROCK LLC
3605 Dehesa Rd, El Cajon (92019-2903)
PHONE.............................619 440-2363
Tom Nelson, *Mgr*
EMP: 44
Web: www.azusaca.gov
SIC: **1422** Crushed and broken limestone
HQ: Azusa Rock, Llc
3901 Fish Canyon Rd
Azusa CA 91702
858 530-9444

(P-372)
CALMAT CO
16101 Hwy 156, Maricopa (93252)
P.O. Box 22800 (93390-2800)
PHONE.............................661 858-2673
Angela Bailey, *Mgr*
EMP: 368
Web: www.vulcanmaterials.com
SIC: **1422** Crushed and broken limestone
HQ: Calmat Co.
1200 Urban Center Dr
Birmingham AL 35242
818 553-8821

1429 Crushed And Broken Stone, Nec

(P-373)
TRIANGLE ROCK PRODUCTS LLC
500 N Brand Blvd Ste 500, Glendale
(91203-3319)

▲ = Import ▼ = Export
◆ = Import/Export

PHONE..................818 553-8820
Stanley G Bass, *Pr*
EMP: 184 **EST:** 1978
SQ FT: 20,000
SALES (est): 804.46K **Publicly Held**
SIC: 1429 1442 2951 3273 Igneus rock, crushed and broken-quarrying; Construction sand and gravel; Asphalt paving mixtures and blocks; Ready-mixed concrete
HQ: Calmat Co.
1200 Urban Center Dr
Birmingham AL 35242
818 553-8821

1442 Construction Sand And Gravel

(P-374)
ENNISS INC
12535 Vigilante Rd, Lakeside (92040-1167)
P.O. Box 1769 (92040-0917)
PHONE..................619 561-1101
David Von Bhren, *Pr*
D Lois Miller, *
EMP: 40 **EST:** 2002
SQ FT: 4,700
SALES (est): 9.43MM **Privately Held**
Web: www.ennissinc.com
SIC: 1442 4212 3271 4953 Sand mining; Local trucking, without storage; Architectural concrete: block, split, fluted, screen, etc.; Recycling, waste materials

(P-375)
GAIL MATERIALS INC
10060 Dawson Canyon Rd, Corona (92883-2112)
PHONE..................951 667-6106
▲ **EMP:** 24 **EST:** 1987
SQ FT: 5,000
SALES (est): 3.74MM **Privately Held**
Web: www.gailmaterials.net
SIC: 1442 Construction sand and gravel

(P-376)
PTI SAND & GRAVEL INC
14925 River Rd, Eastvale (92880-8935)
P.O. Box 6019 (92860-8034)
PHONE..................951 272-0140
Michael Ellena, *Pr*
Mark Horner, *
EMP: 28 **EST:** 1948
SALES (est): 4.15MM **Privately Held**
Web: www.ptisag.com
SIC: 1442 Construction sand and gravel

1446 Industrial Sand

(P-377)
PIONEER SANDS LLC
31302 Ortega Hwy, San Juan Capistrano (92675)
PHONE..................949 728-0171
Mike Miclette, *Brnch Mgr*
EMP: 32
SALES (corp-wide): 344.58B **Publicly Held**
SIC: 1446 Silica sand mining
HQ: Pioneer Sands Llc
777 Hidden Rdg
Irving TX 75038
972 444-9001

(P-378)
PIONEER SANDS LLC
9952 Enos Lane, Bakersfield (93314)
PHONE..................661 746-5789

Donna Bartlett, *Brnch Mgr*
EMP: 29
SALES (corp-wide): 344.58B **Publicly Held**
Web: www.pwgillibrand.com
SIC: 1446 Silica mining
HQ: Pioneer Sands Llc
777 Hidden Rdg
Irving TX 75038
972 444-9001

(P-379)
PW GILLIBRAND CO INC (PA)
4537 Ish Dr, Simi Valley (93063-7667)
P.O. Box 1019 (93062-1019)
PHONE..................805 526-2195
Celine Gillibrand, *CEO*
Richard Valencia, *
Jim Costello, *
EMP: 48 **EST:** 1957
SQ FT: 11,000
SALES (est): 24.25MM
SALES (corp-wide): 24.25MM **Privately Held**
Web: www.pwgillibrand.com
SIC: 1446 Grinding sand mining

1474 Potash, Soda, And Borate Minerals

(P-380)
5E BORON AMERICAS LLC
27555 Hector Rd, Newberry Springs (92365-8905)
PHONE..................442 292-2120
Michael Schlumpberger, *CEO*
EMP: 38
Web: www.5eadvancedmaterials.com
SIC: 1474 Borate compounds (natural) mining
HQ: 5e Boron Americas, Llc
9329 Mariposa Rd Ste 210
Hesperia CA 92344
419 371-3331

1479 Chemical And Fertilizer Mining

(P-381)
SEARLES VALLEY MINERALS INC
80201 Trona Rd, Trona (93562)
PHONE..................760 372-2259
Burnell Blanchard, *VP*
EMP: 122
Web: www.svminerals.com
SIC: 1479 Salt and sulfur mining
HQ: Searles Valley Minerals Inc.
9401 Indian Creek Pkwy
Overland Park KS 66210

(P-382)
SEARLES VALLEY MINERALS INC
13068 Main St, Trona (93562-1911)
PHONE..................760 672-2053
EMP: 122
Web: www.svminerals.com
SIC: 1479 Salt and sulfur mining
HQ: Searles Valley Minerals Inc.
9401 Indian Creek Pkwy
Overland Park KS 66210

1481 Nonmetallic Mineral Services

(P-383)
MP MINE OPERATIONS LLC
67750 Bailey Rd, Mountain Pass (92366)
PHONE..................702 277-0848
James H Litinsky, *CEO*
Michael Rosethal, *
EMP: 108 **EST:** 2017
SALES (est): 63.28MM
SALES (corp-wide): 253.44MM **Publicly Held**
SIC: 1481 1099 Mine exploration, nonmetallic minerals; Rare-earth ores mining
PA: Mp Materials Corp.
1700 S Pvlion Ctr Dr Ste
702 844-6111

1499 Miscellaneous Nonmetallic Mining

(P-384)
ATLAS LITHIUM CORPORATION
433 N Camden Dr Ste 810, Beverly Hills (90210-4412)
PHONE..................833 661-7900
Marc Fogassa, *Ch*
Tiago Moreira De Miranda, *Principal Accounting Officer*
Brian W Bernier, *Investor Relations Vice President*
Joel De Paiva Monteiro Esg, *Operations*
Areli Nogueira Da Silva Jr Geol, *MINERAL EXPLORATION*
EMP: 76 **EST:** 2012
SIC: 1499 Diamond mining, industrial

(P-385)
DICAPERL CORPORATION (DH)
Also Called: Grefco Dicaperl
23705 Crenshaw Blvd Ste 101, Torrance (90505-5278)
PHONE..................610 667-6640
Ray Perelman, *CEO*
Glenn Jones, *
Mike Cull, *
Barry Katz, *
▼ **EMP:** 90 **EST:** 1992
SQ FT: 5,000
SALES (est): 1.99MM **Privately Held**
Web: www.dicalite.com
SIC: 1499 3677 Perlite mining; Filtration devices, electronic
HQ: Grefco Minerals Inc.
1 Bala Ave Ste 310
Bala Cynwyd PA 19004
610 660-8820

(P-386)
IMERYS MINERALS CALIFORNIA INC (HQ)
2500 San Miguelito Rd, Lompoc (93436-9743)
P.O. Box 519 (93438-0519)
PHONE..................805 736-1221
Douglas A Smith, *Pr*
John Oskam, *
John Leichty, *
◆ **EMP:** 67 **EST:** 1991
SQ FT: 11,600
SALES (est): 24.79MM
SALES (corp-wide): 34.61MM **Privately Held**
Web: www.imerys.com
SIC: 1499 3295 Diatomaceous earth mining; Minerals, ground or treated

PA: Imerys Filtration Minerals, Inc.
2500 San Miguelito Rd
805 736-1221

1521 Single-family Housing Construction

(P-387)
A CLARK/MCCARTHY JOINT VENTURE
18201 Von Karman Ave Ste 800, Irvine (92612-1092)
PHONE..................714 429-9779
EMP: 1125
SIC: 1521 Single-family housing construction

(P-388)
APTIM FEDERAL SERVICES LLC
1230 Columbia St Ste 1200, San Diego (92101-8517)
PHONE..................619 239-1690
Eric Malcolm, *Brnch Mgr*
EMP: 455
SALES (corp-wide): 2.37B **Privately Held**
Web: www.aptim.com
SIC: 1521 Single-family housing construction
HQ: Aptim Federal Services, Llc
1200 Brickyard Ln Ste 202
Baton Rouge LA 70802
225 932-2500

(P-389)
ATI RESTORATION LLC
1175 Hall Ave, Riverside (92509-1870)
PHONE..................951 682-9200
Larry Hampton, *Mgr*
EMP: 143
Web: www.atirestoration.com
SIC: 1521 Repairing fire damage, single-family houses
PA: Ati Restoration, Llc
3360 E La Palma Ave

(P-390)
AZ CONSTRUCTION INC (PA)
Also Called: Ace Fence Company
727 Glendora Ave, La Puente (91744-4014)
PHONE..................626 333-0727
Amy Tsui, *Pr*
America Tang, *VP*
EMP: 114 **EST:** 2013
SALES (est): 2.22MM
SALES (corp-wide): 2.22MM **Privately Held**
Web: www.acefencecompany.com
SIC: 1521 Single-family housing construction

(P-391)
BROOKFELD STHLAND HOLDINGS LLC
Also Called: Brookfield Residential
3200 Park Center Dr Ste 1000, Costa Mesa (92626-7228)
PHONE..................714 427-6868
EMP: 160 **EST:** 1996
SALES (est): 5.95MM
SALES (corp-wide): 69.83B **Privately Held**
SIC: 1521 Single-family housing construction
HQ: Brookfield Homes (Us) Llc
3201 Jermantown Rd
Fairfax VA 22030
703 270-1400

(P-392)
BROWNCO CONSTRUCTION CO INC
Also Called: Brownco Construction

P
R
O
D
U
C
T
S

&

S
V
C
S

1000 E Katella Ave, Anaheim (92805-6617)
PHONE....................714 935-9600
Scot Alan Brown, *Pr*
Jeff Radtke, *
EMP: 87 **EST:** 1999
SQ FT: 15,000
SALES (est): 24.04MM **Privately Held**
Web: www.browncoinc.com
SIC: 1521 Single-family housing construction

(P-393)
CALVILLO CONSTRUCTION CORP
Also Called: Tiling and Stone Counter Tops
1133 Brooks St Ste C, Ontario
(91762-3662)
PHONE....................310 985-3911
Luciano Calvillo, *Owner*
Luciano Calvillo, *Pr*
EMP: 26 **EST:** 2011
SALES (est): 1.56MM **Privately Held**
Web: www.calvilloconstructioncorp.com
SIC: 1521 1522 1411 1743 Single-family housing construction; Hotel/motel and multi-family home construction; Limestone and marble dimension stone; Tile installation, ceramic

(P-394)
CHAMPION HOME BUILDERS INC
299 N Smith Ave, Corona (92878-3241)
PHONE....................951 256-4617
EMP: 104
SALES (corp-wide): 2.02B **Publicly Held**
Web: www.championhomes.com
SIC: 1521 2451 New construction, single-family houses; Mobile homes, except recreational
HQ: Champion Home Builders, Inc.
755 W Big Beavr Rd # 1000
Troy MI 48084
248 614-8200

(P-395)
COASTLINE CNSTR & AWNG CO INC
5742 Research Dr, Huntington Beach
(92649-1617)
PHONE....................714 891-9798
John W Almquist, *Pr*
EMP: 100 **EST:** 1980
SQ FT: 1,600
SALES (est): 4.63MM **Privately Held**
Web: www.coastlineconawn.com
SIC: 1521 Mobile home repair, on site

(P-396)
COUNTY OF RIVERSIDE
Facilities Mgmt
3450 14th St, Riverside (92501-3862)
PHONE....................951 955-4800
Michael Sylvester, *Dir*
EMP: 95
SALES (corp-wide): 5.07B **Privately Held**
Web: www.rivco.org
SIC: 1521 9532 7349 Single-family housing construction; Urban and community development; Building maintenance services, nec
PA: County Of Riverside
4080 Lemon St Fl 11
951 955-1110

(P-397)
DEMPSEY CONSTRUCTION INC
1835 Aston Ave, Carlsbad (92008-7310)
PHONE....................760 918-6900
John Dempsey, *Pr*

EMP: 87 **EST:** 2010
SALES (est): 16.25MM **Privately Held**
Web: www.dempseyconstruction.com
SIC: 1521 Single-family housing construction

(P-398)
DENNIS ALLEN ASSOCIATES (PA)
Also Called: Allen Associates
201 N Milpas St, Santa Barbara
(93103-3201)
PHONE....................805 884-8777
Dennis W Allen, *Pr*
Ian Cronshaw, *
Jennifer Cushnie, *
EMP: 95 **EST:** 1983
SALES (est): 9.52MM **Privately Held**
Web: www.buildallen.com
SIC: 1521 1542 General remodeling, single-family houses; Commercial and office buildings, renovation and repair

(P-399)
DISASTER RSTRTION PRFSSNALS IN
Also Called: Service Master By ARS
1517 W 130th St, Gardena (90249-2103)
PHONE....................310 301-8030
Ahmad Elzarou, *CEO*
EMP: 80 **EST:** 2003
SALES (est): 8.91MM **Privately Held**
SIC: 1521 7299 1542 Repairing fire damage, single-family houses; Home improvement and renovation contractor agency; Commercial and office building contractors

(P-400)
EBC INC (PA)
Also Called: Ellis Building Contractors
219 Manhattan Beach Blvd Ste 3,
Manhattan Beach (90266-5324)
PHONE....................310 753-6407
Brad Ellis, *Pr*
Patricia Ellis, *
EMP: 95 **EST:** 1980
SALES (est): 2.34MM
SALES (corp-wide): 2.34MM **Privately Held**
SIC: 1521 1542 New construction, single-family houses; Commercial and office building, new construction

(P-401)
ELEVEN WESTERN BUILDERS INC (PA)
2862 Executive Pl, Escondido
(92029-1524)
PHONE....................760 796-6346
Rick W Backus, *CEO*
Richard Huey, *
EMP: 82 **EST:** 1983
SQ FT: 20,000
SALES (est): 134.04MM
SALES (corp-wide): 134.04MM **Privately Held**
Web: www.ewbinc.com
SIC: 1521 New construction, single-family houses

(P-402)
EXCEL CONTRACTORS INC
Also Called: Progression Drywall
348 E Avenue K8 Ste B, Lancaster
(93535-4514)
PHONE....................661 942-6944
John Rockey, *Pr*
Rose Rockey, *
EMP: 100 **EST:** 1987
SALES (est): 18.65MM **Privately Held**

SIC: 1521 1742 1542 Single-family home remodeling, additions, and repairs; Drywall; Commercial and office building, new construction

(P-403)
FERREIRA CONSTRUCTION CO INC
10370 Commerce Center Dr Ste 200,
Rancho Cucamonga (91730-5806)
PHONE....................909 606-5900
Brandon Tensick, *VP*
EMP: 524
SALES (corp-wide): 600MM **Privately Held**
Web: www.ferreiraconstruction.com
SIC: 1521 Single-family housing construction
PA: Ferreira Construction Co., Inc.
31 Tannery Rd
908 534-8655

(P-404)
FORT HILL CONSTRUCTION (PA)
12711 Ventura Blvd Ste 390, Studio City
(91604-2491)
PHONE....................323 656-7425
George Peper, *Pr*
Mike Mc Grail, *
Gordon Foote, *
Joseph Goldfarb, *
James Kweskin, *
▲ **EMP:** 70 **EST:** 1971
SQ FT: 4,000
SALES (est): 7.05MM
SALES (corp-wide): 7.05MM **Privately Held**
Web: www.forthill.com
SIC: 1521 New construction, single-family houses

(P-405)
GENERATION CONSTRUCTION INC
15650 El Prado Rd, Chino (91710-9108)
P.O. Box 991 (91708-0991)
PHONE....................909 923-2077
Antwan De Paul, *Pr*
EMP: 150 **EST:** 1986
SALES (est): 5.48MM **Privately Held**
Web: www.gconstruction.com
SIC: 1521 Single-family housing construction

(P-406)
GOLDEN ARROW CONSTRUCTION INC
Also Called: Five Star Labor
21213b Hawthorne Blvd Pmb 5402,
Torrance (90503-5501)
PHONE....................310 523-9056
Jill Bird, *Pr*
EMP: 206 **EST:** 1992
SQ FT: 2,000
SALES (est): 437.12K **Privately Held**
SIC: 1521 7361 Single-family housing construction; Employment agencies

(P-407)
GRAY CONSTRUCTION INC
2070 N Tustin Ave, Santa Ana
(92705-7827)
PHONE....................714 491-1315
Bob Moore, *Brnch Mgr*
EMP: 103
SALES (corp-wide): 623.17MM **Privately Held**
Web: www.gray.com
SIC: 1521 Single-family housing construction
HQ: Gray Construction, Inc.
10 Quality St

Lexington KY 40507
859 281-5000

(P-408)
INNOVATIVE COMMUNITIES INC (PA)
1282 Pacific Oaks Pl, Escondido
(92029-2917)
PHONE....................760 690-5225
Thomas P Dobron, *Pr*
EMP: 93 **EST:** 1990
SQ FT: 4,698
SALES (est): 1.21MM
SALES (corp-wide): 1.21MM **Privately Held**
Web: www.innovative-resort.com
SIC: 1521 Single-family housing construction

(P-409)
JF SHEA CONSTRUCTION INC (HQ)
Also Called: Shea Homes For Active Adults
655 Brea Canyon Rd, Walnut (91789-3078)
P.O. Box 489 (91788-0489)
PHONE....................909 594-9500
▲ **EMP:** 200 **EST:** 1958
SALES (est): 613.04MM
SALES (corp-wide): 2.1B **Privately Held**
Web: www.sheahomes.com
SIC: 1521 1622 6512 New construction, single-family houses; Tunnel construction; Commercial and industrial building operation
PA: J. F. Shea Co., Inc.
655 Brea Canyon Rd
909 594-9500

(P-410)
JMH ENGINEERING AND CNSTR
2825 Temple Ave, Signal Hill (90755-2212)
PHONE....................562 317-1700
EMP: 80
SALES (corp-wide): 2.03MM **Privately Held**
Web: www.jmheandc.com
SIC: 1521 Single-family housing construction
PA: Jmh Engineering And Construction
3291 Wendy Way
562 547-8270

(P-411)
JR CONSTRUCTION INC
8123 Engineer Rd, San Diego
(92111-1907)
PHONE....................858 505-4760
Ramon B Camacho, *Pr*
EMP: 70 **EST:** 1992
SALES (est): 4.82MM **Privately Held**
SIC: 1521 Single-family housing construction

(P-412)
K A R CONSTRUCTION INC
1306 Brooks St, Ontario (91762-3611)
PHONE....................909 988-5054
Kurt Alan Rothweiler, *Prin*
EMP: 70 **EST:** 2010
SALES (est): 12.06MM **Privately Held**
Web: www.karconstruction.com
SIC: 1521 Single-family housing construction

(P-413)
KATERRA CONSTRUCTION LLC
1950 W Corporate Way, Anaheim
(92801-5373)
PHONE....................720 449-3909
EMP: 728
SALES (corp-wide): 1.13B **Privately Held**
Web: www.katerra.com

SIC: **1521** Single-family housing construction
HQ: Katerra Construction Llc
2494 Sand Hill Rd Ste 100
Menlo Park CA 94025
650 422-3572

(P-414)
KB HOME GRATER LOS ANGELES INC (HQ)
10990 Wilshire Blvd Ste 700, Los Angeles (90024-3913)
PHONE...............................310 231-4000
Jeffrey Mezge, *Pr*
EMP: 90 **EST:** 1957
SQ FT: 40,000
SALES (est): 30.58MM
SALES (corp-wide): 6.38B **Publicly Held**
Web: www.smarthome-losangeles.info
SIC: **1521** 1522 Single-family home remodeling, additions, and repairs; Multi-family dwelling construction, nec
PA: Kb Home
10990 Wilshire Blvd Fl 7
310 231-4000

(P-415)
KB HOME GRATER LOS ANGELES INC
36310 Inland Valley Dr, Wildomar (92595-7595)
PHONE...............................951 691-5300
George Brenner, *Mgr*
EMP: 164
SALES (corp-wide): 6.38B **Publicly Held**
Web: www.kbhome.com
SIC: **1521** 1522 Single-family home remodeling, additions, and repairs; Multi-family dwelling construction, nec
HQ: Kb Home Greater Los Angeles Inc.
10990 Wilshire Blvd # 700
Los Angeles CA 90024
310 231-4000

(P-416)
KOLOA PACIFIC CONSTRUCTION INC
12700 Stowe Dr Ste 260, Poway (92064-8870)
PHONE...............................858 486-7800
Ernest H Grabbe Junior, *Prin*
EMP: 114 **EST:** 2009
SALES (est): 37.16MM **Privately Held**
Web: www.koloapacific.com
SIC: **1521** Single-family housing construction

(P-417)
LARGO CONCRETE INC
591 Camino De La Reina Ste 620, San Diego (92108-3108)
PHONE...............................619 356-2142
EMP: 110
Web: www.largoconcrete.com
SIC: **1521** Single-family housing construction
PA: Largo Concrete, Inc.
2741 Walnut Ave Fl 1

(P-418)
MB BUILDERS INC
Also Called: General Contracting
403 S Las Posas Rd, San Marcos (92078-4067)
PHONE...............................760 410-1442
Mike Bowling, *Prin*
EMP: 75 **EST:** 2002
SALES (est): 7.96MM **Privately Held**
SIC: **1521** New construction, single-family houses

(P-419)
MC&A USA LLC
19700 Mariner Ave, Torrance (90503-1648)
PHONE...............................504 267-8145
EMP: 99 **EST:** 2019
SALES (est): 362.92K **Privately Held**
SIC: **1521** Single-family housing construction

(P-420)
MGB CONSTRUCTION INC
91 Commercial Ave, Riverside (92507-1111)
PHONE...............................951 342-0303
Emily Beach, *Pr*
Emilly Beach, *
EMP: 150 **EST:** 2001
SALES (est): 9.51MM **Privately Held**
Web: www.mgbconstruction.net
SIC: **1521** Single-family housing construction

(P-421)
MILENDER WHITE INC
1401 Dove St Ste 500, Newport Beach (92660-2420)
PHONE...............................303 216-0420
EMP: 96
SALES (corp-wide): 725.44K **Privately Held**
Web: www.milenderwhite.com
SIC: **1521** Single-family housing construction
HQ: Milender White Inc.
12655 W 54th Dr
Arvada CO 80002
303 216-0420

(P-422)
NHS WESTERN DIVISION INC
Also Called: Fixd Construction Co.
115 S Palm Ave, Ontario (91762-3847)
PHONE...............................909 947-9931
Damien Melle, *CEO*
Mia Melle, *
EMP: 89 **EST:** 2012
SALES (est): 4.91MM **Privately Held**
SIC: **1521** Single-family housing construction

(P-423)
PACIFIC CAST CNSTR WTRPROOFING
390 Oak Ave Ste A, Carlsbad (92008-2967)
PHONE...............................760 298-3170
James Schilling, *Pr*
EMP: 23 **EST:** 2012
SALES (est): 2.53MM **Privately Held**
Web: www.pacificcoastcorporate.com
SIC: **1521** 1389 Single-family housing construction; Construction, repair, and dismantling services

(P-424)
ROMERO GENERAL CNSTR CORP
8320 Nelson Way, Escondido (92026-5211)
PHONE...............................760 715-0154
Jerusha Finster, *Brnch Mgr*
EMP: 102
Web: www.romerogc.com
SIC: **1521** Single-family housing construction
PA: Romero General Construction Corp.
2150 N Cntre Cy Pkwy Ste

(P-425)
SEARS HOME IMPRV PDTS INC
Also Called: Sears
730 S Orange Ave, West Covina (91790-2613)
PHONE...............................626 671-1892
EMP: 119
SALES (corp-wide): 4.18B **Privately Held**

Web: www.searshomeservices.com
SIC: **1521** General remodeling, single-family houses
HQ: Sears Home Improvement Products, Inc.
1024 Florida Central Pkwy
Longwood FL 32750
407 767-0990

(P-426)
SEARS HOME IMPRV PDTS INC
Also Called: Sears
2900 N Bellflower Blvd, Long Beach (90815-1149)
PHONE...............................562 485-4904
EMP: 119
SALES (corp-wide): 4.18B **Privately Held**
Web: www.searshomeservices.com
SIC: **1521** General remodeling, single-family houses
HQ: Sears Home Improvement Products, Inc.
1024 Florida Central Pkwy
Longwood FL 32750
407 767-0990

(P-427)
SEARS HOME IMPRV PDTS INC
Also Called: Sears
5665 Rosemead Blvd, Temple City (91780-1804)
PHONE...............................626 988-9134
EMP: 119
SALES (corp-wide): 4.18B **Privately Held**
Web: www.searshomeservices.com
SIC: **1521** General remodeling, single-family houses
HQ: Sears Home Improvement Products, Inc.
1024 Florida Central Pkwy
Longwood FL 32750
407 767-0990

(P-428)
SEATTLE TNNEL PRTNERS A JINT V
555 Anton Blvd Ste 1000, Costa Mesa (92626-7019)
PHONE...............................206 971-8701
▲ **EMP:** 300 **EST:** 2010
SALES (est): 472.21K **Privately Held**
SIC: **1521** Single-family home remodeling, additions, and repairs

(P-429)
SERVICMASTER OPCO HOLDINGS LLC
Servicmster Rcvery Svcs By Rgh
13758 Amarillo Ave, Chino (91710-7038)
PHONE...............................951 840-0134
EMP: 854
SALES (corp-wide): 157.41MM **Privately Held**
Web: www.servicemaster.com
SIC: **1521** Single-family home remodeling, additions, and repairs
PA: Servicemaster Opco Holdings Llc
1 Glenlake Pkwy Ste 1400
888 937-3783

(P-430)
SHIMMICK CONSTRUCTION CO INC
16481 Scientific Bldg 2, Irvine (92618-4394)
PHONE...............................510 777-5000
Trina Clay, *Prin*
EMP: 110
SALES (corp-wide): 632.81MM **Publicly Held**

Web: www.shimmick.com
SIC: **1521** Single-family housing construction
HQ: Shimmick Construction Company Incorporated
530 Technology Dr Ste 300
Irvine CA 92618

(P-431)
SHIMMICK CONSTRUCTION CO INC
1999 Avenue Of The Stars Ste 2600, Los Angeles (90067-6033)
PHONE...............................310 663-8924
EMP: 110
SALES (corp-wide): 632.81MM **Publicly Held**
Web: www.shimmick.com
SIC: **1521** Single-family housing construction
HQ: Shimmick Construction Company Incorporated
530 Technology Dr Ste 300
Irvine CA 92618

(P-432)
SILVERADO FRAMING & CNSTR
Also Called: Residential Framer
3091 E La Cadena Dr, Riverside (92507-2630)
P.O. Box 2941 (92516-2941)
PHONE...............................951 352-1100
Ed Solis, *Pr*
EMP: 100 **EST:** 2011
SQ FT: 2,500
SALES (est): 543.66K **Privately Held**
Web: www.silveradoframing.com
SIC: **1521** Single-family housing construction

(P-433)
SUPERIOR CONSTRUCTION INC
265 N Joy St, Corona (92879-0600)
P.O. Box 1148 (92878-1148)
PHONE...............................951 808-8780
Kenneth Day, *Pr*
EMP: 100 **EST:** 1976
SQ FT: 3,000
SALES (est): 9.05MM **Privately Held**
Web: www.superiorconstruction.com
SIC: **1521** 1542 New construction, single-family houses; Commercial and office building, new construction

(P-434)
TRICON AMERICAN HOMES LLC
15771 Red Hill Ave, Tustin (92780-7303)
P.O. Box 15086 (92735-0086)
PHONE...............................844 874-2661
Kevin Baldridge, *Managing Member*
EMP: 177 **EST:** 2012
SALES (est): 35.69MM
SALES (corp-wide): 8.93B **Privately Held**
Web: www.triconresidential.com
SIC: **1521** Single-family home remodeling, additions, and repairs
HQ: Tricon Residential Inc
801-7 St Thomas St
Toronto ON M5S 2
416 925-7228

(P-435)
ULTIMATE BUILDERS INC
23679 Calabasas Rd, Calabasas (91302-1502)
PHONE...............................818 481-2627
EMP: 85
SALES (corp-wide): 8.46MM **Privately Held**
Web: www.repipe1.com
SIC: **1521** New construction, single-family houses
PA: Ultimate Builders, Inc.
19326 Ventura Blvd # 201

PRODUCTS & SVCS

818 342-2568

480 840-8100

510 636-2100

(P-451)

(P-436)

ULTIMATE REMOVAL INC
Also Called: Ultimate Demo
2168 Pomona Blvd, Pomona (91768-3332)
P.O. Box 1220 (91769-1220)
PHONE..............................909 524-0800
John W Welch, *Pr*
Patrick Coleman, *
EMP: 124 EST: 1995
SQ FT: 9,900
SALES (est): 9.8MM **Privately Held**
Web: www.ultimateremoval.com
SIC: **1521** Single-family housing construction

(P-437)

US BEST REPAIR SERVICE INC
Also Called: US Best Repairs
1652 Edinger Ave Ste E, Tustin
(92780-6530)
PHONE..............................888 750-2378
Mark Zaverl, *CEO*
EMP: 101 EST: 2008
SALES (est): 11.24MM **Privately Held**
Web: www.usbestrepairs.com
SIC: **1521 1522 1542** Single-family home
remodeling, additions, and repairs;
Remodeling, multi-family dwellings;
Commercial and office buildings, renovation
and repair

(P-438)

WARMINGTON RESIDENTIAL CAL INC
3090 Pullman St, Costa Mesa
(92626-5901)
PHONE..............................714 557-5511
James Warmington Junior, *Pr*
Matt Tingler, *
Mike Riddlesberger, *
EMP: 150 EST: 2003
SALES (est): 9.91MM **Privately Held**
Web: www.homesbywarmington.com
SIC: **1521** New construction, single-family
houses

(P-439)

WEST COAST ARBORISTS INC
8163 Commercial St, La Mesa
(91942-2928)
PHONE..............................858 566-4204
EMP: 116
SALES (corp-wide): 47.18MM **Privately Held**
Web: www.westcoastarborists.com
SIC: **1521 0783** Single-family home
remodeling, additions, and repairs;
Ornamental shrub and tree services
PA: West Coast Arborists, Inc.
2200 E Via Burton
714 991-1900

(P-440)

WILLIAM LYON HOMES (HQ)
4695 Macarthur Ct Ste 800, Newport Beach
(92660-1863)
PHONE..............................949 833-3600
Matthew Zaist, *Pr*
William Lyon, *
Brian Doyle, *
Colin Severn, *
Jason Liljestrom, *Corporate Secretary*
EMP: 77 EST: 1956
SALES (est): 2.09B
SALES (corp-wide): 7.42B **Publicly Held**
Web: www.lyonhomes.com
SIC: **1521** New construction, single-family
houses
PA: Taylor Morrison Home Corporation
4900 N Scttsdale Rd Ste 2

1522 Residential Construction, Nec

(P-441)

716 MANAGEMENT INC
Also Called: Brentwood Builders
3900 W Alameda Ave # 120, Burbank
(91505-4316)
PHONE..............................818 471-4956
EMP: 70 EST: 2016
SALES (est): 5.1MM **Privately Held**
Web: www.brentwood.builders
SIC: **1522 1542 1531 1521** Residential
construction, nec; Restaurant construction;
Single-family home remodeling, additions,
and repairs

(P-442)

BERNARDS BUILDERS INC
555 1st St, San Fernando (91340-3051)
PHONE..............................818 898-1521
Doug Bernards, *Ch*
Jeffrey G Bernards, *
Greg Simons, *
Ken Menager, *
John Kramer, *
EMP: 330 EST: 2013
SALES (est): 5.18MM
SALES (corp-wide): 98.91MM **Privately Held**
SIC: **1522** Residential construction, nec
PA: Bernards Bros. Inc.
555 First St
818 898-1521

(P-443)

BLH CONSTRUCTION COMPANY
20750 Ventura Blvd Ste 155, Woodland Hills
(91364-6202)
PHONE..............................818 905-3837
Charles Brumbaugh, *CEO*
Brian Holland, *
EMP: 150 EST: 2001
SALES (est): 23.31MM **Privately Held**
SIC: **1522** Apartment building construction

(P-444)

COBALT CONSTRUCTION COMPANY
Also Called: Cobalt Southwest Company
2259 Ward Ave Ste 200, Simi Valley
(93065-1880)
P.O. Box 802018 (91380-2018)
PHONE..............................805 577-6222
Darin Kruse, *CEO*
▲ EMP: 70 EST: 1978
SQ FT: 43,000
SALES (est): 6.55MM **Privately Held**
Web: www.cobaltcc.com
SIC: **1522 8711 1542** Multi-family dwellings,
new construction; Construction and civil
engineering; Commercial and office
building, new construction

(P-445)

CONDON-JOHNSON & ASSOC INC
3434 Grove St, Lemon Grove (91945-1812)
PHONE..............................858 530-9165
George Burr, *Genl Mgr*
EMP: 100
SALES (corp-wide): 85.75MM **Privately Held**
Web: www.condon-johnson.com
SIC: **1522** Residential construction, nec
PA: Condon-Johnson & Associates, Inc.
480 Roland Way Ste 200

(P-446)

FAIRFIELD DEVELOPMENT INC (PA)
Also Called: Ffd II
5355 Mira Sorrento Pl Ste 100, San Diego
(92121-3812)
PHONE..............................858 457-2123
Christopher E Hashioka, *Prin*
James L Bosler, *
Ted Bradford, *
Jay Walker, *
Alan G Bear, *
▲ EMP: 225 EST: 1985
SALES (est): 22.41MM
SALES (corp-wide): 22.41MM **Privately Held**
Web: www.fairfieldresidential.com
SIC: **1522** Multi-family dwelling construction,
nec

(P-447)

G TECH CONSTRUCTION
1291 Simpson Way, Escondido
(92029-1434)
PHONE..............................858 224-2909
George Stepanians, *Owner*
EMP: 121 EST: 1980
SQ FT: 2,000
SALES (est): 1.65MM **Privately Held**
SIC: **1522 1542** Residential construction, nec
; Nonresidential construction, nec

(P-448)

KENNARD DEVELOPMENT GROUP
Also Called: Kdg Construction Consulting
1025 N Brand Blvd Ste 300, Glendale
(91202-3633)
PHONE..............................818 241-0800
Lydia Kennard, *CEO*
Jeffrey Lilly, *
EMP: 98 EST: 1980
SQ FT: 2,500
SALES (est): 8.03MM **Privately Held**
Web: www.kdgcc.com
SIC: **1522 1541 1623 1611** Residential
construction, nec; Industrial buildings and
warehouses; Water, sewer, and utility lines;
Highway and street construction

(P-449)

OLEN RESIDENTIAL REALTY CORP (HQ)
Also Called: Olen Companies, The
7 Corporate Plaza Dr, Newport Beach
(92660-7904)
PHONE..............................949 644-6536
Igor M Olenicoff, *Pr*
EMP: 70 EST: 1992
SALES (est): 47.7MM **Privately Held**
Web: www.olen.com
SIC: **1522** Multi-family dwellings, new
construction
PA: Olen Properties Corp.
7 Corporate Plaza Dr

(P-450)

REBCO COMMUNITIES INC
Also Called: Warmington Homes California
3090 Pullman St, Costa Mesa
(92626-5901)
P.O. Box 2946 (92628-2946)
PHONE..............................714 557-5511
EMP: 310
SIC: **1522** Residential construction, nec

REGIS CONTRACTORS LP
18825 Bardeen Ave, Irvine (92612-1520)
PHONE..............................949 253-0455
Jackie Mcdade, *Pt*
EMP: 122 EST: 1995
SQ FT: 18,000
SALES (est): 619.68K
SALES (corp-wide): 95.9MM **Privately Held**
SIC: **1522** Apartment building construction
PA: Sares Regis Group Residential, Inc.
3501 Jamboree Rd Ste 300
949 756-5959

(P-452)

SBHIS
740 Bay Blvd, Chula Vista (91910-5254)
PHONE..............................619 427-2689
EMP: 71 EST: 2014
SALES (est): 2.27MM **Privately Held**
Web: www.sbhis.net
SIC: **1522** Residential construction, nec

(P-453)

TRI POINTE HOMES INC
Also Called: TRI POINTE HOMES, INC.
57 Furlong, Irvine (92602-1812)
PHONE..............................714 389-5933
Paul Faubion, *Brnch Mgr*
EMP: 132
SALES (corp-wide): 3.67B **Publicly Held**
Web: www.tripointehomes.com
SIC: **1522** Residential construction, nec
HQ: Tri Pointe Homes Holdings, Inc.
3161 Mchelson Dr Ste 1500
Irvine CA 92612

(P-454)

TRI POINTE HOMES HOLDINGS INC (HQ)
Also Called: Tri Pointe
3161 Michelson Dr Ste 1500, Irvine
(92612-4414)
P.O. Box 57088 (92619)
PHONE..............................949 438-1400
Douglas Bauer, *CEO*
Barry S Sternlicht, *
Douglas F Bauer, *
Thomas J Mitchell, *Pr*
Michael D Grubbs, *CFO*
EMP: 118 EST: 2009
SALES (est): 1.38B
SALES (corp-wide): 3.67B **Publicly Held**
Web: www.tripointehomes.com
SIC: **1522** Residential construction, nec
PA: Tri Pointe Homes, Inc.
940 Suthwood Blvd Ste 200
775 413-1030

(P-455)

VAN DAELE HOMES INC
391 N Main St, Corona (92878-4001)
PHONE..............................951 354-2121
Michael B Van Daele, *CEO*
EMP: 78 EST: 1985
SALES (est): 2.95MM **Privately Held**
Web: www.vandaele.com
SIC: **1522** Residential construction, nec

(P-456)

WALTON CONSTRUCTION INC
Also Called: Walton Construction Services
358 E Foothill Blvd Ste 100, San Dimas
(91773-1264)
PHONE..............................909 267-7777
Blake Jackson, *Pr*
E Lee Jackson, *
Rick Walker, *
David Jackson, *

EMP: 80 EST: 2004
SQ FT: 8,000
SALES (est): 20.11MM Privately Held
Web: www.waltonci.com
SIC: 1522 1542 Apartment building construction; Commercial and office building contractors

(P-457)
WERMERS MULTI-FAMILY CORP
Also Called: Wermers
5120 Shoreham Pl Ste 150, San Diego (92122-5959)
PHONE..................858 535-1475
Thomas W Wermers, *Pr*
Jeff Bunker, *
Barry Weber, *
Richard Wood, *
Tom Wermers, *
EMP: 130 EST: 1997
SQ FT: 7,000
SALES (est): 21.72MM Privately Held
Web: www.wermerscompanies.com
SIC: 1522 Hotel/motel and multi-family home construction

(P-458)
WESTERN NATIONAL PRPTS LLC (PA)
Also Called: Arkebauer Properties
8 Executive Cir, Irvine (92614-6746)
P.O. Box 19528 (92623-9528)
PHONE..................949 862-6200
David Stone, *Ch Bd*
Michael K Hayde, *
Rex Delong, *
Debra Meute, *
Jeffrey R Scott, *
▲ EMP: 129 EST: 1981
SQ FT: 37,000
SALES (est): 23.42MM
SALES (corp-wide): 23.42MM Privately Held
Web: www.wng.com
SIC: 1522 6513 6512 6531 Apartment building construction; Apartment building operators; Nonresidential building operators ; Real estate agents and managers

---
1531 Operative Builders

(P-459)
BEAZER MORTGAGE CORPORATION
Also Called: Beazer
1800 E Imperial Hwy Ste 200, Brea (92821-6072)
PHONE..................714 480-1635
John Short, *Mgr*
EMP: 100
SALES (corp-wide): 2.33B Publicly Held
Web: www.beazer.com
SIC: 1531 Speculative builder, single-family houses
HQ: Beazer Mortgage Corporation
2002 Summit Blvd
Brookhaven GA 30319

(P-460)
DR HORTON INC
8501 Fallbrook Ave Ste 270, West Hills (91304-3268)
PHONE..................818 334-1955
EMP: 74
SALES (corp-wide): 36.8B Publicly Held
Web: www.drhorton.com
SIC: 1531 Speculative builder, single-family houses
PA: D.R. Horton, Inc.
1341 Horton Cir

817 390-8200

(P-461)
FIELDSTONE COMMUNITIES INC (PA)
16 Technology Dr Ste 125, Irvine (92618-2325)
PHONE..................949 790-5400
William H Mcfarland, *CEO*
Frank Foster, *
Peter Ochs, *
David Langlois, *
Alan Arthur, *
EMP: 130 EST: 1986
SQ FT: 15,000
SALES (est): 8.72MM Privately Held
SIC: 1531 Speculative builder, single-family houses

(P-462)
KB HOME (PA)
10990 Wilshire Blvd Fl 7, Los Angeles (90024-3907)
PHONE..................310 231-4000
Jeffrey T Mezger, *Ch Bd*
Robert Mcgibney, *Pr*
Jeff J Kaminski, *Ex VP*
Brian J Woram, *Ex VP*
Albert Z Praw, *Executive Real Estate Vice President*
EMP: 100 EST: 1957
SALES (est): 6.38B
SALES (corp-wide): 6.38B Publicly Held
Web: www.kbhome.com
SIC: 1531 Operative builders

(P-463)
LENNAR CORPORATION
15131 Alton Pkwy Ste 190, Irvine (92618-2386)
PHONE..................949 349-8000
Jonathan Jaffe, *COO*
EMP: 100
SALES (corp-wide): 34.23B Publicly Held
Web: www.lennar.com
SIC: 1531 Speculative builder, single-family houses
PA: Lennar Corporation
5505 Waterford Dst Dr
305 559-4000

(P-464)
LEWIS COMPANIES (PA)
1156 N Mountain Ave, Upland (91786-3633)
PHONE..................909 985-0971
Richard A Lewis, *Pr*
Goldy S Lewis, *
Robert E Lewis, *
Roger G Lewis, *
Randall W Lewis, *
EMP: 200 EST: 1973
SALES (est): 1.81MM
SALES (corp-wide): 1.81MM Privately Held
Web: www.lewisgroupofcompanies.com
SIC: 1531 Operative builders

(P-465)
THE RYLAND GROUP INC
3011 Townsgate Rd Ste 200, Westlake Village (91361-5878)
PHONE..................805 367-3800
▼ EMP: 1502
SIC: 1531 1521 6162 Operative builders; Single-family housing construction; Mortgage bankers and loan correspondents

(P-466)
TRI POINTE HOMES INC
Also Called: Tri Pointe Homes, Inc.
5 Peters Canyon Rd Ste 100, Irvine (92606-1792)
PHONE..................949 478-8600
Sarah Shahin, *Off Mgr*
EMP: 132
SALES (corp-wide): 3.67B Publicly Held
Web: www.tripointehomes.com
SIC: 1531 Speculative builder, single-family houses
HQ: Tri Pointe Homes Holdings, Inc.
3161 Mchelson Dr Ste 1500
Irvine CA 92612

(P-467)
VAN DAELE DEVELOPMENT CORP
Also Called: Van Daele Homes
391 N Main St, Corona (92878-4001)
PHONE..................951 354-6800
Michael B Van Daele, *CEO*
Jeff Hack, *
Michael Van Daele, *Prin*
EMP: 110 EST: 1987
SALES (est): 15.91MM Privately Held
Web: www.vandaele.com
SIC: 1531 Speculative builder, single-family houses

(P-468)
WARMINGTON HOMES (PA)
3090 Pullman St, Costa Mesa (92626-7936)
PHONE..................714 434-4435
Timothy P Hogan, *Pr*
James P Warmington, *Ch Bd*
Michael Riddlesperger, *CFO*
▲ EMP: 120 EST: 1972
SQ FT: 40,000
SALES (est): 7.19MM
SALES (corp-wide): 7.19MM Privately Held
Web: www.homesbywarmington.com
SIC: 1531 Speculative builder, single-family houses

(P-469)
WARMINGTON HOMES
15615 Alton Pkwy Ste 150, Irvine (92618-7302)
PHONE..................949 679-3100
EMP: 127
SALES (corp-wide): 7.19MM Privately Held
Web: www.homesbywarmington.com
SIC: 1531 Speculative builder, single-family houses
PA: Warmington Homes
3000 Pullman St
714 434-4435

1541 Industrial Buildings And Warehouses

(P-470)
AMAYA CURIEL CORPORATION
Also Called: Amaya Curiel Y CIA S.A.
9775 Marconi Dr Ste G, San Diego (92154-7267)
PHONE..................619 661-1230
Roberto Curiel, *Prin*
EMP: 900 EST: 1972
SALES (est): 9.91MM Privately Held
SIC: 1541 Warehouse construction

(P-471)
AMERICAN DE ROSA LAMPARTS LLC
Also Called: Luminance
10650 4th St, Rancho Cucamonga (91730-5918)
PHONE..................800 777-4440
EMP: 95
SALES (corp-wide): 19.21MM Privately Held
Web: luminance.us.com
SIC: 1541 Industrial buildings and warehouses
HQ: American De Rosa Lamparts, Llc
370 Falls Commerce Pkwy
Cuyahoga Falls OH 44224

(P-472)
BAKELL LLC
Also Called: Jdi Distribution
824 Lytle St, Redlands (92374-6230)
PHONE..................800 292-2137
Deborah Blevins, *Managing Member*
Justin Jordan, *
EMP: 65 EST: 2015
SALES (est): 4.58MM Privately Held
Web: www.bakell.com
SIC: 1541 5149 2051 3299 Food products manufacturing or packing plant construction ; Baking supplies; Bakery: wholesale or wholesale/retail combined; Mica products

(P-473)
BETHLEHEM CONSTRUCTION INC
425 J St, Wasco (93280-2335)
PHONE..................661 758-1001
Michael J Addleman, *Brnch Mgr*
EMP: 86
SALES (corp-wide): 32.84MM Privately Held
Web: www.bethlehemconstruction.com
SIC: 1541 1542 Warehouse construction; Commercial and office building, new construction
PA: Bethlehem Construction Incorporated
5505 Titchenal Way
509 782-1001

(P-474)
BIOTIX
6995 Calle De Linea Ste 106, San Diego (92154-8015)
PHONE..................858 875-5479
Mel Johnson, *Mgr*
EMP: 27
Web: www.biotix.com
SIC: 1541 2869 Industrial buildings and warehouses; Laboratory chemicals, organic
HQ: Biotix
10030 Scripps Summit Ct # 130
San Diego CA 92131
858 875-7696

(P-475)
CALIFORNIA SHTMTL WORKS INC
Also Called: California Sheet Metal
1020 N Marshall Ave, El Cajon (92020-1829)
PHONE..................619 562-7010
Robin Hoffos, *Pr*
Joe Isom, *
▲ EMP: 90 EST: 1913
SQ FT: 15,000
SALES (est): 41.52MM Privately Held
Web: www.califsheetmetal.com

SIC: **1541** 3444 Renovation, remodeling and repairs: industrial buildings; Sheet metalwork

(P-476)
CLARK CNSTR GROUP - CAL INC
18201 Von Karman Ave Ste 800, Irvine (92612-1092)
PHONE.....................714 754-0764
Richard M Heim, *Pr*
EMP: 450 **EST:** 2012
SALES (est): 34.03MM
SALES (corp-wide): 1.66B **Privately Held**
SIC: **1541** 1542 Industrial buildings and warehouses; Nonresidential construction, nec
HQ: Clark Construction Group, Llc
7900 Westpark Dr Ste T300
Mclean VA 22102
301 272-8100

(P-477)
CMC REBAR WEST
7326 Mission Gorge Rd, San Diego (92120-1224)
PHONE.....................858 737-7700
EMP: 121
SALES (corp-wide): 1.56B **Privately Held**
Web: www.cmc.com
SIC: **1541** Steel building construction
HQ: Cmc Rebar West
3880 Murphy Canyon Rd # 100
San Diego CA 92123

(P-478)
CMC REBAR WEST
10840 Norwalk Blvd, Santa Fe Springs (90670-3826)
PHONE.....................714 692-7082
Lee Albright, *Brnch Mgr*
EMP: 73
SALES (corp-wide): 1.56B **Privately Held**
Web: www.cmc.com
SIC: **1541** Industrial buildings and warehouses
HQ: Cmc Rebar West
3880 Murphy Canyon Rd # 100
San Diego CA 92123

(P-479)
EDNA H PAGEL INC
Also Called: Sweetener Products
2050 E 38th St, Vernon (90058-1615)
P.O. Box 58426 (90058-0426)
PHONE.....................323 234-2200
EMP: 96
SIC: **1541** 5153 4213 Food products manufacturing or packing plant construction ; Soybeans; Trucking, except local

(P-480)
FRIZE CORPORATION
16605 Gale Ave, City Of Industry (91745-1802)
PHONE.....................800 834-2127
James N Frize, *Pr*
EMP: 80 **EST:** 1981
SQ FT: 25,000
SALES (est): 36.61MM **Privately Held**
Web: www.frizecorp.com
SIC: **1541** 1542 Industrial buildings and warehouses; Commercial and office building contractors

(P-481)
FULLMER CONSTRUCTION
1725 S Grove Ave, Ontario (91761-4530)
PHONE.....................909 947-9467
Robert A Fullmer, *Pr*

Gary Fullmer, *
Brad Anderson, *
James Fullmer, *
Gered Yetter, *
◆ **EMP:** 120 **EST:** 1946
SQ FT: 20,000
SALES (est): 41.15MM **Privately Held**
Web: www.fullmerco.com
SIC: **1541** Industrial buildings, new construction, nec

(P-482)
GRAY WEST CONSTRUCTION INC
Also Called: GRAY WC
2070 N Tustin Ave, Santa Ana (92705-7827)
PHONE.....................714 491-1317
Brian Silver, *CEO*
EMP: 175 **EST:** 1999
SALES (est): 24.97MM **Privately Held**
SIC: **1541** Renovation, remodeling and repairs: industrial buildings

(P-483)
GRIMMWAY ENTERPRISES INC
Grimmway Farm
12020 Malaga Rd, Arvin (93203-9527)
PHONE.....................661 854-6240
EMP: 251
SALES (corp-wide): 577.4MM **Privately Held**
Web: www.grimmway.com
SIC: **1541** 1542 Industrial buildings and warehouses; Nonresidential construction, nec
PA: Grimmway Enterprises, Inc.
12064 Buena Vista Blvd
800 301-3101

(P-484)
H C OLSEN CNSTR CO INC
710 Los Angeles Ave, Monrovia (91016-4250)
PHONE.....................626 359-8900
Linda Jacqueline Pearson, *CEO*
Karl Pearson, *
EMP: 75 **EST:** 1946
SQ FT: 12,800
SALES (est): 20.44MM **Privately Held**
Web: www.hcolsen.com
SIC: **1541** Industrial buildings, new construction, nec

(P-485)
HAL HAYS CONSTRUCTION INC (PA)
4181 Latham St, Riverside (92501-1729)
PHONE.....................951 788-0703
Kirby Hays, *CEO*
Hal Hays, *
EMP: 113 **EST:** 1990
SQ FT: 28,400
SALES (est): 56.37MM **Privately Held**
Web: www.halhays.com
SIC: **1541** 1542 1623 1629 Industrial buildings and warehouses; Commercial and office buildings, renovation and repair; Water, sewer, and utility lines; Dams, waterways, docks, and other marine construction

(P-486)
HEIL CONSTRUCTION INC
701 S Myrtle Ave, Monrovia (91016-3422)
PHONE.....................626 303-7141
EMP: 70

SIC: **1541** 1542 8741 Industrial buildings and warehouses; Commercial and office building contractors; Business management

(P-487)
ISEC INCORPORATED
10105 Carroll Canyon Rd, San Diego (92131-1109)
PHONE.....................858 279-9085
Louis L Anderson, *Pr*
EMP: 103
SALES (corp-wide): 317.22MM **Privately Held**
Web: www.isecinc.com
SIC: **1541** Industrial buildings, new construction, nec
PA: Isec, Incorporated
6000 Grnwood Plz Blvd Ste
303 790-1444

(P-488)
KEVCON INC
10679 Westview Pkwy, San Diego (92126-2961)
PHONE.....................760 432-0307
Kevin Kutina, *Pr*
EMP: 84 **EST:** 1988
SQ FT: 600
SALES (est): 5.26MM **Privately Held**
Web: www.kevcon.us
SIC: **1541** 1542 8741 Industrial buildings and warehouses; Commercial and office building contractors; Management services

(P-489)
KUSTOM KANOPIES INC
210 Senior Cir, Lompoc (93436-1491)
PHONE.....................801 399-3400
TOLL FREE: 800
Wesley R Robison, *Pr*
Ronald E Schwartz, *
Sharee Robison, *
EMP: 30 **EST:** 1987
SQ FT: 56,000
SALES (est): 541.36K **Privately Held**
SIC: **1541** 5999 3444 Industrial buildings and warehouses; Awnings; Sheet metalwork

(P-490)
LEDCOR CMI INC
6405 Mira Mesa Blvd Ste 100, San Diego (92121-4120)
PHONE.....................602 595-3017
David W Lede, *Ch*
Cliff Lede, *Vice Chairman*
EMP: 82 **EST:** 2003
SALES (est): 3.31MM **Privately Held**
Web: www.ledcor.com
SIC: **1541** 1611 1629 1623 Industrial buildings and warehouses; Highway and street construction; Mine loading and discharging station construction; Pipeline construction, nsk

(P-491)
MAINTENANCE RESOURCE INC
Also Called: Facilities Resource Group
1151 N Del Rio Pl, Ontario (91764-4505)
PHONE.....................616 406-0004
John N Weeber, *CEO*
John N Weeber, *Pr*
Brad Kirk, *
▲ **EMP:** 75 **EST:** 1999
SALES (est): 10.09MM **Privately Held**
Web: www.webfrg.com
SIC: **1541** 1711 1731 Renovation, remodeling and repairs: industrial buildings; Plumbing, heating, air-conditioning; Electrical work

(P-492)
MILLIE AND SEVERSON INC
3601 Serpentine Dr, Los Alamitos (90720-2440)
PHONE.....................562 493-3611
Scott Feest, *Pr*
Brian Cresap, *Prin*
Robert E Wissmann, *
John Grossman, *
Mark Huber, *
EMP: 75 **EST:** 1945
SQ FT: 15,000
SALES (est): 24.56MM **Privately Held**
Web: www.mandsinc.com
SIC: **1541** Industrial buildings, new construction, nec
PA: Severson Group Incorporated
3601 Serpentine Dr

(P-493)
MINSHEW BROTHERS STL CNSTR INC
12578 Vigilante Rd, Lakeside (92040-1112)
P.O. Box 1000 (92040-0902)
EMP: 105 **EST:** 1992
SQ FT: 22,000
SALES (est): 9.99MM **Privately Held**
SIC: **1541** 1791 Steel building construction; Structural steel erection

(P-494)
MORLEY BUILDERS INC (PA)
Also Called: Benchmark Contractors
3330 Ocean Park Blvd, Santa Monica (90405-3202)
PHONE.....................310 399-1600
EMP: 140 **EST:** 1984
SALES (est): 92.7MM
SALES (corp-wide): 92.7MM **Privately Held**
Web: www.morleybuilders.com
SIC: **1541** 1522 1542 1771 Industrial buildings and warehouses; Multi-family dwelling construction, nec; Commercial and office building contractors; Concrete work

(P-495)
OLTMANS CONSTRUCTION CO (PA)
10005 Mission Mill Rd, Whittier (90601-1739)
P.O. Box 985 (90608-0985)
PHONE.....................562 948-4242
Joseph O Oltmans Ii, *Ch Bd*
John Gormly, *
Charles Roy, *SERV*
Jim Woodside, *
Gerald Singh, *
▼ **EMP:** 85 **EST:** 1932
SQ FT: 33,000
SALES (est): 153.33K
SALES (corp-wide): 153.33K **Privately Held**
Web: www.oltmans.com
SIC: **1541** 1542 Industrial buildings, new construction, nec; Commercial and office building, new construction

(P-496)
OLTMANS CONSTRUCTION CO
270 Conejo Ridge Ave Ste 210, Thousand Oaks (91361-4957)
PHONE.....................805 495-9553
Robert Larson, *Mgr*
EMP: 438
SQ FT: 2,600
SALES (corp-wide): 153.33K **Privately Held**
Web: www.oltmans.com

SIC: **1541** 1542 Industrial buildings and warehouses; Nonresidential construction, nec

PA: The Oltmans Construction Co
10005 Mission Mill Rd
562 948-4242

(P-497)
PURE SIMPLE FOODS LLC
Also Called: Lark Ellen Farm
420 Bryant Cir Ste B, Ojai (93023-4209)
PHONE..............................805 272-8448
Kelley D'angelo, *CEO*
EMP: 25 **EST:** 2021
SALES (est): 3.43MM **Privately Held**
SIC: **1541** 5149 2068 Food products manufacturing or packing plant construction ; Health foods; Nuts: dried, dehydrated, salted or roasted

(P-498)
RQ CONSTRUCTION LLC
1620 Faraday Ave, Carlsbad (92008-7313)
PHONE..............................760 631-7707
George H Rogers Iii, *CEO*
Craig Shadle, *CFO*
Mary Baker, *Sec*
EMP: 170 **EST:** 1996
SALES (est): 218.46MM **Privately Held**
Web: www.rqconstruction.com
SIC: **1541** Industrial buildings, new construction, nec

(P-499)
RUSSELL HOBBS INC
2301 W San Bernardino Ave, Redlands (92374-5007)
PHONE..............................909 792-8257
Russell Hobbs, *Brnch Mgr*
EMP: 197
SALES (corp-wide): 2.96B **Publicly Held**
SIC: **1541** Industrial buildings and warehouses
HQ: Russell Hobbs, Inc.
3633 S Flamingo Rd
Miramar FL 33027
954 883-1000

(P-500)
SHIMS BARGAIN INC
Also Called: JC Sales
7030 E Slauson Ave, Commerce (90040-3621)
PHONE..............................323 726-8800
Andy Kim, *Mgr*
EMP: 116
Web: www.jcsalesweb.com
SIC: **1541** Industrial buildings and warehouses
PA: Shims Bargain, Inc.
2600 S Soto St

(P-501)
SMITH MCHNCL-LCTRICAL-PLUMBING
Also Called: Smith Electric Service
1340 W Betteravia Rd, Santa Maria (93455-1030)
PHONE..............................805 621-5000
Michael Brannon, *Pr*
Larry Brannon, *
EMP: 150 **EST:** 1980
SQ FT: 10,000
SALES (est): 46.92MM **Privately Held**
Web: www.smithmep.com
SIC: **1541** 1711 1731 1542 Industrial buildings, new construction, nec; Plumbing, heating, air-conditioning; Fire detection and burglar alarm systems specialization; Nonresidential construction, nec

(P-502)
SPECTRUM CNSTR GROUP INC
14252 Culver Dr Ste 356, Irvine (92604-0317)
PHONE..............................949 246-9749
Bisher Aljazzar, *CEO*
EMP: 99 **EST:** 2016
SALES (est): 23.55MM **Privately Held**
Web: www.spectrumcgi.com
SIC: **1541** 1622 1542 1611 Steel building construction; Bridge, tunnel, and elevated highway construction; Commercial and office building, new construction; Highway and street construction

(P-503)
SQUARE H BRANDS INC
3615 E Vernon Ave, Vernon (90058-1815)
PHONE..............................323 267-4600
Bobby Codilla, *Prin*
EMP: 100
SALES (corp-wide): 24.28MM **Privately Held**
Web: www.hoffybrand.com
SIC: **1541** Food products manufacturing or packing plant construction
PA: Square H Brands, Inc.
2731 S Soto St
323 267-4600

(P-504)
STANTRU RESOURCES INC
Also Called: Stantru Reinforcing Steel
11175 Redwood Ave, Fontana (92337-7137)
P.O. Box 310189 (92331-0189)
PHONE..............................909 587-1441
Ida Ichen, *Pr*
William M Klorman, *
EMP: 83 **EST:** 1991
SALES (est): 4.06MM **Privately Held**
Web: www.stantru.com
SIC: **1541** 1542 Industrial buildings, new construction, nec; Commercial and office building, new construction

(P-505)
SUNNY SERVICE GROUP LLC
Also Called: Probio Medicine Corp
192 Technology Dr Ste T, Irvine (92618-2414)
PHONE..............................323 818-2625
Dzmitry Mikhnavets, *Managing Member*
EMP: 45 **EST:** 2016
SALES (est): 311.72K **Privately Held**
Web: www.probiomed.org
SIC: **1541** 7389 2499 Food products manufacturing or packing plant construction ; Labeling bottles, cans, cartons, etc.; Food handling and processing products, wood

(P-506)
SYNEAR FOODS USA LLC
Also Called: Synear Foods
9601 Canoga Ave, Chatsworth (91311-4115)
PHONE..............................818 341-3588
EMP: 36 **EST:** 2015
SALES (est): 49.08MM **Privately Held**
Web: www.synearusa.com
SIC: **1541** 2038 Food products manufacturing or packing plant construction ; Breakfasts, frozen and packaged
PA: Zhengzhou Synear Food Co., Ltd.
No. 13 Yingcai Street, Huiji District

(P-507)
T B PENICK & SONS INC
13280 Evening Creek Dr S Ste 100, San Diego (92128-4109)

PHONE..............................858 558-1800
Marc E Penick, *CEO*
Timothy Penick, *Pr*
John T Boyd, *CFO*
Keely Prochaska Ctrl, *Prin*
EMP: 150 **EST:** 1905
SQ FT: 30,000
SALES (est): 116.67MM **Privately Held**
Web: www.tbpenick.com
SIC: **1541** 1542 Industrial buildings and warehouses; Nonresidential construction, nec

(P-508)
TAISEI CONSTRUCTION CORPORATION
970 W 190th St Ste 920, Torrance (90502-1063)
PHONE..............................714 886-1530
▲ **EMP:** 120
SIC: **1541** 1542 Industrial buildings and warehouses; Nonresidential construction, nec

(P-509)
TRI-TECH RESTORATION CO INC
3301 N San Fernando Blvd, Burbank (91504-2531)
PHONE..............................818 565-3900
Armine Bakmazian, *Pr*
Michael Boyd, *
EMP: 70 **EST:** 1995
SQ FT: 35,000
SALES (est): 16.31MM **Privately Held**
Web: www.tritechrestoration.com
SIC: **1541** Industrial buildings and warehouses

(P-510)
UNIVERSAL DUST CLLCTR MFG SUP (PA)
Also Called: UDC
1041 N Kraemer Pl, Anaheim (92806-2611)
PHONE..............................714 630-8588
Theresa A Shaffer, *CEO*
Curt Schendel, *
George G Shaffer, *
Deborah Huerta, *
EMP: 89 **EST:** 1984
SQ FT: 30,000
SALES (est): 25.21MM
SALES (corp-wide): 25.21MM **Privately Held**
Web: www.udccorporation.com
SIC: **1541** Industrial buildings, new construction, nec

(P-511)
UPRITE CONSTRUCTION CORP
Also Called: General Contractor
2211 Michelson Dr Ste 350, Irvine (92612-1390)
PHONE..............................949 877-8877
Robert Dellaringa, *CEO*
Joe Martino, *
Phil Tanghal, *
Jay Olson, *
Tracy Zalke, *
EMP: 78 **EST:** 1991
SQ FT: 3,500
SALES (est): 34.58MM **Privately Held**
Web: www.upriteco.com
SIC: **1541** 5082 Warehouse construction; General construction machinery and equipment

(P-512)
WEST COAST DISTRIBUTION INC
4440 E 26th St, Vernon (90058-4318)
PHONE..............................323 588-6508
Kelly Wicker, *Brnch Mgr*
EMP: 82
SALES (corp-wide): 4.55MM **Privately Held**
Web: www.montagefulfillment.com
SIC: **1541** 4789 Industrial buildings and warehouses; Pipeline terminal facilities, independently operated
PA: West Coast Distribution, Inc.
2602 E 37th St
323 588-6508

1542 Nonresidential Construction, Nec

(P-513)
2H CONSTRUCTION INC
2653 Walnut Ave, Signal Hill (90755-1830)
PHONE..............................562 424-5567
Sean Hitchcock, *Pr*
Ronald Compton, *
Ericka Hitchcock, *
EMP: 70 **EST:** 1997
SQ FT: 8,000
SALES (est): 28.05MM **Privately Held**
Web: www.2hconstruction.com
SIC: **1542** Commercial and office building, new construction

(P-514)
ABHE & SVOBODA INC
880 Tavern Rd, Alpine (91901-3810)
PHONE..............................619 659-1320
David Grant, *Mgr*
EMP: 85
SALES (corp-wide): 1.96MM **Privately Held**
Web: www.abheonline.com
SIC: **1542** Commercial and office building, new construction
PA: Abhe & Svoboda, Inc.
18100 Dairy Ln
952 447-6025

(P-515)
AIS CONSTRUCTION COMPANY
7015 Vista Del Rincon Dr, Ventura (93001-9758)
P.O. Box 4209 (93403-4209)
PHONE..............................805 928-9467
Andy Sheaffer, *Pr*
EMP: 85 **EST:** 1996
SQ FT: 4,000
SALES (est): 7.87MM **Privately Held**
Web: www.aisconstruction.com
SIC: **1542** Commercial and office building contractors

(P-516)
ANDERSON BURTON CNSTR INC (PA)
121 Nevada St, Arroyo Grande (93420-2609)
PHONE..............................805 481-5096
Joann Anderson, *Pr*
EMP: 99 **EST:** 1999
SQ FT: 5,000
SALES (est): 39MM **Privately Held**
Web: www.andersonburton.com
SIC: **1542** 1522 Commercial and office building, new construction; Residential construction, nec

(P-517)
ANDREW L YOUNGQUIST CNSTR INC
3187 Red Hill Ave Ste 200, Costa Mesa (92626-3454)
PHONE..................949 862-5611
Andrew L Youngquist, *Ch Bd*
James Lefler, *
Richard Lee Youngquist, *
EMP: 90 **EST:** 1996
SQ FT: 10,319
SALES (est): 4.26MM **Privately Held**
SIC: 1542 1522 8741 Commercial and office building contractors; Residential construction, nec; Construction management

(P-518)
AUSTIN COMMERCIAL LP
402 W Broadway Ste 400, San Diego (92101-3554)
PHONE..................619 446-5637
James Cole, *Off Mgr*
EMP: 73
SALES (corp-wide): 2.22B **Privately Held**
Web: www.austin-ind.com
SIC: 1542 Commercial and office building, new construction
HQ: Austin Commercial, Lp
3535 Travis St Ste 300
Dallas TX 75204
214 443-5500

(P-519)
AUSTIN COMMERCIAL LP
5901 W Century Blvd Ste 600, Los Angeles (90045-5442)
PHONE..................310 421-0269
Clive Buchan, *Brnch Mgr*
EMP: 73
SALES (corp-wide): 2.22B **Privately Held**
Web: www.austin-ind.com
SIC: 1542 Commercial and office building, new construction
HQ: Austin Commercial, Lp
3535 Travis St Ste 300
Dallas TX 75204
214 443-5500

(P-520)
BALFOUR BEATTY CNSTR LLC
13520 Evening Creek Dr N Ste 270, San Diego (92128-8105)
PHONE..................858 635-7400
EMP: 100
SALES (corp-wide): 9.96B **Privately Held**
Web: www.balfourbeattyus.com
SIC: 1542 Commercial and office building, new construction
HQ: Balfour Beatty Construction, Llc
3100 Mckinnon St 3rd Fl
Dallas TX 75201
214 451-1000

(P-521)
BARNHART INC
10620 Treena St Ste 300, San Diego (92131-1141)
P.O. Box 270399 (92198-2399)
PHONE..................858 635-7400
◆ **EMP:** 291
SIC: 1542 8741 Commercial and office building, new construction; Construction management

(P-522)
BERGMAN KPRS LLC (PA)
2850 Saturn St Ste 100, Brea (92821-1701)
PHONE..................714 924-7000
Mark C Bergman, *Prin*

Joel H Stensby, *
Lev Rabinovich, *
Paul Kristedja, *
EMP: 125 **EST:** 1982
SQ FT: 7,500
SALES (est): 16.5MM
SALES (corp-wide): 16.5MM **Privately Held**
Web: www.bergmankprs.com
SIC: 1542 Restaurant construction

(P-523)
BOMEL CONSTRUCTION CO INC
939 E Francis St, Ontario (91761-5631)
PHONE..................909 923-3319
Richard Laughlin, *Mgr*
EMP: 106
SALES (corp-wide): 63.12MM **Privately Held**
Web: www.bomelconstruction.com
SIC: 1542 Commercial and office building, new construction
PA: Bomel Construction Co., Inc.
96 Corporate Park Ste 100
714 921-1660

(P-524)
BR BUILDING RESOURCES CO
2247 Lindsay Way, Glendora (91740-5398)
P.O. Box 2090 (91740)
PHONE..................626 963-4880
Gary Pellant, *Pr*
Juan Banos, *
Jose Banos, *
Vanessa Banos, *
Ramon Banos, *
EMP: 120 **EST:** 2009
SQ FT: 9,000
SALES (est): 28MM **Privately Held**
Web: www.brco.com
SIC: 1542 Commercial and office buildings, renovation and repair

(P-525)
BYCOR GENERAL CONTRACTORS INC
Also Called: Bycor General Contractors
6490 Marindustry Dr, San Diego (92121-5297)
PHONE..................858 587-1901
Scott Kaats, *CEO*
Richard A Byer, *
EMP: 90 **EST:** 1975
SQ FT: 10,041
SALES (est): 118.05MM **Privately Held**
Web: www.bycor.com
SIC: 1542 Commercial and office building, new construction

(P-526)
C W DRIVER INCORPORATED
Also Called: C. W. DRIVER, INCORPORATED
7588 Metropolitan Dr, San Diego (92108-4401)
PHONE..................619 696-5100
Joe Grosshart, *Dir*
EMP: 107
SALES (corp-wide): 77.45MM **Privately Held**
Web: www.cwdriver.com
SIC: 1542 Commercial and office building, new construction
PA: C.W. Driver, Llc
468 N Rosemead
626 351-8800

(P-527)
CALIFORNIA STRL CONCEPTS INC

28358 Constellation Rd Ste 660, Valencia (91355-5040)
PHONE..................661 257-6903
Jeffrey Horne, *CEO*
Penny Horne, *
EMP: 85 **EST:** 2006
SALES (est): 14.03MM **Privately Held**
Web: www.cscbuilding.net
SIC: 1542 Commercial and office building, new construction

(P-528)
CASTLE & COOKE INVESTMENTS INC
1 Dole Dr, Westlake Village (91362-7300)
PHONE..................310 208-3636
David H Murdock, *CEO*
EMP: 200 **EST:** 2008
SALES (est): 4.9MM **Privately Held**
SIC: 1542 7011 7359 1522 Commercial and office building, new construction; Resort hotel; Equipment rental and leasing, nec; Hotel/motel, new construction

(P-529)
CIRKS CONSTRUCTION INC
Also Called: Kds Construction
507 W Blueridge Ave, Orange (92865-4205)
PHONE..................877 632-6717
EMP: 70
SALES (corp-wide): 208.37MM **Privately Held**
SIC: 1542 Commercial and office building, new construction
PA: Cirks Construction Inc.
1927 N Glassell St
714 632-6717

(P-530)
CLARK CNSTR GROUP - CAL LP
18201 Von Karman Ave Ste 800, Irvine (92612-1092)
PHONE..................714 429-9779
Richard M Heim, *CEO*
EMP: 393 **EST:** 2004
SQ FT: 5,000
SALES (est): 7.47MM
SALES (corp-wide): 1.66B **Privately Held**
SIC: 1542 Commercial and office building, new construction
HQ: Clark Construction Group, Llc
7900 Westpark Dr Ste T300
Mclean VA 22102
301 272-8100

(P-531)
CLAY CORONA COMPANY (PA)
22079 Knabe Rd, Corona (92883-7111)
PHONE..................951 277-2667
Gerald K Deleo, *Pr*
Craig Deleo, *
Joyce Deleo, *
EMP: 23 **EST:** 1947
SALES (est): 9.48MM
SALES (corp-wide): 9.48MM **Privately Held**
Web: www.coronaclayco.com
SIC: 1542 3295 8711 1794 Commercial and office building contractors; Minerals, ground or treated; Construction and civil engineering; Excavation work

(P-532)
COLOMBO CONSTRUCTION CO INC
3211 Rio Mirada Dr, Bakersfield (93308-4945)
PHONE..................661 316-0100
EMP: 75 **EST:** 1946

SALES (est): 25.25MM **Privately Held**
Web: www.colomboconstruction.com
SIC: 1542 1541 Commercial and office building, new construction; Industrial buildings, new construction, nec

(P-533)
CREW BUILDERS INC
8130 Commercial St, La Mesa (91942-2926)
P.O. Box 6205 (92166-0205)
PHONE..................619 587-2033
Jeff D Salewsky, *CEO*
Jon Archer, *
EMP: 120 **EST:** 2006
SALES (est): 27.33MM **Privately Held**
Web: www.crewbuilders.com
SIC: 1542 Commercial and office building, new construction

(P-534)
DPR CONSTRUCTION A GEN PARTNR
5010 Shoreham Pl Ste 100, San Diego (92122-6900)
PHONE..................858 646-0757
Peter Salvati, *Dir*
EMP: 244
Web: www.dpr.com
SIC: 1542 Commercial and office building, new construction
HQ: Dpr Construction, A General Partnership
1450 Veterans Blvd
Redwood City CA 94063

(P-535)
DPR CONSTRUCTION A GEN PARTNR
88 W Colorado Blvd Ste 301, Pasadena (91105-3703)
PHONE..................626 463-1265
Dal Swain, *Brnch Mgr*
EMP: 101
Web: www.dpr.com
SIC: 1542 Commercial and office building, new construction
HQ: Dpr Construction, A General Partnership
1450 Veterans Blvd
Redwood City CA 94063

(P-536)
ENGEL HOLDINGS INC
Also Called: Cabrillo Hoist
14754 Ceres Ave, Fontana (92335-4205)
P.O. Box 3179 (91729-3179)
PHONE..................866 950-9862
Conal Molloy, *Pr*
▲ **EMP:** 103 **EST:** 1977
SQ FT: 2,000
SALES (est): 9.23MM
SALES (corp-wide): 2.16B **Privately Held**
Web: www.safwayatlantic.com
SIC: 1542 Commercial and office building contractors
HQ: Safway Atlantic, Llc
700 Commercial Ave
Carlstadt NJ 07072
201 636-5500

(P-537)
ENVIRONMENTAL CONSTRUCTION INC
21550 Oxnard St Ste 1060, Woodland Hills (91367-7123)
PHONE..................818 449-8920
Farid Soroudi, *CEO*
Zia Abhari, *

▲ = Import ▼ = Export
◆ = Import/Export

EMP: 90 **EST:** 2004
SQ FT: 2,500
SALES (est): 23.79MM **Privately Held**
Web:
www.environmentalconstructioninc.com
SIC: 1542 Commercial and office building contractors

(P-538)

ERICKSON-HALL CONSTRUCTION CO (PA)

500 Corporate Dr, Escondido (92029-1517)
PHONE...................760 796-7700
Dave Erickson, *CEO*
Mike Hall, *
Mike Conroy, *
Mat Gates, *
EMP: 86 **EST:** 1998
SALES (est): 40.45MM
SALES (corp-wide): 40.45MM **Privately Held**
Web: www.ericksonhall.com
SIC: 1542 Commercial and office building, new construction

(P-539)

FJ WILLERT CONTRACTING CO

1869 Nirvana Ave, Chula Vista (91911-6117)
PHONE...................619 421-1980
Fred M Willert, *Pr*
EMP: 110 **EST:** 1972
SQ FT: 11,748
SALES (est): 44.08MM **Privately Held**
Web: www.fjwillert.com
SIC: 1542 Commercial and office building, new construction

(P-540)

GRANI INSTALLATION INC (PA)

5411 Commercial Dr, Huntington Beach (92649-1231)
PHONE...................714 898-0441
Gregory A Grani, *CEO*
EMP: 100 **EST:** 1973
SQ FT: 6,000
SALES (est): 23.05MM
SALES (corp-wide): 23.05MM **Privately Held**
Web: www.grani.biz
SIC: 1542 1742 Commercial and office buildings, renovation and repair; Acoustical and ceiling work

(P-541)

HAMANN CONSTRUCTION

1000 Pioneer Way, El Cajon (92020-1923)
PHONE...................619 440-7424
Jeffrey C Hamann, *CEO*
Jeffrey C Hamann, *Pr*
Gregg Hamann, *
EMP: 75 **EST:** 1954
SQ FT: 15,000
SALES (est): 42.19MM **Privately Held**
Web: www.hamannco.com
SIC: 1542 Commercial and office building, new construction

(P-542)

HAR-BRO LLC (HQ)

2750 Signal Pkwy, Signal Hill (90755-2207)
PHONE...................562 528-8000
EMP: 80 **EST:** 1956
SALES (est): 49.46MM
SALES (corp-wide): 161.86MM **Privately Held**
Web: www.goblusky.com

SIC: 1542 1521 1522 Commercial and office building, new construction; New construction, single-family houses; Apartment building construction
PA: Blusky Restoration Contractors, Llc
9110 E Nchols Ave Ste 180
303 789-4258

(P-543)

HARVEY USA LLC

Also Called: Harvey General Contracting
9455 Ridgehaven Ct Ste 200, San Diego (92123-1649)
PHONE...................858 769-4000
Stephen Harvey, *CEO*
Paul J Pietsch, *
Debra Gillespie, *
EMP: 125 **EST:** 2005
SALES (est): 23.24MM **Privately Held**
Web: www.harveyusa.com
SIC: 1542 Commercial and office building, new construction

(P-544)

HEALTHCARE DESIGN & CNSTR LLC

Also Called: Hdc
18302 Irvine Blvd Ste 120, Tustin (92780-3436)
PHONE...................714 245-0144
Scot Berlinski, *Pr*
EMP: 73 **EST:** 2013
SALES (est): 22MM **Privately Held**
Web: www.hdcbuilders.com
SIC: 1542 Hospital construction

(P-545)

HENSEL PHELPS CONSTRUCTION CO

Also Called: Hensel Phelps
18850 Von Karman Ave Ste 100, Irvine (92612-1598)
PHONE...................626 636-4449
EMP: 77
SALES (corp-wide): 6.9B **Privately Held**
Web: www.henselphelps.com
SIC: 1542 Commercial and office building, new construction
PA: Hensel Phelps Construction Co.
420 6th Ave
970 352-6565

(P-546)

HITT CONTRACTING INC

3733 Motor Ave Ste 200, Los Angeles (90034-6403)
PHONE...................424 326-1042
EMP: 250
SALES (corp-wide): 1.22B **Privately Held**
Web: www.hitt.com
SIC: 1542 1531 Nonresidential construction, nec; Operative builders
PA: Hitt Contracting, Inc.
2900 Fairview Park Dr
703 846-9000

(P-547)

HOLBROOK CONSTRUCTION INC

9814 Norwalk Blvd Ste 200, Santa Fe Springs (90670-2992)
PHONE...................714 523-1150
Laurence A Holbrook, *Pr*
EMP: 75 **EST:** 1985
SQ FT: 3,000
SALES (est): 8.57MM **Privately Held**
Web: www.holbrookconstruction.net
SIC: 1542 Commercial and office building, new construction

(P-548)

HOUALLA ENTERPRISES LTD

Also Called: Metro Bldrs & Engineers Group
2610 Avon St, Newport Beach (92663-4706)
PHONE...................949 515-4350
Fouad Houalla, *Pr*
▲ **EMP:** 85 **EST:** 1987
SQ FT: 1,200
SALES (est): 20.15MM **Privately Held**
Web: www.metrobuilders.com
SIC: 1542 Commercial and office building, new construction

(P-549)

INTERIOR EXPERTS GEN BLDRS INC

4534 Carter Ct, Chino (91710-5060)
PHONE...................909 203-4922
Adam Lopez, *Pr*
Shane Loomis, *
EMP: 125 **EST:** 1992
SQ FT: 9,000
SALES (est): 8.9MM **Privately Held**
Web: www.interiorexpertsgc.com
SIC: 1542 Nonresidential construction, nec

(P-550)

JOHN M FRANK CONSTRUCTION INC

Also Called: John M Frank Service Group
913 E 4th St, Santa Ana (92701-4748)
PHONE...................714 210-3600
John M Frank, *CEO*
Laurie Dawson, *
EMP: 80 **EST:** 1984
SALES (est): 23.86MM **Privately Held**
Web: www.johnmfrankconstruction.com
SIC: 1542 5411 5812 Commercial and office building, new construction; Supermarkets; Family restaurants

(P-551)

JONES BROTHERS CNSTR CORP (PA)

Also Called: Peck Jones Construction
1601 Cloverfield Blvd, Santa Monica (90404-4082)
PHONE...................310 470-1885
J Gregory Jones, *Pr*
EMP: 98 **EST:** 1923
SALES (est): 2.37MM
SALES (corp-wide): 2.37MM **Privately Held**
SIC: 1542 Commercial and office building contractors

(P-552)

KIEWIT CORPORATION

Also Called: Measure of Excellence Cabinets
12700 Stowe Dr Ste 180, Poway (92064-8883)
PHONE...................858 208-4285
EMP: 80
SALES (corp-wide): 17.08B **Privately Held**
SIC: 1542 Commercial and office building contractors
HQ: Kiewit Corporation
3555 Farnam St Ste 1000
Omaha NE 68102
402 342-2052

(P-553)

KOLL CONSTRUCTION LP

4343 Von Karman Ave Ste 150, Newport Beach (92660-1200)
PHONE...................949 833-3030
Donald M Koll, *Managing Member*
EMP: 100 **EST:** 1996

SALES (est): 8.39MM **Privately Held**
SIC: 1542 Nonresidential construction, nec

(P-554)

KPRS CONSTRUCTION SERVICES INC (PA)

Also Called: Kprs
2850 Saturn St Ste 110, Brea (92821-1701)
PHONE...................714 672-0800
Joel H Stensby, *Pr*
Paul Kristedja, *
Lev Rabinovich, *
EMP: 91 **EST:** 1995
SQ FT: 31,000
SALES (est): 807.36MM
SALES (corp-wide): 807.36MM **Privately Held**
Web: www.kprsinc.com
SIC: 1542 8711 Commercial and office building, new construction; Building construction consultant

(P-555)

LMC HLLYWOOD HGHLAND HLDNGS LL

Also Called: Lennar Multi Family Community
20 Enterprise, Aliso Viejo (92656-7104)
PHONE...................949 448-1600
Todd Farrell, *CEO*
EMP: 500 **EST:** 2013
SALES (est): 5.37MM **Privately Held**
SIC: 1542 Commercial and office building contractors

(P-556)

MCCARTHY BLDG COMPANIES INC

20401 Sw Birch St Ste 200, Newport Beach (92660-1796)
PHONE...................949 851-8383
EMP: 347
SALES (corp-wide): 6.35B **Privately Held**
Web: www.mccarthy.com
SIC: 1542 1541 Institutional building construction; Industrial buildings, new construction, nec
HQ: Mccarthy Building Companies, Inc.
12851 Manchester Rd
Saint Louis MO 63131
314 968-3300

(P-557)

MCCARTHY BLDG COMPANIES INC

Southern California Division
20401 Sw Birch St Ste 300, Newport Beach (92660 1708)
PHONE...................949 851-8383
Randy Highland, *Brnch Mgr*
EMP: 75
SALES (corp-wide): 6.35B **Privately Held**
Web: www.mccarthy.com
SIC: 1542 Commercial and office building, new construction
HQ: Mccarthy Building Companies, Inc.
12851 Manchester Rd
Saint Louis MO 63131
314 968-3300

(P-558)

MCCARTHY BLDG COMPANIES INC

1113 S Bush St, Orange (92868-4222)
PHONE...................949 851-8383
Pat Peterson, *Brnch Mgr*
EMP: 78
SALES (corp-wide): 6.35B **Privately Held**
Web: www.mccarthy.com

PRODUCTS & SVCS

SIC: 1542 Commercial and office building, new construction
HQ: Mccarthy Building Companies, Inc.
12851 Manchester Rd
Saint Louis MO 63131
314 968-3300

(P-559)
MCCARTHY BLDG COMPANIES INC
515 S Flower St Ste 3600, Los Angeles (90071-2221)
PHONE............................213 655-1100
EMP: 416
SALES (corp-wide): 6.35B **Privately Held**
Web: www.mccarthy.com
SIC: 1542 Commercial and office building contractors
HQ: Mccarthy Building Companies, Inc.
12851 Manchester Rd
Saint Louis MO 63131
314 968-3300

(P-560)
MERUELO ENTERPRISES INC (PA)
9550 Firestone Blvd Ste 105, Downey (90241-5560)
PHONE............................562 745-2300
Alex Meruelo, *CEO*
Al Stoller, *
Joe Marchica, *
EMP: 501 **EST:** 1986
SALES (est): 464.46MM
SALES (corp-wide): 464.46MM **Privately Held**
Web: www.merueloenterprises.com
SIC: 1542 Nonresidential construction, nec

(P-561)
NEVELL GROUP INC (PA)
Also Called: N G I
3001 Enterprise St Ste 200, Brea (92821-6210)
PHONE............................714 579-7501
Michael J Nevell, *Pr*
Bruce Pasqua, *
Bryan Bodine, *
Chris Taylor, *
EMP: 125 **EST:** 2002
SQ FT: 35,000
SALES (est): 51.92MM
SALES (corp-wide): 51.92MM **Privately Held**
Web: www.nevellgroup.com
SIC: 1542 Commercial and office building, new construction

(P-562)
NEVELL GROUP INC
Also Called: Nevell Group Inc San Diego
3284 Grey Hawk Ct, Carlsbad (92010-6651)
PHONE............................760 598-3501
Greg Thomas, *Brnch Mgr*
EMP: 388
SALES (corp-wide): 51.92MM **Privately Held**
Web: www.nevellgroup.com
SIC: 1542 Commercial and office building, new construction
PA: The Nevell Group Inc
3001 Enterprise St
714 579-7501

(P-563)
PACIFIC BUILDING GROUP (PA)
9752 Aspen Creek Ct Ste 100, San Diego (92126-1082)
PHONE............................858 552-0600

Gregory A Rogers, *CEO*
Jim Roherty, *
Ron Maize, *
Lisa Hitt, *
William Hansen, *
▲ **EMP:** 98 **EST:** 1984
SQ FT: 17,880
SALES (est): 47.6MM
SALES (corp-wide): 47.6MM **Privately Held**
Web: www.pacificbuildinggroup.com
SIC: 1542 Commercial and office building, new construction

(P-564)
PARKCO BUILDING COMPANY
24795 State Highway 74, Perris (92570-8759)
PHONE............................714 444-1441
W Adrian Hoyle, *Pr*
EMP: 99 **EST:** 2013
SALES (est): 8.29MM **Privately Held**
Web: www.parkcobuilding.com
SIC: 1542 1771 1799 Commercial and office building, new construction; Foundation and footing contractor; Erection and dismantling of forms for poured concrete

(P-565)
PCL CONSTRUCTION SERVICES INC
4690 Executive Dr Ste 100, San Diego (92121-3073)
PHONE............................858 657-3400
EMP: 90
SALES (corp-wide): 5.99B **Privately Held**
Web: www.pcl.com
SIC: 1542 Commercial and office building, new construction
HQ: Pcl Construction Services, Inc.
2000 S Colo Blvd Ste 2-50
Denver CO 80222
303 365-6500

(P-566)
PCL CONSTRUCTION SERVICES INC
655 N Central Ave Ste 1600, Glendale (91203-1438)
PHONE............................818 246-3481
Dale Kain, *Mgr*
EMP: 191
SQ FT: 17,619
SALES (corp-wide): 5.99B **Privately Held**
Web: www.pcl.com
SIC: 1542 Commercial and office building, new construction
HQ: Pcl Construction Services, Inc.
2000 S Colo Blvd Ste 2-50
Denver CO 80222
303 365-6500

(P-567)
PCL INDUSTRIAL SERVICES INC
1500 S Union Ave, Bakersfield (93307-4144)
PHONE............................661 832-3995
Joe W Carrieri, *CEO*
Gary L Basher, *
EMP: 300 **EST:** 2002
SALES (est): 92.36MM **Privately Held**
SIC: 1542 Commercial and office building, new construction

(P-568)
PCN3 INC
11082 Winners Cir Ste B, Los Alamitos (90720-2893)
PHONE............................562 493-4124
Brian Abghari, *Pr*

Brian Abghari, *CEO*
EMP: 75 **EST:** 1999
SQ FT: 2,000
SALES (est): 2.15MM **Privately Held**
Web: www.pcn3.com
SIC: 1542 Commercial and office building, new construction

(P-569)
PENWAL INDUSTRIES INC
10611 Acacia St, Rancho Cucamonga (91730-5410)
PHONE............................909 466-1555
Chris A Pennington, *Prin*
▲ **EMP:** 100 **EST:** 1981
SQ FT: 65,000
SALES (est): 20.73MM **Privately Held**
Web: www.penwal.com
SIC: 1542 3999 8742 3993 Shopping center construction; Advertising display products; Management consulting services; Signs and advertising specialties

(P-570)
PERRY COAST CONSTRUCTION INC
Also Called: West Coast Construction
3811 Wacker Dr, Jurupa Valley (91752-1142)
PHONE............................951 774-0677
Robert Perry, *Pr*
Erin Perry, *
Britney Perry, *
EMP: 105 **EST:** 2012
SALES (est): 21.35MM **Privately Held**
Web: www.wcconcrete.com
SIC: 1542 Restaurant construction

(P-571)
PHILMONT MANAGEMENT INC
3450 Wilshire Blvd Ste 850, Los Angeles (90010-2211)
PHONE............................213 380-0159
Monica Nam, *Pr*
EMP: 99 **EST:** 1997
SQ FT: 6,000
SALES (est): 10.43MM **Privately Held**
Web: www.philmontinc.com
SIC: 1542 Commercial and office building, new construction

(P-572)
PLATINUM CONSTRUCTION INC
865 S East St, Anaheim (92805-5356)
PHONE............................714 527-0700
Darrin W Streilein, *Pr*
EMP: 100 **EST:** 2005
SALES (est): 12.97MM **Privately Held**
SIC: 1542 1541 1742 Commercial and office building contractors; Steel building construction; Plastering, drywall, and insulation

(P-573)
PNG BUILDERS
Also Called: General Contractor
2392 S Bateman Ave, Duarte (91010-3312)
PHONE............................626 256-9539
Steven Mathison, *CEO*
Louie Garcia, *
Michelle Mcneal, *Prin*
Gina Bockhold, *
EMP: 70 **EST:** 1959
SQ FT: 33,000
SALES (est): 151.56MM **Privately Held**
Web: www.pacific-inc.com
SIC: 1542 1522 Commercial and office building contractors; Residential construction, nec

(P-574)
PR CONSTRUCTION INC
1995 N Batavia St, Orange (92865-4107)
PHONE............................714 637-7848
Sean Brennan, *CEO*
Sean Brennan, *Pr*
Chris Harris, *
EMP: 72 **EST:** 1990
SQ FT: 11,500
SALES (est): 47.84MM **Privately Held**
Web: www.prconstruction.net
SIC: 1542 1531 Nonresidential construction, nec

(P-575)
R J LANTHIER COMPANY INC
485 Corporate Dr, Escondido (92029-1507)
PHONE............................760 738-9798
EMP: 80
SIC: 1542 1711 Nonresidential construction, nec; Warm air heating and air conditioning contractor

(P-576)
RBA BUILDERS INC
16490 Harbor Blvd Ste A, Fountain Valley (92708-1392)
PHONE............................714 895-9000
Robert Anderson, *CEO*
EMP: 82 **EST:** 2007
SALES (est): 49.78MM **Privately Held**
Web: www.rbabuildersinc.com
SIC: 1542 Commercial and office building, new construction

(P-577)
RD OLSON CONSTRUCTION INC
400 Spectrum Center Dr Ste 1200, Irvine (92618-5022)
PHONE............................949 474-2001
EMP: 125 **EST:** 1979
SALES (est): 4.26MM
SALES (corp-wide): 41.12MM **Privately Held**
Web: www.rdolson.com
SIC: 1542 1522 Commercial and office buildings, renovation and repair; Hotel/motel and multi-family home construction
PA: The Robert D Olson Corporation
400 Spectrum Center Dr # 12
949 474-2001

(P-578)
RESOURCE ENVIRONMENTAL INC
13100 Alondra Blvd Ste 108, Cerritos (90703-2262)
PHONE............................562 468-7000
Richard Miller, *CEO*
Jared Sloan Cooper, *
EMP: 75 **EST:** 2005
SALES (est): 29.37MM **Privately Held**
Web: www.resourceenvironmental.com
SIC: 1542 Nonresidential construction, nec

(P-579)
ROBERT CLAPPER CNSTR SVCS INC
Also Called: RC Construction Services
700 New York St, Redlands (92374-2921)
PHONE............................909 829-3688
Robert W Clapper, *Prin*
Rebecca Clapper, *
EMP: 100 **EST:** 1994
SALES (est): 15.1MM **Privately Held**
Web: www.rcconstruction.com
SIC: 1542 1771 Commercial and office building, new construction; Concrete work

(P-580)
RUDOLPH AND SLETTEN INC
2855 Michelle Ste 350, Irvine (92606-1013)
PHONE..................................949 252-1919
Eric Lascurain, *Dir*
EMP: 184
SALES (corp-wide): 3.88B **Publicly Held**
Web: www.rsconstruction.com
SIC: 1542 1541 Commercial and office
  building, new construction; Industrial
  buildings and warehouses
HQ: Rudolph And Sletten, Inc.
  120 Constitution Dr
  Menlo Park CA 94025
  650 216-3600

(P-581)
SAN-MAR CONSTRUCTION CO INC
4875 E La Palma Ave Ste 602, Anaheim
(92807-1955)
PHONE..................................714 693-5400
Sandra Drew, *CEO*
EMP: 200 **EST:** 1993
SQ FT: 3,000
SALES (est): 22.06MM **Privately Held**
Web: www.san-mar.com
SIC: 1542 Commercial and office building,
  new construction

(P-582)
SHAWMUT WOODWORKING & SUP INC
Also Called: Shawmut Design and Cnstr
11390 W Olympic Blvd Fl 2, Los Angeles
(90064-1607)
PHONE..................................323 602-1000
Leonard Porzio, *Prin*
EMP: 145
SALES (corp-wide): 278.72MM **Privately Held**
Web: www.shawmut.com
SIC: 1542 Commercial and office building,
  new construction
PA: Shawmut Woodworking & Supply, Inc.
  560 Harrison Ave
  617 622-7000

(P-583)
SIERRA PACIFIC CONSTRS INC
Also Called: Sierra Pacific Constructors
22212 Ventura Blvd Ste 300, Woodland Hills
(91364-1530)
PHONE..................................747 888-5000
Cary Gerhardt, *Prin*
Cary Gerhardt, *CEO*
Ken Laspada, *
EMP: 99 **EST:** 1983
SQ FT: 13,500
SALES (est): 46.03MM **Privately Held**
Web: www.spcinc.com
SIC: 1542 Commercial and office buildings,
  renovation and repair

(P-584)
SILVER CREEK INDUSTRIES LLC
2830 Barrett Ave, Perris (92571-3258)
PHONE..................................951 943-5393
Brett D Bashaw, *CEO*
Micheal Rhodes, *
EMP: 175 **EST:** 2005
SQ FT: 25,000
SALES (est): 91.07MM **Privately Held**
Web: www.silvercreekmodular.com
SIC: 1542 2452 Commercial and office
  building contractors; Prefabricated wood
  buildings

(P-585)
SINANIAN DEVELOPMENT INC
Also Called: Sinanian
18980 Ventura Blvd Ste 200, Tarzana
(91356-3228)
PHONE..................................818 996-9666
Antranik Sinanian, *CEO*
Andy Sinanian, *
Sinan Sinanian, *
Harry Sinanian, *Stockholder*
EMP: 70 **EST:** 1981
SQ FT: 4,000
SALES (est): 25.09MM **Privately Held**
Web: www.sinanian.com
SIC: 1542 1522 6552 Commercial and office
  building, new construction; Residential
  construction, nec; Subdividers and
  developers, nec

(P-586)
SNYDER LANGSTON HOLDINGS LLC
Also Called: Snyder Langston
17962 Cowan, Irvine (92614-6036)
PHONE..................................949 863-9200
TOLL FREE: 800
Stephen Jones Senior, *Ch*
John Rochford, *
Jason Rich, *
Gary Campanaro, *
EMP: 175 **EST:** 1986
SQ FT: 16,000
SALES (est): 51.48MM **Privately Held**
Web: www.snyderlangston.com
SIC: 1542 8742 1522 Commercial and office
  building, new construction; Real estate
  consultant; Residential construction, nec

(P-587)
SOLPAC INC
Also Called: Soltek Pacific
2424 Congress St, San Diego
(92110-2819)
PHONE..................................619 296-6247
Stephen W Thompson, *CEO*
Dave Carlin, *
John Myers, *
Kevin Cammall, *
EMP: 121 **EST:** 1994
SQ FT: 7,386
SALES (est): 16.3MM **Privately Held**
Web: www.soltekpacific.com
SIC: 1542 Commercial and office building,
  new construction

(P-588)
SOUTH COAST PIERING INC
Also Called: Saber
7301 Madison St, Paramount (90723-4029)
PHONE..................................800 922-2488
Franz M Froehlich, *CEO*
EMP: 70 **EST:** 2003
SALES (est): 15.06MM **Privately Held**
Web: www.saberfoundations.com
SIC: 1542 Commercial and office buildings,
  renovation and repair

(P-589)
STREAMLINE FINISHES INC
26429 Rancho Pkwy S Ste 140, Lake Forest
(92630-8330)
PHONE..................................949 600-8964
William Seidel, *Pr*
EMP: 80 **EST:** 2004
SQ FT: 6,000
SALES (est): 19.64MM **Privately Held**
Web: www.streamlinefinishes.com
SIC: 1542 Commercial and office building
  contractors

(P-590)
SUMMER SYSTEMS INC
28942 Hancock Pkwy, Valencia
(91355-1069)
PHONE..................................661 257-4419
Don London, *Pr*
Connie London, *
EMP: 80 **EST:** 1988
SQ FT: 20,000
SALES (est): 26.58MM **Privately Held**
Web: www.summersystems.net
SIC: 1542 Nonresidential construction, nec

(P-591)
TECHNO COATINGS INC
785 E Debra Ln, Anaheim (92805-6334)
PHONE..................................714 774-4671
Michael Birney, *Brnch Mgr*
EMP: 75
SALES (corp-wide): 41.05MM **Privately
Held**
Web: www.technocoatings.com
SIC: 1542 Commercial and office buildings,
  renovation and repair
PA: Techno Coatings, Inc.
  1391 S Allec St
  714 635-1130

(P-592)
TECHNO COATINGS INC
795 E Debra Ln, Anaheim (92805-6334)
PHONE..................................714 774-4671
Michael Birney, *Pr*
EMP: 75
SALES (corp-wide): 41.05MM **Privately
Held**
Web: www.technocoatings.com
SIC: 1542 1629 1721 1799 Commercial and
  office buildings, renovation and repair;
  Blasting contractor, except building
  demolition; Painting and paper hanging;
  Coating of concrete structures with plastic
PA: Techno Coatings, Inc.
  1391 S Allec St
  714 635-1130

(P-593)
TECHNO COATINGS INC (PA)
Also Called: Techno West
1391 S Allec St, Anaheim (92805-6304)
PHONE..................................714 635-1130
EMP: 200 **EST:** 1974
SALES (est): 41.05MM
SALES (corp-wide): 41.05MM **Privately
Held**
Web: www.technocoatings.com
SIC: 1542 1629 1721 1799 Commercial and
  office buildings, renovation and repair;
  Blasting contractor, except building
  demolition; Painting and paper hanging;
  Coating of concrete structures with plastic

(P-594)
TRITON STRUCTURAL CONCRETE INC
15435 Innovation Dr Ste 225, San Diego
(92128-3445)
PHONE..................................858 866-2450
Tim Penick, *CEO*
John Boyd, *
EMP: 250 **EST:** 2007
SALES (est): 21.25MM **Privately Held**
Web: www.tritonstructural.com
SIC: 1542 Commercial and office building,
  new construction

(P-595)
TURNER CONSTRUCTION COMPANY
1900 S State College Blvd Ste 200,
Anaheim (92806-6197)
PHONE..................................714 940-9000
Bernie Morrissey, *VP*
EMP: 300
Web: www.turnerconstruction.com
SIC: 1542 Commercial and office building,
  new construction
HQ: Turner Construction Company Inc
  66 Hudson Blvd East
  New York NY 10001
  212 229-6000

(P-596)
TUTOR PERINI CORPORATION (PA)
Also Called: Tutor Perini
15901 Olden St, Sylmar (91342-1051)
PHONE..................................818 362-8391
Ronald N Tutor, *Ch Bd*
Gary G Smalley, *Pr*
Ryan J Soroka, *Sr VP*
Ghassan M Ariqat, *Ex VP*
Henry Dieu, *PAO*
▲ **EMP:** 160 **EST:** 1894
SALES (est): 3.88B
SALES (corp-wide): 3.88B **Publicly Held**
Web: www.tutorperini.com
SIC: 1542 8741 1611 1791 Commercial and
  office building contractors; Construction
  management; Concrete construction:
  roads, highways, sidewalks, etc.; Structural
  steel erection

(P-597)
TUTOR-SALIBA CORPORATION (HQ)
15901 Olden St, Rancho Cascades
(91342-1051)
PHONE..................................818 362-8391
Ronald N Tutor, *CEO*
David L Randall, *Sr VP*
William B Sparks, *
Jack Frost, *
John D Barrett, *
▲ **EMP:** 100 **EST:** 2003
SQ FT: 20,000
SALES (est): 33.83MM
SALES (corp-wide): 3.88B **Publicly Held**
Web: www.tutorperini.com
SIC: 1542 1629 7353 1799 Commercial and
  office building, new construction; Subway
  construction; Cranes and aerial lift
  equipment, rental or leasing; Rigging and
  scaffolding
PA: Tutor Perini Corporation
  15901 Olden St
  818 362-8391

(P-598)
TUTOR-SALIBA PERINI
15901 Olden St, Sylmar (91342-1051)
PHONE..................................818 362-8391
EMP: 7733
SIC: 1542 1611 1622 Specialized public
  building contractors; Highway and street
  construction; Bridge, tunnel, and elevated
  highway construction

(P-599)
USS CAL BUILDERS INC
8031 Main St, Stanton (90680-2452)
PHONE..................................714 828-4882
Allen Othman, *CEO*
Jennifer Hotrum, *
Eric Othman, *
EMP: 135 **EST:** 1992
SALES (est): 28.11MM **Privately Held**
Web: www.usscalbuilders.com

PRODUCTS & SVCS

SIC: 1542 Specialized public building
contractors

(P-600)
WALSH CONSTRUCTION COMPANY
1260 Corona Pointe Ct Ste 201, Corona
(92879-5008)
PHONE.....................951 336-7040
EMP: 212
SALES (corp-wide): 3.62B **Privately Held**
Web: www.walshconstruction.com
SIC: 1542 Commercial and office building,
new construction
HQ: Walsh Construction Company
5960 N Broadway St
Chicago IL 60660
312 563-5400

(P-601)
WE ONEIL CONSTRUCTION CO CAL
Also Called: W E O'Neil Construction
9485 Haven Ave Ste 101, Rancho
Cucamonga (91730-5877)
PHONE.....................909 466-5300
John Finn, *Brnch Mgr*
EMP: 161
SALES (corp-wide): 233.95MM **Privately
Held**
Web: www.weoneil.com
SIC: 1542 1541 1522 1521 Commercial and
office building, new construction; Industrial
buildings and warehouses; Residential
construction, nec; New construction, single-
family houses
HQ: W.E. O'neil Construction Co Of
California
909 N Pcf Cast Hwy Ste 40
El Segundo CA 90245
310 643-7900

(P-602)
WEBCOR CONSTRUCTION LP
Also Called: Webcor Builders
2150 W Washington St Ste 308, San Diego
(92110-2047)
PHONE.....................619 798-3891
Matt Rosie, *CEO*
EMP: 131
Web: www.webcor.com
SIC: 1542 Nonresidential construction, nec
HQ: Webcor Construction L.P.
207 King St Ste 300
San Francisco CA 94107

(P-603)
WEBCOR CONSTRUCTION LP
Also Called: Webcor Builders
333 S Grand Ave Ste 4400, Los Angeles
(90071-1548)
PHONE.....................213 239-2800
Leo Bandini, *Mgr*
EMP: 131
Web: www.webcor.com
SIC: 1542 Commercial and office building,
new construction
HQ: Webcor Construction L.P.
207 King St Ste 300
San Francisco CA 94107

(P-604)
WEST PACIFIC SERVICES INC
4445 Eastgate Mall Ste 200, San Diego
(92121-1979)
PHONE.....................888 401-0188
Joshua L Prado, *CEO*
EMP: 138 EST: 2009
SALES (est): 9.3MM **Privately Held**

SIC: 1542 Nonresidential construction, nec

(P-605)
WHITING-TURNER CONTRACTING CO
250 Commerce Ste 150, Irvine
(92602-1345)
PHONE.....................949 863-0800
Len Cannatelli Junior, *Ex VP*
EMP: 330
SALES (corp-wide): 8.62B **Privately Held**
Web: www.whiting-turner.com
SIC: 1542 1541 Commercial and office
building, new construction; Industrial
buildings and warehouses
PA: The Whiting-Turner Contracting
Company
300 E Joppa Rd
410 821-1100

1611 Highway And Street Construction

(P-606)
ADOPT-A-HIGHWAY MAINTENANCE
Also Called: Adopt-A-Beach
3158 Red Hill Ave Ste 200, Costa Mesa
(92626-3416)
PHONE.....................800 200-0003
Peter Morin, *CEO*
Patricia Nelson, *
Dennis Day, *
Dan Day, *
EMP: 104 EST: 1990
SQ FT: 6,000
SALES (est): 24.03MM **Privately Held**
Web: www.adoptahighway.com
SIC: 1611 4959 Highway and street
maintenance; Sanitary services, nec

(P-607)
ALL AMERICAN ASPHALT
All American Service and Sup
1776 All American Way, Corona
(92879-2070)
P.O. Box 2229 (92878-2229)
PHONE.....................951 736-7617
Kim Mcguire Managing, *Brnch Mgr*
EMP: 179
SALES (corp-wide): 91.09MM **Privately
Held**
Web: www.allamericanasphalt.com
SIC: 1611 Highway and street paving
contractor
PA: All American Asphalt
400 E 6th St
951 736-7600

(P-608)
ATKINSON CONSTRUCTION INC
611 Anton Blvd, Costa Mesa (92626-7005)
PHONE.....................303 410-2540
John O'keefe, *Pr*
EMP: 450 EST: 2004
SALES (est): 10.34MM
SALES (corp-wide): 1.66B **Privately Held**
Web: www.atkn.com
SIC: 1611 1622 Highway and street
construction; Bridge, tunnel, and elevated
highway construction
HQ: Clark Construction Group, Llc
7900 Westpark Dr Ste T300
Mclean VA 22102
301 272-8100

(P-609)
BEADOR CONSTRUCTION CO INC
2900 Bristol St, Costa Mesa (92626-5981)
PHONE.....................951 674-7352
David A Beador, *Pr*
EMP: 80 EST: 1996
SALES (est): 21.93MM **Privately Held**
SIC: 1611 General contractor, highway and
street construction

(P-610)
BENS ASPHALT & MAINT CO INC
Also Called: Medina Construction
2537 Rubidoux Blvd, Riverside
(92509-2142)
PHONE.....................951 248-1103
EMP: 90
Web: www.bensasphalt.com
SIC: 1611 Surfacing and paving
PA: Ben's Asphalt & Maintenance
Company, Inc.
2200 S Yale St Ste A

(P-611)
BRUTOCO ENGINEERING & CONSTRUCTION INC
Also Called: Brutoco Engineering
1272 Center Court Dr Ste 101, Covina
(91724-3667)
EMP: 200 EST: 1967
SALES (est): 4.97MM **Privately Held**
Web: www.brutoco.net
SIC: 1611 1629 1622 General contractor,
highway and street construction; Dams,
waterways, docks, and other marine
construction; Bridge construction

(P-612)
CITY OF SAN DIEGO
2781 Caminito Chollas, San Diego
(92105-5039)
PHONE.....................619 527-7482
Mario Sierra, *Dir*
EMP: 207
SALES (corp-wide): 2.9B **Privately Held**
Web: www.sandiego.gov
SIC: 1611 9199 Highway and street
maintenance; General government
administration
PA: City Of San Diego
202 C St
619 236-6330

(P-613)
DENNIS M MCCOY & SONS INC
32107 Lindero Canyon Rd Ste 212,
Westlake Village (91361-4255)
PHONE.....................818 874-3872
Dennis Mccoy, *CEO*
Morgan Mccoy, *Pr*
EMP: 75 EST: 1994
SQ FT: 3,000
SALES (est): 11.47MM **Privately Held**
Web: www.mccoyandsons.com
SIC: 1611 Grading

(P-614)
EAGLE PAVING LLC
Also Called: Toro Engineering
13915 Danielson St Ste 201, Poway
(92064-8884)
PHONE.....................858 486-6400
Joel Batule, *Managing Member*
Joel Batule, *Pr*
James B Bostick, *
EMP: 75 EST: 2006
SQ FT: 3,920
SALES (est): 16.06MM **Privately Held**

Web: www.eaglepaving.us
SIC: 1611 Surfacing and paving

(P-615)
EBS GENERAL ENGINEERING INC
1345 Quarry St Ste 101, Corona
(92879-1734)
PHONE.....................951 279-6869
Joseph Nanci, *Pr*
EMP: 90 EST: 1994
SQ FT: 4,000
SALES (est): 17.67MM **Privately Held**
Web: www.ebs-inc.us
SIC: 1611 Highway and street construction

(P-616)
FOOTHILL / ESTRN TRNSP CRRDOR
Also Called: Transportation Corridor Agency
125 Pacifica Ste 100, Irvine (92618-3324)
PHONE.....................949 754-3400
Michael Kraman, *CEO*
Amy Potter, *
EMP: 70 EST: 1986
SQ FT: 10,000
SALES (est): 209.38MM **Privately Held**
Web: www.thetollroads.com
SIC: 1611 General contractor, highway and
street construction

(P-617)
GRANITE CONSTRUCTION COMPANY
Also Called: Southern California Regional
38000 Monroe St, Indio (92203-9500)
PHONE.....................760 775-7500
Jay Mcquillen, *Mgr*
EMP: 393
Web: www.graniteconstruction.com
SIC: 1611 1771 General contractor, highway
and street construction; Concrete work
HQ: Granite Construction Company
585 W Beach St
Watsonville CA 95076
831 724-1011

(P-618)
GRANITE CONSTRUCTION COMPANY
5335 Debbie Rd, Santa Barbara
(93111-2001)
P.O. Box 6744 (93160-6744)
PHONE.....................805 964-9951
Bruce Mcgowan, *Mgr*
EMP: 169
SQ FT: 65,396
Web: www.graniteconstruction.com
SIC: 1611 General contractor, highway and
street construction
HQ: Granite Construction Company
585 W Beach St
Watsonville CA 95076
831 724-1011

(P-619)
GRANITE CONSTRUCTION INC
213 Columbia Way, Lancaster
(93535-5335)
PHONE.....................805 667-8210
EMP: 100
Web: www.graniteconstruction.com
SIC: 1611 General contractor, highway and
street construction
PA: Granite Construction Incorporated
585 W Beach St

(P-620)
GRIFFITH COMPANY
1128 Carrier Parkway Ave, Bakersfield (93308-9666)
P.O. Box 70157 (93387-0157)
PHONE...............................661 392-6640
Rus Grigg, *Mgr*
EMP: 341
SALES (corp-wide): 350MM **Privately Held**
Web: www.griffithcompany.net
SIC: 1611 General contractor, highway and street construction
PA: Griffith Company
    3050 E Birch St
    714 984-5500

(P-621)
GRIFFITH COMPANY (PA)
Also Called: Tahoe Stag
3050 E Birch St, Brea (92821-6248)
PHONE...............................714 984-5500
Jamie Angus, *Pr*
Jim Waltze, *
Thomas L Foss, *
Ryan Aukerman, *
Steve Ruelas, *
EMP: 187 **EST:** 1922
SQ FT: 100,000
SALES (est): 350MM
SALES (corp-wide): 350MM **Privately Held**
Web: www.griffithcompany.net
SIC: 1611 General contractor, highway and street construction

(P-622)
HARDY & HARPER INC
32 Rancho Cir, Lake Forest (92630-8325)
PHONE...............................714 444-1851
Daniel Thomas Maas, *CEO*
Fred T Maas Senior, *Dir*
EMP: 200 **EST:** 1946
SALES (est): 2.56MM **Privately Held**
Web: www.hardyandharper.com
SIC: 1611 2951 Surfacing and paving; Asphalt paving mixtures and blocks

(P-623)
HARPER FEDERAL CNSTR LLC
14130 Biscayne Pl, Poway (92064-6640)
PHONE...............................619 543-1296
Jeffrey A Harper, *Managing Member**
Ronald D Harper, *
EMP: 80 **EST:** 2007
SALES (est): 8.42MM **Privately Held**
SIC: 1611 1711 1751 1742 Grading; Plumbing, heating, air-conditioning; Carpentry work; Plastering, drywall, and insulation

(P-624)
HILLCREST CONTRACTING INC
1467 Circle City Dr, Corona (92879-1668)
P.O. Box 1898 (91718)
PHONE...............................951 273-9600
Glenn J Salsbury, *Pr*
E G Lindholm, *
EMP: 75 **EST:** 1984
SQ FT: 11,600
SALES (est): 20.52MM **Privately Held**
Web: www.hillcrestcontracting.com
SIC: 1611 General contractor, highway and street construction

(P-625)
IES COMMERCIAL INC
Also Called: Ies
6885 Flanders Dr Ste A, San Diego (92121-2933)
PHONE...............................858 210-4900
Brad Sandman, *Prin*
EMP: 131
Web: www.iescomm.com
SIC: 1611 7812 1623 7382 General contractor, highway and street construction; Audio-visual program production; Cable laying construction; Security systems services
HQ: Ies Commercial, Inc.
    2801 South Fair Lane
    Tempe AZ 85282
    480 379-6200

(P-626)
INTERNATIONAL PAVING SVCS INC
Also Called: I P S
1199 Opal Ave, Mentone (92359-1284)
P.O. Box 10458 (92423-0458)
PHONE...............................909 794-2101
Brent Rieger, *Pr*
EMP: 80 **EST:** 2007
SALES (est): 8.5MM **Privately Held**
Web: www.ipspaving.com
SIC: 1611 Surfacing and paving

(P-627)
JACOBSSON ENGRG CNSTR INC
72310 Varner Rd, Thousand Palms (92276-3362)
P.O. Box 14430 (92255-4430)
PHONE...............................760 345-8700
Dan Jacobsson, *Pr*
Ingeborg Jacobsson, *
EMP: 75 **EST:** 1991
SQ FT: 9,000
SALES (est): 1.44MM **Privately Held**
Web: www.jacobssoninc.com
SIC: 1611 Highway and street construction

(P-628)
JB BOSTICK LLC (PA)
2870 E La Cresta Ave, Anaheim (92806-1816)
PHONE...............................714 238-2121
James B Bostick, *Pr*
Jerry Hamlin, *
EMP: 75 **EST:** 1964
SQ FT: 2,870
SALES (est): 2.04MM
SALES (corp-wide): 2.04MM **Privately Held**
Web: www.jbbostick.com
SIC: 1611 1771 Grading; Concrete work

(P-629)
KEC ENGINEERING
26320 Lester Cir, Corona (92883-6399)
P.O. Box 909 (92878-0909)
PHONE...............................951 734-3010
James Elfring, *Pr*
Les Card, *
Scott Pfeiffer, *Ex VP*
EMP: 110 **EST:** 1953
SALES (est): 22.91MM **Privately Held**
Web: www.kecengineering.com
SIC: 1611 General contractor, highway and street construction

(P-630)
KIEWIT INFRASTRUCTURE WEST CO
10704 Shoemaker Ave, Santa Fe Springs (90670-4040)
PHONE...............................562 946-1816
Ken Riley, *Mgr*
EMP: 125

SQ FT: 12,514
SALES (corp-wide): 10.41B **Privately Held**
Web: www.kiewit.com
SIC: 1611 1542 1541 General contractor, highway and street construction; Nonresidential construction, nec; Industrial buildings and warehouses
HQ: Kiewit Infrastructure West Co.
    2200 Columbia House Blvd
    Vancouver WA 98661
    402 342-2052

(P-631)
LARRY JACINTO CONSTRUCTION INC
9555 N Wabash Ave, Redlands (92374-2714)
P.O. Box 615 (92359-0615)
PHONE...............................909 794-2151
Larry Frankland Jacinto, *CEO*
EMP: 80 **EST:** 1971
SQ FT: 8,500
SALES (est): 9.36MM **Privately Held**
Web: www.larryjacintoconstruction.com
SIC: 1611 Grading

(P-632)
LB3 ENTERPRISES INC
12485 Highway 67 # 3, Lakeside (92040-1158)
P.O. Box 130 (92022)
PHONE...............................619 579-6161
Lawrence Lee Brown, *Pr*
Debra Brown, *
EMP: 90 **EST:** 2004
SALES (est): 67.83MM **Privately Held**
Web: www.lb3enterprises.com
SIC: 1611 1623 7389 Grading; Water, sewer, and utility lines; Business services, nec

(P-633)
MACRO-Z-TECHNOLOGY COMPANY (PA)
Also Called: M Z T
841 E Washington Ave, Santa Ana (92701-3878)
PHONE...............................714 564-1130
Bryan J Zatica, *CEO*
EMP: 97 **EST:** 1989
SQ FT: 3,000
SALES (est): 27.86MM **Privately Held**
Web: www.mztco.com
SIC: 1611 1542 8711 Concrete construction: roads, highways, sidewalks, etc.; Commercial and office building contractors; Engineering services

(P-634)
MAMCO INC (PA)
Also Called: Alabbasi
764 Ramona Expy Ste C, Perris (92571-9716)
PHONE...............................951 776-9300
Marwan Alabbasi, *CEO*
Elizabeth Alabbasi, *
Rumzi Alabbasi, *
EMP: 116 **EST:** 2002
SQ FT: 2,200
SALES (est): 33.61MM **Privately Held**
Web: www.alabbasi.biz
SIC: 1611 General contractor, highway and street construction

(P-635)
MANERI TRAFFIC CONTROL INC
Also Called: M T C
4949 2nd St, Fallbrook (92028-9790)
PHONE...............................951 695-5104
Maria Maneri, *CEO*
Johnny Maneri, *

EMP: 70 **EST:** 2007
SQ FT: 900
SALES (est): 1.54MM **Privately Held**
Web: www.maneridirect.com
SIC: 1611 7389 Highway and street sign installation; Flagging service (traffic control)

(P-636)
MARATHON GENERAL INC
1728 Mission Rd, Escondido (92029-1111)
PHONE...............................760 738-9714
Mark Miller, *Pr*
Steven Gallant, *
Donald Tolen, *
EMP: 80 **EST:** 1988
SQ FT: 3,000
SALES (est): 18.9MM **Privately Held**
Web: www.mgipaving.com
SIC: 1611 General contractor, highway and street construction

(P-637)
MATICH CORPORATION (PA)
1596 E Harry Shepard Blvd, San Bernardino (92408-0197)
P.O. Box 10 (92346-1010)
PHONE...............................909 382-7400
Stephen A Matich, *CEO*
Martin A Matich, *
Randall Valadez, *
Robert M Matich, *
Patrick A Matich, *
EMP: 60 **EST:** 1918
SQ FT: 10,000
SALES (est): 48.1MM
SALES (corp-wide): 48.1MM **Privately Held**
Web: www.matichcorp.com
SIC: 1611 2951 General contractor, highway and street construction; Asphalt paving mixtures and blocks

(P-638)
MYERS & SONS CONSTRUCTION LP
5777 W Century Blvd Ste 600, Los Angeles (90045-5636)
PHONE...............................424 227-3285
EMP: 161
Web: www.myers-sons.com
SIC: 1611 Highway and street construction
PA: Myers & Sons Construction, L.P.
    45 Morrison Ave

(P-639)
NATIONAL PAVING COMPANY INC
4361 Fort Dr, Riverside (92509-6784)
P.O. Box 3649 (92519-3649)
PHONE...............................951 369-1332
Richard J Lindholm, *Pr*
Lawrence Spicher, *
EMP: 78 **EST:** 1986
SQ FT: 4,000
SALES (est): 9.72MM **Privately Held**
Web: www.nationalpaving.com
SIC: 1611 Highway and street paving contractor

(P-640)
OTAY RIVER CONSTRUCTORS LLC
860 Harold Pl, Chula Vista (91914-3550)
P.O. Box 600 (92346-0600)
PHONE...............................619 397-7500
Rich Linford, *Pr*
▲ **EMP:** 130 **EST:** 2002
SQ FT: 17,000
SALES (est): 2.57MM **Privately Held**

SIC: 1611 Highway and street construction

(P-641)
PALP INC
Also Called: Excel Paving Co
2230 Lemon Ave, Long Beach
(90806-5124)
P.O. Box 16405 (90806-0995)
PHONE.....................562 599-5841
Curtis P Brown, *CEO*
George Mcrae, *Sr VP*
Bruce Flatt, *
Michelle Drakulich, *
EMP: 225 EST: 1976
SQ FT: 11,000
SALES (est): 23.58MM **Privately Held**
Web: www.excelpavingcompany.com
SIC: 1611 8711 Highway and street paving
   contractor; Engineering services

(P-642)
PAVER DECOR MASONRY INC
Also Called: Alpha & Omega Pavers
987 Calimesa Blvd, Calimesa (92320-1138)
P.O. Box 727 (92320-0727)
PHONE.....................909 795-8474
Adam Cuevas, *Pr*
Mary Cuevas, *
EMP: 25 EST: 1995
SQ FT: 2,500
SALES (est): 8.69MM **Privately Held**
Web: www.paverdecor.com
SIC: 1611 3531 Highway and street paving
   contractor; Pavers

(P-643)
RICK HAMM CONSTRUCTION INC
201 W Carleton Ave, Orange (92867-3607)
PHONE.....................714 532-0815
Rick Hamm, *Pr*
Llana Hamm, *
EMP: 90 EST: 1977
SQ FT: 25,000
SALES (est): 19.49MM **Privately Held**
Web: www.rickhamm.com
SIC: 1611 1771 1791 1741 General
   contractor, highway and street construction;
   Patio construction, concrete; Precast
   concrete structural framing or panels,
   placing of; Masonry and other stonework

(P-644)
RIVERSIDE CONSTRUCTION COMPANY INC
4225 Garner Rd, Riverside (92501-1057)
P.O. Box 1146 (92502-1146)
PHONE.....................951 682-8308
EMP: 150 EST: 1966
SALES (est): 22.61MM **Privately Held**
Web: www.rivconstruct.com
SIC: 1611 General contractor, highway and
   street construction

(P-645)
RJ NOBLE COMPANY (PA)
15505 E Lincoln Ave, Orange (92865-1015)
P.O. Box 620 (92856-9020)
PHONE.....................714 637-1550
Michael J Carver, *Pr*
Craig Porter, *
James N Ducote, *
EMP: 144 EST: 1950
SQ FT: 5,500
SALES (est): 30.81MM
SALES (corp-wide): 30.81MM **Privately Held**
Web: www.rjnoblecompany.com
SIC: 1611 Highway and street paving
   contractor

(P-646)
ROMERO GENERAL CNSTR CORP (PA)
Also Called: Romero Construction
2150 N Centre City Pkwy Ste I, Escondido
(92026-1347)
PHONE.....................760 489-8412
Keith Reilly, *Pr*
EMP: 73 EST: 1992
SQ FT: 3,500
SALES (est): 9.39MM **Privately Held**
Web: www.romerogc.com
SIC: 1611 Highway and street paving
   contractor

(P-647)
RSVC COMPANY
Also Called: Reliable Service Company
3051 Myers St Ste B, Riverside
(92503-5525)
P.O. Box 7189 (92513-7189)
PHONE.....................951 684-6578
Mark David Aldaco, *Pr*
Mark David Aldaco, *CEO*
Keith Gruber, *
EMP: 188 EST: 2004
SALES (est): 48.53MM **Privately Held**
Web: www.rsvc.com
SIC: 1611 8741 8712 General contractor,
   highway and street construction;
   Management services; Architectural
   services

(P-648)
SEMA CONSTRUCTION INC
320 Goddard Ste 150, Irvine (92618-4630)
PHONE.....................949 470-0500
Steve Mills, *Mgr*
EMP: 100
Web: www.sema.inc
SIC: 1611 1771 Highway and street
   construction; Concrete work
PA: Sema Construction, Inc.
   7353 S Eagle St

(P-649)
SKANSKA USA CIVL W CAL DST INC (DH)
1995 Agua Mansa Rd, Riverside
(92509-2405)
PHONE.....................951 684-5360
Richard Cavallero, *CEO*
Michael Aparicio, *
Todd Sutton, *
Joseph Nogues, *
Michael Cobelli, *
EMP: 700 EST: 1919
SQ FT: 15,000
SALES (est): 139.9MM
SALES (corp-wide): 115.37MM **Privately Held**
Web: usa.skanska.com
SIC: 1611 1622 1629 8711 General
   contractor, highway and street construction;
   Bridge construction; Dam construction;
   Engineering services
HQ: Skanska Usa Civil Inc.
   7520 Astoria Blvd Ste 200
   East Elmhurst NY 11370
   718 340-0777

(P-650)
SUPERIOR PAVING COMPANY INC
Also Called: United Paving Company
1880 N Delilah St, Corona (92879-1892)
PHONE.....................951 739-9200
Sabas Trujillo, *CEO*
EMP: 85 EST: 2008

SQ FT: 3,000
SALES (est): 25.33MM **Privately Held**
Web: www.united-paving.com
SIC: 1611 Highway and street paving
   contractor

1622 Bridge, Tunnel, And Elevated Highway

(P-651)
FLATIRON WEST INC
16341 Chino Corona Rd, Chino
(91708-9233)
PHONE.....................909 597-8413
Thomas J Rademacher, *CEO*
EMP: 160
Web: www.flatironcorp.com
SIC: 1622 1611 Bridge construction;
   Highway and street construction
HQ: Flatiron West, Inc.
   12121 Scripps Summit Dr # 400
   San Diego CA 92131

(P-652)
FLUOR DANIEL CONSTRUCTION CO (DH)
Also Called: FLUOR DANIEL
INTERCONTINENTAL
3 Polaris Way, Aliso Viejo (92656-5338)
P.O. Box 5014 (77487)
PHONE.....................949 349-2000
Paul Buckham, *Pr*
EMP: 500 EST: 1953
SALES (est): 3.38MM
SALES (corp-wide): 15.47B **Publicly Held**
SIC: 1622 Bridge, tunnel, and elevated
   highway construction
HQ: Fluor Enterprises, Inc.
   6700 Las Colinas Blvd
   Irving TX 75039
   469 398-7000

(P-653)
HAZARD CONSTRUCTION COMPANY
Also Called: Hazard Construction
10529 Vine St Ste 1, Lakeside
(92040-2446)
P.O. Box 229000 (92192-9000)
PHONE.....................858 587-3600
Jason Mordhorst, *Pr*
Klaus Guttau, *VP*
EMP: 100 EST: 1926
SALES (est): 43.95MM **Privately Held**
Web: www.hazardconstruction.com
SIC: 1622 1611 Bridge construction;
   Highway and street construction

(P-654)
MCM CONSTRUCTION INC
19010 Slover Ave, Bloomington
(92316-2459)
PHONE.....................909 875-0533
Nella Flores, *Brnch Mgr*
EMP: 77
SALES (corp-wide): 33.93MM **Privately Held**
Web: www.mcmconstructioninc.com
SIC: 1622 Bridge construction
PA: M.C.M. Construction, Inc.
   6413 32nd St
   916 334-1221

(P-655)
OC 405 PARTNERS JOINT VENTURE
3100 W Lake Center Dr Ste 200, Santa Ana
(92704-6917)

PHONE.....................858 251-2200
Ashok Patel, *Pt*
Tony Bagheri, *
Luigi Realini, *
Loris Paravano, *
EMP: 75 EST: 2016
SQ FT: 69,000
SALES (est): 61.08MM **Privately Held**
Web: www.oc405partners.com
SIC: 1622 Bridge construction
HQ: Ohla Usa, Inc.
   75-20 Astria Blvd Ste 150
   East Elmhurst NY 11370

(P-656)
STEVE P RADOS INC
1638 Pioneer Way, El Cajon (92020-1636)
PHONE.....................619 328-1360
Steve Rados, *Mgr*
EMP: 110
SALES (corp-wide): 54.82MM **Privately Held**
Web: www.rados.com
SIC: 1622 Highway construction, elevated
HQ: Steve P Rados Inc
   2002 E Mcfadden Ave # 200
   Santa Ana CA 92705
   714 835-4612

1623 Water, Sewer, And Utility Lines

(P-657)
A & H COMMUNICATIONS INC
15 Chrysler, Irvine (92618-2009)
PHONE.....................949 250-4555
Brian Elliott, *Pr*
Brett Howard, *
EMP: 250 EST: 2000
SALES (est): 24.44MM **Privately Held**
Web: www.aandh.com
SIC: 1623 Cable laying construction

(P-658)
AIRX UTILITY SURVEYORS INC (PA)
785 E Mission Rd # 100, San Marcos
(92069-1903)
PHONE.....................760 480-2347
Gail Mcmorran, *Pr*
EMP: 55 EST: 1999
SALES (est): 9.17MM
SALES (corp-wide): 9.17MM **Privately Held**
Web: www.airxutility.com
SIC: 1623 1389 3272 1611 Underground
   utilities contractor; Testing, measuring,
   surveying, and analysis services;
   Monuments, concrete; Highway and street
   construction

(P-659)
ARB INC (HQ)
Also Called: ARB Industrial
26000 Commercentre Dr, Lake Forest
(92630-8816)
PHONE.....................949 598-9242
Tom Mccormick, *CEO*
Scott Summers, *
Timothy Healy, *
John P Schauerman, *
John M Perisich, *
▲ EMP: 140 EST: 1960
SALES (est): 458.68MM **Publicly Held**
Web: www.prim.com
SIC: 1623 1629 Oil and gas line and
   compressor station construction; Industrial
   plant construction
PA: Primoris Services Corporation
   2300 N Field St Ste 1900

▲ = Import ▼ = Export
◆ = Import/Export

(P-660)

ARIZONA PIPELINE COMPANY (PA)

17372 Lilac St, Hesperia (92345-5162)
P.O. Box 401865 (92340-1865)
PHONE.................................760 244-8212
Lowell Duane Moyers, *Ch*
Nina Moyers, *
Phyliss Moyers, *
Tom Seals, *
EMP: 400 **EST:** 1979
SQ FT: 5,000
SALES (est): 53.94MM
SALES (corp-wide): 53.94MM **Privately Held**
Web: www.arizonapipeline.com
SIC: 1623 Pipeline construction, nsk

(P-661)

ARIZONA PIPELINE COMPANY

1745 Sampson Ave, Corona (92879-1864)
PHONE.................................951 270-3100
John Guzlow, *Div Mgr*
EMP: 200
SALES (corp-wide): 53.94MM **Privately Held**
Web: www.arizonapipeline.com
SIC: 1623 8711 Underground utilities contractor; Engineering services
PA: Arizona Pipeline Company
17372 Lilac St
760 244-8212

(P-662)

BALI CONSTRUCTION INC

9852 Joe Vargas Way, South El Monte (91733-3108)
PHONE.................................626 442-8003
Ted Polich Iii, *Pr*
Michael E Brooks, *
EMP: 100 **EST:** 1987
SQ FT: 7,000
SALES (est): 58.08MM **Privately Held**
Web: www.baliconstruction.com
SIC: 1623 Underground utilities contractor

(P-663)

BLOIS CONSTRUCTION INC

3201 Sturgis Rd, Oxnard (93030-8931)
P.O. Box 672 (93032-0672)
PHONE.................................805 485-0011
James B Blois, *Pr*
Steve Woodworth, *
Dan Schultz, *
EMP: 150 **EST:** 1965
SQ FT: 10,000
SALES (est): 22.92MM **Privately Held**
Web: www.bloisconstruction.com
SIC: 1623 Underground utilities contractor

(P-664)

BOUDREAU PIPELINE CORPORATION

Also Called: A & B Equipment
463 N Smith Ave, Corona (92878-4305)
PHONE.................................951 493-6780
Alan J Boudreau, *CEO*
Christie Boudreau, *
Ron Jacobson, *
EMP: 300 **EST:** 2000
SQ FT: 14,000
SALES (est): 66.84MM **Privately Held**
Web: www.boudreaupipeline.com
SIC: 1623 Pipeline construction, nsk

(P-665)

BURTECH PIPELINE INCORPORATED

Also Called: Burtech Plumbing

1325 Pipeline Dr, Vista (92081-8835)
PHONE.................................760 634-2822
Dominic J Burtech, *Pr*
Julie Burtech, *
EMP: 70 **EST:** 1994
SALES (est): 25.25MM **Privately Held**
Web: www.burtechpipeline.com
SIC: 1623 Water main construction

(P-666)

CA STATION MANAGEMENT INC

3200 E Guasti Rd Ste 100, Ontario (91761-8661)
PHONE.................................909 245-6251
Taqi Chaudry, *CEO*
EMP: 250 **EST:** 2016
SALES (est): 4.86MM **Privately Held**
SIC: 1623 7389 8082 Underground utilities contractor; Telephone answering service; Home health care services

(P-667)

CAMERON INTRSTATE PIPELINE LLC

488 8th Ave, San Diego (92101-7123)
PHONE.................................619 696-3110
Ryan O'neal, *VP*
EMP: 200 **EST:** 2005
SALES (est): 28.44MM **Privately Held**
Web: www.semprainfrastructure.com
SIC: 1623 Oil and gas pipeline construction

(P-668)

CASS CONSTRUCTION INC (PA)

Also Called: Cass
1100 Wagner Dr, El Cajon (92020-3047)
P.O. Box 309 (92022-0309)
PHONE.................................619 590-0929
Jimmie Nelson, *Ch Bd*
Kyle P Nelson, *
Laura Nelson, *
EMP: 345 **EST:** 1974
SQ FT: 5,700
SALES (est): 43.87MM
SALES (corp-wide): 43.87MM **Privately Held**
Web: www.cassarrieta.com
SIC: 1623 1611 Underground utilities contractor; Grading

(P-669)

CONSTRUCTION SPECIALTY SVC INC

Also Called: C S S
4550 Buck Owens Blvd, Bakersfield (93308-4948)
P.O. Box 9429 (93389-9429)
PHONE.................................661 864-7573
Daniel I George, *Pr*
Denise George, *
EMP: 53 **EST:** 2008
SQ FT: 1,000
SALES (est): 9.48MM **Privately Held**
Web: www.cssincorp.biz
SIC: 1623 3271 Pipeline construction, nsk; Concrete block and brick

(P-670)

DIVERSIFIED UTILITY SVCS INC

3105 Unicorn Rd, Bakersfield (93308-6858)
P.O. Box P.O. Box 80417 (93380-0417)
PHONE.................................661 325-3212
Leigh Ann Anderson, *CEO*
Steven S Anderson, *
William Mitchell, *Stockholder*
Cody Anderson, *Stockholder*
EMP: 272 **EST:** 1997
SALES (est): 19.38MM **Privately Held**
Web: www.diversifiedutilityservices.com

SIC: 1623 Underground utilities contractor

(P-671)

DOTY BROS EQUIPMENT CO (HQ)

11232 Firestone Blvd, Norwalk (90650-2201)
PHONE.................................562 864-6566
EMP: 100 **EST:** 1931
SALES (est): 26.72MM
SALES (corp-wide): 464.46MM **Privately Held**
Web: www.dotybros.com
SIC: 1623 Pipeline construction, nsk
PA: Meruelo Enterprises, Inc.
9550 Firestone Blvd # 105
562 745-2300

(P-672)

GENERAL PRODUCTION SVC CAL INC

Also Called: G P S
1333 Kern St, Taft (93268-9700)
P.O. Box 344 (93268-0344)
PHONE.................................661 765-5330
Charles Beard, *CEO*
Oreste Risi, *
EMP: 180 **EST:** 1967
SALES (est): 17.86MM **Privately Held**
Web: www.genprod.com
SIC: 1623 Oil and gas pipeline construction

(P-673)

HCI LLC (HQ)

Also Called: H C I
6830 Airport Dr, Riverside (92504-1904)
P.O. Box 5389 (92860)
PHONE.................................951 520-4200
George Blanco, *Managing Member*
Simon Wachsberg, *
◆ **EMP:** 300 **EST:** 1981
SALES (est): 43.17MM
SALES (corp-wide): 97.99MM **Privately Held**
Web: www.hci-inc.com
SIC: 1623 Telephone and communication line construction
PA: Lombardy Holdings, Inc.
151 Kalmus Dr Ste F6
951 808-4550

(P-674)

HENKELS & MCCOY INC

2840 Ficus St, Pomona (91766-6501)
PHONE.................................909 517-3011
Michael Giarratano, *Sr VP*
EMP: 300
SALES (corp-wide): 12B **Publicly Held**
Web: www.henkels.com
SIC: 1623 Electric power line construction
HQ: Henkels & Mccoy, Inc
985 Jolly Rd
Blue Bell PA 19422
215 283-7600

(P-675)

HERMAN WEISSKER INC (HQ)

1645 Brown Ave, Riverside (92509-1859)
PHONE.................................951 826-8800
Luis Alberto Armona, *CEO*
Ron Politte, *
Marty Mayeda, *
EMP: 176 **EST:** 1959
SQ FT: 12,000
SALES (est): 35.33MM
SALES (corp-wide): 464.46MM **Privately Held**
Web: www.hermanweissker.com
SIC: 1623 1731 Underground utilities contractor; Electrical work

SIC: 1623 Underground utilities contractor

PA: Meruelo Enterprises, Inc.
9550 Firestone Blvd # 105
562 745-2300

(P-676)

HP COMMUNICATIONS INC (PA)

13341 Temescal Canyon Rd, Corona (92883-4980)
PHONE.................................951 572-1200
Nicholas Goldman, *Pr*
Ahmad Olomi, *
Chris Price, *
EMP: 83 **EST:** 1998
SQ FT: 130,680
SALES (est): 102.71MM
SALES (corp-wide): 102.71MM **Privately Held**
Web: www.hpcomminc.com
SIC: 1623 Communication line and transmission tower construction

(P-677)

HP COMMUNICATIONS INC

15453 Olde Highway 80, El Cajon (92021-2409)
PHONE.................................951 579-8339
Dustin Walters, *Rgnl Mgr*
EMP: 79
SALES (corp-wide): 102.71MM **Privately Held**
Web: www.hpcomminc.com
SIC: 1623 Communication line and transmission tower construction
PA: Hp Communications, Inc.
13341 Temescal Canyon Rd
951 572-1200

(P-678)

HP COMMUNICATIONS INC

1931 Mateo St, Los Angeles (90021-2832)
PHONE.................................951 457-0133
Ralph Ochoa, *Rgnl Mgr*
EMP: 79
SALES (corp-wide): 102.71MM **Privately Held**
Web: www.hpcomminc.com
SIC: 1623 Communication line and transmission tower construction
PA: Hp Communications, Inc.
13341 Temescal Canyon Rd
951 572-1200

(P-679)

IRISH COMMUNICATION COMPANY (DH)

2649 Stingle Ave, Rosemead (91770-3326)
P.O. Box 457 (91770-0457)
PHONE.................................626 288-6170
Gregory C Warde, *CEO*
Dan Mitchell, *
Pat D Furnare, *
Larry Manke Rcdd, *VP*
Dennis Brackney, *
EMP: 100 **EST:** 1985
SQ FT: 9,000
SALES (est): 12.55MM
SALES (corp-wide): 92.22MM **Privately Held**
Web: www.irishteam.com
SIC: 1623 8748 1731 Telephone and communication line construction; Telecommunications consultant; Communications specialization
HQ: Irish Construction
2641 River Ave
Rosemead CA 91770
626 288-8530

P R O D U C T S & S V C S

(P-680)
IRISH CONSTRUCTION (HQ)
2641 River Ave, Rosemead (91770-3392)
P.O. Box 579 (91770-0579)
PHONE.............................626 288-8530
Gregory C Warde, *Ch Bd*
William E Wilbanks, *
Randall W Dale, *
Jerry L Olmscheid, *
Ken West, *
EMP: 150 **EST:** 1947
SQ FT: 15,000
SALES (est): 36.01MM
SALES (corp-wide): 92.22MM **Privately Held**
Web: www.irishteam.com
SIC: 1623 Telephone and communication line construction
PA: Manhattan Capital Corporation
　　2641 River Ave
　　626 288-8530

(P-681)
JR FILANC CNSTR CO INC (PA)
740 N Andreasen Dr, Escondido (92029-1414)
PHONE.............................760 941-7130
Mark E Filanc, *CEO*
Vincent L Diaz, *
Linda Stangel, *
EMP: 100 **EST:** 1952
SQ FT: 13,200
SALES (est): 59.46MM
SALES (corp-wide): 59.46MM **Privately Held**
Web: www.filanc.com
SIC: 1623 1629 Pumping station construction; Waste water and sewage treatment plant construction

(P-682)
K S FABRICATION & MACHINE INC
Also Called: KS Fabrication & Machine
6205 District Blvd, Bakersfield (93313-2141)
P.O. Box 41630 (93384-1630)
PHONE.............................661 617-1700
Kevin S Small, *CEO*
Becky Scott, *
EMP: 150 **EST:** 1999
SALES (est): 10.2MM **Privately Held**
Web: www.ksilp.com
SIC: 1623 Water, sewer, and utility lines

(P-683)
KANA PIPELINE INC
12620 Magnolia Ave, Riverside (92503-4636)
PHONE.............................714 986-1400
Dan Locke, *Pr*
EMP: 100 **EST:** 1984
SQ FT: 55,000
SALES (est): 24.07MM **Privately Held**
Web: www.kanapipeline.com
SIC: 1623 1629 Water main construction; Drainage system construction

(P-684)
KS INDUSTRIES LP (PA)
Also Called: K S I
6205 District Blvd, Bakersfield (93313-2141)
P.O. Box 41630 (93384-1630)
PHONE.............................661 617-1700
Kevin Small, *Pt*
EMP: 2000 **EST:** 1979
SQ FT: 20,000
SALES (est): 490.64MM
SALES (corp-wide): 490.64MM **Privately Held**

Web: www.ksilp.com
SIC: 1623 Water, sewer, and utility lines

(P-685)
LOMBARDY HOLDINGS INC (PA)
151 Kalmus Dr Ste F6, Costa Mesa (92626-5965)
P.O. Box 1080 (92247-1080)
PHONE.............................951 808-4550
Marc Laulhere, *CEO*
Pam Laulhere, *
EMP: 200 **EST:** 1940
SQ FT: 80,000
SALES (est): 97.99MM
SALES (corp-wide): 97.99MM **Privately Held**
SIC: 1623 5211 Telephone and communication line construction; Electrical construction materials

(P-686)
MURRIETA DEVELOPMENT COMPANY INC
42540 Rio Nedo, Temecula (92590-3727)
PHONE.............................951 719-1680
EMP: 126 **EST:** 1981
SALES (est): 22.5MM **Privately Held**
Web: www.murrietadevelopment.com
SIC: 1623 Water, sewer, and utility lines

(P-687)
NTS INC
Also Called: Newberry Technical Services
8200 Stockdale Hwy Ste M10306, Bakersfield (93311-1091)
PHONE.............................661 588-8514
EMP: 425
Web: www.ntsinc.com
SIC: 1623 1541 1771 Pipeline construction, nsk; Industrial buildings, new construction, nec; Concrete work

(P-688)
ORION CONSTRUCTION CORPORATION
2185 La Mirada Dr, Vista (92081-8830)
PHONE.............................760 597-9660
Richard Dowsing, *CEO*
Mark Dowsing, *
EMP: 80 **EST:** 1987
SQ FT: 7,000
SALES (est): 28.35MM **Privately Held**
Web: www.orionconstruction.com
SIC: 1623 1629 1542 Water, sewer, and utility lines; Industrial plant construction; Nonresidential construction, nec

(P-689)
PRECISION PIPELINE LLC
10400 Trademark St, Rancho Cucamonga (91730-5826)
PHONE.............................909 229-6858
EMP: 441
SALES (corp-wide): 12B **Publicly Held**
Web: www.precisionwest.com
SIC: 1623 Pipeline construction, nsk
HQ: Precision Pipeline Llc
　　3314 56th St
　　Eau Claire WI 54703
　　715 874-4510

(P-690)
S E C C CORPORATION (PA)
502 N Sheridan St, Corona (92878-4022)
PHONE.............................909 393-5419
Michael C Aranda, *Pr*
Mary Aranda, *
EMP: 75 **EST:** 1995
SALES (est): 47.44MM **Privately Held**

Web: www.secc-corp.com
SIC: 1623 Telephone and communication line construction

(P-691)
S E PIPE LINE CONSTRUCTION CO
11832 Bloomfield Ave, Santa Fe Springs (90670-4610)
PHONE.............................562 868-9771
Charles Rikel, *Pr*
James Doulames, *VP*
Thomas Tustin, *Sec*
EMP: 100 **EST:** 1946
SQ FT: 5,000
SALES (est): 24.54MM **Privately Held**
Web: www.sepipeline.com
SIC: 1623 Gas main construction

(P-692)
SCHILLING PARADISE CORP
487 Vernon Way, El Cajon (92020-1932)
PHONE.............................619 449-4141
Jeff Platt, *Pr*
Michael Manos, *
EMP: 175 **EST:** 2009
SALES (est): 7.69MM **Privately Held**
Web: www.schillingcorp.com
SIC: 1623 1731 Underground utilities contractor; General electrical contractor

(P-693)
SCW CONTRACTING CORPORATION
2525 Old Highway 395, Fallbrook (92028-8794)
PHONE.............................760 728-1308
Jeffrey Dean Scrape, *CEO*
Susanne Scrape, *
EMP: 70 **EST:** 1980
SQ FT: 3,000
SALES (est): 1.88MM **Privately Held**
Web: www.scwcompanies.com
SIC: 1623 1791 3449 Underground utilities contractor; Structural steel erection; Miscellaneous metalwork

(P-694)
SHOFFEITT PIPELINE INC
15801 Rockfield Blvd Ste L, Irvine (92618-2869)
PHONE.............................949 581-1600
Kathy Shoffeitt, *Pr*
John Shoffeitt, *
John Shoffeitt Junior, *Sec*
EMP: 80 **EST:** 2013
SQ FT: 3,200
SALES (est): 8.63MM **Privately Held**
Web: shoffeitt-pipeline-inc.hub.biz
SIC: 1623 Underground utilities contractor

(P-695)
SOLEX CONTRACTING INC
42146 Remington Ave, Temecula (92590-2547)
PHONE.............................951 308-1706
Jerry Allen, *Pr*
EMP: 110 **EST:** 2004
SQ FT: 12,000
SALES (est): 29.59MM **Privately Held**
Web: www.solexcontracting.com
SIC: 1623 1542 1541 Communication line and transmission tower construction; Commercial and office building, new construction; Renovation, remodeling and repairs: industrial buildings

(P-696)
SOUTHWEST CONTRACTORS (PA)
Also Called: Bowman Pipeline Contractors
136 Allen Rd # 100, Bakersfield (93314-3710)
PHONE.............................661 588-0484
Floyd E Bowman Junior, *CEO*
Kathy Bowman, *
EMP: 25 **EST:** 1981
SALES (est): 23.28MM
SALES (corp-wide): 23.28MM **Privately Held**
Web: www.southwestcontractors.net
SIC: 1623 3443 Oil and gas pipeline construction; Industrial vessels, tanks, and containers

(P-697)
SPINIELLO COMPANIES
2650 Pomona Blvd, Pomona (91768-3220)
PHONE.............................909 629-1000
Priscilla Moyer, *Mgr*
EMP: 182
SALES (corp-wide): 40.99MM **Privately Held**
Web: www.spiniello.com
SIC: 1623 Underground utilities contractor
PA: Spiniello Companies
　　354 Eisenhower Pkwy # 1200
　　973 808-8383

(P-698)
SUKUT CONSTRUCTION LLC
4010 W Chandler Ave, Santa Ana (92704-5202)
PHONE.............................714 540-5351
Michael Crawford, *Prin*
Paul Kuliev, *
EMP: 99 **EST:** 2014
SALES (est): 12.1MM **Privately Held**
Web: www.sukut.com
SIC: 1623 1629 1611 Water, sewer, and utility lines; Earthmoving contractor; Grading

(P-699)
T C CONSTRUCTION COMPANY INC
Also Called: Tc Construction Company
10540 Prospect Ave, Santee (92071-4591)
PHONE.............................619 448-4560
Terry W Cameron, *CEO*
Austin Cameron, *
Derek Franken, *
Jack Gieffels, *
Darren Tharp, *
EMP: 230 **EST:** 1976
SQ FT: 16,000
SALES (est): 62.22MM **Privately Held**
Web: www.tcincsd.com
SIC: 1623 1611 Underground utilities contractor; Highway and street paving contractor

(P-700)
THERMAL ENERGY SOLUTIONS INC
100 Quantico Ave, Bakersfield (93307-2839)
PHONE.............................661 489-4100
Nelson Ivan Ayala, *CEO*
Gabriela Lopez De Ayala, *
Nelson Ayala, *
EMP: 27 **EST:** 2008
SALES (est): 5.11MM **Privately Held**
Web: www.thermalenergyinc.com

▲ = Import ▼ = Export
◆ = Import/Export

SIC: 1623 1711 3494 7699 Oil and gas line and compressor station construction; Process piping contractor; Line strainers, for use in piping systems; Tank and boiler cleaning service

(P-701)
TURN AROUND COMMUNICATIONS INC
100 N Barranca St Ste 260, West Covina (91791-1637)
P.O. Box 6121 (91734-2121)
PHONE....................................626 443-2400
Sayeid Kouhkan, *Pr*
EMP: 170 **EST:** 2002
SALES (est): 20.16MM **Privately Held**
Web:
www.turnaroundcommunications.net
SIC: 1623 Telephone and communication line construction

(P-702)
VADNAIS TRENCHLESS SVCS INC
11858 Bernardo Plaza Ct Ste 100, San Diego (92128-2440)
PHONE....................................858 550-1460
Paul Vadnais, *CEO*
Jeff Anderson, *
Jesse Mangan, *
▲ **EMP:** 100 **EST:** 1964
SALES (est): 2.33MM **Privately Held**
Web: www.vadnaiscorp.com
SIC: 1623 Sewer line construction

(P-703)
VALVERDE CONSTRUCTION INC
10936 Shoemaker Ave, Santa Fe Springs (90670-4533)
P.O. Box 3223 (90670-0223)
PHONE....................................562 906-1826
Joe A Valverde, *Pr*
Joe A Valverde, *Pr*
Edward Valverde, *
Rose Valverde, *
Christopher Valverde, *
EMP: 135 **EST:** 1972
SQ FT: 9,000
SALES (est): 48.7MM **Privately Held**
Web: valverde.webflow.io
SIC: 1623 Water main construction

(P-704)
VCI CONSTRUCTION LLC (HQ)
1921 W 11th St Ste A, Upland (91786-3508)
PHONE....................................909 946-0905
John Xanthos, *Pr*
Logan Teal, *
Vic Marovish, *
EMP: 100 **EST:** 1998
SQ FT: 29,500
SALES (est): 43.85MM
SALES (corp-wide): 4.18B **Publicly Held**
Web: www.vcicom.com
SIC: 1623 Underground utilities contractor
PA: Dycom Industries, Inc.
11780 Us Hwy 1 Ste 600
561 627-7171

(P-705)
W A RASIC CNSTR CO INC (PA)
4150 Long Beach Blvd, Long Beach (90807-2650)
PHONE....................................562 928-6111
Peter L Rasic, *CEO*
EMP: 147 **EST:** 1978
SQ FT: 8,500
SALES (est): 49.96MM
SALES (corp-wide): 49.96MM **Privately Held**

Web: www.warasic.com
SIC: 1623 Sewer line construction

(P-706)
W M LYLES CO
42142 Roick Dr, Temecula (92590-3695)
P.O. Box 1347 (92564-1347)
PHONE....................................951 296-2354
EMP: 113
SALES (corp-wide): 17.85MM **Privately Held**
Web: www.wmlylesco.com
SIC: 1623 Water, sewer, and utility lines
HQ: W. M. Lyles Co.
525 W Alluvial Ave
Fresno CA 93711
559 441-1900

(P-707)
WEST TECH CONTRACTING INC
568 N Tulip St, Escondido (92025-2533)
PHONE....................................760 233-2570
EMP: 70 **EST:** 1991
SALES (est): 15.13MM **Privately Held**
Web: www.west-techcontracting.com
SIC: 1623 Oil and gas pipeline construction

1629 Heavy Construction, Nec

(P-708)
ARB INC
2130 La Mirada Dr, Vista (92081-8815)
PHONE....................................619 295-2754
Tim Burkes, *Mgr*
EMP: 273
Web: www.prim.com
SIC: 1629 Industrial plant construction
HQ: Arb, Inc.
26000 Commercentre Dr
Lake Forest CA 92630
949 598-9242

(P-709)
BEMUS LANDSCAPE INC
951 Calle Negocio Ste D, San Clemente (92673-6280)
P.O. Box 74268 (92673)
PHONE....................................714 557-7910
William Howard Bemus, *Pr*
Jonathon Parry, *
Martine Bemus, *
EMP: 300 **EST:** 1973
SQ FT: 7,000
SALES (est): 24.24MM **Privately Held**
Web: www.bemus.com
SIC: 1629 0782 Drainage system construction; Landscape contractors

(P-710)
CURTIN MARITIME CORP
725 Pier T Ave, Long Beach (90802-6234)
P.O. Box 2531 (90801)
PHONE....................................562 983-7257
Martin Jeremiah Curtin Junior, *CEO*
Kelly Curtin, *
EMP: 326 **EST:** 1997
SQ FT: 65,340
SALES (est): 98.89MM **Privately Held**
Web: www.curtinmaritime.com
SIC: 1629 4492 Marine construction; Tugboat service

(P-711)
ENVIROGENICS SYSTEMS COMPANY
9255 Telstar Ave, El Monte (91731-2845)
PHONE....................................818 573-9220
Doctor Fadi Abbash, *Pr*
R Kadaj, *

EMP: 100 **EST:** 1967
SQ FT: 91,000
SALES (est): 1.39MM **Privately Held**
SIC: 1629 Industrial plant construction

(P-712)
FOUNDATION PILE INC
8375 Almeria Ave, Fontana (92335-3283)
P.O. Box 97 (94561-0097)
PHONE....................................909 350-1584
Derek Halecky, *CEO*
Peter Brandl, *
Dermot Fallon, *
Earl Robbins, *
Nikki Sjoblom, *
EMP: 97 **EST:** 1978
SALES (est): 15.7MM
SALES (corp-wide): 49.44MM **Privately Held**
Web:
www.foundationconstructorsinc.com
SIC: 1629 1794 Pile driving contractor; Excavation and grading, building construction
PA: Foundation Constructors, Inc.
81 Big Break Rd
925 754-6633

(P-713)
FRONTIER-KEMPER CONSTRUCTORS INC (HQ)
Also Called: Fkc-Lake Shore
15900 Olden St, Rancho Cascades (91342-1051)
P.O. Box 6690 (47719-0690)
PHONE....................................818 362-2062
▲ **EMP:** 70 **EST:** 1972
SALES (est): 92.91MM
SALES (corp-wide): 3.88B **Publicly Held**
Web: www.frontierkemper.com
SIC: 1629 Earthmoving contractor
PA: Tutor Perini Corporation
15901 Olden St
818 362-8391

(P-714)
HELLAS CONSTRUCTION INC
5135 Avenida Encinas Ste A, Carlsbad (92008-4341)
PHONE....................................760 891-8090
James Towsley, *Owner*
EMP: 387
Web: www.hellasconstruction.com
SIC: 1629 Athletic and recreation facilities construction
HQ: Hellas Construction, Inc.
12000 W Parmer Ln
Cedar Park TX 78613
800 233-5714

(P-715)
HERZOG CONTRACTING CORP
3760 Kilroy Airport Way Ste 120, Long Beach (90806-2455)
P.O. Box 1089 (64502-1089)
PHONE....................................562 595-7414
Jennifer Lord, *Brnch Mgr*
EMP: 88
SALES (corp-wide): 433.21MM **Privately Held**
Web: www.herzog.com
SIC: 1629 1611 4953 Railroad and railway roadbed construction; Highway and street paving contractor; Sanitary landfill operation
HQ: Herzog Contracting Corp.
600 S Riverside Rd
Saint Joseph MO 64507
816 233-9001

(P-716)
IRWIN INDUSTRIES INC
2301 Rosecrans Ave Ste 3185, El Segundo (90245-4918)
P.O. Box 8678 (25303-0678)
PHONE....................................704 457-5117
EMP: 710
SIC: 1629 1731 1796 7353 Power plant construction; Electric power systems contractors; Power generating equipment installation; Heavy construction equipment rental

(P-717)
MANSON CONSTRUCTION CO
340 Golden Shore Ste 310, Long Beach (90802-4229)
PHONE....................................562 983-2340
Tim Henson, *Brnch Mgr*
EMP: 70
SALES (corp-wide): 487.77MM **Privately Held**
Web: www.mansonconstruction.com
SIC: 1629 Marine construction
HQ: Manson Construction Co.
5209 E Marginal Way S
Seattle WA 98134
206 762-0850

(P-718)
SHIMMICK CONSTRUCTION CO INC (HQ)
Also Called: Transprttion Oprtons MGT Slton
530 Technology Dr Ste 300, Irvine (92618-1350)
PHONE....................................949 591-5922
EMP: 93 **EST:** 1990
SQ FT: 30,000
SALES (est): 632.81MM
SALES (corp-wide): 632.81MM **Publicly Held**
Web: www.shimmick.com
SIC: 1629 1623 Earthmoving contractor; Sewer line construction
PA: Shimmick Corporation
530 Technology Dr Ste 300
510 777-5000

(P-719)
SKANSKA USA CVIL W RCKY MTN DS (DH)
Also Called: Skanska Rocky Mountain Dst
1995 Agua Mansa Rd, Riverside (92509-2405)
PHONE....................................970 565-8000
Curtis Broughton, *Sr VP*
Curtis Broughton, *Sr VP*
David Sltton, *
Chris Eastin, *
Emeric Ondeck, *
EMP: 70 **EST:** 1950
SQ FT: 22,500
SALES (est): 8MM
SALES (corp-wide): 115.37MM **Privately Held**
SIC: 1629 1611 1711 Dam construction; General contractor, highway and street construction; Mechanical contractor
HQ: Skanska Usa Civil Inc.
7520 Astoria Blvd Ste 200
East Elmhurst NY 11370
718 340-0777

(P-720)
SLATER INC
11045 Rose Ave, Fontana (92337-7051)
P.O. Box 759 (92334-0759)
PHONE....................................909 822-6800
Phillip S Slater, *CEO*
Steve David, *VP*

Edward Johnson, *CFO*
EMP: 97 **EST:** 1981
SQ FT: 6,000
SALES (est): 7.88MM **Privately Held**
Web: www.slaterinc.com
SIC: 1629 8711 Drainage system
construction; Engineering services

(P-721)
TIMEC COMPANIES INC
Also Called: Timec
2997 E Maria St, E Rncho Dmngz
(90221-5801)
PHONE.....................310 885-4710
Craig Crowder, *CEO*
EMP: 230
Web: www.timec.com
SIC: 1629 Industrial plant construction
HQ: Timec Companies Inc
473 E Channel Rd
Benicia CA 94510
707 642-2222

(P-722)
VISTA STEEL CO INC
Also Called: VISTA STEEL CO INC
331 W Lewis St, Ventura (93001-1394)
PHONE.....................805 653-1189
John Swaffar, *Brnch Mgr*
EMP: 24
SALES (corp-wide): 1.87MM **Privately
Held**
Web: www.vistasteelco.com
SIC: 1629 3449 Dams, waterways, docks,
and other marine construction;
Miscellaneous metalwork
PA: Vista Steel Company
6100 Frncis Btllo Rd Ste
805 964-4732

(P-723)
WARREN COLLINS AND ASSOC
INC (PA)
Also Called: Collins Company
300 E Eucalyptus Ave, Ontario (91762)
PHONE.....................909 548-6708
Larry W Collins, *Pr*
Nancy Collins, *
▲ **EMP:** 23 **EST:** 1975
SQ FT: 8,000
SALES (est): 2.13MM
SALES (corp-wide): 2.13MM **Privately
Held**
Web: www.collinscompany.com
SIC: 1629 3949 1799 3446 Athletic and
recreation facilities construction; Sporting
and athletic goods, nec; Scaffolding;
Scaffolds, mobile or stationary: metal

1711 Plumbing, Heating, Air-
conditioning

(P-724)
10X HVAC OF CA LLC
Also Called: General AC & Plbg
31170 Reserve Dr, Thousand Palms
(92276-6653)
PHONE.....................760 343-7488
Patrick Somers, *Pr*
EMP: 75 **EST:** 2022
SALES (est): 2.94MM **Privately Held**
Web: www.callthegeneral.com
SIC: 1711 Plumbing, heating, air-conditioning

(P-725)
20/20 PLUMBING & HEATING
INC
674 Rancheros Dr, San Marcos
(92069-3005)

PHONE.....................760 535-3101
EMP: 103
SALES (corp-wide): 62.12MM **Privately
Held**
Web: www.2020ph.com
SIC: 1711 Plumbing contractors
PA: 20/20 Plumbing & Heating, Inc.
7343 Orangewood Dr Ste B
951 396-2020

(P-726)
20/20 PLUMBING & HEATING
INC (PA)
Also Called: Honeywell Authorized Dealer
7343 Orangewood Dr Ste B, Riverside
(92504-1053)
PHONE.....................951 396-2020
Thomas Lew Baker, *CEO*
EMP: 97 **EST:** 2014
SALES (est): 62.12MM
SALES (corp-wide): 62.12MM **Privately
Held**
Web: www.2020ph.com
SIC: 1711 Plumbing contractors

(P-727)
A & D FIRE PROTECTION INC
7130 Convoy Ct, San Diego (92111-1019)
PHONE.....................619 258-7697
Andrew R Otero, *Pr*
EMP: 80 **EST:** 1988
SQ FT: 10,000
SALES (est): 4.7MM **Privately Held**
Web: www.hillerfire.com
SIC: 1711 1542 Fire sprinkler system
installation; Nonresidential construction, nec

(P-728)
A O REED & CO LLC
4777 Ruffner St, San Diego (92111-1578)
P.O. Box 85226 (92186)
PHONE.....................858 565-4131
Steve Andrade, *Ch Bd*
David Clarkin, *
Craig Koehler, *
EMP: 500 **EST:** 1914
SQ FT: 55,000
SALES (est): 148.26MM **Privately Held**
Web: www.aoreed.com
SIC: 1711 Mechanical contractor

(P-729)
ACCO ENGINEERED SYSTEMS
INC (PA)
Also Called: Acco
888 E Walnut St, Pasadena (91101-1895)
PHONE.....................818 244-6571
EMP: 900 **EST:** 1934
SALES (est): 1.51B
SALES (corp-wide): 1.51B **Privately Held**
Web: www.accoes.com
SIC: 1711 7623 3448 Process piping
contractor; Air conditioning repair;
Buildings, portable: prefabricated metal

(P-730)
ACH MECHANICAL
CONTRACTORS INC
411 Business Center Ct, Redlands
(92373-8084)
P.O. Box 8234 (92375-1434)
PHONE.....................909 307-2850
Hector Vargas, *
EMP: 80 **EST:** 2000
SQ FT: 14,450
SALES (est): 1.86MM **Privately Held**
Web: www.achmechanical.com
SIC: 1711 Mechanical contractor

(P-731)
AIR-TRO INCORPORATED
Also Called: Air-Tro Air Conditioning & Htg
1630 S Myrtle Ave, Monrovia (91016-4634)
PHONE.....................626 357-3535
EMP: 70 **EST:** 1969
SALES (est): 9.51MM **Privately Held**
Web: www.airtro.com
SIC: 1711 Warm air heating and air
conditioning contractor

(P-732)
ALL TMPERATURES
CONTROLLED INC
Also Called: Honeywell Authorized Dealer
9720 Topanga Canyon Pl, Chatsworth
(91311-4134)
PHONE.....................818 882-1478
George Mego, *Pr*
EMP: 72 **EST:** 1978
SQ FT: 13,481
SALES (est): 10.4MM **Privately Held**
Web:
www.alltemperaturescontrolled.com
SIC: 1711 Warm air heating and air
conditioning contractor

(P-733)
ALPHA MECHANICAL INC
4990 Greencraig Ln Ste A, San Diego
(92123-1673)
PHONE.....................858 278-3500
Boris Barshak, *Brnch Mgr*
EMP: 137
Web: www.alphamechanical.com
SIC: 1711 Mechanical contractor
PA: Alpha Mechanical, Inc.
1866 Friendship Dr

(P-734)
ALPHA MECHANICAL HEATING
& AIR CONDITIONING INC
4885 Greencraig Ln, San Diego
(92123-1664)
PHONE.....................858 279-1300
EMP: 250
SIC: 1711 Sprinkler contractors

(P-735)
AMERICAN BEECH SOLAR LLC
18575 Jamboree Rd Ste 850, Irvine
(92612-2558)
PHONE.....................949 398-3915
Frederick Robinson, *Managing Member*
EMP: 80 **EST:** 2016
SALES (est): 939.12K **Privately Held**
SIC: 1711 Solar energy contractor

(P-736)
AMPAM PARKS MECHANICAL
INC (PA)
17036 Avalon Blvd, Carson (90746-1206)
PHONE.....................310 835-1532
Chris Kennedy, *CEO*
John D Parks, *VP*
James C Wright, *CFO*
Chris Kennedy, *Ex VP*
▲ **EMP:** 725 **EST:** 1999
SQ FT: 16,000
SALES (est): 99.28MM
SALES (corp-wide): 99.28MM **Privately
Held**
Web: www.ampam.com
SIC: 1711 Plumbing contractors

(P-737)
AMS AMERICAN MECH SVCS
MD INC

2116 E Walnut Ave, Fullerton (92831-4845)
PHONE.....................714 888-6820
Charles S Knight, *Genl Mgr*
EMP: 170
SALES (corp-wide): 1.52B **Privately Held**
Web: www.aeservices.us
SIC: 1711 Mechanical contractor
HQ: Ams American Mechanical Services Of
Maryland, Inc.
13300 Mid Atlantic Blvd
Laurel MD 20708
301 206-5070

(P-738)
ANDERSEN COMMERCIAL
PLBG INC
1608 Yeager Ave, La Verne (91750-5853)
PHONE.....................909 599-5950
Paul Andersen, *CEO*
Duane Kerr, *
EMP: 101 **EST:** 1993
SQ FT: 2,000
SALES (est): 11.64MM **Privately Held**
Web: www.andersenplumbing.com
SIC: 1711 Plumbing contractors

(P-739)
APEX MECHANICAL SYSTEMS
INC
7440 Trade St Ste A, San Diego
(92121-3412)
PHONE.....................858 536-8700
Randall E Melhouse, *CEO*
Kathy Draper, *
David R Draper, *
Blaine Stratton, *Stockholder*
Edward Draper, *Stockholder*
EMP: 79 **EST:** 2003
SALES (est): 12.18MM **Privately Held**
Web: www.apexmech.com
SIC: 1711 Mechanical contractor

(P-740)
API GROUP LIFE SAFETY USA
LLC
3720 Industry Ave Ste 107, Lakewood
(90712-4135)
PHONE.....................562 279-0770
Wesley Sue, *Mgr*
EMP: 81
SALES (corp-wide): 6.93B **Publicly Held**
Web: www.wsfp.com
SIC: 1711 Fire sprinkler system installation
HQ: Api Group Life Safety Usa Llc
7026 S Tucson Way
Centennial CO 80112
303 792-0022

(P-741)
ARROWHEAD BRASS &
PLUMBING LLC
5147 Alhambra Ave, Los Angeles
(90032-3413)
PHONE.....................800 332-4267
Fred Schneider, *CEO*
▲ **EMP:** 80 **EST:** 1936
SQ FT: 35,000
SALES (est): 7.11MM **Privately Held**
Web: www.arrowheadbrass.com
SIC: 1711 Plumbing contractors

(P-742)
ASI HASTINGS INC
Also Called: Asi Heating, Air and Solar
4870 Viewridge Ave Ste 200, San Diego
(92123-1671)
PHONE.....................619 590-9300
TOLL FREE: 800
Philip Justo, *Pr*

Kenneth Justo, *
EMP: 120 **EST:** 1952
SQ FT: 2,000
SALES (est): 15.39MM
SALES (corp-wide): 97.38MM **Privately Held**
Web: www.asiheatingandair.com
SIC: 1711 Heating systems repair and maintenance
PA: Service Champions, Llc
3150 E Birch St
714 777-7777

(P-743)
ASSOCIATE MECH CONTRS INC
622 S Vinewood St, Escondido (92029-1925)
PHONE.....................760 294-3517
Richard Reinholz, *Pr*
Laura Reinholz, *Corporate Secretary*
Christina Payne, *
EMP: 150 **EST:** 2011
SALES (est): 26.56MM **Privately Held**
Web: www.amechinc.com
SIC: 1711 Mechanical contractor

(P-744)
ASTRO MECHANICAL CONTRACTORS INC
603 S Marshall Ave, El Cajon (92020-4214)
PHONE.....................619 442-9686
EMP: 85 **EST:** 1960
SALES (est): 9.47MM **Privately Held**
Web: www.astro-mech.com
SIC: 1711 1542 Plumbing contractors; Nonresidential construction, nec

(P-745)
ATLAS MECHANICAL INC (PA)
Also Called: Honeywell Authorized Dealer
8260 Camino Santa Fe Ste B, San Diego (92121-3255)
PHONE.....................858 554-0700
EMP: 74 **EST:** 1991
SALES (est): 35.68MM **Privately Held**
Web: www.atlasmechanical.com
SIC: 1711 3531 Ventilation and duct work contractor; Construction machinery

(P-746)
AWHAP ACQUISITION CORP
28358 Constellation Rd Ste 698, Valencia (91355-5044)
PHONE.....................888 611-4328
Alex Stuckey, *CEO*
EMP: 152 **EST:** 2020
SALES (est): 7.79MM **Privately Held**
SIC: 1711 Plumbing, heating, air-conditioning

(P-747)
BARR ENGINEERING INC
19 Castano, Rcho Sta Marg (92688-1662)
PHONE.....................562 944-1722
Peter Buongiorno, *Pr*
Pamela Price-recchia, *Sec*
Mike Buongiorno, *
EMP: 82 **EST:** 1958
SALES (est): 21.69MM **Privately Held**
Web: www.barrengineering.com
SIC: 1711 Warm air heating and air conditioning contractor

(P-748)
BCM CUSTOMER SERVICE
12155 Kirkham Rd, Poway (92064-6870)
PHONE.....................858 679-5757
Brian R Cox, *CEO*
EMP: 90 **EST:** 1996
SQ FT: 30,000
SALES (est): 4.66MM **Privately Held**

SIC: 1711 1796 Plumbing, heating, air-conditioning; Installing building equipment

(P-749)
BERNEL INC
Also Called: Vfs Fire Protection Services
501 W Southern Ave, Orange (92865-3217)
PHONE.....................714 778-6070
Randy Roland Nelson, *CEO*
Kevin Berthoud, *
Mario Lopez, *
EMP: 140 **EST:** 1994
SQ FT: 7,800
SALES (est): 19.74MM **Privately Held**
Web: www.vfsfire.com
SIC: 1711 7382 Fire sprinkler system installation; Security systems services

(P-750)
BILL HOWE PLUMBING INC
Also Called: Am-PM Sewer & Drain Cleaning
9210 Sky Park Ct Ste 200, San Diego (92123-4478)
PHONE.....................800 245-5469
William Howe, *Pr*
Tina Howe, *
EMP: 85 **EST:** 1982
SALES (est): 24.6MM **Privately Held**
Web: www.billhowe.com
SIC: 1711 Plumbing contractors

(P-751)
BONESO BROTHERS CNSTR INC
1446 Spring St, Paso Robles (93446-2171)
PHONE.....................805 227-4450
Steve Boneso, *Pr*
Rob Boneso, *
EMP: 80 **EST:** 1999
SALES (est): 40MM **Privately Held**
Web: www.bonesobrothersconstruction.com
SIC: 1711 1542 Mechanical contractor; Nonresidential construction, nec

(P-752)
BREEZE AIR CONDITIONING LLC
75145 Saint Charles Pl Ste A, Palm Desert (92211-9048)
PHONE.....................760 346-0855
Joe Coker, *Managing Member*
EMP: 59 **EST:** 1980
SQ FT: 33,000
SALES (est): 4.48MM **Privately Held**
Web: www.breezeac.com
SIC: 1711 3444 5075 3433 Warm air heating and air conditioning contractor; Sheet metalwork; Warm air heating and air conditioning; Logo, gas fireplace

(P-753)
BRIGHTVIEW LANDSCAPE DEV INC
2000 S Yale St, Santa Ana (92704-3934)
PHONE.....................714 546-7975
Gins Garmann, *Mgr*
EMP: 143
SALES (corp-wide): 2.77B **Publicly Held**
Web: www.brightview.com
SIC: 1711 0781 Irrigation sprinkler system installation; Landscape services
HQ: Brightview Landscape Development, Inc.
27001 Agoura Rd Ste 350
Calabasas CA 91301
818 223-8500

(P-754)
BRIGHTVIEW LANDSCAPE DEV INC
13691 Vaughn St, San Fernando (91340-3072)
PHONE.....................818 838-4700
Greg Motschenbacher, *Brnch Mgr*
EMP: 71
SALES (corp-wide): 2.77B **Publicly Held**
Web: www.brightview.com
SIC: 1711 0781 Irrigation sprinkler system installation; Landscape services
HQ: Brightview Landscape Development, Inc.
27001 Agoura Rd Ste 350
Calabasas CA 91301
818 223-8500

(P-755)
BROMIC HEATING PTY LIMITED
7595 Irvine Center Dr Ste 100, Irvine (92618-2958)
PHONE.....................855 552-7432
EMP: 100 **EST:** 2017
SALES (est): 4.49MM **Privately Held**
Web: www.bromic.com
SIC: 1711 Mechanical contractor

(P-756)
BRYMAX CONSTRUCTION SVCS INC
7436 Lorge Cir, Huntington Beach (92647-3619)
PHONE.....................949 200-9619
Brooke Willems, *CEO*
Michael Willems, *
Steve Sylvester, *
Tony Teriitehau, *
EMP: 79 **EST:** 2015
SALES (est): 25.32MM **Privately Held**
Web: www.brymaxservices.com
SIC: 1711 5075 5065 4225 Plumbing, heating, air-conditioning; Warm air heating and air conditioning; Electronic parts and equipment, nec; General warehousing and storage

(P-757)
C & L REFRIGERATION CORP
Also Called: Honeywell Authorized Dealer
4111 N Palm St, Fullerton (92835-1025)
P.O. Box 2319 (92822-2319)
PHONE.....................800 901-4822
Ronald J Cassell, *CEO*
Ronald J Cassell Junior, *CEO*
Denise Lowe, *CFO*
Larry Jaslove, *
EMP: 150 **EST:** 1978
SQ FT: 18,000
SALES (est): 50.97MM **Privately Held**
Web: www.clrefrigeration.com
SIC: 1711 Refrigeration contractor

(P-758)
CALVIN DUBOIS
Also Called: Sun Energy Construction
9057 Arrow Rte, Rancho Cucamonga (91730-4452)
PHONE.....................909 222-6662
Dennis Jay, *
Calvin Dubois, *
EMP: 73 **EST:** 2018
SALES (est): 10.96MM **Privately Held**
Web: www.sunenergyco.com
SIC: 1711 Solar energy contractor

(P-759)
CASCADE THERMAL SOLUTIONS LLC (PA)
1890 Cordell Ct Ste 102, El Cajon (92020-0913)
PHONE.....................619 562-8852
Romulo Lambert Smith, *CEO*

Romulo Lambert Smith, *Pr*
Kay Smith, *
EMP: 49 **EST:** 1989
SQ FT: 55,000
SALES (est): 19.03MM **Privately Held**
Web: www.fullspectrumlabservices.com
SIC: 1711 3821 7699 Refrigeration contractor ; Laboratory apparatus and furniture; Scientific equipment repair service

(P-760)
CFP FIRE PROTECTION INC
153 Technology Dr Ste 200, Irvine (92618-2461)
PHONE.....................949 727-3277
Matt Krofcheck, *Pr*
Josh Hobgood, *
EMP: 100 **EST:** 2002
SQ FT: 21,960
SALES (est): 7.12MM **Privately Held**
Web: www.cfpfire.com
SIC: 1711 Fire sprinkler system installation
PA: Mx Holdings Us, Inc.
153 Technology Dr Ste 200

(P-761)
CHRISTIAN BROTHERS MECHANICAL SERVICES INC
Also Called: CB Controls
11140 Thurston Ln, Jurupa Valley (91752-1426)
PHONE.....................951 361-2247
EMP: 110 **EST:** 1985
SALES (est): 18.35MM **Privately Held**
Web: www.cbhvac.com
SIC: 1711 Warm air heating and air conditioning contractor

(P-762)
CIRCULATING AIR INC (PA)
Also Called: Honeywell Authorized Dealer
7337 Varna Ave, North Hollywood (91605-4009)
PHONE.....................818 764-0530
TOLL FREE: 800
Joseph Gallagher, *Ex VP*
Susan Gallagher, *
Marcy Ahlstrom, *
EMP: 100 **EST:** 1965
SQ FT: 13,000
SALES (est): 24.86MM
SALES (corp-wide): 24.86MM **Privately Held**
Web: www.circulatingair.com
SIC: 1711 Mechanical contractor

(P-763)
CIRCULATING AIR INC
1109 W Columbia Way, Lancaster (93534-8146)
PHONE.....................661 942-2048
Joe Galleger, *Mgr*
EMP: 71
SALES (corp-wide): 24.86MM **Privately Held**
Web: www.circulatingair.com
SIC: 1711 Warm air heating and air conditioning contractor
PA: Circulating Air, Inc.
7337 Varna Ave
818 764-0530

(P-764)
CLAY DUNN ENTERPRISES INC
Also Called: Air-TEC
1606 E Carson St, Carson (90745-2504)
P.O. Box 5444 (90749-5444)
PHONE.....................310 549-1698
Clayton N Dunn, *Pr*
Hayley Amberg, *

EMP: 138 **EST:** 1969
SQ FT: 18,000
SALES (est): 18.72MM **Privately Held**
Web: www.airtecperforms.com
SIC: 1711 Warm air heating and air
  conditioning contractor

(P-765)

CONTROL AIR CONDITIONING CORPORATION

Also Called: Honeywell Authorized Dealer
5200 E La Palma Ave, Anaheim
(92807-2019)
PHONE....................714 777-8600
EMP: 360
SIC: 1711 3444 Warm air heating and air
  conditioning contractor; Ducts, sheet metal

(P-766)

COOLSYS COML INDUS SLTIONS INC (DH)

145 S State College Blvd Ste 200, Brea
(92821-5806)
PHONE....................714 510-9609
Bradley Norman Howard, *Ch Bd*
Scott Rosner, *
Andrew Mandell, *
EMP: 103 **EST:** 1995
SALES (est): 480.58MM
SALES (corp-wide): 3.63B **Publicly Held**
Web: www.sourcerefrigeration.com
SIC: 1711 Refrigeration contractor
HQ: Coolsys, Inc.
  145 S State Cllege Blvd S
  Brea CA 92821
  714 510-9577

(P-767)

COSCO FIRE PROTECTION INC

Also Called: 76
4990 Greencraig Ln, San Diego
(92123-1673)
PHONE....................858 444-2000
Alexander Hernandez, *Mgr*
EMP: 86
Web: www.coscofire.com
SIC: 1711 Fire sprinkler system installation
HQ: Cosco Fire Protection, Inc.
  29222 Rancho Viejo Rd # 205
  San Juan Capistrano CA 92675

(P-768)

COUNTYWIDE MECH SYSTEMS LLC

1400 N Johnson Ave Ste 114, El Cajon
(92020-1651)
PHONE....................619 449-9900
Paul Duke, *Pr*
David Cimpl, *
EMP: 230 **EST:** 2011
SQ FT: 5,000
SALES (est): 42.44MM
SALES (corp-wide): 281.74MM **Privately
Held**
Web: www.countywidems.com
SIC: 1711 Mechanical contractor
PA: Modigent, Llc
  3930 E Watkins St Ste 300
  888 293-5334

(P-769)

COUTS HEATING & COOLING INC

1693 Rimpau Ave, Corona (92881-3202)
PHONE....................951 278-5560
EMP: 160 **EST:** 1978
SALES (est): 27.77MM **Privately Held**
Web: www.couts.com

SIC: 1711 Warm air heating and air
  conditioning contractor

(P-770)

CRITCHFELD MECH INC STHERN CAL

15391 Springdale St, Huntington Beach
(92649-1100)
PHONE....................949 390-2900
Mike Pearlman, *CEO*
EMP: 100 **EST:** 2004
SALES (est): 5.06MM **Privately Held**
Web: www.cmihvac.com
SIC: 1711 Warm air heating and air
  conditioning contractor

(P-771)

DAVE WILLIAMS PLBG & ELEC INC

75140 Saint Charles Pl Ste C, Palm Desert
(92211-9044)
PHONE....................760 296-1397
Daniel Williams, *Pr*
Dave Williams, *
EMP: 110 **EST:** 2008
SALES (est): 8.41MM **Privately Held**
Web: www.dwpeinc.com
SIC: 1711 Plumbing contractors

(P-772)

DESERT MECHANICAL INC

Also Called: Dmi
15870 Olden St, Rancho Cascades
(91342-1241)
PHONE....................702 873-7333
Casey M Condron, *Pr*
Alex L Hodson, *
Andre Burnthon, *
Joseph Guglielmo, *
Dan Naylor, *
EMP: 1100 **EST:** 1977
SQ FT: 25,000
SALES (est): 12.14MM
SALES (corp-wide): 3.88B **Publicly Held**
Web: www.lvdmi.com
SIC: 1711 Plumbing contractors
PA: Tutor Perini Corporation
  15901 Olden St
  818 362-8391

(P-773)

DYNAMIC PLUMBING SYSTEMS INC

5920 Winterhaven Ave, Riverside
(92504-1048)
PHONE....................951 343-1200
EMP: 306
SIC: 1711 Plumbing contractors

(P-774)

ECB CORP (PA)

Also Called: Omniduct
6400 Artesia Blvd, Buena Park
(90620-1006)
PHONE....................714 385-8900
Robert Brumleu, *Pr*
▲ **EMP:** 100 **EST:** 1980
SQ FT: 56,000
SALES (est): 21.5MM
SALES (corp-wide): 21.5MM **Privately
Held**
Web: www.omniduct.com
SIC: 1711 3444 Ventilation and duct work
  contractor; Ducts, sheet metal

(P-775)

EMCOR GROUP INC

3233 Enterprise St, Brea (92821-6239)
PHONE....................714 993-9500

EMP: 77
SALES (corp-wide): 12.58B **Publicly Held**
Web: www.emcorgroup.com
SIC: 1711 Mechanical contractor
PA: Emcor Group, Inc.
  301 Merritt 7
  203 849-7800

(P-776)

EMCOR SVCS INTGRATED SOLUTIONS

2 Cromwell, Irvine (92618-1816)
PHONE....................513 679-3325
Mike Biox, *Pr*
EMP: 169 **EST:** 2010
SALES (est): 2.5MM
SALES (corp-wide): 12.58B **Publicly Held**
Web: www.mesaenergy.com
SIC: 1711 Mechanical contractor
PA: Emcor Group, Inc.
  301 Merritt 7
  203 849-7800

(P-777)

ENERGY ENTERPRISES USA INC (PA)

Also Called: Canopy Energy
6842 Van Nuys Blvd Ste 800, Van Nuys
(91405-4660)
PHONE....................424 339-0005
Lior Agam, *CEO*
EMP: 100 **EST:** 2011
SQ FT: 11,000
SALES (est): 4.09MM
SALES (corp-wide): 4.09MM **Privately
Held**
Web: www.canopyenergy.com
SIC: 1711 Solar energy contractor

(P-778)

ESS LLC

Also Called: Evergreen Solar Services
5227 Dantes View Dr, Agoura Hills
(91301-2313)
PHONE....................888 303-6424
Jacob Stephens, *Pr*
Eliahu Arbib, *Prin*
Shaul Arbiv, *Prin*
EMP: 100 **EST:** 2011
SALES (est): 1.25MM **Privately Held**
SIC: 1711 Solar energy contractor

(P-779)

FREEDOM FOREVER LLC (PA)

Also Called: Freedom Forever
43445 Business Park Dr Ste 104, Temecula
(92590-3670)
PHONE....................888 557-6431
Brett Leon Bouchy, *CEO*
EMP: 88 **EST:** 2016
SALES (est): 227.62MM
SALES (corp-wide): 227.62MM **Privately
Held**
Web: www.freedomforever.com
SIC: 1711 Solar energy contractor

(P-780)

FREEDOM SOLAR SERVICES

Also Called: Freedom Forever
43445 Business Park Dr Ste 110, Temecula
(92590-3671)
PHONE....................888 557-6431
Brett Leon Bouchy, *CEO*
EMP: 150 **EST:** 2012
SALES (est): 2.01MM **Privately Held**
Web: www.freedomforever.com
SIC: 1711 Solar energy contractor

(P-781)

FRONTIER MECHANICAL INC

Also Called: Frontier Plumbing
6309 Seven Seas Ave, Bakersfield
(93308-5133)
PHONE....................661 589-6203
Rick Palmer, *Pr*
Brenda Palmer, *Stockholder*
EMP: 93 **EST:** 1987
SQ FT: 120,000
SALES (est): 6.7MM **Privately Held**
Web: www.frontier-plumbing.com
SIC: 1711 1521 Plumbing contractors; New
  construction, single-family houses

(P-782)

GENERAL UNDGRD FIRE PRTCTION I

701 W Grove Ave, Orange (92865-3213)
P.O. Box 29830 (92809-0194)
PHONE....................714 632-8646
Robert Anderson, *CEO*
Terry Householder, *
Karla Distrola, *
EMP: 110 **EST:** 1985
SQ FT: 8,000
SALES (est): 2.58MM **Privately Held**
Web: www.gufpinc.com
SIC: 1711 Fire sprinkler system installation

(P-783)

GRAYCON INC

232 S 8th Ave, City Of Industry
(91746-3200)
PHONE....................626 961-9640
Wayne Lyons, *Pr*
Erik Peterson, *
EMP: 75 **EST:** 1968
SQ FT: 12,000
SALES (est): 9.76MM **Privately Held**
Web: www.graycon.net
SIC: 1711 Mechanical contractor

(P-784)

GREATER SAN DIEGO AC CO INC

Also Called: Honeywell Authorized Dealer
3883 Ruffin Rd Ste C, San Diego
(92123-4813)
PHONE....................619 469-7818
Randy Baillargeon, *Pr*
Ryan Baillargeon, *
EMP: 115 **EST:** 1993
SQ FT: 8,500
SALES (est): 21.8MM **Privately Held**
Web: www.gsdac.com
SIC: 1711 Warm air heating and air
  conditioning contractor

(P-785)

H L MOE CO INC (PA)

Also Called: Keefe Plumbing Services
526 Commercial St, Glendale (91203-2861)
PHONE....................818 572-2100
Martha Tennyson, *CEO*
Michael C Davis, *
Bernice Davis, *
Richard Herrea, *
Robert Francis, *
EMP: 130 **EST:** 1927
SALES (est): 21.94MM
SALES (corp-wide): 21.94MM **Privately
Held**
Web: www.moeplumbing.com
SIC: 1711 Plumbing contractors

(P-786)

HELIX MECHANICAL INC

1100 N Magnolia Ave Ste L, El Cajon
(92020-1953)

PHONE..................619 440-1518
Stephen Baker, *CEO*
Michael Hurley, *
Patrick Harrelson, *
EMP: 109 **EST:** 2003
SALES (est): 15.84MM **Privately Held**
Web: www.helixmechanical.com
SIC: 1711 1751 Mechanical contractor;
Carpentry work

(P-787)
HPS MECHANICAL INC (PA)
3100 E Belle Ter, Bakersfield (93307-6830)
PHONE...................661 397-2121
Les Denherder, *Pr*
Scott Denherder, *
EMP: 127 **EST:** 1959
SALES (est): 50.85MM
SALES (corp-wide): 50.85MM **Privately Held**
Web: www.hpsmechanical.com
SIC: 1711 Plumbing contractors

(P-788)
INDUSTRIAL COML SYSTEMS INC
Also Called: San Marcos Mechanical
1165 Joshua Way, Vista (92081-7840)
PHONE...................760 300-4094
Robin Sides, *Pr*
Matt Harbin, *
Cindy Sides, *
EMP: 160 **EST:** 1982
SQ FT: 15,000
SALES (est): 30.36MM **Privately Held**
Web: www.1ics.net
SIC: 1711 Ventilation and duct work contractor

(P-789)
INFINITY PLUMBING DESIGNS INC
9182 Stellar Ct, Corona (92883-4923)
PHONE...................951 737-4436
Andrew D Carlson, *Pr*
EMP: 300 **EST:** 2006
SQ FT: 5,925
SALES (est): 25.57MM **Privately Held**
Web: www.infinityplumbingdesigns.com
SIC: 1711 Plumbing contractors

(P-790)
INTEGRATED ENERGY GROUP LLC ✪
Also Called: Ie Construction
3929 E Guasti Rd Ste F, Ontario (91761-1540)
PHONE...................605 381-7859
Josh Tofteland, *Managing Member*
Shane Scaletti, *
EMP: 155 **EST:** 2023
SALES (est): 7.08MM **Privately Held**
SIC: 1711 Solar energy contractor

(P-791)
JACKSON & BLANC
7929 Arjons Dr, San Diego (92126-4301)
PHONE...................858 831-7900
Kirk Jackson, *CEO*
John Fusca, *
▲ **EMP:** 110 **EST:** 1931
SQ FT: 36,000
SALES (est): 65.48MM **Privately Held**
Web: www.jacksonandblanc.com
SIC: 1711 Mechanical contractor

(P-792)
K & S AIR CONDITIONING INC
Also Called: K&S

143 E Meats Ave, Orange (92865-3309)
PHONE...................714 685-0077
Steven Patz, *Pr*
Renee Patz, *
EMP: 140 **EST:** 1952
SQ FT: 18,000
SALES (est): 24.58MM **Privately Held**
Web: www.kandsair.com
SIC: 1711 Warm air heating and air conditioning contractor

(P-793)
KEN STARR INC
Also Called: Home Comfort USA
1120 N Tustin Ave, Anaheim (92807-1712)
PHONE...................714 632-8789
Ken Starr, *Pr*
Paul Buono, *
EMP: 80 **EST:** 2011
SQ FT: 9,000
SALES (est): 13.99MM **Privately Held**
Web: www.homecomfortusa.com
SIC: 1711 Warm air heating and air conditioning contractor

(P-794)
KINCAID INDUSTRIES INC
31065 Plantation Dr, Thousand Palms (92276-6623)
PHONE...................760 343-5457
Scott Kincaid, *CEO*
EMP: 79 **EST:** 1995
SQ FT: 7,000
SALES (est): 9.79MM **Privately Held**
Web: www.kincaidindustries.com
SIC: 1711 Plumbing contractors

(P-795)
LDI MECHANICAL INC (PA)
Also Called: Honeywell Authorized Dealer
1587 E Bentley Dr, Corona (92879-1738)
PHONE...................951 340-9685
Lloyd Smith, *Pr*
Mike Smith, *
Robert Smith, *
Steve Buren, *
Jeff Minarik, *
EMP: 155 **EST:** 1985
SQ FT: 38,000
SALES (est): 94.22MM
SALES (corp-wide): 94.22MM **Privately Held**
Web: www.ldimechanical.com
SIC: 1711 Mechanical contractor

(P-796)
LITE SOLAR CORP
Also Called: Lite Solar
3553 Atlantic Ave, Long Beach (90807-5606)
PHONE...................562 256-1249
EMP: 150
Web: www.litesolar.com
SIC: 1711 Solar energy contractor

(P-797)
LOZANO PLUMBING SERVICES INC
Also Called: Plumbing Master
3615 Presley Ave, Riverside (92507-4448)
P.O. Box 53137 (92517-4137)
PHONE...................951 683-4840
Andrew Lozano, *Pr*
Felipe Lozano, *
Andrew Lozano, *Sec*
EMP: 130 **EST:** 2004
SALES (est): 13.56MM **Privately Held**
Web: www.plumbingmaster.com
SIC: 1711 Plumbing contractors

(P-798)
LPSH HOLDINGS INC
Also Called: Horizon Solar Power
3570 W Florida Ave Ste 168, Hemet (92545-3518)
PHONE...................951 926-1176
Zachary Allman, *Acctg Mgr*
EMP: 461
SALES (corp-wide): 15.16MM **Privately Held**
SIC: 1711 Solar energy contractor
PA: Lpsh Holdings, Inc.
7100 W Florida Ave
855 647-5061

(P-799)
M & M PLUMBING INC
6782 Columbus St, Riverside (92504-1118)
PHONE...................951 354-5388
Robert Malcom, *Pr*
Glenn Malcolm, *
EMP: 80 **EST:** 2002
SALES (est): 4.7MM **Privately Held**
Web: www.mmplumbing.net
SIC: 1711 Plumbing contractors

(P-800)
MAINSTREAM ENERGY CORPORATION
Also Called: Rec Solar
775 Fiero Ln Ste 200, San Luis Obispo (93401-7904)
PHONE...................805 528-9705
EMP: 493
Web: www.mainstreamenergy.com
SIC: 1711 5049 Solar energy contractor;
Scientific and engineering equipment and supplies

(P-801)
MARCOS M URIARTE
Also Called: Plumbing Solution Specialist
28202 Cabot Rd Ste 300, Laguna Niguel (92677-1249)
P.O. Box 17022 (92817-7022)
PHONE...................714 326-1064
Marcos M Uriarte, *Owner*
EMP: 75 **EST:** 2010
SALES (est): 4.72MM **Privately Held**
Web:
www.plumbingsolutionspecialist.com
SIC: 1711 Plumbing contractors

(P-802)
MDDR INC
Also Called: Econo Air
1921 Petra Ln, Placentia (92870-6749)
PHONE...................714 792-1993
Michael Richards, *Pr*
Rhonda Richards, *
EMP: 110 **EST:** 1991
SALES (est): 23.89MM **Privately Held**
Web: www.myeconoair.com
SIC: 1711 1731 Warm air heating and air conditioning contractor; Electrical work

(P-803)
MEMEGED TEVUOT SHEMESH (PA)
Also Called: Titan Solar
5550 Topanga Canyon Blvd Ste 280, Woodland Hills (91367-7471)
PHONE...................866 575-1211
Ofir Haimoff, *Pr*
EMP: 152 **EST:** 2011
SQ FT: 20,000
SALES (est): 2.02MM
SALES (corp-wide): 2.02MM **Privately Held**

SIC: 1711 5074 Solar energy contractor;
Heating equipment and panels, solar

(P-804)
MENIFEE VALLEY AC INC
3875 Industrial Ave, Hemet (92545-9789)
PHONE...................888 785-6125
Michael Mccarthy, *Pr*
John R Lawson, *
Michael Mccarthy, *CFO*
EMP: 75 **EST:** 1998
SALES (est): 9.48MM **Privately Held**
Web: www.mvac-inc.com
SIC: 1711 Warm air heating and air conditioning contractor

(P-805)
MESA ENERGY SYSTEMS INC (HQ)
Also Called: Emcor Services Mesa Energy
2 Cromwell, Irvine (92618-1816)
PHONE...................949 460-0460
Robert A Lake, *Pr*
Charles G Fletcher Junior, *VP*
Michael Ecshner, *
Kip Bagley, *
Steve Hunt, *
EMP: 210 **EST:** 1984
SQ FT: 55,000
SALES (est): 114.02MM
SALES (corp-wide): 12.58B **Publicly Held**
Web: www.mesaenergy.com
SIC: 1711 7623 Warm air heating and air conditioning contractor; Refrigeration service and repair
PA: Emcor Group, Inc.
301 Merritt 7
203 849-7800

(P-806)
MILLENNIUM FIRE PRTECTION CORP
2218 Faraday Ave Ste 120, Carlsbad (92008-7234)
PHONE...................760 722-2722
Stan Butts, *CEO*
Brian Richardson, *
EMP: 75 **EST:** 2005
SALES (est): 11.91MM **Privately Held**
Web: mfpc.us
SIC: 1711 8711 7389 Fire sprinkler system installation; Fire protection engineering; Fire protection service other than forestry or public

(P-807)
MUIR-CHASE PLUMBING CO INC
Also Called: M C
4530 Brazil St Ste 1, Los Angeles (90039-1000)
PHONE...................818 500-1940
Don Chase, *Pr*
Jay Chase, *
James M Muir, *
Grant Muir, *
Gail Comstock, *
EMP: 90 **EST:** 1975
SQ FT: 5,000
SALES (est): 23.76MM **Privately Held**
Web: www.muirchase.com
SIC: 1711 7699 Plumbing contractors; Sewer cleaning and rodding

(P-808)
MULTI MECHANICAL INC
Also Called: Honeywell Authorized Dealer
469 Blaine St, Corona (92879-1304)
PHONE...................714 632-7404

P R O D U C T S & S V C S

Brandon Abblitt, *CEO*
EMP: 75 **EST:** 2003
SALES (est): 9.36MM
SALES (corp-wide): 99.28MM **Privately Held**
Web: www.multimechanical.com
SIC: 1711 Mechanical contractor
PA: Ampam Parks Mechanical, Inc.
17036 Avalon Blvd
310 835-1532

(P-809)
MURRAY PLUMBING AND HTG CORP (PA)
Also Called: Murray Company
18414 S Santa Fe Ave, E Rncho Dmngz (90221-5612)
PHONE..................310 637-1500
Kevan Steffey, *Ch*
James De Flavio, *
EMP: 250 **EST:** 1913
SQ FT: 26,000
SALES (est): 354.84MM
SALES (corp-wide): 354.84MM **Privately Held**
Web: www.murraycompany.com
SIC: 1711 Plumbing contractors

(P-810)
NATIONAL AIR INC
Also Called: National Air and Energy
2053 Kurtz St, San Diego (92110-2014)
PHONE..................619 299-2500
Jared M Wells, *CEO*
EMP: 110 **EST:** 1995
SQ FT: 10,500
SALES (est): 24.49MM **Privately Held**
Web: www.natlair.com
SIC: 1711 Mechanical contractor

(P-811)
NEW POWER INC
887 Marlborough Ave, Riverside (92507-2133)
PHONE..................800 980-9825
Thomas Shaffer, *Pr*
Matt Collins, *
EMP: 83 **EST:** 2009
SALES (est): 1.94MM **Privately Held**
Web: www.newpower.company
SIC: 1711 Solar energy contractor

(P-812)
NEXGEN AC & HTG LLC
Also Called: Nexgen Air Conditioning & Plbg
700 N Valley St Ste K, Anaheim (92801-3824)
PHONE..................760 616-5870
Ismael Valdez, *CEO*
Yanela Valdez, *
EMP: 84 **EST:** 2015
SALES (est): 1.87MM
SALES (corp-wide): 215.03MM **Privately Held**
Web: www.nexgenairandplumbing.com
SIC: 1711 Warm air heating and air conditioning contractor
PA: Wrench Group Llc
1819 Main St Ste 1300
941 477-3771

(P-813)
NP MECHANICAL INC
9129 Stellar Ct, Corona (92883-4924)
P.O. Box 309 (92878-0309)
PHONE..................951 667-4220
Cecil J Hallinan, *CEO*
Richard Hallinan, *
EMP: 400 **EST:** 2005
SALES (est): 45.66MM **Privately Held**

Web: www.npmechanicalinc.net
SIC: 1711 Mechanical contractor

(P-814)
ONE CALL PLUMBER SANTA BARBARA
1016 Cliff Dr Apt 309, Santa Barbara (93109-1784)
PHONE..................805 364-6337
EMP: 100 **EST:** 2017
SALES (est): 537.89K **Privately Held**
Web: www.plumbersinsantabarbara.com
SIC: 1711 Plumbing contractors

(P-815)
PACIFIC RIM MECH CONTRS INC (PA)
Also Called: Honeywell Authorized Dealer
9125 Rehco Rd, San Diego (92121-2270)
PHONE..................858 974-6500
Joseph Mucher, *CEO*
Eric Bader, *
Theodore J Keenan, *
Brian Turner, *
Colin Cook, *
EMP: 400 **EST:** 2002
SQ FT: 50,000
SALES (est): 227.5MM
SALES (corp-wide): 227.5MM **Privately Held**
Web: www.prmech.com
SIC: 1711 Mechanical contractor

(P-816)
PACIFIC RIM MECH CONTRS INC
1701 E Edinger Ave Ste F2, Santa Ana (92705-5028)
PHONE..................714 285-2600
John Heusner, *Mgr*
EMP: 250
SALES (corp-wide): 227.5MM **Privately Held**
Web: www.prmech.com
SIC: 1711 Mechanical contractor
PA: Pacific Rim Mechanical Contractors, Inc.
9125 Rehco Rd
858 974-6500

(P-817)
PAN-PACIFIC MECHANICAL LLC
Also Called: Pan-Pacific Plumbing & Mech
11622 El Camino Real Ste 100, San Diego (92130-2051)
PHONE..................858 764-2464
EMP: 425
SALES (corp-wide): 405.33MM **Privately Held**
Web: www.ppmechanical.com
SIC: 1711 Mechanical contractor
PA: Pan-Pacific Mechanical Llc
18250 Euclid St
949 474-9170

(P-818)
PAN-PACIFIC MECHANICAL LLC (PA)
Also Called: Pan-Pacific Mechanical
18250 Euclid St, Fountain Valley (92708-6112)
PHONE..................949 474-9170
Reed Mcmackin, *CEO*
Cindy Lanette Mcmackin, *Pr*
Rex Mcmackin, *VP*
Joe Koh, *
Jon Houchin, *
▲ **EMP:** 150 **EST:** 1947
SQ FT: 60,000
SALES (est): 405.33MM

SALES (corp-wide): 405.33MM **Privately Held**
Web: www.ppmechanical.com
SIC: 1711 Plumbing contractors

(P-819)
PIPE RESTORATION INC
Also Called: Ace Duraflo Pipe Restoration
2926 W Pendleton Ave, Santa Ana (92704-4939)
PHONE..................714 564-7600
Larry Gillanders, *CEO*
Mike Carper, *
EMP: 70 **EST:** 2001
SALES (est): 8.84MM **Privately Held**
Web: www.pri-corp.com
SIC: 1711 Plumbing contractors

(P-820)
PLUMBING PIPING & CNSTR INC
5950 Lakeshore Dr, Cypress (90630-3371)
PHONE..................714 821-0490
Bruce Cook Junior, *Pr*
EMP: 100 **EST:** 1960
SQ FT: 12,600
SALES (est): 13.25MM **Privately Held**
Web: www.1ppc.com
SIC: 1711 Plumbing, heating, air-conditioning

(P-821)
PPC ENTERPRISES INC
Also Called: Premier Plumbing Company
5920 Rickenbacker Ave, Riverside (92504-1042)
PHONE..................951 354-5402
Jeffrey Geiger, *Pr*
Dawn Geiger, *
EMP: 125 **EST:** 1982
SQ FT: 10,000
SALES (est): 9.36MM **Privately Held**
Web: www.premierplumbingcompany.com
SIC: 1711 Plumbing contractors

(P-822)
PRECISE AIR SYSTEMS INC
Also Called: Hvac Installation and Repair
5467 W San Fernando Rd, Los Angeles (90039-1014)
P.O. Box 39609 (90039-0609)
PHONE..................818 646-9757
TOLL FREE: 877
Fred Khachekian, *Pr*
EMP: 91 **EST:** 1975
SQ FT: 3,200
SALES (est): 18.5MM **Privately Held**
Web: www.preciseairsystems.com
SIC: 1711 Warm air heating and air conditioning contractor

(P-823)
PRO TRAFFIC SERVICES INC
321 Hunter St, Ramona (92065-3005)
PHONE..................760 906-6961
Janet Andrews, *Pr*
Neil Treffers, *
Greg Wakeman, *
EMP: 99 **EST:** 2018
SALES (est): 2.61MM **Privately Held**
Web: www.ptats.com
SIC: 1711 Plumbing, heating, air-conditioning

(P-824)
PRO-CRAFT CONSTRUCTION INC
500 Iowa St Ste 100, Redlands (92373-8068)
PHONE..................909 790-5222
Timothy Mcfayden, *Pr*
Susan Mc Fayden, *

EMP: 142 **EST:** 2006
SALES (est): 24.6MM **Privately Held**
Web: www.procraftci.com
SIC: 1711 Plumbing contractors

(P-825)
R & R MECHANICAL CONTRACTORS INC
1400 N Johnson Ave Ste 114, El Cajon (92020-1651)
PHONE..................619 449-9900
EMP: 100 **EST:** 1998
SALES (est): 2.41MM **Privately Held**
SIC: 1711 Mechanical contractor

(P-826)
RAWLINGS MECHANICAL CORP (PA)
11615 Pendleton St, Sun Valley (91352-2502)
P.O. Box 703 (91353-0703)
PHONE..................323 875-2040
Robert S Bratton, *Pr*
Rex Horney, *
Patricia Wood, *
EMP: 74 **EST:** 1953
SQ FT: 22,000
SALES (est): 22.17MM
SALES (corp-wide): 22.17MM **Privately Held**
Web: www.rawlingsmechanical.com
SIC: 1711 Mechanical contractor

(P-827)
RC MAINTENANCE HOLDINGS INC
569 Bateman Cir, Corona (92878-4012)
PHONE..................951 903-6303
Richard Collins Junior, *Pr*
Christine Meva, *Acctg Mgr*
EMP: 130 **EST:** 2020
SALES (est): 22.14MM **Privately Held**
Web: www.rcstoremaintenance.com
SIC: 1711 Plumbing, heating, air-conditioning

(P-828)
REC SOLAR COMMERCIAL CORP
Also Called: Rec Solar
3450 Broad St Ste 105, San Luis Obispo (93401-7214)
PHONE..................844 732-7652
Matt Walz, *CEO*
Gary Morris, *
EMP: 200 **EST:** 2013
SQ FT: 15,000
SALES (est): 45.84MM **Privately Held**
Web: www.recsolar.com
SIC: 1711 Solar energy contractor

(P-829)
RELIABLE ENERGY MANAGEMENT INC
Also Called: Honeywell Authorized Dealer
6829 Walthall Way, Paramount (90723-2028)
PHONE..................562 984-5511
George R Garcia, *Pr*
Judy Garcia, *
EMP: 80 **EST:** 1995
SALES (est): 27.64MM **Privately Held**
Web: www.relenergy.com
SIC: 1711 Warm air heating and air conditioning contractor

(P-830)
RESIDENTIAL FIRE SYSTEMS INC

8085 E Crystal Dr, Anaheim (92807-2523)
PHONE..........................714 666-8450
Ty Maley, *Pr*
Cesar Anchondo, *
Jack Maley, *
Ruben Hernandez, *
EMP: 75 **EST:** 2000
SQ FT: 6,200
SALES (est): 8.93MM **Privately Held**
Web: www.resfire.com
SIC: 1711 5063 Fire sprinkler system
  installation; Signaling equipment, electrical

(P-831)
RIGHT ANGLE SOLUTIONS INC
6315 Pedley Rd, Jurupa Valley
(92509-6007)
P.O. Box 965 (91752-0965)
PHONE..........................951 934-3081
Duane Eric Cook, *CEO*
EMP: 25 **EST:** 2009
SALES (est): 10MM **Privately Held**
Web: www.rightanglesolutionsinc.com
SIC: 1711 3569 4959 8744 Plumbing
  contractors; Filters and strainers, pipeline;
  Environmental cleanup services; Facilities
  support services

(P-832)
RLH FIRE PROTECTION INC (PA)
4300 Stine Rd Ste 800, Bakersfield
(93313-2354)
P.O. Box 42470 (93384)
PHONE..........................661 322-9344
Michael Norton, *CEO*
Jason Norton, *
Gary Stites, *
Geoff Kallenberger, *
Gregg Fulton, *
EMP: 75 **EST:** 1984
SQ FT: 8,000
SALES (est): 42.31MM
SALES (corp-wide): 42.31MM **Privately
Held**
Web: www.rlhfp.com
SIC: 1711 1542 Fire sprinkler system
  installation; Nonresidential construction, nec

(P-833)
S S W MECHANICAL CNSTR INC
Also Called: Ssw
670 S Oleander Rd, Palm Springs
(92264-1502)
P.O. Box 3160 (92263-3160)
PHONE..........................760 327-1481
Sean Wood, *Pr*
W T Hayes, *
EMP: 140 **EST:** 1996
SQ FT: 7,000
SALES (est): 6.53MM **Privately Held**
Web: www.sswmechanical.com
SIC: 1711 Plumbing contractors

(P-834)
SCHMIDT FIRE PROTECTION CO INC
4760 Murphy Canyon Rd Ste 100, San
Diego (92123-4334)
PHONE..........................858 279-6122
John J Durso, *Pr*
Greg Konold, *
John J Durso, *VP*
EMP: 72 **EST:** 1969
SQ FT: 13,800
SALES (est): 9.66MM **Privately Held**
Web: www.schmidtfireprotection.com
SIC: 1711 Fire sprinkler system installation

(P-835)
SDG ENTERPRISES
Also Called: Century West Plumbing
822 Hampshire Rd Ste H, Westlake Village
(91361-2850)
PHONE..........................805 777-7978
Nick Simili, *Pr*
Robert Garcia, *
Vincent Simili, *
Vincent Dipinto, *
EMP: 100 **EST:** 1999
SQ FT: 3,000
SALES (est): 10.17MM **Privately Held**
SIC: 1711 Plumbing contractors

(P-836)
SERVICE GENIUS LOS ANGELES INC
8925 Fullbright Ave, Chatsworth
(91311-6124)
PHONE..........................818 200-3379
William Monk, *Pr*
EMP: 100 **EST:** 2018
SALES (est): 1.18MM **Privately Held**
Web: www.servicegenius.com
SIC: 1711 Warm air heating and air
  conditioning contractor

(P-837)
SHELDON MECHANICAL CORPORATION
26015 Avenue Hall, Santa Clarita
(91355-1241)
PHONE..........................661 286-1361
Dan Boute, *Pr*
Stanley Nisenson, *
Beverly Nisenson, *
Chrystal Bout'e, *
EMP: 80 **EST:** 1984
SQ FT: 45,000
SALES (est): 12.74MM **Privately Held**
Web: www.sheldonmech.com
SIC: 1711 Mechanical contractor

(P-838)
SHERWOOD MECHANICAL INC
6630 Top Gun St, San Diego (92121-4112)
PHONE..........................858 679-3000
Mitch Roberts, *Pr*
James Robert, *
Bill Smyth, *
EMP: 100 **EST:** 2003
SALES (est): 21.63MM **Privately Held**
Web: www.sherwoodmechanical.com
SIC: 1711 Mechanical contractor

(P-839)
SKYPOWER HOLDINGS LLC
4700 Wilshire Blvd, Los Angeles
(90010-3853)
PHONE..........................323 860-4900
Kerry Adler, *CEO*
Avi Shemesh, *Pr*
EMP: 101 **EST:** 2010
SALES (est): 1.84MM **Privately Held**
Web: www.cimgroup.com
SIC: 1711 Solar energy contractor

(P-840)
SMART ENERGY SOLAR INC
Also Called: Smart Energy USA
1641 Comm St, Corona (92880)
PHONE..........................800 405-1978
Leo Joaquin Bautista, *Prin*
EMP: 120 **EST:** 2013
SALES (est): 3.63MM **Privately Held**
Web: www.smartenergyusa.com
SIC: 1711 Solar energy contractor

(P-841)
SOLAR SPECTRUM LLC
Also Called: Sungevity
27368 Via Industria Ste 101, Temecula
(92590-4852)
PHONE..........................844 777-6527
Patrick Mcgivern, *CEO*
William Nettles, *
David White, *
EMP: 266 **EST:** 2017
SALES (est): 13.55MM **Privately Held**
Web: www.fora.tv
SIC: 1711 8713 Solar energy contractor;
  Surveying services

(P-842)
SOLCIUS LLC
Also Called: SOLCIUS LLC
12155 Magnolia Ave Ste 12b/C, Riverside
(92503-4967)
PHONE..........................951 772-0030
EMP: 227
SALES (corp-wide): 69.13MM **Privately
Held**
Web: www.solcius.com
SIC: 1711 Solar energy contractor
PA: Solcius, Llc
  1555 N Freedom Blvd
  800 960-4150

(P-843)
SOUTH COAST MECHANICAL INC
800 E Orangethorpe Ave, Anaheim
(92801-1123)
PHONE..........................714 738-6644
James Reynolds, *CEO*
Zoltan Bulgozdi, *
EMP: 75 **EST:** 2004
SALES (est): 21.97MM **Privately Held**
Web: www.scfacilityservices.com
SIC: 1711 7699 Mechanical contractor;
  Industrial machinery and equipment repair

(P-844)
STERLING PLUMBING INC
3111 W Central Ave, Santa Ana
(92704-5302)
PHONE..........................714 641-5480
Rodney Robbins, *Pr*
Leslie Schaefer, *
EMP: 100 **EST:** 2003
SALES (est): 11.89MM **Privately Held**
Web: www.sterlingplumbinginc.com
SIC: 1711 Plumbing contractors

(P-845)
SUN SOLAR ENERGY SOLUTIONS INC
12625 Jomani Dr, Bakersfield (93312-3444)
PHONE..........................661 379-7000
Scott Ryan, *Prin*
Jeffrey Periera, *Prin*
EMP: 92 **EST:** 2011
SALES (est): 12.29MM **Privately Held**
Web: www.sunpowerbysunsolar.com
SIC: 1711 Solar energy contractor

(P-846)
SUNBELT CONTROLS INC
735 N Todd Ave, Azusa (91702-2244)
PHONE..........................626 610-2340
Jim Boyd, *Brnch Mgr*
EMP: 79
SALES (corp-wide): 1.51B **Privately Held**
Web: www.sunbeltcontrols.com
SIC: 1711 Mechanical contractor
HQ: Sunbelt Controls, Inc.
  4511 Willow Rd Ste 4

Pleasanton CA 94588

(P-847)
SUTTLES PLUMBING & MECH CORP
2267 Agate Ct, Simi Valley (93065-1843)
PHONE..........................818 718-9779
Stephanie Aguilar, *Pr*
Bryan Suttles, *
Stephen Suttles, *
Sheralyn Suttles, *
EMP: 75 **EST:** 1970
SQ FT: 6,000
SALES (est): 5.44MM **Privately Held**
Web: www.suttlesplumbing.com
SIC: 1711 Plumbing contractors

(P-848)
TRILOGY PLUMBING INC
1525 S Sinclair St, Anaheim (92806-5934)
PHONE..........................714 441-2952
Dennis Burk, *Pr*
Linda Burk, *
EMP: 250 **EST:** 2003
SQ FT: 18,000
SALES (est): 6.5MM **Privately Held**
Web: www.trilogyplumbing.com
SIC: 1711 Septic system construction

(P-849)
TRUE AIR MECHANICAL INC
Also Called: True Home Heating and AC
1801 California Ave, Corona (92881-7251)
PHONE..........................888 316-0642
Scott Flora, *CEO*
EMP: 180 **EST:** 2010
SALES (est): 25.33MM **Privately Held**
Web: www.truehomehvac.com
SIC: 1711 Warm air heating and air
  conditioning contractor

(P-850)
UNIVERSITY MARELICH MECH INC
1000 N Kraemer Pl, Anaheim (92806-2610)
PHONE..........................714 632-2600
Scott Baker, *Sr VP*
Walter S Baker, *
John R Wycoff, *
John Ellis, *
EMP: 184 **EST:** 2005
SQ FT: 24,384
SALES (est): 2.2MM
SALES (corp-wide): 12.58B **Publicly Held**
SIC: 1711 Mechanical contractor
PA: Emcor Group, Inc.
  301 Merritt 7
  203 849-7800

(P-851)
WALTER ANDERSON PLUMBING INC
Also Called: Anderson Plbg Htg A Condition
1830 John Towers Ave, El Cajon
(92020-1134)
PHONE..........................619 449-7646
Mary Jean Anderson, *CEO*
Kyle Anderson, *
EMP: 125 **EST:** 1978
SQ FT: 10,000
SALES (est): 22.99MM
SALES (corp-wide): 447.19MM **Privately
Held**
Web:
www.andersonplumbingheatingandair.com
SIC: 1711 Plumbing contractors
PA: Essential Services Intermediate
  Holding Corporation
  3416 Robards Ct
  502 657-1903

(P-852)
WEST COAST AC CO INC
1155 Pioneer Way Ste 101, El Cajon
(92020-1964)
PHONE..................619 561-8000
David Dudley, *CEO*
Colin Fisher, *
James Clower, *
EMP: 150 **EST:** 1960
SQ FT: 24,000
SALES (est): 21.63MM **Privately Held**
Web: www.wcac.com
SIC: 1711 Warm air heating and air conditioning contractor

(P-853)
WESTERN ALLIED CORPORATION
Also Called: Honeywell Authorized Dealer
12046 Florence Ave, Santa Fe Springs
(90670-4406)
P.O. Box 3628 (90670-1628)
PHONE..................562 944-6341
Howell L Poe, *CEO*
EMP: 45 **EST:** 1960
SQ FT: 15,000
SALES (est): 36.08MM **Privately Held**
Web: www.wasocal.com
SIC: 1711 3433 3432 Warm air heating and air conditioning contractor; Heating equipment, except electric; Plumbing fixture fittings and trim

(P-854)
WESTERN FIRE PROTECTION INC (PA)
13630 Danielson St, Poway (92064-6830)
PHONE..................858 513-4949
EMP: 91 **EST:** 1989
SALES (est): 13.12MM **Privately Held**
Web: www.westernfireprotection.com
SIC: 1711 Fire sprinkler system installation

(P-855)
XCEL MECHANICAL SYSTEMS INC
1710 W 130th St, Gardena (90249-2004)
PHONE..................310 660-0090
Kevin Michel, *Pr*
EMP: 175 **EST:** 1996
SQ FT: 10,000
SALES (est): 41.89MM **Privately Held**
Web: www.xcelmech.com
SIC: 1711 Mechanical contractor

(P-856)
ZERO ENERGY CONTRACTING INC
13850 Cerritos Corporate Dr Ste D, Cerritos
(90703-2467)
PHONE..................626 701-3180
Michael Murphy, *Ch Bd*
Paul Hanson, *
Jerry Suk, *
Joseph Power Cbd, *Prin*
EMP: 125 **EST:** 2010
SQ FT: 8,000
SALES (est): 3.13MM **Privately Held**
SIC: 1711 Solar energy contractor

(P-857)
ZERO ENERGY CONTRACTING LLC
13850 Cerritos Corporate Dr Ste D, Cerritos
(90703-2467)
PHONE..................626 701-3180
EMP: 93 **EST:** 2009
SALES (est): 9.9MM **Privately Held**

SIC: 1711 Solar energy contractor

1721 Painting And Paper Hanging

(P-858)
ADVANCED INDUSTRIAL SVCS INC
Also Called: Advanced Industrial Svcs Cal
7831 Alondra Blvd, Paramount
(90723-5005)
PHONE..................562 940-8305
Rex Johnston Junior, *Pr*
EMP: 85 **EST:** 2007
SALES (est): 1.84MM **Privately Held**
Web: www.ais-york.com
SIC: 1721 Industrial painting

(P-859)
ARENA PAINTING CONTRACTORS INC
525 E Alondra Blvd, Gardena (90248-2903)
PHONE..................310 316-2446
Wilson Grant, *CEO*
Guy Grant Ii, *Pr*
EMP: 100 **EST:** 1982
SQ FT: 10,000
SALES (est): 11.5MM **Privately Held**
Web: www.arenapainting.biz
SIC: 1721 Commercial painting

(P-860)
BORBON INCORPORATED
2560 W Woodland Dr, Anaheim
(92801-2636)
PHONE..................714 994-0170
David Morales, *Pr*
EMP: 120 **EST:** 1974
SALES (est): 12.73MM **Privately Held**
Web: www.borbon.net
SIC: 1721 Exterior residential painting contractor

(P-861)
EMPCC INC
Also Called: Empire Community Painting
1682 Langley Ave Fl 2, Irvine (92614-5620)
PHONE..................888 278-8200
Jason Reid, *Pr*
Jeff Gunhus, *
Matt Stewart, *
Spencer Pepe, *
Tracy Meneses, *
EMP: 284 **EST:** 2003
SQ FT: 1,000
SALES (est): 1.1MM **Privately Held**
SIC: 1721 Painting and paper hanging
PA: Mjp Empire, Inc.
1682 Langley Ave Fl 2

(P-862)
GENERAL COATINGS CORPORATION
600 W Freedom Ave, Orange (92865-2537)
PHONE..................858 587-1277
Craig Kinsman, *Brnch Mgr*
EMP: 83
SQ FT: 7,047
SALES (corp-wide): 35.9MM **Privately Held**
Web: www.gencoat.com
SIC: 1721 Painting and paper hanging
PA: General Coatings Corporation
6711 Nancy Rdg Dr
858 587-1277

(P-863)
GENERAL COATINGS CORPORATION (PA)
6711 Nancy Ridge Dr, San Diego
(92121-2231)
PHONE..................858 587-1277
Craig A Kinsman, *CEO*
Andrew Fluken, *
EMP: 250 **EST:** 1987
SQ FT: 14,000
SALES (est): 35.9MM
SALES (corp-wide): 35.9MM **Privately Held**
Web: www.gencoat.com
SIC: 1721 1799 Painting and paper hanging; Waterproofing

(P-864)
GENERAL COATINGS CORPORATION
1230 Carbide Dr, Corona (92881-7268)
PHONE..................909 204-4150
Craig Kinsman, *Owner*
EMP: 84
SALES (corp-wide): 35.9MM **Privately Held**
Web: www.gencoat.com
SIC: 1721 Painting and paper hanging
PA: General Coatings Corporation
6711 Nancy Ridg Dr
858 587-1277

(P-865)
GPS PAINTING WALLCOVERING INC
1307 E Saint Gertrude Pl Ste C, Santa Ana
(92705-5228)
PHONE..................714 730-8904
Eliot Schneider, *Pr*
EMP: 100 **EST:** 2001
SALES (est): 9.89MM **Privately Held**
Web:
www.gpspaintingandwallcovering.com
SIC: 1721 Painting and paper hanging

(P-866)
HARRIS & RUTH PAINTING CONTG (PA)
28408 Lorna Ave, West Covina (91790)
PHONE..................626 960-4004
Terry Cairy, *Pr*
Mark Heydorff, *
Bruce Boyer, *
EMP: 70 **EST:** 1970
SQ FT: 1,000
SALES (est): 6.25MM
SALES (corp-wide): 6.25MM **Privately Held**
Web: www.harris-ruthpainting.com
SIC: 1721 Exterior commercial painting contractor

(P-867)
J M V B INC
Also Called: Spc Building Services
12118 Severn Way, Riverside (92503-4804)
P.O. Box 614 (92856-6614)
PHONE..................714 288-9797
Benjamin J Rodriguez, *Pr*
EMP: 80 **EST:** 1993
SALES (est): 2.67MM **Privately Held**
Web: www.spcbs.com
SIC: 1721 Painting and paper hanging

(P-868)
LEADING EDGE AVIATION SVCS INC
5251 California Ave Ste 170, Irvine
(92617-3077)

PHONE..................714 556-0576
EMP: 800
SIC: 1721 4581 3721 Aircraft painting; Aircraft maintenance and repair services; Motorized aircraft

(P-869)
PBC PAVERS INC
Also Called: Peterson Bros Construction
2929 E White Star Ave, Anaheim
(92806-2628)
PHONE..................714 278-0488
Robert Peterson, *Pr*
Eldin Peterson, *
▲ **EMP:** 80 **EST:** 1995
SALES (est): 2.81MM **Privately Held**
Web: www.pbccompanies.com
SIC: 1721 Pavement marking contractor

(P-870)
PRIMECO
220 Oceanside Blvd, Oceanside
(92054-4903)
PHONE..................760 967-8278
Brett Musgrove, *Pr*
Stacey Musgrove, *
EMP: 90 **EST:** 1992
SQ FT: 2,100
SALES (est): 12.62MM **Privately Held**
Web: www.primeco.com
SIC: 1721 1542 Residential painting; Commercial and office building contractors

(P-871)
RC WENDT PAINTING INC
21612 Surveyor Cir, Huntington Beach
(92646-7068)
PHONE..................714 960-2700
Robert C Wendt, *Pr*
Scott Wendt, *
Jeri Wendt, *
EMP: 110 **EST:** 1980
SALES (est): 5.96MM **Privately Held**
Web: www.wendtcompanies.com
SIC: 1721 Residential painting

(P-872)
RTE ENTERPRISES INC
Also Called: Color Concepts
21530 Roscoe Blvd, Canoga Park
(91304-4144)
PHONE..................818 999-5300
Ron Evenhaim, *Pr*
EMP: 100 **EST:** 1987
SQ FT: 2,000
SALES (est): 2.31MM **Privately Held**
Web: www.ceocolorcon1.com
SIC: 1721 1742 Painting and paper hanging; Plastering, drywall, and insulation

(P-873)
SANDERS & WOHRMAN CORPORATION
709 N Poplar St, Orange (92868-1013)
PHONE..................714 919-0446
John Thomas Wohrman, *Prin*
Todd Wohrman, *
EMP: 150 **EST:** 1979
SQ FT: 12,000
SALES (est): 23.36MM **Privately Held**
Web: www.swcoatings.com
SIC: 1721 Residential painting

(P-874)
VERTEX COATINGS INC
1291 W State St, Ontario (91762-4015)
PHONE..................909 923-5795
Russ Phillips, *Pr*
Stacy Phillips, *Corporate Secretary*
EMP: 74 **EST:** 1990

SQ FT: 11,000
SALES (est): 13.37MM **Privately Held**
Web: www.vertexcoatings.com
SIC: 1721 Commercial painting

(P-875)
WEST COAST INTERIORS INC
Also Called: West Coast Painting
1610 W Linden St, Riverside (92507-6810)
PHONE..............................951 778-3592
Mark Herbert, *CEO*
Dan Slavin, *Marketing**
Santos Garcia, *
Colleen Butler, *
Keith Caneva, *Corporate Controller**
EMP: 600 EST: 1968
SQ FT: 8,000
SALES (est): 6.03MM **Privately Held**
Web: www.wcdp.com
SIC: 1721 Wallcovering contractors

1731 Electrical Work

(P-876)
4LIBERTY INC
7675 Dagget St Ste 200, San Diego
(92111-2256)
PHONE..............................619 400-1000
Sharelynn Moore, *CEO*
Liberty E Mann, *
EMP: 85 EST: 2010
SALES (est): 11.54MM **Privately Held**
Web: www.4liberty.com
SIC: 1731 Telephone and telephone
equipment installation

(P-877)
A M ORTEGA CONSTRUCTION INC (PA)
Also Called: Western Rim Pipeline
10125 Channel Rd, Lakeside (92040-1703)
PHONE..............................619 390-1988
Archie Maurice Ortega, *Pr*
Linda Ortega, *
EMP: 110 EST: 1974
SQ FT: 10,000
SALES (est): 42.92MM
SALES (corp-wide): 42.92MM **Privately Held**
Web: www.amortega.com
SIC: 1731 Electrical work

(P-878)
AAA ELCTRCAL CMMUNICATIONS INC (PA)
Also Called: AAA Facility Services
25007 Anza Dr, Valencia (91355-3414)
PHONE..............................800 892-4784
Joann Katinos, *CEO*
Brian Higgins, *Pr*
EMP: 133 EST: 1995
SQ FT: 6,000
SALES (est): 34.13MM **Privately Held**
Web: www.aaafacilityservices.com
SIC: 1731 1711 7349 1721 General
electrical contractor; Plumbing, heating, air-
conditioning; Building maintenance
services, nec; Commercial painting

(P-879)
ACS COMMUNICATIONS INC
Also Called: Fiber Optic Technologies
680 Knox St Ste 150, Torrance
(90502-1325)
PHONE..............................310 767-2145
Robby Sawyer, *Pr*
EMP: 101
SIC: 1731 Communications specialization
HQ: Acs Communications, Inc.
2535 Brockton Dr Ste 400

Austin TX 78758
512 837-4400

(P-880)
AJ KIRKWOOD & ASSOCIATES INC
4300 N Harbor Blvd, Fullerton
(92835-1091)
PHONE..............................714 505-1977
Arch Kirkwood, *Ch*
James Klassen, *
Michael Hewson, *
Aidan Culligan, *
Sam Sandoval, *
EMP: 500 EST: 1996
SALES (est): 76.11MM **Privately Held**
Web: www.ajk-a.com
SIC: 1731 8748 7389 General electrical
contractor; Communications consulting;
Design services

(P-881)
ALBD ELECTRIC AND CABLE
Also Called: A Lighting By Design
1031 S Leslie St, La Habra (90631-6843)
PHONE..............................949 440-1216
Chad Lambert, *CEO*
James Black, *
EMP: 100 EST: 2002
SALES (est): 28.02MM **Privately Held**
Web: www.albdinc.com
SIC: 1731 3651 General electrical contractor
; Household audio and video equipment

(P-882)
ALLTECH INDUSTRIES INC
301 E Pomona Blvd, Monterey Park
(91755-7300)
PHONE..............................323 450-2168
Hilda Perez, *Pr*
EMP: 30 EST: 2010
SQ FT: 2,000
SALES (est): 519.29K **Privately Held**
Web:
alltechindustriesinc.wordpress.com
SIC: 1731 7381 3669 7382 Fire detection
and burglar alarm systems specialization;
Security guard service; Burglar alarm
apparatus, electric; Fire alarm maintenance
and monitoring

(P-883)
AMERICAN SOLAR DIRECT INC
11766 Wilshire Blvd Ste 500, Los Angeles
(90025-6551)
PHONE..............................424 214-6700
EMP: 107
SIC: 1731 Electrical work

(P-884)
ANDERSON & HOWARD ELECTRIC INC
Also Called: Anderson Howard
15 Chrysler, Irvine (92618-2009)
PHONE..............................949 250-4555
Greg Elliott, *Pr*
Brian E Elliott, *
Tom Howard, *
Charles B Howard, *
EMP: 210 EST: 1967
SALES (est): 49.9MM **Privately Held**
Web: www.aandh.com
SIC: 1731 General electrical contractor

(P-885)
ARDENT COMPANIES INC
4842 Airport Dr, Bakersfield (93308-9796)
PHONE..............................661 633-1465
Glenn Dubuc, *Dist Mgr*

EMP: 75
SALES (corp-wide): 12.58B **Publicly Held**
Web: www.theardentcompanies.com
SIC: 1731 General electrical contractor
HQ: Ardent Companies, Inc.
4824 Rosedale Ln
Bakersfield CA 93314
661 633-1465

(P-886)
BAKER ELECTRIC & RENEWABLES LLC
1298 Pacific Oaks Pl, Escondido
(92029-2900)
PHONE..............................760 745-2001
EMP: 586 EST: 1938
SALES (est): 97.86MM **Privately Held**
Web: www.baker-electric.com
SIC: 1731 8711 General electrical contractor
; Engineering services

(P-887)
BERGELECTRIC CORP (PA)
3182 Lionshead Ave, Carlsbad
(92010-4701)
PHONE..............................760 638-2374
Edward Billig, *CEO*
Ron Wood, *
Steve Buhr, *
Steve Parks, *
▲ EMP: 100 EST: 1946
SALES (est): 779.21MM
SALES (corp-wide): 779.21MM **Privately Held**
Web: www.bergelectric.com
SIC: 1731 General electrical contractor

(P-888)
BERGELECTRIC CORP
3182 Lionshead Ave, Carlsbad
(92010-4701)
PHONE..............................760 746-1003
Edward Billig, *Pr*
EMP: 760
SALES (corp-wide): 779.21MM **Privately Held**
Web: www.bergelectric.com
SIC: 1731 General electrical contractor
PA: Bergelectric Corp.
3182 Lionshead Ave
760 638-2374

(P-889)
BERGELECTRIC CORP
2210 Meyers Ave, Escondido (92029-1003)
PHONE..............................760 746-1003
Thomas R Anderson, *Ch Bd*
EMP: 117
SALES (corp-wide): 779.21MM **Privately Held**
Web: www.bergelectric.com
SIC: 1731 General electrical contractor
PA: Bergelectric Corp.
3182 Lionshead Ave
760 638-2374

(P-890)
BERGELECTRIC CORP
955 Borra Pl, Escondido (92029-2011)
PHONE..............................760 291-8100
Thomas R Anderson, *Ch Bd*
EMP: 93
SALES (corp-wide): 779.21MM **Privately Held**
Web: www.bergelectric.com
SIC: 1731 General electrical contractor
PA: Bergelectric Corp.
3182 Lionshead Ave
760 638-2374

(P-891)
BERGELECTRIC CORP
15776 Gateway Cir, Tustin (92780-6469)
PHONE..............................949 250-7005
Mark Bauer, *Mgr*
EMP: 100
SALES (corp-wide): 779.21MM **Privately Held**
Web: www.bergelectric.com
SIC: 1731 General electrical contractor
PA: Bergelectric Corp.
3182 Lionshead Ave
760 638-2374

(P-892)
BRIGGS ELECTRIC INC (PA)
14381 Franklin Ave, Tustin (92780-7010)
PHONE..............................714 544-2500
Jeff Perry, *
Thomas J Perry, *
Todd Perry, *
▲ EMP: 100 EST: 1946
SQ FT: 5,500
SALES (est): 51.07MM
SALES (corp-wide): 51.07MM **Privately Held**
Web: www.briggselectric.com
SIC: 1731 General electrical contractor

(P-893)
BUILDING ELCTRONIC CONTRLS INC (PA)
2246 Lindsay Way, Glendora (91740-5398)
PHONE..............................909 305-1600
Richard Taylor, *Pr*
Shelley Taylor, *
EMP: 48 EST: 1996
SQ FT: 13,000
SALES (est): 18.43MM **Privately Held**
Web: www.becinc.net
SIC: 1731 3699 General electrical contractor
; Security control equipment and systems

(P-894)
C G SYSTEMS LLC
Also Called: California Gate Entry Systems
1470 N Hundley St, Anaheim (92806-1322)
PHONE..............................714 632-8882
Kevin Squire, *CEO*
EMP: 27 EST: 1982
SALES (est): 6.22MM **Privately Held**
Web: www.californiagate.com
SIC: 1731 3699 3315 5731 Fire detection
and burglar alarm systems specialization;
Security devices; Fence gates, posts, and
fittings: steel; Video cameras, recorders,
and accessories

(P-895)
C T AND F INC
7228 Scout Ave, Bell Gardens
(90201-4998)
PHONE..............................562 927-2339
EMP: 80
Web: www.ctandf.net
SIC: 1731 General electrical contractor

(P-896)
CALENERGY LLC
7030 Gentry Rd, Calipatria (92233-9720)
PHONE..............................402 231-1527
Bill Fehrman, *Pr*
EMP: 350 EST: 2013
SALES (est): 9.97MM **Privately Held**
SIC: 1731 Electric power systems contractors

(P-897)
CAROL ELECTRIC COMPANY INC

P R O D U C T S & S V C S

3822 Cerritos Ave, Los Alamitos
(90720-2420)
PHONE....................562 431-1870
John R Fuqua, *Ch Bd*
Allen Moffitt, *
Brian Moffitt, *
EMP: 90 EST: 1979
SQ FT: 10,000
SALES (est): 17.4MM Privately Held
Web: www.carolelectric.com
SIC: 1731 General electrical contractor

(P-898)
CBR ELECTRIC INC
22 Rancho Cir, Lake Forest (92630-8325)
PHONE....................949 455-0331
Cary Raffety, *Pr*
EMP: 150 EST: 1989
SQ FT: 4,000
SALES (est): 2.02MM Privately Held
Web: www.cbrelectric.com
SIC: 1731 General electrical contractor

(P-899)
CITY-WIDE ELECTRONIC SYSTEMS INC
440 Highland Ave, El Cajon (92020-5209)
P.O. Box 2069 (92021-0069)
PHONE....................619 444-0219
EMP: 100
SIC: 1731 General electrical contractor

(P-900)
COMET ELECTRIC INC
21625 Prairie St, Chatsworth (91311-5833)
PHONE....................818 340-0965
Adam Saitman, *CEO*
Steve Goad, *VP*
Keith Berson, *Ex VP*
Jason Pennington, *CFO*
EMP: 150 EST: 1993
SQ FT: 12,000
SALES (est): 49.66MM
SALES (corp-wide): 121.07MM Privately Held
Web: www.cometelectric.com
SIC: 1731 General electrical contractor
PA: Valley Electric Co. Of Mt. Vernon, Inc.,
1100 Merrill Creek Pkwy
425 407-0832

(P-901)
COMMUNCTION WIRG SPCALISTS INC
Also Called: C W S
8909 Complex Dr Ste F, San Diego
(92123-1418)
PHONE....................858 278-4545
Eric Templin, *Pr*
Richard Templin, *
Donna Templin, *Stockholder*
EMP: 80 EST: 1991
SQ FT: 5,500
SALES (est): 8.93MM Privately Held
Web: www.cwssandiego.com
SIC: 1731 Telephone and telephone
equipment installation

(P-902)
COMMUNICATION TECH SVCS LLC
1590 S Milliken Ave Ste H, Ontario
(91761-2326)
PHONE....................508 382-2700
Chris Ungson, *Brnch Mgr*
EMP: 266
Web: www.cts1.com

SIC: 1731 8748 Voice, data, and video
wiring contractor; Communications
consulting
PA: Communication Technology Services,
Llc
33 Locke Dr Ste 201

(P-903)
CONTRA COSTA ELECTRIC INC
3208 Landco Dr, Bakersfield (93308-6156)
PHONE....................661 322-4036
Richard Trainer, *Mgr*
EMP: 104
SALES (corp-wide): 12.58B Publicly Held
Web: www.ccelectric.com
SIC: 1731 General electrical contractor
HQ: Contra Costa Electric, Inc.
825 Howe Rd
Martinez CA 94553
925 229-4250

(P-904)
COOPER LIGHTING LLC
285 Rood Rd Ste 101, Calexico
(92231-9535)
PHONE....................760 357-4760
EMP: 94
Web: www.cooperlighting.com
SIC: 1731 Lighting contractor
HQ: Cooper Lighting, Llc
1121 Hwy 74 S
Peachtree City GA 30269
770 486-4800

(P-905)
CROSSTOWN ELEC & DATA INC
5454 Diaz St, Baldwin Park (91706-2026)
PHONE....................626 813-6693
Dave Heermance, *CEO*
EMP: 100 EST: 1998
SQ FT: 2,500
SALES (est): 2.86MM Privately Held
Web: www.crosstowndata.com
SIC: 1731 General electrical contractor

(P-906)
CSI ELECTRICAL CONTRACTORS INC
41769 11th St W Ste B, Palmdale
(93551-1418)
PHONE....................661 723-0869
Roland Tamayo, *Brnch Mgr*
EMP: 448
SALES (corp-wide): 3.64B Publicly Held
Web: www.csielectric.com
SIC: 1731 General electrical contractor
HQ: Csi Electrical Contractors, Inc.
10623 Fulton Wells Ave
Santa Fe Springs CA 90670

(P-907)
CSI ELECTRICAL CONTRACTORS INC (HQ)
Also Called: C S I
10623 Fulton Wells Ave, Santa Fe Springs
(90670-3741)
P.O. Box 2887 (90670-0887)
PHONE....................562 946-0700
Steven M Watts, *Pr*
Paul Pica, *Pr*
Rick Yauney, *CFO*
William T Macnider, *Sec*
Andrew Soffa, *Ex VP*
EMP: 150 EST: 1990
SQ FT: 49,044
SALES (est): 146.31MM
SALES (corp-wide): 3.64B Publicly Held
Web: www.csielectric.com
SIC: 1731 General electrical contractor
PA: Myr Group Inc.
12121 Grant St Unit 610

303 286-8000

(P-908)
CSI ELECTRICAL CONTRACTORS INC
310 Via Vera Cruz Ste 106, San Marcos
(92078-2631)
PHONE....................760 227-0577
Steve Watts, *Brnch Mgr*
EMP: 449
SALES (corp-wide): 3.64B Publicly Held
Web: www.csielectric.com
SIC: 1731 General electrical contractor
HQ: Csi Electrical Contractors, Inc.
10623 Fulton Wells Ave
Santa Fe Springs CA 90670

(P-909)
DONCO & SONS INC
Also Called: Donco Associates & Sons
2871 E Blue Star St, Anaheim
(92806-2508)
PHONE....................714 779-0099
Donavon W Fink, *Pr*
Mark Fink, *
Dave Fink, *
Diane Fink, *
EMP: 28 EST: 1980
SALES (est): 5.45MM Privately Held
Web: www.donco.com
SIC: 1731 3993 Electrical work; Electric signs

(P-910)
DYNALECTRIC COMPANY
1111 Pioneer Way, El Cajon (92020-1964)
PHONE....................619 328-4007
Daivd Rispolrch, *Mgr*
EMP: 300
SALES (corp-wide): 12.58B Publicly Held
Web: www.dyna-sd.com
SIC: 1731 General electrical contractor
HQ: Dynalectric Company
22930 Shaw Rd Ste 100
Dulles VA 20166
703 288-2866

(P-911)
ECLIPSE LIGHTING & ELECTRICAL
935 E Discovery Ln, Anaheim (92801-1147)
PHONE....................714 871-9366
Cory Kruip, *Pr*
Cory Kruip, *CEO*
EMP: 76 EST: 2012
SALES (est): 9.01MM Privately Held
Web: www.eclipselightingservices.com
SIC: 1731 General electrical contractor

(P-912)
ELECTRICAL & INSTRUMENTATION UNLIMITED OF CALIFORNIA INC
Also Called: Eiu of California
6950 District Blvd, Bakersfield
(93313-2072)
P.O. Box 40878 (93384-0878)
EMP: 200
SIC: 1731 General electrical contractor

(P-913)
ELECTRONIC CONTROL SYSTEMS LLC
Also Called: Albireo Energy
12575 Kirkham Ct Ste 1, Poway
(92064-8844)
PHONE....................858 513-1911
Dan Coler, *Managing Member*
EMP: 145 EST: 1996

SQ FT: 17,000
SALES (est): 41.25MM
SALES (corp-wide): 135.55MM Privately Held
Web: www.albireoenergy.com
SIC: 1731 7382 Energy management
controls; Security systems services
PA: Albireo Energy, Llc
3 Ethel Rd Ste 300
732 512-9100

(P-914)
ELITE ELECTRIC
9415 Bellegrave Ave, Riverside
(92509-2741)
PHONE....................951 681-5811
Carl Eric Dawson, *Pr*
EMP: 80 EST: 1978
SQ FT: 1,720
SALES (est): 11.11MM Privately Held
Web: www.elite-electricinc.com
SIC: 1731 General electrical contractor

(P-915)
ENERGY WATCH
3555 Landco Dr, Bakersfield (93308-6169)
PHONE....................661 324-0930
Stefanie Doubert, *Mgr*
EMP: 90 EST: 2005
SALES (est): 501.88K Privately Held
Web: www.kernenergywatch.com
SIC: 1731 General electrical contractor

(P-916)
EV CONNECT INC
26521 Rancho Pkwy S, Lake Forest
(92630-8329)
PHONE....................888 780-0062
Bassem Ammouri, *CEO*
Jordan Ramer, *
David Hughes, *
Patrick Macdonald-king, *COO*
Rose Devries, *
EMP: 86 EST: 2010
SALES (est): 27.38MM
SALES (corp-wide): 1.09K Privately Held
Web: www.evconnect.com
SIC: 1731 5072 8748 Electrical work;
Hardware; Business consulting, nec
PA: Schneider Electric Se
Null
146046982

(P-917)
FAITH ELECTRIC LLC
1980 Orange Tree Ln Ste 106, Redlands
(92374-2803)
PHONE....................909 767-2682
Elijah Adams, *Managing Member*
EMP: 200 EST: 2014
SQ FT: 5,000
SALES (est): 80MM Privately Held
Web: www.faithelectricllc.com
SIC: 1731 General electrical contractor

(P-918)
FISHEL COMPANY
5878 Autoport Mall, San Diego
(92121-2514)
PHONE....................858 658-0830
Sal Padula, *Brnch Mgr*
EMP: 149
SALES (corp-wide): 758.15MM Privately Held
Web: www.teamfishel.com
SIC: 1731 1623 Telephone and telephone
equipment installation; Water main
construction
PA: The Fishel Company
1366 Dublin Rd

614 274-8100

(P-919)
FISK ELECTRIC COMPANY
15870 Olden St, Rancho Cascades
(91342-1241)
PHONE................................818 884-1166
Orvil Anthony, *Sr VP*
EMP: 165
SALES (corp-wide): 3.88B **Publicly Held**
Web: www.fiskcorp.com
SIC: 1731 General electrical contractor
HQ: Fisk Electric Company
10855 Westview Dr
Houston TX 77043
713 868-6111

(P-920)
FOSHAY ELECTRIC CO INC
950 Industrial Blvd, Chula Vista
(91911-1608)
PHONE................................858 277-7676
Theresa M Faucher, *Pr*
Mark Faucher, *
Michael Beringhaus, *
EMP: 100 **EST:** 1947
SALES (est): 8.52MM **Privately Held**
Web: www.foshayelectric.com
SIC: 1731 General electrical contractor

(P-921)
GOULD ELECTRIC INC
12975 Brookprinter Pl Ste 280, Poway
(92064-8895)
P.O. Box 504377 (92150-4377)
PHONE................................858 486-1727
EMP: 125
Web: www.gouldelect.com
SIC: 1731 General electrical contractor

(P-922)
GREGG ELECTRIC INC
608 W Emporia St, Ontario (91762-3709)
PHONE................................909 983-1794
Randall F Fehlman, *Pr*
James Fehlman, *
Victoria Mensen, *
EMP: 150 **EST:** 1961
SQ FT: 15,000
SALES (est): 7.58MM **Privately Held**
Web: www.greggelectric.com
SIC: 1731 General electrical contractor

(P-923)
HELIX ELECTRIC INC
13100 Alondra Blvd Ste 108, Cerritos
(90703-2262)
P.O. Box 85298 (92186-5298)
PHONE................................562 941-7200
Acey Long, *VP*
EMP: 907
SALES (corp-wide): 487.17MM **Privately Held**
Web: www.helixelectric.com
SIC: 1731 General electrical contractor
PA: Helix Electric, Inc.
6795 Flanders Dr
858 535-0505

(P-924)
HELIX ELECTRIC INC (PA)
Also Called: Helix Renewables
6795 Flanders Dr, San Diego (92121-2903)
P.O. Box 85298 (92186-5298)
PHONE................................858 535-0505
EMP: 220 **EST:** 1985
SALES (est): 487.17MM
SALES (corp-wide): 487.17MM **Privately Held**
Web: www.helixelectric.com

SIC: 1731 General electrical contractor

(P-925)
HMT ELECTRIC INC
2340 Meyers Ave, Escondido (92029-1008)
PHONE................................858 458-9771
Brian Hudak, *CEO*
EMP: 85 **EST:** 2007
SQ FT: 2,000
SALES (est): 33.37MM **Privately Held**
Web: www.hmtelectric.com
SIC: 1731 General electrical contractor

(P-926)
INTERIOR ELECTRIC INCORPORATED
747 N Main St, Orange (92868-1105)
PHONE................................714 771-9098
Mark Beverly, *Pr*
Mark Maskevich, *
Chad Stewart, *
Gus Baquerizo, *
Glen Nielsen, *
EMP: 75 **EST:** 1987
SQ FT: 10,000
SALES (est): 3.14MM **Privately Held**
Web: www.ie-systems.net
SIC: 1731 General electrical contractor

(P-927)
IPITEK INC
Also Called: Ipitek
2461 Impala Dr, Carlsbad (92010-7227)
P.O. Box 130878 (92013-0878)
PHONE................................760 438-1010
Michael M Salour, *Ch Bd*
EMP: 170 **EST:** 1982
SQ FT: 40,000
SALES (est): 7.72MM **Privately Held**
SIC: 1731 Fiber optic cable installation

(P-928)
JEEVA CORPORATION
Also Called: Satellite Pros
750 E E St Unit B, Ontario (91764-3821)
PHONE................................909 238-4073
Orlando Uranga, *CEO*
Rita Uranga, *
EMP: 70 **EST:** 2011
SQ FT: 1,800
SALES (est): 1.75MM **Privately Held**
Web: www.greenjeeva.com
SIC: 1731 Cable television installation

(P-929)
JMG SECURITY SYSTEMS INC
17150 Newhope St Ste 109, Fountain Valley
(92708-4273)
PHONE................................714 545-8882
TOLL FREE: 800
Ken Jacobs, *CEO*
Michael Christensen, *
Gil Ledesma, *
Sue Tjelmeland, *
Gary Beale, *
EMP: 70 **EST:** 1987
SQ FT: 14,000
SALES (est): 19.64MM **Privately Held**
Web: www.jmgsecurity.com
SIC: 1731 5063 Safety and security
specialization; Burglar alarm systems

(P-930)
JOHNSON-PELTIER
Also Called: Johnson-Peltier
12021 Shoemaker Ave, Santa Fe Springs
(90670-4718)
PHONE................................562 944-3408
EMP: 75 **EST:** 1957
SALES (est): 1.31MM **Privately Held**

Web: www.johnson-peltier.com
SIC: 1731 General electrical contractor

(P-931)
KDC INC (HQ)
Also Called: Kdc Systems
4462 Corporate Center Dr, Los Alamitos
(90720-2539)
PHONE................................714 828-7000
Earnest Lee Brown, *Pr*
Ben Martin, *
Dusty Lord, *
EMP: 207 **EST:** 1976
SQ FT: 57,000
SALES (est): 31.89MM
SALES (corp-wide): 12.58B **Publicly Held**
Web: www.kdc-systems.com
SIC: 1731 1611 3823 General electrical
contractor; General contractor, highway and
street construction; Process control
instruments
PA: Emcor Group, Inc.
301 Merritt 7
203 849-7800

(P-932)
KITE ELECTRIC INCORPORATED
Also Called: K E
2 Thomas, Irvine (92618-2512)
PHONE................................949 380-7471
Tracy Adams, *Pr*
EMP: 120 **EST:** 2000
SALES (est): 10.78MM **Privately Held**
Web: www.kiteelectric.com
SIC: 1731 Electrical work

(P-933)
LASER ELECTRIC INC
650 Opper St, Escondido (92029-1020)
PHONE................................760 658-6626
Denise Hartnett, *Pr*
Denise Hartnett, *CEO*
Kevin Hartnett, *
EMP: 120 **EST:** 1987
SQ FT: 11,000
SALES (est): 39.9MM **Privately Held**
Web: www.laserelectric.com
SIC: 1731 General electrical contractor

(P-934)
LEED ELECTRIC INC
13138 Arctic Cir, Santa Fe Springs
(90670-5508)
PHONE................................562 270-9500
Seth Jamali Dinan, *Pr*
EMP: 135 **EST:** 1979
SQ FT: 8,480
SALES (est): 21.38MM **Privately Held**
Web: www.leedelectric.com
SIC: 1731 General electrical contractor

(P-935)
LION SHIELD PROTECTION INC
93 Plateau, Aliso Viejo (92656-8027)
PHONE................................949 334-7905
Keith Fowler, *CEO*
EMP: 95 **EST:** 2021
SALES (est): 964.85K **Privately Held**
SIC: 1731 Safety and security specialization

(P-936)
LITTLEJOHN-REULAND CORPORATION
4575 Pacific Blvd, Vernon (90058-2207)
P.O. Box 58487 (90058-0487)
PHONE................................323 587-5255
Richard Pena, *Pr*
Dolores Robinson, *
Barry Mileski, *
EMP: 45 **EST:** 1926

SQ FT: 50,000
SALES (est): 10.03MM **Privately Held**
Web: www.littlejohn-reuland.com
SIC: 1731 7694 5063 5511 General
electrical contractor; Armature rewinding
shops; Electrical supplies, nec; New and
used car dealers

(P-937)
MARK LAND ELECTRIC INC
7876 Deering Ave, Canoga Park
(91304-5005)
PHONE................................818 883-5110
Lloyd Saitman, *CEO*
Stewart Franklin, *
John Bennet, *
EMP: 99 **EST:** 1981
SQ FT: 10,000
SALES (est): 24.07MM **Privately Held**
Web: www.lmela.com
SIC: 1731 General electrical contractor

(P-938)
MB HERZOG ELECTRIC INC
15709 Illinois Ave, Paramount
(90723-4112)
PHONE................................562 531-2002
Ryan M Herzog, *CEO*
Kevin Ryan, *
EMP: 200 **EST:** 1974
SQ FT: 6,200
SALES (est): 23.12MM **Privately Held**
Web: www.herzogelectric.com
SIC: 1731 General electrical contractor

(P-939)
MEDLEY COMMUNICATIONS INC (PA)
43015 Black Deer Loop Ste 203, Temecula
(92590-3575)
PHONE................................951 245-5200
Darrin Medley, *Pr*
EMP: 175 **EST:** 1985
SALES (est): 2.34MM **Privately Held**
Web: www.medleycom.com
SIC: 1731 8748 Cable television installation;
Communications consulting

(P-940)
MOBIZ IT INC
Also Called: Mobiz
1175 Idaho St Ste 103, Redlands
(92374-4591)
PHONE................................909 453-6700
Hamad Riaz, *CEO*
EMP: 100 **EST:** 2017
SALES (est): 30MM **Privately Held**
Web: www.mobizino.com
SIC: 1731 8742 7373 7371 Electrical work;
Management consulting services; Systems
integration services; Computer software
systems analysis and design, custom

(P-941)
MORROW-MEADOWS CORPORATION
13000 Kirkham Way Ste 101, Poway
(92064-7148)
PHONE................................858 974-3650
Gary Dadmon, *Mgr*
EMP: 327
SALES (corp-wide): 540.72MM **Privately Held**
Web: www.morrow-meadows.com
SIC: 1731 General electrical contractor
PA: Morrow-Meadows Corporation
231 Benton Ct
858 974-3650

(P-942)
MORROW-MEADOWS
CORPORATION (PA)
Also Called: Cherry City Electric
231 Benton Ct, City Of Industry
(91789-5213)
PHONE..................858 974-3650
Robert E Meadows, *VP*
EMP: 850 **EST:** 1964
SQ FT: 55,000
SALES (est): 540.72MM
SALES (corp-wide): 540.72MM **Privately
Held**
Web: www.morrow-meadows.com
SIC: 1731 General electrical contractor

(P-943)
NAZZARENO ELECTRIC CO INC
1250 E Gene Autry Way, Anaheim
(92805-6716)
PHONE..................714 712-4744
Paul Rick Nazzareno, *Pr*
EMP: 75 **EST:** 1993
SQ FT: 10,000
SALES (est): 4.19MM **Privately Held**
Web: www.nazzareno.com
SIC: 1731 General electrical contractor

(P-944)
NEAL ELECTRIC CORP (HQ)
5928 Balfour Ct, Carlsbad (92008-7304)
P.O. Box 1655 (92074-1655)
PHONE..................858 513-2525
Daniel Zupp, *Pr*
Luis Armona, *
Casimier Wesolowski, *
Harry Schirer, *
Alex Meruelo, *
EMP: 75 **EST:** 2008
SALES (est): 54.46MM
SALES (corp-wide): 464.46MM **Privately
Held**
Web: www.nealelectric.com
SIC: 1731 General electrical contractor
PA: Meruelo Enterprises, Inc.
9550 Firestone Blvd # 105
562 745-2300

(P-945)
NWEC NEVADA INC
Also Called: New Wave Electric
1232 Distribution Way, Vista (92081-8816)
PHONE..................760 757-0187
John Lisowski, *Pr*
John J Lisowski, *
EMP: 75 **EST:** 2011
SALES (est): 2.03MM **Privately Held**
SIC: 1731 General electrical contractor

(P-946)
OBRYANT ELECTRIC INC (PA)
9314 Eton Ave, Chatsworth (91311-5809)
PHONE..................818 407-1986
Cathy O'bryant, *Pr*
Steve O'bryant, *Sec*
EMP: 120 **EST:** 1978
SQ FT: 25,000
SALES (est): 21.3MM
SALES (corp-wide): 21.3MM **Privately
Held**
Web: www.obryantelectric.com
SIC: 1731 General electrical contractor

(P-947)
PACIFIC COAST CABLING INC
(PA)
Also Called: PCC Network Solutions
20717 Prairie St, Chatsworth (91311-6011)
PHONE..................818 407-1911

EMP: 51 **EST:** 1985
SALES (est): 31.46MM
SALES (corp-wide): 31.46MM **Privately
Held**
Web: www.pccinc.com
SIC: 1731 3613 Computer installation;
Control panels, electric

(P-948)
PARADISE ELECTRIC INC
697 Greenfield Dr, El Cajon (92021-2983)
PHONE..................619 449-4141
Mike Manos, *Pr*
Jeff Platt, *
EMP: 217 **EST:** 1988
SQ FT: 7,000
SALES (est): 1.59MM
SALES (corp-wide): 29.28MM **Privately
Held**
Web: www.schillingcorp.com
SIC: 1731 General electrical contractor
HQ: Builders Tradesource Corp
697 Greenfield Dr
El Cajon CA 92021

(P-949)
PATRIC COMMUNICATIONS INC
(PA)
Also Called: Advanced Electronic Solutions
15215 Alton Pkwy Ste 200, Irvine
(92618-2613)
PHONE..................619 579-2898
Sean P Mcdermott, *Pr*
Richard P Apgar, *
Kathy Alford, *
EMP: 70 **EST:** 1981
SALES (est): 9.91MM **Privately Held**
SIC: 1731 1751 3699 Fire detection and
burglar alarm systems specialization;
Carpentry work; Security devices

(P-950)
PAVLETICH ELC
CMMNICATIONS INC (PA)
Also Called: Pavletich Electric
6308 Seven Seas Ave, Bakersfield
(93308-5132)
PHONE..................661 589-9473
John Pavletich, *CEO*
Scott Pavletich, *
EMP: 89 **EST:** 1994
SQ FT: 15,000
SALES (est): 15.14MM **Privately Held**
Web: www.pavelectric.com
SIC: 1731 General electrical contractor

(P-951)
PINNACLE NETWORKING SVCS
INC
Also Called: PINNACLE COMMUNICATION
SERVICE
730 Fairmont Ave, Glendale (91203-1078)
PHONE..................818 241-6009
Avo Amirian, *CEO*
Joe Licursi, *
EMP: 130 **EST:** 1994
SQ FT: 10,000
SALES (est): 23.73MM **Privately Held**
Web: www.pinnacleinc.com
SIC: 1731 8748 Communications
specialization; Telecommunications
consultant

(P-952)
PIVOT INTERIORS INC
Pivot Interiors-Receiving Only
3200 Park Center Dr Ste 100, Costa Mesa
(92626-7104)
PHONE..................949 988-5400

Ken Baugh, *CEO*
EMP: 178
SALES (corp-wide): 38.16MM **Privately
Held**
Web: www.pivotinteriors.com
SIC: 1731 Electrical work
PA: Pivot Interiors, Inc.
3355 Scott Blvd Ste 110
408 432-5600

(P-953)
PORTERMATT ELECTRIC INC
5431 Production Dr, Huntington Beach
(92649-1524)
PHONE..................714 596-8788
Tim Matthews, *Pr*
John F Porter Iii, *VP*
EMP: 90 **EST:** 1998
SQ FT: 5,300
SALES (est): 33.09MM **Privately Held**
Web: www.portermatt.com
SIC: 1731 1799 General electrical contractor
; Athletic and recreation facilities
construction

(P-954)
PROFESSNAL ELEC CNSTR
SVCS INC
Also Called: Pecs
9112 Santa Anita Ave, Rancho Cucamonga
(91730-6143)
PHONE..................909 373-4100
Lori Casey, *CEO*
Robert W Casey, *
EMP: 102 **EST:** 2007
SQ FT: 15,000
SALES (est): 21.52MM **Privately Held**
Web: www.pecs.biz
SIC: 1731 8711 1542 General electrical
contractor; Engineering services;
Nonresidential construction, nec

(P-955)
PYRO-COMM SYSTEMS INC (PA)
Also Called: Pyro
15215 Alton Pkwy, Irvine (92618-2359)
PHONE..................714 902-8000
Michael Donahue, *Pr*
Nanci Donahue, *
EMP: 150 **EST:** 1980
SALES (est): 38.45MM
SALES (corp-wide): 38.45MM **Privately
Held**
Web: www.pyrocomm.com
SIC: 1731 5063 Fire detection and burglar
alarm systems specialization; Fire alarm
systems

(P-956)
ROSENDIN ELECTRIC INC
1730 S Anaheim Way, Anaheim
(92805-6537)
PHONE..................714 739-1334
Cliff Thompson, *Brnch Mgr*
EMP: 668
SALES (corp-wide): 2.06B **Privately Held**
Web: www.rosendin.com
SIC: 1731 General electrical contractor
PA: Rosendin Electric, Inc.
880 Mabury Rd
408 286-2800

(P-957)
RYE ELECTRIC INC
28202 Cabot Rd Ste 300, Laguna Niguel
(92677-1249)
PHONE..................949 441-0545
Christopher Golden, *Pr*
EMP: 75 **EST:** 2018
SALES (est): 12.9MM **Privately Held**

Web: www.ryecompany.com
SIC: 1731 General electrical contractor

(P-958)
SBE ELECTRICAL
CONTRACTING INC
2817 Mcgaw Ave, Irvine (92614-5835)
PHONE..................714 544-5066
Jeffery S Wilson, *CEO*
EMP: 105 **EST:** 2016
SALES (est): 5.03MM **Privately Held**
Web: www.sbeoc.com
SIC: 1731 General electrical contractor

(P-959)
SEAL ELECTRIC INC
1162 Greenfield Dr, El Cajon (92021-3314)
PHONE..................619 449-7323
Frank Bongiovanni, *Pr*
EMP: 145 **EST:** 1996
SQ FT: 5,000
SALES (est): 8.1MM **Privately Held**
Web: www.sealelectric.com
SIC: 1731 General electrical contractor

(P-960)
SFADIA INC
Also Called: Green Energy Innovations
8485 Artesia Blvd Ste A, Buena Park
(90621-4194)
PHONE..................323 622-1930
Pilje Park, *Pr*
Pil Soon Um, *
▲ **EMP:** 86 **EST:** 2010
SALES (est): 8.93MM **Privately Held**
Web: www.geinnovationsinc.com
SIC: 1731 Energy management controls

(P-961)
SOLRITE ELECTRIC LLC
330 Rancheros Dr Ste 116, San Marcos
(92069-2939)
PHONE..................833 765-6682
EMP: 110 **EST:** 2017
SALES (est): 28.52MM **Privately Held**
Web: www.gosolnova.com
SIC: 1731 Electrical work

(P-962)
SOUND RIVER CORPORATION
Also Called: Atk Audiotek
28238 Avenue Crocker, Valencia
(91355-1248)
PHONE..................661 705-3700
Michael M Macdonald, *Pr*
James Harmala, *
John M Stewart, *
EMP: 85 **EST:** 1983
SQ FT: 25,000
SALES (est): 24.1MM **Privately Held**
Web: www.atkaudiotek.com
SIC: 1731 7359 Voice, data, and video
wiring contractor; Sound and lighting
equipment rental

(P-963)
SOUTHERN CONTRACTING
COMPANY
559 N Twin Oaks Valley Rd, San Marcos
(92069-1798)
P.O. Box 445 (92079-0445)
PHONE..................760 744-0760
Timothy R Mcbride, *CEO*
Richard W Mc Bride, *
Tim Mc Bride, *
▲ **EMP:** 125 **EST:** 1963
SQ FT: 8,400
SALES (est): 49.96MM **Privately Held**
Web: www.southerncontracting.com

SIC: 1731 General electrical contractor

(P-964)

SPECIALTY CONSTRUCTION INC

645 Clarion Ct, San Luis Obispo
(93401-8177)
PHONE.................................805 543-1706
Rudolph Bachmann, *Pr*
Jeffrey Martin, *
Chris Teaford, *
Doug Clay, *
Steve Haymaker, *
EMP: 100 EST: 1992
SQ FT: 8,000
SALES (est): 22.56MM **Privately Held**
Web: www.specialtyconstruction.com
SIC: 1731 Telephone and telephone
equipment installation

(P-965)

SPECTRA INDUSTRIAL SVCS INC

Also Called: Spectra Industrial Electric
21818 S Wilmington Ave Ste 402, Carson
(90810-1642)
PHONE.................................310 835-0808
Michael J Merrill, *Pr*
Richard Mangan, *
EMP: 70 EST: 1989
SQ FT: 20,000
SALES (est): 9.9MM **Privately Held**
Web: www.braggcompanies.com
SIC: 1731 Access control systems
specialization

(P-966)

STC NETCOM INC (PA)

Also Called: Centerline
11611 Industry Ave, Fontana (92337-6931)
PHONE.................................951 685-8181
Giuseppe Floro, *Pr*
Jeffry Kinne, *
Shawnda Letourneau, *
EMP: 70 EST: 1990
SQ FT: 6,000
SALES (est): 8.14MM **Privately Held**
Web: www.stcnetcom.com
SIC: 1731 Fiber optic cable installation

(P-967)

STEINY AND COMPANY INC

221 N Ardmore Ave, Los Angeles
(90004-4503)
PHONE.................................213 382-2331
EMP: 300
Web: www.steinyco.com
SIC: 1731 General electrical contractor

(P-968)

SUN ELECTRIC LP

2101 S Yale St Ste B, Santa Ana
(92704-4424)
PHONE.................................714 210-3744
Jeffery J Ber Bernardino, *Ltd Pt*
EMP: 100 EST: 2003
SALES (est): 668.06K **Privately Held**
SIC: 1731 General electrical contractor

(P-969)

SUNSHINE COMMUNICATIONS SE INC

350 Cypress Ln Ste D, El Cajon
(92020-1664)
P.O. Box 3509 (33572-1005)
PHONE.................................619 448-7600
Robert Straub, *CEO*
EMP: 235 EST: 1998
SALES (est): 9.22MM **Privately Held**

Web: www.sunshinecom.com
SIC: 1731 Cable television installation

(P-970)

SUNWEST ELECTRIC INC

3064 E Mariloma, Anaheim (92806-1810)
PHONE.................................714 630-8700
Brien Pariseau, *Pr*
Doug Lyvers, *
EMP: 175 EST: 1985
SQ FT: 20,000
SALES (est): 21.05MM **Privately Held**
Web: www.sunwestelectric.net
SIC: 1731 Electrical work

(P-971)

SUPERIOR ELEC MECH & PLBG INC

8613 Helms Ave, Rancho Cucamonga
(91730-4521)
PHONE.................................909 357-9400
David A Stone Junior, *CEO*
Walt Schobel, *
Pam Metzer, *
EMP: 291 EST: 2001
SQ FT: 50,000
SALES (est): 22.18MM **Privately Held**
Web: www.superioremp.com
SIC: 1731 1711 General electrical contractor
; Mechanical contractor

(P-972)

T MCGEE ELECTRIC INC

2390 S Reservoir St, Pomona
(91766-6410)
P.O. Box 1111 (91708-1111)
PHONE.................................909 591-6461
Trent L Mc Gee, *Pr*
EMP: 100 EST: 1986
SALES (est): 10.07MM **Privately Held**
Web: www.tmcgeeelectric.com
SIC: 1731 General electrical contractor

(P-973)

TAFT ELECTRIC COMPANY (PA)

1694 Eastman Ave, Ventura (93003-5782)
P.O. Box 3416 (93006-3416)
PHONE.................................805 642-0121
James Marsh, *Pr*
Carol A Smith, *
Jeff Wofford, *
EMP: 209 EST: 1942
SQ FT: 40,000
SALES (est): 99.9MM
SALES (corp-wide): 99.9MM **Privately Held**
Web: www.taftelectric.com
SIC: 1731 1629 General electrical contractor
; Waste water and sewage treatment plant
construction

(P-974)

TRI-SIGNAL INTEGRATION INC (PA)

Also Called: Honeywell Authorized Dealer
28110 Avenue Stanford Unit D, Santa
Clarita (91355-1161)
PHONE.................................818 566-8558
Robert Mckibben, *Pr*
Rett Hicks, *
Michael Swisher, *
Dennis Furden, *
EMP: 100 EST: 1998
SQ FT: 16,000
SALES (est): 27.78MM
SALES (corp-wide): 27.78MM **Privately Held**
Web: www.tri-signal.com
SIC: 1731 Fire detection and burglar alarm
systems specialization

(P-975)

TRL SYSTEMS INCORPORATED

Also Called: T R L
9531 Milliken Ave, Rancho Cucamonga
(91730-6006)
PHONE.................................909 390-8392
Lynn Purdy, *Ch*
Mark L Purdy, *
EMP: 100 EST: 1980
SQ FT: 14,000
SALES (est): 40.65MM **Privately Held**
Web: www.trlsystems.com
SIC: 1731 General electrical contractor

(P-976)

VECTOR RESOURCES INC (PA)

Also Called: Vectorusa
20917 Higgins Ct, Torrance (90501-1723)
PHONE.................................310 436-1000
TOLL FREE: 800
David Zukerman, *Pr*
Robert Messinger, *
John Schuman, *Dist Vice President*
Jeffrey Zukerman, *
EMP: 167 EST: 1988
SALES (est): 60.03MM
SALES (corp-wide): 60.03MM **Privately Held**
Web: www.vectorusa.com
SIC: 1731 3651 7373 Communications
specialization; Clock radio and telephone
combinations; Systems engineering,
computer related

(P-977)

WEST COAST LTG & ENRGY INC

18550 Minthorn St, Lake Elsinore
(92530-2784)
PHONE.................................951 296-0680
Johnny Odell Leach, *Pr*
Johnny Odell Leach, *Pr*
Tammy Leach, *
EMP: 90 EST: 1994
SQ FT: 2,646
SALES (est): 8.51MM **Privately Held**
Web: www.wcleinc.com
SIC: 1731 General electrical contractor

(P-978)

WORLDWIND SERVICES LLC

Also Called: World Wind & Solar
1222 Vine St Ste 301, Paso Robles
(93446-2333)
PHONE.................................661 822-4877
Mark Mclanahan, *CEO*
Kristin Osborn, *
Matthew Gillette, *
EMP: 700 EST: 2007
SALES (est): 14.54MM
SALES (corp-wide): 477.32MM **Privately Held**
Web: www.worldwindsolar.com
SIC: 1731 1389 8742 Electrical work;
Construction, repair, and dismantling
services; Maintenance management
consultant
HQ: Pearce Services, Llc
1222 Vine St
Paso Robles CA 93446
805 467-2528

(P-979)

X3 MANAGEMENT SERVICES INC

Also Called: X3 Engineering & Construction
325 Market Pl, Escondido (92029-1302)
P.O. Box 460669 (92046-0669)
PHONE.................................760 597-9336
David G Cranford, *CEO*
Arlette Zuniga, *

EMP: 85 EST: 2005
SALES (est): 22.84MM **Privately Held**
Web: www.x3corp.net
SIC: 1731 1531 1541 1711 Electrical work;
Operative builders; Industrial buildings and
warehouses; Solar energy contractor

1741 Masonry And Other Stonework

(P-980)

B&B INDUSTRIAL SERVICES INC (PA)

14549 Manzanita Dr, Fontana
(92335-5378)
PHONE.................................909 428-3167
Lyndon Brewer, *Pr*
Ted Brewer, *
Tim Brewer, *
EMP: 261 EST: 1993
SQ FT: 12,000
SALES (est): 5.75MM **Privately Held**
Web: www.bb-industrial.com
SIC: 1741 Refractory or acid brick masonry

(P-981)

DESIGN MASONRY INC

20703 Santa Clara St, Canyon Country
(91351-2424)
PHONE.................................661 252-2784
Scott Floyd, *Pr*
Randall Carpenter, *
EMP: 70 EST: 2009
SALES (est): 12.03MM **Privately Held**
Web: www.designmasonry.com
SIC: 1741 Stone masonry

(P-982)

FRANK S SMITH MASONRY INC

2830 Pomona Blvd, Pomona (91768-3224)
PHONE.................................909 468-0525
Frank E Smith, *Pr*
Brian E Smith, *
Kevin J Smith, *
EMP: 100 EST: 1938
SQ FT: 54,000
SALES (est): 9.63MM **Privately Held**
Web: www.franksmithmasonry.com
SIC: 1741 Bricklaying

(P-983)

GBC CONCRETE MASNRY CNSTR INC

561 Birch St, Lake Elsinore (92530-2732)
PHONE.................................951 245-2355
Tom Daniel, *Pr*
EMP: 170 EST: 1985
SQ FT: 8,000
SALES (est): 23.25MM **Privately Held**
Web: www.gbcconstruction.com
SIC: 1741 1771 Foundation building;
Concrete work

(P-984)

HBA INCORPORATED

512 E Vermont Ave, Anaheim (92805-5603)
P.O. Box 25861 (92825-5861)
PHONE.................................714 635-8602
Gerald G Pyle, *Pr*
Joe Alessandrini, *
EMP: 100 EST: 2006
SALES (est): 11.32MM **Privately Held**
Web: www.hbabuild.com
SIC: 1741 Masonry and other stonework

(P-985)

J GINGER MASONRY LP (PA)

8188 Lincoln Ave Ste 100, Riverside
(92504-4329)

PHONE..............................951 688-5050
John L Ginger, *Ltd Pt*
EMP: 265 **EST:** 1978
SALES (est): 23.13MM **Privately Held**
Web: www.jgingermasonry.com
SIC: 1741 Masonry and other stonework

(P-986)
MASONRY CONCEPTS INC
15408 Comet St, Santa Fe Springs
(90670-5534)
PHONE..............................562 802-3700
Dana Kemp, *Pr*
Ronald O Udall, *
Peter Sturdivant, *
Russell Knight, *
EMP: 100 **EST:** 1983
SQ FT: 10,000
SALES (est): 17.18MM **Privately Held**
Web: www.masonry-concepts.com
SIC: 1741 Masonry and other stonework

(P-987)
MASONRY GROUP NEVADA INC
8188 Lincoln Ave Ste 99, Riverside
(92504-4329)
PHONE..............................951 509-5300
EMP: 99
SALES (est): 1.15MM **Privately Held**
SIC: 1741 Masonry and other stonework

(P-988)
SPECTRA COMPANY
Also Called: Spectra Historic Construction
2510 Supply St, Pomona (91767-2113)
PHONE..............................909 599-0760
Ray Adamyk, *CEO*
Ann Dresselhaus, *
▲ **EMP:** 125 **EST:** 1985
SQ FT: 7,000
SALES (est): 13.21MM **Privately Held**
Web: www.spectracompany.com
SIC: 1741 1771 1743 1721 Masonry and
other stonework; Concrete work; Terrazzo,
tile, marble and mosaic work; Painting and
paper hanging

(P-989)
SUPERIOR MASONRY WALLS LTD
300 W Olive St Ste A, Colton (92324-1765)
PHONE..............................909 370-1800
Daniel Lee, *Pr*
EMP: 75 **EST:** 2011
SALES (est): 4.65MM **Privately Held**
Web: www.superiormasonrywalls.com
SIC: 1741 Masonry and other stonework

(P-990)
VARIATIONS IN STONE INC
360 La Perle Pl, Costa Mesa (92627-7749)
PHONE..............................949 438-8337
Joseph Dorando, *CFO*
James Joseph Dorando, *
EMP: 75 **EST:** 2015
SALES (est): 524.97K **Privately Held**
SIC: 1741 Masonry and other stonework

(P-991)
VINCENT CONTRACTORS INC
Also Called: Vincent Scaffolding
4501 E La Palma Ave Ste 200, Anaheim
(92807-1950)
PHONE..............................714 660-0165
Justin Erdtsieck, *Pr*
Kenny Vo, *
EMP: 430 **EST:** 2016
SQ FT: 5,538
SALES (est): 23.86MM **Privately Held**

SIC: 1741 1742 Masonry and other
stonework; Plastering, drywall, and
insulation

(P-992)
WIRTZ QUALITY INSTALLATIONS
7932 Armour St, San Diego (92111-3718)
PHONE..............................858 569-3816
Victor Fox, *Pr*
Ida Wirtz, *
John Wirtz, *
Ryan Wilson, *
EMP: 85 **EST:** 2009
SALES (est): 8.5MM **Privately Held**
Web: www.wirtzquality.com
SIC: 1741 1752 1743 1799 Masonry and
other stonework; Floor laying and floor
work, nec; Terrazzo, tile, marble and
mosaic work; Cleaning building exteriors,
nec

1742 Plastering, Drywall, And Insulation

(P-993)
A A GONZALEZ INC
13264 Ralston Ave, Rancho Cascades
(91342-7607)
P.O. Box 408 (91341-0408)
PHONE..............................818 367-2242
Albert Gonzales, *Pr*
Aida Lepe, *
EMP: 100 **EST:** 1992
SALES (est): 6.3MM **Privately Held**
Web: www.aagonz.com
SIC: 1742 Plastering, drywall, and insulation

(P-994)
ALAN SMITH POOL PLASTERING INC
Also Called: H2o Leak Pros
227 W Carleton Ave, Orange (92867-3607)
PHONE..............................714 628-9494
Stephen Scherer, *Pr*
Teresa Smith, *
Alan Smith, *
▲ **EMP:** 78 **EST:** 1981
SQ FT: 5,000
SALES (est): 24.79MM **Privately Held**
Web: www.alansmithpools.com
SIC: 1742 Plastering, plain or ornamental

(P-995)
ALL WALL INC
46150 Commerce St Ste 102, Indio
(92201-3418)
PHONE..............................760 600-5108
Saul M Gonzalez, *Pr*
Yvette Ambriz, *
Saul Miranda, *
EMP: 89 **EST:** 2012
SALES (est): 4.41MM **Privately Held**
Web: www.allwalldi.com
SIC: 1742 1721 7389 Drywall; Exterior
residential painting contractor; Business
Activities at Non-Commercial Site

(P-996)
ANCCA CORPORATION
Also Called: N-U Enterprise
7 Goddard, Irvine (92618-4600)
PHONE..............................949 553-0084
Nicole Hunt, *Sec*
EMP: 99 **EST:** 2008
SALES (est): 2.48MM **Privately Held**
SIC: 1742 Plastering, drywall, and insulation

(P-997)
BERGER BROS INC
154 N Aspan Ave, Azusa (91702-4224)
PHONE..............................626 334-2699
EMP: 350
Web: www.bergerbro.com
SIC: 1742 Plastering, plain or ornamental

(P-998)
BEST INTERIORS INC (PA)
2100 E Via Burton, Anaheim (92806-1219)
PHONE..............................714 490-7999
Dennis Ayres, *Pr*
Michael Herrig, *
EMP: 150 **EST:** 1986
SQ FT: 20,000
SALES (est): 22.24MM
SALES (corp-wide): 22.24MM **Privately Held**
Web: www.bestinteriors.net
SIC: 1742 Drywall

(P-999)
BEST INTERIORS INC
4395 Murphy Canyon Rd, San Diego
(92123-4337)
PHONE..............................858 715-3760
EMP: 80
SALES (corp-wide): 22.24MM **Privately Held**
Web: www.bestinteriors.net
SIC: 1742 Drywall
PA: Best Interiors, Inc.
2100 E Via Burton
714 490-7999

(P-1000)
BRADY COMPANY/SAN DIEGO INC
8100 Center St, La Mesa (91942-2925)
P.O. Box 968 (91944-0968)
PHONE..............................619 462-2600
Scott Brady, *CEO*
EMP: 300 **EST:** 1946
SQ FT: 4,000
SALES (est): 2.21MM **Privately Held**
Web: www.brady.com
SIC: 1742 1542 Plastering, plain or
ornamental; Commercial and office
buildings, renovation and repair

(P-1001)
BRADY SOCAL INCORPORATED
8100 Center St, La Mesa (91942-2925)
PHONE..............................619 462-2600
Ricky Marshall, *Pr*
Scott Brady, *
EMP: 99 **EST:** 2009
SALES (est): 7.84MM **Privately Held**
Web: www.brady.com
SIC: 1742 1751 Drywall; Window and door
installation and erection

(P-1002)
CALDERON DRYWALL CONTRS INC
1931 E Meats Ave Trlr 127, Orange
(92865-4002)
PHONE..............................714 696-2977
EMP: 84
SALES (corp-wide): 4.81MM **Privately Held**
SIC: 1742 Drywall
PA: Calderon Drywall Contractors Inc.
2085 N Nordic St
714 900-1863

(P-1003)
CAPITAL DRYWALL LP
333 S Grand Ave Ste 4070, Los Angeles
(90071-1544)
PHONE..............................909 599-6818
Frank Scardino, *Pr*
Art Toscano, *
Angela Gates, *
EMP: 249 **EST:** 1980
SQ FT: 8,000
SALES (est): 2.45MM **Privately Held**
SIC: 1742 Drywall
PA: U.S. Builder Services, Llc
272 E Deerpath Ste 308

(P-1004)
CASTON INC
354 S Allen St, San Bernardino
(92408-1508)
PHONE..............................909 381-1619
James I Malachowski Junior, *Pr*
EMP: 100 **EST:** 2010
SALES (est): 11.15MM **Privately Held**
Web: www.castoninc.com
SIC: 1742 Drywall

(P-1005)
CHURCH & LARSEN INC
16103 Avenida Padilla, Irwindale
(91702-3223)
PHONE..............................626 303-8741
Raymond W Larsen, *Pr*
Kenneth R Larsen, *
Kenneth P Larsen, *
EMP: 250 **EST:** 1980
SQ FT: 10,800
SALES (est): 9.54MM **Privately Held**
Web: www.churchandlarsen.com
SIC: 1742 Drywall

(P-1006)
ELLJAY ACOUSTICS INC
511 Cameron St, Placentia (92870-6425)
PHONE..............................714 961-1173
Ronald B Bishop, *Pr*
EMP: 70 **EST:** 1966
SQ FT: 6,900
SALES (est): 5.75MM **Privately Held**
Web: www.elljay.com
SIC: 1742 Acoustical and ceiling work

(P-1007)
FARWEST INSULATION CONTRACTING
Also Called: Pacific Insulation
2741 Yates Ave, Commerce (90040-2623)
PHONE..............................310 634-2800
Linda Chadarria, *Mgr*
EMP: 91
SALES (corp-wide): 25.73MM **Privately Held**
Web: www.farwestinsulation.com
SIC: 1742 Insulation, buildings
PA: Farwest Insulation Contracting, Inc
1220 S Sherman St
714 520-5600

(P-1008)
FIVE STAR PLASTERING INC
23022 La Cadena Dr Ste 200, Laguna Hills
(92653-1362)
PHONE..............................949 683-5091
Thomas Blythe, *Pr*
EMP: 100 **EST:** 2010
SALES (est): 3.86MM **Privately Held**
Web: www.fivestarplastering.com
SIC: 1742 Drywall

(P-1009)
FUTURE ENERGY CORPORATION
4120 Avenida De La Plata, Oceanside (92056-6001)
PHONE...............................760 477-9700
Jeffrey Adkins, *Brnch Mgr*
EMP: 70
SALES (corp-wide): 6.23MM **Privately Held**
Web: www.futureenergysavers.com
SIC: 1742 1521 Acoustical and insulation work; Single-family home remodeling, additions, and repairs
PA: Future Energy Corporation
8980 Grant Line Rd
800 985-0733

(P-1010)
HI-TEMP INSULATION INC
4700 Calle Alto, Camarillo (93012-8489)
PHONE...............................805 484-2774
Sieg Borck, *CEO*
Fecialita Allen, *
▲ **EMP:** 410 **EST:** 1964
SQ FT: 100,000
SALES (est): 48.41MM **Privately Held**
Web: www.hi-tempinsulation.com
SIC: 1742 Insulation, buildings

(P-1011)
INFINITY DRYWALL CONTG INC
237 Glider Cir, Corona (92878-5034)
PHONE...............................714 634-2255
Dennis Lafreniere, *Pr*
Liza Lafreniere, *
EMP: 200 **EST:** 2006
SALES (est): 39MM **Privately Held**
Web: www.infinitydw.com
SIC: 1742 1751 Drywall; Framing contractor

(P-1012)
JADE INC
11126 Sepulveda Blvd Ste B, Mission Hills (91345-1130)
PHONE...............................818 365-7137
Steven Arteaga, *CEO*
Jay Arteaga, *
Michelle Vojtech, *
Cheryl Taylor, *
Gail De Ande, *
EMP: 75 **EST:** 1974
SQ FT: 5,000
SALES (est): 4.98MM **Privately Held**
Web: www.jadedrywall.com
SIC: 1742 Drywall

(P-1013)
JOHN JORY CORPORATION (PA)
2180 N Glassell St, Orange (92865-3308)
P.O. Box 6050 (92863-6050)
PHONE...............................714 279-7901
Kenneth Johnson, *CEO*
Jack Jory, *
EMP: 385 **EST:** 1965
SALES (est): 7.32MM
SALES (corp-wide): 7.32MM **Privately Held**
Web: www.johnjorycorp.com
SIC: 1742 Drywall

(P-1014)
MARTIN BROS/MARCOWALL INC (PA)
17104 S Figueroa St, Gardena (90248-3021)
P.O. Box 2089 (90247-0089)
PHONE...............................310 532-5335
Mohammad Chahine, *CEO*

EMP: 110 **EST:** 1966
SQ FT: 6,000
SALES (est): 20.54MM
SALES (corp-wide): 20.54MM **Privately Held**
Web: www.martinbros.net
SIC: 1742 Drywall

(P-1015)
MARTIN INTEGRATED SYSTEMS
Also Called: Martin Integrated
1525 W Orange Grove Ave Ste D, Orange (92868-1109)
PHONE...............................714 998-9100
Cory Hovivian, *Pr*
Marshall Hovivian, *
Anne Reizer, *
EMP: 30 **EST:** 1989
SALES (est): 3.47MM **Privately Held**
Web: www.martinintegrated.com
SIC: 1742 3446 3296 Acoustical and ceiling work; Acoustical suspension systems, metal ; Acoustical board and tile, mineral wool

(P-1016)
MOWERY THOMASON INC
1225 N Red Gum St, Anaheim (92806-1821)
PHONE...............................714 666-1717
Robert J Heimerl, *Pr*
Todd Heimerl, *
Toni Heimerl, *
EMP: 175 **EST:** 1957
SQ FT: 8,000
SALES (est): 18.02MM **Privately Held**
Web: www.mowerythomason.com
SIC: 1742 Drywall

(P-1017)
OJ INSULATION LP (HQ)
Also Called: Abco Insulation
600 S Vincent Ave, Azusa (91702-5145)
PHONE...............................800 707-9278
Pamela A Henson, *Pt*
EMP: 148 **EST:** 2006
SQ FT: 12,000
SALES (est): 22.6MM
SALES (corp-wide): 2.78B **Publicly Held**
Web: www.ojinc.com
SIC: 1742 1751 1741 Insulation, buildings; Carpentry work; Masonry and other stonework
PA: Installed Building Products, Inc.
495 S High St Ste 50
614 221-3399

(P-1018)
ORANGE COUNTY PLST CO INC
3191 Airport Loop Dr Ste B1, Costa Mesa (92626-3404)
PHONE...............................714 957-1971
Robert G Smith, *Pr*
EMP: 128 **EST:** 1995
SALES (est): 4.17MM **Privately Held**
SIC: 1742 Plastering, plain or ornamental

(P-1019)
ORANGE COUNTY THERMAL INDS INC (PA)
1940 N Glassell St, Orange (92865-4314)
PHONE...............................714 279-9416
Eduardo Olivares, *Pr*
EMP: 51 **EST:** 2010
SQ FT: 10,000
SALES (est): 8.06MM
SALES (corp-wide): 8.06MM **Privately Held**
Web: www.teamocti.com
SIC: 1742 3296 Insulation, buildings; Acoustical board and tile, mineral wool

(P-1020)
PACIFIC BUILDING GROUP
13541 Stoney Creek Rd, San Diego (92129-2050)
PHONE...............................858 552-0600
Jim Roherty, *Brnch Mgr*
EMP: 92
SALES (corp-wide): 47.6MM **Privately Held**
Web: www.pacificbuildinggroup.com
SIC: 1742 Acoustical and ceiling work
PA: Pacific Building Group
9752 Aspen Creek Ct # 100
858 552-0600

(P-1021)
PACIFIC SYSTEMS INTERIORS INC
190 E Arrow Hwy Ste D, San Dimas (91773-3314)
PHONE...............................310 436-6820
Michelle Orr Mcneal, *Dir*
EMP: 150 **EST:** 1987
SQ FT: 30,000
SALES (est): 39.51MM **Privately Held**
Web: www.psi.builders
SIC: 1742 1542 Drywall; Nonresidential construction, nec

(P-1022)
PADILLA CONSTRUCTION COMPANY
Also Called: Garris Plastering
1620 N Brian St, Orange (92867-3422)
PHONE...............................714 685-8500
Ralph Padilla, *Prin*
EMP: 250 **EST:** 1963
SALES (est): 5.51MM **Privately Held**
Web: www.padillaconstruction.com
SIC: 1742 Plastering, drywall, and insulation

(P-1023)
PETROCHEM INSULATION INC
Also Called: Petrochem
3117 E South St, Long Beach (90805-3742)
PHONE...............................310 638-6663
Erich Freudenthaler, *Mgr*
EMP: 111
SALES (corp-wide): 2.72B **Privately Held**
Web: www.petrocheminc.com
SIC: 1742 3531 Insulation, buildings; Construction machinery
HQ: Petrochem Insulation, Inc.
1501 W Ftnhead Pkwy # 550
Tempe AZ 85282
707 644-7455

(P-1024)
PROWALL LATH AND PLASTER
360 S Spruce St, Escondido (92025-4052)
P.O. Box 3058 (92033-3058)
PHONE...............................760 480-9001
Mary Kathawa, *Pr*
EMP: 99 **EST:** 2009
SALES (est): 2.42MM **Privately Held**
Web: www.prowalllathandplaster.net
SIC: 1742 Plastering, plain or ornamental

(P-1025)
QUALITY PRODUCTION SVCS INC
18711 S Broadwick St, Compton (90220-6427)
PHONE...............................310 406-3350
Arshak George Kctoyantz, *Pr*
EMP: 100 **EST:** 1995
SALES (est): 9.35MM **Privately Held**
Web: www.qpscompany.com
SIC: 1742 Drywall

(P-1026)
ROYAL WEST DRYWALL INC
2008 2nd St, Norco (92860-2804)
PHONE...............................951 271-4600
Paul Diguiseppe, *CEO*
EMP: 100 **EST:** 1988
SQ FT: 20,473
SALES (est): 4.3MM **Privately Held**
Web: www.royalwestdrywall.com
SIC: 1742 Drywall

(P-1027)
RUTHERFORD CO INC (PA)
2107 Crystal St, Los Angeles (90039-2901)
PHONE...............................323 666-5284
Paul Rutherford, *Pr*
Sheila Rutherford, *
Brad Rutherford, *
James Rutherford, *
EMP: 100 **EST:** 1970
SQ FT: 15,000
SALES (est): 9.17MM
SALES (corp-wide): 9.17MM **Privately Held**
Web: www.rutherfordco.net
SIC: 1742 Plastering, plain or ornamental

(P-1028)
SIERRA LATHING COMPANY INC
1189 Leiske Dr, Rialto (92376-8633)
PHONE...............................909 421-0211
Gary K Waldron, *CEO*
Connie Waldron, *
EMP: 200 **EST:** 1958
SQ FT: 10,000
SALES (est): 3.33MM **Privately Held**
SIC: 1742 1751 Drywall; Framing contractor

(P-1029)
SPECIALTY TEAM PLASTERING INC
4652 Vintage Ranch Ln, Santa Barbara (93110-2079)
PHONE...............................805 966-3858
Jaime Melgosa, *Pr*
Robin Melgosa, *
EMP: 130 **EST:** 1993
SQ FT: 1,000
SALES (est): 8.1MM **Privately Held**
Web: www.specialtyteamplastering.com
SIC: 1742 Plastering, plain or ornamental

(P-1030)
STANDARD DRYWALL INC (HQ)
Also Called: S D I
9831 Channel Rd, Lakeside (92040-3173)
PHONE...............................619 443-7034
Robert E Caya, *CEO*
Blaine Caya, *
EMP: 300 **EST:** 1956
SALES (est): 50MM **Privately Held**
Web: www.standarddrywall.com
SIC: 1742 Drywall
PA: E M P Interiors Inc
9831 Channel Rd

(P-1031)
SUNSHINE METAL CLAD INC
7201 Edison Hwy, Bakersfield (93307-9011)
PHONE...............................661 366-0575
James R Eudy, *Pr*
Linda Payne, *
▲ **EMP:** 100 **EST:** 1979
SQ FT: 50,000
SALES (est): 4.75MM **Privately Held**
Web: www.smcinsulation.com
SIC: 1742 Insulation, buildings

(P-1032)
SUPERIOR WALL SYSTEMS INC
Also Called: Sws
1232 E Orangethorpe Ave, Fullerton
(92831-5224)
PHONE...............714 278-0000
Ronald Lee Hudson, *CEO*
Greg Smith, *
EMP: 500 EST: 1979
SQ FT: 40,000
SALES (est): 9.77MM **Privately Held**
Web: www.superiorwallsystems.com
SIC: 1742 Drywall

(P-1033)
TEMECULA VALLEY DRYWALL INC
Also Called: Timberlake Painting
41228 Raintree Ct, Murrieta (92562-7089)
PHONE...............951 600-1742
Doug A Misemer, *CEO*
Lorry Hales, *
Sandy Villella, *
EMP: 75 EST: 1990
SQ FT: 8,000
SALES (est): 8.55MM **Privately Held**
Web: www.tvdrywall.com
SIC: 1742 1721 Drywall; Painting and paper
hanging

(P-1034)
THERMO POWER INDUSTRIES
Also Called: Thermo Power Industries
10570 Humbolt St, Los Alamitos
(90720-2439)
PHONE...............562 799-0087
Edward Lydic, *CEO*
John G Carroll, *
EMP: 50 EST: 1986
SQ FT: 5,500
SALES (est): 5.87MM **Privately Held**
Web: www.thermopowerindustries.com
SIC: 1742 1721 3479 Insulation, buildings;
Commercial painting; Coating, rust
preventive

(P-1035)
WEST COAST DRYWALL & CO INC
Also Called: West Coast Drywall & Paint
1610 W Linden St, Riverside (92507-6810)
PHONE...............951 778-3592
Mark Herbert, *CEO*
Dan Slavin, *
Santos Garcia, *
Colleen Butler, *
Keith Caneva, *Corporate Controller*
EMP: 400 EST: 2002
SQ FT: 18,962
SALES (est): 22.11MM **Privately Held**
Web: www.westcoastpainting.com
SIC: 1742 Drywall

1743 Terrazzo, Tile, Marble, Mosaic Work

(P-1036)
ALEXS TILE WORKS INC
5920 Matthews St, Goleta (93117-3922)
P.O. Box 810 (93102-0810)
PHONE...............805 967-5308
Vitali Drohomyrecky, *Pr*
Ruthe Drohomyrecky, *
Leonid Bondarenko, *
EMP: 25 EST: 1989
SALES (est): 2.48MM **Privately Held**
Web: www.alexstile.com

SIC: 1743 3272 Tile installation, ceramic;
Floor slabs and tiles, precast concrete

(P-1037)
CERAMIC TILE ART INC
11601 Pendleton St, Sun Valley
(91352-2502)
PHONE...............818 767-9088
Itamar Levy, *Pr*
▲ EMP: 75 EST: 1993
SALES (est): 2.82MM **Privately Held**
Web: www.ceramictileart.us
SIC: 1743 Tile installation, ceramic

(P-1038)
COASTAL TILE INC
Also Called: Coastal The
13226 Moorpark St Apt 104, Sherman Oaks
(91423-5177)
PHONE...............818 988-6134
Ronig Yemini, *Pr*
Eyal Reguev, *
▲ EMP: 100 EST: 1993
SALES (est): 3.91MM **Privately Held**
SIC: 1743 Tile installation, ceramic

(P-1039)
ELEGANZA TILES INC (PA)
3125 E Coronado St, Anaheim
(92806-1915)
PHONE...............714 224-1700
Miauw K Darmawan, *CEO*
Vonny Purnama, *VP*
◆ EMP: 70 EST: 2002
SALES (est): 20.17MM
SALES (corp-wide): 20.17MM **Privately Held**
Web: www.eleganzatiles.com
SIC: 1743 Tile installation, ceramic

(P-1040)
JEFFREY COURT INC
Also Called: Jeffrey Court
620 Parkridge Ave, Norco (92860-3124)
PHONE...............951 340-3383
▲ EMP: 77 EST: 1991
SALES (est): 4.82MM **Privately Held**
Web: www.jeffreycourt.com
SIC: 1743 Tile installation, ceramic

(P-1041)
MANTELS & MORE CORP
2909 Tanager Ave, Commerce
(90040-2723)
PHONE...............323 869-9764
Raffi Gourdikian, *CEO*
Tahlene Gourkikian, *
EMP: 43 EST: 1999
SQ FT: 25,000
SALES (est): 1.86MM **Privately Held**
SIC: 1743 3281 Terrazzo, tile, marble and
mosaic work; Granite, cut and shaped

(P-1042)
PARAGON INDUSTRIES INC
Also Called: Bedrosian's Tile
16450 Foothill Blvd Ste 100, Sylmar
(91342-1087)
PHONE...............818 833-0550
Josie Cox, *Brnch Mgr*
EMP: 32
SQ FT: 108,362
SALES (corp-wide): 251.57MM **Privately Held**
Web: www.bedrosians.com
SIC: 1743 3253 5032 5211 Tile installation,
ceramic; Ceramic wall and floor tile;
Ceramic wall and floor tile, nec; Tile,
ceramic
PA: Paragon Industries, Inc.
4285 N Golden State Blvd

559 275-5000

(P-1043)
TILE & MARBLE DESIGN CO INC
Also Called: Marbleworks
7421 Vincent Cir, Huntington Beach
(92648-1246)
PHONE...............714 847-6472
David Blataric, *CEO*
EMP: 32 EST: 2005
SALES (est): 3.2MM **Privately Held**
SIC: 1743 3281 Tile installation, ceramic;
Marble, building: cut and shaped

1751 Carpentry Work

(P-1044)
ARCHITECTURAL WOODWORKING CO
582 Monterey Pass Rd, Monterey Park
(91754-2485)
PHONE...............626 570-4125
John K Jack Heydorff, *Pr*
John F Heydorff, *Stockholder*
Richard A Schaub, *
Edward Illig, *
Thomas C Heydorff, *
EMP: 100 EST: 1963
SQ FT: 60,000
SALES (est): 4.69MM **Privately Held**
Web: www.awcla.com
SIC: 1751 2431 Carpentry work; Millwork

(P-1045)
CLEAR VIEW WINDOWS & DOORS INC
28106 Avenue Crocker, Santa Clarita
(91355-1207)
P.O. Box 802242 (91380-2242)
PHONE...............661 257-5050
EMP: 70
SIC: 1751 5031 Window and door
(prefabricated) installation; Metal doors,
sash and trim

(P-1046)
CLOSET WORLD INC
14438 Don Julian Rd, City Of Industry
(91746-3101)
PHONE...............626 855-0846
EMP: 85
Web: www.closetworld.com
SIC: 1751 5211 Cabinet building and
installation; Closets, interiors and
accessories
PA: Closet World, Inc.
3860 Capitol Ave

(P-1047)
COMMERCIAL WOOD PRODUCTS COMPANY
Also Called: Cwp
10019 Yucca Rd, Adelanto (92301-2242)
PHONE...............760 246-4530
EMP: 115
Web: www.commercialwood.com
SIC: 1751 Cabinet building and installation

(P-1048)
CRAFTSMAN LATH AND PLASTER INC
8325 63rd St, Riverside (92509-6004)
PHONE...............951 685-9922
Kevin Tunstill, *Pr*
EMP: 350 EST: 2015
SALES (est): 4.49MM **Privately Held**
Web: www.craftsmanlp.com
SIC: 1751 Carpentry work

(P-1049)
CWP CABINETS INC
15447 Anacapa Rd Ste 102, Victorville
(92392-2481)
PHONE...............760 246-4530
Michael Rodriguez, *CEO*
EMP: 115 EST: 2011
SALES (est): 1.34MM **Privately Held**
SIC: 1751 2434 2541 5712 Cabinet building
and installation; Wood kitchen cabinets;
Wood partitions and fixtures; Cabinet work,
custom

(P-1050)
GRESEAN INDUSTRIES INC
6320 Caballero Blvd, Buena Park
(90620-1126)
P.O. Box 928 (92075-0928)
EMP: 25 EST: 1986
SALES (est): 2.73MM **Privately Held**
Web: www.cabinetsystems.com
SIC: 1751 2421 Cabinet and finish carpentry
; Flooring (dressed lumber), softwood

(P-1051)
HAKES SASH & DOOR INC
31945 Corydon St, Lake Elsinore
(92530-8524)
PHONE...............951 674-2414
Allen J Hakes, *Pr*
EMP: 190 EST: 2005
SQ FT: 2,000
SALES (est): 9.54MM **Privately Held**
Web: www.hakesdoor.net
SIC: 1751 3442 5211 Window and door
installation and erection; Window and door
frames; Sash, wood or metal

(P-1052)
HOME ORGANIZERS INC
Also Called: Closet World, The
3860 Capitol Ave, City Of Industry
(90601-1733)
PHONE...............562 699-9945
Frank Melkonian, *Pr*
EMP: 660 EST: 2001
SALES (est): 11.12MM **Privately Held**
Web: www.closetworld.com
SIC: 1751 2541 Cabinet building and
installation; Cabinets, lockers, and shelving

(P-1053)
ISEC INCORPORATED
Also Called: Intermountain Specialty Eqp
20 Centerpointe Dr Ste 140, La Palma
(90623-2563)
PHONE...............714 761-5151
Greg Timmerman, *VP*
EMP: 133
SQ FT: 5,000
SALES (corp-wide): 317.22MM **Privately Held**
Web: www.isecinc.com
SIC: 1751 Cabinet and finish carpentry
PA: Isec, Incorporated
6000 Grnwood Plz Blvd Ste
303 790-1444

(P-1054)
ISEC INCORPORATED
2363 Teller Rd Ste 106, Newbury Park
(91320-6058)
PHONE...............805 375-6957
Kevin Zimmerman, *Brnch Mgr*
EMP: 74
SALES (corp-wide): 317.22MM **Privately Held**
Web: www.isecinc.com
SIC: 1751 Cabinet and finish carpentry
PA: Isec, Incorporated
6000 Grnwood Plz Blvd Ste

303 790-1444

(P-1055)
LAURENCE-HOVENIER INC
179 N Maple St, Corona (92878-3260)
PHONE...................................951 736-2990
Ronald Laurence, *Pr*
Fred Hovenier, *
EMP: 190 **EST:** 1979
SQ FT: 6,000
SALES (est): 8.36MM **Privately Held**
Web: www.framingcontractors.com
SIC: 1751 Framing contractor

(P-1056)
LOZANO CASEWORKS INC
242 W Hanna St, Colton (92324-2772)
PHONE...................................909 783-7530
EMP: 70
SIC: 1751 2522 Cabinet building and
installation; Cabinets, office: except wood

(P-1057)
NORCAL INC
Also Called: Seeley Brothers
1400 Moonstone, Brea (92821-2801)
PHONE...................................714 224-3949
Michael Seeley, *Pt*
Phil Norys, *
Joe Calvillo, *
EMP: 175 **EST:** 1987
SQ FT: 62,000
SALES (est): 21.82MM **Privately Held**
Web: www.seeleybros.com
SIC: 1751 Finish and trim carpentry

(P-1058)
PRIME TECH CABINETS INC
2215 S Standard Ave, Santa Ana
(92707-3036)
PHONE...................................949 757-4900
Hassan Farjamrad, *Pr*
Zora Farjamrad, *
EMP: 110 **EST:** 1988
SALES (est): 9.78MM **Privately Held**
Web: www.ptcabinets.com
SIC: 1751 Cabinet building and installation

(P-1059)
RANCH HOUSE DOORS INC
Also Called: R H D
1527 Pomona Rd, Corona (92878-4359)
PHONE...................................951 278-2884
Michael James Neal, *CEO*
Cristian Neal, *
Sandra Neal, *
EMP: 70 **EST:** 1997
SQ FT: 33,000
SALES (est): 9.14MM **Privately Held**
Web: www.ranchhousedoors.com
SIC: 1751 Garage door, installation or
erection

(P-1060)
ROY E WHITEHEAD INC
Also Called: Rew
2245 Via Cerro, Riverside (92509-2421)
PHONE...................................951 682-1490
David Whitehead, *CEO*
Chris Bagley, *
Dan Gilley, *
Byron Mitchell, *
Dennis Whitehead, *
EMP: 75 **EST:** 1955
SQ FT: 36,000
SALES (est): 5.21MM **Privately Held**
Web: www.royewhitehead.com
SIC: 1751 Cabinet building and installation

(P-1061)
SURECRAFT SUPPLY INC
2875 Executive Pl, Escondido
(92029-1524)
EMP: 131
Web: www.surecraft.com
SIC: 1751 Carpentry work

(P-1062)
TAYLOR TRIM & SUPPLY INC
Also Called: Finish Carpentry
2342 Meyers Ave, Escondido (92029-1008)
PHONE...................................760 740-2000
Timothy P Taylor, *CEO*
Sarah Garcia, *
Marlene Taylor, *
▲ **EMP:** 75 **EST:** 1990
SQ FT: 13,200
SALES (est): 15.75MM **Privately Held**
Web: www.taylortrim.com
SIC: 1751 Finish and trim carpentry

(P-1063)
TRIMCO FINISH INC
3130 W Harvard St, Santa Ana
(92704-3937)
PHONE...................................714 708-0300
EMP: 160
Web: www.trimcofinish.com
SIC: 1751 Finish and trim carpentry

(P-1064)
TWR ENTERPRISES INC
1661 Railroad St, Corona (92878-5003)
PHONE...................................951 279-2000
Thomas W Rhodes, *Pr*
EMP: 200 **EST:** 1985
SQ FT: 20,000
SALES (est): 7.76MM **Privately Held**
Web: www.twrframing.com
SIC: 1751 Framing contractor

(P-1065)
VORTEX INDUSTRIES LLC (PA)
Also Called: Vortex Doors
20 Odyssey, Irvine (92618-3144)
PHONE...................................714 434-8000
Elizabeth Turner Everett, *CEO*
▲ **EMP:** 25 **EST:** 1937
SQ FT: 10,000
SALES (est): 144.97MM
SALES (corp-wide): 144.97MM **Privately
Held**
Web: www.vortexdoors.com
SIC: 1751 3441 7699 Garage door,
installation or erection; Fabricated structural
metal; Door and window repair

(P-1066)
WESLAR INC
28310 Constellation Rd, Valencia
(91355-5078)
PHONE...................................661 702-1362
Larry Kern, *Pr*
Wes Toy, *
EMP: 100 **EST:** 1981
SQ FT: 5,500
SALES (est): 6.6MM **Privately Held**
SIC: 1751 Framing contractor

(P-1067)
WIN-DOR INC (PA)
450 Delta Ave, Brea (92821-2935)
PHONE...................................714 576-2030
TOLL FREE: 800
Gary Templin, *CEO*
Wolfgang Wirthgen, *
EMP: 170 **EST:** 1994
SQ FT: 73,000

SALES (est): 46.75MM **Privately Held**
Web: www.windorsystems.com
SIC: 1751 3446 Window and door
(prefabricated) installation; Guards, made
from pipe

1752 Floor Laying And Floor Work, Nec

(P-1068)
HOME CARPET INVESTMENT INC (PA)
Also Called: Americas Finest Carpet
Company
730 Design Ct Ste 401, Chula Vista
(91911-6160)
PHONE...................................619 262-8040
Carlos Ledesma, *CEO*
EMP: 81 **EST:** 1998
SQ FT: 2,500
SALES (est): 9.76MM **Privately Held**
Web: www.americasfinestcarpet.com
SIC: 1752 7217 Carpet laying; Carpet and
upholstery cleaning

(P-1069)
HY-TECH TILE INC
1130 Palmyrita Ave Ste 350, Riverside
(92507-1706)
P.O. Box 5577 (92517-5577)
PHONE...................................951 788-0550
Brian Lyman, *Pr*
Tom Shoemaker, *
Cristina Olteanu, *
Narcis Postolache, *
EMP: 110 **EST:** 1994
SQ FT: 12,000
SALES (est): 13.33MM **Privately Held**
Web: www.hytechtile.com
SIC: 1752 1743 Ceramic floor tile installation
; Terrazzo, tile, marble and mosaic work

(P-1070)
J W FLOOR COVERING INC (PA)
Also Called: J. W. Floor Covering
9881 Carroll Centre Rd, San Diego
(92126-4554)
PHONE...................................858 536-8565
John Wallace, *Owner*
John S Wallace, *
Gary Grado, *
EMP: 140 **EST:** 1983
SQ FT: 20,500
SALES (est): 15.41MM
SALES (corp-wide): 15.41MM **Privately
Held**
Web: www.jwfloor.com
SIC: 1752 Floor laying and floor work, nec

1761 Roofing, Siding, And Sheetmetal Work

(P-1071)
A PREMAN ROOFING INC
Also Called: A Preman Roofing
875 34th St, San Diego (92102-3331)
PHONE...................................619 276-1700
Aaron Preman, *CEO*
EMP: 75 **EST:** 2003
SALES (est): 29.93MM **Privately Held**
Web: www.premanroofing.com
SIC: 1761 1711 Roofing contractor; Solar
energy contractor

(P-1072)
ACTION ROOFING COMPANY LLC

Also Called: Action Roofing
534 E Ortega St, Santa Barbara
(93103-3016)
PHONE...................................805 966-3696
John J Martin Junior, *Pr*
Peggy Martin, *
Steve Martin, *
Sharon Fritz, *
EMP: 70 **EST:** 1985
SQ FT: 5,000
SALES (est): 7.38MM **Privately Held**
Web: www.aroofing.com
SIC: 1761 Roofing contractor

(P-1073)
BEST CONTRACTING SERVICES INC (PA)
Also Called: Construction
19027 S Hamilton Ave, Gardena
(90248-4408)
PHONE...................................310 328-9176
Sean Tabazadeh, *CEO*
Modjtaba Tabazadeh, *
Fatemeh Tabazadeh, *
▲ **EMP:** 400 **EST:** 1982
SQ FT: 57,000
SALES (est): 99.21MM
SALES (corp-wide): 99.21MM **Privately
Held**
Web: www.bestcontracting.com
SIC: 1761 Roofing contractor

(P-1074)
BLIGH ROOF CO
Also Called: Bligh Pacific
11043 Forest Pl, Santa Fe Springs
(90670-3905)
P.O. Box 3083 (90670-0083)
PHONE...................................562 944-9753
EMP: 75 **EST:** 1976
SALES (est): 7.27MM **Privately Held**
Web: www.bligh.com
SIC: 1761 Roofing contractor

(P-1075)
CHALLENGER SHEET METAL INC
9353 Abraham Way Ste A, Santee
(92071-5641)
PHONE...................................619 596-8040
Joel Quinonez, *CEO*
Robert Basso, *
▲ **EMP:** 80 **EST:** 1987
SQ FT: 18,000
SALES (est): 7.18MM **Privately Held**
Web: www.challengersm.com
SIC: 1761 Sheet metal work, nec

(P-1076)
CMF INC
Also Called: Custom Metal Fabricators
1317 W Grove Ave, Orange (92865-4137)
PHONE...................................714 637-2409
David Duclett, *CEO*
Mark Allen, *
Darren Sagert, *
EMP: 100 **EST:** 1956
SQ FT: 11,000
SALES (est): 31.58MM **Privately Held**
Web: www.cmfinc.com
SIC: 1761 Sheet metal work, nec

(P-1077)
DANNY LETNER INC
Also Called: Letner Roofing Company
1490 N Glassell St, Orange (92867-3612)
PHONE...................................714 633-0030
EMP: 230 **EST:** 1957
SALES (est): 48.05MM **Privately Held**
Web: www.letner.com

SIC: 1761 Roofing contractor

(P-1078)
DRI COMMERCIAL CORPORATION
Also Called: D R I
2081 Business Center Dr Ste 195, Irvine (92612-1116)
PHONE.....................949 266-1900
EMP: 159
Web: www.dricommercial.com
SIC: 1761 Roofing contractor

(P-1079)
DRI COMPANIES
2081 Business Center Dr Ste 195, Irvine (92612-1116)
PHONE.....................949 266-1900
EMP: 264
Web: www.dricompanies.com
SIC: 1761 Roofing contractor

(P-1080)
DUKE PACIFIC INC
13950 Monte Vista Ave, Chino (91710-5535)
P.O. Box 1800 (91708-1800)
PHONE.....................909 591-0191
Gregory C Severson, Pr
Judith E Braaten, *
EMP: 100 EST: 1958
SQ FT: 10,000
SALES (est): 4.6MM Privately Held
Web: www.dukepacific.com
SIC: 1761 Roofing contractor

(P-1081)
EBERHARD
15220 Raymer St, Van Nuys (91405-1065)
PHONE.....................818 782-4604
Brian Lee Mowatt, CEO
Dave Stefko, Sr VP
EMP: 150 EST: 1976
SALES (est): 8.16MM Privately Held
Web: www.eberhardco.com
SIC: 1761 1799 Roofing contractor; Waterproofing

(P-1082)
EDJE-ENTERPRISES
18500 Pasadena St Ste B, Lake Elsinore (92530-2775)
PHONE.....................951 245-7070
Edward Joseph Jennen, CEO
Maryjane Jennen, *
EMP: 82 EST: 2006
SALES (est): 2.45MM Privately Held
Web: www.edje-enterprises.com
SIC: 1761 Architectural sheet metal work

(P-1083)
EHMCKE SHEET METAL CORP
840 W 19th St, National City (91950-5406)
P.O. Box 13010 (92170-3010)
PHONE.....................619 477-6484
John F Cornell, CEO
Dennis Isaacs, *
Dennis Stainbrook, *
Richard Parra, *
▲ EMP: 55 EST: 1927
SQ FT: 25,000
SALES (est): 9.66MM Privately Held
Web: www.ehmckesheetmetal.com
SIC: 1761 8712 3446 Sheet metal work, nec; Architectural services; Architectural metalwork

(P-1084)
GES SHEET METAL INC
14531 Fontlee Ln, Fontana (92335-2557)
PHONE.....................909 598-3332
Michelle Lee, Pr
Glenn E Schuske Junior, CEO
Tootie Schuske, *
Glenn E Schushke Senior, Stockholder
EMP: 70 EST: 1972
SQ FT: 10,500
SALES (est): 6.89MM Privately Held
Web: www.gessheetmetal.com
SIC: 1761 1791 Architectural sheet metal work; Structural steel erection

(P-1085)
HERBERT MALARKEY ROOFING CO
9301 Garfield Ave, South Gate (90280-3804)
PHONE.....................562 806-8000
John Stromme, Mgr
EMP: 72
Web: www.malarkeyroofing.com
SIC: 1761 Roofing contractor
HQ: Herbert Malarkey Roofing Company
3131 N Columbia Blvd
Portland OR 97217
503 283-1191

(P-1086)
HOWARD ROOFING COMPANY INC
245 N Mountain View Ave, Pomona (91767-5629)
PHONE.....................909 622-5598
Larry K Malekow, Pr
Ron A Malekow, *
Mitch T Caldwell, *
EMP: 70 EST: 1977
SQ FT: 27,000
SALES (est): 9.36MM Privately Held
Web: www.howardroofing.com
SIC: 1761 Roofing contractor

(P-1087)
KAISER AIR CONDITIONING AND SHEET METAL INC
Also Called: Kaiser Air Conditioning
600 Pacific Ave, Oxnard (93030-7318)
PHONE.....................805 988-1800
EMP: 25 EST: 1981
SALES (est): 7.97MM Privately Held
Web: www.kaiserac.com
SIC: 1761 1711 3444 Architectural sheet metal work; Warm air heating and air conditioning contractor; Sheet metalwork

(P-1088)
LA ROCQUE BETTER ROOFS INC
9077 Arrow Rte Ste 100, Rancho Cucamonga (91730-4430)
PHONE.....................909 476-2699
Guy D Larocque, Pr
Linda Robinson, *
EMP: 75 EST: 1984
SALES (est): 6.8MM Privately Held
Web: www.larocquebetterroofs.com
SIC: 1761 Roofing contractor

(P-1089)
LEONARD ROOFING INC
43280 Business Park Dr Ste 107, Temecula (92590-3676)
PHONE.....................951 506-3811
Bruce S Leonard, Pr
▲ EMP: 156 EST: 2004
SALES (est): 47.05MM Privately Held

SIC: 1761 Roofing contractor

(P-1090)
PACIFIC STRUCFRAME LLC
1600 Chicago Ave Ste R11, Riverside (92507-2040)
PHONE.....................951 405-8536
John B Hanna, Pr
EMP: 91 EST: 2017
SQ FT: 2,000
SALES (est): 9.54MM Privately Held
Web: www.pacificstrucframe.com
SIC: 1761 Roofing, siding, and sheetmetal work

(P-1091)
PERFORMANCE SHEETS LLC
440 Baldwin Park Blvd, City Of Industry (91746-1407)
PHONE.....................626 333-0195
Mike Crosson, Pr
Michael Feterik, Managing Member*
Greg Hall, Managing Member*
Forest Felvey, *
▲ EMP: 125 EST: 2006
SALES (est): 28.07MM Privately Held
Web: www.performancesheets.net
SIC: 1761 Sheet metal work, nec
HQ: Smurfit Kappa North America Llc
125 E John Crptr Fwy Ste
Irving TX 75062
800 306-8326

(P-1092)
PETERSEN-DEAN INC
Also Called: Petersendean
2210 S Dupont Dr, Anaheim (92806-6104)
PHONE.....................714 629-9670
Greg O'donnell, Brnch Mgr
EMP: 105
Web: www.petersendean.com
SIC: 1761 Roofing contractor
PA: Petersen-Dean, Inc.
6950 Preston Ave

(P-1093)
PLATINUM ROOFING INC
11500 W Olympic Blvd Ste 530, Los Angeles (90064-1676)
PHONE.....................408 280-5028
Bill Shevlin, CEO
Sean Marzola, *
EMP: 80 EST: 2000
SALES (est): 9.64MM Privately Held
Web: www.platinumroofinginc.com
SIC: 1761 Roofing contractor

(P-1094)
ROYAL WESTLAKE ROOFING LLC
Also Called: Boral Industries
3093 Industry St Ste A, Oceanside (92054-4895)
PHONE.....................760 967-0827
Jose Davila, Mgr
EMP: 122
Web: www.westlakeroyalroofing.com
SIC: 1761 Roofing contractor
HQ: Royal Westlake Roofing Llc
2801 Post Oak Blvd # 600
Houston TX 77056
800 658-8004

(P-1095)
SBB ROOFING INC (PA)
Also Called: Bilt-Well Roofing & Mtl Co
3310 Verdugo Rd, Los Angeles (90065-2845)
P.O. Box 65827 (90065-0827)
PHONE.....................323 254-2888

Bruce Radenbaugh, Pr
Steven Radenbaugh, *
EMP: 180 EST: 1984
SQ FT: 5,000
SALES (est): 4.07MM
SALES (corp-wide): 4.07MM Privately Held
Web: www.biltwellroofing.com
SIC: 1761 Roofing contractor

(P-1096)
SOUTHWEST SPECIALTY CONTRS LLC
Also Called: Southwest Specialty Contrs
705 E Harrison St Ste 100, Corona (92879-1398)
PHONE.....................951 987-8008
EMP: 87
SALES (corp-wide): 26.58MM Privately Held
Web: www.swscontractors.com
SIC: 1761 1799 1742 Ceilings, metal: erection and repair; Insulation of pipes and boilers; Acoustical and insulation work
PA: Southwest Specialty Contractors Llc
5990 S Buffalo Dr
702 382-7972

(P-1097)
STANDARD BLDG SOLUTIONS INC
Also Called: GAF Materials
6505 Zerker Rd, Shafter (93263-9614)
PHONE.....................661 387-1110
Phil Halpin, Genl Mgr
EMP: 100
SALES (corp-wide): 6.35B Privately Held
Web: www.gaf.com
SIC: 1761 Roofing contractor
HQ: Standard Building Solutions Inc.
1 Campus Dr
Parsippany NJ 07054

(P-1098)
TINCO SHEET METAL INC
958 N Eastern Ave, Los Angeles (90063-1308)
PHONE.....................323 263-0511
Brian Powell, Pr
Michael Nevarez, *
Laura Nevarez, *
Jim Stock, *
▲ EMP: 250 EST: 2003
SQ FT: 18,000
SALES (est): 38MM Privately Held
Web: www.tincosheetmetal.com
SIC: 1761 Roofing contractor

(P-1099)
WEISS SHEET METAL COMPANY
Also Called: Metcoe Skylight Specialites
1715 W 135th St, Gardena (90249-2507)
PHONE.....................310 354-2700
Andre Sarai, Pr
Steve Linder, *
Morris Saraie, *
▼ EMP: 45 EST: 1937
SQ FT: 33,000
SALES (est): 8.82MM Privately Held
Web: www.metcoe.com
SIC: 1761 3211 Skylight installation; Skylight glass

(P-1100)
WESTERN PACIFIC ROOFING CORP
3462 E La Campana Way, Palm Springs (92262-5416)
PHONE.....................661 273-1336

Sig Hall, *Mgr*
EMP: 110
SALES (corp-wide): 11.85MM **Privately Held**
Web: www.westpacroof.com
SIC: 1761 1799 Roofing contractor; Waterproofing
PA: Western Pacific Roofing Corp.
2229 E Avenue Q
661 273-1336

1771 Concrete Work

(P-1101)
ARCIERO BROTHERS INC
5614 E La Palma Ave, Anaheim (92807-2110)
PHONE..............................714 238-6600
EMP: 130
SIC: 1771 Concrete repair

(P-1102)
ASACRETE INC
7117 Valjean Ave, Van Nuys (91406-3917)
PHONE..............................818 398-3400
Saeid Alavi, *Pr*
EMP: 200 **EST:** 2017
SALES (est): 45MM **Privately Held**
Web: www.asacrete.com
SIC: 1771 Concrete work

(P-1103)
B & M CONTRACTORS INC
4473 Cochran St, Simi Valley (93063-3065)
PHONE..............................805 581-5480
Dave Moore, *Pr*
Randall Bilsland, *
EMP: 70 **EST:** 2000
SALES (est): 1.55MM **Privately Held**
Web: www.bamconcrete.com
SIC: 1771 Concrete work

(P-1104)
BAYMARR CONSTRUCTORS INC
6950 Mcdivitt Dr, Bakersfield (93313-2046)
P.O. Box 22074 (93390-2074)
PHONE..............................661 395-1676
Eric Recktenwald, *CEO*
Jack Whitney, *
Pat Howes, *
EMP: 111 **EST:** 1988
SQ FT: 10,000
SALES (est): 9.42MM **Privately Held**
Web: www.baymarr.com
SIC: 1771 Concrete work

(P-1105)
BEDROCK COMPANY
2970 Myers St, Riverside (92503-5524)
PHONE..............................951 273-1931
Glenn E Jackson Junior, *CEO*
Carlene Jackson, *Corporate Secretary**
EMP: 70 **EST:** 1993
SQ FT: 5,000
SALES (est): 18.26MM **Privately Held**
Web: www.thebedrockco.com
SIC: 1771 Concrete work

(P-1106)
BEN F SMITH INC
Also Called: Concrete Construction
8655 Miramar Pl Ste B, San Diego (92121-2567)
PHONE..............................858 271-4320
Stuart Shelton, *Mgr*
EMP: 180
SALES (corp-wide): 8.67MM **Privately Held**
Web: www.benfsmithinc.com
SIC: 1771 Concrete work
PA: Ben F. Smith, Inc.
4420 Baldwin Ave
626 444-2543

(P-1107)
CASPER COMPANY
3825 Bancroft Dr, Spring Valley (91977-2122)
PHONE..............................619 589-6001
Roger Casper, *CEO*
William R Haithcock, *
Ken S Ringer, *
Greg T Casper, *
Steven Casper, *
EMP: 143 **EST:** 1984
SQ FT: 6,000
SALES (est): 23.71MM **Privately Held**
Web: www.caspercompany.com
SIC: 1771 Concrete work

(P-1108)
CELL-CRETE CORPORATION (PA)
Also Called: Cell-Crete
135 Railroad Ave, Monrovia (91016-4652)
PHONE..............................626 357-3500
EMP: 80 **EST:** 1965
SALES (est): 51.69MM
SALES (corp-wide): 51.69MM **Privately Held**
Web: www.cell-crete.com
SIC: 1771 Flooring contractor

(P-1109)
CEMENT CUTTING INC
3610 Hancock St Frnt, San Diego (92110-4335)
PHONE..............................619 296-9592
Harold O Grafton, *CEO*
John Gregory Becker, *
Steven Morgan, *
Steve Quinn, *
EMP: 80 **EST:** 1977
SQ FT: 7,000
SALES (est): 1.87MM **Privately Held**
Web: www.cementcutting.com
SIC: 1771 Concrete work

(P-1110)
CENTURY WEST CONCRETE INC
9782 Indiana Ave, Riverside (92503-5563)
PHONE..............................951 712-4065
Esteban Damian C Diaz, *CEO*
EMP: 310 **EST:** 2014
SALES (est): 7.45MM **Privately Held**
Web: www.centurywestconcrete.com
SIC: 1771 Concrete work

(P-1111)
COFFMAN SPECIALTIES INC (PA)
9685 Via Excelencia Ste 200, San Diego (92126-7500)
PHONE..............................858 536-3100
Colleen Coffman, *Pr*
Kevin Coffman, *
EMP: 247 **EST:** 1990
SQ FT: 6,000
SALES (est): 109.12MM **Privately Held**
Web: www.coffmanspecialties.com
SIC: 1771 Concrete work

(P-1112)
CORNERSTONE CONCRETE INC
255 Benjamin Dr, Corona (92879-6509)
PHONE..............................951 279-2221

Matthew R Valente, *Prin*
EMP: 87 **EST:** 2011
SALES (est): 5.6MM **Privately Held**
Web: www.contractorsincollaboration.com
SIC: 1771 Concrete work

(P-1113)
CRAWFORD ASSOCIATES
2635 E Chanslor Way, Blythe (92225-9805)
P.O. Box 807 (92226-0807)
PHONE..............................760 922-6804
Bill Crawford, *Pt*
Tommy Crawford, *Pt*
Cody Crawford, *Pt*
EMP: 27 **EST:** 1975
SQ FT: 1,500
SALES (est): 5.96MM **Privately Held**
Web: www.crawfordconcrete.com
SIC: 1771 3273 Concrete work; Ready-mixed concrete

(P-1114)
DEMCON CONCRETE CONTRS INC
Also Called: Demcon Concrete Contractor
13795 Blaisdell Pl Ste 202, Poway (92064-8896)
PHONE..............................858 748-5090
Derek Leffler, *Pr*
Edwin Stougton, *
Mike Wildley, *
Diane Leffler, *
EMP: 75 **EST:** 2000
SALES (est): 1.61MM **Privately Held**
Web: www.demconconcrete.com
SIC: 1771 Concrete work

(P-1115)
EKEDAL CONCRETE INC
19600 Fairchild Ste 123, Irvine (92612-2509)
PHONE..............................949 729-8082
Dave Ekedal, *Pr*
Ryan Ekedal, *
EMP: 100 **EST:** 1974
SALES (est): 5.78MM **Privately Held**
Web: www.ekedalconcrete.com
SIC: 1771 Concrete work

(P-1116)
GENERAL PAVEMENT MANAGEMENT INC
Also Called: GPM
850 Lawrence Dr Ste 100, Thousand Oaks (91320-1508)
PHONE..............................805 933-0909
EMP: 85 **EST:** 1957
SALES (est): 31.61MM **Privately Held**
Web: www.gpmpavement.com
SIC: 1771 1721 1611 Blacktop (asphalt) work ; Pavement marking contractor; Surfacing and paving

(P-1117)
GONSALVES & SANTUCCI INC
Also Called: Conco Cement Co
13052 Dahlia St, Fontana (92337-6926)
PHONE..............................909 350-0474
Steve Gonzales, *Pr*
EMP: 475
SALES (corp-wide): 164.76MM **Privately Held**
Web: www.conconow.com
SIC: 1771 Concrete pumping
PA: Gonsalves & Santucci, Inc.
5141 Commercial Cir
925 685-6799

(P-1118)
GUY YOCOM CONSTRUCTION INC (PA)
3299 Horseless Carriage Dr Ste H, Norco (92860-3604)
PHONE..............................951 284-3456
Guy W Yocom, *Prin*
Richard Majestic, *
Dave Kent, *
Greg Wilson, *
Shirley Kowalke, *
EMP: 212 **EST:** 1978
SQ FT: 41,000
SALES (est): 44.6MM
SALES (corp-wide): 44.6MM **Privately Held**
Web: www.yocominc.com
SIC: 1771 Concrete work

(P-1119)
HB PARKCO CONSTRUCTION INC (PA)
24795 State Highway 74, Perris (92570-8759)
PHONE..............................714 567-4752
Brett D Behrns, *VP*
W Adrian Hoyle, *
Micheal Barry, *
EMP: 394 **EST:** 2002
SALES (est): 2.56K
SALES (corp-wide): 2.56K **Privately Held**
Web: www.hbparkco.com
SIC: 1771 Parking lot construction

(P-1120)
HEIDI CORPORATION
Also Called: Donald J Schefflers Cnstr
727 N Vernon Ave, Azusa (91702-2232)
PHONE..............................626 333-6317
Donald J Scheffler, *Pr*
▲ **EMP:** 75 **EST:** 1990
SQ FT: 15,000
SALES (est): 1.46MM **Privately Held**
Web: www.donaldschefflerconstruction.com
SIC: 1771 Concrete work

(P-1121)
INLAND CC INC
Also Called: ICC
7010 Wyndham Hill Dr, Riverside (92506-7506)
PHONE..............................909 355-1318
Marvin Hawkins, *CEO*
Karen Hawkins, *
EMP: 150 **EST:** 1995
SALES (est): 9.9MM **Privately Held**
Web: www.inlandconcrete.net
SIC: 1771 Foundation and footing contractor

(P-1122)
JEZOWSKI & MARKEL CONTRS INC
749 N Poplar St, Orange (92868-1013)
PHONE..............................714 978-2222
Leonard Michael Barth, *Prin*
Joseph Dean, *
Dorothy Destefano, *
EMP: 145 **EST:** 1953
SQ FT: 4,500
SALES (est): 24.5MM **Privately Held**
Web: www.jmcontractors.com
SIC: 1771 Foundation and footing contractor

(P-1123)
JT WIMSATT CONTG CO INC (PA)
28064 Avenue Stanford Unit B, Valencia (91355-1160)
PHONE..............................661 775-8090

PRODUCTS & SVCS

John Ewing Wimsatt, *CEO*
John E Wimsatt Iii, *Pr*
Tricia Wimsatt, *
EMP: 270 **EST:** 1992
SALES (est): 38.45MM **Privately Held**
Web: www.jtwimsatt.com
SIC: 1771 Concrete work

(P-1124)
LARGO CONCRETE INC
1690 W Foothill Blvd Ste B, Upland
(91786-8433)
PHONE.....................909 981-7844
Paul Burkel, *Prin*
EMP: 219
Web: www.largoconcrete.com
SIC: 1771 Concrete work
PA: Largo Concrete, Inc.
       2741 Walnut Ave Fl 1

(P-1125)
LARGO CONCRETE INC (PA)
2741 Walnut Ave Ste 110, Tustin
(92780-7040)
PHONE.....................714 731-3600
EMP: 70 **EST:** 1989
SALES (est): 150.81MM **Privately Held**
Web: www.largoconcrete.com
SIC: 1771 Concrete work

(P-1126)
MORLEY CONSTRUCTION COMPANY (HQ)
3330 Ocean Park Blvd, Santa Monica
(90405-3202)
PHONE.....................310 399-1600
Mark Benjamin, *Pr*
Mark Benjamin, *Ch Bd*
Bert Lewitt, *
Reginald Jackson, *
Tod Paris, *
▲ **EMP:** 80 **EST:** 1947
SQ FT: 20,000
SALES (est): 21.69MM
SALES (corp-wide): 92.7MM **Privately Held**
Web: www.morleyconcrete.com
SIC: 1771 1522 1542 Concrete work;
   Condominium construction; Commercial
   and office building, new construction
PA: Morley Builders, Inc.
       3330 Ocean Park Blvd
       310 399-1600

(P-1127)
NED L WEBSTER CONCRETE CNSTR
8800 Grimes Canyon Rd, Moorpark
(93021-9768)
PHONE.....................805 529-4900
Ned Webster, *Prin*
EMP: 75 **EST:** 2000
SALES (est): 4.92MM **Privately Held**
SIC: 1771 Concrete work

(P-1128)
NMN CONSTRUCTION INC
2741 Walnut Ave Ste 110, Tustin
(92780-7040)
PHONE.....................714 389-2104
Kenneth Long, *CEO*
EMP: 100 **EST:** 1994
SALES (est): 4.08MM **Privately Held**
SIC: 1771 Driveway, parking lot, and
   blacktop contractors

(P-1129)
PACIFIC PAVINGSTONE INC
Also Called: Pacific Outdoor Living

8309 Tujunga Ave Unit 201, Sun Valley
(91352-3216)
PHONE.....................818 244-4000
Terry Morrill, *Pr*
Trent Morrill, *
Chad Morrill, *
EMP: 115 **EST:** 1999
SALES (est): 12.69MM **Privately Held**
Web: www.jacksturf.com
SIC: 1771 Driveway contractor

(P-1130)
PACIFIC STHWEST STRUCTURES INC
7845 Lemon Grove Way Ste A, Lemon
Grove (91945-1880)
PHONE.....................619 469-2323
Daniel Fitzgerald, *Pr*
EMP: 150 **EST:** 1995
SQ FT: 7,500
SALES (est): 14.6MM **Privately Held**
Web: www.pssiconcrete.com
SIC: 1771 Concrete work

(P-1131)
PACIFIC STRUCTURES SC INC (PA)
Also Called: Pacific Structures
1212 Abbot Kinney Blvd Apt A, Venice
(90291-2301)
PHONE.....................415 970-5434
Ross Edwards, *Ch Bd*
David E Williams, *Pr*
Ron Marano, *CFO*
Eric Horn, *Treas*
Scott Brauninger, *Dir*
EMP: 249 **EST:** 2008
SALES (est): 20.26MM
SALES (corp-wide): 20.26MM **Privately Held**
Web: www.pacific-structures.com
SIC: 1771 Concrete work

(P-1132)
PENHALL HOLDING COMPANY
1801 W Penhall Way, Anaheim
(92801-6700)
PHONE.....................714 772-6450
Kathy Wall, *Sec*
EMP: 94 **EST:** 2010
SALES (est): 8.75MM **Privately Held**
Web: www.penhall.com
SIC: 1771 Concrete work

(P-1133)
PETERSON BROTHERS CNSTR INC
Also Called: Pbc Companies
2929 E White Star Ave, Anaheim
(92806-2628)
PHONE.....................714 278-0488
Elden Peterson, *CEO*
Robert K Peterson, *
Patrick Burns, *
Mike Hoefnagels, *
Jack Saldate, *
▲ **EMP:** 600 **EST:** 1983
SALES (est): 38.06MM **Privately Held**
Web: www.pbccompanies.com
SIC: 1771 3531 1741 Concrete work; Pavers
   ; Concrete block masonry laying

(P-1134)
SANTA ANA CREEK DEVELOPMENT COMPANY
Also Called: Mark Company
2288 N Batavia St, Orange (92865-3106)
PHONE.....................714 685-3462
EMP: 100 **EST:** 1964

SALES (est): 24.97MM **Privately Held**
Web: www.themarkco.com
SIC: 1771 1611 1623 Concrete work;
   Grading; Pipeline construction, nsk

(P-1135)
SOUTHLAND PAVING INC
361 N Hale Ave, Escondido (92029-1798)
PHONE.....................760 747-6895
Richard Fleck, *CEO*
Daniel Devlin, *
Robert Kennedy, *
Anne Fleck, *
EMP: 75 **EST:** 1983
SQ FT: 35,000
SALES (est): 24.66MM **Privately Held**
Web: www.southlandpaving.com
SIC: 1771 2951 Blacktop (asphalt) work;
   Asphalt paving mixtures and blocks

(P-1136)
STRUCTRAL PRSRVTION SYSTEMS LL
11800 Monarch St, Garden Grove
(92841-2113)
PHONE.....................714 891-9080
Mike Szoke, *Mgr*
EMP: 248
Web: www.structural.net
SIC: 1771 Concrete repair
HQ: Structural Preservation Systems, Llc
       10150 Old Columbia Rd
       Columbia MD 21046

(P-1137)
SUPERIOR GUNITE (PA)
12306 Van Nuys Blvd, Sylmar
(91342-6086)
PHONE.....................818 896-9199
Anthony L Federico, *Pr*
David Bowers, *
Steve Crawford, *
EMP: 145 **EST:** 1964
SQ FT: 5,000
SALES (est): 39.75MM
SALES (corp-wide): 39.75MM **Privately Held**
Web: www.shotcrete.com
SIC: 1771 Gunite contractor

(P-1138)
TEAM C CONSTRUCTION
1272 Greenfield Dr, El Cajon (92021-3316)
PHONE.....................619 579-6572
David Clarke, *Pr*
EMP: 70 **EST:** 1995
SQ FT: 2,000
SALES (est): 6.14MM **Privately Held**
Web: www.teamcconstruction.com
SIC: 1771 Concrete work

(P-1139)
TEAM FINISH INC
155 Arovista Cir Ste A, Brea (92821-3842)
PHONE.....................714 671-9190
Thomas M Stangl, *Pr*
Mary Stangl, *
EMP: 80 **EST:** 1996
SQ FT: 1,200
SALES (est): 10.81MM **Privately Held**
SIC: 1771 Concrete work

(P-1140)
UNITED BROTHERS CONCRETE INC
73700 Dinah Shore Dr, Palm Desert
(92211-0813)
PHONE.....................760 346-1013
Lauro Barcenas, *Pr*

Luis Barcenas, *
Oscar Barcenas, *
EMP: 150 **EST:** 1999
SALES (est): 4.87MM **Privately Held**
SIC: 1771 Concrete work

(P-1141)
Z-BEST CONCRETE INC
2575 Main St, Riverside (92501-2238)
PHONE.....................951 774-1870
Roger Crott, *Pr*
Jerry Faust, *
EMP: 80 **EST:** 1989
SQ FT: 2,400
SALES (est): 13.71MM **Privately Held**
SIC: 1771 1741 Concrete work; Masonry
   and other stonework

1781 Water Well Drilling

(P-1142)
BRAX COMPANY INC
Also Called: Frederick Pump Company
31248 Valley Center Rd, Valley Center
(92082-6757)
PHONE.....................760 749-2209
Steven Tweed, *Pr*
EMP: 37 **EST:** 1985
SQ FT: 3,000
SALES (est): 10.23MM **Privately Held**
Web: www.braxcompany.com
SIC: 1781 5084 3563 Water well drilling;
   Water pumps (industrial); Air and gas
   compressors

(P-1143)
GREGG DRILLING LLC
2726 Walnut Ave, Signal Hill (90755-1832)
PHONE.....................562 427-6899
John Gregg, *Pr*
Patrick Keating, *
Chris Christensen, *
Sonja De Keyser-meurs, *Sec*
EMP: 160 **EST:** 2018
SQ FT: 17,000
SALES (est): 9.88MM **Privately Held**
Web: www.greggdrilling.com
SIC: 1781 Water well drilling

(P-1144)
KENAI DRILLING LIMITED
2651 Patton Way, Bakersfield (93308-5745)
PHONE.....................661 587-0117
Gene Kramer, *Bmch Mgr*
EMP: 131
Web: www.kenaidrilling.com
SIC: 1781 Servicing, water wells
PA: Kenai Drilling Limited
       6430 Cat Canyon Rd

(P-1145)
YELLOW JACKET DRLG SVCS LLC
9460 Lucas Ranch Rd, Rancho Cucamonga
(91730-5743)
PHONE.....................909 989-8563
EMP: 86
SALES (corp-wide): 21.45MM **Privately Held**
Web: www.yellowjacketdrilling.com
SIC: 1781 Water well drilling
PA: Yellow Jacket Drilling Services, Llc
       3922 E Univ Dr Ste 1
       602 453-3252

(P-1146)
ZIM INDUSTRIES INC
Bakersfield Well & Pump Co
7212 Fruitvale Ave, Bakersfield
(93308-9529)

PHONE..............................661 393-9661
John Zimmerer, *Mgr*
EMP: 140
SALES (corp-wide): 19.33MM **Privately Held**
Web: www.zimindustries.com
SIC: 1781 7699 Servicing, water wells;
Pumps and pumping equipment repair
PA: Zim Industries, Inc.
4532 E Jefferson Ave
559 834-1551

1791 Structural Steel Erection

(P-1147)
ALLIED STEEL CO INC
1027 Palmyrita Ave, Riverside
(92507-1701)
PHONE..............................951 241-7000
Brian P Chapman, *Pr*
Perry K Chapman, *
Nicky Chapman, *
Jeanette Chapman, *
EMP: 60 **EST:** 1944
SQ FT: 48,000
SALES (est): 6.7MM **Privately Held**
Web: www.alliedsteelco.com
SIC: 1791 3441 Structural steel erection;
Fabricated structural metal

(P-1148)
ANVIL STEEL CORPORATION
Also Called: Anvil Iron
134 W 168th St, Gardena (90248-2729)
PHONE..............................310 329-5811
Gerry Bustrum, *CEO*
Paul Schifino, *
Mike Norton, *
▲ **EMP:** 90 **EST:** 1973
SQ FT: 4,000
SALES (est): 22.21MM **Privately Held**
Web: www.anvilsteel.com
SIC: 1791 Iron work, structural

(P-1149)
ARTIMEX IRON INC
315 Cypress Ln, El Cajon (92020-1695)
PHONE..............................619 444-3155
EMP: 116 **EST:** 1973
SALES (est): 4.06MM **Privately Held**
Web: www.artimexiron.com
SIC: 1791 Iron work, structural

(P-1150)
BAPKO METAL INC
721 S Parker St Ste 300, Orange
(92000-4702)
PHONE..............................714 639-9380
Fred Bagatourian, *Pr*
Heather Wiliams, *
Clint Rieber, *
EMP: 80 **EST:** 1978
SALES (est): 22.73MM **Privately Held**
Web: www.bapko.com
SIC: 1791 3441 Structural steel erection;
Fabricated structural metal

(P-1151)
CAL-STATE STEEL CORPORATION
1397 Lynnmere Dr, Thousand Oaks
(91360-1946)
PHONE..............................310 632-2772
Salvador Valenzuelam, *CEO*
Les Furdek, *
David Olson, *
▲ **EMP:** 150 **EST:** 1963
SQ FT: 10,000
SALES (est): 2.62MM **Privately Held**

Web: www.calstatesteel.com
SIC: 1791 Iron work, structural

(P-1152)
COAST IRON & STEEL CO
12300 Lakeland Rd, Santa Fe Springs
(90670-3869)
P.O. Box 2846 (90670-0846)
PHONE..............................562 946-4421
Greg White, *Pr*
Cyndi White Cramer, *Stockholder*
Carrie White, *Stockholder*
Jared White, *Stockholder*
Duane Westrup, *
▲ **EMP:** 50 **EST:** 1953
SQ FT: 360,000
SALES (est): 10.34MM **Privately Held**
Web: www.rsac.com
SIC: 1791 3441 Structural steel erection;
Fabricated structural metal

(P-1153)
HEAVY METAL STEEL COMPANY INC
Also Called: Heavy Metal Steel
12130 Lomica Dr, San Diego (92128-2716)
PHONE..............................858 433-4800
Linda Rosenberg, *Pr*
Linda D Rosenberg, *
Arnold Rosenberg, *
EMP: 25 **EST:** 2014
SALES (est): 2MM **Privately Held**
Web: www.heavymetalsteel.com
SIC: 1791 3449 Structural steel erection;
Fabricated bar joists and concrete
reinforcing bars

(P-1154)
INTEGRITY REBAR PLACERS
1345 Nandina Ave, Perris (92571-9402)
PHONE..............................951 696-6843
Kenneth Negrete, *Pr*
Richard Rabay, *
Mario Duran, *Prin*
▲ **EMP:** 200 **EST:** 2005
SALES (est): 8.49MM **Privately Held**
Web: www.integrityrebarplacers.com
SIC: 1791 Structural steel erection

(P-1155)
KCB TOWERS INC
27260 Meines St, Highland (92346-4223)
P.O. Box 100 (92346-0100)
PHONE..............................909 862-0322
S Lynn Bogh, *CEO*
Miles Bogh, *
Sharon Bogh, *
EMP: 100 **EST:** 1982
SQ FT: 12,000
SALES (est): 7.14MM **Privately Held**
Web: www.kcbtowers.com
SIC: 1791 3441 Concrete reinforcement,
placing of; Fabricated structural metal

(P-1156)
LEGACY REINFORCING STEEL LLC
1057 Tierra Del Rey Ste F, Chula Vista
(91910-7882)
PHONE..............................619 646-0205
Brian Briggs, *Pr*
EMP: 75 **EST:** 2019
SALES (est): 2.65MM **Privately Held**
SIC: 1791 3449 Structural steel erection;
Bars, concrete reinforcing: fabricated steel

(P-1157)
M BAR C CONSTRUCTION INC
1770 La Costa Meadows Dr, San Marcos
(92078-5106)

PHONE..............................760 744-4131
Michael Jason Ianni, *CEO*
EMP: 85 **EST:** 2005
SALES (est): 63.87MM **Privately Held**
Web: www.mbarcconstruction.com
SIC: 1791 1623 Structural steel erection;
Electric power line construction

(P-1158)
MARTINEZ STEEL CORPORATION
1500 S Haven Ave Ste 150, Ontario
(91761-2971)
PHONE..............................909 946-0686
Harry Williams, *CEO*
Debbie Martinez, *
Joe Martinez, *
EMP: 200 **EST:** 1994
SALES (est): 26.18MM **Privately Held**
Web: www.martinezsteel.com
SIC: 1791 Structural steel erection

(P-1159)
MILLENNIUM REINFORCING INC
1046 Calle Recodo, San Clemente
(92673-6261)
P.O. Box 73698 (92673-0124)
PHONE..............................949 361-9730
Matthew Taylor, *CEO*
EMP: 265 **EST:** 2009
SALES (est): 8.11MM **Privately Held**
Web: www.millenniumreinforcing.com
SIC: 1791 Structural steel erection

(P-1160)
QUALITY REINFORCING INC
13275 Gregg St, Poway (92064-7120)
PHONE..............................858 748-8400
Bryan Miller, *Pr*
▲ **EMP:** 85 **EST:** 1987
SQ FT: 5,000
SALES (est): 2.3MM **Privately Held**
Web: www.qualityreinforcing.com
SIC: 1791 Concrete reinforcement, placing of

(P-1161)
R & B REINFORCING STEEL CORP
13581 5th St, Chino (91710-5166)
PHONE..............................909 591-1726
David Mcdaniel, *CEO*
Robert Bessette, *
Nancy Bessette, *
EMP: 80 **EST:** 1983
SQ FT: 30,000
SALES (est): 3.61MM **Privately Held**
Web: www.rbsteel.net
SIC: 1791 Iron work, structural

(P-1162)
REBAR ENGINEERING INC
10706 Painter Ave, Santa Fe Springs
(90670-4581)
P.O. Box 3986 (90670-1986)
PHONE..............................562 946-2461
Charles L Krebs, *Pr*
Jack Garroutte, *
EMP: 250 **EST:** 1963
SQ FT: 6,500
SALES (est): 21.68MM **Privately Held**
Web: www.rebarengineering.com
SIC: 1791 Concrete reinforcement, placing of

(P-1163)
RIKA CORPORATION
Also Called: Diversified Metal Works
332 W Brenna Ln, Orange (92867-5637)
PHONE..............................949 830-9050
John E Ferguson, *CEO*

Justin Ferguson, *
▲ **EMP:** 100 **EST:** 1977
SQ FT: 8,000
SALES (est): 3.92MM **Privately Held**
Web: www.dmwk.com
SIC: 1791 Structural steel erection

1793 Glass And Glazing Work

(P-1164)
ELICC AMERICAS CORPORATION
13475 Danielson St Ste 250, Poway
(92064-8859)
PHONE..............................760 233-0066
Yizeng Li, *CEO*
Ethan Li, *CEO*
Helen Fang, *
Rick Eckstrom, *
EMP: 160 **EST:** 2015
SALES (est): 14.16MM **Privately Held**
Web: www.eliccgroup.com
SIC: 1793 Glass and glazing work

(P-1165)
GIROUX GLASS INC (PA)
Also Called: Giroux
850 W Washington Blvd Ste 200, Los
Angeles (90015-3359)
PHONE..............................213 747-7406
Nataline Lomedico, *CEO*
Anne-merelie Murrell, *Ch Bd*
Stephanie Lamb, *
Robert Bob Burkhammer, *Ex VP*
Bob Linford, *
▲ **EMP:** 120 **EST:** 1946
SALES (est): 77.6MM
SALES (corp-wide): 77.6MM **Privately Held**
Web: www.girouxglass.com
SIC: 1793 Glass and glazing work

(P-1166)
RYNOCLAD TECHNOLOGIES INC
780 E Francis St Ste M, Ontario
(91761-5553)
PHONE..............................951 264-3441
Victor Wright, *CEO*
Troy Thomas, *
EMP: 200 **EST:** 2011
SALES (est): 25MM **Privately Held**
Web: www.rynoclad.com
SIC: 1793 Glass and glazing work

(P-1167)
TOWER GLASS INC
9570 Pathway St Ste A, Santee
(92071-4100)
PHONE..............................619 596-6199
Evelyn Dee Swaim, *CEO*
Barry Swaim, *
EMP: 100 **EST:** 1989
SQ FT: 15,000
SALES (est): 8.05MM **Privately Held**
Web: www.towerglass.com
SIC: 1793 Glass and glazing work

(P-1168)
WALTERS & WOLF GLASS COMPANY
1975 Puddingstone Dr, La Verne
(91750-5818)
PHONE..............................909 392-1961
Tom Lackey, *Brnch Mgr*
EMP: 83
SALES (corp-wide): 86.87MM **Privately Held**
Web: www.waltersandwolf.com

SIC: **1793** Glass and glazing work
PA: Walters & Wolf Glass Company
41450 Boscell Rd
510 490-1115

(P-1169)
WOODBRIDGE GLASS INC
3441 W Macarthur Blvd, Santa Ana
(92704-6805)
PHONE...............714 838-4444
Virginia Siciliani, *Pr*
John Siciliani, *
Jim Siciliani, *
▲ **EMP: 205 EST:** 1981
SALES (est): 47.51MM **Privately Held**
Web: www.woodbridgeglass.com
SIC: 1793 5231 Glass and glazing work;
Glass, leaded or stained

1794 Excavation Work

(P-1170)
CALEX ENGINEERING INC
Also Called: Calex Engineering Co.
23651 Pine St, Newhall (91321-3106)
PHONE...............661 254-1866
Ryan Seitz, *Pr*
Mike Neilson, *
EMP: 70 EST: 1975
SQ FT: 1,800
SALES (est): 33.69MM **Privately Held**
Web: www.calex.net
SIC: 1794 Excavation work

(P-1171)
GUINN CORPORATION
6533 Rosedale Hwy, Bakersfield
(93308-5903)
P.O. Box 1339 (93302-1339)
PHONE...............661 325-6109
Gary Guinn, *CEO*
Tim Guinn, *
Jeff Affonso, *
EMP: 75 EST: 1952
SQ FT: 3,600
SALES (est): 9.31MM **Privately Held**
Web: www.guinnconstruction.com
SIC: 1794 Excavation and grading, building
construction

(P-1172)
LOVCO CONSTRUCTION INC
Also Called: Lovco Construction
1300 E Burnett St, Signal Hill (90755-3512)
P.O. Box 90335 (90809-0335)
PHONE...............562 595-1601
Terry C Lovingier, *Pr*
Steve Barnett, *
Katie Lovingier, *
Matt Lovinger, *
Mike Mcgougan, *VP*
EMP: 125 EST: 1988
SQ FT: 2,500
SALES (est): 22.19MM **Privately Held**
Web: www.lovcoconstruction.com
SIC: 1794 1771 1611 Excavation and
grading, building construction; Concrete
work; Highway and street construction

(P-1173)
MGE UNDERGROUND INC
2501 Golden Hill Rd, Paso Robles
(93446-6391)
P.O. Box P.O. Box 4189 (93447-4189)
PHONE...............805 238-3510
Michael Joe Goldstein, *Pr*
Summer Golstein, *
EMP: 372 EST: 1997
SALES (est): 80.36MM **Privately Held**

Web: www.mgeunderground.com
SIC: 1794 Excavation work

(P-1174)
REED THOMAS COMPANY INC
1025 N Santiago St, Santa Ana
(92701-3800)
PHONE...............714 558-7691
Harvey T Biegle, *Pr*
EMP: 90 EST: 1981
SQ FT: 8,800
SALES (est): 8.8MM **Privately Held**
Web: www.reedthomas.com
SIC: 1794 Excavation and grading, building
construction

(P-1175)
STURGEON SON GRADING & PAV INC (PA)
3511 Gilmore Ave, Bakersfield
(93308-6205)
P.O. Box 2840 (93303-2840)
PHONE...............661 322-4408
John E Powell, *CEO*
Oliver Sturgeon, *
Paul Sturgeon, *
EMP: 180 EST: 1927
SQ FT: 3,500
SALES (est): 12.92MM
SALES (corp-wide): 12.92MM **Privately
Held**
Web: www.sturgeonservices.com
SIC: 1794 8711 Excavation work;
Engineering services

(P-1176)
SUKUT CONSTRUCTION INC
4010 W Chandler Ave, Santa Ana
(92704-5274)
PHONE...............714 540-5351
Steve Yurosek, *Pr*
Michael Crawford, *
Myron Sukut, *
Paul Kuliev, *
▲ **EMP: 200 EST:** 1968
SQ FT: 12,000
SALES (est): 100.18MM **Privately Held**
Web: www.sukut.com
SIC: 1794 1611 1623 1629 Excavation and
grading, building construction; General
contractor, highway and street construction;
Water and sewer line construction; Dams,
waterways, docks, and other marine
construction

(P-1177)
TIDWELL EXCAV ACQUISITION INC
Also Called: Tidwell Excavating
1691 Los Angeles Ave, Ventura
(93004-3213)
PHONE...............805 647-4707
Alex Miruello, *Pr*
Timothy Wayne Goodwin, *
Louis Armona, *
EMP: 90 EST: 1956
SALES (est): 9.78MM
SALES (corp-wide): 464.46MM **Privately
Held**
Web: www.tidwell-inc.com
SIC: 1794 Excavation and grading, building
construction
PA: Meruelo Enterprises, Inc.
9550 Firestone Blvd # 105
562 745-2300

1795 Wrecking And Demolition Work

(P-1178)
AMERICAN WRECKING INC
2459 Lee Ave, South El Monte
(91733-1407)
PHONE...............626 350-8303
Jose Luis Galaviz, *Pr*
Robert Hall, *
Warne Galaviz, *
Jay Gonzalez, *
EMP: 100 EST: 1989
SQ FT: 1,000
SALES (est): 20.47MM **Privately Held**
Web: www.americanwreckinginc.com
SIC: 1795 Demolition, buildings and other
structures

(P-1179)
CLAUSS CONSTRUCTION
9911 Maine Ave, Lakeside (92040-3107)
PHONE...............619 390-4940
Joshua Clauss, *CEO*
Patrick Michael Clauss, *
EMP: 80 EST: 1991
SALES (est): 17.18MM **Privately Held**
Web: www.claussconstruction.com
SIC: 1795 1629 4959 Wrecking and
demolition work; Earthmoving contractor;
Toxic or hazardous waste cleanup

(P-1180)
DANNY RYAN PRECISION CONTG INC
Also Called: Precision Contracting
16782 Millikan Ave, Irvine (92606-5010)
PHONE...............949 642-6664
Danny Ryan, *Pr*
EMP: 90 EST: 1991
SALES (est): 11.42MM **Privately Held**
Web: www.adepprecision.com
SIC: 1795 1799 Demolition, buildings and
other structures; Asbestos removal and
encapsulation

(P-1181)
EMPIRE DEMOLITION INC
137 N Joy St, Corona (92879-1321)
P.O. Box 129 (92878-0129)
PHONE...............909 393-8300
Kris Huff, *CEO*
Collin Cumbee, *
EMP: 100 EST: 1997
SALES (est): 11.13MM **Privately Held**
Web: www.empiredemolition.com
SIC: 1795 Demolition, buildings and other
structures

(P-1182)
GD HEIL INC
1031 Segovia Cir, Placentia (92870-7137)
PHONE...............714 687-9100
James A Langford, *CEO*
James A Langford, *CEO*
Gary Heil, *
Steve Mc Clain, *
Laura Heil, *
EMP: 160 EST: 1992
SQ FT: 20,770
SALES (est): 8.66MM **Privately Held**
Web: www.gdheil.com
SIC: 1795 Demolition, buildings and other
structures

(P-1183)
GGG DEMOLITION INC (PA)
1130 W Trenton Ave, Orange (92867-3536)

PHONE...............714 699-9350
Gregg Miller, *Sec*
EMP: 96 EST: 2012
SALES (est): 2.29MM
SALES (corp-wide): 2.29MM **Privately
Held**
Web: www.gggdemo.com
SIC: 1795 Demolition, buildings and other
structures

(P-1184)
INTERIOR RMOVAL SPECIALIST INC
8990 Atlantic Ave, South Gate
(90280-3505)
PHONE...............323 357-6900
Carlos Herrera, *CEO*
Isabel Herrera, *
EMP: 150 EST: 1994
SALES (est): 225 **Privately Held**
Web: www.irsdemo.com
SIC: 1795 Demolition, buildings and other
structures

(P-1185)
MILLER ENVIRONMENTAL INC
1130 W Trenton Ave, Orange (92867-3536)
PHONE...............714 385-0099
Gregg Miller, *Pr*
Rob Schaefer, *
Mindy Peek, *General*
EMP: 150 EST: 1999
SQ FT: 3,000
SALES (est): 16.52MM **Privately Held**
Web: www.millerenvironmental.com
SIC: 1795 4953 Demolition, buildings and
other structures; Hazardous waste
collection and disposal

(P-1186)
NORTHSTAR DEMOLITION AND REMEDIATION LP
404 N Berry St, Brea (92821-3104)
EMP: 476
SALES (est): 92.89MM **Privately Held**
SIC: 1795 1799 8744 Demolition, buildings
and other structures; Decontamination
services; Environmental remediation

1796 Installing Building Equipment

(P-1187)
CLASSIC INSTALLS INC
41755 Elm St, Murrieta (92562-1419)
PHONE...............951 678-9906
Dirk Steffen, *CEO*
EMP: 70 EST: 2007
SALES (est): 11.04MM **Privately Held**
Web: www.classicinstalls.com
SIC: 1796 Installing building equipment

(P-1188)
CURRENT HOME INC
Also Called: Current Home
7100 W Florida Ave, Hemet (92545-3410)
PHONE...............866 454-6073
Brian Walrod, *CEO*
EMP: 75 EST: 2019
SALES (est): 9.93MM **Privately Held**
Web: www.currenthome.com
SIC: 1796 Power generating equipment
installation

(P-1189)
MAINTECH RESOURCES INC
5042 Northwestern Way, Westminster
(92683-2729)

▲ = Import ▼ = Export
◆ = Import/Export

PHONE.................................562 804-0664
John Ellen, *Pr*
EMP: 36 **EST:** 1984
SALES (est): 2.46MM **Privately Held**
Web: www.maintech-hq.com
SIC: 1796 1731 8711 3498 Installing building equipment; General electrical contractor; Structural engineering; Coils, pipe; fabricated from purchased pipe

(P-1190)
PERFORMANCE CONTRACTING INC
4955 E Landon Dr, Anaheim (92807-1972)
PHONE.................................913 310-7120
William Massey, *Mgr*
EMP: 99
SALES (corp-wide): 1.11B **Privately Held**
Web: www.performancecontracting.com
SIC: 1796 Installing building equipment
HQ: Performance Contracting, Inc.
   11145 Thompson Ave
   Lenexa KS 66219
   913 888-8600

(P-1191)
UNITED RIGGERS & ERECTORS INC (PA)
4188 Valley Blvd, Walnut (91789-1446)
P.O. Box 728 (91789)
PHONE.................................909 978-0400
Brian D Kelley, *CEO*
Thomas J Kruss, *
EMP: 100 **EST:** 1966
SQ FT: 58,000
SALES (est): 11.88MM
SALES (corp-wide): 11.88MM **Privately Held**
Web: www.ure-inc.com
SIC: 1796 Machinery installation

(P-1192)
WEST COAST IRON INC
Also Called: Westcoast Iron
9302 Jamacha Rd, Spring Valley (91977-4297)
PHONE.................................619 464-8456
EMP: 75 **EST:** 1988
SALES (est): 18.68MM **Privately Held**
Web: www.westcoastiron.com
SIC: 1796 1541 3441 Installing building equipment; Steel building construction; Building components, structural steel

---
1799 Special Trade Contractors, Nec

(P-1193)
A-1 ENTERPRISES INC
Also Called: A-1 Fence
2831 E La Cresta Ave, Anaheim (92806-1817)
PHONE.................................714 630-3390
TOLL FREE: 800
Norman Shepherd, *Pr*
James Sypitkowski, *
EMP: 45 **EST:** 1953
SQ FT: 39,000
SALES (est): 9.56MM **Privately Held**
Web: www.a1fence.com
SIC: 1799 3446 Fence construction; Acoustical suspension systems, metal

(P-1194)
ANTIS ROOFG WATERPROOFING LLC
Also Called: Antis Roofing
2649 Campus Dr, Irvine (92612-1601)

PHONE.................................949 461-9222
EMP: 124 **EST:** 1988
SALES (est): 10.32MM **Privately Held**
Web: www.antisroofing.com
SIC: 1799 1761 Waterproofing; Roofing contractor

(P-1195)
ATI RESTORATION LLC (PA)
Also Called: ATI
3360 E La Palma Ave, Anaheim (92806-2814)
PHONE.................................714 283-9990
Gary Moore, *CEO*
Ryan Moore, *
Jeff Moore, *
Scott Moore, *OF OPRS & ENVIRONMENTAL HEALTH SERVICES*
Yun Kim, *
▲ **EMP:** 128 **EST:** 1989
SQ FT: 57,000
SALES (est): 287.11MM **Privately Held**
Web: www.atirestoration.com
SIC: 1799 1541 1742 1731 Antenna installation; Industrial buildings and warehouses; Plastering, drywall, and insulation; Electrical work

(P-1196)
ATI RSTRTION SPRING VLY CA INC
Also Called: J&M Keystone, Inc.
2709 Via Orange Way Ste A, Spring Valley (91978-1708)
PHONE.................................619 466-9876
David Carpenter, *CEO*
Kevin Casenhiser, *
Gary Moore, *
Ryan Moore, *
Jeffrey Moore, *
EMP: 117 **EST:** 1991
SQ FT: 9,100
SALES (est): 17.4MM **Privately Held**
Web: www.jmkeystone.com
SIC: 1799 1542 8744 7349 Steam cleaning of building exteriors; Commercial and office buildings, renovation and repair; Environmental remediation; Air duct cleaning
PA: Ati Restoration, Llc
   3360 E La Palma Ave

(P-1197)
CALIFORNIA CLOSET COMPANY INC
Also Called: California Closet Co
5921 Skylab Rd, Huntington Beach (92647-2002)
PHONE.................................714 899-4905
Mike Cassidy, *Genl Mgr*
EMP: 115
SALES (corp-wide): 4.33B **Privately Held**
Web: www.californiaclosets.com
SIC: 1799 Closet organizers, installation and design
HQ: California Closet Company, Inc.
   2001 W Phelps Rd Ste 1
   Phoenix AZ 85023
   510 763-2033

(P-1198)
CLOSET FACTORY INC (PA)
12800 S Bdwy, Los Angeles (90061)
PHONE.................................310 516-7000
John La Barbera, *CEO*
Greg Stein, *
Kathryn La Barbera, *
EMP: 117 **EST:** 1983
SQ FT: 40,000
SALES (est): 62.42MM

SALES (corp-wide): 62.42MM **Privately Held**
Web: www.closetfactory.com
SIC: 1799 Closet organizers, installation and design

(P-1199)
COURTNEY INC (PA)
16781 Millikan Ave, Irvine (92606-5009)
PHONE.................................949 222-2050
George Courtney, *CEO*
Mildred Courtney, *
EMP: 80 **EST:** 1994
SALES (est): 50.73MM **Privately Held**
Web: www.courtneyinc.com
SIC: 1799 Waterproofing

(P-1200)
CROWN FENCE CO
12070 Telegraph Rd Ste 340, Santa Fe Springs (90670-8216)
PHONE.................................562 864-5177
TOLL FREE: 800
Eric Fiedler, *Prin*
Chris E Nickelatti, *Prin*
Lief Nicolaisen, *Prin*
Eric W Fiedler, *
Doug Eustace, *Prin*
▲ **EMP:** 96 **EST:** 1923
SALES (est): 20.38MM **Privately Held**
Web: www.crownfence.com
SIC: 1799 5039 Fence construction; Wire fence, gates, and accessories

(P-1201)
D&A ENDEAVORS INC
Also Called: SERVPRO of Beverly Hills
11400 W Olympic Blvd, Los Angeles (90064-1550)
PHONE.................................310 390-7540
Arezo Jeffries, *CEO*
Daniel Jeffries, *
EMP: 80 **EST:** 2014
SALES (est): 4.56MM **Privately Held**
Web: www.servprobeverlyhillswestwood.com
SIC: 1799 8744 7349 1741 Construction site cleanup; Environmental remediation; Building maintenance services, nec; Tuckpointing or restoration

(P-1202)
EXCEL MDULAR SCAFFOLD LSG CORP
2555 Birch St, Vista (92081-8433)
PHONE.................................760 598-0050
Benjamin Bartlett, *Brnch Mgr*
EMP: 1197
Web: www.excelscaffold.com
SIC: 1799 Rigging and scaffolding
PA: Excel Modular Scaffold And Leasing Corporation
   720 Washington St Unit 5

(P-1203)
FENCECORP INC
3045 Industry St, Oceanside (92054-4834)
PHONE.................................760 721-2101
Gary Hansen, *Prin*
EMP: 85
SALES (corp-wide): 56MM **Privately Held**
Web: www.fencecorp.us
SIC: 1799 Fence construction
HQ: Fencecorp, Inc.
   18440 Van Buren Blvd
   Riverside CA 92508

(P-1204)
FENCECORP INC (HQ)
18440 Van Buren Blvd, Riverside (92508-9258)
PHONE.................................951 686-3170
T Perrry Massie, *CEO*
Dale Marriott, *
Floyd Nixon, *
Gary Hansen, *
EMP: 170 **EST:** 2006
SQ FT: 5,000
SALES (est): 8.76MM
SALES (corp-wide): 56MM **Privately Held**
Web: www.fencecorp.us
SIC: 1799 Fence construction
PA: Fenceworks, Llc
   870 Main St
   951 788-5620

(P-1205)
FENCEWORKS LLC (PA)
Also Called: Golden State Fence Co.
870 Main St, Riverside (92501-1016)
PHONE.................................951 788-5620
Jason Ostrander, *CEO*
Mel Kay, *
▲ **EMP:** 250 **EST:** 1998
SQ FT: 20,000
SALES (est): 56MM
SALES (corp-wide): 56MM **Privately Held**
Web: www.fenceworks.us
SIC: 1799 Fence construction

(P-1206)
G W SURFACES (PA)
Also Called: Showershapes
2432 Palma Dr, Ventura (93003-5732)
PHONE.................................805 642-5004
James A Garver, *Pr*
Georgann Garver, *
Tidus Gutierrez, *
EMP: 100 **EST:** 1976
SQ FT: 30,000
SALES (est): 9.69MM
SALES (corp-wide): 9.69MM **Privately Held**
Web: www.gwsurfaces.com
SIC: 1799 Counter top installation

(P-1207)
GREGG DRILLING & TESTING INC (PA)
2726 Walnut Ave, Signal Hill (90755-1832)
PHONE.................................562 427-6899
John M Gregg, *Pr*
Patrick Keating, *
Chris Christensen, *
▲ **EMP:** 71 **EST:** 1085
SQ FT: 17,000
SALES (est): 24.59MM
SALES (corp-wide): 24.59MM **Privately Held**
Web: www.greggdrilling.com
SIC: 1799 1781 Core drilling and cutting; Water well drilling

(P-1208)
HARTMARK CAB DESIGN & MFG INC
Also Called: Hartmark Cabinet Design
3575 Grapevine St, Jurupa Valley (91752-3505)
P.O. Box 54204 (92619-4204)
PHONE.................................909 591-9153
Gary Allen Hartmark, *Pr*
Gary Allen Hartmark, *Pr*
Marnell Hartmark, *
EMP: 45 **EST:** 1986
SQ FT: 44,000
SALES (est): 16.27MM **Privately Held**

Web: www.hartmark.com
SIC: 1799 2434 1751 Kitchen cabinet installation; Wood kitchen cabinets; Cabinet and finish carpentry

(P-1209)
HERZOG CONTRACTING CORP
2155 Hancock St, San Diego (92110-2012)
PHONE..................................619 849-6990
EMP: 87
SALES (corp-wide): 433.21MM **Privately Held**
Web: www.herzog.com
SIC: 1799 Antenna installation
HQ: Herzog Contracting Corp.
600 S Riverside Rd
Saint Joseph MO 64507
816 233-9001

(P-1210)
IN-LINE FENCE & RAILING CO INC
Also Called: In-Line Construction
1307 Walnut St, Ramona (92065-1840)
P.O. Box 2637 (92065-0945)
PHONE..................................760 789-0282
David Ortiz, Pr
EMP: 28 EST: 1998
SALES (est): 3.61MM **Privately Held**
Web: www.inlinerail.com
SIC: 1799 1611 3441 1542 Fence construction; General contractor, highway and street construction; Building components, structural steel; Commercial and office building, new construction

(P-1211)
JEFFRIES GLOBAL INC
Also Called: SERVPRO Jeffries Global
8484 Wilshire Blvd Ste 605, Beverly Hills (90211-3214)
PHONE..................................888 255-3488
Daniel Jeffries, Prin
EMP: 85 EST: 2020
SALES (est): 4.67MM **Privately Held**
SIC: 1799 Asbestos removal and encapsulation

(P-1212)
KELLER NORTH AMERICA INC
1780 E Lemonwood Dr, Santa Paula (93060-9510)
PHONE..................................805 933-1331
Alan Ringen, Brnch Mgr
EMP: 95
Web: www.keller-na.com
SIC: 1799 Building site preparation
HQ: Keller North America, Inc.
7550 Teague Rd Ste 300
Hanover MD 21076
410 551-8200

(P-1213)
KING SUPPLY COMPANY LLC
6340 Valley View St, Buena Park (90620-1032)
PHONE..................................714 670-8980
Michelle Mccloud, Brnch Mgr
EMP: 79
Web: www.kingmetals.com
SIC: 1799 Ornamental metal work
PA: King Supply Company, Llc
9611 E R L Thornton Fwy

(P-1214)
LAYFIELD USA CORPORATION (DH)
10038 Marathon Pkwy, Lakeside (92040-2771)

PHONE..................................619 562-1200
Thomas Rose, CEO
Rob Rempel, *
Steve Palubiski, *
▲ EMP: 100 EST: 2004
SALES (est): 51.97MM
SALES (corp-wide): 3.77MM **Privately Held**
Web: www.layfieldgroup.com
SIC: 1799 Building board-up contractor
HQ: Layfield Group Limited
11120 Silversmith Pl
Richmond BC V7A 5
604 275-5588

(P-1215)
M GAW INC
Also Called: Jet Sets
6910 Farmdale Ave, North Hollywood (91605-6210)
PHONE..................................818 503-7997
Michael Gaw, Pr
EMP: 90 EST: 1991
SQ FT: 15,000
SALES (est): 9.24MM **Privately Held**
Web: www.jetsets.com
SIC: 1799 Prop, set or scenery construction, theatrical

(P-1216)
MISSION POOLS OF ESCONDIDO
Also Called: Mission Pools of Lake Forest
27439 Bostik Ct, Temecula (92590-3698)
PHONE..................................949 588-0100
Don Ogden, Mgr
EMP: 105
SALES (corp-wide): 24.07MM **Privately Held**
Web: www.missionpools.com
SIC: 1799 Swimming pool construction
PA: Mission Pools Of Escondido
755 W Grand Ave
760 743-2605

(P-1217)
MP AERO LLC
7701 Woodley Ave, Van Nuys (91406-1732)
PHONE..................................818 901-9828
EMP: 85 EST: 2013
SQ FT: 165,000
SALES (est): 10.62MM **Privately Held**
Web: www.mpaero.com
SIC: 1799 3721 Renovation of aircraft interiors; Research and development on aircraft by the manufacturer

(P-1218)
NAVAL COATING INC
2080 Cambridge Ave, Cardiff By The Sea (92007-1708)
PHONE..................................619 234-8366
Alan Lerchbacker, Pr
EMP: 149 EST: 1969
SALES (est): 3.32MM **Privately Held**
Web: www.navalcoating.us
SIC: 1799 1721 2851 Sandblasting of building exteriors; Industrial painting; Paints and allied products

(P-1219)
PACIFIC AQUASCAPE INC
17520 Newhope St Ste 120, Fountain Valley (92708-8203)
PHONE..................................714 843-5734
Johan Perslow, Ch
Cory M Severson, *
Bob Lobo, *
Kevin Curran, *

EMP: 75 EST: 1994
SQ FT: 21,000
SALES (est): 10.43MM **Privately Held**
Web: www.pacificaquascape.com
SIC: 1799 Swimming pool construction

(P-1220)
PARKING NETWORK INC
1625 W Olympic Blvd Ste 1010, Los Angeles (90015-3853)
PHONE..................................213 613-1500
Frank Zelaya, CEO
Rose Zelaya, *
EMP: 120 EST: 2001
SALES (est): 9.84MM **Privately Held**
Web: www.parkingnetwork.net
SIC: 1799 8748 Parking lot maintenance; Business consulting, nec

(P-1221)
PENHALL COMPANY
Also Called: Penhall San Diego 202
5775 Eastgate Dr, San Diego (92121-2803)
PHONE..................................858 550-1111
Keith Martin, Mgr
EMP: 87
SQ FT: 6,609
Web: www.penhall.com
SIC: 1799 1741 1795 Building site preparation; Masonry and other stonework; Wrecking and demolition work
PA: Penhall Company
1212 Corporate Dr Ste 500

(P-1222)
PROFORM INTERIOR CNSTR INC
663 33rd St Ste C, San Diego (92102-3300)
PHONE..................................619 881-0041
James Pettit, Pr
Reid Schneider, *
EMP: 73 EST: 2014
SQ FT: 5,000
SALES (est): 5.07MM **Privately Held**
Web: www.proforminteriors.com
SIC: 1799 Home/office interiors finishing, furnishing and remodeling

(P-1223)
PSG FENCING CORPORATION
330 Main St, Riverside (92501-1028)
PHONE..................................951 275-9252
EMP: 83
Web: www.psgfencinginc.com
SIC: 1799 Fence construction
PA: P.S.G. Fencing Corporation
1218 D St

(P-1224)
REPUBLIC FENCE CO INC (PA)
11309 Danube Ave, Granada Hills (91344-4323)
PHONE..................................818 341-5323
David Woolf, Pr
Bonnie Woolf, *
EMP: 26 EST: 1973
SQ FT: 11,000
SALES (est): 4.31MM
SALES (corp-wide): 4.31MM **Privately Held**
Web: www.republicfenceco.com
SIC: 1799 3312 5085 Fence construction; Structural shapes and pilings, steel; Fasteners and fastening equipment

(P-1225)
REY-CREST ROOFG WATERPROOFING
Also Called: Rey-Crest Roofg Waterproofing
3065 Verdugo Rd, Los Angeles (90065-2014)

PHONE..................................323 257-9329
George Reyes, Pr
Georgia Reyes, *
EMP: 80 EST: 1969
SQ FT: 10,000
SALES (est): 8.84MM **Privately Held**
Web: www.rey-crestroofing.com
SIC: 1799 1761 Waterproofing; Roofing contractor

(P-1226)
SIGNATURE PARKING LLC
Also Called: Signature Parking
1482 E Valley Rd Ste 311, Santa Barbara (93108-1200)
PHONE..................................805 969-7275
Michael Holmstrom, Prin
EMP: 78 EST: 2011
SALES (est): 176.9K **Privately Held**
Web: www.signatureparking.com
SIC: 1799 Parking facility equipment and maintenance

(P-1227)
TEAM WEST CONTRACTING CORP
2733 S Vista Ave, Bloomington (92316-3269)
PHONE..................................951 340-3426
Dawn Lilly, Prin
Jerry R Pacheco, *
Stephen Knehans, *
EMP: 92 EST: 2009
SQ FT: 7,200
SALES (est): 8.54MM **Privately Held**
Web: www.twc-corp.com
SIC: 1799 Fence construction

(P-1228)
TESERRA (PA)
Also Called: California Pools
86100 Avenue 54, Coachella (92236-3813)
P.O. Box 1280 (92236-1280)
PHONE..................................760 340-9000
Bob Smith, Pr
James Harebottle, *
EMP: 399 EST: 1985
SQ FT: 10,000
SALES (est): 21.92MM
SALES (corp-wide): 21.92MM **Privately Held**
Web: www.teserraoutdoors.com
SIC: 1799 Swimming pool construction

(P-1229)
TLS PRODUCTIONS INC
6 Venture, Irvine (92618-3340)
PHONE..................................810 220-8577
William Ross, Pr
Brad Hayes, *
EMP: 24 EST: 1996
SALES (est): 3.81MM **Privately Held**
Web: www.tlsproductionsinc.com
SIC: 1799 3648 7922 Rigging, theatrical; Stage lighting equipment; Lighting, theatrical

(P-1230)
TURN KEY SCAFFOLD LLC
410 W 30th St, National City (91950-7269)
P.O. Box 120340 (91912-3440)
PHONE..................................619 642-0880
Alvin Ruis Iii, Pr
EMP: 106 EST: 2017
SALES (est): 5.26MM **Privately Held**
Web: www.tksscaffold.com
SIC: 1799 Scaffolding

▲ = Import ▼ = Export
◆ = Import/Export

(P-1231)
WASHINGTON ORNA IR WORKS INC (PA)
Also Called: Washington Iron Works
17926 S Broadway, Gardena (90248-3540)
P.O. Box 460 (90247-0846)
PHONE..............................310 327-8660
Daniel Welsh, *CEO*
Tom Pederson, *
Luke Welsh, *
Chris Powell, *
EMP: 97 **EST:** 1966
SQ FT: 141,240
SALES (est): 25.46MM
SALES (corp-wide): 25.46MM **Privately Held**
SIC: 1799 3446 Ornamental metal work; Architectural metalwork

(P-1232)
WATERPRFING ROFG SOLUTIONS INC
11041 Santa Monica Blvd Ste 306, Los Angeles (90025-3523)
PHONE..............................310 571-0892
Homayoun Kazemi, *CEO*
Mauricio Barahona, *
EMP: 72 **EST:** 2001
SALES (est): 11MM **Privately Held**
Web: www.wandrsolutions.com
SIC: 1799 Waterproofing

(P-1233)
WAYNE PERRY INC (PA)
8281 Commonwealth Ave, Buena Park (90621-2537)
PHONE..............................714 826-0352
Wayne Perry, *Pr*
Adam Leiter, *
Ron Perry, *
Greg Nicholson, *
Daniel Mcgill, *VP*
EMP: 185 **EST:** 1969
SQ FT: 4,000
SALES (est): 25.01MM
SALES (corp-wide): 25.01MM **Privately Held**
Web: www.wpinc.com
SIC: 1799 8711 Decontamination services; Engineering services

(P-1234)
WEST COAST COUNTERTOPS INC
1200 Marlborough Ave Ste B, Riverside (92507-2158)
PHONE..............................951 719-3670
▲ **EMP:** 90 **EST:** 1990
SALES (est): 2.66MM **Privately Held**
SIC: 1799 5211 Counter top installation; Counter tops

(P-1235)
WEST COAST FIRESTOPPING INC
1130 W Trenton Ave, Orange (92867-3536)
PHONE..............................714 935-1104
Karl Stoll, *Pr*
EMP: 80 **EST:** 2007
SALES (est): 8.65MM **Privately Held**
Web: www.westcoastfirestop.com
SIC: 1799 Fireproofing buildings

(P-1236)
WOODS MAINTENANCE SERVICES INC
Also Called: Hydro-Pressure Systems
7250 Coldwater Canyon Ave, North Hollywood (91605-4203)
PHONE..............................818 764-2515
Barry Woods, *Pr*
Barry Woods, *Pr*
Diane Woods, *
Jeff Woods, *
Josh Woods, *
EMP: 135 **EST:** 1975
SALES (est): 5.06MM **Privately Held**
Web: www.graffiticontrol.com
SIC: 1799 Cleaning building exteriors, nec

(P-1237)
YYK ENTERPRISES OPERATIONS LLC (PA)
3475 E St, San Diego (92102-3335)
PHONE..............................619 474-6229
Ted Kines, *CEO*
Steve Johnstone, *
EMP: 190 **EST:** 1981
SQ FT: 4,000
SALES (est): 9.58MM
SALES (corp-wide): 9.58MM **Privately Held**
Web: www.yykenterprises.com
SIC: 1799 1721 3731 Sandblasting of building exteriors; Ship painting; Shipbuilding and repairing

---

2011 Meat Packing Plants

(P-1238)
BURNETT & SON MEAT CO INC
Also Called: Burnett Fine Foods
1420 S Myrtle Ave, Monrovia (91016-4153)
PHONE..............................626 357-2165
Donald L Burnett, *Pr*
▲ **EMP:** 80 **EST:** 1978
SQ FT: 20,000
SALES (est): 23.89MM **Privately Held**
Web: www.burnettandson.com
SIC: 2011 Meat by-products, from meat slaughtered on site

(P-1239)
CARGILL MEAT SOLUTIONS CORP
Cargill Food Distribution
10602 N Trademark Pkwy Ste 500, Rancho Cucamonga (91730-5937)
PHONE..............................909 476-3120
Guy Milam, *Genl Mgr*
EMP: 58
SALES (corp-wide): 159.59B **Privately Held**
Web: www.cargill.com
SIC: 2011 Meat by-products, from meat oloughtorod on cito
HQ: Cargill Meat Solutions Corp
825 E Douglas Ave
Wichita KS 67202
316 462-7279

(P-1240)
CARGILL MEAT SOLUTIONS CORP
13034 Excelsior Dr, Norwalk (90650-6867)
PHONE..............................562 345-5240
EMP: 43
SALES (corp-wide): 159.59B **Privately Held**
Web: distributors.cargill.com
SIC: 2011 Meat packing plants
HQ: Cargill Meat Solutions Corp
825 E Douglas Ave
Wichita KS 67202
316 462-7279

(P-1241)
CLOUGHERTY PACKING LLC (DH)
Also Called: Smithfield Foods
3049 E Vernon Ave, Los Angeles (90058-1800)
P.O. Box 58870 (90058-0870)
PHONE..............................323 583-4621
Kenneth J Baptist, *Pr*
EMP: 300 **EST:** 1937
SQ FT: 1,000,000
SALES (est): 65.83MM **Privately Held**
Web: farmerjohn.sfdbrands.com
SIC: 2011 2013 Meat packing plants; Sausages and other prepared meats
HQ: Smithfield Foods, Inc.
200 Commerce St
Smithfield VA 23430
757 365-3000

(P-1242)
FIRSTCLASS FOODS - TROJAN INC
Also Called: First Class Foods
12500 Inglewood Ave, Hawthorne (90250-4217)
P.O. Box 2397 (90251-2397)
PHONE..............................310 676-2500
Salomon Benzimra, *Pr*
Felix Benzimra, *VP Sls*
Albert Benzimra, *Sec*
Lucy Benzimra, *CFO*
EMP: 135 **EST:** 1963
SQ FT: 45,000
SALES (est): 28.77MM **Publicly Held**
SIC: 2011 5147 Meat packing plants; Meats and meat products
HQ: Us Foods, Inc.
9399 W Higgins Rd Ste 500
Rosemont IL 60018

(P-1243)
HEATHERFIELD FOODS INC
Also Called: Villa Roma Sausage Co
1150 Brooks St, Ontario (91762-3606)
PHONE..............................877 460-3060
EMP: 25 **EST:** 1987
SALES (est): 9.9MM **Privately Held**
Web: www.villaromasausage.com
SIC: 2011 Sausages, from meat slaughtered on site

(P-1244)
JOBBERS MEAT PACKING CO LLC
Also Called: Wilmar
3336 Fruitland Ave, Vernon (90058-3714)
P.O. Box 58368 (90058)
PHONE..............................323 585-6328
Martin Evanson, *CEO*
EMP: 234 **EST:** 1978
SQ FT: 19,000
SALES (est): 25.04MM
SALES (corp-wide): 63.43MM **Privately Held**
SIC: 2011 Beef products, from beef slaughtered on site
PA: Hv Randall Foods Llc
2900 Ayers
323 261-6565

(P-1245)
NAGLES VEAL INC
1411 E Base Line St, San Bernardino (92410-4113)
PHONE..............................909 383-7075
Michael Lemler, *Pr*
▲ **EMP:** 50 **EST:** 1983
SQ FT: 12,500
SALES (est): 4.18MM **Privately Held**
Web: www.nagleveal.com
SIC: 2011 Veal, from meat slaughtered on site

(P-1246)
OLLI SALUMERIA AMERICANA LLC
1301 Rocky Point Dr, Oceanside (92056-5864)
▲ **EMP:** 65 **EST:** 2010
SALES (est): 25.13MM **Privately Held**
Web: www.olli.com
SIC: 2011 Meat packing plants

(P-1247)
OWB PACKERS LLC
57 Shank Rd, Brawley (92227-9616)
PHONE..............................760 351-2700
Eric W Brandt, *Managing Member*
EMP: 79 **EST:** 2016
SALES (est): 10.35MM **Privately Held**
Web: www.owbpackers.com
SIC: 2011 Meat packing plants

(P-1248)
PACIFIC PRIME MEATS LLC ✪
3501 E Vernon Ave, Vernon (90058-1813)
PHONE..............................310 523-3664
Paul Guiliano, *CEO*
Dawn Allen, *
EMP: 100 **EST:** 2024
SALES (est): 7MM **Privately Held**
SIC: 2011 Meat packing plants

(P-1249)
R B R MEAT COMPANY INC
Also Called: Rightway
5151 Alcoa Ave, Vernon (90058-3715)
P.O. Box 58225 (90058-0225)
PHONE..............................323 973-4868
Irwin Miller, *Pr*
Larry Vanden Bos, *
James Craig, *
EMP: 23 **EST:** 1951
SQ FT: 65,000
SALES (est): 10.43MM **Privately Held**
SIC: 2011 Meat packing plants

(P-1250)
SERV-RITE MEAT COMPANY INC
Also Called: Packers Bar M
2515 N San Fernando Rd, Los Angeles (90065-1325)
P.O. Box 65026 (90065-0026)
PHONE..............................323 227-1911
Gary Marks, *CEO*
Norman Marks, *
Norma Marks, *
EMP: 55 **EST:** 1976
SQ FT: 55,000
SALES (est): 10.79MM **Privately Held**
Web: www.bar-m.com
SIC: 2011 Meat packing plants

(P-1251)
SSRE HOLDINGS LLC
Also Called: Signature Fresh
18901 Railroad St, City Of Industry (91748-1322)
PHONE..............................800 314-2098
Stanley J Wetch, *Managing Member*
Stanley Joseph Wetch, *Managing Member*
EMP: 100 **EST:** 2014
SALES (est): 3.01MM **Privately Held**
SIC: 2011 Meat by-products, from meat slaughtered on site

(P-1252)
VIZ CATTLE CORPORATION
Also Called: Sukarne
17800 Castleton St Ste 435, City Of Industry
(91748-5748)
PHONE.....................310 884-5260
Edwin Botero, *CEO*
Eddy Gutierrez, *
▲ **EMP:** 39 **EST:** 1992
SALES (est): 11.29MM **Privately Held**
SIC: 2011 5154 Meat packing plants; Cattle
HQ: Grupo Viz, S.A.P.I. De C.V.
    Av. Diana Tang No. 59 - A
    Culiacan SIN 80199

(P-1253)
WEST LAKE FOOD
CORPORATION (PA)
Also Called: Tay Ho
301 N Sullivan St, Santa Ana (92703-3417)
PHONE.....................714 973-2286
Jayce Yenson, *CEO*
Chieu Nguyen, *
Chuong Nguyen, *
Jayce Yenson, *Sec*
◆ **EMP:** 39 **EST:** 1986
SALES (est): 7.89MM
SALES (corp-wide): 7.89MM **Privately Held**
SIC: 2011 Beef products, from beef
    slaughtered on site

2013 Sausages And Other Prepared Meats

(P-1254)
ARIES BEEF LLC
17 W Magnolia Blvd, Burbank
(91502-1781)
PHONE.....................818 526-4855
Steven Zoll, *Managing Member*
EMP: 36 **EST:** 2021
SALES (est): 17.3MM
SALES (corp-wide): 143.99MM **Privately Held**
SIC: 2013 Sausages and other prepared
    meats
PA: United Deli Holdings Llc
    1143 W Lake St

(P-1255)
BOYD SPECIALTIES LLC
1016 E Cooley Dr Ste N, Colton
(92324-3962)
PHONE.....................909 219-5120
Jae Boyd, *CEO*
▲ **EMP:** 64 **EST:** 2008
SQ FT: 10,000
SALES (est): 11.55MM **Privately Held**
Web: www.boydspecialtiesjerky.com
SIC: 2013 Snack sticks, including jerky: from
    purchased meat

(P-1256)
CTI FOODS AZUSA LLC
1120 W Foothill Blvd, Azusa (91702-2818)
PHONE.....................626 633-1609
Robert Horowitz, *CEO*
Horst Sieben, *CFO*
Pam Cardinale, *Dir Fin*
▲ **EMP:** 220 **EST:** 1998
SQ FT: 115,000
SALES (est): 24.29MM
SALES (corp-wide): 972MM **Privately Held**
SIC: 2013 Cooked meats, from purchased
    meat
HQ: Cti Foods Holding Co., Llc
    2106 E State Hwy 114 Ste

Southlake TX 76092

(P-1257)
DEREK AND CONSTANCE LEE
CORP (PA)
Also Called: Great River Food
19355 San Jose Ave, City Of Industry
(91748-1420)
PHONE.....................909 595-8831
Derek E Lee, *Pr*
Eric Lee, *
▲ **EMP:** 95 **EST:** 1985
SQ FT: 50,000
SALES (est): 14.7MM
SALES (corp-wide): 14.7MM **Privately Held**
Web: www.greatriverfood.com
SIC: 2013 1541 Sausages and other
    prepared meats; Food products
    manufacturing or packing plant construction

(P-1258)
FORMOSA MEAT COMPANY INC
Also Called: Universal Meat Company
10646 Fulton Ct, Rancho Cucamonga
(91730-4848)
PHONE.....................909 987-0470
Cheng-ting Shih, *VP*
Hsiu-o Kan, *Treas*
▲ **EMP:** 40 **EST:** 1995
SQ FT: 23,000
SALES (est): 1.63MM **Privately Held**
Web: www.formosa.com
SIC: 2013 Snack sticks, including jerky: from
    purchased meat

(P-1259)
GAYTAN FOODS LLC
15430 Proctor Ave, City Of Industry
(91745-1024)
P.O. Box 3385 (91744-0385)
PHONE.....................626 330-4553
EMP: 100
Web: www.benestarbrands.com
SIC: 2013 2099 2022 2011 Sausages and
    other prepared meats; Food preparations,
    nec; Cheese; natural and processed; Meat
    packing plants

(P-1260)
KITCHEN CUTS LLC
6045 District Blvd, Maywood (90270-3560)
PHONE.....................323 560-7415
Raul Tapia Senior, *CEO*
EMP: 68 **EST:** 2011
SALES (est): 8.49MM
SALES (corp-wide): 87.04MM **Privately Held**
Web: www.kitchen-cuts.com
SIC: 2013 Beef stew, from purchased meat
PA: Tapia Enterprises, Inc.
    6067 District Blvd
    323 560-7415

(P-1261)
KRUSE AND SON INC
235 Kruse Ave, Monrovia (91016-4899)
P.O. Box 945 (91017-0945)
PHONE.....................626 358-4536
David R Kruse, *CEO*
EMP: 25 **EST:** 1949
SQ FT: 20,000
SALES (est): 16.15MM **Privately Held**
Web: www.kruseandson.com
SIC: 2013 Ham, smoked: from purchased
    meat

(P-1262)
LA ESPANOLA MEATS INC
25020 Doble Ave, Harbor City
(90710-3155)
PHONE.....................310 539-0455
Alex Motamedi, *CEO*
Juana Faraone, *
Frank Faraone, *
◆ **EMP:** 25 **EST:** 1975
SQ FT: 8,800
SALES (est): 6.9MM **Privately Held**
Web: www.laespanolameats.com
SIC: 2013 5421 Sausages and related
    products, from purchased meat; Meat
    markets, including freezer provisioners

(P-1263)
OLD BBH INC
280 10th Ave, San Diego (92101-7406)
P.O. Box 85362 (92186-5362)
PHONE.....................858 715-4000
◆ **EMP:** 550
Web: www.bumblebee.com
SIC: 2013 2032 2033 Beef stew, from
    purchased meat; Chili, with or without meat:
    packaged in cans, jars, etc.; Vegetables
    and vegetable products, in cans, jars, etc.

(P-1264)
PAMPANGA FOOD COMPANY
INC
1835 N Orangethorpe Park Ste A, Anaheim
(92801-1143)
PHONE.....................714 773-0537
Ray Reyes, *Pr*
Coni Reyes, *VP*
EMP: 30 **EST:** 1984
SQ FT: 11,000
SALES (est): 13.84MM **Privately Held**
Web: www.pampangafood.com
SIC: 2013 5812 8742 2011 Sausages and
    other prepared meats; Eating places; Food
    and beverage consultant; Sausages, from
    meat slaughtered on site

(P-1265)
PAPA CANTELLAS
INCORPORATED
Also Called: Papa Cantella's Sausage Plant
3341 E 50th St, Vernon (90058-3003)
PHONE.....................323 584-7272
Thomas P Cantella, *CEO*
Chris Stafford, *
EMP: 60 **EST:** 1981
SQ FT: 13,000
SALES (est): 13.3MM **Privately Held**
Web: www.papacantella.com
SIC: 2013 Sausages, from purchased meat

(P-1266)
POCINO FOODS COMPANY
14250 Lomitas Ave, City Of Industry
(91746-3014)
P.O. Box 2219 (91746-0219)
PHONE.....................626 968-8000
Naoki Higuchi, *CEO*
Luciana Obrien, *
▲ **EMP:** 100 **EST:** 1933
SQ FT: 70,000
SALES (est): 60.29MM **Privately Held**
Web: www.pocinofoods.com
SIC: 2013 Sausages, from purchased meat
PA: Zensho Holdings Co., Ltd.
    2-18-1, Konan

(P-1267)
PROVENA FOODS INC (HQ)
5010 Eucalyptus Ave, Chino (91710-9216)
PHONE.....................909 627-1082

Theodore L Arena, *Pr*
Santo Zito, *
Ronald A Provera, *
Thomas J Mulroney, *CAO*
▲ **EMP:** 60 **EST:** 1960
SALES (est): 24.3MM
SALES (corp-wide): 11.92B **Publicly Held**
SIC: 2013 2032 2098 Sausages and other
    prepared meats; Canned specialties;
    Macaroni and spaghetti
PA: Hormel Foods Corporation
    1 Hormel Pl
    507 437-5611

(P-1268)
RAEMICA INC
Also Called: Far West Meats
7759 Victoria Ave, Highland (92346-5637)
P.O. Box 190 (92324-0190)
PHONE.....................909 864-1990
Thomas R Serrato, *CEO*
Wade Snyder, *
Michael Serrato, *
EMP: 41 **EST:** 1978
SQ FT: 35,000
SALES (est): 2.38MM **Privately Held**
Web: www.farwestmeat.com
SIC: 2013 5421 Cured meats, from
    purchased meat; Meat markets, including
    freezer provisioners

(P-1269)
RICE FIELD CORPORATION
14500 Valley Blvd, City Of Industry
(91746-2918)
PHONE.....................626 968-6917
Derek Lee, *Pr*
▲ **EMP:** 120 **EST:** 1997
SQ FT: 100,000
SALES (est): 9.28MM **Privately Held**
Web: www.ricefieldcorporation.com
SIC: 2013 Sausages and other prepared
    meats

(P-1270)
SETTLERS JERKY INC
307 Paseo Sonrisa, Walnut (91789-2721)
PHONE.....................909 444-3999
Cherron L Hart, *CEO*
Aaron J Anderson, *
EMP: 27 **EST:** 2011
SQ FT: 20,000
SALES (est): 6.52MM **Privately Held**
Web: www.settlersjerky.com
SIC: 2013 Snack sticks, including jerky: from
    purchased meat

(P-1271)
SQUARE H BRANDS INC (PA)
Also Called: Hoffy
2731 S Soto St, Vernon (90058-8026)
PHONE.....................323 267-4600
Henry Haskell, *CEO*
William Hannigan, *CFO*
◆ **EMP:** 50 **EST:** 1995
SQ FT: 100,000
SALES (est): 24.28MM
SALES (corp-wide): 24.28MM **Privately Held**
Web: www.hoffybrand.com
SIC: 2013 Sausages, from purchased meat

(P-1272)
STAR FOOD SNACKS INTL INC
Also Called: Star Food Snacks
125 E Laurel St, Colton (92324-2462)
PHONE.....................909 825-8882
Aida Hawa, *CEO*
Waleed Saab, *
Asber Hawa, *

▲ = Import ▼ = Export
◆ = Import/Export

EMP: 80 EST: 2010
SALES (est): 3.28MM **Privately Held**
Web: www.enjoybeefjerky.com
SIC: 2013 Beef, dried: from purchased meat

(P-1273)
SWIFT BEEF COMPANY
Also Called: Jbs Case Ready
15555 Meridian Pkwy, Riverside
(92518-3046)
PHONE..........................951 571-2237
Andre Nogueira, *CEO*
EMP: 200 **EST:** 2015
SALES (est): 49.99MM **Publicly Held**
SIC: 2013 Beef, dried: from purchased meat
HQ: Jbs Usa Food Company
1770 Promontory Cir
Greeley CO 80634
970 506-8000

(P-1274)
T&J SAUSAGE KITCHEN INC
Also Called: T & J Sausage Kitchen
2831 E Miraloma Ave, Anaheim
(92806-1804)
PHONE..........................714 632-8350
Tom Drozdowski, *CEO*
David Armendariz, *
EMP: 45 **EST:** 1984
SQ FT: 20,000
SALES (est): 9.22MM **Privately Held**
Web: www.tandjsausage.com
SIC: 2013 Sausages and other prepared
meats

(P-1275)
YONEKYU USA INC
611 N 20th St, Montebello (90640-3135)
PHONE..........................323 581-4194
Osamu Saito, *Pr*
Kenji Ikeda, *
Don Ferris, *
▼ **EMP:** 52 **EST:** 1992
SALES (est): 2.27MM **Privately Held**
Web: www.yqusa.com
SIC: 2013 Sausages, from purchased meat
HQ: Yonekyu Corp. Inc.
1259, Terabayashi, Okanomiya
Numazu SZO 410-0

2015 Poultry Slaughtering And Processing

(P-1276)
COMMODITY SALES CO
517 S Clarence St, Los Angeles
(90033-4225)
PHONE..........................323 980-5463
William T Zant, *Pr*
EMP: 120 **EST:** 1067
SQ FT: 14,522
SALES (est): 2.48MM **Privately Held**
SIC: 2015 5144 5142 Poultry slaughtering
and processing; Poultry and poultry
products; Packaged frozen goods

(P-1277)
FOSTER POULTRY FARMS
Also Called: FOSTER POULTRY FARMS
1805 N Santa Fe Ave, Compton
(90221-1009)
PHONE..........................310 223-1499
Ronald Altman, *Brnch Mgr*
EMP: 480
SALES (corp-wide): 1.25B **Privately Held**
Web: www.fosterfarms.com
SIC: 2015 Poultry slaughtering and
processing
PA: Foster Poultry Farms, Llc
1000 Davis St

209 394-7901

(P-1278)
GLENOAKS FOOD INC
11030 Randall St, Sun Valley (91352-2621)
PHONE..........................818 768-9091
John J Fallon Iii, *CEO*
Marvin Caeser, *Stockholder**
Katty Majailovic, *Stockholder**
John J Fallon Iii, *Pr*
EMP: 40 **EST:** 1996
SQ FT: 30,000
SALES (est): 4.51MM **Privately Held**
Web: www.jcrivers.com
SIC: 2015 2013 3999 2091 Poultry
slaughtering and processing; Beef, dried:
from purchased meat; Pet supplies; Fish,
dried

(P-1279)
INGENUE INC
Also Called: Qc Poultry
1111 W Olympic Blvd, Montebello
(90640-5123)
P.O. Box 17238 (92817-7238)
PHONE..........................323 726-8084
Nick Macis, *Pr*
Michelle Macis, *Sec*
EMP: 100 **EST:** 1998
SQ FT: 10,000
SALES (est): 17.13MM **Privately Held**
Web: www.qcpoultry.com
SIC: 2015 Poultry slaughtering and
processing

(P-1280)
KIFUKI USA CO INC (HQ)
15547 1st St, Irwindale (91706-6201)
PHONE..........................626 334-8090
Kuniaki Ishikaiwa, *Pr*
▲ **EMP:** 90 **EST:** 1989
SQ FT: 52,000
SALES (est): 52.69MM **Privately Held**
Web: kifukiusa.openfos.com
SIC: 2015 2013 2035 Eggs, processed:
dehydrated; Beef, dried: from purchased
meat; Seasonings and sauces, except
tomato and dry
PA: Kewpie Corporation
1-4-13, Shibuya

(P-1281)
LOS ANGELES POULTRY CO INC
4816 Long Beach Ave, Los Angeles
(90058-1915)
P.O. Box 58328 (90058-0328)
PHONE..........................323 232-1019
David Dahan, *Pr*
Dror Dahan, *
EMP: 88 **EST:** 1988
SQ FT: 32,000
SALES (est): 7.03MM **Privately Held**
Web: www.lapoultry.com
SIC: 2015 Poultry slaughtering and
processing

(P-1282)
WESTERN SUPREME INC
Also Called: California Poultry
846 Produce Ct, Los Angeles (90021-1832)
P.O. Box 21441 (90021-0441)
PHONE..........................213 627-3861
Frank Fogarty, *Pr*
Marlene Fogarty, *
EMP: 125 **EST:** 1991
SQ FT: 10,000
SALES (est): 9.81MM **Privately Held**
SIC: 2015 Chicken slaughtering and
processing

2021 Creamery Butter

(P-1283)
VENTURA FOODS LLC
Also Called: Saffola Quality Foods
2900 Jurupa St, Ontario (91761-2915)
PHONE..........................323 262-9157
Tom Bospic, *Mgr*
EMP: 42
Web: www.venturafoods.com
SIC: 2021 2035 5199 2079 Creamery butter;
Dressings, salad: raw and cooked (except
dry mixes); Oils, animal or vegetable;
Edible fats and oils
PA: Ventura Foods, Llc
40 Pointe Dr

2022 Cheese; Natural And Processed

(P-1284)
ARIZA CHEESE CO INC
7602 Jackson St, Paramount (90723-4912)
PHONE..........................562 630-4144
Fatima Cristina Ariza, *CEO*
Ausencio Ariza, *
EMP: 40 **EST:** 1970
SQ FT: 8,000
SALES (est): 2.72MM **Privately Held**
Web: www.arizacheeseco.com
SIC: 2022 Natural cheese

(P-1285)
ARIZA GLOBAL FOODS INC
7602 Jackson St, Paramount (90723-4912)
PHONE..........................562 630-4144
Pablo Gonzalez, *CEO*
EMP: 23 **EST:** 2015
SALES (est): 885.19K **Privately Held**
SIC: 2022 Cheese; natural and processed

(P-1286)
EINSTEIN NOAH REST GROUP INC
Also Called: Noah's New York Bagels
16304 Beach Blvd, Westminster
(92683-7857)
PHONE..........................714 847-4609
Fransico Valdez, *Mgr*
EMP: 195
Web: www.bagelbrands.com
SIC: 2022 5812 Spreads, cheese; Cafe
PA: Einstein Noah Restaurant Group, Inc.
555 Zang St Ste 300

(P-1287)
KAROUN DAIRIES INC (PA)
Also Called: Karoun Cheese
13023 Arroyo St, San Fernando
(91340-1540)
PHONE..........................818 767-7000
Anto Baghdassarian, *Pr*
Ohan Baghdassarian, *
Rostom Baghdassarian, *
Seta Baghdassarian, *
Tsolak Khatcherian, *
▲ **EMP:** 40 **EST:** 1991
SQ FT: 70,000
SALES (est): 43.03MM **Privately Held**
Web: www.karouncheese.com
SIC: 2022 5143 Natural cheese; Cheese

(P-1288)
LIFE IS LIFE LLC
Also Called: Parmela Creamery
2611 Cottonwood Ave, Moreno Valley
(92553-8089)

PHONE..........................310 584-7541
Ryan Hayes Salomone, *Managing Member*
EMP: 28 **EST:** 2012
SALES (est): 10.71MM **Privately Held**
SIC: 2022 Imitation cheese

(P-1289)
SAPUTO CHEESE USA INC
5611 Imperial Hwy, South Gate
(90280-7419)
PHONE..........................562 862-7686
Rick Mckenney, *Brnch Mgr*
EMP: 527
SALES (corp-wide): 3.79B **Privately Held**
Web: www.saputo.com
SIC: 2022 5143 Natural cheese; Cheese
HQ: Saputo Cheese Usa Inc.
10700 W Res Dr Ste 400
Milwaukee WI 53226

(P-1290)
SIERRA CHEESE MANUFACTURING COMPANY INC
Also Called: Sierra
916 S Santa Fe Ave, Compton
(90221-4392)
PHONE..........................310 635-1216
EMP: 39 **EST:** 1959
SALES (est): 4.77MM **Privately Held**
Web: www.sierracheese.com
SIC: 2022 Natural cheese

2023 Dry, Condensed, Evaporated Products

(P-1291)
ARMOR DERMALOGICS LLC
9151 Atlanta Ave Unit 5864, Huntington
Beach (92615-2436)
PHONE..........................714 202-6424
EMP: 50 **EST:** 2018
SALES (est): 306.03K **Privately Held**
SIC: 2023 Dietary supplements, dairy and
non-dairy based

(P-1292)
BETTER NUTRITIONALS LLC
3380 Horseless Carriage Rd, Norco
(92860-3635)
PHONE..........................310 356-9019
Roger Tyre, *Brnch Mgr*
EMP: 100
SALES (corp-wide): 34.31MM **Privately Held**
SIC: 2023 Dietary supplements, dairy and
non-dairy based
PA: Better Nutritionals, Llc
3390 Hrseless Carriage Dr
310 356-9019

(P-1293)
BETTER NUTRITIONALS LLC
3350 Horseless Carriage Rd, Norco
(92860-3635)
PHONE..........................310 356-9019
Roger Tyre, *Brnch Mgr*
EMP: 100
SALES (corp-wide): 34.31MM **Privately Held**
SIC: 2023 Dietary supplements, dairy and
non-dairy based
PA: Better Nutritionals, Llc
3390 Hrseless Carriage Dr
310 356-9019

PRODUCTS & SVCS

(P-1294)
BETTER NUTRITIONALS LLC
17120 S Figueroa St Ste B, Gardena
(90248-3024)
PHONE.................310 356-9019
Sharon Hoffman, *Brnch Mgr*
EMP: 50
SALES (corp-wide): 34.31MM **Privately Held**
Web: www.betternutritionals.com
SIC: 2023 Dietary supplements, dairy and non-dairy based
PA: Better Nutritionals, Llc
3390 Hrseless Carriage Dr
310 356-9019

(P-1295)
BETTER NUTRITIONALS LLC (PA)
3390 Horseless Carriage Dr, Norco
(92860-3635)
PHONE.................310 356-9019
Sharon Hoffman, *CEO*
▼ **EMP:** 30 **EST:** 2015
SQ FT: 100,000
SALES (est): 34.31MM
SALES (corp-wide): 34.31MM **Privately Held**
SIC: 2023 Dietary supplements, dairy and non-dairy based

(P-1296)
BIO-NUTRITIONAL RES GROUP INC
Also Called: Power Crunch
6 Morgan Ste 100, Irvine (92618-1920)
P.O. Box 3669 (90510-3669)
PHONE.................714 427-6990
Kevin Lawrence, *CEO*
Karen L Stensby, *
Curtis Steinhaus, *
EMP: 185 **EST:** 1991
SQ FT: 3,000
SALES (est): 49.64MM **Privately Held**
Web: www.powercrunch.com
SIC: 2023 Dietary supplements, dairy and non-dairy based

(P-1297)
EL INDIO SHOPS INCORPORATED
Also Called: El Indio Mexican Restaurant
3695 India St, San Diego (92103-4799)
PHONE.................619 299-0333
Ralph R Pesqueira Junior, *Pr*
Eva Sanchez, *
EMP: 55 **EST:** 1940
SQ FT: 10,000
SALES (est): 4.56MM **Privately Held**
Web: www.elindiosandiego.net
SIC: 2023 5812 Evaporated buttermilk; Mexican restaurant

(P-1298)
FEIHE INTERNATIONAL INC (PA)
2275 Huntington Dr Pmb 278, San Marino
(91108-2640)
PHONE.................626 757-8885
You-bin Leng, *Pr*
Hua Liu, *
EMP: 1932 **EST:** 1985
SALES (est): 362.97MM **Privately Held**
SIC: 2023 Dry, condensed and evaporated dairy products

(P-1299)
KERRY INC
64405 Lincoln St, Mecca (92254-6501)
P.O. Box 398 (92254-0398)

PHONE.................760 396-2116
Darren Worden, *Pr*
EMP: 63
Web: www.kerry.com
SIC: 2023 Dry, condensed and evaporated dairy products
HQ: Kerry Inc.
3400 Millington Rd
Beloit WI 53511
608 363-1200

(P-1300)
LIEF ORGANICS LLC (PA)
Also Called: Lief Labs
28903 Avenue Paine, Valencia
(91355-4169)
PHONE.................661 775-2500
Adel Villalobos, *CEO*
Adel Villalobos, *Pr*
Steve Chopp, *
Victor Leyson, *
Nathan Cox, *Development*
EMP: 25 **EST:** 2008
SALES (est): 43.84MM
SALES (corp-wide): 43.84MM **Privately Held**
Web: www.lieforganics.com
SIC: 2023 Dietary supplements, dairy and non-dairy based

(P-1301)
NATURALIFE ECO VITE LABS
Also Called: Paragon Laboratories
20433 Earl St, Torrance (90503-2414)
PHONE.................310 370-1563
Jay Kaufman, *CEO*
Richard Kaufman, *
Claire Kaufman, *
Steven Billis, *
▲ **EMP:** 100 **EST:** 1971
SQ FT: 25,000
SALES (est): 25.51MM **Privately Held**
Web: www.paragonlabsusa.com
SIC: 2023 2844 2834 5122 Dietary supplements, dairy and non-dairy based; Toilet preparations; Suppositories; Vitamins and minerals

(P-1302)
NESTLE USA INC
3285 De Forest Cir, Jurupa Valley
(91752-3239)
PHONE.................877 463-7853
EMP: 71
Web: www.nestleusa.com
SIC: 2023 Evaporated milk
HQ: Nestle Usa, Inc.
1812 N Moore St
Arlington VA 22209
800 225-2270

(P-1303)
NESTLE USA INC
7301 District Blvd, Bakersfield
(93313-2042)
PHONE.................661 398-3536
EMP: 170
Web: www.nestleusa.com
SIC: 2023 Evaporated milk
HQ: Nestle Usa, Inc.
1812 N Moore St
Arlington VA 22209
800 225-2270

(P-1304)
NESTLE USA INC
800 N Brand Blvd, Glendale (91203-1245)
PHONE.................818 549-6000
EMP: 157
Web: www.nestle.com

SIC: 2023 Evaporated milk
HQ: Nestle Usa, Inc.
1812 N Moore St
Arlington VA 22209
800 225-2270

(P-1305)
NOVOTECH NUTRACEUTICALS INC
Also Called: Manufacturer
4987 Olivas Park Dr, Ventura (93003-7667)
PHONE.................805 676-1098
Jennifer L Li, *Pr*
Jennifer Lihhwa Li, *CEO*
EMP: 42 **EST:** 2007
SALES (est): 5.94MM **Privately Held**
Web: www.novotechnutra.com
SIC: 2023 2833 2911 2048 Dietary supplements, dairy and non-dairy based; Vitamins, natural or synthetic: bulk, uncompounded; Mineral oils, natural; Mineral feed supplements

(P-1306)
PHARMACHEM LABORATORIES LLC
Also Called: PHARMACHEM LABORATORIES, LLC
2929 E White Star Ave, Anaheim
(92806-2628)
PHONE.................714 630-6000
George Joseph, *VP*
EMP: 42
SALES (corp-wide): 2.11B **Publicly Held**
Web: www.ashland.com
SIC: 2023 Dietary supplements, dairy and non-dairy based
HQ: Pharmachem Laboratories Llc
265 Harrison Tpke
Kearny NJ 07032

(P-1307)
PROLACTA BIOSCIENCE INC
1800 Highland Ave, Duarte (91010-2837)
PHONE.................626 599-9260
Scott A Elster, *CEO*
EMP: 304
SALES (corp-wide): 91.91MM **Privately Held**
Web: www.prolacta.com
SIC: 2023 Dried and powdered milk and milk products
PA: Prolacta Bioscience, Inc.
757 Baldwin Pk Blvd
626 599-9260

(P-1308)
UQORA INC
4250 Executive Sq, La Jolla (92037-1482)
PHONE.................888 313-1372
Vivian Rhoads, *Pr*
Jenna Ryan, *
Spencer Gordon, *
EMP: 43 **EST:** 2017
SALES (est): 23.57MM **Privately Held**
Web: www.uqora.com
SIC: 2023 Dietary supplements, dairy and non-dairy based
HQ: Pharmavite Llc
8531 Fallbrook Ave
West Hills CA 91304
818 221-6200

(P-1309)
VITAMIN FRIENDS LLC
17120 S Figueroa St Ste B, Gardena
(90248-3024)
PHONE.................310 356-9018
Sharon Hoffman, *Pr*
▲ **EMP:** 25 **EST:** 2012

SQ FT: 5,000
SALES (est): 1.87MM **Privately Held**
Web: www.vitaminfriends.com
SIC: 2023 Dietary supplements, dairy and non-dairy based

(P-1310)
VITAWEST NUTRACEUTICALS INC
Also Called: Chocolates and Health
1502 Arrow Hwy, La Verne (91750-5318)
PHONE.................888 557-8012
Iraiz Gomez, *CEO*
EMP: 25 **EST:** 2016
SALES (est): 2.13MM **Privately Held**
Web: www.vitawestnutra.com
SIC: 2023 Dietary supplements, dairy and non-dairy based

(P-1311)
WELLINGTON FOODS INC (PA)
1930 California Ave, Corona (92881-6491)
PHONE.................951 547-7000
Anthony E Hamack Senior, *Ch*
Tony Mauer, *CFO*
▲ **EMP:** 144 **EST:** 1974
SQ FT: 50,000
SALES (est): 27.28MM
SALES (corp-wide): 27.28MM **Privately Held**
Web: www.wellingtonfoods.com
SIC: 2023 Dietary supplements, dairy and non-dairy based

(P-1312)
YBCC INC
17800 Castleton St Ste 386, City Of Industry
(91748-1791)
PHONE.................626 213-3945
Xiuhua Song, *Pr*
EMP: 38 **EST:** 1986
SALES (est): 352.06K **Privately Held**
SIC: 2023 Dietary supplements, dairy and non-dairy based

2024 Ice Cream And Frozen Deserts

(P-1313)
BERENICE 2 AM CORP
Also Called: Bobboi Natural Gelato
8008 Girard Ave Ste 150, La Jolla
(92037-4159)
PHONE.................858 255-8693
Andrea Racca, *CEO*
Andrea Racca, *Ofcr*
EMP: 50 **EST:** 2014
SQ FT: 900
SALES (est): 1.83MM **Privately Held**
Web: www.bobboi.com
SIC: 2024 Ice cream and frozen deserts

(P-1314)
BIG TRAIN INC
Also Called: Big T Industries
25392 Commercentre Dr, Lake Forest
(92630-8823)
PHONE.................949 340-8800
◆ **EMP:** 150
Web: www.kerryfoodservice.com
SIC: 2024 2086 Ice cream and frozen deserts ; Fruit drinks (less than 100% juice): packaged in cans, etc.

(P-1315)
BROTHERS INTL DESSERTS (PA)
Also Called: Brothers Desserts

3400 W Segerstrom Ave, Santa Ana
(92704-6405)
PHONE..............................949 655-0080
Gary M Winkler, *CEO*
▲ **EMP:** 200 **EST:** 1974
SALES (est): 44.34MM
SALES (corp-wide): 44.34MM **Privately Held**
Web: www.brothersdesserts.com
SIC: 2024 Ice cream, bulk

(P-1316)
DANONE US LLC
3500 Barranca Pkwy Ste 240, Irvine
(92606-8231)
PHONE..............................949 474-9670
John Mastrotaolo, *Dir*
EMP: 43
SALES (corp-wide): 967.79MM **Privately Held**
Web: www.dannon.com
SIC: 2024 Ice cream and frozen deserts
HQ: Danone Us, Llc
    1 Maple Ave
    White Plains NY 10605
    914 872-8400

(P-1317)
FARCHITECTURE BB LLC
Also Called: Coolhaus
8588 Washington Blvd, Culver City
(90232-7463)
PHONE..............................917 701-2777
Natasha Case, *Managing Member*
Daniel Fishman, *
EMP: 30 **EST:** 2009
SALES (est): 4.94MM **Privately Held**
SIC: 2024 Ice cream, packaged: molded, on sticks, etc.

(P-1318)
HIGH ROAD CRAFT ICE CREAM INC (PA)
12243 Branford St, Sun Valley
(91352-1010)
PHONE..............................678 701-7623
Keith M Schroeder, *CEO*
Nicki Schroeder, *CMO*
Christian Rodrigue, *
Justine Zarch, *Chief Supply Chain Officer*
Danielle O'connor, *CFO*
EMP: 25 **EST:** 2010
SALES (est): 20.81MM **Privately Held**
Web: www.highroadcraft.com
SIC: 2024 Ice cream and frozen deserts

(P-1319)
MACKIE INTERNATIONAL INC (PA)
Also Called: Sun Ice USA
4193 Flat Rock Dr Ste 200, Riverside
(92505-7113)
PHONE..............................951 346-0530
Ernesto U Dacay Junior, *Pr*
◆ **EMP:** 40 **EST:** 1983
SALES (est): 4.8MM
SALES (corp-wide): 4.8MM **Privately Held**
Web: www.mackieinternational.net
SIC: 2024 2086 5199 Ices, flavored (frozen dessert); Fruit drinks (less than 100% juice): packaged in cans, etc.; Baskets

(P-1320)
TROPICALE FOODS LLC (PA)
1237 W State St, Ontario (91762-4015)
P.O. Box 2224 (91708)
PHONE..............................909 635-1000
Steven C Schiller, *CEO*
▲ **EMP:** 46 **EST:** 1999
SALES (est): 181.55MM

SALES (corp-wide): 181.55MM **Privately Held**
Web: www.tropicalefoods.com
SIC: 2024 Ice milk, packaged: molded, on sticks, etc.

(P-1321)
WE THE PIE PEOPLE LLC
Also Called: Jc's Pie Pops
9909 Topanga Canyon Blvd # 159, Chatsworth (91311-3602)
PHONE..............................818 349-1880
Jennifer Constantine, *Managing Member*
Thomas Spler, *
▲ **EMP:** 50 **EST:** 2012
SALES (est): 769.51K **Privately Held**
Web: www.piepops.com
SIC: 2024 Nondairy based frozen desserts

(P-1322)
ZIEGENFELDER COMPANY
12262 Colony Ave, Chino (91710-2095)
PHONE..............................909 509-0493
Donovan Arriaga, *Dir*
EMP: 65
Web: www.twinpops.com
SIC: 2024 Fruit pops, frozen
HQ: The Ziegenfelder Company
    87 18th St
    Wheeling WV 26003
    304 232-6360

(P-1323)
ZIEGENFELDER COMPANY
12290 Colony Ave, Chino (91710-2095)
PHONE..............................909 590-0493
Allan Hawthorne, *Brnch Mgr*
EMP: 65
Web: www.twinpops.com
SIC: 2024 Ice cream, packaged: molded, on sticks, etc.
HQ: The Ziegenfelder Company
    87 18th St
    Wheeling WV 26003
    304 232-6360

2026 Fluid Milk

(P-1324)
AYO FOODS LLC
Also Called: Ayo Food
927 Main St, Delano (93215-1729)
P.O. Box 1987 (93216-1987)
PHONE..............................661 345-5457
Matt Billings, *Managing Member*
EMP: 50 **EST:** 2018
SALES (est): 100K **Privately Held**
Web: www.ayoyogurt.com
SIC: 2026 Yogurt

(P-1325)
BERKELEY FARMS LLC
Also Called: Buds Ice Cream San Francisco
17637 E Valley Blvd, City Of Industry
(91744-5731)
P.O. Box 4616 (94540-4616)
PHONE..............................510 265-8600
▲ **EMP:** 400
Web: www.berkeleyfarms.com
SIC: 2026 0241 5143 Fluid milk; Dairy farms; Butter

(P-1326)
CALIFORNIA DAIRIES INC
11709 Artesia Blvd, Artesia (90701-3803)
PHONE..............................562 809-2595
Joe Heffington, *Brnch Mgr*
EMP: 65
SALES (corp-wide): 3.32B **Privately Held**

Web: www.californiadairies.com
SIC: 2026 Milk processing (pasteurizing, homogenizing, bottling)
PA: California Dairies, Inc.
    2000 N Plz Dr
    559 625-2200

(P-1327)
DAIRY FARMERS AMERICA INC
4375 N Ventura Ave, Ventura (93001-1124)
PHONE..............................805 653-0042
Kevin Clark, *Mgr*
EMP: 26
SALES (corp-wide): 21.72B **Privately Held**
Web: www.dfamilk.com
SIC: 2026 2022 2021 2023 Milk processing (pasteurizing, homogenizing, bottling); Natural cheese; Creamery butter; Condensed milk
PA: Dairy Farmers Of America, Inc.
    1405 N 98th St
    816 801-6455

(P-1328)
DEAN SOCAL LLC
Also Called: Swiss Dairy
17637 E Valley Blvd, City Of Industry
(91744-5731)
PHONE..............................951 734-3950
EMP: 140
SIC: 2026 Fluid milk

(P-1329)
FARMDALE CREAMERY LLC
Also Called: Farmdale
1049 W Base Line St, San Bernardino
(92411-2310)
PHONE..............................909 888-4938
Norman R Shotts Ii, *CEO*
Nicholas J Sibilio, *
Norman R Shotts Iii, *Genl Mgr*
Michael Shotts, *General Vice President*
Florence Shotts, *
▲ **EMP:** 100 **EST:** 1978
SQ FT: 110,000
SALES (est): 7.34MM **Privately Held**
Web: www.farmdale.net
SIC: 2026 2022 Buttermilk, cultured; Natural cheese

(P-1330)
GENERAL MILLS INC
Also Called: General Mills
1055 Sandhill Ave, Carson (90746-1312)
P.O. Box 4589 (90749-4589)
PHONE..............................310 605-6108
Jeff Crandle, *Mgr*
EMP: 08
SQ FT: 62,497
SALES (corp-wide): 19.86B **Publicly Held**
Web: www.generalmills.com
SIC: 2026 2041 Yogurt; Flour mixes
PA: General Mills, Inc.
    1 General Mills Blvd
    763 764-7600

(P-1331)
GOOD CULTURE LLC
22 Corporate Park, Irvine (92606-3117)
PHONE..............................949 545-9945
Jesse Merrill, *Managing Member*
Anders Eisner, *Managing Member*
EMP: 25 **EST:** 2014
SALES (est): 2MM **Privately Held**
Web: www.goodculture.com
SIC: 2026 2023 Fluid milk; Dry, condensed and evaporated dairy products

(P-1332)
HERITAGE DISTRIBUTING COMPANY (PA)
Also Called: Rex Creamery
5743 Smithway St Ste 105, Commerce
(90040-1548)
P.O. Box 668 (90241-0668)
PHONE..............................323 838-1225
Ted S Degroot, *Pr*
EMP: 24 **EST:** 1998
SALES (est): 68.56MM **Privately Held**
SIC: 2026 Milk processing (pasteurizing, homogenizing, bottling)

(P-1333)
PAC FILL INC
Also Called: Sun Dairy Co
5471 W San Fernando Rd, Los Angeles
(90039-1014)
PHONE..............................818 409-0117
Vahik Sarkissian, *CEO*
Edward Sarkissian, *
Jerry Nicoghosian, *
EMP: 25 **EST:** 1977
SQ FT: 22,000
SALES (est): 9.23MM **Privately Held**
Web: www.sundairy.com
SIC: 2026 2086 Yogurt; Carbonated soft drinks, bottled and canned

(P-1334)
PARAMOUNT DAIRY INC
15255 Texaco Ave, Paramount
(90723-3917)
PHONE..............................562 361-1800
Phillip C Chang, *Brnch Mgr*
EMP: 135
SALES (corp-wide): 3.07MM **Privately Held**
Web: www.paramount-dairy.com
SIC: 2026 Yogurt
PA: Paramount Dairy, Inc.
    17801 Cartwright Rd
    949 265-8077

(P-1335)
STREMICKS HERITAGE FOODS LLC (HQ)
Also Called: Heritage Foods
4002 Westminster Ave, Santa Ana
(92703-1310)
PHONE..............................714 775-5000
Louis J Stremick, *Managing Member*
Michael W Malone, *
Jack P Noenickx, *Managing Member*
▼ **EMP:** 300 **EST:** 1916
SALES (est): 574.58MM
SALES (corp-wide): 21.72B **Privately Held**
Web: www.heritage-foods.com
SIC: 2026 Cream, sour
PA: Dairy Farmers Of America, Inc.
    1405 N 98th St
    816 801-6455

(P-1336)
WIN SOON INC
Also Called: Epoca Yocool
4569 Firestone Blvd, South Gate
(90280-3343)
PHONE..............................323 564-5070
Junsang Lee, *Pr*
Jun Sang Lee, *
▲ **EMP:** 52 **EST:** 1993
SQ FT: 7,000
SALES (est): 8.66MM **Privately Held**
Web: www.winsoonepoca.com
SIC: 2026 5149 Yogurt; Soft drinks

2032 Canned Specialties

(P-1337)
BELLISSIMO DISTRIBUTION LLC
Also Called: Greco and Sons
1389 Park Center Dr, Vista (92081-8338)
PHONE..............................760 292-9100
EMP: 48
SALES (corp-wide): 78.84B **Publicly Held**
Web: www.grecoandsons.com
SIC: 2032 Italian foods, nec: packaged in cans, jars, etc.
HQ: Bellissimo Distribution, Llc
　　1550 Hecht Dr
　　Bartlett IL 60103

(P-1338)
CAER INC
Also Called: Yumi
8070 Melrose Ave, Los Angeles (90046-7015)
PHONE..............................415 879-9864
Angela Sutherland, *CEO*
Evelyn Rusli, *
▲ EMP: 27 EST: 2015
SALES (est): 5.86MM **Privately Held**
Web: www.helloyumi.com
SIC: 2032 7389 Baby foods, including meats: packaged in cans, jars, etc.; Business Activities at Non-Commercial Site

(P-1339)
CORN MAIDEN FOODS INC
24201 Frampton Ave, Harbor City (90710-2105)
PHONE..............................310 784-0400
Pascal Dropsy, *Pr*
EMP: 65 EST: 1995
SQ FT: 40,000
SALES (est): 3.49MM **Privately Held**
Web: www.commaidenfoods.com
SIC: 2032 Canned specialties

(P-1340)
DOLORES CANNING CO INC
1020 N Eastern Ave, Los Angeles (90063-3214)
P.O. Box 63187 (90063-0187)
PHONE..............................323 263-9155
David Munoz, *Pr*
Steve A Munoz, *
Frank T Munoz, *
EMP: 25 EST: 1956
SQ FT: 5,000
SALES (est): 6.09MM **Privately Held**
Web: www.dolorescanning.com
SIC: 2032 2011 Mexican foods, nec: packaged in cans, jars, etc.; Meat packing plants

(P-1341)
JUANITAS FOODS
Also Called: Pico Pica Foods
645 George De La Torre Jr Ave, Wilmington (90744-6055)
P.O. Box 847 (90748-0847)
PHONE..............................310 834-5339
Aaron De La Torre, *CEO*
Mark De La Torre, *
James Steveson, *
EMP: 125 EST: 1946
SQ FT: 85,000
SALES (est): 43MM **Privately Held**
Web: www.juanitas.com
SIC: 2032 Mexican foods, nec: packaged in cans, jars, etc.

(P-1342)
KRAFT HEINZ FOODS COMPANY
Heinz
2450 White Rd, Irvine (92614-6250)
PHONE..............................949 250-4080
Dan Foss, *Brnch Mgr*
EMP: 26
SALES (corp-wide): 26.64B **Publicly Held**
Web: www.kraftheinzcompany.com
SIC: 2032 2035 Soups, except seafood: packaged in cans, jars, etc.; Seasonings and sauces, except tomato and dry
HQ: Kraft Heinz Foods Company
　　1 Ppg Pl Ste 3400
　　Pittsburgh PA 15222
　　412 456-5700

(P-1343)
SALICO FARMS INC
4231 Us Highway 86 Ste 4, Brawley (92227-9648)
P.O. Box 1531 (92227-0229)
PHONE..............................760 344-5375
Niaz Mohamed Junior, *Pr*
Sara Ann Mohamed, *
Martin Mohamed, *
EMP: 120 EST: 1981
SQ FT: 2,400
SALES (est): 472.61K **Privately Held**
SIC: 2032 Beans and bean sprouts, canned, jarred, etc.

(P-1344)
SHINE FOOD INC (PA)
19216 Normandie Ave, Torrance (90502-1011)
PHONE..............................310 329-3829
Stephen Y S Lee, *CEO*
Tracy Lee, *
▲ EMP: 50 EST: 1986
SQ FT: 30,000
SALES (est): 13.37MM
SALES (corp-wide): 13.37MM **Privately Held**
Web: www.shinefoods.com
SIC: 2032 Canned specialties

(P-1345)
SUPERIOR QUALITY FOODS INC
Also Called: Superior Touch
2355 E Francis St, Ontario (91761-7727)
P.O. Box 908 (30162-0908)
PHONE..............................909 923-4733
▲ EMP: 63
SIC: 2032 2034 Canned specialties; Dried and dehydrated soup mixes

(P-1346)
T & T FOODS INC
Also Called: Colonel Lee's Enterprises
3080 E 50th St, Vernon (90058-2918)
PHONE..............................323 588-2158
Michelle Ma, *CEO*
David Ma, *VP*
EMP: 50 EST: 1967
SQ FT: 19,000
SALES (est): 4.88MM **Privately Held**
Web: www.tandtfoods.net
SIC: 2032 2099 Ethnic foods, canned, jarred, etc.; Food preparations, nec

(P-1347)
WING HING FOODS LLC
Also Called: Wing Hing
1659 E 23rd St, Los Angeles (90011-1803)
PHONE..............................323 232-8899
▲ EMP: 90
Web: www.winghing.com
SIC: 2032 Ethnic foods, canned, jarred, etc.

2033 Canned Fruits And Specialties

(P-1348)
ASEPTIC TECHNOLOGY LLC
Also Called: Aseptic Technology
24855 Corbit Pl, Yorba Linda (92887-5543)
PHONE..............................714 694-0168
Julie Hodson, *
Noel Calma, *
Clay White, *
Lan Pham, *
EMP: 117 EST: 2013
SQ FT: 59,300
SALES (est): 6.53MM **Privately Held**
Web: www.asepticllc.com
SIC: 2033 Canned fruits and specialties

(P-1349)
BEAUMONT JUICE LLC
Also Called: Perricone Juices
550 B St, Beaumont (92223-2672)
PHONE..............................951 769-7171
Robert Paul Rovzar, *CEO*
Thomas M Carmody, *
Joe Perricone, *
Paul Golub, *
▲ EMP: 98 EST: 1994
SQ FT: 30,000
SALES (est): 37.91MM
SALES (corp-wide): 37.91MM **Privately Held**
Web: www.perriconefarms.com
SIC: 2033 Fruit juices: fresh
PA: G B & P Citrus Co Inc
　　1601 E Olympic Blvd Ste 1
　　213 312-1380

(P-1350)
HK CANNING INC (PA)
130 N Garden St, Ventura (93001-2529)
PHONE..............................805 652-1392
Henry Knaust, *Pr*
Carol Knaust, *VP*
EMP: 39 EST: 1996
SQ FT: 91,552
SALES (est): 3.35MM **Privately Held**
SIC: 2033 Vegetables: packaged in cans, jars, etc.

(P-1351)
J M SMUCKER COMPANY
800 Commercial Ave, Oxnard (93030-7234)
P.O. Box 5161 (93031-5161)
PHONE..............................805 487-5483
Al Yamamoto, *Mgr*
EMP: 47
SQ FT: 20,000
SALES (corp-wide): 8.18B **Publicly Held**
Web: www.smuckers.com
SIC: 2033 Canned fruits and specialties
PA: The J M Smucker Company
　　1 Strawberry Ln
　　330 682-3000

(P-1352)
KRAFT HEINZ FOODS COMPANY
Also Called: Kraft Foods
1500 E Walnut Ave, Fullerton (92831-4731)
PHONE..............................714 870-8235
Robert Pech, *Brnch Mgr*
EMP: 43
SQ FT: 2,878
SALES (corp-wide): 26.64B **Publicly Held**
Web: www.kraftheinzcompany.com
SIC: 2033 Canned fruits and specialties
HQ: Kraft Heinz Foods Company
　　1 Ppg Pl Ste 3400
　　Pittsburgh PA 15222
　　412 456-5700

(P-1353)
LUDFORDS INC
3038 Pleasant St, Riverside (92507-5554)
PHONE..............................909 948-0797
EMP: 40 EST: 1926
SALES (est): 35.84MM **Privately Held**
Web: www.ludfordsinc.com
SIC: 2033 Fruit juices: packaged in cans, jars, etc.

(P-1354)
NASCO GOURMET FOODS INC
Also Called: Platinum Distribution
22720 Savi Ranch Pkwy, Yorba Linda (92887-4608)
PHONE..............................714 279-2100
Burhan Nasser, *Pr*
Jerry Pascoe, *
Mary Beth Nasser, *
EMP: 90 EST: 1990
SQ FT: 42,000
SALES (est): 3.67MM
SALES (corp-wide): 44.16MM **Privately Held**
Web: www.nasserco.com
SIC: 2033 Seasonings, tomato: packaged in cans, jars, etc.
PA: Nasser Company, Inc.
　　22720 Savi Ranch Pkwy
　　714 279-2100

(P-1355)
REFRESCO BEVERAGES US INC
Also Called: Crosby Fruit Products
11751 Pacific Ave, Fontana (92337-6961)
PHONE..............................951 685-0481
Kirk Karassa, *Brnch Mgr*
EMP: 150
SQ FT: 99,500
Web: www.refresco-na.com
SIC: 2033 Fruit juices: packaged in cans, jars, etc.
HQ: Refresco Beverages Us Inc.
　　8112 Woodland Ctr Blvd
　　Tampa FL 33614

(P-1356)
SATICOY FOODS CORPORATION
554 Todd Rd, Santa Paula (93060-9725)
P.O. Box 4547 (93007-0547)
PHONE..............................805 647-5266
EMP: 40 EST: 1967
SALES (est): 12.19MM
SALES (corp-wide): 63.59MM **Privately Held**
SIC: 2033 Vegetables: packaged in cans, jars, etc.
PA: Moody Dunbar, Inc.
　　2000 Waters Edge Dr # 21
　　423 952-0100

(P-1357)
SUNDOWN FOODS USA INC
Also Called: Sundown Foods
10891 Business Dr, Fontana (92337-8235)
PHONE..............................909 606-6797
Jeff Wartell, *Pr*
▲ EMP: 30 EST: 1998
SALES (est): 4.14MM **Privately Held**
Web: www.sundownfoods.com
SIC: 2033 Vegetables and vegetable products, in cans, jars, etc.

(P-1358)
SUNNYGEM LLC (PA)
Also Called: Sunnygem
500 N F St, Wasco (93280-1435)
PHONE..............................661 758-0491
John Vidovich, *Managing Member*
Ajit Sidhu, *

◆ **EMP:** 116 **EST:** 2005
SQ FT: 270,000
SALES (est): 41.45MM **Privately Held**
Web: www.sunnygem.com
SIC: 2033 3556 Fruit juices: fresh; Juice extractors, fruit and vegetable: commercial type

(P-1359)
TROPICAL PRESERVING CO INC
5 Lewiston Ct, Ladera Ranch (92694-0532)
PHONE..................213 748-5108
Ronald Randall, *Pr*
EMP: 23 **EST:** 1928
SALES (est): 1.96MM **Privately Held**
Web: www.tropicalpreserving.com
SIC: 2033 Jams, jellies, and preserves, packaged in cans, jars, etc.

(P-1360)
VITA JUICE CORPORATION
10725 Sutter Ave, Pacoima (91331-2596)
PHONE..................818 899-1195
EMP: 100
SIC: 2033 Fruit juices: concentrated, hot pack

(P-1361)
VITA-PAKT CITRUS PRODUCTS CO (PA)
10000 Stockdale Hwy Ste 390, Bakersfield (93311-3601)
P.O. Box 309 (91723-0309)
PHONE..................626 332-1101
James R Boyles, *CEO*
Lloyd Shimizu, *
◆ **EMP:** 50 **EST:** 1957
SALES (est): 47.18MM
SALES (corp-wide): 47.18MM **Privately Held**
Web: www.vita-pakt.com
SIC: 2033 2037 Apple sauce: packaged in cans, jars, etc.; Fruit juices, frozen

(P-1362)
VIVE ORGANIC INC
2554 Lincoln Blvd Ste 772, Venice (90291-5043)
PHONE..................877 774-9291
Wyatt Taubman, *CEO*
EMP: 35 **EST:** 2015
SALES (est): 5.27MM
SALES (corp-wide): 59.64MM **Privately Held**
Web: www.viveorganic.com
SIC: 2033 Fruit juices: packaged in cans, jars, etc.
PA: Suja Life, Llc
3841 Ocean Ranch Blvd
855 879-7852

(P-1363)
WALKER FOODS INC
Also Called: La Flora Del Sur
237 N Mission Rd, Los Angeles (90033-2103)
PHONE..................323 268-5191
Robert L Walker Junior, *Pr*
Denise Walker, *
EMP: 65 **EST:** 1914
SQ FT: 150,000
SALES (est): 15.06MM **Privately Held**
Web: www.walkerfoods.net
SIC: 2033 2032 2099 Canned fruits and specialties; Canned specialties; Ready-to-eat meals, salads, and sandwiches

2034 Dehydrated Fruits, Vegetables, Soups

(P-1364)
AMERICAN FOOD INGREDIENTS INC
4021 Avenida De La Plata Ste 501, Oceanside (92056-5849)
PHONE..................760 967-6287
Karen Koppenhaver, *CEO*
▲ **EMP:** 30 **EST:** 1993
SQ FT: 2,000
SALES (est): 7.73MM **Privately Held**
Web: www.americanfoodingredients.com
SIC: 2034 Dried and dehydrated vegetables

(P-1365)
INLAND EMPIRE FOODS INC (PA)
5425 Wilson St, Riverside (92509-2434)
PHONE..................951 682-8222
Mark H Sterner, *Pr*
Paul Stiritz, *
▼ **EMP:** 35 **EST:** 1985
SQ FT: 85,000
SALES (est): 10.57MM
SALES (corp-wide): 10.57MM **Privately Held**
Web: www.inlandempirefoods.com
SIC: 2034 Vegetables, dried or dehydrated (except freeze-dried)

(P-1366)
NAMAR FOODS
Also Called: Namar Company
6830 Walthall Way, Paramount (90723-2028)
PHONE..................562 531-2744
EMP: 38 **EST:** 1962
SALES (est): 5.11MM **Privately Held**
Web: www.namar.com
SIC: 2034 Dried and dehydrated fruits, vegetables and soup mixes

2035 Pickles, Sauces, And Salad Dressings

(P-1367)
GEDNEY FOODS COMPANY
12243 Branford St, Sun Valley (91352-1010)
P.O. Box 8 (55318-0008)
PHONE..................952 448-2612
Charles Weil, *CEO*
Barry Stecter, *
Carl Tuttle, *
James R Cook, *Technology Vice President*
▲ **EMP:** 125 **EST:** 1881
SALES (est): 2.32MM **Privately Held**
Web: www.gedneyfoods.com
SIC: 2035 Pickles, vinegar

(P-1368)
GFF INC
Also Called: Girard Food Service
145 Willow Ave, City Of Industry (91746-2047)
PHONE..................323 232-6255
Emanuel Marti, *CEO*
Bill Perry, *Pr*
William Perry, *Pr*
▲ **EMP:** 89 **EST:** 1981
SQ FT: 92,000
SALES (est): 47.43MM **Privately Held**
Web: www.girardsdressings.com
SIC: 2035 Pickles, sauces, and salad dressings

PA: Haco Holding Ag
Worbstrasse 262

(P-1369)
LEE KUM KEE (USA) FOODS INC (PA)
14455 Don Julian Rd, City Of Industry (91746-3102)
PHONE..................626 709-1888
Simon Wu, *Pr*
Dickson Chan, *
EMP: 99 **EST:** 1996
SQ FT: 54,000
SALES (est): 17.13MM
SALES (corp-wide): 17.13MM **Privately Held**
Web: corporate.lkk.com
SIC: 2035 Seasonings and sauces, except tomato and dry

(P-1370)
MOREHOUSE FOODS INC
760 Epperson Dr, City Of Industry (91748-1336)
PHONE..................626 854-1655
David L Latter Senior, *Ch*
David L Latter Junior, *Pr*
◆ **EMP:** 50 **EST:** 1898
SQ FT: 65,000
SALES (est): 10.08MM **Privately Held**
Web: www.morehousefoods.com
SIC: 2035 5149 Mustard, prepared (wet); Seasonings, sauces, and extracts

(P-1371)
PACIFICA FOODS LLC
Also Called: Stir Foods
1581 N Main St, Orange (92867-3439)
PHONE..................951 371-3123
Ming Milton Liu, *
EMP: 140 **EST:** 2000
SALES (est): 60MM
SALES (corp-wide): 249.44MM **Privately Held**
Web: www.stirfoods.com
SIC: 2035 5149 2033 Seasonings and sauces, except tomato and dry; Sauces; Tomato products, packaged in cans, jars, etc.
PA: Corona-Orange Foods Intermediate Holdings Llc
1581 N Main St
714 637-6050

(P-1372)
Q & B FOODS INC (DH)
15547 1st St, Irwindale (91706-6201)
PHONE..................020 304-0090
Kuniaki Ishikaiwa, *Pr*
Jerry Shepherd, *Ex VP*
Akio Okumura, *CEO*
◆ **EMP:** 69 **EST:** 1982
SQ FT: 52,000
SALES (est): 41.31MM **Privately Held**
Web: www.qbfoods.com
SIC: 2035 Dressings, salad: raw and cooked (except dry mixes)
HQ: Kifuki U.S.A. Co., Inc.
15547 1st St
Irwindale CA 91706

(P-1373)
VANLAW FOOD PRODUCTS INC (HQ)
Also Called: Coron-Rnge Fods Intrmdate Hldn
2325 Moore Ave, Fullerton (92833-2510)
P.O. Box 2388 (92837-0388)
PHONE..................714 870-9091
EMP: 72 **EST:** 1945
SALES (est): 50.27MM

SALES (corp-wide): 249.44MM **Privately Held**
Web: www.stirfoods.com
SIC: 2035 2087 Pickles, sauces, and salad dressings; Syrups, drink
PA: Corona-Orange Foods Intermediate Holdings Llc
1581 N Main St
714 637-6050

2037 Frozen Fruits And Vegetables

(P-1374)
CANADAS FINEST FOODS INC
Also Called: Reliant Foodservice
26090 Ynez Rd, Temecula (92591-6000)
PHONE..................951 296-1040
David Canada, *Pr*
▲ **EMP:** 70 **EST:** 1996
SQ FT: 102,000
SALES (est): 2.06MM **Privately Held**
Web: 051ef4c.netsolhost.com
SIC: 2037 2024 Fruit juices; Dairy based frozen desserts

(P-1375)
DOLE PACKAGED FOODS LLC (HQ)
Also Called: Glacier Foods Division
1 Baxter Way, Westlake Village (91362-3889)
P.O. Box 5700 (91359-5700)
PHONE..................800 232-8888
David A Delorenzo, *Managing Member*
Gregory Costley, *Managing Member*
Ann Wiese, *
Jim Johnston, *
Tim Nelson, *
◆ **EMP:** 550 **EST:** 1967
SQ FT: 81,000
SALES (est): 256.93MM **Privately Held**
Web: www.dolesunshine.com
SIC: 2037 Fruits, quick frozen and cold pack (frozen)
PA: Itochu Corporation
2-5-1, Kitaaoyama

(P-1376)
IMPERIAL VALLEY FOODS INC
1961 Buchanan Ave, Calexico (92231-4306)
P.O. Box 233 Paulin Ave (92231)
PHONE..................760 203-1896
Gustavo Caballero, *CEO*
Gustavo Caballero Junior, *Pr*
Fornando Cabolloro, *
Edna Cabellero, *
▲ **EMP:** 300 **EST:** 2006
SALES (est): 5.36MM **Privately Held**
SIC: 2037 Frozen fruits and vegetables

(P-1377)
J HELLMAN FROZEN FOODS INC (PA)
1601 E Olympic Blvd Ste 200, Los Angeles (90021-1941)
P.O. Box 86267 (90086-0267)
PHONE..................213 243-9105
Tracy Hellman, *CEO*
Bryce Hellman, *
EMP: 50 **EST:** 1990
SQ FT: 21,000
SALES (est): 4.92MM
SALES (corp-wide): 4.92MM **Privately Held**
Web: www.jhellmanfrozenfoods.com
SIC: 2037 Frozen fruits and vegetables

(P-1378)

LANGER JUICE COMPANY INC

16185 Stephens St, City Of Industry
(91744)
PHONE...............................626 336-3100
EMP: 300 **EST:** 2016
SALES (est): 1.78MM **Privately Held**
Web: www.langers.com
SIC: 2037 Fruit juices

(P-1379)

LIVE FRESH CORPORATION

1055 E Cooley Ave, San Bernardino
(92408-2819)
PHONE...............................909 478-0895
▲ **EMP:** 180 **EST:** 1993
SALES (est): 1.08MM **Privately Held**
SIC: 2037 Fruit juices

(P-1380)

SUNSATION INC

100 S Cambridge Ave, Claremont
(91711-4842)
PHONE...............................909 542-0280
Perry Eichor, *CEO*
Perry Eichor, *Pr*
David Bryant, *
Saul Kusnier, *Prin*
EMP: 48 **EST:** 2003
SQ FT: 30,000
SALES (est): 6.08MM **Privately Held**
SIC: 2037 Fruit juices

(P-1381)

VENTURA COASTAL LLC (PA)

2325 Vista Del Mar Dr, Ventura
(93001-3700)
P.O. Box 69 (93002-0069)
PHONE...............................805 653-7000
Donald Dames, *
Bill Borgers, *Managing Member*
Rolph Scherer, *
Don Uhlrich, *
◆ **EMP:** 50 **EST:** 1951
SQ FT: 25,000
SALES (est): 31.97K
SALES (corp-wide): 31.97K **Privately Held**
Web: www.venturacoastal.com
SIC: 2037 Fruit juice concentrates, frozen

(P-1382)

WM BOLTHOUSE FARMS INC (HQ)

Also Called: Bolthouse Farms
7200 E Brundage Ln, Bakersfield
(93307-3099)
PHONE...............................800 467-4683
Jeffrey Dunn, *CEO*
Mike Rosenthal, *CFO*
Matthew Ayres, *
◆ **EMP:** 1000 **EST:** 1970
SQ FT: 700,000
SALES (est): 562.6MM
SALES (corp-wide): 562.6MM **Privately Held**
Web: www.bolthouse.com
SIC: 2037 0161 2033 2099 Fruit juices;
   Carrot farm; Vegetable juices: packaged in
   cans, jars, etc.; Sauce, gravy, dressing, and
   dip mixes
PA: Generis Holdings, Lp
   7200 E Brundage Ln
   661 366-7209

2038 Frozen Specialties, Nec

(P-1383)

AJINOMOTO FOODS NORTH AMER INC (DH)

4200 Concours Ste 100, Ontario
(91764-4982)
PHONE...............................909 477-4700
Sumio Maeda, *Pr*
Taro Komura, *
James Caltabiano, *
Daniel O'brien, *CIO*
Brett Buatti Csco, *Prin*
▲ **EMP:** 100 **EST:** 2015
SQ FT: 56,000
SALES (est): 721.28MM **Privately Held**
Web: www.ajinomotofoods.com
SIC: 2038 2037 Frozen specialties, nec;
   Frozen fruits and vegetables
HQ: Ajinomoto North America Holdings, Inc.
   7124 N Marine Dr
   Portland OR 97203
   503 505-5783

(P-1384)

AJINOMOTO FOODS NORTH AMER INC

Also Called: Windsor Foods
4200 Concours Ste 100, Ontario
(91764-4982)
PHONE...............................909 477-4700
Steve Charles, *Mgr*
EMP: 244
Web: www.ajinomotofoods.com
SIC: 2038 5142 Frozen specialties, nec;
   Packaged frozen goods
HQ: Ajinomoto Foods North America, Inc.
   4200 E Concours Ste 100
   Ontario CA 91764

(P-1385)

ASTROCHEF LLC

Also Called: Pegasus Foods
1111 Mateo St, Los Angeles (90021-1717)
P.O. Box 86404 (90086-0404)
PHONE...............................213 627-9860
Jim Zaferis, *CEO*
Evangelos Ambatielos, *
Steve Koufoudakis, *
EMP: 55 **EST:** 1998
SQ FT: 60,000
SALES (est): 9.81MM **Privately Held**
Web: www.pegasusfoodsinc.com
SIC: 2038 Frozen specialties, nec

(P-1386)

CARDENAS MARKETS LLC

1621 E Francis St, Ontario (91761-8324)
PHONE...............................909 923-7426
Javier Ramirez, *COO*
EMP: 200
SALES (corp-wide): 142.12MM **Privately Held**
Web: www.cardenasmarkets.com
SIC: 2038 5411 Frozen specialties, nec;
   Grocery stores
HQ: Cardenas Markets Llc
   2501 E Guasti Rd
   Ontario CA 91761
   909 923-7426

(P-1387)

CRAVE FOODS INC

Also Called: Crave Foods
2043 Imperial St, Los Angeles
(90021-3203)
PHONE...............................562 900-7272
Shaheda Sayed, *Pr*
Riaz A Surti, *

▲ **EMP:** 40 **EST:** 1992
SQ FT: 20,000
SALES (est): 3.54MM **Privately Held**
Web: www.cravefoods.com
SIC: 2038 Frozen specialties, nec

(P-1388)

CULINARY BRANDS INC (PA)

3280 E 44th St, Vernon (90058-2426)
PHONE...............................626 289-3000
Frank Calma, *Pr*
Mohsen Ganeian, *Prin*
EMP: 41 **EST:** 2011
SQ FT: 2,000
SALES (est): 8.29MM
SALES (corp-wide): 8.29MM **Privately Held**
Web: www.culinaryinternational.com
SIC: 2038 Frozen specialties, nec

(P-1389)

DEL REAL LLC (PA)

Also Called: Del Real Foods
11041 Inland Ave, Jurupa Valley
(91752-1155)
PHONE...............................951 681-0395
Michael Axelrod, *CEO*
Jesus Cardenas, *Pr*
Jose Cardenas, *VP*
Viviano Del Villar Junior, *COO*
Manuel Martinez, *CFO*
EMP: 72 **EST:** 2003
SQ FT: 175,000
SALES (est): 104.79MM
SALES (corp-wide): 104.79MM **Privately Held**
Web: www.delrealfoods.com
SIC: 2038 Ethnic foods, nec, frozen

(P-1390)

DON MIGUEL MEXICAN FOODS INC (HQ)

Also Called: Don Miguel Foods
333 S Anita Dr Ste 1000, Orange
(92868-3318)
PHONE...............................714 385-4500
Jeff Frank, *CEO*
Saralyn Brown, *
Mike Elliott, *
Terry Girch, *
Michael Chaignot, *
▲ **EMP:** 45 **EST:** 1908
SQ FT: 80,000
SALES (est): 86.25MM **Privately Held**
Web: www.donmiguel.com
SIC: 2038 Frozen specialties, nec
PA: Megamex Foods, Llc
   333 S Anita Dr Ste 1000

(P-1391)

EXCELLINE FOOD PRODUCTS LLC

833 N Hollywood Way, Burbank
(91505-2814)
PHONE...............................818 701-7710
EMP: 29 **EST:** 1979
SQ FT: 23,000
SALES (est): 2.56MM **Privately Held**
Web: www.excellinefoods.com
SIC: 2038 Ethnic foods, nec, frozen

(P-1392)

GOLDEN STATE FOODS CORP

640 S 6th Ave, City Of Industry
(91746-3086)
PHONE...............................626 465-7500
Chad Buechel, *Brnch Mgr*
EMP: 350
SALES (corp-wide): 1.5MM **Privately Held**
Web: www.goldenstatefoods.com

SIC: 2038 2087 2026 2051 Frozen
   specialties, nec; Flavoring extracts and
   syrups, nec; Fluid milk; Bread, cake, and
   related products
PA: Golden State Foods Corp.
   18301 Von Krman Ave Ste 1
   949 247-8000

(P-1393)

HARVEST FARMS INC

45000 Yucca Ave, Lancaster (93534-2526)
PHONE...............................661 945-3636
Craig Shugert, *CEO*
Eric Shiring, *
▲ **EMP:** 100 **EST:** 1947
SQ FT: 18,000
SALES (est): 19.81MM
SALES (corp-wide): 519.54MM **Privately Held**
Web: www.harvestfarms.com
SIC: 2038 5144 Lunches, frozen and
   packaged; Poultry and poultry products
HQ: Good Source Solutions, Inc.
   3115 Melrose Dr Ste 160
   Carlsbad CA 92010
   858 455-4800

(P-1394)

LA MEXICANA LLC

6535 Caballero Blvd Unit A, Buena Park
(90620-8106)
PHONE...............................323 277-3660
Angelo Fraggos, *CEO*
EMP: 40 **EST:** 2006
SALES (est): 1MM
SALES (corp-wide): 471.74MM **Privately Held**
SIC: 2038 Ethnic foods, nec, frozen
PA: Blue Point Capital Partners Llc
   127 Public Sq Ste 5100
   216 535-4700

(P-1395)

LA MOUSSE DESSERTS INC

Also Called: La Mousse
18211 S Broadway, Gardena (90248-3535)
PHONE...............................310 478-6051
Leah Noble, *Pr*
EMP: 29 **EST:** 2017
SQ FT: 11,000
SALES (est): 5.91MM **Privately Held**
Web: www.lamoussedesserts.com
SIC: 2038 Frozen specialties, nec

(P-1396)

LANGLOIS FANCY FROZEN FOODS INC

2975 Laguna Canyon Rd, Laguna Beach
(92651-1148)
PHONE...............................949 497-1741
EMP: 49 **EST:** 1951
SALES (est): 4.49MM **Privately Held**
Web: www.langloisfoods.com
SIC: 2038 Dinners, frozen and packaged

(P-1397)

NESTLE USA INC

Also Called: Nestle Dist Ctr & Logistics
3450 Dulles Dr, Jurupa Valley (91752-3242)
PHONE...............................951 360-7200
Dean Ingram, *Brnch Mgr*
EMP: 291
Web: www.nestleusa.com
SIC: 2038 Frozen specialties, nec
HQ: Nestle Usa, Inc.
   1812 N Moore St
   Arlington VA 22209
   800 225-2270

(P-1398)
PICTSWEET COMPANY
732 Hanson Way, Santa Maria
(93458-9710)
P.O. Box 5878 (93456-5878)
PHONE..............................805 928-4414
Thomas Kerulas, *Brnch Mgr*
EMP: 300
SALES (corp-wide): 403.32MM **Privately Held**
Web: www.pictsweetfarms.com
SIC: 2038 2099 Frozen specialties, nec; Food preparations, nec
PA: The Pictsweet Company
10 Pictsweet Dr
731 663-7600

(P-1399)
REAL VISION FOODS LLC
Also Called: Real Vision Foods
72 Knollglen, Irvine (92614-7485)
PHONE..............................253 228-5050
Joseph H Ertman, *Pr*
Joseph Ertman, *
EMP: 50 EST: 2019
SALES (est): 1.05MM **Privately Held**
Web: www.realvisionfoods.com
SIC: 2038 Snacks, incl. onion rings, cheese sticks, etc.

(P-1400)
SHINE FOOD INC
Jesse Lord
21100 S Western Ave, Torrance (90501-1700)
PHONE..............................310 533-6010
John Freschi, *Mgr*
EMP: 90
SALES (corp-wide): 13.37MM **Privately Held**
Web: www.shinefoods.com
SIC: 2038 2053 2052 2051 Frozen specialties, nec; Frozen bakery products, except bread; Cookies and crackers; Bread, cake, and related products
PA: Shine Food, Inc.
19216 Normandie Ave
310 329-3829

(P-1401)
SPECIALTY BRANDS INCORPORATED
4200 Concours Ste 100, Ontario (91764-4982)
P.O. Box 51467 (91761-1057)
PHONE..............................909 477-4851
EMP: 1900
SIC: 2038 5142 Frozen specialties, nec; Packaged frozen goods

(P 1402)
STIR FOODS LLC
1851 N Delilah St, Corona (92879-1800)
PHONE..............................714 871-9231
Phil Decarion, *CEO*
EMP: 27
SALES (corp-wide): 249.44MM **Privately Held**
Web: www.stirfoods.com
SIC: 2038 2099 Frozen specialties, nec; Food preparations, nec
HQ: Stir Foods, Llc
1581 N Main St
Orange CA 92867

(P-1403)
TAWA SUPERMARKET INC (PA)
Also Called: 99 Ranch Market
6281 Regio Ave, Buena Park (90620-1023)
PHONE..............................714 521-8899

Chang Hua K Chen, *CEO*
▲ EMP: 122 EST: 1985
SQ FT: 117,000
SALES (est): 490.41MM
SALES (corp-wide): 490.41MM **Privately Held**
Web: www.99ranch.com
SIC: 2038 5411 Breakfasts, frozen and packaged; Supermarkets, chain

(P-1404)
WINDSOR QUALITY FOOD COMPANY LTD
Also Called: Windsor Foods
4200 Concours Ste 100, Ontario (91764-4982)
PHONE..............................713 843-5200
EMP: 3300
Web: www.ajinomotofoods.com
SIC: 2038 Frozen specialties, nec

2041 Flour And Other Grain Mill Products

(P-1405)
GENERAL MILLS INC
Also Called: General Mills
4309 Fruitland Ave, Vernon (90058-3176)
PHONE..............................323 584-3433
Jeff Shapiro, *Brnch Mgr*
EMP: 26
SQ FT: 81,186
SALES (corp-wide): 19.86B **Publicly Held**
Web: www.generalmills.com
SIC: 2041 Flour mills, cereal (except rice)
PA: General Mills, Inc.
1 General Mills Blvd
763 764-7600

(P-1406)
PILLSBURY COMPANY LLC
Also Called: Pillsbury
220 S Kenwood St Ste 202, Glendale (91205-1671)
PHONE..............................818 522-3952
Linda Goodman, *Brnch Mgr*
EMP: 32
SALES (corp-wide): 19.86B **Publicly Held**
Web: www.lgpillsbury.com
SIC: 2041 Doughs and batters
HQ: The Pillsbury Company Llc
1 General Mills Blvd
Minneapolis MN 55426

(P-1407)
SING KUNG CORP
12061 Clark St, Arcadia (91006-5829)
PHONE..............................626 358-5838
Louis Choy, *Pr*
◆ EMP: 25 EST: 1997
SQ FT: 7,000
SALES (est): 2.1MM **Privately Held**
Web: www.singkung.com
SIC: 2041 Flour and other grain mill products

(P-1408)
SUNOPTA GRAINS AND FOODS INC
12128 Center St, South Gate (90280-8046)
PHONE..............................323 774-6000
EMP: 62
SALES (corp-wide): 630.3MM **Publicly Held**
Web: www.sunopta.com
SIC: 2041 5153 Flour and other grain mill products; Grains
HQ: Sunopta Grains And Foods Inc.
7078 Shady Oak Rd

Eden Prairie MN 55344

(P-1409)
THE SWEET LIFE ENTERPRISES INC
Also Called: Aryzta Sweet Life
2350 Pullman St, Santa Ana (92705-5507)
PHONE..............................949 261-7400
EMP: 115
Web: www.sweetlifeinc.com
SIC: 2041 5149 Doughs and batters; Crackers, cookies, and bakery products

2043 Cereal Breakfast Foods

(P-1410)
CALIFRNIA NUTRITIONAL PDTS INC
64405 Lincoln St, Mecca (92254-6501)
PHONE..............................760 625-3884
Minh Tuan Nguyen, *CEO*
Roy Nguyen, *
Douglas Scott Scharinger, *
EMP: 65 EST: 2022
SALES (est): 5.5MM **Privately Held**
SIC: 2043 Cereal breakfast foods

(P-1411)
EAST WEST TEA COMPANY LLC
Also Called: Golden Temple
1616 Preuss Rd, Los Angeles (90035-4212)
PHONE..............................310 275-9891
Gurudhan S Khalsa, *Mgr*
EMP: 226
SALES (corp-wide): 63.9MM **Privately Held**
Web: www.yogiproducts.com
SIC: 2043 2099 2064 8721 Cereal breakfast foods; Tea blending; Candy and other confectionery products; Billing and bookkeeping service
PA: East West Tea Company, Llc
1325 Westec Dr
800 964-4832

(P-1412)
INTELLIGENT BLENDS LLC
5330 Eastgate Mall, San Diego (92121-2804)
PHONE..............................858 888-7937
Michael Ishayik, *Pr*
▲ EMP: 38 EST: 2013
SALES (est): 15.05MM **Privately Held**
Web: www.intelligentblends.com
SIC: 2043 Cereal breakfast foods

2044 Rice Milling

(P-1413)
MARS FOOD US LLC
Also Called: Uncle Ben's
6875 Pacific View Dr, Los Angeles (90068-1831)
PHONE..............................562 616-7347
EMP: 34
SALES (corp-wide): 42.84B **Privately Held**
SIC: 2044 Rice milling
HQ: Mars Food Us, Llc
2001 E Cashdan St Ste 201
Rancho Dominguez CA 90220
310 933-0670

2045 Prepared Flour Mixes And Doughs

(P-1414)
LANGLOIS COMPANY
Also Called: Langlois Flour Company
10810 San Sevaine Way, Jurupa Valley (91752-1116)
PHONE..............................951 360-3900
Richard W Langlois, *Pr*
Sally Langlois, *
Lynn Langlois Nye, *
▼ EMP: 50 EST: 1950
SQ FT: 48,000
SALES (est): 7.88MM **Privately Held**
Web: www.langloiscompany.com
SIC: 2045 2035 2079 2099 Blended flour: from purchased flour; Mayonnaise; Vegetable refined oils (except corn oil); Gelatin dessert preparations

(P-1415)
POPLA INTERNATIONAL INC
1740 S Sacramento Ave, Ontario (91761-7744)
PHONE..............................909 923-6899
Mike Shinozaki, *Pr*
Ashley Shinozaki, *
◆ EMP: 41 EST: 1986
SQ FT: 8,000
SALES (est): 4.17MM **Privately Held**
Web: www.popla.com
SIC: 2045 Prepared flour mixes and doughs

2047 Dog And Cat Food

(P-1416)
ARTHUR DOGSWELL LLC (PA)
Also Called: Dogswell
11301 W Olympic Blvd Ste 520, Los Angeles (90064-1653)
PHONE..............................888 559-8833
Brad Casper, *Managing Member*
Gianmarco Giannini, *Managing Member*
Berenice Officer, *
▲ EMP: 33 EST: 2003
SQ FT: 2,000
SALES (est): 21.2MM
SALES (corp-wide): 21.2MM **Privately Held**
Web: www.dogswell.com
SIC: 2047 5149 Dog food; Pet foods

(P-1417)
HONEST KITCHEN INC
1705 Hancock St Ste 100, San Diego (92110-2051)
PHONE..............................619 544-0018
Michael Greenwell, *CEO*
Jacob Fuller, *CFO*
Nathan Kredich, *COO*
Mike Steck, *Mktg Dir*
Kirk Jensen, *COO*
EMP: 73 EST: 2002
SALES (est): 20.68MM **Privately Held**
Web: www.thehonestkitchen.com
SIC: 2047 Dog and cat food

(P-1418)
J&R TAYLOR BROTHERS ASSOC INC
Also Called: Premium Pet Foods
16321 Arrow Hwy, Irwindale (91706-2018)
PHONE..............................626 334-9301
Rick Taylor, *Pr*
◆ EMP: 58 EST: 1967
SALES (est): 1.38MM
SALES (corp-wide): 3.2B **Publicly Held**

PRODUCTS & SVCS

SIC: **2047** 2048 Dog food; Prepared feeds, nec
PA: Central Garden & Pet Company
1340 Treat Blvd Ste 600
925 948-4000

(P-1419)
KRUSE PET HOLDINGS LLC (PA)
Also Called: Perfection Pet Brands
1609 W Highway 246, Buellton (93427-9478)
PHONE....................559 302-4880
Kevin Kruse, *CEO*
Jeremy Wilhelm, *Pr*
Mike Gagene, *VP*
Brian Ubegin, *CFO*
EMP: 29 **EST:** 2011
SALES (est): 76.3MM
SALES (corp-wide): 76.3MM **Privately Held**
Web: www.perfectionpetfoods.com
SIC: **2047** Dog food

(P-1420)
MARS PETCARE US INC
2765 Lexington Way, San Bernardino (92407-1842)
PHONE....................909 887-8131
Ed.Skokan, *Mgr*
EMP: 50
SQ FT: 76,000
SALES (corp-wide): 42.84B **Privately Held**
Web: www.marspetcare.com
SIC: **2047** 2048 Dog food; Prepared feeds, nec
HQ: Mars Petcare Us, Inc.
2013 Ovation Pkwy
Franklin TN 37067
615 807-4626

(P-1421)
MARS PETCARE US INC
13243 Nutro Way, Victorville (92395-7789)
PHONE....................760 261-7900
EMP: 60
SALES (corp-wide): 42.84B **Privately Held**
Web: www.marspetcare.com
SIC: **2047** Cat food
HQ: Mars Petcare Us, Inc.
2013 Ovation Pkwy
Franklin TN 37067
615 807-4626

(P-1422)
NESTLE PURINA PETCARE COMPANY
800 N Brand Blvd Fl 5, Glendale (91203-4281)
PHONE....................314 982-1000
EMP: 46
Web: www.purina.com
SIC: **2047** Dog and cat food
HQ: Nestle Purina Petcare Company
800 Chouteau Ave
Saint Louis MO 63102
314 982-1000

(P-1423)
NESTLE PURINA PETCARE COMPANY
Also Called: Nestle Purina Factory
1710 Golden Cat Rd, Maricopa (93252)
PHONE....................661 769-8261
Mike Ashmore, *Mgr*
EMP: 103
Web: www.purina.com
SIC: **2047** Dog and cat food
HQ: Nestle Purina Petcare Company
800 Chouteau Ave

Saint Louis MO 63102
314 982-1000

2048 Prepared Feeds, Nec

(P-1424)
A SHOC BEVERAGE LLC
844 Production Pl, Newport Beach (92663-2810)
PHONE....................949 490-1612
Lance Collins, *Managing Member*
Kyle Ostrowsky, *
EMP: 50 **EST:** 2018
SALES (est): 11.06MM **Privately Held**
Web: www.drinkaccelerator.com
SIC: **2048** Mineral feed supplements

(P-1425)
CANINE CAVIAR PET FOODS INC
Also Called: Canine Caviar
4131 Tigris Way, Riverside (92503-4844)
P.O. Box 5872 (92860-8029)
PHONE....................714 223-1800
Jeff Baker, *Pr*
Gary Ward, *
◆ **EMP:** 30 **EST:** 1996
SQ FT: 6,000
SALES (est): 5.56MM **Privately Held**
Web: www.caninecaviar.com
SIC: **2048** Canned pet food (except dog and cat)

(P-1426)
GARMON CORPORATION (PA)
Also Called: Naturvet
27461 Via Industria, Temecula (92590-3752)
PHONE....................888 628-8783
Scott Garmon, *CEO*
Debra O'brien, *CFO*
Jodi Hoefler, *Sec*
▲ **EMP:** 60 **EST:** 1979
SQ FT: 18,500
SALES (est): 24.1MM
SALES (corp-wide): 24.1MM **Privately Held**
Web: www.naturvet.com
SIC: **2048** Feed supplements

(P-1427)
HARBOR GREEN GRAIN LP
13181 Crossroads Pkwy N Ste 200, City Of Industry (91746-3451)
PHONE....................310 991-8089
Shing Lo, *Pr*
Zach Xu, *CEO*
Kevin Yoon, *COO*
◆ **EMP:** 45 **EST:** 2014
SALES (est): 2.42MM **Privately Held**
SIC: **2048** Alfalfa, cubed

(P-1428)
INTERNATIONAL PROCESSING CORP (DH)
233 Wilshire Blvd Ste 310, Santa Monica (90401-1206)
P.O. Box 2211 (90407-2211)
PHONE....................310 458-1574
Bob Mcmullen, *Pr*
EMP: 25 **EST:** 1953
SALES (est): 3.02MM
SALES (corp-wide): 203.79MM **Privately Held**
SIC: **2048** Prepared feeds, nec
HQ: Reconserve, Inc.
2811 Wlshire Blvd Ste 410
Santa Monica CA 90403
310 458-1574

(P-1429)
LEGACY EPOCH LLC
21011 Warner Center Ln Ste A, Woodland Hills (91367-6509)
PHONE....................844 673-7305
Shawn Lipman, *CEO*
Gary Puterman, *
Robert Roizen, *
Brian Roizen, *Chief Architect**
Igor Roizen, *Chief Scientist**
EMP: 83 **EST:** 2015
SALES (est): 11.31MM
SALES (corp-wide): 309.39MM **Publicly Held**
Web: www.feedonomics.com
SIC: **2048** Chicken feeds, prepared
PA: Bigcommerce Holdings, Inc.
11305 Four Pnts Dr Bldg I
512 865-4500

(P-1430)
NATURAL BALANCE PET FOODS LLC (PA)
19425 Soledad Canyon Rd # 302, Canyon Country (91351-2632)
P.O. Box 397 (91785-0397)
PHONE....................800 829-4493
Brian Connolly, *CEO*
▲ **EMP:** 65 **EST:** 1989
SQ FT: 55,000
SALES (est): 26.42MM **Privately Held**
Web: www.naturalbalanceinc.com
SIC: **2048** 5199 Prepared feeds, nec; Pet supplies

(P-1431)
NATURAL BALANCE PET FOODS LLC
1224 Montague Unit 1, Pacoima (91331)
PHONE....................800 829-4493
EMP: 68
Web: www.naturalbalanceinc.com
SIC: **2048** Prepared feeds, nec
PA: Natural Balance Pet Foods, Llc
19425 Soledad Cyn Rd #302

(P-1432)
RECONSERVE INC (HQ)
Also Called: Dext Company
2811 Wilshire Blvd Ste 410, Santa Monica (90403-4805)
P.O. Box 2211 (90407-2211)
PHONE....................310 458-1574
Meyer Luskin, *CEO*
David Luskin, *
EMP: 25 **EST:** 1966
SQ FT: 5,000
SALES (est): 99.3MM
SALES (corp-wide): 203.79MM **Privately Held**
Web: www.reconserve.com
SIC: **2048** Livestock feeds
PA: Scope Industries
2811 Wilshire Blvd # 410
310 458-1574

(P-1433)
STAR MILLING CO
23901 Water St, Perris (92570-9094)
P.O. Box 1987 (92572-1987)
PHONE....................951 657-3143
William R Cramer Junior, *Pr*
Paul R Cramer, *
Greg W Carls, *
◆ **EMP:** 99 **EST:** 1952
SALES (est): 26.43MM **Privately Held**
Web: www.starmilling.com
SIC: **2048** Poultry feeds

(P-1434)
SUN-GRO COMMODITIES INC (PA)
34575 Famoso Rd, Bakersfield (93308-9769)
PHONE....................661 393-2612
Donald G Smith, *CEO*
Scott Smith, *
Lori Melendez, *
Wendy Smith, *
EMP: 25 **EST:** 1974
SQ FT: 1,400
SALES (est): 4.97MM
SALES (corp-wide): 4.97MM **Privately Held**
Web: www.sun-gro.com
SIC: **2048** 4212 Livestock feeds; Local trucking, without storage

2051 Bread, Cake, And Related Products

(P-1435)
BAKED IN THE SUN
Also Called: S & S Bakery
2560 Progress St, Vista (92081-8465)
PHONE....................760 591-9045
EMP: 250
Web: www.bakedinthesun.com
SIC: **2051** Bagels, fresh or frozen

(P-1436)
BAKERS KNEADED LLC
148 W 132nd St Ste D, Los Angeles (90061-1649)
PHONE....................310 819-8700
Carlos Enriquez, *CEO*
Carlos Enriquez, *Managing Member*
Paul Cox, *
EMP: 28 **EST:** 2017
SALES (est): 2.73MM **Privately Held**
SIC: **2051** Bread, all types (white, wheat, rye, etc); fresh or frozen

(P-1437)
BESTWAY SANDWICHES INC (PA)
Also Called: Bestway Foods
28209 Avenue Stanford, Valencia (91355-3984)
PHONE....................818 361-1800
Khachatur Budagyan, *CEO*
EMP: 46 **EST:** 2008
SALES (est): 12.2MM **Privately Held**
SIC: **2051** Bread, all types (white, wheat, rye, etc); fresh or frozen

(P-1438)
BUBBLES BAKING COMPANY
15215 Keswick St, Van Nuys (91405-1014)
P.O. Box 2a (93287-0002)
PHONE....................818 786-1700
FAX: 818 786-3617
EMP: 50
SQ FT: 23,000
SALES (est): 13.38MM **Privately Held**
SIC: **2051** Cakes, bakery: except frozen

(P-1439)
CALIFORNIA CHURROS CORPORATION
751 Via Lata, Colton (92324-3930)
PHONE....................909 370-4777
Jorge D Martinez, *CEO*
Jorge D Martinez Senior, *Pr*
Eva A Martinez, *
Frank Ruvalcaba, *
EMP: 264 **EST:** 1980

SQ FT: 54,800
SALES (est): 8.34MM
SALES (corp-wide): 1.57B **Publicly Held**
Web: www.churros.com
SIC: 2051 Pastries, e.g. danish: except frozen
HQ: J & J Snack Foods Corp. Of California
5353 Downey Rd
Los Angeles CA 90058
323 581-0171

(P-1440)
DANISH BAKING CO INC
Also Called: Bubbles Baking Company
15215 Keswick St, Van Nuys (91405-1014)
PHONE..............................818 786-1700
EMP: 70
SIC: 2051 Bread, cake, and related products

(P-1441)
DAWN FOOD PRODUCTS INC
15601 Mosher Ave Ste 230, Tustin (92780-6426)
PHONE..............................714 258-1223
Joe Barsoppi, *Genl Mgr*
EMP: 150
SALES (corp-wide): 1.73B **Privately Held**
Web: www.dawnfoods.com
SIC: 2051 Pastries, e.g. danish: except frozen
HQ: Dawn Food Products, Inc.
3333 Sargent Rd
Jackson MI 49201

(P-1442)
DISTINCT INDULGENCE INC
Also Called: Mrs Appletree's Bakery
5018 Lante St, Baldwin Park (91706-1839)
PHONE..............................818 546-1700
Robert W Gray, *Pr*
Suzanne Gray, *
▲ **EMP:** 38 **EST:** 1985
SQ FT: 10,000
SALES (est): 8.28MM **Privately Held**
Web: www.mrsappletree.com
SIC: 2051 5499 Bakery: wholesale or wholesale/retail combined; Health and dietetic food stores

(P-1443)
EL METATE INC
Also Called: El Metate Market
817 W 19th St, Costa Mesa (92627-3518)
PHONE..............................949 646-9362
Brian Murrieta, *Brnch Mgr*
EMP: 190
SALES (corp-wide): 3.68MM **Privately Held**
Web: www.elmetate.com
SIC: 2051 2052 2099 5812 Breads, rolls, and buns; Cookies; Tortillas, fresh or refrigerated; Mexican restaurant
PA: El Metate, Inc.
838 E 1st St
714 542-3913

(P-1444)
EL SEGUNDO BREAD BAR LLC
Also Called: Bread Bar
701 E El Segundo Blvd, El Segundo (90245-4108)
PHONE..............................310 615-9898
Myrna Al-midani, *Managing Member*
▲ **EMP:** 32 **EST:** 2004
SQ FT: 8,000
SALES (est): 2.57MM **Privately Held**
Web: www.breadbar.la
SIC: 2051 5149 Bread, all types (white, wheat, rye, etc); fresh or frozen; Bakery products

(P-1445)
FIESTA MEXICAN FOODS INC
979 G St, Brawley (92227-2615)
PHONE..............................760 344-3580
Raymond Armenta, *Pr*
EMP: 30 **EST:** 1956
SQ FT: 4,000
SALES (est): 2.5MM **Privately Held**
SIC: 2051 2099 Pastries, e.g. danish: except frozen; Tortillas, fresh or refrigerated

(P-1446)
FLOWERS BAKERIES SLS SOCAL LLC ✪
10625 Poplar Ave, Fontana (92337-7335)
PHONE..............................702 281-4797
Mallyn Kong, *Admn*
EMP: 34 **EST:** 2024
SALES (est): 2.46MM **Privately Held**
SIC: 2051 Bread, all types (white, wheat, rye, etc); fresh or frozen

(P-1447)
FLOWERS BKG CO HENDERSON LLC
21540 Blythe St, Canoga Park (91304-4910)
PHONE..............................818 884-8970
EMP: 72
SALES (corp-wide): 5.09B **Publicly Held**
Web: www.flowersfoods.com
SIC: 2051 Breads, rolls, and buns
HQ: Flowers Baking Co. Of Henderson, Llc
501 Conestoga Way
Henderson NV 89002
702 567-6401

(P-1448)
FLOWERS BKG CO HENDERSON LLC
3800 W Century Blvd, Inglewood (90303-1011)
PHONE..............................310 695-9846
EMP: 72
SALES (corp-wide): 5.09B **Publicly Held**
Web: www.flowersfoods.com
SIC: 2051 Breads, rolls, and buns
HQ: Flowers Baking Co. Of Henderson, Llc
501 Conestoga Way
Henderson NV 89002
702 567-6401

(P-1449)
FLOWERS BKG CO HENDERSON LLC
7311 Doig Dr, Garden Grove (92841-1806)
PHONE..............................702 281-4797
EMP: 72
SALES (corp-wide): 5.09B **Publicly Held**
Web: www.flowersfoods.com
SIC: 2051 Breads, rolls, and buns
HQ: Flowers Baking Co. Of Henderson, Llc
501 Conestoga Way
Henderson NV 89002
702 567-6401

(P-1450)
FOOD FOR LIFE BAKING CO INC (PA)
Also Called: Natural Food Mill
2991 Doherty St, Corona (92879-5811)
P.O. Box 1434 (92878-1434)
PHONE..............................951 279-5090
R James Torres, *Pr*
Charles Torres, *
▲ **EMP:** 100 **EST:** 1970
SQ FT: 170,000
SALES (est): 36.34MM

SALES (corp-wide): 36.34MM **Privately Held**
Web: www.foodforlife.com
SIC: 2051 Bakery: wholesale or wholesale/retail combined

(P-1451)
FRESH START BAKERIES INC
Also Called: Fresh Start Bakeries N Amer
145 S State College Blvd Ste 200, Brea (92821-5806)
PHONE..............................714 256-8900
▲ **EMP:** 600
SIC: 2051 Bread, cake, and related products

(P-1452)
FRISCO BAKING COMPANY INC
Also Called: Frisco Baking Company
621 W Avenue 26, Los Angeles (90065-1095)
PHONE..............................323 225-6111
Aldo Pricco Junior, *CEO*
James Pricco, *
Ronald Perata, *
John Pricco, *
Mary Anne Fetter, *
EMP: 115 **EST:** 1938
SQ FT: 18,000
SALES (est): 5.8MM **Privately Held**
Web: www.friscobakingcompany.com
SIC: 2051 Bread, all types (white, wheat, rye, etc); fresh or frozen

(P-1453)
GALASSOS BAKERY (PA)
10820 San Sevaine Way, Mira Loma (91752-1116)
PHONE..............................951 360-1211
Jeannette Galasso, *CEO*
Jeannette Galasso, *Pr*
Mark Bailey, *
Pearl Denault, *
Rick Vargas, *Operations*
EMP: 180 **EST:** 1968
SQ FT: 110,000
SALES (est): 24.63MM
SALES (corp-wide): 24.63MM **Privately Held**
Web: www.galassos.com
SIC: 2051 Bread, cake, and related products

(P-1454)
GIULIANO-PAGANO CORPORATION
Also Called: Giuliano's Bakery
1264 E Walnut St, Carson (90746-1319)
PHONE..............................310 537-7700
Nancy Ritmire Giuliano, *Ch Bd*
Gregory Ritmire, *
EMP: 100 **EST:** 1952
SQ FT: 40,000
SALES (est): 1.69MM **Privately Held**
Web: www.giulianos.com
SIC: 2051 Bakery: wholesale or wholesale/retail combined

(P-1455)
GLOBAL IMPACT INV PARTNERS LLC
1410 Westwood Blvd Apt 260, Los Angeles (90024-4981)
PHONE..............................310 592-2000
EMP: 25 **EST:** 2014
SQ FT: 16,400
SALES (est): 283.46K **Privately Held**
SIC: 2051 Cakes, bakery: except frozen

(P-1456)
GOLD COAST BAKING COMPANY LLC (PA)
Also Called: Kanan Baking Company
21250 Califa St Ste 104, Woodland Hills (91367-5040)
PHONE..............................818 575-7280
Edward H Rogers Iii, *CEO*
EMP: 57 **EST:** 2003
SQ FT: 60,000
SALES (est): 104.72MM **Privately Held**
Web: www.goldcoastbakery.com
SIC: 2051 Bakery: wholesale or wholesale/retail combined

(P-1457)
GOLD COAST BAKING COMPANY LLC
1590 E Saint Gertrude Pl, Santa Ana (92705-5310)
PHONE..............................714 545-2253
Eli Cooperstein, *Mgr*
EMP: 26
Web: www.goldcoastbakery.com
SIC: 2051 Bread, cake, and related products
PA: Gold Coast Baking Company, Llc
21250 Califa St Ste 104

(P-1458)
HANNAHMAX BAKING INC
14601 S Main St, Gardena (90248-1916)
PHONE..............................310 380-6778
Joanne Adirim, *CEO*
Stuart Scwartz, *
EMP: 145 **EST:** 1993
SQ FT: 15,000
SALES (est): 1.59MM **Privately Held**
Web: www.hannahmax.com
SIC: 2051 Bakery: wholesale or wholesale/retail combined

(P-1459)
LAVASH CORPORATION OF AMERICA
Also Called: Toneonel Lavash
2835 Newell St, Los Angeles (90039-3817)
PHONE..............................323 663-5249
Edmond Hartounin, *Pr*
EMP: 25 **EST:** 1980
SQ FT: 10,000
SALES (est): 3MM **Privately Held**
Web: www.organicflatbread.net
SIC: 2051 Bakery: wholesale or wholesale/retail combined

(P-1460)
LITTLE BROTHERS BAKERY LLC
Also Called: Little Brothers Bakery
320 W Alondra Blvd, Gardena (90248-2423)
PHONE..............................310 225-3790
Paul C Giuliano, *Managing Member*
Anthony S Giuliano, *
Joann Giuliano, *
▲ **EMP:** 65 **EST:** 1999
SQ FT: 15,000
SALES (est): 10.19MM **Privately Held**
Web: www.littlebrothersbakery.com
SIC: 2051 5149 Bakery: wholesale or wholesale/retail combined; Bakery products

(P-1461)
MOCHI ICE CREAM COMPANY LLC (PA)
Also Called: Mikawaya
5563 Alcoa Ave, Vernon (90058-3730)
PHONE..............................323 587-5504
Jerry Bucan, *CEO*
Joel Friedman, *Ofcr*

PRODUCTS & SVCS

◆ EMP: 30 EST: 1910
SQ FT: 10,000
SALES (est): 19.62MM
SALES (corp-wide): 19.62MM **Privately Held**
Web: www.mymochi.com
SIC: **2051** 2024 5451 Cakes, pies, and pastries; Ice cream and frozen deserts; Ice cream (packaged)

(P-1462)
NOUSHIG INC
Also Called: Amoretti
451 Lombard St, Oxnard (93030-5143)
PHONE.................................805 983-2903
Jack Barsoumian, *CEO*
Hayop L Barsoumian, *
Maral Barsoumian, *
◆ **EMP: 50 EST: 1998**
SQ FT: 10,000
SALES (est): 10.86MM **Privately Held**
Web: www.amoretti.com
SIC: **2051** 5149 Bread, cake, and related products; Soft drinks

(P-1463)
ROSSMOOR PASTRIES MGT INC
2325 Redondo Ave, Signal Hill (90755-4019)
PHONE.................................562 498-2253
Charles Feder, *CEO*
Janice Ahlgren, *
EMP: 80 EST: 2000
SALES (est): 2.14MM **Privately Held**
Web: www.rossmoorpastries.com
SIC: **2051** Bread, cake, and related products

(P-1464)
SGB BETTER BAKING CO LLC
14528 Blythe St, Van Nuys (91402-6006)
PHONE.................................818 787-9992
Chris Botticella, *CEO*
Ash Aghasi, *
EMP: 57 EST: 2019
SALES (est): 1.54MM
SALES (corp-wide): 22.41MM **Privately Held**
SIC: **2051** 5149 Bakery: wholesale or wholesale/retail combined; Bakery products
PA: Surge Global Bakeries Holdings Llc
13336 Paxton St
818 896-0525

(P-1465)
SGB BUBBLES BAKING CO LLC
15215 Keswick St, Van Nuys (91405-1014)
PHONE.................................818 786-1700
Lewis Sharp, *
EMP: 100 EST: 2019
SQ FT: 50,000
SALES (est): 1.26MM **Privately Held**
SIC: **2051** 5461 Bread, cake, and related products; Retail bakeries

(P-1466)
SUGAR FOODS LLC
6190 E Slauson Ave, Commerce (90040-3010)
PHONE.................................323 727-8290
Harland Gray, *Mgr*
EMP: 100
SALES (corp-wide): 677.96MM **Privately Held**
Web: www.sugarfoods.com
SIC: **2051** 2052 2099 Bread, cake, and related products; Cookies and crackers; Food preparations, nec
HQ: Sugar Foods Llc
3059 Townsgate Rd Ste 101
Westlake Village CA 91361
805 396-5000

(P-1467)
TALLGRASS PICTURES LLC
Also Called: Izola
710 13th St Ste 300, San Diego (92101-7351)
PHONE.................................619 227-2701
Jeffrey Lamont Brown, *Managing Member*
EMP: 29 EST: 2004
SALES (est): 2.5MM **Privately Held**
Web: www.izolabakery.com
SIC: **2051** Bakery: wholesale or wholesale/retail combined

(P-1468)
UNITED STATES BAKERY
Also Called: Franz Family Bakeries
457 E Martin Luther King Jr Blvd, Los Angeles (90011-5650)
PHONE.................................323 232-6124
EMP: 24
SALES (corp-wide): 497.81MM **Privately Held**
Web: www.franzbakery.com
SIC: **2051** Bread, cake, and related products
PA: United States Bakery
315 Ne 10th Ave
503 232-2191

(P-1469)
VBC HOLDINGS INC
134 Main St, El Segundo (90245-3801)
PHONE.................................310 322-7357
James N Desisto, *CEO*
Larry De Sisto, *
EMP: 40 EST: 1959
SQ FT: 35,000
SALES (est): 1.07MM **Privately Held**
Web: www.venicebakery.com
SIC: **2051** 5149 Bread, all types (white, wheat, rye, etc); fresh or frozen; Baking supplies

(P-1470)
VURGER CO (USA) CORP
1800 Century Park E Ste 600, Los Angeles (90067-1508)
PHONE.................................929 318-9546
Rachel Hugh, *CEO*
EMP: 50 EST: 2022
SALES (est): 803.26K **Privately Held**
SIC: **2051** Bakery: wholesale or wholesale/retail combined

(P-1471)
WESTERN BAGEL BAKING CORP
21749 Ventura Blvd, Woodland Hills (91364-1835)
PHONE.................................818 887-5451
Tim Brennen, *Prin*
EMP: 24
SALES (corp-wide): 44.04MM **Privately Held**
Web: www.westernbagel.com
SIC: **2051** 5461 Bagels, fresh or frozen; Bagels
PA: Western Bagel Baking Corp
7814 Sepulveda Blvd
818 786-5847

(P-1472)
WESTERN BAGEL BAKING CORP (PA)
7814 Sepulveda Blvd, Van Nuys (91405-1062)
PHONE.................................818 786-5847
Steven Ustin, *Pr*
▼ **EMP: 225 EST: 1946**
SQ FT: 23,500

SALES (est): 44.04MM
SALES (corp-wide): 44.04MM **Privately Held**
Web: www.westernbagel.com
SIC: **2051** 5461 Bagels, fresh or frozen; Bagels

(P-1473)
YAMAZAKI BAKING CO LTD
335 E 2nd St Ste 223, Los Angeles (90012-4220)
PHONE.................................323 581-5218
Yoshinaga Nagano, *Admn*
EMP: 33
Web: www.yamazakipan.co.jp
SIC: **2051** Bakery: wholesale or wholesale/retail combined
PA: Yamazaki Baking Co., Ltd.
3-10-1, Iwamotocho

2052 Cookies And Crackers

(P-1474)
ADRIENNES GOURMET FOODS
849 Ward Dr, Santa Barbara (93111-2920)
PHONE.................................805 964-6848
▲ **EMP: 60**
SIC: **2052** 2099 2098 Cookies and crackers; Food preparations, nec; Macaroni and spaghetti

(P-1475)
AMAYS BAKERY & NOODLE CO INC (PA)
837 E Commercial St, Los Angeles (90012-3413)
PHONE.................................213 626-2713
Kee Hom, *CEO*
▲ **EMP: 63 EST: 1968**
SQ FT: 20,000
SALES (est): 1.5MM
SALES (corp-wide): 1.5MM **Privately Held**
Web: www.amaysbakery.com
SIC: **2052** 2098 Cookies; Noodles (e.g. egg, plain, and water), dry

(P-1476)
ASPIRE BAKERIES HOLDCO LLC (HQ)
6701 Center Dr W Ste 850, Los Angeles (90045-1695)
PHONE.................................844 992-7747
Tyson Yu, *Pr*
Didier Vinamont, *
Chris Woo, *
EMP: 135 EST: 2021
SALES (est): 1.62B
SALES (corp-wide): 1.78B **Privately Held**
SIC: **2052** 2053 2051 Cookies; Frozen bakery products, except bread; Cakes, pies, and pastries
PA: Goldberg Lindsay & Co. Llc
630 Fifth Ave 30th Fl
212 651-1100

(P-1477)
ASPIRE BAKERIES LLC (DH)
6701 Center Dr W Ste 850, Los Angeles (90045-1695)
PHONE.................................844 992-7747
Tyson Yu, *CEO*
◆ **EMP: 235 EST: 1977**
SQ FT: 90,000
SALES (est): 1.6B
SALES (corp-wide): 1.78B **Privately Held**
Web: www.aspirebakeries.com
SIC: **2052** 2053 2051 Cookies; Frozen bakery products, except bread; Cakes, pies, and pastries

HQ: Aspire Bakeries Holdings Llc
6701 Center Dr W Ste 850
Los Angeles CA 90045
844 992-7747

(P-1478)
ASPIRE BAKERIES LLC
15963 Strathern St, Van Nuys (91406-1313)
PHONE.................................818 904-8230
Marcus Garcia, *Brnch Mgr*
EMP: 325
SALES (corp-wide): 1.78B **Privately Held**
Web: www.aspirebakeries.com
SIC: **2052** Cookies
HQ: Aspire Bakeries Llc
6701 Center Dr W Ste 850
Los Angeles CA 90045
844 992-7747

(P-1479)
ASPIRE BAKERIES LLC
357 W Santa Ana Ave, Bloomington (92316-2901)
PHONE.................................714 478-4656
Armando Villalpando, *Mgr*
EMP: 126
SALES (corp-wide): 1.78B **Privately Held**
Web: www.aspirebakeries.com
SIC: **2052** Cookies
HQ: Aspire Bakeries Llc
6701 Center Dr W Ste 850
Los Angeles CA 90045
844 992-7747

(P-1480)
BETTER BAKERY LLC
Also Called: Better Bakery Co
444 E Santa Clara St, Ventura (93001-2749)
PHONE.................................661 294-9882
EMP: 212
Web: www.betterbakery.com
SIC: **2052** Bakery products, dry

(P-1481)
BISCOMERICA CORP
565 West Slover Ave, Rialto (92377)
P.O. Box 1070 (92376)
PHONE.................................909 877-5997
Nadi Soltan, *Ch Bd*
Ayad Fargo, *
◆ **EMP: 252 EST: 1979**
SQ FT: 250,000
SALES (est): 55.15MM **Privately Held**
Web: www.biscomericacorp.com
SIC: **2052** 2064 Cookies; Candy and other confectionery products

(P-1482)
BLOOMFIELD BAKERS
Also Called: Bloomfield Bakers
10711 Bloomfield St, Los Alamitos (90720-2503)
PHONE.................................626 610-2253
William R Ross, *Genl Pt*
Gary Marx, *Brnch Mgr*
▼ **EMP: 600 EST: 1992**
SQ FT: 75,000
SALES (est): 19.29MM
SALES (corp-wide): 3.43B **Publicly Held**
Web: www.barbakers.com
SIC: **2052** 2064 Cookies; Candy and other confectionery products
HQ: Treehouse Private Brands, Inc.
2021 Spring Rd Ste 600
Oak Brook IL 60523

(P-1483)

CHARLIES SPECIALTIES INC
501 Airpark Dr, Fullerton (92833-2501)
PHONE..................724 346-2350
Jay Thier, *Pr*
Edward G Byrnes Junior, *Ch*
Thomas C Byrnes, *
EMP: 93 **EST:** 1967
SALES (est): 1.31MM
SALES (corp-wide): 38.32MM **Privately Held**
Web: www.bkcompany.com
SIC: 2052 5149 5142 2045 Cookies; Groceries and related products, nec; Packaged frozen goods; Prepared flour mixes and doughs
PA: Byrnes And Kiefer Company
131 Kline Ave
724 538-5200

(P-1484)

CRUMBL COOKIES
23702 El Toro Rd Ste B, Lake Forest (92630-8905)
PHONE..................949 519-0791
Spencer Hanks, *Owner*
EMP: 70 **EST:** 2021
SALES (est): 1.7MM **Privately Held**
Web: www.crumblcookies.com
SIC: 2052 Cookies

(P-1485)

D F STAUFFER BISCUIT CO INC
Laguna Cookie Company
4041 W Garry Ave, Santa Ana (92704-6315)
PHONE..................714 546-6855
Albert Ovalle, *Mgr*
EMP: 50
Web: www.meijiamerica.com
SIC: 2052 Cookies
HQ: D F Stauffer Biscuit Co Inc
360 S Belmont St
York PA 17403
717 815-4600

(P-1486)

DIBELLA BAKING COMPANY INC
Also Called: Dibella
3524 Seagate Way Ste 110, Oceanside (92056-2673)
PHONE..................951 797-4144
EMP: 65
Web: www.dibellafamiglia.com
SIC: 2052 Cookies

(P-1487)

ELEMENTS FOOD GROUP INC
5560 Brooks St, Montclair (91763-4522)
P.O. Box 4020 (92661-4020)
PHONE..................909 983-2011
Wayne Sorensen, *Pr*
EMP: 60 **EST:** 2004
SQ FT: 23,000
SALES (est): 506.35K **Privately Held**
Web: www.elementsfoods.com
SIC: 2052 2038 Bakery products, dry; Breakfasts, frozen and packaged

(P-1488)

FANTASY COOKIE CORPORATION (PA)
Also Called: Fantasy Cookie Company
12322 Gladstone Ave, Sylmar (91342-5318)
PHONE..................818 361-6901
▲ **EMP:** 33 **EST:** 1979
SALES (est): 11.57MM
SALES (corp-wide): 11.57MM **Privately Held**

Web: www.fantasycookie.com
SIC: 2052 Cookies and crackers

(P-1489)

J & J SNACK FOODS CORP CAL (HQ)
5353 S Downey Rd, Los Angeles (90058-3725)
PHONE..................323 581-0171
Dan Fachner, *Ch Bd*
Ken Plunk, *
Lynwood Mallard, *CMO**
Michael Pollner, *
Steve Every, *
▲ **EMP:** 96 **EST:** 1978
SQ FT: 132,000
SALES (est): 103.41MM
SALES (corp-wide): 1.57B **Publicly Held**
Web: www.jjsnack.com
SIC: 2052 5149 Pretzels; Cookies
PA: J&J Snack Foods Corp.
350 Fellowship Rd
856 665-9533

(P-1490)

LAGUNA COOKIE COMPANY INC
4041 W Garry Ave, Santa Ana (92704-6315)
PHONE..................714 546-6855
Takeshi Izumi, *CEO*
EMP: 100 **EST:** 1981
SQ FT: 55,000
SALES (est): 11.13MM **Privately Held**
SIC: 2052 Cookies
HQ: D F Stauffer Biscuit Co Inc
360 S Belmont St
York PA 17403
717 815-4600

(P-1491)

PHENIX GOURMET LLC
Also Called: Monaco Baking Company
4225 N Palm St, Fullerton (92835-1045)
PHONE..................562 404-5028
▲ **EMP:** 135
SIC: 2052 Cookies

(P-1492)

SOUTH COAST BAKING LLC (DH)
Also Called: South Coast Baking Co.
1711 Kettering, Irvine (92614-5615)
PHONE..................949 851-9654
Kent Hayden, *CEO*
Rick Ptak, *
◆ **EMP:** 55 **EST:** 2011
SALES (est): 88.26MM **Privately Held**
SIC: 2052 5149 Cookies; Cookies
HQ: South Coast Baking Nwa, Llc
800 S 40th St
Springdale AR

2053 Frozen Bakery Products, Except Bread

(P-1493)

BONERTS INCORPORATED
Also Called: Bonert's Slice of Pie
3144 W Adams St, Santa Ana (92704-5808)
PHONE..................714 540-3535
Tim Rooney, *Mgr*
EMP: 50
Web: www.bonertspies.com
SIC: 2053 2051 Frozen bakery products, except bread; Bread, cake, and related products
PA: Bonert's Incorporated
273 S Canon Dr

(P-1494)

NEMOS BAKERY INC (HQ)
Also Called: Ne-Mo's
416 N Hale Ave, Escondido (92029-1496)
PHONE..................760 741-5725
Phillip S Estes, *CEO*
Bob Yurick, *VP*
Sam Delucca Junior, *Sr VP*
James M Shorin, *Sec*
Michael J Chaignot, *CFO*
▲ **EMP:** 70 **EST:** 1975
SALES (est): 24.63MM **Privately Held**
Web: www.nemosbakery.com
SIC: 2053 Cakes, bakery: frozen
PA: Horizon Holdings, Llc
1 Bush St

(P-1495)

OPERA PATISSERIE
Also Called: Opera Patisserie
8480 Redwood Creek Ln, San Diego (92126-1067)
PHONE..................858 536-5800
Diane Anderson, *Prin*
Vincent Garcia, *
EMP: 61 **EST:** 2002
SQ FT: 9,000
SALES (est): 5.19MM **Privately Held**
Web: www.operapatisserie.com
SIC: 2053 5812 Pastries, e.g. danish: frozen; Cafe

(P-1496)

RICH PRODUCTS CORPORATION
3401 W Segerstrom Ave, Santa Ana (92704-6404)
PHONE..................714 338-1145
EMP: 28
SALES (corp-wide): 4.81B **Privately Held**
Web: www.richs.com
SIC: 2053 Frozen bakery products, except bread
PA: Rich Products Corporation
1 Robert Rich Way
716 878-8000

2061 Raw Cane Sugar

(P-1497)

AZUMEX CORP
2320 Paseo De Las Americas, San Diego (92154-7276)
PHONE..................619 710-8855
Fabian Gomez-ibarra, *CEO*
EMP: 28 **EST:** 2011
SALES (est): 4.20MM **Privately Held**
Web: www.azumexsugar.com
SIC: 2061 Granulated cane sugar

2063 Beet Sugar

(P-1498)

SPRECKELS SUGAR COMPANY INC
395 W Keystone Rd, Brawley (92227-9739)
P.O. Box 581 (92227-0581)
PHONE..................760 344-3110
John Richmond, *Pr*
John Richmond, *CEO*
Neil Rudeen, *
Jeff Plathe, *
▲ **EMP:** 260 **EST:** 1905
SALES (est): 23.88MM
SALES (corp-wide): 112.01MM **Privately Held**
Web: www.spreckelssugar.com

SIC: 2063 Beet sugar, from beet sugar refinery
PA: Southern Minnesota Beet Sugar Cooperative
83550 County Rd 21
320 329-8305

2064 Candy And Other Confectionery Products

(P-1499)

180 SNACKS INC
Also Called: Mareblu Naturals
1173 N Armando St, Anaheim (92806-2609)
PHONE..................714 238-1192
Michael Kim, *Pr*
Katherine Kim, *
▲ **EMP:** 47 **EST:** 2004
SALES (est): 9.16MM **Privately Held**
Web: www.180snacks.com
SIC: 2064 2034 2068 Granola and muesli, bars and clusters; Dried and dehydrated fruits; Salted and roasted nuts and seeds

(P-1500)

ADAMS AND BROOKS INC
4345 Hallmark Pkwy, San Bernardino (92407-1829)
P.O. Box 9940 (92427-0940)
PHONE..................909 880-2305
▲ **EMP:** 160 **EST:** 1932
SALES (est): 23MM **Privately Held**
Web: www.adams-brooks.com
SIC: 2064 Nuts, candy covered

(P-1501)

CALIFORNIA SNACK FOODS INC
Also Called: California Candy
2131 Tyler Ave, South El Monte (91733-2754)
PHONE..................626 444-4508
Murl W Nelson, *CEO*
Steve Nelson, *
Paul Mullen, *
Mary Nelson, *
EMP: 45 **EST:** 1961
SQ FT: 30,000
SALES (est): 6.91MM **Privately Held**
Web: www.californiasnackfoods.com
SIC: 2064 2024 2099 2051 Fruits candied, crystallized, or glazed; Juice pops, frozen; Popcorn, packaged: except already popped ; Cakes, pies, and pastries

(P-1502)

CHOCOLATES A LA CARTE INC
24836 Avenue Rockefeller, Valencia (91355-3467)
PHONE..................661 257-3700
▲ **EMP:** 165
Web: www.candymaker.com
SIC: 2064 2066 Chocolate candy, except solid chocolate; Chocolate and cocoa products

(P-1503)

FOOD TECHNOLOGY AND DESIGN LLC (PA)
Also Called: Food Pharma
10012 Painter Ave, Santa Fe Springs (90670-3016)
PHONE..................562 944-7821
Glen Marinelli, *Managing Member*
Remmell Gopez, *Managing Member*
EMP: 27 **EST:** 2001
SQ FT: 20,000

PRODUCTS & SVCS

SALES (est): 16.28MM
SALES (corp-wide): 16.28MM **Privately Held**
Web: www.foodpharma.com
SIC: 2064 Candy and other confectionery products

(P-1504)
GENESIS FOODS CORPORATION
Also Called: Garvey Nut & Candy
8825 Mercury Ln, Pico Rivera (90660-6707)
PHONE..............................323 890-5890
TOLL FREE: 800
▲ **EMP:** 60
Web: www.garveycandy.com
SIC: 2064 5149 Candy and other confectionery products; Cookies

(P-1505)
HIRA PARIS INC
Also Called: Andy Anand Chocolates
3811 Schaefer Ave Ste B, Chino (91710-5400)
PHONE..............................909 634-3900
Thaminder Singh Anand, *Pr*
Sing Datu, *VP*
EMP: 200 **EST:** 2020
SALES (est): 2.19MM **Privately Held**
Web: www.andyanand.com
SIC: 2064 5149 Candy bars, including chocolate covered bars; Chocolate

(P-1506)
HOTLIX (PA)
Also Called: Hotlix Candy
966 Griffin St, Grover Beach (93433-3019)
P.O. Box 447 (93483-0447)
PHONE..............................805 473-0596
Larry Peterman, *Pr*
▼ **EMP:** 25 **EST:** 1983
SQ FT: 1,500
SALES (est): 3.74MM
SALES (corp-wide): 3.74MM **Privately Held**
Web: www.hotlix.com
SIC: 2064 Lollipops and other hard candy

(P-1507)
INW LIVING ECOLOGY OPCO LLC (HQ)
Also Called: Interntnal Ntrtn Wllness Hldng
240 Crouse Dr, Corona (92879-8093)
PHONE..............................951 371-4982
Aman Chogle, *Managing Member*
EMP: 28 **EST:** 2020
SALES (est): 1.81MM
SALES (corp-wide): 539.78MM **Privately Held**
Web: www.inwmfg.com
SIC: 2064 2023 Granola and muesli, bars and clusters; Dietary supplements, dairy and non-dairy based
PA: International Nutrition & Wellness Holdings, Llc
1270 Champion Cir
972 490-3300

(P-1508)
LB BEADELS LLC
70 Atlantic Ave, Long Beach (90802-5202)
PHONE..............................562 726-1700
Joshua Beadel, *Prin*
EMP: 32 **EST:** 2013
SALES (est): 4.93MM **Privately Held**
Web: www.the-breakfast-bar.com
SIC: 2064 Breakfast bars

(P-1509)
MAVE ENTERPRISES INC
Also Called: It's Delish
11555 Cantara St Ste B-E, North Hollywood (91605-1652)
P.O. Box 480620 (90048-1620)
PHONE..............................818 767-4533
Amy Grawitzky, *CEO*
Moshe Grawitzky, *
Rochell Legarreta, *
▲ **EMP:** 35 **EST:** 1992
SQ FT: 35,000
SALES (est): 8.08MM **Privately Held**
Web: www.itsdelish.com
SIC: 2064 2099 2033 2068 Candy and other confectionery products; Seasonings and spices; Canned fruits and specialties; Salted and roasted nuts and seeds

(P-1510)
MCKEEVER DANLEE CONFECTIONARY
760 N Mckeever Ave, Azusa (91702-2349)
PHONE..............................626 334-8964
Gerald Morris, *Pr*
Brian Halpert, *
David A Pistole, *
EMP: 103 **EST:** 1994
SQ FT: 10,000
SALES (est): 963.87K
SALES (corp-wide): 179.18MM **Privately Held**
SIC: 2064 Candy and other confectionery products
HQ: Morris National, Inc.
760 N Mckeever Ave
Azusa CA 91702
626 385-2000

2066 Chocolate And Cocoa Products

(P-1511)
VERY SPECIAL CHOCOLATS INC
760 N Mckeever Ave, Azusa (91702-2349)
PHONE..............................626 334-7838
Gerry Morris Zubatoff, *CEO*
Gerald Morris, *
Bram Morris, *
David Pistole, *
▲ **EMP:** 171 **EST:** 1986
SQ FT: 40,000
SALES (est): 3.6MM
SALES (corp-wide): 179.18MM **Privately Held**
SIC: 2066 Chocolate and cocoa products
HQ: Morris National, Inc.
760 N Mckeever Ave
Azusa CA 91702
626 385-2000

2068 Salted And Roasted Nuts And Seeds

(P-1512)
MELLACE FAMILY BRANDS CAL INC
6195 El Camino Real, Carlsbad (92009-1602)
P.O. Box 22831 (92192-2831)
PHONE..............................760 448-1940
V Pulla, *Pr*
J Pulla, *
Vincent Cosentino, *
EMP: 50 **EST:** 2011
SQ FT: 50,000

SALES (est): 922.07K
SALES (corp-wide): 394.19MM **Privately Held**
SIC: 2068 Salted and roasted nuts and seeds
PA: Johnvince Foods
555 Steeprock Dr
416 663-6146

(P-1513)
MFB LIQUIDATION INC
Also Called: Mama Mellaces Old World Treats
6195 El Camino Real, Carlsbad (92009-1602)
PHONE..............................760 448-1940
▲ **EMP:** 50 **EST:** 1962
SALES (est): 1.16MM **Privately Held**
SIC: 2068 Salted and roasted nuts and seeds

(P-1514)
MIXED NUTS INC
7909 Crossway Dr, Pico Rivera (90660-4449)
PHONE..............................323 587-6887
Vanik Hartounian, *Pr*
◆ **EMP:** 25 **EST:** 1986
SALES (est): 6.96MM **Privately Held**
Web: www.mixednutsinc.com
SIC: 2068 5145 Nuts: dried, dehydrated, salted or roasted; Nuts, salted or roasted

(P-1515)
NEW CENTURY SNACKS LLC
5560 E Slauson Ave, Commerce (90040-2921)
PHONE..............................323 278-9578
▲ **EMP:** 25
SIC: 2068 2099 Salted and roasted nuts and seeds; Food preparations, nec

(P-1516)
PRIMEX FARMS LLC (PA)
16070 Wildwood Rd, Wasco (93280-9210)
PHONE..............................661 758-7790
Ali Amin, *CEO*
Ignasius Handoko, *
EMP: 30 **EST:** 2002
SQ FT: 136,837
SALES (est): 264.21MM
SALES (corp-wide): 264.21MM **Privately Held**
Web: www.primex.us
SIC: 2068 Nuts: dried, dehydrated, salted or roasted

(P-1517)
SNAK CLUB LLC
Also Called: New Century Snacks
5560 E Slauson Ave, Commerce (90040-2921)
PHONE..............................323 278-9578
Farhad Morshed, *Pr*
EMP: 117
SALES (corp-wide): 118.93MM **Privately Held**
Web: www.snakclub.com
SIC: 2068 2099 Salted and roasted nuts and seeds; Food preparations, nec
HQ: Snak Club, Llc
607 N Nash St
El Segundo CA 90245
310 322-4400

(P-1518)
TORN & GLASSER INC
1845 Mount Vernon Ave, Pomona (91768-3348)
PHONE..............................909 706-4100
Greg Glasser, *Pr*
EMP: 25
SALES (corp-wide): 129.37MM **Privately Held**

Web: www.tornandglasser.com
SIC: 2068 Salted and roasted nuts and seeds
PA: Torn & Glasser, Inc.
1622 E Olympic Blvd
213 593-1332

(P-1519)
WONDERFUL PSTCHIOS ALMONDS LLC (HQ)
Also Called: Paramount Farms
11444 W Olympic Blvd Fl 10, Los Angeles (90064-1557)
P.O. Box 200937 (75320)
PHONE..............................310 966-5700
Stewart Resnick, *Pr*
Michael Hohmann, *
Craig B Cooper, *Senior Vice President Managing*
Bill Phillimore, *
◆ **EMP:** 25 **EST:** 1989
SQ FT: 15,000
SALES (est): 915.31MM
SALES (corp-wide): 2.04B **Privately Held**
Web: www.wonderful.com
SIC: 2068 Salted and roasted nuts and seeds
PA: The Wonderful Company Llc
11444 W Olympic Blvd Fl 1
310 966-5700

2076 Vegetable Oil Mills, Nec

(P-1520)
SMART FOODS LLC
3398 Leonis Blvd, Vernon (90058-3014)
PHONE..............................800 284-2250
◆ **EMP:** 25 **EST:** 2015
SALES (est): 3.11MM **Privately Held**
Web: www.avocadooilusa.com
SIC: 2076 2046 Vegetable oil mills, nec; Corn oil, refined

2077 Animal And Marine Fats And Oils

(P-1521)
BAKER COMMODITIES INC
3001 Sierra Pine Ave, Vernon (90058-4120)
PHONE..............................323 318-8260
EMP: 28
SALES (corp-wide): 153.63MM **Privately Held**
Web: www.bakercommodities.com
SIC: 2077 Animal and marine fats and oils
PA: Baker Commodities, Inc.
4020 Bandini Blvd
323 268-2801

(P-1522)
BAKER COMMODITIES INC (PA)
Also Called: Grease Company, The
4020 Bandini Blvd, Vernon (90058-4274)
PHONE..............................323 268-2801
TOLL FREE: 800
James M Andreoli, *Pr*
Mitchel Ebright, *
Denis Luckey, *
◆ **EMP:** 150 **EST:** 1948
SQ FT: 12,000
SALES (est): 153.63MM
SALES (corp-wide): 153.63MM **Privately Held**
Web: www.bakercommodities.com
SIC: 2077 2048 Tallow rendering, inedible; Poultry feeds

(P-1523)
D & D SERVICES INC
Also Called: D & D Cremations Service
4105 Bandini Blvd, Vernon (90058-4208)
P.O. Box 55338 (91385-0338)
PHONE.................................323 261-4176
William M Gorman, *Pr*
Vincent Gorman, *
Roseanne Gorman, *
EMP: 41 **EST:** 1967
SQ FT: 100,000
SALES (est): 4.67MM **Privately Held**
SIC: 2077 Animal and marine fats and oils

(P-1524)
DARLING INGREDIENTS INC
2626 E 25th St, Los Angeles (90058-1212)
P.O. Box 58725 (90058-0725)
PHONE.................................323 583-6311
Thomas Nunley, *Genl Mgr*
EMP: 44
SALES (corp-wide): 6.79B **Publicly Held**
Web: www.darlingii.com
SIC: 2077 2048 Animal and marine fats and
oils; Prepared feeds, nec
PA: Darling Ingredients Inc.
5601 N Macarthur Blvd
972 717-0300

2079 Edible Fats And Oils

(P-1525)
COAST PACKING COMPANY
3275 E Vernon Ave, Vernon (90058-1820)
P.O. Box 58918 (90058-0918)
PHONE.................................323 277-7700
EMP: 60 **EST:** 1922
SALES (est): 22.23MM **Privately Held**
Web: www.coastpacking.com
SIC: 2079 Edible fats and oils

(P-1526)
LIBERTY VEGETABLE OIL COMPANY
15760 Ventura Blvd, Encino (91436-3000)
P.O. Box 4207 (90703-4207)
PHONE.................................562 921-3567
Irwin Field, *Pr*
Ronald Field, *
◆ **EMP:** 40 **EST:** 1948
SALES (est): 5.36MM **Privately Held**
Web: www.libertyvegetableoil.com
SIC: 2079 Olive oil

(P-1527)
VENTURA FOODS LLC (PA)
Also Called: Lou Ana Foods
40 Pointe Dr, Brea (92821-3652)
PHONE.................................714 257-3700
Christopher Furman, *Pr*
Rebecca J Walsh, *
Andy Euser, *CAO**
Erika Noonburg-morgan, *Ex VP*
Luis Andrade, *Executive Commercial Vice
President**
◆ **EMP:** 200 **EST:** 1996
SALES (est): 2.05B **Privately Held**
Web: www.venturafoods.com
SIC: 2079 2035 Vegetable shortenings
(except corn oil); Pickles, sauces, and
salad dressings

(P-1528)
VENTURA FOODS LLC
2900 Jurupa St, Ontario (91761-2915)
PHONE.................................714 257-3700
Wayne Kess, *Mgr*
EMP: 68
Web: www.venturafoods.com

SIC: 2079 2035 Vegetable shortenings
(except corn oil); Pickles, sauces, and
salad dressings
PA: Ventura Foods, Llc
40 Pointe Dr

(P-1529)
WILSEY FOODS INC
40 Pointe Dr, Brea (92821-3652)
PHONE.................................714 257-3700
Takashi Fukunaga, *CEO*
Steve Takagi, *
Hiro Matsumura, *
◆ **EMP:** 1000 **EST:** 1919
SQ FT: 103,378
SALES (est): 4.08MM **Privately Held**
Web: www.venturafoods.com
SIC: 2079 5149 Cooking oils, except corn:
vegetable refined; Shortening, vegetable
HQ: Mbk Usa Holdings, Llc
200 Park Ave Fl 36
New York NY 10166
212 878-6773

2082 Malt Beverages

(P-1530)
ANGEL CITY PUBLIC HSE & BREWRY
216 S Alameda St, Los Angeles
(90012-4201)
PHONE.................................562 983-6880
Vincent Barrios, *Prin*
▲ **EMP:** 24 **EST:** 2013
SALES (est): 826.51K **Privately Held**
Web: www.angelcitybrewery.com
SIC: 2082 Beer (alcoholic beverage)

(P-1531)
ANHEUSER-BUSCH LLC
Also Called: Anheuser-Busch
2800 S Reservoir St, Pomona
(91766-6525)
PHONE.................................951 782-3935
TOLL FREE: 800
Yo Sanchez, *Mgr*
EMP: 115
SALES (corp-wide): 1.7B **Privately Held**
Web: www.budweisertours.com
SIC: 2082 Beer (alcoholic beverage)
HQ: Anheuser-Busch, Llc
1 Busch Pl
Saint Louis MO 63118
800 342-5283

(P-1532)
ANHEUSER-BUSCH LLC
Also Called: Anheuser-Busch
12065 Pike St, Santa Fe Springs
(90670-2064)
P.O. Box 3088 (90670 1988)
PHONE.................................562 699-3424
EMP: 32
SALES (corp-wide): 1.7B **Privately Held**
Web: www.anheuser-busch.com
SIC: 2082 5181 Malt beverage products;
Beer and ale
HQ: Anheuser-Busch, Llc
1 Busch Pl
Saint Louis MO 63118
800 342-5283

(P-1533)
ANHEUSER-BUSCH LLC
Also Called: Anheuser-Busch
20499 S Reeves Ave, Carson (90810-1011)
PHONE.................................310 761-4600
Damian Bonnenfant, *Mgr*
EMP: 48

SALES (corp-wide): 1.7B **Privately Held**
Web: www.budweisertours.com
SIC: 2082 Beer (alcoholic beverage)
HQ: Anheuser-Busch, Llc
1 Busch Pl
Saint Louis MO 63118
800 342-5283

(P-1534)
ANHEUSER-BUSCH LLC
Also Called: Anheuser-Busch
5959 Santa Fe St, San Diego (92109-1623)
P.O. Box 80758 (92138-0758)
PHONE.................................858 581-7000
Denise Cooper, *Genl Mgr*
EMP: 54
SALES (corp-wide): 1.7B **Privately Held**
Web: www.budweisertours.com
SIC: 2082 Beer (alcoholic beverage)
HQ: Anheuser-Busch, Llc
1 Busch Pl
Saint Louis MO 63118
800 342-5283

(P-1535)
ASSOCIATED MICROBREWERIES INC
9675 Scranton Rd, San Diego
(92121-1761)
PHONE.................................858 587-2739
Bryan King, *Brnch Mgr*
EMP: 89
SALES (corp-wide): 22.36MM **Privately
Held**
Web: www.karlstrauss.com
SIC: 2082 Beer (alcoholic beverage)
PA: Associated Microbreweries, Inc.
5985 Santa Fe St
858 273-2739

(P-1536)
ASSOCIATED MICROBREWERIES INC (PA)
Also Called: Karl Strauss Brewery Garden
5985 Santa Fe St, San Diego (92109-1623)
PHONE.................................858 273-2739
Christopher W Cramer, *Pr*
Matthew H Rattner, *
EMP: 50 **EST:** 1988
SQ FT: 2,000
SALES (est): 22.36MM
SALES (corp-wide): 22.36MM **Privately
Held**
Web: www.karlstrauss.com
SIC: 2082 5812 Beer (alcoholic beverage);
Eating places

(P-1537)
ASSOCIATED MICROBREWERIES INC
Also Called: Karl Strauss Brewery & Rest
1157 Columbia St, San Diego (92101-3511)
PHONE.................................619 234-2739
Shawn Phaby, *Mgr*
EMP: 90
SALES (corp-wide): 22.36MM **Privately
Held**
Web: www.karlstrauss.com
SIC: 2082 5812 Beer (alcoholic beverage);
Eating places
PA: Associated Microbreweries, Inc.
5985 Santa Fe St
858 273-2739

(P-1538)
ASSOCIATED MICROBREWERIES INC
901 S Coast Dr Ste A, Costa Mesa
(92626-7790)

PHONE.................................714 546-2739
David Sadeler, *Mgr*
EMP: 86
SALES (corp-wide): 22.36MM **Privately
Held**
Web: www.karlstrauss.com
SIC: 2082 Beer (alcoholic beverage)
PA: Associated Microbreweries, Inc.
5985 Santa Fe St
858 273-2739

(P-1539)
ASSOCTED MCRBRWRIES LTD A CAL
Also Called: Karl Strauss Brewing Company
5985 Santa Fe St, San Diego (92109-1623)
PHONE.................................858 273-2739
Christopher W Cramer, *Prin*
EMP: 27 **EST:** 1988
SALES (est): 1.51MM **Privately Held**
Web: www.karlstrauss.com
SIC: 2082 Beer (alcoholic beverage)

(P-1540)
FIRESTONE WALKER INC
1332 Vendels Cir, Paso Robles
(93446-3802)
PHONE.................................805 226-8514
Adam Firestone, *Brnch Mgr*
EMP: 86
SALES (corp-wide): 97.18MM **Privately
Held**
Web: www.firestonewalker.com
SIC: 2082 Beer (alcoholic beverage)
PA: Firestone Walker, Inc.
1400 Ramada Dr
805 225-5911

(P-1541)
FIRESTONE WALKER INC (PA)
Also Called: Firestone Walker Brewing Co
1400 Ramada Dr, Paso Robles
(93446-3993)
PHONE.................................805 225-5911
David Walker, *CEO*
Adam Firestone, *
◆ **EMP:** 156 **EST:** 1997
SALES (est): 97.18MM
SALES (corp-wide): 97.18MM **Privately
Held**
Web: www.firestonewalker.com
SIC: 2082 Beer (alcoholic beverage)

(P-1542)
FIRESTONE WALKER INC
Also Called: Firestone Walker Brewing Co
620 Mcmurray Rd, Buellton (93427-2511)
PHONE.................................805 254-4205
Patrick Mcalary, *Genl Mgr*
EMP: 86
SALES (corp-wide): 97.18MM **Privately
Held**
Web: www.firestonewalker.com
SIC: 2082 Beer (alcoholic beverage)
PA: Firestone Walker, Inc.
1400 Ramada Dr
805 225-5911

(P-1543)
HOME BREW MART INC
9045 Carroll Way, San Diego (92121-2405)
PHONE.................................858 790-6900
Jim Buechler, *CEO*
Jack White, *
Yuseff Cherney, *
Rick Morgan, *
Julie Buechler, *
▲ **EMP:** 425 **EST:** 1992
SQ FT: 107,000
SALES (est): 6.98MM

SALES (corp-wide): 9.96B **Publicly Held**
Web: www.ballastpoint.com
SIC: 2082 5999 Ale (alcoholic beverage);
Alcoholic beverage making equipment and
supplies
PA: Constellation Brands, Inc.
50 E Broad St
585 678-7100

(P-1544)
JDZ INC
Also Called: Alesmith Brewing Company
9990 Alesmith Ct, San Diego (92126-4200)
P.O. Box 993 (92038-0993)
PHONE..............................858 549-9888
Peter Zien, *CEO*
EMP: 54 **EST:** 2014
SALES (est): 4.79MM **Privately Held**
SIC: 2082 Beer (alcoholic beverage)

(P-1545)
KARL STRAUSS BREWING
COMPANY (PA)
5985 Santa Fe St, San Diego (92109-1623)
P.O. Box 5965 (92109)
PHONE..............................858 273-2739
Chris Cramer, *CEO*
Matt Rattner, *Prin*
EMP: 50 **EST:** 1989
SALES (est): 15.92MM **Privately Held**
Web: www.karlstrauss.com
SIC: 2082 Beer (alcoholic beverage)

(P-1546)
KINGS & CONVICTS BP LLC
2215 India St, San Diego (92101-1725)
PHONE..............................619 255-7213
EMP: 210
SALES (corp-wide): 116.07MM **Privately**
Held
Web: www.ballastpoint.com
SIC: 2082 Malt beverages
HQ: Kings & Convicts Bp, Llc
9045 Carroll Way
San Diego CA 92121
858 790-6900

(P-1547)
KINGS & CONVICTS BP LLC
5401 Linda Vista Rd Ste 406, San Diego
(92110-2402)
PHONE..............................619 295-2337
Jim Johnson, *Brnch Mgr*
EMP: 54
SALES (corp-wide): 116.07MM **Privately**
Held
Web: www.ballastpoint.com
SIC: 2082 Malt beverages
HQ: Kings & Convicts Bp, Llc
9045 Carroll Way
San Diego CA 92121
858 790-6900

(P-1548)
LA QUINTA BREWING
COMPANY LLC
74714 Technology Dr, Palm Desert
(92211-5803)
PHONE..............................760 200-2597
Scott Stokes, *Managing Member*
Scott Stoaks, *
EMP: 55 **EST:** 2013
SALES (est): 4.8MM **Privately Held**
Web: www.laquintabrewing.com
SIC: 2082 5813 Beer (alcoholic beverage);
Beer garden (drinking places)

(P-1549)
OTAY LAKES BREWERY LLC
Also Called: Novo Brasil Brewing Co.
901 Lane Ave Ste 100, Chula Vista
(91914-3536)
PHONE..............................619 768-0172
EMP: 38 **EST:** 2014
SALES (est): 6.49MM **Privately Held**
Web: www.novobrew.com
SIC: 2082 Ale (alcoholic beverage)

(P-1550)
POWER BRANDS CONSULTING
LLC
Also Called: Bevpack
5805 Sepulveda Blvd Ste 501, Van Nuys
(91411-2551)
PHONE..............................818 989-9646
EMP: 40 **EST:** 2006
SQ FT: 5,000
SALES (est): 8.53MM **Privately Held**
Web: www.powerbrands.us
SIC: 2082 8742 Malt beverage products;
Food and beverage consultant

(P-1551)
PROST LLC
Also Called: Bolt Brewery
8179 Center St, La Mesa (91942-2907)
PHONE..............................619 954-4189
EMP: 25 **EST:** 2013
SALES (est): 931.3K **Privately Held**
SIC: 2082 Malt beverages

(P-1552)
PURE PROJECT LLC
1305 Hot Springs Way, Vista (92081-7876)
PHONE..............................760 552-7873
Mat Robar, *Managing Member*
EMP: 67 **EST:** 2015
SALES (est): 6MM **Privately Held**
Web: www.purebrewing.org
SIC: 2082 Beer (alcoholic beverage)

(P-1553)
STONE BREWING CO LLC
2816 Historic Decatur Rd Ste 116, San
Diego (92106-6164)
PHONE..............................619 269-2100
EMP: 219
Web: www.stonebrewing.com
SIC: 2082 Malt beverages
HQ: Stone Brewing Co., Llc
1999 Citracado Pkwy
Escondido CA 92029

(P-1554)
STONE BREWING CO LLC
1977 Citracado Pkwy, Escondido
(92029-4158)
PHONE..............................760 294-7899
EMP: 219
Web: www.stonebrewing.com
SIC: 2082 Malt beverages
HQ: Stone Brewing Co., Llc
1999 Citracado Pkwy
Escondido CA 92029

(P-1555)
TAPROOM BEER CO
2000 El Cajon Blvd, San Diego
(92104-1007)
PHONE..............................619 539-7738
Kevin Conover, *Pt*
EMP: 30 **EST:** 2020
SALES (est): 585.28K **Privately Held**
Web: www.taproombeerco.com
SIC: 2082 Beer (alcoholic beverage)

(P-1556)
TEMBLOR BREWING LLC
3200 Buck Owens Blvd, Bakersfield
(93308-6318)
PHONE..............................661 489-4855
Donald Bynum, *CEO*
EMP: 49 **EST:** 2014
SQ FT: 19,000
SALES (est): 4.15MM **Privately Held**
Web: www.temblorbrewing.com
SIC: 2082 5813 Ale (alcoholic beverage);
Bars and lounges

2083 Malt

(P-1557)
GREAT WESTERN MALTING CO
995 Joshua Way Ste B, Vista (92081-7856)
PHONE..............................360 991-0888
Mike O'toole, *Pr*
EMP: 99
Web: www.greatwesternmalting.com
SIC: 2083 Malt
HQ: Great Western Malting Co.
1705 Nw Harborside Dr
Vancouver WA 98660
360 693-3661

2084 Wines, Brandy, And Brandy Spirits

(P-1558)
ALMA ROSA WINERY
VINEYARDS LLC
1607 Mission Dr Ste 300, Solvang
(93463-3640)
PHONE..............................805 688-9090
J Richard Sanford, *Managing Member*
EMP: 26 **EST:** 2006
SALES (est): 1.18MM **Privately Held**
Web: www.almarosawinery.com
SIC: 2084 Wines

(P-1559)
BOTTAIA WINES LP
35601 Rancho California Rd, Temecula
(92591-4024)
PHONE..............................951 252-1799
EMP: 40 **EST:** 2016
SALES (est): 5.09MM **Privately Held**
Web: www.bottaiawinery.com
SIC: 2084 Wines

(P-1560)
CALLAWAY VINEYARD &
WINERY
32720 Rancho California Rd, Temecula
(92591-4925)
P.O. Box 9014 (92589-9014)
PHONE..............................951 676-4001
Mike Jellison, *Pr*
▲ **EMP:** 70 **EST:** 1969
SALES (est): 4.23MM **Privately Held**
Web: www.callawaywinery.com
SIC: 2084 Wine cellars, bonded: engaged in
blending wines

(P-1561)
CORBETT VINEYARDS LLC
Also Called: Kitchen and Rail
2195 Corbett Canyon Rd, Arroyo Grande
(93420-4974)
PHONE..............................805 782-9463
William Swanson, *Managing Member*
Bill Swanson, *
Rob Rossi, *
▲ **EMP:** 25 **EST:** 2008

SALES (est): 1.83MM **Privately Held**
Web: www.coewine.com
SIC: 2084 Wines

(P-1562)
COURTSIDE CELLARS LLC (PA)
Also Called: Tolosa Winery
4910 Edna Rd, San Luis Obispo
(93401-7938)
PHONE..............................805 782-0500
James Efird, *
Robin Baggett, *
▲ **EMP:** 30 **EST:** 1998
SQ FT: 70,000
SALES (est): 10.2MM
SALES (corp-wide): 10.2MM **Privately**
Held
Web: www.tolosawinery.com
SIC: 2084 Wines

(P-1563)
CYDEA INC
Also Called: Beveragefactory.com
8510 Miralani Dr, San Diego (92126-4351)
PHONE..............................800 710-9939
Craig Costanzo, *CEO*
Michael Costanzo, *
Barbara Costanzo, *
◆ **EMP:** 49 **EST:** 1997
SQ FT: 12,000
SALES (est): 9.13MM **Privately Held**
Web: www.beveragefactory.com
SIC: 2084 2082 5046 5078 Wines, brandy,
and brandy spirits; Beer (alcoholic
beverage); Coffee brewing equipment and
supplies; Refrigeration equipment and
supplies

(P-1564)
DAOU VINEYARDS LLC
Also Called: Daou Vineyards
2740 Hidden Mountain Rd, Paso Robles
(93446-8712)
PHONE..............................805 226-5460
Ben Dollard, *Brnch Mgr*
EMP: 29
Web: www.daouvineyards.com
SIC: 2084 Wines
PA: Daou Vineyards, Llc
2777 Hidden Mountain Rd

(P-1565)
EOS ESTATE WINERY
Also Called: Eos
2300 Airport Rd, Paso Robles
(93446-8549)
P.O. Box 1287 (93447-1287)
PHONE..............................805 239-2562
TOLL FREE: 800
Frank Arciero, *Pt*
Phil Arciero, *Pt*
Fern Underwood, *Pt*
▲ **EMP:** 47 **EST:** 1986
SALES (est): 875.23K **Privately Held**
Web: www.eosvintage.com
SIC: 2084 0172 3172 Wines; Grapes;
Personal leather goods, nec

(P-1566)
EUROPA VILLAGE LLC
Also Called: Europa Village
33475 La Serena Way, Temecula
(92591-5104)
PHONE..............................951 506-1818
John Goldsmith, *General*
▲ **EMP:** 140
SALES (corp-wide): 10.43MM **Privately**
Held
Web: www.europavillage.com
SIC: 2084 Wines

▲ = Import ▼ = Export
◆ = Import/Export

PA: Europa Village Llc
41150 Vua Europa •
951 506-1818

(P-1567)
F KORBEL & BROS
Also Called: Heck Cellars
15401 Bear Mountain Winery Rd, Arvin
(93203-9743)
PHONE..............................661 854-6137
Tambra Wood, *Mgr*
EMP: 23
SQ FT: 250,000
SALES (corp-wide): 42.09MM **Privately Held**
Web: www.korbel.com
SIC: 2084 0172 Wines; Grapes
PA: F. Korbel & Bros.
13250 River Rd
707 824-7000

(P-1568)
FALKNER WINERY INC
40620 Calle Contento, Temecula
(92591-5041)
PHONE..............................951 676-6741
Ray Falkner, *CEO*
Loretta Falkner, *
EMP: 65 **EST:** 1993
SALES (est): 5.05MM **Privately Held**
Web: www.falknerwinery.com
SIC: 2084 7299 Wines; Banquet hall facilities

(P-1569)
FIRESTONE VINEYARD LP
Also Called: Curtis Winery
5000 Zaca Station Rd, Los Olivos
(93441-4566)
P.O. Box 244 (93441-0244)
PHONE..............................805 688-3940
Michael L Gravelle, *Pt*
Adam Firestone, *Pt*
▲ **EMP:** 85 **EST:** 1976
SQ FT: 45,000
SALES (est): 1.85MM
SALES (corp-wide): 69.09MM **Privately Held**
Web: www.firestonewine.com
SIC: 2084 0172 Wines; Grapes
HQ: Foley Family Wines, Inc.
200 Concourse Blvd
Santa Rosa CA 95403

(P-1570)
FLOOD RANCH COMPANY
Also Called: Rancho Sisquoc Winery
6600 Foxen Canyon Rd, Santa Maria
(93454-9656)
PHONE..............................805 937-3616
Ed A Holt, *Mgr*
EMP: 33
SALES (corp-wide): 4.59MM **Privately Held**
Web: www.ranchosisquoc.com
SIC: 2084 Wines
PA: Flood Ranch Company
870 Market St Ste 1100
415 982-5645

(P-1571)
FOLEY FMLY WINES HOLDINGS INC
90 Easy St, Buellton (93427-9566)
PHONE..............................805 450-7225
EMP: 93
SALES (corp-wide): 69.09MM **Privately Held**
Web: www.foleyfoodandwinesociety.com
SIC: 2084 Wines
PA: Foley Family Wines Holdings, Inc.
200 Concourse Blvd

707 708-7600

(P-1572)
FOXEN VINEYARD INC
Also Called: Foxen Canyon Winery & Vineyard
7600 Foxen Canyon Rd, Santa Maria
(93454-9170)
PHONE..............................805 937-4251
Richard Dore, *Pr*
William Wathen, *
EMP: 35 **EST:** 1987
SQ FT: 4,000
SALES (est): 4.98MM **Privately Held**
Web: www.foxenvineyard.com
SIC: 2084 Wines

(P-1573)
GALLO VINEYARDS INC
5595 Creston Rd, Paso Robles
(93446-9480)
PHONE..............................209 394-6281
Allan Reynolds, *Dir*
Javier Pulido, *Mgr*
EMP: 143 **EST:** 2000
SQ FT: 2,624
SALES (est): 4.66MM **Privately Held**
Web: www.gallo.com
SIC: 2084 Wines

(P-1574)
GIUMARRA VINEYARDS CORPORATION
11220 Edison Hwy, Bakersfield
(93307-8431)
P.O. Box 1968 (93303-1968)
PHONE..............................661 395-7000
EMP: 130
SALES (corp-wide): 72.36MM **Privately Held**
Web: www.giumarravineyards.com
SIC: 2084 Wines, brandy, and brandy spirits
PA: Giumarra Vineyards Corporation
11220 Edison Hwy
661 395-7000

(P-1575)
J LOHR WINERY CORPORATION
6169 Airport Rd, Paso Robles
(93446-9547)
PHONE..............................805 239-8900
J Lohr, *Owner*
EMP: 31
SALES (corp-wide): 25.35MM **Privately Held**
Web: www.jlohr.com
SIC: 2084 Wines
PA: J. Lohr Winery Corporation
1000 Lenzen Ave
408 288-5057

(P-1576)
JAMES TOBIN CELLARS INC
8950 Union Rd, Paso Robles (93446-9356)
PHONE..............................805 239-2204
Tobin J Shumrick, *Pr*
Claire Silver, *Stockholder*
EMP: 23 **EST:** 1987
SQ FT: 10,000
SALES (est): 4.59MM **Privately Held**
Web: www.tobinjames.com
SIC: 2084 Wines

(P-1577)
LAETITIA VINEYARD & WINERY INC
Also Called: Laetitia Winery
453 Laetitia Vineyard Dr, Arroyo Grande
(93420-9701)

PHONE..............................805 481-1772
Selim K Zilkha, *Pr*
▲ **EMP:** 65 **EST:** 1994
SALES (est): 4.04MM **Privately Held**
Web: www.laetitiawine.com
SIC: 2084 Wines

(P-1578)
LEONESSE CELLARS LLC
38311 De Portola Rd, Temecula
(92592-8923)
P.O. Box 1371 (92593-1371)
PHONE..............................951 302-7601
Gary Winder, *Managing Member*
Michael Rennie, *
▲ **EMP:** 25 **EST:** 2003
SQ FT: 6,000
SALES (est): 5MM **Privately Held**
Web: www.leonesscellars.com
SIC: 2084 Wines

(P-1579)
LORIMAR WINERY
42031 Main St Ste C, Temecula
(92590-2792)
PHONE..............................951 240-5177
Lawrie Lipton, *Prin*
EMP: 28 **EST:** 1997
SALES (est): 1.33MM **Privately Held**
Web: www.lorimarwinery.com
SIC: 2084 Wines

(P-1580)
LOUIDAR LLC
Also Called: Mount Palomar Winery
33820 Rancho California Rd, Temecula
(92591-4930)
P.O. Box 891510 (92589-1510)
PHONE..............................951 676-5047
Peter Poole, *Prin*
Louis Darwish, *Managing Member*
EMP: 30 **EST:** 1997
SQ FT: 4,000
SALES (est): 4.33MM **Privately Held**
Web: www.mountpalomarwinery.com
SIC: 2084 Wines

(P-1581)
PHASE 2 CELLARS LLC
Also Called: Bezel
4910 Edna Rd, San Luis Obispo
(93401-7938)
PHONE..............................805 782-0300
Kenneth Robin Baggett, *Managing Member*
EMP: 28 **EST:** 2015
SALES (est): 5.79MM **Privately Held**
Web: www.phase2cellars.com
SIC: 2084 Wines

(P-1582)
RBZ VINEYARDS LLC
Also Called: Sextant Wines
2324 W Highway 46, Paso Robles
(93446-8602)
P.O. Box 391 (93447-0391)
PHONE..............................805 542-0133
Craig Stoller, *Prin*
EMP: 30 **EST:** 2006
SALES (est): 4.36MM **Privately Held**
Web: www.sextantwines.com
SIC: 2084 Wines

(P-1583)
ROLLING HILLS VINEYARD INC
4213 Pascal Pl, Pls Vrds Pnsl
(90274-3943)
PHONE..............................310 541-5098
EMP: 23
SALES (corp-wide): 211.41K **Privately Held**

SIC: 2084 Wines, brandy, and brandy spirits
PA: Rolling Hills Vineyard, Inc.
6200 E Canyon Rim Rd # 201

(P-1584)
SAN ANTONIO WINERY INC (PA)
Also Called: San Antonio Gift Shop
737 Lamar St, Los Angeles (90031-2591)
PHONE..............................323 223-1401
Santo Riboli, *CEO*
Maddelena Riboli, *
Cathey Riboli, *Asst Tr*
◆ **EMP:** 101 **EST:** 1917
SQ FT: 310,000
SALES (est): 19.74MM
SALES (corp-wide): 19.74MM **Privately Held**
Web: www.sanantoniowinery.com
SIC: 2084 5182 5812 Wines; Wine; Eating places

(P-1585)
SOUTH COAST WINERY INC
Also Called: South Coast Winery Resort Spa
34843 Rancho California Rd, Temecula
(92591-4006)
PHONE..............................951 587-9463
James A Carter, *Pr*
▲ **EMP:** 32 **EST:** 2001
SALES (est): 11.2MM
SALES (corp-wide): 24.46MM **Privately Held**
Web: www.southcoastwinery.com
SIC: 2084 7011 7991 Wines; Resort hotel; Spas
PA: Spruce Grove, Inc.
3719 S Plaza Dr
714 546-4255

(P-1586)
TEMECULA VALLEY WINERY MGT LLC
Also Called: Leonesse Cellars
27495 Diaz Rd, Temecula (92590-3414)
PHONE..............................951 699-8896
EMP: 56 **EST:** 2008
SQ FT: 40,000
SALES (est): 11.86MM **Privately Held**
Web: www.tvwinerymanagement.com
SIC: 2084 Wines

(P-1587)
TERRAVANT WINE COMPANY LLC
Also Called: Terravant Wine
35 Industrial Way, Buellton (93427-9565)
PHONE..............................805 688-4245
Lew Eisaguirre, *Pr*
Diane Turner, *
Fred Kayne, *Managing Member*
Eric J Guerra, *
▲ **EMP:** 110 **EST:** 2006
SQ FT: 25,000
SALES (est): 23.54MM **Privately Held**
Web: www.summerlandwinebrands.com
SIC: 2084 Wines

(P-1588)
THE WONDERFUL COMPANY LLC (PA)
Also Called: Teleflora
11444 W Olympic Blvd Fl 10, Los Angeles
(90064-1557)
P.O. Box 30119 (90030-0119)
PHONE..............................310 966-5700
◆ **EMP:** 250 **EST:** 2010
SALES (est): 2.04B
SALES (corp-wide): 2.04B **Privately Held**
Web: www.wonderful.com

PRODUCTS & SVCS

SIC: 2084 0723 Wines; Fruit crops market preparation services

(P-1589)
THORNTON WINERY
Also Called: Cafe Champagne
32575 Rancho California Rd, Temecula (92591-4935)
P.O. Box 9008 (92589-9008)
PHONE.................951 699-0099
John M Thornton, *Ch Bd*
Steve Thornton, *
EMP: 98 **EST:** 1975
SQ FT: 41,000
SALES (est): 4.89MM **Privately Held**
Web: www.thorntonwine.com
SIC: 2084 5812 5947 Wine cellars, bonded; engaged in blending wines; Eating places; Gift shop

(P-1590)
TOOTH AND NAIL WINERY
3090 Anderson Rd, Paso Robles (93446-9616)
PHONE.................805 369-6100
Kim Walker, *Pr*
EMP: 23 **EST:** 2014
SALES (est): 1.23MM **Privately Held**
Web: www.toothandnailwine.com
SIC: 2084 Wines

(P-1591)
TREANA WINERY LLC
Also Called: Liberty School
4280 Second Wind Way, Paso Robles (93447)
P.O. Box 3260 (93447-3260)
PHONE.................805 237-2932
Charles Wagner, *
▲ **EMP:** 30 **EST:** 1996
SALES (est): 6.85MM **Privately Held**
Web: www.hopefamilywines.com
SIC: 2084 Wines

(P-1592)
VINTAGE WINE ESTATES INC CA
3070 Limestone Way Unit C, Paso Robles (93446-5988)
PHONE.................805 503-9660
EMP: 23
SALES (corp-wide): 283.23MM **Privately Held**
Web: www.vintagewineestates.com
SIC: 2084 Wines
HQ: Vintage Wine Estates, Inc. (Ca)
     205 Concourse Blvd
     Santa Rosa CA 95403

(P-1593)
WIENS CELLARS LLC
35055 Via Del Ponte, Temecula (92592-8022)
PHONE.................951 694-9892
EMP: 45 **EST:** 2001
SALES (est): 4.65MM **Privately Held**
Web: www.wienscellars.com
SIC: 2084 Wines

(P-1594)
WILSON CREEK WNERY VNYARDS INC
Also Called: Wilson Creek Winery
35960 Rancho California Rd, Temecula (92591-5088)
PHONE.................951 699-9463
William J Wilson, *CEO*
Michael Wilson, *
Craig Johns, *
EMP: 110 **EST:** 2000
SQ FT: 6,000

SALES (est): 24.19MM **Privately Held**
Web: www.wilsoncreekwinery.com
SIC: 2084 8999 Wines; Personal services

(P-1595)
WINC INC
927 S Santa Fe Ave, Los Angeles (90021-1726)
PHONE.................855 282-5829
Alexander Oxman, *CEO*
EMP: 146 **EST:** 2007
SALES (est): 2.47MM **Privately Held**
Web: www.winc.com
SIC: 2084 Wines

2085 Distilled And Blended Liquors

(P-1596)
BOOCHERY INC
Also Called: Boochcraft
684 Anita St Ste F, Chula Vista (91911-7170)
PHONE.................619 207-0530
Michael Kent, *CEO*
Adam Hiner, *
Andrew Clark, *
Michael Kent, *Sec*
EMP: 65 **EST:** 2015
SQ FT: 5,000
SALES (est): 10.81MM **Privately Held**
Web: www.boochcraft.com
SIC: 2085 Distilled and blended liquors

(P-1597)
HAMMOND INC WHICH WILL DO BUS
404 S Coast Hwy, Oceanside (92054-4007)
PHONE.................925 381-5392
Nicholas Hammond, *Pr*
EMP: 25 **EST:** 2018
SALES (est): 2.35MM **Privately Held**
Web: www.paccoastspirits.com
SIC: 2085 Ethyl alcohol for beverage purposes

(P-1598)
SAZERAC COMPANY INC
Barton Brands of California
2202 E Del Amo Blvd, Carson (90749)
P.O. Box 6263 (90749-6263)
PHONE.................310 604-8717
Michael Dominick, *Mgr*
EMP: 55
SALES (corp-wide): 1.28B **Privately Held**
Web: www.sazerac.com
SIC: 2085 Distilled and blended liquors
PA: Sazerac Company, Inc.
     101 Magazine St Fl 5
     866 729-3722

(P-1599)
STILLHOUSE LLC
8201 Beverly Blvd Ste 300, Los Angeles (90048-4542)
PHONE.................323 498-1111
Brad Beckerman, *CEO*
Paul Sheppard, *COO*
EMP: 32 **EST:** 2009
SALES (est): 1.51MM **Privately Held**
Web: www.stillhouse.com
SIC: 2085 Corn whiskey
PA: Bacardi Limited
     C/O Conyers Corporate Services
     (Bermuda) Limited

2086 Bottled And Canned Soft Drinks

(P-1600)
AMERICAN BOTTLING COMPANY
Also Called: Dr Pepper Snapple Group
1188 Mt Vernon Ave, Riverside (92507-1829)
PHONE.................951 341-7500
Vince Spurgeon, *Mgr*
EMP: 79
Web: www.keurigdrpepper.com
SIC: 2086 5149 Soft drinks: packaged in cans, bottles, etc.; Soft drinks
HQ: The American Bottling Company
     6425 Hall Of Fame Ln
     Frisco TX 75034

(P-1601)
AMERICAN BOTTLING COMPANY
Also Called: 7 Up / R C Bottling Co
3220 E 26th St, Vernon (90058-8008)
PHONE.................323 268-7779
Russ Wolfe, *Contrlr*
EMP: 115
Web: www.keurigdrpepper.com
SIC: 2086 5149 Soft drinks: packaged in cans, bottles, etc.; Groceries and related products, nec
HQ: The American Bottling Company
     6425 Hall Of Fame Ln
     Frisco TX 75034

(P-1602)
AMERICAN BOTTLING COMPANY
1166 Arroyo St, San Fernando (91340-1824)
PHONE.................818 898-1471
Ed Nemecek, *Brnch Mgr*
EMP: 79
Web: www.keurigdrpepper.com
SIC: 2086 5149 Soft drinks: packaged in cans, bottles, etc.; Soft drinks
HQ: The American Bottling Company
     6425 Hall Of Fame Ln
     Frisco TX 75034

(P-1603)
AMERICAN BOTTLING COMPANY
230 E 18th St, Bakersfield (93305-5609)
PHONE.................661 323-7921
Brian Sutton, *Mgr*
EMP: 79
Web: www.keurigdrpepper.com
SIC: 2086 5149 Soft drinks: packaged in cans, bottles, etc.; Soft drinks
HQ: The American Bottling Company
     6425 Hall Of Fame Ln
     Frisco TX 75034

(P-1604)
AMERICAN BOTTLING COMPANY
618 Hanson Way, Santa Maria (93458-9734)
PHONE.................805 928-1001
Richard Roese, *Brnch Mgr*
EMP: 51
Web: www.keurigdrpepper.com
SIC: 2086 Soft drinks: packaged in cans, bottles, etc.
HQ: The American Bottling Company
     6425 Hall Of Fame Ln
     Frisco TX 75034

(P-1605)
AMERICAN BOTTLING COMPANY
1166 Arroyo St, Orange (92865)
PHONE.................714 974-8560
Mark Jones, *Mgr*
EMP: 185
Web: www.keurigdrpepper.com
SIC: 2086 5149 Soft drinks: packaged in cans, bottles, etc.; Soft drinks
HQ: The American Bottling Company
     6425 Hall Of Fame Ln
     Frisco TX 75034

(P-1606)
AMERIPEC INC
6965 Aragon Cir, Buena Park (90620-1118)
PHONE.................714 690-9191
Ping C Wu, *CEO*
Ed Muratori, *
EMP: 150 **EST:** 1988
SQ FT: 215,000
SALES (est): 2.56MM **Privately Held**
Web: www.ameripec.com
SIC: 2086 Carbonated soft drinks, bottled and canned
HQ: President Global Corporation
     6965 Aragon Cir
     Buena Park CA 90620

(P-1607)
AQUAHYDRATE INC
5870 W Jefferson Blvd Ste D, Los Angeles (90016-3159)
P.O. Box 69798 (90069-0798)
PHONE.................310 559-5058
John Cochran, *CEO*
David Loewen, *
Mark Loeffler, *
Mark Wahlberg, *
Matthew Howison, *
◆ **EMP:** 38 **EST:** 2003
SALES (est): 3.04MM **Privately Held**
Web: www.aquahydrate.com
SIC: 2086 Mineral water, carbonated: packaged in cans, bottles, etc.

(P-1608)
BEVERAGES & MORE INC
Also Called: Bevmo
28011 Greenfield Dr, Laguna Niguel (92677-4428)
PHONE.................949 643-3020
Christoph Killin, *Brnch Mgr*
EMP: 137
SALES (corp-wide): 1.61B **Privately Held**
Web: www.bevmo.com
SIC: 2086 5149 5921 Bottled and canned soft drinks; Beverages, except coffee and tea; Beer (packaged)
HQ: Beverages & More, Inc.
     1401 Wllow Pass Rd Ste 90
     Concord CA 94520

(P-1609)
BLK INTERNATIONAL LLC
12410 Clark St, Santa Fe Springs (90670-3916)
PHONE.................424 282-3443
Sara Bergstein, *CEO*
Jacqueline Wilkie, *
Louise Wilkie, *
John Kim, *
EMP: 27 **EST:** 2016
SALES (est): 1.44MM **Privately Held**
Web: www.getblk.com
SIC: 2086 Water, natural: packaged in cans, bottles, etc.

(P-1610)
BOTTLING GROUP LLC
Also Called: Pepsico
6659 Sycamore Canyon Blvd, Riverside
(92507-0733)
PHONE..................951 697-3200
Jon Hess, *Prin*
EMP: 55 **EST:** 2011
SALES (est): 19.61MM **Privately Held**
Web: www.pepsico.com
SIC: 2086 Carbonated soft drinks, bottled
and canned

(P-1611)
**CALIFORNIA SPIRITS COMPANY
LLC**
2946 Norman Strasse Rd, San Marcos
(92069-5933)
PHONE..................619 677-7066
Sam Alexander, *Managing Member*
Kyle Clarke, *Managing Member**
Casey Miles, *Managing Member**
Justin Wilkinson, *Managing Member**
EMP: 30 **EST:** 2016
SALES (est): 5.7MM **Privately Held**
Web: www.calspirits.com
SIC: 2086 Carbonated soft drinks, bottled
and canned

(P-1612)
CCE
1334 S Central Ave, Los Angeles
(90021-2210)
PHONE..................213 744-8909
EMP: 28 **EST:** 2011
SALES (est): 158.19K **Privately Held**
SIC: 2086 Bottled and canned soft drinks

(P-1613)
**CHAMELEON BEVERAGE
COMPANY INC (PA)**
6444 E 26th St, Commerce (90040-3214)
PHONE..................323 724-8223
Derek Reineman, *CEO*
Walter Corrigan, *
◆ **EMP:** 68 **EST:** 1995
SQ FT: 100,000
SALES (est): 12.42MM **Privately Held**
Web: www.chameleonbeverage.com
SIC: 2086 5149 Water, natural: packaged in
cans, bottles, etc.; Soft drinks

(P-1614)
COCA-COLA COMPANY
Also Called: Coca-Cola
1650 S Vintage Ave, Ontario (91761-3656)
PHONE..................909 975-5200
Melvin Robinson, *Mgr*
EMP: 63
SALES (corp-wide): 45.75B **Publicly Held**
Web: www.coca-colacompany.com
SIC: 2086 Bottled and canned soft drinks
PA: The Coca-Cola Company
1 Coca Cola Plz Nw
404 676-2121

(P-1615)
**CRYSTAL GEYSER WATER
COMPANY**
1233 E California Ave, Bakersfield
(93307-1205)
PHONE..................661 323-6296
Gerhard Gaugel, *Brnch Mgr*
EMP: 46
Web: www.crystalgeyser.com
SIC: 2086 5141 2099 2033 Mineral water,
carbonated: packaged in cans, bottles, etc.;
Groceries, general line; Food preparations,
nec; Canned fruits and specialties

HQ: Crystal Geyser Water Company
501 Washington St
Calistoga CA 94515
888 424-1977

(P-1616)
**CRYSTAL GEYSER WATER
COMPANY**
2351 E Brundage Ln Ste A, Bakersfield
(93307-3063)
PHONE..................661 321-0896
Robert Hofferd, *Mgr*
EMP: 46
Web: www.crystalgeyserwatercompany.com
SIC: 2086 Mineral water, carbonated:
packaged in cans, bottles, etc.
HQ: Crystal Geyser Water Company
501 Washington St
Calistoga CA 94515
888 424-1977

(P-1617)
DRINKPAK LLC
21375 Needham Ranch Pkwy, Santa Clarita
(91321-5528)
PHONE..................833 376-5725
Nathaniel Patena, *Managing Member*
Jon Ballas, *
Ben Rush, *
EMP: 600 **EST:** 2020
SALES (est): 74MM **Privately Held**
Web: www.drinkpak.com
SIC: 2086 Carbonated beverages,
nonalcoholic: pkged. in cans, bottles

(P-1618)
**FAST TRACK ENERGY DRINK
LLC**
8447 Wilshire Blvd Ste 401, Beverly Hills
(90211-3209)
PHONE..................310 281-2045
Brian Slover Senior, *Pr*
EMP: 25 **EST:** 2010
SALES (est): 366.71K **Privately Held**
SIC: 2086 Carbonated beverages,
nonalcoholic: pkged. in cans, bottles

(P-1619)
GENIUS PRODUCTS NT INC
556 N Diamond Bar Blvd Ste 101, Diamond
Bar (91765-1054)
PHONE..................510 671-0219
Chris Clifford, *CEO*
EMP: 110 **EST:** 2019
SALES (est): 1.23MM **Privately Held**
SIC: 2086 Carbonated beverages,
nonalcoholic: pkged. in cans, bottles

(P-1620)
GTS LIVING FOODS LLC (PA)
Also Called: Synergy Beverages
4415 Bandini Blvd, Los Angeles
(90058-4309)
P.O. Box 2352 (90213)
PHONE..................323 581-7787
Kim Bates, *CMO**
EMP: 700 **EST:** 1994
SALES (est): 172.15MM **Privately Held**
Web: www.gtslivingfoods.com
SIC: 2086 Bottled and canned soft drinks

(P-1621)
KEVITA INC (HQ)
Also Called: Kevita
2220 Celsius Ave Ste A, Oxnard
(93030-5181)
PHONE..................805 200-2250
Chakra Earthsong, *CEO*
Cynthia Nastanski, *

Ada Cheng, *
EMP: 58 **EST:** 2009
SQ FT: 17,000
SALES (est): 21.55MM **Publicly Held**
Web: www.kevita.com
SIC: 2086 Bottled and canned soft drinks
PA: Pepsico, Inc.
700 Anderson Hill Rd
914 253-2000

(P-1622)
**LIQUID DEATH MOUNTAIN
WATER**
1447 2nd St Ste 200, Santa Monica
(90401-3404)
PHONE..................818 521-5500
EMP: 35 **EST:** 2022
SALES (est): 7.1MM **Privately Held**
Web: www.liquiddeath.com
SIC: 2086 Water, natural: packaged in cans,
bottles, etc.

(P-1623)
**MONSTER BEVERAGE 1990
CORPORATION**
1 Monster Way, Corona (92879-7101)
PHONE..................951 739-6200
◆ **EMP:** 2001
SIC: 2086 Soft drinks: packaged in cans,
bottles, etc.

(P-1624)
**MONSTER BEVERAGE
COMPANY**
1990 Pomona Rd, Corona (92878-4355)
PHONE..................866 322-4466
Mark Hall, *Prin*
EMP: 25 **EST:** 2010
SALES (est): 3.24MM
SALES (corp-wide): 7.14B **Publicly Held**
Web: www.monsterbevcorp.com
SIC: 2086 Soft drinks: packaged in cans,
bottles, etc.
PA: Monster Beverage Corporation
1 Monster Way
951 739-6200

(P-1625)
**MONSTER BEVERAGE
CORPORATION (PA)**
Also Called: Monster
1 Monster Way, Corona (92879-7101)
PHONE..................951 739-6200
Rodney C Sacks, *Ch Bd*
Hilton H Schlosberg, *
Thomas J Kelly, *CFO*
EMP: 2367 **EST:** 1985
SALES (est): 7.14B
SALES (corp-wide): 7.14B **Publicly Held**
Web: www.monsterbevcorp.com
SIC: 2086 Carbonated beverages,
nonalcoholic: pkged. in cans, bottles

(P-1626)
ORANGE BANG INC
13115 Telfair Ave, Sylmar (91342-3574)
PHONE..................818 833-1000
David Fox, *Pr*
EMP: 40 **EST:** 1971
SQ FT: 33,000
SALES (est): 2.3MM **Privately Held**
Web: www.orangebang.com
SIC: 2086 Soft drinks: packaged in cans,
bottles, etc.

(P-1627)
P-AMERICAS LLC
Also Called: Pepsico
4375 N Ventura Ave, Ventura (93001-1124)
P.O. Box 25070 (93002-5070)
PHONE..................805 641-4200
Daniel Sassen, *Brnch Mgr*
EMP: 42
SALES (corp-wide): 86.39B **Publicly Held**
Web: www.pepsico.com
SIC: 2086 Carbonated soft drinks, bottled
and canned
HQ: P-Americas Llc
1 Pepsi Way
Somers NY 10589
336 896-5740

(P-1628)
PEPSI-COLA BOTTLING GROUP
Also Called: Pepsico
215 E 21st St, Bakersfield (93305-5115)
PHONE..................661 635-1100
Steve Longfield, *Brnch Mgr*
EMP: 62
SALES (corp-wide): 86.39B **Publicly Held**
Web: www.pepsi-ny.com
SIC: 2086 Carbonated soft drinks, bottled
and canned
HQ: Pepsi-Cola Bottling Group
700 Anderson Hill Rd
Purchase NY 10577

(P-1629)
**PEPSI-COLA METRO BTLG CO
INC**
Also Called: Pepsi-Cola
2471 Nadeau St, Mojave (93501-1507)
PHONE..................661 824-2051
Blaine Sherritt, *Mgr*
EMP: 33
SALES (corp-wide): 86.39B **Publicly Held**
Web: www.pepsico.com
SIC: 2086 5149 Bottled and canned soft
drinks; Soft drinks
HQ: Pepsi-Cola Metropolitan Bottling
Company, Inc.
700 Anderson Hill Rd
Purchase NY 10577
914 767-6000

(P-1630)
**PEPSI-COLA METRO BTLG CO
INC**
Also Called: Pepsi-Cola
1200 Arroyo St, San Fernando
(91340-1545)
PHONE..................818 898-3829
Bob Simpson, *Brnch Mgr*
EMP: 59
SALES (corp-wide): 86.39B **Publicly Held**
Web: www.pepsico.com
SIC: 2086 Carbonated soft drinks, bottled
and canned
HQ: Pepsi-Cola Metropolitan Bottling
Company, Inc.
700 Anderson Hill Rd
Purchase NY 10577
914 767-6000

(P-1631)
**PEPSI-COLA METRO BTLG CO
INC**
Also Called: Pepsico
27717 Aliso Creek Rd, Aliso Viejo
(92656-3804)
PHONE..................949 643-5700
Natolie Daniel, *Mgr*
EMP: 92
SALES (corp-wide): 86.39B **Publicly Held**

Web: www.pepsico.com
SIC: 2086 Carbonated soft drinks, bottled and canned
HQ: Pepsi-Cola Metropolitan Bottling Company, Inc.
700 Anderson Hill Rd
Purchase NY 10577
914 767-6000

(P-1632)
PEPSI-COLA METRO BTLG CO INC
Also Called: Pepsi-Cola
6261 Caballero Blvd, Buena Park (90620-1123)
PHONE...........................714 522-9635
Margaret Gramann, *Mgr*
EMP: 123
SALES (corp-wide): 86.39B **Publicly Held**
Web: www.pepsico.com
SIC: 2086 5149 Carbonated soft drinks, bottled and canned; Soft drinks
HQ: Pepsi-Cola Metropolitan Bottling Company, Inc.
700 Anderson Hill Rd
Purchase NY 10577
914 767-6000

(P-1633)
PEPSI-COLA METRO BTLG CO INC
Also Called: Pepsico
2345 Thompson Way, Santa Maria (93455-1050)
PHONE...........................805 739-2160
Joe Pearson, *Brnch Mgr*
EMP: 52
SALES (corp-wide): 86.39B **Publicly Held**
Web: www.pepsico.com
SIC: 2086 Carbonated soft drinks, bottled and canned
HQ: Pepsi-Cola Metropolitan Bottling Company, Inc.
700 Anderson Hill Rd
Purchase NY 10577
914 767-6000

(P-1634)
PEPSI-COLA METRO BTLG CO INC
Also Called: Pepsico
10057 Marathon Pkwy, Lakeside (92040-2771)
PHONE...........................858 560-6735
Art Brennan, *Brnch Mgr*
EMP: 82
SALES (corp-wide): 86.39B **Publicly Held**
Web: www.pepsico.com
SIC: 2086 Carbonated soft drinks, bottled and canned
HQ: Pepsi-Cola Metropolitan Bottling Company, Inc.
700 Anderson Hill Rd
Purchase NY 10577
914 767-6000

(P-1635)
PEPSI-COLA METRO BTLG CO INC
Also Called: Pepsi-Cola
19700 Figueroa St, Carson (90745-1003)
PHONE...........................310 327-4222
Stefan Freeman, *Mgr*
EMP: 205
SALES (corp-wide): 86.39B **Publicly Held**
Web: www.pepsico.com
SIC: 2086 5149 Carbonated soft drinks, bottled and canned; Soft drinks

HQ: Pepsi-Cola Metropolitan Bottling Company, Inc.
700 Anderson Hill Rd
Purchase NY 10577
914 767-6000

(P-1636)
PEPSICO
1650 E Central Ave, San Bernardino (92408-2611)
PHONE...........................562 818-9429
EMP: 30 **EST:** 2015
SALES (est): 1.08MM **Privately Held**
Web: www.pepsico.com
SIC: 2086 Carbonated soft drinks, bottled and canned

(P-1637)
PEPSICO INC
Also Called: Pepsico
4416 Azusa Canyon Rd, Baldwin Park (91706-2797)
PHONE...........................626 338-5531
Kip Zaughan, *Mgr*
EMP: 23
SALES (corp-wide): 86.39B **Publicly Held**
Web: www.pepsico.com
SIC: 2086 Carbonated soft drinks, bottled and canned
PA: Pepsico, Inc.
700 Anderson Hill Rd
914 253-2000

(P-1638)
PURE-FLO WATER CO (PA)
Also Called: Pure Flo Water
2169 Orange Ave, Escondido (92029-4302)
P.O. Box 660579 (75266-0579)
PHONE...........................619 596-4130
Braian Grant, *CEO*
Marian Grant, *
EMP: 75 **EST:** 1969
SALES (est): 5.47MM
SALES (corp-wide): 5.47MM **Privately Held**
Web: www.water.com
SIC: 2086 Water, natural: packaged in cans, bottles, etc.

(P-1639)
RED BULL MEDIA HSE N AMER INC
1630 Stewart St Ste A, Santa Monica (90404-4020)
PHONE...........................310 393-4647
Jennifer Barney, *Brnch Mgr*
EMP: 54
SALES (corp-wide): 11.47B **Privately Held**
SIC: 2086 Carbonated beverages, nonalcoholic: pkged. in cans, bottles
HQ: Red Bull Media House North America, Inc.
1740 Stewart St
Santa Monica CA 90404
310 393-4647

(P-1640)
REFRESCO BEVERAGES US INC
Also Called: San Bernardino Canning Co.
499 E Mill St, San Bernardino (92408-1523)
PHONE...........................909 915-1430
Ed Williams, *Mgr*
EMP: 24
SQ FT: 76,180
Web: www.refresco-na.com
SIC: 2086 5149 Carbonated beverages, nonalcoholic: pkged. in cans, bottles; Soft drinks
HQ: Refresco Beverages Us Inc.
8112 Woodland Ctr Blvd

Tampa FL 33614

(P-1641)
REYES COCA-COLA BOTTLING LLC
Also Called: Coca-Cola
17220 Nutro Way, Victorville (92395-7714)
PHONE...........................760 241-2653
Rose Wols, *Mgr*
EMP: 28
SALES (corp-wide): 850.14MM **Privately Held**
Web: www.reyescocacola.com
SIC: 2086 Bottled and canned soft drinks
PA: Reyes Coca-Cola Bottling, L.L.C.
3 Park Plz Ste 600
213 744-8616

(P-1642)
REYES COCA-COLA BOTTLING LLC
Also Called: Coca-Cola
1000 Fairway Dr, Santa Maria (93455-1512)
PHONE...........................805 614-3702
Dan Suchecki, *Mgr*
EMP: 28
SALES (corp-wide): 850.14MM **Privately Held**
Web: www.reyescocacola.com
SIC: 2086 Bottled and canned soft drinks
PA: Reyes Coca-Cola Bottling, L.L.C.
3 Park Plz Ste 600
213 744-8616

(P-1643)
REYES COCA-COLA BOTTLING LLC
Also Called: Coca-Cola
5335 Walker St, Ventura (93003-7406)
PHONE...........................805 644-2211
Jim Donelson, *Mgr*
EMP: 35
SALES (corp-wide): 850.14MM **Privately Held**
Web: www.reyescocacola.com
SIC: 2086 5149 Bottled and canned soft drinks; Groceries and related products, nec
PA: Reyes Coca-Cola Bottling, L.L.C.
3 Park Plz Ste 600
213 744-8616

(P-1644)
REYES COCA-COLA BOTTLING LLC
4320 Ride St, Bakersfield (93313-4831)
PHONE...........................661 324-6531
Ed Shell, *Mgr*
EMP: 97
SALES (corp-wide): 850.14MM **Privately Held**
Web: www.reyescocacola.com
SIC: 2086 Bottled and canned soft drinks
PA: Reyes Coca-Cola Bottling, L.L.C.
3 Park Plz Ste 600
213 744-8616

(P-1645)
REYES COCA-COLA BOTTLING LLC
666 Union St, Montebello (90640-6624)
PHONE...........................323 278-2600
Gary Drees, *Mgr*
EMP: 230
SQ FT: 127,556
SALES (corp-wide): 850.14MM **Privately Held**
Web: www.reyescocacola.com

SIC: 2086 Bottled and canned soft drinks
PA: Reyes Coca-Cola Bottling, L.L.C.
3 Park Plz Ste 600
213 744-8616

(P-1646)
REYES COCA-COLA BOTTLING LLC
Also Called: Coca-Cola
1338 E 14th St, Los Angeles (90021-2344)
PHONE...........................213 744-8659
Perry Fitch, *Genl Mgr*
EMP: 28
SALES (corp-wide): 850.14MM **Privately Held**
Web: www.reyescocacola.com
SIC: 2086 Bottled and canned soft drinks
PA: Reyes Coca-Cola Bottling, L.L.C.
3 Park Plz Ste 600
213 744-8616

(P-1647)
REYES COCA-COLA BOTTLING LLC
Also Called: Coca-Cola
700 W Grove Ave, Orange (92865-3214)
PHONE...........................714 974-1901
Thomas Murphy, *Brnch Mgr*
EMP: 70
SQ FT: 7,043
SALES (corp-wide): 850.14MM **Privately Held**
Web: www.reyescocacola.com
SIC: 2086 Bottled and canned soft drinks
PA: Reyes Coca-Cola Bottling, L.L.C.
3 Park Plz Ste 600
213 744-8616

(P-1648)
REYES COCA-COLA BOTTLING LLC (PA)
Also Called: Coca-Cola
3 Park Plz Ste 600, Irvine (92614-2575)
PHONE...........................213 744-8616
James Quincy, *CEO*
Nehal Desai, *
◆ **EMP:** 300 **EST:** 1902
SQ FT: 80,000
SALES (est): 850.14MM
SALES (corp-wide): 850.14MM **Privately Held**
Web: www.reyescocacola.com
SIC: 2086 Bottled and canned soft drinks

(P-1649)
REYES COCA-COLA BOTTLING LLC
Also Called: Coca-Cola
86375 Industrial Way, Coachella (92236-2729)
PHONE...........................760 396-4500
Andrell Gritley, *Genl Mgr*
EMP: 70
SALES (corp-wide): 850.14MM **Privately Held**
Web: www.reyescocacola.com
SIC: 2086 Bottled and canned soft drinks
PA: Reyes Coca-Cola Bottling, L.L.C.
3 Park Plz Ste 600
213 744-8616

(P-1650)
REYES COCA-COLA BOTTLING LLC
Also Called: Coca-Cola
11900 Cabernet Dr, Fontana (92337-7707)
PHONE...........................909 980-3121
Sid Campa, *Mgr*
EMP: 181

SALES (corp-wide): 850.14MM **Privately Held**
Web: www.reyescocacola.com
SIC: **2086** 5149 Bottled and canned soft drinks; Groceries and related products, nec
PA: Reyes Coca-Cola Bottling, L.L.C.
3 Park Plz Ste 600
213 744-8616

(P-1651)

REYES COCA-COLA BOTTLING LLC

Also Called: Coca-Cola
5255 Federal Blvd, San Diego (92105-5710)
PHONE..............................619 266-6300
Randy Cleveland, *Mgr*
EMP: 376
SALES (corp-wide): 850.14MM **Privately Held**
Web: www.reyescocacola.com
SIC: **2086** 5149 Bottled and canned soft drinks; Groceries and related products, nec
PA: Reyes Coca-Cola Bottling, L.L.C.
3 Park Plz Ste 600
213 744-8616

(P-1652)

REYES COCA-COLA BOTTLING LLC

Also Called: Coca-Cola
8729 Cleta St, Downey (90241-5202)
PHONE..............................562 803-8100
Kim Curtis, *Mgr*
EMP: 90
SQ FT: 76,395
SALES (corp-wide): 850.14MM **Privately Held**
Web: www.coca-cola.com
SIC: **2086** 5149 Bottled and canned soft drinks; Groceries and related products, nec
PA: Reyes Coca-Cola Bottling, L.L.C.
3 Park Plz Ste 600
213 744-8616

(P-1653)

SBM DAIRIES INC

Also Called: Heartland Farms
17851 Railroad St, City Of Industry (91748-1118)
PHONE..............................626 923-3000
▼ EMP: 300
Web: www.gcd.com
SIC: **2086** 2026 2033 Fruit drinks (less than 100% juice): packaged in cans, etc.; Fluid milk; Canned fruits and specialties

(P-1654)

SHASTA BEVERAGES INC

14405 Artesia Blvd, La Mirada (90638-5886)
PHONE..............................714 523-2280
Bruce Mcdowell, *Mgr*
EMP: 66
SALES (corp-wide): 1.19B **Publicly Held**
Web: www.shastapop.com
SIC: **2086** 5149 Soft drinks: packaged in cans, bottles, etc.; Soft drinks
HQ: Shasta Beverages, Inc.
26901 Indl Blvd
Hayward CA 94545
954 581-0922

(P-1655)

STRATUS GROUP DUO LLC

4401 S Downey Rd, Vernon (90058-2518)
PHONE..............................323 581-3663
Dara Killilea, *Managing Member*
EMP: 30 EST: 2018
SALES (est): 833.97K **Privately Held**

SIC: **2086** Bottled and canned soft drinks

(P-1656)

UNIX PACKAGING LLC (PA)

Also Called: Mammoth Water
9 Minson Way, Montebello (90640-6744)
PHONE..............................213 627-5050
Bobby Melamed, *CEO*
Shawn Arianpour, *
Kourosh Melamed, *
▲ EMP: 100 EST: 2010
SQ FT: 125,000
SALES (est): 90.43MM
SALES (corp-wide): 90.43MM **Privately Held**
Web: www.unixpackaging.com
SIC: **2086** Pasteurized and mineral waters, bottled and canned

(P-1657)

WISER FOODS INC

5405 E Village Rd Unit 8219, Long Beach (90808-7010)
P.O. Box 8219 (90808-0219)
PHONE..............................310 895-0888
Jeri Powers, *CEO*
Jeri Diane Powers, *
EMP: 100 EST: 2017
SALES (est): 890.62K **Privately Held**
Web: www.wiserfoods.global
SIC: **2086** 5169 1541 8742 Bottled and canned soft drinks; Alcohols; Food products manufacturing or packing plant construction ; Administrative services consultant

(P-1658)

ZEVIA LLC

15821 Ventura Blvd Ste 145, Encino (91436-5201)
PHONE..............................310 202-7000
Padraic Spence, *Managing Member*
EMP: 75 EST: 2007
SALES (est): 110.03MM
SALES (corp-wide): 166.42MM **Publicly Held**
Web: www.zevia.com
SIC: **2086** Bottled and canned soft drinks
PA: Zevia Pbc
15821 Vntura Blvd Ste 135
424 343-2654

(P-1659)

ZEVIA PBC (PA)

Also Called: Zevia
15821 Ventura Blvd Ste 135, Encino (91436-4787)
PHONE..............................424 343-2654
Amy Taylor, *Pr*
Padraic L Spence, *Non-Executive Chairman of the Board*
Girish Satya, *CAO*
Alfred A Guarino, *CCO*
Lorna R Simms, *Corporate Secretary*
EMP: 40 EST: 2007
SQ FT: 20,185
SALES (est): 166.42MM
SALES (corp-wide): 166.42MM **Publicly Held**
Web: www.zevia.com
SIC: **2086** Bottled and canned soft drinks

2087 Flavoring Extracts And Syrups, Nec

(P-1660)

AMERICAN FRUITS & FLAVORS LLC (HQ)

Also Called: Juice Division
10725 Sutter Ave, Pacoima (91331-2553)

P.O. Box 331060 (91333-1060)
PHONE..............................818 899-9574
Jack Haddad, *
◆ EMP: 125 EST: 1975
SQ FT: 10,000
SALES (est): 40.37MM
SALES (corp-wide): 7.14B **Publicly Held**
Web: www.americanfruits-flavors.com
SIC: **2087** Concentrates, drink
PA: Monster Beverage Corporation
1 Monster Way
951 739-6200

(P-1661)

AMERICAN FRUITS & FLAVORS LLC

Also Called: Weber
9345 Santa Anita Ave, Rancho Cucamonga (91730-6126)
PHONE..............................909 291-2620
Brian Maton, *Mgr*
EMP: 48
SALES (corp-wide): 7.14B **Publicly Held**
Web: www.americanfruits-flavors.com
SIC: **2087** Concentrates, drink
HQ: American Fruits And Flavors, Llc
10725 Sutter Ave
Pacoima CA 91331
818 899-9574

(P-1662)

AMERICAN FRUITS & FLAVORS LLC

400 S Central Ave, Los Angeles (90013-1712)
PHONE..............................213 624-1831
Terry Miller, *Mgr*
EMP: 64
SALES (corp-wide): 7.14B **Publicly Held**
Web: www.americanfruits-flavors.com
SIC: **2087** Concentrates, drink
HQ: American Fruits And Flavors, Llc
10725 Sutter Ave
Pacoima CA 91331
818 899-9574

(P-1663)

AMERICAN FRUITS & FLAVORS LLC

Also Called: Ability
22560 Lucerne St, Carson (90745-4303)
PHONE..............................310 522-1844
Ricardo Velasquez, *Mgr*
EMP: 55
SALES (corp-wide): 7.14B **Publicly Held**
Web: www.americanfruits-flavors.com
SIC: **2087** Concentrates, drink
HQ: American Fruits And Flavors, Llc
10725 Sutter Ave
Pacoima CA 91331
818 899-9574

(P-1664)

AMERICAN FRUITS & FLAVORS LLC

Also Called: Lineage
3001 Sierra Pine Ave, Vernon (90058-4120)
PHONE..............................323 881-8321
Julio Tovar, *Mgr*
EMP: 47
SALES (corp-wide): 7.14B **Publicly Held**
Web: www.americanfruits-flavors.com
SIC: **2087** Concentrates, drink
HQ: American Fruits And Flavors, Llc
10725 Sutter Ave
Pacoima CA 91331
818 899-9574

(P-1665)

AMERICAN FRUITS & FLAVORS LLC

13530 Rosecrans Ave, Santa Fe Springs (90670-5023)
PHONE..............................562 320-2802
Michael Mallette, *Mgr*
EMP: 34
SALES (corp-wide): 7.14B **Publicly Held**
Web: www.americanfruits-flavors.com
SIC: **2087** Concentrates, drink
HQ: American Fruits and Flavors, Llc
10725 Sutter Ave
Pacoima CA 91331
818 899-9574

(P-1666)

AMERICAN FRUITS & FLAVORS LLC

1527 Knowles Ave, Los Angeles (90063-1606)
PHONE..............................818 899-9574
Daron Canales, *Mgr*
EMP: 25
SALES (corp-wide): 7.14B **Publicly Held**
Web: www.americanfruits-flavors.com
SIC: **2087** Concentrates, drink
HQ: American Fruits And Flavors, Llc
10725 Sutter Ave
Pacoima CA 91331
818 899-9574

(P-1667)

AMERICAN FRUITS & FLAVORS LLC

1565 Knowles Ave, Los Angeles (90063-1606)
PHONE..............................818 899-9574
Daron Canales, *Mgr*
EMP: 25
SALES (corp-wide): 7.14B **Publicly Held**
Web: www.americanfruits-flavors.com
SIC: **2087** Concentrates, drink
HQ: American Fruits And Flavors, Llc
10725 Sutter Ave
Pacoima CA 91331
818 899-9574

(P-1668)

BETTER BEVERAGES INC (PA)

Also Called: Chem-Mark of Orange County
10624 Midway Ave, Cerritos (90703-1581)
P.O. Box 1399 (90707-1399)
PHONE..............................562 924-8321
H Ronald Harris, *CEO*
Tricia Harris, *
William Kendig, *General Vice President*
Patrick Dickson, *
▲ EMP: 40 EST: 1946
SQ FT: 15,000
SALES (est): 8.26MM
SALES (corp-wide): 8.26MM **Privately Held**
Web: www.betbev.com
SIC: **2087** 7359 5169 Beverage bases; Equipment rental and leasing, nec; Industrial gases

(P-1669)

BI NUTRACEUTICALS INC

2384 E Pacifica Pl, Rancho Dominguez (90220-6214)
PHONE..............................310 669-2100
◆ EMP: 120
Web: www.botanicals.com
SIC: **2087** 2833 5122 5149 Flavoring extracts and syrups, nec; Medicinals and botanicals; Vitamins and minerals; Seasonings, sauces, and extracts

(P-1670)
BLUE PACIFIC FLAVORS INC
1354 Marion Ct, City Of Industry
(91745-2418)
PHONE..................626 934-0099
Donald F Wilkes, Pr
▲ EMP: 35 EST: 1993
SQ FT: 40,000
SALES (est): 9.05MM Privately Held
Web: www.bluepacificflavors.com
SIC: 2087 2869 Extracts, flavoring;
Perfumes, flavorings, and food additives

(P-1671)
BYRNES & KIEFER CO
501 Airpark Dr, Fullerton (92833-2501)
PHONE..................714 554-4000
EMP: 55 EST: 2012
SALES (est): 2.47MM Privately Held
Web: www.bkcompany.com
SIC: 2087 Colorings, confectioners'

(P-1672)
**CALIFRNIA CSTM FRITS
FLVORS LL (PA)**
Also Called: California Cstm Frt & Flavors
15800 Tapia St, Irwindale (91706-2178)
PHONE..................626 736-4130
Mike Mulhausen, Pr
◆ EMP: 35 EST: 1984
SALES (est): 27.98MM
SALES (corp-wide): 27.98MM Privately
Held
Web: www.ccff.com
SIC: 2087 2033 2099 5083 Extracts, flavoring
; Fruits: packaged in cans, jars, etc.; Food
preparations, nec; Dairy machinery and
equipment

(P-1673)
**CARMI FLVR & FRAGRANCE CO
INC (PA)**
Also Called: Carmi Flavors
6030 Scott Way, Commerce (90040-3516)
PHONE..................323 888-9240
Eliot Carmi, Pr
▲ EMP: 40 EST: 1980
SQ FT: 35,000
SALES (est): 19.68MM
SALES (corp-wide): 19.68MM Privately
Held
Web: www.carmiflavors.com
SIC: 2087 2844 Extracts, flavoring;
Perfumes, cosmetics and other toilet
preparations

(P-1674)
CUSTOM INGREDIENTS INC (PA)
Also Called: Custom Flavors
160 Calle Iglesia Ste 102, San Clemente
(92672-7551)
PHONE..................949 276-7995
Michael L Wendling, CEO
Steven Bishop, CFO
Alexander Wendling, Pr
EMP: 24 EST: 2000
SALES (est): 21.22MM Privately Held
Web: www.customflavors.com
SIC: 2087 Beverage bases, concentrates,
syrups, powders and mixes

(P-1675)
**DELANO GROWERS GRAPE
PRODUCTS**
32351 Bassett Ave, Delano (93215-9699)
PHONE..................661 725-3255
Jim Cesare, Pr
▲ EMP: 55 EST: 1940
SQ FT: 40,000

SALES (est): 8.82MM Privately Held
Web:
www.delanogrowersgrapeproducts.com
SIC: 2087 Concentrates, drink

(P-1676)
DR SMOOTHIE BRANDS LLC
Also Called: Sunny Sky Products
1730 Raymer Ave, Fullerton (92833-2530)
PHONE..................714 449-9787
Sam Lteif, CEO
▼ EMP: 25 EST: 2006
SQ FT: 30,000
SALES (est): 2.53MM
SALES (corp-wide): 42.45MM Privately
Held
Web: www.drsmoothie.com
SIC: 2087 Beverage bases, concentrates,
syrups, powders and mixes
PA: Juice Tyme, Inc.
4401 S Oakley Ave
773 579-1291

(P-1677)
DRYWATER INC
3901 Westerly Pl Ste 111, Newport Beach
(92660-2306)
PHONE..................844 434-0829
Bryan Appio, CEO
EMP: 25 EST: 2021
SALES (est): 2.49MM Privately Held
Web: www.drywater.com
SIC: 2087 Beverage bases

(P-1678)
FLAVOR HOUSE INC
16378 Koala Rd, Adelanto (92301-3916)
PHONE..................760 246-9131
Richard Staley, Owner
Richard Staley, Pr
▲ EMP: 45 EST: 1977
SQ FT: 23,600
SALES (est): 7.35MM Privately Held
Web: www.flavorhouseinc.com
SIC: 2087 Flavoring extracts and syrups, nec

(P-1679)
FLAVOR INFUSION LLC
Also Called: Fisa
332 Forest Ave Ste 19, Laguna Beach
(92651-2100)
PHONE..................949 715-4369
◆ EMP: 40
SIC: 2087 Syrups, drink

(P-1680)
FLAVOR PRODUCERS LLC (PA)
Also Called: Flavor Producers
8521 Fallbrook Ave Ste 380, West Hills
(91304-3239)
PHONE..................661 257-3400
EMP: 47 EST: 1981
SALES (est): 57.58MM
SALES (corp-wide): 57.58MM Privately
Held
Web: www.flavorproducers.com
SIC: 2087 Concentrates, flavoring (except
drink)

(P-1681)
FROZEN BEAN INC
9238 Bally Ct, Rancho Cucamonga
(91730-5313)
PHONE..................855 837-6936
John Bae, CEO
▼ EMP: 30 EST: 2011
SALES (est): 5.39MM Privately Held
Web: www.thefrozenbean.com
SIC: 2087 Beverage bases, concentrates,
syrups, powders and mixes

(P-1682)
**GOLDEN STATE FOODS CORP
(PA)**
Also Called: Golden State Foods
18301 Von Karman Ave Ste 1100, Irvine
(92612-0133)
PHONE..................949 247-8000
Brian Dick, Pr
John E Page, *
Ed Rodriguez, Chief Human Resources
Officer*
William Sanderson, *
Brad Tingey, *
◆ EMP: 35 EST: 1969
SALES (est): 1.5MM
SALES (corp-wide): 1.5MM Privately Held
Web: www.goldenstatefoods.com
SIC: 2087 5142 5148 5149 Syrups, drink;
Packaged frozen goods; Vegetables;
Condiments

(P-1683)
**HERBALIFE MANUFACTURING
LLC (DH)**
800 W Olympic Blvd Ste 406, Los Angeles
(90015-1367)
PHONE..................866 866-4744
Richard Caloca, *
◆ EMP: 52 EST: 2008
SQ FT: 145,000
SALES (est): 49.5MM Privately Held
Web: www.herbalife.com
SIC: 2087 2023 Beverage bases,
concentrates, syrups, powders and mixes;
Dietary supplements, dairy and non-dairy
based
HQ: Herbalife International, Inc.
800 W Olympic Blvd Ste 40
Los Angeles CA 90015
310 410-9600

(P-1684)
J & J PROCESSING INC
Also Called: Custom Foods
14715 Anson Ave, Santa Fe Springs
(90670-5305)
PHONE..................562 926-2333
James B Nelson, CEO
Paul Nelson, *
▲ EMP: 50 EST: 1972
SQ FT: 44,000
SALES (est): 8.65MM Privately Held
Web: www.custom-foods.com
SIC: 2087 2041 2099 Beverage bases; Flour
and other grain mill products; Seasonings:
dry mixes

(P-1685)
**JAVO BEVERAGE COMPANY
INC**
1311 Specialty Dr, Vista (92081-8521)
PHONE..................760 560-5286
Dennis Riley, Pr
Dennis Riley, Pr
Gerry Anderson, CFO
Chris Johnson, Ex VP
▲ EMP: 100 EST: 2002
SQ FT: 39,000
SALES (est): 39.27MM
SALES (corp-wide): 33.16MM Privately
Held
Web: www.javobeverage.com
SIC: 2087 Extracts, flavoring
HQ: Florida Food Products, Llc
1025 Grnwood Blvd Ste 500
Lake Mary FL 32746
855 337-1633

(P-1686)
KEY ESSENTIALS INC
Also Called: Agilex Flavors & Fragrances
1916 S Tubeway Ave, Commerce
(90040-1612)
▲ EMP: 60
SIC: 2087 Flavoring extracts and syrups, nec

(P-1687)
METAROM USA INC
1725 Gillespie Way Ste 101, El Cajon
(92020-1044)
PHONE..................619 449-0299
Christophe Dugas, Pr
Brandon Brown, *
EMP: 46 EST: 2016
SALES (est): 2.85MM Privately Held
SIC: 2087 Extracts, flavoring

(P-1688)
**NEWPORT FLAVORS &
FRAGRANCES**
Also Called: Nature's Flavors
833 N Elm St, Orange (92867-7909)
PHONE..................714 771-2200
William R Sabo, CEO
Jeanne A Rossman, *
▲ EMP: 30 EST: 1984
SALES (est): 6.49MM Privately Held
Web: www.newportflavors.com
SIC: 2087 Extracts, flavoring

(P-1689)
SCISOREK & SON FLAVORS INC
Also Called: S&S Flavours
2951 Enterprise St, Brea (92821-6212)
PHONE..................714 524-0550
Mark Tuerffs, Pr
Dan Hart, *
EMP: 50 EST: 1928
SQ FT: 33,000
SALES (est): 6.23MM Privately Held
Web: www.ssflavors.com
SIC: 2087 Extracts, flavoring

(P-1690)
SUNOPTA FRUIT GROUP INC
12128 Center St, South Gate (90280-8046)
P.O. Box 2218 (90280-9218)
PHONE..................323 774-6000
◆ EMP: 62
SIC: 2087 Flavoring extracts and syrups, nec

(P-1691)
T HASEGAWA USA INC (HQ)
14017 183rd St, Cerritos (90703-7000)
PHONE..................714 522-1900
Tom Damiano, CEO
Tokujiro Hasegawa, *
▲ EMP: 50 EST: 1978
SQ FT: 56,000
SALES (est): 68.18MM Privately Held
Web: www.thasegawa.com
SIC: 2087 Extracts, flavoring
PA: T.Hasegawa Co., Ltd.
4-4-14, Nihombashihoncho

(P-1692)
UNITED BRANDS COMPANY INC
5930 Cornerstone Ct W Ste 170, San Diego
(92121-3772)
PHONE..................619 461-5220
Michael Michail, Pr
Philip W Oneil, CRO
EMP: 43 EST: 2001
SQ FT: 1,800
SALES (est): 2.18MM Privately Held
Web: www.unitedbrandsco.com

SIC: 2087 2082 Beverage bases; Ale
   (alcoholic beverage)

(P-1693)
WEIDER HEALTH AND FITNESS
21100 Erwin St, Woodland Hills
(91367-3772)
PHONE..............................818 884-6800
Eric Weider, *Pr*
George Lengvari, *
Bernard J Cartoon, *
Lian Katz, *
Tonja Fuller, *
EMP: 466 **EST:** 1940
SQ FT: 6,000
SALES (est): 5.22MM **Privately Held**
SIC: 2087 7991 7999 Beverage bases,
   concentrates, syrups, powders and mixes;
   Physical fitness facilities; Physical fitness
   instruction

2091 Canned And Cured Fish And Seafoods

(P-1694)
AQUAMAR INC
10888 7th St, Rancho Cucamonga
(91730-5421)
PHONE..............................909 481-4700
Hugo Yamakawa, *Pr*
Taka Iwasaki, *
◆ **EMP:** 150 **EST:** 1987
SQ FT: 42,000
SALES (est): 24.99MM **Privately Held**
Web: www.aquamarseafood.com
SIC: 2091 2092 Shellfish, canned and cured;
   Fresh or frozen packaged fish
PA: Lm Foods, Llc
   100 Raskulinecz Rd

(P-1695)
BUMBLE BEE FOODS LLC
13100 Arctic Cir, Santa Fe Springs
(90670-5508)
PHONE..............................562 483-7474
Jan Tharp, *Brnch Mgr*
EMP: 41
Web: www.thebumblebeecompany.com
SIC: 2091 Canned and cured fish and
   seafoods
HQ: Bumble Bee Foods, Llc
   280 10th Ave
   San Diego CA 92101
   800 800-8572

(P-1696)
BUMBLE BEE SEAFOODS LP
280 10th Ave, San Diego (92101-7406)
P.O. Box 85362 (92186-5362)
PHONE..............................050 715-4000
Christopher Lischewsky, *Pr*
◆ **EMP:** 150 **EST:** 1997
SALES (est): 18.34MM **Privately Held**
Web: www.bumblebee.com
SIC: 2091 2047 Tuna fish: packaged in
   cans, jars, etc.; Dog and cat food

(P-1697)
PACIFIC AMERICAN FISH CO INC (PA)
Also Called: Pafco
5525 S Santa Fe Ave, Vernon
(90058-3523)
PHONE..............................323 319-1551
Peter Huh, *CEO*
Paul Huh, *
◆ **EMP:** 150 **EST:** 1977
SQ FT: 100,000
SALES (est): 52.71MM

SALES (corp-wide): 52.71MM **Privately Held**
Web: www.pafco.net
SIC: 2091 5146 Fish, filleted (boneless);
   Fish, fresh

(P-1698)
SOUTHWIND FOODS LLC (PA)
Also Called: Great Amercn Seafood Import Co
20644 S Fordyce Ave, Carson
(90810-1018)
P.O. Box 86021 (90086)
PHONE..............................323 262-8222
Sebastiano Buddy Galletti, *CEO*
Jim Lee, *
Paul Galletti, *
Sam Galletti, *
Salvatori Perri, *
▲ **EMP:** 125 **EST:** 1999
SQ FT: 80,000
SALES (est): 136.02MM
SALES (corp-wide): 136.02MM **Privately Held**
Web: www.southwindfoods.com
SIC: 2091 Seafood products: packaged in
   cans, jars, etc.

(P-1699)
YAMASA ENTERPRISES
Also Called: Yamasa Fish Cake
515 Stanford Ave, Los Angeles
(90013-2189)
PHONE..............................213 626-2211
Frank Kawana, *CEO*
Yuji Kawana, *
Sachie Kawana, *
▲ **EMP:** 27 **EST:** 1939
SQ FT: 20,000
SALES (est): 4.77MM **Privately Held**
Web: www.yamasafishcake.com
SIC: 2091 Fish and seafood cakes:
   packaged in cans, jars, etc.

2092 Fresh Or Frozen Packaged Fish

(P-1700)
ADVANCED FRESH CNCPTS FRNCHISE
Also Called: Afcfc
19700 Mariner Ave, Torrance (90503-1648)
PHONE..............................310 604-3200
Jeffery Seiler, *CEO*
▲ **EMP:** 60 **EST:** 2002
SALES (est): 9.03MM
SALES (corp-wide): 48.2MM **Privately Held**
Web: www.advancedfreshconcepts.com
SIC: 2092 6794 Fresh or frozen packaged
   fish; Franchises, selling or licensing
PA: Advanced Fresh Concepts Corp
   19205 S Laurel Park Rd
   310 604-3630

(P-1701)
ATLANTIS SEAFOOD LLC
Also Called: Seacatch Seafoods
10501 Valley Blvd Ste 1820, El Monte
(91731-3623)
PHONE..............................626 626-4900
EMP: 85
SIC: 2092 Seafoods, frozen: prepared

(P-1702)
BLUE NALU INC
Also Called: Bluenalu
6060 Nancy Ridge Dr Ste 100, San Diego
(92121-3218)
PHONE..............................858 703-8703

Henry Louis Cooperhouse, *CEO*
Chris Somogyi, *
Deja Westerson, *
EMP: 42 **EST:** 2017
SALES (est): 11.85MM **Privately Held**
Web: www.bluenalu.com
SIC: 2092 Fresh or frozen packaged fish

(P-1703)
CFWF INC
842 Flint Ave, Wilmington (90744-3739)
PHONE..............................310 221-6280
▲ **EMP:** 102
SIC: 2092 5146 Fresh or frozen packaged
   fish; Fish and seafoods

(P-1704)
ETHOS SEAFOOD GROUP LLC
18531 S Broadwick St, Rancho Dominguez
(90220-6440)
PHONE..............................312 858-3474
EMP: 54 **EST:** 2012
SALES (est): 1.79MM
SALES (corp-wide): 142.04MM **Privately Held**
Web: www.smseafoodcr.com
SIC: 2092 5146 Fresh or frozen packaged
   fish; Fish and seafoods
PA: Santa Monica Seafood Company
   18531 S Broadwick St
   310 886-7900

(P-1705)
FISH HOUSE FOODS INC
1263 Linda Vista Dr, San Marcos
(92078-3827)
PHONE..............................760 597-1270
Ron Butler, *Pr*
Ronald J Butler, *
Rex Butler, *
Karen Butler, *
EMP: 240 **EST:** 1985
SQ FT: 52,000
SALES (est): 1.15MM
SALES (corp-wide): 2.24MM **Privately Held**
Web: www.fishhousefoods.com
SIC: 2092 5149 Seafoods, fresh: prepared;
   Groceries and related products, nec
PA: The Fish House Vera Cruz Inc
   3585 Main St Ste 212
   760 744-8000

(P-1706)
FISHERMANS PRIDE PRCESSORS INC
Also Called: Neptune Foods
4510 3 Alameda St, Vernon (90050-2011)
PHONE..............................323 232-1980
Howard Choi, *CEO*
Hector Poon, *
◆ **EMP:** 300 **EST:** 1954
SQ FT: 125,000
SALES (est): 24.26MM **Privately Held**
SIC: 2092 Fresh or frozen packaged fish

(P-1707)
INLAND COLD STORAGE
2356 Fleetwood Dr, Riverside (92509-2409)
PHONE..............................951 369-0230
EMP: 38 **EST:** 2013
SALES (est): 259.82K **Privately Held**
Web: www.inlandcold.com
SIC: 2092 Fresh or frozen packaged fish

(P-1708)
J DELUCA FISH COMPANY INC
Also Called: Nautilus Seafood
505 E Harry Bridges Blvd, Wilmington
(90744-6607)

PHONE..............................310 221-6500
Wayne Berman, *Brnch Mgr*
EMP: 38
SALES (corp-wide): 23.11MM **Privately Held**
Web: www.jdelucafishco.com
SIC: 2092 Fresh or frozen packaged fish
PA: J Deluca Fish Company, Inc.
   2194 Signal Pl
   310 684-5180

(P-1709)
NIKKO ENTERPRISE CORPORATION
Also Called: Hanna Fuji Sushi
13168 Sandoval St, Santa Fe Springs
(90670-6600)
PHONE..............................562 941-6080
Tlang T Mawii, *CEO*
Robby Sharma, *
Sein Myint, *Stockholder**
EMP: 23 **EST:** 1995
SQ FT: 5,000
SALES (est): 902.79K **Privately Held**
Web: www.necsushi.com
SIC: 2092 Fresh or frozen fish or seafood
   chowders, soups, and stews

(P-1710)
OCEAN DIRECT LLC (HQ)
Also Called: Boardwalk Solutions
13771 Gramercy Pl, Gardena (90249-2470)
PHONE..............................424 266-9300
▼ **EMP:** 184 **EST:** 2003
SQ FT: 20,000
SALES (est): 41.4MM
SALES (corp-wide): 113.36MM **Privately Held**
Web: www.oceandirect.com
SIC: 2092 2022 2037 2033 Fresh or frozen
   fish or seafood chowders, soups, and stews
   ; Natural cheese; Frozen fruits and
   vegetables; Vegetables and vegetable
   products, in cans, jars, etc.
PA: Richmond Wholesale Meat, Llc
   2920 Regatta Blvd
   510 233-5111

(P-1711)
SANTA MONICA SEAFOOD COMPANY (PA)
Also Called: Santa Monica Seafood
18531 S Broadwick St, Rancho Dominguez
(90220-6440)
PHONE..............................310 886-7900
TOLL FREE: 888
Roger O'brien, *CEO*
Michael Cigliano Ii, *VP*
▲ **EMP:** 100 **EST:** 1939
SQ FT: 65,000
SALES (est): 142.04MM
SALES (corp-wide): 142.04MM **Privately Held**
Web: www.santamonicaseafood.com
SIC: 2092 5146 Seafoods, frozen: prepared;
   Seafoods

(P-1712)
SIMPLY FRESH LLC
Also Called: Rojo's
11215 Knott Ave Ste A, Cypress
(90630-5495)
PHONE..............................714 562-5000
Dale Jabour, *CEO*
▼ **EMP:** 160 **EST:** 1987
SQ FT: 20,000
SALES (est): 27.3MM
SALES (corp-wide): 113.55MM **Privately Held**
Web: www.simplyff.com

SIC: 2092 Fresh or frozen packaged fish
PA: Lakeview Farms, Llc
1600 Gressel Dr
419 695-9925

(P-1713)
STATE FISH CO INC
624 W 9th St Ste 100, San Pedro
(90731-7288)
PHONE...............................310 547-9530
◆ EMP: 230
Web: www.statefish.com
SIC: 2092 5146 Fresh or frozen packaged
fish; Fish, frozen, unpackaged

2095 Roasted Coffee

(P-1714)
APFFELS COFFEE INC
Also Called: Apffels Coffee
12115 Pacific St, Santa Fe Springs
(90670-2989)
P.O. Box 2506 (90670-0506)
PHONE...............................562 309-0400
Darryl Blunk, CEO
Alvin Apffel, *
Edward Apffel, *
Mike Rogers, *
◆ EMP: 37 EST: 1914
SQ FT: 100,000
SALES (est): 4.03MM Privately Held
Web: www.apffels.com
SIC: 2095 5149 Coffee roasting (except by
wholesale grocers); Coffee, green or
roasted

(P-1715)
CAFFE DAMORE INC
1916 S Tubeway Ave, Commerce
(90040-1612)
▲ EMP: 105
Web: www.kerryfoodservice.com
SIC: 2095 5046 Instant coffee; Coffee
brewing equipment and supplies

(P-1716)
EBERINE ENTERPRISES INC
Also Called: Euro Coffee
3360 Fruitland Ave, Los Angeles
(90058-3714)
PHONE...............................323 587-1111
▲ EMP: 29 EST: 1983
SALES (est): 3.08MM Privately Held
Web: www.eurocoffee.com
SIC: 2095 Roasted coffee

(P-1717)
EQUAL EXCHANGE INC
2920 Norman Strasse Rd, San Marcos
(92069-5935)
PHONE...............................619 335-6259
Nanelle Newbom, Mgr
EMP: 79
SALES (corp-wide): 1.57MM Privately
Held
Web: shop.equalexchange.coop
SIC: 2095 Coffee roasting (except by
wholesale grocers)
PA: Equal Exchange, Inc.
3401 Se 17th Ave
503 847-2000

(P-1718)
F GAVINA & SONS INC
Also Called: Gavia
2700 Fruitland Ave, Vernon (90058-2893)
PHONE...............................323 582-0671
Pedro Gavina, Pr
Francisco M Gavina, *

Leonora Gavina, *
Jose Gavina, *
▲ EMP: 295 EST: 1870
SQ FT: 239,000
SALES (est): 32.94MM Privately Held
Web: www.gavina.com
SIC: 2095 Coffee roasting (except by
wholesale grocers)

(P-1719)
**GROUNDWORK COFFEE
ROASTERS LLC**
Also Called: Groundwork Coffee
5457 Cleon Ave, North Hollywood
(91601-2834)
PHONE...............................818 506-6020
EMP: 160 EST: 2011
SQ FT: 4,650
SALES (est): 16.69MM Privately Held
Web: www.groundworkcoffee.com
SIC: 2095 5812 5149 Roasted coffee;
Contract food services; Coffee, green or
roasted

(P-1720)
SON OF A BARISTA USA LLC
5125 Wheeler Ridge Rd, Arvin
(93203-9629)
PHONE...............................323 788-8718
EMP: 37
SALES (corp-wide): 962.14K Privately
Held
SIC: 2095 Roasted coffee
PA: Son Of A Barista Usa, Llc
5401 S Soto St
323 780-8250

2096 Potato Chips And Similar Snacks

(P-1721)
**ANITAS MEXICAN FOODS CORP
(PA)**
3454 N Mike Daley Dr, San Bernardino
(92407-1890)
PHONE...............................909 884-8706
Ricardo Alvarez, Pr
Ricardo Robles, *
Rene Robles, *
Jacqueline Robles, *
▲ EMP: 57 EST: 1936
SQ FT: 330,000
SALES (est): 49.19MM
SALES (corp-wide): 49.19MM Privately
Held
Web: www.anitasmfc.com
SIC: 2096 Potato chips and similar snacks

(P-1722)
ANITAS MEXICAN FOODS CORP
3392 N Mike Daley Dr, San Bernardino
(92407-1892)
PHONE...............................909 884-8706
EMP: 35
SALES (corp-wide): 49.19MM Privately
Held
Web: www.anitasmfc.com
SIC: 2096 Potato chips and similar snacks
PA: Anita's Mexican Foods Corp.
3454 N Mike Daley Dr
909 884-8706

(P-1723)
GRUMA CORPORATION
Also Called: Mission Foods
11559 Jersey Blvd Ste A, Rancho
Cucamonga (91730-4924)
PHONE...............................909 980-3566

Victor Cervantes, Manager
EMP: 85
Web: www.missionfoods.com
SIC: 2096 Tortilla chips
HQ: Gruma Corporation
5601 Executive Dr Ste 800
Irving TX 75038
972 232-5000

(P-1724)
GRUMA CORPORATION
Also Called: Mission Foods
5505 E Olympic Blvd, Commerce
(90022-5129)
PHONE...............................323 803-1400
Bob Solano, Brnch Mgr
EMP: 500
Web: www.missionfoods.com
SIC: 2096 Tortilla chips
HQ: Gruma Corporation
5601 Executive Dr Ste 800
Irving TX 75038
972 232-5000

(P-1725)
KING HENRYS INC
Also Called: Manufacturing
29124 Hancock Pkwy 1, Valencia
(91355-1066)
PHONE...............................818 536-3692
Trina Davidian, CEO
◆ EMP: 45 EST: 1989
SQ FT: 44,000
SALES (est): 11.67MM Privately Held
Web: www.kinghenrys.com
SIC: 2096 2064 Cheese curls and puffs;
Breakfast bars

(P-1726)
MARQUEZ MARQUEZ INC
Also Called: Marquez & Marquez Food PR
11821 Industrial Ave, South Gate
(90280-7914)
PHONE...............................562 408-0960
Elias Marquez, Pr
EMP: 29 EST: 1993
SALES (est): 2.33MM Privately Held
Web: www.marquezmarquez.com
SIC: 2096 2041 Corn chips and other corn-
based snacks; Flour

(P-1727)
**RUDOLPH FOODS COMPANY
INC**
920 W Fourth St, Beaumont (92223-2675)
PHONE...............................909 388-2202
Fransico Quirarte, Mgr
EMP: 123
SALES (corp-wide): 131.1MM Privately
Held
Web: www.rudolphfoods.com
SIC: 2096 Pork rinds
PA: Rudolph Foods Company, Inc.
6575 Bellefontaine Rd
909 383-7463

(P-1728)
SNACK IT FORWARD LLC
Also Called: World Peas Brand
6080 Center Dr Ste 600, Los Angeles
(90045-1540)
PHONE...............................310 242-5517
Nick Desai, CEO
Bryan Cameron, COO
EMP: 23 EST: 2011
SQ FT: 500
SALES (est): 6.79MM Privately Held
Web: www.snackitforward.com
SIC: 2096 Cheese curls and puffs

(P-1729)
SNAK-KING LLC (PA)
16150 Stephens St, City Of Industry
(91745-1718)
PHONE...............................626 336-7711
◆ EMP: 500 EST: 1978
SALES (est): 174.35MM
SALES (corp-wide): 174.35MM Privately
Held
Web: www.snakking.com
SIC: 2096 Potato chips and similar snacks

2097 Manufactured Ice

(P-1730)
ARCTIC GLACIER USA INC
17011 Central Ave, Carson (90746-1303)
PHONE...............................310 638-0321
Sharon Cooper, Mgr
EMP: 200
SALES (corp-wide): 253.92MM Privately
Held
Web: www.arcticglacier.com
SIC: 2097 Manufactured ice
HQ: Arctic Glacier U.S.A., Inc.
307 23rd Street Ext
Pittsburgh PA 15215
800 562-1990

(P-1731)
**MOUNTAIN WATER ICE
COMPANY INC (PA)**
17011 Central Ave, Carson (90746-1303)
PHONE...............................310 638-0321
EMP: 54 EST: 1925
SALES (est): 4.83MM
SALES (corp-wide): 4.83MM Privately
Held
SIC: 2097 Manufactured ice

2098 Macaroni And Spaghetti

(P-1732)
MARUCHAN INC
1902 Deere Ave, Irvine (92606-4819)
PHONE...............................949 789-2300
Shino Saki, Mgr
EMP: 220
Web: www.maruchan.com
SIC: 2098 5146 Noodles (e.g. egg, plain,
and water), dry; Fish, cured
HQ: Maruchan, Inc.
15800 Laguna Canyon Rd
Irvine CA 92618
949 789-2300

(P-1733)
**NISSIN FOODS USA COMPANY
INC (DH)**
2001 W Rosecrans Ave, Gardena
(90249-2931)
PHONE...............................310 327-8478
Brian Huff, Pr
Takahiro Enomoto, *
◆ EMP: 200 EST: 1970
SQ FT: 200,000
SALES (est): 123.55MM Privately Held
Web: www.nissinfoods.com
SIC: 2098 2038 Noodles (e.g. egg, plain,
and water), dry; Ethnic foods, nec, frozen
HQ: Nissin Food Products Co., Ltd.
6-28-1, Shinjuku
Shinjuku-Ku TKY 160-0

(P-1734)
PEKING NOODLE CO INC
1514 N San Fernando Rd, Los Angeles
(90065-1282)

▲ = Import ▼ = Export
◆ = Import/Export

PHONE..................323 223-0897
Frank Tong, *Pr*
Stephen Tong, *
Donna Tong, *
▲ EMP: 40 EST: 1928
SQ FT: 40,000
SALES (est): 5.94MM **Privately Held**
Web: www.pekingnoodle.com
SIC: 2098 2052 Noodles (e.g. egg, plain, and water), dry; Cookies and crackers

(P-1735)
SANYO FOODS CORP AMERICA (DH)
Also Called: Yorba Linda Country Club
11955 Monarch St, Garden Grove
(92841-2194)
PHONE..................714 891-3671
Yuko Takahashi, *CEO*
Yumei Mugita, *
◆ EMP: 30 EST: 1978
SQ FT: 130,000
SALES (est): 13.18MM **Privately Held**
Web: www.sanyofoodsamerica.com
SIC: 2098 7997 Noodles (e.g. egg, plain, and water), dry; Golf club, membership
HQ: Sanyo Foods Co., Ltd.
1-1-1, Higashihama
Ichikawa CHI 272-0

2099 Food Preparations, Nec

(P-1736)
ALBANY FARMS INC
625 Fair Oaks Ave Ste 125, South
Pasadena (91030-2688)
PHONE..................213 330-6573
William Saller, *CEO*
EMP: 39
SALES (corp-wide): 1.5MM **Privately Held**
Web: www.albanyfarms.com
SIC: 2099 Food preparations, nec
PA: Albany Farms Inc.
10680 W Pico Blvd Ste 230
877 832-8269

(P-1737)
ALFRED LOUIE INCORPORATED
4501 Shepard St, Bakersfield (93313-2310)
PHONE..................661 831-2520
Victor Louie, *Pr*
Gordon Louie, *Sec*
Samuel Louie, *Stockholder*
Maryann Louie, *Stockholder*
EMP: 26 EST: 1979
SQ FT: 28,000
SALES (est): 2.97MM **Privately Held**
SIC: 2099 0182 Noodles, fried (Chinese); Bean sprouts, grown under cover

(P-1738)
AMERICAN YEAST CORPORATION
5455 District Blvd, Bakersfield
(93313-2123)
PHONE..................661 834-1050
Lloyd Fry, *Mgr*
EMP: 28
SALES (corp-wide): 3.14MM **Privately Held**
SIC: 2099 Food preparations, nec
HQ: American Yeast Corporation
8215 Beachwood Rd
Baltimore MD 21222
410 477-3700

(P-1739)
AREVALO TORTILLERIA INC
3033 Supply Ave, Commerce (90040-2709)

P.O. Box 788 (90078-0788)
PHONE..................323 888-1711
Edward Arello, *Mgr*
EMP: 30
SALES (corp-wide): 18.86MM **Privately Held**
Web: www.arevalos.com
SIC: 2099 Tortillas, fresh or refrigerated
PA: Arevalo Tortilleria, Inc.
1537 W Mines Ave
323 888-1711

(P-1740)
AREVALO TORTILLERIA INC (PA)
1537 W Mines Ave, Montebello
(90640-5414)
P.O. Box 788 (90640-0788)
PHONE..................323 888-1711
Jose Luis Arevalo, *CEO*
Emilia Arevalo, *
▲ EMP: 82 EST: 1985
SQ FT: 20,000
SALES (est): 18.86MM
SALES (corp-wide): 18.86MM **Privately Held**
Web: www.arevalos.com
SIC: 2099 Food preparations, nec

(P-1741)
ASIANA CUISINE ENTERPRISES INC
Also Called: Ace Sushi
22771 S Western Ave Ste 100, Torrance
(90501-5196)
PHONE..................310 327-2223
Harlan Chin, *Pr*
Gary Chin, *
▲ EMP: 560 EST: 1990
SQ FT: 6,000
SALES (est): 23.02MM **Privately Held**
Web: www.acesushi.com
SIC: 2099 5812 8741 Ready-to-eat meals, salads, and sandwiches; Fast food restaurants and stands; Management services

(P-1742)
BCD FOOD INC
320 W Carob St, Compton (90220-5211)
PHONE..................310 323-1200
Tae Ro Lee, *Pr*
▲ EMP: 40 EST: 2006
SALES (est): 2.21MM **Privately Held**
SIC: 2099 Box lunches, for sale off premises

(P-1743)
BENEVOLENCE FOOD PRODUCTS LLC
Also Called: Bfp
2761 Saturn St Ste D, Brea (92821-6707)
PHONE..................888 832-3738
EMP: 24 EST: 2010
SALES (est): 343.91K **Privately Held**
SIC: 2099 Food preparations, nec

(P-1744)
BEST FORMULATIONS LLC (HQ)
Also Called: Best Formulations
17758 Rowland St, City Of Industry
(91748-1148)
PHONE..................626 912-9998
Jeffrey Goh, *CEO*
Eugene Ung, *Executive Manager*
Kelly Ung, *
◆ EMP: 39 EST: 1984
SQ FT: 50,000
SALES (est): 106.95MM **Privately Held**
Web: www.bestformulations.com

SIC: 2099 8748 5149 2834 Food preparations, nec; Business consulting, nec ; Health foods; Pharmaceutical preparations
PA: Sirio Pharma Co., Ltd.
No.83, Taishan Rd.

(P-1745)
BEST FORMULATIONS LLC
938 Radecki Ct, City Of Industry
(91748-1132)
PHONE..................626 912-9998
EMP: 111
Web: www.bestformulations.com
SIC: 2099 8748 5149 2834 Food preparations, nec; Business consulting, nec ; Health foods; Pharmaceutical preparations
HQ: Best Formulations Llc
17758 Rowland St
City Of Industry CA 91748
626 912-9998

(P-1746)
BITCHIN INC (PA)
Also Called: Bitchin Sauce
6211 Yarrow Dr Ste C, Carlsbad
(92011-1539)
PHONE..................760 224-7447
Starr Edwards, *CEO*
Harrison Edwards, *CMO*
EMP: 30 EST: 2012
SALES (est): 10.16MM
SALES (corp-wide): 10.16MM **Privately Held**
Web: www.bitchinsauce.com
SIC: 2099 Sauce, gravy, dressing, and dip mixes

(P-1747)
BITCHIN SAUCE LLC
Also Called: Bitchin' Sauce
4509 Adams St, Carlsbad (92008-4208)
P.O. Box 130610 (92013-0610)
PHONE..................737 248-2446
Starr Edwards, *CEO*
Starr Edwards, *Ch Bd*
EMP: 75 EST: 2020
SALES (est): 2.61MM
SALES (corp-wide): 10.16MM **Privately Held**
Web: www.bitchinsauce.com
SIC: 2099 Sauce, gravy, dressing, and dip mixes
PA: Bitchin' Inc.
6211 Yarrow Dr Ste C
760 224-7447

(P-1748)
BRISTOL FARMS (HQ)
915 E 230th St, Carson (90745-5005)
PHONE..................310 233-4700
Adam Caldecott, *CEO*
EMP: 100 EST: 1982
SQ FT: 73,667
SALES (est): 94.53MM **Privately Held**
Web: www.bristolfarms.com
SIC: 2099 5411 Ready-to-eat meals, salads, and sandwiches; Grocery stores, chain
PA: The Endeavour Capital Fund Limited Partnership
920 Sw 6th Ave Ste 1400

(P-1749)
C & F FOODS INC
12400 Wilshire Blvd Ste 1180, Los Angeles
(90025-1058)
PHONE..................626 723-1000
◆ EMP: 400
Web: www.cnf-foods.com
SIC: 2099 Food preparations, nec

(P-1750)
CALAVO GROWERS INC (PA)
Also Called: Calavo
1141 Cummings Rd Ste A, Santa Paula
(93060-9118)
PHONE..................805 525-1245
Lecil Cole, *Pr*
Steven Hollister, *Ch Bd*
Danny Dumas, *Sr VP*
Shawn Munsell, *CFO*
EMP: 132 EST: 1924
SALES (est): 971.95MM
SALES (corp-wide): 971.95MM **Publicly Held**
Web: www.calavo.com
SIC: 2099 5148 Salads, fresh or refrigerated; Fruits

(P-1751)
CAMINO REAL FOODS INC (PA)
Also Called: Camino Real Kitchens
2638 E Vernon Ave, Los Angeles
(90058-1825)
P.O. Box 30729 (90030-0729)
PHONE..................323 585-6599
Rob Cross, *Pr*
Richard Lunsford, *
EMP: 150 EST: 1980
SALES (est): 55.44MM
SALES (corp-wide): 55.44MM **Privately Held**
Web: www.caminorealkitchens.com
SIC: 2099 Food preparations, nec

(P-1752)
CARGILL MEAT SOLUTIONS CORP
3501 E Vernon Ave, Vernon (90058-1813)
PHONE..................515 735-9800
Hans Kabat, *Pr*
EMP: 216
SALES (corp-wide): 159.59B **Privately Held**
Web: www.cargill.com
SIC: 2099 Food preparations, nec
HQ: Cargill Meat Solutions Corp
825 E Douglas Ave
Wichita KS 67202
316 462-7279

(P-1753)
CEDARLANE NATURAL FOODS INC (PA)
Also Called: Cedarlane Foods
717 E Artesia Blvd Ste A, Carson
(90746-1228)
PHONE..................310 886-7720
Robert Atallah, *CEO*
Neil Holmes, *
▲ EMP: 100 EST: 1981
SALES (est): 81.29MM
SALES (corp-wide): 81.29MM **Privately Held**
Web: www.cedarlanefoods.com
SIC: 2099 Food preparations, nec

(P-1754)
CHEF MERITO LLC (PA)
Also Called: Merito.com
7915 Sepulveda Blvd, Van Nuys
(91405-1032)
PHONE..................818 787-0100
Margaret Crow, *CEO*
Jose J Corugedo, *
Natt Hasson, *
▲ EMP: 43 EST: 1985
SQ FT: 30,000
SALES (est): 26.51MM
SALES (corp-wide): 26.51MM **Privately Held**

Web: www.chefmerito.com
SIC: 2099 2033 2032 2044 Spices, including grinding; Jellies, edible, including imitation: in cans, jars, etc.; Soups, except seafood: packaged in cans, jars, etc.; Enriched rice (vitamin and mineral fortified)

(P-1755)
CHEFMASTER
501 Airpark Dr, Fullerton (92833-2501)
PHONE..............................714 554-4000
Aaron G Byrnes, *Pr*
▲ **EMP:** 35 **EST:** 1939
SALES (est): 6.66MM **Privately Held**
Web: www.chefmaster.com
SIC: 2099 Sugar powdered, from purchased ingredients

(P-1756)
CJ FOODS INC (HQ)
Also Called: CJ America
4 Centerpointe Dr Ste 100, La Palma
(90623-1074)
PHONE..............................714 367-7200
Pious Jung, *CEO*
EMP: 78 **EST:** 1995
SALES (est): 48.39MM **Privately Held**
Web: www.cjfoods.com
SIC: 2099 Food preparations, nec
PA: Cj Cheiljedang Corporation
330 Dongho-Ro, Jung-Gu

(P-1757)
COSMOS FOOD CO INC
17501 Mondino Dr, Rowland Heights
(91748-4160)
PHONE..............................323 221-9142
David Kim, *Pr*
EMP: 45 **EST:** 1971
SALES (est): 4.52MM **Privately Held**
Web: www.cosmosfood.com
SIC: 2099 5149 Tortillas, fresh or refrigerated ; Groceries and related products, nec

(P-1758)
CREATIVE FOODS LLC
12622 Poway Rd # A, Poway (92064-4451)
PHONE..............................858 748-0070
Frank Interlandi, *Managing Member*
EMP: 25 **EST:** 2007
SALES (est): 562.88K **Privately Held**
SIC: 2099 5812 Food preparations, nec; Eating places

(P-1759)
CULINARY INTERNATIONAL
LLC (PA)
3280 E 44th St, Vernon (90058-2426)
PHONE..............................626 289-3000
EMP: 249 **EST:** 2017
SALES (est): 23.83MM
SALES (corp-wide): 23.83MM **Privately Held**
Web: www.culinaryinternational.com
SIC: 2099 2038 5149 Food preparations, nec ; Ethnic foods, nec, frozen; Natural and organic foods

(P-1760)
CULINARY SPECIALTIES INC
Also Called: Culinary Specialties
1231 Linda Vista Dr, San Marcos
(92078-3809)
PHONE..............................760 744-8220
Chris Schragner, *Pr*
Patrick O Farrell, *
EMP: 53 **EST:** 1997
SQ FT: 6,400
SALES (est): 7.94MM **Privately Held**
Web: www.culinaryspecialties.net

SIC: 2099 2038 Emulsifiers, food; Frozen specialties, nec

(P-1761)
CURATION FOODS INC (HQ)
2811 Airpark Dr, Santa Maria (93455-1417)
P.O. Box 727 (93434)
PHONE..............................800 454-1355
◆ **EMP:** 80 **EST:** 1979
SQ FT: 200,000
SALES (est): 67.97MM
SALES (corp-wide): 128.26MM **Publicly Held**
Web: www.apioinc.com
SIC: 2099 0723 Food preparations, nec; Vegetable packing services
PA: Lifecore Biomedical, Inc.
3515 Lyman Blvd
952 368-4300

(P-1762)
DELORI-NUTIFOOD PRODUCTS
INC
Also Called: Delori Foods
17043 Green Dr, City Of Industry
(91745-1812)
P.O. Box 92668 (91715-2668)
PHONE..............................626 965-3006
Jaime Brown, *CEO*
Blanca Brown, *
▲ **EMP:** 32 **EST:** 1991
SALES (est): 4.86MM **Privately Held**
Web: www.deloriproducts.com
SIC: 2099 Jelly, corncob (gelatin)

(P-1763)
DIANAS MEXICAN FOOD PDTS
INC
2905 Durfee Ave, El Monte (91732-3517)
PHONE..............................626 444-0555
Samuel Magana, *Owner*
EMP: 59
SQ FT: 13,530
SALES (corp-wide): 23.78MM **Privately Held**
Web: www.dianas.net
SIC: 2099 5812 Tortillas, fresh or refrigerated ; Mexican restaurant
PA: Diana's Mexican Food Products, Inc.
16330 Pioneer Blvd
562 926-5802

(P-1764)
DIANAS MEXICAN FOOD PDTS
INC (PA)
Also Called: La Bonita
16330 Pioneer Blvd, Norwalk (90650-7095)
P.O. Box 369 (90651-0369)
PHONE..............................562 926-5802
Samuel Magana, *CEO*
Hortensia Magana, *
EMP: 50 **EST:** 1975
SQ FT: 4,068
SALES (est): 23.78MM
SALES (corp-wide): 23.78MM **Privately Held**
Web: www.dianas.net
SIC: 2099 5812 Tortillas, fresh or refrigerated ; Ethnic food restaurants

(P-1765)
DIVINE PASTA COMPANY
140 W Providencia Ave, Burbank
(91502-2121)
P.O. Box 15425 (90209-1425)
PHONE..............................818 559-7440
EMP: 42
SIC: 2099 Pasta, rice, and potato, packaged combination products

(P-1766)
EARTH ISLAND LLC (HQ)
Also Called: Follow Your Heart
9201 Owensmouth Ave, Chatsworth
(91311-5854)
P.O. Box 9400 (91309)
PHONE..............................818 725-2820
▲ **EMP:** 35 **EST:** 1988
SALES (est): 11.79MM
SALES (corp-wide): 967.79MM **Privately Held**
Web: www.followyourheart.com
SIC: 2099 Food preparations, nec
PA: Danone
17 Boulevard Haussmann
149485000

(P-1767)
EARTHRISE NUTRITIONALS LLC
113 E Hoober Rd, Calipatria (92233-9703)
P.O. Box 270 (92233-0270)
PHONE..............................760 348-5027
Jose Perez, *Mgr*
EMP: 29
Web: www.earthrise.com
SIC: 2099 Chicory root, dried
HQ: Earthrise Nutritionals Llc
3333 Michelson Dr Ste 300
Irvine CA 92612
949 623-0980

(P-1768)
EL GALLITO MARKET INC
12242 Valley Blvd, El Monte (91732-3108)
PHONE..............................626 442-1190
Sandra Veisaga, *Pr*
Mario Rodriguez, *
EMP: 35 **EST:** 1974
SQ FT: 1,200
SALES (est): 2.36MM **Privately Held**
Web: www.elgallitomkt.com
SIC: 2099 5421 5411 Tortillas, fresh or refrigerated; Meat and fish markets; Grocery stores

(P-1769)
ESPERANZAS TORTILLERIA
750 Rock Springs Rd, Escondido
(92025-1625)
PHONE..............................760 743-5908
Victor Martinez, *Pr*
Teresa Martinez, *
Hugo Martinez, *
Leonor Batista, *
EMP: 46 **EST:** 1980
SALES (est): 1.77MM **Privately Held**
Web: www.esperanzastortilleria.com
SIC: 2099 Tortillas, fresh or refrigerated

(P-1770)
EVERSON SPICE COMPANY INC
2667 Gundry Ave, Long Beach
(90755-1808)
PHONE..............................562 595-4785
Kim Everson, *CEO*
Ken Hopkins, *
Thomas L Everson, *Prin*
▲ **EMP:** 35 **EST:** 1987
SQ FT: 35,000
SALES (est): 5.6MM **Privately Held**
Web: www.eversonspice.com
SIC: 2099 Spices, including grinding

(P-1771)
EVERYTABLE PBC
Also Called: Everytable
3650 W Martin Luther King Jr Blvd, Los
Angeles (90008-1700)
PHONE..............................323 296-0311
EMP: 38

SALES (corp-wide): 70.66MM **Privately Held**
Web: www.everytable.com
SIC: 2099 Box lunches, for sale off premises
PA: Everytable, Pbc
18901 Railroad St
917 319-6156

(P-1772)
F I O IMPORTS INC
Also Called: Contessa Premium Foods
5980 Alcoa Ave, Vernon (90058-3925)
PHONE..............................323 263-5100
Dirk Leuenberger, *Pr*
Bob Nielsen, *CFO*
EMP: 180 **EST:** 2002
SALES (est): 24.31MM **Privately Held**
SIC: 2099 Food preparations, nec
HQ: Aqua Star (Usa), Corp.
2025 First Ave
Seattle WA 98121
800 232-6280

(P-1773)
FAMILY LOOMPYA
CORPORATION
2626 Southport Way Ste F, National City
(91950-8753)
PHONE..............................619 477-2125
Alen Enriquez, *Pr*
▲ **EMP:** 25 **EST:** 1973
SQ FT: 10,000
SALES (est): 3.94MM **Privately Held**
Web: www.familyloompya.com
SIC: 2099 5149 Food preparations, nec; Specialty food items

(P-1774)
FIVE STAR GOURMET FOODS
INC (PA)
3880 Ebony St, Ontario (91761-1500)
PHONE..............................909 390-0032
Tal Shoshan, *CEO*
Michelle Eoff, *Ex VP*
Masha Simonian, *CFO*
Michael Solomon, *Pr*
EMP: 199 **EST:** 1999
SQ FT: 130,000
SALES (est): 52.52MM
SALES (corp-wide): 52.52MM **Privately Held**
Web: www.fivestargourmetfoods.com
SIC: 2099 Ready-to-eat meals, salads, and sandwiches

(P-1775)
FOODOLOGY LLC
Also Called: Sproutime
8920 Norris Ave, Sun Valley (91352-2740)
PHONE..............................818 252-1888
EMP: 75 **EST:** 1980
SQ FT: 20,000
SALES (est): 1.48MM **Privately Held**
SIC: 2099 Ready-to-eat meals, salads, and sandwiches

(P-1776)
FOODS ON FLY LLC
7004 Carroll Rd, San Diego (92121-2213)
PHONE..............................858 404-0642
Peter Didomizio, *Managing Member*
Budy Kubursi, *
EMP: 38 **EST:** 2019
SALES (est): 2.41MM **Privately Held**
SIC: 2099 Sandwiches, assembled and packaged: for wholesale market

(P-1777)
FRESH & READY FOODS LLC (PA)
1145 Arroyo St Ste B, San Fernando (91340-1842)
PHONE..................818 837-7600
Art Sezgin, *Pr*
John Saladino, *
EMP: 99 **EST:** 2015
SALES (est): 23.22MM
SALES (corp-wide): 23.22MM **Privately Held**
Web: www.freshandreadyfoods.com
SIC: 2099 Salads, fresh or refrigerated

(P-1778)
FRESHREALM INC (PA)
1330 Calle Avanzado, San Clemente (92673-6351)
P.O. Box 5317 (92674-5317)
PHONE..................800 264-1297
Michael R Lippold, *CEO*
Salomi Varma, *
EMP: 125 **EST:** 2013
SQ FT: 5,000
SALES (est): 212.4MM
SALES (corp-wide): 212.4MM **Privately Held**
Web: www.freshrealm.com
SIC: 2099 Food preparations, nec

(P-1779)
FUJI FOOD PRODUCTS INC (PA)
14420 Bloomfield Ave, Santa Fe Springs (90670-5410)
PHONE..................562 404-2590
Farrell Hirsch, *CEO*
Javier Aceves, *
▲ **EMP:** 100 **EST:** 2010
SALES (est): 46.24MM
SALES (corp-wide): 46.24MM **Privately Held**
Web: www.fujisansushi.com
SIC: 2099 Food preparations, nec

(P-1780)
FUJI FOOD PRODUCTS INC
8660 Miramar Rd Ste N, San Diego (92126-4362)
PHONE..................619 268-3118
Kenny Sung, *Brnch Mgr*
EMP: 150
SALES (corp-wide): 46.24MM **Privately Held**
Web: www.fujisansushi.com
SIC: 2099 Food preparations, nec
PA: Fuji Food Products, Inc.
14420 Bloomfield Ave
562 404-2590

(P-1781)
FUJI NATURAL FOODS INC (HQ)
13500 S Hamner Ave, Ontario (91761-2605)
P.O. Box 3728 (91761-0973)
PHONE..................909 947-1008
Katsuhiro Nakagawa, *CEO*
Ikuzo Sugiyama, *
◆ **EMP:** 72 **EST:** 1979
SQ FT: 65,000
SALES (est): 9.09MM **Privately Held**
Web: www.fujinf.com
SIC: 2099 Food preparations, nec
PA: Taiyo Foodstuffs Industry Co., Ltd.
2618-6, Naegicho

(P-1782)
GOLD COAST INGREDIENTS INC
2429 Yates Ave, Commerce (90040-1917)
PHONE..................323 724-8935

Clarence H Brasher, *CEO*
James A Sgro, *
Laurie Goddard, *
◆ **EMP:** 53 **EST:** 1985
SQ FT: 50,000
SALES (est): 20.06MM **Privately Held**
Web: www.goldcoastinc.com
SIC: 2099 Almond pastes

(P-1783)
GOLD STAR FOODS INC (HQ)
3781 E Airport Dr, Ontario (91761-1558)
P.O. Box 4328 (91761-8828)
PHONE..................909 843-9600
Sean Leer, *Pr*
C Scott Salmon, *Strategy Vice President*
Joe Villarreal, *
Greg Johnson, *
Les Wong, *
▲ **EMP:** 64 **EST:** 2007
SQ FT: 38,000
SALES (est): 329.25MM
SALES (corp-wide): 519.54MM **Privately Held**
Web: www.goldstarfoods.com
SIC: 2099 Ready-to-eat meals, salads, and sandwiches
PA: Highview Capital, Llc
11755 Wlshire Blvd Ste 14
310 806-9780

(P-1784)
GOLDEN SPECIALTY FOODS LLC
14605 Best Ave, Norwalk (90650-5258)
PHONE..................562 802-2537
Philip Pisciotta, *CEO*
Philip Pisciotta, *Managing Member*
Jeff Chan, *
Deryk Howard, *
◆ **EMP:** 25 **EST:** 1979
SQ FT: 31,000
SALES (est): 5.06MM **Privately Held**
Web: www.goldenspecialtyfoods.com
SIC: 2099 2032 Food preparations, nec; Canned specialties

(P-1785)
GOODMAN FOOD PRODUCTS INC (PA)
Also Called: Don Lee Farms
200 E Beach Ave Fl 1, Inglewood (90302-3404)
PHONE..................310 674-3180
Donald Goodman, *CEO*
▲ **EMP:** 250 **EST:** 1982
SQ FT: 55,000
SALES (est): 49.19MM
SALES (corp-wide): 49.19MM **Privately Held**
Web: www.donleefarms.com
SIC: 2099 Food preparations, nec

(P-1786)
GPDE SLVA SPCES INCRPORATION (PA)
Also Called: Peterson's Spices
8531 Loch Lomond Dr, Pico Rivera (90660-2509)
PHONE..................562 407-2643
Ravi De Silva, *Pr*
Rupa De Silva, *
Binuka De Silva, *
Nalin Kulasooriya, *
◆ **EMP:** 80 **EST:** 2008
SQ FT: 60,000
SALES (est): 19.85MM **Privately Held**
Web: www.cinnamononline.com
SIC: 2099 5149 Chili pepper or powder; Spices and seasonings

(P-1787)
HALIBURTON INTERNATIONAL FOODS INC
3855 Jurupa St, Ontario (91761-1404)
PHONE..................909 428-8520
▲ **EMP:** 278 **EST:** 1992
SALES (est): 49.38MM **Privately Held**
Web: www.haliburton.net
SIC: 2099 Food preparations, nec

(P-1788)
HESPERIA UNIFIED SCHOOL DST
Also Called: Hesperia Usd Food Service
11176 G Ave, Hesperia (92345-8315)
PHONE..................760 948-1051
Janet Clesceri, *Brnch Mgr*
EMP: 63
SALES (corp-wide): 450.24MM **Privately Held**
Web: www.cottonwoodelementary.org
SIC: 2099 8322 8299 Box lunches, for sale off premises; Geriatric social service; Arts and crafts schools
PA: Hesperia Unified School District
15576 Main St
760 244-4411

(P-1789)
HONEY BENNETTS FARM
3176 Honey Ln, Fillmore (93015-2026)
PHONE..................805 521-1375
Gilebert Vannoy, *Pr*
Ann Lindsay Bennett, *
EMP: 25 **EST:** 1978
SQ FT: 20,000
SALES (est): 2.66MM **Privately Held**
Web: www.bennetthoney.com
SIC: 2099 5191 0279 Honey, strained and bottled; Farm supplies; Apiary (bee and honey farm)

(P-1790)
HOUSE FOODS AMERICA CORP (HQ)
Also Called: Hinoichi Tofu
7351 Orangewood Ave, Garden Grove (92841-1411)
PHONE..................714 901-4350
Atsushi Tomohara, *Pr*
Masakazu Nishida, *
▲ **EMP:** 41 **EST:** 1947
SQ FT: 30,000
SALES (est): 74.4MM **Privately Held**
Web: www.house-foods.com
SIC: 2099 Food preparations, nec
PA: House Foods Group Inc.
1-5-7, Mikuriyasakaemachi

(P-1791)
HUSKS UNLIMITED (PA)
9925 Airway Rd # C, San Diego (92154-7932)
PHONE..................619 476-8301
Luis Duenas, *CEO*
Eric Brenk, *Pr*
EMP: 30 **EST:** 2012
SALES (est): 10.96MM
SALES (corp-wide): 10.96MM **Privately Held**
Web: www.husksunlimitedinc.com
SIC: 2099 0723 5159 2013 Food preparations, nec; Corn drying services; Corn husks; Cooked meats, from purchased meat

(P-1792)
IMPERFECT FOODS INC (HQ)
Also Called: Imperfect Produce

351 Cheryl Ln, Walnut (91789-3003)
PHONE..................510 595-6683
Abhi Ramesh, *CEO*
EMP: 75 **EST:** 2017
SALES (est): 24.28MM
SALES (corp-wide): 25MM **Privately Held**
Web: www.imperfectfoods.com
SIC: 2099 Vegetables, peeled for the trade
PA: Misfits Market, Inc.
7481 Coca Cola Dr
678 559-7970

(P-1793)
INTERNTIONAL TEA IMPORTERS INC (PA)
Also Called: India Tea Importers
2140 Davie Ave, Commerce (90040-1706)
PHONE..................562 801-9600
Brendan Shah, *CEO*
Bianca Shah, *
Reena Shah, *
◆ **EMP:** 32 **EST:** 1992
SQ FT: 21,500
SALES (est): 9.68MM **Privately Held**
Web: www.teavendor.com
SIC: 2099 5149 Tea blending; Coffee and tea

(P-1794)
JAYONE FOODS INC
7212 Alondra Blvd, Paramount (90723-3902)
PHONE..................562 633-7400
Seung Hoon Lee, *Pr*
Chil Park, *
◆ **EMP:** 50 **EST:** 1999
SQ FT: 28,000
SALES (est): 8.94MM **Privately Held**
Web: www.jayonefoods.com
SIC: 2099 Food preparations, nec

(P-1795)
JIMENES FOOD INC
7046 Jackson St, Paramount (90723-4835)
PHONE..................562 602-2505
Reyna Jimenez, *Pr*
Juan Jimenez, *
EMP: 30 **EST:** 1998
SQ FT: 11,000
SALES (est): 8MM **Privately Held**
Web: www.juanjs.com
SIC: 2099 Tortillas, fresh or refrigerated

(P-1796)
JSL FOODS INC (PA)
3550 Pasadena Ave, Los Angeles (90031-1946)
PHONE..................323 223-2484
Teiji Kawana, *Pr*
Koji Kawana, *
◆ **EMP:** 71 **EST:** 1990
SALES (est): 60.68MM **Privately Held**
Web: www.jslfoods.com
SIC: 2099 5142 2052 Pasta, uncooked: packaged with other ingredients; Packaged frozen goods; Cookies

(P-1797)
KATE FARMS INC
101 Innovation Pl, Santa Barbara (93108-2268)
P.O. Box 50840 (93150)
PHONE..................805 845-2446
Richard Laver, *Pr*
Richard Laver, *Prin*
Michelle Laver, *
Tom Beecher, *Executive Corporate Development Vice President*
EMP: 123 **EST:** 2015
SALES (est): 40.72MM **Privately Held**
Web: www.katefarms.com

PRODUCTS & SVCS

SIC: 2099 Ready-to-eat meals, salads, and sandwiches

(P-1798)
KTS KITCHENS INC
1065 E Walnut St Ste C, Carson
(90746-1384)
PHONE...............................310 764-0850
Kathleen D Taggares, *CEO*
Joan Paris, *
EMP: 250 EST: 1987
SALES (est): 20.32MM **Privately Held**
Web: www.ktskitchens.com
SIC: 2099 2035 Pizza, refrigerated: except frozen; Dressings, salad: raw and cooked (except dry mixes)

(P-1799)
LA BARCA TORTILLERIA INC
3047 Whittier Blvd, Los Angeles
(90023-1651)
P.O. Box 23548 (90023-0548)
PHONE...............................323 268-1744
Jose Luis Arevalo, *CEO*
Antonio Arevalo, *
Alexander Arevalo, *
EMP: 50 EST: 1988
SQ FT: 6,000
SALES (est): 4.6MM **Privately Held**
SIC: 2099 Tortillas, fresh or refrigerated

(P-1800)
LA COLONIAL TORTILLA PDTS INC
Also Called: La Colonial Mexican Foods
543 Monterey Pass Rd, Monterey Park
(91754-2416)
PHONE...............................626 289-3647
Daniel Robles, *Pr*
EMP: 185 EST: 1950
SQ FT: 27,000
SALES (est): 7.95MM **Privately Held**
Web: www.lacolonial-la.com
SIC: 2099 Tortillas, fresh or refrigerated

(P-1801)
LA FE TORTILLERIA INC (PA)
Also Called: La Fe Tortilleria Factory
1512 Linda Vista Dr, San Marcos
(92078-3808)
P.O. Box 787 (92079-0787)
PHONE...............................760 752-8350
Jesus Martinez, *Pr*
Isabel Delgado, *
Hoxsie Smith, *
Andrea Smith, *
EMP: 30 EST: 2005
SQ FT: 4,000
SALES (est): 2.25MM
SALES (corp-wide): 2.25MM **Privately Held**
Web: www.lafetortilleria.com
SIC: 2099 5812 5046 5461 Tortillas, fresh or refrigerated; Mexican restaurant; Bakery equipment and supplies; Retail bakeries

(P-1802)
LA FORTALEZA INC
525 N Ford Blvd, Los Angeles
(90022-1104)
PHONE...............................323 261-1211
Hermila Josefina Ortiz, *CEO*
David Ortiz, *
Ramiro Ortiz Junior, *VP*
EMP: 98 EST: 1990
SQ FT: 40,000
SALES (est): 10.08MM **Privately Held**
Web: www.lafortalezaproducts.net
SIC: 2099 2096 Tortillas, fresh or refrigerated ; Potato chips and similar snacks

(P-1803)
LA GLORIA FOODS CORP (PA)
Also Called: La Gloria Tortilleria
3455 E 1st St, Los Angeles (90063-2945)
PHONE...............................323 262-0410
Maria De La Luz Vera, *CEO*
▼ EMP: 80 EST: 1954
SQ FT: 8,000
SALES (est): 4.45MM
SALES (corp-wide): 4.45MM **Privately Held**
Web: www.lagloriafoods.com
SIC: 2099 5461 5812 Tortillas, fresh or refrigerated; Bread; Mexican restaurant

(P-1804)
LABRUCHERIE PRODUCE LLC
1407 S La Brucherie Rd, El Centro
(92243-9677)
PHONE...............................760 352-2170
Jean Labrucherie, *Managing Member*
Tim Labrucherie, *Prin*
EMP: 42 EST: 2011
SALES (est): 11.3MM
SALES (corp-wide): 11.3MM **Privately Held**
Web: www.lbproduce.com
SIC: 2099 0191 Vegetables, peeled for the trade; General farms, primarily crop
PA: Tjl Capital, Inc.
1407 S La Brucherie Rd
760 352-2170

(P-1805)
LASSONDE PAPPAS AND CO INC
1755 E Acacia St, Ontario (91761-7702)
PHONE...............................909 923-4041
Rick Jochums, *Mgr*
EMP: 31
SALES (corp-wide): 402.06MM **Privately Held**
Web: www.lassondepappas.com
SIC: 2099 Food preparations, nec
HQ: Lassonde Pappas And Company, Inc.
3 Executive Campus
Cherry Hill NJ 08002
856 455-1000

(P-1806)
LEHMAN FOODS INC
Also Called: Fresh & Ready
1145 Arroyo St Ste B, San Fernando
(91340-1842)
PHONE...............................818 837-7600
Charles Lehman, *CEO*
Art Sezgin, *
Harry Iknadosian, *
Lisa Lehman, *
Cameron Childs, *
EMP: 25 EST: 1990
SQ FT: 15,000
SALES (est): 6.29MM **Privately Held**
SIC: 2099 Salads, fresh or refrigerated

(P-1807)
LETS DO LUNCH
Also Called: Integrated Food Service
310 W Alondra Blvd, Gardena
(90248-2423)
PHONE...............................310 523-3664
Paul G Giuliano, *CEO*
Paul G Giuliano, *Pr*
Jon Sugimoto, *
David Watzke, *
▲ EMP: 300 EST: 1991
SQ FT: 57,000
SALES (est): 50.06MM **Privately Held**
Web: www.integratedfoodservice.com

SIC: 2099 Sandwiches, assembled and packaged: for wholesale market

(P-1808)
LEY GRAND FOODS CORPORATION
287 S 6th Ave, La Puente (91746-2916)
PHONE...............................626 336-2244
Frank Chen, *Pr*
J J Chen, *Sec*
Chien Chen, *VP*
▲ EMP: 23 EST: 1989
SQ FT: 4,000
SALES (est): 2.46MM **Privately Held**
Web: www.leygrandfoods.com
SIC: 2099 Food preparations, nec

(P-1809)
LIVING WELLNESS PARTNERS LLC
Also Called: Buddha Teas
3305 Tyler St, Carlsbad (92008-3056)
PHONE...............................800 642-3754
John Boyd, *CEO*
Nicholas Narier, *
EMP: 30 EST: 2013
SQ FT: 10,000
SALES (est): 4.53MM **Privately Held**
Web: www.buddhateas.com
SIC: 2099 Tea blending

(P-1810)
LOS PERICOS FOOD PRODUCTS LLC
2301 Valley Blvd, Pomona (91768-1105)
PHONE...............................909 623-5625
Marcelino Ortega, *Pt*
Luis Ortega, *Pt*
Guadalupe Ortega, *Pt*
EMP: 46 EST: 1962
SQ FT: 20,000
SALES (est): 2.51MM **Privately Held**
Web: www.lospericosfood.com
SIC: 2099 Tortillas, fresh or refrigerated

(P-1811)
MARS FOOD US LLC (HQ)
Also Called: Mars Food North America
2001 E Cashdan St Ste 201, Rancho Dominguez (90220-6438)
PHONE...............................310 933-0670
Vincent Howell, *Managing Member*
◆ EMP: 500 EST: 1936
SALES (est): 221.15MM
SALES (corp-wide): 42.84B **Privately Held**
SIC: 2099 Food preparations, nec
PA: Mars, Incorporated
6885 Elm St
703 821-4900

(P-1812)
MARUCHAN INC (HQ)
15800 Laguna Canyon Rd, Irvine
(92618-3103)
PHONE...............................949 789-2300
Noritaka Sumimoto, *CEO*
Mutsuhiko Oda, *
◆ EMP: 450 EST: 1972
SQ FT: 300,000
SALES (est): 243.06MM **Privately Held**
Web: www.maruchan.com
SIC: 2099 Food preparations, nec
PA: Toyo Suisan Kaisha, Ltd.
2-13-40, Konan

(P-1813)
MARUKAN VINEGAR U S A INC
7755 Monroe St, Paramount (90723-5020)
PHONE...............................562 630-6060

Yasuo Sasada, *Ch Bd*
EMP: 42
Web: www.marukan-usa.com
SIC: 2099 Vinegar
HQ: Marukan Vinegar (U. S. A.) Inc.
16203 Vermont Ave
Paramount CA 90723
562 630-6060

(P-1814)
MCI FOODS INC
Also Called: Los Cabos Mexican Foods
13013 Molette St, Santa Fe Springs
(90670-5521)
PHONE...............................562 977-4000
Daniel Southard, *Pr*
Alberta Southard, *
John M Southard, *
EMP: 140 EST: 1970
SQ FT: 15,000
SALES (est): 22.81MM **Privately Held**
Web: www.loscabosmexicanfoods.com
SIC: 2099 Food preparations, nec

(P-1815)
MCK ENTERPRISES INC
Also Called: Valley Spuds
910 Commercial Ave, Oxnard (93030-7232)
PHONE...............................805 483-5292
Evelyn Gardiner, *Pr*
Al Melino, *
Travis Dergan, *
Evelyn Gardner, *
EMP: 87 EST: 2004
SQ FT: 60,000
SALES (est): 2MM **Privately Held**
Web: www.valleyspuds.com
SIC: 2099 Food preparations, nec

(P-1816)
MINSLEY INC (PA)
989 S Monterey Ave, Ontario (91761-3463)
PHONE...............................909 458-1100
Song Tae Jin, *CEO*
▲ EMP: 23 EST: 2002
SQ FT: 42,000
SALES (est): 5.21MM **Privately Held**
Web: www.minsley.com
SIC: 2099 Pasta, rice, and potato, packaged combination products

(P-1817)
MIZKAN AMERICA INC
Also Called: Indian Summer
10037 8th St, Rancho Cucamonga
(91730-5210)
PHONE...............................909 484-8743
Pete Marsing, *Brnch Mgr*
EMP: 92
SQ FT: 58,500
Web: www.mizkan.com
SIC: 2099 Vinegar
HQ: Mizkan America, Inc.
1661 Fhanville Dr Ste 200
Mount Prospect IL 60056
847 590-0059

(P-1818)
MOJAVE FOODS CORPORATION
6000 E Slauson Ave, Commerce
(90040-3008)
PHONE...............................323 890-8900
EMP: 104
SALES (corp-wide): 6.66B **Publicly Held**
SIC: 2099 Butter, renovated and processed
HQ: Mojave Foods Corporation
6200 E Slauson Ave
Los Angeles CA 90040
323 890-8900

(P-1819)
MOJAVE FOODS CORPORATION (HQ)
6200 E Slauson Ave, Los Angeles (90040-3012)
PHONE...................323 890-8900
Richard D Lipka, *CEO*
Craig M Berger, *
◆ **EMP:** 96 **EST:** 1953
SQ FT: 110,000
SALES (est): 32.29MM
SALES (corp-wide): 6.66B **Publicly Held**
SIC: 2099 Butter, renovated and processed
PA: Mccormick & Company Incorporated
  24 Schilling Rd Ste 1
  410 771-7301

(P-1820)
MR TORTILLA INC
1112 Arroyo St, San Fernando (91340-1850)
PHONE...................818 233-8932
Anthony Alcazar, *CEO*
Ronald Alcazar, *
EMP: 50 **EST:** 2012
SALES (est): 1.7MM **Privately Held**
Web: www.mrtortilla.com
SIC: 2099 Tortillas, fresh or refrigerated

(P-1821)
MRS FOODS INCORPORATED (PA)
Also Called: La Rancherita Tortilleria Deli
4406 W 5th St, Santa Ana (92703-3224)
PHONE...................714 554-2791
Laura Perez, *Pr*
Shirley Serna, *
Roxana Perez, *
▲ **EMP:** 40 **EST:** 1981
SQ FT: 4,000
SALES (est): 1.78MM
SALES (corp-wide): 1.78MM **Privately Held**
SIC: 2099 5812 Tortillas, fresh or refrigerated; Fast-food restaurant, independent

(P-1822)
NATREN INC
3105 Willow Ln, Thousand Oaks (91361-4919)
PHONE...................805 371-4737
Yordan Trenev, *CEO*
Natasha Trenev, *
Odessa Braza, *
EMP: 60 **EST:** 1983
SQ FT: 22,000
SALES (est): 8.31MM **Privately Held**
Web: www.natren.com
SIC: 2099 8011 Food preparations, nec; Offices and clinics of medical doctors

(P-1823)
NATURES FLAVORS
833 N Elm St, Orange (92867-7909)
PHONE...................714 744-3700
Bill Sabo, *Prin*
▲ **EMP:** 23 **EST:** 1998
SALES (est): 1.78MM **Privately Held**
Web: www.naturesflavors.com
SIC: 2099 Food preparations, nec

(P-1824)
NINA MIA INC
Also Called: Pasta Mia
826 Enterprise Way, Fullerton (92831-5015)
PHONE...................714 773-5588
Diego Mazza, *Pr*
▲ **EMP:** 80 **EST:** 1984
SQ FT: 32,000

SALES (est): 14.99MM **Privately Held**
Web: www.pastamia.com
SIC: 2099 Pasta, uncooked: packaged with other ingredients

(P-1825)
NINAS MEXICAN FOODS INC
20631 Valley Blvd Ste A, Walnut (91789-2751)
PHONE...................909 468-5888
Ruben Vasquez, *Pr*
▲ **EMP:** 40 **EST:** 1989
SQ FT: 14,000
SALES (est): 2.09MM **Privately Held**
SIC: 2099 Tortillas, fresh or refrigerated

(P-1826)
ORGANIC MILLING INC (PA)
505 W Allen Ave, San Dimas (91773-1487)
PHONE...................800 638-8686
Wolfgang Buehler, *CEO*
Lupe Martinez, *
EMP: 89 **EST:** 2009
SALES (est): 10.66MM **Privately Held**
Web: www.organicmilling.com
SIC: 2099 Food preparations, nec

(P-1827)
ORGANIC MILLING CORPORATION
505 W Allen Ave, San Dimas (91773-1487)
PHONE...................909 599-0961
◆ **EMP:** 33
Web: www.organicmilling.com
SIC: 2099 Food preparations, nec

(P-1828)
OSI INDUSTRIES LLC
1155 Mt Vernon Ave, Riverside (92507-1830)
PHONE...................951 684-4500
Sheldon Lavin, *CEO*
▲ **EMP:** 341
Web: www.osigroup.com
SIC: 2099 Ready-to-eat meals, salads, and sandwiches
HQ: Osi Industries, Llc
  1225 Corp Blvd Ste 105
  Aurora IL 60505
  630 851-6600

(P-1829)
OUT OF SHELL LLC
Also Called: Ling's
9658 Remer St, South El Monte (91733-3033)
PHONE...................626 401-1923
Bing Yang, *
EMP: 200 **EST:** 1999
SALES (est): 14.12MM **Privately Held**
Web: www.outoftheshell.com
SIC: 2099 Food preparations, nec

(P-1830)
OVERHILL FARMS INC (DH)
Also Called: Chicago Brothers
2727 E Vernon Ave, Vernon (90058-1822)
P.O. Box 58806 (90058-0806)
PHONE...................323 582-9977
James Rudis, *Pr*
Robert C Bruning, *
Robert A Olivarez, *
Rick Alvarez, *
EMP: 113 **EST:** 1995
SQ FT: 170,000
SALES (est): 81.4MM **Privately Held**
Web: www.overhillfarms.com
SIC: 2099 Food preparations, nec
HQ: Bellisio Foods, Inc
  701 N Wash St Ste 400

Minneapolis MN 55401

(P-1831)
PACIFIC SPICE COMPANY INC
Also Called: Pacific Natural Spices
6430 E Slauson Ave, Commerce (90040-3108)
PHONE...................323 726-9190
Gershon Schlussel, *CEO*
Gershon D Schlussel, *
Akiba E Schlussel, *
Sharon Schlussel, *
◆ **EMP:** 130 **EST:** 1966
SQ FT: 150,000
SALES (est): 23.1MM **Privately Held**
Web: www.pacificspice.com
SIC: 2099 5149 Spices, including grinding; Spices and seasonings

(P-1832)
PALERMO FAMILY LP (PA)
Also Called: Divine Pasta Company
140 W Providencia Ave, Burbank (91502-2121)
PHONE...................213 542-3300
Alexander Palermo, *Prin*
EMP: 27 **EST:** 1991
SQ FT: 30,000
SALES (est): 4.36MM **Privately Held**
Web: www.divinepasta.com
SIC: 2099 Pasta, rice, and potato, packaged combination products

(P-1833)
PASSPORT FOOD GROUP LLC
Also Called: Wing Hing Noodle Company
2539 E Philadelphia St, Ontario (91761-7774)
PHONE...................909 627-7312
▲ **EMP:** 150
SIC: 2099 Pasta, rice, and potato, packaged combination products

(P-1834)
PASSPORT FOODS (SVC) LLC
2539 E Philadelphia St, Ontario (91761-7774)
PHONE...................909 627-7312
Mark Thomson, *CEO*
EMP: 150 **EST:** 2019
SALES (est): 5.43MM **Privately Held**
SIC: 2099 Pasta, rice, and potato, packaged combination products

(P-1835)
PENGUIN NATURAL FOODS INC
5659 Mansfield Way, Bell (90201-6300)
PHONE...................323 488-6000
EMP: 28
Web: www.penguinfoods.com
SIC: 2099 Food preparations, nec
PA: Penguin Natural Foods, Inc.
  4400 Alcoa Ave

(P-1836)
PENGUIN NATURAL FOODS INC (PA)
4400 Alcoa Ave, Vernon (90058-2412)
PHONE...................323 727-7980
▲ **EMP:** 45 **EST:** 1993
SALES (est): 13.73MM **Privately Held**
Web: www.penguinfoods.com
SIC: 2099 Pasta, rice, and potato, packaged combination products

(P-1837)
PENSIEVE FOODS
Also Called: Eatgud
1782 Industrial Way, Los Angeles (90023-4319)

P.O. Box 995 (91711-0995)
PHONE...................323 938-8666
David Alan Medak, *Managing Member*
EMP: 45 **EST:** 2015
SALES (est): 2.48MM **Privately Held**
SIC: 2099 2037 Food preparations, nec; Frozen fruits and vegetables

(P-1838)
QUOC VIET FOODS (PA)
Also Called: Cafvina Coffee & Tea
12221 Monarch St, Garden Grove (92841-2906)
PHONE...................714 283-3663
Tuan Nguyen, *CEO*
Tuan Nguyen, *Pr*
Theresa Nguyen, *Ex VP*
Kim Vu, *Stockholder*
Khanh Nguyen, *Stockholder*
▲ **EMP:** 32 **EST:** 2002
SQ FT: 2,000
SALES (est): 18.03MM
SALES (corp-wide): 18.03MM **Privately Held**
Web: www.quocviet.com
SIC: 2099 2095 5149 2034 Seasonings and spices; Coffee roasting (except by wholesale grocers); Coffee and tea; Soup mixes

(P-1839)
READY PAC FOODS INC (HQ)
4401 Foxdale St, Irwindale (91706-2161)
PHONE...................626 856-8686
Mary Thompson, *CEO*
Tim Clark, *
Jay Ellis, *SO*
Dan Redfern, *
Scott Mcguire, *SCO*
◆ **EMP:** 2000 **EST:** 2000
SQ FT: 135,000
SALES (est): 973.11MM
SALES (corp-wide): 2.67MM **Privately Held**
Web: www.readypac.com
SIC: 2099 5148 Salads, fresh or refrigerated; Vegetables, fresh
PA: Bonduelle
  La Woestyne
  328426060

(P-1840)
READY PAC PRODUCE INC (DH)
Also Called: Ready Pac Foods
4401 Foxdale St, Irwindale (91706-2161)
PHONE...................800 800-4088
Tony Sarsam, *CEO*
Jay Ellis, *Sls Mgr*
Bob Estes, *CIO*
Dan Redfern, *CFO*
Tristan Simpson, *CMO*
▲ **EMP:** 32 **EST:** 1909
SQ FT: 480,000
SALES (est): 78.85MM
SALES (corp-wide): 2.67MM **Privately Held**
Web: www.readypac.com
SIC: 2099 5148 Salads, fresh or refrigerated; Fresh fruits and vegetables
HQ: Ready Pac Foods, Inc.
  4401 Foxdale St
  Irwindale CA 91706
  626 856-8686

(P-1841)
REYNALDOS MEXICAN FOOD CO LLC (PA)
3301 E Vernon Ave, Vernon (90058-1809)
PHONE...................562 803-3188
Douglas Reed, *CFO*

Marisol Scrugham, *
Al Soto, *Managing Member**
EMP: 160 **EST:** 2006
SALES (est): 31.26MM **Privately Held**
Web: www.sabrosurafoods.com
SIC: 2099 Food preparations, nec

(P-1842)
RICH PRODUCTS CORPORATION
12805 Busch Pl, Santa Fe Springs
(90670-3023)
PHONE.................562 946-6396
Mike Ball, *Mgr*
EMP: 106
SALES (corp-wide): 4.81B **Privately Held**
Web: www.richs.com
SIC: 2099 2051 Desserts, ready-to-mix;
   Bread, cake, and related products
PA: Rich Products Corporation
   1 Robert Rich Way
   716 878-8000

(P-1843)
RISVOLDS INC
1234 W El Segundo Blvd, Gardena
(90247-1593)
PHONE.................323 770-2674
Tim Brandon, *CEO*
Ed Scoullar, *
EMP: 65 **EST:** 1937
SQ FT: 30,000
SALES (est): 9.1MM **Privately Held**
Web: www.risvolds.com
SIC: 2099 Salads, fresh or refrigerated

(P-1844)
ROMEROS FOOD PRODUCTS INC (PA)
15155 Valley View Ave, Santa Fe Springs
(90670-5323)
PHONE.................562 802-1858
Richard Scandalito, *CEO*
Leon Romero Senior, *Pr*
Raul Romero Senior, *VP*
Leon S Romero, *
EMP: 100 **EST:** 1971
SQ FT: 20,000
SALES (est): 21.87MM
SALES (corp-wide): 21.87MM **Privately Held**
Web: www.romerosfood.com
SIC: 2099 2096 5461 Tortillas, fresh or
   refrigerated; Tortilla chips; Retail bakeries

(P-1845)
ROSKAM BAKING COMPANY LLC
505 W Allen Ave, San Dimas (91773-1445)
PHONE.................909 599-0961
Robert Roskam, *Pr*
EMP: 140
SALES (corp-wide): 280.97MM **Privately Held**
Web: www.roskamfoods.com
SIC: 2099 Food preparations, nec
PA: Roskam Baking Company, Llc
   4880 Corp Exch Blvd Se
   616 574-5757

(P-1846)
ROSKAM BAKING COMPANY LLC
305 S Acacia St Ste A, San Dimas
(91773-2928)
PHONE.................909 305-0185
Lupe Martinez, *Brnch Mgr*
EMP: 317
SALES (corp-wide): 280.97MM **Privately Held**

Web: www.organicmilling.com
SIC: 2099 Food preparations, nec
PA: Roskam Baking Company, Llc
   4880 Corp Exch Blvd Se
   616 574-5757

(P-1847)
RUIZ MEXICAN FOODS INC (PA)
Also Called: Ruiz Flour Tortillas
1200 Marlborough Ave Ste A, Riverside
(92507-2158)
PHONE.................909 947-7811
Dolores C Ruiz, *CEO*
▼ **EMP:** 120 **EST:** 1976
SQ FT: 38,000
SALES (est): 3.64MM
SALES (corp-wide): 3.64MM **Privately Held**
Web: www.ruizflourtortillas.com
SIC: 2099 3556 Tortillas, fresh or refrigerated
   ; Food products machinery

(P-1848)
SABATER USA INC (PA)
Also Called: Npms Natural Products Mil Svcs
14824 S Main St, Gardena (90248-1919)
PHONE.................310 518-2227
Jose Sabater Sanchez, *CEO*
David Solomon, *
▲ **EMP:** 33 **EST:** 1999
SQ FT: 80,000
SALES (est): 8.6MM
SALES (corp-wide): 8.6MM **Privately Held**
Web: www.bdsnatural.com
SIC: 2099 5149 Seasonings and spices;
   Natural and organic foods

(P-1849)
SAUER BRANDS INC
184 Suburban Rd, San Luis Obispo
(93401-7502)
PHONE.................805 597-8900
William W Lovette, *CEO*
EMP: 65
SALES (corp-wide): 700.62MM **Privately Held**
Web: www.sauerbrandsinc.com
SIC: 2099 Seasonings and spices
PA: Sauer Brands, Inc.
   2000 W Broad St
   804 359-5786

(P-1850)
SHORE FRONT LLC
3973 Trolley Ct, Brea (92823-1054)
PHONE.................714 612-3751
Anil Kumar, *
Ajay Maini, *CEO*
EMP: 40 **EST:** 2009
SALES (est): 1.95MM **Privately Held**
Web: www.subway.com
SIC: 2099 5812 Ready-to-eat meals, salads,
   and sandwiches; Eating places

(P-1851)
SILAO TORTILLERIA INC
Also Called: Silao Tortilleria
18316 Senteno St, Rowland Heights
(91748-4433)
PHONE.................626 961-0761
Leandro Espinosa Senior, *Pr*
Leandro Espinosa Junior, *VP*
EMP: 44 **EST:** 1955
SALES (est): 4.21MM **Privately Held**
SIC: 2099 Tortillas, fresh or refrigerated

(P-1852)
SINCERE ORIENT COMMERCIAL CORP
Also Called: Sincere Orient Food Company

15222 Valley Blvd, City Of Industry
(91746-3323)
PHONE.................626 333-8882
Andy Khun, *Pr*
▲ **EMP:** 70 **EST:** 1984
SQ FT: 12,000
SALES (est): 5.61MM **Privately Held**
Web: www.sincereorient.com
SIC: 2099 Pasta, rice, and potato, packaged
   combination products

(P-1853)
SONORA MILLS FOODS INC (PA)
Also Called: Pop Chips
3064 E Maria St, E Rncho Dmngz
(90221-5804)
PHONE.................310 639-5333
Patrick Turpin, *CEO*
Martin Basch, *
▲ **EMP:** 191 **EST:** 1991
SQ FT: 80,000
SALES (est): 22.58MM
SALES (corp-wide): 22.58MM **Privately Held**
SIC: 2099 Food preparations, nec

(P-1854)
SOUP BASES LOADED INC
2355 E Francis St, Ontario (91761-7727)
PHONE.................909 230-6890
Alan Portney, *Pr*
EMP: 45 **EST:** 1997
SQ FT: 27,000
SALES (est): 10.28MM **Privately Held**
Web: www.soupbasesloaded.com
SIC: 2099 2034 Seasonings: dry mixes;
   Dried and dehydrated soup mixes

(P-1855)
SOUTHWEST PRODUCTS LLC
8411 Siempre Viva Rd, San Diego
(92154-6299)
PHONE.................619 263-8000
▲ **EMP:** 250
Web: www.assemblysystems.com
SIC: 2099 Tortillas, fresh or refrigerated

(P-1856)
SOYFOODS OF AMERICA
1091 Hamilton Rd, Duarte (91010-2743)
PHONE.................626 358-3836
Ka Nin Lee, *Pr*
EMP: 27 **EST:** 1981
SQ FT: 15,000
SALES (est): 3.1MM **Privately Held**
Web: www.soyfoods-usa.com
SIC: 2099 Food preparations, nec

(P-1857)
STANESS JONEKOS ENTPS INC
Also Called: Eat Like A Woman
4000 W Magnolia Blvd Ste D, Burbank
(91505-2827)
PHONE.................818 606-2710
Staness Jonekos, *Owner*
EMP: 27 **EST:** 1988
SALES (est): 239.42K **Privately Held**
Web: www.eatlikeawoman.com
SIC: 2099 Food preparations, nec

(P-1858)
SUNRISE GROWERS INC
Also Called: Oxnard 2 Warehouse
2640 Sturgis Rd, Oxnard (93030-7931)
PHONE.................612 619-9545
Jill Barnett, *Pr*
EMP: 1120 **EST:** 2011
SALES (est): 2.41MM
SALES (corp-wide): 630.3MM **Publicly Held**

SIC: 2099 Food preparations, nec
HQ: Sunopta Foods Inc.
   7078 Shady Oak Rd
   Eden Prairie MN 55344

(P-1859)
TAMPICO SPICE CO INCORPORATED
Also Called: Tampico Spice Company
5901 S Central Ave # 5941, Los Angeles
(90001-1128)
P.O. Box 1229 (90001-0229)
PHONE.................323 235-3154
George Martinez, *CEO*
Delia Navarro, *Sec*
▲ **EMP:** 40 **EST:** 1946
SQ FT: 150,000
SALES (est): 8.37MM **Privately Held**
Web: www.tampicospice.com
SIC: 2099 Spices, including grinding

(P-1860)
TATTOOED CHEF INC (PA)
6305 Alondra Blvd, Paramount
(90723-3750)
PHONE.................562 602-0822
Salvatore Galletti, *CEO*
Salvatore Galletti, *Ch Bd*
Gaspare Guarrasi, *COO*
Stephanie Dieckmann, *CFO*
Matthew Williams, *CGO*
EMP: 28 **EST:** 2018
SALES (est): 230.93MM
SALES (corp-wide): 230.93MM **Publicly Held**
Web: www.tattooedchef.com
SIC: 2099 Food preparations, nec

(P-1861)
THE HUNTER SPICE INC
184 Suburban Rd, San Luis Obispo
(93401-7502)
P.O. Box 8110 (93403-8110)
PHONE.................805 597-8900
▲ **EMP:** 65
Web: www.sauers.com
SIC: 2099 Seasonings and spices

(P-1862)
TRIPLE H FOOD PROCESSORS LLC
5821 Wilderness Ave, Riverside
(92504-1004)
PHONE.................951 352-5700
Richard J Harris, *
▲ **EMP:** 60 **EST:** 1976
SQ FT: 120,000
SALES (est): 17.18MM **Privately Held**
Web: www.triplehfoods.com
SIC: 2099 2035 2033 Food preparations, nec
   ; Pickles, sauces, and salad dressings;
   Jams, jellies, and preserves, packaged in
   cans, jars, etc.

(P-1863)
TU MADRE ROMANA INC
13633 S Western Ave, Gardena
(90249-2503)
P.O. Box 1275 (90249-0275)
PHONE.................323 321-6041
EMP: 215
Web: www.ramonas.com
SIC: 2099 5812 Tortillas, fresh or refrigerated
   ; Delicatessen (eating places)

(P-1864)
UCE HOLDINGS INC
411 Center St, Los Angeles (90012-3435)
PHONE.................213 217-4235

Gary Kawaguchi, *CEO*
Edward Shelley, *
◆ **EMP:** 87 **EST:** 2006
SQ FT: 45,000
SALES (est): 47.28K **Privately Held**
Web: www.uppercrustent.com
SIC: 2099 Bread crumbs, except made in
bakeries

(P-1865)
VILLAGE GREEN FOODS INC
1732 Kaiser Ave, Irvine (92614-5706)
PHONE............................949 261-0111
EMP: 25 **EST:** 1970
SALES (est): 3.19MM **Privately Held**
Web: www.villagegreenfoods.com
SIC: 2099 Food preparations, nec

(P-1866)
WORLDWIDE SPECIALTIES INC
Also Called: California Specialty Farms
2420 Modoc St, Los Angeles (90021-2916)
PHONE............................323 587-2200
Mady Joes, *Mgr*
EMP: 120
Web: www.newcsf.com
SIC: 2099 Almond pastes
PA: Worldwide Specialties, Inc.
2421 E 16th St 1

2111 Cigarettes

(P-1867)
HOOK IT UP
1513 S Grand Ave, Santa Ana
(92705-4410)
PHONE............................714 600-0100
Zack Zakari, *CEO*
EMP: 23 **EST:** 2014
SQ FT: 5,000
SALES (est): 461.15K **Privately Held**
SIC: 2111 Cigarettes

(P-1868)
R J REYNOLDS TOBACCO COMPANY
8380 Miramar Mall Ste 117, San Diego
(92121-2549)
PHONE............................858 625-8453
Ken Stevens, *Prin*
EMP: 95
Web: www.rjrt.com
SIC: 2111 Cigarettes
HQ: R. J. Reynolds Tobacco Company
401 N Main St
Winston Salem NC 27101
336 741-5000

2211 Broadwoven Fabric Mills, Cotton

(P-1869)
ALSTYLE APPAREL LLC
1501 E Cerritos Ave, Anaheim
(92805-6400)
PHONE............................714 765-0400
EMP: 1163 **EST:** 2014
SALES (est): 1.06MM
SALES (corp-wide): 3.2B **Privately Held**
SIC: 2211 Apparel and outerwear fabrics,
cotton
HQ: Alstyle Apparel & Activewear
Management Co.
1501 E Cerritos Ave
Anaheim CA 92805
714 765-0400

(P-1870)
AVITEX INC (PA)
Also Called: Veratex
20362 Plummer St, Chatsworth
(91311-5371)
PHONE............................818 994-6487
Avi Cohen, *CEO*
▲ **EMP:** 250 **EST:** 1992
SQ FT: 15,000
SALES (est): 2.53MM **Privately Held**
Web: www.veratex.com
SIC: 2211 5131 Sheets, bedding and table
cloths: cotton; Linen piece goods, woven

(P-1871)
BABYLON INTERNATIONAL LLC
16520 Bake Pkwy Ste 230, Irvine
(92618-4689)
PHONE............................323 433-4104
Ayse G Erkovan, *Opers Mgr*
EMP: 50 **EST:** 2005
SALES (est): 1.61MM **Privately Held**
SIC: 2211 Twills, drills, denims and other
ribbed fabrics: cotton

(P-1872)
BONDED FIBERLOFT INC
2748 Tanager Ave, Commerce
(90040-2798)
PHONE............................323 726-7820
Mark Bidner, *CEO*
Mike Wood, *CFO*
EMP: 299 **EST:** 1998
SQ FT: 96,000
SALES (est): 491.96K **Privately Held**
SIC: 2211 2823 2299 Broadwoven fabric
mills, cotton; Cellulosic manmade fibers;
Batts and batting: cotton mill waste and
related material
PA: Western Synthetic Fiber Inc
2 Atlantic Ave Fl 4

(P-1873)
BTS TRADING INC
Also Called: Manufacture
2052 E Vernon Ave, Vernon (90058-1613)
PHONE............................213 800-6755
Euisoo Kim, *Pr*
EMP: 35 **EST:** 2020
SALES (est): 553.95K **Privately Held**
SIC: 2211 Apparel and outerwear fabrics,
cotton

(P-1874)
CENTRIC BRANDS INC
Also Called: Joe's Dsert Hlls Prmium Otlets
48650 Seminole Dr Ste 170, Cabazon
(92230-2118)
PHONE............................951 797-5077
EMP: 39
Web: www.centricbrands.com
SIC: 2211 Denims
PA: Centric Brands Llc
350 5th Ave Fl 6

(P-1875)
CENTRIC BRANDS INC
Also Called: CENTRIC BRANDS INC.
5630 Paseo Del Norte Ste 144, Carlsbad
(92008-4470)
PHONE............................760 603-8520
EMP: 39
Web: www.joesjeans.com
SIC: 2211 Denims
PA: Centric Brands Llc
350 5th Ave Fl 6

(P-1876)
COLORMAX INDUSTRIES INC (PA)
1627 Paloma St, Los Angeles
(90021-3013)
PHONE............................213 748-6600
Gholamreza Amighi, *Pr*
Goodarz Haydarzadeh, *
EMP: 25 **EST:** 1988
SQ FT: 64,000
SALES (est): 1.25MM
SALES (corp-wide): 1.25MM **Privately Held**
SIC: 2211 2269 2261 2254 Broadwoven
fabric mills, cotton; Finishing plants, nec;
Finishing plants, cotton; Dyeing and
finishing knit underwear

(P-1877)
CREATIVE COSTUMING DESIGNS INC
Also Called: Creative Costuming & Designs
15402 Electronic Ln, Huntington Beach
(92649-1334)
PHONE............................714 895-0982
Noreen Roberts, *Pr*
Noreen Roberts, *CEO*
Kevin Roberts, *
EMP: 35 **EST:** 2009
SQ FT: 5,300
SALES (est): 2.49MM **Privately Held**
Web: www.creative-costuming.com
SIC: 2211 Apparel and outerwear fabrics,
cotton

(P-1878)
FACTORY ONE STUDIO INC
6700 Avalon Blvd Ste 101, Los Angeles
(90003-1920)
PHONE............................323 752-1670
Steve C Rhee, *CEO*
EMP: 52 **EST:** 2017
SALES (est): 1.8MM **Privately Held**
Web: www.factoryonestudio.com
SIC: 2211 Denims

(P-1879)
FIRST FINISH INC
11126 Wright Rd, Lynwood (90262-3122)
PHONE............................310 631-6717
Keyomars Fard, *Pr*
▲ **EMP:** 25 **EST:** 2003
SQ FT: 10,000
SALES (est): 1.09MM **Privately Held**
SIC: 2211 Jean fabrics

(P-1880)
G KAGAN AND SONS INC (PA)
Also Called: Kagan Trim Center
3957 S Hill St, Los Angeles (90037-1313)
PHONE............................323 583-1400
Jed Kagan, *Pr*
Rod Kagan, *
◆ **EMP:** 25 **EST:** 1946
SQ FT: 50,000
SALES (est): 2.08MM
SALES (corp-wide): 2.08MM **Privately Held**
Web: www.kagantrim.com
SIC: 2211 Apparel and outerwear fabrics,
cotton

(P-1881)
HIDDEN JEANS INC
Also Called: Cello Jeans
7210 Dominion Cir, Commerce
(90040-3647)
PHONE............................213 746-4223
Kenny Park, *CEO*

Adam Lee, *
◆ **EMP:** 30 **EST:** 2007
SQ FT: 4,000
SALES (est): 4.92MM **Privately Held**
Web: www.hiddenjeans.com
SIC: 2211 2339 Denims; Jeans: women's,
misses', and juniors'

(P-1882)
KNIT GENERATION GROUP INC
3818 S Broadway, Los Angeles
(90037-1412)
PHONE............................213 221-5081
Joseph Dania, *CEO*
EMP: 25 **EST:** 2013
SALES (est): 2.38MM **Privately Held**
Web: www.knitgeneration.net
SIC: 2211 Broadwoven fabric mills, cotton

(P-1883)
LINKSOUL LLC
530 S Coast Hwy, Oceanside (92054-4009)
PHONE............................760 231-7069
Dave Seymour Cfo, *COO*
EMP: 29 **EST:** 2013
SALES (est): 2.52MM **Privately Held**
Web: www.linksoul.com
SIC: 2211 Apparel and outerwear fabrics,
cotton

(P-1884)
MASTERPIECE ARTIST CANVAS LLC
Also Called: Canvas Concepts
1401 Air Wing Rd, San Diego (92154-7705)
PHONE............................619 710-2500
John M Sooklaris, *Pr*
◆ **EMP:** 50 **EST:** 1965
SQ FT: 1,000
SALES (est): 2.44MM **Privately Held**
Web: www.masterpiecearts.com
SIC: 2211 Canvas

(P-1885)
PJY LLC
Also Called: Intimo Industry
3251 Leonis Blvd, Vernon (90058-3018)
PHONE............................323 583-7737
Ryan Fisher, *CEO*
▲ **EMP:** 40 **EST:** 2001
SALES (est): 5.69MM **Privately Held**
Web: www.intimoindustry.com
SIC: 2211 Long cloth, cotton

(P-1886)
SOCAL GARMENT WORKS LLC
4700 S Boyle Ave Ste G, Vernon
(90058-3032)
PHONE............................323 300-5717
Michael Burns, *Managing Member*
Joseph Burns, *Managing Member*
Sho Kato, *Managing Member*
EMP: 43 **EST:** 2020
SALES (est): 1.1MM **Privately Held**
SIC: 2211 2221 Apparel and outerwear
fabrics, cotton; Apparel and outerwear
fabric, manmade fiber or silk

(P-1887)
STANZINO INC (PA)
Also Called: Apparel House USA
16325 S Avalon Blvd, Gardena
(90248-2909)
PHONE............................213 746-8822
David Ghods, *CEO*
EMP: 25 **EST:** 2011
SALES (est): 3.85MM
SALES (corp-wide): 3.85MM **Privately Held**

SIC: 2211 Apparel and outerwear fabrics, cotton

(P-1888)
STANZINO INC
17937 Santa Rita St, Encino (91316-3602)
PHONE....................818 602-5171
David Ghods, *Brnch Mgr*
EMP: 120
SALES (corp-wide): 3.85MM **Privately Held**
SIC: 2211 Apparel and outerwear fabrics, cotton
PA: Stanzino, Inc.
16325 S Avalon Blvd
213 746-8822

(P-1889)
TWIN DRAGON MARKETING INC (PA)
Also Called: Tdmi
14600 S Broadway, Gardena (90248-1812)
PHONE....................310 715-7070
Dominic Poon, *CEO*
Joseph Tse, *Treas*
◆ EMP: 49 EST: 1980
SQ FT: 39,000
SALES (est): 21.88MM
SALES (corp-wide): 21.88MM **Privately Held**
Web: www.tdmi-us.com
SIC: 2211 Denims

(P-1890)
XCVI LLC (PA)
15236 Burbank Blvd, Sherman Oaks (91411-3504)
PHONE....................213 749-2661
Alon Zeltzer, *CEO*
Mordechia Zelter, *
Gita Zeltzer, *
▲ EMP: 60 EST: 1996
SALES (est): 9.68MM
SALES (corp-wide): 9.68MM **Privately Held**
Web: www.xcvi.com
SIC: 2211 Apparel and outerwear fabrics, cotton

2221 Broadwoven Fabric Mills, Manmade

(P-1891)
DAE SHIN USA INC
610 N Gilbert St, Fullerton (92833-2555)
PHONE....................714 578-8900
Jae Weon Lee, *CEO*
▲ EMP: 100 EST: 1999
SQ FT: 10,000
SALES (est): 5.93MM **Privately Held**
SIC: 2221 Textile mills, broadwoven: silk and manmade, also glass
PA: Daeshin Textile Co., Ltd.
16 Haean-Ro 397beon-Gil, Danwon-Gu

(P-1892)
DOOL FNA INC
Also Called: Grand Textile
16624 Edwards Rd, Cerritos (90703-2438)
PHONE....................562 483-4100
Jae Weon Lee, *CEO*
▲ EMP: 120 EST: 1999
SALES (est): 3.11MM **Privately Held**
SIC: 2221 Textile mills, broadwoven: silk and manmade, also glass

(P-1893)
FABRICMATE SYSTEMS INC
Also Called: Fabricmate
2781 Golf Course Dr Unit A, Ventura (93003-7939)
PHONE....................805 642-7470
Craig Lanuza, *Pr*
Manoj Pradhan, *
▲ EMP: 30 EST: 1995
SQ FT: 16,116
SALES (est): 4.92MM **Privately Held**
Web: www.fabricmate.com
SIC: 2221 Upholstery, tapestry, and wall covering fabrics

(P-1894)
FABTEX INC
Also Called: Ft Textiles
615 S State College Blvd, Fullerton (92831-5115)
PHONE....................714 538-0877
William P Friese, *Brnch Mgr*
EMP: 105
SALES (corp-wide): 49.37MM **Privately Held**
Web: www.fabtex.com
SIC: 2221 2515 2392 2391 Draperies and drapery fabrics, manmade fiber and silk; Mattresses and bedsprings; Household furnishings, nec; Curtains and draperies
PA: Fabtex, Inc.
111 Woodbine Ln
800 778-2791

(P-1895)
GROUND CONTROL BUSINESS MGT (DH)
Also Called: Savitsky Stin Bcon Bcci A Cal
2049 Century Park E Ste 1400, Los Angeles (90067-3116)
PHONE....................310 315-6200
Chris Bucci, *CEO*
EMP: 23 EST: 1997
SALES (est): 20.94MM **Privately Held**
Web: www.gcbm.com
SIC: 2221 Satins
HQ: Nfp Corp.
200 Park Ave Fl 32
New York NY 10166
212 301-4001

(P-1896)
JUICY COUTURE INC
1580 Jesse St, Los Angeles (90021-1317)
PHONE....................888 824-8826
Pamela Levy, *CEO*
Edgar O Huber, *Pr*
Lisa Rodericks, *
Ellen Rodriguez, *
▲ EMP: 160 EST: 1990
SALES (est): 48.81K **Publicly Held**
Web: www.juicycouture.com
SIC: 2221 Broadwoven fabric mills, manmade
HQ: Kate Spade Holdings Llc
5822 Haverford Ave Ste 2
Philadelphia PA 19131
212 354-4900

(P-1897)
S&B DEVELOPMENT GROUP LLC
1901 Avenue Of The Stars 235, Los Angeles (90067-6001)
PHONE....................213 446-2818
Nathalio Ortez, *CEO*
EMP: 48 EST: 2008
SQ FT: 50,000
SALES (est): 703.71K **Privately Held**

SIC: 2221 5023 Broadwoven fabric mills, manmade; Sheets, textile

2231 Broadwoven Fabric Mills, Wool

(P-1898)
CALIFORNIA INDUSTRIAL FABRICS
2325 Marconi Ct, San Diego (92154-7241)
PHONE....................619 661-7166
TOLL FREE: 800
Michael Kent Lindsey, *Pr*
Patrick Dickey, *
Erin Mcnamara, *CFO*
◆ EMP: 30 EST: 1978
SQ FT: 24,000
SALES (est): 5.66MM **Privately Held**
Web: www.cifabrics.com
SIC: 2231 Broadwoven fabric mills, wool

(P-1899)
CMK MANUFACTURING LLC
Also Called: Green Dragon
10375 Wilshire Blvd Apt 2h, Los Angeles (90024-4714)
▲ EMP: 31 EST: 2003
SALES (est): 656.64K **Privately Held**
Web: www.freesocietyclothing.com
SIC: 2231 5632 Cloth, wool: mending; Apparel accessories

(P-1900)
COMFORT INDUSTRIES INC
301 W Las Tunas Dr, San Gabriel (91776-1201)
PHONE....................562 692-8288
Kevin D.o.s., *CEO*
Ken Quach, *
Mike D.o.s., *Treas*
Kevin Deal, *
◆ EMP: 35 EST: 1998
SALES (est): 821.69K **Privately Held**
SIC: 2231 Upholstery fabrics, wool

(P-1901)
FAM LLC (PA)
Also Called: Fam Brands
5553 Bandini Blvd B, Bell (90201-6421)
PHONE....................323 888-7755
Frank Zarabi, *Pr*
Rich Campanelli, *
Rich Lyons, *
Nazy Salamat, *
Carrie Henley, *
▲ EMP: 64 EST: 1985
SQ FT: 75,000
SALES (est): 77.14MM **Privately Held**
Web: www.fambrands.com
SIC: 2231 2221 Apparel and outerwear broadwoven fabrics; Apparel and outerwear fabric, manmade fiber or silk

(P-1902)
LEKOS DYE & FINISHING INC (PA)
3131 E Harcourt St, Compton (90221-5505)
P.O. Box 2245 (90621)
PHONE....................310 763-0900
Ilgun Lee, *Pr*
▲ EMP: 64 EST: 2003
SQ FT: 72,000
SALES (est): 10.85MM
SALES (corp-wide): 10.85MM **Privately Held**
SIC: 2231 Dyeing and finishing: wool or similar fibers

(P-1903)
ROSHAN TRADING INC
Also Called: Envirofabrics
3631 Union Pacific Ave, Los Angeles (90023-3255)
PHONE....................213 622-9904
David Roshan, *CEO*
◆ EMP: 40 EST: 1986
SALES (est): 5.08MM **Privately Held**
Web: www.lagunafabrics.com
SIC: 2231 5131 Broadwoven fabric mills, wool; Textiles, woven, nec

(P-1904)
TRI-STAR DYEING & FINSHG INC
15125 Marquardt Ave, Santa Fe Springs (90670-5705)
PHONE....................562 483-0123
Jang You, *Prin*
▲ EMP: 63 EST: 2006
SQ FT: 60,000
SALES (est): 2.81MM **Privately Held**
Web: www.tristar-df.com
SIC: 2231 Dyeing and finishing: wool or similar fibers

2241 Narrow Fabric Mills

(P-1905)
CHUA & SONS CO INC
Also Called: Reliable Tape Products
3300 E 50th St, Vernon (90058-3004)
P.O. Box 58261 (90058-0261)
PHONE....................323 588-8044
Shirley Chua, *Pr*
▲ EMP: 23 EST: 1984
SQ FT: 67,000
SALES (est): 778.13K **Privately Held**
SIC: 2241 Fabric tapes

(P-1906)
HOLLYWOOD RIBBON INDUSTRIES INC
9000 Rochester Ave, Rancho Cucamonga (91730-5522)
P.O. Box 428 (18603-0428)
PHONE....................323 266-0670
◆ EMP: 400
Web: www.hollywoodribbon.com
SIC: 2241 Ribbons, nec

(P-1907)
UNIVERSAL ELASTIC & GARMENT SUPPLY INC
2200 S Alameda St, Vernon (90058-1308)
PHONE....................213 748-2995
▲ EMP: 23 EST: 1991
SALES (est): 2.18MM **Privately Held**
Web: www.universalelastic.com
SIC: 2241 5131 Narrow fabric mills; Piece goods and notions

2252 Hosiery, Nec

(P-1908)
GILDAN USA INC
Also Called: GILDAN USA INC.
28200 Highway 189, Lake Arrowhead (92352-9700)
PHONE....................909 485-1475
EMP: 46
SALES (corp-wide): 3.2B **Privately Held**
Web: www.gildancorp.com
SIC: 2252 Hosiery, nec
HQ: Gildan Usa Llc
1980 Clements Ferry Rd
Charleston SC 29492

▲ = Import ▼ = Export
◆ = Import/Export

(P-1909)

K B SOCKS INC (DH)

Also Called: K Bell

550 N Oak St, Inglewood (90302-2942)

PHONE....................310 670-3235

▲ EMP: 51 EST: 1985

SALES (est): 2.37MM

SALES (corp-wide): 3.26B **Privately Held**

Web: www.kbellsocks.com

SIC: 2252 Socks

HQ: Renfro Llc

661 Linville Rd

Mount Airy NC 27030

336 719-8000

(P-1910)

UNIVERSAL HOSIERY INC

28337 Constellation Rd, Valencia

(91355-5048)

PHONE....................661 702-8444

Johnathan Ekizian, *Pr*

▲ EMP: 75 EST: 1994

SQ FT: 44,000

SALES (est): 3.2MM **Privately Held**

Web: www.universalhosiery.com

SIC: 2252 Socks

2253 Knit Outerwear Mills

(P-1911)

BALBOA MANUFACTURING CO LLC (PA)

Also Called: Bobster Eyewear

4909 Murphy Canyon Rd Ste 310, San Diego (92123-4301)

PHONE....................858 715-0060

John Smaller, *Managing Member*

Jennifer Struebing, *

▲ EMP: 26 EST: 1996

SQ FT: 40,000

SALES (est): 2.43MM **Privately Held**

Web: www.bobster.com

SIC: 2253 2211 Hats and headwear, knit; Apparel and outerwear fabrics, cotton

(P-1912)

BYER CALIFORNIA

Alfred Paquette Division

1201 Rio Vista Ave, Los Angeles

(90023-2609)

PHONE....................323 780-7615

Jan Shostak, *Mgr*

EMP: 114

SQ FT: 10,000

SALES (corp-wide): 124.12MM **Privately Held**

Web: www.byrca.com

SIC: 2253 2339 2335 Dresses, knit; Women's and misses' outerwear, nec; Women's, junior's, and misses' dresses

PA: Byer California

66 Potrero Ave

415 626-7844

(P-1913)

CREW KNITWEAR LLC

2155 E 7th St Ste 125, Los Angeles

(90023-1031)

PHONE....................323 526-3888

Fredrick Ken, *Mgr*

EMP: 66

Web: www.crewknitwear.com

SIC: 2253 Dresses, knit

PA: Crew Knitwear, Llc

660 S Myers St

(P-1914)

CUT AND SEW CO INC

1939 S Susan St, Santa Ana (92704-3901)

PHONE....................714 981-7244

Arturo Martinez, *CEO*

EMP: 107 EST: 2020

SALES (est): 3.35MM **Privately Held**

SIC: 2253 T-shirts and tops, knit

(P-1915)

DELTA PACIFIC ACTIVEWEAR INC

331 S Hale Ave, Fullerton (92831-4805)

PHONE....................714 871-9281

Imran Parekh, *Pr*

▲ EMP: 80 EST: 1998

SALES (est): 1.25MM **Privately Held**

Web: www.delpacific.com

SIC: 2253 2331 2321 T-shirts and tops, knit; Women's and misses' blouses and shirts; Men's and boy's furnishings

(P-1916)

FANTASY ACTIVEWEAR INC (PA)

Also Called: Fantasy Manufacturing

5383 Alcoa Ave, Vernon (90058-3734)

PHONE....................213 705-4111

Anwar Gajiani, *CEO*

Yassmin Gajiani, *

▲ EMP: 38 EST: 1991

SQ FT: 20,000

SALES (est): 3.52MM **Privately Held**

SIC: 2253 2331 2321 T-shirts and tops, knit; Women's and misses' blouses and shirts; Men's and boy's furnishings

(P-1917)

FANTASY DYEING & FINISHING INC

5383 Alcoa Ave, Vernon (90058-3734)

PHONE....................323 983-9988

Anwar M Gajiani, *CEO*

EMP: 36 EST: 2003

SALES (est): 1.56MM **Privately Held**

SIC: 2253 Dyeing and finishing knit outerwear, excl. hosiery and glove

(P-1918)

FORTUNE SWIMWEAR LLC (HQ)

Also Called: Palisades Beach Club

2340 E Olympic Blvd Ste A, Los Angeles (90021-2544)

PHONE....................310 733-2130

Stephen Soller, *Managing Member*

Craig Soller, *

Gary Bub, *

Ann Kennedy, *

◆ EMP: 30 EST: 2002

SQ FT: 10,000

SALES (est): 34.7MM **Privately Held**

Web: www.fortuneswimwear.com

SIC: 2253 2335 Bathing suits and swimwear, knit; Women's, junior's, and misses' dresses

PA: Coast Style Group, Llc

860 S Los Angeles St # 540

(P-1919)

INSTA-LETTERING MACHINE CO (PA)

Also Called: Insta Graphic Systems

13925 166th St, Cerritos (90703-2431)

P.O. Box 7900 (90702-7900)

PHONE....................562 404-3000

◆ EMP: 90 EST: 1959

SALES (est): 8.72MM

SALES (corp-wide): 8.72MM **Privately Held**

Web: www.instagraph.com

SIC: 2253 2752 2396 T-shirts and tops, knit; Transfers, decalcomania or dry; lithographed; Screen printing on fabric articles

(P-1920)

ISIQALO LLC

Also Called: Spectra USA

5610 Daniels St, Chino (91710-9024)

PHONE....................714 683-2820

Nick Agakanian, *

▼ EMP: 350 EST: 2012

SALES (est): 8.81MM **Privately Held**

Web: www.spectrausa.net

SIC: 2253 5136 5137 2321 T-shirts and tops, knit; Men's and boy's clothing; Women's and children's clothing; Sport shirts, men's and boys': from purchased materials

(P-1921)

LATIGO INC

4371 E 49th St, Vernon (90058-3122)

PHONE....................323 583-8000

Mandana Vasseghi, *CEO*

Nazanine Farshidan, *

EMP: 30 EST: 2011

SQ FT: 18,000

SALES (est): 1.92MM **Privately Held**

Web: www.latigousa.com

SIC: 2253 Knit outerwear mills

(P-1922)

LSPACE AMERICA LLC

Also Called: L Space

14420 Myford Rd, Irvine (92606-1017)

PHONE....................949 750-2292

Lauren Kula, *

◆ EMP: 62 EST: 2008

SALES (est): 5.9MM **Privately Held**

Web: www.lspace.com

SIC: 2253 2331 Bathing suits and swimwear, knit; Women's and misses' blouses and shirts

(P-1923)

MAD ENGINE GLOBAL LLC (HQ)

Also Called: Mad Engine

1017 Grandview Ave, Glendale (91201-2205)

PHONE....................858 558-5270

Danish Gajiani, *CEO*

Faizan Bakali, *

Christine Bettles, *

Oliver Calder, *

◆ EMP: 54 EST: 1987

SALES (est): 638.25MM

SALES (corp-wide): 638.25MM **Privately Hold**

Web: www.madengine.com

SIC: 2253 2261 T-shirts and tops, knit; Screen printing of cotton broadwoven fabrics

PA: Mad Acquisition Corporation

360 N Crescent Dr

858 558-5270

(P-1924)

STUDIO9D8 INC

9743 Alesia St, South El Monte (91733-3008)

PHONE....................626 350-0832

Ann Lem, *CEO*

EMP: 30 EST: 2011

SALES (est): 2.52MM **Privately Held**

Web: www.studio9d8.com

SIC: 2253 2515 T-shirts and tops, knit; Studio couches

(P-1925)

SUNSETS INC

Also Called: Sunsets Separates

24511 Frampton Ave, Harbor City (90710-2108)

PHONE....................310 784-3600

▲ EMP: 35 EST: 1984

SALES (est): 5.39MM **Privately Held**

Web: www.sunsetsinc.com

SIC: 2253 Bathing suits and swimwear, knit

2257 Weft Knit Fabric Mills

(P-1926)

SHARA-TEX INC

3338 E Slauson Ave, Vernon (90058-3915)

PHONE....................323 587-7200

Shahram Fahimian, *Ch Bd*

S Tony Souferian, *

▲ EMP: 45 EST: 1989

SQ FT: 55,000

SALES (est): 2.8MM **Privately Held**

Web: www.shara-tex.com

SIC: 2257 Weft knit fabric mills

(P-1927)

TENENBLATT CORPORATION

Also Called: Antex Knitting Mills

3750 Broadway Pl, Los Angeles (90007-4400)

PHONE....................323 232-2061

William Tenenblatt, *Pr*

Anna Tenenblatt, *

◆ EMP: 104 EST: 1973

SQ FT: 60,000

SALES (est): 1.41MM

SALES (corp-wide): 66.31MM **Privately Held**

SIC: 2257 Dyeing and finishing circular knit fabrics

PA: Matchmaster Dyeing & Finishing, Inc.

3750 S Broadway

323 232-2061

2259 Knitting Mills, Nec

(P-1928)

AZITEX TRADING CORP

Also Called: Azitex Knitting Mills

1850 E 15th St, Los Angeles (90021-2820)

PHONE....................213 745-7072

Michael Azizi, *Pr*

Mozie Azizi, *

Andrew Azizi, *

▲ EMP: 60 EST: 1986

SQ FT: 50,000

SALES (est): 2.52MM **Privately Held**

Web: azitex-trading-co-knitting-mills.business.site

SIC: 2259 2253 Convertors, knit goods; Knit outerwear mills

(P-1929)

PIERCAN USA INC

160 Bosstick Blvd, San Marcos (92069-5930)

PHONE....................760 599-4543

Vincent Lucas, *CEO*

Vincent Lucas, *Pr*

Gean-christopher Lucas, *Treas*

Antoine Dobrowolski, *

▲ EMP: 62 EST: 1995

SALES (est): 10.05MM **Privately Held**

Web: www.piercanusa.com

SIC: 2259 3842 3089 2673 Work gloves, knit; Gloves, safety; Gloves or mittens, plastics; Plastic and pliofilm bags

(P-1930)
SAS TEXTILES INC
3100 E 44th St, Vernon (90058-2406)
PHONE....................323 277-5555
Sohrab Sassounian, *Pr*
Soheil Sassounian, *
Albert Sassounian, *
▲ **EMP:** 70 **EST:** 1991
SQ FT: 40,000
SALES (est): 9.5MM **Privately Held**
Web: www.sastextile.com
SIC: **2259** 2257 7389 Convertors, knit goods
; Weft knit fabric mills; Textile and apparel
services

2261 Finishing Plants, Cotton

(P-1931)
**CAITAC GARMENT
PROCESSING INC**
14725 S Broadway, Gardena (90248-1813)
PHONE....................310 217-9888
Muneyuki Ishii, *CEO*
Azusa Sahara, *
▲ **EMP:** 270 **EST:** 1991
SQ FT: 200,000
SALES (est): 23.61MM **Privately Held**
Web: www.caitacgarment.com
SIC: **2261** 2339 2325 5651 Screen printing
of cotton broadwoven fabrics; Women's
and misses' outerwear, nec; Men's and
boy's trousers and slacks; Jeans stores
PA: Caitac Holdings Corp.
3-12, Showacho, Kita-Ku

(P-1932)
CUSTOM LOGOS INC
7889 Clairemont Mesa Blvd, San Diego
(92111-1618)
PHONE....................858 277-1886
▲ **EMP:** 44 **EST:** 1982
SALES (est): 13.86MM **Privately Held**
Web: www.customlogos.com
SIC: **2261** Screen printing of cotton
broadwoven fabrics

(P-1933)
HARRYS DYE AND WASH INC
Also Called: Harry's Dye & Wash
1015 E Orangethorpe Ave, Anaheim
(92801-1135)
PHONE....................714 446-0300
Harry Choung, *Pr*
Kang Ho Lee, *
EMP: 30 **EST:** 1994
SQ FT: 20,000
SALES (est): 2.02MM **Privately Held**
SIC: **2261** 2269 Finishing plants, cotton;
Finishing plants, nec

(P-1934)
SILK SCREEN SHIRTS INC
Also Called: SSS
6185 El Camino Real, Carlsbad
(92009-1602)
PHONE....................760 233-3900
Stephen H Taylor, *Pr*
Laura D Wile, *
William Regan, *
▲ **EMP:** 30 **EST:** 1969
SQ FT: 20,000
SALES (est): 4.42MM **Privately Held**
Web: www.silkscreenshirtsinc.com
SIC: **2261** 2396 Screen printing of cotton
broadwoven fabrics; Automotive and
apparel trimmings

(P-1935)
SUPER DYEING LLC
Also Called: Super Dyeing and Finishing
8825 Millergrove Dr, Santa Fe Springs
(90670-2003)
PHONE....................562 692-9500
▲ **EMP:** 75 **EST:** 1995
SALES (est): 1.91MM **Privately Held**
Web: www.superdyeing.com
SIC: **2261** Dyeing cotton broadwoven fabrics

(P-1936)
TOMORROWS LOOK INC
Also Called: Dimensions In Screen Printing
17462 Von Karman Ave, Irvine
(92614-6206)
PHONE....................949 596-8400
Steven E Mellgren, *CEO*
Torrey Mellgren, *
EMP: 70 **EST:** 1986
SQ FT: 36,000
SALES (est): 7.39MM **Privately Held**
SIC: **2261** Screen printing of cotton
broadwoven fabrics

(P-1937)
**WASHINGTON GRMENT DYG
FNSHG IN**
1332 E 18th St, Los Angeles (90021-3027)
PHONE....................213 747-1111
Pradip Shah, *Mgr*
EMP: 35
SALES (corp-wide): 1.34MM **Privately
Held**
Web: www.washingtongarment.com
SIC: **2261** 2262 Finishing plants, cotton;
Finishing plants, manmade
PA: Washington Garment Dyeing &
Finishing, Inc.
1341 E Washington Blvd
213 747-1111

2262 Finishing Plants, Manmade

(P-1938)
INX PRINTS INC
1802 Kettering, Irvine (92614-5618)
PHONE....................949 660-9190
Harold A Haase Junior, *CEO*
David Van Steenhuyse, *
▼ **EMP:** 100 **EST:** 2004
SQ FT: 26,000
SALES (est): 15.72MM **Privately Held**
Web: inx-prints-inc.hub.biz
SIC: **2262** Screen printing: manmade fiber
and silk broadwoven fabrics

(P-1939)
**WASHINGTON GARMENT
DYEING (PA)**
1341 E Washington Blvd, Los Angeles
(90021-3037)
PHONE....................213 747-1111
Vijay Shah, *Pr*
Pradip Shah, *
EMP: 25 **EST:** 1988
SQ FT: 20,000
SALES (est): 1.34MM
SALES (corp-wide): 1.34MM **Privately
Held**
Web: www.washingtongarment.com
SIC: **2262** 2261 2269 Dyeing: manmade
fiber and silk broadwoven fabrics; Dyeing
cotton broadwoven fabrics; Finishing
plants, nec

2269 Finishing Plants, Nec

(P-1940)
EXPO DYEING & FINISHING INC
8898 Los Coyotes Ct Unit 320, Buena Park
(90621-3875)
PHONE....................714 220-9583
Eduardo J Kim, *Pr*
▲ **EMP:** 170 **EST:** 1987
SALES (est): 8.06MM **Privately Held**
Web: www.expodye.com
SIC: **2269** Dyeing: raw stock, yarn, and
narrow fabrics

(P-1941)
GEARMENT INC (PA)
Also Called: Gearment
14801 Able Ln Ste 102, Huntington Beach
(92647-2059)
PHONE....................866 236-5476
Ton Le, *Pr*
Tom Le, *Pr*
Sang D.o.s., *CMO*
EMP: 195 **EST:** 2016
SALES (est): 33.6MM
SALES (corp-wide): 33.6MM **Privately
Held**
Web: www.gearment.com
SIC: **2269** Printing of narrow fabrics

(P-1942)
**MATCHMASTER DYG & FINSHG
INC (PA)**
Also Called: Antex Knitting Mills
3750 S Broadway, Los Angeles
(90007-4436)
PHONE....................323 232-2061
William Tenenblatt, *Pr*
◆ **EMP:** 250 **EST:** 1977
SQ FT: 66,000
SALES (est): 66.31MM
SALES (corp-wide): 66.31MM **Privately
Held**
Web: www.antex.com
SIC: **2269** Dyeing: raw stock, yarn, and
narrow fabrics

(P-1943)
**PACIFIC COAST BACH LABEL
INC**
3015 S Grand Ave, Los Angeles
(90007-3814)
PHONE....................213 612-0314
Dan Finnegan, *Pr*
▲ **EMP:** 23 **EST:** 1989
SALES (est): 429.7K **Privately Held**
Web: www.pcblabel.com
SIC: **2269** 2679 Labels, cotton: printed;
Labels, paper: made from purchased
material

(P-1944)
**PACIFIC CONTNTL TEXTILES
INC**
Also Called: Pct
2880 E Ana St, Compton (90221-5602)
P.O. Box 1330 (90801)
PHONE....................310 639-1500
Edmund Kim, *CEO*
◆ **EMP:** 98 **EST:** 1983
SALES (est): 5.98MM
SALES (corp-wide): 23.03MM **Privately
Held**
SIC: **2269** 2329 Finishing plants, nec; Men's
and boys' sportswear and athletic clothing
PA: Edmund Kim International, Inc.
2880 E Ana St
310 604-1100

(P-1945)
REZEX CORPORATION
Also Called: Geltman Industries
1930 E 51st St, Vernon (90058-2804)
EMP: 25 **EST:** 1981
SALES (est): 2.85MM **Privately Held**
Web: www.geltman.com
SIC: **2269** Finishing plants, nec

2273 Carpets And Rugs

(P-1946)
**AMERICAN COVER DESIGN 26
INC**
2131 E 52nd St, Vernon (90058-3498)
PHONE....................323 582-8666
Daniel Mahgerefteh, *CEO*
Elyas Myers, *
EMP: 25 **EST:** 2001
SALES (est): 6.76MM **Privately Held**
Web: www.americancoverdesign.com
SIC: **2273** 5023 Rugs, machine woven; Rugs

(P-1947)
ATLAS CARPET MILLS INC
3201 S Susan St, Santa Ana (92704-6838)
P.O. Box 11467 (36671-0467)
PHONE....................323 724-7930
James Horwich, *Pr*
Ada Horwich, *
Stan Dunford, *
Mark Hesther, *
Markos Varpas, *
▲ **EMP:** 229 **EST:** 1969
SALES (est): 3.72MM
SALES (corp-wide): 276.34MM **Publicly
Held**
Web: www.atlascarpetmills.com
SIC: **2273** Rugs, tufted
HQ: Tdg Operations, Llc
716 Bill Myles Dr
Saraland AL 36571
251 679-3512

(P-1948)
BENTLEY MILLS INC (PA)
Also Called: Bentley Mills
14641 Don Julian Rd, City Of Industry
(91746-3106)
PHONE....................626 333-4585
Jay Brown, *Pr*
Nancy Agger-nielsen, *CFO*
◆ **EMP:** 250 **EST:** 1980
SQ FT: 390,000
SALES (est): 99.82MM
SALES (corp-wide): 99.82MM **Privately
Held**
Web: www.bentleymills.com
SIC: **2273** 2299 Carpets, textile fiber;
Batting, wadding, padding and fillings

(P-1949)
**CATALINA CARPET MILLS INC
(PA)**
Also Called: Catalina Home
14418 Best Ave, Santa Fe Springs
(90670-5133)
PHONE....................562 926-5811
Duane Jensen, *Pr*
Jack Heinrich, *
▲ **EMP:** 38 **EST:** 1975
SQ FT: 60,000
SALES (est): 9.4MM
SALES (corp-wide): 9.4MM **Privately Held**
Web: www.catalinahome.com
SIC: **2273** 5023 Finishers of tufted carpets
and rugs; Floor coverings

(P-1950)

DURKAN PATTERNED CARPETS INC

3633 Lenawee Ave # 120, Los Angeles (90016-4319)
PHONE.................................310 838-2898
Kathy Stein, *Mgr*
EMP: 248
SIC: 2273 Carpets, hand and machine made
HQ: Durkan Patterned Carpets, Inc.
121 Goodwill Dr
Dalton GA 30721
706 278-7037

(P-1951)

FABRICA INTERNATIONAL INC

Also Called: Fabrica Fine Carpet
3201 S Susan St, Santa Ana (92704-6838)
P.O. Box 2007 (30722-2007)
PHONE.................................949 261-7181
Greg Uttecht, *Pr*
Jon A Faulkner, *
▲ EMP: 167 EST: 1974
SQ FT: 107,000
SALES (est): 7.21MM
SALES (corp-wide): 276.34MM **Publicly Held**
SIC: 2273 Carpets, hand and machine made
PA: The Dixie Group Inc
475 Reed Rd
706 876-5800

(P-1952)

INTERFACEFLOR LLC

1111 S Grand Ave Ste 103, Los Angeles (90015-2164)
PHONE.................................213 741-2139
EMP: 81
SALES (corp-wide): 1.26B **Publicly Held**
Web: www.interface.com
SIC: 2273 Finishers of tufted carpets and rugs
HQ: Interfaceflor, Llc
1503 Orchard Hill Rd
Lagrange GA 30240

(P-1953)

MARSPRING CORPORATION (PA)

Also Called: Marflex
4920 S Boyle Ave, Vernon (90058-3017)
P.O. Box 58643 (90058-0643)
PHONE.................................323 589-5637
Ronald J Greitzer, *Pr*
Stan Greitzer, *
▲ EMP: 34 EST: 1950
SQ FT: 54,008
SALES (est): 6.62MM
SALES (corp-wide): 6.62MM **Privately Held**
Web: www.reliancecarpetcushion.com
SIC: 2273 Carpets, textile fiber

(P-1954)

MOHAWK INDUSTRIES INC

9687 Transportation Way, Fontana (92335-2604)
PHONE.................................909 357-1064
Lisa Gomez, *Brnch Mgr*
EMP: 26
Web: www.mohawkind.com
SIC: 2273 3253 Finishers of tufted carpets and rugs; Ceramic wall and floor tile
PA: Mohawk Industries, Inc.
160 S Industrial Blvd

(P-1955)

ROYALTY CARPET MILLS INC

Also Called: Royalty

17111 Red Hill Ave, Irvine (92614-5607)
PHONE.................................949 474-4000
▲ EMP: 800
SIC: 2273 Carpets, hand and machine made

(P-1956)

SHAW INDUSTRIES GROUP INC

Also Called: Carriage Carpet Mills
11411 Valley View St, Cypress (90630-5368)
PHONE.................................562 430-4445
Stan Diehl, *Mgr*
EMP: 30
SALES (corp-wide): 364.48B **Publicly Held**
Web: www.shawinc.com
SIC: 2273 5713 5023 Finishers of tufted carpets and rugs; Floor covering stores; Homefurnishings
HQ: Shaw Industries Group, Inc.
616 E Walnut Ave
Dalton GA 30722
706 278-3812

(P-1957)

STANTON CARPET CORP

Also Called: Hibernia Woolen Mills
2209 Pine Ave, Manhattan Beach (90266-2832)
PHONE.................................562 945-8711
Debbie Dearo, *Mgr*
EMP: 50
SALES (corp-wide): 49.28MM **Privately Held**
Web: www.stantoncarpet.com
SIC: 2273 Carpets and rugs
PA: Stanton Carpet Corp.
100 Snnyside Blvd Ste 100
516 822-5878

2295 Coated Fabrics, Not Rubberized

(P-1958)

AOC LLC

Also Called: AOC California Plant
19991 Seaton Ave, Perris (92570-8724)
PHONE.................................951 657-5161
John Mulrine, *Mgr*
EMP: 100
Web: www.aocresins.com
SIC: 2295 2821 5169 Resin or plastic coated fabrics; Plastics materials and resins; Synthetic resins, rubber, and plastic materials
PA: Aoc, Llc
955 Hwy. 57

(P-1959)

CALIFORNIA COMBINING CORP

5607 S Santa Fe Ave, Vernon (90058-3525)
P.O. Box 509 (90280-0509)
PHONE.................................323 589-5727
Charlette Heller, *CEO*
Vincent Rosato, *
Kathy Diaz, *
▲ EMP: 37 EST: 1947
SQ FT: 68,000
SALES (est): 2.53MM **Privately Held**
Web: www.flamelaminatingcorp.com
SIC: 2295 Coated fabrics, not rubberized

(P-1960)

J MILLER CANVAS LLC

2429 S Birch St, Santa Ana (92707-3406)
PHONE.................................714 641-0052
EMP: 26 EST: 2018
SALES (est): 2.35MM **Privately Held**

Web: www.jmillercanvas.com
SIC: 2295 Waterproofing fabrics, except rubberizing

(P-1961)

SOLECTA INC (PA)

4113 Avenida De La Plata, Oceanside (92056-6002)
PHONE.................................760 630-9643
Jim Ford, *CEO*
Michael Ahearn, *
▲ EMP: 24 EST: 2014
SALES (est): 11.03MM
SALES (corp-wide): 11.03MM **Privately Held**
Web: www.solecta.com
SIC: 2295 Chemically coated and treated fabrics

2297 Nonwoven Fabrics

(P-1962)

TEXOLLINI INC

2575 E El Presidio St, Long Beach (90810-1114)
PHONE.................................310 537-3400
Daniel Kadisha, *Pr*
◆ EMP: 250 EST: 1989
SQ FT: 200,000
SALES (est): 22.96MM **Privately Held**
Web: www.texollini.com
SIC: 2297 2262 2269 2221 Nonwoven fabrics ; Dyeing: manmade fiber and silk broadwoven fabrics; Finishing plants, nec; Broadwoven fabric mills, manmade

---

2298 Cordage And Twine

(P-1963)

LIFT-IT MANUFACTURING CO INC

Also Called: Lift It
1603 W 2nd St, Pomona (91766-1252)
PHONE.................................909 469-2251
▲ EMP: 46 EST: 1979
SALES (est): 6.47MM **Privately Held**
Web: www.lift-it.com
SIC: 2298 Slings, rope

2299 Textile Goods, Nec

(P-1964)

ALANIC INTERNATIONAL CORP

Also Called: Dioz Group, The
9730 Wilshire Blvd Ph, Beverly Hills (90211-2709)
PHONE.................................855 525-2642
Farhan Beig, *Pr*
Johnny Beig, *CEO*
Tony Beig, *Sr VP*
▲ EMP: 38 EST: 2013
SALES (est): 7.55MM **Privately Held**
Web: www.alanic.com
SIC: 2299 2329 2339 Broadwoven fabrics: linen, jute, hemp, and ramie; Athletic clothing, except uniforms: men's, youths' and boys'; Athletic clothing: women's, misses', and juniors'

(P-1965)

AMERICAN DAWN INC (PA)

Also Called: ADI
401 W Artesia Blvd, Compton (90220-5518)
PHONE.................................800 821-2221
Adnan Rawjee, *Pr*
Mahmud G Rawjee, *
◆ EMP: 60 EST: 1980

SQ FT: 212,000
SALES (est): 25.02MM
SALES (corp-wide): 25.02MM **Privately Held**
Web: www.americandawn.com
SIC: 2299 5023 5131 2393 Linen fabrics; Linens and towels; Textiles, woven, nec; Cushions, except spring and carpet: purchased materials

(P-1966)

AMERICAN FOAM FIBER & SUPS INC (PA)

Also Called: Foam Depot
255 S 7th Ave Ste A, City Of Industry (91746-3256)
PHONE.................................626 969-7268
Jack Hung, *Pr*
Irene Hung, *VP*
▲ EMP: 26 EST: 2006
SALES (est): 3.82MM **Privately Held**
Web: www.affsinc.com
SIC: 2299 Hair, curled: for upholstery, pillow, and quilt filling

(P-1967)

AMPM MAINTENANCE CORPORATION

1010 E 14th St, Los Angeles (90021-2212)
PHONE.................................424 230-1300
Mohammad Saderi, *Pr*
EMP: 48 EST: 2020
SALES (est): 165.06K **Privately Held**
Web: www.ampmmaintenance.com
SIC: 2299 Textile goods, nec

(P-1968)

AMRAPUR OVERSEAS INCORPORATED (PA)

Also Called: Colonial Home Textiles
1560 E 6th St Ste 101, Corona (92879-1712)
PHONE.................................714 893-8808
Chandru H Wadhwani, *CEO*
Laxmi Wadhwani, *
◆ EMP: 25 EST: 1983
SQ FT: 130,000
SALES (est): 9.2MM
SALES (corp-wide): 9.2MM **Privately Held**
Web: www.amrapur.com
SIC: 2299 2269 5023 Linen fabrics; Linen fabrics: dyeing, finishing, and printing; Linens and towels

(P-1969)

DECCOFELT CORPORATION

555 S Vermont Ave, Glendora (91741-6206)
P.O. Box 156 (91740-0156)
PHONE.................................626 963-8511
Gerald L Heinrich, *CEO*
▲ EMP: 24 EST: 1951
SQ FT: 33,000
SALES (est): 4.69MM **Privately Held**
Web: www.deccofelt.com
SIC: 2299 Felts and felt products

(P-1970)

ETRADE 24 INC

16600 Calneva Dr, Encino (91436-4130)
PHONE.................................818 712-0574
EMP: 25 EST: 2018
SALES (est): 2.06MM **Privately Held**
Web: us.etrade.com
SIC: 2299 2326 7389 Batting, wadding, padding and fillings; Medical and hospital uniforms, men's; Brokers' services

PRODUCTS & SVCS

(P-1971)
J H TEXTILES INC
2301 E 55th St, Vernon (90058-3435)
PHONE..............................323 585-4124
Jong Soon Hur, *CEO*
▲ **EMP: 25 EST:** 2003
SQ FT: 80,000
SALES (est): 1MM **Privately Held**
Web: www.jhtextilesinc.com
SIC: 2299 Textile mill waste and remnant
processing

(P-1972)
NEW HAVEN COMPANIES INC
13571 Vaughn St Unit E, San Fernando
(91340-3006)
PHONE..............................818 686-7020
Alex Franco, *Mgr*
EMP: 55
Web: www.newhaven-usa.com
SIC: 2299 3537 2298 2273 Batting, wadding,
padding and fillings; Industrial trucks and
tractors; Cordage and twine; Carpets and
rugs
PA: The New Haven Companies Inc
3951 Sw 30th Ave

(P-1973)
REDWOOD WELLNESS LLC
1950 W Corporate Way, Anaheim
(92801-5373)
PHONE..............................323 843-2676
Robert Rosenheck, *CEO*
EMP: 38 **EST:** 2017
SALES (est): 3.41MM **Privately Held**
SIC: 2299 Hemp yarn, thread, roving, and
textiles

2311 Men's And Boy's Suits And Coats

(P-1974)
AMWEAR USA INC
Also Called: Tactsquad
250 Benjamin Dr, Corona (92879-6508)
PHONE..............................800 858-6755
Hong Li Hawkins, *CEO*
Hang Guo, *Prin*
EMP: 34 **EST:** 2017
SALES (est): 1.6MM **Privately Held**
Web: www.tactsquad.com
SIC: 2311 5699 Men's and boys' uniforms;
Uniforms

(P-1975)
BARCO UNIFORMS INC
350 W Rosecrans Ave, Gardena
(90248-1728)
PHONE..............................310 323-7315
Ron Wagensiel, *CEO*
Danny Robertson, *
David Ayers, *
Kathy Peterson, *
David Aquino, *
◆ **EMP:** 372 **EST:** 1929
SQ FT: 74,000
SALES (est): 32.56MM **Privately Held**
Web: www.barcomade.com
SIC: 2311 2326 2337 Men's and boys'
uniforms; Men's and boy's work clothing;
Uniforms, except athletic: women's,
misses', and juniors'

(P-1976)
BLUE SPHERE INC
Also Called: Lucky-13 Apparel
10869 Portal Dr, Los Alamitos
(90720-2508)

PHONE..............................714 953-7555
Robert Kloetzly, *Pr*
▲ **EMP:** 30 **EST:** 1989
SALES (est): 748.18K **Privately Held**
Web: www.bluespheremfg.com
SIC: 2311 2331 2369 Men's and boy's suits
and coats; Women's and misses' blouses
and shirts; Girl's and children's outerwear,
nec

(P-1977)
NEW CHEF FASHION INC
3223 E 46th St, Los Angeles (90058-2407)
PHONE..............................323 581-0300
Chantal Salama, *CEO*
Guy Lucien Salama, *
▲ **EMP:** 70 **EST:** 1989
SALES (est): 8.66MM **Privately Held**
Web: www.newchef.com
SIC: 2311 2339 2326 5137 Men's and boys'
uniforms; Women's and misses' outerwear,
nec; Men's and boy's work clothing;
Uniforms, women's and children's

(P-1978)
NO SECOND THOUGHTS INC
Also Called: Nst
1333 30th St Ste D, San Diego
(92154-3487)
PHONE..............................619 428-5992
Audrey Swirsky, *Pr*
Onnie Ramos, *
EMP: 52 **EST:** 1999
SALES (est): 2.2MM **Privately Held**
Web: www.nst2.com
SIC: 2311 2329 2326 Men's and boys'
uniforms; Men's and boys' sportswear and
athletic clothing; Medical and hospital
uniforms, men's

(P-1979)
STRINGKING INC (PA)
19100 S Vermont Ave, Gardena
(90248-4413)
PHONE..............................310 503-8901
Jake Mccampbell, *CEO*
EMP: 23 **EST:** 2020
SALES (est): 50MM
SALES (corp-wide): 50MM **Privately Held**
Web: www.stringking.com
SIC: 2311 Men's and boys' uniforms

(P-1980)
TYLER TRAFFICANTE INC (PA)
Also Called: Richard Tyler
700 S Palm Ave, Alhambra (91803-1528)
PHONE..............................323 869-9299
Lisa Trafficante, *Pr*
Richard Tyler, *
EMP: 23 **EST:** 1986
SQ FT: 30,000
SALES (est): 3.83MM
SALES (corp-wide): 3.83MM **Privately Held**
Web: www.hbpta.org
SIC: 2311 2335 5611 5621 Tailored suits and
formal jackets; Gowns, formal; Suits, men's
; Dress shops

2321 Men's And Boy's Furnishings

(P-1981)
COTTON LINKS LLC
2990 Grace Ln, Costa Mesa (92626-4120)
PHONE..............................714 444-4700
Robby Khalek, *Managing Member*
EMP: 25 **EST:** 2011
SALES (est): 1.64MM **Privately Held**

Web: www.clca.co
SIC: 2321 Men's and boy's furnishings

(P-1982)
CREATIVE DESIGN INDUSTRIES
2587 Otay Center Dr, San Diego
(92154-7612)
PHONE..............................619 710-2525
Sylvia Habchi, *Pt*
Elie Habchi, *
▲ **EMP:** 125 **EST:** 1982
SQ FT: 15,000
SALES (est): 1.76MM **Privately Held**
SIC: 2321 5137 Men's and boy's furnishings;
Sportswear, women's and children's

(P-1983)
DISTRO WORLDWIDE LLC
Also Called: Get Primped
3400 S Main St, Los Angeles (90007-4412)
PHONE..............................818 849-0953
Jessica Raben, *Managing Member*
EMP: 25 **EST:** 2020
SALES (est): 466.96K **Privately Held**
SIC: 2321 Men's and boys' dress shirts

(P-1984)
JL DESIGN ENTERPRISES INC
Also Called: Jl Racing.com
37407 Industry Way, Murrieta (92563-3103)
PHONE..............................714 479-0240
Jolene Sparza, *Pr*
Kenneth Mills, *
▲ **EMP:** 63 **EST:** 1983
SALES (est): 3.91MM **Privately Held**
Web: www.jlrowing.com
SIC: 2321 Sport shirts, men's and boys':
from purchased materials

(P-1985)
JUST FOR FUN INC
Also Called: Jff Uniforms
557 Van Ness Ave, Torrance (90501-1424)
P.O. Box 9012 (90508-9012)
PHONE..............................310 320-1327
Corinne Stolz, *Pr*
Gary Stolz, *
▲ **EMP:** 24 **EST:** 1975
SQ FT: 11,000
SALES (est): 877.79K **Privately Held**
Web: www.jffuniforms.com
SIC: 2321 2337 2339 2326 Uniform shirts:
made from purchased materials; Uniforms,
except athletic: women's, misses', and
juniors'; Women's and misses' outerwear,
nec; Men's and boy's work clothing

(P-1986)
LISA FACTORY INC
144 N Swall Dr, Beverly Hills (90211-1943)
PHONE..............................213 536-5326
Abrar Ahmed, *CEO*
EMP: 52 **EST:** 2020
SALES (est): 48.66MM **Privately Held**
SIC: 2321 5199 Men's and boys' dress shirts
; General merchandise, non-durable

(P-1987)
TEXTILE UNLIMITED CORPORATION (PA)
20917 Higgins Ct, Torrance (90501-1723)
PHONE..............................310 263-7400
James Y Kim, *CEO*
Sam Lee, *Pr*
Stanley Kim, *Pr*
Yumi Park, *Sec*
◆ **EMP:** 61 **EST:** 1994
SALES (est): 1.84MM **Privately Held**
Web: www.tuc.net

SIC: 2321 2339 2329 2331 Men's and boy's
furnishings; Women's and misses' athletic
clothing and sportswear; Men's and boys'
athletic uniforms; Women's and misses'
blouses and shirts

(P-1988)
TOP HEAVY CLOTHING COMPANY INC (PA)
28381 Vincent Moraga Dr, Temecula
(92590-3653)
PHONE..............................951 442-8839
Tadd D Chilcott, *Pr*
Douglas Lo, *
▲ **EMP:** 65 **EST:** 1995
SQ FT: 40,000
SALES (est): 1.94MM **Privately Held**
Web: www.topheavyclothing.com
SIC: 2321 Men's and boys' dress shirts

2323 Men's And Boy's Neckwear

(P-1989)
ARMY OF HAPPY LLC
4580 Euclid Ave, San Diego (92115-3223)
PHONE..............................704 517-9890
Sean Brunle, *Prin*
EMP: 46 **EST:** 2013
SALES (est): 287.49K **Privately Held**
SIC: 2323 Men's and boy's neckwear

2325 Men's And Boy's Trousers And Slacks

(P-1990)
AG ADRIANO GOLDSCHMIED INC (PA)
Also Called: AG Jeans
2741 Seminole Ave Ste A, South Gate
(90280-5550)
PHONE..............................323 357-1111
U Yul Ku, *CEO*
Adriano Suarez, *
▲ **EMP:** 48 **EST:** 2000
SQ FT: 150,000
SALES (est): 22.87MM
SALES (corp-wide): 22.87MM **Privately
Held**
Web: www.agjeans.com
SIC: 2325 2339 5136 5137 Men's and boy's
trousers and slacks; Women's and misses'
outerwear, nec; Men's and boy's clothing;
Women's and children's clothing

(P-1991)
RCRV INC (PA)
Also Called: Rock Revival
4715 S Alameda St, Vernon (90058-2014)
PHONE..............................323 235-8070
Eric S Choi, *Pr*
Young S Cho, *
Kheim Nguyen, *Design Vice President*
◆ **EMP:** 23 **EST:** 2008
SQ FT: 70,000
SALES (est): 1.56MM
SALES (corp-wide): 1.56MM **Privately
Held**
Web: www.rockrevival.com
SIC: 2325 5699 Men's and boys' jeans and
dungarees; Customized clothing and
apparel

(P-1992)
ROB INC
Also Called: Robin's Jeans
6760 Foster Bridge Blvd, Bell Gardens
(90201-2030)

▲ = Import ▼ = Export
◆ = Import/Export

PHONE..............................562 806-5589
Robert Chretien, *CEO*
Gilberto Jimenez, *
◆ **EMP:** 90 **EST:** 2005
SQ FT: 26,000
SALES (est): 9.62MM **Privately Held**
Web: www.robinsjean.com
SIC: 2325 2339 2369 Jeans: men's, youths', and boys'; Women's and misses' culottes, knickers and shorts; Shorts (outerwear): girls' and children's

(P-1993)
TRUE RELIGION APPAREL INC (HQ)
Also Called: True Religion Brand Jeans
500 W 190th St Ste 300, Gardena (90248-4269)
PHONE..............................855 928-6124
Michael Buckley, *CEO*
Lynne Koplin, *Pr*
Peter F Collins, *CFO*
Kelly Gvildys, *VP Opers*
David Chiovetti, *Sr VP*
▲ **EMP:** 300 **EST:** 2005
SALES (est): 270.02MM
SALES (corp-wide): 350MM **Privately Held**
Web: www.truereligion.com
SIC: 2325 2339 2369 Men's and boy's trousers and slacks; Women's and misses' outerwear, nec; Jeans: girls', children's, and infants'
PA: Trlg Corporate Holdings, Llc
1888 Rosecrans Ave
323 266-3072

2326 Men's And Boy's Work Clothing

(P-1994)
FIGS INC
Also Called: Figs
2834 Colorado Ave Ste 100, Santa Monica (90404-3644)
PHONE..............................424 300-8330
Catherine Spear, *CEO*
Heather Hasson, *
Sarah Oughtred, *CFO*
▲ **EMP:** 354 **EST:** 2013
SALES (est): 545.65MM **Privately Held**
Web: www.wearfigs.com
SIC: 2326 5699 Work apparel, except uniforms; Work clothing

(P-1995)
IMAGE APPAREL FOR BUSINESS INC
1618 E Edinger Ave, Santa Ana (92705-5019)
PHONE..............................714 541-5247
Keith Knerr, *CEO*
Robert Duffield, *
EMP: 25 **EST:** 2009
SALES (est): 2.87MM **Privately Held**
Web: www.ia4biz.com
SIC: 2326 2339 2353 7213 Men's and boy's work clothing; Uniforms, athletic: women's, misses', and juniors'; Uniform hats and caps ; Linen supply

(P-1996)
IMAGE SOLUTIONS APPAREL INC
Also Called: Image Solutions
19571 Magellan Dr, Torrance (90502-1136)
PHONE..............................310 464-8991
Christopher Kelley, *Pr*
Paula Fox, *

▲ **EMP:** 111 **EST:** 1997
SQ FT: 4,500
SALES (est): 24.41MM **Privately Held**
Web: www.eimagesolutions.com
SIC: 2326 2337 Work uniforms; Uniforms, except athletic: women's, misses', and juniors'

(P-1997)
LA TRIUMPH INC
Also Called: Medgear
13336 Alondra Blvd, Cerritos (90703-2205)
PHONE..............................562 404-7657
Hasina Lakhani, *CEO*
Amin Lakhani, *
▲ **EMP:** 24 **EST:** 2003
SQ FT: 40,000
SALES (est): 2.39MM **Privately Held**
Web: www.pacuniforms.com
SIC: 2326 Medical and hospital uniforms, men's

(P-1998)
MED COUTURE INC
Also Called: Peaches
15301 Ventura Blvd, Sherman Oaks (91403-3102)
PHONE..............................214 231-2500
Barry Rothschild, *Pr*
Mark Wilcoxson, *
◆ **EMP:** 87 **EST:** 1987
SALES (est): 22.53MM **Privately Held**
Web: www.medcouture.com
SIC: 2326 Work uniforms

(P-1999)
OFFLINE INC (PA)
Also Called: Inspira
2931 S Alameda St, Vernon (90058-1326)
PHONE..............................213 742-9001
Charles Park, *Pr*
Karen Park, *CFO*
▲ **EMP:** 45 **EST:** 2002
SALES (est): 9.22MM
SALES (corp-wide): 9.22MM **Privately Held**
Web: www.offlineinc.com
SIC: 2326 2342 Industrial garments, men's and boys'; Foundation garments, women's

(P-2000)
PPD HOLDING LLC (PA)
10119 Jefferson Blvd, Culver City (90232-3519)
PHONE..............................310 733-2100
Paige Adams-geller, *Chief Design Officer*
EMP: 63 **EST:** 2012
SALES (est): 49.17MM
SALES (corp-wide): 49.17MM **Privately Held**
SIC: 2326 2331 6719 Men's and boy's work clothing; Women's and misses' blouses and shirts; Investment holding companies, except banks

(P-2001)
ROF LLC
Also Called: Ring of Fire
7800 Airport Business Pkwy, Van Nuys (91406-1731)
PHONE..............................818 933-4000
Eran Bitton, *
▲ **EMP:** 45 **EST:** 2007
SQ FT: 60,000
SALES (est): 4.97MM **Privately Held**
Web: www.ringoffireclothing.com
SIC: 2326 5651 5136 Men's and boy's work clothing; Jeans stores; Men's and boy's outerwear

(P-2002)
STRATEGIC DISTRIBUTION L P
Also Called: Cherokee Uniforms
15301 Ventura Blvd, Sherman Oaks (91403-3102)
▲ **EMP:** 240 **EST:** 2003
SALES (est): 36.27MM
SALES (corp-wide): 609.92MM **Privately Held**
Web: www.strategicpartners.net
SIC: 2326 2337 3143 3144 Work uniforms; Uniforms, except athletic: women's, misses', and juniors'; Men's footwear, except athletic; Women's footwear, except athletic
HQ: Careismatic Brands, Llc
15301 Ventura Blvd
Sherman Oaks CA 91403

2329 Men's And Boy's Clothing, Nec

(P-2003)
4 WHAT ITS WORTH INC (PA)
Also Called: Tyte Jeans
5815 Smithway St, Commerce (90040-1605)
PHONE..............................323 728-4503
Alden J Halpern, *Dir*
Kyle Soladay, *CFO*
◆ **EMP:** 50 **EST:** 1993
SQ FT: 38,000
SALES (est): 15.35MM **Privately Held**
Web: www.rewash.com
SIC: 2329 5961 5651 5699 Knickers, dress (separate): men's and boys'; Electronic shopping; Jeans stores; Designers, apparel

(P-2004)
A AND G INC (HQ)
Also Called: Alstyle Apparel
11296 Harrel St, Jurupa Valley (91752-3715)
PHONE..............................714 765-0400
Keith S Walters, *Pr*
Keith S Walters, *Prin*
Michael D Magill Same, *Sec*
◆ **EMP:** 627 **EST:** 1978
SALES (est): 17.04MM
SALES (corp-wide): 3.2B **Privately Held**
Web: www.americanapparel.com
SIC: 2329 2253 Athletic clothing, except uniforms: men's, youths' and boys'; T-shirts and tops, knit
PA: Les Vetements De Sport Gildan Inc
600 Boul De Maisonneuve O 33eme Etage
514 735-2023

(P-2005)
ANDARI FASHION INC
Also Called: Andari
9626 Telstar Ave, El Monte (91731-3004)
PHONE..............................626 575-2759
Wei Chen Wang, *Pr*
Lillian Wang, *
Charles Chang, *
◆ **EMP:** 120 **EST:** 1991
SQ FT: 50,000
SALES (est): 5.81MM **Privately Held**
Web: www.andari.com
SIC: 2329 2339 2253 5199 Sweaters and sweater jackets, men's and boys'; Women's and misses' accessories; Sweaters and sweater coats, knit; Art goods and supplies

(P-2006)
ASHWORTH INC
Also Called: Ashworth Studio

2765 Loker Ave W, Carlsbad (92010-6601)
PHONE..............................760 438-6610
◆ **EMP:** 598
Web: www.ashworth-golf.com
SIC: 2329 2339 2353 Men's and boys' sportswear and athletic clothing; Athletic clothing: women's, misses', and juniors'; Hats, caps, and millinery

(P-2007)
BIRDWELL ENTERPRISES INC
Also Called: Birdwell Beach Britches
8801 Research Dr, Irvine (92618-4236)
PHONE..............................714 557-7040
Vivian Richardson, *Pr*
William Robert Mann, *
EMP: 25 **EST:** 1962
SALES (est): 2.39MM **Privately Held**
Web: www.birdwellbeachbritches.com
SIC: 2329 2339 2326 Bathing suits and swimwear: men's and boys'; Women's and misses' outerwear, nec; Men's and boy's work clothing

(P-2008)
BOA INC
580 W Lambert Rd Ste L, Brea (92821-3913)
PHONE..............................714 256-8960
David Fleming, *Pr*
Pamela Fleming, *
▲ **EMP:** 34 **EST:** 1992
SQ FT: 6,000
SALES (est): 2.66MM **Privately Held**
Web: www.boausa.com
SIC: 2329 2337 2339 Men's and boys' sportswear and athletic clothing; Women's and misses' suits and coats; Women's and misses' outerwear, nec

(P-2009)
DC SHOES LLC (HQ)
Also Called: DC
5600 Argosy Ave Ste 100, Huntington Beach (92649-1063)
PHONE..............................714 889-4206
Arne Arens, *CEO*
Francis Roy, *CFO*
Maryn Miller, *Sec*
◆ **EMP:** 87 **EST:** 1993
SQ FT: 100,000
SALES (est): 9.63MM **Privately Held**
Web: www.dcshoes.com
SIC: 2329 5136 5137 5139 Men's and boys' sportswear and athletic clothing; Men's and boy's clothing; Women's and children's clothing; Footwear
PA: Authentic Brands Group Llc
1411 Broadway Fl 21

(P-2010)
FEAR OF GOD LLC
558 S Alameda St, Los Angeles (90013-1726)
PHONE..............................213 235-7985
Bastien Daguzan, *CEO*
Jerry Manuel, *Managing Member*
EMP: 39 **EST:** 2011
SALES (est): 5.56MM **Privately Held**
Web: www.fearofgod.com
SIC: 2329 Sweaters and sweater jackets, men's and boys'

(P-2011)
FETISH GROUP INC (PA)
Also Called: Tag Rag
1013 S Los Angeles St Ste 700, Los Angeles (90015-1793)
PHONE..............................323 587-7873
Raphael Sabbah, *CEO*

Orly Dahan, *
▲ **EMP:** 39 **EST:** 1986
SQ FT: 28,000
SALES (est): 2.3MM
SALES (corp-wide): 2.3MM **Privately Held**
Web: www.goldhawkclothing.com
SIC: 2329 2339 2369 Men's and boys' sportswear and athletic clothing; Women's and misses' athletic clothing and sportswear; Girl's and children's outerwear, nec

(P-2012)
GLOBAL CASUALS INC
18505 S Broadway, Gardena (90248-4632)
PHONE..................................310 817-2828
Jack Tsao, *Genl Mgr*
▲ **EMP:** 41 **EST:** 1995
SQ FT: 2,000
SALES (est): 423.63K
SALES (corp-wide): 49.41MM **Privately Held**
SIC: 2329 Men's and boys' sportswear and athletic clothing
PA: Seattle Pacific Industries, Inc.
1633 Wstlake Ave N Ste 30
253 872-8822

(P-2013)
HURLEY INTERNATIONAL LLC (PA)
Also Called: Hurley
3080 Bristol St, Costa Mesa (92626-3093)
PHONE..................................855 655-2515
Adrian L Bell, *
Ann M Miller, *
◆ **EMP:** 200 **EST:** 2001
SALES (est): 47.52MM
SALES (corp-wide): 47.52MM **Privately Held**
Web: www.hurley.com
SIC: 2329 5137 Knickers, dress (separate): men's and boys'; Women's and children's clothing

(P-2014)
JH DESIGN GROUP
940 W Washington Blvd, Los Angeles (90015-3312)
PHONE..................................213 747-5700
▲ **EMP:** 60 **EST:** 1987
SALES (est): 1.63MM **Privately Held**
Web: www.shopjhdesign.com
SIC: 2329 2337 Jackets (suede, leatherette, etc.), sport: men's and boys'; Women's and misses' capes and jackets

(P-2015)
JOE WELLS ENTERPRISES INC
Also Called: Max Muscle
1500 S Sunkist St Ste D, Anaheim (92806-5815)
P.O. Box 825 (92781-0825)
◆ **EMP:** 26
Web: www.maxmuscle.com
SIC: 2329 2023 2339 6794 Men's and boys' sportswear and athletic clothing; Dietary supplements, dairy and non-dairy based; Sportswear, women's; Franchises, selling or licensing

(P-2016)
JS APPAREL INC
1751 E Del Amo Blvd, Carson (90746-2938)
PHONE..................................310 631-6333
Ki S Kim, *CEO*
▲ **EMP:** 99 **EST:** 2004
SALES (est): 1.4MM **Privately Held**
Web: www.jsapparel.net

SIC: 2329 2339 Men's and boys' sportswear and athletic clothing; Women's and misses' outerwear, nec

(P-2017)
KORAL LLC
Also Called: Koral Activewear
1334 3rd Street Promenade Ste 200, Santa Monica (90401-1361)
PHONE..................................323 391-1060
Marcelo Kugel, *Managing Member*
Peter Koral, *
Liz Hampshire, *
Ilana Kugel, *
EMP: 36 **EST:** 2002
SALES (est): 808.38K **Privately Held**
Web: www.koral.com
SIC: 2329 2339 Men's and boys' sportswear and athletic clothing; Women's and misses' athletic clothing and sportswear

(P-2018)
L A CSTM AP & PROMOTIONS INC (PA)
2680 Temple Ave, Long Beach (90806-2209)
PHONE..................................562 595-1770
Chris Roybal, *Pr*
EMP: 33 **EST:** 1984
SQ FT: 10,000
SALES (est): 5.26MM **Privately Held**
Web: www.lacustomapparel.com
SIC: 2329 5136 Athletic clothing, except uniforms: men's, youths' and boys'; Men's and boy's clothing

(P-2019)
LEEMARC INDUSTRIES LLC
Also Called: Canari
340 Rancheros Dr Ste 172, San Marcos (92069-2980)
PHONE..................................760 598-0505
Christopher Robinson, *Managing Member*
▲ **EMP:** 55 **EST:** 2000
SALES (est): 5.32MM **Privately Held**
Web: www.canari.com
SIC: 2329 2339 Athletic clothing, except uniforms: men's, youths' and boys'; Women's and misses' outerwear, nec

(P-2020)
LIQUID GRAPHICS INC
2701 S Harbor Blvd Unit A, Santa Ana (92704-5839)
PHONE..................................949 486-3588
Josh Merrell, *Pr*
Mark Hyman, *
◆ **EMP:** 130 **EST:** 1997
SQ FT: 100,000
SALES (est): 21.79MM **Privately Held**
Web: www.liquidgraphicsmfg.com
SIC: 2329 Men's and boys' sportswear and athletic clothing

(P-2021)
MORTEX CORPORATION
Also Called: Mortex Apparel
40 E Verdugo Ave, Burbank (91502-1931)
P.O. Box 127 (27591-0127)
EMP: 225
SIC: 2329 2339 5699 Men's and boys' sportswear and athletic clothing; Sportswear, women's; Sports apparel

(P-2022)
NAUTICA OPCO LLC
950 Barrington Ave, Ontario (91764-5111)
PHONE..................................909 297-7243
EMP: 315
SALES (corp-wide): 3.08B **Privately Held**

SIC: 2329 2834 5136 5137 Men's and boys' sportswear and athletic clothing; Pharmaceutical preparations; Men's and boys' sportswear and work clothing; Women's and children's lingerie and undergarments
HQ: Nautica Opco Llc
125 Chubb Ave Fl 5
Lyndhurst NJ 07071
866 376-4184

(P-2023)
PATAGONIA INC (HQ)
Also Called: Great Pacific Patagonia
259 W Santa Clara St, Ventura (93001-2545)
P.O. Box 150 (93002-0150)
PHONE..................................805 643-8616
◆ **EMP:** 500 **EST:** 1979
SALES (est): 342.14MM
SALES (corp-wide): 415.44MM **Privately Held**
Web: www.patagonia.com
SIC: 2329 2339 Athletic clothing, except uniforms: men's, youths' and boys'; Athletic clothing: women's, misses', and juniors'
PA: Patagonia Works
259 W Santa Clara St
805 643-8616

(P-2024)
SPEEDO USA INC
Also Called: Speedo USA
6251 Katella Ave, Cypress (90630-5234)
PHONE..................................657 465-3800
Jim Gerson, *Pr*
◆ **EMP:** 400 **EST:** 1990
SQ FT: 10,000
SALES (est): 17.93MM **Privately Held**
Web: us.speedo.com
SIC: 2329 2339 2321 3949 Athletic clothing, except uniforms: men's, youths' and boys'; Bathing suits: women's, misses', and juniors'; Men's and boys' sports and polo shirts; Water sports equipment
HQ: Pentland Capital Limited
8 Manchester Square
London W1U 3
207 535-3820

(P-2025)
SPIRIT CLOTHING COMPANY (PA)
Also Called: Spirit Active Wear
2211 E 37th St, Los Angeles (90058-1427)
PHONE..................................213 784-0251
TOLL FREE: 800
Jake Ptasznik, *CEO*
▼ **EMP:** 102 **EST:** 1983
SQ FT: 19,000
SALES (est): 9.71MM
SALES (corp-wide): 9.71MM **Privately Held**
Web: www.spiritjersey.com
SIC: 2329 5651 5621 Men's and boys' sportswear and athletic clothing; Unisex clothing stores; Ready-to-wear apparel, women's

(P-2026)
SPIRIT CLOTHING COMPANY
2137 E 37th St, Vernon (90058-1416)
PHONE..................................213 784-5372
EMP: 70
SALES (corp-wide): 9.71MM **Privately Held**
Web: www.spiritjersey.com
SIC: 2329 5651 Men's and boys' sportswear and athletic clothing; Unisex clothing stores
PA: Spirit Clothing Company
2211 E 37th St

213 784-0251

(P-2027)
SPORTSROBE INC
8654 Hayden Pl, Culver City (90232-2902)
PHONE..................................310 559-3999
Allen Ruegsegger, *Pr*
Mary Ann Ruegsegger, *
EMP: 49 **EST:** 1979
SQ FT: 14,000
SALES (est): 535.57K **Privately Held**
SIC: 2329 Baseball uniforms: men's, youths', and boys'

(P-2028)
STREAMLINE DSIGN SLKSCREEN INC (PA)
Also Called: Old Guys Rule
1299 S Wells Rd, Ventura (93004-1901)
PHONE..................................805 884-1025
Thom Hill, *CEO*
▲ **EMP:** 60 **EST:** 1995
SQ FT: 33,000
SALES (est): 1.41MM **Privately Held**
Web: www.oldguysrule.com
SIC: 2329 5136 5611 Men's and boys' sportswear and athletic clothing; Men's and boy's clothing; Men's and boys' clothing stores

(P-2029)
THIRTY THREE THREADS INC (PA)
Also Called: Toesox
1330 Park Center Dr, Vista (92081-8300)
PHONE..................................877 486-3769
Barry Buchholtz, *CEO*
Joseph Patterson, *Dir*
Deedee Wilson, *Dir*
▲ **EMP:** 34 **EST:** 2004
SALES (est): 10.8MM
SALES (corp-wide): 10.8MM **Privately Held**
Web: www.thirtythreethreads.com
SIC: 2329 2252 Athletic clothing, except uniforms: men's, youths' and boys'; Socks

(P-2030)
TRAVISMATHEW LLC (HQ)
15202 Graham St, Huntington Beach (92649-1109)
PHONE..................................562 799-6900
Ryan Ellis, *CEO*
▲ **EMP:** 38 **EST:** 2007
SALES (est): 37.91MM
SALES (corp-wide): 4.28B **Publicly Held**
Web: www.travismathew.com
SIC: 2329 5699 5651 5661 Athletic clothing, except uniforms: men's, youths' and boys'; Sports apparel; Unisex clothing stores; Men's shoes
PA: Topgolf Callaway Brands Corp.
2180 Rutherford Rd
760 931-1771

(P-2031)
WATERFRONT DESIGN GROUP LLC
122 E Washington Blvd, Los Angeles (90015-3601)
PHONE..................................213 746-5800
EMP: 23 **EST:** 2001
SALES (est): 275.57K **Privately Held**
SIC: 2329 Men's and boys' sportswear and athletic clothing

(P-2032)
ZK ENTERPRISES INC
Also Called: Unique Sales

4368 District Blvd, Vernon (90058-3124)
PHONE..................213 622-7012
Ron Kelfer, *Pr*
Kathy Kelfer, *
EMP: 40 **EST:** 1985
SQ FT: 13,000
SALES (est): 1.59MM **Privately Held**
Web: www.uniquesalesco.com
SIC: 2329 2339 Athletic clothing, except
uniforms: men's, youths' and boys'; Jogging
and warmup suits; women's, misses', and
juniors'

2331 Women's And Misses' Blouses And Shirts

(P-2033)
ALPINESTARS USA
Also Called: Alpinestars USA
2780 W 237th St, Torrance (90505-5270)
PHONE..................310 891-0222
Giovanni Mazzarolo, *CEO*
▲ **EMP:** 82 **EST:** 1986
SQ FT: 28,380
SALES (est): 9.27MM
SALES (corp-wide): 333.6MM **Privately Held**
Web: www.asbydf.com
SIC: 2331 2326 3751 5571 Women's and
misses' blouses and shirts; Men's and boy's
work clothing; Motorcycle accessories;
Motorcycle parts and accessories
HQ: Alpinestars Spa
Viale Enrico Fermi 5
Asolo TV 31011
042 352-9571

(P-2034)
BLUPRINT CLOTHING CORP
4851 S Santa Fe Ave, Vernon
(90058-2103)
PHONE..................323 780-4347
Ju Hyun Kim, *CEO*
Liz Lee, *
▲ **EMP:** 75 **EST:** 2005
SALES (est): 30MM **Privately Held**
Web: www.bluprintcorp.com
SIC: 2331 Women's and misses' blouses
and shirts

(P-2035)
FORTUNE CASUALS LLC (PA)
Also Called: Judy Ann
10119 Jefferson Blvd, Culver City
(90232-3519)
PHONE..................310 733-2100
Fred Kayne, *Managing Member*
◆ **EMP:** 100 **EST:** 1999
SQ FT: 40,000
SALES (est): 2.21MM
SALES (corp-wide): 2.21MM **Privately Held**
SIC: 2331 2339 2321 T-shirts and tops,
women's: made from purchased materials;
Slacks: women's, misses', and juniors';
Men's and boy's furnishings

(P-2036)
GLORIA LANCE INC (PA)
Also Called: Electric Designs
15616 S Broadway, Gardena (90248-2211)
P.O. Box 3941 (90247-7519)
PHONE..................310 767-4400
Robert Hempling, *Pr*
Zvia Hempling, *
Miguel Lopez, *
Gloria Lopez, *
◆ **EMP:** 90 **EST:** 1983
SQ FT: 25,000

SALES (est): 4.49MM
SALES (corp-wide): 4.49MM **Privately Held**
SIC: 2331 2339 2335 Blouses, women's and
juniors': made from purchased material;
Sportswear, women's; Bridal and formal
gowns

(P-2037)
GURU KNITS INC
Also Called: Antex Knitting Mills
225 W 38th St, Los Angeles (90037-1405)
PHONE..................323 235-9424
Kevin Port, *CEO*
William Tenenblatt, *
◆ **EMP:** 60 **EST:** 2007
SALES (est): 4.08MM **Privately Held**
Web: www.aceross.com
SIC: 2331 2361 Women's and misses'
blouses and shirts; Blouses: girls',
children's, and infants'

(P-2038)
HARARI INC (PA)
9646 Brighton Way, Los Angeles (90016)
PHONE..................323 734-5302
EMP: 45 **EST:** 1979
SALES (est): 1.29MM
SALES (corp-wide): 1.29MM **Privately Held**
Web: www.harariinc.com
SIC: 2331 5621 Women's and misses'
blouses and shirts; Women's clothing stores

(P-2039)
HARKHAM INDUSTRIES INC (PA)
Also Called: Jonathan Martin
857 S San Pedro St Ste 300, Los Angeles
(90014-2435)
PHONE..................323 586-4600
Uri Harkham, *Pr*
◆ **EMP:** 50 **EST:** 1974
SQ FT: 140,000
SALES (est): 4.5MM
SALES (corp-wide): 4.5MM **Privately Held**
Web: www.jonathanmartin.com
SIC: 2331 2335 2337 2339 Blouses,
women's and juniors': made from
purchased material; Women's, junior's, and
misses' dresses; Skirts, separate: women's,
misses', and juniors'; Women's and misses'
outerwear, nec

(P-2040)
JUDY ANN OF CALIFORNIA INC
Also Called: Landing Gear
1936 Mateo St, Los Angeles (90021-2833)
PHONE..................213 623-9233
Michael Geller, *Pr*
EMP: 150 **EST:** 1985
SALES (est): 2.31MM **Privately Held**
SIC: 2331 2339 T-shirts and tops, women's:
made from purchased materials; Slacks:
women's, misses', and juniors'

(P-2041)
K TOO
Also Called: K-Too
800 E 12th St Ste 117, Los Angeles
(90021-2199)
PHONE..................213 747-7766
Jae Hee Kim, *CEO*
Kelley Kim, *
◆ **EMP:** 41 **EST:** 2007
SALES (est): 2.55MM **Privately Held**
Web: www.ktoousa.com
SIC: 2331 Women's and misses' blouses
and shirts

(P-2042)
KANDY KISS OF CALIFORNIA INC
14761 Califa St, Van Nuys (91411-3107)
▲ **EMP:** 60
Web: www.perfectdomain.com
SIC: 2331 2335 2361 Women's and misses'
blouses and shirts; Women's, junior's, and
misses' dresses; Shirts: girls', children's,
and infants'

(P-2043)
KSM GARMENT INC
Also Called: Alex and Jane
5613 Maywood Ave, Maywood
(90270-2503)
PHONE..................323 585-8811
EMP: 42
SIC: 2331 Women's and misses' blouses
and shirts

(P-2044)
LA MAMBA LLC
150 N Myers St, Los Angeles (90033-2109)
PHONE..................323 526-3526
Fabian Oberfeld, *Managing Member*
Denni Kopelan, *
Stephen Brown, *
▲ **EMP:** 31 **EST:** 2008
SALES (est): 3.36MM **Privately Held**
SIC: 2331 Blouses, women's and juniors':
made from purchased material

(P-2045)
LEEBE APPAREL INC
Also Called: Leebe
3499 S Main St, Los Angeles (90007-4413)
PHONE..................323 897-5585
Won Joo Lee, *Pr*
▲ **EMP:** 25 **EST:** 2007
SQ FT: 8,000
SALES (est): 895.68K **Privately Held**
Web: www.leebeapparel.com
SIC: 2331 Women's and misses' blouses
and shirts

(P-2046)
LF SPORTSWEAR INC (PA)
Also Called: Furst
13336 Beach Ave, Marina Del Rey
(90292-5622)
PHONE..................310 437-4100
Phillip L Furst, *CEO*
Marsha Furst, *
Steve Katz, *
◆ **EMP:** 30 **EST:** 1980
SALES (est): 9.4MM
SALES (corp-wide): 9.4MM **Privately Held**
Web: www.lfstores.com
SIC: 2331 5137 2211 Women's and misses'
blouses and shirts; Women's and children's
dresses, suits, skirts, and blouses; Denims

(P-2047)
MF INC
Also Called: Welovefine
2010 E 15th St, Los Angeles (90021-2823)
PHONE..................213 627-2498
Danish Gajiani, *CEO*
Faizan Bakali, *Pr*
Bill Bussiere, *CFO*
Dean Allen, *CMO*
◆ **EMP:** 120 **EST:** 1999
SQ FT: 700,000
SALES (est): 3.55MM
SALES (corp-wide): 638.25MM **Privately Held**

SIC: 2331 2253 T-shirts and tops, women's:
made from purchased materials; T-shirts
and tops, knit
HQ: Mad Engine Global, Llc
1017 Grandview Ave
Glendale CA 91201
858 558-5270

(P-2048)
MONROW LLC
Also Called: Monrow
1404 S Main St Ste C, Los Angeles
(90015-2566)
PHONE..................213 741-6007
Megan George, *Pr*
EMP: 29 **EST:** 2007
SALES (est): 4.19MM **Privately Held**
Web: www.monrow.com
SIC: 2331 T-shirts and tops, women's: made
from purchased materials

(P-2049)
MXF DESIGNS INC
Also Called: Nally & Millie
5327 Valley Blvd, Los Angeles
(90032-3930)
PHONE..................323 266-1451
James Park, *Pr*
Nally Park, *Stockholder*
▼ **EMP:** 95 **EST:** 1994
SALES (est): 2.46MM **Privately Held**
Web: www.nallyandmillie.com
SIC: 2331 Blouses, women's and juniors':
made from purchased material

(P-2050)
MYMICHELLE COMPANY LLC (HQ)
Also Called: My Michelle
13077 Temple Ave, La Puente
(91746-1418)
PHONE..................626 934-4166
Arthur Gordon, *Pr*
Arthur Gordon, *Pr*
Roger D Joseph, *
◆ **EMP:** 300 **EST:** 1948
SQ FT: 600,000
SALES (est): 2.44MM
SALES (corp-wide): 373.66MM **Privately Held**
SIC: 2331 2337 2335 2361 Blouses,
women's and juniors': made from
purchased material; Skirts, separate:
women's, misses', and juniors';
Dresses,paper, cut and sewn; Blouses:
girls', children's, and infants'
PA: Kellwood Company, Llc
13071 Temple Ave
626 934-4122

(P-2051)
NOTHING TO WEAR INC (PA)
Also Called: Figure 8
630 Maple Ave, Torrance (90503-5001)
PHONE..................310 328-0408
Cindy Nunes Freeman, *Pr*
Darrin Freeman, *
◆ **EMP:** 35 **EST:** 1991
SQ FT: 18,000
SALES (est): 2.19MM **Privately Held**
Web: www.goldensunbrand.com
SIC: 2331 2335 2339 Women's and misses'
blouses and shirts; Women's, junior's, and
misses' dresses; Women's and misses'
accessories

(P-2052)
PAIGE LLC (HQ)
Also Called: Paige Premium Denim
10119 Jefferson Blvd, Culver City
(90232-3519)

PHONE...................................310 733-2100
Paige Adams-geller, *Chief Design Officer*
Walter Lacher, *
Michael Henschel, *
Caroline Blanchard, *
◆ **EMP:** 150 **EST:** 2004
SQ FT: 40,000
SALES (est): 49.17MM
SALES (corp-wide): 49.17MM **Privately Held**
Web: www.paige.com
SIC: 2331 2326 Women's and misses' blouses and shirts; Men's and boy's work clothing
PA: Ppd Holding, Llc
    10119 Jefferson Blvd
    310 733-2100

(P-2053)
PROJECT SOCIAL T LLC
615 S Clarence St, Los Angeles (90023-1107)
PHONE...................................323 266-4500
Mike Chodler, *Managing Member*
EMP: 30 **EST:** 2011
SALES (est): 2.96MM **Privately Held**
Web: www.projectsocialt.com
SIC: 2331 5137 5621 Women's and misses' blouses and shirts; Women's and children's clothing; Women's clothing stores

(P-2054)
STONY APPAREL CORP (PA)
Also Called: Eyeshadow
1201 S Grand Ave, Los Angeles (90015-2105)
PHONE...................................323 981-9080
Lu Kong, *CEO*
Anthony Millar, *CFO*
Sarah Van Zee, *Sec*
▲ **EMP:** 175 **EST:** 1996
SALES (est): 32.12MM **Privately Held**
Web: www.stonyapparel.com
SIC: 2331 2335 7389 Women's and misses' blouses and shirts; Women's, junior's, and misses' dresses; Apparel designers, commercial

(P-2055)
TIANELLO INC
Also Called: Tianello By Steve Barraza
138 W 38th St, Los Angeles (90037-1404)
PHONE...................................323 231-0599
Steven Barraza, *Pr*
▲ **EMP:** 185 **EST:** 1992
SQ FT: 25,000
SALES (est): 1.55MM **Privately Held**
Web: www.tianello.com
SIC: 2331 5621 2339 Women's and misses' blouses and shirts; Women's clothing stores ; Women's and misses' outerwear, nec

(P-2056)
UNGER FABRIK LLC (PA)
18525 Railroad St, City Of Industry (91748-1316)
PHONE...................................626 469-8080
Yongbin Luo, *CEO*
◆ **EMP:** 110 **EST:** 1998
SQ FT: 300,000
SALES (est): 5.56MM
SALES (corp-wide): 5.56MM **Privately Held**
Web: www.oneworldapparel.com
SIC: 2331 Women's and misses' blouses and shirts

2335 Women's, Junior's, And Misses' Dresses

(P-2057)
AGS USA LLC
Also Called: American Garment Sewing
1210 Rexford Ave, Pasadena (91107-1713)
PHONE...................................323 588-2200
▲ **EMP:** 150
Web: www.agsusallc.com
SIC: 2335 2326 2331 2339 Women's, junior's, and misses' dresses; Men's and boy's work clothing; Women's and misses' blouses and shirts; Jeans: women's, misses', and juniors'

(P-2058)
AQUARIUS RAGS LLC (PA)
Also Called: ABS By Allen Schwartz
15821 Ventura Blvd Ste 270, Encino (91436-4775)
PHONE...................................213 895-4400
Allen Schwartz, *Managing Member*
▲ **EMP:** 75 **EST:** 2003
SALES (est): 5.35MM
SALES (corp-wide): 5.35MM **Privately Held**
SIC: 2335 Women's, junior's, and misses' dresses

(P-2059)
AVALON APPAREL LLC
1901 W Center St, Colton (92324-6509)
PHONE...................................323 440-4344
EMP: 93
Web: www.avalonapparel.com
SIC: 2335 Ensemble dresses: women's, misses', and juniors'
PA: Avalon Apparel, Llc
    2520 W 6th St

(P-2060)
AVALON APPAREL LLC (PA)
Also Called: Disorderly Kids
2520 W 6th St, Los Angeles (90057-3174)
PHONE...................................323 581-3511
Elliot Schutzer, *Managing Member*
Jason Schutzer, *
Jill Grossman, *
Terri Cohen, *
EMP: 165 **EST:** 2004
SQ FT: 5,000
SALES (est): 24.58MM **Privately Held**
Web: www.avalonapparel.com
SIC: 2335 Ensemble dresses: women's, misses', and juniors'

(P-2061)
CALIFORNIA BLUE APPAREL INC
Also Called: Ever Blue
245 W 28th St, Los Angeles (90007-3312)
PHONE...................................213 745-5400
▲ **EMP:** 30
Web: www.californiablue.com
SIC: 2335 2339 2331 Women's, junior's, and misses' dresses; Women's and misses' outerwear, nec; Women's and misses' blouses and shirts

(P-2062)
CAROL ANDERSON INC (PA)
Also Called: Carol Anderson By Invitation
18700 S Laurel Park Rd, Rancho Dominguez (90220-6003)
PHONE...................................310 638-3333
Jan Janura, *Pr*
Carol M Anderson, *

Jan A Janura, *
◆ **EMP:** 25 **EST:** 1977
SQ FT: 50,000
SALES (est): 4.69MM
SALES (corp-wide): 4.69MM **Privately Held**
Web: www.cabionline.com
SIC: 2335 2339 Women's, junior's, and misses' dresses; Shorts (outerwear): women's, misses', and juniors'

(P-2063)
CHOON INC (PA)
Also Called: Pezeme
1443 E 4th St, Los Angeles (90033-4214)
PHONE...................................213 225-2500
Choon S Nakamura, *Pr*
Daniel Nakamura, *
◆ **EMP:** 31 **EST:** 1972
SALES (est): 2.32MM
SALES (corp-wide): 2.32MM **Privately Held**
Web: www.choon.com
SIC: 2335 Women's, junior's, and misses' dresses

(P-2064)
COMPLETE CLOTHING COMPANY (PA)
Also Called: Willow
4950 E 49th St, Vernon (90058-2736)
PHONE...................................213 892-1188
Eleanor M Sanchez, *CEO*
▲ **EMP:** 43 **EST:** 1995
SQ FT: 30,000
SALES (est): 10.67MM **Privately Held**
Web: www.shopwillow.com
SIC: 2335 2339 2337 2331 Women's, junior's, and misses' dresses; Sportswear, women's; Women's and misses' suits and coats; Women's and misses' blouses and shirts

(P-2065)
J C TRIMMING COMPANY INC
Also Called: JC Industries
3800 S Hill St, Los Angeles (90037-1416)
PHONE...................................323 235-4458
Eric Shin, *CEO*
◆ **EMP:** 65 **EST:** 1993
SALES (est): 4.45MM **Privately Held**
SIC: 2335 2326 Women's, junior's, and misses' dresses; Men's and boy's work clothing

(P-2066)
JODI KRISTOPHER LLC (PA)
Also Called: City Triangles
1950 Naomi Ave, Los Angeles (90011-1342)
PHONE...................................323 890-8000
Adir Haroni, *CEO*
Juduth Naka, *
▲ **EMP:** 83 **EST:** 1990
SQ FT: 100,000
SALES (est): 23.55MM **Privately Held**
Web: www.davidkristopher.com
SIC: 2335 Women's, junior's, and misses' dresses

(P-2067)
JWC STUDIO INC (PA)
Also Called: Johnny Was Showroom
2423 E 23rd St, Los Angeles (90058-1201)
PHONE...................................323 231-8222
Eli Levite, *Pr*
▼ **EMP:** 26 **EST:** 1994
SQ FT: 30,000
SALES (est): 2.3MM
SALES (corp-wide): 2.3MM **Privately Held**

Web: www.johnnywas.com
SIC: 2335 Women's, junior's, and misses' dresses

(P-2068)
L A GLO INC
Also Called: Roberta
1451 Hi Point St, Los Angeles (90035-4100)
PHONE...................................323 932-0091
Elaine Johnson, *Pr*
Alan Johnson, *
▲ **EMP:** 50 **EST:** 1979
SQ FT: 25,000
SALES (est): 1.35MM **Privately Held**
SIC: 2335 Women's, junior's, and misses' dresses

(P-2069)
PRIVATE BRAND MDSG CORP
Also Called: Jody of California
214 W Olympic Blvd, Los Angeles (90015-1693)
P.O. Box 260923 (91426-0923)
PHONE...................................213 749-0191
William Berman, *Pr*
Rochelle Berman, *
John Berman, *
EMP: 23 **EST:** 1954
SQ FT: 6,000
SALES (est): 1.33MM **Privately Held**
Web: privatebm.openfos.com
SIC: 2335 2339 Women's, junior's, and misses' dresses; Sportswear, women's

(P-2070)
PROMISES PROMISES INC
3121 S Grand Ave, Los Angeles (90007-3816)
PHONE...................................213 749-7725
Eugene M Hardy, *CEO*
Sean Hardy, *
▲ **EMP:** 29 **EST:** 1978
SALES (est): 2.3MM **Privately Held**
SIC: 2335 Women's, junior's, and misses' dresses

(P-2071)
ST JOHN KNITS INTL INC
Also Called: St John Boutiques
17421 Derian Ave, Irvine (92614-5817)
PHONE...................................949 863-1171
Kelly Gray, *Mgr*
EMP: 4000
SALES (corp-wide): 239.44MM **Privately Held**
Web: www.stjohnknits.com
SIC: 2335 Women's, junior's, and misses' dresses
HQ: St. John Knits International, Incorporated
    5515 E La Palma Ave
    Anaheim CA 92807
    949 863-1171

(P-2072)
SUBLITEX INC
Also Called: Sublitex Sublimation Tech
1515 E 15th St, Los Angeles (90021-2711)
PHONE...................................323 582-9596
EMP: 35 **EST:** 2008
SALES (est): 3.4MM **Privately Held**
SIC: 2335 7389 Women's, junior's, and misses' dresses; Printing broker

(P-2073)
TLMF INC
Also Called: Big Strike
1515 E 15th St, Los Angeles (90021-2711)
PHONE...................................212 764-2334

▲ = Import ▼ = Export
◆ = Import/Export

▲ **EMP:** 100
Web: www.heartsoul.org
SIC: 2335 2337 Women's, junior's, and misses' dresses; Women's and misses' suits and coats

(P-2074)
TRINITY SPORTS INC
2067 E 55th St, Vernon (90058-3441)
PHONE.................323 277-9288
▲ **EMP:** 300
Web: www.trinitysportsinc.com
SIC: 2335 2339 2325 Women's, junior's, and misses' dresses; Women's and misses' outerwear, nec; Men's and boy's trousers and slacks

(P-2075)
TRIXXI CLOTHING COMPANY INC (PA)
Also Called: Ash & Violet
6817 E Acco St, Commerce (90040-1901)
PHONE.................323 585-4200
Annette Soufrine, *CEO*
Leslie Flores, *
▲ **EMP:** 49 **EST:** 2001
SQ FT: 35,000
SALES (est): 3.08MM
SALES (corp-wide): 3.08MM **Privately Held**
Web: www.trixxi.com
SIC: 2335 2331 Women's, junior's, and misses' dresses; Blouses, women's and juniors': made from purchased material

2337 Women's And Misses' Suits And Coats

(P-2076)
KOMAROV ENTERPRISES INC
Also Called: Kisca
10939 Venice Blvd, Los Angeles (90034-7015)
PHONE.................213 244-7000
Dimitri Komarov, *Pr*
Dimitri Leiberman, *
Shelley Komvarov, *
▲ **EMP:** 75 **EST:** 1997
SALES (est): 9.52MM **Privately Held**
Web: www.komarov.com
SIC: 2337 2331 Women's and misses' suits and coats; Women's and misses' blouses and shirts

(P-2077)
R B III ASSOCIATES INC
Also Called: Teamwork Athletic Apparel
2386 Faraday Ave Ste 125, Carlsbad (92008-7263)
PHONE.................760 471-5370
Matthew Lehrer, *CEO*
Dave Caserta, *
Andy Lehrer, *
▲ **EMP:** 150 **EST:** 1976
SALES (est): 24.58MM **Privately Held**
SIC: 2337 2329 Uniforms, except athletic: women's, misses', and juniors'; Men's and boys' athletic uniforms

(P-2078)
TOPSON DOWNS CALIFORNIA INC
Also Called: TOPSON DOWNS OF CALIFORNIA, INC.
3545 Motor Ave, Los Angeles (90034-4806)
PHONE.................310 558-0300
Kris Scott, *Brnch Mgr*
EMP: 131

SALES (corp-wide): 45.02MM **Privately Held**
Web: www.topsondowns.com
SIC: 2337 5621 Women's and misses' suits and coats; Ready-to-wear apparel, women's
PA: Topson Downs Of California, Llc
3840 Watseka Ave
310 558-0300

2339 Women's And Misses' Outerwear, Nec

(P-2079)
AARON CORPORATION
Also Called: J P Sportswear
2645 Industry Way, Lynwood (90262-4007)
PHONE.................323 235-5959
Paul Shechet, *Pr*
Francisco Balleste, *
▲ **EMP:** 170 **EST:** 1955
SALES (est): 3.38MM **Privately Held**
Web: www.jpsportswear.us
SIC: 2339 Women's and misses' athletic clothing and sportswear

(P-2080)
APPAREL PROD SVCS GLOBL LLC (PA)
Also Called: APS Global
8954 Lurline Ave, Chatsworth (91311-6103)
P.O. Box 5011 (91365-5011)
PHONE.................818 700-3700
◆ **EMP:** 42 **EST:** 2013
SQ FT: 15,000
SALES (est): 5.56MM **Privately Held**
SIC: 2339 2329 Women's and misses' athletic clothing and sportswear; Men's and boys' sportswear and athletic clothing

(P-2081)
BB CO INC
Also Called: Wild Lizard
1753 E 21st St, Los Angeles (90058-1006)
PHONE.................213 550-1158
Kyoung K Frazier, *Pr*
Kyoung K Frazier, *Pr*
Cecy Mendoza, *
▲ **EMP:** 30 **EST:** 1998
SQ FT: 22,000
SALES (est): 7.5MM **Privately Held**
SIC: 2339 Women's and misses' athletic clothing and sportswear

(P-2082)
BE BOP CLOTHING
Also Called: Rebel Jeans
5833 Avalon Blvd, Los Angeles (90003-1307)
PHONE.................323 846-0121
Guillermo Granados, *Pr*
Marcus Sphatt, *
Michael Harb, *
EMP: 350 **EST:** 1987
SQ FT: 100,000
SALES (est): 19.8MM **Privately Held**
SIC: 2339 Sportswear, women's

(P-2083)
BOARDRIDERS WHOLESALE LLC
Dakine
6201 Oak Cyn Ste 100, Irvine (92618-5232)
PHONE.................949 916-3060
EMP: 45
SALES (corp-wide): 106.29MM **Privately Held**
Web: www.quiksilver.com

SIC: 2339 2331 Women's and misses' outerwear, nec; Women's and misses' blouses and shirts
PA: Boardriders Wholesale, Llc
5600 Argosy Ave Ste 100

(P-2084)
CARBON 38 INC
2866 Westbrook Ave, Los Angeles (90046-1249)
PHONE.................888 723-5838
Katherine Johnson, *CEO*
EMP: 90 **EST:** 2012
SALES (est): 7.86MM
SALES (corp-wide): 25.07MM **Privately Held**
Web: www.carbon38.com
SIC: 2339 Sportswear, women's
PA: Bc Brands, Llc
38 E 29th St

(P-2085)
CITIZENS OF HUMANITY LLC (PA)
Also Called: Goldsign
5715 Bickett St, Huntington Park (90255-2624)
PHONE.................323 923-1240
Jerome Dahan, *CEO*
Amy Williams, *Pr*
◆ **EMP:** 158 **EST:** 2005
SQ FT: 70,000
SALES (est): 47.21MM
SALES (corp-wide): 47.21MM **Privately Held**
Web: www.citizensofhumanity.com
SIC: 2339 Jeans: women's, misses', and juniors'

(P-2086)
CLOTHING ILLUSTRATED INC (PA)
Also Called: Love Stitch
836 Traction Ave, Los Angeles (90013-1816)
PHONE.................213 403-9950
Danny Hanasab Foruzesh, *CEO*
▲ **EMP:** 35 **EST:** 2002
SALES (est): 9.58MM **Privately Held**
Web: www.shoplovestitch.com
SIC: 2339 Women's and misses' accessories

(P-2087)
CREW KNITWEAR LLC (PA)
Also Called: Hiatus
660 S Myers St, Los Angeles (90023-1015)
PHONE.................323 526-3888
Paricia Franklin, *CEO*
Chris Y Jung, *Pr*
Peter Jung, *CFO*
▲ **EMP:** 58 **EST:** 2001
SQ FT: 39,000
SALES (est): 13.6MM **Privately Held**
Web: www.crewknitwear.com
SIC: 2339 Women's and misses' outerwear, nec

(P-2088)
DAKINE EQUIPMENT LLC
19400 Harborgate Way, Torrance (90501-1354)
PHONE.................424 276-3618
Shane Wallace, *
EMP: 25 **EST:** 2018
SALES (est): 4.19MM
SALES (corp-wide): 4.91MM **Privately Held**
SIC: 2339 2329 Snow suits: women's, misses', and juniors'; Ski and snow clothing: men's and boys'

PA: Jr286, Inc.
20100 S Vermont Ave
877 464-5301

(P-2089)
DAVID GRMENT CTNG FSING SVC IN
Also Called: Clothng/Pparel/Uniform/ppe Mfg
5008 S Boyle Ave, Vernon (90058-3904)
PHONE.................323 216-1574
Mario Alvarado, *CEO*
David Alvarado, *
Mario Alvarado, *VP*
▲ **EMP:** 45 **EST:** 1987
SQ FT: 15,000
SALES (est): 1.67MM **Privately Held**
SIC: 2339 2326 2329 Women's and misses' athletic clothing and sportswear; Men's and boy's work clothing; Men's and boys' sportswear and athletic clothing

(P-2090)
DDA HOLDINGS INC
Also Called: A Commom Thread
834 S Broadway Ste 600, Los Angeles (90014-3217)
PHONE.................213 624-5200
Anthony Graham, *CEO*
Sandra Balestier, *
▲ **EMP:** 25 **EST:** 2007
SQ FT: 15,000
SALES (est): 8.47MM **Privately Held**
Web: www.ddaholdings.com
SIC: 2339 Women's and misses' athletic clothing and sportswear

(P-2091)
DESIGN TODAYS INC (PA)
11707 Cetona Way, Porter Ranch (91326-4604)
PHONE.................213 745-3091
Sung Ok Hong, *Pr*
EMP: 26 **EST:** 1987
SALES (est): 1.02MM **Privately Held**
SIC: 2339 Women's and misses' outerwear, nec

(P-2092)
DMBM LLC
2445 E 12th St Ste C, Los Angeles (90021-2954)
PHONE.................714 321-6032
David Chong, *Owner*
EMP: 23
SIC: 2339 2369 Women's and misses' outerwear, nec; Girl's and children's outerwear, nec
PA: Dmbm, Llc
2701 S Santa Fe Ave

(P-2093)
DNAM APPAREL INDUSTRIES LLC
Also Called: Ed Hardy
4938 Triggs St, Commerce (90022-4832)
PHONE.................323 859-0114
Henri Levy, *Managing Member*
Michael Cohen, *
▲ **EMP:** 32 **EST:** 2004
SALES (est): 1.22MM **Privately Held**
SIC: 2339 5137 Service apparel, washable: women's; Women's and children's clothing

(P-2094)
ESKA INC
1370 Mirasol St, Los Angeles (90023-3109)
PHONE.................323 846-3700
Suk Cho, *Pr*
EMP: 25 **EST:** 2014

SALES (est): 983.78K **Privately Held**
SIC: **2339** Athletic clothing: women's, misses', and juniors'

(P-2095)
EV R INC
Also Called: Skinny Minnie
3400 Slauson Ave, Maywood (90270-2525)
PHONE..................................323 312-5400
▲ EMP: 50
SIC: **2339** Athletic clothing: women's, misses', and juniors'

(P-2096)
FINESSE APPAREL INC
Also Called: Finesse
815 Fairview Ave Unit 101, South Pasadena (91030-2490)
PHONE..................................213 747-7077
▲ EMP: 45
Web: www.finesseusa.com
SIC: **2339** Women's and misses' athletic clothing and sportswear

(P-2097)
GAZE USA INC
2011 E 25th St, Vernon (90058-1127)
PHONE..................................213 622-0022
Ji S Hong, *CEO*
Stephen S Whang, *
EMP: 25 EST: 2010
SALES (est): 816.98K **Privately Held**
SIC: **2339 5651 3999** Women's and misses' athletic clothing and sportswear; Unisex clothing stores; Bristles, dressing of

(P-2098)
GOOD AMERICAN LLC (PA)
1601 Vine St, Los Angeles (90028-8806)
P.O. Box 888 (90232-0888)
PHONE..................................213 357-5100
Emma Grede, *CEO*
Khloe Kardashian, *
EMP: 42 EST: 2016
SALES (est): 19.95MM
SALES (corp-wide): 19.95MM **Privately Held**
Web: www.goodamerican.com
SIC: **2339 5137 5621** Jeans: women's, misses', and juniors'; Women's and children's clothing; Women's clothing stores

(P-2099)
HEARTS DELIGHT
4035 N Ventura Ave, Ventura (93001-1163)
PHONE..................................805 648-7123
Deborah Mesker, *Owner*
EMP: 27 EST: 1986
SQ FT: 2,000
SALES (est): 765.29K **Privately Held**
Web: shop.heartsdelightclothiers.com
SIC: **2339 5621** Women's and misses' outerwear, nec; Boutiques

(P-2100)
HEATHER BY BORDEAUX INC
Also Called: Bordeaux
5983 Malburg Way, Vernon (90058-3945)
PHONE..................................213 622-0555
Afshin Raminfar, *CEO*
▲ EMP: 39 EST: 2003
SALES (est): 2.88MM **Privately Held**
Web: www.heatherfashion.com
SIC: **2339** Service apparel, washable: women's

(P-2101)
IT JEANS INC
Also Called: It Campus

2425 E 38th St, Vernon (90058-1708)
PHONE..................................323 588-2156
▲ EMP: 23
Web: www.itjeans.com
SIC: **2339 2369** Jeans: women's, misses', and juniors'; Girl's and children's outerwear, nec

(P-2102)
J & F DESIGN INC
Also Called: Next Generation
2042 Garfield Ave, Commerce (90040-1804)
PHONE..................................323 526-4444
Jack Farshi, *Pr*
◆ EMP: 75 EST: 1991
SQ FT: 100,000
SALES (est): 18MM **Privately Held**
Web: www.bobbyjackbrand.com
SIC: **2339** Sportswear, women's

(P-2103)
JANIN
10031 Hunt Ave, South Gate (90280-6310)
PHONE..................................323 564-0995
Jose Estevez, *Owner*
EMP: 210 EST: 1987
SQ FT: 10,000
SALES (est): 821.28K **Privately Held**
SIC: **2339** Neckwear and ties: women's, misses', and juniors'

(P-2104)
JAYA APPAREL GROUP LLC (PA)
2761 Fruitland Ave Fl 2, Los Angeles (90058-3607)
PHONE..................................323 584-3500
Jane Siskin, *Managing Member*
Don Lewis, *
Jalal Elbasri, *
◆ EMP: 67 EST: 2005
SALES (est): 24.28MM
SALES (corp-wide): 24.28MM **Privately Held**
Web: www.jayaapparelgroup.com
SIC: **2339 2337** Women's and misses' jackets and coats, except sportswear; Women's and misses' suits and skirts

(P-2105)
JD/CMC INC
Also Called: Color ME Cotton
2834 E 11th St, Los Angeles (90023-3406)
PHONE..................................818 767-2260
Mari Tatevosian, *Pr*
Anait Grigorian, *
◆ EMP: 35 EST: 1991
SQ FT: 12,000
SALES (est): 2.15MM **Privately Held**
Web: www.cmcclick.com
SIC: **2339** Women's and misses' outerwear, nec

(P-2106)
JNJ APPAREL INC
18788 Fairfield Rd, Porter Ranch (91326-3922)
PHONE..................................323 584-9700
Chan Hyoung Park, *Pr*
▲ EMP: 30 EST: 2001
SALES (est): 604.29K **Privately Held**
SIC: **2339** Women's and misses' athletic clothing and sportswear

(P-2107)
JOLYN CLOTHING COMPANY LLC
16390 Pacific Coast Hwy Ste 201, Huntington Beach (92649-1851)
PHONE..................................714 794-2149

Warren Lief Pedersen, *Pr*
Ann Dawson, *
Brandon Molina, *
EMP: 30 EST: 2007
SALES (est): 3.03MM **Privately Held**
Web: www.jolyn.com
SIC: **2339 5621** Women's and misses' athletic clothing and sportswear; Women's sportswear

(P-2108)
JOWETT GARMENTS FACTORY INC
Also Called: Jowett Group
10359 Rush St, South El Monte (91733-3341)
PHONE..................................626 350-0515
◆ EMP: 40
Web: www.jowett.com
SIC: **2339** Athletic clothing: women's, misses', and juniors'

(P-2109)
JT DESIGN STUDIO INC (PA)
Also Called: 860, Shameless, Hot Wire
860 S Los Angeles St Ste 912, Los Angeles (90014-3319)
PHONE..................................213 891-1500
Ted Cooper, *Pr*
Robert Grossman, *
▲ EMP: 24 EST: 1998
SALES (est): 2.97MM
SALES (corp-wide): 2.97MM **Privately Held**
Web: www.jtdesignstudio.com
SIC: **2339** Women's and misses' athletic clothing and sportswear

(P-2110)
JUST FOR WRAPS INC (PA)
Also Called: A-List
4871 S Santa Fe Ave, Vernon (90058-2103)
PHONE..................................213 239-0503
Vrajesh Lal, *CEO*
Rakesh Lal, *
▲ EMP: 130 EST: 1980
SALES (est): 9.93MM
SALES (corp-wide): 9.93MM **Privately Held**
Web: muralsjustforkids.weebly.com
SIC: **2339 2335 2337** Sportswear, women's; Women's, junior's, and misses' dresses; Women's and misses' suits and coats

(P-2111)
KAYO OF CALIFORNIA (PA)
Also Called: Kayo Clothing Company
11854 Alameda St, Lynwood (90262-4019)
PHONE..................................323 233-6107
Jack Ostrovsky, *Ch Bd*
Jeffrey Michaels, *
Jonathan Kaye, *
Annabelle Wall, *
▲ EMP: 45 EST: 1968
SALES (est): 7.93MM
SALES (corp-wide): 7.93MM **Privately Held**
Web: www.kayo.com
SIC: **2339 2337** Sportswear, women's; Skirts, separate: women's, misses', and juniors'

(P-2112)
KIM & CAMI PRODUCTIONS INC
2950 Leonis Blvd, Vernon (90058-2916)
PHONE..................................323 584-1300
Kimberly A Hiatt, *Pr*
Cami Gasmer, *
▲ EMP: 40 EST: 1999

SQ FT: 1,000
SALES (est): 2.41MM **Privately Held**
SIC: **2339** Sportswear, women's

(P-2113)
KLK FORTE INDUSTRY INC (PA)
Also Called: Honey Punch
1535 Rio Vista Ave, Los Angeles (90023-2619)
PHONE..................................323 415-9181
Katherine Kim, *CEO*
◆ EMP: 45 EST: 2012
SQ FT: 30,000
SALES (est): 1.79MM
SALES (corp-wide): 1.79MM **Privately Held**
SIC: **2339** Women's and misses' outerwear, nec

(P-2114)
KORAL INDUSTRIES LLC (PA)
Also Called: Koral Los Angeles
1334 3rd Street Promenade Ste 200, Santa Monica (90401-1361)
PHONE..................................323 585-5343
Peter Koral, *
▲ EMP: 31 EST: 2012
SALES (est): 8.71MM
SALES (corp-wide): 8.71MM **Privately Held**
Web: www.koral.com
SIC: **2339** Service apparel, washable: women's

(P-2115)
L&L MANUFACTURING CO INC
Also Called: L & L Distributors
12400 Wilshire Blvd Ste 360, Los Angeles (90025-1059)
EMP: 270
SIC: **2339 2329 2369 8741** Sportswear, women's; Men's and boys' sportswear and athletic clothing; Girl's and children's outerwear, nec; Management services

(P-2116)
LAT LLC
Also Called: G Girl Clothing
2618 Fruitland Ave, Vernon (90058-2220)
PHONE..................................323 233-3017
Simon Cho, *Managing Member*
Sung H Cho, *
▲ EMP: 40 EST: 1999
SALES (est): 3.04MM **Privately Held**
Web: www.latapparel.com
SIC: **2339** Women's and misses' outerwear, nec

(P-2117)
LEE THOMAS INC (PA)
13800 S Figueroa St, Los Angeles (90061-1026)
PHONE..................................310 532-7560
Lee Opolinsky, *Pr*
Thomas Mahoney, *
EMP: 30 EST: 1981
SQ FT: 45,000
SALES (est): 2.27MM
SALES (corp-wide): 2.27MM **Privately Held**
SIC: **2339** Women's and misses' athletic clothing and sportswear

(P-2118)
LEFTY PRODUCTION CO LLC
318 W 9th St Ste 1010, Los Angeles (90015-1546)
PHONE..................................323 515-9266
Marta Abrams, *Managing Member*
EMP: 36 EST: 2012

SALES (est): 561.67K **Privately Held**
Web: www.leftyproductionco.com
SIC: 2339 Athletic clothing: women's,
misses', and juniors'

(P-2119)
MARIKA LLC
5553 Bandini Blvd B, Bell (90201-6421)
PHONE.............................323 888-7755
▲ **EMP:** 100 **EST:** 1982
SQ FT: 160,000
SALES (est): 3.83MM **Privately Held**
Web: www.marika.com
SIC: 2339 5137 Athletic clothing: women's,
misses', and juniors'; Women's and
children's outerwear

(P-2120)
MAX LEON INC (PA)
Also Called: Max Studio.com
3100 New York Dr Ste 100, Pasadena
(91107-1554)
P.O. Box 70879 (91117)
PHONE.............................626 797-6886
Leon Max, *CEO*
Ernest E Hoffer, *
Kerri Specker, *
▲ **EMP:** 85 **EST:** 1979
SQ FT: 65,000
SALES (est): 24.43MM
SALES (corp-wide): 24.43MM **Privately
Held**
Web: www.maxstudio.com
SIC: 2339 5632 Sportswear, women's;
Apparel accessories

(P-2121)
MGT INDUSTRIES INC (PA)
Also Called: California Dynasty
13889 S Figueroa St, Los Angeles
(90061-1025)
PHONE.............................310 516-5900
Jeffrey P Mirvis, *CEO*
Alessandra Strahl, *
Mike Brooks, *
Phil Nathanson, *
▲ **EMP:** 68 **EST:** 1983
SQ FT: 82,000
SALES (corp-wide): 4.18K **Privately Held**
Web: www.mgtind.com
SIC: 2339 Women's and misses' outerwear,
nec

(P-2122)
MONTEREY CANYON LLC (PA)
1515 E 15th St, Los Angeles (90021-2711)
PHONE.............................213 741-0209
Richard Sneider, *
▲ **EMP:** 70 **EST:** 1977
SALES (est): 5.41MM
SALES (corp-wide): 5.41MM **Privately
Held**
SIC: 2339 Sportswear, women's

(P-2123)
NEW FASHION PRODUCTS INC
3600 E Olympic Blvd, Los Angeles
(90023-3121)
PHONE.............................310 354-0090
▲ **EMP:** 170 **EST:** 1975
SALES (est): 3.59MM **Privately Held**
SIC: 2339 2325 Slacks: women's, misses',
and juniors'; Men's and boy's trousers and
slacks

(P-2124)
PACIFIC ATHLETIC WEAR INC
7340 Lampson Ave, Garden Grove
(92841-2902)

PHONE.............................714 751-8006
John Hillenbrand, *Pr*
Gabriela Hillenbrand, *
▲ **EMP:** 70 **EST:** 1994
SALES (est): 10.03MM **Privately Held**
Web: www.pacificathleticwear.com
SIC: 2339 Uniforms, athletic: women's,
misses', and juniors'

(P-2125)
PATTERSON KINCAID LLC
5175 S Soto St, Vernon (90058-3620)
PHONE.............................323 584-3559
Jane Siskin, *Managing Member*
Jilali Elbasri, *
◆ **EMP:** 32 **EST:** 2010
SQ FT: 35,000
SALES (est): 1.05MM
SALES (corp-wide): 24.28MM **Privately
Held**
SIC: 2339 Women's and misses' outerwear,
nec
PA: Jaya Apparel Group Llc
2761 Frtland Ave Fl 2 Ste
323 584-3500

(P-2126)
PIET RETIEF INC
Also Called: Peter Cohen Companies
1914 6th Ave, Los Angeles (90018-1124)
PHONE.............................323 732-8312
Peter Cohen, *Pr*
Lee Stuart Cox, *
Anna Cohen, *
EMP: 34 **EST:** 1983
SQ FT: 4,800
SALES (est): 1.37MM **Privately Held**
SIC: 2339 Sportswear, women's

(P-2127)
POINT CONCEPTION INC
Also Called: Kechika
23121 Arroyo Vis Ste A, Rcho Sta Marg
(92688-2633)
PHONE.............................949 589-6890
Jeff Jung, *CEO*
Jamie Jung, *
Victoria Jung, *
◆ **EMP:** 35 **EST:** 1979
SQ FT: 20,000
SALES (est): 974.67K **Privately Held**
Web: www.kechika.com
SIC: 2339 Bathing suits: women's, misses',
and juniors'

(P-2128)
RAJ MANUFACTURING LLC
Also Called: Rajswim
2712 Dow Ave, Tustin (92780-7210)
PHONE.............................714 838-3110
Barinder Bhathal, *Pr*
Jennifer Renish, *Contrlr*
EMP: 25 **EST:** 2006
SALES (est): 2.14MM **Privately Held**
Web: www.rajswim.com
SIC: 2339 Bathing suits: women's, misses',
and juniors'

(P-2129)
RHAPSODY CLOTHING INC
Also Called: Epilogue and Arrested
810 E Pico Blvd Ste 24, Los Angeles
(90021-2375)
PHONE.............................213 614-8887
Bryan Kang, *CEO*
Yoon Mi Kang, *VP*
▲ **EMP:** 65 **EST:** 1994
SALES (est): 1.26MM **Privately Held**
Web: www.rhapsodyclothing.com

SIC: 2339 Shorts (outerwear): women's,
misses', and juniors'

(P-2130)
ROTAX INCORPORATED
Also Called: Gamma
2940 Leonis Blvd, Vernon (90058-2916)
P.O. Box 58071 (90058-0071)
PHONE.............................323 589-5999
Arthur Torssien, *Pr*
Ripsick Kepenekian, *
▲ **EMP:** 40 **EST:** 1993
SALES (est): 1.93MM **Privately Held**
Web: www.rotax1.com
SIC: 2339 2329 Women's and misses'
outerwear, nec; Men's and boys'
sportswear and athletic clothing

(P-2131)
SECOND GENERATION INC
Also Called: Fish Bowl
21650 Oxnard St Ste 500, Woodland Hills
(91367-4911)
▲ **EMP:** 68 **EST:** 1996
SQ FT: 11,000
SALES (est): 3.18MM **Privately Held**
Web: www.bebopjeans.com
SIC: 2339 5621 Women's and misses'
athletic clothing and sportswear; Women's
clothing stores

(P-2132)
SOLOW
2907 Glenview Ave, Los Angeles
(90039-2823)
PHONE.............................323 664-7772
▲ **EMP:** 30 **EST:** 1999
SQ FT: 20,000
SALES (est): 662.01K **Privately Held**
SIC: 2339 Sportswear, women's

(P-2133)
ST JOHN KNITS INC (DH)
Also Called: St John Knits
5515 E La Palma Ave Ste 100, Anaheim
(92807-2127)
PHONE.............................877 750-1171
Andy Lew, *CEO*
Andrew Wong, *
Christina Zabat-fran, *Sec*
EMP: 262 **EST:** 1962
SALES (est): 59MM
SALES (corp-wide): 239.44MM **Privately
Held**
Web: www.stjohncafe.com
SIC: 2339 2253 2389 Women's and misses'
accessories; Knit outerwear mills; Men's
miscellaneous accessories
HQ: St. John Knits International,
Incorporated
5515 E La Palma Ave
Anaheim CA 92807
949 863-1171

(P-2134)
ST JOHN KNITS INTL INC (HQ)
Also Called: St John Knits
5515 E La Palma Ave, Anaheim
(92807-2127)
PHONE.............................949 863-1171
Geoffroy Van Raemdonck, *CEO*
Glenn Mcmahon, *CEO*
Bernd Beetz, *
Tammy Storino, *
Bruce Fetter, *
◆ **EMP:** 150 **EST:** 1962
SALES (est): 239.44MM
SALES (corp-wide): 239.44MM **Privately
Held**
Web: www.stjohnknits.com

SIC: 2339 Sportswear, women's
PA: Gray Vestar Investors Llc
17622 Armstrong Ave
949 863-1171

(P-2135)
TCJ MANUFACTURING LLC
Also Called: Velvet Heart
2744 E 11th St, Los Angeles (90023-3404)
PHONE.............................213 488-8400
▲ **EMP:** 43 **EST:** 2008
SALES (est): 2.84MM **Privately Held**
Web: www.velveteheart.com
SIC: 2339 Athletic clothing: women's,
misses', and juniors'

(P-2136)
TCW TRENDS INC
2886 Columbia St, Torrance (90503-3808)
PHONE.............................310 533-5177
Charanjiv Mansingh, *CEO*
▲ **EMP:** 28 **EST:** 2001
SQ FT: 10,000
SALES (est): 4.95MM **Privately Held**
Web: www.tcwusa.com
SIC: 2339 2326 5137 Aprons, except rubber
or plastic: women's, misses', juniors'; Men's
and boy's work clothing; Coordinate sets:
women's, children's, and infants'

(P-2137)
TEMPTED APPAREL CORP
4516 Loma Vista Ave, Vernon
(90058-2602)
PHONE.............................323 859-2480
Don X Ho, *CEO*
Tsun Kit Luk, *
▲ **EMP:** 58 **EST:** 1996
SALES (est): 1.99MM **Privately Held**
Web: www.temptedapparel.com
SIC: 2339 Women's and misses' outerwear,
nec

(P-2138)
THE ORIGINAL CULT INC
Also Called: Lip Service
40 E Verdugo Ave, Burbank (91502-1931)
PHONE.............................323 260-7308
▲ **EMP:** 71
SIC: 2339 2311 2399 Women's and misses'
outerwear, nec; Men's and boy's suits and
coats; Emblems, badges, and insignia

(P-2139)
**TOAD & CO INTERNATIONAL
INC (PA)**
Also Called: Toad & Co
2020 Alameda Padre Serra Ste 125, Santa
Barbara (93103-1768)
P.O. Box 21508 (93121-1508)
PHONE.............................800 865-8623
Gordon Seabury, *Pr*
▲ **EMP:** 35 **EST:** 1991
SQ FT: 7,000
SALES (est): 17.72MM **Privately Held**
Web: www.toadandco.com
SIC: 2339 2329 Women's and misses'
athletic clothing and sportswear; Men's and
boys' sportswear and athletic clothing

(P-2140)
TREIVUSH INDUSTRIES INC
Also Called: B B Blu
940 W Washington Blvd, Los Angeles
(90015-3312)
PHONE.............................213 745-7774
Menachem Treivush, *Pr*
EMP: 100 **EST:** 1983
SQ FT: 125,000
SALES (est): 2.18MM **Privately Held**

PRODUCTS & SVCS

Web: www.treivush.com
SIC: 2339 5137 Sportswear, women's;
Sportswear, women's and children's

(P-2141)
VICTORY PROFESSIONAL PDTS INC
Also Called: Victory Koredrry
5601 Engineer Dr, Huntington Beach
(92649-1123)
PHONE....................714 887-0621
Marc V Spitaleri, *CEO*
Marc Spitaleri, *
▲ EMP: 28 EST: 1979
SQ FT: 8,500
SALES (est): 3MM Privately Held
Web: www.victorybuiltusa.com
SIC: 2339 2329 2393 Women's and misses'
athletic clothing and sportswear; Men's and
boys' sportswear and athletic clothing;
Textile bags

(P-2142)
W & W CONCEPT INC
Also Called: Perseption
4890 S Alameda St, Vernon (90058-2806)
PHONE....................323 803-3090
Wonsook Chong, *Pr*
Jay Joo, *
▲ EMP: 55 EST: 1996
SQ FT: 45,000
SALES (est): 8.3MM Privately Held
Web: www.perseption.com
SIC: 2339 5137 Sportswear, women's;
Women's and children's outerwear

(P-2143)
YMI JEANSWEAR INC
1015 Wall St Ste 115, Los Angeles
(90015-2392)
PHONE....................213 746-6681
Ronan Vered, *Bmch Mgr*
EMP: 54
SALES (corp-wide): 7.52MM Privately
Held
Web: www.ymijeans.com
SIC: 2339 2325 Jeans: women's, misses',
and juniors'; Men's and boys' jeans and
dungarees
PA: Y.M.I Jeanswear, Inc.
1155 S Boyle Ave
323 581-7700

(P-2144)
ZOOEY APPAREL INC
1526 Cloverfield Blvd Ste C, Santa Monica
(90404-3773)
PHONE....................310 315-2880
Alice Heller, *Pr*
Viet D.o.s., *COO*
EMP: 24 EST: 2003
SQ FT: 5,000
SALES (est): 285.74K Privately Held
SIC: 2339 Women's and misses' outerwear,
nec

2341 Women's And Children's Underwear

(P-2145)
402 SHOES INC
Also Called: Trashy Lingerie
402 N La Cienega Blvd, West Hollywood
(90048-1907)
PHONE....................323 655-5437
Mitchell Shrier, *Pr*
Tracy Shrier, *
EMP: 23 EST: 1974
SQ FT: 6,000

SALES (est): 832.64K Privately Held
Web: www.trashy.com
SIC: 2341 5632 2322 Women's and
children's nightwear; Lingerie and corsets
(underwear); Men's and boy's underwear
and nightwear

(P-2146)
AFR APPAREL INTERNATIONAL INC
Also Called: Parisa Lingerie & Swim Wear
25365 Prado De La Felicidad, Calabasas
(91302-3652)
PHONE....................818 773-5000
Amir Moghadam, *Pr*
Brenda J Moghadam, *
▲ EMP: 60 EST: 1992
SALES (est): 25MM Privately Held
Web: www.parisausa.com
SIC: 2341 2342 2369 5137 Women's and
children's nightwear; Bras, girdles, and
allied garments; Bathing suits and
swimwear: girls', children's, and infants';
Lingerie

(P-2147)
CHARLES KOMAR & SONS INC
Also Called: Komar Distribution Services
11850 Riverside Dr, Jurupa Valley
(91752-1001)
PHONE....................951 934-1377
Lisa Casillas, *Bmch Mgr*
EMP: 307
SALES (corp-wide): 359.75MM Privately
Held
Web: www.komarbrands.com
SIC: 2341 Women's and children's
underwear
PA: Charles Komar & Sons, Inc.
90 Hudson St Fl 9
212 725-1500

(P-2148)
DELTA GALIL USA INC
777 S Alameda St Fl 3, Los Angeles
(90021-1657)
PHONE....................213 488-4859
EMP: 307
Web: www.deltagalil.com
SIC: 2341 Women's and children's
undergarments
HQ: Delta Galil Usa Inc.
1 Harmon Plz Fl 5
Secaucus NJ 07094
201 902-0055

(P-2149)
GUESS INC (PA)
Also Called: GUESS?
1444 S Alameda St, Los Angeles
(90021-2433)
PHONE....................213 765-3100
Carlos Alberini, *CEO*
Alex Yemenidjian, *Non-Executive Chairman of the Board*
Paul Marciano, *CCO*
Dennis Secor, *Interim Chief Financial Officer*
Fabrice Benarouche, *CAO*
◆ EMP: 700 EST: 1981
SQ FT: 341,700
SALES (est): 2.78B
SALES (corp-wide): 2.78B Publicly Held
Web: www.guess.com
SIC: 2341 2325 2369 6794 Women's and
children's underwear; Men's and boy's
trousers and slacks; Girl's and children's
outerwear, nec; Copyright buying and
licensing

(P-2150)
HONEST COMPANY INC (PA)
Also Called: Honest
12130 Millennium Ste 500, Los Angeles
(90094-2946)
PHONE....................310 917-9199
Nikolaos Vlahos, *CEO*
Carla Vernon, *CEO*
James D White, *Ch Bd*
Rick Rexing, *CRO*
▲ EMP: 156 EST: 2011
SQ FT: 46,518
SALES (est): 344.37M Publicly Held
Web: www.honest.com
SIC: 2341 2833 5961 Panties: women's,
misses', children's, and infants'; Vitamins,
natural or synthetic: bulk, uncompounded;
Catalog and mail-order houses

(P-2151)
NATIONAL CORSET SUPPLY HOUSE (PA)
Also Called: Louden Madelon
3240 E 26th St, Vernon (90058-8008)
PHONE....................323 261-0265
Roy Schlobohm, *CEO*
◆ EMP: 65 EST: 1948
SQ FT: 25,000
SALES (est): 6.24MM
SALES (corp-wide): 6.24MM Privately
Held
Web: www.shirleyofhollywood.com
SIC: 2341 5137 Women's and children's
undergarments; Corsets

(P-2152)
SELECTRA INDUSTRIES CORP
5166 Alcoa Ave, Vernon (90058-3716)
PHONE....................323 581-8500
John Neman, *Pr*
Mark Neman, *
Malek Neman, *
▲ EMP: 85 EST: 2000
SQ FT: 30,000
SALES (est): 4.77MM Privately Held
Web: www.selectraindustries.com
SIC: 2341 2339 Women's and children's
underwear; Sportswear, women's

2342 Bras, Girdles, And Allied Garments

(P-2153)
BRAGEL INTERNATIONAL INC
Also Called: Brava
3383 Pomona Blvd, Pomona (91768-3297)
PHONE....................909 598-8808
Clotilde Chen, *CEO*
Alice Chen, *
Kenny Chen, *Stockholder*
▲ EMP: 45 EST: 1989
SQ FT: 30,000
SALES (est): 5.03MM Privately Held
Web: www.bragel.com
SIC: 2342 Brassieres

(P-2154)
FOH GROUP INC (PA)
Also Called: Fredericks.com
6255 W Sunset Blvd Ste 2212, Los Angeles
(90028-7403)
◆ EMP: 38 EST: 1935
SQ FT: 23,000
SALES (est): 24.88MM
SALES (corp-wide): 24.88MM Privately
Held

SIC: 2342 2339 5621 5632 Bras, girdles,
and allied garments; Women's and misses'
outerwear, nec; Women's clothing stores;
Women's accessory and specialty stores

(P-2155)
NOBBE ORTHOPEDICS INC
3010 State St, Santa Barbara (93105-3304)
PHONE....................805 687-7508
Ralph W Nobbe, *Pr*
Rolf Schiefel, *
Erwin Nobbe, *
EMP: 29 EST: 1964
SQ FT: 2,850
SALES (est): 2.49MM
SALES (corp-wide): 1.12B Privately Held
Web: www.nobbeorthopedics.com
SIC: 2342 5999 Corsets and allied garments
; Orthopedic and prosthesis applications
PA: Hanger, Inc.
10910 Domain Dr Ste 300
512 777-3800

2353 Hats, Caps, And Millinery

(P-2156)
AGRON INC (PA)
2440 S Sepulveda Blvd Ste 201, Los
Angeles (90064-1748)
PHONE....................310 473-7223
Wade Siegel, *Pr*
Anton Schiff, *
◆ EMP: 57 EST: 1989
SQ FT: 10,000
SALES (est): 10.11MM Privately Held
Web: sales.agron.com
SIC: 2353 2393 3949 3171 Hats, caps, and
millinery; Canvas bags; Sporting and
athletic goods, nec; Women's handbags
and purses

(P-2157)
AUGUST HAT COMPANY INC (PA)
Also Called: August Accessories
2021 Calle Yucca, Thousand Oaks
(91360-2257)
PHONE....................805 983-4651
Roque Valladares, *Pr*
Ann Valladares, *Sec*
▲ EMP: 23 EST: 1990
SALES (est): 1.66MM Privately Held
SIC: 2353 2381 2339 Hats, caps, and
millinery; Fabric dress and work gloves;
Scarves, hoods, headbands, etc.: women's

(P-2158)
CALI-FAME LOS ANGELES INC
Also Called: Kennedy Athletics
20934 S Santa Fe Ave, Carson
(90810-1131)
PHONE....................310 747-5263
Michael G Kennedy, *CEO*
Brian Kennedy, *
Timothy Kennedy, *
Linelle Kennedy, *
▲ EMP: 92 EST: 1925
SQ FT: 30,000
SALES (est): 9.11MM Privately Held
Web: www.caliheadwear.com
SIC: 2353 Uniform hats and caps

(P-2159)
LEGENDARY HOLDINGS INC
Also Called: Legendary Headwear
2295 Paseo De Las Americas Ste 19, San
Diego (92154-7909)
PHONE....................619 872-6100

◆ **EMP:** 38
Web: www.legendaryholdings.com
SIC: 2353 Hats, caps, and millinery

(P-2160)
MAGIC APPAREL GROUP INC
Also Called: Magic Apparel & Magic
Headwear
1100 W Walnut St, Compton (90220-5114)
P.O. Box 2308 (90274-8308)
PHONE..............................310 223-4000
◆ **EMP:** 30
SIC: 2353 Baseball caps

(P-2161)
NIKE INC
Nike
20001 Ellipse, Foothill Ranch (92610-3001)
PHONE..............................949 616-4042
Matt Ross, *Mgr*
EMP: 27
SALES (corp-wide): 51.36B **Publicly Held**
Web: www.nike.com
SIC: 2353 5137 5136 Baseball caps;
Women's and children's clothing; Men's and
boy's clothing
PA: Nike, Inc.
1 Sw Bowerman Dr
503 671-6453

2361 Girl's And Children's Dresses, Blouses

(P-2162)
ALL ACCESS APPAREL INC (PA)
Also Called: Self Esteem
1515 Gage Rd, Montebello (90640-6613)
PHONE..............................323 889-4300
Richard Clareman, *CEO*
Andrea Rankin, *
Michael Conway, *
◆ **EMP:** 130 **EST:** 1997
SQ FT: 122,000
SALES (est): 17.6MM **Privately Held**
Web: www.selfesteemclothing.com
SIC: 2361 2335 2331 Girl's and children's
dresses, blouses; Women's, junior's, and
misses' dresses; Women's and misses'
blouses and shirts

(P-2163)
AST SPORTSWEAR INC (PA)
2701 E Imperial Hwy, Brea (92821-6713)
P.O. Box 17219 (92817-7219)
PHONE..............................714 223-2030
Shoaib Dadabhoy, *CEO*
Taher Dadabhoy, *Sec*
Abdul Rashid, *COO*
▲ **EMP:** 85 **EST:** 1995
SQ FT: 42,000
SALES (est): 18.52MM **Privately Held**
Web: www.astsportswear.com
SIC: 2361 2331 5699 T-shirts and tops:
girls', children's, and infants'; T-shirts and
tops, women's: made from purchased
materials; Sports apparel

(P-2164)
EVY OF CALIFORNIA INC
2042 Garfield Ave, Commerce
(90040-1804)
P.O. Box 812030 (90081-0018)
PHONE..............................213 746-4647
▲ **EMP:** 140
Web: www.evy.com
SIC: 2361 2369 Dresses: girls', children's,
and infants'; Warm-up, jogging, and sweat
suits: girls' and children's

(P-2165)
KWDZ MANUFACTURING LLC (PA)
337 S Anderson St, Los Angeles
(90033-3742)
PHONE..............................323 526-3526
Gene Bonilla, *
◆ **EMP:** 75 **EST:** 1999
SQ FT: 45,000
SALES (est): 1.7MM
SALES (corp-wide): 1.7MM **Privately Held**
Web: www.calfashion.org
SIC: 2361 T-shirts and tops: girls', children's,
and infants'

(P-2166)
LEIGH JERRY CALIFORNIA INC (PA)
Also Called: Jerry Leigh Entertainment AP
7860 Nelson Rd, Van Nuys (91402-6044)
PHONE..............................818 909-6200
Andrew Leigh, *CEO*
Barbara Leigh, *
◆ **EMP:** 245 **EST:** 1962
SQ FT: 40,000
SALES (est): 95.93MM
SALES (corp-wide): 95.93MM **Privately Held**
Web: www.jerryleigh.com
SIC: 2361 5137 Girl's and children's
dresses, blouses; Sportswear, women's
and children's

(P-2167)
MISYD CORP (PA)
Also Called: Ruby Rox
30 Fremont Pl, Los Angeles (90005-3858)
PHONE..............................213 742-1800
Robert Borman, *Pr*
Joseph Hanasab, *
▲ **EMP:** 79 **EST:** 1993
SQ FT: 35,000
SALES (est): 2.32MM **Privately Held**
Web: www.misyd.com
SIC: 2361 Shirts: girls', children's, and
infants'

2369 Girl's And Children's Outerwear, Nec

(P-2168)
BODYWAVES INC (PA)
Also Called: Aks, Amy K Su
12362 Knott St, Garden Grove
(92841-2802)
PHONE..............................714 898-9900
EMP: 47 **EST:** 1986
SALES (est): 3.16MM
SALES (corp-wide): 3.16MM **Privately Held**
Web: www.elleven.com
SIC: 2369 2335 2331 2325 Girl's and
children's outerwear, nec; Dresses,paper,
cut and sewn; Women's and misses'
blouses and shirts; Men's and boy's
trousers and slacks

(P-2169)
FRANKIES BIKINIS LLC
Also Called: Frankies Bikinis
4030 Del Rey Ave, Venice (90292-5602)
PHONE..............................323 354-4133
Francheska Aiello, *CEO*
Miriam Aiello, *
Frank Messmann, *
EMP: 36 **EST:** 2013
SALES (est): 5.68MM **Privately Held**
Web: www.frankiesbikinis.com

SIC: 2369 Bathing suits and swimwear:
girls', children's, and infants'

(P-2170)
GRACING BRAND MANAGEMENT INC
Also Called: Gbm
1108 W Valley Blvd Ste 660, Alhambra
(91803)
PHONE..............................626 297-2472
Sabrina Yam, *CEO*
Vico Yam, *
EMP: 492 **EST:** 2017
SALES (est): 1.34MM **Privately Held**
SIC: 2369 5137 5131 2211 Bathing suits and
swimwear: girls', children's, and infants';
Swimsuits: women's, children's, and infants'
; Trimmings, apparel; Apparel and
outerwear fabrics, cotton

(P-2171)
MANHATTAN BEACHWEAR LLC (PA)
10855 Business Center Dr Ste C, Cypress
(90630-5252)
PHONE..............................657 384-2110
EMP: 65 **EST:** 2020
SALES (est): 24.1MM
SALES (corp-wide): 24.1MM **Privately Held**
Web: www.mbwswim.com
SIC: 2369 2329 Bathing suits and swimwear:
girls', children's, and infants'; Bathing suits
and swimwear: men's and boys'

(P-2172)
THE LUNADA BAY CORPORATION (PA)
Also Called: Becca
2000 E Winston Rd, Anaheim (92806-5546)
PHONE..............................714 490-1313
▲ **EMP:** 49 **EST:** 1980
SALES (est): 12.73MM
SALES (corp-wide): 12.73MM **Privately Held**
Web: www.lunadabayswim.com
SIC: 2369 Bathing suits and swimwear:
girls', children's, and infants'

(P-2173)
TRLG CORPORATE HOLDINGS LLC (PA)
1888 Rosecrans Ave, Manhattan Beach
(90266-3712)
PHONE..............................323 266-3072
Dalli Snyder, *CFO*
Alan Weiss, *VP*
Eugene Davis, *Dir*
Steve Perrella, *Dir*
◆ **EMP:** 101 **EST:** 2017
SQ FT: 119,000
SALES (est): 350MM
SALES (corp-wide): 350MM **Privately Held**
Web: deluxeductcleaners.yolasite.com
SIC: 2369 2325 2339 Girl's and children's
outerwear, nec; Men's and boy's trousers
and slacks; Women's and misses'
outerwear, nec

(P-2174)
UN DEUX TROIS INC (PA)
2301 E 7th St, Los Angeles (90023-1035)
PHONE..............................323 588-1067
Colin Shorkend, *Pr*
Cydney Shorkend, *
Beverly Shorkend, *
Erin Shorkend, *
▲ **EMP:** 24 **EST:** 1988

SALES (est): 4.97MM **Privately Held**
SIC: 2369 5137 Girl's and children's
outerwear, nec; Fur clothing, women's and
children's

(P-2175)
VESTURE GROUP INCORPORATED
Also Called: Pinky Los Angeles
3405 W Pacific Ave, Burbank (91505-1555)
PHONE..............................818 842-0200
Robert Galishoff, *CEO*
Gayle Lupacchini, *
▲ **EMP:** 72 **EST:** 2007
SQ FT: 3,500
SALES (est): 9.41MM **Privately Held**
Web: www.vesturegroupinc.com
SIC: 2369 2335 Skirts: girls', children's, and
infants'; Women's, junior's, and misses'
dresses

2381 Fabric Dress And Work Gloves

(P-2176)
SVO ENTERPRISE LLC
9854 Baldwin Pl, El Monte (91731-2202)
PHONE..............................626 406-4770
Scott Streitfld C.p.a., *Admn*
EMP: 25 **EST:** 2013
SALES (est): 482.66K **Privately Held**
Web: www.svoenterprises.com
SIC: 2381 Fabric dress and work gloves

2384 Robes And Dressing Gowns

(P-2177)
TERRY TOWN CORPORATION
8851 Kerns St Ste 100, San Diego
(92154-6298)
PHONE..............................619 421-5354
Saip Ereren, *CEO*
◆ **EMP:** 100 **EST:** 1988
SALES (est): 33.19MM **Privately Held**
Web: www.terrytown.com
SIC: 2384 5023 5719 Bathrobes, men's and
women's: made from purchased materials;
Linens and towels; Bedding (sheets,
blankets, spreads, and pillows)

2386 Leather And Sheep-lined Clothing

(P-2178)
CHROME HEARTS LLC (PA)
Also Called: Chrome Hearts
915 N Mansfield Ave, Los Angeles
(90038-2311)
PHONE..............................323 957-7544
Richard Stark, *Managing Member*
Robert Bowman, *
Mario D Lejtman, *
▲ **EMP:** 50 **EST:** 2005
SQ FT: 50,000
SALES (est): 21.87MM
SALES (corp-wide): 21.87MM **Privately Held**
Web: www.chromehearts.com
SIC: 2386 3911 2511 2371 Leather and
sheep-lined clothing; Jewelry, precious
metal; Wood household furniture; Fur goods

(P-2179)
DISTINCTIVE INDS TEXAS INC
9419 Ann St, Santa Fe Springs
(90670-2613)
PHONE.....................323 889-5766
Dwight Forrester, *Brnch Mgr*
EMP: 30
Web: www.distinctiveindustries.com
SIC: 2386 Coats and jackets, leather and
sheep-lined
PA: Distinctive Industries Of Texas, Inc.
4516 Seton Center Pkwy # 13

(P-2180)
FLIGHT SUITS
Also Called: Gibson & Barnes
1900 Weld Blvd Ste 140, El Cajon
(92020-0503)
PHONE.....................619 440-2700
▲ EMP: 100 EST: 1977
SALES (est): 15.33MM Privately Held
Web: www.gibson-barnes.com
SIC: 2386 Coats and jackets, leather and
sheep-lined

(P-2181)
KRASNES INC
Also Called: Cop Shopper
2222 Commercial St, San Diego
(92113-1111)
PHONE.....................619 232-2066
Jerry Krasne, *Pr*
Gail Wilson, *
Kurt Krasne, *
▲ EMP: 90 EST: 1947
SQ FT: 28,000
SALES (est): 1.51MM Privately Held
Web: www.triplek.com
SIC: 2386 3484 Leather and sheep-lined
clothing; Small arms

(P-2182)
SCULLY SPORTSWEAR INC (PA)
Also Called: Scully Leather Wear
1701 Pacific Ave, Oxnard (93033-2745)
PHONE.....................805 483-6339
Daniel Scully Iii, *CEO*
Robert Swink, *
▲ EMP: 50 EST: 1906
SQ FT: 80,000
SALES (est): 10.39MM
SALES (corp-wide): 10.39MM Privately
Held
Web: www.scullyleather.com
SIC: 2386 5099 Coats and jackets, leather
and sheep-lined; Luggage

2387 Apparel Belts

(P-2183)
SHIRINIAN-SHAW INC
Also Called: Lejon Tulliani
1229 Railroad St, Corona (92882-1838)
PHONE.....................951 736-1229
John W Shirinian, *Pr*
Jack Shirinian, *
▲ EMP: 40 EST: 1968
SQ FT: 33,000
SALES (est): 10.68MM Privately Held
Web: www.lejon.com
SIC: 2387 3172 Apparel belts; Personal
leather goods, nec

2389 Apparel And Accessories, Nec

(P-2184)
ACADEMIC CH CHOIR GWNS MFG INC
Also Called: Academic Cap & Gown
8944 Mason Ave, Chatsworth (91311-6107)
PHONE.....................818 886-8697
TOLL FREE: 800
Michael Cronan, *Pr*
Mike Cronan, *
Evelyn Cronan, *
Mark Cronan, *
◆ EMP: 30 EST: 1947
SQ FT: 13,000
SALES (est): 1.34MM Privately Held
Web: www.academicapparel.com
SIC: 2389 2353 Clergymen's vestments;
Hats, caps, and millinery

(P-2185)
AHS TRINITY GROUP INC (PA)
11041 Vanowen St, North Hollywood
(91605-6314)
PHONE.....................818 508-2105
Eddie Marks, *Pr*
Bill Haber, *CFO*
EMP: 25 EST: 1989
SALES (est): 8.87MM Privately Held
Web: www.westerncostume.com
SIC: 2389 7299 6512 Costumes; Costume
rental; Commercial and industrial building
operation

(P-2186)
ANAYA BROTHERS CUTTING LLC
3130 Leonis Blvd, Vernon (90058-3012)
PHONE.....................323 582-5758
Martin Anaya Junior, *Owner*
EMP: 90
SALES (est): 4.82MM Privately Held
SIC: 2389 Apparel and accessories, nec

(P-2187)
APP WINDDOWN LLC (HQ)
Also Called: American Apparel
747 Warehouse St, Los Angeles
(90021-1106)
P.O. Box 5129 (39047-5129)
◆ EMP: 141 EST: 2005
SALES (est): 42.13MM
SALES (corp-wide): 3.2B Privately Held
Web:
www.greenmanairductcleaning.com
SIC: 2389 2311 2331 Men's miscellaneous
accessories; Men's and boy's suits and
coats; Women's and misses' blouses and
shirts
PA: Les Vetements De Sport Gildan Inc
600 Boul De Maisonneuve O 33eme
Etage
514 735-2023

(P-2188)
CALIFRNIA CSTUME CLLCTIONS INC (PA)
Also Called: California Costume Int'l
210 S Anderson St, Los Angeles
(90033-3205)
PHONE.....................323 262-8383
Tak Kwan Woo, *CEO*
Peter Woo, *Pr*
Charles C K Woo, *Sec*
◆ EMP: 280 EST: 1992
SQ FT: 300,000
SALES (est): 24.56MM Privately Held

Web: www.californiacostumes.com
SIC: 2389 5699 Costumes; Costumes,
masquerade or theatrical

(P-2189)
CHARADES LLC
20579 Valley Blvd, Walnut (91789-2730)
PHONE.....................626 435-0077
▲ EMP: 240 EST: 2000
SALES (est): 2MM Privately Held
Web: www.rubies.com
SIC: 2389 Costumes

(P-2190)
CONQUER NATION INC
Also Called: Conquer Nation Staffing
2651 E 12th St, Los Angeles (90023-2618)
PHONE.....................310 651-5555
Jerry Saeedian, *CEO*
EMP: 142 EST: 2022
SALES (est): 1.99MM Privately Held
Web: www.conquernation.com
SIC: 2389 Hospital gowns

(P-2191)
DECKERS OUTDOOR CORPORATION (PA)
Also Called: DECKERS
250 Coromar Dr, Goleta (93117-3697)
PHONE.....................805 967-7611
Stefano Caroti, *Pr*
Michael F Devine Iii, *Ch Bd*
Steven J Fasching, *CFO*
Angela Ogbechie, *Chief Supply Chain
Officer*
Thomas Garcia, *Chief*
▲ EMP: 2751 EST: 1975
SALES (est): 4.29B
SALES (corp-wide): 4.29B Publicly Held
Web: www.deckers.com
SIC: 2389 2339 3021 Men's miscellaneous
accessories; Women's and misses'
accessories; Sandals, rubber

(P-2192)
DIAMOND COLLECTION LLC
Also Called: Charades
20579 Valley Blvd, Walnut (91789-2730)
PHONE.....................626 435-0077
EMP: 30 EST: 2016
SALES (est): 400.89K Privately Held
SIC: 2389 5137 Costumes; Dresses

(P-2193)
DIANA DID-IT DESIGNS INC
Also Called: Princess Paradise
20579 Valley Blvd, Walnut (91789-2730)
PHONE.....................970 226-5062
Diana Clements, *Pr*
Brad Clements, *
◆ EMP: 26 EST: 1980
SALES (est): 351.16K Privately Held
Web: www.rubies.com
SIC: 2389 7299 Costumes; Costume rental

(P-2194)
DISGUISE INC (HQ)
12120 Kear Pl, Poway (92064-7132)
PHONE.....................858 391-3600
Stephen Berman, *CEO*
Benoit Pousset, *Pr*
◆ EMP: 69 EST: 1987
SQ FT: 206,000
SALES (est): 27.92MM Publicly Held
Web: www.disguise.com
SIC: 2389 7299 Costumes; Costume rental
PA: Jakks Pacific, Inc.
2951 28th St

(P-2195)
H&M FASHION USA INC
4413 Patterson Ave, Perris (92571-9717)
PHONE.....................909 990-7815
EMP: 196
SALES (corp-wide): 1.38B Privately Held
SIC: 2389 Apparel for handicapped
PA: H&M Fashion Usa, Inc.
300 Lighting Way Ste 100
551 254-2700

(P-2196)
LOS ANGELES APPAREL INC (PA)
Also Called: La Apparel
1020 E 59th St, Los Angeles (90001-1010)
PHONE.....................213 275-3120
Dov Charney, *CEO*
Morris Charney, *Dir*
David Nisenbaum, *Dir*
EMP: 104 EST: 2016
SALES (est): 33.41MM
SALES (corp-wide): 33.41MM Privately
Held
Web: www.losangelesapparel.net
SIC: 2389 Uniforms and vestments

(P-2197)
LOS ANGELES APPAREL INC
Also Called: La Apparel
647 E 59th St, Los Angeles (90001-1001)
PHONE.....................213 275-3120
EMP: 173
SALES (corp-wide): 33.41MM Privately
Held
Web: www.losangelesapparel.net
SIC: 2389 Uniforms and vestments
PA: Los Angeles Apparel, Inc.
1020 E 59th St
213 275-3120

(P-2198)
MDC INTERIOR SOLUTIONS LLC
Also Called: Komar Apparel Supply
6900 E Washington Blvd, Los Angeles
(90040-1908)
PHONE.....................800 621-4006
Gary Rothschild, *Mgr*
EMP: 23
SALES (corp-wide): 26.25MM Privately
Held
Web: www.mdcwall.com
SIC: 2389 Men's miscellaneous accessories
PA: Mdc Interior Solutions, Llc
400 High Grove Blvd
847 437-4000

(P-2199)
ML KISHIGO MFG CO LLC
11250 Slater Ave, Fountain Valley
(92708-5421)
PHONE.....................949 852-1963
Loren H Wall, *CEO*
Karen Wall, *
▲ EMP: 86 EST: 1971
SALES (est): 14.09MM
SALES (corp-wide): 14.7B Privately Held
Web: www.catricking.com
SIC: 2389 5099 Men's miscellaneous
accessories; Safety equipment and supplies
PA: Bunzl Public Limited Company
York House
208 560-1244

(P-2200)
R & R INDUSTRIES INC
204 Avenida Fabricante, San Clemente
(92672-7538)
PHONE.....................800 234-5611
Robert Pare, *Pr*

Roger Poulin, *
▲ **EMP:** 30 **EST:** 1978
SQ FT: 8,150
SALES (est): 3.61MM **Privately Held**
Web: www.rrind.com
SIC: 2389 2759 Uniforms and vestments;
Promotional printing

(P-2201)
**RG COSTUMES &
ACCESSORIES INC**
726 Arrow Grand Cir, Covina (91722-2147)
PHONE..............................626 858-9559
Roger Lee, *Pr*
Michael Lee, *
◆ **EMP:** 30 **EST:** 1982
SQ FT: 21,000
SALES (est): 747.44K **Privately Held**
Web: www.rgcostume.com
SIC: 2389 7299 Costumes; Costume rental

(P-2202)
**WALT DSNEY IMGNRING RES
DEV IN**
Also Called: Disney
1200 N Miller St Unit D, Anaheim
(92806-1954)
PHONE..............................714 781-3152
Mark Hollingworth, *Brnch Mgr*
EMP: 36
SALES (corp-wide): 91.36B **Publicly Held**
Web: www.disneyimaginations.com
SIC: 2389 Masquerade costumes
HQ: Walt Disney Imagineering Research &
Development, Inc.
1401 Flower St
Glendale CA 91201
818 544-6500

2391 Curtains And Draperies

(P-2203)
AMTEX CALIFORNIA INC
Also Called: Ameritex International
113 S Utah St, Los Angeles (90033-3213)
PHONE..............................323 859-2200
Saq Hafeez, *Pr*
Alia Hafeez, *
◆ **EMP:** 45 **EST:** 1991
SQ FT: 40,000
SALES (est): 1.85MM **Privately Held**
Web:
ameritexinternational.americommerce.com
SIC: 2391 2392 5023 Draperies, plastic and
textile: from purchased materials;
Bedspreads and bed sets: made from
purchased materials; Curtains

(P-2204)
SEW WHAT INC
Also Called: Rent What
1978 E Gladwick St, Compton
(90220-6201)
PHONE..............................310 639-6000
Megan Duckett, *Pr*
Adam Duckett, *
◆ **EMP:** 35 **EST:** 1997
SQ FT: 15,000
SALES (est): 4.85MM **Privately Held**
Web: www.sewwhatinc.com
SIC: 2391 5049 Curtains and draperies;
Theatrical equipment and supplies

(P-2205)
**SUPERIOR WINDOW
COVERINGS INC**
7683 N San Fernando Rd, Burbank
(91505-1073)
PHONE..............................818 762-6685

Marco Bonilla, *Pr*
▲ **EMP:** 35 **EST:** 1979
SQ FT: 4,000
SALES (est): 2.4MM **Privately Held**
Web: www.superiorshades.com
SIC: 2391 2591 Draperies, plastic and
textile: from purchased materials; Blinds
vertical

2392 Household Furnishings, Nec

(P-2206)
ANATOMIC GLOBAL INC
1241 Old Temescal Rd Ste 103, Corona
(92881-7266)
PHONE..............................800 874-7237
▲ **EMP:** 115 **EST:** 1991
SALES (est): 1.54MM **Privately Held**
SIC: 2392 Bedspreads and bed sets: made
from purchased materials

(P-2207)
**BRENTWOOD ORIGINALS INC
(PA)**
Also Called: Brentwood Originals
3780 Kilroy Airport Way Ste 540, Long
Beach (90806-2459)
PHONE..............................310 637-6804
Joy Stewart, *CEO*
Loren Sweet, *
Bill Bronstein, *
Craig Torrey, *
Tom Rose, *
◆ **EMP:** 35 **EST:** 1958
SALES (est): 109.45MM
SALES (corp-wide): 109.45MM **Privately
Held**
Web: www.brentwoodoriginals.com
SIC: 2392 Cushions and pillows

(P-2208)
COOP HOME GOODS LLC
Also Called: Coop
9 Executive Cir, Irvine (92614-6734)
PHONE..............................888 316-1886
Zachary Kramer, *Managing Member*
EMP: 50 **EST:** 2021
SALES (est): 4.75MM **Privately Held**
Web: www.coopsleepgoods.com
SIC: 2392 Pillows, bed: made from
purchased materials

(P-2209)
CUSTOM QUILTING INC
2832 Walnut Ave Ste D, Tustin
(92780-7002)
PHONE..............................714 731-7271
Alfredo Zermeno, *Owner*
Elda Zermeno, *
EMP: 28 **EST:** 1983
SALES (est): 689.37K **Privately Held**
Web: www.customquiltinginc.com
SIC: 2392 5719 Bedspreads and bed sets:
made from purchased materials; Bedding
(sheets, blankets, spreads, and pillows)

(P-2210)
INSTANT TUCK INC
9663 Santa Monica Blvd, Beverly Hills
(90210-4303)
PHONE..............................310 955-8824
Adrian Gluck, *CEO*
EMP: 30 **EST:** 2019
SALES (est): 472.88K **Privately Held**
SIC: 2392 Mattress pads

(P-2211)
JOMAR TABLE LINENS INC
Also Called: Linen Lovers
4000 E Airport Dr Ste A, Ontario
(91761-1592)
PHONE..............................909 390-1444
EMP: 80 **EST:** 1982
SALES (est): 1.71MM **Privately Held**
Web: www.jomaronline.com
SIC: 2392 7336 Tablecloths: made from
purchased materials; Silk screen design

(P-2212)
KIDS LINE LLC
10541 Humbolt St, Los Alamitos
(90720-5401)
P.O. Box 16712 (92623-6712)
PHONE..............................310 660-0110
◆ **EMP:** 140
SIC: 2392 Blankets, comforters and beddings

(P-2213)
LA PILLOW & FIBER INC
7633 Bequette Ave, Pico Rivera
(90660-4501)
PHONE..............................323 724-7969
EMP: 57
SALES (corp-wide): 6.86MM **Privately
Held**
SIC: 2392 Cushions and pillows
PA: L.A. Pillow & Fiber, Inc.
2331 S Tubeway Ave
323 724-7969

(P-2214)
LAMBS & IVY INC
Also Called: Bed Time Originals
2042 E Maple Ave, El Segundo
(90245-5008)
PHONE..............................310 322-3800
Barbara Laiken, *Pr*
Cathy Ravdin, *
◆ **EMP:** 39 **EST:** 1980
SQ FT: 30,000
SALES (est): 5.57MM **Privately Held**
Web: www.lambsivy.com
SIC: 2392 Blankets, comforters and beddings

(P-2215)
LOFTA
9225 Brown Deer Rd, San Diego
(92121-2268)
PHONE..............................858 299-8000
Jay B Levitt, *CEO*
EMP: 35 **EST:** 2016
SALES (est): 11.09MM **Publicly Held**
Web: www.lofta.com
SIC: 2392 Mattress pads
HQ: Apria, Inc.
7353 Company Dr
Indianapolis IN 46237
800 990-9799

(P-2216)
MATTEO LLC
1000 E Cesar E Chavez Ave, Los Angeles
(90033-1204)
PHONE..............................213 617-2813
Matthew Lenoci, *Managing Member*
▲ **EMP:** 50 **EST:** 1996
SQ FT: 25,000
SALES (est): 2.76MM **Privately Held**
Web: www.matteola.com
SIC: 2392 Blankets, comforters and beddings

(P-2217)
**MICRONOVA MANUFACTURING
INC**
3431 Lomita Blvd, Torrance (90505-5010)

PHONE..............................310 784-6990
Audrey J Reynolds Lowman, *CEO*
▲ **EMP:** 30 **EST:** 1984
SQ FT: 28,310
SALES (est): 7.37MM **Privately Held**
Web: www.micronova-mfg.com
SIC: 2392 Mops, floor and dust

(P-2218)
**NORTHWESTERN CONVERTING
CO**
Also Called: Premier Mop & Broom
2395 Railroad St, Corona (92878-5411)
P.O. Box 78328 (92877-0144)
PHONE..............................800 959-3402
Tom Buckles, *Pr*
Thomas M Buckles, *
▲ **EMP:** 100 **EST:** 1935
SALES (est): 10.27MM **Privately Held**
Web: northwesternc.openfos.com
SIC: 2392 Household furnishings, nec

(P-2219)
OMNIA LEATHER MOTION INC
Also Called: Cathy Ireland Home
4950 Edison Ave, Chino (91710-5713)
PHONE..............................909 393-4400
Peter Zolferino, *Pr*
Luie Nastri, *
▲ **EMP:** 200 **EST:** 1989
SALES (est): 10.4MM **Privately Held**
Web: www.omnialeather.com
SIC: 2392 Household furnishings, nec

(P-2220)
**PACIFIC CAST FTHER CUSHION
LLC (HQ)**
Also Called: Pacific Coast Feather Cushion
7600 Industry Ave, Pico Rivera
(90660-4302)
PHONE..............................562 801-9995
Neil Puro, *Managing Member*
◆ **EMP:** 110 **EST:** 1986
SALES (est): 12.84MM
SALES (corp-wide): 46.93MM **Privately
Held**
Web: www.pcfcushion.com
SIC: 2392 Cushions and pillows
PA: Pacific Coast Feather, Llc
901 W Yamato Rd Ste 250
206 624-1057

(P-2221)
PACIFIC URETHANES LLC
Also Called: Pacific Urethanes
1671 Champagne Ave Ste A, Ontario
(91761-3660)
PHONE..............................909 390-8400
Darrell Nance, *Managing Member*
Neil Silverman, *
▲ **EMP:** 200 **EST:** 2010
SQ FT: 250,000
SALES (est): 23.84MM
SALES (corp-wide): 5.15B **Publicly Held**
Web: www.pacificurethanes.com
SIC: 2392 5021 Blankets, comforters and
beddings; Beds and bedding
PA: Leggett & Platt, Incorporated
1 Leggett Rd
417 358-8131

(P-2222)
PARACHUTE HOME INC
3525 Eastham Dr, Culver City
(90232-2440)
PHONE..............................310 903-0353
Ariel Kaye, *CEO*
Jeff Barker, *
EMP: 250 **EST:** 2013
SQ FT: 13,000

SALES (est): 57.14MM **Privately Held**
Web: www.parachutehome.com
SIC: 2392 5719 Sheets, fabric: made from
   purchased materials; Bedding (sheets,
   blankets, spreads, and pillows)

(P-2223)
PRO-MART INDUSTRIES INC
Also Called: Promart Dazz
17421 Von Karman Ave, Irvine
(92614-6205)
PHONE.................................949 428-7700
Azad Sabounjian, *CEO*
▲ **EMP:** 40 **EST:** 1970
SQ FT: 120,000
SALES (est): 10.26MM **Privately Held**
Web: www.shopsmartdesign.com
SIC: 2392 1799 5085 Bags, laundry: made
   from purchased materials; Closet
   organizers, installation and design; Bins
   and containers, storage

(P-2224)
**RELIANCE UPHOLSTERY SUP
CO INC**
Also Called: Reliance Carpet Cushion
4920 S Boyle Ave, Huntington Park (90255)
P.O. Box 58584 (90058-0584)
PHONE.................................323 321-2300
Ronald J Greitzer, *CEO*
Stanley Grietzer, *
Sheldon P Wallach, *
EMP: 95 **EST:** 1931
SQ FT: 360,000
SALES (est): 3.44MM **Privately Held**
Web: www.reliancecarpetcushion.com
SIC: 2392 Linings, carpet: textile, except felt

(P-2225)
**UNIVERSAL CUSHION
COMPANY INC (PA)**
Also Called: Cloud Nine Comforts
1610 Mandeville Canyon Rd, Los Angeles
(90049-2524)
PHONE.................................323 887-8000
Sharyl G Bloom, *Pr*
Sharyl Bloom, *
▲ **EMP:** 34 **EST:** 1989
SALES (est): 1.27MM **Privately Held**
Web: www.cloudninecomforts.com
SIC: 2392 2221 2211 Cushions and pillows;
   Comforters and quilts, manmade fiber and
   silk; Sheets and sheetings, cotton

(P-2226)
VFT INC
Also Called: Vertical Fiber Technologies
1040 S Vail Ave, Montebello (90640-6020)
PHONE.................................323 728-2280
John Chang, *Pr*
▲ **EMP:** 40 **EST:** 1998
SQ FT: 70,000
SALES (est): 5.77MM **Privately Held**
SIC: 2392 Household furnishings, nec

2393 Textile Bags

(P-2227)
ACTION BAG & COVER INC
18401 Mount Langley St, Fountain Valley
(92708-6904)
PHONE.................................714 965-7777
Byung Ki Lee, *Pr*
▲ **EMP:** 80 **EST:** 1978
SQ FT: 15,000
SALES (est): 2.22MM **Privately Held**
Web: www.actionbaginc.com
SIC: 2393 Canvas bags

(P-2228)
CTA MANUFACTURING INC
Also Called: Bagmasters
1160 California Ave, Corona (92881-3324)
PHONE.................................951 280-2400
Richard Whittier, *Pr*
Gayne Whittier, *
▲ **EMP:** 40 **EST:** 1922
SQ FT: 23,000
SALES (est): 5.1MM **Privately Held**
Web: www.bagmasters.com
SIC: 2393 Textile bags

(P-2229)
GMI INC
Also Called: GARY MANUFACTURING
2626 Southport Way Ste E, National City
(91950-8754)
PHONE.................................619 429-4479
Kathryn Smith, *CEO*
Andrea Beagle, *
EMP: 26 **EST:** 2022
SALES (est): 272.42K **Privately Held**
SIC: 2393 2392 2394 2385 Textile bags;
   Tablecloths: made from purchased materials
   ; Liners and covers, fabric: made from
   purchased materials; Diaper covers,
   waterproof: made from purchased materials

(P-2230)
GOLD CREST INDUSTRIES INC
1018 E Acacia St, Ontario (91761-4553)
P.O. Box 939 (91769-0939)
PHONE.................................909 930-9069
Jose Garcia, *Pr*
EMP: 40 **EST:** 1963
SQ FT: 14,000
SALES (est): 2.47MM **Privately Held**
Web: www.goldcrestind.com
SIC: 2393 3999 2392 Cushions, except
   spring and carpet: purchased materials;
   Umbrellas, garden or wagon; Household
   furnishings, nec

(P-2231)
**OUTDOOR RCRTION GROUP
HLDNGS L (PA)**
Also Called: Outdoor Products
3450 Mount Vernon Dr, Los Angeles
(90008-4936)
PHONE.................................323 226-0830
Andrew Altshule, *CEO*
Joel Altshule, *
George Aba, *
◆ **EMP:** 37 **EST:** 1946
SQ FT: 90,000
SALES (est): 14MM
SALES (corp-wide): 14MM **Privately Held**
Web: www.outdoorproducts.com
SIC: 2393 3949 Textile bags; Camping
   equipment and supplies

2394 Canvas And Related
Products

(P-2232)
A&R TARPAULINS INC
Also Called: AR Tech Aerospace
16246 Valley Blvd, Fontana (92335-7831)
P.O. Box 1400 (92334-1400)
PHONE.................................909 829-4444
Carmen Weisbart, *Pr*
Bud Weisbart, *
Charles Rosselet, *
EMP: 34 **EST:** 1977
SQ FT: 15,000
SALES (est): 7.53MM **Privately Held**
Web: www.artarpaulins.com

SIC: 2394 Awnings, fabric: made from
   purchased materials

(P-2233)
**A-AZTEC RENTS & SELLS INC
(PA)**
Also Called: Aztec Tents
2665 Columbia St, Torrance (90503-3801)
PHONE.................................310 347-3010
TOLL FREE: 800
Chuck Miller, *CEO*
Alex Kouzmanoff, *
◆ **EMP:** 125 **EST:** 1967
SQ FT: 70,000
SALES (est): 9.31MM
SALES (corp-wide): 9.31MM **Privately
Held**
Web: www.aztectent.com
SIC: 2394 Canvas and related products

(P-2234)
CANVAS CONCEPTS INC
649 Anita St Ste A2, Chula Vista
(91911-4658)
PHONE.................................619 424-3428
Robert A Mackenzie, *Pr*
Anton Silvernagel, *
Olivia Appel, *
EMP: 34 **EST:** 2000
SQ FT: 9,600
SALES (est): 901.24K **Privately Held**
Web: www.canvasstore.com
SIC: 2394 Awnings, fabric: made from
   purchased materials

(P-2235)
CANVAS SPECIALTY INC
1309 S Eastern Ave, Commerce
(90040-5610)
▲ **EMP:** 25 **EST:** 1942
SQ FT: 84,000
SALES (est): 829.03K **Privately Held**
Web: www.can-spec.com
SIC: 2394 5199 Tarpaulins, fabric: made
   from purchased materials; Canvas products

(P-2236)
CARAVAN CANOPY INTL INC
Also Called: Caravan Canopy
17510-17512 Studebaker Rd, Cerritos
(90703)
PHONE.................................714 367-3000
Lindy Jung Park, *CEO*
David Hudrlik, *
◆ **EMP:** 70 **EST:** 1999
SQ FT: 50,000
SALES (est): 9.76MM **Privately Held**
Web: www.caravancanopy.com
SIC: 2394 3444 2392 Canvas and related
   products; Awnings and canopies; Chair
   covers and pads: made from purchased
   materials

(P-2237)
EIDE INDUSTRIES INC
Also Called: Awnings.com
16215 Piuma Ave, Cerritos (90703-1528)
PHONE.................................562 402-8335
Don Araiza, *Pr*
Jesus Borrego, *
Dan Neill, *
Joe Belli, *
◆ **EMP:** 80 **EST:** 1938
SQ FT: 41,000
SALES (est): 11.24MM **Privately Held**
Web: www.eideindustries.com
SIC: 2394 Tents: made from purchased
   materials

(P-2238)
FRAMETENT INC
Also Called: Central Tent
26480 Summit Cir, Santa Clarita
(91350-2991)
PHONE.................................661 290-3375
Nattha Chunapongse, *Pr*
◆ **EMP:** 30 **EST:** 1994
SALES (est): 1.94MM **Privately Held**
SIC: 2394 5999 Tents: made from purchased
   materials; Tents

(P-2239)
GMA COVER CORP
1170 Somera Rd, Los Angeles
(90077-2628)
▲ **EMP:** 179
SIC: 2394 3812 Canvas and related products
   ; Defense systems and equipment

(P-2240)
INTERNATIONAL E-Z UP INC (PA)
1900 2nd St, Norco (92860-2803)
PHONE.................................800 742-3363
Leonardo Pais, *CEO*
Katie Melzer, *
◆ **EMP:** 89 **EST:** 1983
SQ FT: 115,000
SALES (est): 24.62MM
SALES (corp-wide): 24.62MM **Privately
Held**
Web: www.ezup.com
SIC: 2394 5999 Shades, canvas: made from
   purchased materials; Tents

(P-2241)
ROLL-RITE LLC
Also Called: Pulltarps Manufacturing
1404 N Marshall Ave, El Cajon
(92020-1521)
PHONE.................................619 449-8860
EMP: 48
Web: www.rollrite.com
SIC: 2394 3479 Tarpaulins, fabric: made
   from purchased materials; Bonderizing of
   metal or metal products
HQ: Roll-Rite Llc
   650 Industrial Dr
   Gladwin MI 48624

(P-2242)
STARK MFG CO
Also Called: Stark Awning & Canvas
76 Broadway, Chula Vista (91910-1422)
PHONE.................................619 425-5880
Turner Stark, *Ch*
EMP: 29 **EST:** 1953
SQ FT: 3,500
SALES (est): 2.62MM **Privately Held**
Web: www.starkmfgco.com
SIC: 2394 3444 Awnings, fabric: made from
   purchased materials; Sheet metalwork

(P-2243)
SUPERIOR AWNING INC
14555 Titus St, Panorama City
(91402-4920)
PHONE.................................818 780-7200
Brian Hotchkiss, *Pr*
Julie Hotchkiss, *
EMP: 40 **EST:** 1984
SQ FT: 11,776
SALES (est): 8.38MM **Privately Held**
Web: www.superiorawning.com
SIC: 2394 5999 3444 Awnings, fabric: made
   from purchased materials; Awnings; Sheet
   metalwork

▲ = Import   ▼ = Export
◆ = Import/Export

(P-2244)
TRANSPORTATION EQUIPMENT INC
Also Called: Pulltarps Manufacturing
1404 N Marshall Ave, El Cajon
(92020-1521)
PHONE..............................619 449-8860
TOLL FREE: 800
▲ EMP: 48
Web: www.pulltarps.com
SIC: 2394 3479 Tarpaulins, fabric: made from purchased materials; Bonderizing of metal or metal products

2395 Pleating And Stitching

(P-2245)
AMERICAN QUILTING COMPANY INC
Also Called: Antaky Quilting Company
1540 Calzona St, Los Angeles
(90023-3254)
PHONE..............................323 233-2500
Derek Antaky, CEO
Elias Antaky Junior, VP
▲ EMP: 30 EST: 1917
SALES (est): 2.06MM Privately Held
Web: www.antakyquilting.com
SIC: 2395 Quilting: for the trade

(P-2246)
ENRICH ENTERPRISES INC ✪
Also Called: National Emblem
3925 E Vernon St, Long Beach
(90815-1727)
PHONE..............................310 515-5055
Rich Rozycki, CEO
EMP: 25 EST: 2024
SALES (est): 4.67MM Privately Held
SIC: 2395 Embroidery and art needlework

(P-2247)
J & M RICHMAN CORPORATION
1501 Beach St, Montebello (90640-5431)
PHONE..............................800 422-9646
James D Richman, Pr
Tom Shapiro, *
Maury Rice, *
EMP: 25 EST: 1992
SALES (est): 3.92MM Privately Held
Web: www.academydesign.co
SIC: 2395 5999 3448 Quilted fabrics or cloth ; Awnings; Buildings, portable: prefabricated metal

(P-2248)
LA PALM FURNITURES & ACC INC (PA)
Also Called: Royal Plasticware
1650 W Artesia Blvd, Gardena
(90248-3217)
PHONE..............................310 217-2700
Dorra Ngan, CEO
Donna Sada, VP
Gino Lam, Dir
John Lee, Dir
Shawn Morse, Sls Dir
▲ EMP: 27 EST: 1996
SQ FT: 30,000
SALES (est): 4.23MM
SALES (corp-wide): 4.23MM Privately Held
Web: www.nationalemblem.com
SIC: 2395 Embroidery products, except Schiffli machine

(P-2249)
LAKESHIRTS LLC
Also Called: Yesterdays Sportswear

1400 Railroad St Ste 104, Paso Robles
(93446-1771)
PHONE..............................805 239-1290
Mark Fritz, Brnch Mgr
EMP: 45
SALES (corp-wide): 33.08MM Privately Held
Web: www.yessport.com
SIC: 2395 Embroidery and art needlework
PA: Lakeshirts Llc
750 Randolph Rd
800 627-2780

(P-2250)
MANHATTAN STITCHING CO INC
Also Called: Manhattan Stitching Co
8362 Artesia Blvd Ste E, Buena Park
(90621-4179)
PHONE..............................714 521-9479
Maxine Jossel, Pr
Lynne Miller, *
Cory Miller, *
EMP: 37 EST: 2005
SQ FT: 750
SALES (est): 1.85MM Privately Held
Web: www.manhattanstitching.com
SIC: 2395 Embroidery products, except Schiffli machine; Promotional printing ; Advertising, promotional, and trade show services

(P-2251)
MELMARC PRODUCTS INC
752 S Campus Ave, Ontario (91761-1728)
PHONE..............................714 549-2170
Brian Hirth, Pr
Leila Drager, *
Harish Naran, *
▲ EMP: 160 EST: 1987
SQ FT: 85,000
SALES (est): 24.5MM Privately Held
Web: www.melmarc.com
SIC: 2395 2396 Pleating and stitching; Screen printing on fabric articles

(P-2252)
MODERN EMBROIDERY INC
3701 W Moore Ave, Santa Ana
(92704-6836)
PHONE..............................714 436-9960
Gene Lee, Pr
EMP: 42 EST: 1996
SALES (est): 3.59MM Privately Held
Web: www.modernembroidery.com
SIC: 2395 Embroidery and art needlework

(P-2253)
NATIONAL EMBLEM INC (PA)
3925 E Vernon St, Long Beach
(90815-1727)
P.O. Box 15680 (90815-0680)
PHONE..............................310 515-5055
TOLL FREE: 800
Milton H Lubin Senior, Pr
Milton H Lubin Junior, VP
▲ EMP: 250 EST: 1972
SQ FT: 60,000
SALES (est): 4.09MM
SALES (corp-wide): 4.09MM Privately Held
Web: www.nationalemblem.com
SIC: 2395 2396 Emblems, embroidered; Automotive and apparel trimmings

(P-2254)
OUTLOOK RESOURCES INC
Also Called: Leftbank Art
14930 Alondra Blvd, La Mirada
(90638-5752)
PHONE..............................562 623-9328

Chris Hyun, Pr
◆ EMP: 100 EST: 2008
SALES (est): 13.25MM Privately Held
Web: www.leftbankart.com
SIC: 2395 5999 Pleating and stitching; Art dealers

(P-2255)
REBECCA INTERNATIONAL INC
4587 E 48th St, Vernon (90058-3201)
PHONE..............................323 973-2602
Eli Kahen, Owner
EMP: 25 EST: 2015
SQ FT: 1,500
SALES (est): 801.72K Privately Held
Web: www.rebeccainternational.com
SIC: 2395 2759 7299 Embroidery products, except Schiffli machine; Screen printing; Stitching services

2396 Automotive And Apparel Trimmings

(P-2256)
ABSOLUTE SCREENPRINT INC
333 Cliffwood Park St, Brea (92821-4104)
P.O. Box 9069 (92822-9069)
PHONE..............................714 529-2120
Steven Restivo, CEO
Andrea Restivo, *
▲ EMP: 250 EST: 1991
SQ FT: 65,000
SALES (est): 24.87MM Privately Held
Web: www.absolutescreenprint.com
SIC: 2396 3993 2759 Screen printing on fabric articles; Signs and advertising specialties; Screen printing

(P-2257)
ATELIER LUXURY GROUP LLC
Also Called: Amiri
1330 Channing St, Los Angeles
(90021-2411)
PHONE..............................310 751-2444
Michael Amiri, Managing Member
EMP: 45 EST: 2019
SQ FT: 30,000
SALES (est): 13.58MM Privately Held
SIC: 2396 2311 2321 2331 Apparel and other linings, except millinery; Men's and boy's suits and coats; Men's and boy's furnishings; Women's and misses' blouses and shirts

(P-2258)
D AND J MARKETING INC
Also Called: DJM Suspension
580 W 184th St, Gardena (90248-4202)
PHONE..............................310 538-1583
Jeffery J Ullmann, Pr
Mark Dunham, *
▲ EMP: 32 EST: 1985
SQ FT: 18,000
SALES (est): 2.07MM Privately Held
Web: www.djmsuspension.com
SIC: 2396 2531 3714 Automotive trimmings, fabric; Public building and related furniture; Motor vehicle parts and accessories

(P-2259)
DISTINCTIVE INDUSTRIES
Also Called: Specialty Division
10618 Shoemaker Ave, Santa Fe Springs
(90670-4038)
PHONE..............................800 421-9777
Dwight Forrister, CEO
Aaron Forrister, *
▲ EMP: 410 EST: 1969
SQ FT: 110,000

SALES (est): 3.72MM Privately Held
Web: www.distinctiveindustries.com
SIC: 2396 3086 Automotive trimmings, fabric ; Plastics foam products
PA: Distinctive Industries Of Texas, Inc.
4516 Seton Center Pkwy # 13

(P-2260)
FOUR SEASONS DESIGN INC (PA)
2451 Britannia Blvd, San Diego
(92154-7405)
PHONE..............................619 761-5151
John Borsini, Pr
▲ EMP: 25 EST: 2000
SALES (est): 20.15MM
SALES (corp-wide): 20.15MM Privately Held
Web: www.fourseasonsdesign.com
SIC: 2396 Screen printing on fabric articles

(P-2261)
GRAPHIC PRINTS INC
Also Called: Pipeline
904 Silver Spur Rd Ste 415, Rolling Hills Estate (90274-3800)
P.O. Box 459 (90248)
PHONE..............................310 870-1239
Alan Greenberg, CEO
Tamotsu Inouye, *
Richard Greenberg, *
EMP: 45 EST: 1971
SQ FT: 22,000
SALES (est): 3.18MM Privately Held
Web: www.pipelinegear.com
SIC: 2396 2339 2329 Screen printing on fabric articles; Women's and misses' athletic clothing and sportswear; Men's and boys' sportswear and athletic clothing

(P-2262)
I D BRAND LLC
3185 Airway Ave Ste A, Costa Mesa
(92626-4601)
PHONE..............................949 422-7057
▲ EMP: 44 EST: 1995
SQ FT: 6,400
SALES (est): 2.81MM Privately Held
Web: www.brandid.com
SIC: 2396 Apparel findings and trimmings

(P-2263)
KAMM INDUSTRIES INC
Also Called: Prp Seats
43352 Business Park Dr, Temecula
(92590-3665)
PHONE..............................800 317-6253
Aaron Wedeking, CEO
Mike Doherty, *
▲ EMP: 43 EST: 2009
SALES (est): 5.38MM Privately Held
Web: www.prpseats.com
SIC: 2396 Automotive trimmings, fabric

(P-2264)
KAPAN - KENT COMPANY INC
3540 Seagate Way Ste 100, Oceanside
(92056-6039)
PHONE..............................760 631-1716
Arnold Kapen Senior, Pr
▲ EMP: 35 EST: 1958
SALES (est): 4.02MM Privately Held
Web: www.kapankent.com
SIC: 2396 3231 Screen printing on fabric articles; Decorated glassware: chipped, engraved, etched, etc.

(P-2265)
ORBO MANUFACTURING INC
1000 S Euclid St, La Habra (90631-6806)
PHONE..............................562 222-4535
Roberto Galvez, *CEO*
EMP: 25 EST: 2021
SALES (est): 920.32K **Privately Held**
SIC: 2396 Furniture trimmings, fabric

(P-2266)
SIMSO TEX SUBLIMATION (PA)
Also Called: Simso Tex
3028 E Las Hermanas St, Compton
(90221-5511)
PHONE..............................310 885-9717
Joe Simsoly, *CEO*
Eli Simsollo, *
Kaden Simsollo, *
▲ EMP: 36 EST: 2001
SQ FT: 38,000
SALES (est): 3.18MM
SALES (corp-wide): 3.18MM **Privately Held**
SIC: 2396 Fabric printing and stamping

(P-2267)
SMOOTHREADS INC
Also Called: 2.95 Guys
13750 Stowe Dr Ste A, Poway
(92064-8828)
PHONE..............................800 536-5959
Lance Beesley, *Pr*
▲ EMP: 28 EST: 1987
SQ FT: 12,000
SALES (est): 2.3MM **Privately Held**
Web: www.295guys.com
SIC: 2396 2395 Screen printing on fabric
articles; Embroidery products, except
Schiffli machine

(P-2268)
TESCA USA INC
Also Called: Tesca
333 S Grand Ave Ste 4100, Los Angeles
(90071-1571)
PHONE..............................586 991-0744
Christopher Glinka, *Genl Mgr*
EMP: 43 EST: 2004
SALES (est): 8.03MM **Privately Held**
Web: www.tescagroup.com
SIC: 2396 3089 3465 3714 Automotive
trimmings, fabric; Injection molding of
plastics; Automotive stampings; Automotive
wiring harness sets

(P-2269)
WESTIN AUTOMOTIVE
PRODUCTS INC (PA)
Also Called: Westin
320 W Covina Blvd, San Dimas
(91773-2907)
PHONE..............................626 960-6762
Robert West, *CEO*
▲ EMP: 35 EST: 1994
SQ FT: 10,000
SALES (est): 15.59MM **Privately Held**
Web: www.westinautomotive.com
SIC: 2396 Automotive and apparel trimmings

2399 Fabricated Textile Products, Nec

(P-2270)
ACTION EMBROIDERY CORP
(PA)
Also Called: Action
1315 Brooks St, Ontario (91762-3612)
PHONE..............................909 983-1359

Ira Newman, *Pr*
Steven Mendelow, *
Ozzie Silna Stkhlr, *Prin*
▲ EMP: 120 EST: 1986
SQ FT: 12,000
SALES (est): 9.24MM
SALES (corp-wide): 9.24MM **Privately Held**
Web: www.actionembroiderycorp.com
SIC: 2399 2395 Emblems, badges, and
insignia: from purchased materials; Pleating
and stitching

(P-2271)
AIRBORNE SYSTEMS N AMER CA INC
3100 W Segerstrom Ave, Santa Ana
(92704-5812)
PHONE..............................714 662-1400
Bryce Wiedeman, *Pr*
Sean P Maroney, *
Halle F Terrion, *
Terrance M Paradie, *
▼ EMP: 200 EST: 1919
SQ FT: 160,000
SALES (est): 48.12MM
SALES (corp-wide): 7.94B **Publicly Held**
Web: www.airborne-sys.com
SIC: 2399 Parachutes
HQ: Airborne Systems North America Inc.
5800 Magnolia Ave
Pennsauken NJ 08109
856 663-1275

(P-2272)
AUTOLIV ASP INC
Also Called: Autoliv Akr Fcilty -Casa Whse
9355 Airway Rd, San Diego (92154-7931)
PHONE..............................619 662-8018
Alberto Garcia, *Brnch Mgr*
EMP: 45
SALES (corp-wide): 10.47B **Publicly Held**
SIC: 2399 Seat belts, automobile and aircraft
HQ: Autoliv Asp, Inc.
1320 Pacific Dr
Auburn Hills MI 48326

(P-2273)
AUTOLIV SAFETY
TECHNOLOGY INC
2475 Paseo De Las Americas Ste A, San
Diego (92154-7255)
PHONE..............................619 662-8000
Bradley J Murray, *Pr*
Anthony J Nellis, *
Raymond B Pekar, *
EMP: 1003 EST: 1989
SALES (est): 3.14MM
SALES (corp-wide): 10.47B **Publicly Held**
Web: www.autoliv.com
SIC: 2399 Seat belts, automobile and aircraft
PA: Autoliv, Inc.
3350 Airport Rd
801 629-9800

(P-2274)
DISPLAY FABRICATION GROUP INC
1231 N Miller St Ste 100, Anaheim
(92806-1950)
PHONE..............................714 373-2100
Luis Ocampo, *Pr*
Luis Ocampo, *Pr*
◆ EMP: 50 EST: 2002
SQ FT: 100,000
SALES (est): 5.08MM **Privately Held**
Web: www.displayfg.com
SIC: 2399 Belting, fabric: made from
purchased materials

(P-2275)
EEVELLE LLC
5928 Balfour Ct, Carlsbad (92008-7304)
PHONE..............................760 434-2231
Charles Mckee, *Managing Member*
▲ EMP: 24 EST: 1994
SALES (est): 4.28MM **Privately Held**
Web: www.eevelle.com
SIC: 2399 Automotive covers, except seat
and tire covers

(P-2276)
EXXEL OUTDOORS INC
343 Baldwin Park Blvd, City Of Industry
(91746-1406)
PHONE..............................626 369-7278
EMP: 158
SALES (corp-wide): 91.88MM **Privately Held**
Web: www.exxel.com
SIC: 2399 Sleeping bags
PA: Exxel Outdoors, Inc.
300 American Blvd
205 486-5258

(P-2277)
FXC CORPORATION
Guardian Parachute Division
3050 Red Hill Ave, Costa Mesa
(92626-4524)
PHONE..............................714 557-8032
Frank X Chevrier, *Mgr*
EMP: 64
SALES (corp-wide): 11.45MM **Privately Held**
Web: www.fxcguardian.com
SIC: 2399 3429 Parachutes; Parachute
hardware
PA: Fxc Corporation
3050 Red Hill Ave
714 556-7400

(P-2278)
HITEX DYEING & FINISHING INC
355 Vineland Ave, City Of Industry
(91746-2321)
PHONE..............................626 363-0160
Young C Kim, *Pr*
▲ EMP: 25 EST: 2010
SALES (est): 466.71K **Privately Held**
Web: www.hitexdye.com
SIC: 2399 2257 Nets, launderers and dyers;
Dyeing and finishing circular knit fabrics

(P-2279)
JUANITA F WADE
Also Called: Seaborn Canvas
435 N Harbor Blvd Ste B1, San Pedro
(90731-2271)
PHONE..............................310 519-1208
Juanita F Wade, *Owner*
Juanita Wade, *Owner*
▼ EMP: 25 EST: 1987
SQ FT: 5,000
SALES (est): 516.02K **Privately Held**
SIC: 2399 2394 Banners, pennants, and
flags; Canvas and related products

(P-2280)
PRESTIGE FLAG & BANNER CO INC
Also Called: Prestige Flag
591 Camino De La Reina Ste 917, San
Diego (92108-3146)
PHONE..............................619 497-2220
▼ EMP: 100 EST: 1991
SALES (est): 4.5MM **Privately Held**
Web: www.prestigeflag.com
SIC: 2399 Flags, fabric

(P-2281)
VANGUARD INDUSTRIES EAST INC
2440 Impala Dr, Carlsbad (92010-7226)
PHONE..............................800 433-1334
William M Gershen, *Brnch Mgr*
EMP: 30
SALES (corp-wide): 12.95MM **Privately Held**
Web: www.vanguardmil.com
SIC: 2399 Military insignia, textile
PA: Vanguard Industries East, Inc.
1172 Azalea Garden Rd
757 665-8405

(P-2282)
VANGUARD INDUSTRIES WEST INC (PA)
2440 Impala Dr, Carlsbad (92010-7226)
PHONE..............................760 438-4437
William M Gershen, *Pr*
Michael Harrison, *
Bill Gershen,. *
▲ EMP: 107 EST: 1980
SQ FT: 36,000
SALES (est): 8.92MM
SALES (corp-wide): 8.92MM **Privately Held**
Web: www.vanguardmil.com
SIC: 2399 2395 Military insignia, textile;
Pleating and stitching

(P-2283)
WESSCO INTL LTD A CAL LTD PRTN (PA)
Also Called: Wessco International
11400 W Olympic Blvd Ste 450, Los
Angeles (90064-1585)
PHONE..............................310 477-4272
Robert Bregman, *Pr*
Tyler Shepodd, *CFO*
Nick Bregman, *COO*
◆ EMP: 54 EST: 1979
SQ FT: 7,000
SALES (est): 60MM
SALES (corp-wide): 60MM **Privately Held**
Web: www.wessco.net
SIC: 2399 2393 3161 2273 Sleeping bags;
Textile bags; Traveling bags; Bathmats and
sets, textile

2411 Logging

(P-2284)
WELL ANALYSIS
CORPORATION INC (PA)
Also Called: Welaco
5500 Woodmere Dr, Bakersfield
(93313-2776)
P.O. Box 20008 (93390-0008)
PHONE..............................661 283-9510
Judy L Bebout, *CEO*
Brenda Muniozguren, *
Robert Muniozguren, *
Dan Bebout, *
▲ EMP: 26 EST: 1989
SQ FT: 1,400
SALES (est): 4.88MM **Privately Held**
Web: www.welacogroup.com
SIC: 2411 1389 Logging; Oil field services,
nec

▲ = Import ▼ = Export
◆ = Import/Export

2421 Sawmills And Planing Mills, General

(P-2285)
ARTESIA SAWDUST PRODUCTS INC
13434 S Ontario Ave, Ontario (91761-7956)
PHONE...............................909 947-5983
TOLL FREE: 800
Brigitte De Laura-espinoza, *Pr*
Anthony Espinoza, *
EMP: 35 EST: 1960
SQ FT: 2,700
SALES (est): 4.4MM **Privately Held**
Web: www.artesiasawdust.com
SIC: 2421 Sawdust and shavings

(P-2286)
HMR BUILDING SYSTEMS LLC
620 Newport Center Dr Fl 12, Newport Beach (92660-6420)
PHONE...............................951 749-4700
▲ EMP: 75 EST: 2008
SQ FT: 90,000
SALES (est): 688.35K **Privately Held**
SIC: 2421 Building and structural materials, wood
PA: Rsi Holding Llc
620 Nwport Ctr Dr 12th Fl

(P-2287)
STRATA FOREST PRODUCTS INC (PA)
Also Called: Profile Planing Mill
2600 S Susan St, Santa Ana (92704-5816)
PHONE...............................714 751-0800
TOLL FREE: 800
Richard W Hormuth, *Pr*
John Hormuth, *
▲ EMP: 50 EST: 1991
SQ FT: 38,000
SALES (est): 8.61MM
SALES (corp-wide): 8.61MM **Privately Held**
Web: www.strataforest.com
SIC: 2421 Planing mills, nec

2426 Hardwood Dimension And Flooring Mills

(P-2288)
FURNITURE TECHNOLOGIES INC
17227 Columbus St, Adelanto (92301)
P.O. Box 1076 (92301-1076)
PHONE...............................760 246-9180
Kenneth Drum, *CEO*
EMP: 24 EST: 1990
SQ FT: 31,000
SALES (est): 2.88MM **Privately Held**
Web: www.ftical.com
SIC: 2426 Furniture stock and parts, hardwood

(P-2289)
HARDWOOD FLRG LIQUIDATORS INC (PA)
Also Called: Republic Flooring
7227 Telegraph Rd, Montebello (90640-6512)
PHONE...............................323 201-4200
Eliyahu Shuat, *CEO*
▲ EMP: 100 EST: 2008
SALES (est): 76.09MM
SALES (corp-wide): 76.09MM **Privately Held**

Web: www.republicfloor.com
SIC: 2426 Flooring, hardwood

(P-2290)
HOGUE BROS INC
Also Called: Hogue Grips
550 Linne Rd, Paso Robles (93446-8454)
P.O. Box 1138 (93447-1138)
PHONE...............................805 239-1440
▲ EMP: 36
Web: www.hogueinc.com
SIC: 2426 3489 Hardwood dimension and flooring mills; Guns, howitzers, mortars, and related equipment

(P-2291)
PARQUET BY DIAN
16601 S Main St, Gardena (90248-2722)
PHONE...............................310 527-3779
Anatoli Efros, *CEO*
Dima Efros, *Pr*
EMP: 92 EST: 1993
SALES (est): 5.19MM **Privately Held**
Web: www.parquet.com
SIC: 2426 Parquet flooring, hardwood

(P-2292)
RTMEX INC
Also Called: Best Redwood
1202 Piper Ranch Rd, San Diego (92154-7714)
P.O. Box 8662 (91912-8662)
PHONE...............................619 391-9913
Jorje Sampietro, *Pr*
EMP: 108 EST: 2010
SQ FT: 15,000
SALES (est): 1.88MM **Privately Held**
Web: www.best-redwood.com
SIC: 2426 Carvings, furniture: wood

(P-2293)
WEST COAST FURN FRAMERS INC
24006 Tahquitz Rd, Apple Valley (92307-2236)
PHONE...............................760 669-5275
Katelynn Galiana-baca, *Pr*
Katelynn Baca, *
Javier Galiana, *
EMP: 27 EST: 2017
SALES (est): 2.39MM **Privately Held**
SIC: 2426 Frames for upholstered furniture, wood

2431 Millwork

(P-2294)
ABC CUSTOM WOOD SHUTTERS INC
Also Called: Golden West Shutters
20561 Pascal Way, Lake Forest (92630-8119)
PHONE...............................949 595-0300
David Harris, *VP*
John Stahman, *
EMP: 35 EST: 1991
SALES (est): 874.78K **Privately Held**
Web: www.gwshutters.com
SIC: 2431 Door shutters, wood

(P-2295)
ANDERCO INC
540 Airpark Dr, Fullerton (92833-2503)
PHONE...............................714 446-9508
Peter Johnson, *Pr*
Ralph Johnson, *
▲ EMP: 50 EST: 1983
SQ FT: 70,000

SALES (est): 7.03MM
SALES (corp-wide): 183.49MM **Privately Held**
SIC: 2431 5031 Door frames, wood; Doors and windows
HQ: Metrie Inc.
2200 140th Ave E Ste 600
Sumner WA 98390
253 470-5050

(P-2296)
ARCHITCTRAL MLLWK SNTA BARBARA
Also Called: Manufacturers of Wood Products
8 N Nopal St, Santa Barbara (93103-3317)
P.O. Box 4699 (93140-4699)
PHONE...............................805 965-7011
Thomas G Mathews, *Pr*
Glenice Mathews, *
Joseph J Mathews, *
Ronald Mathews, *Stockholder*
EMP: 40 EST: 1968
SQ FT: 10,000
SALES (est): 4.87MM **Privately Held**
Web: www.archmill.com
SIC: 2431 Millwork

(P-2297)
ART GLASS ETC INC
Also Called: AG Millworks
3111 Golf Course Dr, Ventura (93003-7604)
PHONE...............................805 644-4494
Rachid El Etel, *Pr*
Aida El Etel, *
▲ EMP: 50 EST: 1986
SALES (est): 4.55MM **Privately Held**
Web: www.agmillworks.com
SIC: 2431 Doors and door parts and trim, wood

(P-2298)
AVALON SHUTTERS INC
3407 N Perris Blvd, Perris (92571-3100)
PHONE...............................909 937-4900
Douglas Noel Serbin, *Pr*
Douglas Noel Serbin, *CEO*
▲ EMP: 90 EST: 1986
SQ FT: 85,000
SALES (est): 14.73MM **Privately Held**
Web: www.avalonshutters.com
SIC: 2431 Window shutters, wood

(P-2299)
CALIFRNIA DLUXE WNDOWS INDS IN (PA)
20735 Superior St, Chatsworth (91311-4416)
PHONE...............................818 349-5566
Aaron Adirim, *Pr*
EMP: 46 EST: 1999
SQ FT: 60,000
SALES (est): 12.36MM
SALES (corp-wide): 12.36MM **Privately Held**
Web: www.cdwindows.com
SIC: 2431 2824 Windows and window parts and trim, wood; Vinyl fibers

(P-2300)
CANYON GRAPHICS INC
3738 Ruffin Rd, San Diego (92123-1812)
PHONE...............................858 646-0444
Scott Moncrieff, *CEO*
EMP: 60 EST: 1981
SALES (est): 9.26MM **Privately Held**
Web: www.canyongraphics.com
SIC: 2431 2754 Moldings and baseboards, ornamental and trim; Labels: gravure printing

(P-2301)
CONTRACTORS WARDROBE INC (PA)
Also Called: Contractors Wardrobe
26121 Avenue Hall, Valencia (91355-3490)
P.O. Box 800790 (91380)
PHONE...............................661 257-1177
▲ EMP: 200 EST: 1972
SALES (est): 81.02MM
SALES (corp-wide): 81.02MM **Privately Held**
Web: www.cwdoors.com
SIC: 2431 3088 Doors, wood; Shower stalls, fiberglass and plastics

(P-2302)
DANMER INC
Also Called: Danmer Custom Shutters
8000 Woodley Ave, Van Nuys (91406-1226)
PHONE...............................516 670-5125
▲ EMP: 250
Web: www.danmer.com
SIC: 2431 5023 Window shutters, wood; Window covering parts and accessories

(P-2303)
DECORE-ATIVE SPC NC LLC (PA)
2772 Peck Rd, Monrovia (91016-5005)
PHONE...............................626 254-9191
Jack Lansford Senior, *CEO*
Jack Lansford Junior, *Pr*
Eric Lansford, *
Billie Lansford, *
▲ EMP: 650 EST: 1969
SALES (est): 95.6MM
SALES (corp-wide): 95.6MM **Privately Held**
Web: www.decore.com
SIC: 2431 Millwork

(P-2304)
DECORE-ATIVE SPC NC LLC
4414 Azusa Canyon Rd, Irwindale (91706-2740)
PHONE...............................626 960-7731
David Thompson, *Brnch Mgr*
EMP: 111
SALES (corp-wide): 95.6MM **Privately Held**
Web: www.decore.com
SIC: 2431 Millwork
PA: Decore-Ative Specialties Nc Llc
2772 Peck Rd
626 254-9191

(P-2305)
ECMD INC
10863 Jersey Blvd 100, Rancho Cucamonga (91730-5151)
PHONE...............................909 980-1775
EMP: 47
SALES (corp-wide): 186.49MM **Privately Held**
Web: www.ecmd.com
SIC: 2431 Moldings, wood: unfinished and prefinished
PA: Ecmd, Inc.
2 Grandview St
336 667-5976

(P-2306)
FINELINE WOODWORKING INC
Also Called: Fineline Architectural Mllwk
1139 Baker St, Costa Mesa (92626-4114)
PHONE...............................714 540-5468
Marc Butman, *CEO*
Jon Muller, *

Tom Crone, *
Julie Butman, *OF EVENTS & SOCIAL MEDIA*
EMP: 60 **EST:** 2006
SQ FT: 20,000
SALES (est): 6.44MM **Privately Held**
Web: www.finelinewood.com
SIC: 2431 Millwork

(P-2307)
GL WOODWORKING INC
Also Called: Millers Woodworking
14341 Franklin Ave, Tustin (92780-7010)
PHONE..............................949 515-2192
Grant Miller, *Owner*
EMP: 63 **EST:** 2004
SALES (est): 7.02MM **Privately Held**
SIC: 2431 Millwork

(P-2308)
HALEY BROS INC (HQ)
6291 Orangethorpe Ave, Buena Park (90620-1377)
PHONE..............................714 670-2112
Thomas J Cobb, *CEO*
Thomas Cobb, *Sec*
▲ **EMP:** 90 **EST:** 1987
SQ FT: 24,000
SALES (est): 18.16MM
SALES (corp-wide): 103.78MM **Privately Held**
Web: www.haleybros.com
SIC: 2431 Doors, wood
PA: T. M. Cobb Company
500 Palmyrita Ave
951 248-2400

(P-2309)
HALEY BROS INC
1575 Riverview Dr, San Bernardino (92408-2922)
PHONE..............................800 854-5951
EMP: 110
SALES (corp-wide): 103.78MM **Privately Held**
Web: www.haleybros.com
SIC: 2431 Doors, wood
HQ: Haley Bros., Inc.
6291 Orangethorpe Ave
Buena Park CA 90620

(P-2310)
HIGHLAND LUMBER SALES INC
300 E Santa Ana St, Anaheim (92805-3953)
PHONE..............................714 778-2293
Richard Phillips, *Pr*
Daniel Lobue, *
▲ **EMP:** 31 **EST:** 1991
SQ FT: 2,000
SALES (est): 8.52MM **Privately Held**
Web: www.highlandlumber.com
SIC: 2431 5031 2493 5211 Millwork; Lumber: rough, dressed, and finished; Reconstituted wood products; Lumber products

(P-2311)
JELD-WEN INC
Also Called: International Wood Products
3760 Convoy St Ste 111, San Diego (92111-3743)
PHONE..............................800 468-3667
Hugo Hernadez, *Off Mgr*
EMP: 140
Web: www.jeld-wen.ca
SIC: 2431 Doors, wood
HQ: Jeld-Wen, Inc.
2645 Silver Crescent Dr
Charlotte NC 28273
800 535-3936

(P-2312)
LEEPERS WOOD TURNING CO INC (PA)
Also Called: Leeper's Stair Products
341 Bonnie Cir Ste 104, Corona (92878-5195)
P.O. Box 17098 (90807-7098)
PHONE..............................562 422-6525
Michael Skinner, *Pr*
Barbara Skinner, *
Molly Rubio, *
◆ **EMP:** 38 **EST:** 1946
SQ FT: 29,000
SALES (est): 1.82MM
SALES (corp-wide): 1.82MM **Privately Held**
Web: www.ljsmith.com
SIC: 2431 Staircases and stairs, wood

(P-2313)
MILLCRAFT INC
2850 E White Star Ave, Anaheim (92806-2517)
PHONE..............................714 632-9621
Lars Eppick, *Pr*
Ray Pfeifer, *
Philip De Marco, *
Reginald Skipcott, *
EMP: 70 **EST:** 1983
SQ FT: 34,000
SALES (est): 1.28MM **Privately Held**
Web: www.millcraft.com
SIC: 2431 2434 Doors, wood; Wood kitchen cabinets

(P-2314)
MILLWORKS BY DESIGN INC
4525 Runway St, Simi Valley (93063-3479)
PHONE..............................818 597-1326
Daniel S Parish, *CEO*
Zachary D Eglit, *Pr*
▲ **EMP:** 43 **EST:** 2007
SALES (est): 2.46MM **Privately Held**
Web: www.millworksbydesign.com
SIC: 2431 Millwork

(P-2315)
MTD KITCHEN INC
13213 Sherman Way, North Hollywood (91605-4649)
PHONE..............................818 764-2254
Gil Alkoby, *CEO*
EMP: 85 **EST:** 2012
SALES (est): 10.54MM **Privately Held**
Web: www.mtdkitchen.com
SIC: 2431 2441 1799 2434 Millwork; Cases, wood; Kitchen cabinet installation; Vanities, bathroom: wood

(P-2316)
NORTHWESTERN INC
10153-1/2 Riverside Dr #250, Toluca Lake (91602-2561)
PHONE..............................818 786-1581
▲ **EMP:** 40
SIC: 2431 Woodwork, interior and ornamental, nec

(P-2317)
NOVO MANUFACTURING LLC
Also Called: Lj Smith Stair Systems
341 Bonnie Cir Ste 104, Corona (92878-5195)
PHONE..............................951 479-4620
Rob Brown, *CEO*
EMP: 59
SALES (corp-wide): 2.58B **Privately Held**
Web: www.ljsmith.com
SIC: 2431 Millwork
HQ: Novo Manufacturing, Llc
35280 Scio-Bowerston Rd

Bowerston OH 44695
740 269-2221

(P-2318)
NOVO MANUFACTURING LLC
25956 Commercentre Dr, Lake Forest (92630-8815)
PHONE..............................949 609-0544
Danny Umemoto, *Mgr*
EMP: 47
SALES (corp-wide): 2.58B **Privately Held**
Web: www.ljsmith.com
SIC: 2431 Millwork
HQ: Novo Manufacturing, Llc
35280 Scio-Bowerston Rd
Bowerston OH 44695
740 269-2221

(P-2319)
OHLINE CORPORATION
1930 W 139th St, Gardena (90249-2490)
PHONE..............................310 327-4630
EMP: 33
SIC: 2431 Door shutters, wood

(P-2320)
OLD ENGLISH MIL WOODWORKS INC (PA)
Also Called: Old English Mil & Woodworks
27772 Avenue Scott, Santa Clarita (91355-3417)
PHONE..............................661 294-9171
Lay Cho, *Pr*
Edmond Cho, *
EMP: 30 **EST:** 1977
SQ FT: 30,000
SALES (est): 1.09MM
SALES (corp-wide): 1.09MM **Privately Held**
Web: www.oldenglishmilling.com
SIC: 2431 2439 1751 Staircases and stairs, wood; Structural wood members, nec; Carpentry work

(P-2321)
ORANGE WOODWORKS INC
1215 N Parker St, Orange (92867-4613)
PHONE..............................714 997-2600
Jeff Mcmillian, *Pr*
EMP: 45 **EST:** 1984
SQ FT: 120,000
SALES (est): 2.46MM **Privately Held**
Web: www.orangewoodworks.com
SIC: 2431 Millwork

(P-2322)
PACIFIC ARCHTECTURAL MLLWK INC
1435 Pioneer St, Brea (92821-3721)
PHONE..............................562 905-9282
EMP: 27
SALES (est): 1.4MM **Privately Held**
Web: www.pacmillwork.com
SIC: 2431 Millwork

(P-2323)
PACIFIC ARCHTECTURAL MLLWK INC
101 E Commwl Ave Ste A, Fullerton (92832)
PHONE..............................714 525-2059
EMP: 62
Web: www.pacmillwork.com
SIC: 2431 Window shutters, wood
PA: Pacific Architectural Millwork, Inc.
101 E Commwl Ave Ste A

(P-2324)
PACIFIC ARCHTECTURAL MLLWK INC
Also Called: Reveal Windows & Doors
1031 S Leslie St, La Habra (90631-6843)
PHONE..............................562 905-3200
John Higman, *CEO*
Roy Gustin, *
Alice Vanberpool, *
◆ **EMP:** 100 **EST:** 2007
SALES (est): 9.04MM **Privately Held**
Web: www.pacmillwork.com
SIC: 2431 Planing mill, millwork

(P-2325)
QUALITY SHUTTERS INC
3359 Chicago Ave Ste A, Riverside (92507-6820)
PHONE..............................951 683-4939
Agustin Flores, *Owner*
EMP: 49 **EST:** 2002
SALES (est): 1.81MM **Privately Held**
SIC: 2431 Window frames, wood

(P-2326)
RENAISSNCE FRNCH DORS SASH INC (PA)
Also Called: Renaissance Doors & Windows
38 Segada, Rcho Sta Marg (92688-2744)
PHONE..............................714 578-0090
Michael Jenkins, *Pr*
Thomas Jenkins, *
James Jenkins, *
EMP: 129 **EST:** 1982
SQ FT: 75,000
SALES (est): 2.84MM
SALES (corp-wide): 2.84MM **Privately Held**
Web: www.renaissancewindowsanddoors.com
SIC: 2431 Doors, wood

(P-2327)
SOUTH COAST STAIRS INC
30251 Tomas, Rcho Sta Marg (92688-2123)
PHONE..............................949 858-1685
Chris Galloway, *Pr*
Mary Galloway, *
Tamera Selchau, *
EMP: 40 **EST:** 1980
SQ FT: 2,000
SALES (est): 2.78MM **Privately Held**
Web: www.scstairs.com
SIC: 2431 2439 5211 Staircases and stairs, wood; Structural wood members, nec; Millwork and lumber

(P-2328)
T M COBB COMPANY (PA)
Also Called: Haley Bros
500 Palmyrita Ave, Riverside (92507-1196)
PHONE..............................951 248-2400
Jeffrey Cobb, *Pr*
Thomas J Cobb, *
▲ **EMP:** 23 **EST:** 1947
SALES (est): 103.78MM
SALES (corp-wide): 103.78MM **Privately Held**
Web: www.tmcobb.com
SIC: 2431 3442 Door frames, wood; Window and door frames

(P-2329)
TABER COMPANY INC
121 Waterworks Way Ste 100, Irvine (92618-7719)
PHONE..............................714 543-7100
Brian Taber, *Pr*

EMP: 65 **EST:** 2002
SALES (est): 22.63MM **Privately Held**
Web: www.taberco.net
SIC: 2431 Millwork

(P-2330)
TALBERT ARCHTCTRAL PANL DOOR I
711 S Stimson Ave, City Of Industry (91745-1627)
PHONE..............................714 671-9700
Jeff Tustin, *Pr*
Nick Parrino, *
Angie Talbert, *Corporate Secretary**
Heidi Gordon Ctrl, *Prin*
EMP: 65 **EST:** 2005
SALES (est): 18MM **Privately Held**
Web: www.talbertusa.com
SIC: 2431 Millwork

(P-2331)
THE ENKEBOLL CO
Also Called: Enkeboll Design
16506 Avalon Blvd, Carson (90746-1096)
PHONE..............................310 532-1400
EMP: 27 **EST:** 1955
SALES (est): 2.44MM **Privately Held**
Web: www.enkebolldesigns.com
SIC: 2431 Ornamental woodwork: cornices, mantels, etc.

(P-2332)
TRINITY WOODWORKS INC
2620 Temple Heights Dr, Oceanside (92056-3512)
PHONE..............................760 639-5351
Jeffrey D Hollenbeck, *CEO*
EMP: 23 **EST:** 2011
SALES (est): 4.21MM **Privately Held**
Web: www.trinitywoodworksinc.com
SIC: 2431 Millwork

(P-2333)
W B POWELL INC
630 Parkridge Ave, Norco (92860-3124)
PHONE..............................951 270-0095
Charles G Mayhew, *CEO*
Chuck Mayhew, *
Doug Westra, *
EMP: 57 **EST:** 1993
SALES (est): 9.93MM
SALES (corp-wide): 44.51MM **Privately Held**
Web: www.wbpowell.com
SIC: 2431 2439 Millwork; Structural wood members, nec
PA: Plymold, Inc.
615 Centennial Dr
507 789-5111

(P-2334)
WESTERN INTEGRATED MTLS INC (PA)
3310 E 59th St, Long Beach (90805-4504)
PHONE..............................562 634-2823
Larry Farrah, *Pr*
Edward G Farrah, *
Jim Halbrook, *
Alex Rojas, *
Debra Price, *
▲ **EMP:** 30 **EST:** 1975
SQ FT: 20,000
SALES (est): 5.36MM
SALES (corp-wide): 5.36MM **Privately Held**
Web: www.aluminumdoorframes.com
SIC: 2431 3442 Millwork; Window and door frames

(P-2335)
WOODWORK PIONEERS CORP
1757 S Claudina Way, Anaheim (92805-6544)
PHONE..............................714 991-1017
Karina Avalos, *Pr*
EMP: 50 **EST:** 2016
SALES (est): 749.13K **Privately Held**
Web: www.woodworkpioneers.com
SIC: 2431 Millwork

2434 Wood Kitchen Cabinets

(P-2336)
ACCURATE LAMINATED PDTS INC
1826 Dawns Way, Fullerton (92831-5323)
PHONE..............................714 632-2773
Daniel Dunn, *Pr*
Patricia Dunn, *
EMP: 30 **EST:** 1989
SQ FT: 5,000
SALES (est): 4.99MM **Privately Held**
Web: www.accuratelaminated.com
SIC: 2434 Wood kitchen cabinets

(P-2337)
AMERICAN WOODMARK CORPORATION
Also Called: RSI Home Products
400 E Orangethorpe Ave, Anaheim (92801-1046)
PHONE..............................714 449-2200
EMP: 266
SALES (corp-wide): 1.85B **Publicly Held**
Web: www.americanwoodmark.com
SIC: 2434 Vanities, bathroom: wood
PA: American Woodmark Corporation
561 Shady Elm Rd
540 665-9100

(P-2338)
ARTCRAFTERS CABINETS
5446 Cleon Ave, North Hollywood (91601-2897)
PHONE..............................818 752-8960
Jack R Walter, *Pr*
Sharon E Walter, *
EMP: 50 **EST:** 1949
SQ FT: 20,000
SALES (est): 2.34MM **Privately Held**
Web: www.artcrafter.com
SIC: 2434 2521 2431 Wood kitchen cabinets ; Wood office furniture; Millwork

(P-2339)
B YOUNG ENTERPRISES INC
Also Called: Mission Vly Cab / Counter Tecn
12254 Iavelli Way, Poway (92064-6818)
PHONE..............................858 748-0935
EMP: 75
SIC: 2434 2521 5031 5211 Wood kitchen cabinets; Cabinets, office: wood; Kitchen cabinets; Cabinets, kitchen

(P-2340)
BROMACK COMPANY
3005 Humboldt St, Los Angeles (90031-1830)
PHONE..............................323 227-5000
Kurt Webster, *Managing Member*
Kurt Webster, *Prin*
Brown Mcpherson Iii, *Prin*
EMP: 24 **EST:** 2010
SALES (est): 1.02MM **Privately Held**
Web: www.bromack.com
SIC: 2434 Wood kitchen cabinets

(P-2341)
CABINETS 2000 LLC
11100 Firestone Blvd, Norwalk (90650-2269)
PHONE..............................562 868-0909
Afshin Abdollahi, *CEO*
Nematollah Abdollahi, *
Sherwood Prusso, *
Sue Abdollahi, *
Frank Hamadani, *
EMP: 180 **EST:** 1988
SQ FT: 103,000
SALES (est): 27.21MM
SALES (corp-wide): 2.54B **Privately Held**
Web: www.cabinets2000.com
SIC: 2434 1751 Wood kitchen cabinets; Cabinet and finish carpentry
PA: Cabinetworks Group, Inc.
20000 Victor Pkwy
734 205-4600

(P-2342)
CABINETS BY PRCISION WORKS INC
Also Called: Precision Works
81101 Indio Blvd Ste D22, Indio (92201-1922)
PHONE..............................760 342-1133
Pierre Letellier, *Pr*
Katherine Letellier, *
EMP: 50 **EST:** 1993
SQ FT: 16,000
SALES (est): 4.8MM **Privately Held**
Web: www.cabinetsbyprecision.com
SIC: 2434 2431 Wood kitchen cabinets; Millwork

(P-2343)
CALIFORNIA WOODWORKING INC
1726 Ives Ave, Oxnard (93033-4072)
PHONE..............................805 982-9090
Edward Vickery, *Pr*
Lucas Vickery, *
Susan Vickery, *
EMP: 30 **EST:** 1990
SQ FT: 8,000
SALES (est): 2.31MM **Privately Held**
Web: www.calwoodinc.com
SIC: 2434 Wood kitchen cabinets

(P-2344)
CALIFRNIA DSGNERS CHICE CSTM C
547 Constitution Ave Ste F, Camarillo (93012-8572)
PHONE..............................805 987-5820
Mark Mulchay, *Pr*
Russell Leavitt, *
EMP: 38 **EST:** 1989
SALES (est): 5.85MM **Privately Held**
Web: www.cdcc-inc.com
SIC: 2434 Wood kitchen cabinets

(P-2345)
CORONA MILLWORKS COMPANY (PA)
5572 Edison Ave, Chino (91710-6936)
PHONE..............................909 606-3288
Jose Corona, *CEO*
▲ **EMP:** 63 **EST:** 1995
SQ FT: 8,700
SALES (est): 24.9MM
SALES (corp-wide): 24.9MM **Privately Held**
Web: www.coronamillworks.com
SIC: 2434 Wood kitchen cabinets

(P-2346)
DREES WOOD PRODUCTS INC
14020 Orange Ave, Paramount (90723-2018)
PHONE..............................562 633-7337
Ed Drees, *CEO*
EMP: 100 **EST:** 1982
SALES (est): 6.09MM **Privately Held**
Web: www.dreeswoodproducts.com
SIC: 2434 Wood kitchen cabinets

(P-2347)
ELITE STONE GROUP INC
1205 S Dupont Ave, Ontario (91761-1536)
PHONE..............................909 629-6988
Yiyong Huang, *CEO*
EMP: 30 **EST:** 2015
SALES (est): 2.47MM **Privately Held**
Web: www.elitestonegroup.com
SIC: 2434 5032 1741 Wood kitchen cabinets ; Building stone; Stone masonry

(P-2348)
EXCEL CABINETS INC
225 Jason Ct, Corona (92879-6199)
PHONE..............................951 279-4545
Charles W Ketzel, *CEO*
Kevin Ketzel, *
Sandra Ketzel, *
▲ **EMP:** 35 **EST:** 1990
SALES (est): 7.45MM **Privately Held**
Web: www.excelcabinetsinc.com
SIC: 2434 Wood kitchen cabinets

(P-2349)
FINISHING TOUCH MOULDING INC
Also Called: Finishing Touch Millwork
6190 Corte Del Cedro, Carlsbad (92011-1515)
PHONE..............................760 444-1019
Roland Chaney, *Pr*
EMP: 55 **EST:** 2013
SALES (est): 4.82MM **Privately Held**
Web: www.ftmillwork.com
SIC: 2434 1751 Wood kitchen cabinets; Carpentry work

(P-2350)
I AND E CABINETS INC
14660 Raymer St, Van Nuys (91405-1217)
PHONE..............................818 933-6480
Israel Chlomovitz, *CEO*
Ettie Chlomovitz, *
EMP: 34 **EST:** 1981
SQ FT: 9,000
SALES (est): 2.4MM **Privately Held**
Web: www.iecabinets.com
SIC: 2434 Wood kitchen cabinets

(P-2351)
K & Z CABINET CO INC
1450 S Grove Ave, Ontario (91761-4523)
PHONE..............................909 947-3567
Dennis Chan, *Pr*
EMP: 60 **EST:** 1975
SQ FT: 59,000
SALES (est): 4.85MM **Privately Held**
Web: www.kzcabt.com
SIC: 2434 2431 Wood kitchen cabinets; Millwork

(P-2352)
KOBIS WINDOWS & DOORS MFG INC
7326 Laurel Canyon Blvd, North Hollywood (91605-3710)
PHONE..............................818 764-6400
Kobi Louria, *CEO*

▲ **EMP:** 25 **EST:** 1999
SALES (est): 2.62MM **Privately Held**
Web: www.kobiwindows.net
SIC: 2434 2431 1522 Vanities, bathroom: wood; Millwork; Residential construction, nec

(P-2353)
MASTERBRAND CABINETS LLC
3700 S Riverside Ave, Colton (92324-3329)
PHONE..................951 682-1535
Michael Mejia, *Mgr*
EMP: 46
SALES (corp-wide): 2.73B **Publicly Held**
Web: www.masterbrand.com
SIC: 2434 Wood kitchen cabinets
HQ: Masterbrand Cabinets Llc
3300 Entp Pkwy Ste 300
Beachwood OH 44122
812 482-2527

(P-2354)
MCCONNELL CABINETS INC
Also Called: Coastal Wood Products
13110 Louden Ln, City Of Industry (91746-1507)
PHONE..................626 937-2200
▲ **EMP:** 740
Web: www.mcconnellinc.com
SIC: 2434 Wood kitchen cabinets

(P-2355)
MIKADA CABINETS LLC
Also Called: Mikada Cabinets
11777 San Vicente Blvd Ste 777, Los Angeles (90049-5067)
EMP: 60 **EST:** 1965
SALES (est): 2.33MM **Privately Held**
Web: www.mikadacabinets.com
SIC: 2434 Wood kitchen cabinets

(P-2356)
N K CABINETS INC
Also Called: Universal Custom Cabinets
13290 Paxton St, Pacoima (91331-2356)
PHONE..................818 897-7909
Arno Yesayan, *CEO*
Norik Kayramanyon, *
EMP: 34 **EST:** 1995
SALES (est): 2.18MM **Privately Held**
Web: www.nkcabinets.com
SIC: 2434 2521 3843 2599 Wood kitchen cabinets; Cabinets, office: wood; Cabinets, dental; Cabinets, factory

(P-2357)
PROFESSIONAL CABINET SOLUTIONS
2111 Eastridge Ave, Riverside (92507-0778)
PHONE..................909 614-2900
M Scott Culbreth, *CEO*
Paul Joachimczyk, *CFO*
EMP: 250 **EST:** 1996
SALES (est): 9.28MM
SALES (corp-wide): 1.85B **Publicly Held**
Web: www.pcscabinetry.com
SIC: 2434 Wood kitchen cabinets
HQ: Rsi Home Products Llc
400 E Orangethorpe Ave
Anaheim CA 92801
714 449-2200

(P-2358)
QUALITY CABINET AND FIXTURE CO (HQ)
7955 Saint Andrews Ave, San Diego (92154-8224)
PHONE..................619 266-1011

Donald Paradise, *Ch Bd*
Tim Paradise, *
Andrew Meek, *
Nicholas P Willems, *
Mike Bonde, *
▲ **EMP:** 23 **EST:** 1966
SQ FT: 55,000
SALES (est): 2.08MM
SALES (corp-wide): 20.34MM **Privately Held**
Web: www.glennrieder.com
SIC: 2434 Wood kitchen cabinets
PA: Glenn Rieder, Llc
6520 W Becher Pl
414 449-2888

(P-2359)
REBORN CABINETS LLC (PA)
Also Called: Reborn Bath Solutions
5515 E La Palma Ave Ste 250, Anaheim (92807-2131)
PHONE..................714 630-2220
TOLL FREE: 800
Vincent Nardolillo, *Managing Member*
Anthony Nardolillo, *
EMP: 484 **EST:** 1983
SALES (est): 114.99MM
SALES (corp-wide): 114.99MM **Privately Held**
Web: www.reborncabinets.com
SIC: 2434 2431 Wood kitchen cabinets; Millwork

(P-2360)
ROBERT C WORTH INC
15846 Liggett St, North Hills (91343-3142)
PHONE..................661 942-6601
Robert C Worth, *Prin*
EMP: 60 **EST:** 2011
SALES (est): 1.77MM **Privately Held**
Web: www.worthcabinets.com
SIC: 2434 Wood kitchen cabinets

(P-2361)
ROYAL CABINETS INC
Also Called: Royal Cabinets
1299 E Phillips Blvd, Pomona (91766-5429)
PHONE..................909 629-8565
Clay Smith, *Pr*
Bill Roan, *
▲ **EMP:** 600 **EST:** 1984
SQ FT: 70,000
SALES (est): 19.15MM **Privately Held**
Web: www.royalcabinets.com
SIC: 2434 2511 Wood kitchen cabinets; Wood household furniture

(P-2362)
ROYAL INDUSTRIES INC
Also Called: Royal Cabinets
1299 E Phillips Blvd, Pomona (91766-5429)
PHONE..................909 629-8565
Clay R Smith, *Ch Bd*
Eric Vanderheyden, *
Gary Silverman, *
William Roan, *
Gustavo Danjoi, *
EMP: 130 **EST:** 1985
SALES (est): 11.23MM **Privately Held**
Web: www.royalcabinets.com
SIC: 2434 Vanities, bathroom: wood

(P-2363)
SOUTHCOAST CABINET INC (PA)
755 Pinefalls Ave, Walnut (91789-3027)
PHONE..................909 594-3089
Dante M Senese, *CEO*
John Lopez, *
EMP: 42 **EST:** 1983

SQ FT: 108,000
SALES (est): 10.57MM
SALES (corp-wide): 10.57MM **Privately Held**
Web: www.southcoastcabinet.com
SIC: 2434 Wood kitchen cabinets

(P-2364)
TESSA MIA CORP
9565 Vassar Ave, Chatsworth (91311-4141)
PHONE..................877 740-5757
Zack Kami, *CEO*
Yom Tov Yohanan, *
EMP: 27 **EST:** 2019
SALES (est): 5.5MM **Privately Held**
SIC: 2434 Wood kitchen cabinets

(P-2365)
ULTRA BUILT KITCHENS INC
1814 E 43rd St, Los Angeles (90058-1517)
PHONE..................323 232-3362
Iris Yanes, *Pr*
Eduardo Yanes, *
Daisy Blanco, *
EMP: 28 **EST:** 1993
SQ FT: 18,000
SALES (est): 2.35MM **Privately Held**
Web: www.ultrabuiltkitchens.net
SIC: 2434 Vanities, bathroom: wood

(P-2366)
VCSD INC
Also Called: Valley Cabinet
585 Vernon Way, El Cajon (92020-1934)
PHONE..................619 579-6886
Larry Doyle, *Pr*
Susan Raymond, *
EMP: 49 **EST:** 2011
SALES (est): 5.08MM **Privately Held**
Web: www.vcsdinc.com
SIC: 2434 Wood kitchen cabinets

(P-2367)
W L RUBOTTOM CO
320 W Lewis St, Ventura (93001-1335)
PHONE..................805 648-6943
Gary Mccoy, *Pr*
Lawrence Rubottom, *
EMP: 55 **EST:** 1946
SQ FT: 40,000
SALES (est): 5.01MM **Privately Held**
Web: www.wlrubottom.com
SIC: 2434 Wood kitchen cabinets

(P-2368)
WYNDHAM COLLECTION LLC
1175 Aviation Pl, San Fernando (91340-1460)
PHONE..................888 522-8476
Martin Symes, *Managing Member*
EMP: 26 **EST:** 2011
SQ FT: 100,000
SALES (est): 5.92MM **Privately Held**
Web: www.wyndhamcollection.com
SIC: 2434 Vanities, bathroom: wood

2435 Hardwood Veneer And Plywood

(P-2369)
G - L VENEER CO INC (PA)
2224 E Slauson Ave, Huntington Park (90255-2793)
PHONE..................323 582-5203
▲ **EMP:** 96 **EST:** 1977
SALES (est): 21.28MM
SALES (corp-wide): 21.28MM **Privately Held**

Web: www.glveneer.com
SIC: 2435 Hardwood veneer and plywood

(P-2370)
GENERAL VENEER MFG CO
8652 Otis St, South Gate (90280-3292)
P.O. Box 1607 (90280-1607)
PHONE..................323 564-2661
William Dewitt, *Pr*
Ed Bewitt, *
Douglas Bradley, *
EMP: 50 **EST:** 1942
SQ FT: 200,000
SALES (est): 8.74MM **Privately Held**
Web: www.generalveneer.com
SIC: 2435 3365 Hardwood veneer and plywood; Aerospace castings, aluminum

(P-2371)
PLYCRAFT INDUSTRIES INC
Also Called: Concepts & Wood
2100 E Slauson Ave, Huntington Park (90255-2727)
PHONE..................323 587-8101
Ashley Joffe, *Pr*
Nathan Joffe, *
Donald R Greenberg, *
▲ **EMP:** 180 **EST:** 1979
SQ FT: 71,187
SALES (est): 4.55MM **Privately Held**
Web: www.plycraft.com
SIC: 2435 Plywood, hardwood or hardwood faced

(P-2372)
SWANER HARDWOOD CO INC (PA)
5 W Magnolia Blvd, Burbank (91502-1776)
PHONE..................818 953-5350
Gary Swaner, *Pr*
Keith M Swaner, *
Beverly Swaner, *
Stephen Haag, *
▲ **EMP:** 70 **EST:** 1967
SQ FT: 4,500
SALES (est): 21.83MM
SALES (corp-wide): 21.83MM **Privately Held**
Web: www.swanerhardwood.com
SIC: 2435 5031 Hardwood veneer and plywood; Lumber: rough, dressed, and finished

2439 Structural Wood Members, Nec

(P-2373)
CALIFORNIA TRUSFRAME LLC
23447 Cajalco Rd, Perris (92570-8435)
PHONE..................951 657-7491
EMP: 206
SALES (corp-wide): 17.1B **Publicly Held**
Web: www.bldr.com
SIC: 2439 Trusses, wooden roof
HQ: California Trusframe, Llc
23665 Cajalco Rd
Perris CA 92570

(P-2374)
CALIFORNIA TRUSFRAME LLC (HQ)
Also Called: Ctf
23665 Cajalco Rd, Perris (92570-8181)
PHONE..................951 350-4880
Shawn Overholtzer, *Pr*
Steve Stroder, *
Mark Rome, *
EMP: 90 **EST:** 2011

▲ = Import ▼ = Export
◆ = Import/Export

SALES (est): 52.82MM
SALES (corp-wide): 17.1B **Publicly Held**
Web: www.bldr.com
SIC: 2439 Trusses, wooden roof
PA: Builders Firstsource, Inc.
6031 Cnnection Dr Ste 400
214 880-3500

(P-2375)
CALIFORNIA TRUSS COMPANY (PA)

23665 Cajalco Rd, Perris (92570-8181)
PHONE..............................951 657-7491
Kenneth M Cloyd, *Pr*
Mike Ruede, *VP*
Jim Butler, *CFO*
EMP: 87 **EST:** 1970
SQ FT: 5,000
SALES (est): 4.86MM
SALES (corp-wide): 4.86MM **Privately Held**
Web: www.caltruss.com
SIC: 2439 Trusses, wooden roof

(P-2376)
GOLDENWOOD TRUSS CORPORATION

11032 Nardo St, Ventura (93004-3210)
PHONE..............................805 659-2520
Kevin Tollefson, *Pr*
Darin Ranson, *
Myron Hodgson, *
EMP: 80 **EST:** 1998
SALES (est): 9.74MM **Privately Held**
Web: www.goldenwoodtruss.com
SIC: 2439 Trusses, wooden roof

(P-2377)
HANSON TRUSS INC

13950 Yorba Ave, Chino (91710-5520)
PHONE..............................909 591-9256
Donald R Hanson, *Pr*
Tom Hanson, *
EMP: 300 **EST:** 1985
SQ FT: 4,000
SALES (est): 10.44MM **Privately Held**
Web: www.hansontruss.com
SIC: 2439 Trusses, wooden roof

(P-2378)
HESPERIA HOLDING INC

9780 E Ave, Hesperia (92345-6174)
PHONE..............................760 244-8787
William Nalls, *Pr*
Mark Presgraves, *
Don Shimp, *
EMP: 74 **EST:** 2000
SALES (est): 1.73MM **Privately Held**
Web: www.capitalholdingsinc.com
SIC: 2439 Structural wood members, nec

(P-2379)
INLAND TRUSS INC (PA)

275 W Rider St, Perris (92571-3225)
PHONE..............................951 300-1758
Dan Irwin, *Pr*
Ernie Castro, *
EMP: 66 **EST:** 1991
SQ FT: 1,200
SALES (est): 7MM **Privately Held**
Web: www.inlandempiretruss.com
SIC: 2439 Trusses, wooden roof

(P-2380)
SIMPSON STRONG-TIE COMPANY INC

12246 Holly St, Riverside (92509-2314)
PHONE..............................714 871-8373
Dave Bastian, *Brnch Mgr*

EMP: 250
SQ FT: 40,845
SALES (corp-wide): 2.21B **Publicly Held**
Web: www.strongtie.com
SIC: 2439 3429 Structural wood members, nec; Hardware, nec
HQ: Simpson Strong-Tie Company Inc.
5956 W Las Positos Blvd
Pleasanton CA 94588
925 560-9000

(P-2381)
SPATES FABRICATORS INC

Also Called: Spates Fabricators
85435 Middleton St, Thermal (92274-9619)
PHONE..............................760 397-4122
Tom Spates, *Pr*
David Spates, *
Frankie Spates, *
EMP: 51 **EST:** 1976
SQ FT: 40,000
SALES (est): 9.52MM **Privately Held**
Web: www.spates.com
SIC: 2439 Trusses, except roof: laminated lumber

(P-2382)
T L TIMMERMAN CNSTR INC

Also Called: Timco
9845 Santa Fe Ave E, Hesperia (92345-6216)
P.O. Box 402563 (92340-2563)
PHONE..............................760 244-2532
Timothy L Timmerman, *Pr*
Anita Timmerman, *
EMP: 30 **EST:** 1976
SQ FT: 7,700
SALES (est): 2.15MM **Privately Held**
SIC: 2439 Trusses, wooden roof

2441 Nailed Wood Boxes And Shook

(P-2383)
BASAW MANUFACTURING INC (PA)

Also Called: Basaw Manufacturing
11323 Hartland St, North Hollywood (91605-6310)
PHONE..............................818 765-6650
Robert Allen, *Pr*
Hugh Mullen, *
Eleazar Padilla, *
Jorge Cea, *
Martha Rivera, *
▲ **EMP:** 32 **EST:** 1990
SALES (est): 0.51MM
SALES (corp-wide): 9.51MM **Privately Held**
Web: www.basaw.com
SIC: 2441 7389 Shipping cases, wood: nailed or lock corner; Packaging and labeling services

(P-2384)
CAL-COAST PKG & CRATING INC

2040 E 220th St, Carson (90810-1603)
PHONE..............................310 518-7215
Dale Loughry, *Pr*
▲ **EMP:** 35 **EST:** 1957
SQ FT: 58,000
SALES (est): 2.55MM **Privately Held**
Web: www.calcoastpacking.com
SIC: 2441 2449 Shipping cases, wood: nailed or lock corner; Wood containers, nec

2448 Wood Pallets And Skids

(P-2385)
ARNIES SUPPLY SERVICE LTD (PA)

1541 N Ditman Ave, Los Angeles (90063-2501)
P.O. Box 26 (91754-0026)
PHONE..............................323 263-1696
Arnold Espino, *Pr*
Madeline Espino, *
Maria Espino, *
EMP: 25 **EST:** 1975
SALES (est): 4.4MM
SALES (corp-wide): 4.4MM **Privately Held**
Web: www.arniessupply.com
SIC: 2448 Pallets, wood

(P-2386)
COMMERCIAL LBR & PALLET CO INC (PA)

135 Long Ln, City Of Industry (91746-2699)
PHONE..............................626 968-0631
Raymond Gutierrez, *Pr*
EMP: 150 **EST:** 1941
SQ FT: 10,000
SALES (est): 24.18MM
SALES (corp-wide): 24.18MM **Privately Held**
Web: www.clcpallets.com
SIC: 2448 5031 Pallets, wood; Lumber: rough, dressed, and finished

(P-2387)
E VASQUEZ DISTRIBUTORS INC

Also Called: Oxnard Pallet Company
4524 E Pleasant Valley Rd, Oxnard (93033-2309)
P.O. Box 1748 (93032-1748)
PHONE..............................805 487-8458
Elias Vasquez Junior, *Pr*
Beatrice Vasquez, *
EMP: 30 **EST:** 1989
SQ FT: 480
SALES (est): 3.99MM **Privately Held**
Web: www.oxnardpalletco.com
SIC: 2448 4214 Pallets, wood; Local trucking with storage

(P-2388)
G C PALLETS INC

5490 26th St, Riverside (92509-2212)
PHONE..............................909 357-8515
Mayra Gaona, *CEO*
Sebastian Gaona, *
EMP: 30 **EST:** 2001
SALES (est): 2.45MM **Privately Held**
Web: www.gcpalletsusa.com
SIC: 2448 Pallets, wood

(P-2389)
IFCO SYSTEMS US LLC

8950 Rochester Ave Ste 150, Rancho Cucamonga (91730-5541)
PHONE..............................909 484-4332
Mike Ellis, *Prin*
EMP: 56
Web: www.ifco.com
SIC: 2448 Pallets, wood
PA: Ifco Systems Us, Llc
3030 N Rcky Pt Dr Ste 300

(P-2390)
PALLET MASTERS INC

655 E Florence Ave, Los Angeles (90001-2319)
PHONE..............................323 758-1713
Stephen H Anderson, *Pr*

EMP: 55 **EST:** 1991
SQ FT: 105,000
SALES (est): 1.69MM **Privately Held**
Web: www.palletmasters.com
SIC: 2448 2441 2439 Pallets, wood; Boxes, wood; Structural wood members, nec

(P-2391)
RAMIREZ PALLETS INC

8431 Sultana Ave, Fontana (92335-3298)
PHONE..............................909 822-2066
Cresencio Ramirez, *Pr*
EMP: 35 **EST:** 1977
SALES (est): 2.58MM **Privately Held**
Web: www.ramirezpallets.com
SIC: 2448 Pallets, wood

(P-2392)
SATCO INC (PA)

Also Called: Satco
1601 E El Segundo Blvd, El Segundo (90245-4334)
PHONE..............................310 322-4719
Glenn M Proctor, *CEO*
Vincent Voong, *
Richard Weis, *
▲ **EMP:** 125 **EST:** 1968
SQ FT: 27,000
SALES (est): 30.19MM
SALES (corp-wide): 30.19MM **Privately Held**
Web: www.satco-inc.com
SIC: 2448 3537 Pallets, wood and metal combination; Containers (metal), air cargo

(P-2393)
VOTAW WOOD PRODUCTS INC

Also Called: Pomona Box Co
301 W Imperial Hwy, La Habra (90631-7263)
P.O. Box 536 (90633-0536)
PHONE..............................714 871-0932
EMP: 30 **EST:** 1929
SALES (est): 2.23MM **Privately Held**
Web: www.pomonabox.com
SIC: 2448 2441 5085 Pallets, wood; Boxes, wood; Boxes, crates, etc., other than paper

2449 Wood Containers, Nec

(P-2394)
GREIF INC

6001 S Eastern Ave, Commerce (90040-3413)
PHONE..............................323 724-7500
EMP: 26
SALES (corp-wide): 5.22B **Publicly Held**
Web: www.greif.com
SIC: 2449 2655 Shipping cases and drums, wood: wirebound and plywood; Fiber cans, drums, and similar products
PA: Greif, Inc.
425 Winter Rd
740 549-6000

(P-2395)
PICNIC AT ASCOT INC

3237 W 131st St, Hawthorne (90250-5514)
PHONE..............................310 674-3098
Paul Whitlock, *Pr*
Jill Brown, *
◆ **EMP:** 30 **EST:** 1992
SQ FT: 20,000
SALES (est): 3.78MM **Privately Held**
Web: www.picnicatascot.com
SIC: 2449 5947 Baskets: fruit and vegetable, round stave, till, etc.; Gift, novelty, and souvenir shop

2451 Mobile Homes

(P-2396)
CAVCO INDUSTRIES INC
Also Called: Fleetwood Homes
7007 Jurupa Ave, Riverside (92504-1015)
P.O. Box 49991 (92514-1991)
PHONE..............................951 688-5353
Mike Hayes, *Brnch Mgr*
EMP: 46
SALES (corp-wide): 1.79B **Publicly Held**
Web: www.cavco.com
SIC: 2451 2452 Mobile homes;
Prefabricated buildings, wood
PA: Cavco Industries, Inc.
3636 N Centl Ave Ste 1200
602 256-6263

(P-2397)
D-MAC INC
1105 E Discovery Ln, Anaheim
(92801-1121)
PHONE..............................714 808-3918
David A Wade, *Prin*
EMP: 26 **EST:** 1998
SALES (est): 1.77MM **Privately Held**
Web: www.d-macinc.com
SIC: 2451 5039 5032 Mobile home frames;
Structural assemblies, prefabricated: non-
wood; Paving materials

(P-2398)
DVELE INC
25525 Redlands Blvd, Loma Linda
(92354-2009)
P.O. Box 1710 (92354-0150)
PHONE..............................909 796-2561
EMP: 45
SALES (corp-wide): 8.07MM **Privately
Held**
Web: www.dvele.com
SIC: 2451 2452 Mobile homes, except
recreational; Prefabricated buildings, wood
PA: Dvele, Inc.
5521 La Jolla Blvd
805 323-3711

(P-2399)
DVELE OMEGA CORPORATION
Also Called: Hallmark Southwest
25525 Redlands Blvd, Loma Linda
(92354-2009)
P.O. Box 1710 (92354-0150)
PHONE..............................909 796-2561
Luca Brammer, *Pr*
EMP: 100 **EST:** 2018
SQ FT: 5,000
SALES (est): 12.27MM **Privately Held**
Web: www.dvele.com
SIC: 2451 2452 Mobile homes, personal or
private use; Prefabricated wood buildings

(P-2400)
**FLEETWOOD HOMES
CALIFORNIA INC (DH)**
Also Called: Fleetwood Homes
7007 Jurupa Ave, Riverside (92504-1015)
P.O. Box 7638 (92513-7638)
PHONE..............................951 351-2494
Elvin Smith, *Pr*
Boyd R Plowman, *
Forrest D Theobald, *
Lyle N Larkin, *
Roger L Howsmon, *
▲ **EMP:** 176 **EST:** 1963
SQ FT: 262,900
SALES (est): 10.39MM **Privately Held**
SIC: 2451 Mobile homes
HQ: Fleetwood Enterprises, Inc.
1351 Pomona Rd Ste 230

Corona CA 92882
951 354-3000

(P-2401)
NEXTMOD INC
6361 Box Springs Blvd, Riverside
(92507-0716)
P.O. Box 2008 (91709-0067)
PHONE..............................909 740-3120
Melina Corona, *CEO*
Sean Khan, *
Elvia Chavez, *
EMP: 45 **EST:** 2012
SALES (est): 1.3MM **Privately Held**
Web: www.nextmodinc.com
SIC: 2451 7519 Mobile buildings: for
commercial use; Mobile offices and
commercial units, rental

(P-2402)
SKYLINE HOMES INC
499 W Esplanade Ave, San Jacinto
(92583-5001)
P.O. Box 670 (92581-0670)
PHONE..............................951 654-9321
Jim Claverie, *Genl Mgr*
EMP: 115
SALES (corp-wide): 2.02B **Publicly Held**
Web: www.skylinehomes.com
SIC: 2451 Mobile homes
HQ: Skyline Homes, Inc.
2520 Bypass Rd
Elkhart IN 46514
574 294-6521

2452 Prefabricated Wood Buildings

(P-2403)
**APPLIED POLYTECH SYSTEMS
INC**
Also Called: A P S
26000 Springbrook Ave Ste 102, Santa
Clarita (91350-2592)
PHONE..............................818 504-9261
Christine Wagner, *Pr*
EMP: 30 **EST:** 1988
SQ FT: 6,000
SALES (est): 772.85K **Privately Held**
Web: www.apsincprecast.com
SIC: 2452 Prefabricated wood buildings

(P-2404)
PLH PRODUCTS INC
10541 Calle Lee Ste 119, Los Alamitos
(90720-6782)
PHONE..............................714 739-6622
Seung Woo Lee, *Ch Bd*
Kyung Min Park, *
Won Yong Lee, *
◆ **EMP:** 405 **EST:** 1992
SALES (est): 24.43MM **Privately Held**
Web: www.plhproducts.com
SIC: 2452 2449 5999 Sauna rooms,
prefabricated, wood; Hot tubs, wood;
Sauna equipment and supplies

(P-2405)
WALDEN STRUCTURES INC
1000 Bristol St N # 126, Newport Beach
(92660-8916)
PHONE..............................909 389-9100
Charlie Walden, *Owner*
Michael J Dominici, *
Curtis H Claire, *
EMP: 400 **EST:** 1996
SQ FT: 150,000
SALES (est): 48.47MM **Privately Held**
Web: www.silvercreekmodular.com

SIC: 2452 Modular homes, prefabricated,
wood

2491 Wood Preserving

(P-2406)
**HOOVER TREATED WOOD PDTS
INC**
Also Called: Hoover Treated Wood Pdts Plant
5601 District Blvd, Bakersfield
(93313-2129)
PHONE..............................661 833-0429
EMP: 23
SALES (corp-wide): 4.41B **Publicly Held**
Web: www.frtw.com
SIC: 2491 Structural lumber and timber,
treated wood
HQ: Hoover Treated Wood Products, Inc.
154 Wire Rd
Thomson GA 30824
706 595-5058

(P-2407)
**WEST COAST WOOD
PRESERVING LLC**
5601 District Blvd, Bakersfield
(93313-2129)
PHONE..............................661 833-0429
▲ **EMP:** 125
SIC: 2491 Preserving (creosoting) of wood

2499 Wood Products, Nec

(P-2408)
ALACO LADDER COMPANY
5167 G St, Chino (91710-5143)
PHONE..............................909 591-7561
Gil Jacobs, *Pr*
Mario Garcia, *
▼ **EMP:** 25 **EST:** 1946
SQ FT: 26,000
SALES (est): 669.22K
SALES (corp-wide): 6.72MM **Privately
Held**
Web: www.alacoladder.com
SIC: 2499 3354 3499 Ladders, wood;
Aluminum extruded products; Metal ladders
PA: B, E & P Enterprises, Llc
5167 G St
909 591-7561

(P-2409)
B E & P ENTERPRISES LLC (PA)
Also Called: Alaco Ladder Company
5167 G St, Chino (91710-5143)
PHONE..............................909 591-7561
Fred Evans, *
Gil Jacobs, *
Stephen Bernstein, *
EMP: 24 **EST:** 1946
SALES (est): 4.72MM
SALES (corp-wide): 4.72MM **Privately
Held**
Web: www.alacoladder.com
SIC: 2499 3499 3354 Ladders, wood;
Ladders, portable: metal; Aluminum
extruded products

(P-2410)
BRENT-WOOD PRODUCTS INC
17071 Hercules St, Hesperia (92345-7621)
P.O. Box 17037 (90807-7037)
PHONE..............................800 400-7335
Lawrence D Hobbs, *CEO*
Birgitta Olin, *
Anna Pinili, *
▼ **EMP:** 30 **EST:** 1963
SQ FT: 26,000

SALES (est): 1.34MM **Privately Held**
Web: www.brent-wood.com
SIC: 2499 Reels, plywood

(P-2411)
CRI 2000 LP (PA)
Also Called: Lso
2245 San Diego Ave Ste 125, San Diego
(92110-2072)
PHONE..............................619 542-1975
Mitchell G Lynn, *Pt*
◆ **EMP:** 50 **EST:** 2002
SQ FT: 10,000
SALES (est): 10.42MM **Privately Held**
Web: www.cri2000.com
SIC: 2499 5112 5049 5092 Picture frame
molding, finished; Office supplies, nec;
School supplies; Arts and crafts equipment
and supplies

(P-2412)
LARSON-JUHL US LLC
Also Called: Larson Picture Frames
12206 Bell Ranch Dr, Santa Fe Springs
(90670-3361)
PHONE..............................562 946-6873
Anthony Eikenberry, *Mgr*
EMP: 31
SALES (corp-wide): 364.48B **Publicly
Held**
Web: www.artmaterialsservice.com
SIC: 2499 Picture frame molding, finished
HQ: Larson-Juhl Us L L C
990 Pchtree Indus Blvd Un
Suwanee GA 30024
770 279-5200

(P-2413)
OUTDOOR DIMENSIONS LLC
5325 E Hunter Ave, Anaheim (92807-2054)
PHONE..............................714 578-9555
Brian Pickler, *Managing Member*
Donald Pickler, *
Brian Pickler, *VP*
EMP: 160 **EST:** 1974
SQ FT: 80,000
SALES (est): 39.28MM **Privately Held**
Web: www.outdoordimensions.com
SIC: 2499 3993 3281 Signboards, wood;
Signs and advertising specialties; Cut stone
and stone products

(P-2414)
**PACIFIC PANEL PRODUCTS
CORP**
Also Called: Pacific Panel Products
15601 Arrow Hwy, Irwindale (91706-2004)
P.O. Box 2204 (91706-1126)
PHONE..............................626 851-0444
Jon R Dickey, *CEO*
▲ **EMP:** 39 **EST:** 1994
SQ FT: 79,800
SALES (est): 6.13MM **Privately Held**
Web: www.pacificpanel.com
SIC: 2499 Decorative wood and woodwork

(P-2415)
PRO TOUR MEMORABILIA LLC
Also Called: Ptm Images
700 N San Vicente Blvd Ste G696, West
Hollywood (90069-5073)
P.O. Box 15084 (90209-1084)
PHONE..............................424 303-7200
◆ **EMP:** 25 **EST:** 1995
SQ FT: 8,000
SALES (est): 998.88K **Privately Held**
Web: pro-tour-memorabilia-llc.hub.biz
SIC: 2499 Picture and mirror frames, wood

(P-2416)
QUALITY FIRST WOODWORKS INC
1264 N Lakeview Ave, Anaheim
(92807-1831)
PHONE..............................714 632-0480
Mark Nappy, *Pr*
Chad Nappy, *
EMP: 115 EST: 1989
SQ FT: 30,000
SALES (est): 10.53MM **Privately Held**
Web: www.qfwinc.com
SIC: 2499 1751 Decorative wood and
   woodwork; Cabinet building and installation

(P-2417)
ROMA MOULDING INC
6230 N Irwindale Ave, Irwindale
(91702-3208)
PHONE..............................626 334-2539
Jon Mathews, *Opers Mgr*
EMP: 44
SALES (corp-wide): 28.86MM **Privately Held**
Web: www.romamoulding.com
SIC: 2499 5023 Picture frame molding,
   finished; Frames and framing, picture and
   mirror
PA: Roma Moulding Inc
   360 Hanlan Rd
   905 850-1500

(P-2418)
UNIVERSITY FRAMES INC
Also Called: Campus Images
3060 E Miraloma Ave, Anaheim
(92806-1810)
PHONE..............................714 575-5100
John G Winn, *CEO*
Diane Winn, *
▲ EMP: 50 EST: 1996
SQ FT: 20,000
SALES (est): 5.01MM **Privately Held**
Web: www.universityframes.com
SIC: 2499 5999 Picture frame molding,
   finished; Picture frames, ready made

2511 Wood Household Furniture

(P-2419)
BAU FURNITURE MFG INC
21 Kelly Ln, Ladera Ranch (92694-1463)
PHONE..............................949 643-2729
Thomas Bau, *Pr*
Linda Bau, *
EMP: 52 EST: 1978
SALES (est): 589.1K **Privately Held**
SIC: 2511 2512 2521 Tables, household:
   wood; Upholstered household furniture;
   Tables, office: wood

(P-2420)
BIG TREE FURNITURE & INDS INC (PA)
760 S Vail Ave, Montebello (90640-4954)
PHONE..............................310 894-7500
Joe Ho, *CEO*
◆ EMP: 47 EST: 1985
SALES (est): 8.58MM **Privately Held**
SIC: 2511 Wood household furniture

(P-2421)
BROWNWOOD FURNITURE INC
9805 6th St Ste 104, Rancho Cucamonga
(91730-5751)
PHONE..............................909 945-5613
Rick Vartanian, *Pr*

Pat Eberly, *
Jose Navarro, *
◆ EMP: 150 EST: 1979
SQ FT: 107,000
SALES (est): 5.36MM **Privately Held**
Web: www.brownwoodfurniture.com
SIC: 2511 Wood bedroom furniture

(P-2422)
DOREL HOME FURNISHINGS INC
5400 Shea Center Dr, Ontario
(91761-7892)
PHONE..............................909 390-5705
EMP: 67
SALES (corp-wide): 1.39B **Privately Held**
Web: www.ameriwoodhome.com
SIC: 2511 Console tables: wood
HQ: Dorel Home Furnishings, Inc.
   410 E 1st St S
   Wright City MO 63390
   636 745-3351

(P-2423)
DOUG MOCKETT & COMPANY INC
1915 Abalone Ave, Torrance (90501-3706)
P.O. Box 3333 (90266-1333)
PHONE..............................310 318-2491
Tyra Cunningham, *Pr*
Susan Darby Gordon, *
Sonia Marie H Mockett, *
◆ EMP: 65 EST: 1984
SALES (est): 12.96MM **Privately Held**
Web: www.mockett.com
SIC: 2511 5072 Unassembled or unfinished
   furniture, household: wood; Furniture
   hardware, nec

(P-2424)
FREMARC INDUSTRIES INC (PA)
Also Called: Fremarc Designs
18810 San Jose Ave, City Of Industry
(91748-1325)
P.O. Box 1086 (91788-1086)
PHONE..............................626 965-0802
Maurice M Donenfeld, *Pr*
Harriette Donenfeld, *
▲ EMP: 78 EST: 1971
SQ FT: 45,000
SALES (est): 1.62MM
SALES (corp-wide): 1.62MM **Privately Held**
Web: www.fremarc.com
SIC: 2511 Wood household furniture

(P-2425)
FURNITURE TECHNICS INC
Also Called: Furniture Techniques
2900 Supply Ave, Commerce (90040-2708)
PHONE..............................562 802-0261
Cesar Rousseau, *Pr*
Ricardo Flores, *
EMP: 25 EST: 1988
SALES (est): 823.21K **Privately Held**
SIC: 2511 2426 Wood household furniture;
   Furniture stock and parts, hardwood

(P-2426)
HOLLYWOOD CHAIRS (PA)
Also Called: Totally Bamboo
120 W Grand Ave Ste 102, Escondido
(92025-2642)
PHONE..............................760 471-6600
Joanne Sullivan, *CEO*
Thomas Sullivan, *Sec*
◆ EMP: 24 EST: 1999
SQ FT: 10,000
SALES (est): 6.86MM **Privately Held**
Web: www.totallybamboo.com

SIC: 2511 Wood household furniture

(P-2427)
JP PRODUCTS LLC
2054 Davie Ave, Commerce (90040-1705)
PHONE..............................310 237-6237
Patrick Mooney, *Managing Member*
Jacqueline Mooney, *Managing Member*
EMP: 46 EST: 2010
SQ FT: 35,000
SALES (est): 1.11MM **Privately Held**
SIC: 2511 Wood household furniture

(P-2428)
LAUREN ANTHONY & CO INC
11425 Woodside Ave Ste B, Santee
(92071-4726)
PHONE..............................619 590-1141
Randy T Passanisi, *Pr*
EMP: 23 EST: 2004
SALES (est): 233.05K **Privately Held**
Web: www.anthonylauren.com
SIC: 2511 Wood household furniture

(P-2429)
LEGACY COMMERCIAL HOLDINGS INC
Also Called: Armen Living
28939 Avenue Williams, Valencia
(91355-4183)
PHONE..............................818 767-6626
Kevin Kevonian, *Pr*
Kevon Kevonian, *Pr*
Honigsfeld Lee, *VP*
▲ EMP: 35 EST: 2007
SALES (est): 6.75MM **Privately Held**
Web: www.armenliving.com
SIC: 2511 2514 2531 2521 Kitchen and
   dining room furniture; Metal lawn and
   garden furniture; Public building and related
   furniture; Wood office furniture

(P-2430)
MIKHAIL DARAFEEV INC (PA)
5075 Edison Ave, Chino (91710-5716)
PHONE..............................909 613-1818
Antonina Darafeev, *Pr*
Paul Darafeev, *
George Darafeev, *
▲ EMP: 50 EST: 1957
SALES (est): 9.95MM
SALES (corp-wide): 9.95MM **Privately Held**
Web: www.darafeev.com
SIC: 2511 Stools, household: wood

(P-2431)
MORETTIS DESIGN COLLECTION INC
16926 Keegan Ave Ste C, Carson
(90746-1322)
PHONE..............................310 638-5555
Mori Afshar, *Pr*
▲ EMP: 30 EST: 1992
SALES (est): 691.66K **Privately Held**
Web: www.morettisdesign.com
SIC: 2511 Wood household furniture

(P-2432)
NOVA LIFESTYLE INC (PA)
6565 E Washington Blvd, Commerce
(90040-1821)
PHONE..............................323 888-9999
Thanh H Lam, *Ch Bd*
Min Su, *Corporate Secretary*
Jeffery Chuang, *CFO*
Mark Chapman, *VP Mktg*
Steven Qiang Liu, *VP*
EMP: 24 EST: 2011

SALES (est): 11.09MM
SALES (corp-wide): 11.09MM **Publicly Held**
Web: www.novalifestyle.com
SIC: 2511 2512 Wood household furniture;
   Upholstered household furniture

(P-2433)
RADFORD CABINETS INC
216 E Avenue K8, Lancaster (93535-4527)
PHONE..............................661 729-8931
Steven Radford, *Pr*
Robert Mendoza, *
Sharon Radford, *
EMP: 70 EST: 1992
SQ FT: 20,000
SALES (est): 6.57MM **Privately Held**
Web: www.radfordcabinetsinc.com
SIC: 2511 2434 2521 Kitchen and dining
   room furniture; Wood kitchen cabinets;
   Cabinets, office: wood

(P-2434)
RUSS BASSETT CORP
Also Called: Group Five
8189 Byron Rd, Whittier (90606-2615)
PHONE..............................562 945-2445
Mike Dressendorfer, *CEO*
Peter Fink, *
▲ EMP: 115 EST: 1959
SQ FT: 112,000
SALES (est): 21.9MM **Privately Held**
Web: www.russbassett.com
SIC: 2511 Wood household furniture

(P-2435)
SAN DIEGO ARCFT INTERIORS INC
2381 Boswell Rd, Chula Vista
(91914-3509)
PHONE..............................619 474-1997
Juan Carlos Vasquez, *Pr*
▲ EMP: 23 EST: 2009
SALES (est): 2.63MM **Privately Held**
Web: www.sdaircraftinteriors.com
SIC: 2511 Chairs, household, except
   upholstered: wood

(P-2436)
SANDBERG FURNITURE MFG CO INC (PA)
Also Called: Sandberg Furniture
5705 Alcoa Ave, Vernon (90058-3794)
P.O. Box 58291 (90058-0291)
PHONE..............................323 582-0711
John Sandberg, *CEO*
Mark Nixon, *Sr VP*
▲ EMP: 225 EST: 1918
SALES (est): 24.72MM
SALES (corp-wide): 24.72MM **Privately Held**
Web: www.sandbergfurniture.com
SIC: 2511 Wood bedroom furniture

(P-2437)
TREND MANOR FURN MFG CO INC
17047 Gale Ave, City Of Industry
(91745-1887)
PHONE..............................626 964-6493
Theodore Vecchione, *Pr*
▲ EMP: 42 EST: 1946
SQ FT: 63,000
SALES (est): 2.83MM **Privately Held**
Web: www.trendmanor.com
SIC: 2511 Wood household furniture

(P-2438)
WHALEN LLC (DH)
Also Called: Whalen Furniture Manufacturing
1578 Air Wing Rd, San Diego (92154-7706)
PHONE.........................619 423-9948
Jose Luis Laparte, *Pr*
David Levinson, *
◆ **EMP:** 26 **EST:** 1991
SQ FT: 100,000
SALES (est): 24.78MM **Privately Held**
Web: www.whalenfurniture.com
SIC: 2511 Wood household furniture
HQ: Li & Fung Development (China) Limited
10/F Lifung Twr
Cheung Sha Wan KLN

2512 Upholstered Household Furniture

(P-2439)
A RUDIN INC (PA)
Also Called: A Rudin Designs
6062 Alcoa Ave, Vernon (90058-3902)
PHONE.........................323 589-5547
Arnold Rudin, *Pr*
Ralph Rudin, *
◆ **EMP:** 92 **EST:** 1918
SQ FT: 117,000
SALES (est): 8.06MM
SALES (corp-wide): 8.06MM **Privately Held**
Web: www.arudin.com
SIC: 2512 5021 Upholstered household furniture; Household furniture

(P-2440)
ARDMORE HOME DESIGN INC (PA)
Also Called: Pigeon and Poodle
918 S Stimson Ave, City Of Industry (91745-1640)
PHONE.........................626 803-7769
Chris Dewitt, *CEO*
Oscar Yague, *
◆ **EMP:** 49 **EST:** 2012
SALES (est): 22.93MM
SALES (corp-wide): 22.93MM **Privately Held**
Web: www.madegoods.com
SIC: 2512 Upholstered household furniture

(P-2441)
BJ LIQUIDATION INC
Also Called: Burton James
428 Turnbull Canyon Rd, City Of Industry (91745-1011)
PHONE.........................626 961-7221
Harold Zoref, *CEO*
Norman Zoref, *
EMP: 80 **EST:** 1983
SQ FT: 28,000
SALES (est): 5.65MM **Privately Held**
Web: www.burtonjames.com
SIC: 2512 Upholstered household furniture

(P-2442)
CISCO BROS CORP (PA)
Also Called: Cisco & Brothers Designs
474 S Arroyo Pkwy, Pasadena (91105-2530)
PHONE.........................323 778-8612
Francisco Pinedo, *CEO*
Alba E Pinedo, *
◆ **EMP:** 145 **EST:** 1993
SALES (est): 31.43MM **Privately Held**
Web: www.ciscohome.net
SIC: 2512 Upholstered household furniture

(P-2443)
COMMERCIAL INTR RESOURCES INC
Also Called: Contract Resources
6077 Rickenbacker Rd, Commerce (90040-3031)
PHONE.........................562 926-5885
Roberta Tuchman, *CEO*
Stanley Rice, *
Barbara Rice, *
Stephanie Lesko, *
EMP: 65 **EST:** 1982
SQ FT: 28,000
SALES (est): 1.42MM **Privately Held**
Web: www.villahallmark.com
SIC: 2512 Upholstered household furniture

(P-2444)
DELLAROBBIA INC (PA)
119 Waterworks Way, Irvine (92618-3110)
PHONE.........................949 251-9532
David Soonlan, *Pr*
Sunee Soonlan, *
▲ **EMP:** 48 **EST:** 1979
SQ FT: 27,000
SALES (est): 673K
SALES (corp-wide): 673K **Privately Held**
Web: www.dellarobbia.com
SIC: 2512 Upholstered household furniture

(P-2445)
E J LAUREN LLC
Also Called: Ejl
2690 Pellissier Pl, City Of Industry (90601-1507)
PHONE.........................562 803-1113
Antonio Ocampo, *Managing Member*
◆ **EMP:** 50 **EST:** 2009
SALES (est): 2.33MM **Privately Held**
Web: www.ejlauren.com
SIC: 2512 Upholstered household furniture

(P-2446)
ELITE LEATHER LLC
1620 5th Ave Ste 400, San Diego (92101-2738)
PHONE.........................909 548-8600
▲ **EMP:** 100
Web: www.oneforvictory.com
SIC: 2512 Living room furniture: upholstered on wood frames

(P-2447)
GOMEN FURNITURE MFG INC
11612 Wright Rd, Lynwood (90262-3945)
PHONE.........................310 635-4894
Leonardo Gonzalez, *Pr*
▲ **EMP:** 30 **EST:** 1990
SALES (est): 1.22MM **Privately Held**
Web: www.gomenfurnmfg.com
SIC: 2512 7641 Upholstered household furniture; Upholstery work

(P-2448)
HARBOR FURNITURE MFG INC (PA)
Also Called: Harbor House
15817 Whitepost Ln, La Mirada (90638-3126)
PHONE.........................323 636-1201
Malcolm Tuttleton Junior, *Pr*
Brent Tuttleton, *
▲ **EMP:** 25 **EST:** 1929
SALES (est): 1.9MM
SALES (corp-wide): 1.9MM **Privately Held**
SIC: 2512 2511 6514 2521 Upholstered household furniture; Wood household furniture; Dwelling operators, except apartments; Wood office furniture

(P-2449)
HUNTINGTON INDUSTRIES INC
12520 Chadron Ave, Hawthorne (90250-4808)
PHONE.........................323 772-5575
▲ **EMP:** 150
SIC: 2512 Upholstered household furniture

(P-2450)
LITTLE CASTLE FURNITURE CO INC
301 Todd Ct, Oxnard (93030-5192)
P.O. Box 4254 (91359-1254)
PHONE.........................805 278-4646
Kayvan Torabian, *Pr*
▲ **EMP:** 35 **EST:** 1998
SQ FT: 9,000
SALES (est): 7.64MM **Privately Held**
Web: www.littlecastleinc.com
SIC: 2512 Upholstered household furniture

(P-2451)
M&J DESIGN INC
Also Called: M&J Design Furniture
1303 S Claudina St, Anaheim (92805-6235)
PHONE.........................714 687-9918
Jorge Mojica, *CEO*
EMP: 23 **EST:** 2018
SALES (est): 2.71MM **Privately Held**
Web: www.mjdesignus.com
SIC: 2512 2541 5712 Upholstered household furniture; Wood partitions and fixtures; Custom made furniture, except cabinets

(P-2452)
MARGE CARSON INC (PA)
555 W 5th St, Los Angeles (90013-1010)
P.O. Box 1283 (91769-1283)
PHONE.........................626 571-1111
James Labarge, *CEO*
Dominic Ching, *
▲ **EMP:** 82 **EST:** 1951
SALES (est): 9.82MM
SALES (corp-wide): 9.82MM **Privately Held**
Web: www.margecarson.com
SIC: 2512 2511 Living room furniture: upholstered on wood frames; Wood household furniture

(P-2453)
MARLIN DESIGNS LLC
13845 Alton Pkwy Ste C, Irvine (92618-1643)
PHONE.........................949 637-7257
Ronald Whitlock, *Managing Member*
EMP: 150 **EST:** 1995
SALES (est): 2.03MM **Privately Held**
Web: www.marlin-designs.com
SIC: 2512 Upholstered household furniture

(P-2454)
MARTIN/BRATTRUD INC
1231 W 134th St, Gardena (90247-1902)
PHONE.........................323 770-4171
Allan G Stratford, *Pr*
Patrick Baxter, *
EMP: 95 **EST:** 1946
SQ FT: 38,000
SALES (est): 9.12MM **Privately Held**
Web: www.martinbrattrud.com
SIC: 2512 2511 Upholstered household furniture; Tables, household: wood

(P-2455)
MINSON CORPORATION
Also Called: Mallin Casual Furniture
11701 Wilshire Blvd Ste 15a, Los Angeles (90025-1599)
PHONE.........................323 513-1041
▲ **EMP:** 300
Web: www.minson.com
SIC: 2512 2514 Wood upholstered chairs and couches; Lawn furniture: metal

(P-2456)
NEW CLASSIC HM FURNISHING INC (PA)
Also Called: New Classic Furniture
7351 Mcguire Ave, Fontana (92336-1668)
PHONE.........................909 484-7676
Jean Tong, *CEO*
◆ **EMP:** 44 **EST:** 2001
SALES (est): 104.06MM
SALES (corp-wide): 104.06MM **Privately Held**
Web: www.newclassicfurniture.com
SIC: 2512 5023 Living room furniture: upholstered on wood frames; Decorative home furnishings and supplies

(P-2457)
R C FURNITURE INC
1111 Jellick Ave, City Of Industry (91748-1212)
PHONE.........................626 964-4100
Rene Cazares, *Pr*
▲ **EMP:** 81 **EST:** 1986
SQ FT: 25,000
SALES (est): 1.67MM **Privately Held**
Web: www.renecazares.com
SIC: 2512 5021 Upholstered household furniture; Furniture

(P-2458)
ROBERT MICHAEL LTD
10035 Geary Ave, Santa Fe Springs (90670-3237)
P.O. Box 2397 (90670-0397)
PHONE.........................562 758-6789
◆ **EMP:** 263
Web: www.robertmichaellimited.com
SIC: 2512 Upholstered household furniture

(P-2459)
ROYAL CUSTOM DESIGNS LLC
Also Called: Custom Furniture Designs, LLC
13951 Monte Vista Ave, Chino (91710-5536)
PHONE.........................909 591-8990
Jeff Sladick, *Pr*
▲ **EMP:** 133 **EST:** 1970
SQ FT: 35,000
SALES (est): 11.45MM
SALES (corp-wide): 11.45MM **Privately Held**
Web: www.royalcustomdesigns.com
SIC: 2512 Upholstered household furniture
PA: Makers & Craftsmen Llc
396 E Jefferson Ave
909 525-5181

(P-2460)
STITCH INDUSTRIES INC
Also Called: Joybird
767 S Alameda St Ste 360, Los Angeles (90021-1665)
PHONE.........................888 282-0842
Kurt L Darrow, *CEO*
EMP: 50 **EST:** 2013
SALES (est): 27.55MM
SALES (corp-wide): 2.05B **Publicly Held**
Web: www.joybird.com
SIC: 2512 5961 5712 Upholstered household furniture; Catalog and mail-order houses; Furniture stores
PA: La-Z-Boy Incorporated
1 Lazboy Dr
734 242-1444

▲ = Import ▼ = Export
◆ = Import/Export

(P-2461)

TERRA FURNITURE INC

1950 Salto Dr, Hacienda Heights
(91745-4209)
▲ **EMP:** 41 **EST:** 1964
SALES (est): 932.61K **Privately Held**
Web: www.terrafurniture.com
SIC: 2512 2514 2522 2511 Upholstered
household furniture; Metal household
furniture; Office furniture, except wood;
Wood lawn and garden furniture

(P-2462)

YEN-NHAI INC

Also Called: Nathan Anthony Furniture
4940 District Blvd, Vernon (90058-2718)
PHONE......................323 584-1315
Khai Mai, *Pr*
EMP: 40 **EST:** 1995
SALES (est): 3.65MM **Privately Held**
Web: www.nafurniture.com
SIC: 2512 Upholstered household furniture

2514 Metal Household Furniture

(P-2463)

ATLANTIC REPRESENTATIONS INC (PA)

Also Called: Snowsound USA
10018 Santa Fe Springs Rd, Santa Fe
Springs (90670-2922)
P.O. Box 2399 (90670-0399)
PHONE......................562 903-9550
Shahriar Dardashti, *Pr*
Farnaz Dardashti, *
Leo Dardashti, *
▲ **EMP:** 30 **EST:** 1984
SQ FT: 150,000
SALES (est): 8.62MM **Privately Held**
Web: www.snowsoundusa.com
SIC: 2514 2511 Metal household furniture;
Wood household furniture

(P-2464)

ATLAS SURVIVAL SHELTERS LLC

7407 Telegraph Rd, Montebello
(90640-6515)
PHONE......................323 727-7084
Ronal D Hubbard, *Managing Member*
EMP: 25 **EST:** 2011
SQ FT: 30,000
SALES (est): 2.34MM **Privately Held**
Web: www.atlassurvivalshelters.com
SIC: 2614 Beds, including folding and
cabinet, household: metal

(P-2465)

CASUALWAY USA LLC

Also Called: Casualway Home & Garden
1623 Lola Way, Oxnard (93030-5080)
PHONE......................805 660-7408
Guoxiang Wu, *Pr*
Ralph Ybarra, *VP*
EMP: 99
SALES (est): 492.58K **Privately Held**
SIC: 2514 Garden furniture, metal

(P-2466)

DOUGLAS FURNITURE OF CALIFORNIA LLC

809 Tyburn Rd, Palos Verdes Estates
(90274-2843)
PHONE......................310 749-0003
▲ **EMP:** 2400

SIC: 2514 2512 Dinette sets: metal;
Recliners: upholstered on wood frames

(P-2467)

EARTHLITE LLC (DH)

Also Called: Earthlite
990 Joshua Way, Vista (92081-7855)
P.O. Box 51245 (90051-5545)
PHONE......................760 599-1112
James Chenevey, *CEO*
Philippe Barret, *
Tara Grodjesk, *WELLNESS*
◆ **EMP:** 86 **EST:** 1987
SQ FT: 68,000
SALES (est): 42.65MM
SALES (corp-wide): 47.43MM **Privately
Held**
Web: www.earthlite.com
SIC: 2514 5091 2531 Tables, household:
metal; Spa equipment and supplies; Chairs,
portable folding
HQ: Earthlite Holdings, Llc
150 E 58th St Fl 37
New York NY 10155
212 317-2004

(P-2468)

ELLIOTTS DESIGNS INC

2473 E Rancho Del Amo Pl, Compton
(90220-6311)
PHONE......................310 631-4931
Elliott Jones, *Pr*
Julie Jones, *
EMP: 30 **EST:** 1974
SQ FT: 127,000
SALES (est): 399.15K **Privately Held**
SIC: 2514 5021 Beds, including folding and
cabinet, household: metal; Furniture

(P-2469)

GRACO CHILDRENS PRODUCTS INC

17182 Nevada St, Victorville (92394-7806)
PHONE......................770 418-7200
EMP: 293
SALES (corp-wide): 8.13B **Publicly Held**
SIC: 2514 Juvenile furniture, household:
metal
HQ: Graco Children's Products Inc.
6655 Pachtree Dunwoody Rd
Atlanta GA 30328
770 418-7200

(P-2470)

JBI LLC

Also Called: Buchbinder, Jay Industries
18521 S Santa Fe Ave, Compton
(90221-5624)
PHONE......................310 537-2910
Claudio Luna, *Mgr*
EMP: 48
SALES (corp-wide): 25.21MM **Privately
Held**
Web: www.jbi-interiors.com
SIC: 2514 2221 2511 Tables, household:
metal; Fiberglass fabrics; Wood household
furniture
PA: Jbi, Llc
2650 E El Presidio St
310 886-8034

(P-2471)

MURRAYS IRON WORKS INC (PA)

7355 E Slauson Ave, Commerce
(90040-3626)
PHONE......................323 521-1100
▲ **EMP:** 165 **EST:** 1966
SALES (est): 2.54MM
SALES (corp-wide): 2.54MM **Privately
Held**

Web: www.murraysiw.com
SIC: 2514 3446 5021 5961 Metal household
furniture; Fences or posts, ornamental iron
or steel; Furniture; Furniture and
furnishings, mail order

(P-2472)

RSI HOME PRODUCTS INC

RSI HOME PRODUCTS, INC.
620 Newport Center Dr Ste 1030, Newport
Beach (92660-8048)
PHONE......................949 720-1116
Terri Stevens, *Brnch Mgr*
EMP: 184
SALES (corp-wide): 1.85B **Publicly Held**
Web: www.americanwoodmark.com
SIC: 2514 2541 1751 Metal household
furniture; Wood partitions and fixtures;
Cabinet and finish carpentry
HQ: Rsi Home Products Llc
400 E Orangethorpe Ave
Anaheim CA 92801
714 449-2200

(P-2473)

RSI HOME PRODUCTS LLC (HQ)

Also Called: RSI
400 E Orangethorpe Ave, Anaheim
(92801-1046)
PHONE......................714 449-2200
Alex Calabrese, *CEO*
Jeff Hoeft, *
David Lowrie, *
▲ **EMP:** 700 **EST:** 1994
SQ FT: 675,000
SALES (est): 559.01MM
SALES (corp-wide): 1.85B **Publicly Held**
Web: www.americanwoodmark.com
SIC: 2514 2541 3281 2434 Kitchen cabinets:
metal; Counter and sink tops; Cut stone
and stone products; Wood kitchen cabinets
PA: American Woodmark Corporation
561 Shady Elm Rd
540 665-9100

(P-2474)

SANDUSKY LEE LLC

16125 Widmere Rd, Arvin (93203-9307)
P.O. Box 517 (93203-0517)
PHONE......................661 854-5551
Jim Coontz, *Brnch Mgr*
EMP: 26
SALES (corp-wide): 279.66MM **Privately
Held**
Web: www.sanduskycabinets.com
SIC: 2514 2522 Metal household furniture;
Office furniture, except wood
HQ: Sandusky Lee Llc
80 Keystone St
Littlestown PA 17340
717 359-4111

(P-2475)

TROPITONE FURNITURE CO INC (DH)

5 Marconi, Irvine (92618-2594)
PHONE......................949 595-2010
Randy Danielson, *Ex VP*
◆ **EMP:** 300 **EST:** 1954
SQ FT: 100,000
SALES (est): 100MM
SALES (corp-wide): 141.25MM **Privately
Held**
Web: www.tropitone.com
SIC: 2514 2522 Garden furniture, metal;
Office furniture, except wood
HQ: Jordan Brown Inc
475 W Town Pl Ste 200
Saint Augustine FL 32092

(P-2476)

WESLEY ALLEN INC

Also Called: Iron Beds of America
1001 E 60th St, Los Angeles (90001-1098)
PHONE......................323 231-4275
Victor Sawan, *CEO*
▲ **EMP:** 150 **EST:** 1976
SQ FT: 100,000
SALES (est): 19.05MM **Privately Held**
Web: www.wesleyallen.com
SIC: 2514 Metal household furniture

2515 Mattresses And Bedsprings

(P-2477)

ADVANCED INNVTIVE RCVERY TECH

3401 Space Center Ct Ste 811b, Jurupa
Valley (91752-1132)
PHONE......................949 273-8100
Brad Bannister, *Mgr*
EMP: 30
SALES (corp-wide): 14.06MM **Privately
Held**
Web: www.airtechfoam.com
SIC: 2515 Mattresses, containing felt, foam
rubber, urethane, etc.
PA: Advanced Innovative Recovery
Technologies, Inc.
23615 El Toro Rd
949 273-8100

(P-2478)

AMERICAN NATIONAL MFG INC

252 Mariah Cir, Corona (92879-1751)
PHONE......................951 273-7888
Eve Miller, *Pr*
Craig Miller, *VP*
◆ **EMP:** 65 **EST:** 1993
SQ FT: 75,000
SALES (est): 8.59MM **Privately Held**
Web: www.americannationalmfg.com
SIC: 2515 5712 Mattresses and bedsprings;
Furniture stores

(P-2479)

AMF SUPPORT SURFACES INC (DH)

1691 N Delilah St, Corona (92879-1885)
PHONE......................951 549-6800
Fredrick Kohnke, *CEO*
Curt Wyatt, *
Charles C Wyatt, *
Carole A Wyatt, *
▲ **FMP:** 162 **EST:** 1932
SQ FT: 40,000
SALES (est): 9.42MM
SALES (corp-wide): 14.81B **Publicly Held**
SIC: 2515 Mattresses, containing felt, foam
rubber, urethane, etc.
HQ: Anodyne Medical Device, Inc.
1069 State Road 46 E
Batesville IN 47006

(P-2480)

BANNER MATTRESS INC

1501 E Cooley Dr Ste B, Colton
(92324-3991)
PHONE......................909 835-4200
▲ **EMP:** 57
Web: www.bannermattressonline.com
SIC: 2515 5021 Bedsprings, assembled;
Mattresses

(P-2481)

BRENTWOOD HOME LLC (PA)

Also Called: Silverrest

---

621 Burning Tree Rd, Fullerton
(92833-1448)
PHONE..................562 949-3759
Vy Nguyen, *CEO*
EMP: 128 **EST:** 2015
SQ FT: 80,000
SALES (est): 26.71MM
SALES (corp-wide): 26.71MM **Privately Held**
Web: www.brentwoodhome.com
SIC: 2515 5021 5712 Mattresses, containing felt, foam rubber, urethane, etc.; Mattresses ; Mattresses

(P-2482)
ES KLUFT & COMPANY INC (DH)
Also Called: Aireloom
11096 Jersey Blvd Ste 101, Rancho Cucamonga (91730-5158)
PHONE..................909 373-4211
Jon Stowe, *CEO*
Brad Goodshaw, *CFO*
◆ **EMP:** 174 **EST:** 2004
SALES (est): 110.87MM **Privately Held**
Web: www.aireloom.com
SIC: 2515 Mattresses, innerspring or box spring
HQ: Vi - Spring Limited
Ernesettle Lane
Plymouth PL5 2
175 236-6311

(P-2483)
G & M MATTRESS AND FOAM CORPORATION
Also Called: Fun Furnishings
10606 7th St, Rancho Cucamonga (91730-5438)
P.O. Box 7220 (91750-7220)
PHONE..................909 593-1000
EMP: 80 **EST:** 1987
SALES (est): 6.07MM **Privately Held**
SIC: 2515 Mattresses, containing felt, foam rubber, urethane, etc.

(P-2484)
GATEWAY MATTRESS CO INC
624 S Vail Ave, Montebello (90640-4992)
PHONE..................323 725-1923
EMP: 65 **EST:** 1961
SALES (est): 6.41MM **Privately Held**
Web: www.gatewaymattress.com
SIC: 2515 Mattresses, innerspring or box spring

(P-2485)
GOLDEN MATTRESS CO INC
11680 Wright Rd, Lynwood (90262-3945)
PHONE..................323 887-1888
San Dang, *CEO*
Phuc Nguyen, *
◆ **EMP:** 52 **EST:** 1980
SALES (est): 1.13MM **Privately Held**
Web: www.goldenmattressus.com
SIC: 2515 5021 Mattresses and foundations; Mattresses

(P-2486)
IDEAL MATTRESS COMPANY INC
1901 Main St, San Diego (92113-2129)
PHONE..................619 595-0003
Jesse Hernandez, *Pr*
John Hernandez, *
Patrick Goularte, *
Estella Goularte, *
EMP: 25 **EST:** 1929
SQ FT: 10,000
SALES (est): 388.95K **Privately Held**
SIC: 2515 Mattresses, containing felt, foam rubber, urethane, etc.

(P-2487)
LEGGETT & PLATT INCORPORATED
Also Called: Lpcc 6008
1050 S Dupont Ave, Ontario (91761-1578)
PHONE..................909 937-1010
Barry Kubasak, *Mgr*
EMP: 96
SALES (corp-wide): 5.15B **Publicly Held**
Web: www.leggett.com
SIC: 2515 Mattresses, innerspring or box spring
PA: Leggett & Platt, Incorporated
1 Leggett Rd
417 358-8131

(P-2488)
MARSPRING CORPORATION
Also Called: Los Angeles Fiber Co
5190 S Santa Fe Ave, Vernon (90058-3532)
P.O. Box 58643 (90058-0643)
PHONE..................310 484-6849
Ronald Greitzer, *Pr*
EMP: 56
SALES (corp-wide): 6.62MM **Privately Held**
Web: www.reliancecarpetcushion.com
SIC: 2515 Spring cushions
PA: Marspring Corporation
4920 S Boyle Ave
323 589-5637

(P-2489)
PURA NATURALS INC
3401 Space Center Ct Ste 811a, Jurupa Valley (91752-1130)
PHONE..................949 273-8100
Brad Bannister, *Mgr*
EMP: 30
SALES (corp-wide): 14.06MM **Privately Held**
Web: www.puranaturalsproducts.com
SIC: 2515 Mattresses, containing felt, foam rubber, urethane, etc.
HQ: Pura Naturals, Inc.
23615 El Toro Rd Ste X300
Lake Forest CA 92630
949 273-8100

(P-2490)
SERTA SIMMONS BEDDING LLC
23700 Cactus Ave, Moreno Valley (92553-8900)
PHONE..................951 807-8467
Stephanie Mckibbon, *Brnch Mgr*
EMP: 50
SALES (corp-wide): 4.59B **Privately Held**
Web: www.sertasimmons.com
SIC: 2515 Mattresses and bedsprings
HQ: Serta Simmons Bedding, Llc
2451 Industry Ave
Doraville GA 30360

(P-2491)
SKY RIDER EQUIPMENT CO INC
1180 N Blue Gum St, Anaheim (92806-2409)
PHONE..................714 632-6890
Martin Villegas, *CEO*
Carl Gray, *
Dev Donnelley, *
Karl Keranen, *
▲ **EMP:** 30 **EST:** 1984
SQ FT: 12,000
SALES (est): 5.37MM **Privately Held**
Web: www.sky-rider.com
SIC: 2515 7349 5719 Foundations and platforms; Window cleaning; Window shades, nec

(P-2492)
SOUTH BAY INTERNATIONAL INC
Also Called: Cariloha
8570 Hickory Ave, Rancho Cucamonga (91739-9632)
PHONE..................909 718-5000
Guohai Tang, *Pr*
Daniella Serven, *
Weijun She, *
Wendiao Hou, *
▲ **EMP:** 25 **EST:** 1993
SALES (est): 50.07MM **Privately Held**
Web: www.southbayinternational.com
SIC: 2515 Mattresses and bedsprings

(P-2493)
STRESS-O-PEDIC MATTRESS CO INC
Also Called: Stress-O-Pedic
2060 S Wineville Ave Ste A, Ontario (91761-3633)
PHONE..................909 605-2010
▲ **EMP:** 58
Web: www.stressopedic.com
SIC: 2515 Mattresses, innerspring or box spring

(P-2494)
TEMPO INDUSTRIES INC
2137 E 55th St, Vernon (90058-3439)
P.O. Box 1822 (91353-1822)
PHONE..................415 552-8074
▲ **EMP:** 134
Web: www.tempofurniture.com
SIC: 2515 Sleep furniture

(P-2495)
VISIONARY SLEEP LLC
2060 S Wineville Ave Ste A, Ontario (91761-3633)
PHONE..................909 605-2010
Carter Gronbach, *Mgr*
EMP: 58
SALES (corp-wide): 7.4MM **Privately Held**
SIC: 2515 Mattresses, innerspring or box spring
PA: Visionary Sleep, Llc
1721 Moon Lake Blvd # 205
812 945-4155

(P-2496)
WIDLY INC
Also Called: American Furniture Alliance
785 E Harrison St Ste 100, Corona (92879-1350)
PHONE..................951 279-0900
▲ **EMP:** 130
SIC: 2515 5021 Mattresses and bedsprings; Furniture

2517 Wood Television And Radio Cabinets

(P-2497)
ANA GLOBAL LLC (PA)
2360 Marconi Ct, San Diego (92154-7241)
PHONE..................619 482-9990
▲ **EMP:** 90 **EST:** 1953
SALES (est): 9.69MM
SALES (corp-wide): 9.69MM **Privately Held**
Web: www.anaglb.com
SIC: 2517 5999 Television cabinets, wood; Medical apparatus and supplies

(P-2498)
GILBERT MARTIN WDWKG CO INC (PA)
Also Called: Martin Furniture
2345 Britannia Blvd, San Diego (92154-8313)
PHONE..................800 268-5669
Gilbert Martin, *CEO*
Mark Mitchell, *CFO*
◆ **EMP:** 30 **EST:** 1980
SQ FT: 210,000
SALES (est): 10.01MM
SALES (corp-wide): 10.01MM **Privately Held**
Web: www.martinfurniture.com
SIC: 2517 2511 2521 5021 Home entertainment unit cabinets, wood; Wood household furniture; Wood office furniture; Furniture

---

2519 Household Furniture, Nec

(P-2499)
ARKTURA LLC (HQ)
966 Sandhill Ave, Carson (90746-1217)
PHONE..................310 532-1050
Chris Kabatsi, *Managing Member*
▲ **EMP:** 30 **EST:** 2008
SALES (est): 10.35MM
SALES (corp-wide): 1.3B **Publicly Held**
Web: www.arktura.com
SIC: 2519 Furniture, household: glass, fiberglass, and plastic
PA: Armstrong World Industries, Inc.
2500 Columbia Ave
717 397-0611

(P-2500)
CALIFRNIA FURN COLLECTIONS INC
Also Called: Artifacts International
150 Reed Ct Ste A, Chula Vista (91911-5890)
PHONE..................619 621-2455
Eric Vogt, *Pr*
EMP: 114 **EST:** 1986
SQ FT: 40,000
SALES (est): 1.5MM **Privately Held**
Web: www.artifactsinternational.com
SIC: 2519 2514 2511 2512 Household furniture, except wood or metal: upholstered ; Metal household furniture; Wood household furniture; Upholstered household furniture

(P-2501)
DON ALDERSON ASSOCIATES INC
3327 La Cienega Pl, Los Angeles (90016-3116)
PHONE..................310 837-5141
Juan Guardado, *Prin*
EMP: 40 **EST:** 1979
SALES (est): 580.16K **Privately Held**
SIC: 2519 Household furniture, except wood or metal: upholstered

(P-2502)
NEXT DAY FRAME INC
11560 Wright Rd, Lynwood (90262-3944)
PHONE..................310 886-0851
Nancy Abelar, *CEO*
EMP: 65 **EST:** 2012
SALES (est): 2.17MM **Privately Held**
SIC: 2519 Household furniture, except wood or metal: upholstered

▲ = Import ▼ = Export
◆ = Import/Export

(P-2503)

NICHOLAS MICHAEL DESIGNS LLC

2330 Raymer Ave, Fullerton (92833-2515)
PHONE.................................714 562-8101
Michael A Cimarusti Senior, *CEO*
Michael J Cimarusti I, *
▲ **EMP:** 120 **EST:** 2003
SALES (est): 21.79MM **Privately Held**
Web: www.mndca.com
SIC: 2519 Household furniture, except wood
  or metal: upholstered

2521 Wood Office Furniture

(P-2504)

A M CABINETS INC (PA)

239 E Gardena Blvd, Gardena
  (90248-2813)
PHONE.................................310 532-1919
Alex H Mc Kay Junior, *CEO*
Alex H Mc Kay Junior, *Pr*
Nancy Wolfinger, *
EMP: 88 **EST:** 1975
SQ FT: 35,000
SALES (est): 14.89MM
SALES (corp-wide): 14.89MM **Privately Held**
Web: www.amcabinets.com
SIC: 2521 2434 2541 Wood office furniture;
  Wood kitchen cabinets; Counters or
  counter display cases, wood

(P-2505)

BLEAU CONSULTING INC (PA)

555 Raven St, San Diego (92102-4523)
PHONE.................................619 263-5550
Ron P Montbleau, *Pr*
Marti Montbleau, *
David Zammit, *
Barton Ward, *
EMP: 57 **EST:** 1980
SQ FT: 32,000
SALES (est): 25.72MM
SALES (corp-wide): 25.72MM **Privately Held**
Web: www.montbleau.com
SIC: 2521 1751 2434 Wood office furniture;
  Cabinet building and installation; Wood
  kitchen cabinets

(P-2506)

CASEWORX INC (PA)

Also Called: Caseworx
1130 Research Dr, Redlands (92374-4562)
PHONE.................................909 799-8550
Bruce Humphrey, *Pr*
Gregg Schneider, *Sec*
▲ **EMP:** 25 **EST:** 1992
SQ FT: 28,000
SALES (est): 4.81MM **Privately Held**
Web: www.caseworx.com
SIC: 2521 Cabinets, office: wood

(P-2507)

CRI SUB 1 (DH)

Also Called: E O C
1715 S Anderson Ave, Compton
  (90220-5005)
PHONE.................................310 537-1657
Ken Bodger, *CEO*
Richard L Sinclair Junior, *Pr*
Charles Hess, *VP*
▲ **EMP:** 27 **EST:** 1969
SQ FT: 120,000
SALES (est): 1.79MM
SALES (corp-wide): 11.48MM **Privately Held**

SIC: 2521 Cabinets, office: wood
HQ: Chromcraft Revington, Inc.
  140 Bradford Dr Ste A
  West Berlin NJ 08091

(P-2508)

DESKMAKERS INC

6525 Flotilla St, Commerce (90040-1713)
PHONE.................................323 264-2260
Philip Polishook, *CEO*
John Bornstein, *
◆ **EMP:** 50 **EST:** 1982
SQ FT: 105,000
SALES (est): 12.55MM **Privately Held**
Web: www.deskmakers.com
SIC: 2521 Desks, office: wood

(P-2509)

FORTRESS INC

Also Called: Off Broadway
1721 Wright Ave, La Verne (91750-5841)
PHONE.................................909 593-8600
Donald I Wolper, *Pr*
▲ **EMP:** 35 **EST:** 1959
SQ FT: 100
SALES (est): 6.66MM **Privately Held**
Web: www.fortresseating.com
SIC: 2521 2522 Chairs, office: padded,
  upholstered, or plain: wood; Chairs, office:
  padded or plain: except wood

(P-2510)

NAKAMURA-BEEMAN INC

8520 Wellsford Pl, Santa Fe Springs
  (90670-2226)
PHONE.................................562 696-1400
Mike Beeman, *Pr*
EMP: 40 **EST:** 1978
SQ FT: 20,000
SALES (est): 4.91MM **Privately Held**
Web: www.nbifixtures.com
SIC: 2521 3429 2541 Wood office furniture;
  Cabinet hardware; Display fixtures, wood

(P-2511)

NEW MAVERICK DESK INC

Also Called: Maverick Desk
15100 S Figueroa St, Gardena
  (90248-1724)
PHONE.................................310 217-1554
John Long, *CEO*
Ted Jaroszewicz, *
Rich Mealey, *
▲ **EMP:** 150 **EST:** 1997
SQ FT: 1,000
SALES (est): 20.65MM **Privately Held**
Web: www.maverickdesk.com
SIC: 2521 Wood office furniture
HQ: Workstream Inc.
  3158 Production Dr
  Fairfield OH 45014

(P-2512)

NORSTAR OFFICE PRODUCTS INC (PA)

Also Called: Boss
5353 Jillson St, Commerce (90040-2115)
PHONE.................................323 262-1919
William W Huang, *Pr*
◆ **EMP:** 40 **EST:** 1991
SQ FT: 150,000
SALES (est): 37.35MM **Privately Held**
Web: www.boss-chair.com
SIC: 2521 2522 Chairs, office: padded,
  upholstered, or plain: wood; Chairs, office:
  padded or plain: except wood

(P-2513)

OFFICE CHAIRS INC

Also Called: Oci
14815 Radburn Ave, Santa Fe Springs
  (90670-5319)
PHONE.................................562 802-0464
Sharon Klapper, *Pr*
Donald J Simek, *
Joseph J Klapper Junior, *Sec*
▲ **EMP:** 60 **EST:** 1974
SQ FT: 60,000
SALES (est): 2.92MM **Privately Held**
Web: www.ocicontract.com
SIC: 2521 2512 Wood office furniture;
  Chairs: upholstered on wood frames

(P-2514)

OFS BRANDS HOLDINGS INC

5559 Mcfadden Ave, Huntington Beach
  (92649-1317)
P.O. Box 100 (47542-0100)
PHONE.................................714 903-2257
Craig Baker, *Pr*
EMP: 550 **EST:** 2018
SALES (est): 2.5MM
SALES (corp-wide): 228.87MM **Privately Held**
SIC: 2521 Wood office furniture
PA: Ofs Brands Holdings Inc.
  1204 E 6th St
  800 521-5381

(P-2515)

PARKINSON ENTERPRISES INC

Also Called: Salman
135 S State College Blvd Ste 625, Brea
  (92821-5811)
PHONE.................................714 626-0275
Michael Parkinson, *CEO*
Carolyn Parkinson, *
EMP: 70 **EST:** 1993
SQ FT: 75,000
SALES (est): 2.69MM **Privately Held**
SIC: 2521 Wood office furniture

(P-2516)

RBF LIFESTYLE HOLDINGS LLC

Also Called: Beverly Furniture
1441 W 2nd St, Pomona (91766-1202)
PHONE.................................626 333-5700
▲ **EMP:** 45
SIC: 2521 2511 Chairs, office: padded,
  upholstered, or plain: wood; Dining room
  furniture: wood

(P-2517)

S & H CABINETS AND MFG INC

10800 Mulberry Ave, Fontana
  (92337-7027)
PHONE.................................909 357-0551
Michael Hansen, *CEO*
EMP: 40 **EST:** 1954
SQ FT: 22,000
SALES (est): 4.87MM **Privately Held**
Web: www.shcabinets.com
SIC: 2521 2541 2431 Cabinets, office: wood;
  Table or counter tops, plastic laminated;
  Millwork

(P-2518)

SPACESTOR INC

16411 Carmenita Rd, Cerritos
  (90703-2216)
PHONE.................................310 410-0220
Charles Hubert Kingston, *CEO*
▲ **EMP:** 23 **EST:** 2013
SALES (est): 24.74MM **Privately Held**
Web: www.spacestor.com

SIC: 2521 2522 5712 Wood office furniture;
  Office furniture, except wood; Office
  furniture

(P-2519)

STOLO CABINETS INC (PA)

Also Called: Stolo Custom Cabinets
860 Challenger St, Brea (92821-2946)
PHONE.................................714 529-7303
Gary Stolo, *VP*
Justin Stolo, *
Robert F Stolo, *
EMP: 45 **EST:** 1953
SQ FT: 15,000
SALES (est): 9.55MM
SALES (corp-wide): 9.55MM **Privately Held**
Web: www.stolocabinets.com
SIC: 2521 Cabinets, office: wood

2522 Office Furniture, Except Wood

(P-2520)

ANGELL & GIROUX INC

2727 Alcazar St, Los Angeles (90033-1196)
P.O. Box 33156 (90033)
PHONE.................................323 269-8596
Richard M Hart, *CEO*
Carol A Hart, *
Kenneth Hart, *
EMP: 52 **EST:** 1956
SQ FT: 13,000
SALES (est): 5.41MM **Privately Held**
Web: www.angellandgiroux.com
SIC: 2522 3479 Cabinets, office: except
  wood; Painting, coating, and hot dipping

(P-2521)

ARTE DE MEXICO INC (PA)

1000 Chestnut St, Burbank (91506-1623)
PHONE.................................818 753-4559
Gerald J Stoffers, *CEO*
▲ **EMP:** 90 **EST:** 1982
SQ FT: 103,000
SALES (est): 8.01MM
SALES (corp-wide): 8.01MM **Privately Held**
Web: www.artedemexico.com
SIC: 2522 3645 Office furniture, except wood
  ; Residential lighting fixtures

(P-2522)

CARTERS METAL FABRICATORS INC

935 W 5th St, Azusa (91702-3311)
PHONE.................................626 815-4225
EMP: 30
Web: www.cartersmetal.com
SIC: 2522 Office furniture, except wood

(P-2523)

CRAFTWOOD INDUSTRIES INC

222 Shelbourne, Irvine (92620-2176)
P.O. Box 2068 (49422-2068)
PHONE.................................616 796-1209
Terry W Beckering, *Pr*
Roger Steensma, *
Kathy Prominski, *Corporate Secretary*
EMP: 35 **EST:** 1995
SALES (est): 1.45MM **Privately Held**
Web: www.craftwoodindustries.com
SIC: 2522 2531 2426 2511 Office furniture,
  except wood; Public building and related
  furniture; Hardwood dimension and flooring
  mills; Wood household furniture

(P-2524)
ELITE MFG CORP
Also Called: Elite Modern
12143 Altamar Pl, Santa Fe Springs
(90670-2501)
PHONE.................888 354-8356
Peter Luong, *CEO*
Robinson Ho, *
▲ **EMP:** 102 **EST:** 1988
SQ FT: 62,000
SALES (est): 16.12MM **Privately Held**
Web: www.elitemodern.com
SIC: 2522 2514 Office furniture, except wood
; Metal household furniture

(P-2525)
ERGOCRAFT CONTRACT SOLUTIONS
Also Called: Ergocraft Office Furniture
6055 E Washington Blvd Ste 500,
Commerce (90040-2426)
▲ **EMP:** 25 **EST:** 2001
SALES (est): 1.37MM **Privately Held**
Web: www.ecs-designs.com
SIC: 2522 Office furniture, except wood

(P-2526)
EXEMPLIS LLC (PA)
Also Called: Sitonit
6415 Katella Ave, Cypress (90630-5245)
PHONE.................714 995-4800
Paul Devries, *CEO*
Mike Mekjian, *
Patrick Sommerfield, *
◆ **EMP:** 40 **EST:** 1996
SQ FT: 20,000
SALES (est): 157.5MM **Privately Held**
Web: www.exemplis.com
SIC: 2522 Chairs, office: padded or plain:
except wood

(P-2527)
EXEMPLIS LLC
Also Called: Sit On It
6280 Artesia Blvd, Buena Park
(90620-1004)
PHONE.................714 995-4800
Paul Devries, *Mgr*
EMP: 132
Web: www.exemplis.com
SIC: 2522 2521 2512 Chairs, office: padded
or plain: except wood; Wood office furniture
; Upholstered household furniture
PA: Exemplis Llc
6415 Katella Ave

(P-2528)
EXEMPLIS LLC
Also Called: Ideon
6280 Artesia Blvd, Buena Park
(90620-1004)
PHONE.................714 898-5500
Craig Dumity, *Dir*
EMP: 38
Web: www.exemplis.com
SIC: 2522 5021 Chairs, office: padded or
plain: except wood; Furniture
PA: Exemplis Llc
6415 Katella Ave

(P-2529)
HIGHMARK SMART RELIABLE SEATING INC
Also Called: Highmark
5559 Mcfadden Ave, Huntington Beach
(92649-1317)
PHONE.................714 903-2257
◆ **EMP:** 200

SIC: 2522 Chairs, office: padded or plain:
except wood

(P-2530)
KORDEN INC
601 S Milliken Ave Ste H, Ontario
(91761-8103)
PHONE.................909 988-8979
Barjona S Meek, *Prin*
Thomas Mc Cormick, *Pr*
Jim Ethridge, *Ex VP*
EMP: 25 **EST:** 1949
SALES (est): 7.79MM **Privately Held**
Web: www.modernspace.com
SIC: 2522 Stools, office: except wood

(P-2531)
MCDOWELL CRAIG OFF SYSTEMS INC
Also Called: McDowell-Craig Office Furn
13146 Firestone Blvd, Norwalk (90650)
P.O. Box 349 (90651-0349)
PHONE.................562 921-4441
Brent G Mcdowell, *Pr*
Jeffrey C Mcdowell, *Sec*
EMP: 70 **EST:** 1995
SQ FT: 117,000
SALES (est): 2.49MM **Privately Held**
Web: www.mcdowellcraig.com
SIC: 2522 Office furniture, except wood

(P-2532)
SUPER STRUCT BLDG SYSTEMS INC
1251 Montalvo Way Ste F, Palm Springs
(92263)
P.O. Box 1014 (92247-1014)
PHONE.................760 322-2522
John G Kalogeris, *Pr*
Chris Kalogeris, *
EMP: 40 **EST:** 1960
SQ FT: 10,000
SALES (est): 598.29K **Privately Held**
SIC: 2522 2439 Panel systems and
partitions, office: except wood; Trusses,
wooden roof

(P-2533)
VERSA PRODUCTS (PA)
Also Called: Versatables.com
14105 Avalon Blvd, Los Angeles
(90061-2637)
PHONE.................310 353-7100
Christopher Laudadio, *CEO*
▲ **EMP:** 108 **EST:** 2000
SQ FT: 35,000
SALES (est): 21.68MM
SALES (corp-wide): 21.68MM **Privately Held**
Web: www.versatables.com
SIC: 2522 Office desks and tables, except
wood

(P-2534)
X-CHAIR LLC
6415 Katella Ave Ste 200, Cypress
(90630-5245)
PHONE.................844 492-4247
Anthony Mazlish, *Managing Member*
EMP: 39 **EST:** 2015
SALES (est): 2.4MM **Privately Held**
Web: www.xchair.com
SIC: 2522 Office furniture, except wood
PA: Exemplis Llc
6415 Katella Ave

2531 Public Building And Related Furniture

(P-2535)
AEROFOAM INDUSTRIES INC
Also Called: Quality Foam Packaging
31855 Corydon St, Lake Elsinore
(92530-8501)
PHONE.................951 245-4429
Noel Castellon, *Pr*
Noel Castellon Junior, *VP*
Jim Barrett, *
Ruth Castellon, *
Darlene Garay, *
▲ **EMP:** 80 **EST:** 2010
SQ FT: 150,000
SALES (est): 9.82MM **Privately Held**
Web: www.aerofoams.com
SIC: 2531 Seats, aircraft

(P-2536)
AIRO INDUSTRIES COMPANY
429 Jessie St, San Fernando (91340-2541)
PHONE.................818 838-1008
Bahram Salem, *Pr*
Mike Salem, *
▲ **EMP:** 25 **EST:** 1989
SQ FT: 20,000
SALES (est): 2.69MM **Privately Held**
Web: www.airoindustries.com
SIC: 2531 4581 Seats, aircraft; Aircraft
upholstery repair

(P-2537)
CLARIOS LLC
Also Called: Johnson Controls
2100 Chicago Ave, Riverside (92507-2202)
PHONE.................951 222-0284
EMP: 23
SALES (corp-wide): 69.83B **Privately Held**
Web: www.clarios.com
SIC: 2531 Public building and related
furniture
HQ: Clarios, Llc
5757 N Green Bay Ave Flor
Glendale WI 53209

(P-2538)
CLARIOS LLC
Also Called: Johnson Controls
39312 Leopard St Ste A, Palm Desert
(92211-1129)
PHONE.................760 200-5225
EMP: 38
SALES (corp-wide): 69.83B **Privately Held**
Web: www.clarios.com
SIC: 2531 Seats, automobile
HQ: Clarios, Llc
5757 N Green Bay Ave Flor
Glendale WI 53209

(P-2539)
CLARIOS LLC
Also Called: Johnson Controls
4100 Guardian St, Simi Valley
(93063-6717)
PHONE.................805 522-5555
Dimitri Dorfan, *Mgr*
EMP: 36
SALES (corp-wide): 69.83B **Privately Held**
Web: www.clarios.com
SIC: 2531 Seats, automobile
HQ: Clarios, Llc
5757 N Green Bay Ave Flor
Glendale WI 53209

(P-2540)
COD USA INC
Also Called: Creative Outdoor Distrs USA
25954 Commercentre Dr, Lake Forest
(92630-8815)
PHONE.................949 381-7367
Heather Smulson, *Pr*
Brian Horowitz, *CEO*
Barbara Tolbert, *COO*
◆ **EMP:** 23 **EST:** 2016
SQ FT: 34,000
SALES (est): 1.15MM **Privately Held**
SIC: 2531 Chairs, portable folding

(P-2541)
ECR4KIDS LP
Also Called: Early Childhood Resources
5630 Kearny Mesa Rd Ste B, San Diego
(92111-1323)
PHONE.................619 323-2005
Lee Siegel, *Pt*
◆ **EMP:** 25 **EST:** 2003
SALES (est): 5.26MM **Privately Held**
Web: www.ecr4kids.com
SIC: 2531 3944 2511 5021 Chairs, table and
arm; Craft and hobby kits and sets;
Children's wood furniture; Chairs
PA: Cri 2000, L.P.
2245 San Diego Ave # 125

(P-2542)
EUROTEC SEATING INCORPORATED
1000 S Euclid St, La Habra (90631-6806)
PHONE.................562 806-6171
◆ **EMP:** 50
SIC: 2531 Seats, automobile

(P-2543)
HOLGUIN & HOLGUIN INC
Also Called: Seating Resource
968 W Foothill Blvd, Azusa (91702-2842)
PHONE.................626 815-0168
Gilda Vega, *Pr*
John H Holguin, *
EMP: 45 **EST:** 1994
SQ FT: 25,000
SALES (est): 1.57MM **Privately Held**
Web: www.seatingresource.com
SIC: 2531 Public building and related
furniture

(P-2544)
J L FURNISHINGS LLC
Also Called: J L F/Lone Meadow
1620 5th Ave Ste 400, San Diego
(92101-2738)
PHONE.................310 605-6600
◆ **EMP:** 300
Web: www.thestandardbyrcd.com
SIC: 2531 2521 Chairs, table and arm;
Wood office chairs, benches and stools

(P-2545)
JOHNSON CONTROLS INC
Also Called: Johnson Controls
12393 Slauson Ave, Whittier (90606-2824)
PHONE.................562 698-8301
Stephen Roell, *Brnch Mgr*
EMP: 27
Web: www.johnsoncontrols.com
SIC: 2531 1711 Seats, automobile; Warm air
heating and air conditioning contractor
HQ: Johnson Controls, Inc.
5757 N Green Bay Ave
Milwaukee WI 53209
866 496-1999

(P-2546)

JOHNSON CONTROLS INC

Also Called: Johnson Controls
5770 Warland Dr Ste A, Cypress
(90630-5047)
PHONE...............................562 594-3200
Dough Beebe, *Mgr*
EMP: 150
Web: www.johnsoncontrols.com
SIC: 2531 1711 5075 5065 Seats, automobile
; Heating systems repair and maintenance;
Warm air heating and air conditioning;
Electronic parts and equipment, nec
HQ: Johnson Controls, Inc.
5757 N Green Bay Ave
Milwaukee WI 53209
866 496-1999

(P-2547)

JOSEPH MANUFACTURING CO INC

Also Called: Mortech Manufacturing
411 N Aerojet Dr, Azusa (91702-3253)
PHONE...............................626 334-1471
Gino Joseph, *Pr*
Gino Joseph, *CEO*
Paul Joseph, *
Christy Haines, *
◆ **EMP:** 82 **EST:** 1986
SQ FT: 43,000
SALES (est): 11.64MM **Privately Held**
Web: www.mortechmfg.com
SIC: 2531 5087 Altars and pulpits; Funeral
director's equipment and supplies

(P-2548)

KRUEGER INTERNATIONAL INC

16510 Bake Pkwy Ste 100, Irvine
(92618-5606)
PHONE...............................949 748-7000
EMP: 44
SALES (corp-wide): 484.48MM **Privately
Held**
Web: www.ki.com
SIC: 2531 School furniture
PA: Krueger International, Inc.
1330 Bellevue St
920 468-8100

(P-2549)

LOUIS SARDO UPHOLSTERY INC (PA)

Also Called: Sardo Bus & Coach Upholstery
512 W Rosecrans Ave, Gardena
(90248-1515)
PHONE...............................310 327-0532
Louis Sardo, *Pr*
Jeanie Sardo, *
EMP: 55 **EST:** 1916
SQ FT: 10,000
SALES (est): 5MM
SALES (corp-wide): 5MM **Privately Held**
Web: www.sardobus.com
SIC: 2531 3713 7641 Seats, automobile;
Truck and bus bodies; Reupholstery and
furniture repair

(P-2550)

ORBO CORPORATION (PA)

Also Called: Eurotec Seating
1000 S Euclid St, La Habra (90631-6806)
PHONE...............................562 806-6171
Oscar Galvez, *Pr*
EMP: 37 **EST:** 2001
SALES (est): 1.86MM
SALES (corp-wide): 1.86MM **Privately
Held**
Web: www.4seating.com
SIC: 2531 Seats, automobile

(P-2551)

PACIFIC HOSPITALITY DESIGN INC

Also Called: PH Design
2620 S Malt Ave, Commerce (90040-3206)
PHONE...............................323 278-7998
Gilberto Martinez, *CEO*
Ana Martinez, *
EMP: 25 **EST:** 1979
SQ FT: 14,000
SALES (est): 2.31MM **Privately Held**
Web: www.phdesign.com
SIC: 2531 Public building and related
furniture

(P-2552)

SEATING CONCEPTS LLC

4229 Ponderosa Ave Ste B, San Diego
(92123-1519)
PHONE...............................619 491-3159
Juan Carlos Letayf, *Managing Member*
Bill Overton, *
Jose Letayf, *
◆ **EMP:** 30 **EST:** 1982
SALES (est): 3.57MM **Privately Held**
Web: www.scicustom.com
SIC: 2531 5021 Theater furniture; Chairs

(P-2553)

TALIMAR SYSTEMS INC

3105 W Alpine St, Santa Ana (92704-6911)
PHONE...............................714 557-4884
David G Wesdell, *Pr*
▲ **EMP:** 37 **EST:** 1988
SQ FT: 11,000
SALES (est): 4.77MM **Privately Held**
Web: www.talimarsystems.com
SIC: 2531 5712 7389 5932 Public building
and related furniture; Furniture stores;
Merchandise liquidators; Office furniture,
secondhand

(P-2554)

VILLA FURNITURE MFG CO

Also Called: Villa International
16440 Manning Way, Cerritos (90703-2225)
PHONE...............................714 535-7272
Andrew M Greenthal, *Pr*
▲ **EMP:** 125 **EST:** 1949
SALES (est): 9.91MM **Privately Held**
Web: www.villainternational.com
SIC: 2531 2522 Vehicle furniture; Office
furniture, except wood

(P-2555)

VIRCO MFG CORPORATION (PA)

2027 Harpers Way, Torrance (90501-1524)
PHONE...............................310 533-0474
Robert A Virtue, *Ch Bd*
Douglas A Virtue, *
J Scott Bell, *Sr VP*
Robert E Dose, *Sr VP*
Patricia Quinones, *Sr VP*
◆ **EMP:** 88 **EST:** 1950
SQ FT: 560,000
SALES (est): 269.12MM
SALES (corp-wide): 269.12MM **Publicly
Held**
Web: www.virco.com
SIC: 2531 2522 2511 School furniture; Office
furniture, except wood; Wood household
furniture

2541 Wood Partitions And Fixtures

(P-2556)

AMTREND CORPORATION

1458 Manhattan Ave, Fullerton
(92831-5222)
PHONE...............................714 630-2070
Hamid A Malik, *Pr*
Javeeda Malik, *
EMP: 85 **EST:** 1980
SQ FT: 45,000
SALES (est): 16.52MM **Privately Held**
Web: www.amtrend.com
SIC: 2541 2521 7641 2512 Wood partitions
and fixtures; Wood office furniture;
Upholstery work; Upholstered household
furniture

(P-2557)

BLOCK TOPS INC (PA)

Also Called: Top Source, The
1321 S Sunkist St, Anaheim (92806-5614)
PHONE...............................714 978-5080
Vanessa Bates, *CEO*
Nate Kolenski, *
▲ **EMP:** 34 **EST:** 1977
SQ FT: 10,000
SALES (est): 7.19MM
SALES (corp-wide): 7.19MM **Privately
Held**
Web: www.blocktops.com
SIC: 2541 2519 3281 2821 Table or counter
tops, plastic laminated; Furniture,
household: glass, fiberglass, and plastic;
Cut stone and stone products; Plastics
materials and resins

(P-2558)

BRISTOL OMEGA INC

9441 Opal Ave Ste 2, Mentone
(92359-9900)
PHONE...............................909 794-6862
Ralf G Zacky, *CEO*
EMP: 27 **EST:** 1993
SALES (est): 2.03MM **Privately Held**
Web: www.bristolomega.com
SIC: 2541 1611 Wood partitions and fixtures;
General contractor, highway and street
construction

(P-2559)

CCM ENTERPRISES (PA)

10848 Wheatlands Ave, Santee
(92071-2855)
PHONE...............................619 562-2605
Cody L Nosko, *CEO*
Duane Nosco, *
Virginia Jaggi, *
EMP: 60 **EST:** 1995
SQ FT: 67,543
SALES (est): 2.13MM **Privately Held**
Web: www.ccmmfg.com
SIC: 2541 1799 Counter and sink tops;
Kitchen and bathroom remodeling

(P-2560)

CK MANUFACTURING & TRADING INC

Also Called: Kosakura Associates
3 Holland, Irvine (92618-2506)
P.O. Box 1190 (75483-1190)
PHONE...............................949 529-3400
▲ **EMP:** 35
SIC: 2541 Display fixtures, wood

(P-2561)

COLUMBIA SHOWCASE & CAB CO INC

11034 Sherman Way Ste A, Sun Valley
(91352-4915)
PHONE...............................818 765-9710
Samuel M Patterson Junior, *CEO*
▲ **EMP:** 125 **EST:** 1950
SQ FT: 170,000
SALES (est): 8.6MM **Privately Held**
SIC: 2541 1542 Cabinets, except
refrigerated: show, display, etc.: wood;
Commercial and office building contractors

(P-2562)

COMPATICO INC

1901 S Archibald Ave, Ontario
(91761-8548)
PHONE...............................616 940-1772
John Rea, *Pr*
Richard Posthumus, *
William Boer, *
Cheryl Daniels, *
Carrie Boer, *
◆ **EMP:** 45 **EST:** 1989
SALES (est): 1.55MM **Privately Held**
Web: www.compatico.com
SIC: 2541 Wood partitions and fixtures

(P-2563)

EUROPEAN WHOLESALE COUNTER

10051 Prospect Ave, Santee (92071-4321)
PHONE...............................619 562-0565
Pete Sciarrino, *CEO*
EMP: 150 **EST:** 2008
SQ FT: 40,000
SALES (est): 3.59MM **Privately Held**
Web: www.europeancompany.com
SIC: 2541 1799 Counter and sink tops;
Counter top installation

(P-2564)

F-J-E INC

Also Called: Jf Fixtures & Design
546 W Esther St, Long Beach
(90813-1529)
PHONE...............................562 437-7466
Frank Ernandes, *Pr*
Barbara Ernandes, *
EMP: 25 **EST:** 1983
SQ FT: 26,000
SALES (est): 1.99MM **Privately Held**
Web: www.jffixtures.com
SIC: 2541 2542 Store fixtures, wood;
Fixtures, store: except wood

(P-2565)

IDEAL PRODUCTS INC

4025 Garner Rd, Riverside (92501-1043)
P.O. Box 4090 (91761-1006)
PHONE...............................951 727-8600
Robert L Martin Junior, *CEO*
Virginia Martin, *
EMP: 35 **EST:** 1976
SALES (est): 5.6MM **Privately Held**
Web: www.idealockers.com
SIC: 2541 Lockers, except refrigerated: wood

(P-2566)

IVARS DISPLAY (PA)

Also Called: Ivar's Displays
2314 E Locust Ct, Ontario (91761-7613)
PHONE...............................909 923-2761
Ivan Gundersen, *CFO*
Karl Gundersen, *
Linda Pulice, *
Jason Gundersen, *
▲ **EMP:** 87 **EST:** 1966
SQ FT: 95,000
SALES (est): 18.21MM
SALES (corp-wide): 18.21MM **Privately
Held**
Web: www.ivarsdisplay.com
SIC: 2541 2542 Store fixtures, wood;
Shelving, office and store, except wood

PRODUCTS & SVCS

(P-2567)

JUDITH VON HOPF INC
1525 W 13th St Ste H, Upland
(91786-7528)
PHONE....................909 481-1884
Judith P Hopf, *CEO*
▲ **EMP:** 25 **EST:** 1976
SALES (est): 1.12MM **Privately Held**
Web: www.judithvonhopf.com
SIC: 2541 Display fixtures, wood

(P-2568)

KILLION INDUSTRIES INC (PA)
1380 Poinsettia Ave, Vista (92081-8504)
PHONE....................760 727-5102
Richard W Killion, *Pr*
Larry Edward, *
◆ **EMP:** 80 **EST:** 1981
SQ FT: 185,000
SALES (est): 23.59MM
SALES (corp-wide): 23.59MM **Privately
Held**
Web: www.killionindustries.com
SIC: 2541 Store and office display cases
and fixtures

(P-2569)

LA CABINET & MILLWORK INC
Also Called: Bromack
3005 Humboldt St, Los Angeles
(90031-1830)
PHONE....................323 227-5000
EMP: 25 **EST:** 2005
SQ FT: 17,000
SALES (est): 3.71MM **Privately Held**
SIC: 2541 1799 2434 1751 Counters or
counter display cases, wood; Counter top
installation; Wood kitchen cabinets;
Carpentry work

(P-2570)

**LEONARDS CARPET SERVICE
INC (PA)**
Also Called: Xgrass Turf Direct
1121 N Red Gum St, Anaheim
(92806-2582)
PHONE....................714 630-1930
Leonard Nagel, *Pr*
Joel Nagel, *
▲ **EMP:** 75 **EST:** 1970
SQ FT: 52,000
SALES (est): 23.06MM
SALES (corp-wide): 23.06MM **Privately
Held**
Web: www.leonardscarpetservice.com
SIC: 2541 1771 1799 Table or counter tops,
plastic laminated; Flooring contractor;
Artificial turf installation

(P-2571)

NICO NAT MFG CORP
Also Called: Niconat Manufacturing
2624 Yates Ave, Commerce (90040-2622)
PHONE....................323 721-1900
Jose Valdez, *CEO*
Francisco Valdez, *Stockholder*
EMP: 45 **EST:** 2008
SALES (est): 9.42MM **Privately Held**
Web: www.niconatmfg.com
SIC: 2541 Store and office display cases
and fixtures

(P-2572)

OMNI ENCLOSURES INC
Also Called: Omni Pacific
505 Raleigh Ave, El Cajon (92020-3139)
PHONE....................619 579-6664
Thomas P Burke, *Pr*
▲ **EMP:** 27 **EST:** 1981
SQ FT: 20,000

SALES (est): 8.75MM **Privately Held**
Web: www.omnilabsolutions.com
SIC: 2541 Office fixtures, wood

(P-2573)

SPOONERS WOODWORKS INC
Also Called: Spooners Woodworks
12460 Kirkham Ct, Poway (92064-6819)
PHONE....................858 679-9086
Tom Spooner, *Admn*
Thomas Spooner, *
Stephen Spooner, *
Valerie Spooner, *
Rosemary Spooner, *
EMP: 120 **EST:** 1979
SQ FT: 22,000
SALES (est): 23.76MM **Privately Held**
Web: www.spoonerwoodworks.com
SIC: 2541 Store fixtures, wood

(P-2574)

TEMEKA ADVERTISING INC
Also Called: Temeka Group
9073 Pulsar Ct, Corona (92883-7357)
PHONE....................951 277-2525
Michael D Wilson, *CEO*
Paul Mieboer, *Stockholder*
Marlene Kelly, *
▲ **EMP:** 55 **EST:** 1991
SQ FT: 24,000
SALES (est): 10.27MM **Privately Held**
Web: www.temekagroup.com
SIC: 2541 Store and office display cases
and fixtures

(P-2575)

YOSHIMASA DISPLAY CASE INC
Also Called: Yoshimasa
10808 Weaver Ave, South El Monte
(91733-2751)
PHONE....................213 637-9999
Toro Hayashi, *Pr*
Michael Y Yoo, *
Alma Kim Oprtn, *Mgr*
▲ **EMP:** 35 **EST:** 2011
SALES (est): 1.56MM **Privately Held**
Web: www.yoshimasausa.com
SIC: 2541 3564 Store and office display
cases and fixtures; Aircurtains (blower)

2542 Partitions And Fixtures, Except Wood

(P-2576)

**ADVANCED EQUIPMENT
CORPORATION (PA)**
2401 W Commonwealth Ave, Fullerton
(92833-2999)
PHONE....................714 635-5350
Wesley B Dickson, *Ch*
W Scott Dickson, *Senior President*
W Dickson, *
Bryan Dickson, *
Frank Manning, *
◆ **EMP:** 50 **EST:** 1957
SQ FT: 51,000
SALES (est): 15.89MM
SALES (corp-wide): 15.89MM **Privately
Held**
Web: www.advancedequipment.com
SIC: 2542 2541 Partitions for floor
attachment, prefabricated: except wood;
Wood partitions and fixtures

(P-2577)

**BOBRICK WASHROOM
EQUIPMENT INC (HQ)**
Also Called: Gamco

6901 Tujunga Ave, North Hollywood
(91605-5882)
PHONE....................818 764-1000
◆ **EMP:** 100 **EST:** 1906
SALES (est): 129.48MM
SALES (corp-wide): 132.97MM **Privately
Held**
Web: www.bobrick.com
SIC: 2542 Partitions for floor attachment,
prefabricated: except wood
PA: The Bobrick Corporation
6901 Tujunga Ave
818 764-1000

(P-2578)

CTA FIXTURES INC
5721 Santa Ana St Ste B, Ontario
(91761-8617)
PHONE....................909 390-6744
Carlos Gutierrez, *CEO*
▲ **EMP:** 62 **EST:** 1994
SQ FT: 90,000
SALES (est): 1.5MM **Privately Held**
Web: www.ctafixtures.com
SIC: 2542 Partitions and fixtures, except
wood

(P-2579)

CUTTING EDGE CREATIVE LLC
9944 Flower St, Bellflower (90706-5411)
PHONE....................562 907-7007
Jennifer Franklin, *Managing Member*
Ward Lookabaugh, *
▲ **EMP:** 75 **EST:** 1996
SALES (est): 1.8MM **Privately Held**
SIC: 2542 3496 7319 Racks, merchandise
display or storage: except wood;
Miscellaneous fabricated wire products;
Display advertising service

(P-2580)

FELBRO INC
3666 E Olympic Blvd, Los Angeles
(90023-3147)
PHONE....................323 263-8686
Howard Feldner, *Ch Bd*
Norman Feldner, *
Jeffrey Feldner, *
▲ **EMP:** 180 **EST:** 1945
SQ FT: 75,000
SALES (est): 8.59MM **Privately Held**
Web: www.felbrodisplays.com
SIC: 2542 Racks, merchandise display or
storage: except wood

(P-2581)

**FIELD MANUFACTURING CORP
(PA)**
1751 Torrance Blvd Ste N, Torrance
(90501-1726)
PHONE....................310 781-9292
Patrick Field, *Pr*
▲ **EMP:** 36 **EST:** 1955
SQ FT: 20,000
SALES (est): 8.23MM
SALES (corp-wide): 8.23MM **Privately
Held**
Web: www.field-manufacturing.com
SIC: 2542 3089 Partitions and fixtures,
except wood; Injection molding of plastics

(P-2582)

IDX LOS ANGELES LLC
Also Called: West Coast Mfg & Whsng
5005 E Philadelphia St, Ontario
(91761-2816)
PHONE....................909 212-8333
Graham Fownes, *Genl Mgr*
◆ **EMP:** 109 **EST:** 2012
SALES (est): 24.8MM

SALES (corp-wide): 7.22B **Publicly Held**
Web: www.idxcorporation.com
SIC: 2542 Partitions and fixtures, except
wood
PA: Ufp Industries, Inc.
2801 E Beltline Ave Ne
616 364-6161

(P-2583)

K-JACK ENGINEERING CO INC
5672 Buckingham Dr, Huntington Beach
(92649-1160)
P.O. Box 2320 (90249)
PHONE....................310 327-8389
▲ **EMP:** 60 **EST:** 1963
SALES (est): 1.85MM **Privately Held**
Web: www.kjack.com
SIC: 2542 Racks, merchandise display or
storage: except wood

(P-2584)

LIBERTY DIVERSIFIED INTL INC
Also Called: Liberty Packaging
13100 Danielson St, Poway (92064-6840)
PHONE....................858 391-7302
EMP: 245
SALES (corp-wide): 1.02B **Privately Held**
Web: www.libertydiversified.com
SIC: 2542 5112 3089 2952 Fixtures, office:
except wood; Stationery and office supplies
; Plastics containers, except foam; Roofing
materials
PA: Liberty Diversified International, Inc.
5600 Highway 169 N
763 536-6600

(P-2585)

LLC WALKER WEST
Also Called: Impac International
5500 Jurupa St, Ontario (91761-3668)
PHONE....................800 767-9378
Kory Levoy, *Brnch Mgr*
EMP: 53
Web: www.premierenclosuresystems.com
SIC: 2542 3444 Cabinets: show, display, or
storage: except wood; Sheet metalwork
PA: Walker West, Llc
1555 S Vintage Ave

(P-2586)

**PACIFIC MANUFACTURING MGT
INC**
Also Called: Greneker Solutions
3110 E 12th St, Los Angeles (90023-3616)
PHONE....................323 263-9000
Erik Johnson, *Pr*
Steven Beckman, *
▲ **EMP:** 60 **EST:** 2003
SQ FT: 60,000
SALES (est): 4.63MM **Privately Held**
Web: www.greneker.com
SIC: 2542 2541 Fixtures: display, office, or
store: except wood; Display fixtures, wood

(P-2587)

RAP SECURITY INC
4630 Cecilia St, Cudahy (90201-5814)
PHONE....................323 560-3493
Angelo Palmer, *Pr*
Bob Palmer, *
◆ **EMP:** 55 **EST:** 1984
SQ FT: 40,000
SALES (est): 2.02MM **Privately Held**
SIC: 2542 Fixtures, store: except wood

(P-2588)

RAPID RACK HOLDINGS INC
1370 Valley Vista Dr Ste 100, Diamond Bar
(91765-3921)
EMP: 618

Web: www.rapidrack.com

SIC: 2542 Postal lock boxes, mail racks, and related products

(P-2589)

RAPID RACK INDUSTRIES INC

1370 Valley Vista Dr Ste 100, Diamond Bar (91765-3921)

▲ EMP: 75

SIC: 2542 Partitions and fixtures, except wood

(P-2590)

REEVE STORE EQUIPMENT COMPANY (PA)

9131 Bermudez St, Pico Rivera (90660-4507)

PHONE..............................562 949-2535

TOLL FREE: 800

John Frackelton, *Pr*

Robert Frackelton, *

Mary Ann Crysler, *

▲ EMP: 100 EST: 1932

SQ FT: 170,000

SALES (est): 16.22MM

SALES (corp-wide): 16.22MM **Privately Held**

Web: www.reeveco.com

SIC: 2542 3471 Counters or counter display cases, except wood; Electroplating of metals or formed products

(P-2591)

SALSBURY INDUSTRIES INC (PA)

Also Called: Salsbury Industries

18300 Central Ave, Carson (90746-4008)

PHONE..............................800 624-5269

TOLL FREE: 800

Dennis Fraher, *Pr*

Brian Fraher, *VP*

John Fraher, *Ch*

Michael N Lobasso, *CFO*

◆ EMP: 250 EST: 1936

SQ FT: 600,000

SALES (est): 47.42MM **Privately Held**

Web: www.mailboxes.com

SIC: 2542 Locker boxes, postal service: except wood

(P-2592)

SALSBURY INDUSTRIES INC

1010 E 62nd St, Los Angeles (90001-1510)

PHONE..............................323 846-6700

EMP: 95

Web: www.salsburyindustries.com

SIC: 2542 Locker boxes, postal service: except wood

PA: Salsbury Industries, Inc.
18300 Central Ave

(P-2593)

SPECTRUM INTL HOLDINGS

14421 Bonelli St, City Of Industry (91746-3021)

PHONE..............................626 333-7225

Matthew Harrison, *Ch Bd*

Robert A Davies, *

EMP: 620 EST: 1997

SALES (est): 2.66MM **Privately Held**

SIC: 2542 Postal lock boxes, mail racks, and related products

(P-2594)

STEVES PLATING CORPORATION

3111 N San Fernando Blvd, Burbank (91504-2527)

PHONE..............................818 842-2184

Terry Knezevich, *CEO*

Roger C Knezevich, *

EMP: 140 EST: 1956

SQ FT: 80,000

SALES (est): 2.21MM **Privately Held**

Web: www.stevesplating.com

SIC: 2542 3446 3471 7692 Fixtures, store: except wood; Ladders, for permanent installation: metal; Plating of metals or formed products; Welding repair

(P-2595)

TEICHMAN ENTERPRISES INC

Also Called: T & H Store Fixtures

6100 Bandini Blvd, Commerce (90040-3112)

PHONE..............................323 278-9000

Ruth Teichman, *Pr*

Steve Teichman, *

Bernard Teichman, *

Sidney Teichman, *

Alan Teichman, *

▲ EMP: 50 EST: 1956

SALES (est): 5.16MM **Privately Held**

Web: www.teichman.net

SIC: 2542 Fixtures: display, office, or store: except wood

(P-2596)

THE BOBRICK CORPORATION (PA)

6901 Tujunga Ave, North Hollywood (91605-5882)

PHONE..............................818 764-1000

◆ EMP: 100 EST: 1906

SALES (est): 132.97MM

SALES (corp-wide): 132.97MM **Privately Held**

Web: www.bobrick.com

SIC: 2542 Partitions for floor attachment, prefabricated: except wood

(P-2597)

UNIWEB INC (PA)

Also Called: Uniweb

222 S Promenade Ave, Corona (92879-1743)

PHONE..............................951 279-7999

Karl F Weber, *CEO*

▲ EMP: 90 EST: 1979

SQ FT: 170,000

SALES (est): 14.27MM

SALES (corp-wide): 14.27MM **Privately Held**

Web: www.uniwebinc.com

SIC: 2542 Fixtures: display, office, or store: except wood

(P-2598)

WESTERN PCF STOR SOLUTIONS INC (PA)

300 E Arrow Hwy, San Dimas (91773-3339)

PHONE..............................909 451-0303

Tom Rogers, *Pr*

Peter G Dunn, *

Angie Bosley, *

Soheir Hakim, *

Paul Bautista, *

EMP: 100 EST: 1985

SQ FT: 165,000

SALES (est): 24.79MM

SALES (corp-wide): 24.79MM **Privately Held**

Web: www.wpss.com

SIC: 2542 Shelving, office and store, except wood

2591 Drapery Hardware And Blinds And Shades

(P-2599)

ALL STRONG INDUSTRY (USA) INC (PA)

326 Paseo Tesoro, Walnut (91789-2725)

PHONE..............................909 598-6494

Pei-hsiang Hsu, *Ch Bd*

Frank Hsu, *

◆ EMP: 30 EST: 1992

SQ FT: 52,000

SALES (est): 7.29MM **Privately Held**

SIC: 2591 Mini blinds

(P-2600)

CENTURY BLINDS INC

300 S Promenade Ave, Corona (92879-1754)

P.O. Box 77940 (92877-0131)

PHONE..............................951 734-3762

Mitch Shapiro, *CEO*

▲ EMP: 100 EST: 1992

SALES (est): 4.99MM **Privately Held**

Web: www.altawindowfashions.com

SIC: 2591 3429 5719 5023 Blinds vertical; Hardware, nec; Vertical blinds; Vertical blinds

HQ: Hunter Douglas Scandinavia Ab Kristineholmsvagen 14a AlingsAs 441 3 32277500

(P-2601)

HD WINDOW FASHIONS INC (DH)

Also Called: M & B Window Fashions

1818 Oak St, Los Angeles (90015-3302)

PHONE..............................213 749-6333

Wayne Gourlay, *Pr*

Dominique Au Yeung, *

▲ EMP: 500 EST: 1975

SQ FT: 200,000

SALES (est): 2.54MM **Privately Held**

SIC: 2591 Mini blinds

HQ: Hunter Douglas Inc. 55 W 46th St 27th Fl New York NY 10036 845 664-7000

(P-2602)

HUNTER DOUGLAS INC

Hunter Douglas Contract

9900 Gidley St, El Monte (91731-1112)

PHONE..............................858 679-7500

Rich Ries, *Brnch Mgr*

EMP: 276

Web: www.hunterdouglasarchitectural.com

SIC: 2591 3446 Drapery hardware and window blinds and shades; Architectural metalwork

HQ: Hunter Douglas Inc. 55 W 46th St 27th Fl New York NY 10036 845 664-7000

(P-2603)

JC WINDOW FASHIONS INC

Also Called: JC Window Fashions

2438 Peck Rd, Whittier (90601-1604)

PHONE..............................909 364-8888

Jennifer Chiao, *CEO*

▲ EMP: 28 EST: 2011

SALES (est): 4.79MM **Privately Held**

Web: www.jcwindowfashions.com

SIC: 2591 Drapery hardware and window blinds and shades

(P-2604)

KITTRICH CORPORATION (PA)

1585 W Mission Blvd, Pomona (91766-1233)

PHONE..............................714 736-1000

Robert Friedland, *CEO*

◆ EMP: 130 EST: 1978

SQ FT: 237,000

SALES (est): 125.59MM

SALES (corp-wide): 125.59MM **Privately Held**

Web: www.kittrich.com

SIC: 2591 2392 2381 Blinds vertical; Household furnishings, nec; Fabric dress and work gloves

(P-2605)

L C PRINGLE SALES INC (PA)

Also Called: Pringle's Draperies

12020 Western Ave, Garden Grove (92841-2913)

PHONE..............................714 892-1524

Larry C Pringle, *Pr*

Carolyn Pringle, *

Curtis L Pringle, *

Susan Pringle Kusinsky, *

Pamela Pringle Skinner, *

EMP: 30 EST: 1968

SQ FT: 11,000

SALES (est): 2.57MM

SALES (corp-wide): 2.57MM **Privately Held**

Web: www.pringlesdraperies.com

SIC: 2591 7216 2391 7211 Blinds vertical; Drapery, curtain drycleaning; Draperies, plastic and textile: from purchased materials ; Power laundries, family and commercial

(P-2606)

ROBERSON CONSTRUCTION

Also Called: Architectural Window Shades

22 Central Ct, Pasadena (91105-2060)

P.O. Box 3286 (91731)

PHONE..............................626 578-1936

▲ EMP: 35

Web: www.openinfo.com

SIC: 2591 Window shades

(P-2607)

SHEWARD & SON & SONS (PA)

Also Called: Solar Shading Systems

14352 Chambers Rd, Tustin (92780-6912)

PHONE..............................714 556-6055

▲ EMP: 25 EST: 1986

SALES (est): 5.21MM

SALES (corp-wide): 5.21MM **Privately Held**

Web: www.shewards.com

SIC: 2591 1799 2221 1752 Curtain and drapery rods, poles, and fixtures; Window treatment installation; Draperies and drapery fabrics, manmade fiber and silk; Carpet laying

(P-2608)

SHOWDOGS INC

Also Called: Wholesale Shade

168 S Pacific St, San Marcos (92078-2527)

PHONE..............................760 603-3269

Patrick Howe, *Pr*

EMP: 30 EST: 2013

SQ FT: 10,000

SALES (est): 2.32MM **Privately Held**

Web: www.wholesaleshade.com

SIC: 2591 Blinds vertical

2599 Furniture And Fixtures, Nec

(P-2609)
ALEGACY FDSRVICE PDTS GROUP IN
Also Called: Alegacy
12683 Corral Pl, Santa Fe Springs (90670-4748)
PHONE..................562 320-3100
Jesse Gross, *Prin*
Brett Gross, *
Eric Gross, *
◆ **EMP:** 60 **EST:** 2000
SQ FT: 130,000
SALES (est): 9.66MM **Privately Held**
Web: www.alegacy.com
SIC: 2599 3263 Carts, restaurant equipment; Cookware, fine earthenware

(P-2610)
COMMERCIAL CSTM STING UPHL INC
12601 Western Ave, Garden Grove (92841-4014)
PHONE..................714 850-0520
Robert Francis, *CEO*
Lynn D.o.s., *Sec*
▲ **EMP:** 90 **EST:** 1988
SQ FT: 50,000
SALES (est): 21.05MM **Privately Held**
Web: www.ccs-ind.com
SIC: 2599 Restaurant furniture, wood or metal

(P-2611)
ERGONOM CORPORATION (PA)
Also Called: E R G International
361 Bernoulli Cir, Oxnard (93030-5164)
PHONE..................805 981-9978
George Zaki, *CEO*
Roy Zaki, *
▲ **EMP:** 90 **EST:** 1981
SALES (est): 24.86MM
SALES (corp-wide): 24.86MM **Privately Held**
Web: www.erginternational.com
SIC: 2599 2531 Hospital furniture, except beds; School furniture

(P-2612)
ERGONOM CORPORATION
Also Called: Erg International
390 Lombard St, Oxnard (93030-7209)
PHONE..................805 981-9978
Roy Zaki, *Pr*
EMP: 70
SALES (corp-wide): 24.86MM **Privately Held**
Web: www.erginternational.com
SIC: 2599 2531 Hospital furniture, except beds; School furniture
PA: Ergonom Corporation
361 Bernoulli Cir
805 981-9978

(P-2613)
FORBES INDUSTRIES DIV
1933 E Locust St, Ontario (91761-7608)
PHONE..................909 923-4559
Tim Sweetland, *Pr*
Peter Sweetland, *
▼ **EMP:** 210 **EST:** 1919
SQ FT: 110,000
SALES (est): 3.96MM
SALES (corp-wide): 48.01MM **Privately Held**
Web: www.forbesindustries.com

SIC: 2599 Carts, restaurant equipment
PA: The Winsford Corporation
1933 E Locust St
909 923-4559

(P-2614)
JBI LLC (PA)
Also Called: Jbi Interiors
2650 E El Presidio St, Long Beach (90810-1115)
PHONE..................310 886-8034
Pete Jensen, *Music Manager*
Bonnie Holt, *
Michael Buchbinder, *
Gregg Buchbinder, *
◆ **EMP:** 200 **EST:** 1968
SQ FT: 270,000
SALES (est): 25.21MM
SALES (corp-wide): 25.21MM **Privately Held**
Web: www.jbi-interiors.com
SIC: 2599 5046 Restaurant furniture, wood or metal; Restaurant equipment and supplies, nec

(P-2615)
STAINLESS FIXTURES INC
1250 E Franklin Ave, Pomona (91766-5449)
PHONE..................909 622-1615
Randy Rodriguez, *Pr*
EMP: 35 **EST:** 1989
SQ FT: 36,000
SALES (est): 1.63MM **Privately Held**
SIC: 2599 Restaurant furniture, wood or metal

(P-2616)
TAHITI CABINETS INC
5419 E La Palma Ave, Anaheim (92807-2022)
PHONE..................714 693-0618
Mark Ramsey, *Pr*
Doreen Ramsey, *
EMP: 58 **EST:** 1975
SQ FT: 32,000
SALES (est): 3.12MM **Privately Held**
Web: www.tahiticabinets.com
SIC: 2599 2431 2434 Cabinets, factory; Millwork; Wood kitchen cabinets

(P-2617)
TRESTON IAC LLC
8175 E Brookdale Ln, Anaheim (92807-2526)
PHONE..................714 990-8997
EMP: 28
Web: www.iacindustries.com
SIC: 2599 Bar furniture
HQ: Treston Iac Llc
3831 S Bullard Ave
Goodyear AZ 85338
714 989-5363

(P-2618)
WESTERN MILL FABRICATORS INC
670 S Jefferson St Ste B, Placentia (92870-6638)
PHONE..................714 993-3667
Kimball Boyack, *CEO*
EMP: 30 **EST:** 1987
SALES (est): 506.44K **Privately Held**
Web: www.wmfinc.com
SIC: 2599 Bar, restaurant and cafeteria furniture

2611 Pulp Mills

(P-2619)
NEW GREEN DAY LLC
1710 E 111th St, Los Angeles (90059-1910)
P.O. Box 72147 (90002-0147)
PHONE..................323 566-7603
Brian Kelly, *CEO*
David Holt, *
Kirk Sanford, *Managing Member*
Daniel Montoya, *
Randi Yamamoto, *
EMP: 25 **EST:** 2004
SQ FT: 25,000
SALES (est): 5.06MM **Privately Held**
Web: www.ngdla.com
SIC: 2611 Pulp manufactured from waste or recycled paper

2621 Paper Mills

(P-2620)
ALLIED WEST PAPER CORP
11101 Etiwanda Ave Unit 100, Fontana (92337-6986)
PHONE..................909 349-0710
Ray Ovanessian, *CEO*
Mike Ovanessian, *
Eric Ovanessian, *
◆ **EMP:** 95 **EST:** 1989
SQ FT: 300,000
SALES (est): 40.47MM **Privately Held**
Web: www.alliedwestpaper.com
SIC: 2621 Paper mills

(P-2621)
CROWN PAPER CONVERTING INC
Also Called: Crown Paper Converting
1380 S Bon View Ave, Ontario (91761-4403)
P.O. Box 3277 (91761-0928)
PHONE..................909 923-5226
Bruce Hale, *Prin*
Lisa Hale, *
EMP: 40 **EST:** 1983
SQ FT: 34,000
SALES (est): 1.8MM **Privately Held**
Web: www.crownpaperconverting.com
SIC: 2621 Paper mills

(P-2622)
DYNAMIC RESOURCES INC
7894 Dagget St Ste 202e, San Diego (92111-2323)
PHONE..................619 268-3070
Kwang Kim, *CFO*
Cheong Won Bae, *CEO*
EMP: 60 **EST:** 2010
SQ FT: 9,000
SALES (est): 769.86K **Privately Held**
Web: www.dynamicresources.biz
SIC: 2621 2672 Lithograph paper; Adhesive papers, labels, or tapes: from purchased material

(P-2623)
ENVELOPMENTS INC
13091 Sandhurst Pl, Santa Ana (92705-2135)
PHONE..................714 569-3300
Mark A Smith, *CEO*
Holly Jakobs, *
Deborah Hefter, *
▲ **EMP:** 39 **EST:** 1993
SALES (est): 1.6MM **Privately Held**
Web: www.envelopments.com

SIC: 2621 5112 Stationary, envelope and tablet papers; Stationery

(P-2624)
FRINGE STUDIO LLC
6029 W Slauson Ave, Culver City (90230-6507)
P.O. Box 3663 (90230)
PHONE..................310 390-9900
Scott Kingsland, *Managing Member*
▲ **EMP:** 30 **EST:** 2004
SALES (est): 2.42MM **Privately Held**
Web: www.fringestudio.com
SIC: 2621 3999 Stationary, envelope and tablet papers; Pet supplies
PA: Punch Studio, Llc
6025 W Slauson Ave

(P-2625)
HARVARD LABEL LLC
Also Called: Harvard Card Systems
111 Baldwin Park Blvd, City Of Industry (91746-1402)
PHONE..................626 333-8881
Michael Tang, *CEO*
David Banducci, *
▲ **EMP:** 115 **EST:** 1996
SQ FT: 125,000
SALES (est): 24.81MM **Privately Held**
SIC: 2621 2675 2752 Greeting card paper; Stencil cards, die-cut: made from purchased materials; Cards, lithographed
PA: Plasticard - Locktech International, Llc
1220 Trade Dr

(P-2626)
INTERNATIONAL PAPER COMPANY
International Paper
601 E Ball Rd, Anaheim (92805-5910)
PHONE..................714 776-6060
Terry Tockey, *Brnch Mgr*
EMP: 117
SALES (corp-wide): 18.92B **Publicly Held**
Web: www.internationalpaper.com
SIC: 2621 Paper mills
PA: International Paper Company
6400 Poplar Ave
901 419-7000

(P-2627)
INTERNATIONAL PAPER COMPANY
Also Called: International Paper
9211 Norwalk Blvd, Santa Fe Springs (90670-2923)
PHONE..................562 692-9465
Lee Bekiarian, *Brnch Mgr*
EMP: 64
SALES (corp-wide): 18.92B **Publicly Held**
Web: www.internationalpaper.com
SIC: 2621 Paper mills
PA: International Paper Company
6400 Poplar Ave
901 419-7000

(P-2628)
INTERNATIONAL PAPER COMPANY
Also Called: International Paper
1350 E 223rd St, Carson (90745-4381)
PHONE..................310 549-5525
Melanie Kastner, *Brnch Mgr*
EMP: 91
SALES (corp-wide): 18.92B **Publicly Held**
Web: www.internationalpaper.com
SIC: 2621 Paper mills
PA: International Paper Company
6400 Poplar Ave

901 419-7000

(P-2629)
INTERNATIONAL PAPER COMPANY
Also Called: International Paper
19615 S Susana Rd, Compton
(90221-5717)
PHONE..............................310 639-2310
Joseph Winters, *Genl Mgr*
EMP: 38
SALES (corp-wide): 18.92B **Publicly Held**
Web: www.internationalpaper.com
SIC: 2621 Paper mills
PA: International Paper Company
6400 Poplar Ave
901 419-7000

(P-2630)
LD PRODUCTS INC
Also Called: 4inkjets
2501 E 28th St, Signal Hill (90755-2138)
PHONE..............................888 321-2552
Aaron Leon, *CEO*
Patrick Devane, *
◆ **EMP:** 193 **EST:** 1999
SALES (est): 36.58MM **Privately Held**
Web: www.ldproducts.com
SIC: 2621 5045 Stationary, envelope and
tablet papers; Printers, computer

(P-2631)
NEW-INDY CONTAINERBOARD LLC (DH)
Also Called: International Paper
3500 Porsche Way Ste 150, Ontario
(91764-4969)
P.O. Box 519 (93044-0519)
PHONE..............................909 296-3400
Richard Hartman, *CEO*
Mike Conkey, *
▲ **EMP:** 95 **EST:** 2012
SALES (est): 319.18MM
SALES (corp-wide): 587.57MM **Privately Held**
Web: www.newindycontainerboard.com
SIC: 2621 Paper mills
HQ: New-Indy Containerboard Hold Co Llc
1 Patriot Pl
Foxborough MA 02035

(P-2632)
NEW-INDY ONTARIO LLC
Also Called: New-Indy Containerboard
5100 Jurupa St, Ontario (91761-3618)
PHONE..............................909 390-1055
Richard Hartman, *CEO*
Mike Conkey, *
EMP: 110 **EST:** 2012
SALES (est): 56.01MM
SALES (corp-wide): 587.57MM **Privately Held**
Web: www.newindycontainerboard.com
SIC: 2621 Paper mills
HQ: New-Indy Containerboard Llc
3500 Porsche Wy Ste 150
Ontario CA 91764
909 296-3400

(P-2633)
NEW-INDY OXNARD LLC
Also Called: New-Indy Containerboard
5936 Perkins Rd, Oxnard (93033-9044)
P.O. Box 519 (93044-0519)
PHONE..............................805 986-3881
Richard Hartman, *CEO*
Mike Conkey, *
▲ **EMP:** 224 **EST:** 2012
SALES (est): 18.14MM
SALES (corp-wide): 587.57MM **Privately Held**

Web: www.newindycontainerboard.com
SIC: 2621 Paper mills
HQ: New-Indy Containerboard Llc
3500 Porsche Wy Ste 150
Ontario CA 91764
909 296-3400

(P-2634)
PACON INC
4249 Puente Ave, Baldwin Park
(91706-3420)
PHONE..............................626 814-4654
Robert M Austin, *CEO*
Michael Austin, *
◆ **EMP:** 103 **EST:** 1977
SQ FT: 44,000
SALES (est): 20.6MM **Privately Held**
Web: www.paconinc.com
SIC: 2621 Paper mills

(P-2635)
PAPER SURCE CONVERTING MFG INC
Also Called: Soft-Touch Tissue
4800 S Santa Fe Ave, Vernon
(90058-2104)
PHONE..............................323 583-3800
Jacob Khobian, *CEO*
Jonathan Khodabakhsh, *
Fery Khodabakhsh, *
▲ **EMP:** 50 **EST:** 1996
SQ FT: 55,000
SALES (est): 26.7MM **Privately Held**
Web: www.papersourcemfg.com
SIC: 2621 Tissue paper

(P-2636)
SAN DIEGO DAILY TRANSCRIPT
Also Called: Daily Transcript
34 Emerald Gln, Laguna Niguel
(92677-9379)
P.O. Box 85469 (92186-5469)
PHONE..............................619 232-4381
Ed Frederickson, *Pr*
EMP: 63 **EST:** 1886
SQ FT: 30,000
SALES (est): 2.88MM
SALES (corp-wide): 3.92MM **Privately Held**
SIC: 2621 4813 Printing paper; Online
service providers
PA: Calcomco, Inc.
5544 S Red Pine Cir
313 885-9228

(P-2637)
SAPPI NORTH AMERICA INC
21700 Copley Dr Ste 165, Diamond Bar
(91765-4434)
PHONE..............................714 456-0600
Bront Domichoal, *Brnch Mgr*
EMP: 51
Web: www.sappi.com
SIC: 2621 Paper mills
HQ: Sappi North America, Inc.
255 State St Ste 4
Boston MA 02109
617 423-7300

(P-2638)
SOLUT INC
4645 North Ave Ste 102, Oceanside
(92056-3593)
PHONE..............................760 758-7240
EMP: 43
Web: www.gosolut.com
SIC: 2621 2656 Packaging paper; Sanitary
food containers
PA: Solut , Inc.
7787 Graphics Way

Web: www.newindycontainerboard.com
SIC: 2621 Paper mills
HQ: New-Indy Containerboard Llc
3500 Porsche Wy Ste 150
Ontario CA 91764
909 296-3400

(P-2639)
SPECIALTY PAPER MILLS INC
8844 Millergrove Dr, Santa Fe Springs
(90670-2004)
P.O. Box 3188 (90670-0188)
PHONE..............................562 692-8737
Ronald Gabriel, *Pr*
Aldo De Soto, *
Agnes Gabriel, *
EMP: 200 **EST:** 1959
SQ FT: 45,000
SALES (est): 2.42MM
SALES (corp-wide): 15.93MM **Privately Held**
Web: www.gabrielcontainer.com
SIC: 2621 2631 Paper mills; Paperboard mills
PA: Gabriel Container
8844 Millergrove Dr
562 699-1051

2631 Paperboard Mills

(P-2640)
CALIFRNIA TRADE CONVERTERS INC
9816 Variel Ave, Chatsworth (91311-4316)
PHONE..............................818 899-1455
Carlos Martinez, *Pr*
EMP: 25 **EST:** 1997
SALES (est): 2.02MM **Privately Held**
SIC: 2631 2675 Paperboard mills; Paper die-cutting

(P-2641)
ONE UP MANUFACTURING LLC
550 E Airline Way, Gardena (90248-2502)
PHONE..............................310 749-8347
Nielson Ballon, *Managing Member*
Kavish Mehta, *
Nathan Miller, *
EMP: 25 **EST:** 2017
SALES (est): 3.46MM **Privately Held**
SIC: 2631 Container, packaging, and boxboard

(P-2642)
PREFERRED PRINTING & PACKAGING INC
1493 E Philadelphia St, Ontario
(91761-5729)
PHONE..............................909 923-2053
EMP: 30 **EST:** 1991
SALES (est): 4.99MM **Privately Held**
Web: www.preferredpnp.com
SIC: 2631 Folding boxboard

(P-2643)
SONOCO PRODUCTS COMPANY
Also Called: Sonoco Industrial Products Div
166 Baldwin Park Blvd, City Of Industry
(91746-1498)
PHONE..............................626 369-6611
Dhamo Srinivasan, *Mgr*
EMP: 93
SALES (corp-wide): 6.78B **Publicly Held**
Web: www.sonoco.com
SIC: 2631 2611 Paperboard mills; Pulp mills
PA: Sonoco Products Company
1 N 2nd St
843 383-7000

(P-2644)
SONOCO PRODUCTS COMPANY
12851 Leyva St, Norwalk (90650-6853)
PHONE..............................562 921-0881
Jeff Blaine, *Mgr*
EMP: 63

SQ FT: 164,934
SALES (corp-wide): 6.78B **Publicly Held**
Web: www.sonoco.com
SIC: 2631 2655 Paperboard mills; Fiber
cans, drums, and similar products
PA: Sonoco Products Company
1 N 2nd St
843 383-7000

(P-2645)
TAYLORD PRODUCTS INTL INC (PA)
4505 Lister St, San Diego (92110-3333)
PHONE..............................619 247-6544
Adela S Taylor, *CEO*
Thomas N Taylor, *Pr*
EMP: 155 **EST:** 1990
SALES (est): 4.19MM
SALES (corp-wide): 4.19MM **Privately Held**
SIC: 2631 Container, packaging, and boxboard

(P-2646)
UNION CARBIDE CORPORATION
19206 Hawthorne Blvd, Torrance
(90503-1590)
PHONE..............................310 214-5300
Patrick E Gottschalk, *Prin*
EMP: 34
SQ FT: 15,269
SALES (corp-wide): 44.62B **Publicly Held**
Web: www.unioncarbide.com
SIC: 2631 Latex board
HQ: Union Carbide Corporation
7501 State Hwy 185 N
Seadrift TX 77983
361 553-2997

(P-2647)
WRKCO INC
1025 W 190th St Ste 450, Gardena
(90248-4339)
PHONE..............................310 532-8988
EMP: 32
SIC: 2631 Paperboard mills
HQ: Wrkco Inc.
1000 Abrnthy Rd Ne Ste 12
Atlanta GA 30328
770 448-2193

(P-2648)
WRKCO INC
14103 Borate St, Santa Fe Springs
(90670-5342)
PHONE..............................770 448-2193
EMP: 27
SIC: 2631 Paperboard mills
HQ: Wrkco Inc.
1000 Abrnthy Rd Ne Ste 12
Atlanta GA 30328
770 448-2193

(P-2649)
ZAPP PACKAGING INC
1921 S Business Pkwy, Ontario
(91761-8539)
PHONE..............................909 930-1500
Vincent Randazzo, *CEO*
William L Finn, *
Bruce Altshuler, *
▲ **EMP:** 60 **EST:** 1931
SQ FT: 80,000
SALES (est): 6.61MM **Privately Held**
Web: www.autajon.com
SIC: 2631 Folding boxboard

PRODUCTS & SVCS

2652 Setup Paperboard Boxes

(P-2650)
MOZAIK LLC
245 W Carl Karcher Way, Anaheim (92801-2499)
PHONE.....................562 207-1900
Sharon Carton Ctrl, *Prin*
▲ **EMP:** 24 **EST:** 2006
SQ FT: 27,000
SALES (est): 8.12MM **Privately Held**
Web: www.mozaik.net
SIC: 2652 Filing boxes, paperboard: made from purchased materials

2653 Corrugated And Solid Fiber Boxes

(P-2651)
ABEX DISPLAY SYSTEMS INC (PA)
Also Called: Abex Exhibit Systems
355 Parkside Dr, San Fernando (91340-3036)
PHONE.....................800 537-0231
Robbie Blumenfeld, *Pr*
Max Candiotty, *
◆ **EMP:** 105 **EST:** 1982
SQ FT: 85,000.
SALES (est): 2.78MM
SALES (corp-wide): 2.78MM **Privately Held**
Web: www.abex.com
SIC: 2653 2541 Display items, solid fiber: made from purchased materials; Store and office display cases and fixtures

(P-2652)
ADVANCE PAPER BOX COMPANY
Also Called: Packaging Spectrum
6100 S Gramercy Pl, Los Angeles (90047-1397)
PHONE.....................323 750-2550
Martin Gardner, *CEO*
Martin Gardner, *Pr*
Nick Silk, *
Carlo Mendoza, *
Devan Gardner, *
▲ **EMP:** 250 **EST:** 1924
SQ FT: 500,000
SALES (est): 23.18MM **Privately Held**
Web: www.advancepaperbox.com
SIC: 2653 3082 2657 Boxes, corrugated: made from purchased materials; Unsupported plastics profile shapes; Folding paperboard boxes

(P-2653)
ANDROP PACKAGING INC
Also Called: Ontario Foam Products
4400 E Francis St, Ontario (91761-2327)
PHONE.....................909 605-8842
Cesar Flores, *Pr*
▲ **EMP:** 23 **EST:** 1974
SQ FT: 52,000
SALES (est): 8.63MM **Privately Held**
Web: www.androppkg.com
SIC: 2653 3086 Boxes, corrugated: made from purchased materials; Plastics foam products

(P-2654)
BAY CITIES CONTAINER CORP (PA)
Also Called: Bay Cities Packaging & Design

5138 Industry Ave, Pico Rivera (90660-2550)
PHONE.....................562 948-3751
Greg A Tucker, *CEO*
Patrick Donohoe, *
Michael Musgrave, *
▲ **EMP:** 96 **EST:** 1956
SALES (est): 150.82MM
SALES (corp-wide): 150.82MM **Privately Held**
Web: www.bay-cities.com
SIC: 2653 3993 5113 Boxes, corrugated: made from purchased materials; Signs and advertising specialties; Corrugated and solid fiber boxes

(P-2655)
BLOWER-DEMPSAY CORPORATION (PA)
Also Called: Pak West Paper & Packaging
4042 W Garry Ave, Santa Ana (92704-6300)
PHONE.....................714 481-3800
James Blower, *Pr*
Linda Dempsay, *
Serge Poirier, *
▲ **EMP:** 217 **EST:** 1973
SQ FT: 190,000
SALES (est): 107.24MM
SALES (corp-wide): 107.24MM **Privately Held**
Web: pakwest.blowerdempsay.com
SIC: 2653 Boxes, corrugated: made from purchased materials

(P-2656)
BOXES R US INC
Also Called: Ultimate Paper Box Company
15051 Don Julian Rd, City Of Industry (91746-3302)
PHONE.....................626 820-5410
Janak P Patel, *Pr*
Dipak Patel, *
▲ **EMP:** 70 **EST:** 1996
SQ FT: 38,000
SALES (est): 9.64MM **Privately Held**
SIC: 2653 Boxes, corrugated: made from purchased materials

(P-2657)
CALIFORNIA BOX COMPANY (PA)
13901 Carmenita Rd, Santa Fe Springs (90670-4916)
PHONE.....................562 921-1223
▲ **EMP:** 67 **EST:** 1990
SALES (est): 78.02MM
SALES (corp-wide): 78.02MM **Privately Held**
Web: www.calbox.com
SIC: 2653 Corrugated and solid fiber boxes

(P-2658)
CD CONTAINER INC
Also Called: Carton Design
7343 Paramount Blvd, Pico Rivera (90660-3713)
PHONE.....................562 948-1910
Juan De La Cruz, *Pr*
Juan De La Cruz, *Pr*
Jose De La Cruz, *
▲ **EMP:** 70 **EST:** 1987
SQ FT: 46,000
SALES (est): 9.46MM **Privately Held**
Web: www.cdcontainerinc.com
SIC: 2653 Boxes, corrugated: made from purchased materials

(P-2659)
CFLUTE CORP
Also Called: Montebello Container
13220 Molette St, Santa Fe Springs (90670-5526)
P.O. Box 788 (90637-0788)
PHONE.....................562 404-6221
▲ **EMP:** 170
Web: www.montcc.com
SIC: 2653 Boxes, corrugated: made from purchased materials

(P-2660)
COMMANDER PACKAGING WEST INC
602 S Rockefeller Ave Ste D, Ontario (91761-8191)
PHONE.....................714 921-9350
Joseph F Kindlon, *Ch Bd*
Brian R Webber, *
EMP: 37 **EST:** 1987
SQ FT: 48,000
SALES (est): 866.79K **Privately Held**
SIC: 2653 7389 5113 Boxes, corrugated: made from purchased materials; Packaging and labeling services; Corrugated and solid fiber boxes
PA: Cano Container Corporation
3920 Enterprise Ct Ste A

(P-2661)
CORRUGADOS DE BAJA CALIFORNIA
2475 Paseo De Las A, San Diego (92154)
PHONE.....................619 662-8672
Smurfit Kappa, *Owner*
EMP: 900 **EST:** 2008
SALES (est): 39.19MM **Privately Held**
SIC: 2653 Corrugated and solid fiber boxes

(P-2662)
CROCKETT GRAPHICS INC (PA)
Also Called: Folding Cartons
980 Avenida Acaso, Camarillo (93012-8759)
PHONE.....................805 987-8577
Edward Randall Crockett, *Pr*
Edward Randall Crockett, *Pr*
Rod K Rieth, *
▲ **EMP:** 60 **EST:** 1994
SALES (est): 17.11MM
SALES (corp-wide): 17.11MM **Privately Held**
Web: www.garedgraphics.com
SIC: 2653 Corrugated boxes, partitions, display items, sheets, and pad

(P-2663)
ECKO PRODUCTS GROUP LLC
Also Called: Ecko Print & Packaging
740 S Milliken Ave Ste C, Ontario (91761-7842)
P.O. Box 4117 (91761-1007)
PHONE.....................909 628-5678
Eric Rogers, *CFO*
Christopher Hively, *Pr*
◆ **EMP:** 23 **EST:** 2002
SQ FT: 17,000
SALES (est): 5.41MM **Privately Held**
Web: www.eckopg.com
SIC: 2653 5085 2759 Boxes, corrugated: made from purchased materials; Abrasives and adhesives; Commercial printing, nec

(P-2664)
EMPIRE CONTAINER CORPORATION
1161 E Walnut St, Carson (90746-1382)
PHONE.....................310 537-8190

Donald Simmons, *Pr*
Gregory V Hall, *
Patrick Fox, *Stockholder*
▲ **EMP:** 66 **EST:** 1970
SQ FT: 61,000
SALES (est): 2.49MM **Privately Held**
Web: www.empirecfs.com
SIC: 2653 3578 Boxes, corrugated: made from purchased materials; Point-of-sale devices

(P-2665)
FLEETWOOD FIBRE LLC
Also Called: Fleetwood Fibre Pkg & Graphics
15250 Don Julian Rd, City Of Industry (91745-1001)
PHONE.....................626 968-8503
EMP: 225 **EST:** 1952
SALES (est): 24.05MM
SALES (corp-wide): 792.6MM **Privately Held**
Web: www.goldenwestpackaging.com
SIC: 2653 Boxes, corrugated: made from purchased materials
PA: Golden West Packaging Group Llc
15250 Don Julian Rd
888 501-5893

(P-2666)
FRUIT GROWERS SUPPLY COMPANY (PA)
Also Called: Fgs Packing Services
27770 Entertainment Dr Ste 120, Valencia (91355-1093)
PHONE.....................888 997-4855
Jim Phillips, *CEO*
Charles Boyce, *
William O Knox, *
◆ **EMP:** 50 **EST:** 1907
SQ FT: 10,000
SALES (est): 122.9MM
SALES (corp-wide): 122.9MM **Privately Held**
Web: www.fruitgrowerssupply.com
SIC: 2653 0811 5191 2448 Boxes, corrugated: made from purchased materials; Timber tracts; Farm supplies; Pallets, wood

(P-2667)
GABRIEL CONTAINER (PA)
Also Called: Recycled Paper Products
8844 Millergrove Dr, Santa Fe Springs (90670-2013)
P.O. Box 3188 (90670-0188)
PHONE.....................562 699-1051
Ronald H Gabriel, *Pr*
Agnes Gabriel, *
▲ **EMP:** 199 **EST:** 1935
SQ FT: 72,000
SALES (est): 15.93MM
SALES (corp-wide): 15.93MM **Privately Held**
Web: www.gabrielcontainer.com
SIC: 2653 2621 Boxes, corrugated: made from purchased materials; Paper mills

(P-2668)
GENERAL CONTAINER
235 Radio Rd, Corona (92879-1725)
PHONE.....................714 562-8700
Tim G Black, *CEO*
Scott Black, *
EMP: 72 **EST:** 1976
SALES (est): 19.64MM
SALES (corp-wide): 50.43MM **Privately Held**
Web: www.gcbox.com
SIC: 2653 Boxes, corrugated: made from purchased materials

▲ = Import ▼ = Export
◆ = Import/Export

PA: U.S. Display Group, Inc.
810 S Washington St
931 455-9585

(P-2669)

GLOBAL PACKAGING SOLUTIONS INC

6259 Progressive Dr Ste 200, San Diego
(92154-6644)
PHONE.................................619 710-2661
Jawed Ghias, *CEO*
Anila Parikh, *
Rajnikanth Parikh, *
Tariq Butt, *
Henry Romo, *Stockholder*
▲ **EMP:** 280 **EST:** 2006
SALES (est): 8.19MM **Privately Held**
Web: www.globsoln.com
SIC: 2653 3089 Corrugated and solid fiber boxes; Injection molding of plastics
PA: Global Packaging Solutions, S.A. De C.V.
Calle 7 Norte No.108

(P-2670)

GOLDEN WEST PACKG GROUP LLC (PA)

15250 Don Julian Rd, City Of Industry
(91745-1001)
PHONE.................................888 501-5893
Mark J Favre, *CEO*
Brad Jordan, *
Brian Mcdonnell, *CFO*
EMP: 381 **EST:** 2017
SALES (est): 792.6MM
SALES (corp-wide): 792.6MM **Privately Held**
Web: www.goldenwestpackaging.com
SIC: 2653 Boxes, corrugated: made from purchased materials

(P-2671)

GOLDENCORR SHEETS LLC

13890 Nelson Ave, City Of Industry
(91746-2050)
P.O. Box 90968 (91715-0968)
PHONE.................................626 369-6446
Tom Anderson, *Managing Member*
John Webb, *Managing Member*
Glen Tucker, *Managing Member*
Jeffrey Erseluis, *Managing Member*
John Perullo, *
▲ **EMP:** 150 **EST:** 1999
SALES (est): 26.57MM **Privately Held**
Web: www.goldencorr.net
SIC: 2653 Corrugated boxes, partitions, display items, sheets, and pad

(P-2672)

HERITAGE CONTAINER INC

4777 Felspar St, Riverside (92509-3040)
P.O. Box 605 (91752-0605)
PHONE.................................951 360-1900
Richard Gabriel, *CEO*
Thomas Gabriel, *
Nancy Zuniga, *
EMP: 100 **EST:** 1988
SQ FT: 95,000
SALES (est): 16.5MM **Privately Held**
Web: www.heritagecontainer.com
SIC: 2653 5199 Boxes, corrugated: made from purchased materials; Packaging materials

(P-2673)

HERITAGE PAPER CO (HQ)

2400 S Grand Ave, Santa Ana
(92705-5211)
PHONE.................................714 540-9737
Ron Scagliotti, *CEO*

Lenet Derksen, *
▲ **EMP:** 75 **EST:** 1976
SQ FT: 150,000
SALES (est): 2.33MM
SALES (corp-wide): 52.87MM **Privately Held**
Web: www.heritagepaper.net
SIC: 2653 5199 Boxes, corrugated: made from purchased materials; Packaging materials
PA: Pioneer Packing, Inc.
2430 S Grand Ave
714 540-9751

(P-2674)

HOOVER CONTAINERS INC

19570 San Jose Ave, City Of Industry
(91748-1404)
P.O. Box 10366 (92838-6366)
PHONE.................................909 444-9454
▲ **EMP:** 60
SIC: 2653 5113 Boxes, corrugated: made from purchased materials; Corrugated and solid fiber boxes

(P-2675)

HPI LIQUIDATIONS INC

13100 Danielson St, Poway (92064-6840)
PHONE.................................858 391-7302
EMP: 245
SIC: 2653 5199 Boxes, corrugated: made from purchased materials; Packaging materials

(P-2676)

INTERNATIONAL PAPER COMPANY

Also Called: International Paper
11211 Greenstone Ave, Santa Fe Springs
(90670-4616)
PHONE.................................323 946-6100
Marc Bailey, *Genl Mgr*
EMP: 24
SALES (corp-wide): 18.92B **Publicly Held**
Web: www.internationalpaper.com
SIC: 2653 Boxes, corrugated: made from purchased materials
PA: International Paper Company
6400 Poplar Ave
901 419-7000

(P-2677)

JELLCO CONTAINER INC

1151 N Tustin Ave, Anaheim (92807-1736)
PHONE.................................714 666-2728
Jeff Erselius, *Pr*
Rick Leininger, *
EMP: 72 **EST:** 1077
SQ FT: 42,000
SALES (est): 10.44MM **Privately Held**
Web: www.jellco.com
SIC: 2653 Boxes, corrugated: made from purchased materials

(P-2678)

JKV INC

Also Called: Atlantic Box & Carton Company
8343 Loch Lomond Dr, Pico Rivera
(90660-2507)
PHONE.................................562 948-3000
Michael Valov, *Pr*
Jack Valov, *
Elena Valov, *
EMP: 40 **EST:** 1971
SQ FT: 30,000
SALES (est): 6.31MM **Privately Held**
Web: www.atlanticboxncarton.com
SIC: 2653 Boxes, corrugated: made from purchased materials

(P-2679)

LIBERTY CONTAINER COMPANY

Also Called: Key Container
4224 Santa Ana St, South Gate
(90280-2557)
PHONE.................................323 564-4211
Robert J Watts, *Pr*
William J Watts, *
▲ **EMP:** 110 **EST:** 1956
SQ FT: 300,000
SALES (est): 20.42MM **Privately Held**
Web: www.keycontainer.com
SIC: 2653 Boxes, corrugated: made from purchased materials

(P-2680)

LIFOAM INDUSTRIES LLC

15671 Industry Ln, Huntington Beach
(92649-1536)
PHONE.................................714 891-5035
EMP: 48
SALES (corp-wide): 708.32MM **Privately Held**
Web: www.lifoam.com
SIC: 2653 Corrugated and solid fiber boxes
HQ: Lifoam Industries, Llc
1303 S Batesville Rd
Greer SC 29650
410 889-1023

(P-2681)

MARFRED INDUSTRIES

Also Called: Amatix
12708 Branford St, Sun Valley (91353)
▲ **EMP:** 300
SIC: 2653 5113 Boxes, solid fiber: made from purchased materials; Shipping supplies

(P-2682)

NUMATECH WEST (KMP) LLC

Also Called: Kmp Numatech Pacific
1201 E Lexington Ave, Pomona
(91766-5520)
P.O. Box 357 (92871-0357)
PHONE.................................909 706-3627
John Neate, *Managing Member*
▲ **EMP:** 100 **EST:** 1986
SQ FT: 65,000
SALES (est): 2.36MM
SALES (corp-wide): 2.36MM **Privately Held**
SIC: 2653 Boxes, corrugated: made from purchased materials
PA: Nw Packaging Llc
1201 E Lexington Ave
909 706-3627

(P-2683)

PACIFIC QUALITY PACKAGING CORP

680 Neptune Ave, Brea (92821-2909)
PHONE.................................714 257-1234
Frederick H Chau, *Pr*
▲ **EMP:** 65 **EST:** 1984
SQ FT: 44,000
SALES (est): 8.04MM **Privately Held**
SIC: 2653 3993 Boxes, corrugated: made from purchased materials; Signs and advertising specialties

(P-2684)

PACKAGING CORPORATION AMERICA

Also Called: PCA/Los Angeles 349
4240 Bandini Blvd, Vernon (90058-4215)
PHONE.................................323 263-7581
Mark Beyma, *Brnch Mgr*
EMP: 91
SALES (corp-wide): 8.48B **Publicly Held**

Web: www.packagingcorp.com
SIC: 2653 Boxes, corrugated: made from purchased materials
PA: Packaging Corporation Of America
1 N Field Ct
847 482-3000

(P-2685)

PACKAGING CORPORATION AMERICA

Also Called: PCA/South Gate 378
9700 E Frontage Rd Ste 20, South Gate
(90280-5421)
PHONE.................................562 927-7741
Eric Thorntoon, *Brnch Mgr*
EMP: 114
SALES (corp-wide): 8.48B **Publicly Held**
Web: www.packagingcorp.com
SIC: 2653 Boxes, corrugated: made from purchased materials
PA: Packaging Corporation Of America
1 N Field Ct
847 482-3000

(P-2686)

PACKAGING CORPORATION AMERICA

Also Called: San Bernardino Sheet Plant
879 E Rialto Ave, San Bernardino
(92408-1202)
PHONE.................................909 888-7008
EMP: 24
SALES (corp-wide): 8.48B **Publicly Held**
Web: www.packagingcorp.com
SIC: 2653 Boxes, corrugated: made from purchased materials
PA: Packaging Corporation Of America
1 N Field Ct
847 482-3000

(P-2687)

PNC PROACTIVE NTHRN CONT LLC

Also Called: Proactive Northern Container
602 S Rockefeller Ave Ste A, Ontario
(91761-8191)
PHONE.................................909 390-5624
Gary Hartog, *Managing Member*
▲ **EMP:** 44 **EST:** 2005
SQ FT: 362,000
SALES (est): 1.92MM **Privately Held**
SIC: 2653 Boxes, corrugated: made from purchased materials
PA: Fourth Third Llc
375 Park Ave Ste 3304

(P-2688)

RELIABLE CONTAINER CORPORATION

9206 Santa Fe Springs Rd, Santa Fe Springs (90670-2618)
PHONE.................................562 861-6226
EMP: 275
SIC: 2653 5113 Boxes, corrugated: made from purchased materials; Corrugated and solid fiber boxes

(P-2689)

SOUTHLAND BOX COMPANY

4201 Fruitland Ave, Vernon (90058-3118)
P.O. Box 512214 (90051-0214)
PHONE.................................323 583-2231
▲ **EMP:** 170 **EST:** 1945
SALES (est): 69.74MM **Privately Held**
Web: www.southlandbox.com
SIC: 2653 5113 Corrugated boxes, partitions, display items, sheets, and pad; Corrugated and solid fiber boxes
PA: Tomoku Co., Ltd.
2-2-2, Marunouchi

PRODUCTS & SVCS

(P-2690)

SOUTHLAND CONTAINER CORP

Also Called: Concept Packaging Group
1600 Champagne Ave, Ontario
(91761-3612)
PHONE..................................909 937-9781
Tom Heinz, *Brnch Mgr*
EMP: 259
SALES (corp-wide): 93.13MM **Privately Held**
Web: www.southlandcontainer.com
SIC: 2653 Boxes, corrugated: made from purchased materials
PA: Southland Container Corporation
60 Fairview Church Rd
864 578-0085

(P-2691)

ST WORTH CONTAINER LLC

727 S Wanamaker Ave, Ontario
(91761-8116)
PHONE..................................909 390-4550
EMP: 82 EST: 1994
SALES (est): 14.75MM **Privately Held**
Web: www.goldenwestpackaging.com
SIC: 2653 Corrugated boxes, partitions, display items, sheets, and pad

(P-2692)

TRIPLE A CONTAINERS INC

16069 Shoemaker Ave, Cerritos
(90703-2234)
P.O. Box 6111 (90702-6111)
PHONE..................................562 404-7433
EMP: 88 EST: 1957
SALES (est): 2.47MM **Privately Held**
Web: www.newindypackaging.com
SIC: 2653 3993 Corrugated boxes, partitions, display items, sheets, and pad; Signs and advertising specialties

(P-2693)

WESTERN CORRUGATED DESIGN INC

8741 Pioneer Blvd, Santa Fe Springs
(90670-2021)
PHONE..................................562 695-9295
John Brendlinger, *CEO*
▲ EMP: 50 EST: 2004
SALES (est): 7.54MM **Privately Held**
Web: www.wcd1.com
SIC: 2653 Boxes, corrugated: made from purchased materials

(P-2694)

WESTROCK RKT LLC

Also Called: Alliance Display & Packaging
100 E Tujunga Ave Ste 102, Burbank
(91502-1963)
PHONE..................................818 729-0610
Allen Kinder, *Brnch Mgr*
EMP: 51
Web: www.westrock.com
SIC: 2653 Boxes, corrugated: made from purchased materials
HQ: Westrock Rkt, Llc
1000 Abernathy Rd Ste 125
Atlanta GA 30328
770 448-2193

(P-2695)

WESTROCK RKT LLC

749 N Poplar St, Orange (92868-1013)
PHONE..................................714 978-2895
Bob Appoloney, *Brnch Mgr*
EMP: 29
Web: www.westrock.com
SIC: 2653 Boxes, corrugated: made from purchased materials
HQ: Westrock Rkt, Llc
1000 Abernathy Rd Ste 125

Atlanta GA 30328
770 448-2193

2655 Fiber Cans, Drums, And Similar Products

(P-2696)

PLASTOPAN INDUSTRIES INC (PA)

Also Called: Plastopan
812 E 59th St, Los Angeles (90001-1006)
PHONE..................................323 231-2225
Ronald D Miller, *Pr*
Catherine M Bump, *
Sofia G Miller, *
Martin L Miller, *
EMP: 30 EST: 1992
SQ FT: 48,000
SALES (est): 5.55MM **Privately Held**
SIC: 2655 Fiber cans, drums, and similar products

(P-2697)

SGL COMPOSITES INC (DH)

1551 W 139th St, Gardena (90249-2603)
PHONE..................................424 329-5250
David Otterson, *CEO*
Jeff Schade, *
▼ EMP: 90 EST: 1995
SALES (est): 49.48MM
SALES (corp-wide): 1.18B **Privately Held**
Web: www.sglcarbon.com
SIC: 2655 Fiber cans, drums, and similar products
HQ: Sgl Carbon, Llc
10715 Dvid Tylor Dr Ste 4
Charlotte NC 28262
704 593-5100

(P-2698)

SPIRAL PPR TUBE & CORE CO INC

5200 Industry Ave, Pico Rivera
(90660-2506)
PHONE..................................562 801-9705
George Hibard, *CEO*
Summer Hibard, *
▲ EMP: 45 EST: 1949
SQ FT: 40,000
SALES (est): 1.41MM **Privately Held**
Web: www.spiralpaper.com
SIC: 2655 Fiber cans, drums, and similar products

(P-2699)

TUBE-TAINER INC

8174 Byron Rd, Whittier (90606-2616)
PHONE..................................562 945-3711
Mike Mundia, *Pr*
▲ EMP: 45 EST: 1967
SQ FT: 44,000
SALES (est): 9.75MM **Privately Held**
Web: www.tubetainer.com
SIC: 2655 Tubes, fiber or paper: made from purchased material

2656 Sanitary Food Containers

(P-2700)

FINELINE SETTINGS LLC

2041 S Turner Ave Unit 30, Ontario
(91761-8510)
PHONE..................................845 369-6100
Abraham Feig, *Brnch Mgr*
▲ EMP: 26
SALES (corp-wide): 384.87MM **Privately Held**

Web: www.finelinesettings.com
SIC: 2656 Sanitary food containers
HQ: Fineline Settings, Llc
135 Crotty Rd Ste 1
Middletown NY 10941
845 369-6100

2657 Folding Paperboard Boxes

(P-2701)

ABSOLUTE PACKAGING INC

1201 N Miller St, Anaheim (92806-1933)
PHONE..................................714 630-3020
Ramin Kohan, *Pr*
EMP: 35 EST: 2020
SALES (est): 2.64MM **Privately Held**
Web: www.absolutepackaginginc.com
SIC: 2657 5199 Folding paperboard boxes; Packaging materials

(P-2702)

YAVAR MANUFACTURING CO INC

Also Called: National Packaging Products
1900 S Tubeway Ave, Commerce
(90040-1612)
PHONE..................................323 722-2040
Massoud Afari, *CEO*
Ben Afari, *
▲ EMP: 48 EST: 1998
SQ FT: 50,000
SALES (est): 14.43MM **Privately Held**
Web: www.nationalpkg.com
SIC: 2657 2631 Folding paperboard boxes; Folding boxboard

2671 Paper; Coated And Laminated Packaging

(P-2703)

AMCOR FLEXIBLES LLC

Also Called: Amcor Flexibles Healthcare
5416 Union Pacific Ave, Commerce
(90022-5117)
PHONE..................................323 721-6777
Graeme Liebelt, *Brnch Mgr*
EMP: 1217
SALES (corp-wide): 14.69B **Privately Held**
SIC: 2671 2621 2821 3081 Plastic film, coated or laminated for packaging; Packaging paper; Plastics materials and resins; Packing materials, plastics sheet
HQ: Amcor Flexibles Llc
3 Parkway N Ste 300
Deerfield IL 60015
224 313-7000

(P-2704)

AUDIO VIDEO COLOR CORPORATION (PA)

17707 S Santa Fe Ave, E Rncho Dmngz
(90221-5419)
PHONE..................................424 213-7500
Kali J Limath, *CEO*
Guy Marrom, *
Michael Baker, *Prin*
▲ EMP: 145 EST: 1990
SQ FT: 78,000
SALES (est): 15.02MM **Privately Held**
Web: www.avccorp.com
SIC: 2671 Paper; coated and laminated packaging

(P-2705)

BAY CITIES CONTAINER CORP

9206 Santa Fe Springs Rd, Santa Fe
Springs (90670-2618)

PHONE..................................562 551-2946
Greg Tucker, *CEO*
EMP: 32
SALES (corp-wide): 150.82MM **Privately Held**
Web: www.bay-cities.com
SIC: 2671 Paper; coated and laminated packaging
PA: Bay Cities Container Corp
5138 Industry Ave
562 948-3751

(P-2706)

DREAMFIELDS CALIFORNIA LLC

65000 Two Bunch Palms Trl, Desert Hot
Springs (92240-5429)
PHONE..................................310 691-9739
Scot Garrambone, *CFO*
Sebastian Solano, *Managing Member**
Lukasz Tracz, *Managing Member**
EMP: 300 EST: 2022
SALES (est): 4.33MM **Privately Held**
SIC: 2671 Paper; coated and laminated packaging

(P-2707)

FEDERATED DIVERSIFIED SLS INC

Also Called: FDS Manufacturing Company
Svcs
2200 S Reservoir St, Pomona
(91766-6408)
P.O. Box 45 (91769-0045)
PHONE..................................909 591-1733
Robert B Stevenson, *CEO*
EMP: 89 EST: 1957
SALES (est): 3.89MM **Privately Held**
SIC: 2671 2631 2653 3086 Paper; coated and laminated packaging; Container, packaging, and boxboard; Corrugated and solid fiber boxes; Cups and plates, foamed plastics

(P-2708)

GLOBAL LINK SOURCING INC

41690 Corporate Center Ct, Murrieta
(92562-7084)
PHONE..................................951 698-1977
Jullie Annet, *Pr*
▲ EMP: 70 EST: 2006
SQ FT: 80,000
SALES (est): 2.21MM **Privately Held**
Web: www.globallinksourcing.com
SIC: 2671 Paper; coated and laminated packaging

(P-2709)

LACERTA GROUP LLC

20650 Prairie St, Chatsworth (91311-6008)
PHONE..................................508 339-3312
EMP: 75
SIC: 2671 Thermoplastic coated paper for packaging
PA: Lacerta Group, Llc
360 Forbes Blvd

(P-2710)

PGAC CORP (PA)

Also Called: Pgi
9630 Ridgehaven Ct Ste B, San Diego
(92123-5605)
PHONE..................................858 560-8213
Mark Grantham, *Pr*
Florentina Shields, *
EMP: 75 EST: 1975
SALES (est): 19.79MM **Privately Held**
Web: www.pgisd.com
SIC: 2671 Paper, coated or laminated for packaging

(P-2711)
PRECISION LABEL LLC
659 Benet Rd, Oceanside (92058-1208)
P.O. Box 766 (92075-0766)
PHONE..............................760 757-7533
Robert A Wilcox, *Pr*
EMP: 30 **EST:** 1991
SQ FT: 7,000
SALES (est): 8.95MM
SALES (corp-wide): 4.71B **Privately Held**
Web: www.p-label.com
SIC: 2671 2759 Paper; coated and laminated packaging; Labels and seals: printing, nsk
HQ: Inovar Packaging Group, Llc
9001 Sterling St
Irving TX 75063

(P-2712)
THERMECH CORPORATION
Also Called: Thermech Engineering
1773 W Lincoln Ave Ste I, Anaheim (92801-6713)
PHONE..............................714 533-3183
Jim Shah, *CEO*
Richard Gorman, *
EMP: 23 **EST:** 1949
SQ FT: 24,000
SALES (est): 5.1MM **Privately Held**
Web: www.thermech.com
SIC: 2671 3083 Paper; coated and laminated packaging; Plastics finished products, laminated

(P-2713)
TRIUNE ENTERPRISES INC
Also Called: Triune Enterprises Mfg
13711 S Normandie Ave, Gardena (90249-2609)
PHONE..............................310 719-1600
John Christman, *CEO*
Sidney Arouh, *VP*
Donald Alhanati, *Sec*
◆ **EMP:** 23 **EST:** 1996
SQ FT: 29,000
SALES (est): 1.65MM **Privately Held**
Web: www.triuneent.com
SIC: 2671 5162 Plastic film, coated or laminated for packaging; Plastics materials and basic shapes

(P-2714)
VINYL TECHNOLOGY LLC (PA)
200 Railroad Ave, Monrovia (91016-4643)
PHONE..............................626 443-5257
Carlos A Mollura, *Ch Bd*
Daniel Mullora, *
Carlos Mollura Junior, *VP*
Rodney Mollura, *
Haydee Mollura, *
◆ **EMP:** 199 **EST:** 1981
SQ FT: 68,000
SALES (est): 46.38MM
SALES (corp-wide): 46.38MM **Privately Held**
Web: www.vinyltechnology.com
SIC: 2671 7389 Plastic film, coated or laminated for packaging; Sewing contractor

---

2672 Paper; Coated And Laminated, Nec

(P-2715)
AVERY DENNISON CORPORATION
2900 Bradley St, Pasadena (91107-1560)
PHONE..............................626 304-2000
Dave Edwards, *VP*
EMP: 120

SQ FT: 67,580
SALES (corp-wide): 8.36B **Publicly Held**
Web: www.averydennison.com
SIC: 2672 2679 Adhesive papers, labels, or tapes: from purchased material; Labels, paper: made from purchased material
PA: Avery Dennison Corporation
8080 Norton Pkwy
440 534-6000

(P-2716)
AVERY DENNISON CORPORATION
11195 Eucalyptus St, Rancho Cucamonga (91730-3836)
PHONE..............................909 987-4631
Marta E Corfaelb, *Mgr*
EMP: 62
SALES (corp-wide): 8.36B **Publicly Held**
Web: www.averydennison.com
SIC: 2672 Tape, pressure sensitive: made from purchased materials
PA: Avery Dennison Corporation
8080 Norton Pkwy
440 534-6000

(P-2717)
AVERY DENNISON CORPORATION
50 Pointe Dr, Brea (92821-3648)
PHONE..............................714 674-8500
Rick Alonzo, *Mgr*
EMP: 400
SALES (corp-wide): 8.36B **Publicly Held**
Web: www.averydennison.com
SIC: 2672 3081 3497 2678 Adhesive papers, labels, or tapes: from purchased material; Unsupported plastics film and sheet; Metal foil and leaf; Stationery products
PA: Avery Dennison Corporation
8080 Norton Pkwy
440 534-6000

(P-2718)
AVERY DENNISON FOUNDATION
207 N Goode Ave Ste 500, Glendale (91203-1301)
PHONE..............................626 304-2000
Alicia Maddox, *Pr*
EMP: 26 **EST:** 1978
SALES (est): 448.1K **Privately Held**
SIC: 2672 Paper; coated and laminated, nec

(P-2719)
BECKERS FABRICATION INC
Also Called: B F I Labels
22465 La Palma Ave, Yorba Linda (92887-3803)
PHONE..............................714 692-1600
Mark Becker, *CEO*
Dan Becker, *
EMP: 24 **EST:** 1981
SQ FT: 6,500
SALES (est): 5.71MM **Privately Held**
Web: www.beckersfab.com
SIC: 2672 2759 Paper; coated and laminated, nec; Screen printing

(P-2720)
CINTON LLC
Also Called: West Coast Labels
620 Richfield Rd, Placentia (92870-6727)
PHONE..............................714 961-8808
Salvatore Scaffide, *Pr*
Romona Scaffide, *
Cindi Montgomery, *
EMP: 46 **EST:** 1972
SQ FT: 23,000
SALES (est): 9.63MM **Privately Held**

Web: www.fortissolutionsgroup.com
SIC: 2672 2679 Paper; coated and laminated, nec; Labels, paper: made from purchased material
PA: Fortis Solutions Group, Llc
2505 Hawkeye Ct

(P-2721)
CLARIANT CORPORATION
926 S 8th St, Colton (92324-3500)
P.O. Box 610 (92324-0610)
PHONE..............................909 825-1793
Kenneth Golder, *Pr*
EMP: 32
Web: www.clariant.com
SIC: 2672 7389 5199 Paper; coated and laminated, nec; Packaging and labeling services; Packaging materials
HQ: Clariant Corporation
500 E Morehead St Ste 400
Charlotte NC 28202
704 331-7000

(P-2722)
EDWARDS ASSOC CMMNICATIONS INC (PA)
Also Called: Edwards Label
2277 Knoll Dr Ste A, Ventura (93003-5878)
PHONE..............................805 658-2626
Joel Horacio Gomez-avila, *Pr*
John Edwards, *
EMP: 150 **EST:** 1984
SQ FT: 44,000
SALES (est): 17.08MM
SALES (corp-wide): 17.08MM **Privately Held**
Web: www.edwardslabel.com
SIC: 2672 Labels (unprinted), gummed: made from purchased materials

(P-2723)
FELIX SCHOELLER NORTH AMER INC
1260 N Lakeview Ave, Anaheim (92807-1831)
PHONE..............................315 298-8425
EMP: 25
SALES (corp-wide): 29.22MM **Privately Held**
Web: www.felix-schoeller.com
SIC: 2672 Paper; coated and laminated, nec
HQ: Felix Schoeller North America Inc.
179 County Route 2a
Pulaski NY 13142
315 298-8425

(P-2724)
HARRIS INDUSTRIES INC (PA)
5181 Argosy Ave, Huntington Beach (92649-1058)
P.O. Box 3209 (92005-3209)
PHONE..............................714 898-8048
William Helzer, *Pr*
Gail Helzer, *
◆ **EMP:** 50 **EST:** 1987
SQ FT: 25,000
SALES (est): 9.97MM
SALES (corp-wide): 9.97MM **Privately Held**
Web: www.harrisind.com
SIC: 2672 Tape, pressure sensitive: made from purchased materials

(P-2725)
PRECISION DYNAMICS CORPORATION (HQ)
Also Called: Pdc-Identicard
25124 Springfield Ct Ste 200, Valencia (91355-1087)

PHONE..............................818 897-1111
J Michael Nauman, *CEO*
Robin Barber, *
Robert Case, *
John Park, *
◆ **EMP:** 161 **EST:** 1956
SQ FT: 75,000
SALES (est): 34.6MM
SALES (corp-wide): 1.34B **Publicly Held**
Web: www.pdcorp.com
SIC: 2672 2754 5047 3069 Adhesive papers, labels, or tapes: from purchased material; Labels: gravure printing; Instruments, surgical and medical; Tape, pressure sensitive: rubber
PA: Brady Corporation
6555 W Good Hope Rd
414 358-6600

(P-2726)
SC LIQUIDATION COMPANY LLC
566 Vanguard Way, Brea (92821-3928)
PHONE..............................714 482-1006
EMP: 103
Web: www.spinps.com
SIC: 2672 Labels (unprinted), gummed: made from purchased materials
HQ: Sc Liquidation Company, Llc
550 Summit Ave
Troy OH 45373
937 332-6500

(P-2727)
SEAL METHODS INC (PA)
11915 Shoemaker Ave, Santa Fe Springs (90670-4717)
P.O. Box 2604 (90670-0604)
PHONE..............................562 944-0291
Darin Welter, *CEO*
Geraldine Welter, *
Douglas Kraus, *
◆ **EMP:** 90 **EST:** 1974
SQ FT: 75,000
SALES (est): 35.55MM
SALES (corp-wide): 35.55MM **Privately Held**
Web: www.sealmethodsinc.com
SIC: 2672 3053 5085 Masking tape: made from purchased materials; Gaskets, all materials; Gaskets

---

2673 Bags: Plastic, Laminated, And Coated

(P-2728)
BAGCRAFTPAPERCON III LLC
515 Turnbull Canyon Rd, City Of Industry (91745-1118)
PHONE..............................626 961-6766
EMP: 122
SALES (corp-wide): 32.64B **Publicly Held**
Web: www.novolex.com
SIC: 2673 Plastic bags: made from purchased materials
HQ: Bagcraftpapercon Iii, Llc
3436 Tringdon Way Ste 100
Charlotte NC 28277
800 845-6051

(P-2729)
CALIFORNIA PLASTIX INC
1319 E 3rd St, Pomona (91766-2212)
PHONE..............................909 629-8288
Danny Farshadfar, *Pr*
Touraj Tour, *
▼ **EMP:** 25 **EST:** 1994
SQ FT: 44,000
SALES (est): 4MM **Privately Held**
Web: www.californiaplastix.com

PRODUCTS & SVCS

SIC: 2673 3089 Garment and wardrobe bags, (plastic film); Extruded finished plastics products, nec

(P-2730)
CROWN POLY INC
Also Called: Pull-N-Pac
5700 Bickett St, Huntington Park
(90255-2625)
PHONE..............................323 585-5522
Ebrahim Simhaee, *CEO*
◆ **EMP:** 150 **EST:** 1991
SQ FT: 40,000
SALES (est): 25.6MM **Privately Held**
Web: www.crownpoly.com
SIC: 2673 Plastic bags: made from purchased materials

(P-2731)
DURABAG COMPANY INC
Also Called: Superpak
1432 Santa Fe Dr, Tustin (92780-6417)
PHONE..............................714 259-8811
Frank C S Huang, *VP*
Daniel Huang, *
Feng Jung Huang, *
▲ **EMP:** 70 **EST:** 1985
SQ FT: 150,000
SALES (est): 9.02MM **Privately Held**
Web: www.durabag.net
SIC: 2673 Food storage and frozen food bags, plastic

(P-2732)
GREAT AMERICAN PACKAGING
4361 S Soto St, Vernon (90058-2311)
PHONE..............................323 582-2247
Greg Gurewitz, *Pr*
Marlene Gurewitz, *
Bruce Carter, *
Bob Clarke, *
Fito Perez Outside Sales, *Prin*
EMP: 50 **EST:** 1966
SQ FT: 40,000
SALES (est): 8.97MM **Privately Held**
Web: www.greatampack.com
SIC: 2673 3081 3082 Plastic bags: made from purchased materials; Plastics film and sheet; Unsupported plastics profile shapes

(P-2733)
LIBERTY PACKG & EXTRUDING INC
Also Called: Liberty Film
3015 Supply Ave, Commerce (90040-2709)
PHONE..............................323 722-5124
Derek De Heras, *CEO*
Derek De Heras, *Pr*
Bonnie Hudson, *
Mary Hudson, *
Mary Anne Bove, *
EMP: 40 **EST:** 1986
SQ FT: 25,000
SALES (est): 5.11MM **Privately Held**
Web: www.libertypkg.com
SIC: 2673 7389 Plastic and pliofilm bags; Packaging and labeling services

(P-2734)
MERCURY PLASTICS INC (HQ)
14825 Salt Lake Ave, City Of Industry
(91746-3131)
PHONE..............................626 961-0165
Benjamin Deutsch, *CEO*
Stanley Tzenkov, *
Kamyar Mirdamadi, *
Yathira Munoz, *
▲ **EMP:** 415 **EST:** 1987
SQ FT: 140,000
SALES (est): 92.41MM **Privately Held**

Web: www.mercplastics.com
SIC: 2673 2759 3089 Plastic bags: made from purchased materials; Bags, plastic, printing, nsk; Plastics containers, except foam
PA: Alpha Industries Management, Inc. 2919 Center Port Cir

(P-2735)
MOHAWK WESTERN PLASTICS INC
1496 Arrow Hwy, La Verne (91750-5297)
P.O. Box 463 (91750-0463)
PHONE..............................909 593-7547
John R Mordoff, *CEO*
J Christopher Mordoff, *
EMP: 40 **EST:** 1965
SQ FT: 28,000
SALES (est): 10.66MM **Privately Held**
Web: www.mohawkwestern.com
SIC: 2673 3081 Plastic bags: made from purchased materials; Unsupported plastics film and sheet

(P-2736)
NORMAN PAPER AND FOAM CO INC
Also Called: Norman International
4501 S Santa Fe Ave, Vernon
(90058-2129)
PHONE..............................323 582-7132
Norman Levine, *Pr*
Dawnn Winter, *
Christopher Werner, *
Ellen Levine, *
▲ **EMP:** 23 **EST:** 1980
SQ FT: 40,000
SALES (est): 6.76MM **Privately Held**
Web: www.normaninternational.com
SIC: 2673 2671 3086 Bags: plastic, laminated, and coated; Paper; coated and laminated packaging; Packaging and shipping materials, foamed plastics

(P-2737)
NOVOLEX BAGCRAFT INC
Also Called: Zenith Specialty Bag
17625 Railroad St, Rowland Heights
(91748-1110)
PHONE..............................626 912-2481
Stanley Bikulege, *Mgr*
EMP: 43
SALES (corp-wide): 32.64B **Publicly Held**
Web: www.novolex.com
SIC: 2673 2674 Bags: plastic, laminated, and coated; Bags: uncoated paper and multiwall
HQ: Novolex Bagcraft, Inc.
101 E Carolina Ave
Hartsville SC 29550
800 845-6051

(P-2738)
REPUBLIC BAG INC (PA)
580 E Harrison St, Corona (92879-1344)
PHONE..............................951 734-9740
Richard Schroeder, *CEO*
Steven Fritz, *
Mark Teo, *
▲ **EMP:** 80 **EST:** 1976
SQ FT: 59,000
SALES (est): 18.95MM
SALES (corp-wide): 18.95MM **Privately Held**
Web: www.republicbag.com
SIC: 2673 Plastic bags: made from purchased materials

(P-2739)
SUN PLASTICS INC
7140 E Slauson Ave, Commerce
(90040-3663)
PHONE..............................323 888-6999
Vahan Bagamian, *Pr*
Movses Shrikian, *
EMP: 50 **EST:** 1979
SQ FT: 60,000
SALES (est): 8.75MM **Privately Held**
Web: www.sunplastics.com
SIC: 2673 Plastic bags: made from purchased materials

(P-2740)
SUNSHINE FPC INC
Also Called: Sunshine
1600 Gage Rd, Montebello (90640-6616)
PHONE..............................323 721-8168
▲ **EMP:** 65 **EST:** 1981
SALES (est): 8.99MM **Privately Held**
Web: www.sunshinefpc.com
SIC: 2673 Plastic bags: made from purchased materials

(P-2741)
THE HEAT FACTORY INC
2793 Loker Ave W, Carlsbad (92010-6601)
PHONE..............................760 893-8300
Chris Treptow, *CEO*
▲ **EMP:** 35 **EST:** 1980
SALES (est): 2.51MM **Privately Held**
Web: shop.heatfactory.com
SIC: 2673 2381 Bags: plastic, laminated, and coated; Fabric dress and work gloves

(P-2742)
WESTERN STATES PACKAGING INC
13276 Paxton St, Pacoima (91331-2356)
PHONE..............................818 686-6045
Richard Joyce, *Pr*
Mark Pickrell, *
▲ **EMP:** 50 **EST:** 1995
SQ FT: 35,000
SALES (est): 8.18MM **Privately Held**
Web: www.wspusa.com
SIC: 2673 5113 5162 Plastic bags: made from purchased materials; Bags, paper and disposable plastic; Plastics materials, nec

2674 Bags: Uncoated Paper And Multiwall

(P-2743)
ENDPAK PACKAGING INC
9101 Perkins St, Pico Rivera (90660-4512)
PHONE..............................562 801-0281
Edgar A Garcia, *CEO*
Carlos Garcia, *
EMP: 90 **EST:** 1992
SQ FT: 45,600
SALES (est): 17.91MM **Privately Held**
Web: www.endpak.com
SIC: 2674 5199 Paper bags: made from purchased materials; Packaging materials

(P-2744)
PACOBOND INC
9344 Glenoaks Blvd, Sun Valley
(91352-1533)
PHONE..............................818 768-5002
Arsine Seraydarian, *CEO*
Gerard Seradarian, *
▲ **EMP:** 50 **EST:** 1985
SALES (est): 2.17MM **Privately Held**
Web: www.pacobond.com

SIC: 2674 5162 Shopping bags: made from purchased materials; Plastics materials, nec

2675 Die-cut Paper And Board

(P-2745)
K & D GRAPHICS
Also Called: K & D Graphics Prtg & Packg
1432 N Main St Ste C, Orange
(92867-3450)
PHONE..............................714 639-8900
Don Chew, *CEO*
Kim Chew, *
Montri Chew, *
Bebe Chew, *
Gus Chew, *
▲ **EMP:** 48 **EST:** 1981
SQ FT: 75,500
SALES (est): 9.07MM **Privately Held**
Web: www.kdgpp.com
SIC: 2675 2752 Die-cut paper and board; Offset printing

(P-2746)
PRESENTATION FOLDER INC
1130 N Main St, Orange (92867-3421)
PHONE..............................714 289-7000
Joseph Tardie Junior, *Pr*
Joseph Tardie Senior, *VP*
◆ **EMP:** 45 **EST:** 1988
SQ FT: 70,000
SALES (est): 8.56MM **Privately Held**
Web: www.presentationfolder.com
SIC: 2675 2759 2672 Folders, filing, die-cut: made from purchased materials; Embossing on paper; Paper; coated and laminated, nec

2676 Sanitary Paper Products

(P-2747)
PRINCESS PAPER INC
4455 Fruitland Ave, Vernon (90058-3222)
PHONE..............................323 588-4777
Abraham Hakimi, *Pr*
▲ **EMP:** 45 **EST:** 1989
SQ FT: 150,000
SALES (est): 4.69MM **Privately Held**
Web: www.princesspaper.com
SIC: 2676 Towels, napkins, and tissue paper products

(P-2748)
PROCTER & GAMBLE PAPER PDTS CO
Also Called: Procter & Gamble
800 N Rice Ave, Oxnard (93030-8910)
PHONE..............................805 485-8871
Shirley Boone, *Mgr*
EMP: 2621
SALES (corp-wide): 84.04B **Publicly Held**
Web: us.pg.com
SIC: 2676 Towels, paper: made from purchased paper
HQ: The Procter & Gamble Paper Products Company
1 Procter And Gamble Plz
Cincinnati OH 45202
513 983-1100

(P-2749)
UI MEDICAL LLC
1670 W Park Ave, Redlands (92373-8048)
PHONE..............................562 453-1515
Joseph Baum Harris, *Ex Dir*
Wade Johnson, *
Nicolas Soichet, *
Christian Bluhm, *

Aaron Johnson, *
EMP: 25 **EST:** 2016
SALES (est): 1.59MM **Privately Held**
Web: www.quickchange.com
SIC: 2676 Diapers, paper (disposable): made from purchased paper

2677 Envelopes

(P-2750)
INLAND ENVELOPE COMPANY
Also Called: Alna Envelope Company
150 N Park Ave, Pomona (91768-3835)
PHONE..............................909 622-2016
Bernard Kloenne, *CEO*
Otilia Kloenne, *Corporate Secretary*
EMP: 55 **EST:** 1966
SQ FT: 45,000
SALES (est): 16.61MM **Privately Held**
Web: www.inlandenvelope.com
SIC: 2677 Envelopes

(P-2751)
LA ENVELOPE INCORPORATED
1053 S Vail Ave, Montebello (90640-6019)
PHONE..............................323 838-9300
Gary T Earls, *Pr*
Louise Earls, *
EMP: 35 **EST:** 1986
SQ FT: 25,000
SALES (est): 6.46MM **Privately Held**
Web: www.laenvelope.com
SIC: 2677 2752 Envelopes; Offset printing

(P-2752)
SEABOARD ENVELOPE CO INC
15601 Cypress Ave, Irwindale (91706-2120)
P.O. Box 721 (92625-0721)
PHONE..............................626 960-4559
Ronald Neidringhaus, *Pr*
Richard Riggle, *
Valerie Niedringhaus, *Prin*
EMP: 25 **EST:** 1939
SQ FT: 72,000
SALES (est): 872.08K **Privately Held**
Web: www.seaboardenvelope.com
SIC: 2677 Envelopes

(P-2753)
SOUTHLAND ENVELOPE LLC
8830 Siempre Viva Rd, San Diego (92154-6278)
P.O. Box 1570 (92040-0913)
PHONE..............................619 449-3553
David Gonzalez, *CEO*
Frank Soloman Junior, *Pr*
Rita Soloman, *
EMP: 115 **EST:** 1970
SQ FT: 80,000
SALES (est): 24.5MM **Privately Held**
Web: www.marketing.com
SIC: 2677 Envelopes

(P-2754)
VISION ENVELOPE & PRTG CO INC (PA)
13707 S Figueroa St, Los Angeles (90061-1045)
PHONE..............................310 324-7062
Mark Fisher, *Prin*
Michael J Leeny, *
Ericka Fisher, *Prin*
Joe Barretto, *Prin*
Kraig Herrera, *Prin*
EMP: 50 **EST:** 1993
SQ FT: 45,000
SALES (est): 2.43MM **Privately Held**
Web: www.vision-envelope.com

SIC: 2677 2752 Envelopes; Offset printing

2678 Stationery Products

(P-2755)
AVERY DENNISON OFFICE PRODUCTS CO INC
Also Called: Dennison Division
50 Pointe Dr, Brea (92821-3652)
▼ **EMP:** 2410
SIC: 2678 3951 2672 2891 Notebooks: made from purchased paper; Markers, soft tip (felt, fabric, plastic, etc.); Labels (unprinted), gummed: made from purchased materials; Adhesives

(P-2756)
AVERY DNNSON RET INFO SVCS LLC (HQ)
207 N Goode Ave Fl 6, Glendale (91203-1364)
PHONE..............................626 304-2000
EMP: 51 **EST:** 2008
SALES (est): 23.41MM
SALES (corp-wide): 8.36B **Publicly Held**
SIC: 2678 3497 Notebooks: made from purchased paper; Metal foil and leaf
PA: Avery Dennison Corporation
8080 Norton Pkwy
440 534-6000

(P-2757)
AVERY PRODUCTS CORPORATION (DH)
Also Called: ID&c
50 Pointe Dr, Brea (92821-3648)
PHONE..............................714 674-8500
Mark Cooper, *CEO*
Jeff Lattanzio, *
Bohdan Sirota, *
◆ **EMP:** 101 **EST:** 2012
SALES (est): 325.82MM
SALES (corp-wide): 4.84B **Privately Held**
Web: www.avery.com
SIC: 2678 3951 2672 2891 Notebooks: made from purchased paper; Markers, soft tip (felt, fabric, plastic, etc.); Labels (unprinted), gummed: made from purchased materials; Adhesives
HQ: Ccl Industries Corporation
161 Worcester Rd Ste 403
Framingham MA 01701

(P-2758)
AVERY PRODUCTS CORPORATION
6987 Calle De Linea Ste 101, San Diego (92154-8016)
PHONE..............................619 671-1022
Geoff Martin, *Pr*
EMP: 117
SALES (corp-wide): 4.84B **Privately Held**
Web: www.avery.com
SIC: 2678 Stationery products
HQ: Avery Products Corporation
50 Pointe Dr
Brea CA 92821
714 674-8500

(P-2759)
BAVARIAN NORDIC INC
6275 Nancy Ridge Dr Ste 110, San Diego (92121-2245)
PHONE..............................919 600-1260
EMP: 25 **EST:** 2005
SALES (est): 5.23MM **Privately Held**
SIC: 2678 Stationery products

(P-2760)
COAST INDEX CO INC
Also Called: Coast Index 965
850 Lawrence Dr, Newbury Park (91320-1508)
PHONE..............................805 499-6844
EMP: 75 **EST:** 1982
SALES (est): 1.96MM **Privately Held**
Web: www.coastindex.com
SIC: 2678 2782 Stationery: made from purchased materials; Library binders, looseleaf

(P-2761)
TREE HOUSE PAD & PAPER INC
2341 Pomona Rd Ste 108, Corona (92878-4373)
PHONE..............................800 213-4184
David Moncrief, *Pr*
Darrin Monroe, *
EMP: 55 **EST:** 1998
SQ FT: 50,000
SALES (est): 10.63MM **Privately Held**
Web: www.treehousepaper.com
SIC: 2678 Stationery products

2679 Converted Paper Products, Nec

(P-2762)
88 SPECIAL SWEET INC
10488 Hickson St, El Monte (91731-4900)
PHONE..............................909 525-7055
Stella Sotoodeh, *CEO*
EMP: 78 **EST:** 2005
SALES (est): 2.56MM **Privately Held**
Web: www.stellateaproducts.com
SIC: 2679 Cups, pressed and molded pulp: made from purchased material

(P-2763)
A PLUS LABEL INC
3215 W Warner Ave, Santa Ana (92704-5314)
PHONE..............................714 229-9811
Nick Phan, *Pr*
EMP: 50 **EST:** 1995
SQ FT: 6,400
SALES (est): 4.31MM **Privately Held**
Web: apluslabel.wpcomstaging.com
SIC: 2679 Tags and labels, paper

(P-2764)
ARTISSIMO DESIGNS LLC (HQ)
2100 E Grand Ave Ste 400, El Segundo (90245-5169)
PHONE..............................310 906-3700
Ravi Bhagavatula, *Managing Member*
▲ **EMP:** 50 **EST:** 2015
SQ FT: 13,000
SALES (est): 41.71MM
SALES (corp-wide): 42.13MM **Privately Held**
SIC: 2679 Wallboard, decorated: made from purchased material
PA: Excelsior Capital Partners, Llc
4695 Mcarthur Crt Ste 370
949 566-8110

(P-2765)
CALPACO PAPERS INC (PA)
3155 Universe Dr, Jurupa Valley (91752-3252)
PHONE..............................323 767-2800
Paul Maier, *Pr*
Francis A Maier, *
▲ **EMP:** 136 **EST:** 1968
SQ FT: 606,000

SALES (est): 1.83MM
SALES (corp-wide): 1.83MM **Privately Held**
Web: www.actfulfillment.com
SIC: 2679 5111 Paper products, converted, nec; Printing and writing paper

(P-2766)
DIGITAL LABEL SOLUTIONS LLC
1177 N Grove St, Anaheim (92806-2110)
PHONE..............................714 982-5000
Joel H Mark, *CEO*
Sandy Petersen, *
Suzie Dobyns, *
EMP: 29 **EST:** 2006
SALES (est): 1.71MM **Privately Held**
Web: www.digitallabelsolutions.com
SIC: 2679 Tags and labels, paper
PA: Brook & Whittle Limited
20 Carter Dr

(P-2767)
ENCORR SHEETS LLC
5171 E Francis St, Ontario (91761-3661)
PHONE..............................626 523-4661
EMP: 44 **EST:** 2016
SALES (est): 2.41MM **Privately Held**
Web: www.encorrsheetsllc.com
SIC: 2679 Corrugated paper: made from purchased material

(P-2768)
FDS MANUFACTURING COMPANY (PA)
2200 S Reservoir St, Pomona (91766-6408)
P.O. Box 3120 (91769-3120)
PHONE..............................909 591-1733
Robert B Stevenson, *CEO*
Samuel B Stevenson, *
Chuck O'connor, *VP*
Kevin Stevenson, *
▲ **EMP:** 100 **EST:** 1950
SQ FT: 240,000
SALES (est): 21.08MM
SALES (corp-wide): 21.08MM **Privately Held**
Web: www.fdsmfg.com
SIC: 2679 3089 Corrugated paper: made from purchased material; Plastics containers, except foam

(P-2769)
GOLDEN KRAFT INC
15500 Valley View Ave, La Mirada (90638-5230)
PHONE..............................562 926-8888
Dan August, *Genl Mgr*
▲ **EMP:** 273 **EST:** 1982
SQ FT: 63,200
SALES (est): 4.25MM
SALES (corp-wide): 64.37B **Privately Held**
SIC: 2679 2631 Corrugated paper: made from purchased material; Paperboard mills
HQ: Georgia-Pacific Corrugated Iii Llc
5645 W 82nd St
Indianapolis IN 46278

(P-2770)
P & R PAPER SUPPLY CO INC
1350 Piper Ranch Rd, San Diego (92154-7708)
PHONE..............................619 671-2400
Bruce Overmeyer, *Mgr*
EMP: 180
SALES (corp-wide): 1.65B **Privately Held**
Web: www.prpaper.com
SIC: 2679 2621 Paper products, converted, nec; Paper mills

HQ: P. & R. Paper Supply Company, Inc.
1898 E Colton Ave
Redlands CA 92374
909 389-1807

(P-2771)
PACIFIC PPRBD CONVERTING LLC (PA)
Also Called: Pacific Paper
8865 Utica Ave Ste A, Rancho Cucamonga
(91730-5144)
PHONE...................909 476-6466
William F Donahue, *Managing Member*
EMP: 24 EST: 2016
SALES (est): 14.94MM
SALES (corp-wide): 14.94MM **Privately Held**
Web: www.pacificpaper.com
SIC: 2679 Paperboard products, converted, nec

(P-2772)
PRIME CONVERTING CORPORATION
9121 Pittsburgh Ave Ste 100, Rancho Cucamonga (91730-5550)
P.O. Box 3207 (91729-3207)
PHONE...................909 476-9500
Robert J Nielsen, *Pr*
▲ EMP: 24 EST: 2003
SALES (est): 1.94MM **Privately Held**
Web: www.primecc.com
SIC: 2679 Paper products, converted, nec

(P-2773)
PROGRESSIVE LABEL INC
2545 Yates Ave, Commerce (90040-2619)
P.O. Box 911430 (90091-1238)
PHONE...................323 415-9770
Gus Garcia, *Pr*
Adam Flores, *
Julie Lawrence, *
David Lawrence, *Stockholder*
▲ EMP: 39 EST: 1988
SQ FT: 18,000
SALES (est): 4.48MM **Privately Held**
Web: www.progressivelabel.com
SIC: 2679 2672 2671 2241 Tags and labels, paper; Paper; coated and laminated, nec; Paper; coated and laminated packaging; Narrow fabric mills

(P-2774)
SUMMIT ENTERPRISES INC
Also Called: Summit Erosion Control
2471 Montecito Rd Ste A, Ramona (92065-1641)
P.O. Box 880335 (92168-0335)
PHONE...................858 679-2100
Larry Holley, *CEO*
Timothy R Binder, *
EMP: 50 EST: 2005
SALES (est): 9.14MM **Privately Held**
Web: www.summiterosion.com
SIC: 2679 Book covers, paper

(P-2775)
TAGTIME USA INC
4601 District Blvd, Vernon (90058-2731)
PHONE...................323 587-1555
Cort Johnson, *Pr*
Darryl Rudnick, *
Mindy Knox, *
David Scott, *
▲ EMP: 480 EST: 2001
SQ FT: 23,000
SALES (est): 16.66MM **Privately Held**
Web: www.tagtimeusa.com
SIC: 2679 Labels, paper: made from purchased material

(P-2776)
TEKNI-PLEX INC
Also Called: Natvar
19555 Arenth Ave, City Of Industry (91748-1403)
PHONE...................909 589-4366
Joleen Kennelley, *Brnch Mgr*
EMP: 97
SALES (corp-wide): 996.3MM **Privately Held**
Web: www.tekni-plex.com
SIC: 2679 3061 Egg cartons, molded pulp: made from purchased material; Medical and surgical rubber tubing (extruded and lathe-cut)
PA: Tekni-Plex, Inc.
460 E Swedesford Rd # 300
484 690-1520

(P-2777)
THOMPSON PIPE GROUP INC (PA)
3011 N Laurel Ave, Rialto (92377-3725)
PHONE...................909 822-0200
Kenneth D Thompson, *CEO*
EMP: 26 EST: 2018
SALES (est): 30.07MM
SALES (corp-wide): 30.07MM **Privately Held**
Web: www.thompsonpipegroup.com
SIC: 2679 Pipes and fittings, fiber: made from purchased material

(P-2778)
W/S PACKAGING GROUP INC
W/S Packaging Fullerton
531 Airpark Dr, Fullerton (92833-2501)
PHONE...................714 992-2574
Mathew Edwards, *Genl Mgr*
EMP: 28
SALES (corp-wide): 14.54B **Privately Held**
SIC: 2679 2671 2759 Labels, paper: made from purchased material; Paper; coated and laminated packaging; Labels and seals: printing, nsk
HQ: W/S Packaging Group, Inc.
2571 S Hemlock Rd
Green Bay WI 54229
800 818-5481

2711 Newspapers

(P-2779)
ANTELOPE VALLEY NEWSPAPERS INC
Also Called: Antelope Valley Press
44939 10th St W, Lancaster (93534-2313)
PHONE...................661 940-1000
Tammy Valdes, *Mgr*
EMP: 29
SALES (corp-wide): 9.82MM **Privately Held**
Web: www.avpress.com
SIC: 2711 7313 2741 Newspapers: publishing only, not printed on site; Newspaper advertising representative; Miscellaneous publishing
PA: Antelope Valley Newspapers Inc.
37404 Sierra Hwy
661 273-2700

(P-2780)
ASIA-PACIFIC CALIFORNIA INC
Also Called: The China Press
1710 S Del Mar Ave, San Gabriel (91776-3852)
PHONE...................626 281-8500
Non Hiand, *Genl Mgr*
EMP: 35

SIC: 2711 Newspapers, publishing and printing
PA: Asia-Pacific California, Inc.
2121 W Mission Rd Ste 207

(P-2781)
ASSOCIATED DESERT NEWSPAPER (DH)
Also Called: Imperial Valley Press
205 N 8th St, El Centro (92243-2301)
P.O. Box 2641 (92244-2641)
PHONE...................760 337-3400
Mayer Malone, *Pr*
David Leone, *
Teresa Zimmer, *
Clifford James, *
John Yanni, *
EMP: 40 EST: 1950
SQ FT: 30,000
SALES (est): 5.7MM
SALES (corp-wide): 3.28B **Publicly Held**
Web: www.ivpressonline.com
SIC: 2711 Newspapers, publishing and printing
HQ: Schurz Communications, Inc.
1301 E Douglas Rd Ste 200
Mishawaka IN 46545
574 247-7237

(P-2782)
ASSOCIATED STUDENTS UCLA
Also Called: Asucla Publications
308 Westwood Plz Ste 118, Los Angeles (90095-8355)
PHONE...................310 825-2787
Arvli Ward, *Mgr*
EMP: 152
SALES (corp-wide): 55.96MM **Privately Held**
Web: www.asucla.ucla.edu
SIC: 2711 2741 2721 Newspapers: publishing only, not printed on site; Miscellaneous publishing; Periodicals
PA: Associated Students U.C.L.A.
308 Westwood Plz
310 794-8836

(P-2783)
CALIFORNIA COMMUNITY NEWS LLC
Also Called: Burbank Leader
221 N Brand Blvd Fl 2, Glendale (91203-2609)
PHONE...................818 843-8700
Danette Goulet, *Mgr*
EMP: 56
SIC: 2711 Newspapers: publishing only, not printed on site
HQ: California Community News, Llc
2000 E 8th St
Los Angeles CA 90021

(P-2784)
CALIFORNIA COMMUNITY NEWS LLC (DH)
2000 E 8th St, Los Angeles (90021-2474)
PHONE...................626 388-1017
Eddy Hartenstein, *Pr*
Judy Kendall, *
Julie Xanders, *
EMP: 349 EST: 1993
SALES (est): 5.27MM **Privately Held**
SIC: 2711 Newspapers, publishing and printing
HQ: Tribune Publishing Company
1000 Albion Ave
Schaumburg IL 60193
312 222-9100

(P-2785)
CALIFORNIA NEWSPPR SVC BUR INC
Also Called: California Newspaper Service
915 E 1st St, Los Angeles (90012-4000)
P.O. Box 60460 (90060-0460)
PHONE...................213 229-5500
EMP: 23 EST: 1990
SALES (est): 2.26MM
SALES (corp-wide): 67.71MM **Publicly Held**
Web: www.journaltech.com
SIC: 2711 Newspapers, publishing and printing
PA: Daily Journal Corporation
915 E 1st St
213 229-5300

(P-2786)
CALIFRNIA NWSPAPERS LTD PARTNR (DH)
Also Called: Inland Valley Daily Bulletin
605 E Huntington Dr Ste 100, Monrovia (91016-6353)
P.O. Box 1259 (91722-0259)
PHONE...................626 962-8811
Ron Hasse, *Pr*
Mark Welches, *VP*
EMP: 450 EST: 1997
SALES (est): 15.7MM
SALES (corp-wide): 556.09MM **Privately Held**
Web: www.sgvtribune.com
SIC: 2711 Newspapers, publishing and printing
HQ: Medianews Group, Inc.
5990 Washington St
Denver CO 80216

(P-2787)
CALIFRNIA NWSPAPERS LTD PARTNR
Also Called: Inland Valley Daily Bulletin
3200 E Guasti Rd Ste 100, Ontario (91761-8661)
PHONE...................909 987-6397
Bob Balzer, *Mgr*
EMP: 350
SALES (corp-wide): 556.09MM **Privately Held**
Web: www.sgvtribune.com
SIC: 2711 Newspapers, publishing and printing
HQ: California Newspapers Limited Partnership
605 E Huntington Dr # 100
Monrovia CA 91016
626 962-8811

(P-2788)
CALIFRNIA NWSPAPERS LTD PARTNR
Also Called: Redlands Daily Facts
19 E Citrus Ave Ste 102, Redlands (92373-4763)
PHONE...................909 793-3221
Peggy Del Torro, *Mgr*
EMP: 350
SQ FT: 8,301
SALES (corp-wide): 556.09MM **Privately Held**
Web: www.sgvtribune.com
SIC: 2711 7313 Newspapers, publishing and printing; Newspaper advertising representative
HQ: California Newspapers Limited Partnership
605 E Huntington Dr # 100
Monrovia CA 91016
626 962-8811

(P-2789)

CHURM PUBLISHING INC (PA)
Also Called: O.C. Metro Magazine
1451 Quail St Ste 201, Newport Beach
(92660-2741)
PHONE.....................714 796-7000
Steve Churm, *Pr*
Peter Churm, *
Brian O'neill, *CFO*
EMP: 47 **EST:** 1982
SQ FT: 7,000
SALES (est): 669.76K
SALES (corp-wide): 669.76K **Privately Held**
Web: www.ocmetro.com
SIC: 2711 Newspapers, publishing and printing

(P-2790)

COAST NEWS INC
Also Called: Beach News
531 Encinitas Blvd Ste 204, Encinitas
(92024-3773)
P.O. Box 232550 (92023-2550)
PHONE.....................760 436-9737
James Kydd, *CEO*
EMP: 34 **EST:** 1987
SALES (est): 1.4MM **Privately Held**
Web: www.thecoastnews.com
SIC: 2711 2741 Newspapers, publishing and printing; Miscellaneous publishing

(P-2791)

COMMUNITY MEDIA CORPORATION (PA)
Also Called: San Dego Nghborhood Newspapers
15005 S Vermont Ave, Gardena
(90247-3004)
PHONE.....................714 220-0292
Kathy Verdugo, *Pr*
EMP: 37 **EST:** 1993
SALES (est): 4.65MM **Privately Held**
Web: www.communitymedius.com
SIC: 2711 Newspapers, publishing and printing

(P-2792)

CYCLE NEWS INC (PA)
Also Called: CN Publishing Group
17771 Mitchell N, Irvine (92614-6028)
PHONE.....................949 863-7082
Sharon Clayton, *Pr*
EMP: 32 **EST:** 1965
SQ FT: 10,000
SALES (est): 4.75MM
SALES (corp-wide): 4.75MM **Privately Held**
Web: www.cyclenews.com
SIC: 2711 Newspapers, publishing and printing

(P-2793)

DAILY JOURNAL CORPORATION (PA)
915 E 1st St, Los Angeles (90012-4042)
PHONE.....................213 229-5300
Steven Myhill-jones, *Interim Chief Executive Officer*
Tu To, *CFO*
EMP: 69 **EST:** 1888
SQ FT: 34,000
SALES (est): 67.71MM
SALES (corp-wide): 67.71MM **Publicly Held**
Web: www.dailyjournal.com
SIC: 2711 2721 7313 7372 Newspapers, publishing and printing; Magazines: publishing and printing; Newspaper advertising representative; Prepackaged software

(P-2794)

DESERT SUN PUBLISHING CO (DH)
Also Called: Desert Sun The
750 N Gene Autry Trl, Palm Springs
(92262-5463)
P.O. Box 2734 (92263-2734)
PHONE.....................760 322-8889
EMP: 200 **EST:** 1974
SQ FT: 30,621
SALES (est): 2.73MM
SALES (corp-wide): 2.66B **Publicly Held**
Web: www.desertsun.com
SIC: 2711 Newspapers, publishing and printing
HQ: Gannett Media Corp.
7950 Jones Branch Dr
Mclean VA 22102
703 854-6000

(P-2795)

E Z BUY & E Z SELL RECYCL CORP (DH)
Also Called: Recycler Classified
4954 Van Nuys Blvd Ste 201, Sherman Oaks (91403-1759)
PHONE.....................310 886-7808
Niki Ruokosuo, *Pr*
Jim Fullmer, *
EMP: 200 **EST:** 1973
SQ FT: 13,000
SALES (est): 1.51MM
SALES (corp-wide): 4.93B **Publicly Held**
Web: recyclerclassifieds.blogspot.com
SIC: 2711 2741 Newspapers: publishing only, not printed on site; Miscellaneous publishing
HQ: Tribune Media Company
515 N State St Ste 2400
Chicago IL 60654
312 222-3394

(P-2796)

EL CLASIFICADO (PA)
11205 Imperial Hwy, Norwalk (90650-2229)
PHONE.....................323 837-4095
Martha C Dela Torre, *Pr*
Gil Garcia, *
Joseph Badame, *
EMP: 42 **EST:** 1988
SALES (est): 24.96MM **Privately Held**
Web: www.elclasificado.com
SIC: 2711 Newspapers, publishing and printing

(P-2797)

FREEDOM COMMUNICATIONS INC
Also Called: Freedom Newspapers
625 N Grand Ave, Santa Ana (92701-4347)
P.O. Box 11450 (92711-1450)
PHONE.....................714 796-7000
▲ **EMP:** 7542
SIC: 2711 2721 7313 2741 Newspapers, publishing and printing; Periodicals; Newspaper advertising representative; Miscellaneous publishing

(P-2798)

GARDENA VALLEY NEWS INC
Also Called: Valley News Gardens
15005 S Vermont Ave, Gardena
(90247-3004)
P.O. Box 219 (90248-0219)
PHONE.....................310 329-6351
George D Algie, *Pr*
Ruriko Yatabe, *
EMP: 40 **EST:** 1904
SQ FT: 8,200

SALES (est): 695.81K **Privately Held**
Web: www.gardenavalleynews.org
SIC: 2711 Commercial printing and newspaper publishing combined

(P-2799)

GATEHOUSE MEDIA LLC
Also Called: Victorville Daily Press
13891 Park Ave, Victorville (92392-2435)
PHONE.....................760 241-7744
EMP: 31
SALES (corp-wide): 2.66B **Publicly Held**
Web: www.vvdailypress.com
SIC: 2711 Commercial printing and newspaper publishing combined
HQ: Gatehouse Media, Llc
175 Sllys Trl Fl 3 Corp C
Pittsford NY 14534
585 598-0030

(P-2800)

GRACE COMMUNICATIONS INC (PA)
Also Called: Metropolitan News Company
210 S Spring St, Los Angeles (90012-3710)
P.O. Box 86308 (90086-0308)
PHONE.....................213 628-4384
Joann W Grace, *Pr*
Roger M Grace, *
EMP: 43 **EST:** 1901
SQ FT: 21,000
SALES (est): 8.87MM
SALES (corp-wide): 8.87MM **Privately Held**
Web: www.mnc.net
SIC: 2711 Newspapers, publishing and printing

(P-2801)

HARRELL HOLDINGS (PA)
1707 Eye St Ste 102, Bakersfield
(93301-5208)
P.O. Box 440 (93302-0440)
PHONE.....................661 322-5627
Richard Beene, *Pr*
Virginia Fritts Moorhouse, *
Gizel Bermudez, *
Michelle Hirst, *
Logan Molen, *
EMP: 188 **EST:** 1897
SALES (est): 13.61MM
SALES (corp-wide): 13.61MM **Privately Held**
Web: www.bakersfield.com
SIC: 2711 Commercial printing and newspaper publishing combined

(P-2802)

HI-DESERT PUBLISHING COMPANY
Also Called: Yuciapa & Calimesa News Mirror
35154 Yucaipa Blvd, Yucaipa (92399-4339)
P.O. Box 760 (92399-0760)
PHONE.....................909 795-8145
Jerry Bean, *Mgr*
EMP: 27
SALES (corp-wide): 21.91MM **Privately Held**
Web: www.newsmirror.net
SIC: 2711 Newspapers, publishing and printing
HQ: Hi-Desert Publishing Company
56445 29 Palms Hwy
Yucca Valley CA 92284

(P-2803)

HI-DESERT PUBLISHING COMPANY
Also Called: Mountain News & Shopper

28200 Highway 189 Bldg O-1, Lake Arrowhead (92352-9700)
P.O. Box 2410 (92352-2410)
PHONE.....................909 336-3555
Harry Bradley, *Mgr*
EMP: 41
SALES (corp-wide): 21.91MM **Privately Held**
Web: www.hidesertstar.com
SIC: 2711 Commercial printing and newspaper publishing combined
HQ: Hi-Desert Publishing Company
56445 29 Palms Hwy
Yucca Valley CA 92284

(P-2804)

HI-DESERT PUBLISHING COMPANY (HQ)
56445 29 Palms Hwy, Yucca Valley
(92284-2861)
PHONE.....................760 365-3315
Cindy Melland, *Publisher*
Stacy Moore, *
EMP: 70 **EST:** 1990
SALES (est): 4.17MM
SALES (corp-wide): 21.91MM **Privately Held**
Web: www.hidesertstar.com
SIC: 2711 Newspapers, publishing and printing
PA: Brehm Communications, Inc.
16644 W Bernardo Dr # 300
858 451-6200

(P-2805)

INVESTORS BUSINESS DAILY INC (HQ)
5900 Wilshire Blvd Ste 2950, Los Angeles
(90036-5041)
PHONE.....................800 831-2525
William O'neil, *Pr*
Kathy Sherman, *
Edward Skolarus, *CDO*
▲ **EMP:** 200 **EST:** 1984
SQ FT: 180,000
SALES (est): 11.48MM
SALES (corp-wide): 335.64MM **Privately Held**
Web: www.investors.com
SIC: 2711 Newspapers, publishing and printing
PA: Data Analysis Inc.
12655 Beatrice St
310 448-6800

(P-2806)

JOONG-ANG DAILY NEWS CAL INC
Also Called: JOONG-ANG DAILY NEWS CALIFORNIA, INC.
7750 Dagget St Ste 208, San Diego
(92111-2236)
PHONE.....................858 573-1111
Kwong Luk Chang, *Brnch Mgr*
▲ **EMP:** 56
Web: www.koreadaily.com
SIC: 2711 Newspapers, publishing and printing
HQ: Joongangilbo Usa, Inc.
690 Wilshire Pl
Los Angeles CA 90005
213 368-2512

(P-2807)

JOONGANGILBO USA INC (DH)
Also Called: Joong-Ang Daily News Cal Inc
690 Wilshire Pl, Los Angeles (90005-3930)
PHONE.....................213 368-2512
Kae Hong Ko, *CEO*
In Taek Park, *

PRODUCTS & SVCS

◆ **EMP:** 200 **EST:** 1974
SQ FT: 70,000
SALES (est): 20.81MM **Privately Held**
Web: www.koreadaily.com
SIC: 2711 Commercial printing and
newspaper publishing combined
HQ: Joongang Ilbo Co.,Ltd.
48-6 Sangamsan-Ro, Mapo-Gu
Seoul 03909

(P-2808)
KAAR DRECT MAIL
FLFILLMENT LLC
1225 Exposition Way Ste 160, San Diego
(92154-6667)
PHONE..............................619 382-3670
EMP: 25 **EST:** 2013
SALES (est): 4.95MM **Privately Held**
Web: www.kaardm.com
SIC: 2711 5963 2752 8742 Commercial
printing and newspaper publishing
combined; Direct sales, telemarketing;
Publication printing, lithographic; Marketing
consulting services

(P-2809)
LA OPINION LP (HQ)
Also Called: Lozano Enterprises
915 Wilshire Blvd Ste 915, Los Angeles
(90017-3474)
P.O. Box 71847 (90071-0847)
PHONE..............................213 891-9191
Monica C Lozano, *CEO*
EMP: 54 **EST:** 1926
SALES (est): 3.9MM
SALES (corp-wide): 19.49MM **Privately
Held**
Web: www.laopinion.com
SIC: 2711 Newspapers, publishing and
printing
PA: Impremedia, Llc
41 Flatbush Ave Ste 1
212 807-4600

(P-2810)
LA OPINION LP
210 E Washington Blvd, Los Angeles
(90015-3603)
PHONE..............................213 896-2222
Carlos Marina, *Mgr*
EMP: 359
SALES (corp-wide): 19.49MM **Privately
Held**
Web: www.laopinion.com
SIC: 2711 Newspapers, publishing and
printing
HQ: La Opinion, L.P.
915 Wilshire Blvd Ste 915 # 915
Los Angeles CA 90017
213 891-9191

(P-2811)
LA TIMES
202 W 1st St Ste 500, Los Angeles
(90012-4401)
PHONE..............................213 237-2279
Raymond Jansen, *CEO*
EMP: 38 **EST:** 2008
SALES (est): 3.12MM **Privately Held**
Web: www.onnitimessquare.com
SIC: 2711 Newspapers, publishing and
printing

(P-2812)
LATINA & ASSOCIATES INC (PA)
Also Called: El Latino Newspaper
1031 Bay Blvd, Chula Vista (91911-1625)
P.O. Box 120550 (92112-0550)
PHONE..............................619 426-1491
Fanny Miller, *CEO*

EMP: 25 **EST:** 1985
SALES (est): 831.55K
SALES (corp-wide): 831.55K **Privately
Held**
Web: www.ellatinoonline.com
SIC: 2711 Newspapers: publishing only, not
printed on site

(P-2813)
LOS ANGELES SENTINEL INC
Also Called: La Sentinel Newspaper
3800 Crenshaw Blvd, Los Angeles
(90008-1813)
PHONE..............................323 299-3800
Jennifer Thomas, *Pr*
Brik Booker, *
EMP: 51 **EST:** 1933
SALES (est): 1.11MM **Privately Held**
Web: www.lasentinel.net
SIC: 2711 Newspapers, publishing and
printing

(P-2814)
LOS ANGLES TMES
CMMNCTIONS LLC (PA)
Also Called: Los Angeles Times
2300 E Imperial Hwy, El Segundo
(90245-2813)
PHONE..............................213 237-5000
Ross Levinsohn, *CEO*
Scott Mckibben, *Pr*
Don Reis S, *VP*
▲ **EMP:** 3956 **EST:** 1884
SQ FT: 162,000
SALES (est): 216MM
SALES (corp-wide): 216MM **Privately
Held**
Web: www.latimes.com
SIC: 2711 Newspapers, publishing and
printing

(P-2815)
MAMMOTH MEDIA INC
1447 2nd St, Santa Monica (90401-3404)
PHONE..............................832 315-0833
Benoit Vatere, *CEO*
Mike Jones, *
EMP: 64 **EST:** 2016
SALES (est): 2.18MM **Privately Held**
Web: www.mammoth.la
SIC: 2711 Newspapers

(P-2816)
METROPOLITAN NEWS
COMPANY
Also Called: Riverside Blltin Jrupa This We
3540 12th St, Riverside (92501-3802)
P.O. Box 60859 (90060-0859)
PHONE..............................951 369-5890
Roger Gray, *Pr*
EMP: 29 **EST:** 1998
SALES (est): 167.25K **Privately Held**
Web: www.mnc.net
SIC: 2711 Newspapers, publishing and
printing

(P-2817)
NATIONAL MEDIA INC (HQ)
Also Called: Beach Reporter
609 Deep Valley Dr Ste 200, Rllng Hls Est
(90274-3614)
P.O. Box 2609 (90274-8609)
PHONE..............................310 377-6877
Stephen C Laxineta, *Pr*
Simon M Tam, *
William Dean Singleton, *
EMP: 30 **EST:** 1983
SQ FT: 12,000
SALES (est): 4.27MM
SALES (corp-wide): 556.09MM **Privately
Held**

Web: www.dailybreeze.com
SIC: 2711 Newspapers: publishing only, not
printed on site
PA: Digital First Media, Llc
101 W Colfax Ave Fl 11
303 954-6360

(P-2818)
NGUOI VIET VTNAMESE
PEOPLE INC (PA)
Also Called: Nguoi Viet Newspaper
14771 Moran St, Westminster
(92683-5553)
PHONE..............................714 892-9414
Dat Pham, *Ch*
Hoang Tong, *
Dieu Le, *
▲ **EMP:** 30 **EST:** 1978
SQ FT: 10,000
SALES (est): 2.44MM
SALES (corp-wide): 2.44MM **Privately
Held**
Web: www.nguoi-viet.com
SIC: 2711 5994 2741 Newspapers:
publishing only, not printed on site; News
dealers and newsstands; Miscellaneous
publishing

(P-2819)
NORTH COUNTY TIMES
28441 Rancho California Rd Ste 103,
Temecula (92590-3618)
PHONE..............................951 676-4315
Claude Reinke, *Mgr*
EMP: 45
SALES (corp-wide): 611.38MM **Publicly
Held**
Web: www.caseybrownco.com
SIC: 2711 Newspapers, publishing and
printing
HQ: North County Times
350 Camino De La Reina
San Diego CA 92108
800 533-8830

(P-2820)
NORTH COUNTY TIMES (DH)
Also Called: Californian, The
350 Camino De La Reina, San Diego
(92108-3007)
PHONE..............................800 533-8830
▲ **EMP:** 250 **EST:** 1962
SQ FT: 45,000
SALES (est): 1.17MM
SALES (corp-wide): 611.38MM **Publicly
Held**
Web: www.caseybrownco.com
SIC: 2711 Newspapers, publishing and
printing
HQ: Lee Publications, Inc.
4600 E 53rd St
Davenport IA 52807
563 383-2100

(P-2821)
NORTHEAST NEWSPAPERS INC
621 W Beverly Blvd, Montebello
(90640-3623)
PHONE..............................213 727-1117
Art Aguilar, *Pr*
Tom Morrison, *
EMP: 32 **EST:** 1905
SALES (est): 2.58MM **Privately Held**
SIC: 2711 Newspapers, publishing and
printing

(P-2822)
PASADENA NEWSPAPERS INC
(PA)
Also Called: Pasadena Star-News

605 E Huntington Dr Ste 100, Monrovia
(91016-6353)
PHONE..............................626 578-6300
Dean Singleton, *Pr*
▲ **EMP:** 190 **EST:** 1884
SALES (est): 827.87K **Privately Held**
Web: www.pasadenastarnews.com
SIC: 2711 7313 Commercial printing and
newspaper publishing combined;
Newspaper advertising representative

(P-2823)
PRESS-ENTERPRISE COMPANY
(PA)
3450 14th St, Riverside (92501-3862)
P.O. Box 792 (92502-0792)
PHONE..............................951 684-1200
Ronald Redfern, *Pr*
Kathy Weiermiller, *VP*
Sue Barry, *VP*
Ed Lasak, *CFO*
▲ **EMP:** 700 **EST:** 2011
SQ FT: 190,000
SALES (est): 18.62MM
SALES (corp-wide): 18.62MM **Privately
Held**
Web: www.pressenterprise.com
SIC: 2711 Commercial printing and
newspaper publishing combined

(P-2824)
SAN DIEGO UNION-TRIBUNE
LLC
San Diego Union Tribune
1920 Main St, Irvine (92614-7209)
P.O. Box 120191 (92112-0191)
PHONE..............................619 299-3131
Roy E Gene Bell, *CEO*
EMP: 39
Web: www.sandiegouniontribune.com
SIC: 2711 7313 Newspapers: publishing
only, not printed on site; Newspaper
advertising representative
PA: The San Diego Union-Tribune Llc
600 B St Ste 1201

(P-2825)
SAN DIEGO UNION-TRIBUNE
LLC (PA)
Also Called: San Diego Union Tribune, The
600 B St Ste 1201, San Diego
(92101-4505)
P.O. Box 120191 (92112-0191)
PHONE..............................619 299-3131
Jeff Light, *Pr*
EMP: 600 **EST:** 2009
SALES (est): 11.96MM **Privately Held**
Web: www.sandiegouniontribune.com
SIC: 2711 7313 7383 Newspapers:
publishing only, not printed on site;
Newspaper advertising representative;
News reporting services for newspapers
and periodicals

(P-2826)
SANTA BARBARA
INDEPENDENT INC
Also Called: Independent
1715 State St, Santa Barbara (93101-2521)
PHONE..............................805 965-5205
M Partridge Poette, *Pr*
Marianne Partridge Poette, *
Brandi Rivera, *
EMP: 40 **EST:** 1984
SALES (est): 2.19MM **Privately Held**
Web: www.independent.com
SIC: 2711 Newspapers, publishing and
printing

(P-2827)

SIGNAL

Also Called: Newhall Signal
26330 Diamond Pl Ste 100, Santa Clarita
(91350-5819)
P.O. Box 801870 (91380-1870)
PHONE................................661 259-1234
Charles Morris, *Pr*
EMP: 29 **EST:** 1919
SQ FT: 32,000
SALES (est): 2.02MM
SALES (corp-wide): 44.73MM **Privately Held**
Web: www.signalscv.com
SIC: 2711 Newspapers, publishing and printing
PA: Morris Multimedia, Inc.
    27 Abercorn St
    912 233-1281

(P-2828)

SING TAO NEWSPAPERS LTD

Also Called: Sing Tao Nwspapers Los Angeles
17059 Green Dr, City Of Industry
(91745-1812)
PHONE................................626 956-8200
Sau K Cheung, *Mgr*
EMP: 52
Web: std.stheadline.com
SIC: 2711 Newspapers, publishing and printing
HQ: Sing Tao Limited
    8/F Sing Tao News Corporation Bldg
    Tseung Kwan O NT

(P-2829)

SLO NEW TIMES INC

Also Called: New Times Media Group
1010 Marsh St, San Luis Obispo
(93401-3630)
PHONE................................805 546-8208
Bob Rucker, *CEO*
EMP: 24 **EST:** 1987
SALES (est): 788.07K **Privately Held**
Web: www.newtimesslo.com
SIC: 2711 Newspapers, publishing and printing

(P-2830)

SUN CMPANY OF SAN BRNRDINO CAL (HQ)

Also Called: San Bernardino County Sun, The
4030 Georgia Blvd, San Bernardino
(92407-1847)
PHONE................................909 889-9666
Bob Balzer, *Pr*
Douglass I I Mccorkindale, *Prin*
EMP: 400 **EST:** 1964
SQ FT: 110,000
SALES (est): 140.1MM
SALES (corp-wide): 2.66B **Publicly Held**
Web: www.sbsun.com
SIC: 2711 Newspapers, publishing and printing
PA: Gannett Co., Inc.
    1675 Broadway Fl 23
    703 854-6000

(P-2831)

TAKE A BREAK PAPER

1048 W Gardena Blvd, Gardena
(90247-4956)
PHONE................................323 333-7773
Albert Moran, *Pt*
EMP: 30 **EST:** 2013
SALES (est): 198.49K **Privately Held**
Web: www.takeabreakpaper.com
SIC: 2711 Newspapers, publishing and printing

(P-2832)

THE KOREA TIMES LOS ANGELES INC (PA)

Also Called: Korea Times
3731 Wilshire Blvd Ste 1000, Los Angeles
(90010-2828)
PHONE................................323 692-2000
▲ **EMP:** 200 **EST:** 1969
SALES (est): 23.89MM
SALES (corp-wide): 23.89MM **Privately Held**
Web: www.koreatimes.com
SIC: 2711 Newspapers, publishing and printing

(P-2833)

THEWRAP

2260 S Centinela Ave Ste 150, Los Angeles
(90064-1007)
PHONE................................424 273-4787
EMP: 41 **EST:** 2016
SALES (est): 1.17MM **Privately Held**
Web: www.thewrap.com
SIC: 2711 Newspapers

(P-2834)

TRIBE MDIA CORP A CAL NNPRFIT

Also Called: Jewish Journal, The
3250 Wilshire Blvd, Los Angeles
(90010-1577)
PHONE................................213 368-1661
Rob Eshman, *Publisher*
EMP: 27 **EST:** 1985
SQ FT: 4,500
SALES (est): 773.01K **Privately Held**
Web: www.jewishjournal.com
SIC: 2711 Newspapers, publishing and printing

(P-2835)

VILLAGE NEWS INC

Also Called: Fallbrook Bonsall Village News
41740 Enterprise Cir S, Temecula
(92590-4881)
PHONE................................760 451-3488
Julie Reeder, *Pr*
Michelle Howard, *Advt Dir*
EMP: 33 **EST:** 1997
SQ FT: 1,500
SALES (est): 2.35MM **Privately Held**
Web: www.villagenews.com
SIC: 2711 Newspapers, publishing and printing

(P-2836)

VOICE OF SAN DIEGO

110 W A St Ste 650, San Diego
(92101-3708)
PHONE................................619 325-0525
Scott Lewis, *CEO*
Julianne Markow, *COO*
EMP: 24 **EST:** 2004
SALES (est): 2.34MM **Privately Held**
Web: www.voiceofsandiego.org
SIC: 2711 Newspapers: publishing only, not printed on site

(P-2837)

WAVE COMMUNITY NEWSPAPERS INC (PA)

Also Called: The Wave
1007 N Sepulveda Blvd, Manhattan Beach
(90266-5964)
PHONE................................323 290-3000
Pluria Marshall, *Pr*
Andy Wiedlin, *Chief Business Officer**
▲ **EMP:** 30 **EST:** 1970
SALES (est): 4.92MM

SALES (corp-wide): 4.92MM **Privately Held**
SIC: 2711 Commercial printing and newspaper publishing combined

(P-2838)

WESTERN OUTDOORS PUBLICATIONS (PA)

Also Called: Western Outdoor News
901 Calle Amanecer Ste 115, San Clemente
(92673-4216)
P.O. Box 73370 (92673-0113)
PHONE................................949 366-0030
Robert Twilegar, *Pr*
Lori Twilegar, *
EMP: 28 **EST:** 1953
SALES (est): 2.38MM
SALES (corp-wide): 2.38MM **Privately Held**
Web: www.wonews.com
SIC: 2711 2721 Newspapers: publishing only, not printed on site; Periodicals

(P-2839)

WICK COMMUNICATIONS CO

Also Called: Kern Valley Sun
6404 Lake Isabella Blvd, Lake Isabella
(93240-9475)
P.O. Box 3074 (93240-3074)
PHONE................................760 379-3667
Cliff Urfeth, *Mgr*
EMP: 27
SALES (corp-wide): 37.72MM **Privately Held**
Web: www.wickcommunications.com
SIC: 2711 Newspapers, publishing and printing
HQ: Wick Communications Co.
    333 W Wilcox Dr Ste 302
    Sierra Vista AZ 85635
    520 458-0200

(P-2840)

WORLD JOURNAL LA LLC (HQ)

1588 Corporate Center Dr, Monterey Park
(91754-7624)
PHONE................................323 268-4982
James Guon, *CEO*
▲ **EMP:** 170 **EST:** 1981
SQ FT: 45,000
SALES (est): 6.03MM **Privately Held**
SIC: 2711 Newspapers, publishing and printing
PA: United Daily News Co., Ltd.
    No. 369, Datong Rd., Sec. 1

2721 Periodicals

(P-2841)

ADAMS TRADE PRESS LP (PA)

Also Called: Adams Business Media
420 S Palm Canyon Dr, Palm Springs
(92262-7304)
PHONE................................760 318-7000
Mark Adams, *Pt*
EMP: 30 **EST:** 1994
SQ FT: 2,000
SALES (est): 1.01MM **Privately Held**
SIC: 2721 Magazines: publishing only, not printed on site

(P-2842)

ADVANSTAR COMMUNICATIONS INC

2525 Main St Ste 300, Irvine (92614-6680)
PHONE................................714 513-8400
FAX: 714 513-8403
EMP: 80
SALES (corp-wide): 1.06B **Privately Held**

SIC: 2721 7389 Magazines: publishing only, not printed on site; Trade show arrangement
HQ: Advanstar Communications Inc.
    2501 Colorado Ave Ste 280
    Santa Monica CA 90404
    310 857-7500

(P-2843)

AEROTECH NEWS AND REVIEW INC (PA)

Also Called: Astro News
220 E Avenue K4 Ste 4, Lancaster
(93535-4687)
P.O. Box 1332 (93584-1332)
PHONE................................661 945-5634
Paul Kinison, *Pr*
EMP: 42 **EST:** 1986
SALES (est): 911.65K
SALES (corp-wide): 911.65K **Privately Held**
Web: www.aerotechnews.com
SIC: 2721 2741 2752 Trade journals: publishing only, not printed on site; Miscellaneous publishing; Commercial printing, lithographic

(P-2844)

BBM FAIRWAY INC (PA)

3520 Challenger St, Torrance (90503-1640)
P.O. Box 2703 (90509-2703)
EMP: 120 **EST:** 1961
SALES (est): 7.75MM
SALES (corp-wide): 7.75MM **Privately Held**
Web: www.bobit.com
SIC: 2721 7319 8742 Magazines: publishing only, not printed on site; Media buying service; Marketing consulting services

(P-2845)

BOBIT BUSINESS MEDIA INC

21250 Hawthorne Blvd Ste 360, Torrance
(90503-5540)
PHONE................................310 533-2400
Richard Rivera, *CEO*
EMP: 223 **EST:** 2018
SALES (est): 2.79MM
SALES (corp-wide): 957.36MM **Privately Held**
Web: www.bobit.com
SIC: 2721 Magazines: publishing only, not printed on site
PA: Gemspring Capital, Llc
    54 Wilton Rd
    203 842-8886

(P-2846)

CBJ LP

Also Called: San Fernando Valley Bus Jurnl
11150 Santa Monica Blvd Ste 350, Los
Angeles (90025-3385)
PHONE................................818 676-1750
Pegi Matsuda, *Mgr*
EMP: 76
SALES (corp-wide): 23.64MM **Privately Held**
Web: www.sfvbj.com
SIC: 2721 Magazines: publishing only, not printed on site
PA: Cbj, L.P.
    7101 College Blvd # 1100
    913 451-9000

(P-2847)

CBJ LP

Also Called: Los Angeles Business Journal
11150 Santa Monica Blvd, Los Angeles
(90025-3380)
PHONE................................323 549-5225
Matt Toledo, *Brnch Mgr*

EMP: 40
SALES (corp-wide): 23.64MM **Privately Held**
Web: www.labusinessjournal.com
SIC: 2721 2711 8742 Periodicals, publishing only; Newspapers; General management consultant
PA: Cbj, L.P.
7101 College Blvd # 1100
913 451-9000

(P-2848)
CBJ LP
Also Called: Orange County Business Journal
18500 Von Karman Ave Ste 150, Irvine (92612-0508)
PHONE..............................949 833-8373
Janet Cox, *Mgr*
EMP: 40
SALES (corp-wide): 23.64MM **Privately Held**
Web: www.ocbj.com
SIC: 2721 2711 7313 Trade journals: publishing only, not printed on site; Newspapers; Newspaper advertising representative
PA: Cbj, L.P.
7101 College Blvd # 1100
913 451-9000

(P-2849)
CBJ LP
Also Called: San Diego Business Journal
4909 Murphy Canyon Rd Ste 200, San Diego (92123-5381)
PHONE..............................858 277-6359
Armon Mills, *Prin*
EMP: 25
SQ FT: 10,000
SALES (corp-wide): 23.64MM **Privately Held**
Web: www.sdbj.com
SIC: 2721 2741 2711 Trade journals: publishing and printing; Miscellaneous publishing; Newspapers
PA: Cbj, L.P.
7101 College Blvd # 1100
913 451-9000

(P-2850)
CLIQUE BRANDS INC
Also Called: Who What Wear
750 N San Vicente Blvd Ste 800, West Hollywood (90069-5788)
PHONE..............................310 623-6916
Katherine Power, *CEO*
Hilary Kerr, *Pr*
Mika Onishi, *COO*
David Thomas, *Dir*
EMP: 32 **EST:** 2007
SQ FT: 2,200
SALES (est): 4.89MM **Privately Held**
SIC: 2721 5621 Magazines: publishing only, not printed on site; Women's specialty clothing stores

(P-2851)
CREATIVE AGE PUBLICATIONS INC
Also Called: Nailpro
15975 High Knoll Rd, Encino (91436-3426)
PHONE..............................818 782-7328
Deborah Carver, *Pr*
Mindy Rosiejka, *
EMP: 50 **EST:** 1972
SALES (est): 4.13MM **Privately Held**
Web: www.creativeage.com
SIC: 2721 2731 Magazines: publishing only, not printed on site; Book publishing

(P-2852)
CURTCO ROBB MEDIA LLC (PA)
29160 Heathercliff Rd Ste 200, Malibu (90265-6306)
PHONE..............................310 589-7700
Stephen Colvin, *CEO*
William J Curtis, *
Christopher Fabian, *
David Arnold, *
EMP: 30 **EST:** 2001
SALES (est): 5.1MM
SALES (corp-wide): 5.1MM **Privately Held**
Web: www.curtco.com
SIC: 2721 Magazines: publishing and printing

(P-2853)
DESERT PUBLICATIONS INC (PA)
Also Called: Desert Grafics
303 N Indian Canyon Dr, Palm Springs (92262-6015)
P.O. Box 2724 (92263-2724)
PHONE..............................760 325-2333
Franklin Jones, *VP*
EMP: 47 **EST:** 1965
SQ FT: 25,000
SALES (est): 4.19MM
SALES (corp-wide): 4.19MM **Privately Held**
Web: www.palmspringslife.com
SIC: 2721 7311 Magazines: publishing only, not printed on site; Advertising agencies

(P-2854)
DISNEY PUBLISHING WORLDWIDE (DH)
Also Called: Disney Editions
500 S Buena Vista St, Burbank (91521-0001)
PHONE..............................212 633-4400
R Russell Hampton Junior, *Ch*
▲ **EMP:** 100 **EST:** 1992
SALES (est): 5.63MM
SALES (corp-wide): 91.36B **Publicly Held**
Web: jobs.disneycareers.com
SIC: 2721 Magazines: publishing only, not printed on site
HQ: Disney Enterprises, Inc.
500 S Buena Vista St
Burbank CA 91521
818 560-1000

(P-2855)
DUNCAN MCINTOSH COMPANY INC (PA)
Also Called: Sea Magazine
18475 Bandilier Cir, Fountain Valley (92708-7012)
P.O. Box 1337 (92659-0337)
PHONE..............................949 660-6150
Duncan R Mcintosh, *CEO*
Teresa Mcintosh, *Sec*
EMP: 35 **EST:** 1967
SQ FT: 15,728
SALES (est): 5.36MM
SALES (corp-wide): 5.36MM **Privately Held**
Web: www.duncanmcintoshco.com
SIC: 2721 7389 Magazines: publishing and printing; Trade show arrangement

(P-2856)
EMERALD X LLC
Also Called: Vnu Business
31910 Del Obispo St Ste 200, San Juan Capistrano (92675-3195)
PHONE..............................949 226-5754
Denise Bashem, *Brnch Mgr*
EMP: 30

SALES (corp-wide): 385.6MM **Publicly Held**
Web: www.emeraldx.com
SIC: 2721 7389 Trade journals: publishing only, not printed on site; Promoters of shows and exhibitions
HQ: Emerald X, Llc
31910 Del Obspo St Ste 20
San Juan Capistrano CA 92675

(P-2857)
ENTREPRENEUR MEDIA LLC (PA) ✪
Also Called: Entrepeneur Magazine
1651 E 4th St Ste 125, Santa Ana (92701-5141)
P.O. Box 19787 (92623-9787)
PHONE..............................949 261-2325
Ryan Shea, *CEO*
Bill Shaw, *
Chris Damore, *
Michael Le Du, *
▲ **EMP:** 80 **EST:** 2023
SQ FT: 30,000
SALES (est): 18.87MM **Privately Held**
Web: www.entrepreneur.com
SIC: 2721 Magazines: publishing only, not printed on site

(P-2858)
GOLD PROSPECTORS ASSN AMER LLC
Also Called: Gold Prospectors Assn Amer
25819 Jefferson Ave Ste 110, Murrieta (92562-6965)
P.O. Box 891509 (92589-1509)
PHONE..............................951 699-4749
Thomas Massie, *Managing Member*
Richard Dixon, *Managing Member*
EMP: 30 **EST:** 1966
SALES (est): 2.39MM **Privately Held**
Web: www.goldprospectors.org
SIC: 2721 4833 Magazines: publishing only, not printed on site; Television broadcasting stations

(P-2859)
HAYMARKET WORLDWIDE INC
17030 Red Hill Ave, Irvine (92614-5626)
PHONE..............................949 417-6700
Peter Foubister, *CEO*
▲ **EMP:** 24 **EST:** 1992
SQ FT: 4,000
SALES (est): 272.27K
SALES (corp-wide): 226.37MM **Privately Held**
SIC: 2721 Magazines: publishing only, not printed on site
HQ: Haymarket Media, Inc.
275 7th Ave Fl 10
New York NY 10001
646 638-6000

(P-2860)
ID MATTERS LLC
7060 Hollywood Blvd 8th Fl, Los Angeles (90028-6021)
PHONE..............................323 822-4800
Kelly Novak, *Managing Member*
EMP: 36 **EST:** 2012
SALES (est): 1.11MM **Privately Held**
SIC: 2721 Magazines: publishing and printing

(P-2861)
INLAND EMPIRE MEDIA GROUP INC
Also Called: Inland Empire Magazine
36095 Monte De Oro Rd, Temecula (92592-8123)

PHONE..............................951 682-3026
Don Lorenzi, *Pr*
Don Lorenzi, *Pr*
Richard Lorenzi, *Sec*
EMP: 31 **EST:** 1972
SALES (est): 921.52K **Privately Held**
Web: www.inlandempiremagazine.com
SIC: 2721 Magazines: publishing and printing

(P-2862)
KELLEY BLUE BOOK CO INC (DH)
195 Technology Dr, Irvine (92618-2402)
P.O. Box 19691 (92623)
PHONE..............................949 770-7704
Jared Rowe, *CEO*
John Morrison, *
EMP: 92 **EST:** 1926
SALES (est): 25.19MM
SALES (corp-wide): 16.61B **Privately Held**
Web: www.kbb.com
SIC: 2721 Trade journals: publishing only, not printed on site
HQ: Autotrader.Com, Inc.
6205 Pachtree Dunwoody Rd
Atlanta GA 30328
404 568-8000

(P-2863)
L F P INC (PA)
Also Called: Flynt, Larry Publishing
8484 Wilshire Blvd Ste 900, Beverly Hills (90211-3218)
PHONE..............................323 651-3525
Larry Flynt, *Ch Bd*
Michael H Klein, *
▲ **EMP:** 100 **EST:** 1976
SQ FT: 10,000
SALES (est): 33.18MM
SALES (corp-wide): 33.18MM **Privately Held**
Web: www.hustlermagazine.com
SIC: 2721 Magazines: publishing only, not printed on site

(P-2864)
LANDSCAPE COMMUNICATIONS INC
Also Called: Landscape Contract National
14771 Plaza Dr Ste A, Tustin (92780-2779)
P.O. Box 1126 (92781-1126)
PHONE..............................714 979-5276
George Schmok, *Pr*
EMP: 25 **EST:** 1991
SQ FT: 1,618
SALES (est): 3.11MM **Privately Held**
Web: www.landscapearchitect.com
SIC: 2721 Trade journals: publishing only, not printed on site

(P-2865)
MNM CORPORATION (PA)
Also Called: Apparel Newsgroup, The
110 E 9th St Ste A777, Los Angeles (90079-1777)
PHONE..............................213 627-3737
Martin Wernicke, *CEO*
▲ **EMP:** 25 **EST:** 1985
SQ FT: 11,000
SALES (est): 963.99K
SALES (corp-wide): 963.99K **Privately Held**
Web: www.apparelnews.net
SIC: 2721 8721 Magazines: publishing only, not printed on site; Accounting, auditing, and bookkeeping

(P-2866)

OMICS GROUP INC

5716 Corsa Ave Ste 110, Westlake Village
(91362-7354)
PHONE..................650 268-9744
Srinu B Gedela, *Brnch Mgr*
EMP: 460
SALES (corp-wide): 791.73K **Privately Held**
Web: www.omicsonline.org
SIC: 2721 Trade journals: publishing and printing
PA: Omics Group Inc
2360 Corp Cir Ste 400
888 843-8169

(P-2867)

ORANGE COAST MAGAZINE LLC

Also Called: Orange Coast Magazine
5900 Wilshire Blvd # 10, Los Angeles
(90036-5013)
PHONE..................949 862-1133
Gary Thoe, *Pr*
EMP: 61 **EST:** 1975
SALES (corp-wide): 39.71MM **Privately Held**
Web: www.orangecoast.com
SIC: 2721 5812 Magazines: publishing only, not printed on site; Eating places
HQ: Emmis Publishing, L.P.
40 Monument Cir Ste 100
Indianapolis IN 46204

(P-2868)

PAISANO PUBLICATIONS LLC (PA)

Also Called: V Twin Magazine
28210 Dorothy Dr, Agoura Hills
(91301-2693)
PHONE..................818 889-8740
John Lagana, *CEO*
John Lagana, *Publisher*
Joseph Teresi, *
Robert Davis, *
EMP: 60 **EST:** 1971
SQ FT: 40,000
SALES (est): 1.24MM
SALES (corp-wide): 1.24MM **Privately Held**
Web: www.v-twin.com
SIC: 2721 Magazines: publishing only, not printed on site

(P-2869)

PAISANO PUBLICATIONS INC

Also Called: V/ Twins
28210 Dorothy Dr, Agoura Hills
(91301-2693)
P.O. Box 3000 (91376-3000)
PHONE..................818 889-8740
Bill Prather, *Pr*
Allen Ribakoff, *
Joseph Teresi, *
Robert Davis, *
EMP: 52 **EST:** 1993
SALES (est): 941.32K
SALES (corp-wide): 1.24MM **Privately Held**
SIC: 2721 7812 Magazines: publishing and printing; Commercials, television: tape or film
PA: Paisano Publications, Llc
28210 Dorothy Dr
818 889-8740

(P-2870)

PARTNER CONCEPTS INC

811 Camino Viejo, Santa Barbara
(93108-2313)
PHONE..................805 745-7199
William J Kasch, *Pr*
William L Coulson, *
EMP: 75 **EST:** 1983
SALES (est): 18.57MM **Privately Held**
SIC: 2721 Magazines: publishing only, not printed on site

(P-2871)

PLAYBOY ENTERPRISES INC

10960 Wilshire Blvd Fl 22, Los Angeles
(90024-3808)
PHONE..................310 424-1800
John Luther, *Mgr*
EMP: 79
SALES (corp-wide): 142.95MM **Publicly Held**
Web: www.powersergefitness.com
SIC: 2721 Magazines: publishing and printing
HQ: Playboy Enterprises, Inc.
10960 Wlshire Blvd Ste 22
Los Angeles CA 90024
310 424-1800

(P-2872)

PUBLISHERS DEVELOPMENT CORP

Also Called: American Handgunner and Guns
225 W Valley Pkwy Ste 100, Escondido
(92025-2613)
PHONE..................858 605-0200
Thomas Von Rosen, *CEO*
Thomas M Hollander, *
EMP: 40 **EST:** 1941
SALES (est): 1.39MM **Privately Held**
Web: www.americanhandgunner.com
SIC: 2721 Magazines: publishing only, not printed on site

(P-2873)

QG PRINTING CORP

6688 Box Springs Blvd, Riverside
(92507-0726)
PHONE..................951 571-2500
Ken Eazell, *Mgr*
EMP: 51
SALES (corp-wide): 2.96B **Publicly Held**
SIC: 2721 2752 Periodicals; Commercial printing, lithographic
HQ: Qg Printing Corp.
N61w23044 Harrys Way
Sussex WI 53089

(P-2874)

RECRUITMENT SERVICES INC

Also Called: Working Nurse
3600 Wilshire Blvd Ste 1526, Los Angeles
(90010-2619)
PHONE..................213 364-1960
Randy Goldring, *Pr*
EMP: 33 **EST:** 2008
SALES (est): 194.64K **Privately Held**
Web: www.workingnurse.com
SIC: 2721 Periodicals

(P-2875)

ROBB CURTCO MEDIA LLC

22741 Pacific Coast Hwy Ste 401, Malibu
(90265-5876)
PHONE..................310 589-7700
EMP: 33
SALES (corp-wide): 5.1MM **Privately Held**
Web: www.curtco.com
SIC: 2721 Magazines: publishing and printing
PA: Curtco Robb Media Llc
29160 Heathercliff Rd # 1

310 589-7700

(P-2876)

SAN DIEGO MAGAZINE PUBG CO

Also Called: San Diego Magazine
1230 Columbia St Ste 800, San Diego
(92101-3571)
PHONE..................619 230-9292
James Fitzpatrick, *CEO*
Claire Johnson, *
EMP: 30 **EST:** 1948
SALES (est): 2.49MM
SALES (corp-wide): 11.2MM **Privately Held**
Web: www.sandiegomagazine.com
SIC: 2721 Magazines: publishing only, not printed on site
PA: Curtco, Publishing
29160 Heathercliff Rd # 1
310 589-7700

(P-2877)

TL ENTERPRISES LLC

Also Called: Highways Magazine
2750 Park View Ct Ste 240, Oxnard
(93036-5458)
PHONE..................805 981-8393
EMP: 200
Web: rv.campingworld.com
SIC: 2721 Magazines: publishing only, not printed on site

(P-2878)

UBM CANON LLC (DH)

2901 28th St Ste 100, Santa Monica
(90405-2975)
PHONE..................310 445-4200
Sally Shankland, *CEO*
Scott Schulman, *
Sally Shankland, *Pr*
Stephen Corrick, *
Fred Gysi, *
EMP: 31 **EST:** 1996
SQ FT: 50,000
SALES (est): 5.88MM
SALES (corp-wide): 3.98B **Privately Held**
Web: www.informamarkets.com
SIC: 2721 7389 Magazines: publishing only, not printed on site; Trade show arrangement
HQ: Informa Tech Holdings Llc
1983 Marcus Ave Ste 250
New Hyde Park NY 11042
516 562-7800

(P-2879)

WORLD HISTORY GROUP LLC

Also Called: Historynet
9720 Wilshire Blvd, Beverly Hills
(90212-2021)
PHONE..................703 779-8322
EMP: 27 **EST:** 2015
SALES (est): 198.99K **Privately Held**
Web: www.historynet.com
SIC: 2721 7389 Magazines: publishing only, not printed on site; Business services, nec

---

2731 Book Publishing

(P-2880)

80LV LLC

15260 Ventura Blvd Ste 2230, Sherman Oaks (91403-5356)
PHONE..................818 435-6613
EMP: 38 **EST:** 2015
SALES (est): 247.44K **Privately Held**
Web: www.80.lv
SIC: 2731 Book publishing

(P-2881)

ABC - CLIO INC (HQ)

Also Called: ABC-Clio
75 Aero Camino, Goleta (93117-3134)
P.O. Box 1911 (93116-1911)
PHONE..................805 968-1911
Ronald Boehm, *CEO*
EMP: 115 **EST:** 1955
SALES (est): 21.96MM
SALES (corp-wide): 434.48MM **Privately Held**
Web: www.abc-clio.com
SIC: 2731 Books, publishing only
PA: Bloomsbury Publishing Plc
50 Bedford Square
207 631-5600

(P-2882)

ACCESS BOOKS

1800 Century Park E Ste 600, Los Angeles
(90067-1508)
PHONE..................310 920-1694
Mark Constantino, *Pr*
Mark Constantino, *Pr*
EMP: 148 **EST:** 1999
SQ FT: 36,000
SALES (est): 697.48K **Privately Held**
Web: www.accessbooks.net
SIC: 2731 Book publishing

(P-2883)

AVN MEDIA NETWORK INC

Also Called: Adult Video News
9400 Penfield Ave, Chatsworth
(91311-6549)
PHONE..................818 718-5788
Tony Rios, *CEO*
EMP: 30 **EST:** 1982
SQ FT: 15,000
SALES (est): 2.42MM **Privately Held**
Web: www.avn.com
SIC: 2731 2721 Book publishing; Periodicals

(P-2884)

BERTELSMANN INC

Also Called: Arvato Services
29011 Commerce Center Dr, Valencia
(91355-4195)
PHONE..................661 702-2700
Janet Adams, *Mgr*
EMP: 9820
SALES (corp-wide): 54.57MM **Privately Held**
Web: www.arvato.com
SIC: 2731 Books, publishing only
HQ: Bertelsmann, Inc.
1745 Broadway
New York NY 10019
212 782-1000

(P-2885)

BRIDGE PUBLICATIONS INC (PA)

Also Called: Bpi Records
5600 E Olympic Blvd, Commerce
(90022-5128)
PHONE..................323 888-6200
Blake Silber, *CEO*
Lis Astrupgaard, *
Marilyn Pisani, *
Suzanne Riley, *
▲ **EMP:** 40 **EST:** 1981
SQ FT: 15,000
SALES (est): 20.95MM
SALES (corp-wide): 20.95MM **Privately Held**
Web: www.bridgepub.com
SIC: 2731 3652 Books, publishing only; Prerecorded records and tapes

PRODUCTS & SVCS

(P-2886)
CPP/BELWIN INC
16320 Roscoe Blvd Ste 100, Van Nuys
(91406-1216)
P.O. Box 10003 (91410-0003)
PHONE.....................818 891-5999
Steven Manus, *Pr*
▲ **EMP:** 57 **EST:** 1988
SQ FT: 142,000
SALES (est): 481.55K **Privately Held**
SIC: 2731 Book music: publishing only, not
　printed on site
PA: Alfred Music Group Inc.
　16320 Roscoe Blvd Ste 100

(P-2887)
CREATIVE TEACHING PRESS INC (PA)
11145 Knott Ave, Cypress (90630-5140)
PHONE.....................714 799-2100
James M Connelly, *CEO*
Luella Connelly, *
Susan Connelly, *
Patrick Connelly, *
◆ **EMP:** 95 **EST:** 1965
SALES (est): 5.46MM
SALES (corp-wide): 5.46MM **Privately Held**
Web: www.creativeteaching.com
SIC: 2731 Books, publishing only

(P-2888)
DAWN SIGN PRESS INC
6130 Nancy Ridge Dr, San Diego
(92121-3223)
PHONE.....................858 625-0600
Joe Dannis, *CEO*
Thomas Schlegel, *
Tina Jo Breindel, *
◆ **EMP:** 28 **EST:** 1977
SQ FT: 16,500
SALES (est): 2.46MM **Privately Held**
Web: www.dawnsign.com
SIC: 2731 Books, publishing only

(P-2889)
EDUCATIONAL IDEAS INCORPORATED
Also Called: Ballard & Tighe Publishers
950 W Central Ave, Brea (92821-2261)
P.O. Box 219 (92822-0219)
PHONE.....................714 990-4332
Dorothy Roberts, *Ch Bd*
Mark Espinola, *CEO*
Kent Roberts, *Sec*
◆ **EMP:** 48 **EST:** 1976
SALES (est): 2.77MM **Privately Held**
Web: www.ballard-tighe.com
SIC: 2731 Books, publishing only

(P-2890)
HOUGHTON MIFFLIN HARCOURT PUBG
Also Called: Harcourt Trade Publishers
525 B St Ste 1900, San Diego
(92101-4495)
PHONE.....................617 351-5000
Barbara Fisch, *Brnch Mgr*
EMP: 26
SALES (corp-wide): 1.97B **Privately Held**
Web: www.hmhco.com
SIC: 2731 Textbooks: publishing only, not
　printed on site
HQ: Houghton Mifflin Harcourt Publishing
　Company
　125 High St Ste 900
　Boston MA 02110
　617 351-5000

(P-2891)
JUDY O PRODUCTIONS INC
4858 W Pico Blvd Ste 331, Los Angeles
(90019-4225)
PHONE.....................323 938-8513
Judy Ostarch, *Pr*
▲ **EMP:** 28 **EST:** 1999
SALES (est): 503.12K **Privately Held**
SIC: 2731 Book publishing

(P-2892)
MANSON WESTERN LLC
Also Called: Western Psychological Services
625 Alaska Ave, Torrance (90503-5124)
PHONE.....................424 201-8800
EMP: 117 **EST:** 1996
SALES (est): 32.55MM **Privately Held**
Web: www.wpspublish.com
SIC: 2731 Book publishing

(P-2893)
NARCOTICS ANNYMOUS WRLD SVCS I (PA)
Also Called: WORLD SERVICE OFFICE
19737 Nordhoff Pl, Chatsworth
(91311-6606)
P.O. Box 9999 (91409-9099)
PHONE.....................818 773-9999
Anthony Edmondson, *CEO*
▲ **EMP:** 44 **EST:** 1953
SQ FT: 35,000
SALES (est): 9.92MM
SALES (corp-wide): 9.92MM **Privately Held**
Web: www.naws.org
SIC: 2731 Books, publishing only

(P-2894)
PLURAL PUBLISHING INC
9177 Aero Dr, San Diego (92123-2400)
PHONE.....................858 492-1555
Sadanand Singh, *Pr*
▲ **EMP:** 23 **EST:** 2004
SALES (est): 1.51MM **Privately Held**
Web: www.pluralpublishing.com
SIC: 2731 Textbooks: publishing only, not
　printed on site

(P-2895)
SAGE PUBLICATIONS INC (PA)
Also Called: Cq Press Fairfax Co
2455 Teller Rd, Thousand Oaks
(91320-2234)
PHONE.....................805 499-0721
▲ **EMP:** 104 **EST:** 1965
SALES (est): 89.37MM
SALES (corp-wide): 89.37MM **Privately Held**
Web: us.sagepub.com
SIC: 2731 Book publishing

(P-2896)
TEACHER CREATED RESOURCES INC
Also Called: Blue Star Education
12621 Western Ave, Garden Grove
(92841-4014)
PHONE.....................714 230-7060
Darin Smith, *Pr*
Sarah Fournier, *
◆ **EMP:** 103 **EST:** 2004
SALES (est): 24.2MM **Privately Held**
Web: www.teachercreated.com
SIC: 2731 Books, publishing and printing

(P-2897)
THE FULL VOID 2 INC
Also Called: Alfred Music Publishing
16320 Roscoe Blvd Ste 100, Van Nuys
(91406-1216)

P.O. Box 10003 (91410-0003)
PHONE.....................818 891-5999
◆ **EMP:** 275
SIC: 2731 Book publishing

(P-2898)
TOKYOPOP INC (PA)
4136 Del Rey Ave, Marina Del Rey
(90292-5604)
PHONE.....................323 920-5967
Stuart J Levy, *Pr*
John Parker, *
Victor Chin, *
◆ **EMP:** 66 **EST:** 1997
SALES (est): 5.28MM
SALES (corp-wide): 5.28MM **Privately Held**
Web: www.tokyopop.com
SIC: 2731 3652 7812 7371 Books,
　publishing only; Compact laser discs,
　prerecorded; Video tape production;
　Custom computer programming services

(P-2899)
WALTER FOSTER PUBLISHING INC
6 Orchard Ste 100, Lake Forest
(92630-8351)
PHONE.....................949 380-7510
▲ **EMP:** 26
Web: www.walterfoster.com
SIC: 2731 Books, publishing only

(P-2900)
WEST PUBLISHING CORPORATION
Also Called: The Rutter Group
5161 Lankershim Blvd, North Hollywood
(91601-4962)
PHONE.....................800 747-3161
William Rutter, *Brnch Mgr*
EMP: 1607
SALES (corp-wide): 10.66B **Publicly Held**
Web: home.westacademic.com
SIC: 2731 8111 Book publishing; General
　practice attorney, lawyer
HQ: West Publishing Corporation
　2900 Ames Crssing Rd Ste
　Eagan MN 55121
　651 687-7000

2741 Miscellaneous Publishing

(P-2901)
AIO ACQUISITION INC (HQ)
Also Called: Personnel Concepts
3200 E Guasti Rd Ste 300, Ontario
(91761-8661)
P.O. Box 5750 (60197)
PHONE.....................800 333-3795
▲ **EMP:** 92 **EST:** 1989
SALES (est): 20.83MM
SALES (corp-wide): 1.34B **Publicly Held**
Web: www.personnelconcepts.com
SIC: 2741 7319 Posters: publishing and
　printing; Circular and handbill distribution
PA: Brady Corporation
　6555 W Good Hope Rd
　414 358-6600

(P-2902)
ALG INC
120 Broadway Ste 200, Santa Monica
(90401-2385)
P.O. Box 61207 (93160-1207)
PHONE.....................424 258-8026
James Nguyen, *Pr*

Michael Guthrie, *
Jeff Swart, *
Scott Watkinson, *
Bernard Brenner, *
EMP: 97 **EST:** 1972
SALES (est): 2.31MM **Publicly Held**
Web: www.automotiveleaseguide.com
SIC: 2741 Guides: publishing only, not
　printed on site
PA: Truecar, Inc.
　225 Snta Mnica Blvd Fl 12

(P-2903)
AMERICAN SOC CMPSERS ATHORS PB
Also Called: Ascap
7920 W Sunset Blvd Ste 300, Los Angeles
(90046-3300)
PHONE.....................323 883-1000
Daniel Gonzales, *Genl Mgr*
EMP: 131
SALES (corp-wide): 49.06MM **Privately Held**
Web: www.ascap.com
SIC: 2741 Miscellaneous publishing
PA: American Society Of Composers,
　Authors And Publishers
　250 W 57th St Ste 1300
　212 621-6000

(P-2904)
ASSOCIATED DESERT SHOPPERS INC (DH)
Also Called: The White Sheet
73400 Highway 111, Palm Desert
(92260-3908)
PHONE.....................760 346-1729
Harold Paradis, *Pr*
Esperanza Barrett, *
Rey Verdugo Senior, *Dir Opers*
EMP: 75 **EST:** 1987
SQ FT: 4,000
SALES (est): 4.34MM
SALES (corp-wide): 3.28B **Publicly Held**
Web: www.greenandwhitesheet.com
SIC: 2741 7313 Shopping news: publishing
　and printing; Newspaper advertising
　representative
HQ: Schurz Communications, Inc.
　1301 E Douglas Rd Ste 200
　Mishawaka IN 46545
　574 247-7237

(P-2905)
C PUBLISHING LLC
Also Called: C Magazine
1543 7th St Ste 202, Santa Monica
(90401-2645)
PHONE.....................310 393-3800
Jennifer Smith Hale, *Managing Member*
Jennifer Smith Hale, *Mgr*
Jenny Murray, *IN*
Lesley Canpoy, *Publisher*
EMP: 25 **EST:** 2005
SALES (est): 1.2MM **Privately Held**
Web: www.magazinec.com
SIC: 2741 Miscellaneous publishing

(P-2906)
CHINESE OVERSEAS MKTG SVC CORP (PA)
Also Called: Chinese Consumer Yellow Pages
3940 Rosemead Blvd, Rosemead
(91770-1952)
PHONE.....................626 280-8588
Alan Kao, *Pr*
Gorden Kao, *Dir*
▲ **EMP:** 60 **EST:** 1982
SQ FT: 9,298
SALES (est): 4.76MM

▲ = Import ▼ = Export
◆ = Import/Export

SALES (corp-wide): 4.76MM **Privately Held**
Web: www.ccyp.com
SIC: 2741 7389 8742 Directories, telephone: publishing only, not printed on site; Trade show arrangement; Marketing consulting services

(P-2907)
COGNELLA INC
Also Called: University Readers
320 S Cedros Ave Ste 400, Solana Beach (92075-1996)
PHONE..................858 552-1120
Bassin Hamadeh, *CEO*
EMP: 65 EST: 1997
SQ FT: 8,000
SALES (est): 8.06MM **Privately Held**
Web: www.cognella.com
SIC: 2741 Miscellaneous publishing

(P-2908)
COLBI TECHNOLOGIES INC
13891 Newport Ave Ste 150, Tustin (92780-7897)
PHONE..................714 505-9544
Charles Olsen, *Prin*
Larry Goshorn, *
Francisco Javier Oseguera, *
Jamin Boggs, *
Lettie Cowie, *
EMP: 43 EST: 2008
SALES (est): 1.35MM **Privately Held**
Web: www.colbitech.com
SIC: 2741 Miscellaneous publishing

(P-2909)
CORWIN PRESS INC
2455 Teller Rd, Newbury Park (91320-2218)
PHONE..................805 499-9734
Douglas Rife, *Pr*
Leigh Peake, *
Johnnie A James, *
EMP: 47 EST: 1990
SALES (est): 3.75MM
SALES (corp-wide): 89.37MM **Privately Held**
Web: us.corwin.com
SIC: 2741 Miscellaneous publishing
PA: Sage Publications, Inc.
2455 Teller Rd
805 499-0721

(P-2910)
DAISY PUBLISHING COMPANY INC
Also Called: Hi Torque Publications
25233 Anza Dr, Santa Clarita (91355-1289)
P.O. Box 957 (91380-9057)
PHONE..................661 295-1910
Roland Hinz, *Pr*
Lila Hinz, *
EMP: 55 EST: 1969
SQ FT: 16,000
SALES (est): 4.12MM **Privately Held**
Web: www.hi-torque.com
SIC: 2741 Miscellaneous publishing

(P-2911)
DANIELS INC (PA)
Also Called: Big Nickel
74745 Leslie Ave, Palm Desert (92260-2030)
PHONE..................801 621-3355
Daniel Murphy, *Pr*
Dennis Porter, *
EMP: 23 EST: 1968
SQ FT: 10,000
SALES (est): 430.08K

SALES (corp-wide): 430.08K **Privately Held**
Web: www.danielsdki.com
SIC: 2741 Shopping news: publishing and printing

(P-2912)
DIVERSIFIED PRINTERS INC
12834 Maxwell Dr, Tustin (92782-0914)
PHONE..................714 994-3400
Kenneth Bittner, *Pr*
Jerry Tominaga, *
Paul R Nassar, *
EMP: 51 EST: 1986
SQ FT: 105,000
SALES (est): 891.92K **Privately Held**
SIC: 2741 2759 2789 Directories, nec: publishing and printing; Commercial printing, nec; Bookbinding and related work

(P-2913)
ELECTRIC SOLIDUS LLC
26565 Agoura Rd Ste 200, Calabasas (91302-1990)
PHONE..................917 692-7764
EMP: 25 EST: 2019
SALES (est): 1.09MM **Privately Held**
SIC: 2741 Internet publishing and broadcasting

(P-2914)
ELSEVIER INC
Also Called: Elsevier
10620 Treena St, San Diego (92131-1140)
PHONE..................619 231-6616
Kristen Chrisman, *Brnch Mgr*
EMP: 67
SALES (corp-wide): 11.42B **Privately Held**
Web: www.elsevier.com
SIC: 2741 Miscellaneous publishing
HQ: Elsevier Inc.
230 Park Ave Fl 7
New York NY 10169
212 309-8100

(P-2915)
ELSEVIER INC
Also Called: Elsevier Academic Press
525 B St, San Diego (92101-4401)
PHONE..................619 231-6616
EMP: 30
SALES (corp-wide): 11.42B **Privately Held**
Web: www.elsevier.com
SIC: 2741 Technical manuals: publishing only, not printed on site
HQ: Elsevier Inc.
230 Park Ave Fl 7
New York NY 10169
212 309-8100

(P-2916)
G R LEONARD & CO INC
Also Called: Leonard's Guide
181 N Vermont Ave, Glendora (91741-3321)
PHONE..................847 797-8101
David Ercolani, *CEO*
Ahmed Hawari, *
Elizabeth Stern, *
▲ EMP: 26 EST: 1912
SALES (est): 2.19MM **Privately Held**
Web: www.leonardsguide.com
SIC: 2741 Directories, nec: publishing only, not printed on site

(P-2917)
GLOBAL COMPLIANCE INC
Also Called: Compliance Poster
438 W Chestnut Ave Ste A, Monrovia (91016-1129)

P.O. Box 607 (91017-0607)
PHONE..................626 303-6855
Patricia A Blum, *Pr*
EMP: 25 EST: 1990
SALES (est): 2.13MM **Privately Held**
Web: www.accupostdocs.com
SIC: 2741 Posters: publishing and printing

(P-2918)
GOOD WORLDWIDE LLC
6380 Wilshire Blvd # 15, Los Angeles (90048-5003)
PHONE..................323 206-6495
Michelle Medlock, *Mgr*
EMP: 44 EST: 2010
SALES (est): 1.3MM **Privately Held**
Web: www.good.is
SIC: 2741 Miscellaneous publishing

(P-2919)
GRAPHIQ LLC
101a Innovation Pl, Santa Barbara (93108-2268)
P.O. Box 1259 (93067-1259)
PHONE..................805 335-2433
Kevin Oconnor, *Pr*
Scott Leonard, *
EMP: 120 EST: 2009
SALES (est): 9.26MM **Publicly Held**
Web: www.graphiq.com
SIC: 2741 4813 Internet publishing and broadcasting; Web search portals
PA: Amazon.Com, Inc.
410 Terry Ave N

(P-2920)
GREAT EASTERN ENTERTAINMENT CO
610 W Carob St, Compton (90220-5210)
PHONE..................310 638-5058
Kent Hsu, *Pr*
▲ EMP: 24 EST: 1995
SQ FT: 6,000
SALES (est): 4.72MM **Privately Held**
Web: www.geanimation.com
SIC: 2741 Posters: publishing and printing

(P-2921)
HANLEY WOOD MEDIA INC (HQ)
Also Called: Zonda Media
4000 Macarthur Blvd Ste 400, Newport Beach (92660-2543)
PHONE..................202 736-3300
Jeffrey Meyers, *CEO*
EMP: 24 EST: 2013
SALES (est): 39.77MM
SALES (corp-wide): 179.03MM **Privately Held**
Web: www.jlconline.com
SIC: 2741 Business service newsletters: publishing and printing
PA: Hw Holdco, Llc
1 Thomas Cir Nw # 600
202 452-0800

(P-2922)
INFORMA BUSINESS MEDIA INC
Sourceesb
16815 Von Karman Ave # 150, Irvine (92606-2406)
PHONE..................949 252-1146
EMP: 30
SALES (corp-wide): 3.12B **Privately Held**
SIC: 2741 Directories, nec: publishing only, not printed on site
HQ: Informa Business Media, Inc.
605 3rd Ave
New York NY 10158
212 204-4200

(P-2923)
JUMPER MEDIA LLC
Also Called: Jumper Media
1719 Alta La Jolla Dr, La Jolla (92037-7103)
PHONE..................831 333-6202
Colton Bollinger, *CEO*
EMP: 99 EST: 2016
SALES (est): 5.53MM **Privately Held**
Web: www.jumpermedia.co
SIC: 2741 Internet publishing and broadcasting

(P-2924)
JUNGOTV LLC
1800 Vine St, Los Angeles (90028-5250)
PHONE..................650 207-6227
George Chung, *CEO*
EMP: 60 EST: 2015
SALES (est): 945.26K **Privately Held**
Web: www.jungotv.com
SIC: 2741 Internet publishing and broadcasting

(P-2925)
LA XPRESS AIR & HEATING SVCS
6400 E Washington Blvd Ste 121, Commerce (90040-1820)
PHONE..................310 856-9678
Jesus A Chavez, *CEO*
EMP: 67 EST: 2013
SALES (est): 1.08MM **Privately Held**
Web: www.laxpressairheating.com
SIC: 2741 Miscellaneous publishing

(P-2926)
MARCOA MEDIA LLC (PA)
9955 Black Mountain Rd, San Diego (92126-4514)
P.O. Box 509100 (92150-9100)
PHONE..................858 635-9627
Michael Martella, *Managing Member*
Matt Benedict, *
EMP: 40 EST: 1967
SQ FT: 40,000
SALES (est): 3.91MM
SALES (corp-wide): 3.91MM **Privately Held**
Web: www.mybaseguide.com
SIC: 2741 Atlas, map, and guide publishing

(P-2927)
NATIONAL APPRAISAL GUIDES INC
Also Called: Nada Appraisal Guide
3186 Airway Ave Ste K, Costa Mesa (92626-4650)
PHONE..................714 556-8511
Donald D Christy Junior, *Pr*
Jody Christy, *
Robin Lewis, *
EMP: 33 EST: 1968
SQ FT: 20,000
SALES (est): 2.18MM **Privately Held**
Web: www.jdpower.com
SIC: 2741 Guides: publishing and printing

(P-2928)
NEIL A KJOS MUSIC COMPANY (PA)
Also Called: Kjos Music
4382 Jutland Dr, San Diego (92117-3642)
P.O. Box 178270 (92177-8270)
PHONE..................858 270-9800
Neil A Kjos Junior, *Ch Bd*
Ryan Nowlin, *
Barbara G Kjos, *
▲ EMP: 40 EST: 1985

SQ FT: 72,000
SALES (est): 4.21MM
SALES (corp-wide): 4.21MM **Privately Held**
Web: www.kjos.com
SIC: 2741 Music, book: publishing and printing

(P-2929)
NETMARBLE US INC
600 Wilshire Blvd Ste 1100, Los Angeles (90005-3983)
PHONE.................................213 222-7712
Chul Min Sim, *CEO*
EMP: 66 **EST:** 2012
SQ FT: 2,500
SALES (est): 2.36MM **Privately Held**
SIC: 2741 5734 Miscellaneous publishing; Software, computer games
PA: Netmarble Corporation
　　G-Tower

(P-2930)
NETWORK TELEVISION TIME INC
3929 Clearford Ct, Westlake Village (91361-4106)
PHONE.................................877 468-8899
Bruce Arditte, *Pr*
EMP: 26 **EST:** 1999
SQ FT: 200
SALES (est): 384.33K **Privately Held**
SIC: 2741 7374 7371 Internet publishing and broadcasting; Data processing and preparation; Custom computer programming services

(P-2931)
NEXTCLIENTCOM INC
25000 Avenue Stanford, Valencia (91355-4553)
PHONE.................................661 222-7755
EMP: 30 **EST:** 2000
SALES (est): 2.07MM **Privately Held**
Web: www.nextclient.com
SIC: 2741 8742 7336 Newsletter publishing; Marketing consulting services; Commercial art and graphic design

(P-2932)
OWSLA TOURING LLC
16000 Ventura Blvd Ste 600, Encino (91436-2753)
PHONE.................................818 385-1933
Tim Smith, *Prin*
EMP: 29 **EST:** 2013
SALES (est): 882.91K **Privately Held**
SIC: 2741 Miscellaneous publishing

(P-2933)
PARROT COMMUNICATIONS INTL INC
Also Called: Parrot Media Network
25461 Rye Canyon Rd, Valencia (91355-1206)
PHONE.................................818 567-4700
Robert W Mertz, *CEO*
▲ **EMP:** 50 **EST:** 1989
SALES (est): 4.1MM **Privately Held**
Web: www.parrotmedia.com
SIC: 2741 7331 4822 7375 Directories, nec: publishing only, not printed on site; Direct mail advertising services; Facsimile transmission services; Information retrieval services

(P-2934)
PENNYSAVER USA PUBLISHING LLC
Also Called: Original Pennysaver, The
2830 Orbiter St, Brea (92821-6224)
P.O. Box 8900 (92822-8900)
PHONE.................................866 640-3900
EMP: 1000
Web: www.pennysaverusa.com
SIC: 2741 Shopping news: publishing only, not printed on site

(P-2935)
PLANETIZEN INC
Also Called: Planetizen
3530 Wilshire Blvd Ste 1285, Los Angeles (90010-2341)
PHONE.................................877 260-7526
Chris Steins, *Pr*
EMP: 32 **EST:** 2011
SALES (est): 199.35K **Privately Held**
Web: www.planetizen.com
SIC: 2741 Internet publishing and broadcasting

(P-2936)
PLAYBOY ENTERPRISES INTL INC
Also Called: Peei
10960 Wilshire Blvd Ste 2200, Los Angeles (90024-3702)
PHONE.................................310 424-1800
Christopher Pachler, *Ex VP*
Christopher Pachler, *CAO*
Hugh Heffner, *Chief Creative Officer*
EMP: 100 **EST:** 1964
SALES (est): 12.01MM
SALES (corp-wide): 142.95MM **Publicly Held**
Web: www.playboy.com
SIC: 2741 Miscellaneous publishing
HQ: Playboy Enterprises, Inc.
　　10960 Wlshire Blvd Ste 22
　　Los Angeles CA 90024
　　310 424-1800

(P-2937)
POLLSTAR LLC
Also Called: Pollstar.com
1100 Glendon Ave Ste 2100, Los Angeles (90024-3592)
PHONE.................................559 271-7900
Gary Bongiovanni, *Pr*
Gary Smith, *
EMP: 58 **EST:** 1981
SALES (est): 3.25MM **Privately Held**
Web: store.pollstar.com
SIC: 2741 Miscellaneous publishing

(P-2938)
PROTOTYPE INDUSTRIES INC (PA)
26035 Acero Ste 100, Mission Viejo (92691-7951)
PHONE.................................949 680-4890
Irene Grigoriadis, *CEO*
EMP: 28 **EST:** 1991
SQ FT: 4,000
SALES (est): 453.84K **Privately Held**
Web: www.prototypeindustries.com
SIC: 2741 2752 Miscellaneous publishing; Offset printing

(P-2939)
RASPADOXPRESS
8610 Van Nuys Blvd, Panorama City (91402-7205)
PHONE.................................818 892-6969
Oscar Limon, *Brnch Mgr*
EMP: 77
SALES (corp-wide): 1.42MM **Privately Held**
Web: www.raspadoxpress.com

SIC: 2741 Miscellaneous publishing
PA: Raspadoxpress
　　9765 Laurel Canyon Blvd
　　818 890-4111

(P-2940)
REAL MARKETING
8470 Redwood Creek Ln Ste 200, San Diego (92126-1000)
PHONE.................................858 847-0335
David Collins, *Pr*
▼ **EMP:** 28 **EST:** 2007
SALES (est): 8.51MM **Privately Held**
Web: www.realmarketing4you.com
SIC: 2741 2759 2721 Newsletter publishing; Promotional printing; Magazines: publishing and printing

(P-2941)
RIYE GROUP LLC
2110 W 103rd St, Los Angeles (90047-4113)
PHONE.................................820 203-9215
Lanon Johnson, *Pr*
EMP: 49 **EST:** 2021
SALES (est): 150.2K **Privately Held**
SIC: 2741 8742 8741 7514 Internet publishing and broadcasting; Marketing consulting services; Administrative management; Passenger car rental

(P-2942)
SUPERBAM INC
214 Main St, El Segundo (90245-3803)
PHONE.................................310 845-5784
Rian Bosak, *CEO*
EMP: 27 **EST:** 2018
SALES (est): 783.65K **Privately Held**
Web: www.superbam.com
SIC: 2741 Internet publishing and broadcasting

(P-2943)
SUPERMEDIA LLC
Also Called: Verizon
3131 Katella Ave, Los Alamitos (90720-2335)
P.O. Box 3770 (90720-0377)
PHONE.................................562 594-5101
Del Humenik, *Mgr*
EMP: 50
SQ FT: 150,078
SALES (corp-wide): 916.96MM **Publicly Held**
SIC: 2741 7372 2791 Directories, telephone: publishing only, not printed on site; Prepackaged software; Typesetting
HQ: Supermedia Llc
　　2200 W Airfield Dr
　　Dfw Airport TX 75261
　　972 453-7000

(P-2944)
TABOR COMMUNICATIONS INC
Also Called: Hpcwire
8445 Camino Santa Fe Ste 101, San Diego (92121-2649)
PHONE.................................858 625-0070
Debra Goldfarb, *Pr*
Thomas Taber, *Ch Bd*
Lara Kisielewska, *CMO*
EMP: 24 **EST:** 2002
SQ FT: 15,000
SALES (est): 4.19MM **Privately Held**
Web: www.hpcwire.com
SIC: 2741 Miscellaneous publishing

(P-2945)
TEACHER CREATED MATERIALS INC

SIC: 2741 Miscellaneous publishing

5301 Oceanus Dr, Huntington Beach (92649-1030)
P.O. Box 1040 (92647-1040)
PHONE.................................714 891-2273
Rachelle Cracchiolo, *CEO*
Corinne Burton, *
Deanne Mendoza, *
Rich Levitt, *
◆ **EMP:** 110 **EST:** 1979
SQ FT: 10,000
SALES (est): 24.31MM **Privately Held**
Web: www.teachercreatedmaterials.com
SIC: 2741 Miscellaneous publishing

(P-2946)
TECHTURE INC
Also Called: Estech Digital
1010 Wilshire Blvd Apt 1206, Los Angeles (90017-5668)
PHONE.................................323 347-6209
Muhammad Zubair Khan, *Pr*
Chris M Joseph, *
EMP: 35 **EST:** 2021
SALES (est): 379.2K **Privately Held**
Web: www.techture.co
SIC: 2741 Internet publishing and broadcasting

(P-2947)
THOMSON REUTERS CORPORATION
3280 Motor Ave Ste 200, Los Angeles (90034-3700)
PHONE.................................310 287-2360
Ayanna Chambliss, *Brnch Mgr*
EMP: 29
SQ FT: 900
SALES (corp-wide): 10.66B **Publicly Held**
Web: www.thomsonreuters.com
SIC: 2741 Miscellaneous publishing
HQ: Thomson Reuters Corporation
　　333 Bay St
　　Toronto ON M5H 2
　　416 687-7500

(P-2948)
THOMSON REUTERS CORPORATION
163 Albert Pl, Costa Mesa (92627-1744)
PHONE.................................949 400-7782
EMP: 26
SALES (corp-wide): 10.66B **Publicly Held**
Web: www.thomsonreuters.com
SIC: 2741 Miscellaneous publishing
HQ: Thomson Reuters Corporation
　　333 Bay St
　　Toronto ON M5H 2
　　416 687-7500

(P-2949)
TRANSWESTERN PUBLISHING COMPANY LLC
Also Called: Transwestern Publishing
8344 Clairemont Mesa Blvd, San Diego (92111-1307)
PHONE.................................858 467-2800
EMP: 1869
SIC: 2741 Directories, telephone: publishing and printing

(P-2950)
UNIVERSAL MUS GROUP DIST CORP (DH)
Also Called: Umgd
2220 Colorado Ave, Santa Monica (90404-3506)
PHONE.................................310 235-4700
Jim Urie, *Pr*
Kevin Lipson, *

EMP: 76 **EST:** 1989
SALES (est): 14.91MM **Privately Held**
Web: www.universalmusic.com
SIC: 2741 Miscellaneous publishing
HQ: Vivendi Holding I Llc
1755 Broadway Fl 2
New York NY 10019
212 445-3800

(P-2951)
UNIVERSAL MUSIC PUBLISHING INC
Also Called: Universal Christian Music Pubg
1601 Cloverfield Blvd, Santa Monica
(90404-4082)
PHONE..............................310 235-4700
Jody Gerson, *CEO*
EMP: 87 **EST:** 1999
SALES (est): 5.03MM **Privately Held**
Web: www.spandaubalIetstore.com
SIC: 2741 Miscellaneous publishing
HQ: Universal Music Group, Inc.
2220 Colorado Ave
Santa Monica CA 90404
310 865-0770

(P-2952)
UPPER DECK COMPANY (PA)
5830 El Camino Real, Carlsbad
(92008-8816)
PHONE..............................800 873-7332
Jason Masherah, *Pr*
Don Utic, *Treas*
EMP: 30 **EST:** 2003
SQ FT: 33,424
SALES (est): 25.3MM **Privately Held**
Web: www.upperdeck.com
SIC: 2741 Music, book: publishing and printing

(P-2953)
WARNER CHAPPELL MUSIC INC (DH)
Also Called: Warner Geometric Music
777 S Santa Fe Ave, Los Angeles
(90021-1750)
PHONE..............................310 441-8600
Cameron Strang, *CEO*
Ira Pianko, *
Jay Morgenstern, *
Brian Roberts, *
Scott Francis, *
EMP: 110 **EST:** 1984
SALES (est): 9.69MM **Publicly Held**
Web: www.warnerrecords.com
SIC: 2741 Music book and sheet music publishing
HQ: Warner Music Inc
1633 Broadway
New York NY 10019

(P-2954)
WB MUSIC CORP (DH)
Also Called: Wc Music Corp.
10585 Santa Monica Blvd Ste 200, Los
Angeles (90025-4926)
PHONE..............................310 441-8600
Leslie Bider, *CEO*
EMP: 125 **EST:** 1994
SALES (est): 1.86MM **Publicly Held**
SIC: 2741 Music, sheet: publishing only, not printed on site
HQ: Warner Music Inc.
1633 Broadway
New York NY 10019

(P-2955)
WEBTOON ENTERTAINMENT INC (PA)

5700 Wilshire Blvd Ste 220, Los Angeles
(90036-7205)
PHONE..............................323 297-3410
Junkoo Kim, *Ch Bd*
David J Lee, *
Yongsoo Kim, *CSO*
Chankyu Park, *
Hyeeun Son, *CDO*
EMP: 739 **EST:** 2016
SQ FT: 22,296
SALES (est): 14.01MM
SALES (corp-wide): 14.01MM **Publicly Held**
Web: apply.workable.com
SIC: 2741 Miscellaneous publishing

(P-2956)
WEST PUBLISHING CORPORATION
2801 Camino Del Rio S, San Diego
(92108-3800)
PHONE..............................619 296-7862
Wes Askins, *Brnch Mgr*
EMP: 516
SALES (corp-wide): 10.66B **Publicly Held**
Web: store.legal.thomsonreuters.com
SIC: 2741 Miscellaneous publishing
HQ: West Publishing Corporation
2900 Ames Crssing Rd Ste
Eagan MN 55121
651 687-7000

(P-2957)
YAMAGATA AMERICA INC
3760 Convoy St Ste 219, San Diego
(92111-3744)
PHONE..............................858 751-1010
Yasuhide Fujimoto, *Pr*
EMP: 101 **EST:** 2009
SQ FT: 4,630
SALES (est): 804.67K **Privately Held**
Web: www.yamagatadsa.com
SIC: 2741 Technical manuals: publishing and printing
HQ: Yamagata Holdings America, Inc.
3760 Convoy St Ste 219
San Diego CA 92111

2752 Commercial Printing, Lithographic

(P-2958)
ACE COMMERCIAL INC
Also Called: Press Colorcom
10310 Pioneer Blvd Ste 1, Santa Fe Springs
(90670-3737)
PHONE..............................562 946 6664
Andrew H Choi, *CEO*
EMP: 40 **EST:** 1988
SQ FT: 22,000
SALES (est): 3.95MM **Privately Held**
Web: www.acecommercial.com
SIC: 2752 7331 2791 2789 Offset printing;
Direct mail advertising services; Typesetting
; Bookbinding and related work

(P-2959)
ADVANCED COLOR GRAPHICS
Also Called: Acg Ecopack
1921 S Business Pkwy, Ontario
(91761-8539)
PHONE..............................909 930-1500
Steve Thompson, *Pr*
Mike Mullens, *
EMP: 60 **EST:** 1992
SQ FT: 70,000
SALES (est): 1.39MM **Privately Held**
SIC: 2752 Offset printing

(P-2960)
AMERICAN PCF PRTRS COLLEGE INC
Also Called: Kenny The Printer
675 N Main St, Orange (92868-1103)
PHONE..............................949 250-3212
TOLL FREE: 800
David Smith, *CEO*
Cal Laird, *
EMP: 36 **EST:** 1981
SALES (est): 3.99MM **Privately Held**
Web: www.westprint.com
SIC: 2752 Offset printing

(P-2961)
AMERICHIP INC (PA)
Also Called: Americhip
19032 S Vermont Ave, Gardena
(90248-4412)
PHONE..............................310 323-3697
Timothy Clegg, *CEO*
Kevin Clegg, *Pr*
John Clegg, *VP*
Primoz Samardzija, *Ex VP*
Francis Logan, *Corporate Counsel*
▲ **EMP:** 45 **EST:** 1995
SQ FT: 30,000
SALES (est): 4.35MM
SALES (corp-wide): 4.35MM **Privately Held**
Web: www.americhip.com
SIC: 2752 Promotional printing, lithographic

(P-2962)
ANCHORED PRINTS
Also Called: Roots Fulfillment
1199 N Grove St, Anaheim (92806-2110)
PHONE..............................714 929-9317
Samuel I Schinhofen, *CEO*
Samuel Schinhofen, *CEO*
EMP: 23 **EST:** 2018
SALES (est): 2.5MM **Privately Held**
Web: home.anchoredprints.com
SIC: 2752 Commercial printing, lithographic

(P-2963)
ANDERSON LA INC
Also Called: Anderson Printing
3550 Tyburn St, Los Angeles (90065-1427)
PHONE..............................323 460-4115
▲ **EMP:** 95
SIC: 2752 2759 Commercial printing, lithographic; Letterpress printing

(P-2964)
APPLE GRAPHICS INC
3550 Tyburn St, Los Angeles (90065-1427)
PHONE..............................626 301-4287
EMP: 50
SIC: 2752 2791 2789 Lithographing on metal
; Typesetting; Bookbinding and related work

(P-2965)
AVION GRAPHICS INC
27192 Burbank, Foothill Ranch
(92610-2503)
PHONE..............................949 472-0438
Craig Greiner, *Pr*
Michele Morris, *
Mary Kay Swanson, *Stockholder*
EMP: 33 **EST:** 1984
SQ FT: 6,800
SALES (est): 6.12MM **Privately Held**
Web: www.aviongraphics.com
SIC: 2752 7336 3993 5999 Decals,
lithographed; Commercial art and graphic
design; Signs and advertising specialties;
Decals

(P-2966)
AZALEA SYSTEMS CORP INC
Also Called: Handbill Printers
820 E Parkridge Ave, Corona (92879-6611)
PHONE..............................951 547-5910
Ralph Azar, *Pr*
EMP: 26 **EST:** 2018
SALES (est): 5.28MM **Privately Held**
SIC: 2752 Offset printing

(P-2967)
B AND Z PRINTING INC
1300 E Wakeham Ave # B, Santa Ana
(92705-4145)
PHONE..............................714 892-2000
Frank Buono, *Pr*
James Zimmer, *
EMP: 45 **EST:** 1984
SQ FT: 40,000
SALES (est): 947.08K **Privately Held**
Web: www.bandzprinting.com
SIC: 2752 2789 Offset printing; Bookbinding
and related work

(P-2968)
BARRYS PRINTING INC
Also Called: All About Printing
9005 Eton Ave Ste D, Canoga Park
(91304-6534)
PHONE..............................818 998-8600
Barry Shapiro, *CEO*
EMP: 30 **EST:** 1996
SALES (est): 1.01MM **Privately Held**
Web: barrysprinting.mfgpages.com
SIC: 2752 7334 Offset printing;
Photocopying and duplicating services

(P-2969)
BERT-CO INDUSTRIES INC
Also Called: Bert-Co
2150 S Parco Ave, Ontario (91761-5768)
P.O. Box 4150 (91761-1068)
PHONE..............................323 669-5700
▲ **EMP:** 154
SIC: 2752 Commercial printing, lithographic

(P-2970)
BIG HORN WEALTH MANAGEMENT INC
2577 Research Dr, Corona (92882-7607)
PHONE..............................951 273-7900
▲ **EMP:** 64
SIC: 2752 Offset printing

(P-2971)
BOONE PRINTING & GRAPHICS INC
70 S Kellogg Ave Ste 8, Goleta
(93117-6408)
PHONE..............................805 683-2340
Andrew Ochsner, *Pr*
Dave Tanner, *
Jim Petrini Acctn, *Mgr*
EMP: 52 **EST:** 1988
SQ FT: 15,000
SALES (est): 8.85MM **Privately Held**
Web: www.boonegraphics.net
SIC: 2752 Offset printing

(P-2972)
BOSS LITHO INC
1544 Hauser Blvd, Los Angeles
(90019-3940)
PHONE..............................626 912-7088
Jean Paul Nataf, *Pr*
EMP: 48 **EST:** 2010
SALES (est): 4.16MM **Privately Held**
Web: www.bosslitho.com
SIC: 2752 Offset printing

PRODUCTS & SVCS

(P-2973)
BREHM COMMUNICATIONS INC (PA)
Also Called: B C I
16644 W Bernardo Dr Ste 300, San Diego (92127-1901)
P.O. Box 28429 (92198-0429)
PHONE..............................858 451-6200
Bill Brehm Junior, *Pr*
Tom Taylor, *
Mona Brehm, *
W J Brehm, *
EMP: 29 **EST:** 1919
SQ FT: 6,000
SALES (est): 21.91MM
SALES (corp-wide): 21.91MM **Privately Held**
Web: www.brehmcommunications.com
SIC: 2752 2711 Offset printing; Commercial printing and newspaper publishing combined

(P-2974)
C4 LITHO LLC
27020 Daisy Cir, Yorba Linda (92887-4233)
PHONE..............................714 259-1073
Su T Dang, *Managing Member*
EMP: 24 **EST:** 2006
SALES (est): 965.57K **Privately Held**
Web: www.c4usa.com
SIC: 2752 Offset printing

(P-2975)
CAL SOUTHERN GRAPHICS CORP (HQ)
Also Called: California Graphics
9655 De Soto Ave, Chatsworth (91311-5013)
PHONE..............................310 559-3600
Timothy Toomey, *CEO*
▲ **EMP:** 91 **EST:** 1959
SALES (est): 9.72MM
SALES (corp-wide): 25.12MM **Privately Held**
Web: www.socalgraph.com
SIC: 2752 2759 2754 Lithographing on metal; Commercial printing, nec; Commercial printing, gravure
PA: Gpa Printing Ca Llc
9655 De Soto Ave
818 237-9771

(P-2976)
CALIFORNIA OFFSET PRINTERS INC (PA)
Also Called: Cop Communications
5075 Brooks St, Montclair (91763-4804)
PHONE..............................818 291-1100
TOLL FREE: 800
John Hedlund, *Ch Bd*
William R Rittwage, *Pr*
EMP: 68 **EST:** 1962
SQ FT: 55,000
SALES (est): 11.72MM
SALES (corp-wide): 11.72MM **Privately Held**
Web: www.copprints.com
SIC: 2752 2741 2721 Offset printing; Miscellaneous publishing; Periodicals

(P-2977)
CDR GRAPHICS INC (PA)
1207 E Washington Blvd, Los Angeles (90021-3035)
P.O. Box 15311 (90015-0311)
PHONE..............................310 474-7600
Homan Hadawi, *Pr*
EMP: 23 **EST:** 2010
SALES (est): 2.33MM

SALES (corp-wide): 2.33MM **Privately Held**
Web: www.cdrgraphics.com
SIC: 2752 Offset printing

(P-2978)
CHROMATIC INC LITHOGRAPHERS
127 Concord St, Glendale (91203-2456)
PHONE..............................818 242-5785
Keith Sevigny, *Pr*
Michael Sevigny, *
Mary Gene Sevigny, *
Marlene Lunn, *
▲ **EMP:** 32 **EST:** 1969
SALES (est): 1.63MM **Privately Held**
Web: www.chromaticinc.com
SIC: 2752 Offset printing

(P-2979)
CLASSIC LITHO & DESIGN INC
340 Maple Ave, Torrance (90503-2600)
PHONE..............................310 224-5200
Masoud Nikravan, *CEO*
Firouzeh Nikravan, *
EMP: 30 **EST:** 1976
SQ FT: 12,500
SALES (est): 5.21MM **Privately Held**
Web: www.classiclitho.com
SIC: 2752 Offset printing

(P-2980)
CLEAR IMAGE PRINTING INC
12744 San Fernando Rd, Sylmar (91342-3853)
PHONE..............................818 547-4684
Anthony Toven, *Pr*
EMP: 28 **EST:** 2007
SQ FT: 18,000
SALES (est): 5.04MM **Privately Held**
Web: www.clearimageprinting.com
SIC: 2752 Offset printing

(P-2981)
COLOR INC
1600 Flower St, Glendale (91201-2319)
PHONE..............................818 240-1350
Barry D Hamm, *Pr*
James E Hamm, *
EMP: 35 **EST:** 1968
SQ FT: 16,000
SALES (est): 2.54MM **Privately Held**
Web: www.colorincorporated.com
SIC: 2752 2796 Color lithography; Platemaking services

(P-2982)
COLOR WEST INC
Also Called: Color West Printing & Packg
2228 N Hollywood Way, Burbank (91505-1112)
P.O. Box 10879 (91510-0879)
PHONE..............................818 840-8881
EMP: 170
Web: www.colorwestprinting.com
SIC: 2752 Commercial printing, lithographic

(P-2983)
COLORFX INC
11050 Randall St, Sun Valley (91352-2621)
P.O. Box 12357 (91224-5357)
PHONE..............................818 767-7671
Razmik Avedissian, *CEO*
Arby Avedissian, *
Yolanda Avedissian, *
EMP: 50 **EST:** 1996
SQ FT: 28,000
SALES (est): 1.26MM **Privately Held**
Web: www.colorfxweb.com
SIC: 2752 Offset printing

(P-2984)
COLOUR CONCEPTS INC
Also Called: Partner Printing
1225 Los Angeles St, Glendale (91204-2403)
EMP: 150 **EST:** 1989
SQ FT: 36,000
SALES (est): 2.44MM **Privately Held**
Web: www.partnerprinting.com
SIC: 2752 7371 Offset printing; Computer software development

(P-2985)
CONTINENTAL GRAPHICS CORP
Also Called: Continental Data Graphics
4000 N Lakewood Blvd, Long Beach (90808-1700)
PHONE..............................714 503-4200
Steve Meade, *Mgr*
EMP: 67
SALES (corp-wide): 77.79B **Publicly Held**
Web: www.cdgnow.com
SIC: 2752 Promotional printing, lithographic
HQ: Continental Graphics Corporation
4060 N Lkwood Blvd Bldg 8
Long Beach CA 90808
714 503-4200

(P-2986)
CONTINENTAL GRAPHICS CORP
Also Called: Continental Data Graphics
222 N Pacific Coast Hwy Ste 300, El Segundo (90245-5614)
PHONE..............................310 662-2307
Mike Parvin, *Mgr*
EMP: 67
SALES (corp-wide): 77.79B **Publicly Held**
Web: www.cdgnow.com
SIC: 2752 7336 Promotional printing, lithographic; Graphic arts and related design
HQ: Continental Graphics Corporation
4060 N Lkwood Blvd Bldg 8
Long Beach CA 90808
714 503-4200

(P-2987)
CONTINENTAL GRAPHICS CORP
Also Called: Continental Data Graphics
4060 N Lakewood Blvd Bldg 801, Long Beach (90808-1700)
PHONE..............................714 827-1752
Warren Smith, *Mgr*
EMP: 67
SALES (corp-wide): 77.79B **Publicly Held**
Web: www.cdgnow.com
SIC: 2752 7336 Promotional printing, lithographic; Graphic arts and related design
HQ: Continental Graphics Corporation
4060 N Lkwood Blvd Bldg 8
Long Beach CA 90808
714 503-4200

(P-2988)
CONTINENTAL GRAPHICS CORP
Also Called: Continental Engineering Svcs
6910 Carroll Rd, San Diego (92121-2211)
PHONE..............................858 552-6520
Manuel Defaria, *Brnch Mgr*
EMP: 67
SALES (corp-wide): 77.79B **Publicly Held**
Web: services.boeing.com
SIC: 2752 7336 Promotional printing, lithographic; Graphic arts and related design
HQ: Continental Graphics Corporation
4060 N Lkwood Blvd Bldg 8
Long Beach CA 90808
714 503-4200

(P-2989)
CONTINENTAL GRAPHICS CORP
Also Called: Continental Data Graphics
9302 Pittsburgh Ave Ste 100, Rancho Cucamonga (91730-5564)
PHONE..............................909 758-9800
Steve Meade, *Brnch Mgr*
EMP: 67
SALES (corp-wide): 77.79B **Publicly Held**
Web: services.boeing.com
SIC: 2752 7336 Promotional printing, lithographic; Graphic arts and related design
HQ: Continental Graphics Corporation
4060 N Lkwood Blvd Bldg 8
Long Beach CA 90808
714 503-4200

(P-2990)
CORPORATE GRAPHICS INTL INC
Also Called: Corporate Graphics West
4909 Alcoa Ave, Vernon (90058-3022)
PHONE..............................323 826-3440
Robert Gonynor, *Genl Mgr*
EMP: 65
SALES (corp-wide): 3.81B **Privately Held**
Web: www.taylor.com
SIC: 2752 2759 Offset printing; Embossing on paper
HQ: Corporate Graphics International, Inc.
1750 Tower Blvd
North Mankato MN 56003

(P-2991)
COYLE REPRODUCTIONS INC (PA)
2850 Orbiter St, Brea (92821-6224)
PHONE..............................866 269-5373
Frank T Cutrone Junior, *CEO*
Frank T Cutrone, *Ch Bd*
EMP: 112 **EST:** 1963
SQ FT: 85,000
SALES (est): 11.25MM
SALES (corp-wide): 11.25MM **Privately Held**
Web: www.coylerepro.com
SIC: 2752 2759 Offset printing; Screen printing

(P-2992)
CREATIVE PRESS LLC (PA)
Also Called: Creative Press
1350 S Caldwell Cir, Anaheim (92805-6408)
PHONE..............................714 774-5060
EMP: 29 **EST:** 2007
SQ FT: 31,000
SALES (est): 11.46MM **Privately Held**
Web: www.creativepressinc.net
SIC: 2752 2791 2789 Offset printing; Typesetting; Bookbinding and related work

(P-2993)
CREATIVE PRESS LLC
1600 E Ball Rd, Anaheim (92805-5990)
PHONE..............................714 774-5060
EMP: 36
Web: www.creativepressinc.net
SIC: 2752 2791 2789 Offset printing; Typesetting; Bookbinding and related work
PA: Creative Press, L.L.C.
1350 S Caldwell Cir

(P-2994)
CRESCENT INC
Also Called: Print Printing
670 S Jefferson St, Placentia (92870-6638)
PHONE..............................714 992-6030
Reza Mohkami, *Pr*

▲ = Import ▼ = Export
◆ = Import/Export

Ira Heshmati, *
Tahereh Mohkami, *
EMP: 25 **EST:** 1980
SALES (est): 2.04MM **Privately Held**
Web: www.printprinting.com
SIC: 2752 7549 Offset printing; Do-it-
yourself garages

(P-2995)
CRESTEC USA INC
Also Called: Crestec Los Angeles
2410 Mira Mar Ave, Long Beach
(90815-1756)
PHONE..................................310 327-9000
Takeomi Kurisawa, *CEO*
Mike Burk, *
▲ **EMP:** 50 **EST:** 1967
SALES (est): 8.74MM **Privately Held**
Web: www.crestecusa.com
SIC: 2752 Offset printing
PA: Crestec Inc.
69, Higashimikatacho, Chuo-Ku

(P-2996)
CYU LITHOGRAPHICS INC
Also Called: Choice Lithographics
6951 Oran Cir, Buena Park (90621-3305)
PHONE..................................888 878-9898
Michael Wang, *Pr*
▲ **EMP:** 25 **EST:** 1983
SQ FT: 13,000
SALES (est): 2.41MM **Privately Held**
SIC: 2752 2721 Color lithography;
Magazines: publishing only, not printed on
site

(P-2997)
D & J PRINTING INC
Also Called: Bang Printing
600 W Technology Dr, Palmdale
(93551-3748)
PHONE..................................661 265-1995
EMP: 64
SALES (corp-wide): 611.15MM **Privately
Held**
Web: www.sheridan.com
SIC: 2752 Offset printing
HQ: D. & J. Printing, Inc.
3323 Oak St
Brainerd MN 56401
218 829-2877

(P-2998)
D & R SCREEN PRINTING INC
7314 Pierce Ave, Whittier (90602-1111)
PHONE..................................562 458-6443
Jose D Rios, *Pr*
EMP: 31 **EST:** 2008
SALES (est): 1.15MM **Privately Held**
SIC: 2752 Commercial printing, lithographic

(P-2999)
DAVID B ANDERSON
Also Called: Central Coast Printing
174 Suburban Rd Ste 100, San Luis Obispo
(93401-7522)
PHONE..................................805 489-0661
David B Anderson, *Owner*
EMP: 26 **EST:** 1978
SALES (est): 1.37MM **Privately Held**
Web: www.boonegraphics.net
SIC: 2752 Offset printing

(P-3000)
DELTA PRINTING SOLUTIONS
INC
28210 Avenue Stanford, Valencia
(91355-3983)
PHONE..................................661 257-0584
Tony Richardson, *Pr*

EMP: 130 **EST:** 2003
SQ FT: 100,000
SALES (est): 2.03MM **Privately Held**
Web: www.deltaprintingsolutions.com
SIC: 2752 Offset printing

(P-3001)
DIGITAL PRINTING SYSTEMS
INC (PA)
2350 Panorama Ter, Los Angeles
(90039-2536)
PHONE..................................626 815-1888
Donald J Nores, *Ch*
Donald J Nores, *Ch Bd*
Peter Young, *
Jim Nores, *
Joyce Nores, *
◆ **EMP:** 68 **EST:** 1971
SALES (est): 2.13MM
SALES (corp-wide): 2.13MM **Privately
Held**
Web: www.southlandprinting.com
SIC: 2752 Offset printing

(P-3002)
DIGITAL SUPERCOLOR INC
Also Called: Supercolor
PHONE..................................949 622-0010
▲ **EMP:** 55
Web: www.supercolor.com
SIC: 2752 7336 2759 Commercial printing,
lithographic; Commercial art and graphic
design; Commercial printing, nec

(P-3003)
DIGITALPRO INC (PA)
Also Called: Dpi Direct
13257 Kirkham Way, Poway (92064-7115)
PHONE..................................858 874-7750
Sam Mousavi, *CEO*
Paul Moebius, *Sec*
EMP: 35 **EST:** 2001
SQ FT: 38,000
SALES (est): 2.77MM
SALES (corp-wide): 2.77MM **Privately
Held**
Web: www.dpidirect.com
SIC: 2752 Offset printing

(P-3004)
DOT PRINTER INC (PA)
2424 Mcgaw Ave, Irvine (92614-5834)
PHONE..................................949 474-1100
Bruce M Carson, *Pr*
Jim Voss, *
Stan Lowe, *
▲ **EMP:** 95 **EST:** 1980
SQ FT: 40,000
SALES (est): 29.08MM
SALES (corp-wide): 29.08MM **Privately
Hold**
Web: www.thedotcorp.com
SIC: 2752 2732 3555 Offset printing; Book
printing; Printing trades machinery

(P-3005)
ECLIPSE PRTG & GRAPHICS
LLC
Also Called: James Litho
9145 Milliken Ave, Rancho Cucamonga
(91730-5509)
PHONE..................................909 390-2452
Jeffrey James, *Managing Member*
Sue James, *
EMP: 23 **EST:** 1999
SALES (est): 4.47MM **Privately Held**
Web: www.jameslitho.com
SIC: 2752 Offset printing

(P-3006)
ELUM DESIGNS INC
Also Called: Elum
8969 Kenamar Dr Ste 113, San Diego
(92121-2441)
PHONE..................................858 650-3586
Bradley Foster, *CEO*
Melissa Foster, *
Craig Ross, *
▲ **EMP:** 27 **EST:** 2002
SALES (est): 2.27MM **Privately Held**
Web: www.elumdesigns.com
SIC: 2752 Offset printing

(P-3007)
FISHER PRINTING INC (PA)
2257 N Pacific St, Orange (92865-2615)
PHONE..................................714 998-9200
Thomas Fischer, *Ch*
Will Fischer, *
Tom Scarpati, *
EMP: 150 **EST:** 1933
SQ FT: 60,000
SALES (est): 47.46K
SALES (corp-wide): 47.46K **Privately Held**
Web: www.gofisher.net
SIC: 2752 Offset printing

(P-3008)
GRAPHIC COLOR SYSTEMS INC
Also Called: Continental Colorcraft
1166 W Garvey Ave, Monterey Park
(91754-2511)
PHONE..................................323 283-3000
Andy Scheidegger, *Pr*
Linda Clarke, *
Maria Donhauser, *
EMP: 52 **EST:** 1968
SQ FT: 28,000
SALES (est): 4.97MM **Privately Held**
Web: www.continentalcolorcraft.com
SIC: 2752 2796 2791 2759 Offset printing;
Color separations, for printing; Typesetting;
Commercial printing, nec

(P-3009)
GRAPHIC VISIONS INC
7119 Fair Ave, North Hollywood
(91605-6304)
PHONE..................................818 845-8393
Randall Avazian, *CEO*
Kenneth Langer, *
▲ **EMP:** 23 **EST:** 1940
SALES (est): 4.36MM **Privately Held**
Web: www.graphicvisionsla.com
SIC: 2752 Offset printing

(P-3010)
GW REED PRINTING INC
4071 Greystone Dr, Ontario (91761-3100)
PHONE..................................909 947-0599
EMP: 40
SIC: 2752 7336 Offset printing; Commercial
art and graphic design

(P-3011)
HANDBILL PRINTERS LP
Also Called: Handbill Printers
820 E Parkridge Ave, Corona (92879-6611)
PHONE..................................951 547-5910
Don J Messick, *Pr*
Kenneth Messick, *Pt*
Michael Messick, *Pt*
Mark Messick, *Pt*
Dane Messick, *Pt*
EMP: 45 **EST:** 1984
SQ FT: 62,500
SALES (est): 2.04MM **Privately Held**
Web: www.handbillprinters.com

SIC: 2752 7336 Offset printing; Graphic arts
and related design

(P-3012)
HARMAN PRESS INC
Also Called: Harman Envelopes
6840 Vineland Ave, North Hollywood
(91605-6409)
PHONE..................................818 432-0570
Jay Goldner, *Pr*
Phillip Goldner, *
Deborah Goldner-watson, *Sec*
EMP: 38 **EST:** 1963
SQ FT: 10,000
SALES (est): 2.26MM **Privately Held**
Web: www.harmanpress.com
SIC: 2752 Offset printing

(P-3013)
IKONICK LLC
705 W 9th St Apt 1404, Los Angeles
(90015-1696)
PHONE..................................516 680-7765
Mark Mastrandrea, *Pr*
EMP: 35 **EST:** 2017
SALES (est): 675.54K **Privately Held**
Web: www.ikonick.com
SIC: 2752 7336 Commercial printing,
lithographic; Commercial art and graphic
design

(P-3014)
IMAGIC
2810 N Lima St, Burbank (91504-2510)
PHONE..................................818 333-1670
EMP: 59
SIC: 2752 Commercial printing, lithographic

(P-3015)
IMPACT PRINTING & GRAPHICS
15150 Sierra Bonita Ln, Chino
(91710-8903)
PHONE..................................909 614-1678
Bill Mcginley, *Pr*
EMP: 25 **EST:** 1995
SQ FT: 14,000
SALES (est): 3.79MM **Privately Held**
Web: www.impactpkgco.com
SIC: 2752 Offset printing

(P-3016)
IMPRESS COMMUNICATIONS
LLC
9320 Lurline Ave, Chatsworth (91311-6041)
PHONE..................................818 701-8800
Paul Marino, *CEO*
▲ **EMP:** 92 **EST:** 1974
SQ FT: 50,000
SALES (est): 10.5MM **Privately Held**
Web: www.impress1.com
SIC: 2752 7336 7319 Offset printing;
Commercial art and graphic design; Display
advertising service

(P-3017)
INK & COLOR INC
Also Called: Acuprint
5920 Bowcroft St, Los Angeles
(90016-4302)
PHONE..................................310 280-6060
Saman Sowlaty, *CEO*
Mojgan Sowalty, *
▲ **EMP:** 30 **EST:** 1985
SQ FT: 17,000
SALES (est): 4.58MM **Privately Held**
Web: www.acuprint.net
SIC: 2752 Offset printing

(P-3018)
INK SPOT INC
9737 Bell Ranch Dr, Santa Fe Springs
(90670-2951)
PHONE..................626 338-4500
Somsak Reuanglith, *CEO*
EMP: 26 EST: 2004
SALES (est): 4.66MM **Privately Held**
Web: www.inkspotinc.com
SIC: 2752 Offset printing

(P-3019)
INKWRIGHT LLC
5822 Research Dr, Huntington Beach
(92649-1348)
PHONE..................714 892-3300
EMP: 30 EST: 2010
SALES (est): 4.17MM **Privately Held**
Web: www.inkwright.com
SIC: 2752 Offset and photolithographic
printing

(P-3020)
INLAND LITHO LLC
Also Called: Inland Group
4305 E La Palma Ave, Anaheim
(92807-1843)
PHONE..................714 993-6000
Steve Urbanovitch, *Managing Member*
EMP: 60 EST: 1984
SQ FT: 40,000
SALES (est): 9.16MM **Privately Held**
Web: www.inlandgroupllc.com
SIC: 2752 Offset printing

(P-3021)
INSTANT WEB LLC
Also Called: Iwco Direct - Downey
7300 Flores St, Downey (90242-4010)
PHONE..................562 658-2020
Jake Hertel, *Brnch Mgr*
EMP: 129
SALES (corp-wide): 6.55B **Privately Held**
Web: www.iwco.com
SIC: 2752 Commercial printing, lithographic
HQ: Instant Web, Llc
7951 Powers Blvd
Chanhassen MN 55317
952 474-0961

(P-3022)
INSUA GRAPHICS
INCORPORATED
9121 Glenoaks Blvd, Sun Valley
(91352-2612)
PHONE..................818 767-7007
Jose Miguel Insua, *CEO*
Eric Insua, *
Albert Insua, *
◆ EMP: 35 EST: 1996
SQ FT: 28,000
SALES (est): 6.22MM **Privately Held**
Web: www.insua.com
SIC: 2752 Offset printing

(P-3023)
INTEGRATED
COMMUNICATIONS INC
208 N Broadway, Santa Ana (92701-4863)
PHONE..................310 851-8066
Peter Levshin, *CEO*
David Humphrey, *
▲ EMP: 24 EST: 1986
SALES (est): 2.34MM **Privately Held**
Web: www.icla.com
SIC: 2752 Commercial printing, lithographic

(P-3024)
INTERLINK INC
Also Called: Precision Plastics Packaging
3845 E Coronado St, Anaheim
(92807-1649)
PHONE..................714 905-7700
Bob Bhagat, *Pr*
Hathin Bhagat, *
▲ EMP: 85 EST: 1963
SQ FT: 50,000
SALES (est): 11.23MM **Privately Held**
Web: www.pppc.com
SIC: 2752 Commercial printing, lithographic

(P-3025)
K-1 PACKAGING GROUP
Also Called: K-1 Packaging Group
2001 W Mission Blvd, Pomona
(91766-1020)
PHONE..................626 964-9384
EMP: 134
Web: www.k1packaging.com
SIC: 2752 Offset and photolithographic
printing
PA: K-1 Packaging Group Llc
17989 Arenth Ave

(P-3026)
K-1 PACKAGING GROUP LLC
(PA)
17989 Arenth Ave, City Of Industry
(91748-1126)
PHONE..................626 964-9384
Mike Tsai, *Pr*
◆ EMP: 77 EST: 1992
SALES (est): 23.05MM **Privately Held**
Web: www.k1packaging.com
SIC: 2752 Offset and photolithographic
printing

(P-3027)
KELMSCOTT
COMMUNICATIONS LLC
Also Called: Orange County Printing
2485 Da Vinci, Irvine (92614-5844)
PHONE..................949 475-1900
Paz Calaci, *Brnch Mgr*
EMP: 320
SALES (corp-wide): 15B **Privately Held**
Web: www.rrd.com
SIC: 2752 Offset printing
HQ: Kelmscott Communications Llc
5858 Westheimer Rd # 410
Houston TX 77057
713 787-0977

(P-3028)
KINDRED LITHO
INCORPORATED
10833 Bell Ct, Rancho Cucamonga
(91730-4835)
PHONE..................909 944-4015
Kurt Kindred, *Pr*
Cherie Kindred, *Sec*
EMP: 36 EST: 1971
SQ FT: 8,000
SALES (est): 1.18MM **Privately Held**
Web: www.kindredcorp.com
SIC: 2752 Offset printing

(P-3029)
KOVIN CORPORATION INC
Also Called: Neb Cal Printing
9240 Mira Este Ct, San Diego
(92126-6336)
PHONE..................858 558-0100
Mervin Kodesh, *Pr*
Sandra Kodesh, *
Debbie Dykstra, *

EMP: 30 EST: 1984
SQ FT: 10,000
SALES (est): 2.08MM **Privately Held**
SIC: 2752 2789 Offset printing; Bookbinding
and related work

(P-3030)
L & L PRINTERS CARLSBAD
LLC
Also Called: Specialist Media Group
6200 Yarrow Dr, Carlsbad (92011-1537)
PHONE..................760 477-0321
William Anderson, *Pr*
EMP: 50 EST: 2006
SALES (est): 5.02MM **Privately Held**
Web: www.llprinters.com
SIC: 2752 Offset printing

(P-3031)
LA PRINTING & GRAPHICS INC
Also Called: L A Press
13951 S Main St, Los Angeles
(90061-2140)
PHONE..................310 527-4526
Kevin Sheu Chhim Kaing, *CEO*
Sheu C Kevin Kaing, *
Lor Yik, *Corporate Secretary*
EMP: 26 EST: 1989
SQ FT: 32,000
SALES (est): 2.22MM **Privately Held**
SIC: 2752 Offset printing

(P-3032)
LABOR LAW CENTER INC
Also Called: Laborlawcenter.com
3501 W Garry Ave, Santa Ana
(92704-6422)
PHONE..................800 745-9970
Duyen La, *Pr*
EMP: 25 EST: 2004
SALES (est): 4.61MM **Privately Held**
Web: www.laborlawcenter.com
SIC: 2752 Commercial printing, lithographic

(P-3033)
LEGAL VISION GROUP LLC
2030 Paddock Ln, Norco (92860-2663)
PHONE..................310 945-5550
EMP: 30 EST: 2018
SALES (est): 521.33K **Privately Held**
Web: www.legalvisiongroup.com
SIC: 2752 7389 7374 7335 Commercial
printing, lithographic; Mailing and
messenger services; Data processing and
preparation; Commercial photography

(P-3034)
LESTER LITHOGRAPH INC
1128 N Gilbert St, Anaheim (92801-1412)
PHONE..................714 491-3981
Robert Miller, *CEO*
Georgiana Lester, *
Larry Lester, *
Larita Miller, *
James Jim Witt, *VP*
EMP: 50 EST: 1980
SQ FT: 25,000
SALES (est): 4.31MM **Privately Held**
Web: www.lesterlitho.com
SIC: 2752 Offset printing

(P-3035)
LICHER DIRECT MAIL INC
980 Seco St, Pasadena (91103-2897)
PHONE..................626 795-3333
Wayne Licher Senior, *Pr*
Wayne Licher Junior, *VP*
Besse Licher, *Sec*
EMP: 35 EST: 1946
SQ FT: 17,000

SALES (est): 5.35MM **Privately Held**
Web: www.licherdm.com
SIC: 2752 7331 Offset printing; Direct mail
advertising services

(P-3036)
LITHOGRAPHIX INC (PA)
12250 Crenshaw Blvd, Hawthorne
(90250-3332)
PHONE..................323 770-1000
Herbert Zebrack, *Pr*
Jeffrey Zebrack, *
Victor Wolfe, *
▲ EMP: 305 EST: 1949
SQ FT: 250,000
SALES (est): 45.78MM
SALES (corp-wide): 45.78MM **Privately
Held**
Web: lithographix.com.lithographix.com
SIC: 2752 2759 Offset printing; Commercial
printing, nec

(P-3037)
MADISN/GRHAM CLOR
GRAPHICS INC
Also Called: Colorgraphics
150 N Myers St, Los Angeles (90033-2109)
PHONE..................323 261-7171
Cappy Childs, *CEO*
Arthur Bell, *
Chris Madison, *
Terry Bell, *
▲ EMP: 380 EST: 1953
SQ FT: 96,000
SALES (est): 2.47MM **Privately Held**
Web: www.advantageinc.com
SIC: 2752 2796 Offset printing;
Graphic arts and related design;
Platemaking services

(P-3038)
MAIL HANDLING GROUP INC
Also Called: Mail Handling Services
2840 Madonna Dr, Fullerton (92835-1830)
PHONE..................952 975-5000
Brian Ostenso, *President COOC*
Michael Murphy, *
EMP: 120 EST: 1977
SALES (est): 1.87MM **Privately Held**
SIC: 2752 7331 7374 Offset printing; Mailing
service; Data processing service

(P-3039)
MAN-GROVE INDUSTRIES INC
Also Called: Lithocraft Co
1201 N Miller St, Anaheim (92806-1933)
PHONE..................714 630-3020
EMP: 64
Web: www.lithocraft-files.com
SIC: 2752 Offset printing

(P-3040)
MARINA GRAPHIC CENTER INC
Also Called: Brotherwise Games
12901 Cerise Ave, Hawthorne
(90250-5520)
PHONE..................310 970-1777
EMP: 115 EST: 1964
SALES (est): 8.13MM **Privately Held**
Web: www.marinagraphics.com
SIC: 2752 Offset printing

(P-3041)
MARRS PRINTING INC
Also Called: Mars Printing and Packaging
860 Tucker Ln, City Of Industry
(91789-2914)
PHONE..................909 594-9459
Walter H Marrs, *CEO*
Scott Marrs, *

Teresa Grisby, *
Jackie Marrs, *
EMP: 82 **EST:** 1971
SQ FT: 27,000
SALES (est): 9.96MM **Privately Held**
Web: www.marrs.com
SIC: 2752 Offset printing

(P-3042)
MATSUDA HOUSE PRINTING INC
Also Called: B & G House of Printing
1825 W 169th St Ste A, Gardena
(90247-5270)
PHONE..........................310 532-1533
Benjamin Matsuda, *CEO*
Darren Matsuda, *
Patsy Matsuda, *
▲ **EMP:** 31 **EST:** 1975
SALES (est): 2.35MM **Privately Held**
Web: www.bgprinting.com
SIC: 2752 Lithographing on metal

(P-3043)
MERIDIAN GRAPHICS INC
2652 Dow Ave, Tustin (92780-7208)
PHONE..........................949 833-3500
David R Melin, *Pr*
Paul Valencia, *
David Melin, *
Craig Miller, *
▲ **EMP:** 65 **EST:** 2000
SQ FT: 40,000
SALES (est): 3.84MM **Privately Held**
Web: www.mglitho.com
SIC: 2752 2759 Offset printing; Letterpress printing

(P-3044)
MIDNIGHT OIL AGENCY LLC
Also Called: Midnight Oil Agency, Inc.
3800 W Vanowen St Ste 101, Burbank
(91505-1173)
PHONE..........................818 295-6100
EMP: 285 **EST:** 1989
SALES (est): 17.06MM
SALES (corp-wide): 430.34MM **Privately Held**
Web: www.moagency.com
SIC: 2752 8742 Commercial printing, lithographic; Marketing consulting services
PA: The Imagine Group Llc
1000 Valley Park Dr
800 942-7088

(P-3045)
MODERN PRINTING & MAILING INC
3535 Enterprise St, San Diego
(92110-3211)
PHONE..........................619 222-0535
Steve Hire, *Pr*
Alice Hire, *
EMP: 28 **EST:** 1962
SQ FT: 12,000
SALES (est): 663.34K **Privately Held**
Web: modern-printing-and-mailing-in-san-diego-ca.cityfos.com
SIC: 2752 7331 2759 Offset printing; Mailing service; Commercial printing, nec

(P-3046)
MOLINO COMPANY
Also Called: Melcast
13712 Alondra Blvd, Cerritos (90703-2316)
PHONE..........................323 726-1000
Melchor Castano, *Pr*
EMP: 85 **EST:** 1976
SQ FT: 200,000

SALES (est): 6.22MM **Privately Held**
SIC: 2752 Offset printing

(P-3047)
MONARCH LITHO INC (PA)
1501 Date St, Montebello (90640-632*)
PHONE..........................323 727-0300
Robert Lopez, *CEO*
George Lopez, *VP*
Victor Neri, *Sec*
EMP: 50 **EST:** 1974
SQ FT: 153,000
SALES (est): 18.21MM
SALES (corp-wide): 18.21MM **Privately Held**
Web: www.monarchlitho.com
SIC: 2752 Offset printing

(P-3048)
NATIONAL GRAPHICS LLC
Also Called: Jano Graphics
200 N Elevar St, Oxnard (93030-7969)
PHONE..........................805 644-9212
Mike Scher, *Pr*
EMP: 40 **EST:** 1960
SALES (est): 1.82MM **Privately Held**
Web: www.janoprint.com
SIC: 2752 Offset printing

(P-3049)
NEYENESCH PRINTERS INC
2750 Kettner Blvd, San Diego
(92101-1295)
P.O. Box 81184 (92138-1184)
PHONE..........................619 297-2281
Carl A Bentley, *CEO*
Clifford Neyenesch, *
Dave Pauley, *
Kandy Neyenesch, *
EMP: 70 **EST:** 1899
SQ FT: 30,000
SALES (est): 18.65MM **Privately Held**
Web: www.neyenesch.com
SIC: 2752 Offset printing

(P-3050)
NIKNEJAD INC
Also Called: Colornet Press
6855 Hayvenhurst Ave, Van Nuys
(91406-4718)
PHONE..........................310 477-0407
Kamran Niknejad, *Pr*
Rashid Yassamy, *
Sima Fouladi, *
EMP: 40 **EST:** 1981
SQ FT: 5,000
SALES (est): 4.81MM **Privately Held**
Web: www.colornetpress.com
SIC: 2752 7336 2791 Offset printing; Graphic arts and related design; Typesetting

(P-3051)
NO BOUNDARIES INC
Also Called: Greenbox Art and Culture
789 Gateway Center Way, San Diego
(92102-4539)
PHONE..........................619 266-2349
Thomas Capp, *CEO*
Karen Capp, *
▲ **EMP:** 50 **EST:** 2002
SQ FT: 3,500
SALES (est): 1.81MM **Privately Held**
Web: www.shopgreenboxart.com
SIC: 2752 Offset printing

(P-3052)
OCPC INC
Also Called: The Orange County Printing Co
2485 Da Vinci, Irvine (92614-5844)
PHONE..........................949 475-1900

Miguel Jacobowitz, *Prin*
EMP: 60 **EST:** 1986
SQ FT: 18,000
SALES (est): 5.46MM **Privately Held**
Web: www.rrd.com
SIC: 2752 Offset printing

(P-3053)
ONEIL DIGITAL SOLUTIONS LLC (HQ)
Also Called: Oneil Data Systems
12655 Beatrice St, Los Angeles
(90066-7300)
P.O. Box 941507 (75094-1507)
PHONE..........................972 881-1282
Elizabeth Smith, *Contrlr*
▲ **EMP:** 155 **EST:** 2011
SALES (est): 103.47MM
SALES (corp-wide): 335.64MM **Privately Held**
Web: www.oneildigitalsolutions.com
SIC: 2752 5045 7389 Commercial printing, lithographic; Computer software; Mailbox rental and related service
PA: Data Analysis Inc.
12655 Beatrice St
310 448-6800

(P-3054)
PACER PRINT
4101 Guardian St, Simi Valley
(93063-3382)
PHONE..........................888 305-3144
Peter Varady, *CEO*
Naomi Gonzalez, *
EMP: 35 **EST:** 2016
SALES (est): 7.27MM **Privately Held**
Web: www.pacerprint.com
SIC: 2752 Offset printing

(P-3055)
PACIFIC WEST LITHO INC
Also Called: Pacific West
3291 E Miraloma Ave, Anaheim
(92806-1910)
PHONE..........................714 579-0868
Chang Che Chou, *CEO*
EMP: 70 **EST:** 1984
SQ FT: 24,000
SALES (est): 6.39MM **Privately Held**
Web: www.pacificwestlitho.com
SIC: 2752 Lithographing on metal

(P-3056)
PACKAGING MANUFACTURING INC
2285 Michael Faraday Dr Ste 12, San Diego
(92154-7926)
PHONE..........................619 498-9199
Salvatore Anza, *CEO*
Jim Belcher, *
Gayle Cronin, *
EMP: 240 **EST:** 2009
SALES (est): 30MM **Privately Held**
Web: www.pmpackaging.com
SIC: 2752 Commercial printing, lithographic

(P-3057)
PDF PRINT COMMUNICATIONS INC (PA)
2630 E 28th St, Long Beach (90755-2202)
PHONE..........................562 426-6978
Kevin J Mullaney, *Pr*
EMP: 52 **EST:** 1973
SQ FT: 23,000
SALES (est): 16.91MM
SALES (corp-wide): 16.91MM **Privately Held**
Web: www.pdfpc.com

SIC: 2752 2761 Offset printing; Manifold business forms

(P-3058)
PEGASUS INTERPRINT INC
7111 Hayvenhurst Ave, Van Nuys
(91406-3807)
PHONE..........................800 926-9873
▲ **EMP:** 24
SIC: 2752 Offset printing

(P-3059)
PGI PACIFIC GRAPHICS INTL
Also Called: Pgi
14938 Nelson Ave, City Of Industry
(91744-4330)
PHONE..........................626 336-7707
Yvonne Castillo Wasson, *CEO*
Ricardo Wasson, *
EMP: 25 **EST:** 1989
SQ FT: 17,000
SALES (est): 4.6MM **Privately Held**
Web: www.pacgraphics.com
SIC: 2752 2759 8742 7331 Offset printing; Commercial printing, nec; Marketing consulting services; Mailing service

(P-3060)
PHOENIX MARKETING SERVICES INC
651 Wharton Dr, Claremont (91711-4819)
PHONE..........................909 399-4000
▲ **EMP:** 95
Web: www.phoenixmarketing.net
SIC: 2752 5199 Offset printing; Advertising specialties

(P-3061)
PJ PRINTERS INC
1530 Lakeview Loop, Anaheim
(92807-1819)
PHONE..........................714 779-8484
EMP: 45 **EST:** 1983
SALES (est): 7.02MM **Privately Held**
Web: www.pjprinters.com
SIC: 2752 Commercial printing, lithographic

(P-3062)
PM CORPORATE GROUP INC (PA)
Also Called: PM Packaging
2285 Michael Faraday Dr Ste 12, San Diego
(92154-7926)
PHONE..........................800 343-3139
Salvatore Anza, *CEO*
Jim Belcher, *Pr*
Gaylo Cronin, *COO*
EMP: 56 **EST:** 2007
SALES (est): 150.21MM
SALES (corp-wide): 150.21MM **Privately Held**
Web: www.pmpackaging.com
SIC: 2752 Offset printing

(P-3063)
POSTAL INSTANT PRESS INC (HQ)
Also Called: PIP Printing
26722 Plaza, Mission Viejo (92691-8051)
P.O. Box 9077 (92690-9077)
PHONE..........................949 348-5000
Don F Lowe, *CEO*
Dan F Lowe, *
Richard Low, *
Thomas Muller, *
Dan Conger, *
EMP: 40 **EST:** 1996
SQ FT: 25,000
SALES (est): 2.61MM

P R O D U C T S & S V C S

SALES (corp-wide): 19.99MM **Privately Held**
Web: www.pip.com
SIC: 2752 6159 Offset printing; Machinery and equipment finance leasing
PA: Franchise Services, Inc.
26722 Plaza
949 348-5400

(P-3064)
PRECISION LITHO INC
Also Called: Rrd Pckaging Solutions - Vista
1185 Joshua Way, Vista (92081-7892)
PHONE..............................760 727-9400
Daniel Knotts, *Pr*
Elif Sagsen-ercel, *Ex VP*
EMP: 35 EST: 1981
SQ FT: 40,000
SALES (est): 2.34MM
SALES (corp-wide): 15B **Privately Held**
Web: www.plitho.com
SIC: 2752 Offset printing
HQ: Consolidated Graphics, Inc.
5858 Westheimer Rd # 200
Houston TX 77057

(P-3065)
PRECISION OFFSET INC
Also Called: Precision Services Group
15201 Woodlawn Ave, Tustin (92780-6418)
PHONE..............................949 752-1714
Lawrence Smith, *CEO*
EMP: 75 EST: 1979
SQ FT: 15,000
SALES (est): 10.54MM **Privately Held**
Web: www.precisionservicesgroup.com
SIC: 2752 Offset printing

(P-3066)
PRIMARY COLOR SYSTEMS CORP
3500 W Burbank Blvd, Burbank (91505-2268)
PHONE..............................818 643-5944
EMP: 53
SALES (corp-wide): 47.93MM **Privately Held**
Web: www.pchagencyla.com
SIC: 2752 Offset printing
PA: Primary Color Systems Corporation
11130 Holder St Ste 210
949 660-7080

(P-3067)
PRINTIVITY LLC
Also Called: Printivity
8840 Kenamar Dr Ste 405, San Diego (92121-2450)
PHONE..............................877 649-5463
Lawrence Chou, *CEO*
EMP: 30 EST: 2010
SALES (est): 7.13MM **Privately Held**
Web: www.printivity.com
SIC: 2752 2711 2721 Offset printing; Commercial printing and newspaper publishing combined; Magazines: publishing and printing

(P-3068)
PRINTRUNNER LLC
Also Called: U-Nited Printing and Copy Ctr
8000 Haskell Ave, Van Nuys (91406-1321)
PHONE..............................888 296-5760
Dean Rabbani, *Managing Member*
Mike Zaya, *
Adam Berger, *
Kamie Davison, *
EMP: 23 EST: 1999
SQ FT: 50,000
SALES (est): 1.23MM **Privately Held**

Web: www.printrunner.com
SIC: 2752 Offset printing

(P-3069)
PRINTS 4 LIFE
43145 Business Ctr Pkwy, Lancaster (93535-4564)
PHONE..............................661 942-2233
EMP: 27
Web: www.learn4life.org
SIC: 2752 Commercial printing, lithographic

(P-3070)
PRO DOCUMENT SOLUTIONS INC (PA)
Also Called: Pro Vote Solutions
1760 Commerce Way, Paso Robles (93446-3620)
PHONE..............................805 238-6680
George Phillips, *CEO*
Brad Stier, *
Noal Phillips, *
Molly Comin, *
Diana Phillips, *
▲ EMP: 43 EST: 1979
SQ FT: 35,000
SALES (est): 10.09MM
SALES (corp-wide): 10.09MM **Privately Held**
Web: www.prodocumentsolutions.com
SIC: 2752 Forms, business: lithographed

(P-3071)
PROGRAPHICS INC
9200 Lower Azusa Rd, Rosemead (91770-1593)
PHONE..............................626 287-0417
Christina Stevens, *CEO*
Timothy Stevens, *
Jaime Colacio, *
EMP: 28 EST: 1967
SQ FT: 23,000
SALES (est): 2.45MM **Privately Held**
Web: www.prographicsllc.com
SIC: 2752 Offset printing

(P-3072)
PRPCO
Also Called: Poor Richard's Press
2226 Beebee St, San Luis Obispo (93401-5505)
PHONE..............................805 543-6844
Todd P Ventura, *Pr*
Richard C Blake, *
Mary Monroe, *
EMP: 35 EST: 2000
SALES (est): 4.08MM **Privately Held**
Web: www.prpco.com
SIC: 2752 Offset printing

(P-3073)
Q TEAM
Also Called: Ryan Press
6400 Dale St, Buena Park (90621-3115)
PHONE..............................714 228-4465
Mike Quibodeaux, *CEO*
Donna Quibodeaux, *
Mike Quibodeaux, *VP*
James Quibodeaux, *
EMP: 45 EST: 1980
SQ FT: 13,000
SALES (est): 4.84MM **Privately Held**
Web: www.ryanpress.com
SIC: 2752 Offset printing

(P-3074)
QG PRINTING IL LLC
Also Called: Quad Graphics
6688 Box Springs Blvd, Riverside (92507-0726)

PHONE..............................951 571-2500
Georg Decker, *Brnch Mgr*
EMP: 123
SALES (corp-wide): 2.96B **Publicly Held**
SIC: 2752 Offset printing
HQ: Qg Printing Ii Llc
N61w23044 Harrys Way
Sussex WI 53089

(P-3075)
QUAD/GRAPHICS INC
Also Called: QUAD/GRAPHICS INC.
6688 Box Springs Blvd, Riverside (92507-0726)
PHONE..............................951 689-1122
Uli Oels, *Genl Mgr*
EMP: 62
SALES (corp-wide): 2.96B **Publicly Held**
Web: www.quad.com
SIC: 2752 7336 Offset printing; Commercial art and graphic design
PA: Quad/Graphics, Inc.
N61 W23044 Harry's Way
414 566-6000

(P-3076)
QUEEN BEACH PRINTERS INC
937 Pine Ave, Long Beach (90813-4375)
P.O. Box 540 (90801-0540)
PHONE..............................562 436-8201
Nicholas W Edwards, *CEO*
William L Edwards Senior, *Pr*
William L Edwards Junior, *VP*
Virginia Noyes, *
EMP: 30 EST: 1944
SQ FT: 25,000
SALES (est): 2.41MM **Privately Held**
Web: www.qbprinters.com
SIC: 2752 7336 Offset printing; Commercial art and graphic design

(P-3077)
ROBO 3D INC
Also Called: Robo 3d Printer
5070 Santa Fe St Ste C, San Diego (92109-1610)
PHONE..............................844 476-2233
Braydon Moreno, *CEO*
Randall Waynick, *
▲ EMP: 25 EST: 2013
SALES (est): 3.76MM **Privately Held**
Web: www.robo3d.com
SIC: 2752 Commercial printing, lithographic

(P-3078)
RUSH PRESS INC
Also Called: Arts & Crafts Press
955 Gateway Center Way, San Diego (92102-4542)
PHONE..............................619 296-7874
EMP: 48
Web: www.rushpress.com
SIC: 2752 Offset printing

(P-3079)
SAN DIEGUITO PUBLISHERS INC
Also Called: San Dieguito Printers
1880 Diamond St, San Marcos (92078-5100)
P.O. Box 885 (92075-0885)
PHONE..............................760 593-5139
▲ EMP: 59 EST: 1964
SALES (est): 1.64MM **Privately Held**
Web: www.sd-print.com
SIC: 2752 Offset printing

(P-3080)
SCHOLASTIC SPORTS INC
4878 Ronson Ct Ste Kl, San Diego (92111-1806)

PHONE..............................858 496-9221
EMP: 90
SQ FT: 5,500
SALES (est): 867.63K **Privately Held**
SIC: 2752 Commercial printing, lithographic

(P-3081)
SIR SPEEDY INC (HQ)
Also Called: Sir Speedy
26722 Plaza, Mission Viejo (92691-8051)
P.O. Box 9077 (92690-9077)
PHONE..............................949 348-5000
Don Lowe, *CEO*
Richard Lowe, *
Dan Conger, *
EMP: 43 EST: 1968
SQ FT: 44,000
SALES (est): 7.99MM
SALES (corp-wide): 19.99MM **Privately Held**
Web: www.sirspeedy.com
SIC: 2752 Commercial printing, lithographic
PA: Franchise Services, Inc.
26722 Plaza
949 348-5400

(P-3082)
SOUTHWEST OFFSET PRTG CO INC (PA)
13650 Gramercy Pl, Gardena (90249-2453)
PHONE..............................310 965-9154
Greg Mcdonald, *CEO*
Jennifer Mcdonald, *VP*
Art Spear, *
▲ EMP: 275 EST: 1986
SQ FT: 45,000
SALES (est): 42.54MM
SALES (corp-wide): 42.54MM **Privately Held**
Web: www.southwestoffset.com
SIC: 2752 Offset printing

(P-3083)
SPORT CARD CO LLC
5830 El Camino Real, Carlsbad (92008-8816)
PHONE..............................800 873-7332
Richard Mc William, *CEO*
Jason Masherah, *
Roz Nowicki, *
◆ EMP: 400 EST: 1988
SQ FT: 247,000
SALES (est): 19MM **Privately Held**
Web: www.upperdeck.com
SIC: 2752 5947 Souvenir cards, lithographed ; Gift, novelty, and souvenir shop

(P-3084)
SS WHITTIER LLC
Also Called: Sir Speedy
7240 Greenleaf Ave, Whittier (90602-1312)
PHONE..............................562 698-7513
George Coriaty, *Owner*
EMP: 32 EST: 1979
SQ FT: 12,000
SALES (est): 4.64MM **Privately Held**
Web: www.sswhittier.com
SIC: 2752 7334 Commercial printing, lithographic; Photocopying and duplicating services

(P-3085)
SUPERIOR LITHOGRAPHICS INC
3055 Bandini Blvd, Vernon (90058-4109)
PHONE..............................323 263-8400
Douglas Rawson, *CEO*
Carol Rawson, *
▲ EMP: 90 EST: 1982
SQ FT: 60,000

▲ = Import ▼ = Export
◆ = Import/Export

SALES (est): 19.68MM **Privately Held**
Web: www.superiorlithographics.com
SIC: 2752 Offset printing

(P-3086)
TAILGATE PRINTING INC
Also Called: Hip Hop Royalty
2930 S Fairview St, Santa Ana
(92704-6503)
PHONE.............................714 966-3035
Maria C Vega, *CEO*
EMP: 90 EST: 2008
SQ FT: 80,000
SALES (est): 7.76MM **Privately Held**
Web: www.tailgatela.com
SIC: 2752 Offset printing

(P-3087)
TAJEN GRAPHICS INC
Also Called: Apollo Printing & Graphics
2100 W Lincoln Ave Ste B, Anaheim
(92801-5642)
PHONE.............................714 527-3122
Dhansukhlal Ratanjee, *Pr*
Ken Ratanjee, *
EMP: 30 EST: 1977
SQ FT: 1,800
SALES (est): 3.22MM **Privately Held**
Web: www.apganaheim.com
SIC: 2752 2791 Offset printing; Typesetting,
computer controlled

(P-3088)
TECHNOLOGY TRAINING CORP
Also Called: Avalon Communications
3238 W 131st St, Hawthorne (90250-5517)
PHONE.............................310 644-7777
Richard D Lytle, *Pr*
EMP: 54
SALES (corp-wide): 4.84MM **Privately Held**
Web: www.ttcus.com
SIC: 2752 7331 3577 Offset printing; Direct
mail advertising services; Computer
peripheral equipment, nec
PA: Technology Training Corp
369 Van Ness Way Ste 735
310 320-8110

(P-3089)
THE LIGATURE INC (HQ)
Also Called: Echelon Fine Printing
4909 Alcoa Ave, Vernon (90058-3022)
PHONE.............................323 585-6000
Linda H Pennell, *
Denyse Owens, *
Dave Meyer, *
Tom Clifford, *
EMP: 50 EST: 1920
SQ FT: 47,415
SALES (est): 6.93MM
SALES (corp-wide): 3.81B **Privately Held**
Web: www.echelonprint.com
SIC: 2752 2759 Offset printing; Invitation
and stationery printing and engraving
PA: Taylor Corporation
1725 Roe Crest Dr
507 625-2828

(P-3090)
TREND OFFSET PRINTING
SERVICES INC (HQ)
Also Called: Trend Offset Printing
3701 Catalina St, Los Alamitos
(90720-2402)
P.O. Box 3008 (90720-1308)
PHONE.............................562 598-2446
◆ EMP: 41 EST: 1986
SALES (est): 85.58MM
SALES (corp-wide): 487.58MM **Privately
Held**

Web: www.mittera.com
SIC: 2752 Offset printing
PA: Mittera Group, Inc.
5085 Ne 17th St
515 343-5359

(P-3091)
TREND OFFSET PRINTING
SVCS INC
Also Called: TREND OFFSET PRINTING
SERVICES INCORPORATED
3791 Catalina St, Los Alamitos
(90720-2402)
PHONE.............................562 598-2446
Paul Rhilindger, *Mgr*
EMP: 425
SALES (corp-wide): 487.58MM **Privately
Held**
Web: www.mittera.com
SIC: 2752 2732 Offset printing; Books,
printing and binding
HQ: Trend Offset Printing Services, Inc.
3701 Catalina St
Los Alamitos CA 90720
562 598-2446

(P-3092)
TYPECRAFT INC
Also Called: Typecraft Wood & Jones
2040 E Walnut St, Pasadena (91107-5804)
PHONE.............................626 795-8093
D Harry Montgomery, *Pr*
Jeffrey J Gish, *
EMP: 38 EST: 1947
SQ FT: 19,000
SALES (est): 4.23MM **Privately Held**
Web: www.typecraft.com
SIC: 2752 Offset printing

(P-3093)
ULTIMATE PRINT SOURCE INC
Also Called: Printing 4him
2070 S Hellman Ave, Ontario (91761-8018)
PHONE.............................909 947-5292
Jeffrey J Ferrazzano, *CEO*
Desiree Ferrazzano, *
Edith Le Leux, *
Jon Le Leux, *
EMP: 30 EST: 1987
SQ FT: 20,000
SALES (est): 4.74MM **Privately Held**
Web: www.ultimateprintsource.com
SIC: 2752 Offset printing

(P-3094)
UNI-SPORT INC
16933 Gramercy Pl, Gardena (90247-5207)
PHONE.............................310 217-4587
Thomas Hebert, *Pr*
◆ EMP: 25 EST: 2006
SQ FT: 10,000
SALES (est): 2.25MM **Privately Held**
Web: www.uni-sport.com
SIC: 2752 Commercial printing, lithographic

(P-3095)
V3 PRINTING CORPORATION
Also Called: V 3
200 N Elevar St, Oxnard (93030-7969)
PHONE.............................805 981-2600
David Wilson, *Pr*
Michael Szanger, *
EMP: 80 EST: 1959
SQ FT: 4,000
SALES (est): 9MM **Privately Held**
Web: www.printv3.com
SIC: 2752 Lithographing on metal

(P-3096)
VALLEY BUSINESS PRINTERS
INC
Also Called: Valley Printers
6355 Topanga Canyon Blvd Ste 225,
Woodland Hills (91367-2118)
PHONE.............................818 362-7771
Michael Flannery, *CEO*
Bruce Bolkin, *
Karen S Flannery, *
▲ EMP: 92 EST: 1965
SALES (est): 1.28MM **Privately Held**
Web: www.valleyprinters.net
SIC: 2752 2759 Offset printing; Commercial
printing, nec

(P-3097)
VDP DIRECT LLC (PA)
5520 Ruffin Rd Ste 111, San Diego
(92123-1320)
P.O. Box 910027 (92191-0027)
PHONE.............................858 300-4510
EMP: 24 EST: 2004
SQ FT: 12,500
SALES (est): 901.53K
SALES (corp-wide): 901.53K **Privately
Held**
Web: www.vdpdirect.com
SIC: 2752 Offset printing

(P-3098)
VENTURA PRINTING INC (PA)
Also Called: V3
200 N Elevar St, Oxnard (93030-7969)
PHONE.............................805 981-2600
David Wilson, *Pr*
▲ EMP: 99 EST: 1946
SALES (est): 4.26MM
SALES (corp-wide): 4.26MM **Privately
Held**
Web: www.nationalgraphics.com
SIC: 2752 Offset printing

(P-3099)
VOMELA SPECIALTY COMPANY
Also Called: Vomela
9810 Bell Ranch Dr, Santa Fe Springs
(90670-2952)
PHONE.............................562 944-3853
Loren Maxwell, *Brnch Mgr*
EMP: 126
SALES (corp-wide): 258.06MM **Privately
Held**
Web: www.vomela.com
SIC: 2752 7336 Poster and decal printing,
lithographic; Commercial art and graphic
design
PA: Vomela Specialty Company
845 Minnehaha Ave E
651 228-2200

(P-3100)
WEBER PRINTING COMPANY
INC
1124 E Del Amo Blvd, Long Beach
(90807-1010)
PHONE.............................310 639-5064
Richard M Weber, *Pr*
Steven Weber, *
Lynda Slack, *
EMP: 35 EST: 1946
SQ FT: 30,000
SALES (est): 2.84MM **Privately Held**
Web: www.weberprint.com
SIC: 2752 Offset printing

(P-3101)
WESTROCK CP LLC
MPS Corona

2577 Research Dr, Corona (92882-7607)
PHONE.............................951 273-7900
EMP: 64
Web: www.westrock.com
SIC: 2752 Offset printing
HQ: Westrock Cp, Llc
1000 Abernathy Rd Ste 125
Atlanta GA 30328

(P-3102)
WOODRIDGE PRESS INC
2485 Da Vinci, Irvine (92614-5844)
PHONE.............................949 475-1900
EMP: 50
Web: www.woodridgepress.com
SIC: 2752 2796 Offset printing; Platemaking
services

(P-3103)
WS PACKAGING-BLAKE
PRINTERY
Also Called: Poor Richards Press
2224 Beebee St, San Luis Obispo
(93401-5505)
PHONE.............................805 543-6844
Bruce Dickinson, *Brnch Mgr*
EMP: 34
SQ FT: 3,500
SALES (corp-wide): 14.54B **Privately Held**
SIC: 2752 2621 2791 Offset printing;
Wrapping paper; Typesetting, computer
controlled
HQ: Ws Packaging-Blake Printery
2222 Beebee St
San Luis Obispo CA 93401
805 543-6843

(P-3104)
WTPC INC
Also Called: World Trade Printing Company
12082 Western Ave, Garden Grove
(92841-2913)
PHONE.............................714 903-2500
Joe Ratanjee, *CEO*
▲ EMP: 30 EST: 1991
SQ FT: 25,000
SALES (est): 14.46MM **Privately Held**
Web: www.wtpcenter.com
SIC: 2752 Offset printing

(P-3105)
ZOO PRINTING INC (PA)
Also Called: Zoo Printing Trade Printer
1225 Los Angeles St, Glendale
(91204-2403)
PHONE.............................310 253-7751
Dan Doron, *Pr*
Marla Camins, *
▲ EMP: 43 EST: 2001
SALES (est): 9.93MM
SALES (corp-wide): 9.93MM **Privately
Held**
Web: www.zooprinting.com
SIC: 2752 Offset printing

(P-3106)
ZUZA LLC
2304 Faraday Ave, Carlsbad (92008-7216)
PHONE.............................760 494-9000
Philip M Lurie, *CEO*
Philip M Lurie, *Pr*
Martin Solarish, *
EMP: 72 EST: 1992
SQ FT: 23,000
SALES (est): 15.49MM **Privately Held**
Web: www.zuzaprint.com
SIC: 2752 Offset printing

PRODUCTS & SVCS

2754 Commercial Printing, Gravure

(P-3107)
KMR LABEL LLC
Also Called: Axiom Label Group
1360 W Walnut Pkwy, Compton
(90220-5029)
PHONE..................310 603-8910
EMP: 50
Web: www.resourcelabel.com
SIC: 2754 2752 Labels: gravure printing;
Commercial printing, lithographic

(P-3108)
ONEIL CAPITAL MANAGEMENT INC
12655 Beatrice St, Los Angeles
(90066-7300)
PHONE..................310 448-6400
William O Neil, *CEO*
▲ EMP: 152 EST: 1973
SQ FT: 70,000
SALES (est): 25.29MM
SALES (corp-wide): 335.64MM **Privately Held**
Web: www.oneildigitalsolutions.com
SIC: 2754 2732 2741 2711 Catalogs:
gravure printing, not published on site;
Book printing; Miscellaneous publishing;
Newspapers
PA: Data Analysis Inc.
12655 Beatrice St
310 448-6800

(P-3109)
RESOURCE LABEL GROUP LLC
Also Called: Axiom Label & Packaging
1360 W Walnut Pkwy, Compton
(90220-5029)
PHONE..................310 603-8910
Kieron Delahunt, *Brnch Mgr*
EMP: 50
Web: www.resourcelabel.com
SIC: 2754 2752 Labels: gravure printing;
Commercial printing, lithographic
PA: Resource Label Group, Llc
2550 Mridian Blvd Ste 370

(P-3110)
STUART F COOPER CO
1565 E 23rd St, Los Angeles (90011-1801)
P.O. Box 11306 (90011-0306)
PHONE..................213 747-7141
EMP: 150
SIC: 2754 Announcements: gravure printing

2759 Commercial Printing, Nec

(P-3111)
4 OVER LLC (HQ)
Also Called: 4 Over
1225 Los Angeles St, Glendale
(91204-2403)
PHONE..................818 246-1170
Zarik Megerdichian, *CEO*
Tina Hartounian, *
▲ EMP: 50 EST: 2000
SALES (est): 172.36MM
SALES (corp-wide): 172.36MM **Privately Held**
Web: www.4over.com
SIC: 2759 7336 Commercial printing, nec;
Commercial art and graphic design
PA: Four Cents Holdings, Llc
1225 Los Angeles St

(P-3112)
ABC IMAGING OF WASHINGTON
17240 Red Hill Ave, Irvine (92614-5628)
PHONE..................949 419-3728
EMP: 23
SALES (corp-wide): 129.31MM **Privately Held**
Web: www.abcimaging.com
SIC: 2759 Commercial printing, nec
PA: Abc Imaging Of Washington, Inc
5290 Shawnee Rd Ste 300
202 429-8870

(P-3113)
ADCRAFT PRODUCTS CO INC
Also Called: Adcraft Labels
1230 S Sherman St, Anaheim
(92805-6455)
PHONE..................714 776-1230
Randy C Mottram, *Pr*
Keith A Mottram, *
EMP: 27 EST: 1977
SALES (est): 7.87MM **Privately Held**
Web: www.adcraftlabels.com
SIC: 2759 Labels and seals: printing, nsk

(P-3114)
ADVANCED WEB OFFSET INC
Also Called: Awo
2260 Oak Ridge Way, Vista (92081-8341)
PHONE..................760 727-1700
Stephen F Shoemaker, *Pr*
David Altomare, *
EMP: 75 EST: 1989
SQ FT: 65,000
SALES (est): 8.37MM **Privately Held**
Web: www.awoink.com
SIC: 2759 2752 Newspapers: printing, nsk;
Offset and photolithographic printing

(P-3115)
AMERICAN FOOTHILL PUBG CO INC
10009 Commerce Ave, Tujunga
(91042-2303)
PHONE..................818 352-7878
Doris Horwith, *Pr*
Douglas Horwith, *
EMP: 40 EST: 1920
SQ FT: 13,000
SALES (est): 2.32MM **Privately Held**
Web:
www.americanfoothillpublishing.com
SIC: 2759 Newspapers: printing, nsk

(P-3116)
AMERICAN ZABIN INTL INC
3933 S Hill St, Los Angeles (90037-1313)
PHONE..................213 746-3770
Alan Faiola, *CEO*
Alan Faiola, *CFO*
Steven Garfinkle, *
Eric Sedso, *Marketing*
◆ EMP: 32 EST: 1993
SQ FT: 18,000
SALES (est): 2.89MM **Privately Held**
Web: www.zabin.com
SIC: 2759 Tags: printing, nsk

(P-3117)
ARACA MERCHANDISE LP
Araca Ink
459 Park Ave, San Fernando (91340-2525)
PHONE..................818 743-5400
Judy Courney, *Mgr*
EMP: 97
Web: www.araca.com
SIC: 2759 Screen printing
HQ: Araca Merchandise L.P.
545 W 45th St Fl 10

New York NY 10036

(P-3118)
ARTISAN NAMEPLATE AWARDS CORP
Also Called: Weber Precision Graphics
2730 S Shannon St, Santa Ana
(92704-5232)
PHONE..................714 556-6222
Henry G Weber, *Pr*
Margaret Weber, *
EMP: 33 EST: 1972
SQ FT: 12,160
SALES (est): 4.65MM **Privately Held**
Web: www.weberpg.com
SIC: 2759 3479 Labels and seals: printing,
nsk; Coating of metals with plastic or resins

(P-3119)
ARTISAN SCREEN PRINTING INC
1055 W 5th St, Azusa (91702-3313)
PHONE..................626 815-2700
Vasant N Doabria, *Pr*
Praful Bajaria, *
C P Kheni, *
▲ EMP: 120 EST: 2004
SQ FT: 90,000
SALES (est): 3.52MM **Privately Held**
Web: www.artisanscreen.com
SIC: 2759 Screen printing

(P-3120)
BLACKBURN ALTON INVSTMENTS LLC
Also Called: Foster Print
700 E Alton Ave, Santa Ana (92705-5610)
PHONE..................714 731-2000
EMP: 34 EST: 2011
SALES (est): 1.64MM **Privately Held**
SIC: 2759 Commercial printing, nec

(P-3121)
BLC WC INC (PA)
Also Called: Imperial Marking Systems
13260 Moore St, Cerritos (90703-2228)
PHONE..................562 926-1452
TOLL FREE: 800
Ernest Wong, *Pr*
Donald Ingle, *
Timothy Koontz, *
EMP: 120 EST: 1989
SQ FT: 60,000
SALES (est): 11.19MM
SALES (corp-wide): 11.19MM **Privately Held**
Web: www.resourcelabel.com
SIC: 2759 Labels and seals: printing, nsk

(P-3122)
BRETKERI CORPORATION
Also Called: So Cal Graphics
8316 Clairemont Mesa Blvd Ste 105, San
Diego (92111-1316)
P.O. Box 720386 (92172-0386)
PHONE..................858 292-4919
Bret Catcott, *Pr*
Keri Catcott, *Sec*
EMP: 26 EST: 1982
SQ FT: 4,500
SALES (est): 2.93MM **Privately Held**
Web: www.socalgraphics.com
SIC: 2759 7336 Commercial printing, nec;
Graphic arts and related design

(P-3123)
BRIXEN & SONS INC
2100 S Fairview St, Santa Ana
(92704-4516)

PHONE..................714 566-1444
Martin Corey Brixen, *Pr*
Son Nguyen, *
▲ EMP: 27 EST: 1992
SQ FT: 32,000
SALES (est): 4.71MM **Privately Held**
Web: www.brixen.com
SIC: 2759 3993 Screen printing; Signs and
advertising specialties

(P-3124)
BROOK & WHITTLE LIMITED
Also Called: Label Impressions
1177 N Grove St, Anaheim (92806-2110)
PHONE..................714 634-3466
Remy Zada, *Brnch Mgr*
EMP: 42
Web: www.brookandwhittle.com
SIC: 2759 Labels and seals: printing, nsk
PA: Brook & Whittle Limited
20 Carter Dr

(P-3125)
BROWNTROUT PUBLISHERS INC (PA)
Also Called: Browntrout
201 Continental Blvd Ste 200, El Segundo
(90245-4514)
PHONE..................310 607-9010
William Michael Brown, *CEO*
Gray Peterson, *
Neal Potter, *
▲ EMP: 40 EST: 1993
SQ FT: 11,000
SALES (est): 7.95MM **Privately Held**
Web: www.browntrout.com
SIC: 2759 Calendars: printing, nsk

(P-3126)
C T L PRINTING INDS INC
Also Called: Cal Tape & Label
1741 W Lincoln Ave Ste A, Anaheim
(92801-6716)
PHONE..................714 635-2980
James Edward Hudson, *CEO*
J J Hudson, *
Dave Adams, *
EMP: 25 EST: 1960
SQ FT: 8,950
SALES (est): 1.73MM **Privately Held**
Web: ctlprintingindustries.openfos.com
SIC: 2759 Labels and seals: printing, nsk

(P-3127)
CCL LABEL INC
Pharmaceutical Label Systems
576 College Commerce Way, Upland
(91786-4377)
PHONE..................909 608-2655
Kieorn Delahunt, *Brnch Mgr*
EMP: 95
SQ FT: 43,000
SALES (corp-wide): 4.84B **Privately Held**
Web: www.cclind.com
SIC: 2759 Labels and seals: printing, nsk
HQ: Ccl Label, Inc.
161 Worcester Rd Ste 403
Framingham MA 01701
508 872-4511

(P-3128)
CCL LABEL (DELAWARE) INC
576 College Commerce Way, Upland
(91786-4377)
PHONE..................909 608-2260
Kieron Delahunt, *Mgr*
EMP: 253
SALES (corp-wide): 4.84B **Privately Held**
SIC: 2759 Labels and seals: printing, nsk
HQ: Ccl Label (Delaware), Inc.
15 Controls Dr

▲ = Import ▼ = Export
◆ = Import/Export

Shelton CT 06484
203 926-1253

(P-3129)
COASTAL TAG & LABEL INC
13233 Barton Cir, Whittier (90605-3255)
P.O. Box 3303 (90670-1303)
PHONE.....................562 946-4318
Fred Elhami, *Pr*
Ruth Elhami, *
EMP: 94 **EST:** 1982
SALES (est): 2.91MM **Privately Held**
SIC: 2759 2672 2671 Labels and seals:
printing, nsk; Paper; coated and laminated,
nec; Paper; coated and laminated
packaging
PA: A F E Industries, Inc.
13233 Barton Cir

(P-3130)
COLMOL INC
Also Called: King Graphics
8517 Production Ave, San Diego
(92121-2204)
PHONE.....................858 693-7575
Sean P Mundy, *CEO*
▲ **EMP:** 45 **EST:** 1991
SQ FT: 14,000
SALES (est): 4.77MM **Privately Held**
Web: www.kinggraph.com
SIC: 2759 Screen printing

(P-3131)
CONSOLIDATED GRAPHICS INC
Anderson La
3550 Tyburn St, Los Angeles (90065-1427)
PHONE.....................323 460-4115
Luke Westlake, *Grp VP*
EMP: 111
SALES (corp-wide): 15B **Privately Held**
Web: www.rrd.com
SIC: 2759 2752 Commercial printing, nec;
Offset printing
HQ: Consolidated Graphics, Inc.
5858 Westheimer Rd # 200
Houston TX 77057

(P-3132)
CORPORATE IMPRESSIONS LA INC
Also Called: Dorado Pkg
10742 Burbank Blvd, North Hollywood
(91601-2516)
PHONE.....................818 761-9295
Jennifer L Freund, *Pr*
EMP: 27 **EST:** 1982
SQ FT: 10,000
SALES (est): 2.39MM **Privately Held**
Web: www.impressionsla.com
SIC: 2759 7389 Screen printing; Packaging
and labeling services

(P-3133)
COSMO FIBER CORPORATION (PA)
1802 Santo Domingo Ave, Duarte
(91010-2933)
PHONE.....................626 256-6098
Sidney Ru, *Pr*
Sissy Ru, *Sec*
◆ **EMP:** 25 **EST:** 1990
SQ FT: 4,000
SALES (est): 4.55MM **Privately Held**
Web: www.cosmopromos.com
SIC: 2759 7389 Promotional printing;
Advertising, promotional, and trade show
services

(P-3134)
CR & A CUSTOM APPAREL INC
Also Called: Cr & A Custom
312 W Pico Blvd, Los Angeles
(90015-2437)
PHONE.....................213 749-4440
Masoud Rad, *COO*
Carmen Rad, *Pr*
Dino Maquiddang, *
◆ **EMP:** 30 **EST:** 1993
SQ FT: 26,500
SALES (est): 5.87MM **Privately Held**
Web: www.cracustom.com
SIC: 2759 Posters, including billboards:
printing, nsk

(P-3135)
DEAN HESKETH COMPANY INC
Also Called: Mpressions
2551 W La Palma Ave, Anaheim
(92801-2622)
PHONE.....................714 236-2138
Matthew Hesketh, *Pr*
▲ **EMP:** 35 **EST:** 1956
SQ FT: 6,000
SALES (est): 1.67MM **Privately Held**
Web: www.mpressions.graphics
SIC: 2759 Commercial printing, nec

(P-3136)
DIGITAL ROOM HOLDINGS INC (HQ)
Also Called: New Printing
8000 Haskell Ave, Van Nuys (91406-1321)
PHONE.....................310 575-4440
Michael Turner, *CEO*
Brett Zane, *
▲ **EMP:** 63 **EST:** 2016
SALES (est): 100.86MM **Publicly Held**
Web: www.digitalroominc.com
SIC: 2759 7336 Commercial printing, nec;
Graphic arts and related design
PA: Sycamore Partners Management, L.P.
9 W 57th St Ste 3100

(P-3137)
DM LUXURY LLC
875 Prospect St Ste 300, La Jolla
(92037-4264)
PHONE.....................858 366-9721
EMP: 107
SALES (corp-wide): 46.69MM **Privately Held**
Web: www.modernluxurymedia.com
SIC: 2759 Advertising literature: printing, nsk
PA: Dm Luxury, Llc
3414 Peachtree Rd Ne # 48
404 443-1180

(P-3138)
EXPRESS BUSINESS SYSTEMS INC
Also Called: Express
9155 Trade Pl, San Diego (92126-4377)
P.O. Box 537 (92038-0537)
PHONE.....................858 549-9828
Briggs Keiffer, *Pr*
Maureen O'malley, *Sec*
EMP: 37 **EST:** 1987
SQ FT: 7,000
SALES (est): 6.37MM **Privately Held**
Web: www.expresscorp.com
SIC: 2759 3993 2672 2671 Labels and
seals: printing, nsk; Signs and advertising
specialties; Paper; coated and laminated,
nec; Paper; coated and laminated
packaging

(P-3139)
G-2 GRAPHIC SERVICE INC
5510 Cleon Ave, North Hollywood
(91601-2835)
PHONE.....................818 623-3100
John C Beard, *CEO*
Joe Cotrupe, *
Pamela Beard-cotrupe, *VP*
Scott Dewinkeleer, *
◆ **EMP:** 52 **EST:** 1969
SQ FT: 35,000
SALES (est): 9.55MM **Privately Held**
Web: www.g2online.com
SIC: 2759 7331 Commercial printing, nec;
Direct mail advertising services

(P-3140)
GRAPHIC TRENDS INCORPORATED
7301 Adams St, Paramount (90723-4007)
PHONE.....................562 531-2339
Kieu V Tran, *Prin*
EMP: 40 **EST:** 1983
SQ FT: 20,984
SALES (est): 4.85MM **Privately Held**
Web: www.graphictrends.net
SIC: 2759 7336 Screen printing; Graphic
arts and related design

(P-3141)
GRAPHICS 2000 LLC
1600 E Valencia Dr, Fullerton (92831-4735)
PHONE.....................714 879-1188
EMP: 54
SIC: 2759 2396 Letterpress and screen
printing; Automotive and apparel trimmings

(P-3142)
GREAT WESTERN PACKAGING LLC
8230 Haskell Ave 8240, Van Nuys
(91406-1322)
PHONE.....................818 464-3800
Michael C Warner, *Managing Member*
Victoria Warner Kaplan, *
EMP: 68 **EST:** 1970
SALES (est): 2.37MM **Privately Held**
Web: www.greatwesternpackaging.com
SIC: 2759 Commercial printing, nec

(P-3143)
HEARTLAND LABEL PRINTERS LLC
9817 7th St Ste 703, Rancho Cucamonga
(91730-7802)
PHONE.....................909 243-7151
John Wojcik, *Prin*
EMP: 575
Web: www.hrtlp.com
SIC: 2759 Labels and seals: printing, nsk
HQ: Heartland Label Printers, Llc
1700 Stephen St
Little Chute WI 54140
920 687-4145

(P-3144)
HUDSON PRINTING INC
Also Called: Hudson Printing
2780 Loker Ave W, Carlsbad (92010-6611)
PHONE.....................760 602-1260
James Fairweather, *Pr*
Tom Fairweather, *VP*
Anne Fairweather, *Treas*
EMP: 23 **EST:** 2004
SQ FT: 6,000
SALES (est): 5.41MM **Privately Held**
Web: www.hudsonsd.com
SIC: 2759 2752 Screen printing; Offset
printing

(P-3145)
ID SUPPLY
3183 Red Hill Ave, Costa Mesa
(92626-3401)
PHONE.....................949 287-9200
Brandon Ruddach, *CEO*
Brandon Rudach, *
EMP: 49 **EST:** 2017
SALES (est): 5.2MM **Privately Held**
Web: www.idsupplyco.com
SIC: 2759 Screen printing

(P-3146)
INK FX CORPORATION
513 S La Serena Dr, Covina (91723-3202)
PHONE.....................909 673-1950
Joe Metz, *Pr*
Mike Machrone, *
EMP: 25 **EST:** 1993
SALES (est): 2.35MM **Privately Held**
Web: www.inkfx.com
SIC: 2759 Screen printing

(P-3147)
INTERNTIONAL COLOR POSTERS INC
Also Called: ICP West
8081 Orangethorpe Ave, Buena Park
(90621-3801)
PHONE.....................949 768-1005
Eric Guerineau, *Pr*
▲ **EMP:** 33 **EST:** 1985
SQ FT: 26,000
SALES (est): 1.81MM **Privately Held**
SIC: 2759 Screen printing

(P-3148)
INVESTMENT ENTERPRISES INC (PA)
Also Called: A2z Color Graphics
8230 Haskell Ave Ste 8240, Van Nuys
(91406-1322)
PHONE.....................818 464-3800
Michael Warner, *Pr*
Denise Scanlon, *
Jack Wickson, *
EMP: 43 **EST:** 1970
SALES (est): 2.29MM
SALES (corp-wide): 2.29MM **Privately Held**
SIC: 2759 Magazines: printing, nsk

(P-3149)
IRIS GROUP INC
Also Called: Modern Postcard
1675 Faraday Ave, Carlsbad (92008-7314)
PHONE.....................760 431-1103
Steve Hoffman, *CEO*
EMP: 250 **EST:** 1977
SQ FT: 75,000
SALES (est): 17.97MM **Privately Held**
Web: www.modernpostcard.com
SIC: 2759 5961 Commercial printing, nec;
Mail order house, nec

(P-3150)
KIERAN LABEL CORP
2321 Siempre Viva Ct Ste 101, San Diego
(92154-6301)
PHONE.....................619 449-4457
Denis Vanier, *CEO*
William Walker, *
Bill Walker, *
▲ **EMP:** 44 **EST:** 1979
SALES (est): 1.46MM **Privately Held**
Web: www.kieranlabel.com
SIC: 2759 Commercial printing, nec
PA: I.D. Images Llc
1120 W 130th St

(P-3151)
L A SUPPLY CO
Also Called: Label House
4241 E Brickell St, Ontario (91761-1512)
PHONE.....................949 470-9900
Randolph William Austin, *CEO*
▲ EMP: 31 EST: 1947
SALES (est): 773.81K **Privately Held**
SIC: 2759 2752 2672 2396 Labels and seals: printing, nsk; Commercial printing, lithographic; Paper; coated and laminated, nec; Automotive and apparel trimmings

(P-3152)
LABEL IMPRESSIONS INC
1831 W Sequoia Ave, Orange
(92868-1017)
PHONE.....................714 634-3466
EMP: 42
SIC: 2759 Labels and seals: printing, nsk

(P-3153)
LABELTRONIX LLC (HQ)
Also Called: Rethink Label Systems
2419 E Winston Rd, Anaheim (92806-5544)
PHONE.....................800 429-4321
▲ EMP: 73 EST: 1993
SQ FT: 48,000
SALES (est): 15.75MM
SALES (corp-wide): 94.14MM **Privately Held**
Web: www.awtlabelpack.com
SIC: 2759 Labels and seals: printing, nsk
PA: Advanced Web Technologies, Inc.
600 Hoover St Ne Ste 500
612 706-3700

(P-3154)
LEGION CREATIVE GROUP
500 N Brand Blvd Ste 1800, Glendale
(91203-3305)
PHONE.....................323 498-1100
Kathleen Fliller, *Owner*
EMP: 25 EST: 2015
SALES (est): 6.7MM **Privately Held**
Web: www.legioncreative.us
SIC: 2759 Advertising literature: printing, nsk

(P-3155)
MILLION CORPORATION
Also Called: Able Card Corporation
1300 W Optical Dr Ste 600, Irwindale
(91702-3285)
PHONE.....................626 969-1888
Herman Ho, *CEO*
Hector Dominguez, *
Donny Yu, *
EMP: 70 EST: 1989
SQ FT: 45,000
SALES (est): 7.93MM **Privately Held**
Web: www.ablecard.com
SIC: 2759 Commercial printing, nec
PA: First Nations Capital Partners, Llc
7676 Hazard Center Dr # 5

(P-3156)
NOWDOCS INTERNATIONAL INC
Also Called: Nowdocs
3230 E Imperial Hwy Ste 302, Brea
(92821-6747)
PHONE.....................714 986-1559
EMP: 24
SIC: 2759 Commercial printing, nec

(P-3157)
OPTEC LASER SYSTEMS LLC
11622 El Camino Real Ste 100, San Diego
(92130-2051)
PHONE.....................858 220-1070
EMP: 25 EST: 2017
SALES (est): 900.51K **Privately Held**
Web: www.optec-laser-systems.com
SIC: 2759 Laser printing

(P-3158)
ORANGE CIRCLE STUDIO CORP (PA)
Also Called: Studio OH
2 Technology Dr, Irvine (92618-5317)
PHONE.....................949 727-0800
Kelly Carioti, *CEO*
Daniel H Whang, *Sec*
Scott Whang, *Ch*
◆ EMP: 77 EST: 2009
SALES (est): 38.5MM
SALES (corp-wide): 38.5MM **Privately Held**
Web: www.studiooh.com
SIC: 2759 5112 5199 2086 Calendars: printing, nsk; Social stationery and greeting cards; Candles; Bottled and canned soft drinks

(P-3159)
ORBITEL INTERNATIONAL LLC
Also Called: Weddingolala
15304 Valley Blvd, City Of Industry
(91746-3324)
PHONE.....................626 369-7050
▲ EMP: 25 EST: 2008
SALES (est): 243.22K **Privately Held**
SIC: 2759 5199 Invitations: printing, nsk; Party favors, balloons, hats, etc.

(P-3160)
ORORA VISUAL LLC
1600 E Valencia Dr, Fullerton (92831-4735)
PHONE.....................714 879-2400
James R Hamel, *Pr*
▲ EMP: 100 EST: 1987
SALES (est): 10.03MM **Privately Held**
Web: www.ororagroup.com
SIC: 2759 Screen printing

(P-3161)
PRIMARY COLOR SYSTEMS CORP (PA)
11130 Holder St Ste 210, Cypress
(90630-5162)
PHONE.....................949 660-7080
Daniel Hirt, *CEO*
Michael Hirt, *
▲ EMP: 305 EST: 1984
SQ FT: 40,000
SALES (est): 47.93MM
SALES (corp-wide): 47.93MM **Privately Held**
Web: www.primarycolor.com
SIC: 2759 2752 Commercial printing, nec; Offset printing

(P-3162)
PRIMARY COLOR SYSTEMS CORP
401 Coral Cir, El Segundo (90245-4622)
PHONE.....................310 841-0250
Ed Philipps, *Brnch Mgr*
EMP: 53
SALES (corp-wide): 47.93MM **Privately Held**
Web: www.primarycolor.com
SIC: 2759 2752 Commercial printing, nec; Commercial printing, lithographic
PA: Primary Color Systems Corporation
11130 Holder St Ste 210
949 660-7080

(P-3163)
PROGRAPHICS SCREENPRINTING INC
1975 Diamond St, San Marcos
(92078-5122)
PHONE.....................760 744-4555
Bruce Heid, *Pr*
Barbara Heid, *
EMP: 41 EST: 1989
SQ FT: 18,000
SALES (est): 2.68MM **Privately Held**
Web: www.prografx.com
SIC: 2759 3993 2396 5112 Screen printing; Signs and advertising specialties; Automotive and apparel trimmings; Pens and/or pencils

(P-3164)
PROGROUP
Also Called: Pro Group
17622 Armstrong Ave, Irvine (92614-5728)
PHONE.....................949 748-5400
Cindy Kennedy, *Pr*
Thomas Brian Kennedy, *
EMP: 25 EST: 2008
SALES (est): 10.34MM **Privately Held**
Web: professionalreprographic.mfgpages.com
SIC: 2759 Commercial printing, nec

(P-3165)
PROGRSSIVE INTGRATED SOLUTIONS
Also Called: Progressive Manufacturing
3291 E Miraloma Ave, Anaheim
(92806-1910)
PHONE.....................714 237-0980
Rodney Dean Boehme, *Pr*
EMP: 76 EST: 1988
SALES (est): 2.35MM **Privately Held**
Web: www.progressiveusa.com
SIC: 2759 2752 Envelopes: printing, nsk; Offset printing

(P-3166)
R R DONNELLEY & SONS COMPANY
Also Called: R R Donnelley
955 Gateway Center Way, San Diego
(92102-4542)
PHONE.....................619 527-4600
Boyd Richardson, *Brnch Mgr*
EMP: 39
SALES (corp-wide): 15B **Privately Held**
Web: www.rrd.com
SIC: 2759 Commercial printing, nec
HQ: R. R. Donnelley & Sons Company
35 W Wacker Dr
Chicago IL 60601
312 326-8000

(P-3167)
R R DONNELLEY & SONS COMPANY
Los Angeles Manufacturing Div
19681 Pacific Gateway Dr, Torrance
(90502-1164)
PHONE.....................310 516-3100
Barbara Dowell, *Dir*
EMP: 70
SQ FT: 80,000
SALES (corp-wide): 15B **Privately Held**
Web: www.rrd.com
SIC: 2759 2752 Publication printing; Commercial printing, lithographic
HQ: R. R. Donnelley & Sons Company
35 W Wacker Dr
Chicago IL 60601
312 326-8000

(P-3168)
RESOURCE LABEL GROUP LLC
1511 E Edinger Ave, Santa Ana
(92705-4907)
PHONE.....................714 619-7100
Robert Simko, *Mgr*
EMP: 80
Web: www.resourcelabel.com
SIC: 2759 2752 Commercial printing, nec; Commercial printing, lithographic
PA: Resource Label Group, Llc
2550 Mridian Blvd Ste 370

(P-3169)
RESPONSE ENVELOPE INC (PA)
1340 S Baker Ave, Ontario (91761-7742)
PHONE.....................909 923-5855
Jonas Ulrich, *CEO*
Philip Ulrich, *
▲ EMP: 104 EST: 1986
SQ FT: 85,000
SALES (est): 1.9MM
SALES (corp-wide): 1.9MM **Privately Held**
Web: www.marketing.com
SIC: 2759 2677 Envelopes: printing, nsk; Envelopes

(P-3170)
RETAIL PRINT MEDIA INC
Also Called: RPM Media
2355 Crenshaw Blvd Ste 135, Torrance
(90501-3341)
PHONE.....................424 488-6950
Raymond Young, *CEO*
Karli Sikich, *
EMP: 35 EST: 2015
SALES (est): 2.02MM **Privately Held**
Web: www.retailprintmedia.com
SIC: 2759 7371 Advertising literature: printing, nsk; Computer software writing services

(P-3171)
RJ ACQUISITION CORP (PA)
Also Called: Ad Art Company
3260 E 26th St, Los Angeles (90058-8008)
PHONE.....................323 318-1107
Joe M Demarco, *Pr*
Roger Keech, *
Eddie Leon, *Prin*
Jose Puentes Plant, *Prin*
▲ EMP: 215 EST: 1944
SQ FT: 200,000
SALES (est): 28.7MM
SALES (corp-wide): 28.7MM **Privately Held**
Web: www.adartco.com
SIC: 2759 Screen printing

(P-3172)
ROBINSON PRINTING INC
Also Called: Robinson Printing
42685 Rio Nedo, Temecula (92590-3711)
PHONE.....................951 296-0300
David Robinson, *CEO*
Mike Robinson, *
▲ EMP: 38 EST: 1981
SQ FT: 24,000
SALES (est): 2.78MM **Privately Held**
Web: www.robinsonprinting.com
SIC: 2759 2621 Screen printing; Packaging paper

(P-3173)
SAFE PUBLISHING COMPANY
400 Del Norte Blvd, Oxnard (93030-7997)
PHONE.....................805 973-1300
John Gooden, *Pr*
EMP: 70 EST: 1976
SQ FT: 96,000

SALES (est): 1.39MM **Privately Held**
SIC: **2759** 8748 8742 8741 Promotional printing; Business consulting, nec; Management consulting services; Management services

(P-3174)
SAN BRNRDINO CMNTY COLLEGE DST
Also Called: Print Shop
701 S Mount Vernon Ave, San Bernardino (92410-2798)
PHONE..............................909 888-6511
Louie Chavira, *Supervisor*
EMP: 85
SALES (corp-wide): 46.53MM **Privately Held**
Web: www.sbccd.edu
SIC: **2759** Commercial printing, nec
PA: San Bernardino Community College District
550 E Hsptlity Ln Ste 200
909 382-4000

(P-3175)
SHORETT PRINTING INC (PA)
Also Called: Crown Printers
250 W Rialto Ave, San Bernardino (92408-1017)
PHONE..............................714 545-4689
Charles D Shorett Junior, *CEO*
John Shorett, *
EMP: 30 EST: 1970
SALES (est): 6.4MM
SALES (corp-wide): 6.4MM **Privately Held**
Web: www.crownconnect.com
SIC: **2759** 2752 Commercial printing, nec; Offset printing

(P-3176)
SUPACOLOR USA INC
Also Called: Supacolor
12705 Daphne Ave, Hawthorne (90250-3311)
PHONE..............................844 973-2862
Ramneek Walia, *CEO*
EMP: 91 EST: 2019
SALES (est): 9.9MM **Privately Held**
Web: www.supacolor.com
SIC: **2759** Letterpress and screen printing

(P-3177)
SUPER COLOR DIGITAL LLC (PA)
Also Called: Super Color Digital
16761 Hale Ave, Irvine (92606-5006)
PHONE..............................949 622-0010
Peyman Rashtchi, *Managing Member*
▲ EMP: 25 EST: 2006
SQ FT: 48,043
SALES (est): 43.33MM **Privately Held**
Web: www.supercolor.com
SIC: **2759** Commercial printing, nec

(P-3178)
SUPERIOR PRINTING INC
Also Called: Superior Press
9440 Norwalk Blvd, Santa Fe Springs (90670-2928)
PHONE..............................888 590-7998
Robert Traut, *Pr*
Kevin Traut, *
Jason Traut, *
EMP: 95 EST: 1953
SQ FT: 32,000
SALES (est): 20.15MM **Privately Held**
Web: www.superiorpress.com
SIC: **2759** 5112 Commercial printing, nec; Business forms

(P-3179)
TARGET MDIA PRTNERS INTRCTIVE (HQ)
Also Called: Target Mdia Prtners Intractive
5200 Lankershim Blvd Ste 350, North Hollywood (91601-3100)
PHONE..............................323 930-3123
Dave Duckwitz, *CEO*
EMP: 35 EST: 1998
SALES (est): 7.31MM
SALES (corp-wide): 24.96MM **Privately Held**
Web: www.targetmediapartners.com
SIC: **2759** 7331 Commercial printing, nec; Direct mail advertising services
PA: Responselogix, Inc.
6900 E Camelback Rd
888 713-8958

(P-3180)
TAYLOR DIGITAL
101 W Avenida Vista Hermosa Ste 122, San Clemente (92672-7707)
PHONE..............................949 391-3333
EMP: 24 EST: 2019
SALES (est): 1.21MM **Privately Held**
SIC: **2759** Commercial printing, nec

(P-3181)
TAYLOR GRAPHICS INC
1582 Browning, Irvine (92606-4807)
PHONE..............................949 752-5200
Dean S Taylor, *CEO*
Carla Spicer, *
EMP: 23 EST: 1950
SQ FT: 7,500
SALES (est): 2.86MM **Privately Held**
SIC: **2759** Screen printing

(P-3182)
TEC COLOR CRAFT (PA)
Also Called: TEC Color Craft Products
1860 Wright Ave, La Verne (91750-5824)
PHONE..............................909 392-9000
Edgar A Frenkiel, *CEO*
▲ EMP: 40 EST: 1960
SQ FT: 8,000
SALES (est): 5.39MM
SALES (corp-wide): 5.39MM **Privately Held**
Web: www.teccolorcraft.com
SIC: **2759** Screen printing

(P-3183)
TEE STYLED INC
4640 E La Palma Ave, Anaheim (92807-1910)
PHONE..............................323 983-9988
Anwar Gajiani, *Pr*
EMP: 41 EST: 2019
SALES (est): 1.05MM **Privately Held**
Web: www.teestyled.com
SIC: **2759** Screen printing
PA: Fantasy Activewear, Inc.
5383 Alcoa Ave

(P-3184)
THE/STUDIO
360 E 2nd St Ste 800, Los Angeles (90012-4607)
PHONE..............................213 233-1633
EMP: 29 EST: 2018
SALES (est): 1.63MM **Privately Held**
Web: www.thestudio.com
SIC: **2759** Screen printing

(P-3185)
VITACHROME GRAPHICS GROUP INC
Also Called: Vitachrome Graphics
3710 Park Pl, Montrose (91020-1623)
P.O. Box 2924 (90670-0924)
PHONE..............................818 957-0900
Gary Durbin, *Pr*
Tony Won, *
EMP: 45 EST: 1971
SQ FT: 43,000
SALES (est): 1.29MM **Privately Held**
Web: www.adahotelsigns.com
SIC: **2759** Decals: printing, nsk

(P-3186)
VOMAR PRODUCTS INC
Also Called: Vomar
7800 Deering Ave, Canoga Park (91304-5005)
PHONE..............................818 610-5115
Paul Van Ostrand, *CEO*
Herbert Paul Van Ostrand, *
Jason Van Ostrand, *
EMP: 38 EST: 1961
SQ FT: 29,000
SALES (est): 6MM **Privately Held**
Web: www.vomarproducts.com
SIC: **2759** 3993 Commercial printing, nec; Name plates: except engraved, etched, etc.: metal

(P-3187)
WES GO INC
Also Called: GP Color Imaging Group
8211 Lankershim Blvd, North Hollywood (91605-1614)
PHONE..............................818 504-1200
Wesley Adams, *CEO*
Thomas Wilhelm, *
▲ EMP: 24 EST: 2001
SALES (est): 4.45MM **Privately Held**
Web: www.gpcolor.com
SIC: **2759** Posters, including billboards: printing, nsk

(P-3188)
WESTERN STATES ENVELOPE CORP
2301 Raymer Ave, Fullerton (92833-2514)
P.O. Box 2607 (92837)
PHONE..............................714 449-0909
Lisa Hoehle, *Pr*
EMP: 60 EST: 1968
SQ FT: 24,000
SALES (est): 1.09MM **Privately Held**
Web: www.wseca.com
SIC: **2759** Commercial printing, nec

(P-3189)
WILSONS ART STUDIO INC
Also Called: Solutions Unlimited
501 S Acacia Ave, Fullerton (92831-5101)
PHONE..............................714 870-7030
William L Goetsch, *Pr*
N Jim Goetsch, *
Roberta C Goetsch, *
EMP: 63 EST: 1958
SQ FT: 50,000
SALES (est): 4.49MM **Privately Held**
Web: www.solutions-unlimited.net
SIC: **2759** 2396 Screen printing; Automotive and apparel trimmings

---

2761 Manifold Business Forms

(P-3190)
APPERSON INC (PA)
17315 Studebaker Rd Ste 211, Cerritos (90703-2508)
P.O. Box 480309 (28269-5338)
PHONE..............................562 356-3333
Kelly Doherty, *CEO*
Brian Apperson, *
William Apperson, *
▲ EMP: 70 EST: 1955
SQ FT: 80,080
SALES (est): 9.86MM
SALES (corp-wide): 9.86MM **Privately Held**
Web: www.apperson.com
SIC: **2761** Continuous forms, office and business

(P-3191)
BESTFORMS INC
1135 Avenida Acaso, Camarillo (93012-8740)
PHONE..............................805 388-0503
Joe Valdez, *Pr*
Patrick Valdez, *
EMP: 48 EST: 1985
SQ FT: 31,000
SALES (est): 3.78MM **Privately Held**
Web: www.bestforms.com
SIC: **2761** Manifold business forms

(P-3192)
COMPLYRIGHT DIST SVCS INC
3451 Jupiter Ct, Oxnard (93030-8957)
PHONE..............................805 981-0992
Richard Roddis, *CEO*
EMP: 44 EST: 2006
SALES (est): 10.92MM
SALES (corp-wide): 3.81B **Privately Held**
Web: www.complyrightdealer.com
SIC: **2761** Manifold business forms
PA: Taylor Corporation
1725 Roe Crest Dr
507 625-2828

(P-3193)
NBS SYSTEMS INC (PA)
2477 E Orangethorpe Ave, Fullerton (92831-5303)
PHONE..............................217 999-3472
Bill Gascon, *Pr*
EMP: 35 EST: 1963
SALES (est): 2.1MM
SALES (corp-wide): 2.1MM **Privately Held**
Web: www.nbschecks.com
SIC: **2761** 2759 Continuous forms, office and business; Commercial printing, nec

(P-3194)
PRINTEGRA CORP
23281 La Palma Ave, Yorba Linda (92887-4768)
PHONE..............................714 602-2221
Terri Reynolds, *Mgr*
EMP: 65
SQ FT: 38,000
SALES (corp-wide): 420.11MM **Publicly Held**
Web: www.printegra.com
SIC: **2761** 2782 Continuous forms, office and business; Blankbooks and looseleaf binders
HQ: Printegra Corp
1560 Westfork Dr
Lithia Springs GA 30122
770 319-9500

(P-3195)
TST/IMPRESO INC
10589 Business Dr, Fontana (92337-8223)
PHONE..............................909 357-7190
▲ EMP: 42
SALES (corp-wide): 45.42MM **Privately Held**
Web: www.tstimpreso.com

SIC: 2761 Manifold business forms
HQ: Tst/Impreso, Inc.
652 Southwestern Blvd
Coppell TX 75019
972 462-0100

(P-3196)
WRIGHT BUSINESS GRAPHICS LLC
Also Called: Wright Business Graphics Calif
13602 12th St Ste A, Chino (91710-5200)
P.O. Box 20489 (97294-0489)
PHONE..................................909 614-6700
Gene Snitker, *Prin*
EMP: 28
SALES (corp-wide): 420.11MM **Publicly Held**
Web: www.wrightbg.com
SIC: 2761 Manifold business forms
HQ: Wright Business Graphics Llc
18440 Ne San Rafael St
Portland OR 97230
800 547-8397

2782 Blankbooks And Looseleaf Binders

(P-3197)
CHECKWORKS INC
315 Cloverleaf Dr Ste J, Baldwin Park
(91706-6510)
P.O. Box 60065 (91716-0065)
PHONE..................................626 333-1444
Aloysius J Uniack, *Pr*
Aloysius J Uniack, *
Christen Mc Kiernan, *
EMP: 55 EST: 1995
SQ FT: 15,000
SALES (est): 4.52MM **Privately Held**
Web: www.checkworks.com
SIC: 2782 Checkbooks

(P-3198)
CONTINENTAL BDR SPECIALTY CORP (PA)
407 W Compton Blvd, Gardena
(90248-1703)
PHONE..................................310 324-8227
Andrew Lisardi, *CEO*
Jack Gray, *
▼ EMP: 120 EST: 1978
SQ FT: 31,000
SALES (est): 4.41MM
SALES (corp-wide): 4.41MM **Privately Held**
Web: www.continentalbinder.com
SIC: 2782 2759 2675 2396 Looseleaf binders and devices; Commercial printing, nec; Die-cut paper and board; Automotive and apparel trimmings

(P-3199)
HANOVER ACCESSORIES CORP
6049 E Slauson Ave, Commerce
(90040-3007)
▲ EMP: 120
SIC: 2782 Library binders, looseleaf

(P-3200)
PIONEER PHOTO ALBUMS INC (PA)
9801 Deering Ave, Chatsworth
(91311-4398)
P.O. Box 2497 (91313-2497)
PHONE..................................818 882-2161
Shell Plutsky, *CEO*
Jason Reubens, *
Rick Collies, *

◆ EMP: 150 EST: 1972
SQ FT: 100,000
SALES (est): 16.64MM
SALES (corp-wide): 16.64MM **Privately Held**
Web: www.pioneerphotoalbums.com
SIC: 2782 Albums

2789 Bookbinding And Related Work

(P-3201)
B J BINDERY INC
833 S Grand Ave, Santa Ana (92705-4117)
PHONE..................................714 835-7342
Naresh Arya, *CEO*
Renu Arya, *
▲ EMP: 80 EST: 1970
SQ FT: 29,000
SALES (est): 4.34MM **Privately Held**
Web: www.bjbindery.com
SIC: 2789 Binding only: books, pamphlets, magazines, etc.

(P-3202)
KATER-CRAFTS INCORPORATED
Also Called: Book Binders
3205 Weldon Ave, Los Angeles
(90065-2312)
PHONE..................................562 692-0665
Bruce Kavin, *Pr*
Richard Kavin, *
EMP: 40 EST: 1948
SALES (est): 1.32MM **Privately Held**
Web: www.katercrafts.com
SIC: 2789 Binding only: books, pamphlets, magazines, etc.

(P-3203)
ROSS BINDERY INC
15310 Spring Ave, Santa Fe Springs
(90670-5644)
PHONE..................................562 623-4565
George Jackson, *CEO*
▲ EMP: 120 EST: 1969
SQ FT: 65,000
SALES (est): 7.97MM **Privately Held**
Web: www.rossbindery.com
SIC: 2789 Pamphlets, binding

2791 Typesetting

(P-3204)
CASTLE PRESS
1128 N Gilbert St, Anaheim (92801-1401)
PHONE..................................800 794-0858
Jay Bautista, *Mgr*
EMP: 23 EST: 2016
SALES (est): 1.27MM **Privately Held**
Web: www.castlepress.com
SIC: 2791 Typesetting

(P-3205)
DT123 (PA)
13035 Hartsook St, Sherman Oaks
(91423-1616)
PHONE..................................213 488-1230
David Richard Tobman, *CEO*
Ann Tobman, *
EMP: 37 EST: 1949
SALES (est): 4.88MM
SALES (corp-wide): 4.88MM **Privately Held**
Web: www.automation-123.com
SIC: 2791 2796 2759 2732 Typesetting; Platemaking services; Commercial printing, nec; Book printing

2796 Platemaking Services

(P-3206)
FLEXLINE INCORPORATED
3727 S Meyler St, San Pedro (90731-6431)
PHONE..................................562 921-4141
John Bateman, *Pr*
William Hall, *
EMP: 28 EST: 1991
SALES (est): 654.1K **Privately Held**
SIC: 2796 2759 3555 Platemaking services; Commercial printing, nec; Printing plates

2812 Alkalies And Chlorine

(P-3207)
ARKEMA INC
Also Called: Arkema Coating Resins
19206 Hawthorne Blvd, Torrance
(90503-1505)
PHONE..................................310 214-5327
EMP: 43
SALES (corp-wide): 134.78MM **Privately Held**
Web: www.arkema.com
SIC: 2812 2819 2869 2899 Chlorine, compressed or liquefied; Industrial inorganic chemicals, nec; Industrial organic chemicals, nec; Metal treating compounds
HQ: Arkema Inc.
900 1st Ave
King Of Prussia PA 19406
610 205-7000

(P-3208)
HASA INC (PA)
23119 Drayton St, Saugus (91350-2599)
P.O. Box 761 (90213)
PHONE..................................661 259-5848
EMP: 95 EST: 1964
SALES (est): 149.04MM
SALES (corp-wide): 149.04MM **Privately Held**
Web: www.hasa.com
SIC: 2812 Chlorine, compressed or liquefied

(P-3209)
OLIN CHLOR ALKALI LOGISTICS
Also Called: Chlor Alkali Products & Vinyls
11600 Pike St, Santa Fe Springs
(90670-2938)
PHONE..................................562 692-0510
John Bilac, *Brnch Mgr*
EMP: 94
SALES (corp-wide): 6.83B **Publicly Held**
Web: www.olinchloralkali.com
SIC: 2812 Alkalies and chlorine
HQ: Olin Chlor Alkali Logistics Inc
490 Stuart Rd Ne
Cleveland TN 37312
423 336-4850

2813 Industrial Gases

(P-3210)
AIR LIQUID HEALTHCARE
12460 Arrow Rte, Rancho Cucamonga
(91739-9682)
PHONE..................................909 899-4633
Gerald Berger, *Prin*
EMP: 28 EST: 2004
SALES (est): 2.61MM **Privately Held**
SIC: 2813 8099 Oxygen, compressed or liquefied; Health and allied services, nec

(P-3211)
AIR LIQUIDE ELECTRONICS US LP
1502 W Anaheim St, Wilmington
(90744-2303)
PHONE..................................310 549-7079
EMP: 3930
SALES (corp-wide): 114.13MM **Privately Held**
Web: www.airliquide.com
SIC: 2813 3564 8631 2819 Industrial gases; Blowers and fans; Labor organizations; Industrial inorganic chemicals, nec
HQ: Air Liquide Electronics U.S. Lp
9101 Lyndon B Jhnson Fwy
Dallas TX 75243
972 301-5200

(P-3212)
AIR PRODUCTS AND CHEMICALS INC
Air Products
1969 Palomar Oaks Way, Carlsbad
(92011-1307)
PHONE..................................760 931-9555
EMP: 85
SALES (corp-wide): 12.1B **Publicly Held**
Web: www.airproducts.com
SIC: 2813 3625 2899 2865 Industrial gases; Relays and industrial controls; Chemical preparations, nec; Cyclic crudes and intermediates
PA: Air Products And Chemicals, Inc.
1940 Air Products Blvd
610 481-4911

(P-3213)
AIRGAS INC
Also Called: Airgas
3737 Worsham Ave, Long Beach
(90808-1774)
P.O. Box 93500 (90809-3500)
PHONE..................................510 429-4216
EMP: 43
SALES (corp-wide): 114.13MM **Privately Held**
Web: www.airgas.com
SIC: 2813 Industrial gases
HQ: Airgas, Inc.
259 N Rdnor Chster Rd Ste
Radnor PA 19087
610 687-5253

(P-3214)
AIRGAS USA LLC
8832 Dice Rd, Santa Fe Springs
(90670-2516)
PHONE..................................562 945-1383
Rafael Motta, *Brnch Mgr*
EMP: 45
SQ FT: 29,887
SALES (corp-wide): 114.13MM **Privately Held**
Web: www.airgas.com
SIC: 2813 5084 Industrial gases; Industrial machinery and equipment
HQ: Airgas Usa, Llc
259 N Rdnor Chster Rd Ste
Radnor PA 19087
216 642-6600

(P-3215)
AIRGAS USA LLC
9756 Santa Fe Springs Rd, Santa Fe
Springs (90670-2920)
PHONE..................................562 906-8700
Cynthia Aragundi, *Mgr*
EMP: 23
SALES (corp-wide): 114.13MM **Privately Held**

Web: www.airgas.com
SIC: 2813 5169 Industrial gases; Oxygen
HQ: Airgas Usa, Llc
  259 N Rdnor Chster Rd Ste
  Radnor PA 19087
  216 642-6600

(P-3216)
LINDE INC
Praxair
5705 E Airport Dr, Ontario (91761-8611)
PHONE..................................909 390-0283
M M Stenberg, *Brnch Mgr*
EMP: 33
Web: www.lindeus.com
SIC: 2813 Industrial gases
HQ: Linde Inc.
  10 Riverview Dr
  Danbury CT 06810
  203 837-2000

(P-3217)
MESSER LLC
660 Baldwin Park Blvd, City Of Industry
(91746-1501)
PHONE..................................626 855-8366
Mike Colvin, *Brnch Mgr*
EMP: 35
SALES (corp-wide): 2.29B **Privately Held**
Web: www.messeramericas.com
SIC: 2813 Nitrogen
HQ: Messer Llc
  200 Smrst Corp Blvd # 7000
  Bridgewater NJ 08807
  800 755-9277

(P-3218)
MESSER LLC
Also Called: Cryostar USA
13117 Meyer Rd, Whittier (90605-3555)
PHONE..................................562 903-1290
Mark Sutton, *Brnch Mgr*
EMP: 45
SALES (corp-wide): 2.29B **Privately Held**
Web: www.messeramericas.com
SIC: 2813 3561 Oxygen, compressed or
  liquefied; Pumps and pumping equipment
HQ: Messer Llc
  200 Smrst Corp Blvd # 7000
  Bridgewater NJ 08807
  800 755-9277

(P-3219)
MESSER LLC
2535 Del Amo Blvd, Torrance (90503-1706)
PHONE..................................310 533-8394
Jason Lacasella, *Brnch Mgr*
EMP: 100
SALES (corp-wide): 2.29B **Privately Held**
Web: www.messeramericas.com
SIC: 2813 Carbon dioxide
HQ: Messer Llc
  200 Smrst Corp Blvd # 7000
  Bridgewater NJ 08807
  800 755-9277

(P-3220)
NEON ROSE INC
Also Called: Neon Rose
5158 Bristol Rd, San Diego (92116-2130)
PHONE..................................619 218-6103
Erin Cutler, *Prin*
EMP: 26 EST: 2018
SALES (est): 286.52K **Privately Held**
Web: www.neonroseagency.com
SIC: 2813 Neon

(P-3221)
PLZ CORP
840 Tourmaline Dr, Newbury Park
(91320-1205)

PHONE..................................805 498-4531
James Seastrom, *Brnch Mgr*
EMP: 43
SALES (corp-wide): 766.3MM **Privately Held**
Web: www.plzcorp.com
SIC: 2813 Aerosols
PA: Plz Corp.
  2651 Wrrnville Rd Ste 300
  630 628-3000

2816 Inorganic Pigments

(P-3222)
OXERRA AMERICAS LLC
Davis Colors
3700 E Olympic Blvd, Los Angeles
(90023-3123)
P.O. Box 23100 (90023-0100)
PHONE..................................323 269-7311
Nick Paris, *VP*
EMP: 70
SQ FT: 540,000
Web: americas.oxerra.com
SIC: 2816 2865 Inorganic pigments; Cyclic
  crudes and intermediates
HQ: Oxerra Americas, Llc
  10001 Wdloch Frest Dr Ste
  The Woodlands TX 77380
  281 465-6700

(P-3223)
RYVEC INC
251 E Palais Rd, Anaheim (92805-6239)
PHONE..................................714 520-5592
Michael Ryan, *CEO*
Aristeo Figueroa, *CFO*
◆ EMP: 23 EST: 1982
SQ FT: 43,000
SALES (est): 1.56MM **Privately Held**
Web: www.ryvec.com
SIC: 2816 2865 2821 Color pigments; Dyes
  and pigments; Polyurethane resins

(P-3224)
SOLOMON COLORS INC
1371 Laurel Ave, Rialto (92376-3011)
PHONE..................................909 873-9444
Jeff Bowers, *Brnch Mgr*
EMP: 31
SQ FT: 80,000
SALES (corp-wide): 74.83MM **Privately Held**
Web: www.solomoncolors.com
SIC: 2816 Inorganic pigments
PA: Solomon Colors, Inc.
  4050 Color Plant Rd
  217 522-3112

(P-3225)
SPECTRA COLOR INC
9116 Stellar Ct, Corona (92883-4923)
P.O. Box 79527 (92877-0184)
PHONE..................................951 277-0200
Robert Shedd, *Pr*
John Shedd, *
▲ EMP: 42 EST: 1976
SQ FT: 40,000
SALES (est): 8.91MM **Privately Held**
Web: www.spectracolor.com
SIC: 2816 3089 2821 Color pigments;
  Coloring and finishing of plastics products;
  Plastics materials and resins

2819 Industrial Inorganic Chemicals, Nec

(P-3226)
ADVANCED CHEMICAL TECHNOLOGY
Also Called: Advanced Chemical Technology
3540 E 26th St, Vernon (90058-4103)
PHONE..................................800 527-9607
Daniel Anthony Earley, *CEO*
EMP: 40 EST: 1996
SALES (est): 2.69MM **Privately Held**
Web: www.actglobal.net
SIC: 2819 2899 5169 Industrial inorganic
  chemicals, nec; Antiscaling compounds,
  boiler; Anti-corrosion products

(P-3227)
AMBER CHEMICAL INC
5201 Boylan St, Bakersfield (93308-4567)
PHONE..................................661 325-2072
▲ EMP: 24 EST: 1983
SALES (est): 8.27MM **Privately Held**
Web: www.amberchem.com
SIC: 2819 5169 Industrial inorganic
  chemicals, nec; Industrial chemicals

(P-3228)
CALIFORNIA SILICA PRODUCTS LLC
12808 Rancho Rd, Adelanto (92301-2719)
PHONE..................................909 947-0028
Randall Humphreys, *Brnch Mgr*
EMP: 84
SALES (corp-wide): 813.38K **Privately Held**
Web: www.calsilica.net
SIC: 2819 Silica compounds
PA: California Silica Products, Llc
  1420 S Bon View Ave
  760 885-5358

(P-3229)
CALIFORNIA SULPHUR COMPANY
2250 E Pacific Coast Hwy, Wilmington
(90744-2917)
P.O. Box 176 (90748-0176)
PHONE..................................562 437-0768
John Babbitt, *Prin*
▼ EMP: 28 EST: 1958
SQ FT: 900
SALES (est): 6.8MM **Privately Held**
Web:
www.california-sulphur-company.com
SIC: 2810 Industrial inorganic chemicals, nec

(P-3230)
CAR SOUND EXHAUST SYSTEM INC
Environmental Catalyst Tech
1901 Corporate Centre Dr, Oceanside
(92056-5831)
PHONE..................................949 888-1625
EMP: 165
SALES (corp-wide): 89.19MM **Privately Held**
Web: www.magnaflow.com
SIC: 2819 Catalysts, chemical
PA: Car Sound Exhaust System, Inc.
  1901 Corporate Centre
  949 858-5900

(P-3231)
CARBOMER INC
6324 Ferris Sq Ste B, San Diego
(92121-3238)

P.O. Box 261026 (92196-1026)
PHONE..................................858 552-0992
Manssur Yalpani, *Pr*
EMP: 85 EST: 1995
SALES (est): 4.45MM **Privately Held**
Web: www.carbomer.com
SIC: 2819 Industrial inorganic chemicals, nec

(P-3232)
CARBON ACTIVATED CORPORATION (PA)
2250 S Central Ave, Compton
(90220-5311)
PHONE..................................310 885-4555
◆ EMP: 50 EST: 1993
SALES (est): 28.6MM **Privately Held**
Web: www.activatedcarbon.com
SIC: 2819 5074 Charcoal (carbon), activated
  ; Water purification equipment

(P-3233)
CDTI ADVANCED MATERIALS INC (PA)
Also Called: Cdti
1641 Fiske Pl, Oxnard (93033-1862)
PHONE..................................805 639-9458
Matthew Beale, *Pr*
Lon E Bell, *
Peter J Chase, *
Tracy A Kern, *Corporate Secretary**
Stephen J Golden, *
EMP: 47 EST: 1994
SALES (est): 22.85MM **Privately Held**
Web: www.cdti.com
SIC: 2819 3823 Catalysts, chemical;
  Process control instruments

(P-3234)
CHAMPIONX LLC
Also Called: Nalco Champion
6321 District Blvd, Bakersfield
(93313-2143)
PHONE..................................661 834-0454
Tom Pappas, *Mgr*
EMP: 30
SQ FT: 5,000
SALES (corp-wide): 3.76B **Publicly Held**
Web: www.championx.com
SIC: 2819 7349 Industrial inorganic
  chemicals, nec; Chemical cleaning services
HQ: Championx Llc
  2445 Tech Frest Blvd Bldg
  The Woodlands TX 77381
  281 632-6500

(P-3235)
ECO SERVICES OPERATIONS CORP
20720 S Wilmington Ave, Long Beach
(90810-1034)
PHONE..................................310 885-6719
Stephen Caro, *Brnch Mgr*
EMP: 51
SALES (corp-wide): 691.12MM **Publicly Held**
Web: www.pqcorp.com
SIC: 2819 Sulfuric acid, oleum
HQ: Eco Services Operations Corp.
  300 Lindenwood Dr
  Malvern PA 19355
  610 251-9118

(P-3236)
ELEMENTIS SPECIALTIES INC
31763 Mountain View Rd, Newberry Springs
(92365-9763)
PHONE..................................760 257-9112
Mike Mcgath, *Mgr*
EMP: 80

SALES (corp-wide): 713.4MM **Privately Held**
Web: www.elementis.com
SIC: 2819 Industrial inorganic chemicals, nec
HQ: Elementis Specialties, Inc.
469 Old Trenton Rd
East Windsor NJ 08512

(P-3237)
ENERGY SOLUTIONS (US) LLC
Also Called: Marchem Solvay Group
20851 S Santa Fe Ave, Long Beach
(90810-1130)
PHONE.................310 669-5300
Maria Johnson, *Mgr*
EMP: 352
SALES (corp-wide): 8.01MM **Privately Held**
Web: www.solvay.com
SIC: 2819 Industrial inorganic chemicals, nec
HQ: Solvay Usa Llc
504 Carnegie Ctr
Princeton NJ 08540
609 860-4000

(P-3238)
HELLS KITCHEN GEOTHERMAL LLC
124 W 9th St Ste 101, Imperial
(92251-1383)
PHONE.................760 604-0433
Rodney Grahame Colwell, *CEO*
James Turner, *COO*
Jeffrey Garber, *VP*
EMP: 26 **EST:** 2016
SALES (est): 10.52MM **Privately Held**
Web: www.cthermal.com
SIC: 2819 4939 Industrial inorganic chemicals, nec; Combination utilities, nec

(P-3239)
JM HUBER MICROPOWDERS INC
Also Called: Nutri Granulations
16024 Phoebe Ave, La Mirada
(90638-5606)
PHONE.................714 994-7855
Mike Marberry, *Pr*
EMP: 35
SQ FT: 45,000
SALES (corp-wide): 1.24B **Privately Held**
Web: www.nutrigranulations.com
SIC: 2819 Industrial inorganic chemicals, nec
HQ: J.M. Huber Micropowders Inc.
3100 Cumberland Blvd Se # 600
Atlanta GA 30339
732 549-8600

(P-3240)
KEMIRA WATER SOLUTIONS INC
14000 San Bernardino Ave, Fontana
(92335-5258)
PHONE.................909 350-5678
Keith Heasley, *Mgr*
EMP: 46
SALES (corp-wide): 3.68B **Privately Held**
Web: www.californiasteel.com
SIC: 2819 Industrial inorganic chemicals, nec
HQ: Kemira Water Solutions, Inc.
200 Gllria Pkwy Se Ste 15
Atlanta GA 30339

(P-3241)
MARCHEM TECHNOLOGIES LLC
20851 S Santa Fe Ave, Carson
(90810-1130)
PHONE.................310 638-9352
◆ **EMP:** 30

Web: www.marchemtechnologies.com
SIC: 2819 2899 Industrial inorganic chemicals, nec; Chemical preparations, nec

(P-3242)
MORAVEK BIOCHEMICALS INC (PA)
Also Called: Moravek
577 Mercury Ln, Brea (92821-4831)
P.O. Box 1716 (92822-1716)
PHONE.................714 990-2018
Paul Moravek, *Pr*
Joseph Moravek, *
Helen Moravek, *
▲ **EMP:** 25 **EST:** 1976
SQ FT: 6,000
SALES (est): 8.57MM
SALES (corp-wide): 8.57MM **Privately Held**
Web: www.moravek.com
SIC: 2819 Industrial inorganic chemicals, nec

(P-3243)
OMYA CALIFORNIA INC
Also Called: O M Y A
7299 Crystal Creek Rd, Lucerne Valley
(92356-8646)
PHONE.................760 248-7306
▲ **EMP:** 100
SIC: 2819 8741 3281 Calcium compounds and salts, inorganic, nec; Management services; Cut stone and stone products

(P-3244)
OMYA INC
7299 Crystal Creek Rd, Lucerne Valley
(92356-8646)
PHONE.................760 248-5200
Rainer Seidler, *CEO*
EMP: 100
Web: www.omya.com
SIC: 2819 8741 3281 Calcium compounds and salts, inorganic, nec; Management services; Cut stone and stone products
HQ: Omya Inc.
9987 Carver Rd Ste 300
Cincinnati OH 45242
513 387-4600

(P-3245)
PHIBRO-TECH INC
8851 Dice Rd, Santa Fe Springs
(90670-2515)
PHONE.................562 698-8036
Mark Alling, *Mgr*
EMP: 50
SALES (corp-wide): 1.02B **Publicly Held**
Web: www.pahc.com
SIC: 2819 2899 Inorganic metal compounds or salts, nec; Chemical preparations, nec
HQ: Phibro-Tech, Inc.
300 Frank W Burr Blvd
Teaneck NJ 07666

(P-3246)
PQ LLC
8401 Quartz Ave, South Gate (90280-2536)
PHONE.................323 326-1100
Jim Olivier, *Mgr*
EMP: 107
SALES (corp-wide): 461.02MM **Privately Held**
Web: www.pqcorp.com
SIC: 2819 Industrial inorganic chemicals, nec
PA: Pq Llc
300 Lindenwood Dr
610 651-4200

(P-3247)
SINGOD INVESTORS VI LLC
Also Called: Element Anheim Rsort Cnvntion
1600 S Clementine St, Anaheim
(92802-2901)
PHONE.................714 326-7800
Padmesh Patel, *Prin*
EMP: 55 **EST:** 2016
SALES (est): 6.9MM **Privately Held**
Web: www.marriott.com
SIC: 2819 Elements

(P-3248)
SOLVAY AMERICA INC
Also Called: SOLVAY AMERICA, INC.
1440 N Kraemer Blvd, Anaheim
(92806-1404)
PHONE.................714 688-4403
Michele Jenkins, *Brnch Mgr*
EMP: 116
SALES (corp-wide): 120.79MM **Privately Held**
Web: www.solvay.com
SIC: 2819 Industrial inorganic chemicals, nec
HQ: Solvay America Llc
3737 Buffalo Spdwy Ste 80
Houston TX 77098
713 525-4000

(P-3249)
SOLVAY AMERICA INC
Also Called: SOLVAY AMERICA, INC.
645 N Cypress St, Orange (92867-6603)
PHONE.................225 361-3376
EMP: 52
SALES (corp-wide): 120.79MM **Privately Held**
Web: www.solvay.com
SIC: 2819 Industrial inorganic chemicals, nec
HQ: Solvay America Llc
3737 Buffalo Spdwy Ste 80
Houston TX 77098
713 525-4000

(P-3250)
SOLVAY AMERICA INC
Also Called: SOLVAY AMERICA, INC.
12801 Ann St, Santa Fe Springs
(90670-3025)
PHONE.................562 906-3300
EMP: 90
SALES (corp-wide): 120.79MM **Privately Held**
Web: www.solvay.com
SIC: 2819 Industrial inorganic chemicals, nec
HQ: Solvay America Llc
3737 Buffalo Spdwy Ste 80
Houston TX 77098
713 525-4000

(P-3251)
SOLVAY AMERICA LLC
1191 N Hawk Cir, Anaheim (92807-1723)
PHONE.................713 525-4000
EMP: 82
SALES (corp-wide): 120.79MM **Privately Held**
Web: www.solvay.com
SIC: 2819 Industrial inorganic chemicals, nec
HQ: Solvay America Llc
3737 Buffalo Spdwy Ste 80
Houston TX 77098
713 525-4000

(P-3252)
SOLVAY CHEMICALS INC
645 N Cypress St, Orange (92867-6603)
PHONE.................714 744-5610
EMP: 27
SALES (corp-wide): 120.79MM **Privately Held**

Web: www.solvay.com
SIC: 2819 Industrial inorganic chemicals, nec
HQ: Solvay Chemicals, Inc.
1201 Fannin St Ste 262
Houston TX 77002
713 525-6500

(P-3253)
SPECIALTY MINERALS INC
Minerals Technology
6565 Meridian Rd, Lucerne Valley
(92356-8602)
P.O. Box 558 (92356-0558)
PHONE.................760 248-5300
Doug Mayger, *Brnch Mgr*
EMP: 150
Web: www.mineralstech.com
SIC: 2819 Industrial inorganic chemicals, nec
HQ: Specialty Minerals Inc.
622 Third Ave 38th Fl
New York NY 10017

(P-3254)
US BORAX INC
14486 Borax Rd, Boron (93516-2017)
PHONE.................760 762-7000
Joe A Carrabba, *Brnch Mgr*
EMP: 900
SALES (corp-wide): 54.04B **Privately Held**
Web: www.borax.com
SIC: 2819 Industrial inorganic chemicals, nec
HQ: U.S. Borax Inc.
200 E Randolph St # 7100
Chicago IL 60601
773 270-6500

(P-3255)
VENUS LABORATORIES INC
Earth Friendly Products
11150 Hope St, Cypress (90630-5236)
PHONE.................714 891-3100
Firas Jamal, *Mgr*
EMP: 70
SALES (corp-wide): 76.72MM **Privately Held**
Web: www.ecos.com
SIC: 2819 2844 2842 2841 Industrial inorganic chemicals, nec; Perfumes, cosmetics and other toilet preparations; Polishes and sanitation goods; Soap and other detergents
PA: Venus Laboratories, Inc.
111 S Rohlwing Rd
630 595-1900

2821 Plastics Materials And Resins

(P-3256)
ALPHA CORPORATION OF TENNESSEE
Also Called: Alpha-Owens Corning
19991 Seaton Ave, Perris (92570-8724)
PHONE.................951 657-5161
John Mulrine, *Mgr*
EMP: 136
SALES (corp-wide): 1.49MM **Privately Held**
Web: www.aocresins.com
SIC: 2821 Polyethylene resins
HQ: The Alpha Corporation Of Tennessee
955 Highway 57
Piperton TN 38017
901 854-2800

(P-3257)
AMERICAS STYRENICS LLC
305 Crenshaw Blvd, Torrance (90503-1701)
PHONE.................424 488-3757

Brad Crocker, *Brnch Mgr*
EMP: 83
SALES (corp-wide): 7.42B **Privately Held**
Web: www.amsty.com
SIC: 2821 Plastics materials and resins
HQ: Americas Styrenics Llc
24 Waterway Ave Ste 1200
The Woodlands TX 77380

(P-3258)
APTCO LLC (PA)
31381 Pond Rd Bldg 2, Mc Farland
(93250-9795)
PHONE............................661 792-2107
Jim Banuelos, *Managing Member*
◆ **EMP:** 99 EST: 1996
SALES (est): 16.07MM **Privately Held**
Web: www.aptcollc.com
SIC: 2821 Thermoplastic materials

(P-3259)
BDC EPOXY SYSTEMS INC
12903 Sunshine Ave, Santa Fe Springs
(90670-4732)
P.O. Box 2445 (90670-0445)
PHONE............................562 944-6177
Fred Benson, *CEO*
Matt Benson, *
Laura Benson, *
▲ **EMP:** 27 EST: 1976
SQ FT: 15,000
SALES (est): 5.28MM **Privately Held**
Web: www.bdcepoxysystems.com
SIC: 2821 Epoxy resins

(P-3260)
BJB ENTERPRISES INC
14791 Franklin Ave, Tustin (92780-7215)
PHONE............................714 734-8450
Brian Stransky, *Pr*
EMP: 27 EST: 1970
SQ FT: 38,000
SALES (est): 7.16MM **Privately Held**
Web: www.bjbenterprises.com
SIC: 2821 3087 5162 Polyurethane resins;
Custom compound purchased resins;
Plastics materials and basic shapes

(P-3261)
COMPOSITES HORIZONS LLC (DH)
1629 W Industrial Park St, Covina
(91722-3418)
PHONE............................626 331-0861
Renee Fahmy, *
▲ **EMP:** 140 EST: 1974
SQ FT: 25,000
SALES (est): 23.75MM
SALES (corp-wide): 364.48B **Publicly Held**
Web: www.pccstructurals.com
SIC: 2821 3844 3728 Plastics materials and
resins; X-ray apparatus and tubes; Aircraft
parts and equipment, nec
HQ: Precision Castparts Corp.
5885 Meadows Rd Ste 620
Lake Oswego OR 97035
503 946-4800

(P-3262)
CROSSFIELD PRODUCTS CORP (PA)
Also Called: Dex-O-Tex Division
3000 E Harcourt St, Compton (90221-5589)
PHONE............................310 886-9100
Richard Watt, *Ch Bd*
W Brad Watt, *
Ronald Borum, *
◆ **EMP:** 47 EST: 1938
SQ FT: 23,000

SALES (est): 23.79MM
SALES (corp-wide): 23.79MM **Privately Held**
Web: www.crossfieldproducts.com
SIC: 2821 Plastics materials and resins

(P-3263)
DOW COMPANY FOUNDATION
Dow Chemical
11266 Jersey Blvd, Rancho Cucamonga
(91730-5114)
P.O. Box 748 (91729-0748)
PHONE............................909 476-4127
Steve Rynders, *Prin*
EMP: 159
SALES (corp-wide): 44.62B **Publicly Held**
Web: corporate.dow.com
SIC: 2821 Thermoplastic materials
HQ: Dow Company Foundation
2030 Dow Center
Midland MI 48674
989 636-1000

(P-3264)
ECOWISE INC
13538 Excelsior Dr Unit B, Santa Fe
Springs (90670-5616)
PHONE............................626 759-3997
Sheng Xu, *Pr*
EMP: 30 EST: 2019
SALES (est): 5.93MM **Privately Held**
Web: www.ecowisepcr.com
SIC: 2821 Polyethylene resins

(P-3265)
ELASCO INC
Also Called: E Sales
11377 Markon Dr, Garden Grove
(92841-1402)
PHONE............................714 373-4767
Henry Larrucea, *Pr*
Janet Lurrucea, *
Gary Stull, *
David Schindler, *
▲ **EMP:** 100 EST: 1979
SQ FT: 28,000
SALES (est): 4.68MM **Privately Held**
Web: www.elascourethane.com
SIC: 2821 2891 2822 Polyurethane resins;
Adhesives and sealants; Synthetic rubber

(P-3266)
ELASCO URETHANE INC
11377 Markon Dr, Garden Grove
(92841-1402)
PHONE............................714 895-7031
John Frasco, *CEO*
EMP: 04 EST: 2014
SALES (est): 3.84MM **Privately Held**
Web: www.elascourethane.com
SIC: 2821 2891 2822 Polyurethane resins;
Adhesives and sealants; Synthetic rubber

(P-3267)
FERCO COLOR INC (PA)
Also Called: Ferco Plastic Products
5498 Vine St, Chino (91710-5247)
PHONE............................909 930-0773
Jennifer Thaw, *Pr*
EMP: 48 EST: 1989
SQ FT: 20,000
SALES (est): 1.2MM **Privately Held**
Web: www.fercocolor.com
SIC: 2821 2865 Polyethylene resins; Color
pigments, organic

(P-3268)
HOFFMAN PLASTIC COMPOUNDS INC
16616 Garfield Ave, Paramount
(90723-5399)

PHONE............................323 636-3346
Ronald P Hoffman, *Pr*
Susan Hoffman, *
▲ **EMP:** 66 EST: 1976
SQ FT: 46,000
SALES (est): 15.93MM **Privately Held**
Web: www.hoffmanplastic.com
SIC: 2821 3087 Polyvinyl chloride resins,
PVC; Custom compound purchased resins

(P-3269)
HOLCIM SOLUTIONS & PDTS US LLC
Pacific Polymers
12271 Monarch St, Garden Grove
(92841-2906)
PHONE............................714 898-0025
Robert Seiple, *Brnch Mgr*
EMP: 27
Web: www.holcimacs.com
SIC: 2821 2822 2851 2891 Plastics
materials and resins; Synthetic rubber;
Paints and allied products; Adhesives and
sealants
HQ: Holcim Solutions And Products Us, Llc
26 Century Blvd Ste 205
Nashville TN 37214

(P-3270)
HUNTSMAN ADVANCED MATERIALS AM
Also Called: Huntsman
5121 W San Fernando Rd, Los Angeles
(90039-1011)
PHONE............................818 265-7221
Glenn Bauernschmidt, *Mgr*
EMP: 120
SALES (corp-wide): 6.11B **Publicly Held**
Web: www.huntsman.com
SIC: 2821 Plastics materials and resins
HQ: Huntsman Advanced Materials
Americas Llc
10003 Woodloch Forest Dr
The Woodlands TX 77380
281 719-6000

(P-3271)
INDORAMA VNTRES SSTNBLE SLTION
11591 Etiwanda Ave, Fontana
(92337-6927)
PHONE............................951 727-8318
John Wang, *CEO*
EMP: 39 EST: 2018
SALES (est): 23.76MM **Privately Held**
Web: www.indoramaventures.com
SIC: 2821 Plastics materials and resins
HQ: Indorama Ventures Public Company
Limited
75/102 Soi Sukhumvit 19 (Vadhana),
Asok Road
Vadhana 10110

(P-3272)
INDUSPAC CALIFORNIA INC
Also Called: Pacific Foam
1550 Champagne Ave, Ontario
(91761-3600)
PHONE............................909 390-4422
Keith Tatum, *Genl Mgr*
EMP: 30
Web: induspac.squarespace.com
SIC: 2821 Polyethylene resins
HQ: Induspac California, Inc.
38505 Cherry St Ste H
Newark CA 94560

(P-3273)
INEOS COMPOSITES US LLC
6608 E 26th St, Los Angeles (90040-3216)
P.O. Box 22118 (90022-0118)
PHONE............................323 767-1300
Reid Mork, *Brnch Mgr*
EMP: 60
SQ FT: 45,845
SALES (corp-wide): 929.29K **Privately Held**
Web: www.ineos.com
SIC: 2821 Plastics materials and resins
HQ: Ineos Composites Us, Llc
955 Yard St # 400
Columbus OH 43212
614 790-9299

(P-3274)
INEOS POLYPROPYLENE LLC
Also Called: Ineos
2384 E 223rd St, Carson (90810-1615)
PHONE............................310 847-8523
Jim Ratcliffe, *Ch*
▲ **EMP:** 25 EST: 1998
SALES (est): 24.42MM
SALES (corp-wide): 929.29K **Privately Held**
Web: www.ineos.com
SIC: 2821 Plastics materials and resins
HQ: Ineos Usa Llc
2600 S Shore Blvd Ste 500
League City TX 77573

(P-3275)
J-M MANUFACTURING COMPANY INC
Also Called: JM Eagle
23711 Rider St, Perris (92570-7114)
PHONE............................951 657-7400
Robert Johnson, *Mgr*
EMP: 40
SALES (corp-wide): 304.63MM **Privately Held**
Web: www.jmeagle.com
SIC: 2821 Polyvinyl chloride resins, PVC
PA: J-M Manufacturing Company, Inc.
5200 W Century Blvd
310 693-8200

(P-3276)
J-M MANUFACTURING COMPANY INC
10990 Hemlock Ave, Fontana
(92337-7250)
PHONE............................909 822-3009
Stephen Yang, *Mgr*
EMP: 95
SQ FT: 72,000
SALES (corp-wide): 304.63MM **Privately Held**
Web: www.jmeagle.com
SIC: 2821 3084 5051 3085 Polyvinyl
chloride resins, PVC; Plastics pipe; Pipe
and tubing, steel; Plastics bottles
PA: J-M Manufacturing Company, Inc.
5200 W Century Blvd
310 693-8200

(P-3277)
JOES PLASTICS INC
Also Called: Joes Plastics
5725 District Blvd, Vernon (90058-5590)
PHONE............................323 771-8433
Joe La Fountain Junior, *CEO*
▼ **EMP:** 40 EST: 1974
SQ FT: 130,000
SALES (est): 2.34MM **Privately Held**
SIC: 2821 Plastics materials and resins

(P-3278)
MAPEI CORPORATION
5415 Industrial Pkwy, San Bernardino
(92407-1803)
PHONE.....................909 475-4100
Jose Granillo, *Mgr*
EMP: 62
SALES (corp-wide): 4.55B **Privately Held**
Web: www.mapei.com
SIC: 2821 Acrylic resins
HQ: Mapei Corporation
1144 E Newport Ctr Dr
Deerfield Beach FL 33442
954 246-8888

(P-3279)
MER-KOTE PRODUCTS INC
4125 E La Palma Ave Ste 250, Anaheim
(92807-1869)
P.O. Box 17866 (92817-7866)
PHONE.....................714 778-2266
EMP: 30
SIC: 2821 Thermoplastic materials

(P-3280)
MULTI-PLASTICS INC
Also Called: Multi Plastics
11625 Los Nietos Rd, Santa Fe Springs
(90670-2009)
PHONE.....................562 692-1202
Rafael Enriquez, *Brnch Mgr*
EMP: 36
SALES (corp-wide): 107.83MM **Privately Held**
Web: www.multi-plastics.com
SIC: 2821 Plastics materials and resins
PA: Multi-Plastics, Inc.
7770 N Central Dr
740 548-4894

(P-3281)
MUM INDUSTRIES INC
2320 Meyers Ave, Escondido (92029-1006)
PHONE.....................800 729-1314
EMP: 61
SALES (corp-wide): 6.33MM **Privately Held**
Web: www.mumindustries.com
SIC: 2821 Plasticizer/additive based plastic materials
PA: Mum Industries Inc.
8989 Tyler Blvd
440 269-4966

(P-3282)
NATURAL ENVMTL PROTECTION CO
Also Called: Nepco
750 S Reservoir St, Pomona (91766-3815)
PHONE.....................909 620-8028
Young Su Shin, *Pr*
▲ **EMP:** 31 **EST:** 2006
SQ FT: 3,600
SALES (est): 3.05MM **Privately Held**
SIC: 2821 Polystyrene resins
PA: Kumsung Industrial Co.Ltd
57-6 Gubong-Gil, Donghwa-Myeon

(P-3283)
NEW TECHNOLOGY PLASTICS INC
7110 Fenwick Ln, Westminster
(92683-5248)
PHONE.....................562 941-6034
Gregory A Nelson, *CEO*
EMP: 35 **EST:** 1996
SALES (est): 9.93MM **Privately Held**
Web: www.newtechnologyplastics.com

SIC: 2821 5162 Molding compounds, plastics
; Plastics materials and basic shapes

(P-3284)
ORION PLASTICS CORPORATION
700 W Carob St, Compton (90220-5225)
PHONE.....................310 223-0370
Patricia Conkling, *Prin*
▲ **EMP:** 75 **EST:** 2000
SQ FT: 60,000
SALES (est): 2.29MM **Privately Held**
Web: www.orionplastics.net
SIC: 2821 Plastics materials and resins

(P-3285)
PERFORMANCE MATERIALS CORP (HQ)
Also Called: Tencate Performance Composite
1150 Calle Suerte, Camarillo (93012-8051)
PHONE.....................805 482-1722
Thomas W Smith, *Pr*
◆ **EMP:** 100 **EST:** 1986
SQ FT: 50,000
SALES (est): 23.82MM **Privately Held**
Web: www.toraytac.com
SIC: 2821 Plastics materials and resins
PA: Toray Industries, Inc.
2-1-1, Nihombashimuromachi

(P-3286)
PEXCO AEROSPACE INC
5451 Argosy Ave, Huntington Beach
(92649-1038)
PHONE.....................714 894-9922
Julio Cuevas, *Manager*
EMP: 40
SALES (corp-wide): 7.94B **Publicly Held**
Web: www.pexcoaerospace.com
SIC: 2821 Plastics materials and resins
HQ: Pexco Aerospace, Inc.
2405 S 3rd Ave
Union Gap WA 98903

(P-3287)
PLASKOLITE WEST LLC
Also Called: Continental Acrylics
2225 E Del Amo Blvd, Compton
(90220-6303)
PHONE.....................310 637-2103
Rick Larkin, *CFO*
▲ **EMP:** 30 **EST:** 2000
SALES (est): 9.44MM
SALES (corp-wide): 542.25MM **Privately Held**
SIC: 2821 Acrylic resins
PA: Plaskolite, Llc
400 W Ntnwide Blvd Ste 40
614 294-3281

(P-3288)
PROFESSIONAL PLASTICS INC (PA)
1810 E Valencia Dr, Fullerton (92831-4847)
PHONE.....................714 446-6500
TOLL FREE: 800
EMP: 50 **EST:** 1984
SALES (est): 110.43MM
SALES (corp-wide): 110.43MM **Privately Held**
Web: www.professionalplastics.com
SIC: 2821 5162 3083 3081 Plastics materials and resins; Plastics materials and basic shapes; Laminated plastics plate and sheet; Plastics film and sheet

(P-3289)
QYCELL CORPORATION
600 Etiwanda Ave, Ontario (91761-8635)

PHONE.....................909 390-6644
Grant Kesler, *CEO*
▲ **EMP:** 25 **EST:** 1990
SQ FT: 45,000
SALES (est): 8.09MM **Privately Held**
Web: www.qycellfoam.com
SIC: 2821 Plastics materials and resins

(P-3290)
ROCK WEST COMPOSITES INC (PA)
Also Called: Performance Plastics
7625 Panasonic Way, San Diego
(92154-8204)
PHONE.....................858 537-6260
James P Gormican, *CEO*
EMP: 51 **EST:** 2006
SALES (est): 51.31MM **Privately Held**
Web: www.rockwestcomposites.com
SIC: 2821 Plastics materials and resins

(P-3291)
SAINT-GOBAIN PRFMCE PLAS CORP
7301 Orangewood Ave, Garden Grove
(92841-1411)
PHONE.....................714 893-0470
Greg Maki, *Brnch Mgr*
EMP: 190
SALES (corp-wide): 402.18MM **Privately Held**
Web: plastics.saint-gobain.com
SIC: 2821 Plastics materials and resins
HQ: Saint-Gobain Performance Plastics
Corporation
20 Moores Rd
Malvern PA 19355
440 836-6900

(P-3292)
SAINT-GOBAIN PRFMCE PLAS CORP
Also Called: High Performance Seals
7301 Orangewood Ave, Garden Grove
(92841-1411)
PHONE.....................714 630-5818
Thomas Kinisky, *CEO*
EMP: 91
SALES (corp-wide): 402.18MM **Privately Held**
Web: plastics.saint-gobain.com
SIC: 2821 Plastics materials and resins
HQ: Saint-Gobain Performance Plastics
Corporation
20 Moores Rd
Malvern PA 19355
440 836-6900

(P-3293)
SPHERE ALLIANCE INC
Also Called: Advanced Aircraft Seal
3087 12th St, Riverside (92507-4904)
PHONE.....................951 352-2400
Daryl Silva, *CEO*
EMP: 37 **EST:** 2011
SALES (est): 3.85MM **Privately Held**
SIC: 2821 Plastics materials and resins

(P-3294)
STEPAN COMPANY
Also Called: Anaheim Plant
1208 N Patt St, Anaheim (92801-2549)
PHONE.....................714 776-9870
Tom Szczeblowski, *Mgr*
EMP: 247
SQ FT: 10,412
SALES (corp-wide): 2.33B **Publicly Held**
Web: www.stepan.com

SIC: 2821 2843 Plastics materials and resins
; Surface active agents
PA: Stepan Company
1101 Skokie Blvd Ste 500
847 446-7500

(P-3295)
TA AEROSPACE CO
Also Called: Ta Division
28065 Franklin Pkwy, Valencia
(91355-4117)
PHONE.....................661 702-0448
Jim Sweeney, *Pr*
EMP: 180
SQ FT: 78,124
SALES (corp-wide): 7.94B **Publicly Held**
Web: www.transdigm.com
SIC: 2821 3429 Elastomers, nonvulcanizable (plastics); Clamps, metal
HQ: Ta Aerospace Co.
28065 Franklin Pkwy
Valencia CA 91355
661 775-1100

(P-3296)
TAMMY TAYLOR NAILS INC
2001 E Deere Ave, Santa Ana
(92705-5724)
PHONE.....................949 250-9287
Tammy Taylor, *Pr*
▼ **EMP:** 45 **EST:** 1982
SQ FT: 11,500
SALES (est): 5.5MM **Privately Held**
Web: www.tammytaylornails.com
SIC: 2821 7231 5087 Acrylic resins; Beauty shops; Beauty parlor equipment and supplies

(P-3297)
TECHMER PM INC
18420 S Laurel Park Rd, Compton
(90220-6015)
PHONE.....................310 632-9211
John R Manuck, *Pr*
◆ **EMP:** 500 **EST:** 1982
SQ FT: 40,000
SALES (est): 14.27MM **Privately Held**
Web: www.techmerpm.com
SIC: 2821 Plastics materials and resins

(P-3298)
TEKNOR APEX COMPANY
Maclin Company
420 S 6th Ave, City Of Industry
(91746-3128)
P.O. Box 2307 (91746-0307)
PHONE.....................626 968-4656
Tony Patrizio, *Mgr*
EMP: 104
SALES (corp-wide): 731.88MM **Privately Held**
Web: www.teknorapex.com
SIC: 2821 3081 3089 Vinyl resins, nec; Unsupported plastics film and sheet; Plastics processing
PA: Teknor Apex Company
505 Central Ave
401 725-8000

(P-3299)
TEKNOR COLOR COMPANY
Also Called: Teknor Apex
420 S 6th Ave, City Of Industry
(91746-3128)
P.O. Box 2307 (91746-0307)
PHONE.....................626 336-7709
Tony Patrizio, *Genl Mgr*
EMP: 30
SALES (corp-wide): 731.88MM **Privately Held**

▲ = Import ▼ = Export
◆ = Import/Export

Web: www.teknorapex.com
SIC: 2821 3089 Plastics materials and resins
; Plastics processing
HQ: Teknor Color Company Llc
505 Central Ave
Pawtucket RI 02861

(P-3300)
UREMET CORPORATION
7012 Belgrave Ave, Garden Grove
(92841-2808)
PHONE...................657 257-4027
Steve Zamollo, *CEO*
Mark Moore, *
John Cockriel, *
▲ EMP: 26 EST: 1989
SQ FT: 9,500
SALES (est): 13.28MM Privately Held
Web: www.uremet.com
SIC: 2821 Polyurethane resins

(P-3301)
US BLANKS LLC (PA)
14700 S San Pedro St, Gardena
(90248-2001)
P.O. Box 486 (90248-0486)
PHONE...................310 225-6774
Kimberly Thress, *
▲ EMP: 48 EST: 2006
SALES (est): 15.52MM
SALES (corp-wide): 15.52MM Privately
Held
Web: www.usblanks.com
SIC: 2821 Plastics materials and resins

(P-3302)
XERXES CORPORATION
1210 N Tustin Ave, Anaheim (92807-1637)
PHONE...................714 630-0012
Rudy Tapia, *Mgr*
EMP: 119
SALES (corp-wide): 673.6MM Privately
Held
Web: www.xerxes.com
SIC: 2821 5999 3444 Polystyrene resins;
Fiberglass materials, except insulation;
Sheet metalwork
HQ: Xerxes Corporation
7901 Xerxes Ave S
Minneapolis MN 55431
952 887-1890

2822 Synthetic Rubber

(P-3303)
ARNCO
5141 Firestone Pl, South Gate
(90280-3535)
PHONE...................323 249-7500
◆ EMP: 50 EST: 1971
SALES (est): 2.66MM Privately Held
SIC: 2822 2821 3089 5084 Synthetic rubber;
Plastics materials and resins; Casting of
plastics; Paint spray equipment, industrial

(P-3304)
CRITICALPOINT CAPITAL LLC
Arlon Materials For Elec Div
9433 Hyssop Dr, Rancho Cucamonga
(91730-6107)
PHONE...................909 987-9533
Roy Baulmer, *Brnch Mgr*
EMP: 100
SALES (corp-wide): 19.26MM Privately
Held
Web: www.criticalpointpartners.com
SIC: 2822 3672 2821 Silicone rubbers;
Printed circuit boards; Plastics materials
and resins

PA: Criticalpoint Capital, Llc
2101 Rosecrans Ave
310 321-4400

2824 Organic Fibers, Noncellulosic

(P-3305)
MATCHES INC
1700 E Araby St Ste 64, Palm Springs
(92264)
PHONE...................760 899-1919
Jinle Chen, *Ch Bd*
Zhimeng Zhao, *CAO*
Xiqing Zhang, *COO*
EMP: 359 EST: 2009
SALES (est): 901.82K Privately Held
SIC: 2824 Polyester fibers

(P-3306)
ST PAUL BRANDS INC
11842 Monarch St, Garden Grove
(92841-2113)
PHONE...................714 903-1000
Jimmy Ngo, *Pr*
Henry Smith, *
Fred Evans, *
▲ EMP: 25 EST: 2004
SALES (est): 2.35MM Privately Held
Web: probactive.en.ec21.com
SIC: 2824 Protein fibers

(P-3307)
TURNER FIBERFILL INC
1600 Date St, Montebello (90640-6371)
P.O. Box 460 (90640-0460)
PHONE...................323 724-7957
Paul Turner, *Pr*
▲ EMP: 35 EST: 2003
SALES (est): 2.42MM Privately Held
SIC: 2824 Polyester fibers

2833 Medicinals And Botanicals

(P-3308)
ALLERMED LABORATORIES INC
7203 Convoy Ct, San Diego (92111-1020)
PHONE...................858 292-1060
H S Nielsen, *Pr*
EMP: 30 EST: 1972
SQ FT: 20,000
SALES (est): 5.22MM Privately Held
Web: www.stallergenesgreer.com
SIC: 2833 2836 Medicinals and botanicals;
Biological products, except diagnostic

(P-3309)
AMASS BRANDS INC
860 E Stowell Rd, Santa Maria
(93454-7006)
PHONE...................619 204-2560
Mark Thomas Lynn, *CEO*
EMP: 34 EST: 2019
SALES (est): 8.56MM Privately Held
Web: www.amass.com
SIC: 2833 Alkaloids and other botanical
based products

(P-3310)
B & C NUTRITIONAL PRODUCTS INC
Also Called: Merical
2995 E Miraloma Ave, Anaheim
(92806-1805)
PHONE...................714 238-7225

EMP: 77
SIC: 2833 2048 2834 Medicinals and
botanicals; Prepared feeds, nec; Vitamin
preparations

(P-3311)
BIO-RAD LABORATORIES INC
Bio-RAD E C S
9500 Jeronimo Rd, Irvine (92618-2017)
PHONE...................949 598-1200
Kelly Knapps, *Brnch Mgr*
EMP: 187
SALES (corp-wide): 2.8B Publicly Held
Web: www.bio-rad.com
SIC: 2833 2835 Medicinals and botanicals;
Diagnostic substances
PA: Bio-Rad Laboratories, Inc.
1000 Alfred Nobel Dr
510 724-7000

(P-3312)
CARGILL INCORPORATED
Also Called: Cargill
600 N Gilbert St, Fullerton (92833-2555)
PHONE...................714 449-6708
Steve Hoemoller, *Mgr*
EMP: 48
SALES (corp-wide): 159.59B Privately
Held
Web: www.cargill.com
SIC: 2833 2079 5199 Vegetable oils,
medicinal grade: refined or concentrated;
Edible fats and oils; Oils, animal or
vegetable
PA: Cargill, Incorporated
15407 Mcginty Rd W
800 227-4455

(P-3313)
CHROMADEX CORPORATION (PA)
Also Called: Chromadex
10900 Wilshire Blvd Ste 600, Los Angeles
(90024-6534)
PHONE...................310 388-6706
Robert Fried, *CEO*
Frank L Jaksch Junior, *Ex Ch Bd*
James Lee, *Interim CAO*
Carlos Lopez, *Sr VP*
Ozan Pamir, *CFO*
EMP: 31 EST: 2000
SQ FT: 10,000
SALES (est): 83.57MM
SALES (corp-wide): 83.57MM Publicly
Held
Web: www.chromadex.com
SIC: 2833 Medicinals and botanicals

(P-3314)
ESMOND NATURAL INC
Also Called: Hopkins Labratory Co
5316 Irwindale Ave, Irwindale (91706-2034)
PHONE...................626 337-1588
Paul C Wei, *CEO*
Lindey Tseng, *
Midori H Wei, *Sec*
▲ EMP: 25 EST: 1994
SALES (est): 5.23MM Privately Held
Web: www.esmondnatural.com
SIC: 2833 Vitamins, natural or synthetic:
bulk, uncompounded

(P-3315)
EVOLIFE SCIENTIFIC LLC
3150 Long Beach Blvd, Long Beach
(90807-5061)
PHONE...................888 750-0310
EMP: 23 EST: 2019
SALES (est): 1.42MM Privately Held
Web: www.evolifescientific.com

SIC: 2833 Medicinals and botanicals

(P-3316)
EXCELSIOR NUTRITION INC
Also Called: 4excelsior
1206 N Miller St Unit D, Anaheim
(92806-1960)
PHONE...................657 999-5188
Lin Yisheng, *Pr*
Jian Wu, *
EMP: 61 EST: 2014
SQ FT: 78,000
SALES (est): 10.36MM Privately Held
Web: www.4excelsior.com
SIC: 2833 Medicinals and botanicals

(P-3317)
GREEN STAR LABS INC
Also Called: Covalent Cbd
4075 Ruffin Rd, San Diego (92123-1817)
PHONE...................619 489-9020
Sandro Piancone, *CEO*
Brooke Dang, *
EMP: 50 EST: 2022
SALES (est): 5MM
SALES (corp-wide): 5.1MM Publicly Held
Web: www.greenstarlabs.net
SIC: 2833 Medicinals and botanicals
HQ: The Hempacco Co Inc
9925 Airway Rd
San Diego CA 92154
619 779-0715

(P-3318)
J & D LABORATORIES INC
2710 Progress St, Vista (92081-8449)
PHONE...................760 734-6800
David Wood, *CEO*
Fon Wong, *CFO*
▲ EMP: 300 EST: 1988
SQ FT: 32,000
SALES (est): 10.33MM
SALES (corp-wide): 203.23MM Privately
Held
Web: www.capteksoftgel.com
SIC: 2833 2834 Vitamins, natural or
synthetic: bulk, uncompounded;
Pharmaceutical preparations
HQ: Captek Softgel International, Inc.
16218 Arthur St
Cerritos CA 90703

(P-3319)
MIDNIGHT MANUFACTURING LLC
Also Called: Loud Mfg
2535 Conejo Spectrum St Bldg 4,
Thousand Oaks (91320-1453)
PHONE...................714 833-6130
Kevin A Shaw, *Pr*
EMP: 25 EST: 2019
SALES (est): 5.59MM Privately Held
Web: www.midnightmanufacturing.com
SIC: 2833 Medicinals and botanicals

(P-3320)
MRO MARYRUTH LLC
1171 S Robertson Blvd Ste 148, Los
Angeles (90035-1403)
PHONE...................424 343-6650
Colleen Boehmer, *Managing Member*
Mary Boehmer, *
Dave Hsu, *
EMP: 195 EST: 2021
SALES (est): 2.29MM Privately Held
SIC: 2833 Medicinals and botanicals

(P-3321)

MYCELIUM ENTERPRISES LLC ✪

10632 Trask Ave, Garden Grove
(92843-2496)
PHONE....................657 251-0016
Andrew Boyd Jones, *Managing Member*
Matthew Rhoden, *Managing Member*
Heather Norris, *
EMP: 25 **EST:** 2023
SALES (est): 1.04MM **Privately Held**
SIC: 2833 Medicinals and botanicals

(P-3322)

NATURAL ALTERNATIVES INTL INC (PA)

Also Called: NAI
1535 Faraday Ave, Carlsbad (92008-7319)
PHONE....................760 736-7700
Mark A Ledoux, *Ch Bd*
Kenneth E Wolf, *Pr*
Michael E Fortin, *CFO*
▲ **EMP:** 178 **EST:** 1980
SQ FT: 20,981
SALES (est): 113.8MM
SALES (corp-wide): 113.8MM **Publicly Held**
Web: www.nai-online.com
SIC: 2833 2834 Medicinals and botanicals; Pharmaceutical preparations

(P-3323)

NU-HEALTH PRODUCTS CO

Also Called: Nu Health Products
20875 Currier Rd, Walnut (91789-3081)
PHONE....................909 869-0666
Lynn Leung, *Pr*
▲ **EMP:** 25 **EST:** 1991
SQ FT: 12,000
SALES (est): 2.15MM **Privately Held**
Web: www.nu-health.com
SIC: 2833 2048 5149 Vitamins, natural or synthetic: bulk, uncompounded; Prepared feeds, nec; Organic and diet food

(P-3324)

ORGAIN LLC

16631 Millikan Ave, Irvine (92606-5028)
P.O. Box 4918 (92616-4918)
PHONE....................888 881-4246
Andrew Abraham, *CEO*
EMP: 47 **EST:** 2019
SALES (est): 36.76MM **Privately Held**
Web: www.orgain.com
SIC: 2833 5499 Medicinals and botanicals; Health and dietetic food stores
PA: Nestle S.A.
　　Avenue Nestle 55

(P-3325)

ORGANIC BY NATURE INC (PA)

Also Called: Organic
2610 Homestead Pl, Rancho Dominguez (90220-5610)
PHONE....................562 901-0177
Amy L Venner Hamdi, *CEO*
David Sandoval, *
▲ **EMP:** 35 **EST:** 1993
SQ FT: 30,000
SALES (est): 10.32MM **Privately Held**
Web: www.organicbynatureinc.com
SIC: 2833 Adrenal derivatives

(P-3326)

PALETTE LIFE SCIENCES INC (PA)

27 E Cota St Ste 402, Santa Barbara (93101-7603)
PHONE....................805 869-7020
Per Lango, *CEO*
Hank Courson, *
EMP: 71 **EST:** 2018
SALES (est): 5.44MM
SALES (corp-wide): 5.44MM **Privately Held**
Web: www.palettelifesciences.com
SIC: 2833 Medicinal chemicals

(P-3327)

PHARMAVITE LLC (DH)

8531 Fallbrook Ave, West Hills (91304-3232)
PHONE....................818 221-6200
Jeff Boutelle, *CEO*
Tobe Cohen, *SPECIALTY BRANDS*
Christine Burdick-bell J.d., *Ex VP*
Rhonda Hoffman, *CGO*
Jerome Metivier, *
▲ **EMP:** 300 **EST:** 1971
SQ FT: 45,000
SALES (est): 519.52MM **Privately Held**
Web: www.pharmavite.com
SIC: 2833 2834 Vitamins, natural or synthetic: bulk, uncompounded; Pharmaceutical preparations
HQ: Otsuka America, Inc.
　　1 Embrcadero Ctr Ste 2020
　　San Francisco CA 94111

(P-3328)

PROMEGA BIOSCIENCES LLC

277 Granada Dr, San Luis Obispo (93401-7396)
PHONE....................805 544-8524
EMP: 55 **EST:** 1999
SQ FT: 40,000
SALES (est): 21.39MM
SALES (corp-wide): 743.96MM **Privately Held**
Web: www.promega.com
SIC: 2833 2835 Medicinal chemicals; Diagnostic substances
PA: Promega Corporation
　　2800 Woods Hollow Rd
　　608 274-4330

(P-3329)

RON TEEGUARDEN ENTERPRISES INC (PA)

Also Called: Dragon Herbs
10940 Wilshire Blvd, Los Angeles (90024-3915)
PHONE....................323 556-8188
Ron Teagarden, *Pr*
Yanlin Teegarden, *
◆ **EMP:** 23 **EST:** 1994
SALES (est): 4.8MM
SALES (corp-wide): 4.8MM **Privately Held**
Web: www.dragonherbs.com
SIC: 2833 5122 Drugs and herbs: grading, grinding, and milling; Medicinals and botanicals

(P-3330)

S&B PHARMA INC

Also Called: Norac Pharma
405 S Motor Ave, Azusa (91702-3232)
PHONE....................626 334-2908
Doctor Daniel Levin, *Pr*
▲ **EMP:** 66 **EST:** 2012
SALES (est): 10.36MM **Privately Held**
Web: www.noracpharma.com
SIC: 2833 8731 2834 Medicinals and botanicals; Commercial physical research; Pharmaceutical preparations
PA: Alkem Laboratories Limited
　　Devashish Building, Alkem House,

(P-3331)

SAPPHIRE ENERGY INC

10996 Torreyana Rd Ste 280, San Diego (92121-1161)
PHONE....................858 768-4700
James Levine, *CEO*
Thomas Willardson, *CFO*
EMP: 55 **EST:** 2007
SALES (est): 4.31MM **Privately Held**
Web: www.sapphireenergy.com
SIC: 2833 Medicinals and botanicals

(P-3332)

STAUBER CALIFORNIA INC

Also Called: Stauber USA
4120 N Palm St, Fullerton (92835-1026)
PHONE....................714 441-3900
▲ **EMP:** 95
SIC: 2833 Medicinals and botanicals

(P-3333)

STAUBER PRFMCE INGREDIENTS INC (HQ)

Also Called: Stauber
4120 N Palm St, Fullerton (92835-1026)
PHONE....................714 441-3900
Patrick Hawkins, *CEO*
Dan Stauber, *Chief Brand Officer*
EMP: 66 **EST:** 1969
SALES (est): 34.06MM
SALES (corp-wide): 919.16MM **Publicly Held**
Web: www.stauberusa.com
SIC: 2833 Medicinals and botanicals
PA: Hawkins, Inc.
　　2381 Rosegate
　　612 331-6910

(P-3334)

VYTALOGY WELLNESS LLC

15233 Ventura Blvd, Sherman Oaks (91403-2201)
PHONE....................818 867-4440
Nina Barton, *Managing Member*
EMP: 130 **EST:** 2021
SALES (est): 14.75MM **Privately Held**
Web: www.natrol.com
SIC: 2833 Vitamins, natural or synthetic: bulk, uncompounded

2834 Pharmaceutical Preparations

(P-3335)

A Q PHARMACEUTICALS INC

11555 Monarch St Ste C, Garden Grove (92841-1814)
PHONE....................714 903-1000
Tracy Nguyen, *Pr*
Henry Smith, *
▲ **EMP:** 30 **EST:** 2001
SQ FT: 3,000
SALES (est): 3.97MM **Privately Held**
Web: www.aqpharmaceuticals.com
SIC: 2834 Pharmaceutical preparations

(P-3336)

ABBOTT LABORATORIES

15900 Valley View Ct, Sylmar (91342-3577)
PHONE....................818 493-2388
Dee Vetter, *Prin*
EMP: 25
SALES (corp-wide): 40.11B **Publicly Held**
Web: www.abbott.com
SIC: 2834 Pharmaceutical preparations
PA: Abbott Laboratories
　　100 Abbott Park Rd
　　224 667-6100

(P-3337)

ABBOTT VASCULAR INC

26531 Ynez Rd, Temecula (92591-4630)
PHONE....................951 941-2400
Ronald Dollens, *Brnch Mgr*
EMP: 500
SALES (corp-wide): 40.11B **Publicly Held**
Web: www.cardiovascular.abbott
SIC: 2834 Pharmaceutical preparations
HQ: Abbott Vascular Inc.
　　3200 Lakeside Dr
　　Santa Clara CA 95054
　　408 845-3000

(P-3338)

ABRAXIS BIOSCIENCE LLC (DH)

11755 Wilshire Blvd Fl 20, Los Angeles (90025-1543)
PHONE....................800 564-0216
EMP: 232 **EST:** 2007
SALES (est): 16.97MM
SALES (corp-wide): 45.01B **Publicly Held**
Web: www.celgene.com
SIC: 2834 Pharmaceutical preparations
HQ: Abraxis Bioscience, Inc.
　　86 Morris Ave
　　Summit NJ 07901

(P-3339)

ACADIA PHARMACEUTICALS INC (PA)

Also Called: Acadia
12830 El Camino Real Ste 400, San Diego (92130-2976)
PHONE....................858 558-2871
Catherine Owen Adams, *CEO*
Stephen R Biggar, *Non-Executive Chairman of the Board*
Mark C Schneyer, *Ex VP*
Jennifer J Rhodes, *CLO*
Elizabeth H Z Thompson, *Ex VP*
▲ **EMP:** 563 **EST:** 1993
SQ FT: 67,000
SALES (est): 726.44MM **Publicly Held**
Web: www.acadia.com
SIC: 2834 Pharmaceutical preparations

(P-3340)

ACTAVIS LLC

311 Bonnie Cir, Corona (92878-5182)
P.O. Box 1149 (92878-1149)
PHONE....................909 270-1400
Allen Chao, *Brnch Mgr*
EMP: 79
Web: www.actavis.com
SIC: 2834 Pharmaceutical preparations
HQ: Actavis Llc
　　1150 S Northpoint Blvd
　　Waukegan IL 60085
　　862 261-7000

(P-3341)

ADAM NUTRITION INC

11010 Hopkins St Ste B, Jurupa Valley (91752-3279)
PHONE....................951 361-1120
◆ **EMP:** 130
Web: www.adamnutrition.com
SIC: 2834 Vitamin, nutrient, and hematinic preparations for human use

(P-3342)

AEGIS LIFE INC

Also Called: Aegis Biodefense
3033 Science Park Rd Ste 270, San Diego (92121-1168)
PHONE....................650 666-5287
Hong Jiang, *COO*
John Lewis, *CEO*
EMP: 30 **EST:** 2020

▲ = Import　▼ = Export
◆ = Import/Export

SALES (est): 885.44K **Privately Held**
Web: www.aegis.life
SIC: 2834 Pharmaceutical preparations

(P-3343)
AGOURON PHARMACEUTICALS INC (HQ)
10777 Science Center Dr, San Diego (92121-1111)
PHONE..............................858 622-3000
Catherine Mackey Ph.d., *Sr VP*
EMP: 50 **EST:** 1984
SALES (est): 3.92MM
SALES (corp-wide): 58.5B **Publicly Held**
Web: www.agi.org
SIC: 2834 5122 8731 Pharmaceutical preparations; Pharmaceuticals; Commercial physical research
PA: Pfizer Inc.
66 Hudson Blvd E
212 733-2323

(P-3344)
AKCEA THERAPEUTICS INC (HQ)
Also Called: Akcea Therapeutics
2850 Gazelle Ct, Carlsbad (92010)
PHONE..............................617 207-0202
Brett Monia, *Pr*
Elizabeth Hougen, *Treas*
Melissa Yoon, *Sec*
Michael Pollock, *Chief Commercial Officer*
Tracy Berns, *Chief Compliance Officer*
EMP: 69 **EST:** 2017
SALES (est): 488.54MM
SALES (corp-wide): 787.65MM **Publicly Held**
Web: www.ionispharma.com
SIC: 2834 8731 Pharmaceutical preparations; Biological research
PA: Ionis Pharmaceuticals, Inc.
2855 Gazelle Ct
760 931-9200

(P-3345)
ALLERGAN SALES LLC (DH)
2525 Dupont Dr, Irvine (92612-1599)
P.O. Box 19534 (92623-9534)
PHONE..............................862 261-7000
Brenton L Saunders, *Ch*
William Meury, *CCO**
Matthew M Walsh, ***
A Robert D Bailey, *CLO**
Karen L Ling, *Chief Human Resource Officer**
▲ **EMP:** 600 **EST:** 1986
SQ FT: 10,000
SALES (est): 372.19MM
SALES (corp-wide): 54.32B **Publicly Held**
Web: www.abbvie.com
SIC: 2834 Pharmaceutical preparations
HQ: Allergan, Inc.
1 N Waukegan Rd
North Chicago IL 60064
862 261-7000

(P-3346)
ALLERGAN SPCLTY THRPEUTICS INC
Also Called: Allergan
2525 Dupont Dr, Irvine (92612-1599)
PHONE..............................714 246-4500
David Pyott, *Pr*
EMP: 1500 **EST:** 1997
SALES (est): 481.05MM
SALES (corp-wide): 54.32B **Publicly Held**
Web: www.allergandatalabs.com
SIC: 2834 Pharmaceutical preparations
HQ: Allergan, Inc.
1 N Waukegan Rd

North Chicago IL 60064
862 261-7000

(P-3347)
ALLERGAN USA INC (DH)
Also Called: Pacific Communications
18581 Teller Ave, Irvine (92612-1627)
P.O. Box 19534 (92623-9534)
PHONE..............................714 427-1900
David E I Pyott, *CEO*
Craig Sullivan, *Pr*
Jeffrey L Edwards, *VP*
Douglas S Ingram, *Sec*
James M Hindman, *Treas*
EMP: 67 **EST:** 2007
SALES (est): 471.46MM
SALES (corp-wide): 54.32B **Publicly Held**
Web: www.pacificcommunications.com
SIC: 2834 Druggists' preparations (pharmaceuticals)
HQ: Allergan, Inc.
1 N Waukegan Rd
North Chicago IL 60064
862 261-7000

(P-3348)
AMARE GLOBAL LP
17872 Gillette Ave Ste 100, Irvine (92614-6573)
PHONE..............................888 898-8551
Jared Turner, *CEO*
Hiep Tran, *Ch*
Gabriel Sanchez, *OF SALES*
EMP: 27 **EST:** 2017
SALES (est): 2.71MM **Privately Held**
SIC: 2834 Vitamin preparations

(P-3349)
AMBIT BIOSCIENCES CORPORATION
10201 Wateridge Cir Ste 200, San Diego (92121-5806)
PHONE..............................858 334-2100
Michael A Martino, *Pr*
Faheem Hasnain, *Ch Bd*
Alan Fuhrman, *CFO*
Annette North, *Sr VP*
Mario Orlando, *Sr VP*
EMP: 53 **EST:** 2000
SQ FT: 20,000
SALES (est): 6.5MM **Privately Held**
Web: www.ambitbio.com
SIC: 2834 Pharmaceutical preparations
PA: Daiichi Sankyo Company, Limited
3-5-1, Nihombashihoncho

(P-3350)
AMBRX INC (PA)
10975 N Torrey Pines Rd Ste 100, La Jolla (92037-1051)
PHONE..............................858 875-2400
Tiecheng Qiao, *CEO*
John D Diekman, ***
John W Wallen Iii, *VP*
Ho Cho, ***
Simon Allen, *Chief Business Officer**
EMP: 56 **EST:** 2003
SALES (est): 25MM
SALES (corp-wide): 25MM **Privately Held**
Web: www.ambrx.com
SIC: 2834 Druggists' preparations (pharmaceuticals)

(P-3351)
AMGEN INC
1840 De Havilland Dr, Newbury Park (91320-1789)
PHONE..............................805 447-1000
Gordon M Binder, *Mgr*
EMP: 169

North Chicago IL 60064
862 261-7000

SALES (corp-wide): 28.19B **Publicly Held**
Web: www.amgen.com
SIC: 2834 Pharmaceutical preparations
PA: Amgen Inc.
1 Amgen Center Dr
805 447-1000

(P-3352)
AMGEN USA INC (HQ)
1 Amgen Center Dr, Thousand Oaks (91320-1799)
PHONE..............................805 447-1000
Kevin W Sharer, *CEO*
EMP: 96 **EST:** 2010
SALES (est): 27.37MM
SALES (corp-wide): 28.19B **Publicly Held**
Web: www.amgen.com
SIC: 2834 Pharmaceutical preparations
PA: Amgen Inc.
1 Amgen Center Dr
805 447-1000

(P-3353)
AMPHASTAR PHARMACEUTICALS INC (PA)
Also Called: AMPHASTAR
11570 6th St, Rancho Cucamonga (91730-6025)
PHONE..............................909 980-9484
Jack Yongfeng Zhang, *CSO*
Jack Yongfeng Zhang, *CSO*
Mary Ziping Luo, *Chief Scientist**
William J Peters, ***
▲ **EMP:** 102 **EST:** 1996
SQ FT: 267,674
SALES (est): 644.39MM
SALES (corp-wide): 644.39MM **Publicly Held**
Web: www.amphastar.com
SIC: 2834 Pharmaceutical preparations

(P-3354)
AMYLIN OHIO LLC
9360 Towne Centre Dr, San Diego (92121-3057)
PHONE..............................858 552-2200
EMP: 1300
SIC: 2834 Pharmaceutical preparations

(P-3355)
ANAPTYSBIO INC (PA)
Also Called: ANAPTYSBIO
10770 Wateridge Cir Ste 210, San Diego (92121-5801)
PHONE..............................858 362-6295
John Orwin, *Ch Bd*
Hamza Suria, *Pr*
Eric Loumeau, *COO*
Dennis Mulroy, *CFO*
Paul F Lizzul, *CMO*
EMP: 116 **EST:** 2005
SQ FT: 45,000
SALES (est): 17.16MM **Publicly Held**
Web: www.anaptysbio.com
SIC: 2834 Pharmaceutical preparations

(P-3356)
ANCHEN PHARMACEUTICALS INC
5 Goodyear, Irvine (92618-2000)
PHONE..............................949 639-8100
Phillip Brancazio, *Brnch Mgr*
EMP: 236
SALES (corp-wide): 711.66K **Privately Held**
Web: www.parpharm.com
SIC: 2834 Druggists' preparations (pharmaceuticals)
HQ: Anchen Pharmaceuticals, Inc.
300 Tice Blvd Ste 230

Woodcliff Lake NJ 07677
949 639-8100

(P-3357)
AOE INTERNATIONAL INC
20611 Belshaw Ave, Carson (90746-3507)
▲ **EMP:** 35 **EST:** 1998
SQ FT: 12,500
SALES (est): 839.73K **Privately Held**
SIC: 2834 Vitamin, nutrient, and hematinic preparations for human use

(P-3358)
APPLIED MLECULAR EVOLUTION INC (HQ)
10300 Campus Point Dr Ste 200, San Diego (92121-1504)
PHONE..............................858 597-4990
Thomas Bumol, *Pr*
EMP: 50 **EST:** 1990
SQ FT: 43,000
SALES (est): 3.03MM
SALES (corp-wide): 34.12B **Publicly Held**
SIC: 2834 Pharmaceutical preparations
PA: Eli Lilly And Company
1 Lilly Corporate Ctr
317 276-2000

(P-3359)
ARCTURUS THRPTICS HOLDINGS INC (PA)
Also Called: ARCTURUS
10628 Science Center Dr Ste 250, San Diego (92121-1132)
PHONE..............................858 900-2660
Joseph E Payne, *Pr*
Peter Farrell, *Ch Bd*
Andy Sassine, *CFO*
Padmanabh Chivukula, *CSO*
Lance Kurata, *CLO*
EMP: 26 **EST:** 2013
SQ FT: 24,700
SALES (est): 166.8MM
SALES (corp-wide): 166.8MM **Publicly Held**
Web: www.arcturusrx.com
SIC: 2834 Pharmaceutical preparations

(P-3360)
ARDEA BIOSCIENCES INC
9390 Towne Centre Dr Ste 100, San Diego (92121-3026)
PHONE..............................858 625-0787
EMP: 25 **EST:** 2019
SALES (est): 2.94MM **Privately Held**
SIC: 2834 Pharmaceutical preparations

(P-3361)
ARROWHEAD PHARMACEUTICALS INC (PA)
Also Called: Arrowhead
177 E Colorado Blvd Ste 700, Pasadena (91105-1976)
PHONE..............................626 304-3400
Christopher Anzalone, *Pr*
Douglass Given, ***
Kenneth A Myszkowski, *CFO*
Patrick O'brien, *COO*
Javier San Martin, *CMO*
EMP: 137 **EST:** 1989
SQ FT: 49,000
SALES (est): 3.55MM **Publicly Held**
Web: www.arrowheadpharma.com
SIC: 2834 8731 Pharmaceutical preparations; Biological research

(P-3362)
AUSPEX PHARMACEUTICALS INC

3333 N Torrey Pines Ct Ste 400, La Jolla
(92037-1022)
P.O. Box 49272 (90049-0272)
PHONE..................................858 558-2400
Larry Downey, *Pr*
Deborah A Griffin, *
Austin D Kim, *
EMP: 30 **EST:** 2001
SALES (est): 2.38MM **Privately Held**
Web: www.tevapharm.com
SIC: 2834 Pharmaceutical preparations
PA: Teva Pharmaceutical Industries Limited
124 Dvora Hanevia

(P-3363)
AVANIR PHARMACEUTICALS INC (DH)

30 Enterprise Ste 200, Aliso Viejo
(92656-7112)
PHONE..................................949 389-6700
Rohan Palekar, *Pr*
Gregory J Flesher, *Sr VP*
Joao Siffert, *Sr VP*
Christine G Ocampo, *VP*
EMP: 67 **EST:** 1988
SALES (est): 64.98MM **Privately Held**
Web: www.otsuka-us.com
SIC: 2834 Pharmaceutical preparations
HQ: Otsuka Pharmaceutical Co., Ltd.
2-16-4, Konan
Minato-Ku TKY 108-0

(P-3364)
AVID BIOSERVICES INC (PA)

Also Called: Avid Bioservices
14191 Myford Rd, Tustin (92780-7020)
PHONE..................................714 508-6100
Nicholas S Green, *Pr*
Joseph Carleone, *Non-Executive Chairman of the Board*
Daniel R Hart, *CFO*
Matthew Kwietniak, *CCO*
Mark R Ziebell, *Corporate Secretary*
EMP: 120 **EST:** 1981
SALES (est): 139.91MM
SALES (corp-wide): 139.91MM **Publicly Held**
Web: www.avidbio.com
SIC: 2834 Pharmaceutical preparations

(P-3365)
AVID BIOSERVICES INC

14272 Franklin Ave Ste 115, Tustin
(92780-7064)
PHONE..................................714 508-6000
Steven W King, *Pr*
EMP: 97
SALES (corp-wide): 139.91MM **Publicly Held**
Web: www.avidbio.com
SIC: 2834 Pharmaceutical preparations
PA: Avid Bioservices, Inc.
14191 Myford Rd
714 508-6100

(P-3366)
AVID BIOSERVICES INC

14282 Franklin Ave, Tustin (92780-7009)
PHONE..................................714 508-6166
EMP: 48
SALES (corp-wide): 139.91MM **Publicly Held**
Web: www.avidbio.com
SIC: 2834 Pharmaceutical preparations
PA: Avid Bioservices, Inc.
14191 Myford Rd
714 508-6100

(P-3367)
AVIDITY BIOSCIENCES INC (PA)

Also Called: AVIDITY BIOSCIENCES
10578 Science Center Dr Ste 125, San
Diego (92121-1145)
PHONE..................................858 401-7900
Sarah Boyce, *Pr*
Troy Wilson, *
Joseph Baroldi, *COO*
Michael F Maclean, *CFO*
Arthur A Levin, *CSO*
EMP: 23 **EST:** 2012
SQ FT: 8,561
SALES (est): 9.56MM
SALES (corp-wide): 9.56MM **Publicly Held**
Web: www.aviditybiosciences.com
SIC: 2834 Pharmaceutical preparations

(P-3368)
BACHEM AMERICAS INC

Also Called: Bachem Vista BSD
1271 Avenida Chelsea, Vista (92081-8315)
PHONE..................................888 422-2436
Brian Gregg, *Pr*
EMP: 45
Web: www.bachem.com
SIC: 2834 Pharmaceutical preparations
HQ: Bachem Americas, Inc.
3132 Kashiwa St
Torrance CA 90505
310 784-4440

(P-3369)
BACHEM AMERICAS INC

3131 Fujita St, Torrance (90505-4006)
PHONE..................................424 347-5600
EMP: 45
Web: www.bachem.com
SIC: 2834 Pharmaceutical preparations
HQ: Bachem Americas, Inc.
3132 Kashiwa St
Torrance CA 90505
310 784-4440

(P-3370)
BAXALTA US INC

4501 Colorado Blvd, Los Angeles
(90039-1103)
PHONE..................................818 240-5600
Raul Navarro, *Brnch Mgr*
EMP: 694
SIC: 2834 Pharmaceutical preparations
HQ: Baxalta Us Inc.
1200 Lakeside Dr
Bannockburn IL

(P-3371)
BEAUTY & HEALTH INTERNATIONAL

7541 Anthony Ave, Garden Grove
(92841-4005)
P.O. Box 890 (92684-0890)
PHONE..................................714 903-9730
Charles G Myung, *Pr*
▲ **EMP:** 50 **EST:** 1993
SQ FT: 12,000
SALES (est): 2.31MM **Privately Held**
SIC: 2834 2844 5122 5149 Vitamin
preparations; Cosmetic preparations;
Vitamins and minerals; Health foods

(P-3372)
BEST FORMULATIONS LLC

17775 Rowland St, City Of Industry
(91748-1138)
PHONE..................................626 912-9998
EMP: 111
Web: www.bestformulations.com

SIC: 2834 Pharmaceutical preparations
HQ: Best Formulations Llc
17758 Rowland St
City Of Industry CA 91748
626 912-9998

(P-3373)
BF SUMA PHARMACEUTICALS INC

5001 Earle Ave, Rosemead (91770-1169)
PHONE..................................626 285-8366
Chak Yeung Chan, *Pr*
Annie Cheng, *Contrlr*
▲ **EMP:** 50 **EST:** 2006
SQ FT: 10,000
SALES (est): 6.63MM **Privately Held**
SIC: 2834 Pharmaceutical preparations

(P-3374)
BIMEDA INC

5539 Ayon Ave, Irwindale (91706-2057)
PHONE..................................626 815-1680
Tim Tynan, *Brnch Mgr*
EMP: 187
SALES (corp-wide): 3.51B **Privately Held**
Web: www.bimedaus.com
SIC: 2834 3841 Veterinary pharmaceutical
preparations; Surgical and medical
instruments
HQ: Bimeda Inc.
475 N Martingale Rd # 120
Schaumburg IL 60173
630 928-0361

(P-3375)
BIOMED CALIFORNIA INC

Also Called: Soleo Health
721 S Glasgow Ave Ste C, Inglewood
(90301-3016)
PHONE..................................310 665-1121
John Ginzler, *CFO*
Drew Walk, *CEO*
EMP: 57 **EST:** 2007
SALES (est): 2.74MM **Privately Held**
SIC: 2834 5912 Druggists' preparations
(pharmaceuticals); Drug stores and
proprietary stores
HQ: Biomed Healthcare, Inc.
950 Calcon Hook Rd Ste 19
Sharon Hill PA 19079
888 244-2340

(P-3376)
BIORX PHARMACEUTICALS INC

Also Called: Biorx Laboratories
6320 Chalet Dr, Commerce (90040-3706)
PHONE..................................323 725-3100
Amin Jack, *Pr*
EMP: 32 **EST:** 2010
SALES (est): 2.4MM **Privately Held**
Web: www.biorxlabs.com
SIC: 2834 2844 Pharmaceutical preparations
; Perfumes, cosmetics and other toilet
preparations

(P-3377)
CAPRICOR

8700 Beverly Blvd, West Hollywood
(90048-1804)
PHONE..................................310 423-2104
EMP: 38 **EST:** 2018
SALES (est): 5.93MM **Privately Held**
Web: www.capricor.com
SIC: 2834 Pharmaceutical preparations

(P-3378)
CAPTEK MIDCO INC

2710 Progress St, Vista (92081-8449)
PHONE..................................760 734-6800
EMP: 66

SALES (corp-wide): 203.23MM **Privately Held**
Web: www.capteksoftgel.com
SIC: 2834 Pharmaceutical preparations
HQ: Captek Midco, Inc.
16218 Arthur St
Cerritos CA 90703
562 921-9511

(P-3379)
CAPTEK SOFTGEL INTL INC (DH)

16218 Arthur St, Cerritos (90703-2131)
PHONE..................................562 921-9511
Carl Randall Bridges, *CEO*
Danielle Conner, *
Jan Fuh Miller, *
▲ **EMP:** 300 **EST:** 1995
SQ FT: 90,000
SALES (est): 203.23MM
SALES (corp-wide): 203.23MM **Privately Held**
Web: www.capteksoftgel.com
SIC: 2834 Vitamin, nutrient, and hematinic
preparations for human use
HQ: Captek Midco, Inc.
16218 Arthur St
Cerritos CA 90703
562 921-9511

(P-3380)
CAPTEK SOFTGEL INTL INC

Also Called: Captek Pharma
14535 Industry Cir, La Mirada (90638-5814)
PHONE..................................657 325-0412
Paul Hwang, *Genl Mgr*
EMP: 50
SALES (corp-wide): 203.23MM **Privately Held**
Web: www.capteksoftgel.com
SIC: 2834 Pharmaceutical preparations
HQ: Captek Softgel International, Inc.
16218 Arthur St
Cerritos CA 90703

(P-3381)
CARDIFF ONCOLOGY INC

Also Called: CARDIFF ONCOLOGY
11055 Flintkote Ave, San Diego
(92121-1220)
PHONE..................................858 952-7570
Mark Erlander, *CEO*
Rodney S Markin, *
James Levine, *
Tod Smeal, *CSO*
EMP: 32 **EST:** 2002
SALES (est): 488K **Privately Held**
Web: www.cardiffoncology.com
SIC: 2834 2836 Pharmaceutical preparations
; Biological products, except diagnostic

(P-3382)
CARLSBAD TECHNOLOGY INC

Also Called: Carlsbad Tech
5923 Balfour Ct, Carlsbad (92008-7304)
PHONE..................................760 431-8284
Robert Wan, *CEO*
EMP: 70
Web: www.carlsbadtech.com
SIC: 2834 Druggists' preparations
(pharmaceuticals)
HQ: Carlsbad Technology Inc.
5922 Frnsworth Ct Ste 101
Carlsbad CA 92008

(P-3383)
CARLSBAD TECHNOLOGY INC (DH)

Also Called: Carlsbad Tech
5922 Farnsworth Ct Ste 101, Carlsbad
(92008-7398)

PHONE..............................760 431-8284
Robert Wan, *CEO*
Andy Cheng, *
▲ **EMP:** 30 **EST:** 1990
SQ FT: 27,000
SALES (est): 23.67MM **Privately Held**
Web: www.carlsbadtech.com
SIC: 2834 Druggists' preparations
(pharmaceuticals)
HQ: Yung Shin Pharm. Ind. Co., Ltd.
No. 1191, Sec. 1, Zhongshan Rd.
Taichung City 43700

(P-3384)
CATALENT PHARMA
SOLUTIONS INC
Also Called: Pharmatek
7330 Carroll Rd Ste 200, San Diego
(92121-2364)
PHONE..............................858 805-6383
EMP: 200
Web: www.catalent.com
SIC: 2834 Pharmaceutical preparations
HQ: Catalent Pharma Solutions, Inc.
14 Schoolhouse Rd
Somerset NJ 08873

(P-3385)
CATALENT PHARMA
SOLUTIONS INC
8926 Ware Ct, San Diego (92121-2222)
PHONE..............................877 587-1835
EMP: 51
Web: www.catalent.com
SIC: 2834 Pharmaceutical preparations
HQ: Catalent Pharma Solutions, Inc.
14 Schoolhouse Rd
Somerset NJ 08873

(P-3386)
CELGENE CORPORATION
Also Called: Celgene Signal Research
10300 Campus Point Dr Ste 100, San Diego
(92121-1504)
PHONE..............................858 795-4961
Alan Lewis, *Brnch Mgr*
EMP: 32
SALES (corp-wide): 45.01B **Publicly Held**
Web: www.bms.com
SIC: 2834 Pharmaceutical preparations
HQ: Celgene Corporation
86 Morris Ave
Summit NJ 07901
908 673-9000

(P-3387)
CH LABORATORIES INC (PA)
1243 W 130th St, Gardena (90247-1501)
PHONE..............................310 516-8273
Brid Nolan, *Pr*
EMP: 24 **EST:** 2001
SQ FT: 30,000
SALES (est): 2.46MM
SALES (corp-wide): 2.46MM **Privately**
Held
Web: www.chlabs.com
SIC: 2834 Vitamin preparations

(P-3388)
CONTINENTAL VITAMIN CO INC
Also Called: Cvc Specialties
4510 S Boyle Ave, Vernon (90058-2418)
PHONE..............................323 581-0176
Ron Beckenfeld, *Pr*
Lillian Beckenfeld, *
EMP: 60 **EST:** 1969
SQ FT: 80,000
SALES (est): 9.54MM **Privately Held**
Web: www.cvc4health.com

SIC: 2834 5122 Vitamin preparations;
Vitamins and minerals

(P-3389)
COSMEDX SCIENCE INC
3550 Vine St Ste 210, Riverside
(92507-4175)
P.O. Box 1925 (92878-1925)
PHONE..............................951 371-0509
▲ **EMP:** 50
Web: www.cosmedxscience.com
SIC: 2834 Dermatologicals

(P-3390)
COUGAR BIOTECHNOLOGY INC
10990 Wilshire Blvd Ste 1200, Los Angeles
(90024-3919)
PHONE..............................310 943-8040
Alan H Auerbach, *Pr*
Charles Eyler, *VP Fin*
Gloria Lee Md, *Clinical Vice President*
Arie S Belldegrun Md, *Ch Bd*
EMP: 58 **EST:** 2003
SQ FT: 7,300
SALES (est): 2.38MM
SALES (corp-wide): 85.16B **Publicly Held**
Web: www.pumabiotechnology.com
SIC: 2834 Drugs affecting neoplasms and
endocrine systems
PA: Johnson & Johnson
1 Johnson & Johnson Plz
732 524-0400

(P-3391)
CRINETICS
PHARMACEUTICALS INC (PA)
Also Called: Crinetics
6055 Lusk Blvd, San Diego (92121-2700)
PHONE..............................858 450-6464
R Scott Struthers, *Pr*
Wendell Wierenga, *Ch Bd*
Jeff Knight, *COO*
Marc Wilson, *CFO*
Alan Krasner, *CMO*
EMP: 60 **EST:** 2008
SALES (est): 4.01MM **Publicly Held**
Web: www.crinetics.com
SIC: 2834 Pharmaceutical preparations

(P-3392)
CV SCIENCES INC (PA)
9530 Padgett St Ste 107, San Diego
(92126-4449)
PHONE..............................866 290-2157
Joseph Dowling, *CEO*
Michael Mona Iii, *Pr*
Joerg Grasser, *CFO*
EMP: 30 **EST:** 2013
SALES (est): 16MM
SALES (corp-wide): 16MM **Privately Held**
Web: www.cvsciences.com
SIC: 2834 Pharmaceutical preparations

(P-3393)
CYMBIOTIKA LLC (PA)
5825 Oberlin Dr Ste 5, San Diego
(92121-3777)
PHONE..............................770 910-4945
Shahab Elmi, *CEO*
EMP: 32 **EST:** 2018
SALES (est): 3.39MM
SALES (corp-wide): 3.39MM **Privately**
Held
Web: www.cymbiotika.com
SIC: 2834 Pharmaceutical preparations

(P-3394)
CYMBIOTIKA LLC
8885 Rehco Rd, San Diego (92121-3261)
PHONE..............................949 652-8177

Anya Bytnar, *Mgr*
EMP: 58
SALES (corp-wide): 3.39MM **Privately**
Held
Web: www.cymbiotika.com
SIC: 2834 Pharmaceutical preparations
PA: Cymbiotika Llc
5825 Oberlin Dr Ste 5
770 910-4945

(P-3395)
DENDREON
PHARMACEUTICALS LLC (HQ)
1700 Saturn Way, Seal Beach
(90740-5618)
PHONE..............................562 252-7500
Jason Oneill, *CEO*
Matthew Kemp, *CCO**
Christina Yi, *
Chris Carr, *
EMP: 50 **EST:** 2015
SALES (est): 115.38MM **Privately Held**
Web: www.dendreon.com
SIC: 2834 Pharmaceutical preparations
PA: Nanjing Xinjiekou Department Store
Co., Ltd.
No.1, Zhongshan South Road, Qinhuai
District

(P-3396)
DESIGN THERAPEUTICS INC
Also Called: DESIGN THERAPEUTICS
6005 Hidden Valley Rd Ste 110, Carlsbad
(92011-4223)
PHONE..............................858 293-4900
Pratik Shah, *Ch Bd*
Sean Jeffries, *COO*
Jae B Kim, *CMO*
EMP: 124 **EST:** 2017
SQ FT: 17,270
Web: www.designtx.com
SIC: 2834 Pharmaceutical preparations

(P-3397)
DNIB UNWIND INC
333 S Grand Ave Ste 4070, Los Angeles
(90071-1544)
PHONE..............................213 617-2717
EMP: 114
SIC: 2834 Pharmaceutical preparations

(P-3398)
EARTHRISE NUTRITIONALS
LLC (HQ)
3333 Michelson Dr Ste 300, Irvine
(92612-1683)
PHONE..............................949 623-0980
Ichi Kato, *
▲ **EMP:** 25 **EST:** 1987
SALES (est): 21.94MM **Privately Held**
Web: www.earthrise.com
SIC: 2834 2023 Tablets, pharmaceutical;
Dietary supplements, dairy and non-dairy
based
PA: Dic Corporation
3-7-20, Nihombashi

(P-3399)
EDWARDS LIFESCIENCES LLC
(HQ)
1 Edwards Way, Irvine (92614-5688)
PHONE..............................949 250-2500
Michael A Mussallem, *Managing Member*
▲ **EMP:** 1700 **EST:** 1958
SALES (est): 488.01MM
SALES (corp-wide): 6B **Publicly Held**
Web: www.edwards.com
SIC: 2834 Pharmaceutical preparations
PA: Edwards Lifesciences Corp
1 Edwards Way

949 250-2500

(P-3400)
ELITRA PHARMACEUTICALS
3510 Dunhill St Ste A, San Diego
(92121-1201)
PHONE..............................858 410-3030
Paul R Hamelin, *CEO*
Harry Hixson Junior, *Ch Bd*
J Gordon Foulkes, *Senior Vice President*
Research & Development
EMP: 65 **EST:** 1997
SQ FT: 35,735
SALES (est): 686.93K **Privately Held**
Web: www.elitra.net
SIC: 2834 8731 Pharmaceutical preparations
; Commercial physical research

(P-3401)
EQUILLIUM INC (PA)
2223 Avenida De La Playa Ste 105, La Jolla
(92037-3217)
PHONE..............................858 412-1200
Bruce D Steel, *Pr*
Daniel M Bradbury, *Ex Ch Bd*
Stephen Connelly, *CSO*
Christine Zedelmayer, *Sr VP*
Jason A Keyes, *CFO*
EMP: 31 **EST:** 2017
SQ FT: 1,750
SALES (est): 36.08MM
SALES (corp-wide): 36.08MM **Publicly**
Held
Web: www.equilliumbio.com
SIC: 2834 2836 Pharmaceutical preparations
; Biological products, except diagnostic

(P-3402)
ERASCA INC
Also Called: Erasca
3115 Merryfield Row Ste 300, San Diego
(92121-1174)
PHONE..............................858 465-6511
Jonathan E Lim, *Ch Bd*
David M Chacko, *Chief Business Officer*
Ebun S Garner, *Corporate Secretary*
Shannon R Morris, *CMO*
EMP: 126 **EST:** 2018
SQ FT: 77,828
Web: www.erasca.com
SIC: 2834 Pharmaceutical preparations

(P-3403)
EVOLUS INC (PA)
Also Called: Evolus
520 Newport Center Dr Ste 1200, Newport
Beach (92660-7022)
PHONE..............................949 284-4555
David Moatazedi, *Pr*
Vikram Malik, *Ch Bd*
Sandra Beaver, *CFO*
Rui Avelar, *Chief Medical Officer*
Tomoko Yamagishi-dressler, *CMO*
EMP: 251 **EST:** 2012
SQ FT: 17,758
SALES (est): 202.09MM **Publicly Held**
Web: www.evolus.com
SIC: 2834 Pharmaceutical preparations

(P-3404)
FORMEX LLC
9601 Jeronimo Rd, Irvine (92618-2025)
PHONE..............................858 529-6600
Cyrus K Mirsaidi, *Pr*
Ian Wisenberg, *
J Blair West, *CSO**
EMP: 32 **EST:** 2013
SALES (est): 4.49MM **Privately Held**
Web: www.formexllc.com

PRODUCTS & SVCS

SIC: 2834 8731 8071 Tablets,
pharmaceutical; Biological research;
Testing laboratories
PA: Bioduro Llc
11011 Torreyana Rd

(P-3405)
GENENTECH INC
1 Antibody Way, Oceanside (92056-5701)
PHONE..............................760 231-2440
Amr Elkhayat, *Dir*
EMP: 5051
Web: www.gene.com
SIC: 2834 Pharmaceutical preparations
HQ: Genentech, Inc.
1 Dna Way Stop 258a
South San Francisco CA 94080
650 225-1000

(P-3406)
GENOMICS INST OF NVRTIS RES FN
10675 John J Hopkins Dr, San Diego
(92121-1127)
PHONE..............................858 812-1805
Genevieve Welch, *Prin*
EMP: 64 EST: 2013
SALES (est): 3.51MM **Privately Held**
Web: www.novartis.com
SIC: 2834 Pharmaceutical preparations

(P-3407)
GENVIVO INC
1981 E Locust St, Ontario (91761-7608)
PHONE..............................626 441-6695
Chris Bergman, *Brnch Mgr*
EMP: 38
SALES (corp-wide): 6.66MM **Privately Held**
Web: www.genvivoinc.com
SIC: 2834 Pharmaceutical preparations
PA: Genvivo, Inc.
475 Huntington Dr
626 441-6695

(P-3408)
GENZYME CORPORATION
Also Called: Genzyme Genetics
655 E Huntington Dr, Monrovia
(91016-3636)
PHONE..............................626 471-9922
Jane Willis, *Brnch Mgr*
EMP: 77
Web: www.genzyme.com
SIC: 2834 Pharmaceutical preparations
HQ: Genzyme Corporation
450 Water St
Cambridge MA 02141
617 252-7500

(P-3409)
GILEAD PALO ALTO INC
Also Called: Gilead Scientist
550 Cliffside Dr, San Dimas (91773-2978)
PHONE..............................909 394-4000
Chris Beley, *CEO*
EMP: 125
SALES (corp-wide): 27.12B **Publicly Held**
Web: www.gilead.com
SIC: 2834 Pharmaceutical preparations
HQ: Alto Gilead Palo Inc
333 Lakeside Dr
Foster City CA 94404

(P-3410)
GILEAD PALO ALTO INC
4049 Avenida De La Plata, Oceanside
(92056-5802)
PHONE..............................760 945-7701
EMP: 125

SALES (corp-wide): 27.12B **Publicly Held**
Web: www.gilead.com
SIC: 2834 Pharmaceutical preparations
HQ: Alto Gilead Palo Inc
333 Lakeside Dr
Foster City CA 94404

(P-3411)
GILEAD SCIENCES INC
1800 Wheeler St, La Verne (91750-5801)
PHONE..............................650 522-2771
Michael Lee, *Prin*
EMP: 99 EST: 1987
SALES (est): 22.58MM **Privately Held**
Web: www.gilead.com
SIC: 2834 Pharmaceutical preparations

(P-3412)
GMP LABORATORIES AMERICA INC (PA)
Also Called: Gmp Labratories of America
2931 E La Jolla St, Anaheim (92806-1306)
PHONE..............................714 630-2467
Mohammad Ishaq, *CEO*
Suhail Ishaq, *
▲ EMP: 92 EST: 1994
SQ FT: 90,000
SALES (est): 23MM **Privately Held**
Web: www.gmplabs.com
SIC: 2834 Pharmaceutical preparations

(P-3413)
GOSSAMER BIO INC (PA)
3013 Science Park Rd Ste 200, San Diego
(92121-1101)
PHONE..............................858 684-1300
Faheem Hasnain, *Ch Bd*
Bryan Giraudo, *CFO*
Richard Aranda, *CMO*
Bob Smith, *CCO*
Christian Waage, *Ex VP*
EMP: 30 EST: 2015
SQ FT: 63,667
Web: www.gossamerbio.com
SIC: 2834 Pharmaceutical preparations

(P-3414)
GREENWICH BIOSCIENCES LLC (DH)
Also Called: Greenwich Biosciences, Inc.
5750 Fleet St Ste 200, Carlsbad
(92008-4709)
PHONE..............................760 795-2200
Julian Gangolli, *Pr*
Justin Gover, *
Scott Giacobello, *
EMP: 23 EST: 2013
SQ FT: 4,911
SALES (est): 19.51MM **Privately Held**
Web: www.jazzpharma.com
SIC: 2834 Pharmaceutical preparations
HQ: Gw Pharmaceuticals Limited
Sovereign House
Cambridge CAMBS
122 326-6800

(P-3415)
GUCKENHEIMER ENTERPRISES INC
4010 Ocean Ranch Blvd, Oceanside
(92056-5700)
PHONE..............................760 414-3659
EMP: 74
SALES (corp-wide): 44.25MM **Privately Held**
Web: www.gilead.com
SIC: 2834 Pharmaceutical preparations
PA: Guckenheimer Enterprises, Inc.
1850 Gateway Dr Ste 500

650 592-3800

(P-3416)
GYRE THERAPEUTICS INC (PA)
12730 High Bluff Dr Ste 250, San Diego
(92130-3023)
PHONE..............................650 266-8674
Charles Wu, *CEO*
Ying Luo, *Ch Bd*
Songjiang Ma, *Pr*
Ruoyu Chen, *Interim Chief Financial Officer*
Weiguo Ye, *COO*
EMP: 450 EST: 2002
SALES (est): 113.45MM **Publicly Held**
Web: www.catalystbiosciences.com
SIC: 2834 Pharmaceutical preparations

(P-3417)
H J HARKINS COMPANY INC
Also Called: Pharma Pac
1400 W Grand Ave Ste F, Grover Beach
(93433-4221)
PHONE..............................805 929-1333
Norma Jean Erenius, *CEO*
Charles Smith, *
EMP: 50 EST: 1984
SQ FT: 10,000
SALES (est): 2.24MM **Privately Held**
Web: www.pharmapac.com
SIC: 2834 Pharmaceutical preparations

(P-3418)
HARPERS PHARMACY INC
Also Called: Ameripharma
132 S Anita Dr Ste 210, Orange
(92868-3317)
PHONE..............................877 778-3773
Andrew A Harper, *CEO*
Gor Mnatsakanyan, *
EMP: 187 EST: 2016
SALES (est): 14.07MM **Privately Held**
Web: www.ameripharma.com
SIC: 2834 Pharmaceutical preparations

(P-3419)
HERON THERAPEUTICS INC (PA)
Also Called: Heron Therapeutics
4242 Campus Point Ct Ste 200, San Diego
(92121-1513)
PHONE..............................858 251-4400
Craig Collard, *CEO*
Adam Morgan, *
Ira Duarte, *Ex VP*
William Forbes, *CDO*
Brett Fleshman, *Chief Business Officer*
EMP: 122 EST: 1983
SQ FT: 52,148
SALES (est): 127.04MM
SALES (corp-wide): 127.04MM **Publicly Held**
Web: www.herontx.com
SIC: 2834 Pharmaceutical preparations

(P-3420)
HIKMA PHARMACEUTICALS USA INC
2325 Camino Vida Roble Ste B, Carlsbad
(92011-1567)
PHONE..............................760 683-0901
Sigurdur Olafsson, *Brnch Mgr*
EMP: 45
SALES (corp-wide): 2.88B **Privately Held**
Web: www.hikma.com
SIC: 2834 Pharmaceutical preparations
HQ: Hikma Pharmaceuticals Usa Inc.
200 Connell Dr Ste Fl 4
Berkeley Heights NJ 07922
908 673-1030

(P-3421)
HYLANDS CONSUMER HEALTH INC (PA)
Also Called: Hyland's Homeopathic
13301 S Main St, Los Angeles
(90061-1611)
P.O. Box 61067 (90061-0067)
PHONE..............................310 768-0700
Daniel Krombach, *Pr*
Daniel M Krombach, *
Will Righeimer, *
Dan Krombach, *
Stephen Schnack, *
▲ EMP: 300 EST: 1903
SQ FT: 150
SALES (est): 96.52MM
SALES (corp-wide): 96.52MM **Privately Held**
Web: www.hylands.com
SIC: 2834 5912 Pharmaceutical preparations
; Drug stores

(P-3422)
IMPRIMISRX LLC
Also Called: Imprimisrx
1000 Aviara Dr Ste 220, Carlsbad
(92011-4218)
PHONE..............................844 446-6979
EMP: 121 EST: 2019
SALES (est): 17.1MM **Publicly Held**
Web: www.imprimisrx.com
SIC: 2834 Pharmaceutical preparations
PA: Harrow, Inc.
102 Woodmont Blvd Ste 610

(P-3423)
INNOCOLL BIOTHERAPEUTICS NA
5163 Lakeview Canyon Rd, Westlake
Village (91362-5212)
PHONE..............................484 406-5200
Louis Pascarella, *CEO*
EMP: 100 EST: 2015
SALES (est): 2.42MM **Privately Held**
Web: www.innocoll.com
SIC: 2834 Pharmaceutical preparations

(P-3424)
INOVA DIAGNOSTICS INC
9889 Willow Creek Rd, San Diego
(92131-1119)
PHONE..............................858 586-9900
EMP: 143
Web: www.werfen.com
SIC: 2834 Pharmaceutical preparations
HQ: Inova Diagnostics, Inc.
9900 Old Grove Rd
San Diego CA 92131
858 586-9900

(P-3425)
INSTACURE HEALING PRODUCTS
235 N Moorpark Rd Unit 2022, Thousand
Oaks (91360-4311)
PHONE..............................818 222-9600
David Traub, *Owner*
EMP: 33 EST: 2015
SQ FT: 6,000
SALES (est): 476.4K **Privately Held**
Web: www.instacure.net
SIC: 2834 Lip balms

(P-3426)
INTERNATIONAL VITAMIN CORP
Also Called: Adam Nutrition
1 Park Plz Ste 800, Irvine (92614-5998)
PHONE..............................949 664-5500
Iliu Elisara, *Brnch Mgr*

EMP: 125
Web: www.ivcinc.com
SIC: 2834 Vitamin, nutrient, and hematinic preparations for human use
PA: International Vitamin Corporation
4695 Mcarthur Ct Ste 1400

(P-3427)
INTERNATIONAL VITAMIN CORPORAT (PA)
Also Called: I V C
4695 Macarthur Ct Ste 1400, Newport Beach (92660-8896)
PHONE...........................949 664-5500
John Torphy, *CEO*
Bing Ma, *CFO*
Bence Rabo, *
▲ **EMP:** 72 **EST:** 2009
SQ FT: 166,000
SALES (est): 619.44MM **Privately Held**
Web: www.ivcinc.com
SIC: 2834 5149 8099 Vitamin preparations; Organic and diet food; Nutrition services

(P-3428)
INTERNTNAL MDCTION SYSTEMS LTD
Also Called: IMS
1886 Santa Anita Ave, South El Monte (91733-3414)
PHONE...........................626 442-6757
Jack Zhang, *CEO*
William Peters, *
Mary Luo Zhang, *
▲ **EMP:** 720 **EST:** 1963
SALES (est): 28.78MM
SALES (corp-wide): 644.39MM **Publicly Held**
Web: www.amphastar.com
SIC: 2834 2833 3841 Drugs acting on the central nervous system & sense organs; Anesthetics, in bulk form; Surgical and medical instruments
PA: Amphastar Pharmaceuticals Inc
11570 6th St
909 980-9484

(P-3429)
IONIS PHARMACEUTICALS INC
2282 Faraday Ave, Carlsbad (92008-7208)
PHONE...........................760 603-3567
Stanley Crooke, *Brnch Mgr*
EMP: 96
SALES (corp-wide): 787.65MM **Publicly Held**
Web: www.ionispharma.com
SIC: 2834 Pharmaceutical preparations
PA: Ionis Pharmaceuticals, Inc
2855 Gazelle Ct
760 931-9200

(P-3430)
IONIS PHARMACEUTICALS INC
1896 Rutherford Rd, Carlsbad (92008-7326)
PHONE...........................760 931-9200
Alfred Chappell, *Brnch Mgr*
EMP: 100
SALES (corp-wide): 787.65MM **Publicly Held**
Web: www.ionispharma.com
SIC: 2834 Pharmaceutical preparations
PA: Ionis Pharmaceuticals, Inc.
2855 Gazelle Ct
760 931-9200

(P-3431)
IONIS PHARMACEUTICALS INC (PA)
Also Called: Ionis
2855 Gazelle Ct, Carlsbad (92010-6670)
PHONE...........................760 931-9200
Brett P Monia, *CEO*
Joseph Loscalzo, *Non-Executive Chairman of the Board*
Elizabeth L Hougen, *Ex VP*
Joseph T Baroldi, *Chief Business Officer*
C Frank Bennett, *CSO*
▲ **EMP:** 566 **EST:** 1989
SALES (est): 787.65MM
SALES (corp-wide): 787.65MM **Publicly Held**
Web: www.ionispharma.com
SIC: 2834 8731 3845 Pharmaceutical preparations; Medical research, commercial ; Electromedical equipment

(P-3432)
ISTA PHARMACEUTICALS INC
50 Technology Dr, Irvine (92618-2301)
P.O. Box 25169 (18002-5169)
PHONE...........................949 788-6000
EMP: 330
SIC: 2834 Pharmaceutical preparations

(P-3433)
JANSSEN RESEARCH & DEV LLC
3210 Merryfield Row, San Diego (92121-1126)
PHONE...........................858 450-2000
Steve Schuetzle, *Mgr*
EMP: 228
SALES (corp-wide): 85.16B **Publicly Held**
Web: www.janssen.com
SIC: 2834 Pharmaceutical preparations
HQ: Janssen Research & Development, Llc
920 Us Highway 202
Raritan NJ 08869
908 704-4000

(P-3434)
JANUX THERAPEUTICS INC
Also Called: Janux
10955 Vista Sorrento Pkwy Ste 200, San Diego (92130-8699)
PHONE...........................858 751-4493
David Campbell, *Pr*
Ron Barrett, *Ch Bd*
Tommy Diraimondo, *CSO*
EMP: 69 **EST:** 2017
SALES (est): 8.08MM **Privately Held**
Web: www.januxrx.com
SIC: 2834 Pharmaceutical preparations

(P-3435)
JARROW INDUSTRIES LLC (PA)
12246 Hawkins St, Santa Fe Springs (90670-3365)
PHONE...........................562 906-1919
Jarrow Rogovin, *Ch Bd*
Mohammed Khalid, *
Ben Khowong, *
David Chen, *
▲ **EMP:** 74 **EST:** 2000
SQ FT: 125,000
SALES (est): 24.41MM
SALES (corp-wide): 24.41MM **Privately Held**
Web: www.jarrowindustries.com
SIC: 2834 Vitamin preparations

(P-3436)
KATE SOMERVILLE SKINCARE LLC (HQ)
Also Called: Kate Smrvlle Skin Hlth Experts
2121 Park Pl Ste 100, El Segundo (90245-4180)
PHONE...........................323 655-7546
Stuart Hill, *CEO*
Ambrus Seres, *
Lina Goodnight Ctrl, *Prin*
Kate Somerville, *
Michelle Taylor, *
▲ **EMP:** 51 **EST:** 2005
SALES (est): 24.1MM
SALES (corp-wide): 64.79B **Privately Held**
Web: www.katesomerville.com
SIC: 2834 5122 Pharmaceutical preparations ; Toiletries
PA: Unilever Plc
Unilever House

(P-3437)
KC PHARMACEUTICALS INC (PA)
3420 Pomona Blvd, Pomona (91768-3236)
PHONE...........................909 598-9499
Lieutenant Khouw, *Ch Bd*
Doctor Pramuditya Oen, *CEO*
Joseph Sutedjo, *
▲ **EMP:** 62 **EST:** 1987
SQ FT: 20,000
SALES (est): 44.57MM
SALES (corp-wide): 44.57MM **Privately Held**
Web: www.kc-ph.com
SIC: 2834 Solutions, pharmaceutical

(P-3438)
KINDEVA DRUG DELIVERY LP
Also Called: 3m/Pharmaceuticals
19901 Nordhoff St, Northridge (91324-3213)
P.O. Box 1001 (91328-1001)
PHONE...........................818 341-1300
Carol Beesley, *Brnch Mgr*
EMP: 400
Web: www.kindevadd.com
SIC: 2834 Pharmaceutical preparations
PA: Kindeva Drug Delivery L.P.
42 Water St W Bldg 75

(P-3439)
KURA ONCOLOGY INC (PA)
12730 High Bluff Dr Ste 400, San Diego (92130-2079)
PHONE...........................858 500-8800
Troy E Wilson, *Ch Bd*
Kathleen Ford, *COO*
Teresa Bair, *CLO*
Stephen Dale, *Chief Medical Officer*
Brian Powl, *Chief Commercial Officer*
EMP: 36 **EST:** 2007
SQ FT: 13,420
Web: www.kuraoncology.com
SIC: 2834 Pharmaceutical preparations

(P-3440)
KYOWA KIRIN INC
9420 Athena Cir, La Jolla (92037-1387)
PHONE...........................858 952-7000
Steve Schaefer, *Brnch Mgr*
EMP: 50
Web: kkna.kyowakirin.com
SIC: 2834 Pharmaceutical preparations
HQ: Kyowa Kirin, Inc.
510 Carnegie Ctr Ste 600
Princeton NJ 08540
609 919-1100

(P-3441)
KYTHERA BIOPHARMACEUTICALS INC
30930 Russell Ranch Rd Fl 3, Westlake Village (91362-7378)
PHONE...........................818 587-4500
A Robert D Bailey, *Pr*
John W Smither, *CFO*
Elisabeth A Sandoval, *CCO*
Frederick Beddingfield Iii, *CMO*
EMP: 106 **EST:** 2005
SQ FT: 33,198
SALES (est): 25.08MM
SALES (corp-wide): 54.32B **Publicly Held**
Web: www.mykybella.com
SIC: 2834 Dermatologicals
HQ: Allergan Unlimited Company
Clonshaugh Business & Technology Park
Coolock D17 E

(P-3442)
LEINER HEALTH PRODUCTS INC (DH)
Also Called: Leiner Health Products
901 E 233rd St, Carson (90745-6204)
PHONE...........................631 200-2000
Jeffrey A Nagel, *CEO*
Michael Collins, *
Harvey Kamil, *
◆ **EMP:** 200 **EST:** 1952
SQ FT: 488,000
SALES (est): 22.13MM **Privately Held**
Web: www.leiner.com
SIC: 2834 5122 Vitamin, nutrient, and hematinic preparations for human use; Vitamins and minerals
HQ: Nhs U.S., Llc
1041 Us-202
Bridgewater NJ 08807
800 422-2752

(P-3443)
LEINER HEALTH PRODUCTS INC
Also Called: Leiner Health Products
7366 Orangewood Ave, Garden Grove (92841-1412)
PHONE...........................714 898-9936
James Smith, *Mgr*
EMP: 217
Web: www.leiner.com
SIC: 2834 2844 2833 5122 Vitamin, nutrient, and hematinic preparations for human use; Perfumes, cosmetics and other toilet preparations; Medicinals and botanicals; Vitamins and minerals
HQ: Leiner Health Products, Inc.
901 E 233rd St
Carson CA 90745
631 200-2000

(P-3444)
LONGBOARD PHARMACEUTICALS INC
Also Called: LONGBOARD
4275 Executive Sq Ste 950, La Jolla (92037-9208)
PHONE...........................858 789 9283
Kevin R Lind, *Pr*
Paul J Sekhri, *
Brandi L Roberts, *Ex VP*
Randall E Kaye, *Chief Medical Officer*
EMP: 50 **EST:** 2020
SQ FT: 9,289
SALES (est): 1.24MM **Privately Held**
Web: www.longboardpharma.com
SIC: 2834 Pharmaceutical preparations

(P-3445)
LOREM CYTORI USA INC
8659 Production Ave, San Diego (92121-2206)
PHONE...........................858 746-8696
Jonathan Soneff, *CEO*
EMP: 41 **EST:** 2019
SALES (est): 868.85K **Privately Held**
Web: www.cytori.com

PRODUCTS & SVCS

SIC: 2834 Pharmaceutical preparations

(P-3446)
MANNKIND CORPORATION
30930 Russell Ranch Rd Ste 300,
Westlake Village (91362-7379)
PHONE..............................818 661-5000
EMP: 303
SALES (corp-wide): 198.96MM **Publicly Held**
Web: www.mannkindcorp.com
SIC: 2834 Pharmaceutical preparations
PA: Mannkind Corporation
  1 Casper St Ste 330
  818 661-5000

(P-3447)
MARAVAI LFSCENCES HOLDINGS INC (PA)
Also Called: Maravai Lifesciences
10770 Wateridge Cir Ste 200, San Diego
(92121-5801)
PHONE..............................858 546-0004
William Martin Iii, *CEO*
R Andrew Eckert, *Ch Bd*
Eric Tardif, *Pr*
Kevin Herde, *CFO*
Brian Neel Coo Nucleic Acid Production, *Prin*
EMP: 27 EST: 2014
SQ FT: 119,000
SALES (est): 288.94MM
SALES (corp-wide): 288.94MM **Publicly Held**
Web: www.maravai.com
SIC: 2834 Pharmaceutical preparations

(P-3448)
MCKENNA LABS INC (PA)
1601 E Orangethorpe Ave, Fullerton
(92831-5230)
PHONE..............................714 687-6888
Dennis Alexander Owen, *Pr*
◆ EMP: 38 EST: 1998
SQ FT: 62,000
SALES (est): 42.48MM
SALES (corp-wide): 42.48MM **Privately Held**
Web: www.mckennalabs.com
SIC: 2834 2844 Pharmaceutical preparations
; Perfumes, cosmetics and other toilet
preparations

(P-3449)
MED-PHARMEX INC
2727 Thompson Creek Rd, Pomona
(91767-1861)
PHONE..............................909 593-7875
Paul Hays, *CEO*
▲ EMP: 117 EST: 1982
SQ FT: 18,000
SALES (est): 29.54MM
SALES (corp-wide): 355.83K **Privately Held**
Web: www.medpharmex.com
SIC: 2834 Pharmaceutical preparations
HQ: Dechra Pharmaceuticals Limited
  24 Cheshire Business Park
  Northwich CW9 7

(P-3450)
MEI PHARMA INC
Also Called: MEI Pharma
11455 El Camino Real Ste 250, San Diego
(92130-2088)
PHONE..............................858 369-7100
Frederick W Driscoll, *Ch Bd*
EMP: 46 EST: 2002
SQ FT: 45,100
SALES (est): 65.3MM **Privately Held**

Web: www.meipharma.com
SIC: 2834 Pharmaceutical preparations

(P-3451)
METACRINE INC
Also Called: Metacrine
3985 Sorrento Valley Blvd Ste C, San Diego
(92121-1497)
PHONE..............................858 369-7800
Preston Klassen, *Pr*
Richard Heyman, *
Patricia Millican, *CFO*
Hubert Chen, *CMO*
EMP: 32 EST: 2014
SQ FT: 20,475
Web: www.metacrine.com
SIC: 2834 Pharmaceutical preparations

(P-3452)
MURAD LLC (HQ)
2121 Park Pl Fl 1, El Segundo
(90245-4843)
PHONE..............................310 726-0600
Elizabeth Ashmun, *
▲ EMP: 160 EST: 1990
SQ FT: 8,000
SALES (est): 52.4MM
SALES (corp-wide): 64.79B **Privately Held**
Web: www.murad.com
SIC: 2834 5122 Vitamin, nutrient, and
hematinic preparations for human use;
Pharmaceuticals
PA: Unilever Plc
  Unilever House

(P-3453)
MURAD LLC
Also Called: Murad
8207 W 3rd St, Los Angeles (90048-4302)
PHONE..............................310 906-3100
EMP: 104
SALES (corp-wide): 64.79B **Privately Held**
Web: www.murad.com
SIC: 2834 Pharmaceutical preparations
HQ: Murad, Llc
  2121 Park Pl Ste 1
  El Segundo CA 90245

(P-3454)
NATALS INC
Also Called: Ritual
1370 N St Andrews Pl, Los Angeles
(90028-8529)
PHONE..............................323 475-6033
Katerina Schneider, *CEO*
Elizabeth Reifsnyder, *
EMP: 110 EST: 2015
SALES (est): 10.19MM **Privately Held**
Web: www.ritual.com
SIC: 2834 Vitamin preparations

(P-3455)
NATIONAL RESILIENCE INC (PA)
Also Called: Resilience
3115 Merryfield Row Ste 200, San Diego
(92121-1174)
PHONE..............................888 737-2460
William S Marth, *Pr*
Sandy Mahatme, *Pr*
Elliot Menschik, *Chief Digital Officer*
Georgeta Puscalau, *Chief Quality Officer*
EMP: 23 EST: 2020
SALES (est): 535.8MM
SALES (corp-wide): 535.8MM **Privately Held**
Web: www.resilience.com
SIC: 2834 Pharmaceutical preparations

(P-3456)
NATROL INC
21411 Prairie St, Chatsworth (91311-5829)
PHONE..............................818 739-6000
◆ EMP: 230
SIC: 2834 2833 Vitamin, nutrient, and
hematinic preparations for human use;
Medicinals and botanicals

(P-3457)
NATROL LLC (PA)
15233 Ventura Blvd Fl 900, Sherman Oaks
(91403-2250)
PHONE..............................800 262-8765
Nina Barton, *CEO*
◆ EMP: 130 EST: 2014
SALES (est): 85.54MM
SALES (corp-wide): 85.54MM **Privately Held**
Web: www.natrol.com
SIC: 2834 Pharmaceutical preparations

(P-3458)
NBTY MANUFACTURING LLC
Also Called: Omni-Pak Industries
5115 E La Palma Ave, Anaheim
(92807-2018)
PHONE..............................714 765-8323
Steve Cahillane, *CEO*
Harvey Kamil, *Managing Member*
Scott Rudolph, *
Hans Lindgren, *
▼ EMP: 224 EST: 1978
SALES (est): 11.07MM **Privately Held**
SIC: 2834 Vitamin preparations
HQ: Nhs U.S., Llc
  1041 Us-202
  Bridgewater NJ 08807
  800 422-2752

(P-3459)
NEURELIS INC (PA)
3430 Carmel Mountain Rd Ste 300, San
Diego (92121-1071)
PHONE..............................858 251-2111
Craig Chambliss, *CEO*
George Stuart, *CFO*
Charles Dewildt, *Chief Commercial Officer*
Brittany Bradrick, *CFO*
Adrian L Rabinowicz, *CMO*
EMP: 30 EST: 2008
SQ FT: 100
SALES (est): 12.17MM
SALES (corp-wide): 12.17MM **Privately Held**
Web: www.neurelis.com
SIC: 2834 Druggists' preparations
(pharmaceuticals)

(P-3460)
NEW GENERATION WELLNESS INC (PA)
Also Called: Nexgen Pharma
46 Corporate Park Ste 200, Irvine
(92606-3120)
P.O. Box 19516 (92623-9516)
PHONE..............................949 863-0340
Kyle Brown, *Pr*
Mark Nishi, *
Chris Limer, *OF DIETARY SUPPLEMENT*
EMP: 190 EST: 1935
SQ FT: 50,000
SALES (est): 52.38MM
SALES (corp-wide): 52.38MM **Privately Held**
Web: www.newgenerationwellness.com
SIC: 2834 Pharmaceutical preparations

(P-3461)
NHK LABORATORIES INC (PA)
12230 Florence Ave, Santa Fe Springs
(90670-3806)
PHONE..............................562 903-5835
Karim Amirul, *CEO*
Nasima A Karim, *
Mohammad H Haque, *
Shafiel Ahmed, *
▲ EMP: 35 EST: 1987
SQ FT: 90,000
SALES (est): 21.21MM **Privately Held**
Web: www.nhklabs.com
SIC: 2834 5122 Vitamin preparations;
Vitamins and minerals

(P-3462)
NHK LABORATORIES INC
10603 Norwalk Blvd, Santa Fe Springs
(90670-3821)
PHONE..............................562 204-5002
Shafiel Ahmed, *CEO*
EMP: 55
Web: www.nhklabs.com
SIC: 2834 5122 Vitamin preparations;
Vitamins and minerals
PA: Nhk Laboratories, Inc.
  12230 Florence Ave

(P-3463)
NURA USA LLC
Also Called: Nura
2652 White Rd, Irvine (92614-6248)
PHONE..............................949 946-5700
Lily Ruan, *Pr*
EMP: 30 EST: 2018
SALES (est): 8.14MM **Privately Held**
Web: www.nurausa.com
SIC: 2834 Vitamin preparations

(P-3464)
NUTRAWISE HEALTH & BEAUTY LLC
Also Called: Nutrawise
9600 Toledo Way, Irvine (92618-1808)
PHONE..............................888 271-8976
Darren Rude, *CEO*
Patty Terzo-rude, *Pr*
EMP: 95 EST: 2010
SQ FT: 130,000
SALES (est): 37.44MM
SALES (corp-wide): 492.26MM **Privately Held**
Web: www.youtheory.com
SIC: 2834 Vitamin, nutrient, and hematinic
preparations for human use
PA: Jamieson Wellness Inc
  1 Adelaide St E Suite 2200
  416 960-0052

(P-3465)
ONYX PHARMACEUTICALS INC
1 Amgen Center Dr, Newbury Park
(91320-1730)
PHONE..............................650 266-0000
Pablo Cagnoni, *Pr*
Bob Goeltz, *Ex Dir*
Matthew K Fust, *Ex VP*
Suzanne M Shema, *Ex VP*
Helen Torley, *Ex VP*
EMP: 741 EST: 2013
SQ FT: 297,111
SALES (est): 26.92MM
SALES (corp-wide): 28.19B **Publicly Held**
SIC: 2834 8049 Drugs affecting parasitic and
infective diseases; Occupational therapist
PA: Amgen Inc.
  1 Amgen Center Dr
  805 447-1000

(P-3466)
OREXIGEN THERAPEUTICS INC
Also Called: Orexigen
3344 N Torrey Pines Ct Ste 200, La Jolla
(92037-1024)
PHONE...................858 875-8600
Thomas P Lynch, *Pr*
Thomas P Lynch, *Pr*
Lota S Zoth, *
EMP: 100 **EST:** 2003
SQ FT: 29,935
SALES (est): 5.9MM
SALES (corp-wide): 47.13MM **Privately Held**
Web: www.curraxpharma.com
SIC: 2834 Pharmaceutical preparations
HQ: Nalpropion Pharmaceuticals, Llc
155 Franklin Rd Ste 450
Brentwood TN 37027
800 793-2145

(P-3467)
OTONOMY INC
Also Called: Otonomy
4796 Executive Dr, San Diego
(92121-3090)
PHONE...................619 323-2200
David A Weber, *Pr*
Jay Lichter, *
Paul E Cayer, *Chief Business Officer*
EMP: 56 **EST:** 2008
SQ FT: 62,000
SALES (est): 125K **Privately Held**
Web: www.otonomy.com
SIC: 2834 Pharmaceutical preparations

(P-3468)
P & L DEVELOPMENT LLC
Also Called: Pl Development
11865 Alameda St, Lynwood (90262-4022)
PHONE...................323 567-2482
Jim Smith, *Genl Mgr*
EMP: 110
Web: www.pldevelopments.com
SIC: 2834 2841 2844 Pharmaceutical
preparations; Soap and other detergents;
Perfumes, cosmetics and other toilet
preparations
PA: P & L Development, Llc
200 Hicks St

(P-3469)
PACIFIC PHARMA INC
18600 Von Karman Ave, Irvine
(92612-1513)
PHONE...................714 246-4600
Roger Maffia, *Dir*
EMP: 2000 **EST:** 1997
SALES (est): 1.52MM
SALES (corp-wide): 54.32B **Publicly Held**
SIC: 2834 Pharmaceutical preparations
HQ: Allergan, Inc.
1 N Waukegan Rd
North Chicago IL 60064
862 261-7000

(P-3470)
PACIFIC SHORE HOLDINGS INC
Also Called: Nature-Cide
8236 Remmet Ave, Canoga Park
(91304-4156)
PHONE...................818 998-0996
Matthew Mills, *Pr*
Jennifer Mills, *
Ronald J Tchorzewski, *
David E Toomey, *
▲ **EMP:** 24 **EST:** 1981
SQ FT: 13,000
SALES (est): 5.25MM
SALES (corp-wide): 5.25MM **Privately
Held**

Web: www.pac-sh.com
SIC: 2834 2879 Pharmaceutical preparations
; Pesticides, agricultural or household
PA: X Med Inc
8236 Remmet Ave
818 349-2870

(P-3471)
**PACIRA PHARMACEUTICALS
INC**
10578 Science Center Dr, San Diego
(92121-1143)
PHONE...................858 625-2424
Chuck Laranjeira, *Pr*
EMP: 73 **EST:** 2022
SALES (est): 3.31MM **Publicly Held**
Web: www.pacira.com
SIC: 2834 Pharmaceutical preparations
PA: Pacira Biosciences, Inc.
5401 W Knnedy Blvd Lncoln

(P-3472)
PFENEX INC
Also Called: Pfenex
10790 Roselle St, San Diego (92121-1508)
PHONE...................858 352-4400
Evert B Schimmelpennink, *
Evert B Schimmelpennink, *
Jason Grenfell-gardner, *Ch Bd*
Shawn A Scranton, *Sr VP*
Patrick K Lucy, *Chief Business Officer*
EMP: 81 **EST:** 2009
SQ FT: 46,959
SALES (est): 9.84MM
SALES (corp-wide): 131.31MM **Publicly
Held**
Web: www.pelicanexpression.com
SIC: 2834 Pharmaceutical preparations
PA: Ligand Pharmaceuticals Incorporated
555 Heritage Dr Ste 200
858 550-7500

(P-3473)
PFIZER INC
Also Called: Pfizer
10777 Science Center Dr, San Diego
(92121-1111)
PHONE...................858 622-3000
Karen Katen, *Brnch Mgr*
EMP: 92
SALES (corp-wide): 58.5B **Publicly Held**
Web: www.pfizer.com
SIC: 2834 Pharmaceutical preparations
PA: Pfizer Inc.
66 Hudson Blvd E
212 733-2323

(P-3474)
PFIZER INC
Also Called: Pfizer
10646 Science Center Dr, San Diego
(92121-1150)
PHONE...................858 622-3001
Mary Mateja, *Mgr*
EMP: 57
SALES (corp-wide): 58.5B **Publicly Held**
Web: www.pfizer.com
SIC: 2834 Pharmaceutical preparations
PA: Pfizer Inc.
66 Hudson Blvd E
212 733-2323

(P-3475)
**PHARMACEUTIC LITHO LABEL
INC**
3990 Royal Ave, Simi Valley (93063-3380)
PHONE...................805 285-5162
Timothy Laurence, *Pr*
Tom Moore, *Pr*
Rick Machale, *VP*

▲ **EMP:** 85 **EST:** 1964
SQ FT: 32,000
SALES (est): 21.15MM **Privately Held**
Web: www.resourcelabel.com
SIC: 2834 Pharmaceutical preparations
PA: Resource Label Group, Llc
2550 Mridian Blvd Ste 370

(P-3476)
PHARMION CORPORATION
12481 High Bluff Dr Ste 200, San Diego
(92130-3583)
PHONE...................858 335-5744
Jeffry Howbert, *Brnch Mgr*
EMP: 48
SALES (corp-wide): 45.01B **Publicly Held**
Web: www.bms.com
SIC: 2834 Pharmaceutical preparations
HQ: Pharmion Corporation
86 Morris Ave
Summit NJ 07901
908 673-9000

(P-3477)
**POLYPEPTIDE LABS SAN
DIEGO LLC**
9395 Cabot Dr, San Diego (92126-4310)
PHONE...................858 408-0808
EMP: 72 **EST:** 1986
SQ FT: 43,000
SALES (est): 9.12MM **Privately Held**
Web: www.polypeptide.com
SIC: 2834 2833 8731 Pharmaceutical
preparations; Medicinals and botanicals;
Biotechnical research, commercial
HQ: Polypeptide Laboratories Inc.
365 Maple Ave
Torrance CA 90503

(P-3478)
**PRESCIENT HOLDINGS GROUP
LLC**
10181 Scripps Gateway Ct, San Diego
(92131-5152)
PHONE...................858 790-7004
Christine Nguyen, *Pr*
Debra Minich, *Dir*
Ethan Dargie, *VP*
Mike Schneider, *VP*
Vasu Bobba, *VP*
EMP: 39 **EST:** 2021
SALES (est): 986.07K **Privately Held**
Web: www.prescientholdingsgroup.com
SIC: 2834 Pharmaceutical preparations

(P-3479)
PRIMAPHARMA INC
3443 Tripp Ct, San Diego (92121-1032)
PHONE...................858 259-0969
Mark Livingston, *Pr*
Tony Dziabo, *
Larry Braga, *
Nayaz Ahmed, *
Arshad Chaudry, *
EMP: 35 **EST:** 2015
SQ FT: 24,000
SALES (est): 5.2MM **Privately Held**
Web: www.primapharma.net
SIC: 2834 Pharmaceutical preparations

(P-3480)
**PROMETHEUS BIOSCIENCES
INC**
3050 Science Park Rd, San Diego
(92121-1102)
PHONE...................858 422-4300
Mark C Mckenna, *Ch Bd*
Keith W Marshall, *CFO*
Mark Stenhouse, *COO*

EMP: 72 **EST:** 2016
SALES (est): 6.81MM
SALES (corp-wide): 60.12B **Publicly Held**
Web: www.prometheuslabs.com
SIC: 2834 Pharmaceutical preparations
PA: Merck & Co., Inc.
126 E Lincoln Ave
908 740-4000

(P-3481)
**PROMETHEUS LABORATORIES
INC (PA)**
9410 Carroll Park Dr, San Diego
(92121-5201)
PHONE...................858 824-0895
Warren Cresswell, *CEO*
Peter Westlake, *CFO*
Robert Carlson, *VP*
Bruce M Wagman, *VP*
Larry Mimms Ph.d., *VP*
EMP: 405 **EST:** 1996
SQ FT: 99,000
SALES (est): 33.67MM **Privately Held**
Web: www.prometheuslabs.com
SIC: 2834 8011 Pharmaceutical preparations
; Offices and clinics of medical doctors

(P-3482)
PROTAB LABORATORIES (PA)
25892 Towne Centre Dr, Foothill Ranch
(92610-3409)
PHONE...................949 635-1930
Min W Chen, *CEO*
Randy L Pollan, *VP*
Shafiqul Islam, *VP*
Joanne Hsu, *Dir Opers*
▲ **EMP:** 65 **EST:** 2004
SALES (est): 31.26MM **Privately Held**
Web: www.protablabs.com
SIC: 2834 2023 Vitamin preparations;
Dietary supplements, dairy and non-dairy
based

(P-3483)
PROTAB LABORATORIES
30321 Esperanza, Rcho Sta Marg
(92688-2119)
PHONE...................949 713-1301
Son Dao, *Brnch Mgr*
EMP: 85
Web: www.protablabs.com
SIC: 2834 Pharmaceutical preparations
PA: Protab Laboratories
25892 Towne Centre Dr

(P-3484)
**PUMA BIOTECHNOLOGY INC
(PA)**
Also Called: Puma Biotechnology
10880 Wilshire Blvd Ste 2150, Los Angeles
(90024-4100)
P.O. Box 64945 (55164-0945)
PHONE...................424 248-6500
Alan H Auerbach, *Ch Bd*
Maximo F Nougues, *CFO*
Alvin Wong, *CSO*
Jeff Ludwig, *CCO*
Douglas Hunt, *Regional AFF MED AFF
PHARMA*
EMP: 185 **EST:** 2007
SQ FT: 65,656
SALES (est): 235.64MM
SALES (corp-wide): 235.64MM **Publicly
Held**
Web: www.pumabiotechnology.com
SIC: 2834 Pharmaceutical preparations

P R O D U C T S   &   S V C S

(P-3485)
PURETEK CORPORATION (PA)
1145 Arroyo St Ste D, San Fernando
(91340-1839)
PHONE..................818 361-3316
Barry Pressman, *CEO*
◆ **EMP:** 50 **EST:** 1991
SQ FT: 114,000
SALES (est): 55.92MM **Privately Held**
Web: www.puretekcorp.com
SIC: 2834 Pharmaceutical preparations

(P-3486)
PURETEK CORPORATION
7900 Nelson Rd Unit A, Panorama City
(91402-6828)
PHONE..................818 361-3949
Jeff Pressman, *Brnch Mgr*
EMP: 130
Web: www.puretekcorp.com
SIC: 2834 2844 Pharmaceutical preparations
; Cosmetic preparations
PA: Puretek Corporation
1145 Arroyo Ave Unit D

(P-3487)
QUOREX PHARM INC (PA)
2232 Rutherford Rd, Carlsbad
(92008-8814)
PHONE..................760 602-1910
Robert Robb, *Pr*
Robert Robb, *Pr*
Jeffrey Stein, *Chief Scientist**
Krzysztof Appelt, *Technology**
Gary J G Atkinson, *CFO*
EMP: 42 **EST:** 1999
SQ FT: 23,500
SALES (est): 1.99MM
SALES (corp-wide): 1.99MM **Privately Held**
SIC: 2834 Pharmaceutical preparations

(P-3488)
RANIR LLC
Also Called: Dr. Fresh
6 Centerpointe Dr Ste 640, La Palma
(90623-2587)
PHONE..................866 373-7374
Kevin Parekh, *Brnch Mgr*
EMP: 34
Web: www.perrigo.com
SIC: 2834 Pharmaceutical preparations
HQ: Ranir, Llc
4701 E Paris Ave Se
Grand Rapids MI 49512
616 698-8880

(P-3489)
RECEPTOS INC
3033 Science Park Rd Ste 300, San Diego
(92121-1168)
PHONE..................858 652-5700
Faheem Hasnain, *Pr*
Marcus F Boehm, *
Graham Cooper, *
Shiela Gujrathi, *CMO**
Robert J Peach, *CSO**
EMP: 32 **EST:** 2009
SALES (est): 7.27MM
SALES (corp-wide): 45.01B **Publicly Held**
Web: www.celgene.com
SIC: 2834 Pharmaceutical preparations
HQ: Celgene Corporation
86 Morris Ave
Summit NJ 07901
908 673-9000

(P-3490)
REDWOOD SCIENTIFIC TECH INC
245 E Main St Ste 115, Alhambra
(91801-7507)
PHONE..................310 693-5401
Jason E Cardiff, *Pr*
Eunjung Cardiff, *
Jacques Poujade, *
Rhonda Pearlman, *
M Salah Zaki, *CMO**
EMP: 24 **EST:** 2014
SALES (est): 933.91K **Privately Held**
SIC: 2834 Druggists' preparations
(pharmaceuticals)

(P-3491)
REMPEX PHARMACEUTICALS INC
3013 Science Park Rd 1st Fl, San Diego
(92121-1101)
PHONE..................858 875-2840
Stuart Kingsley, *Pr*
William Oconner, *
EMP: 40 **EST:** 2013
SQ FT: 60
SALES (est): 3.13MM **Privately Held**
SIC: 2834 Pharmaceutical preparations
HQ: The Medicines Company
8 Sylvan Way
Parsippany NJ 07054
973 290-6000

(P-3492)
RESILIENCE US INC (HQ)
3115 Merryfield Row Ste 200, San Diego
(92121-1174)
PHONE..................984 202-0854
Sandy Mahatme, *Pr*
EMP: 23 **EST:** 2020
SALES (est): 98.63MM
SALES (corp-wide): 535.8MM **Privately Held**
SIC: 2834 3559 Pharmaceutical preparations
; Pharmaceutical machinery
PA: National Resilience, Inc.
3115 Mrryfeld Row Ste 200
888 737-2460

(P-3493)
ROBINSON PHARMA INC
3300 W Segerstrom Ave, Santa Ana
(92704-6403)
PHONE..................714 241-0235
Gulfam Sheikh, *Mgr*
EMP: 120
Web: www.robinsonpharma.com
SIC: 2834 Medicines, capsuled or ampuled
PA: Robinson Pharma, Inc.
3330 S Harbor Blvd

(P-3494)
ROBINSON PHARMA INC (PA)
3330 S Harbor Blvd, Santa Ana
(92704-6831)
PHONE..................714 241-0235
Tuong Nguyen, *CEO*
Tam Nguyen, *
Elaine Phan, *
◆ **EMP:** 310 **EST:** 1989
SQ FT: 124,000
SALES (est): 91.87MM **Privately Held**
Web: www.robinsonpharma.com
SIC: 2834 Medicines, capsuled or ampuled

(P-3495)
ROBINSON PHARMA INC
3701 W Warner Ave, Santa Ana
(92704-5218)
PHONE..................714 241-0235
Tam H Nguyen, *CEO*
EMP: 121
Web: www.robinsonpharma.com

SIC: 2834 7389 Pharmaceutical preparations
; Packaging and labeling services
PA: Robinson Pharma, Inc.
3330 S Harbor Blvd

(P-3496)
S K LABORATORIES INC
Also Called: S K Labs
5420 E La Palma Ave, Anaheim
(92807-2023)
PHONE..................714 695-9800
Bansi Patel, *Pr*
Ramila B Patel, *
▲ **EMP:** 100 **EST:** 1992
SQ FT: 60,000
SALES (est): 25MM **Privately Held**
Web: www.sklabs.com
SIC: 2834 Pharmaceutical preparations

(P-3497)
SAMSON PHARMACEUTICALS INC
5635 Smithway St, Commerce
(90040-1545)
PHONE..................323 722-3066
Jay Kassir, *Pr*
▲ **EMP:** 40 **EST:** 2001
SALES (est): 6.16MM **Privately Held**
Web: www.samsonpharmaceutical.com
SIC: 2834 Pharmaceutical preparations

(P-3498)
SAPU BIOSCIENCE LLC
10840 Thornmint Rd Ste 118, San Diego
(92127-2404)
PHONE..................650 635-7018
Vuong Trieu, *Managing Member*
Chao Hsiao, *
EMP: 25 **EST:** 2022
SALES (est): 5.49MM **Privately Held**
SIC: 2834 Pharmaceutical preparations

(P-3499)
SENTYNL THERAPEUTICS INC
420 Stevens Ave Ste 200, Solana Beach
(92075-2078)
PHONE..................888 227-8725
Matt Heck, *CEO*
Daniel Stokely, *
Michael Hercz, *General**
Darren Pincus, *
Shawn Scranton, *
EMP: 30 **EST:** 2011
SALES (est): 6.4MM **Privately Held**
Web: www.sentynl.com
SIC: 2834 Pharmaceutical preparations
HQ: Zydus Lifesciences Limited
Zydus Corporate Park Scheme No. 63,
Survey No. 536,
Ahmedabad GJ 38248

(P-3500)
SHIRE
1445 Lawrence Dr, Newbury Park
(91320-1311)
PHONE..................805 372-3000
John Sandstrom, *Prin*
EMP: 43 **EST:** 2018
SALES (est): 1.07MM **Privately Held**
Web: www.takeda.com
SIC: 2834 Pharmaceutical preparations

(P-3501)
SHIRE RGENERATIVE MEDICINE INC
Also Called: Advanced Biohealing.com
11095 Torreyana Rd, San Diego
(92121-1104)
PHONE..................858 754-5396

EMP: 50
SIC: 2834 Pharmaceutical preparations
HQ: Shire Regenerative Medicine, Inc.
36 Church Ln
Westport CT 06880
877 422-4463

(P-3502)
SICOR INC (HQ)
19 Hughes, Irvine (92618-1902)
PHONE..................949 455-4700
Carlo Salvi, *Vice Chairman*
▲ **EMP:** 800 **EST:** 1986
SQ FT: 170,000
SALES (est): 17.49MM **Privately Held**
Web: www.tevausa.com
SIC: 2834 8731 Drugs acting on the
cardiovascular system, except diagnostic;
Medical research, commercial
PA: Teva Pharmaceutical Industries Limited
124 Dvora Hanevia

(P-3503)
SIGNAL PHARMACEUTICALS LLC
10300 Campus Point Dr Ste 100, San Diego
(92121-1504)
PHONE..................858 795-4700
Alan J Lewis Ph.d., *Pr*
Shripad Bhagwat, *Drug Discovery Vice President**
David R Webb, *Research Vice President**
EMP: 134 **EST:** 1992
SQ FT: 78,202
SALES (est): 40.2MM
SALES (corp-wide): 45.01B **Publicly Held**
SIC: 2834 Pharmaceutical preparations
HQ: Celgene Corporation
86 Morris Ave
Summit NJ 07901
908 673-9000

(P-3504)
SIMPSON INDUSTRIES INC
Also Called: Simpsonsimpson Industries
20611 Belshaw Ave, Carson (90746-3507)
PHONE..................310 605-1224
Rick Simpson, *CEO*
Robert Simpson, *
EMP: 35 **EST:** 2011
SALES (est): 4.07MM **Privately Held**
Web: www.simpsonindustries.com
SIC: 2834 Proprietary drug products

(P-3505)
SKINMEDICA INC
18655 Teller Ave, Irvine (92612-1610)
P.O. Box 19534 (92623-9534)
PHONE..................760 929-2600
▲ **EMP:** 275
Web: www.skinmedica.com
SIC: 2834 2844 Dermatologicals; Perfumes,
cosmetics and other toilet preparations

(P-3506)
SOCIETAL CDMO SAN DIEGO LLC
6828 Nancy Ridge Dr Ste 100, San Diego
(92121-2224)
PHONE..................858 623-1520
J David Enloe Junior, *Pr*
Ryan Lake, *
Scott Rizzo, *
EMP: 55 **EST:** 2015
SQ FT: 24,100
SALES (est): 10.92MM **Privately Held**
SIC: 2834 Druggists' preparations
(pharmaceuticals)
HQ: Societal Cdmo, Inc.
490 Lapp Rd

▲ = Import ▼ = Export
◆ = Import/Export

Malvern PA 19355

(P-3507)
SPYGLASS PHARMA INC
27061 Aliso Creek Rd Ste 100, Aliso Viejo
(92656-5322)
PHONE..............................949 284-6904
Patrick Mooney, *CEO*
Margot Goodkin, *CMO*
James Dennewill, *CFO*
EMP: 23 **EST:** 2019
SALES (est): 3.56MM **Privately Held**
Web: www.spyglasspharma.com
SIC: 2834 Pharmaceutical preparations

(P-3508)
ST JUDE MEDICAL LLC
Also Called: Sjm Facility
2375 Morse Ave, Irvine (92614-6233)
PHONE..............................949 769-5000
EMP: 24
SALES (corp-wide): 40.11B **Publicly Held**
Web: www.cardiovascular.abbott
SIC: 2834 Pharmaceutical preparations
HQ: St. Jude Medical, Llc
1 Saint Jude Medical Dr
Saint Paul MN 55117
651 756-2000

(P-3509)
STA PHARMACEUTICAL US LLC
6114 Nancy Ridge Dr, San Diego
(92121-3223)
PHONE..............................609 606-6499
Chen Hui, *CFO*
EMP: 40 **EST:** 2016
SALES (est): 5.48MM **Privately Held**
Web: www.stapharma.com
SIC: 2834 Pharmaceutical preparations

(P-3510)
STERISYN INC
Also Called: Sterisyn Scientific
11969 Challenger Ct, Moorpark
(93021-7119)
PHONE..............................805 991-9694
Julie Anne, *Admn*
Timothy Henry, *CEO*
EMP: 30 **EST:** 2015
SALES (est): 789.15K **Privately Held**
Web: www.sterisyn.com
SIC: 2834 Pharmaceutical preparations

(P-3511)
SYNTHORX INC
Also Called: Synthorx
11099 N Torrey Pines Rd Ste 190, La Jolla
(92037-1029)
PHONE..............................858 352-5100
John Reed, *Pr*
Marie Dehans, *
EMP: 38 **EST:** 2014
SQ FT: 8,636
SALES (est): 7.66MM **Publicly Held**
Web: www.synthorx.com
SIC: 2834 8731 Pharmaceutical preparations
; Biotechnical research, commercial
HQ: Aventis Inc.
55 Corporate Dr
Bridgewater NJ 08807

(P-3512)
TEVA PARENTERAL MEDICINES INC
19 Hughes, Irvine (92618-1902)
P.O. Box 57049 (92618)
PHONE..............................949 455-4700
Phillip Frost, *Ch Bd*
Amir Elstein, *
Karin Shanahan, *

Nir Baron, *
Iris Beck-codner, *VP*
▲ **EMP:** 830 **EST:** 1990
SQ FT: 148,000
SALES (est): 30.16MM **Privately Held**
SIC: 2834 Pills, pharmaceutical
HQ: Teva Pharmaceuticals Usa, Inc.
400 Interpace Pkwy Bldg A
Parsippany NJ 07054
215 591-3000

(P-3513)
TRAVERE THERAPEUTICS INC (PA)
Also Called: Travere
3611 Valley Centre Dr Ste 300, San Diego
(92130-3331)
PHONE..............................888 969-7879
Eric Dube, *Pr*
Gary Lyons, *Ch Bd*
Christopher Cline, *CFO*
Peter Heerma, *CCO*
Elizabeth E Reed, *Corporate Secretary*
EMP: 334 **EST:** 2008
SQ FT: 149,123
SALES (est): 145.24MM **Publicly Held**
Web: www.travere.com
SIC: 2834 8731 Pharmaceutical preparations
; Biotechnical research, commercial

(P-3514)
TRIUS THERAPEUTICS LLC
4747 Executive Dr Ste 1100, San Diego
(92121-3114)
PHONE..............................858 452-0370
Jeffrey Stein, *Pr*
John P Schmid, *
Michael Morneau, *CAO*
Kenneth Bartizal, *Chief Development Officer*
John Finn, *
EMP: 152 **EST:** 2007
SQ FT: 39,000
SALES (est): 4.15MM
SALES (corp-wide): 60.12B **Publicly Held**
Web: www.triusrx.com
SIC: 2834 Antibiotics, packaged
HQ: Cubist Pharmaceuticals Llc
2000 Galloping Hill Road
Kenilworth NJ 07033

(P-3515)
TYRA BIOSCIENCES INC
Also Called: TYRA
2656 State St, Carlsbad (92008-1626)
PHONE..............................619 728-4760
Todd Harris, *Pr*
Robert More, *
Daniel Bensen, *COO*
Alan Fuhrman, *CFO*
Hiroomi Tada, *CMO*
EMP: 49 **EST:** 2018
SQ FT: 4,734
Web: www.tyra.bio
SIC: 2834 Pharmaceutical preparations

(P-3516)
UNITED PHARMA LLC
2317 Moore Ave, Fullerton (92833-2510)
PHONE..............................714 738-8999
Bill Wang, *Pr*
▲ **EMP:** 130 **EST:** 2006
SQ FT: 53,000
SALES (est): 24.18MM **Privately Held**
Web: www.unitedpharmallc.com
SIC: 2834 Pharmaceutical preparations

(P-3517)
VERTEX PHRMCTCALS SAN DEGO LLC (HQ)

3215 Merryfield Row, San Diego
(92121-1126)
PHONE..............................858 404-6600
Joshua S Boger, *Managing Member*
Ian F Smith, *
▲ **EMP:** 235 **EST:** 2001
SQ FT: 81,000
SALES (est): 32.85MM **Publicly Held**
Web: www.vrtx.com
SIC: 2834 Pharmaceutical preparations
PA: Vertex Pharmaceuticals Incorporated
50 Northern Ave

(P-3518)
VIKING THERAPEUTICS INC (PA)
9920 Pacific Heights Blvd Ste 350, San
Diego (92121-4306)
PHONE..............................858 704-4660
Brian Lian, *Pr*
Lawson Macartney, *Ch Bd*
Marianne Mancini, *COO*
Greg Zante, *CFO*
EMP: 26 **EST:** 2012
SQ FT: 7,940
Web: www.vikingtherapeutics.com
SIC: 2834 Pharmaceutical preparations

(P-3519)
VIRACTA THERAPEUTICS INC (PA)
Also Called: Viracta
2533 S Coast Highway 101 Ste 210, Cardiff
(92007-2133)
PHONE..............................858 400-8470
Mark Rothera, *Pr*
Roger Pomerantz, *Ch Bd*
Melody Burcar, *VP Fin*
Michael Faerm, *CFO*
Darrel Cohen, *Chief Medical Officer*
EMP: 35 **EST:** 1998
SQ FT: 5,337
SALES (est): 4.09MM
SALES (corp-wide): 4.09MM **Publicly Held**
Web: www.sunesis.com
SIC: 2834 Pharmaceutical preparations

(P-3520)
VITATECH NUTRITIONAL SCIENCES INC
2802 Dow Ave, Tustin (92780-7212)
PHONE..............................714 832-9700
▲ **EMP:** 285
SIC: 2834 Vitamin preparations

(P-3521)
WACKER BIOTECH US INC
10390 Pacific Center Ct, San Diego
(92121-4340)
PHONE..............................858 875-4700
Doctor Philippe Cronet, *CEO*
Keith Hall, *
EMP: 24 **EST:** 2018
SQ FT: 68,400
SALES (est): 9.07MM
SALES (corp-wide): 6.96B **Privately Held**
Web: www.wacker.com
SIC: 2834 Pharmaceutical preparations
HQ: Wacker Chemical Corporation
3301 Sutton Rd
Adrian MI 49221
517 264-8500

(P-3522)
WAKUNAGA OF AMERICA CO LTD (HQ)
Also Called: Kyolic
23501 Madero, Mission Viejo (92691-2764)

PHONE..............................949 855-2776
Kazuhiko Nomura, *Pr*
Hiyoshi Sakai, *
◆ **EMP:** 64 **EST:** 1972
SQ FT: 36,000
SALES (est): 31.86MM **Privately Held**
Web: www.kyolic.com
SIC: 2834 Pharmaceutical preparations
PA: Wakunaga Pharmaceutical Co., Ltd.
13-4, Arakicho

(P-3523)
WEST COAST LABORATORIES INC
156 E 162nd St, Gardena (90248-2802)
PHONE..............................310 527-6163
Maurice Ovadia, *Mgr*
EMP: 35
SQ FT: 4,000
SALES (corp-wide): 10.66MM **Privately Held**
Web: www.westcoastlabsinc.com
SIC: 2834 Vitamin preparations
PA: West Coast Laboratories, Inc.
116 E Alondra Blvd
323 321-4774

(P-3524)
XENCOR INC
Also Called: Xencor
465 N Halstead St Ste 200, Pasadena
(91107-3291)
PHONE..............................626 305-5900
Bassil I Dahiyat, *Pr*
John R Desjarlais, *CSO*
Nancy K Valente, *CDO*
Bart Jan Cornelissen, *Sr VP*
Celia E Eckert, *Corporate Secretary*
EMP: 256 **EST:** 1997
SQ FT: 83,083
SALES (est): 168.34MM **Privately Held**
Web: www.xencor.com
SIC: 2834 Pharmaceutical preparations

(P-3525)
YOUCARE PHARMA (USA) INC
132 Business Center Dr, Corona
(92878-3224)
P.O. Box 668 (92878-0668)
PHONE..............................951 258-3114
Weishi Yu, *CEO*
EMP: 60 **EST:** 2015
SQ FT: 160,000
SALES (est): 2.43MM **Privately Held**
SIC: 2834 Pharmaceutical preparations
PA: Youcare Pharmaceutical Group Co.,
Ltd
No. 6, Hongda Middle Road, Economic
And Technological Area

(P-3526)
ZENTALIS PHARMACEUTICALS INC (PA)
Also Called: Zentalis
10275 Science Center Dr Ste 100, San
Diego (92121-1171)
PHONE..............................858 263-4333
Julie Eastland, *Pr*
David M Johnson, *Ch Bd*
Iris Roth, *COO*
Kevin D Bunker, *CSO*
Andrea Paul, *Corporate Secretary*
EMP: 110 **EST:** 2014
SQ FT: 4,115
Web: www.zentalis.com
SIC: 2834 Pharmaceutical preparations

PRODUCTS & SVCS

(P-3527)
ZP OPCO INC
Also Called: Zosano
34790 Ardentech Ct, Los Angeles
(90071-3152)
PHONE..................510 745-1200
Konstantinos Alataris, CEO
Konstantinos Alataris, Pr
Winnie W Tso, CFO
EMP: 32 EST: 2006
SALES (est): 448.57K
SALES (corp-wide): 785K Privately Held
SIC: 2834 Pharmaceutical preparations
PA: Zosano Pharma Corporation
34790 Ardentech Ct
510 745-1200

2835 Diagnostic Substances

(P-3528)
ACON LABORATORIES INC (PA)
9440 Carroll Park Dr, San Diego
(92121-5201)
PHONE..................858 875-8000
Jinn-nan Lin, Pr
▲ EMP: 46 EST: 1999
SQ FT: 36,000
SALES (est): 19.24MM Privately Held
Web: www.aconlabs.com
SIC: 2835 Diagnostic substances

(P-3529)
ALERE INC
9975 Summers Ridge Rd, San Diego
(92121-2997)
PHONE..................858 805-2000
Sabina Roaldset, Brnch Mgr
EMP: 54
SALES (corp-wide): 40.11B Publicly Held
Web: www.globalpointofcare.abbott
SIC: 2835 Diagnostic substances
HQ: Alere Inc.
51 Sawyer Rd Ste 200
Waltham MA 02453
781 647-3900

(P-3530)
ALERE SAN DIEGO INC (DH)
9942 Mesa Rim Rd, San Diego
(92121-2910)
PHONE..................858 805-2000
Christopher Scoggins, CEO
Karen Peterson, *
▲ EMP: 97 EST: 1988
SQ FT: 350,000
SALES (est): 92.79MM
SALES (corp-wide): 40.11B Publicly Held
Web: www.globalpointofcare.abbott
SIC: 2835 Diagnostic substances
HQ: Alere Inc.
51 Sawyer Rd Ste 200
Waltham MA 02453
781 647-3900

(P-3531)
ALERE SAN DIEGO INC
828 Towne Center Dr, Pomona
(91767-5900)
PHONE..................858 805-2000
EMP: 453
SALES (corp-wide): 40.11B Publicly Held
Web: www.globalpointofcare.abbott
SIC: 2835 In vitro diagnostics
HQ: Alere San Diego, Inc.
9942 Mesa Rim Rd
San Diego CA 92121
858 805-2000

(P-3532)
ALERE SAN DIEGO INC
Also Called: Immunalysis
829 Towne Center Dr, Pomona
(91767-5901)
PHONE..................909 482-0840
Bob Funck, Brnch Mgr
EMP: 453
SALES (corp-wide): 40.11B Publicly Held
Web: www.globalpointofcare.abbott
SIC: 2835 3841 Diagnostic substances;
Diagnostic apparatus, medical
HQ: Alere San Diego, Inc.
9942 Mesa Rim Rd
San Diego CA 92121
858 805-2000

(P-3533)
ALFA SCIENTIFIC DESIGNS INC
13200 Gregg St, Poway (92064-7121)
PHONE..................858 513-3888
Chai Bunyagidj, CEO
Chai Bunyagidj, Pr
Naishu Wang, *
Angela Shen, *
Claudia Shen, *
▲ EMP: 94 EST: 1996
SQ FT: 39,000
SALES (est): 18.89MM Privately Held
Web: www.alfascientific.com
SIC: 2835 Diagnostic substances

(P-3534)
BIOCELL LABORATORIES INC
2001 E University Dr, Rancho Dominguez
(90220-6411)
PHONE..................310 537-3300
▲ EMP: 35 EST: 1972
SALES (est): 2.43MM Privately Held
Web: www.biocell.com
SIC: 2835 2836 Diagnostic substances;
Biological products, except diagnostic

(P-3535)
BIOSERV CORPORATION
Also Called: Bioserve
9380 Judicial Dr, San Diego (92121-3830)
PHONE..................917 817-1326
Henry Ji Ph.d., Pr
Kevin Herde, *
EMP: 27 EST: 2016
SALES (est): 5MM
SALES (corp-wide): 62.84MM Publicly
Held
Web: www.bioservamerica.com
SIC: 2835 2834 Diagnostic substances;
Pharmaceutical preparations
PA: Sorrento Therapeutics, Inc.
4955 Directors Pl
858 203-4100

(P-3536)
BIOSOURCE INTERNATIONAL INC
5791 Van Allen Way, Carlsbad
(92008-7321)
PHONE..................805 659-5759
Terrance J Bieker, Pr
Alan Edrick, Ex VP
Kevin J Reagan Ph.d., Executive Technical
Vice President
Jean-pierre L Conte, Ch Bd
Jozef Vangenechten, Executive
Commercial Vice President
EMP: 26 EST: 1989
SQ FT: 51,821
SALES (est): 1.39MM Privately Held
SIC: 2835 Diagnostic substances

(P-3537)
DERMTECH INC (PA)
12340 El Camino Real, San Diego
(92130-3078)
PHONE..................866 450-4223
Bret Christensen, Pr
Matthew Posard, Non-Executive Chairman
of the Board
Kevin Sun, CFO
Claudia Ibarra, COO
Todd Wood, Chief Commercial Officer
EMP: 207 EST: 1995
SQ FT: 28,655
SALES (est): 15.3MM
SALES (corp-wide): 15.3MM Publicly
Held
Web: www.dermtechstratum.com
SIC: 2835 8071 Diagnostic substances;
Testing laboratories

(P-3538)
DIASORIN MOLECULAR LLC
11331 Valley View St, Cypress
(90630-5300)
PHONE..................562 240-6500
Carlo Rosa, CEO
EMP: 200 EST: 2016
SALES (est): 34.34MM Privately Held
Web: int.diasorin.com
SIC: 2835 5047 In vitro diagnostics;
Diagnostic equipment, medical
HQ: Diasorin Inc.
1951 Northwestern Ave
Stillwater MN 55082
651 439-9710

(P-3539)
EPICUREN DISCOVERY
31 Journey Ste 100, Aliso Viejo
(92656-3334)
PHONE..................949 588-5807
Colleen Lohrman, Pr
▲ EMP: 65 EST: 1999
SALES (est): 8.7MM Privately Held
Web: www.epicuren.com
SIC: 2835 Enzyme and isoenzyme
diagnostic agents

(P-3540)
GATEWAY GENOMICS LLC
11436 Sorrento Valley Rd, San Diego
(92121-1349)
P.O. Box 99129 (92169-1129)
PHONE..................858 886-7250
Christopher Jacob, CEO
EMP: 53 EST: 2018
SALES (est): 3.67MM Publicly Held
Web: www.myriad.com
SIC: 2835 Microbiology and virology
diagnostic products
PA: Myriad Genetics, Inc.
322 North 2200 West

(P-3541)
GEN-PROBE INCORPORATED
10210 Genetic Center Dr, San Diego
(92121-4394)
PHONE..................858 410-8000
EMP: 74
SALES (corp-wide): 4.03B Publicly Held
Web: www.gen-probe.com
SIC: 2835 In vitro diagnostics
HQ: Gen-Probe Incorporated
250 Campus Dr
Marlborough MA 01752
508 263-8937

(P-3542)
INOVA DIAGNOSTICS INC
9675 Businesspark Ave, San Diego
(92131-1644)
PHONE..................858 586-9900
Roger Ingles, Brnch Mgr
EMP: 143
Web: www.werfen.com
SIC: 2835 Diagnostic substances
HQ: Inova Diagnostics, Inc.
9900 Old Grove Rd
San Diego CA 92131
858 586-9900

(P-3543)
LEHMAN MILLET INCORPORATED
Also Called: Leham Millet West
3 Macarthur Pl Ste 700, Santa Ana
(92707-6078)
PHONE..................714 850-7900
Bruce Lehman, CEO
EMP: 49
SALES (corp-wide): 15.2MM Privately
Held
Web: www.precisioneffect.com
SIC: 2835 Diagnostic substances
HQ: Lehman Millet Incorporated
101 Tremont St Ste 205
Boston MA 02108
617 722-0019

(P-3544)
LIFE TECHNOLOGIES CORPORATION (HQ)
Also Called: Thermo Fisher Scientific
5781 Van Allen Way, Carlsbad
(92008-7321)
P.O. Box 1039 (92018-1039)
PHONE..................760 603-7200
Seth Hoogasian, CEO
Mark P Stevenson, *
John A Cottingham, CLO*
◆ EMP: 140 EST: 1997
SALES (est): 888.72MM
SALES (corp-wide): 42.86B Publicly Held
Web: www.thermofisher.com
SIC: 2835 2836 Diagnostic substances;
Biological products, except diagnostic
PA: Thermo Fisher Scientific Inc.
168 3rd Ave
781 622-1000

(P-3545)
MOLECULAR PROBES INC
5781 Van Allen Way, Carlsbad
(92008-7321)
PHONE..................760 603-7200
EMP: 31
SALES (corp-wide): 42.86B Publicly Held
SIC: 2835 Diagnostic substances
HQ: Molecular Probes, Inc.
29851 Willow Creek Rd
Eugene OR 97402
760 603-7200

(P-3546)
ORTHO-CLINICAL DIAGNOSTICS INC
612 W Katella Ave Ste B, Orange
(92867-4608)
PHONE..................714 639-2323
Robert Black, Brnch Mgr
EMP: 27
SQ FT: 2,200
SALES (corp-wide): 3B Publicly Held
Web: www.orthoclinicaldiagnostics.com
SIC: 2835 Blood derivative diagnostic agents
HQ: Ortho-Clinical Diagnostics, Inc.
1001 Us Hwy 202
Raritan NJ 08869
908 218-8000

▲ = Import ▼ = Export
◆ = Import/Export

(P-3547)

PACIFIC BIOTECH INC

10165 Mckellar Ct, San Diego
(92121-4201)
PHONE..................858 552-1100
Wayne Kay, *Pr*
EMP: 43 **EST:** 1981
SQ FT: 70,000
SALES (est): 4.87MM
SALES (corp-wide): 3B **Publicly Held**
SIC: 2835 Pregnancy test kits
HQ: Quidel Corporation
9975 Summers Ridge Rd
San Diego CA 92121
858 552-1100

(P-3548)

QUANTIMETRIX

2005 Manhattan Beach Blvd, Redondo
Beach (90278-1205)
PHONE..................310 536-0006
Monty Ban, *Pr*
Edward Cleek, *
Abdee Akhavan, *
EMP: 70 **EST:** 1974
SQ FT: 86,400
SALES (est): 8.77MM **Privately Held**
Web: www.quantimetrix.com
SIC: 2835 Diagnostic substances

(P-3549)

QUIDEL CORPORATION

10165 Mckellar Ct, San Diego
(92121-4299)
PHONE..................858 552-1100
EMP: 26
SALES (corp-wide): 3B **Publicly Held**
Web: www.quidelortho.com
SIC: 2835 Diagnostic substances
HQ: Quidel Corporation
9975 Summers Ridge Rd
San Diego CA 92121
858 552-1100

(P-3550)

QUIDEL CORPORATION (HQ)

9975 Summers Ridge Rd, San Diego
(92121-2997)
PHONE..................858 552-1100
Randall J Steward, *CFO*
Robert J Bujarski, *Senior Vice President
Business Development*
Werner Kroll, *Senior Vice President
Research & Development*
EMP: 90 **EST:** 1977
SQ FT: 30,000
SALES (est): 1.7B
SALES (corp-wide): 3B **Publicly Held**
Web: www.quidelortho.com
SIC: 2835 Pregnancy test kits
PA: Quidelortho Corporation
9975 Summers Ridge Rd
858 552-1100

(P-3551)

QUIDELORTHO CORPORATION (PA)

9975 Summers Ridge Rd, San Diego
(92121-2997)
PHONE..................858 552-1100
Brian J Blaser, *Pr*
Kenneth F Buechler, *Non-Executive
Chairman of the Board*
Robert J Bujarski, *Pr*
Joseph M Busky, *CFO*
Michael S Iskra, *CCO*
EMP: 39 **EST:** 2021
SALES (est): 3B
SALES (corp-wide): 3B **Publicly Held**
Web: www.quidelortho.com

SIC: 2835 Pregnancy test kits

(P-3552)

RESPONSE GENETICS INC

1640 Marengo St Ste 7, Los Angeles
(90033-1057)
PHONE..................323 224-3900
EMP: 113
Web: www.responsegenetics.com
SIC: 2835 Diagnostic substances

(P-3553)

SYNTRON BIORESEARCH INC

2774 Loker Ave W, Carlsbad (92010-6610)
PHONE..................760 930-2200
Charles Yu, *Pr*
▲ **EMP:** 278 **EST:** 1986
SALES (est): 18.83MM **Privately Held**
Web: www.syntron.net
SIC: 2835 5122 Diagnostic substances;
Biologicals and allied products

(P-3554)

TECO DIAGNOSTICS

Also Called: Lab Health Medical
1268 N Lakeview Ave, Anaheim
(92807-1831)
PHONE..................714 693-7788
K C Chen, *Pr*
◆ **EMP:** 70 **EST:** 1985
SQ FT: 40,000
SALES (est): 9.65MM **Privately Held**
Web: www.tecodiagnostics.com
SIC: 2835 5049 Diagnostic substances;
Laboratory equipment, except medical or
dental

2836 Biological Products, Except Diagnostic

(P-3555)

AMBRX BIOPHARMA INC

Also Called: Ambrx
10975 N Torrey Pines Rd, La Jolla
(92037-1051)
PHONE..................858 875-2400
Daniel J Oconnor, *CEO*
EMP: 70 **EST:** 2015
SQ FT: 36,172
SALES (est): 2.44MM
SALES (corp-wide): 85.16B **Publicly Held**
Web: www.ambrx.com
SIC: 2836 Biological products, except
diagnostic
PA: Johnson & Johnson
1 Johnson & Johnson Plz
732 524-0400

(P-3556)

AMERICAN PEPTIDE COMPANY INC

1271 Avenida Chelsea, Vista (92081-8315)
PHONE..................408 733-7604
▲ **EMP:** 86
SIC: 2836 5169 Biological products, except
diagnostic; Chemicals and allied products,
nec

(P-3557)

AMGEN INC (PA)

Also Called: Amgen
1 Amgen Center Dr, Thousand Oaks
(91320-1799)
PHONE..................805 447-1000
Robert A Bradway, *Ch Bd*
Esteban Santos, *Operations*
Peter H Griffith, *Ex VP*
Jonathan P Graham, *Ex VP*

David M Reese, *Ex VP*
◆ **EMP:** 1942 **EST:** 1980
SALES (est): 28.19B
SALES (corp-wide): 28.19B **Publicly Held**
Web: www.amgen.com
SIC: 2836 Biological products, except
diagnostic

(P-3558)

ARK ANIMAL HEALTH INC

4955 Directors Pl, San Diego (92121-3836)
PHONE..................858 203-4100
EMP: 30 **EST:** 2017
SALES (est): 810.28K
SALES (corp-wide): 62.84MM **Publicly
Held**
Web: www.arkanimalhealth.com
SIC: 2836 Biological products, except
diagnostic
PA: Sorrento Therapeutics, Inc.
4955 Directors Pl
858 203-4100

(P-3559)

ARMATA PHARMACEUTICALS INC (PA)

Also Called: Armata Pharmaceuticals
5005 Mcconnell Ave, Los Angeles
(90066-6715)
PHONE..................310 665-2928
Todd R Patrick, *CEO*
Brian Varnum, *CDO*
Steve R Martin, *CFO*
Duane Morris, *VP*
EMP: 24 **EST:** 1989
SQ FT: 35,500
SALES (est): 5.51MM **Publicly Held**
Web: www.armatapharma.com
SIC: 2836 Biological products, except
diagnostic

(P-3560)

ARTIVA BIOTHERAPEUTICS INC

5505 Morehouse Dr Ste 100, San Diego
(92121-1720)
PHONE..................858 267-4467
Fred Aslan, *Pr*
Brian Daniels, *
Neha Krishnamohan, *Ex VP*
Christopher P Horan, *Chief Technician*
Thorsten Graef, *CMO*
EMP: 81 **EST:** 2019
SQ FT: 51,621
SALES (est): 33.49MM **Privately Held**
Web: www.artivabio.com
SIC: 2836 Biological products, except
diagnostic

(P-3561)

ATARA BIOTHERAPEUTICS INC (PA)

Also Called: Atara Bio
2380 Conejo Spectrum St Ste 200,
Thousand Oaks (91320-1444)
PHONE..................805 623-4211
Anhco Nguyen, *Pr*
Pascal Touchon, *
Eric Hyllengren, *CFO*
Amar Murugan, *CLO*
Jill Henrich, *Ex VP*
EMP: 160 **EST:** 2012
SQ FT: 51,160
SALES (est): 8.57MM
SALES (corp-wide): 8.57MM **Publicly
Held**
Web: www.atarabio.com
SIC: 2836 8731 Biological products, except
diagnostic; Biotechnical research,
commercial

(P-3562)

ATYR PHARMA INC (PA)

Also Called: Atyr Pharma
10240 Sorrento Valley Rd Ste 300, San
Diego (92121-1605)
PHONE..................858 731-8389
Sanjay S Shukla, *Pr*
Timothy P Coughlin, *Ch Bd*
Jill M Broadfoot, *CFO*
Nancy E Denyes, *Corporate Secretary*
Danielle Campbell, *Pers/VP*
EMP: 58 **EST:** 2005
SQ FT: 23,696
SALES (est): 353K **Publicly Held**
Web: www.atyrpharma.com
SIC: 2836 2834 Biological products, except
diagnostic; Pharmaceutical preparations

(P-3563)

BACHEM AMERICAS INC

3031 Fujita St, Torrance (90505-4004)
PHONE..................310 539-4171
EMP: 45
Web: www.bachem.com
SIC: 2836 Biological products, except
diagnostic
HQ: Bachem Americas, Inc.
3132 Kashiwa St
Torrance CA 90505
310 784-4440

(P-3564)

BACHEM AMERICAS INC

3152 Kashiwa St, Torrance (90505-4011)
PHONE..................310 784-4440
EMP: 45
Web: www.bachem.com
SIC: 2836 2834 Biological products, except
diagnostic; Pharmaceutical preparations
HQ: Bachem Americas, Inc.
3132 Kashiwa St
Torrance CA 90505
310 784-4440

(P-3565)

BACHEM AMERICAS INC (DH)

Also Called: Bachem California
3132 Kashiwa St, Torrance (90505-4087)
PHONE..................310 784-4440
Brian Gregg, *CEO*
Michael Brenk, *
Najib Masloub, *
▲ **EMP:** 25 **EST:** 1971
SQ FT: 70,000
SALES (est): 104.75MM **Privately Held**
Web: www.bachem.com
SIC: 2836 2834 Biological products, except
diagnostic; Pharmaceutical preparations
HQ: Bachem Holding Ag
Hauptstrasse 144
Bubendorf BL 4416

(P-3566)

BIOATLA INC

Also Called: Bioatla
11085 Torreyana Rd, San Diego
(92121-1104)
PHONE..................858 558-0708
Jay M Short, *Ch Bd*
Richard A Waldron, *CFO*
Eric Sievers, *CMO*
Christian Vasquez, *CAO*
EMP: 65 **EST:** 2007
SQ FT: 43,377
Web: www.bioatla.com
SIC: 2836 Biological products, except
diagnostic

(P-3567)

CAMBRIDGE EQUITIES LP

9922 Jefferson Blvd, Culver City
(90232-3506)
PHONE.................858 350-2300
EMP: 46 **EST:** 2011
SALES (est): 1.38MM **Privately Held**
SIC: 2836 Biological products, except
diagnostic

(P-3568)

CG ONCOLOGY INC

Also Called: Cg Oncology
400 Spectrum Center Dr Ste 2040, Irvine
(92618-5024)
PHONE.................949 409-3700
Arthur Kuan, *Ch Bd*
Ambaw Bellete, *Pr*
Corleen Roche, *CFO*
Vijay Kasturi, *CMO*
EMP: 61 **EST:** 2010
SQ FT: 1,249
SALES (est): 204K **Privately Held**
Web: www.cgoncology.com
SIC: 2836 Biological products, except
diagnostic

(P-3569)

CIDARA THERAPEUTICS INC (PA)

Also Called: Cidara
6310 Nancy Ridge Dr Ste 101, San Diego
(92121-3209)
PHONE.................858 752-6170
Jeffrey L Stein, *Pr*
Daniel D Burgess, *Ch Bd*
Preetam Shah, *Chief Business Officer*
Paul Daruwala, *COO*
Taylor Sandison, *CMO*
EMP: 51 **EST:** 2012
SQ FT: 29,638
SALES (est): 63.91MM
SALES (corp-wide): 63.91MM **Publicly Held**
Web: www.cidara.com
SIC: 2836 8731 Biological products, except
diagnostic; Biotechnical research,
commercial

(P-3570)

CLINIQA CORPORATION (HQ)

Also Called: Cliniqa
495 Enterprise St, San Marcos
(92078-4364)
PHONE.................760 744-1900
Kevin Gould, *Pr*
C Granger Haugh, *
Dean Harriman, *
Shing Kwan, *
Larry Beaty, *
▼ **EMP:** 29 **EST:** 1976
SQ FT: 25,000
SALES (est): 20.7MM
SALES (corp-wide): 1.16B **Publicly Held**
Web: www.cliniqa.com
SIC: 2836 Biological products, except
diagnostic
PA: Bio-Techne Corporation
614 Mckinley Pl Ne
612 379-8854

(P-3571)

CLINIQA CORPORATION

258 La Moree Rd, San Marcos
(92078-4381)
PHONE.................760 744-1900
Charles G Haugh, *CEO*
EMP: 58
SALES (corp-wide): 1.16B **Publicly Held**
Web: www.cliniqa.com

SIC: 2836 Biological products, except
diagnostic
HQ: Cliniqa Corporation
495 Enterprise St
San Marcos CA 92078
760 744-1900

(P-3572)

EMD MILLIPORE CORPORATION

Also Called: Bioscience Research Reagents
28820 Single Oak Dr, Temecula
(92590-3607)
PHONE.................951 676-8080
John Ambroziak, *Mgr*
EMP: 69
SALES (corp-wide): 22.82B **Privately Held**
Web: www.emdmillipore.com
SIC: 2836 2835 3826 Biological products,
except diagnostic; Diagnostic substances;
Liquid testing apparatus
HQ: Emd Millipore Corporation
400 Summit Dr
Burlington MA 01803
800 645-5476

(P-3573)

FUJIFILM DSYNTH BTCHNLGIES CAL

2430 Conejo Spectrum St, Thousand Oaks
(91320-1445)
PHONE.................914 789-8100
Martin Meeson, *Pr*
Gerry Farrell, *COO*
Hideru Sato, *Treas*
Steve Lee, *Sec*
EMP: 29
SALES (est): 23.55MM **Privately Held**
Web: www.fujifilmdiosynth.com
SIC: 2836 Biological products, except
diagnostic
HQ: Fujifilm Diosynth Biotechnologies Uk
Limited
New Billingham House
Billingham TS23

(P-3574)

FUJIFILM DSYNTH BTCHNLGIES USA

2430 Conejo Spectrum St, Thousand Oaks
(91320-1445)
PHONE.................805 699-5579
Takatoshi Ishikawa, *Brnch Mgr*
EMP: 134
Web: www.atarabio.com
SIC: 2836 Biological products, except
diagnostic
HQ: Fujifilm Diosynth Biotechnologies
U.S.A., Inc.
101 J Morris Comns Ln
Morrisville NC 27560

(P-3575)

FUJIFILM IRVINE SCIENTIFIC INC (DH)

Also Called: Irvine Scientific
1830 E Warner Ave, Santa Ana
(92705-5505)
PHONE.................949 261-7800
Yutaka Yamaguchi, *CEO*
Judy Malillo, *
Ryo Iguchi, *
▲ **EMP:** 44 **EST:** 1970
SQ FT: 20,000
SALES (est): 93.57MM **Privately Held**
Web: www.irvinesci.com
SIC: 2836 5047 Blood derivatives; Medical
laboratory equipment
HQ: Fujifilm Holdings America Corporation
200 Summit Lake Dr
Valhalla NY 10595

(P-3576)

GB007 INC

3013 Science Park Rd, San Diego
(92121-1101)
PHONE.................858 684-1300
Sheila Gujrathi, *CEO*
EMP: 99 **EST:** 2004
SALES (est): 482.6K **Publicly Held**
Web: www.gossamerbio.com
SIC: 2836 Biological products, except
diagnostic
PA: Gossamer Bio, Inc.
3013 Scence Pk Rd Ste 200
858 684-1300

(P-3577)

GRIFOLS BIOLOGICALS LLC (DH)

5555 Valley Blvd, Los Angeles
(90032-3520)
PHONE.................323 225-2221
David Bell, *
Max Debrouwer, *
Willie Zuniga, *
▲ **EMP:** 67 **EST:** 2003
SALES (est): 185.52MM **Privately Held**
Web: www.grifols.com
SIC: 2836 2834 Plasmas; Pharmaceutical
preparations
HQ: Grifols Shared Services North
America, Inc.
2410 Lillyvale Ave
Los Angeles CA 90032
323 225-2221

(P-3578)

GRIFOLS USA LLC

Also Called: Access Biologicals
995 Park Center Dr, Vista (92081-8312)
PHONE.................760 931-8444
EMP: 71
Web: www.grifols.com
SIC: 2836 Biological products, except
diagnostic
HQ: Grifols Usa, Llc
2410 Grifols Way
Los Angeles CA 90032
323 225-2221

(P-3579)

HALOZYME THERAPEUTICS INC (PA)

Also Called: Halozyme
12390 El Camino Real, San Diego
(92130-3162)
PHONE.................858 794-8889
Helen I Torley, *Pr*
Jeffrey W Henderson, *Ch Bd*
Nicole Labrosse, *Sr VP*
Mark Snyder, *CCO*
Michael J Labarre, *Sr VP*
EMP: 62 **EST:** 1998
SALES (est): 829.25MM
SALES (corp-wide): 829.25MM **Publicly Held**
Web: www.halozyme.com
SIC: 2836 2834 Biological products, except
diagnostic; Pharmaceutical preparations

(P-3580)

IMMUNITYBIO INC (PA)

Also Called: Immunitybio
3530 John Hopkins Ct, San Diego
(92121-1121)
PHONE.................844 696-5235
Richard Adcock, *Pr*
Patrick Soon-shiong, *Ex Ch Bd*
David Sachs, *CFO*
Barry J Simon, *CORP AFFAIRS*
EMP: 51 **EST:** 2002

SQ FT: 44,681
SALES (est): 622K **Publicly Held**
Web: www.immunitybio.com
SIC: 2836 Biological products, except
diagnostic

(P-3581)

INHIBRX INC (HQ)

Also Called: Inhibrx
11025 N Torrey Pines Rd Ste 200, La Jolla
(92037-1030)
PHONE.................858 795-4220
Mark P Lappe, *Pr*
Kelly Deck, *CFO*
Klaus W Wagner, *CMO*
Brendan P Eckelman, *CSO*
David Matly, *CCO*
EMP: 127 **EST:** 2010
SQ FT: 34,000
SALES (est): 1.8MM **Publicly Held**
Web: www.inhibrx.com
SIC: 2836 Biological products, except
diagnostic
PA: Sanofi
46 Avenue De La Grande Armee

(P-3582)

INHIBRX BIOSCIENCES INC ✪

11025 N Torrey Pines Rd Ste 140, La Jolla
(92037-1030)
PHONE.................858 795-4220
Mark P Lappe, *Ch Bd*
Kelly D Deck, *CFO*
Brendan P Eckelman, *CSO*
EMP: 163 **EST:** 2024
SQ FT: 43,000
SALES (est): 11.5MM **Privately Held**
SIC: 2836 Biological products, except
diagnostic

(P-3583)

MINDERA CORP

1221 Liberty Way, Vista (92081-8368)
PHONE.................858 810-6070
Frank Stubbe, *Admn*
Philippe Nore, *
EMP: 30 **EST:** 2014
SALES (est): 6.43MM **Privately Held**
Web: www.minderadx.com
SIC: 2836 Biological products, except
diagnostic

(P-3584)

NEUROCRINE BIOSCIENCES INC (PA)

Also Called: Neurocrine
6027 Edgewood Bend Ct, San Diego
(92130-8235)
PHONE.................858 617-7600
Kyle Gano, *Pr*
William H Rastetter, *
Matthew C Abernethy, *CFO*
Julie S Cooke, *Chief Human Resource Officer*
Darin M Lippoldt, *CLO*
EMP: 236 **EST:** 1992
SQ FT: 141,000
SALES (est): 1.89B **Publicly Held**
Web: www.neurocrine.com
SIC: 2836 Biological products, except
diagnostic

(P-3585)

POSEIDA THERAPEUTICS INC (PA)

Also Called: POSEIDA
9390 Towne Centre Dr Ste 200, San Diego
(92121-3026)
PHONE.................858 779-3100
Kristin Yarema, *Pr*

Mark J Gergen, *Ex Ch Bd*
Harry J Leonhardt, *CCO*
Johanna M Mylet, *CFO*
Syed Rizvi, *CMO*
EMP: 329 **EST:** 2014
SQ FT: 87,000
SALES (est): 64.7MM
SALES (corp-wide): 64.7MM **Publicly Held**
Web: www.poseida.com
SIC: 2836 2834 Biological products, except diagnostic; Pharmaceutical preparations

(P-3586)
PROLACTA BIOSCIENCE INC (PA)
757 Baldwin Park Blvd, City Of Industry (91746-1504)
PHONE..............................626 599-9260
Scott A Elster, *CEO*
Scott A Elster, *CEO*
Joseph Fournell, *VP*
Alan Kofsky, *VP*
Tami D Ciranna, *CFO*
▼ **EMP:** 132 **EST:** 1999
SQ FT: 65,000
SALES (est): 91.91MM
SALES (corp-wide): 91.91MM **Privately Held**
Web: www.prolacta.com
SIC: 2836 Biological products, except diagnostic

(P-3587)
SORRENTO THERAPEUTICS INC (PA)
4955 Directors Pl, San Diego (92121-3836)
PHONE..............................858 203-4100
Henry Ji, *Ch Bd*
EMP: 64 **EST:** 2006
SQ FT: 30,000
SALES (est): 62.84MM
SALES (corp-wide): 62.84MM **Publicly Held**
Web: www.sorrentotherapeutics.com
SIC: 2836 Biological products, except diagnostic

(P-3588)
TARSUS PHARMACEUTICALS INC
15440 Laguna Canyon Rd Ste 160, Irvine (92618-2143)
PHONE..............................949 409-9820
Bobak Azamian, *Pr*
Michael Ackermann, *
Jeff Farrow, *CSO*
Seshadri Neervannan, *COO*
Aziz Mottiwala, *CCO*
EMP: 244 **EST:** 2016
SQ FT: 10,879
SALES (est): 17.45MM **Privately Held**
Web: www.tarsusrx.com
SIC: 2836 Biological products, except diagnostic

2841 Soap And Other Detergents

(P-3589)
ALL ONE GOD FAITH INC (PA)
Also Called: Dr. Bronners Magic Soaps
1335 Park Center Dr, Vista (92081-8357)
P.O. Box 1958 (92085-1958)
PHONE..............................844 937-2551
David Bronner, *CEO*
Michael Bronner, *
Trudy Bronner, *
◆ **EMP:** 170 **EST:** 1973

SQ FT: 126,000
SALES (est): 41.33MM **Privately Held**
Web: www.drbronner.com
SIC: 2841 2834 2844 Soap: granulated, liquid, cake, flaked, or chip; Lip balms; Lotions, shaving

(P-3590)
ALL ONE GOD FAITH INC
Also Called: Dr. Bronners Magic Soaps
1225 Park Center Dr Ste D, Vista (92081-8353)
PHONE..............................760 599-4010
David Bronner, *CEO*
EMP: 70
Web: www.drbronner.com
SIC: 2841 Soap: granulated, liquid, cake, flaked, or chip
PA: All One God Faith, Inc.
1335 Park Ctr Dr

(P-3591)
BRADFORD SOAP MEXICO INC
1778 Zinetta Rd Ste G, Calexico (92231-9510)
PHONE..............................760 768-4539
John Howland, *CEO*
EMP: 493
SALES (corp-wide): 227.55MM **Privately Held**
Web: www.bradfordsoap.com
SIC: 2841 Soap: granulated, liquid, cake, flaked, or chip
HQ: Bradford Soap Mexico, Inc.
200 Providence St
West Warwick RI 02893
401 821-2141

(P-3592)
GENLABS (PA)
5568 Schaefer Ave, Chino (91710-9041)
P.O. Box 1697 (91708-1697)
PHONE..............................909 591-8451
EMP: 135 **EST:** 1968
SALES (est): 33.04MM
SALES (corp-wide): 33.04MM **Privately Held**
Web: www.genlabscorp.com
SIC: 2841 2869 8071 5169 Soap and other detergents; Laboratory chemicals, organic; Testing laboratories; Chemicals and allied products, nec

(P-3593)
GOODWIN AMMONIA COMPANY LLC
Also Called: The Goodwin Company
12301 Monarch St, Garden Grove (92841-2908)
PHONE..............................714 894-0531
Tom Goodwin, *Pr*
EMP: 68
SALES (corp-wide): 52.56MM **Privately Held**
Web: www.goodwininc.com
SIC: 2841 Soap and other detergents
PA: The Goodwin Ammonia Company Llc
12361 Monarch St
714 894-0531

(P-3594)
MISSION KLEENSWEEP PROD INC
Also Called: Mission Laboratories
13644 Live Oak Ln, Baldwin Park (91706-1317)
PHONE..............................323 223-1405
TOLL FREE: 888
Helen Rosenbaum, *Pr*
EMP: 53 **EST:** 1936

SQ FT: 75,000
SALES (est): 5MM **Privately Held**
SIC: 2841 2842 Soap and other detergents; Polishes and sanitation goods

(P-3595)
PANROSA ENTERPRISES INC
550 Monica Cir, Corona (92878-5496)
PHONE..............................951 339-5888
Peter Chengjian Pan, *Pr*
Jingwen Zhao, *
Chenyang Sun, *
▲ **EMP:** 60 **EST:** 2003
SALES (est): 5.49MM **Privately Held**
Web: www.panrosa.com
SIC: 2841 Soap and other detergents

2842 Polishes And Sanitation Goods

(P-3596)
3D/INTERNATIONAL INC
20724 Centre Pointe Pkwy Unit 1, Santa Clarita (91350-2980)
PHONE..............................661 250-2020
Tony Goren, *Mgr*
EMP: 146
SALES (corp-wide): 5.44B **Publicly Held**
Web: www.3dproducts.com
SIC: 2842 Automobile polish
HQ: 3d/International, Inc.
2200 West Loop S Ste 200
Houston TX 77027
713 871-7000

(P-3597)
AMREP INC
1555 S Cucamonga Ave, Ontario (91761-4512)
PHONE..............................770 422-2071
William Redmond, *Pr*
EMP: 285
SALES (corp-wide): 978.45MM **Privately Held**
Web: www.amrepproducts.com
SIC: 2842 Specialty cleaning
HQ: Amrep, Inc.
600 Galleria Pkwy Se
Atlanta GA 30339
877 428-9937

(P-3598)
AWESOME PRODUCTS INC (PA)
Also Called: La's Totally Awesome
6370 Altura Blvd, Buena Park (90620-1001)
PHONE..............................714 562-8873
Luksarang D Hardas, *CEO*
◆ **EMP:** 125 **EST:** 1983
SQ FT: 250,000
SALES (est): 80.68MM
SALES (corp-wide): 80.68MM **Privately Held**
Web: www.lastotallyawesome.com
SIC: 2842 Cleaning or polishing preparations, nec

(P-3599)
B&D INVESTMENT PARTNERS INC (PA)
20950 Centre Pointe Pkwy, Santa Clarita (91350-2975)
◆ **EMP:** 48 **EST:** 1960
SQ FT: 100,000
SALES (est): 23.25MM
SALES (corp-wide): 23.25MM **Privately Held**
Web: www.bc-labs.com

SIC: 2842 2844 Cleaning or polishing preparations, nec; Perfumes, cosmetics and other toilet preparations

(P-3600)
BURNS ENVIRONMENTAL SVCS INC
19360 Rinaldi St Ste 381, Northridge (91326-1607)
PHONE..............................800 577-4009
EMP: 42 **EST:** 2005
SALES (est): 397.67K **Privately Held**
Web: www.burns-enviro.com
SIC: 2842 Polishes and sanitation goods

(P-3601)
CILAJET LLC
16425 Ishida Ave, Gardena (90248-2924)
PHONE..............................310 320-8000
Jaci Warren, *Pr*
EMP: 25 **EST:** 2006
SALES (est): 3.49MM **Privately Held**
Web: www.cilajet.com
SIC: 2842 7542 Automobile polish; Washing and polishing, automotive

(P-3602)
CLOROX MANUFACTURING COMPANY
Also Called: Clorox
2300 W San Bernardino Ave, Redlands (92374-5000)
PHONE..............................909 307-2756
EMP: 50
SALES (corp-wide): 7.09B **Publicly Held**
Web: www.thecloroxcompany.com
SIC: 2842 Polishes and sanitation goods
HQ: Clorox Manufacturing Company
1221 Broadway
Oakland CA 94612

(P-3603)
FLO-KEM INC
19402 S Susana Rd, Compton (90221-5798)
PHONE..............................310 632-7124
EMP: 48
Web: www.flo-kem.com
SIC: 2842 Cleaning or polishing preparations, nec

(P-3604)
GPS ASSOCIATES INC
1803 Carnegie Ave, Santa Ana (92705-5502)
PHONE..............................949 408-3162
Joe Parisi, *CEO*
Renee Gaudreau, *
EMP: 49 **EST:** 1993
SALES (est): 1.85MM
SALES (corp-wide): 1.85MM **Publicly Held**
Web: www.guardrxhandsanitizer.com
SIC: 2842 Sanitation preparations, disinfectants and deodorants
PA: Mountain High Acquisitions Corp.
4350 Executive Dr Ste 200
760 402-5105

(P-3605)
GRANITE GOLD INC
12780 Danielson Ct Ste A, Poway (92064-8857)
PHONE..............................858 499-8933
Lenny Sciarrino, *CEO*
Scott Martin, *COO*
Leonard Pellegrino, *VP*
EMP: 91 **EST:** 2002
SALES (est): 7.26MM **Privately Held**

Web: www.granitegold.com
SIC: 2842 Cleaning or polishing
preparations, nec

(P-3606)
GRANITIZE PRODUCTS INC
Also Called: Granitize Aviation Intl
11022 Vulcan St, South Gate (90280-7621)
P.O. Box 2306 (90280-9306)
PHONE..................562 923-5438
Tony Raymondo, *CEO*
Betty Raymondo, *
◆ EMP: 75 EST: 1930
SQ FT: 30,000
SALES (est): 19.81MM Privately Held
Web: www.granitize.com
SIC: 2842 Automobile polish

(P-3607)
JASON MARKK INC (PA)
15325 Blackburn Ave, Norwalk
(90650-6842)
PHONE..................213 687-7060
Jason M Angsuvarn, *CEO*
▲ EMP: 32 EST: 2007
SALES (est): 5.76MM
SALES (corp-wide): 5.76MM Privately
Held
Web: www.jasonmarkk.com
SIC: 2842 Shoe polish or cleaner

(P-3608)
KIK-SOCAL INC
Also Called: Kik
9028 Dice Rd, Santa Fe Springs
(90670-2520)
PHONE..................562 946-6427
Jeffrey M Nodland, *CEO*
Stratis Katsiris, *
William Smith, *
Ben W Kaak, *
EMP: 3000 EST: 1995
SQ FT: 3,000,000
SALES (est): 24.04MM
SALES (corp-wide): 771.06MM Privately
Held
SIC: 2842 Bleaches, household: dry or liquid
HQ: Kik International Llc
1725 N Brown Rd
Lawrenceville GA 30043

(P-3609)
LAB CLEAN INC
3627 Briggeman Dr, Los Alamitos
(90720-2475)
PHONE..................714 689-0063
Mark Cunningham, *CEO*
Mark Cunningham, *Managing Member*
Matthew Bays, *
EMP: 25 EST: 2005
SQ FT: 40,000
SALES (est): 2.29MM Privately Held
Web: www.lab-clean.com
SIC: 2842 Cleaning or polishing
preparations, nec

(P-3610)
LMC ENTERPRISES (PA)
Also Called: Chemco Products Company
6401 Alondra Blvd, Paramount
(90723-3758)
PHONE..................562 602-2116
Elaine S Cooper, *CEO*
Janis Utz, *
John D Grimes, *
EMP: 70 EST: 1962
SQ FT: 15,000
SALES (est): 41.67MM
SALES (corp-wide): 41.67MM Privately
Held

Web: www.chemcoprod.com
SIC: 2842 Cleaning or polishing
preparations, nec

(P-3611)
LMC ENTERPRISES
Also Called: Flo-Kem
19402 S Susana Rd, Compton
(90221-5712)
PHONE..................310 632-7124
Elaine Cooper, *CEO*
EMP: 50
SQ FT: 20,000
SALES (corp-wide): 41.67MM Privately
Held
Web: www.chemcoprod.com
SIC: 2842 Cleaning or polishing
preparations, nec
PA: Lmc Enterprises
6401 E Alondra Blvd
562 602-2116

(P-3612)
MAINTEX INC (PA)
13300 Nelson Ave, City Of Industry
(91746-1516)
P.O. Box 7110 (91744-7110)
PHONE..................800 446-1888
TOLL FREE: 800
▲ EMP: 140 EST: 1960
SALES (est): 66.69MM
SALES (corp-wide): 66.69MM Privately
Held
Web: www.maintex.com
SIC: 2842 5087 Cleaning or polishing
preparations, nec; Janitors' supplies

(P-3613)
MEGUIARS INC (HQ)
Also Called: Brilliant Solutions
213 Technology Dr, Irvine (92618-2437)
PHONE..................949 752-8000
Barry J Meguiar, *Pr*
Michael W Meguiar, *
Catherine E Bayless, *
◆ EMP: 50 EST: 1901
SALES (est): 49.16MM
SALES (corp-wide): 32.68B Publicly Held
Web: www.meguiars.com
SIC: 2842 Cleaning or polishing
preparations, nec
PA: 3m Company
3m Center
651 733-1110

(P-3614)
MORGAN GALLACHER INC
Also Called: Custom Chemical Formulators
8707 Millergrove Dr, Santa Fe Springs
(90670-2001)
PHONE..................562 695-1232
Harriet Von Luft, *Ch Bd*
David M Smith, *
Tam Sarmiento, *
▼ EMP: 46 EST: 1964
SQ FT: 100,000
SALES (est): 8.63MM Privately Held
Web: www.morgan-gallacher.com
SIC: 2842 5169 Cleaning or polishing
preparations, nec; Industrial chemicals

(P-3615)
MPM BUILDING SERVICES INC
Also Called: Mpm & Associates
7011 Hayvenhurst Ave Ste F, Van Nuys
(91406-3822)
PHONE..................818 708-9676
Paul Davis, *Pr*
Mike Danesh, *VP*
EMP: 25 EST: 1975

SQ FT: 35,000
SALES (est): 890.5K Privately Held
Web: www.mpmco.com
SIC: 2842 Polishes and sanitation goods

(P-3616)
OIL-DRI CORPORATION AMERICA
950 Petroleum Club Rd, Taft (93268-9748)
P.O. Box 1277 (93268-1277)
PHONE..................661 765-7194
EMP: 43
SALES (corp-wide): 437.59MM Publicly
Held
Web: www.oildri.com
SIC: 2842 Sweeping compounds, oil or
water absorbent, clay or sawdust
PA: Oil-Dri Corporation Of America
410 N Mich Ave Ste 400
312 321-1515

(P-3617)
OLYMPUS WATER HOLDINGS IV LP (PA)
360 N Crescent Dr Bldg S, Beverly Hills
(90210-2529)
PHONE..................310 739-6325
Mary Ann Sigler, *Pr*
EMP: 23 EST: 2020
SALES (est): 17.33MM
SALES (corp-wide): 17.33MM Privately
Held
SIC: 2842 Polishes and sanitation goods

(P-3618)
PEERLESS MATERIALS COMPANY
4442 E 26th St, Vernon (90058-4318)
P.O. Box 33228 (90033)
PHONE..................323 266-0313
Louis J Buty, *Pr*
Peter H Pritchard, *
▲ EMP: 40 EST: 1967
SQ FT: 35,000
SALES (est): 7.39MM Privately Held
Web: www.americantex.com
SIC: 2842 Sweeping compounds, oil or
water absorbent, clay or sawdust

(P-3619)
SOAPTRONIC LLC
19771 Pauling, Foothill Ranch
(92610-2606)
PHONE..................949 465-8955
Horst Binderbauer, *Managing Member*
◆ EMP: 25 EST: 1998
SALES (est): 5.05MM Privately Held
Web: www.germstar.com
SIC: 2842 2841 Sanitation preparations,
disinfectants and deodorants; Soap and
other detergents

(P-3620)
SUNSHINE MAKERS INC (PA)
Also Called: Simple Green
15922 Pacific Coast Hwy, Huntington Beach
(92649-1894)
PHONE..................562 795-6000
Bruce P Fabrizio, *
Bruce P Fabrizio, *
Rose Concilia, *
Jeffrey Hyder, *
Patrick Sheehan, *
▼ EMP: 51 EST: 1981
SQ FT: 25,000
SALES (est): 26.08MM
SALES (corp-wide): 26.08MM Privately
Held
Web: www.simplegreen.com

SIC: 2842 Cleaning or polishing
preparations, nec

(P-3621)
SUSTAINABLE CARE COMPANY INC ✪
633 W 5th St Fl 28, Los Angeles
(90071-3502)
PHONE..................310 210-7090
Mark Sorensen, *CEO*
Thomas Riebs, *
EMP: 25 EST: 2024
SALES (est): 825.06K Privately Held
SIC: 2842 Polishes and sanitation goods

(P-3622)
SYNSUS PRVATE LBEL PRTNERS LLC
980 Rancheros Dr, San Marcos
(92069-3029)
PHONE..................713 714-0225
Greg Crawrford, *Brnch Mgr*
EMP: 59
SALES (corp-wide): 51.41MM Privately
Held
Web: www.synsus.com
SIC: 2842 Polishes and sanitation goods
PA: Synsus Private Label Partners, Llc
18211 Katy Fwy Ste 325
713 714-0225

(P-3623)
US CONTINENTAL MARKETING INC (PA)
Also Called: U.S. Continental
310 Reed Cir, Corona (92879-1349)
PHONE..................951 808-8888
David Lee Williams, *Pr*
◆ EMP: 81 EST: 1988
SQ FT: 40,000
SALES (est): 22.78MM Privately Held
Web: www.uscontinental.com
SIC: 2842 Leather dressings and finishes

2843 Surface Active Agents

(P-3624)
CHEMEOR INC
727 Arrow Grand Cir, Covina (91722-2148)
PHONE..................626 966-3808
Yongchun Tang, *Ch Bd*
Pat Mills, *
Patrick Shuler, *
Carl Aften, *
▲ EMP: 40 EST: 2005
SQ FT: 16,000
SALES (est): 9.29MM Privately Held
Web: www.chemeor.com
SIC: 2843 1389 2911 Surface active agents;
Chemically treating wells; Aromatic
chemical products

(P-3625)
HENKEL US OPERATIONS CORP
21551 Prairie St, Chatsworth (91311-5831)
PHONE..................818 435-0889
EMP: 41
SALES (corp-wide): 23.39B Privately Held
Web: www.henkel-northamerica.com
SIC: 2843 Surface active agents
HQ: Henkel Us Operations Corporation
1 Henkel Way
Rocky Hill CT 06067
860 571-5100

(P-3626)
HENKEL US OPERATIONS CORP
20021 S Susana Rd, Compton
(90221-5721)

PHONE.................................562 297-6840
Tam Nguyen, *Brnch Mgr*
EMP: 175
SALES (corp-wide): 23.39B Privately Held
Web: www.henkel.com
SIC: 2843 Surface active agents
HQ: Henkel Us Operations Corporation
   1 Henkel Way
   Rocky Hill CT 06067
   860 571-5100

(P-3627)
JUSTICE BROS DIST CO INC
Also Called: Justice Bros-J B Car Care Pdts
2734 Huntington Dr, Duarte (91010-2301)
PHONE.................................626 359-9174
Edward R Justice Senior, *Ch Bd*
Edward R Justice Junior, *Pr*
▲ EMP: 25 EST: 1947
SQ FT: 33,000
SALES (est): 5.22MM Privately Held
Web: www.justicebrothers.com
SIC: 2843 2899 Surface active agents;
   Chemical preparations, nec

2844 Toilet Preparations

(P-3628)
ADONIS INC
475 N Sheridan St, Corona (92878-4021)
PHONE.................................951 432-3960
Helga Arminak, *CEO*
EMP: 42 EST: 2020
SQ FT: 73,200
SALES (est): 9.01MM Privately Held
Web:
www.adoniscontractmanufacturer.com
SIC: 2844 Perfumes, cosmetics and other
   toilet preparations

(P-3629)
ALASTIN SKINCARE INC
5999 Avenida Encinas, Carlsbad
(92008-4431)
PHONE.................................844 858-7546
Amber Edwards, *CEO*
Alan Widgerow, *CMO*
John Garruto, *
Tom Christenson, *
Cam Garner, *Ch Bd*
EMP: 150 EST: 2015
SALES (est): 32.27MM Privately Held
Web: www.alastin.com
SIC: 2844 Perfumes, cosmetics and other
   toilet preparations

(P-3630)
AMERICAN INTL INDS INC
Also Called: Aii Beauty
2220 Gaspar Ave, Commerce
(90040-1516)
PHONE.................................323 728-2999
David Eisenstein, *CEO*
◆ EMP: 1100 EST: 1998
SQ FT: 224,000
SALES (est): 9.53MM Privately Held
Web: www.aiibeauty.com
SIC: 2844 Perfumes, cosmetics and other
   toilet preparations

(P-3631)
ARCHIPELAGO INC
Also Called: Archipelago Botanicals
1548 18th St, Santa Monica (90404-3404)
PHONE.................................213 743-9200
David Klass, *CEO*
Gregory Corzine, *
◆ EMP: 110 EST: 1994
SALES (est): 7.61MM Privately Held

Web: www.shoparchipelago.com
SIC: 2844 3999 Perfumes, cosmetics and
   other toilet preparations; Candles

(P-3632)
AWARE PRODUCTS LLC
Also Called: Voyant Beauty
9250 Mason Ave, Chatsworth (91311-6005)
PHONE.................................818 206-6700
Richard Mcevoy, *CEO*
Bill Saracco, *
▲ EMP: 150 EST: 1973
SQ FT: 60,000
SALES (est): 44.89MM
SALES (corp-wide): 771.06MM Privately
Held
SIC: 2844 Hair preparations, including
   shampoos
HQ: Voyant Beauty Holdings, Inc.
   6710 River Rd
   Hodgkins IL 60525
   708 482-8881

(P-3633)
BBEAUTIFUL LLC
Also Called: Chrislie Formulations
1361 Mountain View Cir, Azusa
(91702-1649)
PHONE.................................626 610-2332
◆ EMP: 40
SIC: 2844 5999 Cosmetic preparations;
   Cosmetics

(P-3634)
BLUEFIELD ASSOCIATES INC
5430 Brooks St, Montclair (91763-4520)
PHONE.................................909 476-6027
Iheatu N Obioha, *CEO*
Chimere K Obioha, *
Tembi Sukuta, *
◆ EMP: 30 EST: 1986
SQ FT: 30,000
SALES (est): 2.5MM Privately Held
Web: www.bluefieldinc.com
SIC: 2844 5122 Cosmetic preparations;
   Cosmetics, perfumes, and hair products

(P-3635)
BOTANX LLC
3357 E Miraloma Ave Ste 156, Anaheim
(92806-1937)
PHONE.................................714 854-1601
James Mcgee, *Managing Member*
▲ EMP: 50 EST: 2005
SALES (est): 5.21MM Privately Held
Web: www.botanx.com
SIC: 2844 Cosmetic preparations

(P-3636)
BRIGHT INNOVATION LABS
Also Called: Bocchi Laboratories
26421 Ruether Ave, Santa Clarita
(91350-2621)
PHONE.................................661 252-3807
Robert J Bocchi, *Managing Member*
EMP: 154
SQ FT: 86,200
SALES (corp-wide): 225.12MM Privately
Held
Web: www.brightinnovationlabs.com
SIC: 2844 Perfumes, cosmetics and other
   toilet preparations
HQ: Shadow Holdings, Llc
   9200 Smiths Mill Rd
   New Albany OH 43054
   614 741-7458

(P-3637)
CALI CHEM INC
Also Called: Be Beauty

14271 Corporate Dr Ste B, Garden Grove
(92843-5000)
PHONE.................................714 265-3740
Tung Doan, *CEO*
Duc Doan, *
Amy Doan, *
▲ EMP: 25 EST: 2005
SQ FT: 50,000
SALES (est): 7.1MM Privately Held
Web: www.bebeautyproducts.com
SIC: 2844 Face creams or lotions

(P-3638)
COLONIAL ENTERPRISES INC
690 Knox St Ste 200, Torrance
(90502-1323)
PHONE.................................909 822-8700
Louis Navarro, *COO*
EMP: 40 EST: 1977
SALES (est): 4.92MM Privately Held
SIC: 2844 2087 Shampoos, rinses,
   conditioners: hair; Powders, drink

(P-3639)
COOLA LLC
Also Called: Coola Suncare
6023 Innovation Way Ste 110, Carlsbad
(92009-1789)
PHONE.................................760 940-2125
Eric Mccue, *CEO*
Christopher Birchby, *CCO*
Ron Wangerin, *
EMP: 56 EST: 2004
SALES (est): 8.05MM Privately Held
Web: www.coola.com
SIC: 2844 5722 Suntan lotions and oils;
   Suntanning equipment and supplies

(P-3640)
COSMETIC GROUP USA INC
12708 Branford St, Pacoima (91331-4203)
PHONE.................................818 767-2889
Andrea Chuchvara, *CEO*
Judy Zegarelli, *
▼ EMP: 180 EST: 1984
SQ FT: 80,000
SALES (est): 18.46MM Privately Held
Web: www.cosmeticgroupusa.com
SIC: 2844 Cosmetic preparations

(P-3641)
COSMETIC TECHNOLOGIES LLC
2585 Azurite Cir, Newbury Park
(91320-1202)
PHONE.................................805 376-9960
▲ EMP: 60
Web: www.cosmetictechnologies.com
SIC: 2844 Cosmetic preparations

(P-3642)
COSMO INTERNATIONAL CORP
Also Called: Cosmo International Fragrances
9200 W Sunset Blvd Ste 401, West
Hollywood (90069-3506)
PHONE.................................310 271-1100
Axel Van Liempt, *Brnch Mgr*
EMP: 63
SALES (corp-wide): 49.87MM Privately
Held
Web: www.cosmo-fragrances.com
SIC: 2844 Perfumes, natural or synthetic
PA: Cosmo International Corp
   1341 W Newport Center Dr
   954 798-4500

(P-3643)
COSRICH GROUP INC
12243 Branford St, Sun Valley
(91352-1010)
PHONE.................................818 686-2500

EMP: 35
SALES (corp-wide): 1.71B Privately Held
Web: www.ouchiesonline.com
SIC: 2844 Perfumes, cosmetics and other
   toilet preparations
HQ: Cosrich Group, Inc.
   51 La France Ave 55
   Bloomfield NJ 07003
   866 771-7473

(P-3644)
DEN-MAT CORPORATION
21515 Vanowen St Ste 200, Canoga Park
(91303-2715)
PHONE.................................800 445-0345
Robert Brennis, *Mgr*
EMP: 179
SALES (corp-wide): 167.38MM Privately
Held
Web: www.denmat.com
SIC: 2844 Toothpastes or powders,
   dentifrices
HQ: Den-Mat Corporation
   236 S Broadway St
   Orcutt CA 93455
   805 922-8491

(P-3645)
DEN-MAT CORPORATION (DH)
236 S Bdwy, Orcutt (93455-4605)
PHONE.................................805 922-8491
Robert L Ibsen, *CEO*
Noreen Freitas, *
▲ EMP: 500 EST: 1972
SQ FT: 2,500
SALES (est): 3.91MM
SALES (corp-wide): 167.38MM Privately
Held
Web: www.denmat.com
SIC: 2844 3843 Toothpastes or powders,
   dentifrices; Dental materials
HQ: Den-Mat Holdings, Llc
   1017 W Central Ave
   Lompoc CA 93436

(P-3646)
DERMALOGICA LLC (HQ)
Also Called: Dermal Group, The
1535 Beachey Pl, Carson (90746-4005)
PHONE.................................310 900-4000
Aurelian Lis, *Pr*
Jane Wurwand, *
◆ EMP: 150 EST: 1983
SQ FT: 52,000
SALES (est): 100.72MM
SALES (corp-wide): 64.79B Privately Held
Web: www.dermalogica.com
SIC: 2844 Cosmetic preparations
PA: Unilever Plc
   Unilever House

(P-3647)
DIAMOND WIPES INTL INC
4200 E Mission Blvd, Ontario (91761-2952)
PHONE.................................909 230-9888
EMP: 135
SALES (corp-wide): 51.1MM Privately
Held
Web: www.diamondwipes.com
SIC: 2844 Towelettes, premoistened
PA: Diamond Wipes International, Inc.
   4651 Schaefer Ave
   909 230-9888

(P-3648)
DIAMOND WIPES INTL INC
13775 Ramona Ave, Chino (91710-5405)
PHONE.................................909 230-9888
EMP: 68
SALES (corp-wide): 51.1MM Privately
Held

PRODUCTS & SVCS

Web: www.diamondwipes.com
SIC: 2844 Towelettes, premoistened
PA: Diamond Wipes International, Inc.
4651 Schaefer Ave
909 230-9888

(P-3649)
DIAMOND WIPES INTL INC (PA)
Also Called: Diamond Wipes
4651 Schaefer Ave, Chino (91710-5542)
PHONE.............................909 230-9888
Steve Gallo, *CEO*
Jessica Chang Lum, *
Vivian Kul, *
Neville Kadimi, *
▲ EMP: 100 EST: 1994
SALES (est): 51.1MM
SALES (corp-wide): 51.1MM **Privately Held**
Web: www.diamondwipes.com
SIC: 2844 Towelettes, premoistened

(P-3650)
DR SQUATCH LLC
4065 Glencoe Ave Apt 300b, Marina Del Rey (90292-6079)
PHONE.............................631 229-7068
Josh Friedman, *Pr*
Daniel Larson, *
EMP: 250 EST: 2013
SALES (est): 96.12MM **Privately Held**
Web: www.drsquatch.com
SIC: 2844 7389 Perfumes, cosmetics and other toilet preparations; Business Activities at Non-Commercial Site

(P-3651)
EVERBRANDS INC
11791 Monarch St, Garden Grove (92841-1818)
PHONE.............................855 595-2999
Michael Florman, *CEO*
Joshua Wallace, *
EMP: 45 EST: 2013
SQ FT: 6,000
SALES (est): 7.99MM **Privately Held**
Web: www.eversmilewhite.com
SIC: 2844 Oral preparations

(P-3652)
GAR LABORATORIES INC
1844 Massachusetts Ave, Riverside (92507-2662)
PHONE.............................951 788-0700
▲ EMP: 110 EST: 1978
SALES (est): 22.48MM **Privately Held**
Web: www.garlabs.com
SIC: 2844 Perfumes, cosmetics and other toilet preparations

(P-3653)
GIOVANNI COSMETICS INC
Also Called: Giovanni Hair Care & Cosmetics
2064 E University Dr, Rancho Dominguez (90220-6419)
P.O. Box 6990 (90212-6990)
PHONE.............................310 952-9960
Giovanni J Guidotti, *CEO*
Arthur Guidotti, *
◆ EMP: 56 EST: 1979
SALES (est): 12.89MM **Privately Held**
Web: www.giovannicosmetics.com
SIC: 2844 5122 5999 Cosmetic preparations; Cosmetics, perfumes, and hair products; Cosmetics

(P-3654)
GLAM AND GLITS NAIL DESIGN INC
Also Called: Kiara Sky Professional Nails

8700 Swigert Ct Unit 209, Bakersfield (93311-9696)
PHONE.............................661 393-4800
Khoa Duong, *CEO*
▲ EMP: 65 EST: 2013
SALES (est): 7.35MM **Privately Held**
Web: www.glamandglits.com
SIC: 2844 Manicure preparations

(P-3655)
GRAHAM WEBB INTERNATIONAL INC (HQ)
6109 De Soto Ave, Woodland Hills (91367-3709)
PHONE.............................760 918-3600
Rick Kornbluth, *Pr*
Thomas P Baumann, *VP*
EMP: 70 EST: 1989
SQ FT: 30,000
SALES (est): 2.44MM **Publicly Held**
SIC: 2844 Hair preparations, including shampoos
PA: Coty Inc.
350 5th Ave

(P-3656)
HAIN CELESTIAL GROUP INC
Also Called: Jason's Natural
5630 Rickenbacker Rd, Bell (90201-6412)
PHONE.............................323 859-0553
David Vazquez, *Brnch Mgr*
EMP: 150
Web: www.hain.com
SIC: 2844 Perfumes, cosmetics and other toilet preparations
PA: The Hain Celestial Group Inc
221 River St Ste 12

(P-3657)
HENKEL US OPERATIONS CORP
Joico Laboratories Division
5800 Bristol Pkwy, Culver City (90230-6696)
PHONE.............................626 321-4100
Annie Hu, *Brnch Mgr*
EMP: 29
SALES (corp-wide): 23.39B **Privately Held**
Web: www.joico.com
SIC: 2844 Hair preparations, including shampoos
HQ: Henkel Us Operations Corporation
1 Henkel Way
Rocky Hill CT 06067
860 571-5100

(P-3658)
HENKEL US OPERATIONS CORP
12155 Paine Pl, Poway (92064-7154)
PHONE.............................203 655-8911
Tracy Henslin, *Brnch Mgr*
EMP: 46
SALES (corp-wide): 23.39B **Privately Held**
Web: www.henkel.com
SIC: 2844 Hair preparations, including shampoos
HQ: Henkel Us Operations Corporation
1 Henkel Way
Rocky Hill CT 06067
860 571-5100

(P-3659)
HUNTER VAUGHAN LLC
Also Called: H2v By Burke Williams
450 N Oak St, Inglewood (90302-3315)
PHONE.............................626 534-7050
William K Armour, *CEO*
EMP: 250 EST: 2001
SALES (est): 448.69K **Privately Held**
Web: www.burkewilliams.com

SIC: 2844 Perfumes, cosmetics and other toilet preparations

(P-3660)
IDA CLASSIC INC (PA)
9530 De Soto Ave, Chatsworth (91311-5010)
PHONE.............................818 773-9042
Ida Csiszar, *CEO*
Steve Csiszar, *
Frank Csiszar, *
▲ EMP: 125 EST: 1988
SQ FT: 70,000
SALES (est): 20.86MM **Privately Held**
Web: www.classiccosmetics.com
SIC: 2844 Cosmetic preparations

(P-3661)
INSPARATION INC
Also Called: Brian Guy Electric Ltg Svcs Co
11950 Hertz Ave, Moorpark (93021-7145)
PHONE.............................805 553-0820
Lori Guy, *CEO*
EMP: 38 EST: 1987
SALES (est): 5.18MM **Privately Held**
Web: www.insparation.com
SIC: 2844 Cosmetic preparations

(P-3662)
JOICO LABORATORIES INC
5800 Bristol Pkwy, Culver City (90230-6696)
PHONE.............................626 321-4100
Sara Jones, *Pr*
Akira Mochizuki, *
Takahiro Iwabuchi, *
▲ EMP: 28 EST: 1976
SALES (est): 2.1MM **Privately Held**
Web: www.joico.com
SIC: 2844 Hair preparations, including shampoos

(P-3663)
KDC/ONE CHATSWORTH INC
Also Called: Cosmetic Laboratories-America
20320 Prairie St, Chatsworth (91311-6026)
PHONE.............................818 709-1345
Nicholas Whitley, *CEO*
EMP: 199
SALES (corp-wide): 2.66B **Privately Held**
Web: www.kdc-one.com
SIC: 2844 Cosmetic preparations
HQ: Kdc/One Chatsworth, Inc.
20245 Sunburst St
Chatsworth CA 91311
818 709-1345

(P-3664)
KDC/ONE CHATSWORTH INC (DH)
20245 Sunburst St, Chatsworth (91311-6219)
PHONE.............................818 709-1345
Nicholas Whitley, *CEO*
EMP: 99 EST: 2020
SALES (est): 96.64MM
SALES (corp-wide): 2.66B **Privately Held**
Web: www.kdc-one.com
SIC: 2844 Shampoos, rinses, conditioners: hair
HQ: Kdc Us Holdings, Inc.
4400 S Hamilton Rd
Groveport OH 43125

(P-3665)
KENVUE BRANDS LLC
Also Called: Neutrogena
5760 W 96th St, Los Angeles (90045-5544)
PHONE.............................310 642-1150
EMP: 227

SALES (corp-wide): 15.44B **Publicly Held**
Web: www.neutrogena.com
SIC: 2844 Perfumes, cosmetics and other toilet preparations
HQ: Kenvue Brands Llc
1 Kenvue Way
Summit NJ 07901
908 874-1000

(P-3666)
KIM LAUBE & COMPANY INC
Also Called: Kelco
2221 Statham Blvd, Oxnard (93033-3913)
PHONE.............................805 240-1300
Kim E Laube, *Pr*
▲ EMP: 40 EST: 1982
SALES (est): 4.96MM **Privately Held**
Web: www.kimlaubeco.com
SIC: 2844 3999 Hair preparations, including shampoos; Hair clippers for human use, hand and electric

(P-3667)
KUM KANG TRADING USA INC
Also Called: Black N Gold
6433 Alondra Blvd, Paramount (90723-3758)
PHONE.............................562 531-6111
Yoon Oh, *Pr*
◆ EMP: 25 EST: 1987
SQ FT: 20,000
SALES (est): 994.86K **Privately Held**
SIC: 2844 Hair preparations, including shampoos

(P-3668)
LEE PHARMACEUTICALS
1434 Santa Anita Ave, South El Monte (91733-3312)
PHONE.............................626 442-3141
Ronald G Lee, *CEO*
Mike Agresti, *
▲ EMP: 82 EST: 1971
SALES (est): 2.33MM **Privately Held**
Web: www.leepharmaceuticals.com
SIC: 2844 2834 3843 Manicure preparations; Pharmaceutical preparations; Enamels, dentists'

(P-3669)
MASTEY DE PARIS INC
24841 Avenue Tibbitts, Valencia (91355-3405)
PHONE.............................661 257-4814
Stephen Mastey, *Pr*
Lesley Mastey, *
Henri Mastey, *
EMP: 50 EST: 1976
SALES (est): 2.1MM **Privately Held**
Web: www.mastey.com
SIC: 2844 Hair preparations, including shampoos

(P-3670)
MERLE NORMAN COSMETICS INC (PA)
Also Called: Merle Norman Cosmetics
9130 Bellanca Ave, Los Angeles (90045-4772)
PHONE.............................310 641-3000
Jack B Nethercutt, *Ch Bd*
Amy Hackbart, *
Michael Cassidy, *
Helen Nethercutt, *
Rick Rosa, *
▲ EMP: 345 EST: 1974
SQ FT: 354,000
SALES (est): 39.64MM
SALES (corp-wide): 39.64MM **Privately Held**

Web: www.merlenorman.com
SIC: **2844** 5999 Cosmetic preparations;
Cosmetics

(P-3671)
NATURAL THOUGHTS INCORPORATED
Also Called: Biotone Professional Products
4757 Old Cliffs Rd, San Diego
(92120-1134)
PHONE...............................619 582-0027
▲ **EMP:** 38 **EST:** 1978
SALES (est): 5.02MM **Privately Held**
Web: www.biotone.com
SIC: **2844** 5122 Cosmetic preparations;
Drugs, proprietaries, and sundries

(P-3672)
NEUTRADERM INC
20660 Nordhoff St, Chatsworth
(91311-6114)
PHONE...............................818 534-3190
Samuel D Raoof, *CEO*
Toora J Raoof, *
▲ **EMP:** 25 **EST:** 2003
SALES (est): 11.54MM **Privately Held**
Web: www.neutraderm.com
SIC: **2844** Cosmetic preparations

(P-3673)
NYX LOS ANGELES INC
Also Called: Nyx Cosmetics
588 Crenshaw Blvd, Torrance (90503-1705)
PHONE...............................323 869-9420
◆ **EMP:** 140
SIC: **2844** 5122 Perfumes, cosmetics and
other toilet preparations; Cosmetics

(P-3674)
O P I PRODUCTS INC (HQ)
13034 Saticoy St, North Hollywood
(91605-3510)
PHONE...............................818 759-8688
Jules Kaufman, *CEO*
John Heffner, *
Susan Weiss-fischmann, *Ex VP*
Eric Schwartz, *
William Halfacre, *Executive Sales &
Marketing Vice President*
◆ **EMP:** 500 **EST:** 1981
SQ FT: 250,000
SALES (est): 22.31MM **Publicly Held**
Web: www.opi.com
SIC: **2844** Perfumes, cosmetics and other
toilet preparations
PA: Coty Inc.
350 5th Ave

(P-3675)
ORLY INTERNATIONAL INC (PA)
Also Called: Sparitual
7710 Haskell Ave, Van Nuys (91406-1905)
PHONE...............................818 994-1001
Jeff Pink, *Pr*
◆ **EMP:** 99 **EST:** 1977
SQ FT: 65,000
SALES (est): 24.85MM
SALES (corp-wide): 24.85MM **Privately
Held**
Web: www.orlybeauty.com
SIC: **2844** Cosmetic preparations

(P-3676)
PACIFIC WORLD CORPORATION (PA)
757 S Alameda St Ste 280, Los Angeles
(90021-1674)
PHONE...............................949 598-2400
William George, *CEO*

Stuart Noyes, *
Bart Dibie, *
Justin Martini, *
Bob Nabholz, *
◆ **EMP:** 99 **EST:** 1947
SALES (est): 30.53MM
SALES (corp-wide): 30.53MM **Privately
Held**
Web: www.pacificworldcorp.com
SIC: **2844** 3421 3999 5199 Cosmetic
preparations; Clippers, fingernail and toenail
; Fingernails, artificial; General
merchandise, non-durable

(P-3677)
PANGAEA HOLDINGS INC
Also Called: Lumin
1968 S Coast Hwy Pmb 3080, Laguna
Beach (92651-3681)
PHONE...............................402 704-7546
Ingrid Jackel, *CEO*
Richard Hong, *
EMP: 24 **EST:** 2018
SALES (est): 1.78MM **Privately Held**
Web: www.pmall.shop
SIC: **2844** Perfumes, cosmetics and other
toilet preparations

(P-3678)
PERSON & COVEY INC
616 Allen Ave, Glendale (91201-2014)
P.O. Box 25018 (91221-5018)
PHONE...............................818 937-5000
Lorne Person Junior, *CEO*
Lorne Person Senior, *Ch Bd*
Sue Person, *
EMP: 45 **EST:** 1941
SQ FT: 36,000
SALES (est): 9.42MM **Privately Held**
Web: www.personandcovey.com
SIC: **2844** 2834 Cosmetic preparations;
Dermatologicals

(P-3679)
PHYSICIANS FORMULA INC (DH)
22067 Ferrero, City Of Industry
(91789-5214)
PHONE...............................626 334-3395
Ingrid Jackel, *CEO*
Jeff Rogers, *
Rick Kirchhoff, *
Joseph J Jaeger, *
Richard John Almeida External Reporting,
Mgr
▲ **EMP:** 57 **EST:** 1980
SQ FT: 82,800
SALES (est): 22.27MM
SALES (corp-wide): 270.93MM **Privately
Held**
Web: www.physiciansformula.com
SIC: **2844** Cosmetic preparations
HQ: Physicians Formula Holdings, Inc.
22067 Ferrero
Walnut CA 91789

(P-3680)
PHYSICIANS FORMULA COSMT INC
22067 Ferrero, City Of Industry
(91789-5214)
PHONE...............................626 334-3395
Jeffrey P Rogers, *Pr*
Joseph J Jaeger, *CFO*
EMP: 56 **EST:** 1937
SALES (est): 2.47MM
SALES (corp-wide): 270.93MM **Privately
Held**
Web: www.physiciansformula.com

SIC: **2844** Cosmetic preparations
HQ: Physicians Formula, Inc.
22067 Ferrero
City Of Industry CA 91789
626 334-3395

(P-3681)
PLZ CORP
2375 3rd St, Riverside (92507-3306)
PHONE...............................951 683-2912
Marcelo Jimenez, *Brnch Mgr*
EMP: 126
SALES (corp-wide): 766.3MM **Privately
Held**
Web: www.plzcorp.com
SIC: **2844** Cosmetic preparations
PA: Plz Corp.
2651 Wrrnville Rd Ste 300
630 628-3000

(P-3682)
PLZ CORP
14425 Yorba Ave, Chino (91710-5733)
PHONE...............................909 393-9475
Mikel Pruett, *Brnch Mgr*
EMP: 64
SALES (corp-wide): 766.3MM **Privately
Held**
Web: www.plzcorp.com
SIC: **2844** Cosmetic preparations
PA: Plz Corp.
2651 Wrrnville Rd Ste 300
630 628-3000

(P-3683)
PLZ CORP
2321 3rd St, Riverside (92507-3306)
PHONE...............................951 683-2912
Ian Sishman, *Mgr*
EMP: 86
SALES (corp-wide): 766.3MM **Privately
Held**
Web: www.plzcorp.com
SIC: **2844** 5122 5087 Cosmetic preparations
; Cosmetics, perfumes, and hair products;
Beauty parlor equipment and supplies
PA: Plz Corp.
2651 Wrrnvlle Rd Stre 300 300 Stre
630 628-3000

(P-3684)
PROLABS FACTORY INC
15001 Oxnard St, Van Nuys (91411-2613)
P.O. Box 492419 (90049-8419)
PHONE...............................818 646-3677
EMP: 26 **EST:** 2020
SALES (est): 790.63K **Privately Held**
SIC: **2844** Cosmetic preparations

(P-3685)
REVLON INC
Creative Nail Design
1125 Joshua Way Ste 12, Vista
(92081-7840)
PHONE...............................619 372-1379
Jim Northstrum, *Brnch Mgr*
EMP: 74
Web: www.revlon.com
SIC: **2844** Cosmetic preparations
HQ: Revlon, Inc.
55 Water St
New York NY 10041

(P-3686)
SHARPMART LLC ✪
Also Called: S&H
3911 Cleveland Ave Unit 33748, San Diego
(92103-3402)
PHONE...............................619 278-1473
Sudarshan Sharma, *Pr*

EMP: 25 **EST:** 2023
SALES (est): 368.19K **Privately Held**
SIC: **2844** 5961 Perfumes, cosmetics and
other toilet preparations; Cosmetics and
perfumes, mail order

(P-3687)
SOLEVY CO LLC
Also Called: VI Degrees Collective
28918 Hancock Pkwy, Valencia
(91355-1070)
PHONE...............................661 622-4880
Solomon Levy, *Pr*
EMP: 60 **EST:** 2017
SALES (est): 1.57MM **Privately Held**
SIC: **2844** Perfumes, cosmetics and other
toilet preparations

(P-3688)
SPATZ CORPORATION
Also Called: Spatz Laboratories
1600 Westar Dr, Oxnard (93033-2423)
PHONE...............................805 487-2122
Joel Lynn Nelson, *CEO*
Laura Nelson, *
George Jefferson, *
John Nelson, *
▲ **EMP:** 145 **EST:** 1954
SQ FT: 62,000
SALES (est): 44.34MM **Privately Held**
Web: www.spatzlabs.com
SIC: **2844** 3089 Cosmetic preparations;
Plastics containers, except foam

(P-3689)
STILA STYLES LLC (HQ)
Also Called: Stila Cosmetics
801 N Brand Blvd Ste 910, Glendale
(91203)
PHONE...............................866 784-5201
Lynn Tilton, *CEO*
Desiree Tordecilla, *CMO CCO*
Sarah Lucero, *OF EDUCATION AND
ARTISTRY*
▲ **EMP:** 44 **EST:** 2009
SALES (est): 19.97MM
SALES (corp-wide): 1.17K **Privately Held**
Web: www.stilacosmetics.com
SIC: **2844** Cosmetic preparations
PA: Patriarch Partners, Llc
1 Liberty Plz Rm 3500
212 825-0550

(P-3690)
SUNEVA MEDICAL INC (PA)
5870 Pacific Center Blvd, San Diego
(92121-4204)
PHONE...............................858 650-0000
Patricia Altavilla, *CEO*
Joseph A Newcomb, *
Stewart M Brown, *
Nicola Selley, *
Brian Pilcher, *CSO*
EMP: 42 **EST:** 2009
SALES (est): 15.41MM
SALES (corp-wide): 15.41MM **Privately
Held**
Web: www.sunevamedical.com
SIC: **2844** 3842 Cosmetic preparations;
Cosmetic restorations

(P-3691)
TRADEMARK COSMETICS LLC
545 Columbia Ave, Riverside (92507-2183)
PHONE...............................951 683-2631
Kristopher Dover, *CEO*
Joy Boiani, *
▲ **EMP:** 38 **EST:** 1994
SQ FT: 160,000
SALES (est): 2.54MM

SALES (corp-wide): 59.19MM **Privately Held**
Web: www.trademarkcosmetics.com
SIC: **2844** 7231 5999 5122 Hair preparations, including shampoos; Beauty shops; Cosmetics; Cosmetics
PA: Truarc Partners, Lp
　　545 Madison Ave
　　212 508-3300

(P-3692)
TU-K INDUSTRIES LLC
5702 Firestone Pl, South Gate (90280-3714)
PHONE..................................562 927-3365
Arman Cornell, *Prin*
Alpin K Kaler, *
Eleanor Kaler, *
▲ EMP: 50 EST: 1970
SQ FT: 40,000
SALES (est): 5.32MM **Privately Held**
Web: www.tukindustries.com
SIC: **2844** Cosmetic preparations

(P-3693)
UNIVERSAL PACKG SYSTEMS INC (PA)
Also Called: Paklab
14570 Monte Vista Ave, Chino (91710-5743)
PHONE..................................909 517-2442
Jeffery Morlando, *CEO*
Alan Kristel, *
William Wachtel, *
◆ EMP: 750 EST: 1987
SALES (est): 379.38MM
SALES (corp-wide): 379.38MM **Privately Held**
Web: www.paklab.com
SIC: **2844** 7389 3565 2671 Cosmetic preparations; Packaging and labeling services; Bottling machinery: filling, capping, labeling; Plastic film, coated or laminated for packaging

(P-3694)
USP INC
Also Called: Enjoy Haircare
1818 Ord Way, Oceanside (92056-1502)
PHONE..................................760 842-7700
Patrick Dockry, *Prin*
Gordon Fletcher, *
▲ EMP: 60 EST: 1995
SQ FT: 60,000
SALES (est): 8.58MM **Privately Held**
Web: www.enjoyhaircare.com
SIC: **2844** Hair preparations, including shampoos

(P-3695)
VEGE - KURL INC
Also Called: Vege-Tech Company
412 W Cypress St, Glendale (91204-2402)
PHONE..................................818 956-5582
Eric W Huffman, *Pr*
Helen Huffman, *
EMP: 60 EST: 1959
SALES (est): 9.8MM **Privately Held**
Web: www.vegelabs.com
SIC: **2844** 2833 5122 Shampoos, rinses, conditioners: hair; Medicinals and botanicals ; Cosmetics, perfumes, and hair products

(P-3696)
WELLA CORPORATION (HQ)
4500 Park Granada # 100, Calabasas (91302-1665)
PHONE..................................800 422-2336
◆ EMP: 250 EST: 1935
SALES (est): 32.47MM **Publicly Held**

Web: us.wella.professionalstore.com
SIC: **2844** Toilet preparations
PA: Kkr & Co. Inc.
　　30 Hudson Yards

(P-3697)
WESTRIDGE LABORATORIES INC
1671 E Saint Andrew Pl, Santa Ana (92705-4932)
PHONE..................................714 259-9400
Gregg Richard Haskell, *CEO*
John Speelman, *
▲ EMP: 28 EST: 1993
SALES (est): 5.18MM **Privately Held**
Web: www.idlube.com
SIC: **2844** Cosmetic preparations

(P-3698)
WESTWOOD LABORATORIES LLC (PA)
710 S Ayon Ave, Azusa (91702-5123)
PHONE..................................626 969-3305
Paul Schirmer, *CEO*
Brian Surpia Ctrl, *Prin*
▲ EMP: 25 EST: 2004
SALES (est): 12.06MM **Privately Held**
Web: www.westwoodlabs.com
SIC: **2844** Perfumes, cosmetics and other toilet preparations

(P-3699)
WESTWOOD LABORATORIES LLC
766 S Ayon Ave, Azusa (91702-5112)
PHONE..................................626 969-3305
Arnel Garcia, *Mgr*
EMP: 25
Web: www.westwoodlabs.com
SIC: **2844** Perfumes, cosmetics and other toilet preparations
PA: Westwood Laboratories, Llc
　　710 S Ayon Ave

(P-3700)
YG LABORATORIES INC
Also Called: Youthglow
11520 Warner Ave, Fountain Valley (92708-2512)
PHONE..................................714 474-2800
EMP: 28 EST: 1977
SALES (est): 4.05MM **Privately Held**
Web: www.yglabs.com
SIC: **2844** Cosmetic preparations

(P-3701)
YOUTH TO PEOPLE INC
888 N Douglas St, El Segundo (90245-2839)
PHONE..................................309 648-5500
Joseph Cloyes, *CEO*
Greg Gonzalez, *
EMP: 95 EST: 2018
SALES (est): 8.8MM
SALES (corp-wide): 6.5B **Privately Held**
Web: www.youthtothepeople.com
SIC: **2844** Lotions, shaving
PA: L'oreal
　　14 Rue Royale
　　140206000

(P-3702)
ZO SKIN HEALTH INC (DH)
9685 Research Dr, Irvine (92618-4657)
PHONE..................................949 988-7524
Mark Williams, *CEO*
Kevin Cornett, *
▲ EMP: 80 EST: 2006
SQ FT: 12,000

SALES (est): 24.04MM
SALES (corp-wide): 8.02B **Publicly Held**
Web: www.zoskinhealth.com
SIC: **2844** Face creams or lotions
HQ: Blackstone Tactical Opportunities Advisors L.L.C.
　　345 Park Ave
　　New York NY 10154
　　212 583-5000

───────────────

2851 Paints And Allied Products

(P-3703)
BEHR HOLDINGS CORPORATION (HQ)
3400 W Segerstrom Ave, Santa Ana (92704-6405)
PHONE..................................714 545-7101
Jeff Filley, *Pr*
EMP: 26 EST: 1997
SALES (est): 1.5B
SALES (corp-wide): 7.97B **Publicly Held**
Web: www.behr.com
SIC: **2851** Paints and paint additives
PA: Masco Corporation
　　17450 College Pkwy
　　313 274-7400

(P-3704)
BEHR PROCESS LLC (DH)
Also Called: Behr Paint Company
1801 E Saint Andrew Pl, Santa Ana (92705-5044)
PHONE..................................714 545-7101
Megan Selby, *Pr*
Jonathan Sullivan, *
John G Sznewajs, *
Lawrence F Leaman, *
▼ EMP: 700 EST: 1947
SQ FT: 220,000
SALES (est): 1.5B
SALES (corp-wide): 7.97B **Publicly Held**
Web: www.behr.com
SIC: **2851** Paints and paint additives
HQ: Behr Holdings Corporation
　　3400 W Segerstrom Ave
　　Santa Ana CA 92704

(P-3705)
BEHR SALES INC (HQ)
Also Called: Behr Holdings
3400 W Segerstrom Ave, Santa Ana (92704-6405)
PHONE..................................714 545-7101
Jeffrey D Filley, *CEO*
Jonathan M Sullivan, *
Anthony Demiro, *
EMP: 169 EST: 1948
SQ FT: 54,000
SALES (est): 127.41MM
SALES (corp-wide): 7.97B **Publicly Held**
Web: www.behr.com
SIC: **2851** Paints and paint additives
PA: Masco Corporation
　　17450 College Pkwy
　　313 274-7400

(P-3706)
CARDINAL INDUSTRIAL FINISHES (PA)
1329 Potrero Ave Ca, South El Monte (91733-3088)
P.O. Box 9296 (91733)
PHONE..................................626 444-9274
Lawrence C Felix, *CEO*
◆ EMP: 100 EST: 1952
SQ FT: 50,000
SALES (est): 24.25MM

SALES (corp-wide): 24.25MM **Privately Held**
Web: www.cardinalpaint.com
SIC: **2851** Lacquers, varnishes, enamels, and other coatings

(P-3707)
CARDINAL PAINT AND POWDER INC
15010 Don Julian Rd, City Of Industry (91746-3301)
PHONE..................................626 937-6767
Stanley W Ekstrom, *Brnch Mgr*
EMP: 143
SALES (corp-wide): 95.19MM **Privately Held**
Web: www.cardinalpaint.com
SIC: **2851** Paints and allied products
PA: Cardinal Paint And Powder, Inc.
　　1900 Aerojet Way
　　702 852-2333

(P-3708)
CARDINAL PAINT AND POWDER INC
1329 Potrero Ave, South El Monte (91733-3012)
PHONE..................................626 444-9274
EMP: 53 EST: 2016
SALES (est): 5.01MM **Privately Held**
Web: www.cardinalpaint.com
SIC: **2851** Paints and allied products

(P-3709)
COMMERCE COATING SERVICES INC
20725 S Western Ave Ste 144, Torrance (90501-1884)
PHONE..................................310 345-1979
Chris Palicke, *Pr*
Rene Ditton, *
EMP: 60 EST: 2018
SALES (est): 3.99MM **Privately Held**
Web: www.commercecoatingservices.com
SIC: **2851** Paints and allied products

(P-3710)
CONSOLIDATED COLOR CORPORATION
12316 Carson St, Hawaiian Gardens (90716-1604)
PHONE..................................562 420-7714
Michael J Muldoon, *Pr*
Deborah Muldown, *
EMP: 25 EST: 1993
SQ FT: 30,000
SALES (est): 2.78MM **Privately Held**
Web: www.consolidatedcolorcorp.com
SIC: **2851** 2865 Paints and paint additives; Cyclic crudes and intermediates

(P-3711)
DURA TECHNOLOGIES INC
2720 S Willow Ave Ste A, Bloomington (92316-3259)
P.O. Box 333 (92316-0333)
PHONE..................................909 877-8477
Douglas L Dennis, *Pr*
Gina L Dennis, *
▲ EMP: 150 EST: 1977
SQ FT: 14,000
SALES (est): 4.39MM **Privately Held**
SIC: **2851** Paints and allied products

(P-3712)
ENNIS TRAFFIC SAFETY SOLUTIONS
Also Called: Colorama Paints

6624 Stanford Ave, Los Angeles
(90001-1538)
P.O. Box 1496 (90001-0496)
PHONE....................323 758-1147
EMP: 48
SIC: 2851 Paints and allied products

(P-3713)
EPMAR CORPORATION
9930 Painter Ave, Whittier (90605-2759)
PHONE....................562 946-8781
Peter Weissman, Pr
Joe Matrange, *
◆ EMP: 38 EST: 1980
SQ FT: 26,000
SALES (est): 10.18MM
SALES (corp-wide): 1.95B Publicly Held
Web: www.epmar.com
SIC: 2851 2891 2821 3087 Epoxy coatings;
Adhesives and sealants; Plastics materials
and resins; Custom compound purchased
resins
PA: Quaker Chemical Corporation
901 E Hector St
610 832-4000

(P-3714)
FRAZEE INDUSTRIES INC
Also Called: Frazee Paint & Wallcovering
6625 Miramar Rd, San Diego (92121-2508)
PHONE....................858 626-3600
EMP: 900
Web: www.sherwin-williams.com
SIC: 2851 5198 5231 Paints, waterproof;
Paints; Paint

(P-3715)
FSI COATING TECHNOLOGIES INC
45 Parker Ste 100, Irvine (92618-1658)
PHONE....................949 540-1140
Antonios Grigoriou, Pr
Richard Chang, CFO
EMP: 24 EST: 1986
SALES (est): 2.6MM Privately Held
Web: www.fsicti.com
SIC: 2851 Lacquers, varnishes, enamels,
and other coatings
HQ: Sdc Technologies, Inc.
45 Parker Ste 100
Irvine CA 92618
714 939-8300

(P-3716)
LAIRD COATINGS CORPORATION
Also Called: Coatings Resource
15541 Commerce Ln, Huntington Beach
(92649-1601)
PHONE....................714 894-5252
Jeff Laird, CEO
▲ EMP: 51 EST: 1976
SQ FT: 17,500
SALES (est): 9.83MM Privately Held
Web: www.coatingsresource.com
SIC: 2851 2865 Paints and paint additives;
Dyes, synthetic organic

(P-3717)
MICROBLEND INC
Also Called: Microblend Technologies
543 Country Club Dr, Simi Valley
(93065-0637)
PHONE....................330 998-4602
John E Tyson, CEO
Melvin J Sauder, *
Dan Trevino, *
John Bond, *
Jennifer Haslip, *
◆ EMP: 46 EST: 2014

SALES (est): 4.22MM Privately Held
Web: www.microblend.com
SIC: 2851 Paints and paint additives

(P-3718)
OLIVE REFINISH
19014 Pacific Coast Hwy, Malibu
(90265-5406)
PHONE....................805 273-5072
Albert Banoun, Owner
EMP: 25 EST: 2004
SALES (est): 536.84K Privately Held
Web: www.oliverefinish.com
SIC: 2851 Paints and allied products

(P-3719)
PPG INDUSTRIES INC
11601 United St, Mojave (93501-7048)
PHONE....................661 824-4532
Michelle Brown, Mgr
EMP: 24
SALES (corp-wide): 17.65B Publicly Held
Web: www.ppg.com
SIC: 2851 Paints and allied products
PA: Ppg Industries, Inc.
1 Ppg Pl
412 434-3131

(P-3720)
RHINO LININGS CORPORATION (PA)
9747 Businesspark Ave, San Diego
(92131-1661)
PHONE....................858 450-0441
Pierre M Gagnon, CEO
Russel Lewis, *
Sandra S Roberts, *
◆ EMP: 65 EST: 1988
SQ FT: 20,000
SALES (est): 53.3MM
SALES (corp-wide): 53.3MM Privately Held
Web: www.rhinolinings.com
SIC: 2851 Coating, air curing

(P-3721)
SIERRACIN CORPORATION (HQ)
12780 San Fernando Rd, Sylmar
(91342-3796)
PHONE....................818 741-1656
Barry N Gillespie, CEO
David B Navikas, *
Michael H Mcgarry, Ex VP
Frank S Sklarsky, *
Viktoras R Sekmakas, *
▲ EMP: 550 EST: 1952
SQ FT: 287,000
SALES (est): 60.14MM
SALES (corp-wide): 17.65B Publicly Held
Web: www.ppgaerospace.com
SIC: 2851 Paints and allied products
PA: Ppg Industries, Inc.
1 Ppg Pl
412 434-3131

(P-3722)
SPECIALIZED MILLING CORP
Also Called: Specialty Finishes
10330 Elm Ave, Fontana (92337-7319)
PHONE....................909 357-7890
Jack Neems, Pr
Seymour S Neems, Ch Bd
Adele Neems, Treas
EMP: 50 EST: 1968
SQ FT: 11,000
SALES (est): 2.5MM Privately Held
SIC: 2851 Paints and allied products

2865 Cyclic Crudes And Intermediates

(P-3723)
COLOR SCIENCE INC
Also Called: C S I
1230 E Glenwood Pl, Santa Ana
(92707-3000)
PHONE....................714 434-1033
Jocelyn Eubank, CEO
Mark Hoffenberg, *
EMP: 45 EST: 1989
SQ FT: 9,000
SALES (est): 22.22MM
SALES (corp-wide): 24.9MM Privately Held
Web: www.modifiedplastics.com
SIC: 2865 Color pigments, organic
PA: Modified Plastics, Inc.
1240 E Glenwood Pl
714 546-4667

2869 Industrial Organic Chemicals, Nec

(P-3724)
AEROJET ROCKETDYNE DE INC (DH)
Also Called: Aerojet Rocketdyne
8900 De Soto Ave, Canoga Park
(91304-1967)
P.O. Box 7922 (91309-7922)
PHONE....................818 586-1000
Eileen P Drake, CEO
Pete Gleszer, *
Jerry Tucker, *
▲ EMP: 417 EST: 2005
SALES (est): 403.12MM
SALES (corp-wide): 19.42B Publicly Held
Web: www.l3harris.com
SIC: 2869 3724 Rocket engine fuel, organic;
Aircraft engines and engine parts
HQ: Aerojet Rocketdyne Holdings, Inc.
222 N Pcf Cast Hwy Ste 50
El Segundo CA 90245
310 252-8100

(P-3725)
AEROJET ROCKETDYNE DE INC
8495 Carla Ln, West Hills (91304-3201)
PHONE....................818 586-9629
EMP: 140
SALES (corp-wide): 19.42B Publicly Held
Web: www.l3harris.com
SIC: 2869 3724 Rocket engine fuel, organic;
Aircraft engines and engine parts
HQ: Inc Aerojet Rocketdyne Of De
8900 De Soto Ave
Canoga Park CA 91304
818 586-1000

(P-3726)
AEROJET ROCKETDYNE DE INC
9001 Lurline Ave, Chatsworth (91311-6122)
P.O. Box 7922 (91309-7922)
PHONE....................818 586-1000
Helen Lubin, Brnch Mgr
EMP: 115
SALES (corp-wide): 19.42B Publicly Held
Web: www.l3harris.com
SIC: 2869 3724 Rocket engine fuel, organic;
Aircraft engines and engine parts
HQ: Inc Aerojet Rocketdyne Of De
8900 De Soto Ave
Canoga Park CA 91304
818 586-1000

(P-3727)
AVIENT COLORANTS USA LLC
14355 Ramona Ave, Chino (91710-5740)
PHONE....................909 606-1325
Mike Urbano, Brnch Mgr
EMP: 64
Web: www.avient.com
SIC: 2869 Industrial organic chemicals, nec
HQ: Avient Colorants Usa Llc
85 Industrial Dr
Holden MA 01520
877 546-2885

(P-3728)
BASF CORPORATION
138 E Meats Ave, Orange (92865-3310)
PHONE....................714 921-1430
John Zomer, Mgr
EMP: 127
SQ FT: 10,000
SALES (corp-wide): 74.89B Privately Held
Web: www.basf.com
SIC: 2869 2821 Industrial organic chemicals,
nec; Plastics materials and resins
HQ: Basf Corporation
100 Park Ave
Florham Park NJ 07932
800 962-7831

(P-3729)
BASF CORPORATION
6700 8th St, Buena Park (90620-1097)
PHONE....................714 521-6085
Tim Stmarseille, Mgr
EMP: 29
SALES (corp-wide): 74.89B Privately Held
Web: www.basf.com
SIC: 2869 Industrial organic chemicals, nec
HQ: Basf Corporation
100 Park Ave
Florham Park NJ 07932
800 962-7831

(P-3730)
BASF ENZYMES LLC (DH)
3550 John Hopkins Ct, San Diego
(92121-1121)
PHONE....................858 431-8520
◆ EMP: 78 EST: 1992
SALES (est): 12.07MM
SALES (corp-wide): 74.89B Privately Held
Web: nutrition.basf.com
SIC: 2869 Industrial organic chemicals, nec
HQ: Basf Corporation
100 Park Ave
Florham Park NJ 07932
800 962-7831

(P-3731)
BIOTIX (HQ)
10030 Scripps Summit Ct Ste 130, San
Diego (92131-3979)
PHONE....................858 875-7696
Paul Nowak, CEO
Tony Altig, *
Ron Perkins, *
Celia Reyes, *
Mickie Henshall, *
◆ EMP: 28 EST: 2006
SALES (est): 20.77MM Privately Held
Web: www.biotix.com
SIC: 2869 Laboratory chemicals, organic
PA: Biotix Holdings, Inc.
10636 Scripps Summit Ct

(P-3732)
CHEMLOGICS GROUP LLC
Also Called: Envirochem Technologies
7305 Morro Rd Ste 200, Atascadero
(93422-4445)

PHONE..................805 591-3314
EMP: 35
SIC: 2869 Industrial organic chemicals, nec

(P-3733)
FIRMENICH
424 S Atchison St, Anaheim (92805-4045)
PHONE..................714 535-2871
EMP: 89
SALES (est): 38.34MM **Privately Held**
Web: www.firmenich.com
SIC: 2869 Industrial organic chemicals, nec

(P-3734)
INTERNATIONAL ACADEMY OF FIN (PA)
Also Called: Cordova Industries
13177 Foothill Blvd, Sylmar (91342-4830)
P.O. Box 922079 (91392-2079)
PHONE..................818 361-7724
Sam Cordova, *Pr*
Steven M Cordova, *
Rodrick Cordova, *
Sam Scott Cordova, *
Steven Schector, *
EMP: 24 EST: 1963
SQ FT: 6,000
SALES (est): 1.69MM **Privately Held**
SIC: 2869 3944 2879 Alcohols, industrial: denatured (non-beverage); Video game machines, except coin-operated; Insecticides, agricultural or household

(P-3735)
PROVIVI INC
1701 Colorado Ave, Santa Monica (90404-3436)
PHONE..................310 828-2307
Pedro S L Coelho, *CEO*
Peter Meinhold, *
Eduardo Sein, *
Teri Quinn Gray, *
EMP: 75 EST: 2012
SALES (est): 12.86MM **Privately Held**
Web: www.provivi.com
SIC: 2869 Laboratory chemicals, organic

(P-3736)
SAINT-GOBAIN CERAMICS PLAS INC
Innovative Organics Division
4905 E Hunter Ave, Anaheim (92807-2058)
PHONE..................714 701-3900
Robert E Futrell Junior, *Brnch Mgr*
EMP: 188
SALES (corp-wide): 402.18MM **Privately Held**
Web: www.saint-gobain.com
SIC: 2869 2899 Industrial organic chemicals, nec; Chemical preparations, nec
HQ: Saint-Gobain Ceramics & Plastics, Inc.
3840 Fishcreek Rd
Stow OH 44224

(P-3737)
STRATOS RENEWABLES CORPORATION
Also Called: A Development Stage Company
9440 Santa Monica Blvd Ste 401, Beverly Hills (90210-4607)
PHONE..................310 402-5901
Thomas Snyder, *Pr*
Julio Cesar Alonso, *
Valerie Broadbent, *
Jorge Eduardo Aza, *
Sanjay Pai, *Chief Strategy Officer*
EMP: 28 EST: 2004
SALES (est): 4.01MM **Privately Held**
Web: www.stratosrenewables.com

SIC: 2869 0133 Ethyl alcohol, ethanol; Sugarcane and sugar beets

(P-3738)
SUGAR FOODS LLC (HQ)
Also Called: Sugar Foods
3059 Townsgate Rd Ste 101, Westlake Village (91361-2936)
PHONE..................805 396-5000
Marty Wilson, *Pr*
Donald G Tober, *
Stephen Odell, *
Jack Vivinetto, *
◆ EMP: 34 EST: 1961
SQ FT: 10,000
SALES (est): 510.8MM
SALES (corp-wide): 677.96MM **Privately Held**
Web: www.sugarfoods.com
SIC: 2869 2023 2099 2068 Sweeteners, synthetic; Cream substitutes; Sugar; Salted and roasted nuts and seeds
PA: Ppc Investment Partners Lp
110 N Wacker Dr Ste 4400
312 447-6050

(P-3739)
TASTEPOINT INC
Also Called: Tastepoint By Iff
790 E Harrison St, Corona (92879-1348)
PHONE..................951 734-6620
EMP: 188
SALES (corp-wide): 11.48B **Publicly Held**
Web: www.tastepoint.com
SIC: 2869 Flavors or flavoring materials, synthetic
HQ: Tastepoint Inc.
7800 Holstein Ave
Philadelphia PA 19153
215 365-7800

(P-3740)
USL PARALLEL PRODUCTS CAL
12281 Arrow Rte, Rancho Cucamonga (91739-9601)
PHONE..................909 980-1200
Gene Kiesel, *CEO*
Ken Reese, *
Jim Russell, *
Bob Pasma, *
Tim Cusson, *
▲ EMP: 35 EST: 1981
SQ FT: 6,000
SALES (est): 4.8MM
SALES (corp-wide): 87.06MM **Privately Held**
Web: www.parallelproducts.com
SIC: 2869 Alcohols, industrial: denatured (non-beverage)
PA: Parallel Environmental Services Corporation
401 Industry Rd
502 471-2444

(P-3741)
UTAK LABORATORIES INC
25020 Avenue Tibbitts, Valencia (91355-3447)
PHONE..................661 294-3935
James D Plutchak, *CEO*
EMP: 26 EST: 1974
SQ FT: 12,000
SALES (est): 9.82MM **Privately Held**
Web: www.utak.com
SIC: 2869 Industrial organic chemicals, nec

(P-3742)
VERENIUM CORPORATION
3550 John Hopkins Ct, San Diego (92121-1121)

P.O. Box 685 (07932-0685)
PHONE..................858 431-8500
▲ EMP: 111
Web: nutrition.basf.com
SIC: 2869 Industrial organic chemicals, nec

(P-3743)
WACKER CHEMICAL CORPORATION
Also Called: Precision Silicones
13910 Oaks Ave, Chino (91710-7010)
PHONE..................909 590-8822
Sudipta Das, *Brnch Mgr*
EMP: 70
SALES (corp-wide): 6.96B **Privately Held**
Web: www.wacker.com
SIC: 2869 5169 Silicones; Industrial chemicals
HQ: Wacker Chemical Corporation
3301 Sutton Rd
Adrian MI 49221
517 264-8500

2873 Nitrogenous Fertilizers

(P-3744)
GRO-POWER INC
15065 Telephone Ave, Chino (91710-9614)
PHONE..................909 393-3744
Brent Holden, *Pr*
▼ EMP: 25 EST: 1966
SALES (est): 4.12MM **Privately Held**
Web: www.gropower.com
SIC: 2873 0782 0721 Fertilizers: natural (organic), except compost; Lawn and garden services; Crop planting and protection

(P-3745)
HYPONEX CORPORATION
Also Called: Scotts- Hyponex
12273 Brown Ave, Jurupa Valley (92509-1828)
PHONE..................909 597-2811
Roclund White, *Brnch Mgr*
EMP: 217
SALES (corp-wide): 3.55B **Publicly Held**
Web: www.suntreksolar.com
SIC: 2873 Fertilizers: natural (organic), except compost
HQ: Hyponex Corporation
14111 Scottslawn Rd
Marysville OH 43040
937 644-0011

(P-3746)
RENTECH NTRGN PASADENA SPA LLC
10877 Wilshire Blvd Ste 710, Los Angeles (90024-4364)
PHONE..................310 571-9805
EMP: 44 EST: 1987
SALES (est): 919.67K **Publicly Held**
SIC: 2873 Nitrogenous fertilizers
HQ: Cvr Nitrogen, Lp
10877 Wilshire Blvd Fl 10
Los Angeles CA 90024
310 571-9800

(P-3747)
SCOTTS COMPANY LLC
742 Industrial Way, Shafter (93263-4018)
PHONE..................661 387-9555
Aaron Leach, *Brnch Mgr*
EMP: 23
SALES (corp-wide): 3.55B **Publicly Held**
Web: www.scotts.com
SIC: 2873 Fertilizers: natural (organic), except compost

HQ: The Scotts Company Llc
14111 Scottslawn Rd
Marysville OH 43040
937 644-0011

(P-3748)
WHITTIER FERTILIZER COMPANY
9441 Kruse Rd, Pico Rivera (90660-1492)
PHONE..................562 699-3461
Robert Osborn, *CEO*
Janet Osborn, *
▲ EMP: 51 EST: 1930
SQ FT: 20,000
SALES (est): 9.92MM **Privately Held**
Web: www.whittierfertilizer.com
SIC: 2873 5261 2875 Fertilizers: natural (organic), except compost; Garden supplies and tools, nec; Fertilizers, mixing only

---

2875 Fertilizers, Mixing Only

(P-3749)
JH BIOTECH INC (PA)
Also Called: Jh Biotech
4951 Olivas Park Dr, Ventura (93003-7667)
P.O. Box 3538 (93006)
PHONE..................805 650-8933
Hsinhung John Hsu, *Pr*
◆ EMP: 23 EST: 1986
SQ FT: 3,000
SALES (est): 15.43MM
SALES (corp-wide): 15.43MM **Privately Held**
Web: www.jhbiotech.com
SIC: 2875 Fertilizers, mixing only

2879 Agricultural Chemicals, Nec

(P-3750)
AMERICAN VANGUARD CORPORATION (PA)
Also Called: Avd
4695 Macarthur Ct, Newport Beach (92660-1882)
PHONE..................949 260-1200
Douglas A Kaye Iii, *CEO*
Eric G Wintemute, *Ch Bd*
David T Johnson, *VP*
◆ EMP: 67 EST: 1969
SQ FT: 19,953
SALES (est): 579.37MM
SALES (corp-wide): 579.37MM **Publicly Held**
Web: www.american-vanguard.com
SIC: 2879 Pesticides, agricultural or household

(P-3751)
AMVAC CHEMICAL CORPORATION (HQ)
4695 Macarthur Ct Ste 1200, Newport Beach (92660-8859)
PHONE..................323 264-3910
Eric G Wintemute, *Ch*
Bob Trogele, *
David T Johnson, *
Glen Johnson, *
Cindy Baker Smith, *
◆ EMP: 36 EST: 1945
SQ FT: 152,000
SALES (est): 95.98MM
SALES (corp-wide): 579.37MM **Publicly Held**
Web: www.amvac-chemical.com
SIC: 2879 Pesticides, agricultural or household

PA: American Vanguard Corporation
4695 Macarthur Ct
949 260-1200

(P-3752)
CERTIS USA LLC
Also Called: Thermo Trilogy
720 5th St, Wasco (93280-1420)
PHONE..................................661 758-8471
Michael Hillberry, *Prin*
EMP: 40
Web: www.certisbio.com
SIC: 2879 5191 Pesticides, agricultural or
household; Insecticides
HQ: Certis U.S.A. L.L.C.
9145 Guilford Rd Ste 175
Columbia MD 21046

(P-3753)
CIBUS INC
Also Called: Cibus
6455 Nancy Ridge Dr, San Diego
(92121-2249)
PHONE..................................858 450-0008
Rory Riggs, *Ch Bd*
Gerhard Prante, *
Peter Beetham, *
Cornelis Broos, *Interim Chief Financial
Officer*
Greg Gocal, *CSO*
EMP: 183 **EST:** 2010
SQ FT: 53,423
SALES (est): 1.82MM **Privately Held**
Web: www.calyxt.com
SIC: 2879 8731 0721 Agricultural chemicals,
nec; Agricultural research; Crop planting
and protection

(P-3754)
ECOSMART TECHNOLOGIES INC
1585 W Mission Blvd, Pomona
(91766-1233)
PHONE..................................770 667-0006
EMP: 25
SIC: 2879 Insecticides and pesticides

(P-3755)
GROW MORE INC
15600 New Century Dr, Gardena
(90248-2129)
PHONE..................................310 515-1700
John Atwill Ii, *CEO*
◆ **EMP:** 62 **EST:** 1918
SQ FT: 43,560
SALES (est): 1.74MM **Privately Held**
Web: www.growmore.com
SIC: 2879 2899 2873 2869 Agricultural
chemicals, nec; Chemical preparations, nec
; Nitrogenous fertilizers; Industrial organic
chemicals, nec

(P-3756)
MONSANTO COMPANY
Also Called: Monsanto
2700 Camino Del Sol, Oxnard
(93030-7967)
PHONE..................................805 827-2341
EMP: 23
SALES (corp-wide): 51.78B **Privately Held**
Web: www.monsanto.com
SIC: 2879 Agricultural chemicals, nec
HQ: Monsanto Technology Llc.
800 North Lindbergh Blvd
Saint Louis MO 63167
314 694-1000

2891 Adhesives And Sealants

(P-3757)
AC PRODUCTS INC
Also Called: Quaker
9930 Painter Ave, Whittier (90605-2759)
PHONE..................................714 630-7311
Peter Weissman, *Pr*
Joseph Matrange, *
Hugh H Muller, *
Sheldon I Weinstein, *
◆ **EMP:** 35 **EST:** 1972
SQ FT: 28,000
SALES (est): 11.58MM
SALES (corp-wide): 1.95B **Publicly Held**
Web: www.acpmaskants.com
SIC: 2891 2952 8731 Adhesives and
sealants; Coating compounds, tar;
Chemical laboratory, except testing
PA: Quaker Chemical Corporation
901 E Hector St
610 832-4000

(P-3758)
ADVANCED CHEMISTRY & TECHNOLOGY INC
Also Called: AC Tech
7341 Anaconda Ave, Garden Grove
(92841-2921)
PHONE..................................714 373-8118
▲ **EMP:** 70
Web: www.actechaero.com
SIC: 2891 Sealants

(P-3759)
ADVANTAGE ADHESIVES INC
1420 S Vintage Ave, Ontario (91761-3646)
PHONE..................................909 204-4990
Greg Lane, *Pr*
▲ **EMP:** 26 **EST:** 1998
SALES (est): 8.95MM **Privately Held**
Web: www.advantageadhesives.com
SIC: 2891 Adhesives

(P-3760)
AXIOM MATERIALS INC
2320 Pullman St, Santa Ana (92705-5507)
PHONE..................................949 623-4400
Murat Oguz Arca, *CEO*
Olcay Demirkesen, *
▲ **EMP:** 35 **EST:** 2009
SQ FT: 15,000
SALES (est): 18.58MM **Privately Held**
Web: www.axiommaterials.com
SIC: 2891 2295 Epoxy adhesives; Resin or
plastic coated fabrics
HQ: Kordsa, Inc.
4501 N Access Rd
Chattanooga TN 37415
423 643 8300

(P-3761)
BOSTIK INC
27460 Bostik Ct, Temecula (92590-3698)
PHONE..................................951 296-6425
Ed Lui, *Brnch Mgr*
EMP: 46
SALES (corp-wide): 134.78MM **Privately
Held**
Web: www.bostik.com
SIC: 2891 2899 Adhesives; Chemical
preparations, nec
HQ: Bostik, Inc.
11320 W Watertwn Plnk Rd
Wauwatosa WI 53226
414 774-2250

(P-3762)
CUSTOM BUILDING PRODUCTS LLC (DH)
Also Called: C-Cure
7711 Center Ave Ste 500, Huntington Beach
(92647-3076)
PHONE..................................800 272-8786
Don Devine, *CEO*
Thomas Peck Junior, *Pr*
Marc Powell, *
◆ **EMP:** 65 **EST:** 2005
SQ FT: 15,000
SALES (est): 386.06MM **Privately Held**
Web: www.custombuildingproducts.com
SIC: 2891 Adhesives and sealants
HQ: The Quikrete Companies Llc
5 Concourse Pkwy Ste 1900
Atlanta GA 30328
404 634-9100

(P-3763)
CUSTOM BUILDING PRODUCTS LLC
6511 Salt Lake Ave, Bell (90201-2198)
PHONE..................................323 582-0846
Tom Milan, *Manager*
EMP: 141
Web: www.custombuildingproducts.com
SIC: 2891 3273 2899 5032 Adhesives and
sealants; Ready-mixed concrete; Chemical
preparations, nec; Ceramic wall and floor
tile, nec
HQ: Custom Building Products Llc
7711 Center Ave Ste 500
Huntington Beach CA 92647
800 272-8786

(P-3764)
DESMOND VENTURES INC
17451 Von Karman Ave, Irvine
(92614-6205)
P.O. Box 19507 (92623-9507)
PHONE..................................949 474-0400
▲ **EMP:** 135
SIC: 2891 2851 Adhesives and sealants;
Lacquers, varnishes, enamels, and other
coatings

(P-3765)
ESSENTRA INTERNATIONAL LLC
Also Called: Duraco Express
21303 Ferrero, Walnut (91789-5231)
PHONE..................................708 315-7498
EMP: 1150
SALES (corp-wide): 394.25MM **Privately
Held**
Web: www.essentra.com
SIC: 2891 Adhesives and sealants
HQ: Essentra International Llc
2 Westbrook Corp Ctr
Westchester IL 60154
866 800-0775

(P-3766)
FLAMEMASTER CORPORATION
Also Called: Chemseal
13576 Desmond St, Pacoima (91331-2315)
P.O. Box 4510 (91333-4500)
PHONE..................................818 890-1401
Joshua Mazin, *Pr*
▲ **EMP:** 28 **EST:** 1942
SALES (est): 5.72MM **Privately Held**
Web: www.flamemaster.com
SIC: 2891 Sealants

(P-3767)
GENERAL SEALANTS
300 Turnbull Canyon Rd, City Of Industry
(91745-1009)

P.O. Box 3855 (91744-0855)
PHONE..................................626 961-0211
Bradley Boyle, *Pr*
Patricia Boyle, *
Patrick Boyle, *
◆ **EMP:** 120 **EST:** 1964
SQ FT: 96,000
SALES (est): 19.45MM **Privately Held**
Web: www.generalsealants.com
SIC: 2891 Adhesives

(P-3768)
HENKEL CHEMICAL MANAGEMENT LLC
Also Called: Henkel Electronic Mtls LLC
14000 Jamboree Rd, Irvine (92606-1730)
PHONE..................................888 943-6535
Benoit Pouliquen, *VP*
Alan P Syzdek, *
Paul R Berry, *
EMP: 170 **EST:** 2010
SQ FT: 75,000
SALES (est): 4.31MM
SALES (corp-wide): 23.39B **Privately Held**
Web: www.henkel.com
SIC: 2891 Adhesives
PA: Henkel Ag & Co. Kgaa
Henkelstr. 67
2117970

(P-3769)
HENKEL US OPERATIONS CORP
Dexter Electronics Mtls Div
15051 Don Julian Rd, City Of Industry
(91746-3302)
P.O. Box 1282 (91749-1282)
PHONE..................................626 968-6511
Jim Dehart, *Mgr*
EMP: 60
SALES (corp-wide): 23.39B **Privately Held**
Web: www.henkel.com
SIC: 2891 Adhesives
HQ: Henkel Us Operations Corporation
1 Henkel Way
Rocky Hill CT 06067
860 571-5100

(P-3770)
INTERNATIONAL COATINGS CO INC (PA)
Also Called: International Coatings
13929 166th St, Cerritos (90703-2431)
PHONE..................................562 926-1010
Stephen W Kahane, *CEO*
Herbert A Wells, *
Janet Wells, *
◆ **EMP:** 40 **EST:** 1957
SQ FT: 50,000
SALES (est): 15.32MM
SALES (corp-wide): 15.32MM **Privately
Held**
Web: www.iccink.com
SIC: 2891 2899 3555 2893 Adhesives; Ink or
writing fluids; Printing trades machinery;
Printing ink

(P-3771)
IPS CORPORATION (HQ)
Also Called: Weld-On Adhesives
455 W Victoria St, Compton (90220-6064)
PHONE..................................310 898-3300
Tracy Bilbrough, *CEO*
Will Barton, *
Gary Rosenfield, *
◆ **EMP:** 180 **EST:** 1953
SQ FT: 22,000
SALES (est): 717.97MM **Privately Held**
Web: www.ipscorp.com
SIC: 2891 Adhesives, plastic
PA: Centerbridge Partners, L.P.
375 Park Ave Fl 12 C

PRODUCTS & SVCS

(P-3772)
MITSUBISHI CHEMICAL CRBN FBR
Also Called: Mitsubishi Chemical Carbon Fiber and Composites, Inc.
1822 Reynolds Ave, Irvine (92614-5714)
PHONE.....................800 929-5471
Takashi Sasaki, *VP*
EMP: 110
Web: www.mccfc.com
SIC: 2891 5169 Adhesives; Chemical additives
HQ: Mitsubishi Chemical Carbon Fiber And Composites, Inc
5900 88th St
Sacramento CA 95828

(P-3773)
PACER TECHNOLOGY (HQ)
Also Called: Super Glue
3281 E Guasti Rd Ste 260, Ontario (91761-7642)
PHONE.....................909 987-0550
E T Gravette, *CEO*
Ronald T Gravette, *
Kristine Wright, *
James Gallagher, *
Marsha Gravette, *
◆ **EMP:** 107 **EST:** 1975
SQ FT: 47,700
SALES (est): 24.1MM
SALES (corp-wide): 24.1MM **Privately Held**
Web: www.supergluecorp.com
SIC: 2891 3089 3085 Adhesives and sealants; Plastics containers, except foam; Plastics bottles
PA: Cyan Holding Corporation
9420 Santa Anita Ave
909 987-0550

(P-3774)
PACKAGING SYSTEMS INC
26435 Summit Cir, Santa Clarita (91350-2991)
PHONE.....................661 253-5700
Raymond J Gray, *CEO*
Steve Gray, *
Patricia Gray, *
▼ **EMP:** 42 **EST:** 1976
SQ FT: 25,700
SALES (est): 15.05MM **Privately Held**
Web: www.pkgsys.net
SIC: 2891 Adhesives and sealants

(P-3775)
PRC - DESOTO INTERNATIONAL INC (HQ)
Also Called: PPG Aerospace
24811 Avenue Rockefeller, Valencia (91355-3468)
PHONE.....................661 678-4209
Michael H Mcgarry, *Pr*
Barry Gillespie, *
David P Morris, *
John Machin, *
Donna Lee Walker, *Tax Administration Vice President*
▲ **EMP:** 320 **EST:** 1945
SQ FT: 200,000
SALES (est): 138.57MM
SALES (corp-wide): 17.65B **Publicly Held**
Web: www.ppgaerospace.com
SIC: 2891 3089 Sealing compounds, synthetic rubber or plastic; Plastics containers, except foam
PA: Ppg Industries, Inc.
1 Ppg Pl
412 434-3131

(P-3776)
PRC - DESOTO INTERNATIONAL INC
Also Called: PPG Aerospace
11601 United St, Mojave (93501-7048)
PHONE.....................661 824-4532
Dave Richardson, *Brnch Mgr*
EMP: 130
SALES (corp-wide): 17.65B **Publicly Held**
Web: guide13227.guidechem.com
SIC: 2891 Sealing compounds, synthetic rubber or plastic
HQ: Prc - Desoto International, Inc.
24811 Ave Rockefeller
Valencia CA 91355
661 678-4209

(P-3777)
QSPAC INDUSTRIES INC (PA)
Also Called: Quality Service Pac Industry
15020 Marquardt Ave, Santa Fe Springs (90670-5704)
PHONE.....................562 407-3868
Jow-lin Tang, *Pr*
Wu-hsiung Chung, *CFO*
Vic Lee, *
◆ **EMP:** 52 **EST:** 2009
SQ FT: 96,000
SALES (est): 2.18MM **Privately Held**
Web: www.qspac.com
SIC: 2891 Adhesives

(P-3778)
SEAL FOR LIFE INDUSTRIES LLC (HQ)
2290 Enrico Fermi Dr Ste 22, San Diego (92154-7228)
PHONE.....................619 671-0932
Jeffrey Oravitz, *CEO*
Dirk Totte, *Pr*
Mauricio Perini, *CFO*
▲ **EMP:** 44 **EST:** 2012
SQ FT: 260,831
SALES (est): 51.99MM
SALES (corp-wide): 23.39B **Privately Held**
Web: www.sealforlife.com
SIC: 2891 2952 Sealing compounds, synthetic rubber or plastic; Coating compounds, tar
PA: Henkel Ag & Co. Kgaa
Henkelstr. 67
2117970

(P-3779)
SIGNATURE FLEXIBLE PACKG LLC (PA)
Also Called: Dazpak Flexible Packaging
19310 San Jose Ave, City Of Industry (91748-1419)
PHONE.....................909 598-7844
Adrian Backer, *Pr*
Jeff Sewel, *
Kelly Redding, *
▲ **EMP:** 50 **EST:** 1954
SALES (est): 30.99MM
SALES (corp-wide): 30.99MM **Privately Held**
Web: www.dazpak.com
SIC: 2891 2673 Adhesives and sealants; Bags: plastic, laminated, and coated

(P-3780)
STIC-ADHESIVE PRODUCTS CO INC
3950 Medford St, Los Angeles (90063-1675)
PHONE.....................323 268-2956
Junho Suh, *Pr*
EMP: 150 **EST:** 1975

SQ FT: 75,000
SALES (est): 9.5MM **Privately Held**
Web: www.milspeccoating.com
SIC: 2891 2851 Adhesives; Paints and allied products

(P-3781)
TEC SPECIALTY PRODUCTS LLC ✪
1230 Rosecrans Ave Ste 520, Manhattan Beach (90266-2562)
PHONE.....................801 897-5514
Christopher Sznewajs, *Managing Member*
EMP: 250 **EST:** 2024
SALES (est): 1.77MM **Privately Held**
SIC: 2891 Adhesives and sealants

(P-3782)
TECHNICOTE INC
1587 E Bentley Dr Ste 101, Corona (92879-1788)
PHONE.....................951 372-0627
George Parker, *Mgr*
EMP: 40
SALES (corp-wide): 62.09MM **Privately Held**
Web: www.technicote.com
SIC: 2891 2675 Adhesives; Die-cut paper and board
PA: Technicote, Inc.
6206 Wolf Creek Pike
800 358-4448

2892 Explosives

(P-3783)
TELEDYNE REYNOLDS INC
1001 Knox St, Torrance (90502-1030)
PHONE.....................310 823-5491
EMP: 250
SIC: 2892 3489 3678 3643 Explosives; Ordnance and accessories, nec; Electronic connectors; Current-carrying wiring services

2893 Printing Ink

(P-3784)
GANS INK AND SUPPLY CO INC (PA)
Also Called: Gans Digital
1441 Boyd St, Los Angeles (90033-3714)
P.O. Box 33806 (90033-0806)
PHONE.....................323 264-2200
Jeffrey Koppelman, *Pr*
◆ **EMP:** 50 **EST:** 1950
SQ FT: 28,000
SALES (est): 20.46MM
SALES (corp-wide): 20.46MM **Privately Held**
Web: www.gansink.com
SIC: 2893 Printing ink

(P-3785)
INK SYSTEMS INC (PA)
2311 S Eastern Ave, Commerce (90040-1430)
PHONE.....................323 720-4000
▲ **EMP:** 55 **EST:** 1985
SALES (est): 24.96MM
SALES (corp-wide): 24.96MM **Privately Held**
Web: www.inksystems.com
SIC: 2893 Printing ink

(P-3786)
SUN CHEMICAL CORPORATION
General Printing Ink Division
12963 Park St, Santa Fe Springs (90670-4083)

PHONE.....................562 946-2327
Paul Stack, *Mgr*
EMP: 27
Web: www.sunchemical.com
SIC: 2893 5084 Printing ink; Printing trades machinery, equipment, and supplies
HQ: Sun Chemical Corporation
35 Waterview Blvd
Parsippany NJ 07054
973 404-6000

2895 Carbon Black

(P-3787)
ALDILA MATERIALS TECH CORP (DH)
13450 Stowe Dr, Poway (92064-6860)
PHONE.....................858 486-6970
Pete Matthewson, *Pr*
▼ **EMP:** 33 **EST:** 1997
SALES (est): 3.17MM **Privately Held**
Web: www.aldila.com
SIC: 2895 Carbon black
HQ: Aldila, Inc.
1945 Kellogg Ave
Carlsbad CA 92008
858 513-1801

2899 Chemical Preparations, Nec

(P-3788)
ACORN ENGINEERING COMPANY (PA)
Also Called: Morris Group International
15125 Proctor Ave, City Of Industry (91746-3327)
P.O. Box 3527 (91744-0527)
PHONE.....................800 488-8999
Donald E Morris, *CEO*
William D Morris, *
Kristin E Kahle, *
Randal Morris, *
Barrett Morris, *
◆ **EMP:** 702 **EST:** 1955
SQ FT: 120,000
SALES (est): 99.75MM
SALES (corp-wide): 99.75MM **Privately Held**
Web: www.acorneng.com
SIC: 2899 3431 Distilled water; Drinking fountains, metal

(P-3789)
AMERICAN CONSUMER PRODUCTS LLC
120 E 8th St Ste 908, Los Angeles (90014-3332)
PHONE.....................323 289-6610
David Molayem, *Pr*
David Molayem, *
Kam Jahanbigloo, *
Daryoosh Molayem, *
◆ **EMP:** 73 **EST:** 1999
SALES (est): 1.31MM
SALES (corp-wide): 17.62MM **Privately Held**
Web: *
www.american-consumer-products.com
SIC: 2899 2844 2834 Chemical preparations, nec; Cosmetic preparations; Pharmaceutical preparations
PA: Tabletops Unlimited, Inc.
23000 Avalon Blvd
310 549-6000

(P-3790)

AT APOLLO TECHNOLOGIES LLC

31441 Santa Margarita Pkwy Ste A219, Rcho Sta Marg (92688-1836)
PHONE.................................949 888-0573
Austin Browning, *Managing Member*
EMP: 23 EST: 1980
SALES (est): 2.25MM **Privately Held**
Web: www.apolloh2o.com
SIC: 2899 Water treating compounds

(P-3791)

CALIFORNIA RESPIRATORY CARE

16055 Ventura Blvd # 715, Encino (91436-2601)
PHONE.................................818 379-9999
EMP: 55
SALES (est): 4.18MM **Privately Held**
SIC: 2899 5047 5169 Chemical preparations, nec; Medical and hospital equipment; Oxygen

(P-3792)

CHEMDIV INC

Also Called: Chemical Diversity Labs
12730 High Bluff Dr, San Diego (92130-2075)
PHONE.................................858 794-4860
Nikolay P Savchuk, *CEO*
A Ivachtchenko, *Ch*
EMP: 40 EST: 1995
SALES (est): 9.74MM **Privately Held**
Web: www.chemdiv.com
SIC: 2899 Chemical preparations, nec

(P-3793)

CHEMTREAT INC

Also Called: Trident Technologies
8885 Rehco Rd, San Diego (92121-3261)
PHONE.................................804 935-2000
EMP: 94
SALES (corp-wide): 5.02B **Publicly Held**
Web: www.chemtreat.com
SIC: 2899 Water treating compounds
HQ: Chemtreat, Inc.
5640 Cox Rd
Glen Allen VA 23060
804 935-2000

(P-3794)

COATINC UNITED STATES INC

325 W Washington St Ste 2340, San Diego (92103-1946)
PHONE.................................619 638-7261
Paul Mcsweeney, *CEO*
EMP: 42 EST: 2014
SALES (est): 166.04K **Privately Held**
Web: www.coatinc.com
SIC: 2800 Fluxes: brazing, soldering, galvanizing, and welding

(P-3795)

CUTWATER SPIRITS LLC (HQ)

9750 Distribution Ave, San Diego (92121-2310)
PHONE.................................858 672-3848
EMP: 79 EST: 2016
SALES (est): 14.42MM
SALES (corp-wide): 1.7B **Privately Held**
Web: www.cutwaterspirits.com
SIC: 2899 Distilled water
PA: Anheuser-Busch Inbev
Grand-Place 1
25049660

(P-3796)

CYTEC ENGINEERED MATERIALS INC

645 N Cypress St, Orange (92867-6603)
PHONE.................................714 630-9400
Ron Martin, *Brnch Mgr*
EMP: 130
SQ FT: 300,000
SALES (corp-wide): 8.01MM **Privately Held**
Web: www.syensqo.com
SIC: 2899 Chemical preparations, nec
HQ: Cytec Engineered Materials Inc.
2085 E Tech Cir Ste 102
Tempe AZ 85284

(P-3797)

EVONIK CORPORATION

Also Called: Air Products
3305 E 26th St, Vernon (90058-4101)
PHONE.................................323 264-0311
William Ayacha, *Brnch Mgr*
EMP: 79
SALES (corp-wide): 16.59B **Privately Held**
Web: corporate.evonik.com
SIC: 2899 2891 2821 Chemical preparations, nec; Adhesives and sealants; Plastics materials and resins
HQ: Evonik Corporation
2 Turner Pl
Piscataway NJ 08854
732 981-5060

(P-3798)

FIRMENICH INCORPORATED

Also Called: Firmenich
424 S Atchison St, Anaheim (92805-4045)
PHONE.................................714 535-2871
EMP: 246
Web: www.firmenich.com
SIC: 2899 2869 Essential oils; Perfumes, flavorings, and food additives
HQ: Firmenich Incorporated
250 Plainsboro Rd
Plainsboro NJ 08536
609 452-1000

(P-3799)

FIRMENICH INCORPORATED

10636 Scripps Summit Ct, San Diego (92131-3965)
PHONE.................................858 646-8323
Kym Coleman, *Brnch Mgr*
EMP: 59
Web: www.firmenich.com
SIC: 2899 Essential oils
HQ: Firmenich Incorporated
250 Plainsboro Rd
Plainsboro NJ 08536
609 452-1000

(P-3800)

GGTW LLC

Also Called: South Bay Salt Works
1470 Bay Blvd, Chula Vista (91911-3942)
PHONE.................................619 423-3388
Glenn Warner, *Owner*
Tracy Strahl, *Prin*
▼ EMP: 24 EST: 1930
SALES (est): 4.17MM **Privately Held**
SIC: 2899 Salt

(P-3801)

HEMOSURE INC

5358 Irwindale Ave, Baldwin Park (91706-2086)
PHONE.................................888 436-6787
Doctor John Wan, *Pr*
Sherry Wang, *
EMP: 40 EST: 2003

SALES (est): 3.98MM **Privately Held**
Web: www.hemosure.com
SIC: 2899 3841 Chemical preparations, nec; Surgical and medical instruments
PA: W.H.P.M. Inc.
5358 Irwindale Ave

(P-3802)

HOME & BODY COMPANY (PA)

Also Called: Direct Chemicals
5800 Skylab Rd, Huntington Beach (92647-2054)
PHONE.................................714 842-8000
Hazem H Haddad, *Pr*
Nadene Haddad, *
▲ EMP: 349 EST: 1997
SALES (est): 41.68MM
SALES (corp-wide): 41.68MM **Privately Held**
Web: www.homeandbodyco.com
SIC: 2899 2842 2841 2844 Essential oils; Bleaches, household: dry or liquid; Textile soap; Face creams or lotions

(P-3803)

HYDRANAUTICS (DH)

401 Jones Rd, Oceanside (92058-1216)
PHONE.................................760 901-2500
Masaaki Ando, *Pr*
Michael Concannon, *
Randolph Truby, *
Marek Wilf, *
Norio Ikeyama, *
◆ EMP: 400 EST: 1987
SQ FT: 150,000
SALES (est): 106.12MM **Privately Held**
Web: www.membranes.com
SIC: 2899 3589 Chemical preparations, nec; Water treatment equipment, industrial
HQ: Nitto Americas, Inc.
400 Frank W Burr Blvd Ste
Teaneck NJ 07666
510 445-5400

(P-3804)

INDIO PRODUCTS INC

Cultural Heritage Candle Co
5331 E Slauson Ave, Commerce (90040-2916)
PHONE.................................323 720-9117
Marty Mayer, *Owner*
EMP: 33
SALES (corp-wide): 26.98MM **Privately Held**
Web: www.indioproducts.com
SIC: 2899 3999 5199 5049 Incense; Candles ; Candles; Religious supplies
PA: Indio Products, Inc.
12910 Mulberry Dr Unit A
323 720-1188

(P-3805)

INSULTECH LLC (PA)

Also Called: Insultech
3530 W Garry Ave, Santa Ana (92704-6423)
PHONE.................................714 384-0506
Ryan Barto, *Managing Member*
◆ EMP: 45 EST: 1994
SQ FT: 30,000
SALES (est): 15.61MM **Privately Held**
Web: www.insultech.com
SIC: 2899 Insulating compounds

(P-3806)

INX INTERNATIONAL INK CO

13821 Marquardt Ave, Santa Fe Springs (90670-5016)
PHONE.................................562 404-5664
Elvis Tran, *Mgr*

EMP: 30
Web: www.inxinternational.com
SIC: 2899 2893 Ink or writing fluids; Printing ink
HQ: Inx International Ink Co.
150 N Mrtngale Rd Ste 700
Schaumburg IL 60173
630 382-1800

(P-3807)

KEMIRA WATER SOLUTIONS INC

Also Called: Kemiron Pacific
14000 San Bernardino Ave, Fontana (92335-5258)
PHONE.................................909 350-5678
Hailu Mequira, *Mgr*
EMP: 35
SALES (corp-wide): 3.68B **Privately Held**
Web: www.kemira.com
SIC: 2899 Water treating compounds
HQ: Kemira Water Solutions, Inc.
200 Gllria Pkwy Se Ste 15
Atlanta GA 30339

(P-3808)

KIK POOL ADDITIVES INC

5160 E Airport Dr, Ontario (91761-7824)
PHONE.................................909 390-9912
John A Christensen, *Pr*
David M Christensen, *VP*
Debra Schonk, *VP*
Brian Patterson, *CFO*
Chet Yoakum, *VP*
▲ EMP: 140 EST: 1958
SALES (est): 16.87MM **Privately Held**
Web: www.kem-tek.com
SIC: 2899 3089 7389 5169 Chemical preparations, nec; Plastics hardware and building products; Packaging and labeling services; Swimming pool and spa chemicals

(P-3809)

L M SCOFIELD COMPANY (DH)

12767 Imperial Hwy, Santa Fe Springs (90670-4711)
PHONE.................................323 720-3000
Phillip J Arnold, *Pr*
◆ EMP: 50 EST: 1915
SQ FT: 36,000
SALES (est): 9.46MM **Privately Held**
Web: usa.sika.com
SIC: 2899 Concrete curing and hardening compounds
HQ: Sika Corporation
201 Polito Ave
Lyndhurst NJ 07071
201 933-8800

(P-3810)

LG NANOH2O LLC

Also Called: Lg Nanoh2o, Inc.
21250 Hawthorne Blvd Ste 330, Torrance (90503-5541)
PHONE.................................424 218-4000
Jeff Green, *CEO*
Michael Demartino, *VP*
John Markovich, *CFO*
Doug Barnes, *COO*
Cj Kurth, *VP*
▲ EMP: 35 EST: 2005
SQ FT: 2,000
SALES (est): 7.3MM **Privately Held**
SIC: 2899 Distilled water
PA: Lg Chem, Ltd.
128 Yeoui-Daero, Yeongdeungpo-Gu

(P-3811)

LUBRIZOL GLOBAL MANAGEMENT INC

3115 Propeller Dr, Paso Robles
(93446-8524)
PHONE..................805 239-1550
Daniel Mccornack, *Prin*
EMP: 24
SALES (corp-wide): 364.48B **Publicly Held**
Web: www.lubrizol.com
SIC: 2899 Chemical preparations, nec
HQ: Lubrizol Global Management, Inc.
　9911 Brecksville Rd
　Cleveland OH 44141
　216 447-5000

(P-3812)
MASTER BUILDERS LLC
Degussa Construction
9060 Haven Ave, Rancho Cucamonga
(91730-5405)
PHONE..................909 987-1758
Dave Lougheed, *Mgr*
EMP: 878
Web: master-builders-solutions.basf.us
SIC: 2899 Chemical preparations, nec
HQ: Master Builders, Llc
　23700 Chagrin Blvd
　Beachwood OH 44122
　800 228-3318

(P-3813)
MATSUI INTERNATIONAL CO INC (HQ)
Also Called: Unimark
1501 W 178th St, Gardena (90248-3203)
PHONE..................310 767-7812
Masa Matsui, *Pr*
Yoshi Haga, *
◆ **EMP:** 32 **EST:** 1987
SQ FT: 30,000
SALES (est): 24.62MM **Privately Held**
Web: www.matsui-color.com
SIC: 2899 Ink or writing fluids
PA: Matsui Shikiso Chemical Co., Ltd.
　64, Kamikazansakuradani, Yamashina-Ku

(P-3814)
MEDICAL CHEMICAL CORPORATION
Also Called: M C C
19250 Van Ness Ave, Torrance
(90501-1102)
P.O. Box 6217 (90504-0217)
PHONE..................310 787-6800
Emmanuel Didier, *Pr*
Patrick Braden, *
Andy Rocha, *
Kris Kontis, *
◆ **EMP:** 45 **EST:** 1954
SALES (est): 7.86MM **Privately Held**
Web: www.med-chem.com
SIC: 2899 2841 Chemical preparations, nec;
　Soap and other detergents

(P-3815)
MOC PRODUCTS COMPANY INC (PA)
Also Called: Auto Edge Solutions
12306 Montague St, Pacoima
(91331-2279)
PHONE..................818 794-3500
Mark Waco, *CEO*
Dave Waco, *
◆ **EMP:** 75 **EST:** 1954
SQ FT: 100,000
SALES (est): 52.48MM
SALES (corp-wide): 52.48MM **Privately Held**
Web: www.mocproducts.com

SIC: 2899 7549 5169 Corrosion preventive
lubricant; Automotive maintenance services
; Chemicals and allied products, nec

(P-3816)
MORTON SALT INC
1050 Pier F Ave, Long Beach (90802-6215)
P.O. Box 2289 (90801-2289)
PHONE..................562 437-0071
Ken Dobson, *Brnch Mgr*
EMP: 86
SALES (corp-wide): 3.82B **Privately Held**
Web: www.mortonsalt.com
SIC: 2899 Salt
HQ: Morton Salt, Inc.
　444 W Lake St Ste 3000
　Chicago IL 60606

(P-3817)
PHIBRO ANIMAL HEALTH CORP
Phibro-Tech
8851 Dice Rd, Santa Fe Springs
(90670-2515)
PHONE..................562 698-8036
Mark Alling, *Mgr*
EMP: 56
SALES (corp-wide): 1.02B **Publicly Held**
Web: www.pahc.com
SIC: 2899 2819 Chemical preparations, nec;
Industrial inorganic chemicals, nec
HQ: Phibro Animal Health Corporation
　300 Frank W Burr Blvd Ste
　Teaneck NJ 07666
　201 329-7300

(P-3818)
PRESTONE PRODUCTS CORPORATION
Also Called: Kik Custom Products
19500 Mariner Ave, Torrance (90503-1644)
PHONE..................424 271-4836
Raymond Yu, *Manager*
EMP: 30
Web: www.prestone.com
SIC: 2899 5531 5169 Antifreeze compounds
; Automotive parts; Anti-freeze compounds
HQ: Prestone Products Llc
　6250 N River Rd Ste 6000
　Rosemont IL 60018

(P-3819)
RELTON CORPORATION
317 Rolyn Pl, Arcadia (91007-2838)
P.O. Box 60019 (91066-6019)
PHONE..................800 423-1505
William Kinard, *Ch*
Wm Craig Kinard, *
Craig Kinard, *
Kevin Kinard, *
Chris Kinard, *
◆ **EMP:** 65 **EST:** 1946
SQ FT: 20,000
SALES (est): 9.03MM **Privately Held**
Web: www.relton.com
SIC: 2899 3423 3546 2992 Chemical
preparations, nec; Masons' hand tools;
Power-driven handtools; Lubricating oils
and greases

(P-3820)
SIGMA-ALDRICH CORPORATION
Also Called: Safc Pharma
6211 El Camino Real, Carlsbad
(92009-1604)
PHONE..................760 710-6213
Tim Quinn, *Mgr*
EMP: 50
SALES (corp-wide): 22.82B **Privately Held**
Web: www.sigmaaldrich.com

SIC: 2899 Chemical preparations, nec
HQ: Sigma-Aldrich Corporation
　3050 Spruce St
　Saint Louis MO 63103
　314 771-5765

(P-3821)
TORAY MEMBRANE USA INC (DH)
13435 Danielson St, Poway (92064-6825)
PHONE..................858 218-2360
Steve Cappos, *CEO*
Tak Wakisaka, *
Gabriel Juarez, *
◆ **EMP:** 85 **EST:** 2006
SQ FT: 90,000
SALES (est): 25.57MM **Privately Held**
Web: www.water.toray
SIC: 2899 Water treating compounds
HQ: Toray Holding (U.S.A.), Inc.
　461 5th Ave Fl 9
　New York NY 10017
　212 697-8150

(P-3822)
VEOLIA WTS USA INC
Also Called: GE Water & Process Tech
8.5 Miles Nw Avila Beach, Avila Beach
(93424)
PHONE..................805 545-3743
EMP: 90
Web: www.watertechnologies.com
SIC: 2899 Water treating compounds
HQ: Veolia Wts Usa, Inc.
　3600 Horizon Blvd
　Trevose PA 19053
　866 439-2837

2911 Petroleum Refining

(P-3823)
CASTAIC TRUCK STOP INC
31611 Castaic Rd, Castaic (91384-3939)
PHONE..................661 295-1374
Sarkis Khrimian, *Pr*
Refe Dimmuck, *
EMP: 26 **EST:** 1994
SQ FT: 2,000
SALES (est): 3.92MM **Privately Held**
Web: www.castaictruckstop.com
SIC: 2911 7389 5812 Diesel fuels; Flea
market; American restaurant

(P-3824)
DE MENNO-KERDOON TRADING CO (HQ)
2000 N Alameda St, Compton
(90222-2799)
PHONE..................310 537-7100
Jim Ennis, *COO*
Jay Demel, *
EMP: 149 **EST:** 1990
SQ FT: 60,000
SALES (est): 38.18MM
SALES (corp-wide): 128.17MM **Privately Held**
SIC: 2911 Oils, fuel
PA: World Oil Marketing Company
　9302 Garfield Ave
　562 928-0100

(P-3825)
KERN OIL & REFINING CO (HQ)
Also Called: Kern Energy
7724 E Panama Ln, Bakersfield
(93307-9210)
PHONE..................661 845-0761
EMP: 125 **EST:** 1971
SALES (est): 53.04MM

SALES (corp-wide): 86.86MM **Privately Held**
Web: www.kernenergy.com
SIC: 2911 Petroleum refining
PA: Casey Company
　180 E Ocean Blvd Ste 1010
　562 436-9685

(P-3826)
MTS SOLUTIONS LLC ✪
7131 Charity Ave, Bakersfield
(93308-5870)
PHONE..................661 589-5804
EMP: 36 **EST:** 2023
SALES (est): 5.62MM **Privately Held**
Web: www.mts-stim.com
SIC: 2911 Petroleum refining

(P-3827)
NEW LEAF BIOFUEL LLC
2285 Newton Ave, San Diego (92113-3619)
PHONE..................619 236-8500
Jennifer Case, *Pt*
Nicole Kennard, *Managing Member*
▲ **EMP:** 35 **EST:** 2006
SALES (est): 6.14MM **Privately Held**
Web: www.newleafbiofuel.com
SIC: 2911 8742 Diesel fuels; Restaurant and
food services consultants

(P-3828)
PARAMOUNT PETROLEUM CORP (DH)
Also Called: Paramount Asphalt
14700 Downey Ave, Paramount
(90723-4526)
PHONE..................562 531-2060
W S Lovejoy, *CEO*
◆ **EMP:** 155 **EST:** 1980
SQ FT: 6,000
SALES (est): 23.09MM
SALES (corp-wide): 16.92B **Publicly Held**
Web: www.alon.com
SIC: 2911 Petroleum refining
HQ: Alon Usa Energy, Inc.
　310 Seven Springs Way # 500
　Brentwood TN 37027

(P-3829)
SACAHN JV
15916 Bernardo Center Dr, San Diego
(92127-1828)
PHONE..................858 924-1110
EMP: 99 **EST:** 2014
SQ FT: 3,000
SALES (est): 4.22MM **Privately Held**
SIC: 2911 Oils, fuel

(P-3830)
SAN JOAQUIN REFINING CO INC
3500 Shell St, Bakersfield (93388)
P.O. Box 5576 (93388-5576)
PHONE..................661 327-4257
Kenneth E Fait, *Ch Bd*
Majid Mojibi, *
Dorothy A Gribben, *
EMP: 130 **EST:** 1979
SQ FT: 15,000
SALES (est): 47.17MM **Privately Held**
Web: www.sjr.com
SIC: 2911 Oils, fuel

(P-3831)
TESORO REFINING & MKTG CO LLC
5905 N Paramount Blvd, Long Beach
(90805-3709)
PHONE..................562 728-2215

▲ = Import ▼ = Export
◆ = Import/Export

EMP: 86
SIC: 2911 5541 Petroleum refining; Gasoline service stations
HQ: Tesoro Refining & Marketing Company Llc
19100 Ridgewood Pkwy
San Antonio TX 78259
210 626-6000

(P-3832)
TORRANCE REFINING COMPANY LLC
3700 W 190th St, Torrance (90504-5733)
PHONE................................310 212-2800
Thomas J Nimbley, *CEO*
EMP: 600 **EST:** 2015
SALES (est): 72.92MM
SALES (corp-wide): 46.78B **Privately Held**
Web: www.pbfenergy.com
SIC: 2911 2992 Petroleum refining; Lubricating oils
HQ: Pbf Energy Western Region Llc
3760 Kilroy Arprt Way Ste
Long Beach CA 90806
973 455-7500

(P-3833)
TRICOR REFINING LLC
1134 Manor St, Bakersfield (93308-3553)
P.O. Box 5877 (93388-5877)
PHONE................................661 393-7110
Majid Mojibi, *Managing Member**
Don Brookes, *Managing Member**
Kenneth E Fait, *Managing Member**
EMP: 28 **EST:** 2001
SALES (est): 9.74MM **Privately Held**
Web: www.tricorrefining.com
SIC: 2911 Oils, fuel

(P-3834)
ULTRAMAR INC
Also Called: Village Center Ultramar
9508 E Palmdale Blvd, Palmdale (93591-2202)
PHONE................................661 944-2496
Ken Berglund, *Mgr*
EMP: 66
SALES (corp-wide): 144.77B **Publicly Held**
Web: www.valero.com
SIC: 2911 Petroleum refining
HQ: Ultramar Inc.
1 Valero Way
San Antonio TX 78249
210 345-2000

(P-3835)
VALERO REF COMPANY-CALIFORNIA
Also Called: Valero
2401 E Anaheim St, Wilmington (90744-4009)
PHONE................................562 491-6754
Mark Thair, *Mgr*
EMP: 1167
SALES (corp-wide): 144.77B **Publicly Held**
Web: www.valero.com
SIC: 2911 Petroleum refining
HQ: Valero Refining Company-California
1 Valero Way
San Antonio TX 78249
210 345-2000

(P-3836)
WD-40 COMPANY
Also Called: Hdp Holdings
9715 Businesspark Ave, San Diego (92131-1642)
PHONE................................619 275-1400

Garry Ridge, *Pr*
EMP: 233
SALES (corp-wide): 590.56MM **Publicly Held**
Web: www.wd40company.com
SIC: 2911 Oils, lubricating
PA: Wd-40 Company
9715 Businesspark Ave
619 275-1400

2951 Asphalt Paving Mixtures And Blocks

(P-3837)
GOLDSTAR ASPHALT PRODUCTS INC
1354 Jet Way, Perris (92571-7466)
PHONE................................951 940-1610
Jeff S Nelson, *Pr*
EMP: 32 **EST:** 1997
SALES (est): 2.51MM **Privately Held**
Web: www.goldstarasphalt.com
SIC: 2951 Asphalt paving mixtures and blocks

(P-3838)
NPG INC (PA)
Also Called: Goldstar Asphalt Products
1354 Jet Way, Perris (92571-7466)
P.O. Box 1515 (92572-1515)
PHONE................................951 940-0200
Jeff Nelson, *Pr*
Sharon Nelson, *
EMP: 54 **EST:** 1962
SQ FT: 6,900
SALES (est): 22.79MM **Privately Held**
Web: www.goldstarasphalt.com
SIC: 2951 1799 1771 Asphalt and asphaltic paving mixtures (not from refineries); Parking lot maintenance; Driveway, parking lot, and blacktop contractors

(P-3839)
PAVEMENT RECYCLING SYSTEMS INC
Also Called: West Coast Milling
48028 90th St W, Lancaster (93536-9366)
PHONE................................661 948-5599
Steve Ward, *Mgr*
EMP: 60
Web: www.pavementrecycling.com
SIC: 2951 1611 Asphalt paving mixtures and blocks; Surfacing and paving
PA: Pavement Recycling Systems, Inc.
10240 San Sevaine Way

2952 Asphalt Felts And Coatings

(P-3840)
FONTANA PAPER MILLS INC
13733 Valley Blvd, Fontana (92335-5268)
P.O. Box 339 (92334-0339)
PHONE................................909 823-4100
George Thagard Iii, *Pr*
Jeff Thagard, *
Ray G Thagard Junior, *Sec*
EMP: 56 **EST:** 1967
SQ FT: 28,000
SALES (est): 13.06MM **Privately Held**
Web: www.fontanaroof.com
SIC: 2952 2621 Roofing materials; Felts, building

(P-3841)
HCO HOLDING II CORPORATION
999 N Pacific Coast Hwy Ste 800, El Segundo (90245-2716)

PHONE................................310 955-9200
Brian C Strauss, *Pr*
EMP: 560 **EST:** 2005
SALES (est): 3.85MM
SALES (corp-wide): 249.72MM **Privately Held**
SIC: 2952 2821 2891 Roof cement: asphalt, fibrous, or plastic; Polyurethane resins; Sealants
HQ: Hco Holding I Corporation
999 N Splveda Blvd Ste 80
El Segundo CA 90245
323 583-5000

(P-3842)
HENRY COMPANY LLC (HQ)
Also Called: Henry Building Products
999 N Pacific Coast Hwy Ste 800, El Segundo (90245-2716)
PHONE................................310 955-9200
Frank Ready, *Pr*
Jason Peel, *
◆ **EMP:** 100 **EST:** 1981
SALES (est): 212.61MM
SALES (corp-wide): 4.59B **Publicly Held**
Web: www.henry.com
SIC: 2952 2821 2891 Roof cement: asphalt, fibrous, or plastic; Polyurethane resins; Sealants
PA: Carlisle Companies Incorporated
16430 N Scttsdale Rd Ste
480 781-5000

(P-3843)
HNC PARENT INC (PA)
999 N Pacific Coast Hwy Ste 800, El Segundo (90245-2716)
PHONE................................310 955-9200
Rob Newbold, *Prin*
EMP: 100 **EST:** 2012
SALES (est): 249.72MM
SALES (corp-wide): 249.72MM **Privately Held**
SIC: 2952 2821 2891 Roof cement: asphalt, fibrous, or plastic; Polyurethane resins; Sealants

(P-3844)
JAMES HARDIE TRADING CO INC
26300 La Alameda Ste 400, Mission Viejo (92691-8372)
PHONE................................949 582-2378
Bryon G Borgardt, *Pr*
EMP: 160 **EST:** 1995
SALES (est): 17.15MM **Privately Held**
Web: www.jameshardie.com
SIC: 2952 Siding materials
HQ: James Hardie Transition Co., Inc.
26300 La Alameda Ste 400
Mission Viejo CA 92691
949 348-1800

(P-3845)
LUNDAY-THAGARD COMPANY
9301 Garfield Ave, South Gate (90280-3804)
P.O. Box 1519 (90280-1519)
PHONE................................562 928-6990
John Todorovich, *VP Opers*
EMP: 369
SALES (corp-wide): 128.17MM **Privately Held**
SIC: 2952 2951 Roofing materials; Asphalt paving mixtures and blocks
HQ: Lunday-Thagard Company
9302 Garfield Ave
South Gate CA 90280
562 928-7000

(P-3846)
OWENS CORNING SALES LLC
Also Called: Owens Corning
1501 N Tamarind Ave, Compton (90222-4130)
P.O. Box 5665 (90224-5665)
PHONE................................310 631-1062
David Randalph, *Brnch Mgr*
EMP: 102
Web: www.owenscorning.com
SIC: 2952 2951 1761 Roofing felts, cements, or coatings, nec; Asphalt paving mixtures and blocks; Roofing, siding, and sheetmetal work
HQ: Owens Corning Sales, Llc
1 Owens Corning Pkwy
Toledo OH 43659
419 248-8000

2992 Lubricating Oils And Greases

(P-3847)
AOCLSC INC
Also Called: Aocusa
3365 E Slauson Ave, Vernon (90058-3914)
PHONE................................562 776-4000
Stephen Milam, *CEO*
EMP: 30
SALES (corp-wide): 50.84MM **Privately Held**
SIC: 2992 Lubricating oils and greases
HQ: Aoclsc, Inc.
1601 Mccloskey Blvd
Tampa FL 33605
813 248-1988

(P-3848)
AOCLSC INC
Also Called: Aocusa
8015 Paramount Blvd, Pico Rivera (90660-4811)
PHONE................................813 248-1988
Harry Barkett, *Brnch Mgr*
EMP: 150
SALES (corp-wide): 50.84MM **Privately Held**
SIC: 2992 Lubricating oils
HQ: Aoclsc, Inc.
1601 Mccloskey Blvd
Tampa FL 33605
813 248-1988

(P-3849)
CHEM ARROW CORP
13643 Live Oak Ln, Irwindale (91706-1317)
P.O. Box 2366 (91706-1198)
PHONE................................626 358-2255
Alphonse Spalding, *Ch Bd*
Hemith Mitchello, *
▼ **EMP:** 25 **EST:** 1977
SQ FT: 36,000
SALES (est): 11.18MM **Privately Held**
Web: www.chemarrow.com
SIC: 2992 2899 Lubricating oils; Fuel tank or engine cleaning chemicals

(P-3850)
CHEMTOOL INCORPORATED
1300 Goodrick Dr, Tehachapi (93561-1508)
PHONE................................661 823-7190
Bill Hart, *Mgr*
EMP: 125
SALES (corp-wide): 364.48B **Publicly Held**
Web: www.chemtool.com

SIC: 2992 2899 5172 Oils and greases, blending and compounding; Chemical preparations, nec; Lubricating oils and greases
HQ: Chemtool Incorporated
29400 Lakeland Blvd
Wickliffe OH 44092
815 957-4140

(P-3851)
DEMENNO/KERDOON HOLDINGS (DH)
Also Called: Demenno-Kerdoon
9302 Garfield Ave, South Gate (90280-3805)
PHONE...............................562 231-1550
Robert Roth, *Ch Bd*
Bruce Demenno, *
Steve Kerdoon, *
EMP: 67 **EST:** 1971
SQ FT: 21,000
SALES (est): 20.12MM
SALES (corp-wide): 128.17MM **Privately Held**
Web: www.worldoilcorp.com
SIC: 2992 2911 Oils and greases, blending and compounding; Petroleum refining
HQ: De Menno-Kerdoon Trading Company
2000 N Alameda Street
Compton CA 90222

(P-3852)
DEMENNO/KERDOON HOLDINGS
Also Called: D K Environmental
3650 E 26th St, Vernon (90058-4104)
PHONE...............................323 268-3387
Rodney Ananda, *Mgr*
EMP: 27
SALES (corp-wide): 128.17MM **Privately Held**
Web: www.worldoilcorp.com
SIC: 2992 4953 Oils and greases, blending and compounding; Refuse systems
HQ: Demenno/Kerdoon Holdings
9302 Garfield Ave
South Gate CA 90280
562 231-1550

(P-3853)
EVERGREEN HOLDINGS INC
18952 Macarthur Blvd Ste 410, Irvine (92612-1402)
PHONE...............................949 757-7770
▲ **EMP:** 189
SIC: 2992 4953 Re-refining lubricating oils and greases, nec; Liquid waste, collection and disposal

(P-3854)
EVERGREEN OIL INC (HQ)
Also Called: Evergreen Environmental Svcs
18025 S Broadway, Gardena (90248-3539)
PHONE...............................949 757-7770
Jake Voogd, *CEO*
George Lamont, *Ex VP*
Obert Gwaltney, *VP Opers*
Jesus Romero, *VP*
EMP: 23 **EST:** 1983
SALES (est): 23.19MM
SALES (corp-wide): 5.41B **Publicly Held**
SIC: 2992 2911 4953 Lubricating oils and greases; Petroleum refining; Refuse systems
PA: Clean Harbors, Inc.
42 Longwater Dr
781 792-5000

(P-3855)
EZ LUBE LLC
532 W Florida Ave, Hemet (92543-4007)
PHONE...............................951 766-1996
Richie Berling, *Mgr*
EMP: 72
SALES (corp-wide): 21.83MM **Privately Held**
Web: www.ezlube.com
SIC: 2992 Lubricating oils
PA: Ez Lube, Llc
3540 Howard Way Ste 200

(P-3856)
LUBECO INC
6859 Downey Ave, Long Beach (90805-1967)
PHONE...............................562 602-1791
Steven Rossi, *Pr*
EMP: 45 **EST:** 1958
SQ FT: 20,000
SALES (est): 5.33MM **Privately Held**
Web: www.lubecoinc.com
SIC: 2992 2851 Lubricating oils and greases ; Paints and allied products

(P-3857)
LUBRICATING SPECIALTIES COMPANY
Also Called: AOC USA
8015 Paramount Blvd, Pico Rivera (90660-4888)
PHONE...............................562 776-4000
◆ **EMP:** 170
SIC: 2992 Lubricating oils

(P-3858)
SOUTH WEST LUBRICANTS INC
Also Called: Maxima Racing Oils
9266 Abraham Way, Santee (92071-5611)
PHONE...............................619 449-5000
Daniel J Massie, *CEO*
◆ **EMP:** 54 **EST:** 1979
SQ FT: 50,000
SALES (est): 11.62MM **Privately Held**
Web: www.maximausa.com
SIC: 2992 5172 Lubricating oils and greases ; Lubricating oils and greases

(P-3859)
WD-40 COMPANY (PA)
9715 Businesspark Ave, San Diego (92131-1642)
PHONE...............................619 275-1400
Steven A Brass, *Pr*
Eric P Etchart, *Non-Executive Chairman of the Board*
Sara K Hyzer, *VP Fin*
Phenix Q Kiamilev, *Corporate Secretary*
Jeffrey G Lindeman, *Chief Human Resources Officer*
EMP: 133 **EST:** 1953
SALES (est): 590.56MM
SALES (corp-wide): 590.56MM **Publicly Held**
Web: www.wd40company.com
SIC: 2992 2851 Lubricating oils; Removers and cleaners

2999 Petroleum And Coal Products, Nec

(P-3860)
LUNDAY-THAGARD COMPANY (HQ)
Also Called: Ltr
9302 Garfield Ave, South Gate (90280-3805)

P.O. Box 1519 (90280-1519)
PHONE...............................562 928-7000
Bernard B Roth, *Ch Bd*
Robert Roth, *
Steve Roth, *
Bert Wootan, *
Peter Stockhausen, *
EMP: 106 **EST:** 1937
SQ FT: 16,000
SALES (est): 17.74MM
SALES (corp-wide): 128.17MM **Privately Held**
SIC: 2999 2951 2911 Coke; Paving blocks; Gases and liquefied petroleum gases
PA: World Oil Marketing Company
9302 Garfield Ave
562 928-0100

(P-3861)
RENTECH INC (PA)
10880 Wilshire Blvd Ste 1101, Los Angeles (90024-4112)
PHONE...............................310 571-9800
Keith Forman, *Pr*
Halbert S Washburn, *
Keith B Forman, *
Paul M Summers, *
Colin M Morris, *
EMP: 50 **EST:** 1981
SQ FT: 600
SALES (est): 31.25MM
SALES (corp-wide): 31.25MM **Privately Held**
Web: www.rentechinc.com
SIC: 2999 2873 6794 Waxes, petroleum: not produced in petroleum refineries; Nitrogenous fertilizers; Patent buying, licensing, leasing

3011 Tires And Inner Tubes

(P-3862)
BIG BRAND TIRE & SERVICE
Also Called: Big Brand Tire & Svc - Menifee
26920 Newport Rd, Menifee (92584-9076)
PHONE...............................951 679-6266
EMP: 99 **EST:** 2020
SALES (est): 2.65MM **Privately Held**
SIC: 3011 Automobile tires, pneumatic

(P-3863)
BRIDGESTONE AMERICAS INC
Also Called: Firestone Cmplete Auto Care 79
3690 Murphy Canyon Rd, San Diego (92123-4455)
PHONE...............................858 874-3109
EMP: 29
Web: www.bridgestoneamericas.com
SIC: 3011 Tires and inner tubes
HQ: Bridgestone Americas, Inc.
200 4th Ave S Ste 100
Nashville TN 37201
615 937-1000

(P-3864)
DESSER TIRE & RUBBER CO LLC (DH)
Also Called: Desser Tire & Rubber Co
6900 W Acco St, Montebello (90640-5435)
P.O. Box 1028 (90640-1028)
PHONE...............................323 721-4900
◆ **EMP:** 35 **EST:** 1995
SALES (est): 22.97MM
SALES (corp-wide): 860.49MM **Publicly Held**
Web: www.desser.com
SIC: 3011 Airplane tires, pneumatic
HQ: Desser Holding Company, Llc
6900 W Acco St
Montebello CA 90640
323 721-4900

(P-3865)
HSB HOLDINGS INC
14050 Day St, Moreno Valley (92553-9106)
PHONE...............................951 214-6590
Ohannes Beudjekian, *Ch Bd*
Sarkis Beudjeaian, *
▲ **EMP:** 40 **EST:** 1989
SQ FT: 80,000
SALES (est): 5.25MM **Privately Held**
Web: www.basrecycling.com
SIC: 3011 Tires, cushion or solid rubber

(P-3866)
YOKOHAMA CORP NORTH AMERICA (HQ)
Also Called: Yokohama Tire
1 Macarthur Pl, Santa Ana (92707-5927)
PHONE...............................540 389-5426
Yasuo Tominaga, *CEO*
Takaharu Fushimi, *
◆ **EMP:** 250 **EST:** 1917
SALES (est): 792.7MM **Privately Held**
Web: www.yokohamatire.com
SIC: 3011 5014 Tires and inner tubes; Tires and tubes
PA: Yokohama Rubber Company, Limited, The
2-1, Oiwake

3021 Rubber And Plastics Footwear

(P-3867)
K-SWISS INC
12450 Philadelphia Ave, Eastvale (91752-3230)
PHONE...............................951 361-7501
EMP: 42
Web: www.kswiss.com
SIC: 3021 Rubber and plastics footwear
HQ: K-Swiss Inc.
101 N Brand Blvd
Glendale CA 91203
323 675-2700

(P-3868)
K-SWISS INC (DH)
Also Called: K-Swiss
101 N Brand Blvd Ste 1700, Glendale (91203-2628)
PHONE...............................323 675-2700
Holly Li, *CEO*
Barney Waters, *CMO**
◆ **EMP:** 30 **EST:** 1990
SALES (est): 35.56MM **Privately Held**
Web:
SIC: 3021 5661 Rubber and plastics footwear ; Children's shoes
HQ: Xtep International Holdings Limited
Rm A 27/F Billion Ctr Twr A
Kowloon Bay KLN

(P-3869)
K-SWISS SALES CORP
101 N Brand Blvd, Glendale (91203-2639)
PHONE...............................323 675-2700
Cheryl Kuchinka, *Pr*
EMP: 127 **EST:** 1999
SALES (est): 1.95MM **Privately Held**
Web: www.kswiss.com
SIC: 3021 Rubber and plastics footwear
HQ: K-Swiss Inc.
101 N Brand Blvd
Glendale CA 91203
323 675-2700

▲ = Import ▼ = Export
◆ = Import/Export

(P-3870)
PLS DIABETIC SHOE COMPANY INC
21500 Osborne St, Canoga Park (91304-1522)
PHONE..............................818 734-7080
Ambartsum Kumuryan, *Pr*
Konstandin Kumuryan, *
▲ **EMP:** 32 **EST:** 2004
SQ FT: 24,031
SALES (est): 1.66MM **Privately Held**
Web: www.pedorthiclab.com
SIC: 3021 Shoes, rubber or plastic molded to fabric

(P-3871)
PRINCIPLE PLASTICS
1136 W 135th St, Gardena (90247-1919)
P.O. Box 2408 (90247-0408)
PHONE..............................310 532-3411
David Hoyt, *Pr*
Robert Hoyt, *
▲ **EMP:** 27 **EST:** 1948
SQ FT: 28,000
SALES (est): 5.18MM **Privately Held**
Web: www.sloggers.com
SIC: 3021 3949 2519 Galoshes, plastic; Golf equipment; Lawn and garden furniture, except wood and metal

(P-3872)
VANS INC (DH)
Also Called: Vans Shoes
1588 S Coast Dr, Costa Mesa (92626-1533)
PHONE..............................714 755-4000
Arthur I Carver, *Senior Vice President Global Operations*
Robert L Nagel, *
Craig E Gosselin, *
Scott J Blechman, *
Marissa Pardini, *PRODUCT Merchandising*
▲ **EMP:** 279 **EST:** 1987
SQ FT: 185,000
SALES (est): 495.69MM
SALES (corp-wide): 10.45B **Publicly Held**
Web: www.vans.com
SIC: 3021 2321 2329 2325 Canvas shoes, rubber soled; Men's and boys' sports and polo shirts; Men's and boys' sportswear and athletic clothing; Slacks, dress: men's, youths', and boys'
HQ: Vf Outdoor, Llc
1551 Wewatta St
Denver CO 80202
855 500-8639

3052 Rubber And Plastics Hose And Beltings

(P-3873)
NORTH AMERICAN FIRE HOSE CORP
Also Called: Nafhc
910 Noble Way, Santa Maria (93454-1506)
P.O. Box 1968 (93456-1968)
PHONE..............................805 922-7076
Michael S Aubuchon, *CEO*
Virginia Aubuchon, *
▲ **EMP:** 55 **EST:** 1980
SQ FT: 43,000
SALES (est): 6.4MM **Privately Held**
Web: www.nafhc.com
SIC: 3052 Fire hose, rubber

(P-3874)
PARKER-HANNIFIN CORPORATION
Also Called: Parker Service Center
8460 Kass Dr, Buena Park (90621-3808)
PHONE..............................714 522-8840
Chris Wright, *Brnch Mgr*
EMP: 69
SALES (corp-wide): 19.93B **Publicly Held**
Web: www.parker.com
SIC: 3052 3429 Rubber and plastics hose and beltings; Hardware, nec
PA: Parker-Hannifin Corporation
6035 Parkland Blvd
216 896-3000

(P-3875)
SANISURE INC (HQ)
Also Called: Sani-Tech West, Inc.
1020 Flynn Rd, Camarillo (93012-8705)
PHONE..............................805 389-0400
Richard J Shor, *Pr*
Sherry Maxson, *
EMP: 61 **EST:** 1991
SQ FT: 27,000
SALES (est): 59.92MM
SALES (corp-wide): 5.01B **Privately Held**
Web: www.sani-techwest.com
SIC: 3052 3053 Rubber hose; Gasket materials
PA: 3i Group Plc
16 Palace Street
207 975-3131

(P-3876)
TK PAX INC
Also Called: P A X Industries
1545 Macarthur Blvd, Costa Mesa (92626-1407)
PHONE..............................714 850-1330
Tom Kawaguchi, *Pr*
Randy Tamura, *
▲ **EMP:** 30 **EST:** 1985
SALES (est): 4.62MM **Privately Held**
Web: www.paxindustries.com
SIC: 3052 3053 Rubber hose; Gaskets, all materials

(P-3877)
TTI FLOOR CARE NORTH AMER INC
13055 Valley Blvd, Fontana (92335-2603)
PHONE..............................440 996-2802
Ross Verrocchi, *Mgr*
EMP: 100
Web: www.ttifloorcare.com
SIC: 3052 5722 Vacuum cleaner hose, plastic; Vacuum cleaners
HQ: Tti Floor Care North America, Inc.
8405 Ibm Dr
Charlotte NC 28262

3053 Gaskets; Packing And Sealing Devices

(P-3878)
ABLE INDUSTRIAL PRODUCTS INC (PA)
2006 S Baker Ave, Ontario (91761-7709)
PHONE..............................909 930-1585
Gilbert J Martinez, *CEO*
Debbie Viramontes, *
Gloria Martinez, *CTRL*
▲ **EMP:** 30 **EST:** 1974
SQ FT: 21,120
SALES (est): 16.99MM
SALES (corp-wide): 16.99MM **Privately Held**
Web: www.able123.com
SIC: 3053 3069 5085 Gaskets, all materials; Weather strip, sponge rubber; Industrial supplies

(P-3879)
BRYANT RUBBER CORP (PA)
1580 W Carson St, Long Beach (90810-1455)
PHONE..............................310 530-2530
Steven Bryant, *Prin*
Steven Bryant, *Prin*
Robert Tracewell, *Prin*
Brogan Bryant, *Prin*
Tracy Hunter, *
EMP: 37 **EST:** 1971
SALES (est): 24.17MM
SALES (corp-wide): 24.17MM **Privately Held**
Web: www.bryantrubber.com
SIC: 3053 Gaskets; packing and sealing devices

(P-3880)
BRYANT RUBBER CORP
Also Called: Ingla Rubber Products
1083 W 251st St., Bellflower (90706)
PHONE..............................310 530-2530
Jack Klimek, *Brnch Mgr*
EMP: 113
SALES (corp-wide): 24.17MM **Privately Held**
Web: www.bryantrubber.com
SIC: 3053 3061 Gaskets; packing and sealing devices; Mechanical rubber goods
PA: Bryant Rubber Corp.
1580 W Carson St
310 530-2530

(P-3881)
CANNON GASKET INC
7784 Edison Ave, Fontana (92336-3635)
PHONE..............................909 355-1547
Billy Cannon, *Pr*
Billy Jr P Cannon, *
Candy Houle, *
▲ **EMP:** 27 **EST:** 1971
SQ FT: 10,000
SALES (est): 2.39MM **Privately Held**
Web: www.cannongasket.com
SIC: 3053 Gaskets, all materials

(P-3882)
CHAVERS GASKET CORPORATION
23325 Del Lago Dr, Laguna Hills (92653-1309)
PHONE..............................949 472-8118
Riley Cole, *CEO*
Christopher Cole, *
EMP: 25 **EST:** 1986
SQ FT: 13,000
SALES (est): 4.47MM **Privately Held**
Web: www.chaversgasket.com
SIC: 3053 Gaskets, all materials

(P-3883)
CIASONS INDUSTRIAL INC
1615 Boyd St, Santa Ana (92705-5103)
PHONE..............................714 259-0838
Paul Hsieh, *Pr*
Grace S P Hsieh, *
Samuel Hsieh, *
▲ **EMP:** 30 **EST:** 1985
SQ FT: 25,000
SALES (est): 2MM **Privately Held**
Web: www.ciasons.com
SIC: 3053 3563 Packing: steam engines, pipe joints, air compressors, etc.; Air and gas compressors

(P-3884)
D W MACK CO INC
900 W 8th St, Azusa (91702-2216)
P.O. Box 1247 (91017-1247)

PHONE..............................626 969-1817
Danny J Mack, *Pr*
Joseph Demarco, *
Dennis S Mack, *
▲ **EMP:** 40 **EST:** 1979
SALES (est): 5.33MM **Privately Held**
Web: www.dwmack.com
SIC: 3053 Gaskets, all materials

(P-3885)
DAN-LOC GROUP LLC
Also Called: Dan-Loc Bolt & Gasket
20444 Tillman Ave, Carson (90746-3516)
PHONE..............................310 538-2822
Rudy Estrada, *Brnch Mgr*
EMP: 66
SALES (corp-wide): 23.23MM **Privately Held**
Web: www.danlocgroup.com
SIC: 3053 3452 Gaskets and sealing devices; Bolts, nuts, rivets, and washers
PA: Dan-Loc Group, Llc
725 N Drennan St
713 356-3500

(P-3886)
DAR-KEN INC
Also Called: K & S Enterprises
10515 Rancho Rd, Adelanto (92301-3414)
PHONE..............................760 246-4010
Ken Mc Gilp, *Pt*
Darla Mc Gilp, *
EMP: 32 **EST:** 1965
SQ FT: 10,000
SALES (est): 3.27MM **Privately Held**
Web: www.ksentusa.com
SIC: 3053 3728 Gaskets; packing and sealing devices; Aircraft parts and equipment, nec

(P-3887)
FREUDENBERG-NOK GENERAL PARTNR
Also Called: International Seal Company
2041 E Wilshire Ave, Santa Ana (92705-4726)
PHONE..............................714 834-0602
John Hudspeth, *Mgr*
EMP: 150
SQ FT: 28,928
SALES (corp-wide): 12.96B **Privately Held**
Web: www.fst.com
SIC: 3053 Gaskets and sealing devices
HQ: Freudenberg-Nok General Partnership
47774 W Anchor Ct
Plymouth MI 48170
734 451-0020

(P-3888)
GASKET MANUFACTURING CO
8427 Scoura Way, Santa Fe Springs (90670-2215)
PHONE..............................310 217-5600
TOLL FREE: 800
Maureen E Labor, *CEO*
Dewain R Butler, *
Maureen E Labor, *Pr*
Vince Labor, *
EMP: 33 **EST:** 1937
SALES (est): 5.69MM **Privately Held**
Web: www.gasketmfg.com
SIC: 3053 Gaskets, all materials
PA: Gasket Associates Lp
10816 Kurt St

(P-3889)
HDZ BROTHERS INC
1924 E Mcfadden Ave, Santa Ana (92705-4705)
PHONE..............................714 953-4010

Zeferino Hernandez, *Pr*
EMP: 23 **EST:** 2007
SALES (est) 532.57K **Privately Held**
SIC: 3053 Gaskets; packing and sealing
devices

(P-3890)
HUTCHINSON SEAL CORPORATION (DH)
Also Called: National O Rings
11634 Patton Rd, Downey (90241-5212)
PHONE.....................248 375-4190
Christian Groche, *Pr*
▲ **EMP:** 120 **EST:** 1996
SQ FT: 125,000
SALES (est): 6.37MM
SALES (corp-wide): 7.88B **Privately Held**
Web: www.hutchinson-seal.com
SIC: 3053 Gaskets and sealing devices
HQ: Hutchinson Corporation
460 Fuller Ave Ne
Grand Rapids MI 49503
616 459-4541

(P-3891)
INDUSTRIAL GASKET AND SUP CO
Also Called: Gasketfab Division
2702 Dashwood St, Lakewood
(90712-2136)
P.O. Box 4138 (90510-4138)
PHONE.....................310 530-1771
William P Hynes, *Pr*
Kevin P Treacy, *VP*
Theresa Holmes, *Sec*
EMP: 23 **EST:** 1970
SALES (est): 2.41MM **Privately Held**
SIC: 3053 5085 Gaskets, all materials;
Gaskets

(P-3892)
INERTECH SUPPLY INC
Also Called: Inertech
641 Monterey Pass Rd, Monterey Park
(91754-2418)
PHONE.....................626 282-2000
James Huang, *Pr*
Charlie C Miskell, *
Bruce Wang, *
Walter Lee, *
▲ **EMP:** 75 **EST:** 1991
SQ FT: 14,000
SALES (est): 4.6MM **Privately Held**
Web: www.inertech.com
SIC: 3053 5085 2891 Gasket materials;
Gaskets; Adhesives and sealants

(P-3893)
J MILLER CO INC
Also Called: Miller Gasket Co
11537 Bradley Ave, San Fernando
(91340-2519)
PHONE.....................818 837-0181
TOLL FREE: 800
Dennis D Miller, *Pr*
Elaine Miller, *
▲ **EMP:** 35 **EST:** 1961
SQ FT: 20,000
SALES (est): 2.41MM **Privately Held**
Web: www.millergasket.com
SIC: 3053 Gaskets, all materials

(P-3894)
KIRKHILL INC
Also Called: Haskon, Div of
300 E Cypress St, Brea (92821-4097)
PHONE.....................714 529-4901
Michael Harden, *Brnch Mgr*
EMP: 700
SALES (corp-wide): 7.94B **Publicly Held**

Web: www.kirkhill.com
SIC: 3053 3728 2822 Gaskets; packing and
sealing devices; Aircraft parts and
equipment, nec; Synthetic rubber
HQ: Kirkhill Inc.
300 E Cypress St
Brea CA 92821
714 529-4901

(P-3895)
LGG INDUSTRIAL INC
15500 Blackburn Ave, Norwalk
(90650-6845)
PHONE.....................562 802-7782
EMP: 74
SALES (corp-wide): 437.91MM **Privately Held**
Web: www.lggindustrial.com
SIC: 3053 3965 3052 2992 Gaskets, all
materials; Fasteners; Heater hose, rubber;
Lubricating oils
PA: Lgg Industrial, Inc.
650 Washington Rd Ste 500
800 937-9070

(P-3896)
PARCO LLC (DH)
1801 S Archibald Ave, Ontario
(91761-7677)
PHONE.....................909 947-2200
Adam Morrison Burgener, *CEO*
Angie Garcia, *VP*
▲ **EMP:** 113 **EST:** 1989
SALES (est): 54.03MM **Privately Held**
Web: www.parcoinc.com
SIC: 3053 Gaskets; packing and sealing
devices
HQ: Datwyler Schweiz Ag
Militarstrasse 7
Schattdorf UR 6467

(P-3897)
REAL SEAL CO INC
Also Called: Real Seal
1971 Don Lee Pl, Escondido (92029-1141)
PHONE.....................760 743-7263
Patrick Thomas Tobin, *CEO*
Rose Ann Tobin, *
◆ **EMP:** 25 **EST:** 1970
SQ FT: 22,000
SALES (est): 2.59MM **Privately Held**
Web: www.real-seal.com
SIC: 3053 5085 Oil seals, rubber; Industrial
supplies

(P-3898)
RPM PRODUCTS INC (PA)
Also Called: Rubber Plastic & Metal Pdts
23201 Antonio Pkwy, Rancho Santa Margari
(92688-2653)
PHONE.....................949 888-8543
Mark Paolella, *Pr*
Suzanne Paolella, *
▲ **EMP:** 35 **EST:** 1994
SALES (est): 3.92MM **Privately Held**
Web: www.rpmproducts.com
SIC: 3053 3089 5085 Gaskets and sealing
devices; Injection molding of plastics;
Gaskets and seals

(P-3899)
SEAL SCIENCE INC (HQ)
Also Called: S S I
3701 E Conant St, Long Beach
(90808-1783)
PHONE.....................949 253-3130
Frederick E Tuliper, *CEO*
Patricia Tuliper, *
▲ **EMP:** 68 **EST:** 1985
SALES (est): 16.33MM

SALES (corp-wide): 150.17MM **Privately Held**
Web: www.sealscience.com
SIC: 3053 3089 3061 Gaskets, all materials;
Injection molding of plastics; Mechanical
rubber goods
PA: Sanders Industries Holdings, Inc.
3701 E Conant St
562 354-2920

(P-3900)
SEWING COLLECTION INC (PA)
3113 E 26th St, Vernon (90058-8006)
PHONE.....................323 264-2223
Touraj Tour, *Pr*
Houshang Tour, *VP*
◆ **EMP:** 47 **EST:** 1991
SQ FT: 135,000
SALES (est): 27.06MM
SALES (corp-wide): 27.06MM **Privately Held**
Web: www.sewingcollection.com
SIC: 3053 5199 4953 Packing materials;
Packaging materials; Recycling, waste
materials

(P-3901)
SPIRA MANUFACTURING CORP
650 Jessie St, San Fernando (91340-2233)
PHONE.....................818 764-8222
George M Kunkel, *Pr*
Bonnie Paul, *
Michael Kunkel, *
Wendy Kunkel, *
EMP: 30 **EST:** 1972
SQ FT: 15,000
SALES (est): 5.34MM **Privately Held**
Web: www.spira-emi.com
SIC: 3053 Gaskets, all materials

(P-3902)
SWABPLUS INC
9669 Hermosa Ave, Rancho Cucamonga
(91730-5813)
PHONE.....................909 987-7898
Tom Y Lee, *CEO*
Garry Tsaur, *
Eddy C Wan, *
▲ **EMP:** 41 **EST:** 1998
SALES (est): 1.12MM **Privately Held**
SIC: 3053 Packing materials

(P-3903)
WEST COAST GASKET CO
300 Ranger Ave, Brea (92821-6217)
PHONE.....................714 869-0123
Louis Russell, *Prin*
Jean Grey, *
EMP: 75 **EST:** 1979
SQ FT: 50,000
SALES (est): 9.43MM **Privately Held**
Web: www.westcoastgasket.com
SIC: 3053 3061 3469 5085 Gaskets, all
materials; Mechanical rubber goods; Metal
stampings, nec; Industrial supplies

3061 Mechanical Rubber Goods

(P-3904)
OMNI SEALS INC
11031 Jersey Blvd Ste A, Rancho
Cucamonga (91730-5150)
PHONE.....................909 946-0181
EMP: 68
SIC: 3061 Mechanical rubber goods

(P-3905)
R D RUBBER TECHNOLOGY CORP
12870 Florence Ave, Santa Fe Springs
(90670-4540)
PHONE.....................562 941-4800
Walter V Hopkins Junior, *Pr*
Rosanne Dukowitz, *
EMP: 27 **EST:** 1986
SQ FT: 15,600
SALES (est): 3.7MM **Privately Held**
Web: www.rdrubber.com
SIC: 3061 Mechanical rubber goods

(P-3906)
RUBBERCRAFT CORP CAL LTD (HQ)
Also Called: Rubber Teck Division
3701 E Conant St, Long Beach
(90808-1783)
PHONE.....................562 354-2800
Marc Sanders, *CEO*
Eric Sanders, *
EMP: 238 **EST:** 1984
SQ FT: 40,000
SALES (est): 48.96MM
SALES (corp-wide): 150.17MM **Privately Held**
Web: www.rubbercraft.com
SIC: 3061 Appliance rubber goods
(mechanical)
PA: Sanders Industries Holdings, Inc.
3701 E Conant St
562 354-2920

3069 Fabricated Rubber Products, Nec

(P-3907)
3M COMPANY
Also Called: 3M
1601 S Shamrock Ave, Monrovia
(91016-4283)
PHONE.....................626 358-0136
Bob Palmer, *Mgr*
EMP: 46
SALES (corp-wide): 32.68B **Publicly Held**
Web: www.3m.com
SIC: 3069 Rubber coated fabrics and clothing
PA: 3m Company
3m Center
651 733-1110

(P-3908)
AMES RUBBER MFG CO INC
Also Called: Ames Industrial
4516 Brazil St, Los Angeles (90039-1002)
PHONE.....................818 240-9313
TOLL FREE: 800
Timothy L Brown, *CEO*
Pat Brown, *
▲ **EMP:** 30 **EST:** 1954
SQ FT: 20,000
SALES (est): 4.59MM **Privately Held**
Web: www.amesrubberonline.com
SIC: 3069 3061 Medical and laboratory
rubber sundries and related products;
Mechanical rubber goods

(P-3909)
CALIFORNIA GASKET AND RBR CORP (PA)
533 W Collins Ave, Orange (92867-5509)
PHONE.....................714 202-8500
Scott H Franklin, *VP*
Armando Rodriguez, *
EMP: 25 **EST:** 1942
SQ FT: 51,000

SALES (est): 5.74MM
SALES (corp-wide): 5.74MM **Privately Held**
Web: www.californiagasket.com
SIC: **3069** 3053 3469 3061 Molded rubber products; Gaskets; packing and sealing devices; Metal stampings, nec; Appliance rubber goods (mechanical)

(P-3910)
COI RUBBER PRODUCTS INC
19255 San Jose Ave Unit D-1, City Of Industry (91748-1418)
PHONE.....................................626 965-9966
David Chao, *CEO*
EMP: 450 EST: 2013
SQ FT: 2,500
SALES (est): 2.39MM **Privately Held**
Web: www.coirubber.com
SIC: **3069** Medical and laboratory rubber sundries and related products

(P-3911)
FLEX COMPANY
318 Lincoln Blvd Ste 204, Venice (90291-2865)
PHONE.....................................424 209-2711
Lauren Schulte, *CEO*
Brian Wang, *
EMP: 30 EST: 2015
SQ FT: 4,500
SALES (est): 7.2MM **Privately Held**
Web: www.flexfits.com
SIC: **3069** 5999 5122 Birth control devices, rubber; Toiletries, cosmetics, and perfumes; Drugs, proprietaries, and sundries

(P-3912)
GOOD-WEST RUBBER CORP (PA)
Also Called: Goodyear Rbr Co Southern Cal
9615 Feron Blvd, Rancho Cucamonga (91730-4503)
PHONE.....................................909 987-1774
Christian Groche, *Pr*
Harold W Sears, *
Patrick Sears, *
Fred Ledesma, *
▲ EMP: 145 EST: 1961
SQ FT: 56,000
SALES (est): 19.69MM
SALES (corp-wide): 19.69MM **Privately Held**
Web: www.goodyearrubber.com
SIC: **3069** 3061 5531 Molded rubber products; Mechanical rubber goods; Automotive tires

(P-3913)
HEXPOL COMPOUNDING CA INC (DH)
Also Called: Valley Processing
2500 E Thompson St, Long Beach (90805-1836)
PHONE.....................................626 961-0311
Tracy Garrison, *Pr*
Ernie Ulmer, *CFO*
EMP: 93 EST: 2011
SALES (est): 38MM
SALES (corp-wide): 6.47MM **Privately Held**
Web: www.hexpol.com
SIC: **3069** Custom compounding of rubber materials
HQ: Hexpol Holding Inc.
14330 Kinsman Rd
Burton OH 44021
440 834-4644

(P-3914)
HITT COMPANIES
Also Called: Hitt Marking Devices I D Tech
3231 W Macarthur Blvd, Santa Ana (92704-6801)
PHONE.....................................714 979-1405
Harold G Hitt, *Pr*
Ken Hitt, *
Heidi Hitt, *
▲ EMP: 24 EST: 1987
SQ FT: 10,000
SALES (est): 4.4MM **Privately Held**
Web: www.thehittcompanies.com
SIC: **3069** 3993 5199 Stationer's rubber sundries; Signs and advertising specialties; Badges

(P-3915)
HUTCHINSON AROSPC & INDUST INC
Also Called: Barry Controls Aerospace
4510 W Vanowen St, Burbank (91505-1135)
P.O. Box 7710 (91510-7710)
PHONE.....................................818 843-1000
Grant Hintze, *CEO*
EMP: 156
SALES (corp-wide): 7.88B **Privately Held**
Web: www.hutchinsonai.com
SIC: **3069** Molded rubber products
HQ: Hutchinson Aerospace & Industry, Inc.
82 South St
Hopkinton MA 01748
508 417-7000

(P-3916)
INNOCOR WEST LLC
300 S Tippecanoe Ave 310, San Bernardino (92408-2605)
PHONE.....................................909 307-3737
Carol S Eicher, *CEO*
Doug Vaughan, *CFO*
▲ EMP: 556 EST: 2003
SQ FT: 150,000
SALES (est): 2.08MM **Privately Held**
SIC: **3069** 5021 Pillows, sponge rubber; Mattresses
HQ: Innocor, Inc.
200 Schulz Dr Ste 2
Red Bank NJ 07701

(P-3917)
INTERNATIONAL RUBBER PDTS INC (HQ)
Also Called: Irp
1035 Calle Amanecer, San Clemente (92673-6260)
PHONE.....................................909 947-1244
Rich Mcmanus, *CEO*
▲ EMP: 58 EST: 2003
SQ FT: 45,000
SALES (est): 29.52MM
SALES (corp-wide): 150.17MM **Privately Held**
Web: www.irpi.com
SIC: **3069** Medical and laboratory rubber sundries and related products
PA: Sanders Industries Holdings, Inc.
3701 E Conant St
562 354-2920

(P-3918)
JJ ACQUISITIONS LLC
8501 Fallbrook Ave Ste 370, West Hills (91304-3242)
PHONE.....................................818 772-0100
Matthew Matsudaira, *Managing Member*
EMP: 41 EST: 2014
SALES (est): 7MM **Privately Held**
SIC: **3069** Toys, rubber

(P-3919)
JOHNSON DOC ENTERPRISES
11933 Vose St, North Hollywood (91605-5750)
PHONE.....................................818 764-1543
Ronald Braverman, *Pr*
Chad Braverman, *Dir*
◆ EMP: 31 EST: 1987
SALES (est): 728.54K **Privately Held**
Web: www.docjohnson.com
SIC: **3069** Toys, rubber

(P-3920)
KIRKHILL INC
1451 S Carlos Ave, Ontario (91761-7676)
P.O. Box 7012 (90242-7012)
PHONE.....................................562 803-1117
Robert L Harold, *Ch*
Bruce Mekjian, *
Arlene Hite, *
Gary Riopelle, *
EMP: 95 EST: 1941
SALES (est): 1.9MM **Privately Held**
Web: www.kirkhill.com
SIC: **3069** Acid bottles, rubber

(P-3921)
KIRKHILL RUBBER COMPANY
2500 E Thompson St, Long Beach (90805-1836)
PHONE.....................................562 803-1117
David Schlothauer, *Pr*
Edward Reker, *
EMP: 99 EST: 2018
SALES (est): 19.97MM
SALES (corp-wide): 6.47MM **Privately Held**
Web: www.kirkhill.com
SIC: **3069** Medical and laboratory rubber sundries and related products
HQ: Hexpol Holding Inc.
14330 Kinsman Rd
Burton OH 44021
440 834-4644

(P-3922)
KMC ACQUISITION LLC (PA)
Also Called: Kirkhill Manufacturing Company
1451 S Carlos Ave, Ontario (91761-7676)
PHONE.....................................562 396-0121
▲ EMP: 49 EST: 1996
SALES (est): 24.5MM **Privately Held**
Web: www.rubbersales.com
SIC: **3069** Molded rubber products

(P-3923)
LEONARDS MOLDED PRODUCTS INC
25031 Anza Dr, Valencia (91355-3414)
PHONE.....................................661 253-2227
Randy Smith, *Pr*
Randy Smith, *Pr*
Frank Smith, *
EMP: 25 EST: 1984
SQ FT: 5,000
SALES (est): 2.43MM **Privately Held**
Web: www.lmrubber.com
SIC: **3069** Molded rubber products

(P-3924)
MITCHELL RUBBER PRODUCTS LLC (PA)
1880 Iowa Ave Ste 400, Riverside (92507-7405)
P.O. Box 7577 (92658-7577)
PHONE.....................................951 681-5655
Theodore Ballou, *CEO*
Mark Mitchell, *Corporate Secretary*
◆ EMP: 120 EST: 1967

SALES (est): 9.86MM
SALES (corp-wide): 9.86MM **Privately Held**
Web: www.mitchellrubber.com
SIC: **3069** 2891 2822 Mats or matting, rubber, nec; Adhesives and sealants; Synthetic rubber

(P-3925)
MODUS ADVANCED INC
2772 Loker Ave W, Carlsbad (92010-6610)
PHONE.....................................925 960-8700
Richard Mackirdy Junior, *CEO*
Don E Ulery, *
Natalia Spruiell, *
▲ EMP: 53 EST: 1976
SALES (est): 14.66MM **Privately Held**
Web: www.modusadvanced.com
SIC: **3069** 3599 3053 Molded rubber products; Machine and other job shop work; Gaskets; packing and sealing devices

(P-3926)
NEWBY RUBBER INC
320 Industrial St, Bakersfield (93307-2706)
PHONE.....................................661 327-5137
TOLL FREE: 800
Kelly Newby, *Pr*
Lori Newby, *
▼ EMP: 25 EST: 1958
SQ FT: 80,000
SALES (est): 4.39MM **Privately Held**
Web: www.newbyrubber.com
SIC: **3069** Molded rubber products

(P-3927)
NUSIL TECHNOLOGY LLC (DH)
Also Called: Nusil
1050 Cindy Ln, Carpinteria (93013-2906)
PHONE.....................................805 684-8780
◆ EMP: 400 EST: 1980
SALES (est): 131.69MM
SALES (corp-wide): 6.97B **Publicly Held**
Web: nusil.avantorsciences.com
SIC: **3069** Medical and laboratory rubber sundries and related products
HQ: Avantor Performance Materials, Llc
100 Mtsnford Rd Bldg 1 St
Radnor PA 19087
610 573-2600

(P-3928)
OXYSTRAP INTERNATIONAL INC
8705 Complex Dr, San Diego (92123-1401)
PHONE.....................................800 699-6901
Bruce L Gertsch, *CEO*
EMP: 28 EST: 2015
SALES (est): 588.5K **Privately Held**
Web: www.oxystrap.com
SIC: **3069** 2326 3949 Medical and laboratory rubber sundries and related products; Medical and hospital uniforms, men's; Team sports equipment

(P-3929)
PMR PRECISION MFG & RBR CO INC
1330 Etiwanda Ave, Ontario (91761-8605)
PHONE.....................................909 605-7525
Samuel Surh, *Pr*
George Surh, *
EMP: 30 EST: 1996
SQ FT: 36,800
SALES (est): 2.2MM **Privately Held**
Web: www.pmrubbertech.com
SIC: **3069** 2295 Rubberized fabrics; Coated fabrics, not rubberized

PRODUCTS & SVCS

(P-3930)

PROMOTONAL DESIGN CONCEPTS INC

Also Called: Creative Inflatables

9872 Rush St, South El Monte (91733-2635)

PHONE..................626 579-4454

Adam Melendez, *CEO*

◆ **EMP:** 71 **EST:** 1984

SALES (est): 2MM **Privately Held**

Web: www.promotionaldesigngroup.com

SIC: 3069 7389 5092 2394 Balloons, advertising and toy: rubber; Balloons, novelty and toy; Toy novelties and amusements; Canvas and related products

(P-3931)

R & R RUBBER MOLDING INC

2444 Loma Ave, South El Monte (91733-1416)

P.O. Box 3533 (91733-0533)

PHONE..................626 575-8105

Richard P Norman, *Pr*

EMP: 35 **EST:** 1977

SQ FT: 6,100

SALES (est): 1.86MM **Privately Held**

Web: www.rrrubber.com

SIC: 3069 Molded rubber products

(P-3932)

R & S PROCESSING CO INC

15712 Illinois Ave, Paramount (90723-4113)

P.O. Box 2037 (90723-8037)

PHONE..................562 531-0738

Karen A Kelly, *Pr*

Linda M Inga, *

Anthony J Inga, *

EMP: 73 **EST:** 1959

SQ FT: 53,000

SALES (est): 5.2MM **Privately Held**

Web: www.rsprocessing.com

SIC: 3069 Reclaimed rubber (reworked by manufacturing processes)

(P-3933)

ROGERS CORPORATION

Also Called: Diversified Silicone

13937 Rosecrans Ave, Santa Fe Springs (90670-5209)

PHONE..................562 404-8942

Brian Lindey, *Genl Mgr*

EMP: 60

SALES (corp-wide): 908.4MM **Publicly Held**

Web: www.rogerscorp.com

SIC: 3069 Bags, rubber or rubberized fabric

PA: Rogers Corporation

2225 W Chandler Blvd

480 917-6000

(P-3934)

RUBBER-CAL INC

18424 Mount Langley St, Fountain Valley (92708-6905)

PHONE..................714 772-3000

EMP: 39 **EST:** 2019

SALES (est): 3.63MM **Privately Held**

Web: www.rubbercal.com

SIC: 3069 Fabricated rubber products, nec

(P-3935)

S & H RUBBER CO

1141 E Elm Ave, Fullerton (92831-5023)

PHONE..................714 525-0277

Stephen Haney, *Pr*

Mike Haney, *Mgr*

EMP: 28 **EST:** 1967

SQ FT: 5,406

SALES (est): 3.14MM **Privately Held**

Web: www.shrubber.com

SIC: 3069 Washers, rubber

(P-3936)

SFRLC INC

12306 Washington Blvd, Whittier (90606-2503)

PHONE..................562 693-2776

William Krames, *Pr*

Mike Peterman, *

EMP: 50 **EST:** 1966

SQ FT: 30,000

SALES (est): 2.16MM **Privately Held**

Web: www.santaferubber.com

SIC: 3069 Molded rubber products

(P-3937)

SHERCON LLC

Also Called: Shercon, Inc.

18704 S Ferris Pl, Rancho Dominguez (90220-6400)

▲ **EMP:** 60 **EST:** 1966

SQ FT: 50,000

SALES (est): 1.5MM

SALES (corp-wide): 2.26B **Privately Held**

Web: www.caplugs.com

SIC: 3069 3089 2672 Tape, pressure sensitive: rubber; Injection molded finished plastics products, nec; Paper; coated and laminated, nec

HQ: Caplugs, Inc.

2150 Elmwood Ave

Buffalo NY 14207

716 876-9855

(P-3938)

SPANGLER INDUSTRIES INC

Also Called: A S I American

1711 N Delilah St, Corona (92879-1865)

P.O. Box 1445 (92878-1445)

PHONE..................951 735-5000

Bernard D Spangler, *Pr*

Greg Spangler, *

EMP: 165 **EST:** 1970

SQ FT: 37,897

SALES (est): 8.53MM **Privately Held**

SIC: 3069 Rubber bands

(P-3939)

TA AEROSPACE CO (DH)

28065 Franklin Pkwy, Valencia (91355-4117)

PHONE..................661 775-1100

Carol Marinello, *Pr*

▲ **EMP:** 250 **EST:** 1919

SQ FT: 100,000

SALES (est): 193.2MM

SALES (corp-wide): 7.94B **Publicly Held**

Web: www.taaerospace.com

SIC: 3069 Reclaimed rubber and specialty rubber compounds

HQ: Esterline Technologies Corp

1350 Euclid Ave Ste 1600

Cleveland OH 44114

216 706-2960

(P-3940)

TIMEMED LABELING SYSTEMS INC (DH)

27770 Entertainment Dr Ste 200, Valencia (91355-1094)

PHONE..................818 897-1111

Cecil Kost, *CEO*

Mark Segal, *

Tracey Carpentier, *

EMP: 100 **EST:** 1953

SQ FT: 75,000

SALES (est): 4.7MM

SALES (corp-wide): 1.34B **Publicly Held**

Web: www.pdchealthcare.com

SIC: 3069 Tape, pressure sensitive: rubber

HQ: Precision Dynamics Corporation

25124 Sprngfeld Ct Ste 20

Valencia CA 91355

818 897-1111

(P-3941)

VIP RUBBER COMPANY INC (PA)

540 S Cypress St, La Habra (90631-6127)

PHONE..................562 905-3456

Bernardyne Louise Campana, *Pr*

Howard Vipperman, *

Deena Campana, *

Kathy Leclair, *

Thomas Leclair, *

▲ **EMP:** 107 **EST:** 1970

SQ FT: 58,000

SALES (est): 23.69MM

SALES (corp-wide): 23.69MM **Privately Held**

Web: www.viprubber.com

SIC: 3069 3089 3061 Rubber hardware; Plastics hardware and building products; Mechanical rubber goods

(P-3942)

WEST AMERICAN RUBBER CO LLC (PA)

Also Called: Warco

1337 W Braden Ct, Orange (92868-1123)

P.O. Box 6146 (92863-6146)

PHONE..................714 532-3355

Tim Hemstreet, *Managing Member*

▲ **EMP:** 124 **EST:** 1910

SQ FT: 12,500

SALES (est): 48.04MM

SALES (corp-wide): 48.04MM **Privately Held**

Web: www.warco.com

SIC: 3069 3061 3053 Sheets, hard rubber; Mechanical rubber goods; Gaskets, all materials

(P-3943)

WEST AMERICAN RUBBER CO LLC

Also Called: Warco

750 N Main St, Orange (92868-1184)

P.O. Box 6146 (92863-6146)

PHONE..................714 532-3355

Renan Mendez, *Com Operations Vice President*

EMP: 165

SALES (corp-wide): 48.04MM **Privately Held**

Web: www.warco.com

SIC: 3069 Sheets, hard rubber

PA: West American Rubber Company Llc

1337 Braden Ct

714 532-3355

3081 Unsupported Plastics Film And Sheet

(P-3944)

ARLON GRAPHICS LLC (HQ)

200 Boysenberry Ln, Placentia (92870-6413)

PHONE..................714 985-6300

Andrew Mcneill, *Pr*

Andrew Huddlestone, *Area President*

Rich Trombino, *

Chad Russell, *

◆ **EMP:** 148 **EST:** 2011

SALES (est): 28.75MM

SALES (corp-wide): 314.36MM **Privately Held**

Web: www.arlon.com

SIC: 3081 Vinyl film and sheet

PA: Flexcon Company, Inc.

1 Flexcon Industrial Park

508 885-8200

(P-3945)

ARVINYL LAMINATES LP

233 N Sherman Ave, Corona (92882-1844)

PHONE..................951 371-7800

Andy Peters, *Pt*

EMP: 51 **EST:** 2011

SALES (est): 9.91MM **Privately Held**

Web: www.arvinyl.com

SIC: 3081 Vinyl film and sheet

(P-3946)

BERRY GLOBAL FILMS LLC

14000 Monte Vista Ave, Chino (91710-5537)

PHONE..................909 517-2872

J Brendan Barba, *Pr*

EMP: 149

SQ FT: 63,480

Web: www.berryglobal.com

SIC: 3081 2673 Polyethylene film; Bags: plastic, laminated, and coated

HQ: Berry Global Films, Llc

95 Chestnut Ridge Rd

Montvale NJ 07645

201 641-6600

(P-3947)

DELSTAR HOLDING CORP

9225 Isaac St, Santee (92071-5615)

PHONE..................619 258-1503

Scott Anglin, *Brnch Mgr*

▲ **EMP:** 26

Web: www.swmintl.com

SIC: 3081 Polypropylene film and sheet

HQ: Delstar Holding Corp.

100 N Point Ctr E Ste 600

Alpharetta GA 30022

800 514-0186

(P-3948)

DELSTAR TECHNOLOGIES INC

Also Called: Swm

1306 Fayette St, El Cajon (92020-1513)

PHONE..................619 258-1503

Mark Laughlin, *Mgr*

EMP: 50

Web: www.delstarinc.com

SIC: 3081 Polypropylene film and sheet

HQ: Delstar Technologies, Inc.

601 Industrial Dr

Middletown DE 19709

302 378-8888

(P-3949)

FLEXCON COMPANY INC

12840 Reservoir St, Chino (91710-2944)

PHONE..................909 465-0408

David R Trujillo, *Mgr*

EMP: 40

SALES (corp-wide): 314.36MM **Privately Held**

Web: www.flexcon.com

SIC: 3081 2679 Plastics film and sheet; Labels, paper: made from purchased material

PA: Flexcon Company, Inc.

1 Flexcon Industrial Park

508 885-8200

(P-3950)

GRAFFITI SHIELD INC

2940 E La Palma Ave Ste D, Anaheim (92806-2619)

PHONE..................714 575-1100

Jeffrey Green, *CEO*

EMP: 24 EST: 2013
SALES (est): 6.11MM Privately Held
Web: www.graffiti-shield.com
SIC: 3081 Floor or wall covering, unsupported plastics

(P-3951)
MERCURY PLASTICS INC
Poly Pak Packaging Division
2939 E Washington Blvd, Los Angeles (90023-4218)
PHONE.............................323 264-2400
Benjamin Deutsch, Brnch Mgr
EMP: 95
Web: www.polypak.com
SIC: 3081 2677 Polyethylene film; Envelopes
HQ: Mercury Plastics, Inc.
    14825 Salt Lake Ave
    City Of Industry CA 91746
    626 961-0165

(P-3952)
MONTEBELLO PLASTICS LLC
601 W Olympic Blvd, Montebello (90640-5229)
P.O. Box 789 (90640-0789)
PHONE.............................323 728-6814
EMP: 50 EST: 1982
SQ FT: 25,000
SALES (est): 3.46MM Privately Held
Web: www.montebelloplastics.com
SIC: 3081 2673 3089 Packing materials, plastics sheet; Trash bags (plastic film): made from purchased materials; Extruded finished plastics products, nec

(P-3953)
OCEANIA INC
14209 Gannet St, La Mirada (90638-5220)
PHONE.............................562 926-8886
Tai Leong, CEO
Angela Leung, *
▲ EMP: 30 EST: 2014
SALES (est): 1.79MM Privately Held
SIC: 3081 Plastics film and sheet

(P-3954)
PLASTICS FAMILY HOLDINGS INC
Also Called: Eplastics
5535 Ruffin Rd, San Diego (92123-1314)
PHONE.............................858 560-1551
Nate Gardner, Brnch Mgr
EMP: 58
Web: www.lairdplastics.com
SIC: 3081 3082 5162 2541 Unsupported plastics film and sheet; Unsupported plastics profile shapes, Plastics materials and basic shapes; Wood partitions and fixtures
HQ: Plastics Family Holdings, Inc
    5800 Campus Cir Dr E Ste 1
    Irving TX 75063
    469 299-7000

(P-3955)
POLY PAK AMERICA INC
2939 E Washington Blvd, Los Angeles (90023-4277)
PHONE.............................323 264-2400
TOLL FREE: 800
EMP: 95
Web: www.polypak.com
SIC: 3081 2677 Polyethylene film; Envelopes

(P-3956)
PROVIDIEN THERMOFORMING LLC
Also Called: Providien Thermoforming, Inc.

6740 Nancy Ridge Dr, San Diego (92121-2230)
PHONE.............................858 850-1591
Jeffrey S Goble, CEO
Jenny Ames, *
Frank Ames Junior, Sec
Paul Jazwin, *
▲ EMP: 48 EST: 1982
SQ FT: 25,500
SALES (est): 20.42MM
SALES (corp-wide): 4.59B Publicly Held
Web: www.providienmedical.com
SIC: 3081 Unsupported plastics film and sheet
HQ: Providien, Llc
    6740 Nancy Ridge Dr
    San Diego CA 92121

(P-3957)
SAINT-GOBAIN SOLAR GARD LLC (DH)
Also Called: Saint-Gobain Performance Plas
4540 Viewridge Ave, San Diego (92123-1637)
P.O. Box 2864 (52733-2864)
PHONE.............................866 300-2674
M Shawn Puccio, *
◆ EMP: 88 EST: 2001
SQ FT: 65,000
SALES (est): 48.04MM
SALES (corp-wide): 402.18MM Privately Held
Web: www.solargard.com
SIC: 3081 5162 3479 Plastics film and sheet ; Plastics film; Coating of metals and formed products
HQ: Saint-Gobain Performance Plastics Corporation
    20 Moores Rd
    Malvern PA 19355
    440 836-6900

(P-3958)
SOLVAY DRAKA INC (DH)
6900 Elm St, Commerce (90040-2625)
PHONE.............................323 725-7010
▲ EMP: 120 EST: 1986
SALES (est): 40.32MM
SALES (corp-wide): 2.67MM Privately Held
Web: www.renolit.com
SIC: 3081 3087 Vinyl film and sheet; Custom compound purchased resins
HQ: Renolit Se
    Horchheimer Str. 50
    Worms RP 67547
    62413030

(P-3959)
TRM MANUFACTURING INC
375 Trm Cir, Corona (92879-1758)
P.O. Box 77520 (92877-0117)
PHONE.............................951 256-8550
Ted Moore, Pr
Anaisa Moore, *
▲ EMP: 200 EST: 1978
SQ FT: 200,000
SALES (est): 83.74MM Privately Held
Web: www.trmmfg.com
SIC: 3081 Polyethylene film

(P-3960)
W PLASTICS INC
Also Called: Western Plastics Temecula
41573 Dendy Pkwy Ste 2543, Temecula (92590-3757)
PHONE.............................800 442-9727
Michael T F Cunningham, Pr
Patrick Cunningham, VP
Thomas C Cunningham, Treas

◆ EMP: 35 EST: 1991
SQ FT: 65,000
SALES (est): 5.05MM Privately Held
Web: www.wplastics.com
SIC: 3081 1799 Plastics film and sheet; Food service equipment installation

3082 Unsupported Plastics Profile Shapes

(P-3961)
BIRD B GONE LLC
1921 E Edinger Ave, Santa Ana (92705-4720)
PHONE.............................949 472-3122
Bruce Alan Donoho, CEO
Julianne Donoho, *
David Smith, *
◆ EMP: 86 EST: 1992
SQ FT: 7,100
SALES (est): 15.9MM Privately Held
Web: www.birdbgone.com
SIC: 3082 Unsupported plastics profile shapes
HQ: Pelsis Limited
    Sterling House
    Knaresborough HG5 8
    800 988-5359

(P-3962)
JSN PACKAGING PRODUCTS INC
9700 Jeronimo Rd, Irvine (92618-2019)
PHONE.............................949 458-0050
Jim Nagel, Pr
Sandra Nagel, *
James H Nagel Junior, CEO
EMP: 65 EST: 1985
SALES (est): 9.57MM Privately Held
Web: www.jsn.com
SIC: 3082 3089 Tubes, unsupported plastics ; Caps, plastics

3083 Laminated Plastics Plate And Sheet

(P-3963)
ALCHEM PLASTICS INC
Also Called: Spartech Plastics
14263 Gannet St, La Mirada (90638-5220)
PHONE.............................714 523-2260
▲ EMP: 130
SIC: 3083 Thermoplastics laminates: rods, tubes, plates, and sheet

(P-3964)
JOHNSON LAMINATING COATING INC
20631 Annalee Ave, Carson (90746-3576)
PHONE.............................310 635-4929
Scott Davidson, Pr
▲ EMP: 75 EST: 1960
SQ FT: 50,000
SALES (est): 9.52MM Privately Held
Web: www.johnsonlaminating.com
SIC: 3083 3081 2891 1541 Laminated plastics sheets; Unsupported plastics film and sheet; Adhesives and sealants; Food products manufacturing or packing plant construction

(P-3965)
LITE EXTRUSIONS MFG INC
Also Called: Lite Extrusions
15025 S Main St, Gardena (90248-1922)
PHONE.............................323 770-4298
Paul Puga, Pr

William Puga, *
Barbara Puga, *
EMP: 30 EST: 1973
SQ FT: 23,500
SALES (est): 2.2MM Privately Held
Web: www.liteextrusions.com
SIC: 3083 Thermoplastics laminates: rods, tubes, plates, and sheet

(P-3966)
NELCO PRODUCTS INC
1100 E Kimberly Ave, Anaheim (92801-1101)
PHONE.............................714 879-4293
▲ EMP: 135
Web: www.nelcoproducts.com
SIC: 3083 Laminated plastics plate and sheet

(P-3967)
PLASTICS RESEARCH CORPORATION
Also Called: PRC
1400 S Campus Ave, Ontario (91761-4330)
PHONE.............................909 391-9050
Gene Gregory, CEO
Robert Black, *
Michael Maedel, *
▲ EMP: 100 EST: 1972
SQ FT: 105,000
SALES (est): 9.79MM Privately Held
Web: www.prccal.com
SIC: 3083 Laminated plastics plate and sheet

(P-3968)
PLASTIFAB INC
Also Called: Plastifab/Leed Plastics
1425 Palomares St, La Verne (91750-5294)
PHONE.............................909 596-1927
Rick Donnelly, Pr
EMP: 30 EST: 1977
SQ FT: 15,000
SALES (est): 4.62MM Privately Held
Web: www.plastifabonline.com
SIC: 3083 5162 3089 Laminated plastics sheets; Plastics sheets and rods; Plastics processing

(P-3969)
PTM & W INDUSTRIES INC
10640 Painter Ave, Santa Fe Springs (90670-4092)
PHONE.............................562 946-4511
Charles E Owen, CEO
William Ryan, *
▲ EMP: 25 EST: 1959
SQ FT: 25,000
SALES (est): 4.76MM Privately Held
Web: www.ptm-w.com
SIC: 3083 2992 2891 2851 Plastics finished products, laminated; Lubricating oils and greases; Adhesives and sealants; Paints and allied products

(P-3970)
REPET INC
14207 Monte Vista Ave, Chino (91710-5724)
PHONE.............................909 594-5333
Shubin Zhao, Pr
▲ EMP: 145 EST: 2009
SALES (est): 6.44MM Privately Held
Web: www.repetinc.com
SIC: 3083 Plastics finished products, laminated

(P-3971)
SIMMONS FAMILY CORPORATION
Also Called: Teklam

PRODUCTS & SVCS

350 W Rincon St, Corona (92880-2004)
PHONE..............................951 278-4563
▲ EMP: 80
SIC: 3083 Laminated plastics plate and sheet

(P-3972)
VANDERVEER INDUSTRIAL PLAS LLC
Also Called: Vanderveer Industrial Plastics
515 S Melrose St, Placentia (92870-6337)
PHONE..............................714 579-7700
Greg Geiss, *Managing Member*
EMP: 46 EST: 2012
SQ FT: 29,000
SALES (est): 6.51MM
SALES (corp-wide): 46.29MM **Privately Held**
Web: www.vanderveerplastics.com
SIC: 3083 Laminated plastics plate and sheet
PA: The Gund Company Inc
9333 Dielman Indus Dr
314 423-5200

3084 Plastics Pipe

(P-3973)
EXCALIBUR EXTRUSION INC
110 E Crowther Ave, Placentia
(92870-5637)
PHONE..............................714 528-8834
EMP: 50
Web: www.viprubber.com
SIC: 3084 3089 Plastics pipe; Fittings for pipe, plastics

(P-3974)
HANCOR INC
140 Vineland Rd, Bakersfield (93307-9515)
PHONE..............................661 366-1520
James Tingle, *Mgr*
EMP: 52
SALES (corp-wide): 2.87B **Publicly Held**
Web: www.adspipe.com
SIC: 3084 5051 Plastics pipe; Pipe and tubing, steel
HQ: Hancor, Inc.
4640 Trueman Blvd
Hilliard OH 43026
614 658-0050

(P-3975)
J-M MANUFACTURING COMPANY INC (PA)
Also Called: JM Eagle
5200 W Century Blvd, Los Angeles
(90045-5928)
PHONE..............................310 693-8200
Walter Wang, *Ch*
Shirley Wang, *
◆ EMP: 150 EST: 1982
SQ FT: 24,000
SALES (est): 304.63MM
SALES (corp-wide): 304.63MM **Privately Held**
Web: www.jmeagle.com
SIC: 3084 2821 3082 Plastics pipe; Polyvinyl chloride resins, PVC; Unsupported plastics profile shapes

(P-3976)
KAKUICHI AMERICA INC
23540 Telo Ave, Torrance (90505-4013)
PHONE..............................310 539-1590
Yasuo Ogami, *CEO*
Kenichi Tanaka, *
▲ EMP: 100 EST: 1973
SQ FT: 110,000
SALES (est): 10.25MM **Privately Held**
Web: www.pacificecho.com

SIC: 3084 Plastics pipe
HQ: Kakuichi Co., Ltd.
1415, Midoricho, Tsuruga
Nagano NAG 380-0

(P-3977)
PACIFIC PLASTICS INC
111 S Berry St, Brea (92821-4827)
PHONE..............................714 990-9050
Anayat Raminfar, *Pr*
Farhad Bahremand, *
Rahim Arian, *
John Ramin, *
Ata Ramin, *
▲ EMP: 71 EST: 1980
SQ FT: 32,000
SALES (est): 11.9MM **Privately Held**
Web: www.pacificplastics.us
SIC: 3084 Plastics pipe

(P-3978)
PW EAGLE INC
Also Called: JM Eagle
5200 W Century Blvd, Los Angeles
(90045-5928)
PHONE..............................800 621-4404
▼ EMP: 1087
SIC: 3084 Plastics pipe

(P-3979)
SPEARS MANUFACTURING CO
15860 Olden St, Rancho Cascades
(91342-1241)
PHONE..............................818 364-1611
EMP: 26
SALES (corp-wide): 1.37B **Privately Held**
Web: www.spearsmfg.net
SIC: 3084 Plastics pipe
PA: Spears Manufacturing Co.
15853 Olden St
818 364-1611

(P-3980)
VALENCIA PIPE COMPANY
Also Called: Home-Flex
28305 Livingston Ave, Valencia
(91355-4164)
PHONE..............................661 257-3923
Andrew Dervin, *CEO*
Curt Meyer, *
Peter Dervin, *
Uriel Sandoval, *
▲ EMP: 28 EST: 2007
SALES (est): 15.19MM **Privately Held**
Web: www.valenciapipe.com
SIC: 3084 5074 3479 3312 Plastics pipe; Pipes and fittings, plastic; Coating or wrapping steel pipe; Galvanized pipes, plates, sheets, etc.: iron and steel

---

3085 Plastics Bottles

(P-3981)
ALTIUM PACKAGING LLC
Mayfair Plastics
1500 E 223rd St, Carson (90745-4316)
PHONE..............................310 952-8736
Larry Lindsey, *Mgr*
EMP: 85
SALES (corp-wide): 15.9B **Publicly Held**
Web: www.altiumpkg.com
SIC: 3085 2656 Plastics bottles; Sanitary food containers
HQ: Altium Packaging Llc
2500 Windy Ridge Pkwy Se # 1400
Atlanta GA 30339
678 742-4600

(P-3982)
CLASSIC CONTAINERS INC
1700 S Hellman Ave, Ontario (91761-7638)
PHONE..............................909 930-3610
Manny G Hernandez Senior, *CEO*
Ernie Hernandez, *
Maria Hernandez, *
Manny Hernandez Junior, *Treas*
EMP: 280 EST: 1988
SQ FT: 60,000
SALES (est): 22.4MM **Privately Held**
Web: www.classiccontainers.com
SIC: 3085 3089 5085 Plastics bottles; Plastics containers, except foam; Industrial supplies

(P-3983)
MUNCHKIN INC (PA)
Also Called: Curio Home Goods
7835 Gloria Ave, Van Nuys (91406-1822)
PHONE..............................800 344-2229
Steven Dunn, *CEO*
Andrew Keimach, *
David Dunn, *
Gary Rolfes, *
Jeff Hale, *
◆ EMP: 123 EST: 1991
SQ FT: 63,000
SALES (est): 48.13MM **Privately Held**
Web: www.munchkin.com
SIC: 3085 3069 5999 Plastics bottles; Teething rings, rubber; Infant furnishings and equipment

(P-3984)
MUNCHKIN INC
27334 San Bernardino Ave, Redlands
(92374-5051)
PHONE..............................818 893-5000
Steven Dunn, *Brnch Mgr*
EMP: 36
Web: www.munchkin.com
SIC: 3085 Plastics bottles
PA: Munchkin, Inc.
7835 Gloria Ave

(P-3985)
NARAYAN CORPORATION
Also Called: Plastic Processing Co
13432 Estrella Ave, Gardena (90248-1513)
PHONE..............................310 719-7330
Harshad Desai, *Pr*
▲ EMP: 37 EST: 2002
SALES (est): 1.67MM **Privately Held**
Web: www.plasticprocessing.net
SIC: 3085 3089 Plastics bottles; Bottle caps, molded plastics

(P-3986)
PLASCOR INC
972 Columbia Ave, Riverside (92507-2140)
PHONE..............................951 328-1010
David Harrigan, *Pr*
▼ EMP: 135 EST: 1993
SQ FT: 50,000
SALES (est): 8.73MM **Privately Held**
Web: www.plascorinc.net
SIC: 3085 Plastics bottles

(P-3987)
PLAXICON HOLDING CORPORATION
Also Called: Plaxicon Co
10660 Acacia St, Rancho Cucamonga
(91730-5409)
PHONE..............................909 944-6868
Bill Williams, *CEO*
EMP: 323 EST: 1983
SQ FT: 150,000
SALES (est): 1.99MM **Privately Held**

SIC: 3085 3089 Plastics bottles; Plastics containers, except foam
PA: Graham Packaging Company Europe Llc
700 Indian Springs Dr # 100

(P-3988)
POLY-TAINER INC (PA)
Also Called: Custom Molded Devices
450 W Los Angeles Ave, Simi Valley
(93065-1646)
PHONE..............................805 526-3424
TOLL FREE: 800
Julie Williams, *CEO*
Paul Strong, *Pr*
Stephanie Strong, *VP*
Tim Williams, *CFO*
▲ EMP: 120 EST: 1970
SQ FT: 95,000
SALES (est): 47.83MM
SALES (corp-wide): 47.83MM **Privately Held**
Web: www.polytainer.com
SIC: 3085 Plastics bottles

(P-3989)
POLYCYCLE SOLUTIONS LLC
4516 Azusa Canyon Rd, Irwindale
(91706-2742)
PHONE..............................626 856-2100
▲ EMP: 60
SIC: 3085 Plastics bottles

(P-3990)
RING CONTAINER TECH LLC
8275 Almeria Ave, Fontana (92335-3280)
PHONE..............................909 350-8416
Fred Miller, *Brnch Mgr*
EMP: 56
SQ FT: 60,800
SALES (corp-wide): 2.25B **Privately Held**
Web: www.ringcontainer.com
SIC: 3085 3411 3089 Plastics bottles; Food containers, metal; Blow molded finished plastics products, nec
HQ: Ring Container Technologies, Llc.
1 Industrial Park
Oakland TN 38060
800 280-7464

3086 Plastics Foam Products

(P-3991)
ABAD FOAM INC
6560 Caballero Blvd, Buena Park
(90620-1130)
PHONE..............................714 994-2223
Cesar Chavez, *CEO*
▲ EMP: 50 EST: 1974
SALES (est): 10.19MM **Privately Held**
Web: www.ibscomfort.com
SIC: 3086 Plastics foam products

(P-3992)
ALTIUM PACKAGING LP
Also Called: A Division Continental Can Co
1217 E Saint Gertrude Pl, Santa Ana
(92707-3029)
PHONE..............................714 241-6640
Cesare Calabrese, *Brnch Mgr*
EMP: 37
SALES (corp-wide): 15.9B **Publicly Held**
Web: www.altiumpkg.com
SIC: 3086 3085 Plastics foam products; Plastics bottles
HQ: Altium Packaging Lp
3101 Towercreek Pkwy
Atlanta GA 30339
678 742-4600

▲ = Import ▼ = Export
◆ = Import/Export

(P-3993)
AMFOAM INC (PA)
Also Called: American Foam & Packaging
15110 S Broadway, Gardena (90248-1822)
PHONE.................310 327-4003
Brian Leecing, *Pr*
Alex Gelbard, *
▲ **EMP:** 45 **EST:** 1993
SQ FT: 42,000
SALES (est): 1.6MM **Privately Held**
Web: www.amfoaminc.com
SIC: 3086 5199 Packaging and shipping
materials, foamed plastics; Foam rubber

(P-3994)
ATLAS ROOFING CORPORATION
2335 Roll Dr Ste 4121, San Diego
(92154-7298)
PHONE.................626 334-5358
Edith Villegas, *Mgr*
EMP: 26
Web: www.achfoam.com
SIC: 3086 Insulation or cushioning material,
foamed plastics
HQ: Atlas Roofing Corporation
2100 Riveredge Pkwy
Atlanta GA 30328
800 388-6134

(P-3995)
CARPENTER CO
Also Called: Carpenter E R Co
7809 Lincoln Ave, Riverside (92504-4497)
P.O. Box 7788 (92513-7788)
PHONE.................951 354-7550
Jim Nanfeldt, *Mgr*
EMP: 45
SALES (corp-wide): 506.96MM **Privately Held**
Web: www.carpenter.com
SIC: 3086 2821 7389 5033 Insulation or
cushioning material, foamed plastics;
Plastics materials and resins; Furniture
finishing; Insulation materials
PA: Carpenter Co.
5016 Monument Ave
804 359-0800

(P-3996)
CLEAN CUT TECHNOLOGIES LLC
1145 N Ocean Cir, Anaheim (92806-1939)
PHONE.................714 864-3500
EMP: 100
Web: www.oliverhcp.com
SIC: 3086 Packaging and shipping
materials, foamed plastics

(P-3997)
DART CONTAINER CORP CALIFORNIA (PA)
Also Called: Dtx
150 S Maple Center, Corona (92880)
PHONE.................951 735-8115
Keith Clark, *CEO* *
Sujith Chandran, *
▲ **EMP:** 300 **EST:** 1937
SQ FT: 50,000
SALES (est): 34.69MM
SALES (corp-wide): 34.69MM **Privately Held**
SIC: 3086 Cups and plates, foamed plastics

(P-3998)
FIVE STAR FOOD CONTAINERS INC
250 Eastgate Rd, Barstow (92311-3224)
PHONE.................626 437-6219
Larry Luc, *Pr*

▲ **EMP:** 60 **EST:** 2016
SALES (est): 2.32MM **Privately Held**
SIC: 3086 Plastics foam products

(P-3999)
FOAM FACTORY INC
17515 S Santa Fe Ave, Compton
(90221-5400)
PHONE.................310 603-9808
Felipe Alcazar, *Pr*
▼ **EMP:** 45 **EST:** 1989
SQ FT: 40,000
SALES (est): 5.38MM **Privately Held**
SIC: 3086 3069 5199 5087 Insulation or
cushioning material, foamed plastics; Foam
rubber; Foams and rubber; Upholsterers'
equipment and supplies

(P-4000)
FOAM MOLDERS AND SPECIALTIES
20004 State Rd, Cerritos (90703-6456)
PHONE.................562 924-7757
EMP: 50
SALES (corp-wide): 15.38MM **Privately Held**
Web: www.foammolders.com
SIC: 3086 Packaging and shipping
materials, foamed plastics
PA: Foam Molders And Specialties
11110 Business Cir
562 924-7757

(P-4001)
FOAM MOLDERS AND SPECIALTIES (PA)
Also Called: Foam Specialties
11110 Business Cir, Cerritos (90703-5523)
PHONE.................562 924-7757
Daniel M Doke, *Pr*
Dan Doke, *
Rory Strammer, *
Roberta J Doke, *
Norman Himel, *
▲ **EMP:** 50 **EST:** 1973
SQ FT: 35,600
SALES (est): 15.38MM
SALES (corp-wide): 15.38MM **Privately Held**
Web: www.foammolders.com
SIC: 3086 3089 Plastics foam products;
Thermoformed finished plastics products,
nec

(P-4002)
FOAM-CRAFT INC
2441 Cypress Way, Fullerton (92831-5103)
PHONE.................714 459-9971
Bruce Schneider, *Pr*
Michael Blatt, *
▲ **EMP:** 165 **EST:** 1965
SQ FT: 110,000
SALES (est): 3.87MM
SALES (corp-wide): 495.02MM **Privately Held**
SIC: 3086 Plastics foam products
PA: Future Foam, Inc.
1610 Ave N
712 323-9122

(P-4003)
FOAMEX LP
Also Called: Foamex
1400 E Victoria Ave, San Bernardino
(92408-2924)
PHONE.................909 824-8981
Ron Paez, *Mgr*
EMP: 24
Web: www.fxi.com

SIC: 3086 Carpet and rug cushions, foamed
plastics
PA: Foamex L.P.
100 W Matsonford Rd # 5

(P-4004)
FUTURE FOAM INC
2451 Cypress Way, Fullerton (92831-5103)
PHONE.................714 871-2344
Randall Lake, *Mgr*
EMP: 30
SALES (corp-wide): 495.02MM **Privately Held**
Web: www.futurefoam.com
SIC: 3086 Insulation or cushioning material,
foamed plastics
PA: Future Foam, Inc.
1610 Ave N
712 323-9122

(P-4005)
FUTURE FOAM INC
Also Called: Future Foam
2441 Cypress Way, Fullerton (92831-5103)
PHONE.................714 459-9971
EMP: 165
SALES (corp-wide): 495.02MM **Privately Held**
Web: www.futurefoam.com
SIC: 3086 Plastics foam products
PA: Future Foam, Inc.
1610 Ave N
712 323-9122

(P-4006)
HUHTAMAKI INC
4209 Noakes St, Commerce (90023-4024)
PHONE.................323 269-0151
Mark Pettigrew, *Brnch Mgr*
EMP: 119
SALES (corp-wide): 4.53B **Privately Held**
Web: www.huhtamaki.com
SIC: 3086 3089 2657 2656 Cups and plates,
foamed plastics; Plastics containers, except
foam; Folding paperboard boxes; Sanitary
food containers
HQ: Huhtamaki, Inc.
9201 Packaging Dr
De Soto KS 66018
913 583-3025

(P-4007)
MARKO FOAM PRODUCTS INC
Also Called: Marko Foam Products
7441 Vincent Cir, Huntington Beach
(92648-1246)
PHONE.................949 417-3307
Robert Brown, *Brnch Mgr*
EMP: 75
SALES (corp-wide): 22.66MM **Privately Held**
Web: www.markofoam.com
SIC: 3086 2821 Packaging and shipping
materials, foamed plastics; Plastics
materials and resins
PA: Marko Foam Products, Inc
2940 Directors Row
801 972-1354

(P-4008)
NORTH AMRCN FOAM PPR CNVERTERS
11835 Wicks St, Sun Valley (91352-1906)
PHONE.................818 255-3383
Bijan Toobian, *CEO*
Haydeh Toobian, *
▲ **EMP:** 25 **EST:** 1998
SQ FT: 30,000
SALES (est): 4.87MM **Privately Held**

SIC: 3086 2672 5087 Plastics foam products
; Paper; coated and laminated, nec;
Laundry equipment and supplies

(P-4009)
PLASTIC SERVICES AND PRODUCTS
Also Called: General Plastics
12243 Branford St, Sun Valley
(91352-1010)
P.O. Box 1367 (91353-1367)
PHONE.................818 896-1101
◆ **EMP:** 3000
SIC: 3086 3674 2865 2816 Plastics foam
products; Semiconductors and related
devices; Food dyes or colors, synthetic;
Color pigments

(P-4010)
PMC GLOBAL INC (PA)
12243 Branford St, Sun Valley
(91352-1010)
PHONE.................818 896-1101
Philip Kamins, *CEO*
Gary Kamins, *
Thian Cheong, *
Steven Cohen, *
◆ **EMP:** 75 **EST:** 1996
SALES (est): 1.71B
SALES (corp-wide): 1.71B **Privately Held**
Web: www.pmcglobalinc.com
SIC: 3086 3674 2865 2816 Plastics foam
products; Semiconductors and related
devices; Food dyes or colors, synthetic;
Color pigments

(P-4011)
PMC LEADERS IN CHEMICALS INC (HQ)
12243 Branford St, Sun Valley
(91352-1010)
PHONE.................818 896-1101
Gary Kamins, *Pr*
EMP: 200 **EST:** 1992
SQ FT: 180,000
SALES (est): 10.28MM
SALES (corp-wide): 1.71B **Privately Held**
Web: www.pmcglobalinc.com
SIC: 3086 5169 Plastics foam products;
Chemicals and allied products, nec
PA: Pmc Global, Inc.
12243 Branford St
818 896-1101

(P-4012)
POMONA QUALITY FOAM LLC
1279 Philadelphia St, Pomona
(91766-5536)
PHONE.................909 628-7844
EMP: 67 **EST:** 2015
3Q FT: 70,000
SALES (est): 5.77MM **Privately Held**
Web: www.pomonaqualityfoam.com
SIC: 3086 Plastics foam products

(P-4013)
PREMIER PACKAGING LLC
10700 Business Dr Ste 100, Fontana
(92337-8201)
PHONE.................909 749-5123
EMP: 36
Web: www.prempack.com
SIC: 3086 5085 5113 Packaging and
shipping materials, foamed plastics;
Packing, industrial; Corrugated and solid
fiber boxes
PA: Premier Packaging, Llc
4301 Produce Rd

(P-4014)
QUALITY FOAM PACKAGING INC
31855 Corydon St, Lake Elsinore (92530-8501)
PHONE.....................951 245-4429
Noel A Castellon, *Pr*
Ruth Castellon, *Sec*
James Barrett, *VP*
▲ EMP: 25 EST: 1973
SQ FT: 56,000
SALES (est): 16.08MM Privately Held
Web: www.qualityfoam.com
SIC: 3086 Packaging and shipping materials, foamed plastics

(P-4015)
SEALED AIR CORPORATION
Also Called: Special Products Group
2311 Boswell Rd Ste 8, Chula Vista (91914-3512)
PHONE.....................619 421-9003
David Rader, *Mgr*
EMP: 25
SALES (corp-wide): 5.49B Publicly Held
Web: www.sealedair.com
SIC: 3086 Packaging and shipping materials, foamed plastics
PA: Sealed Air Corporation
2415 Cascade Pointe Blvd
980 221-3235

(P-4016)
SEALED AIR CORPORATION
Packaging Products Div
19440 Arenth Ave, City Of Industry (91748-1424)
PHONE.....................909 594-1791
EMP: 126
SALES (corp-wide): 5.49B Publicly Held
Web: www.sealedair.com
SIC: 3086 Packaging and shipping materials, foamed plastics
PA: Sealed Air Corporation
2415 Cascade Pointe Blvd
980 221-3235

(P-4017)
SLEEPCOMP WEST LLC
Also Called: Latexco West
10006 Santa Fe Springs Rd, Santa Fe Springs (90670-2922)
PHONE.....................562 946-3222
Roger Coffey, *Pr*
▲ EMP: 40 EST: 2002
SQ FT: 53,000
SALES (est): 2.04MM Privately Held
Web: www.novaya-comfort.com
SIC: 3086 Plastics foam products

(P-4018)
SPECIALTY ENTERPRISES CO
Also Called: Seco Industries
6858 E Acco St, Commerce (90040-1902)
PHONE.....................323 726-9721
Charles De Heras, *Pr*
▲ EMP: 100 EST: 1983
SQ FT: 60,000
SALES (est): 23.69MM Privately Held
Web: www.specialtyenterprises.com
SIC: 3086 3565 Plastics foam products; Packaging machinery
HQ: Cnh Industrial America Llc
700 State St
Racine WI 53404
630 887-2233

(P-4019)
SPORTS VENUE PADDING INC
Also Called: Artistic Coverings
14135 Artesia Blvd, Cerritos (90703-7025)
PHONE.....................562 404-9343
Troy Robinson, *CEO*
Michelle Robinson, *
Ken Robinson, *
▲ EMP: 30 EST: 2000
SALES (est): 5.1MM Privately Held
Web: www.sportsvenuepadding.com
SIC: 3086 3949 2759 7941 Padding, foamed plastics; Track and field athletic equipment; Commercial printing, nec; Sports field or stadium operator, promoting sports events

(P-4020)
STYROTEK INC
345 Road 176, Delano (93215-9471)
P.O. Box 2870 (93303-2870)
PHONE.....................661 725-4957
Martin Caratan, *Pr*
Dale Arthur, *
▲ EMP: 110 EST: 1973
SQ FT: 18,500
SALES (est): 3.9MM Privately Held
Web: www.styrotek.com
SIC: 3086 Packaging and shipping materials, foamed plastics

(P-4021)
UFP TECHNOLOGIES INC
20211 S Susana Rd, Compton (90221-5725)
PHONE.....................714 662-0277
Richard Tunila, *Brnch Mgr*
EMP: 50
SALES (corp-wide): 400.07MM Publicly Held
Web: www.ufpt.com
SIC: 3086 Packaging and shipping materials, foamed plastics
PA: Ufp Technologies, Inc.
100 Hale St
978 352-2200

(P-4022)
WALTER N COFFMAN INC
5180 Naranja St, San Diego (92114-3515)
PHONE.....................619 266-2642
Walter N Coffman, *CEO*
EMP: 70 EST: 2000
SALES (est): 5.38MM Privately Held
Web: www.wncfoam.com
SIC: 3086 Cups and plates, foamed plastics

3088 Plastics Plumbing Fixtures

(P-4023)
AQUATIC CO
Lasco Bathware
8101 E Kaiser Blvd Ste 200, Anaheim (92808-2287)
PHONE.....................714 993-1220
Scott Hartman, *Mgr*
EMP: 110
SQ FT: 5,000
SALES (corp-wide): 594.73MM Privately Held
Web: www.aquaticbath.com
SIC: 3088 1711 5211 Shower stalls, fiberglass and plastics; Plumbing, heating, air-conditioning; Bathroom fixtures, equipment and supplies
HQ: Aquatic Co.
665 Industrial Rd
Savannah TN 38372

(P-4024)
AQUATIC CO
1700 N Delilah St, Corona (92879-1893)
PHONE.....................714 993-1220
Gary Anderson, *Pr*
EMP: 340
SALES (corp-wide): 594.73MM Privately Held
Web: www.aquaticbath.com
SIC: 3088 Plastics plumbing fixtures
HQ: Aquatic Co.
665 Industrial Rd
Savannah TN 38372

(P-4025)
EUROTECH SHOWERS INC
Also Called: Eurotech Luxury Shower Doors
23552 Commerce Center Dr Ste B, Laguna Hills (92653-1514)
PHONE.....................949 716-4099
James Simmons, *Pr*
EMP: 25 EST: 2006
SQ FT: 2,800
SALES (est): 2.21MM Privately Held
Web: www.eurotechshowers.com
SIC: 3088 Shower stalls, fiberglass and plastics

(P-4026)
FIBER CARE BATHS INC
9832 Yucca Rd Ste A, Adelanto (92301-2471)
PHONE.....................760 246-0019
Harry R Kilpatrick, *CEO*
Kaye Allen, *
EMP: 275 EST: 1996
SQ FT: 6,000
SALES (est): 2.64MM Privately Held
Web: www.fibercarebaths.com
SIC: 3088 Shower stalls, fiberglass and plastics

(P-4027)
JACUZZI PRODUCTS CO (DH)
13925 City Center Dr Ste 200, Chino Hills (91709-5438)
PHONE.....................909 606-1416
Thomas D Koos, *CEO*
Philip Weeks, *
▲ EMP: 120 EST: 1959
SALES (est): 65.57MM
SALES (corp-wide): 430.34K Privately Held
Web: www.jacuzzi.com
SIC: 3088 Tubs (bath, shower, and laundry), plastics
HQ: Jacuzzi Inc.
17872 Gllette Ave Ste 300
Irvine CA 92614
909 606-7733

(P-4028)
JACUZZI PRODUCTS CO
14525 Monte Vista Ave, Chino (91710-5721)
PHONE.....................909 548-7732
Jim Barry, *Mgr*
EMP: 340
SALES (corp-wide): 430.34K Privately Held
Web: www.jacuzzi.com
SIC: 3088 5091 Tubs (bath, shower, and laundry), plastics; Fitness equipment and supplies
HQ: Jacuzzi Products Co.
13925 City Center Dr # 200
Chino Hills CA 91709
909 606-1416

(P-4029)
KING BROS ENTERPRISES LLC
29101 The Old Rd, Valencia (91355-1014)
P.O. Box 9203 (91392-9203)
PHONE.....................661 257-3262
▲ EMP: 125
SIC: 3088 5169 Plastics plumbing fixtures; Synthetic resins, rubber, and plastic materials

(P-4030)
LE ELEGANT BATH INC
Also Called: American Bath Factory
13405 Estelle St, Corona (92879-1877)
P.O. Box 127 (92878-0127)
PHONE.....................951 734-0238
Richard Wheeler, *Pr*
Debbie Wheeler, *
◆ EMP: 120 EST: 1984
SQ FT: 18,000
SALES (est): 9.33MM Privately Held
Web: www.americanbathfactory.com
SIC: 3088 Tubs (bath, shower, and laundry), plastics

(P-4031)
VANTAGE ASSOCIATES INC
Glassform
1565 Macarthur Blvd, Costa Mesa (92626-1407)
PHONE.....................800 995-8322
Paul Roy, *CEO*
EMP: 25
SALES (corp-wide): 24.86MM Privately Held
Web: www.vantageassoc.com
SIC: 3088 2519 Plastics plumbing fixtures; Fiberglass and plastic furniture
PA: Vantage Associates Inc.
1565 Macarthur Blvd
619 477-6940

(P-4032)
WATKINS MANUFACTURING CORP
1325 Hot Springs Way, Vista (92081-8360)
PHONE.....................760 598-6464
EMP: 289
SALES (corp-wide): 7.97B Publicly Held
Web: www.hotspring.com
SIC: 3088 Hot tubs, plastics or fiberglass
HQ: Watkins Manufacturing Corporation
1280 Park Center Dr
Vista CA 92081
760 598-6464

3089 Plastics Products, Nec

(P-4033)
10 DAY PARTS INC
Also Called: Westfall Technik
20109 Paseo Del Prado, Walnut (91789-2665)
PHONE.....................951 279-4810
Brian Laibach, *Dir.Opers*
EMP: 35 EST: 2018
SALES (est): 9.93MM
SALES (corp-wide): 500.49MM Privately Held
Web: www.westfalltechnik.com
SIC: 3089 Injection molding of plastics
PA: Westfall Technik, Llc
9280 S Kyrene Rd
702 659-9898

(P-4034)
A & S MOLD AND DIE CORP
9705 Eton Ave, Chatsworth (91311-4306)
PHONE.....................818 341-5393

Arno Adlhoch, *CEO*
Karen Adlhoch, *
▲ **EMP:** 90 **EST:** 1969
SQ FT: 35,000
SALES (est): 4.49MM **Privately Held**
Web: www.aandsmold.com
SIC: 3089 3544 Injection molding of plastics;
Special dies, tools, jigs, and fixtures

(P-4035)
A&A GLOBAL IMPORTS LLC
(PA)
Also Called: A&A Fulfillment Center
1801 E 41st St, Vernon (90058-1533)
PHONE...................................888 315-2453
David Aryan, *Pr*
Brian Anowns, *
James Bunting, *
Adam Wolf, *
▲ **EMP:** 59 **EST:** 2011
SALES (est): 10.72MM
SALES (corp-wide): 10.72MM **Privately
Held**
Web: www.aaglobalimports.com
SIC: 3089 3999 Injection molded finished
plastics products, nec

(P-4036)
ACORN-GENCON PLASTICS
LLC
13818 Oaks Ave, Chino (91710-7008)
PHONE...................................909 591-8461
Donald E Morris, *Managing Member*
▲ **EMP:** 68 **EST:** 2001
SQ FT: 94,000
SALES (est): 4.3MM
SALES (corp-wide): 99.75MM **Privately
Held**
Web: www.acorn-gencon.com
SIC: 3089 3088 3821 3082 Injection molded
finished plastics products, nec; Plastics
plumbing fixtures; Laboratory apparatus
and furniture; Unsupported plastics profile
shapes
HQ: Acorn Plastics, Inc.
13818 Oaks Ave
Chino CA 91710
909 591-8461

(P-4037)
ADVANCED CMPSITE PDTS
TECH INC
Also Called: Acpt
15602 Chemical Ln, Huntington Beach
(92649-1507)
PHONE...................................714 895-5544
James C Leslie Ii, *Pr*
EMP: 45 **EST:** 1904
SQ FT: 25,300
SALES (est): 8.77MM **Privately Held**
Web: www.acpt.com
SIC: 3089 8748 Hardware, plastics;
Business consulting, nec

(P-4038)
ADVANCED MATERIALS INC
(HQ)
20211 S Susana Rd, Compton
(90221-5725)
PHONE...................................310 537-5444
Steve Scott, *Pr*
◆ **EMP:** 29 **EST:** 1959
SQ FT: 56,000
SALES (est): 5.09MM
SALES (corp-wide): 400.07MM **Publicly
Held**
SIC: 3089 Injection molding of plastics
PA: Ufp Technologies, Inc.
100 Hale St
978 352-2200

(P-4039)
AKRA PLASTIC PRODUCTS INC
1504 E Cedar St, Ontario (91761-5761)
PHONE...................................909 930-1999
Alexander Semeczko, *CEO*
R Wayne Callaway, *
Bentley Callaway, *
Alex Semeczko, *
EMP: 37 **EST:** 1972
SQ FT: 36,000
SALES (est): 6.62MM **Privately Held**
Web: www.akraplastics.com
SIC: 3089 2821 2542 5063 Plastics
processing; Plastics materials and resins;
Office and store showcases and display
fixtures; Lighting fixtures, commercial and
industrial

(P-4040)
ALLTEC INTEGRATED MFG INC
Also Called: New Age Enclosures
2240 S Thornburg St, Santa Maria
(93455-1248)
PHONE...................................805 595-3500
Randall Dennis, *CEO*
◆ **EMP:** 40 **EST:** 2002
SQ FT: 13,500
SALES (est): 9.89MM **Privately Held**
Web: www.alltecmfg.com
SIC: 3089 2821 Injection molding of plastics;
Plastics materials and resins

(P-4041)
ALTIUM HOLDINGS LLC
Also Called: California Plastics
12165 Madera Way, Riverside
(92503-4849)
PHONE...................................951 340-9390
Steve Thompson, *Mgr*
EMP: 1104
SALES (corp-wide): 77.81MM **Privately
Held**
Web: www.altiumpkg.com
SIC: 3089 Plastics containers, except foam
PA: Altium Holdings Llc
2500 Wndy Rdge Pkwy Ste 1
678 742-4600

(P-4042)
ALTIUM PACKAGING
Also Called: ALTIUM PACKAGING
4516 Azusa Canyon Rd, Irwindale
(91706-2742)
PHONE...................................626 856-2100
EMP: 60
SALES (corp-wide): 15.9B **Publicly Held**
Web: www.altiumpkg.com
SIC: 3089 Plastics containers, except foam
HQ: Altium Packaging Llc
2500 Windy Ridge Pkwy Se # 1400
Atlanta GA 30339
678 742-4600

(P-4043)
ALTIUM PACKAGING LLC
Also Called: Reid Plastics Customer Svcs
1070 Samuelson St, City Of Industry
(91748-1219)
PHONE...................................888 425-7343
Fred Braham, *Prin*
EMP: 70
SALES (corp-wide): 15.9B **Publicly Held**
Web: www.altiumpkg.com
SIC: 3089 3085 Plastics containers, except
foam; Plastics bottles
HQ: Altium Packaging Llc
2500 Windy Ridge Pkwy Se # 1400
Atlanta GA 30339
678 742-4600

(P-4044)
ALTIUM PACKAGING LP
Envision Plastics
14312 Central Ave, Chino (91710-5752)
PHONE...................................909 590-7334
EMP: 50
SALES (corp-wide): 15.9B **Publicly Held**
Web: www.altiumpkg.com
SIC: 3089 Plastics containers, except foam
HQ: Altium Packaging Lp
3101 Towercreek Pkwy
Atlanta GA 30339
678 742-4600

(P-4045)
AMA PLASTICS
1100 Citrus St, Riverside (92507-1731)
PHONE...................................951 734-5600
Mark Atchinson, *CEO*
Gary Atchinson, *
◆ **EMP:** 393 **EST:** 1971
SQ FT: 92,000
SALES (est): 49.55MM
SALES (corp-wide): 500.49MM **Privately
Held**
Web: www.westfalltechnik.com
SIC: 3089 3544 Molding primary plastics;
Forms (molds), for foundry and plastics
working machinery
PA: Westfall Technik, Llc
9280 S Kyrene Rd
702 659-9898

(P-4046)
AMERICAN INTEGRITY CORP
13510 Central Rd, Apple Valley
(92308-6561)
P.O. Box 999 (92307-0017)
PHONE...................................760 247-1082
EMP: 50
Web: www.americaninintegrity.com
SIC: 3089 5211 Window frames and sash,
plastics; Lumber and other building
materials

(P-4047)
AMERICAN PLASTIC
PRODUCTS INC
9243 Glenoaks Blvd, Sun Valley
(91352-2614)
PHONE...................................818 504-1073
Roupen Yegavian, *Pr*
Varosh Petrosian, *
▲ **EMP:** 75 **EST:** 1991
SQ FT: 35,000
SALES (est): 1.32MM **Privately Held**
Web:
www.americanplacticproductcinc.com
SIC: 3089 Injection molding of plastics

(P-4048)
AMS PLASTICS INC
Also Called: Westfall Technik
1100 Citrus St, Riverside (92507-1731)
PHONE...................................951 734-5600
Jim Henke, *Brnch Mgr*
EMP: 393
Web: www.westfalltechnik.com
SIC: 3089 Molding primary plastics
PA: Ams Plastics, Inc.
20109 Paseo Del Prado

(P-4049)
AMS PLASTICS INC (PA)
Also Called: Westfall Technik
20109 Paseo Del Prado, Walnut
(91789-2665)
PHONE...................................619 713-2000
Adolfo Arellano, *CEO*
Diane L Plein, *Sec*

▲ **EMP:** 43 **EST:** 1983
SALES (est): 10.67MM **Privately Held**
Web: www.westfalltechnik.com
SIC: 3089 Injection molding of plastics

(P-4050)
ANAHEIM CUSTOM
EXTRUDERS INC
Also Called: Ace
1360 N Mccan St, Anaheim (92806-1316)
PHONE...................................714 693-8508
TOLL FREE: 800
William A Czapar, *Ch Bd*
Chrintina Smith, *
EMP: 48 **EST:** 1977
SALES (est): 7.46MM **Privately Held**
Web: www.acextrusions.com
SIC: 3089 3082 Extruded finished plastics
products, nec; Unsupported plastics profile
shapes

(P-4051)
APON INDUSTRIES CORP
10005 Marconi Dr Ste 2, San Diego
(92154-5208)
▲ **EMP:** 200 **EST:** 1998
SALES (est): 2.05MM **Privately Held**
Web: www.aponindustries.com
SIC: 3089 Injection molding of plastics

(P-4052)
ARGEE MFG CO SAN DIEGO INC
Also Called: Argee
9550 Pathway St, Santee (92071-4169)
PHONE...................................619 449-5050
Robert Goldman, *Pr*
Ruth Goldman, *
▲ **EMP:** 75 **EST:** 1961
SQ FT: 65,000
SALES (est): 5.07MM **Privately Held**
Web: www.argeecorp.com
SIC: 3089 Plastics hardware and building
products

(P-4053)
ARLON LLC
Arlon Adhesives-Films Division
2811 S Harbor Blvd, Santa Ana
(92704-5805)
P.O. Box 5260 (92704-0260)
PHONE...................................714 540-2811
Elmer Pruim, *Pr*
EMP: 150
SQ FT: 124,478
SALES (corp-wide): 908.4MM **Publicly
Held**
Web: www.arlonecp.com
SIC: 3009 3001 2072 Plastics hardware and
building products; Unsupported plastics film
and sheet; Paper, coated and laminated,
nec
HQ: Arlon Llc
1100 Governor Lea Rd
Bear DE 19701

(P-4054)
ARMORCAST PRODUCTS
COMPANY INC
500 S Dupont Ave, Ontario (91761-1508)
PHONE...................................909 390-1365
Paul Boghossian, *Brnch Mgr*
EMP: 40
SALES (corp-wide): 5.37B **Publicly Held**
Web: www.armorcastprod.com
SIC: 3089 5092 Plastics processing; Toys,
nec
HQ: Armorcast Products Company, Inc.
9140 Lurline Ave
Chatsworth CA 91311
818 982-3600

PRODUCTS & SVCS

(P-4055)
ARTHURMADE PLASTICS INC
Also Called: Kirk Containers
2131 Garfield Ave, City Of Commerce
(90040-1805)
PHONE..................................323 721-7325
Kirk Marounian, *Pr*
Silva Marounian, *
Arthur Marounian, *
EMP: 75 **EST:** 1984
SQ FT: 20,000
SALES (est): 1.4MM **Privately Held**
SIC: 3089 Injection molding of plastics

(P-4056)
AXIUM PACKAGING LLC
5701 Clark St, Ontario (91761-3640)
PHONE..................................909 969-0766
Kulwinder Singh, *Mgr*
EMP: 578
Web: www.axiumpackaging.com
SIC: 3089 Plastics containers, except foam
PA: Axium Packaging Llc
   9005 Smiths Mill Rd

(P-4057)
B & S PLASTICS INC
Also Called: Waterway Plastics
2200 Sturgis Rd, Oxnard (93030-8978)
PHONE..................................805 981-0262
Bill Spears, *CEO*
Sandy Spears, *
◆ **EMP:** 105 **EST:** 1973
SQ FT: 240,000
SALES (est): 43.56MM **Privately Held**
Web: www.waterwayplastics.com
SIC: 3089 Injection molding of plastics

(P-4058)
B AND P PLASTICS INC
Also Called: Advance Plastics
225 W 30th St, National City (91950-7203)
PHONE..................................619 477-1893
Bruce Browne, *Pr*
Patricia Browne, *
▲ **EMP:** 35 **EST:** 1974
SQ FT: 10,000
SALES (est): 12.34MM **Privately Held**
Web: www.advanceplastics.com
SIC: 3089 3061 Molding primary plastics;
   Mechanical rubber goods

(P-4059)
BACE MANUFACTURING INC
(HQ)
Also Called: Spm
3125 E Coronado St, Anaheim
(92806-1915)
PHONE..................................714 630-6002
Richard R Harris, *Pr*
Shannon White, *
EMP: 700 **EST:** 1989
SQ FT: 200,000
SALES (est): 11.78MM
SALES (corp-wide): 28.39MM **Privately Held**
SIC: 3089 Injection molding of plastics
PA: Medplast Group, Inc.
   7865 Northcourt Rd # 100
   480 553-6400

(P-4060)
BANDLOCK CORPORATION
1734 S Vineyard Ave, Ontario
(91761-7746)
PHONE..................................909 947-7500
EMP: 68

SIC: 3089 3492 3082 Extruded finished
   plastics products, nec; Hose and tube
   couplings, hydraulic/pneumatic;
   Unsupported plastics profile shapes

(P-4061)
BARBER-WEBB COMPANY INC
(PA)
12912 Lakeland Rd, Santa Fe Springs
(90670-4517)
PHONE..................................541 488-4821
TOLL FREE: 800
Donald B Barber Junior, *Pr*
Brian Barber, *
James Barber, *
Wr Greenbecker, *
▼ **EMP:** 30 **EST:** 1945
SALES (est): 4.55MM
SALES (corp-wide): 4.55MM **Privately Held**
Web: www.barber-webb.com
SIC: 3089 Plastics processing

(P-4062)
BARNES PLASTICS INC
Also Called: Barnes Plastics
18903 Anelo Ave, Gardena (90248-4598)
PHONE..................................310 329-6301
Charles Walker, *CEO*
Scott Piepmeyer, *
▲ **EMP:** 30 **EST:** 1930
SQ FT: 30,000
SALES (est): 4.46MM **Privately Held**
Web: www.barnesplastics.com
SIC: 3089 Injection molding of plastics

(P-4063)
BEEMAK PLASTICS LLC
Also Called: Beemak-Idl Display Products
1515 S Harris Ct, Anaheim (92806-5932)
PHONE..................................800 421-4393
John Davis, *Managing Member*
Fred Garcy, *
Winfred Ross, *
▲ **EMP:** 100 **EST:** 1951
SALES (est): 25MM
SALES (corp-wide): 475.79MM **Privately Held**
Web: www.beemak.com
SIC: 3089 Injection molding of plastics
HQ: Deflecto, Llc
   7035 E 86th St
   Indianapolis IN 46250
   317 849-9555

(P-4064)
BENT MANUFACTURING CO INC
Also Called: Bent Manufacturing Company
17311 Nichols Ln, Huntington Beach
(92647-5721)
PHONE..................................714 842-0600
EMP: 85
Web: www.bentmfg.com
SIC: 3089 3069 Blow molded finished
   plastics products, nec; Hard rubber and
   molded rubber products

(P-4065)
BERICAP LLC
Also Called: Bericap
1671 Champagne Ave Ste B, Ontario
(91761-3650)
PHONE..................................909 390-5518
Steve Buckley, *Pr*
Steve Buckley, *Managing Member*
David Andison, *
▲ **EMP:** 67 **EST:** 2001
SALES (est): 4.98MM
SALES (corp-wide): 2.67MM **Privately Held**

Web: www.bericap.com
SIC: 3089 Injection molding of plastics
HQ: Bericap Holding Gmbh
   Kirchstr. 5
   Budenheim RP 55257
   613929020

(P-4066)
BERRY GLOBAL INC
14000 Monte Vista Ave, Chino
(91710-5537)
PHONE..................................909 465-9055
Salama Elsayed, *Brnch Mgr*
EMP: 200
Web: www.berryglobal.com
SIC: 3089 3081 Bottle caps, molded plastics;
   Unsupported plastics film and sheet
HQ: Berry Global, Inc.
   101 Oakley St
   Evansville IN 47710

(P-4067)
BERRY GLOBAL INC
4875 E Hunter Ave, Anaheim (92807-2005)
PHONE..................................714 777-5200
Don Parodi, *Mgr*
EMP: 57
Web: www.berryglobal.com
SIC: 3089 3081 Bottle caps, molded plastics;
   Unsupported plastics film and sheet
HQ: Berry Global, Inc.
   101 Oakley St
   Evansville IN 47710

(P-4068)
BH-TECH INC
5425 Oberlin Dr Ste 207, San Diego
(92121-1843)
PHONE..................................858 694-0900
Seung Hoon Han, *CEO*
Woo Hyuk Choi, *CFO*
EMP: 700 **EST:** 2018
SALES (est): 6.47MM **Privately Held**
SIC: 3089 Injection molding of plastics

(P-4069)
BLOW MOLDED PRODUCTS INC
Also Called: Bmp
4720 Felspar St, Riverside (92509-3068)
PHONE..................................951 360-6055
EMP: 40
Web: www.blowmoldedproducts.com
SIC: 3089 Injection molding of plastics

(P-4070)
BM EXTRUSION INC
1575 Omaha Ct, Riverside (92507-2444)
PHONE..................................951 782-9020
Bacilio Mejia, *Pr*
EMP: 24 **EST:** 2006
SALES (est): 1.75MM **Privately Held**
SIC: 3089 Plastics containers, except foam

(P-4071)
BOMATIC INC (DH)
Also Called: Bmi
43225 Business Park Dr, Temecula
(92590-3648)
PHONE..................................909 947-3900
Kjeld R Hestehave, *Pr*
Borge Hestehave, *
Mary Ann, *
Kirk Franks, *
Kresten Hestehave, *
▲ **EMP:** 40 **EST:** 1969
SQ FT: 35,000
SALES (est): 21.72MM **Privately Held**
Web: www.bomatic.com
SIC: 3089 Plastics containers, except foam
HQ: Universal Packaging West, Inc.
   43225 Business Park Dr

Temecula CA 92590
909 947-3900

(P-4072)
BOMATIC INC
2181 E Francis St, Ontario (91761-7723)
PHONE..................................909 947-3900
Back Melon, *Mgr*
EMP: 60
Web: www.bomatic.com
SIC: 3089 Plastics containers, except foam
HQ: Bomatic, Inc.
   43225 Business Park Dr
   Temecula CA 92590
   909 947-3900

(P-4073)
BOTTLEMATE INC (PA)
2095 Leo Ave, Commerce (90040-1626)
PHONE..................................323 887-9009
Kai-win Chuang, *CEO*
Anderson Chuang, *
Mei-li Chang, *Sec*
▲ **EMP:** 23 **EST:** 1982
SQ FT: 25,000
SALES (est): 2.7MM **Privately Held**
Web: www.bottlemate.com
SIC: 3089 5162 Blow molded finished
   plastics products, nec; Plastics products,
   nec

(P-4074)
BRADLEY MANUFACTURING CO
INC
Also Called: Bradley's Plastic Bag Co
9368 Stewart And Gray Rd, Downey
(90241-5316)
PHONE..................................562 923-5556
Keith Smith, *Pr*
Richard Lane, *
EMP: 28 **EST:** 1933
SALES (est): 2.36MM **Privately Held**
Web: www.bradleypackaging.com
SIC: 3089 3069 3083 2673 Plastics
   processing; Tubing, rubber; Laminated
   plastics plate and sheet; Bags: plastic,
   laminated, and coated

(P-4075)
C & G PLASTICS
Also Called: C & G Mercury Plastics
12729 Foothill Blvd, Sylmar (91342-5314)
PHONE..................................818 837-3773
Greg Leighton, *Pr*
▲ **EMP:** 25 **EST:** 1963
SQ FT: 6,000
SALES (est): 4.5MM **Privately Held**
Web: www.cgplastics.net
SIC: 3089 Injection molding of plastics

(P-4076)
C & R MOLDS INC
2737 Palma Dr, Ventura (93003-7651)
P.O. Box 5644 (93005-0644)
PHONE..................................805 658-7098
Randall Ohnemus, *Pr*
Marla Ohnemus, *
▲ **EMP:** 24 **EST:** 1984
SQ FT: 12,000
SALES (est): 5.11MM **Privately Held**
Web: www.crmolds.com
SIC: 3089 3544 Injection molding of plastics;
   Special dies, tools, jigs, and fixtures

(P-4077)
C-PAK INDUSTRIES INC
4925 Hallmark Pkwy, San Bernardino
(92407-1870)
PHONE..................................909 880-6017
Arch Young, *Pr*

▲ = Import ▼ = Export
◆ = Import/Export

EMP: 28 EST: 1999
SQ FT: 25,000
SALES (est): 5.01MM **Privately Held**
Web: www.c-pak.net
SIC: **3089** Injection molding of plastics

(P-4078)
CAMBRO MANUFACTURING COMPANY
7601 Clay Ave, Huntington Beach (92648-2219)
PHONE...........................714 848-1555
David Capestro, *Mgr*
EMP: 244
SALES (corp-wide): 307.89MM **Privately Held**
Web: www.cambro.com
SIC: **3089** Plastics containers, except foam
PA: Cambro Manufacturing Company Inc
5801 Skylab Rd
714 848-1555

(P-4079)
CAMBRO MANUFACTURING COMPANY
Also Called: Cambro Manufacturing
5801 Skylab Rd, Huntington Beach (92647-2051)
PHONE...........................714 848-1555
Argyle Campbell, *Pr*
EMP: 69
SALES (corp-wide): 307.89MM **Privately Held**
Web: www.cambro.com
SIC: **3089** Trays, plastics
PA: Cambro Manufacturing Company Inc
5801 Skylab Rd
714 848-1555

(P-4080)
CAMBRO MANUFACTURING COMPANY (PA)
Also Called: Cambro
5801 Skylab Rd, Huntington Beach (92647-2051)
P.O. Box 2000 (92647-2000)
PHONE...........................714 848-1555
Argyle Campbell, *CEO*
◆ **EMP:** 500 **EST:** 1951
SQ FT: 300,000
SALES (est): 307.89MM
SALES (corp-wide): 307.89MM **Privately Held**
Web: www.cambro.com
SIC: **3089** Trays, plastics

(P-4081)
CANYON PLASTICS LLC
28455 Livingston Ave, Valencia (91355-4173)
PHONE...........................800 350-6325
TOLL FREE: 800
Karshan A Gajera, *CEO*
▲ **EMP:** 78 **EST:** 1982
SQ FT: 110,950
SALES (est): 17.37MM **Privately Held**
Web: www.canyonplastics.com
SIC: **3089 3544** Plastics containers, except foam; Forms (molds), for foundry and plastics working machinery

(P-4082)
CAPLUGS INC
Also Called: Caplugs
18704 S Ferris Pl, Rancho Dominguez (90220-6400)
PHONE...........................310 537-2300
Fred Karam, *Brnch Mgr*
EMP: 60

SALES (corp-wide): 2.26B **Privately Held**
Web: www.caplugs.com
SIC: **3089** Injection molding of plastics
HQ: Caplugs, Inc.
2150 Elmwood Ave
Buffalo NY 14207
716 876-9855

(P-4083)
CARR MANAGEMENT INC
22324 Temescal Canyon Rd, Corona (92883-4622)
PHONE...........................951 277-4800
Nick Rende, *Brnch Mgr*
EMP: 70
Web: www.carrmanagement.com
SIC: **3089** Plastics containers, except foam
PA: Carr Management, Inc.
1 Tara Blvd Ste 303

(P-4084)
CARSON INDUSTRIES LLC
Also Called: Oldcastle Prcast Enclsure Slto
2434 Rubidoux Blvd, Riverside (92509-2144)
P.O. Box 99697 (60696-7497)
PHONE...........................951 788-9720
◆ **EMP:** 3000
SIC: **3089** Boxes, plastics

(P-4085)
CCI INDUSTRIES INC (PA)
Also Called: Cool Curtain CCI
350 Fischer Ave Ste A, Costa Mesa (92626-4508)
PHONE...........................714 662-3879
Michael Robinson, *Pr*
▲ **EMP:** 27 **EST:** 1976
SQ FT: 15,000
SALES (est): 2.75MM
SALES (corp-wide): 2.75MM **Privately Held**
Web: www.coolcurtain.com
SIC: **3089 3564 3496** Doors, folding: plastics or plastics coated fabric; Aircurtains (blower); Grilles and grillework, woven wire

(P-4086)
CCL TUBE INC (HQ)
2250 E 220th St, Carson (90810-1638)
PHONE...........................310 635-4444
Andreas Iseli, *CEO*
◆ **EMP:** 98 **EST:** 1984
SQ FT: 300,000
SALES (est): 44.41MM
SALES (corp-wide): 4.84B **Privately Held**
Web: www.ccltube.com
SIC: **3089** Injection molded finished plastics products, nec
PA: Ccl Industries Inc.
111 Gordon Baker Rd Suite 801
416 756-8500

(P-4087)
CERTIFIED THERMOPLASTICS INC
Also Called: Certified Thermoplastics LLC
26381 Ferry Ct, Santa Clarita (91350-2998)
PHONE...........................661 222-3006
Robert Duncan, *Pr*
▲ **EMP:** 35 **EST:** 1978
SQ FT: 30,000
SALES (est): 7.56MM
SALES (corp-wide): 756.99MM **Publicly Held**
Web: www.ctplastics.com
SIC: **3089** Injection molding of plastics
HQ: Ducommun Labarge Technologies, Inc.
1601 E Broadway Rd
Phoenix AZ 85040
480 998-0733

(P-4088)
CHARMAINE PLASTICS INC
Also Called: Craftech
2941 E La Jolla St, Anaheim (92806-1306)
PHONE...........................714 630-8117
John Butler, *Pr*
Alfredo Bonetto, *
John Ayers, *
Douglas Barker, *Product Vice President*
Steven Lawson, *
▲ **EMP:** 88 **EST:** 1979
SQ FT: 35,000
SALES (est): 20.54MM
SALES (corp-wide): 43.66MM **Privately Held**
Web: www.craftechcorp.com
SIC: **3089 3559** Injection molding of plastics; Plastics working machinery
PA: Sage Park Acq. Ct Llc
725 Cool Sprng Blvd Ste 2
615 637-8030

(P-4089)
CHUBBY GORILLA INC (PA)
4320 N Harbor Blvd, Fullerton (92835-1091)
PHONE...........................844 365-5218
Ibraheem Hamsa Aboabdo, *CEO*
Eyad Aboabdo, *
EMP: 27 **EST:** 2015
SALES (est): 7.49MM
SALES (corp-wide): 7.49MM **Privately Held**
Web: www.chubbygorilla.com
SIC: **3089** Closures, plastics

(P-4090)
CLEAR-AD INC
Also Called: Brochure Holders 4u
2410 W 3rd St, Santa Ana (92703-3519)
PHONE...........................866 627-9718
Juan Diaz, *CEO*
John Diaz, *Prin*
Bruce Kelly, *
EMP: 30 **EST:** 1972
SQ FT: 17,006
SALES (est): 4.71MM **Privately Held**
Web: www.brochureholders4u.com
SIC: **3089 3544 3993 3061** Injection molded finished plastics products, nec; Forms (molds), for foundry and plastics working machinery; Displays and cutouts, window and lobby; Medical and surgical rubber tubing (extruded and lathe-cut)

(P-4091)
CODAN US CORPORATION
Also Called: Codan US
3501 W Sunflower Ave, Santa Ana (92704-6923)
PHONE...........................714 545-2111
Mike Thompson, *Pr*
▲ **EMP:** 100 **EST:** 1971
SALES (est): 21.28MM
SALES (corp-wide): 64.2K **Privately Held**
Web: www.codanusa.com
SIC: **3089** Molding primary plastics
PA: Codan Holding Gmbh & Co. Kg
Stig Husted-Andersen Str. 11
43635111

(P-4092)
COOL-PAK LLC
Also Called: Bunzl Agrclture Group Chstrfel
401 N Rice Ave, Oxnard (93030-7936)
PHONE...........................805 981-2434
Nick Weber, *
Jim Borchard, *
Derek Goodin, *
Patrick Larmon, *

▲ **EMP:** 85 **EST:** 2001
SQ FT: 124,000
SALES (est): 14.46MM
SALES (corp-wide): 14.7B **Privately Held**
Web: www.cool-pak.com
SIC: **3089** Plastics containers, except foam
HQ: Bunzl Distribution Usa, Llc
1 Cityplace Dr Ste 200
Saint Louis MO 63141

(P-4093)
CORNUCOPIA TOOL & PLASTICS INC
448 Sherwood Rd, Paso Robles (93446-3554)
P.O. Box 1915 (93447-1915)
PHONE...........................805 238-7660
Larry Horn, *Pr*
Art Horn, *
EMP: 47 **EST:** 1969
SQ FT: 20,000
SALES (est): 9.21MM **Privately Held**
Web: www.cornucopiaplastics.com
SIC: **3089 3544** Injection molding of plastics; Industrial molds

(P-4094)
COUNTY PLASTICS CORP
Also Called: Chemtainer Industries
135 E Stanley St, Compton (90220-5604)
PHONE...........................310 635-5400
George Karathanas, *Mgr*
EMP: 23
SALES (corp-wide): 21.53MM **Privately Held**
Web: www.chemtainer.com
SIC: **3089 2821** Plastics and fiberglass tanks; Plastics materials and resins
PA: County Plastics Corp.
361 Neptune Ave
631 422-8300

(P-4095)
CPD INDUSTRIES
Also Called: Custom Packaging Design
4665 State St, Montclair (91763-6130)
PHONE...........................909 465-5596
Carlos Hurtado, *Pr*
Sergio Briceno, *
EMP: 29 **EST:** 1985
SQ FT: 22,000
SALES (est): 4.49MM **Privately Held**
Web: www.cpdindustries.com
SIC: **3089** Plastics containers, except foam

(P-4096)
CREU LLC
12750 Daltic Ct, Rancho Cucamonga (91739-8957)
PHONE...........................909 483-4888
Anthony Quezada, *CEO*
EMP: 25 **EST:** 2014
SALES (est): 2.1MM **Privately Held**
SIC: **3089 5063** Automotive parts, plastic; Lighting fixtures

(P-4097)
DACHA ENTERPRISES INC
1915 Elise Cir, Corona (92879-1882)
PHONE...........................951 273-7777
EMP: 77
SALES (corp-wide): 36.4MM **Privately Held**
Web: www.accentplastics.com
SIC: **3089** Injection molding of plastics
HQ: Dacha Enterprises, Inc.
13948 Mountain Ave
Chino CA 91710
951 273-7777

(P-4098)

DAMAR PLASTICS MANUFACTURING INC

Also Called: Damar Plastics
1035 Pioneer Way Ste 160, El Cajon
(92020-1978)
PHONE..............................619 283-2300
EMP: 45 **EST:** 2013
SALES (est): 5.01MM **Privately Held**
Web: www.damarplastics.com
SIC: 3089 Plastics processing

(P-4099)

DELAMO MANUFACTURING INC

7171 Telegraph Rd, Montebello
(90640-6511)
PHONE..............................323 936-3566
Fred Morad, *CEO*
EMP: 80 **EST:** 2008
SQ FT: 120,000
SALES (est): 2.86MM **Privately Held**
Web: www.delamo-mfg.com
SIC: 3089 Plastics kitchenware, tableware, and houseware

(P-4100)

DELFIN DESIGN & MFG INC

15672 Producer Ln, Huntington Beach
(92649-1310)
PHONE..............................949 888-4644
John M Rief, *Pr*
Paul Iverson, *
Rita Williams, *
▲ **EMP:** 28 **EST:** 1991
SALES (est): 1.76MM
SALES (corp-wide): 19.62MM **Privately Held**
Web: www.delfinfs.com
SIC: 3089 3083 Thermoformed finished plastics products, nec; Plastics finished products, laminated
HQ: Steelite International U.S.A. Inc.
154 Keystone Dr
New Castle PA 16105

(P-4101)

DESIGN WEST TECHNOLOGIES INC

2701 Dow Ave, Tustin (92780-7209)
PHONE..............................714 731-0201
Ryan Hur, *Pr*
▲ **EMP:** 65 **EST:** 1994
SQ FT: 60,000
SALES (est): 16.26MM **Privately Held**
Web: www.dwtusa.com
SIC: 3089 8711 Injection molded finished plastics products, nec; Electrical or electronic engineering

(P-4102)

DIAL INDUSTRIES INC

Also Called: All-Power Plastcs Div Dial
3616 Noakes St, Los Angeles
(90023-3200)
PHONE..............................323 263-6878
Richard Oxford, *Pr*
EMP: 100
SALES (corp-wide): 10.12MM **Privately Held**
Web: www.dialind.com
SIC: 3089 3354 Plastics kitchenware, tableware, and houseware; Aluminum extruded products
PA: Dial Industries, Inc.
3628 Noakes St
323 263-6878

(P-4103)

DIAL INDUSTRIES INC (PA)

3628 Noakes St, Los Angeles
(90023-3222)
PHONE..............................323 263-6878
▲ **EMP:** 80 **EST:** 1968
SALES (est): 4.05MM
SALES (corp-wide): 4.05MM **Privately Held**
Web: www.dialind.com
SIC: 3089 Plastics kitchenware, tableware, and houseware

(P-4104)

DISPENSING DYNAMICS INTL INC (PA)

Also Called: Perrin Craft
1940 Diamond St, San Marcos
(92078-5120)
PHONE..............................626 961-3691
Dean Debuhr, *Ch*
Larry Maccormack, *
Scott Strachan, *
Michael Severyn, *
Rocky Wilske, *
◆ **EMP:** 99 **EST:** 1932
SALES (est): 23.51MM
SALES (corp-wide): 23.51MM **Privately Held**
Web: www.dispensingdynamics.com
SIC: 3089 3993 Injection molding of plastics; Signs and advertising specialties

(P-4105)

DISTINCTIVE PLASTICS INC

1385 Decision St, Vista (92081-8523)
PHONE..............................760 599-9100
Timothy Curnutt, *Pr*
Violeta Curnutt, *
▲ **EMP:** 62 **EST:** 1982
SQ FT: 44,500
SALES (est): 8.68MM **Privately Held**
Web: www.dpi-tech.com
SIC: 3089 3312 Injection molding of plastics; Tool and die steel

(P-4106)

DIVERSIFIED PLASTICS INC

Also Called: Pacific Plas Injection Molding
1333 Keystone Way, Vista (92081-8311)
PHONE..............................760 598-5333
Rob Gilman, *Genl Mgr*
EMP: 30
SALES (corp-wide): 11.23MM **Privately Held**
Web: www.divplast.com
SIC: 3089 3544 Injection molding of plastics; Industrial molds
PA: Diversified Plastics, Inc.
8617 Xylon Ct
763 424-2525

(P-4107)

DOREL JUVENILE GROUP INC

9950 Calabash Ave, Fontana (92335-5210)
PHONE..............................909 428-0295
Carrisa John, *Prin*
EMP: 122
SALES (corp-wide): 1.39B **Privately Held**
Web: na.doreljuvenile.com
SIC: 3089 Plastics kitchenware, tableware, and houseware
HQ: Dorel Juvenile Group, Inc.
2525 State St
Columbus IN 47201
800 457-5276

(P-4108)

DOREL JUVENILE GROUP INC

Also Called: Cosco Home & Office Products
5400 Shea Center Dr, Ontario
(91761-7892)
PHONE..............................909 390-5705
Rick Mc Cook, *Mgr*
EMP: 140
SALES (corp-wide): 1.39B **Privately Held**
Web: www.dorel.com
SIC: 3089 Plastics kitchenware, tableware, and houseware
HQ: Dorel Juvenile Group, Inc.
2525 State St
Columbus IN 47201
800 457-5276

(P-4109)

DPP 2020 INC (DH)

533 E Third St, Beaumont (92223-2715)
P.O. Box 2097 (92223-0997)
PHONE..............................951 845-3161
Kevin Rost, *CEO*
Monica Rost, *
◆ **EMP:** 31 **EST:** 1974
SQ FT: 150,000
SALES (est): 19.81MM **Privately Held**
Web: www.duraplastics.com
SIC: 3089 Fittings for pipe, plastics
HQ: Tigre Sa Participacoes
Rua Xavantes 54
Joinvile SC 89203

(P-4110)

EDCO PLASTICS INC

2110 E Winston Rd, Anaheim (92806-5534)
PHONE..............................714 772-1986
Edward A Contreras, *Pr*
Maria Contreras, *
▲ **EMP:** 49 **EST:** 1984
SQ FT: 25,000
SALES (est): 4.93MM **Privately Held**
Web: www.edcoplastics.com
SIC: 3089 Molding primary plastics

(P-4111)

EDRIS PLASTICS MFG INC

4560 Pacific Blvd, Vernon (90058-2208)
PHONE..............................323 581-7000
Hovanes Hovik Issagholian, *CEO*
▲ **EMP:** 26 **EST:** 1991
SQ FT: 27,000
SALES (est): 4.82MM **Privately Held**
Web: www.edrisplastics.com
SIC: 3089 Injection molding of plastics

(P-4112)

ENGINEERING MODEL ASSOC INC (PA)

Also Called: Ema
1020 Wallace Way, City Of Industry
(91748-1027)
PHONE..............................626 912-7011
John Jay Wanderman, *Pr*
John Jay Wanderman, *Pr*
Leon Katz, *
EMP: 25 **EST:** 1955
SQ FT: 28,000
SALES (est): 9.43MM
SALES (corp-wide): 9.43MM **Privately Held**
SIC: 3089 5162 Plastics processing; Plastics products, nec

(P-4113)

ENVISION PLASTICS INDUSTRIES LLC

Also Called: Envision Plastics
14312 Central Ave, Chino (91710-5752)
PHONE..............................909 590-7334
EMP: 50
SIC: 3089 Lamp bases and shades, plastics

(P-4114)

EXPANDED RUBBER & PLASTICS CORP

Also Called: Erp
19200 S Laurel Park Rd, Rancho
Dominguez (90220-6008)
PHONE..............................310 324-6692
EMP: 37 **EST:** 1957
SALES (est): 5.91MM **Privately Held**
Web: www.expandedrubber.com
SIC: 3089 3086 5088 Molding primary plastics; Plastics foam products; Aircraft and space vehicle supplies and parts

(P-4115)

EXTRUMED INC (DH)

Also Called: Vesta
547 Trm Cir, Corona (92879-1768)
PHONE..............................951 547-7400
Phil Estes, *Pr*
Chris Guglielmi, *
Eric R Schnur, *
EMP: 28 **EST:** 1990
SQ FT: 53,000
SALES (est): 19.27MM
SALES (corp-wide): 364.48B **Publicly Held**
SIC: 3089 Injection molding of plastics
HQ: Vesta Intermediate Funding, Inc.
9900 S 57th St
Franklin WI 53132
414 423-0550

(P-4116)

FISCHER MOLD INCORPORATED

393 Meyer Cir, Corona (92879-1078)
PHONE..............................951 279-1140
Robert Fischer, *Pr*
Eleanor Fischer, *
▲ **EMP:** 60 **EST:** 1969
SQ FT: 32,000
SALES (est): 9.19MM **Privately Held**
Web: www.fischermold.com
SIC: 3089 3544 Injection molding of plastics; Special dies, tools, jigs, and fixtures

(P-4117)

FIT-LINE INC

Also Called: Fit-Line Global
2901 S Tech Center Dr, Santa Ana
(92705-5657)
PHONE..............................714 549-9091
Ronni Levinson, *CEO*
▼ **EMP:** 50 **EST:** 1993
SQ FT: 4,500
SALES (est): 5.53MM **Privately Held**
Web: www.fit-lineglobal.com
SIC: 3089 Fittings for pipe, plastics

(P-4118)

FLUIDMASTER INC (PA)

30800 Rancho Viejo Rd, San Juan
Capistrano (92675-1570)
PHONE..............................949 728-2000
Robert Anderson Schoepe, *CEO*
Michael Draves, *
Robert Connell, *
Derek Baker, *
◆ **EMP:** 98 **EST:** 1957
SALES (est): 42.94MM
SALES (corp-wide): 42.94MM **Privately Held**
Web: www.fluidmaster.com
SIC: 3089 3432 1711 Injection molding of plastics; Plumbing fixture fittings and trim; Plumbing contractors

(P-4119)
FORMULA PLASTICS INC
451 Tecate Rd Ste 2b, Tecate (91980)
PHONE..........................866 307-1362
Alexander Mora, *CEO*
Elias Mora, *
Joe Mora, *
Monica Mora, *
▲ EMP: 500 EST: 1984
SQ FT: 20,000
SALES (est): 1.75MM **Privately Held**
Web: www.formulaplastics.com
SIC: 3089 Injection molding of plastics

(P-4120)
FRUTH CUSTOM PLASTICS INC
Also Called: Cal-AZ Sales & Marketing
701 Richfield Rd, Placentia (92870-6729)
P.O. Box 807 (92811-0807)
PHONE..........................714 993-9955
EMP: 80 EST: 1980
SALES (est): 8.76MM **Privately Held**
Web: www.fruth.com
SIC: 3089 3081 2673 Plastics containers,
except foam; Plastics film and sheet;
Plastic bags: made from purchased
materials
HQ: C. P. Converters, Inc.
15 Grumbacher Rd
York PA 17406
717 764-1193

(P-4121)
G B REMANUFACTURING INC
2040 E Cherry Industrial Cir, Long Beach
(90805-4410)
PHONE..........................562 272-7333
Michael J Kitching, *CEO*
F William Kitching, *
Patricia Kitching, *
▲ EMP: 70 EST: 1986
SQ FT: 26,400
SALES (est): 9.8MM **Privately Held**
Web: www.gbreman.com
SIC: 3089 Injection molded finished plastics
products, nec

(P-4122)
GARY MANUFACTURING INC
2626 Southport Way Ste E, National City
(91950-8754)
PHONE..........................619 429-4479
Brian Smith, *Pr*
Helen Smith, *
▲ EMP: 35 EST: 1958
SQ FT: 10,000
SALES (est): 4.89MM **Privately Held**
Web: www.garymanufacturing.com
SIC: 3089 2392 5162 2673 Plastics
containers, except foam; Napkins, fabric
and nonwoven: made from purchased
materials; Plastics materials and basic
shapes; Bags: plastic, laminated, and
coated

(P-4123)
GEMINI FILM & BAG INC (PA)
Also Called: Gemini Plastics
3574 Fruitland Ave, Maywood
(90270-2008)
P.O. Box 806 (92811-0806)
PHONE..........................323 582-0901
James Fruth, *Pr*
Brian Kunisch, *
EMP: 25 EST: 1966
SQ FT: 12,000
SALES (est): 925.8K
SALES (corp-wide): 925.8K **Privately Held**

SIC: 3089 8742 Extruded finished plastics
products, nec; Manufacturing management
consultant

(P-4124)
GEO PLASTICS
2200 E 52nd St, Vernon (90058-3446)
PHONE..........................323 277-8106
Michael Abraham Morris, *CEO*
Justin Hunt, *
▲ EMP: 27 EST: 1992
SALES (est): 4.91MM **Privately Held**
Web: www.geoplastics.com
SIC: 3089 Extruded finished plastics
products, nec

(P-4125)
GETPART LA INC
Also Called: Fitparts
13705 Cimarron Ave, Gardena
(90249-2463)
PHONE..........................424 331-9599
Ilya S Shchelokov, *CEO*
EMP: 23 EST: 2016
SALES (est): 3.53MM **Privately Held**
Web: www.fitparts.com
SIC: 3089 Automotive parts, plastic

(P-4126)
GIBRALTAR PLASTIC PDTS CORP
12885 Foothill Blvd, Sylmar (91342-5384)
PHONE..........................818 365-9318
Harvey J Jacobs, *Pr*
EMP: 25 EST: 1964
SQ FT: 30,000
SALES (est): 4.75MM **Privately Held**
Web: www.gibraltarplastic.com
SIC: 3089 Injection molded finished plastics
products, nec

(P-4127)
GILL CORPORATION (PA)
4056 Easy St, El Monte (91731-1054)
PHONE..........................626 443-6094
Stephen E Gill, *Ch*
William Heinze, *
Irv Freund, *Business Development*
Don Clark, *
◆ EMP: 236 EST: 1945
SQ FT: 390,000
SALES (est): 225.82MM
SALES (corp-wide): 225.82MM **Privately
Held**
Web: www.mcgillcorp.com
SIC: 3089 3469 3272 2448 Laminating of
plastics; Honeycombed metal; Panels and
sections, prefabricated concrete; Cargo
containers, wood and metal combination

(P-4128)
GKN ARSPACE TRNSPRNCY SYSTEMS
12122 Western Ave, Garden Grove
(92841-2915)
PHONE..........................714 893-7531
John Danley, *CEO*
Mike Mccann Ceo Aeostructures N
America, *Prin*
Joakim Anderson, *Chief Executive Officer
Engine Systems*
Gavin Wesson, *
Russ Dunn, *Technology*
▲ EMP: 360 EST: 1946
SQ FT: 324,000
SALES (est): 26.21MM
SALES (corp-wide): 6.06B **Privately Held**
Web: www.gknaerospace.com

SIC: 3089 3231 3827 3728 Windows, plastics
; Mirrors, truck and automobile: made from
purchased glass; Optical instruments and
lenses; Aircraft parts and equipment, nec
HQ: Gkn America Corp.
1180 Pchtree St Ne Ste 24
Atlanta GA 30309
630 972-9300

(P-4129)
GT STYLING CORP
2830 E Via Martens, Anaheim
(92806-1751)
PHONE..........................714 644-9214
Gregory Allen Knox, *CEO*
Jodee Jensen Smith, *Ex VP*
EMP: 27 EST: 2001
SALES (est): 2.33MM **Privately Held**
Web: www.gtsstyling.com
SIC: 3089 Molding primary plastics

(P-4130)
HEE ENVIRONMENTAL ENGINEERING LLC
16605 Koala Rd, Adelanto (92301-3925)
PHONE..........................760 530-1409
EMP: 38
SIC: 3089 Plastics and fiberglass tanks

(P-4131)
HI-REL PLASTICS & MOLDING CORP
7575 Jurupa Ave, Riverside (92504-1012)
PHONE..........................951 354-0258
Rakesh Bajaria, *CEO*
Rick Bajria, *
Harry Thummer, *
Dennis Sovalia, *
▲ EMP: 50 EST: 1984
SQ FT: 15,000
SALES (est): 4.54MM **Privately Held**
Web: www.hirelplastics.com
SIC: 3089 3549 3599 Injection molded
finished plastics products, nec; Assembly
machines, including robotic; Machine shop,
jobbing and repair

(P-4132)
HIGHLAND PLASTICS INC
Also Called: Hi-Plas
3650 Dulles Dr, Mira Loma (91752-3260)
PHONE..........................951 360-9587
James L Nelson, *Prin*
William B Warren, *
◆ EMP: 130 EST: 1974
SQ FT: 150,000
SALES (est): 11.51MM **Privately Held**
SIC: 3089 Injection molding of plastics

(P-4133)
HOOD MANUFACTURING INC
Also Called: Thermobile
2621 S Birch St, Santa Ana (92707-3410)
PHONE..........................714 979-7681
Michael Hood, *Pr*
Patrica Hood, *
Michele Rauschenbach, *CIO*
EMP: 60 EST: 1948
SQ FT: 24,000
SALES (est): 7.28MM **Privately Held**
Web: www.hoodmfg.com
SIC: 3089 3585 Injection molded finished
plastics products, nec; Refrigeration and
heating equipment

(P-4134)
HOOSIER INC
1152 California Ave, Corona (92881-3324)
P.O. Box 78926 (92877)

PHONE..........................951 272-3070
Robert G Simms, *CEO*
EMP: 80 EST: 1979
SQ FT: 45,000
SALES (est): 9.78MM **Privately Held**
Web: www.hoosierinc.com
SIC: 3089 Injection molding of plastics

(P-4135)
HOUSEWARES INTERNATIONAL INC
Also Called: American Household Company
1933 S Broadway Ste 867, Los Angeles
(90007-4523)
PHONE..........................323 581-3000
Kamyar Solouki, *CEO*
Sean Solouki, *
◆ EMP: 35 EST: 1988
SALES (est): 5.33MM **Privately Held**
Web: www.housewaresintl.com
SIC: 3089 5023 Kitchenware, plastics;
Kitchenware

(P-4136)
HUSKY INJECTION MLDING SYSTEMS
3505 Cadillac Ave Ste N4, Costa Mesa
(92626-1433)
PHONE..........................714 545-8200
Michael Smith, *Mgr*
EMP: 53
SQ FT: 6,501
Web: www.husky.co
SIC: 3089 Injection molding of plastics
HQ: Husky Injection Molding Systems, Inc.
288 North Rd
Milton VT 05468
802 859-8000

(P-4137)
HUSKY INJCTION MLDING SYSTEMS
5245 Maureen Ln, Moorpark (93021-7125)
PHONE..........................805 523-9593
EMP: 53
Web: www.husky.co
SIC: 3089 Injection molding of plastics
HQ: Husky Injection Molding Systems, Inc.
288 North Rd
Milton VT 05468
802 859-8000

(P-4138)
IDEMIA AMERICA CORP
3150 E Ana St, Compton (90221-5607)
PHONE..........................310 884-7900
Eric Daniele, *Dir*
EMP: 161
SALES (corp-wide): 4.59B **Privately Held**
Web: www.idemia.com
SIC: 3089 3083 Identification cards, plastics;
Plastics finished products, laminated
HQ: Idemia America Corp.
11951 Freedom Dr Ste 1800
Reston VA 20190
703 775-7800

(P-4139)
INLINE PLASTICS INC
1950 S Baker Ave, Ontario (91761-7755)
PHONE..........................909 923-1033
Kelly Orr, *CEO*
Alfredo Perez, *
EMP: 25 EST: 1996
SQ FT: 21,000
SALES (est): 5.16MM **Privately Held**
Web: www.inlineplasticsinc.com
SIC: 3089 Injection molding of plastics

(P-4140)
INTERTRADE INDUSTRIES LTD
14600 Hoover St, Westminster
(92683-5346)
PHONE..............................714 894-5566
EMP: 56 EST: 1975
SALES (est): 2.67MM **Privately Held**
SIC: **3089** Plastics boats and other marine
   equipment
PA: American Innotek, Inc.
   2655 Vista Pacific Dr

(P-4141)
IPS INDUSTRIES INC
Also Called: Spectrum Bags
12641 166th St, Cerritos (90703-2101)
PHONE..............................562 623-2555
Frank Su, *CEO*
Peter Hii, *
David Silva, *
Ben Tran, *
Betty Green, *
◆ EMP: 80 EST: 1990
SQ FT: 150,000
SALES (est): 21.08MM **Privately Held**
Web: www.ipspi.com
SIC: **3089** 3629 Battery cases, plastics or
   plastics combination; Battery chargers,
   rectifying or nonrotating

(P-4142)
**J & L CSTM PLSTIC EXTRSONS
INC**
850 Lawson St, City Of Industry
(91748-1103)
PHONE..............................626 442-0711
Edwin Woo, *CEO*
Louis Salmon, *
Jaime Lizarraga, *
EMP: 30 EST: 1974
SALES (est): 3.11MM **Privately Held**
Web: www.jlplastic.com
SIC: **3089** Plastics hardware and building
   products

(P-4143)
J A ENGLISH II INC
Also Called: Pacific Plstcs-Njction Molding
1333 Keystone Way, Vista (92081-8311)
PHONE..............................760 598-5333
▲ EMP: 25
Web: www.divplast.com
SIC: **3089** 3544 Injection molding of plastics;
   Industrial molds

(P-4144)
JACOBSON PLASTICS INC
1401 Freeman Ave, Long Beach
(90804-2518)
PHONE..............................562 433-4911
Jeff Jacobson, *Pr*
▲ EMP: 75 EST: 1962
SQ FT: 25,000
SALES (est): 3.13MM **Privately Held**
Web: www.jacobsonplastics.com
SIC: **3089** 3544 Injection molding of plastics;
   Special dies, tools, jigs, and fixtures

(P-4145)
**JASON TOOL AND
ENGINEERING INC**
7101 Honold Cir, Garden Grove
(92841-1424)
PHONE..............................714 895-5067
Jack Winterswyk, *Pr*
Curtis H Thompson, *
▲ EMP: 30 EST: 1979
SQ FT: 30,000
SALES (est): 5.13MM **Privately Held**

Web: www.jasontool.com
SIC: **3089** 3544 Injection molding of plastics;
   Dies, plastics forming

(P-4146)
JB PLASTICS INC
1921 E Edinger Ave, Santa Ana
(92705-4720)
PHONE..............................714 541-8500
Joseph N Chiodo, *Pr*
Bruce Donoho, *
EMP: 45 EST: 2000
SQ FT: 30,000
SALES (est): 7.95MM **Privately Held**
Web: www.jb-plastics.com
SIC: **3089** Injection molding of plastics

(P-4147)
JET PLASTICS (PA)
941 N Eastern Ave, Los Angeles
(90063-1395)
PHONE..............................323 268-6706
TOLL FREE: 800
Lee R Johnson, *Pr*
Lee Johnson, *
Lon Johnson, *
Lowel Johnson, *
◆ EMP: 50 EST: 1948
SQ FT: 30,000
SALES (est): 8.69MM
SALES (corp-wide): 8.69MM **Privately
Held**
Web: www.jetplastics.com
SIC: **3089** Injection molding of plastics

(P-4148)
JG PLASTICS GROUP LLC
335 Fischer Ave, Costa Mesa (92626-4522)
PHONE..............................714 751-4266
◆ EMP: 50 EST: 1975
SQ FT: 32,000
SALES (est): 9.99MM **Privately Held**
Web: www.jgplastics.com
SIC: **3089** 3544 Injection molding of plastics;
   Special dies, tools, jigs, and fixtures

(P-4149)
JSN INDUSTRIES INC
9700 Jeronimo Rd, Irvine (92618-2019)
PHONE..............................949 458-0050
James N Nagel Junior, *CEO*
Sandra Nagel, *
EMP: 70 EST: 1984
SQ FT: 65,000
SALES (est): 8.37MM **Privately Held**
Web: www.jsn.com
SIC: **3089** Injection molding of plastics

(P-4150)
KARAT PACKAGING INC (PA)
Also Called: KARAT
6185 Kimball Ave, Chino (91708-9126)
PHONE..............................626 965-8882
Alan Yu, *Ch Bd*
Jian Guo, *CFO*
Marvin Cheng, *VP Mfg*
Daniel Quire, *CRO*
EMP: 26 EST: 2000
SALES (est): 405.65MM
SALES (corp-wide): 405.65MM **Publicly
Held**
Web: www.irkarat.com
SIC: **3089** 5113 Plastics containers, except
   foam; Disposable plates, cups, napkins,
   and eating utensils

(P-4151)
KAS ENGINEERING INC (PA)
1714 14th St, Santa Monica (90404-4341)
PHONE..............................310 450-8925

EMP: 24 EST: 1958
SALES (est): 5.17MM
SALES (corp-wide): 5.17MM **Privately
Held**
Web: www.kasengineering.com
SIC: **3089** 3541 Injection molding of plastics;
   Machine tools, metal cutting type

(P-4152)
KELCOURT PLASTICS INC (DH)
Also Called: Kelpac Medical
1000 Calle Recodo, San Clemente
(92673-6225)
PHONE..............................949 361-0774
John Wolf, *CEO*
Rob Bonatakis, *
▲ EMP: 80 EST: 1982
SQ FT: 20,000
SALES (est): 26.88MM
SALES (corp-wide): 2.93B **Publicly Held**
Web: www.spectrumplastics.com
SIC: **3089** Injection molding of plastics
HQ: Ppc Industries Inc.
   10101 78th Ave
   Pleasant Prairie WI 53158
   262 947-0900

(P-4153)
**KEPNER PLAS FABRICATORS
INC**
3131 Lomita Blvd, Torrance (90505-5158)
PHONE..............................562 543-4472
James Garrett Iii, *CEO*
James Garrett, *CEO*
Frank Meyers, *
Meryl Bayley, *
▲ EMP: 26 EST: 1960
SQ FT: 50,000
SALES (est): 3.29MM **Privately Held**
Web: www.elastec.com
SIC: **3089** Injection molding of plastics

(P-4154)
KING BROS INDUSTRIES
29101 The Old Rd, Valencia (91355-1014)
◆ EMP: 170
Web: www.kbico.com
SIC: **3089** Plastics hardware and building
   products

(P-4155)
KING PLASTICS INC
840 N Elm St, Orange (92867-7908)
P.O. Box 6229 (92863-6229)
PHONE..............................714 997-7540
Larry E Lathrum, *CEO*
◆ EMP: 96 EST: 1962
SQ FT: 100,000
SALES (est): 15.01MM **Privately Held**
Web: www.kingplastics.com
SIC: **3089** Plastics kitchenware, tableware,
   and houseware

(P-4156)
KUI CO INC
266 Calle Pintoresco, San Clemente
(92672-7504)
PHONE..............................949 369-7949
Terry Daum, *Pr*
Sandy Daum, *
EMP: 40 EST: 1996
SQ FT: 14,800
SALES (est): 4.44MM **Privately Held**
Web: www.kuicoinc.com
SIC: **3089** Plastics processing

(P-4157)
**L & H MOLD & ENGINEERING
INC (PA)**

Also Called: L & H Molds
140 Atlantic St, Pomona (91768-3285)
PHONE..............................909 930-1547
Stan Hillary, *CEO*
Steve Hillary, *Pr*
Brenda Bishop, *Sec*
EMP: 23 EST: 1974
SQ FT: 6,000
SALES (est): 2.52MM
SALES (corp-wide): 2.52MM **Privately
Held**
SIC: **3089** Injection molding of plastics

(P-4158)
LAMSCO WEST INC
29101 The Old Rd, Santa Clarita
(91355-1014)
PHONE..............................661 295-8620
Steve Griffith, *Pr*
Scott Wilkinson, *
Rick Casillas, *
EMP: 99 EST: 1993
SQ FT: 31,280
SALES (est): 22.68MM
SALES (corp-wide): 145.58MM **Privately
Held**
Web: www.lamscowest.com
SIC: **3089** Injection molding of plastics
HQ: Avantus Aerospace, Inc.
   29101 The Old Rd
   Valencia CA 91355
   661 295-8620

(P-4159)
LEADING INDUSTRY INC
Also Called: Pinnacle Plastic Containers
1151 Pacific Ave, Oxnard (93033-2472)
PHONE..............................805 385-4100
◆ EMP: 100
Web: www.perfectdomain.com
SIC: **3089** Plastics processing

(P-4160)
**LEHRER BRLLNPRFKTION
WERKS INC**
Also Called: Lbi - USA
20801 Nordhoff St, Chatsworth
(91311-5925)
P.O. Box 3519 (91313-3519)
PHONE..............................818 407-1890
Keith Lehrer, *Pr*
Chett Lehrer, *
▲ EMP: 65 EST: 1949
SQ FT: 38,000
SALES (est): 3.01MM **Privately Held**
SIC: **3089** Cases, plastics

(P-4161)
LLC WALKER WEST
1555 S Vintage Ave, Ontario (91761-3655)
PHONE..............................909 390-4300
Frank San Roman, *CEO*
Frank San Roman, *Managing Member*
EMP: 175 EST: 1954
SALES (est): 3.02MM **Privately Held**
SIC: **3089** Automotive parts, plastic

(P-4162)
MARINE FENDERS INTL INC
452 W Valley Blvd, Rialto (92376-7718)
PHONE..............................310 834-7037
Gerald Thermos, *CEO*
Gerald Thermos, *Pr*
◆ EMP: 35 EST: 2004
SALES (est): 1.6MM **Privately Held**
Web: www.marinefendersintl.com
SIC: **3089** Plastics boats and other marine
   equipment

(P-4163)
MARTIN CHANCEY CORPORATION
Also Called: Taral Plastics
525 Malloy Ct, Corona (92878-4045)
PHONE.................510 972-6300
Chancey Price Martin, *CEO*
Emily Martin, *
▲ **EMP: 25 EST:** 2003
SALES (est): 5.5MM **Privately Held**
Web: www.taralplastics.com
SIC: 3089 5085 Jars, plastics; Plastic bottles

(P-4164)
MEDEGEN LLC (DH)
4501 E Wall St, Ontario (91761-8143)
P.O. Box 515111 (90051-5111)
PHONE.................909 390-9080
Michael E Stanley, *
W Mark Dorris, *
Paul M Ellis, *
Jeffrey S Goble, *
▲ **EMP: 50 EST:** 2001
SQ FT: 3,000
SALES (est): 29.64MM
SALES (corp-wide): 20.18B **Publicly Held**
Web: www.medegenmed.com
SIC: 3089 Injection molded finished plastics products, nec
HQ: Carefusion Corporation
3750 Torrey View Ct
San Diego CA 92130

(P-4165)
MEDEGEN INC
930 S Wanamaker Ave, Ontario
(91761-8151)
PHONE.................909 390-9080
▲ **EMP:** 180
SIC: 3089 3544 Injection molded finished plastics products, nec; Special dies, tools, jigs, and fixtures

(P-4166)
MEDWAY PLASTICS CORPORATION
2250 E Cherry Industrial Cir, Long Beach
(90805-4414)
PHONE.................562 630-1175
Thomas Hutchinson Junior, *CEO*
Mary Hutchinson, *
Gerry Hutchinson, *
Rick Hutchinson, *
Sheryl Mcdaniel, *VP*
◆ **EMP: 141 EST:** 1974
SALES (est): 23.1MM **Privately Held**
Web: www.medwayplastics.com
SIC: 3089 Injection molding of plastics

(P-4167)
MERGER SUB GOTHAM 2 LLC
6261 Katella Ave Ste 250, Cypress
(90630-5200)
PHONE.................714 462-4603
Nicholas Kovacevich, *CEO*
EMP: 109 EST: 2021
SALES (est): 2.16MM
SALES (corp-wide): 65.37MM **Publicly Held**
SIC: 3089 5085 Plastics containers, except foam; Industrial supplies
PA: Greenlane Holdings, Inc.
1095 Brken Sund Pkwy Ste
877 292-7660

(P-4168)
MERRICK ENGINEERING INC (PA)
1275 Quarry St, Corona (92879-1707)

PHONE.................951 737-6040
Abraham M Abdi, *Pr*
Katina Brown, *
Mina Abdi, *
◆ **EMP: 250 EST:** 1971
SQ FT: 150,000
SALES (est): 39.41MM
SALES (corp-wide): 39.41MM **Privately Held**
Web: www.merrickengineering.com
SIC: 3089 Injection molding of plastics

(P-4169)
MI TECHNOLOGIES INC
Also Called: Lutema
2215 Paseo De Las Americas Ste 30, San
Diego (92154-7801)
PHONE.................619 710-2637
Amir Tafreshi, *CEO*
John Celms, *
Ali Irani-tehrani, *Prin*
▲ **EMP: 700 EST:** 2004
SQ FT: 8,000
SALES (est): 15.93MM **Privately Held**
Web: www.discount-merchant.com
SIC: 3089 3672 5731 3999 Injection molding of plastics; Printed circuit boards; Consumer electronic equipment, nec; Barber and beauty shop equipment

(P-4170)
MILGARD MANUFACTURING LLC
Also Called: Milgard Windows
26879 Diaz Rd, Temecula (92590-3470)
PHONE.................480 763-6000
Cory Hall, *Brnch Mgr*
EMP: 249
SALES (corp-wide): 822.1MM **Privately Held**
Web: www.milgard.com
SIC: 3089 3442 5211 3231 Windows, plastics; Sash, door or window: metal; Door and window products; Products of purchased glass
HQ: Milgard Manufacturing Llc
1498 Pacific Ave Fl 4
Tacoma WA 98402
253 922-4343

(P-4171)
MISSION PLASTICS INC
1930 S Parco Ave, Ontario (91761-8312)
PHONE.................909 947-7287
Patrick Dauphinee, *CEO*
Charles Montes, *
▲ **EMP: 120 EST:** 1982
SQ FT: 20,000
SALES (est): 1.41MM **Privately Held**
Web: www.missionplastics.com
SIC: 3089 Injection molding of plastics

(P-4172)
MODERN CONCEPTS INC
3121 E Ana St, E Rncho Dmngz
(90221-5606)
PHONE.................310 637-0013
Richard J Warpack, *Pr*
◆ **EMP: 60 EST:** 1983
SQ FT: 42,000
SALES (est): 7.25MM **Privately Held**
SIC: 3089 3087 Coloring and finishing of plastics products; Custom compound purchased resins

(P-4173)
MODIFIED PLASTICS INC (PA)
1240 E Glenwood Pl, Santa Ana
(92707-3000)
PHONE.................714 546-4667

Robert Estep, *CEO*
Jocelyn Eubank, *
▲ **EMP: 27 EST:** 1976
SQ FT: 18,000
SALES (est): 22.22MM
SALES (corp-wide): 22.22MM **Privately Held**
Web: www.modifiedplastics.com
SIC: 3089 Injection molding of plastics

(P-4174)
MOLDED FIBER GL COMPANIES - W
Also Called: M F G West
9400 Holly Rd, Adelanto (92301-3900)
P.O. Box 675 (44005-0675)
PHONE.................760 246-4042
Richard Morrison, *CEO*
Dave Denny, *
Jim Sommer, *
▲ **EMP: 100 EST:** 1958
SQ FT: 66,000
SALES (est): 8.76MM
SALES (corp-wide): 360.86MM **Privately Held**
Web: www.moldedfiberglass.com
SIC: 3089 Air mattresses, plastics
PA: Molded Fiber Glass Companies
2925 Mfg Pl
440 997-5851

(P-4175)
MOLDING CORPORATION AMERICA
10349 Norris Ave, Pacoima (91331-2220)
PHONE.................818 890-7877
Mark Hurley, *CEO*
Sandra Rinder, *VP*
▲ **EMP: 50 EST:** 1967
SQ FT: 59,000
SALES (est): 5.62MM **Privately Held**
Web: www.moldingcorp.com
SIC: 3089 Injection molding of plastics

(P-4176)
NATIONAL DIVERSIFIED SALES INC (HQ)
Also Called: Nds
21300 Victory Blvd Ste 215, Woodland Hills
(91367-7721)
P.O. Box 339 (93247-0339)
PHONE.................559 562-9888
Michael Gummeson, *Pr*
Randall Stott, *
Josie Malonado, *
◆ **EMP: 200 EST:** 1978
SQ FT: 5,000
SALES (est): 210.51MM **Privately Held**
Web: www.ndspro.com
SIC: 3089 Plastics hardware and building products
PA: Norma Group Se
Edisonstr. 4

(P-4177)
NEOPACIFIC HOLDINGS INC
Also Called: Pro-Action Products
14940 Calvert St, Van Nuys (91411-2603)
PHONE.................818 786-2900
Steve Chan, *Pr*
▲ **EMP: 48 EST:** 1981
SQ FT: 24,000
SALES (est): 8.04MM **Privately Held**
Web: www.proactionproducts.com
SIC: 3089 Injection molding of plastics

(P-4178)
NEW WEST PRODUCTS INC
Also Called: ITW Space Bag

7520 Airway Rd Ste 1, San Diego
(92154-8304)
PHONE.................619 671-9022
◆ **EMP:** 46
Web: www.ziploc.com
SIC: 3089 2673 Plastics containers, except foam; Bags: plastic, laminated, and coated

(P-4179)
NEWELL BRANDS INC
17182 Nevada St, Victorville (92394-7806)
PHONE.................760 246-2700
EMP: 35
SALES (corp-wide): 8.13B **Publicly Held**
Web: www.newellbrands.com
SIC: 3089 Plastics kitchenware, tableware, and houseware
PA: Newell Brands Inc.
6655 Pachtree Dunwoody Rd
770 418-7000

(P-4180)
NEWLIGHT TECHNOLOGIES INC
Also Called: Aircarbon
14382 Astronautics Ln, Huntington Beach
(92647-2081)
PHONE.................714 556-4500
Mark Herrema, *CEO*
Kenton Kimmel, *
Evan Creelman, *
EMP: 29 EST: 2007
SALES (est): 11.62MM **Privately Held**
Web: www.newlight.com
SIC: 3089 Plastics processing

(P-4181)
NEWPORT LAMINATES INC
3121 W Central Ave, Santa Ana
(92704-5302)
PHONE.................714 545-8335
Brad A Bollman, *Pr*
Wendy Bollman, *
EMP: 40 EST: 1974
SQ FT: 24,000
SALES (est): 4.26MM **Privately Held**
Web: www.newportlaminates.com
SIC: 3089 Fiber, vulcanized

(P-4182)
NORCO INJECTION MOLDING INC
Also Called: Norco Plastics
14325 Monte Vista Ave, Chino
(91710-5726)
P.O. Box 2528 (91708-2528)
PHONE.................909 393-4000
Jack Williams, *Pr*
John Williams, *CFO*
▲ **EMP: 100 EST:** 1974
SQ FT: 45,000
SALES (est): 2.28MM **Privately Held**
Web: www.niminc.com
SIC: 3089 3544 Injection molding of plastics; Special dies, tools, jigs, and fixtures

(P-4183)
NORCO PLASTICS INC
14325 Monte Vista Ave, Chino
(91710-5726)
P.O. Box 2528 (91708-2528)
PHONE.................909 393-4000
John Williams, *CEO*
▲ **EMP: 90 EST:** 2010
SALES (est): 9.33MM **Privately Held**
Web: www.norcoplastics.com
SIC: 3089 Plastics containers, except foam

(P-4184)
NORTON PACKAGING INC
5800 S Boyle Ave, Vernon (90058-3927)
PHONE..........................323 588-6167
Joe Schrick, *Brnch Mgr*
EMP: 25
SALES (corp-wide): 32.65MM **Privately Held**
Web: www.nortonpackaging.com
SIC: 3089 5162 Plastics containers, except foam; Resins
PA: Norton Packaging, Inc.
20670 Corsair Blvd
510 786-1922

(P-4185)
NUBS PLASTICS INC
991 Park Center Dr, Vista (92081-8312)
PHONE..........................760 598-2525
Niyogi Ramolia, *Pr*
▼ EMP: 30 EST: 1993
SQ FT: 13,000
SALES (est): 4.84MM **Privately Held**
Web: www.nubsplasticsinc.com
SIC: 3089 Injection molding of plastics

(P-4186)
NUCONIC PACKAGING LLC
4889 Loma Vista Ave, Vernon
(90058-3216)
PHONE..........................323 588-9033
Alan Franz, *CEO*
Christopher Winkler, *
Skip Farber, *
Jason Farber, *
▲ EMP: 31 EST: 2008
SQ FT: 30,000
SALES (est): 4.6MM **Privately Held**
Web: www.easypak.com
SIC: 3089 4783 Plastics containers, except foam; Packing and crating

(P-4187)
NYPRO INC
Also Called: Nypro Healthcare Baja
505 Main St Rm 107, Chula Vista
(91911-6059)
PHONE..........................619 498-9250
Gregg Lambert, *Genl Mgr*
EMP: 75
SALES (corp-wide): 28.88B **Publicly Held**
Web: www.nypromold.com
SIC: 3089 3559 Injection molding of plastics; Robots, molding and forming plastics
HQ: Nypro Inc.
101 Union St
Clinton MA 01510
978 365-9721

(P-4188)
NYPRO SAN DIEGO INC
505 Main St, Chula Vista (91911-6059)
PHONE..........................619 482-7033
Gordon Lankton, *Sec*
Ernie Rice, *
▼ EMP: 80 EST: 1988
SQ FT: 66,000
SALES (est): 5.26MM
SALES (corp-wide): 28.88B **Publicly Held**
SIC: 3089 Injection molding of plastics
HQ: Nypro Inc.
101 Union St
Clinton MA 01510
978 365-9721

(P-4189)
OMNI RESOURCE RECOVERY INC
1495 N 8th St Ste 150, Colton
(92324-1451)

PHONE..........................909 327-2900
EMP: 250
Web: www.omnirecovery.com
SIC: 3089 Extruded finished plastics products, nec

(P-4190)
PACTIV LLC
2024 Norris Rd, Bakersfield (93308-2238)
PHONE..........................661 392-4000
Steve Stewart, *Mgr*
EMP: 103
Web: www.pactivevergreen.com
SIC: 3089 3086 Kitchenware, plastics; Plastics foam products
HQ: Pactiv Llc
1900 W Field Ct
Lake Forest IL 60045
847 482-2000

(P-4191)
PARADIGM PACKAGING EAST LLC
Also Called: Paradigm Packaging West
9595 Utica Ave, Rancho Cucamonga
(91730-5921)
P.O. Box 10 (91785-0010)
PHONE..........................909 985-2750
Steve Costecki, *Mgr*
EMP: 27
SALES (corp-wide): 112.7MM **Privately Held**
SIC: 3089 Plastics containers, except foam
HQ: Paradigm Packaging East Llc
141 5th St
Saddle Brook NJ 07663
201 909-3400

(P-4192)
PARAMOUNT PANELS INC (PA)
Also Called: California Plasteck
1531 E Cedar St, Ontario (91761-5762)
PHONE..........................909 947-8008
Arthur G Thorne, *Pr*
John G Thorne, *
EMP: 32 EST: 1962
SQ FT: 12,000
SALES (est): 3.77MM
SALES (corp-wide): 3.77MM **Privately Held**
Web: www.paramountpanels.com
SIC: 3089 3812 3728 Plastics processing; Search and navigation equipment; Aircraft parts and equipment, nec

(P-4193)
PC VAUGHAN MFG CORP
Also Called: Rostar Filters
1278 Mercantile St, Oxnard (93030-7522)
PHONE..........................805 278-2555
Jeff Starin, *CEO*
Jeff Starin, *Pr*
EMP: 65 EST: 1979
SQ FT: 40,000
SALES (est): 4.94MM **Privately Held**
Web: www.rostarfilters.com
SIC: 3089 3569 3714 5085 Automotive parts, plastic; Filters; Filters: oil, fuel, and air, motor vehicle; Filters, industrial

(P-4194)
PEERLESS INJECTION MOLDING LLC
Also Called: Proplas Technologies
14321 Corp Dr, Garden Grove (92843)
PHONE..........................714 689-1920
Scott Taylor, *Pr*
▲ EMP: 50 EST: 1977
SQ FT: 51,112
SALES (est): 9.65MM

SALES (corp-wide): 39.28MM **Privately Held**
SIC: 3089 Injection molding of plastics
PA: Comar, Inc.
201 Laurel Rd Fl 2
856 692-6100

(P-4195)
PERFORMNCE ENGINEERED PDTS INC
Also Called: Honor Plastics
3270 Pomona Blvd, Pomona (91768-3282)
PHONE..........................909 594-7487
Dinesh Savalia, *CEO*
EMP: 48 EST: 2016
SQ FT: 42,000
SALES (est): 9MM **Privately Held**
Web: www.honorplastics.com
SIC: 3089 Injection molding of plastics

(P-4196)
PINNPACK CAPITAL HOLDINGS LLC
Also Called: Pinnpack Packaging
1151 Pacific Ave, Oxnard (93033-2472)
PHONE..........................805 385-4100
Iraj Maroofian, *CEO*
Irage Barkohanai, *
Sriram Kailasam, *
EMP: 205 EST: 2021
SALES (est): 50.91MM **Privately Held**
Web: www.pinnpack.com
SIC: 3089 Plastics containers, except foam

(P-4197)
PLAINFIELD MOLDING INC
Also Called: Plainfield Companies
135 S State College Blvd Ste 200, Brea
(92821-5805)
PHONE..........................815 436-7806
EMP: 69
SIC: 3089 Molding primary plastics

(P-4198)
PLAINFIELD TOOL AND ENGINEERING INC
Also Called: Plainfield Stamping-Illinois
135 South College Blvd Ste 200, Brea
(92821)
PHONE..........................815 436-5671
▲ EMP: 305
SIC: 3089 3469 Injection molding of plastics; Metal stampings, nec

(P-4199)
PLASTIC AND METAL CENTER INC
23162 La Cadena Dr, Laguna Hills
(92653-1405)
PHONE..........................949 770-0610
Faramarz Khaladj, *Pr*
Fred Carr, *
Denise Khaladj, *
EMP: 25 EST: 1993
SQ FT: 20,000
SALES (est): 2.5MM **Privately Held**
Web: www.plastic-metal.com
SIC: 3089 Injection molding of plastics

(P-4200)
PLASTIC MOLDED COMPONENTS INC
Also Called: P M C
5920 Lakeshore Dr, Cypress (90630-3371)
PHONE..........................714 229-0133
EMP: 40 EST: 1979
SALES (est): 1.22MM **Privately Held**

Web:
www.moldedplasticcomponents.com
SIC: 3089 Molding primary plastics

(P-4201)
PLASTIC TECHNOLOGIES INC
Also Called: Blow Molded Products
4720 Felspar St, Riverside (92509-3068)
PHONE..........................951 360-6055
Meir Ben-david, *Pr*
Diane Ben-david, *VP*
EMP: 50 EST: 2018
SALES (est): 5.02MM **Privately Held**
Web: www.blowmoldedproducts.com
SIC: 3089 Injection molding of plastics

(P-4202)
PLASTICS DEVELOPMENT CORP
960 Calle Negocio, San Clemente
(92673-6201)
PHONE..........................949 492-0217
Inder Jain, *Pr*
Sanie Jain, *
Vijay Jain, *
▲ EMP: 23 EST: 1969
SQ FT: 7,000
SALES (est): 2.37MM **Privately Held**
Web: www.plasticsdev.com
SIC: 3089 Injection molding of plastics

(P-4203)
PLASTICS PLUS TECHNOLOGY INC
1495 Research Dr, Redlands (92374-4584)
PHONE..........................909 747-0555
Kathy Bodor, *CEO*
EMP: 33 EST: 1980
SQ FT: 35,000
SALES (est): 4.1MM **Privately Held**
Web: www.plasticsplus.com
SIC: 3089 3544 Injection molding of plastics; Forms (molds), for foundry and plastics working machinery

(P-4204)
PLASTPRO 2000 INC (PA)
Also Called: Plastpro Doors
5200 W Century Blvd, Los Angeles
(90045-5928)
PHONE..........................310 693-8600
Shirley Wang, *CEO*
Shirley Wang, *Pr*
Johnny Mai, *CFO*
◆ EMP: 126 EST: 1994
SALES (est): 22.63MM **Privately Held**
Web: www.plastproinc.com
SIC: 3089 Fiberglass doors

(P-4205)
POLYMER LOGISTICS INC
1725 Sierra Ridge Dr, Riverside
(92507-7133)
PHONE..........................951 567-2900
Albert Terrazas, *Brnch Mgr*
EMP: 57
SALES (corp-wide): 217.91MM **Privately Held**
Web: www.toscaltd.com
SIC: 3089 5085 5162 Pallets, plastics; Boxes, crates, etc., other than paper; Plastics materials and basic shapes
HQ: Polymer Logistics, Inc.
1175 Peachtree St Ne # 1900
Atlanta GA 30361

(P-4206)
PRC COMPOSITES LLC (PA)
1400 S Campus Ave, Ontario (91761-4330)

PHONE..................909 391-2006
John Upsher, *Managing Member*
Gene Gregory, *
EMP: 79 **EST:** 2014
SALES (est): 18.14MM
SALES (corp-wide): 18.14MM **Privately Held**
Web: www.prccal.com
SIC: 3089 Plastics containers, except foam

(P-4207)
PRECISE AEROSPACE MFG LLC
Also Called: Precise Plastic Products
22951 La Palma Ave, Yorba Linda
(92887-6701)
PHONE..................951 898-0500
Ronnie E Harwood, *CEO*
Roxanne Abdi, *
▲ **EMP:** 42 **EST:** 1965
SQ FT: 39,000
SALES (est): 11.32MM **Privately Held**
Web: www.precisemfg.com
SIC: 3089 3544 Molding primary plastics;
Industrial molds

(P-4208)
PREPRODUCTION PLASTICS INC
Also Called: P P I
210 Teller St, Corona (92879-1886)
PHONE..................951 340-9680
Koby Loosen, *Pr*
Ron Loosen, *
Barbara Loosen, *
▲ **EMP:** 50 **EST:** 1978
SQ FT: 45,000
SALES (est): 8.44MM **Privately Held**
Web: www.ppiplastics.com
SIC: 3089 3544 Molding primary plastics;
Forms (molds), for foundry and plastics
working machinery

(P-4209)
PRES-TEK PLASTICS INC (PA)
10700 7th St, Rancho Cucamonga
(91730-5404)
PHONE..................909 360-1600
Donna C Pursell, *CEO*
EMP: 27 **EST:** 2005
SALES (est): 23.72MM
SALES (corp-wide): 23.72MM **Privately Held**
Web: www.prestekplastics.com
SIC: 3089 Injection molding of plastics

(P-4210)
PRINCE LIONHEART INC (PA)
2421 Westgate Rd, Santa Maria
(93455-1075)
PHONE..................805 922-2250
Kelly Griffiths, *CEO*
Debbie Di Nardi, *
▲ **EMP:** 40 **EST:** 1973
SQ FT: 80,000
SALES (est): 12.1MM
SALES (corp-wide): 12.1MM **Privately Held**
Web: www.princelionheart.com
SIC: 3089 Injection molding of plastics

(P-4211)
PRO DESIGN GROUP INC
438 E Alondra Blvd, Gardena (90248-2902)
PHONE..................310 767-1032
Chris Raab, *Pr*
Christopher Allen Raab, *
Maria Chandler, *
▲ **EMP:** 35 **EST:** 1990
SQ FT: 50,000
SALES (est): 4.55MM **Privately Held**

Web: www.theprodesigngroup.com
SIC: 3089 Plastics kitchenware, tableware,
and houseware

(P-4212)
PROULX MANUFACTURING INC
Also Called: Universal Products
11433 6th St, Rancho Cucamonga
(91730-6024)
PHONE..................909 980-0662
Richard A Proulx, *CEO*
Lorraine Proulx, *
Raymond E Proulx, *
◆ **EMP:** 45 **EST:** 1970
SALES (est): 6.5MM **Privately Held**
Web: www.proulxmfg.com
SIC: 3089 Plastics hardware and building
products

(P-4213)
PROVIDIEN INJCTION MOLDING INC
Also Called: Pedi
6740 Nancy Ridge Dr, San Diego
(92121-2230)
PHONE..................760 931-1844
Jeffrey S Goble, *CEO*
Richard D Witchey Junior, *Pr*
Louise Witchey, *
Paul Jazwin, *
◆ **EMP:** 74 **EST:** 1985
SALES (est): 11.87MM
SALES (corp-wide): 4.59B **Publicly Held**
Web: www.providienmedical.com
SIC: 3089 Injection molded finished plastics
products, nec
HQ: Witco Industries, Inc.
2731 Loker Ave W
Carlsbad CA 92010

(P-4214)
R V BEST INC
Also Called: Shademaster Products
9335 Stevens Rd, Santee (92071-2809)
PHONE..................619 448-7300
Steven Smoot, *Pr*
Mike Scheller, *
Dan Smoot, *
EMP: 45 **EST:** 1983
SQ FT: 15,000
SALES (est): 1.53MM **Privately Held**
SIC: 3089 5999 Awnings, fiberglass and
plastics combination; Awnings

(P-4215)
RAKAR INCORPORATED
1680 Universe Cir, Oxnard (93033-2441)
PHONE..................805 487-2721
Theresa Padilla, *CEO*
EMP: 48 **EST:** 1951
SALES (est): 9.05MM **Privately Held**
Web: www.rakarinc.com
SIC: 3089 3544 Injection molding of plastics;
Forms (molds), for foundry and plastics
working machinery

(P-4216)
RAMKO INJECTION INC
3551 Tanya Ave, Hemet (92545-9447)
PHONE..................951 929-0360
Robert G Andrei, *Pr*
EMP: 100 **EST:** 2007
SALES (est): 1.5MM **Privately Held**
Web: www.ramko-inj.com
SIC: 3089 3364 Blow molded finished
plastics products, nec; Nonferrous die-
castings except aluminum

(P-4217)
RAMTEC ASSOCIATES INC
Also Called: Con-Tech Plastics
3200 E Birch St Ste B, Brea (92821-6287)
PHONE..................714 996-7477
Ralph Riehl, *Pr*
Vernon Meurer, *
▲ **EMP:** 28 **EST:** 1984
SQ FT: 35,000
SALES (est): 4.61MM **Privately Held**
SIC: 3089 Molding primary plastics

(P-4218)
RAY PRODUCTS COMPANY INC
1700 Chablis Ave, Ontario (91761-3610)
PHONE..................888 776-9014
EMP: 50 **EST:** 1949
SALES (est): 8.17MM **Privately Held**
Web: www.rayplastics.com
SIC: 3089 Thermoformed finished plastics
products, nec

(P-4219)
REEVES EXTRUDED PRODUCTS INC
1032 Stockton Ave, Arvin (93203-2330)
PHONE..................661 854-5970
Matthew Cobbs, *CEO*
Steve Reeves, *
Beverly Palmer, *
Sandy Shelton, *
EMP: 75 **EST:** 1967
SQ FT: 45,000
SALES (est): 4.66MM **Privately Held**
Web: www.reevesextruded.com
SIC: 3089 Injection molding of plastics

(P-4220)
REHAU CONSTRUCTION LLC
1250 Corona Pointe Ct Ste 301, Corona
(92879-1780)
PHONE..................951 549-9017
Joe Lepire, *Mgr*
EMP: 67
Web: www.rehau.com
SIC: 3089 Plastics processing
HQ: Rehau Construction Llc
1501 Edwards Ferry Rd Ne
Leesburg VA 20176

(P-4221)
REHRIG PACIFIC COMPANY (HQ)
4010 E 26th St, Los Angeles (90058-4477)
PHONE..................323 262-5145
William J Rehrig, *Pr*
Michael J Doka, *
James L Drew, *
Rajesh Luhar, *
◆ **EMP:** 150 **EST:** 1997
SQ FT: 200,000
SALES (est): 402.13MM **Privately Held**
Web: www.rehrigpacific.com
SIC: 3089 2821 Cases, plastics; Plasticizer/
additive based plastic materials
PA: Rehrig Pacific Holdings, Inc.
900 Corporate Center Dr

(P-4222)
REHRIG PACIFIC HOLDINGS INC (PA)
900 Corporate Center Dr, Monterey Park
(91754-7620)
PHONE..................323 262-5145
William J Rehrig, *CEO*
Michael J Doka, *Pr*
William Widmann, *VP*
James L Drew, *CFO*
Muriel Kiser, *Sec*
EMP: 99 **EST:** 1998

SALES (est): 438.07MM **Privately Held**
Web: www.rehrigpacific.com
SIC: 3089 2821 Cases, plastics; Plasticizer/
additive based plastic materials

(P-4223)
REINHOLD INDUSTRIES INC (DH)
12827 Imperial Hwy, Santa Fe Springs
(90670-4761)
PHONE..................562 944-3281
Clarence Hightower, *CEO*
Carl Walker, *
▲ **EMP:** 145 **EST:** 1984
SQ FT: 130,000
SALES (est): 22.37MM **Publicly Held**
Web: www.reinhold-ind.com
SIC: 3089 3764 2531 Molding primary
plastics; Space propulsion units and parts;
Seats, aircraft
HQ: Reinhold Holdings, Inc.
12827 E Imperial Hwy
Santa Fe Springs CA 90670

(P-4224)
RESINART CORPORATION
Also Called: Resinart Plastics
1621 Placentia Ave, Costa Mesa
(92627-4311)
PHONE..................949 642-3665
Gary Uecker, *Pr*
Gene Chandler, *
Frank Uecker, *
EMP: 40 **EST:** 1969
SQ FT: 15,000
SALES (est): 3.45MM **Privately Held**
Web: www.resinart.com
SIC: 3089 Molding primary plastics

(P-4225)
RONCO PLASTICS INC
Also Called: Ronco Plastics
15022 Parkway Loop Ste B, Tustin
(92780-6529)
PHONE..................714 259-1385
Raul L Barajas, *Pr*
Ronald L Pearson, *
EMP: 28 **EST:** 1976
SQ FT: 28,000
SALES (est): 4.84MM **Privately Held**
Web: www.ronco-plastics.com
SIC: 3089 Plastics containers, except foam

(P-4226)
RONFORD PRODUCTS INC
1116 E 2nd St, Pomona (91766-2114)
PHONE..................909 622-7446
Carl Higgins, *Mgr*
EMP: 28
SALES (corp-wide): 2.13MM **Privately Held**
SIC: 3089 5093 Injection molding of plastics;
Plastics scrap
PA: Ronford Products, Inc.
16616 Garfield Ave
562 408-1081

(P-4227)
ROTATIONAL MOLDING INC
Also Called: R M I
17038 S Figueroa St, Gardena
(90248-3089)
PHONE..................310 327-5401
Mario Poma, *CEO*
Douglas Russell, *
EMP: 80 **EST:** 2010
SALES (est): 4.21MM **Privately Held**
Web: www.rotationalmoldinginc.com
SIC: 3089 Plastics containers, except foam
PA: Tank Holding Corp.
6400 N 60th St

(P-4228)

ROTO DYNAMICS INC

1925 N Lime St, Orange (92865-4123)
PHONE.....................714 685-0183
Rishi Saran, *Pr*
Yogindra Saran, *
Rishi Saran, *VP*
EMP: 24 **EST:** 2005
SALES (est): 2.9MM **Privately Held**
Web: www.rotodynamics.com
SIC: 3089 3949 Plastics containers, except foam; Cases, gun and rod (sporting equipment)

(P-4229)

ROYAL INTERPACK NORTH AMER INC

475 Palmyrita Ave, Riverside (92507-1812)
PHONE.....................951 787-6925
Radhika Shah, *CEO*
Tee Komsan, *
Visnau Chawla, *
Kunal Sidhpura, *
Abu Hossain, *
▲ **EMP:** 45 **EST:** 2011
SALES (est): 1.69MM **Privately Held**
Web: www.royalinterpack.com
SIC: 3089 Thermoformed finished plastics products, nec

(P-4230)

RPLANET ERTH LOS ANGLES HLDNGS

5300 S Boyle Ave, Vernon (90058-3921)
PHONE.....................833 775-2638
EMP: 51 **EST:** 2015
SALES (est): 14.16MM **Privately Held**
Web: www.rplanetearth.com
SIC: 3089 Injection molding of plastics

(P-4231)

RPM PLASTIC MOLDING INC

2821 E Miraloma Ave, Anaheim (92806-1804)
PHONE.....................714 630-9300
Michael Ferik, *CEO*
Phil Hothan, *
▲ **EMP:** 25 **EST:** 1995
SALES (est): 4.66MM **Privately Held**
Web: www.rpmselect.com
SIC: 3089 Injection molding of plastics

(P-4232)

RSK TOOL INCORPORATED

410 W Carob St, Compton (90220-5213)
PHONE.....................310 537-3302
Ronald Kohagura, *Pr*
Virginia Kohagura, *
Mark Kohagura, *
EMP: 35 **EST:** 1974
SQ FT: 27,000
SALES (est): 2.48MM **Privately Held**
Web: www.rsktool.com
SIC: 3089 Injection molding of plastics

(P-4233)

S&B INDUSTRY INC

Also Called: Fxp Technologies
105 S Puente St, Brea (92821-3844)
PHONE.....................909 569-4155
Paul H Shiung, *Pr*
EMP: 39
SIC: 3089 Injection molded finished plastics products, nec
HQ: S&B Industry, Inc.
    13301 Pk Vsta Blvd Ste 10
    Fort Worth TX 76177

(P-4234)

SAGE PLASTICS LONG BEACH CORP

2210 E Artesia Blvd, Long Beach (90805-1739)
PHONE.....................562 423-3900
Jeff Vice, *Pr*
Miguel Garcia, *Sec*
EMP: 80 **EST:** 2003
SQ FT: 20,000
SALES (est): 8.89MM **Privately Held**
Web: california-plastic-containers-inc.hub.biz
SIC: 3089 Injection molding of plastics

(P-4235)

SAN DIEGO ACE INC

5363 Sweetwater Trl, San Diego (92130-5040)
P.O. Box 486 (91980-0486)
PHONE.....................619 206-7339
Kyung Min Kim, *CEO*
▲ **EMP:** 200 **EST:** 1992
SALES (est): 4.3MM **Privately Held**
Web: www.sandiegoace.com
SIC: 3089 Molding primary plastics

(P-4236)

SANDIA PLASTICS INC

Also Called: Ultimate Solutions
15571 Container Ln, Huntington Beach (92649-1530)
PHONE.....................714 901-8400
William Allan, *CEO*
Bisson Monty, *
Tim Petersen, *
Christina Limon, *
▲ **EMP:** 31 **EST:** 1996
SQ FT: 2,500
SALES (est): 6.86MM **Privately Held**
Web: www.sandiaplastics.com
SIC: 3089 Injection molded finished plastics products, nec

(P-4237)

SERCO MOLD INC (PA)

Also Called: Serpac Electronic Enclosures
2009 Wright Ave, La Verne (91750-5812)
PHONE.....................626 331-0517
Patricia Ann Serio, *CEO*
Don Serio Junior, *VP*
▲ **EMP:** 38 **EST:** 1978
SQ FT: 85,000
SALES (est): 7.85MM
SALES (corp-wide): 7.85MM **Privately Held**
Web: www.serpac.com
SIC: 3089 3544 5999 Injection molding of plastics; Industrial molds; Electronic parts and equipment

(P-4238)

SETCO LLC

4875 E Hunter Ave, Anaheim (92807-2005)
PHONE.....................812 424-2904
Patty Harper, *Brnch Mgr*
EMP: 150
Web: www.berryglobal.com
SIC: 3089 Plastics containers, except foam
HQ: Setco, Llc
    101 Oakley St
    Evansville IN 47710
    812 424-2904

(P-4239)

SIERRACIN/SYLMAR CORPORATION

Also Called: PPG Aerospace
12780 San Fernando Rd, Sylmar (91342-3796)

PHONE.....................818 362-6711
Barry Gillespie, *CEO*
◆ **EMP:** 600 **EST:** 1952
SQ FT: 300,000
SALES (est): 62.73MM
SALES (corp-wide): 17.65B **Publicly Held**
Web: www.ppgaerospace.com
SIC: 3089 3812 3621 3231 Windshields, plastics; Search and navigation equipment; Motors and generators; Products of purchased glass
PA: Ppg Industries, Inc.
    1 Ppg Pl
    412 434-3131

(P-4240)

SKB CORPORATION (PA)

434 W Levers Pl, Orange (92867-3605)
PHONE.....................714 637-1252
Steven A Kottman, *CEO*
David Sanderson, *
Don Weber, *
◆ **EMP:** 350 **EST:** 1975
SALES (est): 46.72MM
SALES (corp-wide): 46.72MM **Privately Held**
Web: www.skbcases.com
SIC: 3089 3161 Cases, plastics; Luggage

(P-4241)

SMART LLC

Also Called: Chemical Guys
3501 Sepulveda Blvd, Torrance (90505-2537)
PHONE.....................866 822-3670
David Knotek, *CEO*
Paul Schneider, *
▼ **EMP:** 40 **EST:** 2003
SALES (est): 27.68MM **Privately Held**
Web: www.chemicalguys.com
SIC: 3089 5013 Automotive parts, plastic; Automotive supplies and parts

(P-4242)

SNAPWARE CORPORATION

Also Called: Corningware Corelle & More
2325 Cottonwood Ave, Riverside (92508-2309)
PHONE.....................951 361-3100
Kris Malkoski, *CEO*
Ken Tran, *
Grant Hartman, *
◆ **EMP:** 180 **EST:** 1991
SALES (est): 11.27MM
SALES (corp-wide): 994.64MM **Privately Held**
Web: www.snapware.com
SIC: 3089 Plastics kitchenware, tableware, and houseware
HQ: Instant Brands Llc
    3025 Hghland Pkwy Ste 700
    Downers Grove IL 60515
    847 233-8600

(P-4243)

SOL-PAK THERMOFORMING INC

3388 Fruitland Ave, Vernon (90058-3714)
PHONE.....................323 582-3333
Moussa Soleimani-kashi, *Pr*
Joseph Soleimani, *VP*
Joubin Soleimani-kashi, *CFO*
▲ **EMP:** 23 **EST:** 2004
SALES (est): 4.62MM **Privately Held**
Web: www.solpak.com
SIC: 3089 Plastics containers, except foam

(P-4244)

SONFARREL

3000 E La Jolla St, Anaheim (92806-1310)

PHONE.....................714 630-7280
EMP: 25 **EST:** 1955
SALES (est): 4.5MM **Privately Held**
Web: www.sonfarrel.com
SIC: 3089 Injection molding of plastics

(P-4245)

SOUTHERN CALIFORNIA PLAS INC

3122 Maple St, Santa Ana (92707-4408)
PHONE.....................714 751-7084
Anthony Codet, *Pr*
▲ **EMP:** 54 **EST:** 1995
SQ FT: 240,000
SALES (est): 7.9MM **Privately Held**
SIC: 3089 Injection molding of plastics

(P-4246)

SP CRAFTECH I LLC

Also Called: Craftech
2941 E La Jolla St, Anaheim (92806-1306)
PHONE.....................714 630-8117
Thomas Stenglein, *Prin*
Allen Webb, *Prin*
Robert Joubran, *Prin*
EMP: 38 **EST:** 2021
SALES (est): 9.79MM **Privately Held**
Web: www.craftechcorp.com
SIC: 3089 Injection molding of plastics

(P-4247)

SPIN PRODUCTS INC

13878 Yorba Ave, Chino (91710-5518)
PHONE.....................909 590-7000
Paul Burlingham, *Pr*
William Burlingham, *
▲ **EMP:** 24 **EST:** 1996
SQ FT: 96,000
SALES (est): 4.87MM **Privately Held**
Web: www.spinproducts.com
SIC: 3089 Plastics containers, except foam

(P-4248)

STAR PLASTIC DESIGN

25914 President Ave, Harbor City (90710-3333)
PHONE.....................310 530-7119
Dana Maltun, *Pr*
▲ **EMP:** 60 **EST:** 1980
SQ FT: 25,000
SALES (est): 2.43MM **Privately Held**
Web: www.starplastic.com
SIC: 3089 Injection molding of plastics

(P-4249)

STAR SHIELD SOLUTIONS LLC

4315 Santa Ana St, Ontario (91761-7872)
P.O. Box 968 (91743)
PHONE.....................866 662-4477
Gil Stanfill, *Managing Member*
EMP: 60 **EST:** 2007
SALES (est): 5.88MM **Privately Held**
Web: www.starshieldsolutions.com
SIC: 3089 7389 Automotive parts, plastic; Financial services

(P-4250)

STEWARD PLASTICS INC

Also Called: Smooth-Bor Plastics
23322 Del Lago Dr, Laguna Hills (92653-1310)
PHONE.....................949 581-9530
▼ **EMP:** 75 **EST:** 1971
SALES (est): 10.06MM **Privately Held**
Web: www.smoothborplastics.com
SIC: 3089 Plastics processing

(P-4251)

STONE CANYON INDUSTRIES LLC
1875 Century Park E Ste 320, Los Angeles (90067-2539)
PHONE...................310 570-4869
James H Fordyce, *CEO*
Adam Cohn, *
Michael Neumann, *
Sascha Kaeser, *
Shawn Malleck, *
EMP: 2708 EST: 2014
SALES (est): 25.86MM **Privately Held**
Web: www.scihinc.com
SIC: 3089 3411 Plastics containers, except foam; Metal cans

(P-4252)

STRAND ART COMPANY INC
4700 E Hunter Ave, Anaheim (92807-1919)
PHONE...................714 777-0444
Kevin Strand, *Pr*
Vicky Strand, *
▲ EMP: 50 EST: 1974
SQ FT: 10,480
SALES (est): 2.1MM **Privately Held**
Web: www.strandart.com
SIC: 3089 Injection molded finished plastics products, nec

(P-4253)

SYNTECH DEVELOPMENT & MFG INC (PA)
Also Called: S D M
13948 Mountain Ave, Chino (91710-9018)
PHONE...................909 465-5554
Harry N Herbert, *CEO*
Bob Hobbs, *
Eddie Montelongo, *
EMP: 23 EST: 1998
SQ FT: 11,000
SALES (est): 36.4MM
SALES (corp-wide): 36.4MM **Privately Held**
Web: www.sdmplastics.com
SIC: 3089 Injection molding of plastics

(P-4254)

TALCO PLASTICS INC
3270 E 70th St, Long Beach (90805-1821)
PHONE...................562 630-1224
Ajit Ferera, *Mgr*
EMP: 64
SALES (corp-wide): 23.05MM **Privately Held**
Web: www.talcoplastics.com
SIC: 3089 4953 Extruded finished plastics products, nec; Recycling, waste materials
PA: Talco Plastics, Inc.
1000 W Rincon St
061 631 2000

(P-4255)

TAMSHELL CORP
Also Called: Tamshell
545 Monica Cir, Corona (92878-5447)
PHONE...................951 272-9395
John Hernandez, *Pr*
Art Pierce, *
EMP: 95 EST: 1979
SALES (est): 20.25MM **Privately Held**
Web: www.tamshell.com
SIC: 3089 Caps, plastics

(P-4256)

TENMA AMERICA CORPORATION
333 H St Ste 5000, Chula Vista (91910-5561)

PHONE...................619 754-2250
Kan Kaneko, *CEO*
Takayoshi Hirayama, *Pr*
Hitoshi Nakamura, *VP*
Minoru Watanaba, *Sec*
▲ EMP: 168 EST: 1996
SALES (est): 9.9MM **Privately Held**
Web: www.nket.net
SIC: 3089 Molding primary plastics
PA: Tenma Corporation
1-63-6, Akabane

(P-4257)

THERMODYNE INTERNATIONAL LTD
1841 S Business Pkwy, Ontario (91761-8537)
PHONE...................909 923-9945
Gary S Ackerman, *Ch Bd*
Scott Ackerman, *
◆ EMP: 110 EST: 1967
SQ FT: 57,500
SALES (est): 3.88MM **Privately Held**
Web: www.thermodyne.com
SIC: 3089 3694 Plastics containers, except foam; Engine electrical equipment

(P-4258)

THREE-D PLASTICS INC (PA)
Also Called: Three-D Traffics Works
430 N Varney St, Burbank (91502-1732)
PHONE...................323 849-1316
Frank J Dvoracek, *CEO*
Joseph Dvoracek, *
Kathleen D Trumbo, *
EMP: 35 EST: 1968
SQ FT: 40,000
SALES (est): 4.68MM
SALES (corp-wide): 4.68MM **Privately Held**
Web: www.3dplastics.com
SIC: 3089 Injection molding of plastics

(P-4259)

TNT PLASTIC MOLDING INC (PA)
725 E Harrison St, Corona (92879-1350)
PHONE...................951 808-9700
Diane Mixson, *Pr*
John Chadwick, *
Lynn Chadwick, *
Doug Chadwick, *
Dennis Chadwick, *
▲ EMP: 80 EST: 1979
SQ FT: 30,000
SALES (est): 24.69MM
SALES (corp-wide): 24.69MM **Privately Held**
Web: www.tntplasticmolding.com
SIC: 3089 Injection molding of plastics

(P-4260)

TOTEX MANUFACTURING INC
3050 Lomita Blvd, Torrance (90505-5103)
PHONE...................310 326-2028
Tommy Tong, *Pr*
▲ EMP: 70 EST: 1998
SALES (est): 11.17MM **Privately Held**
Web: www.totexmfg.com
SIC: 3089 5063 Battery cases, plastics or plastics combination; Batteries, dry cell

(P-4261)

TRELLBORG SLING SLTIONS US INC
3077 Rollie Gates Dr, Paso Robles (93446-9500)
PHONE...................805 239-4284
EMP: 49

SALES (corp-wide): 60.4MM **Privately Held**
Web: www.trelleborg.com
SIC: 3089 Plastics processing
HQ: Trelleborg Sealing Solutions Us, Inc.
2531 Bremer Rd
Fort Wayne IN 46803
260 749-9631

(P-4262)

TRIM-LOK INC (PA)
6855 Hermosa Cir, Buena Park (90620-1151)
P.O. Box 6180 (90622-6180)
PHONE...................714 562-0500
Gary Whitener, *Pr*
◆ EMP: 178 EST: 1971
SQ FT: 57,000
SALES (est): 51.5MM
SALES (corp-wide): 51.5MM **Privately Held**
Web: www.trimlok.com
SIC: 3089 Molding primary plastics

(P-4263)

TRINITY INTERNATIONAL INDS LLC
1041 E 230th St, Carson (90745-5007)
PHONE...................800 985-5506
Cze Chao Tam, *CEO*
▲ EMP: 33 EST: 2007
SQ FT: 35,000
SALES (est): 11.14MM **Privately Held**
Web: www.trinityii.com
SIC: 3089 2511 2542 Organizers for closets, drawers, etc.: plastics; Storage chests, household: wood; Racks, merchandise display or storage: except wood

(P-4264)

TRU-FORM PLASTICS INC
14600 Hoover St, Westminster (92683-5346)
PHONE...................310 327-9444
Douglas W Sahm Senior, *CEO*
John D Evans, *
Anita Lorber, *
Clauve Hurwicz, *
▲ EMP: 35 EST: 1956
SQ FT: 1,000
SALES (est): 5.19MM **Privately Held**
Web: www.tru-formplastics.com
SIC: 3089 Plastics processing

(P-4265)

TST MOLDING LLC
Also Called: All Amrcan Injction Mlding Svc
42022 Avenida Alvarado, Temecula (92590-3445)
PHONE...................951 296-6200
Terry Voss, *Managing Member*
EMP: 27 EST: 2009
SALES (est): 4.54MM **Privately Held**
Web: www.tstmolding.com
SIC: 3089 Injection molding of plastics

(P-4266)

UFO INC
2110 Belgrave Ave, Huntington Park (90255-2713)
P.O. Box 58192 (90058-0192)
PHONE...................323 588-5450
Efi Youavian, *Pr*
Efraim Youavian, *
▲ EMP: 50 EST: 1982
SQ FT: 65,000
SALES (est): 1.31MM **Privately Held**
Web: www.ufobrand.com

SIC: 3089 2842 5199 Sponges, plastics; Polishes and sanitation goods; Foams and rubber

(P-4267)

US POLYMERS INC (PA)
Also Called: Duramax Building Products
1057 S Vail Ave, Montebello (90640-6019)
PHONE...................323 728-3023
Viken Ohanesian, *CEO*
Jacques Ohanesian, *
Vram Ohanesian, *
Haigan Ohanesian, *
◆ EMP: 100 EST: 1983
SQ FT: 70,000
SALES (est): 24.57MM
SALES (corp-wide): 24.57MM **Privately Held**
Web: www.uspolymersinc.com
SIC: 3089 3084 Shutters, plastics; Plastics pipe

(P-4268)

V-T INDUSTRIES INC
9818 Firestone Blvd, Downey (90241-5595)
PHONE...................714 521-2008
EMP: 69
SALES (corp-wide): 434.93MM **Privately Held**
Web: www.vtindustries.com
SIC: 3089 3083 4213 2435 Plastics hardware and building products; Plastics finished products, laminated; Trucking, except local; Hardwood veneer and plywood
PA: V-T Industries Inc.
1000 Industrial Park Rd
712 368-4381

(P-4269)

VANTAGE ASSOCIATES INC
12333 Los Nietos Rd, Santa Fe Springs (90670-2911)
PHONE...................562 968-1400
Paul Roy, *CEO*
EMP: 65
SQ FT: 20,000
SALES (corp-wide): 24.86MM **Privately Held**
Web: www.vantageassoc.com
SIC: 3089 2499 5085 3621 Plastics processing; Spools, reels, and pulleys: wood; Industrial supplies; Motors and generators
PA: Vantage Associates Inc.
1565 Macarthur Blvd
619 477-6940

(P-4270)

VINVENTIONS USA LLC (PA)
888 Prospect St, La Jolla (92037-4260)
PHONE...................919 460-2200
Lars Von Kantzow, *Managing Member*
Peter A Schmitt, *Managing Member**
◆ EMP: 230 EST: 1998
SALES (est): 23.47MM
SALES (corp-wide): 23.47MM **Privately Held**
Web: us.vinventions.com
SIC: 3089 Caps, plastics

(P-4271)

VPET USA LLC
12925b Marlay Ave, Fontana (92337-6939)
PHONE...................909 605-1668
Jeffrey Kellar, *CEO*
Steven Saull, *
EMP: 96 EST: 2019
SALES (est): 2.18MM **Privately Held**
Web: www.vpetusa.com

SIC: 3089 Plastics containers, except foam

(P-4272)
WADDINGTON NORTH AMERICA INC
Also Called: Wna City of Industry
1135 Samuelson St, City Of Industry
(91748-1222)
PHONE.................................626 913-4022
Mike Evans, Pr
EMP: 112
SALES (corp-wide): 32.64B **Publicly Held**
Web: www.novolex.com
SIC: 3089 Plastics kitchenware, tableware, and houseware
HQ: Waddington North America, Inc.
3436 Tringdon Way Ste 100
Charlotte NC 28277

(P-4273)
WCP WEST COAST GLASS LLC
Also Called: West Coast Vinyl Windows
17730 Crusader Ave, Cerritos
(90703-2629)
PHONE.................................562 653-9797
Charles Neubauer, Pr
▲ **EMP:** 95 **EST:** 1988
SQ FT: 50,000
SALES (est): 7.29MM
SALES (corp-wide): 11.29MM **Privately Held**
Web: www.westcoastglass.com
SIC: 3089 3211 Windows, plastics; Insulating glass, sealed units
HQ: Agnora Ltd
200 Mountain Rd
Collingwood ON L9Y 4
705 444-6654

(P-4274)
WEST-BAG INC
1161 Monterey Pass Rd, Monterey Park
(91754-3614)
PHONE.................................323 264-0750
Luis Michel, Pr
Sixto Michel, *
EMP: 30 **EST:** 1977
SQ FT: 12,000
SALES (est): 2.47MM **Privately Held**
Web: www.west-bag.com
SIC: 3089 5149 Food casings, plastics; Sausage casings

(P-4275)
WESTERN CASE INCORPORATED
231 E Alessandro Blvd, Riverside
(92508-5084)
PHONE.................................951 214-6380
TOLL FREE: 877
Paul F Queyrel, CEO
Mario Robles, Prin
▲ **EMP:** 60 **EST:** 1981
SALES (est): 13.47MM **Privately Held**
Web: www.westerncase.com
SIC: 3089 3544 3444 Cases, plastics; Special dies, tools, jigs, and fixtures; Sheet metalwork

3111 Leather Tanning And Finishing

(P-4276)
ANDREW ALEXANDER INC
Also Called: Falltech
1306 S Alameda St, Compton
(90221-4803)
PHONE.................................323 752-0066

Michael Dancyger, Pr
Jeff Crosson, *
◆ **EMP:** 100 **EST:** 1992
SQ FT: 100,000
SALES (est): 24.92MM **Privately Held**
Web: www.falltech.com
SIC: 3111 Harness leather

(P-4277)
CUSTOMFAB INC
7345 Orangewood Ave, Garden Grove
(92841-1411)
PHONE.................................714 891-9119
Donald Alhanati, Pr
▲ **EMP:** 250 **EST:** 1991
SQ FT: 47,000
SALES (est): 14.47MM **Privately Held**
Web: www.customfabusa.com
SIC: 3111 3842 Accessory products, leather; Surgical appliances and supplies

(P-4278)
HERITAGE LEATHER COMPANY INC
4011 E 52nd St, Maywood (90270-2205)
PHONE.................................323 983-0420
Jose C Munoz, CEO
Gustavo Gonzalez, *
▲ **EMP:** 30 **EST:** 2000
SQ FT: 5,000
SALES (est): 546.15K **Privately Held**
Web: www.heritageleather.com
SIC: 3111 Belting leather

(P-4279)
LA LA LAND PRODUCTION & DESIGN
1701 S Santa Fe Ave, Los Angeles
(90021-2904)
PHONE.................................323 406-9223
Alexander M Zar, CEO
EMP: 45 **EST:** 2006
SQ FT: 30,000
SALES (est): 4.7MM **Privately Held**
Web: www.lalaland-design.com
SIC: 3111 Accessory products, leather

3131 Footwear Cut Stock

(P-4280)
CYDWOQ INC
2102 Kenmere Ave, Burbank (91504-3413)
PHONE.................................818 848-8307
Rafi Balouzian, Pr
Richard Delamarter, Stockholder*
◆ **EMP:** 28 **EST:** 1996
SQ FT: 15,000
SALES (est): 1.82MM **Privately Held**
Web: www.cydwoq.com
SIC: 3131 3199 Laces, shoe and boot: leather; Leather belting and strapping

(P-4281)
SOLE SOCIETY GROUP INC
11248 Playa Ct # B, Culver City
(90230-6127)
P.O. Box 5206 (90231)
PHONE.................................310 220-0808
Andy Solomon, Managing Member
Talitha Peters, *
▲ **EMP:** 200 **EST:** 2011
SALES (est): 1.66MM
SALES (corp-wide): 3.07B **Publicly Held**
Web: www.solesociety.com
SIC: 3131 5661 5621 Boot and shoe accessories; Men's boots; Ready-to-wear apparel, women's
HQ: Vcs Group Llc
1370 Ave Of The Americas

New York NY 10019
646 898-1050

3143 Men's Footwear, Except Athletic

(P-4282)
CAREISMATIC BRANDS LLC (DH)
Also Called: Cherokee Uniform
15301 Ventura Blvd, Sherman Oaks
(91403-3102)
PHONE.................................818 671-2128
Sidharth Lakhani, CEO
Robert Pierpoint, *
Kent Percy, CRO*
◆ **EMP:** 203 **EST:** 1995
SQ FT: 140,000
SALES (est): 189.35MM
SALES (corp-wide): 609.92MM **Privately Held**
Web: www.careismatic.com
SIC: 3143 3144 5139 2339 Men's footwear, except athletic; Women's footwear, except athletic; Shoes; Women's and misses' outerwear, nec
HQ: Careismatic Group Ii, Inc.
1119 Colorado Ave
Santa Monica CA 90401
818 671-2100

3144 Women's Footwear, Except Athletic

(P-4283)
ALPARGATAS USA INC
Also Called: Havaianas
513 Boccaccio Ave, Venice (90291-4806)
PHONE.................................646 277-7171
Marcio Moura, CEO
Afonso Fugiyama, *
◆ **EMP:** 30 **EST:** 2006
SALES (est): 7.8MM **Privately Held**
SIC: 3144 Women's footwear, except athletic
PA: Alpargatas Sa
Av. Das Nacoes Unidas 14261

(P-4284)
EVOLUTION DESIGN LAB INC
Also Called: Jellypop
144 W Colorado Blvd, Pasadena
(91105-1949)
PHONE.................................626 960-8388
Jennet Chow, CEO
▲ **EMP:** 25 **EST:** 2009
SALES (est): 3.51MM **Privately Held**
Web: www.jellypop-shoes.com
SIC: 3144 5139 Women's footwear, except athletic; Shoes

(P-4285)
IMPO INTERNATIONAL LLC
Also Called: Chili's
3510 Black Rd, Santa Maria (93455-5927)
P.O. Box 639 (93456-0639)
PHONE.................................805 922-7753
Laura Ann Hopkins, Managing Member
◆ **EMP:** 24 **EST:** 1968
SQ FT: 30,000
SALES (est): 4.78MM **Privately Held**
Web: www.impo.com
SIC: 3144 Boots, canvas or leather: women's

(P-4286)
MILLENNIAL BRANDS LLC
126 W 9th St, Los Angeles (90015-1500)
PHONE.................................925 230-0617

Catalin Gaitanaru, Prin
EMP: 27
SIC: 3144 Women's footwear, except athletic
PA: Millennial Brands Llc
2002 Diablo Rd

(P-4287)
SURGEON WORLDWIDE INC
3855 S Hill St, Los Angeles (90037-1415)
PHONE.................................707 501-7962
Mariko Chambrone, VP
EMP: 27 **EST:** 2018
SALES (est): 1.83MM **Privately Held**
SIC: 3144 3143 Women's footwear, except athletic; Men's footwear, except athletic

3149 Footwear, Except Rubber, Nec

(P-4288)
SKECHERS USA INC (PA)
Also Called: Skechers
228 Manhattan Beach Blvd Ste 200, Manhattan Beach (90266-5356)
PHONE.................................310 318-3100
Robert Greenberg, Ch Bd
Michael Greenberg, *
John Vandemore, CFO
David Weinberg, *
Philip Paccione, Corporate Secretary
▲ **EMP:** 80 **EST:** 1992
SQ FT: 213,000
SALES (est): 8B **Publicly Held**
Web: www.skechers.com
SIC: 3149 3021 Athletic shoes, except rubber or plastic; Shoes, rubber or plastic molded to fabric

(P-4289)
SOLE TECHNOLOGY INC (PA)
Also Called: Etnies
26921 Fuerte, Lake Forest (92630-8149)
PHONE.................................949 460-2020
Pierre Senizergues, Pr
Paul Migaki, COO
◆ **EMP:** 95 **EST:** 1996
SALES (est): 38.68MM **Privately Held**
Web: www.soletechnology.com
SIC: 3149 5139 Athletic shoes, except rubber or plastic; Footwear

3161 Luggage

(P-4290)
AMERICAN TRAVELER INC
9509 Feron Blvd, Rancho Cucamonga
(91730-4541)
PHONE.................................909 466-4000
Scott Oh, CEO
June Yi, *
EMP: 25 **EST:** 2009
SALES (est): 1.26MM **Privately Held**
Web: www.americantravelerinc.com
SIC: 3161 Luggage

(P-4291)
ANVIL CASES INC
1242 E Edna Pl Unit B, Covina
(91724-2540)
PHONE.................................626 968-4100
Joseph Calzone, Pr
Vincent Calzone, *
▲ **EMP:** 125 **EST:** 1952
SALES (est): 5.27MM
SALES (corp-wide): 20.3MM **Privately Held**
Web: www.calzoneandanvil.com

▲ = Import ▼ = Export
◆ = Import/Export

SIC: 3161 Musical instrument cases
PA: Calzone, Ltd.
225 Black Rock Ave
203 367-5766

(P-4292)
ENCORE CASES INC
8600 Tamarack Ave, Sun Valley
(91352-2504)
PHONE..............................818 768-8803
Gary A Peterson, *Pr*
▲ EMP: 27 EST: 1988
SALES (est): 2.35MM **Privately Held**
Web: www.encorecases.com
SIC: 3161 Cases, carrying, nec

(P-4293)
G & G QUALITY CASE CO INC
2025 E 25th St, Vernon (90058-1127)
P.O. Box 58541 (90058-0541)
PHONE..............................323 233-2482
Efren Guzman, *Pr*
Ben Germain, *
Maria Germain, *
▲ EMP: 70 EST: 1978
SQ FT: 13,500
SALES (est): 2.13MM **Privately Held**
Web: www.ggqualitycase.com
SIC: 3161 Musical instrument cases

(P-4294)
HAMMITT INC
2101 Pacific Coast Hwy, Hermosa Beach
(90254-2796)
PHONE..............................310 292-5200
Anthony Drockton, *Ch*
Andrew Forbes, *
▲ EMP: 51 EST: 2008
SQ FT: 3,600
SALES (est): 26.5MM **Privately Held**
Web: www.hammitt.com
SIC: 3161 3171 Traveling bags; Women's
handbags and purses

(P-4295)
HSIAO & MONTANO INC
Also Called: Odyssey Innovative Designs
809 W Santa Anita Ave, San Gabriel
(91776-1016)
PHONE..............................626 588-2528
Mario Montano, *CEO*
John Hsiao, *
▲ EMP: 50 EST: 1995
SALES (est): 1.64MM **Privately Held**
Web: www.odysseygear.com
SIC: 3161 3648 5084 1751 Musical
instrument cases; Lighting equipment, nec;
Woodworking machinery; Cabinet and
finish carpentry

(P-4296)
JAN-AL INNERPRIZES INC
Also Called: Jan-Al Cases
3339 Union Pacific Ave, Los Angeles
(90023-3812)
P.O. Box 23337 (90023-0337)
PHONE..............................323 260-7212
Miriam Alejandro, *Pr*
Jan Michael Alejandro, *
▲ EMP: 30 EST: 1983
SQ FT: 16,000
SALES (est): 2.56MM **Privately Held**
Web: www.janalcase.com
SIC: 3161 Luggage

(P-4297)
NATUS INC
4522 Katella Ave Ste 200, Los Alamitos
(90720-2624)
PHONE..............................626 355-3746

Jimmy Chen, *Pr*
◆ EMP: 90 EST: 2009
SALES (est): 595.82K **Privately Held**
SIC: 3161 Suitcases

(P-4298)
OGIO INTERNATIONAL INC (HQ)
Also Called: Ogio
2180 Rutherford Rd, Carlsbad
(92008-7328)
PHONE..............................801 619-4100
Anthony Palma, *CEO*
Michael Pratt, *
▲ EMP: 23 EST: 1989
SQ FT: 70,000
SALES (est): 805.55K
SALES (corp-wide): 4.28B **Publicly Held**
Web: www.ogio.com
SIC: 3161 2393 Traveling bags; Textile bags
PA: Topgolf Callaway Brands Corp.
2180 Rutherford Rd
760 931-1771

(P-4299)
OGIO INTERNATIONAL INC
Also Called: Ogio Powersports
508 Constitution Ave, Camarillo
(93012-8510)
PHONE..............................800 326-6325
EMP: 77
SALES (corp-wide): 4.28B **Publicly Held**
Web: www.ogio.com
SIC: 3161 Luggage
HQ: Ogio International, Inc.
2180 Rutherford Rd
Carlsbad CA 92008
801 619-4100

(P-4300)
SANDPIPER OF CALIFORNIA INC
687 Anita St Ste A, Chula Vista
(91911-4693)
P.O. Box 489 (91908-0489)
PHONE..............................619 424-2222
EMP: 54
SIC: 3161 Luggage

(P-4301)
TARGUS US LLC
1211 N Miller St, Anaheim (92806-1933)
PHONE..............................714 765-5555
Mikel Williams, *CEO*
Victor Streufert, *CFO*
EMP: 52 EST: 2015
SQ FT: 200,656
SALES (est): 2.44MM **Publicly Held**
Web: us.targus.com
SIC: 3161 Cases, carrying, nec
HQ: B. Riley Principal Investments, Llc
11100 Santa Monica Blvd
Los Angeles CA 90025
310 966-1444

(P-4302)
**TRAVELERS CHOICE
TRAVELWARE**
Also Called: Golden Pacific
2805 S Reservoir St, Pomona
(91766-6526)
PHONE..............................909 529-7688
Roger Yang, *CEO*
Annie Yang, *CFO*
▲ EMP: 55 EST: 1993
SQ FT: 12,000
SALES (est): 3.44MM **Privately Held**
Web: www.travelerchoice.com
SIC: 3161 5948 Luggage; Luggage and
leather goods stores

3171 Women's Handbags And Purses

(P-4303)
ISABELLE HANDBAG INC
3155 Bandini Blvd Unit A, Vernon
(90058-4134)
PHONE..............................323 277-9888
Roye Xu, *Pr*
James Li, *VP*
▲ EMP: 35 EST: 2011
SQ FT: 2,000
SALES (est): 354.41K **Privately Held**
Web: www.emperiahandbags.com
SIC: 3171 5632 Handbags, women's;
Handbags

(P-4304)
SBNW LLC (PA)
5600 W Adams Blvd, Los Angeles
(90016-2562)
PHONE..............................213 234-5122
Jason Rimokh, *
EMP: 110 EST: 2018
SALES (est): 992.61K
SALES (corp-wide): 992.61K **Privately
Held**
SIC: 3171 Handbags, women's

3172 Personal Leather Goods, Nec

(P-4305)
LEATHER PRO INC
Also Called: Turtleback Case
12900 Bradley Ave, Sylmar (91342-3829)
PHONE..............................818 833-8822
Brian Eremita, *Pr*
Al Eremita, *
▲ EMP: 24 EST: 2001
SQ FT: 13,000
SALES (est): 2.19MM **Privately Held**
Web: www.turtlebackcase.com
SIC: 3172 Personal leather goods, nec

(P-4306)
MALIBU LEATHER INC
510 W 6th St Ste 1002, Los Angeles
(90014-1311)
PHONE..............................310 985-0707
Allen Cinoglu, *Pr*
EMP: 125 EST: 2009
SQ FT: 12,000
SALES (est): 6.8MM **Privately Held**
SIC: 3172 5199 5948 Personal leather
goods, nec; Leather, leather goods, and furs
; Luggage and leather goods stores

(P-4307)
RIDGE WALLET LLC
Also Called: Ridge Wallet, The
2448 Main St, Santa Monica (90405-3516)
PHONE..............................818 636-2832
Daniel Kane, *Managing Member*
EMP: 61 EST: 2016
SALES (est): 4.78MM **Privately Held**
Web: www.ridge.com
SIC: 3172 Wallets

3199 Leather Goods, Nec

(P-4308)
AKER INTERNATIONAL INC
Also Called: Aker Leather Products
2248 Main St Ste 4, Chula Vista
(91911-3932)

PHONE..............................619 423-5182
Kamuran Aker, *CEO*
Laurie Aker, *
Levent Aker, *
▲ EMP: 30 EST: 1981
SQ FT: 10,000
SALES (est): 3.44MM **Privately Held**
Web: www.akerleather.com
SIC: 3199 Holsters, leather

(P-4309)
**CUSTOM LEATHERCRAFT MFG
LLC**
Also Called: CLC Work Gear
5701 S Eastern Ave, Commerce
(90040-2973)
◆ EMP: 73 EST: 1983
SALES (est): 24.98MM **Privately Held**
Web: www.goclc.com
SIC: 3199 2394 3111 Leather belting and
strapping; Canvas and related products;
Glove leather
HQ: Hultafors Group Ab
J A Wettergrens Gata 7, Inga
VAstra Frolunda 421 3
337237400

(P-4310)
ELEANOR RIGBY LEATHER CO
Also Called: Coda Mexico
4660 La Jolla Village Dr Ste 500 Pmb
50054, San Diego (92122-4605)
PHONE..............................619 356-5590
Peter Robinson, *CEO*
▲ EMP: 70 EST: 2011
SQ FT: 2,000
SALES (est): 4.74MM **Privately Held**
Web: www.eleanorrigbyhome.com
SIC: 3199 Leather garments

(P-4311)
YATES GEAR INC ✪
330 N Brand Blvd Ste 700, Glendale
(91203-2336)
PHONE..............................530 222-4606
Jeffrey Morris, *CEO*
Kyle E Renninger, *CFO*
Thomas A Burger Junior, *Sec*
▲ EMP: 55 EST: 2024
SALES (est): 3.71MM
SALES (corp-wide): 496.65MM **Privately
Held**
Web: www.yatesgear.com
SIC: 3199 3842 Safety belts, leather;
Personal safety equipment
PA: Gridiron Capital, Llc
220 Elm St Fl 2
203 972-1100

3211 Flat Glass

(P-4312)
BUDGET ENTERPRISES LLC
Also Called: Solar Art
23042 Mill Creek Dr, Laguna Hills
(92653-1214)
PHONE..............................949 697-9544
Matthew Darienzo, *CEO*
EMP: 25 EST: 2014
SALES (est): 5.22MM **Privately Held**
Web: www.solarart.com
SIC: 3211 Construction glass

(P-4313)
**CARDINAL GLASS INDUSTRIES
INC**
Also Called: Cardinal C G
24100 Cardinal Ave, Moreno Valley
(92551-9545)

PHONE...................951 485-9007
Scott Paisley, *Brnch Mgr*
EMP: 157
SALES (corp-wide): 1B Privately Held
Web: www.cardinalcorp.com
SIC: 3211 5039 3229 Flat glass; Glass construction materials; Pressed and blown glass, nec
PA: Cardinal Glass Industries Inc
775 Pririe Ctr Dr Ste 200
952 229-2600

(P-4314)
CEVIANS LLC (PA)
3193 Red Hill Ave, Costa Mesa (92626-3432)
PHONE...................714 619-5135
Eric Lemay, *Pr*
EMP: 84 EST: 2014
SALES (est): 15.21MM
SALES (corp-wide): 15.21MM Privately Held
Web: www.cevians.com
SIC: 3211 Flat glass

(P-4315)
CL SOLUTIONS LLC
1900 S Susan St, Santa Ana (92704-3924)
PHONE...................714 597-6499
Corre Marie Myer, *CEO*
EMP: 57 EST: 2011
SALES (est): 3.43MM Privately Held
Web:
www.transparentarmorsolutions.com
SIC: 3211 Flat glass

(P-4316)
INTERNATIONAL SKYLIGHTS
Also Called: Acralight International
1831 Ritchey St, Santa Ana (92705-5138)
PHONE...................800 325-4355
EMP: 110
Web: www.acralightsolar.com
SIC: 3211 Skylight glass

(P-4317)
MEDILAND CORPORATION
Also Called: Premium Windows
15 Longitude Way, Corona (92881-4911)
PHONE...................562 630-9696
Carlos Landazuri, *CEO*
Jose Medina, *Corporate Secretary**
▲ EMP: 79 EST: 2005
SALES (est): 8.46MM Privately Held
Web: www.premiumwindows.com
SIC: 3211 3645 Window glass, clear and colored; Garden, patio, walkway and yard lighting fixtures: electric

(P-4318)
SUNDOWN LIQUIDATING CORP (PA)
Also Called: Bristolite
401 Goetz Ave, Santa Ana (92707-3709)
PHONE...................714 540-8950
Randolph Heartfield, *CEO*
Rick Beets, *
◆ EMP: 92 EST: 1970
SQ FT: 100,000
SALES (est): 4.1MM
SALES (corp-wide): 4.1MM Privately Held
SIC: 3211 Skylight glass

(P-4319)
US HORIZON MANUFACTURING INC
'Also Called: U.S. Horizon Mfg
28539 Industry Dr, Valencia (91355-5424)
PHONE...................661 775-1675

Donald E Friest, *CEO*
Garrett A Russell, *
▲ EMP: 39 EST: 1998
SQ FT: 44,000
SALES (est): 11.74MM
SALES (corp-wide): 34.95B Privately Held
Web: www.ushorizon.com
SIC: 3211 3429 Plate and sheet glass; Hardware, nec
HQ: C. R. Laurence Co., Inc.
2503 E Vernon Ave
Los Angeles CA 90058
323 588-1281

3221 Glass Containers

(P-4320)
ACME VIAL & GLASS CO
Also Called: Acme Vial
1601 Commerce Way, Paso Robles (93446-3626)
PHONE...................805 239-2666
Debra C Knowles, *Pr*
Kay Anderson, *
▲ EMP: 25 EST: 1942
SALES (est): 4.54MM Privately Held
Web: acmevialglassa.openfos.com
SIC: 3221 3231 5113 Vials, glass; Products of purchased glass; Industrial and personal service paper

(P-4321)
PACIFIC VIAL MFG INC
2738 Supply Ave, Commerce (90040-2704)
PHONE...................323 721-7004
Steven Oh, *Prin*
▲ EMP: 40 EST: 2001
SQ FT: 30,000
SALES (est): 12.89MM Privately Held
Web: www.pacificvial.com
SIC: 3221 Vials, glass

(P-4322)
PACKLINE USA LLC
9555 Hyssop Dr, Rancho Cucamonga (91730-6124)
PHONE...................909 392-8000
Amir Tamshe, *Managing Member*
EMP: 50 EST: 2018
SALES (est): 10.02MM Privately Held
Web: www.packlineusa.com
SIC: 3221 3089 Bottles for packing, bottling, and canning: glass; Plastics containers, except foam

---

3229 Pressed And Blown Glass, Nec

(P-4323)
APUTURE IMAGING INDUSTRIES
1715 N Gower St, Los Angeles (90028-5405)
PHONE...................626 295-6133
Bob Meesterman, *Sls Dir*
EMP: 25 EST: 2015
SALES (est): 773.66K Privately Held
Web: www.aputure.com
SIC: 3229 Glass lighting equipment parts

(P-4324)
CARLEY (PA)
1502 W 228th St, Torrance (90501-5105)
PHONE...................310 325-8474
James A Carley, *Pr*
▲ EMP: 225 EST: 1974
SQ FT: 14,000
SALES (est): 7.82MM
SALES (corp-wide): 7.82MM Privately Held

Web: www.carleylamps.com
SIC: 3229 3646 3641 Lamp parts and shades, glass; Commercial lighting fixtures; Electric lamps

(P-4325)
DONOCO INDUSTRIES INC
Also Called: Encore Plastics
5642 Research Dr Ste B, Huntington Beach (92649-1634)
P.O. Box 3208 (92605-3208)
PHONE...................714 893-7889
Richard Harvey, *CEO*
Donald Okada, *
George West, *
EMP: 25 EST: 1993
SQ FT: 12,000
SALES (est): 1.91MM Privately Held
Web: www.encoreplastics.com
SIC: 3229 Tableware, glass or glass ceramic

(P-4326)
GLAS WERK INC
29710 Avenida De Las Bandera, Rancho Santa Margari (92688-2614)
PHONE...................949 766-1296
Maik Mike Bollhorn, *Pr*
▲ EMP: 26 EST: 1987
SQ FT: 6,000
SALES (est): 2.55MM Privately Held
Web: www.glaswerk.com
SIC: 3229 Scientific glassware

(P-4327)
IFIBER OPTIX INC
14450 Chambers Rd, Tustin (92780-6914)
PHONE...................714 665-9796
Sanjeev Jaiswal, *Pr*
▲ EMP: 25 EST: 2000
SQ FT: 5,731
SALES (est): 2.86MM Privately Held
Web: www.ifiberoptix.com
SIC: 3229 Fiber optics strands

(P-4328)
PERFORMANCE COMPOSITES INC
1418 S Alameda St, Compton (90221-4802)
PHONE...................310 328-6661
Francis Hu, *CEO*
EMP: 106 EST: 1994
SQ FT: 46,000
SALES (est): 22.36MM Privately Held
Web: www.performancecomposites.com
SIC: 3229 3624 3544 Glass fiber products; Carbon and graphite products; Special dies, tools, jigs, and fixtures

(P-4329)
SHAMIR INSIGHT INC
Also Called: Shamir
9938 Via Pasar, San Diego (92126-4559)
PHONE...................858 514-8330
Raanan Naftalovich, *CEO*
Richard Dailey, *
Joyce Hornaday, *
▲ EMP: 77 EST: 1997
SALES (est): 19.3MM
SALES (corp-wide): 7.66MM Privately Held
Web: www.rcpvrewards.com
SIC: 3229 Optical glass
HQ: Shamir Optical Industry Ltd
Kibbutz
Shamir 12135

(P-4330)
ZEONS INC
291 S La Cienega Blvd Ste 102, Beverly Hills (90211-3308)
PHONE...................323 302-8299
Naved Jafry, *Pr*
EMP: 312 EST: 2014
SQ FT: 3,500
SALES (est): 3.45MM Privately Held
SIC: 3229 1629 6211 Insulators, electrical: glass; Power plant construction; Investment certificate sales

---

3231 Products Of Purchased Glass

(P-4331)
CHAM-CAL ENGINEERING CO
12722 Western Ave, Garden Grove (92841-4017)
PHONE...................714 898-9721
▲ EMP: 85 EST: 1970
SALES (est): 9.17MM Privately Held
Web: www.chamcal.com
SIC: 3231 8711 Mirrors, truck and automobile: made from purchased glass; Engineering services

(P-4332)
DENNIS DIGIORGIO
Also Called: Oc Direct Shower Door
333 City Blvd W Ste 1700, Orange (92868-5905)
PHONE...................714 408-7527
Dennis Digiorgio, *Owner*
EMP: 43 EST: 2010
SALES (est): 1MM Privately Held
Web: www.ocframeless.com
SIC: 3231 Products of purchased glass

(P-4333)
GAFFOGLIO FMLY MTLCRAFTERS INC (PA)
Also Called: Camera Ready Cars
11161 Slater Ave, Fountain Valley (92708-4921)
PHONE...................714 444-2000
George Gaffoglio, *CEO*
Ruben Gaffoglio, *
Mike Alexander, *
EMP: 103 EST: 1979
SQ FT: 94,000
SALES (est): 11.42MM
SALES (corp-wide): 11.42MM Privately Held
Web: www.metalcrafters.com
SIC: 3231 3711 3365 Mirrors, truck and automobile: made from purchased glass; Automobile assembly, including specialty automobiles; Aerospace castings, aluminum

(P-4334)
GLASSWERKS LA INC (HQ)
Also Called: Glasswerks Group
8600 Rheem Ave, South Gate (90280-3333)
PHONE...................888 789-7810
Randy Steinberg, *CEO*
Ruben Huerta, *Sec*
Edwin Rosengrant, *VP Sls*
Michael Torres, *CFO*
▲ EMP: 280 EST: 1949
SQ FT: 100,000
SALES (est): 41.8MM Privately Held
Web: www.glasswerks.com
SIC: 3231 3211 Mirrored glass; Flat glass
PA: Gwla Acquisition Corp.
8600 Rheem Ave

(P-4335)
GP MERGER SUB INC
Also Called: Glaspro
9401 Ann St, Santa Fe Springs
(90670-2613)
PHONE..................................562 946-7722
Joseph Green, *Pr*
Jim Martineau, *
Jeff Brown, *
◆ EMP: 85 EST: 1986
SQ FT: 75,000
SALES (est): 11.84MM Privately Held
Web: www.glas-pro.com
SIC: 3231 Laminated glass: made from
purchased glass

(P-4336)
INVENIOS LLC
320 N Nopal St, Santa Barbara
(93103-3225)
PHONE..................................805 962-3333
Paul Then, *Pr*
EMP: 83 EST: 2017
SALES (est): 10.65MM
SALES (corp-wide): 12.59B Publicly Held
Web: www.invenios.com
SIC: 3231 Products of purchased glass
PA: Corning Incorporated
1 Riverfront Plz
607 974-9000

(P-4337)
JUDSON STUDIOS INC
200 S Avenue 66, Los Angeles
(90042-3632)
PHONE..................................323 255-0131
David Judson, *Pr*
EMP: 27 EST: 1897
SQ FT: 10,000
SALES (est): 2.27MM Privately Held
Web: www.judsonstudios.com
SIC: 3231 Stained glass: made from
purchased glass

(P-4338)
LARRY MTHVIN INSTALLATIONS INC (HQ)
Also Called: L M I
501 Kettering Dr, Ontario (91761-8150)
PHONE..................................909 563-1700
Larry Methvin, *CEO*
▲ EMP: 200 EST: 1975
SQ FT: 28,000
SALES (est): 22.86MM
SALES (corp-wide): 3.47B Publicly Held
Web: www.larrymethvin.com
SIC: 3231 3431 1751 Doors, glass: made
from purchased glass; Shower stalls, metal;
Carpentry work
PA: Patrick Industries, Inc.
107 W Franklin St
574 294-7511

(P-4339)
LIPPERT COMPONENTS MFG INC
Hehr Glass Co
1021 Walnut Ave, Pomona (91766-6528)
PHONE..................................909 628-5557
Pete Adams, *Mgr*
EMP: 50
SALES (corp-wide): 3.78B Publicly Held
Web: corporate.lippert.com
SIC: 3231 5231 Doors, glass: made from
purchased glass; Glass
HQ: Lippert Components Manufacturing,
Inc.
3501 County Rd 6 E
Elkhart IN 46514
574 535-1125

(P-4340)
MILGARD MANUFACTURING LLC
Also Called: Milgard-Simi Valley
355 E Easy St, Simi Valley (93065-1801)
PHONE..................................805 581-6325
Wayne Ramay, *Brnch Mgr*
EMP: 100
SALES (corp-wide): 822.1MM Privately
Held
Web: www.milgard.com
SIC: 3231 Products of purchased glass
HQ: Milgard Manufacturing Llc
1498 Pacific Ave Fl 4
Tacoma WA 98402
253 922-4343

(P-4341)
NEW GLASPRO INC
9401 Ann St, Santa Fe Springs
(90670-2613)
PHONE..................................800 776-2368
Joseph Green, *Pr*
EMP: 23 EST: 2005
SALES (est): 1.19MM Privately Held
Web: www.glas-pro.com
SIC: 3231 Products of purchased glass

(P-4342)
PACIFIC ARTGLASS CORPORATION
Also Called: Pacific Glass
125 W 157th St, Gardena (90248-2225)
PHONE..................................310 516-7828
John Williams, *Pr*
▲ EMP: 23 EST: 1976
SQ FT: 18,000
SALES (est): 2.37MM Privately Held
Web: www.pacificartglass.com
SIC: 3231 5231 Products of purchased glass
; Glass, leaded or stained

(P-4343)
PRL GLASS SYSTEMS INC
14760 Don Julian Rd, City Of Industry
(91746-3107)
PHONE..................................877 775-2586
EMP: 74
Web: www.prlglass.com
SIC: 3231 Products of purchased glass
PA: Prl Glass Systems, Inc.
13644 Nelson Ave

(P-4344)
PRL GLASS SYSTEMS INC (PA)
Also Called: P R L
13644 Nelson Ave, City Of Industry
(91746-2336)
PHONE..................................626 961-5890
◆ EMP: 200 EST: 1989
SALES (est): 51.31MM Privately Held
Web: www.prlglass.com
SIC: 3231 3354 Products of purchased glass
; Aluminum extruded products

(P-4345)
RAYOTEK SCIENTIFIC LLC
Also Called: Rayotek Scientific
8845 Rehco Rd, San Diego (92121-3261)
PHONE..................................858 558-3671
William Raggio, *Pr*
Jessica Yadley, *
EMP: 30 EST: 1996
SQ FT: 30,000
SALES (est): 8.35MM
SALES (corp-wide): 10.31MM Privately
Held
Web: www.rayotek.com

SIC: 3231 8748 Products of purchased glass
; Business consulting, nec
PA: Mcdanel Advanced Ceramic
Technologies, Llc
510 9th Ave
724 843-8300

(P-4346)
SREAM INC
12869 Temescal Canyon Rd Ste A, Corona
(92883-4021)
PHONE..................................951 245-6999
Jarir Farraj, *CEO*
Steve Rodriguez, *
EMP: 34 EST: 2013
SALES (est): 2.5MM Privately Held
Web: www.liquidsciglass.com
SIC: 3231 5231 Products of purchased glass
; Glass

(P-4347)
TOTAL MONT LLC
Also Called: Western States Glass
790 W 12th St, Long Beach (90813-2810)
PHONE..................................562 983-1374
EMP: 44 EST: 2020
SALES (est): 7.37MM Privately Held
SIC: 3231 3211 Insulating glass: made from
purchased glass; Tempered glass

(P-4348)
TRIVIEW GLASS INDUSTRIES LLC
Also Called: Triview
279 Shawnan Ln, La Habra (90631-8087)
PHONE..................................626 363-7980
Alexander A Kastaniuk, *CEO*
▲ EMP: 99 EST: 2008
SALES (est): 10.82MM Privately Held
Web: trivew-glass.squarespace.com
SIC: 3231 Products of purchased glass

(P-4349)
TWED-DELLS INC
Also Called: California Glass & Mirror Div
1900 S Susan St, Santa Ana (92704-3924)
PHONE..................................714 754-6900
Corey M Myer Junior, *Pr*
Gayle Myer, *
▲ EMP: 38 EST: 1980
SQ FT: 45,000
SALES (est): 5.6MM Privately Held
Web: www.tbmglass.com
SIC: 3231 Mirrored glass

(P-4350)
ZADRO PRODUCTS INC
14462 Astronautics Ln Ste 101, Huntington
Beach (92647-2077)
PHONE..................................714 892-9200
Zlatko Zadro, *Pr*
Becky Zadro, *
◆ EMP: 35 EST: 1986
SQ FT: 22,000
SALES (est): 7.51MM Privately Held
Web: www.zadroinc.com
SIC: 3231 3641 Mirrored glass; Electric
lamps

3241 Cement, Hydraulic

(P-4351)
CALPORTLAND COMPANY
Also Called: Oro Grande Cement Plant
19409 National Trails Hwy, Oro Grande
(92368-9705)
PHONE..................................760 245-5321
EMP: 58
Web: www.calportland.com

SIC: 3241 3273 5032 Portland cement;
Ready-mixed concrete; Brick, stone, and
related material
HQ: Calportland Company
2025 E Financial Way
Glendora CA 91741

(P-4352)
CALPORTLAND COMPANY (DH)
Also Called: Arizona Portland Cement
2025 E Financial Way, Glendora
(91741-4692)
P.O. Box 371534 (89137-1534)
PHONE..................................626 852-6200
Michio Kimura, *Ch Bd*
Allen Hamblen, *
James A Repman, *
James A Wendoll, *
John Renninger, *
▲ EMP: 77 EST: 1891
SQ FT: 28,000
SALES (est): 864.13MM Privately Held
Web: www.calportland.com
SIC: 3241 3273 5032 Portland cement;
Ready-mixed concrete; Brick, stone, and
related material
HQ: Taiheiyo Cement U.S.A., Inc.
2025 E Fincl Way Ste 200
Glendora CA 91741
626 852-6200

(P-4353)
CALPORTLAND COMPANY
Also Called: California Portland Cement
9350 Oak Creek Rd, Mojave (93501-7738)
PHONE..................................661 824-2401
Bruce Shaffer, *Brnch Mgr*
EMP: 130
Web: www.calportland.com
SIC: 3241 5032 5211 Masonry cement;
Brick, stone, and related material; Cement
HQ: Calportland Company
2025 E Financial Way
Glendora CA 91741

(P-4354)
CTS CEMENT MANUFACTURING CORP (PA)
12442 Knott St, Garden Grove
(92841-2832)
PHONE..................................714 379-8260
Walter J Hoyle, *CEO*
▼ EMP: 45 EST: 1978
SQ FT: 14,000
SALES (est): 35.68MM
SALES (corp-wide): 35.68MM Privately
Held
Web: www.ctscement.com
SIC: 3241 Cement, hydraulic

(P-4355)
JAMES HARDIE BUILDING PDTS INC
26300 La Alameda Ste 400, Mission Viejo
(92691-8372)
PHONE..................................949 348-1800
Louis Gries, *Pr*
EMP: 86
SQ FT: 97,250
Web: www.jameshardie.com
SIC: 3241 Natural cement
HQ: James Hardie Building Products Inc.
303 E Wacker Dr
Chicago IL 60601
312 291-5072

(P-4356)
MITSUBISHI CEMENT CORPORATION

1150 Pier F Ave, Long Beach (90802-6252)
PHONE..............................562 495-0600
Marty Marcum, *Mgr*
EMP: 428
Web: www.mitsubishicement.com
SIC: 3241 Cement, hydraulic
HQ: Mitsubishi Cement Corporation
   151 Cassia Way
   Henderson NV 89014
   702 932-3900

(P-4357)
MITSUBISHI CEMENT CORPORATION
5808 State Highway 18, Lucerne Valley
(92356-8179)
PHONE..............................760 248-7373
Jim Russell, *Brnch Mgr*
EMP: 175
Web: www.mitsubishicement.com
SIC: 3241 Portland cement
HQ: Mitsubishi Cement Corporation
   151 Cassia Way
   Henderson NV 89014
   702 932-3900

(P-4358)
NATIONAL CEMENT COMPANY INC (HQ)
15821 Ventura Blvd Ste 475, Encino
(91436-2935)
PHONE..............................818 728-5200
James E Rotch, *Ch Bd*
▲ **EMP:** 38 **EST:** 1920
SQ FT: 11,446
SALES (est): 452.77MM
SALES (corp-wide): 632.96MM **Privately Held**
Web: www.nationalcement.com
SIC: 3241 3273 Portland cement; Ready-mixed concrete
PA: Vicat
   Les Trois Vallons
   474275900

(P-4359)
RIVERSIDE CEMENT HOLDINGS COMPANY
Also Called: Txi Riverside Cement
1500 Rubidoux Blvd, Riverside
(92509-1840)
P.O. Box 832 (92502-0832)
PHONE..............................951 774-2500
▲ **EMP:** 380
SIC: 3241 3272 Natural cement; Concrete products, nec

3251 Brick And Structural Clay Tile

(P-4360)
ARTO BRICK / CALIFORNIA PAVERS
Also Called: Arto Brick and Cal Pavers
15209 S Broadway, Gardena (90248-1823)
PHONE..............................310 768-8500
Arto Alajian, *CEO*
EMP: 40 **EST:** 1966
SQ FT: 18,000
SALES (est): 4.53MM **Privately Held**
Web: www.arto.com
SIC: 3251 Brick and structural clay tile

3253 Ceramic Wall And Floor Tile

(P-4361)
OCEANSIDE GLASSTILE COMPANY (PA)
Also Called: Mandala
2445 Grand Ave, Vista (92081-7806)
PHONE..............................760 929-4000
Sean M Gildea, *CEO*
Jim Jensen, *
John Marckx, *
Rick Blacklock, *
Jeff Nibler, *
◆ **EMP:** 375 **EST:** 1992
SQ FT: 48,000
SALES (est): 33.6MM **Privately Held**
Web: www.glasstile.com
SIC: 3253 5032 Mosaic tile, glazed and unglazed: ceramic; Tile, clay or other ceramic, excluding refractory

3259 Structural Clay Products, Nec

(P-4362)
UNITED STATES TILE CO
909 Railroad St, Corona (92882-1906)
PHONE..............................951 739-4613
◆ **EMP:** 125
SIC: 3259 Roofing tile, clay

3261 Vitreous Plumbing Fixtures

(P-4363)
TUBULAR SPECIALTIES MFG INC
Also Called: T S M
13011 S Spring St, Los Angeles
(90061-1685)
PHONE..............................310 515-4801
Marcia Lynn Hemphill, *CEO*
L C Huntley, *
Arif Mansuri, *
▲ **EMP:** 62 **EST:** 1966
SQ FT: 38,000
SALES (est): 4.11MM **Privately Held**
Web: www.calltsm.com
SIC: 3261 2656 3446 Bathroom accessories/fittings, vitreous china or earthenware; Sanitary food containers; Railings, prefabricated metal

3264 Porcelain Electrical Supplies

(P-4364)
MAGNET SALES & MFG CO INC (HQ)
Also Called: Integrated Magnetics
11250 Playa Ct, Culver City (90230-6127)
PHONE..............................310 391-7213
TOLL FREE: 800
Anil Nanji, *Pr*
Anil Nanji, *Pr*
Gary Hooper, *
▲ **EMP:** 75 **EST:** 1936
SQ FT: 45,000
SALES (est): 18.77MM
SALES (corp-wide): 46.01MM **Privately Held**
Web: www.intemag.com

SIC: 3264 3621 Porcelain electrical supplies; Servomotors, electric
PA: Integrated Technologies Group, Inc.
   11250 Playa Ct
   310 391-7213

(P-4365)
PRECISION FRRITES CERAMICS INC
5432 Production Dr, Huntington Beach
(92649-1525)
PHONE..............................714 901-7622
Frank Hong, *CEO*
Myung Sook Hong, *
Sung Mo Hong, *Pr*
Ji Soo Lee, *General Vice President*
EMP: 99 **EST:** 1975
SQ FT: 23,811
SALES (est): 5.19MM **Privately Held**
Web: www.semiceramic.com
SIC: 3264 3674 3599 Porcelain electrical supplies; Semiconductors and related devices; Machine shop, jobbing and repair

3269 Pottery Products, Nec

(P-4366)
BERNEY-KARP INC
3350 E 26th St, Vernon (90058-4145)
PHONE..............................323 260-7122
Morry Karp, *Pr*
Anna Ramos, *
▲ **EMP:** 74 **EST:** 1970
SQ FT: 80,000
SALES (est): 4.8MM **Privately Held**
Web: berneykarp.openfos.com
SIC: 3269 Pottery cooking and kitchen articles

(P-4367)
HAGEN-RENAKER INC (PA)
914 W Cienega Ave, San Dimas
(91773-2415)
P.O. Box 41324 (90853-1324)
PHONE..............................909 599-2341
Susan Renaker Nikas, *Pr*
Mary Lou Salas, *
EMP: 80 **EST:** 1946
SQ FT: 88,964
SALES (est): 5.32MM
SALES (corp-wide): 5.32MM **Privately Held**
Web: www.hagenrenaker.com
SIC: 3269 0181 Figures: pottery, china, earthenware, and stoneware; Nursery stock, growing of

(P-4368)
SANTA BARBARA DESIGN STUDIO (PA)
1600 Pacific Ave, Oxnard (93033-2746)
P.O. Box 6087 (93160-6087)
PHONE..............................805 966-3883
Raymond Markow, *CEO*
◆ **EMP:** 53 **EST:** 1972
SQ FT: 2,400
SALES (est): 3.38MM
SALES (corp-wide): 3.38MM **Privately Held**
Web: www.sb-designstudio.com
SIC: 3269 5719 Art and ornamental ware, pottery; Pottery

3271 Concrete Block And Brick

(P-4369)
AIR-VOL BLOCK INC
1 Suburban Rd, San Luis Obispo
(93401-7523)
P.O. Box 931 (93406-0931)
PHONE..............................805 543-1314
Robert J Miller, *Pr*
Richard Ayres, *
EMP: 40 **EST:** 1962
SQ FT: 1,400
SALES (est): 5.87MM **Privately Held**
Web: www.airvolblock.com
SIC: 3271 Blocks, concrete or cinder: standard

(P-4370)
ANGELUS BLOCK CO INC (PA)
11374 Tuxford St, Sun Valley (91352-2678)
PHONE..............................714 637-8594
Mario Antonini, *Pr*
Edward Antonini, *
▲ **EMP:** 50 **EST:** 1946
SQ FT: 2,000
SALES (est): 24.19MM
SALES (corp-wide): 24.19MM **Privately Held**
Web: www.angelusblock.com
SIC: 3271 Concrete block and brick

(P-4371)
ORCO BLOCK & HARDSCAPE (PA)
11100 Beach Blvd, Stanton (90680-3219)
PHONE..............................714 527-2239
Richard J Muth, *CEO*
Mary M Muth, *
EMP: 60 **EST:** 1946
SQ FT: 5,000
SALES (est): 23.6MM
SALES (corp-wide): 23.6MM **Privately Held**
Web: www.orco.com
SIC: 3271 Architectural concrete: block, split, fluted, screen, etc.

(P-4372)
RCP BLOCK & BRICK INC (PA)
8240 Broadway, Lemon Grove
(91945-2004)
P.O. Box 579 (91946-0579)
PHONE..............................619 460-9101
Michael Finch, *CEO*
Charles T Finch, *
Eugene M Chubb, *
EMP: 57 **EST:** 1947
SQ FT: 4,000
SALES (est): 23.09MM
SALES (corp-wide): 23.09MM **Privately Held**
Web: www.rcpblock.com
SIC: 3271 5211 5032 Blocks, concrete or cinder: standard; Masonry materials and supplies; Concrete building products

(P-4373)
RCP BLOCK & BRICK INC
8755 N Magnolia Ave, Santee
(92071-4594)
PHONE..............................619 448-2240
Randy Scott, *Brnch Mgr*
EMP: 40
SALES (corp-wide): 23.09MM **Privately Held**
Web: www.rcpblock.com

SIC: **3271** 5032 5211 Blocks, concrete or cinder: standard; Concrete and cinder block ; Lumber and other building materials
PA: Rcp Block & Brick, Inc.
8240 Broadway
619 460-9101

(P-4374)
RCP BLOCK & BRICK INC
75 N 4th Ave, Chula Vista (91910-1007)
PHONE...............................619 474-1516
Tim Ostrom, *Mgr*
EMP: 41
SALES (corp-wide): 23.09MM **Privately Held**
Web: www.rcpblock.com
SIC: **3271** 5032 5211 Blocks, concrete or cinder: standard; Concrete and cinder block ; Concrete and cinder block
PA: Rcp Block & Brick, Inc.
8240 Broadway
619 460-9101

(P-4375)
RCP BLOCK & BRICK INC
577 N Vulcan Ave, Encinitas (92024-2120)
PHONE...............................760 753-1164
Chico Savage, *Mgr*
EMP: 41
SALES (corp-wide): 23.09MM **Privately Held**
Web: www.rcpblock.com
SIC: **3271** 5211 Blocks, concrete or cinder: standard; Lumber and other building materials
PA: Rcp Block & Brick, Inc.
8240 Broadway
619 460-9101

(P-4376)
WESTERN STATES WHOLESALE INC
Also Called: Patio Industries
1600 E Francis St, Ontario (91761-5720)
P.O. Box 3340 (91761-0934)
PHONE...............................909 947-0028
Randy Humphries, *Pr*
EMP: 145
Web: www.wswcorp.com
SIC: **3271** Blocks, concrete or cinder: standard
PA: Western States Wholesale, Inc.
1420 S Bon View Ave

(P-4377)
WESTERN STATES WHOLESALE INC (PA)
Also Called: C-Cure
1420 S Bon View Ave, Ontario (91761-4405)
P.O. Box 3340 (91761-0934)
PHONE...............................909 947-0028
Randall Humphreys, *CEO*
Robert Humphreys, *
Donna Humphreys, *
▲ **EMP:** 70 **EST:** 1995
SQ FT: 60,000
SALES (est): 29.54MM **Privately Held**
Web: www.wswcorp.com
SIC: **3271** 5072 5032 5211 Concrete block and brick; Bolts; Drywall materials; Lumber products

---

3272 Concrete Products, Nec

(P-4378)
ACKER STONE INDUSTRIES INC (DH)
13296 Temescal Canyon Rd, Corona (92883-5299)
PHONE...............................951 674-0047
Giora Ackerstein, *Ch Bd*
▲ **EMP:** 50 **EST:** 1987
SQ FT: 14,000
SALES (est): 22.42MM **Privately Held**
Web: www.ackerstone.com
SIC: **3272** 3271 Concrete products, precast, nec; Paving blocks, concrete
HQ: Ackerstein Zvi Ltd.
103 Medinat Hayehudim
Herzliya 46766

(P-4379)
AMERON INTERNATIONAL CORP
Also Called: Ameron Protective Coatings
1020 B St, Fillmore (93015-1024)
PHONE...............................425 258-2616
William Miner, *Brnch Mgr*
EMP: 115
SALES (corp-wide): 8.58B **Publicly Held**
SIC: **3272** Cylinder pipe, prestressed or pretensioned concrete
HQ: Ameron International Corporation
7909 Parkwood Circle Dr
Houston TX 77036
713 375-3700

(P-4380)
AMERON INTERNATIONAL CORP
Ameron Pole Products & Systems
1020 B St, Fillmore (93015-1024)
PHONE...............................805 524-0223
West Allison, *Mgr*
EMP: 100
SALES (corp-wide): 8.58B **Publicly Held**
SIC: **3272** 3648 3646 3441 Concrete products, precast, nec; Lighting equipment, nec; Commercial lighting fixtures; Fabricated structural metal
HQ: Ameron International Corporation
7909 Parkwood Circle Dr
Houston TX 77036
713 375-3700

(P-4381)
AVILAS GARDEN ART (PA)
14608 Merrill Ave, Fontana (92335-4219)
PHONE...............................909 350-4546
Ralph G Avila, *Owner*
EMP: 60 **EST:** 1981
SQ FT: 7,000
SALES (est): 519.27K
SALES (corp-wide): 519.27K **Privately Held**
Web: www.avilasgardenart.com
SIC: **3272** 5261 5211 5199 Precast terrazzo or concrete products; Lawn ornaments; Masonry materials and supplies; Statuary

(P-4382)
CLARK - PACIFIC CORPORATION
9367 Holly Rd, Adelanto (92301-3910)
PHONE...............................626 962-8755
EMP: 36
SALES (corp-wide): 243.72MM **Privately Held**
Web: www.clarkpacific.com
SIC: **3272** 5032 Concrete products, precast, nec; Brick, stone, and related material
PA: Clark - Pacific Corporation
710 Riverpoint Ct # 100
916 371-0305

(P-4383)
CLARK - PACIFIC CORPORATION
Also Called: Tecon Pacific
4684 Ontario Mills Pkwy Ste 200, Ontario (91764-5151)
PHONE...............................909 823-1433
Donald Clark, *Owner*
EMP: 49
SALES (corp-wide): 243.72MM **Privately Held**
Web: www.clarkpacific.com
SIC: **3272** 5211 Concrete products, precast, nec; Masonry materials and supplies
PA: Clark - Pacific Corporation
710 Riverpoint Ct # 100
916 371-0305

(P-4384)
CORESLAB STRUCTURES LA INC
150 W Placentia Ave, Perris (92571-3200)
PHONE...............................951 943-9119
Mario Franciosa, *CEO*
Lou Franciosa, *
Robert H Konoske, *General Vice President*
Jorgen Clausen, *
EMP: 200 **EST:** 1955
SQ FT: 25,000
SALES (est): 21.21MM
SALES (corp-wide): 27.34MM **Privately Held**
Web: www.coreslab.com
SIC: **3272** Concrete products, precast, nec
HQ: Coreslab Holdings U S Inc
1-332 Jones Rd
Stoney Creek ON L8E 5
905 643-0220

(P-4385)
CREATIVE STONE MFG INC (PA)
Also Called: Coronado Stone Products
342 W Perry St, Perris (92571-9723)
PHONE...............................800 847-8663
Melton Bacon, *Pr*
Scott Ebersole, *VP*
Bob Ratkovic, *Mgr*
◆ **EMP:** 180 **EST:** 1962
SALES (est): 29.14MM
SALES (corp-wide): 29.14MM **Privately Held**
Web: www.coronado.com
SIC: **3272** Siding, precast stone

(P-4386)
DCC GENERAL ENGRG CONTRS INC
2180 Meyers Ave, Escondido (92029-1001)
PHONE...............................760 480-7400
Frank D'agostini, *Pr*
Scott Woods, *
EMP: 75 **EST:** 1982
SQ FT: 2,100
SALES (est): 9.09MM **Privately Held**
Web: www.dccengineering.com
SIC: **3272** 1771 3531 Concrete products, nec ; Curb and sidewalk contractors; Asphalt plant, including gravel-mix type

(P-4387)
ELDORADO STONE LLC (DH)
3817 Ocean Ranch Blvd Ste 114, Oceanside (92056-8607)
P.O. Box 2289 (92079-2289)
PHONE...............................800 925-1491
Donald P Newman, *Managing Member*
◆ **EMP:** 50 **EST:** 2000
SALES (est): 63.06MM **Privately Held**
Web: www.eldoradostone.com
SIC: **3272** Concrete products, precast, nec
HQ: Headwaters Incorporated
10701 S Rver Front Pkwy
South Jordan UT 84095

(P-4388)
ELK CORPORATION OF TEXAS
Also Called: Elk
6200 Zerker Rd, Shafter (93263-9612)
PHONE...............................661 391-3900
Gus Freshwater, *Brnch Mgr*
EMP: 140
SALES (corp-wide): 6.35B **Privately Held**
SIC: **3272** 2952 Precast terrazzo or concrete products; Asphalt felts and coatings
HQ: Elk Corporation Of Texas
14911 Quorum Dr Ste 600
Dallas TX 75254

(P-4389)
FARLEY PAVING STONE CO INC
Also Called: Farley Interlocking Pav Stones
39301 Badger St, Palm Desert (92211-1161)
P.O. Box 10946 (92255-0946)
PHONE...............................760 773-3960
Shon Farley, *VP*
Charissa Farley, *
Hector Gonzalez, *
EMP: 70 **EST:** 1985
SALES (est): 4.07MM **Privately Held**
Web: www.farleypavers.com
SIC: **3272** 3531 3281 Paving materials, prefabricated concrete; Pavers; Curbing, paving, and walkway stone

(P-4390)
FIORE STONE INC
1814 Commercenter W Ste E, San Bernardino (92408-3332)
PHONE...............................909 424-0221
Bruce Raabe, *Pr*
EMP: 45 **EST:** 2009
SALES (est): 4.95MM **Privately Held**
Web: www.fiorestone.com
SIC: **3272** Concrete products, precast, nec

(P-4391)
FORMS AND SURFACES COMPANY LLC
Also Called: Lightform
6395 Cindy Ln, Carpinteria (93013-2909)
PHONE...............................805 684-8626
EMP: 150 **EST:** 1975
SQ FT: 63,000
SALES (est): 1.09MM **Privately Held**
Web: www.forms-surfaces.com
SIC: **3272** 3531 3446 3429 Building materials, except block or brick: concrete; Construction machinery; Architectural metalwork; Hardware, nec

(P-4392)
FORTERRA PIPE & PRECAST LLC
Also Called: South Coast Materials Co
9229 Harris Plant Rd, San Diego (92145-0001)
P.O. Box 639069 (92163-9069)
PHONE...............................858 715-5600
Carol Hartwig, *Brnch Mgr*
EMP: 42
Web: www.forterrabp.com
SIC: **3272** Concrete products, nec
HQ: Forterra Pipe & Precast, Llc
511 E John Crptr Fwy Ste
Irving TX 75062
469 458-7973

(P-4393)
FORTERRA PIPE & PRECAST LLC
26380 Palomar Rd, Sun City (92585-9811)
PHONE...............................951 523-7039

EMP: 44
Web: www.rinkerpipe.com
SIC: 3272 Concrete products, nec
HQ: Forterra Pipe & Precast, Llc
　　511 E John Crptr Fwy Ste
　　Irving TX 75062
　　469 458-7973

(P-4394)
GOLDEN EMPIRE CON PDTS INC
Also Called: Structurecast
8261 Mccutchen Rd, Bakersfield
(93311-9407)
PHONE..............................661 833-4490
Brent Dezember, *Pr*
Ann Dzember, *
EMP: 65 **EST:** 1997
SQ FT: 10,000
SALES (est): 10.04MM **Privately Held**
Web: www.structurecast.com
SIC: 3272 1791 Precast terrazzo or concrete
　products; Precast concrete structural
　framing or panels, placing of

(P-4395)
HANSON ROOF TILE INC
10651 Elm Ave, Fontana (92337-7324)
P.O. Box 660225 (75266-0225)
PHONE..............................888 509-4787
▲ **EMP:** 422
SIC: 3272 Roofing tile and slabs, concrete

(P-4396)
HEADWATERS INCORPORATED
1345 Philadelphia St, Pomona
(91766-5564)
PHONE..............................909 627-9066
Jim Johnson, *Mgr*
EMP: 26
Web: www.ecomaterial.com
SIC: 3272 Concrete products, nec
HQ: Headwaters Incorporated
　　10701 S Rver Front Pkwy
　　South Jordan UT 84095

(P-4397)
J & R CONCRETE PRODUCTS INC
440 W Markham St, Perris (92571-8138)
PHONE..............................951 943-5855
Raul Ramirez, *Pr*
EMP: 42 **EST:** 1981
SQ FT: 40,000
SALES (est): 4.7MM **Privately Held**
Web: www.jrconcreteproducts.com
SIC: 3272 Meter boxes, concrete

(P-4398)
JENSEN ENTERPRISES INC
Also Called: Jensen Precast
14221 San Bernardino Ave, Fontana
(92335-5232)
PHONE..............................909 357-7264
TOLL FREE: 800
Carol Kohanle, *Mgr*
EMP: 300
SALES (corp-wide): 237.25MM **Privately Held**
Web: www.jensenprecast.com
SIC: 3272 7699 5211 5039 Concrete
　products, precast, nec; Waste cleaning
　services; Masonry materials and supplies;
　Septic tanks
PA: Jensen Enterprises, Inc.
　　9895 Double R Blvd
　　775 352-2700

(P-4399)
KTI INCORPORATED
Also Called: Rialto Concrete Products
3011 N Laurel Ave, Rialto (92377-3725)
PHONE..............................909 434-1888
Kenneth D Thompson, *CEO*
Daniel J Deming, *
Jerry Cowden, *
EMP: 100 **EST:** 1987
SQ FT: 400
SALES (est): 11.03MM **Privately Held**
Web: www.thompsonpipegroup.com
SIC: 3272 Concrete products, precast, nec

(P-4400)
MCFIEBOW INC (PA)
17025 S Main St, Gardena (90248-3125)
PHONE..............................310 327-7474
Gordon S Mcwilliams, *CEO*
Paul Mitchell, *
EMP: 50 **EST:** 1963
SQ FT: 15,000
SALES (est): 9.93MM
SALES (corp-wide): 9.93MM **Privately Held**
Web: www.stepstoneinc.com
SIC: 3272 Concrete products, precast, nec

(P-4401)
MCFIEBOW INC
13238 S Figueroa St, Los Angeles
(90061-1140)
PHONE..............................310 327-7474
Kelsy Carrington, *Brnch Mgr*
EMP: 25
SALES (corp-wide): 9.93MM **Privately Held**
Web: www.stepstoneinc.com
SIC: 3272 Concrete products, precast, nec
PA: Mcfiebow Inc.
　　17025 S Main St
　　310 327-7474

(P-4402)
MID-STATE CONCRETE PDTS INC
1625 E Donovan Rd Ste C, Santa Maria
(93454-2519)
P.O. Box 219 (93456-0219)
PHONE..............................805 928-2855
TOLL FREE: 800
Ralph Vander Veen, *Pr*
Pat Vander Veen, *
EMP: 23 **EST:** 1975
SQ FT: 2,000
SALES (est): 4.91MM **Privately Held**
Web: www.midstateconcrete.com
SIC: 3272 Concrete products, precast, nec

(P-4403)
NEWBASIS LLC
2626 Kansas Ave, Riverside (92507-2600)
PHONE..............................951 787-0600
EMP: 150 **EST:** 2020
SALES (est): 31.04MM
SALES (corp-wide): 31.04MM **Privately Held**
Web: www.newbasis.com
SIC: 3272 Concrete products, nec
PA: Capital Precast Holdings, Llc
　　250 W Nottingham Dr # 120

(P-4404)
NEWBASIS WEST LLC
2626 Kansas Ave, Riverside (92507-2600)
PHONE..............................951 787-0600
Jennifer Ewing, *
Kim Ruiz, *
◆ **EMP:** 115 **EST:** 1989
SALES (est): 24.81MM

SALES (corp-wide): 24.81MM **Privately Held**
Web: www.newbasis.com
SIC: 3272 Manhole covers or frames,
　concrete
PA: Echo Rock Ventures, Inc.
　　370 Hammond Dr
　　530 823-9600

(P-4405)
NEWMAN AND SONS INC (PA)
2655 1st St Ste 210, Simi Valley
(93065-1578)
PHONE..............................805 522-1646
Dennis L Newman, *Pr*
EMP: 40 **EST:** 1938
SQ FT: 12,500
SALES (est): 672.65K
SALES (corp-wide): 672.65K **Privately Held**
Web: www.newmanandsons.com
SIC: 3272 Paving materials, prefabricated
　concrete

(P-4406)
OLDCAST PRECAST (DH)
Also Called: Riverside Foundary
2434 Rubidoux Blvd, Riverside
(92509-2144)
PHONE..............................951 788-9720
Thomas D Lynch, *Ch Bd*
John R Waren, *
EMP: 35 **EST:** 1966
SQ FT: 7,000
SALES (est): 2.05MM
SALES (corp-wide): 34.95B **Privately Held**
Web: www.inland-concrete.com
SIC: 3272 3271 Concrete products, precast,
　nec; Concrete block and brick
HQ: Oldcastle Infrastructure, Inc.
　　7000 Central Pkwy Ste 800
　　Atlanta GA 30328
　　770 270-5000

(P-4407)
OLDCASTLE INFRASTRUCTURE INC
19940 Hansen Ave, Nuevo (92567-9649)
PHONE..............................951 928-8713
EMP: 30
SALES (corp-wide): 34.95B **Privately Held**
Web: www.oldcastleinfrastructure.com
SIC: 3272 Concrete products, nec
HQ: Oldcastle Infrastructure, Inc.
　　7000 Central Pkwy Ste 800
　　Atlanta GA 30328
　　770 270-5000

(P-4408)
OLDCASTLE INFRASTRUCTURE INC
Also Called: Utility Vault
10650 Hemlock Ave, Fontana
(92337-7296)
P.O. Box 310039 (92331-0039)
PHONE..............................909 428-3700
Glenn Scheaffer, *Mgr*
EMP: 49
SALES (corp-wide): 34.95B **Privately Held**
Web: locator.oldcastleinfrastructure.com
SIC: 3272 Concrete products, precast, nec
HQ: Oldcastle Infrastructure, Inc.
　　7000 Central Pkwy Ste 800
　　Atlanta GA 30328
　　770 270-5000

(P-4409)
OLDCASTLE INFRASTRUCTURE INC

Also Called: Utility Vault
2512 Harmony Grove Rd, Escondido
(92029-2800)
PHONE..............................951 683-8200
EMP: 50
SALES (corp-wide): 29.71B **Privately Held**
SIC: 3272 3446 Concrete products, precast,
　nec; Open flooring and grating for
　construction
HQ: Oldcastle Infrastructure, Inc.
　　7000 Cntl Prkaway Ste 800
　　Atlanta GA 30328
　　470 602-2000

(P-4410)
PACIFIC STONE DESIGN INC
1201 E Wakeham Ave, Santa Ana
(92705-4145)
PHONE..............................714 836-5757
Scott Sterling, *Pr*
Kathy Sterling, *
EMP: 45 **EST:** 1996
SQ FT: 40,000
SALES (est): 4.33MM **Privately Held**
Web: www.pacificstone.net
SIC: 3272 Concrete products, precast, nec

(P-4411)
PARAGON BUILDING PRODUCTS INC (PA)
2191 5th St Ste 111, Norco (92860-1966)
P.O. Box 99 (92860-0099)
PHONE..............................951 549-1155
Jeffrey M Goodman, *Pr*
Jack Goodman, *
Richard Goodman, *
▲ **EMP:** 25 **EST:** 1984
SQ FT: 16,500
SALES (est): 24.85MM
SALES (corp-wide): 24.85MM **Privately Held**
Web: www.paragonbp.us
SIC: 3272 3271 5032 Dry mixture concrete;
　Concrete block and brick; Brick, stone, and
　related material

(P-4412)
PRE-CON PRODUCTS
240 W Los Angeles Ave, Simi Valley
(93065-1695)
P.O. Box 940669 (93094-0669)
PHONE..............................805 527-0841
EMP: 70 **EST:** 1964
SALES (est): 5.66MM **Privately Held**
Web: www.preconproducts.com
SIC: 3272 Pipe, concrete or lined with
　concrete

(P-4413)
PRECAST INNOVATIONS INC
1670 N Main St, Orange (92867-3405)
PHONE..............................714 921-4060
Chester Valdovinos, *Pr*
EMP: 28 **EST:** 2011
SQ FT: 20,000
SALES (est): 4.01MM **Privately Held**
Web: www.precastinnovations.com
SIC: 3272 1791 Concrete products, precast,
　nec; Precast concrete structural framing or
　panels, placing of

(P-4414)
PRIME FORMING & CNSTR SUPS INC
Also Called: Fitzgerald Formliners
1500a E Chestnut Ave, Santa Ana
(92701-6321)
PHONE..............................714 547-6710
Edward Fitzgerald, *Pr*
EMP: 46 **EST:** 1988

▲ = Import ▼ = Export
◆ = Import/Export

SQ FT: 30,000
SALES (est): 8.76MM **Privately Held**
Web: www.formliners.com
SIC: 3272 Concrete products, nec

(P-4415)
PRO-CAST PRODUCTS INC (PA)
27417 3rd St, Highland (92346-4258)
P.O. Box 602 (92346-0602)
PHONE..................................909 793-7602
TOLL FREE: 800
EMP: 49 EST: 1987
SALES (est): 7.24MM
SALES (corp-wide): 7.24MM **Privately Held**
Web: www.procastproducts.com
SIC: 3272 Concrete products, nec

(P-4416)
QUICK CRETE PRODUCTS CORP
731 Parkridge Ave, Norco (92860-3149)
P.O. Box 639 (92860-0639)
PHONE..................................951 737-6240
EMP: 180 EST: 1976
SALES (est): 24.38MM **Privately Held**
Web: www.quickcrete.com
SIC: 3272 Concrete products, precast, nec

(P-4417)
QUIKRETE CALIFORNIA LLC (DH)
Also Called: Quikrete
3940 Temescal Canyon Rd, Corona (92883-5618)
PHONE..................................951 277-3155
John O Winshester, *Managing Member*
EMP: 43 EST: 2004
SALES (est): 27.68MM **Privately Held**
SIC: 3272 Concrete products, nec
HQ: The Quikrete Companies Llc
5 Concourse Pkwy Ste 1900
Atlanta GA 30328
404 634-9100

(P-4418)
QUIKRETE COMPANIES LLC
Also Called: True Cast Concrete Products
11145 Tuxford St, Sun Valley (91352-2632)
PHONE..................................323 875-1367
Greg Gibhel, *Principal B*
EMP: 34
Web: www.quikrete.com
SIC: 3272 3271 5211 Steps, prefabricated concrete; Concrete block and brick; Masonry materials and supplies
HQ: The Quikrete Companies Llc
5 Concourse Pkwy Ste 1900
Atlanta GA 30328
404 634-9100

(P-4419)
RMR PRODUCTS INC (PA)
11011 Glenoaks Blvd Ste 1, Pacoima (91331-1634)
PHONE..................................818 890-0896
David Mckendrick, *CEO*
Jim Mckendrick, *Pr*
EMP: 25 EST: 1984
SQ FT: 3,200
SALES (est): 726.24K
SALES (corp-wide): 726.24K **Privately Held**
Web: www.chimneyproductsinc.com
SIC: 3272 Chimney caps, concrete

(P-4420)
ROYAL WESTLAKE ROOFING LLC
Also Called: Monier Lifetile

3511 N Riverside Ave, Rialto (92377-3803)
PHONE..................................909 822-4407
Kevin O Neil, *Mgr*
EMP: 29
Web: www.westlakeroyalroofing.com
SIC: 3272 3251 5032 2952 Roofing tile and slabs, concrete; Brick clay: common face, glazed, vitrified, or hollow; Cinders; Asphalt felts and coatings
HQ: Royal Westlake Roofing Llc
2801 Post Oak Blvd # 600
Houston TX 77056
800 658-8004

(P-4421)
SAN DIEGO PRECAST CONCRETE INC (DH)
Also Called: US Concrete Precast
2735 Cactus Rd, San Diego (92154-8024)
PHONE..................................619 240-8000
Douglas Mclaughlin, *Pr*
EMP: 28 EST: 1999
SQ FT: 1,600
SALES (est): 3.62MM **Publicly Held**
Web: www.sandiego.gov
SIC: 3272 3281 Meter boxes, concrete; Urns, cut stone
HQ: U.S. Concrete, Inc.
331 N Main St
Euless TX 76039
817 835-4105

(P-4422)
SOUTHWEST CONCRETE PRODUCTS
519 S Benson Ave, Ontario (91762-4002)
PHONE..................................909 983-9789
Bob Dzajkich, *Pr*
Eileen Dzajkich, *
Natalie Dzajkich, *
▲ EMP: 27 EST: 1966
SQ FT: 25,000
SALES (est): 4.08MM **Privately Held**
SIC: 3272 5032 Manhole covers or frames, concrete; Brick, stone, and related material

(P-4423)
SPEC FORMLINERS INC
1038 E 4th St, Santa Ana (92701-4751)
P.O. Box 10277 (92711-0277)
PHONE..................................714 429-9500
Stephen A Deering, *CEO*
Anthony Zaha, *
EMP: 26 EST: 1996
SQ FT: 23,000
SALES (est): 6.4MM **Privately Held**
Web: www.specformliners.com
SIC: 3272 Concrete products, nec

(P-4424)
W R MEADOWS INC
Also Called: W. R. Meadows Southern Cai
2300 Valley Blvd, Pomona (91768-1168)
P.O. Box 667 (91788-0667)
PHONE..................................909 469-2606
Michael Knapp, *Brnch Mgr*
EMP: 27
SALES (corp-wide): 26.89K **Privately Held**
Web: www.wrmeadows.com
SIC: 3272 3444 2899 2891 Concrete products, nec; Concrete forms, sheet metal; Chemical preparations, nec; Adhesives and sealants
PA: W. R. Meadows, Inc.
300 Industrial Dr
800 342-5976

3273 Ready-mixed Concrete

(P-4425)
A & A READY MIXED CONCRETE INC (PA)
Also Called: A&A Concrete Supply
4621 Teller Ave Ste 130, Newport Beach (92660-2165)
PHONE..................................949 253-2800
Kurt Caillier, *Pr*
Randy Caillier, *
▲ EMP: 45 EST: 1956
SQ FT: 8,000
SALES (est): 49.53MM
SALES (corp-wide): 49.53MM **Privately Held**
Web: www.aareadymix.com
SIC: 3273 Ready-mixed concrete

(P-4426)
ALLIANCE READY MIX INC
310 James Way Ste 210, Pismo Beach (93449-2877)
P.O. Box 1163 (93421-1163)
PHONE..................................805 556-3015
Brandt Robertson, *Brnch Mgr*
EMP: 27
SIC: 3273 Ready-mixed concrete
PA: Alliance Ready Mix, Inc.
915 Sheridan Rd

(P-4427)
ALPHA MATERIALS INC
6170 20th St, Riverside (92509-2031)
PHONE..................................951 788-5150
Brian Oaks, *Pr*
EMP: 36 EST: 2002
SQ FT: 1,200
SALES (est): 8.46MM **Privately Held**
Web: www.alpha-materials-inc.com
SIC: 3273 Ready-mixed concrete

(P-4428)
ARROW TRANSIT MIX
507 E Avenue L12, Lancaster (93535-5417)
P.O. Box 6677 (93539-6677)
PHONE..................................661 945-7600
H D Follendore, *Pr*
Christine Follendore, *
EMP: 35 EST: 1998
SQ FT: 7,200
SALES (est): 5.96MM **Privately Held**
Web: www.arrowtransitmix.com
SIC: 3273 Ready-mixed concrete

(P-4429)
ASSOCIATED READY MIX CON INC
Also Called: ASSOCIATED READY MIX CONCRETE, INC.
8946 Bradley Ave, Sun Valley (91352-2601)
PHONE..................................818 504-3100
Tim Sullivan, *Mgr*
EMP: 77
Web: www.aareadymix.com
SIC: 3273 Ready-mixed concrete
PA: Associated Ready Mixed Concrete, Inc.
4621 Teller Ave Ste 130

(P-4430)
ASSOCIATED READY MIXED CON INC (PA)
4621 Teller Ave Ste 130, Newport Beach (92660-2165)
PHONE..................................949 253-2800
Kurt Caillier, *Pr*

Randy Caillier, *
Chris Pizano, *
EMP: 40 EST: 1996
SALES (est): 17.83MM **Privately Held**
Web: www.assocrmc.com
SIC: 3273 Ready-mixed concrete

(P-4431)
BENDER READY MIX INC
Also Called: Bender Ready Mix Concrete
516 S Santa Fe St, Santa Ana (92705-4142)
PHONE..................................714 560-0744
Sarah Bender, *CEO*
Greg Bender, *Pr*
EMP: 28 EST: 2007
SALES (est): 4.74MM **Privately Held**
Web: www.benderreadymix.com
SIC: 3273 Ready-mixed concrete

(P-4432)
CALPORTLAND
2025 E Financial Way, Glendora (91741-4692)
P.O. Box 371534 (89137-1534)
PHONE..................................760 343-3403
Terri Stelter, *Pr*
Diane Sarauer, *VP*
Debra Rubenzer, *Sec*
EMP: 59 EST: 1973
SQ FT: 480
SALES (est): 2.3MM **Privately Held**
Web: www.calportland.com
SIC: 3273 Ready-mixed concrete

(P-4433)
CAPITAL READY MIX INC
11311 Pendleton St, Sun Valley (91352-1530)
PHONE..................................818 771-1122
Tigran Aneian, *CEO*
EMP: 32 EST: 2014
SALES (est): 6.29MM **Privately Held**
SIC: 3273 Ready-mixed concrete

(P-4434)
CEMEX CEMENT INC
25220 Black Mountain Quarry Rd, Apple Valley (92307-9341)
PHONE..................................760 381-7616
Luis Lopez, *Brnch Mgr*
EMP: 200
SIC: 3273 Ready-mixed concrete
HQ: Cemex Cement, Inc.
10100 Katy Fwy Ste 300
Houston TX 77043
713 650-6200

(P-4435)
CEMEX MATERIALS LLC
1205 S Rancho Ave, Colton (92324-3342)
PHONE..................................909 825-1500
Lindsey Hank, *Mgr*
EMP: 100
SIC: 3273 Ready-mixed concrete
HQ: Cemex Materials Llc
1720 Cntrpark Dr E Ste 10
West Palm Beach FL 33401
561 833-5555

(P-4436)
CONCRETE HOLDING CO CAL INC
15821 Ventura Blvd Ste 475, Encino (91436-4778)
PHONE..................................818 788-4228
Don Unmacht, *Pr*
Dominique Bidet, *
EMP: 702 EST: 1988
SQ FT: 4,000

SALES (est): 1.41MM
SALES (corp-wide): 632.96MM **Privately Held**
Web: www.nationalcement.com
SIC: 3273 Ready-mixed concrete
HQ: National Cement Company, Inc.
15821 Ventura Blvd # 475
Encino CA 91436
818 728-5200

(P-4437)
DIVERSIFIED MINERALS INC
Also Called: Dmi Ready Mix
1100 Mountain View Ave Ste F, Oxnard (93030-7213)
PHONE..................................805 247-1069
James W Price, *Pr*
Sharron Price, *
▲ **EMP: 44 EST:** 1990
SQ FT: 44,482
SALES (est): 9.73MM **Privately Held**
Web: www.dmicement.com
SIC: 3273 4013 3531 3241 Ready-mixed concrete; Railroad terminals; Bituminous, cement and concrete related products and equip.; Pozzolana cement

(P-4438)
E-Z MIX INC (PA)
11450 Tuxford St, Sun Valley (91352-2638)
PHONE..................................818 768-0568
William Frenzel, *CEO*
Sunjiv Parekh, *
EMP: 33 **EST:** 1992
SQ FT: 50,000
SALES (est): 10.85MM **Privately Held**
Web: www.ezmixinc.com
SIC: 3273 Ready-mixed concrete

(P-4439)
GARY BALE REDI-MIX CON INC
16131 Construction Cir W, Irvine (92606-4410)
PHONE..................................949 786-9441
Kyle Goerlitz, *CEO*
EMP: 80 **EST:** 1968
SALES (est): 5.11MM **Privately Held**
Web: www.garybaleredimix.com
SIC: 3273 Ready-mixed concrete

(P-4440)
GIBSON & SCHAEFER INC (PA)
1126 Rock Wood Rd, Heber (92249)
P.O. Box 1539 (92249-1539)
PHONE..................................619 352-3535
Don Gibson, *Pr*
P M Schaefer, *
Maria Schaefer, *
Rhoberta Gibson, *
EMP: 50 **EST:** 1989
SQ FT: 1,440
SALES (est): 10.1MM **Privately Held**
Web: www.gibsonandschaeferinc.com
SIC: 3273 5032 Ready-mixed concrete; Gravel

(P-4441)
HI-GRADE MATERIALS CO
6500 E Avenue T, Littlerock (93543-1722)
P.O. Box 1050 (93543-1050)
PHONE..................................661 533-3100
Rod Elderton, *Mgr*
EMP: 88
SALES (corp-wide): 49.72MM **Privately Held**
Web: www.robar.com
SIC: 3273 Ready-mixed concrete
HQ: Hi-Grade Materials Co.
17671 Bear Valley Rd
Hesperia CA
760 244-9325

(P-4442)
HOLLIDAY TRUCKING INC
2300 W Base Line St, San Bernardino (92410-1002)
PHONE..................................888 273-2200
Frederick N Holliday, *Brnch Mgr*
EMP: 60
SALES (corp-wide): 3.96MM **Privately Held**
Web: www.hollidayrock.com
SIC: 3273 Ready-mixed concrete
PA: Holliday Trucking Inc.
1401 N Benson Ave
909 982-1553

(P-4443)
HOLLIDAY TRUCKING INC (PA)
1401 N Benson Ave, Upland (91786-2166)
PHONE..................................909 982-1553
Frederick N Holliday, *Pr*
Penny Holliday, *
John Holliday, *
Ronald Chambers, *
EMP: 60 **EST:** 1964
SQ FT: 2,000
SALES (est): 3.96MM
SALES (corp-wide): 3.96MM **Privately Held**
Web: www.hollidayrock.com
SIC: 3273 4212 Ready-mixed concrete; Local trucking, without storage

(P-4444)
LEBATA INC
Also Called: A & A Ready Mix Concrete
4621 Teller Ave Ste 130, Newport Beach (92660-2165)
PHONE..................................949 253-2800
Kurt Caillier, *Pr*
EMP: 30 **EST:** 1987
SALES (est): 5.1MM **Privately Held**
SIC: 3273 Ready-mixed concrete

(P-4445)
NATIONAL CEMENT CO CAL INC (DH)
15821 Ventura Blvd Ste 475, Encino (91436-2935)
PHONE..................................818 728-5200
Steven Weiss, *Pr*
Pragati Kapoor, *CFO*
Dominique Bidet, *VP*
▲ **EMP:** 37 **EST:** 1987
SQ FT: 12,000
SALES (est): 61.15MM
SALES (corp-wide): 632.96MM **Privately Held**
Web: www.nationalcement.com
SIC: 3273 Ready-mixed concrete
HQ: National Cement Company, Inc.
15821 Ventura Blvd # 475
Encino CA 91436
818 728-5200

(P-4446)
NATIONAL CEMENT COMPANY INC
2626 E 26th St, Vernon (90058-1218)
PHONE..................................323 923-4466
EMP: 78
SALES (corp-wide): 632.96MM **Privately Held**
Web: www.nationalcement.com
SIC: 3273 Ready-mixed concrete
HQ: National Cement Company, Inc.
15821 Ventura Blvd # 475
Encino CA 91436
818 728-5200

(P-4447)
PACIFIC AGGREGATES INC
28251 Lake St, Lake Elsinore (92530-1635)
PHONE..................................951 245-2460
Kai Chin, *CEO*
Dale Kline, *
▲ **EMP:** 75 **EST:** 2002
SQ FT: 1,000
SALES (est): 11.57MM
SALES (corp-wide): 372.87MM **Privately Held**
Web: www.pacificaggregates.com
SIC: 3273 Ready-mixed concrete
PA: Castle & Cooke, Inc.
10000 Stockdale Hwy # 300
818 879-6700

(P-4448)
ROBAR ENTERPRISES INC (PA)
17671 Bear Valley Rd, Hesperia (92345-4902)
PHONE..................................760 244-5456
Jonathan D Hove, *CEO*
Robert E Hove, *
Al Calvanico, *
EMP: 150 **EST:** 1981
SQ FT: 26,000
SALES (est): 49.72MM
SALES (corp-wide): 49.72MM **Privately Held**
Web: www.robarenterprises.com
SIC: 3273 5051 3441 Ready-mixed concrete; Steel; Building components, structural steel

(P-4449)
ROBERTSONS RDYMX LTD A CAL LTD (PA)
Also Called: Robertson's
200 S Main St Ste 200, Corona (92882-2212)
P.O. Box 3600 (92878-3600)
PHONE..................................951 493-6500
TOLL FREE: 800
Jon Troesh, *Pt*
▲ **EMP:** 85 **EST:** 1991
SQ FT: 22,008
SALES (est): 458.49MM
SALES (corp-wide): 458.49MM **Privately Held**
Web: www.rrmca.com
SIC: 3273 3531 5032 2951 Ready-mixed concrete; Bituminous, cement and concrete related products and equip.; Asphalt mixture ; Asphalt paving mixtures and blocks

(P-4450)
ROBERTSONS RDYMX LTD A CAL LTD
27401 3rd St, Highland (92346-4242)
PHONE..................................909 425-2930
Dennis Troesh, *Pr*
EMP: 153
SALES (corp-wide): 458.49MM **Privately Held**
Web: www.rrmca.com
SIC: 3273 Ready-mixed concrete
PA: Robertson's Ready Mix, Ltd., A California Limited Partnership
200 S Main St Ste 200
951 493-6500

(P-4451)
ROBERTSONS READY MIX LTD
9635 C Ave, Hesperia (92345-6047)
PHONE..................................760 244-7239
EMP: 61
SALES (corp-wide): 458.49MM **Privately Held**
Web: www.rrmca.com

SIC: 3273 Ready-mixed concrete
PA: Robertson's Ready Mix, Ltd., A California Limited Partnership
200 S Main St Ste 200
951 493-6500

(P-4452)
ROBERTSONS READY MIX LTD
Also Called: Miramar Plant 33
5692 Eastgate Dr, San Diego (92121-2816)
PHONE..................................800 834-7557
EMP: 102
SALES (corp-wide): 458.49MM **Privately Held**
Web: www.rrmca.com
SIC: 3273 Ready-mixed concrete
PA: Robertson's Ready Mix, Ltd., A California Limited Partnership
200 S Main St Ste 200
951 493-6500

(P-4453)
ROBERTSONS READY MIX LTD
1310 Simpson Way, Escondido (92029-1377)
PHONE..................................951 685-4600
EMP: 61
SALES (corp-wide): 458.49MM **Privately Held**
Web: www.rrmca.com
SIC: 3273 Ready-mixed concrete
PA: Robertson's Ready Mix, Ltd., A California Limited Partnership
200 S Main St Ste 200
951 493-6500

(P-4454)
ROBERTSONS READY MIX LTD
7900 Moss Ave, California City (93505-4311)
PHONE..................................760 373-4815
EMP: 92
SALES (corp-wide): 458.49MM **Privately Held**
Web: www.rrmca.com
SIC: 3273 Ready-mixed concrete
PA: Robertson's Ready Mix, Ltd., A California Limited Partnership
200 S Main St Ste 200
951 493-6500

(P-4455)
RWH INC
Also Called: Holiday Transportation
15115 Oxnard St, Van Nuys (91411-2615)
PHONE..................................818 782-2350
TOLL FREE: 800
EMP: 30 **EST:** 1964
SALES (est): 4.3MM **Privately Held**
Web: www.bonanzaconcrete.com
SIC: 3273 4212 Ready-mixed concrete; Local trucking, without storage

(P-4456)
SUPERIOR READY MIX CONCRETE LP
802 E Main St, El Centro (92243-9474)
P.O. Box 400 (92244-0400)
PHONE..................................760 352-4341
Donald Lee, *Brnch Mgr*
EMP: 70
SALES (corp-wide): 205.26MM **Privately Held**
Web: www.superiorrm.com
SIC: 3273 Ready-mixed concrete
PA: Superior Ready Mix Concrete L.P.
1564 Mission Rd
760 745-0556

▲ = Import ▼ = Export
◆ = Import/Export

(P-4457)

SUPERIOR READY MIX CONCRETE LP

Also Called: Srm Contracting & Paving
7192 Mission Gorge Rd, San Diego
(92120-1131)
PHONE.....................619 265-0955
Brent Cooper, *Brnch Mgr*
EMP: 70
SALES (corp-wide): 205.26MM **Privately Held**
Web: www.superiorrm.com
SIC: 3273 Ready-mixed concrete
PA: Superior Ready Mix Concrete L.P.
1564 Mission Rd
760 745-0556

(P-4458)

SUPERIOR READY MIX CONCRETE LP

Also Called: Canyon Rock & Asphalt
7500 Mission Gorge Rd, San Diego
(92120-1304)
PHONE.....................619 265-0296
Tracy Mall, *Mgr*
EMP: 70
SALES (corp-wide): 205.26MM **Privately Held**
Web: www.superiorrm.com
SIC: 3273 Ready-mixed concrete
PA: Superior Ready Mix Concrete L.P.
1564 Mission Rd
760 745-0556

(P-4459)

SUPERIOR READY MIX CONCRETE LP

Also Called: TTT Concrete
12494 Highway 67, Lakeside (92040-1133)
PHONE.....................619 443-7510
Jerry Anderson, *Mgr*
EMP: 71
SQ FT: 3,200
SALES (corp-wide): 205.26MM **Privately Held**
Web: www.superiorrm.com
SIC: 3273 Ready-mixed concrete
PA: Superior Ready Mix Concrete L.P.
1564 Mission Rd
760 745-0556

(P-4460)

SUPERIOR READY MIX CONCRETE LP (PA)

Also Called: Southland Ready Mix Concrete
1564 Mission Rd, Escondido (92029-1194)
PHONE.....................760 746 0666
Donald Lee, *Pr*
EMP: 50 **EST:** 1957
SALES (est): 205.26MM
SALES (corp-wide): 205.26MM **Privately Held**
Web: www.superiorrm.com
SIC: 3273 1611 5032 Ready-mixed concrete
; Surfacing and paving; Gravel

(P-4461)

SUPERIOR READY MIX CONCRETE LP

Also Called: Superior Ready Mix Concrete
24635 Temescal Canyon Rd, Corona
(92883-5422)
PHONE.....................951 277-3553
Justine Moss, *Brnch Mgr*
EMP: 71
SALES (corp-wide): 205.26MM **Privately Held**
Web: www.superiorrm.com

SIC: 3273 Ready-mixed concrete
PA: Superior Ready Mix Concrete L.P.
1564 Mission Rd
760 745-0556

(P-4462)

SUPERIOR READY MIX CONCRETE LP

Also Called: Hemet Ready Mix
1130 N State St, Hemet (92543-1510)
PHONE.....................951 658-9225
Wayne Heckerman, *Prin*
EMP: 71
SALES (corp-wide): 205.26MM **Privately Held**
Web: www.superiorrm.com
SIC: 3273 5211 Ready-mixed concrete;
Masonry materials and supplies
PA: Superior Ready Mix Concrete L.P.
1564 Mission Rd
760 745-0556

(P-4463)

SUPERIOR READY MIX CONCRETE LP

Also Called: Superior Ready Mix Concrete
72270 Varner Rd, Thousand Palms
(92276-3341)
PHONE.....................760 343-3418
Mark Higgins, *Mgr*
EMP: 71
SALES (corp-wide): 205.26MM **Privately Held**
Web: www.superiorrm.com
SIC: 3273 Ready-mixed concrete
PA: Superior Ready Mix Concrete L.P.
1564 Mission Rd
760 745-0556

(P-4464)

SUPERIOR READY MIX CONCRETE LP

Also Called: American Ready Mix
1564 Mission Rd, Escondido (92029-1194)
PHONE.....................760 728-1128
Greg Sage, *Mgr*
EMP: 71
SALES (corp-wide): 205.26MM **Privately Held**
Web: www.superiorrm.com
SIC: 3273 1442 Ready-mixed concrete;
Construction sand and gravel
PA: Superior Ready Mix Concrete L.P.
1564 Mission Rd
760 745-0556

(P-4465)

VULCAN MATERIALS CO

849 W Washington Ave, Escondido
(92025-1634)
PHONE.....................760 737-3486
TOLL FREE: 800
A F Gerstell, *Pr*
EMP: 215 **EST:** 1957
SALES (est): 531.78K **Publicly Held**
SIC: 3273 Ready-mixed concrete
HQ: Calmat Co.
1200 Urban Center Dr
Birmingham AL 35242
818 553-8821

(P-4466)

WESTWOOD BUILDING MATERIALS CO

15708 Inglewood Ave, Lawndale
(90260-2544)
PHONE.....................310 643-9158
Craig St John, *Pr*
Liza Peitzmeier, *

EMP: 36 **EST:** 1941
SQ FT: 23,500
SALES (est): 9.39MM **Privately Held**
Web: www.westwoodbm.com
SIC: 3273 Ready-mixed concrete

3275 Gypsum Products

(P-4467)

PABCO BUILDING PRODUCTS LLC

Also Called: Pabco Paper
4460 Pacific Blvd, Vernon (90058-2206)
PHONE.....................323 581-6113
Phil Bonnell, *Pr*
EMP: 134
SALES (corp-wide): 1.21B **Privately Held**
Web: www.pabcogypsum.com
SIC: 3275 Gypsum products
HQ: Pabco Building Products, Llc
10811 International Dr
Rancho Cordova CA 95670
510 792-1577

(P-4468)

PROFORM FINISHING PRODUCTS LLC

1850 Pier B St, Long Beach (90813-2604)
P.O. Box 1888 (90801-1888)
PHONE.....................562 435-4465
Tim Fout, *Mgr*
EMP: 39
SALES (corp-wide): 795.88MM **Privately Held**
Web: www.nationalgypsum.com
SIC: 3275 Gypsum products
HQ: Proform Finishing Products, Llc
2001 Rexford Rd
Charlotte NC 28211

(P-4469)

UNITED STATES GYPSUM COMPANY

401 Van Ness Ave, Torrance (90501-1422)
PHONE.....................908 232-8900
Matt Craig, *Mgr*
EMP: 100
SQ FT: 71,800
SALES (corp-wide): 16B **Privately Held**
Web: www.usg.com
SIC: 3275 Gypsum products
HQ: United States Gypsum Company
550 W Adams St
Chicago IL 60661
312 606-4000

(P-4470)

UNITED STATES GYPSUM COMPANY

3810 Evan Hewes Hwy, Imperial
(92251-9529)
P.O. Box 2450 (92244-2450)
PHONE.....................760 358-3200
George Keelan, *Dir Fin*
EMP: 107
SALES (corp-wide): 16B **Privately Held**
Web: www.usg.com
SIC: 3275 Gypsum products
HQ: United States Gypsum Company
550 W Adams St
Chicago IL 60661
312 606-4000

3281 Cut Stone And Stone Products

(P-4471)

BEST-WAY MARBLE & TILE CO INC

Also Called: Best Way Marble
5037 Telegraph Rd, Los Angeles
(90022-4922)
PHONE.....................323 266-6794
Shelley Herrera, *Pr*
◆ **EMP:** 28 **EST:** 1981
SQ FT: 16,000
SALES (est): 2.66MM **Privately Held**
Web: www.bestwaymarble.com
SIC: 3281 1743 Table tops, marble; Marble
installation, interior

(P-4472)

CARNEVALE & LOHR INC

6521 Clara St, Bell Gardens (90201-5634)
PHONE.....................562 927-8311
Louie Carnevale, *CEO*
Edmund B Lohr Iv, *Prin*
David Carnevale, *
Michael Carnevale, *
▲ **EMP:** 33 **EST:** 1958
SALES (est): 4.01MM **Privately Held**
Web: www.carnevaleandlohr.com
SIC: 3281 1741 Cut stone and stone
products; Marble masonry, exterior
construction

(P-4473)

COAST FLAGSTONE CO

1810 Colorado Ave, Santa Monica
(90404-3412)
PHONE.....................310 829-4010
Timothy Wang, *Owner*
EMP: 70 **EST:** 2010
SALES (est): 986.4K **Privately Held**
Web: www.bourgetbros.com
SIC: 3281 Flagstones

(P-4474)

KAMMERER ENTERPRISES INC

Also Called: American Marble
1280 N Melrose Dr, Vista (92083-3469)
PHONE.....................760 560-0550
William S Kammerer, *CEO*
Bill Kammerer, *
Karl Miethke, *
▲ **EMP:** 100 **EST:** 1985
SALES (est): 10.67MM **Privately Held**
Web: www.amarble.com
SIC: 3281 Curbing, granite or stone

(P-4475)

L&S STONE LLC (DH)

Also Called: L & S Stone and Fireplace Shop
1370 Grand Ave Ste B, San Marcos
(92078-2404)
PHONE.....................760 736-3232
◆ **EMP:** 50 **EST:** 1970
SQ FT: 35,000
SALES (est): 1.28MM **Privately Held**
Web: www.eldoradostone.com
SIC: 3281 Cut stone and stone products
HQ: Eldorado Stone Llc
3817 Ocean Ranch Blvd
Oceanside CA 92056
800 925-1491

(P-4476)

RUGGERI MARBLE AND GRANITE INC

25028 Vermont Ave, Harbor City
(90710-3116)

PHONE.................310 513-2155
Andre Ruggeri, *Pr*
Robert Ruggeri, *
◆ **EMP:** 80 **EST:** 1991
SALES (est): 4.6MM **Privately Held**
Web: www.ruggerimarble.com
SIC: 3281 5032 Marble, building: cut and
shaped; Ceramic wall and floor tile, nec

(P-4477)
SAMPLE TILE AND STONE INC
1410 Richardson St, San Bernardino
(92408-2962)
PHONE.................951 776-8562
Curtis Sample, *CEO*
EMP: 45 **EST:** 2011
SQ FT: 13,500
SALES (est): 6.07MM **Privately Held**
Web: www.sampletileandstone.com
SIC: 3281 5032 1411 1743 Cut stone and
stone products; Limestone; Limestone and
marble dimension stone; Terrazzo, tile,
marble and mosaic work

(P-4478)
STANDRIDGE GRANITE CORPORATION
9437 Santa Fe Springs Rd, Santa Fe
Springs (90670-2684)
PHONE.................562 946-6334
Deborah Deleon, *Pr*
EMP: 30 **EST:** 1965
SQ FT: 24,000
SALES (est): 4.88MM **Privately Held**
Web: www.standridgegranite.com
SIC: 3281 1411 Granite, cut and shaped;
Dimension stone

(P-4479)
SULLIVANS STONE FACTORY INC
83778 Avenue 45, Indio (92201-3310)
PHONE.................760 347-5535
Robert J Sullivan, *Pr*
▲ **EMP:** 25 **EST:** 2004
SALES (est): 2.41MM **Privately Held**
Web: www.sullivansstonefactory.com
SIC: 3281 Granite, cut and shaped

(P-4480)
WESTLAKE ROYAL STONE LLC
3817 Ocean Ranch Blvd, Oceanside
(92056-8607)
PHONE.................800 255-1727
Michael Mildenhall, *Managing Member*
EMP: 83 **EST:** 2006
SALES (est): 4.56MM **Publicly Held**
Web: www.elevatewithstone.com
SIC: 3281 Building stone products
HQ: Westlake Pipe & Fittings Corporation
2801 Post Oak Blvd Ste 60
Houston TX 77056

3291 Abrasive Products

(P-4481)
BUFF AND SHINE MFG INC
2139 E Del Amo Blvd, Rancho Dominguez
(90220-6301)
PHONE.................310 886-5111
Richard Umbrell, *Pr*
Elizabeth Umbrell, *
◆ **EMP:** 40 **EST:** 1987
SQ FT: 25,792
SALES (est): 4.22MM **Privately Held**
Web: www.buffandshine.com
SIC: 3291 Buffing or polishing wheels,
abrasive or nonabrasive

(P-4482)
CRATEX MANUFACTURING CO INC
Also Called: Cratex
328 Encinitas Blvd Ste 200, Encinitas
(92024-8704)
PHONE.................760 942-2877
Allen R Mccasland, *CEO*
Barbara Mccasland, *Sec*
▲ **EMP:** 75 **EST:** 1946
SALES (est): 3.7MM **Privately Held**
Web: www.cratex.com
SIC: 3291 Wheels, grinding: artificial

(P-4483)
JASON INCORPORATED
Jackson Lea Division
13006 Philadelphia St Ste 305, Whittier
(90601-4250)
PHONE.................562 921-9821
Ron Locher, *Brnch Mgr*
EMP: 25
SQ FT: 30,000
SALES (corp-wide): 173.28MM **Privately
Held**
Web: www.osborn.com
SIC: 3291 2273 3599 Buffing or polishing
wheels, abrasive or nonabrasive;
Automobile floor coverings, except rubber
or plastic; Custom machinery
PA: Jason Incorporated
833 E Michigan St Ste 900

(P-4484)
MAVERICK ABRASIVES CORPORATION
4340 E Miraloma Ave, Anaheim
(92807-1886)
PHONE.................714 854-9531
Rami Aryan, *Pr*
◆ **EMP:** 60 **EST:** 1997
SQ FT: 15,000
SALES (est): 9.83MM **Privately Held**
Web: www.maverickabrasives.com
SIC: 3291 Abrasive products

(P-4485)
TECHNIFEX PRODUCTS LLC
25261 Rye Canyon Rd, Valencia
(91355-1203)
PHONE.................661 294-3800
Joe Ortiz, *VP*
▲ **EMP:** 25 **EST:** 1999
SALES (est): 4.87MM **Privately Held**
Web: www.technifex.com
SIC: 3291 Steel wool

(P-4486)
YEAGER ENTERPRISES CORP
Also Called: Pasco
7100 Village Dr, Buena Park (90621-2261)
PHONE.................714 994-2040
Joseph O'mera, *CEO*
David M Yeager, *
Joan F Yeager, *
▲ **EMP:** 81 **EST:** 1920
SQ FT: 55,000
SALES (est): 1.34MM **Privately Held**
SIC: 3291 Abrasive products

3295 Minerals, Ground Or Treated

(P-4487)
3M COMPANY
Also Called: 3M
18750 Minnesota Rd, Corona (92881-4313)
PHONE.................951 737-3441

Flees Peter, *Brnch Mgr*
EMP: 47
SALES (corp-wide): 32.68B **Publicly Held**
Web: www.3m.com
SIC: 3295 2952 Roofing granules; Asphalt
felts and coatings
PA: 3m Company
3m Center
651 733-1110

(P-4488)
JON BROOKS INC (PA)
Also Called: Laguna Clay Company
14400 Lomitas Ave, City Of Industry
(91746-3018)
PHONE.................626 330-0631
Jon Brooks, *Pr*
Laurie Brooks, *
◆ **EMP:** 100 **EST:** 1981
SQ FT: 117,000
SALES (est): 20.91MM
SALES (corp-wide): 20.91MM **Privately
Held**
Web: www.lagunaclay.com
SIC: 3295 5085 Clay, ground or otherwise
treated; Refractory material

(P-4489)
SGL TECHNIC LLC (DH)
Also Called: Inc Polycarbon
28176 Avenue Stanford, Valencia
(91355-1119)
PHONE.................661 257-0500
Ken Mamon, *Pr*
Brian Green, *VP*
▲ **EMP:** 48 **EST:** 1967
SQ FT: 130,000
SALES (est): 13.74MM
SALES (corp-wide): 1.18B **Privately Held**
Web: www.sglcarbon.com
SIC: 3295 3624 Graphite, natural: ground,
pulverized, refined, or blended; Carbon and
graphite products
HQ: Sgl Carbon, Llc
10715 Dvid Tylor Dr Ste 4
Charlotte NC 28262
704 593-5100

3296 Mineral Wool

(P-4490)
C A SCHROEDER INC (PA)
Also Called: Casco Mfg
1318 1st St, San Fernando (91340-2804)
PHONE.................818 365-9561
Susan A Knudsen, *CEO*
Clifford A Schroeder, *
EMP: 42 **EST:** 1969
SQ FT: 18,500
SALES (est): 7.17MM
SALES (corp-wide): 7.17MM **Privately
Held**
Web: www.casco-flex.com
SIC: 3296 3585 3444 3433 Fiberglass
insulation; Refrigeration and heating
equipment; Sheet metalwork; Heating
equipment, except electric

(P-4491)
CONSOLIDATED FIBRGLS PDTS CO
Also Called: Conglas
3801 Standard St, Bakersfield
(93308-5230)
PHONE.................661 323-6026
Daron J Thomas, *CEO*
Jack Pfeffer, *
EMP: 60 **EST:** 1972
SQ FT: 20,000
SALES (est): 4.33MM **Privately Held**

SIC: 3296 Fiberglass insulation

(P-4492)
JOHNS MANVILLE CORPORATION
4301 Firestone Blvd, South Gate
(90280-3318)
PHONE.................323 568-2220
Rudi Bianchi, *Mgr*
EMP: 54
SALES (corp-wide): 364.48B **Publicly
Held**
Web: www.jm.com
SIC: 3296 Mineral wool
HQ: Johns Manville Corporation
717 17th St
Denver CO 80202
303 978-2000

(P-4493)
KAINALU BLUE INC
4675 North Ave, Oceanside (92056-3511)
PHONE.................760 806-6400
Robin Gray, *Pr*
EMP: 30 **EST:** 1965
SQ FT: 30,000
SALES (est): 4.62MM **Privately Held**
Web: www.lamvin.com
SIC: 3296 3275 Acoustical board and tile,
mineral wool; Gypsum products

(P-4494)
ROCK STRUCTURES-RIP RAP
11126 Silverton Ct, Corona (92881-5626)
PHONE.................951 371-1112
Antonio Paredes, *Owner*
EMP: 30 **EST:** 2003
SQ FT: 3,500
SALES (est): 2.34MM **Privately Held**
SIC: 3296 Insulation: rock wool, slag, and
silica minerals

(P-4495)
SOUND SEAL INC
Lamvin
4675 North Ave, Oceanside (92056-3511)
PHONE.................760 806-6400
Robin Gray, *Mgr*
EMP: 25
Web: www.soundseal.com
SIC: 3296 3275 Acoustical board and tile,
mineral wool; Gypsum products
HQ: Sound Seal, Inc.
50 Hp Almgren Dr
Agawam MA 01001
413 789-1770

(P-4496)
USMPC BUYER INC
Also Called: Isolatek International
4062 Georgia Blvd, San Bernardino
(92407-1847)
PHONE.................909 473-3027
Adrienne Bowen, *Brnch Mgr*
EMP: 41
SALES (corp-wide): 28.2MM **Privately
Held**
Web: www.isolatek.com
SIC: 3296 Mineral wool insulation products
PA: Usmpc Buyer Inc.
41 Furnace St
973 347-1200

3299 Nonmetallic Mineral Products,

(P-4497)
3M TECHNICAL CERAMICS INC (HQ)

1922 Barranca Pkwy, Irvine (92606-4826)
PHONE..................................949 862-9600
Joel P Moskowitz, *CEO*
Jerrold J Pellizzon, *Corporate Secretary*
Thomas A Cole, *
Terry M Hart, *
David P Reed, *Assistant Corporate Secretary*
◆ EMP: 78 EST: 1987
SQ FT: 99,000
SALES (est): 284.05MM
SALES (corp-wide): 32.68B **Publicly Held**
Web: www.ceradyne.com
SIC: 3299 3671 Ceramic fiber; Cathode ray tubes, including rebuilt
PA: 3m Company
   3m Center
   651 733-1110

(P-4498)
3M TECHNICAL CERAMICS INC
17466 Daimler St, Irvine (92614-5514)
PHONE..................................949 756-0642
Joel Moskowitz, *Brnch Mgr*
EMP: 25
SQ FT: 33,965
SALES (corp-wide): 32.68B **Publicly Held**
Web: www.ceradyne.com
SIC: 3299 3264 Ceramic fiber; Porcelain electrical supplies
HQ: 3m Technical Ceramics, Inc.
   1922 Barranca Pkwy
   Irvine CA 92606
   949 862-9600

(P-4499)
ALS GARDEN ART INC (PA)
311 W Citrus St, Colton (92324-1412)
PHONE..................................909 424-0221
Donald Bracci, *Pr*
EMP: 290 EST: 1949
SQ FT: 305,000
SALES (est): 1.21MM
SALES (corp-wide): 1.21MM **Privately Held**
Web: www.alsgardenart.com
SIC: 3299 3272 Statuary: gypsum, clay, papier mache, metal, etc.; Concrete products, nec

(P-4500)
BURLINGAME INDUSTRIES INC
Also Called: Eagle Roofing Products Co
2352 N Locust Ave, Rialto (92377-5000)
PHONE..................................909 355-7000
Robert Burlingame, *Pr*
EMP: 109
SQ FT: 76,704
SALES (corp-wide): 54.45MM **Privately Held**
Web: www.eagleroofing.com
SIC: 3299 3272 2952 Tile, sand lime; Concrete products, nec; Asphalt felts and coatings
PA: Burlingame Industries, Incorporated
   3546 N Riverside Ave
   909 355-7000

(P-4501)
CERADYNE ESK LLC
3169 Red Hill Ave M, Costa Mesa (92626-3419)
PHONE..................................714 549-0421
Joel P Moskowitz, *CEO*
Jason Smith, *CFO*
EMP: 27 EST: 2004
SALES (est): 9.43MM
SALES (corp-wide): 32.68B **Publicly Held**
SIC: 3299 Ceramic fiber
HQ: 3m Technical Ceramics, Inc.
   1922 Barranca Pkwy

Irvine CA 92606
949 862-9600

(P-4502)
FOUNDRY SERVICE & SUPPLIES INC
2029 S Parco Ave, Ontario (91761-5700)
PHONE..................................909 284-5000
Curt Parnell, *CEO*
Joel Leathers, *
◆ EMP: 24 EST: 1962
SQ FT: 40,000
SALES (est): 2.72MM **Privately Held**
Web: www.foundryservice.com
SIC: 3299 Art goods: plaster of paris, papier mache, and scagliola

(P-4503)
OMEGA PRODUCTS CORP (HQ)
Also Called: Omega Products International
1681 California Ave, Corona (92881-3375)
P.O. Box 77220 (92877-0107)
PHONE..................................951 737-7447
Michael G Dawe, *CEO*
Todd Martin, *
▲ EMP: 60 EST: 1973
SQ FT: 11,000
SALES (est): 47.21MM
SALES (corp-wide): 73.27MM **Privately Held**
Web: www.omega-products.com
SIC: 3299 2899 Stucco; Chemical preparations, nec
PA: Opal Service, Inc.
   282 S Anita Dr
   714 935-0900

(P-4504)
OMEGA PRODUCTS CORP
282 S Anita Dr 3rd Fl, Orange (92868-3308)
P.O. Box 1149 (92856-0149)
PHONE..................................714 935-0900
Todd Martin, *Mgr*
EMP: 26
SALES (corp-wide): 73.27MM **Privately Held**
Web: www.omega-products.com
SIC: 3299 Stucco
HQ: Omega Products Corp.
   1681 California Ave
   Corona CA 92881
   951 737-7447

(P-4505)
OPAL SERVICE INC (PA)
282 S Anita Dr, Orange (92868-3308)
P.O. Box 1149 (92856-0149)
PHONE..................................714 935-0900
Kenneth R Thompson, *CEO*
▲ EMP: 30 EST: 1962
SQ FT: 1,200
SALES (est): 73.27MM
SALES (corp-wide): 73.27MM **Privately Held**
SIC: 3299 5031 5211 Stucco; Doors and windows; Lumber and other building materials

(P-4506)
PAREX USA INC (DH)
2150 Eastridge Ave, Riverside (92507-0720)
PHONE..................................714 778-2266
Rodrigo Lacerda, *Pr*
◆ EMP: 30 EST: 1926
SALES (est): 100.66MM **Privately Held**
Web: www.parexusa.com
SIC: 3299 5031 Stucco; Building materials, interior

HQ: Sika France
   84 Rue Edouard Vaillant
   Le Bourget IDF 93350
   149928000

(P-4507)
ROLLS-ROYCE HIGH TEMPERATURE COMPOSITES INC
Also Called: Rolls-Royce Htc
5730 Katella Ave, Cypress (90630-5005)
PHONE..................................714 375-4085
EMP: 50 EST: 1992
SALES (est): 9.44MM
SALES (corp-wide): 20.55B **Privately Held**
SIC: 3299 Mica products
HQ: Rolls-Royce North America (Usa) Holdings Co.
   1900 Rston Mtro Plz Ste 4
   Reston VA 20190
   703 834-1700

3312 Blast Furnaces And Steel Mills

(P-4508)
2ND SOURCE WIRE & CABLE INC
Also Called: 2nd Source Wire & Cable
20445 E Walnut Dr N, Walnut (91789-2918)
PHONE..................................714 482-2866
Donna Silvers, *Pr*
Danny Chargualaf, *
Cathy Moorhead, *
Lois Ginn, *
EMP: 65 EST: 1989
SALES (est): 4.63MM
SALES (corp-wide): 1.89B **Privately Held**
Web: www.alignprecision.com
SIC: 3312 3399 Pipes and tubes; Brads: aluminum, brass, or other nonferrous metal or wire
HQ: Align Precision - Anaheim, Inc.
   7100 Belgrave Ave
   Garden Grove CA 92841

(P-4509)
AMERICAN PLANT SERVICES INC (PA)
6242 N Paramount Blvd, Long Beach (90805-3714)
P.O. Box 727 (90801-0727)
PHONE..................................562 630-1773
George M Bragg, *Pr*
Mary-ann Pool, *Sec*
EMP: 24 EST: 1981
SALES (est): 1.25MM
SALES (corp-wide): 1.25MM **Privately Held**
SIC: 3312 Blast furnaces and steel mills

(P-4510)
ARTSONS MANUFACTURING COMPANY
11121 Garfield Ave, South Gate (90280-7505)
PHONE..................................323 773-3469
Jeffery A Winders, *CEO*
Jeffrey A Winders, *
Steve Winders, *
Art L Winders, *
▲ EMP: 28 EST: 1958
SALES (est): 1.59MM **Privately Held**
Web: www.artsonswire.com
SIC: 3312 Wire products, steel or iron

(P-4511)
B-METAL HOLDING COMPANY INC
12790 Holly St, Riverside (92509-2364)
PHONE..................................951 367-1510
EMP: 27
SALES (corp-wide): 524.41MM **Privately Held**
Web: www.borrmannmetals.com
SIC: 3312 Iron and steel products, hot-rolled
HQ: B-Metal Holding Company, Inc.
   110 W Olive Ave
   Burbank CA 91502
   818 846-7171

(P-4512)
BROWN-PACIFIC INC
Also Called: B P W
13639 Bora Dr, Santa Fe Springs (90670-5010)
PHONE..................................562 921-3471
Ron R Nagele, *CEO*
Claudia Nagele, *
Kenneth Brown, *
EMP: 32 EST: 1967
SQ FT: 35,000
SALES (est): 4.53MM **Privately Held**
Web: www.brownpacific.com
SIC: 3312 3355 3357 3356 Bar, rod, and wire products; Wire, aluminum: made in rolling mills; Nonferrous wiredrawing and insulating; Nonferrous rolling and drawing, nec

(P-4513)
CALIFORNIA AMFORGE CORPORATION
Also Called: California Amforge
750 N Vernon Ave, Azusa (91702-2231)
PHONE..................................626 334-4931
William Taylor, *Brnch Mgr*
EMP: 102
SQ FT: 20,000
SALES (corp-wide): 23.95MM **Privately Held**
Web: www.cal-amforge.com
SIC: 3312 3462 Forgings, iron and steel; Iron and steel forgings
PA: California Amforge Corporation
   750 N Vernon Ave
   626 334-4931

(P-4514)
CALIFORNIA STEEL INDS INC (HQ)
Also Called: Si
14000 San Bernardino Ave, Fontana (92335-5259)
P.O. Box 5080 (92334-5080)
PHONE..................................909 350-6300
Marcelo Botelho, *Pr*
Ricardo Bernardes, *Executive Commercial Vice President*
Brett Guge, *Executive Vice President Finance & Administration*
▲ EMP: 238 EST: 1983
SALES (est): 439.17MM
SALES (corp-wide): 34.71B **Publicly Held**
Web: www.californiasteel.com
SIC: 3312 3317 Slabs, steel; Pipes, wrought: welded, lock joint, or heavy riveted
PA: Nucor Corporation
   1915 Rexford Rd
   704 366-7000

(P-4515)
CALPIPE INDUSTRIES LLC
923 Calpipe Rd, Santa Paula (93060-9155)
PHONE..................................562 803-4388

Francisco Hernandez, *Prin*
EMP: 38
Web: www.atkore.com
SIC: 3312 Pipes and tubes
HQ: Calpipe Industries, Llc
16100 Lathrop Ave
Harvey IL 60426

(P-4516)
EASYFLEX INC
Also Called: Easyflex
2700 N Main St Ste 800, Santa Ana
(92705-6672)
PHONE....................888 577-8999
Mary Sunmin Kim, *Pr*
◆ **EMP:** 25 **EST:** 2005
SALES (est): 2.49MM **Privately Held**
Web: www.easyflexusa.com
SIC: 3312 Stainless steel

(P-4517)
HARDY FRAMES INC
Also Called: My Tech USA
250 Klug Cir, Corona (92878-5409)
PHONE....................951 245-9525
Clifford Grant, *Brnch Mgr*
EMP: 100
SALES (corp-wide): 3.9MM **Privately Held**
Web: www.hardyframe.com
SIC: 3312 Stainless steel
PA: Hardy Frames, Inc.
555 S Promenade Ave # 104
805 477-0793

(P-4518)
INTERNATIONAL MFG TECH INC (DH)
Also Called: Nassco
2798 Harbor Dr, San Diego (92113-3650)
PHONE....................619 544-7741
Willam J Cuddy, *CEO*
James C Scott, *
▲ **EMP:** 57 **EST:** 1990
SALES (est): 47.05MM
SALES (corp-wide): 42.27B **Publicly Held**
SIC: 3312 3731 Structural and rail mill products; Shipbuilding and repairing
HQ: Nassco Holdings Incorporated
2798 East Harbor Dr
San Diego CA 92106

(P-4519)
INTERSTATE STEEL CENTER CO INC
7001 S Alameda St, Los Angeles
(90001-2204)
PHONE....................323 583-0855
Leon Banks, *Pr*
William Korth, *
EMP: 50 **EST:** 1972
SQ FT: 53,000
SALES (est): 7.4MM **Privately Held**
Web: www.interstateleveling.com
SIC: 3312 5051 Blast furnaces and steel mills; Iron and steel (ferrous) products

(P-4520)
LEXANI WHEEL CORPORATION
Also Called: Lexani
1121 Olympic Dr, Corona (92881-3391)
PHONE....................951 808-4220
Frank J Hodges, *CEO*
◆ **EMP:** 33 **EST:** 1996
SQ FT: 35,000
SALES (est): 4.96MM **Privately Held**
Web: www.lexani.com
SIC: 3312 Wheels

(P-4521)
PASO ROBLES TANK INC (HQ)
825 26th St, Paso Robles (93446-1242)
P.O. Box 3229 (93447-3229)
PHONE....................805 227-1641
Shawn P Owens, *CEO*
Shane P Wombles, *
Eduardo Peralta, *
▲ **EMP:** 63 **EST:** 2000
SALES (est): 46.24MM
SALES (corp-wide): 61.08MM **Privately Held**
Web: www.pasoroblestank.com
SIC: 3312 3443 Blast furnaces and steel mills; Tanks, standard or custom fabricated: metal plate
PA: Associated Construction And Engineering, Inc.
23232 Peralta Dr Ste 206
949 455-2682

(P-4522)
PRICE INDUSTRIES INC
Also Called: International Iron Products
10883 Thornmint Rd, San Diego
(92127-2403)
PHONE....................858 673-4451
Kenneth Alan Price, *Pr*
Barbara Price, *
EMP: 75 **EST:** 1968
SQ FT: 4,000
SALES (est): 8.73MM **Privately Held**
Web: www.priceindustries.com
SIC: 3312 3441 1791 5072 Structural and rail mill products; Fabricated structural metal; Structural steel erection; Bolts, nuts, and screws

(P-4523)
RTM PRODUCTS INC
13120 Arctic Cir, Santa Fe Springs
(90670-5508)
PHONE....................562 926-2400
Robert M Thierjung, *Prin*
EMP: 23 **EST:** 2007
SALES (est): 4.08MM **Privately Held**
Web: www.rtmproducts.com
SIC: 3312 Tool and die steel and alloys

(P-4524)
SAN DEGO PRCSION MACHINING INC
9375 Ruffin Ct, San Diego (92123-5304)
PHONE....................858 499-0379
William Matteson, *CEO*
EMP: 40 **EST:** 1971
SQ FT: 23,000
SALES (est): 4.34MM **Privately Held**
Web: www.sdpm.com
SIC: 3312 3599 Stainless steel; Machine shop, jobbing and repair

(P-4525)
SEARING INDUSTRIES INC (PA)
Also Called: Searing Industries
8901 Arrow Rte, Rancho Cucamonga
(91730-4410)
P.O. Box 3059 (91729-3059)
PHONE....................909 948-3030
Lee Searing, *CEO*
Jim Searing, *Prin*
Mmargaret Cantu, *VP Fin*
◆ **EMP:** 120 **EST:** 1985
SQ FT: 265,000
SALES (est): 23.05MM
SALES (corp-wide): 23.05MM **Privately Held**
Web: www.searingindustries.com
SIC: 3312 3317 Tubes, steel and iron; Steel pipe and tubes

(P-4526)
STATE PIPE & SUPPLY INC
Westcoast Pipe Lining Division
2180 N Locust Ave, Rialto (92377-4166)
PHONE....................909 356-5670
Kenneth Walker, *Mgr*
EMP: 50
Web: www.statepipe.com
SIC: 3312 Blast furnaces and steel mills
HQ: State Pipe & Supply, Inc.
183 S Cedar Ave
Rialto CA 92376
909 877-9999

(P-4527)
TAMCO (HQ)
Also Called: CMC Steel California
5425 Industrial Pkwy, San Bernardino
(92407-1803)
PHONE....................909 899-0660
Chia Yuan Wang, *CEO*
Harley Scardoelli, *
Vilmar Babot, *
◆ **EMP:** 50 **EST:** 1974
SALES (est): 35.89MM
SALES (corp-wide): 7.93B **Publicly Held**
Web: www.asgsales.com
SIC: 3312 Blast furnaces and steel mills
PA: Commercial Metals Company
6565 N Mcrthur Blvd Ste 8
214 689-4300

(P-4528)
WEST CAST STL PROC HLDINGS LLC (PA)
13568 Vintage Pl, Chino (91710-5243)
PHONE....................909 393-8405
Erik Gamm, *CEO*
Ron Searcy, *Pr*
EMP: 25 **EST:** 2021
SALES (est): 59.06MM
SALES (corp-wide): 59.06MM **Privately Held**
Web: www.steelcousa.com
SIC: 3312 6719 3444 5075 Stainless steel; Investment holding companies, except banks; Elbows, for air ducts, stovepipes, etc.: sheet metal; Warm air heating and air conditioning

(P-4529)
WHEEL AND TIRE CLUB INC
Also Called: Discounted Wheel Warehouse
1909 S Susan St Ste D, Santa Ana
(92704-3901)
PHONE....................800 901-6003
Naeem Niamat, *CEO*
◆ **EMP:** 35 **EST:** 2013
SQ FT: 42,000
SALES (est): 3.95MM **Privately Held**
Web: www.discountedwheelwarehouse.com
SIC: 3312 5013 5014 Locomotive wheels, rolled; Wheels, motor vehicle; Tires and tubes

3313 Electrometallurgical Products

(P-4530)
NIKON AM SYNERGY INC
3550 E Carson St, Long Beach
(90808-2330)
PHONE....................310 607-0188
Thomas David Mckee, *CEO*
Gary Handley, *
EMP: 30 **EST:** 2013
SALES (est): 16.58MM **Privately Held**
Web: www.morf3d.com

SIC: 3313 3499 Alloys, additive, except copper: not made in blast furnaces; Fire- or burglary-resistive products
PA: Nikon Corporation
1-5-20, Nishioi

(P-4531)
R D MATHIS COMPANY
2840 Gundry Ave, Signal Hill (90755-1893)
P.O. Box 92916 (90809-2916)
PHONE....................562 426-7049
Robert Lumley, *Pr*
Kirk Bennett, *
Barbara Bennett, *
EMP: 25 **EST:** 1963
SQ FT: 10,000
SALES (est): 2.7MM **Privately Held**
Web: www.rdmathis.com
SIC: 3313 8711 3567 3443 Molybdenum silicon, not made in blast furnaces; Engineering services; Industrial furnaces and ovens; Fabricated plate work (boiler shop)

3315 Steel Wire And Related Products

(P-4532)
BARRETTE OUTDOOR LIVING INC
1151 Palmyrita Ave, Riverside
(92507-1703)
PHONE....................800 336-2383
Rick Paulson, *Mgr*
EMP: 30
SALES (corp-wide): 34.95B **Privately Held**
Web: www.barretteoutdoorliving.com
SIC: 3315 Fence gates, posts, and fittings: steel
HQ: Barrette Outdoor Living, Inc.
7830 Freeway Cir
Middleburg Heights OH 44130
440 891-0790

(P-4533)
DAVIS WIRE CORPORATION (HQ)
5555 Irwindale Ave, Irwindale (91706-2046)
PHONE....................626 969-7651
Jim Baske, *Pr*
Emily Heisley, *
▲ **EMP:** 150 **EST:** 1927
SQ FT: 265,000
SALES (est): 36.65MM **Privately Held**
Web: www.daviswire.com
SIC: 3315 Wire, ferrous/iron
PA: The Heico Companies L L C
70 W Madison Ste 5600

(P-4534)
DAYTON SUPERIOR CORPORATION
6001 20th St, Riverside (92509-2030)
PHONE....................951 782-9517
Jeffrey Bokn, *Brnch Mgr*
EMP: 26
SALES (corp-wide): 7.35B **Privately Held**
Web: www.daytonsuperior.com
SIC: 3315 Steel wire and related products
HQ: Dayton Superior Corporation
1125 Byers Rd
Miamisburg OH 45342
937 866-0711

(P-4535)
HAMROCK INC
3019 Wilshire Blvd, Santa Monica
(90403-2301)

PHONE..................562 944-0255
Stephen R Hamrock, *Prin*
Michael E Hamrock, *Prin*
▲ **EMP:** 250 **EST:** 1976
SALES (est): 2.97MM **Privately Held**
Web: www.hamrockmusic.com
SIC: 3315 2542 3496 3317 Wire and
  fabricated wire products; Racks,
  merchandise display or storage: except
  wood; Miscellaneous fabricated wire
  products; Steel pipe and tubes

(P-4536)
INWESCO INCORPORATED (HQ)
746 N Coney Ave, Azusa (91702-2239)
PHONE..................626 334-7115
David L Morris, *CEO*
EMP: 65 **EST:** 1967
SQ FT: 30,000
SALES (est): 25MM
SALES (corp-wide): 34.95B **Privately Held**
Web: www.inwesco.com
SIC: 3315 Steel wire and related products
PA: Crh Public Limited Company
  Stonemason S Way
  14041000

(P-4537)
MERCHANTS METALS LLC
Also Called: Merchants Metals
6466 Mission Blvd, Riverside (92509-4195)
PHONE..................951 686-1888
Rob Sisco, *Mgr*
EMP: 96
SQ FT: 8,750
SALES (corp-wide): 1.09B **Privately Held**
Web: www.merchantsmetals.com
SIC: 3315 3496 Fence gates, posts, and
  fittings: steel; Miscellaneous fabricated wire
  products
HQ: Merchants Metals Llc
  3 Ravinia Dr Ste 1750
  Atlanta GA 30346
  770 741-0300

(P-4538)
MK MAGNETICS INC
17030 Muskrat Ave, Adelanto (92301-2258)
PHONE..................760 246-6373
Lill Runge, *Pr*
Magne Stangenes, *
John Stangenes, *
Jay Runge, *Corporate Secretary**
Karen Warren, *
▲ **EMP:** 53 **EST:** 2003
SQ FT: 45,000
SALES (est): 5.4MM
SALES (corp-wide): 23.07MM **Privately Held**
Web: www.mkmagnetics.com
SIC: 3315 Steel wire and related products
PA: Stangenes Industries, Inc.
  1052 E Meadow Cir
  650 855-9926

(P-4539)
NATIONAL WIRE AND CABLE CORPORATION
Also Called: National Wire and Cable
136 N San Fernando Rd, Los Angeles
(90031-1780)
P.O. Box 31307 (90031-0307)
PHONE..................323 225-5611
EMP: 170 **EST:** 1952
SALES (est): 22.05MM **Privately Held**
Web: www.nationalwire.com
SIC: 3315 5031 Cable, steel: insulated or
  armored; Molding, all materials

(P-4540)
PRO DETENTION INC
Also Called: Viking Products
2238 N Glassell St Ste E, Orange
(92865-2742)
PHONE..................714 881-3680
Mike Peterson, *CEO*
▲ **EMP:** 70 **EST:** 2012
SALES (est): 9.11MM **Privately Held**
SIC: 3315 Wire and fabricated wire products

(P-4541)
SOUTH BAY WIRE & CABLE CO LLC (PA)
54125 Maranatha Dr, Idyllwild
(92549-0075)
P.O. Box 67 (92549-0067)
PHONE..................951 659-2183
EMP: 80 **EST:** 2021
SALES (est): 10.08MM
SALES (corp-wide): 10.08MM **Privately Held**
Web: www.southbaycable.com
SIC: 3315 Wire and fabricated wire products

(P-4542)
TREE ISLAND WIRE (USA) INC
K-Lath
3880 W Valley Blvd, Pomona (91769)
PHONE..................909 595-6617
Ken Stufford, *Mgr*
EMP: 115
SALES (corp-wide): 185.25MM **Privately Held**
Web: www.treeisland.com
SIC: 3315 Wire, steel: insulated or armored
HQ: Tree Island Wire (Usa), Inc.
  3880 Valley Blvd
  Walnut CA 91789

(P-4543)
TREE ISLAND WIRE (USA) INC
Industrial Alloys
13470 Philadelphia Ave, Fontana
(92337-7700)
PHONE..................909 594-7511
Rebecca Kalis, *Brnch Mgr*
EMP: 115
SALES (corp-wide): 185.25MM **Privately Held**
Web: www.treeisland.com
SIC: 3315 Wire, steel: insulated or armored
HQ: Tree Island Wire (Usa), Inc.
  3880 Valley Blvd
  Walnut CA 91789

(P-4544)
TREE ISLAND WIRE (USA) INC (DH)
Also Called: TI Wire
3880 Valley Blvd, Walnut (91789-1515)
P.O. Box 90100 (92427-1100)
PHONE..................909 594-7511
Amar S Doman, *Ch Bd*
Nancy Davies, *CEO*
Brian Liu, *CFO*
Stephen Ogden, *VP*
▲ **EMP:** 250 **EST:** 1980
SALES (est): 24MM
SALES (corp-wide): 185.25MM **Privately Held**
Web: www.treeisland.com
SIC: 3315 Steel wire and related products
HQ: Tree Island Industries Ltd
  3933 Boundary Rd
  Richmond BC
  604 524-3744

(P-4545)
US HANGER COMPANY LLC
17501 S Denver Ave, Gardena
(90248-3410)
PHONE..................310 323-8030
Gene Livshin, *Managing Member*
▲ **EMP:** 47 **EST:** 2008
SALES (est): 3.69MM **Privately Held**
SIC: 3315 5199 Hangers (garment), wire;
  Clothes hangers

(P-4546)
WIRETECH INC (PA)
6440 Canning St, Commerce (90040-3122)
PHONE..................323 722-4933
William Hillpot, *CEO*
Irene Sanchez, *
Garry Goodson, *
Simon Correa, *
▲ **EMP:** 87 **EST:** 2001
SALES (est): 26.22MM
SALES (corp-wide): 26.22MM **Privately Held**
Web:
wiretechincorporated.wordpress.com
SIC: 3315 Steel wire and related products

3317 Steel Pipe And Tubes

(P-4547)
CALIFORNIA STEEL INDS INC
1 California Steel Way, Fontana (92335)
PHONE..................909 350-6300
Kyle Schulty, *Brnch Mgr*
EMP: 429
SALES (corp-wide): 34.71B **Publicly Held**
Web: www.californiasteel.com
SIC: 3317 5051 Pipes, wrought: welded, lock
  joint, or heavy riveted; Iron and steel
  (ferrous) products
HQ: California Steel Industries, Inc.
  14000 San Bernardino Ave
  Fontana CA 92335
  909 350-6300

(P-4548)
INTERNATIONAL CONSULTING UNLTD
Also Called: Kns Industrial Supply
13045 Park St, Santa Fe Springs
(90670-4005)
PHONE..................714 449-3318
Karen Scott, *CEO*
EMP: 25 **EST:** 2016
SALES (est): 6.54MM **Privately Held**
Web: www.knsindustrialsupplies.com
SIC: 3317 Steel pipe and tubes

(P-4549)
K-TUBE CORPORATION
Also Called: K Tube Technologies
13400 Kirkham Way Frnt, Poway
(92064-7167)
PHONE..................858 513-9229
Greg May, *CEO*
EMP: 100 **EST:** 1982
SQ FT: 75,000
SALES (est): 23.54MM
SALES (corp-wide): 1.61B **Privately Held**
Web: www.k-tube.com
SIC: 3317 Tubing, mechanical or
  hypodermic sizes: cold drawn stainless
PA: Cook Group Incorporated
  750 Daniels Way
  812 339-2235

(P-4550)
MARUICHI AMERICAN CORPORATION
11529 Greenstone Ave, Santa Fe Springs
(90670-4697)
PHONE..................562 903-8600
Wataru Morita, *Pr*
Teruo Horikawa, *
Takehiko Katsumata, *
Makoto Ishikawa, *
Takuhiro Ishihara, *
▲ **EMP:** 96 **EST:** 1978
SQ FT: 240,000
SALES (est): 21.97MM **Privately Held**
Web: www.macsfs.com
SIC: 3317 Pipes, seamless steel
PA: Maruichi Steel Tube Ltd.
  5-1-60, Namba, Chuo-Ku

(P-4551)
NORTHWEST PIPE COMPANY
12351 Rancho Rd, Adelanto (92301-2711)
PHONE..................760 246-3191
Charles Koenig, *VP*
EMP: 154
SALES (corp-wide): 444.36MM **Publicly Held**
Web: www.nwpipe.com
SIC: 3317 3321 Pipes, wrought: welded, lock
  joint, or heavy riveted; Gray and ductile iron
  foundries
PA: Northwest Pipe Company
  201 Ne Pk Plz Dr Ste 100
  360 397-6250

(P-4552)
NUCOR WAREHOUSE SYSTEMS INC (HQ)
3851 S Santa Fe Ave, Vernon
(90058-1712)
PHONE..................323 588-4261
TOLL FREE: 800
Dave Olmstead, *Pr*
Steve Rogers, *VP*
Sturgeon Baker, *Contrlr*
Matthew Devries, *Supply Chain Manager*
◆ **EMP:** 177 **EST:** 1985
SQ FT: 285,000
SALES (est): 158.73MM
SALES (corp-wide): 34.71B **Publicly Held**
Web: www.nucorwarehousesystems.com
SIC: 3317 Tubes, seamless steel
PA: Nucor Corporation
  1915 Rexford Rd
  704 366-7000

(P-4553)
PRIMUS PIPE AND TUBE INC (DH)
5855 Obispo Ave, Long Beach
(90805-3715)
PHONE..................562 808-8000
Tommy Grahn, *Pr*
Chris Podsaid, *VP*
Karl Almond, *VP Fin*
Roy Harrison, *VP Opers*
Scott Templeton, *Ex VP*
▲ **EMP:** 51 **EST:** 1967
SQ FT: 120,000
SALES (est): 24.51MM **Privately Held**
Web: www.primuspipeandtube.com
SIC: 3317 Steel pipe and tubes
HQ: Ta Chen International, Inc.
  5860 N Paramount Blvd
  Long Beach CA 90805
  562 808-8000

PRODUCTS & SVCS

(P-4554)

ROSCOE MOSS MANUFACTURING CO (PA)

Also Called: Roscoe Moss Company
4360 Worth St, Los Angeles (90063-2573)
P.O. Box 31064 (90031-0064)
PHONE..................................323 261-4185
Roscoe Moss Junior, *Ch Bd*
George E Moss, *
Robert A Vanvaler, *
Tony Creque, *
Regis Coyle, *Corporate Secretary*
◆ **EMP:** 90 **EST:** 1913
SQ FT: 20,000
SALES (est): 21.74MM
SALES (corp-wide): 21.74MM **Privately Held**
Web: www.roscoemoss.com
SIC: 3317 Well casing, wrought: welded,
lock joint, or heavy riveted

(P-4555)

VALLEY METALS LLC

Also Called: Leggett & Platt 0768
13125 Gregg St, Poway (92064-7122)
P.O. Box 85402 (92186-5402)
PHONE..................................858 513-1300
Kirk Nelson, *Managing Member*
EMP: 40 **EST:** 1946
SQ FT: 47,700
SALES (est): 15.13MM
SALES (corp-wide): 5.15B **Publicly Held**
Web: www.leggettaerospace.com
SIC: 3317 Tubes, wrought: welded or lock
joint
HQ: Western Pneumatic Tube Company, Llc
835 6th St S
Kirkland WA 98033
425 822-8271

3321 Gray And Ductile Iron Foundries

(P-4556)

ALHAMBRA FOUNDRY COMPANY LTD

Also Called: Afco
1147 S Meridian Ave, Alhambra
(91803-1218)
P.O. Box 469 (91802-0469)
PHONE..................................626 289-4294
Arzhang Baghkhanian, *CEO*
James Wright, *
Mike Smalski, *
▲ **EMP:** 46 **EST:** 1984
SQ FT: 48,370
SALES (est): 885 **Privately Held**
Web: www.ejco.com
SIC: 3321 3312 5051 Gray iron castings, nec
; Structural shapes and pilings; steel; Iron
and steel (ferrous) products

(P-4557)

GLOBE IRON FOUNDRY INC

5649 Randolph St, Commerce
(90040-3489)
PHONE..................................323 723-8983
John M Pratto, *Pr*
Othon Garcia, *
John Pratto Junior, *VP Prd*
Jeff Pratto, *
EMP: 70 **EST:** 1929
SQ FT: 58,000
SALES (est): 8.59MM **Privately Held**
Web: www.globeiron.com
SIC: 3321 3543 3369 Gray iron castings, nec
; Industrial patterns; Nonferrous foundries,
nec

(P-4558)

JDH PACIFIC INC (PA)

1818 E Orangethorpe Ave, Fullerton
(92831-5324)
PHONE..................................562 926-8088
Donald Hu, *CEO*
▲ **EMP:** 30 **EST:** 1989
SALES (est): 24.88MM **Privately Held**
Web: www.jdhpacific.com
SIC: 3321 3324 3599 3462 Gray iron
castings, nec; Commercial investment
castings, ferrous; Crankshafts and
camshafts, machining; Iron and steel
forgings

(P-4559)

PACIFIC ALLOY CASTING COMPANY INC

5900 Firestone Blvd Fl 1, South Gate
(90280-3797)
PHONE..................................562 928-1387
EMP: 120 **EST:** 1937
SALES (est): 17.06MM **Privately Held**
Web: www.pacificalloy.com
SIC: 3321 Gray and ductile iron foundries

(P-4560)

THOMPSON GUNDRILLING INC

13840 Saticoy St, Van Nuys (91402-6582)
PHONE..................................323 873-4045
Michael Thompson, *Pr*
Robert Thompson, *
EMP: 39 **EST:** 1973
SQ FT: 32,000
SALES (est): 2.81MM **Privately Held**
Web: www.thompsongundrilling.com
SIC: 3321 Gray and ductile iron foundries

3322 Malleable Iron Foundries

(P-4561)

STEVEN HANDELMAN STUDIOS INC (PA)

716 N Milpas St, Santa Barbara
(93103-3029)
PHONE..................................805 884-9070
Steven Handelman, *Owner*
EMP: 41 **EST:** 1973
SALES (est): 2.28MM
SALES (corp-wide): 2.28MM **Privately Held**
Web: www.lightingshs.com
SIC: 3322 Malleable iron foundries

3324 Steel Investment Foundries

(P-4562)

CAST PARTS INC

Also Called: Cpp-City of Industry
16800 Chestnut St, City Of Industry
(91748-1017)
PHONE..................................626 937-3444
David Atwood, *Brnch Mgr*
EMP: 231
SALES (corp-wide): 957.88MM **Privately Held**
Web: www.cppcorp.com
SIC: 3324 Aerospace investment castings,
ferrous
HQ: Cast Parts, Inc.
4200 Valley Blvd
Walnut CA 91789
909 595-2252

(P-4563)

CAST PARTS INC (HQ)

Also Called: Cpp-Pomona
4200 Valley Blvd, Walnut (91789-1408)
PHONE..................................909 595-2252
James Stewart, *CEO*
Steve Clodfelter, *
Ali Ghavami, *
Anthony Klemenc, *
EMP: 185 **EST:** 2000
SQ FT: 300,000
SALES (est): 37.66MM
SALES (corp-wide): 957.88MM **Privately Held**
SIC: 3324 3365 Steel investment foundries;
Aluminum foundries
PA: Consolidated Precision Products Corp.
1621 Euclid Ave Ste 1850
216 453-4800

(P-4564)

HOWMET CORPORATION

900 E Watson Center Rd, Carson
(90745-4201)
PHONE..................................310 847-8152
EMP: 1088
SALES (corp-wide): 6.64B **Publicly Held**
Web: www.howmet.com
SIC: 3324 Commercial investment castings,
ferrous
HQ: Howmet Corporation
3850 White Lake Dr
Whitehall MI 49461
231 894-5686

(P-4565)

HOWMET GLOBL FSTNING SYSTEMS I

Rosan / Eagle Products
800 S State College Blvd, Fullerton
(92831-5334)
PHONE..................................714 871-1550
Craig Brown, *Mgr*
EMP: 100
SALES (corp-wide): 6.64B **Publicly Held**
SIC: 3324 3365 Aerospace investment
castings, ferrous; Aerospace castings,
aluminum
HQ: Howmet Global Fastening Systems Inc.
3990a Heritage Oak Ct
Simi Valley CA 93063
805 426-2270

(P-4566)

LISI AEROSPACE NORTH AMER INC

2602 Skypark Dr, Torrance (90505-5314)
PHONE..................................310 326-8110
Christian Darville, *CEO*
◆ **EMP:** 900 **EST:** 2009
SALES (est): 29.28MM
SALES (corp-wide): 2.67MM **Privately Held**
Web: www.lisi-aerospace.com
SIC: 3324 Aerospace investment castings,
ferrous
HQ: Lisi Aerospace
42 A 52
Paris 12 IDF 75012
140198200

(P-4567)

MILLER CASTINGS INC (PA)

2503 Pacific Park Dr, Whittier (90601-1680)
PHONE..................................562 695-0461
Hadi Khandehroo, *Pr*
Ralph Miller, *
Hadi Khandehroo, *CEO*
▲ **EMP:** 328 **EST:** 1973
SQ FT: 40,000

SALES (est): 49.35MM
SALES (corp-wide): 49.35MM **Privately Held**
Web: www.millercastings.com
SIC: 3324 Steel investment foundries

(P-4568)

NET SHAPES INC (PA)

1336 E Francis St Ste B, Ontario
(91761-5723)
PHONE..................................909 947-3231
Joseph S Cannone, *Pr*
James Cannone, *VP*
EMP: 63 **EST:** 1986
SQ FT: 43,500
SALES (est): 8.89MM
SALES (corp-wide): 8.89MM **Privately Held**
Web: www.netshapes.com
SIC: 3324 Steel investment foundries

(P-4569)

PAC-RANCHO INC (HQ)

Also Called: Cpp Rancho Cucamonga
11000 Jersey Blvd, Rancho Cucamonga
(91730-5103)
PHONE..................................909 987-4721
James Stewart, *CEO*
EMP: 102 **EST:** 1984
SQ FT: 55,000
SALES (est): 23.85MM
SALES (corp-wide): 957.88MM **Privately Held**
SIC: 3324 3354 3369 Commercial
investment castings, ferrous; Aluminum
extruded products; Nonferrous foundries,
nec
PA: Consolidated Precision Products Corp.
1621 Euclid Ave Ste 1850
216 453-4800

3325 Steel Foundries, Nec

(P-4570)

CWI STEEL TECHNOLOGIES CORPORATION

2415 Campus Dr Ste 100, Irvine
(92612-8529)
PHONE..................................949 476-7600
EMP: 48
SIC: 3325 Steel foundries, nec

(P-4571)

DAMERON ALLOY FOUNDRIES (PA)

6330 Gateway Dr Ste B, Cypress
(90630-4836)
PHONE..................................310 631-5165
John W Dameron, *Pr*
Augustin Huerta, *
▲ **EMP:** 100 **EST:** 1946
SQ FT: 5,000
SALES (est): 23.95MM
SALES (corp-wide): 23.95MM **Privately Held**
Web: www.dameron.net
SIC: 3325 3324 Steel foundries, nec;
Commercial investment castings, ferrous

(P-4572)

WCS EQUIPMENT HOLDINGS LLC (HQ)

Also Called: Steelco USA
13568 Vintage Pl, Chino (91710-5243)
PHONE..................................909 393-8405
Erik Gamm, *CEO*
EMP: 36 **EST:** 2006
SALES (est): 49.58MM
SALES (corp-wide): 59.06MM **Privately Held**

Web: www.steelcousa.com
SIC: 3325 Steel foundries, nec
PA: West Coast Steel & Processing
Holdings, Llc
13568 Vintage Pl
909 393-8405

(P-4573)
WCS EQUIPMENT HOLDINGS LLC
Also Called: Deluxe Building Products
1350 E Lexington Ave, Pomona
(91766-5521)
PHONE.................909 993-5700
EMP: 59
SALES (corp-wide): 59.06MM **Privately Held**
Web: www.deluxebuildingproducts.com
SIC: 3325 Steel foundries, nec
HQ: Wcs Equipment Holdings, Llc
13568 Vintage Pl
Chino CA 91710

3331 Primary Copper

(P-4574)
CORRPRO COMPANIES INC
23309 La Palma Ave, Yorba Linda
(92887-4773)
PHONE.................562 944-1636
Randy Galinski, *Prin*
EMP: 24
SALES (corp-wide): 1.48B **Privately Held**
Web: www.corrpro.com
SIC: 3331 1799 Cathodes (primary), copper;
Corrosion control installation
HQ: Corrpro Companies, Inc.
580 Goddard Ave
Chesterfield MO 63005
636 530-8000

3334 Primary Aluminum

(P-4575)
ALUMINUM PRECISION PDTS INC (PA)
3333 W Warner Ave, Santa Ana
(92704-5898)
PHONE.................714 546-8125
Gregory S Keeler, *Pr*
Roark Keeler, *VP*
Simona Manoiu, *CFO*
◆ **EMP:** 550 **EST:** 1965
SALES (est): 37.3MM
SALES (corp-wide): 37.3MM **Privately Held**
Web: www.aluminumprecision.com
SIC: 3334 Primary aluminum

(P-4576)
HOWMET AEROSPACE INC
3016 Lomita Blvd, Torrance (90505-5103)
PHONE.................212 836-2674
EMP: 356
SALES (corp-wide): 6.64B **Publicly Held**
Web: www.howmet.com
SIC: 3334 Primary aluminum
PA: Howmet Aerospace Inc.
201 Isabella St Ste 200
412 553-1950

(P-4577)
INOVATIV INC
1500 W Mckinley St, Azusa (91702-3218)
PHONE.................626 969-5300
Patrick Blewett, *CEO*
Tracy Barbosa, *
EMP: 40 **EST:** 2013

SALES (est): 6.22MM **Privately Held**
Web: www.inovativ.com
SIC: 3334 Primary aluminum

(P-4578)
MAURICE & MAURICE ENGRG INC
17579 Mesa St Ste B4, Hesperia
(92345-8308)
P.O. Box 403682 (92340-3682)
PHONE.................760 949-5151
Jennifer Thomas, *CEO*
Aron Maurice, *
Jennifer Maurice, *
EMP: 27 **EST:** 1973
SQ FT: 22,000
SALES (est): 2.63MM **Privately Held**
SIC: 3334 Primary aluminum

3339 Primary Nonferrous Metals, Nec

(P-4579)
ARGEN CORPORATION (PA)
Also Called: Jelenko
8515 Miralani Dr, San Diego (92126-4352)
PHONE.................858 455-7900
Anton Woolf, *CEO*
Jackie Woolf, *
Paul Cascone, *
Joel Freedman, *
Andrea Ravid, *
▲ **EMP:** 203 **EST:** 1963
SQ FT: 39,609
SALES (est): 75.94MM
SALES (corp-wide): 75.94MM **Privately Held**
Web: www.argen.com
SIC: 3339 3843 Precious metals; Dental
equipment and supplies

(P-4580)
COMMODITY RESOURCE ENVMTL INC
Also Called: Commodity Rsource
Enviromental
11847 United St, Mojave (93501-7047)
PHONE.................661 824-2416
Mike Kelsey, *Mgr*
EMP: 40
SALES (corp-wide): 9.46MM **Privately Held**
Web: www.creweb.com
SIC: 3339 3341 Precious metals; Secondary
nonferrous metals
PA: Commodity Resource &
Environmental, Inc.
116 E Prospect Ave
818 843-2811

(P-4581)
PCC ROLLMET INC
1822 Deere Ave, Irvine (92606-4817)
PHONE.................949 221-5333
Ken Buck, *Pr*
Mark Donegan, *Ch Bd*
Emi Donis, *VP*
Shawn Hagel, *CFO*
EMP: 70 **EST:** 2011
SALES (est): 22.38MM
SALES (corp-wide): 364.48B **Publicly Held**
Web: www.rollmetusa.com
SIC: 3339 Nickel refining (primary)
HQ: Precision Castparts Corp.
5885 Meadows Rd Ste 620
Lake Oswego OR 97035
503 946-4800

3341 Secondary Nonferrous Metals

(P-4582)
CERTIFIED ALLOY PRODUCTS INC
3245 Cherry Ave, Long Beach
(90807-5213)
P.O. Box 90 (90801-0090)
PHONE.................562 595-6621
▲ **EMP:** 110 **EST:** 1943
SALES (est): 34.84MM
SALES (corp-wide): 388.18K **Privately Held**
Web: www.doncasters.com
SIC: 3341 3313 3325 3312 Nickel smelting
and refining (secondary); Ferroalloys; Steel
foundries, nec; Blast furnaces and steel
mills
HQ: Doncasters Limited
1 Park Row
Leeds LS1 5
133 286-4900

(P-4583)
DAVID H FELL & CO INC (PA)
6009 Bandini Blvd, Los Angeles
(90040-2967)
PHONE.................323 722-9992
TOLL FREE: 800
Larry Fell, *Ch*
Lawrence Fell, *
Sondra Fell, *
▼ **EMP:** 24 **EST:** 1973
SQ FT: 18,000
SALES (est): 5.38MM
SALES (corp-wide): 5.38MM **Privately Held**
Web: www.dhfco.com
SIC: 3341 5094 Secondary precious metals;
Bullion, precious metals

(P-4584)
GEMINI INDUSTRIES INC
2311 Pullman St, Santa Ana (92705-5585)
PHONE.................949 250-4011
M Elguindy, *CEO*
Diana Keiffer, *Sec*
▲ **EMP:** 75 **EST:** 1973
SALES (est): 4.22MM **Privately Held**
Web: www.gemini-catalyst.com
SIC: 3341 Secondary precious metals

(P-4585)
HERAEUS PRCOUS MTLS N AMER LLC (DH)
15524 Carmenita Rd, Santa Fe Springs
(90670-5610)
PHONE.................562 921-7464
Andre Christl, *Managing Member*
Uve Kupka, *
◆ **EMP:** 200 **EST:** 1970
SQ FT: 71,000
SALES (est): 32.26MM
SALES (corp-wide): 2.67MM **Privately Held**
Web: www.heraeus-hpmn.com
SIC: 3341 2899 Gold smelting and refining
(secondary); Chemical preparations, nec
HQ: Heraeus Holding Gesellschaft Mit
Beschrankter Haftung
Heraeusstr. 12-14
Hanau HE 63450
6181350

(P-4586)
JOHNSON MATTHEY INC
Also Called: Noble Metals

12205 World Trade Dr, San Diego
(92128-3766)
P.O. Box Orld Trade (92128)
PHONE.................858 716-2400
Steve Hill, *Brnch Mgr*
EMP: 204
SALES (corp-wide): 16.3B **Privately Held**
Web: www.matthey.com
SIC: 3341 Secondary nonferrous metals
HQ: Johnson Matthey Inc.
435 Devon Park Dr Ste 600
Wayne PA 19087
610 971-3000

(P-4587)
TEXAS TST INC
13428 Benson Ave, Chino (91710-5258)
PHONE.................951 685-2155
◆ **EMP:** 50
Web: www.tst-inc.com
SIC: 3341 Aluminum smelting and refining
(secondary)

(P-4588)
TST INC (PA)
Also Called: Alpase
13428 Benson Ave, Chino (91710-5258)
PHONE.................951 685-2155
Andrew G Stein, *CEO*
Robert A Stein, *
Greg Levine, *
James Davidson, *
◆ **EMP:** 260 **EST:** 1961
SQ FT: 123,000
SALES (est): 36.95MM
SALES (corp-wide): 36.95MM **Privately Held**
Web: www.tst-inc.com
SIC: 3341 5093 Aluminum smelting and
refining (secondary); Metal scrap and waste
materials

3353 Aluminum Sheet, Plate, And Foil

(P-4589)
ALUM-A-FOLD PACIFIC INC
Also Called: AFP
3730 Capitol Ave, City Of Industry
(90601-1731)
PHONE.................562 699-4550
▲ **EMP:** 45
Web: www.perfectdomain.com
SIC: 3353 Aluminum sheet, plate, and foil

(P-4590)
HOWMET AEROSPACE INC
Also Called: Howmet Aerospace Inc
1550 Gage Rd, Montebello (90640-6614)
PHONE.................323 728-3001
EMP: 135
SALES (corp-wide): 6.64B **Publicly Held**
Web: www.howmet.com
SIC: 3353 Aluminum sheet and strip
PA: Howmet Aerospace Inc.
201 Isabella St Ste 200
412 553-1950

(P-4591)
MATERIAL SCIENCES CORPORATION
Also Called: MSC-La
3730 Capitol Ave, City Of Industry
(90601-1731)
PHONE.................562 699-4550
Patrick Murley, *CEO*
EMP: 45
SALES (corp-wide): 120.84MM **Privately Held**

Web: www.materialsciencescorp.com
SIC: **3353** Aluminum sheet, plate, and foil
PA: Material Sciences Corporation
6855 Commerce Blvd
734 207-4444

(P-4592)
SOUTHWIRE COMPANY LLC
Southwire Master Service Ctr
9199 Cleveland Ave Ste 100, Rancho Cucamonga (91730-8559)
PHONE..............................909 989-2888
David Jordan, *Brnch Mgr*
EMP: 95
SALES (corp-wide): 1.7B **Privately Held**
Web: www.southwire.com
SIC: **3353** Aluminum sheet and strip
PA: Southwire Company, Llc
One Southwire Dr
770 832-4529

(P-4593)
SOUTHWIRE INC
Also Called: Alflex
20250 S Alameda St, Compton (90221-6207)
PHONE..............................310 886-8300
Jorge Eulloqui, *Mgr*
EMP: 500
SALES (corp-wide): 1.7B **Privately Held**
Web: www.southwire.com
SIC: **3353** 3644 3315 Coils, sheet aluminum; Electric conduits and fittings; Cable, steel: insulated or armored
HQ: Southwire Inc
11695 Pacific Ave
Fontana CA 92337
310 884-8500

(P-4594)
TCI TEXARKANA INC
Also Called: Texarkana Aluminum
5855 Obispo Ave, Long Beach (90805-3715)
PHONE..............................562 808-8000
Johnny Hsieh, *CEO*
James Chang, *VP*
Andrew Chang, *Contrlr*
EMP: 100 EST: 2018
SALES (est): 2.54MM **Privately Held**
SIC: **3353** Coils, sheet aluminum
HQ: Ta Chen International, Inc.
5860 N Paramount Blvd
Long Beach CA 90805
562 808-8000

3354 Aluminum Extruded Products

(P-4595)
ANAHEIM EXTRUSION CO INC
1330 N Kraemer Blvd, Anaheim (92806-1401)
P.O. Box 6380 (92816-0380)
PHONE..............................714 630-3111
EMP: 80 EST: 1974
SALES (est): 5.08MM **Privately Held**
Web: www.anaheimextrude.com
SIC: **3354** Aluminum extruded products
HQ: Universal Molding Company
9151 Imperial Hwy
Downey CA 90242
310 886-1750

(P-4596)
FRY REGLET CORPORATION (PA)
14013 Marquardt Ave, Santa Fe Springs (90670-5018)

P.O. Box 665 (90637-0665)
PHONE..............................800 237-9773
Stephen Reed, *CEO*
Avon M Hall, *
James Tuttle, *
EMP: 75 EST: 1945
SQ FT: 20,000
SALES (est): 35.64MM
SALES (corp-wide): 35.64MM **Privately Held**
Web: www.fryreglet.com
SIC: **3354** Aluminum extruded products

(P-4597)
GLOBAL TRUSS AMERICA LLC
Also Called: Global Truss
4295 Charter St, Vernon (90058-2520)
PHONE..............................323 415-6225
Charles Davies, *Managing Member*
Kenneth Kahn, *
◆ EMP: 55 EST: 2004
SQ FT: 60,000
SALES (est): 6.98MM **Privately Held**
Web: www.globaltruss.com
SIC: **3354** Aluminum extruded products

(P-4598)
HYDRO EXTRUSION USA LLC
18111 Railroad St, City Of Industry (91748-1216)
PHONE..............................626 964-3411
Matt Zundel, *Sls Dir*
EMP: 300
Web: www.hydro.com
SIC: **3354** Aluminum extruded products
HQ: Hydro Extrusion Usa, Llc
6250 N River Rd Ste 5000
Rosemont IL 60018

(P-4599)
KAISER ALUMINUM CORPORATION
6250 Bandini Blvd, Commerce (90040-3168)
PHONE..............................323 726-8011
EMP: 74
SALES (corp-wide): 3.09B **Publicly Held**
Web: www.kaiseraluminum.com
SIC: **3354** Aluminum extruded products
PA: Kaiser Aluminum Corporation
1550 W Mcewen Dr Ste 500
629 252-7040

(P-4600)
LUXFER INC
1995 3rd St, Riverside (92507-3483)
PHONE..............................951 684-5110
Brian Mcguire, *Mgr*
EMP: 31
SALES (corp-wide): 405MM **Privately Held**
Web: www.luxfercylinders.com
SIC: **3354** 3728 Aluminum extruded products; Aircraft parts and equipment, nec
HQ: Luxfer Inc.
3016 Kansas Ave Bldg 1
Riverside CA 92507
951 684-5110

(P-4601)
MERIT ALUMINUM INC (PA)
2480 Railroad St, Corona (92880)
PHONE..............................951 735-1770
Michael Rapport, *CEO*
Evan Rapport, *
▲ EMP: 122 EST: 1990
SQ FT: 58,000
SALES (est): 24.18MM **Privately Held**
Web: www.meritaluminum.com

SIC: **3354** Aluminum extruded products

(P-4602)
NEAL FEAY COMPANY
Also Called: Troy Metal Products
133 S La Patera Ln, Goleta (93117-3291)
PHONE..............................805 967-4521
Neal C Rasmussen, *CEO*
N J Rasmussen, *
Alex Rasmussen, *
EMP: 60 EST: 1944
SQ FT: 50,000
SALES (est): 3.9MM **Privately Held**
Web: www.nealfeay.com
SIC: **3354** Tube, extruded or drawn, aluminum; Electronic enclosures, stamped or pressed metal

(P-4603)
PENGCHENG ALUMINUM ENTERPRISE INC USA
Also Called: Zhong W Ang Group
19605 E Walnut Dr N, Walnut (91789-2815)
PHONE..............................909 598-7933
▲ EMP: 30
Web: www.pcaus.com
SIC: **3354** Aluminum extruded products

(P-4604)
PRL ALUMINUM INC
14760 Don Julian Rd, City Of Industry (91746-3107)
PHONE..............................626 968-7507
Roberto Landeros, *CEO*
EMP: 100 EST: 2004
SALES (est): 8.07MM **Privately Held**
Web: www.architecturalglassandmetal.com
SIC: **3354** Aluminum extruded products
PA: Prl Glass Systems, Inc.
13644 Nelson Ave

(P-4605)
SAMUEL SON & CO (USA) INC
Also Called: Sierra Aluminum
2345 Fleetwood Dr, Riverside (92509-2410)
PHONE..............................951 781-7800
EMP: 24
SALES (corp-wide): 1.54B **Privately Held**
Web: www.samuel.com
SIC: **3354** Aluminum extruded products
HQ: Samuel, Son & Co. (Usa) Inc.
1401 Davey Rd Ste 300
Woodridge IL 60517
800 323-4424

(P-4606)
SIERRA ALUMINUM COMPANY
2345 Fleetwood Dr, Riverside (92509-2426)
PHONE..............................951 781-7800
▲ EMP: 24
Web: www.samuel.com
SIC: **3354** Aluminum extruded products

(P-4607)
SUN VALLEY PRODUCTS INC (HQ)
4626 Sperry St, Los Angeles (90039-1018)
PHONE..............................818 247-8350
Jennifer K Hillman, *Pr*
Rosanne M Kusar, *
Angelica K Clark, *
EMP: 40 EST: 1960
SQ FT: 64,980
SALES (est): 3.16MM
SALES (corp-wide): 4.35MM **Privately Held**
Web: www.sunvalleyextrusion.com

SIC: **3354** Aluminum extruded products
PA: Darfield Industries, Inc.
4626 Sperry St
818 247-8350

(P-4608)
SUPERIOR METAL SHAPES INC
4730 Eucalyptus Ave, Chino (91710-9255)
PHONE..............................909 947-3455
David A Stockton, *Pr*
EMP: 40 EST: 1983
SQ FT: 64,000
SALES (est): 4.68MM **Privately Held**
Web: www.superiormetalshapes.net
SIC: **3354** Shapes, extruded aluminum, nec

(P-4609)
TRULITE GL ALUM SOLUTIONS LLC
19430 San Jose Ave, City Of Industry (91748-1421)
PHONE..............................800 877-8439
Elizabeth Hemsing, *Mgr*
EMP: 72
Web: www.trulite.com
SIC: **3354** Aluminum extruded products
PA: Trulite Glass & Aluminum Solutions, Llc
1750 Funders Pkwy Ste 154

(P-4610)
UNIVERSAL MLDING EXTRUSION INC (DH)
Also Called: Umex
9151 Imperial Hwy, Downey (90242-2808)
PHONE..............................562 401-1015
Dominick L Baione, *CEO*
◆ EMP: 41 EST: 1988
SALES (est): 49.51MM **Privately Held**
Web: www.umextrude.com
SIC: **3354** Aluminum extruded products
HQ: Universal Molding Company
9151 Imperial Hwy
Downey CA 90242
310 886-1750

(P-4611)
US POLYMERS INC
5910 Bandini Blvd, Commerce (90040-2963)
PHONE..............................323 727-6888
Vram Ohanesiam, *Mgr*
EMP: 100
SALES (corp-wide): 24.57MM **Privately Held**
Web: www.uspolymersinc.com
SIC: **3354** 5719 Aluminum extruded products; Window furnishings
PA: U.S. Polymers, Inc.
1057 S Vail Ave
323 728-3023

(P-4612)
VISION SYSTEMS INC
11322 Woodside Ave N, Santee (92071-4728)
PHONE..............................619 258-7300
Fred W Witte, *Pr*
James Schlereth, *
▲ EMP: 60 EST: 1984
SQ FT: 32,000
SALES (est): 19.28MM **Privately Held**
Web: www.visionsystems.com
SIC: **3354** 3442 Aluminum extruded products; Window and door frames

(P-4613)
VISTA METALS CORP (PA)
13425 Whittram Ave, Fontana (92335-2999)

PHONE..................909 823-4278
Andrew Primack, *CEO*
Raymond Alpert, *
Steve Chevlin, *
Robert Praefke, *
◆ **EMP: 235 EST: 1968**
SQ FT: 17,000
SALES (est): 30.25MM
SALES (corp-wide): 30.25MM Privately Held
Web: www.vistametals.com
SIC: 3354 3341 Aluminum extruded products ; Aluminum smelting and refining (secondary)

3355 Aluminum Rolling And Drawing, Nec

(P-4614)
ARCADIA PRODUCTS LLC (HQ)
Also Called: Arcadia Norcal
2301 E Vernon Ave, Los Angeles (90023)
PHONE...................323 771-9819
James Schladen, *CEO*
Khan Chow, *CFO*
▲ **EMP: 250 EST: 1985**
SQ FT: 50,000
SALES (est): 71.39MM
SALES (corp-wide): 719.19MM Publicly Held
Web: www.arcadiainc.com
SIC: 3355 Extrusion ingot, aluminum: made in rolling mills
PA: Dmc Global Inc.
   11800 Ridge Pkwy Ste 300
   303 665-5700

(P-4615)
METALS USA BUILDING PDTS LP (DH)
Also Called: Metals USA
955 Columbia St, Brea (92821-2923)
PHONE...............713 946-9000
Charles Canning, *Pt*
Robert Mcpherson, *Pt*
▲ **EMP: 700 EST: 1960**
SQ FT: 60,000
SALES (est): 31.78MM
SALES (corp-wide): 14.81B Publicly Held
Web: www.metalsusa.com
SIC: 3355 5031 1542 Structural shapes, rolled, aluminum; Building materials, exterior ; Commercial and office buildings, renovation and repair
HQ: Metals Usa, Inc.
   800 W Cypress Creed Rd St
   Fort Lauderdale FL 33309
   215 673-3595

(P-4616)
METALS USA BUILDING PDTS LP
1951 S Parco Ave Ste C, Ontario (91761-8315)
PHONE..................800 325-1305
Steve Brang, *Mgr*
EMP: 88
SALES (corp-wide): 14.81B Publicly Held
Web: www.metalsusa.com
SIC: 3355 Structural shapes, rolled, aluminum
HQ: Metals Usa Building Products Lp
   955 Columbia St
   Brea CA 92821
   713 946-9000

3356 Nonferrous Rolling And Drawing, Nec

(P-4617)
DYNAMET INCORPORATED
16052 Beach Blvd Ste 221, Huntington Beach (92647-3855)
PHONE...................714 375-3150
Tom Proteau, *Mgr*
EMP: 32
SALES (corp-wide): 2.76B Publicly Held
Web: www.carpentertechnology.com
SIC: 3356 Titanium and titanium alloy bars, sheets, strip, etc.
HQ: Dynamet Incorporated
   195 Museum Rd
   Washington PA 15301
   724 228-1000

(P-4618)
INTERSPACE BATTERY INC (PA)
2009 W San Bernardino Rd, West Covina (91790-1091)
PHONE...................626 813-1234
Paul Godber, *Ch Bd*
Donald W Godber, *Pr*
EMP: 23 EST: 1970
SQ FT: 36,000
SALES (est): 1.68MM
SALES (corp-wide): 1.68MM Privately Held
Web: www.concordebattery.com
SIC: 3356 3691 Battery metal; Storage batteries

(P-4619)
NEW CNTURY MTALS SOUTHEAST INC
Also Called: Rti Los Angeles
15723 Shoemaker Ave, Norwalk (90650-6863)
PHONE...................562 356-6804
Jeremy S Halford, *CEO*
Marie T Batz, *
EMP: 229 EST: 1998
SALES (est): 2.18MM
SALES (corp-wide): 6.64B Publicly Held
SIC: 3356 Titanium
HQ: Rmi Titanium Company, Llc
   1000 Warren Ave
   Niles OH 44446
   330 652-9952

(P-4620)
OCEANIA INTERNATIONAL LLC
Also Called: Stanford Advanced Materials
23661 Birtcher Dr, Lake Forest (92630-1770)
PHONE...................949 407-8904
Alexander Chen, *CEO*
Alexander Chen, *Managing Member*
▲ **EMP: 40 EST: 2012**
SALES (est): 3.69MM Privately Held
Web: www.samaterials.com
SIC: 3356 3313 Titanium and titanium alloy bars, sheets, strip, etc.; Ferromolybdenum

(P-4621)
P KAY METAL INC (PA)
Also Called: P K Metal
2448 E 25th St, Los Angeles (90058-1234)
PHONE...................323 585-5058
Larry Kay, *Pr*
Sharon Kay, *
Cindy Flame, *
▲ **EMP: 44 EST: 1977**
SALES (est): 10.77MM
SALES (corp-wide): 10.77MM Privately Held

Web: www.pkaymetal.com
SIC: 3356 Lead and lead alloy bars, pipe, plates, shapes, etc.

(P-4622)
UMC ACQUISITION CORP (PA)
Also Called: Universal Molding Company
9151 Imperial Hwy, Downey (90242-2808)
PHONE...................562 940-0300
Dominick L Baione, *Ch Bd*
Edward L Koch Iii, *Pr*
EMP: 50 EST: 1998
SALES (est): 102.03MM Privately Held
Web: www.universalmold.com
SIC: 3356 3354 3471 3479 Nonferrous rolling and drawing, nec; Aluminum extruded products; Anodizing (plating) of metals or formed products; Aluminum coating of metal products

(P-4623)
UNIVERSAL MOLDING COMPANY (HQ)
9151 Imperial Hwy, Downey (90242-2808)
PHONE...................310 886-1750
Dominick L Baione, *Ch Bd*
EMP: 160 EST: 1952
SQ FT: 62,000
SALES (est): 98.46MM Privately Held
Web: www.universalmold.com
SIC: 3356 3354 3448 3471 Nonferrous rolling and drawing, nec; Aluminum extruded products; Screen enclosures; Anodizing (plating) of metals or formed products
PA: Umc Acquisition Corp.
   9151 E Imperial Hwy

(P-4624)
VSMPO-TIRUS US INC
Also Called: West Coast Service Center
2850 E Cedar St, Ontario (91761-8514)
PHONE...................909 230-9020
Dave Richardson, *Mgr*
EMP: 53
Web: www.vsmpo-tirus.com
SIC: 3356 Titanium
HQ: Vsmpo-Tirus, U.S., Inc.
   401 Riverport Dr
   Leetsdale PA 15056
   720 746-1023

3357 Nonferrous Wiredrawing And Insulating

(P-4625)
BELDEN INC
Also Called: Coast Custom Cable
1048 E Burgrove St, Carson (90746-3514)
PHONE...................310 639-9473
Michael Dugar, *Brnch Mgr*
EMP: 750
SALES (corp-wide): 2.51B Publicly Held
Web: www.alphawire.com
SIC: 3357 3699 Coaxial cable, nonferrous; Electrical equipment and supplies, nec
PA: Belden Inc.
   1 N Brentwood Blvd Fl 15
   314 854-8000

(P-4626)
BRIDGEWAVE COMMUNICATIONS INC
17034 Camino San Bernardo, San Diego (92127-5708)
PHONE...................408 567-6900
Amir Makleff, *Pr*
John Keating, *

▲ **EMP: 25 EST: 1998**
SALES (est): 4.29MM Privately Held
Web: www.bridgewave.com
SIC: 3357 3229 Communication wire; Pressed and blown glass, nec

(P-4627)
BROADATA COMMUNICATIONS INC
2545 W 237th St Ste K, Torrance (90505-5229)
PHONE...................310 530-1416
David Faulkner, *CEO*
Freddie Lin, *
Patty Shaw, *
German Lopez, *
◆ **EMP: 40 EST: 2000**
SQ FT: 10,000
SALES (est): 12.08MM Privately Held
Web: www.broadatacom.com
SIC: 3357 3663 Fiber optic cable (insulated); Television broadcasting and communications equipment

(P-4628)
CALIFORNIA FINE WIRE CO (PA)
338 S 4th St, Grover Beach (93433-1999)
P.O. Box 446 (93483-0446)
PHONE...................805 489-5144
EMP: 36 EST: 1961
SALES (est): 10.4MM
SALES (corp-wide): 10.4MM Privately Held
Web: www.calfinewire.com
SIC: 3357 3315 3466 3341 Nonferrous wiredrawing and insulating; Wire, ferrous/ iron; Closures, stamped metal; Secondary nonferrous metals

(P-4629)
CALIFORNIA INSULATED WIRE &
3050 N California St, Burbank (91504-2004)
PHONE...................818 569-4930
Bill Boyd, *Pr*
Micheal Boyd, *
Bruce Boyd, *
Lois Boyd, *
EMP: 60 EST: 1978
SQ FT: 26,000
SALES (est): 8.72MM Privately Held
Web: www.ciwinc.com
SIC: 3357 Communication wire

(P-4630)
CALMONT ENGRG & ELEC CORP (PA)
Also Called: Calmont Wire & Cable
420 E Alton Ave, Santa Ana (92707-4278)
PHONE...................714 549-0336
Barbara Monteleone, *Pr*
Blanche F Chilcote, *
EMP: 36 EST: 1970
SQ FT: 24,000
SALES (est): 5.41MM
SALES (corp-wide): 5.41MM Privately Held
Web: www.calmont.com
SIC: 3357 3061 Nonferrous wiredrawing and insulating; Medical and surgical rubber tubing (extruded and lathe-cut)

(P-4631)
CENTURY WIRE & CABLE INC
5701 S Eastern Ave, Commerce (90040-2973)
PHONE...................800 999-5566
David Lifschitz, *CEO*
Carl Tom, *
Rowdy Oxford, *

William Suddarth, *
EMP: 100 **EST:** 1982
SALES (est): 8.93MM
SALES (corp-wide): 127.37MM **Privately Held**
Web: www.centurywire.com
SIC: 3357 5063 Nonferrous wiredrawing and insulating; Electrical apparatus and equipment
HQ: Gehr Industries, Inc.
5701 S Eastern Ave
Commerce CA 90040
323 728-5558

(P-4632)
FIBEROPTIC SYSTEMS INC
60 Moreland Rd Ste A, Simi Valley (93065-1643)
PHONE...........................805 579-6600
Sanford S Stark, *Pr*
Kathy Hanau, *
EMP: 29 **EST:** 1982
SQ FT: 14,000
SALES (est): 6.21MM **Privately Held**
Web: www.fiberopticsystems.com
SIC: 3357 3229 Fiber optic cable (insulated); Fiber optics strands

(P-4633)
GEHR INDUSTRIES INC (HQ)
Also Called: Gehr Group
5701 S Eastern Ave, Commerce (90040-2973)
PHONE...........................323 728-5558
David Lifschitz, *CEO*
Carlton Tom, *
Mark Goldman, *
William Suddarth, *
Maximilian Paetzold, *
▲ **EMP:** 140 **EST:** 1966
SALES (est): 57.64MM
SALES (corp-wide): 127.37MM **Privately Held**
Web: www.gehrindustries.com
SIC: 3357 5063 5072 5085 Nonferrous wiredrawing and insulating; Electrical apparatus and equipment; Hardware; Industrial supplies
PA: The Gehr Group Inc
5701 S Eastern Ave
323 728-5558

(P-4634)
JEB HOLDINGS CORP
42033 Rio Nedo, Temecula (92590-3705)
P.O. Box 67 (92549-0067)
PHONE...........................951 296-9900
Gordon Brown, *Pr*
EMP: 23
SALES (corp-wide): 8.59MM **Privately Held**
Web: www.southbaycable.com
SIC: 3357 Nonferrous wiredrawing and insulating
PA: Jeb Holdings Corp.
54125 Maranatha Dr
951 659-2183

(P-4635)
OKONITE COMPANY INC
2900 Skyway Dr, Santa Maria (93455-1897)
PHONE...........................805 922-6682
Rick Flory, *Brnch Mgr*
EMP: 125
SQ FT: 10,000
SALES (corp-wide): 55.09MM **Privately Held**
Web: www.okonite.com
SIC: 3357 Nonferrous wiredrawing and insulating

PA: The Okonite Company Inc
102 Hilltop Rd
201 825-0300

(P-4636)
PRECISION FIBER PRODUCTS INC
Also Called: Pfp
642 Palomar St, Chula Vista (91911-2626)
PHONE...........................408 946-4040
Ray Pierce, *Pr*
◆ **EMP:** 30 **EST:** 2003
SALES (est): 3.47MM **Privately Held**
Web: www.precisionfiberproducts.com
SIC: 3357 Fiber optic cable (insulated)

(P-4637)
PRIME WIRE & CABLE INC
11701 6th St, Rancho Cucamonga (91730-6030)
PHONE...........................323 266-2010
EMP: 104
Web: www.primewirecable.com
SIC: 3357 Nonferrous wiredrawing and insulating
HQ: Prime Wire & Cable, Inc.
1330 Valley Vista Dr
Diamond Bar CA 91765
888 445-9955

(P-4638)
QPC FIBER OPTIC LLC
27612 El Lazo, Laguna Niguel (92677-3913)
PHONE...........................949 361-8855
Steven J Wilkes, *Pr*
David Olsen, *
EMP: 30 **EST:** 1999
SQ FT: 1,400
SALES (est): 9.54MM **Privately Held**
Web: www.qpcfiber.com
SIC: 3357 Fiber optic cable (insulated)

(P-4639)
SUPERIOR ESSEX INC
5250 Ontario Mills Pkwy Ste 300, Ontario (91764-5131)
PHONE...........................909 481-4804
Victor Alegria, *Brnch Mgr*
EMP: 103
Web: www.superioressex.com
SIC: 3357 Nonferrous wiredrawing and insulating
HQ: Superior Essex Inc.
5770 Pwers Frry Rd Nw Ste
Atlanta GA 30327
770 657-6000

(P-4640)
WINCHSTER INTRCNNECT CM CA INC
Also Called: C B S
1810 Diamond St, San Marcos (92078-5100)
PHONE...........................800 848-4257
Lewis Brian Falk, *CEO*
Donald Falk, *
Shannon Baroni, *
▲ **EMP:** 175 **EST:** 1965
SQ FT: 40,000
SALES (est): 46.8MM **Privately Held**
Web: www.falmat.com
SIC: 3357 5063 Nonferrous wiredrawing and insulating; Wire and cable
HQ: Aptiv Corporation
5725 Innovation Dr
Troy MI 48098

(P-4641)
WIRE TECHNOLOGY CORPORATION
9527 Laurel St, Los Angeles (90002-2653)
P.O. Box 1608 (90280-1608)
PHONE...........................310 635-6935
Rachel Mendoza, *Pr*
Darlene Delange, *
Robert Mendoza, *
EMP: 25 **EST:** 1970
SQ FT: 4,000
SALES (est): 3.02MM **Privately Held**
Web: www.wiretechnologycorp.com
SIC: 3357 Nonferrous wiredrawing and insulating

3363 Aluminum Die-castings

(P-4642)
AEROTEC ALLOYS INC
10632 Alondra Blvd, Norwalk (90650-5301)
PHONE...........................562 809-1378
Robert W Franklin, *CEO*
Mitchell Frahm, *
EMP: 50 **EST:** 1986
SQ FT: 18,000
SALES (est): 7.11MM **Privately Held**
Web: www.aerotecalloys.com
SIC: 3363 3312 3365 3325 Aluminum die-castings; Blast furnaces and steel mills; Aluminum foundries; Steel foundries, nec

(P-4643)
ALLOY DIE CASTING CO (PA)
Also Called: ADC Aerospace
6550 Caballero Blvd, Buena Park (90620-1130)
PHONE...........................714 521-9800
Rick Simpson, *CEO*
Eric Sanders, *Pr*
Wim Huijs, *VP*
Maeli Garcia, *Dir*
EMP: 135 **EST:** 1939
SQ FT: 55,000
SALES (est): 23.12MM
SALES (corp-wide): 23.12MM **Privately Held**
Web: www.adc-aerospace.com
SIC: 3363 Aluminum die-castings

(P-4644)
ALUMINUM DIE CASTING CO INC
10775 San Sevaine Way, Jurupa Valley (91752-1146)
PHONE...........................951 681-3900
Steve Bennett, *CEO*
Rudy Bennett, *
James Bennett, *Stockholder*
EMP: 65 **EST:** 1950
SQ FT: 31,000
SALES (est): 3.39MM **Privately Held**
Web: www.adc3900.com
SIC: 3363 3364 Aluminum die-castings; Nonferrous die-castings except aluminum

(P-4645)
EDELBROCK FOUNDRY CORP
1320 S Buena Vista St, San Jacinto (92583-4665)
PHONE...........................951 654-6677
Otis Victor Edelbrock, *Pr*
Ronald L Webb, *
Nancy Edelbrock, *
Aristedes Seles, *
Camme Edelbrock, *
EMP: 38 **EST:** 1938
SQ FT: 75,000
SALES (est): 4.34MM **Privately Held**
Web: www.edelbrockfoundry.com

SIC: 3363 3365 3325 Aluminum die-castings ; Aluminum foundries; Steel foundries, nec
HQ: Edelbrock, Llc
8649 Hacks Cross Rd
Olive Branch MS 38654
310 781-2222

(P-4646)
HYATT DIE CAST AND ENGINEERING CORPORATION - SOUTH (PA)
4656 Lincoln Ave, Cypress (90630-2650)
P.O. Box 728 (90630-0728)
PHONE...........................714 826-7550
EMP: 80 **EST:** 1956
SALES (est): 24.28MM
SALES (corp-wide): 24.28MM **Privately Held**
Web: www.hyattdiecast.com
SIC: 3363 Aluminum die-castings

(P-4647)
HYATT DIE CAST ENGRG CORP - S
12250 Industry St, Garden Grove (92841-2816)
PHONE...........................714 622-2131
Mike Senter, *Brnch Mgr*
EMP: 35
SALES (corp-wide): 24.28MM **Privately Held**
Web: www.hyattdiecast.com
SIC: 3363 Aluminum die-castings
PA: Hyatt Die Cast And Engineering Corporation - South
4656 Lincoln Ave
714 826-7550

(P-4648)
KENWALT DIE CASTING CORP
Also Called: Kenwait Die Casting Company
8719 Bradley Ave, Sun Valley (91352-2799)
PHONE...........................818 768-5800
TOLL FREE: 800
Ken Zaucha Senior, *Pr*
Rose Zaucha, *Stockholder*
▼ **EMP:** 25 **EST:** 1974
SQ FT: 20,000
SALES (est): 3.55MM **Privately Held**
Web: www.kenwalt.com
SIC: 3363 Aluminum die-castings

(P-4649)
MAGNESIUM ALLOY PDTS CO INC
2420 N Alameda St, Compton (90222-2895)
P.O. Box 4668 (90224-4668)
PHONE...........................310 605-1440
J W Long, *Pr*
M B Long, *
EMP: 46 **EST:** 1945
SQ FT: 90,000
SALES (est): 4.39MM **Privately Held**
Web: www.magnesiumalloy.com
SIC: 3363 Aluminum die-castings

(P-4650)
MAGNESIUM ALLOY PRODUCTS CO LP
2420 N Alameda St, Compton (90222-2804)
PHONE...........................323 636-2276
Richard Killen, *Pt*
James Long, *Pt*
EMP: 50 **EST:** 1956
SALES (est): 2.29MM **Privately Held**
Web: www.magnesiumalloy.com

SIC: **3363** Aluminum die-castings

(P-4651)
PACIFIC DIE CASTING CORP
6155 S Eastern Ave, Commerce
(90040-3401)
PHONE..............................323 725-1308
Jeff Orlandini, *VP*
Sonny Yun, *Stockholder**
▲ **EMP:** 150 **EST:** 1954
SQ FT: 8,000
SALES (est): 6.65MM **Privately Held**
Web: www.pacdiecast.com
SIC: **3363** Aluminum die-castings

(P-4652)
RANGERS DIE CASTING CO
10828 Alameda St, Lynwood (90262-1721)
P.O. Box 127 (90262-0127)
PHONE..............................310 764-1800
EMP: 40
Web: www.rangersdiecasting.com
SIC: **3363** 3544 3599 Aluminum die-castings
; Special dies, tools, jigs, and fixtures;
Machine and other job shop work

(P-4653)
SEA SHIELD MARINE PRODUCTS INC
Also Called: American Zinc Enterprises
20832 Currier Rd, Walnut (91789-3017)
PHONE..............................909 594-2507
Wendell Walter Godwin, *CEO*
Shelley Lopez, *
Alicia Vongoeben, *
▲ **EMP:** 45 **EST:** 1971
SQ FT: 25,000
SALES (est): 4.36MM **Privately Held**
Web: www.seashieldmarine.com
SIC: **3363** 3364 Aluminum die-castings;
Magnesium and magnesium-base alloy die-
castings

(P-4654)
VENUS ALLOYS INC (PA)
1415 S Allec St, Anaheim (92805-6306)
PHONE..............................714 635-8800
E K Venugopal, *Pr*
Kousalya Venugopal, *
EMP: 24 **EST:** 1989
SQ FT: 20,000
SALES (est): 4.58MM **Privately Held**
SIC: **3363** 3364 Aluminum die-castings;
Brass and bronze die-castings

3364 Nonferrous Die-castings Except Aluminum

(P-4655)
ALCAST MFG INC
2910 Fisk Ln, Redondo Beach
(90278-5437)
PHONE..............................310 542-3581
EMP: 30
SALES (corp-wide): 9.6MM **Privately Held**
Web: www.alcast-foundry.com
SIC: **3364** 3363 Brass and bronze die-
castings; Aluminum die-castings
PA: Alcast Mfg, Inc.
7355 E Slauson Ave
310 542-3581

(P-4656)
AMERICAN DIE CASTING INC
14576 Fontlee Ln, Fontana (92335-2599)
PHONE..............................909 356-7768
TOLL FREE: 800
Walter Mueller, *Pr*

Jeffrey Mueller, *
Marjorie Mueller, *
EMP: 50 **EST:** 1992
SQ FT: 20,000
SALES (est): 4.67MM **Privately Held**
Web: www.americandiecasting.com
SIC: **3364** 3363 Zinc and zinc-base alloy die-
castings; Aluminum die-castings

(P-4657)
CALIFORNIA DIE CASTING INC
1820 S Grove Ave, Ontario (91761-5613)
PHONE..............................909 947-9947
Dan C Lane, *Pr*
Jerry C Holland, *
Roy Herring, *
EMP: 49 **EST:** 1996
SQ FT: 3,000
SALES (est): 8.52MM **Privately Held**
Web: www.caldiecast.com
SIC: **3364** 3363 Nonferrous die-castings
except aluminum; Aluminum die-castings

(P-4658)
DEL MAR INDUSTRIES (PA)
Also Called: Del Mar Die Casting Co
12901 S Western Ave, Gardena
(90249-1917)
P.O. Box 881 (90294-0881)
PHONE.......................... (323) 321-0600
Doctor Taylor, *CEO*
Louis A Cuhrt, *
Judith Taylor, *
Susan Davis, *Stockholder**
EMP: 100 **EST:** 1968
SQ FT: 68,000
SALES (est): 2.05MM
SALES (corp-wide): 2.05MM **Privately Held**
Web: www.delmarindustries.com
SIC: **3364** Zinc and zinc-base alloy die-
castings

(P-4659)
DYNACAST LLC
Also Called: Dynacast, LLC
25952 Commercentre Dr, Lake Forest
(92630-8815)
PHONE..............................949 707-1211
John Hess, *Brnch Mgr*
EMP: 140
SALES (corp-wide): 1.08B **Privately Held**
Web: www.dynacast.com
SIC: **3364** Nonferrous die-castings except
aluminum
HQ: Dynacast Us Holdings, Inc.
14045 Balntyn Corp Pl
Charlotte NC 28277
704 927-2790

(P-4660)
FTG AEROSPACE INC (DH)
20740 Marilla St, Chatsworth (91311-4407)
PHONE..............................818 407-4024
Michael Labrador, *Pr*
▼ **EMP:** 42 **EST:** 2011
SQ FT: 13,000
SALES (est): 24.49MM
SALES (corp-wide): 98.06MM **Privately Held**
Web: www.ftgcorp.com
SIC: **3364** Nonferrous die-castings except
aluminum
HQ: Firan Technology Group (Usa)
Corporation
20750 Marilla St
Chatsworth CA 91311
818 407-4024

(P-4661)
VERTECHS ENTERPRISES INC (PA)
1071 Industrial Pl, El Cajon (92020-3107)
PHONE..............................858 578-3900
Geosef Straza, *CEO*
George C Straza, *
▲ **EMP:** 46 **EST:** 2007
SALES (est): 1.62MM **Privately Held**
Web: www.vertechsusa.com
SIC: **3364** 3724 3544 Copper and copper
alloy die-castings; Aircraft engines and
engine parts; Die sets for metal stamping
(presses)

(P-4662)
WHITEFOX DEFENSE TECH INC
854 Monterey St, San Luis Obispo
(93401-3225)
PHONE..............................805 225-4506
Mark Kulam, *Pr*
EMP: 28 **EST:** 2016
SALES (est): 5.81MM **Privately Held**
Web: www.whitefoxdefense.com
SIC: **3364** Nonferrous die-castings except
aluminum

3365 Aluminum Foundries

(P-4663)
AEROL CO INC
Also Called: Aerol Co
19560 S Rancho Way, Rancho Dominguez
(90220-6038)
PHONE..............................310 762-2660
▲ **EMP:** 36
Web: www.aerol.com
SIC: **3365** 2821 3714 3728 Aluminum
foundries; Plastics materials and resins;
Motor vehicle parts and accessories;
Wheels, aircraft

(P-4664)
ALCAST MFG INC (PA)
7355 E Slauson Ave, Commerce
(90040-3626)
PHONE..............................310 542-3581
Kiwon Ban, *CEO*
Soo Ban, *Treas*
Lily Martinez, *
▲ **EMP:** 25 **EST:** 1986
SALES (est): 9.6MM
SALES (corp-wide): 9.6MM **Privately Held**
Web: www.alcast-foundry.com
SIC: **3365** 3366 3544 3369 Aluminum and
aluminum-based alloy castings; Brass
foundry, nec; Special dies, tools, jigs, and
fixtures; Nonferrous foundries, nec

(P-4665)
ALUMISTAR INC
Also Called: Pacific Cast Products
520 S Palmetto Ave, Ontario (91762-4121)
PHONE..............................562 633-6673
Peter Lake, *Pr*
▲ **EMP:** 26 **EST:** 1982
SALES (est): 2.54MM **Privately Held**
Web: www.pacificcastproducts.com
SIC: **3365** Aluminum and aluminum-based
alloy castings

(P-4666)
BUDDY BAR CASTING LLC
10801 Sessler St, South Gate
(90280-7222)
PHONE..............................562 861-9664
Ky Fell, *CEO*
Edward W Barksdale Senior, *Prin*
Bill Fell, *

Mike Mckeen, *VP*
John Fell, *
▲ **EMP:** 130 **EST:** 1953
SQ FT: 25,000
SALES (est): 8.43MM **Privately Held**
Web: www.buddybarcasting.com
SIC: **3365** Aluminum foundries

(P-4667)
CALIDAD INC
1730 S Balboa Ave, Ontario (91761-7773)
PHONE..............................909 947-3937
Don Cornell, *Pr*
Daniel Garcia, *
EMP: 30 **EST:** 1986
SQ FT: 10,000
SALES (est): 2.67MM **Privately Held**
Web: www.calidadinc.com
SIC: **3365** 3324 Aluminum foundries; Steel
investment foundries

(P-4668)
CONSOLDTED PRECISION PDTS CORP
705 Industrial Way, Port Hueneme
(93041-3505)
PHONE..............................805 488-6451
EMP: 88
SALES (corp-wide): 957.88MM **Privately Held**
Web: www.cppcorp.com
SIC: **3365** Aluminum foundries
PA: Consolidated Precision Products Corp.
1621 Euclid Ave Ste 1850
216 453-4800

(P-4669)
CONSOLDTED PRECISION PDTS CORP
Also Called: Cpp - Pomona
4200 West Valley Blvd, Pomona (91769)
PHONE..............................909 595-2252
James Stewart, *CEO*
EMP: 93
SALES (corp-wide): 957.88MM **Privately Held**
Web: www.cppcorp.com
SIC: **3365** 3324 Aluminum foundries; Steel
investment foundries
PA: Consolidated Precision Products Corp.
1621 Euclid Ave Ste 1850
216 453-4800

(P-4670)
CONSOLIDATED FOUNDRIES INC
Also Called: Cpp Cudahy
8333 Wilcox Ave, Cudahy (90201-5919)
P.O. Box 1099 (90201)
PHONE..............................323 773-2363
Steve Gallardo, *Brnch Mgr*
EMP: 121
SALES (corp-wide): 957.88MM **Privately Held**
Web: www.cppcorp.com
SIC: **3365** 3324 Aluminum foundries; Steel
investment foundries
HQ: Consolidated Foundries, Inc.
1621 Euclid Ave Ste 1850
Cleveland OH 44115

(P-4671)
CYTEC ENGINEERED MATERIALS INC
Also Called: Solvay Composite Materials
1440 N Kraemer Blvd, Anaheim
(92806-1404)
PHONE..............................714 632-1174
Ron Martin, *Brnch Mgr*

PRODUCTS & SVCS

EMP: 125
SQ FT: 135,055
SALES (corp-wide): 8.01MM **Privately Held**
Web: www.syensqo.com
SIC: 3365 2891 2851 2823 Aerospace castings, aluminum; Adhesives and sealants ; Paints and allied products; Cellulosic manmade fibers
HQ: Cytec Engineered Materials Inc.
2085 E Tech Cir Ste 102
Tempe AZ 85284

(P-4672)
DC PARTNERS INC (PA)
Also Called: Soligen 2006
1356 N Santiago St, Santa Ana (92701-2515)
PHONE..............................714 558-9444
Yehoram Uziel, *Pr*
Alecia Wagner, *
EMP: 32 **EST:** 2005
SALES (est): 4.07MM **Privately Held**
Web: www.soligen2006.com
SIC: 3365 3599 Aluminum foundries; Machine and other job shop work

(P-4673)
EMPLOYEE OWNED PCF CAST PDTS I
Also Called: Aluminum Casting Company
520 S Palmetto Ave, Ontario (91762-4121)
PHONE..............................562 633-6673
Alex B Hall, *Pr*
EMP: 24 **EST:** 2000
SALES (est): 983.13K **Privately Held**
SIC: 3365 Aluminum and aluminum-based alloy castings

(P-4674)
GC INTERNATIONAL INC (PA)
Also Called: Alj
4671 Calle Carga, Camarillo (93012-8560)
PHONE..............................805 389-4631
Mark Griffith, *Pr*
Richard R Carlson, *Pr*
Mark R Griffith, *VP*
Terry Carlson, *VP*
F Willard Griffith, *CEO*
▼ **EMP:** 43 **EST:** 1975
SQ FT: 45,000
SALES (est): 9.92MM
SALES (corp-wide): 9.92MM **Privately Held**
Web: www.aljcast.com
SIC: 3365 3695 3369 3061 Aluminum and aluminum-based alloy castings; Magnetic disks and drums; Lead, zinc, and white metal; Appliance rubber goods (mechanical)

(P-4675)
GRISWOLD INDUSTRIES (PA)
Also Called: Cla-Val Co
1701 Placentia Ave, Costa Mesa (92627-4416)
P.O. Box 1325 (92659-0325)
PHONE..............................949 722-4800
◆ **EMP:** 420 **EST:** 1936
SALES (est): 85.81MM
SALES (corp-wide): 85.81MM **Privately Held**
Web: www.cla-val.com
SIC: 3365 3366 3492 3325 Aluminum foundries; Brass foundry, nec; Control valves, fluid power: hydraulic and pneumatic ; Steel foundries, nec

(P-4676)
MAGPARTS (HQ)
Also Called: Cpp-Azusa

1545 W Roosevelt St, Azusa (91702-3281)
P.O. Box 1099 (90201-7099)
PHONE..............................626 334-7897
Richard H Emerson, *Pr*
L Scott Donald Mac, *VP*
Ellen E Skatvold, *
EMP: 108 **EST:** 1958
SQ FT: 100,000
SALES (est): 19.03MM
SALES (corp-wide): 957.88MM **Privately Held**
Web: www.perfectdomain.com
SIC: 3365 3369 Aluminum and aluminum-based alloy castings; Magnesium and magnes.-base alloy castings, exc. die-casting
PA: Consolidated Precision Products Corp.
1621 Euclid Ave Ste 1850
216 453-4800

(P-4677)
SONFARREL AEROSPACE LLC
3010 E La Jolla St, Anaheim (92806-1324)
PHONE..............................714 630-7280
Jeffrey Greer, *CEO*
Ken Anderson, *
EMP: 96 **EST:** 2018
SALES (est): 10.43MM **Privately Held**
Web: www.son-aero.com
SIC: 3365 Aerospace castings, aluminum

(P-4678)
SUPERNAL LLC
15555 Laguna Canyon Rd, Irvine (92618-7722)
PHONE..............................202 422-3275
Jaiwon Shin, *Brnch Mgr*
EMP: 139
Web: www.supernal.aero
SIC: 3365 Aerospace castings, aluminum
HQ: Supernal, Llc
1101 16th St Nw
Washington DC 20036
202 422-3175

3366 Copper Foundries

(P-4679)
FLEETWOOD CONTINENTAL INC
19451 S Susana Rd, Compton (90221-5713)
PHONE..............................310 609-1477
David J Forster, *Pr*
▲ **EMP:** 75 **EST:** 1965
SQ FT: 5,000
SALES (est): 9.65MM **Privately Held**
Web: www.fleetcon.com
SIC: 3366 3823 3561 3523 Castings (except die), nec, bronze; Turbine flow meters, industrial process type; Pumps and pumping equipment; Farm machinery and equipment

(P-4680)
GALAXY DIE AND ENGINEERING INC
Also Called: Galaxy Bearing Company
24910 Avenue Tibbitts, Valencia (91355-3426)
PHONE..............................661 775-9301
Jawahar Saini, *Pr*
Hamid Baig, *
Sooltan Ali Bhoy, *
Malkiat Saini, *Stockholder*
EMP: 40 **EST:** 1958
SQ FT: 30,000
SALES (est): 5.75MM **Privately Held**
Web: www.galaxybearing.com

SIC: 3366 3575 Bushings and bearings; Computer terminals

(P-4681)
HILLER COMPANIES LLC
Also Called: Hiller Marine
7070 Convoy Ct, San Diego (92111-1017)
PHONE..............................858 899-5008
EMP: 32
SALES (corp-wide): 179.36MM **Privately Held**
SIC: 3366 Propellers
PA: The Hiller Companies, Llc
3751 Joy Springs Dr
251 661-1275

(P-4682)
MONTCLAIR BRONZE INC
2535 E 57th St, Huntington Park (90255-2520)
P.O. Box 2009 (91763-0509)
PHONE..............................909 986-2664
Dan Griffiths, *
Wayne Freeberg, *.
Thomas Freeberg, *
EMP: 30 **EST:** 1963
SALES (est): 5.21MM **Privately Held**
Web: www.montclairbronze.com
SIC: 3366 3599 Bronze foundry, nec; Machine shop, jobbing and repair

(P-4683)
PAC FOUNDRIES INC
Also Called: Cpp-Port Hueneme
705 Industrial Way, Port Hueneme (93041-3505)
PHONE..............................805 986-1308
James Stewart, *CEO*
EMP: 176 **EST:** 1978
SALES (est): 9.9MM
SALES (corp-wide): 957.88MM **Privately Held**
Web: www.cppcorp.com
SIC: 3366 Copper foundries
PA: Consolidated Precision Products Corp.
1621 Euclid Ave Ste 1850
216 453-4800

3369 Nonferrous Foundries, Nec

(P-4684)
ALLIEDSIGNAL AROSPC SVC CORP (HQ)
Also Called: Allied Signal Aerospace
2525 W 190th St, Torrance (90504-6002)
PHONE..............................310 323-9500
Bernd F Kessler, *Pr*
Mary Beth Orson, *
James V Gelly, *
EMP: 53 **EST:** 2003
SALES (est): 14.93MM
SALES (corp-wide): 36.66B **Publicly Held**
SIC: 3369 3822 3812 3769 Nonferrous foundries, nec; Environmental controls; Search and navigation equipment; Space vehicle equipment, nec
PA: Honeywell International Inc.
855 S Mint St
704 627-6200

(P-4685)
CAST PARTNER INC
4658 W Washington Blvd, Los Angeles (90016-1743)
PHONE..............................323 876-9000
Fridlizius Theo, *Pr*
EMP: 29 **EST:** 2013
SALES (est): 2.21MM **Privately Held**

Web: www.castpartner.com
SIC: 3369 Nonferrous foundries, nec

(P-4686)
CAST-RITE INTERNATIONAL INC (PA)
515 E Airline Way, Gardena (90248-2501)
PHONE..............................310 532-2080
Donald E Dehaan, *CEO*
Wynn Chapman, *
Howard Watkins, *
◆ **EMP:** 90 **EST:** 1961
SQ FT: 59,330
SALES (est): 7.59MM
SALES (corp-wide): 7.59MM **Privately Held**
Web: www.cast-rite.com
SIC: 3369 Zinc and zinc-base alloy castings, except die-castings

(P-4687)
DECCO CASTINGS INC
1410 Hill St, El Cajon (92020-5749)
PHONE..............................818 416-0068
Colm Plunkett, *Brnch Mgr*
EMP: 30
SALES (corp-wide): 11.3MM **Privately Held**
Web: www.deccocastings.com
SIC: 3369 Nonferrous foundries, nec
PA: Decco Castings, Inc.
1596 Pioneer Way
619 444-9437

(P-4688)
FENICO PRECISION CASTINGS INC
7805 Madison St, Paramount (90723-4220)
PHONE..............................562 634-5000
Don Tomeo, *Pr*
Sherry Tomeo, *
▲ **EMP:** 75 **EST:** 1987
SQ FT: 20,000
SALES (est): 4.83MM **Privately Held**
Web: www.fenicocastings.com
SIC: 3369 3366 3324 3322 Machinery castings, exc. die, nonferrous, exc. alum. copper; Copper foundries; Steel investment foundries; Malleable iron foundries

(P-4689)
FS - PRECISION TECH CO LLC
3025 E Victoria St, Compton (90221-5616)
PHONE..............................310 638-0595
Israel M Sanchez, *
▲ **EMP:** 100 **EST:** 2004
SALES (est): 24.83MM **Privately Held**
Web: www.fs-precision.com
SIC: 3369 Titanium castings, except die-casting

(P-4690)
INTERNATIONAL DIE CASTING INC
515 E Airline Way, Gardena (90248-2501)
PHONE..............................310 324-2278
▲ **EMP:** 38 **EST:** 1977
SALES (est): 3.25MM
SALES (corp-wide): 7.59MM **Privately Held**
Web: www.internationaldiecasting.com
SIC: 3369 2842 3364 Zinc and zinc-base alloy castings, except die-castings; Metal polish; Nonferrous die-castings except aluminum
PA: Cast-Rite International, Inc.
515 E Airline Way
310 532-2080

(P-4691)

ORLANDINI ENTPS PCF DIE CAST

Also Called: Pacific Die Casting
6155 S Eastern Ave, Commerce
(90040-3401)
PHONE..................................323 725-1332
Jeff Orlandini, *Pr*
Vincent Orlandini, *
▲ **EMP:** 125 **EST:** 1955
SQ FT: 45,000
SALES (est): 2.17MM **Privately Held**
Web: www.pacdiecast.com
SIC: 3369 3363 Machinery castings, exc. die, nonferrous, exc. alum. copper; Aluminum die-castings

(P-4692)

PANKL AEROSPACE SYSTEMS

16615 Edwards Rd, Cerritos (90703-2437)
PHONE..................................562 207-6300
Horst Rieger, *CEO*
Barry Calvert, *
Wolfgang Plasser, *
Harry Glieder, *
EMP: 75 **EST:** 2000
SQ FT: 63,040
SALES (est): 21.15MM
SALES (corp-wide): 3.83B **Privately Held**
Web: www.pankl.com
SIC: 3369 3724 Aerospace castings, nonferrous: except aluminum; Aircraft engines and engine parts
HQ: Pankl Holdings, Inc.
1902 Mcgaw Ave
Irvine CA 92614

(P-4693)

TECHNI-CAST CORP

Also Called: Techni Cast Corp
11220 Garfield Ave, South Gate
(90280-7586)
PHONE..................................562 923-4585
Bryn Jhan Van Hiel Ii, *Pr*
Donald Van Hiel, *
Lynne Van Hiel, *
Elaine M Kay, *
▲ **EMP:** 80 **EST:** 1954
SQ FT: 60,000
SALES (est): 9.88MM **Privately Held**
Web: www.techni-cast.com
SIC: 3369 3599 3364 3325 Lead, zinc, and white metal; Machine shop, jobbing and repair; Nonferrous die-castings except aluminum; Steel foundries, nec

---

3398 Metal Heat Treating

(P-4694)

ACCURATE STEEL TREATING INC

10008 Miller Way, South Gate
(90280-5496)
PHONE..................................562 927-6528
Ronald Loyns, *Pr*
Mike Bastin, *
EMP: 38 **EST:** 1962
SQ FT: 10,000
SALES (est): 4.59MM **Privately Held**
Web: www.accuratesteeltreating.com
SIC: 3398 Metal heat treating

(P-4695)

AEROCRAFT HEAT TREATING CO INC

15701 Minnesota Ave, Paramount
(90723-4120)
PHONE..................................562 674-2400
David W Dickson, *CEO*

Robert Lyddon, *
EMP: 57 **EST:** 1957
SQ FT: 18,000
SALES (est): 4.31MM
SALES (corp-wide): 364.48B **Publicly Held**
Web: www.aerocraft-ht.com
SIC: 3398 Metal heat treating
HQ: Precision Castparts Corp.
5885 Meadows Rd Ste 620
Lake Oswego OR 97035
503 946-4800

(P-4696)

AREMAC HEAT TREATING INC

330 S 9th Ave, City Of Industry
(91746-3311)
P.O. Box 90068 (91715-0068)
PHONE..................................626 333-3898
B E Kopaskie, *Pr*
Bernard E Kopaskie, *
Doctor Butler, *VP*
Jan Kopaskie, *
EMP: 38 **EST:** 1967
SQ FT: 14,000
SALES (est): 1.27MM **Privately Held**
Web: www.aremac.com
SIC: 3398 Metal heat treating

(P-4697)

ASTRO ALUMINUM TREATING CO

11040 Palmer Ave, South Gate
(90280-7497)
PHONE..................................562 923-4344
Mark R Dickson, *Pr*
Mike Burns, *
EMP: 90 **EST:** 1977
SQ FT: 4,800
SALES (est): 19.09MM **Privately Held**
Web: www.astroaluminum.com
SIC: 3398 Metal heat treating

(P-4698)

BODYCOTE THERMAL PROC INC

9921 Romandel Ave, Santa Fe Springs
(90670-3441)
PHONE..................................562 946-1717
Manuel Granillo, *Prin*
EMP: 48
SALES (corp-wide): 1B **Privately Held**
Web: www.bodycote.com
SIC: 3398 Metal heat treating
HQ: Bodycote Thermal Processing, Inc.
12750 Merit Dr Ste 1400
Dallas TX 75251
214 904-2420

(P-4699)

BODYCOTE THERMAL PROC INC

515 W Apra St, Compton (90220-5523)
PHONE..................................714 893-6561
Manuel Granillo, *Brnch Mgr*
EMP: 34
SALES (corp-wide): 1B **Privately Held**
Web: www.bodycote.com
SIC: 3398 Metal heat treating
HQ: Bodycote Thermal Processing, Inc.
12750 Merit Dr Ste 1400
Dallas TX 75251
214 904-2420

(P-4700)

BODYCOTE USA INC

2900 S Sunol Dr, Vernon (90058-4315)
PHONE..................................323 264-0111
EMP: 2260
SQ FT: 31,717
SALES (corp-wide): 1B **Privately Held**
Web: www.bodycote.com

SIC: 3398 Metal heat treating
HQ: Bodycote Usa, Inc.
12750 Merit Dr Ste 1400
Dallas TX 75251
214 904-2420

(P-4701)

BURBANK STEEL TREATING INC

415 S Varney St, Burbank (91502-2194)
PHONE..................................818 842-0975
Mildred Bennett, *Ch Bd*
Larry Bennett, *
Kenneth Bennett, *
EMP: 45 **EST:** 1969
SQ FT: 16,000
SALES (est): 5.16MM **Privately Held**
Web: www.burbanksteel.com
SIC: 3398 Metal heat treating

(P-4702)

CONTINENTAL HEAT TREATING INC

10643 Norwalk Blvd, Santa Fe Springs
(90670-3821)
PHONE..................................562 944-8808
James Stull, *Pr*
Shaun Radford, *
Laura Rubio, *
Don Lowman, *
Dennis Hugie, *
EMP: 62 **EST:** 1957
SQ FT: 20,000
SALES (est): 9.92MM **Privately Held**
Web: www.continentalht.com
SIC: 3398 Metal heat treating

(P-4703)

KITTYHAWK INC (PA)

11651 Monarch St, Garden Grove
(92841-1816)
PHONE..................................714 895-5024
Brandon Creason, *Pr*
Daniel Bednar, *
EMP: 50 **EST:** 1995
SALES (est): 6.38MM
SALES (corp-wide): 6.38MM **Privately Held**
Web: www.kittyhawkinc.com
SIC: 3398 Metal heat treating

(P-4704)

KITTYHAWK PRODUCTS CA LLC

11651 Monarch St, Garden Grove
(92841-1816)
PHONE..................................714 895-5024
Brandon Creason, *Prin*
Kimberly Dickerson, *Prin*
Daniel Bednar, *Prin*
EMP: 25 **EST:** 2019
SALES (est): 345.5K **Privately Held**
Web: www.kittyhawkinc.com
SIC: 3398 Metal heat treating

(P-4705)

KPI SERVICES INC

Also Called: Kittyhawk Products
11651 Monarch St, Garden Grove
(92841-1816)
PHONE..................................714 895-5024
Charles Barre, *CEO*
Dennis Poor, *
Steve Belloise, *
Dee Dee Poor, *
Lois Barre, *
▲ **EMP:** 35 **EST:** 1995
SQ FT: 12,500
SALES (est): 7.33MM **Privately Held**
Web: www.kittyhawkinc.com

SIC: 3398 Metal heat treating

(P-4706)

METAL IMPROVEMENT COMPANY LLC

Also Called: Para Tech Coating
35 Argonaut Ste A1, Laguna Hills
(92656-4151)
PHONE..................................949 855-8010
Bill Gleason, *Mgr*
EMP: 30
SALES (corp-wide): 2.85B **Publicly Held**
Web: www.imrtest.com
SIC: 3398 Shot peening (treating steel to reduce fatigue)
HQ: Metal Improvement Company, Llc
80 Route 4 E Ste 310
Paramus NJ 07652
201 843-7800

(P-4707)

METAL IMPROVEMENT COMPANY LLC

2588 Industry Way Ste A, Lynwood
(90262-4015)
PHONE..................................323 585-2168
Amando Yanez, *Mgr*
EMP: 95
SQ FT: 28,260
SALES (corp-wide): 2.85B **Publicly Held**
Web: www.imrtest.com
SIC: 3398 Shot peening (treating steel to reduce fatigue)
HQ: Metal Improvement Company, Llc
80 Route 4 E Ste 310
Paramus NJ 07652
201 843-7800

(P-4708)

METAL IMPROVEMENT COMPANY LLC

E/M Coatings Solutions
6940 Farmdale Ave, North Hollywood
(91605-6210)
PHONE..................................818 983-1952
Brent Taylor, *Brnch Mgr*
EMP: 85
SALES (corp-wide): 2.85B **Publicly Held**
Web: www.imrtest.com
SIC: 3398 Shot peening (treating steel to reduce fatigue)
HQ: Metal Improvement Company, Llc
80 Route 4 E Ste 310
Paramus NJ 07652
201 843-7800

(P-4709)

METAL IMPROVEMENT COMPANY LLC

E/M Coatings Services
20751 Superior St, Chatsworth
(91311-4416)
PHONE..................................818 407-6280
Brent Taylor, *Brnch Mgr*
EMP: 96
SALES (corp-wide): 2.85B **Publicly Held**
Web: www.imrtest.com
SIC: 3398 Shot peening (treating steel to reduce fatigue)
HQ: Metal Improvement Company, Llc
80 Route 4 E Ste 310
Paramus NJ 07652
201 843-7800

(P-4710)

NEWTON HEAT TREATING CO INC

19235 E Walnut Dr N, City Of Industry
(91748-1494)

P.O. Box 8010　(91748-0010)
PHONE..................626 964-6528
Greg Newton, *Pr*
Linda Malcor, *
EMP: 71 **EST:** 1968
SQ FT: 1,900
SALES (est): 8.67MM **Privately Held**
Web: www.newtonheattreating.com
SIC: 3398 8734 3444　Metal heat treating; X-ray inspection service, industrial; Sheet metalwork

(P-4711)
PRO TECH THERMAL SERVICES
1954 Tandem, Norco (92860-3607)
PHONE..................951 272-5808
Brian Grier, *Pr*
Nathan Smith, *
Carolyn Dearborn, *
EMP: 33 **EST:** 1997
SQ FT: 4,000
SALES (est): 6.97MM **Privately Held**
Web: www.protechthermal.com
SIC: 3398　Metal heat treating

(P-4712)
QUALITY HEAT TREATING INC
3305 Burton Ave, Burbank (91504-3199)
PHONE..................818 840-8212
James G Stull, *Pr*
EMP: 34 **EST:** 1945
SQ FT: 20,000
SALES (est): 7.42MM **Privately Held**
Web: www.qualityht.com
SIC: 3398 3471　Metal heat treating; Sand blasting of metal parts

(P-4713)
SOLAR ATMOSPHERES INC
8606 Live Oak Ave, Fontana (92335-3172)
PHONE..................909 217-7400
EMP: 24
Web: www.solaratm.com
SIC: 3398　Annealing of metal
PA: Solar Atmospheres, Inc.
　　1969 Clearview Rd

(P-4714)
TEAM INC
Also Called: Team Industrial Services
1515 240th St, Harbor City (90710-1308)
PHONE..................310 514-2312
Bill Pigeon, *Mgr*
EMP: 25
SALES (corp-wide): 862.62MM **Publicly Held**
Web: www.teaminc.com
SIC: 3398 3567　Metal heat treating; Heating units and devices, industrial: electric
HQ: Team, Inc.
　　5095 Paris St
　　Denver CO 80239

(P-4715)
THERMAL-VAC TECHNOLOGY INC
Also Called: City Steel Heat Treating
1221 W Struck Ave, Orange (92867-3531)
PHONE..................714 997-2601
Steve Driscol, *CEO*
Aaron Anderson, *
Jennider Kovatch, *
EMP: 41 **EST:** 1985
SQ FT: 26,800
SALES (est): 8.71MM **Privately Held**
Web: www.thermalvac.com
SIC: 3398　Brazing (hardening) of metal

(P-4716)
TRIW1969 INC
877 Vernon Way, El Cajon (92020-1940)
PHONE..................619 593-3636
Derick Dennis, *Pr*
Chris Constable, *
EMP: 33 **EST:** 1969
SQ FT: 29,500
SALES (est): 4.32MM **Privately Held**
Web: www.certifiedmetalcraft.com
SIC: 3398　Brazing (hardening) of metal
PA: Solar Atmospheres, Inc.
　　1969 Clearview Rd

(P-4717)
VALLEY METAL TREATING INC
355 Se End Ave, Pomona (91766-2312)
PHONE..................909 623-6316
James G Stull, *Pr*
EMP: 38 **EST:** 1986
SQ FT: 8,000
SALES (est): 2.55MM **Privately Held**
Web: www.valleymt.net
SIC: 3398　Metal heat treating

3399 Primary Metal Products

(P-4718)
MICRO SURFACE ENGR INC (PA)
Also Called: Ball TEC
1550 E Slauson Ave, Los Angeles (90011-5099)
P.O. Box 58611 (90011)
PHONE..................323 582-7348
TOLL FREE: 800
Eugene A Gleason Junior, *Pr*
Helen Gleason, *
Eugene A Gleason Iii, *Sec*
EMP: 35 **EST:** 1952
SQ FT: 46,000
SALES (est): 9.4MM
SALES (corp-wide): 9.4MM **Privately Held**
Web: www.precisionballs.com
SIC: 3399　Steel balls

(P-4719)
PRECISION PWDRED MET PARTS INC
145 Atlantic St, Pomona (91768-3286)
PHONE..................909 595-5656
Maurice Bridgman, *Pr*
David Connelly, *
▲ **EMP:** 48 **EST:** 1978
SQ FT: 25,000
SALES (est): 2.84MM **Privately Held**
Web: www.precisionpm.com
SIC: 3399　Powder, metal

3411 Metal Cans

(P-4720)
CONTAINER SUPPLY COMPANY INCORPORATED
Also Called: C S C
12571 Western Ave, Garden Grove (92841-4012)
P.O. Box 5367 (92846-0367)
PHONE..................714 892-8321
▲ **EMP:** 105 **EST:** 1947
SALES (est): 21.09MM **Privately Held**
Web: www.containersupplycompany.com
SIC: 3411 2656　Food and beverage containers; Sanitary food containers

(P-4721)
METAL CONTAINER CORPORATION
7155 Central Ave, Riverside (92504-1400)
PHONE..................951 354-0444
Bob Parker, *Brnch Mgr*
EMP: 158
SALES (corp-wide): 1.7B **Privately Held**
Web: www.metal-containers.com
SIC: 3411　Can lids and ends, metal
HQ: Metal Container Corporation
　　3636 S Geyer Rd Ste 100
　　Saint Louis MO 63127
　　314 577-2000

(P-4722)
METAL CONTAINER CORPORATION
10980 Inland Ave, Jurupa Valley (91752-1127)
PHONE..................951 360-4500
Otto Sosapavon, *Prin*
EMP: 158
SALES (corp-wide): 1.7B **Privately Held**
Web: www.metal-containers.com
SIC: 3411　Aluminum cans
HQ: Metal Container Corporation
　　3636 S Geyer Rd Ste 100
　　Saint Louis MO 63127
　　314 577-2000

(P-4723)
SILGAN CAN COMPANY
Also Called: Silgan
21600 Oxnard St Ste 1600, Woodland Hills (91367-3609)
PHONE..................818 348-3700
EMP: 166
SIC: 3411 2032　Metal cans; Canned specialties

(P-4724)
SILGAN CONTAINERS CORPORATION (DH)
Also Called: Silgan
21600 Oxnard St Ste 1600, Woodland Hills (91367-3609)
PHONE..................818 710-3700
Anthony J Allott, *CEO*
Thomas J Snyder, *Ch Bd*
R Phillip Silver, *V Ch Bd*
James D Beam, *Pr*
Joseph Heaney, *VP*
◆ **EMP:** 100 **EST:** 1987
SALES (est): 478.49MM **Publicly Held**
Web: www.silgancontainers.com
SIC: 3411　Food containers, metal
HQ: Silgan Containers Llc
　　21600 Oxnard St Ste 1600
　　Woodland Hills CA 91367
　　818 710-3700

(P-4725)
SILGAN CONTAINERS LLC (HQ)
21600 Oxnard St Ste 1600, Woodland Hills (91367-3609)
PHONE..................818 710-3700
Thomas Snyder, *Pr*
Joseph Heaney, *
Anthony Cost, *
Richard Brewer, *
Michael Beninato, *Supply Chain Management Vice-President*
◆ **EMP:** 100 **EST:** 1997
SALES (est): 1.63B **Publicly Held**
Web: www.silgancontainers.com
SIC: 3411　Food containers, metal
PA: Silgan Holdings Inc.
　　4 Landmark Sq Ste 400

(P-4726)
SILGAN CONTAINERS MFG CORP (DH)
Also Called: Silgan
21600 Oxnard St Ste 1600, Woodland Hills (91367-3609)
PHONE..................818 710-3700
Thomas Snyder, *Prin*
EMP: 70 **EST:** 1997
SALES (est): 668.67MM **Publicly Held**
Web: www.silgancontainers.com
SIC: 3411　Metal cans
HQ: Silgan Containers Llc
　　21600 Oxnard St Ste 1600
　　Woodland Hills CA 91367
　　818 710-3700

(P-4727)
VAN CAN COMPANY
13230 Evening Creek Dr S Ste 212, San Diego (92128-4106)
PHONE..................858 391-8084
▲ **EMP:** 200
Web: www.vancan.com
SIC: 3411　Tin cans

3412 Metal Barrels, Drums, And Pails

(P-4728)
GREIF INC
8250 Almeria Ave, Fontana (92335-3279)
PHONE..................909 350-2112
Andy Wade, *Mgr*
EMP: 54
SQ FT: 73,320
SALES (corp-wide): 5.22B **Publicly Held**
Web: www.greif.com
SIC: 3412 2674 2655 2449　Drums, shipping: metal; Bags: uncoated paper and multiwall; Fiber cans, drums, and similar products; Wood containers, nec
PA: Greif, Inc.
　　425 Winter Rd
　　740 549-6000

3421 Cutlery

(P-4729)
KAI USA LTD
6031 Malburg Way, Vernon (90058-3947)
PHONE..................323 589-2600
EMP: 28
Web: zt.kaiusa.com
SIC: 3421　Carving sets
HQ: Kai U.S.A., Ltd.
　　18600 Sw Teton Ave
　　Tualatin OR 97062
　　503 682-1966

(P-4730)
NADOLIFE INC
1025 Orange Ave, Coronado (92118-3405)
PHONE..................619 522-0077
EMP: 28
SALES (corp-wide): 2.89MM **Privately Held**
SIC: 3421　Table and food cutlery, including butchers'
PA: Nadolife, Inc.
　　2709 Newton Ave
　　619 522-6890

(P-4731)
PACIUGO
122 Main St Ste 122, Huntington Beach (92648-5126)

PHONE..................714 536-5388
EMP: 25 **EST:** 2009
SALES (est): 1.45MM **Privately Held**
SIC: 3421 Table and food cutlery, including butchers'

(P-4732)
PHC SHARP HOLDINGS INC (HQ)
17819 Gillette Ave, Irvine (92614-6501)
PHONE..................714 662-1033
Mark Marinovich, *CEO*
Joe Garavaglia, *CFO*
EMP: 23 **EST:** 2006
SQ FT: 27,000
SALES (est): 9.99MM
SALES (corp-wide): 19.68MM **Privately Held**
SIC: 3421 Cutlery
PA: Levine Leichtman Capital Partners, Llc
345 N Maple Dr Ste 300
310 275-5335

3423 Hand And Edge Tools, Nec

(P-4733)
ADVANCED CUTTING TOOLS INC
17741 Metzler Ln, Huntington Beach (92647-6246)
PHONE..................714 842-9376
Stjepan Herceg, *Pr*
EMP: 30 **EST:** 1987
SQ FT: 10,200
SALES (est): 2.64MM **Privately Held**
Web: www.actincorporated.com
SIC: 3423 3545 5251 Hand and edge tools, nec; Machine tool accessories; Tools'

(P-4734)
ALLEGION ACCESS TECH LLC
15750 Jurupa Ave, Fontana (92337-7329)
PHONE..................909 628-9272
John Rapisarda, *Mgr*
EMP: 32
Web: www.stanleyaccess.com
SIC: 3423 Hand and edge tools, nec
HQ: Allegion Access Technologies Llc
65 Scott Swamp Rd
Farmington CT 06032

(P-4735)
ALLEGION ACCESS TECH LLC
8380 Camino Santa Fe Ste 100, San Diego (92121-2657)
PHONE..................858 431-5940
Michael Hecker, *Brnch Mgr*
EMP: 32
Web: www.stanleyaccess.com
SIC: 3423 Hand and edge tools, nec
HQ: Allegion Access Technologies Llc
65 Scott Swamp Rd
Farmington CT 06032

(P-4736)
AUGERSCOPE INC
Also Called: Marco Products
10375 Wilshire Blvd Apt 1b, Los Angeles (90024-4712)
▲ **EMP:** 45 **EST:** 1924
SALES (est): 1.07MM **Privately Held**
SIC: 3423 Plumbers' hand tools

(P-4737)
CALIFORNIA FLEXRAKE CORP
Also Called: Flexrake
9620 Gidley St, Temple City (91780-4215)

P.O. Box 1289 (91780-1289)
PHONE..................626 443-4026
John P Mcguire, *Pr*
▲ **EMP:** 25 **EST:** 1946
SALES (est): 2.31MM **Privately Held**
Web: www.flexrake.com
SIC: 3423 Garden and farm tools, including shovels

(P-4738)
CRAFTSMAN UNITY LLC
2273 E Via Burton, Anaheim (92806-1222)
PHONE..................714 776-8995
Justin Hennings, *Managing Member*
EMP: 175 **EST:** 1986
SALES (est): 9.66MM **Privately Held**
Web: www.craftsmancuttingdies.com
SIC: 3423 Cutting dies, except metal cutting

(P-4739)
FUN PROPERTIES INC
Also Called: PEC Tool
2645 Maricopa St, Torrance (90503-5144)
PHONE..................310 787-4500
Richard A Luboviski, *CEO*
Sandy Luboviski, *
Bernard Brooks, *
◆ **EMP:** 60 **EST:** 1960
SQ FT: 68,000
SALES (est): 5.02MM **Privately Held**
Web: www.pec.tools
SIC: 3423 Hand and edge tools, nec

(P-4740)
HALEX CORPORATION (DH)
4200 Santa Ana St Ste A, Ontario (91761-1539)
PHONE..................909 629-6219
Mark Chichak, *Pr*
◆ **EMP:** 43 **EST:** 2002
SALES (est): 4.61MM
SALES (corp-wide): 402.18MM **Privately Held**
Web: www.traxxcorp.com
SIC: 3423 Carpet layers' hand tools
HQ: Gcp Applied Technologies Inc.
2325 Lkeview Pkwy Ste 400
Alpharetta GA 30009
617 876-1400

(P-4741)
KAL-CAMERON MANUFACTURING CORP (HQ)
Also Called: Pro American Premium Tools
4265 Puente Ave, Baldwin Park (91706-3420)
PHONE..................626 338-7308
John Toshima, *Ch Dd*
EMP: 100 **EST:** 1983
SQ FT: 32,000
SALES (est): 3.98MM
SALES (corp-wide): 8.76MM **Privately Held**
SIC: 3423 Mechanics' hand tools
PA: American Kal Enterprises, Inc.
4265 Puente Ave
626 338-7308

(P-4742)
MONSTER TOOL LLC
2470 Ash St U 2, Vista (92081-8461)
PHONE..................760 477-1000
Richard Mcintyre, *Pr*
Kevin Zimmerman, *CFO*
EMP: 150 **EST:** 2021
SALES (est): 5.82MM
SALES (corp-wide): 12.03B **Privately Held**
Web: www.monstertool.com
SIC: 3423 Hand and edge tools, nec
PA: Sandvik Ab
Spangvagen 10

26260000

(P-4743)
PACIFIC HANDY CUTTER INC (DH)
Also Called: PHC
170 Technology Dr, Irvine (92618-2401)
PHONE..................714 662-1033
Mark Marinovich, *CEO*
▲ **EMP:** 34 **EST:** 1960
SALES (est): 9.99MM
SALES (corp-wide): 19.68MM **Privately Held**
Web: www.phcsafety.com
SIC: 3423 3421 Hand and edge tools, nec; Cutlery
HQ: Phc Sharp Holdings, Inc.
17819 Gillette Ave
Irvine CA 92614
714 662-1033

(P-4744)
PHC MERGER INC
Also Called: PHC
17819 Gillette Ave, Irvine (92614-6501)
PHONE..................714 662-1033
▲ **EMP:** 50
Web: www.phcsafety.com
SIC: 3423 3421 Hand and edge tools, nec; Cutlery

(P-4745)
PRODUCTS ENGINEERING CORP
Also Called: PEC
2645 Maricopa St, Torrance (90503-5144)
PHONE..................310 787-4500
Hongguang Ren, *Pr*
Jianhua Ren, *
EMP: 49 **EST:** 1961
SALES (est): 4.35MM **Privately Held**
Web: www.pec.tools
SIC: 3423 3596 4731 Hand and edge tools, nec; Scales and balances, except laboratory; Freight transportation arrangement

(P-4746)
TOUGHBUILT INDUSTRIES INC (PA)
Also Called: Toughbuilt
8669 Research Dr, Irvine (92618-4204)
PHONE..................949 528-3100
Michael Panosian, *Ch Bd*
Martin Galstyan, *CFO*
Joshua Keeler, *CDO*
Zareh Khachatoorian, *COO*
EMP: 255 **EST:** 2012
SQ FT: 15,500
SALES (est): 95.25MM
SALES (corp-wide): 95.25MM **Publicly Held**
Web: www.toughbuilt.com
SIC: 3423 3429 3069 Hand and edge tools, nec; Hardware, nec; Kneeling pads, rubber

3425 Saw Blades And Handsaws

(P-4747)
HILTI US MANUFACTURING INC
Also Called: Dbi
6601 Darin Way, Cypress (90630-5130)
P.O. Box 21148 (74121-1148)
PHONE..................714 230-7410
EMP: 30 **EST:** 1984
SALES (est): 3.48MM **Privately Held**
SIC: 3425 Saw blades and handsaws
HQ: Hilti, Inc.
5400 S 122nd East Ave

Tulsa OK 74146
800 879-8000

(P-4748)
WESTERN SAW MANUFACTURERS INC
Also Called: Western Saw
3200 Camino Del Sol, Oxnard (93030-8998)
PHONE..................805 981-0999
Kevin Baron, *CEO*
Frank Baron, *
Kraig Baron, *
Nancy Pounds, *
◆ **EMP:** 50 **EST:** 1930
SQ FT: 70,000
SALES (est): 9.67MM **Privately Held**
Web: www.westernsaw.com
SIC: 3425 3546 Saw blades and handsaws; Power-driven handtools

3429 Hardware, Nec

(P-4749)
ACCURIDE INTERNATIONAL INC (PA)
12311 Shoemaker Ave, Santa Fe Springs (90670-4721)
PHONE..................562 903-0200
Scott E Jordan, *CEO*
Jeffrey A Dunlap, *
Jerome Barr, *
Kent A Jordan, *
▲ **EMP:** 47 **EST:** 1966
SALES (est): 69.27MM
SALES (corp-wide): 69.27MM **Privately Held**
Web: www.accuride.com
SIC: 3429 Cabinet hardware

(P-4750)
ACTRON MANUFACTURING INC
1841 Railroad St, Corona (92878-5012)
PHONE..................951 371-0885
Frank Rechberg, *CEO*
Dow Rechberg, *
EMP: 93 **EST:** 1971
SQ FT: 30,000
SALES (est): 16.66MM **Privately Held**
Web: www.actronmfginc.com
SIC: 3429 Aircraft hardware

(P-4751)
ALARIN AIRCRAFT HINGE INC
Also Called: Commerce
6231 Randolph St, Commerce (90040-3514)
PHONE..................323 725-1666
Gregory A Sanders, *Pr*
EMP: 25 **EST:** 1988
SQ FT: 11,000
SALES (est): 6.73MM **Privately Held**
Web: www.alarin.com
SIC: 3429 3728 Aircraft hardware; Aircraft parts and equipment, nec

(P-4752)
ASCO SINTERING CO
2750 Garfield Ave, Commerce (90040-2610)
P.O. Box 911157 (90091-1157)
PHONE..................323 725-3550
Neil Moore, *CEO*
Robert Lebrun, *VP*
▲ **EMP:** 33 **EST:** 1971
SQ FT: 69,000
SALES (est): 7.77MM **Privately Held**
Web: www.ascosintering.com

(PA)=Parent Co (HQ)=Headquarters
✪ = New Business established in last 2 years

SIC: 3429 3714 Hardware, nec; Motor vehicle parts and accessories

(P-4753)
ASSA ABLOY ACC DOOR CNTRLS GRO
Also Called: Markar & Pemko Products
4226 Transport St, Ventura (93003-5627)
PHONE...................................805 642-2600
EMP: 108
SIC: 3429 3466 Locks or lock sets; Crowns and closures
HQ: Assa Abloy Accessories And Door Controls Group, Inc.
1902 Airport Rd
Monroe NC 28110
877 974-2255

(P-4754)
AUTOMOTIVE RACING PRODUCTS INC
Also Called: A R P
1760 E Lemonwood Dr, Santa Paula (93060-9510)
PHONE...................................805 525-1497
Michael Holzapsel, Brnch Mgr
EMP: 87
SALES (corp-wide): 59.57K Privately Held
Web: www.arp-bolts.com
SIC: 3429 Hardware, nec
PA: Automotive Racing Products, Inc.
1863 Eastman Ave
805 339-2200

(P-4755)
AUTOMOTIVE RACING PRODUCTS INC (PA)
Also Called: A R P
1863 Eastman Ave, Ventura (93003-8084)
PHONE...................................805 339-2200
Gary Holzapfel, CEO
Mike Holzapfel, *
Robert Flourin, *
Kelly Schau, *
▲ EMP: 65 EST: 1975
SQ FT: 10,000
SALES (est): 59.57K
SALES (corp-wide): 59.57K Privately Held
Web: www.arp-bolts.com
SIC: 3429 3714 3452 Hardware, nec; Motor vehicle parts and accessories; Bolts, nuts, rivets, and washers

(P-4756)
AVANTUS AEROSPACE INC
14957 Gwenchris Ct, Paramount (90723-3423)
PHONE...................................562 633-6626
Brian Williams, Brnch Mgr
EMP: 50
SALES (corp-wide): 145.58MM Privately Held
Web: www.calscrew.net
SIC: 3429 3452 Metal fasteners; Bolts, nuts, rivets, and washers
HQ: Avantus Aerospace, Inc.
29101 The Old Rd
Valencia CA 91355
661 295-8620

(P-4757)
AVIBANK MFG INC
Avk Industrial Products
25323 Rye Canyon Rd, Valencia (91355-1205)
PHONE...................................661 257-2329
James M Wolpert, Genl Mgr
EMP: 85
SQ FT: 23,000

SALES (corp-wide): 364.48B Publicly Held
Web: www.avibank.com
SIC: 3429 3541 3452 Hardware, nec; Machine tools, metal cutting type; Bolts, nuts, rivets, and washers
HQ: Avibank Mfg., Inc.
11500 Sherman Way
North Hollywood CA 91605
818 392-2100

(P-4758)
B & B SPECIALTIES INC (PA)
4321 E La Palma Ave, Anaheim (92807-1887)
PHONE...................................714 985-3000
Bruce Borchardt, Pr
▲ EMP: 90 EST: 1971
SQ FT: 40,000
SALES (est): 22.69MM
SALES (corp-wide): 22.69MM Privately Held
Web: www.bbspecialties.com
SIC: 3429 3452 Metal fasteners; Bolts, nuts, rivets, and washers

(P-4759)
BALDWIN HARDWARE CORPORATION (DH)
Also Called: Baldwin Brass
19701 Da Vinci, Lake Forest (92610-2622)
PHONE...................................949 672-4000
David R Lumley, CEO
◆ EMP: 816 EST: 1944
SQ FT: 300,000
SALES (est): 11.25MM
SALES (corp-wide): 2.96B Publicly Held
Web: www.baldwinhardware.com
SIC: 3429 Builders' hardware
HQ: Spectrum Brands, Inc.
3001 Deming Way
Middleton WI 53562
608 275-3340

(P-4760)
BIRMINGHAM FASTENER & SUP INC
Also Called: Pacific Coast Bolt
12748 Florence Ave, Santa Fe Springs (90670-3906)
PHONE...................................562 944-9549
Brad Tinney, Brnch Mgr
EMP: 38
SALES (corp-wide): 193.68MM Privately Held
Web: www.bhamfast.com
SIC: 3429 Hardware, nec
PA: Birmingham Fastener & Supply, Inc.
931 Ave W
205 595-3511

(P-4761)
CAL-JUNE INC (PA)
Also Called: Jim-Buoy
5238 Vineland Ave, North Hollywood (91601-3221)
P.O. Box 9551 (91609-1551)
PHONE...................................323 877-4164
James H Robertson, Pr
Jennifer D Jacobson, *
Melini Robertson, *
Andrea Robertson, *
◆ EMP: 30 EST: 1966
SQ FT: 3,000
SALES (est): 5.42MM
SALES (corp-wide): 5.42MM Privately Held
Web: www.jimbuoy.com
SIC: 3429 Marine hardware

(P-4762)
CALIFORNIA SCREW PRODUCTS CORP
14950 Gwenchris Ct, Paramount (90723-3423)
P.O. Box 228 (90723-0228)
PHONE...................................562 633-6626
Dan Strangio, CEO
Dennis Suedkamp, *
EMP: 75 EST: 1966
SQ FT: 20,000
SALES (est): 9.37MM Privately Held
Web: www.calscrew.net
SIC: 3429 3452 Metal fasteners; Bolts, nuts, rivets, and washers

(P-4763)
CONSOLIDATED AEROSPACE MFG LLC
630 E Lambert Rd, Brea (92821-4119)
PHONE...................................714 989-2802
EMP: 82 EST: 2014
SALES (est): 5.1MM Privately Held
Web: www.camaerospace.com
SIC: 3429 Metal fasteners

(P-4764)
CRD MFG INC
615 Fee Ana St, Placentia (92870-6704)
PHONE...................................714 871-3300
Timothy Carroll, CEO
EMP: 25 EST: 2011
SALES (est): 2.49MM Privately Held
Web: www.crdmfg.com
SIC: 3429 3699 Motor vehicle hardware; Welding machines and equipment, ultrasonic

(P-4765)
DARNELL-ROSE INC
1205 Via Roma, Colton (92324-3909)
PHONE...................................626 912-1688
Brent Bargar, Pr
John Posen, *
Robbie Mccullah, VP Opers
EMP: 40 EST: 1984
SALES (est): 2.73MM Privately Held
Web: www.casters.com
SIC: 3429 Aircraft & marine hardware, inc. pulleys & similar items

(P-4766)
DOVAL INDUSTRIES INC
Also Called: Doval Industries Co
3961 N Mission Rd, Los Angeles (90031-2931)
PHONE...................................323 226-0335
Cruz Sandoval, CEO
▲ EMP: 65 EST: 1985
SALES (est): 1.86MM Privately Held
Web: www.doval.com
SIC: 3429 5072 2759 Keys, locks, and related hardware; Hardware; Screen printing

(P-4767)
FORESPAR PRODUCTS CORP
Also Called: Tea Tree Essentials
22322 Gilberto, Rancho Santa Margari (92688-2110)
PHONE...................................949 858-8820
◆ EMP: 60 EST: 1964
SALES (est): 3.36MM Privately Held
Web: www.forespar.com
SIC: 3429 Marine hardware

(P-4768)
FRAMELESS HARDWARE COMPANY LLC

Also Called: Fhc
4361 Firestone Blvd, South Gate (90280-3340)
PHONE...................................888 295-4531
Donald Friese Junior, Managing Member
EMP: 47 EST: 2020
SALES (est): 1.4MM Privately Held
Web: www.fhc-usa.com
SIC: 3429 1793 2591 Builders' hardware; Glass and glazing work; Drapery hardware and window blinds and shades

(P-4769)
HAMPTON PRODUCTS INTL CORP (PA)
50 Icon, Foothill Ranch (92610-3000)
PHONE...................................800 562-5625
Gregory J Gluchowski, Pr
▲ EMP: 175 EST: 1973
SQ FT: 160,000
SALES (est): 32.34MM
SALES (corp-wide): 32.34MM Privately Held
Web: www.hamptonproducts.com
SIC: 3429 Padlocks

(P-4770)
HARTWELL CORPORATION (DH)
Also Called: Hasco
900 Richfield Rd, Placentia (92870-6788)
PHONE...................................714 993-4200
Dain Miller, Pr
▲ EMP: 200 EST: 1957
SQ FT: 134,000
SALES (est): 68.68MM
SALES (corp-wide): 7.94B Publicly Held
Web: www.hartwellcorp.com
SIC: 3429 Aircraft hardware
HQ: Mckechnie Aerospace Investments, Inc.
20 Pacifica Ste 200
Irvine CA

(P-4771)
HODGE PRODUCTS INC
Also Called: Lock People, The
7365 Mission Gorge Rd Ste F, San Diego (92120-1274)
P.O. Box 1326 (92022)
PHONE...................................800 778-2217
Anthony A Hodge, CEO
Allan Hodge, *
▲ EMP: 25 EST: 1971
SALES (est): 5.34MM Privately Held
Web: www.hpionline.com
SIC: 3429 5099 Locks or lock sets; Locks and lock sets

(P-4772)
HOLLYWOOD BED SPRING MFG INC (PA)
Also Called: Hollywood Bed & Spring Mfg
5959 Corvette St, Commerce (90040-1601)
PHONE...................................323 887-9500
Larry Harrow, CEO
Jason Harrow, *
Andrea Harrow, *
◆ EMP: 78 EST: 1945
SQ FT: 55,000
SALES (est): 17.5MM
SALES (corp-wide): 17.5MM Privately Held
Web: www.hollywoodbed.com
SIC: 3429 2515 2511 2514 Hardware, nec; Mattresses and bedsprings; Wood household furniture; Frames for box springs or bedsprings: metal

(P-4773)
INSPIRED FLIGHT TECH INC
Also Called: Inspired Flight
225 Suburban Rd Ste A, San Luis Obispo
(93401-7547)
PHONE...............................805 776-3640
Richard Stollmeyer, *CEO*
Marcus Stollmeyer, *
EMP: 34 EST: 2017
SALES (est): 3.63MM **Privately Held**
Web: www.inspiredflight.com
SIC: 3429 Aircraft hardware

(P-4774)
J & M PRODUCTS INC
1647 Truman St, San Fernando
(91340-3119)
PHONE...............................818 837-0205
EMP: 97 EST: 1995
SALES (est): 16.69MM **Privately Held**
Web: www.jmproducts.com
SIC: 3429 3679 Hardware, nec; Harness
assemblies, for electronic use: wire or cable

(P-4775)
JONATHAN ENGNRED SLUTIONS CORP (HQ)
250 Commerce Ste 100, Irvine
(92602-1341)
PHONE...............................714 665-4400
Jack Frickel, *Pr*
Jason Ciancarulo, *
▲ EMP: 44 EST: 1954
SQ FT: 120,000
SALES (est): 99.21MM
SALES (corp-wide): 397.46MM **Privately Held**
Web: www.jonathanengr.com
SIC: 3429 3562 Hardware, nec; Ball
bearings and parts
PA: Jll Partners, Llc
300 Park Ave 18th Fl
212 286-8600

(P-4776)
KWIKSET CORPORATION
Also Called: Spectrum Brands Hdwr HM Imprv
19701 Da Vinci, Foothill Ranch
(92610-2622)
P.O. Box 620992 (53562-0992)
PHONE...............................949 672-4000
▲ EMP: 3200
Web: www.kwikset.com
SIC: 3429 Keys, locks, and related hardware

(P-4777)
LIGHT COMPOSITE CORPORATION
Also Called: Forespar
22322 Gilberto, Rcho Sta Marg
(92688-2102)
PHONE...............................949 858-8820
Robert R Foresman, *Pr*
Juin Foresman, *Prin*
Marilyn Holst, *Sec*
▼ EMP: 25 EST: 1991
SALES (est): 902.06K **Privately Held**
Web: www.forespar.com
SIC: 3429 Marine hardware

(P-4778)
LUCKY LINE PRODUCTS INC
7890 Dunbrook Rd, San Diego
(92126-4369)
PHONE...............................858 549-6699
◆ EMP: 26 EST: 1948
SALES (est): 6.51MM **Privately Held**
Web: www.luckyline.com

SIC: 3429 3993 Keys, locks, and related
hardware; Signs and advertising specialties

(P-4779)
M A G ENGINEERING MFG CO
Also Called: M.A.g Engineering & Mfg
17305 Demler St, Irvine (92614)
▲ EMP: 40 EST: 1968
SALES (est): 3.7MM **Privately Held**
SIC: 3429 Locks or lock sets

(P-4780)
MCMAHON STEEL COMPANY INC
1880 Nirvana Ave, Chula Vista
(91911-6118)
PHONE...............................619 671-9700
Derek J Mcmahon, *Pr*
Kevin Mcmahon, *VP*
EMP: 120 EST: 1970
SQ FT: 14,300
SALES (est): 7.7MM **Privately Held**
Web: www.mcmahonsteel.com
SIC: 3429 1791 3441 Hardware, nec;
Structural steel erection; Fabricated
structural metal

(P-4781)
MOELLER MFG & SUP LLC
630 E Lambert Rd, Brea (92821-4119)
PHONE...............................714 999-5551
Stevens Chevillotte, *Pr*
Peter George, *
EMP: 45 EST: 1978
SALES (est): 14MM
SALES (corp-wide): 15.78B **Publicly Held**
SIC: 3429 3452 Aircraft hardware; Washers,
metal
HQ: Consolidated Aerospace
Manufacturing, Llc
1425 S Acacia Ave
Fullerton CA 92831
714 989-2797

(P-4782)
MONADNOCK COMPANY
Also Called: Lisi Aerospace
16728 Gale Ave, City Of Industry
(91745-1803)
PHONE...............................626 964-6581
Christian Darville, *CEO*
Michael Reyes, *
▼ EMP: 190 EST: 1987
SQ FT: 90,000
SALES (est): 25.82MM
SALES (corp-wide): 2.67MM **Privately Held**
SIC: 3429 Aircraft hardware
HQ: Lisi Aerospace
42 A 52
Paris 12 IDF 75012
140198200

(P-4783)
MONOGRAM AEROSPACE FAS INC
3423 Garfield Ave, Commerce
(90040-3103)
PHONE...............................323 722-4760
John P Schaefer, *CEO*
David Adler, *
▲ EMP: 250 EST: 1990
SQ FT: 97,500
SALES (est): 36.42MM
SALES (corp-wide): 893.55MM **Publicly Held**
Web: www.trsaero.com
SIC: 3429 3452 Hardware, nec; Bolts, metal
PA: Trimas Corporation
38505 Wodward Ave Ste 200

248 631-5450

(P-4784)
NATIONAL MANUFACTURING CO
Also Called: Stanley National Hardware
19701 Da Vinci, Lake Forest (92610-2622)
PHONE...............................800 346-9445
◆ EMP: 1660 EST: 1901
SALES (est): 3.94MM
SALES (corp-wide): 15.78B **Publicly Held**
SIC: 3429 Builders' hardware
PA: Stanley Black & Decker, Inc.
1000 Stanley Dr
860 225-5111

(P-4785)
ORION ORNAMENTAL IRON INC
6918 Tujunga Ave, North Hollywood
(91605-6212)
PHONE...............................818 752-0688
Sunil Patel, *CEO*
Atul Patel, *
▲ EMP: 40 EST: 1983
SQ FT: 30,000
SALES (est): 5.41MM **Privately Held**
Web: www.ironartbyorion.com
SIC: 3429 Builders' hardware

(P-4786)
PACIFIC LOCK COMPANY (PA)
25605 Hercules St, Valencia (91355-5051)
PHONE...............................661 294-3707
Gregory B Waugh, *Pr*
Joshua Fleagane, *
Patty Yang, *
▲ EMP: 29 EST: 1998
SQ FT: 18,000
SALES (est): 6.72MM **Privately Held**
Web: www.paclock.com
SIC: 3429 3699 5099 Keys and key blanks;
Security devices; Locks and lock sets

(P-4787)
SATURN FASTENERS INC
425 S Varney St, Burbank (91502-2193)
PHONE...............................818 973-1807
Raymond David Barker Junior, *C*
Laura Elaine Barker, *
Raymond.D Barker Junior, *Pr*
▼ EMP: 112 EST: 1989
SQ FT: 38,000
SALES (est): 12.38MM **Privately Held**
Web: www.saturnfasteners.com
SIC: 3429 5085 5072 3452 Metal fasteners;
Industrial supplies; Bolts, nuts, and screws;
Bolts, nuts, rivets, and washers
HQ: Acument Global Technologies, Inc.
6125 18 Mile Rd
Sterling Heights MI 48314
586 997-5600

(P-4788)
SNAPNRACK INC
775 Fiero Ln Ste 200, San Luis Obispo
(93401-7904)
PHONE...............................877 732-2860
Lyn Cowgill, *Off Mgr*
EMP: 26 EST: 2014
SALES (est): 977.53K **Privately Held**
Web: www.snapnrack.com
SIC: 3429 Clamps, couplings, nozzles, and
other metal hose fittings

(P-4789)
SPEP ACQUISITION CORP (PA)
Also Called: Sierra Pacific Engrg & Pdts
4041 Via Oro Ave, Long Beach
(90810-1458)
P.O. Box 5246 (90749-5246)
PHONE...............................310 608-0693

Barry Stein, *Pr*
Larry Mirick, *
◆ EMP: 70 EST: 1986
SQ FT: 48,300
SALES (est): 20.69MM
SALES (corp-wide): 20.69MM **Privately Held**
Web: www.spep.com
SIC: 3429 8711 5072 Hardware, nec;
Engineering services; Hardware

(P-4790)
STAR DIE CASTING INC
12209 Slauson Ave, Santa Fe Springs
(90670-2605)
PHONE...............................562 698-0627
Jer Ming Yu, *Pr*
Mei H Yu, *VP*
▲ EMP: 80 EST: 1980
SQ FT: 13,290
SALES (est): 1.43MM **Privately Held**
Web: www.stargroupglobal.com
SIC: 3429 3364 3544 Builders' hardware;
Nonferrous die-castings except aluminum;
Special dies and tools

(P-4791)
TOP LINE MFG INC
Also Called: Sroodtuo
7032 Alondra Blvd, Paramount
(90723-3926)
P.O. Box 739 (90723-0739)
PHONE...............................562 633-0605
Anne Graffy, *CEO*
▲ EMP: 29 EST: 1982
SQ FT: 20,000
SALES (est): 7.11MM **Privately Held**
Web: www.toplinemfg.com
SIC: 3429 Motor vehicle hardware

(P-4792)
TOWNSTEEL INC
17901 Railroad St, City Of Industry
(91748-1113)
PHONE...............................626 965-8917
Lydia Meng, *Pr*
Shien Cheng Meng, *VP*
◆ EMP: 100 EST: 2001
SQ FT: 10,000
SALES (est): 9.12MM **Privately Held**
Web: www.townsteel.com
SIC: 3429 Door locks, bolts, and checks

(P-4793)
UMPCO INC
7100 Lampson Ave, Garden Grove
(92841-3914)
P.O. Box 5158 (92846-0158)
PHONE...............................714 897-3531
Dan Miller, *CEO*
EMP: 75 EST: 1963
SQ FT: 60,000
SALES (est): 9.27MM **Privately Held**
Web: www.umpco.com
SIC: 3429 Clamps, metal

(P-4794)
VIT PRODUCTS INC
2063 Wineridge Pl, Escondido
(92029-1931)
PHONE...............................760 480-6702
Don Pagano, *Pr*
Arthur Arns, *
EMP: 36 EST: 1972
SQ FT: 24,000
SALES (est): 4.06MM **Privately Held**
Web: www.vitproducts.com
SIC: 3429 2295 Clamps, couplings, nozzles,
and other metal hose fittings; Coated
fabrics, not rubberized

PRODUCTS & SVCS

(P-4795)
W & F MFG INC
10635 Keswick St, Sun Valley
(91352-4610)
P.O. Box 1219 (91353-1219)
PHONE..................................818 394-6060
▲ **EMP:** 50
SIC: 3429 Door opening and closing
devices, except electrical

(P-4796)
WINFIELD LOCKS INC
Also Called: Computerized Security Systems
1721 Whittier Ave, Costa Mesa
(92627-4580)
PHONE..................................949 722-5400
John Kimes, *Pr*
EMP: 5006 **EST:** 1977
SQ FT: 30,000
SALES (est): 2.14MM
SALES (corp-wide): 7.97B **Publicly Held**
Web: www.zeusbeard.com
SIC: 3429 Locks or lock sets
HQ: Masco Building Products Corp.
17450 College Pkwy
Livonia MI 48152
313 274-7400

(P-4797)
YOUNG ENGINEERS INC
25841 Commercentre Dr, Lake Forest
(92630-8812)
P.O. Box 278 (92609-0278)
PHONE..................................949 581-9411
Pat Wells, *Pr*
EMP: 64 **EST:** 1963
SQ FT: 26,000
SALES (est): 9.37MM
SALES (corp-wide): 218.18MM **Privately
Held**
Web: www.youngengineers.com
SIC: 3429 Aircraft hardware
PA: Novaria Group, L.L.C.
6685 Iron Horse Blvd
214 707-8980

3431 Metal Sanitary Ware

(P-4798)
HYDRO SYSTEMS INC (PA)
29132 Avenue Paine, Valencia
(91355-5402)
PHONE..................................661 775-0686
Scott G Steinhardt, *Pr*
Dave Ortwein, *
Larry Burroughs, *
EMP: 95 **EST:** 1979
SQ FT: 90,000
SALES (est): 18.92MM
SALES (corp-wide): 18.92MM **Privately
Held**
Web: www.hydrosystem.com
SIC: 3431 3432 3088 Bathtubs: enameled
iron, cast iron, or pressed metal; Plumbing
fixture fittings and trim; Plastics plumbing
fixtures

(P-4799)
MAG AEROSPACE INDUSTRIES
LLC
Also Called: Monogram Systems
1500 Glenn Curtiss St, Carson
(90746-4012)
P.O. Box 11189 (90749)
PHONE..................................801 400-7944
Sebastien Weber, *Pr*
Mark Scott, *
David Conrad, *
Mike Nieves, *SUPPLY CHAIN**

Tim Birbeck, *
◆ **EMP:** 350 **EST:** 1989
SQ FT: 150,000
SALES (est): 99.67MM
SALES (corp-wide): 940.23MM **Privately
Held**
SIC: 3431 3728 Plumbing fixtures: enameled
iron, cast iron,or pressed metal; Aircraft
parts and equipment, nec
PA: Safran
2 Boulevard Du General Martial Valin

(P-4800)
SEACHROME CORPORATION
Also Called: Seachrome
1906 E Dominguez St, Long Beach
(90810-1002)
PHONE..................................310 427-8010
Sam C Longo Junior, *CEO*
▲ **EMP:** 112 **EST:** 1983
SQ FT: 50,000
SALES (est): 22.1MM **Privately Held**
Web: www.seachrome.com
SIC: 3431 5072 3842 3429 Bathroom
fixtures, including sinks; Builders' hardware,
nec; Surgical appliances and supplies;
Hardware, nec

3432 Plumbing Fixture
Fittings And Trim

(P-4801)
BRASSTECH INC
1301 E Wilshire Ave, Santa Ana
(92705-4420)
PHONE..................................714 796-9278
EMP: 250
SALES (corp-wide): 7.97B **Publicly Held**
Web: www.brasstech.com
SIC: 3432 Plumbing fixture fittings and trim
HQ: Brasstech, Inc.
2001 Carnegie Ave
Santa Ana CA 92705
949 417-5207

(P-4802)
BRASSTECH INC (HQ)
Also Called: Newport Brass
2001 Carnegie Ave, Santa Ana
(92705-5531)
PHONE..................................949 417-5207
Jonathan Wood, *CEO*
John G Sznewajs, *
Kenneth G Cole, *
Kathleen S Rodes, *
◆ **EMP:** 90 **EST:** 1987
SQ FT: 70,000
SALES (est): 82.87MM
SALES (corp-wide): 7.97B **Publicly Held**
Web: www.brasstech.com
SIC: 3432 Plumbing fixture fittings and trim
PA: Masco Corporation
17450 College Pkwy
313 274-7400

(P-4803)
CALIFORNIA FAUCETS INC (PA)
Also Called: Pvd Coatings
5271 Argosy Ave, Huntington Beach
(92649-1015)
PHONE..................................800 822-8855
Jeffrey Howard Silverstein, *CEO*
Sonia Silverstein, *
◆ **EMP:** 36 **EST:** 1988
SALES (est): 23.27MM **Privately Held**
Web: www.calfaucets.com
SIC: 3432 Faucets and spigots, metal and
plastic

(P-4804)
CALIFORNIA FAUCETS INC
5231 Argosy Ave, Huntington Beach
(92649-1015)
PHONE..................................657 400-1639
Blas Ramierez, *Brnch Mgr*
EMP: 39
Web: www.calfaucets.com
SIC: 3432 Faucets and spigots, metal and
plastic
PA: California Faucets, Inc.
5271 Argosy Dr

(P-4805)
PRICE PFISTER INC
Also Called: Price Pfister Brass Mfg
19701 Da Vinci, Lake Forest (92610-2622)
P.O. Box 620992 (53562-0992)
PHONE..................................949 672-4000
▲ **EMP:** 2300
SALES (est): 128.86MM **Privately Held**
Web: www.pfisterfaucets.com
SIC: 3432 Faucets and spigots, metal and
plastic

(P-4806)
RAIN BIRD CORPORATION
Also Called: Rain Bird Golf Division
970 W Sierra Madre Ave, Azusa
(91702-1873)
PHONE..................................626 812-3400
Matt Circle, *Mgr*
EMP: 69
SALES (corp-wide): 433.78MM **Privately
Held**
Web: www.rainbird.com
SIC: 3432 3494 3433 Plumbing fixture
fittings and trim; Valves and pipe fittings,
nec; Heating equipment, except electric
PA: Rain Bird Corporation
970 W Sierra Madre Ave
626 812-3400

(P-4807)
SANTEC INC
3501 Challenger St Fl 2, Torrance
(90503-1697)
PHONE..................................310 542-0063
Nicolas Chen, *CEO*
James S Chen, *
▲ **EMP:** 50 **EST:** 1981
SQ FT: 32,000
SALES (est): 5.51MM **Privately Held**
Web: www.santecfaucet.com
SIC: 3432 Faucets and spigots, metal and
plastic

3433 Heating Equipment,
Except Electric

(P-4808)
AMERICAN SOLAR LLC
8484 Wilshire Blvd Ste 630, Beverly Hills
(90211-3215)
PHONE..................................323 250-1307
Meir Yaniv, *CEO*
EMP: 30 **EST:** 2020
SALES (est): 916.76K **Privately Held**
Web: www.americansolar.net
SIC: 3433 Solar heaters and collectors

(P-4809)
CAPITAL COOKING EQUIPMENT
INC
Also Called: Capital Cooking
1025 E Bedmar St, Carson (90746-3601)
PHONE..................................562 903-1168
Roberto Bernal, *

Alejandro Bernal, *
Porfiro Guzman, *
Rafael Romero, *
▲ **EMP:** 47 **EST:** 2001
SALES (est): 4.66MM **Privately Held**
Web: www.capital-cooking.com
SIC: 3433 3631 Stoves, wood and coal
burning; Gas ranges, domestic

(P-4810)
EMPIRE PRODUCTS INC
5061 Brooks St, Montclair (91763-4835)
PHONE..................................909 399-3355
Robert Beck, *Ch Bd*
EMP: 57 **EST:** 1982
SQ FT: 6,000
SALES (est): 476.13K **Privately Held**
SIC: 3433 3429 3631 Logs, gas fireplace;
Fireplace equipment, hardware: andirons,
grates, screens; Household cooking
equipment

(P-4811)
INDEPENDENT ENERGY
SOLUTIONS INC
663 S Rancho Santa Fe Rd Ste 682, San
Marcos (92078-3973)
PHONE..................................760 752-9706
▲ **EMP:** 42
Web: www.indenergysolutions.com
SIC: 3433 Heating equipment, except electric

(P-4812)
OMC-THC LIQUIDATING INC
12131 Community Rd, Poway
(92064-8893)
PHONE..................................858 486-8846
Frank Polese, *Prin*
EMP: 23 **EST:** 2005
SALES (est): 962.37K **Privately Held**
Web: www.fralock.com
SIC: 3433 Heating equipment, except electric

(P-4813)
RASMUSSEN IRON WORKS INC
12028 Philadelphia St, Whittier
(90601-3925)
PHONE..................................562 696-8718
Theodore Rasmussen, *Pr*
T E Rasmussen, *
▲ **EMP:** 62 **EST:** 1907
SQ FT: 40,000
SALES (est): 4.81MM **Privately Held**
Web: www.radiantpatioheater.com
SIC: 3433 Logs, gas fireplace

(P-4814)
RAYPAK INC (DH)
2151 Eastman Ave, Oxnard (93030-5194)
PHONE..................................805 278-5300
Kevin Mcdonald, *VP*
◆ **EMP:** 320 **EST:** 1949
SQ FT: 250,000
SALES (est): 48.03MM **Privately Held**
Web: www.raypak.com
SIC: 3433 Heaters, swimming pool: oil or gas
HQ: Rheem Manufacturing Company Inc
1100 Abrnathy Rd Ste 1700
Atlanta GA 30328
770 351-3000

3441 Fabricated Structural Metal

(P-4815)
AEC - ABLE ENGINEERING COMPANY INC
600 Pine Ave, Goleta (93117-3831)
PHONE..........................805 685-2262
EMP: 120
SIC: 3441 3769 Fabricated structural metal; Space vehicle equipment, nec

(P-4816)
ANDERSON CHRNESKY STRL STL INC
Also Called: Acss
353 Risco Cir, Beaumont (92223-2676)
PHONE..........................951 769-5700
Kevin Charneskey, *Pr*
Kevin Charnesky, *
EMP: 85 EST: 1984
SQ FT: 6,600
SALES (est): 36.73MM **Privately Held**
Web: www.acssteelinc.com
SIC: 3441 Fabricated structural metal

(P-4817)
BAY CITY MARINE INC (PA)
1625 Cleveland Ave, National City (91950-4212)
PHONE..........................619 477-3991
Paul Ralph, *CEO*
Michelle Ralph, *
Timothy Dernbach, *
Steve Johnston, *
EMP: 24 EST: 1971
SQ FT: 11,000
SALES (est): 8.73MM
SALES (corp-wide): 8.73MM **Privately Held**
Web: www.baycmarine.com
SIC: 3441 3731 7699 Fabricated structural metal; Military ships, building and repairing; Boat repair

(P-4818)
BELLOWS MFG & RES INC
864 Arroyo St, San Fernando (91340-1832)
PHONE..........................818 838-1333
Arteom Art Bulgadarian, *CEO*
Kent L Fortin, *
EMP: 30 EST: 2005
SQ FT: 28,000
SALES (est): 8.68MM **Privately Held**
Web: www.bellowsmfg.com
SIC: 3441 3724 3764 Fabricated structural metal; Aircraft engines and engine parts; Propulsion units for guided missiles and space vehicles

(P-4819)
BLUE STAR STEEL INC
12122 Industry Rd, Lakeside (92040-1736)
PHONE..........................619 448-5520
Rodney Walker, *Pr*
EMP: 45 EST: 1962
SALES (est): 4.33MM **Privately Held**
Web: www.bluestarsteelinc.com
SIC: 3441 Fabricated structural metal

(P-4820)
BOYD CORPORATION (PA)
Also Called: Boyd Construction
5832 Ohio St, Yorba Linda (92886-5323)
P.O. Box 6012 (92816-0012)
PHONE..........................714 533-2375
Mitch Aiello, *Pr*
EMP: 29 EST: 1980

SALES (est): 9.77MM
SALES (corp-wide): 9.77MM **Privately Held**
Web: www.boydcorp.com
SIC: 3441 2891 Fabricated structural metal; Adhesives

(P-4821)
BRUNTON ENTERPRISES INC
Also Called: Plas-Tal Manufacturing Co
8815 Sorensen Ave, Santa Fe Springs (90670-2636)
PHONE..........................562 945-0013
Sean P Brunton, *CEO*
John W Brunton Junior, *Pr*
EMP: 125 EST: 1947
SQ FT: 45,000
SALES (est): 10.78MM **Privately Held**
Web: www.plas-tal.com
SIC: 3441 Fabricated structural metal

(P-4822)
C A BUCHEN CORP
9231 Glenoaks Blvd, Sun Valley (91352-2688)
PHONE..........................818 767-5408
John Oster, *CEO*
Ryan Chapman, *
EMP: 25 EST: 1962
SQ FT: 22,500
SALES (est): 2.53MM **Privately Held**
Web: www.cabuchen.com
SIC: 3441 1791 3312 Fabricated structural metal; Structural steel erection; Galvanized pipes, plates, sheets, etc.: iron and steel

(P-4823)
CAMPBELL CERTIFIED INC
1629 Ord Way, Oceanside (92056-3599)
PHONE..........................760 722-9353
Mark Anthony Campbell, *CEO*
Linzie Walker, *
EMP: 30 EST: 1991
SQ FT: 45,000
SALES (est): 3.72MM **Privately Held**
Web: www.campbellcertified.com
SIC: 3441 Fabricated structural metal

(P-4824)
CAPITOL STEEL FABRICATORS INC
3522 Greenwood Ave, Commerce (90040-3319)
P.O. Box 640 (91017-0640)
PHONE..........................323 721-5460
James Moreland, *Pr*
Janice Moreland, *
Eric Jonkey, *Stockholder*
EMP: 25 EST: 1984
SALES (est): 8.77MM **Privately Held**
Web: www.capitolsteel.com
SIC: 3441 Fabricated structural metal

(P-4825)
CARROLL METAL WORKS INC
740 W 16th St, National City (91950-4205)
PHONE..........................619 477-9125
Pat Carroll, *Pr*
EMP: 95 EST: 1984
SQ FT: 11,500
SALES (est): 4.82MM **Privately Held**
Web: www.carrollmetalworks.com
SIC: 3441 Fabricated structural metal

(P-4826)
COLUMBIA ALUMINUM PRODUCTS LLC
1150 W Rincon St, Corona (92878-9601)
PHONE..........................323 728-7361

Drew D Mumford, *Managing Member*
Grant Palenske, *
▲ EMP: 70 EST: 1989
SALES (est): 8.61MM **Privately Held**
Web: www.columbiaaluminumproductsllc.com
SIC: 3441 Fabricated structural metal

(P-4827)
COLUMBIA STEEL INC
2175 N Linden Ave, Rialto (92377-4445)
PHONE..........................909 874-8840
Gustavo Waldemar Theisen, *CEO*
William Young, *
Luis Theisen, *
Charmaine Helenihi, *
EMP: 75 EST: 1975
SQ FT: 63,384
SALES (est): 25.8MM **Privately Held**
Web: www.csirialto.com
SIC: 3441 Building components, structural steel

(P-4828)
COMMERCIAL SHTMTL WORKS INC
Also Called: CSM Metal Fabricating & Engrg
1800 S San Pedro St, Los Angeles (90015-3780)
PHONE..........................213 748-7321
Jack L Gardener, *CEO*
▲ EMP: 27 EST: 1916
SQ FT: 22,000
SALES (est): 5.58MM **Privately Held**
Web: www.csmworks.com
SIC: 3441 Fabricated structural metal

(P-4829)
CRAFTECH METAL FORMING INC
24100 Water Ave Ste B, Perris (92570-6738)
PHONE..........................951 940-6444
Richard L Shaw, *Pr*
EMP: 40 EST: 1996
SQ FT: 26,000
SALES (est): 4.66MM **Privately Held**
Web: www.craftechmetal.com
SIC: 3441 3499 3444 Fabricated structural metal; Fire- or burglary-resistive products; Sheet metalwork

(P-4830)
CROSNO CONSTRUCTION INC
819 Sheridan Rd, Arroyo Grande (93420-5833)
PHONE..........................805 343-7437
Wade Crosno, *Pr*
Wade Crosno, *Pr*
Jaime Crosno, *
EMP: 48 EST: 2004
SQ FT: 5,000
SALES (est): 8.64MM **Privately Held**
Web: www.crosnoconstruction.com
SIC: 3441 Fabricated structural metal

(P-4831)
D & M STEEL INC
13020 Pierce St, Pacoima (91331-2528)
PHONE..........................818 896-2070
Michael Atia, *Pr*
David Dagni, *
EMP: 37 EST: 1980
SQ FT: 16,500
SALES (est): 6.19MM **Privately Held**
Web: www.d-msteel.com
SIC: 3441 Fabricated structural metal

(P-4832)
EAST CAST REPR FABRICATION LLC
Also Called: West Coast Operations
280 Trousdale Dr Ste E, Chula Vista (91910-1079)
PHONE..........................619 591-9577
Brett Baker, *Prin*
EMP: 29
SALES (corp-wide): 24.39MM **Privately Held**
Web: www.ecrfab.com
SIC: 3441 Fabricated structural metal
PA: East Coast Repair & Fabrication, L.L.C.
1201 Terminal Ave
757 455-9600

(P-4833)
EW CORPRTION INDUS FABRICATORS (PA)
1002 E Main St, El Centro (92243)
P.O. Box 2189 (92244-2189)
PHONE..........................760 337-0020
Tiberio R Esparza, *Pr*
◆ EMP: 69 EST: 1973
SQ FT: 100,000
SALES (est): 4.98MM
SALES (corp-wide): 4.98MM **Privately Held**
Web: www.ewcorporation.com
SIC: 3441 Fabricated structural metal

(P-4834)
FABCO STEEL FABRICATION INC
14688 San Bernardino Ave, Fontana (92335-5319)
P.O. Box 8636 (91701-0636)
PHONE..........................909 350-1535
John E Schick, *Pr*
Rich Schick, *
EMP: 35 EST: 1979
SQ FT: 30,000
SALES (est): 1.27MM **Privately Held**
Web: www.fabcosteel.com
SIC: 3441 Fabricated structural metal

(P-4835)
FABRICATION TECH INDS INC
2200 Haffley Ave, National City (91950-6418)
P.O. Box 1447 (91951-1447)
PHONE..........................619 477-4141
Joey Houshar, *Ch Bd*
Martha Houshar, *
▲ EMP: 75 EST: 1994
SQ FT: 50,000
SALES (est): 9.11MM **Privately Held**
Web: www.ftisd.com
SIC: 3441 Fabricated structural metal

(P-4836)
FREEBERG INDUS FBRICATION CORP
Also Called: Freeberg Industrial
2874 Progress Pl, Escondido (92029-1516)
PHONE..........................760 737-7614
Marc Brown, *Pr*
James R St John, *
EMP: 85 EST: 1992
SQ FT: 128,000
SALES (est): 23.39MM **Privately Held**
Web: www.freeberg.com
SIC: 3441 3444 Fabricated structural metal; Sheet metalwork

PRODUCTS & SVCS

(P-4837)

HITECH METAL FABRICATION CORP

Also Called: H M F
1705 S Claudina Way, Anaheim
(92805-6544)
PHONE..............................714 635-3505
Ba V Nguyen, *Pr*
Matthew Vu, *
EMP: 60 EST: 1989
SQ FT: 42,850
SALES (est): 7.6MM Privately Held
Web: www.hmfcorp.com
SIC: 3441 Fabricated structural metal

(P-4838)

HOMESTEAD SHEET METAL

9031 Memory Ln, Spring Valley
(91977-2152)
PHONE..............................619 469-4373
George Tomlanovich, *Pr*
Chuck Highfill, *Sec*
EMP: 27 EST: 1996
SQ FT: 5,625
SALES (est): 4.01MM Privately Held
Web: www.homesteadsheetmetal.com
SIC: 3441 Fabricated structural metal

(P-4839)

J L M C INC

1944 S Bon View Ave, Ontario
(91761-5503)
P.O. Box 3817 (91761-0979)
PHONE..............................909 947-2980
EMP: 35 EST: 1984
SALES (est): 2.04MM Privately Held
Web: www.jlmc.com
SIC: 3441 Fabricated structural metal

(P-4840)

JCI METAL PRODUCTS (PA)

6540 Federal Blvd, Lemon Grove
(91945-1311)
PHONE..............................619 229-8206
Marcel Becker, *CEO*
Mark Withers, *
Rich Bartlett, *
Lorey Topham, *
EMP: 57 EST: 1984
SQ FT: 21,000
SALES (est): 3.09MM Privately Held
SIC: 3441 1761 Fabricated structural metal
for ships; Architectural sheet metal work

(P-4841)

JOHASEE REBAR INC

Also Called: Johasee Rebar
26365 Earthmover Cir, Corona
(92883-5270)
PHONE..............................661 589-0972
Mike Hill Senior, *CEO*
Tamara L Chapman, *
Michael Hill Junior, *COO*
EMP: 47 EST: 1979
SALES (est): 3.96MM
SALES (corp-wide): 3.49MM Privately
Held
SIC: 3441 1791 Fabricated structural metal;
Concrete reinforcement, placing of
PA: Lms Holdings (Ab) Ltd
7452 132 St
604 598-9930

(P-4842)

KATCH INC

520 Hofgaarden St, City Of Industry
(91744-5529)
PHONE..............................626 369-0958
John Zheng, *CEO*
Son T Nguyen, *

EMP: 25 EST: 2003
SQ FT: 20,000
SALES (est): 4.09MM Privately Held
Web: www.integralfab.com
SIC: 3441 Fabricated structural metal

(P-4843)

KERN STEEL FABRICATION INC (PA)

627 Williams St, Bakersfield (93305-5437)
PHONE..............................661 327-9588
Tom Champness, *CEO*
Ali E Champness, *
Samuel E Champness, *
◆ EMP: 54 EST: 1959
SQ FT: 50,000
SALES (est): 22.92MM
SALES (corp-wide): 22.92MM Privately
Held
Web: www.kernsteel.com
SIC: 3441 3728 4581 3412 Fabricated
structural metal; Aircraft parts and
equipment, nec; Aircraft maintenance and
repair services; Metal barrels, drums, and
pails

(P-4844)

KUMAR INDUSTRIES

4775 Chino Ave, Chino (91710-5130)
PHONE..............................909 591-0722
EMP: 23 EST: 1980
SALES (est): 11.01MM Privately Held
Web: www.kumarindustries.net
SIC: 3441 Building components, structural
steel

(P-4845)

LEXINGTON ACQUISITION INC

Also Called: Lexington
11125 Vanowen St, North Hollywood
(91605-6316)
PHONE..............................818 768-5768
EMP: 145
SIC: 3441 Fabricated structural metal

(P-4846)

LIGHTCAP INDUSTRIES INC

Also Called: JC Supply & Manufacturing
1612 S Cucamonga Ave, Ontario
(91761-4513)
PHONE..............................909 930-3772
EMP: 50
SIC: 3441 3479 Building components,
structural steel; Painting, coating, and hot
dipping

(P-4847)

M W REID WELDING INC

Also Called: South Bay Welding
781 Oconner St, El Cajon (92020-1644)
PHONE..............................619 401-5880
Bruce A Reid, *Pr*
Timothy Hill, *
Timothy Fair, *
Susan Reid, *
EMP: 78 EST: 1965
SQ FT: 25,000
SALES (est): 8.44MM Privately Held
Web: www.southbaywelding.com
SIC: 3441 Fabricated structural metal

(P-4848)

MADISON INC OF OKLAHOMA

18000 Studebaker Rd, Cerritos
(90703-2679)
PHONE..............................918 224-6990
John Samuel Frey, *Pr*
Robert E Hansen, *
Barbara Cruncleton, *
EMP: 67 EST: 1946

SALES (est): 9.15MM
SALES (corp-wide): 44.99MM Privately
Held
SIC: 3441 1541 3448 3444 Fabricated
structural metal; Prefabricated building
erection, industrial; Prefabricated metal
buildings and components; Sheet metalwork
PA: John S. Frey Enterprises
1900 E 64th St
323 583-4061

(P-4849)

MAYA STEEL FABRICATIONS INC

301 E Compton Blvd, Gardena
(90248-2015)
PHONE..............................310 532-8830
Meir Amsalam, *CEO*
Yechiel Yogev, *
Sara Haddad, *
EMP: 64 EST: 1982
SQ FT: 65,000
SALES (est): 8.81MM Privately Held
Web: www.mayasteel.com
SIC: 3441 Building components, structural
steel

(P-4850)

MCCAIN MANUFACTURING INC

2633 Progress St, Vista (92081-8402)
P.O. Box 2307 (92067)
PHONE..............................760 295-9290
Jeffrey Lynn Mccain, *CEO*
EMP: 61 EST: 2016
SALES (est): 5.1MM Privately Held
SIC: 3441 Fabricated structural metal

(P-4851)

MCM FABRICATORS INC

Also Called: Global Fabricators
720 Commerce Way, Shafter (93263-9530)
P.O. Box 80247 (93380-0247)
PHONE..............................661 589-2774
Jim L Moses, *Pr*
Gary E Moses, *
Bill Chaney, *
EMP: 140 EST: 1982
SQ FT: 12,000
SALES (est): 6.1MM Privately Held
SIC: 3441 Fabricated structural metal

(P-4852)

MCWHIRTER STEEL INC

42211 7th St E, Lancaster (93535-5400)
PHONE..............................661 951-8998
David Mcwhirter, *Pr*
Angela Mcwhirter, *CFO*
Nathan Mcwhirter, *Dir*
EMP: 95 EST: 1992
SQ FT: 21,000
SALES (est): 14.14MM Privately Held
Web: www.mcwhirtersteel.com
SIC: 3441 1791 Fabricated structural metal;
Structural steel erection

(P-4853)

MEDSCO FABRICATION & DIST INC

938 N Eastern Ave, Los Angeles
(90063-1308)
PHONE..............................323 263-0511
Michael Nevarez, *Ch Bd*
Brian Powell, *Pr*
Jim Stock, *CFO*
John Millan, *COO*
Laura Nevarez, *Sec*
EMP: 56 EST: 2001
SALES (est): 4.93MM Privately Held
Web: www.medscofabrication.com

SIC: 3441 Fabricated structural metal

(P-4854)

MERRIMANS INCORPORATED

32195 Dunlap Blvd, Yucaipa (92399-1728)
P.O. Box 547 (92320-0547)
PHONE..............................909 795-5301
TOLL FREE: 800
Tod Merriman, *Pr*
Janice Merriman, *
Lisa Merriman, *
Elaine Onken, *
EMP: 30 EST: 1965
SQ FT: 5,000
SALES (est): 1.62MM Privately Held
Web: www.merrimansinc.com
SIC: 3441 5271 1521 Building components,
structural steel; Mobile home parts and
accessories; General remodeling, single-
family houses

(P-4855)

METAL SUPPLY LLC

11810 Center St, South Gate (90280-7832)
PHONE..............................562 634-9940
TOLL FREE: 800
Dion Genchi, *Pr*
Bruce E Hubert, *
▼ EMP: 63 EST: 1961
SQ FT: 50,000
SALES (est): 3.74MM Privately Held
Web: www.metalsupply.com
SIC: 3441 5051 Fabricated structural metal;
Iron and steel (ferrous) products

(P-4856)

METALS USA BUILDING PDTS LP

6450 Caballero Blvd Ste A, Buena Park
(90620-1007)
PHONE..............................714 522-7852
Tom Bush, *Brnch Mgr*
EMP: 103
SALES (corp-wide): 14.81B Publicly Held
Web: www.metalsusa.com
SIC: 3441 3444 Fabricated structural metal;
Sheet metalwork
HQ: Metals Usa Building Products Lp
955 Columbia St
Brea CA 92821
713 946-9000

(P-4857)

MITCHELL FABRICATION

Also Called: Amazing Steel
4564 Mission Blvd, Montclair (91763-6106)
PHONE..............................909 590-0393
Jim Mitchell, *Pr*
▲ EMP: 30 EST: 1985
SQ FT: 35,000
SALES (est): 3.9MM Privately Held
Web: www.mitchellamazing.com
SIC: 3441 Fabricated structural metal

(P-4858)

PACIFIC MARITIME INDS CORP

Also Called: P M I
1790 Dornoch Ct, San Diego (92154-7206)
PHONE..............................619 575-8141
John Atkinson, *CEO*
▲ EMP: 110 EST: 1995
SQ FT: 38,000
SALES (est): 20.11MM Privately Held
Web: pacificmaritimeindm.openfos.com
SIC: 3441 Fabricated structural metal

(P-4859)

PARCELL STEEL CORP

Also Called: Parcell Steel
26365 Earthmover Cir, Corona
(92883-5270)

PHONE..................951 471-3200
EMP: 140
Web: www.parcellsteel.com
SIC: 3441 Fabricated structural metal

(P-4860)
PRECISION WELDING INC
241 Enterprise Pkwy, Lancaster
(93534-7201)
PHONE..................661 729-3436
David R Jones, *Pr*
David Jones, *Pr*
EMP: 23 **EST:** 1995
SQ FT: 10,000
SALES (est): 3.96MM **Privately Held**
Web: www.precisionweldingla.com
SIC: 3441 1799 Fabricated structural metal;
Welding on site

(P-4861)
PREMIER STEEL STRUCTURES INC
13345 Estelle St, Corona (92879-1881)
PHONE..................951 356-6655
Armando Rodarte, *Pr*
EMP: 30 **EST:** 2016
SALES (est): 5.71MM **Privately Held**
Web:
www.psspremiersteelstructures.com
SIC: 3441 Fabricated structural metal

(P-4862)
R & D STEEL INC
7930 E Tarma St, Long Beach
(90808-3140)
PHONE..................310 631-6183
Joie A Dunyon, *Pr*
Jim Dunyon, *
▲ **EMP:** 30 **EST:** 1979
SALES (est): 2.52MM **Privately Held**
Web: www.rdsteelinc.com
SIC: 3441 Fabricated structural metal

(P-4863)
R & I INDUSTRIES INC
Also Called: R & I
1876 S Taylor Ave, Ontario (91761-5556)
PHONE..................909 923-7747
William Franklin Rowan Senior, *CEO*
William Franklin Rowan Junior, *VP*
Ardith Rowan, *
EMP: 40 **EST:** 1978
SQ FT: 12,000
SALES (est): 6.76MM **Privately Held**
Web: www.rimetal.com
SIC: 3441 Building components, structural
steel

(P-4864)
RICHARDSON STEEL INC
9102 Harness St Ste A, Spring Valley
(91977-3924)
PHONE..................619 697-5892
John Richardson, *Pr*
Lance Richardson, *
Natalie N Lautner, *
EMP: 32 **EST:** 1993
SQ FT: 5,000
SALES (est): 4.62MM **Privately Held**
Web: www.richardsonsteelinc.com
SIC: 3441 Fabricated structural metal

(P-4865)
RND CONTRACTORS INC
14796 Jurupa Ave Ste A, Fontana
(92337-7232)
PHONE..................909 429-8500
Nancy Sauter, *Pr*
EMP: 40 **EST:** 2007
SALES (est): 9.62MM **Privately Held**

Web: www.uia.net
SIC: 3441 Fabricated structural metal

(P-4866)
S & R ARCHITECTURAL METALS INC
2609 W Woodland Dr, Anaheim
(92801-2627)
PHONE..................714 226-0108
EMP: 45
SIC: 3441 Fabricated structural metal

(P-4867)
SCHROEDER IRON CORPORATION
8417 Beech Ave, Fontana (92335-1200)
PHONE..................909 428-6471
Linda Schroeder, *Pr*
EMP: 30 **EST:** 1993
SQ FT: 23,000
SALES (est): 9.75MM **Privately Held**
Web: www.schroederiron.com
SIC: 3441 Building components, structural
steel

(P-4868)
SO-CAL STRL STL FBRICATION INC
130 S Spruce Ave, Rialto (92376-9005)
PHONE..................909 877-1299
Craig B Yates, *CEO*
Kim Yates, *
EMP: 50 **EST:** 1995
SQ FT: 40,000
SALES (est): 9.26MM **Privately Held**
SIC: 3441 Fabricated structural metal

(P-4869)
SOUTH BAY FOUNDRY INC (HQ)
895 Inland Center Dr, San Bernardino
(92408-1828)
PHONE..................909 383-1823
Bill Rogers, *Pr*
Russell Goodsell, *
▲ **EMP:** 35 **EST:** 1990
SQ FT: 12,002
SALES (est): 23.55MM
SALES (corp-wide): 46.84MM **Privately
Held**
Web: www.southbayfoundry.com
SIC: 3441 3322 Fabricated structural metal;
Malleable iron foundries
PA: Olympic Foundry Inc.
5200 Airport Way S
206 764-6200

(P-4870)
SPARTAN INC
3030 M St, Bakersfield (93301-2137)
PHONE..................661 327-1205
John Wood, *Pr*
Louis Stern, *
John D Clemmey, *
Teresa Wood, *
▼ **EMP:** 65 **EST:** 2002
SQ FT: 125,000
SALES (est): 9.49MM **Privately Held**
Web: www.spartaninc.net
SIC: 3441 8711 Fabricated structural metal;
Engineering services

(P-4871)
STEEL-TECH INDUSTRIAL CORP
1268 Sherborn St, Corona (92879-2090)
PHONE..................951 270-0144
Michael R Black, *Pr*
Braebon Black, *
Linda Black, *
Elise Roberts, *

EMP: 47 **EST:** 1984
SQ FT: 15,000
SALES (est): 8.96MM **Privately Held**
Web: www.steeltech.org
SIC: 3441 Fabricated structural metal

(P-4872)
STRUCTURAL STL FABRICATORS INC
10641 Sycamore Ave, Stanton
(90680-2639)
P.O. Box 707 (90680-0707)
PHONE..................714 761-1695
Rex Shaw, *Pr*
Maureen Shaw, *
EMP: 25 **EST:** 1983
SQ FT: 3,600
SALES (est): 5.53MM **Privately Held**
SIC: 3441 Fabricated structural metal

(P-4873)
TITAN METAL FABRICATORS INC (PA)
Also Called: Titan
352 Balboa Cir, Camarillo (93012-8644)
PHONE..................805 487-5050
Steve Muscarella, *Pr*
Tom Muscarella, *
▲ **EMP:** 69 **EST:** 1998
SQ FT: 15,000
SALES (est): 20.85MM
SALES (corp-wide): 20.85MM **Privately
Held**
Web: www.titanmf.com
SIC: 3441 Fabricated structural metal

(P-4874)
TOBIN STEEL COMPANY INC
817 E Santa Ana Blvd, Santa Ana
(92701-3909)
P.O. Box 717 (92702-0717)
PHONE..................714 541-2268
Linda A Robin, *CEO*
Carl Tobin, *
Steve Tobin, *
Jim Tobin, *
EMP: 65 **EST:** 1978
SQ FT: 20,000
SALES (est): 9.44MM **Privately Held**
Web: www.tobinsteel.com
SIC: 3441 Building components, structural
steel

(P-4875)
TOLAR MANUFACTURING CO INC
258 Mariah Cir, Corona (92879-1751)
PHONE..................951 808-0081
Gary Tolar, *Pr*
Rhonda Tolar, *
▲ **EMP:** 40 **EST:** 1991
SQ FT: 22,000
SALES (est): 8.58MM **Privately Held**
Web: www.tolarmfg.com
SIC: 3441 3599 3448 Fabricated structural
metal; Machine shop, jobbing and repair;
Prefabricated metal buildings and
components

(P-4876)
TRUSSWORKS INTERNATIONAL INC
1275 E Franklin Ave, Pomona
(91766-5450)
PHONE..................714 630-2772
Michael Farrell, *Pr*
Ali Shantyaei, *
EMP: 60 **EST:** 2007
SALES (est): 9.21MM **Privately Held**

Web: www.twifab.com
SIC: 3441 3446 1791 Fabricated structural
metal; Architectural metalwork; Building
front installation, metal

(P-4877)
V & F FABRICATION COMPANY INC
13902 Seaboard Cir, Garden Grove
(92843-3910)
PHONE..................714 265-0630
Vinh Nguyen, *Pr*
Vinh Van Nguyen, *
Senator Truong, *Sec*
▲ **EMP:** 35 **EST:** 1989
SALES (est): 4.71MM **Privately Held**
SIC: 3441 3599 3769 3444 Fabricated
structural metal; Machine shop, jobbing and
repair; Space vehicle equipment, nec;
Sheet metalwork

(P-4878)
VISTA STEEL COMPANY (PA)
6100 Francis Botello Rd Ste C, Goleta
(93117-3264)
PHONE..................805 964-4732
Maria Di Maggio, *Pr*
EMP: 50 **EST:** 1969
SQ FT: 600
SALES (est): 1.87MM
SALES (corp-wide): 1.87MM **Privately
Held**
Web: www.vistasteelco.com
SIC: 3441 Fabricated structural metal

(P-4879)
WADCO INDUSTRIES INC
Also Called: Wadco Steel Sales
2625 S Willow Ave, Bloomington
(92316-3258)
PHONE..................909 874-7800
David D Scheibel, *CEO*
Salvador Arratia, *
Anthony Salazar, *
Scott Brown, *
EMP: 47 **EST:** 1979
SQ FT: 50,000
SALES (est): 1.71MM **Privately Held**
Web: www.wadcoindustries.com
SIC: 3441 5051 Building components,
structural steel; Steel

(P-4880)
WESTCO INDUSTRIES INC
Also Called: Corbell Products
2625 S Willow Ave, Bloomington
(92316-3258)
PHONE..................909 874-0700
David Schibel, *Pr*
▲ **EMP:** 25 **EST:** 2005
SQ FT: 25,000
SALES (est): 1.6MM **Privately Held**
Web: www.westcoind.com
SIC: 3441 Fabricated structural metal

(P-4881)
WESTERN BAY SHEET METAL INC
1410 Hill St, El Cajon (92020-5749)
PHONE..................619 233-1753
James Lozano, *Pr*
Roy Lozano, *
Helena Lopez, *
▲ **EMP:** 45 **EST:** 1981
SQ FT: 9,800
SALES (est): 3.76MM **Privately Held**
Web: www.westernbay.net
SIC: 3441 3444 Fabricated structural metal;
Sheet metalwork

PRODUCTS & SVCS

(P-4882)
ZIA AAMIR
Also Called: Bridge Metals
2043 Imperial St, Los Angeles
(90021-3203)
PHONE..............................714 337-7861
Aamir Zia, *Owner*
EMP: 25 **EST:** 2017
SALES (est): 1.53MM **Privately Held**
Web: www.bridgemetals.com
SIC: 3441 Fabricated structural metal

3442 Metal Doors, Sash, And Trim

(P-4883)
ACTIVE WINDOW PRODUCTS
Also Called: Z Industries
5431 W San Fernando Rd, Los Angeles
(90039-1088)
P.O. Box 39125 (90039-0125)
PHONE..............................323 245-5185
TOLL FREE: 800
Michael Schoenfeld, *Pr*
Rosa Castro, *
▲ **EMP:** 53 **EST:** 1952
SQ FT: 96,000
SALES (est): 7.45MM **Privately Held**
Web: www.activewindowproducts.com
SIC: 3442 Storm doors or windows, metal

(P-4884)
AIR LOUVERS INC
6285 Randolph St, Commerce
(90040-3514)
PHONE..............................800 554-6077
EMP: 50
SALES (corp-wide): 142.69MM **Privately Held**
Web: www.activarcpg.com
SIC: 3442 Metal doors, sash, and trim
HQ: Air Louvers, Inc.
9702 Newton Ave S
Bloomington MN 55431
800 554-6077

(P-4885)
CRYSTAL PCF WIN & DOOR SYS LLC
Also Called: Crystal
1850 Atlanta Ave, Riverside (92507-2476)
PHONE..............................951 779-9300
Thomas C Chen, *Managing Member*
EMP: 102 **EST:** 2010
SALES (est): 23.79MM **Privately Held**
Web: www.cpwds.com
SIC: 3442 Window and door frames

(P-4886)
DOOR COMPONENTS INC
Also Called: DCI Hollow Metal On Demand
7980 Redwood Ave, Fontana (92336-1638)
PHONE..............................909 770-5700
Robert Briggs, *Pr*
Ronald Green, *
EMP: 200 **EST:** 1981
SQ FT: 45,000
SALES (est): 28.07MM **Privately Held**
Web: www.doorcomponents.com
SIC: 3442 Metal doors

(P-4887)
ELIZABETH SHUTTERS INC
Also Called: Elizabeth Shutters
525 S Rancho Ave, Colton (92324-3240)
P.O. Box 1345 (92324)
PHONE..............................909 825-1531
Dean Frost, *CEO*

Maren Frost, *
Maggie Castaneda, *Accounts Payable*
EMP: 45 **EST:** 1996
SQ FT: 51,000
SALES (est): 4.86MM **Privately Held**
Web: www.elizabethshutters.com
SIC: 3442 5023 5211 2431 Shutters, door or window: metal; Window furnishings; Door and window products; Millwork

(P-4888)
EUROLINE STEEL WINDOWS
Also Called: Euroline Steel Windows & Doors
22600 Savi Ranch Pkwy Ste E, Yorba Linda
(92887-4616)
PHONE..............................877 590-2741
Elyas Balta, *CEO*
▲ **EMP:** 54 **EST:** 2013
SALES (est): 7.54MM **Privately Held**
Web: www.eurolinesteelwindows.com
SIC: 3442 Window and door frames

(P-4889)
HEHR INTERNATIONAL INC
Also Called: Hehr International Polymers
P.O. Box 39160 (90039-0160)
PHONE..............................323 663-1261
▲ **EMP:** 199
Web: www.hehr-international.com
SIC: 3442 Window and door frames

(P-4890)
J T WALKER INDUSTRIES INC
Also Called: Rite Screen
9322 Hyssop Dr, Rancho Cucamonga
(91730-6103)
PHONE..............................909 481-1909
Dan Harvey, *Pr*
EMP: 4277
SQ FT: 36,929
SALES (corp-wide): 23.69MM **Privately Held**
SIC: 3442 Screen and storm doors and windows
PA: J. T. Walker Industries, Inc.
1310 N Hercules Ave
727 461-0501

(P-4891)
KAWNEER COMPANY INC
925 Marlborough Ave, Riverside
(92507-2138)
PHONE..............................951 410-4779
EMP: 89
SALES (corp-wide): 8.96B **Privately Held**
Web: www.kawneer.us
SIC: 3442 Metal doors, sash, and trim
HQ: Kawneer Company, Inc.
555 Guthridge Ct
Norcross GA 30092
770 449-5555

(P-4892)
KRIEGER SPECIALITY PDTS LLC (DH)
Also Called: Krieger Steel Products
4880 Gregg Rd, Pico Rivera (90660-2107)
PHONE..............................562 695-0645
Robert J Mccluney, *Pr*
A W Mc Cluney, *Ch Bd*
William Mc Cluney, *Ex VP*
James Mc Cluney, *Stockholder*
Charles Mc Cluney, *Stockholder*
EMP: 58 **EST:** 1974
SQ FT: 39,000
SALES (est): 9.41MM **Privately Held**
Web: www.kriegerproducts.com
SIC: 3442 1751 Metal doors; Window and door (prefabricated) installation
HQ: Schlage Lock Company Llc
11819 N Pennsylvania St

Carmel IN 46032
317 810-3700

(P-4893)
LAWRENCE ROLL UP DOORS INC (PA)
4525 Littlejohn St, Baldwin Park
(91706-2239)
PHONE..............................626 962-4163
TOLL FREE: 800
Paul Weston Freberg, *CEO*
◆ **EMP:** 35 **EST:** 1925
SQ FT: 35,000
SALES (est): 17.42MM
SALES (corp-wide): 17.42MM **Privately Held**
Web: www.lawrencedoors.com
SIC: 3442 3446 Rolling doors for industrial buildings or warehouses, metal; Architectural metalwork

(P-4894)
MILLWORKS ETC INC
Also Called: Steel Works Etc
2230 Statham Blvd Ste 100, Oxnard
(93033-3909)
PHONE..............................805 499-3400
Robin W Shattuck, *CEO*
◆ **EMP:** 25 **EST:** 1985
SALES (est): 5.98MM **Privately Held**
Web: www.millworksetc.com
SIC: 3442 Window and door frames

(P-4895)
MNM MANUFACTURING INC
3019 E Harcourt St, Compton (90221-5503)
PHONE..............................310 898-1099
Matt Klein, *Pr*
Elizabeth Klein, *
Marlene Klein, *
EMP: 60 **EST:** 1980
SQ FT: 24,000
SALES (est): 4.53MM **Privately Held**
Web: www.mnmmfg.com
SIC: 3442 Sash, door or window: metal

(P-4896)
MULHOLLAND SECURITY CTRS LLC
Also Called: Mulholland Brand
21260 Deering Ct, Canoga Park
(91304-5015)
PHONE..............................800 562-5770
Avi Ben David, *CEO*
Henry Zimmerman, *Pr*
Eyal Sibrower, *COO*
Avi 'coby' Jacoby, *CFO*
EMP: 65 **EST:** 2018
SALES (est): 7.6MM **Privately Held**
Web: www.mulhollandbrand.com
SIC: 3442 7699 Garage doors, overhead: metal; Locksmith shop

(P-4897)
OMNIMAX INTERNATIONAL LLC
Also Called: Alumax Building Products
28921 Us Highway 74, Sun City
(92585-9675)
PHONE..............................951 928-1000
Mitchell B Lewis, *CEO*
EMP: 62
Web: www.omnimax.com
SIC: 3442 3444 5999 Casements, aluminum; Sheet metalwork; Awnings
HQ: Omnimax International, Llc
30 Technlogy Pkwy S Ste 4
Peachtree Corners GA 30092
770 449-7066

(P-4898)
PEMKO MANUFACTURING CO
4226 Transport St, Ventura (93003-5627)
P.O. Box 3780 (93006-3780)
PHONE..............................800 283-9988
◆ **EMP:** 250
SIC: 3442 Weather strip, metal

(P-4899)
R & S AUTOMATION INC
283 W Bonita Ave, Pomona (91767-1848)
PHONE..............................800 962-3111
Jerry Bradfield, *Mgr*
EMP: 27
SALES (corp-wide): 5.23MM **Privately Held**
Web: www.rsoperators.com
SIC: 3442 3446 5031 5063 Metal doors; Grillwork, ornamental metal; Doors, nec; Motor controls, starters and relays: electric
PA: R & S Automation, Inc.
2041 W Avenue 140th
510 357-4110

(P-4900)
S E - G I PRODUCTS INC
20521 Teresita Way, Lake Forest
(92630-8142)
PHONE..............................949 297-8530
EMP: 180 **EST:** 1976
SALES (est): 10.81MM
SALES (corp-wide): 1.62B **Privately Held**
SIC: 3442 Sash, door or window: metal
HQ: Truck Accessories Group, Llc
28858 Ventura Dr
Elkhart IN 46517
574 522-5337

(P-4901)
SAN JOAQUIN WINDOW INC
Also Called: ATI Windows
1455 Columbia Ave, Riverside
(92507-2013)
PHONE..............................909 946-3697
Stephen Schwartz, *CEO*
Daniel Schwartz, *
EMP: 120 **EST:** 1992
SQ FT: 190,000
SALES (est): 15.14MM **Privately Held**
SIC: 3442 5211 Metal doors, sash, and trim; Door and window products

(P-4902)
SDS INDUSTRIES INC
Also Called: Timely Prefinished Steel
10241 Norris Ave, Pacoima (91331-2218)
PHONE..............................818 492-3500
EMP: 130 **EST:** 1973
SALES (est): 21.7MM **Privately Held**
Web: www.timelyframes.com
SIC: 3442 Window and door frames

(P-4903)
SOLATUBE INTERNATIONAL INC (DH)
Also Called: Solatube
2210 Oak Ridge Way, Vista (92081-8341)
PHONE..............................888 765-2882
Robert E Westfall Junior, *CEO*
Francisco Lopez, *
▲ **EMP:** 100 **EST:** 1995
SQ FT: 105,000
SALES (est): 38.22MM **Privately Held**
Web: www.solatube.com
SIC: 3442 Metal doors, sash, and trim
HQ: Kingspan Light & Air Llc
28662 N Ballard Dr
Lake Forest IL 60045
847 816-1060

(P-4904)

TORRANCE STEEL WINDOW CO INC

1819 Abalone Ave, Torrance (90501-3704)
PHONE.................................310 328-9181
Dong K Lim, *Pr*
▲ **EMP:** 30 **EST:** 1964
SQ FT: 32,000
SALES (est): 3.68MM **Privately Held**
Web: www.torrancesteelwindow.com
SIC: 3442 Window and door frames

(P-4905)

WINDOW ENTERPRISES INC

Also Called: Torrence Aluminum Window
430 Nevada St, Redlands (92373-4244)
PHONE.................................951 943-4894
▲ **EMP:** 30 **EST:** 1970
SALES (est): 1MM **Privately Held**
SIC: 3442 Storm doors or windows, metal

3443 Fabricated Plate Work (boiler shop)

(P-4906)

AAR MANUFACTURING INC

Also Called: Telair International
2220 E Cerritos Ave, Anaheim
(92806-5709)
PHONE.................................714 634-8807
EMP: 150
SALES (corp-wide): 1.77B **Publicly Held**
SIC: 3443 Containers, shipping (bombs, etc.): metal plate
HQ: Aar Manufacturing, Inc.
1100 N Wood Dale Rd
Wood Dale IL 60191
630 227-2000

(P-4907)

ACD LLC (DH)

Also Called: Nikkiso Acd
2321 Pullman St, Santa Ana (92705-5512)
PHONE.................................949 261-7533
Peter Wagner, *CEO*
James Estes, *
◆ **EMP:** 49 **EST:** 1978
SQ FT: 52,000
SALES (est): 47.65MM **Privately Held**
Web: www.nikkisoceig.com
SIC: 3443 3559 Cryogenic tanks, for liquids and gases; Cryogenic machinery, industrial
HQ: Cryogenic Industries, Inc.
27710 Jffrson Ave Ste 301
Temecula CA 92590
951 677-2081

(P-4908)

AJAX BOILER INC

Also Called: Ace Boiler
2701 S Harbor Blvd, Santa Ana
(92704-5838)
PHONE.................................714 437-9050
▼ **EMP:** 68
Web: www.aceheaters.com
SIC: 3443 Fabricated plate work (boiler shop)

(P-4909)

BA HOLDINGS INC (DH)

3016 Kansas Ave Bldg 1, Riverside
(92507-3445)
PHONE.................................951 684-5110
John S Rhodes, *CEO*
EMP: 30 **EST:** 1996
SALES (est): 64.36MM
SALES (corp-wide): 405MM **Privately Held**
Web: www.mediluxcylinders.com

SIC: 3443 3728 Cylinders, pressure: metal plate; Aircraft parts and equipment, nec
HQ: Luxfer Overseas Holdings Limited
Anchorage Gateway, 5 Anchorage
Quay
Salford LANCS M50 3

(P-4910)

BASIC INDUSTRIES INTL INC (PA)

Also Called: Pacific Metal Products
10850 Wilshire Blvd Ste 760, Los Angeles
(90024-4709)
PHONE.................................951 226-1500
John Wallace, *Pr*
Steven W Burge, *
EMP: 50 **EST:** 2000
SALES (est): 3.01MM
SALES (corp-wide): 3.01MM **Privately Held**
Web: www.biidemexico.com
SIC: 3443 3446 Fabricated plate work (boiler shop); Architectural metalwork

(P-4911)

CJI PROCESS SYSTEMS INC

Also Called: Lee Ray Sandblasting
12000 Clark St, Santa Fe Springs
(90670-3709)
PHONE.................................562 777-0614
Archie Cholakian, *Pr*
John Cholakian, *
▼ **EMP:** 70 **EST:** 1982
SQ FT: 35,000
SALES (est): 8.88MM **Privately Held**
Web: www.cjiprocesssystems.com
SIC: 3443 3441 3444 Tanks, lined: metal plate; Fabricated structural metal; Sheet metalwork

(P-4912)

COMMERCIAL METAL FORMING INC

Also Called: Commercial Metal Forming
341 W Collins Ave, Orange (92867-5505)
PHONE.................................714 532-6321
William Kowal, *Pr*
Donald E Washdewicz, *VP*
▲ **EMP:** 25 **EST:** 2003
SALES (est): 4.45MM **Privately Held**
Web: www.cmforming.com
SIC: 3443 Fabricated plate work (boiler shop)

(P-4913)

CONSOLIDATED FABRICATORS CORP (PA)

Also Called: Confab
14620 Arminta St, Van Nuys (91402-5993)
PHONE.................................800 635-8335
Michael J Melideo, *CEO*
Jeff Lombardi, *
▲ **EMP:** 110 **EST:** 1974
SQ FT: 150,000
SALES (est): 26.61MM
SALES (corp-wide): 26.61MM **Privately Held**
Web: www.con-fab.com
SIC: 3443 5051 3444 Dumpsters, garbage; Steel; Studs and joists, sheet metal

(P-4914)

COOK AND COOK INCORPORATED

Also Called: Royal Welding & Fabricating
1000 E Elm Ave, Fullerton (92831-5022)
PHONE.................................714 680-6669
Wallace F Cook, *Pr*
Patricia Cook, *
EMP: 30 **EST:** 1967

SQ FT: 30,000
SALES (est): 4.74MM **Privately Held**
Web: www.royalwelding.com
SIC: 3443 3599 3444 Industrial vessels, tanks, and containers; Amusement park equipment; Sheet metalwork

(P-4915)

HYUNDAI TRANSLEAD (HQ)

8880 Rio San Diego Dr Ste 600, San Diego
(92108-1640)
PHONE.................................619 574-1500
Sean Kenney, *CEO*
Glen Harney, *
Jangsoo Choi, *
Hae Sung Park, *
▲ **EMP:** 87 **EST:** 1989
SALES (est): 440.44MM **Privately Held**
Web: www.translead.com
SIC: 3443 3715 3412 Industrial vessels, tanks, and containers; Semitrailers for truck tractors; Metal barrels, drums, and pails
PA: Hyundai Motor Company
12 Heolleung-Ro, Seocho-Gu

(P-4916)

MELCO STEEL INC

1100 W Foothill Blvd, Azusa (91702-2818)
PHONE.................................626 334-7875
Michel Kashou, *Pr*
Mazin Kashou, *
Joann Reese, *
EMP: 30 **EST:** 1971
SQ FT: 25,500
SALES (est): 4.43MM **Privately Held**
Web: www.melcosteel.com
SIC: 3443 Vessels, process or storage (from boiler shops): metal plate

(P-4917)

OMEGA II INC

Also Called: Omega Industrial Marine
3525 Main St, Chula Vista (91911-5830)
PHONE.................................619 920-6650
Greg Lewis, *CEO*
Nicholas Ruiz, *MNG*
EMP: 39 **EST:** 1986
SALES (est): 3.82MM **Privately Held**
Web: www.omegaindustrial.net
SIC: 3443 1542 1629 1541 Air coolers, metal plate; Nonresidential construction, nec ; Marine construction; Industrial buildings and warehouses

(P-4918)

PACIFIC STEAM EQUIPMENT INC

Also Called: P S E Boilers
11748 Slauson Ave, Santa Fe Springs
(90670-2227)
PHONE.................................562 906-9292
William S M Shanahan Md, *Pr*
Shin Duk David Kang, *VP*
▲ **EMP:** 25 **EST:** 1954
SQ FT: 22,500
SALES (est): 3.67MM **Privately Held**
Web: www.pacificsteam.com
SIC: 3443 5074 3582 2841 Tanks, standard or custom fabricated: metal plate; Plumbing and hydronic heating supplies; Commercial laundry equipment; Soap and other detergents

(P-4919)

PACIFIC TANK & CNSTR INC

17995 E Highway 46, Shandon
(93461-9636)
PHONE.................................805 237-2929
Tom Yanaga, *Mgr*
EMP: 30

Web: www.pacifictank.net
SIC: 3443 Fabricated plate work (boiler shop)
PA: Pacific Tank & Construction, Inc.
31551 Avnida Los Cerritos

(P-4920)

PARKER-HANNIFIN CORPORATION

Hydraulic Accumulator Division
14087 Borate St, Santa Fe Springs
(90670-5336)
PHONE.................................562 404-1938
Mark Gagnon, *Brnch Mgr*
EMP: 53
SALES (corp-wide): 19.93B **Publicly Held**
Web: www.parker.com
SIC: 3443 3052 2822 Fabricated plate work (boiler shop); Rubber and plastics hose and beltings; Synthetic rubber
PA: Parker-Hannifin Corporation
6035 Parkland Blvd
216 896-3000

(P-4921)

PLUCKYS DUMP RENTAL LLC

10136 Bowman Ave, South Gate
(90280-6233)
PHONE.................................323 540-3510
EMP: 45 **EST:** 2021
SALES (est): 1.08MM **Privately Held**
SIC: 3443 Dumpsters, garbage

(P-4922)

PROTEC ARISAWA AMERICA INC

2455 Ash St, Vista (92081-8424)
PHONE.................................760 599-4800
Lee Hancock, *Pr*
◆ **EMP:** 50 **EST:** 2005
SALES (est): 9.35MM **Privately Held**
Web: www.protec-arisawa.com
SIC: 3443 Process vessels, industrial: metal plate

(P-4923)

RITE ENGINEERING & MANUFACTURING CORPORATION

5832 Garfield Ave, Commerce
(90040-3605)
PHONE.................................562 862-2135
EMP: 25 **EST:** 1952
SALES (est): 5.96MM **Privately Held**
Web: www.riteboiler.com
SIC: 3443 Boilers: industrial, power, or marine

(P-4924)

ROY E HANSON JR MFG (PA)

Also Called: Hanson Tank
1600 E Washington Blvd, Los Angeles
(90021-3123)
P.O. Box 30507 (90030-0507)
PHONE.................................213 747-7514
Jonathan Goss, *CEO*
Johnathan Goss, *
Cliff Jones, *
Thys Dorenbosch, *
Dorothy Griffen, *
▼ **EMP:** 80 **EST:** 1932
SQ FT: 55,000
SALES (est): 10.18MM
SALES (corp-wide): 10.18MM **Privately Held**
Web: www.hansontank.com
SIC: 3443 Fuel tanks (oil, gas, etc.), metal plate

(P-4925)
S BRAVO SYSTEMS INC
Also Called: Bravo Support
2929 Vail Ave, Los Angeles (90040-2615)
PHONE..............................323 888-4133
Paola Bravo Recendez, *CEO*
▲ EMP: 26 EST: 1986
SQ FT: 40,000
SALES (est): 10MM Privately Held
Web: www.sbravo.com
SIC: 3443 Containers, shipping (bombs, etc.): metal plate

(P-4926)
SID E PARKER BOILER MFG CO INC
Also Called: Parker Boiler Co
5930 Bandini Blvd, Commerce (90040-2998)
PHONE..............................323 727-9800
Sid D Danenhauer, *Ch Bd*
Greg G Danenhauer, *
Ed Marchak, *
◆ EMP: 66 EST: 1939
SQ FT: 80,000
SALES (est): 9.23MM Privately Held
Web: www.parkerboiler.com
SIC: 3443 3433 Boilers: industrial, power, or marine; Heating equipment, except electric

(P-4927)
SOUTH GATE ENGINEERING LLC
13477 Yorba Ave, Chino (91710-5055)
PHONE..............................909 628-2779
William Paolino, *Managing Member*
EMP: 115 EST: 1947
SALES (est): 22.09MM Privately Held
Web: www.southgateengineering.com
SIC: 3443 Vessels, process or storage (from boiler shops): metal plate

(P-4928)
SPX FLOW US LLC
Also Called: A P V Crepaco
26561 Rancho Pkwy S, Lake Forest (92630-8301)
PHONE..............................949 455-8150
Brian Ahern, *Mgr*
EMP: 39
SALES (corp-wide): 1.78B Privately Held
SIC: 3443 Fabricated plate work (boiler shop)
HQ: Spx Flow Us, Llc
135 Mt Read Blvd
Rochester NY 14611
585 436-5550

(P-4929)
STRUCTURAL COMPOSITES INDS LLC (DH)
Also Called: SCI
336 Enterprise Pl, Pomona (91768-3244)
PHONE..............................909 594-7777
Ken Miller, *Managing Member*
◆ EMP: 49 EST: 2007
SALES (est): 3.46MM
SALES (corp-wide): 405MM Privately Held
SIC: 3443 Tanks, lined: metal plate
HQ: Luxfer Inc.
3016 Kansas Ave Bldg 1
Riverside CA 92507
951 684-5110

(P-4930)
SUPERIOR TANK CO INC (PA)
Also Called: Stci
9500 Lucas Ranch Rd, Rancho Cucamonga (91730-5724)

PHONE..............................909 912-0580
Jesus Eric Marquez, *Pr*
George Marquez, *
Lewis A Marquez, *
◆ EMP: 50 EST: 1984
SQ FT: 53,392
SALES (est): 44.83MM
SALES (corp-wide): 44.83MM Privately Held
Web: www.superiortank.com
SIC: 3443 3494 1791 1794 Fuel tanks (oil, gas, etc.), metal plate; Valves and pipe fittings, nec; Structural steel erection; Excavation work

(P-4931)
TAIT & ASSOCIATES INC
2131 S Dupont Dr, Anaheim (92806-6102)
PHONE..............................714 560-8222
Jim Streipz, *Brnch Mgr*
EMP: 49
SALES (corp-wide): 23.79MM Privately Held
Web: www.tait.com
SIC: 3443 Fuel tanks (oil, gas, etc.), metal plate
PA: Tait & Associates, Inc.
701 N Park Center Dr
866 584-0283

(P-4932)
THERMLLY ENGNRED MNFCTRED PDTS
Also Called: T E M P
543 W 135th St, Gardena (90248-1505)
PHONE..............................310 523-9934
Robert Greenwood, *Pr*
Binh Vinh, *
▲ EMP: 27 EST: 1994
SQ FT: 50,000
SALES (est): 5.08MM Privately Held
Web: www.tempinc.com
SIC: 3443 Heat exchangers, condensers, and components

(P-4933)
WATERCREST INC
4850 E Airport Dr, Ontario (91761-7818)
PHONE..............................909 390-3944
Jeremiah B Robins, *CEO*
Gary F Johnson, *Pr*
▲ EMP: 28 EST: 1996
SQ FT: 29,000
SALES (est): 3.26MM Privately Held
Web: www.yinluntdi.com
SIC: 3443 Heat exchangers, condensers, and components

(P-4934)
WELLS STRUTHERS CORPORATION
Also Called: Tei Struthers Wells
10375 Slusher Dr, Santa Fe Springs (90670-3748)
PHONE..............................814 726-1000
John C Wallace, *Pr*
John M Carey, *
Burton M Abrams, *
EMP: 30 EST: 1937
SQ FT: 30,000
SALES (est): 597.46K Privately Held
SIC: 3443 Heat exchangers, plate type

(P-4935)
WORTHINGTON CYLINDER CORP
336 Enterprise Pl, Pomona (91768-3244)
PHONE..............................909 594-7777
EMP: 154

SALES (corp-wide): 1.25B Publicly Held
Web: www.worthingtonenterprises.com
SIC: 3443 Cylinders, pressure: metal plate
HQ: Worthington Cylinder Corporation
200 W Wlson Bridge Rd
Worthington OH 43085
614 840-3210

3444 Sheet Metalwork

(P-4936)
A-1 METAL PRODUCTS INC
2707 Supply Ave, Commerce (90040-2703)
PHONE..............................323 721-3334
Jerry Calsbeek, *Pr*
Patricia Calsbeek, *
EMP: 24 EST: 1952
SQ FT: 40,000
SALES (est): 3.11MM Privately Held
Web: www.a1metalproducts.com
SIC: 3444 Sheet metal specialties, not stamped

(P-4937)
ABLE SHEET METAL INC (PA)
614 N Ford Blvd, Los Angeles (90022-1195)
PHONE..............................323 269-2181
Dmitri Triphon, *CEO*
Gurgen Tovmasyan, *General Vice President*
◆ EMP: 40 EST: 2001
SQ FT: 25,000
SALES (est): 7.98MM
SALES (corp-wide): 7.98MM Privately Held
Web: www.ablemetal.com
SIC: 3444 Sheet metal specialties, not stamped

(P-4938)
ADAMS-CAMPBELL COMPANY LTD (PA)
Also Called: Accent Ceilings
15343 Proctor Ave, City Of Industry (91745-1022)
P.O. Box 3867 (91744-0867)
PHONE..............................626 330-3425
EMP: 74 EST: 1909
SALES (est): 12MM
SALES (corp-wide): 12MM Privately Held
Web: www.adamscampbell.com
SIC: 3444 3469 3431 Sheet metalwork; Metal stampings, nec; Metal sanitary ware

(P-4939)
ADVANCED METAL MFG INC
49 Strathearn Pl, Simi Valley (93065-1653)
PHONE..............................805 322-4161
Scott Stewart, *CEO*
Gina Stewart Ctrl, *Prin*
▲ EMP: 30 EST: 2010
SALES (est): 5.1MM Privately Held
Web: www.advancedmetalmfg.com
SIC: 3444 Sheet metalwork

(P-4940)
AERO ARC
16634 S Figueroa St, Gardena (90248-2627)
PHONE..............................310 324-3400
EMP: 38 EST: 1984
SALES (est): 8.68MM Privately Held
Web: www.aeroarc.com
SIC: 3444 3498 Sheet metalwork; Fabricated pipe and fittings

(P-4941)
AERO BENDING COMPANY
560 Auto Center Dr Ste A, Palmdale (93551-4485)
PHONE..............................661 948-2363
Robert Burns, *Pr*
EMP: 80 EST: 1944
SQ FT: 26,000
SALES (est): 1.45MM Privately Held
Web: www.aerobendingco.com
SIC: 3444 5088 Sheet metalwork; Aircraft engines and engine parts

(P-4942)
AERO PRECISION ENGINEERING
11300 Hindry Ave, Los Angeles (90045-6228)
PHONE..............................310 642-9747
Sherry L Martinez, *Pr*
Tom Segotta, *
EMP: 45 EST: 1984
SQ FT: 55,000
SALES (est): 10.27MM Privately Held
Web: www.aeroprecisioneng.com
SIC: 3444 3599 Sheet metal specialties, not stamped; Machine shop, jobbing and repair

(P-4943)
ALL-WAYS METAL INC
401 E Alondra Blvd, Gardena (90248-2901)
PHONE..............................310 217-1177
Shirley Pickens, *Pr*
Scott Pickens, *
EMP: 30 EST: 1983
SQ FT: 29,000
SALES (est): 2.6MM Privately Held
Web: www.allwaysmetal.com
SIC: 3444 Sheet metal specialties, not stamped

(P-4944)
ALLIANCE METAL PRODUCTS INC
20844 Plummer St, Chatsworth (91311-5004)
PHONE..............................818 709-1204
Dan L Rowlett Junior, *CEO*
EMP: 212 EST: 2002
SQ FT: 2,000
SALES (est): 3.44MM Privately Held
Web: www.alliancemp.com
SIC: 3444 Sheet metal specialties, not stamped

(P-4945)
AMD INTERNATIONAL TECH LLC
Also Called: International Rite-Way Pdts
1725 S Campus Ave, Ontario (91761-4346)
PHONE..............................909 985-8300
EMP: 25 EST: 1994
SQ FT: 17,000
SALES (est): 3.67MM Privately Held
Web: www.intlrwp.com
SIC: 3444 1761 Sheet metal specialties, not stamped; Sheet metal work, nec

(P-4946)
AMERICAN AIRCRAFT PRODUCTS INC
Also Called: A A P
15411 S Broadway, Gardena (90248-2207)
PHONE..............................310 532-7434
Gerald R Tupper, *Pr*
EMP: 67 EST: 1975
SQ FT: 54,000
SALES (est): 9.77MM Privately Held
Web: www.americanaircraft.com
SIC: 3444 3599 Sheet metalwork; Machine shop, jobbing and repair

(P-4947)

AMERICAN RANGE CORPORATION
13592 Desmond St, Pacoima (91331-2315)
PHONE................................818 897-0808
Lorne G Deacon, *Pr*
Cindy M Cervantes, *
▲ **EMP:** 120 **EST:** 1989
SQ FT: 125,000
SALES (est): 22.74MM
SALES (corp-wide): 48.03MM **Privately Held**
Web: www.americanrange.com
SIC: 3444 3631 Hoods, range: sheet metal; Household cooking equipment
PA: Hatco Corporation
635 S 28th St
414 671-6350

(P-4948)

AMF ANAHEIM LLC
2100 E Orangewood Ave, Anaheim (92806-6108)
PHONE................................714 363-9206
▲ **EMP:** 120
SIC: 3444 Sheet metalwork

(P-4949)

ANOROC PRECISION SHTMTL INC
Also Called: Anoroc
19122 S Santa Fe Ave, Compton (90221-5910)
PHONE................................310 515-6015
Roxanne Zavala, *CEO*
Pete Corona, *Lending Vice President**
EMP: 25 **EST:** 1978
SQ FT: 15,000
SALES (est): 2.06MM **Privately Held**
Web: www.anoroc.com
SIC: 3444 Sheet metal specialties, not stamped

(P-4950)

AP PRECISION METALS INC
1185 Park Center Dr, Vista (92081-8343)
PHONE................................619 628-0003
Lane A Litke, *CEO*
Victor B Miller, *
Susan D Miller, *
EMP: 35 **EST:** 2000
SALES (est): 13.43MM **Privately Held**
Web: www.apprecision.com
SIC: 3444 Sheet metalwork

(P-4951)

ARMORCAST PRODUCTS COMPANY INC (DH)
9140 Lurline Ave, Chatsworth (91311-5923)
PHONE................................818 982-3600
▲ **EMP:** 220 **EST:** 1972
SALES (est): 42.41MM
SALES (corp-wide): 5.37B **Publicly Held**
Web: www.armorcastprod.com
SIC: 3444 3089 Sheet metalwork; Plastics processing
HQ: Hubbell Lenoir City, Inc.
3621 Industrial Park Dr
Lenoir City TN 37771
865 986-9726

(P-4952)

ARRK NORTH AMERICA INC
4660 La Jolla Village Dr Ste 100, San Diego (92122-4604)
PHONE................................858 552-1587
Carlos Herrera, *Pr*
Koji Tsujino, *
Takuya Kasai, *

▲ **EMP:** 145 **EST:** 1984
SALES (est): 17.46MM **Privately Held**
Web: www.arrk.com
SIC: 3444 Sheet metalwork
HQ: Arrk Corporation
2-2-9, Minamihonmachi, Chuo-Ku
Osaka OSK 541-0

(P-4953)

ARTISTIC WELDING
Also Called: Precision Sheet Metal
505 E Gardena Blvd, Gardena (90248-2915)
PHONE................................310 515-4922
George R Sandoval, *Pr*
Mary Sandoval, *
EMP: 65 **EST:** 1974
SQ FT: 85,000
SALES (est): 4.5MM **Privately Held**
Web: www.artistic-welding.com
SIC: 3444 Sheet metalwork

(P-4954)

ASM CONSTRUCTION INC
Also Called: American Sheet Metal
1947 John Towers Ave, El Cajon (92020-1117)
PHONE................................619 449-1966
Robert Burner, *Pr*
Ron Burner Junior, *CFO*
EMP: 41 **EST:** 1993
SQ FT: 9,000
SALES (est): 2.37MM **Privately Held**
SIC: 3444 Sheet metalwork

(P-4955)

BASMAT INC (PA)
Also Called: McStarlite
1531 240th St, Harbor City (90710-1308)
PHONE................................310 325-2063
John W Basso, *CEO*
John Allen Basso, *
Sharon Stelter, *
▲ **EMP:** 100 **EST:** 1952
SQ FT: 42,000
SALES (est): 19.67MM
SALES (corp-wide): 19.67MM **Privately Held**
Web: www.mcstarlite.com
SIC: 3444 Sheet metalwork

(P-4956)

BAY CITIES TIN SHOP INC
Also Called: Bay Cities Metal Products
301 E Alondra Blvd, Gardena (90248-2809)
PHONE................................310 660-0351
Majid Abai, *CEO*
Henry Kamberg, *
Gary Mugford, *
Debra Childress, *
EMP: 170 **EST:** 1958
SALES (est): 17.53MM **Privately Held**
Web: www.bcmet.com
SIC: 3444 Sheet metal specialties, not stamped

(P-4957)

BAY SHEET METAL INC
9343 Bond Ave Ste C, El Cajon (92021-2839)
PHONE................................619 401-9270
Michael Hayes, *Pr*
EMP: 28 **EST:** 2000
SALES (est): 3.49MM **Privately Held**
Web: www.westernbay.net
SIC: 3444 Sheet metalwork

(P-4958)

BEND-TEK INC (PA)
2205 S Yale St, Santa Ana (92704-4426)

PHONE................................714 210-8966
Melinda Nguyen, *CEO*
Mac Le, *Ofcr*
Eric Tran, *CFO*
EMP: 46 **EST:** 1999
SQ FT: 7,000
SALES (est): 7.72MM
SALES (corp-wide): 7.72MM **Privately Held**
Web: www.bendtekinc.com
SIC: 3444 Pipe, sheet metal

(P-4959)

BOOZAK INC
Also Called: K Squared Metals
508 Chaney St Ste A, Lake Elsinore (92530-2797)
PHONE................................951 245-6045
Kevin Kluzak, *Pr*
Kevin Booth, *
EMP: 45 **EST:** 2004
SALES (est): 2.35MM **Privately Held**
SIC: 3444 Sheet metal specialties, not stamped

(P-4960)

BROADWAY AC HTG & SHTMTL
Also Called: Broadway Sheet Metal
7855 Burnet Ave, Van Nuys (91405-1010)
PHONE................................818 781-1477
Alexander Merzel, *Pr*
Vince Lombardo, *
Anna Merzel, *
EMP: 35 **EST:** 1926
SQ FT: 7,000
SALES (est): 2.08MM **Privately Held**
Web: www.broadwaysm.com
SIC: 3444 Sheet metalwork

(P-4961)

C&O MANUFACTURING COMPANY INC
9640 Beverly Rd, Pico Rivera (90660-2137)
PHONE................................562 692-7525
Cesar Gonzalez, *Pr*
Oscar Valdez, *
EMP: 67 **EST:** 1995
SQ FT: 22,000
SALES (est): 9.27MM **Privately Held**
Web: www.cnomfg.com
SIC: 3444 Sheet metal specialties, not stamped

(P-4962)

CAL PAC SHEET METAL INC
Also Called: Cal Pac Sheet Metal
2720 S Main St Ste B, Santa Ana (92707-3404)
PHONE................................714 979-2733
Marushkah Kurtz, *CEO*
Bob Catalano, *
Carolyn Miller, *
EMP: 40 **EST:** 1977
SQ FT: 5,000
SALES (est): 4.53MM **Privately Held**
Web: www.calpacsheetmetal.com
SIC: 3444 Sheet metal specialties, not stamped

(P-4963)

CALIFORNIA CHASSIS INC
3356 E La Palma Ave, Anaheim (92806-2814)
PHONE................................714 666-8511
EMP: 110 **EST:** 1947
SALES (est): 1.7MM
SALES (corp-wide): 2.89MM **Privately Held**

SIC: 3444 2522 Metal housings, enclosures, casings, and other containers; Office furniture, except wood
PA: Arroyo Holdings Inc
898 N Fair Oaks Ave
626 765-9340

(P-4964)

CAPTIVE-AIRE SYSTEMS INC
1123 Washington Ave, Santa Monica (90403-4159)
PHONE................................310 876-8505
EMP: 23
SALES (corp-wide): 485.13MM **Privately Held**
Web: www.captiveaire.com
SIC: 3444 Sheet metalwork
PA: Captive-Aire Systems, Inc.
4641 Pragon Pk Rd Ste 104
919 882-2410

(P-4965)

CARLA SENTER
Also Called: Swift Fab
515 E Alondra Blvd, Gardena (90248-2903)
PHONE................................310 366-7295
Carla Senter, *Owner*
Robert Senter, *Owner*
EMP: 26 **EST:** 1988
SQ FT: 6,000
SALES (est): 2.65MM **Privately Held**
Web: www.swiftfab.com
SIC: 3444 Sheet metal specialties, not stamped

(P-4966)

CARTEL INDUSTRIES LLC
Also Called: Cartel Industries
17152 Armstrong Ave, Irvine (92614-5718)
PHONE................................949 474-3200
Gant Penick, *
▲ **EMP:** 49 **EST:** 1971
SQ FT: 30,000
SALES (est): 9.68MM **Privately Held**
Web: www.cartelind.com
SIC: 3444 Sheet metal specialties, not stamped

(P-4967)

CASTLE INDUSTRIES INC OF CALIFORNIA
Also Called: M.C. Gill
4056 Easy St, El Monte (91731-1054)
PHONE................................909 390-0899
EMP: 48
SIC: 3444 Sheet metalwork

(P-4968)

CEMCO LLC (DH)
Also Called: Cemco Steel
13191 Crossroads Pkwy N Ste 325, City Of Industry (91746-3438)
PHONE................................800 775-2362
Tom Porter, *Pr*
Toshihiko Iizuka, *
◆ **EMP:** 68 **EST:** 1973
SQ FT: 40,000
SALES (est): 78.14MM **Privately Held**
Web: www.cemcosteel.com
SIC: 3444 Sheet metalwork
HQ: Shoji Jfe America Holdings Inc
301 E Ocean Blvd Ste 1750
Long Beach CA 90802
562 637-3500

(P-4969)

CLARKWESTERN DIETRICH BUILDING
Also Called: Clarkdietrich Building Systems

6510 General Rd, Riverside (92509-0103)
PHONE...................................951 360-3500
Clark Dietrich, *Owner*
EMP: 40
SALES (corp-wide): 1.25B Publicly Held
Web: www.clarkdietrich.com
SIC: 3444 8711 3081 Studs and joists, sheet metal; Engineering services; Vinyl film and sheet
HQ: Clarkwestern Dietrich Building Systems Llc
9050 Cntre Pnte Dr Ste 40
West Chester OH 45069

(P-4970)
COAST SHEET METAL INC
990 W 17th St, Costa Mesa (92627-4403)
PHONE...................................949 645-2224
Wayne Chambers, *Pr*
Marna Chambers, *
EMP: 35 EST: 1960
SQ FT: 3,800
SALES (est): 2.65MM Privately Held
Web: www.coastsheetmetal.com
SIC: 3444 Sheet metalwork

(P-4971)
COMPUMERIC ENGINEERING INC
Also Called: Bearsaver
1390 S Milliken Ave, Ontario (91761-1585)
PHONE...................................909 605-7666
Jeannie Hankins, *CEO*
EMP: 45 EST: 1989
SQ FT: 30,000
SALES (est): 4.73MM Privately Held
Web: www.compumeric.com
SIC: 3444 Sheet metalwork

(P-4972)
COMPUTER METAL PRODUCTS CORP
Also Called: Vline Industries
370 E Easy St, Simi Valley (93065-1802)
PHONE...................................805 520-6966
Jim Visage, *Pr*
Karen Bender, *
EMP: 90 EST: 1971
SQ FT: 25,000
SALES (est): 5.31MM Privately Held
Web: www.computermetal.com
SIC: 3444 Sheet metalwork

(P-4973)
CONCISE FABRICATORS INC
Also Called: Concise Fabricators
7550 Panasonic Way, San Diego (92154-8207)
PHONE...................................520 746-3226
James Dean Johnson, *Pr*
Bill Maples, *
▼ EMP: 50 EST: 1981
SQ FT: 120,000
SALES (est): 3.31MM Privately Held
SIC: 3444 Sheet metalwork
PA: Blackbird Management Group, Llc
240 E Illinois St # 2004

(P-4974)
COWELCO
Also Called: Cowelco Steel Contractors
1634 W 14th St, Long Beach (90813-1205)
PHONE...................................562 432-5766
EMP: 50 EST: 1947
SALES (est): 4.68MM Privately Held
Web: www.cowelco.com
SIC: 3444 3441 3443 1791 Sheet metalwork ; Fabricated structural metal; Fabricated plate work (boiler shop); Structural steel erection

(P-4975)
COY INDUSTRIES INC
Also Called: E R C Company
2970 E Maria St, E Rncho Dmngz (90221-5802)
PHONE...................................310 603-2970
Michael Coy, *Pr*
James Patrick Coy, *
EMP: 95 EST: 1972
SQ FT: 50,000
SALES (est): 10.36MM Privately Held
Web: www.ercco.com
SIC: 3444 3469 Sheet metal specialties, not stamped; Metal stampings, nec

(P-4976)
DANRICH WELDING CO INC
155 N Eucla Ave, San Dimas (91773-2587)
PHONE...................................562 634-4811
Richard Schenk, *Pr*
EMP: 26 EST: 1970
SALES (est): 1.26MM Privately Held
Web: www.danrichwelding.com
SIC: 3444 7692 Sheet metalwork; Welding repair

(P-4977)
DAVE WHIPPLE SHEET METAL INC
1077 N Cuyamaca St, El Cajon (92020-1803)
PHONE...................................619 562-6962
Dave Whipple Senior, *Pr*
Carol Whipple, *
EMP: 34 EST: 1993
SQ FT: 9,000
SALES (est): 4.94MM Privately Held
Web: www.whipplesm.com
SIC: 3444 Sheet metalwork

(P-4978)
DECRA ROOFING SYSTEMS INC (DH)
Also Called: Decra
1230 Railroad St, Corona (92882-1837)
PHONE...................................951 272-8180
Willard C Hudson Junior, *Pr*
◆ EMP: 70 EST: 1998
SQ FT: 60,000
SALES (est): 25.14MM Privately Held
Web: www.decra.com
SIC: 3444 Metal roofing and roof drainage equipment
HQ: Fletcher Building Holdings Usa, Inc.
1230 Railroad St
Corona CA 92882
951 272-8180

(P-4979)
DELAFOIL HOLDINGS INC (PA)
18500 Von Karman Ave Ste 450, Irvine (92612-0504)
PHONE...................................949 752-4580
Drew Adams, *Dir*
EMP: 230 EST: 1999
SALES (est): 1.67MM
SALES (corp-wide): 1.67MM Privately Held
SIC: 3444 Radiator shields or enclosures, sheet metal

(P-4980)
DIMIC STEEL TECH INC
145 N 8th Ave, Upland (91786-5402)
PHONE...................................909 946-6767
Miles Dimic, *Pr*
Anna Dimic, *
▲ EMP: 24 EST: 1973
SQ FT: 45,000

SALES (est): 3.33MM Privately Held
Web: www.dimicsteeltech.com
SIC: 3444 Sheet metal specialties, not stamped

(P-4981)
DUR-RED PRODUCTS
5634 Costa Dr, Chino Hills (91709-3996)
PHONE...................................323 771-9000
Russell Smith, *Pr*
Linda Harrison, *
EMP: 50 EST: 1961
SALES (est): 1.73MM Privately Held
Web: www.activarcpg.com
SIC: 3444 3446 Sheet metalwork; Architectural metalwork

(P-4982)
DYNAMO AVIATION INC
9601 Mason Ave # A, Chatsworth (91311-5207)
P.O. Box 14040 (91409)
PHONE...................................818 785-9561
Masoud S Rabadi, *CEO*
Robin C Scott, *
Lary Hockens, *CAO*
Christopher Rabadi, *
Riley Drake, *Finance*
EMP: 86 EST: 1986
SQ FT: 27,000
SALES (est): 18.54MM Privately Held
Web: www.dynamoaviation.com
SIC: 3444 Sheet metalwork

(P-4983)
EQUIPMENT DESIGN & MFG INC
119 Explorer St, Pomona (91768-3278)
PHONE...................................909 594-2229
Rick Clewett, *CEO*
Steve Clewett, *
Ryan Clewett, *
EMP: 55 EST: 1976
SQ FT: 27,400
SALES (est): 6.43MM Privately Held
Web: www.equipmentdesign.net
SIC: 3444 Sheet metalwork

(P-4984)
ESM AEROSPACE INC
1203 W Isabel St, Burbank (91506-1407)
PHONE...................................818 841-3653
Jerome Flament, *Pr*
Rina Flament, *
EMP: 25 EST: 2005
SQ FT: 8,900
SALES (est): 2.96MM Privately Held
Web: www.esmaerospace.com
SIC: 3444 Casings, sheet metal

(P-4985)
EXCEL SHEET METAL INC (PA)
Also Called: Excel Bridge Manufacturing Co.
12001 Shoemaker Ave, Santa Fe Springs (90670-4718)
PHONE...................................562 944-0701
Craig E Vasquez, *CEO*
Jeffrey Vasquez, *
▼ EMP: 53 EST: 1952
SQ FT: 16,000
SALES (est): 2.7MM
SALES (corp-wide): 2.7MM Privately Held
Web: www.excelsheetmetal.com
SIC: 3444 1622 Sheet metalwork; Bridge construction

(P-4986)
FABRICATION CONCEPTS CORPORATION
Also Called: Fabcon
1800 E Saint Andrew Pl, Santa Ana (92705-5043)

PHONE...................................714 881-2000
◆ EMP: 180
Web: www.fabcon.com
SIC: 3444 Sheet metalwork

(P-4987)
FLETCHER BLDG HOLDINGS USA INC (DH)
1230 Railroad St, Corona (92882-1837)
PHONE...................................951 272-8180
Willard Hudson, *Pr*
John Miller, *
Steve Jones, *
◆ EMP: 70 EST: 1998
SQ FT: 60,000
SALES (est): 25.41MM Privately Held
Web: www.decra.com
SIC: 3444 Metal roofing and roof drainage equipment
HQ: Fletcher Building (Australia) Pty Ltd
1035 Nudgee Road
Banyo QLD 4014

(P-4988)
GAINES MANUFACTURING INC
12200 Kirkham Rd, Poway (92064-6806)
PHONE...................................858 486-7100
Ted Gaines, *Prin*
EMP: 40 EST: 1989
SQ FT: 23,000
SALES (est): 2.73MM Privately Held
Web: www.gainesmfg.com
SIC: 3444 Mail (post office) collection or storage boxes, sheet metal

(P-4989)
GREAT PACIFIC ELBOW LLC
Also Called: Great Pacific Elbow Company
13900 Sycamore Way, Chino (91710-7016)
PHONE...................................909 606-5551
Erik Gamm, *CEO*
Ron Searcy, *Pr*
EMP: 25 EST: 2021
SALES (est): 4.94MM
SALES (corp-wide): 59.06MM Privately Held
Web: www.greatpacificelbow.com
SIC: 3444 3827 Elbows, for air ducts, stovepipes, etc.: sheet metal; Telescopes: elbow, panoramic, sighting, fire control, etc.
PA: West Coast Steel & Processing Holdings, Llc
13568 Vintage Pl
909 393-8405

(P-4990)
HALLMARK METALS INC
600 W Foothill Blvd, Glendora (91741-2403)
PHONE...................................626 335-1263
Scott Schoenick, *Pr*
Joseph Allen Zerucha, *
David Peifer, *
Candice Schoenick, *
Marina Carmona, *
EMP: 28 EST: 1959
SQ FT: 23,000
SALES (est): 4.42MM Privately Held
Web: www.hallmarkmetals.com
SIC: 3444 3469 Sheet metalwork; Machine parts, stamped or pressed metal

(P-4991)
HAMILTON METALCRAFT INC
848 N Fair Oaks Ave, Pasadena (91103-3046)
PHONE...................................626 795-4811
Sandra Stahler, *Pr*
EMP: 25 EST: 1966
SQ FT: 10,000

▲ = Import ▼ = Export
◆ = Import/Export

SALES (est): 2.15MM **Privately Held**
Web: www.hmetal.com
SIC: **3444** Casings, sheet metal

(P-4992)
INTERNATIONAL WEST INC
Also Called: Continental Industries
1025 N Armando St, Anaheim
(92806-2606)
PHONE..............................714 632-9190
Jeffery Aaron Hayden, *Pr*
Tami Hayden, *
EMP: 31 EST: 1985
SQ FT: 8,500
SALES (est): 5.56MM **Privately Held**
Web: www.continental-ind.com
SIC: **3444** Sheet metalwork

(P-4993)
JBW PRECISION INC
2650 Lavery Ct, Newbury Park
(91320-1581)
PHONE..............................805 499-1973
David Ogden, *Pr*
Jack Ogden, *
Dawn Spalding, *
EMP: 23 EST: 1969
SQ FT: 2,500
SALES (est): 4.18MM **Privately Held**
Web: www.jbwprecision.com
SIC: **3444** Sheet metal specialties, not
stamped

(P-4994)
JEFFREY FABRICATION LLC
Also Called: C & J Metal Prducts
6323 Alondra Blvd, Paramount
(90723-3750)
PHONE..............................562 634-3101
Lilly Chang, *Managing Member*
EMP: 50 EST: 2011
SALES (est): 2.56MM **Privately Held**
Web: www.cjmetals.com
SIC: **3444** Sheet metalwork

(P-4995)
KB SHEETMETAL FABRICATION INC
17371 Mount Wynne Cir # B, Fountain
Valley (92708-4107)
PHONE..............................714 979-1780
Cong Nguyen, *Pr*
EMP: 25 EST: 2001
SQ FT: 12,000
SALES (est): 4.81MM **Privately Held**
Web: www.kb-sheetmetal.com
SIC: **3444** 3441 Sheet metalwork;
Fabricated structural metal

(P-4996)
L & T PRECISION LLC
12105 Kirkham Rd, Poway (92064-6870)
PHONE..............................858 513-7874
Loc Nguyen, *Pr*
Loc Nguyen, *Pr*
Tho Nguyen, *
Tien D Nguyen, *
EMP: 110 EST: 1984
SQ FT: 48,000
SALES (est): 18.78MM **Privately Held**
Web: www.ltprecision.com
SIC: **3444** 3599 Sheet metal specialties, not
stamped; Machine and other job shop work

(P-4997)
LLC WALKER WEST
Impac International
11445 Pacific Ave, Fontana (92337-8227)
PHONE..............................951 685-9660
Kory Lavoy, *Div Mgr*

EMP: 52
Web: www.impac-international.com
SIC: **3444** 3315 Housings for business
machines, sheet metal; Steel wire and
related products
PA: Walker West, Llc
1555 S Vintage Ave

(P-4998)
LYNAM INDUSTRIES INC
13050 Santa Ana Ave, Fontana
(92337-6948)
PHONE..............................951 360-1919
EMP: 28
Web: www.lynaminc.com
SIC: **3444** Sheet metalwork
PA: Lynam Industries, Inc.
11027 Jasmine St

(P-4999)
LYNAM INDUSTRIES INC (PA)
11027 Jasmine St, Fontana (92337-6955)
PHONE..............................951 360-1919
Troy Lindstrom, *Pr*
Greg Traeger Pe, *Dir*
▲ EMP: 57 EST: 1989
SQ FT: 39,000
SALES (est): 2.17MM **Privately Held**
Web: www.lynaminc.com
SIC: **3444** Sheet metal specialties, not
stamped

(P-5000)
M-5 STEEL MFG INC (PA)
1353 Philadelphia St, Pomona
(91766-5554)
PHONE..............................323 263-9383
Douglas Linkon, *CEO*
▲ EMP: 46 EST: 1970
SALES (est): 5.43MM
SALES (corp-wide): 5.43MM **Privately
Held**
Web: www.m5steel.com
SIC: **3444** 3443 Gutters, sheet metal;
Fabricated plate work (boiler shop)

(P-5001)
MARATHON FINISHING SYSTEMS INC
Also Called: Manufacturing
42355 Rio Nedo, Temecula (92590-3701)
PHONE..............................310 791-5601
Christian Rerucha, *Pr*
▲ EMP: 25 EST: 2004
SALES (est): 2.59MM **Privately Held**
Web: www.marathonspraybooths.com
SIC: **3444** Booths, spray: prefabricated
sheet metal

(P-5002)
MARINE & REST FABRICATORS INC
3768 Dalbergia St, San Diego
(92113-3815)
PHONE..............................619 232-7267
Carlos Velazquez, *Pr*
EMP: 44 EST: 1986
SQ FT: 7,600
SALES (est): 4.44MM **Privately Held**
Web: www.mrf.bz
SIC: **3444** 3731 Restaurant sheet metalwork
; Military ships, building and repairing

(P-5003)
MAYONI ENTERPRISES
10320 Glenoaks Blvd, Pacoima
(91331-1699)
PHONE..............................818 896-0026
Isaac Benyehuda, *CEO*

Isaac Glazer, *
EMP: 60 EST: 1984
SQ FT: 17,000
SALES (est): 3.89MM **Privately Held**
Web: www.mayoni.com
SIC: **3444** 3581 Sheet metal specialties, not
stamped; Automatic vending machines

(P-5004)
MEADOWS SHEET METAL AND AC INC
Also Called: Meadows Mechanical
333 Crown Vista Dr, Gardena (90248-1705)
PHONE..............................310 615-1125
Madonna Rose, *CEO*
Thomas Nolan, *
Dennis Johnson, *
EMP: 50 EST: 1949
SQ FT: 5,000
SALES (est): 9.58MM **Privately Held**
SIC: **3444** 1711 Sheet metalwork; Heating
and air conditioning contractors

(P-5005)
METAL ENGINEERING INC
1642 S Sacramento Ave, Ontario
(91761-8052)
PHONE..............................626 334-1819
Arthur A Valenzuela, *Pr*
EMP: 23 EST: 2002
SQ FT: 14,000
SALES (est): 1.05MM **Privately Held**
Web: www.metaleng.com
SIC: **3444** 1761 Awnings and canopies;
Sheet metal work, nec

(P-5006)
METAL MASTER INC
4611 Overland Ave, San Diego
(92123-1233)
PHONE..............................858 292-8880
Benito Garrido, *Pr*
Donald Wagner, *
Dianne Yeaman, *
EMP: 41 EST: 1987
SQ FT: 30,000
SALES (est): 4.36MM **Privately Held**
Web: www.metalmasterinc.com
SIC: **3444** 3541 Sheet metalwork; Milling
machines

(P-5007)
METAL-FAB SERVICES INDUST INC
2500 E Miraloma Way, Anaheim
(92806-1608)
PHONE..............................714 630-7771
Carlos Mondragon, *Pr*
▲ EMP: 34 EST: 2003
SQ FT: 28,000
SALES (est): 5.96MM **Privately Held**
Web: www.metalfabsi.com
SIC: **3444** Sheet metal specialties, not
stamped

(P-5008)
MMP SHEET METAL INC
501 Commercial Way, La Habra
(90631-6170)
PHONE..............................562 691-1055
Frank Varanelli, *Pr*
EMP: 30 EST: 1977
SQ FT: 8,500
SALES (est): 2.29MM **Privately Held**
Web: www.mmp-sheetmetal.com
SIC: **3444** Sheet metal specialties, not
stamped

(P-5009)
MODULAR METAL FABRICATORS INC
24600 Nandina Ave, Moreno Valley
(92551-9518)
PHONE..............................951 242-3154
E E Gearing, *CEO*
Don Gearing, *
Mike Beam, *
John Wingate, *
Pat Geary, *
▲ EMP: 130 EST: 1970
SQ FT: 200,000
SALES (est): 21.24MM **Privately Held**
SIC: **3444** Pipe, sheet metal

(P-5010)
MS INDUSTRIAL SHTMTL INC
Also Called: Baghouse and Indus Shtmtl Svcs
1731 Pomona Rd, Corona (92878-4363)
PHONE..............................951 272-6610
Nancy Nicola, *CEO*
Warren Lampkin, *
Dan Suffel, *
EMP: 130 EST: 1985
SQ FT: 35,000
SALES (est): 24MM **Privately Held**
Web: www.1888baghouse.com
SIC: **3444** Sheet metalwork

(P-5011)
ORECO DUCT SYSTEMS INC
5119 Azusa Canyon Rd, Baldwin Park
(91706-1833)
P.O. Box 1460 (91706-7460)
PHONE..............................626 337-8832
Robert I Havai, *Pr*
EMP: 110 EST: 1985
SQ FT: 57,600
SALES (est): 759.07K **Privately Held**
Web: www.orecoduct.com
SIC: **3444** Sheet metalwork

(P-5012)
OXNARD PRCSION FABRICATION INC
Also Called: O P F
2200 Teal Club Rd, Oxnard (93030-8640)
PHONE..............................805 985-0447
David Garza, *Pr*
David Garza, *Pr*
Robert Valles, *
EMP: 30 EST: 1987
SQ FT: 107,000
SALES (est): 3.87MM **Privately Held**
Web: www.opfmfg.com
SIC: **3444** 3469 3443 Sheet metal
specialties, not stamped, Metal stampings,
nec; Fabricated plate work (boiler shop)

(P-5013)
PACIFIC AWARD METALS INC
Also Called: Award Metals
10302 Birtcher Dr, Jurupa Valley
(91752-1829)
PHONE..............................360 694-9530
Mark Shaff, *Mgr*
EMP: 40
SALES (corp-wide): 1.38B **Publicly Held**
Web:
www.gibraltarbuildingproducts.com
SIC: **3444** 3443 Concrete forms, sheet metal
; Fabricated plate work (boiler shop)
HQ: Pacific Award Metals, Inc.
1450 Virginia Ave
Baldwin Park CA 91706
626 814-4410

(P-5014)
PACIFIC AWARD METALS INC (HQ)
Also Called: Award Metals
1450 Virginia Ave, Baldwin Park
(91706-5819)
PHONE..........................626 814-4410
Brian J Lipke, CEO
W Brent Taylor, *
Frank Fulford, *
EMP: 100 EST: 2001
SQ FT: 110,000
SALES (est): 48.48MM
SALES (corp-wide): 1.38B Publicly Held
Web:
www.gibraltarbuildingproducts.com
SIC: 3444 3312 Sheet metalwork; Blast
furnaces and steel mills
PA: Gibraltar Industries, Inc.
3556 Lake Shore Rd
716 826-6500

(P-5015)
PACIFIC MARINE SHEET METAL CORPORATION
Also Called: Southwest Manufacturing Svcs
2650 Jamacha Rd Ste 147 Pmb, El Cajon
(92019-4319)
PHONE..........................858 869-8900
◆ EMP: 200
SIC: 3444 Sheet metalwork

(P-5016)
PARIS PRECISION LLC
1650 Ramada Dr, Paso Robles
(93446-5976)
PHONE..........................805 239-2500
EMP: 150
SIC: 3444 Sheet metalwork

(P-5017)
PCI INDUSTRIES INC
6501 Potello St, Commerce (90040)
PHONE..........................323 728-0004
Greg Skilley, VP
EMP: 28
SALES (corp-wide): 45.1MM Privately
Held
Web: www.pottorff.com
SIC: 3444 3564 Metal ventilating equipment;
Filters, air: furnaces, air conditioning
equipment, etc.
PA: Pci Industries, Inc.
5101 Blue Mound Rd
817 509-2300

(P-5018)
PCI INDUSTRIES INC
Pottorff
700 S Vail Ave, Montebello (90640-4954)
PHONE..........................323 889-6770
EMP: 28
SALES (corp-wide): 45.1MM Privately
Held
Web: www.pottorff.com
SIC: 3444 Sheet metalwork
PA: Pci Industries, Inc.
5101 Blue Mound Rd
817 509-2300

(P-5019)
PINNACLE PRECISION SHTMTL CORP
Fabnet
5410 E La Palma Ave, Anaheim
(92807-2023)
PHONE..........................714 777-3129
Robert F Denham, Brnch Mgr
EMP: 88

SALES (corp-wide): 48.83MM Privately
Held
Web: www.pinnaclemetal.com
SIC: 3444 3599 Metal housings, enclosures,
casings, and other containers; Machine
shop, jobbing and repair
HQ: Pinnacle Precision Sheet Metal
Corporation
5410 E La Palma Ave
Anaheim CA 92807
714 777-3129

(P-5020)
PINNACLE PRECISION SHTMTL CORP (HQ)
5410 E La Palma Ave, Anaheim
(92807-2023)
PHONE..........................714 777-3129
David Oddo, Pr
Brian Mclaughlin, VP
Paul Oddo, Stockholder*
EMP: 61 EST: 1973
SALES (est): 27.14MM
SALES (corp-wide): 48.83MM Privately
Held
Web: www.pinnaclemetal.com
SIC: 3444 Sheet metalwork
PA: The Partner Companies Llc
155 N Wacker Dr Ste 4670
312 883-7266

(P-5021)
PLENUMS PLUS LLC
67 Brisbane St, Chula Vista (91910-1065)
PHONE..........................619 422-5515
EMP: 75 EST: 1986
SALES (est): 5.39MM Privately Held
Web: www.plenumsplus.com
SIC: 3444 Sheet metalwork

(P-5022)
PNA CONSTRUCTION TECH INC
301 Espee St Ste E, Bakersfield
(93301-2659)
PHONE..........................661 326-1700
Matt Wilen, Prin
EMP: 33
SALES (corp-wide): 5.83MM Privately
Held
Web: www.pna-inc.com
SIC: 3444 Concrete forms, sheet metal
PA: P.N.A. Construction Technologies, Inc.
1349 W Bryn Mawr Ave
770 668-9500

(P-5023)
PRECISE INDUSTRIES INC
610 Neptune Ave, Brea (92821-2909)
PHONE..........................714 482-2333
Terry D Wells, Pr
Robert L Wells, *
▲ EMP: 120 EST: 2004
SQ FT: 78,000
SALES (est): 12.13MM Privately Held
Web: www.preciseind.com
SIC: 3444 3679 3599 Sheet metalwork;
Electronic circuits; Machine and other job
shop work

(P-5024)
PRISM AEROSPACE
3087 12th St, Riverside (92507-4904)
PHONE..........................951 582-2850
Eng Tan, CEO
Peng Tan, *
EMP: 50 EST: 2014
SQ FT: 100,000
SALES (est): 8.17MM Privately Held
Web: www.prismaerospace.com

SIC: 3444 3812 Forming machine work,
sheet metal; Aircraft/aerospace flight
instruments and guidance systems

(P-5025)
QUALITY FABRICATION INC (PA)
4020 Garner Rd, Riverside (92501-1006)
PHONE..........................818 407-5015
Pradeep Kumar, CEO
▲ EMP: 99 EST: 1980
SALES (est): 14.95MM
SALES (corp-wide): 14.95MM Privately
Held
Web: www.quality-fab.com
SIC: 3444 Sheet metal specialties, not
stamped

(P-5026)
R & D METAL FABRICATORS INC
Also Called: R&D Metal
5250 Rancho Rd, Huntington Beach
(92647-2052)
PHONE..........................714 891-4878
EMP: 36 EST: 1971
SALES (est): 5.78MM Privately Held
Web: www.rdmetal.com
SIC: 3444 Sheet metalwork

(P-5027)
RAH INDUSTRIES INC (PA)
24800 Avenue Rockefeller, Valencia
(91355-3467)
PHONE..........................661 295-5190
EMP: 185 EST: 1971
SALES (est): 21.83MM
SALES (corp-wide): 21.83MM Privately
Held
Web: www.rah-ind.com
SIC: 3444 3599 Sheet metalwork; Machine
shop, jobbing and repair

(P-5028)
RAMDA METAL SPECIALTIES INC
Also Called: Ramda Metal Specialties
13012 Crenshaw Blvd, Gardena
(90249-1544)
PHONE..........................310 538-2136
Daniel Guevara, CEO
EMP: 25 EST: 1985
SQ FT: 25,000
SALES (est): 4.12MM Privately Held
Web: www.ramda.com
SIC: 3444 Metal housings, enclosures,
casings, and other containers

(P-5029)
RIGOS EQUIPMENT MFG LLC
Also Called: Rigos Sheet Metal
14501 Joanbridge St, Baldwin Park
(91706-1749)
PHONE..........................626 813-6621
EMP: 23 EST: 1977
SQ FT: 3,600
SALES (est): 4.91MM Privately Held
Web: www.rigosequipment.com
SIC: 3444 Sheet metalwork

(P-5030)
ROBERT F CHAPMAN INC
43100 Exchange Pl, Lancaster
(93535-4524)
PHONE..........................661 940-9482
Tim Mitchell, CEO
John H Mitchell, *
Paulette Mitchell, *
EMP: 53 EST: 1959
SQ FT: 62,000
SALES (est): 4.92MM Privately Held
Web: www.robertfchapman.com

SIC: 3444 3549 Sheet metalwork;
Metalworking machinery, nec

(P-5031)
ROMLA CO
Also Called: Romla Ventilator Co
9668 Heinrich Hertz Dr Ste D, San Diego
(92154-7919)
PHONE..........................619 946-1224
Ronald W Haneline, CEO
Robert Haneline, *
Bob Haneline, *
▲ EMP: 33 EST: 1945
SQ FT: 18,000
SALES (est): 6.52MM Privately Held
Web: www.romlair.com
SIC: 3444 Metal ventilating equipment

(P-5032)
SA SERVING LINES INC
Also Called: G A Systems
226 W Carleton Ave, Orange (92867-3608)
PHONE..........................714 848-7529
Steve Aderson, CEO
Pat Devalle, CFO
Virginia Anderson, Sec
EMP: 29 EST: 2011
SALES (est): 1.66MM Privately Held
Web: www.gasystemsmfg.com
SIC: 3444 Metal housings, enclosures,
casings, and other containers

(P-5033)
SHEET METAL ENGINEERING
1780 Voyager Ave, Simi Valley
(93063-3301)
PHONE..........................805 306-0390
Kenneth Chamberlain, Pr
Kenneth Chamberlain, Pr
David Reed, *
Kathy Chou, *
EMP: 25 EST: 1983
SQ FT: 21,000
SALES (est): 2.4MM Privately Held
Web: www.sheetmetaleng.com
SIC: 3444 1799 Sheet metal specialties, not
stamped; Welding on site

(P-5034)
SMS FABRICATIONS INC
11698 Warm Springs Rd, Riverside
(92505-5862)
PHONE..........................951 351-6828
Michael A Uranga, CEO
Sandy Sligar, *
Scott Sligar, *
EMP: 36 EST: 2003
SALES (est): 3.54MM Privately Held
Web: www.sheetmetalspecialists.com
SIC: 3444 Sheet metalwork

(P-5035)
SPAN-O-MATIC INC
825 Columbia St, Brea (92821-2917)
PHONE..........................714 256-4700
Wolfgang Arnold, Pr
Lynda Arnold, *
Erik A Arnold, *
Carl Arnold, *
EMP: 40 EST: 1972
SQ FT: 50,000
SALES (est): 4.39MM Privately Held
Web: www.spanomatic.com
SIC: 3444 Sheet metalwork

(P-5036)
SPEC-BUILT SYSTEMS INC
2150 Michael Faraday Dr, San Diego
(92154-7903)
P.O. Box 531581 (92153)

▲ = Import ▼ = Export
◆ = Import/Export

PHONE..............................619 661-8100
Randy Eifler, *Pr*
EMP: 75 **EST:** 1986
SQ FT: 25,000
SALES (est): 19.94MM **Privately Held**
Web: www.specbuilt.com
SIC: 3444 Sheet metalwork

(P-5037)
SPECIALTY FABRICATIONS INC
2674 Westhills Ct, Simi Valley
(93065-6234)
PHONE..............................805 579-9730
Mark Zimmerman, *Pr*
Randy Zimmerman, *
EMP: 49 **EST:** 1978
SQ FT: 80,000
SALES (est): 2.15MM **Privately Held**
Web: www.specfabinc.com
SIC: 3444 3599 Sheet metalwork; Machine
and other job shop work

(P-5038)
SPRAY ENCLOSURE TECH INC
Also Called: Spray Tech
1427 N Linden Ave, Rialto (92376-8601)
PHONE..............................909 419-7011
Tyler Rand, *Pr*
▲ **EMP:** 30 **EST:** 1994
SQ FT: 59,000
SALES (est): 10.31MM **Privately Held**
Web: www.spraytech.com
SIC: 3444 Booths, spray: prefabricated
sheet metal

(P-5039)
STEELDYNE INDUSTRIES
Also Called: ABC Sheet Metal
2871 E La Cresta Ave, Anaheim
(92806-1817)
PHONE..............................714 630-6200
Jeff Duveneck, *Pr*
Richard Duveneck, *
EMP: 40 **EST:** 1995
SQ FT: 20,000
SALES (est): 10.17MM **Privately Held**
Web: www.abcsheetmetal.com
SIC: 3444 Sheet metal specialties, not
stamped

(P-5040)
STEIN INDUSTRIES INC (PA)
4005 Artesia Ave, Fullerton (92833-2519)
PHONE..............................714 522-4560
Rudi Steinhilber, *CEO*
Theodore Steinhilber, *
Dave Spivy, *
EMP: 30 **EST:** 1982
SQ FT: 30,800
SALES (est): 4.3MM
SALES (corp-wide): 4.3MM **Privately Held**
Web: www.stein-industries.com
SIC: 3444 2599 Sheet metalwork; Work
benches, factory

(P-5041)
STOLL METALCRAFT INC
24808 Anza Dr, Valencia (91355-1258)
PHONE..............................661 295-0401
Gunter Stoll, *Pr*
EMP: 105 **EST:** 1973
SQ FT: 45,000
SALES (est): 24.7MM **Privately Held**
Web: www.stoll-metalcraft.com
SIC: 3444 Sheet metal specialties, not
stamped

(P-5042)
STRETCH FORMING CORPORATION

Also Called: Sfc
804 S Redlands Ave, Perris (92570-2478)
PHONE..............................951 443-0911
Brian D Geary, *Owner*
Brian D Geary, *CEO*
▲ **EMP:** 85 **EST:** 2009
SQ FT: 97,000
SALES (est): 14.27MM **Privately Held**
Web: www.stretchformingcorp.com
SIC: 3444 Sheet metalwork

(P-5043)
SUPERIOR DUCT FABRICATION INC
1683 Mount Vernon Ave, Pomona
(91768-3300)
PHONE..............................909 620-8565
Mike Hilgert, *CEO*
Kerry Bootke, *
◆ **EMP:** 107 **EST:** 2002
SQ FT: 3,900
SALES (est): 19.01MM **Privately Held**
Web: www.sdfab.com
SIC: 3444 Ducts, sheet metal

(P-5044)
T & F SHEET MTLS FAB MCHNING I
15607 New Century Dr, Gardena
(90248-2128)
PHONE..............................310 516-8548
Thomas Medina, *Pr*
Hector Medina, *
EMP: 32 **EST:** 2005
SQ FT: 9,800
SALES (est): 3.55MM **Privately Held**
Web: www.tnfsheetmetal.com
SIC: 3444 Sheet metalwork

(P-5045)
TFC MANUFACTURING INC
4001 Watson Plaza Dr, Lakewood
(90712-4034)
PHONE..............................562 426-9559
Majid Shahbazi, *Pr*
Hamid Sharifat, *
EMP: 81 **EST:** 1999
SQ FT: 28,500
SALES (est): 10.07MM **Privately Held**
Web: www.tfcmfg.com
SIC: 3444 Sheet metalwork

(P-5046)
TIDE ROCK HOLDINGS LLC (PA)
343 S Highway 101 Ste 200, Solana Beach
(92075-1879)
PHONE..............................858 204-7438
Ryan Peddycord, *CEO*
EMP: 216 **EST:** 2013
SALES (est): 68.36MM
SALES (corp-wide): 68.36MM **Privately Held**
Web: www.tiderock.com
SIC: 3444 Sheet metalwork

(P-5047)
TREND TECHNOLOGIES LLC (DH)
Also Called: Trend Technologies
4626 Eucalyptus Ave, Chino (91710-9215)
P.O. Box 51 5001 (90051-5001)
PHONE..............................909 597-7861
Earl Payton, *Managing Member*
▲ **EMP:** 220 **EST:** 2002
SQ FT: 125,000
SALES (est): 145.24MM **Privately Held**
Web: www.trendtechnologies.com

SIC: **3444** 3469 3499 3089 Metal housings,
enclosures, casings, and other containers;
Electronic enclosures, stamped or pressed
metal; Aquarium accessories, metal;
Injection molding of plastics
HQ: Ttl Holdings, Llc
4626 Eucalyptus Ave
Chino CA 91710
909 597-7861

(P-5048)
TRI PRECISION SHEETMETAL INC
1104 N Armando St, Anaheim
(92806-2609)
PHONE..............................714 632-8838
Leonardo Cortes, *CEO*
Ross Morrow, *
Rob Morrow, *
EMP: 40 **EST:** 1988
SALES (est): 5.15MM **Privately Held**
Web: www.triprecision.com
SIC: 3444 3542 Sheet metalwork; Sheet
metalworking machines

(P-5049)
TRIO METAL STAMPING INC
Also Called: Trio Metal Stamping
15318 Proctor Ave, City Of Industry
(91745-1023)
PHONE..............................626 336-1228
Damian Rickard, *CEO*
Georgia Boris, *
EMP: 53 **EST:** 1947
SQ FT: 75,000
SALES (est): 4.92MM **Privately Held**
Web: www.triometalstamping.com
SIC: 3444 3469 Sheet metalwork; Stamping
metal for the trade

(P-5050)
TRU-DUCT INC
2515 Industry St, Oceanside (92054-4807)
PHONE..............................619 660-3858
Drew E Miles, *CEO*
EMP: 45 **EST:** 1991
SALES (est): 9.76MM **Privately Held**
Web: www.tru-duct.com
SIC: 3444 Ducts, sheet metal

(P-5051)
US PRECISION SHEET METAL INC
Also Called: U S Precision Manufacturing
4020 Garner Rd, Riverside (92501-1006)
PHONE..............................951 276-2611
Amanda Hawkins, *CEO*
Ray Mayo, *
Sal Giulano, *
EMP: 68 **EST:** 1981
SQ FT: 25,000
SALES (est): 7.31MM **Privately Held**
Web: www.usprecision.net
SIC: 3444 Sheet metal specialties, not
stamped

(P-5052)
VALLEY PRECISION MET PDTS INC
Also Called: Valley Precision Metal Pdts
27771 Avenue Hopkins, Valencia
(91355-1223)
PHONE..............................661 607-0100
Howard Vermillion Junior, *Pr*
Jon Cantor, *
EMP: 30 **EST:** 1948
SQ FT: 5,800
SALES (est): 4.69MM **Privately Held**
Web: www.veiaerospace.com

SIC: **3444** Sheet metalwork

(P-5053)
VERSAFAB CORP (PA)
15919 S Broadway, Gardena (90248-2489)
PHONE..............................800 421-1822
Edward Penfold Junior, *Ch Bd*
Joe Flynn, *Pr*
EMP: 40 **EST:** 1982
SQ FT: 35,000
SALES (est): 5.05MM
SALES (corp-wide): 5.05MM **Privately Held**
Web: www.versafabcorp.com
SIC: 3444 3465 3496 3469 Sheet metalwork
; Moldings or trim, automobile: stamped
metal; Miscellaneous fabricated wire
products; Metal stampings, nec

(P-5054)
VERSAFORM CORPORATION
Also Called: Sonaca North America
1377 Specialty Dr, Vista (92081-8521)
PHONE..............................760 599-4477
Ronals S Saks, *Pr*
EMP: 73 **EST:** 1974
SQ FT: 24,000
SALES (est): 3.69MM **Privately Held**
Web: www.lmiaerospace.com
SIC: 3444 3549 3398 Forming machine
work, sheet metal; Metalworking machinery,
nec; Metal heat treating
HQ: Lmi Aerospace, Inc.
3600 Mueller Rd
Saint Charles MO 63301
636 946-6525

(P-5055)
VTS SHEETMETAL SPECIALIST CO
13831 Seaboard Cir, Garden Grove
(92843-3908)
PHONE..............................714 237-1420
Thomas Bonnett, *Pr*
Tom Bonnett, *
Sa H Vo, *Sec*
EMP: 31 **EST:** 1986
SQ FT: 21,300
SALES (est): 4.86MM **Privately Held**
Web: www.vtsfab.com
SIC: 3444 Metal housings, enclosures,
casings, and other containers

(P-5056)
WCS EQUIPMENT HOLDINGS LLC
Also Called: Steelco USA
13006 14th St, Chino (91710-4305)
PHONE..............................909 393-8405
Erik Gamm, *Prin*
EMP: 59
SALES (corp-wide): 59.06MM **Privately Held**
Web: www.steelcousa.com
SIC: 3444 Sheet metalwork
HQ: Wcs Equipment Holdings, Llc
13568 Vintage Pl
Chino CA 91710

(P-5057)
WILL-MANN INC
225 E Santa Fe Ave, Fullerton
(92832-1917)
P.O. Box 976 (92836-0976)
PHONE..............................714 870-0350
Manfred Frischmuth, *Pr*
Lore Frischmuth, *
Sabina Andrassy, *
EMP: 40 **EST:** 1968
SQ FT: 30,000

SALES (est): 4.56MM **Privately Held**
Web: www.will-mann.com
SIC: 3444 7692 3471 Sheet metal
specialties, not stamped; Welding repair;
Plating and polishing

3446 Architectural Metalwork

(P-5058)
ADF INCORPORATED
Also Called: Able Design and Fabrication
1550 W Mahalo Pl, Rancho Dominguez
(90220-5422)
PHONE..............................310 669-9700
Lou Mannick, *Pr*
EMP: 30 EST: 1993
SQ FT: 23,000
SALES (est): 3.81MM
SALES (corp-wide): 46.29MM **Privately
Held**
Web: www.adfvisual.com
SIC: 3446 Partitions and supports/studs,
including acoustical systems
PA: Peerless Industries, Inc.
2300 White Oak Cir
630 375-5100

(P-5059)
**ALABAMA METAL INDUSTRIES
CORP**
Also Called: Amico Fontana
11093 Beech Ave, Fontana (92337-7268)
P.O. Box 310353 (92331-0353)
PHONE..............................909 350-9280
Lilly Mc Donalds, *Brnch Mgr*
EMP: 25
SALES (corp-wide): 92.55MM **Privately
Held**
Web: www.amicoglobal.com
SIC: 3446 Open flooring and grating for
construction
PA: Alabama Metal Industries Corporation
3245 Fayette Ave
205 787-2611

(P-5060)
**CLARK STEEL FABRICATORS
INC**
12610 Vigilante Rd, Lakeside (92040-1113)
P.O. Box 1370 (92040-0910)
PHONE..............................619 390-1502
Kimberley L Clark, *Pr*
Kevin B Clark, *
EMP: 45 EST: 1977
SQ FT: 12,500
SALES (est): 7.68MM **Privately Held**
Web: www.clarksteelfab.com
SIC: 3446 3441 Architectural metalwork;
Fabricated structural metal

(P-5061)
DENNISON INC
Also Called: Maxxon Company
17901 Railroad St, City Of Industry
(91748-1113)
PHONE..............................626 965-8917
Dennis Ma, *CEO*
◆ EMP: 47 EST: 1990
SQ FT: 26,000
SALES (est): 2MM **Privately Held**
SIC: 3446 Architectural metalwork

(P-5062)
**EUROCRAFT ARCHTECTURAL
MET INC**
5619 Watcher St, Bell Gardens
(90201-1632)
PHONE..............................323 771-1323
John Fechter, *Pr*

EMP: 30 EST: 1976
SQ FT: 30,000
SALES (est): 4.36MM **Privately Held**
Web: www.eurocraftmetal.com
SIC: 3446 Architectural metalwork

(P-5063)
FORMS AND SURFACES INC
6395 Cindy Ln, Carpinteria (93013-2909)
PHONE..............................805 684-8626
George Hickmann, *Brnch Mgr*
EMP: 80
SALES (corp-wide): 94.26MM **Privately
Held**
Web: www.forms-surfaces.com
SIC: 3446 Architectural metalwork
PA: Forms And Surfaces, Inc.
30 Pine St
412 781-9003

(P-5064)
HART & COOLEY INC
Also Called: HART & COOLEY, INC.
10855 Philadelphia Ave Ste B, Jurupa
Valley (91752-3289)
PHONE..............................951 332-5132
EMP: 44
Web: www.hartandcooley.com
SIC: 3446 Architectural metalwork
HQ: Hart & Cooley Llc
4460 44th St Se Ste F
Grand Rapids MI 49512
800 433-6341

(P-5065)
J TALLEY CORPORATION (PA)
Also Called: Talley Metal Fabrication
989 W 7th St, San Jacinto (92582-3813)
P.O. Box 850 (92581-0850)
PHONE..............................951 654-2123
Joe Brown Talley, *CEO*
EMP: 86 EST: 1963
SQ FT: 13,400
SALES (est): 6.79MM
SALES (corp-wide): 6.79MM **Privately
Held**
Web: www.talleymetalfabrication.com
SIC: 3446 3444 Railings, prefabricated metal
; Culverts, flumes, and pipes

(P-5066)
**JANSEN ORNAMENTAL SUPPLY
CO**
10926 Schmidt Rd, El Monte (91733-2791)
PHONE..............................626 442-0271
Mike Jansen, *CEO*
Harry Jansen, *
John Jansen, *
▲ EMP: 30 EST: 1960
SQ FT: 22,000
SALES (est): 2.51MM **Privately Held**
Web: www.jansensupply.com
SIC: 3446 Architectural metalwork

(P-5067)
K & J WIRE PRODUCTS CORP
1220 N Lance Ln, Anaheim (92806-1812)
PHONE..............................714 816-0360
Klaus Borutzki, *Pr*
Barbara Borutzki, *
EMP: 25 EST: 1989
SQ FT: 21,000
SALES (est): 952.89K **Privately Held**
Web: www.kjwire.com
SIC: 3446 3496 5046 3315 Architectural
metalwork; Miscellaneous fabricated wire
products; Store fixtures and display
equipment; Wire and fabricated wire
products

(P-5068)
LAVI INDUSTRIES LLC (PA)
27810 Avenue Hopkins, Valencia
(91355-3409)
PHONE..............................877 275-5284
Gavriel Lavi, *Pr*
Susan Lavi, *
◆ EMP: 80 EST: 1979
SQ FT: 80,000
SALES (est): 19.06MM
SALES (corp-wide): 19.06MM **Privately
Held**
Web: www.lavi.com
SIC: 3446 Railings, banisters, guards, etc:
made from metal pipe

(P-5069)
**LNI CUSTOM MANUFACTURING
INC**
15542 Broadway Center St, Gardena
(90248-2137)
PHONE..............................310 978-2000
Scott Blakely, *CEO*
EMP: 50 EST: 1995
SALES (est): 9.48MM **Privately Held**
Web: www.lnisigns.com
SIC: 3446 5046 Architectural metalwork;
Neon signs

(P-5070)
**PARAMOUNT METAL & SUPPLY
INC**
8140 Rosecrans Ave, Paramount
(90723-2754)
PHONE..............................562 634-8180
Vincent Jue, *CEO*
George Jue, *
Helen Jue, *
EMP: 25 EST: 1955
SQ FT: 80,000
SALES (est): 2.18MM **Privately Held**
Web: www.paramountmetals.com
SIC: 3446 Architectural metalwork

(P-5071)
SECURUS INC
Also Called: Holdrite
14284 Danielson St, Poway (92064-8885)
◆ EMP: 50 EST: 1983
SQ FT: 46,000
SALES (est): 2.31MM **Privately Held**
SIC: 3446 3351 3431 5162 Acoustical
suspension systems, metal; Tubing, copper
and copper alloy; Plumbing fixtures:
enameled iron, cast iron,or pressed metal;
Plastics materials and basic shapes
PA: Reliance Worldwide Corporation
Limited
Level 32 140 William Street

(P-5072)
**TJS METAL MANUFACTURING
INC**
10847 Drury Ln, Lynwood (90262-1833)
PHONE..............................310 604-1545
Jose Antonio Gallegos, *CEO*
EMP: 26 EST: 1999
SQ FT: 30,000
SALES (est): 4.23MM **Privately Held**
Web: www.tjsmetal.com
SIC: 3446 Architectural metalwork

(P-5073)
**WASHINGTON ORNA IR WORKS
INC**
Production Steel
17913 S Main St, Gardena (90248-3520)
PHONE..............................310 327-8660
Luke Welsh, *Mgr*

EMP: 23
SALES (corp-wide): 25.46MM **Privately
Held**
SIC: 3446 1542 Architectural metalwork;
Nonresidential construction, nec
PA: Washington Ornamental Iron Works
Inc.
17926 S Broadway St
310 327-8660

3448 Prefabricated Metal
Buildings

(P-5074)
**ALLIED MDULAR BLDG
SYSTEMS INC (PA)**
642 W Nicolas Ave, Orange (92868-1316)
PHONE..............................714 516-1188
Kevin Peithman, *CEO*
Raj Singh, *
Cathy Peithman, *
Richard Navarro, *
EMP: 38 EST: 1996
SQ FT: 35,000
SALES (est): 14.08MM **Privately Held**
Web: www.alliedmodular.com
SIC: 3448 Prefabricated metal buildings

(P-5075)
BIG ENTERPRISES
9702 Rush St, El Monte (91733-1731)
PHONE..............................626 448-1449
EMP: 49 EST: 1971
SALES (est): 8.5MM **Privately Held**
Web: www.bigbooth.com
SIC: 3448 Buildings, portable: prefabricated
metal

(P-5076)
CRATE MODULAR INC
3025 E Dominguez St, Carson
(90810-1437)
PHONE..............................310 405-0829
Rich Rozycki, *CEO*
Natasaha Deski, *
Moises Bada, *
EMP: 99 EST: 2018
SALES (est): 17.29MM **Privately Held**
Web: www.cratemodular.com
SIC: 3448 Prefabricated metal buildings and
components

(P-5077)
FCP INC (PA)
23100 Wildomar Trl, Wildomar
(92595-9699)
P.O. Box 1555 (92595-1555)
PHONE..............................951 678-4571
Russell J Greer, *CEO*
Barret Hilzer, *
EMP: 84 EST: 1982
SQ FT: 200,000
SALES (est): 6.5MM
SALES (corp-wide): 6.5MM **Privately Held**
Web: www.fcpbarns.com
SIC: 3448 1541 Prefabricated metal
components; Steel building construction

(P-5078)
GCN SUPPLY LLC
9070 Bridgeport Pl, Rancho Cucamonga
(91730-5530)
PHONE..............................909 643-4603
Gustavo Chona Senior, *Managing Member*
EMP: 50 EST: 2015
SALES (est): 1.4MM **Privately Held**
Web: www.gcnsupply.com

SIC: **3448** 2671 Prefabricated metal buildings and components; Plastic film, coated or laminated for packaging

(P-5079)

H ROBERTS CONSTRUCTION
2165 W Gaylord St, Long Beach (90813-1033)
PHONE............................562 590-4825
Kathleen F Roberts, *Pr*
EMP: 51 EST: 1988
SQ FT: 1,100
SALES (est): 1.93MM **Privately Held**
Web: www.robertsconstructionllc.net
SIC: **3448** Buildings, portable: prefabricated metal

(P-5080)

JOHN L CONLEY INC
Also Called: Conleys Greenhouse Mfg & Sales
4344 Mission Blvd, Montclair (91763-6038)
PHONE............................909 627-0981
John L Conley, *CEO*
Tom Conley, *
Dean Conley, *
Howard Davis, *
◆ EMP: 75 EST: 1946
SALES (est): 8.75MM **Privately Held**
Web: www.conleys.com
SIC: **3448** 3441 Greenhouses, prefabricated metal; Fabricated structural metal

(P-5081)

JTS MODULAR INC
7001 Mcdivitt Dr Ste B, Bakersfield (93313-2030)
P.O. Box 41765 (93384-1765)
PHONE............................661 835-9270
Dene Hurlbert, *Pr*
John Hurlbert, *
Lee Hawkins, *
Phillip Engler, *
EMP: 50 EST: 2000
SQ FT: 4,000
SALES (est): 8.5MM **Privately Held**
Web: www.jtsmodular.com
SIC: **3448** Prefabricated metal buildings and components

(P-5082)

MADISON INDUSTRIES (HQ)
17201 Darwin Ave, Hesperia (92345-5178)
PHONE............................562 484-5099
John Frey Junior, *Pr*
John Samuel Frey, *
Grace Lee, *Corporate Controller*
EMP: 28 EST: 1974
SALES (est): 11.51MM
SALES (corp-wide): 44.99MM **Privately Held**
Web: www.madisonind.com
SIC: **3448** 3441 1542 Prefabricated metal buildings and components; Fabricated structural metal; Nonresidential construction, nec
PA: John S. Frey Enterprises
1900 E 64th St
323 583-4061

(P-5083)

MCELROY METAL MILL INC
Also Called: McElroy Metal
17031 Koala Rd, Adelanto (92301-2246)
PHONE............................760 246-5545
Pete Nadler, *Mgr*
EMP: 37
SQ FT: 37,700
SALES (corp-wide): 40.53MM **Privately Held**

Web: www.mcelroymetal.com
SIC: **3448** Prefabricated metal components
PA: Mcelroy Metal Mill, Inc.
1500 Hamilton Rd
318 747-8000

(P-5084)

MOBILE MODULAR MANAGEMENT CORP
Also Called: Trs Rentelco
11450 Mission Blvd, Jurupa Valley (91752-1015)
PHONE............................800 819-1084
Thomas Sanders, *Mgr*
EMP: 112
SALES (corp-wide): 831.84MM **Publicly Held**
Web: www.mgrc.com
SIC: **3448** 7519 Prefabricated metal buildings and components; Trailer rental
HQ: Mobile Modular Management Corporation
5700 Las Positas Rd
Livermore CA 94551
925 443-8052

(P-5085)

MORIN CORPORATION
Also Called: Morin West
10707 Commerce Way, Fontana (92337-8216)
PHONE............................909 428-3747
Ilhan Eser, *VP*
EMP: 40
Web: www.morincorp.com
SIC: **3448** Prefabricated metal buildings and components
HQ: Morin Corporation
685 Middle St Ste 1
Bristol CT 06010

(P-5086)

ORANGE COUNTY ERECTORS INC
517 E La Palma Ave, Anaheim (92801-2536)
PHONE............................714 502-8455
Richard Lewis, *CEO*
Sandra Lewis, *
EMP: 50 EST: 1975
SQ FT: 80,000
SALES (est): 10.04MM **Privately Held**
Web: www.ocerectors.com
SIC: **3448** 3441 1791 Buildings, portable: prefabricated metal; Fabricated structural metal; Structural steel erection

(P-5087)

PROGRESSIVE MARKETING PDTS INC
Also Called: Progressive Marketing
4571 Avenida Del Este, Yorba Linda (92886-3002)
PHONE............................714 888-1700
Leonard Dozier, *CEO*
Scott Hillstrom, *Dir*
Sam Malik, *Ex VP*
Tiffany Dozier, *Ex VP*
◆ EMP: 80 EST: 1977
SALES (est): 4.61MM **Privately Held**
Web: www.premiermounts.com
SIC: **3448** Prefabricated metal buildings and components

(P-5088)

STELL INDUSTRIES INC
Also Called: C-Thru Sunrooms
1951 S Parco Ave Ste B, Ontario (91761-8315)

PHONE............................951 369-8777
Gary P Stell Junior, *CEO*
Jason S Albany, *
Mike Leigh, *
EMP: 50 EST: 1947
SALES (est): 2.27MM **Privately Held**
SIC: **3448** Sunrooms, prefabricated metal

(P-5089)

UNITED CARPORTS LLC
7280 Sycamore Canyon Blvd Ste 1, Riverside (92508-2316)
PHONE............................800 757-6742
Ryan Spates, *Pr*
Ryan Spates, *Managing Member*
Garrett Spates, *
EMP: 28 EST: 2011
SQ FT: 5,000
SALES (est): 6.64MM **Privately Held**
Web: www.unitedcarports.com
SIC: **3448** Prefabricated metal buildings and components

3449 Miscellaneous Metalwork

(P-5090)

AMC MACHINING INC
1540 Commerce Way, Paso Robles (93446-3524)
P.O. Box 665 (93447-0665)
PHONE............................805 238-5452
Alex Camp, *Pr*
EMP: 35 EST: 2007
SQ FT: 10,000
SALES (est): 6.07MM **Privately Held**
Web: www.amcmachining.com
SIC: **3449** Miscellaneous metalwork

(P-5091)

ARCHITECTURAL ENTERPRISES INC
Also Called: Hi-Tech Iron Works
5821 Randolph St, Commerce (90040-3415)
PHONE............................323 268-4000
Kevin Drake, *Pr*
John S Lee, *
Alma Gutierrez, *
EMP: 40 EST: 1984
SQ FT: 20,000
SALES (est): 6.19MM **Privately Held**
SIC: **3449** Miscellaneous metalwork

(P-5092)

C&K FORM FABRICATION INC
370 N 9th St, Colton (92324-2909)
P.O. Box 431 (92324-0431)
PHONE............................909 825-1882
Kyle A Payson, *CEO*
EMP: 41 EST: 2016
SALES (est): 2.28MM
SALES (corp-wide): 25.12MM **Privately Held**
SIC: **3449** Miscellaneous metalwork
PA: Squires Lumber Company
370 N 9th St
909 825-1882

(P-5093)

CMC STEEL US LLC
Also Called: Gerdau Ameristeel
5425 Industrial Pkwy, San Bernardino (92407-1803)
PHONE............................909 646-7827
EMP: 42
SALES (corp-wide): 7.93B **Publicly Held**
Web: www.cmc.com

SIC: **3449** Bars, concrete reinforcing: fabricated steel
HQ: Cmc Steel Us, Llc
6565 N Mcrthur Blvd Ste 8
Irving TX 75039
214 689-4300

(P-5094)

FAB SERVICES WEST INC
10007 Elm Ave, Fontana (92335-6318)
PHONE............................909 350-7500
EMP: 77 EST: 2011
SALES (est): 4.79MM **Privately Held**
SIC: **3449** Miscellaneous metalwork
HQ: Fab Holding Llc
3335 Susan St
Costa Mesa CA 92626
949 236-5520

(P-5095)

H WAYNE LEWIS INC
Also Called: Amber Steel Co.
312 S Willow Ave, Rialto (92376-6313)
P.O. Box 900 (92377-0900)
PHONE............................909 874-2213
H Wayne Lewis, *CEO*
Dan Bergen, *
Janet Lewis, *
Kriss Lewis, *
EMP: 40 EST: 1983
SQ FT: 8,100
SALES (est): 4.55MM **Privately Held**
Web: www.ambersteelco.com
SIC: **3449** Bars, concrete reinforcing: fabricated steel

(P-5096)

INNOVATIVE METAL INDS INC
Also Called: Southwest Data Products
1330 Riverview Dr, San Bernardino (92408-2944)
PHONE............................909 796-6200
Kelly Brodhagan, *CEO*
▲ EMP: 100 EST: 2006
SQ FT: 150,000
SALES (est): 23.97MM
SALES (corp-wide): 34.71B **Publicly Held**
Web: www.imiac.com
SIC: **3449** Curtain wall, metal
PA: Nucor Corporation
1915 Rexford Rd
704 366-7000

(P-5097)

JLJ REBAR EXTREME INC
1532 Wall Ave, San Bernardino (92404-5018)
PHONE............................909 381-9177
Jose Luis Jaime, *CEO*
EMP: 50 EST: 2019
SALES (est): 3.74MM **Privately Held**
SIC: **3449** Bars, concrete reinforcing: fabricated steel

(P-5098)

KING WIRE PARTITIONS INC
Also Called: A A A Partitions
6044 N Figueroa St, Los Angeles (90042-4232)
PHONE............................323 256-4848
Max Behshid, *Pr*
Millie Behshid, *
Farid Behshid, *
▲ EMP: 30 EST: 1978
SQ FT: 24,000
SALES (est): 1.12MM **Privately Held**
Web: www.kingwireusa.com
SIC: **3449** 5046 3496 Miscellaneous metalwork; Partitions; Miscellaneous fabricated wire products

(P-5099)
NORTH STAR ACQUISITION INC
Also Called: North Star Company
14912 S Broadway, Gardena (90248-1818)
PHONE..................310 515-2200
EMP: 63 **EST:** 1950
SALES (est): 4.09MM **Privately Held**
Web: www.northstarcompany.com
SIC: 3449 3444 3321 3316 Custom roll
formed products; Sheet metalwork; Gray
and ductile iron foundries; Cold finishing of
steel shapes

(P-5100)
PACIFIC STEEL GROUP LLC (PA)
Also Called: Psg
4805 Murphy Canyon Rd, San Diego
(92123-4324)
PHONE..................858 251-1100
Eric Benson, *Prin*
Eric Benson, *CEO*
John Scurlock, *
Monica Kamoss, *
EMP: 114 **EST:** 2014
SQ FT: 26,000
SALES (est): 123.74MM
SALES (corp-wide): 123.74MM **Privately
Held**
Web: www.pacificsteelgroup.com
SIC: 3449 Bars, concrete reinforcing:
fabricated steel

(P-5101)
TAMCO
Also Called: Gerdau Rancho Cucamonga
1000 Quail St Ste 260, Newport Beach
(92660-2784)
P.O. Box 13158 (92658-5087)
PHONE..................949 552-9714
EMP: 300
SALES (corp-wide): 7.93B **Publicly Held**
Web: www.asgsales.com
SIC: 3449 Bars, concrete reinforcing:
fabricated steel
HQ: Tamco
5425 Industrial Pkwy
San Bernardino CA 92407
909 899-0660

3451 Screw Machine Products

(P-5102)
ABEL AUTOMATICS LLC
Also Called: Abel Reels
165 N Aviador St, Camarillo (93010-8484)
PHONE..................805 388-3721
David Dragoo, *Ch Bd*
◆ **EMP:** 30 **EST:** 1980
SQ FT: 16,000
SALES (est): 2.44MM **Privately Held**
Web: www.abelreels.com
SIC: 3451 3949 Screw machine products;
Reels, fishing

(P-5103)
ALGER PRECISION MACHINING LLC
724 S Bon View Ave, Ontario (91761-1913)
PHONE..................909 986-4591
Duane Femrite, *Prin*
Jim Hemingway, *Prin*
Danny Hankla, *Prin*
▲ **EMP:** 160 **EST:** 1986
SQ FT: 35,000
SALES (est): 23.2MM **Privately Held**
Web: www.algerprecision.com
SIC: 3451 Screw machine products

(P-5104)
BALDA HK PLASTICS INC
Also Called: H K Prcision Turning Machining
3229 Roymar Rd, Oceanside (92058-1311)
PHONE..................760 757-1100
Dan Wannigen, *Mgr*
EMP: 40
SQ FT: 9,808
SALES (corp-wide): 2.67MM **Privately
Held**
SIC: 3451 3544 3089 Screw machine
products; Special dies and tools; Injection
molded finished plastics products, nec
HQ: Balda Precision, Inc.
3233 Roymar Rd
Oceanside CA 92058
760 757-1100

(P-5105)
BALDA PRECISION INC (DH)
Also Called: HK Precision Turning Machining
3233 Roymar Rd, Oceanside (92058-1311)
PHONE..................760 757-1100
EMP: 80 **EST:** 1974
SALES (est): 18.8MM
SALES (corp-wide): 2.67MM **Privately
Held**
SIC: 3451 3544 3089 Screw machine
products; Special dies and tools; Injection
molded finished plastics products, nec
HQ: Clere Ag
Schluterstr. 45
Berlin BE 10707
302 130-0430

(P-5106)
DESIGNED METAL CONNECTIONS INC
Also Called: DMC
623 E Artesia Blvd, Carson (90746-1201)
PHONE..................310 323-6200
EMP: 25
SALES (corp-wide): 364.48B **Publicly
Held**
Web: www.pccfluidfittings.com
SIC: 3451 Screw machine products
HQ: Designed Metal Connections, Inc.
14800 S Figueroa St
Gardena CA 90248
310 323-6200

(P-5107)
FASTENER INNOVATION TECH INC
Also Called: F I T
19300 S Susana Rd, Compton
(90221-5711)
PHONE..................310 538-1111
Larry Valeriano, *Pr*
EMP: 99 **EST:** 1979
SQ FT: 65,000
SALES (est): 15.95MM
SALES (corp-wide): 145.58MM **Privately
Held**
Web: www.fitfastener.com
SIC: 3451 3728 3452 3429 Screw machine
products; Aircraft parts and equipment, nec;
Bolts, nuts, rivets, and washers; Hardware,
nec
HQ: Avantus Aerospace, Inc.
29101 The Old Rd
Valencia CA 91355
661 295-8620

(P-5108)
GT PRECISION INC
Also Called: Alard Machine Products
1629 W 132nd St, Gardena (90249-2005)
PHONE..................310 323-4374
Gregg Thompson, *CEO*

▲ **EMP:** 107 **EST:** 1967
SQ FT: 11,700
SALES (est): 23.08MM **Privately Held**
Web: www.alardmachine.com
SIC: 3451 Screw machine products

(P-5109)
ONYX INDUSTRIES INC (PA)
Also Called: Quad R Tech
1227 254th St, Harbor City (90710-2912)
PHONE..................310 539-8830
Vladimir Reil, *CEO*
▲ **EMP:** 100 **EST:** 1978
SQ FT: 30,000
SALES (est): 18.41MM
SALES (corp-wide): 18.41MM **Privately
Held**
Web: www.onyxindustries.com
SIC: 3451 Screw machine products

(P-5110)
ONYX INDUSTRIES INC
521 W Rosecrans Ave, Gardena
(90248-1514)
PHONE..................310 851-6161
Siamak Maghoul, *Brnch Mgr*
EMP: 100
SALES (corp-wide): 18.41MM **Privately
Held**
Web: www.studex.com
SIC: 3451 Screw machine products
PA: Onyx Industries Inc.
1227 254th St
310 539-8830

(P-5111)
PACIFIC PRECISION INC
1318 Palomares St, La Verne (91750-5232)
PHONE..................909 392-5610
EMP: 40 **EST:** 1981
SALES (est): 9.38MM **Privately Held**
Web: www.pacificprecisioninc.com
SIC: 3451 Screw machine products

(P-5112)
PRICE MANUFACTURING CO INC
372 N Smith Ave, Corona (92878-4371)
P.O. Box 1209 (92878-1209)
PHONE..................951 371-5660
Robert P Schiffmacher, *CEO*
Ively Schiffmacher, *
EMP: 32 **EST:** 1979
SQ FT: 15,600
SALES (est): 5.55MM **Privately Held**
Web: www.pricemfg.com
SIC: 3451 Screw machine products

(P-5113)
SORENSON ENGINEERING INC (PA)
32032 Dunlap Blvd, Yucaipa (92399-1767)
PHONE..................909 795-2434
David L Sorenson, *Pr*
Paul Sewell, *
◆ **EMP:** 161 **EST:** 1956
SQ FT: 61,000
SALES (est): 46.64MM
SALES (corp-wide): 46.64MM **Privately
Held**
Web: www.sorensoneng.com
SIC: 3451 Screw machine products

(P-5114)
SWISS-MICRON INC
22361 Gilberto Ste A, Rcho Sta Marg
(92688-2103)
PHONE..................949 589-0430
Kurt Sollberger, *CEO*
Beverley Sollberger, *
EMP: 53 **EST:** 1984

SQ FT: 16,000
SALES (est): 4.78MM **Privately Held**
Web: www.swissmicron.com
SIC: 3451 Screw machine products

(P-5115)
TL MACHINE INC
14272 Commerce Dr, Garden Grove
(92843-4942)
PHONE..................714 554-4154
Thanh X Ly, *Pr*
Thanh Ly, *
Tuyen Ly, *
Quang Ly, *
▲ **EMP:** 90 **EST:** 2001
SQ FT: 39,126
SALES (est): 14.53MM **Privately Held**
Web: www.tlmachine.com
SIC: 3451 3561 3593 3728 Screw machine
products; Pumps and pumping equipment;
Fluid power cylinders and actuators;
Aircraft parts and equipment, nec

(P-5116)
WYATT PRECISION MACHINE INC
3301 E 59th St, Long Beach (90805-4503)
PHONE..................562 634-0524
Dennis Allison, *Pr*
Paul Layton, *
Allen Harmon, *
EMP: 47 **EST:** 1952
SQ FT: 14,000
SALES (est): 5.29MM **Privately Held**
Web: www.wyattprecisionmachine.com
SIC: 3451 Screw machine products

3452 Bolts, Nuts, Rivets, And Washers

(P-5117)
3-V FASTENER CO INC
630 E Lambert Rd, Brea (92821-4119)
PHONE..................949 888-7700
Peter George, *CEO*
EMP: 56 **EST:** 1982
SQ FT: 18,500
SALES (est): 23.26MM
SALES (corp-wide): 15.78B **Publicly Held**
SIC: 3452 Bolts, metal
HQ: Consolidated Aerospace
Manufacturing, Llc
1425 S Acacia Ave
Fullerton CA 92831
714 989-2797

(P-5118)
ANILLO INDUSTRIES LLC
Also Called: Anillo Industries
2090 N Glassell St, Orange (92865-3306)
P.O. Box 5586 (92863-5586)
PHONE..................714 637-7000
Kurt Hilton Koch, *Pr*
Mark Koch, *VP*
EMP: 28 **EST:** 1957
SQ FT: 80,000
SALES (est): 5.63MM
SALES (corp-wide): 40.07MM **Privately
Held**
Web: www.anilloinc.com
SIC: 3452 3325 3499 3429 Washers;
Bushings, cast steel: except investment;
Shims, metal; Hardware, nec
PA: Novaria Holdings, Llc
809 W Vickery Blvd
817 381-3810

(P-5119)
AZTEC MANUFACTURING INC
(PA)
Also Called: Aztec Washer Company
13821 Danielson St, Poway (92064-6891)
PHONE................................858 513-4350
▲ **EMP: 25 EST:** 1970
SALES (est): 24.82MM
SALES (corp-wide): 24.82MM **Privately Held**
Web: www.aztecwasher.com
SIC: 3452 Washers

(P-5120)
BRILES AEROSPACE LLC
1559 W 135th St, Gardena (90249-2219)
PHONE................................424 320-3817
Richard Alessi, *CEO*
Richard Alessi, *Managing Member*
Daniel Yoon, *
EMP: 80 EST: 2012
SQ FT: 22,000
SALES (est): 1.76MM **Privately Held**
Web: www.brilesaerospace.com
SIC: 3452 Bolts, nuts, rivets, and washers

(P-5121)
BRISTOL INDUSTRIES LLC
630 E Lambert Rd, Brea (92821-4119)
PHONE................................714 990-4121
EMP: 152 EST: 1973
SALES (est): 47.7MM
SALES (corp-wide): 15.78B **Publicly Held**
Web: www.bristolindustries.com
SIC: 3452 Bolts, nuts, rivets, and washers
HQ: Consolidated Aerospace
Manufacturing, Llc
1425 S Acacia Ave
Fullerton CA 92831
714 989-2797

(P-5122)
CBS FASTENERS LLC
1345 N Brasher St, Anaheim (92807-2046)
PHONE................................714 779-6368
Vic Luna, *Pr*
Gerald Bozarth, *
EMP: 49 EST: 1978
SQ FT: 10,400
SALES (est): 9.12MM **Privately Held**
Web: www.cbsfasteners.com
SIC: 3452 Bolts, metal

(P-5123)
DGL HOLDINGS INC
3850 E Miraloma Ave, Anaheim
(92806-2108)
PHONE................................714 630-7040
George Hennes, *Pr*
David Boehm, *
EMP: 50 EST: 1969
SQ FT: 35,500
SALES (est): 2.76MM **Privately Held**
Web: www.mwcomponents.com
SIC: 3452 Bolts, nuts, rivets, and washers

(P-5124)
DOUBLECO INCORPORATED
Also Called: R & D Fasteners
9444 9th St, Rancho Cucamonga
(91730-4509)
P.O. Box 250 (91785-0250)
PHONE................................909 481-0799
Craig Scheu, *Pr*
EMP: 100 EST: 1986
SQ FT: 30,000
SALES (est): 23.62MM **Privately Held**
Web: www.rdfast.com

SIC: 3452 5072 Bolts, metal; Bolts

(P-5125)
DUPREE INC
Also Called: Stake Fastener
14395 Ramona Ave, Chino (91710-5740)
P.O. Box 1797 (91708-1797)
PHONE................................909 597-4889
Jim Pon, *Pr*
James D Dupree, *
▲ **EMP: 31 EST:** 1958
SQ FT: 60,000
SALES (est): 4.57MM **Privately Held**
Web: www.dupreeinc.com
SIC: 3452 6512 Bolts, metal; Commercial
and industrial building operation

(P-5126)
FEDERAL MANUFACTURING
CORP
9825 De Soto Ave, Chatsworth
(91311-4412)
PHONE................................818 341-9825
Helen Rainey, *Pr*
Arthur Rainey, *
Paul Rainey, *
EMP: 42 EST: 1951
SQ FT: 36,000
SALES (est): 6.51MM **Privately Held**
Web: www.federalmanufacturing.com
SIC: 3452 3812 3462 3429 Bolts, metal;
Search and navigation equipment; Iron and
steel forgings; Hardware, nec

(P-5127)
GOLDEN BOLT LLC
9361 Canoga Ave, Chatsworth
(91311-5879)
PHONE................................818 626-8261
EMP: 79 EST: 2016
SALES (est): 5.14MM **Privately Held**
Web: www.goldenboltllc.com
SIC: 3452 Bolts, metal

(P-5128)
HI-SHEAR CORPORATION (DH)
2600 Skypark Dr, Torrance (90505-5373)
PHONE................................310 326-8110
Christian Darville, *CEO*
▲ **EMP: 600 EST:** 1943
SQ FT: 180,000
SALES (est): 128.01MM
SALES (corp-wide): 2.67MM **Privately Held**
Web: www.hi-shear.com
SIC: 3452 3429 Bolts, nuts, rivets, and
washers; Aircraft hardware
HQ: Lisi Aerospace
42 A 52
Paris 12 IDF 75012
140198200

(P-5129)
HUCK INTERNATIONAL INC
Also Called: Arconic Fastening Systems
900 E Watson Center Rd, Carson
(90745-4201)
PHONE................................310 830-8200
Jim Dawn, *Mgr*
EMP: 203
SALES (corp-wide): 6.64B **Publicly Held**
Web: www.howmet.com
SIC: 3452 Nuts, metal
HQ: Huck International, Inc.
3724 E Columbia St
Tucson AZ 85714
520 519-7400

(P-5130)
INSTRUMENT BEARING
FACTORY USA
19360 Rinaldi St, Northridge (91326-1607)
PHONE................................818 989-5052
EMP: 50
SQ FT: 30,000
SALES (est): 2.67MM **Privately Held**
SIC: 3452 5085 Bolts, metal; Industrial
supplies

(P-5131)
KING HOLDING CORPORATION
360 N Crescent Dr, Beverly Hills
(90210-4874)
PHONE................................586 254-3900
EMP: 7970
SIC: 3452 3465 3469 3089 Bolts, nuts,
rivets, and washers; Automotive stampings;
Metal stampings, nec; Injection molded
finished plastics products, nec

(P-5132)
MS AEROSPACE INC
13928 Balboa Blvd, Sylmar (91342-1086)
PHONE................................818 833-9095
Michel Szostak, *CEO*
Jerome Taieb, *
Jim Cole, *General Vice President*
EMP: 302 EST: 1992
SALES (est): 48.59MM **Privately Held**
Web: www.msaerospace.com
SIC: 3452 3728 Bolts, nuts, rivets, and
washers; Aircraft parts and equipment, nec

(P-5133)
NYLOK LLC
Also Called: Nylok Western Fastener
313 N Euclid Way, Anaheim (92801-6738)
PHONE................................714 635-3993
Scott Plantiga, *Mgr*
EMP: 45
SALES (corp-wide): 23.23MM **Privately Held**
Web: www.nylok.com
SIC: 3452 Bolts, nuts, rivets, and washers
PA: Nylok, Llc
15260 Hallmark Ct
586 786-0100

(P-5134)
PAUL R BRILES INC
Also Called: Pb Fasteners
1700 W 132nd St, Gardena (90249-2008)
PHONE................................310 323-6222
▲ **EMP:** 1262
Web: www.pccfasteners.com
SIC: 3452 Bolts, nuts, rivets, and washers

(P-5135)
POWER FASTENERS INC
650 E 60th St, Los Angeles (90001-1012)
P.O. Box 512056 (90051-0056)
PHONE................................323 232-4362
Patrick Harrington, *Pr*
▲ **EMP: 30 EST:** 1991
SQ FT: 35,000
SALES (est): 831.13K **Privately Held**
Web: 041d6c8.netsolhost.com
SIC: 3452 3448 Bolts, nuts, rivets, and
washers; Prefabricated metal components

(P-5136)
RISCO INC
390 Risco Cir, Beaumont (92223-2676)
PHONE................................951 769-2899
Joseph A Frainee Ii, *CEO*
Cynthia R Frainee, *
EMP: 30 EST: 1964

SQ FT: 30,000
SALES (est): 3.93MM **Privately Held**
Web: www.risco-fasteners.com
SIC: 3452 Bolts, metal

(P-5137)
SUNLAND AEROSPACE
FASTENERS
12920 Pierce St, Pacoima (91331-2526)
PHONE................................818 485-8929
Anik Khochou, *Admn*
Jack Wilson, *
EMP: 80 EST: 2012
SQ FT: 11,000
SALES (est): 1.79MM **Privately Held**
Web: www.sunlandaerospace.com
SIC: 3452 Bolts, nuts, rivets, and washers

(P-5138)
TWIST TITE MFG INC
13344 Cambridge St, Santa Fe Springs
(90670-4904)
PHONE................................562 229-0990
Spiro Aykias, *CEO*
Martha Leonard, *
EMP: 32 EST: 1994
SQ FT: 18,200
SALES (est): 1.77MM **Privately Held**
Web: www.twisttite.com
SIC: 3452 Bolts, nuts, rivets, and washers

(P-5139)
VALLEY-TODECO INC
Also Called: Arconic Fastening Systems
135 N Unruh Ave, City Of Industry
(91744-4427)
PHONE................................800 992-4444
Jim Cotello, *Pr*
▲ **EMP: 130 EST:** 1995
SALES (est): 12.07MM
SALES (corp-wide): 6.64B **Publicly Held**
SIC: 3452 5085 Bolts, nuts, rivets, and
washers; Fasteners, industrial: nuts, bolts,
screws, etc.
HQ: Howmet Global Fastening Systems Inc.
3990a Heritage Oak Ct
Simi Valley CA 93063
805 426-2270

3462 Iron And Steel Forgings

(P-5140)
ADVANCED STRUCTURAL TECH
INC
Also Called: Asa
950 Richmond Ave, Oxnard (93030-7212)
PHONE................................805 204-9133
Robert Melsness, *Pr*
Douglas Jones, *
▼ **EMP: 135 EST:** 2009
SALES (est): 23.97MM **Privately Held**
Web: www.astforgetech.com
SIC: 3462 Aircraft forgings, ferrous

(P-5141)
FORGED METALS INC
10685 Beech Ave, Fontana (92337-7212)
PHONE................................909 350-9260
Torben Kaese, *CEO*
◆ **EMP: 200 EST:** 1982
SQ FT: 4,800
SALES (est): 24.06MM
SALES (corp-wide): 6.64B **Publicly Held**
SIC: 3462 Iron and steel forgings
PA: Howmet Aerospace Inc.
201 Isabella St Ste 200
412 553-1950

PRODUCTS & SVCS

(P-5142)

INDEPENDENT FORGE COMPANY

692 N Batavia St, Orange (92868-1282)
PHONE.................714 997-7337
Rosemary Ruiz, *Pr*
Joe Ramirez, *
Gloria Lopez, *
▲ EMP: 40 EST: 1975
SQ FT: 11,900
SALES (est): 4.62MM **Privately Held**
Web: www.independentforge.com
SIC: 3462 Iron and steel forgings

(P-5143)

JMMCA INC (PA)

Also Called: Pmp Forge
850 W Bradley Ave, El Cajon (92020-1218)
PHONE.................619 448-2711
James Matarese, *CEO*
Betty Matarese, *
▲ EMP: 83 EST: 1963
SQ FT: 92,000
SALES (est): 18.37MM
SALES (corp-wide): 18.37MM **Privately Held**
Web: www.pmpforge.com
SIC: 3462 Iron and steel forgings

(P-5144)

MATTCO FORGE INC

7530 Jackson St, Paramount (90723-4910)
PHONE.................562 634-8635
Denis B Brady, *CEO*
EMP: 34
SALES (corp-wide): 40.39MM **Privately Held**
Web: www.mattcoforge.com
SIC: 3462 Iron and steel forgings
HQ: Mattco Forge, Inc.
16443 Minnesota Ave
Paramount CA 90723
562 634-8635

(P-5145)

PACIFIC FORGE INC

10641 Etiwanda Ave, Fontana (92337-6991)
PHONE.................909 390-0701
Ronald D Browne, *Pr*
Jacqueline Dyer, *
EMP: 55 EST: 1955
SQ FT: 34,816
SALES (est): 1.9MM
SALES (corp-wide): 474.53MM **Privately Held**
Web: www.pacificforge.com
SIC: 3462 3463 Iron and steel forgings;
Nonferrous forgings
PA: Avis Industrial Corporation
1909 S Main St
765 998-8100

(P-5146)

PERFORMANCE FORGE INC

7401 Telegraph Rd, Montebello (90640-6500)
PHONE.................323 722-3460
Wayne Ramay, *Pr*
EMP: 30 EST: 2012
SALES (est): 5.5MM **Privately Held**
Web: www.performance-forge.com
SIC: 3462 Iron and steel forgings

(P-5147)

PREMIER GEAR & MACHINING INC

2360 Pomona Rd, Corona (92880)
P.O. Box 2799 (92878-2799)

PHONE.................951 278-5505
Steve Golden, *Pr*
Huy Nguyen, *
EMP: 25 EST: 1986
SQ FT: 21,000
SALES (est): 7.5MM **Privately Held**
Web: www.premiergearinc.com
SIC: 3462 3599 Iron and steel forgings;
Machine shop, jobbing and repair

(P-5148)

PRESS FORGE COMPANY

7700 Jackson St, Paramount (90723-5073)
P.O. Box 1432 (90723-1432)
PHONE.................562 531-4962
Jeffrey M Carlton, *CEO*
Michael Buxton, *
Mike Buxton, *
▲ EMP: 80 EST: 1978
SQ FT: 32,726
SALES (est): 21.04MM
SALES (corp-wide): 364.48B **Publicly Held**
Web: www.pressforge.com
SIC: 3462 Iron and steel forgings
HQ: Precision Castparts Corp.
5885 Meadows Rd Ste 620
Lake Oswego OR 97035
503 946-4800

(P-5149)

RUBICON GEAR INC

Also Called: Rubicon Gear
225 Citation Cir, Corona (92878-5023)
PHONE.................951 356-3800
Cheryl A Edwards, *Ch Bd*
Ryan B Edwards, *
Frank Salazar, *
EMP: 68 EST: 1970
SQ FT: 25,000
SALES (est): 8.34MM **Privately Held**
Web: www.rubicon-gear.com
SIC: 3462 Gears, forged steel

(P-5150)

TIMKEN GEARS & SERVICES INC

Also Called: Philadelphia Gear
12935 Imperial Hwy, Santa Fe Springs (90670-4715)
PHONE.................310 605-2600
Tony Tartaglio, *Brnch Mgr*
EMP: 29
SALES (corp-wide): 4.77B **Publicly Held**
Web: www.philagear.com
SIC: 3462 Gear and chain forgings
HQ: Timken Gears & Services Inc.
935 1st Ave Ste 200
King Of Prussia PA 19406

(P-5151)

VI-STAR GEAR CO INC

7312 Jefferson St, Paramount (90723-4094)
PHONE.................323 774-3750
Thomas R Redfield, *Pr*
Chris Redfield, *
EMP: 30 EST: 1960
SQ FT: 12,000
SALES (est): 5.71MM **Privately Held**
Web: www.vistargear.com
SIC: 3462 3728 Iron and steel forgings;
Gears, aircraft power transmission

3463 Nonferrous Forgings

(P-5152)

ALUM-ALLOY CO INC

603 S Hope Ave, Ontario (91761-1824)
PHONE.................909 986-0410

David Howell, *CEO*
Marilyn Howell, *
Clark Howell, *
EMP: 40 EST: 1961
SQ FT: 20,000
SALES (est): 1.22MM **Privately Held**
Web: www.lynwoodpattern.com
SIC: 3463 3365 Aluminum forgings;
Aluminum foundries

(P-5153)

CARLTON FORGE WORKS LLC

Also Called: Carlton Forge Works
7743 Adams St, Paramount (90723-4200)
PHONE.................562 633-1131
◆ EMP: 300 EST: 1929
SALES (est): 50.31MM
SALES (corp-wide): 364.48B **Publicly Held**
Web: www.cfworks.com
SIC: 3463 3462 Nonferrous forgings; Iron and steel forgings
HQ: Precision Castparts Corp.
5885 Meadows Rd Ste 620
Lake Oswego OR 97035
503 946-4800

(P-5154)

CONTINENTAL FORGE COMPANY LLC

412 E El Segundo Blvd, Compton (90222-2317)
PHONE.................310 603-1014
Olivier Jarrault, *CEO*
Peter Manos, *
EMP: 90 EST: 1968
SQ FT: 27,000
SALES (est): 10.65MM
SALES (corp-wide): 170.38MM **Privately Held**
Web: www.cforge.com
SIC: 3463 Aluminum forgings
HQ: Forged Solutions Group Limited
Dale Road North
Matlock DE4 2
792 065-5762

(P-5155)

GEL INDUSTRIES INC

Also Called: Quality Aluminum Forge Div
810 N Lemon St, Orange (92867-6616)
PHONE.................714 639-8191
EMP: 150
SIC: 3463 Aluminum forgings

(P-5156)

LINDSEY MANUFACTURING CO

Also Called: Lindsey Systems
760 N Georgia Ave, Azusa (91702-2249)
P.O. Box 877 (91702-0877)
PHONE.................626 969-3471
Keith E Lindsey, *Pr*
Frederick Findley, *
Lela Lindsey, *
▲ EMP: 110 EST: 1947
SQ FT: 60,000
SALES (est): 15.17MM **Privately Held**
Web: www.lindsey-usa.com
SIC: 3463 3644 Pole line hardware forgings, nonferrous; Noncurrent-carrying wiring devices

(P-5157)

LUXFER INC

Superform USA
6825 Jurupa Ave, Riverside (92504-1039)
PHONE.................951 351-4100
Michael Reynolds, *VP*
EMP: 38
SALES (corp-wide): 405MM **Privately Held**

Web: www.luxfercylinders.com
SIC: 3463 Aluminum forgings
HQ: Luxfer Inc.
3016 Kansas Ave Bldg 1
Riverside CA 92507
951 684-5110

(P-5158)

QUALITY ALUMINUM FORGE LLC

794 N Cypress St, Orange (92867-6606)
PHONE.................714 639-8191
EMP: 186
SALES (corp-wide): 87.02MM **Publicly Held**
Web: www.sifco.com
SIC: 3463 Aluminum forgings
HQ: Quality Aluminum Forge, Llc
793 N Cypress St
Orange CA 92867
714 639-8191

(P-5159)

QUALITY ALUMINUM FORGE LLC (HQ)

793 N Cypress St, Orange (92867-5596)
PHONE.................714 639-8191
EMP: 44 EST: 2011
SALES (est): 40.36MM
SALES (corp-wide): 87.02MM **Publicly Held**
Web: www.sifco.com
SIC: 3463 Aluminum forgings
PA: Sifco Industries, Inc.
970 E 64th St
216 881-8600

(P-5160)

SHULTZ STEEL COMPANY LLC

Also Called: S S
5321 Firestone Blvd, South Gate (90280-3629)
PHONE.................323 357-3200
◆ EMP: 490 EST: 1956
SALES (est): 74.94MM
SALES (corp-wide): 364.48B **Publicly Held**
Web: www.shultzsteel.com
SIC: 3463 3462 Aircraft forgings, nonferrous; Aircraft forgings, ferrous
HQ: Precision Castparts Corp.
5885 Meadows Rd Ste 620
Lake Oswego OR 97035
503 946-4800

(P-5161)

STS METALS INC (PA)

Also Called: Sierra Alloys Company
5467 Ayon Ave, Irwindale (91706-2044)
PHONE.................626 969-6711
Craig Culaciati, *CEO*
Ed Brennan, *VP*
Jeff Augustyn, *Ex VP*
▲ EMP: 52 EST: 1974
SQ FT: 75,000
SALES (est): 17.23MM
SALES (corp-wide): 17.23MM **Privately Held**
Web: www.sierraalloys.com
SIC: 3463 3494 3312 Nonferrous forgings; Valves and pipe fittings, nec; Blast furnaces and steel mills

(P-5162)

WEBER METALS INC (HQ)

16706 Garfield Ave, Paramount (90723-5315)
PHONE.................562 602-0260
John R Creed, *CEO*
Paul Dennis, *

◆ **EMP: 39 EST:** 1962
SQ FT: 270,000
SALES (est): 66.09MM
SALES (corp-wide): 3.59B **Privately Held**
Web: www.webermetals.com
SIC: 3463 Aluminum forgings
PA: Otto Fuchs Beteiligungen Kg
Derschlager Str. 26
2354730

(P-5163)
WEBER METALS INC
233 E Manville St, Compton (90220-5602)
PHONE..............................562 543-3316
EMP: 461
SALES (corp-wide): 3.59B **Privately Held**
Web: www.webermetals.com
SIC: 3463 Aluminum forgings
HQ: Weber Metals, Inc.
16706 Garfield Ave
Paramount CA 90723
562 602-0260

(P-5164)
WJB BEARINGS INC
535 Brea Canyon Rd, City Of Industry
(91789-3001)
PHONE..............................909 598-6238
John Jun Jiang, *CEO*
▲ **EMP: 25 EST:** 1992
SQ FT: 30,000
SALES (est): 4.87MM **Privately Held**
Web: www.wjbgroup.us
SIC: 3463 5085 Bearing and bearing race
forgings, nonferrous; Bearings

3465 Automotive Stampings

(P-5165)
T-REX TRUCK PRODUCTS INC
Also Called: T-Rex Grilles
2365 Railroad St, Corona (92878-5411)
PHONE..............................800 287-5900
Behrouz Mizban, *Pr*
▼ **EMP: 55 EST:** 1995
SQ FT: 45,000
SALES (est): 3.63MM **Privately Held**
Web: www.trexbillet.com
SIC: 3465 Automotive stampings

(P-5166)
TROY SHEET METAL WORKS INC (PA)
Also Called: Troy Products
1024 S Vail Ave, Montebello (90640-6020)
PHONE..............................323 720-4100
Carl Moses Kahalewai, *CEO*
Paul Alvarado, *Stockholder**
Carol Stewart, *Stockholder**
Marci Norkin, *Stockholder**
Rigo Guadiana, *
EMP: 73 EST: 1930
SQ FT: 16,000
SALES (est): 10.81MM
SALES (corp-wide): 10.81MM **Privately Held**
Web: www.troyproducts.com
SIC: 3465 3444 3714 3564 Automotive
stampings; Sheet metalwork; Motor vehicle
parts and accessories; Blowers and fans

3469 Metal Stampings, Nec

(P-5167)
A & J MANUFACTURING COMPANY
70 Icon, Foothill Ranch (92610-3000)
PHONE..............................714 544-9570

Barry Lyerly, *CEO*
Janice Lyerly, *
EMP: 32 EST: 1954
SQ FT: 40,000
SALES (est): 4.14MM **Privately Held**
Web: www.aj-racks.com
SIC: 3469 Electronic enclosures, stamped or
pressed metal

(P-5168)
A-W ENGINEERING COMPANY INC
8528 Dice Rd, Santa Fe Springs
(90670-2590)
PHONE..............................562 945-1041
Guy Hansen, *Pr*
Anthony Giangrande, *
EMP: 36 EST: 1965
SQ FT: 38,000
SALES (est): 5.14MM **Privately Held**
Web: www.aw-eng.com
SIC: 3469 3544 Stamping metal for the trade
; Special dies and tools

(P-5169)
ACRONTOS MANUFACTURING INC
Also Called: AI Industries
1641 E Saint Gertrude Pl, Santa Ana
(92705-5311)
PHONE..............................714 850-9133
Ngoc V Hoang, *Pr*
EMP: 30 EST: 1991
SQ FT: 22,000
SALES (est): 2MM **Privately Held**
SIC: 3469 3599 3441 Stamping metal for the
trade; Machine and other job shop work;
Fabricated structural metal

(P-5170)
ACTION STAMPING INC
119 Explorer St, Pomona (91768-3278)
P.O. Box 778 (91740-0778)
PHONE..............................626 914-7466
Henry Reynolds, *CEO*
Terry Reynolds, *
▲ **EMP: 42 EST:** 1982
SALES (est): 2MM **Privately Held**
Web: www.actionstamping.com
SIC: 3469 Stamping metal for the trade

(P-5171)
ALL NEW STAMPING CO
10801 Lower Azusa Rd, El Monte
(91731-1307)
P.O. Box 5948 (91734-1948)
PHONE..............................626 443-8813
TOLL FREE: 800
Donald Schuil, *Pr*
Robert Larson, *
EMP: 150 EST: 1962
SQ FT: 40,000
SALES (est): 12.33MM **Privately Held**
Web: www.allnewstamping.com
SIC: 3469 3441 3444 Stamping metal for the
trade; Fabricated structural metal; Sheet
metal specialties, not stamped

(P-5172)
APT METAL FABRICATORS INC
11164 Bradley Ave, Pacoima (91331-2484)
PHONE..............................818 896-7478
Dennis M Vigo, *Pr*
Susan Vigo, *
▼ **EMP: 26 EST:** 1975
SQ FT: 18,000
SALES (est): 2.75MM **Privately Held**
Web: www.aptmetal.com
SIC: 3469 Stamping metal for the trade

(P-5173)
ASCENT MANUFACTURING LLC
2545 W Via Palma, Anaheim (92801-2624)
PHONE..............................714 540-6414
Travis Mullen, *CEO*
David Kramer, *
EMP: 34 EST: 2001
SQ FT: 17,000
SALES (est): 2.92MM **Privately Held**
Web: www.ascentmfg.com
SIC: 3469 1796 Machine parts, stamped or
pressed metal; Machinery installation

(P-5174)
BANDEL MFG INC
4459 Alger St, Los Angeles (90039-1292)
PHONE..............................818 246-7493
Jeannie Finley, *Pr*
Ed Finley, *
Chester Carlson, *
EMP: 23 EST: 1947
SQ FT: 15,000
SALES (est): 2.74MM **Privately Held**
Web: www.bandel.com
SIC: 3469 Stamping metal for the trade

(P-5175)
BINDER METAL PRODUCTS INC
14909 S Broadway, Gardena (90248-1817)
P.O. Box 2306 (90247-0306)
PHONE..............................800 233-0896
Steve Binder, *Pr*
Adam Binder, *
Ana Weber, *
▲ **EMP: 75 EST:** 1925
SQ FT: 35,000
SALES (est): 9.25MM **Privately Held**
Web: www.bindermetal.com
SIC: 3469 Stamping metal for the trade

(P-5176)
BLOOMERS METAL STAMPINGS INC
28615 Braxton Ave, Valencia (91355-4112)
PHONE..............................661 257-2955
Matt Holland, *CEO*
Perry Bloomer, *
Ella H Bloomer, *
EMP: 30 EST: 1976
SQ FT: 25,000
SALES (est): 3.93MM **Privately Held**
Web: www.bloomersmetal.com
SIC: 3469 Stamping metal for the trade

(P-5177)
BRAXTON CARIBBEAN MFG CO INC
2641 Walnut Ave, Tustin (92780-7005)
P.O. Box 425 (92781-0425)
PHONE..............................714 508-3570
Thomas Ordway, *Pr*
Robert Dionne, *
Joesph Triano, *
EMP: 62 EST: 1972
SALES (est): 3.68MM **Privately Held**
Web: www.braxtonmfg.com
SIC: 3469 Stamping metal for the trade

(P-5178)
CARAN PRECISION ENGINEERING & MANUFACTURING CORP (PA)
2830 Orbiter St, Brea (92821-6224)
PHONE..............................714 447-5400
▲ **EMP: 98 EST:** 1964
SALES (est): 23.83MM
SALES (corp-wide): 23.83MM **Privately Held**
Web: www.caranprecision.com

SIC: 3469 Metal stampings, nec

(P-5179)
CYGNET STMPING FABG INC A SWAN (PA)
613 Justin Ave, Glendale (91201-2326)
PHONE..............................818 240-7574
Marko Swan, *Pr*
E Michael Swan, *
John Swan, *
EMP: 29 EST: 1976
SQ FT: 28,000
SALES (est): 5.11MM
SALES (corp-wide): 5.11MM **Privately Held**
Web: www.cygnetstamping.com
SIC: 3469 Stamping metal for the trade

(P-5180)
DAVID ENGINEERING & MFG INC
Also Called: David Engineering & Mfg
1230 Quarry St, Corona (92879-1708)
P.O. Box 77035 (92877-0101)
PHONE..............................951 735-5200
Mike David, *CEO*
Michael David, *
EMP: 30 EST: 2003
SALES (est): 6.49MM **Privately Held**
Web: www.davidengineering.com
SIC: 3469 3544 Stamping metal for the trade
; Special dies and tools

(P-5181)
DAYTON ROGERS OF CALIFORNIA INC
13630 Saticoy St, Van Nuys (91402-6302)
PHONE..............................763 784-7714
EMP: 158
SIC: 3469 Stamping metal for the trade

(P-5182)
DIVERSIFIED TOOL & DIE
2585 Birch St, Vista (92081-8433)
PHONE..............................760 598-9100
Ernst Wilms, *CEO*
Rosa Wilms, *
EMP: 30 EST: 1972
SQ FT: 33,000
SALES (est): 4.64MM **Privately Held**
Web: www.stamping.com
SIC: 3469 3544 Stamping metal for the trade
; Special dies and tools

(P-5183)
EAGLEWARE MANUFACTURING CO INC
12683 Corral Pl, Santa Fe Springs
(90670-4748)
PHONE..............................562 320-3100
Brett L Gross, *Pr*
Eric Gross, *
▲ **EMP: 32 EST:** 1963
SQ FT: 130,000
SALES (est): 2.29MM **Privately Held**
SIC: 3469 3421 Stamping metal for the trade
; Cutlery

(P-5184)
ELIXIR INDUSTRIES
24800 Chrisanta Dr Ste 210, Mission Viejo
(92691-4842)
PHONE..............................949 860-5000
◆ **EMP:** 64
Web: www.elixirind.com
SIC: 3469 Metal stampings, nec

PRODUCTS & SVCS

(P-5185)
ENTERPRISES INDUSTRIES INC
7500 Tyrone Ave, Van Nuys (91405-1447)
PHONE...............................818 989-6103
Tony Magnome, *Pr*
Rolando Loera, *
Livino D Ribaya Junior, *VP Mfg*
Frank Ramirez Iii, *VP Engg*
Charles E Shaw, *
EMP: 130 **EST:** 1971
SALES (est): 1.13MM **Privately Held**
SIC: 3469 Stamping metal for the trade

(P-5186)
FALLBROOK INDUSTRIES INC
Also Called: Standish Precision Products
323 Industrial Way Ste 1, Fallbrook
(92028-2357)
PHONE...............................760 728-7229
Michael Standish, *Pr*
Dennis Standish, *
▲ **EMP:** 25 **EST:** 1973
SQ FT: 15,000
SALES (est): 3.6MM **Privately Held**
Web: www.standishproducts.com
SIC: 3469 Stamping metal for the trade

(P-5187)
FRED R RIPPY INC
12450 Whittier Blvd, Whittier (90602-1017)
PHONE...............................562 698-9801
▼ **EMP:** 35 **EST:** 1950
SALES (est): 7.08MM **Privately Held**
Web: www.frrippy.com
SIC: 3469 Metal stampings, nec

(P-5188)
FTR ASSOCIATES INC
11862 Burke St, Santa Fe Springs
(90670-2536)
PHONE...............................562 945-7504
EMP: 32 **EST:** 1986
SALES (est): 4.75MM **Privately Held**
Web: www.ftrmetalproducts.com
SIC: 3469 Metal stampings, nec

(P-5189)
GLOBAL PCCI (GPC) (PA)
Also Called: Gpc
2465 Campus Dr Ste 100, Irvine
(92612-1502)
PHONE...............................757 637-9000
Sherri Bovino, *Pt*
EMP: 120 **EST:** 1989
SQ FT: 10,000
SALES (est): 17.65MM **Privately Held**
SIC: 3469 4499 Metal stampings, nec;
　Salvaging, distressed vessels and cargoes

(P-5190)
HANMAR LLC (PA)
Also Called: Metalite Manufacturing
11441 Bradley Ave, Pacoima (91331-2304)
PHONE...............................818 890-2802
John Schachtner, *CEO*
Hannes Michael Schachtner, *
EMP: 49 **EST:** 1969
SQ FT: 25,000
SALES (est): 17MM
SALES (corp-wide): 17MM **Privately Held**
Web: www.metalite.net
SIC: 3469 Spinning metal for the trade

(P-5191)
HI TECH HONEYCOMB INC
9355 Ruffin Ct, San Diego (92123-5304)
PHONE...............................858 974-1600
Joao J Costa, *CEO*
John J Costa, *

Selma Costa, *
John Costa, *
EMP: 136 **EST:** 1989
SQ FT: 20,000
SALES (est): 20.93MM **Privately Held**
Web: www.hitechhoneycomb.com
SIC: 3469 Honeycombed metal

(P-5192)
HOUSTON BAZZ CO
Also Called: Bazz Houston Co
12700 Western Ave, Garden Grove
(92841-4082)
PHONE...............................714 898-2666
Javier Castro, *Pr*
Chester O Houston, *
▲ **EMP:** 85 **EST:** 1957
SQ FT: 50,000
SALES (est): 23.33MM **Privately Held**
Web: www.bhisolutions.com
SIC: 3469 3495 3493 Machine parts,
　stamped or pressed metal; Mechanical
　springs, precision; Steel springs, except
　wire

(P-5193)
IMPERIAL CAL PRODUCTS INC
425 Apollo St, Brea (92821-3110)
PHONE...............................714 990-9100
Shari Bittel, *Pr*
Kathy Flentye, *
▲ **EMP:** 35 **EST:** 1961
SQ FT: 35,000
SALES (est): 5.11MM **Privately Held**
Web: www.imperialhoods.com
SIC: 3469 Kitchen fixtures and equipment:
　metal, except cast aluminum

(P-5194)
INNOVATIVE STAMPING INC
Also Called: Innovative Systems
2068 E Gladwick St, Compton
(90220-6299)
P.O. Box 5327 (90224-5327)
PHONE...............................310 537-6996
Gerald L Czaban, *Pr*
Kim Stevenson, *
▼ **EMP:** 32 **EST:** 1976
SQ FT: 128,000
SALES (est): 4.7MM **Privately Held**
Web: www.innovative-sys.com
SIC: 3469 Stamping metal for the trade

(P-5195)
KAGA (USA) INC
2620 S Susan St, Santa Ana (92704-5816)
PHONE...............................714 540-2697
Masaaki Nozaki, *Pr*
Takashi Nozaki, *
Nobuharu Nozaki, *
Fumio Shiina, *
▲ **EMP:** 30 **EST:** 1981
SQ FT: 38,400
SALES (est): 5.82MM **Privately Held**
Web: www.kagainc.com
SIC: 3469 Stamping metal for the trade
PA: Kaga,Inc.
　140, Ni, Ota, Tsubatamachi

(P-5196)
KB DELTA INC
Also Called: KB Delta Comprsr Valve Parts
3155 Fujita St, Torrance (90505-4006)
PHONE...............................310 530-1539
Boris Giourof, *CEO*
Katarina Giourof, *
◆ **EMP:** 37 **EST:** 1982
SALES (est): 5.57MM **Privately Held**
Web: www.kbdelta.com

SIC: 3469 5085 7699 Machine parts,
　stamped or pressed metal; Industrial
　supplies; Compressor repair

(P-5197)
KITCOR CORPORATION
9959 Glenoaks Blvd, Sun Valley
(91352-1085)
PHONE...............................323 875-2820
Kent Kitchen, *Prin*
Kent Kitchen, *
Alice Kitchen, *
Jim Kitchen, *
Bob Kitchen, *
EMP: 35 **EST:** 1943
SQ FT: 42,000
SALES (est): 8.24MM **Privately Held**
Web: www.kitcor.com
SIC: 3469 Kitchen fixtures and equipment:
　metal, except cast aluminum

(P-5198)
LARRY SPUN PRODUCTS INC
1533 S Downey Rd, Los Angeles
(90023-4042)
PHONE...............................323 881-6300
Hilario F Hurtado, *CEO*
EMP: 49 **EST:** 1958
SQ FT: 6,000
SALES (est): 4.95MM **Privately Held**
Web: www.larryspunproducts.com
SIC: 3469 Stamping metal for the trade

(P-5199)
LOCK-RIDGE TOOL COMPANY
INC
145 N 8th Ave, Upland (91786-5402)
PHONE...............................909 865-8309
Keith Clark, *Pr*
Ashford Clark, *
Penney Clark, *
▲ **EMP:** 52 **EST:** 1962
SALES (est): 8.97MM **Privately Held**
Web: www.lockridgetool.com
SIC: 3469 Stamping metal for the trade

(P-5200)
LUPPEN HOLDINGS INC (PA)
Also Called: Metal Products Engineering
3050 Leonis Blvd, Vernon (90058-2914)
PHONE...............................323 581-8121
TOLL FREE: 800
Luppe R Luppen, *Ch Bd*
Paula Luppen, *
Ray Woodmansee, *
▲ **EMP:** 23 **EST:** 1940
SQ FT: 40,000
SALES (est): 688.31K
SALES (corp-wide): 688.31K **Privately
Held**
Web: www.metalproductseng.com
SIC: 3469 3578 3596 Stamping metal for the
　trade; Change making machines; Scales
　and balances, except laboratory

(P-5201)
METALITE MANUFACTURING
COMPANY
Also Called: Metalite Mfg Companys
11441 Bradley Ave, Pacoima (91331-2304)
PHONE...............................818 890-2802
Hanness Schachtner, *CEO*
Jan Schacatner, *
EMP: 41 **EST:** 1923
SQ FT: 58,000
SALES (est): 2.74MM
SALES (corp-wide): 17MM **Privately Held**
Web: www.metalite.net
SIC: 3469 Stamping metal for the trade
PA: Hanmar, Llc
　11441 Bradley Ave

818 890-2802

(P-5202)
METCO MANUFACTURING INC
Also Called: Metco Fourslide Manufacturing
17540 S Denver Ave, Gardena
(90248-3411)
PHONE...............................310 516-6547
Jack Bishop, *Pr*
Darryl Scholl, *
Shirley Bishop, *
Dana Beisel, *
EMP: 29 **EST:** 1980
SQ FT: 11,200
SALES (est): 4.83MM **Privately Held**
Web: www.metcofourslide.com
SIC: 3469 Stamping metal for the trade

(P-5203)
MICRO MATRIX SYSTEMS
Also Called: M M S
1899 Salem Ct, Claremont (91711-2638)
PHONE...............................909 626-8544
Grant P Zarbock, *CEO*
Kerry Zarbock, *
▲ **EMP:** 25 **EST:** 1968
SALES (est): 2.49MM **Privately Held**
Web: www.mmsys.biz
SIC: 3469 Stamping metal for the trade

(P-5204)
NANOPRECISION PRODUCTS
INC
802 Calle Plano, Camarillo (93012-8557)
PHONE...............................310 597-4991
Michael K Barnoski, *CEO*
EMP: 25 **EST:** 2002
SALES (est): 2.22MM **Privately Held**
Web: www.nanoprecision.com
SIC: 3469 3721 Stamping metal for the trade
　; Research and development on aircraft by
　the manufacturer

(P-5205)
NATIONAL METAL STAMPINGS
INC
42110 8th St E, Lancaster (93535-5413)
PHONE...............................661 945-1157
William T Bloomer, *Pr*
Madeleine J Bloomer, *
▲ **EMP:** 70 **EST:** 1979
SQ FT: 20,000
SALES (est): 9.91MM **Privately Held**
Web: www.nationalmetal.com
SIC: 3469 Stamping metal for the trade

(P-5206)
NELLXO LLC
5990 Bald Eagle Dr, Fontana (92336-4573)
PHONE...............................909 320-8501
EMP: 37 **EST:** 2021
SALES (est): 606.86K **Privately Held**
SIC: 3469 7389 Household cooking and
　kitchen utensils, metal; Business Activities
　at Non-Commercial Site

(P-5207)
PACIFIC METAL STAMPINGS INC
28415 Witherspoon Pkwy, Valencia
(91355-4174)
PHONE...............................661 257-7656
Brian Schlotfelt, *CEO*
Scott Schlotfelt, *
▲ **EMP:** 30 **EST:** 1954
SQ FT: 21,000
SALES (est): 6.76MM **Privately Held**
Web: www.pacificmetalstampings.com
SIC: 3469 Stamping metal for the trade

(P-5208)
PACIFIC PRECISION METALS INC
Also Called: Tubing Seal Cap Co
1100 E Orangethorpe Ave Ste 253,
Anaheim (92801-1164)
P.O. Box 51481 (91761)
PHONE.....................951 226-1500
Ajay N Thakkar, Pr
EMP: 200 EST: 1987
SQ FT: 2,063
SALES (est): 20.05MM Privately Held
Web: www.pacificprecisioninc.com
SIC: 3469 3429 2599 8711 Stamping metal
for the trade; Door locks, bolts, and checks;
Cabinets, factory; Machine tool design
PA: Triyar Sv, Llc
10850 Wilshire Blvd

(P-5209)
PRECISION RESOURCE INC
Also Called: Precision Resource Cal Div
5803 Engineer Dr, Huntington Beach
(92649-1127)
PHONE.....................714 891-4439
Robert Fitzgerald, Prin
EMP: 104
SQ FT: 27,000
SALES (corp-wide): 147.25MM Privately
Held
Web: www.precisionresource.com
SIC: 3469 3544 Stamping metal for the trade
; Special dies, tools, jigs, and fixtures
PA: Precision Resource, Inc.
25 Forest Pkwy
203 925-0012

(P-5210)
PROTOTYPE & SHORT-RUN SVCS INC
Also Called: Pass
1310 W Collins Ave, Orange (92867-5415)
PHONE.....................714 449-9661
Jack Mc Devitt, Pr
EMP: 25 EST: 1989
SQ FT: 6,700
SALES (est): 6.02MM
SALES (corp-wide): 10.07MM Privately
Held
Web: www.prototype-shortrun.com
SIC: 3469 Stamping metal for the trade
PA: Apl Manufacturing Inc
1310 W Collins Ave
714 542-1942

(P-5211)
RESEARCH TOOL & DIE WORKS LLC
Also Called: RT&d
17124 Keegan Ave, Carson (90746-1379)
PHONE.....................310 630 5722
EMP: 66 EST: 1952
SALES (est): 7.73MM
SALES (corp-wide): 653.43MM Privately
Held
Web: www.fairbanksmorsedefense.com
SIC: 3469 Metal stampings, nec
HQ: Fairbanks Morse, Llc
701 White Ave
Beloit WI 53511
800 356-6955

(P-5212)
SERRA MANUFACTURING CORP (PA)
3039 E Las Hermanas St, Compton
(90221-5575)
PHONE.....................310 537-4560
Sylvia G Hernandez, Ch Bd

John B Hernandez, *
Kris Hernandez, *
EMP: 53 EST: 1959
SQ FT: 23,916
SALES (est): 8.52MM
SALES (corp-wide): 8.52MM Privately
Held
Web: www.serramfg.com
SIC: 3469 Stamping metal for the trade

(P-5213)
SOUTHWEST GREENE INTL INC
Also Called: Greene Group Industries
4055b Calle Platino, Oceanside
(92056-5805)
PHONE.....................760 639-4960
Alexis Willingham, Pr
▲ EMP: 100 EST: 1997
SQ FT: 80,000
SALES (est): 18.38MM Privately Held
Web: www.greenegroup.com
SIC: 3469 Metal stampings, nec

(P-5214)
SPOTTER GLOBAL INC
1204 N Miller St Unit A, Anaheim
(92806-1958)
PHONE.....................515 817-3726
Luke Zhao, CEO
EMP: 140 EST: 2021
SALES (est): 2MM Privately Held
SIC: 3469 5064 Household cooking and
kitchen utensils, metal; Electric household
appliances, nec

(P-5215)
STEICO INDUSTRIES INC
Also Called: Steico
1814 Ord Way, Oceanside (92056-1502)
PHONE.....................760 438-8015
Troy Steiner, CEO
▲ EMP: 230 EST: 2001
SQ FT: 52,000
SALES (est): 51.17MM
SALES (corp-wide): 1.2B Privately Held
Web: www.steicoindustries.com
SIC: 3469 5051 Metal stampings, nec;
Metals service centers and offices
HQ: Senior Operations Llc
300 E Devon Ave
Bartlett IL 60103
630 372-3500

(P-5216)
SUNSTONE COMPONENTS GROUP INC (HQ)
Also Called: Sun Stone Sales
42136 Avenida Alvarado, Temecula
(92590-3400)
PHONE.....................951 296-5010
Bradway B Adams, CEO
David Bernard, *
EMP: 41 EST: 1990
SALES (est): 9.89MM
SALES (corp-wide): 27.84MM Privately
Held
Web: www.4scg.com
SIC: 3469 Metal stampings, nec
PA: Pancon Corporation
350 Revolutionary Dr
781 297-6000

(P-5217)
TEAM MANUFACTURING INC
2625 Homestead Pl, Rancho Dominguez
(90220-5610)
PHONE.....................310 639-0251
Ed Ellis, CEO
James Cheatham, *
▲ EMP: 50 EST: 1975

SQ FT: 34,000
SALES (est): 4.86MM Privately Held
Web: www.teammfg.com
SIC: 3469 3544 Stamping metal for the trade
; Die sets for metal stamping (presses)

(P-5218)
TRU-FORM INDUSTRIES INC (PA)
Also Called: Tru Form Industries
14511 Anson Ave, Santa Fe Springs
(90670-5393)
PHONE.....................562 802-2041
Vernon M Hildebrandt, CEO
▲ EMP: 69 EST: 1974
SQ FT: 50,000
SALES (est): 8.55MM
SALES (corp-wide): 8.55MM Privately
Held
Web: www.tru-form.com
SIC: 3469 3496 3429 Metal stampings, nec;
Clips and fasteners, made from purchased
wire; Hardware, nec

(P-5219)
USG CEILINGS PLUS LLC
6711 E Washington Blvd, Commerce
(90040-1801)
PHONE.....................323 724-8166
Nancy Mercolino, Pr
EMP: 24 EST: 2017
SALES (est): 10.1MM
SALES (corp-wide): 16B Privately Held
Web: www.usg.com
SIC: 3469 Architectural panels or parts,
porcelain enameled
HQ: Usg Corporation
550 W Adams St
Chicago IL 60661
312 436-4000

(P-5220)
VANGUARD TOOL & MFG CO INC
Also Called: Vanguard Tool & Manufacturing
8388 Utica Ave, Rancho Cucamonga
(91730-3849)
PHONE.....................909 980-9392
Robert A Scudder, Pr
Connie Scudder, *
EMP: 49 EST: 1970
SQ FT: 47,000
SALES (est): 8.86MM Privately Held
Web: www.vanguardtoolmfg.net
SIC: 3469 Stamping metal for the trade

(P-5221)
WALKER SPRING & STAMPING CORP
Also Called: Walker
1555 S Vintage Ave, Ontario (91761-3055)
PHONE.....................909 390-4300
Lang Walker, Ch Bd
Bruce Walker, Pr
James D Walker Junior, VP Mfg
Randy Walker, VP Sls
Carmen Prieto, Sec
▲ EMP: 110 EST: 1954
SQ FT: 108,000
SALES (est): 19.83MM Privately Held
SIC: 3469 3495 Stamping metal for the trade
; Precision springs

(P-5222)
WEST COAST MANUFACTURING INC
Also Called: West Coast Manufacturing
11822 Western Ave, Stanton (90680-3438)
PHONE.....................714 897-4221

Patrick Hundley, Pr
Minerva Hundley, *
▲ EMP: 26 EST: 1993
SQ FT: 8,000
SALES (est): 11.19MM Privately Held
Web: www.westcoastmfg.com
SIC: 3469 Machine parts, stamped or
pressed metal

(P-5223)
WEST COAST METAL STAMPING INCORPORATED
550 W Crowther Ave, Placentia
(92870-6312)
PHONE.....................714 792-0322
EMP: 32 EST: 1966
SALES (est): 6.71MM Privately Held
Web: www.wcmetalstamping.com
SIC: 3469 Stamping metal for the trade

3471 Plating And Polishing

(P-5224)
AAA PLATING & INSPECTION INC
424 E Dixon St, Compton (90222-1420)
PHONE.....................323 979-8930
Gerald Wahlin, CEO
Charles Schwan, *
EMP: 95 EST: 1958
SQ FT: 50,000
SALES (est): 8.7MM Privately Held
Web: www.aaaplating.com
SIC: 3471 8734 Anodizing (plating) of metals
or formed products; Metallurgical testing
laboratory

(P-5225)
ACCURATE PLATING COMPANY
2811 Alcazar St, Los Angeles (90033-1108)
P.O. Box 33348 (90033-0348)
PHONE.....................323 268-8567
Dennis Orr, Pr
Rigo Rodriguez, *
EMP: 30 EST: 1949
SQ FT: 18,000
SALES (est): 3.47MM Privately Held
Web: www.accurateplatingco.com
SIC: 3471 Electroplating of metals or formed
products

(P-5226)
ALCO PLATING CORP (PA)
Also Called: Modern Plating
1400 Long Beach Ave, Los Angeles
(90021-2794)
PHONE.....................213 749-7501
E Edward Chuck Manzetti, Pr
Emil Edward Chuck Manzetti, Pr
David Manzetti, *
▲ EMP: 50 EST: 1929
SQ FT: 65,000
SALES (est): 3.17MM
SALES (corp-wide): 3.17MM Privately
Held
Web: www.alconickelchrome.com
SIC: 3471 Electroplating of metals or formed
products

(P-5227)
ALERT PLATING COMPANY
Also Called: Alert Plating
9939 Glenoaks Blvd, Sun Valley
(91352-1023)
PHONE.....................818 771-9304
David La Liberte, Pr
Maurice La Liberte, *
Shirley La Liberte, *
Ed Lee, *

PRODUCTS & SVCS

EMP: 45 EST: 1968
SQ FT: 22,000
SALES (est): 4.37MM **Privately Held**
SIC: 3471 Finishing, metals or formed
products

(P-5228)
ALL METALS PROCESSING OF SAN DIEGO INC
Also Called: AMC
8401 Standustrial St, Stanton (90680-2688)
PHONE..................714 828-8238
EMP: 120
Web: www.allmetalsprocessing.com
SIC: 3471 3479 8734 Electroplating of
metals or formed products; Enameling,
including porcelain, of metal products; X-
ray inspection service, industrial

(P-5229)
ALL MTALS PROC ORANGE CNTY LLC
8401 Standustrial St, Stanton (90680-2688)
PHONE..................714 828-8238
Scott Christman, CFO
Bob Wolfsberger, *
Rose Blikian, *
Michael Coburn, *
Derek Watson, *
EMP: 125 EST: 2015
SALES (est): 19.36MM **Privately Held**
Web: www.allmetalsprocessing.com
SIC: 3471 3479 8734 Electroplating of
metals or formed products; Enameling,
including porcelain, of metal products; X-
ray inspection service, industrial

(P-5230)
ALLBLACK CO INC
8155 Byron Rd, Whittier (90606-2615)
PHONE..................562 946-2955
Juan F Guerrero, Pr
Lorena Guerrero, *
▲ EMP: 39 EST: 1992
SQ FT: 12,000
SALES (est): 4.63MM **Privately Held**
Web: www.allblackco-inc.com
SIC: 3471 Electroplating of metals or formed
products

(P-5231)
ALPHA POLISHING CORPORATION (PA)
Also Called: General Plating
1313 Mirasol St, Los Angeles (90023-3108)
PHONE..................323 263-7593
TOLL FREE: 800
Alan Olick, Pr
Alan Olick, Pr
Trinidad Gonzales, *
EMP: 60 EST: 1940
SQ FT: 7,500
SALES (est): 2.45MM
SALES (corp-wide): 2.45MM **Privately
Held**
Web: www.generalplatingco.net
SIC: 3471 3911 Plating of metals or formed
products; Pins (jewelry), precious metal

(P-5232)
ANAPLEX CORPORATION
15547 Garfield Ave, Paramount
(90723-4033)
PHONE..................714 522-4481
Carmen Campbell, CEO
Bernie Kerper, *
EMP: 48 EST: 1962
SQ FT: 38,000
SALES (est): 4.88MM **Privately Held**

Web: www.anaplexcorp.com
SIC: 3471 Electroplating of metals or formed
products

(P-5233)
ANODIZING INDUSTRIES INC
5222 Alhambra Ave, Los Angeles
(90032-3403)
P.O. Box 32459 (90032-0459)
PHONE..................323 227-4916
Eugene J Golling, Pr
Amir Afshar, *
▲ EMP: 30 EST: 1980
SQ FT: 8,000
SALES (est): 3.01MM **Privately Held**
Web: www.anodizingindustries.com
SIC: 3471 3479 2396 Anodizing (plating) of
metals or formed products; Painting of
metal products; Automotive and apparel
trimmings

(P-5234)
ANODYNE INC
2230 S Susan St, Santa Ana (92704-4493)
PHONE..................714 549-3321
Ralph Adams, Pr
Patti Kientz, *
EMP: 49 EST: 1960
SQ FT: 30,000
SALES (est): 3.71MM **Privately Held**
Web: www.anodyne.aero
SIC: 3471 8734 Anodizing (plating) of metals
or formed products; Testing laboratories

(P-5235)
ASSOCIATED PLATING COMPANY
9636 Ann St, Santa Fe Springs
(90670-2995)
PHONE..................562 946-5525
Michael Evans, Pr
Jon Shulkin, Stockholder*
▲ EMP: 26 EST: 1952
SQ FT: 18,000
SALES (est): 2.39MM **Privately Held**
Web: www.associatedplating.com
SIC: 3471 Finishing, metals or formed
products

(P-5236)
AUTOMATION PLATING CORPORATION
927 Thompson Ave, Glendale
(91201-2011)
PHONE..................323 245-4951
Peter K Wiggins, *
Edward Lee, *
Pat Kinzy, *
Marcia Mitchell, *
EMP: 40 EST: 1941
SQ FT: 65,000
SALES (est): 5.06MM **Privately Held**
Web: www.apczinc.com
SIC: 3471 Plating of metals or formed
products

(P-5237)
BARRY AVENUE PLATING CO INC
2210 Barry Ave, Los Angeles (90064-1488)
PHONE..................310 478-0078
Chuck Kearsley, Pr
Charles B Kearsley Iv, Pr
Kenneth F Kearsley, *
▼ EMP: 88 EST: 1951
SQ FT: 26,000
SALES (est): 10.36MM **Privately Held**
Web: www.barryavenueplating.com

SIC: 3471 Electroplating of metals or formed
products

(P-5238)
BHC INDUSTRIES INC
239 E Greenleaf Blvd, Compton
(90220-4913)
PHONE..................310 632-2000
Gary Barken, Pr
EMP: 25 EST: 2000
SQ FT: 20,000
SALES (est): 719.37K **Privately Held**
Web: www.barkenshardchrome.com
SIC: 3471 Electroplating of metals or formed
products

(P-5239)
BLACK OXIDE INDUSTRIES INC
Also Called: Black Oxide
1745 N Orangethorpe Park Ste A, Anaheim
(92801-1172)
PHONE..................714 870-9610
Pete Mata, Pr
Edward Mata, *
Evelyn Mata, *
EMP: 35 EST: 1974
SALES (est): 2MM **Privately Held**
Web: www.blackoxideindustries.com
SIC: 3471 3479 Electroplating of metals or
formed products; Coating of metals and
formed products

(P-5240)
BODYCOTE THERMAL PROC INC
3370 Benedict Way, Huntington Park
(90255-4517)
PHONE..................323 583-1231
Chris Hall, Brnch Mgr
EMP: 87
SQ FT: 16,694
SALES (corp-wide): 1B **Privately Held**
Web: www.bodycote.com
SIC: 3471 3398 Plating and polishing; Metal
heat treating
HQ: Bodycote Thermal Processing, Inc.
12750 Merit Dr Ste 1400
Dallas TX 75251
214 904-2420

(P-5241)
BOWMAN PLATING CO INC
2631 E 126th St, Compton (90222-1599)
P.O. Box 5205 (90224-5205)
PHONE..................310 639-4343
Mac Esfandi, Pr
Rashel Esfandi, *
John Esfandi, Stockholder*
Cyrus Gipoor, Stockholder*
EMP: 150 EST: 1952
SALES (est): 8.51MM **Privately Held**
Web: www.bowmanplating.com
SIC: 3471 Electroplating of metals or formed
products

(P-5242)
BOWMAN-FIELD INC
Also Called: Chrome Nickel Plating
2800 Martin Luther King Jr Blvd, Lynwood
(90262-1829)
PHONE..................310 638-8519
Hector Flores, Pr
Ron Storer, *
▲ EMP: 60 EST: 1946
SQ FT: 20,000
SALES (est): 1.03MM **Privately Held**
Web: www.chrome1.com
SIC: 3471 3714 Chromium plating of metals
or formed products; Motor vehicle parts and
accessories

(P-5243)
BRONZE-WAY PLATING CORPORATION (PA)
3301 E 14th St, Los Angeles (90023-3893)
PHONE..................323 266-6933
Sarkis Mikhael-fard, Pr
Benjamin Mikhael-fard, VP
Fiyodor Mikhael-fard, VP
Fred Mikhael-fard, VP
EMP: 44 EST: 1956
SQ FT: 27,000
SALES (est): 549.68K
SALES (corp-wide): 549.68K **Privately
Held**
Web: www.generalplatingco.net
SIC: 3471 Electroplating of metals or formed
products

(P-5244)
CAL-AURUM INDUSTRIES
Also Called: Cal-Aurum
15632 Container Ln, Huntington Beach
(92649-1533)
PHONE..................714 898-0996
Paul A Ginder, Pr
Chuck Tygard, *
EMP: 35 EST: 1971
SQ FT: 25,000
SALES (est): 5.05MM **Privately Held**
Web: www.cal-aurum.com
SIC: 3471 Electroplating of metals or formed
products

(P-5245)
CAL-TRON PLATING INC
11919 Rivera Rd, Santa Fe Springs
(90670-2209)
PHONE..................562 945-1181
Carl Troncale Junior, CEO
Carl Troncale Senior, Ch Bd
EMP: 45 EST: 1961
SQ FT: 15,000
SALES (est): 2.98MM **Privately Held**
Web: www.cal-tronplating.com
SIC: 3471 Electroplating of metals or formed
products

(P-5246)
CERTIFIED STEEL TREATING CORP
2454 E 58th St, Vernon (90058-3592)
PHONE..................323 583-8711
Janice Davis, Pr
Pauline Nicolls, Stockholder*
Jeff Davis, *
EMP: 42 EST: 1947
SQ FT: 30,000
SALES (est): 7.5MM **Privately Held**
SIC: 3471 3398 Sand blasting of metal parts;
Annealing of metal

(P-5247)
CHROMAL PLATING COMPANY
Also Called: Chromal Plating & Grinding
1748 Workman St, Los Angeles
(90031-3395)
PHONE..................323 222-0119
Ethel Bokelman, Pr
Ray F Bokelman Junior, VP
Diane L Remilinger, *
Robin Bokelman, *
Robin Ospoin, *
EMP: 28 EST: 1946
SQ FT: 20,625
SALES (est): 2.51MM **Privately Held**
Web: www.chromal.com
SIC: 3471 3999 Electroplating of metals or
formed products; Grinding and pulverizing
of materials, nec

(P-5248)

CHROME TECH INC

2310 Cape Cod Way, Santa Ana
(92703-3562)
PHONE.....................714 543-4092
EMP: 107
Web: www.chrometechwheels.com
SIC: 3471 Plating and polishing

(P-5249)

COAST PLATING INC (PA)

Also Called: Valence Los Angeles
128 W 154th St, Gardena (90248-2202)
PHONE.....................323 770-0240
EMP: 50 **EST:** 1965
SALES (est): 5.11MM
SALES (corp-wide): 5.11MM **Privately Held**
Web: www.coastplating.com
SIC: 3471 Plating of metals or formed products

(P-5250)

COAST TO COAST MET FINSHG CORP

401 S Raymond Ave, Alhambra
(91803-1532)
PHONE.....................626 282-2122
Gildardo Bernal, *Pr*
David Bernal, *
EMP: 25 **EST:** 1978
SQ FT: 20,000
SALES (est): 2.08MM **Privately Held**
Web: www.ctclightingmfg.com
SIC: 3471 3646 3645 Finishing, metals or formed products; Commercial lighting fixtures; Residential lighting fixtures

(P-5251)

COASTLINE METAL FINISHING CORP

7061 Patterson Dr, Garden Grove
(92841-1414)
PHONE.....................714 895-9099
Tracy Glende, *CEO*
Jamie Mitchell, *
Matthew Alty, *
EMP: 83 **EST:** 1987
SQ FT: 18,600
SALES (est): 8.26MM **Privately Held**
Web: www.valencesurfacetech.com
SIC: 3471 Finishing, metals or formed products

(P-5252)

CONNELL PROCESSING INC (PA)

3094 N Avon St, Burbank (91504-2003)
PHONE.....................818 845-7661
Stephen Lee, *Pr*
David Augustine, *
EMP: 27 **EST:** 1946
SQ FT: 25,000
SALES (est): 2.81MM
SALES (corp-wide): 2.81MM **Privately Held**
Web: www.connellprocessing.com
SIC: 3471 Electroplating of metals or formed products

(P-5253)

DANCO ANODIZING INC (PA)

Also Called: Danco Metal Surfacing
44 La Porte St, Arcadia (91006-2827)
P.O. Box 660727 (91066-0727)
PHONE.....................626 445-3303
Sherri Vivian Scherer, *Pr*
David Tatge, *
EMP: 40 **EST:** 1971

SQ FT: 10,000
SALES (est): 15.68MM
SALES (corp-wide): 15.68MM **Privately Held**
Web: www.danco.net
SIC: 3471 Electroplating of metals or formed products

(P-5254)

DANCO ANODIZING INC

Also Called: Danco
1750 E Monticello Ct, Ontario (91761-7740)
PHONE.....................909 923-0562
Joe Galvan, *Mgr*
EMP: 102
SALES (corp-wide): 15.68MM **Privately Held**
Web: www.danco.net
SIC: 3471 Anodizing (plating) of metals or formed products
PA: Danco Anodizing, Inc.
44 La Porte St
626 445-3303

(P-5255)

E M E INC

Also Called: Electro Machine & Engrg Co
500 E Pine St, Compton (90222-2818)
P.O. Box 4998 (90224-4998)
PHONE.....................310 639-1621
Wesley Turnbow, *CEO*
Randy Turnbow, *
Steven Turnbow, *
EMP: 125 **EST:** 1962
SQ FT: 65,000
SALES (est): 10.97MM **Privately Held**
Web: www.emeplating.com
SIC: 3471 2899 Anodizing (plating) of metals or formed products; Chemical preparations, nec

(P-5256)

ELECTRODE TECHNOLOGIES INC

Also Called: Reid Metal Finishing
3110 W Harvard St Ste 14, Santa Ana
(92704-3940)
PHONE.....................714 549-3771
Tim A Grandcolas, *Pr*
Ivan Padron, *
▲ **EMP:** 40 **EST:** 1978
SQ FT: 10,000
SALES (est): 7.43MM **Privately Held**
Web: www.rmfusa.com
SIC: 3471 Finishing, metals or formed products

(P-5257)

ELECTROLIZING INC

1947 Hooper Ave, Los Angeles
(90011-1354)
P.O. Box 11900 (90011-0900)
PHONE.....................213 749-7876
Susan B Grant, *Pr*
Jack Morgan, *
EMP: 26 **EST:** 1947
SQ FT: 10,000
SALES (est): 2.68MM **Privately Held**
Web: www.electrolizingofla.com
SIC: 3471 Electroplating of metals or formed products

(P-5258)

ELECTROLURGY INC

1121 Duryea Ave, Irvine (92614-5584)
PHONE.....................949 250-4494
Eron G Eklund, *Pr*
June Eklund, *
Sean Eklund, *
Stefni Gritten, *

EMP: 68 **EST:** 1969
SQ FT: 25,000
SALES (est): 8.3MM **Privately Held**
Web: www.electrolurgy.com
SIC: 3471 3429 Electroplating of metals or formed products; Marine hardware

(P-5259)

ELECTRONIC PRECISION SPC INC

545 Mercury Ln, Brea (92821-4831)
PHONE.....................714 256-8950
Thomas Olszewski, *CEO*
Henry Brown, *
EMP: 34 **EST:** 1980
SQ FT: 4,000
SALES (est): 5.14MM **Privately Held**
Web: www.elecprec.com
SIC: 3471 Electroplating of metals or formed products

(P-5260)

ELITE METAL FINISHING LLC (PA)

Also Called: Metal Finishing Pntg Lab Tstg
540 Spectrum Cir, Oxnard (93030-8988)
PHONE.....................805 983-4320
Joel Clemons, *Pt*
Joe Hansen, *
George Hansen, *
EMP: 109 **EST:** 2001
SQ FT: 55,000
SALES (est): 20.1MM
SALES (corp-wide): 20.1MM **Privately Held**
Web: www.elitemetalfinishing.com
SIC: 3471 8734 Plating of metals or formed products; Testing laboratories

(P-5261)

FLARE GROUP

1571 Macarthur Blvd, Costa Mesa
(92626-1407)
PHONE.....................714 549-0202
EMP: 25
SALES (est): 1.04MM **Privately Held**
SIC: 3471 Plating and polishing

(P-5262)

GENES PLATING WORKS INC (PA)

3498 E 14th St, Los Angeles (90023-3819)
PHONE.....................323 269-8748
Harry W Levy, *Pr*
John F Whitney, *VP*
EMP: 30 **EST:** 2002
SQ FT: 13,000
SALES (est): 1.31MM
SALES (corp-wide): 1.31MM **Privately Held**
Web: www.lombardtechnologies.com
SIC: 3471 Plating of metals or formed products

(P-5263)

GEORGE INDUSTRIES (HQ)

4116 Whiteside St, Los Angeles
(90063-1692)
PHONE.....................323 264-6660
Jeff Briggs, *Pr*
EMP: 40 **EST:** 1953
SQ FT: 38,200
SALES (est): 5.46MM
SALES (corp-wide): 4.17B **Publicly Held**
Web: www.valmontcoatings.com
SIC: 3471 3479 Anodizing (plating) of metals or formed products; Aluminum coating of metal products
PA: Valmont Industries, Inc.
15000 Valmont Plz

402 963-1000

(P-5264)

GLOBAL METAL SOLUTIONS INC

2150 Mcgaw Ave, Irvine (92614-0912)
PHONE.....................949 872-2995
Mario Robles, *Pr*
Mario Robles, *Pr*
Thomas Linovitz, *
EMP: 35 **EST:** 2016
SALES (est): 8.41MM **Privately Held**
Web: www.gms1.net
SIC: 3471 Polishing, metals or formed products

(P-5265)

GSP METAL FINISHING INC

16520 S Figueroa St, Gardena
(90248-2625)
PHONE.....................818 744-1328
Mike Palatas, *VP*
EMP: 35 **EST:** 2019
SALES (est): 2.46MM **Privately Held**
Web: www.gspmf.com
SIC: 3471 Electroplating of metals or formed products

(P-5266)

HIGHTOWER PLATING & MFG CO LLC

Also Called: Anillo Industries
2090 N Glassell St, Orange (92865-3391)
P.O. Box 5586 (92863-5586)
PHONE.....................714 637-9110
Kurt Koch, *Pr*
Mark Koch, *
EMP: 50 **EST:** 1957
SQ FT: 8,000
SALES (est): 2.06MM **Privately Held**
SIC: 3471 Plating of metals or formed products

(P-5267)

HIXSON METAL FINISHING

829 Production Pl, Newport Beach
(92663-2809)
PHONE.....................800 900-9798
Carl Blazik, *Prin*
Douglas Greene, *
EMP: 69 **EST:** 1960
SQ FT: 38,000
SALES (est): 5.76MM **Privately Held**
Web: www.hmfgroup.com
SIC: 3471 Finishing, metals or formed products

(P-5268)

INTERNATIONAL PLATING SVC LLC (PA)

4045 Bonita Rd Ste 309, Bonita
(91902-1337)
P.O. Box 210310 (91921-0310)
PHONE.....................619 454-2135
Guillermo A Fernandez, *Managing Member*
Jeffrey Robert Adams, *
EMP: 34 **EST:** 1996
SQ FT: 500
SALES (est): 2.33MM
SALES (corp-wide): 2.33MM **Privately Held**
Web: www.platinadorabaja.com
SIC: 3471 Electroplating of metals or formed products

(P-5269)

INVECO INC

Also Called: Mighty Green
440 Fair Dr Ste 200, Costa Mesa
(92626-6222)

PHONE..................949 378-3850
Dennis D'alessio, *Pr*
EMP: 30 **EST:** 2013
SALES (est): 18MM **Privately Held**
SIC: 3471 Cleaning, polishing, and finishing

(P-5270)
JCR AIRCRAFT DEBURRING LLC
Also Called: Jcr Deburring
221 Foundation Ave, La Habra
(90631-6812)
PHONE..................714 870-4427
Juan Carlos Ruiz, *CEO*
Juan Carlos Ruiz, *Managing Member*
Omar Ruiz, *
EMP: 80 **EST:** 1986
SALES (est): 10.62MM **Privately Held**
Web: www.jcrindustries.com
SIC: 3471 3541 3444 3542 Electroplating of
metals or formed products; Deburring
machines; Forming machine work, sheet
metal; Machine tools, metal forming type

(P-5271)
JD PROCESSING INC
2220 Cape Cod Way, Santa Ana
(92703-3563)
PHONE..................714 972-8161
Thomas Scimeca, *CEO*
EMP: 50 **EST:** 2014
SALES (est): 4.77MM **Privately Held**
Web: www.jdprocessinginc.com
SIC: 3471 3559 Anodizing (plating) of metals
or formed products; Anodizing equipment

(P-5272)
KRYLER CORP
Also Called: Pecific Grinding
1217 E Ash Ave, Fullerton (92831-5019)
PHONE..................714 871-9611
Chet Krygier Senior, *Pr*
Phyllis Krygier, *
EMP: 30 **EST:** 1977
SQ FT: 900
SALES (est): 2.42MM **Privately Held**
Web: www.krylercorporation.com
SIC: 3471 Electroplating of metals or formed
products

(P-5273)
MAIN STEEL LLC
3100 Jefferson St, Riverside (92504-4339)
PHONE..................951 231-4949
Mike Folley, *Brnch Mgr*
EMP: 63
SALES (corp-wide): 1.54B **Privately Held**
Web: www.mainsteel.com
SIC: 3471 Polishing, metals or formed
products
HQ: Main Steel, Llc
2200 E Pratt Blvd
Elk Grove Village IL 60007
847 916-1220

(P-5274)
METAL CHEM INC
Also Called: Metal Chem
21514 Nordhoff St, Chatsworth
(91311-5822)
PHONE..................818 727-9951
Carlos Pongo, *Pr*
EMP: 30 **EST:** 1997
SALES (est): 6.15MM **Privately Held**
Web: www.metalcheminc.com
SIC: 3471 3443 Plating of metals or formed
products; Fabricated plate work (boiler
shop)

(P-5275)
METAL SURFACES INTL LLC
6060 Shull St, Bell Gardens (90201-6237)
P.O. Box 5001 (90202-5001)
PHONE..................562 927-1331
Olaf Schubert, *Pr*
Charles K Bell, *
Sam Bell, *
EMP: 150 **EST:** 1954
SQ FT: 85,000
SALES (est): 18.65MM **Privately Held**
Web: www.metalsurfaces.com
SIC: 3471 Electroplating of metals or formed
products

(P-5276)
MORRELLS ELECTRO PLATING INC
Also Called: Morrell's Metal Finishing
436 E Euclid Ave, Compton (90222-2810)
P.O. Box 3085 (90223-3085)
PHONE..................310 639-1024
Cyrus Gipoor, *Pr*
EMP: 30 **EST:** 1948
SQ FT: 20,000
SALES (est): 4.6MM **Privately Held**
Web: www.morrellsplating.com
SIC: 3471 Electroplating of metals or formed
products

(P-5277)
MULTICHROME COMPANY INC (PA)
Also Called: Microplate
1013 W Hillcrest Blvd, Inglewood
(90301-2019)
PHONE..................310 216-1086
Steven A Peterman, *Pr*
EMP: 26 **EST:** 1962
SQ FT: 5,000
SALES (est): 2.36MM
SALES (corp-wide): 2.36MM **Privately Held**
Web: www.multiplate.com
SIC: 3471 Electroplating of metals or formed
products

(P-5278)
NASMYTH TMF INC
29102 Hancock Pkwy, Valencia
(91355-1066)
PHONE..................818 954-9504
Peter Smith, *CEO*
EMP: 54 **EST:** 2014
SQ FT: 10,000
SALES (est): 6.22MM
SALES (corp-wide): 248.37K **Privately Held**
Web: www.technicalmetalfinishing.com
SIC: 3471 3479 Anodizing (plating) of metals
or formed products; Coating of metals and
formed products
HQ: Ngl Realisations Limited
Nasmyth House
Coventry W MIDLANDS CV7 9

(P-5279)
OLD SPC INC
202 W 140th St, Los Angeles (90061-1006)
PHONE..................310 533-0748
Mary Mcmeans, *CEO*
Donna Martinez, *VP*
Jesus Diaz, *Sec*
EMP: 25 **EST:** 1999
SQ FT: 60,000
SALES (est): 3.3MM **Privately Held**
Web: www.spectrumplating.com
SIC: 3471 Electroplating of metals or formed
products

(P-5280)
OMNI METAL FINISHING INC (PA)
11639 Coley River Cir, Fountain Valley
(92708-4216)
PHONE..................714 979-9414
Victor M Salazar, *Pr*
Ramiro Salazar, *
Filiberto Hernandez, *
EMP: 99 **EST:** 1980
SQ FT: 34,000
SALES (est): 15.79MM
SALES (corp-wide): 15.79MM **Privately Held**
Web: www.omnimetal.com
SIC: 3471 Electroplating of metals or formed
products

(P-5281)
OPTI-FORMS INC
42310 Winchester Rd, Temecula
(92590-4810)
PHONE..................951 296-1300
Kevin Thompson, *Pr*
Robert Brunson, *
Clint Tinker, *
EMP: 45 **EST:** 1984
SQ FT: 61,000
SALES (est): 9.96MM **Privately Held**
Web: www.optiforms.com
SIC: 3471 3827 Plating of metals or formed
products; Optical instruments and lenses

(P-5282)
PENTRATE METAL PROCESSING
3517 E Olympic Blvd, Los Angeles
(90023-3976)
PHONE..................323 269-2121
John J Grana, *Pr*
Vincent Grana, *
Nick Grana, *
Nick Gran, *Genl Mgr*
EMP: 30 **EST:** 1945
SQ FT: 18,000
SALES (est): 3.03MM **Privately Held**
Web: www.pentrate.com
SIC: 3471 Electroplating of metals or formed
products

(P-5283)
PLASMA RGGEDIZED SOLUTIONS INC
5452 Business Dr, Huntington Beach
(92649-1226)
PHONE..................714 893-6063
Bob Marla, *Brnch Mgr*
EMP: 27
Web: www.plasmarugged.com
SIC: 3471 3479 Electroplating and plating;
Coating of metals and formed products
PA: Plasma Ruggedized Solutions, Inc.
2284 Ringwood Ave Ste A

(P-5284)
PLATERONICS PROCESSING INC
Also Called: Plateronics Processing
9164 Independence Ave, Chatsworth
(91311-5902)
PHONE..................818 341-2191
Joseph Roter, *Pr*
Marvin Roter, *
Lee F Roter, *
EMP: 35 **EST:** 1959
SQ FT: 6,500
SALES (est): 3MM **Privately Held**
Web: www.plateronics.com

SIC: 3471 5051 Finishing, metals or formed
products; Metals service centers and offices

(P-5285)
PRECISION ANODIZING & PLTG INC
Also Called: P A P
1601 N Miller St, Anaheim (92806-1469)
PHONE..................714 996-1601
Jose A Salazar, *CEO*
EMP: 89 **EST:** 1971
SQ FT: 44,000
SALES (est): 9.94MM **Privately Held**
Web:
www.precisionanodizingandplating.com
SIC: 3471 Electroplating of metals or formed
products

(P-5286)
QUAKER CITY PLATING
Also Called: Quaker City Plating & Silvrsm
11729 Washington Blvd, Whittier
(90606-2613)
P.O. Box 2406 (90610-2406)
PHONE..................562 945-3721
Michael Crain, *Mng Pt*
Angelo Dirado, *Mng Pt*
▲ **EMP:** 220 **EST:** 1937
SQ FT: 48,000
SALES (est): 23.36MM **Privately Held**
Web: www.qcpent.com
SIC: 3471 Plating of metals or formed
products

(P-5287)
RAVLICH ENTERPRISES LLC (PA)
Also Called: Neutronic Stamping & Plating
100 Business Center Dr, Corona
(92878-3224)
PHONE..................714 964-8900
Anthony Ravlich, *CEO*
Nicholas Ravlich, *CFO*
EMP: 27 **EST:** 2003
SQ FT: 27,000
SALES (est): 10.45MM
SALES (corp-wide): 10.45MM **Privately Held**
Web: www.neutronicstamping.com
SIC: 3471 3469 Electroplating of metals or
formed products; Metal stampings, nec

(P-5288)
RAVLICH ENTERPRISES LLC
Also Called: Spectrum Plating Company
202 W 140th St, Los Angeles (90061-1006)
PHONE..................310 533-0748
Anthony Ravlich, *Brnch Mgr*
EMP: 41
SALES (corp-wide): 10.45MM **Privately Held**
Web: www.neutronicstamping.com
SIC: 3471 Plating and polishing
PA: Ravlich Enterprises, Llc
100 Business Center Dr
714 964-8900

(P-5289)
REAL PLATING INC
1245 W 2nd St, Pomona (91766-1310)
PHONE..................909 623-2304
Juan Real, *CEO*
EMP: 25 **EST:** 2007
SQ FT: 5,264
SALES (est): 2.05MM **Privately Held**
Web: www.realplating.com
SIC: 3471 Electroplating of metals or formed
products

(P-5290)

SAFE PLATING INC
18001 Railroad St, City Of Industry
(91748-1215)
PHONE..............................626 810-1872
Magdy Seif, *Pr*
Mario Gomez, *
EMP: 58 EST: 1979
SQ FT: 35,000
SALES (est): 4.81MM **Privately Held**
Web: www.safeplatinginc.com
SIC: 3471 Electroplating of metals or formed
products

(P-5291)

SANTA ANA PLATING (PA)
1726 E Rosslynn Ave, Fullerton
(92831-5111)
PHONE..............................310 923-8305
Tony Kakuk, *Pr*
EMP: 55 EST: 1954
SQ FT: 17,100
SALES (est): 952.53K
SALES (corp-wide): 952.53K **Privately
Held**
SIC: 3471 Finishing, metals or formed
products

(P-5292)

SANTOSHI CORPORATION
Also Called: Entrance Tech
2439 Seaman Ave, El Monte (91733-1936)
PHONE..............................626 444-7118
Hershad Shah, *Pr*
Raksha Shah, *
EMP: 33 EST: 1971
SQ FT: 15,000
SALES (est): 6.36MM **Privately Held**
Web: www.alumacoat.com
SIC: 3471 Coloring and finishing of
aluminum or formed products

(P-5293)

SCHMIDT INDUSTRIES INC
Also Called: Prime Plating
11321 Goss St, Sun Valley (91352-3206)
P.O. Box 1843 (91353-1843)
PHONE..............................818 768-9100
Fred Schmidt, *Pr*
Jennifer Schmidt, *
EMP: 90 EST: 1986
SQ FT: 30,000
SALES (est): 1.24MM **Privately Held**
Web: www.prime-plating.com
SIC: 3471 Electroplating of metals or formed
products

(P-5294)

SHEFFIELD PLATERS INC
9850 Waples St, San Diego (92121-2921)
PHONE..............................858 546-8484
Dale Watkins Junior, *Pr*
Mark Watkins, *
Shelley Watkins, *Stockholder*
EMP: 85 EST: 1946
SQ FT: 20,000
SALES (est): 4.75MM **Privately Held**
Web: www.sheffieldplaters.com
SIC: 3471 Plating of metals or formed
products

(P-5295)

SHEILA STREET PROPERTIES
INC (PA)
5900 Sheila St, Commerce (90040-2403)
P.O. Box 911458 (90091-1238)
PHONE..............................323 838-9208
EMP: 51 EST: 1931
SALES (est): 13MM
SALES (corp-wide): 13MM **Privately Held**

Web: www.valleyplating.com
SIC: 3471 Plating of metals or formed
products

(P-5296)

SOUTHERN CALIFORNIA
PLATING CO
3261 National Ave, San Diego
(92113-2636)
PHONE..............................619 231-1481
Paul Hummell Junior, *Pr*
EMP: 30 EST: 1946
SQ FT: 13,000
SALES (est): 1.5MM **Privately Held**
Web: www.socalplating.com
SIC: 3471 Electroplating of metals or formed
products

(P-5297)

SYMCOAT METAL PROCESSING
INC
7887 Dunbrook Rd Ste C, San Diego
(92126-4382)
PHONE..............................858 451-3313
Sylvia Twiggs, *Pr*
Michelle Kanganis, *VP*
EMP: 24 EST: 1994
SQ FT: 12,000
SALES (est): 967.55K **Privately Held**
SIC: 3471 3341 Finishing, metals or formed
products; Secondary nonferrous metals

(P-5298)

TECHNIC INC
1170 N Hawk Cir, Anaheim (92807-1789)
PHONE..............................714 632-0200
Mike Chicos, *Mgr*
EMP: 30
SALES (corp-wide): 91.24MM **Privately
Held**
Web: www.technic.com
SIC: 3471 2899 3678 3672 Plating of metals
or formed products; Plating compounds;
Electronic connectors; Printed circuit boards
PA: Technic, Inc.
47 Molter St
401 781-6100

(P-5299)

TEMECULA QUALITY PLATING
INC
42147 Roick Dr, Temecula (92590-3695)
PHONE..............................951 296-9875
Duc Vo, *Pr*
Dat Vo, *
EMP: 32 EST: 2011
SALES (est): 1.82MM **Privately Held**
Web: www.temeculaplating.com
SIC: 3471 Electroplating of metals or formed
products

(P-5300)

TRIDENT PLATING INC
10046 Romandel Ave, Santa Fe Springs
(90670-3424)
PHONE..............................562 906-2556
Maty Rodriguez, *Pr*
Juan Carlos Rodriguez, *
Ian Holmber, *
EMP: 28 EST: 1981
SQ FT: 18,197
SALES (est): 2.46MM **Privately Held**
Web: www.tridentplating.com
SIC: 3471 Electroplating of metals or formed
products

(P-5301)

TRIUMPH PROC - EMBEE DIV
INC

2158 S Hathaway St, Santa Ana
(92705-5249)
PHONE..............................714 546-9842
EMP: 400
SALES (est): 10.75MM **Privately Held**
SIC: 3471 Electroplating and plating

(P-5302)

TRIUMPH PROCESSING INC
Also Called: Valence Lynwood
2605 Industry Way, Lynwood (90262-4007)
PHONE..............................323 563-1338
Peter Labarbera, *CEO*
Richard C III, *
EMP: 103 EST: 1968
SQ FT: 140,000
SALES (est): 20.15MM
SALES (corp-wide): 138.9MM **Privately
Held**
Web: www.valencesurfacetech.com
SIC: 3471 3398 3356 Anodizing (plating) of
metals or formed products; Metal heat
treating; Nonferrous rolling and drawing, nec
PA: Valence Surface Technologies Llc
300 Cntnntal Blvd Ste 600
888 540-0878

(P-5303)

ULTRAMET
12173 Montague St, Pacoima
(91331-2295)
PHONE..............................818 899-0236
Andrew Duffy, *CEO*
Walter Abrams, *
Richard B Kaplan, *Stockholder*
James Kaplan, *Stockholder*
▲ EMP: 79 EST: 1970
SQ FT: 43,000
SALES (est): 7.67MM **Privately Held**
Web: www.ultramet.com
SIC: 3471 8731 Electroplating and plating;
Commercial physical research

(P-5304)

VALEX CORP (HQ)
6080 Leland St, Ventura (93003-7605)
PHONE..............................805 658-0944
▲ EMP: 83 EST: 1976
SALES (est): 36.16MM
SALES (corp-wide): 14.81B **Publicly Held**
Web: www.valex.com
SIC: 3471 3317 3494 Polishing, metals or
formed products; Steel pipe and tubes;
Valves and pipe fittings, nec
PA: Reliance, Inc.
16100 N 71st St Ste 400
480 564-5700

3479 Metal Coating And
Allied Services

(P-5305)

ABACUS POWDER COATING
1829 Tyler Ave, South El Monte
(91733-3617)
PHONE..............................626 443-7556
Esther Davidoff, *Pr*
EMP: 25 EST: 2006
SALES (est): 2.44MM **Privately Held**
Web: www.abacuspowder.com
SIC: 3479 Coating of metals and formed
products

(P-5306)

ADFA INCORPORATED
Also Called: A&A Jewelry Supply
319 W 6th St, Los Angeles (90014-1703)
PHONE..............................213 627-8004
Robert Adem, *Pr*

Naim Farah, *
▲ EMP: 45 EST: 1986
SALES (est): 4.4MM **Privately Held**
Web: www.aajewelry.com
SIC: 3479 3548 3172 Engraving jewelry,
silverware, or metal; Electric welding
equipment; Cases, jewelry

(P-5307)

ALPHACOAT FINISHING LLC
9350 Cabot Dr, San Diego (92126-4311)
PHONE..............................949 748-7796
Vaishali Joshi, *
EMP: 28 EST: 2017
SALES (est): 2.5MM **Privately Held**
Web: www.alphacoatfinishing.com
SIC: 3479 Coating of metals and formed
products

(P-5308)

AMADA AMERICA INC
100 S Puente St, Brea (92821-3813)
PHONE..............................714 739-2111
EMP: 64
Web: www.amada.com
SIC: 3479 Aluminum coating of metal
products
HQ: Amada America, Inc.
7025 Firestone Blvd
Buena Park CA 90621
714 739-2111

(P-5309)

AMERICAN ETCHING & MFG
13730 Desmond St, Pacoima (91331-2796)
PHONE..............................323 875-3910
Gary Kipka, *Pr*
EMP: 45 EST: 1972
SQ FT: 20,000
SALES (est): 4.21MM **Privately Held**
Web: www.aemetch.com
SIC: 3479 Etching on metals

(P-5310)

APPLIED COATINGS & LININGS
3224 Rosemead Blvd, El Monte
(91731-2807)
PHONE..............................626 280-6354
EMP: 24
SQ FT: 150,000
SALES (est): 2.7MM **Privately Held**
Web: www.appliedcoatings.com
SIC: 3479 3471 Coating of metals and
formed products; Plating and polishing

(P-5311)

APPLIED POWDERCOAT INC
3101 Camino Del Sol, Oxnard
(93030-8999)
PHONE..............................805 981-1991
Victor Anselmo, *Pr*
J Michael Hagan, *
Deborah Anselmo, *
EMP: 45 EST: 1989
SQ FT: 30,000
SALES (est): 4.17MM **Privately Held**
Web: www.appliedpowder.com
SIC: 3479 Coating of metals and formed
products

(P-5312)

ASTRO CHROME AND POLSG
CORP
8136 Lankershim Blvd, North Hollywood
(91605-1611)
PHONE..............................818 781-1463
Jesse Gonzalez, *Pr*
EMP: 23 EST: 1981
SQ FT: 3,000
SALES (est): 410.01K **Privately Held**

Web: www.astroplating.com
SIC: 3479 Coating of metals and formed products

(P-5313)
ATLAS GALVANIZING LLC
2639 Leonis Blvd, Vernon (90058-2203)
PHONE..................................323 587-6247
Patricia New, *
EMP: 36 EST: 1936
SQ FT: 20,000
SALES (est): 2.79MM Privately Held
Web: www.atlasgalv.com
SIC: 3479 Coating of metals and formed products

(P-5314)
BJS&T ENTERPRISES INC
Also Called: San Diego Powder Coating
1702 N Magnolia Ave, El Cajon (92020-1287)
PHONE..................................619 448-7795
Philip Johnson, Pr
Bob Johnson, *
Stephen Johnson, *
EMP: 50 EST: 2001
SQ FT: 7,000
SALES (est): 4.12MM Privately Held
Web: www.sandiegopowdercoating.com
SIC: 3479 Coating of metals and formed products

(P-5315)
CERTIFIED ENAMELING INC (PA)
Also Called: Certified Archtctral Fbrction
3342 Emery St, Los Angeles (90023-3810)
PHONE..................................323 264-4403
Vicki Ziegel, CEO
Glenn Ziegel, *
EMP: 91 EST: 1953
SQ FT: 50,000
SALES (est): 12MM
SALES (corp-wide): 12MM Privately Held
Web: www.certifiedenameling.com
SIC: 3479 Coating of metals and formed products

(P-5316)
CREST COATING INC
1361 S Allec St, Anaheim (92805-6304)
PHONE..................................714 635-7090
TOLL FREE: 800
Michael D Erickson, CEO
Bonnie George, *
▲ EMP: 60 EST: 1968
SQ FT: 55,000
SALES (est): 9.3MM Privately Held
Web: www.crestcoating.com
SIC: 3479 Coating of metals and formed products

(P-5317)
DENMAC INDUSTRIES INC
7616 Rosecrans Ave, Paramount (90723-2508)
P.O. Box 2144 (90723-8144)
PHONE..................................562 634-2714
Mark Plechot, Pr
Maurice Plechot, *
James Campagna, *
▲ EMP: 40 EST: 1974
SQ FT: 20,000
SALES (est): 4.9MM Privately Held
Web: www.denmac-ind.com
SIC: 3479 Coating of metals and formed products

(P-5318)
DURA COAT PRODUCTS INC (PA)
5361 Via Ricardo, Riverside (92509-2414)
PHONE..................................951 341-6500
Myung K Hong, CEO
Lorrie Y Hong, *
Suzanne Faust, *
◆ EMP: 64 EST: 1986
SQ FT: 29,000
SALES (est): 45.96MM
SALES (corp-wide): 45.96MM Privately Held
Web: www.axalta.com
SIC: 3479 2851 Aluminum coating of metal products; Paints and allied products

(P-5319)
ETS EXPRESS LLC (DH)
Also Called: Ets Express
420 Lombard St, Oxnard (93030-5100)
PHONE..................................805 278-7771
Sharon Eyal, Pr
Taly Eyal, CFO
▲ EMP: 28 EST: 1998
SQ FT: 40,000
SALES (est): 25.24MM Privately Held
Web: www.etsexpress.com
SIC: 3479 3231 Etching and engraving; Cut and engraved glassware: made from purchased glass
HQ: Leedsworld, Inc.
400 Hunt Valley Rd
New Kensington PA 15068
724 334-9000

(P-5320)
FLETCHER COATING CO
Also Called: Fletcher Coating
426 W Fletcher Ave, Orange (92865-2612)
PHONE..................................714 637-4763
Kurtis Breeding, CEO
▲ EMP: 50 EST: 1971
SQ FT: 37,500
SALES (est): 4.78MM Privately Held
Web: www.fletcherkote.com
SIC: 3479 Coating of metals and formed products

(P-5321)
FVO SOLUTIONS INC
Also Called: Foothill Vctonal Opportunities
789 N Fair Oaks Ave, Pasadena (91103-3045)
PHONE..................................626 449-0218
▲ EMP: 75
Web: www.fvosolutions.com
SIC: 3479 3999 Coating of metals and formed products; Gold stamping, except books

(P-5322)
GEMTECH INDS GOOD EARTH MFG
Also Called: Gemtech International
2737 S Garnsey St, Santa Ana (92707-3340)
P.O. Box 15506 (92735-0506)
PHONE..................................714 848-2517
Shig Shiwota, Pr
Maya Shiwota, *
David Shiwota, *
▲ EMP: 24 EST: 1971
SQ FT: 10,500
SALES (est): 2.38MM Privately Held
Web: www.gemtechcoatings.com
SIC: 3479 Coating of metals and formed products

(P-5323)
INLAND POWDER COATING CORP
Also Called: Prs Industries
1656 S Bon View Ave Ste F, Ontario (91761-4419)
P.O. Box 3427 (91761-0943)
PHONE..................................909 947-1122
David Paul Flatten, Pr
Debbie Flatten, *
EMP: 104 EST: 1983
SQ FT: 83,000
SALES (est): 16.91MM Privately Held
Web: www.inlandpowder.com
SIC: 3479 3471 Coating of metals and formed products; Sand blasting of metal parts

(P-5324)
INNOVATIVE COATINGS TECHNOLOGY CORPORATION
Also Called: Incotec
1347 Poole St 106, Mojave (93501-1658)
PHONE..................................661 824-8101
EMP: 127 EST: 1992
SALES (est): 22.04MM Privately Held
Web: www.incoteccorp.com
SIC: 3479 8732 Coating of metals with plastic or resins; Research services, except laboratory

(P-5325)
ISLAND POWDER COATING
Also Called: Powder Coating
1830 Tyler Ave, South El Monte (91733-3618)
PHONE..................................626 279-2460
Joe Graham, Owner
EMP: 30 EST: 1994
SALES (est): 2.17MM Privately Held
Web: www.abacuspowder.com
SIC: 3479 Coating of metals and formed products

(P-5326)
JAN-KENS ENAMELING COMPANY INC
715 E Cypress Ave, Monrovia (91016-4254)
PHONE..................................626 358-1849
EMP: 24
Web: www.jankens.com
SIC: 3479 Coating of metals and formed products

(P-5327)
KENNEDY NAME PLATE CO
4501 Pacific Blvd, Vernon (90058-2207)
PHONE..................................323 585-0121
William J Kennedy Junior, Pr
Mike Kennedy, *
EMP: 25 EST: 1921
SQ FT: 36,000
SALES (est): 2.53MM Privately Held
Web: www.knpco.com
SIC: 3479 7336 3993 3444 Name plates: engraved, etched, etc.; Silk screen design; Signs and advertising specialties; Sheet metalwork

(P-5328)
KENS SPRAY EQUIPMENT LLC
Also Called: Ken's Spray Equipment, Inc.
1900 W Walnut St, Compton (90220-5019)
PHONE..................................310 635-9995
Joseph I Snowden, Pr
EMP: 133 EST: 1979
SALES (est): 29.74MM
SALES (corp-wide): 364.48B Publicly Held

Web: www.pccaero.com
SIC: 3479 Painting of metal products
HQ: Precision Castparts Corp.
5885 Meadows Rd Ste 620
Lake Oswego OR 97035
503 946-4800

(P-5329)
LOS ANGELES GALVANIZING CO
2518 E 53rd St, Huntington Park (90255-2505)
PHONE..................................323 583-2263
Lance Michael Rosenkranz, CEO
Jamie Rosenkranz, *
Tim Rosenkranz, *
Lance Rosenkranz, *
EMP: 58 EST: 1932
SQ FT: 26,000
SALES (est): 9.76MM Privately Held
Web: www.lagalvanizing.com
SIC: 3479 Coating of metals and formed products

(P-5330)
MABEL BAAS INC
Also Called: Royal Coatings
3960 Royal Ave, Simi Valley (93063-3380)
PHONE..................................805 520-8075
Marilyn Teperson, Pr
EMP: 50 EST: 1991
SALES (est): 4.16MM Privately Held
Web: www.royalcoatings.com
SIC: 3479 Coating of metals and formed products

(P-5331)
METAL COATERS CALIFORNIA INC
Also Called: Metal Coaters System
9123 Center Ave, Rancho Cucamonga (91730-5312)
PHONE..................................909 987-4681
Norman C Chambers, CEO
Dick Klein, *
Tom Scarinza, *
EMP: 75 EST: 1998
SALES (est): 2.39MM
SALES (corp-wide): 5.58B Privately Held
Web: www.metalcoaters.com
SIC: 3479 Painting of metal products
HQ: Cornerstone Building Brands, Inc.
5020 Weston Pkwy
Cary NC 27513
281 897-7788

(P-5332)
NELSON NAME PLATE COMPANY (PA)
Also Called: Nelson-Miller
708 Nogales St, City Of Industry (91748-1306)
PHONE..................................323 663-3971
Jim Kaldem, Pr
▲ EMP: 48 EST: 1946
SALES (est): 43.25MM
SALES (corp-wide): 43.25MM Privately Held
Web: www.nelson-miller.co
SIC: 3479 3993 Name plates: engraved, etched, etc.; Signs and advertising specialties

(P-5333)
NM HOLDCO INC
2800 Casitas Ave, Los Angeles (90039-2942)
PHONE..................................323 663-3971
Mark Carroll, Dir
William Mckinley, Dir
EMP: 200 EST: 2011

SALES (est): 877.12K **Privately Held**
SIC: 3479 3993 Name plates: engraved, etched, etc.; Signs and advertising specialties
PA: Superior Capital Partners Llc
418 N Main St

(P-5334)
PARYLENE COATING SERVICES INC
Also Called: Polymer Coating Services
35 Argonaut, Aliso Viejo (92656-4151)
PHONE..............................281 391-7665
EMP: 25
SIC: 3479 Coating of metals and formed products

(P-5335)
PDU LAD CORPORATION (PA)
Also Called: Plastic Dress-Up
11165 Valley Spring Ln, North Hollywood (91602-2646)
P.O. Box 3897 (91733-0897)
PHONE..............................626 442-7711
Loren Funk, CEO
Dennis Funk, *
Allen Greenblat, *
◆ EMP: 38 EST: 1990
SALES (est): 8.8MM **Privately Held**
Web: www.pdu.com
SIC: 3479 Name plates: engraved, etched, etc.

(P-5336)
PELTEK HOLDINGS INC
35 Argonaut Ste A1, Laguna Hills (92656-4151)
PHONE..............................949 855-8010
Jeffrey Stewart, Pr
Paul Stewart, *
Joyce Stewart, *
▲ EMP: 30 EST: 1974
SQ FT: 10,560
SALES (est): 2.33MM **Privately Held**
Web: www.peltekfab.com
SIC: 3479 5169 Bonderizing of metal or metal products; Chemicals and allied products, nec

(P-5337)
PERFORMANCE POWDER INC
2940 E La Jolla St Ste A, Anaheim (92806-1349)
PHONE..............................714 632-0600
Kevin Aaberg, Pr
Robert Goldberg, *
EMP: 29 EST: 1993
SALES (est): 4.71MM **Privately Held**
Web: www.performancepowder.com
SIC: 3479 Coating of metals and formed products

(P-5338)
PLASMA TECHNOLOGY INCORPORATED (PA)
Also Called: P T I
1754 Crenshaw Blvd, Torrance (90501-3384)
PHONE..............................310 320-3373
Robert Donald Dowell, CEO
Burnard Fosket, *
Malcom Jones, *
John Nikitich, *
▲ EMP: 73 EST: 1984
SQ FT: 40,000
SALES (est): 12.34MM
SALES (corp-wide): 12.34MM **Privately Held**
Web: www.ptise.com

SIC: 3479 Coating of metals and formed products

(P-5339)
POWDERCOAT SERVICES LLC
1747 W Lincoln Ave Ste K, Anaheim (92801-6770)
PHONE..............................714 533-2251
Ravi Rao, Pr
▲ EMP: 38 EST: 1981
SQ FT: 75,000
SALES (est): 1.43MM **Privately Held**
Web: www.powdercoatservices.com
SIC: 3479 7211 Coating of metals and formed products; Power laundries, family and commercial

(P-5340)
PROCESSES BY MARTIN INC
12150 Alameda St, Lynwood (90262-4005)
PHONE..............................310 637-1855
Irene Romero, Pr
Cathleen Fuentes, *
EMP: 45 EST: 1993
SQ FT: 200,000
SALES (est): 4.76MM **Privately Held**
Web: www.processesbymartin.com
SIC: 3479 Coating of metals and formed products

(P-5341)
RGF ENTERPRISES INC
220 Citation Cir, Corona (92878-5022)
PHONE..............................951 734-6922
Rodney G Fisher, Pr
EMP: 26 EST: 1976
SQ FT: 15,000
SALES (est): 2.15MM **Privately Held**
Web: www.rgfcoatings.com
SIC: 3479 Coating of metals and formed products

(P-5342)
S C COATINGS CORPORATION
41775 Elm St Ste 302, Murrieta (92562-9267)
PHONE..............................951 461-9777
Michael Podratz, Pr
Victor Lopez, *
EMP: 48 EST: 2000
SALES (est): 4.55MM **Privately Held**
Web: www.sccoatingscorp.com
SIC: 3479 Coating of metals and formed products

(P-5343)
SDC TECHNOLOGIES INC (HQ)
45 Parker Ste 100, Irvine (92618-1658)
PHONE..............................714 939-8300
Richard Chang, Pr
▲ EMP: 25 EST: 1986
SQ FT: 16,800
SALES (est): 52.08MM **Privately Held**
Web: www.sdctech.com
SIC: 3479 Coating of metals and formed products
PA: Mitsui Chemicals, Inc.
2-2-1, Yaesu

(P-5344)
SHMAZE INDUSTRIES INC
Also Called: Shmaze Custom Coatings
20792 Canada Rd, Lake Forest (92630-6732)
PHONE..............................949 583-1448
Michael Shamassian, Pr
Joanne Shamassian, *
EMP: 50 EST: 1987
SQ FT: 21,500
SALES (est): 5.13MM **Privately Held**

Web: www.shmaze.com
SIC: 3479 Coating of metals with plastic or resins

(P-5345)
SOCCO PLASTIC COATING COMPANY
11251 Jersey Blvd, Rancho Cucamonga (91730-5197)
PHONE..............................909 987-4753
Peter M Smits, Pr
Peter M Smits Junior, Pr
Rose Smits, *
EMP: 25 EST: 1945
SQ FT: 60,000
SALES (est): 2.36MM **Privately Held**
Web: www.soccoplastics.com
SIC: 3479 3444 3088 2851 Coating of metals with plastic or resins; Sheet metalwork; Plastics plumbing fixtures; Paints and allied products

(P-5346)
SPECIALTY COATING SYSTEMS INC
4435 E Airport Dr Ste 100, Ontario (91761-7816)
PHONE..............................909 390-8818
Steven Frease, Brnch Mgr
EMP: 99
Web: www.scscoatings.com
SIC: 3479 Coating of metals and formed products
HQ: Specialty Coating Systems, Inc.
7645 Woodland Dr
Indianapolis IN 46278

(P-5347)
STEELSCAPE LLC
11200 Arrow Rte, Rancho Cucamonga (91730-4805)
PHONE..............................909 987-4711
Ron Hurst, Brnch Mgr
EMP: 28
SALES (corp-wide): 83.19MM **Privately Held**
Web: www.steelscape.com
SIC: 3479 Coating of metals and formed products
PA: Steelscape, Llc
222 W Kalama River Rd
360 673-8200

(P-5348)
SUNDIAL INDUSTRIES INC
Also Called: Powder Painting By Sundial
8421 Telfair Ave, Sun Valley (91352-3926)
PHONE..............................010 767-4477
TOLL FREE: 866
Hasu Bhakta, Pr
Naseen Khan, *
Gurtreet Riaz, *
▲ EMP: 30 EST: 1980
SQ FT: 13,000
SALES (est): 2.43MM **Privately Held**
Web: www.sundialpowdercoating.com
SIC: 3479 Coating of metals and formed products

(P-5349)
SUNDIAL POWDER COATINGS INC
Also Called: Bottle Coatings
8421 Telfair Ave, Sun Valley (91352-3926)
PHONE..............................818 767-4477
Hasu Bhakta, CEO
EMP: 25 EST: 1995
SALES (est): 2.61MM **Privately Held**
Web: www.sundialpowdercoating.com

SIC: 3479 Coating of metals and formed products

(P-5350)
TORTOISE INDUSTRIES INC
Also Called: Tortoise Tube
3052 Treadwell St, Los Angeles (90065-1423)
PHONE..............................323 258-7776
EMP: 40 EST: 1981
SALES (est): 2.51MM **Privately Held**
Web: www.tortoiseindustries.com
SIC: 3479 3498 1799 Painting, coating, and hot dipping; Tube fabricating (contract bending and shaping); Exterior cleaning, including sandblasting

(P-5351)
ULTIMATE METAL FINISHING CORP
6150 Sheila St, Commerce (90040-2407)
PHONE..............................323 890-9100
John Ondrasik, Pr
James M Sales, Genl Mgr
EMP: 44 EST: 1983
SQ FT: 4,800
SALES (est): 346K
SALES (corp-wide): 22.58MM **Privately Held**
SIC: 3479 Coating of metals and formed products
PA: Precision Wire Products, Inc.
6150 Sheila St
323 890-9100

(P-5352)
UNITED WESTERN ENTERPRISES INC
Also Called: Uwe
850 Flynn Rd Ste 200, Camarillo (93012-8783)
PHONE..............................805 389-1077
Gerald Williams, Pr
Mike Lynch, *
EMP: 29 EST: 1969
SQ FT: 21,000
SALES (est): 4.99MM
SALES (corp-wide): 4.99MM **Privately Held**
Web: www.uweinc.com
SIC: 3479 Etching, photochemical
PA: Pma Industries
18008 N Black Canyon Hwy
602 607-4155

(P-5353)
VALMONT INDUSTRIES INC
Also Called: Valmont Cings Clwest Glvnlzlng
2226 E Dominguez St, Long Beach (90810-1008)
PHONE..............................310 549-2200
EMP: 50
SALES (corp-wide): 4.17B **Publicly Held**
Web: www.valmontcoatings.com
SIC: 3479 Coating of metals and formed products
PA: Valmont Industries, Inc.
15000 Valmont Plz
402 963-1000

3483 Ammunition, Except For Small Arms, Nec

(P-5354)
FIELD TIME TARGET TRAINING LLC
Also Called: Ft3 Tactical
8230 Electric Ave, Stanton (90680-2640)

PRODUCTS & SVCS

P.O. Box 1219 (90680-1219)
PHONE..................714 677-2841
Michael R Kaplan, *Managing Member*
EMP: 24 **EST:** 2010
SALES (est): 3.6MM **Privately Held**
Web:
www.fieldtimetargetandtraining.com
SIC: 3483 7999 Ammunition, except for
small arms, nec; Shooting range operation

3484 Small Arms

(P-5355)
SAI INDUSTRIES
Also Called: Standard Armament
631 Allen Ave, Glendale (91201-2013)
PHONE..................818 842-6144
Curtis Correll, *CEO*
Gary Correll, *
Marcene Correll, *
Cathy Joens, *
Kriti Ahuja, *
◆ **EMP:** 40 **EST:** 1950
SQ FT: 24,000
SALES (est): 5.79MM **Privately Held**
Web: www.standardarmament.com
SIC: 3484 Guns (firearms) or gun parts, 30
mm. and below

3489 Ordnance And Accessories, Nec

(P-5356)
ARMTEC DEFENSE PRODUCTS CO (DH)
Also Called: Armtec Defense Technologies
85901 Avenue 53, Coachella (92236-2607)
PHONE..................760 398-0143
Robert W Cremin, *CEO*
◆ **EMP:** 330 **EST:** 1968
SQ FT: 108,000
SALES (est): 114.97MM
SALES (corp-wide): 7.94B **Publicly Held**
Web: www.armtecdefense.com
SIC: 3489 Artillery or artillery parts, over 30
mm.
HQ: Esterline Technologies Corp
1350 Euclid Ave Ste 1600
Cleveland OH 44114
216 706-2960

(P-5357)
NETWORKS ELECTRONIC CO LLC
9750 De Soto Ave, Chatsworth
(91311-4485)
PHONE..................818 341-0440
Tamara Marie Christen, *Managing Member*
Andrew Campany, *
▼ **EMP:** 26 **EST:** 2005
SQ FT: 25,000
SALES (est): 5.35MM **Privately Held**
Web: www.networkselectronic.com
SIC: 3489 Ordnance and accessories, nec

(P-5358)
VECTOR LAUNCH LLC (PA)
Also Called: Vector
15261 Connector Ln, Huntington Beach
(92649-1117)
PHONE..................202 888-3063
Jim Penrose, *CEO*
Robert Spalding, *Pr*
Robert Cleave, *CRO*
Stephanie Koster, *CFO*
Eric Besnard, *VP*
EMP: 50 **EST:** 2016
SALES (est): 9.59MM

SALES (corp-wide): 9.59MM **Privately
Held**
Web: www.vector-launch.com
SIC: 3489 Rocket launchers

3491 Industrial Valves

(P-5359)
BERMINGHAM CNTRLS INC A CAL CO (PA)
Also Called: Capital Westward
11144 Business Cir, Cerritos (90703-5523)
PHONE..................562 860-0463
Gregory Gass, *Pr*
Edwin Bonner, *
Kevin Mulholland, *
EMP: 37 **EST:** 1961
SQ FT: 20,000
SALES (est): 1.39MM
SALES (corp-wide): 1.39MM **Privately
Held**
Web: www.bermingham.com
SIC: 3491 3823 5084 Industrial valves;
Process control instruments; Industrial
machinery and equipment

(P-5360)
CIRCOR AEROSPACE INC (DH)
2301 Wardlow Cir, Corona (92878-5101)
P.O. Box 2824 (29304-2824)
PHONE..................951 270-6200
Carl Nasca, *Pr*
Christopher Celtruda, *
Kathy Fazio, *
Michael Dill, *
Renuka Ayer, *
◆ **EMP:** 245 **EST:** 1947
SQ FT: 100,000
SALES (est): 69.36MM **Publicly Held**
Web: www.circoraerospace.com
SIC: 3491 3494 3769 5085 Pressure valves
and regulators, industrial; Plumbing and
heating valves; Space vehicle equipment,
nec; Seals, industrial
HQ: Circor International, Inc.
30 Corporate Dr Ste 200
Burlington MA 01803
781 270-1200

(P-5361)
CRANE INSTRMNTTION SMPLING INC
2301 Wardlow Cir, Corona (92878-5101)
PHONE..................951 270-6200
Andy Brandenburg, *Genl Mgr*
EMP: 80
SALES (corp-wide): 2.09B **Publicly Held**
Web: www.circor.com
SIC: 3491 Industrial valves
HQ: Crane Instrumentation & Sampling, Inc.
405 Centura Ct
Spartanburg SC 29303
864 574-7966

(P-5362)
CURTISS-WRIGHT CORPORATION
1675 Brandywine Ave Ste F, Chula Vista
(91911-6064)
PHONE..................619 482-3405
David Schurra, *Brnch Mgr*
EMP: 85
SALES (corp-wide): 2.85B **Publicly Held**
Web: www.curtisswright.com
SIC: 3491 Industrial valves
PA: Curtiss-Wright Corporation
130 Harbour Pl Dr Ste 300
704 869-4600

(P-5363)
CURTISS-WRIGHT CORPORATION
Also Called: Defense Solutions
28965 Avenue Penn, Santa Clarita
(91355-4185)
PHONE..................661 257-4430
EMP: 56
SALES (corp-wide): 2.85B **Publicly Held**
Web: www.curtisswright.com
SIC: 3491 Industrial valves
PA: Curtiss-Wright Corporation
130 Harbour Pl Dr Ste 300
704 869-4600

(P-5364)
CURTISS-WRIGHT FLOW CONTROL
Penny & Giles
28965 Avenue Penn, Valencia
(91355-4185)
PHONE..................626 851-3100
EMP: 160
SALES (corp-wide): 2.41B **Publicly Held**
SIC: 3491 Industrial valves
HQ: Curtiss-Wright Flow Control
Corporation
1966 Broadhollow Rd Ste E
Farmingdale NY 11735
631 293-3800

(P-5365)
CURTISS-WRIGHT FLOW CTRL CORP
Also Called: Collins Technologies
2950 E Birch St, Brea (92821-6246)
PHONE..................949 271-7500
Glenn Roberts, *Mgr*
EMP: 31
SALES (corp-wide): 2.85B **Publicly Held**
Web: www.curtisswright.com
SIC: 3491 Industrial valves
HQ: Curtiss-Wright Flow Control
Corporation
1966 Broadhollow Rd Ste E
Farmingdale NY 11735
631 293-3800

(P-5366)
IMI CRITICAL ENGINEERING LLC (DH)
Also Called: IMI CCI
22591 Avenida Empresa, Rcho Sta Marg
(92688-2003)
PHONE..................949 858-1877
Kevin Mckown, *Pr*
Abhijit Rao, *CFO*
◆ **EMP:** 365 **EST:** 1961
SQ FT: 75,000
SALES (est): 61.92MM
SALES (corp-wide): 2.74B **Privately Held**
Web: www.retrofit3d.com
SIC: 3491 Process control regulator valves
HQ: Imi Americas Inc.
5400 S Delaware St
Littleton CO 80120
763 488-5400

(P-5367)
JAMES JONES COMPANY
1470 S Vintage Ave, Ontario (91761-3646)
PHONE..................909 418-2558
Jerry Schnelzer, *Genl Mgr*
◆ **EMP:** 3988 **EST:** 1892
SQ FT: 68,000
SALES (est): 3.08MM
SALES (corp-wide): 1.31B **Publicly Held**
Web: www.joneswaterproducts.com

SIC: 3491 3494 Fire hydrant valves; Pipe
fittings
HQ: Mueller Group, Llc
1200 Abrnthy Rd Ne Ste 12
Atlanta GA 30328
770 206-4200

(P-5368)
PACIFIC SEISMIC PRODUCTS INC
233 E Avenue H8, Lancaster (93535-1821)
PHONE..................661 942-4499
Etsuko Ikegaya, *Pr*
Shigeko I Aramaki, *
EMP: 24 **EST:** 1989
SQ FT: 10,000
SALES (est): 1.77MM **Privately Held**
Web: www.pspvalves.com
SIC: 3491 Industrial valves

(P-5369)
RELIANCE WORLDWIDE CORPORATION
2750 E Mission Blvd, Ontario (91761-2909)
PHONE..................770 863-4005
EMP: 60
Web: www.rwc.com
SIC: 3491 Industrial valves
HQ: Reliance Worldwide Corporation
2300 Defoor Hills Rd Nw
Atlanta GA 30318
770 863-4005

(P-5370)
STORM MANUFACTURING GROUP INC
Also Called: Smg
23201 Normandie Ave, Torrance
(90501-5050)
PHONE..................310 326-8287
Dale Philippi, *CEO*
Russell Kneipp, *
Georgia S Claessens, *
Rick Ward, *
◆ **EMP:** 74 **EST:** 1908
SQ FT: 41,936
SALES (est): 6.04MM
SALES (corp-wide): 44.12MM **Privately
Held**
Web: www.getsuperior.com
SIC: 3491 3494 Industrial valves; Sprinkler
systems, field
PA: Storm Industries, Inc.
970 W 190th St
310 534-5232

(P-5371)
WESTERN VALVE INC
Also Called: Western Valve
201 Industrial St, Bakersfield (93307-2703)
P.O. Box 10628 (93389-0628)
PHONE..................661 327-7660
▲ **EMP:** 41 **EST:** 1991
SALES (est): 9.36MM **Privately Held**
Web: www.westernvalve.com
SIC: 3491 Industrial valves

3492 Fluid Power Valves And Hose Fittings

(P-5372)
CRANE CO
Also Called: CRANE CO.
3201 Walnut Ave, Long Beach
(90755-5296)
PHONE..................562 426-2531
Kevin Mckown, *Mgr*
EMP: 110

SALES (corp-wide): 3.37B **Privately Held**
Web: www.craneco.com
SIC: **3492** Fluid power valves and hose
fittings
HQ: Redco Corporation
100 1st Stamford Pl
Stamford CT 06902
203 363-7300

(P-5373)
ELECTROFILM MFG CO LLC
Also Called: Hartzell Aerospace
28510 Industry Dr, Valencia (91355-4100)
PHONE..........................661 257-2242
David Schmidt, *
Joseph W Brown, *
Simon Shackelton, *
EMP: 80 EST: 2008
SQ FT: 43,000
SALES (est): 6.44MM
SALES (corp-wide): 3.28B **Publicly Held**
Web: www.ittaerospace.com
SIC: **3492 3728 3812** Control valves,
aircraft: hydraulic and pneumatic; Aircraft
body and wing assemblies and parts;
Acceleration indicators and systems
components, aerospace
HQ: Itt Aerospace Controls Llc
28150 Industry Dr
Valencia CA 91355
315 568-7258

(P-5374)
FABER ENTERPRISES INC
14800 S Figueroa St, Gardena
(90248-1719)
PHONE..........................310 323-6200
Kevin M Stein, *CEO*
Esther Faber, *
Ronald E Spencer, *
Marilyn Spencer, *
Loretta Appel, *
EMP: 110 EST: 1947
SALES (est): 2.73MM **Privately Held**
Web: www.pccfluidfittings.com
SIC: **3492** Control valves, aircraft: hydraulic
and pneumatic

(P-5375)
**INDUSTRIAL TUBE COMPANY
LLC**
Also Called: Industrial Tube Company
28150 Industry Dr, Valencia (91355-4100)
PHONE..........................661 295-4000
Farrokh Batliwala, *CEO*
EMP: 99 EST: 2008
SQ FT: 28,000
SALES (est): 3.76MM
SALES (corp-wide): 3.28B **Publicly Held**
SIC: **3492 3728 3812** Control valves,
aircraft: hydraulic and pneumatic; Aircraft
body and wing assemblies and parts;
Acceleration indicators and systems
components, aerospace
HQ: Itt Aerospace Controls Llc
28150 Industry Dr
Valencia CA 91355
315 568-7258

(P-5376)
S & H MACHINE INC
9928 Hayward Way, South El Monte
(91733-3114)
PHONE..........................626 448-5062
David Fisher, *Pr*
EMP: 23
SALES (corp-wide): 7.33MM **Privately
Held**
Web: www.shmachine.com

SIC: **3492 3728** Fluid power valves and hose
fittings; Aircraft parts and equipment, nec
PA: S & H Machine, Inc.
900 N Lake St
818 846-9847

(P-5377)
SENIOR OPERATIONS LLC
Senior Aerospace Spencer
28510 Industry Dr, Valencia (91355-5442)
PHONE..........................818 350-8499
Steven Spencer, *Pr*
EMP: 60
SALES (corp-wide): 1.2B **Privately Held**
Web: www.sajetproducts.com
SIC: **3492** Hose and tube fittings and
assemblies, hydraulic/pneumatic
HQ: Senior Operations Llc
300 E Devon Ave
Bartlett IL 60103
630 372-3500

3493 Steel Springs, Except
Wire

(P-5378)
ARGO SPRING MFG CO INC
13930 Shoemaker Ave, Norwalk
(90650-4597)
PHONE..........................800 252-2740
TOLL FREE: 800
Gene Fox, *Pr*
Michael Fox, *
Kay Greathouse, *
▲ EMP: 55 EST: 1966
SQ FT: 20,000
SALES (est): 4.04MM **Privately Held**
Web: www.argospringmfg.com
SIC: **3493 3495 3469 3599** Coiled flat springs
; Wire springs; Stamping metal for the trade
; Custom machinery

(P-5379)
EIBACH INC
Also Called: Eibach Springs, Inc.
264 Mariah Cir, Corona (92879-1706)
PHONE..........................951 256-8300
Greg Cooley, *Pr*
Gary Peek, *
Sieglinde Eibach, *
◆ EMP: 60 EST: 1987
SQ FT: 52,000
SALES (est): 15.49MM
SALES (corp-wide): 116.99MM **Privately
Held**
Web: www.eibach.com
SIC: **3493** Steel springs, except wire
HQ: Heinrich Eibach Gmbh
Am Lennedamm 1
Finnentrop NW 57413
27215110

(P-5380)
JUENGERMANN INC
Also Called: Spring Industries
1899 Palma Dr Ste A, Ventura
(93003-5739)
PHONE..........................805 644-7165
Peter Juengermann, *Pr*
EMP: 40 EST: 1974
SQ FT: 21,600
SALES (est): 4.53MM **Privately Held**
Web: www.springind.com
SIC: **3493 3495** Steel springs, except wire;
Wire springs

(P-5381)
MATTHEW WARREN INC
Also Called: Helical Products

901 W Mccoy Ln, Santa Maria
(93455-1109)
P.O. Box 1069 (93456-1069)
PHONE..........................805 928-3851
Leroy Mcchesney, *Brnch Mgr*
EMP: 30
SALES (corp-wide): 1.05B **Privately Held**
Web: www.mwcomponents.com
SIC: **3493** Helical springs, hot wound:
railroad equip., etc.
HQ: Matthew Warren, Inc.
3426 Tringdon Way Ste 400
Charlotte NC 28277
704 837-0331

(P-5382)
**SUPERSPRINGS
INTERNATIONAL INC**
5251 6th St, Carpinteria (93013-2402)
PHONE..........................805 745-5553
Gerry Lamberti, *CEO*
Ryan Dougan, *
EMP: 32 EST: 1998
SALES (est): 5.03MM **Privately Held**
Web:
www.superspringsinternational.com
SIC: **3493** Automobile springs

3494 Valves And Pipe
Fittings, Nec

(P-5383)
**ALLAN AIRCRAFT SUPPLY CO
LLC**
11643 Vanowen St, North Hollywood
(91605-6128)
PHONE..........................818 765-4992
Robert Kahmann, *Managing Member*
Mary Katz, *Contrlr*
EMP: 45 EST: 1952
SQ FT: 30,000
SALES (est): 9.01MM **Privately Held**
Web: www.allanaircraft.com
SIC: **3494** Pipe fittings

(P-5384)
ANCO INTERNATIONAL INC
Also Called: Anco
19851 Cajon Blvd, San Bernardino
(92407-1828)
PHONE..........................909 887-2521
Marjorie A Nielsen, *Pr*
EMP: 36 EST: 1978
SQ FT: 13,500
SALES (est): 6.39MM **Privately Held**
Web: www.ancointernational.com
SIC: **3494 3599 3402** Valves and pipe
fittings, nec; Machine shop, jobbing and
repair; Fluid power valves and hose fittings

(P-5385)
**CURTISS-WRIGHT FLOW CTRL
CORP (DH)**
Also Called: Paul-Munroe Entertech Division
2950 E Birch St, Brea (92821-6246)
PHONE..........................714 528-1365
Frank U Erlach, *Pr*
Paul Mawn, *VP*
James Leachman, *VP*
Dan Miller, *Genl Mgr*
Jubel Easaw, *Prin*
▲ EMP: 80 EST: 1996
SQ FT: 30,550
SALES (est): 11.36MM
SALES (corp-wide): 2.85B **Publicly Held**
Web: www.curtisswright.com
SIC: **3494 3625** Valves and pipe fittings, nec;
Actuators, industrial

HQ: Curtiss-Wright Flow Control
Corporation
1966 Broadhollow Rd Ste E
Farmingdale NY 11735
631 293-3800

(P-5386)
FEDERAL INDUSTRIES INC
Also Called: FI
645 Hawaii St, El Segundo (90245-4814)
PHONE..........................310 297-4040
Avi Wacht, *Pr*
Asher Bartov, *CEO*
EMP: 23 EST: 1981
SALES (est): 3.34MM **Privately Held**
Web: www.fedindustries.com
SIC: **3494 3728** Valves and pipe fittings, nec;
Aircraft parts and equipment, nec

(P-5387)
**G-G DISTRIBUTION & DEV CO
INC**
Also Called: G/G Industries
28545 Livingston Ave, Valencia
(91355-4166)
PHONE..........................661 257-5700
John Gedney, *Pr*
Mary Ellen, *
Richard Greenberg, *
◆ EMP: 120 EST: 1974
SALES (est): 3MM **Privately Held**
SIC: **3494 3088** Plumbing and heating valves
; Plastics plumbing fixtures

(P-5388)
GRISWOLD CONTROLS LLC (PA)
Also Called: Griswold Controls
1700 Barranca Pkwy, Irvine (92606-4824)
P.O. Box 19612 (92623-9612)
PHONE..........................949 559-6000
Brooks Sherman, *CEO*
◆ EMP: 100 EST: 1960
SALES (est): 21.09MM
SALES (corp-wide): 21.09MM **Privately
Held**
Web: www.griswoldcontrols.com
SIC: **3494 3491** Valves and pipe fittings, nec;
Industrial valves

(P-5389)
**MISSION RUBBER COMPANY
LLC**
1660 Leeson Ln, Corona (92879-2061)
PHONE..........................951 736-1313
EMP: 167
SALES (corp-wide): 66.6MM **Privately
Held**
Web: www.missionrubber.com
SIC: **3494** Couplings, except pressure and
soil pipe
HQ: Mission Rubber Company Llc
1660 Leeson Ln
Corona CA 92879
951 736-1313

(P-5390)
RAIN BIRD CORPORATION (PA)
Also Called: Rain Bird
970 W Sierra Madre Ave, Azusa
(91702-1873)
PHONE..........................626 812-3400
Michael L Donoghue, *CEO*
◆ EMP: 125 EST: 1933
SALES (est): 433.78MM
SALES (corp-wide): 433.78MM **Privately
Held**
Web: www.rainbird.com
SIC: **3494 3432 3523** Sprinkler systems, field
; Lawn hose nozzles and sprinklers; Farm
machinery and equipment

(P-5391)

VACCO INDUSTRIES (DH)
10350 Vacco St, South El Monte
(91733-3399)
PHONE...................626 443-7121
Antonio E Gonzalez, *CEO*
Robert Mc Creadie, *
Paul Rowan, *
EMP: 248 **EST:** 1954
SALES (est): 97.3MM **Publicly Held**
Web: www.vacco.com
SIC: 3494 3492 3728 Valves and pipe
   fittings, nec; Fluid power valves and hose
   fittings; Aircraft parts and equipment, nec
HQ: Esco Technologies Holding Llc
   9900a Clayton Rd
   Saint Louis MO 63124
   314 213-7200

3495 Wire Springs

(P-5392)

**BAL SEAL ENGINEERING LLC
(DH)**
19650 Pauling, Foothill Ranch
(92610-2610)
PHONE...................949 460-2100
Richard Dawson, *CEO*
Peter J Balsells, *Ch*
Jacques Naviaux, *Vice Chairman*
Andrew Wiggins, *Contrlr*
▲ **EMP:** 202 **EST:** 1959
SQ FT: 325,000
SALES (est): 92.5MM
SALES (corp-wide): 775.85MM **Privately
Held**
Web: www.balseal.com
SIC: 3495 3053 Wire springs; Gaskets and
   sealing devices
HQ: Kaman Acquisition Usa, Inc.
   1332 Blue Hills Ave
   Bloomfield CT 06002
   860 243-7100

(P-5393)

BETTS COMPANY
Also Called: Betts Truck Parts
10007 Elm Ave, Fontana (92335-6318)
PHONE...................909 427-9988
TOLL FREE: 800
Dan Paul, *Mgr*
EMP: 26
SALES (corp-wide): 39.88MM **Privately
Held**
Web: www.betts1868.com
SIC: 3495 3493 Wire springs; Automobile
   springs
PA: Betts Company
   2843 S Maple Ave
   559 498-3304

(P-5394)

ICONN ENGINEERING LLC
6882 Preakness Dr, Huntington Beach
(92648-1567)
PHONE...................714 696-8826
Jay Huang, *Pr*
EMP: 25 **EST:** 2011
SALES (est): 387.1K **Privately Held**
Web: www.iconneng.com
SIC: 3495 Wire springs

(P-5395)

MATTHEW WARREN INC
Also Called: Century Spring
5959 Triumph St, Commerce (90040-1609)
PHONE...................800 237-5225
Bill Cook, *Prin*
EMP: 75

SALES (corp-wide): 1.05B **Privately Held**
Web: www.centuryspring.com
SIC: 3495 Wire springs
HQ: Matthew Warren, Inc.
   3426 Tringdon Way Ste 400
   Charlotte NC 28277
   704 837-0331

(P-5396)

NEWCOMB SPRING CORP
Also Called: Newcomb Spring of California
8380 Cerritos Ave, Stanton (90680-2514)
PHONE...................714 995-5341
Robert Guard, *Mgr*
EMP: 25
SALES (corp-wide): 42.63MM **Privately
Held**
Web: www.newcombspring.com
SIC: 3495 3469 5085 Wire springs;
   Stamping metal for the trade; Springs
PA: Newcomb Spring Corp.
   3155 North Point Pkwy G220
   770 981-2803

(P-5397)

ORLANDO SPRING CORP
Also Called: Orlando Precision
5341 Argosy Ave, Huntington Beach
(92649-1036)
PHONE...................562 594-8411
Frank Mauro, *Pr*
Zachary Fischer, *
EMP: 40 **EST:** 1957
SQ FT: 20,000
SALES (est): 8.49MM **Privately Held**
Web: www.orlandospring.com
SIC: 3495 Wire springs

(P-5398)

**PRECISION COIL SPRING
COMPANY**
10107 Rose Ave, El Monte (91731-1898)
PHONE...................626 444-0561
Albert H Goering, *CEO*
Bert Goering, *
Don Adkins, *
William Turek, *VP Mfg*
Gustavo Arenas, *VP Engg*
EMP: 111 **EST:** 1951
SQ FT: 45,000
SALES (est): 8.67MM **Privately Held**
Web: www.pcspring.com
SIC: 3495 Wire springs

(P-5399)

SUPERIOR SPRING COMPANY
1260 S Talt Ave, Anaheim (92806-5533)
PHONE...................714 490-0881
TOLL FREE: 800
Robert De Long Junior, *Pr*
EMP: 25 **EST:** 1958
SQ FT: 17,000
SALES (est): 4.62MM **Privately Held**
Web: www.superiorspring.com
SIC: 3495 Wire springs

3496 Miscellaneous
Fabricated Wire Products

(P-5400)

BEE WIRE & CABLE INC
2850 E Spruce St, Ontario (91761-8550)
PHONE...................909 923-5800
Arjan Bera, *Pr*
Kiran Kaneria, *
Nalin Kaneria, *
▲ **EMP:** 26 **EST:** 1979
SQ FT: 34,400
SALES (est): 3.56MM **Privately Held**

Web: www.beeflex.com
SIC: 3496 Miscellaneous fabricated wire
   products

(P-5401)

**C M C STEEL FABRICATORS
INC**
Also Called: Fontana Steel
1455 Auto Center Dr Ste 200, Ontario
(91761-2239)
P.O. Box 2219 (91729-2219)
PHONE...................909 899-9993
Deborah Marshall, *Brnch Mgr*
EMP: 29
SALES (corp-wide): 7.93B **Publicly Held**
Web: www.cmc.com
SIC: 3496 3441 1791 Miscellaneous
   fabricated wire products; Fabricated
   structural metal; Concrete reinforcement,
   placing of
HQ: C M C Steel Fabricators, Inc.
   1 Steel Mill Dr
   Seguin TX 78155
   830 372-8200

(P-5402)

**CALIFORNIA WIRE PRODUCTS
CORP**
Also Called: Cal-Monarch
1316 Railroad St, Corona (92882-1840)
PHONE...................951 371-7730
John G Frei, *CEO*
Samuel A Agajanian, *
Sam Agajanian, *
▲ **EMP:** 30 **EST:** 1948
SQ FT: 34,000
SALES (est): 2.45MM **Privately Held**
Web: www.cawire.com
SIC: 3496 2542 Screening, woven wire:
   made from purchased wire; Partitions for
   floor attachment, prefabricated: except
   wood

(P-5403)

CIRCLE W ENTERPRISES INC
Also Called: Wirenetics Co
27737 Avenue Hopkins, Valencia
(91355-1223)
PHONE...................661 257-2400
Howard Weiss, *CEO*
Michael Weiss, *
Phyllis G Weiss, *
Mark Lee, *
▲ **EMP:** 50 **EST:** 1969
SQ FT: 65,000
SALES (est): 8.86MM
SALES (corp-wide): 512.41MM **Privately
Held**
SIC: 3496 Miscellaneous fabricated wire
   products
HQ: B.J.G. Electronics, Inc.
   141 Remington Blvd
   Ronkonkoma NY 11779
   631 737-1234

(P-5404)

DHA AMERICA INC
5403 Harvest Run Dr, San Diego
(92130-4879)
PHONE...................858 925-3246
Heon Young Ha, *Pr*
Duck Peerl Ha, *Sec*
▲ **EMP:** 54 **EST:** 1996
SALES (est): 2.55MM **Privately Held**
Web: www.dha-america.com
SIC: 3496 Wire winding
PA: Dae Ha Cable Co.,Ltd.
   2022 Deogyeong-Daero, Giheung-Gu

(P-5405)

EJAY FILTRATION INC
3036 Durahart St, Riverside (92507-3446)
P.O. Box 5268 (92517-5268)
PHONE...................951 683-0805
Jerry Green, *CEO*
Cheryl Young, *
Bob Rostig, *
EMP: 33 **EST:** 1988
SQ FT: 14,000
SALES (est): 4.46MM **Privately Held**
Web: www.ejayfiltration.com
SIC: 3496 Mesh, made from purchased wire

(P-5406)

INNOVIVE LLC (PA)
10019 Waples Ct, San Diego (92121-2962)
PHONE...................858 309-6620
Dee Conger, *CEO*
Joanna Xiong, *
◆ **EMP:** 40 **EST:** 2006
SQ FT: 50,000
SALES (est): 10.28MM **Privately Held**
Web: www.innovive.com
SIC: 3496 Cages, wire

(P-5407)

KEVIN WHALEY
Also Called: Whaley, Kevin Enterprises
9565 Pathway St, Santee (92071-4184)
PHONE...................619 596-4000
Kevin M Whaley, *Owner*
▼ **EMP:** 30 **EST:** 1976
SQ FT: 24,000
SALES (est): 3.3MM **Privately Held**
Web: www.kwcages.com
SIC: 3496 Cages, wire

(P-5408)

PACIFIC WIRE PRODUCTS INC
10725 Vanowen St, North Hollywood
(91605-6402)
PHONE...................818 755-6400
Charles L Swick, *Pr*
EMP: 25 **EST:** 1984
SQ FT: 28,000
SALES (est): 3.44MM **Privately Held**
Web: www.prontoproducts.com
SIC: 3496 Miscellaneous fabricated wire
   products

(P-5409)

PHIFER INCORPORATED
Also Called: Phifer Western
14408 Nelson Ave, City Of Industry
(91744-3513)
PHONE...................626 968-0438
Joel Hartig, *Mgr*
EMP: 59
SQ FT: 23,182
SALES (corp-wide): 286.29MM **Privately
Held**
Web: www.phifer.com
SIC: 3496 Miscellaneous fabricated wire
   products
PA: Phifer Incorporated
   4400 Reese Phifer Ave
   205 345-2120

(P-5410)

**PRECISION WIRE PRODUCTS
INC (PA)**
6150 Sheila St, Commerce (90040-2407)
PHONE...................323 890-9100
Vladimir John Ondrasik Junior, *Prin*
V John Ondrasik, *
◆ **EMP:** 200 **EST:** 1946
SQ FT: 200,000
SALES (est): 22.58MM
SALES (corp-wide): 22.58MM **Privately
Held**

Web: www.precisionwireproducts.com
SIC: 3496 Grocery carts, made from purchased wire

(P-5411)
R & B WIRE PRODUCTS INC
2902 W Garry Ave, Santa Ana (92704-6510)
PHONE..............................714 549-3355
Richard G Rawlins, CEO
◆ EMP: 50 EST: 1948
SQ FT: 20,000
SALES (est): 1.08MM Privately Held
Web: www.rbwire.com
SIC: 3496 Miscellaneous fabricated wire products

(P-5412)
RAMPONE INDUSTRIES LLC
168 E Liberty Ave, Anaheim (92801-1011)
PHONE..............................714 265-0200
Horacio Rampone, Managing Member
▲ EMP: 30 EST: 2003
SALES (est): 4.37MM Privately Held
Web: www.ramponeindustries.com
SIC: 3496 Miscellaneous fabricated wire products

(P-5413)
RAPID MFG A CAL LTD PARTNR (PA)
Also Called: Rapid Manufacturing
8080 E Crystal Dr, Anaheim (92807-2524)
PHONE..............................714 974-2432
Patricia Engler Howard, Genl Pt
Ronald W Howard, *
EMP: 180 EST: 1986
SQ FT: 19,500
SALES (est): 48.66MM
SALES (corp-wide): 48.66MM Privately Held
Web: www.rapidmfg.com
SIC: 3496 Miscellaneous fabricated wire products

(P-5414)
RFC WIRE FORMS INC
Also Called: Rfc Wire Forms
525 Brooks St, Ontario (91762-3702)
PHONE..............................909 467-0559
Donald C Kemby, CEO
Christine Kemby, *
▲ EMP: 70 EST: 1946
SQ FT: 29,000
SALES (est): 2.94MM Privately Held
Web: www.rfcwireforms.com
SIC: 3496 Miscellaneous fabricated wire products

(P-5415)
RPS INC
20331 Corisco St, Chatsworth (91311-6120)
PHONE..............................818 350-8088
Travis Miller, Pr
EMP: 25 EST: 2017
SQ FT: 1,000
SALES (est): 429.95K Privately Held
SIC: 3496 7389 Miscellaneous fabricated wire products; Design services

(P-5416)
TOP-SHELF FIXTURES LLC
5263 Schaefer Ave, Chino (91710-5554)
P.O. Box 2470 (91708-2470)
PHONE..............................909 627-7423
Alonso Munoz, Managing Member
EMP: 95 EST: 2002
SQ FT: 90,000
SALES (est): 20.98MM Privately Held

Web: www.topshelffixtures.com
SIC: 3496 Miscellaneous fabricated wire products

(P-5417)
TREE ISLAND WIRE (USA) INC
Also Called: Tree Island Wire USA
5080 Hallmark Pkwy, San Bernardino (92407-1835)
P.O. Box 90100 (92427-1100)
PHONE..............................909 899-1673
Daryl Young Opts, Mgr
EMP: 115
SALES (corp-wide): 185.25MM Privately Held
Web: www.treeisland.com
SIC: 3496 Miscellaneous fabricated wire products
HQ: Tree Island Wire (Usa), Inc.
3880 Valley Blvd
Walnut CA 91789

(P-5418)
UNITED SUNSHINE AMERICAN INDUSTRIES CORPORATION
Also Called: USA Industries
2808 E Marywood Ln, Orange (92867-1912)
EMP: 25 EST: 1948
SALES (est): 698.27K Privately Held
Web: www.usa-industries.com
SIC: 3496 Fencing, made from purchased wire

(P-5419)
US RIGGING SUPPLY CORP
1600 E Mcfadden Ave, Santa Ana (92705-4310)
PHONE..............................714 545-7444
Richard T Walker, CEO
▲ EMP: 50 EST: 1974
SQ FT: 20,000
SALES (est): 5.68MM Privately Held
Web: www.usrigging.com
SIC: 3496 5051 Miscellaneous fabricated wire products; Rope, wire (not insulated)

(P-5420)
WHITMOR PLSTIC WIRE CABLE CORP (PA)
Also Called: Whitmor Wire and Cable
27737 Avenue Hopkins, Santa Clarita (91355-1223)
PHONE..............................661 257-2400
Michael Weiss, Pr
Jeff Siebert, *
Mark Lee, *
Dwight Van Lake, *
Stella Reaza, *
▼ EMP: 50 EST: 1959
SQ FT: 50,000
SALES (est): 9.22MM
SALES (corp-wide): 9.22MM Privately Held
Web: www.wireandcable.com
SIC: 3496 5063 3357 Cable, uninsulated wire: made from purchased wire; Electrical apparatus and equipment; Nonferrous wiredrawing and insulating

(P-5421)
WHITMOR PLSTIC WIRE CABLE CORP
Also Called: Whitmor Wirenetics
28420 Avenue Stanford, Valencia (91355-3982)
PHONE..............................661 257-2400
Jeff Siebert, VP Mfg
EMP: 42

SALES (corp-wide): 9.22MM Privately Held
Web: www.wireandcable.com
SIC: 3496 5063 Cable, uninsulated wire: made from purchased wire; Electrical apparatus and equipment
PA: Whitmor Plastic Wire And Cable Corp.
27737 Avenue Hopkins
661 257-2400

(P-5422)
WYREFAB INC
15711 S Broadway, Gardena (90248-2401)
P.O. Box 3767 (90247-7467)
PHONE..............................310 523-2147
Charles Nick, Pr
John P Massey, *
EMP: 42 EST: 1948
SQ FT: 55,000
SALES (est): 4.42MM Privately Held
Web: www.wyrefab.com
SIC: 3496 Miscellaneous fabricated wire products

3498 Fabricated Pipe And Fittings

(P-5423)
AEROFIT LLC
1425 S Acacia Ave, Fullerton (92831-5317)
PHONE..............................714 521-5060
Jordan A Law, Managing Member
David A Werner, *
▲ EMP: 150 EST: 1968
SQ FT: 67,000
SALES (est): 22.92MM
SALES (corp-wide): 15.78B Publicly Held
Web: www.aerofit.com
SIC: 3498 Pipe fittings, fabricated from purchased pipe
HQ: Consolidated Aerospace Manufacturing, Llc
1425 S Acacia Ave
Fullerton CA 92831
714 989-2797

(P-5424)
AMERIFLEX INC
Also Called: Mw Components - Corona
2390 Railroad St, Corona (92878-5410)
PHONE..............................951 737-5557
John Bagnuolo, CEO
Chester Kwasniak, CFO
▲ EMP: 76 EST: 1981
SQ FT: 32,000
SALES (est): 7.33MM
SALES (corp-wide): 1.05B Privately Held
Web: www.mwcomponents.com
SIC: 3498 3494 3674 Fabricated pipe and fittings; Valves and pipe fittings, nec; Semiconductors and related devices
HQ: Mw Industries, Inc.
2400 Farrell Rd
Houston TX 77073
800 875-3510

(P-5425)
ASC ENGINEERED SOLUTIONS LLC
2867 Vail Ave, Commerce (90040-2613)
PHONE.................766-0076
EMP: 66
SALES (corp-wide): 836.12MM Privately Held
Web: www.asc-es.com
SIC: 3498 Fabricated pipe and fittings
PA: Asc Engineered Solutions, Llc
2001 Spring Rd Ste 300
800 301-2701

(P-5426)
ASC ENGINEERED SOLUTIONS LLC
551 N Loop Dr, Ontario (91761-8629)
PHONE..............................909 418-3233
Gwyn Lundy, Crdt Mgr
EMP: 52
SALES (corp-wide): 836.12MM Privately Held
Web: www.asc-es.com
SIC: 3498 3321 3317 Fabricated pipe and fittings; Gray and ductile iron foundries; Steel pipe and tubes
PA: Asc Engineered Solutions, Llc
2001 Spring Rd Ste 300
800 301-2701

(P-5427)
BASSANI MANUFACTURING
Also Called: Bassani Exhaust
2900 E La Jolla St, Anaheim (92806-1305)
PHONE..............................714 630-1821
Darryl Bassani, Pr
Becky Bassani, *
▲ EMP: 46 EST: 1969
SQ FT: 20,791
SALES (est): 9.45MM Privately Held
Web: www.bassani.com
SIC: 3498 3599 Fabricated pipe and fittings; Machine shop, jobbing and repair

(P-5428)
BCC DISSOLUTION INC
2929 S Santa Fe Ave, Los Angeles (90058-1425)
P.O. Box 7249 (91327-7249)
PHONE..............................323 583-3444
Ramendra Satyarthi, Pr
▲ EMP: 35 EST: 1982
SQ FT: 65,000
SALES (est): 3.73MM Privately Held
Web: www.bakercouplingcompany.com
SIC: 3498 Couplings, pipe: fabricated from purchased pipe

(P-5429)
CAL PIPE MANUFACTURING INC (PA)
Also Called: Calpipe Security Bollards
12160 Woodruff Ave, Downey (90241-5606)
PHONE..............................562 803-4388
Dan Markus, Pr
Sheri Caine-markus, VP
▲ EMP: 37 EST: 1986
SQ FT: 125,000
SALES (est): 3.08MM
SALES (corp-wide): 3.08MM Privately Held
Web: www.atkore.com
SIC: 3490 Tube fabricating (contract bending and shaping)

(P-5430)
CRYOWORKS INC
3309 Grapevine St, Mira Loma (91752-3503)
PHONE..............................951 360-0920
Timothy L Mast, Pr
Donna J Mast, VP
Tamara Sipos, CFO
EMP: 85 EST: 2009
SALES (est): 10.36MM Privately Held
Web: www.cryoworks.net
SIC: 3498 1711 Fabricated pipe and fittings; Plumbing contractors

(P-5431)
CUNICO CORPORATION
1910 W 16th St, Long Beach (90813-1137)
P.O. Box 9010 (90810-0010)
PHONE..............................562 733-4600
▲ **EMP:** 45 **EST:** 1951
SALES (est): 2.98MM
SALES (corp-wide): 9.45MM **Privately Held**
Web: www.bwxt.com
SIC: 3498 Pipe fittings, fabricated from purchased pipe
PA: Citadel Capital Corporation
1910 W 16th St
562 733-4600

(P-5432)
CUSTOM PIPE & FABRICATION INC (HQ)
10560 Fern Ave, Stanton (90680-2648)
P.O. Box 978 (90680-0978)
PHONE..............................800 553-3058
Danny Daniel, *CEO*
Leonard Shapiro, *Treas*
Jerry Witkow, *Sec*
▲ **EMP:** 60 **EST:** 1972
SQ FT: 8,000
SALES (est): 117.01MM
SALES (corp-wide): 134.62MM **Privately Held**
Web: www.custompipe.com
SIC: 3498 Tube fabricating (contract bending and shaping)
PA: Shapco Inc.
1666 20th St Ste 100
310 264-1666

(P-5433)
EDMUND A GRAY CO (PA)
2277 E 15th St, Los Angeles (90021-2852)
PHONE..............................213 625-0376
Lawrence Gray Junior, *CEO*
Lawrence Gray Iii, *VP*
Patricia Gray, *
▲ **EMP:** 75 **EST:** 1910
SQ FT: 50,000
SALES (est): 13.68MM
SALES (corp-wide): 13.68MM **Privately Held**
Web: www.eagray.com
SIC: 3498 Pipe fittings, fabricated from purchased pipe

(P-5434)
FLEXIBLE METAL INC
Also Called: FMI
1685 Brandywine Ave, Chula Vista (91911-6020)
PHONE..............................734 516-3017
Michael Nocholson, *CEO*
▲ **EMP:** 180 **EST:** 1986
SALES (est): 14.51MM
SALES (corp-wide): 115.37MM **Privately Held**
Web: www.flexiblemetal.com
SIC: 3498 Fabricated pipe and fittings
PA: Hyspan Precision Products, Inc.
1685 Brandywine Ave
619 421-1355

(P-5435)
ILCO INDUSTRIES INC
Also Called: Ilco Industries
1308 W Mahalo Pl, Compton (90220-5418)
PHONE..............................310 631-8655
Elias Awad, *Pr*
EMP: 35 **EST:** 1936
SQ FT: 23,000
SALES (est): 5.84MM **Privately Held**
Web: www.ilcoind.com

(P-5436)
ONE-WAY MANUFACTURING INC
1195 N Osprey Cir, Anaheim (92807-1709)
PHONE..............................714 630-8833
Sue Huang, *CEO*
Ike Huang, *COO*
EMP: 23 **EST:** 2005
SQ FT: 19,400
SALES (est): 6.58MM **Privately Held**
Web: www.onewaymfg.com
SIC: 3498 3599 1541 7692 Tube fabricating (contract bending and shaping); Machine and other job shop work; Truck and automobile assembly plant construction; Welding repair

(P-5437)
RIGHT MANUFACTURING LLC
7949 Stromesa Ct Ste G, San Diego (92126-6338)
PHONE..............................858 566-7002
▲ **EMP:** 30 **EST:** 1971
SQ FT: 15,000
SALES (est): 5.89MM **Privately Held**
Web: www.rightmfg.com
SIC: 3498 3444 Tube fabricating (contract bending and shaping); Sheet metalwork

(P-5438)
RUSSELL FABRICATION CORP
Also Called: American Fabrication
4940 Gilmore Ave, Bakersfield (93308-6150)
PHONE..............................661 861-8495
Kevin Russell, *Pr*
EMP: 45 **EST:** 1985
SALES (est): 4.44MM **Privately Held**
Web: www.americanfabandpowdercoating.com
SIC: 3498 3444 Fabricated pipe and fittings; Sheet metalwork

(P-5439)
WESSEX INDUSTRIES INC
8619 Red Oak St, Rancho Cucamonga (91730-4820)
PHONE..............................562 944-5760
Archie Castillo, *Pr*
Edward Mojica, *
Linne A Castillo, *
EMP: 25 **EST:** 1985
SQ FT: 30,000
SALES (est): 2.44MM **Privately Held**
SIC: 3498 8742 Pipe fittings, fabricated from purchased pipe; Management consulting services

---

3499 Fabricated Metal Products, Nec

(P-5440)
AMERICAN SECURITY PRODUCTS CO
Also Called: Amsec
11925 Pacific Ave, Fontana (92337-8205)
P.O. Box 317001 (92331-7001)
PHONE..............................951 685-9680
David Lazier, *CEO*
Thomas Cassutt, *CFO*
Robert Sallee, *VP*
◆ **EMP:** 237 **EST:** 1946
SQ FT: 150,000
SALES (est): 44.62MM **Privately Held**
Web: www.americansecuritysafes.com

SIC: 3499 1731 Safes and vaults, metal; Safety and security specialization

(P-5441)
ARTISAN HOUSE INC
Also Called: ARTISAN HOUSE, INC
8238 Lankershim Blvd, North Hollywood (91605-1613)
PHONE..............................818 767-7476
Dennis Damore, *Brnch Mgr*
EMP: 30
SALES (corp-wide): 1.45MM **Privately Held**
Web: www.artisanhouse.com
SIC: 3499 Novelties and specialties, metal
PA: Artisan House, Inc.
3750 Cohasset St
818 565-5030

(P-5442)
BEY-BERK INTERNATIONAL (PA)
9145 Deering Ave, Chatsworth (91311-5802)
PHONE..............................818 773-7534
Kurken Y Berksanlar, *Pr*
Serop Beylerian, *
◆ **EMP:** 23 **EST:** 1980
SQ FT: 19,800
SALES (est): 2.88MM
SALES (corp-wide): 2.88MM **Privately Held**
Web: www.bey-berk.com
SIC: 3499 3873 Novelties and giftware, including trophies; Clocks, assembly of

(P-5443)
CHATSWORTH PRODUCTS INC (PA)
Also Called: C P I
4175 Guardian St, Simi Valley (93063-3382)
PHONE..............................818 735-6100
Michael Custer, *CEO*
Larry Renaud, *
Larry Varblow, *
Tom Jorgenson, *
Ted Behrens, *
◆ **EMP:** 25 **EST:** 1990
SALES (est): 107.78MM **Privately Held**
Web: www.chatsworth.com
SIC: 3499 2542 Machine bases, metal; Partitions and fixtures, except wood

(P-5444)
DOT BLUE SAFES CORPORATION
2707 N Garey Ave, Pomona (91767-1809)
PHONE..............................909 445-8888
Berge Jalakian, *CEO*
◆ **EMP:** 42 **EST:** 2004
SQ FT: 90,000
SALES (est): 9.01MM **Privately Held**
Web: www.bluedotsafes.com
SIC: 3499 8741 Safes and vaults, metal; Management services

(P-5445)
ECOOLTHING CORP
Also Called: Cool Things
1321 E Saint Gertrude Pl Ste A, Santa Ana (92705-5241)
P.O. Box 6022 (92616-6022)
PHONE..............................714 368-4791
Connie Wang, *Pr*
Linda Wang, *
▲ **EMP:** 50 **EST:** 2001
SQ FT: 10,000
SALES (est): 2.33MM **Privately Held**

SIC: 3499 5199 Novelties and giftware, including trophies; Gifts and novelties

(P-5446)
EVANS INDUSTRIES INC
Darnell-Rose Div
17915 Railroad St, City Of Industry (91748-1113)
PHONE..............................626 912-1688
Bob Batistic, *Mgr*
EMP: 58
SALES (corp-wide): 16.83MM **Privately Held**
Web: www.mmgmfg.com
SIC: 3499 5072 Wheels: wheelbarrow, stroller, etc.: disc, stamped metal; Casters and glides
HQ: Evans Industries, Inc.
3150 Livernois Rd Ste 170
Troy MI 48083
313 259-2266

(P-5447)
EXECUTIVE SAFE AND SEC CORP
Also Called: Amphion
10722 Edison Ct, Rancho Cucamonga (91730-4845)
PHONE..............................909 947-7020
Scott C Denton, *Pr*
Robyn Denton, *
◆ **EMP:** 30 **EST:** 1999
SQ FT: 11,000
SALES (est): 3.86MM **Privately Held**
Web: www.amphion.biz
SIC: 3499 5072 7382 5099 Safes and vaults, metal; Security devices, locks; Confinement surveillance systems maintenance and monitoring; Locks and lock sets

(P-5448)
INTRA STORAGE SYSTEMS INC
Also Called: Gibo/Kodama Chairs
7100 Honold Cir, Garden Grove (92841-1424)
PHONE..............................714 373-2346
▲ **EMP:** 30 **EST:** 1983
SALES (est): 4MM **Privately Held**
Web: www.intrastorage.com
SIC: 3499 5084 3535 2599 Chair frames, metal; Materials handling machinery; Belt conveyor systems, general industrial use; Factory furniture and fixtures

(P-5449)
L A PROPOINT INC
10870 La Tuna Canyon Rd, Sun Valley (91352-2009)
PHONE..............................818 767-6800
Mark Riddlesperger, *Pr*
James Hartman, *
▼ **EMP:** 30 **EST:** 2002
SQ FT: 28,000
SALES (est): 4.57MM **Privately Held**
Web: www.lapropoint.com
SIC: 3499 3449 Metal household articles; Miscellaneous metalwork

(P-5450)
LAMINATED SHIM COMPANY INC
1691 California Ave, Corona (92881-3375)
PHONE..............................951 273-3900
EMP: 25 **EST:** 1982
SALES (est): 3.45MM **Privately Held**
Web: www.laminatedshim.com
SIC: 3499 Shims, metal

(P-5451)

MAGNETIC COMPONENT ENGRG LLC (PA)

Also Called: M C E
2830 Lomita Blvd, Torrance (90505-5101)
PHONE.................................310 784-3100
Linda Montgomerie, *CEO*
▲ **EMP:** 93 **EST:** 1973
SQ FT: 50,000
SALES (est): 13.38MM
SALES (corp-wide): 13.38MM **Privately Held**
Web: www.mceproducts.com
SIC: 3499 3677 Magnets, permanent: metallic; Electronic coils and transformers

(P-5452)

MATERIAL CONTROL INC

Also Called: Cotterman Company
6901 District Blvd Ste A, Bakersfield (93313-2071)
PHONE.................................661 617-6033
Tony Ortiz, *Brnch Mgr*
EMP: 74
SALES (corp-wide): 42.75MM **Privately Held**
Web: www.cotterman.com
SIC: 3499 Metal ladders
PA: Material Control, Inc.
130 Seltzer Rd
630 892-4274

(P-5453)

PSM INDUSTRIES INC (PA)

14000 Avalon Blvd, Los Angeles (90061-2636)
PHONE.................................888 663-8256
Craig Paullin, *CEO*
Susan Paullin, *
Mary Sherrill, *
▲ **EMP:** 60 **EST:** 1956
SALES (est): 23.24MM
SALES (corp-wide): 23.24MM **Privately Held**
Web: www.psmindustries.com
SIC: 3499 Friction material, made from powdered metal

3511 Turbines And Turbine Generator Sets

(P-5454)

ALTURDYNE POWER SYSTEMS INC

1405 N Johnson Ave, El Cajon (92020-1615)
PHONE.................................619 343-3204
Frank Verbeke, *Pr*
EMP: 30 **EST:** 2013
SQ FT: 3,000
SALES (est): 4.72MM **Privately Held**
Web: www.alturdyne.com
SIC: 3511 1731 Gas turbine generator set units, complete; Electric power systems contractors

(P-5455)

CAPSTONE DSTR SPPORT SVCS CORP (PA)

Also Called: Capstone
16640 Stagg St, Van Nuys (91406-1630)
PHONE.................................818 734-5300
Robert C Flexon, *Pr*
Robert C Flexon, *Pr*
Scott Robinson, *Interim Chief Financial Officer*
John J Juric, *CFO*
◆ **EMP:** 121 **EST:** 1988

SQ FT: 79,000
SALES (est): 69.64MM **Privately Held**
Web: www.capstonegreenenergy.com
SIC: 3511 Turbines and turbine generator sets

(P-5456)

CLIPPER WINDPOWER PLC

Also Called: Clipper Windpower
6305 Carpinteria Ave Ste 300, Carpinteria (93013-2969)
PHONE.................................805 690-3275
Michael Keane, *
EMP: 740 **EST:** 2005
SALES (est): 8.93MM **Privately Held**
SIC: 3511 Turbines and turbine generator sets

(P-5457)

GE RENEWABLES NORTH AMER LLC

13681 Chantico Rd, Tehachapi (93561-8188)
PHONE.................................661 823-6423
Gerlad Turk, *Mgr*
EMP: 212
SALES (corp-wide): 67.95B **Publicly Held**
SIC: 3511 Turbines and turbine generator sets
HQ: Ge Renewables North Amer Llc
8301 Scenic Hwy
Pensacola FL 32514
850 474-4011

(P-5458)

LA TURBINE (HQ)

28557 Industry Dr, Valencia (91355-5424)
PHONE.................................661 294-8290
John Maskaluk, *CEO*
Danny Mascari, *
Christian Maskaluk, *
Idris Kebir, *
Richard Samson, *
▼ **EMP:** 69 **EST:** 2003
SQ FT: 90,000
SALES (est): 19MM **Publicly Held**
Web: www.chartindustries.com
SIC: 3511 Turbines and turbine generator sets and parts
PA: Chart Industries, Inc.
2200 Arprt Indus Dr Ste 1

(P-5459)

MODULAR WIND ENERGY INC

1709 Apollo Ct, Seal Beach (90740-5617)
PHONE.................................562 304-6782
EMP: 53 **EST:** 2007
SALES (est): 1.83MM **Privately Held**
Web: www.modwind.com
SIC: 3511 Turbines and turbine generator sets

(P-5460)

PRECISION ENGINE CONTROLS CORP (DH)

Also Called: Pecc
11661 Sorrento Valley Rd, San Diego (92121-1083)
P.O. Box 7734 (44306-0734)
PHONE.................................858 792-3217
EMP: 102 **EST:** 1992
SALES (est): 12.25MM
SALES (corp-wide): 19.93B **Publicly Held**
SIC: 3511 Gas turbine generator set units, complete
HQ: Meggitt Limited
Ansty Bus.
Coventry W MIDLANDS CV7 9
247 682-6900

(P-5461)

SOLAR TURBINES INCORPORATED (HQ)

2200 Pacific Hwy, San Diego (92101-1773)
P.O. Box 85376 (92186)
PHONE.................................619 544-5352
Derrick York, *Pr*
P Browning, *
Robert May, *
◆ **EMP:** 3890 **EST:** 1927
SQ FT: 1,080,000
SALES (est): 1.88B
SALES (corp-wide): 67.06B **Publicly Held**
Web: www.solarturbines.com
SIC: 3511 Gas turbine generator set units, complete
PA: Caterpillar Inc.
5205 N Ocnnor Blvd Ste 10
972 891-7700

(P-5462)

SOLAR TURBINES INCORPORATED

2660 Sarnen St, San Diego (92154-6216)
PHONE.................................619 544-5321
EMP: 25
SALES (corp-wide): 67.06B **Publicly Held**
Web: www.solarturbines.com
SIC: 3511 Gas turbine generator set units, complete
HQ: Solar Turbines Incorporated
2200 Pacific Hwy
San Diego CA 92101
619 544-5352

(P-5463)

SOLAR TURBINES INCORPORATED

9330 Sky Park Ct, San Diego (92123-4304)
PHONE.................................858 694-6110
Stephen Kanyr, *Prin*
EMP: 200
SALES (corp-wide): 67.06B **Publicly Held**
Web: www.solarturbines.com
SIC: 3511 Gas turbine generator set units, complete
HQ: Solar Turbines Incorporated
2200 Pacific Hwy
San Diego CA 92101
619 544-5352

(P-5464)

SOLAR TURBINES INCORPORATED

9250 Sky Park Ct A, San Diego (92123-5398)
PHONE.................................858 715-2060
EMP: 52
SQ FT: 60,155
SALES (corp-wide): 67.06B **Publicly Held**
Web: www.solarturbines.com
SIC: 3511 Gas turbine generator set units, complete
HQ: Solar Turbines Incorporated
2200 Pacific Hwy
San Diego CA 92101
619 544-5352

(P-5465)

TURBINE REPAIR SERVICES LLC (PA)

1838 E Cedar St, Ontario (91761-7763)
PHONE.................................909 947-2256
Victor M Sanchez, *Managing Member*
Dave Meyer, *
Michael Dorrel, *Managing Member*
Cesar Siordia, *
Danny Sanchez, *
EMP: 39 **EST:** 2000

SQ FT: 12,000
SALES (est): 7.33MM **Privately Held**
Web: www.turbinerepairservices.com
SIC: 3511 Turbines and turbine generator sets

3519 Internal Combustion Engines, Nec

(P-5466)

CUMMINS PACIFIC LLC (HQ)

Also Called: Cummins
1939 Deere Ave, Irvine (92606-4818)
PHONE.................................949 253-6000
TOLL FREE: 800
Mark Yragui, *Pr*
▲ **EMP:** 85 **EST:** 2002
SALES (est): 87.89MM
SALES (corp-wide): 34.06B **Publicly Held**
Web: www.cumminspacific.com
SIC: 3519 5063 7538 Internal combustion engines, nec; Generators; General automotive repair shops
PA: Cummins Inc.
500 Jackson St
812 377-5000

(P-5467)

DETROIT DIESEL CORPORATION

10645 Studebaker Rd 2nd Fl, Downey (90241-3173)
PHONE.................................562 929-7016
Glen Nutting, *VP*
EMP: 53
SALES (corp-wide): 60.75B **Privately Held**
Web: www.demanddetroit.com
SIC: 3519 Engines, diesel and semi-diesel or dual-fuel
HQ: Detroit Diesel Corporation
13400 W Outer Dr
Detroit MI 48239
313 592-5000

(P-5468)

GALE BANKS ENGINEERING

Also Called: Banks Power Products
546 S Duggan Ave, Azusa (91702-5136)
PHONE.................................626 969-9600
Gale C Banks Iii, *Pr*
Vicki L Banks, *
▲ **EMP:** 195 **EST:** 1970
SQ FT: 121,000
SALES (est): 22.57MM **Privately Held**
Web: www.bankspower.com
SIC: 3519 3714 Parts and accessories, internal combustion engines; Motor vehicle parts and accessories

(P-5469)

PACMET AEROSPACE LLC

Also Called: Pacmet Aerospace
224 Glider Cir, Corona (92878-5033)
PHONE.................................909 218-8889
David Janes, *CEO*
David A Janes Junior, *Managing Member*
◆ **EMP:** 76 **EST:** 2005
SQ FT: 45,000
SALES (est): 9.77MM **Privately Held**
Web: www.pacmetaerospace.com
SIC: 3519 Jet propulsion engines

(P-5470)

TRACY INDUSTRIES INC

Also Called: Genuine Parts Distributors
3200 E Guasti Rd Ste 100, Ontario (91761-8661)
P.O. Box 1260 (91762-0260)
PHONE.................................562 692-9034
Timothy Engvall, *CEO*

David Rosenberger, *
Erma Jean Tracy, *
Timothy Engvall, *Treas*
▲ **EMP: 216 EST:** 1946
SALES (est): 3.07MM **Privately Held**
SIC: 3519 7538 Internal combustion
engines, nec; Engine rebuilding: automotive

(P-5471)
TRANSONIC COMBUSTION INC
461 Calle San Pablo, Camarillo
(93012-8506)
PHONE..........................805 465-5145
Wolfgang Bullmer, *Pr*
Timothy Noonan, *
Mike Cheiky, *
EMP: 40 **EST:** 2006
SALES (est): 2.68MM **Privately Held**
Web: www.tscombustion.com
SIC: 3519 Internal combustion engines, nec

3523 Farm Machinery And Equipment

(P-5472)
CAGECO INC
16225 Beaver Rd, Adelanto (92301-3908)
PHONE..........................800 605-4859
Mike Alexander, *Pr*
EMP: 38 **EST:** 2012
SALES (est): 5.65MM **Privately Held**
Web: www.cagecoinc.com
SIC: 3523 Barn, silo, poultry, dairy, and
livestock machinery

(P-5473)
DIG CORPORATION
1210 Activity Dr, Vista (92081-8510).
PHONE..........................760 727-0914
David Levy, *Pr*
Racquell Bibens, *
Greg Smith, *
Duy Johnson, *
◆ **EMP:** 43 **EST:** 1982
SQ FT: 45,000
SALES (est): 11.66MM **Privately Held**
Web: www.digcorp.com
SIC: 3523 Irrigation equipment, self-propelled

(P-5474)
MARIE EDWARD VINEYARDS INC
6901 E Brundage Ln, Bakersfield
(93307-3057)
PHONE..........................661 363-5038
Matthew E Brock, *Pr*
EMP: 35 **EST:** 1988
SALES (est): 1.4MM **Privately Held**
Web: www.brockstrailersinc.com
SIC: 3523 5013 7539 5511 Trailers and
wagons, farm; Trailer parts and accessories
; Trailer repair; Trucks, tractors, and trailers:
new and used

(P-5475)
OLSON IRRIGATION SYSTEMS
Also Called: Olson Industrial Systems
10910 Wheatlands Ave Ste A, Santee
(92071-2867)
P.O. Box 711570 (92072-1570)
PHONE..........................619 562-3100
Donald Olson, *Pr*
Kathleen Baldwin, *
▲ **EMP:** 28 **EST:** 1976
SQ FT: 17,000
SALES (est): 2.53MM **Publicly Held**
SIC: 3523 Sprayers and spraying machines,
agricultural
HQ: Evoqua Water Technologies Llc
210 6th Ave Ste 3300

Pittsburgh PA 15222
724 772-0044

(P-5476)
RAIN BIRD CORPORATION
9491 Ridgehaven Ct, San Diego
(92123-5601)
PHONE..........................619 674-4068
Eileen Collins, *Mgr*
EMP: 59
SALES (corp-wide): 433.78MM **Privately
Held**
Web: www.rainbird.com
SIC: 3523 Farm machinery and equipment
PA: Rain Bird Corporation
970 W Sierra Madre Ave
626 812-3400

(P-5477)
SIGNATURE CONTROL SYSTEMS
16485 Laguna Canyon Rd Ste 130, Irvine
(92618-3848)
PHONE..........................949 580-3640
Brian Smith, *Pr*
◆ **EMP:** 100 **EST:** 2000
SQ FT: 7,000
SALES (est): 5.11MM **Privately Held**
Web: www.signaturecontrolsystems.com
SIC: 3523 Irrigation equipment, self-propelled

(P-5478)
STORM INDUSTRIES INC (PA)
Also Called: Storm
970 W 190th St, Torrance (90502-1000)
PHONE..........................310 534-5232
Dale R Philippi, *CEO*
Guy E Marge, *
Georgia Claessens, *
Jonathan Corbin, *
▲ **EMP:** 100 **EST:** 1977
SALES (est): 44.12MM
SALES (corp-wide): 44.12MM **Privately
Held**
Web: www.stormind.com
SIC: 3523 6552 Irrigation equipment, self-
propelled; Subdividers and developers, nec

(P-5479)
TORO COMPANY
5825 Jasmine St, Riverside (92504-1183)
P.O. Box 489 (92502-0489)
PHONE..........................951 688-9221
Kendrick Melrose, *Mgr*
EMP: 197
SALES (corp-wide): 4.58B **Publicly Held**
Web: www.thetorocompany.com
SIC: 3523 Irrigation equipment, self-propelled
PA: The Toro Company
8111 Lyndale Ave S
952 888-8801

(P-5480)
TORO COMPANY
1588 N Marshall Ave, El Cajon
(92020-1523)
PHONE..........................619 562-2950
Timothy Young, *Mgr*
EMP: 132
SQ FT: 86,578
SALES (corp-wide): 4.58B **Publicly Held**
Web: www.thetorocompany.com
SIC: 3523 Irrigation equipment, self-propelled
PA: The Toro Company
8111 Lyndale Ave S
952 888-8801

3524 Lawn And Garden Equipment

(P-5481)
MCLANE MANUFACTURING INC
6814 Foster Bridge Blvd, Bell Gardens
(90201-2032)
PHONE..........................562 633-8158
Elmer E Malchow, *Ch Bd*
Ronald Mc Lane, *
Olivia Osorio, *
▲ **EMP:** 65 **EST:** 1942
SALES (est): 3.59MM **Privately Held**
Web: www.mclaneedgers.com
SIC: 3524 Lawnmowers, residential: hand or
power

(P-5482)
R&M SUPPLY INC
420 Harley Knox Blvd, Perris (92571-7566)
PHONE..........................951 552-9860
◆ **EMP:** 100
Web: www.randmsupply.com
SIC: 3524 Lawn and garden equipment

(P-5483)
SCOTTS TEMECULA OPERATIONS LLC (DH)
42375 Remington Ave, Temecula
(92590-2512)
PHONE..........................951 719-1700
Jim Hagedorn, *Ch*
Barry Sanders, *Pr*
▲ **EMP:** 41 **EST:** 2001
SQ FT: 400,000
SALES (est): 39.85MM
SALES (corp-wide): 3.55B **Publicly Held**
SIC: 3524 Lawn and garden equipment
HQ: The Scotts Company Llc
14111 Scottslawn Rd
Marysville OH 43040
937 644-0011

(P-5484)
TRU-CUT INC
141 E 157th St, Gardena (90248-2508)
P.O. Box 642475 (90064-8137)
PHONE..........................310 630-0422
Nabi Merchant, *CEO*
▲ **EMP:** 35 **EST:** 1953
SQ FT: 28,620
SALES (est): 2.1MM **Privately Held**
Web: www.trucutmower.com
SIC: 3524 5083 Lawn and garden mowers
and accessories; Lawn and garden
machinery and equipment

(P-5485)
WESTERN CACTUS GROWERS INC
1860 Monte Vista Dr, Vista (92084-7124)
P.O. Box 2018 (92085-2018)
PHONE..........................760 726-1710
Thomas Hans Britsch, *CEO*
Margaret Britsch, *
▲ **EMP:** 25 **EST:** 1974
SQ FT: 6,000
SALES (est): 1.97MM **Privately Held**
SIC: 3524 0181 Lawn and garden equipment
; Florists' greens and flowers

3531 Construction Machinery

(P-5486)
ALTEC INC
1127 Carrier Parkway Ave, Bakersfield
(93308-9666)

PHONE..........................661 679-4177
EMP: 28
SALES (corp-wide): 1.21B **Privately Held**
Web: www.altec.com
SIC: 3531 Construction machinery
PA: Altec, Inc.
210 Inverness Center Dr
205 991-7733

(P-5487)
AMERICAN COMPACTION EQP INC
Also Called: Compaction American
29380 Hunco Way, Lake Elsinore
(92530-2757)
PHONE..........................949 661-2921
Richard S Anderson, *CEO*
Monty Ihde, *
Darryl Kanell, *
Kelly Ihde, *
Mike Shoemaker, *
▲ **EMP:** 24 **EST:** 1987
SQ FT: 8,500
SALES (est): 9.81MM **Privately Held**
Web: www.acewheels.com
SIC: 3531 7353 Soil compactors: vibratory;
Heavy construction equipment rental
HQ: Cascade Corporation
2201 Ne 201st Ave
Fairview OR 97024
503 669-6300

(P-5488)
BLACK DIAMOND BLADE COMPANY (PA)
Also Called: Cutting Edge Supply
234 E O St, Colton (92324-3466)
PHONE..........................800 949-9014
John Brenner, *CEO*
Franklin J Brenner Senior, *Pr*
Hoby Brenner, *Treas*
◆ **EMP:** 35 **EST:** 1950
SQ FT: 16,000
SALES (est): 24.83MM
SALES (corp-wide): 24.83MM **Privately
Held**
Web: www.cuttingedgesupply.com
SIC: 3531 Blades for graders, scrapers,
dozers, and snow plows

(P-5489)
CAVOTEC INET US INC
5665 Corporate Ave, Cypress
(90630-4727)
PHONE..........................714 947-0005
Mike Larkin, *Pr*
Dorothy Chen, *
▼ **EMP:** 70 **EST:** 2011
SALES (est): 7.3MM **Privately Held**
Web: www.cavotec.com
SIC: 3531 Airport construction machinery
HQ: Cavotec Us Holdings, Inc.
5665 Corporate Ave
Cypress CA 90630
714 545-7900

(P-5490)
COUNTY OF LOS ANGELES
Also Called: Public Works, Dept of
14959 Proctor Ave, La Puente
(91746-3206)
PHONE..........................626 968-3312
Mike Lee, *Mgr*
EMP: 30
Web: www.lacounty.info
SIC: 3531 9111 Road construction and
maintenance machinery; Executive offices
PA: County Of Los Angeles
500 W Temple St Ste 437
213 974-1101

▲ = Import ▼ = Export
◆ = Import/Export

(P-5491)
COUNTY OF LOS ANGELES
Also Called: Public Works, Dept of
3637 Winter Canyon Rd, Malibu
(90265-4834)
PHONE...............................310 456-8014
Mark Sanchez, *Mgr*
EMP: 41
Web: www.lacounty.gov
SIC: 3531 9621 Graders, road (construction machinery); Regulation, administration of transportation
PA: County Of Los Angeles
500 W Temple St Ste 437
213 974-1101

(P-5492)
GROUND HOG INC
1470 Victoria Ct, San Bernardino
(92408-2831)
P.O. Box 290 (92402-0290)
PHONE...............................909 478-5700
Edward Carlson, *Pr*
Jack Carlson, *
▼ **EMP:** 25 **EST:** 1948
SQ FT: 52,000
SALES (est): 5.69MM **Privately Held**
Web: www.groundhoginc.com
SIC: 3531 Posthole diggers, powered

(P-5493)
H & L TOOTH COMPANY (PA)
Also Called: H & L Forge Company
1540 S Greenwood Ave, Montebello
(90640-6536)
P.O. Box 48 (74055-0048)
PHONE...............................323 721-5146
Richard L Launder, *Ch Bd*
Brian L Launder, *
▲ **EMP:** 85 **EST:** 1931
SQ FT: 220,000
SALES (est): 1.26MM
SALES (corp-wide): 1.26MM **Privately Held**
Web: www.hltooth.com
SIC: 3531 Bucket or scarifier teeth

(P-5494)
HARCON PRECISION METALS INC
1790 Dornoch Ct, Chula Vista (91910)
PHONE...............................619 423-5544
EMP: 50 **EST:** 1971
SALES (est): 4.55MM **Privately Held**
Web: www.harcon-precision.com
SIC: 3531 3444 Construction machinery; Sheet metalwork

(P-5495)
JLG INDUSTRIES INC
Also Called: Jlg Serviceplus
7820 Lincoln Ave, Riverside (92504-4443)
PHONE...............................951 358-1915
Eric Golden, *Mgr*
EMP: 28
SALES (corp-wide): 9.66B **Publicly Held**
Web: www.jlg.com
SIC: 3531 Cranes, nec
HQ: Jlg Industries, Inc.
1 Jlg Dr
Mc Connellsburg PA 17233
717 485-5161

(P-5496)
MARINE CORPS UNITED STATES
Usmc, Barstow (92311)
PHONE...............................760 577-6716
EMP: 154

Web: www.marines.mil
SIC: 3531 Marine related equipment
HQ: United States Marine Corps
Branch Hlth Clinic Bldg #5
Beaufort SC 29904

(P-5497)
SCHWING AMERICA INC
3351 Grapevine St Bldg A, Jurupa Valley
(91752-3510)
PHONE...............................909 681-6430
Albert Ornelas, *Mgr*
EMP: 244
SALES (corp-wide): 12.98B **Privately Held**
Web: www.schwing.com
SIC: 3531 Bituminous, cement and concrete related products and equip.
HQ: Schwing America, Inc.
5900 Centerville Rd
Saint Paul MN 55127
651 429-0999

(P-5498)
STURGEON SERVICES INTL INC
Ssi
3511 Gilmore Ave, Bakersfield
(93308-6205)
P.O. Box 936 (93302-0936)
PHONE...............................661 322-4408
Ollie Sturgeon, *Brnch Mgr*
EMP: 400
Web: www.sturgeonservices.com
SIC: 3531 Construction machinery
PA: Sturgeon Services International, Inc.
3511 Gilmore Ave

(P-5499)
TRIO ENGINEERED PRODUCTS INC (HQ)
Also Called: Trio
505 W Foothill Blvd, Azusa (91702-2345)
PHONE...............................626 851-3966
Michael Francis Burke, *CEO*
Eugene Xue, *
◆ **EMP:** 25 **EST:** 2002
SALES (est): 4.76MM
SALES (corp-wide): 3.29B **Privately Held**
Web: www.global.weir
SIC: 3531 Construction machinery attachments
PA: Weir Group Plc(The)
1 West Regent Street
141 637-7111

(P-5500)
WESTERN EQUIPMENT MFG INC
Also Called: Western Equipment Mfg
1160 Olympic Dr, Corona (92001-3390)
PHONE...............................951 284-2000
Kenneth R Thompson, *CEO*
William Weihl, *Pr*
▲ **EMP:** 27 **EST:** 2010
SALES (est): 5.5MM **Privately Held**
Web: www.western-emi.com
SIC: 3531 Finishers and spreaders (construction equipment)

3532 Mining Machinery

(P-5501)
POLYALLOYS INJECTED METALS INC
14000 Avalon Blvd, Los Angeles
(90061-2636)
PHONE...............................310 715-9800
Craig Paulin, *CEO*
EMP: 75 **EST:** 2001
SALES (est): 2.64MM
SALES (corp-wide): 23.24MM **Privately Held**

Web: www.psmindustries.com
SIC: 3532 Amalgamators (metallurgical or mining machinery)
PA: Psm Industries, Inc.
14000 Avalon Blvd
888 663-8256

(P-5502)
SPAULDING EQUIPMENT COMPANY (PA)
Also Called: Spaulding Crusher Parts
75 Paseo Adelanto, Perris (92570-9343)
P.O. Box 1807 (92572-1807)
PHONE...............................951 943-4531
George E Spaulding, *Ch Bd*
James Michael Spaulding, *
Norman Vetter, *
Fred Stemrich, *
◆ **EMP:** 47 **EST:** 1966
SALES (est): 5.08MM
SALES (corp-wide): 5.08MM **Privately Held**
Web: www.spauldingequipment.com
SIC: 3532 5082 7699 Mineral beneficiation equipment; Mineral beneficiation machinery ; Industrial machinery and equipment repair

3533 Oil And Gas Field Machinery

(P-5503)
AQUEOS CORPORATION (PA)
418 Chapala St Ste E, Santa Barbara
(93101-8056)
PHONE...............................805 364-0570
Theodore Roche Iv, *Pr*
Bradley Parro, *
Michael Pfau, *
Larry Barels, *
Eric Legendre, *
EMP: 50 **EST:** 2000
SQ FT: 23,000
SALES (est): 38.64MM
SALES (corp-wide): 38.64MM **Privately Held**
Web: www.aqueossubsea.com
SIC: 3533 Oil and gas field machinery

(P-5504)
AQUEOS CORPORATION
2550 Eastman Ave, Ventura (93003-7714)
PHONE...............................805 676-4330
Theodore Roche, *Brnch Mgr*
EMP: 121
SALES (corp-wide): 38.64MM **Privately Held**
Web: www.aqueossubsea.com
SIC: 3533 Oil and gas field machinery
PA: Aqueos Corporation
418 Chapala St Ste F
805 364-0570

(P-5505)
BARDEX CORPORATION (PA)
6338 Lindmar Dr, Goleta (93117-3112)
PHONE...............................805 964-7747
Thomas Miller, *CEO*
◆ **EMP:** 71 **EST:** 1963
SQ FT: 80,000
SALES (est): 20.77MM
SALES (corp-wide): 20.77MM **Privately Held**
Web: www.bardex.com
SIC: 3533 Oil and gas field machinery

(P-5506)
CHANCELLOR OIL TOOLS INC
3521 Gulf St, Bakersfield (93308-5210)
PHONE...............................661 324-2213

EMP: 40
SIC: 3533 Drilling tools for gas, oil, or water wells

(P-5507)
CONTROL SYSTEMS INTL INC
35 Parker, Irvine (92618-1605)
PHONE...............................949 238-4150
Rob Lewis, *Genl Mgr*
EMP: 85
SALES (corp-wide): 7.83B **Privately Held**
Web: www.technipfmc.com
SIC: 3533 Oil and gas field machinery
HQ: Control Systems International, Inc.
8040 Nieman Rd
Shawnee Mission KS 66214
913 599-5010

(P-5508)
DAWSON ENTERPRISES (PA)
Also Called: Cavins Oil Well Tools
2853 Cherry Ave, Signal Hill (90755-1908)
P.O. Box 6039 (90806-0039)
PHONE...............................562 424-8564
James M Dawson, *CEO*
Harry Dawson, *
◆ **EMP:** 36 **EST:** 1928
SQ FT: 19,000
SALES (est): 12.79MM
SALES (corp-wide): 12.79MM **Privately Held**
Web: www.cavins.com
SIC: 3533 7359 Bits, oil and gas field tools: rock; Garage facility and tool rental

(P-5509)
DOWNHOLE STABILIZATION INC
3515 Thomas Way, Bakersfield
(93308-6215)
P.O. Box 2467 (93303-2467)
PHONE...............................661 631-1044
Jim Calanchini, *Pr*
Mike Jarboe, *
Jacob Banducci, *
Diane Calanchini, *
▲ **EMP:** 38 **EST:** 1989
SQ FT: 8,800
SALES (est): 5.04MM **Privately Held**
Web: www.downholestabilization.com
SIC: 3533 5082 3599 1389 Drilling tools for gas, oil, or water wells; Construction and mining machinery; Amusement park equipment; Construction, repair, and dismantling services

(P-5510)
GLOBAL ELASTOMERIC PDTS INC
5551 District Blvd, Bakersfield
(93313-2126)
PHONE...............................661 831-5300
Phil W Embury, *Pr*
Sandy Embury, *
▲ **EMP:** 55 **EST:** 1963
SQ FT: 20,000
SALES (est): 8.36MM **Privately Held**
Web: www.globaleee.com
SIC: 3533 5084 Oil and gas field machinery; Oil refining machinery, equipment, and supplies

(P-5511)
KBA ENGINEERING LLC
2157 Mohawk St, Bakersfield (93308-6020)
P.O. Box 1200 (93302-1200)
PHONE...............................661 323-0487
Richard C Jones, *Managing Member*
EMP: 95 **EST:** 1997
SQ FT: 45,000
SALES (est): 3.3MM **Privately Held**

PRODUCTS & SVCS

Web: www.kbaeng.com
SIC: 3533 3462 Oil and gas field machinery;
Gear and chain forgings

(P-5512)
NOV INC
759 N Eckhoff St, Orange (92868-1005)
P.O. Box 6626 (92863-6626)
PHONE.....................714 978-1900
Owen Unruh, *Prin*
EMP: 23
SALES (corp-wide): 8.58B **Publicly Held**
Web: www.nov.com
SIC: 3533 Oil field machinery and equipment
PA: Nov Inc.
　　10353 Richmond Ave
　　346 223-3000

(P-5513)
SMITH INTERNATIONAL INC
Also Called: Omni Seals
11031 Jersey Blvd Ste A, Rancho
Cucamonga (91730-5150)
PHONE.....................909 906-7900
EMP: 130
Web: www.smithcodevelopment.com
SIC: 3533 Oil and gas field machinery
HQ: Smith International, Llc
　　5599 San Felipe St
　　Houston TX 77056
　　281 443-3370

3534 Elevators And Moving Stairways

(P-5514)
GMS ELEVATOR SERVICES INC
Also Called: Gms Elevator Services
401 Borrego Ct, San Dimas (91773-2971)
PHONE.....................909 599-3904
G Matthew Simpkins, *Pr*
Pamela Simpkins, *
EMP: 35 EST: 1987
SQ FT: 4,000
SALES (est): 5.42MM **Privately Held**
Web: www.gmselevator.com
SIC: 3534 1796 Elevators and equipment;
Elevator installation and conversion

(P-5515)
TL SHIELD & ASSOCIATES INC
Also Called: Inclinator of California
1030 Arroyo St, San Fernando
(91340-1822)
P.O. Box 6845 (91359-6845)
PHONE.....................818 509-8228
Thomas Louis Shield, *Pr*
EMP: 35 EST: 1982
SQ FT: 2,000
SALES (est): 6.62MM **Privately Held**
Web: www.tlshield.com
SIC: 3534 1796 Elevators and equipment;
Elevator installation and conversion

3535 Conveyors And Conveying Equipment

(P-5516)
CONVEYOR SERVICE & ELECTRIC
9550 Ann St, Santa Fe Springs
(90670-2616)
PHONE.....................562 777-1221
Patricia Moseley, *Pt*
Richard Moseley, *Pt*
Efren Alcantar, *Pt*
EMP: 23 EST: 1995

SQ FT: 13,000
SALES (est): 2.6MM **Privately Held**
Web: www.conserel.com
SIC: 3535 1796 Conveyors and conveying
equipment; Machinery installation

(P-5517)
JOSE PEREZ
Also Called: J&E Conveyor Services
41403 Stork Ct, Lake Elsinore
(92532-1665)
PHONE.....................920 318-6527
Jose Perez, *Owner*
EMP: 25 EST: 2022
SALES (est): 1.22MM **Privately Held**
SIC: 3535 7389 Conveyors and conveying
equipment; Business services, nec

(P-5518)
SDI INDUSTRIES INC (DH)
Also Called: Autostore Integrator
24307 Magic Mountain Pkwy # 443,
Valencia (91355-3402)
PHONE.....................818 890-6002
Krish Nathan, *CEO*
Mark Conrad, *
▲ EMP: 150 EST: 1978
SALES (est): 48.64MM
SALES (corp-wide): 2.67MM **Privately Held**
Web: www.sdi.systems
SIC: 3535 3537 8748 8711 Conveyors and
conveying equipment; Industrial trucks and
tractors; Business consulting, nec;
Engineering services
HQ: Element Logic As
　　Dyrskuevegen 26
　　Klofta 2040

(P-5519)
TERRA NOVA TECHNOLOGIES INC
10770 Rockville St Ste A, Santee
(92071-8505)
PHONE.....................619 596-7400
Ronald Kelly, *Pr*
EMP: 80 EST: 2019
SQ FT: 8,366
SALES (est): 2.41MM **Privately Held**
Web: www.tntinc.com
SIC: 3535 8742 Bulk handling conveyor
systems; Industrial consultant
HQ: Cementation Usa Inc.
　　10150 S Cntnnial Pkwy Ste
　　Sandy UT 84070

(P-5520)
TIG/M LLC
21020 Lassen St, Chatsworth (91311-4241)
PHONE.....................818 709-8500
Alvaro Villa, *CEO*
Brad Read, *
David Hall, *
Bradley Read, *
EMP: 30 EST: 2005
SALES (est): 2.07MM **Privately Held**
Web: www.tig-m.com
SIC: 3535 Trolley conveyors

3536 Hoists, Cranes, And Monorails

(P-5521)
CRANEVEYOR CORP (PA)
1524 Potrero Ave, El Monte (91733-3017)
P.O. Box 3727 (91733)
PHONE.....................626 442-1524
Frank Gaetano Trimboli, *CEO*
Hector Valiente, *

John Lehman, *
Greg Bischoff, *
Michael Williams, *
▲ EMP: 67 EST: 1946
SQ FT: 41,200
SALES (est): 28.25MM
SALES (corp-wide): 28.25MM **Privately
Held**
Web: www.craneveyor.com
SIC: 3536 3446 Cranes, overhead traveling;
Railings, banisters, guards, etc: made from
metal pipe

(P-5522)
KONECRANES INC
10310 Pioneer Blvd Ste 2, Santa Fe Springs
(90670-3732)
PHONE.....................562 903-1371
Ari Ramo, *Brnch Mgr*
EMP: 45
Web: www.konecranes.com
SIC: 3536 Hoists, cranes, and monorails
HQ: Konecranes, Inc.
　　4401 Gateway Blvd
　　Springfield OH 45502

(P-5523)
KONECRANES INC
1620 S Carlos Ave, Ontario (91761-7601)
PHONE.....................909 930-0108
Amy Gonzalez, *Brnch Mgr*
EMP: 24
Web: www.konecranes.com
SIC: 3536 Hoists, cranes, and monorails
HQ: Konecranes, Inc.
　　4401 Gateway Blvd
　　Springfield OH 45502

3537 Industrial Trucks And Tractors

(P-5524)
ANCRA INTERNATIONAL LLC (HQ)
Also Called: Delaware Ancra International
601 S Vincent Ave, Azusa (91702-5102)
PHONE.....................626 765-4800
Steve Frediani, *CEO*
Nelson Fong, *
▲ EMP: 130 EST: 1996
SALES (est): 76.8MM **Privately Held**
Web: www.ancraaircraft.com
SIC: 3537 Lift trucks, industrial: fork,
platform, straddle, etc.
PA: The Heico Companies L L C
　　70 W Madison Ste 5600

(P-5525)
ANCRA INTERNATIONAL LLC
Aircraft Systems Division
601 S Vincent Ave, Azusa (91702-5102)
PHONE.....................626 765-4818
Ed Dugic, *Mgr*
EMP: 250
Web: www.ancraaircraft.com
SIC: 3537 2298 Industrial trucks and tractors
; Cargo nets
HQ: Ancra International Llc
　　601 South Vincent Ave
　　Azusa CA 91702

(P-5526)
CONSOLIDATED FRT SYSTEMS LLC
Also Called: CFS
24407 Shoshone Rd, Apple Valley
(92307-6741)
PHONE.....................310 424-9924

Jose Luis Hernandez, *CEO*
EMP: 23 EST: 2020
SALES (est): 3.9MM **Privately Held**
SIC: 3537 Trucks: freight, baggage, etc.:
industrial, except mining

(P-5527)
CROWN EQUIPMENT CORPORATION
Also Called: Crown Lift Trucks
4250 Greystone Dr, Ontario (91761-3104)
PHONE.....................909 923-8357
Mike Lammers, *Mgr*
EMP: 50
SALES (corp-wide): 7.12B **Privately Held**
Web: www.crown.com
SIC: 3537 Lift trucks, industrial: fork,
platform, straddle, etc.
PA: Crown Equipment Corporation
　　44 S Washington St
　　419 629-2311

(P-5528)
CROWN EQUIPMENT CORPORATION
Also Called: Crown Lift Trucks
1300 Palomares St, La Verne (91750-5232)
PHONE.....................626 968-0556
Kevin Mccarthy, *Mgr*
EMP: 27
SQ FT: 28,000
SALES (corp-wide): 7.12B **Privately Held**
Web: www.crown.com
SIC: 3537 Lift trucks, industrial: fork,
platform, straddle, etc.
PA: Crown Equipment Corporation
　　44 S Washington St
　　419 629-2311

(P-5529)
CROWN EQUIPMENT CORPORATION
Also Called: Crown Lift Trucks
4061 Via Oro Ave, Long Beach
(90810-1458)
PHONE.....................310 952-6600
Tom Labrador, *Brnch Mgr*
EMP: 64
SALES (corp-wide): 7.12B **Privately Held**
Web: www.crown.com
SIC: 3537 Lift trucks, industrial: fork,
platform, straddle, etc.
PA: Crown Equipment Corporation
　　44 S Washington St
　　419 629-2311

(P-5530)
GLEASON INDUSTRIAL PDTS INC
Also Called: Milwaukee Hand Truck
10474 Santa Monica Blvd Ste 400, Los
Angeles (90025-6932)
PHONE.....................574 533-1141
Morton Kay, *CEO*
Shirley Kotler, *
Howard Simon, *
▲ EMP: 200 EST: 1891
SQ FT: 200,000
SALES (est): 6.65MM **Privately Held**
SIC: 3537 Industrial trucks and tractors

(P-5531)
J&S GOODWIN INC (HQ)
5753 E Santa Ana Canyon Rd Ste G-355,
Anaheim (92807-3230)
PHONE.....................714 956-4040
Arthur J Goodwin, *CEO*
Sharon Goodwin, *
Mark Mcgregor, *CFO*

Scott Currie, *
Dan Broschak, *
◆ **EMP:** 65 **EST:** 1989
SQ FT: 3,000
SALES (est): 35.64MM
SALES (corp-wide): 8.93B **Publicly Held**
SIC: 3537 5088 5084 Trucks, tractors, loaders, carriers, and similar equipment; Golf carts; Materials handling machinery
PA: Polaris Inc.
2100 Highway 55
763 542-0500

(P-5532)
PAPE MATERIAL HANDLING INC
2600 Peck Rd, City Of Industry (90601-1620)
P.O. Box 60007 (91716-0007)
PHONE....................562 692-9311
Steve Smith, *Mgr*
EMP: 100
Web: www.papemh.com
SIC: 3537 5084 Forklift trucks; Industrial machinery and equipment
HQ: Pape' Material Handling, Inc.
355 Goodpasture Island Rd
Eugene OR 97401

(P-5533)
POWER PT INC (PA)
Also Called: AAA Pallet
1500 Crafton Ave Bldg 100, Mentone (92359-1315)
PHONE....................951 490-4149
Tyson Paulis, *CEO*
EMP: 32 **EST:** 2018
SALES (est): 5.96MM
SALES (corp-wide): 5.96MM **Privately Held**
SIC: 3537 Platforms, stands, tables, pallets, and similar equipment

(P-5534)
POWER PT INC
9292 Nancy St, Cypress (90630-3318)
PHONE....................714 826-7407
Tyson Paulis, *Brnch Mgr*
EMP: 36
SALES (corp-wide): 5.96MM **Privately Held**
SIC: 3537 Platforms, stands, tables, pallets, and similar equipment
PA: Power Pt Inc
1500 Crafton Ave Bldg 100
951 490-4149

(P-5535)
SUPERIOR TRAILER WORKS
13700 Slover Ave, Fontana (92337-7067)
PHONE....................909 350-0185
Jack N Pocock, *CEO*
Jay Pocock, *
▲ **EMP:** 50 **EST:** 1935
SQ FT: 4,000
SALES (est): 4.35MM **Privately Held**
Web: www.superiortrailerworks.com
SIC: 3537 7539 Industrial trucks and tractors; Trailer repair

(P-5536)
TAYLOR-DUNN MANUFACTURING LLC (HQ)
2114 W Ball Rd, Anaheim (92804-5498)
PHONE....................714 956-4040
Keith Simon, *CEO*
◆ **EMP:** 100 **EST:** 1949
SQ FT: 145,000
SALES (est): 23.4MM
SALES (corp-wide): 50.09MM **Privately Held**

Web: www.taylor-dunn.com
SIC: 3537 Trucks, tractors, loaders, carriers, and similar equipment
PA: Waev Inc.
2114 W Ball Rd
714 956-4040

(P-5537)
WAEV INC (PA)
2114 W Ball Rd, Anaheim (92804-5417)
PHONE....................714 956-4040
Keith Simon, *Pr*
Paul Vitrano, *Legal*
Cosmin Batrin, *Sr VP*
Jon Conlon, *Sr VP*
Luke Mulvaney, *Sr VP*
EMP: 48 **EST:** 2021
SALES (est): 50.09MM
SALES (corp-wide): 50.09MM **Privately Held**
Web: www.waevinc.com
SIC: 3537 Trucks, tractors, loaders, carriers, and similar equipment

(P-5538)
WAKOOL TRANSPORT
19130 San Jose Ave, Rowland Heights (91748-1415)
PHONE....................626 723-3100
Willie Wu, *CEO*
Hong Zhu, *
EMP: 72 **EST:** 2022
SALES (est): 3.18MM **Privately Held**
Web: www.wakooltransport.com
SIC: 3537 Trucks: freight, baggage, etc.: industrial, except mining

---

3541 Machine Tools, Metal Cutting Type

(P-5539)
CREMACH TECH INC
Also Called: Creative Machine Technology
400 E Parkridge Ave, Corona (92879-6618)
PHONE....................951 735-3194
Mike Mcneeley, *Brnch Mgr*
EMP: 117
SALES (corp-wide): 16.11B **Publicly Held**
Web: www.cmtus.com
SIC: 3541 Machine tools, metal cutting type
HQ: Cremach Tech, Inc.
369 Meyer Cir
Corona CA 92879

(P-5540)
CREMACH TECH INC (DH)
Also Called: Creative Machine Technology
369 Meyer Cir, Corona (92879-1078)
PHONE....................951 735-3194
Mike Mcneeley, *CEO*
Mike Mcneeley, *Prin*
Jae Wan Choi, *
EMP: 23 **EST:** 2000
SQ FT: 34,000
SALES (est): 23.18MM
SALES (corp-wide): 16.11B **Publicly Held**
Web: www.cmtus.com
SIC: 3541 8711 Machine tools, metal cutting type; Engineering services
HQ: Brooks Instrument Llc
407 W Vine St
Hatfield PA 19440

(P-5541)
DAC INTERNATIONAL INC
Also Called: D A C
6390 Rose Ln, Carpinteria (93013-2998)
PHONE....................805 684-8307
Kenneth R Payne, *Pr*

Joyce Kawachi, *
▲ **EMP:** 34 **EST:** 1999
SQ FT: 17,500
SALES (est): 10.12MM **Privately Held**
Web: www.dac-intl.com
SIC: 3541 Machine tools, metal cutting type

(P-5542)
DEVELOPMENT ASSOCIATES CONTRLS
Also Called: D A C
6390 Rose Ln, Carpinteria (93013-2998)
PHONE....................805 684-8307
Edward W Vernon, *Pr*
EMP: 25 **EST:** 1994
SALES (est): 2.99MM
SALES (corp-wide): 7.66MM **Privately Held**
Web: www.dac-intl.com
SIC: 3541 Lathes, metal cutting and polishing
HQ: Dac Vision Incorporated
3630 W Miller Rd Ste 350
Garland TX 75041
972 677-2700

(P-5543)
DOLLAR SHAVE CLUB INC (HQ)
13335 Maxella Ave, Marina Del Rey (90292-5619)
PHONE....................310 975-8528
Jason Goldberger, *CEO*
Janet Song, *
Danny Miles, *
EMP: 117 **EST:** 2011
SALES (est): 94.1MM
SALES (corp-wide): 64.79B **Privately Held**
Web: us.dollarshaveclub.com
SIC: 3541 3991 2844 Shaving machines (metalworking); Shaving brushes; Shaving preparations
PA: Unilever Plc
Unilever House

(P-5544)
DOWNEY GRINDING CO
12323 Bellflower Blvd, Downey (90242-2829)
P.O. Box 583 (90241-0583)
PHONE....................562 803-5556
Larry Sequeira, *Pr*
Darla Sequeira, *
▲ **EMP:** 26 **EST:** 1960
SQ FT: 27,000
SALES (est): 3.61MM **Privately Held**
Web: www.downeygrinding.com
SIC: 3541 3599 Machine tools, metal cutting type; Machine shop, jobbing and repair

(P-5545)
HAAS AUTOMATION INC (PA)
2800 Sturgis Rd, Oxnard (93030-8901)
PHONE....................805 278-1800
◆ **EMP:** 1521 **EST:** 1983
SALES (est): 437.22MM
SALES (corp-wide): 437.22MM **Privately Held**
Web: www.haascnc.com
SIC: 3541 Machine tools, metal cutting type

(P-5546)
K-V ENGINEERING INC
2411 W 1st St, Santa Ana (92703-3509)
PHONE....................714 229-9977
Duong Vu, *Pr*
Christie Vu, *
EMP: 60 **EST:** 1984
SQ FT: 22,000
SALES (est): 9.13MM **Privately Held**
Web: www.kvengineering.com

SIC: 3541 3542 Milling machines; Machine tools, metal forming type

(P-5547)
KYOCERA TYCOM CORPORATION
Also Called: Kyoceara
3565 Cadillac Ave, Costa Mesa (92626-1401)
PHONE....................714 428-3600
▲ **EMP:** 500
SIC: 3541 3845 3843 3841 Machine tools, metal cutting type; Endoscopic equipment, electromedical, nec; Cutting instruments, dental; Surgical and medical instruments

(P-5548)
MELFRED BORZALL INC
2712 Airpark Dr, Santa Maria (93455-1418)
PHONE....................805 614-4344
Dick Melsheimer, *Prin*
Larry Coots, *Prin*
▲ **EMP:** 40 **EST:** 1946
SQ FT: 30,000
SALES (est): 5.31MM **Privately Held**
Web: www.melfredborzall.com
SIC: 3541 Machine tools, metal cutting type

(P-5549)
R H STRASBAUGH (PA)
Also Called: Strasbaugh
825 Buckley Rd, San Luis Obispo (93401-8192)
PHONE....................805 541-6424
Alan Strasbaugh, *CF*
Brad Diaz, *VP*
Eric Jacobson, *CUST SERV*
Michael Kirkpatrick, *S&M/Dir*
EMP: 50 **EST:** 1964
SQ FT: 135,000
SALES (est): 9.84MM
SALES (corp-wide): 9.84MM **Privately Held**
Web: www.gainliftoff.com
SIC: 3541 3559 5065 Grinding, polishing, buffing, lapping, and honing machines; Semiconductor manufacturing machinery; Electronic parts and equipment, nec

(P-5550)
S L FUSCO INC (PA)
1966 E Via Arado, Rancho Dominguez (90220-6100)
P.O. Box 5924 (90224-5924)
PHONE....................310 868-1010
Jerald C Rosin, *CEO*
Eric Rosin, *
Arlene Rosin, *
Barrie Williams, *
Tom Burke, *
◆ **EMP:** 45 **EST:** 1941
SQ FT: 40,000
SALES (est): 24.65MM
SALES (corp-wide): 24.65MM **Privately Held**
Web: www.slfusco.com
SIC: 3541 Machine tools, metal cutting type

(P-5551)
SAFETY PRODUCTS HOLDINGS LLC
170 Technology Dr, Irvine (92618-2401)
PHONE....................714 662-1033
Andreas Kieper, *of Glbl Sls*
EMP: 50 **EST:** 2016
SALES (est): 3.42MM **Privately Held**
Web: www.phcsafety.com
SIC: 3541 3556 Machine tools, metal cutting type; Cutting, chopping, grinding, mixing, and similar machinery

---

(PA)=Parent Co (HQ)=Headquarters
✪ = New Business established in last 2 years

PA: Bertram Capital Management, Llc
950 Tower Ln Ste 1000

(P-5552)
SHERLINE PRODUCTS INCORPORATED
Also Called: Sherline Products
3235 Executive Rdg, Vista (92081-8527)
PHONE.................................760 727-5181
Joe Martin, *Pr*
Karl W Rohlin Iii, *CEO*
Charla Papp, *
▲ **EMP:** 30 **EST:** 1973
SQ FT: 65,000
SALES (est): 6.04MM **Privately Held**
Web: www.sherlineipd.com
SIC: 3541 3545 Lathes, metal cutting and polishing; Machine tool accessories

(P-5553)
SOUTHWESTERN INDUSTRIES INC (PA)
Also Called: Trak Machine Tools
2615 Homestead Pl, Rancho Dominguez (90220-5610)
P.O. Box 9066 (90224-9066)
PHONE.................................310 608-4422
Stephen F Pinto, *CFO*
Richard W Leonhard, *
John Arroues, *
John Baumhauer, *
Mark Eisen, *
▲ **EMP:** 70 **EST:** 1951
SALES (est): 34.9MM
SALES (corp-wide): 34.9MM **Privately Held**
Web: www.southwesternindustries.com
SIC: 3541 Machine tools, metal cutting type

(P-5554)
US UNION TOOL INC (HQ)
1260 N Fee Ana St, Anaheim (92807-1817)
PHONE.................................714 521-6242
Hideo Hirano, *Pr*
Robert Smallwood, *
▲ **EMP:** 45 **EST:** 1981
SQ FT: 44,000
SALES (est): 5.75MM **Privately Held**
Web: www.uniontool.co.jp
SIC: 3541 Machine tools, metal cutting type
PA: Union Tool Co.
6-17-1, Minamioi

3542 Machine Tools, Metal Forming Type

(P-5555)
ADDITION MANUFACTURING TECHNOLOGIES CA INC
1391 Specialty Dr Ste A, Vista (92081-8521)
PHONE.................................760 597-5220
▲ **EMP:** 35
SIC: 3542 Bending machines

(P-5556)
AMBRIT INDUSTRIES INC
432 Magnolia Ave, Glendale (91204-2406)
PHONE.................................818 243-1224
Paul Yaussi, *Pr*
Louis A Yaussi, *
Michelle Taylor, *
EMP: 38 **EST:** 1946
SQ FT: 9,184
SALES (est): 6.37MM **Privately Held**
Web: www.ambritindustries.com
SIC: 3542 3363 Die casting machines; Aluminum die-castings

(P-5557)
AMERICAN PRECISION HYDRAULICS
Also Called: American Precision Assembly
5601 Research Dr, Huntington Beach (92649-1620)
PHONE.................................714 903-8610
Susan Smith, *Pr*
Steve Smith, *
EMP: 23 **EST:** 1996
SQ FT: 6,500
SALES (est): 2.69MM **Privately Held**
Web: www.americanprecisionassembly.com
SIC: 3542 Presses: hydraulic and pneumatic, mechanical and manual

(P-5558)
ANGELUS MACHINE CORP INTL
4900 Pacific Blvd, Vernon (90058-2214)
PHONE.................................323 583-2171
Maurice Koeberle, *Ch Bd*
Chuck Deane, *
EMP: 45 **EST:** 1910
SQ FT: 295,000
SALES (est): 4.42MM **Privately Held**
SIC: 3542 Metal container making machines: cans, etc.
HQ: Angelus Sanitary Can Machine Company
4900 Pacific Blvd
Vernon CA 90058
314 862-8000

(P-5559)
MEDLIN RAMPS
14903 Marquardt Ave, Santa Fe Springs (90670-5128)
PHONE.................................877 463-3546
Mark Medlin, *Prin*
▲ **EMP:** 42 **EST:** 1990
SQ FT: 10,000
SALES (est): 3.73MM **Privately Held**
Web: www.medlinramps.com
SIC: 3542 5084 3441 Machine tools, metal forming type; Materials handling machinery; Fabricated structural metal

(P-5560)
SAMTECH AUTOMOTIVE USA INC
Also Called: Samtech International
1130 E Dominguez St, Carson (90746-3518)
PHONE.................................310 638-9955
Yoshiki Sakaguchi, *Pr*
Don Zimmerman, *
▲ **EMP:** 50 **EST:** 1996
SQ FT: 27,812
SALES (est): 11.04MM **Privately Held**
Web: www.samtechintl.com
SIC: 3542 Machine tools, metal forming type
PA: Samtech Corp.
1000-18, Emmyocho

(P-5561)
SYNVENTIVE ENGINEERING INC
Also Called: Demand Cnc
3301 Michelson Dr Apt 1534, Irvine (92612-7684)
PHONE.................................312 848-8717
Greg Field, *Pr*
James Bloomfield, *
EMP: 38 **EST:** 2017
SALES (est): 5MM **Privately Held**
SIC: 3542 Machine tools, metal forming type

(P-5562)
UNIVERSAL PUNCH CORP
4001 W Macarthur Blvd, Santa Ana (92704-6307)
P.O. Box 26879 (92799-6879)
PHONE.................................714 556-4488
Kenneth L Williams, *Pr*
Kevin Williams, *
Joan Williams, *
▲ **EMP:** 55 **EST:** 1974
SQ FT: 52,000
SALES (est): 5.47MM **Privately Held**
Web: www.universalpunch.com
SIC: 3542 3545 3544 3452 Punching and shearing machines; Machine tool accessories; Special dies, tools, jigs, and fixtures; Bolts, nuts, rivets, and washers

(P-5563)
US INDUSTRIAL TOOL & SUP CO
Also Called: Usit Co
14083 S Normandie Ave, Gardena (90249-2614)
P.O. Box 2589 (90247-0589)
PHONE.................................310 464-8400
Keith Rowland, *CEO*
▲ **EMP:** 47 **EST:** 1955
SQ FT: 35,000
SALES (est): 4.89MM **Privately Held**
Web: www.ustool.com
SIC: 3542 3546 Machine tools, metal forming type; Power-driven handtools

3544 Special Dies, Tools, Jigs, And Fixtures

(P-5564)
ACE CLEARWATER ENTERPRISES INC
1614 Kona Dr, Compton (90220-5412)
PHONE.................................310 538-5380
James D Dodson, *Brnch Mgr*
EMP: 35
SALES (corp-wide): 19.32MM **Privately Held**
Web: www.aceclearwater.com
SIC: 3544 3728 3769 Special dies, tools, jigs, and fixtures; Aircraft parts and equipment, nec; Space vehicle equipment, nec
PA: Ace Clearwater Enterprises, Inc.
19815 Magellan Dr
310 323-2140

(P-5565)
ADVANCED MACHINING TOOLING INC
Also Called: C S C
13535 Danielson St, Poway (92064-6868)
PHONE.................................858 486-9050
Terry A Deane, *CEO*
Tony Cerda, *
Jodi Deane, *
EMP: 46 **EST:** 1989
SQ FT: 31,000
SALES (est): 7.47MM **Privately Held**
Web: www.amtmfg.com
SIC: 3544 3599 Special dies, tools, jigs, and fixtures; Machine shop, jobbing and repair

(P-5566)
AMBRIT ENGINEERING CORPORATION
2640 Halladay St, Santa Ana (92705-5649)
PHONE.................................714 557-1074
Terrence Saul, *CEO*
John F Mattimoe, *
Thomas W Vickers, *

▲ **EMP:** 65 **EST:** 1972
SQ FT: 32,000
SALES (est): 17.92MM **Privately Held**
Web: www.ambritengineering.com
SIC: 3544 Forms (molds), for foundry and plastics working machinery

(P-5567)
AVIS ROTO DIE CO
1560 N San Fernando Rd, Los Angeles (90065-1225)
P.O. Box 65617 (90065-0617)
PHONE.................................323 255-7070
Avetis Iskanian, *CEO*
EMP: 30 **EST:** 1982
SQ FT: 32,000
SALES (est): 4.62MM **Privately Held**
Web: www.avisrd.com
SIC: 3544 Paper cutting dies

(P-5568)
AW DIE ENGRAVING INC
8550 Roland St, Buena Park (90621-3124)
PHONE.................................714 521-7910
Arnold Werdin, *Pr*
Art Chavez, *
EMP: 30 **EST:** 1972
SQ FT: 9,000
SALES (est): 1.05MM **Privately Held**
Web: www.awdie.com
SIC: 3544 Dies and die holders for metal cutting, forming, die casting

(P-5569)
BALDA C BREWER INC (DH)
Also Called: C Brewer Company
4501 E Wall St, Ontario (91761-8143)
PHONE.................................909 212-0290
Fabio Vanin, *CEO*
Steve Holland, *
Harold Hee, *
Francesco Cavalieri, *
Sergio Stevanato, *
▲ **EMP:** 66 **EST:** 1968
SQ FT: 60,000
SALES (est): 21.18MM
SALES (corp-wide): 2.67MM **Privately Held**
SIC: 3544 3089 Special dies, tools, jigs, and fixtures; Molding primary plastics
HQ: Clere Ag
Schluterstr. 45
Berlin BE 10707
302 130-0430

(P-5570)
CACO-PACIFIC CORPORATION (PA)
813 N Cummings Rd, Covina (91724-2597)
PHONE.................................626 331-3361
Robert G Hoffmann, *Pr*
Manfred Hoffman, *Ch Bd*
Thom Williams, *Sec*
◆ **EMP:** 142 **EST:** 1985
SQ FT: 45,000
SALES (est): 20.83MM
SALES (corp-wide): 20.83MM **Privately Held**
Web: www.cacopacific.com
SIC: 3544 Industrial molds

(P-5571)
CAST-RITE CORPORATION
515 E Airline Way, Gardena (90248-2593)
PHONE.................................310 532-2080
Donald De Haan, *Pr*
Wynn Chapman, *VP*
Howard Watkins, *CFO*
▲ **EMP:** 98 **EST:** 1941
SQ FT: 74,712

SALES (est): 6.24MM
SALES (corp-wide): 23.12MM **Privately Held**
Web: www.cast-rite.com
SIC: **3544** 3471 3363 Special dies and tools; Plating and polishing; Aluminum die-castings
PA: Alloy Die Casting Co.
6550 Caballero Blvd
714 521-9800

(P-5572)
CHARLES MEISNER INC
201 Sierra Pl Ste A, Upland (91786-5668)
PHONE....................909 946-8216
Charles Meisner, *Pr*
Carol Meisner, *
EMP: 25 EST: 1972
SQ FT: 19,000
SALES (est): 2.42MM **Privately Held**
Web: www.charlesmeisnerinc.com
SIC: **3544** 3599 Special dies and tools; Machine shop, jobbing and repair

(P-5573)
COAST AEROSPACE MFG INC
Also Called: Coast Aerospace
950 Richfield Rd, Placentia (92870-6732)
PHONE....................714 893-8066
Louis Ponce, *Pr*
Frank Fleck, *
Steven Castillo, *
David Rodriguez, *Design Vice President*
EMP: 43 EST: 1999
SALES (est): 10.8MM **Privately Held**
Web: www.coastaero.com
SIC: **3544** 3441 3728 3291 Special dies and tools; Fabricated structural metal; Aircraft parts and equipment, nec; Abrasive products

(P-5574)
COLBRIT MANUFACTURING CO INC
9666 Owensmouth Ave Ste G, Chatsworth (91311-8050)
PHONE....................818 709-3608
Gerardo Cruz, *Pr*
Marina Cruz, *
▲ EMP: 30 EST: 1979
SQ FT: 6,000
SALES (est): 5.03MM **Privately Held**
Web: www.colbrit.com
SIC: **3544** Special dies and tools

(P-5575)
CRENSHAW DIE AND MFG CORP
7432 Prince Dr, Huntington Beach (92647-4553)
PHONE....................949 475-5505
TOLL FREE: 800
James V Ireland, *CEO*
Dale Congelliere, *
Sharon Piers, *
EMP: 55 EST: 1962
SQ FT: 38,000
SALES (est): 2.42MM **Privately Held**
Web: www.crenshawdiemfg.com
SIC: **3544** Special dies and tools

(P-5576)
DAUNTLESS INDUSTRIES INC
Also Called: Dauntless Molds
806 N Grand Ave, Covina (91724-2474)
PHONE....................626 966-4494
George R Payton, *Pr*
Norm Holt, *
EMP: 25 EST: 1975
SQ FT: 15,000
SALES (est): 5.36MM **Privately Held**

Web: www.dauntlessmolds.com
SIC: **3544** Special dies and tools

(P-5577)
DAVID ENGINEERING & MANUFACTURING INC
1230 Quarry St, Corona (92879-1708)
PHONE....................951 735-5200
▲ EMP: 30
SIC: **3544** 3469 Special dies and tools; Metal stampings, nec

(P-5578)
EDRO ENGINEERING LLC (DH)
Also Called: Voestalpine High Prfmce Mtls
20500 Carrey Rd, Walnut (91789-2417)
PHONE....................909 594-5751
Terry Henn, *CEO*
Eric Henn, *
Mike Guscott, *
Laurinda Diaz, *Stockholder*
Kevin Ewing, *
◆ EMP: 36 EST: 1976
SQ FT: 60,000
SALES (est): 20.09MM
SALES (corp-wide): 19.29B **Privately Held**
Web: www.edro.com
SIC: **3544** 3599 Special dies and tools; Machine shop, jobbing and repair
HQ: Voestalpine High Performance Metals Llc
2505 Millennium Dr
Elgin IL 60123
877 992-8764

(P-5579)
FAIRWAY INJECTION MOLDS INC
Also Called: Westfall Technik
20109 Paseo Del Prado, Walnut (91789-2665)
PHONE....................909 595-2201
Darrel Zamora, *CEO*
▲ EMP: 54 EST: 1977
SQ FT: 31,147
SALES (est): 9.82MM
SALES (corp-wide): 500.49MM **Privately Held**
Web: www.fairwaymolds.com
SIC: **3544** Industrial molds
PA: Westfall Technik, Llc
9280 S Kyrene Rd
702 659-9898

(P-5580)
FLOTRON
2630 Progress St, Vista (92081-7897)
PHONE....................760 727-2700
Danny K Horrell, *Pr*
EMP: 24 EST: 1991
SQ FT: 25,000
SALES (est): 11.02MM **Privately Held**
Web: www.flotron.com
SIC: **3544** Special dies and tools

(P-5581)
FUSION PRODUCT MFG INC
24024 Humphries Rd Bldg 1, Tecate (91980-4008)
PHONE....................619 819-5521
Adalberto L Ramirez, *Pr*
Jose Ramirez, *
Simon Ramirez, *
▼ EMP: 72 EST: 2004
SQ FT: 36,000
SALES (est): 4.4MM **Privately Held**
Web: www.fusionpm.com
SIC: **3544** Forms (molds), for foundry and plastics working machinery

(P-5582)
GRUBER SYSTEMS INC
29071 The Old Rd, Valencia (91355-1083)
PHONE....................661 257-0464
John Hoskinson, *Ch Bd*
Jim Thiessen, *
Steve Miller, *
Diana Arima, *
Katherine Pavard, *
◆ EMP: 45 EST: 1968
SALES (est): 9.88MM **Privately Held**
Web: www.grubersystems.com
SIC: **3544** 3842 3531 3537 Industrial molds; Whirlpool baths, hydrotherapy equipment; Construction machinery; Industrial trucks and tractors

(P-5583)
HIGHTOWER METAL PRODUCTS LLC
2090 N Glassell St, Orange (92865-3391)
P.O. Box P.O. Box 5586 (92863-5586)
PHONE....................714 637-7000
Kurt Koch, *Pr*
Mark Koch, *
EMP: 66 EST: 1945
SQ FT: 20,000
SALES (est): 4.51MM **Privately Held**
SIC: **3544** Special dies and tools

(P-5584)
HUGHES BROS AIRCRAFTERS INC
11010 Garfield Pl, South Gate (90280-7583)
PHONE....................323 773-4541
Susan Hughes, *Pr*
James P Hughes, *
Michael Hall, *
EMP: 43 EST: 1947
SQ FT: 15,000
SALES (est): 6.65MM **Privately Held**
Web: www.hbai.com
SIC: **3544** 3449 3444 Die sets for metal stamping (presses); Plastering accessories, metal; Sheet metalwork

(P-5585)
IDEA TOOLING AND ENGRG INC
13915 S Main St, Los Angeles (90061-2151)
PHONE....................310 608-7488
Peter Janner, *Pr*
Monica Janner, *
Moe Sumbulan, *
Inga Janner, *
▲ EMP: 56 EST: 1973
SALES (est): 3.78MM **Privately Held**
Web: www.ideatooling.com
SIC: **3544** 3061 Special dies and tools; Mechanical rubber goods

(P-5586)
KINGSON MOLD & MACHINE INC
1350 Titan Way, Brea (92821-3707)
PHONE....................714 871-0221
Gregory S Rex, *CEO*
EMP: 27 EST: 1977
SQ FT: 8,500
SALES (est): 4.99MM **Privately Held**
Web: www.kingsonmold.com
SIC: **3544** 5031 Industrial molds; Molding, all materials

(P-5587)
MAGOR MOLD LLC
420 S Lone Hill Ave, San Dimas (91773-4600)

PHONE....................909 592-3663
Wolfgang Buhler, *Pr*
Martin Schottli, *
▲ EMP: 68 EST: 1967
SQ FT: 15,000
SALES (est): 4.28MM **Privately Held**
Web: www.husky.co
SIC: **3544** Industrial molds

(P-5588)
MARMAN INDUSTRIES INC
1701 Earhart, La Verne (91750-5827)
PHONE....................909 392-2136
EMP: 90 EST: 1985
SALES (est): 15.08MM **Privately Held**
Web: www.marman.com
SIC: **3544** 3089 Industrial molds; Plastics containers, except foam

(P-5589)
MR MOLD & ENGINEERING CORP
1150 Beacon St, Brea (92821-2936)
PHONE....................714 996-5511
Richard Finnie Ii, *Pr*
Marilyn Finnie, *
EMP: 31 EST: 1985
SALES (est): 4.64MM **Privately Held**
Web: www.mrmold.com
SIC: **3544** Special dies and tools

(P-5590)
PACE PUNCHES INC
297 Goddard, Irvine (92618-4604)
PHONE....................949 428-2750
Edward W Pepper, *Pr*
▲ EMP: 55 EST: 1978
SQ FT: 30,000
SALES (est): 4.57MM **Privately Held**
Web: www.pacepunches.com
SIC: **3544** Punches, forming and stamping

(P-5591)
PRECISE DIE AND FINISHING
9400 Oso Ave, Chatsworth (91311-6020)
PHONE....................818 773-9337
David Rewers, *CEO*
EMP: 27 EST: 2016
SQ FT: 15,000
SALES (est): 4.59MM **Privately Held**
Web: www.precisedf.com
SIC: **3544** Special dies and tools

(P-5592)
PRESTIGE MOLD INCORPORATED
11040 Tacoma Dr, Rancho Cucamonga (91730-4857)
PHONE....................909 980-6600
Donna C Pursell. *CEO*
Lance Spangler, *
▲ EMP: 98 EST: 1982
SQ FT: 28,500
SALES (est): 8.21MM
SALES (corp-wide): 9.02MM **Privately Held**
Web: www.prestigemold.com
SIC: **3544** Industrial molds
PA: Pres-Tek Plastics, Inc.
10700 7th St
909 360-1600

(P-5593)
PRODUCT SLINGSHOT INC (DH)
Also Called: Forecast 3d
2221 Rutherford Rd, Carlsbad (92008-8815)
PHONE....................760 929-9380
Corey Douglas Weber, *Pr*

Donovan Weber, *
EMP: 24 **EST:** 1994
SQ FT: 28,000
SALES (est): 44.44MM
SALES (corp-wide): 6.06B **Privately Held**
Web: www.forecast3d.com
SIC: 3544 3082 3089 3555 Industrial molds;
   Unsupported plastics profile shapes;
   Casting of plastics; Printing trades
   machinery
HQ: Gkn Powder Metallurgy Holdings
   Limited
   Rhodium Building,Central Boulevard
   Solihull W MIDLANDS B90 8

(P-5594)
PUNCH PRESS PRODUCTS INC
Also Called: Auto Trend Products
2035 E 51st St, Vernon (90058-2818)
PHONE...................323 581-7151
Delmo Molinari, *Ch*
Cj Matiszik, *Pr*
Helen Wesley, *
Joseph Mcclure, *Genl Mgr*
▲ **EMP:** 67 **EST:** 1953
SQ FT: 150,000
SALES (est): 9.45MM **Privately Held**
Web: www.punch-press.com
SIC: 3544 3469 3471 Special dies and tools;
   Metal stampings, nec; Plating and polishing

(P-5595)
PYRAMID MOLD & TOOL
10155 Sharon Cir, Rancho Cucamonga
(91730-5300)
PHONE...................909 476-2555
Stephen Hoare, *Pr*
Brandan Heyes, *
EMP: 62 **EST:** 1995
SQ FT: 30,300
SALES (est): 8.13MM
SALES (corp-wide): 62.44MM **Privately
Held**
Web: www.pyramidmold.net
SIC: 3544 Industrial molds
PA: Sybridge Technologies U.S. Inc.
   265 Spring Lake Dr
   814 474-9100

(P-5596)
S & S CARBIDE TOOL INC
2830 Via Orange Way Ste D, Spring Valley
(91978-1743)
PHONE...................619 670-5214
Dennis Strong, *Pr*
Gary Stewart, *
EMP: 25 **EST:** 1986
SQ FT: 6,000
SALES (est): 5.76MM **Privately Held**
Web: www.sscarbide.com
SIC: 3544 Special dies and tools

(P-5597)
SANTA FE ENTERPRISES INC
Also Called: SFE
11654 Pike St, Santa Fe Springs
(90670-2938)
PHONE...................562 692-7596
David Warner, *Pr*
Bob Becker, *
EMP: 27 **EST:** 1980
SQ FT: 20,000
SALES (est): 4.83MM **Privately Held**
Web: www.santafeenterprises.com
SIC: 3544 Special dies and tools

(P-5598)
SCHREY & SONS MOLD CO INC
24735 Avenue Rockefeller, Valencia
(91355-3466)

PHONE...................661 294-2260
Walter Schrey, *Pr*
Thomas Schrey, *
William Schrey, *
Gertrude Schrey, *
EMP: 35 **EST:** 1969
SQ FT: 53,000
SALES (est): 6.38MM **Privately Held**
Web: www.schrey.com
SIC: 3544 Industrial molds

(P-5599)
SUPERIOR MOLD CO
3122 Maple St, Santa Ana (92707-4408)
PHONE...................714 751-7084
Codet Anthony, *Prin*
EMP: 27 **EST:** 2012
SALES (est): 3.62MM **Privately Held**
SIC: 3544 Industrial molds

(P-5600)
TEAM TECHNOLOGIES INC
Also Called: Precision Die Cutting, LLC
4675 Vinita Ct, Chino (91710-5731)
PHONE...................626 334-5000
Marshall White, *Brnch Mgr*
EMP: 60
SALES (corp-wide): 261.96MM **Privately
Held**
Web: www.teamtechinc.net
SIC: 3544 Special dies and tools
PA: Team Technologies, Inc.
   5949 Commerce Blvd
   423 587-2199

(P-5601)
UPM INC
Also Called: Universal Plastic Mold
13245 Los Angeles St, Baldwin Park
(91706-2295)
PHONE...................626 962-4001
Jason Dowling, *Pr*
Jason Dowling, *CEO*
Steve Dowling, *
Don Ashleigh, *
◆ **EMP:** 290 **EST:** 1962
SQ FT: 100,000
SALES (est): 29.13MM **Privately Held**
Web: www.upminc.com
SIC: 3544 3089 Forms (molds), for foundry
   and plastics working machinery; Injection
   molding of plastics

(P-5602)
VALCO PLANER WORKS INC
Also Called: Valco Precision Works
6131 Maywood Ave, Huntington Park
(90255-3213)
PHONE...................323 582-6355
Leonel F Valerio, *Pr*
Leonel G Valerio Junior, *VP*
Carlos Valerio, *
▼ **EMP:** 25 **EST:** 1953
SQ FT: 10,000
SALES (est): 4.65MM **Privately Held**
SIC: 3544 3545 Special dies, tools, jigs, and
   fixtures; Machine tool accessories

(P-5603)
WAGNER DIE SUPPLY INC (PA)
2041 Elm Ct, Ontario (91761-7619)
PHONE...................909 947-3044
Ellsworth Knutson, *Pr*
John Knutson, *
Tom Knutson, *
Mike Knutson, *
▲ **EMP:** 36 **EST:** 1947
SALES (est): 5.85MM
SALES (corp-wide): 5.85MM **Privately
Held**

Web: www.wagnerdiesupply.com
SIC: 3544 Dies, steel rule

3545 Machine Tool
Accessories

(P-5604)
AMERICAN QUALITY TOOLS
INC
Also Called: American Quality Tools
12650 Magnolia Ave Ste B, Riverside
(92503-4690)
PHONE...................951 280-4700
Mukesh Aghi, *Pr*
Rakesh Aghi, *
▲ **EMP:** 45 **EST:** 1989
SQ FT: 22,000
SALES (est): 2.28MM **Privately Held**
Web: www.cobracarbide.com
SIC: 3545 Cutting tools for machine tools

(P-5605)
ATS WORKHOLDING LLC (PA)
Also Called: Ats Systems
30222 Esperanza, Rancho Santa Margari
(92688-2121)
PHONE...................800 321-1833
Kenneth Erkenbrack, *Managing Member*
Charles A Goad, *
Wu Robert, *
Carlos Hernandez, *
▲ **EMP:** 43 **EST:** 1981
SQ FT: 22,840
SALES (est): 10.15MM
SALES (corp-wide): 10.15MM **Privately
Held**
Web: www.atssystems.us
SIC: 3545 Milling machine attachments
   (machine tool accessories)

(P-5606)
BARRANCA HOLDINGS LTD
Also Called: Barranca Diamond Products
22815 Frampton Ave, Torrance
(90501-5034)
PHONE...................310 523-5867
Brian Delahaut, *Pr*
▲ **EMP:** 104 **EST:** 1998
SALES (est): 876.4K
SALES (corp-wide): 27.31MM **Privately
Held**
Web: www.barrancadiamond.com
SIC: 3545 Diamond cutting tools for turning,
   boring, burnishing, etc.
PA: Diamond Mk Products Inc
   1315 Storm Pkwy
   310 539-5221

(P-5607)
CAMPBELL ENGINEERING INC
Also Called: Campbell Engineering
20412 Barents Sea Cir, Lake Forest
(92630-8807)
PHONE...................949 859-3306
James J Campbell, *CEO*
Carolyn Campbell, *
EMP: 24 **EST:** 1994
SQ FT: 3,800
SALES (est): 2.9MM **Privately Held**
Web: www.campbellcnc.com
SIC: 3545 3541 Precision measuring tools;
   Lathes, metal cutting and polishing

(P-5608)
CRAIG TOOLS INC
142 Lomita St, El Segundo (90245-4113)
PHONE...................310 322-0614
William B Cleveland, *Pr*
Don Tripler, *

▼ **EMP:** 37 **EST:** 1958
SQ FT: 13,000
SALES (est): 6.78MM **Privately Held**
Web: www.craigtools.com
SIC: 3545 Precision tools, machinists'

(P-5609)
CRITERION MACHINE WORKS
765 W 16th St, Costa Mesa (92627-4302)
EMP: 40 **EST:** 1935
SALES (est): 2.57MM **Privately Held**
Web: www.criterionmachineworks.com
SIC: 3545 Machine tool attachments and
   accessories

(P-5610)
CTE CALIFORNIA TL & ENGRG
INC
Also Called: California Tool & Engineering
7801 Bolero Dr, Jurupa Valley
(92509-5219)
▲ **EMP:** 25 **EST:** 1987
SQ FT: 14,000
SALES (est): 1.77MM **Privately Held**
SIC: 3545 7389 2819 Cutting tools for
   machine tools; Grinding, precision:
   commercial or industrial; Carbides

(P-5611)
CURRY COMPANY LLC
Also Called: Carbro Company
15724 Condon Ave, Lawndale
(90260-2531)
P.O. Box 278 (90260-0278)
PHONE...................310 643-8400
Patrick Curry, *Managing Member*
EMP: 40 **EST:** 2019
SALES (est): 3.23MM
SALES (corp-wide): 21MM **Privately Held**
Web: www.carbrocorp.com
SIC: 3545 End mills
PA: Fullerton Tool Company, Inc.
   121 Perry St
   989 799-4550

(P-5612)
GUHRING INC
15581 Computer Ln, Huntington Beach
(92649-1605)
PHONE...................714 841-3582
EMP: 50
SALES (corp-wide): 1.03B **Privately Held**
Web: www.guhring.com
SIC: 3545 Cutting tools for machine tools
HQ: Guhring, Inc.
   1445 Commerce Ave
   Brookfield WI 53045
   262 784-6730

(P-5613)
KEMPTON MACHINE WORKS
INC
4070 E Leaverton Ct, Anaheim
(92807-1610)
PHONE...................714 990-0596
Greg Kempton, *Pr*
EMP: 29 **EST:** 1983
SQ FT: 14,000
SALES (est): 3.66MM **Privately Held**
Web:
www.kemptonmachineworksinc.com
SIC: 3545 3599 Tools and accessories for
   machine tools; Machine shop, jobbing and
   repair

(P-5614)
KYOCERA SGS PRECISION TLS
INC
Also Called: Kyocera Precision Tools

1814 W Collins Ave, Orange (92867-5425)
PHONE..............................888 848-9266
Csr Paul, Brnch Mgr
EMP: 85
SALES (corp-wide): 36.3MM **Privately Held**
Web: www.kyocera-sgstool.com
SIC: 3545 3541 3845 3843 Machine tool accessories; Machine tools, metal cutting type; Electromedical equipment; Dental equipment and supplies
PA: Kyocera Sgs Precision Tools, Inc.
150 Marc Dr
330 688-6667

(P-5615)
MAKINO INC
17800 Newhope St Ste H, Fountain Valley (92708-5443)
PHONE..............................714 444-4334
Jonathan Haye, Brnch Mgr
EMP: 26
Web: www.makino.com
SIC: 3545 Tools and accessories for machine tools
HQ: Makino Inc.
7680 Innovation Way
Mason OH 45040
513 573-7200

(P-5616)
MEYCO MACHINE AND TOOL INC
11579 Martens River Cir, Fountain Valley (92708-4201)
P.O. Box 9659 (92728-9659)
PHONE..............................714 435-1546
Manuel Gomez, CEO
Victor Salazar, *
Max Gomez, *
Edith Martinez, *
Lorena Estrada, *
EMP: 38 EST: 1996
SQ FT: 12,500
SALES (est): 3.11MM **Privately Held**
Web: www.meycomachine.com
SIC: 3545 Tools and accessories for machine tools

(P-5617)
NORANCO MANUFACTURING (USA) ACQUISITION CORP
Also Called: Noranco Corona Division
345 Cessna Cir Ste 102, Corona (92878-5019)
PHONE..............................951 721-8400
▲ EMP: 125 EST: 2013
SALES (est): 9.25MM
SALES (corp-wide): 364.48B **Publicly Held**
SIC: 3545 3728 Machine tool attachments and accessories; Aircraft parts and equipment, nec
HQ: Noranco Inc
710 Rowntree Dairy Rd
Woodbridge ON L4L 5
905 264-2050

(P-5618)
PENNOYER-DODGE CO
6650 San Fernando Rd, Glendale (91201-1745)
P.O. Box 5105 (91221-1017)
PHONE..............................818 547-2100
Hazel Dodge, Pr
Karen Dodge, *
EMP: 40 EST: 1946
SALES (est): 4.96MM **Privately Held**
Web: www.pdgage.com

SIC: 3545 8734 5084 3643 Gauges (machine tool accessories); Calibration and certification; Instruments and control equipment; Current-carrying wiring services

(P-5619)
PICOSYS INCORPORATED
Also Called: Invenios
320 N Nopal St, Santa Barbara (93103-3225)
PHONE..............................805 962-3333
EMP: 70
SIC: 3545 3821 Precision measuring tools; Micromanipulator

(P-5620)
PIONEER BROACH COMPANY (PA)
6434 Telegraph Rd, Commerce (90040-2593)
PHONE..............................323 728-1263
Gary M Ezor, CEO
Robert Ezor, *
Karin Ezor, *
▲ EMP: 50 EST: 1939
SQ FT: 22,000
SALES (est): 6.04MM
SALES (corp-wide): 6.04MM **Privately Held**
Web: www.pioneerbroach.com
SIC: 3545 3599 3541 Broaches (machine tool accessories); Machine shop, jobbing and repair; Machine tools, metal cutting type

(P-5621)
PRECISION CUTTING TOOLS INC
5572 Fresca Dr, La Palma (90623-1007)
PHONE..............................562 921-7898
Audrey Sheth, CEO
▲ EMP: 30 EST: 1979
SALES (est): 2.17MM **Privately Held**
Web: www.pct-imc.com
SIC: 3545 3541 Cutting tools for machine tools; Drilling machine tools (metal cutting)

(P-5622)
PRECISION CUTTING TOOLS LLC
5572 Fresca Dr, La Palma (90623-1007)
PHONE..............................562 921-7898
Nikhil Sheth, Prin
Mehar Grewal, Prin
Audrey Sheth, Prin
Jacob Harpaz, Prin
EMP: 48 EST: 2018
SALES (est): 4.33MM **Privately Held**
Web: www.pct-imc.com
SIC: 3545 Cutting tools for machine tools

(P-5623)
RAFCO-BRICKFORM LLC (PA)
Also Called: Rafco Products Brickform
11061 Jersey Blvd, Rancho Cucamonga (91730-5135)
PHONE..............................909 484-3399
Robert Freis, Managing Member
Matt Bissantti, Managing Member
▲ EMP: 72 EST: 1973
SQ FT: 79,000
SALES (est): 1.73MM
SALES (corp-wide): 1.73MM **Privately Held**
SIC: 3545 5169 Machine tool accessories; Adhesives, chemical

(P-5624)
SCIENTIFIC CUTTING TOOLS INC
220 W Los Angeles Ave, Simi Valley (93065-1650)

PHONE..............................805 584-9495
Dale Christopher, Pr
Jan Kaye, *
Gary Christopher, *
EMP: 37 EST: 1963
SALES (est): 5.26MM **Privately Held**
Web: www.sct-usa.com
SIC: 3545 Machine tool accessories

(P-5625)
STADCO (HQ)
Also Called: Standard Tool & Die Co
107 S Avenue 20, Los Angeles (90031-1709)
PHONE..............................323 227-8888
Doug Paletz, Pr
Bob Parsi, *
Bret Matta, *
EMP: 86 EST: 1945
SQ FT: 15,000
SALES (est): 29.25MM **Publicly Held**
Web: www.stadco.com
SIC: 3545 3599 Precision tools, machinists'; Machine shop, jobbing and repair
PA: Techprecision Corporation
1 Bella Dr

(P-5626)
STARRETT KINEMETRIC ENGRG INC
26052 Merit Cir Ste 103, Laguna Hills (92653-7004)
PHONE..............................949 348-1213
Douglas Starrett, Pr
EMP: 26 EST: 2007
SALES (est): 5.03MM
SALES (corp-wide): 256.18MM **Privately Held**
Web: www.starrettmetrology.com
SIC: 3545 Machine tool accessories
PA: The L S Starrett Company
121 Crescent St
978 249-3551

(P-5627)
TOOL ALLIANCE CORPORATION
Also Called: Roundtool Laboratories
5372 Mcfadden Ave, Huntington Beach (92649-1239)
PHONE..............................714 373-5864
Keith Dennis, Mgr
EMP: 45
SALES (corp-wide): 5.34MM **Privately Held**
Web: www.toolalliance.com
SIC: 3545 Cutting tools for machine tools
PA: Tool Alliance Corporation
5451 Mcfadden Ave
714 898-9224

(P-5628)
UNITED DRILL BUSHING CORP
Also Called: United California
12200 Woodruff Ave, Downey (90241-5608)
P.O. Box 4250 (90241-1250)
PHONE..............................562 803-1521
Dale L Bethke, Pr
Billie Huckins, *
EMP: 150 EST: 1964
SQ FT: 80,000
SALES (est): 7.04MM **Privately Held**
Web: www.ucc-udb.com
SIC: 3545 3544 Drill bushings (drilling jig); Special dies, tools, jigs, and fixtures

(P-5629)
VERIDIAM INC (DH)
1717 N Cuyamaca St, El Cajon (92020-1110)

PHONE..............................619 448-1000
Brian Joyal, CEO
Jennifer Bowman, *
Robert Oevson, *
Scott Rogow, *
▲ EMP: 53 EST: 1996
SQ FT: 250,000
SALES (est): 64.67MM
SALES (corp-wide): 98MM **Privately Held**
Web: www.veridiam.com
SIC: 3545 3317 3354 3312 Precision tools, machinists'; Tubes, seamless steel; Tube, extruded or drawn, aluminum; Tubes, steel and iron
HQ: Whi Capital Partners
191 N Wacker Dr Ste 1500
Chicago IL 60606

(P-5630)
VIKING PRODUCTS INC
20 Doppler, Irvine (92618-4306)
PHONE..............................949 379-5100
Marc Kaplan, CEO
EMP: 40 EST: 1981
SQ FT: 12,000
SALES (est): 5.02MM **Privately Held**
Web: www.vikingproducts.com
SIC: 3545 Precision measuring tools

(P-5631)
WESTERN GAGE CORPORATION
3316 Maya Linda Ste A, Camarillo (93012-8776)
PHONE..............................805 445-1410
Donald E Moors, Pr
Nanette Moors, *
EMP: 24 EST: 1968
SQ FT: 22,000
SALES (est): 3.65MM **Privately Held**
Web: www.westerngage.com
SIC: 3545 Gauges (machine tool accessories)

(P-5632)
WETMORE TOOL AND ENGRG CO
Also Called: Wetmore Cutting Tools
5091 G St, Chino (91710-5141)
PHONE..............................909 364-1000
Jerome David, CEO
Phil Kurtz, Pr
Mike Gallegos, CFO
Keith Rowland, Ex VP
▲ EMP: 75 EST: 1999
SQ FT: 32,000
SALES (est): 9.03MM
SALES (corp-wide): 12.03B **Privately Held**
Web: www.dormerpramet.com
SIC: 3545 5084 3544 3541 Cutting tools for machine tools; Industrial machinery and equipment; Special dies, tools, jigs, and fixtures; Machine tools, metal cutting type
HQ: Dormer Pramet Ab
Tre Hjartans Vag 2
Halmstad 302 4
35165200

3546 Power-driven Handtools

(P-5633)
BLACK & DECKER CORPORATION
Also Called: Black & Decker
19701 Da Vinci, El Toro (92610-2622)
PHONE..............................949 672-4000
Chris Metz, Mgr
EMP: 26
SALES (corp-wide): 15.78B **Publicly Held**
Web: www.blackanddecker.com

SIC: **3546** 3553 Power-driven handtools;
Woodworking machinery
HQ: The Black & Decker Corporation
701 E Joppa Rd
Towson MD 21286
410 716-3900

(P-5634)

CALIFORNIA AIR TOOLS INC

8560 Siempre Viva Rd, San Diego
(92154-6270)
PHONE.............................866 409-4581
Manuel Gonicman, *CEO*
Larry Cerneka, *Pr*
◆ **EMP:** 30 **EST:** 2002
SQ FT: 10,000
SALES (est): 15MM **Privately Held**
Web: www.californiaairtools.com
SIC: **3546** 3563 5072 Cartridge-activated
hand power tools; Air and gas compressors
; Power tools and accessories

(P-5635)

GEORGE JUE MFG CO INC

Also Called: Paramont Metal & Supply Co
8140 Rosecrans Ave, Paramount
(90723-2794)
PHONE.............................562 634-8181
Vincent Jue, *CEO*
George Jue, *
Elenor Sylva, *
◆ **EMP:** 60 **EST:** 1946
SQ FT: 80,000
SALES (est): 9.47MM **Privately Held**
SIC: **3546** Drills and drilling tools

(P-5636)

MK DIAMOND PRODUCTS INC (PA)

1315 Storm Pkwy, Torrance (90501-5041)
P.O. Box 2803 (90509-2803)
PHONE.............................310 539-5221
Robert J Delahaut, *Pr*
Brian Delahaut, *CFO*
David W Riley, *Sec*
◆ **EMP:** 96 **EST:** 1945
SQ FT: 35,000
SALES (est): 27.31MM
SALES (corp-wide): 27.31MM **Privately Held**
Web: www.mkdiamond.com
SIC: **3546** 3425 Saws and sawing equipment
; Saw blades and handsaws

(P-5637)

SEESCAN INC (PA)

Also Called: Seektech
3855 Ruffin Rd, San Diego (92123-1813)
PHONE.............................858 244-3300
Mark Olsson, *Pr*
John Chew, *
▲ **EMP:** 178 **EST:** 1983
SQ FT: 63,641
SALES (est): 47.11MM
SALES (corp-wide): 47.11MM **Privately Held**
Web: www.seescan.com
SIC: **3546** Power-driven handtools

(P-5638)

ZEPHYR MANUFACTURING CO INC

Also Called: Zephyr Tool Group
201 Hindry Ave, Inglewood (90301-1579)
PHONE.............................310 410-4907
Ray Chin, *VP Fin*
Earl Houston, *
Tom Houstan, *
Robert Szanter, *
▲ **EMP:** 100 **EST:** 1939

SQ FT: 60,000
SALES (est): 3.89MM **Privately Held**
Web: www.zephyrtoolgroup.com
SIC: **3546** 3545 3423 Power-driven
handtools; Machine tool accessories; Hand
and edge tools, nec
PA: Shg Holdings Corp
201 Hindry Ave

3547 Rolling Mill Machinery

(P-5639)

JOHN LIST CORPORATION

Also Called: Protocast
9732 Cozycroft Ave, Chatsworth
(91311-4498)
PHONE.............................818 882-7848
John List, *Pr*
Susan List, *
EMP: 47 **EST:** 1966
SQ FT: 16,000
SALES (est): 8.39MM **Privately Held**
Web: www.protocastjlc.com
SIC: **3547** 3365 3369 3366 Ferrous and
nonferrous mill equipment, auxiliary;
Aluminum and aluminum-based alloy
castings; Nonferrous foundries, nec;
Copper foundries

(P-5640)

OLD COUNTRY MILLWORK INC (PA)

Also Called: O C M
5855 Hooper Ave, Los Angeles
(90001-1280)
PHONE.............................323 234-2940
Gerard J Kilgallon, *CEO*
▲ **EMP:** 24 **EST:** 1984
SQ FT: 36,000
SALES (est): 9.11MM
SALES (corp-wide): 9.11MM **Privately Held**
Web: www.ocmcoil.com
SIC: **3547** 3479 Rolling mill machinery;
Painting, coating, and hot dipping

(P-5641)

VEST TUBE LLC

6023 Alcoa Ave, Los Angeles (90058-3901)
P.O. Box 58827 (90058-0827)
PHONE.............................800 421-6370
Yoshiki Murakami, *Pr*
Sean Mccaughan, *Pr*
Iwaki Sugimoto, *
Tomoya Shiraishi, *
Hideki Matsumoto, *
▲ **EMP:** 77 **EST:** 1970
SQ FT: 312,000
SALES (est): 13.89MM **Privately Held**
Web: www.vesttubellc.com
SIC: **3547** 3317 Rolling mill machinery;
Tubes, wrought: welded or lock joint
HQ: Shoji Jfe America Holdings Inc
301 E Ocean Blvd Ste 1750
Long Beach CA 90802
562 637-3500

3548 Welding Apparatus

(P-5642)

AMADA WELD TECH INC (HQ)

1820 S Myrtle Ave, Monrovia (91016-4833)
PHONE.............................626 303-5676
David Fawcett, *Pr*
Mark G Rodighiero, *
Kunio Minejima, *
James E Malloy, *
David Cielinski, *
◆ **EMP:** 33 **EST:** 1994

SQ FT: 70,000
SALES (est): 50.39MM **Privately Held**
Web: www.amadaweldtech.com
SIC: **3548** 3699 3829 Soldering equipment,
except hand soldering irons; Laser welding,
drilling, and cutting equipment; Measuring
and controlling devices, nec
PA: Amada Co., Ltd.
200, Ishida

(P-5643)

BELHOME INC

Also Called: Technical Devices Company
560 Alaska Ave, Torrance (90503-3904)
P.O. Box 329 (90507-0129)
PHONE.............................310 618-8437
Douglas N Winther, *CEO*
Rey Malazo, *
EMP: 48 **EST:** 1977
SQ FT: 35,000
SALES (est): 2.89MM
SALES (corp-wide): 11.25MM **Privately Held**
Web: www.technicaldev.com
SIC: **3548** 3471 3544 3423 Soldering
equipment, except hand soldering irons;
Cleaning, polishing, and finishing; Special
dies and tools; Hand and edge tools, nec
PA: Winther Technologies, Inc.
560 Alaska Ave
310 618-8437

(P-5644)

BROCO INC

Also Called: Broco
400 S Rockefeller Ave, Ontario
(91761-8144)
PHONE.............................909 483-3222
◆ **EMP:** 25 **EST:** 1968
SALES (est): 11.42MM **Privately Held**
Web: www.broco-rankin.com
SIC: **3548** Welding and cutting apparatus
and accessories, nec

(P-5645)

CREATIVE PATHWAYS INC

20815 Higgins Ct, Torrance (90501-1830)
PHONE.............................310 530-1965
Brent Daldo, *CEO*
Timothy Rohrberg, *
Patrica Rohrberg, *
EMP: 35 **EST:** 1969
SQ FT: 29,000
SALES (est): 8.22MM **Privately Held**
Web: www.creativepathways.com
SIC: **3548** Welding and cutting apparatus
and accessories, nec

(P-5646)

DIAMOND GROUND PRODUCTS INC

2651 Lavery Ct, Newbury Park
(91320-1502)
PHONE.............................805 498-3837
Robert Elizarraz, *CEO*
James C Elizarraz, *
▲ **EMP:** 30 **EST:** 1992
SQ FT: 40,000
SALES (est): 4.92MM **Privately Held**
Web: www.diamondground.com
SIC: **3548** Electrodes, electric welding

(P-5647)

M K PRODUCTS INC

Also Called: Mk Manufacturing
16882 Armstrong Ave, Irvine (92606-4975)
PHONE.............................949 798-1234
Chris Westlake, *Pr*
Dana E Paquin, *
▲ **EMP:** 80 **EST:** 1966

SQ FT: 80,000
SALES (est): 18.57MM **Privately Held**
Web: www.mkproducts.com
SIC: **3548** Electric welding equipment

(P-5648)

OK INTERNATIONAL INC (DH)

Also Called: Metcal
10800 Valley View St, Cypress
(90630-5016)
PHONE.............................714 799-9910
◆ **EMP:** 224 **EST:** 1982
SALES (est): 45.72MM
SALES (corp-wide): 8.44B **Publicly Held**
Web: www.okinternational.com
SIC: **3548** Soldering equipment, except hand
soldering irons
HQ: Dover Engineered Products Segment,
Inc.
3005 Hghland Pkwy Ste 200
Downers Grove IL 60515
630 541-1540

(P-5649)

SSCO MANUFACTURING INC

Also Called: ARC Products
8155 Mercury Ct Ste 100, San Diego
(92111-1227)
PHONE.............................619 628-1022
Victor B Miller, *Pr*
Susan D Miller, *
Lane A Litke, *
EMP: 35 **EST:** 1988
SALES (est): 9.59MM
SALES (corp-wide): 4.19B **Publicly Held**
Web: mechanized.lincolnelectric.com
SIC: **3548** 5085 7629 7699 Electric welding
equipment; Welding supplies; Circuit board
repair; Welding equipment repair
PA: Lincoln Electric Holdings, Inc.
22801 St Clair Ave
216 481-8100

(P-5650)

WINTHER TECHNOLOGIES INC (PA)

Also Called: Technical Devices
560 Alaska Ave, Torrance (90503-3904)
P.O. Box 329 (90507-0129)
PHONE.............................310 618-8437
Douglas N Winther, *Pr*
▲ **EMP:** 46 **EST:** 1986
SQ FT: 32,000
SALES (est): 11.25MM
SALES (corp-wide): 11.25MM **Privately Held**
SIC: **3548** 3544 3542 3471 Soldering
equipment, except hand soldering irons;
Special dies and tools; Machine tools,
metal forming type; Cleaning and descaling
metal products

3549 Metalworking Machinery, Nec

(P-5651)

ADAPT AUTOMATION INC

1661 Palm St Ste A, Santa Ana
(92701-5190)
PHONE.............................714 662-4454
Case Van Mechelen, *Prin*
Case V Mechelen, *
Tim Van Mechelen, *Prin*
Tia V Mechelen, *
Peter Smit, *
EMP: 34 **EST:** 1988
SQ FT: 50,000
SALES (est): 6.78MM **Privately Held**
Web: www.adaptautomation.com

▲ = Import ▼ = Export
◆ = Import/Export

SIC: **3549** Assembly machines, including robotic

(P-5652)
BMCI INC
Also Called: Bergandi Machinery Company
1689 S Parco Ave, Ontario (91761-8308)
P.O. Box 3790 (91761-0977)
PHONE...............................951 361-8000
Scott Barsotti, *Pr*
Jose Garcia, *
Gary Costanzo, *
▼ **EMP: 45 EST: 1994**
SQ FT: 45,000
SALES (est): 4.49MM Privately Held
Web: www.bergandi.com
SIC: **3549 3548** Wiredrawing and fabricating machinery and equipment, ex. die; Welding apparatus

(P-5653)
FOOMA AMERICA INC
12735 Stanhill Dr, La Mirada (90638-1937)
PHONE...............................310 921-0717
Soohyung Kim, *CEO*
EMP: 30 EST: 2019
SALES (est): 1.22MM Privately Held
SIC: **3549** Cutting and slitting machinery

(P-5654)
GOLDEN STATE ENGINEERING INC
15338 Garfield Ave, Paramount (90723-4092)
PHONE...............................562 634-3125
Alexandra Rostovski, *CEO*
Mary Saguini, *
Eugenio Rostovski, *
Tom Scroggin, *
EMP: 120 EST: 1968
SQ FT: 65,000
SALES (est): 20.59MM Privately Held
Web: www.goldenstateeng.com
SIC: **3549 3541 3451 8711** Metalworking machinery, nec; Grinding, polishing, buffing, lapping, and honing machines; Screw machine products; Engineering services

(P-5655)
TELEDYNE SEABOTIX INC
2877 Historic Decatur Rd Ste 100, San Diego (92106-6177)
PHONE...............................619 239-5959
EMP: 68
SIC: **3549** Propeller straightening presses

(P-5656)
UBTECH ROBOTICS CORP
767 S Alameda St Ste 250, Los Angeles (90021-1667)
PHONE...............................213 261-7153
John Rhee, *CEO*
EMP: 30 EST: 2015
SALES (est): 5.46MM Privately Held
Web: www.ubtrobot.com
SIC: **3549** Assembly machines, including robotic
PA: Ubtech Robotics Corp Ltd
  Room 2201, Building C1, Nanshan
  Zhiyuan, No. 1001 Xueyuan Avenue

(P-5657)
WALLNER EXPAC INC (PA)
Also Called: W T E
1274 S Slater Cir, Ontario (91761-1522)
PHONE...............................909 481-8800
Sophia Wallner, *Ch Bd*
Michael Wallner, *
Paul Wallner, *
◆ **EMP: 55 EST: 1959**

SALES (est): 17.8MM
SALES (corp-wide): 17.8MM Privately Held
Web: www.expac.com
SIC: **3549 3542** Metalworking machinery, nec ; Machine tools, metal forming type

---

3554 Paper Industries Machinery

(P-5658)
ELLISON EDUCATIONAL EQP INC (PA)
Also Called: Sizzix
25671 Commercentre Dr, Lake Forest (92630-8801)
PHONE...............................949 598-8822
Richard Birse, *CEO*
Kristin Highberg, *
▲ **EMP: 38 EST: 1981**
SQ FT: 132,000
SALES (est): 12.04MM
SALES (corp-wide): 12.04MM Privately Held
Web: www.ellison.com
SIC: **3554** Cutting machines, paper

3555 Printing Trades Machinery

(P-5659)
4L TECHNOLOGIES INC
Also Called: Catridge Return Center
325 Weakley St, Calexico (92231-9659)
PHONE...............................817 538-0974
EMP: 1047
SALES (corp-wide): 26.47MM Privately Held
Web: www.clovertech.com
SIC: **3555** Printing trades machinery
HQ: 4l Technologies Inc.
  122 W Madison St
  Ottawa IL 61350
  815 431-8100

(P-5660)
CAL PLATE (PA)
17110 Jersey Ave, Artesia (90701-2694)
PHONE...............................562 403-3000
Richard Borelli, *Pr*
EMP: 63 EST: 1966
SQ FT: 33,000
SALES (est): 8.97MM
SALES (corp-wide): 8.97MM Privately Held
Web: www.calplate.com
SIC: **3555 3423 3544** Printing plates; Cutting dies, except metal cutting; Special dies, tools, jigs, and fixtures

(P-5661)
FABRIC8LABS INC
11075 Roselle St, San Diego (92121-1204)
PHONE...............................858 215-1142
Jeff Herman, *CEO*
David Pain, *
EMP: 60 EST: 2016
SALES (est): 7.74MM Privately Held
Web: www.fabric8labs.com
SIC: **3555** Printing trades machinery

(P-5662)
IMPERIAL RUBBER PRODUCTS INC
5691 Gates St, Chino (91710-7603)
PHONE...............................909 393-0528
Ronald Hill, *CEO*

Bob Schwartz, *
Steve Huff, *
▲ **EMP: 35 EST: 1989**
SQ FT: 20,000
SALES (est): 4.69MM Privately Held
Web: www.imperialrubber.com
SIC: **3555** Printing trades machinery

(P-5663)
LITH-O-ROLL CORPORATION
9521 Telstar Ave, El Monte (91731-2994)
P.O. Box 5328 (91734-1328)
PHONE...............................626 579-0340
Rita Sepe, *Pr*
EMP: 50 EST: 1957
SQ FT: 30,000
SALES (est): 9.49MM Privately Held
Web: www.lithoroll.com
SIC: **3555** Printing trades machinery

(P-5664)
PACIFIC BARCODE INC
27531 Enterprise Cir W Ste 201c, Temecula (92590-4888)
PHONE...............................951 587-8717
Michael Meadors, *Pr*
Michael Meadors, *Pr*
Michelle Meadors, *
EMP: 37 EST: 1999
SQ FT: 8,600
SALES (est): 5.03MM Privately Held
Web: www.pacificbarcode.com
SIC: **3555 2759 3565 3577** Printing trades machinery; Commercial printing, nec; Labeling machines, industrial; Bar code (magnetic ink) printers

(P-5665)
PARA-PLATE & PLASTICS CO INC
Also Called: Para Plate
15940 Shoemaker Ave, Cerritos (90703-2200)
PHONE...............................562 404-3434
Shane Pearson, *Pr*
Robert J Clapp, *
John Greenamyer, *
Steve Binnard, *
EMP: 27 EST: 1945
SQ FT: 17,000
SALES (est): 2.49MM Privately Held
Web: www.paraplate.com
SIC: **3555 7336 2796** Printing plates; Commercial art and graphic design; Platemaking services

(P-5666)
RIMA ENTERPRISES INC
Also Called: Rima-System
16417 Ladona Cir, Huntington Beach (92649-2133)
PHONE...............................714 893-4534
Horst K Steinhart, *CEO*
▲ **EMP: 62 EST: 1970**
SALES (est): 2.96MM Privately Held
SIC: **3555** Bookbinding machinery

(P-5667)
THISTLE ROLLER CO INC
209 Van Norman Rd, Montebello (90640-5393)
PHONE...............................323 685-5322
Lizbeth Karpynec, *CEO*
Eric Karpynetz, *
▲ **EMP: 35 EST: 1957**
SQ FT: 45,000
SALES (est): 5.55MM Privately Held
Web: www.thistleroller.com

SIC: **3555** 3312 2796 Printing trades machinery; Blast furnaces and steel mills; Platemaking services

---

3556 Food Products Machinery

(P-5668)
CAPNA FABRICATION
Also Called: Capna Systems
9801 Independence Ave, Chatsworth (91311-4320)
PHONE...............................888 416-6777
Vitaly Mekk, *CEO*
Gene Galyuk, *
EMP: 30 EST: 2017
SALES (est): 7.55MM Privately Held
SIC: **3556** Oilseed crushing and extracting machinery

(P-5669)
CASA HERRERA INC (PA)
2655 Pine St, Pomona (91767-2115)
PHONE...............................909 392-3930
Michael L Herrera, *CEO*
Ronald L Meade, *
Alfred J Herrera, *
Frank J Herrera, *
Susan A Herrera, *
◆ **EMP: 100 EST: 1970**
SQ FT: 100,000
SALES (est): 20.67MM
SALES (corp-wide): 20.67MM Privately Held
Web: www.casaherrera.com
SIC: **3556** Food products machinery

(P-5670)
EBARA MIXERS INC
Also Called: Scott Turbon Mixer Inc.
9351 Industrial Way, Adelanto (92301-3932)
P.O. Box 160 (92301-0160)
PHONE...............................760 246-3430
EMP: 30 EST: 1980
SALES (est): 6.58MM Privately Held
Web: www.haywardgordon.com
SIC: **3556** Cutting, chopping, grinding, mixing, and similar machinery
HQ: Hayward Gordon Us, Inc.
  1541 S 92nd Pl
  Seattle WA 98108
  206 767-5660

(P-5671)
FOTIS AND SON IMPORTS INC (PA)
15451 Electronic Ln, Huntington Beach (92649-1333)
PHONE...............................714 894-9022
Peter Georgatsos, *Pr*
Russ Hillas, *
Laura Georgatsos, *
Eleni Hillas, *
▲ **EMP: 38 EST: 1976**
SQ FT: 34,000
SALES (est): 11.42MM
SALES (corp-wide): 11.42MM Privately Held
Web: www.fotisandsonimports.com
SIC: **3556** Food products machinery

(P-5672)
FRESH VENTURE FOODS LLC
1205 Craig Dr, Santa Maria (93458-4917)
P.O. Box 1023 (93458)
PHONE...............................805 928-3374
John Schaefer, *Managing Member*
Jeff Lundberg, *

P
R
O
D
U
C
T
S

&

S
V
C
S

EMP: 239 EST: 2012
SQ FT: 70
SALES (est): 22.38MM Privately Held
Web: www.freshventurefoods.com
SIC: 3556 Dehydrating equipment, food
processing

(P-5673)
G & I ISLAS INDUSTRIES INC (PA)
Also Called: G & I Industries
12860 Schabarum Ave, Baldwin Park
(91706-6801)
P.O. Box 1262 (91706-7262)
PHONE..................626 960-5020
Gonzalo R Islas, CEO
Sara Islas, *
▲ EMP: 23 EST: 1988
SQ FT: 12,500
SALES (est): 2.73MM
SALES (corp-wide): 2.73MM Privately
Held
Web: www.giislasindustries.com
SIC: 3556 5084 Bakery machinery; Food
industry machinery

(P-5674)
GOLDEN PACIFIC SEAFOODS INC
700 S Raymond Ave, Fullerton
(92831-5233)
PHONE..................714 589-8888
Tony Zavala, Pr
EMP: 45 EST: 2016
SALES (est): 3.6MM Privately Held
SIC: 3556 Meat, poultry, and seafood
processing machinery

(P-5675)
INTERSTATE MEAT CO INC
Also Called: Sterling Pacific Meat Co.
6114 Scott Way, Commerce (90040-3518)
PHONE..................323 838-9400
James T Asher, Pr
EMP: 49 EST: 1996
SALES (est): 10.65MM Privately Held
Web: www.sterlingpacificmeat.com
SIC: 3556 Meat processing machinery

(P-5676)
J C FORD COMPANY (HQ)
Also Called: JC Ford
901 S Leslie St, La Habra (90631-6841)
PHONE..................714 871-7361
Scott D Ruhe, CEO
◆ EMP: 43 EST: 1945
SALES (est): 38.16MM Privately Held
Web: www.jcford.com
SIC: 3556 Food products machinery
PA: Ruhe Corporation
901 S Leslie St

(P-5677)
JOHN BEAN TECHNOLOGIES CORP
1660 Iowa Ave Ste 100, Riverside
(92507-0501)
P.O. Box 5710 (92517-5710)
PHONE..................951 222-2300
Thomas Brickweg, Prin
EMP: 88
Web: www.jbtc.com
SIC: 3556 3542 3523 Dairy and milk
machinery; Nail heading machines; Dairy
equipment (farm), nec
PA: John Bean Technologies Corporation
70 W Madison St Ste 4400

(P-5678)
JUICY WHIP INC (PA)
1668 Curtiss Ct, La Verne (91750-5848)
PHONE..................909 392-7500
TOLL FREE: 800
Gus Stratton, Pr
▲ EMP: 28 EST: 1981
SQ FT: 23,000
SALES (est): 6.37MM
SALES (corp-wide): 6.37MM Privately
Held
Web: www.juicywhip.com
SIC: 3556 2033 Beverage machinery; Fruit
juices: fresh

(P-5679)
LAWRENCE EQUIPMENT LEASING INC (PA)
Also Called: Lawrence Equipment
2034 Peck Rd, El Monte (91733-3727)
PHONE..................626 442-2894
John Lawrence, CEO
Linda Lawrence, *
Glenn Shelton, *
Jack Kirkpatrick, Stockholder*
▲ EMP: 190 EST: 1981
SQ FT: 50,000
SALES (est): 48.74MM
SALES (corp-wide): 48.74MM Privately
Held
Web: www.lawrenceequipment.com
SIC: 3556 Flour mill machinery

(P-5680)
MACHINE BUILDING SPC INC
Also Called: Conveyor Concepts
1977 Blake Ave, Los Angeles (90039-3832)
PHONE..................323 666-8289
Charles Conaway, Ch Bd
Dennis James Conaway, *
Sandra Conaway, *
Sharon Conaway, *
EMP: 25 EST: 1960
SQ FT: 17,000
SALES (est): 3.09MM Privately Held
Web:
www.machinebuildingspecialties.com
SIC: 3556 3535 Bakery machinery; Belt
conveyor systems, general industrial use

(P-5681)
MEMC LIQUIDATING CORPORATION
Also Called: Mc Cann's Engineering & Mfg Co
4570 Colorado Blvd, La Mirada (90638)
P.O. Box 39100 (90039-0100)
PHONE..................818 637-7200
▲ EMP: 250
SIC: 3556 3586 3585 3581 Beverage
machinery; Measuring and dispensing
pumps; Refrigeration and heating
equipment; Automatic vending machines

(P-5682)
PACIFIC PACKAGING MCHY LLC
Also Called: Pack West Machinery
200 River Rd, Corona (92878-1435)
PHONE..................951 393-2200
Gerald Carpino, CEO
Jerry Carpino, *
▲ EMP: 25 EST: 1962
SQ FT: 30,000
SALES (est): 7.55MM Privately Held
Web: www.pacificpak.com
SIC: 3556 3565 Food products machinery;
Packaging machinery
HQ: Pro Mach, Inc.
50 E Rivcenter Blvd Ste 18
Covington KY 41011
513 831-8778

(P-5683)
RESERS FINE FOODS INC
3285 Corporate Vw, Vista (92081-8528)
PHONE..................503 643-6431
EMP: 50
SALES (corp-wide): 347.92MM Privately
Held
Web: www.resers.com
SIC: 3556 Food products machinery
PA: Reser's Fine Foods, Inc.
15570 Sw Jenkins Rd
503 643-6431

(P-5684)
REXNORD INDUSTRIES LLC
Also Called: Industrial Components Div
2175 Union Pl, Simi Valley (93065-1661)
PHONE..................805 583-5514
Dave Kleinhaus, Mgr
EMP: 45
SALES (corp-wide): 6.25B Publicly Held
SIC: 3556 3568 Food products machinery;
Couplings, shaft: rigid, flexible, universal
joint, etc.
HQ: Rexnord Industries, Llc
111 W Michigan St
Milwaukee WI 53203
414 643-3000

(P-5685)
SUPERIOR FOOD MACHINERY INC
8311 Sorensen Ave, Santa Fe Springs
(90670-2125)
PHONE..................562 949-0396
Danny Reyes, Pr
Polo Reyes, Pr
Marc Reyes, VP
EMP: 23 EST: 1975
SQ FT: 14,000
SALES (est): 4.96MM Privately Held
Web: www.superiorinc.com
SIC: 3556 Food products machinery

3559 Special Industry Machinery, Nec

(P-5686)
ACME CRYOGENICS INC
Also Called: Cryogenic Experts
531 Sandy Cir, Oxnard (93036-0971)
PHONE..................805 981-4500
Robert Worcester Junior, Brnch Mgr
EMP: 30
SALES (corp-wide): 8.44B Publicly Held
Web: www.opwces.com
SIC: 3559 Cryogenic machinery, industrial
HQ: Acme Cryogenics, Inc.
2801 Mitchell Ave
Allentown PA 18103
610 966-4488

(P-5687)
AMERGENCE TECHNOLOGY INC
295 Brea Canyon Rd, Walnut (91789-3049)
PHONE..................909 859-8400
Shavonne Tran, Pr
▲ EMP: 29 EST: 2006
SQ FT: 40,000
SALES (est): 868.29K Privately Held
Web: www.amergenceinc.com
SIC: 3559 Recycling machinery

(P-5688)
AMREP MANUFACTURING CO LLC
1555 S Cucamonga Ave, Ontario
(91761-4512)

PHONE..................877 468-9278
Martin Bryant, CEO
EMP: 500 EST: 2019
SALES (est): 10MM Privately Held
Web: www.amrepproducts.com
SIC: 3559 Semiconductor manufacturing
machinery

(P-5689)
AQUA PRO PROPERTIES VII LP
Also Called: Village Marine Technology
2000 W 135th St, Gardena (90249-2456)
PHONE..................310 516-9911
▲ EMP: 256
Web: www.villagemarine.com
SIC: 3559 Desalination equipment

(P-5690)
ASC PROCESS SYSTEMS INC (PA)
Also Called: ASC
28402 Livingston Ave, Valencia
(91355-4172)
PHONE..................818 833-0088
David C Mason, Pr
Dave Mason, *
Gudrun Mason, *
◆ EMP: 240 EST: 1988
SQ FT: 41,000
SALES (est): 39.43MM
SALES (corp-wide): 39.43MM Privately
Held
Web: www.aschome.com
SIC: 3559 3443 3567 Sewing machines and
hat and zipper making machinery;
Fabricated plate work (boiler shop);
Industrial furnaces and ovens

(P-5691)
ASML US INC
Also Called: ASML US, Inc.
1 Viper Way Ste A, Vista (92081-7809)
PHONE..................760 443-6244
Jenna Moggio, Prin
EMP: 310
SALES (corp-wide): 29.96B Privately Held
Web: www.asml.com
SIC: 3559 Semiconductor manufacturing
machinery
HQ: Asml Us, Llc
2625 W Geronimo Pl
Chandler AZ 85224
480 696-2888

(P-5692)
ASML US LLC
17075 Thornmint Ct, San Diego
(92127-2413)
PHONE..................858 385-6500
EMP: 480
SALES (corp-wide): 29.96B Privately Held
Web: www.asml.com
SIC: 3559 Semiconductor manufacturing
machinery
HQ: Asml Us, Llc
2625 W Geronimo Pl
Chandler AZ 85224
480 696-2888

(P-5693)
BARKENS HARDCHROME INC
Also Called: Bhc Industries
239 E Greenleaf Blvd, Compton
(90220-4913)
PHONE..................310 632-2000
Gary Barken, CEO
Carol Barken, VP
EMP: 25 EST: 1942
SQ FT: 60,000
SALES (est): 4.84MM Privately Held

▲ = Import ▼ = Export
◆ = Import/Export

Web: www.barkenshardchrome.com
SIC: **3559** 5082 Metal finishing equipment
for plating, etc.; Oil field equipment

(P-5694)
BENDPAK INC (PA)
30440 Agoura Rd, Agoura Hills
(91301-2145)
PHONE.....................805 933-9970
Jeffrey Kritzer, *Pr*
Donald R Henthorn, *
◆ **EMP:** 98 **EST:** 1965
SALES (est): 26.45MM
SALES (corp-wide): 26.45MM **Privately
Held**
Web: www.bendpak.com
SIC: **3559** 3537 Automotive related
machinery; Industrial trucks and tractors

(P-5695)
BOOM INDUSTRIAL INC
2010 Wright Ave, La Verne (91750-5821)
PHONE.....................909 495-3555
Huiwen Chen, *CEO*
EMP: 60 **EST:** 2016
SALES (est): 2.04MM **Privately Held**
Web: www.boomindustrial.com
SIC: **3559** 3069 Rubber working machinery,
including tires; Rubber automotive products

(P-5696)
COSMODYNE LLC
Also Called: Nikkiso Cosmodyne
3010 Old Ranch Pkwy Ste 300, Seal Beach
(90740-2750)
PHONE.....................562 795-5990
Peter Wagner, *Pr*
◆ **EMP:** 25 **EST:** 1997
SQ FT: 125,000
SALES (est): 16.94MM **Privately Held**
Web: www.nikkisoceig.com
SIC: **3559** 3443 Smelting and refining
machinery and equipment; Cryogenic
tanks, for liquids and gases
HQ: Cryogenic Industries, Inc.
27710 Jfffrson Ave Ste 301
Temecula CA 92590
951 677-2081

(P-5697)
CP MANUFACTURING INC (HQ)
Also Called: CP Manufacturing
6795 Calle De Linea, San Diego
(92154-8017)
PHONE.....................619 477-3175
Robert M Davis, *Pr*
Ruth Davis, *
Theodora Davis Inman, *
Michael W Howard, *
John O Willis, *General Vice President*
▲ **EMP:** 104 **EST:** 1977
SQ FT: 60,572
SALES (est): 25.22MM
SALES (corp-wide): 81.98MM **Privately
Held**
Web: www.cpgrp.com
SIC: **3559** Recycling machinery
PA: Ims Recycling Services, Inc.
2697 Main St
619 231-2521

(P-5698)
CRYOGENIC EXPERTS INC
Also Called: Cexi
531 Sandy Cir, Oxnard (93036-0971)
PHONE.....................805 981-4500
EMP: 30
SIC: **3559** Cryogenic machinery, industrial

(P-5699)
CRYST MARK INC A SWAN
TECHNO C
Also Called: Crystal Mark
613 Justin Ave, Glendale (91201-2326)
PHONE.....................818 240-7520
John Swan, *Pr*
Marko S Swan, *
E Michael Swan, *
Pauline Swan, *
EMP: 40 **EST:** 1968
SQ FT: 18,000
SALES (est): 1.7MM **Privately Held**
Web: www.crystalmarkinc.com
SIC: **3559** 3471 Semiconductor
manufacturing machinery; Sand blasting of
metal parts

(P-5700)
DEK INDUSTRY INC
Also Called: Trademark Plastics, Inc.
807 Palmyrita Ave, Riverside (92507-1805)
PHONE.....................909 941-8810
Alex Wang, *CEO*
Erin Carty, *
Kris Carty, *Sec*
David Carty, *COO*
◆ **EMP:** 150 **EST:** 1988
SQ FT: 100,000
SALES (est): 25.82MM **Privately Held**
Web: www.trademarkplastics.com
SIC: **3559** 3089 Plastics working machinery;
Injection molding of plastics
PA: Zhejiang Gongdong Medical
Technology Co., Ltd.
No.10,Beiyuan Ave.,Huangyan Dist.

(P-5701)
EXCELLON ACQUISITION LLC
(HQ)
Also Called: Excellon Automation Co
16130 Gundry Ave, Paramount
(90723-4831)
PHONE.....................310 668-7700
EMP: 38 **EST:** 1962
SALES (est): 9.91MM
SALES (corp-wide): 10.36MM **Privately
Held**
Web: www.excellon.com
SIC: **3559** Semiconductor manufacturing
machinery
PA: Turning Point Capital, Llc
138 Del Prado St

(P-5702)
FANUC AMERICA
CORPORATION
Also Called: Fanuc Robotics West
25951 Commercentre Dr, Lake Forest
(92630-8805)
PHONE.....................949 595-2700
Mike Hollingsworth, *Mgr*
EMP: 58
Web: www.fanucamerica.com
SIC: **3559** 3548 3569 Metal finishing
equipment for plating, etc.; Electric welding
equipment; Robots, assembly line:
industrial and commercial
HQ: Fanuc America Corporation
3900 W Hamlin Rd
Rochester Hills MI 48309
248 377-7000

(P-5703)
FLIGHT MICROWAVE
CORPORATION
410 S Douglas St, El Segundo
(90245-4628)
PHONE.....................310 607-9819

Rolf Kich, *Pr*
Mike Callas, *
EMP: 26 **EST:** 2004
SQ FT: 8,000
SALES (est): 6.56MM **Publicly Held**
Web: www.flightmicrowave.com
SIC: **3559** Electronic component making
machinery
HQ: Lucix Corporation
800 Avenida Acaso Ste E
Camarillo CA 93012
805 987-6645

(P-5704)
HEXCO INTERNATIONAL
Also Called: Cryogenic Industries
25720 Jefferson Ave, Murrieta
(92562-6929)
PHONE.....................951 677-2081
◆ **EMP:** 117
SIC: **3559** 3561 3443 Cryogenic machinery,
industrial; Pumps and pumping equipment;
Fabricated plate work (boiler shop)

(P-5705)
INDUSTRIAL DYNAMICS CO LTD
(PA)
Also Called: Filtec
3100 Fujita St, Torrance (90505-4007)
P.O. Box 2945 (90509-2945)
PHONE.....................310 325-5633
James Kearbey, *CEO*
▲ **EMP:** 125 **EST:** 1960
SQ FT: 155,000
SALES (est): 27.94MM
SALES (corp-wide): 27.94MM **Privately
Held**
Web: www.filtec.com
SIC: **3559** 3829 Screening equipment,
electric; Measuring and controlling devices,
nec

(P-5706)
INDUSTRIAL TOOLS INC
1800 Avenue Of The Stars, Los Angeles
(90067-4201)
PHONE.....................805 483-1111
Donald O Murphy, *Pr*
John E Anderson, *
Kay Nolan, *
EMP: 50 **EST:** 1961
SALES (est): 4.97MM **Privately Held**
Web: www.iti-abrasives.com
SIC: **3559** 3545 3544 3541 Semiconductor
manufacturing machinery; Machine tool
accessories; Special dies, tools, jigs, and
fixtures; Machine tools, metal cutting type

(P-5707)
INTEGRTED CRYGNIC
SLUTIONS LLC
Also Called: Nikkiso Cryoquip
2835 Progress Pl, Escondido (92029-1516)
PHONE.....................951 234-0899
Peter Wagner, *Managing Member*
EMP: 35 **EST:** 2014
SALES (est): 11.88MM **Privately Held**
Web: www.nikkisoceig.com
SIC: **3559** Cryogenic machinery, industrial

(P-5708)
KVR INVESTMENT GROUP INC
Also Called: Pacific Plating
12113 Branford St, Sun Valley
(91352-5710)
PHONE.....................818 896-1102
Rakesh Bajaria, *Pr*
Ken Pansuria, *
Harry Thummar, *
Benny Kadhrota, *

EMP: 60 **EST:** 1997
SALES (est): 4.67MM **Privately Held**
SIC: **3559** 3471 Metal finishing equipment
for plating, etc.; Plating and polishing

(P-5709)
MEI RIGGING & CRATING LLC
Also Called: Dunkel Bros. Machinery Moving
14555 Alondra Blvd, La Mirada
(90638-5602)
P.O. Box 1630 (97321-0477)
PHONE.....................714 712-5888
Dan Cappello, *Prin*
Sondra Ludwick, *
Seth Christensen, *
Patrick Moore, *
Terry Shain, *
EMP: 60 **EST:** 2018
SALES (est): 5.42MM **Privately Held**
Web: www.dunkelbros.com
SIC: **3559** Special industry machinery, nec

(P-5710)
MERITEK ELECTRONICS CORP
(PA)
Also Called: Ralec USA Electronic Corp
5160 Rivergrade Rd, Baldwin Park
(91706-1406)
PHONE.....................626 373-1728
Pa-shih Oliver Su, *CEO*
◆ **EMP:** 75 **EST:** 1993
SQ FT: 60,000
SALES (est): 20.99MM **Privately Held**
Web: www.meritekusa.com
SIC: **3559** 5065 Electronic component
making machinery; Electronic parts

(P-5711)
MOREHOUSE-COWLES LLC
Also Called: Epworth Morehouse Cowles
13930 Magnolia Ave, Chino (91710-7029)
PHONE.....................909 627-7222
EMP: 25 **EST:** 2004
SALES (est): 5.48MM
SALES (corp-wide): 6.97B **Publicly Held**
Web: www.morehousecowles.com
SIC: **3559** Chemical machinery and
equipment
HQ: Nusil Technology Llc
1050 Cindy Ln
Carpinteria CA 93013
805 684-8780

(P-5712)
MORGAN POLYMER SEALS LLC
3303 2475a Paseo De Las Americas, San
Diego (92154)
PHONE.....................619 498-9221
Kevin A Morgan, *CEO*
Todd Tesky, *VP Sls*
EMP: 400 **EST:** 1007
SALES (est): 3.75MM **Privately Held**
Web: www.morganpolymerseals.com
SIC: **3559** 5211 3663 3365 Automotive
related machinery; Energy conservation
products; Space satellite communications
equipment; Aerospace castings, aluminum

(P-5713)
NEWPORT ELECTRONICS INC
2229 S Yale St, Santa Ana (92704-4401)
PHONE.....................714 540-4914
▲ **EMP:** 90
SIC: **3559** 3829 3822 3825 Electronic
component making machinery;
Temperature sensors, except industrial
process and aircraft; Temperature controls,
automatic; Measuring instruments and
meters, electric

(P-5714)
NORCHEM CORPORATION (PA)
5649 Alhambra Ave, Los Angeles
(90032-3107)
PHONE....................323 221-0221
Gevork Minissian, *CEO*
▲ EMP: 50 EST: 1980
SQ FT: 50,000
SALES (est): 10.63MM
SALES (corp-wide): 10.63MM **Privately Held**
Web: www.norchemcorp.com
SIC: 3559 2842 2841 Chemical machinery and equipment; Laundry cleaning preparations; Soap and other detergents

(P-5715)
PALOMAR TECHNOLOGIES INC (PA)
6305 El Camino Real, Carlsbad
(92009-1606)
PHONE....................760 931-3600
Bruce Hueners, *CEO*
Carl Hempel, *CFO*
EMP: 50 EST: 1975
SQ FT: 40,000
SALES (est): 24.68MM **Privately Held**
Web: www.palomartechnologies.com
SIC: 3559 Semiconductor manufacturing machinery

(P-5716)
PEABODY ENGINEERING & SUP INC
Also Called: Peabody Engineering
13435 Estelle St, Corona (92879-1877)
PHONE....................951 734-7711
Mark Peabody, *CEO*
Larry Peabody, *
◆ EMP: 25 EST: 1952
SQ FT: 32,400
SALES (est): 4.57MM **Privately Held**
Web: www.4peabody.com
SIC: 3559 5084 Chemical machinery and equipment; Industrial machinery and equipment

(P-5717)
PHILLIPS 66 CO CARBON GROUP
2555 Willow Rd, Arroyo Grande
(93420-5731)
PHONE....................805 489-4050
EMP: 26 EST: 2004
SALES (est): 4.08MM **Privately Held**
SIC: 3559 Petroleum refinery equipment

(P-5718)
PROLINE CONCRETE TOOLS INC
4645 North Ave Ste 102, Oceanside
(92056-3593)
PHONE....................760 758-7240
Jeff Irwin, *CEO*
Kellen Irwin, *
Tyler Irwin, *
▼ EMP: 27 EST: 1990
SALES (est): 5.2MM **Privately Held**
Web: www.prolinestamps.com
SIC: 3559 1771 Concrete products machinery; Patio construction, concrete

(P-5719)
RXSAFE LLC
Also Called: Rxsafe
2453 Cades Way Bldg A, Vista
(92081-7858)
PHONE....................760 593-7161
William Holmes, *Managing Member*

Shawn Orr, *
EMP: 68 EST: 2008
SALES (est): 23.02MM **Privately Held**
Web: www.rxsafe.com
SIC: 3559 Pharmaceutical machinery

(P-5720)
STARCO ENTERPRISES INC (PA)
Also Called: Four Star Chemical
3137 E 26th St, Los Angeles (90058-8006)
PHONE....................323 266-7111
George D Stroesenreuther, *CEO*
Ross Sklar, *
▲ EMP: 74 EST: 1973
SQ FT: 25,000
SALES (est): 16.32MM
SALES (corp-wide): 16.32MM **Privately Held**
Web: www.thestarcogroup.com
SIC: 3559 5169 5191 Degreasing machines, automotive and industrial; Specialty cleaning and sanitation preparations; Farm supplies

(P-5721)
SUSS MICROTEC INC (HQ)
2520 Palisades Dr, Corona (92882-0632)
PHONE....................408 940-0300
Frank Averdung, *Pr*
Franz Richter, *
Peter Szafir, *
Stewart Mc C0naughy, *
Stefan Schneidewind, *
EMP: 130 EST: 1980
SALES (est): 23.07MM
SALES (corp-wide): 330.72MM **Privately Held**
Web: www.suss.com
SIC: 3559 3825 3674 Semiconductor manufacturing machinery; Instruments to measure electricity; Semiconductors and related devices
PA: Suss Microtec Se
SchleiBheimer Str. 90
89320070

(P-5722)
TIMEC COMPANIES INC
Also Called: Timec Southern California
6861 Charity Ave, Bakersfield
(93308-5918)
PHONE....................661 322-8177
Will Nord, *Site Superintendent*
EMP: 50
Web: www.timec.com
SIC: 3559 Refinery, chemical processing, and similar machinery
HQ: Timec Companies Inc
473 E Channel Rd
Benicia CA 94510
707 642-2222

(P-5723)
UNITED SURFACE SOLUTIONS LLC
11901 Burke St, Santa Fe Springs
(90670-2507)
PHONE....................562 693-0202
Ken Bagdasarian, *CEO*
EMP: 27 EST: 2010
SQ FT: 20,000
SALES (est): 4.71MM **Privately Held**
Web: www.deburring.com
SIC: 3559 3541 Metal finishing equipment for plating, etc.; Deburring machines

(P-5724)
VIZUALOGIC LLC
1493 E Bentley Dr, Corona (92879-5102)
PHONE....................407 509-3421
Janis Patterson, *
EMP: 200 EST: 2015
SQ FT: 3,000
SALES (est): 4.74MM **Privately Held**
Web: www.vizualogicdirect.com
SIC: 3559 Automotive related machinery

(P-5725)
ZAMBONI COMPANY USA INC
Also Called: Zamboni
15714 Colorado Ave, Paramount
(90723-4211)
PHONE....................562 633-0751
▲ EMP: 35 EST: 1949
SALES (est): 10.67MM **Privately Held**
Web: www.zamboni.com
SIC: 3559 Ice resurfacing machinery

3561 Pumps And Pumping Equipment

(P-5726)
AQUASTAR POOL PRODUCTS INC
Also Called: Aquastar Pool Productions
2340 Palma Dr Ste 104, Ventura
(93003-8091)
PHONE....................877 768-2717
Olaf Mjelde, *CEO*
▲ EMP: 46 EST: 2003
SALES (est): 6.06MM **Privately Held**
Web: www.aquastarpoolproducts.com
SIC: 3561 Pumps, domestic: water or sump

(P-5727)
AQUATEC INTERNATIONAL INC
Also Called: Aquatec Water Systems
17422 Pullman St, Irvine (92614-5527)
PHONE....................949 225-2200
Bryan Hausner, *CEO*
Sami Levi, *
Isak Levi, *
Ivar Schoenmeyr, *
▲ EMP: 95 EST: 1986
SQ FT: 30,000
SALES (est): 22.79MM **Privately Held**
Web: www.aquatec.com
SIC: 3561 Pumps and pumping equipment

(P-5728)
BORIN MANUFACTURING INC
5741 Buckingham Pkwy Ste B, Culver City
(90230-6520)
PHONE....................310 822-1000
Frank William Borin, *CEO*
Gregg Steele, *
EMP: 40 EST: 1976
SALES (est): 9.95MM **Privately Held**
Web: www.borin.com
SIC: 3561 3443 3317 3494 Pumps and pumping equipment; Fabricated plate work (boiler shop); Steel pipe and tubes; Valves and pipe fittings, nec

(P-5729)
CASCADE PUMP COMPANY
10107 Norwalk Blvd, Santa Fe Springs
(90670-3354)
P.O. Box 2767 (90670-0767)
PHONE....................562 946-1414
T W Summerfield, *CEO*
John Summerfield, *
EMP: 60 EST: 1948
SQ FT: 120,000

SALES (est): 9.16MM **Privately Held**
Web: www.cascadepump.com
SIC: 3561 3594 Pumps, domestic: water or sump; Fluid power pumps and motors

(P-5730)
CRYOSTAR USA LLC
13117 Meyer Rd, Whittier (90605-3555)
PHONE....................562 903-1290
▲ EMP: 68 EST: 2014
SALES (est): 11.78MM **Privately Held**
Web: www.cryostar.com
SIC: 3561 Pump jacks and other pumping equipment
HQ: Cryostar Sas
2 Rue De L Industrie
Hesingue 68220
389702727

(P-5731)
FLOWSERVE CORPORATION
Flowserve
27455 Tierra Alta Way Ste C, Temecula
(92590-3498)
PHONE....................951 296-2464
Paul Cortenbach, *Brnch Mgr*
EMP: 87
SALES (corp-wide): 4.32B **Publicly Held**
Web: www.flowserve.com
SIC: 3561 3053 Industrial pumps and parts; Gaskets; packing and sealing devices
PA: Flowserve Corporation
5215 N Ocnnor Blvd Ste 70
972 443-6500

(P-5732)
FLOWSERVE CORPORATION
Flowserve
2300 E Vernon Ave Stop 76, Vernon
(90058-1609)
PHONE....................323 584-1890
Rick Soldo, *Brnch Mgr*
EMP: 342
SALES (corp-wide): 4.32B **Publicly Held**
Web: www.flowserve.com
SIC: 3561 Pumps and pumping equipment
PA: Flowserve Corporation
5215 N Ocnnor Blvd Ste 70
972 443-6500

(P-5733)
FLOWSERVE CORPORATION
Flowserve
1909 E Cashdan St, Compton
(90220-6422)
PHONE....................310 667-4220
Dan Lattimore, *Mgr*
EMP: 79
SALES (corp-wide): 4.32B **Publicly Held**
Web: www.flowserve.com
SIC: 3561 Industrial pumps and parts
PA: Flowserve Corporation
5215 N Ocnnor Blvd Ste 70
972 443-6500

(P-5734)
GRISWOLD PUMP COMPANY
22069 Van Buren St, Grand Terrace
(92313-5607)
PHONE....................909 422-1700
Dale Pavlovich, *Pr*
Edward Vaughn, *VP Engg*
Dave Spitzer, *VP*
Michael Boul, *VP*
◆ EMP: 25 EST: 1996
SQ FT: 25,000
SALES (est): 2.84MM
SALES (corp-wide): 8.44B **Publicly Held**
Web: www.griswoldpump.com

SIC: **3561** 5084 Industrial pumps and parts; Industrial machinery and equipment
HQ: Psg California Llc
  22069 Van Buren St
  Grand Terrace CA 92313
  909 422-1700

(P-5735)
GROVER SMITH MFG CORP
Also Called: Grover Manufacturing
9717 Factorial Way, South El Monte (91733-1724)
P.O. Box 986 (90640-0986)
PHONE.....................323 724-3444
Marilyn Schirmer, *Corporate President*
Marilyn Schirmer, *Pr*
Lino Paras, *
W Michael Meeker, *
▲ **EMP:** 30 **EST:** 1925
SALES (est): 5.88MM **Privately Held**
Web: www.grovermfg.com
SIC: **3561** 3569 Pumps and pumping equipment; Lubrication equipment, industrial

(P-5736)
HASKEL INTERNATIONAL LLC (HQ)
100 E Graham Pl, Burbank (91502-2027)
PHONE.....................818 843-4000
Chris Krieps, *CEO*
Dave Alan Barta, *
Elmer Lee Doty, *
Maria Blase, *
▲ **EMP:** 125 **EST:** 1986
SQ FT: 78,000
SALES (est): 47.09MM
SALES (corp-wide): 6.88B **Publicly Held**
Web: www.haskel.com
SIC: **3561** 3594 5084 5085 Pumps and pumping equipment; Fluid power pumps; Hydraulic systems equipment and supplies; Hose, belting, and packing
PA: Ingersoll Rand Inc.
  525 Harbor Pl Dr Ste 600
  704 896-4000

(P-5737)
MJW INC
Also Called: American Lab and Systems
1328 W Slauson Ave, Los Angeles (90044-2824)
PHONE.....................323 778-8900
Mike Curry, *Pr*
Linda Curry, *
EMP: 65 **EST:** 1978
SQ FT: 30,000
SALES (est): 4.77MM **Privately Held**
Web: modern-jewelry-and-watches.business.site
SIC: **3561** Industrial pumps and parts

(P-5730)
MOLEAER INC
3232 W El Segundo Blvd, Hawthorne (90250-4823)
PHONE.....................424 558-3567
Nicholas Dyner, *CEO*
Warren Russell, *
Bruce Scholten, *
Bryan Brister, *
Hoshang Subawalla, *Chief Business Officer*
EMP: 85 **EST:** 2016
SALES (est): 13.51MM **Privately Held**
Web: www.moleaer.com
SIC: **3561** Pumps and pumping equipment

(P-5739)
PENGUIN PUMPS INCORPORATED

Also Called: Filter Pump Industries
7932 Ajay Dr, Sun Valley (91352-5315)
PHONE.....................818 504-2391
Jerome S Hollander, *Pr*
▲ **EMP:** 50 **EST:** 1972
SQ FT: 20,000
SALES (est): 7.61MM
SALES (corp-wide): 24.11MM **Privately Held**
Web: www.filterpump.com
SIC: **3561** 3569 Pumps and pumping equipment; Filters, general line: industrial
PA: Finish Thompson, Inc.
  921 Greengarden Rd
  814 455-4478

(P-5740)
POLARIS E-COMMERCE INC
1941 E Occidental St, Santa Ana (92705-5115)
PHONE.....................714 907-0582
Insoo Hwang, *CEO*
▲ **EMP:** 25 **EST:** 2010
SALES (est): 2.71MM **Privately Held**
Web: www.officesmartlabels.com
SIC: **3561** Industrial pumps and parts

(P-5741)
PSG CALIFORNIA LLC (HQ)
Also Called: Wilden Pump
22069 Van Buren St, Grand Terrace (92313-5607)
PHONE.....................909 422-1700
Denny L Buskirk, *Managing Member*
Daniel Anderson, *
◆ **EMP:** 295 **EST:** 1998
SQ FT: 153,000
SALES (est): 49.05MM
SALES (corp-wide): 8.44B **Publicly Held**
Web: www.wildenpump.com
SIC: **3561** Industrial pumps and parts
PA: Dover Corporation
  3005 Highland Pkwy
  630 541-1540

(P-5742)
REED LLC
Also Called: Reed Manufacturing
13822 Oaks Ave, Chino (91710-7008)
PHONE.....................909 287-2100
James W Shea, *Managing Member*
Cliff Kao, *VP*
◆ **EMP:** 40 **EST:** 1957
SQ FT: 69,000
SALES (est): 9.93MM **Privately Held**
Web: www.reedpumps.com
SIC: **3561** 3531 Pumps and pumping equipment; Bituminous, cement and concrete related products and equip.

(P-5743)
SCHROFF INC
Also Called: Pep West, Inc.
7328 Trade St, San Diego (92121-3435)
PHONE.....................800 525-4682
Beth Wozniak, *CEO*
Bill Biancaniello, *Pr*
Judy Carle, *VP Fin*
Michael Meyer, *Treas*
▲ **EMP:** 800 **EST:** 2005
SALES (est): 15.89MM **Privately Held**
SIC: **3561** Pumps and pumping equipment
HQ: Schroff, Inc.
  170 Commerce Dr
  Warwick RI 02886
  763 204-7700

(P-5744)
SHURFLO LLC
Also Called: Pentair Water Treatment

3545 Harbor Gtwy S Ste 103, Costa Mesa (92626-1457)
PHONE.....................714 371-1550
▲ **EMP:** 430
Web: www.shurflo.com
SIC: **3561** Pumps and pumping equipment

(P-5745)
TOTAL PROCESS SOLUTIONS LLC
1400 Norris Rd, Bakersfield (93308-2232)
PHONE.....................661 829-7910
Eddie L Rice, *Managing Member*
Stan Ellis, *Managing Member**
Travis Ellis, *Managing Member**
Joey L Taylor, *Managing Member**
EMP: 30 **EST:** 2012
SALES (est): 4.45MM **Privately Held**
SIC: **3561** 3563 Cylinders, pump; Air and gas compressors including vacuum pumps

(P-5746)
XYLEM WATER SOLUTIONS USA INC
17942 Cowan, Irvine (92614-6026)
PHONE.....................949 474-1679
EMP: 53
Web: www.xylem.com
SIC: **3561** Pumps and pumping equipment
HQ: Xylem Water Solutions U.S.A., Inc.
  4828 Parkway Plz Blvd 200
  Charlotte NC 28217

(P-5747)
XYLEM WATER SYSTEMS (CALIFORNIA) INC
830 Bay Blvd Ste 101, Chula Vista (91911-1692)
PHONE.....................619 575-7466
▲ **EMP:** 26
SIC: **3561** 3443 Pumps and pumping equipment; Fabricated plate work (boiler shop)

3562 Ball And Roller Bearings

(P-5748)
CLEAN WAVE MANAGEMENT INC
Also Called: Impact Bearing
1291 Puerta Del Sol, San Clemente (92673-6310)
PHONE.....................949 370-0740
Richard D Kay Junior, *CEO*
Michael Bartlett, *
◆ **EMP:** 30 **EST:** 1006
SQ FT: 20,000
SALES (est): 4.62MM **Privately Held**
Web: www.impactbearing.com
SIC: **3562** Ball bearings and parts

(P-5749)
INDUSTRIAL TCTNICS BRINGS CORP (DH)
18301 S Santa Fe Ave, E Rncho Dmngz (90221-5519)
PHONE.....................310 537-3750
Michael J Hartnett, *CEO*
EMP: 111 **EST:** 1990
SQ FT: 70,000
SALES (est): 42.07MM
SALES (corp-wide): 1.56B **Publicly Held**
Web: www.rbcbearings.com
SIC: **3562** 5085 Roller bearings and parts; Bearings
HQ: Roller Bearing Company Of America, Inc.
  102 Willenbrock Rd

Oxford CT 06478
203 267-7001

(P-5750)
INTEGRATED ENERGY TECHNOLOGIES INC
Also Called: Doncasters Gce Integrated
1478 Santa Sierra Dr, Chula Vista (91913-2862)
PHONE.....................619 421-1151
EMP: 160
SIC: **3562** Casters

(P-5751)
NEXT POINT BEARING GROUP LLC
28364 Avenue Crocker, Valencia (91355-1250)
PHONE.....................818 988-1880
Mark Mickelson, *Managing Member*
John Burroughs, *
▲ **EMP:** 28 **EST:** 2012
SQ FT: 27,000
SALES (est): 8.29MM **Privately Held**
Web: www.nextpointbearing.com
SIC: **3562** 5085 Ball and roller bearings; Bearings

(P-5752)
NMB (USA) INC (HQ)
Also Called: NMB Tech
9730 Independence Ave, Chatsworth (91311-4323)
PHONE.....................818 709-1770
◆ **EMP:** 50 **EST:** 1983
SALES (est): 451.49MM **Privately Held**
Web: www.nmbtc.com
SIC: **3562** 5063 5084 3728 Ball bearings and parts; Motors, electric; Fans, industrial; Aircraft propellers and associated equipment
PA: Minebea Mitsumi Inc.
  1-9-3, Higashishimbashi

(P-5753)
SCHAEFFLER GROUP USA INC
34700 Pacific Coast Hwy Ste 203, Capistrano Beach (92624-1349)
PHONE.....................949 234-9799
Rich Peterson, *Brnch Mgr*
EMP: 29
SALES (corp-wide): 66.25B **Privately Held**
Web: www.schaeffler.us
SIC: **3562** Ball and roller bearings
HQ: Schaeffler Group Usa Inc.
  308 Springhill Farm Rd
  Fort Mill SC 29715
  803 548-8500

(P-5754)
WEARTECH INTERNATIONAL INC
1177 N Grove St, Anaheim (92806-2110)
PHONE.....................714 683-2430
▲ **EMP:** 43
Web: www.weartech.net
SIC: **3562** 3313 3548 3496 Ball bearings and parts; Alloys, additive, except copper: not made in blast furnaces; Welding apparatus; Miscellaneous fabricated wire products

3563 Air And Gas Compressors

(P-5755)
ATLAS COPCO COMPRESSORS LLC
Also Called: Accurate Air Engineering
16207 Carmenita Rd, Cerritos
(90703-2212)
PHONE..............................562 484-6370
John T Lague, *Pr*
EMP: 35
Web: www.accurateair.com
SIC: 3563 Air and gas compressors
HQ: Atlas Copco Compressors Llc
300 Tchnlgy Ctr Way Ste
Rock Hill SC 29730
866 472-1015

(P-5756)
C M AUTOMOTIVE SYSTEMS INC (PA)
5646 W Mission Blvd, Ontario
(91762-4652)
PHONE..............................909 869-7912
Chander Mittal, *Pr*
Sameer Mittal, *CFO*
▲ EMP: 23 EST: 1986
SALES (est): 4.47MM
SALES (corp-wide): 4.47MM **Privately Held**
Web: www.cmautomotive.com
SIC: 3563 Air and gas compressors

(P-5757)
DRESSER-RAND COMPANY
18502 Dominguez Hill Dr, Rancho
Dominguez (90220-6415)
PHONE..............................310 223-0600
EMP: 43
SALES (corp-wide): 73.09B **Privately Held**
SIC: 3563 Air and gas compressors
HQ: Dresser-Rand Company
500 Paul Clark Dr
Olean NY 14870
716 375-3000

(P-5758)
KOBELCO COMPRESSORS AMER INC (DH)
1450 W Rincon St, Corona (92880)
PHONE..............................951 739-3030
Teruhiko Murata, *Pr*
◆ EMP: 260 EST: 1990
SALES (est): 55.25MM **Privately Held**
Web:
www.kobelco-machinery-energy.com
SIC: 3563 Air and gas compressors
including vacuum pumps
HQ: Kobe Steel Usa Holdings Inc.
535 Madison Ave, 5th Fl
New York NY 10022

(P-5759)
KOBELCO COMPRESSORS AMER INC
301 N Smith Ave, Corona (92878-3242)
PHONE..............................951 739-3030
EMP: 75
Web: www.kobelco-machinery-energy.com
SIC: 3563 Air and gas compressors
HQ: Kobelco Compressors America, Inc.
1450 W Rincon St
Corona CA 92880

(P-5760)
NORDSON CORPORATION
2762 Loker Ave W, Carlsbad (92010-6603)
PHONE..............................760 419-6551
Dave Padgett, *Brnch Mgr*
EMP: 81
SALES (corp-wide): 2.69B **Publicly Held**
Web: www.nordson.com
SIC: 3563 Air and gas compressors
PA: Nordson Corporation
28601 Clemens Rd
440 892-1580

(P-5761)
NORDSON CORPORATION
Also Called: Nordon Yestech
2762 Loker Ave W, Carlsbad (92010-6603)
PHONE..............................760 431-1919
Carla Loeffler, *Brnch Mgr*
EMP: 52
SALES (corp-wide): 2.69B **Publicly Held**
Web: www.nordson.com
SIC: 3563 Spraying outfits: metals, paints,
and chemicals (compressor)
PA: Nordson Corporation
28601 Clemens Rd
440 892-1580

(P-5762)
NORDSON CORPORATION
Also Called: Nordson Asymtek
2762 Loker Ave W, Carlsbad (92010-6603)
PHONE..............................760 431-1919
EMP: 212
SALES (corp-wide): 2.69B **Publicly Held**
Web: www.nordson.com
SIC: 3563 Air and gas compressors
PA: Nordson Corporation
28601 Clemens Rd
440 892-1580

(P-5763)
NORDSON MARCH INC
2762 Loker Ave W, Carlsbad (92010-6603)
PHONE..............................925 827-1240
Jerry Wilder, *Brnch Mgr*
EMP: 75
SALES (corp-wide): 2.69B **Publicly Held**
Web: www.nordson.com
SIC: 3563 Air and gas compressors
HQ: March Nordson Inc
2470 Bates Ave Ste A
Concord CA 94520
925 827-1240

(P-5764)
NORDSON TEST INSPTN AMRCAS INC
2762 Loker Ave W, Carlsbad (92010-6603)
PHONE..............................760 918-8471
Don Miller, *Pr*
Christine Schwarzmann, *
Robert E Veillette, *
EMP: 32 EST: 2002
SALES (est): 3.16MM
SALES (corp-wide): 2.69B **Publicly Held**
Web: www.nordson.com
SIC: 3563 Air and gas compressors
PA: Nordson Corporation
28601 Clemens Rd
440 892-1580

(P-5765)
SIEMENS ENERGY INC
18502 S Dominguez Hills Dr, Rancho
Dominguez (90220-6415)
PHONE..............................310 223-0660
EMP: 39
SALES (corp-wide): 38.48B **Privately Held**
Web: www.siemens-energy.com

SIC: 3563 Air and gas compressors
HQ: Siemens Energy, Inc.
4400 N Alafaya Trl
Orlando FL 32826
407 736-2000

3564 Blowers And Fans

(P-5766)
ADWEST TECHNOLOGIES INC (HQ)
Also Called: Adwest
4222 E La Palma Ave, Anaheim
(92807-1816)
PHONE..............................714 632-8595
Brian Cannon, *VP*
Craig Bayer, *
Richard Whitford, *
Maryann Erickson, *
EMP: 35 EST: 1988
SQ FT: 23,500
SALES (est): 4.72MM **Publicly Held**
SIC: 3564 3585 3826 Air purification
equipment; Heating equipment, complete;
Thermal analysis instruments, laboratory
type
PA: Ceco Environmental Corp.
5080 Spectrum Dr Ste 800e

(P-5767)
ATLAS COPCO MAFI-TRENCH CO LLC (DH)
Also Called: Atlas Copco
3037 Industrial Pkwy, Santa Maria
(93455-1807)
PHONE..............................805 928-5757
◆ EMP: 208 EST: 2007
SQ FT: 90,000
SALES (est): 49.9MM **Privately Held**
SIC: 3564 3533 8744 Turbo-blowers,
industrial; Oil and gas field machinery;
Facilities support services
HQ: Atlas Copco North America Llc
6 Century Dr Ste 310
Parsippany NJ 07054

(P-5768)
CAMFIL FARR INC
3625 Del Amo Blvd Ste 260, Torrance
(90503-1688)
PHONE..............................973 616-7300
Frank Shahin, *Prin*
EMP: 35 EST: 2010
SALES (est): 817.3K **Privately Held**
SIC: 3564 Blowers and fans

(P-5769)
ENVION LLC
14724 Ventura Blvd Fl 200, Sherman Oaks
(91403-3514)
PHONE..............................818 217-2500
▲ EMP: 85 EST: 2003
SQ FT: 36,000
SALES (est): 1.84MM
SALES (corp-wide): 3.71MM **Privately Held**
Web: www.envion.com
SIC: 3564 Air purification equipment
PA: Sylmark Inc.
7821 Orion Ave Ste 200
818 217-2000

(P-5770)
HEPA CORPORATION
3071 E Coronado St, Anaheim
(92806-2698)
PHONE..............................714 630-5700
EMP: 100 EST: 1968
SALES (est): 2.2MM **Privately Held**

Web: www.hepa.com
SIC: 3564 Air purification equipment

(P-5771)
IQAIR NORTH AMERICA INC
14351 Firestone Blvd, La Mirada
(90638-5527)
PHONE..............................877 715-4247
Glory Z Dolphin, *CEO*
Frank Hammes, *
▲ EMP: 48 EST: 1991
SQ FT: 40,000
SALES (est): 22.9MM **Privately Held**
Web: www.iqair.com
SIC: 3564 8742 5999 Air cleaning systems;
Materials mgmt. (purchasing, handling,
inventory) consultant; Air purification
equipment
PA: Icleen Entwicklungs- Und
Vertriebsanstalt Fur Umweltprodukte
C/O Jgt Treuunternehmen Reg.

(P-5772)
MACROAIR TECHNOLOGIES INC (PA)
Also Called: Macro Air Technologies
794 S Allen St, San Bernardino
(92408-2210)
P.O. Box 1467 (92324-0805)
PHONE..............................909 890-2270
TOLL FREE: 800
Edward Boyd, *CEO*
◆ EMP: 45 EST: 1979
SQ FT: 15,000
SALES (est): 19MM
SALES (corp-wide): 19MM **Privately Held**
Web: www.macroairfans.com
SIC: 3564 Ventilating fans: industrial or
commercial

(P-5773)
MARS AIR SYSTEMS LLC
Also Called: Mars Air Curtains
14716 S Broadway, Gardena (90248-1814)
PHONE..............................310 532-1555
▼ EMP: 75 EST: 1961
SALES (est): 9.34MM **Privately Held**
Web: www.marsair.com
SIC: 3564 Blowers and fans

(P-5774)
PACWEST AIR FILTER LLC
26550 Adams Ave, Murrieta (92562-7085)
PHONE..............................951 698-2228
Buddy Olds, *Managing Member*
Sarah Olds, *Managing Member*
EMP: 44 EST: 2009
SQ FT: 5,000
SALES (est): 4.74MM **Privately Held**
Web: www.pacwestfilter.com
SIC: 3564 5085 Filters, air: furnaces, air
conditioning equipment, etc.; Filters,
industrial

(P-5775)
QC MANUFACTURING INC
26040 Ynez Rd, Temecula (92591-6033)
PHONE..............................951 325-6340
Dane Stevenson, *Pr*
▲ EMP: 65 EST: 2009
SALES (est): 20.16MM **Privately Held**
Web: www.quietcoolsystems.com
SIC: 3564 Blowers and fans

(P-5776)
ROTRON INCORPORATED
Ametek Rotron
474 Raleigh Ave, El Cajon (92020-3138)
PHONE..............................619 593-7400
Fred Taylor, *Mgr*

▲ = Import ▼ = Export
◆ = Import/Export

EMP: 120
SALES (corp-wide): 6.6B **Publicly Held**
Web: www.rotron.com
SIC: 3564 Blowers and fans
HQ: Rotron Incorporated
　　55 Hasbrouck Ln
　　Woodstock NY 12498
　　845 679-2401

(P-5777)
STANDARD FILTER CORPORATION (PA)
3801 Ocean Ranch Blvd Ste 107,
Oceanside (92056-8603)
PHONE..............................866 443-3615
Tobey Wiik, *Pr*
◆ **EMP:** 26 **EST:** 1973
SALES (est): 6.22MM
SALES (corp-wide): 6.22MM **Privately Held**
Web: www.standardfilter.com
SIC: 3564 5199 Filters, air: furnaces, air conditioning equipment, etc.; Felt

(P-5778)
SUNON INC (PA)
Also Called: Eme Fan & Motor
1760 Yeager Ave, La Verne (91750-5850)
PHONE..............................714 255-0208
Yin Su Hong, *CEO*
▲ **EMP:** 30 **EST:** 1998
SALES (est): 9.25MM
SALES (corp-wide): 9.25MM **Privately Held**
Web: www.sunonusa.com
SIC: 3564 Blowers and fans

(P-5779)
TERRA UNIVERSAL INC (PA)
800 S Raymond Ave, Fullerton (92831-5234)
PHONE..............................714 526-0100
G H Sadaghiani, *CEO*
▲ **EMP:** 99 **EST:** 1975
SQ FT: 88,000
SALES (est): 41.62MM
SALES (corp-wide): 41.62MM **Privately Held**
Web: www.terrauniversal.com
SIC: 3564 3567 3569 3572 Purification and dust collection equipment; Heating units and devices, industrial: electric; Filters; Computer storage devices

(P-5780)
TRI-DIM FILTER CORPORATION
26550 Adams Ave, Murrieta (92562-7085)
PHONE..............................626 826-5003
Scott Breckenridge, *Mgr*
EMP: 30
SALES (corp-wide): 1.42MM **Privately Held**
Web: airfiltration.mann-hummel.com
SIC: 3564 Filters, air: furnaces, air conditioning equipment, etc.
HQ: Tri-Dim Filter Corporation
　　93 Industrial Dr
　　Louisa VA 23093
　　540 967-2600

(P-5781)
VENTUREDYNE LTD
Climet Instruments Company
1320 W Colton Ave, Redlands (92374-2864)
P.O. Box 1760 (92373-0543)
PHONE..............................909 793-2788
Ray Felbinger, *Mgr*
EMP: 65
SALES (corp-wide): 178 **Privately Held**

Web: www.venturedyne.com
SIC: 3564 3829 3825 3823 Blowing fans: industrial or commercial; Measuring and controlling devices, nec; Instruments to measure electricity; Process control instruments
PA: Venturedyne, Ltd.
　　600 College Ave
　　262 691-9900

(P-5782)
VORTECH ENGINEERING INC
Also Called: Vortech
1650 Pacific Ave, Oxnard (93033-2746)
PHONE..............................805 247-0226
Jim Middlebrook, *CEO*
Randolf Riley, *
▲ **EMP:** 42 **EST:** 2001
SALES (est): 10.26MM **Privately Held**
Web: www.vortechsuperchargers.com
SIC: 3564 Blowing fans: industrial or commercial

(P-5783)
VORTOX AIR TECHNOLOGY INC
121 S Indian Hill Blvd, Claremont (91711-4997)
PHONE..............................909 621-3843
EMP: 23 **EST:** 1917
SALES (est): 2.36MM **Privately Held**
Web: www.vortox.com
SIC: 3564 3444 3829 Air cleaning systems; Sheet metalwork; Measuring and controlling devices, nec

(P-5784)
WEMS INC (PA)
Also Called: Wems Electronics
4650 W Rosecrans Ave, Hawthorne (90250-6898)
P.O. Box 528 (90251-0528)
PHONE..............................310 644-0251
Ronald Hood, *CEO*
Nancy Howe, *Information Technology*
Carroll Whitney, *
Charles Wilson, *
EMP: 84 **EST:** 1960
SQ FT: 78,000
SALES (est): 20.45MM
SALES (corp-wide): 20.45MM **Privately Held**
Web: www.wems.com
SIC: 3564 3612 6513 Blowers and fans; Transformers, except electric; Apartment building operators

---

3565 Packaging Machinery

(P-5785)
ACCU-SEAL SENCORPWHITE INC
225 Bingham Dr Ste B, San Marcos (92069-1418)
EMP: 28 **EST:** 1971
SQ FT: 14,000
SALES (est): 7.38MM
SALES (corp-wide): 376.52MM **Privately Held**
Web: www.accu-seal.com
SIC: 3565 Packaging machinery
HQ: Sencorpwhite, Inc.
　　400 Kidds Hill Rd
　　Hyannis MA 02601

(P-5786)
ACCUTEK PACKAGING EQUIPMENT CO (PA)
Also Called: Kiss Packaging Systems
2980 Scott St, Vista (92081-8321)

PHONE..............................760 734-4177
Edward Chocholek, *Prin*
Drew Chocholek, *
Darren Chocholek, *
Drake Chocholek, *
◆ **EMP:** 25 **EST:** 1987
SALES (est): 9.54MM **Privately Held**
Web: www.accutekpackaging.com
SIC: 3565 Packaging machinery

(P-5787)
BELCO PACKAGING SYSTEMS INC
910 S Mountain Ave, Monrovia (91016-3641)
PHONE..............................626 357-9566
TOLL FREE: 800
Helen V Misik, *CEO*
A Michael Misik, *
▲ **EMP:** 25 **EST:** 1959
SQ FT: 35,000
SALES (est): 8.36MM **Privately Held**
Web: www.belcopackaging.com
SIC: 3565 Packing and wrapping machinery

(P-5788)
CAN LINES ENGINEERING INC (PA)
Also Called: C L E
9839 Downey Norwalk Rd, Downey (90241-5502)
PHONE..............................562 861-2996
Donald Koplien, *CEO*
Keenan Koplien, *
Erik Koplien, *
EMP: 89 **EST:** 1960
SQ FT: 40,000
SALES (est): 23.71MM
SALES (corp-wide): 23.71MM **Privately Held**
Web: www.canlines.com
SIC: 3565 3556 Canning machinery, food; Food products machinery

(P-5789)
FUTURE COMMODITIES INTL INC
Also Called: Bestpack Packaging Systems
1425 S Campus Ave, Ontario (91761-4366)
PHONE..............................888 588-2378
David L Lim, *Pr*
Chery Co Lim, *Ex VP*
▲ **EMP:** 27 **EST:** 1984
SQ FT: 27,500
SALES (est): 7.83MM **Privately Held**
Web: www.bestpack.com
SIC: 3565 Packaging machinery

(P-5790)
JACKSAM CORPORATION
Also Called: JACKSAM CORP BLACKOUT
4440 Von Karman Ave Ste 220, Newport Beach (92660-2011)
PHONE..............................800 605-3580
Mark Adams, *Pr*
Michael Sakala, *
EMP: 25 **EST:** 1989
SALES (est): 1.46MM **Privately Held**
Web: www.convectium.com
SIC: 3565 Bottling machinery: filling, capping, labeling

(P-5791)
LABEL-AIRE INC (PA)
Also Called: Label-Aire
550 Burning Tree Rd, Fullerton (92833-1449)
PHONE..............................714 449-5155
▲ **EMP:** 67 **EST:** 1968
SALES (est): 10.59MM
SALES (corp-wide): 10.59MM **Privately Held**

Web: www.label-aire.com
SIC: 3565 Labeling machines, industrial

(P-5792)
M & O PERRY INDUSTRIES INC
Also Called: Perry Industries
412 N Smith Ave, Corona (92878-4303)
PHONE..............................951 734-9838
Phillip Osterhaus, *CEO*
▲ **EMP:** 40 **EST:** 1987
SQ FT: 20,000
SALES (est): 7.67MM **Privately Held**
Web: www.moperry.com
SIC: 3565 8711 7629 5084 Packaging machinery; Engineering services; Electrical repair shops; Conveyor systems

(P-5793)
SYSTEMS TECHNOLOGY INC
Also Called: Delaware Systems Technology
1350 Riverview Dr, San Bernardino (92408-2944)
PHONE..............................909 799-9950
David R Landon, *CEO*
John G Stjohn, *
▲ **EMP:** 65 **EST:** 1998
SQ FT: 43,000
SALES (est): 2.43MM **Privately Held**
Web: www.systems-technology-inc.com
SIC: 3565 Packing and wrapping machinery

(P-5794)
UNITED BAKERY EQUIPMENT CO INC (PA)
Also Called: Hartman Slicer Div
15315 Marquardt Ave, Santa Fe Springs (90670-5709)
PHONE..............................310 635-8121
Dulce Sohm, *CFO*
◆ **EMP:** 99 **EST:** 1966
SALES (est): 19.16MM
SALES (corp-wide): 19.16MM **Privately Held**
Web: www.ubeusa.com
SIC: 3565 3556 Packaging machinery; Bakery machinery

3566 Speed Changers, Drives, And Gears

(P-5795)
MARPLES GEARS INC
1310 Mountain View Cir, Azusa (91702-1648)
PHONE..............................626 570-1744
TOLL FREE: 800
James A Phillips Iv, *CEO*
EMP: 23 **EST:** 1937
SALES (est): 6.28MM **Privately Held**
Web: www.marplesgears.com
SIC: 3566 Speed changers, drives, and gears

(P-5796)
UNIVERSAL MOTION COMPONENTS CO INC
Also Called: U M C
2920 Airway Ave, Costa Mesa (92626-6008)
PHONE..............................714 437-9600
▲ **EMP:** 50 **EST:** 1978
SALES (est): 9.32MM **Privately Held**
Web: www.umcproducts.com
SIC: 3566 5013 3523 3429 Gears, power transmission, except auto; Truck parts and accessories; Irrigation equipment, self-propelled; Marine hardware

PRODUCTS & SVCS

3567 Industrial Furnaces And Ovens

(P-5797)
CIRCLE INDUSTRIAL MFG CORP (PA)
Also Called: Cim Services
1613 W El Segundo Blvd, Compton
(90222-1024)
PHONE.............................310 638-5101
Ronald M La Forest, *Pr*
John La Forest, *
Karen La Forest, *
EMP: 23 EST: 1953
SQ FT: 3,500
SALES (est): 4.94MM
SALES (corp-wide): 4.94MM **Privately Held**
Web: www.circleindustrial.com
SIC: 3567 3542 3535 3444 Industrial furnaces and ovens; Sheet metalworking machines; Conveyors and conveying equipment; Sheet metalwork

(P-5798)
DS FIBERTECH CORP
Also Called: Interntonal Thermoproducts Div
11015 Mission Park Ct, Santee
(92071-5601)
PHONE.............................619 562-7001
Duong Minh Nguyen, *CEO*
Son Dinh Nguyen, *
Eric Ulrich, *
▲ EMP: 45 EST: 1993
SQ FT: 14,000
SALES (est): 4.42MM **Privately Held**
Web: www.dsfibertech.com
SIC: 3567 Heating units and devices, industrial: electric

(P-5799)
HEATER DESIGNS INC
2211 S Vista Ave, Bloomington
(92316-2921)
PHONE.............................909 421-0971
James Fan, *Ch*
Tom Odendahl, *
EMP: 30 EST: 1986
SQ FT: 14,500
SALES (est): 2.96MM **Privately Held**
Web: www.heaterdesigns.com
SIC: 3567 Heating units and devices, industrial: electric

(P-5800)
INDUCTION TECHNOLOGY CORP
22060 Bear Valley Rd, Apple Valley
(92308-7209)
PHONE.............................760 246-7333
EMP: 30 EST: 2019
SALES (est): 3.67MM **Privately Held**
SIC: 3567 Induction heating equipment

(P-5801)
JHAWAR INDUSTRIES LLC
Also Called: G-M Enterprises
525 Klug Cir, Corona (92878-5452)
PHONE.............................951 340-4646
Jean-francois Cloutier, *Managing Member*
▼ EMP: 41 EST: 1975
SQ FT: 50,000
SALES (est): 10.39MM **Privately Held**
SIC: 3567 Vacuum furnaces and ovens

(P-5802)
L C MILLER COMPANY
717 Monterey Pass Rd, Monterey Park
(91754-3606)

PHONE.............................323 268-3611
Dolores Naimy, *Pr*
Victor De Lucia, *
Dave Vito, *
EMP: 27 EST: 1956
SQ FT: 14,000
SALES (est): 4.91MM **Privately Held**
Web: www.lcmiller.com
SIC: 3567 3546 3625 3398 Heating units and devices, industrial: electric; Saws and sawing equipment; Industrial electrical relays and switches; Metal heat treating

(P-5803)
RAMA CORPORATION
600 W Esplanade Ave, San Jacinto
(92583-4999)
PHONE.............................951 654-7351
Peggy Renshaw, *Pr*
EMP: 45 EST: 1947
SQ FT: 25,000
SALES (est): 5.09MM
SALES (corp-wide): 8.78MM **Privately Held**
Web: www.ramacorporation.com
SIC: 3567 3634 Heating units and devices, industrial: electric; Electric housewares and fans
PA: Amark Industries, Inc.
600 W Esplanade Ave
951 654-7351

(P-5804)
W P KEITH CO INC
Also Called: Keith Co
8323 Loch Lomond Dr, Pico Rivera
(90660-2588)
PHONE.............................562 948-3636
Reto Fehr, *CEO*
Carol N Keith, *
Wendell P Keith Junior, *Pr*
▲ EMP: 25 EST: 1954
SQ FT: 19,200
SALES (est): 4.54MM **Privately Held**
Web: www.keithcompany.com
SIC: 3567 Kilns, nsk

3568 Power Transmission Equipment, Nec

(P-5805)
ANACO INC
311 Corporate Terrace Cir, Corona
(92879-6028)
PHONE.............................951 372-2732
Leon Nolen Iii, *Pr*
▲ EMP: 140 EST: 1986
SALES (est): 23.67MM
SALES (corp-wide): 970.37MM **Privately Held**
Web: www.anaco-husky.com
SIC: 3568 Couplings, shaft: rigid, flexible, universal joint, etc.
PA: Mcwane, Inc.
2900 Hwy 280 S Ste 300
205 414-3100

(P-5806)
ATR SALES INC
Also Called: Atra-Flex
110 E Garry Ave, Santa Ana (92707-4201)
PHONE.............................714 432-8411
Jerry Hauck, *CEO*
Raymond Hoyt, *
EMP: 26 EST: 1980
SQ FT: 12,000
SALES (est): 4.38MM **Privately Held**
Web: www.atra-flex.com

SIC: 3568 Couplings, shaft: rigid, flexible, universal joint, etc.
HQ: U.S. Tsubaki Holdings, Inc.
301 E Marquardt Dr
Wheeling IL 60090
847 459-9500

(P-5807)
FORWARD
13020 Pacific Promenade, Los Angeles
(90094-4017)
PHONE.............................310 962-2522
Johnny Ward, *Prin*
EMP: 38 EST: 2011
SALES (est): 1.61MM **Privately Held**
Web: www.foodforward.org
SIC: 3568 Railroad car journal bearings

(P-5808)
HELICAL PRODUCTS COMPANY INC
901 W Mccoy Ln, Santa Maria
(93455-1196)
P.O. Box 1069 (93456-1069)
PHONE.............................805 928-3851
EMP: 120
SIC: 3568 3495 3493 Couplings, shaft: rigid, flexible, universal joint, etc.; Instrument springs, precision; Steel springs, except wire

(P-5809)
HYSPAN PRECISION PRODUCTS INC (PA)
Also Called: Hyspan
1685 Brandywine Ave, Chula Vista
(91911-6097)
PHONE.............................619 421-1355
Eric Barnes, *CEO*
Donald R Heye, *
Phillip Ensz, *
Eric Barnes, *CFO*
◆ EMP: 100 EST: 1974
SQ FT: 54,000
SALES (est): 115.37MM
SALES (corp-wide): 115.37MM **Privately Held**
Web: www.hyspan.com
SIC: 3568 3496 3441 Ball joints, except aircraft and auto; Woven wire products, nec; Expansion joints (structural shapes), iron or steel

(P-5810)
INDU-ELECTRIC NORTH AMER INC (PA)
27756 Avenue Hopkins, Valencia
(91355-1222)
PHONE.............................310 578-2144
Martin Gerber, *CEO*
▲ EMP: 47 EST: 2002
SQ FT: 11,000
SALES (est): 9MM
SALES (corp-wide): 9MM **Privately Held**
Web: www.indu-electric.com
SIC: 3568 5063 Power transmission equipment, nec; Power transmission equipment, electric

(P-5811)
WEST COAST YAMAHA INC
Also Called: West Coast Motor Sports
1622 Illinois Ave, Perris (92571-9374)
PHONE.............................951 943-2061
Gerald Morris Langston, *CEO*
Margret Mckinley, *Sec*
EMP: 25 EST: 1998
SALES (est): 3.2MM **Privately Held**
Web: www.yamaha-motor.com

SIC: 3568 5571 5561 Power transmission equipment, nec; Motorcycle dealers; Recreational vehicle dealers

3569 General Industrial Machinery,

(P-5812)
AVX FILTERS CORPORATION
11144 Penrose St, Sun Valley (91352-2756)
PHONE.............................818 767-6770
John Gilbertson, *Pr*
▲ EMP: 90 EST: 1981
SQ FT: 25,000
SALES (est): 4.29MM **Privately Held**
Web: www.kyocera-avx.com
SIC: 3569 3675 Filters; Electronic capacitors
HQ: Kyocera Avx Components Corporation
1 Avx Blvd
Fountain Inn SC 29644
864 967-2150

(P-5813)
BLUELAB CORPORATION USA INC
437 S Cataract Ave, San Dimas
(91773-2973)
PHONE.............................909 599-1940
Rick Jaries, *Pr*
EMP: 50 EST: 2010
SALES (est): 2.78MM **Privately Held**
SIC: 3569 Testing chambers for altitude, temperature, ordnance, power

(P-5814)
CAMPBELL MEMBRANE TECH INC
1168 N Johnson Ave, El Cajon
(92020-1917)
PHONE.............................619 938-2481
Jeffrey Campbell, *CEO*
◆ EMP: 50 EST: 2007
SALES (est): 4.71MM **Privately Held**
Web: www.campbellsengineering.com
SIC: 3569 Filter elements, fluid, hydraulic line

(P-5815)
CAPSTONE FIRE MANAGEMENT INC (PA)
2240 Auto Park Way, Escondido
(92029-1249)
PHONE.............................760 839-2290
Jerry Dusa, *Pr*
Christopher Dusa, *
Matthew Dusa, *
EMP: 31 EST: 1989
SALES (est): 4.91MM
SALES (corp-wide): 4.91MM **Privately Held**
Web: www.capstonefire.com
SIC: 3569 Firefighting and related equipment

(P-5816)
CLAYTON MANUFACTURING COMPANY (PA)
Also Called: Clayton Industries
17477 Hurley St, City Of Industry
(91744-5106)
PHONE.............................626 443-9381
John Clayton, *Pr*
Boyd A Calvin, *
Phyllis Nielson, *
Alexander Smirnoff, *
Allen L Cluer, *
▲ EMP: 147 EST: 1930
SQ FT: 215,000
SALES (est): 48.23MM
SALES (corp-wide): 48.23MM **Privately Held**

▲ = Import ▼ = Export
◆ = Import/Export

Web: www.claytonindustries.com
SIC: 3569 3829 3511 Generators: steam, liquid oxygen, or nitrogen; Dynamometer instruments; Turbines and turbine generator sets

(P-5817)
CLAYTON MANUFACTURING INC (HQ)
17477 Hurley St, City Of Industry (91744-5106)
PHONE..............................626 443-9381
William Clayton Junior, *CEO*
Boyd A Calvin, *
Allen L Cluer, *
John Clayton, *
▼ **EMP:** 80 **EST:** 1930
SQ FT: 215,000
SALES (est): 4.55MM
SALES (corp-wide): 48.23MM **Privately Held**
Web: www.claytonindustries.com
SIC: 3569 3829 Generators: steam, liquid oxygen, or nitrogen; Dynamometer instruments
PA: Clayton Manufacturing Company
17477 Hurley St
626 443-9381

(P-5818)
DELTA DESIGN INC (HQ)
12367 Crosthwaite Cir, Poway (92064-6817)
PHONE..............................858 848-8000
Samer Aabbani, *Pr*
Charles A Schwan, *
James A Donahue, *
James Mcfarlane, *Sr VP*
Jeff Jose, *
▲ **EMP:** 400 **EST:** 1957
SQ FT: 334,000
SALES (est): 37.41MM
SALES (corp-wide): 636.32MM **Publicly Held**
Web: www.cohu.com
SIC: 3569 3825 3674 Testing chambers for altitude, temperature, ordnance, power; Test equipment for electronic and electrical circuits; Semiconductors and related devices
PA: Cohu, Inc.
12367 Crosthwaite Cir
858 848-8100

(P-5819)
DELTA TAU DATA SYSTEMS INC CAL (HQ)
Also Called: Omron Delta Tau
21314 Lassen St, Chatsworth (91311-4254)
PHONE..............................818 998-2095
Yasuto Ikuta, *Pr*
Tamara Dimitri, *
James Fornear, *
EMP: 129 **EST:** 1976
SALES (est): 21MM **Privately Held**
Web: automation.omron.com
SIC: 3569 7372 3625 3577 Robots, assembly line: industrial and commercial; Prepackaged software; Relays and industrial controls; Computer peripheral equipment, nec
PA: Omron Corporation
801,
Horikawahigashiiruminamifudodocho, Shiokojidoori, Shimogyo-

(P-5820)
ENTEGRIS GP INC
4175 Santa Fe Rd, San Luis Obispo (93401-8159)

PHONE..............................805 541-9299
Bertrand Loy, *Pr*
◆ **EMP:** 130 **EST:** 1975
SQ FT: 50,000
SALES (est): 7.57MM
SALES (corp-wide): 3.52B **Publicly Held**
Web: www.entegris.com
SIC: 3569 Gas producers, generators, and other gas related equipment
PA: Entegris, Inc.
129 Concord Rd
978 436-6500

(P-5821)
FIREBLAST GLOBAL INC
Also Called: Fireblast
41633 Eastman Dr, Murrieta (92562-7054)
PHONE..............................951 277-8319
Richard Egelin, *CEO*
EMP: 25 **EST:** 2000
SALES (est): 6.69MM **Privately Held**
Web: www.fireblast.com
SIC: 3569 8711 Firefighting apparatus; Engineering services

(P-5822)
HONEYBEE ROBOTICS LLC
398 W Washington Blvd Ste 200, Pasadena (91103-2000)
PHONE..............................510 207-4555
Stephen Gorvan, *Brnch Mgr*
EMP: 67
Web: www.honeybeerobotics.com
SIC: 3569 Filters
HQ: Honeybee Robotics, Llc
1830 Lefthand Cir
Longmont CO 80501
303 774-7613

(P-5823)
HONEYBEE ROBOTICS LLC
2408 Lincoln Ave, Altadena (91001-5436)
PHONE..............................303 774-7613
EMP: 67
Web: www.honeybeerobotics.com
SIC: 3569 Filters
HQ: Honeybee Robotics, Llc
1830 Lefthand Cir
Longmont CO 80501
303 774-7613

(P-5824)
INDUSTRIAL FIRE SPRNKLR CO INC
3845 Imperial Ave, San Diego (92113-1702)
PHONE..............................619 266-6030
L David Gandage, *Pr*
EMP: 35 **EST:** 1986
SALES (est): 4.67MM **Privately Held**
Web: www.indfire.net
SIC: 3569 1731 Sprinkler systems, fire: automatic; Fire detection and burglar alarm systems specialization

(P-5825)
JOHNSTON INTERNATIONAL CORPORATION
Also Called: Kingman Industries
14272 Chambers Rd, Tustin (92780-6994)
PHONE..............................714 542-4487
▲ **EMP:** 25 **EST:** 1970
SALES (est): 5MM **Privately Held**
Web: www.plastics.com
SIC: 3569 Assembly machines, non-metalworking

(P-5826)
KNIGHT LLC (HQ)
15340 Barranca Pkwy, Irvine (92618-2215)
PHONE..............................949 595-4800
Don Julienne, *Dir*
Diane Peterson, *Dir*
◆ **EMP:** 100 **EST:** 1972
SQ FT: 46,000
SALES (est): 23.79MM
SALES (corp-wide): 3.27B **Publicly Held**
Web: www.knightequip.com
SIC: 3569 3582 3589 Liquid automation machinery and equipment; Commercial laundry equipment; Dishwashing machines, commercial
PA: Idex Corporation
3100 Sanders Rd Ste 301
847 498-7070

(P-5827)
LUBRICATION SCIENTIFICS LLC
17651 Armstrong Ave, Irvine (92614-5727)
PHONE..............................714 557-0664
Richard Hanley, *Managing Member*
EMP: 48 **EST:** 2014
SALES (est): 5.1MM **Privately Held**
Web: www.lubricationscientifics.com
SIC: 3569 Lubricating equipment

(P-5828)
MYERS MIXERS LLC
8376 Salt Lake Ave, Cudahy (90201-5817)
PHONE..............................323 560-4723
EMP: 41 **EST:** 2014
SALES (est): 5.22MM **Privately Held**
Web: www.myersmixers.com
SIC: 3569 Centrifuges, industrial

(P-5829)
NEWLIFE2 (PA)
4855 Morabito Pl, San Luis Obispo (93401-8748)
PHONE..............................805 549-8093
Kim Boege, *CEO*
EMP: 24 **EST:** 1954
SQ FT: 7,000
SALES (est): 2.97MM
SALES (corp-wide): 2.97MM **Privately Held**
Web: www.tankcleaningmachines.com
SIC: 3569 Liquid automation machinery and equipment

(P-5830)
NORCO INDUSTRIES INC (PA)
Also Called: Flo Dynamics
365 W Victoria St, Compton (90220-6029)
PHONE..............................310 639-4000
◆ **EMP:** 137 **EST:** 1964
SALES (est): 82.94MM
SALES (corp-wide): 82.94MM **Privately Held**
Web: www.norcoind.com
SIC: 3569 2531 5085 3537 Jacks, hydraulic; Seats, automobile; Industrial supplies; Industrial trucks and tractors

(P-5831)
PACIFIC CONSOLIDATED INDS LLC
Also Called: PCI
12201 Magnolia Ave, Riverside (92503-4820)
PHONE..............................951 479-0860
Bob Eng, *Managing Member*
Paul Stevens, *
Robert Eng, *
Alicia Fernandez, *
John Horton, *
◆ **EMP:** 77 **EST:** 2003

SQ FT: 85,000
SALES (est): 23.82MM
SALES (corp-wide): 23.82MM **Privately Held**
Web: www.pcigases.com
SIC: 3569 1382 Gas separators (machinery); Oil and gas exploration services
PA: Pci Holding Company, Inc.
12201 Magnolia Ave
951 479-0860

(P-5832)
PALL CORPORATION
4116 Sorrento Valley Blvd, San Diego (92121-1407)
PHONE..............................858 455-7264
Richard Mc Donald, *Genl Mgr*
EMP: 136
SALES (corp-wide): 23.89B **Publicly Held**
Web: www.pall.com
SIC: 3569 Filters
HQ: Pall Corporation
25 Harbor Park Dr
Port Washington NY 11050
516 484-5400

(P-5833)
PREMIER FILTERS INC
Also Called: OEM
952 N Elm St, Orange (92867-5441)
PHONE..............................657 226-0091
Bob Singh, *CEO*
Bob Singh, *Admn*
EMP: 40 **EST:** 2018
SALES (est): 2.51MM **Privately Held**
Web: www.premieremc.com
SIC: 3569 Filters, general line: industrial

(P-5834)
SEPARATION ENGINEERING INC
931 S Andreasen Dr Ste A, Escondido (92029-1959)
PHONE..............................760 489-0101
Charles E Hull, *Pr*
▲ **EMP:** 28 **EST:** 1980
SQ FT: 20,000
SALES (est): 5.78MM **Privately Held**
SIC: 3569 Filters, general line: industrial

(P-5835)
STEARNS PRODUCT DEV CORP (PA)
Also Called: Doughpro
20281 Harvill Ave, Perris (92570-7235)
PHONE..............................951 657-0379
Steven Raio, *Pr*
▲ **EMP:** 91 **EST:** 1971
SQ FT: 50,000
SALES (est): 21.39MM
SALES (corp-wide): 21.39MM **Privately Held**
Web: www.proluxc.com
SIC: 3569 3444 Assembly machines, non-metalworking; Sheet metalwork

(P-5836)
WASSER FILTRATION INC (PA)
Also Called: Pacific Press
1215 N Fee Ana St, Anaheim (92807-1804)
PHONE..............................714 696-6450
Sean Duby, *Pr*
▲ **EMP:** 70 **EST:** 1987
SQ FT: 20,000
SALES (est): 4.78MM
SALES (corp-wide): 4.78MM **Privately Held**
Web: www.pacpress.com
SIC: 3569 5084 Filters, general line: industrial; Industrial machinery and equipment

(P-5837)

**WESTERN FILTER A DIVISION
OF DONALDSON COMPANY INC**

26235 Technology Dr, Valencia
(91355-1147)
P.O. Box 1299 (55440-1299)
PHONE..............................661 295-0800
▲ EMP: 100
Web: shop.donaldson.com
SIC: 3569 Filters

3571 Electronic Computers

(P-5838)

**ACME PORTABLE MACHINES
INC**

1330 Mountain View Cir, Azusa
(91702-1648)
PHONE..............................626 610-1888
James Cheng, Pr
▲ EMP: 30 EST: 1994
SQ FT: 12,200
SALES (est): 4.59MM Privately Held
Web: www.acmeportable.com
SIC: 3571 Electronic computers

(P-5839)

ALERATEC INC

21722 Lassen St, Chatsworth (91311-3623)
▲ EMP: 24 EST: 2000
SALES (est): 1.74MM Privately Held
Web: www.aleratec.com
SIC: 3571 5045 Electronic computers;
Computer peripheral equipment

(P-5840)

AMERICAN RELIANCE INC

Also Called: Amrel
789 N Fair Oaks Ave, Pasadena
(91103-3045)
PHONE..............................626 443-6818
Edward Chen, CEO
Shelly Chen, *
▲ EMP: 45 EST: 1985
SALES (est): 4.44MM Privately Held
Web: www.amrel.com
SIC: 3571 Electronic computers

(P-5841)

AP LABS INC (PA)

9477 Waples St Ste 150, San Diego
(92121-2937)
PHONE..............................800 822-7522
Thomas Sparrvik, CEO
▲ EMP: 24 EST: 2000
SQ FT: 40,000
SALES (est): 8.94MM
SALES (corp-wide): 8.94MM Privately
Held
Web: www.kontron.com
SIC: 3571 7373 Electronic computers;
Computer integrated systems design

(P-5842)

B-REEL FILMS INC

8383 Wilshire Blvd Ste 1000, Beverly Hills
(90211-2439)
PHONE..............................917 388-3836
Anders Wahlquist, Pr
EMP: 39 EST: 2007
SALES (est): 2MM Privately Held
Web: www.b-reel.com
SIC: 3571 Computers, digital, analog or
hybrid

(P-5843)

**CONTINUOUS COMPUTING
CORP**

Also Called: Ccpu
10431 Wateridge Cir Ste 110, San Diego
(92121-5703)
PHONE..............................858 882-8800
Mike Dagenais, CEO
Ron Pyles, *
Erez Barnavon, *
Robert Telles, *
Michael Coward, *
EMP: 132 EST: 1998
SQ FT: 48,000
SALES (est): 4.85MM Privately Held
SIC: 3571 3661 4812 5045 Computers,
digital, analog or hybrid; Telephone and
telegraph apparatus; Radiotelephone
communication; Computers, peripherals,
and software
HQ: Radisys Corporation
8900 Ne Walker Rd Ste 130
Hillsboro OR 97006
503 615-1100

(P-5844)

**CYBERNET MANUFACTURING
INC**

5 Holland Ste 201, Irvine (92618-2574)
PHONE..............................949 600-8000
Pouran Shoaee, CEO
Joe Divino, *
Tina Jo Wentz, *
◆ EMP: 720 EST: 1996
SALES (est): 21.54MM Privately Held
Web: www.cybernetman.com
SIC: 3571 3577 Electronic computers;
Computer peripheral equipment, nec

(P-5845)

**DYNABOOK AMERICAS INC
(HQ)**

5241 California Ave Ste 100, Irvine
(92617-3052)
PHONE..............................949 583-3000
Ikuaki Takayama, Pr
Takayuki Tono, Sr VP
James Robbins, Genl Mgr
EMP: 298 EST: 2018
SALES (est): 26.28MM Privately Held
Web: us.dynabook.com
SIC: 3571 Electronic computers
PA: Sharp Corporation
1, Takumicho, Sakai-Ku

(P-5846)

**EDGE SOLUTIONS
CONSULTING INC (PA)**

5126 Clareton Dr Ste 160, Agoura Hills
(91301-4529)
P.O. Box 661480 (91066-1480)
PHONE..............................818 591-3500
Marti Reeder, Pr
Marti R Hedge, Pr
EMP: 32 EST: 1999
SQ FT: 600
SALES (est): 8.62MM
SALES (corp-wide): 8.62MM Privately
Held
Web:
www.edgesolutionsandconsulting.com
SIC: 3571 Mainframe computers

(P-5847)

**GARNER HOLT PRODUCTIONS
INC**

Also Called: Garner Holt Productions
1255 Research Dr, Redlands (92374-4541)
PHONE..............................909 799-3030
Garner L Holt, Pr
Michelle Berg, *
EMP: 50 EST: 1977
SQ FT: 50,000

SALES (est): 12.37MM Privately Held
Web: www.garnerholt.com
SIC: 3571 Electronic computers

(P-5848)

GATEWAY INC

Also Called: Gateway
12750 Gateway Park Rd # 124, Poway
(92064-2050)
PHONE..............................858 451-9933
EMP: 46
Web: www.acer.com
SIC: 3571 Personal computers
(microcomputers)
HQ: Gateway, Inc.
7565 Irvine Center Dr # 150
Irvine CA 92618
949 471-7000

(P-5849)

GATEWAY INC (DH)

Also Called: Gateway
7565 Irvine Center Dr Ste 150, Irvine
(92618-4933)
PHONE..............................949 471-7000
Ed Coleman, CEO
Neal E West, Contrlr
John Goldsberry, CFO
Craig Calle, Treas
◆ EMP: 250 EST: 1985
SQ FT: 98,000
SALES (est): 223.23MM Privately Held
Web: www.acer.com
SIC: 3571 3577 Personal computers
(microcomputers); Computer peripheral
equipment, nec
HQ: Acer American Holdings Corp.
1730 N 1st St Ste 400
San Jose CA 95112

(P-5850)

GATEWAY US RETAIL INC

7565 Irvine Center Dr, Irvine (92618-4918)
PHONE..............................949 471-7000
Wayne R Inouye, Pr
Brian Firestone, Executive Strategy Vice
President*
▲ EMP: 29 EST: 1998
SQ FT: 147,000
SALES (est): 1.55MM Privately Held
SIC: 3571 3577 5045 Electronic computers;
Computer peripheral equipment, nec;
Computers, peripherals, and software
HQ: Gateway, Inc.
7565 Irvine Center Dr # 150
Irvine CA 92618
949 471-7000

(P-5851)

HP INC

Also Called: HP
16399 W Bernardo Dr Bldg 61, San Diego
(92127-1801)
PHONE..............................858 924-5117
Philip Liebscher, Brnch Mgr
EMP: 350
SALES (corp-wide): 53.72B Publicly Held
Web: www.hp.com
SIC: 3571 Personal computers
(microcomputers)
PA: Hp Inc.
1501 Page Mill Rd
650 857-1501

(P-5852)

I/O MAGIC CORPORATION

4 Marconi, Irvine (92618-2525)
PHONE..............................949 707-4800
Tony Shahbaz, CEO
Steve Gillings, CFO

EMP: 30 EST: 2000
SALES (est): 3.85MM Privately Held
Web: www.iomagic.com
SIC: 3571 3652 Computers, digital, analog
or hybrid; Compact laser discs, prerecorded

(P-5853)

INNERS TASKS LLC

Also Called: Remstek Corp
27708 Jefferson Ave Ste 201, Temecula
(92590-2641)
PHONE..............................951 225-9696
Jason Patrick, Managing Member
James Stewart, Managing Member
Ryan Wetmore, Managing Member
EMP: 38 EST: 2015
SALES (est): 2.48MM Privately Held
SIC: 3571 Electronic computers

(P-5854)

**INTERNATIONAL BUS MCHS
CORP**

IBM
600 Anton Blvd Ste 400, Costa Mesa
(92626-7677)
PHONE..............................714 472-2237
Jim Steele, Genl Mgr
EMP: 28
SALES (corp-wide): 61.86B Publicly Held
Web: www.ibm.com
SIC: 3571 5045 1731 Computers, digital,
analog or hybrid; Computers, nec;
Computer installation
PA: International Business Machines
Corporation
1 New Orchard Rd
914 499-1900

(P-5855)

**INTERNATIONAL BUS MCHS
CORP**

Also Called: IBM
400 N Brand Blvd Fl 7, Glendale
(91203-2364)
PHONE..............................818 553-8100
EMP: 700
SALES (corp-wide): 61.86B Publicly Held
Web: www.ibm.com
SIC: 3571 Minicomputers
PA: International Business Machines
Corporation
1 New Orchard Rd
914 499-1900

(P-5856)

ISTARUSA GROUP

727 Phillips, Rowland Heights
(91748-1147)
PHONE..............................888 989-1189
Kuo An Wang, CEO
EMP: 28 EST: 2020
SALES (est): 3.35MM Privately Held
Web: www.istarusa.com
SIC: 3571 Electronic computers

(P-5857)

IXI TECHNOLOGY INC

Also Called: Ixi Technology
22705 Savi Ranch Pkwy Ste 200, Yorba
Linda (92887-4604)
PHONE..............................714 221-5000
Michael Carter, CEO
Thomas Bell, *
EMP: 40 EST: 1986
SQ FT: 40,000
SALES (est): 11.68MM Privately Held
SIC: 3571 3672 Electronic computers;
Printed circuit boards

(P-5858)

KEY CODE MEDIA INC (PA)
270 S Flower St, Burbank (91502-2101)
PHONE.............................818 303-3900
Michael Cavanagh, *CEO*
Ka Man Chan, *
EMP: 36 EST: 2001
SQ FT: 13,000
SALES (est): 48.61MM
SALES (corp-wide): 48.61MM **Privately Held**
Web: www.keycodemedia.com
SIC: 3571 Computers, digital, analog or hybrid

(P-5859)

MAGNELL ASSOCIATE INC
Also Called: Newegg.com
17708 Rowland St, City Of Industry (91748-1119)
PHONE.............................626 271-1320
Fred Chang, *Pr*
EMP: 256
SALES (corp-wide): 2.38B **Publicly Held**
Web: www.absgamingpc.com
SIC: 3571 5961 5045 Personal computers (microcomputers); Computers and peripheral equipment, mail order; Computers, peripherals, and software
HQ: Magnell Associate, Inc.
21688 Gtwy Ctr Dr Ste 300
Diamond Bar CA 91765

(P-5860)

MATRI KART
448 W Market St, San Diego (92101-6703)
PHONE.............................858 609-0933
EMP: 50 EST: 2020
SALES (est): 2.59MM **Privately Held**
SIC: 3571 Electronic computers

(P-5861)

MEDIATEK USA INC
1 Ada Ste 200, Irvine (92618-5341)
PHONE.............................408 526-1899
EMP: 147
Web: www.mediatek.com
SIC: 3571 3674 Electronic computers; Semiconductors and related devices
HQ: Mediatek Usa Inc.
2840 Junction Ave
San Jose CA 95134
408 526-1899

(P-5862)

MERCURY COMPUTER SYSTEM INC
1815 Aston Ave Ste 107, Carlsbad (92008-7340)
PHONE.............................760 494-9600
Lance Turner, *CEO*
EMP: 35 EST: 2007
SALES (est): 2.85MM **Privately Held**
SIC: 3571 Electronic computers

(P-5863)

MICRO/SYS INC
158 W Pomona Ave, Monrovia (91016-4558)
PHONE.............................818 244-4600
Susan Wooley, *Pr*
James K Finster, *
EMP: 30 EST: 1976
SALES (est): 4.33MM **Privately Held**
Web: www.embeddedsys.com
SIC: 3571 3674 Electronic computers; Semiconductors and related devices

(P-5864)

PLANTRONICS INC
Ameriphone Products
12082 Western Ave, Garden Grove (92841-2913)
PHONE.............................714 897-0808
George Cheung, *Brnch Mgr*
EMP: 56
SALES (corp-wide): 53.72B **Publicly Held**
Web: www.hp.com
SIC: 3571 Personal computers (microcomputers)
HQ: Plantronics, Inc.
100 Enterprise Way
Scotts Valley CA 95066
831 420-3002

(P-5865)

PREMIO INC (PA)
918 Radecki Ct, City Of Industry (91748-1132)
PHONE.............................626 839-3100
Crystal Tsao, *CEO*
Tom Tsao, *
Ken Szeto, *
Eliza Leung, *
▲ EMP: 120 EST: 1989
SQ FT: 140,000
SALES (est): 41.5MM **Privately Held**
Web: www.premioinc.com
SIC: 3571 7373 7378 Personal computers (microcomputers); Computer integrated systems design; Computer maintenance and repair

(P-5866)

RUGGED SYSTEMS INC
Also Called: Core Systems
13000 Danielson St Ste Q, Poway (92064-6827)
PHONE.............................858 391-1006
Chris O Brien, *CEO*
Chris Alan Schaffner, *
EMP: 156 EST: 2006
SQ FT: 63,000
SALES (est): 10.01MM **Privately Held**
Web: www.ruggedcomputersystems.com
SIC: 3571 7373 Electronic computers; Computer integrated systems design

(P-5867)

SOLARFLARE COMMUNICATIONS INC (DH)
7505 Irvine Center Dr Ste 100, Irvine (92618-3078)
PHONE.............................949 581-6830
Russell Stern, *Pr*
Mary Jane Abalos, *
EMP: 97 EST: 2001
SQ FT: 22,097
SALES (est): 15.97MM
SALES (corp-wide): 22.68B **Publicly Held**
Web: www.xilinx.com
SIC: 3571 Electronic computers
HQ: Xilinx, Inc.
2100 Logic Dr
San Jose CA 95124
408 559-7778

(P-5868)

SOURCE CODE LLC
Also Called: Aberdeen
9808 Alburtis Ave, Santa Fe Springs (90670-3208)
PHONE.............................562 903-1500
EMP: 48
Web: www.thinkmate.com
SIC: 3571 3572 Electronic computers; Computer storage devices
PA: Source Code, Llc
232 Vanderbilt Ave

(P-5869)

SYNERGY MICROSYSTEMS INC
28965 Avenue Penn, Valencia (91355-4185)
PHONE.............................858 452-0020
Chris Wiltsey, *Dir*
EMP: 110 EST: 1985
SALES (est): 3.6MM
SALES (corp-wide): 2.85B **Publicly Held**
Web: www.curtisswright.com
SIC: 3571 Computers, digital, analog or hybrid
HQ: Curtiss-Wright Controls, Inc.
15801 Brixham Hill Ave # 200
Charlotte NC 28277
704 869-4600

(P-5870)

TERADATA OPERATIONS INC (HQ)
17095 Via Del Campo, San Diego (92127-1711)
PHONE.............................937 242-4030
Steve Mcmillan, *Pr*
EMP: 100 EST: 2007
SALES (est): 363.12MM **Publicly Held**
Web: www.teradata.com
SIC: 3571 7379 Electronic computers; Computer related consulting services
PA: Teradata Corporation
17095 Via Del Campo

(P-5871)

TOSHIBA AMER INFO SYSTEMS INC
9740 Irvine Blvd Fl 1, Irvine (92618-1651)
PHONE.............................949 583-3000
Bill Goodwin, *Mgr*
EMP: 120
Web: www.toshiba.com
SIC: 3571 Electronic computers
HQ: Toshiba America Information Systems, Inc.
1251 Ave Of The Amrcas St
New York NY 10020
949 583-3000

3572 Computer Storage Devices

(P-5872)

ADD-ON CMPT PERIPHERALS LLC
Also Called: Addon Networks
15775 Gateway Cir, Tustin (92780-6470)
PHONE.............................949 540-0200
Matt Mccormick, *CEO*
Scott Krzywicki, *
Katie Patton Ctrl, *Prin*
▲ EMP: 73 EST: 1999
SALES (est): 19.59MM
SALES (corp-wide): 12.55B **Publicly Held**
Web: www.addonnetworks.com
SIC: 3572 3577 5045 Computer storage devices; Computer peripheral equipment, nec; Computers and accessories, personal and home entertainment
PA: Amphenol Corporation
358 Hall Ave
203 265-8900

(P-5873)

AFERIN LLC
9808 Alburtis Ave, Santa Fe Springs (90670-3208)
PHONE.............................562 903-1500
▲ EMP: 48

SIC: 3572 3571 Computer storage devices; Electronic computers

(P-5874)

BNL TECHNOLOGIES INC
Also Called: Fantom Drives
22301 S Western Ave Ste 101, Torrance (90501-4155)
PHONE.............................310 320-7272
Hamid Khorsandi, *CEO*
Farhad Fred Bokhoor, *
▲ EMP: 25 EST: 1998
SALES (est): 7.57MM **Privately Held**
Web: www.fantomdrives.com
SIC: 3572 Computer storage devices

(P-5875)

CENTON ELECTRONICS INC (PA)
Also Called: Centon
27 Journey Ste 100, Aliso Viejo (92656-3320)
PHONE.............................949 855-9111
Jennifer Miscione, *CEO*
Gene Miscione, *
Laura Miscione, *
Laura Wellman, *
Janet Miscione, *
◆ EMP: 60 EST: 1978
SQ FT: 20,000
SALES (est): 9.88MM
SALES (corp-wide): 9.88MM **Privately Held**
Web: www.centon.com
SIC: 3572 5734 7379 Computer storage devices; Computer software and accessories; Computer related consulting services

(P-5876)

CERTANCE LLC (HQ)
Also Called: Quantum Corporation
141 Innovation Dr, Irvine (92617-3211)
PHONE.............................949 856-7800
Howard L Matthews, *Pr*
Donald L Waite, *
EMP: 300 EST: 2000
SALES (est): 8.54MM
SALES (corp-wide): 311.6MM **Publicly Held**
Web: www.quantum.com
SIC: 3572 Computer tape drives and components
PA: Quantum Corporation
224 Airport Pkwy Ste 550
408 944-4000

(P-5877)

COMPUCASE CORPORATION
Also Called: Orion Tech
16720 Chestnut St Ste C, City Of Industry (91748-1038)
PHONE.............................626 336-6588
Doung Fu Hsu, *Pr*
Aaron Tao, *
Phillip Liu, *
▲ EMP: 1500 EST: 1995
SQ FT: 30,000
SALES (est): 7.83MM **Privately Held**
Web: www.hecgroupusa.com
SIC: 3572 Computer storage devices
PA: Compucase Enterprise Co., Ltd.
No. 225, Lane 54, Sec. 2, An Ho Rd.

(P-5878)

GLOBAL SILICON ELECTRONICS INC
Also Called: Buslink Media
440 Cloverleaf Dr, Baldwin Park (91706-6500)

PHONE...............626 336-1888
James Djen, *CEO*
Jie Zhu, *
▲ EMP: 39 EST: 2004
SQ FT: 50,000
SALES (est): 2.19MM **Privately Held**
Web: www.buslink.com
SIC: 3572 Computer storage devices

(P-5879)
H CO COMPUTER PRODUCTS (PA)
Also Called: Thinkcp Technologies
16812 Hale Ave, Irvine (92606-5021)
PHONE...............949 833-3222
Ali Hojreh, *CEO*
Mark Hojreh, *
Saed Hojreh, *
Mohammad Hojreh, *
◆ EMP: 25 EST: 1987
SQ FT: 15,600
SALES (est): 10MM **Privately Held**
Web: www.thinkcp.com
SIC: 3572 3577 Computer storage devices; Computer peripheral equipment, nec

(P-5880)
I/OMAGIC CORPORATION (PA)
20512 Crescent Bay Dr, Lake Forest (92630-8847)
PHONE...............949 707-4800
Tony Shahbaz, *Ch Bd*
Tony Shahbaz, *Interim Chief Financial Officer*
Mary St George, *
▲ EMP: 30 EST: 1992
SQ FT: 52,000
SALES (est): 2.05MM **Privately Held**
Web: www.iomagic.com
SIC: 3572 3651 Computer storage devices; Home entertainment equipment, electronic, nec

(P-5881)
KINGSTON TECHNOLOGY COMPANY
17600 Newhope St, Fountain Valley (92708-4298)
PHONE...............310 729-3394
John Tu, *CEO*
EMP: 3000 EST: 1999
SALES (est): 3.31MM **Privately Held**
SIC: 3572 Computer storage devices

(P-5882)
LGARDE INC
15181 Woodlawn Ave, Tustin (92780-6487)
PHONE...............714 259-0771
Gayle D Bilyeu, *Ch Bd*
Constantine Cassapakis, *Pr*
Gordon Veal, *Sec*
Alan R Hirasuna, *Treas*
Mitch Thomas, *Bd of Dir*
EMP: 24 EST: 1971
SQ FT: 19,000
SALES (est): 6.49MM **Privately Held**
Web: www.lgarde.com
SIC: 3572 8731 2822 3769 Tape recorders for computers; Engineering laboratory, except testing; Acrylic rubbers, polyacrylate ; Space vehicle equipment, nec

(P-5883)
NGD SYSTEMS INC
3019 Wilshire Blvd, Santa Monica (90403-2301)
PHONE...............949 870-9148
Mohammad Nader Salessi, *CEO*
EMP: 30 EST: 2016
SALES (est): 4.88MM **Privately Held**

Web: www.ngdsystems.com
SIC: 3572 Computer storage devices

(P-5884)
QUANTUM CORPORATION
141 Innovation Dr Ste 100, Irvine (92617-3212)
PHONE...............949 856-7800
Lisa Ewbank, *Brnch Mgr*
EMP: 37
SALES (corp-wide): 311.6MM **Publicly Held**
Web: www.quantum.com
SIC: 3572 Computer storage devices
PA: Quantum Corporation
224 Airport Pkwy Ste 550
408 944-4000

(P-5885)
RADIAN MEMORY SYSTEMS INC
5010 N Pkwy Ste 205, Calabasas (91302)
PHONE...............818 222-4080
Michael Jadon, *CEO*
Brian Dexheimer, *Board Director*
Ted Samford, *Board Director*
EMP: 26 EST: 2011
SALES (est): 10MM **Privately Held**
Web: www.radianmemory.com
SIC: 3572 Computer storage devices

(P-5886)
SHAXON INDUSTRIES INC
337 W Freedom Ave, Orange (92865-2647)
PHONE...............714 779-1140
Ahmet Erdogan, *CEO*
Yuksel Acik, *
Bahadir Tulunay, *
Bekir Aydinoglu, *
Christina Rodriguez, *
▲ EMP: 85 EST: 1978
SALES (est): 15.45MM **Privately Held**
Web: www.shaxon.com
SIC: 3572 5045 3678 3661 Computer storage devices; Computers and accessories, personal and home entertainment; Electronic connectors; Telephone and telegraph apparatus

(P-5887)
SHOP4TECHCOM
Also Called: Leda Multimedia
13745 Seminole Dr, Chino (91710-5515)
PHONE...............909 248-2725
Danny Wang, *Pr*
▲ EMP: 45 EST: 1999
SQ FT: 25,500
SALES (est): 1.28MM
SALES (corp-wide): 1.28MM **Privately Held**
Web: www.shop4tech.com
SIC: 3572 5731 Computer tape drives and components; Video recorders, players, disc players, and accessories
PA: Plc Multimedia, Inc.
398 Lemon Creek Dr Ste K
909 248-2680

(P-5888)
SILICON TECH INC
Also Called: Silicontech
3009 Daimler St, Santa Ana (92705-5812)
PHONE...............949 476-1130
Manouch Moshayedi, *CEO*
Mike Moshayedi, *
Mark Moshayedi, *
EMP: 409 EST: 1998
SALES (est): 1.89MM
SALES (corp-wide): 13B **Publicly Held**
SIC: 3572 Computer storage devices
HQ: Stec, Inc.
3355 Michelson Dr Ste 100

Irvine CA 92612

(P-5889)
STEC INC (HQ)
3355 Michelson Dr Ste 100, Irvine (92612-5694)
PHONE...............415 222-9996
Stephen D Milligan, *Pr*
▲ EMP: 340 EST: 1990
SQ FT: 73,100
SALES (est): 10.97MM
SALES (corp-wide): 13B **Publicly Held**
SIC: 3572 3674 3577 Computer storage devices; Semiconductors and related devices; Computer peripheral equipment, nec
PA: Western Digital Corporation
5601 Great Oaks Pkwy
408 717-6000

(P-5890)
SYPRIS DATA SYSTEMS INC (HQ)
160 Via Verde, San Dimas (91773-3901)
PHONE...............909 962-9400
Darrell Robertson, *Pr*
▲ EMP: 50 EST: 1957
SQ FT: 30,000
SALES (est): 263.39MM
SALES (corp-wide): 136.22MM **Publicly Held**
SIC: 3572 3651 Computer tape drives and components; Tape recorders: cassette, cartridge or reel: household use
PA: Sypris Solutions, Inc.
101 Bullitt Ln Ste 450
502 329-2000

(P-5891)
US CRITICAL LLC (PA)
Also Called: US Critical
6 Orchard Ste 150, Lake Forest (92630-8352)
PHONE...............949 916-9326
Thomas Horton, *Dir*
John Lightman, *
Kurt Dunteman, *
Angela Lunt, *
EMP: 44 EST: 2013
SQ FT: 12,000
SALES (est): 4.15MM
SALES (corp-wide): 4.15MM **Privately Held**
Web: www.approvednetworks.com
SIC: 3572 Computer disk and drum drives and components

(P-5892)
VIGOBYTE TAPE CORPORATION
2498 Roll Dr Ste 916, San Diego (92154-7213)
PHONE...............866 803-8446
▲ EMP: 700
SIC: 3572 Magnetic storage devices, computer

(P-5893)
WESTERN DIGITAL CORPORATION
Also Called: Fremont Office
3337 Michelson Dr, Irvine (92612-1699)
PHONE...............949 672-7000
EMP: 31
SALES (corp-wide): 13B **Publicly Held**
Web: www.westerndigital.com
SIC: 3572 Disk drives, computer
PA: Western Digital Corporation
5601 Great Oaks Pkwy
408 717-6000

(P-5894)
ZADARA STORAGE INC
6 Venture Ste 140, Irvine (92618-3742)
PHONE...............949 251-0360
Nelson Nahum, *CEO*
Nir Ben Zvi, *
Yair Hershko, *
Vladimir Popovski, *
Doug Jury, *
▲ EMP: 80 EST: 2011
SALES (est): 8.77MM **Privately Held**
Web: www.zadara.com
SIC: 3572 Computer storage devices

3575 Computer Terminals

(P-5895)
IMC NETWORKS CORP (PA)
25531 Commercentre Dr Ste 200, Lake Forest (92630-8874)
PHONE...............949 465-3000
Jerry Roby, *Ch Bd*
Michael Dailey, *
▲ EMP: 40 EST: 1988
SQ FT: 35,000
SALES (est): 9.49MM
SALES (corp-wide): 9.49MM **Privately Held**
Web: www.opm25.com
SIC: 3575 3577 Computer terminals, monitors and components; Computer peripheral equipment, nec

(P-5896)
SMK MANUFACTURING INC
Also Called: SMK
1055 Tierra Del Rey Ste F, Chula Vista (91910-7875)
PHONE...............619 216-6400
Nobuyuki Suzuki, *CEO*
Naomasa Miyata, *VP*
Mathoru Hurukawa, *CFO*
▲ EMP: 50 EST: 1979
SQ FT: 14,688
SALES (est): 21.08MM **Privately Held**
Web: www.smkusa.com
SIC: 3575 Keyboards, computer, office machine
HQ: Smk Electronics Corporation Usa
1055 Tierra Del Rey Ste H
Chula Vista CA 91910
619 216-6400

(P-5897)
TRANSPARENT PRODUCTS INC
28064 Avenue Stanford Unit E, Valencia (91355-1160)
PHONE...............661 294-9787
Fred Bonyadian, *Pr*
John Mcvay, *Pr*
▲ EMP: 50 EST: 1992
SQ FT: 18,000
SALES (est): 8.67MM **Privately Held**
Web: www.touchpage.com
SIC: 3575 7371 Computer terminals, monitors and components; Computer software systems analysis and design, custom

---

3577 Computer Peripheral Equipment, Nec

(P-5898)
ADD-ON CMPT PERIPHERALS INC
15775 Gateway Cir, Tustin (92780-6470)
PHONE...............949 546-8200
James Patton, *CEO*

▲ = Import ▼ = Export
◆ = Import/Export

Matthew Mccormick, *VP*
Brent Loomis, *
Thomas Virden, *
▲ **EMP:** 130 **EST:** 2000
SQ FT: 11,000
SALES (est): 12.17MM **Privately Held**
Web: www.addonnetworks.com
SIC: 3577 5045 Computer peripheral
equipment, nec; Computers, peripherals,
and software

(P-5899)
ALL AMERICAN PRINT SUPPLY CO
17511 Valley View Ave, Cerritos
(90703-7002)
PHONE.................................714 616-5834
EMP: 34 **EST:** 1986
SALES (est): 1.98MM **Privately Held**
Web: www.aaprintsupplyco.com
SIC: 3577 5045 Printers, computer; Printers,
computer

(P-5900)
AMAG TECHNOLOGY INC (DH)
2205 W 126th St Ste B, Hawthorne
(90250-3367)
PHONE.................................310 518-2380
Matt Barnette, *Ch Bd*
N Keith Whitelock, *
Robert A Sawyer Junior, *Pr*
Robert Causee, *
Gary Thorington-jones, *Treas*
▲ **EMP:** 48 **EST:** 1971
SALES (est): 24.89MM
SALES (corp-wide): 2.67MM **Privately Held**
Web: www.amag.com
SIC: 3577 Decoders, computer peripheral
equipment
HQ: G4s Technology Limited
New Challenge House
Tewkesbury GLOS GL20

(P-5901)
APEM INC (HQ)
970 Park Center Dr, Vista (92081-8301)
PHONE.................................978 372-1602
Peter Brouilette, *CEO*
Laurel Pittera, *
Marc Enjalbert, *
◆ **EMP:** 30 **EST:** 2008
SALES (est): 38MM **Privately Held**
Web: www.apem.com
SIC: 3577 3679 Computer peripheral
equipment, nec; Electronic switches
PA: Idec Corporation
2-6-64, Nishimiyahara, Yodogawa-Ku

(P-5902)
APRICORN LLC
12191 Kirkham Rd, Poway (92064-6870)
PHONE.................................858 513-2000
Paul Brown, *Pr*
Michael Gordon, *
▲ **EMP:** 29 **EST:** 1983
SQ FT: 21,000
SALES (est): 7.09MM **Privately Held**
Web: www.apricorn.com
SIC: 3577 5734 Computer peripheral
equipment, nec; Computer and software
stores

(P-5903)
ATELIERE CRTIVE TECH HLDG CORP
315 S Beverly Dr Ste 315, Beverly Hills
(90212-4309)
PHONE.................................855 466-9696
Dan Goman, *CEO*

Rick Capstraw, *CRO*
EMP: 24 **EST:** 2017
SALES (est): 3.68MM **Privately Held**
SIC: 3577 Data conversion equipment,
media-to-media: computer

(P-5904)
BAR CODE SPECIALTIES INC
Also Called: Quest Solution
12272 Monarch St, Garden Grove
(92841-2907)
PHONE.................................877 411-2633
EMP: 30
Web: www.barcodespecialties.com
SIC: 3577 5045 Bar code (magnetic ink)
printers; Computer peripheral equipment

(P-5905)
BELKIN INTERNATIONAL INC (DH)
Also Called: Belkin Components
555 S Aviation Blvd Ste 180, El Segundo
(90245-4852)
PHONE.................................310 751-5100
Steven Malony, *CEO*
Chester Pipkin, *
Jasjit Jay Singh, *
◆ **EMP:** 450 **EST:** 1983
SQ FT: 218,000
SALES (est): 473.4MM **Privately Held**
Web: www.belkin.com
SIC: 3577 5045 5065 Computer peripheral
equipment, nec; Computers and
accessories, personal and home
entertainment; Intercommunication
equipment, electronic
HQ: Foxconn Interconnect Technology
Limited
C/O Conyers Trust Company
(Cayman) Limited
George Town GR CAYMAN KY1-1

(P-5906)
BEST DATA PRODUCTS INC
Also Called: Diamond Multimedia
7801 Alabama Ave, Canoga Park
(91304-4903)
PHONE.................................818 534-1414
Behrouz Zamanzadeh, *CEO*
Bruce Zaman, *
Shirley Zaman, *
▲ **EMP:** 85 **EST:** 1983
SALES (est): 9.88MM **Privately Held**
Web: www.diamondmm.com
SIC: 3577 Computer peripheral equipment,
nec

(P-5907)
BIXOLON AMERICA INC
2575 W 237th St, Torrance (90505-5216)
PHONE.................................858 764-4580
Chan Young Hwang, *CEO*
Yon H Son, *Pr*
◆ **EMP:** 23 **EST:** 2005
SALES (est): 5.19MM **Privately Held**
Web: www.bixolonusa.com
SIC: 3577 Printers, computer
PA: Bixolon Co., Ltd
344 Pangyo-Ro, Bundang-Gu

(P-5908)
CALIFORNIA DIGITAL INC (PA)
6 Saddleback Rd, Rolling Hills
(90274-5141)
P.O. Box 3399 (90510-3399)
PHONE.................................310 217-0500
Terry Reiter, *Pr*
Wade Wood, *
Floyd Pothoven, *
EMP: 67 **EST:** 1973

SQ FT: 30,000
SALES (est): 2.54MM
SALES (corp-wide): 2.54MM **Privately Held**
Web: www.florod.com
SIC: 3577 3571 3699 Computer peripheral
equipment, nec; Mainframe computers;
Electrical equipment and supplies, nec

(P-5909)
CMS PRODUCTS LLC
29620 Skyline Dr, Tehachapi (93561-8571)
PHONE.................................714 424-5520
Les Kristof, *Pr*
EMP: 40 **EST:** 2015
SALES (est): 3.58MM **Privately Held**
Web: www.cmsproducts.com
SIC: 3577 Decoders, computer peripheral
equipment

(P-5910)
CONGATEC INC
6262 Ferris Sq, San Diego (92121-3205)
PHONE.................................858 457-2600
Ronald F Mazza, *Pr*
EMP: 33 **EST:** 2008
SALES (est): 4.45MM
SALES (corp-wide): 355.83K **Privately Held**
Web: www.congatec.com
SIC: 3577 Computer peripheral equipment,
nec
HQ: Congatec Gmbh
Auwiesenstr. 5
Deggendorf BY 94469
991 270-0100

(P-5911)
CS SYSTEMS INC
Also Called: Cs Electronics
16781 Noyes Ave, Irvine (92606-5123)
PHONE.................................949 475-9100
Christian Schwartz, *Pr*
Gayle Schwartz, *
▲ **EMP:** 25 **EST:** 1982
SQ FT: 33,200
SALES (est): 4.97MM **Privately Held**
Web: www.cs-electronics.com
SIC: 3577 3677 Computer peripheral
equipment, nec; Coil windings, electronic

(P-5912)
DELKIN DEVICES INC (PA)
Also Called: Delkin Devices
13350 Kirkham Way, Poway (92064-7117)
PHONE.................................858 391-1234
◆ **EMP:** 100 **EST:** 1986
SALES (est): 13.42MM
SALES (corp-wide): 13.42MM **Privately Held**
Web: www.delkin.com
SIC: 3577 5734 3861 Computer peripheral
equipment, nec; Computer and software
stores; Photographic equipment and
supplies

(P-5913)
DELPHI DISPLAY SYSTEMS INC
3550 Hyland Ave, Costa Mesa
(92626-1438)
PHONE.................................714 825-3400
Ken Neeld, *CEO*
David Skinner, *VP Sls*
Doug Gordon, *Contrlr*
Michael Deson, *CEO*
▲ **EMP:** 55 **EST:** 1997
SQ FT: 10,000
SALES (est): 8.27MM
SALES (corp-wide): 3.87B **Publicly Held**
Web: www.delphidisplay.com

SIC: 3577 Computer peripheral equipment,
nec
PA: Toast, Inc.
333 Summer St
617 297-1005

(P-5914)
EFAXCOM (DH)
Also Called: Jetfax
6922 Hollywood Blvd Fl 5, Los Angeles
(90028-6125)
PHONE.................................323 817-3207
Ronald Brown, *Pr*
John H Harris, *INT'L Operations*
Gary P Kapner, *Vice President North
America*
EMP: 80 **EST:** 1988
SALES (est): 21.9MM
SALES (corp-wide): 1.36B **Publicly Held**
Web: www.ziffdavis.com
SIC: 3577 Computer peripheral equipment,
nec
HQ: J2 Cloud Services, Llc
700 S Flower St Fl 15
Los Angeles CA 90017

(P-5915)
EFAXCOM
Also Called: J2 Global Communications
5385 Hollister Ave Ste 208, Santa Barbara
(93111-2392)
PHONE.................................805 692-0064
Stephen Zendjahas, *Mgr*
EMP: 41
SALES (corp-wide): 1.36B **Publicly Held**
Web: www.ziffdavis.com
SIC: 3577 Computer peripheral equipment,
nec
HQ: Efax.Com
6922 Hollywood Blvd Fl 5
Los Angeles CA 90028
323 817-3207

(P-5916)
EMULEX CORPORATION (DH)
5300 California Ave, Irvine (92617-3038)
▲ **EMP:** 124 **EST:** 1979
SQ FT: 180,000
SALES (est): 31.01MM
SALES (corp-wide): 35.82B **Publicly Held**
Web: www.broadcom.com
SIC: 3577 3661 Input/output equipment,
computer; Telephone and telegraph
apparatus
HQ: Avago Technologies Wireless (U.S.A.)
Manufacturing Llc
4380 Ziegler Rd
Fort Collins CO 80525

(P-5917)
ENCRYPTED ACCESS CORPORATION
1730 Redhill Ave, Irvine (92697-0001)
PHONE.................................714 371-4125
Hirihisa Matsunaga, *Brnch Mgr*
EMP: 110
SIC: 3577 Punch card equipment: readers,
tabulators, sorters, etc.
PA: Encrypted Access Corporation
600 Anton Blvd Fl 11

(P-5918)
EPSON AMERICA INC (DH)
Also Called: Seiko Epson
3131 Katella Ave, Los Alamitos
(90720-2335)
P.O. Box 93012 (90809-3012)
PHONE.................................800 463-7766
John Lang, *Pr*
John D Lang, *

Genevieve Walker, *
◆ **EMP:** 510 **EST:** 1975
SQ FT: 163,000
SALES (est): 359.49MM **Privately Held**
Web: www.epson.com
SIC: 3577 Computer peripheral equipment, nec
HQ: U.S. Epson, Inc.
　3131 Katella Ave
　Los Alamitos CA 90720

(P-5919)
EXCE LP
Also Called: C Enterprises, Inc.
16868 Via Del Campo Ct Ste 200, San Diego (92127-1772)
PHONE..........................858 549-6340
Brian Tauber, *Pr*
Steven Yamasaki, *COO*
EMP: 64 **EST:** 1984
SALES (est): 9.81MM
SALES (corp-wide): 72.17MM **Publicly Held**
Web: www.rfindustries.com
SIC: 3577 5045 3357 3229 Computer peripheral equipment, nec; Computers and accessories, personal and home entertainment; Nonferrous wiredrawing and insulating; Pressed and blown glass, nec
PA: Rf Industries, Ltd.
　16868 Via Del Cmpo Ct Ste
　858 549-6340

(P-5920)
FINIS LLC
3347 Michelson Dr Ste 100, Irvine (92612-0661)
P.O. Box 17192 (92623)
PHONE..........................949 250-4929
EMP: 80 **EST:** 2015
SALES (est): 11.75MM
SALES (corp-wide): 32.46MM **Privately Held**
Web: www.incipio.com
SIC: 3577 Computer peripheral equipment, nec
PA: Incipio Technologies, Inc.
　190 Nwport Ctr Dr Ste 150
　888 893-1638

(P-5921)
HP IT SERVICES INCORPORATED
1506 W Flower Ave, Fullerton (92833-3952)
PHONE..........................714 844-7737
Brian White, *CEO*
EMP: 25 **EST:** 2019
SALES (est): 250K **Privately Held**
Web: www.raditservices.com
SIC: 3577 7372 7382 Computer peripheral equipment, nec; Operating systems computer software; Confinement surveillance systems maintenance and monitoring

(P-5922)
INCIPIO TECHNOLOGIES INC (PA)
Also Called: Incipio Group
　190 Newport Ctr Dr Ste 150, Irvine (92612)
P.O. Box 17192 (92623-7192)
PHONE..........................888 893-1638
Brian Stech, *CEO*
Stephen Finney, *
◆ **EMP:** 26 **EST:** 2000
SALES (est): 32.46MM
SALES (corp-wide): 32.46MM **Privately Held**
Web: www.incipio.com

SIC: 3577 Computer peripheral equipment, nec

(P-5923)
INDUSTRIAL ELCTRNIC ENGNERS IN
Also Called: Iee
13170 Telfair Ave, Sylmar (91342-3573)
PHONE..........................818 787-0311
Thomas Whinfrey, *Pr*
Thomas Whinfrey, *Pr*
Donald G Gumpertz, *Ch*
Alan R Wolen, *Sec*
▲ **EMP:** 100 **EST:** 1947
SALES (est): 22.12MM **Privately Held**
Web: www.ieeinc.com
SIC: 3577 3575 Graphic displays, except graphic terminals; Keyboards, computer, office machine

(P-5924)
INFINEON TECH AMERICAS CORP
Interntnal Rctfier/Hexget Amer
41915 Business Park Dr, Temecula (92590-3637)
PHONE..........................951 375-6008
Marc Rougee, *Brnch Mgr*
EMP: 710
SALES (corp-wide): 16.7B **Privately Held**
Web: www-blue.infineon.com
SIC: 3577 3674 Computer peripheral equipment, nec; Semiconductor circuit networks
HQ: Infineon Technologies Americas Corp.
　101 N Pacific Coast Hwy
　El Segundo CA 90245
　310 726-8200

(P-5925)
INNOVATIVE TECH & ENGRG INC
Also Called: Innov8v
2691 Richter Ave Ste 124, Irvine (92606-5124)
PHONE..........................949 955-2501
Hassan Siddiqi, *Pr*
EMP: 23 **EST:** 1997
SQ FT: 2,200
SALES (est): 728.92K **Privately Held**
Web: www.innov8v.com
SIC: 3577 5961 1731 5999 Computer peripheral equipment, nec; Computers and peripheral equipment, mail order; Safety and security specialization; Audio-visual equipment and supplies

(P-5926)
INTERNET MACHINES CORPORATION (PA)
30501 Agoura Rd Ste 203, Agoura Hills (91301-4389)
PHONE..........................818 575-2100
Christopher Hoogenboom, *CEO*
Christopher Hoogenboom, *Pr*
Frank Knuettel Ii, *CFO*
Chris Haywood, *VP Engg*
Aloke Gupta, *VP Mktg*
EMP: 70 **EST:** 1999
SQ FT: 18,500
SALES (est): 1.17MM
SALES (corp-wide): 1.17MM **Privately Held**
Web: www.internetmachines.com
SIC: 3577 Computer peripheral equipment, nec

(P-5927)
KINGSTON TECHNOLOGY CORP (PA)

17600 Newhope St, Fountain Valley (92708-4298)
PHONE..........................714 435-2600
John Tu, *CEO*
David Sun, *
▲ **EMP:** 500 **EST:** 1987
SALES (est): 1.08B **Privately Held**
Web: www.kingston.com
SIC: 3577 Computer peripheral equipment, nec

(P-5928)
LASERGRAPHICS INC
Also Called: Lasergraphics General Business
20 Ada, Irvine (92618-2303)
PHONE..........................949 753-8282
Mihai Demetrescu Ph.d., *Pr*
Stefan Demetrescu Ph.d., *Senior Vice President Research & Development*
Stefan Demetrescu, *Senior Vice President Research & Development**
David Boyd, *
▲ **EMP:** 40 **EST:** 1981
SQ FT: 20,000
SALES (est): 4.68MM **Privately Held**
Web: www.lasergraphics.com
SIC: 3577 7371 3823 Graphic displays, except graphic terminals; Custom computer programming services; Process control instruments

(P-5929)
LIVESCRIBE INC
930 Roosevelt, Irvine (92620-3664)
▲ **EMP:** 50
Web: www.livescribe.com
SIC: 3577 3951 Computer peripheral equipment, nec; Pens and mechanical pencils

(P-5930)
LOGITECH INC
3 Jenner Ste 180, Irvine (92618-3835)
PHONE..........................510 795-8500
Darrell Bracken, *Brnch Mgr*
EMP: 825
Web: www.logitech.com
SIC: 3577 Computer peripheral equipment, nec
HQ: Logitech Inc.
　3930 N 1st St
　San Jose CA 95134
　510 795-8500

(P-5931)
LOGITECH INC
2053 E Jay St, Ontario (91764-1847)
PHONE..........................972 947-7100
EMP: 260
Web: www.logitech.com
SIC: 3577 Computer peripheral equipment, nec
HQ: Logitech Inc.
　3930 N 1st St
　San Jose CA 95134
　510 795-8500

(P-5932)
LYNN PRODUCTS INC
Also Called: Pureformance Cables
2645 W 237th St, Torrance (90505-5269)
PHONE..........................310 530-5966
Hsinyu Lin, *Pr*
Eric Tseng, *
Chen Huei Tseng, *
Chun Mei Shei, *Treas*
▲ **EMP:** 1000 **EST:** 1982
SQ FT: 35,000
SALES (est): 23.35MM **Privately Held**
Web: www.lynnprod.com

SIC: 3577 3357 Computer peripheral equipment, nec; Fiber optic cable (insulated)

(P-5933)
MAD CATZ INC
Also Called: Mad Catz
10680 Treena St Ste 500, San Diego (92131-2447)
PHONE..........................858 790-5008
▲ **EMP:** 250
SIC: 3577 5734 Computer peripheral equipment, nec; Software, computer games

(P-5934)
MAGMA INC
9918 Via Pasar, San Diego (92126-4559)
PHONE..........................858 530-2511
▲ **EMP:** 30
Web: www.magma.com
SIC: 3577 Computer peripheral equipment, nec

(P-5935)
MAGTEK INC (PA)
1710 Apollo Ct, Seal Beach (90740-5617)
PHONE..........................562 546-6400
Ann Marle Hart, *Pr*
Louis E Struett, *
▲ **EMP:** 200 **EST:** 1972
SQ FT: 48,000
SALES (est): 50.18MM
SALES (corp-wide): 50.18MM **Privately Held**
Web: www.magtek.com
SIC: 3577 3674 Readers, sorters, or inscribers, magnetic ink; Semiconductors and related devices

(P-5936)
MARWAY POWER SYSTEMS INC (PA)
Also Called: Marway Power Solutions
1721 S Grand Ave, Santa Ana (92705-4808)
P.O. Box 30118 (92735-8118)
PHONE..........................714 917-6200
TOLL FREE: 800
Paul Patel, *Pr*
Kevin Jacobs, *
◆ **EMP:** 39 **EST:** 1979
SQ FT: 33,400
SALES (est): 9.7MM
SALES (corp-wide): 9.7MM **Privately Held**
Web: www.marway.com
SIC: 3577 8711 Computer peripheral equipment, nec; Engineering services

(P-5937)
METROMEDIA TECHNOLOGIES INC
311 Parkside Dr, San Fernando (91340-3036)
PHONE..........................818 552-6500
Paul Havig, *Brnch Mgr*
EMP: 26
SALES (corp-wide): 10.3MM **Privately Held**
Web: www.mmt.com
SIC: 3577 Graphic displays, except graphic terminals
PA: Metromedia Technologies, Inc.
　810 7th Ave Fl 29
　212 273-2100

(P-5938)
MOTION ENGINEERING INC (DH)
Also Called: M E I
33 S La Patera Ln, Santa Barbara (93117-3214)

PHONE..................805 696-1200
EMP: 60 **EST:** 1987
SQ FT: 21,000
SALES (est): 3.87MM
SALES (corp-wide): 6.25B **Publicly Held**
Web: www.motioneng.com
SIC: 3577 8711 3823 Computer peripheral equipment, nec; Engineering services; Process control instruments
HQ: Altra Industrial Motion Corp.
    300 Granite St Ste 201
    Braintree MA 02184
    781 917-0600

(P-5939)
MOXA AMERICAS INC
601 Valencia Ave Ste 100, Brea (92823-6357)
PHONE..................714 528-6777
Tein Shun, *CEO*
Ben Chen, *
Tein Shun Chen, *
▲ **EMP:** 50 **EST:** 2002
SQ FT: 8,000
SALES (est): 24.36MM **Privately Held**
Web: www.moxa.com
SIC: 3577 Input/output equipment, computer
PA: Moxa Inc.
    13f, No. 3, Xinbei Blvd., Sec. 4,

(P-5940)
MPD HOLDINGS INC
Also Called: Mousepad Designs
16200 Commerce Way, Cerritos (90703-2324)
PHONE..................213 210-2591
Glenn M Boghosian, *Pr*
▲ **EMP:** 34 **EST:** 1993
SALES (est): 1.21MM **Privately Held**
Web: www.mpdholdings.company
SIC: 3577 2822 Computer peripheral equipment, nec; Ethylene-propylene rubbers, EPDM polymers

(P-5941)
OLEA KIOSKS INC
13845 Artesia Blvd, Cerritos (90703-9000)
PHONE..................562 924-2644
Francisco Olea, *CEO*
Shauna Olea, *
▲ **EMP:** 54 **EST:** 1975
SQ FT: 50,000
SALES (est): 13.91MM **Privately Held**
Web: www.olea.com
SIC: 3577 Computer peripheral equipment, nec

(P-5942)
OMNIPRINT INC
1923 E Deere Ave, Santa Ana (92705-5715)
PHONE..................949 833-0080
Fardin Mostafavi, *Pr*
▲ **EMP:** 24 **EST:** 1984
SQ FT: 22,000
SALES (est): 2.63MM **Privately Held**
Web: www.omniprintinc.com
SIC: 3577 5045 Printers and plotters; Printers, computer

(P-5943)
ONE STOP SYSTEMS INC (PA)
Also Called: Oss
2235 Enterprise St Ste 110, Escondido (92029-2074)
PHONE..................760 745-9883
David Raun, *Pr*
Kenneth Potashner, *Ch Bd*
Daniel Gabel, *CFO*
Jim Ison, *CPO*

EMP: 30 **EST:** 1998
SQ FT: 29,342
SALES (est): 60.9MM
SALES (corp-wide): 60.9MM **Publicly Held**
Web: www.onestopsystems.com
SIC: 3577 3571 Computer peripheral equipment, nec; Electronic computers

(P-5944)
ONE STOP SYSTEMS INC
Also Called: Magma
2235 Enterprise St Ste 110, Escondido (92029-2074)
PHONE..................858 530-2511
Timothy Miller, *Prin*
EMP: 26
SALES (corp-wide): 60.9MM **Publicly Held**
Web: www.onestopsystems.com
SIC: 3577 Computer peripheral equipment, nec
PA: One Stop Systems, Inc.
    2235 Entp St Ste 110
    760 745-9883

(P-5945)
PRINCETON TECHNOLOGY INC
1691 Browning, Irvine (92606-4808)
PHONE..................949 851-7776
Nasir Javed, *CEO*
▲ **EMP:** 30 **EST:** 1990
SQ FT: 14,000
SALES (est): 2.37MM **Privately Held**
Web: www.princetonusa.com
SIC: 3577 5045 3674 Computer peripheral equipment, nec; Computers, peripherals, and software; Semiconductors and related devices

(P-5946)
PRINTRONIX LLC (PA)
7700 Irvine Center Dr Ste 700, Irvine (92618-3042)
PHONE..................714 368-2300
Werner Heid, *CEO*
Sean Irby, *
Bill Matthewes, *
▲ **EMP:** 50 **EST:** 1974
SALES (est): 9.65MM
SALES (corp-wide): 9.65MM **Privately Held**
Web: www.printronix.com
SIC: 3577 Printers, computer

(P-5947)
QUALITYLOGIC INC
2245 1st St Ste 103, Simi Valley (93065-0904)
PHONE..................208 424-1905
Joe Walker, *Mgr*
EMP: 109
SALES (corp-wide): 8.71MM **Privately Held**
Web: www.qualitylogic.com
SIC: 3577 8748 Computer peripheral equipment, nec; Testing services
PA: Qualitylogic, Inc.
    9576 W Emerald St
    208 424-1905

(P-5948)
RAISE 3D TECHNOLOGIES INC
43 Tesla, Irvine (92618-4603)
PHONE..................949 482-2040
Hua Feng, *CEO*
EMP: 23 **EST:** 2018
SALES (est): 9.33MM **Privately Held**
Web: www.raise3d.com

SIC: 3577 7372 7336 Printers, computer; Prepackaged software; Graphic arts and related design
PA: Shanghai Fusion Tech Co., Ltd.
    Room 402,403,404, No.68, 1688 Lane, Guoquan N. Road, Yangpu Dist

(P-5949)
RGB SYSTEMS INC (PA)
Also Called: Extron Electronics
1025 E Ball Rd Ste 100, Anaheim (92805-5957)
PHONE..................714 491-1500
Andrew C Edwards, *CEO*
◆ **EMP:** 185 **EST:** 1983
SQ FT: 160,000
SALES (est): 174.47MM
SALES (corp-wide): 174.47MM **Privately Held**
Web: www.extron.com
SIC: 3577 Computer output to microfilm units

(P-5950)
RICOH PRTG SYSTEMS AMER INC (HQ)
2390 Ward Ave Ste A, Simi Valley (93065-1897)
PHONE..................805 578-4000
Osamu Namikawa, *Pr*
Leonard Stone, *VP*
Hiroyuki Kajiyama, *Pr*
◆ **EMP:** 400 **EST:** 1962
SQ FT: 97,400
SALES (est): 30.72MM **Privately Held**
Web: rpsa.ricoh.com
SIC: 3577 3861 3955 Printers, computer; Toners, prepared photographic (not made in chemical plants); Ribbons, inked: typewriter, adding machine, register, etc.
PA: Ricoh Company, Ltd.
    1-3-6, Nakamagome

(P-5951)
RUGGED INFO TECH EQP CORP
Also Called: Ritec
25 E Easy St, Simi Valley (93065-7707)
PHONE..................805 577-9710
Carl C Stella, *Pr*
Harry P Alteri, *
Vincent Stella, *
Roger Lazer, *
◆ **EMP:** 86 **EST:** 1996
SQ FT: 25,000
SALES (est): 12MM **Privately Held**
Web: www.ritecrugged.com
SIC: 3577 Computer peripheral equipment, nec

(P-5952)
TOPAZ SYSTEMS INC (PA)
Also Called: Fsign Emcee
875 Patriot Dr Ste A, Moorpark (93021-3351)
PHONE..................805 520-8282
Anthony Zank, *Pr*
▲ **EMP:** 25 **EST:** 1995
SQ FT: 16,000
SALES (est): 12.92MM **Privately Held**
Web: www.topazsystems.com
SIC: 3577 7371 Graphic displays, except graphic terminals; Custom computer programming services

(P-5953)
TRI-NET TECHNOLOGY INC
21709 Ferrero, Walnut (91789-5209)
PHONE..................909 598-8818
Tom Chung, *CEO*
Tom Chung, *Pr*
Lisa Chung, *

Akinori Ogawa, *
▲ **EMP:** 100 **EST:** 1992
SQ FT: 35,000
SALES (est): 3.19MM **Privately Held**
Web: www.trinetusa.com
SIC: 3577 3571 Computer peripheral equipment, nec; Electronic computers

(P-5954)
VIEWSONIC CORPORATION (PA)
Also Called: Viewsonic
10 Pointe Dr Ste 200, Brea (92821-7620)
PHONE..................909 444-8888
James Chu, *Ch Bd*
Jeff Volpe, *
Brian Igoe, *
Sung Yi, *
Bonny Cheng, *
◆ **EMP:** 140 **EST:** 1987
SQ FT: 298,050
SALES (est): 81.88MM
SALES (corp-wide): 81.88MM **Privately Held**
Web: www.viewsonic.com
SIC: 3577 3575 5045 Computer peripheral equipment, nec; Computer terminals, monitors and components; Computer peripheral equipment

(P-5955)
WESTERN TELEMATIC INC
5 Sterling, Irvine (92618-2517)
PHONE..................949 586-9950
Daniel Morrison, *CEO*
Herbert Hoover Iii, *Ch Bd*
▲ **EMP:** 50 **EST:** 1964
SQ FT: 24,000
SALES (est): 8.87MM **Privately Held**
Web: www.wti.com
SIC: 3577 5065 Computer peripheral equipment, nec; Electronic parts and equipment, nec

(P-5956)
ZEBRA TECHNOLOGIES CORPORATION
Also Called: Eltron International
30601 Agoura Rd, Agoura Hills (91301-2150)
PHONE..................805 579-1800
Don Skinner, *Brnch Mgr*
EMP: 54
SALES (corp-wide): 4.58B **Publicly Held**
Web: www.zebra.com
SIC: 3577 Bar code (magnetic ink) printers
PA: Zebra Technologies Corporation
    3 Overlook Pt
    847 634-6700

3578 Calculating And Accounting Equipment

(P-5957)
ASTERES INC (PA)
10650 Treena St Ste 105, San Diego (92131-2436)
PHONE..................858 777-8600
Linda Pinney, *CEO*
Martin Bridges, *
▲ **EMP:** 26 **EST:** 2004
SALES (est): 7.73MM
SALES (corp-wide): 7.73MM **Privately Held**
Web: www.asteres.com
SIC: 3578 Cash registers

PRODUCTS & SVCS

(P-5958)
SUZHOU SOUTH
18351 Colima Rd Ste 82, Rowland Heights
(91748-2791)
PHONE.....................626 322-0101
Joel Wynne, *Dir*
EMP: 300 EST: 2017
SALES (est): 2.32MM **Privately Held**
SIC: 3578 Banking machines

3579 Office Machines, Nec

(P-5959)
RICOH ELECTRONICS INC
17482 Pullman St, Irvine (92614-5527)
PHONE.....................714 259-1220
Paul Bakonyi, *Mgr*
EMP: 116
SQ FT: 49,359
Web: rei.ricoh.com
SIC: 3579 3571 Mailing, letter handling, and
addressing machines; Electronic computers
HQ: Ricoh Electronics, Inc.
1125 Hurricane Shoals Rd
Lawrenceville GA 30043
714 566-2500

(P-5960)
SOLARIS PAPER INC
505 N Euclid St Ste 630, Anaheim
(92801-5506)
PHONE.....................714 687-6657
▲ EMP: 197 EST: 2005
SALES (est): 748.42K **Privately Held**
Web: www.solarispaper.com
SIC: 3579 Paper handling machines
HQ: Solaris Paper, Inc.
770 The Cy Dr S Ste 3000
Orange CA 92868

3581 Automatic Vending Machines

(P-5961)
AVT INC
341 Bonnie Cir Ste 102, Corona
(92880-2895)
PHONE.....................951 737-1057
▲ EMP: 38
Web: www.autoretail.com
SIC: 3581 Automatic vending machines

(P-5962)
IMPULSE INDUSTRIES INC
Also Called: Impulse Amusement
9281 Borden Ave, Sun Valley (91352-2034)
PHONE.....................818 767-4258
◆ EMP: 24 EST: 1986
SALES (est): 6.31MM **Privately Held**
Web: www.impulseindustries.com
SIC: 3581 3999 Automatic vending machines
; Coin-operated amusement machines

3582 Commercial Laundry Equipment

(P-5963)
DENIM-TECH LLC
375 E 2nd St Apt 604, Los Angeles
(90012-4154)
PHONE.....................323 277-8998
▲ EMP: 100
Web: www.denim-tech.com
SIC: 3582 Commercial laundry equipment

3585 Refrigeration And Heating Equipment

(P-5964)
ALLIANCE AIR PRODUCTS LLC (DH)
Also Called: Especializados Del Aire
2285 Michael Faraday Dr Ste 15, San Diego
(92154-7926)
PHONE.....................619 428-9688
Luis Plascencia, *Pr*
EMP: 47 EST: 2004
SQ FT: 3,300
SALES (est): 5.74MM **Privately Held**
Web: www.allianceairproducts.com
SIC: 3585 Air conditioning units, complete:
domestic or industrial
HQ: Daikin Applied Americas Inc.
13600 Industrial Pk Blvd
Minneapolis MN 55441
763 553-5330

(P-5965)
ALLIANCE AIR PRODUCTS LLC
9565 Heinrich Hertz Dr Ste 1, San Diego
(92154-7920)
PHONE.....................619 664-0027
EMP: 1053
Web: www.allianceairproducts.com
SIC: 3585 Refrigeration and heating
equipment
HQ: Alliance Air Products, Llc.
2285 Mchael Frday Dr Ste
San Diego CA 92154
619 428-9688

(P-5966)
AMERICAN CONDENSER & COIL LLC
Also Called: American Condenser
1628 W 139th St, Gardena (90249-3003)
PHONE.....................310 327-8600
▲ EMP: 75
Web: www.american-coil.com
SIC: 3585 Air conditioning condensers and
condensing units

(P-5967)
ANTHONY INC (DH)
Also Called: Anthony International
12391 Montero Ave, Sylmar (91342-5370)
PHONE.....................818 365-9451
Jeffrey Clark, *CEO*
Michael Murth, *
David Lautenschaelger, *
Craig Little, *
◆ EMP: 850 EST: 1998
SQ FT: 350,000
SALES (est): 486.02MM
SALES (corp-wide): 8.44B **Publicly Held**
Web: www.anthonyintl.com
SIC: 3585 Refrigeration and heating
equipment
HQ: Dover Refrigeration & Food
Equipment, Inc.
3005 Highland Pkwy # 200
Downers Grove IL 60515
513 878-4400

(P-5968)
ARI INDUSTRIES INC
Also Called: Airdyne Refrigeration
17018 Edwards Rd, Cerritos (90703-2422)
PHONE.....................714 993-3700
R Tony Bedi, *Pr*
Ruth Lee Bedi, *
EMP: 80 EST: 1995
SQ FT: 20,000

SALES (est): 3.1MM **Privately Held**
Web: www.airdyne.com
SIC: 3585 Refrigeration equipment, complete

(P-5969)
CLASSIC TENTS
Also Called: Classic Tents
19119 S Reyes Ave, Compton
(90221-5811)
PHONE.....................310 328-5060
▲ EMP: 45
Web: www.bright.com
SIC: 3585 7359 1731 Air conditioning
equipment, complete; Business machine
and electronic equipment rental services;
General electrical contractor

(P-5970)
COMMERCIAL DISPLAY SYSTEMS LLC
Also Called: C D S
17341 Sierra Hwy, Canyon Country
(91351-1625)
PHONE.....................818 361-8160
Fernando Calderon, *Managing Member*
John T Karnes, *Managing Member**
Duane Beswick, *
EMP: 30 EST: 2002
SQ FT: 17,000
SALES (est): 4.96MM **Privately Held**
Web: www.cdsdoors.net
SIC: 3585 Refrigeration and heating
equipment

(P-5971)
COMPU AIRE INC
8167 Byron Rd, Whittier (90606-2615)
PHONE.....................562 945-8971
Balbir Narang, *Pr*
Robert Narang, *
▲ EMP: 150 EST: 1980
SQ FT: 75,000
SALES (est): 6.44MM **Privately Held**
Web: www.compu-aire.com
SIC: 3585 Air conditioning units, complete:
domestic or industrial

(P-5972)
CROWNTONKA CALIFORNIA INC
Also Called: Thermal Rite
6514 E 26th St, Commerce (90040-3240)
PHONE.....................909 230-6720
Dave Jett, *Genl Mgr*
EMP: 46
Web: www.everidge.com
SIC: 3585 Refrigeration and heating
equipment
HQ: Crowntonka California, Inc.
15600 37th Ave N Ste 100
Minneapolis MN 55446
763 543-2386

(P-5973)
DAIKIN COMFORT TECH MFG LP
15024 Anacapa Rd, Victorville
(92392-2509)
PHONE.....................760 955-7770
Don Johnston, *Brnch Mgr*
EMP: 292
Web: www.goodmanmfg.com
SIC: 3585 Air conditioning equipment,
complete
HQ: Daikin Comfort Technologies
Manufacturing, L.P.
19001 Kermier Rd
Waller TX 77484
877 254-4729

(P-5974)
DATA AIRE INC (HQ)
230 W Blueridge Ave, Orange
(92865-4225)
P.O. Box 7064 (92863)
PHONE.....................800 347-2473
Duncan Moffatt, *Pr*
Edward J Altieri, *
▲ EMP: 60 EST: 1979
SALES (est): 27.32MM
SALES (corp-wide): 496.1MM **Privately
Held**
Web: www.dataaire.com
SIC: 3585 Air conditioning units, complete:
domestic or industrial
PA: Construction Specialties, Inc.
3 Werner Way
908 236-0800

(P-5975)
ELCO RFRGN SOLUTIONS LLC
Also Called: Craft
2554 Commercial St, San Diego
(92113-1132)
PHONE.....................858 888-9447
Dean Rafiee, *Ex Dir*
EMP: 5000 EST: 2014
SALES (est): 9.61MM **Privately Held**
Web: www.icraft.us
SIC: 3585 3499 3999 Refrigeration and
heating equipment; Fire- or burglary-
resistive products; Barber and beauty shop
equipment

(P-5976)
EVERIDGE INC
Also Called: Thermalrite
8886 White Oak Ave, Rancho Cucamonga
(91730-5106)
PHONE.....................909 605-6419
Chris Kahler, *Brnch Mgr*
EMP: 47
Web: www.everidge.com
SIC: 3585 Refrigeration and heating
equipment
PA: Everidge, Inc.
15600 37th Ave N Ste 100

(P-5977)
HUSSMANN CORPORATION
13770 Ramona Ave, Chino (91710-5423)
P.O. Box 5133 (91708-5133)
PHONE.....................909 590-4910
Mike Gleason, *Genl Mgr*
EMP: 350
Web: www.hussmann.com
SIC: 3585 7623 Refrigeration and heating
equipment; Refrigeration service and repair
HQ: Hussmann Corporation
12999 St Charles Rock Rd
Bridgeton MO 63044
314 291-2000

(P-5978)
MESTEK INC
Also Called: Anemostat Products
1220 E Watson Center Rd, Carson
(90745-4206)
PHONE.....................310 835-7500
Chang Hung, *Mgr*
EMP: 200
SALES (corp-wide): 689.94MM **Privately
Held**
Web: www.mestek.com
SIC: 3585 3549 3542 3354 Heating
equipment, complete; Metalworking
machinery, nec; Punching, shearing, and
bending machines; Shapes, extruded
aluminum, nec
PA: Mestek, Inc.
260 N Elm St

413 568-9571

(P-5979)
PAC-REFCO INC
Also Called: Pacific Refrigerator Company
2230 Ottawa Rd Ste A, Apple Valley
(92307)
PHONE................................760 956-8600
John Gomez, *Pr*
Kim Lipka, *
Paul Jett, *
EMP: 25 **EST:** 1944
SQ FT: 25,000
SALES (est): 2.49MM **Privately Held**
SIC: 3585 Refrigeration equipment, complete

(P-5980)
R-COLD INC
1221 S G St, Perris (92570-2477)
PHONE................................951 436-5476
Michael Mulcahy, *Pr*
Ernest Gaston, *
EMP: 65 **EST:** 1982
SQ FT: 28,000
SALES (est): 10.84MM **Privately Held**
Web: www.r-cold.com
SIC: 3585 1541 Refrigeration and heating
equipment; Industrial buildings and
warehouses

(P-5981)
RAHN INDUSTRIES
INCORPORATED (PA)
Also Called: Rahn Industries
2630 Pacific Park Dr, Whittier (90601-1611)
PHONE................................562 908-0680
John Hancock, *Pr*
Jeff Meier, *
Claudia Maytum, *
▲ **EMP:** 46 **EST:** 1979
SQ FT: 25,000
SALES (est): 9.29MM
SALES (corp-wide): 9.29MM **Privately
Held**
Web: www.rahnindustries.com
SIC: 3585 Refrigeration and heating
equipment

(P-5982)
REFRIGERATOR
MANUFACTURERS LLC
Also Called: Airdyne Refrigeration
17018 Edwards Rd, Cerritos (90703-2422)
PHONE................................562 926-2006
Tony Bedi, *Pr*
EMP: 47 **EST:** 2015
SALES (est): 5.99MM **Privately Held**
Web: www.rml-econocold.com
SIC: 3585 Condensers, refrigeration

(P 5083)
SEAWARD PRODUCTS CORP
3721 Capitol Ave, City Of Industry
(90601-1732)
PHONE................................562 699-7997
◆ **EMP:** 55 **EST:** 1975
SALES (est): 465.37K **Privately Held**
SIC: 3585 3634 Heating equipment,
complete; Hot plates, electric

(P-5984)
TEAM AIR INC (PA)
Also Called: Team Air Conditioning Eqp
12771 Brown Ave, Riverside (92509-1831)
PHONE................................909 823-1957
Thirusenthil Nathan, *Pr*
Oliver Corbala, *
EMP: 35 **EST:** 1999
SALES (est): 8.2MM **Privately Held**

Web: www.teamairinc.com
SIC: 3585 Air conditioning equipment,
complete

(P-5985)
THERMOCRAFT
2554 Commercial St, San Diego
(92113-1132)
PHONE................................619 813-2985
Dean Rafiee, *Pr*
Dean Ideen Rafiee, *
EMP: 100 **EST:** 2016
SALES (est): 1.87MM **Privately Held**
SIC: 3585 5078 5031 Refrigeration and
heating equipment; Commercial
refrigeration equipment; Doors, garage

(P-5986)
TRANE US INC
Also Called: Trane
20450 E Walnut Dr N, Walnut (91789-2921)
PHONE................................626 913-7913
EMP: 26
Web: www.trane.com
SIC: 3585 Refrigeration and heating
equipment
HQ: Trane U.S. Inc.
800-E Beaty St
Davidson NC 28036
704 655-4000

(P-5987)
TRANE US INC
Also Called: Trane
3565 Corporate Ct Fl 1, San Diego
(92123-2415)
PHONE................................858 292-0833
Tyler Clemmer, *Brnch Mgr*
EMP: 132
Web: www.trane.com
SIC: 3585 Refrigeration and heating
equipment
HQ: Trane U.S. Inc.
800-E Beaty St
Davidson NC 28036
704 655-4000

(P-5988)
TRANE US INC
Also Called: Southern California Trane
3253 E Imperial Hwy, Brea (92821-6722)
PHONE................................626 913-7123
John Clark, *Brnch Mgr*
EMP: 100
Web: www.trane.com
SIC: 3585 Heating and air conditioning
combination units
HQ: Trane US Inc.
800-E Beaty St
Davidson NC 28036
704 655-4000

(P-5989)
TRUMED SYSTEMS
INCORPORATED
4370 La Jolla Village Dr Ste 200, San Diego
(92122-1250)
PHONE................................844 878-6331
Jesper Jensen, *CEO*
Jesper Jensen, *Pr*
Joe Milkovits, *
Jim Martindale, *Field Operations Vice
President*
EMP: 29 **EST:** 2013
SALES (est): 9.62MM **Privately Held**
Web: www.trumedsystems.com
SIC: 3585 5078 Refrigeration and heating
equipment; Commercial refrigeration
equipment

(P-5990)
UTILITY REFRIGERATOR
12160 Sherman Way, North Hollywood
(91605-5501)
P.O. Box 570782 (91357-0782)
PHONE................................818 764-6200
Michael Michrowski, *Pr*
▲ **EMP:** 25 **EST:** 2007
SALES (est): 4.12MM **Privately Held**
Web: www.utilityrefrigerator.com
SIC: 3585 Parts for heating, cooling, and
refrigerating equipment

(P-5991)
VEGE-MIST INC
Also Called: Alco Designs
407 E Redondo Beach Blvd, Gardena
(90248-2312)
PHONE................................310 353-2300
Samuel Cohen, *CEO*
▲ **EMP:** 61 **EST:** 1988
SQ FT: 8,000
SALES (est): 7.68MM **Privately Held**
Web: www.alcodesigns.com
SIC: 3585 2541 5074 2542 Humidifying
equipment, except portable; Store and
office display cases and fixtures; Water
purification equipment; Partitions and
fixtures, except wood

(P-5992)
WELBILT FDSRVICE
COMPANIES LLC
Also Called: Chester Paul Company
1210 N Red Gum St, Anaheim
(92806-1820)
PHONE................................323 245-3761
EMP: 281
SALES (corp-wide): 4.8B **Privately Held**
Web: direct.welbilt.us
SIC: 3585 Refrigeration and heating
equipment
HQ: Welbilt Foodservice Companies, Llc
2227 Welbilt Blvd
Trinity FL 34655

(P-5993)
WILLIAMS FURNACE CO (DH)
Also Called: Williams Comfort Products
250 W Laurel St, Colton (92324-1435)
PHONE................................562 450-3602
Michael Markowich, *Pr*
James Gidwitz, *
Joseph Sum, *
Mark Nichter, *
Ruth Ann Davis, *
▲ **EMP:** 173 **EST:** 1916
SQ FT: 400,000
SALES (est): 43.34MM
SALES (corp-wide): 113.28MM **Privately
Held**
Web: www.williamscomfort.com
SIC: 3585 3433 Refrigeration and heating
equipment; Heating equipment, except
electric
HQ: Riverbend Industries Inc.
440 S La Salle St # 3100
Chicago IL 60605
312 541-7200

3589 Service Industry
Machinery, Nec

(P-5994)
ADVANCED UV INC (PA)
16350 Manning Way, Cerritos (90703-2224)
PHONE................................562 407-0299
Kiyomitsu Kevin Toma, *CEO*
▲ **EMP:** 25 **EST:** 1996

SQ FT: 30,000
SALES (est): 9.36MM
SALES (corp-wide): 9.36MM **Privately
Held**
Web: www.advanceduv.com
SIC: 3589 Water purification equipment,
household type

(P-5995)
AMIAD USA INC
Also Called: West Coast Sales Office & Whse
1251 Maulhardt Ave, Oxnard (93030-7990)
PHONE................................805 988-3323
EMP: 23
Web: us.amiad.com
SIC: 3589 Water treatment equipment,
industrial
HQ: Amiad U.S.A., Inc.
120 Talbert Rd Ste J
Mooresville NC 28117
704 662-3133

(P-5996)
AMIAD USA INC
Also Called: Amiad Filtration Systems
1251 Maulhardt Ave, Oxnard (93030-7990)
P.O. Box 5547 (93031-5547)
PHONE................................805 988-3323
Tom Akehurst, *Pr*
Issac Orlans, *Stockholder*
▲ **EMP:** 35 **EST:** 1981
SQ FT: 30,000
SALES (est): 3.56MM **Privately Held**
Web: www.amiad.com
SIC: 3589 Water treatment equipment,
industrial
PA: Amiad Water Systems Ltd
Kibbutz

(P-5997)
AMPAC USA INC
5255 State St 5275, Montclair
(91763-6236)
PHONE................................435 291-0961
Hunter Tyson, *Prin*
EMP: 50 **EST:** 2021
SALES (est): 4.62MM **Privately Held**
Web: www.ampac1.com
SIC: 3589 Water purification equipment,
household type

(P-5998)
APPLIED MEMBRANES INC
Also Called: Wateranywhere
2450 Business Park Dr, Vista (92081-8847)
PHONE................................760 727-3711
Gulshan Dhawan, *CEO*
◆ **EMP:** 178 **EST:** 1083
SQ FT: 55,000
SALES (est): 23.81MM **Privately Held**
Web: www.appliedmembranes.com
SIC: 3589 5074 Water purification
equipment, household type; Water heaters
and purification equipment

(P-5999)
AQUA PRODUCTS INC (DH)
2882 Whiptail Loop Ste 100, Carlsbad
(92010-6758)
PHONE................................973 857-2700
Giora Erlich, *Pr*
Joseph Porat, *
Kathleen A Mcclarnon, *Sec*
◆ **EMP:** 24 **EST:** 1964
SALES (est): 6.81MM
SALES (corp-wide): 362.18K **Privately
Held**
Web: www.aquaproducts.com
SIC: 3589 Swimming pool filter and water
conditioning systems

HQ: Foridra Srl
Strada Statale 16 Adriatica 16 17/A
Castelfidardo AN 60022

(P-6000)
AQUAFINE CORPORATION (HQ)
29010 Avenue Paine, Valencia
(91355-4198)
PHONE..............................661 257-4770
Roberta Veloz, *Ch*
Michael Murphy, *
◆ **EMP:** 72 **EST:** 1949
SQ FT: 100,000
SALES (est): 24.33MM
SALES (corp-wide): 23.89B **Publicly Held**
Web: www.trojantechnologies.com
SIC: 3589 Water treatment equipment,
industrial
PA: Danaher Corporation
2200 Pa Ave Nw Ste 800w
202 828-0850

(P-6001)
AQUAMOR LLC (PA)
Also Called: Watersentinel
42188 Rio Nedo, Temecula (92590-3717)
PHONE..............................951 541-9517
▲ **EMP:** 100 **EST:** 2004
SALES (est): 14.91MM
SALES (corp-wide): 14.91MM **Privately
Held**
Web: www.aquamor.com
SIC: 3589 Water filters and softeners,
household type

(P-6002)
**AQUEOUS TECHNOLOGIES
CORP**
1678 N Maple St, Corona (92878-3206)
PHONE..............................909 944-7771
Michael Konrad, *CEO*
▲ **EMP:** 23 **EST:** 1992
SQ FT: 15,000
SALES (est): 4.2MM **Privately Held**
Web: www.aqueoustech.com
SIC: 3589 3829 5084 7699 High pressure
cleaning equipment; Physical property
testing equipment; Cleaning equipment,
high pressure, sand or steam; Industrial
machinery and equipment repair

(P-6003)
AXEON WATER TECHNOLOGIES
40980 County Center Dr Ste 100, Temecula
(92591-6002)
PHONE..............................760 723-5417
Augustin R Pavel, *Pr*
Jeanette Pavel, *
◆ **EMP:** 85 **EST:** 1989
SQ FT: 47,000
SALES (est): 24.17MM **Privately Held**
Web: www.axeonwater.com
SIC: 3589 5999 Water filters and softeners,
household type; Water purification
equipment

(P-6004)
**BLUE DESERT INTERNATIONAL
INC**
Also Called: Hydro Quip
510 N Sheridan St Ste A, Corona
(92878-4024)
PHONE..............................951 273-7575
Christopher W Kuttig, *Pr*
◆ **EMP:** 80 **EST:** 1994
SQ FT: 31,000
SALES (est): 8.14MM **Privately Held**
Web: www.hydroquip.com
SIC: 3589 Swimming pool filter and water
conditioning systems

(P-6005)
**CHEMICAL METHODS ASSOC
LLC (DH)**
Also Called: CMA Dish Machines
17707 Valley View Ave, Cerritos
(90703-7004)
PHONE..............................714 898-8781
Fred G Palmer, *Pr*
▲ **EMP:** 30 **EST:** 1970
SALES (est): 13.4MM
SALES (corp-wide): 4.8B **Privately Held**
Web: www.cmadishmachines.com
SIC: 3589 Dishwashing machines,
commercial
HQ: Ali Group North America Corporation
101 Corporate Woods Pkwy
Vernon Hills IL 60061
847 215-6565

(P-6006)
CITY OF DELANO
Also Called: Delano Waste Water Treatment
1107 Lytle Ave, Delano (93215-9389)
PHONE..............................661 721-3352
Bill Hylton, *Mgr*
EMP: 28
SALES (corp-wide): 39.7MM **Privately
Held**
Web: www.cityofdelano.org
SIC: 3589 Water treatment equipment,
industrial
PA: City Of Delano
1015 11th Ave
661 721-3300

(P-6007)
CITY OF RIVERSIDE
Also Called: Water Treatment Plant
5950 Acorn St, Riverside (92504-1036)
PHONE..............................951 351-6140
Richard Pallante, *Genl Mgr*
EMP: 125
Web: www.riversideca.gov
SIC: 3589 9111 Water treatment equipment,
industrial; Mayors' office
PA: City Of Riverside
3900 Main St 7 Fl
951 826-5311

(P-6008)
CITY OF SANTA MONICA
Also Called: City Snta Mnica Wtr Trtmnt Pla
1228 S Bundy Dr, Los Angeles
(90025-1102)
PHONE..............................310 826-6712
Myriam Cardenas, *Brnch Mgr*
EMP: 236
SQ FT: 2,500
SALES (corp-wide): 546.23MM **Privately
Held**
Web: www.santamonica.gov
SIC: 3589 Sewage and water treatment
equipment
PA: City Of Santa Monica
1685 Main St
310 458-8411

(P-6009)
**CLEAN WATER TECHNOLOGY
INC (HQ)**
Also Called: CWT
13008 S Western Ave, Gardena
(90249-1920)
PHONE..............................310 380-4648
Ariel Lechter, *CEO*
Gerald Friedman, *
▲ **EMP:** 50 **EST:** 1996
SALES (est): 13.83MM
SALES (corp-wide): 149.54MM **Privately
Held**

Web: www.cwt-global.com
SIC: 3589 Water treatment equipment,
industrial
PA: Marvin Engineering Co., Inc.
261 W Beach Ave
310 674-5030

(P-6010)
COMCO INC
2151 N Lincoln St, Burbank (91504-3392)
PHONE..............................818 333-8500
Colin Weightman, *Pr*
EMP: 36 **EST:** 1965
SQ FT: 12,500
SALES (est): 8.03MM **Privately Held**
Web: www.comcoinc.com
SIC: 3589 3291 Sandblasting equipment;
Abrasive products

(P-6011)
**COMPASS WATER SOLUTIONS
INC (HQ)**
15542 Mosher Ave, Tustin (92780-6425)
PHONE..............................949 222-5777
Thomas Farshler, *CEO*
Bill Tidmore, *
▲ **EMP:** 50 **EST:** 1983
SQ FT: 3,000
SALES (est): 11.08MM **Publicly Held**
Web: www.compasswater.com
SIC: 3589 Water treatment equipment,
industrial
PA: Ceco Environmental Corp.
5080 Spectrum Dr Ste 800e

(P-6012)
**DYNAMIC COOKING SYSTEMS
INC**
Also Called: Fisher & Paykel
695 Town Center Dr Ste 180, Costa Mesa
(92626-1902)
PHONE..............................714 372-7000
Laurence Mawhinney, *CEO*
Stuart Broadhurst, *
▲ **EMP:** 700 **EST:** 1987
SQ FT: 140,000
SALES (est): 29.65MM **Privately Held**
SIC: 3589 Cooking equipment, commercial
HQ: Fisher & Paykel Appliances Usa
Holdings Inc.
695 Town Center Dr # 180
Costa Mesa CA 92626

(P-6013)
ENGINEERED FOOD SYSTEMS
2490 Anselmo Dr, Corona (92879-8089)
P.O. Box 28321 (92809-0144)
PHONE..............................714 921-9913
Martin Olguin, *Pr*
Irma Olguin, *
▲ **EMP:** 25 **EST:** 2008
SQ FT: 18,000
SALES (est): 4.51MM **Privately Held**
Web: www.efs-eng.com
SIC: 3589 5084 Food warming equipment,
commercial; Food product manufacturing
machinery

(P-6014)
**FLUIDRA NORTH AMERICA LLC
(HQ)**
Also Called: Zodiac Pool Solutions
2882 Whiptail Loop Ste 100, Carlsbad
(92010-6758)
PHONE..............................760 599-9600
Lennie Rhodes, *Pr*
EMP: 61 **EST:** 2016
SALES (est): 489.08MM **Privately Held**
Web: www.fluidrausa.com

SIC: 3589 Swimming pool filter and water
conditioning systems
PA: Fluidra, Sa
Avenida Alcalde Barnils 69

(P-6015)
GORLITZ SEWER & DRAIN INC
10132 Norwalk Blvd, Santa Fe Springs
(90670-3326)
PHONE..............................562 944-3060
James Kruger, *CEO*
Gerd Kruger, *
Elba Kruger, *
▲ **EMP:** 30 **EST:** 1974
SQ FT: 33,300
SALES (est): 5.06MM **Privately Held**
Web: www.gorlitz.com
SIC: 3589 Sewer cleaning equipment, power

(P-6016)
**J F DUNCAN INDUSTRIES INC
(PA)**
Also Called: Duray
4380 Ayers Ave, Vernon (90058-4306)
PHONE..............................562 862-4269
Johnny F Wong, *CEO*
Don Durward, *
▲ **EMP:** 48 **EST:** 1988
SALES (est): 21.51MM **Privately Held**
Web: www.durayduncan.com
SIC: 3589 Cooking equipment, commercial

(P-6017)
JACUZZI INC (DH)
Also Called: Jacuzzi Outdoor Products
17872 Gillette Ave Ste 300, Irvine
(92614-6573)
PHONE..............................909 606-7733
Roy A Jacuzzi, *Ch Bd*
Thomas Koos, *
Donald C Devine, *
◆ **EMP:** 110 **EST:** 1979
SALES (est): 457.27MM
SALES (corp-wide): 430.34K **Privately
Held**
Web: www.jacuzzi.com
SIC: 3589 3088 Swimming pool filter and
water conditioning systems; Hot tubs,
plastics or fiberglass
HQ: Jacuzzi Brands Llc
17872 Gllette Ave Ste 300
Irvine CA 92614
909 606-1416

(P-6018)
JWC ENVIRONMENTAL INC
Also Called: Disposable Waste System
2600 S Garnsey St, Santa Ana
(92707-3339)
PHONE..............................714 662-5829
Steve Glomb, *CFO*
EMP: 100
SQ FT: 45,637
Web: www.jwce.com
SIC: 3589 Sewage treatment equipment
HQ: Jwc Environmental Inc.
2850 Redhill Ave Ste 125
Santa Ana CA 92705

(P-6019)
**KELLERMYER BERGENSONS
SVCS LLC (PA)**
3605 Ocean Ranch Blvd Ste 200,
Oceanside (92056-2696)
PHONE..............................760 631-5111
Mark Minasian, *CEO*
Christian Cornelius-knudsen, *Pr*
Aj Long, *
Zulfiqar Rashid, *CIO*
Nathaniel Shaw, *Chief Commercial Officer*

EMP: 28 **EST:** 2001
SALES (est): 620.83MM
SALES (corp-wide): 620.83MM **Privately Held**
Web: www.kbs-services.com
SIC: 3589 Commercial cleaning equipment

(P-6020)
MANN+HMMEL WTR FLUID SLTONS IN (DH)
93 S La Patera Ln, Goleta (93117-3246)
PHONE.............................805 964-8003
Peter Knappe, *Pr*
Kevin Edberg, *
◆ **EMP:** 90 **EST:** 1990
SQ FT: 40,000
SALES (est): 29.1MM
SALES (corp-wide): 5.11B **Privately Held**
Web:
water-membrane-solutions.mann-hummel.com
SIC: 3589 Water treatment equipment, industrial
HQ: Mann+Hummel Water & Fluid
Solutions Gmbh
Kasteler Str. 45
Wiesbaden HE 65203
61171187480

(P-6021)
MAR COR PURIFICATION INC
6351 Orangethorpe Ave, Buena Park (90620-1340)
PHONE.............................800 633-3080
Sean West, *Brnch Mgr*
EMP: 27
SIC: 3589 Water treatment equipment, industrial
HQ: Mar Cor Purification, Inc.
4450 Township Line Rd
Skippack PA 19474
800 633-3080

(P-6022)
MAZZEI INJECTOR COMPANY LLC
500 Rooster Dr, Bakersfield (93307-9555)
PHONE.............................661 363-6500
Angelo Mazzei, *CEO*
Geofffrey Whynot, *Pr*
Mary Mazzei, *Bd of Dir*
▲ **EMP:** 24 **EST:** 1978
SALES (est): 2.51MM
SALES (corp-wide): 4.19MM **Privately Held**
Web: www.mazzei.net
SIC: 3589 Water treatment equipment, industrial
PA: Mazzei Injector Corporation
500 Rooster Dr
661 363-6500

(P-6023)
MEISSNER MFG CO INC (PA)
Also Called: Unicel
21701 Prairie St, Chatsworth (91311-5835)
PHONE.............................818 678-0400
EMP: 53 **EST:** 1958
SALES (est): 7.84MM
SALES (corp-wide): 7.84MM **Privately Held**
SIC: 3589 Swimming pool filter and water conditioning systems

(P-6024)
MYTEE PRODUCTS INC
13655 Stowe Dr, Poway (92064-6873)
PHONE.............................858 679-1191
John La Barbera, *Pr*
Paul La Barbera, *

Gina La Barbera, *
◆ **EMP:** 43 **EST:** 1991
SQ FT: 45,000
SALES (est): 8.91MM **Privately Held**
Web: www.mytee.com
SIC: 3589 Commercial cleaning equipment

(P-6025)
N/S CORPORATION (PA)
Also Called: NS Wash Systems
28309 Avenue Crocker, Valencia (91355-1251)
PHONE.............................310 412-7074
G Thomas Ennis Senior, *CEO*
Francis Penggardjaja, *
Lumen Ong, *
◆ **EMP:** 84 **EST:** 1967
SQ FT: 80,000
SALES (est): 20.74MM
SALES (corp-wide): 20.74MM **Privately Held**
Web: www.nswash.com
SIC: 3589 Car washing machinery

(P-6026)
NALCO WTR PRTRTMENT SLTONS LLC
Also Called: Nalco Water
1961 Petra Ln, Placentia (92870-6749)
PHONE.............................714 792-0708
EMP: 28
SALES (corp-wide): 15.32B **Publicly Held**
SIC: 3589 Water treatment equipment, industrial
HQ: Nalco Water Pretreatment Solutions, Llc
1601 W Diehl Rd
Naperville IL 60563
708 754-2550

(P-6027)
PRODUCT SOLUTIONS INC
1182 N Knollwood Cir, Anaheim (92801-1307)
P.O. Box 6601 (92607-6601)
PHONE.............................714 545-9757
Robert Kreaton, *CEO*
Judith Keaton, *
▲ **EMP:** 50 **EST:** 1993
SQ FT: 25,000
SALES (est): 4.76MM **Privately Held**
Web: www.fastproductsolutions.com
SIC: 3589 3631 Commercial cooking and foodwarming equipment; Household cooking equipment

(P-6028)
PRONTO PRODUCTS CO (PA)
9850 Siempre Viva Rd, San Diego (92154-7247)
PHONE.............................619 661-6995
Carlos Matos, *CEO*
William E Parrot, *
Martha J Wagner, *
Barbara Parrot, *
EMP: 39 **EST:** 1962
SALES (est): 4.42MM
SALES (corp-wide): 4.42MM **Privately Held**
Web: www.prontoproducts.com
SIC: 3589 3496 Commercial cooking and foodwarming equipment; Miscellaneous fabricated wire products

(P-6029)
QMP INC
25070 Avenue Tibbitts, Valencia (91355-3447)
PHONE.............................661 294-6860
Freddy Vidal, *Pr*

Irma Vidal, *
▲ **EMP:** 45 **EST:** 1994
SQ FT: 40,000
SALES (est): 4.65MM **Privately Held**
Web: www.qmpusa.com
SIC: 3589 Sewage and water treatment equipment

(P-6030)
SEACO TECHNOLOGIES INC
280 El Cerrito Dr, Bakersfield (93305-1328)
PHONE.............................661 326-1522
Bob Beck, *Brnch Mgr*
EMP: 28
Web: www.seacotech.com
SIC: 3589 Water treatment equipment, industrial
PA: Seaco Technologies, Inc.
3220 Patton Way

(P-6031)
SEWER RODDING EQUIPMENT CO (PA)
Also Called: Flexible Video Systems
3217 Carter Ave, Marina Del Rey (90292-5554)
PHONE.............................310 301-9009
Patrick Crane, *CEO*
EMP: 25 **EST:** 1932
SQ FT: 24,000
SALES (est): 2.28MM
SALES (corp-wide): 2.28MM **Privately Held**
SIC: 3589 Sewer cleaning equipment, power

(P-6032)
SHEPARD BROS INC (PA)
503 S Cypress St, La Habra (90631-6126)
PHONE.............................562 697-1366
Ronald Shepard, *CEO*
Duane Shepard, *
Jon Wynkoop, *
▲ **EMP:** 119 **EST:** 1976
SQ FT: 57,830
SALES (est): 23.33MM
SALES (corp-wide): 23.33MM **Privately Held**
Web: www.shepardbros.com
SIC: 3589 5169 Sewage and water treatment equipment; Chemicals and allied products, nec

(P-6033)
SNOWPURE LLC
Also Called: Snowpure Water Technologies
130 Calle Iglesia Ste A, San Clemente (92672-7535)
P.O. Box 73308 (92673-0113)
PHONE.............................949 240-2188
Michael Snow, *Managing Member*
◆ **EMP:** 30 **EST:** 1979
SALES (est): 7.87MM **Privately Held**
Web: www.snowpure.com
SIC: 3589 5074 Water purification equipment, household type; Water purification equipment

(P-6034)
SPENUZZA INC (HQ)
Also Called: Imperial Coml Cooking Eqp
1128 Sherborn St, Corona (92879-2089)
PHONE.............................951 281-1830
Peter Spenuzza, *CEO*
◆ **EMP:** 71 **EST:** 1957
SQ FT: 100,000
SALES (est): 24.97MM
SALES (corp-wide): 4.04B **Publicly Held**
Web: www.imperialrange.com
SIC: 3589 3556 Cooking equipment, commercial; Food products machinery

PA: The Middleby Corporation
1400 Toastmaster Dr
847 741-3300

(P-6035)
TIMBUCKTOO MANUFACTURING INC
Also Called: T M I
1633 W 134th St, Gardena (90249-2013)
PHONE.............................310 323-1134
Juen Lee, *CEO*
Kyu Lee, *
▲ **EMP:** 43 **EST:** 1974
SQ FT: 50,000
SALES (est): 4.69MM **Privately Held**
Web: www.timbucktoomfg.com
SIC: 3589 Car washing machinery

(P-6036)
VEOLIA WTS SERVICES USA INC
7777 Industry Ave, Pico Rivera (90660-4303)
PHONE.............................562 942-2200
Michael Dimick, *Brnch Mgr*
EMP: 60
SQ FT: 32,091
Web: www.suezwatertechnologies.com
SIC: 3589 Water treatment equipment, industrial
HQ: Veolia Wts Services Usa, Inc.
4545 Patent Rd
Norfolk VA 23502
757 855-9000

(P-6037)
WATER WORKS INC
5490 Complex St Ste 601, San Diego (92123-1126)
PHONE.............................858 499-0119
John Warmes, *Pr*
EMP: 24 **EST:** 2006
SALES (est): 5.79MM **Privately Held**
Web: www.ultrapurewaterworks.com
SIC: 3589 Water treatment equipment, industrial

(P-6038)
YANCHEWSKI & WARDELL ENTPS INC
Also Called: Ecowater Systems
2241 La Mirada Dr, Vista (92081-8828)
PHONE.............................760 754-1960
Ryan Wardell, *Pr*
EMP: 95 **EST:** 2006
SALES (est): 8.15MM **Privately Held**
Web: www.ecowatersocal.com
SIC: 3589 3677 3639 Water purification equipment, household type; Filtration devices, electronic; Hot water heaters, household

(P-6039)
YARDNEY WATER MGT SYSTEMS INC
Also Called: Yardney Water MGT Systems
6666 Box Springs Blvd, Riverside (92507-0736)
PHONE.............................951 656-6716
Chris Phillips, *Pr*
◆ **EMP:** 40 **EST:** 1948
SQ FT: 55,000
SALES (est): 7.15MM **Privately Held**
Web: www.yardneyfilters.com
SIC: 3589 Water treatment equipment, industrial

(P-6040)
ZODIAC POOL SYSTEMS LLC (DH)
Also Called: Jandy Pool Products
2882 Whiptail Loop Ste 100, Carlsbad
(92010-6758)
PHONE...................760 599-9600
Bruce Brooks, *CEO*
Anthony Prudhomme, *
Mike Allanc, *
◆ **EMP:** 250 **EST:** 1999
SALES (est): 489.08MM **Privately Held**
Web: www.fluidrausa.com
SIC: 3589 3999 Swimming pool filter and
    water conditioning systems; Hot tub and
    spa covers
HQ: Fluidra North America Llc
    2882 Whiptail Loop # 100
    Carlsbad CA 92010
    760 599-9600

3592 Carburetors, Pistons, Rings, Valves

(P-6041)
CP-CARRILLO INC (DH)
1902 Mcgaw Ave, Irvine (92614-0910)
PHONE...................949 567-9000
Barry Calvert, *CEO*
Peter Calvert, *
Wolfgang Plasser, *
Harry Glieder, *
▲ **EMP:** 160 **EST:** 2011
SQ FT: 31,840
SALES (est): 16.18MM
SALES (corp-wide): 3.83B **Privately Held**
Web: www.cp-carrillo.com
SIC: 3592 3714 Pistons and piston rings;
    Connecting rods, motor vehicle engine
HQ: Pankl Holdings, Inc.
    1902 Mcgaw Ave
    Irvine CA 92614

(P-6042)
CP-CARRILLO INC
17401 Armstrong Ave, Irvine (92614-5723)
PHONE...................949 567-9000
Barry Calvert, *Managing Member*
EMP: 30
SALES (corp-wide): 3.83B **Privately Held**
Web: www.cp-carrillo.com
SIC: 3592 3714 Pistons and piston rings;
    Connecting rods, motor vehicle engine
HQ: Cp-Carrillo, Inc.
    1902 Mcgaw Ave
    Irvine CA 92614

(P-6043)
PACIFIC PISTON RING CO INC
3620 Eastham Dr, Culver City (90232-2411)
P.O. Box 927 (90232-0927)
PHONE...................310 836-3322
Forest Shannon, *Pr*
Michael Shannon, *
Christina Davis, *
EMP: 58 **EST:** 1921
SQ FT: 35,000
SALES (est): 8.06MM **Privately Held**
Web: www.pacificpistonring.com
SIC: 3592 Pistons and piston rings

(P-6044)
PERFORMANCE MOTORSPORTS INC
5100 Campus Dr Ste 100, Newport Beach
(92660-2191)
PHONE...................714 898-9763
▲ **EMP:** 265

SIC: 3592 Pistons and piston rings

(P-6045)
ROSS RACING PISTONS
625 S Douglas St, El Segundo
(90245-4812)
PHONE...................310 536-0100
Ken Roble, *Pr*
J B Moe Mills, *VP*
Joy Roble, *
EMP: 55 **EST:** 1979
SQ FT: 25,000
SALES (est): 4.89MM **Privately Held**
Web: www.rosspistons.com
SIC: 3592 Pistons and piston rings

(P-6046)
RTR INDUSTRIES LLC (PA)
Also Called: Grant Piston Rings
4430 E Miraloma Ave Ste B, Anaheim
(92807-1840)
PHONE...................714 996-0050
▲ **EMP:** 27 **EST:** 2002
SALES (est): 4.94MM
SALES (corp-wide): 4.94MM **Privately Held**
Web: www.grantpistonrings.com
SIC: 3592 Pistons and piston rings

(P-6047)
SEABISCUIT MOTORSPORTS INC
10800 Valley View St, Cypress
(90630-5016)
PHONE...................714 898-9763
EMP: 30
SALES (corp-wide): 8.44B **Publicly Held**
Web: www.wiseco.com
SIC: 3592 3714 Pistons and piston rings;
    Motor vehicle parts and accessories
HQ: Seabiscuit Motorsports, Inc.
    7201 Industrial Park Blvd
    Mentor OH 44060
    440 951-6600

3593 Fluid Power Cylinders And Actuators

(P-6048)
RTC ARSPACE - CHTSWRTH DIV INC (PA)
20409 Prairie St, Chatsworth (91311-6029)
PHONE...................818 341-3344
James B Hart, *CEO*
Bj Schramm, *Pr*
Bill Hart, *
Elizabeth Hart, *
◆ **EMP:** 84 **EST:** 1958
SQ FT: 42,000
SALES (est): 24.83MM
SALES (corp-wide): 24.83MM **Privately Held**
Web: www.rtcaerospace.com
SIC: 3593 3594 3599 Fluid power cylinders
    and actuators; Fluid power pumps and
    motors; Machine shop, jobbing and repair

3594 Fluid Power Pumps And Motors

(P-6049)
BERNELL HYDRAULICS INC (PA)
8821 Etiwanda Ave, Rancho Cucamonga
(91739-9625)
P.O. Box 417 (91739-0417)
PHONE...................909 899-1751
TOLL FREE: 800

Terrance B Jones Senior, *Ch Bd*
Rhonda A Garness, *
John S Clemons, *
EMP: 28 **EST:** 1977
SALES (est): 15.99MM
SALES (corp-wide): 15.99MM **Privately Held**
Web: www.bernellhydraulics.com
SIC: 3594 5084 3621 3593 Pumps, hydraulic
    power transfer; Hydraulic systems
    equipment and supplies; Motors and
    generators; Fluid power cylinders and
    actuators

(P-6050)
CRISSAIR INC
28909 Avenue Williams, Valencia
(91355-4183)
PHONE...................661 367-3300
Michael Alfred, *Pr*
Patrick Lacanfora, *Sr VP*
Eric Grupp, *VP*
Beverly Miller, *VP*
EMP: 185 **EST:** 1954
SQ FT: 40,000
SALES (est): 45.98MM **Publicly Held**
Web: www.crissair.com
SIC: 3594 3492 Motors, pneumatic; Fluid
    power valves and hose fittings
PA: Esco Technologies Inc.
    9900 A Clayton Rd

(P-6051)
HYPERION MOTORS LLC
1032 W Taft Ave, Orange (92865-4119)
PHONE...................714 363-5858
Angelo Kafantaris, *Prin*
EMP: 50 **EST:** 2011
SALES (est): 4.47MM **Privately Held**
Web: www.hyperion.inc
SIC: 3594 Fluid power pumps and motors

(P-6052)
PARKER-HANNIFIN CORPORATION
Also Called: Cylinder Division
221 Helicopter Cir, Corona (92878-5032)
PHONE...................951 280-3800
Donald P Szmania, *Brnch Mgr*
EMP: 73
SALES (corp-wide): 19.93B **Publicly Held**
Web: www.parker.com
SIC: 3594 3728 3593 Fluid power pumps
    and motors; Aircraft parts and equipment,
    nec; Fluid power cylinders and actuators
PA: Parker-Hannifin Corporation
    6035 Parkland Blvd
    216 896-3000

(P-6053)
PARKER-HANNIFIN CORPORATION
Composite Sealing Systems Div
7664 Panasonic Way, San Diego
(92154-8206)
PHONE...................619 661-7000
Jim Rando, *Mgr*
EMP: 130
SALES (corp-wide): 19.93B **Publicly Held**
Web: www.parker.com
SIC: 3594 Fluid power pumps and motors
PA: Parker-Hannifin Corporation
    6035 Parkland Blvd
    216 896-3000

(P-6054)
WESTERN HYDROSTATICS INC (PA)
1956 Keats Dr, Riverside (92501-1747)

PHONE...................951 784-2133
TOLL FREE: 800
John Starke Scott, *Pr*
Tandy W Scott, *
Barnett Totten, *
▲ **EMP:** 28 **EST:** 1985
SALES (est): 4.44MM
SALES (corp-wide): 4.44MM **Privately Held**
Web: www.weshyd.com
SIC: 3594 7699 5084 Hydrostatic drives
    (transmissions); Hydraulic equipment repair
    ; Hydraulic systems equipment and supplies

3599 Industrial Machinery, Nec

(P-6055)
3-D PRECISION MACHINE INC
42132 Remington Ave, Temecula
(92590-2547)
PHONE...................951 296-5449
Linda Luoma, *Pr*
Roy Luoma, *VP*
EMP: 26 **EST:** 2006
SQ FT: 14,000
SALES (est): 5.14MM **Privately Held**
Web: www.3dprecisionmachine.com
SIC: 3599 Machine shop, jobbing and repair

(P-6056)
3D MACHINE CO INC
4790 E Wesley Dr, Anaheim (92807-1941)
PHONE...................714 777-8985
Maria Falcusan, *Pr*
Constantine Falcusan, *
EMP: 30 **EST:** 1996
SQ FT: 3,300
SALES (est): 4.24MM **Privately Held**
Web: www.3dmachineco.com
SIC: 3599 Machine shop, jobbing and repair

(P-6057)
5TH AXIS INC (PA)
7140 Engineer Rd, San Diego
(92111-1422)
PHONE...................858 505-0432
▲ **EMP:** 200 **EST:** 2005
SQ FT: 21,000
SALES (est): 28MM
SALES (corp-wide): 28MM **Privately Held**
Web: www.5thaxis.com
SIC: 3599 Machine shop, jobbing and repair

(P-6058)
A & B AEROSPACE INC
612 S Ayon Ave, Azusa (91702-5122)
PHONE...................626 334-2976
Kenneth Smith, *Pr*
Malcolm Smith, *
EMP: 35 **EST:** 1950
SQ FT: 23,000
SALES (est): 8.46MM **Privately Held**
Web: www.abaerospace.com
SIC: 3599 Machine shop, jobbing and repair

(P-6059)
A & M ENGINEERING INC
15854 Salvatiera St, Irwindale
(91706-6603)
PHONE...................626 813-2020
Boris Beljak Senior, *Pr*
Boris Beljak Senior, *Pr*
Boris Beljak Junior, *VP*
Roy Beljak, *
Anita Beljak, *
EMP: 80 **EST:** 1973
SQ FT: 25,000
SALES (est): 9.79MM **Privately Held**

Web: www.amengineeringinc.com
SIC: 3599 3812 3537 Machine shop, jobbing
and repair; Search and navigation
equipment; Industrial trucks and tractors

(P-6060)
A & R ENGINEERING CO INC
Also Called: A & R
1053 E Bedmar St, Carson (90746-3601)
PHONE..................................310 603-9060
Murat Sehidoglu, *Pr*
EMP: 72 EST: 1982
SQ FT: 23,334
SALES (est): 9.73MM Privately Held
Web: www.arengr.com
SIC: 3599 Machine shop, jobbing and repair

(P-6061)
A-Z MFG INC
Also Called: AZ Manufacturing
3101 W Segerstrom Ave, Santa Ana
(92704-5811)
PHONE..................................714 444-4446
Ann Lukas, *Prin*
Gary Lukas, *
EMP: 40 EST: 1993
SQ FT: 16,096
SALES (est): 9.66MM Privately Held
Web: www.azmfginc.com
SIC: 3599 Machine shop, jobbing and repair

(P-6062)
**ACCU-TECH LASER
PROCESSING INC**
1175 Linda Vista Dr, San Marcos
(92078-3811)
PHONE..................................760 744-6692
Michael C Gericke, *Pr*
Roger Underwood, *
EMP: 33 EST: 2006
SQ FT: 6,500
SALES (est): 2.67MM Privately Held
Web: www.accutechlaser.com
SIC: 3599 Machine shop, jobbing and repair

(P-6063)
ACE MACHINE SHOP INC
11200 Wright Rd, Lynwood (90262-3124)
P.O. Box 97 (91709)
PHONE..................................310 608-2277
Pedro Gallinucci, *Pr*
Lucia Gallinucci, *
EMP: 70 EST: 1956
SQ FT: 35,000
SALES (est): 6.24MM Privately Held
Web: www.isconcepts.com
SIC: 3599 Machine shop, jobbing and repair

(P-6064)
**ADVANCED JOINING
TECHNOLOGIES INC**
3030 Red Hill Ave, Santa Ana
(92705-5823)
PHONE..................................949 756-8091
EMP: 25
Web: www.ajt-inc.com
SIC: 3599 Machine shop, jobbing and repair

(P-6065)
**ADVANCED MCHNING
SOLUTIONS INC**
3523 Main St Ste 606, Chula Vista
(91911-0803)
PHONE..................................619 671-3055
Pamela Yuhm, *Pr*
EMP: 35 EST: 2005
SALES (est): 2.58MM Privately Held
Web: www.amssd.com

SIC: 3599 Machine shop, jobbing and repair

(P-6066)
AERO CHIP INC
13563 Freeway Dr, Santa Fe Springs
(90670-5633)
PHONE..................................562 404-6300
Solomon M Gavrila, *CEO*
Liviu Pribac, *
EMP: 50 EST: 1988
SQ FT: 17,000
SALES (est): 8.38MM Privately Held
Web: www.aerochip.com
SIC: 3599 Machine shop, jobbing and repair

(P-6067)
**AERO DYNAMIC MACHINING
INC**
7472 Chapman Ave, Garden Grove
(92841-2106)
PHONE..................................714 379-1073
Wendy Nguyen, *Ch Bd*
David Nguyen, *
Wendy Nguyen, *VP*
Kevin Tran, *
▲ EMP: 65 EST: 1998
SALES (est): 10.52MM Privately Held
Web: www.aerodynamicinc.com
SIC: 3599 3499 Machine shop, jobbing and
repair; Fire- or burglary-resistive products

(P-6068)
AERO INDUSTRIES LLC
139 Industrial Way, Buellton (93427-9592)
P.O. Box 198 (93427-0198)
PHONE..................................805 688-6734
Dave Watkins, *Mgr*
EMP: 340 EST: 2007
SALES (est): 2.97MM
SALES (corp-wide): 40.31MM Privately
Held
Web: www.aero-cnc.com
SIC: 3599 Machine shop, jobbing and repair
PA: Gavial Holdings, Inc.
1435 W Mccoy Ln
805 614-0060

(P-6069)
**AERO MECHANISM PRECISION
INC**
21700 Marilla St, Chatsworth (91311-4125)
PHONE..................................818 886-1855
Palminder Sehmbey, *Pr*
EMP: 34 EST: 1996
SQ FT: 8,000
SALES (est): 4.53MM Privately Held
Web: www.aeromechanism.com
SIC: 3599 Machine shop, jobbing and repair

(P-6070)
AERO-K
2040 E Dyer Rd, Santa Ana (92705-5710)
PHONE..................................626 350-5125
Robert Krusic, *Pr*
EMP: 45 EST: 1983
SALES (est): 4.23MM Privately Held
Web: www.aero-k.com
SIC: 3599 Machine shop, jobbing and repair

(P-6071)
**AERODYNAMIC ENGINEERING
INC**
15495 Graham St, Huntington Beach
(92649-1205)
PHONE..................................714 891-2651
Bob Waddell, *
Alfred Mayer, *
Ewald Eisel, *
Mark Schultz, *Manager*

▲ EMP: 40 EST: 1968
SQ FT: 12,000
SALES (est): 4.76MM Privately Held
Web: www.aerodynamic.net
SIC: 3599 3769 Machine shop, jobbing and
repair; Space vehicle equipment, nec

(P-6072)
**AERODYNE PRCSION
MACHINING INC**
5471 Argosy Ave, Huntington Beach
(92649-1038)
PHONE..................................714 891-1311
Raymond Krispel, *Pr*
Otto Schulz, *
Veronica Schultz, *
▲ EMP: 25 EST: 1986
SQ FT: 20,000
SALES (est): 7.73MM Privately Held
Web: www.aerodyneprecision.com
SIC: 3599 Machine shop, jobbing and repair

(P-6073)
AEROTEK INC
2751 Park View Ct Ste 221, Oxnard
(93036-5450)
PHONE..................................805 604-3000
EMP: 1439
SALES (corp-wide): 14.88B Privately Held
Web: www.aerotek.com
SIC: 3599 Machine and other job shop work
HQ: Aerotek, Inc.
7301 Pkwy Dr
Hanover MD 21076
410 694-5100

(P-6074)
ALCO ENGRG & TOOLING CORP
Also Called: Alco Metal Fab
3001 Oak St, Santa Ana (92707-4235)
PHONE..................................714 556-6060
Frank Vallefuoco, *Pr*
Frank Vallefuoco, *CEO*
Tom Hare, *
Angelo D'eramo, *Sec*
EMP: 40 EST: 1944
SQ FT: 32,000
SALES (est): 5.16MM Privately Held
Web: www.alcoge.com
SIC: 3599 Machine shop, jobbing and repair

(P-6075)
ALL STAR PRECISION
8739 Lion St, Rancho Cucamonga
(91730-4428)
PHONE..................................909 944-8373
Scott Jackson, *Owner*
Ron Jackson, *Pt*
EMP: 23 EST: 2004
SALES (est): 3.66MM Privately Held
Web: www.allstarprecision.com
SIC: 3599 Machine shop, jobbing and repair

(P-6076)
ALL SWISS TURNING ✪
7745 Alabama Ave Ste 13, Canoga Park
(91304-6639)
PHONE..................................818 466-3076
Juan R Olivas, *Pr*
EMP: 25 EST: 2024
SALES (est): 1.27MM Privately Held
Web: www.allswissturning.com
SIC: 3599 Machine shop, jobbing and repair

(P-6077)
**ALPHA AVIATION
COMPONENTS INC (PA)**
16772 Schoenborn St, North Hills
(91343-6108)

PHONE..................................818 894-8801
Lidia Gorko, *Pr*
William Tudor, *
EMP: 25 EST: 1954
SQ FT: 18,000
SALES (est): 8.18MM
SALES (corp-wide): 8.18MM Privately
Held
Web: www.alphaaci.com
SIC: 3599 3451 3728 Machine shop, jobbing
and repair; Screw machine products;
Aircraft parts and equipment, nec

(P-6078)
ALTS TOOL & MACHINE INC
10926 Woodside Ave N, Santee
(92071-3272)
P.O. Box 712485 (92072-2485)
PHONE..................................619 562-6653
EMP: 55
Web: www.altstool.com
SIC: 3599 Machine shop, jobbing and repair

(P-6079)
AMERICAN DEBURRING INC
Also Called: A Fab
20742 Linear Ln, Lake Forest (92630-7804)
PHONE..................................949 457-9790
Robert L Campbell, *Pr*
Theresa Cook, *
EMP: 25 EST: 1973
SQ FT: 11,000
SALES (est): 3.2MM Privately Held
Web: www.afabcnc.com
SIC: 3599 Machine shop, jobbing and repair

(P-6080)
ARANDA TOOLING LLC
13950 Yorba Ave, Chino (91710-5520)
PHONE..................................714 379-6565
Pedro Aranda, *Pr*
Martha Aranda, *
▲ EMP: 70 EST: 1976
SQ FT: 60,000
SALES (est): 18.58MM Privately Held
Web: www.arandatooling.com
SIC: 3599 3469 3544 3465 Machine shop,
jobbing and repair; Metal stampings, nec;
Special dies, tools, jigs, and fixtures;
Automotive stampings

(P-6081)
AREMAC ASSOCIATES INC
2004 S Myrtle Ave, Monrovia (91016-4837)
PHONE..................................626 303-8795
Scott Sher, *CEO*
Mariela Vinas, *
EMP: 35 EST: 1963
SQ FT: 12,500
SALES (est): 2.3MM Privately Held
SIC: 3599 3444 Machine shop, jobbing and
repair; Sheet metalwork

(P-6082)
**ARNOLD-GONSALVES ENGRG
INC**
5731 Chino Ave, Chino (91710-5226)
PHONE..................................909 465-1579
Manuel Gonsalves, *Pr*
Mike Arnold, *
EMP: 35 EST: 1969
SQ FT: 10,000
SALES (est): 3.21MM Privately Held
Web: www.arnoldgonsalveseng.com
SIC: 3599 3444 Machine shop, jobbing and
repair; Sheet metal specialties, not stamped

PRODUCTS & SVCS

(P-6083)
ARROW ENGINEERING
4946 Azusa Canyon Rd, Irwindale
(91706-1940)
PHONE...................626 960-2806
John Beaman, *Pr*
Jim Ballantyne, *
EMP: 36 **EST:** 1974
SQ FT: 18,000
SALES (est): 5.66MM **Privately Held**
Web: www.arrow-engineering.com
SIC: 3599 Machine shop, jobbing and repair

(P-6084)
ARROW SCREW PRODUCTS INC
941 W Mccoy Ln, Santa Maria
(93455-1109)
PHONE...................805 928-2269
Robert Vine, *CEO*
Tim Vine, *
Hoang Vine, *
EMP: 33 **EST:** 1956
SQ FT: 10,000
SALES (est): 5.35MM **Privately Held**
Web: www.aspsmca.com
SIC: 3599 3541 Machine shop, jobbing and repair; Machine tools, metal cutting type

(P-6085)
AVATAR MACHINE LLC
18100 Mount Washington St, Fountain
Valley (92708-6121)
PHONE...................714 434-2737
EMP: 23 **EST:** 2008
SALES (est): 9.4MM **Privately Held**
Web: www.avatarmachine.com
SIC: 3599 5049 Machine shop, jobbing and repair; Precision tools

(P-6086)
AXXIS CORPORATION
Also Called: Axxis Arms
1535 Nandina Ave, Perris (92571-7010)
PHONE...................951 436-9921
Brandy Tidball, *Pr*
Brandy Tidball, *Pr*
Susan Tidball, *
Jo Olchawa, *
EMP: 35 **EST:** 2007
SALES (est): 6.2MM **Privately Held**
Web: www.axxiscorp.us
SIC: 3599 Machine shop, jobbing and repair

(P-6087)
AZURE MICRODYNAMICS INC
19652 Descartes, Foothill Ranch
(92610-2600)
PHONE...................949 699-3344
Stanislaw Sulek, *Pr*
Zyta Sulek, *Stockholder*
Oliver Sulek, *
Christopher Hughes, *
EMP: 77 **EST:** 1997
SALES (est): 15.2MM **Privately Held**
Web: www.azuremd.com
SIC: 3599 3544 Machine shop, jobbing and repair; Special dies, tools, jigs, and fixtures

(P-6088)
B & B PIPE AND TOOL CO
2301 Parker Ln, Bakersfield (93308-6006)
PHONE...................661 323-8208
Joe Keller, *Genl Mgr*
EMP: 29
SALES (corp-wide): 7.08MM **Privately Held**
Web: www.bbpipe.com

SIC: 3599 Machine shop, jobbing and repair
PA: B & B Pipe And Tool Co.
3035 Walnut Ave
562 424-0704

(P-6089)
B&B MANUFACTURING CO (PA)
27940 Beale Ct, Santa Clarita
(91355-1210)
PHONE...................661 257-2161
Kenneth Gentry, *CEO*
Fred Duncan, *
▲ **EMP:** 192 **EST:** 1961
SQ FT: 180,000
SALES (est): 21.4MM
SALES (corp-wide): 21.4MM **Privately Held**
Web: www.bbmfg.com
SIC: 3599 Machine shop, jobbing and repair

(P-6090)
BAKERSFIELD MACHINE CO INC
Also Called: BMC Industries
5605 North Chester Ave Ext, Bakersfield
(93308)
P.O. Box 122 (93302-0122)
PHONE...................661 709-1992
John L Meyer, *Pr*
Alfred T Meyer Junior, *VP*
▲ **EMP:** 55 **EST:** 1924
SQ FT: 8,276
SALES (est): 8.97MM **Privately Held**
Web:
www.bakersfieldmachinerymovers.com
SIC: 3599 Machine shop, jobbing and repair

(P-6091)
BARBER WELDING AND MFG CO
7171 Scout Ave, Bell Gardens
(90201-3201)
P.O. Box 635 (92885-0635)
PHONE...................562 928-2570
C Douglas Barber, *CEO*
Yvonne M Barber, *
EMP: 25 **EST:** 1943
SQ FT: 15,000
SALES (est): 2.46MM **Privately Held**
SIC: 3599 3443 Machine shop, jobbing and repair; Tanks for tank trucks, metal plate

(P-6092)
BAUMANN ENGINEERING
212 S Cambridge Ave, Claremont
(91711-4843)
PHONE...................909 621-4181
Fred Baumann, *Pr*
Isolde Doll, *
EMP: 85 **EST:** 1961
SQ FT: 18,057
SALES (est): 5.03MM **Privately Held**
Web: www.becontrols.com
SIC: 3599 Machine shop, jobbing and repair

(P-6093)
BAYLESS MANUFACTURING LLC
Also Called: Fabcon
26140 Avenue Hall, Valencia (91355-4808)
PHONE...................661 257-3373
Robert Lummus, *Pr*
EMP: 235 **EST:** 1978
SALES (est): 8.11MM **Privately Held**
Web: www.fabcon.com
SIC: 3599 3444 Machine shop, jobbing and repair; Sheet metalwork

(P-6094)
BENDER CCP INC
757 Main St Unit 102, Chula Vista
(91911-6168)
PHONE...................619 232-5719
Briana Velasco, *Mgr*
EMP: 42
SALES (corp-wide): 50MM **Privately Held**
Web: www.benderccp.com
SIC: 3599 Custom machinery
PA: Bender Ccp, Inc.
2150 E 37th St
323 232-2371

(P-6095)
BENDER CCP INC (PA)
Also Called: Bender US
2150 E 37th St, Vernon (90058-1417)
P.O. Box 847 (94510)
PHONE...................323 232-2371
Michael Potter, *Pr*
Randall Potter, *
▲ **EMP:** 105 **EST:** 2007
SALES (est): 50MM
SALES (corp-wide): 50MM **Privately Held**
Web: www.benderccp.com
SIC: 3599 3731 Custom machinery; Shipbuilding and repairing

(P-6096)
BERANEK LLC
2340 W 205th St, Torrance (90501-1436)
PHONE...................310 328-9094
Hector Beranek, *Pr*
Sean Holly, *
Christoper Lin, *
Tucker Cowden, *
Stephen Cook, *
EMP: 36 **EST:** 1978
SQ FT: 20,000
SALES (est): 8.38MM
SALES (corp-wide): 13.91MM **Privately Held**
Web: www.beranekinc.com
SIC: 3599 Machine shop, jobbing and repair
PA: J&E Precision Tool Holdings, Llc
107 Valley Rd
413 527-8778

(P-6097)
BMW PRECISION MACHINING INC
2379 Industry St, Oceanside (92054-4803)
PHONE...................760 439-6813
Richard Blakely, *Pr*
EMP: 25 **EST:** 1981
SQ FT: 17,400
SALES (est): 2.57MM **Privately Held**
Web: www.bmwprecision.com
SIC: 3599 Machine shop, jobbing and repair

(P-6098)
BOUDRAUX PRCSION MCHINING CORP
11762 Western Ave Ste G, Stanton
(90680-3481)
PHONE...................714 894-4523
Mike Boudreaux, *Pr*
Steve Boudreaux, *
EMP: 25 **EST:** 1990
SQ FT: 3,750
SALES (est): 849.64K **Privately Held**
Web:
boudreaux-precision-machining-ca.hub.biz
SIC: 3599 Machine shop, jobbing and repair

(P-6099)
BREK MANUFACTURING CO
1513 W 132nd St, Gardena (90249-2287)

PHONE...................310 329-7638
▲ **EMP:** 169 **EST:** 1968
SALES (est): 56.04MM
SALES (corp-wide): 56.04MM **Privately Held**
Web: www.brek.aero
SIC: 3599 Machine shop, jobbing and repair
PA: Aernnova Engineering Us, Inc.
1513 W 132nd St
310 329-7638

(P-6100)
BTL MACHINE
Also Called: Apex Design Tech.
1168 Sherborn St, Corona (92879-2089)
PHONE...................951 808-9929
▲ **EMP:** 65
Web: www.btlmachine.com
SIC: 3599 Machine shop, jobbing and repair

(P-6101)
C & H MACHINE INC
Also Called: Support Equipment
943 S Andreasen Dr, Escondido
(92029-1934)
PHONE...................760 746-6459
Lyle J Anderson, *Ex VP*
Charles Gohlich, *
EMP: 70 **EST:** 1964
SQ FT: 13,000
SALES (est): 7.38MM **Privately Held**
Web: www.c-hmachine.com
SIC: 3599 Machine shop, jobbing and repair

(P-6102)
CAVANAUGH MACHINE WORKS INC
1540 Santa Fe Ave, Long Beach
(90813-1239)
PHONE...................562 437-1126
John Wells, *Pr*
Michael Wells, *
EMP: 40 **EST:** 1946
SQ FT: 19,000
SALES (est): 4.9MM **Privately Held**
Web: www.cavmachine.com
SIC: 3599 3731 3441 Machine shop, jobbing and repair; Shipbuilding and repairing; Fabricated structural metal

(P-6103)
CENTERPOINT MFG CO INC
2625 N San Fernando Blvd, Burbank
(91504-3220)
PHONE...................818 842-2147
John C Rotunno, *Pr*
Carmen Rotunno, *
EMP: 40 **EST:** 1966
SQ FT: 12,000
SALES (est): 5.11MM **Privately Held**
Web: www.centerpointmfgco.com
SIC: 3599 Machine shop, jobbing and repair

(P-6104)
CENTURY PRECISION ENGRG INC
2141 W 139th St, Gardena (90249-2451)
PHONE...................310 538-0015
Myron Yoo, *Pr*
Bruce Lee, *
EMP: 25 **EST:** 1980
SQ FT: 20,000
SALES (est): 3.84MM **Privately Held**
Web: www.centurype.com
SIC: 3599 Machine shop, jobbing and repair

(P-6105)
CJ ADVISORS INC
6900 8th St, Buena Park (90620-1036)

PHONE.....................714 956-3388
Jason Cho, *CEO*
EMP: 23 **EST:** 1993
SALES (est): 1.74MM **Privately Held**
Web: www.hqmachine.com
SIC: 3599 Machine and other job shop work

(P-6106)
CLASSIC WIRE CUT COMPANY INC
28210 Constellation Rd, Valencia
(91355-5000)
PHONE.....................661 257-0558
Brett Bannerman, *Prin*
▲ **EMP:** 150 **EST:** 1984
SQ FT: 80,000
SALES (est): 19.19MM **Privately Held**
Web: www.classicwirecut.com
SIC: 3599 3841 Electrical discharge machining (EDM); Surgical instruments and apparatus

(P-6107)
COAST COMPOSITES LLC
7 Burroughs, Irvine (92618-2804)
PHONE.....................949 455-0665
Brendan Buckel, *Mgr*
EMP: 30
SALES (corp-wide): 7.68MM **Privately Held**
Web: www.ascentaerospace.com
SIC: 3599 Machine shop, jobbing and repair
PA: Coast Composites, Llc
5 Burroughs
949 455-0665

(P-6108)
COMPUTER ASSISTED MFG TECH LLC
Also Called: Camtech
8710 Research Dr 8750, Irvine
(92618-4222)
PHONE.....................949 263-8911
Mike Dennis, *CEO*
EMP: 40 **EST:** 1982
SQ FT: 50,000
SALES (est): 5.69MM
SALES (corp-wide): 5.69MM **Privately Held**
SIC: 3599 Machine shop, jobbing and repair
HQ: Cam Holdco, Llc
8710 Research Dr
Irvine CA

(P-6109)
COREDUX USA LLC
6721 Cobra Way, San Diego (92121-4110)
PHONE.....................858 642-0713
Jan Hennipman, *CEO*
EMP: 100 **EST:** 1988
SQ FT: 23,800
SALES (est): 21.50MM **Privately Held**
Web: www.pyramidprecision.com
SIC: 3599 Machine shop, jobbing and repair

(P-6110)
CRESCO MANUFACTURING INC
Also Called: Crescomfg.com
1614 N Orangethorpe Way, Anaheim
(92801-1227)
PHONE.....................714 525-2326
Jon Spielman, *Pr*
Alberta Spielman, *
EMP: 40 **EST:** 1981
SQ FT: 14,000
SALES (est): 3.67MM **Privately Held**
Web: petespielman.weebly.com
SIC: 3599 Machine shop, jobbing and repair

(P-6111)
CRUSH MASTER GRINDING CORP
Also Called: Evolution Industries
755 Penarth Ave, Walnut (91789-3028)
PHONE.....................909 595-2249
Sherman Durousseau, *Pr*
Jeanne Durousseau, *
EMP: 35 **EST:** 1976
SQ FT: 11,800
SALES (est): 5.29MM **Privately Held**
Web: www.crushmastergrinding.com
SIC: 3599 Machine shop, jobbing and repair

(P-6112)
D MILLS GRNDING MACHINING INC
1738 N Neville St, Orange (92865-4214)
PHONE.....................951 697-6847
Anthony Puccio, *Pr*
Gilles Madelmont, *
Joe Puccio, *
EMP: 150 **EST:** 1973
SALES (est): 2.65MM
SALES (corp-wide): 43.53MM **Privately Held**
Web:
d-mills-grinding-machining-co-inc.hub.biz
SIC: 3599 Grinding castings for the trade
PA: Manufacturing Solutions, Inc.
1738 N Neville St
714 453-0100

(P-6113)
DARMARK CORPORATION
13225 Gregg St, Poway (92064-7120)
PHONE.....................858 679-3970
Darwin Mark Zavadil, *Pr*
Martin T Drake, *
Lori Zavadil, *
Jackie Williams, *
EMP: 90 **EST:** 1979
SQ FT: 28,000
SALES (est): 17.49MM **Privately Held**
Web: www.darmark.com
SIC: 3599 Machine shop, jobbing and repair

(P-6114)
DELAFIELD CORPORATION (PA)
Also Called: Delafield Fluid Technology
1520 Flower Ave, Duarte (91010-2925)
PHONE.....................626 303-0740
Nik Ray, *Pr*
Jim Martin, *
Henry Custodia, *
◆ **EMP:** 120 **EST:** 1949
SQ FT: 90,000
SALES (est): 40.45MM
SALES (corp-wide): 40.45MM **Privately Held**
Web: www.dftcorp.com
SIC: 3599 5085 3498 3492 Hose, flexible metallic; Valves, pistons, and fittings; Tube fabricating (contract bending and shaping); Fluid power valves and hose fittings

(P-6115)
DELTA FABRICATION INC
9600 De Soto Ave, Chatsworth
(91311-5012)
PHONE.....................818 407-4000
Chava Ostrowsky, *CEO*
Joe Ostrowsky, *
EMP: 90 **EST:** 1996
SQ FT: 20,000
SALES (est): 5.24MM **Privately Held**
Web: www.deltahi-tech.com
SIC: 3599 Machine shop, jobbing and repair

(P-6116)
DELTA HI-TECH
9600 De Soto Ave, Chatsworth
(91311-5012)
PHONE.....................818 407-4000
Joe Ostrowsky, *CEO*
Ilan Ostrowsky, *
Gregory Elkhunovich, *
Chava Ostrowsky, *
▲ **EMP:** 130 **EST:** 1985
SQ FT: 40,000
SALES (est): 19.97MM **Privately Held**
Web: www.deltahi-tech.com
SIC: 3599 Machine shop, jobbing and repair

(P-6117)
DIAL PRECISION INC
17235 Darwin Ave, Hesperia (92345-5178)
P.O. Box 402259 (92340-2259)
PHONE.....................760 947-3557
Darryl L Tarullo, *Ch Bd*
Jeff Marousek, *Prin*
Linda James, *Prin*
EMP: 95 **EST:** 1958
SQ FT: 15,000
SALES (est): 4.86MM **Privately Held**
Web: www.dialprecision.com
SIC: 3599 3545 Machine shop, jobbing and repair; Machine tool accessories

(P-6118)
DL HORTON ENTERPRISES INC
Also Called: Warmelin Precision Products
12705 Daphne Ave, Hawthorne
(90250-3311)
PHONE.....................323 777-1700
EMP: 55
SIC: 3599 Machine shop, jobbing and repair

(P-6119)
DOW HYDRAULIC SYSTEMS INC
2895 Metropolitan Pl, Pomona
(91767-1853)
PHONE.....................909 596-6602
Richard P Dow, *Pr*
Ryan K Dow, *
Bryan Dow, *
Keith Dow, *
EMP: 60 **EST:** 1968
SALES (est): 9.33MM **Privately Held**
Web: www.dowhydraulics.com
SIC: 3599 3594 Machine shop, jobbing and repair; Fluid power pumps and motors

(P-6120)
ELY CO INC
3046 Kashiwa St, Torrance (90505-4083)
PHONE.....................310 539-5831
Walter Senff, *CEO*
Kurt Senff, *
Judith Senff, *
Bill Senff, *
EMP: 36 **EST:** 1953
SQ FT: 11,500
SALES (est): 5.28MM **Privately Held**
Web: www.elyco.com
SIC: 3599 Machine shop, jobbing and repair

(P-6121)
ENERGY LINK INDUS SVCS INC
11439 S Enos Ln, Bakersfield (93311-9452)
P.O. Box 10716 (93389-0716)
PHONE.....................661 765-4444
James R Miller Iii, *CEO*
Ray Miller, *
Matt Knight, *Stockholder*
West Moore, *Stockholder*
Joe Yrigoyen Stckhldrs, *Prin*
EMP: 34 **EST:** 2000
SALES (est): 11.9MM **Privately Held**

Web: www.energylink1.com
SIC: 3599 7699 Bellows, industrial: metal; Compressor repair

(P-6122)
EXCEL MANUFACTURING INC
20409 Prairie St, Chatsworth (91311-6029)
PHONE.....................661 257-1900
Susan Halliday, *Pr*
EMP: 46 **EST:** 1992
SQ FT: 14,000
SALES (est): 3MM
SALES (corp-wide): 24.83MM **Privately Held**
Web: www.excelbalermfg.com
SIC: 3599 Machine shop, jobbing and repair
PA: Rtc Aerospace - Chatsworth Division, Inc.
20409 Prairie St
818 341-3344

(P-6123)
FIBREFORM ELECTRONICS INC
Also Called: Fibreform Precision Machining
5341 Argosy Ave, Huntington Beach
(92649-1075)
PHONE.....................714 898-9641
Zachary Fischer, *Ch Bd*
Zachary Fischer, *Ch Bd*
Frank Mauro, *
Todd Crow, *
EMP: 30 **EST:** 1945
SQ FT: 30,000
SALES (est): 4.57MM **Privately Held**
Web: www.fibreformprecision.com
SIC: 3599 Machine shop, jobbing and repair

(P-6124)
FORM GRIND CORPORATION
Also Called: Form Products
30062 Aventura, Rcho Sta Marg
(92688-2010)
PHONE.....................949 858-7000
Ernest Treichler, *CEO*
Gary Treichler, *
Joan Treichler, *
EMP: 27 **EST:** 1963
SQ FT: 30,000
SALES (est): 4.83MM **Privately Held**
Web: www.formgrind.com
SIC: 3599 5084 Machine shop, jobbing and repair; Industrial machinery and equipment

(P-6125)
FORTNER ENG & MFG INC
2927 N Ontario St, Burbank (91504-2017)
P.O. Box 30015 (84130-0015)
PHONE.....................818 240-7740
David W Fortner, *Pr*
EMP: 30 **EST:** 1952
SQ FT: 24,000
SALES (est): 14.54MM **Publicly Held**
Web: www.fortnereng.com
SIC: 3599 Machine shop, jobbing and repair
HQ: Wencor Group, Llc
416 Dividend Dr
Peachtree City GA 30269
678 490-0140

(P-6126)
FORTUNE MANUFACTURING INC
13849 Magnolia Ave, Chino (91710-7028)
PHONE.....................909 591-1547
EMP: 45
SIC: 3599 Machine shop, jobbing and repair

(P-6127)
FRANKLINS INDS SAN DIEGO INC
12135 Dearborn Pl, Poway (92064-7111)

PHONE.............................858 486-9399
Kelly Franklin, *Pr*
EMP: 44 **EST:** 1980
SQ FT: 20,000
SALES (est): 9.22MM **Privately Held**
Web: www.franklin-ind.com
SIC: 3599 Machine shop, jobbing and repair

(P-6128)
FRONTIER ENGRG & MFG TECH INC (PA)
Also Called: Frontier Technologies
800 W 16th St, Long Beach (90813-1413)
PHONE.............................310 767-1227
John Tsai, *CEO*
Steve Hoekstra, *Pr*
▲ **EMP:** 33 **EST:** 1994
SQ FT: 30,000
SALES (est): 10.4MM
SALES (corp-wide): 10.4MM **Privately Held**
Web: www.ftmfg.com
SIC: 3599 8711 Machine shop, jobbing and repair; Engineering services

(P-6129)
FUTURISTICS MACHINE INC
7014 Carroll Rd, San Diego (92121-2213)
PHONE.............................858 450-0644
Mark Mcginn, *CEO*
EMP: 35 **EST:** 2016
SALES (est): 2.54MM **Privately Held**
Web: www.futuristicsmachine.com
SIC: 3599 Machine shop, jobbing and repair

(P-6130)
G V INDUSTRIES INC
1346 Cleveland Ave, National City (91950-4207)
PHONE.............................619 474-3013
Gregory J Verdon, *Pr*
Joseph Verdon, *
Linda Verdon, *Corporate Vice President*
EMP: 38 **EST:** 1978
SQ FT: 14,000
SALES (est): 3.66MM **Privately Held**
Web: www.gvindustries.biz
SIC: 3599 Machine shop, jobbing and repair

(P-6131)
GAMMA AEROSPACE LLC
1461 S Balboa Ave, Ontario (91761-7609)
PHONE.............................310 532-4480
Thomas C Hutton, *Managing Member*
EMP: 32
SALES (corp-wide): 25.21MM **Privately Held**
Web: www.gammaaero.com
SIC: 3599 Machine shop, jobbing and repair
PA: Gamma Aerospace Llc
601 Airport Dr Ste 2718
817 477-2193

(P-6132)
GBF ENTERPRISES INC
2709 Halladay St, Santa Ana (92705-5618)
PHONE.............................714 979-7131
Cheryl Nowak, *Pr*
EMP: 25 **EST:** 1976
SQ FT: 17,000
SALES (est): 5.31MM **Privately Held**
Web: www.gbfenterprises.com
SIC: 3599 Machine shop, jobbing and repair

(P-6133)
GENERAL INDUSTRIAL REPAIR
6865 Washington Blvd, Montebello (90640-5434)
PHONE.............................323 278-0873
Henry Biazus, *Pr*

Richard Biazus, *
EMP: 25 **EST:** 1995
SALES (est): 7.46MM **Privately Held**
Web: www.girepair.us
SIC: 3599 Machine shop, jobbing and repair

(P-6134)
GEORGE FISCHER INC (HQ)
5462 Irwindale Ave Ste A, Baldwin Park (91706-2074)
PHONE.............................626 571-2770
Chris Blumer, *CEO*
Daniel Vaterlaus, *VP*
◆ **EMP:** 239 **EST:** 1954
SALES (est): 314.98MM **Privately Held**
Web: www.georgfischer.com
SIC: 3599 5074 3829 3559 Electrical discharge machining (EDM); Pipes and fittings, plastic; Testing equipment: abrasion, shearing strength, etc.; Foundry machinery and equipment
PA: Georg Fischer Ag
Amsler-Laffon-Strasse 9

(P-6135)
GERMAN MACHINED PRODUCTS INC
Also Called: German Machine Products
1415 W 178th St, Gardena (90248-3201)
PHONE.............................310 532-4480
EMP: 32
SIC: 3599 Machine shop, jobbing and repair

(P-6136)
GLENDEE CORP (PA)
Also Called: Metalagraphics
5390 Gabbert Rd, Moorpark (93021-1772)
PHONE.............................805 523-2422
EMP: 41 **EST:** 1975
SALES (est): 10.92MM
SALES (corp-wide): 10.92MM **Privately Held**
Web: www.mgius.com
SIC: 3599 3444 Machine and other job shop work; Sheet metalwork

(P-6137)
GOLDEN WEST MACHINE INC
9930 Jordan Cir, Santa Fe Springs (90670-3305)
PHONE.............................562 903-1111
Dan Goodman, *Prin*
Al Schlunegger, *
EMP: 35 **EST:** 1982
SQ FT: 25,000
SALES (est): 6.02MM **Privately Held**
Web: www.goldenwestmachine.com
SIC: 3599 7699 Machine shop, jobbing and repair; Industrial machinery and equipment repair

(P-6138)
HALES ENGINEERING COINC
18 Wood Rd, Camarillo (93010-8327)
EMP: 49 **EST:** 1966
SALES (est): 3.65MM **Privately Held**
SIC: 3599 1791 3441 Machine shop, jobbing and repair; Structural steel erection; Fabricated structural metal

(P-6139)
HANSEN ENGINEERING CO
24020 Frampton Ave, Harbor City (90710-2102)
PHONE.............................310 534-3870
EMP: 86 **EST:** 1962
SALES (est): 4.25MM **Privately Held**
Web: www.hansenengineering.com

SIC: 3599 Machine shop, jobbing and repair

(P-6140)
HERA TECHNOLOGIES LLC
1055 E Francis St, Ontario (91761-5633)
PHONE.............................951 751-6191
Didi Truong, *CEO*
Aaron Evans, *
Eugene Chuck, *
EMP: 50 **EST:** 2015
SALES (est): 5.48MM **Privately Held**
Web: www.heratechnologies.com
SIC: 3599 Machine shop, jobbing and repair

(P-6141)
HI-TECH LABELS INCORPORATED
Also Called: Hi-Tech Products
8530 Roland St, Buena Park (90621-3124)
PHONE.............................714 670-2150
Jeffrey T Ruch, *CEO*
▲ **EMP:** 34 **EST:** 1983
SQ FT: 24,000
SALES (est): 6.75MM **Privately Held**
Web: www.hi-tech-products.com
SIC: 3599 Machine shop, jobbing and repair

(P-6142)
HOLLAND & HERRING MFG INC
Also Called: H & H Manufacturing
661 E Monterey Ave, Pomona (91767-5607)
PHONE.............................909 469-4700
Jerry C Holland, *Pr*
Lawrence P Saylor, *Sec*
Debbie Krakowe, *CFO*
Mark B Herring, *Stockholder*
Bruce N Herring, *Stockholder*
EMP: 29 **EST:** 1991
SQ FT: 15,000
SALES (est): 1.02MM **Privately Held**
SIC: 3599 3471 Machine shop, jobbing and repair; Cleaning, polishing, and finishing

(P-6143)
HUGO VENTURE SOLUTIONS CORP
6325 Carpinteria Ave, Carpinteria (93013-2901)
P.O. Box 87 (93014-0087)
PHONE.............................805 684-0935
Alberto Hugo, *CEO*
Roger Hugo, *
Richard Hugo, *
EMP: 43 **EST:** 1961
SQ FT: 12,000
SALES (est): 4.71MM **Privately Held**
Web: www.rinconengineering.com
SIC: 3599 3444 3441 Machine shop, jobbing and repair; Sheet metalwork; Fabricated structural metal

(P-6144)
HYTRON MFG CO INC
15582 Chemical Ln, Huntington Beach (92649-1505)
PHONE.............................714 903-6701
James C Rehling, *Pr*
Robert Rehling, *
Cheryll Rehling, *
Deborah Strickland, *
EMP: 50 **EST:** 1963
SQ FT: 13,370
SALES (est): 3.75MM **Privately Held**
Web: www.hytronmanufacturing.com
SIC: 3599 Machine shop, jobbing and repair

(P-6145)
I COPY INC
Also Called: Ibe Digital
11266 Monarch St Ste B, Garden Grove (92841-1450)
PHONE.............................562 921-0202
Ronald Varing, *Pr*
EMP: 50 **EST:** 2001
SALES (est): 6.25MM **Privately Held**
Web: www.ibedigital.com
SIC: 3599 5044 5999 Amusement park equipment; Duplicating machines; Business machines and equipment

(P-6146)
INTRA AEROSPACE LLC
10671 Civic Center Dr, Rancho Cucamonga (91730-3804)
PHONE.............................909 476-0343
Robert Sayig, *Prin*
EMP: 35 **EST:** 2018
SALES (est): 1.3MM **Privately Held**
Web: www.intra-aerospace.com
SIC: 3599 Machine shop, jobbing and repair

(P-6147)
INTRI-PLEX TECHNOLOGIES INC (HQ)
751 S Kellogg Ave, Goleta (93117-3806)
PHONE.............................805 683-3414
David Dexter, *CEO*
▲ **EMP:** 126 **EST:** 1987
SQ FT: 46,000
SALES (est): 20.93MM
SALES (corp-wide): 21.69MM **Privately Held**
Web: www.intriplex.com
SIC: 3599 Machine shop, jobbing and repair
PA: Ipt Holding Inc
751 S Kellogg Ave
805 683-3414

(P-6148)
J & S INC
229 E Gardena Blvd, Gardena (90248-2800)
PHONE.............................310 719-7144
Joseph Brown, *Pr*
Margaret Brown, *
Sheryl Zamora, *
EMP: 33 **EST:** 1981
SQ FT: 6,141
SALES (est): 3.11MM **Privately Held**
SIC: 3599 Machine shop, jobbing and repair

(P-6149)
J AND K MANUFACTURING INC
14701 Garfield Ave, Paramount (90723-3412)
PHONE.............................562 630-8417
▲ **EMP:** 28 **EST:** 1978
SALES (est): 6.65MM **Privately Held**
SIC: 3599 Machine shop, jobbing and repair

(P-6150)
J I MACHINE COMPANY INC
9720 Distribution Ave, San Diego (92121-2310)
PHONE.............................858 695-1787
Ila Ree Piel, *Pr*
James Piel, *VP*
Mark Jay Piel, *VP*
Wendy Anne Piel, *VP*
▲ **EMP:** 24 **EST:** 1976
SQ FT: 15,400
SALES (est): 3.47MM **Privately Held**
Web: www.jimachine.com

SIC: 3599 3812 Machine shop, jobbing and repair; Search and navigation equipment

(P-6151)
JACO ENGINEERING
879 S East St, Anaheim (92805-5391)
PHONE...............................714 991-1680
H J Meagher, *Pr*
Barbara Meagher, *
EMP: 35 EST: 1964
SQ FT: 10,000
SALES (est): 5.13MM **Privately Held**
Web: www.jacoengineering.com
SIC: 3599 Machine shop, jobbing and repair

(P-6152)
JET CUTTING SOLUTIONS INC
10853 Bell Ct, Rancho Cucamonga (91730-4835)
PHONE...............................909 948-2424
Louis Mammolito, *Pr*
Thomas Ribas, *
Louis Mammooito, *
EMP: 45 EST: 2005
SALES (est): 6.36MM **Privately Held**
Web: www.jetcuttingsolutions.com
SIC: 3599 Machine shop, jobbing and repair

(P-6153)
JMC CLOSING CO LLC
Also Called: Ever-Pac
1499 Palmyrita Ave, Riverside (92507-1600)
PHONE...............................951 278-9900
Ron Vangrouw, *Brnch Mgr*
EMP: 25
SQ FT: 12,400
SALES (corp-wide): 5.97MM **Privately Held**
Web: www.quinncompany.com
SIC: 3599 3444 3441 Machine shop, jobbing and repair; Sheet metalwork; Fabricated structural metal
PA: Jmc Closing Co. Llc
2900 Adams St U C230

(P-6154)
JOHNSON MANUFACTURING INC
15201 Connector Ln, Huntington Beach (92649-1117)
PHONE...............................714 903-0393
Colleen Johnson, *CEO*
Allan Johnson, *
EMP: 35 EST: 1981
SQ FT: 13,000
SALES (est): 4.96MM **Privately Held**
Web: www.johnsonmfginc.com
SIC: 3599 Machine shop, jobbing and repair

(P-6155)
JR MACHINE COMPANY INC
13245 Florence Ave, Santa Fe Springs (90670-4509)
PHONE...............................562 903-9477
Gilbert Reyes, *Pr*
EMP: 29 EST: 1973
SQ FT: 12,000
SALES (est): 2.47MM **Privately Held**
SIC: 3599 Machine shop, jobbing and repair

(P-6156)
K-TECH MACHINE INC
1377 Armorlite Dr, San Marcos (92069-1341)
PHONE...............................800 274-9424
Kenneth Russell, *Pr*
Stuart John Russell, *
EMP: 134 EST: 1990
SQ FT: 16,000
SALES (est): 24.39MM **Privately Held**
Web: www.k-techmachine.com
SIC: 3599 3444 Machine shop, jobbing and repair; Sheet metalwork

(P-6157)
KAP MANUFACTURING INC
327 W Allen Ave, San Dimas (91773-1441)
PHONE...............................909 599-2525
Michael D' Amato, *CFO*
Michael D Amato, *
Kathleen D Amato, *
Bryan D'amato, *VP*
EMP: 27 EST: 1999
SQ FT: 6,000
SALES (est): 4.07MM **Privately Held**
Web: www.kapmfg.com
SIC: 3599 Machine shop, jobbing and repair

(P-6158)
KAY & JAMES INC
Also Called: J&S Machine Works
14062 Balboa Blvd, Sylmar (91342-1005)
PHONE...............................818 998-0357
Kye Sook So, *CEO*
Jung M So, *
EMP: 75 EST: 1981
SQ FT: 25,000
SALES (est): 8.83MM **Privately Held**
SIC: 3599 Machine shop, jobbing and repair

(P-6159)
KEMAC TECHNOLOGY INC
503 S Vincent Ave, Azusa (91702-5131)
PHONE...............................626 334-1519
EMP: 40
Web: www.tecometetch.com
SIC: 3599 3479 Chemical milling job shop; Etching and engraving

(P-6160)
KERLEYLEGACY63 INC
3000-3010 La Jolla St, Anaheim (92806)
PHONE...............................714 630-7286
EMP: 100
SIC: 3599 3469 3444 3061 Machine and other job shop work; Machine parts, stamped or pressed metal; Sheet metalwork; Mechanical rubber goods

(P-6161)
KIMBERLY MACHINE INC
12822 Joy St, Garden Grove (92840-6350)
PHONE...............................714 539-0151
Khanh Cao, *CEO*
Tam Nguyen, *
EMP: 35 EST: 1975
SQ FT: 10,300
SALES (est): 4.3MM **Privately Held**
Web: www.kimberlymachine.com
SIC: 3599 Machine shop, jobbing and repair

(P-6162)
KITCH ENGINEERING INC
12320 Montague St, Pacoima (91331-2213)
PHONE...............................818 897-7133
Steven Kitching, *Pr*
Terry Kitching, *
Kerri Kitching, *
EMP: 30 EST: 1984
SQ FT: 6,000
SALES (est): 4.92MM **Privately Held**
Web: www.kitchengineering.com
SIC: 3599 3751 Machine shop, jobbing and repair; Motorcycles, bicycles and parts

(P-6163)
L A GAUGE COMPANY INC
7440 San Fernando Rd, Sun Valley (91352-4398)
PHONE...............................818 767-7193
Harbans Bawa, *Pr*
EMP: 74 EST: 1954
SQ FT: 26,682
SALES (est): 16.89MM **Privately Held**
Web: www.lagauge.com
SIC: 3599 Machine shop, jobbing and repair

(P-6164)
LANDMARK MFG INC
Also Called: Landmark Motor Cycle ACC
4112 Avenida De La Plata, Oceanside (92056-6099)
PHONE...............................760 941-6626
Tom Allen, *Pr*
Lowell Allen, *VP*
Pat Allen, *Sec*
EMP: 23 EST: 1979
SQ FT: 17,000
SALES (est): 2.56MM **Privately Held**
Web: www.landmarkmfg.com
SIC: 3599 3751 Machine shop, jobbing and repair; Motorcycle accessories

(P-6165)
LASER INDUSTRIES INC
1351 Manhattan Ave, Fullerton (92831-5216)
PHONE...............................714 532-3271
Robert Karim, *Pr*
John Krickl, *
Joseph Butterly, *
Gary Nadau, *
EMP: 65 EST: 1986
SQ FT: 17,500
SALES (est): 11.14MM **Privately Held**
Web: www.laserindustries.com
SIC: 3599 Machine shop, jobbing and repair

(P-6166)
LUSK QUALITY MACHINE PRODUCTS
39457 15th St E, Palmdale (93550-3445)
P.O. Box 901030 (93590-1030)
PHONE...............................661 272-0630
Randall J Lusk, *CEO*
Lloyd Lusk, *
EMP: 27 EST: 1971
SQ FT: 25,000
SALES (est): 4.77MM **Privately Held**
Web: www.luskquality.com
SIC: 3599 3451 Machine shop, jobbing and repair; Screw machine products

(P-6167)
M-INDUSTRIAL ENTERPRISES LLC
Also Called: Project Management
11 Via Onagro, Rcho Sta Marg (92688-4126)
PHONE...............................949 413-7513
Zahid Nazarzai, *Owner*
EMP: 25 EST: 2001
SALES (est): 1.17MM **Privately Held**
SIC: 3599 Industrial machinery, nec

(P-6168)
MALMBERG ENGINEERING INC
655 Deep Valley Dr Ste 125, Rllng Hls Est (90274-3688)
PHONE...............................925 606-6500
▼ EMP: 40
Web: www.malmbergeng.com
SIC: 3599 Custom machinery

(P-6169)
MAR ENGINEERING COMPANY
7350 Greenbush Ave, North Hollywood (91605-4003)
PHONE...............................818 765-4805
Monte Markowitz, *CEO*
Samuel Markowitz, *
Barbara Markowitz, *
EMP: 29 EST: 1957
SQ FT: 12,000
SALES (est): 3.04MM **Privately Held**
Web: www.marengineering.com
SIC: 3599 Machine shop, jobbing and repair

(P-6170)
MARTINEZ AND TUREK INC
Also Called: Martinez & Turek
300 S Cedar Ave, Rialto (92376-9100)
PHONE...............................909 820-6800
Larry Tribe, *Pr*
Donald A Turek, *
Thomas J Martinez, *Testing Vice President*
Laurence Martinez, *
John Romero, *
EMP: 120 EST: 1980
SQ FT: 139,000
SALES (est): 19.67MM **Privately Held**
Web: www.mandtinc.com
SIC: 3599 Machine shop, jobbing and repair

(P-6171)
MATHY MACHINE INC
9315 Wheatlands Rd, Santee (92071-2860)
PHONE...............................619 448-0404
Jay Mathy, *Pr*
EMP: 30 EST: 1979
SQ FT: 14,000
SALES (est): 4.43MM **Privately Held**
Web: www.mathymachine.com
SIC: 3599 Machine shop, jobbing and repair

(P-6172)
MD ENGINEERING INC
1550 Consumer Cir, Corona (92878-3225)
PHONE...............................951 736-5390
Mike Morgan, *Pr*
Ryan Cortes, *
Kurt Bryan Qco, *Prin*
EMP: 37 EST: 1999
SQ FT: 16,000
SALES (est): 5.61MM **Privately Held**
Web: www.mdengineeringonline.com
SIC: 3599 Machine shop, jobbing and repair

(P-6173)
MEDLIN AND SON ENGRG SVC INC
Also Called: Medlin & Sons
12484 Whittier Blvd, Whittier (90602-1017)
PHONE...............................562 464-5889
George W Medlin Ii, *CEO*
Susan Medlin, *
EMP: 45 EST: 1959
SQ FT: 26,000
SALES (est): 4.76MM **Privately Held**
Web: www.medlinandson.com
SIC: 3599 Machine shop, jobbing and repair

(P-6174)
MERRY AN CEJKA
Also Called: Scott Craft Co
4601 Cecilia St, Cudahy (90201-5813)
P.O. Box 430 (90201-0430)
PHONE...............................323 560-3949
Merry An Cejka, *Owner*
Amelia Leal-lee, *Prin*
Robert Cejka, *Prin*
Veronica Zazueta, *Prin*
EMP: 25 EST: 1966
SQ FT: 12,000

PRODUCTS & SVCS

SALES (est): 3.54MM **Privately Held**
Web: www.scottcraftco.com
SIC: 3599 3544 Custom machinery; Special dies, tools, jigs, and fixtures

(P-6175)
METALORE INC
750 S Douglas St, El Segundo (90245-4901)
PHONE...................................310 643-0360
Kenneth Hill, *Pr*
▲ EMP: 30 EST: 1961
SALES (est): 2.39MM **Privately Held**
Web: www.metalore.com
SIC: 3599 Machine shop, jobbing and repair

(P-6176)
METRIC MACHINING (PA)
Also Called: Master Machine Products
3263 Trade Center Dr, Riverside (92507-3432)
PHONE...................................909 947-9222
Drake Archer, *Pr*
Maggie Lopez, *
▲ EMP: 50 EST: 1973
SQ FT: 45,000
SALES (est): 18.19MM
SALES (corp-wide): 18.19MM **Privately Held**
Web: www.metricorp.com
SIC: 3599 Machine shop, jobbing and repair

(P-6177)
MEZIERE ENTERPRISES INC
220 S Hale Ave Ste A, Escondido (92029-1719)
PHONE...................................800 208-1755
Michael Meziere, *Pr*
Don Meziere, *
Dave Meziere, *
▲ EMP: 30 EST: 1980
SQ FT: 15,000
SALES (est): 6.59MM **Privately Held**
Web: www.meziere.com
SIC: 3599 Machine shop, jobbing and repair

(P-6178)
MIKE KENNEY TOOL INC
Also Called: Mkt Innovations
588 Porter Way, Placentia (92870-6453)
PHONE...................................714 577-9262
Mike Kenney, *Pr*
Julie Kenney, *
▲ EMP: 37 EST: 1980
SALES (est): 2.2MM **Privately Held**
Web: www.mkti.com
SIC: 3599 Machine shop, jobbing and repair

(P-6179)
MIKELSON MACHINE SHOP INC
2546 Merced Ave, South El Monte (91733-1924)
PHONE...................................626 448-3920
James Michaelson, *Pr*
James M Mikelson, *
▼ EMP: 23 EST: 1967
SQ FT: 14,000
SALES (est): 4.32MM **Privately Held**
Web: www.mikelson.net
SIC: 3599 Machine shop, jobbing and repair

(P-6180)
MILLER CASTINGS INC
12245 Coast Dr, Whittier (90601-1608)
PHONE...................................562 695-0461
EMP: 42
SALES (corp-wide): 49.35MM **Privately Held**
Web: www.millercastings.com

SIC: 3599 Machine shop, jobbing and repair
PA: Miller Castings, Inc.
2503 Pacific Pk Dr
562 695-0461

(P-6181)
MITCO INDUSTRIES INC (PA)
2235 S Vista Ave, Bloomington (92316-2921)
PHONE...................................909 877-0800
Larry Mitchell, *Pr*
Sammy Mitchell, *
EMP: 26 EST: 1972
SQ FT: 11,000
SALES (est): 4.89MM
SALES (corp-wide): 4.89MM **Privately Held**
Web: vdi.mitcoind.servve.com
SIC: 3599 3533 Machine shop, jobbing and repair; Drilling tools for gas, oil, or water wells

(P-6182)
MKT INNOVATIONS
Also Called: Cooljet Systems
588 Porter Way, Placentia (92870-6453)
PHONE...................................714 524-7668
Mike Kenney, *CEO*
Kathy Jackson, *
▲ EMP: 68 EST: 2002
SALES (est): 4.95MM **Privately Held**
Web: www.mkti.com
SIC: 3599 3523 Machine shop, jobbing and repair; Farm machinery and equipment

(P-6183)
MODERN ENGINE INC
701 Sonora Ave, Glendale (91201-2431)
PHONE...................................818 409-9494
Vachagan Aslanian, *Pr*
Razmik Aslanian, *
Armond Aslanian, *
Nora Aslanian, *
▲ EMP: 43 EST: 1979
SQ FT: 26,000
SALES (est): 4.78MM **Privately Held**
Web: www.meparts.com
SIC: 3599 7539 Machine shop, jobbing and repair; Machine shop, automotive

(P-6184)
MOLNAR ENGINEERING INC
Also Called: Lee's Enterprise
20731 Marilla St, Chatsworth (91311-4408)
PHONE...................................818 993-3495
Laszlo Molnar, *CEO*
Linda D Molnar, *
Tom Molnar, *
Michael Molnar, *
▲ EMP: 37 EST: 1975
SQ FT: 12,000
SALES (est): 6.2MM **Privately Held**
Web: www.leesenterprise.com
SIC: 3599 Machine shop, jobbing and repair

(P-6185)
MOMENI ENGINEERING LLC
Also Called: Essex Industries
5451 Argosy Ave, Huntington Beach (92649-1038)
PHONE...................................714 897-9301
Ahmad Momeni, *Managing Member*
EMP: 28 EST: 1982
SALES (est): 5.63MM **Privately Held**
Web: www.essexindustries.com
SIC: 3599 3841 Machine shop, jobbing and repair; Surgical and medical instruments

(P-6186)
MONO ENGINEERING CORP
20977 Knapp St, Chatsworth (91311-5926)
PHONE...................................818 772-4998
Siamak Morini, *CEO*
EMP: 50 EST: 1994
SQ FT: 40,000
SALES (est): 5.3MM **Privately Held**
Web: www.monoengineering.com
SIC: 3599 3444 8711 Machine shop, jobbing and repair; Sheet metalwork; Industrial engineers

(P-6187)
MOSEYS PRODUCTION MACHINISTS INC (PA)
1550 Lakeview Loop, Anaheim (92807-1819)
PHONE...................................714 693-4840
EMP: 42 EST: 1975
SALES (est): 5.92MM
SALES (corp-wide): 5.92MM **Privately Held**
Web: www.moseys.com
SIC: 3599 Machine shop, jobbing and repair

(P-6188)
MOTORVAC TECHNOLOGIES INC
1431 Village Way, Santa Ana (92705-4714)
PHONE...................................714 558-4822
Mark J Hallsman, *Pr*
John A Rome, *VP*
Gerry Quinn Bdmem, *Prin*
Ron Monark, *Ch Bd*
Stephen Greaves Bdmem, *Prin*
EMP: 30 EST: 1992
SQ FT: 24,360
SALES (est): 3.09MM **Privately Held**
Web: www.cpsproducts.com
SIC: 3599 2899 2842 5013 Gasoline filters, internal combustion engine, except auto; Fuel tank or engine cleaning chemicals; Polishes and sanitation goods; Automotive servicing equipment
PA: Erin Mills International Investment Corp.
C/O Dr. Trevor Carmichael

(P-6189)
NC DYNAMICS INCORPORATED
Also Called: Ncdi
6925 Downey Ave, Long Beach (90805-1823)
PHONE...................................562 634-7392
Kevin Minter, *CEO*
Randall L Bazz, *
▲ EMP: 151 EST: 1979
SALES (est): 9.73MM
SALES (corp-wide): 92.77MM **Privately Held**
Web: www.ncdynamics.com
SIC: 3599 Machine shop, jobbing and repair
PA: Harlow Aerostructures Llc
1501 S Mclean Blvd
316 265-5268

(P-6190)
NC DYNAMICS LLC
Also Called: NC Dynamics
3401 E 69th St, Long Beach (90805-1872)
PHONE...................................562 634-7392
Phillip Friedman, *Managing Member*
EMP: 150 EST: 2017
SALES (est): 9.1MM
SALES (corp-wide): 92.77MM **Privately Held**
Web: www.ncdynamics.com
SIC: 3599 Machine shop, jobbing and repair
PA: Harlow Aerostructures Llc
1501 S Mclean Blvd

316 265-5268

(P-6191)
NELGO INDUSTRIES INC
Also Called: Nelgo Manufacturing
598 Airport Rd, Oceanside (92058-1207)
PHONE...................................760 433-6434
Peter Edward Goethel, *CEO*
EMP: 32 EST: 1966
SALES (est): 4.93MM **Privately Held**
Web: www.nelgo.com
SIC: 3599 Machine shop, jobbing and repair

(P-6192)
NEXT INTENT INC
Also Called: Next Intent
865 Via Esteban, San Luis Obispo (93401-7178)
PHONE...................................805 781-6755
Rodney Babcock, *CEO*
Catherine B Babcock, *
EMP: 30 EST: 1996
SQ FT: 8,500
SALES (est): 4.67MM **Privately Held**
Web: www.nextintent.com
SIC: 3599 Machine shop, jobbing and repair

(P-6193)
NIEDWICK CORPORATION
Also Called: Niedwick Machine Co
967 N Eckhoff St, Orange (92867-5432)
P.O. Box 63851 (92602-6132)
PHONE...................................714 771-9999
Theodore R Niedwick, *Pr*
EMP: 45 EST: 1992
SQ FT: 8,200
SALES (est): 5.2MM **Privately Held**
Web: www.niedwickmachine.com
SIC: 3599 Machine shop, jobbing and repair

(P-6194)
NOROTOS INC
201 E Alton Ave, Santa Ana (92707-4416)
PHONE...................................714 662-3113
Ronald Soto, *Pr*
John Soto, *
▲ EMP: 116 EST: 1985
SQ FT: 12,000
SALES (est): 10.46MM **Privately Held**
Web: www.norotos.com
SIC: 3599 3842 Machine shop, jobbing and repair; Surgical appliances and supplies

(P-6195)
NUSPACE INC (HQ)
4401 E Donald Douglas Dr, Long Beach (90808-1732)
PHONE...................................562 497-3200
Ian Ballinger, *CEO*
Lili Zhou, *
◆ EMP: 25 EST: 1907
SQ FT: 60,000
SALES (est): 2.86MM
SALES (corp-wide): 2.86MM **Privately Held**
Web: www.keyengco.com
SIC: 3599 Air intake filters, internal combustion engine, except auto
PA: Ke Company Acquisition Corp.
4401 E Donald Douglas Dr
562 497-3200

(P-6196)
OEM LLC
311 S Highland Ave, Fullerton (92832-2305)
PHONE...................................714 449-7500
John B Copp, *CEO*
▲ EMP: 23 EST: 1985
SQ FT: 40,000

▲ = Import ▼ = Export
◆ = Import/Export

SALES (est): 2.08MM **Privately Held**
Web: www.oempresssystems.com
SIC: 3599 Machine shop, jobbing and repair

(P-6197)
OMEGA PRECISION
13040 Telegraph Rd, Santa Fe Springs
(90670-4078)
PHONE.................................562 946-2491
Richard Venegas, *CEO*
Joseph M Venegas, *
Richard M Venegas, *
Steve Venegas, *
EMP: 25 **EST:** 1965
SQ FT: 16,332
SALES (est): 2.64MM **Privately Held**
Web: www.omegaprecision.us
SIC: 3599 Machine shop, jobbing and repair

(P-6198)
PARAMOUNT MACHINE CO INC
10824 Edison Ct, Rancho Cucamonga
(91730-3868)
P.O. Box 8068 (91701-0068)
PHONE.................................909 484-3600
Gregory A Harsen, *Pr*
Gail Harsen, *
EMP: 36 **EST:** 1964
SQ FT: 12,000
SALES (est): 5.7MM **Privately Held**
Web: www.paramountmachine.com
SIC: 3599 Machine shop, jobbing and repair

(P-6199)
PARK ENGINEERING AND MFG CO
Also Called: Pem
6430 Roland St, Buena Park (90621-3122)
P.O. Box 2275 (90621-0775)
PHONE.................................714 521-4660
Joanna Tenney, *CEO*
Jeff Tenney, *
EMP: 30 **EST:** 1959
SQ FT: 6,000
SALES (est): 942.66K **Privately Held**
Web: www.roguefishmedia.com
SIC: 3599 Machine shop, jobbing and repair

(P-6200)
PEDAVENA MOULD AND DIE CO INC
12464 Mccann Dr, Santa Fe Springs
(90670-3335)
PHONE.................................310 327-2814
Steve Scardenzan, *Pr*
Paul Weisbrich, *
▲ **EMP:** 28 **EST:** 1964
SQ FT: 12,000
SALES (est): 4.83MM **Privately Held**
Web: www.pmdprecision.com
SIC: 3599 Machine and other job shop work

(P-6201)
PEN MANUFACTURING LLC
Also Called: Pen Manufacturing
1808 N American St, Anaheim
(92801-1001)
PHONE.................................714 992-0950
TOLL FREE: 800
Robert D Pendarvis, *CEO*
Brian Pendarvis, *
EMP: 25 **EST:** 1982
SQ FT: 8,000
SALES (est): 1.07MM **Privately Held**
Web: www.pendarvismanufacturing.com
SIC: 3599 Machine shop, jobbing and repair

(P-6202)
PERFORMANCE MACHINE TECH INC
25141 Avenue Stanford, Valencia
(91355-1227)
PHONE.................................661 294-8617
Dennis Moran, *Pr*
Carolyn Moran, *
EMP: 38 **EST:** 1995
SQ FT: 10,000
SALES (est): 4.98MM **Privately Held**
Web: www.pmtinc.org
SIC: 3599 Machine shop, jobbing and repair

(P-6203)
PL MACHINE CORPORATION
10716 Reagan St, Los Alamitos
(90720-2431)
PHONE.................................714 892-1100
Andrew Dinh, *Ex Dir*
EMP: 25 **EST:** 2009
SALES (est): 5.34MM **Privately Held**
Web: www.plmachinecorp.com
SIC: 3599 Machine shop, jobbing and repair

(P-6204)
PRECISION ARCFT MACHINING INC
Also Called: Pamco
10640 Elkwood St, Sun Valley
(91352-4631)
PHONE.................................818 768-5900
Donald A Pisano, *Pr*
Joyce Pisano, *
Kimberly Pisano, *
▲ **EMP:** 50 **EST:** 1961
SQ FT: 6,500
SALES (est): 6.86MM **Privately Held**
Web: www.pamco-usa.com
SIC: 3599 3678 Machine shop, jobbing and
repair; Electronic connectors

(P-6205)
PRECISION WATERJET INC
Also Called: Precision Machining & Fab
4900 E Hunter Ave, Anaheim (92807-2057)
PHONE.................................888 538-9287
Shane Strowski, *Pr*
EMP: 39 **EST:** 2011
SALES (est): 16.45MM **Privately Held**
Web: www.h2ojet.com
SIC: 3599 Machine shop, jobbing and repair

(P-6206)
PRICE PRODUCTS INCORPORATED
100 State Pl, Escondido (92029-1323)
PHONE.................................760 745-5602
John Price, *Pr*
Robert Price, *
Shirley L Price, *
EMP: 34 **EST:** 1968
SQ FT: 15,000
SALES (est): 5.06MM **Privately Held**
Web: www.priceproducts.com
SIC: 3599 Machine shop, jobbing and repair

(P-6207)
PROCESS FAB INC
13153 Lakeland Rd, Santa Fe Springs
(90670-4520)
P.O. Box 314 (90670)
PHONE.................................562 921-1979
EMP: 180
SIC: 3599 8711 Machine shop, jobbing and
repair; Industrial engineers

(P-6208)
PSCMB REPAIRS INC
Also Called: Quality Industry Repair
12145 Slauson Ave, Santa Fe Springs
(90670-2619)
PHONE.................................626 448-7778
Stephany Castellanos, *CEO*
EMP: 40 **EST:** 2012
SALES (est): 7.32MM **Privately Held**
Web: www.qir-usa.com
SIC: 3599 Machine shop, jobbing and repair

(P-6209)
QUALITY CONTROLLED MFG INC
9429 Abraham Way, Santee (92071-2854)
PHONE.................................619 443-3997
William Grande, *Pr*
James Hiebing, *
Jane Currie, *
EMP: 70 **EST:** 1978
SQ FT: 25,000
SALES (est): 8.73MM **Privately Held**
Web:
www.qualitycontrolledmanufacturinginc.com
SIC: 3599 Machine shop, jobbing and repair

(P-6210)
R & G PRECISION MACHINING INC
2585 Jason Ct, Oceanside (92056-3592)
PHONE.................................760 630-8602
Paul Ryan, *Pr*
Dax Harrison, *
EMP: 25 **EST:** 2004
SALES (est): 4.44MM **Privately Held**
Web: www.rgprecision.com
SIC: 3599 Machine and other job shop work

(P-6211)
RA INDUSTRIES LLC
900 Glenneyre St, Laguna Beach
(92651-2707)
PHONE.................................714 557-2322
Thomas Hyland, *
Carole A Follman, *
◆ **EMP:** 30 **EST:** 1969
SALES (est): 4.93MM **Privately Held**
Web: www.ra-industries.com
SIC: 3599 3593 Machine shop, jobbing and
repair; Fluid power cylinders and actuators

(P-6212)
RALPH E AMES MACHINE WORKS
2301 Dominguez Way, Torrance
(90501-6200)
PHONE.................................310 328-8523
Mike Ames, *Pr*
Ron Ames, *
EMP: 45 **EST:** 1942
SQ FT: 11,000
SALES (est): 8.48MM **Privately Held**
Web: www.amesmachine.com
SIC: 3599 Machine shop, jobbing and repair

(P-6213)
RAMKO MFG INC
3500 Tanya Ave, Hemet (92545-9410)
PHONE.................................951 652-3510
EMP: 100 **EST:** 1981
SALES (est): 1.41MM **Privately Held**
Web: www.ramko.com
SIC: 3599 Machine shop, jobbing and repair

(P-6214)
RAMP ENGINEERING INC
6850 Walthall Way, Paramount
(90723-2028)

PHONE.................................562 531-8030
Mark Scott, *CEO*
Robert C Scott, *
Lisa Scott, *
EMP: 24 **EST:** 1998
SQ FT: 12,000
SALES (est): 2.22MM **Privately Held**
Web: www.rampengineering.com
SIC: 3599 Machine shop, jobbing and repair

(P-6215)
RAPID PRODUCT SOLUTIONS INC
2240 Celsius Ave Ste D, Oxnard
(93030-8015)
PHONE.................................805 485-7234
Max Gerdts, *Pr*
Douglas Wallis, *
Richard Fitch, *
▲ **EMP:** 30 **EST:** 1998
SQ FT: 10,000
SALES (est): 5.05MM **Privately Held**
Web: www.rapid-products.com
SIC: 3599 Machine shop, jobbing and repair

(P-6216)
REID PRODUCTS INC
Also Called: Reid Products
21430 Waalew Rd, Apple Valley
(92307-1026)
P.O. Box 1507 (92307-0028)
PHONE.................................760 240-1355
Kevin Reid, *Pr*
Shelby Reid, *
Lisa Grinser, *
Cliff R Carter, *
EMP: 48 **EST:** 1980
SQ FT: 15,000
SALES (est): 9.69MM **Privately Held**
Web: www.reidproducts.com
SIC: 3599 Machine shop, jobbing and repair

(P-6217)
RESEARCH METAL INDUSTRIES INC
1970 W 139th St, Gardena (90249-2408)
PHONE.................................310 352-3200
Harish Brahmbhatt, *Pr*
◆ **EMP:** 35 **EST:** 1964
SQ FT: 24,000
SALES (est): 11.17MM **Privately Held**
Web: www.researchmetal.com
SIC: 3599 3469 Electrical discharge
machining (EDM); Spinning metal for the
trade

(P-6218)
RINCON ENGINEERING TECH
6325 Carpinteria Ave, Carpinteria
(93013-2901)
PHONE.................................805 684-4144
Edward Avetisian, *Prin*
EMP: 29
SALES (corp-wide): 3.64MM **Privately
Held**
SIC: 3599 Machine shop, jobbing and repair
PA: Rincon Engineering Technologies
3 Caelum Court

(P-6219)
ROBERT H OLIVA INC
Also Called: Romakk Engineering
19863 Nordhoff St, Northridge
(91324-3331)
PHONE.................................818 700-1035
Robert Oliva, *Pr*
Kim Oliva, *
EMP: 25 **EST:** 1975
SQ FT: 4,000
SALES (est): 3.55MM **Privately Held**

Web: www.romakk.com
SIC: 3599 Machine shop, jobbing and repair

(P-6220)
ROBERTS PRECISION ENGRG INC
Also Called: Robert's Engineering
1345 S Allec St, Anaheim (92805-6304)
PHONE..........................714 635-4485
Robert Flores Ii, *Pr*
EMP: 25 EST: 1979
SQ FT: 23,000
SALES (est): 4.2MM **Privately Held**
Web: www.roberts-eng.com
SIC: 3599 Machine shop, jobbing and repair

(P-6221)
ROMEROS ENGINEERING INC
Also Called: American Turn-Key Fabricators
9175 Milliken Ave, Rancho Cucamonga (91730-5509)
PHONE..........................909 481-1170
George Romero, *Pr*
EMP: 25 EST: 2005
SALES (est): 10.43MM **Privately Held**
Web: www.atf1.com
SIC: 3599 Machine and other job shop work

(P-6222)
RONCELLI PLASTICS INC
330 W Duarte Rd, Monrovia (91016-4584)
PHONE..........................800 250-6516
Gino Roncelli, *CEO*
Riley Cole, *
Bingo Roncelli, *
EMP: 151 EST: 1970
SQ FT: 11,000
SALES (est): 24.01MM **Privately Held**
Web: www.roncelli.com
SIC: 3599 Machine shop, jobbing and repair

(P-6223)
RONLO ENGINEERING LTD
955 Flynn Rd, Camarillo (93012-8704)
PHONE..........................805 388-3227
Ronnie Lowe, *CEO*
Rick Slaney, *
Karen Mc Master, *
Tracy Slaney, *
Patricia Lowe Stkhlr, *Prin*
EMP: 30 EST: 1969
SQ FT: 23,650
SALES (est): 6.46MM **Privately Held**
Web: www.ronlo.com
SIC: 3599 Machine shop, jobbing and repair

(P-6224)
S R MACHINING INC
640 Parkridge Ave, Norco (92860-3124)
PHONE..........................951 520-9486
Lawrence T Kaford, *Pr*
EMP: 28 EST: 2003
SALES (est): 3.94MM **Privately Held**
Web: www.srmachining.com
SIC: 3599 Machine shop, jobbing and repair

(P-6225)
S R MACHINING-PROPERTIES LLC
Also Called: S R Machining
640 Parkridge Ave, Norco (92860-3124)
PHONE..........................951 520-9486
Lawrence Kaford, *Pr*
▲ EMP: 134 EST: 1998
SQ FT: 28,000
SALES (est): 4.77MM **Privately Held**
Web: www.srmachining.com

SIC: 3599 3089 Machine shop, jobbing and repair; Injection molding of plastics

(P-6226)
S&S PRECISION MFG INC
2101 S Yale St, Santa Ana (92704-4424)
PHONE..........................714 754-6664
David Mosier, *Pr*
EMP: 45 EST: 1987
SQ FT: 10,000
SALES (est): 4.16MM **Privately Held**
Web: www.ssprecisionmfg.com
SIC: 3599 Machine shop, jobbing and repair

(P-6227)
SANTA FE MACHINE WORKS INC
14578 Rancho Vista Dr, Fontana (92335-4277)
PHONE..........................909 350-6877
Todd Kelly, *Pr*
Dennis Kelly, *
Gilbert Robinson, *
Patricia Kelly, *
Todd Kelly, *Sec*
EMP: 29 EST: 1923
SQ FT: 30,000
SALES (est): 4.45MM **Privately Held**
Web: www.santafemachine.com
SIC: 3599 Machine shop, jobbing and repair

(P-6228)
SAVAGE MACHINING INC
2235 1st St Ste 116, Simi Valley (93065-0903)
PHONE..........................805 584-8047
Wade Savage, *Pr*
EMP: 23 EST: 2001
SALES (est): 4.31MM **Privately Held**
Web: www.savagemachininginc.com
SIC: 3599 Machine shop, jobbing and repair

(P-6229)
SCHNEIDERS MANUFACTURING INC
11122 Penrose St, Sun Valley (91352-2724)
PHONE..........................818 771-0082
Nick Schneider, *Pr*
Tom Schneider, *
Trudy Schneider, *
EMP: 30 EST: 1967
SQ FT: 18,000
SALES (est): 4.06MM **Privately Held**
Web:
www.schneidersmanufacturing.com
SIC: 3599 Machine shop, jobbing and repair

(P-6230)
SCREWMATIC INC
925 W 1st St, Azusa (91702-4222)
P.O. Box 518 (91702-0518)
PHONE..........................626 334-7831
Louis E Zimmerli, *CEO*
Alice Zimmerli, *
Jeff Clow, *
EMP: 65 EST: 1953
SQ FT: 40,000
SALES (est): 4.92MM **Privately Held**
Web: www.screwmaticinc.com
SIC: 3599 Machine shop, jobbing and repair

(P-6231)
SENGA ENGINEERING INC
1525 E Warner Ave, Santa Ana (92705-5419)
PHONE..........................714 549-8011
Roy Jones, *Pr*
EMP: 48 EST: 1976
SQ FT: 25,000

SALES (est): 1.62MM **Privately Held**
Web: www.senga-eng.com
SIC: 3599 Machine shop, jobbing and repair

(P-6232)
SENIOR OPERATIONS LLC
Also Called: Senior Flexonics
9106 Balboa Ave, San Diego (92123-1512)
PHONE..........................858 278-8400
James Young, *VP*
EMP: 70
SALES (corp-wide): 1.2B **Privately Held**
Web: www.sajetproducts.com
SIC: 3599 Bellows, industrial: metal
HQ: Senior Operations Llc
　　300 E Devon Ave
　　Bartlett IL 60103
　　630 372-3500

(P-6233)
SENIOR OPERATIONS LLC
Also Called: Capo Industries Division
790 Greenfield Dr, El Cajon (92021-3101)
PHONE..........................909 627-2723
EMP: 70
SALES (corp-wide): 1.43B **Privately Held**
SIC: 3599 Hose, flexible metallic
HQ: Senior Operations Llc
　　300 E Devon Ave
　　Bartlett IL 60103
　　630 372-3500

(P-6234)
SENIOR OPERATIONS LLC
Also Called: Jet Products
9106 Balboa Ave, San Diego (92123-1512)
PHONE..........................858 278-8400
Damon Evans, *Brnch Mgr*
EMP: 236
SALES (corp-wide): 1.2B **Privately Held**
Web: www.sajetproducts.com
SIC: 3599 Hose, flexible metallic
HQ: Senior Operations Llc
　　300 E Devon Ave
　　Bartlett IL 60103
　　630 372-3500

(P-6235)
SENIOR OPERATIONS LLC
Senior Aerospace
9150 Balboa Ave, San Diego (92123-1512)
PHONE..........................858 278-8400
Willis Fletcher, *Brnch Mgr*
EMP: 151
SALES (corp-wide): 1.2B **Privately Held**
Web: www.sajetproducts.com
SIC: 3599 Machine shop, jobbing and repair
HQ: Senior Operations Llc
　　300 E Devon Ave
　　Bartlett IL 60103
　　630 372-3500

(P-6236)
SERRANO INDUSTRIES INC
9922 Tabor Pl, Santa Fe Springs (90670-3300)
PHONE..........................562 777-8180
Hoberto Serrano, *Pr*
Maria Serrano, *
Bobby Serrano, *
EMP: 34 EST: 1990
SQ FT: 30,000
SALES (est): 4.13MM **Privately Held**
Web: www.serrano-ind.com
SIC: 3599 Machine shop, jobbing and repair

(P-6237)
SHEFFIELD MANUFACTURING INC
9131 Glenoaks Blvd, Sun Valley (91352-2692)

PHONE..........................310 320-1473
EMP: 70
SIC: 3599 3444 3548 3812 Machine shop, jobbing and repair; Sheet metalwork; Electric welding equipment; Search and navigation equipment

(P-6238)
SMI CA INC
Also Called: Saeilo Manufacturing Inds
14340 Iseli Rd, Santa Fe Springs (90670-5204)
PHONE..........................562 926-9407
Katsuhiko Tsukamoto, *CEO*
David Tsukamoto, *
Erik Kawakami, *
EMP: 26 EST: 1999
SQ FT: 10,000
SALES (est): 4.95MM
SALES (corp-wide): 19.09MM **Privately Held**
Web: www.smi-ca.com
SIC: 3599 Machine shop, jobbing and repair
PA: Saeilo Enterprises Inc
　　105 Kahr Ave
　　845 735-6500

(P-6239)
SOLO ENTERPRISE CORP
Also Called: Solo Golf
220 N California Ave, City Of Industry (91744-4384)
P.O. Box 607 (91747-0607)
PHONE..........................626 961-3591
Richard F Mugica, *CEO*
Edward A Mugica, *
EMP: 50 EST: 1966
SQ FT: 20,000
SALES (est): 4.26MM **Privately Held**
Web: www.soloenterprisecorp.com
SIC: 3599 3812 Machine shop, jobbing and repair; Search and navigation equipment

(P-6240)
SONSRAY INC
23935 Madison St, Torrance (90505-6010)
PHONE..........................323 585-1271
Matthew Hoelscher, *Prin*
EMP: 45 EST: 2014
SALES (est): 5.4MM **Privately Held**
Web: www.sonsray.com
SIC: 3599 Industrial machinery, nec

(P-6241)
SOUTHERN CAL TCHNICAL ARTS INC
Also Called: Technical Arts
370 E Crowther Ave, Placentia (92870-6419)
PHONE..........................714 524-2626
John H Robson Iv, *Pr*
John H Robson Iv, *Pr*
Christine Robson, *
Matt Robson, *
Kristi A Robson, *
EMP: 48 EST: 1970
SQ FT: 9,400
SALES (est): 9.94MM
SALES (corp-wide): 489.27MM **Publicly Held**
Web: www.technicalarts.net
SIC: 3599 3827 Machine shop, jobbing and repair; Optical instruments and lenses
PA: Nn, Inc.
　　6210 Ardrey Kell Rd Ste 1
　　980 264-4300

(P-6242)
SPARTAN MANUFACTURING CO
7081 Patterson Dr, Garden Grove (92841-1435)

▲ = Import ▼ = Export
◆ = Import/Export

PHONE..................714 894-1955
R J Horton, *Pr*
Terry Danielson, *
EMP: 26 **EST:** 1957
SQ FT: 16,000
SALES (est): 3.66MM **Privately Held**
Web: www.spartanmfg.com
SIC: 3599 Machine shop, jobbing and repair

(P-6243)
SPEC ENGINEERING COMPANY INC
13754 Saticoy St, Panorama City (91402-6518)
PHONE..................818 780-3045
Gregory Viksman, *Pr*
Anna Viksman, *
EMP: 25 **EST:** 1987
SQ FT: 5,200
SALES (est): 2.74MM **Privately Held**
Web: www.specengco.com
SIC: 3599 3412 Machine shop, jobbing and repair; Metal barrels, drums, and pails

(P-6244)
STINES MACHINE INC
2481 Coral St, Vista (92081-8431)
PHONE..................760 599-9955
Edward L Huston, *Pr*
Tri Tran, *
EMP: 35 **EST:** 1969
SQ FT: 15,000
SALES (est): 2.11MM **Privately Held**
Web: www.stinesmachine.com
SIC: 3599 Machine shop, jobbing and repair

(P-6245)
SUPERIOR THREAD ROLLING CO
12801 Wentworth St, Arleta (91331-4332)
PHONE..................818 504-3626
EMP: 82 **EST:** 1952
SALES (est): 18.28MM **Privately Held**
Web: www.superiorthread.com
SIC: 3599 3542 3429 Machine shop, jobbing and repair; Thread rolling machines; Aircraft hardware

(P-6246)
T/Q SYSTEMS INC
25131 Arctic Ocean Dr, Lake Forest (92630-8852)
PHONE..................949 455-0478
Victor Buytkus, *Pr*
Scott Moebius, *
EMP: 40 **EST:** 1988
SALES (est): 4.65MM **Privately Held**
Web: www.tqsystems.net
SIC: 3599 Machine shop, jobbing and repair

(P-6247)
TECHNIFORM INTERNATIONAL CORP
375 S Cactus Ave, Rialto (92376-6320)
PHONE..................909 877-6886
Richard S Jones, *Pr*
EMP: 176 **EST:** 1989
SQ FT: 60,000
SALES (est): 3.49MM **Privately Held**
Web: www.plantprefab.com
SIC: 3599 3469 3444 Machine shop, jobbing and repair; Metal stampings, nec; Sheet metalwork

(P-6248)
THIESSEN PRODUCTS INC
Also Called: Jim's Machining
555 Dawson Dr Ste A, Camarillo (93012-5085)

PHONE..................805 482-6913
Jim Thiessen, *Pr*
Debra Thiessen, *
Jay R Thiessen, *
EMP: 130 **EST:** 1971
SQ FT: 44,000
SALES (est): 16.05MM **Privately Held**
Web: www.jimsusa.com
SIC: 3599 Machine shop, jobbing and repair

(P-6249)
THOMSON INDUSTRIES INC
Also Called: Thomson Lnear Motion Optimized
2695 Customhouse Ct, San Diego (92154-7645)
PHONE..................619 661-6292
EMP: 30
SALES (corp-wide): 6.25B **Publicly Held**
Web: www.thomsonlinear.com
SIC: 3599 Air intake filters, internal combustion engine, except auto
HQ: Thomson Industries, Inc.
203a W Rock Rd
Radford VA 24141
540 633-3549

(P-6250)
THUNDERBOLT MANUFACTURING INC
641 S State College Blvd, Fullerton (92831-5115)
PHONE..................714 632-0397
Minh Son To, *Pr*
EMP: 26 **EST:** 1990
SQ FT: 5,800
SALES (est): 6.94MM **Privately Held**
Web: www.thunderboltmfg.com
SIC: 3599 Machine shop, jobbing and repair

(P-6251)
TMX ENGINEERING AND MFG CORP
2141 S Standard Ave, Santa Ana (92707-3034)
PHONE..................714 641-5884
Souhil Toubia, *CEO*
Gus Toubia, *
Ali Ossaily, *
Steve Korn, *
Mauricio Escarcega, *
EMP: 75 **EST:** 1985
SQ FT: 23,000
SALES (est): 3.78MM **Privately Held**
Web: www.tmxengineering.com
SIC: 3599 3728 3544 Machine shop, jobbing and repair; Aircraft parts and equipment, nec; Special dies, tools, jigs, and fixtures

(P-6252)
TOMI ENGINEERING INC
414 E Alton Ave, Santa Ana (92707-4242)
PHONE..................714 556-1474
Michael F Falbo, *CEO*
Anthony Falbo, *
EMP: 52 **EST:** 1975
SQ FT: 15,000
SALES (est): 8.37MM **Privately Held**
Web: www.tomiengineering.com
SIC: 3599 Machine shop, jobbing and repair

(P-6253)
TOSCO - TOOL SPECIALTY COMPANY
Also Called: Tool Specialty Co
1011 E Slauson Ave, Los Angeles (90011-5296)
P.O. Box 512157 (90051-0157)
PHONE..................323 232-3561

Jerry Tetzlaff, *Pr*
Ted Tetzlaff, *
▲ **EMP:** 25 **EST:** 1943
SQ FT: 19,500
SALES (est): 2.36MM **Privately Held**
Web: www.toolspecialty.com
SIC: 3599 Machine shop, jobbing and repair

(P-6254)
TOWER INDUSTRIES INC
Also Called: Allied Mechanical Products
1720 S Bon View Ave, Ontario (91761-4411)
PHONE..................909 947-2723
Mark Slater, *Mgr*
EMP: 110
SQ FT: 60,794
SALES (corp-wide): 28.17MM **Privately Held**
Web:
metal-stamping-companies.cmac.ws
SIC: 3599 Machine shop, jobbing and repair
PA: Tower Industries, Inc.
1518 N Endeavor Ln Ste C

(P-6255)
TREPANNING SPECIALITIES INC
Also Called: Trepanning Specialties
16201 Illinois Ave, Paramount (90723-4996)
PHONE..................562 633-8110
Donald B Laughlin, *Pr*
Patricia Laughlin, *
▲ **EMP:** 23 **EST:** 1973
SQ FT: 7,000
SALES (est): 2.92MM **Privately Held**
Web: www.trepanningspec.com
SIC: 3599 Machine shop, jobbing and repair

(P-6256)
TRUE POSITION TECHNOLOGIES LLC
24900 Avenue Stanford, Valencia (91355-1272)
PHONE..................661 294-0030
Allen Sumian, *Pr*
EMP: 82 **EST:** 1990
SQ FT: 25,000
SALES (est): 6.98MM
SALES (corp-wide): 241.4MM **Privately Held**
Web: www.truepositiontech.com
SIC: 3599 Machine shop, jobbing and repair
PA: Hbd Industries, Inc.
565 Metro Pl S Ste 250
614 526-7000

(P-6257)
UNITED PRECISION CORP
20810 Plummer St, Chatsworth (91311-5004)
PHONE..................818 576-9540
Robert Hawrylo, *CEO*
Robert Stanley Hawrylo, *
EMP: 40 **EST:** 2014
SQ FT: 7,500
SALES (est): 7.08MM **Privately Held**
Web: www.upc-usa.com
SIC: 3599 3812 Machine shop, jobbing and repair; Defense systems and equipment

(P-6258)
UNIVERSAL PLANT SVCS CAL INC
20545 Belshaw Ave # A, Carson (90746-3505)
PHONE..................310 618-1600
Stewart Jones, *Brnch Mgr*
EMP: 92
SALES (corp-wide): 273.28MM **Privately Held**

Web: www.universalplant.com
SIC: 3599 Custom machinery
HQ: Universal Plant Services Of California, Inc.
20545a Belshaw Ave
Carson CA 90746
310 618-1600

(P-6259)
UPLAND FAB INC
1445 Brooks St Ste L, Ontario (91762-3665)
PHONE..................909 986-6565
Paul Sapra, *CEO*
Patsy Sapra, *
Steven Sapra, *
Jackson Sapra, *Stockholder*
EMP: 30 **EST:** 1970
SQ FT: 12,000
SALES (est): 4.63MM **Privately Held**
Web: www.uplandfab.com
SIC: 3599 2679 3083 Machine shop, jobbing and repair; Honeycomb core and board: made from purchased material; Plastics finished products, laminated

(P-6260)
V & S ENGINEERING COMPANY LTD
5766 Research Dr, Huntington Beach (92649-1617)
PHONE..................714 898-7869
Dino Dukovic, *Pr*
Dino Dokovic, *Pr*
EMP: 27 **EST:** 1979
SQ FT: 10,000
SALES (est): 581.03K **Privately Held**
Web: www.vseng.biz
SIC: 3599 Machine shop, jobbing and repair

(P-6261)
VALLEY PERFORATING LLC
3201 Gulf St, Bakersfield (93308-4988)
PHONE..................661 324-4964
Mike Dover, *Pr*
Dorothy Reynolds, *
Alice Lomas, *
EMP: 65 **EST:** 1970
SQ FT: 10,440
SALES (est): 5.18MM **Privately Held**
Web: www.valleyperf.com
SIC: 3599 Machine shop, jobbing and repair

(P-6262)
VALLEY TOOL AND MACHINE CO INC
111 Explorer St, Pomona (91768-3278)
PHONE..................909 595-2205
Chuck Rogers, *CEO*
Jim Rogers, *
Nancy Larson, *
EMP: 32 **EST:** 1982
SQ FT: 34,000
SALES (est): 5.11MM **Privately Held**
Web: www.valleytool-inc.com
SIC: 3599 7692 3544 Machine shop, jobbing and repair; Welding repair; Special dies, tools, jigs, and fixtures

(P-6263)
VANDERHORST BROTHERS INDUSTRIES INC
Also Called: V B I
1715 Surveyor Ave, Simi Valley (93063-3374)
PHONE..................805 583-3333
EMP: 60 **EST:** 2000
SALES (est): 11.51MM
SALES (corp-wide): 31.13MM **Privately Held**

Web: www.vbinc.com
SIC: 3599 3542 3728 Machine shop, jobbing and repair; Knurling machines; Aircraft parts and equipment, nec
PA: Rtc Aerospace Llc
7215 45th St Ct E
918 407-0291

(P-6264)
VEECO PROCESS EQUIPMENT INC
Slider Process Division
112 Robin Hill Rd, Goleta (93117-3107)
PHONE.................................805 967-2700
Ed Wagner, *Mgr*
EMP: 52
Web: www.veeco.com
SIC: 3599 3545 3544 3291 Machine shop, jobbing and repair; Machine tool accessories; Special dies, tools, jigs, and fixtures; Abrasive products
HQ: Veeco Process Equipment Inc.
1 Terminal Dr
Plainview NY 11803

(P-6265)
VESCIO THREADING CO
Also Called: Vescio Manufacturing Intl
14002 Anson Ave, Santa Fe Springs (90670-5297)
PHONE.................................562 802-1868
Gregory Vescio, *CEO*
Greg Vescio, *
Robert Vescio, *
Verna Vescio, *
Bob Vescio, *
EMP: 73 EST: 1947
SQ FT: 13,000
SALES (est): 8.9MM **Privately Held**
Web: www.vesciomfg.com
SIC: 3599 Machine shop, jobbing and repair

(P-6266)
VISTA INDUSTRIAL PRODUCTS INC
3210 Executive Rdg, Vista (92081-8527)
PHONE.................................760 599-5050
EMP: 160 EST: 1968
SALES (est): 22.59MM **Privately Held**
Web: www.vista-industrial.com
SIC: 3599 Machine shop, jobbing and repair

(P-6267)
W MACHINE WORKS INC
13814 Del Sur St, San Fernando (91340-3440)
PHONE.................................818 890-8049
Marzel Neckien, *Pr*
Randy Neckien, *
EMP: 45 EST: 1977
SQ FT: 25,000
SALES (est): 9.01MM **Privately Held**
Web: www.wmwcnc.com
SIC: 3599 Machine shop, jobbing and repair

(P-6268)
WAHLCO INC
Also Called: Wahlco
4774 Murrieta St Ste 3, Chino (91710-5155)
PHONE.................................714 979-7300
Alonso Munoz, *CEO*
Robert R Wahler, *
Barry J Southam, *
Dennis Nickel, *
◆ EMP: 106 EST: 1972
SALES (est): 6.53MM **Privately Held**
Web: www.wahlco.com
SIC: 3599 Custom machinery

(P-6269)
WEBER DRILLING CO INC
4028 W 184th St, Torrance (90504-4712)
PHONE.................................310 670-7708
Marlene Wood, *Pr*
Ronald Wood, *
EMP: 25 EST: 1947
SALES (est): 2.35MM **Privately Held**
SIC: 3599 Machine shop, jobbing and repair

(P-6270)
WELDMAC MANUFACTURING COMPANY
1451 N Johnson Ave, El Cajon (92020-1615)
PHONE.................................619 440-2300
Marshall J Rugg, *Pr*
Barbara Bloomfield, *
Robert L Rugg, *
EMP: 122 EST: 1968
SQ FT: 100,000
SALES (est): 13.4MM **Privately Held**
Web: www.weldmac.com
SIC: 3599 3444 7692 Machine shop, jobbing and repair; Sheet metalwork; Brazing

(P-6271)
WELDMAC MANUFACTURING COMPANY
1533 N Johnson Ave, El Cajon (92020-1683)
PHONE.................................619 440-2300
Marshall J Rugg, *CEO*
EMP: 38 EST: 1969
SALES (est): 5.24MM **Privately Held**
Web: www.weldmac.com
SIC: 3599 Machine shop, jobbing and repair

(P-6272)
WEST BOND INC (PA)
1551 S Harris Ct, Anaheim (92806-5932)
PHONE.................................714 978-1551
John C Price, *Pr*
Gary Phillips, *
Phyllis Eppig, *
▼ EMP: 47 EST: 1966
SQ FT: 38,000
SALES (est): 9.98MM
SALES (corp-wide): 9.98MM **Privately Held**
Web: www.westbond.com
SIC: 3599 Machine shop, jobbing and repair

(P-6273)
WESTERN CNC INC
1001 Park Center Dr, Vista (92081-8340)
PHONE.................................760 597-7000
Danny Ashcraft, *Pr*
Carolyn Ashcraft, *
April Ashcraft Ramirez, *
EMP: 100 EST: 1980
SQ FT: 57,000
SALES (est): 12.52MM **Privately Held**
Web: www.westerncnc.com
SIC: 3599 Machine shop, jobbing and repair

(P-6274)
WESTERN PRECISION AERO LLC
11600 Monarch St, Garden Grove (92841-1817)
PHONE.................................714 893-7999
Ed Mckenna, *Managing Member*
Norma Davis, *
EMP: 37 EST: 2009
SQ FT: 16,000
SALES (est): 10.47MM
SALES (corp-wide): 1.56B **Publicly Held**
Web: www.rbcbearings.com

SIC: 3599 Machine shop, jobbing and repair
PA: Rbc Bearings Incorporated
1 Tribiology Ctr
203 267-7001

(P-6275)
WILCOX MACHINE CO
7180 Scout Ave, Bell Gardens (90201-3202)
P.O. Box 2159 (90202-2159)
PHONE.................................562 927-5353
George Schofhauser, *Pr*
Kurt Anderegg, *
Jill Wigney, *
Tom Anderegg, *
◆ EMP: 60 EST: 1955
SALES (est): 7.53MM **Privately Held**
Web: www.wilcoxmachine.com
SIC: 3599 Machine shop, jobbing and repair

(P-6276)
WILLIS MACHINE INC
11000 Alto Dr, Oak View (93022-9569)
PHONE.................................805 604-4500
Harlan Willis, *Pr*
EMP: 23 EST: 1977
SALES (est): 2.52MM **Privately Held**
Web: www.willismachine.com
SIC: 3599 Machine shop, jobbing and repair

(P-6277)
WILSHIRE PRECISION PDTS INC
7353 Hinds Ave, North Hollywood (91605-3704)
PHONE.................................818 765-4571
Thomas G Lewis, *Pr*
Wendy Lewis, *
Dana Lewis, *
Shoshona Lewis, *
EMP: 31 EST: 1951
SQ FT: 10,000
SALES (est): 8.32MM **Privately Held**
Web: www.wilshireprecision.com
SIC: 3599 3621 Machine shop, jobbing and repair; Motors, electric

(P-6278)
WIRE CUT COMPANY INC
6750 Caballero Blvd, Buena Park (90620-1134)
PHONE.................................714 994-1170
Sydney Omar, *Pr*
Sydney Omar, *CEO*
Milton M Thomas, *
Tina Thomas, *
EMP: 30 EST: 1978
SQ FT: 20,000
SALES (est): 4.48MM **Privately Held**
Web: www.wirecutcompany.com
SIC: 3599 Machine shop, jobbing and repair

(P-6279)
YOSMART INC
25172 Arctic Ocean Dr Ste 106, Lake Forest (92630-8851)
PHONE.................................949 825-5958
John Xu, *CEO*
Manxiang Xu, *CEO*
Anqiong Li, *Sec*
Qing Zhao, *
EMP: 29 EST: 2014
SALES (est): 1.5MM **Privately Held**
Web: shop.yosmart.com
SIC: 3599 3824 3699 Water leak detectors; Water meters; Security devices

3612 Transformers, Except Electric

(P-6280)
ABBOTT TECHNOLOGIES INC
8203 Vineland Ave, Sun Valley (91352-3956)
PHONE.................................818 504-0644
Kerima Marie Batte, *CEO*
EMP: 40 EST: 1961
SQ FT: 12,000
SALES (est): 8.24MM **Privately Held**
Web: www.abbott-tech.com
SIC: 3612 3559 3677 Transformers, except electric; Electronic component making machinery; Transformers power supply, electronic type

(P-6281)
ARNOLD MAGNETICS CORPORATION
Also Called: Arnold Magnetics
841 Avenida Acaso Ste A, Camarillo (93012-8798)
PHONE.................................805 484-4221
EMP: 52 EST: 1956
SALES (est): 9.92MM **Privately Held**
Web: www.amcpower.com
SIC: 3612 3679 Transformers, except electric ; Power supplies, all types: static

(P-6282)
CUSTOM MAGNETICS CAL INC
15142 Vista Del Rio Ave, Chino (91710-9694)
PHONE.................................909 620-3877
Christopher Cimino, *CEO*
▲ EMP: 27 EST: 2013
SALES (est): 6.16MM **Privately Held**
Web: www.cmi-power.com
SIC: 3612 Transformers, except electric

(P-6283)
DATATRONICS ROMOLAND INC
Also Called: Datatronics
28151 Us Highway 74, Menifee (92585-8916)
P.O. Box 1579 (92585-1579)
PHONE.................................951 928-7700
Paul Y Siu, *Pr*
Wai M Siu Shui, *
▲ EMP: 70 EST: 1989
SQ FT: 38,800
SALES (est): 16.36MM **Privately Held**
Web: www.datatronics.com
SIC: 3612 3677 Transformers, except electric ; Inductors, electronic

(P-6284)
DOW-ELCO INC
1313 W Olympic Blvd, Montebello (90640-5010)
P.O. Box 669 (90640-0669)
PHONE.................................323 723-1288
Linda Su, *Pr*
Cecile Se Kay, *VP*
Grace Park, *
Ronald Cheung, *
Annie Su, *
EMP: 25 EST: 1946
SQ FT: 8,100
SALES (est): 2.45MM **Privately Held**
SIC: 3612 3829 3061 Vibrators, interrupter; Measuring and controlling devices, nec; Mechanical rubber goods

318   2025 Southern California
Business Directory and Buyers Guide   ▲ = Import ▼ = Export
◆ = Import/Export

(P-6285)
FULHAM CO INC
12705 S Van Ness Ave, Hawthorne
(90250-3322)
PHONE....................323 779-2980
Antony Corrie, *CEO*
James Cooke, *CFO*
Harry Libby, *VP*
Mike Hu, *VP*
Deborah Knuckles, *CFO*
▲ **EMP:** 40 **EST:** 1994
SQ FT: 48,000
SALES (est): 8.52MM **Privately Held**
Web: www.fulham.com
SIC: 3612 Ballasts for lighting fixtures
HQ: Fulham Company Gmbh
Torstr. 138
Berlin BE 10119

(P-6286)
GRAND GENERAL ACCESSORIES LLC
Also Called: Grand General
1965 E Vista Bella Way, Rancho Dominguez
(90220-6106)
PHONE....................310 631-2589
Shu-hui Sophia Lin Huang, *CEO*
Nan-huang Huang, *Sec*
▲ **EMP:** 39 **EST:** 1984
SALES (est): 2.84MM **Privately Held**
Web: www.grandgeneral.com
SIC: 3612 5531 3713 Transformers, except
electric; Truck equipment and parts; Truck
and bus bodies

(P-6287)
JACKSON ENGINEERING CO INC
9411 Winnetka Ave # A, Chatsworth
(91311-6035)
PHONE....................818 886-9567
Ron Jackson, *Pr*
Dennis Elliott, *
EMP: 40 **EST:** 1951
SQ FT: 10,000
SALES (est): 920.19K **Privately Held**
Web: www.jacksonengineering.com
SIC: 3612 Electronic meter transformers

(P-6288)
JUSTIN INC
Also Called: Justin
2663 Lee Ave, El Monte (91733-1411)
PHONE....................626 444-4516
Frank Justin Junior, *Pr*
Jeff Justin, *
Jeffrey Ross Justin, *
EMP: 50 **EST:** 1956
SQ FT: 4,000
SALES (est): 4.16MM **Privately Held**
Web: www.justininc.com
SIC: 3612 Specialty transformers

(P-6289)
MGM TRANSFORMER CO
5701 Smithway St, Commerce
(90040-1583)
PHONE....................323 726-0888
Patrick Gogerchin, *CEO*
Patrick Gogerchin, *Pr*
Luis Otero, *
Bianca Kaveh, *
Sherry Boloury, *
◆ **EMP:** 70 **EST:** 1975
SQ FT: 40,000
SALES (est): 99.19MM **Privately Held**
Web: www.mgmtransformer.com
SIC: 3612 Transformers, except electric

(P-6290)
NUVVE HOLDING CORP (PA)
2488 Historic Decatur Rd Ste 200, San
Diego (92106-6134)
PHONE....................619 456-5161
Gregory Poilasne, *CEO*
Jon M Montgomery, *Interim Chairman of the Board*
Ted Smith, *Pr*
David G Robson, *CFO*
EMP: 38 **EST:** 1996
SALES (est): 8.33MM
SALES (corp-wide): 8.33MM **Publicly Held**
Web: www.nuvve.com
SIC: 3612 Power and distribution
transformers

(P-6291)
OHMEGA SOLENOID CO INC
10912 Painter Ave, Santa Fe Springs
(90670-4529)
P.O. Box 2747 (90670-0747)
PHONE....................562 944-7948
EMP: 47 **EST:** 1967
SALES (est): 5.86MM **Privately Held**
Web: www.ohmegasolenoid.com
SIC: 3612 3679 3677 Power and distribution
transformers; Solenoids for electronic
applications; Electronic coils and
transformers

(P-6292)
ON-LINE POWER INCORPORATED (PA)
Also Called: Power Services
14000 S Broadway, Los Angeles
(90061-1018)
PHONE....................323 721-5017
Abbie Gougerchian, *CEO*
▲ **EMP:** 46 **EST:** 1980
SQ FT: 36,000
SALES (est): 9.49MM
SALES (corp-wide): 9.49MM **Privately Held**
Web: www.onlinepower.com
SIC: 3612 3621 3613 3677 Transformers,
except electric; Motors and generators;
Regulators, power; Electronic coils and
transformers

(P-6293)
ONYX POWER INC
4011 W Carriage Dr, Santa Ana
(92704-6301)
PHONE....................714 513-1500
EMP: 104
SIC: 3612 Power and distribution
transformers

(P-6294)
PACIFIC TRANSFORMER CORP
5399 E Hunter Ave, Anaheim (92807-2054)
PHONE....................714 779-0450
Patrick A Thomas, *CEO*
Justin Richardson, *
▲ **EMP:** 85 **EST:** 1981
SQ FT: 37,000
SALES (est): 14.29MM **Privately Held**
Web: www.pactran.com
SIC: 3612 Power transformers, electric

(P-6295)
PIONEER CUSTOM ELEC PDTS CORP
10640 Springdale Ave, Santa Fe Springs
(90670-3843)
PHONE....................562 944-0626
Geo Murickan, *Pr*

EMP: 68 **EST:** 2013
SALES (est): 3.1MM **Publicly Held**
Web: www.pioneercep.com
SIC: 3612 Electronic meter transformers
PA: Pioneer Power Solutions, Inc.
400 Kelby St Fl 12

(P-6296)
PULSE ELECTRONICS INC (HQ)
15255 Innovation Dr Ste 100, San Diego
(92128-3410)
PHONE....................858 674-8100
Mark Twaalfhoven, *CEO*
Renuka Ayer, *CFO*
John Houston, *
John R D Dickson, *
Mike Bond, *
▲ **EMP:** 270 **EST:** 1955
SQ FT: 49,750
SALES (est): 60MM **Privately Held**
Web: www.pulseelectronics.com
SIC: 3612 3674 3677 Specialty transformers
; Modules, solid state; Filtration devices,
electronic
PA: Yageo Corporation
3f, No.233-1, Pao Chiao Rd.,

(P-6297)
RING LLC (HQ)
Also Called: Ring
12515 Cerise Ave, Hawthorne
(90250-4801)
PHONE....................310 929-7085
Jamie Siminoff, *Managing Member*
▲ **EMP:** 300 **EST:** 2013
SQ FT: 40,000
SALES (est): 49.97MM **Publicly Held**
Web: www.ring.com
SIC: 3612 5065 Doorbell transformers,
electric; Security control equipment and
systems
PA: Amazon.Com, Inc.
410 Terry Ave N

(P-6298)
SEMPRA GLOBAL (HQ)
488 8th Ave, San Diego (92101-7123)
PHONE....................619 696-2000
Mark A Snell, *CEO*
EMP: 60 **EST:** 1997
SALES (est): 1.68MM
SALES (corp-wide): 16.72B **Publicly Held**
Web: www.sempra.com
SIC: 3612 Transformers, except electric
PA: Sempra
488 8th Ave
619 696-2000

(P-6299)
ZETTLER MAGNETICS INC
2410 Birch St, Vista (92081-8472)
PHONE....................949 831-5000
Gunther Rueb, *CEO*
▲ **EMP:** 190 **EST:** 1997
SQ FT: 80,000
SALES (est): 2.28MM **Privately Held**
Web: www.zettlercontrols.com
SIC: 3612 Transformers, except electric
PA: Zettler Components, Inc.
75 Columbia

3613 Switchgear And Switchboard Apparatus

(P-6300)
AEMI HOLDINGS LLC
6610 Cobra Way, San Diego (92121-4107)
PHONE....................858 481-0210
Daniel H Chang, *Pr*

Xiang Ming Li, *Sr VP*
Caili Chang, *
▲ **EMP:** 77 **EST:** 1986
SQ FT: 45,000
SALES (est): 9.21MM **Privately Held**
Web: www.aem-usa.com
SIC: 3613 3677 7699 Fuses and fuse
equipment; Inductors, electronic; Metal
reshaping and replating services

(P-6301)
AGE INCORPORATED
14831 Spring Ave, Santa Fe Springs
(90670-5109)
PHONE....................562 483-7300
Vasken Imasdounian, *Pr*
Daniel Imasdounian, *
Annie Imasdounian, *
▲ **EMP:** 35 **EST:** 1975
SALES (est): 4.2MM **Privately Held**
Web: www.agenameplate.com
SIC: 3613 3625 Control panels, electric;
Electric controls and control accessories,
industrial

(P-6302)
CROWN TECHNICAL SYSTEMS (PA)
13470 Philadelphia Ave, Fontana
(92337-7700)
PHONE....................951 332-4170
Naim Siddiqui, *Pr*
Howard Siddiqui, *VP*
▲ **EMP:** 198 **EST:** 1996
SQ FT: 92,000
SALES (est): 59.3MM **Privately Held**
Web: www.crowntechnicalsystems.com
SIC: 3613 Control panels, electric

(P-6303)
CUSTOM CONTROL SENSORS LLC (PA)
Also Called: Custom Aviation Supply
21111 Plummer St, Chatsworth
(91311-4905)
P.O. Box 3535 (91313-3535)
PHONE....................818 341-4610
Henry P Acuff, *Pr*
Thomas Pilgrim, *
Joann D Acuff, *
EMP: 113 **EST:** 1957
SALES (est): 21.88MM
SALES (corp-wide): 21.88MM **Privately Held**
Web: www.ccsdualsnap.com
SIC: 3613 3643 3625 Switches, electric
power except snap, push button, etc.;
Current-carrying wiring services; Relays
and industrial controls

(P-6304)
DATA LIGHTS RIGGING LLC
Also Called: Ratpac Dimmers
7508 Tyrone Ave, Van Nuys (91405-1447)
PHONE....................818 786-0536
EMP: 31 **EST:** 2014
SALES (est): 1.88MM **Privately Held**
Web: www.ratpaccontrols.com
SIC: 3613 Switchgear and switchboard
apparatus

(P-6305)
ELECTRO SWITCH CORP
Also Called: Digitran
10410 Trademark St, Rancho Cucamonga
(91730-5826)
PHONE....................909 581-0855
Robert M Pineau, *Pr*
EMP: 69
SALES (corp-wide): 39.86MM **Privately Held**

PRODUCTS & SVCS

Web: www.digitran-switches.com
SIC: 3613 3625 Switches, electric power except snap, push button, etc.; Industrial controls: push button, selector switches, pilot
HQ: Electro Switch Corp.
775 Pleasant St Ste 1
Weymouth MA 02189
781 335-1195

(P-6306)
GENERAL SWITCHGEAR INC
14729 Spring Ave, Santa Fe Springs (90670-5107)
EMP: 30 **EST:** 1983
SALES (est): 2.27MM **Privately Held**
SIC: 3613 5063 Switchgear and switchgear accessories, nec; Electrical apparatus and equipment

(P-6307)
HYDRA-ELECTRIC COMPANY (PA)
3151 N Kenwood St, Burbank (91505-1052)
PHONE..................818 843-6211
Tc Queener, *Pr*
Len Torres, *
EMP: 178 **EST:** 1950
SQ FT: 90,000
SALES (est): 22.61MM
SALES (corp-wide): 22.61MM **Privately Held**
Web: www.hydraelectric.com
SIC: 3613 Switches, electric power except snap, push button, etc.

(P-6308)
ICONN INC
Also Called: Iconn Technologies
8909 Irvine Center Dr, Irvine (92618-4249)
PHONE..................800 286-6742
Turker Hidirlar, *CEO*
Jon Harrison, *
Raif Tunc Elmas, *
▲ **EMP:** 56 **EST:** 2007
SQ FT: 9,920
SALES (est): 9.05MM **Privately Held**
Web: www.iconn-ems.com
SIC: 3613 3714 3678 3351 Power connectors, electric; Booster (jump-start) cables, automotive; Electronic connectors; Wire, copper and copper alloy
PA: Cape Ems Berhad
Plo 227a Jalan Cyber 1a

(P-6309)
PHAOSTRON INSTR ELECTRONIC CO
Also Called: Phaostron Instr Electronic Co
717 N Coney Ave, Azusa (91702-2205)
PHONE..................626 969-6801
Paul R Mc Guirk, *Pr*
Andrew Mcguirk, *VP*
Jacqueline Cangialosi, *
EMP: 80 **EST:** 1937
SQ FT: 50,000
SALES (est): 4.35MM **Privately Held**
Web: www.phaostron.com
SIC: 3613 Metering panels, electric
PA: Westbase, Inc.
717 N Coney Ave

(P-6310)
ROMAC SUPPLY CO INC
Also Called: Romac
17722 Neff Ranch Rd, Yorba Linda (92886-9013)
PHONE..................323 721-5810
TOLL FREE: 800

David B Rosenfield, *Pr*
Lisa R Podolsky, *
Phillip Rosenfield, *
Edith Rosenfield, *
Victoria Rosenfield, *
EMP: 60 **EST:** 1955
SALES (est): 5.12MM **Privately Held**
Web: www.tauberaronsinc.com
SIC: 3613 3621 3612 5063 Switchgear and switchgear accessories, nec; Motors and generators; Transformers, except electric; Motors, electric

(P-6311)
STACO SYSTEMS INC (HQ)
Also Called: Staco Switch
7 Morgan, Irvine (92618-2005)
PHONE..................949 297-8700
Patrick Hutchins, *Pr*
Jeffrey Nick, *VP*
Brett Meinsen, *VP Fin*
Tom Lanni, *VP*
Jeff Bowen, *VP Sls*
◆ **EMP:** 69 **EST:** 1957
SQ FT: 35,000
SALES (est): 9.91MM
SALES (corp-wide): 46.24MM **Privately Held**
Web: www.stacosystems.com
SIC: 3613 Switches, electric power except snap, push button, etc.
PA: Components Corporation Of America
5950 Berkshire Ln # 1500
214 969-0166

(P-6312)
W A BENJAMIN ELECTRIC CO
1615 Staunton Ave, Los Angeles (90021-3184)
PHONE..................213 749-7731
D E Benjamin, *Pr*
EMP: 50 **EST:** 1911
SALES (est): 10.27MM **Privately Held**
Web: www.benjaminelectric.com
SIC: 3613 Panelboards and distribution boards, electric

(P-6313)
WEST COAST SWITCHGEAR (DH)
13837 Bettencourt St, Cerritos (90703-1009)
PHONE..................562 802-3441
Alfred P Cisternelli, *CEO*
▲ **EMP:** 93 **EST:** 2003
SQ FT: 20,000
SALES (est): 3.96MM **Privately Held**
Web: www.westcoastswitchgear.com
SIC: 3613 5063 Power circuit breakers; Switchgear
HQ: Resa Power, Llc
8723 Fallbrook Dr
Houston TX 77064
832 900-8340

3621 Motors And Generators

(P-6314)
BARTA - SCHOENEWALD INC (PA)
Also Called: Advanced Motion Controls
3805 Calle Tecate, Camarillo (93012-5068)
PHONE..................805 389-1935
Sandor Barta, *Pr*
Daniel Schoenewald, *
▲ **EMP:** 116 **EST:** 1986
SQ FT: 86,000
SALES (est): 34.72MM
SALES (corp-wide): 34.72MM **Privately Held**

Web: www.a-m-c.com
SIC: 3621 3699 Servomotors, electric; Electrical equipment and supplies, nec

(P-6315)
CAL LLC POWERFLEX SYSTEMS
15445 Innovation Dr, San Diego (92128-3432)
P.O. Box 3155 (94024-0155)
PHONE..................650 469-3392
Raphael Declercq, *CEO*
Bryan Towe, *
EMP: 24 **EST:** 2016
SALES (est): 5.74MM **Privately Held**
Web: www.powerflex.com
SIC: 3621 Generators for gas-electric or oil-electric vehicles
PA: Edf Renewables, Inc.
15445 Innovation Dr

(P-6316)
CALNETIX TECHNOLOGIES LLC (HQ)
16323 Shoemaker Ave, Cerritos (90703-2244)
PHONE..................562 293-1660
Vatche Artinian, *Ch*
Ian Hart, *
Andrea Matiauda, *
Herman Artinian, *UPLING LLC*
Pana Shenoy, *
EMP: 67 **EST:** 2011
SALES (est): 22MM
SALES (corp-wide): 100.4MM **Privately Held**
Web: www.calnetix.com
SIC: 3621 Motors and generators
PA: Calnetix, Inc.
16323 Shoemaker Ave
562 293-1660

(P-6317)
CHARGIE LLC
3947 Landmark St, Culver City (90232-2315)
PHONE..................310 621-0024
Zach Jennings, *Managing Member*
EMP: 61 **EST:** 2020
SALES (est): 4.37MM **Privately Held**
Web: www.chargie.com
SIC: 3621 Electric motor and generator parts

(P-6318)
CMI INTEGRATED TECH INC
11250 Playa Ct, Culver City (90230-6127)
EMP: 35 **EST:** 1989
SQ FT: 6,600
SALES (est): 1.55MM **Privately Held**
SIC: 3621 3825 Electric motor and generator auxiliary parts; Instruments to measure electricity

(P-6319)
COLE INSTRUMENT CORP
2650 S Croddy Way, Santa Ana (92704-5298)
PHONE..................714 556-3100
Ric Garcia, *Pr*
Manuel Garcia, *
Muse Khawaja, *
EMP: 70 **EST:** 1965
SQ FT: 16,000
SALES (est): 8.37MM **Privately Held**
Web: www.cole-switches.com
SIC: 3621 3679 Motors and generators; Electronic switches

(P-6320)
DIRECT DRIVE SYSTEMS INC
621 Burning Tree Rd, Fullerton (92833-1448)
PHONE..................714 872-5500
James Pribble, *CEO*
Michael Slater, *
Robert Clark, *
EMP: 57 **EST:** 2005
SALES (est): 3.69MM
SALES (corp-wide): 7.83B **Privately Held**
SIC: 3621 Electric motor and generator parts
HQ: Fmc Technologies, Inc.
13460 Lockwood Rd
Houston TX 77044
281 591-4000

(P-6321)
EROAD INC
15110 Avenue Of Science Ste 100, San Diego (92128-3405)
P.O. Box 23846 (97281-3846)
PHONE..................503 305-2255
Brian Michie, *Pr*
EMP: 77 **EST:** 2012
SALES (est): 8.41MM **Privately Held**
Web: www.eroad.com
SIC: 3621 Storage battery chargers, motor and engine generator type
PA: Eroad Limited
260 Oteha Valley Road

(P-6322)
GLENTEK INC
208 Standard St, El Segundo (90245-3818)
PHONE..................310 322-3026
Richard Vasak, *CEO*
Helen Sysel, *
◆ **EMP:** 84 **EST:** 1964
SQ FT: 105,000
SALES (est): 11.21MM **Privately Held**
Web: www.glentek.com
SIC: 3621 Motors and generators

(P-6323)
GOHZ INC
23555 Golden Springs Dr Ste K1, Diamond Bar (91765-8100)
PHONE..................800 603-1219
Zhuge Fusheng, *Pr*
EMP: 30 **EST:** 2015
SQ FT: 1,200
SALES (est): 558.71K **Privately Held**
Web: www.gohz.com
SIC: 3621 Frequency converters (electric generators)

(P-6324)
HITACHI AUTOMOTIVE SYSTEMS
Also Called: Los Angeles Plant
6200 Gateway Dr, Cypress (90630-4842)
PHONE..................310 212-0200
EMP: 100
SIC: 3621 3714 Electric motor and generator parts; Motor vehicle parts and accessories
HQ: Hitachi Automotive Systems Americas, Inc.
955 Warwick Rd
Harrodsburg KY 40330
859 734-9451

(P-6325)
INTEGRATED MAGNETICS INC
11250 Playa Ct, Culver City (90230-6127)
PHONE..................310 391-7213
Anil Nanji, *Pr*
EMP: 40 **EST:** 2012
SQ FT: 120,000
SALES (est): 2.28MM
SALES (corp-wide): 46.01MM **Privately Held**

Web: www.intemag.com
SIC: 3621 3679 3764 Rotors, for motors; Cores, magnetic; Rocket motors, guided missiles
PA: Integrated Technologies Group, Inc.
11250 Playa Ct
310 391-7213

(P-6326)
KOLLMORGEN CORPORATION
33 S La Patera Ln, Santa Barbara (93117-3214)
PHONE..................805 696-1236
EMP: 83
SALES (corp-wide): 6.25B Publicly Held
Web: www.kollmorgen.com
SIC: 3621 Servomotors, electric
HQ: Kollmorgen Corporation
203a W Rock Rd
Radford VA 24141
540 639-9045

(P-6327)
LEOCH BATTERY CORPORATION (DH)
20322 Valencia Cir, Lake Forest (92630-8158)
PHONE..................949 588-5853
Hui Peng, *Pr*
Lili Shi, *
◆ EMP: 100 EST: 2003
SALES (est): 52.67MM Privately Held
Web: www.leochamericas.com
SIC: 3621 Storage battery chargers, motor and engine generator type
HQ: Leoch International Technology Limited
C/O Conyers Trust Company (Cayman) Limited
George Town GR CAYMAN KY1-1

(P-6328)
MAC M MC CULLY CORPORATION
Also Called: Mac M McCully Co
5316 Kazuko Ct, Moorpark (93021-1790)
PHONE..................805 529-0661
Guy Mc Cully, *Pr*
EMP: 35 EST: 1979
SALES (est): 5.17MM
SALES (corp-wide): 23.52MM Privately Held
Web: www.windings.com
SIC: 3621 Motors, electric
PA: Careen, Inc.
15 Somsen St
800 795-8533

(P-6329)
NANTENERGY LLC
2040 E Mariposa Ave, El Segundo (90245-5027)
PHONE..................310 905-4866
EMP: 75 EST: 2019
SALES (est): 2.12MM Privately Held
SIC: 3621 8731 Storage battery chargers, motor and engine generator type; Energy research

(P-6330)
RESMED MOTOR TECHNOLOGIES INC
Also Called: Resmed
9540 De Soto Ave, Chatsworth (91311-5010)
PHONE..................818 428-6400
David B Sears, *CEO*
▲ EMP: 170 EST: 2002
SQ FT: 35,000
SALES (est): 49.25MM Publicly Held

SIC: 3621 3714 3841 Coils, for electric motors or generators; Propane conversion equipment, motor vehicle; Surgical and medical instruments
PA: Resmed Inc.
9001 Spectrum Center Blvd

(P-6331)
REULAND ELECTRIC CO (PA)
17969 Railroad St, City Of Industry (91748-1192)
P.O. Box 1464 (91749-1464)
PHONE..................626 964-6411
Noel C Reuland, *Pr*
William Kramer Iii, *VP*
▲ EMP: 130 EST: 1937
SQ FT: 100,000
SALES (est): 50.09MM
SALES (corp-wide): 50.09MM Privately Held
Web: www.reuland.com
SIC: 3621 3566 3363 3625 Motors, electric; Drives, high speed industrial, except hydrostatic; Aluminum die-castings; Electric controls and control accessories, industrial

(P-6332)
SEA ELECTRIC LLC
436 Alaska Ave, Torrance (90503-3902)
PHONE..................424 376-3660
EMP: 29
SALES (est): 10.75MM Privately Held
Web: www.sea-electric.com
SIC: 3621 3711 Motors and generators; Motor vehicles and car bodies

(P-6333)
SKURKA AEROSPACE INC (DH)
4600 Calle Bolero, Camarillo (93012-8575)
P.O. Box 2869 (93011-2869)
PHONE..................805 484-8884
Michael Lisman, *CEO*
Lisa Sabol, *
Halle Terrion, *
EMP: 46 EST: 2004
SQ FT: 70,000
SALES (est): 40.15MM
SALES (corp-wide): 7.94B Publicly Held
Web: www.skurka-aero.com
SIC: 3621 3679 Motors, electric; Transducers, electrical
HQ: Transdigm, Inc.
1350 Euclid Ave
Cleveland OH 44115

(P-6334)
SMI HOLDINGS INC
Also Called: Specialty Motors
28420 Witherspoon Pkwy, Valencia (91355-4167)
PHONE..................800 232-2612
▲ EMP: 25
SIC: 3621 Motors, electric

(P-6335)
THINGAP INC
Also Called: Thingap
4035 Via Pescador, Camarillo (93012-5050)
PHONE..................805 477-9741
John Baumann, *CEO*
EMP: 33 EST: 2012
SALES (est): 4.51MM
SALES (corp-wide): 578.63MM Publicly Held
Web: www.thingap.com
SIC: 3621 Coils, for electric motors or generators
PA: Allient Inc.
495 Commerce Dr Ste 3

716 242-8634

(P-6336)
VALLEY POWER SERVICES INC
425 S Hacienda Blvd, City Of Industry (91745-1123)
PHONE..................909 969-9345
Clark Lee, *Pr*
▲ EMP: 30 EST: 1999
SQ FT: 17,802
SALES (est): 3.98MM Privately Held
Web: www.valleypowersystems.com
SIC: 3621 Motor housings

3624 Carbon And Graphite Products

(P-6337)
ALLIANCE SPACESYSTEMS LLC
4398 Corporate Center Dr, Los Alamitos (90720-2537)
PHONE..................714 226-1400
Rick Byrens, *Pr*
EMP: 155 EST: 1997
SQ FT: 101,000
SALES (est): 21.5MM
SALES (corp-wide): 189.21MM Privately Held
Web: www.appliedcomposites.com
SIC: 3624 Carbon and graphite products
PA: Applied Composites Holdings, Llc
25692 Atlantic Ocean Dr
949 716-3511

(P-6338)
KBR INC
Also Called: Electro-Tech Machining Div
2000 W Gaylord St, Long Beach (90813-1032)
P.O. Box 92610 (14692-0610)
PHONE..................562 436-9281
Ryan Mcmahon, *Pr*
▲ EMP: 32 EST: 1977
SQ FT: 39,000
SALES (est): 5.02MM Privately Held
Web: www.etmgraphite.com
SIC: 3624 Carbon and graphite products

3625 Relays And Industrial Controls

(P-6339)
ABSOLUTE GRAPHIC TECH USA INC
Also Called: Agt
235 Jason Ct, Corona (92879-6199)
PHONE..................909 597-1133
Steven J Barberi, *Pr*
EMP: 49 EST: 2006
SQ FT: 25,800
SALES (est): 9.17MM Privately Held
Web: www.agt-usa.com
SIC: 3625 3577 Industrial electrical relays and switches; Printers and plotters

(P-6340)
ANAHEIM AUTOMATION INC
4985 E Landon Dr, Anaheim (92807-1972)
PHONE..................714 992-6990
Joanne Dargan, *CEO*
Alan Harmon, *
Faithe Reimbold, *
Jhon Witt, *
◆ EMP: 42 EST: 1966
SQ FT: 9,000
SALES (est): 8.73MM Privately Held
Web: www.anaheimautomation.com

SIC: 3625 3545 3566 Control equipment, electric; Machine tool accessories; Speed changers, drives, and gears

(P-6341)
AP PARPRO INC
2700 S Fairview St, Santa Ana (92704-5947)
PHONE..................619 498-9004
Hsiu Pi Wu, *Pr*
Po Ju Shih, *Sec*
EMP: 47 EST: 2005
SALES (est): 5.64MM Privately Held
Web: www.parpro.com
SIC: 3625 Relays and industrial controls

(P-6342)
BALBOA WATER GROUP LLC (HQ)
Also Called: Controlmyspa
2020 Piper Ranch Rd Ste 150, San Diego (92154-6262)
PHONE..................714 384-0384
Eric Kownacki, *CEO*
David J Cline, *
Jean-pierre Parent, *Sr VP*
◆ EMP: 66 EST: 2007
SALES (est): 93.07MM
SALES (corp-wide): 835.6MM Publicly Held
Web: www.balboawater.com
SIC: 3625 3599 Electric controls and control accessories, industrial; Machine shop, jobbing and repair
PA: Helios Technologies, Inc.
7456 16th St E
941 362-1200

(P-6343)
CAL-COMP ELECTRONICS (USA) CO LTD
Also Called: Ccsd
9877 Waples St, San Diego (92121-2922)
PHONE..................858 587-6900
▲ EMP: 299
SIC: 3625 Actuators, industrial

(P-6344)
CONTROL SWITCHES INTL INC
2425 Mira Mar Ave, Long Beach (90815-1757)
P.O. Box 92349 (90809-2349)
PHONE..................562 498-7331
Margerate Turner, *Ex VP*
Peggy Turner, *
Judith Steward, *
Susan Moore, *
Jane Armstrong, *
EMP: 25 EST: 1977
SQ FT: 10,000
SALES (est): 3.49MM
SALES (corp-wide): 7.85MM Privately Held
Web: www.controlswitches.com
SIC: 3625 Switches, electronic applications
PA: Control Switches, Inc.
2425 Mira Mar Ave
562 498-7331

(P-6345)
CRYDOM INC (DH)
2320 Paseo De Las Americas Ste 201, San Diego (92154-7273)
PHONE..................619 210-1590
Bob Ciurczak, *Pr*
▲ EMP: 47 EST: 2005
SQ FT: 20,000
SALES (est): 41.7MM
SALES (corp-wide): 4.05B Privately Held
Web: www.sensata.com

SIC: **3625** 5065 3674 3643 Control equipment, electric; Electronic parts and equipment, nec; Semiconductors and related devices; Current-carrying wiring services

HQ: Sensata Technologies, Inc.
529 Pleasant St
Attleboro MA 02703

(P-6346)
CURTISS-WRGHT CNTRLS ELCTRNIC (DH)
Also Called: Curtiss-Wrght Cntrls Elctrnic
28965 Avenue Penn, Santa Clarita
(91355-4185)
PHONE................................661 257-4430
Thomas P Quinly, *CEO*
David Dietz, *
EMP: 172 EST: 1985
SQ FT: 18,700
SALES (est): 38.8MM
SALES (corp-wide): 2.85B **Publicly Held**
Web: www.curtisswright.com
SIC: **3625** 8731 8711 3769 Relays and industrial controls; Commercial physical research; Consulting engineer; Space vehicle equipment, nec
HQ: Curtiss-Wright Controls, Inc.
15801 Brixham Hill Ave # 200
Charlotte NC 28277
704 869-4600

(P-6347)
DOW-KEY MICROWAVE CORPORATION
Also Called: Dow-Key Microwave
4822 Mcgrath St, Ventura (93003-7718)
PHONE................................805 650-0260
David Wightman, *Pr*
EMP: 150 EST: 1970
SQ FT: 26,000
SALES (est): 26.06MM
SALES (corp-wide): 8.44B **Publicly Held**
Web: www.mpgdover.com
SIC: **3625** 3678 3643 3613 Switches, electronic applications; Electronic connectors; Current-carrying wiring services ; Switchgear and switchboard apparatus
PA: Dover Corporation
3005 Highland Pkwy
630 541-1540

(P-6348)
EATON ELECTRICAL INC
13201 Dahlia St, Fontana (92337-6971)
PHONE................................951 685-5788
EMP: 154
SIC: **3625** Motor controls and accessories
HQ: Eaton Electrical Inc.
1000 Cherrington Pkwy
Moon Township PA 15108

(P-6349)
EMBEDDED SYSTEMS INC
Also Called: Esi Motion
2250a Union Pl, Simi Valley (93065-1660)
PHONE................................805 624-6030
Earnie Beem, *Pr*
Sheila D'angelo, *VP*
EMP: 40 EST: 2005
SALES (est): 8.24MM **Privately Held**
Web: www.esimotion.com
SIC: **3625** Motor starters and controllers, electric

(P-6350)
GENERAL DYNAMICS MISSION
General Dynamics Global
7603 Saint Andrews Ave Ste H, San Diego
(92154-8217)

PHONE................................619 671-5400
Bud Jenkins, *Ofcr*
EMP: 99
SALES (corp-wide): 42.27B **Publicly Held**
Web: www.gdmissionsystems.com
SIC: **3625** 3824 3825 3621 Relays and industrial controls; Fluid meters and counting devices; Instruments to measure electricity; Motors and generators
HQ: General Dynamics Mission Systems, Inc.
12450 Fair Lakes Cir
Fairfax VA 22033
877 449-0600

(P-6351)
ITT CANNON LLC
Also Called: BIW Connector Systems
56 Technology Dr, Irvine (92618-2301)
PHONE................................714 557-4700
Farrokh Batliwala, *Prin*
Farrokh Batliwala, *Pr*
Mary Beth Gustafsson, *
Philip Bordages, *
John Capela, *CAO*
EMP: 132 EST: 2011
SALES (est): 28.52MM
SALES (corp-wide): 3.28B **Publicly Held**
Web: www.ittcannon.com
SIC: **3625** Control equipment, electric
HQ: Itt Industries Holdings, Inc
100 Wshington Blvd Fl 6 Flr 6
Stamford CT 06902
914 641-2000

(P-6352)
ITT LLC
ITT Goulds Pumps
3951 Capitol Ave, City Of Industry
(90601-1734)
P.O. Box 1254 (91749-1254)
PHONE................................562 908-4144
Shashank Patel, *Genl Mgr*
EMP: 75
SQ FT: 85,000
SALES (corp-wide): 3.28B **Publicly Held**
Web: www.itt.com
SIC: **3625** Control equipment, electric
HQ: Itt Llc
1133 Westchester Ave
White Plains NY 10604
914 641-2000

(P-6353)
M W SAUSSE & CO INC (PA)
Also Called: Vibrex
28744 Witherspoon Pkwy, Valencia
(91355-5425)
PHONE................................661 257-3311
Torbjorn Helland, *Pr*
Dan Robinson, *
Paul Azevedo, *
Gregory Hall, *
▲ EMP: 59 EST: 1961
SQ FT: 12,000
SALES (est): 9.82MM
SALES (corp-wide): 9.82MM **Privately Held**
Web: www.vibrex.net
SIC: **3625** Control equipment, electric

(P-6354)
MICROSEMI CORP-POWER MGT GROUP
11861 Western Ave, Garden Grove
(92841-2119)
PHONE................................714 994-6500
James J Peterson, *Pr*
John W Hohener, *
David Goren, *

Rob Warren, *General Vice President*
EMP: 249 EST: 1977
SQ FT: 135,000
SALES (est): 3.89MM
SALES (corp-wide): 7.63B **Publicly Held**
Web: www.microsemi.com
SIC: **3625** 3677 3679 3613 Relays, for electronic use; Electronic transformers; Liquid crystal displays (LCD); Switchgear and switchboard apparatus
HQ: Microsemi Corp.-Power Management Group Holding
11861 Western Ave
Garden Grove CA 92841
714 994-6500

(P-6355)
MOOG INC
Also Called: Moog Jon Street Warehouse
1218 W Jon St, Torrance (90502-1208)
PHONE................................310 533-1178
Alberto Bilalon, *Mgr*
EMP: 500
SALES (corp-wide): 3.32B **Publicly Held**
Web: www.moog.com
SIC: **3625** 8711 3812 Relays and industrial controls; Aviation and/or aeronautical engineering; Aircraft/aerospace flight instruments and guidance systems
PA: Moog Inc.
400 Jamison Rd
716 652-2000

(P-6356)
Q COM INC
17782 Cowan, Irvine (92614-6030)
PHONE................................949 833-1000
Robert Elders, *CEO*
Frederick P Kaiser, *
EMP: 26 EST: 1980
SALES (est): 576.95K **Privately Held**
SIC: **3625** 3822 3564 Control equipment, electric; Environmental controls; Blowers and fans

(P-6357)
RIGHT HAND MANUFACTURING INC
180 Otay Lakes Rd Ste 205, Bonita
(91902-2444)
PHONE................................619 819-5056
▲ EMP: 150 EST: 2003
SALES (est): 790.38K **Privately Held**
Web: www.righthandmanufacturing.com
SIC: **3625** Control circuit devices, magnet and solid state

(P-6358)
ROSEMOUNT ANALYTICAL INC
2400 Barranca Pkwy, Irvine (92606-5018)
Rural Route 22737 (60673-0001)
PHONE................................713 396-8880
◆ EMP: 1100
SIC: **3625** 3825 3823 3564 Relays and industrial controls; Instruments to measure electricity; Process control instruments; Blowers and fans

(P-6359)
S R C DEVICES INCCUSTOMER
6295 Ferris Sq Ste D, San Diego
(92121-3248)
PHONE................................866 772-8668
Richard W Carlyle, *Pr*
Mark Mccabe, *Sr VP*
EMP: 303 EST: 2001
SQ FT: 2,000
SALES (est): 2.76MM **Privately Held**

SIC: **3625** 3643 5065 Switches, electronic applications; Current-carrying wiring services; Electronic parts and equipment, nec

(P-6360)
SOUNDCOAT COMPANY INC
16901 Armstrong Ave, Irvine (92606-4914)
PHONE................................631 242-2200
Clay Simpson, *Brnch Mgr*
EMP: 69
SALES (corp-wide): 130.22MM **Privately Held**
Web: www.soundcoat.com
SIC: **3625** 3086 3296 Noise control equipment; Plastics foam products; Mineral wool
HQ: The Soundcoat Company, Inc.
1 Burt Dr
Deer Park NY 11729
631 242-2200

(P-6361)
SURFACE TECHNOLOGIES CORP
3170 Commercial St, San Diego
(92113-1427)
PHONE................................619 564-8320
Bernard Meartz, *Mgr*
EMP: 31
SQ FT: 29,617
SALES (corp-wide): 24.92MM **Privately Held**
Web: www.surfacetechnologiescorp.com
SIC: **3625** Marine and navy auxiliary controls
PA: Surface Technologies Corporation
2440 Mayport Rd Ste 7
904 241-1501

(P-6362)
SYSTEMS MCHS ATMTN CMPNNTS COR (PA)
Also Called: Smac
5807 Van Allen Way, Carlsbad
(92008-7309)
PHONE................................760 929-7575
Ed Neff, *CEO*
Robert Berry, *
▲ EMP: 165 EST: 1990
SALES (est): 35.4MM **Privately Held**
Web: www.smac-mca.com
SIC: **3625** 2822 3549 Actuators, industrial; Synthetic rubber; Assembly machines, including robotic

(P-6363)
TE CONNECTIVITY CORPORATION
Also Called: Kilovac
550 Linden Ave, Carpinteria (93013-2038)
PHONE................................805 684-4560
Mike Moschitto, *Brnch Mgr*
EMP: 30
SALES (corp-wide): 9.17B **Privately Held**
Web: www.te.com
SIC: **3625** Relays, for electronic use
HQ: Te Connectivity Corporation
1050 Westlakes Dr
Berwyn PA 19312
610 893-9800

(P-6364)
TEAL ELECTRONICS CORPORATION (PA)
10350 Sorrento Valley Rd, San Diego
(92121-1642)
PHONE................................858 558-9000
Glen Kassan, *Ch Bd*
Donald Klein, *CEO*

William Bickel, *VP Fin*
David Nuzzo, *Treas*
◆ **EMP:** 79 **EST:** 1983
SQ FT: 36,059
SALES (est): 6.42MM
SALES (corp-wide): 6.42MM **Privately Held**
SIC: 3625 2631 3612 Noise control equipment; Transformer board; Transformers, except electric

(P-6365)
WOODWARD HRT INC (HQ)
25200 Rye Canyon Rd, Santa Clarita (91355-1204)
PHONE......................661 294-6000
Charles Blankenship, *CEO*
Tom Cromwell, *COO*
Bill Lacey, *CFO*
▲ **EMP:** 650 **EST:** 1954
SQ FT: 200,000
SALES (est): 80.49MM
SALES (corp-wide): 3.32B **Publicly Held**
SIC: 3625 3492 Actuators, industrial; Electrohydraulic servo valves, metal
PA: Woodward, Inc.
1081 Woodward Way
970 482-5811

(P-6366)
ZBE INC
1035 Cindy Ln, Carpinteria (93013-2905)
PHONE......................805 576-1600
Zac Bogart, *Pr*
▲ **EMP:** 45 **EST:** 1980
SQ FT: 7,500
SALES (est): 3.76MM **Privately Held**
Web: www.zbe.com
SIC: 3625 3861 3577 Electric controls and control accessories, industrial; Photographic equipment and supplies; Computer peripheral equipment, nec

---

3629 Electrical Industrial Apparatus

(P-6367)
ARECONT VISION LLC
425 E Colorado St Fl 7, Glendale (91205-5117)
PHONE......................818 937-0700
◆ **EMP:** 103
SIC: 3629 Electronic generation equipment

(P-6368)
AVEOX INC
2205 Ward Ave Ste A, Simi Valley (93065-1864)
PHONE......................805 915-0200
David Palombo, *Pr*
▲ **EMP:** 35 **EST:** 1992
SQ FT: 22,000
SALES (est): 17.3MM **Privately Held**
Web: www.aveox.com
SIC: 3629 Electronic generation equipment

(P-6369)
CAPAX TECHNOLOGIES INC
24842 Avenue Tibbitts, Valencia (91355-3404)
PHONE......................661 257-7666
Jagdish Patel, *Pr*
Nina Patel, *
EMP: 28 **EST:** 1988
SQ FT: 17,000
SALES (est): 2.63MM **Privately Held**
Web: www.capaxtechnologies.com
SIC: 3629 3675 Capacitors, fixed or variable; Electronic capacitors

(P-6370)
COMPOSITE TECHNOLOGY CORP
2026 Mcgaw Ave, Irvine (92614-0911)
PHONE......................949 428-8500
Benton H Wilcoxon, *Ch Bd*
◆ **EMP:** 104 **EST:** 2001
SALES (est): 3.24MM **Privately Held**
SIC: 3629 8711 Mercury arc rectifiers (electrical apparatus); Engineering services

(P-6371)
CONCURRENT HOLDINGS LLC
11150 Santa Monica Blvd Ste 825, Los Angeles (90025-3988)
PHONE......................310 473-3065
Benjamin Teno, *Managing Member*
▲ **EMP:** 750 **EST:** 2012
SALES (est): 2.32MM
SALES (corp-wide): 406.38MM **Privately Held**
SIC: 3629 3679 Electronic generation equipment; Harness assemblies, for electronic use: wire or cable
PA: Balmoral Funds Llc
11150 Snta Mnica Blvd Ste
310 473-3065

(P-6372)
DESCO INDUSTRIES INC (PA)
Also Called: Desco
3651 Walnut Ave, Chino (91710-2904)
PHONE......................909 627-8178
◆ **EMP:** 75 **EST:** 1965
SALES (est): 48.53MM
SALES (corp-wide): 48.53MM **Privately Held**
Web: www.descoindustries.com
SIC: 3629 Static elimination equipment, industrial

(P-6373)
ENGINEERED MAGNETICS INC
Also Called: Aap Division
10524 S La Cienega Blvd, Inglewood (90304-1116)
PHONE......................310 649-9000
Josh Shachar, *Ch Bd*
Kathy Tran, *
Maya Vu, *
Isabella Yi Sha Li, *Dir*
EMP: 26 **EST:** 2000
SQ FT: 57,000
SALES (est): 4.43MM **Privately Held**
Web: www.engineeredmagnetics.net
SIC: 3629 3812 3369 Power conversion units, a.c. to d.c.: static-electric; Missile guidance systems and equipment; Aerospace castings, nonferrous: except aluminum

(P-6374)
EPC POWER CORP (PA)
13250 Gregg St Ste A2, Poway (92064-7164)
PHONE......................858 748-5590
Devin Dilley, *CEO*
Mary Loomas, *CFO*
Allan Abela, *COO*
▼ **EMP:** 113 **EST:** 2010
SQ FT: 10,000
SALES (est): 38.82MM **Privately Held**
Web: www.epcpower.com
SIC: 3629 Battery chargers, rectifying or nonrotating

(P-6375)
IAMPLUS LLC
809 N Cahuenga Blvd, Los Angeles (90038-3703)

PHONE......................323 210-3852
Phil Molyneux, *Pr*
Chandrasekar Rathakrishnan, *Dir*
Rosemary Peschken, *CFO*
EMP: 56 **EST:** 2012
SQ FT: 3,900
SALES (est): 6.28MM
SALES (corp-wide): 9.1MM **Privately Held**
Web: www.iamplus.com
SIC: 3629 Electronic generation equipment
PA: I.Am.Plus Electronics, Inc.
809 N Cahuenga Blvd
323 210-3852

(P-6376)
INTELLIGENT TECHNOLOGIES LLC
Also Called: Itech
9454 Waples St, San Diego (92121-2919)
PHONE......................858 458-1500
Rod Bolton, *Pr*
Frank Cooper, *
▲ **EMP:** 125 **EST:** 1997
SQ FT: 17,846
SALES (est): 23.49MM
SALES (corp-wide): 86.13MM **Privately Held**
Web: www.itecheng.com
SIC: 3629 3356 Battery chargers, rectifying or nonrotating; Battery metal
PA: Universal Power Group, Inc.
120 Dividend Dr Ste 100
469 892-1122

(P-6377)
INTERCONNECT SOLUTIONS CO LLC (PA)
17595 Mount Herrmann St, Fountain Valley (92708-4160)
PHONE......................714 556-7007
Nick Kendall-jones, *CEO*
▲ **EMP:** 70 **EST:** 2018
SQ FT: 15,000
SALES (est): 49.73MM
SALES (corp-wide): 49.73MM **Privately Held**
Web: www.interconnectsolutions.com
SIC: 3629 Electronic generation equipment

(P-6378)
MAXWELL TECHNOLOGIES INC
3912 Calle Fortunada, San Diego (92123-1827)
PHONE......................858 503-3493
EMP: 74
SALES (corp-wide): 96.77B **Publicly Held**
Web: www.maxwell.com
SIC: 3629 Capacitors and condensers
HQ: Maxwell Technologies, Inc.
6155 Crnrstone Ct E Ste 2
San Diego CA 92121
858 503-3300

(P-6379)
Q C M INC
Also Called: Veris Manufacturing
285 Gemini Ave, Brea (92821-3704)
PHONE......................714 414-1173
Jay Cadler, *CEO*
Larry Ching, *
▲ **EMP:** 45 **EST:** 2006
SALES (est): 24.07MM
SALES (corp-wide): 144.18MM **Privately Held**
Web: www.emeraldems.com
SIC: 3629 Electronic generation equipment
PA: Megatronics Us Ultimate Holdco Llc
2243 Lundy Ave
888 706-0230

(P-6380)
SCIENTFIC APPLCTONS RES ASSOC (PA)
Also Called: Sara
6300 Gateway Dr, Cypress (90630-4844)
PHONE......................714 224-4410
Parviz Parhami, *CEO*
James Wes, *
Wes Addington, *
Amy Dockenhorf, *
EMP: 58 **EST:** 1989
SQ FT: 43,000
SALES (est): 41.76MM **Privately Held**
Web: www.sara.com
SIC: 3629 Electronic generation equipment

(P-6381)
SCOTT MFG SOLUTIONS INC
Also Called: Scott Manufacturing Solutions
5051 Edison Ave, Chino (91710-5716)
PHONE......................909 594-9637
Luis Ernesto Lujan, *CEO*
Deborah N Davis, *
Jason J Huitrado, *
▲ **EMP:** 120 **EST:** 1967
SQ FT: 102,660
SALES (est): 21.34MM **Privately Held**
Web: www.scottmfgsolutions.com
SIC: 3629 3613 Electronic generation equipment; Switchgear and switchboard apparatus

(P-6382)
SEACOMP INC (PA)
1525 Faraday Ave Ste 200, Carlsbad (92008-7374)
PHONE......................760 918-6722
Michael Szymanski, *CEO*
Terry Arbaugh, *
Robert Marshal, *
▲ **EMP:** 148 **EST:** 1989
SALES (est): 13.93MM
SALES (corp-wide): 13.93MM **Privately Held**
Web: www.seacomp.com
SIC: 3629 Battery chargers, rectifying or nonrotating

(P-6383)
ZPOWER LLC
5171 Clareton Dr, Agoura Hills (91301-4523)
PHONE......................805 445-7789
Herbert V Weigel Ii, *COO*
Dennis J Dugan, *
Barry A Freeman, *
Damon Mikoy, *
EMP: 210 **EST:** 1996
SALES (est): 14.99MM **Privately Held**
Web: www.riotenergy.com
SIC: 3629 Battery chargers, rectifying or nonrotating

3631 Household Cooking Equipment

(P-6384)
DCEC HOLDINGS INC
Also Called: Twin Eagles, Inc.
13259 166th St, Cerritos (90703-2203)
PHONE......................562 802-3488
Dante L Cantal, *Pr*
Epifania Cantal, *
▲ **EMP:** 101 **EST:** 1999
SQ FT: 45,000
SALES (est): 18.18MM
SALES (corp-wide): 2.84B **Privately Held**
Web: www.twineaglesgrills.com

3631 - Household Cooking Equipment (P-6385)

SIC: 3631 Barbecues, grills, and braziers
(outdoor cooking)
HQ: Dometic Corporation
5600 N River Rd Ste 250
Rosemont IL 60018

(P-6385)
JADE RANGE LLC
Also Called: Jade Products
2650 Orbiter St, Brea (92821-6265)
PHONE...................714 961-2400
Martin M Lindsay, *
▲ EMP: 120 EST: 1998
SALES (est): 22.68MM
SALES (corp-wide): 4.04B **Publicly Held**
Web: www.jaderange.com
SIC: 3631 3589 Household cooking
equipment; Commercial cooking and
foodwarming equipment
PA: The Middleby Corporation
1400 Toastmaster Dr
847 741-3300

(P-6386)
MAGMA PRODUCTS LLC
3940 Pixie Ave, Lakewood (90712-4136)
PHONE...................562 627-0500
James Mashburn, *
◆ EMP: 70 EST: 1976
SQ FT: 22,000
SALES (est): 9.73MM **Privately Held**
Web: www.magmaproducts.com
SIC: 3631 3634 Barbecues, grills, and
braziers (outdoor cooking); Griddles or
grills, electric: household

(P-6387)
MIRAMA ENTERPRISES INC
Also Called: Aroma Housewares
6469 Flanders Dr, San Diego (92121-4104)
PHONE...................858 587-8866
Chung Yuan Peter Chang, CEO
Shiu Run Shirley Chang, *
Tom Kho-hong Kao, Sec
◆ EMP: 68 EST: 1996
SQ FT: 60,000
SALES (est): 13.58MM **Privately Held**
Web: www.aroma-housewares.com
SIC: 3631 Household cooking equipment

(P-6388)
PACIFIC COAST MFG INC
5270 Edison Ave, Chino (91710-5719)
PHONE...................909 627-7040
Bruce Doran, Pr
James Poremba, *
▲ EMP: 72 EST: 2011
SQ FT: 40,000
SALES (est): 9.87MM **Privately Held**
Web: www.pcmbbq.com
SIC: 3631 Barbecues, grills, and braziers
(outdoor cooking)

(P-6389)
RH PETERSON CO (PA)
Also Called: Robert H Peterson Company
14724 Proctor Ave, City Of Industry
(91746-3202)
PHONE...................626 369-5085
◆ EMP: 170 EST: 1949
SALES (est): 22.45MM
SALES (corp-wide): 22.45MM **Privately
Held**
Web: www.rhpeterson.com
SIC: 3631 3433 Barbecues, grills, and
braziers (outdoor cooking); Logs, gas
fireplace

(P-6390)
ROYAL RANGE CALIFORNIA INC
Also Called: Royal Industries
3245 Corridor Dr, Eastvale (91752-1030)
PHONE...................951 360-1600
L Vasan, CEO
Patricia Woods, *
▼ EMP: 65 EST: 1995
SQ FT: 52,000
SALES (est): 9.46MM **Privately Held**
Web: www.royalranges.com
SIC: 3631 Household cooking equipment

(P-6391)
**SUPERIOR EQUIPMENT
SOLUTIONS**
1085 Bixby Dr, City Of Industry
(91745-1704)
PHONE...................323 722-7900
Jeffrey Bernstein, CEO
Stephan Bernstein, *
▲ EMP: 60 EST: 2001
SQ FT: 45,000
SALES (est): 13.99MM **Privately Held**
Web: www.sesbrands.com
SIC: 3631 5046 Household cooking
equipment; Restaurant equipment and
supplies, nec

3632 Household
Refrigerators And Freezers

(P-6392)
**REFRIDERATOR
MANUFACTERS LLC**
17018 Edwards Rd, Cerritos (90703-2422)
PHONE...................562 229-0500
EMP: 42 EST: 2014
SQ FT: 40,000
SALES (est): 1.36MM **Privately Held**
SIC: 3632 Freezers, home and farm

3634 Electric Housewares
And Fans

(P-6393)
BRANDS REPUBLIC INC
10333 Rush St, South El Monte
(91733-3341)
PHONE...................302 401-1195
Asif Kashif, Prin
EMP: 50
SALES (est): 1.6MM **Privately Held**
SIC: 3634 Electric housewares and fans

(P-6394)
**CAPITAL BRANDS
DISTRIBUTION L (PA)**
11601 Wilshire Blvd Ste 2300, Los Angeles
(90025-1759)
PHONE...................800 523-5993
Lenny Sands, *
EMP: 62 EST: 2015
SALES (est): 47.46MM
SALES (corp-wide): 47.46MM **Privately
Held**
Web: www.capitalbrands.com
SIC: 3634 Blenders, electric

(P-6395)
CRYOGENIC INDUSTRIES INC
25720 Jefferson Ave, Murrieta
(92562-6929)
PHONE...................951 677-2060
Peter Wagner, CEO
EMP: 200 EST: 2016

SALES (est): 9.81MM **Privately Held**
Web: www.nikkisoceig.com
SIC: 3634 Vaporizers, electric: household

(P-6396)
FELLOW INDUSTRIES INC
Also Called: Fellow
1342 1/2 Abbot Kinney Blvd, Venice
(90291-3778)
PHONE...................415 649-0361
Jacob Miller, CEO
EMP: 49
SALES (corp-wide): 8.2MM **Privately Held**
Web: www.fellowproducts.com
SIC: 3634 Electric housewares and fans
PA: Fellow Industries Inc.
560 Alabama St.
415 649-0361

(P-6397)
LUMA COMFORT LLC
Also Called: Luma Comfort
6600 Katella Ave, Cypress (90630-5104)
PHONE...................855 963-9247
Luke Peters, Pr
Luke Peters, CEO
Mariella Peters, *
▲ EMP: 50 EST: 2011
SQ FT: 30,000
SALES (est): 2.44MM **Privately Held**
Web: www.lumacomfort.com
SIC: 3634 Electric housewares and fans

(P-6398)
MJC AMERICA LTD (PA)
Also Called: Soleus International
20035 E Walnut Dr N, Walnut (91789-2922)
P.O. Box 472 (91788-0472)
PHONE...................888 876-5387
Simon Chu, CEO
◆ EMP: 35 EST: 1998
SQ FT: 100,000
SALES (est): 3.69MM
SALES (corp-wide): 3.69MM **Privately
Held**
Web: www.soleusair.com
SIC: 3634 Electric housewares and fans

3639 Household Appliances,
Nec

(P-6399)
BRENTWOOD APPLIANCES INC
Also Called: Import
3088 E 46th St, Vernon (90058-2422)
PHONE...................323 266-4600
Poorad Beni Panahi, CEO
Poorad Beni Panahi, CEO
Maurice Araghi, *
John Yadgari, *
◆ EMP: 36 EST: 2009
SQ FT: 65,000
SALES (est): 4.56MM **Privately Held**
Web: www.brentwoodus.com
SIC: 3639 Major kitchen appliances, except
refrigerators and stoves

(P-6400)
BREVILLE USA INC
Also Called: Breville
19400 S Western Ave, Torrance
(90501-1119)
PHONE...................310 755-3000
Stephen Krauss, CEO
Michelle Waters, *
Barbara Dirsa, *
◆ EMP: 50 EST: 1989
SQ FT: 135,000
SALES (est): 24.19MM **Privately Held**

Web: www.breville.com
SIC: 3639 3634 5722 Major kitchen
appliances, except refrigerators and stoves;
Coffee makers, electric: household;
Microwave ovens
HQ: Breville Holdings Pty Limited
G Se 2 170 Bourke Rd
Alexandria NSW 2015

(P-6401)
**HESTAN COMMERCIAL
CORPORATION**
3375 E La Palma Ave, Anaheim
(92806-2815)
P.O. Box 887 (92811-0887)
PHONE...................714 869-2380
Stanley Kin Sui Cheng, CEO
Eric Deng, *
Barry Needleman Ctrl, Prin
▲ EMP: 125 EST: 2013
SQ FT: 70,000
SALES (est): 24.42MM **Privately Held**
Web: commercial.hestan.com
SIC: 3639 Major kitchen appliances, except
refrigerators and stoves
HQ: Meyer Corporation, U.S.
1 Meyer Plz
Vallejo CA 94590
707 551-2800

3641 Electric Lamps

(P-6402)
CANDLE LAMP HOLDINGS LLC
949 S Coast Dr Ste 650, Costa Mesa
(92626-7737)
PHONE...................951 682-9600
Don Hinshaw, CEO
John Clark, Managing Member*
EMP: 310 EST: 2006
SALES (est): 1.37MM **Privately Held**
SIC: 3641 3645 3589 3634 Electric lamps;
Table lamps; Food warming equipment,
commercial; Chafing dishes, electric

(P-6403)
DASOL INC
Also Called: Coronet Lighting
9004 Meredith Pl, Beverly Hills
(90210-1841)
P.O. Box 2065 (90247-0010)
PHONE...................310 327-6700
Sol Smith, Ch Bd
David Smith, *
Mark Smith, *
◆ EMP: 225 EST: 1944
SALES (est): 4.5MM **Privately Held**
SIC: 3641 Electric lamps and parts for
generalized applications

(P-6404)
IWORKS US INC
Also Called: Iworks
2501 S Malt Ave, Commerce (90040-3203)
PHONE...................323 278-8363
Eric Dortch, CEO
◆ EMP: 53 EST: 1988
SQ FT: 35,000
SALES (est): 9.44MM **Privately Held**
Web: www.iworksus.com
SIC: 3641 Electric lamps and parts for
generalized applications

(P-6405)
LEDVANCE LLC
1651 S Archibald Ave, Ontario
(91761-7651)
PHONE...................909 923-3003
Jane Running, Owner

EMP: 23 EST: 2017
SALES (est): 6.51MM **Privately Held**
SIC: 3641 Electric lamps

(P-6406)
LITEGEAR INC
Also Called: Litegear
4406 W Vanowen St, Burbank
(91505-1134)
PHONE..............................818 358-8542
Albert M Demayo, *Pr*
EMP: 45 **EST:** 2006
SALES (est): 7.59MM **Privately Held**
Web: www.litegear.com
SIC: 3641 Electric lamps

(P-6407)
OSRAM SYLVANIA INC
13350 Gregg St Ste 101, Poway
(92064-7137)
PHONE..............................858 748-5077
Dennis Cohen, *Brnch Mgr*
EMP: 88
SALES (corp-wide): 3.9B **Privately Held**
Web: www.sylvania-automotive.com
SIC: 3641 Electric lamps
HQ: Osram Sylvania Inc.
200 Ballardvale St Bldg 2
Wilmington MA 01887
978 570-3000

(P-6408)
TIVOLI LLC
17110 Armstrong Ave, Irvine (92614-5718)
PHONE..............................714 957-6101
Jannhuan Jang, *CEO*
Targetti Poulsen, *Managing Member**
Eric Kramer, *Managing Member**
Susan Larson, *
▲ **EMP:** 50 **EST:** 2003
SALES (est): 9.22MM **Privately Held**
Web: www.tivolilighting.com
SIC: 3641 3646 Tubes, electric light; Ceiling
systems, luminous

(P-6409)
TOLEMAR LLC
6412 Maple Ave, Westminster
(92683-3609)
PHONE..............................657 200-3840
Eric Ison, *Managing Member*
EMP: 45 **EST:** 2017
SALES (est): 1.46MM **Privately Held**
SIC: 3641 Electric lamps

3643 Current-carrying Wiring Devices

(P-6410)
**AERO ELECTRIC CONNECTOR
INC (PA)**
2280 W 208th St, Torrance (90501-1452)
PHONE..............................310 618-3737
Walter Neubauer, *Ch*
Walter Neubauer Junior, *CEO*
EMP: 344 **EST:** 1982
SQ FT: 65,000
SALES (est): 45.47MM
SALES (corp-wide): 45.47MM **Privately
Held**
Web: www.aero-electric.com
SIC: 3643 3678 Connectors and terminals
for electrical devices; Electronic connectors

(P-6411)
AUTOSPLICE PARENT INC (PA)
Also Called: Autosplice
10431 Wateridge Cir Ste 110, San Diego
(92121-5797)

PHONE..............................858 535-0077
Santosh Rao, *CEO*
Ken Krone, *
Jeffrey Cartwright, *
Kevin Barry, *
▲ **EMP:** 200 **EST:** 1954
SQ FT: 20,000
SALES (est): 23.46MM
SALES (corp-wide): 23.46MM **Privately
Held**
Web: www.autosplice.com
SIC: 3643 Electric connectors

(P-6412)
CELESTICA LLC
280 Campillo St Ste G, Calexico
(92231-3200)
PHONE..............................760 357-4880
Michael Garmon, *Brnch Mgr*
EMP: 69
SALES (corp-wide): 7.96B **Privately Held**
Web: www.celestica.com
SIC: 3643 Current-carrying wiring services
HQ: Celestica Llc
400 Glleria Pkwy Ste 1500
Atlanta GA 30339

(P-6413)
**CONNECTEC COMPANY INC
(PA)**
Also Called: MANUFACTURE
1701 Reynolds Ave, Irvine (92614-5711)
PHONE..............................949 252-1077
Rassool Kavezade, *CEO*
Lora Taleb, *
Mike Taleb, *
▲ **EMP:** 74 **EST:** 1988
SQ FT: 12,000
SALES (est): 20.09MM
SALES (corp-wide): 20.09MM **Privately
Held**
Web: www.connectecco.com
SIC: 3643 3678 Electric connectors;
Electronic connectors

(P-6414)
**CTC GLOBAL CORPORATION
(PA)**
Also Called: Ctc Global
2026 Mcgaw Ave, Irvine (92614-0911)
PHONE..............................949 428-8500
J D Sitton, *CEO*
Dean Hagen, *
Anne Mcdowell, *Commercial Vice President*
John Mansfield, *Strategy Vice President**
Eric Johnson, *OF FIELD Technology SRVS**
▲ **EMP:** 146 **EST:** 2011
SALES (est): 34.71MM
SALES (corp-wide): 34.71MM **Privately
Held**
Web: www.ctcglobal.com
SIC: 3643 Power line cable

(P-6415)
DDH ENTERPRISE INC (PA)
2220 Oak Ridge Way, Vista (92081-8341)
PHONE..............................760 599-0171
David Du, *CEO*
Danny Du, *
▲ **EMP:** 100 **EST:** 1988
SQ FT: 42,000
SALES (est): 30.55MM
SALES (corp-wide): 30.55MM **Privately
Held**
Web: www.ddhent.com
SIC: 3643 3644 3699 Current-carrying wiring
services; Noncurrent-carrying wiring devices
; Electrical equipment and supplies, nec

(P-6416)
DMC POWER INC (PA)
623 E Artesia Blvd, Carson (90746-1201)
PHONE..............................310 323-1616
Tony Ward, *CEO*
Michael Yazdanpanah, *
Eben Kane, *
Ed Cox, *
▲ **EMP:** 50 **EST:** 2009
SQ FT: 40,000
SALES (est): 27.99MM **Privately Held**
Web: www.dmcpower.com
SIC: 3643 Current-carrying wiring services

(P-6417)
ELECTRO ADAPTER INC
Also Called: Plating
20640 Nordhoff St, Chatsworth
(91311-6189)
P.O. Box 2560 (91313-2560)
PHONE..............................818 998-1198
Ray Fish, *Pr*
Terrill Fish, *
EMP: 100 **EST:** 1969
SQ FT: 54,000
SALES (est): 11.32MM **Privately Held**
Web: www.electro-adapter.com
SIC: 3643 Electric connectors
PA: Intritec
20640 Nordhoff St

(P-6418)
ESL POWER SYSTEMS INC
2800 Palisades Dr, Corona (92878-9427)
PHONE..............................800 922-4188
Michael Hellmers, *Pr*
David Hellmers, *
◆ **EMP:** 55 **EST:** 1995
SQ FT: 36,000
SALES (est): 15.95MM **Privately Held**
Web: www.eslpwr.com
SIC: 3643 Outlets, electric: convenience

(P-6419)
**FOXLINK INTERNATIONAL INC
(HQ)**
3010 Saturn St Ste 200, Brea (92821-6220)
PHONE..............................714 256-1777
Ching Fan Pu, *CEO*
James Lee, *
▲ **EMP:** 44 **EST:** 1994
SALES (est): 12.81MM **Privately Held**
SIC: 3643 3678 3679 3691 Current-carrying
wiring services; Electronic connectors;
Electronic circuits; Storage batteries
PA: Cheng Uei Precision Industry Co., Ltd.
No.18, Chung Shan Rd.,

(P-6420)
GLENAIR INC (PA)
Also Called: Papi
1211 Air Way, Glendale (91201-2497)
PHONE..............................818 247-6000
EMP: 371 **EST:** 1956
SALES (est): 782.53MM
SALES (corp-wide): 782.53MM **Privately
Held**
Web: www.glenair.com
SIC: 3643 3825 3357 Connectors and
terminals for electrical devices; Test
equipment for electronic and electrical
circuits; Nonferrous wiredrawing and
insulating

(P-6421)
HI REL CONNECTORS INC
Also Called: Hirel Connectors
760 Wharton Dr, Claremont (91711-4800)
PHONE..............................909 626-1820
Fred Baumann, *CEO*

Frederick Bb Baumann, *
EMP: 300 **EST:** 1967
SQ FT: 25,000
SALES (est): 23.04MM **Privately Held**
Web: www.hirelco.net
SIC: 3643 3678 Connectors and terminals
for electrical devices; Electronic connectors

(P-6422)
**JUDCO MANUFACTURING INC
(PA)**
1429 240th St, Harbor City (90710-1306)
P.O. Box 487 (90710-0487)
PHONE..............................310 534-0959
▲ **EMP:** 200 **EST:** 1980
SALES (est): 21.81MM
SALES (corp-wide): 21.81MM **Privately
Held**
Web: www.judco.net
SIC: 3643 Electric switches

(P-6423)
**LYNCOLE GRUNDING
SOLUTIONS LLC**
Also Called: Lyncole Xit Grounding
369 Van Ness Way, Torrance (90501-1489)
PHONE..............................310 214-4000
EMP: 25 **EST:** 1985
SALES (est): 2.67MM **Privately Held**
Web: www.vfclp.com
SIC: 3643 8711 Current-carrying wiring
services; Consulting engineer

(P-6424)
NIVEK INDUSTRIES INC
Also Called: International Component Tech
230 E Dyer Rd Ste K, Santa Ana
(92707-3751)
PHONE..............................714 545-8855
Kevin Pezzolla, *Pr*
EMP: 48 **EST:** 1987
SQ FT: 8,000
SALES (est): 5.29MM **Privately Held**
Web: www.intcomptech.com
SIC: 3643 Current-carrying wiring services

(P-6425)
PLT ENTERPRISES INC
Also Called: So-Cal Value Added
809 Calle Plano, Camarillo (93012-8516)
PHONE..............................805 389-5335
Pamela L Tunis, *Pr*
Peter L Tunis, *
Peter Tunis Junior, *Genl Mgr*
EMP: 75 **EST:** 1996
SQ FT: 41,000
SALES (est): 4.5MM **Privately Held**
SIC: 3643 3679 Current-carrying wiring
services; Harness assemblies, for
electronic use: wire or cable

(P-6426)
**PRECISION STAMPINGS INC
(PA)**
Also Called: P S I
500 Egan Ave, Beaumont (92223-2191)
PHONE..............................951 845-1174
Herman Viets, *Ch Bd*
Steven Morgan, *
Frauke Roth, *Stockholder**
Peter Gailing, *Stockholder**
Herta Viets, *Stockholder**
EMP: 32 **EST:** 1966
SQ FT: 25,000
SALES (est): 8.95MM
SALES (corp-wide): 8.95MM **Privately
Held**
Web: www.precisionstampingsinc.com

SIC: **3643** 5084 7539 Contacts, electrical;
Tool and die makers equipment; Machine
shop, automotive

(P-6427)
SAFRAN USA INC
Also Called: Safran Aerospace
1500 Glenn Curtiss St, Carson
(90746-4012)
PHONE..............................310 884-7198
EMP: 501
SALES (corp-wide): 940.23MM **Privately
Held**
Web: www.safran-group.com
SIC: **3643** 3621 7699 3724 Connectors and
terminals for electrical devices; Motors and
generators; Engine repair and replacement,
non-automotive; Aircraft engines and
engine parts
HQ: Safran Usa, Inc.
700 S Washington St # 320
Alexandria VA 22314
703 351-9898

(P-6428)
SOURIAU USA INC (DH)
1740 Commerce Way, Paso Robles
(93446-3620)
PHONE..............................805 238-2840
Rob Hanes, *Pr*
◆ **EMP:** 46 **EST:** 2003
SQ FT: 55,000
SALES (est): 23.19MM **Privately Held**
Web: usa.souriau.com
SIC: **3643** Bus bars (electrical conductors)
HQ: Eaton Corporation
1000 Eaton Blvd
Cleveland OH 44122
440 523-5000

(P-6429)
SOURIAU USA INC
1750 Commerce Way, Paso Robles
(93446-3620)
PHONE..............................805 226-3573
EMP: 55
SIC: **3643** Current-carrying wiring services
HQ: Souriau Usa, Inc.
1740 Commerce Way
Paso Robles CA 93446
805 238-2840

(P-6430)
SULLINS ELECTRONICS CORP
Also Called: Sullins Connector Solutions
801 E Mission Rd # B, San Marcos
(92069-3002)
PHONE..............................760 744-0125
Kayvan Sullins, *CEO*
▲ **EMP:** 75 **EST:** 1969
SQ FT: 33,000
SALES (est): 8.11MM **Privately Held**
Web: www.sullinscorp.com
SIC: **3643** 3678 Connectors and terminals
for electrical devices; Electronic connectors

(P-6431)
TECHNICAL RESOURCE INDUSTRIES (PA)
Also Called: T R I
12854 Daisy Ct, Yucaipa (92399-2026)
PHONE..............................909 446-1109
Reinhard Thalmayer, *Pr*
EMP: 25 **EST:** 1988
SQ FT: 5,000
SALES (est): 468.89K
SALES (corp-wide): 468.89K **Privately
Held**
SIC: **3643** Electric connectors

(P-6432)
TELEDYNE INSTRUMENTS INC
Also Called: Teledyne Impulse
9855 Carroll Canyon Rd, San Diego
(92131-1103)
PHONE..............................858 842-3100
Kenneth Mendoza, *Fin Mgr*
EMP: 79
SALES (corp-wide): 5.64B **Publicly Held**
Web: www.teledyne.com
SIC: **3643** Electric connectors
HQ: Teledyne Instruments, Inc.
16830 Chestnut St
City Of Industry CA 91748
626 934-1500

(P-6433)
UNIVERSAL SWITCHING CORP
Also Called: U S C
7671 N San Fernando Rd, Burbank
(91505-1073)
PHONE..............................818 785-0200
EMP: 28 **EST:** 1992
SALES (est): 4.68MM **Privately Held**
Web: www.uswi.com
SIC: **3643** Electric switches

3644 Noncurrent-carrying Wiring Devices

(P-6434)
SAF-T-CO SUPPLY
Also Called: All American Pipe Bending
1300 E Normandy Pl, Santa Ana
(92705-4138)
PHONE..............................714 547-9975
Patricia Mcdonald, *Pr*
Robyn Dague, *
Paul Mcdonald, *Sec*
EMP: 50 **EST:** 1987
SQ FT: 24,000
SALES (est): 24.58MM **Privately Held**
Web: www.saftco.com
SIC: **3644** 5063 5032 5074 Noncurrent-
carrying wiring devices; Electrical
apparatus and equipment; Brick, stone, and
related material; Pipes and fittings, plastic

(P-6435)
WESTERN TUBE & CONDUIT CORP (HQ)
2001 E Dominguez St, Long Beach
(90810-1088)
P.O. Box 608 (16161-0608)
PHONE..............................310 537-6300
Barry Zekelman, *CEO*
▲ **EMP:** 88 **EST:** 2004
SQ FT: 420,000
SALES (est): 45.35MM **Privately Held**
Web: www.westerntube.com
SIC: **3644** 3446 3317 Electric conduits and
fittings; Fences or posts, ornamental iron or
steel; Tubing, mechanical or hypodermic
sizes: cold drawn stainless
PA: Zekelman Industries, Inc.
227 W Monroe St Ste 2600

3645 Residential Lighting Fixtures

(P-6436)
ALGER-TRITON INC
Also Called: Alger International
5600 W Jefferson Blvd, Los Angeles
(90016-3131)
PHONE..............................310 229-9500
Mishel Michael, *Prin*

Clark Scott, *Prin*
Michelle Seminaris Bass, *Prin*
Rick Cooley, *Prin*
◆ **EMP:** 28 **EST:** 1993
SALES (est): 3.98MM **Privately Held**
Web: www.studio-at.com
SIC: **3645** Residential lighting fixtures

(P-6437)
AMERICAN NAIL PLATE LTG INC
Also Called: Anp Lighting
9044 Del Mar Ave, Montclair (91763-1627)
PHONE..............................909 982-1807
Harry Foster, *CEO*
Joan Foster, *
Ron Foster, *
Bob Foster, *
▲ **EMP:** 70 **EST:** 1976
SQ FT: 13,000
SALES (est): 8.33MM **Privately Held**
Web: www.anplighting.com
SIC: **3645** 3646 Residential lighting fixtures;
Commercial lighting fixtures

(P-6438)
ANTHONY CALIFORNIA INC (PA)
14485 Monte Vista Ave, Chino
(91710-5728)
PHONE..............................909 627-0351
Kuei-lan Yeh, *CEO*
Cindy Chang, *
◆ **EMP:** 23 **EST:** 1983
SALES (est): 4.79MM
SALES (corp-wide): 4.79MM **Privately
Held**
Web: www.anthonyshowrooms.com
SIC: **3645** 5063 5023 Residential lighting
fixtures; Lighting fixtures; Lamps: floor,
boudoir, desk

(P-6439)
ARTIVA USA INC (PA)
Also Called: Artiva
13901 Magnolia Ave, Chino (91710-7030)
PHONE..............................909 628-1388
Po Y Webb, *Pr*
Gina Yeh, *VP*
▲ **EMP:** 35 **EST:** 2008
SQ FT: 20,000
SALES (est): 2.63MM **Privately Held**
Web: www.artivaus.com
SIC: **3645** 5063 Residential lighting fixtures;
Lighting fixtures

(P-6440)
ARTIVA USA INC
Also Called: Artiva
12866 Ann St Ste 1, Santa Fe Springs
(90670-3064)
PHONE..............................562 298-8968
Jane Wang, *Mgr*
EMP: 42
Web: www.artivaus.com
SIC: **3645** 5063 Residential lighting fixtures;
Lighting fixtures
PA: Artiva Usa Inc.
13901 Magnolia Ave

(P-6441)
BASE LITE CORPORATION
Also Called: Baselite
12260 Eastend Ave, Chino (91710-2008)
PHONE..............................909 444-2776
Moaaa A Teixeira, *CEO*
EMP: 38 **EST:** 1997
SQ FT: 10,000
SALES (est): 4.48MM **Privately Held**
Web: www.baselite.com
SIC: **3645** 3646 Residential lighting fixtures;
Commercial lighting fixtures

(P-6442)
DAB INC
Also Called: Spectrum Lighting
13415 Marquardt Ave, Santa Fe Springs
(90670-5012)
PHONE..............................562 623-4773
David A Boose, *Pr*
▲ **EMP:** 52 **EST:** 1978
SQ FT: 31,000
SALES (est): 2.44MM **Privately Held**
Web: www.scll.com
SIC: **3645** 3648 3646 Residential lighting
fixtures; Decorative area lighting fixtures;
Commercial lighting fixtures

(P-6443)
DMF INC
Also Called: Dmf Lighting
1118 E 223rd St Unit 1, Carson
(90745-4210)
PHONE..............................323 934-7779
Morteza Danesh, *Pr*
Fariba Danesh, *
Michael Danesh, *
▲ **EMP:** 51 **EST:** 1989
SQ FT: 8,000
SALES (est): 15.07MM **Privately Held**
Web: www.dmflighting.com
SIC: **3645** 5063 Residential lighting fixtures;
Lighting fixtures, commercial and industrial

(P-6444)
FEIT ELECTRIC COMPANY INC (PA)
Also Called: Feit Electric
4901 Gregg Rd, Pico Rivera (90660-2108)
PHONE..............................562 463-2852
Aaron Feit, *CEO*
Alan Feit, *
Toby S Feit, *
John Mcmillin, *CFO*
◆ **EMP:** 141 **EST:** 1978
SQ FT: 300,000
SALES (est): 43.92MM
SALES (corp-wide): 43.92MM **Privately
Held**
Web: www.feit.com
SIC: **3645** 3641 5023 3646 Residential
lighting fixtures; Electric light bulbs,
complete; Homefurnishings; Commercial
lighting fixtures

(P-6445)
LIGHTS OF AMERICA INC (PA)
13602 12th St Ste B, Chino (91710-5200)
PHONE..............................909 594-7883
Usman Vakil, *CEO*
Farooq Vakil, *
◆ **EMP:** 500 **EST:** 1977
SQ FT: 210,000
SALES (est): 14.27MM
SALES (corp-wide): 14.27MM **Privately
Held**
Web: www.lightsofamerica.com
SIC: **3645** 3646 3641 Fluorescent lighting
fixtures, residential; Fluorescent lighting
fixtures, commercial; Electric lamps

(P-6446)
MAXIM LIGHTING INTL INC
247 Vineland Ave, City Of Industry
(91746-2319)
PHONE..............................626 956-4200
EMP: 51
SALES (corp-wide): 47.04MM **Privately
Held**
Web: www.maximlighting.com
SIC: **3645** Residential lighting fixtures
PA: Maxim Lighting International, Inc.
253 N Vineland Ave

626 956-4200

(P-6447)
NL&A COLLECTIONS INC
Also Called: Nova
6323 Maywood Ave, Huntington Park
(90255-4531)
P.O. Box 661820 (90066-8820)
PHONE..................................323 277-6266
Daniel Edelist, *Pr*
◆ **EMP:** 40 **EST:** 1980
SQ FT: 48,675
SALES (est): 1.96MM **Privately Held**
Web: www.novaofcalifornia.com
SIC: 3645 5023 Boudoir lamps; Lamps: floor,
boudoir, desk

(P-6448)
PHILIPS NORTH AMERICA LLC
11201 Iberia St Ste A, Jurupa Valley
(91752-3280)
PHONE..................................909 574-1800
Kenneth Parivar, *Brnch Mgr*
EMP: 150
SALES (corp-wide): 18.51B **Privately Held**
Web: usa.philips.com
SIC: 3645 3648 3646 Residential lighting
fixtures; Outdoor lighting equipment; Ceiling
systems, luminous
HQ: Philips North America Llc
222 Jacobs St Fl 3
Cambridge MA 02141
617 245-5900

(P-6449)
TROY-CSL LIGHTING INC
14508 Nelson Ave, City Of Industry
(91744-3514)
P.O. Box 514310 (90051-4310)
PHONE..................................626 336-4511
David Littman, *CEO*
Steve Nadell, *
Anne Wilcox, *
Ian Wilcox, *
◆ **EMP:** 205 **EST:** 1970
SALES (est): 40.47MM **Privately Held**
Web: www.csllighting.com
SIC: 3645 3646 Wall lamps; Ornamental
lighting fixtures, commercial

(P-6450)
VIDESSENCE LLC (PA)
10768 Lower Azusa Rd, El Monte
(91731-1306)
PHONE..................................626 579-0943
Toni Swarens, *Pr*
▲ **EMP:** 25 **EST:** 1951
SQ FT: 35,000
SALES (est): 2.31MM
SALES (corp-wide): 2.31MM **Privately
Held**
Web: www.videssence.tv
SIC: 3645 3648 Residential lighting fixtures;
Stage lighting equipment

(P-6451)
YAWITZ INC
Also Called: Evergreen Lighting
1379 Ridgeway St, Pomona (91768-2701)
PHONE..................................909 865-5599
John Klena, *CEO*
George Cole Iii, *Marketing*
Victor Rosen, *
▲ **EMP:** 42 **EST:** 1997
SQ FT: 23,000
SALES (est): 5.53MM **Privately Held**
Web: www.evergreenlighting.com
SIC: 3645 3646 Fluorescent lighting fixtures,
residential; Fluorescent lighting fixtures,
commercial

3646 Commercial Lighting Fixtures

(P-6452)
ARTE DE MEXICO INC
Also Called: Arte De Mexico
5506 Riverton Ave, North Hollywood
(91601-2815)
PHONE..................................818 753-4510
David Staffers, *Mgr*
EMP: 71
SALES (corp-wide): 8.01MM **Privately
Held**
Web: www.artedemexico.com
SIC: 3646 3446 Commercial lighting fixtures;
Architectural metalwork
PA: Arte De Mexico, Inc.
1000 Chestnut St
818 753-4559

(P-6453)
C W COLE & COMPANY INC
Also Called: Cole Lighting
2560 Rosemead Blvd, South El Monte
(91733-1593)
PHONE..................................626 443-2473
Russell W Cole, *Ch Bd*
Stephen W Cole, *
Donald Cole, *
EMP: 41 **EST:** 1911
SQ FT: 25,000
SALES (est): 3.22MM **Privately Held**
Web: www.colelighting.com
SIC: 3646 Commercial lighting fixtures

(P-6454)
DECO ENTERPRISES INC
Also Called: Deco Lighting
2917 Vail Ave, Commerce (90040-2615)
PHONE..................................323 726-2575
Saman Sinai, *Prin*
Saman Sinai, *CEO*
Ben Peterson, *
Benjamin Pouladian, *
▲ **EMP:** 60 **EST:** 2005
SQ FT: 100,000
SALES (est): 7.7MM **Privately Held**
Web: www.getdeco.com
SIC: 3646 Commercial lighting fixtures

(P-6455)
DSA PHOTOTECH LLC
Also Called: DSA Signage
2321 E Gladwick St, Rancho Dominguez
(90220-6209)
PHONE..................................866 868-1602
▲ **EMP:** 50 **EST:** 1974
SALES (est): 14.07MM **Privately Held**
Web: www.dsasignage.com
SIC: 3646 3648 Commercial lighting fixtures;
Lighting equipment, nec

(P-6456)
**EDISON PRICE LIGHTING INC
(PA)**
Also Called: Epl
5424 E Slauson Ave, Commerce
(90040-2919)
PHONE..................................718 685-0700
Emma Price, *Pr*
Joel R Siegel, *VP*
James D Vizzini, *VP*
Gregory Mortman, *VP*
▲ **EMP:** 119 **EST:** 1952
SALES (est): 7.05MM
SALES (corp-wide): 7.05MM **Privately
Held**
Web: www.epl.com

SIC: **3646** Ceiling systems, luminous

(P-6457)
ENERTRON TECHNOLOGIES INC
3525 Del Mar Heights Rd, San Diego
(92130-2199)
PHONE..................................800 537-7649
Ronald Curley, *Pr*
EMP: 50 **EST:** 1985
SALES (est): 2.34MM **Privately Held**
SIC: 3646 3645 Fluorescent lighting fixtures,
commercial; Fluorescent lighting fixtures,
residential

(P-6458)
FLEXFIRE LEDS INC
Also Called: Evoralight
3554 Business Park Dr Ste F, Costa Mesa
(92626-1423)
PHONE..................................925 273-9080
Brenton Mauriello, *CEO*
EMP: 24 **EST:** 2011
SQ FT: 4,600
SALES (est): 2.22MM **Privately Held**
Web: www.flexfireleds.com
SIC: 3646 5063 Commercial lighting fixtures;
Lighting fixtures

(P-6459)
FLO KINO INC
2840 N Hollywood Way, Burbank
(91505-1023)
PHONE..................................818 767-6528
EMP: 103 **EST:** 1984
SALES (est): 4.81MM **Privately Held**
SIC: 3646 Commercial lighting fixtures

(P-6460)
FLUORESCENT SUPPLY CO INC
Also Called: Fsc
9120 Center Ave, Rancho Cucamonga
(91730-5310)
PHONE..................................909 948-8878
Vincent Alonzi, *Pr*
▲ **EMP:** 48 **EST:** 1969
SQ FT: 80,000
SALES (est): 22.04MM
SALES (corp-wide): 22.04MM **Privately
Held**
Web: www.fsclighting.com
SIC: 3646 3645 Commercial lighting fixtures;
Residential lighting fixtures
PA: Onward Capital Llc
525 W Monroe St Ste 22109
847 983-0869

(P-6461)
FOCUS INDUSTRIES INC
Also Called: Focus Landscape
25301 Commercentre Dr, Lake Forest
(92630-0000)
PHONE..................................949 830-1350
Stan Shibata, *Pr*
June Shibata, *
▲ **EMP:** 100 **EST:** 1989
SQ FT: 40,000
SALES (est): 22.55MM **Privately Held**
Web: www.focusindustries.com
SIC: 3646 5063 Commercial lighting fixtures;
Electrical apparatus and equipment

(P-6462)
HALLMARK LIGHTING LLC
Also Called: Hallmark Lighting
1945 S Tubeway Ave, Commerce
(90040-1611)
PHONE..................................818 885-5010
Christopher Larocca, *CEO*
Robert Godlewski, *
Julie Winfield, *

◆ **EMP:** 80 **EST:** 1978
SALES (est): 5.35MM **Privately Held**
Web: www.hallmarklighting.com
SIC: 3646 3645 3641 Commercial lighting
fixtures; Wall lamps; Electric lamps

(P-6463)
**HI-LITE MANUFACTURING CO
INC**
13450 Monte Vista Ave, Chino
(91710-5149)
PHONE..................................909 465-1999
Dorothy A Ohai, *Pr*
◆ **EMP:** 90 **EST:** 1959
SQ FT: 157,000
SALES (est): 3.61MM **Privately Held**
Web: www.hilitemfg.com
SIC: 3646 3645 Commercial lighting fixtures;
Residential lighting fixtures

(P-6464)
INTENSE LIGHTING LLC
3340 E La Palma Ave, Anaheim
(92806-2814)
PHONE..................................714 630-9877
Roger Weisenaur, *
Kenneth Eidsvold, *
Tom Elam, *Prin*
Allan Gray, *Prin*
◆ **EMP:** 80 **EST:** 2001
SQ FT: 153,000
SALES (est): 22.26MM
SALES (corp-wide): 1.46B **Privately Held**
Web: www.intenselighting.com
SIC: 3646 3645 Commercial lighting fixtures;
Residential lighting fixtures
PA: Leviton Manufacturing Co., Inc.
201 N Service Rd
800 323-8920

(P-6465)
LAMPS PLUS INC
Also Called: Pacific Coast Lighting
4723 Telephone Rd, Ventura (93003-5242)
PHONE..................................805 642-9007
David Hillard, *Mgr*
EMP: 23
SALES (corp-wide): 490.53MM **Privately
Held**
Web: www.lampsplus.com
SIC: 3646 5719 5064 Commercial lighting
fixtures; Lamps and lamp shades; Fans,
household: electric
PA: Lamps Plus, Inc.
20250 Plummer St
818 886-5267

(P-6466)
LF ILLUMINATION LLC
Also Called: Formed Lighting
9200 Deering Ave, Chatsworth
(91311-5803)
PHONE..................................818 885-1335
Loren Kessel, *Pr*
Eileen S Cheng, *
▲ **EMP:** 51 **EST:** 2013
SALES (est): 9.68MM **Privately Held**
Web: www.lfillumination.com
SIC: 3646 3645 5719 Commercial lighting
fixtures; Residential lighting fixtures;
Lighting fixtures

(P-6467)
MODERN WOODWORKS INC
Also Called: Modern Woodworks
7949 Deering Ave, Canoga Park
(91304-5009)
PHONE..................................800 575-3475
George Mekhtarian, *CEO*
Allen Mekhtarian, *

▲ **EMP:** 35 **EST:** 2000
SQ FT: 10,000
SALES (est): 4.04MM **Privately Held**
Web: www.californialightworks.com
SIC: 3646 Commercial lighting fixtures

(P-6468)
NOMOFLO ENTERPRISES INC
Also Called: Kino Flo Lighting Systems
2840 N Hollywood Way, Burbank
(91505-1023)
PHONE....................818 767-6528
Frieder Hochheim, *Pr*
Gary Swink, *VP*
▲ **EMP:** 24 **EST:** 1987
SALES (est): 7.9MM **Privately Held**
Web: www.kinoflo.com
SIC: 3646 Commercial lighting fixtures

(P-6469)
OPTIC ARTS HOLDINGS INC
716 Monterey Pass Rd, Monterey Park
(91754-3607)
PHONE....................213 250-6069
Jason Mullen, *CEO*
Dorian L Hicklin, *
Mason Barker, *
EMP: 47 **EST:** 2011
SQ FT: 15,750
SALES (est): 7.17MM
SALES (corp-wide): 21.63MM **Privately Held**
Web: www.luminii.com
SIC: 3646 3645 3648 Commercial lighting fixtures; Residential lighting fixtures; Decorative area lighting fixtures
PA: Luminii Llc
7777 N Merrimac Ave
224 333-6033

(P-6470)
PACIFIC LTG & STANDARDS CO
2815 Los Flores Blvd, Lynwood
(90262-2416)
PHONE....................310 603-9344
Frank Munoz, *Pr*
Enrique Garcia, *
▲ **EMP:** 34 **EST:** 1982
SQ FT: 17,000
SALES (est): 2.12MM **Privately Held**
Web: www.pacificlighting.com
SIC: 3646 Commercial lighting fixtures

(P-6471)
PRUDENTIAL LIGHTING CORP (PA)
Also Called: P L M
1774 E 21st St, Los Angeles (90058-1082)
P.O. Box 58736 (90058-0736)
PHONE....................213 477-1694
Stanely J Ellis, *CEO*
Jeffrey Ellis, *
Elliot Ellis, *
Jolie Ellis, *
▲ **EMP:** 120 **EST:** 1955
SQ FT: 112,000
SALES (est): 21.31MM
SALES (corp-wide): 21.31MM **Privately Held**
Web: www.prulite.com
SIC: 3646 Fluorescent lighting fixtures, commercial

(P-6472)
SAPPHIRE CHANDELIER LLC
505 Porter Way, Placentia (92870-6454)
PHONE....................714 879-3660
Hector Garibay, *Pt*
Hector Garibay, *Managing Member*
▲ **EMP:** 61 **EST:** 2009

SQ FT: 10,000
SALES (est): 6.88MM **Privately Held**
Web: www.sapphirechandelier.com
SIC: 3646 Commercial lighting fixtures

(P-6473)
SIGNIFY NORTH AMERICA CORP
3350 Enterprise Dr, Bloomington
(92316-3538)
PHONE....................732 563-3000
EMP: 120
Web: www.signify.com
SIC: 3646 Commercial lighting fixtures
HQ: Signify North America Corporation
400 Crossing Blvd Ste 600
Bridgewater NJ 08807
732 563-3000

(P-6474)
SPOTLITE POWER CORPORATION
9937 Jefferson Blvd Ste 110, Culver City
(90232-3529)
PHONE....................310 838-2367
Halston Mikail, *Pr*
▲ **EMP:** 28 **EST:** 2016
SALES (est): 636.19K
SALES (corp-wide): 2.17MM **Privately Held**
SIC: 3646 Commercial lighting fixtures
PA: Spotlite America Corporation
9937 Jefferson Blvd # 110
310 829-0200

(P-6475)
SUN VALLEY LTG STANDARDS INC
Also Called: US Architectural Lighting
660 W Avenue O, Palmdale (93551-3610)
PHONE....................661 233-2000
Joseph Straus, *Pr*
Judith Straus, *VP*
EMP: 52 **EST:** 1984
SQ FT: 30,000
SALES (est): 2.06MM
SALES (corp-wide): 24.01MM **Privately Held**
Web: www.usaltg.com
SIC: 3646 5063 3648 Ornamental lighting fixtures, commercial; Electrical apparatus and equipment; Lighting equipment, nec
PA: U.S. Pole Company, Inc.
660 W Avenue O
800 877-6537

(P-6476)
TOPAZ LIGHTING COMPANY LLC
225 Parkside Dr, San Fernando
(91340-3033)
PHONE....................818 838-3123
EMP: 25
SALES (corp-wide): 1.7B **Privately Held**
Web: www.southwire.com
SIC: 3646 Commercial lighting fixtures
HQ: Topaz Lighting Company Llc
3241 Route 112 Ste 7
Medford NY 11763
800 666-2852

(P-6477)
US ENERGY TECHNOLOGIES INC
Also Called: US Lighting Tech
14370 Myford Road Ste 100, Walnut
(91789)
P.O. Box 365 (90621-0365)
PHONE....................714 617-8800
◆ **EMP:** 50
Web: www.uslightingtech.com

SIC: 3646 Commercial lighting fixtures

(P-6478)
US POLE COMPANY INC (PA)
Also Called: U S Architectural Lighting
660 W Avenue O, Palmdale (93551-3610)
PHONE....................800 877-6537
Joseph Straus, *Pr*
◆ **EMP:** 97 **EST:** 1984
SQ FT: 112,000
SALES (est): 24.01MM
SALES (corp-wide): 24.01MM **Privately Held**
Web: www.usaltg.com
SIC: 3646 Commercial lighting fixtures

(P-6479)
VISION ENGRG MET STAMPING INC
Also Called: Vision Engineering
114 Grand Cypress Ave, Palmdale
(93551-3617)
P.O. Box 901780 (93590-1780)
PHONE....................661 575-0933
Joseph Avila, *CEO*
EMP: 100 **EST:** 1997
SQ FT: 72,000
SALES (est): 2.4MM **Privately Held**
Web: www.visionengineering.com
SIC: 3646 Ceiling systems, luminous

(P-6480)
VISIONAIRE LIGHTING LLC
Also Called: Visionaire Lighting
3780 Kilroy Airport Way, Long Beach
(90806-2457)
PHONE....................310 512-6480
Bryan Fried, *CEO*
Cheryl Moorman, *
◆ **EMP:** 89 **EST:** 2000
SALES (est): 24.64MM **Privately Held**
Web: www.visionairelighting.com
SIC: 3646 Commercial lighting fixtures

(P-6481)
WPMG INC
Also Called: Tempo Industries
1961 Mcgaw Ave, Irvine (92614-0909)
PHONE....................949 442-1601
Dennis Pearson, *CEO*
▲ **EMP:** 31 **EST:** 1986
SQ FT: 27,000
SALES (est): 7.81MM **Privately Held**
Web: www.tempollc.com
SIC: 3646 Commercial lighting fixtures

(P-6482)
YANKON INDUSTRIES INC (PA)
Also Called: Energetic Lighting
13445 12th St, Chino (91710-5206)
PHONE....................909 591-2345
Wei Chen, *CEO*
David Liu, *CEO*
Kristen Tai, *CFO*
▲ **EMP:** 23 **EST:** 2009
SQ FT: 100,627
SALES (est): 8.07MM
SALES (corp-wide): 8.07MM **Privately Held**
Web: www.energeticlighting.com
SIC: 3646 Commercial lighting fixtures

3647 Vehicular Lighting Equipment

(P-6483)
AMP PLUS INC
Also Called: Elco Lighting

2042 E Vernon Ave, Los Angeles
(90058-1613)
PHONE....................323 231-2600
Steve Cohen, *Pr*
◆ **EMP:** 55 **EST:** 1991
SQ FT: 100,000
SALES (est): 8.41MM **Privately Held**
Web: www.elcolighting.com
SIC: 3647 5063 3645 Vehicular lighting equipment; Electrical apparatus and equipment; Residential lighting fixtures

(P-6484)
JKL COMPONENTS CORPORATION
13343 Paxton St, Pacoima (91331-2340)
PHONE....................818 896-0019
Joseph Velas, *Pr*
Kent Koerting, *
EMP: 32 **EST:** 1974
SQ FT: 7,000
SALES (est): 4.46MM **Privately Held**
Web: www.jkllamps.com
SIC: 3647 3827 3699 Automotive lighting fixtures, nec; Optical instruments and lenses ; Electrical equipment and supplies, nec

(P-6485)
KC HILITES INC
13637 Cimarron Ave, Gardena
(90249-2461)
PHONE....................928 635-2607
Michael Dehaas, *Pr*
◆ **EMP:** 36 **EST:** 1970
SQ FT: 25,000
SALES (est): 2.98MM **Privately Held**
Web: www.kchilites.com
SIC: 3647 Vehicular lighting equipment

(P-6486)
SODERBERG MANUFACTURING CO INC
20821 Currier Rd, Walnut (91789-3018)
PHONE....................909 595-1291
B W Soderberg, *CEO*
Kathy Kirkeby, *
Rick Soderberg, *
Kari Levario, *
EMP: 85 **EST:** 1946
SALES (est): 7.62MM **Privately Held**
Web: www.soderberg.aero
SIC: 3647 3812 Aircraft lighting fixtures; Search and navigation equipment

(P-6487)
ZO MOTORS NORTH AMERICA LLC ✪
Also Called: Zm Trucks
21250 Hawthorne Blvd Ste 500, Torrance
(90503-5514)
PHONE....................310 792-7077
Jeroen J De Bris, *Managing Member*
EMP: 50 **EST:** 2023
SALES (est): 2.71MM **Privately Held**
SIC: 3647 Vehicular lighting equipment

3648 Lighting Equipment, Nec

(P-6488)
ALL ACCESS STGING PRDCTONS INC (PA)
1320 Storm Pkwy, Torrance (90501-5041)
PHONE....................310 784-2464
Clive Forrester, *CEO*
Erik Eastland, *
Robert Achlimbari, *
▲ **EMP:** 45 **EST:** 1997
SQ FT: 42,000

SALES (est): 13.74MM
SALES (corp-wide): 13.74MM **Privately Held**
Web: www.allaccessinc.com
SIC: **3648** Stage lighting equipment

(P-6489)
AMERICAN GRIP INC
8468 Kewen Ave, Sun Valley (91352-3118)
PHONE.................................818 768-8922
Lance Snoke, *Pr*
EMP: 25 EST: 1984
SQ FT: 15,000
SALES (est): 5.04MM **Privately Held**
Web: www.americangrip.com
SIC: **3648** 3861 Stage lighting equipment;
Stands, camera and projector

(P-6490)
AMERILLUM LLC
Also Called: Alumen-8
3728 Maritime Way, Oceanside
(92056-2702)
PHONE.................................760 727-7675
Ronald S Lancial, *Managing Member*
Serge Lambert, *
Guy St Pierre, *
▲ EMP: 54 EST: 2010
SQ FT: 27,000
SALES (est): 14.17MM
SALES (corp-wide): 3.84B **Publicly Held**
Web: www.alights.com
SIC: **3648** Lighting equipment, nec
PA: Acuity Brands, Inc.
1170 Pchtree St Ne Ste 23
404 853-1400

(P-6491)
BEGA NORTH AMERICA INC
Also Called: Bega
1000 Bega Way, Carpinteria (93013-2902)
PHONE.................................805 684-0533
Don Kinderdick, *CEO*
◆ EMP: 100 EST: 1985
SQ FT: 60,000
SALES (est): 22.22MM **Privately Held**
Web: www.bega-us.com
SIC: **3648** 3646 Outdoor lighting equipment;
Commercial lighting fixtures

(P-6492)
BIRCHWOOD LIGHTING INC
3340 E La Palma Ave, Anaheim
(92806-2814)
PHONE.................................714 550-7118
EMP: 25 EST: 1993
SQ FT: 1,900
SALES (est): 9.06MM
SALES (corp-wide): 1.46B **Privately Held**
Web: www.birchwoodlighting.com
SIC: **3648** 3646 3645 Decorative area
lighting fixtures; Commercial lighting fixtures
; Residential lighting fixtures
PA: Leviton Manufacturing Co., Inc.
201 N Service Rd
800 323-8920

(P-6493)
BLISS HOLDINGS LLC
745 S Vinewood St, Escondido
(92029-1928)
PHONE.................................626 506-8696
▲ EMP: 50 EST: 2006
SALES (est): 2.11MM **Privately Held**
SIC: **3648** Lighting equipment, nec

(P-6494)
BRIGHTEN CORP
328 S Atlantic Blvd Ste 201, Monterey Park
(91754-3244)

PHONE.................................626 231-6238
Man Kit Lee, *CEO*
EMP: 25 EST: 2020
SALES (est): 1.07MM **Privately Held**
SIC: **3648** Decorative area lighting fixtures

(P-6495)
CLEAR BLUE ENERGY CORP
Also Called: Cbec
17150 Via Del Campo Ste 203, San Diego
(92127-2139)
P.O. Box 532086 (92153)
PHONE.................................858 451-1549
Paul Santina, *CEO*
Jim Kelly, *
EMP: 80 EST: 2009
SALES (est): 9.98MM **Privately Held**
Web: www.cbesco.com
SIC: **3648** 1731 Lighting equipment, nec;
Lighting contractor

(P-6496)
COOPER LIGHTING LLC
Also Called: Cooper Lighting
3350 Enterprise Dr, Bloomington
(92316-3538)
PHONE.................................909 605-6615
John Seiler, *Mgr*
EMP: 502
Web: www.cooperlighting.com
SIC: **3648** Lighting equipment, nec
HQ: Cooper Lighting, Llc
1121 Hwy 74 S
Peachtree City GA 30269
770 486-4800

(P-6497)
DANA CREATH DESIGNS LTD
3030 Kilson Dr, Santa Ana (92707-4203)
PHONE.................................714 662-0111
Dana E Creath, *Pt*
James K Creath, *
Raylene R Creath, *
EMP: 30 EST: 1968
SALES (est): 2.44MM **Privately Held**
Web: www.danacreath.com
SIC: **3648** 3646 3645 Lighting equipment,
nec; Commercial lighting fixtures;
Residential lighting fixtures

(P-6498)
DEEPSEA POWER & LIGHT INC
4033 Ruffin Rd, San Diego (92123-1817)
PHONE.................................858 576-1261
EMP: 23
SIC: **3648** Underwater lighting fixtures

(P-6499)
EEMA INDUSTRIES INC
Also Called: Liton Lighting
5461 W Jefferson Blvd, Los Angeles
(90016-3715)
PHONE.................................323 904-0200
Amir Esmail Zadeh, *Pr*
◆ EMP: 40 EST: 1998
SQ FT: 40,000
SALES (est): 4.32MM **Privately Held**
Web: www.liton.com
SIC: **3648** 5063 Lighting equipment, nec;
Electrical apparatus and equipment

(P-6500)
ELATION LIGHTING INC
Also Called: Elation Professional
6122 S Eastern Ave, Commerce
(90040-3402)
PHONE.................................323 582-3322
Toby Velazquez, *Pr*
Charles J Davies, *
▲ EMP: 60 EST: 1992

SQ FT: 50,000
SALES (est): 4.91MM **Privately Held**
Web: www.elationlighting.com
SIC: **3648** Lighting equipment, nec

(P-6501)
ELITE LIGHTING
Also Called: Elite Lighting
5424 E Slauson Ave, Commerce
(90040-2919)
PHONE.................................323 888-1973
Babak Rashididoust, *CEO*
◆ EMP: 200 EST: 1998
SQ FT: 25,000
SALES (est): 52.36MM **Privately Held**
Web: www.iuseelite.com
SIC: **3648** 3646 3645 Lighting equipment,
nec; Commercial lighting fixtures; Boudoir
lamps

(P-6502)
FOXFURY LLC
Also Called: Foxfury Lighting Solution
3544 Seagate Way, Oceanside
(92056-6041)
PHONE.................................760 945-4231
▲ EMP: 24 EST: 2005
SALES (est): 4.81MM **Privately Held**
Web: www.foxfury.com
SIC: **3648** Lighting equipment, nec

(P-6503)
GALLAGHER RENTAL INC
15701 Heron Ave, La Mirada (90638-5206)
PHONE.................................714 690-1559
Joseph Gallagher, *CEO*
Megan Gallagher, *
EMP: 30 EST: 2012
SALES (est): 3.89MM **Privately Held**
Web: www.gallagherstaging.com
SIC: **3648** Stage lighting equipment

(P-6504)
GREENSHINE NEW ENERGY LLC
23661 Birtcher Dr, Lake Forest
(92630-1770)
PHONE.................................949 609-9636
Alex Chen, *Managing Member*
Scott Douglas, *Genl Mgr*
◆ EMP: 100 EST: 2010
SQ FT: 200
SALES (est): 7.83MM **Privately Held**
Web: www.greenshine-solar.com
SIC: **3648** Lighting equipment, nec

(P-6505)
JIMWAY INC
Also Called: Altair Lighting
20101 S Santa Fe Ave, Compton
(90221-5917)
PHONE.................................310 000-3710
Hsing-min Keng, *CEO*
Irene Wang, *
▲ EMP: 100 EST: 1982
SQ FT: 200,000
SALES (est): 19.89MM **Privately Held**
Web: www.jimway.com
SIC: **3648** 3221 5063 Lighting equipment,
nec; Glass containers; Electrical apparatus
and equipment

(P-6506)
KIM LIGHTING INC
Also Called: Kim Lighting & Mfg
16555 Gale Ave, City Of Industry
(91745-1713)
P.O. Box 1275 (91716)
PHONE.................................626 968-5666
▲ EMP: 550

SIC: **3648** 3646 3317 Outdoor lighting
equipment; Commercial lighting fixtures;
Steel pipe and tubes

(P-6507)
LEDCONN CORP
Also Called: Ledconn
301 Thor Pl, Brea (92821-4133)
PHONE.................................714 256-2111
Tsanyu Wang, *Pr*
Wan Ting Huang, *
▲ EMP: 25 EST: 2008
SQ FT: 2,000
SALES (est): 4.82MM **Privately Held**
Web: www.ledconn.com
SIC: **3648** 3993 7389 Lighting equipment,
nec; Signs and advertising specialties;
Interior decorating

(P-6508)
LIGHT VAST INC
1202 Monte Vista Ave Ste 1, Upland
(91786-8209)
PHONE.................................800 358-0499
Leo Mao, *CEO*
EMP: 24 EST: 2015
SALES (est): 811.93K **Privately Held**
Web: www.lightvast.com
SIC: **3648** Lighting equipment, nec

(P-6509)
LIGHTING CONTROL & DESIGN INC
Also Called: LCD&d
9144 Deering Ave, Chatsworth
(91311-5801)
PHONE.................................323 226-0000
EMP: 46 EST: 1987
SALES (est): 6.1MM
SALES (corp-wide): 3.84B **Publicly Held**
Web: www.acuitybrands.com
SIC: **3648** 3643 5719 Lighting equipment,
nec; Current-carrying wiring services;
Lighting fixtures
PA: Acuity Brands, Inc.
1170 Pchtree St Ne Ste 23
404 853-1400

(P-6510)
MAG INSTRUMENT INC (PA)
2001 S Hellman Ave, Ontario (91761-8019)
P.O. Box 50600 (91761-1083)
PHONE.................................909 947-1006
Anthony Maglica, *CEO*
James Zecchini, *
Thomas K Richardson, *
Malissa Peace, *
Brent Flaharty, *
▲ EMP: 406 EST: 1955
SQ FT: 1,000,000
SALES (est): 46.03MM
SALES (corp-wide): 46.03MM **Privately
Held**
Web: www.maglite.com
SIC: **3648** Flashlights

(P-6511)
MOLE-RICHARDSON CO LTD (PA)
Also Called: Studio Depot
12154 Montague St, Pacoima
(91331-2209)
PHONE.................................323 851-0111
▲ EMP: 100 EST: 1927
SALES (est): 9.65MM
SALES (corp-wide): 9.65MM **Privately
Held**
Web: www.mole.com

SIC: **3648** 3621 3861 3646 Lighting
equipment, nec; Motors and generators;
Photographic equipment and supplies;
Commercial lighting fixtures

(P-6512)
NEW BEDFORD PANORAMEX CORP
Also Called: Nbp
1480 N Claremont Blvd, Claremont
(91711-3538)
PHONE...................................909 982-9806
Steven Robert Ozuna, *Pr*
James Casso, *
Bryce Nielsen, *
EMP: 35 EST: 1966
SQ FT: 65,000
SALES (est): 9.59MM **Privately Held**
Web: www.nbpcorp.com
SIC: **3648** Airport lighting fixtures: runway
approach, taxi, or ramp

(P-6513)
NITERDER TCHNCAL LTG VDEO SYST
Also Called: Niterider
12255 Crosthwaite Cir Ste A, Poway
(92064-8825)
PHONE...................................858 268-9316
Thomas Edward Carroll, *CEO*
Mark Schultz, *
▲ **EMP: 35 EST:** 1989
SALES (est): 5.59MM **Privately Held**
Web: www.niterider.com
SIC: **3648** 3646 Lighting equipment, nec;
Commercial lighting fixtures

(P-6514)
PELICAN PRODUCTS INC (PA)
Also Called: Pelican
23215 Early Ave, Torrance (90505-4002)
PHONE...................................310 326-4700
James Curleigh, *CEO*
Scott Ermeti, *INTL Business*
Dave Pres Biothermal Div Williams, *Prin*
Chris Favreau, *
George Platisa, *
◆ **EMP: 245 EST:** 2007
SQ FT: 150,000
SALES (est): 564.44MM
SALES (corp-wide): 564.44MM **Privately Held**
Web: www.pelican.com
SIC: **3648** 3161 3089 Flashlights; Luggage;
Plastics containers, except foam

(P-6515)
REMOTE OCEAN SYSTEMS INC (PA)
Also Called: R O S
9581 Ridgehaven Ct, San Diego
(92123-1624)
PHONE...................................858 565-8500
Robert Acks, *CEO*
Christine Acks, *
EMP: 34 EST: 1975
SALES (est): 9.47MM
SALES (corp-wide): 9.47MM **Privately Held**
Web: www.rosys.com
SIC: **3648** 3861 3812 3643 Underwater
lighting fixtures; Photographic equipment
and supplies; Search and navigation
equipment; Current-carrying wiring services

(P-6516)
SHIMADA ENTERPRISES INC
Also Called: Celestial Lighting
14009 Dinard Ave, Santa Fe Springs
(90670-4922)

PHONE...................................562 802-8811
Tak Shimada, *Pr*
Mick Shimada, *
▲ **EMP: 30 EST:** 1975
SQ FT: 11,000
SALES (est): 5.29MM **Privately Held**
Web: www.celestiallighting.com
SIC: **3648** Decorative area lighting fixtures

(P-6517)
STERIL-AIRE INC
25060 Avenue Stanford Ste 160, Valencia
(91355-3915)
PHONE...................................818 565-1128
Robert Scheir, *Pr*
◆ **EMP: 23 EST:** 1995
SALES (est): 7.34MM **Privately Held**
Web: www.steril-aire.com
SIC: **3648** Ultraviolet lamp fixtures

(P-6518)
SUREFIRE LLC (PA)
18300 Mount Baldy Cir, Fountain Valley
(92708-6122)
PHONE...................................714 545-9444
Sean Vo, *
Joel Smith, *CAO*
◆ **EMP: 175 EST:** 2000
SQ FT: 45,000
SALES (est): 97.06MM
SALES (corp-wide): 97.06MM **Privately Held**
Web: www.surefire.com
SIC: **3648** 3699 Flashlights; Laser systems
and equipment

(P-6519)
THIN-LITE CORPORATION
530 Constitution Ave, Camarillo
(93012-8595)
PHONE...................................805 987-5021
Alan Griffin, *Pr*
Lilian Cross Szymanek, *
▲ **EMP: 47 EST:** 1970
SQ FT: 27,000
SALES (est): 7.75MM **Privately Held**
Web: www.thinlite.com
SIC: **3648** 3612 3646 Lighting equipment,
nec; Transformers, except electric;
Fluorescent lighting fixtures, commercial

(P-6520)
TOTAL STRUCTURES INC
Also Called: Total Structures
1696 Walter St, Ventura (93003-5619)
PHONE...................................805 676-3322
William Scott Johnson, *CEO*
◆ **EMP: 45 EST:** 1995
SQ FT: 24,000
SALES (est): 4.83MM **Privately Held**
Web: www.totalstructures.com
SIC: **3648** 3441 Lighting equipment, nec;
Fabricated structural metal
HQ: Eurotruss B.V.
Castorweg 2
Leeuwarden FR 8938
582158888

3651 Household Audio And Video Equipment

(P-6521)
ABSOLUTE USA INC
Also Called: Absolute Pro Music
1800 E Washington Blvd, Los Angeles
(90021-3127)
PHONE...................................213 744-0044
Mohammad K Razipour, *Pr*
Sasha Razipour, *

◆ **EMP: 47 EST:** 2002
SQ FT: 35,000
SALES (est): 16MM **Privately Held**
Web: www.absolutepromusic.com
SIC: **3651** Audio electronic systems

(P-6522)
ACTIVEON INC (PA)
10905 Technology Pl, San Diego
(92127-1811)
PHONE...................................858 798-3300
John Lee, *CEO*
Jonathan Zupnik, *VP*
▲ **EMP: 49 EST:** 2006
SALES (est): 1.01MM **Privately Held**
Web: www.activeon.com
SIC: **3651** Household audio and video
equipment

(P-6523)
AL SHELLCO LLC (HQ)
9330 Scranton Rd Ste 600, San Diego
(92121-7706)
PHONE...................................570 296-6444
Mark Lucas, *Managing Member*
Edward Anchel, *
Richard P Horner, *
Ross Gatlin, *
▲ **EMP: 160 EST:** 1953
SQ FT: 120,000
SALES (est): 3.14MM
SALES (corp-wide): 691.84MM **Privately Held**
SIC: **3651** 3577 Radio receiving sets;
Computer peripheral equipment, nec
PA: Prophet Equity Lp
1460 Main St Ste 200
817 898-1500

(P-6524)
ANACOM GENERAL CORPORATION
Also Called: Anacom Medtek
1240 S Claudina St, Anaheim (92805-6232)
PHONE...................................714 774-8484
Daniel S Haines, *Pr*
William K Haines, *
▲ **EMP: 48 EST:** 1967
SQ FT: 20,000
SALES (est): 9.87MM **Privately Held**
Web: www.anacom-medtek.com
SIC: **3651** 3577 Speaker monitors;
Computer peripheral equipment, nec

(P-6525)
ANCHOR AUDIO INC (PA)
5931 Darwin Ct, Carlsbad (92008-7302)
PHONE...................................760 827-7100
Janet Jacobs, *CEO*
David Jacobs, *Pr*
Dwight Garbe, *CFO*
▲ **EMP: 40 EST:** 1973
SQ FT: 31,200
SALES (est): 11.13MM
SALES (corp-wide): 11.13MM **Privately Held**
Web: www.anchoraudio.com
SIC: **3651** Public address systems

(P-6526)
APOGEE ELECTRONICS CORPORATION
Also Called: Apogee Electronics
1715 Berkeley St, Santa Monica
(90404-4104)
PHONE...................................310 584-9394
Betty A Bennett, *CEO*
▲ **EMP: 35 EST:** 1985
SQ FT: 5,000
SALES (est): 4.87MM **Privately Held**

Web: www.apogeedigital.com
SIC: **3651** 3621 8748 Audio electronic
systems; Motors and generators;
Communications consulting

(P-6527)
ARLO TECHNOLOGIES INC (PA)
Also Called: ARLO
2200 Faraday Ave Ste 150, Carlsbad
(92008-7224)
PHONE...................................408 890-3900
Matthew Mcrae, *CEO*
Ralph E Faison, *Ch Bd*
Kurtis Binder, *CFO*
Brian Busse, *Corporate Secretary*
EMP: 86 EST: 2014
SQ FT: 43,500
SALES (est): 491.18MM
SALES (corp-wide): 491.18MM **Publicly Held**
Web: www.arlo.com
SIC: **3651** 7372 Household audio and video
equipment; Application computer software

(P-6528)
AURASOUND INC
1801 E Edinger Ave Ste 190, Santa Ana
(92705-4770)
PHONE...................................949 829-4000
EMP: 72
Web: www.aurasound.com
SIC: **3651** Household audio equipment

(P-6529)
BALTIC LTVIAN UNVRSAL ELEC LLC
Also Called: Blue Microphone
5706 Corsa Ave, Westlake Village
(91362-4057)
PHONE...................................818 879-5200
John Maier, *CEO*
Bart E Thielen, *
Bernard Wise, *
Martin Saulespurens, *
▲ **EMP: 35 EST:** 1998
SALES (est): 2.77MM **Privately Held**
SIC: **3651** 5731 Microphones; Consumer
electronic equipment, nec
PA: Logitech International S.A.
Route De Pampigny 20

(P-6530)
BEATS ELECTRONICS LLC
Also Called: Beats By Dre
8600 Hayden Pl, Culver City (90232-2902)
PHONE...................................424 326-4679
Timothy Cook, *CEO*
▲ **EMP: 500 EST:** 2006
SALES (est): 20.37MM
SALES (corp-wide): 391.04B **Publicly Held**
Web: www.beatsbydre.com
SIC: **3651** 3679 Speaker systems;
Headphones, radio
PA: Apple Inc.
1 Apple Park Way
408 996-1010

(P-6531)
BELKIN INC
Also Called: Belkin
555 S Aviation Blvd, El Segundo
(90245-4852)
PHONE...................................800 223-5546
Chester J Pipkin, *Pr*
George Platisa, *
◆ **EMP: 775 EST:** 2003
SALES (est): 18.66MM **Privately Held**
Web: www.belkin.com

SIC: **3651** Electronic kits for home assembly:
radio, TV, phonograph
HQ: Belkin International, Inc.
555 S Avi Blvd Ste 180
El Segundo CA 90245
310 751-5100

(P-6532)
DANA INNOVATIONS (PA)
Also Called: Sonance
991 Calle Amanecer, San Clemente
(92673-6212)
PHONE.................................949 492-7777
Ari Supran, *CEO*
Scott Struthers, *Pr*
Geoffrey L Spencer, *Sec*
Mike Simmons, *CFO*
◆ **EMP:** 156 **EST:** 1981
SQ FT: 42,320
SALES (est): 49.59MM
SALES (corp-wide): 49.59MM **Privately Held**
Web: www.sonance.com
SIC: **3651** 5731 7629 Speaker systems;
Radio, television, and electronic stores;
Electrical repair shops

(P-6533)
DIGITAL PERIPH SOLUTIONS INC
Also Called: Q-See
160 S Old Springs Rd Ste 220, Anaheim
(92808-1226)
PHONE.................................714 998-3440
Priti Sharma, *Pr*
Rajeev Sharma, *
▲ **EMP:** 40 **EST:** 2002
SQ FT: 30,000
SALES (est): 4.27MM **Privately Held**
Web: www.q-see.com
SIC: **3651** 7382 Video camera-audio
recorders, household use; Confinement
surveillance systems maintenance and
monitoring

(P-6534)
DOREMI LABS INC
Also Called: Doremi
1020 Chestnut St, Burbank (91506-1623)
PHONE.................................818 562-1101
▲ **EMP:** 40
SIC: **3651** Audio electronic systems

(P-6535)
DWI ENTERPRISES
11081 Winners Cir Ste 100, Los Alamitos
(90720-2894)
PHONE.................................714 842 2236
Fred Delgleize, *Pr*
Dan Delgleize, *
Dave Dain, *
Amanda Delgleize, *
◆ **EMP:** 25 **EST:** 1980
SQ FT: 9,500
SALES (est): 2.02MM **Privately Held**
Web: www.dwienterprises.com
SIC: **3651** 3669 Audio electronic systems;
Visual communication systems

(P-6536)
ETI SOUND SYSTEMS INC
Also Called: Eti B Si Professional
5300 Harbor St, Commerce (90040-3927)
PHONE.................................323 835-6660
Eli El-kiss, *Pr*
Avi El-kiss, *VP*
◆ **EMP:** 45 **EST:** 1989
SALES (est): 6.84MM **Privately Held**
Web: www.b-52pro.com

SIC: **3651** Speaker monitors

(P-6537)
FUNAI CORPORATION INC (DH)
12489 Lakeland Rd, Santa Fe Springs
(90670-3938)
PHONE.................................310 787-3000
Yoshihiro Sasaki, *CEO*
Hiroyuki Anabe, *
Ryo Fukuda, *
George Kanazawa, *
Yoichi Kanazawa, *
▲ **EMP:** 25 **EST:** 1991
SALES (est): 12.06MM **Privately Held**
Web: www.funai.us
SIC: **3651** 3955 Television receiving sets;
Print cartridges for laser and other
computer printers
HQ: Funai Group Co., Ltd.
7-7-1, Nakagaito
Daito OSK 574-0

(P-6538)
FUNAI CORPORATION INC
Also Called: Funai Electric Co.
19900 Van Ness Ave, Torrance
(90501-1143)
PHONE.................................201 727-4560
◆ **EMP:** 77
SIC: **3651** Household audio and video
equipment

(P-6539)
HARMAN PROFESSIONAL INC
14780 Bar Harbor Rd, Fontana
(92336-4254)
PHONE.................................844 776-4899
EMP: 159
Web: www.jblpro.com
SIC: **3651** Audio electronic systems
HQ: Harman Professional, Inc.
8500 Balboa Blvd
Northridge CA 91329
818 893-8411

(P-6540)
HARMAN PROFESSIONAL INC
24950 Grove View Rd, Moreno Valley
(92551-9552)
PHONE.................................951 242-2927
EMP: 140
Web: www.jblpro.com
SIC: **3651** Household audio equipment
HQ: Harman Professional, Inc.
8500 Balboa Blvd
Northridge CA 91329
818 893-8411

(P-6541)
HARMAN PROFESSIONAL INC (DH)
Also Called: Harman Professional
8500 Balboa Blvd, Northridge (91329-0003)
P.O. Box 2200 (91329)
PHONE.................................818 893-8411
Brian Divine, *CEO*
◆ **EMP:** 300 **EST:** 2006
SALES (est): 165.47MM **Privately Held**
Web: www.jblpro.com
SIC: **3651** Audio electronic systems
HQ: Harman International Industries
Incorporated
400 Atlantic St Fl 15
Stamford CT 06901
203 328-3500

(P-6542)
HENRYS ADIO VSUAL SLUTIONS INC

Also Called: Audio Images
18002 Cowan, Irvine (92614-6812)
PHONE.................................714 258-7238
Mark Ontiveros, *CEO*
EMP: 30 **EST:** 1998
SALES (est): 5.71MM **Privately Held**
Web: www.audioimages.tv
SIC: **3651** Household audio and video
equipment

(P-6543)
M KLEMME TECHNOLOGY CORP
Also Called: K-Tek
1384 Poinsettia Ave Ste F, Vista
(92081-8505)
PHONE.................................760 727-0593
Brenda L Parker, *Pr*
▲ **EMP:** 26 **EST:** 1996
SALES (est): 3.17MM **Privately Held**
Web: www.ktekpro.com
SIC: **3651** Audio electronic systems

(P-6544)
MARSHALL ELECTRONICS INC (PA)
Also Called: Mogami
20608 Madrona Ave, Torrance
(90503-3715)
PHONE.................................310 333-0606
▲ **EMP:** 90 **EST:** 1979
SALES (est): 12.02MM
SALES (corp-wide): 12.02MM **Privately Held**
Web: www.marshall-usa.com
SIC: **3651** 5961 Electronic kits for home
assembly: radio, TV, phonograph;
Electronic kits and parts, mail order

(P-6545)
MJ BEST VIDEOGRAPHER LLC
14005 S Berendo Ave Apt 3, Gardena
(90247-2248)
PHONE.................................209 208-8432
John S Morris, *CEO*
EMP: 209 **EST:** 2020
SALES (est): 300.82K **Privately Held**
SIC: **3651** Video camera-audio recorders,
household use

(P-6546)
MR DJ INC
1800 E Washington Blvd, Los Angeles
(90021-3127)
PHONE.................................213 744-0044
Mike Razipour, *CEO*
Shahzad Fatemi, *
▲ **EMP:** 50 **EST:** 2009
SALES (est): 1.33MM **Privately Held**
Web: www.mrdjusa.com
SIC: **3651** Audio electronic systems

(P-6547)
PHILIPS
3721 Valley Centre Dr Ste 500, San Diego
(92130-3328)
PHONE.................................916 337-8008
EMP: 81 **EST:** 2018
SALES (est): 4.41MM **Privately Held**
Web: usa.philips.com
SIC: **3651** Household audio and video
equipment

(P-6548)
PIONEER SPEAKERS INC
2050 W 190th St Ste 100, Torrance
(90504-6229)
PHONE.................................310 952-2000
◆ **EMP:** 1250

Web: www.pioneerdj.com
SIC: **3651** Speaker systems

(P-6549)
QSC LLC (PA)
Also Called: Qsc Audio
1675 Macarthur Blvd, Costa Mesa
(92626-1468)
PHONE.................................800 854-4079
Joe Pham, *CEO*
Jatan Shah, *
Barry Ferrell, *
Ray Van Straten, *
Anna Csontos, *
◆ **EMP:** 175 **EST:** 1979
SQ FT: 180,000
SALES (est): 101.64MM
SALES (corp-wide): 101.64MM **Privately Held**
Web: www.qsc.com
SIC: **3651** Household audio equipment

(P-6550)
RENKUS-HEINZ INC (PA)
19201 Cook St, Foothill Ranch
(92610-3501)
PHONE.................................949 588-9997
Harro Heinz, *Ch*
Roscoe L Anthony Iii, *CEO*
Erika Heinz, *
▲ **EMP:** 79 **EST:** 1979
SQ FT: 48,500
SALES (est): 9.86MM
SALES (corp-wide): 9.86MM **Privately Held**
Web: www.renkus-heinz.com
SIC: **3651** Audio electronic systems

(P-6551)
ROCK-OLA MANUFACTURING CORP
Also Called: Antique Apparatus Company
1445 Sepulveda Blvd, Torrance
(90501-5004)
PHONE.................................310 328-1306
Glenn S Streeter, *Pr*
◆ **EMP:** 80 **EST:** 1994
SALES (est): 9.98MM **Privately Held**
Web: www.rock-ola.com
SIC: **3651** Coin-operated phonographs, juke
boxes

(P-6552)
RODE MICROPHONES LLC (DH)
2745 Raymond Ave, Signal Hill
(90755-2129)
P.O. Box 91028 (90809-1028)
PHONE.................................310 328-7456
Mark Ludmer, *CEO*
Peter Freedmon, *
Brian Swboringon, *
▲ **EMP:** 140 **EST:** 2001
SALES (est): 48.01MM **Privately Held**
Web: www.rode.com
SIC: **3651** Microphones
HQ: Freedman Electronics Pty Ltd
107 Carnarvon St
Silverwater NSW 2128

(P-6553)
SANYO MANUFACTURING CORPORATION
2055 Sanyo Ave, San Diego (92154-6234)
P.O. Box 2000 (72336-2000)
PHONE.................................619 661-1134
◆ **EMP:** 100
SIC: **3651** Television receiving sets

(P-6554)

SCOSCHE INDUSTRIES INC
1550 Pacific Ave, Oxnard (93033-2451)
P.O. Box 2901 (93034-2901)
PHONE..............................805 486-4450
Roger J Alves, *CEO*
Scotia Alves, *
Kasidy Alves, *
Vincent Alves, *
Steven Klinger, *
◆ **EMP:** 180 **EST:** 1980
SQ FT: 83,000
SALES (est): 24.51MM **Privately Held**
Web: www.scosche.com
SIC: 3651 Audio electronic systems

(P-6555)

SONOS INC (PA)
Also Called: Sonos
301 Coromar Dr, Goleta (93117-3286)
PHONE..............................805 965-3001
Patrick Spence, *Pr*
Julius Genachowski, *
Saori Casey, *CFO*
Edward Lazarus, *CSO CLO*
Nicholas Millington, *CIO*
◆ **EMP:** 91 **EST:** 2002
SALES (est): 1.52B
SALES (corp-wide): 1.52B **Publicly Held**
Web: www.sonos.com
SIC: 3651 Household audio and video
equipment

(P-6556)

SONY ELECTRONICS INC
Also Called: Sony Style
16530 Via Esprillo, San Diego
(92127-1708)
PHONE..............................858 942-2400
Bill Lunger, *Prin*
EMP: 224
Web: www.sony.com
SIC: 3651 Household audio and video
equipment
HQ: Sony Electronics Inc.
16535 Via Esprillo Bldg 1
San Diego CA 92127
858 942-2400

(P-6557)

SONY ELECTRONICS INC (DH)
16535 Via Esprillo 1, San Diego
(92127-1738)
PHONE..............................858 942-2400
Shigeki Ishizuka, *Pr*
Phil Molyneux, *
Hideki Komiyama, *
Rintaro Miyoshi, *
William A Glaser, *
◆ **EMP:** 1000 **EST:** 1988
SALES (est): 1.41B **Privately Held**
Web: www.sony.com
SIC: 3651 5064 3695 3671 Household audio
and video equipment; Electrical appliances,
television and radio; Video recording tape,
blank; Television tubes
HQ: Sony Corporation Of America
25 Madison Ave Fl 27
New York NY 10010

(P-6558)

SPEAKERCRAFT LLC
12471 Riverside Dr, Mira Loma
(91752-1007)
P.O. Box 9003 (92008)
PHONE..............................951 685-1759
◆ **EMP:** 100
Web: www.speakercraft.com
SIC: 3651 5731 Household audio equipment
; High fidelity stereo equipment

(P-6559)

SYNG INC (PA)
120 Mildred Ave, Venice (90291-4227)
PHONE..............................770 354-0915
Christopher Stringer, *CEO*
Damon Way, *
EMP: 60 **EST:** 2018
SALES (est): 9.51MM
SALES (corp-wide): 9.51MM **Privately
Held**
Web: www.syngspace.com
SIC: 3651 Loudspeakers, electrodynamic or
magnetic

(P-6560)

TECHNICOLOR USA INC
Also Called: Technicolor Connected USA
4049 Industrial Parkway Dr, Lebec
(93243-9719)
PHONE..............................661 496-1309
EMP: 612
Web: www.technicolor.com
SIC: 3651 Household audio and video
equipment
HQ: Technicolor Usa, Inc.
6040 W Sunset Blvd
Hollywood CA 90028
317 587-4287

(P-6561)

TECHNICOLOR USA INC (HQ)
Also Called: Technicolor
6040 W Sunset Blvd, Hollywood
(90028-6402)
P.O. Box 1976 (46206-1976)
PHONE..............................317 587-4287
◆ **EMP:** 800 **EST:** 1987
SALES (est): 576.79MM **Privately Held**
Web: www.technicolor.com
SIC: 3651 3861 3661 Household audio and
video equipment; Cameras, microfilm;
Telephone sets, all types except cellular
radio
PA: Vantiva
10 Boulevard De Grenelle

(P-6562)

TOSHIBA AMER ELCTRNIC
CMPNNTS (DH)
Also Called: Toshiba
5231 California Ave, Irvine (92617-3073)
PHONE..............................949 462-7700
Hideya Yamaguchi, *CEO*
Hitoshi Otsuka, *
Ichiro Hirata, *
Richard Tobias, *
Farhad Mafie, *
◆ **EMP:** 300 **EST:** 1998
SQ FT: 100,000
SALES (est): 66.9MM **Privately Held**
Web: www.toshiba.com
SIC: 3651 3631 3674 3679 Television
receiving sets; Microwave ovens, including
portable: household; Semiconductors and
related devices; Electronic circuits
HQ: Toshiba America Inc
1251 Ave Of Amrcas Ste 41
New York NY 10020
212 596-0600

(P-6563)

TOSHIBA AMERICA INC
5241 California Ave Ste 200, Irvine
(92617-3052)
PHONE..............................212 596-0600
EMP: 1074
Web: www.toshiba.com

SIC: **3651** 3631 5075 3571 Television
receiving sets; Microwave ovens, including
portable: household; Compressors, air
conditioning; Personal computers
(microcomputers)
HQ: Toshiba America Inc
1251 Ave Of Amrcas Ste 41
New York NY 10020
212 596-0600

(P-6564)

ULTIMATE SOUND INC
1200 S Diamond Bar Blvd Ste 200,
Diamond Bar (91765-2298)
PHONE..............................909 861-6200
Robert Chiu, *Pr*
Cindy Chiu, *
◆ **EMP:** 300 **EST:** 1978
SQ FT: 20,000
SALES (est): 5.74MM **Privately Held**
SIC: 3651 5731 Loudspeakers,
electrodynamic or magnetic; Radio,
television, and electronic stores

(P-6565)

VANTAGE POINT PRODUCTS
CORP (PA)
Also Called: Vpt Direct
9234 Hall Rd, Downey (90241-5308)
P.O. Box 2485 (90670-0485)
PHONE..............................562 946-1718
Donald R Burns, *CEO*
Mick Mulcahey, *Pr*
▲ **EMP:** 33 **EST:** 1988
SALES (est): 4.72MM **Privately Held**
Web: www.thinkvp.com
SIC: 3651 Audio electronic systems

(P-6566)

VIZIO INC
2601 S Bdwy Unit B, Los Angeles
(90007-2731)
PHONE..............................213 746-7730
EMP: 122
SALES (corp-wide): 1.68B **Privately Held**
Web: www.vizio.com
SIC: 3651 Television receiving sets
HQ: Vizio, Inc.
39 Tesla
Irvine CA 92618
855 833-3221

(P-6567)

VIZIO INC (HQ)
39 Tesla, Irvine (92618-4603)
PHONE..............................855 833-3221
William Wang, *CEO*
Adam Townsend, *
Jerry Huang, *
◆ **EMP:** 154 **EST:** 2002
SQ FT: 27,300
SALES (est): 90.48MM
SALES (corp-wide): 1.68B **Privately Held**
Web: www.vizio.com
SIC: 3651 Television receiving sets
PA: Vizio Holding Corp.
39 Tesla
949 428-2525

(P-6568)

VIZIO HOLDING CORP (PA)
Also Called: Vizio
39 Tesla, Irvine (92618-4603)
PHONE..............................949 428-2525
William Wang, *Ch Bd*
Ben Wong, *Pr*
Adam Townsend, *CFO*
Michael O'donnell, *CRO*
EMP: 31 **EST:** 2003
SALES (est): 1.68B

SALES (corp-wide): 1.68B **Privately Held**
Web: www.vizio.com
SIC: 3651 Household audio and video
equipment

(P-6569)

VTL AMPLIFIERS INC
4774 Murietta St Ste 10, Chino
(91710-5155)
PHONE..............................909 627-5944
Luke Manley, *Pr*
▲ **EMP:** 24 **EST:** 2000
SQ FT: 6,000
SALES (est): 2.29MM **Privately Held**
Web: www.vtl.com
SIC: 3651 Audio electronic systems

(P-6570)

WIRELESS TECHNOLOGY INC
Also Called: Wti
2064 Eastman Ave Ste 113, Ventura
(93003-7787)
PHONE..............................805 339-9696
Phil Fancher, *CEO*
Arlene Fancher, *
EMP: 30 **EST:** 1987
SQ FT: 7,000
SALES (est): 4.73MM **Privately Held**
Web: www.gotowti.com
SIC: 3651 Household audio and video
equipment

(P-6571)

X HYPER
17600 Newhope St, Fountain Valley
(92708-4220)
P.O. Box 237 (95982-0237)
PHONE..............................530 673-7099
Dennis Eugene Matthews, *Prin*
EMP: 38 **EST:** 2010
SALES (est): 153.7K **Privately Held**
SIC: 3651 Audio electronic systems

3652 Prerecorded Records
And Tapes

(P-6572)

CAPITOL-EMI MUSIC INC
Also Called: E M D
1750b Vine St, Los Angeles (90028-5209)
PHONE..............................323 462-6252
EMP: 1500
SIC: 3652 Compact laser discs, prerecorded

(P-6573)

CPAPERLESS LLC
605 1/2 Orchid Ave, Corona Del Mar
(92625-2461)
P.O. Box 1113 (92625-6113)
PHONE..............................949 510-3365
EMP: 41 **EST:** 2018
SALES (est): 380.87K **Privately Held**
Web: www.safesend.com
SIC: 3652 Prerecorded records and tapes

(P-6574)

DIGITAL FLEX MEDIA INC
Also Called: CD Digital
11150 White Birch Dr, Rancho Cucamonga
(91730-3819)
PHONE..............................909 484-8440
EMP: 90
Web: www.digitalflexmedia.com
SIC: 3652 Compact laser discs, prerecorded

(P-6575)

FEATHERSOFT INC
600 N Mountain Ave Ste C100, Upland
(91786-4359)

▲ = Import ▼ = Export
◆ = Import/Export

PHONE.................925 230-0740
George Varghese, *CEO*
EMP: 29 **EST:** 2018
SALES (est): 286.74K **Privately Held**
Web: www.feathersoft.com
SIC: 3652 Prerecorded records and tapes

(P-6576)
HOLLYWOOD RECORDS INC
Also Called: Andanov Music
500 S Buena Vista St, Burbank
(91521-0002)
PHONE.................818 560-5670
Abbey Konowitch, *Genl Mgr*
EMP: 50 **EST:** 1990
SALES (est): 1.6MM
SALES (corp-wide): 91.36B **Publicly Held**
Web: www.hollywoodrecords.com
SIC: 3652 Prerecorded records and tapes
HQ: Walt Disney Music Company
  500 S Buena Vista St
  Burbank CA 91521
  818 560-1000

(P-6577)
PANASONIC DISC MANUFACTURING CORPORATION OF AMERICA
20000 Mariner Ave Ste 200, Torrance
(90503-1670)
PHONE.................310 783-4800
▲ **EMP:** 200
Web: pdmc.panasonic.com
SIC: 3652 Compact laser discs, prerecorded

(P-6578)
PRECISE MEDIA SERVICES INC
Also Called: Precise-Full Service Media
888 Vintage Ave, Ontario (91764-5392)
PHONE.................909 481-3305
Choy Tim Lee, *CEO*
Robert Miller, *
▲ **EMP:** 25 **EST:** 1991
SQ FT: 112,000
SALES (est): 2.15MM **Privately Held**
Web: www.precisemedia.com
SIC: 3652 7819 Prerecorded records and
tapes; Video tape or disk reproduction

(P-6579)
RAINBO RECORD MFG CORP (PA)
Also Called: Rainbo Records & Cassettes
8960 Eton Ave, Canoga Park (91304-1621)
P.O. Box 280700 (91328-0700)
PHONE.................818 280-1100
Jack Brown, *Prin*
Steve Sheldon, *Prin*
▲ **EMP:** 50 **EST:** 1939
SQ FT: 50,000
SALES (est): 5.05MM
SALES (corp-wide): 5.05MM **Privately Held**
Web: www.urpressing.com
SIC: 3652 5099 Compact laser discs,
prerecorded; Compact discs

(P-6580)
RECORD TECHNOLOGY INC (PA)
486 Dawson Dr Ste 4s, Camarillo
(93012-8049)
PHONE.................805 484-2747
Don Mac Innis, *Pr*
Melodie Mac Innis, *
▲ **EMP:** 24 **EST:** 1972
SQ FT: 30,000
SALES (est): 2.47MM
SALES (corp-wide): 2.47MM **Privately Held**

Web: www.recordtech.com
SIC: 3652 Master records or tapes,
preparation of

3661 Telephone And Telegraph Apparatus

(P-6581)
BALAJI TRADING INC
Also Called: City of Industry
4850 Eucalyptus Ave, Chino (91710-9255)
PHONE.................909 444-7999
Mukesh Batta, *CEO*
▲ **EMP:** 91 **EST:** 2010
SALES (est): 2.51MM **Privately Held**
Web: www.balajiwireless.com
SIC: 3661 Headsets, telephone

(P-6582)
CALIENT TECHNOLOGIES INC (PA)
Also Called: Calient Technologies
120 Cremona Dr Ste 160, Goleta
(93117-3168)
PHONE.................805 695-4800
Arjun Gutpa, *Ofcr*
Kevin Welsh, *
Jitender Miglani, *
Daniel Tardent, *
Jag Setlur, *
▲ **EMP:** 30 **EST:** 1999
SQ FT: 150,000
SALES (est): 21.37MM
SALES (corp-wide): 21.37MM **Privately Held**
Web: www.calient.net
SIC: 3661 Fiber optics communications
equipment

(P-6583)
COASTAL CONNECTIONS
2085 Sperry Ave Ste B, Ventura
(93003-7452)
PHONE.................805 644-5051
Andrew Devine, *Pr*
Nancy Devine, *
◆ **EMP:** 37 **EST:** 2002
SQ FT: 9,000
SALES (est): 2.66MM **Privately Held**
Web: www.coastalcon.com
SIC: 3661 Fiber optics communications
equipment

(P-6584)
EPIC TECHNOLOGIES LLC (HQ)
Also Called: Natel Engineering
9340 Owensmouth Ave, Chatsworth
(91311-6915)
PHONE.................908 707-4085
Sudesh Arora, *Ch*
John J Sammut, *
Robert T Howard, *
Jochen Lipp, *
Marcus Wedner, *
▲ **EMP:** 1750 **EST:** 2004
SQ FT: 52,000
SALES (est): 361.03MM
SALES (corp-wide): 1.43B **Privately Held**
Web: www.neotech.com
SIC: 3661 3577 3679 Telephone and
telegraph apparatus; Computer peripheral
equipment, nec; Electronic circuits
PA: Natel Engineering Company, Llc
  9340 Owensmouth Ave
  818 495-8617

(P-6585)
FRANKLIN WIRELESS CORP
Also Called: FRANKLIN WIRELESS
3940 Ruffin Rd Ste C, San Diego
(92123-1844)
PHONE.................858 623-0000
Ok Chae Kim, *Pr*
Gary Nelson, *
Yun J David Lee, *VP Sls*
Bill Bauer, *Interim Chief Financial Officer*
▲ **EMP:** 69 **EST:** 1981
SALES (est): 30.8MM **Privately Held**
Web: www.franklinwireless.com
SIC: 3661 Fiber optics communications
equipment

(P-6586)
GENERAL PHOTONICS CORP
Also Called: General Photonics
14351 Pipeline Ave, Chino (91710-5642)
PHONE.................909 590-5473
Steve Yao, *Pr*
Bruce Pazouki, *VP*
Helen Ren, *Contrlr*
Shasha Luo, *Acctnt*
▲ **EMP:** 51 **EST:** 1995
SQ FT: 20,000
SALES (est): 8.25MM **Publicly Held**
Web: www.lunainc.com
SIC: 3661 Fiber optics communications
equipment
HQ: Luna Technologies, Inc.
  301 1st St Sw Ste 200
  Roanoke VA 24011
  540 769-8400

(P-6587)
INTERNTNAL CNNCTORS CABLE CORP
Also Called: I C C
1270 N Hancock St, Anaheim (92807-1922)
PHONE.................888 275-4422
Mike Lin, *Pr*
Mike Lin, *Pr*
Eugene Chyun Tsai, *Stockholder*
▲ **EMP:** 110 **EST:** 1984
SQ FT: 38,720
SALES (est): 9.22MM **Privately Held**
Web: www.icc.com
SIC: 3661 5065 Telephone and telegraph
apparatus; Telephone and telegraphic
equipment

(P-6588)
LG-ERICSSON USA INC
20 Mason, Irvine (92618-2706)
PHONE.................877 828-2673
◆ **EMP:** 47
Web: www.lgericssonus.com
SIC: 3661 5065 Telephone sets, all types
except cellular radio; Modems, computer

(P-6589)
NOKIA OF AMERICA CORPORATION
Also Called: Alcatel-Lucent
2000 Corporate Center Dr, Newbury Park
(91320-1400)
PHONE.................818 880-3500
Menandro Canelo, *Ofcr*
EMP: 34
SALES (corp-wide): 24.19B **Privately Held**
Web: www.nokia.com
SIC: 3661 Telephone and telegraph
apparatus
HQ: Nokia Of America Corporation
  600 Mountain Ave Ste 700
  Murray Hill NJ 07974

(P-6590)
RLH INDUSTRIES INC
936 N Main St, Orange (92867-5403)
PHONE.................714 532-1672
James B Harris, *CEO*
Carol E Harris, *
Tristan Harris, *
▲ **EMP:** 40 **EST:** 1988
SQ FT: 16,000
SALES (est): 11.37MM **Privately Held**
Web: www.fiberopticlink.com
SIC: 3661 5065 5999 Telephone and
telegraph apparatus; Communication
equipment; Telephone equipment and
systems

(P-6591)
SONIM TECHNOLOGIES INC (PA)
4445 Eastgate Mall Ste 200, San Diego
(92121-1979)
PHONE.................650 378-8100
Peter Hao Liu, *CEO*
Michael Mulica, *Ch Bd*
Clay Crolius, *CFO*
Charles Becher, *CCO*
▲ **EMP:** 36 **EST:** 1999
SALES (est): 93.63MM
SALES (corp-wide): 93.63MM **Publicly Held**
Web: www.sonimtech.com
SIC: 3661 4812 Telephones and telephone
apparatus; Cellular telephone services

3663 Radio And T.v. Communications Equipment

(P-6592)
ADAPTIVE DIGITAL SYSTEMS INC
20322 Sw Acacia St Ste 200, Newport
Beach (92660-1504)
PHONE.................949 955-3116
Attila W Mathe, *Pr*
Ralph Boehringer, *
Susan Cameron, *
▲ **EMP:** 27 **EST:** 1979
SQ FT: 6,500
SALES (est): 4.02MM **Privately Held**
Web: www.adaptivedigitalsystems.com
SIC: 3663 Marine radio communications
equipment

(P-6593)
AETHERCOMM INC
3205 Lionshead Ave, Carlsbad
(92010-4710)
PHONE.................760 208-6002
William Todd Thornton, *CEO*
Todd Thornton, *
Terri Thornton, *
Richard Martinez, *
Mark Bahu, *
EMP: 125 **EST:** 1999
SQ FT: 46,000
SALES (est): 23.11MM **Privately Held**
Web: www.aethercomm.com
SIC: 3663 Radio and t.v. communications
equipment
HQ: Frontgrade Technologies Llc
  4350 Centennial Blvd
  Colorado Springs CO 80907

(P-6594)
ALE USA INC
Also Called: Alcatel-Lucent Enterprise USA
2000 Corporate Center Dr, Thousand Oaks
(91320-1400)

PHONE..................818 880-3500
Stephan Robineau, *Pr*
Louise Kuphal, *
EMP: 550 **EST:** 2014
SQ FT: 50,000
SALES (est): 61.7MM **Privately Held**
Web: www.al-enterprise.com
SIC: 3663 3613 Mobile communication
equipment; Switchgear and switchboard
apparatus
HQ: China Huaxin Post And
Telecommunications Technology
Co.,Ltd.
Room 1219, Building 4, No. 389
Ningqiao Road, China (Shanghai) P
Shanghai SH 20120
105 852-9297

(P-6595)
ALTINEX INC
Also Called: Air Gap International
500 S Jefferson St, Placentia (92870-6617)
PHONE..................714 990-0877
Jack Gershfeld, *Pr*
▲ **EMP:** 50 **EST:** 1993
SALES (est): 9.82MM **Privately Held**
Web: www.altinex.com
SIC: 3663 3577 3651 5099 Radio and t.v.
communications equipment; Computer
peripheral equipment, nec; Household
audio and video equipment; Video and
audio equipment

(P-6596)
AMPLIFIER TECHNOLOGIES INC (HQ)
901 S Greenwood Ave, Montebello
(90640-5835)
PHONE..................323 278-0001
Morris Kessler, *Pr*
▲ **EMP:** 25 **EST:** 1981
SALES (est): 6.18MM
SALES (corp-wide): 6.18MM **Privately Held**
Web: www.ati-amp.com
SIC: 3663 Television broadcasting and
communications equipment
PA: Macey Investment Corp.
1749 Chapin.Rd
323 278-0001

(P-6597)
ANTCOM CORPORATION
Also Called: Antcom
367 Van Ness Way Ste 602, Torrance
(90501-6246)
PHONE..................310 782-1076
Michael Ritter, *CEO*
Sean Huynh, *VP*
Doug Reid, *Genl Mgr*
Linda Cupchak, *Contrlr*
EMP: 45 **EST:** 1997
SQ FT: 15,000
SALES (est): 9.68MM
SALES (corp-wide): 2.5MM **Privately Held**
Web: www.antcom.com
SIC: 3663 Antennas, transmitting and
communications
HQ: Novatel Inc
10921 14 St Ne
Calgary AB T3K 2
403 295-4500

(P-6598)
ANYDATA CORPORATION
5405 Alton Pkwy, Irvine (92604-3717)
PHONE..................949 900-6040
EMP: 100
SIC: 3663 Mobile communication equipment

(P-6599)
ATX NETWORKS (SAN DIEGO) CORP (DH)
Also Called: Atx Networks San Diego
2800 Whiptail Loop Ste 6, Carlsbad
(92010-6752)
PHONE..................858 546-5050
Dan Whalen, *Pr*
Ian A Lerner, *Chief Product Officer*
Carlos Shteremberg, *
Anthony Tibbs, *
Andrew Isherwood, *
◆ **EMP:** 27 **EST:** 1983
SALES (est): 24.76MM
SALES (corp-wide): 66.29MM **Privately Held**
Web: www.atx.com
SIC: 3663 5065 3678 Radio and t.v.
communications equipment; Electronic
parts and equipment, nec; Electronic
connectors
HQ: Atx Networks Corp
8-1602 Tricont Ave
Whitby ON L1N 7
905 428-6068

(P-6600)
BITTREE INCORPORATED
600 W Elk Ave, Glendale (91204-1404)
P.O. Box 3764 (91221-0764)
PHONE..................818 500-8142
▲ **EMP:** 29 **EST:** 1977
SALES (est): 2.26MM **Privately Held**
Web: www.bittree.com
SIC: 3663 Radio and t.v. communications
equipment

(P-6601)
BOEING SATELLITE SYSTEMS INC (HQ)
Also Called: Boeing
900 N Pacific Coast Hwy, El Segundo
(90245-2710)
P.O. Box 92919 (90009-2919)
PHONE..................310 791-7450
Craig R Cooning, *Pr*
Dave Ryan, *General Vice President*
Charles Toups, *Operations*
◆ **EMP:** 25 **EST:** 1995
SALES (est): 1.23B
SALES (corp-wide): 77.79B **Publicly Held**
Web: www.boeing.com
SIC: 3663 Satellites, communications
PA: The Boeing Company
929 Long Bridge Dr
703 465-3500

(P-6602)
BROADCAST MICROWAVE SVCS LLC (PA)
Also Called: B M S
13475 Danielson St Ste 130, Poway
(92064-8858)
PHONE..................858 391-3050
Harry Davoody, *CEO*
Mike Sieglen, *
Kristina Clark, *
EMP: 109 **EST:** 1982
SQ FT: 37,000
SALES (est): 23.63MM
SALES (corp-wide): 23.63MM **Privately Held**
Web: www.bms-inc.com
SIC: 3663 Microwave communication
equipment

(P-6603)
CENTRON INDUSTRIES INC
441 W Victoria St, Gardena (90248-3528)

PHONE..................310 324-6443
Yong W Kim, *CEO*
Hye S Kim, *Sec*
◆ **EMP:** 37 **EST:** 1984
SQ FT: 10,000
SALES (est): 9.93MM **Privately Held**
Web: www.centronind.com
SIC: 3663 Radio and t.v. communications
equipment

(P-6604)
CPI MALIBU DIVISION
3623 Old Conejo Rd Ste 205, Newbury Park
(91320-0803)
PHONE..................805 383-1829
Joel Littman, *CFO*
EMP: 80 **EST:** 1975
SALES (est): 3.94MM **Privately Held**
SIC: 3663 Antennas, transmitting and
communications
HQ: Communications & Power Industries
Llc
811 Hansen Way
Palo Alto CA 94304

(P-6605)
CPI SATCOM & ANTENNA TECH INC
3111 Fujita St, Torrance (90505-4006)
PHONE..................310 539-6704
Sandra Seto, *Brnch Mgr*
EMP: 270
Web: www.cpii.com
SIC: 3663 Antennas, transmitting and
communications
HQ: Cpi Satcom & Antenna Technologies
Inc.
1700 Cable Dr Ne
Conover NC 28613
704 462-7330

(P-6606)
D X COMMUNICATIONS INC
Also Called: Tpl Communications
8160 Van Nuys Blvd, Panorama City
(91402-4806)
PHONE..................323 256-3000
Richard H Myers, *CEO*
Richard Myers, *
John Ehret, *
EMP: 28 **EST:** 1971
SALES (est): 2.2MM **Privately Held**
Web: www.tplcom.com
SIC: 3663 Satellites, communications

(P-6607)
DENSO WIRELESS SYSTEMS AMERICA INC
2251 Rutherford Rd # 100, Carlsbad
(92008-8815)
PHONE..................760 734-4600
◆ **EMP:** 191
SIC: 3663 3714 Cellular radio telephone;
Motor vehicle electrical equipment

(P-6608)
DJH ENTERPRISES
Also Called: Channel Vision Technology
23011 Moulton Pkwy Ste B6, Laguna Hills
(92653-1222)
PHONE..................714 424-6500
Darrel Eugene Hauk, *Pr*
◆ **EMP:** 35 **EST:** 1993
SALES (est): 6.15MM **Privately Held**
SIC: 3663 Radio and t.v. communications
equipment

(P-6609)
DYNAMIC SCIENCES INTL INC
9400 Lurline Ave Unit B, Chatsworth
(91311-6022)
PHONE..................818 226-6262
Eli Shiri, *Pr*
Robert Cook, *
Oren Shiri, *
EMP: 35 **EST:** 1972
SQ FT: 20,000
SALES (est): 1.32MM **Privately Held**
SIC: 3663 Radio receiver networks

(P-6610)
E-BAND COMMUNICATIONS LLC
82 Coromar Dr, Goleta (93117-3024)
PHONE..................858 408-0660
Jamal Hamdani, *CEO*
Saul Umbrasas, *
Russ Kinsch, *
EMP: 30 **EST:** 2003
SALES (est): 2.32MM
SALES (corp-wide): 27.29MM **Privately Held**
Web: www.e-band.com
SIC: 3663 Carrier equipment, radio
communications
PA: Axxcss Wireless Solutions Inc
82 Coromar Dr
805 968-9621

(P-6611)
ECTRON CORPORATION
9340 Hazard Way Ste B2, San Diego
(92123-1228)
PHONE..................858 278-0600
E Earl Cunningham, *Pr*
Carol C Cunningham, *
Karl E Cunningham, *
EMP: 44 **EST:** 1964
SALES (est): 4.74MM **Privately Held**
Web: www.ectron.com
SIC: 3663 3829 3577 3823 Amplifiers, RF
power and IF; Measuring and controlling
devices, nec; Data conversion equipment,
media-to-media: computer; Process control
instruments

(P-6612)
EEG 3 LLC (DH)
Also Called: Maritime Telecom Netwrk Inc
6080 Center Dr Ste 1200, Los Angeles
(90045-9209)
◆ **EMP:** 200 **EST:** 1990
SALES (est): 30.13MM
SALES (corp-wide): 656.88MM **Privately Held**
SIC: 3663 Satellites, communications
HQ: Emerging Markets Communications,
Llc
1561 E Orangethorpe Ave
Fullerton CA 92831

(P-6613)
EMPOWER RF SYSTEMS INC (PA)
Also Called: Empower Rf
316 W Florence Ave, Inglewood
(90301-1104)
PHONE..................310 412-8100
Barry Phelps, *Ch Bd*
Jon Jacocks, *
Larisa Stanisic, *
EMP: 76 **EST:** 1999
SQ FT: 30,000
SALES (est): 16.8MM
SALES (corp-wide): 16.8MM **Privately Held**
Web: www.empowerrf.com

▲ = Import ▼ = Export
◆ = Import/Export

SIC: 3663 Amplifiers, RF power and IF

(P-6614)
ENSEMBLE COMMUNICATIONS INC
2223 Avenida De La Playa, La Jolla
(92037-3200)
PHONE..............................858 458-1400
Rami Hadar, *Pr*
Sheldon Gilbert, *
EMP: 140 EST: 1997
SQ FT: 63,000
SALES (est): 1.72MM **Privately Held**
SIC: 3663 Radio and t.v. communications
equipment

(P-6615)
FEI-ZYFER INC (HQ)
7321 Lincoln Way, Garden Grove
(92841-1428)
PHONE..............................714 933-4000
Steve Strang, *Pr*
EMP: 32 EST: 1997
SQ FT: 50,000
SALES (est): 11.82MM
SALES (corp-wide): 55.27MM **Publicly Held**
Web: www.fei-zyfer.com
SIC: 3663 Television broadcasting and
communications equipment
PA: Frequency Electronics, Inc.
55 Charles Lindbergh Blvd
516 794-4500

(P-6616)
FLEET MANAGEMENT SOLUTIONS INC
310 Commerce Ste 100, Irvine
(92602-1360)
PHONE..............................800 500-6009
Tony Eales, *CEO*
EMP: 26 EST: 2002
SALES (est): 904.87K
SALES (corp-wide): 3.1B **Publicly Held**
Web:
www.fleetmanagementsolutions.com
SIC: 3663 4899 Radio and t.v.
communications equipment; Satellite earth
stations
HQ: Teletrac Navman (Uk) Ltd
First Floor
Milton Keynes BUCKS MK7 6

(P-6617)
GLOBAL MICROWAVE SYSTEMS INC
Also Called: G M S
1916 Palomar Oaks Way Ste 100, Carlsbad
(92008-5509)
PHONE..............................760 496-0046
EMP: 47
SIC: 3663 7359 Microwave communication
equipment; Business machine and
electronic equipment rental services

(P-6618)
HADRIAN AUTOMATION INC
Also Called: Hadrian
19501 S Western Ave, Torrance (90502)
PHONE..............................503 807-4490
Christopher Power, *CEO*
Lars Lider, *
Sarah Annin, *
Dave Malcher, *Head OF Finance*
EMP: 100 EST: 2018
SALES (est): 10.73MM **Privately Held**
Web: www.hadrian.co
SIC: 3663 Space satellite communications
equipment

(P-6619)
HILLSIDE CAPITAL INC
6222 Fallbrook Ave, Woodland Hills
(91367-1601)
PHONE..............................650 367-2011
Becky Tran, *Pr*
EMP: 115 EST: 2008
SALES (est): 753.64K **Privately Held**
SIC: 3663 Radio and t.v. communications
equipment

(P-6620)
INTERDIGITAL INC
Also Called: INTERDIGITAL, INC.
9276 Scranton Rd Ste 300, San Diego
(92121-7700)
PHONE..............................858 210-4800
Julie Mcdonough, *Brnch Mgr*
EMP: 64
SALES (corp-wide): 549.59MM **Publicly Held**
Web: www.interdigital.com
SIC: 3663 Mobile communication equipment
HQ: Interdigital Wireless, Inc.
200 Bellevue Pkwy Ste 300
Wilmington DE 19809

(P-6621)
KATZ MILLENNIUM SLS & MKTG INC
Also Called: Clear Channel Radio Sales
5700 Wilshire Blvd Ste 100, Los Angeles
(90036-3889)
PHONE..............................323 966-5066
Nathan Brown, *Mgr*
EMP: 227
Web: www.raisingthevolume.com
SIC: 3663 Radio receiver networks
HQ: Katz Millennium Sales & Marketing Inc.
125 W 55th St Frnt 3
New York NY 10019

(P-6622)
L3 TECHNOLOGIES INC
15825 Roxford St, Sylmar (91342-3537)
PHONE..............................818 367-0111
EMP: 91
SALES (corp-wide): 19.42B **Publicly Held**
Web: www.l3harris.com
SIC: 3663 Radio and t.v. communications
equipment
HQ: L3 Technologies, Inc.
600 3rd Ave Fl 34
New York NY 10016
321 727-9100

(P-6623)
L3 TECHNOLOGIES INC
Also Called: L-3 Telemetry & Rf Products
9020 Balboa Ave, San Diego (92123-1510)
PHONE..............................858 279-0411
Burt Smith, *Brnch Mgr*
EMP: 358
SALES (corp-wide): 19.42B **Publicly Held**
Web: www.l3harris.com
SIC: 3663 3669 3812 3679 Telemetering
equipment, electronic; Signaling apparatus,
electric; Search and navigation equipment;
Microwave components
HQ: L3 Technologies, Inc.
600 3rd Ave Fl 34
New York NY 10016
321 727-9100

(P-6624)
L3 TECHNOLOGIES INC
L3 Rccs
10180 Barnes Canyon Rd, San Diego
(92121-2724)
PHONE..............................858 552-9716

Jonathan Roy, *CFO*
EMP: 100
SALES (corp-wide): 19.42B **Publicly Held**
Web: www.l3harris.com
SIC: 3663 Telemetering equipment,
electronic
HQ: L3 Technologies, Inc.
600 3rd Ave Fl 34
New York NY 10016
321 727-9100

(P-6625)
L3 TECHNOLOGIES INC
Also Called: Communction Systms-Wst/
Lnkabit
9020 Balboa Ave, San Diego (92123-1510)
PHONE..............................858 552-9500
Andrew Ivers, *Brnch Mgr*
EMP: 325
SALES (corp-wide): 19.42B **Publicly Held**
Web: www.l3harris.com
SIC: 3663 Space satellite communications
equipment
HQ: L3 Technologies, Inc.
600 3rd Ave Fl 34
New York NY 10016
321 727-9100

(P-6626)
L3 TECHNOLOGIES INC
Also Called: Maripro
7414 Hollister Ave, Goleta (93117-2583)
PHONE..............................805 683-3881
EMP: 90
SALES (corp-wide): 19.42B **Publicly Held**
Web: www.l3harris.com
SIC: 3663 Telemetering equipment,
electronic
HQ: L3 Technologies, Inc.
600 3rd Ave Fl 34
New York NY 10016
321 727-9100

(P-6627)
L3 TECHNOLOGIES INC
602 E Vermont Ave, Anaheim (92805-5607)
PHONE..............................714 758-4222
Robert Vanwechel, *Brnch Mgr*
EMP: 220
SALES (corp-wide): 19.42B **Publicly Held**
Web: www.l3harris.com
SIC: 3663 Telemetering equipment,
electronic
HQ: L3 Technologies, Inc.
600 3rd Ave Fl 34
New York NY 10016
321 727-9100

(P-6628)
L3HARRIS INTERSTATE ELEC CORP
604 E Vermont Ave, Anaheim (92805-5607)
PHONE..............................714 758-3395
Thomas Jackson, *Brnch Mgr*
EMP: 70
SALES (corp-wide): 19.42B **Publicly Held**
Web: www.l3harris.com
SIC: 3663 3621 Telemetering equipment,
electronic; Motors and generators
HQ: L3harris Interstate Electronics
Corporation
602 E Vermont Ave
Anaheim CA 92805
714 758-0500

(P-6629)
LENNTEK CORPORATION
Also Called: Sonix
1610 Lockness Pl, Torrance (90501-5119)
PHONE..............................310 534-2738

Danny Tsai, *Prin*
▲ EMP: 50 EST: 2007
SQ FT: 15,000
SALES (est): 3.11MM **Privately Held**
Web: www.shopsonix.com
SIC: 3663 Mobile communication equipment

(P-6630)
MAINLINE EQUIPMENT INC
Also Called: Mainline
20917 Higgins Ct, Torrance (90501-1723)
PHONE..............................800 444-2288
EMP: 52 EST: 1986
SALES (est): 2.13MM **Privately Held**
Web: www.main-line-inc.com
SIC: 3663 7629 Satellites, communications;
Electrical equipment repair services

(P-6631)
MANLEY LABORATORIES INC
Also Called: Manufacturing
13880 Magnolia Ave, Chino (91710-7027)
PHONE..............................909 627-4256
Eveanna Manley, *Pr*
Eveanna Manley-collins, *Pr*
▲ EMP: 32 EST: 1992
SQ FT: 11,000
SALES (est): 3.97MM **Privately Held**
Web: www.manley.com
SIC: 3663 3651 Radio and t.v.
communications equipment; Audio
electronic systems

(P-6632)
MICRO-MODE PRODUCTS INC
1870 John Towers Ave, El Cajon
(92020-1193)
PHONE..............................619 449-3844
Vincent De Marco, *Pr*
Michael Cuban, *
Ruby Marco, *
EMP: 170 EST: 1971
SALES (est): 22.77MM
SALES (corp-wide): 3.28B **Publicly Held**
Web: www.micromode.com
SIC: 3663 3678 7389 Microwave
communication equipment; Electronic
connectors; Business Activities at Non-
Commercial Site
PA: Itt Inc.
100 Washington Blvd Fl 6
914 641-2000

(P-6633)
MILLENNIUM SPACE SYSTEMS INC (HQ)
2265 E El Segundo Blvd, El Segundo
(90245-4608)
PHONE..............................310 683-5840
Tony Gingiss, *CEO*
Tiffany Cuthric, *
Laura White, *
EMP: 32 EST: 2001
SQ FT: 10,000
SALES (est): 102.37MM
SALES (corp-wide): 77.79B **Publicly Held**
Web: www.millennium-space.com
SIC: 3663 Space satellite communications
equipment
PA: The Boeing Company
929 Long Bridge Dr
703 465-3500

(P-6634)
MISSION MICROWAVE TECH LLC (PA)
6060 Phyllis Dr, Cypress (90630-5243)
PHONE..............................951 893-4925
Francis Auricchio, *CEO*
Michael Delisio, *

PRODUCTS & SVCS

John Ocampo, *
EMP: 70 **EST:** 2014
SALES (est): 10.1MM
SALES (corp-wide): 10.1MM **Privately Held**
Web: www.missionmicrowave.com
SIC: 3663 Satellites, communications

(P-6635)
MOPHIE INC (DH)
15495 Sand Canyon Ave Ste 400, Irvine
(92618-3153)
PHONE.........................888 866-7443
Daniel Huang, *CEO*
▲ **EMP:** 75 **EST:** 2005
SALES (est): 10.05MM
SALES (corp-wide): 92.69MM **Privately Held**
Web: www.zagg.com
SIC: 3663 Mobile communication equipment
HQ: Zagg Inc
　　910 W Lgacy Ctr Way Ste 5
　　Midvale UT 84047

(P-6636)
MOSELEY ASSOCIATES INC (HQ)
Also Called: Moseley
82 Coromar Dr, Goleta (93117-3024)
PHONE.........................805 968-9621
Jamal N Hamdani, *Pr*
Bruce Tarr, *
▲ **EMP:** 92 **EST:** 1961
SQ FT: 56,000
SALES (est): 11.82MM
SALES (corp-wide): 27.29MM **Privately Held**
Web: www.moseleysb.com
SIC: 3663 Radio and t.v. communications equipment
PA: Axxcss Wireless Solutions Inc
　　82 Coromar Dr
　　805 968-9621

(P-6637)
MOTOROLA SLTONS CNNCTIVITY INC (HQ)
42555 Rio Nedo, Temecula (92590-3726)
P.O. Box 9007 (92589)
PHONE.........................951 719-2100
Gino Bonanotte, *CEO*
John Jack Molloy, *Pr*
Andrew Sinclair, *
Uygar Gazioglu, *
Daniel Pekofske, *Care Vice President*
▲ **EMP:** 99 **EST:** 1967
SQ FT: 100,000
SALES (est): 56.28MM
SALES (corp-wide): 9.98B **Publicly Held**
Web: www.motorolasolutions.com
SIC: 3663 Radio and t.v. communications equipment
PA: Motorola Solutions, Inc.
　　500 W Monroe St Ste 4400
　　847 576-5000

(P-6638)
MTI LABORATORY INC
Also Called: Mtil
201 Continental Blvd Ste 300, El Segundo
(90245-4500)
PHONE.........................310 955-3700
Davis Kent, *Pr*
Alister Hsu, *CFO*
▼ **EMP:** 26 **EST:** 2006
SQ FT: 12,000
SALES (est): 6.7MM **Privately Held**
Web: www.mtigroup.com
SIC: 3663 Microwave communication equipment

PA: Microelectronics Technology, Inc.
　　No. 1, Chuangxin 2nd Rd., Science-
　　Based Industrial Park,

(P-6639)
NAVCOM TECHNOLOGY INC (HQ)
20780 Madrona Ave, Torrance
(90503-3777)
PHONE.........................310 381-2000
Tony Thelen, *CEO*
Craig Fawcept, *
Michael Linzy, *
EMP: 100 **EST:** 1997
SQ FT: 55,000
SALES (est): 10.87MM
SALES (corp-wide): 51.72B **Publicly Held**
Web: www.navcomtech.com
SIC: 3663 8748 Satellites, communications; Communications consulting
PA: Deere & Company
　　1 John Deere Pl
　　309 765-8000

(P-6640)
NERDIST CHANNEL LLC
Also Called: Nerdist Industries
2900 W Alameda Ave Unit 1500, Burbank
(91505-4271)
PHONE.........................818 333-2705
EMP: 30 **EST:** 2011
SALES (est): 3.96MM **Privately Held**
Web: www.nerdist.com
SIC: 3663 Digital encoders

(P-6641)
NEXTIVITY INC (PA)
16550 W Bernardo Dr Ste 550, San Diego
(92127-1889)
PHONE.........................858 485-9442
Werner Sievers, *CEO*
Michiel Lotter, *
Carol Lee, *
George Lamb, *
Thomas Cooper, *Business Development*
▲ **EMP:** 49 **EST:** 2006
SALES (est): 34.83MM **Privately Held**
Web: www.nextivityinc.com
SIC: 3663 Airborne radio communications equipment

(P-6642)
NORTHROP GRUMMAN SYSTEMS CORP
Space Systems Division
　1 Space Park Blvd, Redondo Beach
　(90278-1071)
PHONE.........................310 812-5149
EMP: 101
Web: www.northropgrumman.com
SIC: 3663 3674 3679 3761 Airborne radio communications equipment; Semiconductors and related devices; Antennas, satellite: household use; Guided missiles and space vehicles
HQ: Northrop Grumman Systems
　　Corporation
　　2980 Fairview Park Dr
　　Falls Church VA 22042
　　703 280-2900

(P-6643)
OPHIR RF INC
Also Called: Ophir Rf
5300 Beethoven St Fl 3, Los Angeles
(90066-7068)
PHONE.........................310 306-5556
Ilan Israely, *Pr*
Albert Barrios, *
EMP: 42 **EST:** 1992

SQ FT: 11,800
SALES (est): 9.04MM **Privately Held**
Web: www.ophirrf.com
SIC: 3663 Amplifiers, RF power and IF

(P-6644)
PACIFIC WAVE SYSTEMS INC
2525 W 190th St, Torrance (90504-6002)
PHONE.........................714 893-0152
Carl Esposito, *CEO*
John J Tus, *
Victor Jay Miller, *
Robert B Topolski, *
EMP: 68 **EST:** 1992
SALES (est): 3.39MM **Privately Held**
Web: www.pacificwavesystems.com
SIC: 3663 Satellites, communications

(P-6645)
PHONESUIT INC
1431 7th St Ste 201, Santa Monica
(90401-2638)
PHONE.........................310 774-0282
Sumeet Gupta, *CEO*
EMP: 25 **EST:** 2012
SQ FT: 4,000
SALES (est): 2.42MM **Privately Held**
Web: www.phonesuit.com
SIC: 3663 Mobile communication equipment

(P-6646)
PREMIER WIRELESS INC
4010 Watson Plaza Dr Ste 245, Lakewood
(90712-4044)
P.O. Box 1876 (91077-1876)
PHONE.........................925 776-1070
Mike Long, *Pr*
Rowland Lee, *
EMP: 29 **EST:** 1994
SQ FT: 5,000
SALES (est): 2.53MM **Privately Held**
SIC: 3663 4812 Radio and t.v. communications equipment; Cellular telephone services

(P-6647)
QUALCOMM INCORPORATED (PA)
Also Called: Qualcomm
5775 Morehouse Dr, San Diego
(92121-1714)
PHONE.........................858 587-1121
Cristiano R Amon, *Pr*
Mark D Mclaughlin, *Ch Bd*
Akash Palkhiwala, *CFO*
James J Cathey, *CCO*
EMP: 1430 **EST:** 1985
SALES (est): 38.96B
SALES (corp-wide): 38.96B **Publicly Held**
Web: www.qualcomm.com
SIC: 3663 3674 7372 6794 Mobile communication equipment; Semiconductors and related devices; Business oriented computer software; Patent buying, licensing, leasing

(P-6648)
QUALCOMM INCORPORATED
Also Called: Qualcomm
4243 Campus Point Ct, San Diego
(92121-1513)
PHONE.........................858 587-1121
EMP: 279
SALES (corp-wide): 38.96B **Publicly Held**
Web: www.qualcomm.com
SIC: 3663 Radio and t.v. communications equipment
PA: Qualcomm Incorporated
　　5775 Morehouse Dr
　　858 587-1121

(P-6649)
QUALCOMM INCORPORATED
Also Called: Qualcomm
5775 Morehouse Dr, San Diego
(92121-1714)
P.O. Box 10300 (92121)
PHONE.........................202 263-0008
EMP: 25
SALES (corp-wide): 38.96B **Publicly Held**
Web: www.qualcomm.com
SIC: 3663 Radio and t.v. communications equipment
PA: Qualcomm Incorporated
　　5775 Morehouse Dr
　　858 587-1121

(P-6650)
RANTEC MICROWAVE SYSTEMS INC
Microwave Specialty Company
2066 Wineridge Pl, Escondido
(92029-1930)
PHONE.........................760 744-1544
Ben Walpole, *Pr*
EMP: 27
SALES (corp-wide): 12.58MM **Privately Held**
Web: www.rantecantennas.com
SIC: 3663 Radio and t.v. communications equipment
PA: Rantec Microwave Systems, Inc.
　　31186 La Baya Dr
　　818 223-5000

(P-6651)
RAVEON TECHNOLOGIES CORP
2320 Cousteau Ct, Vista (92081-8363)
PHONE.........................760 444-5995
John Richard Sonnenberg, *Pr*
EMP: 37 **EST:** 2003
SQ FT: 7,300
SALES (est): 5.14MM **Privately Held**
Web: www.raveon.com
SIC: 3663 Airborne radio communications equipment

(P-6652)
RAYTHEON APPLIED SGNAL TECH IN
2000 E El Segundo Blvd, El Segundo
(90245-4501)
PHONE.........................310 436-7000
John R Treichler, *CEO*
EMP: 107
SALES (corp-wide): 68.92B **Publicly Held**
Web: www.appsig.com
SIC: 3663 8711 Radio and t.v. communications equipment; Engineering services
HQ: Raytheon Applied Signal Technology, Inc.
　　100 Headquarters Dr
　　San Jose CA 95134
　　408 749-1888

(P-6653)
REMEC BRDBAND WRLESS NTWRKS LL
82 Coromar Dr, Goleta (93117-3024)
PHONE.........................858 312-6900
Jamal Hamdani, *CEO*
Bruce Tarr, *
EMP: 180 **EST:** 2015
SALES (est): 2.29MM
SALES (corp-wide): 27.29MM **Privately Held**
Web: www.sagesat.com
SIC: 3663 Mobile communication equipment
PA: Axxcss Wireless Solutions Inc
　　82 Coromar Dr

▲ = Import ▼ = Export
◆ = Import/Export

805 968-9621

623 300-7000

(P-6654)
REMEC BROADBAND WIRELESS LLC
82 Coromar Dr, Goleta (93117-3024)
PHONE..........................858 312-6900
David K Newman, *Managing Member*
EMP: 102 EST: 2005
SALES (est): 19.75MM **Privately Held**
Web: www.remecbroadband.com
SIC: 3663 Radio and t.v. communications equipment

(P-6655)
ROTATING PRCSION MCHANISMS INC
Also Called: RPM
8750 Shirley Ave, Northridge (91324-3409)
PHONE..........................818 349-9774
Kathy Flynn-nikolai, *CEO*
Daniel P Flynn, *
Jerome Smith, *Stockholder*
EMP: 46 EST: 1986
SQ FT: 40,000
SALES (est): 11.33MM **Privately Held**
Web: www.rpm-psi.com
SIC: 3663 Radio and t.v. communications equipment

(P-6656)
SATELLITE SECURITY CORPORATION
6779 Mesa Ridge Rd Ste 100, San Diego (92121-2996)
PHONE..........................877 437-4199
John Phillips, *CEO*
EMP: 26 EST: 1998
SALES (est): 1.51MM **Privately Held**
Web: www.kratosdefense.com
SIC: 3663 Space satellite communications equipment

(P-6657)
SEASPACE CORPORATION
9155 Brown Deer Rd, San Diego (92121-2260)
PHONE..........................858 746-1100
Eric Park, *CEO*
Erik Park, *
Daniel Lee, *
Jihong Park, *
EMP: 25 EST: 1982
SALES (est): 8.52MM **Privately Held**
Web: www.seaspace.com
SIC: 3663 3829 Satellites, communications; Measuring and controlling devices, nec

(P-6658)
SECURE COMM SYSTEMS INC (HQ)
Also Called: Benchmark Secure Technology
1740 E Wilshire Ave, Santa Ana (92705-4615)
PHONE..........................714 547-1174
Edward Hanrahan, *Pr*
Michael Buseman, *
Roop Lakkaraju, *
Kenneth Dorfman, *
▲ EMP: 147 EST: 2014
SQ FT: 38,000
SALES (est): 104.75MM
SALES (corp-wide): 2.84B **Publicly Held**
Web: www.bench.com
SIC: 3663 3829 3577 3571 Encryption devices; Vibration meters, analyzers, and calibrators; Computer peripheral equipment, nec; Electronic computers
PA: Benchmark Electronics, Inc.
56 S Rockford Dr

(P-6659)
SEKAI ELECTRONICS INC (PA)
38 Waterworks Way, Irvine (92618-3107)
PHONE..........................949 783-5740
Roland Soohoo, *CEO*
EMP: 25 EST: 1982
SQ FT: 7,000
SALES (est): 7.9MM
SALES (corp-wide): 7.9MM **Privately Held**
Web: www.sekai-electronics.com
SIC: 3663 5065 Radio and t.v. communications equipment; Video equipment, electronic

(P-6660)
SILVUS TECHNOLOGIES INC (PA)
10990 Wilshire Blvd Ste 1500, Los Angeles (90024-3957)
PHONE..........................310 479-3333
Babak Daneshrad, *Ch*
Jimi Henderson, *
Weijun Zhu, *
Gorik Hossepian, *
Eduardo Iniguez, *
EMP: 31 EST: 2004
SQ FT: 7,200
SALES (est): 34.21MM
SALES (corp-wide): 34.21MM **Privately Held**
Web: www.silvustechnologies.com
SIC: 3663 8731 Radio and t.v. communications equipment; Commercial physical research

(P-6661)
SPACE MICRO INC
15378 Avenue Of Science Ste 200, San Diego (92128-3451)
PHONE..........................858 332-0700
David Czajkowski, *CEO*
David J Strobel, *
David R Czajkowski, *
Patricia Ellison, *
Michael Jacox, *
EMP: 107 EST: 2002
SALES (est): 20.22MM **Privately Held**
Web: www.spacemicro.com
SIC: 3663 Space satellite communications equipment

(P-6662)
TATUNG COMPANY AMERICA INC (HQ)
2157 Mount Shasta Dr, San Pedro (90732-1334)
PHONE..........................310 637-2105
Huei-jihn Jih, *Pr*
Danny Huang, *
Christina Sun, *
▲ EMP: 98 EST: 1972
SALES (est): 7.19MM **Privately Held**
Web: www.tatungusa.com
SIC: 3663 3575 3944 3651 Television closed circuit equipment; Computer terminals, monitors and components; Video game machines, except coin-operated; Television receiving sets
PA: Tatung Company
22 Chungshan North Road,3rd Sec.,

(P-6663)
TECHNOCONCEPTS INC
6060 Sepulveda Blvd Ste 202, Van Nuys (91411-2512)
PHONE..........................818 988-3364
Antonio Turgeon, *CEO*
Eric Pommer, *

Michael Handelman, *
Richard A Hahn, *
Kevin Worth, *
EMP: 33 EST: 2004
SALES (est): 924.76K **Privately Held**
SIC: 3663 Cellular radio telephone

(P-6664)
TELEMTRY CMMNCTONS SYSTEMS INC
Also Called: TCS
10020 Remmet Ave, Chatsworth (91311-3854)
PHONE..........................818 718-6248
Sarin Michel Roy, *Pr*
Mihail Mateescu, *
EMP: 24 EST: 1999
SQ FT: 14,500
SALES (est): 5.88MM
SALES (corp-wide): 41.45MM **Privately Held**
Web: www.delta-telemetry.com
SIC: 3663 Antennas, transmitting and communications
PA: Delta Information Systems, Inc.
747 Dresher Rd Ste 125
215 657-5270

(P-6665)
THOMSON REUTERS CORPORATION
Also Called: Reuters Television La
5161 Lankershim Blvd, North Hollywood (91601-4962)
PHONE..........................877 518-2761
Kevin Regan, *Brnch Mgr*
EMP: 31
SALES (corp-wide): 10.66B **Publicly Held**
Web: www.thomsonreuters.com
SIC: 3663 Satellites, communications
HQ: Thomson Reuters Corporation
333 Bay St
Toronto ON M5H 2
416 687-7500

(P-6666)
TRANSCOM TELECOMMUNICATION INC
1390 E Burnett St Ste C, Signal Hill (90755-3559)
PHONE..........................562 424-9616
EMP: 27 EST: 2019
SALES (est): 4.97MM **Privately Held**
Web: www.transcomla.com
SIC: 3663 Radio and t.v. communications equipment

(P-6667)
TRICOM RESEARCH INC
17791 Sky Park Cir Ste J, Irvine (92614-6118)
PHONE..........................949 250-6024
◆ EMP: 64
SQ FT: 25,000
SALES (est): 4.22MM **Privately Held**
SIC: 3663 Radio and t.v. communications equipment

(P-6668)
TRICOM RESEARCH INC
17791 Sky Park Cir Ste J, Irvine (92614-6150)
PHONE..........................949 250-6024
Paula Wright, *Pr*
John W Wright, *
EMP: 64 EST: 2012
SALES (est): 3.26MM **Privately Held**
Web: www.tricomresearch.com

SIC: 3663 Radio and t.v. communications equipment

(P-6669)
VIASAT INC (PA)
Also Called: Viasat
6155 El Camino Real, Carlsbad (92009-1602)
PHONE..........................760 476-2200
Mark Dankberg, *Ch Bd*
K Guru Gowrappan, *Pr*
Robert Blair, *Sr VP*
Kevin Harkenrider, *CCO*
Shawn Duffy, *Chief Accounting Officer*
▲ EMP: 1169 EST: 1986
SALES (est): 4.28B
SALES (corp-wide): 4.28B **Publicly Held**
Web: www.viasat.com
SIC: 3663 4899 Space satellite communications equipment; Data communication services

(P-6670)
VIGOR SYSTEMS INC
4660 La Jolla Village Dr Ste 500, San Diego (92122-4605)
PHONE..........................866 748-4467
Magnus Sorlander, *CEO*
Shayna Smith, *
▲ EMP: 35 EST: 2002
SALES (est): 7.75MM **Privately Held**
Web: www.edisen.com
SIC: 3663 Studio equipment, radio and television broadcasting

(P-6671)
W B WALTON ENTERPRISES INC
4185 Hallmark Pkwy, San Bernardino (92407-1832)
P.O. Box 9010 (92427-0010)
PHONE..........................951 683-0930
William B Walton Junior, *Pr*
Jane Walton, *
EMP: 26 EST: 1979
SQ FT: 30,000
SALES (est): 4.94MM **Privately Held**
Web: www.de-ice.com
SIC: 3663 1731 Satellites, communications; Electrical work

(P-6672)
WV COMMUNICATIONS INC
1125 Business Center Cir Ste A, Newbury Park (91320-1186)
PHONE..........................805 376-1820
Uri Yulzari, *CEO*
Jim Iranovich, *VP*
Gerri L Yulzari, *Sec*
▲ EMP: 40 EST: 1998
SQ FT: 18,000
SALES (est): 4.96MM **Privately Held**
Web: www.wv-comm.com
SIC: 3663 Microwave communication equipment

(P-6673)
YAESU USA INC
6125 Phyllis Dr, Cypress (90630-5242)
PHONE..........................714 827-7600
Jun Hasegawa, *CEO*
▲ EMP: 40 EST: 2012
SALES (est): 5.39MM **Privately Held**
Web: www.yaesu.com
SIC: 3663 Radio and t.v. communications equipment

PRODUCTS & SVCS

3669 Communications Equipment, Nec

(P-6674)
71YRS INC (PA)
Also Called: Contract Furn & Ancillary Pdts
6525 Flotilla St, Commerce (90040-1713)
P.O. Box 5769 (90224-5769)
PHONE..............................310 639-0390
◆ EMP: 65 EST: 1952
SALES (est): 10.18MM
SALES (corp-wide): 10.18MM **Privately Held**
Web: www.peterpepper.com
SIC: 3669 Visual communication systems

(P-6675)
BDFCO INC
Also Called: Damac
1926 Kauai Dr, Costa Mesa (92626-3542)
PHONE..............................714 228-2900
Frank J Kubat Junior, *CEO*
Daniel L Davis, *
Robert Mc Clory, *Stockholder*
▲ EMP: 80 EST: 1984
SQ FT: 120,000
SALES (est): 4.41MM **Privately Held**
SIC: 3669 Intercommunication systems, electric

(P-6676)
BLUE SQUIRREL INC
8295 Aero Pl, San Diego (92123-2031)
PHONE..............................858 268-0717
Steve Deal, *CEO*
Dan Patton, *
Larry Cleary, *
Jay Standiford, *
Bill Kepner, *
▲ EMP: 80 EST: 1989
SQ FT: 20,000
SALES (est): 9.66MM **Privately Held**
Web: www.indyme.com
SIC: 3669 3663 Burglar alarm apparatus, electric; Airborne radio communications equipment

(P-6677)
CANOGA PERKINS CORPORATION (HQ)
20600 Prairie St, Chatsworth (91311-6008)
PHONE..............................818 718-6300
Alfred Tim Champion, *Pr*
James Heney, *
◆ EMP: 100 EST: 1965
SQ FT: 64,000
SALES (est): 24.61MM
SALES (corp-wide): 645.5MM **Privately Held**
Web: www.canoga.com
SIC: 3669 Intercommunication systems, electric
PA: Inductotherm Group, Llc
10 Indel Ave
609 267-9000

(P-6678)
COMPUTER SERVICE COMPANY
Also Called: Steiny & Company
210 N Delilah St, Corona (92879-1883)
PHONE..............................951 738-1444
Justin Cataldo, *Mgr*
EMP: 49
SALES (corp-wide): 4.98MM **Privately Held**
SIC: 3669 7629 Traffic signals, electric; Electrical repair shops
PA: Computer Service Company
5463 Diaz St

951 738-1444

(P-6679)
DEI HEADQUARTERS INC
Also Called: Sound United
3002 Wintergreen Dr, Carlsbad (92008-6883)
PHONE..............................760 598-6200
James E Minarik, *Pr*
Kevin P Duffy, *
Veysel P Goker, *
Crystal L Biggs, *
Josh Talge, *CMO*
▲ EMP: 385 EST: 2002
SALES (est): 6.15MM **Privately Held**
SIC: 3669 Burglar alarm apparatus, electric
HQ: Dei Holdings, Inc.
5541 Fermi Ct
Carlsbad CA 92008
760 598-6200

(P-6680)
DEI HOLDINGS INC (HQ)
Also Called: Masimo Consumer
5541 Fermi Ct, Carlsbad (92008-7348)
PHONE..............................760 598-6200
Paul Hataishi, *Pr*
Anthony Blair Tripodi, *COO*
Tom Mcclenahan, *Sec*
◆ EMP: 30 EST: 1999
SQ FT: 198,000
SALES (est): 112.67MM **Privately Held**
Web: www.masimo.com
SIC: 3669 3651 Burglar alarm apparatus, electric; Amplifiers: radio, public address, or musical instrument
PA: Viper Holdings Corporation
200 Clarendon St Fl 54

(P-6681)
ECONOLITE CONTROL PRODUCTS INC (PA)
1250 N Tustin Ave, Anaheim (92807-1617)
P.O. Box 6150 (92816-0150)
PHONE..............................714 630-3700
Michael C Doyle, *Ch*
Christian Haas, *
John Tracey, *
▼ EMP: 160 EST: 1933
SQ FT: 95,000
SALES (est): 90.02MM
SALES (corp-wide): 90.02MM **Privately Held**
Web: www.econolite.com
SIC: 3669 Traffic signals, electric

(P-6682)
ESCO TECHNOLOGIES INC
501 Del Norte Blvd, Oxnard (93030-7983)
PHONE..............................805 604-3875
EMP: 66
Web: www.escotechnologies.com
SIC: 3669 Intercommunication systems, electric
PA: Esco Technologies Inc.
9900 A Clayton Rd

(P-6683)
EXIGENT SENSORS LLC
11441 Markon Dr, Garden Grove (92841-1404)
PHONE..............................949 439-1321
Jeff Buss, *Managing Member*
▲ EMP: 27 EST: 2007
SALES (est): 4.98MM **Privately Held**
SIC: 3669 Fire alarm apparatus, electric

(P-6684)
GENERAL MONITORS INC (DH)
16782 Von Karman Ave Ste 14, Irvine (92606-2417)
PHONE..............................949 581-4464
Richard Lamishaw, *CFO*
◆ EMP: 110 EST: 1961
SALES (est): 47.52MM
SALES (corp-wide): 1.79B **Publicly Held**
Web: www.generalmonitors.com
SIC: 3669 1799 3812 Fire detection systems, electric; Gas leakage detection; Infrared object detection equipment
HQ: Msa Safety Sales, Llc
1000 Cranberry Woods Dr
Cranberry Township PA 16066
800 672-2222

(P-6685)
HONEYWELL SEC AMERICAS LLC
Also Called: Utc, Mas
2955 Red Hill Ave Ste 100, Costa Mesa (92626-1207)
PHONE..............................949 737-7800
Shin Voeks, *Genl Mgr*
EMP: 85
SALES (corp-wide): 36.66B **Publicly Held**
Web: corporate.carrier.com
SIC: 3669 5063 Burglar alarm apparatus, electric; Alarm systems, nec
HQ: Honeywell Security Americas, Llc
855 S Mint St
Charlotte NC 28202

(P-6686)
INDYME SOLUTIONS LLC
8295 Aero Pl Ste 260, San Diego (92123-2029)
PHONE..............................858 268-0717
Joe Joseph Eudano, *CEO*
Bill Kepner, *
James Doss, *
Philip Joostens, *
EMP: 50 EST: 1980
SQ FT: 18,000
SALES (est): 5.95MM **Privately Held**
Web: www.indyme.com
SIC: 3669 Burglar alarm apparatus, electric

(P-6687)
JOHNSON CNTRLS FIRE PRTCTION L
Also Called: Simplexgrinnell
3568 Ruffin Rd, San Diego (92123-2597)
P.O. Box 23080 (92193-3080)
PHONE..............................858 633-9100
Bob Jamieson, *Brnch Mgr*
EMP: 150
SIC: 3669 1731 1711 3873 Emergency alarms; Fire detection and burglar alarm systems specialization; Fire sprinkler system installation; Watches, clocks, watchcases, and parts
HQ: Johnson Controls Fire Protection Lp
6600 Congress Ave
Boca Raton FL 33487
561 988-7200

(P-6688)
MK DAVIDSON INC
3333 W Coast Hwy Ste 200, Newport Beach (92663-4040)
PHONE..............................949 698-2963
Darren Davidson, *CEO*
EMP: 32 EST: 2022
SALES (est): 1.05MM **Privately Held**
Web: www.mkdavidson.com
SIC: 3669 Communications equipment, nec

(P-6689)
PALOMAR PRODUCTS INC
23042 Arroyo Vis, Rcho Sta Marg (92688-2617)
PHONE..............................949 766-5300
Kevin Moschetti, *CEO*
Val Policky, *
Fred Ekstein, *
EMP: 79 EST: 1995
SQ FT: 35,000
SALES (est): 25.04MM
SALES (corp-wide): 7.94B **Publicly Held**
Web: www.palomar.com
SIC: 3669 Intercommunication systems, electric
PA: Transdigm Group Incorporated
1350 Euclid Ave Ste 1600
216 706-2960

(P-6690)
QUALCOMM MEMS TECHNOLOGIES INC
5775 Morehouse Dr, San Diego (92121-1714)
PHONE..............................858 587-1121
Greg Heinzinger, *Sr VP*
Derek Aberle, *
EMP: 25 EST: 1998
SQ FT: 9,000
SALES (est): 6.33MM
SALES (corp-wide): 38.96B **Publicly Held**
SIC: 3669 Visual communication systems
PA: Qualcomm Incorporated
5775 Morehouse Dr
858 587-1121

(P-6691)
RAYTHEON APPLIED SGNAL TECH IN
160 N Riverview Dr Ste 300, Anaheim (92808-2295)
PHONE..............................714 917-0255
John Mcgrory, *Brnch Mgr*
EMP: 107
SALES (corp-wide): 68.92B **Publicly Held**
Web: www.appsig.com
SIC: 3669 Signaling apparatus, electric
HQ: Raytheon Applied Signal Technology, Inc.
100 Headquarters Dr
San Jose CA 95134
408 749-1888

(P-6692)
SIEMENS RAIL AUTOMATION CORP
9568 Archibald Ave, Rancho Cucamonga (91730-5744)
PHONE..............................909 532-5405
Jay Aslam, *Mgr*
EMP: 84
SALES (corp-wide): 84.78B **Privately Held**
Web: www.siemens.com
SIC: 3669 Railroad signaling devices, electric
HQ: Siemens Rail Automation Corporation
2400 Nelson Miller Pkwy
Louisville KY 40223
800 626-2710

(P-6693)
STATEWIDE TRFFIC SFETY SGNS IN (HQ)
2722 S Fairview St Fl 2, Santa Ana (92704-5947)
PHONE..............................949 553-8272
Rob Sehnert, *CEO*
EMP: 39 EST: 1987
SALES (est): 24.12MM
SALES (corp-wide): 539.72MM **Privately Held**

Web: www.statewidess.com
SIC: 3669 Pedestrian traffic control
　equipment
PA: Awp, Inc.
　　4244 Mount Pleasant St Nw
　　330 677-7401

(P-6694)
SYSTECH CORPORATION
Also Called: Systech
118 State Pl Ste 101, Escondido
(92029-1324)
PHONE................................858 674-6500
D Mark Fowler, *Pr*
Don Armerding, *
Jon Goby, *
Cheri Houchin, *
Zenon Barelka, *
▲ **EMP:** 35 **EST:** 1980
SALES (est): 5.61MM **Privately Held**
Web: www.systech.com
SIC: 3669 7371 3661 3577
　Intercommunication systems, electric;
　Custom computer programming services;
　Telephone and telegraph apparatus;
　Computer peripheral equipment, nec

(P-6695)
TACTICAL COMMAND INDS INC
(DH)
4700 E Airport Dr, Ontario (91761-7875)
PHONE................................925 219-1097
Scott O'brien, *CEO*
EMP: 23 **EST:** 1996
SALES (est): 4.43MM
SALES (corp-wide): 482.53MM **Publicly
Held**
Web: www.safariland.com
SIC: 3669 Intercommunication systems,
　electric
HQ: Safariland, Llc
　　13386 International Pkwy
　　Jacksonville FL 32218
　　904 741-5400

(P-6696)
TACTICAL COMMUNICATIONS
CORP
473 Post St, Camarillo (93010-8553)
PHONE................................805 987-4100
Gregory Peacock, *CHBGREGORY
PEACOCK CEO CHBGREGORY
PEACOCK*
EMP: 25 **EST:** 2009
SQ FT: 11,000
SALES (est): 5.2MM **Privately Held**
Web: www.tacticalcommunications.com
SIC: 3669 8999 Intercommunication
　systems, electric; Communication services

(P-6697)
TELLABS ACCESS LLC (HQ)
338 Pier Ave, Hermosa Beach
(90254-3617)
PHONE................................630 798-8671
Mike Dagenais, *Pr*
Robb Warwick, *VP*
Doug Bayerd, *VP*
Jeff Carnes, *VP*
EMP: 44 **EST:** 2014
SALES (est): 16.5MM **Privately Held**
Web: www.tellabs.com
SIC: 3669 Intercommunication systems,
　electric
PA: Marlin Equity Partners, Llc
　　1301 Manhattan Ave

(P-6698)
WALTON ELECTRIC
CORPORATION
755 N Central Ave Ste A, Upland
(91786-9475)
P.O. Box 1599 (91711-8599)
PHONE................................909 981-5051
Tanyon D Dunkley, *CEO*
Don R Davis, *
Ron C Stickel, *
EMP: 150 **EST:** 1985
SQ FT: 10,150
SALES (est): 35.19MM **Privately Held**
Web: www.waltonelectriccorp.com
SIC: 3669 1731 Fire alarm apparatus, electric
　; Electrical work

(P-6699)
ZETTLER COMPONENTS INC
(PA)
75 Columbia, Orange (92868)
PHONE................................949 831-5000
Kurt Rexius, *Genl Mgr*
▲ **EMP:** 250 **EST:** 1996
SQ FT: 27,000
SALES (est): 26MM **Privately Held**
Web: www.zettlercomponents.com
SIC: 3669 5065 5087 Intercommunication
　systems, electric; Intercommunication
　equipment, electronic; Firefighting
　equipment

3671 Electron Tubes

(P-6700)
ECOATM LLC (DH)
10121 Barnes Canyon Rd, San Diego
(92121-2725)
PHONE................................858 999-3200
David Mersten, *
EMP: 250 **EST:** 2008
SALES (est): 105.7MM
SALES (corp-wide): 32.64B **Publicly Held**
Web: www.ecoatm.com
SIC: 3671 Electron tubes
HQ: Apollo Asset Management, Inc.
　　9 W 57th St Fl 42
　　New York NY 10019

(P-6701)
NEWVAC LLC
Also Called: Newvac Division
9330 De Soto Ave, Chatsworth
(91311-4926)
PHONE................................310 990-0401
Garrett Hoffman, *Brnch Mgr*
EMP: 114
SALES (corp-wide): 96.54MM **Privately
Held**
Web: www.ncwvac-llc.com
SIC: 3671 3678 3679 Electron tubes;
　Electronic connectors; Harness assemblies,
　for electronic use: wire or cable
HQ: Newvac, Llc
　　9330 De Soto Ave
　　Chatsworth CA 91311
　　310 525-1205

3672 Printed Circuit Boards

(P-6702)
A & M ELECTRONICS INC
25018 Avenue Kearny, Valencia
(91355-1253)
PHONE................................661 257-3680
Ron Simpson, *Pr*
Tiffiny Simpson, *
EMP: 30 **EST:** 1977

SQ FT: 12,000
SALES (est): 7.32MM **Privately Held**
Web: www.aandmelectronics.com
SIC: 3672 Circuit boards, television and
　radio printed

(P-6703)
ACCU-SEMBLY INC
1835 Huntington Dr, Duarte (91010-2635)
PHONE................................626 357-3447
John Hykes, *CEO*
Marilyn Hykes, *
Jan Shimmin, *Stockholder*
John Shimmin, *Stockholder*
▲ **EMP:** 95 **EST:** 1983
SQ FT: 15,000
SALES (est): 22.18MM **Privately Held**
Web: www.accu-sembly.com
SIC: 3672 Printed circuit boards

(P-6704)
ACCURATE CIRCUIT ENGRG INC
Also Called: Ace
3019 Kilson Dr, Santa Ana (92707-4202)
PHONE................................714 546-2162
Charles Lowe, *CEO*
▲ **EMP:** 70 **EST:** 1984
SQ FT: 15,000
SALES (est): 9.13MM **Privately Held**
Web: www.ace-pcb.com
SIC: 3672 Printed circuit boards

(P-6705)
ACCURATE ENGINEERING INC
8710 Telfair Ave, Sun Valley (91352-2530)
PHONE................................818 768-3919
Shitalkumar Desai, *Pr*
Rush Patel, *
Hiten Golakiea, *
Suresh Jasani, *
Gautam Jasani, *
EMP: 25 **EST:** 1996
SQ FT: 15,000
SALES (est): 2.44MM **Privately Held**
Web: www.accueng.com
SIC: 3672 Printed circuit boards

(P-6706)
ADVANCED CIRCUITS INC
17067 Cantara St, Van Nuys (91406-1112)
PHONE................................818 345-1993
Ralph Richart, *Brnch Mgr*
EMP: 40
Web: www.4pcb.com
SIC: 3672 Printed circuit boards
PA: Advanced Circuits, Inc.
　　21101 E 32nd Pkwy

(P-6707)
AMERICAN CIRCUIT TECH INC
(PA)
5330 E Hunter Ave, Anaheim (92807-2053)
PHONE................................714 777-2480
Ravi Kheni, *Pr*
Giradhar Butani, *
Labheu Zalavadia, *
Kanu Patel, *
EMP: 36 **EST:** 1975
SQ FT: 22,000
SALES (est): 4.33MM
SALES (corp-wide): 4.33MM **Privately
Held**
Web: www.excello.com
SIC: 3672 Circuit boards, television and
　radio printed

(P-6708)
ANC TECHNOLOGY INC
Also Called: Shanghai Anc Electronic Tech
10195 Stockton Rd, Moorpark
(93021-9755)

PHONE................................805 530-3958
Dennis Noble, *CEO*
▲ **EMP:** 100 **EST:** 1994
SQ FT: 60,000
SALES (est): 2.95MM **Privately Held**
Web: www.anctech.com
SIC: 3672 5083 Printed circuit boards;
　Irrigation equipment

(P-6709)
APT ELECTRONICS INC
Also Called: APT Electronics
241 N Crescent Way, Anaheim
(92801-6704)
PHONE................................714 687-6760
Tae Myoung Kim, *CEO*
EMP: 112 **EST:** 1999
SQ FT: 20,000
SALES (est): 24.76MM **Privately Held**
Web: www.aptelectronics.com
SIC: 3672 Printed circuit boards

(P-6710)
ASTRONIC
2 Orion, Aliso Viejo (92656-4200)
PHONE................................949 454-1180
Sang H Choi, *CEO*
Ok Kay Choi, *Sec*
▲ **EMP:** 143 **EST:** 1976
SQ FT: 41,000
SALES (est): 10.16MM **Privately Held**
Web: www.astronic-ems.com
SIC: 3672 1742 Printed circuit boards;
　Acoustical and insulation work

(P-6711)
BENCHMARK ELEC MFG
SLTONS MRPA
Also Called: Benchmark
200 Science Dr, Moorpark (93021-2003)
PHONE................................805 532-2800
Jayne Desorcie, *Pr*
EMP: 523 **EST:** 1986
SALES (est): 18.58MM
SALES (corp-wide): 2.84B **Publicly Held**
Web: www.bench.com
SIC: 3672 Printed circuit boards
HQ: Benchmark Electronics Manufacturing
　　Solutions Inc.
　　5550 Hellyer Ave
　　San Jose CA 95138
　　805 222-1303

(P-6712)
BENCHMARK ELEC PHOENIX
INC
1659 Gailes Blvd, San Diego (92154-8230)
PHONE................................619 397-2402
Roberto Perez, *Brnch Mgr*
EMP: 300
SALES (corp-wide): 2.84B **Publicly Held**
Web: www.bench.com
SIC: 3672 3577 Printed circuit boards;
　Computer peripheral equipment, nec
HQ: Benchmark Electronics Phoenix, Inc.
　　56 S Rockford Dr
　　Tempe AZ 85281
　　623 300-7000

(P-6713)
CAL-COMP USA (SAN DIEGO)
INC
1940 Camino Vida Roble, Carlsbad
(92008-6516)
PHONE................................858 587-6900
Wei-chang Chen, *CEO*
EMP: 215 **EST:** 1995
SQ FT: 65,000
SALES (est): 19.58MM **Privately Held**

Web: www.calcompusa.com
SIC: 3672 Circuit boards, television and radio printed
HQ: Cal-Comp Electronics (Usa) Co., Ltd.
1940 Camino Vida Roble
Carlsbad CA
858 587-6900

(P-6714)
CARTEL ELECTRONICS LLC
Also Called: Apct Orange County
1900 Petra Ln Ste C, Placentia (92870-6758)
PHONE...................714 993-0270
▲ EMP: 85 EST: 1994
SALES (est): 20.69MM
SALES (corp-wide): 87.73MM Privately Held
Web: www.apct.com
SIC: 3672 Printed circuit boards
PA: Apct Holdings, Llc
3495 De La Cruz Blvd
408 727-6442

(P-6715)
CELESTICA AEROSPACE TECH CORP
Also Called: Celestica-Aerospace
895 S Rockefeller Ave Ste 102, Ontario (91761-8182)
PHONE...................512 310-7540
Jeffrey Bain, Pr
Thomas Lovelock, *
Leslie K Sladek, *
▲ EMP: 200 EST: 2002
SQ FT: 55,000
SALES (est): 4.65MM
SALES (corp-wide): 7.96B Privately Held
Web: www.elitehealthchoices.com
SIC: 3672 Printed circuit boards
PA: Celestica Inc
1900-5140 Yonge St
416 448-5800

(P-6716)
CHAD INDUSTRIES INCORPORATED
Also Called: Chad
1565 S Sinclair St, Anaheim (92806-5934)
PHONE...................714 938-0080
Scott W Klimczak, Pr
Wayne Rapp, *
▲ EMP: 40 EST: 1973
SQ FT: 31,000
SALES (est): 4.77MM Privately Held
SIC: 3672 Printed circuit boards

(P-6717)
CIRCUIT SERVICES LLC
Also Called: Career Tech Circuit Services
9134 Independence Ave, Chatsworth (91311-5902)
PHONE...................818 701-5391
Marc Haugen, CEO
EMP: 43 EST: 1998
SALES (est): 32.62MM
SALES (corp-wide): 153.54MM Privately Held
Web: www.careertech-usa.com
SIC: 3672 Printed circuit boards
PA: Fralock Holdings Llc
28525 W Industry Dr
661 702-6999

(P-6718)
CLARITY DESIGN INC
13000 Gregg St Ste B, Poway (92064-7151)
PHONE...................858 746-3500
Thomas H Lupfer, Pr

Thomas H Lupfer, Pr
Robert Melucci, *
◆ EMP: 42 EST: 1991
SALES (est): 8.79MM Privately Held
Web: www.claritydesign.com
SIC: 3672 7373 8711 Circuit boards, television and radio printed; Computer integrated systems design; Engineering services

(P-6719)
COAST TO COAST CIRCUITS INC (PA)
Also Called: Speedy Circuits
5331 Mcfadden Ave, Huntington Beach (92649-1204)
PHONE...................714 891-9441
Edward Porter, CEO
Ronald Scott Lawhead, *
◆ EMP: 41 EST: 1985
SQ FT: 40,000
SALES (est): 13.55MM Privately Held
Web: www.excello.com
SIC: 3672 Circuit boards, television and radio printed

(P-6720)
COPPER CLAD MLTILAYER PDTS INC
Also Called: C C M P
1150 N Hawk Cir, Anaheim (92807-1708)
PHONE...................714 237-1388
Fred Ohanian, Pr
William Schwerter, *
▲ EMP: 25 EST: 1994
SQ FT: 13,200
SALES (est): 673.72K Privately Held
Web: www.ccmpinc.com
SIC: 3672 Printed circuit boards

(P-6721)
CREATION TECH CALEXICO INC (HQ)
Also Called: Aisling Industries
1778 Zinetta Rd Ste F, Calexico (92231-9510)
P.O. Box 1833 (92244)
▲ EMP: 25 EST: 1995
SQ FT: 10,000
SALES (est): 85.94MM
SALES (corp-wide): 656.54MM Privately Held
SIC: 3672 3679 Printed circuit boards; Electronic circuits
PA: Creation Technologies International Inc.
1 Beacon St
877 734-7456

(P-6722)
DE LEON ENTPS ELEC SPCLIST INC
Also Called: De Leon Enterprises
11934 Allegheny St, Sun Valley (91352-1833)
PHONE...................818 252-6690
Miguel De Leon, Pr
▲ EMP: 24 EST: 1994
SQ FT: 11,000
SALES (est): 2.6MM Privately Held
Web: www.deleonenterprises.com
SIC: 3672 Printed circuit boards

(P-6723)
DYNASTY ELECTRONIC COMPANY LLC
Also Called: Dec
1790 E Mcfadden Ave Ste 105, Santa Ana (92705-4638)
PHONE...................714 550-1197

Fredrick Rodenhuis, Managing Member
Mark Clark, *
EMP: 65 EST: 2008
SQ FT: 10,000
SALES (est): 8.57MM Privately Held
Web: www.dec-assembly.com
SIC: 3672 Printed circuit boards

(P-6724)
ELECTRO SURFACE TECH INC
Also Called: E S T
2281 Las Palmas Dr # 101, Carlsbad (92011-1527)
PHONE...................760 431-8306
Hiroo Kirpalani, Pr
EMP: 36 EST: 1989
SQ FT: 31,500
SALES (est): 3.85MM Privately Held
Web: www.est.com
SIC: 3672 Circuit boards, television and radio printed

(P-6725)
ELECTRONIC SURFC MOUNTED INDS
Also Called: Esmi
6731 Cobra Way, San Diego (92121-4110)
PHONE...................858 455-1710
Henry Kim, Pr
Lynn Kim, *
▼ EMP: 40 EST: 1986
SQ FT: 25,000
SALES (est): 5.59MM Privately Held
Web: www.esmiinc.com
SIC: 3672 Printed circuit boards

(P-6726)
EXCELLO CIRCUITS INC
Also Called: Speedy Circuits
5330 E Hunter Ave, Anaheim (92807-2053)
PHONE...................714 993-0560
Rax Ribadia, Pr
Sam Bhayani, *
Rax Ribadia, VP
Tushar Patel, *
EMP: 72 EST: 1992
SQ FT: 11,000
SALES (est): 9.11MM Privately Held
Web: www.excello.com
SIC: 3672 Printed circuit boards

(P-6727)
EXPERT ASSEMBLY SERVICES INC
Also Called: Expert Ems
14312 Chambers Rd Ste B, Tustin (92780-6912)
PHONE...................714 258-8880
Jack Quinn, CEO
EMP: 50 EST: 1997
SALES (est): 12.13MM Privately Held
Web: www.expertassembly.com
SIC: 3672 Printed circuit boards

(P-6728)
FABRICATED COMPONENTS CORP
Also Called: Summit Interconnect Orange
130 W Bristol Ln, Orange (92865-2640)
PHONE...................714 974-8590
Shane Whiteside, Pr
▼ EMP: 140 EST: 1979
SQ FT: 40,000
SALES (est): 9.93MM Privately Held
Web: www.fabricatedcomponents.com
SIC: 3672 Printed circuit boards

(P-6729)
FINE LINE CIRCUITS & TECH INC
594 Apollo St Ste A, Brea (92821-3134)
PHONE...................714 529-2942
Rick Bajaria, Pr
Ken Pansuria, *
Vinny Kathrotia, *
EMP: 30 EST: 1995
SQ FT: 20,000
SALES (est): 4.47MM Privately Held
Web: www.finelinecircuits.com
SIC: 3672 Circuit boards, television and radio printed

(P-6730)
FTG CIRCUITS INC (DH)
20750 Marilla St, Chatsworth (91311-4407)
PHONE...................818 407-4024
Brad Bourne, CEO
Michael Labrador, *
Joe Ricci, *
Ed Hanna, *
▼ EMP: 91 EST: 1956
SQ FT: 38,000
SALES (est): 15.39MM
SALES (corp-wide): 98.06MM Privately Held
Web: www.ftgcorp.com
SIC: 3672 3644 Printed circuit boards; Terminal boards
HQ: Firan Technology Group (Usa) Corporation
20750 Marilla St
Chatsworth CA 91311
818 407-4024

(P-6731)
GAVIAL ENGINEERING & MFG INC
1435 W Mccoy Ln, Santa Maria (93455-1002)
PHONE...................805 614-0060
Don Connors, Pr
Ken Hicks, *
Stanley D Connors, *
EMP: 50 EST: 2012
SQ FT: 25,000
SALES (est): 3.56MM
SALES (corp-wide): 40.31MM Privately Held
Web: www.gavial.com
SIC: 3672 3679 Printed circuit boards; Electronic circuits
PA: Gavial Holdings, Inc.
1435 W Mccoy Ln
805 614-0060

(P-6732)
GEERIRAJ INC
Also Called: Mer-Mar Electronics
7042 Santa Fe Ave E Ste A1, Hesperia (92345-5711)
PHONE...................760 244-6149
Kanjibhai Ghadia, Pr
Suresh Patel, *
EMP: 28 EST: 1974
SQ FT: 22,000
SALES (est): 4.95MM Privately Held
SIC: 3672 Printed circuit boards

(P-6733)
GOLDEN WEST TECHNOLOGY
1180 E Valencia Dr, Fullerton (92831-4627)
PHONE...................714 738-3775
Dan P Rieth, Pr
EMP: 60 EST: 1974
SQ FT: 30,000
SALES (est): 9.21MM Privately Held
Web: www.goldenwesttech.com

▲ = Import ▼ = Export
◆ = Import/Export

SIC: 3672 Printed circuit boards

(P-6734)
GRAPHIC RESEARCH INC
3339 Durham Ct, Burbank (91504-1600)
PHONE...........................818 886-7340
Govind R Vaghashia, *Pr*
Pete Vaghashia, *
▲ EMP: 50 EST: 1966
SALES (est): 3.88MM **Privately Held**
Web: www.graphicresearch.com
SIC: 3672 Printed circuit boards

(P-6735)
HI TECH ELECTRONIC MFG CORP
Also Called: Hitem
1938 Avenida Del Oro, Oceanside (92056-5803)
PHONE...........................858 657-0908
Thai Nguyen, *CEO*
Vinh Lam, *
Tran Vu, *
▲ EMP: 82 EST: 1997
SALES (est): 11MM **Privately Held**
Web: www.hitem.com
SIC: 3672 Circuit boards, television and radio printed

(P-6736)
HUGHES CIRCUITS INC
Also Called: Pcb Fabrication Facility
540 S Pacific St, San Marcos (92078-4050)
PHONE...........................760 744-0300
Barbara Hughes, *Brnch Mgr*
EMP: 126
SALES (corp-wide): 36.08MM **Privately Held**
Web: www.hughescircuits.com
SIC: 3672 Circuit boards, television and radio printed
PA: Hughes Circuits, Inc.
546 S Pacific St
760 744-0300

(P-6737)
HUGHES CIRCUITS INC (PA)
Also Called: Hci
546 S Pacific St, San Marcos (92078-4070)
PHONE...........................760 744-0300
Barbara Hughes, *CEO*
Jerry Hughes, *
Michelle Glatts, *
Joe Hughes, *
Steve Hughes, *
EMP: 99 EST: 1999
SQ FT: 50,000
SALES (est): 36.08MM
SALES (corp-wide): 36.08MM **Privately Held**
Web: www.hughescircuits.com
SIC: 3672 3679 8711 3444 Printed circuit boards; Electronic circuits; Engineering services; Sheet metalwork

(P-6738)
IPC CAL FLEX INC
13337 South St # 307, Cerritos (90703-7308)
PHONE...........................714 952-0373
Scott Kohno, *Pr*
EMP: 25 EST: 1980
SQ FT: 25,000
SALES (est): 1.62MM **Privately Held**
SIC: 3672 Printed circuit boards

(P-6739)
IRVINE ELECTRONICS LLC
Also Called: Irvine Electronics Inc
1601 Alton Pkwy Ste A, Irvine (92606-4843)

PHONE...........................949 250-0315
Jane Zerounian, *Pr*
Onnig Zerounian, *
EMP: 100 EST: 1969
SQ FT: 48,000
SALES (est): 23.38MM
SALES (corp-wide): 912.8MM **Privately Held**
Web: www.volex.com
SIC: 3672 Circuit boards, television and radio printed
PA: Volex Plc
Unit C
203 370-8830

(P-6740)
ISU PETASYS CORP
12930 Bradley Ave, Sylmar (91342-3829)
PHONE...........................818 833-5800
Yong Kyoun Kim, *Pr*
▲ EMP: 95 EST: 1997
SQ FT: 50,000
SALES (est): 21.11MM **Privately Held**
Web: www.isupetasys.com
SIC: 3672 Printed circuit boards
PA: Isu Chemical Co., Ltd.
84 Sapyeong-Daero, Seocho-Gu

(P-6741)
JABIL INC
Also Called: Jabil Chad Automation
1565 S Sinclair St, Anaheim (92806-5934)
PHONE...........................714 938-0080
Babak Naderi, *Dir Opers*
EMP: 50
SALES (corp-wide): 28.88B **Publicly Held**
Web: www.jabil.com
SIC: 3672 Printed circuit boards
PA: Jabil Inc.
10800 Roosevelt Blvd N
727 577-9749

(P-6742)
K L ELECTRONIC INC
3083 S Harbor Blvd, Santa Ana (92704-6448)
PHONE...........................714 751-5611
Khanh Ton, *Pr*
Luon Ton, *Sec*
Michael Ton, *CEO*
EMP: 46 EST: 1981
SQ FT: 4,000
SALES (est): 3.13MM **Privately Held**
Web: www.klelectronics.com
SIC: 3672 Printed circuit boards

(P-6743)
KCA ELECTRONICS INC
Also Called: Summit Interconnect - Anaheim
223 N Crescent Way, Anaheim (92801-6704)
PHONE...........................714 239-2133
Shane Whiteside, *Pr*
▲ EMP: 180 EST: 1992
SQ FT: 60,000
SALES (est): 14.03MM
SALES (corp-wide): 1.78B **Privately Held**
Web: www.kcamerica.com
SIC: 3672 Circuit boards, television and radio printed
HQ: Equity Hci Management L P
1730 Pennsylvania Ave Nw # 525
Washington DC

(P-6744)
LARITECH INC
5898 Condor Dr, Moorpark (93021-2603)
PHONE...........................805 529-5000
William Larrick, *CEO*
Terry Gonzales, *

Joel Butler, *
EMP: 111 EST: 2001
SQ FT: 13,000
SALES (est): 32.82MM **Privately Held**
Web: www.laritech.com
SIC: 3672 Printed circuit boards

(P-6745)
LIFETIME MEMORY PRODUCTS INC
2505 Da Vinci Ste A, Irvine (92614-0170)
P.O. Box 1207 (92652-1207)
PHONE...........................949 794-9000
Paul Columbus, *CEO*
Cameron Hum, *
◆ EMP: 40 EST: 1981
SQ FT: 16,000
SALES (est): 852.13K **Privately Held**
Web: www.lifetimememory.com
SIC: 3672 5045 3674 Printed circuit boards; Computers, peripherals, and software; Semiconductors and related devices

(P-6746)
MARCEL ELECTRONICS INC
130 W Bristol Ln, Orange (92865-2637)
PHONE...........................714 974-8590
EMP: 34 EST: 2014
SALES (est): 5.18MM **Privately Held**
SIC: 3672 Printed circuit boards

(P-6747)
MATRIX USA INC
2730 S Main St, Santa Ana (92707-3435)
PHONE...........................714 825-0404
Kieran Healy, *Pr*
George Potocska, *
Sharon Nioson, *Branch Administrator*
▲ EMP: 25 EST: 2005
SALES (est): 11.37MM
SALES (corp-wide): 9.15MM **Privately Held**
Web: www.matrixelectronics.com
SIC: 3672 Printed circuit boards
HQ: Matrix Electronics Limited
1124 Mid-Way Blvd
Mississauga ON L5T 2
905 670-8400

(P-6748)
MAXTROL CORPORATION
1701 E Edinger Ave Ste B6, Santa Ana (92705-5010)
PHONE...........................714 245-0506
Uri Ranon, *Pr*
Leo Pardo, *
EMP: 40 EST: 1990
SQ FT: 5,000
SALES (est): 2.44MM **Privately Held**
Web: www.maxtrol.com
SIC: 3672 Printed circuit boards

(P-6749)
MERCURY SYSTEMS INC
400 Del Norte Blvd, Oxnard (93030-7997)
PHONE...........................805 388-1345
Deepak Alagh, *Brnch Mgr*
EMP: 110
SALES (corp-wide): 835.27MM **Publicly Held**
Web: www.mrcy.com
SIC: 3672 Printed circuit boards
PA: Mercury Systems, Inc.
50 Minuteman Rd
978 256-1300

(P-6750)
MERCURY SYSTEMS INC
300 Del Norte Blvd, Oxnard (93030-7217)
PHONE...........................805 751-1100

Deepak Alagh, *Brnch Mgr*
EMP: 109
SALES (corp-wide): 835.27MM **Publicly Held**
Web: www.mrcy.com
SIC: 3672 Printed circuit boards
PA: Mercury Systems, Inc.
50 Minuteman Rd
978 256-1300

(P-6751)
MFLEX DELAWARE INC
101 Academy Ste 250, Irvine (92617-3035)
PHONE...........................949 453-6800
Reza A Meshgin, *CEO*
EMP: 4933 EST: 2019
SALES (est): 1.1MM **Privately Held**
SIC: 3672 Printed circuit boards
HQ: Multi-Fineline Electronix, Inc.
101 Academy Ste 250
Irvine CA 92617
949 453-6800

(P-6752)
MODALAI INC
10855 Sorrento Valley Rd Ste 2, San Diego (92121-1629)
PHONE...........................858 247-7053
Charles Sweet Iii, *CEO*
Charles Wheeler Sweet Iii, *CEO*
EMP: 38 EST: 2018
SALES (est): 5.37MM **Privately Held**
Web: www.modalai.com
SIC: 3672 Printed circuit boards

(P-6753)
MULTI-FINELINE ELECTRONIX INC (HQ)
Also Called: Mflex
101 Academy Ste 250, Irvine (92617-3035)
PHONE...........................949 453-6800
Reza Meshgin, *Pr*
Christine Besnard, *
Tom Kampfer, *
Neil Liu, *CIO*
Thomas Lee, *
EMP: 583 EST: 1984
SQ FT: 20,171
SALES (est): 33.12MM **Privately Held**
Web: www.mflex.com
SIC: 3672 Printed circuit boards
PA: Suzhou Dongshan Precision Manufacturing Co., Ltd.
8 Fenghuangshan Road Dongshan Town, Wuzhong District

(P-6754)
MURRIETTA CIRCUITS
5000 E Landon Dr, Anaheim (92807-1978)
PHONE...........................714 970-2430
Andrew Murrietta, *CEO*
Albert G Murrietta, *
Albert A Murrietta, *
Josh Murrietta, *OK Vice President*
Helen Murrietta, *
EMP: 105 EST: 1992
SQ FT: 48,500
SALES (est): 21.95MM **Privately Held**
Web: www.murrietta.com
SIC: 3672 8711 Printed circuit boards; Engineering services

(P-6755)
NASO INDUSTRIES CORPORATION
Also Called: Naso Technologies
3007 Bunsen Ave Ste Q, Ventura (93003-7634)
PHONE...........................805 650-1231
Jahansooz Saleh, *CEO*

Namdar Saleh, *
Bryan Howe, *
Mike White, *
Soraya Saleh, *
EMP: 40 **EST:** 1990
SQ FT: 20,000
SALES (est): 15.68MM **Privately Held**
Web: www.naso.com
SIC: 3672 3599 Printed circuit boards;
Machine shop, jobbing and repair

(P-6756)
NATEL ENGINEERING HOLDINGS INC
9340 Owensmouth Ave, Chatsworth
(91311-6915)
PHONE...........................818 734-6500
EMP: 65 **EST:** 2015
SALES (est): 5.68MM **Privately Held**
Web: www.neotech.com
SIC: 3672 Printed circuit boards

(P-6757)
NEW BRUNSWICK INDUSTRIES INC
5656 La Jolla Blvd, La Jolla (92037-7523)
PHONE...........................619 448-4900
Jim Krehbiel, *Pr*
Sue Harnack, *
Sue Krehbiel, *
EMP: 30 **EST:** 1982
SALES (est): 4.29MM **Privately Held**
Web: www.nbiinc.com
SIC: 3672 Circuit boards, television and
radio printed

(P-6758)
NORTHWEST CIRCUITS CORP
8660 Avenida Costa Blanca, San Diego
(92154-6232)
PHONE...........................619 661-1701
Toribio Lobato, *Pr*
▲ **EMP:** 65 **EST:** 1991
SQ FT: 12,000
SALES (est): 8.66MM **Privately Held**
Web: www.nwcircuits.com
SIC: 3672 Printed circuit boards

(P-6759)
ONCORE MANUFACTURING LLC
Also Called: Oncore Velocity
237 Via Vera Cruz, San Marcos
(92078-2617)
PHONE...........................760 737-6777
Arnulfo Villa, *Prin*
EMP: 110
SALES (corp-wide): 1.43B **Privately Held**
Web: www.neotech.com
SIC: 3672 Printed circuit boards
HQ: Oncore Manufacturing Llc
9340 Owensmouth Ave
Chatsworth CA 91311

(P-6760)
ONCORE MANUFACTURING SVCS INC
Also Called: Neo Tech Natel Epic Oncore
9340 Owensmouth Ave, Chatsworth
(91311-6915)
PHONE...........................510 360-2222
Sudesh Arora, *CEO*
David Brakenwagen, *Sr VP*
Sajjad Malik, *Ex VP*
Magdy Henry, *VP*
Zareen Mohta, *VP*
▲ **EMP:** 230 **EST:** 2007
SALES (est): 88.4MM
SALES (corp-wide): 1.43B **Privately Held**
Web: www.neotech.com

SIC: 3672 Printed circuit boards
PA: Natel Engineering Company, Llc
9340 Owensmouth Ave
818 495-8617

(P-6761)
OSI ELECTRONICS INC (HQ)
12533 Chadron Ave, Hawthorne
(90250-4807)
PHONE...........................310 978-0516
Paul Morben, *Pr*
Bruce Macdonald, *
Lou Campana, *
Alex Colquhoun, *
▲ **EMP:** 52 **EST:** 1995
SQ FT: 60,000
SALES (est): 90.28MM
SALES (corp-wide): 1.54B **Publicly Held**
Web: www.osielectronics.com
SIC: 3672 Printed circuit boards
PA: Osi Systems, Inc.
12525 Chadron Ave
310 978-0516

(P-6762)
PARPRO TECHNOLOGIES INC
Also Called: P T I
2700 S Fairview St, Santa Ana
(92704-5947)
PHONE...........................714 545-8886
Thomas Sparrvik, *CEO*
Keith Knight, *Pr*
Ngathuong Le, *COO*
Eduardo Serrano, *CFO*
EMP: 210 **EST:** 1998
SALES (est): 77.67MM **Privately Held**
Web: www.parpro.com
SIC: 3672 Printed circuit boards
PA: Parpro Corporation
No. 67-1, Dongyuan Rd.

(P-6763)
PHOTO FABRICATORS INC
7648 Burnet Ave, Van Nuys (91405-1043)
PHONE...........................818 781-1010
Steve L Brooks, *Pr*
John R Brooks, *
Susan Brooks, *
▲ **EMP:** 75 **EST:** 1973
SQ FT: 14,000
SALES (est): 8.32MM **Privately Held**
Web: www.photofabricators.com
SIC: 3672 Circuit boards, television and
radio printed

(P-6764)
PIONEER CIRCUITS INC
3021 S Shannon St, Santa Ana
(92704-6320)
PHONE...........................714 641-3132
Robert Lee, *CEO*
James Y Lee, *
EMP: 290 **EST:** 1981
SQ FT: 50,000
SALES (est): 58.9MM **Privately Held**
Web: www.pioneercircuits.com
SIC: 3672 3812 Printed circuit boards;
Defense systems and equipment

(P-6765)
QUALITY SYSTEMS INTGRATED CORP
7098 Miratech Dr Ste 170, San Diego
(92121-3111)
PHONE...........................858 536-3128
EMP: 120
Web: www.qsic.com
SIC: 3672 Printed circuit boards
PA: Quality Systems Integrated Corporation
6740 Top Gun St

(P-6766)
QUALITY SYSTEMS INTGRATED CORP (PA)
Also Called: Quality Systems
6740 Top Gun St, San Diego (92121-4114)
PHONE...........................858 587-9797
Kiem T Le, *CEO*
Minh Nguyen, *Dir*
Hai Bach, *Prin*
Thui Trong, *Prin*
Cecile Le, *CFO*
▲ **EMP:** 155 **EST:** 1994
SQ FT: 50,000
SALES (est): 47.28MM **Privately Held**
Web: www.qsic.com
SIC: 3672 Printed circuit boards

(P-6767)
SAEHAN ELECTRONICS AMERICA INC (PA)
7880 Airway Rd Ste B5g, San Diego
(92154-8308)
PHONE...........................858 496-1500
Bongsu Jeong, *CEO*
John Kim, *Pr*
Bok Geun Song, *CFO*
▲ **EMP:** 53 **EST:** 1994
SALES (est): 2.26MM **Privately Held**
Web: www.saehanusa.com
SIC: 3672 Printed circuit boards

(P-6768)
SANMINA CORPORATION
2945 Airway Ave, Costa Mesa
(92626-6007)
PHONE...........................714 371-2800
Dox Scream, *Mgr*
EMP: 51
SQ FT: 60,580
Web: www.sanmina.com
SIC: 3672 Printed circuit boards
PA: Sanmina Corporation
2700 N 1st St

(P-6769)
SANMINA CORPORATION
Viking Modular Solutions
2950 Red Hill Ave, Costa Mesa
(92626-5935)
PHONE...........................714 913-2200
Hamid Shokrgovar, *Pr*
EMP: 110
Web: www.sanmina.com
SIC: 3672 Printed circuit boards
PA: Sanmina Corporation
2700 N 1st St

(P-6770)
SEMI-KINETICS INC
20191 Windrow Dr Ste A, Lake Forest
(92630-8161)
PHONE...........................949 830-7364
Gary H Gonzalez, *CEO*
▲ **EMP:** 95 **EST:** 1981
SALES (est): 20.71MM
SALES (corp-wide): 75MM **Privately Held**
Web: www.semi-kinetics.com
SIC: 3672 Circuit boards, television and
radio printed
PA: Gonzalez Production Systems, Inc.
1670 Highwood E
248 745-1200

(P-6771)
SMART ELEC & ASSEMBLY INC
Also Called: Smart Electronics
2000 W Corporate Way, Anaheim
(92801-5373)
PHONE...........................714 772-2651

Robert Swelgin, *Pr*
Shou-lee Wang, *CEO*
James Wang, *
Dave Wopschall, *
Getaneh Bekele, *
▲ **EMP:** 120 **EST:** 1994
SQ FT: 34,500
SALES (est): 100.25MM
SALES (corp-wide): 2.84B **Publicly Held**
SIC: 3672 Printed circuit boards
HQ: Secure Communication Systems, Inc.
1740 E Wilshire Ave
Santa Ana CA 92705
714 547-1174

(P-6772)
SOMACIS INC
13500 Danielson St, Poway (92064-6874)
PHONE...........................858 513-2200
Giovanni Tridenti, *CEO*
▲ **EMP:** 120 **EST:** 1970
SQ FT: 76,000
SALES (est): 17.52MM
SALES (corp-wide): 2.67MM **Privately Held**
Web: www.hallmarkcircuits.com
SIC: 3672 Circuit boards, television and
radio printed
HQ: So.Ma.Ci.S. Spa
Via Jesina 17
Castelfidardo AN 60022
071721531

(P-6773)
SOUTH COAST CIRCUITS LLC
Also Called: Summit Interconnect
3506 W Lake Center Dr Ste A, Santa Ana
(92704-6985)
PHONE...........................714 966-2108
Milan Shah, *CEO*
▲ **EMP:** 87 **EST:** 1983
SQ FT: 30,000
SALES (est): 9.5MM
SALES (corp-wide): 1.78B **Privately Held**
Web: www.sccircuits.com
SIC: 3672 Circuit boards, television and
radio printed
HQ: Royal Circuit Solutions, Llc
21 Hamilton Ct
Hollister CA 95023
831 636-7789

(P-6774)
SPECTRUM ASSEMBLY INC
Also Called: Spectrum Electronics
6300 Yarrow Dr Ste 100, Carlsbad
(92011-1542)
PHONE...........................760 930-4000
Ronald Topp, *Pr*
Ronald Tupp, *
Michael Baldwin, *
EMP: 147 **EST:** 1993
SQ FT: 20,000
SALES (est): 24.05MM **Privately Held**
Web: www.saicorp.com
SIC: 3672 3569 3315 3999 Printed circuit
boards; Assembly machines, non-
metalworking; Wire and fabricated wire
products; Barber and beauty shop
equipment

(P-6775)
SUMITRONICS USA INC
9335 Airway Rd Ste 212, San Diego
(92154-7930)
PHONE...........................619 661-0450
Jiro Hashiguchi, *CEO*
Ryuji Sumi, *CFO*
◆ **EMP:** 30 **EST:** 2007
SQ FT: 800
SALES (est): 30.6MM **Privately Held**

Web: www.sumitronics.com
SIC: 3672 Printed circuit boards
HQ: Sumitronics Corporation
1-2-2, Hitotsubashi
Chiyoda-Ku TKY 100-0

(P-6776)
SUMMIT INTERCONNECT INC (HQ)
223 N Crescent Way, Anaheim (92801-6704)
PHONE...............................714 239-2433
Shane Whiteside, Pr
EMP: 150 EST: 2016
SALES (est): 154.36MM
SALES (corp-wide): 1.78B Privately Held
Web: www.summitinterconnect.com
SIC: 3672 Printed circuit boards
PA: Goldberg Lindsay & Co. Llc
630 Fifth Ave 30th Fl
212 651-1100

(P-6777)
TRANSLINE TECHNOLOGY INC
1106 S Technology Cir, Anaheim (92805-6329)
PHONE...............................714 533-8300
Kishor Patel, Pr
Larry Padmani, *
▲ EMP: 33 EST: 1996
SQ FT: 20,000
SALES (est): 4.83MM Privately Held
Web: www.translinetech.com
SIC: 3672 Printed circuit boards

(P-6778)
TRANTRONICS INC
1822 Langley Ave, Irvine (92614-5624)
PHONE...............................949 553-1234
Tom Tran, Pr
EMP: 32 EST: 1997
SALES (est): 9.92MM Privately Held
Web: www.trantronics.com
SIC: 3672 3599 Printed circuit boards; Machine and other job shop work

(P-6779)
TRI-STAR LAMINATES INC
Also Called: Laminating Company of America
20322 Windrow Dr Ste 100, Lake Forest (92630-8150)
PHONE...............................949 587-3200
Patrick Redfern, Pr
EMP: 33 EST: 2000
SQ FT: 50,000
SALES (est): 2.72MM Privately Held
SIC: 3672 Printed circuit boards

(P-6780)
TTM PRINTED CIRCUIT GROUP INC (HQ)
2630 S Harbor Blvd, Santa Ana (92704-5829)
PHONE...............................714 327-3000
Thomas T Edman, Pr
Steve Richards, CFO
▲ EMP: 156 EST: 2006
SALES (est): 26.58MM
SALES (corp-wide): 2.23B Publicly Held
Web: www.ttm.com
SIC: 3672 Printed circuit boards
PA: Ttm Technologies, Inc.
200 Sndpointe Ave Ste 400
714 327-3000

(P-6781)
TTM TECHNOLOGIES INC (PA)
Also Called: TTM
200 Sandpointe Ave Ste 400, Santa Ana (92707-5747)

PHONE...............................714 327-3000
Thomas T Edman, Pr
Rex D Geveden, Non-Executive Chairman of the Board*
Daniel L Boehle, Ex VP
Philip Titterton, Ex VP
Douglas L Soder, Ex VP
EMP: 500 EST: 1978
SQ FT: 14,472
SALES (est): 2.23B
SALES (corp-wide): 2.23B Publicly Held
Web: www.ttm.com
SIC: 3672 Printed circuit boards

(P-6782)
TTM TECHNOLOGIES INC
2630 S Harbor Blvd, Santa Ana (92704-5829)
PHONE...............................714 241-0303
Dale Anderson, Prin
EMP: 300
SALES (corp-wide): 2.23B Publicly Held
Web: www.ttm.com
SIC: 3672 Printed circuit boards
PA: Ttm Technologies, Inc.
200 Sndpointe Ave Ste 400
714 327-3000

(P-6783)
TTM TECHNOLOGIES INC
3140 E Coronado St, Anaheim (92806-1914)
PHONE...............................714 688-7200
EMP: 290
SALES (corp-wide): 2.23B Publicly Held
Web: www.ttm.com
SIC: 3672 Printed circuit boards
PA: Ttm Technologies, Inc.
200 Sndpointe Ave Ste 400
714 327-3000

(P-6784)
TTM TECHNOLOGIES INC
5037 Ruffner St, San Diego (92111-1107)
PHONE...............................858 874-2701
Mark Micale, Mgr
EMP: 149
SALES (corp-wide): 2.23B Publicly Held
Web: www.ttm.com
SIC: 3672 Printed circuit boards
PA: Ttm Technologies, Inc.
200 Sndpointe Ave Ste 400
714 327-3000

(P-6785)
UNITED INTERNATIONAL TECH INC
9207 Deering Ave Ste B, Chatsworth (91311-6960)
PHONE...............................818 772-9400
Edmundo Espindola, CEO
Edmundo Espindolo, *
EMP: 36 EST: 2008
SALES (est): 4.6MM Privately Held
Web: www.uitpcb.com
SIC: 3672 7629 Circuit boards, television and radio printed; Circuit board repair

(P-6786)
VECTOR ELECTRONICS & TECH INC
11115 Vanowen St, North Hollywood (91605-6371)
PHONE...............................818 985-8208
Rakesh Bajaria, CEO
Ken Pansuriah, *
Viny Kathrotia, *
▲ EMP: 25 EST: 2001
SALES (est): 4.06MM Privately Held
Web: www.vectorelect.com

SIC: 3672 Printed circuit boards

(P-6787)
WE IMAGINE INC
9371 Canoga Ave, Chatsworth (91311-5879)
P.O. Box 5696 (91313-5696)
PHONE...............................818 709-0064
EMP: 53 EST: 1974
SALES (est): 5.03MM Privately Held
SIC: 3672 Printed circuit boards

(P-6788)
WFB ARCHIVES INC
13500 Danielson St, Poway (92064-6874)
EMP: 80
SIC: 3672 Printed circuit boards

(P-6789)
WINONICS INC
Also Called: Bench 2 Bench Technologies
1257 S State College Blvd, Fullerton (92831-5336)
PHONE...............................714 626-3755
Tom Sciulli, Genl Mgr
EMP: 120
SALES (corp-wide): 54.55MM Privately Held
Web: www.winonics.com
SIC: 3672 Printed circuit boards
HQ: Winonics Llc
660 N Puente St
Brea CA
714 256-8700

(P-6790)
YUN INDUSTRIAL CO LTD
Also Called: Y I C
161 Selandia Ln, Carson (90746-1412)
PHONE...............................310 715-1898
Ilun Yun, Pr
William Yun, *
Stephen Yun, *
◆ EMP: 40 EST: 1990
SQ FT: 16,000
SALES (est): 10.68MM Privately Held
Web: www.yic-assm.com
SIC: 3672 Printed circuit boards

3674 Semiconductors And Related Devices

(P-6791)
ABSEN INC
20311 Valley Blvd Ste J, Walnut (91789-2658)
PHONE...............................909 480-0129
EMP: 23
SIC: 3674 Light emitting diodes
HQ: Absen Inc.
7120 Lake Ellenor Dr
Orlando FL 32809
407 203-8870

(P-6792)
ACCELERATED MEMORY PROD INC
Also Called: AMP
1317 E Edinger Ave, Santa Ana (92705-4416)
PHONE...............................714 460-9800
Richard Mccauley, Pr
Cathleen Mccauley, VP
◆ EMP: 49 EST: 2007
SQ FT: 10,000
SALES (est): 3.69MM Privately Held
Web: www.ampinc.com

SIC: 3674 Semiconductors and related devices

(P-6793)
ADTECH PHOTONICS INC
Also Called: Adtech Optics
18007 Cortney Ct, City Of Industry (91748-1203)
PHONE...............................626 956-1000
Mary Fong, CEO
EMP: 25 EST: 2012
SALES (est): 2.3MM Privately Held
Web: www.atoptics.com
SIC: 3674 Semiconductors and related devices

(P-6794)
ADVANCED SEMICONDUCTOR INC
Also Called: A S I
24955 Avenue Kearny, Valencia (91355-1252)
PHONE...............................818 982-1200
Fred Golob, CEO
▲ EMP: 58 EST: 1979
SQ FT: 9,000
SALES (est): 3.64MM Privately Held
Web: www.advancedsemiconductor.com
SIC: 3674 Integrated circuits, semiconductor networks, etc.

(P-6795)
ADVANTEST TEST SOLUTIONS INC
26211 Enterprise Way, Lake Forest (92630-8402)
PHONE...............................949 523-6900
Jonathan Sinskie, CEO
Keith Sinskie, CFO
EMP: 66 EST: 2018
SALES (est): 22.4MM Privately Held
Web: www.advantest.com
SIC: 3674 Semiconductors and related devices
HQ: Advantest America, Inc.
3061 Zanker Rd
San Jose CA 95134

(P-6796)
AEROFLEX INCORPORATED
15375 Barranca Pkwy Ste F106, Irvine (92618-2207)
PHONE...............................800 843-1553
Len Burrows, Brnch Mgr
EMP: 225
SALES (corp-wide): 2.67MM Privately Held
Web: www.caes.com
SIC: 3674 Semiconductors and related devices
HQ: Aeroflex Incorporated
2121 Crystal Dr Ste 800
Arlington VA 22202
516 694-6700

(P-6797)
AMERICAN ARIUM
Also Called: Arium
17791 Fitch, Irvine (92614-6019)
PHONE...............................949 623-7090
Larry Traylor, Pr
Diane Dirks, *
EMP: 40 EST: 1977
SQ FT: 32,330
SALES (est): 2.6MM Privately Held
Web: www.asset-intertech.com
SIC: 3674 3577 Microprocessors; Computer peripheral equipment, nec

(P-6798)
AMONIX INC
1709 Apollo Ct, Seal Beach (90740-5617)
PHONE..................562 344-4750
▲ **EMP:** 120
SIC: 3674 Solar cells

(P-6799)
APIC CORPORATION
5800 Uplander Way, Culver City
(90230-6608)
PHONE..................310 642-7975
James Chan, *VP*
Birendra Dutt, *
Koichi Sayano, *
Anguel Nikolov, *
EMP: 58 **EST:** 2001
SQ FT: 14,416
SALES (est): 6.2MM **Privately Held**
Web: www.apichip.com
SIC: 3674 Semiconductors and related
devices

(P-6800)
ARM INC
5375 Mira Sorrento Pl Ste 540, San Diego
(92121-3804)
PHONE..................858 453-1900
Todd Vierra, *Brnch Mgr*
EMP: 1110
SALES (corp-wide): 8.87B **Privately Held**
Web: www.arm.com
SIC: 3674 Integrated circuits, semiconductor
networks, etc.
HQ: Arm, Inc.
120 Rose Orchard Way
San Jose CA 95134

(P-6801)
ASC GROUP INC
12243 Branford St, Sun Valley
(91352-1010)
PHONE..................818 896-1101
Chuck Rogers, *Pr*
EMP: 253 **EST:** 1988
SQ FT: 80,000
SALES (est): 5MM
SALES (corp-wide): 1.71B **Privately Held**
Web: www.pmcglobalinc.com
SIC: 3674 Semiconductors and related
devices
HQ: Pmc, Inc.
12243 Branford St
Sun Valley CA 91352
818 896-1101

(P-6802)
ASI SEMICONDUCTOR INC
Also Called: A S I
24955 Avenue Kearny, Valencia
(91355-1252)
PHONE..................818 982-1200
Steve Golob, *Prin*
Mike Lincoln, *
Fred Golob, *
EMP: 25 **EST:** 2011
SALES (est): 3.78MM **Privately Held**
Web: www.advancedsemiconductor.com
SIC: 3674 Semiconductors and related
devices

(P-6803)
ATOMICA CORP
Also Called: IMT Analytical
75 Robin Hill Rd, Goleta (93117-3108)
PHONE..................805 681-2807
Eric Sigler, *CEO*
Jim Mcgibbon, *CFO*
Chris Gudeman, *
Dave Chrishna, *

EMP: 115 **EST:** 1987
SQ FT: 130,000
SALES (est): 42.81MM **Privately Held**
Web: www.atomica.com
SIC: 3674 Semiconductors and related
devices

(P-6804)
ATTOLLO ENGINEERING LLC
Also Called: Attollo Engineering
160 Camino Ruiz, Camarillo (93012-6700)
PHONE..................805 384-8046
Michael Macdougal, *Pr*
Michael Macdougal, *Owner*
EMP: 52 **EST:** 2012
SALES (est): 5.29MM **Privately Held**
Web: www.attolloengineering.com
SIC: 3674 Semiconductors and related
devices

(P-6805)
**AVID IDNTIFICATION SYSTEMS
INC (PA)**
Also Called: Avid
3185 Hamner Ave, Norco (92860-1937)
PHONE..................951 371-7505
Hannis L Stoddard, *CEO*
Hannis L Stoddard, *Pr*
Peter Troesch, *
▲ **EMP:** 100 **EST:** 1986
SQ FT: 30,000
SALES (est): 12.93MM **Privately Held**
Web: www.avidid.com
SIC: 3674 5999 Semiconductors and related
devices; Pets and pet supplies

(P-6806)
BAYWA RE EPC LLC
17901 Von Karman Ave Ste 1050, Irvine
(92614-5254)
PHONE..................949 398-3915
Baywa R E Solar, *Project LLC*
EMP: 32 **EST:** 2015
SALES (est): 1.05MM **Privately Held**
Web: us.baywa-re.com
SIC: 3674 Solar cells

(P-6807)
BEAM GLOBAL (PA)
5660 Eastgate Dr, San Diego (92121-2816)
PHONE..................858 799-4583
Desmond Wheatley, *Ch Bd*
Katherine Mcdermott, *CFO*
Mark Myers, *COO*
EMP: 103 **EST:** 2006
SQ FT: 53,000
SALES (est): 67.35MM **Publicly Held**
Web: www.beamforall.com
SIC: 3674 Solar cells

(P-6808)
BROADCOM CORPORATION
16340 W Bernardo Dr Bldg A, San Diego
(92127-1802)
PHONE..................858 385-8800
Bell Philip Andrew, *Brnch Mgr*
EMP: 142
SALES (corp-wide): 35.82B **Publicly Held**
Web: www.broadcom.com
SIC: 3674 Integrated circuits, semiconductor
networks, etc.
HQ: Broadcom Corporation
1320 Ridder Park Dr
San Jose CA 95131

(P-6809)
BROADCOM CORPORATION
15101 Alton Pkwy, Irvine (92618-2372)
PHONE..................949 926-5000
EMP: 224

SALES (corp-wide): 35.82B **Publicly Held**
Web: www.broadcom.com
SIC: 3674 Semiconductors and related
devices
HQ: Broadcom Corporation
1320 Ridder Park Dr
San Jose CA 95131

(P-6810)
BROADCOM CORPORATION
Also Called: Broadcom Limited Bldg 2
15191 Alton Pkwy, Irvine (92618-2300)
PHONE..................714 376-5029
EMP: 67
SALES (corp-wide): 35.82B **Publicly Held**
Web: www.broadcom.com
SIC: 3674 Semiconductors and related
devices
HQ: Broadcom Corporation
1320 Ridder Park Dr
San Jose CA 95131

(P-6811)
CAELUX CORPORATION
404 N Halstead St, Pasadena (91107-3124)
PHONE..................626 502-7033
Scott Graybeal, *CEO*
John Iannellli, *Pr*
Jeremy Ferrell, *CFO*
EMP: 27 **EST:** 2014
SALES (est): 7.6MM **Privately Held**
SIC: 3674 Semiconductors and related
devices

(P-6812)
**CLARIPHY COMMUNICATIONS
INC (DH)**
15485 Sand Canyon Ave, Irvine
(92618-3154)
PHONE..................949 861-3074
Nariman Yousefi, *Pr*
William J Ruehle, *
Norman L Swenson, *
EMP: 78 **EST:** 2004
SALES (est): 11.02MM
SALES (corp-wide): 5.51B **Publicly Held**
Web: www.marvell.com
SIC: 3674 Integrated circuits, semiconductor
networks, etc.
HQ: Inphi Corporation
110 Rio Robles
San Jose CA 95134

(P-6813)
CONEXANT HOLDINGS INC
4000 Macarthur Blvd, Newport Beach
(92660-2558)
PHONE..................415 983-2706
EMP: 600
SIC: 3674 5065 Semiconductors and related
devices; Semiconductor devices

(P-6814)
CONEXANT SYSTEMS LLC (HQ)
1901 Main St Ste 300, Irvine (92614-0512)
PHONE..................949 483-4600
Jan Johannessen, *CEO*
EMP: 23 **EST:** 2013
SQ FT: 140,000
SALES (est): 3.13MM
SALES (corp-wide): 959.4MM **Publicly
Held**
SIC: 3674 5065 Semiconductors and related
devices; Semiconductor devices
PA: Synaptics Incorporated
1109 Mckay Dr
408 904-1100

(P-6815)
**COOPER MICROELECTRONICS
INC**
Also Called: CMI
1671 Reynolds Ave, Irvine (92614-5709)
PHONE..................949 553-8352
Kenneth B Cooper Iii, *Pr*
Lily Cooper, *
▲ **EMP:** 37 **EST:** 1985
SQ FT: 10,000
SALES (est): 5.69MM **Privately Held**
Web: www.coopermicro.com
SIC: 3674 7371 Semiconductors and related
devices; Custom computer programming
services

(P-6816)
DATA DEVICE CORPORATION
13000 Gregg St Ste C, Poway
(92064-7151)
PHONE..................858 503-3300
Dan Veenstra, *Brnch Mgr*
EMP: 35
SALES (corp-wide): 7.94B **Publicly Held**
Web: www.ddc-web.com
SIC: 3674 Semiconductors and related
devices
HQ: Data Device Corporation
105 Wilbur Pl
Bohemia NY 11716
631 567-5600

(P-6817)
DAYLIGHT SOLUTIONS INC (DH)
Also Called: Drs Daylight Solutions
16465 Via Esprillo Ste 100, San Diego
(92127-1701)
PHONE..................858 432-7500
Timothy Day, *CEO*
Paul Larson, *Pr*
EMP: 100 **EST:** 2004
SALES (est): 40.72MM
SALES (corp-wide): 16.62B **Publicly Held**
Web: www.daylightsolutions.com
SIC: 3674 5084 3826 Molecular devices,
solid state; Instruments and control
equipment; Analytical instruments
HQ: Leonardo Drs, Inc.
2345 Crystal Dr Ste 1000
Arlington VA 22202
703 416-8000

(P-6818)
DISPLAY PRODUCTS INC
Also Called: Data Display Products
445 S Douglas St, El Segundo
(90245-4630)
PHONE..................310 640-0442
EMP: 48 **EST:** 1970
SALES (est): 5MM **Privately Held**
Web: www.vcclite.com
SIC: 3674 3679 Semiconductors and related
devices; Electronic circuits

(P-6819)
DPA LABS INC
Also Called: Dpa Components International
2251 Ward Ave, Simi Valley (93065-7556)
PHONE..................805 581-9200
Douglas Young, *Pr*
Philip Young, *VP*
EMP: 50 **EST:** 1979
SQ FT: 38,000
SALES (est): 12.15MM **Privately Held**
Web: www.dpaci.com
SIC: 3674 8734 Semiconductors and related
devices; Testing laboratories

(P-6820)
DRS NTWORK IMAGING SYSTEMS LLC
Also Called: Drs Network & Imaging Systems
10600 Valley View St, Cypress
(90630-4833)
PHONE....................714 220-3800
EMP: 100 **EST:** 2009
SALES (est): 23.98MM
SALES (corp-wide): 16.62B **Publicly Held**
Web: www.leonardodrs.com
SIC: 3674 8731 Infrared sensors, solid state;
Commercial physical research
HQ: Leonardo Drs, Inc.
2345 Crystal Dr Ste 1000
Arlington VA 22202
703 416-8000

(P-6821)
EMCORE CORPORATION (PA)
Also Called: Emcore
2015 Chestnut St, Alhambra (91803-1542)
PHONE....................626 293-3400
Jeffrey Rittichier, *CEO*
Stephen L Domenik, *
Tom Minichiello, *CFO*
Iain Black, *Sr VP*
▲ **EMP:** 188 **EST:** 1984
SQ FT: 50,000
SALES (est): 97.72MM
SALES (corp-wide): 97.72MM **Publicly Held**
Web: www.emcore.com
SIC: 3674 3559 Integrated circuits,
semiconductor networks, etc.;
Semiconductor manufacturing machinery

(P-6822)
EPSON ELECTRONICS AMERICA INC (DH)
3131 Katella Ave, Los Alamitos
(90720-2335)
PHONE....................408 922-0200
Koji Abe, *Pr*
Craig Hodowski, *Sec*
▲ **EMP:** 32 **EST:** 1997
SALES (est): 7.67MM **Privately Held**
Web: www.epson.com
SIC: 3674 5065 8731 Semiconductors and
related devices; Electronic parts and
equipment, nec; Commercial physical
research
HQ: U.S. Epson, Inc.
3131 Katella Ave
Los Alamitos CA 90720

(P-6823)
ESSEX ELECTRONICS INC
1130 Mark Ave, Carpinteria (93013-2918)
PHONE....................805 684-7601
Stewart Frioch, *Ch Bd*
Jesse Moore, *CEO*
Fred Zimmermann, *Pr*
Garrett Kaufman, *Pr*
Dean Benjamin, *Prin*
▲ **EMP:** 23 **EST:** 1991
SQ FT: 7,000
SALES (est): 8.35MM **Privately Held**
Web: www.keyless.com
SIC: 3674 Semiconductors and related
devices

(P-6824)
FORMER LUNA SUBSIDIARY INC (HQ)
PHONE....................805 987-0146
EMP: 55 **EST:** 1998
SALES (est): 23.61MM **Publicly Held**

SIC: 3674 Semiconductors and related
devices
PA: Luna Innovations Incorporated
301 1st St Sw Ste 200

(P-6825)
FULCRUM MICROSYSTEMS INC
26630 Agoura Rd, Calabasas (91302-1954)
PHONE....................818 871-8100
Robert R Nunn, *CEO*
Dale Bartos, *
Mike Zeile, *
Uri Cummings, *
EMP: 58 **EST:** 1999
SQ FT: 17,077
SALES (est): 5.6MM
SALES (corp-wide): 54.23B **Publicly Held**
Web: www.fulcrummicro.com
SIC: 3674 Semiconductors and related
devices
PA: Intel Corporation
2200 Mission College Blvd
408 765-8080

(P-6826)
HANWHA ENRGY USA HOLDINGS CORP (HQ)
Also Called: 174 Power Global
400 Spectrum Center Dr Ste 1400, Irvine
(92618-5021)
PHONE....................949 748-5996
Henry Yun, *Pr*
David Kim, *CFO*
EMP: 28 **EST:** 2013
SALES (est): 46.48MM **Privately Held**
Web: www.174powerglobal.com
SIC: 3674 1711 Solar cells; Solar energy
contractor
PA: Hanwha Corporation
86 Cheonggyecheon-Ro, Jung-Gu

(P-6827)
HANWHA Q CELLS USA INC
300 Spectrum Center Dr Ste 500, Irvine
(92618-4989)
PHONE....................706 671-3077
Byeong Young Choi, *CEO*
Hyunkwang Cho, *
EMP: 34 **EST:** 2018
SALES (est): 2.87MM **Privately Held**
Web: www.q-cells.de
SIC: 3674 Solar cells

(P-6828)
INDIE SEMICONDUCTOR INC (PA)
Also Called: INDIE
32 Journey Ste 100, Aliso Viejo
(92656-5329)
PHONE....................949 608-0854
Donald Mcclymont, *CEO*
David Aldrich, *Ch Bd*
Ichiro Aoki, *Pr*
Steven Machuga, *COO*
EMP: 26 **EST:** 2019
SQ FT: 18,000
SALES (est): 223.17MM
SALES (corp-wide): 223.17MM **Publicly Held**
Web: www.indiesemi.com
SIC: 3674 Semiconductors and related
devices

(P-6829)
INFINEON TECH AMERICAS CORP (HQ)
101 N Pacific Coast Hwy, El Segundo
(90245-4318)
PHONE....................310 726-8200

Oleg Khaykin, *CEO*
Ilan Daskal, *
▲ **EMP:** 900 **EST:** 1979
SALES (est): 303.11MM
SALES (corp-wide): 16.7B **Privately Held**
Web: www-blue.infineon.com
SIC: 3674 Integrated circuits, semiconductor
networks, etc.
PA: Infineon Technologies Ag
Am Campeon 1-15
892340

(P-6830)
INFINEON TECH AMERICAS CORP
Crydom Controls
233 Kansas St, El Segundo (90245-4316)
PHONE....................310 726-8000
Derek Lidow, *Mgr*
EMP: 47
SALES (corp-wide): 16.7B **Privately Held**
Web: www-blue.infineon.com
SIC: 3674 Semiconductors and related
devices
HQ: Infineon Technologies Americas Corp.
101 N Pacific Coast Hwy
El Segundo CA 90245
310 726-8200

(P-6831)
INFINEON TECH AMERICAS CORP
1521 E Grand Ave, El Segundo
(90245-4339)
P.O. Box 2788 (91729-2788)
PHONE....................310 252-7116
EMP: 123
SALES (corp-wide): 16.7B **Privately Held**
Web: www-blue.infineon.com
SIC: 3674 Semiconductors and related
devices
HQ: Infineon Technologies Americas Corp.
101 N Pacific Coast Hwy
El Segundo CA 90245
310 726-8200

(P-6832)
INNOPHASE INC
Also Called: Innophase
5880 Oberlin Dr Ste 600, San Diego
(92121-4762)
PHONE....................619 541-8280
Yang Xu, *CEO*
Thomas Lee, *
EMP: 100 **EST:** 2011
SALES (est): 9.66MM **Privately Held**
Web: www.innophaseinc.com
SIC: 3674 Semiconductors and related
devices

(P-6833)
INTEGRA TECHNOLOGIES INC
321 Coral Cir, El Segundo (90245-4620)
PHONE....................310 606-0855
Paul Aken, *Pr*
Jeff Burger, *
EMP: 50 **EST:** 1997
SQ FT: 15,000
SALES (est): 9.43MM **Privately Held**
Web: www.integratech.com
SIC: 3674 Modules, solid state

(P-6834)
INTERCONNECT SYSTEMS INTL LLC (DH)
Also Called: Interconnect Systems, Inc.
741 Flynn Rd, Camarillo (93012-8056)
PHONE....................805 482-2870
Mark Gilliam, *Pr*

William P Miller, *
Glen Griswold, *
Louis Buldain, *
Thomas Casey, *
▲ **EMP:** 90 **EST:** 1987
SQ FT: 48,000
SALES (est): 30.05MM
SALES (corp-wide): 64.37B **Privately Held**
Web: www.isipkg.com
SIC: 3674 Computer logic modules
HQ: Molex, Llc
2222 Wellington Ct
Lisle IL 60532
630 969-4550

(P-6835)
INVENLUX CORPORATION
168 Mason Way Ste B5, City Of Industry
(91746-2339)
PHONE....................626 277-4163
Chunhui Yan, *Pr*
EMP: 23 **EST:** 2008
SQ FT: 18,000
SALES (est): 519.39K **Privately Held**
SIC: 3674 Light emitting diodes

(P-6836)
IQ-ANALOG CORPORATION
12348 High Bluff Dr Ste 110, San Diego
(92130-3547)
PHONE....................858 200-0388
Michael S Kappes, *Pr*
Randy Wayland, *
EMP: 25 **EST:** 2005
SALES (est): 5.39MM **Privately Held**
Web: www.iqanalog.com
SIC: 3674 Semiconductors and related
devices

(P-6837)
IRVINE SENSORS CORPORATION
3000 Airway Ave Ste A1, Costa Mesa
(92626-6033)
PHONE....................714 444-8700
John C Carson, *Pr*
James Justice, *
Anthony Mastrangelo, *
EMP: 43 **EST:** 2013
SALES (est): 5.38MM **Privately Held**
Web: www.irvine-sensors.com
SIC: 3674 8731 Semiconductors and related
devices; Electronic research

(P-6838)
IXYS INTGRTED CRCITS DIV AV IN
145 Columbia, Aliso Viejo (92656-1413)
PHONE....................949 831-4622
Nathan Zommer, *Ch Bd*
Uzi Sasson, *
EMP: 621 **EST:** 1983
SQ FT: 28,000
SALES (est): 4.35MM
SALES (corp-wide): 2.36B **Publicly Held**
SIC: 3674 7389 Microcircuits, integrated
(semiconductor); Design services
HQ: Ixys, Llc
1590 Buckeye Dr
Milpitas CA 95035
408 457-9000

(P-6839)
IXYS LONG BEACH INC (DH)
2500 Mira Mar Ave, Long Beach
(90815-1758)
PHONE....................562 296-6584
Nathan Zommer, *CEO*
Arnold Agbayani, *
▲ **EMP:** 25 **EST:** 1980

SQ FT: 20,000
SALES (est): 11.49MM
SALES (corp-wide): 2.36B Publicly Held
Web: www.littelfuse.com
SIC: 3674 5065 Semiconductors and related devices; Electronic parts and equipment, nec
HQ: Ixys, Llc
1590 Buckeye Dr
Milpitas CA 95035
408 457-9000

(P-6840)
KULR TECHNOLOGY CORPORATION
4863 Shawline St Ste B, San Diego (92111-1435)
PHONE..................408 663-5247
Michael Mo, *CEO*
EMP: 64 EST: 2013
SALES (est): 10MM
SALES (corp-wide): 9.83MM Publicly Held
Web: www.kulrtechnology.com
SIC: 3674 3624 Semiconductors and related devices; Carbon and graphite products
PA: Kulr Technology Group, Inc.
4863 Shawline St Ste B
408 663-5247

(P-6841)
KYOCERA AMERICA INC
8611 Balboa Ave, San Diego (92123-1580)
PHONE..................858 576-2600
▲ EMP: 50
SIC: 3674 Integrated circuits, semiconductor networks, etc.

(P-6842)
KYOCERA INTERNATIONAL INC (HQ)
8611 Balboa Ave, San Diego (92123-1580)
PHONE..................858 576-2600
Robert Whisler, *Vice Chairman*
Nick Huntalas, *
William Edwards, *
George Woodworth, *
Franklin Kim, *
◆ EMP: 100 EST: 1969
SQ FT: 16,000
SALES (est): 113.45MM Privately Held
Web: global.kyocera.com
SIC: 3674 5023 5731 Semiconductors and related devices; Kitchen tools and utensils, nec; Radio, television, and electronic stores
PA: Kyocera Corporation
6, Takedatobadonocho, Fushimi-Ku

(P-6843)
LABARGE/STC INC
600 Anton Blvd, Costa Mesa (92626-7221)
PHONE..................281 207-1400
Anthony J Reardon, *Pr*
Samuel D Williams, *VP*
Weems Turner, *
James S Heiser, *Sec*
EMP: 42 EST: 1985
SALES (est): 1.27MM
SALES (corp-wide): 756.99MM Publicly Held
SIC: 3674 Hybrid integrated circuits
HQ: Ducommun Labarge Technologies, Inc.
689 Craig Rd Ste 200
Saint Louis MO 63141
314 997-0800

(P-6844)
LASER OPERATIONS LLC
Also Called: Qpc Laser
15632 Roxford St, Rancho Cascades (91342-1265)

PHONE..................818 986-0000
Morris Lichtenstein, *Managing Member*
Mikhail Leibov, *
Jeffrey Ungar, *
Elyahu Pendler, *Managing Member*
EMP: 27 EST: 2009
SQ FT: 40,320
SALES (est): 4.53MM Privately Held
Web: www.qpclasers.com
SIC: 3674 Semiconductors and related devices

(P-6845)
LEDTRONICS INC (PA)
23105 Kashiwa Ct, Torrance (90505-4026)
PHONE..................310 534-1505
Pervaiz Lodhie, *Pr*
Almas Lodhie, *
▲ EMP: 40 EST: 1983
SQ FT: 60,000
SALES (est): 20.66MM
SALES (corp-wide): 20.66MM Privately Held
Web: web.ledtronics.com
SIC: 3674 3825 3641 Light emitting diodes; Instruments to measure electricity; Electric lamps

(P-6846)
LOCKWOOD INDUSTRIES LLC (HQ)
Also Called: Fralock
28525 Industry Dr, Valencia (91355-5424)
PHONE..................661 702-6999
Marc Haugen, *CEO*
Bobbi Booher, *
EMP: 105 EST: 1966
SQ FT: 62,500
SALES (est): 49.22MM
SALES (corp-wide): 153.54MM Privately Held
Web: www.fralock.com
SIC: 3674 3842 3089 2891 Semiconductors and related devices; Prosthetic appliances; Plastics containers, except foam; Sealants
PA: Fralock Holdings Llc
28525 W Industry Dr
661 702-6999

(P-6847)
LUXTERA LLC
2320 Camino Vida Roble Ste 100, Carlsbad (92011-1562)
PHONE..................760 448-3520
EMP: 162 EST: 2001
SALES (est): 47.1MM
SALES (corp-wide): 53.8B Publicly Held
Web: www.cisco.com
SIC: 3674 Semiconductors and related devices
PA: Cisco Systems, Inc.
170 W Tasman Dr
408 526-4000

(P-6848)
MARVELL SEMICONDUCTOR INC
15485 Sand Canyon Ave, Irvine (92618-3154)
PHONE..................949 614-7700
Robert E Romney, *Prin*
EMP: 998
SALES (corp-wide): 5.51B Publicly Held
Web: www.marvell.com
SIC: 3674 Semiconductors and related devices
HQ: Marvell Semiconductor, Inc.
5488 Marvell Ln
Santa Clara CA 95054

(P-6849)
MAXLINEAR INC (PA)
5966 La Place Ct Ste 100, Carlsbad (92008-8830)
PHONE..................760 692-0711
Kishore Seendripu, *Ch Bd*
Steven G Litchfield, *CORP*
Connie Kwong, *CAO*
Michael J Lachance, *VP Opers*
▲ EMP: 45 EST: 2003
SQ FT: 68,000
SALES (est): 693.26MM
SALES (corp-wide): 693.26MM Publicly Held
Web: www.maxlinear.com
SIC: 3674 Semiconductors and related devices

(P-6850)
MICRO ANALOG INC
Also Called: Analog
1861 Puddingstone Dr, La Verne (91750-5825)
PHONE..................909 392-8277
Hung T Nguyen, *CEO*
Khanh Van Nguyen, *
▲ EMP: 160 EST: 1991
SQ FT: 27,000
SALES (est): 24.75MM Privately Held
Web: www.micro-analog.com
SIC: 3674 Semiconductors and related devices

(P-6851)
MICROSEMI COMMUNICATIONS INC (DH)
Also Called: Catawba County Schools
4721 Calle Carga, Camarillo (93012-8560)
PHONE..................805 388-3700
Christopher R Gardner, *Pr*
Martin S Mcdermut, *CFO*
Jacob Nielsen, *CIO*
EMP: 53 EST: 1987
SQ FT: 111,000
SALES (est): 33.76MM
SALES (corp-wide): 7.63B Publicly Held
Web: www.microsemi.com
SIC: 3674 Semiconductors and related devices
HQ: Microsemi Corp. -Rf Signal Processing
11861 Western Ave
Garden Grove CA 92841
949 380-6100

(P-6852)
MICROSEMI CORP - ANLOG MXED SG (DH)
Also Called: Linfinity Microelectronics
11861 Western Ave, Garden Grove (92841-2119)
PHONE..................714 898-8121
James Peterson, *CEO*
John Hohener, *CFO*
Paul Pickle, *COO*
Steve Litchfield, *CSO*
EMP: 78 EST: 1968
SALES (est): 16.54MM
SALES (corp-wide): 7.63B Publicly Held
Web: www.microsemi.com
SIC: 3674 Semiconductors and related devices
HQ: Microsemi Corp. -Rf Signal Processing
11861 Western Ave
Garden Grove CA 92841
949 380-6100

(P-6853)
MICROSEMI CORP -RF SIGNAL PROC (HQ)

Also Called: Microsemi
11861 Western Ave, Garden Grove (92841-2119)
PHONE..................949 380-6100
Steve Sanghi, *Ch*
Eric Bjornholt, *
Ganesh Moorthy, *
EMP: 50 EST: 1960
SALES (est): 1.45B
SALES (corp-wide): 7.63B Publicly Held
Web: www.microsemi.com
SIC: 3674 Integrated circuits, semiconductor networks, etc.
PA: Microchip Technology Inc
2355 W Chandler Blvd
480 792-7200

(P-6854)
MICROSEMI CORPORATION
Also Called: Microsemi Corp - Santa Ana
11861 Western Ave, Garden Grove (92841-2119)
PHONE..................714 898-7112
Lane Jorgensen, *Mgr*
EMP: 244
SQ FT: 93,000
SALES (corp-wide): 7.63B Publicly Held
Web: www.microsemi.com
SIC: 3674 Semiconductors and related devices
HQ: Microsemi Corp. -Rf Signal Processing
11861 Western Ave
Garden Grove CA 92841
949 380-6100

(P-6855)
MICROSS HOLDINGS INC
11150 Santa Monica Blvd Ste 750, Los Angeles (90025-0528)
PHONE..................215 997-3200
F Michael Pisch, *CFO*
EMP: 99 EST: 2010
SALES (est): 1.82MM Privately Held
SIC: 3674 Semiconductors and related devices

(P-6856)
MINDSPEED TECHNOLOGIES LLC (HQ)
Also Called: Macom
4000 Macarthur Blvd, Newport Beach (92660-2558)
PHONE..................949 579-3000
Raouf Y Halim, *CEO*
Stephen N Ananias, *
Gerald J Hamilton, *Senior Vice President Worldwide Sales*
Allison K Musetich, *Senior Vice President Human Resources*
Najabat H Bajwa, *
EMP: 54 EST: 2002
SQ FT: 97,000
SALES (est): 22.17MM Publicly Held
Web: www.macom.com
SIC: 3674 Semiconductors and related devices
PA: Macom Technology Solutions Holdings, Inc.
100 Chelmsford St

(P-6857)
MORSE MICRO INC
40 Waterworks Way, Irvine (92618-3107)
PHONE..................949 501-7080
Michael De Nil, *CEO*
EMP: 85 EST: 2019
SALES (est): 5.21MM Privately Held
Web: www.morsemicro.com
SIC: 3674 Integrated circuits, semiconductor networks, etc.

(P-6858)
MRV COMMUNICATIONS INC
Also Called: Mrv
20520 Nordhoff St, Chatsworth
(91311-6113)
PHONE..............................818 773-0900
▲ EMP: 268
SIC: 3674 Integrated circuits, semiconductor
networks, etc.

(P-6859)
NETLIST INC (PA)
Also Called: Netlist
111 Academy Ste 100, Irvine (92617-3046)
PHONE..............................949 435-0025
Chun K Hong, *Pr*
Gail Sasaki, *Corporate Secretary*
EMP: 96 EST: 2000
SQ FT: 14,809
SALES (est): 69.2MM
SALES (corp-wide): 69.2MM **Publicly
Held**
Web: www.netlist.com
SIC: 3674 Semiconductors and related
devices

(P-6860)
NEWPORT FAB LLC
Also Called: Jazz Semiconductor
4321 Jamboree Rd, Newport Beach
(92660-3007)
PHONE..............................949 435-8000
EMP: 99 EST: 2002
SALES (est): 3.84MM **Privately Held**
Web: www.towersemi.com
SIC: 3674 Wafers (semiconductor devices)
HQ: Tower Semiconductor Newport Beach,
Inc.
4321 Jamboree Rd
Newport Beach CA 92660
949 435-8000

(P-6861)
OPENLIGHT PHOTONICS INC
6868 Cortona Dr Ste C, Goleta
(93117-1363)
PHONE..............................805 880-2000
EMP: 33 EST: 2010
SALES (est): 2.46MM **Privately Held**
Web: www.openlightphotonics.com
SIC: 3674 Semiconductors and related
devices

(P-6862)
OPTO DIODE CORPORATION
1260 Calle Suerte, Camarillo (93012-8053)
PHONE..............................805 499-0335
EMP: 40
Web: www.optodiode.com
SIC: 3674 Diodes, solid state (germanium,
silicon, etc.)

(P-6863)
OSI OPTOELECTRONICS INC
Also Called: Advanced Photonix
1240 Avenida Acaso, Camarillo
(93012-8727)
PHONE..............................805 987-0146
Jean-pierre Maufras, *Genl Mgr*
EMP: 50
SALES (corp-wide): 1.54B **Publicly Held**
Web: www.osioptoelectronics.com
SIC: 3674 Semiconductors and related
devices
HQ: Osi Optoelectronics, Inc.
12525 Chadron Ave
Hawthorne CA 90250

(P-6864)
**OSI OPTOELECTRONICS INC
(HQ)**
Also Called: United Detector Technology
12525 Chadron Ave, Hawthorne
(90250-4807)
PHONE..............................310 978-0516
▲ EMP: 70 EST: 1967
SALES (est): 39.7MM
SALES (corp-wide): 1.54B **Publicly Held**
Web: www.osioptoelectronics.com
SIC: 3674 3827 3812 3672 Photoconductive
cells; Optical instruments and lenses;
Search and navigation equipment; Printed
circuit boards
PA: Osi Systems, Inc.
12525 Chadron Ave
310 978-0516

(P-6865)
OSI SYSTEMS INC (PA)
12525 Chadron Ave, Hawthorne
(90250-4807)
PHONE..............................310 978-0516
Deepak Chopra, *Ch Bd*
Alan Edrick, *Ex VP*
Ajay Mehra, *OF OSI SOLUTIONS Business*
Victor Sze, *Ex VP*
Glenn Grindstaff, *Chief Human Resources
Officer*
EMP: 624 EST: 1987
SQ FT: 88,000
SALES (est): 1.54B
SALES (corp-wide): 1.54B **Publicly Held**
Web: www.osi-systems.com
SIC: 3674 3845 Integrated circuits,
semiconductor networks, etc.;
Electromedical equipment

(P-6866)
**OUTSOURCE MANUFACTURING
INC**
2460 Ash St, Vista (92081-8424)
PHONE..............................760 795-1295
▲ EMP: 60
Web: www.outsourcemanufacturing.com
SIC: 3674 Solid state electronic devices, nec

(P-6867)
PIEZO-METRICS INC (PA)
Also Called: Micron Instruments
4584 Runway St, Simi Valley (93063-3449)
PHONE..............................805 522-4676
Herbert Chelner, *Pr*
Sharon Chelner, *
EMP: 25 EST: 1967
SQ FT: 9,000
SALES (est): 3.88MM
SALES (corp-wide): 3.88MM **Privately
Held**
Web: www.microninstruments.com
SIC: 3674 3829 Strain gages, solid state;
Pressure transducers

(P-6868)
PLANSEE USA LLC
Also Called: E/G Electro-Graph
1491 Poinsettia Ave Ste 138, Vista
(92081-8541)
PHONE..............................760 438-9090
EMP: 60
SALES (corp-wide): 242.12K **Privately
Held**
Web: www.plansee.com
SIC: 3674 Semiconductor diodes and
rectifiers
HQ: Plansee Usa Llc
115 Constitution Blvd
Franklin MA 02038
508 553-3800

(P-6869)
POLYFET RF DEVICES INC
1110 Avenida Acaso, Camarillo
(93012-8725)
PHONE..............................805 484-9582
S K Leong, *Pr*
EMP: 25 EST: 1984
SQ FT: 7,500
SALES (est): 5.61MM **Privately Held**
Web: www.polyfet.com
SIC: 3674 Transistors

(P-6870)
PRINTEC HT ELECTRONICS LLC
501 Sally Pl, Fullerton (92831-5014)
PHONE..............................714 484-7597
▲ EMP: 50 EST: 2011
SQ FT: 12,000
SALES (est): 7.58MM **Privately Held**
Web: www.printec-ht.com
SIC: 3674 3629 Modules, solid state;
Electronic generation equipment
PA: Printec H. T. Electronics Corp.
No. 38, Liyan St.

(P-6871)
PSEMI CORPORATION (DH)
9369 Carroll Park Dr, San Diego
(92121-2257)
PHONE..............................858 731-9400
Tatsuo Bizen, *CEO*
James S Cable, *
Takaki Muratajay C Biskupski, *
Takaki Murata, *HIGH PERFORMANCE
ANALOG HP S UNIT*
▲ EMP: 70 EST: 1990
SQ FT: 96,384
SALES (est): 90.4MM **Privately Held**
Web: www.psemi.com
SIC: 3674 Silicon wafers, chemically doped
HQ: Murata Electronics North America, Inc.
3330 Cumberland Blvd Se
Atlanta GA 30339
770 436-1300

(P-6872)
QLOGIC LLC (DH)
15485 Sand Canyon Ave, Irvine
(92618-3154)
PHONE..............................949 389-6000
Arthur Chadwick, *
M Hussain, *
▲ EMP: 138 EST: 1992
SQ FT: 161,000
SALES (est): 41.68MM
SALES (corp-wide): 5.51B **Publicly Held**
Web: www.marvell.com
SIC: 3674 Integrated circuits, semiconductor
networks, etc.
HQ: Cavium, Llc
5488 Marvell Ln
Santa Clara CA 95054

(P-6873)
**QUALCOMM DATACENTER
TECH INC (HQ)**
5775 Morehouse Dr, San Diego
(92121-1714)
PHONE..............................858 567-1121
Dileep Bhandarkar, *Pr*
Anand Chandrasekher, *VP*
EMP: 41 EST: 2016
SALES (est): 6.7MM
SALES (corp-wide): 38.96B **Publicly Held**
SIC: 3674 Integrated circuits, semiconductor
networks, etc.
PA: Qualcomm Incorporated
5775 Morehouse Dr
858 587-1121

(P-6874)
QUALCOMM INCORPORATED
Also Called: Qualcomm
2016 Palomar Airport Rd Ste 100, Carlsbad
(92011-4400)
PHONE..............................858 651-8481
David Lieber, *Prin*
EMP: 27
SALES (corp-wide): 38.96B **Publicly Held**
Web: www.qualcomm.com
SIC: 3674 Integrated circuits, semiconductor
networks, etc.
PA: Qualcomm Incorporated
5775 Morehouse Dr
858 587-1121

(P-6875)
QUALCOMM INCORPORATED
Also Called: Qualcomm
5751 Pacific Center Blvd, San Diego
(92121-4252)
PHONE..............................858 909-0316
Margaret L Johnson, *Brnch Mgr*
EMP: 42
SALES (corp-wide): 38.96B **Publicly Held**
Web: www.qualcomm.com
SIC: 3674 Integrated circuits, semiconductor
networks, etc.
PA: Qualcomm Incorporated
5775 Morehouse Dr
858 587-1121

(P-6876)
QUALCOMM INCORPORATED
Also Called: Qualcomm
10555 Sorrento Valley Rd, San Diego
(92121-1608)
PHONE..............................858 587-1121
Jim Callaghen, *Brnch Mgr*
EMP: 100
SALES (corp-wide): 38.96B **Publicly Held**
Web: www.qualcomm.com
SIC: 3674 Integrated circuits, semiconductor
networks, etc.
PA: Qualcomm Incorporated
5775 Morehouse Dr
858 587-1121

(P-6877)
QUALCOMM INCORPORATED
Also Called: Qualcomm
5525 Morehouse Dr, San Diego
(92121-1710)
PHONE..............................858 587-1121
Derek May, *Sr VP*
EMP: 55
SALES (corp-wide): 38.96B **Publicly Held**
Web: www.qualcomm.com
SIC: 3674 Integrated circuits, semiconductor
networks, etc.
PA: Qualcomm Incorporated
5775 Morehouse Dr
858 587-1121

(P-6878)
QUALCOMM INCORPORATED
Also Called: Qualcomm
9393 Waples St Ste 150, San Diego
(92121-3931)
PHONE..............................858 587-1121
EMP: 106
SALES (corp-wide): 38.96B **Publicly Held**
Web: www.qualcomm.com
SIC: 3674 7372 Integrated circuits,
semiconductor networks, etc.; Prepackaged
software
PA: Qualcomm Incorporated
5775 Morehouse Dr
858 587-1121

(P-6879)
QUALCOMM TECHNOLOGIES INC (HQ)
5775 Morehouse Dr, San Diego
(92121-1714)
P.O. Box 919042 (92191-9042)
PHONE..............................858 587-1121
Cristiano Amon, *CEO*
Kevin Frizzell, *CFO*
Jim Cathey, *CCO*
▲ **EMP: 232 EST:** 2011
SALES (est): 1.88B
SALES (corp-wide): 38.96B **Publicly Held**
Web: www.qualcomm.com
SIC: 3674 7372 6794 Integrated circuits, semiconductor networks, etc.; Business oriented computer software; Patent buying, licensing, leasing
PA: Qualcomm Incorporated
5775 Morehouse Dr
858 587-1121

(P-6880)
QUALCOMM TECHNOLOGIES INC
5745 Pacific Center Blvd, San Diego
(92121-4203)
PHONE..............................858 587-1121
EMP: 27
SALES (corp-wide): 38.96B **Publicly Held**
Web: www.qualcomm.com
SIC: 3674 Integrated circuits, semiconductor networks, etc.
HQ: Qualcomm Technologies, Inc.
5775 Morehouse Dr
San Diego CA 92121
858 587-1121

(P-6881)
QUALCOMM TECHNOLOGIES INC
Also Called: BP
10350 Sorrento Valley Rd, San Diego
(92121-1642)
PHONE..............................858 658-3040
EMP: 24
SALES (corp-wide): 38.96B **Publicly Held**
Web: www.qualcomm.com
SIC: 3674 Integrated circuits, semiconductor networks, etc.
HQ: Qualcomm Technologies, Inc.
5775 Morehouse Dr
San Diego CA 92121
858 587-1121

(P-6882)
QUARTICS INC
15241 Laguna Canyon Rd Ste 200, Irvine
(92618-3146)
P.O. Box 54648 (92619-4648)
PHONE..............................949 679-2672
Sherjil Ahmed, *Pr*
Adeel Ahmed, *
▲ **EMP: 31 EST:** 2005
SALES (est): 1.92MM **Privately Held**
Web: www.quartics.com
SIC: 3674 Semiconductors and related devices

(P-6883)
REVASUM INC
825 Buckley Rd, San Luis Obispo
(93401-8192)
PHONE..............................805 541-6424
Bill Kalenian, *Interim Chief Executive Officer*
Eric Jacobson, *OK Vice President*
Sarah Okada, *
Belinda Reyna, *
Dennis Riccio, *

EMP: 106 EST: 2016
SALES (est): 18.19MM **Privately Held**
Web: www.revasum.com
SIC: 3674 Semiconductors and related devices

(P-6884)
RF DIGITAL CORPORATION
1601 Pacific Coast Hwy Ste 290, Hermosa Beach (90254-3283)
PHONE..............................949 610-0008
Armen Kazanchian, *Pr*
Rod Landers, *
EMP: 103 EST: 1999
SQ FT: 5,000
SALES (est): 2.24MM
SALES (corp-wide): 3.9B **Privately Held**
SIC: 3674 Modules, solid state
HQ: Heptagon Usa, Inc.
465 N Whisman Rd Ste 200
Mountain View CA 94043
650 336-7990

(P-6885)
ROCKLEY PHOTONICS INC (HQ)
17252 Armstrong Ave Ste E, Irvine
(92614-5737)
PHONE..............................626 304-9960
Andrew George Rickman, *CEO*
EMP: 192 EST: 2013
SALES (est): 68.55MM
SALES (corp-wide): 30K **Privately Held**
Web: www.rockleyphotonics.com
SIC: 3674 Semiconductors and related devices
PA: Rockley Photonics Limited
57 Woodstock Road,Clarendon
Business Centre Belsyre Court
186 529-2017

(P-6886)
SANTIER INC
10103 Carroll Canyon Rd, San Diego
(92131-1109)
PHONE..............................858 271-1993
Kevin Cotner, *CEO*
Warren Bartholomew, *
▼ **EMP: 64 EST:** 1991
SQ FT: 23,000
SALES (est): 9.06MM
SALES (corp-wide): 19.17MM **Privately Held**
Web: www.santier.com
SIC: 3674 Semiconductors and related devices
HQ: Egide (Usa), Llc
4 Washington St
Cambridge MD 21613
410 901-6100

(P-6887)
SEMICOA CORPORATION
333 Mccormick Ave, Costa Mesa
(92626-3479)
PHONE..............................714 979-1900
Thomas E Epley, *CEO*
Ramesh Ramchandani, *
Gary B Joyce, *Interim Chief Financial Officer*
Perry Denning, *
▲ **EMP: 60 EST:** 2009
SALES (est): 8.69MM **Privately Held**
Web: www.semicoa.com
SIC: 3674 Semiconductors and related devices

(P-6888)
SEMICONDUCTOR PROCESS EQP LLC
Also Called: Spec

27963 Franklin Pkwy, Valencia
(91355-4110)
PHONE..............................661 257-0934
Arnold Gustin, *CEO*
Robin Douglas, *
Kevin Mcgillivray, *VP*
◆ **EMP: 29 EST:** 1986
SQ FT: 139,000
SALES (est): 9.64MM
SALES (corp-wide): 45.63MM **Privately Held**
Web: www.team-spec.com
SIC: 3674 Semiconductors and related devices
PA: Yield Engineering Systems, Inc.
3178 Laurelview Ct
510 954-6889

(P-6889)
SEMTECH CORPORATION (PA)
Also Called: Semtech
200 Flynn Rd, Camarillo (93012-8790)
PHONE..............................805 498-2111
Hong Q Hou, *Pr*
Rockell N Hankin, *
Mark Lin, *Ex VP*
Asaf Silberstein, *Ex VP*
J Michael Wilson, *Co-Vice President*
▲ **EMP: 180 EST:** 1960
SQ FT: 88,000
SALES (est): 868.76MM
SALES (corp-wide): 868.76MM **Publicly Held**
Web: www.semtech.com
SIC: 3674 Semiconductors and related devices

(P-6890)
SENSEMETRICS INC
750 B St Ste 1630, San Diego
(92101-8131)
P.O. Box 16727 (80216-0727)
PHONE..............................619 738-8300
Cory Stewart Baldwin, *CEO*
EMP: 29 EST: 2014
SALES (est): 3.2MM
SALES (corp-wide): 965.05MM **Publicly Held**
Web: www.infrastructureiot.com
SIC: 3674 Infrared sensors, solid state
PA: Bentley Systems, Incorporated
685 Stockton Dr
610 458-5000

(P-6891)
SILC TECHNOLOGIES INC
181 W Huntington Dr Ste 200, Monrovia
(91016-3494)
PHONE..............................626 375-1231
Bradley Luff, *Prin*
EMP: 52 EST: 2018
SALES (est): 6.67MM **Privately Held**
Web: www.silc.com
SIC: 3674 Semiconductors and related devices

(P-6892)
SIMPLE SOLAR INDUSTRIES LLC
661 Brea Canyon Rd Ste 1, Walnut
(91789-3044)
PHONE..............................844 907-0705
Moe Falah, *Managing Member*
EMP: 50 EST: 2022
SALES (est): 1.27MM **Privately Held**
SIC: 3674 Semiconductors and related devices

(P-6893)
SKYWORKS SOLUTIONS INC
2427 W Hillcrest Dr, Newbury Park
(91320-2202)
PHONE..............................805 480-4400
Michael Gooch, *Mgr*
EMP: 51
SALES (corp-wide): 4.18B **Publicly Held**
Web: www.skyworksinc.com
SIC: 3674 Semiconductors and related devices
PA: Skyworks Solutions, Inc.
5260 California Ave
949 231-3000

(P-6894)
SKYWORKS SOLUTIONS INC
730 Lawrence Dr, Newbury Park
(91320-2207)
PHONE..............................805 480-4227
EMP: 42
SALES (corp-wide): 4.18B **Publicly Held**
Web: www.skyworksinc.com
SIC: 3674 Semiconductors and related devices
PA: Skyworks Solutions, Inc.
5260 California Ave
949 231-3000

(P-6895)
SKYWORKS SOLUTIONS INC (PA)
Also Called: Skyworks
5260 California Ave, Irvine (92617-3228)
PHONE..............................949 231-3000
Liam K Griffin, *Pr*
Robert J Terry, *Sr VP*
Kris Sennesael, *Chief Financial Officer USA*
Reza Kasnavi, *Sr VP*
Carlos S Bori, *Sr VP*
▲ **EMP: 509 EST:** 1962
SQ FT: 218,000
SALES (est): 4.18B
SALES (corp-wide): 4.18B **Publicly Held**
Web: www.skyworksinc.com
SIC: 3674 Integrated circuits, semiconductor networks, etc.

(P-6896)
SOLID STATE DEVICES INC
Also Called: Ssdi
14701 Firestone Blvd, La Mirada
(90638-5918)
PHONE..............................562 404-4474
Arnold N Applebaum, *Pr*
David Franz, *
▲ **EMP: 110 EST:** 1967
SQ FT: 32,000
SALES (est): 20.29MM **Privately Held**
Web: www.ssdi-power.com
SIC: 3674 Diodes, solid state (germanium, silicon, etc.)

(P-6897)
SOURCE PHOTONICS USA INC (PA)
8521 Fallbrook Ave Ste 200, West Hills
(91304-3239)
PHONE..............................818 773-9044
Doug Wright, *CEO*
EMP: 249 EST: 1999
SALES (est): 3.67MM **Privately Held**
Web: www.sourcephotonics.com
SIC: 3674 Semiconductors and related devices

(P-6898)
SST TECHNOLOGIES
Also Called: Sst Vacuum Reflow Systems

▲ = Import ▼ = Export
◆ = Import/Export

6305 El Camino Real, Carlsbad
(92009-1606)
PHONE..................562 803-3361
Anthony Wilson, Pr
Ralph Burroughs, *
◆ EMP: 30 EST: 1969
SALES (est): 4.63MM Privately Held
Web: www.palomartechnologies.com
SIC: 3674 Semiconductors and related
  devices
PA: Palomar Technologies, Inc.
  6305 El Camino Real

(P-6899)
STELLAR MICROELECTRONICS INC
9340 Owensmouth Ave, Chatsworth
(91311-6915)
PHONE..................661 775-3500
Sudesh Arora, Pr
EMP: 239 EST: 1974
SQ FT: 140,000
SALES (est): 17.96MM
SALES (corp-wide): 1.43B Privately Held
Web: www.neotech.com
SIC: 3674 Semiconductors and related
  devices
PA: Natel Engineering Company, Llc
  9340 Owensmouth Ave
  818 495-8617

(P-6900)
STRATEDGE CORPORATION
Also Called: Strat Edge
9424 Abraham Way, Santee (92071-5640)
PHONE..................866 424-4962
Tim Going, Pr
Josie Santos, *
EMP: 40 EST: 1985
SALES (est): 4.65MM Privately Held
Web: www.stratedge.com
SIC: 3674 Semiconductors and related
  devices

(P-6901)
SUBSTANCE ABUSE PROGRAM
1370 S State St Ste A, Hemet (92543)
PHONE..................951 791-3350
Mark Thuve, Mgr
EMP: 30 EST: 2010
SALES (est): 651.45K Privately Held
SIC: 3674 Semiconductors and related
  devices

(P-6902)
SUNCORE INC
15 Hubble Ste 200, Irvine (92618-4268)
PHONE..................949 450-0054
Steven Brimmer, Pr
Donald A Nevins, *
Richard Sanell, *
Arthur Kozak, *
▲ EMP: 31 EST: 2004
SQ FT: 5,000
SALES (est): 1.05MM Privately Held
Web: www.suncoresolar.com
SIC: 3674 5063 5065 Solar cells; Batteries;
  Electronic parts and equipment, nec

(P-6903)
TALMO & CHINN INC
9537 Telstar Ave Ste 131, El Monte
(91731-2912)
PHONE..................626 443-1741
Bruce Talmo, Pr
Martin Chinn, *
EMP: 35 EST: 1972
SQ FT: 9,000
SALES (est): 3.06MM Privately Held

SIC: 3674 Semiconductors and related
devices

(P-6904)
TERIDIAN SEMICONDUCTOR CORP (DH)
6440 Oak Cyn Ste 100, Irvine (92618-5208)
PHONE..................714 508-8800
Mark Casper, CEO
Pete Todd, Worldwide Sales Vice President*
John Silk, *
David Gruetter, *
EMP: 90 EST: 1996
SALES (est): 2.08MM
SALES (corp-wide): 9.43B Publicly Held
Web: www.teridian.com
SIC: 3674 Semiconductors and related
  devices
HQ: Teridian Semiconductor Holdings Corp.
  6440 Oak Cyn Ste 100
  Irvine CA 92618

(P-6905)
TOWER SEMICDTR NEWPORT BCH INC (DH)
Also Called: Towerjazz
4321 Jamboree Rd, Newport Beach
(92660-3007)
PHONE..................949 435-8000
Russell Ellwanger, CEO
Itzhak Edrei, *
Rafi Mor, *
Oren Shirazi, *
▲ EMP: 700 EST: 2002
SQ FT: 300,000
SALES (est): 77.27MM Privately Held
Web: www.towersemi.com
SIC: 3674 Wafers (semiconductor devices)
HQ: Tower Us Holdings Inc.
  4321 Jamboree Rd
  Newport Beach CA 92660

(P-6906)
TRANSPHORM INC (DH)
75 Castilian Dr Ste 200, Goleta
(93117-5580)
PHONE..................805 456-1300
Primit Parikh, *
EMP: 102 EST: 2017
SQ FT: 27,800
SALES (est): 16.51MM Privately Held
Web: www.transphormusa.com
SIC: 3674 Microcircuits, integrated
  (semiconductor)
HQ: Renesas Electronics America Inc.
  6024 Silver Creek Vly Rd
  San Jose CA 95138
  408 284 8200

(P-6907)
TRIDENT SPACE & DEFENSE LLC
Also Called: TCS Space & Component Tech
19951 Mariner Ave, Torrance (90503-1672)
PHONE..................310 214-5500
EMP: 47
Web: www.tridentsd.com
SIC: 3674 3812 8711 Semiconductors and
  related devices; Search and navigation
  equipment; Electrical or electronic
  engineering

(P-6908)
UNIREX CORP
Also Called: Unirex Technologies
2288 E 27th St, Vernon (90058-1131)
PHONE..................323 589-4000
Bijan Neman, Pr
Behzad Neman, *

▲ EMP: 25 EST: 1985
SQ FT: 33,000
SALES (est): 3.46MM Privately Held
Web: www.unirex.com
SIC: 3674 3572 Magnetic bubble memory
  device; Computer storage devices

(P-6909)
US SENSOR CORP
1832 W Collins Ave, Orange (92867-5425)
PHONE..................714 639-1000
Roger W Dankert, CEO
EMP: 100 EST: 1989
SQ FT: 30,000
SALES (est): 10.78MM
SALES (corp-wide): 2.36B Publicly Held
Web: www.littelfuse.com
SIC: 3674 3676 Semiconductors and related
  devices; Thermistors, except temperature
  sensors
PA: Littelfuse, Inc.
  6133 N River Rd Ste 500
  773 628-1000

(P-6910)
VIRTIUM TECHNOLOGY INC
Also Called: Virtium
30052 Tomas, Rcho Sta Marg
(92688-2127)
PHONE..................949 888-2444
▲ EMP: 35
SIC: 3674 Semiconductors and related
  devices

(P-6911)
VISHAY THIN FILM LLC
Also Called: Vishay Spectoral Electronics
4051 Greystone Dr, Ontario (91761-3100)
PHONE..................909 923-3313
EMP: 23 EST: 2006
SALES (est): 461.2K Privately Held
SIC: 3674 Thin film circuits

(P-6912)
VITESSE MANUFACTURING & DEV
Also Called: Vitesse Semiconductor
11861 Western Ave, Garden Grove
(92841-2119)
PHONE..................805 388-3700
Chris Gardner, Pr
EMP: 200 EST: 1984
SALES (est): 15.87MM
SALES (corp-wide): 7.63B Publicly Held
Web: www.microsemi.com
SIC: 3674 Microcircuits, integrated
  (semiconductor)
HQ: Microsemi Communications, Inc.
  4721 Calle Carga
  Camarillo CA 93012
  805 388-3700

(P-6913)
W G HOLT INC
Also Called: Holt Integrated Circuits
101 Columbia, Aliso Viejo (92656-1455)
PHONE..................949 859-8800
David Mead, CEO
EMP: 65 EST: 1976
SALES (est): 8.85MM Privately Held
Web: www.holtic.com
SIC: 3674 Integrated circuits, semiconductor
  networks, etc.

(P-6914)
WELDEX CORPORATION
6751 Katella Ave, Cypress (90630-5105)
PHONE..................714 761-2100
William Jung, CEO
▲ EMP: 300 EST: 1992

SQ FT: 15,000
SALES (est): 8.4MM Privately Held
Web: cms.weldex.com
SIC: 3674 3663 Light emitting diodes;
  Television closed circuit equipment

(P-6915)
WORLDWIDE ENERGY AND MFG USA (PA)
Also Called: Worldwide
1800 S Myrtle Ave, Monrovia (91016-4833)
PHONE..................650 692-7788
John Ballard, Ch Bd
Tiffany Margaret Shum, Dir
▲ EMP: 55 EST: 2000
SALES (est): 4.93MM
SALES (corp-wide): 4.93MM Privately
Held
Web: www.wwmusa.com
SIC: 3674 Semiconductors and related
  devices

(P-6916)
XEL USA INC
Also Called: XEL Group
25231 Paseo De Alicia, Laguna Hills
(92653-4645)
PHONE..................949 425-8686
Paul Kuszka, CEO
EMP: 25 EST: 2008
SALES (est): 836.87K Privately Held
Web: www.xelgroup.com
SIC: 3674 Magnetic bubble memory device

3675 Electronic Capacitors

(P-6917)
GENERAL ATOMICS ELECTRONIC SYSTEMS INC
4949 Greencraig Ln, San Diego
(92123-1675)
P.O. Box 85608 (92186-5608)
PHONE..................858 522-8495
◆ EMP: 300
SIC: 3675 Electronic capacitors

(P-6918)
INCA ONE CORPORATION
1632 1/2 W 134th St, Gardena
(90249-2014)
PHONE..................310 808-0001
Adriana Roberts, Pr
Tupac Roberts, *
▲ EMP: 35 EST: 1971
SALES (est): 1.95MM Privately Held
Web: www.inca-tvlifts.com
SIC: 3675 Electronic capacitors

(P-6919)
JOHANSON TECHNOLOGY INC
4001 Calle Tecate, Camarillo (93012-5087)
PHONE..................805 575-0124
John Petrinec, CEO
▲ EMP: 130 EST: 1991
SQ FT: 30,000
SALES (est): 23.75MM Privately Held
Web: www.johansontechnology.com
SIC: 3675 5065 3674 Electronic capacitors;
  Electronic parts and equipment, nec;
  Semiconductors and related devices
PA: Johanson Ventures, Inc.
  4001 Calle Tecate

(P-6920)
NEWMAR POWER LLC
1580 Sunflower Ave, Costa Mesa
(92626-1511)
PHONE..................800 854-3906

Wolfgang Hombrecher, *Managing Member*
EMP: 250 **EST:** 1979
SALES (est): 26.52MM
SALES (corp-wide): 68.25MM **Privately Held**
Web: www.poweringthenetwork.com
SIC: 3675 3678 3679 Electronic capacitors; Electronic connectors; Electronic switches
PA: Mission Critical Electronics Llc
1580 Sunflower Ave
714 751-0488

3676 Electronic Resistors

(P-6921)
RIEDON INC (PA)
2072 Midwick Dr, Altadena (91001-2825)
▲ **EMP:** 150 **EST:** 1960
SALES (est): 18.61MM **Privately Held**
Web: www.riedon.com
SIC: 3676 Electronic resistors

3677 Electronic Coils And Transformers

(P-6922)
A M I/COAST MAGNETICS INC
Also Called: Coast Magnetics
5333 W Washington Blvd, Los Angeles (90016-1191)
PHONE...............................323 936-6188
Satya Dosaj, *CEO*
Dev Dosaj, *
Phillis Dosaj, *Stockholder**
EMP: 49 **EST:** 1965
SQ FT: 25,000
SALES (est): 4.97MM **Privately Held**
Web: www.coastmagnetics.com
SIC: 3677 3549 Electronic transformers; Coil winding machines for springs

(P-6923)
ALLIED COMPONENTS INTL
2372 Morse Ave, Irvine (92614-6234)
PHONE...............................949 356-1780
Anuj Jain, *CEO*
Rakesh Gupta, *
▲ **EMP:** 25 **EST:** 1992
SALES (est): 4.52MM **Privately Held**
Web: www.alliedcomponents.com
SIC: 3677 Electronic coils and transformers

(P-6924)
ASTRON CORPORATION
9 Autry, Irvine (92618-2768)
PHONE...............................949 458-7277
Loren Pochirowski, *Pr*
William Pochirowski, *
▲ **EMP:** 40 **EST:** 1976
SQ FT: 18,000
SALES (est): 2.19MM **Privately Held**
Web: www.astroncorp.com
SIC: 3677 3679 Transformers power supply, electronic type; Electronic circuits

(P-6925)
BECKER SPECIALTY CORPORATION
15310 Arrow Blvd, Fontana (92335-3249)
PHONE...............................909 356-1095
Jack Mcgrew, *Brnch Mgr*
EMP: 99
SALES (corp-wide): 856.87MM **Privately Held**
SIC: 3677 Electronic coils and transformers
HQ: Becker Specialty Corporation
755 Il Route 83 Ste 223
Bensenville IL 60106

(P-6926)
BOURNS INC (PA)
Also Called: Bourns
1200 Columbia Ave, Riverside (92507-2129)
PHONE...............................951 781-5500
Gordon Bourns, *CEO*
Al Yost, *
James Heiken, *
Gregg Gibbons, *
◆ **EMP:** 171 **EST:** 1952
SQ FT: 205,000
SALES (est): 459.73MM
SALES (corp-wide): 459.73MM **Privately Held**
Web: www.bourns.com
SIC: 3677 3676 3661 3639 Electronic transformers; Electronic resistors; Telephone and telegraph apparatus; Major kitchen appliances, except refrigerators and stoves

(P-6927)
CORONA MAGNETICS INC
Also Called: C M I
201 Corporate Terrace St, Corona (92879-6000)
P.O. Box 1355 (92878-1355)
PHONE...............................951 735-7558
Jay Paasch, *CEO*
Heike Paasch, *
Cory Vila Managing, *Prin*
EMP: 120 **EST:** 1968
SQ FT: 17,000
SALES (est): 4.63MM **Privately Held**
Web: www.corona-magnetics.com
SIC: 3677 3679 Transformers power supply, electronic type; Electronic circuits

(P-6928)
DSPM INC
Also Called: Digital Signal Power Mfg
439 S Stoddard Ave, San Bernardino (92401-2025)
PHONE...............................714 970-2304
Milton Hanson, *Pr*
▲ **EMP:** 30 **EST:** 2003
SQ FT: 30,000
SALES (est): 7.21MM **Privately Held**
Web: www.dspmanufacturing.com
SIC: 3677 Transformers power supply, electronic type

(P-6929)
FILTER CONCEPTS INCORPORATED
22895 Eastpark Dr, Yorba Linda (92887-4653)
PHONE...............................714 545-7003
EMP: 38 **EST:** 1980
SALES (est): 1.98MM **Privately Held**
Web: www.filterconcepts.com
SIC: 3677 Filtration devices, electronic
PA: Astrodyne Corporation
36 Newburgh Rd

(P-6930)
MAGTECH & POWER CONVERSION INC
Also Called: Speciality Labs
1146 E Ash Ave, Fullerton (92831-5018)
PHONE...............................714 451-0106
Viet Pho, *Pr*
Linh Pho, *
EMP: 40 **EST:** 1981
SQ FT: 9,000
SALES (est): 4.99MM **Privately Held**
Web: www.magtechpower.com
SIC: 3677 Electronic transformers

(P-6931)
MEISSNER CORPORATION
1001 Flynn Rd, Camarillo (93012-8706)
PHONE...............................805 388-9911
Christopher A Meissner, *CEO*
EMP: 30 **EST:** 2018
SALES (est): 3.14MM **Privately Held**
SIC: 3677 Filtration devices, electronic

(P-6932)
MIL-SPEC MAGNETICS INC
169 Pacific St, Pomona (91768-3215)
PHONE...............................909 598-8116
Rohan Gunewardena, *Pr*
Shelton Gunewardena, *
Tony Gunewardena, *
Andrew Gunewardena, *
Athula Meepe, *
EMP: 78 **EST:** 1990
SQ FT: 6,000
SALES (est): 12.36MM **Privately Held**
Web: www.milspecmag.com
SIC: 3677 3675 Electronic transformers; Electronic capacitors

(P-6933)
PARKER-HANNIFIN CORPORATION
Also Called: Water Purification
19610 S Rancho Way, Rancho Dominguez (90220-6039)
PHONE...............................310 608-5600
Jaime Garcia, *Prin*
EMP: 150
SALES (corp-wide): 19.93B **Publicly Held**
Web: www.parker.com
SIC: 3677 Filtration devices, electronic
PA: Parker-Hannifin Corporation
6035 Parkland Blvd
216 896-3000

(P-6934)
PAYNE MAGNETICS CORPORATION
854 W Front St, Covina (91722-3614)
PHONE...............................626 332-6207
George Payne, *Ch*
Jon S Payne, *
▲ **EMP:** 100 **EST:** 1982
SQ FT: 6,600
SALES (est): 2.12MM **Privately Held**
Web: www.payne-magnetics.com
SIC: 3677 3699 Electronic transformers; Electrical equipment and supplies, nec

(P-6935)
PREMIER MAGNETICS INC
20381 Barents Sea Cir, Lake Forest (92630-8807)
PHONE...............................949 452-0511
James Earley, *Pr*
▲ **EMP:** 30 **EST:** 1991
SALES (est): 4.99MM **Privately Held**
Web: www.premiermag.com
SIC: 3677 3612 Electronic coils and transformers; Specialty transformers

(P-6936)
RAYCO ELECTRONIC MFG INC
1220 W 130th St, Gardena (90247-1502)
PHONE...............................310 329-2660
Mahendra P Patel, *CEO*
Steve Mardani, *
Mayan Patel, *
EMP: 50 **EST:** 1941
SQ FT: 20,000
SALES (est): 4.81MM **Privately Held**
Web: www.raycoelectronics.com

SIC: 3677 3612 3621 Electronic transformers ; Transformers, except electric; Motors and generators

(P-6937)
ROBERT M HADLEY COMPANY INC
4054 Transport St Ste B, Ventura (93003-8325)
PHONE...............................805 658-7286
E Christopher Waian, *CEO*
Jim Hadley, *
Mary Hadley Waian, *
EMP: 80 **EST:** 1929
SQ FT: 28,000
SALES (est): 4.14MM **Privately Held**
Web: www.rmhco.com
SIC: 3677 Transformers power supply, electronic type

(P-6938)
SI MANUFACTURING INC
Also Called: Standard Industries
1440 S Allec St, Anaheim (92805-6305)
PHONE...............................714 956-7110
James R Reed, *Pr*
Ata Shafizadeh, *
▲ **EMP:** 50 **EST:** 2000
SALES (est): 9.2MM **Privately Held**
Web: www.simfg.com
SIC: 3677 3679 8711 3613 Electronic coils and transformers; Electronic loads and power supplies; Engineering services; Switchgear and switchboard apparatus

(P-6939)
TUR-BO JET PRODUCTS CO INC
5025 Earle Ave, Rosemead (91770-1169)
PHONE...............................626 285-1294
Richard Bloom, *Pr*
Richard L Bloom, *
▲ **EMP:** 95 **EST:** 1945
SQ FT: 27,000
SALES (est): 9.47MM **Privately Held**
Web: www.tbj.aero
SIC: 3677 Coil windings, electronic

(P-6940)
VANGUARD ELECTRONICS COMPANY (PA)
18292 Enterprise Ln, Huntington Beach (92648-1217)
PHONE...............................714 842-3330
EMP: 48 **EST:** 1952
SALES (est): 22.7MM
SALES (corp-wide): 22.7MM **Privately Held**
Web: www.ve1.com
SIC: 3677 Electronic transformers

3678 Electronic Connectors

(P-6941)
AEROFLITE ENTERPRISES INC
261 Gemini Ave, Brea (92821-3704)
PHONE...............................714 773-4251
◆ **EMP:** 52 **EST:** 1977
SALES (est): 4.45MM **Privately Held**
Web: www.aeroflite.com
SIC: 3678 Electronic connectors

(P-6942)
BRANTNER AND ASSOCIATES INC (DH)
Also Called: Te Connectivity MOG
1700 Gillespie Way, El Cajon (92020-1874)
PHONE...............................619 456-6827
Harold G Barksdale, *CEO*

Jean-jacques Fotzeu, *CFO*
▲ **EMP:** 142 **EST:** 1957
SQ FT: 35,000
SALES (est): 18.17MM
SALES (corp-wide): 74.18MM **Privately Held**
Web: www.te.com
SIC: 3678 3643 Electronic connectors; Current-carrying wiring services
HQ: Brantner Holding Llc
    501 Oakside Ave
    Redwood City CA 94063
    650 361-5292

(P-6943)
COMPONENT EQUIPMENT COINC
Also Called: Ceco
3050 Camino Del Sol, Oxnard (93030-7275)
P.O. Box 600 (93066-0600)
PHONE.................................805 988-8004
Bill Rigby, *Pr*
Thomas Conway, *
EMP: 25 **EST:** 1979
SQ FT: 32,000
SALES (est): 2.47MM **Privately Held**
SIC: 3678 Electronic connectors

(P-6944)
CONESYS INC
548 Amapola Ave, Torrance (90501-1472)
PHONE.................................310 212-0065
Teresa Lynn De Foreest, *Admn*
EMP: 64
SALES (corp-wide): 33.1MM **Privately Held**
Web: www.conesys.com
SIC: 3678 Electronic connectors
PA: Conesys, Inc.
    2280 W 208th St
    310 618-3737

(P-6945)
CORSAIR ELEC CONNECTORS INC
17100 Murphy Ave, Irvine (92614-5916)
PHONE.................................949 833-0273
Amir Saket, *Pr*
Steve Simmons, *Finance*
EMP: 140 **EST:** 2009
SQ FT: 34,554
SALES (est): 19.57MM **Privately Held**
Web:
www.corsairelectricalconnectors.com
SIC: 3678 Electronic connectors

(P-6946)
CRISTEK INTERCONNECTS LLC (DH)
Also Called: Cristek
5395 E Hunter Ave, Anaheim (92807-2054)
PHONE.................................714 696-5200
Keith Barclay, *Pr*
EMP: 135 **EST:** 1985
SALES (est): 46.53MM
SALES (corp-wide): 168.44MM **Privately Held**
Web: www.cristek.com
SIC: 3678 Electronic connectors
HQ: Hermetic Solutions Group Inc.
    16 Plains Rd
    Essex CT 06426
    215 645-9420

(P-6947)
DETORONICS CORP
13071 Rosecrans Ave, Santa Fe Springs (90670-4930)
PHONE.................................626 579-7130

Kenneth S Clark, *CEO*
Marcia Baroda, *
EMP: 37 **EST:** 1959
SQ FT: 20,000
SALES (est): 4.66MM **Privately Held**
Web: www.detoronics.com
SIC: 3678 Electronic connectors

(P-6948)
FLEXIBLE MANUFACTURING LLC
Also Called: F M I
1719 S Grand Ave, Santa Ana (92705-4808)
PHONE.................................714 259-7996
Carlos Cortes, *
Bart Pacetti, *
Tom Rendina, *
▲ **EMP:** 100 **EST:** 2001
SQ FT: 15,000
SALES (est): 9.95MM **Privately Held**
Web: www.4fmi.com
SIC: 3678 Electronic connectors

(P-6949)
HOLLAND ELECTRONICS LLC
Also Called: Holland Electronics
2935 Golf Course Dr, Ventura (93003-7604)
PHONE.................................888 628-5411
◆ **EMP:** 48 **EST:** 1998
SALES (est): 9.33MM
SALES (corp-wide): 12.55B **Publicly Held**
Web: www.hollandelectronics.com
SIC: 3678 5063 Electronic connectors; Electrical apparatus and equipment
PA: Amphenol Corporation
    358 Hall Ave
    203 265-8900

(P-6950)
INFINITE ELECTRONICS INTL INC (DH)
17792 Fitch, Irvine (92614-6020)
PHONE.................................949 261-1920
Penny Cotner, *Pr*
Scott Rosner, *
Jim Dauw, *
Terry G Jarniga, *
▲ **EMP:** 51 **EST:** 1972
SQ FT: 40,000
SALES (est): 231.46MM
SALES (corp-wide): 1.84B **Privately Held**
Web: www.infiniteelectronics.com
SIC: 3678 3357 3651 3643 Electronic connectors; Coaxial cable, nonferrous; Household audio and video equipment; Current-carrying wiring services
HQ: Infinite Electronics, Inc.
    17792 Fitch Ave
    Irvine CA 92614
    949 261-1920

(P-6951)
INFINITE ELECTRONICS INTL INC
Pasternack Enterprises
17802 Fitch, Irvine (92614-6002)
PHONE.................................949 261-1920
EMP: 26
SALES (corp-wide): 1.84B **Privately Held**
Web: www.infiniteelectronics.com
SIC: 3678 3651 3357 3643 Electronic connectors; Household audio and video equipment; Coaxial cable, nonferrous; Current-carrying wiring services
HQ: Infinite Electronics International, Inc.
    17792 Fitch
    Irvine CA 92614
    949 261-1920

(P-6952)
J-TECH
548 Amapola Ave, Torrance (90501-1472)
PHONE.................................310 533-6700
Walter Naubauer Junior, *CEO*
EMP: 136 **EST:** 1987
SALES (est): 4.44MM **Privately Held**
SIC: 3678 Electronic connectors

(P-6953)
JOSLYN SUNBANK COMPANY LLC
1740 Commerce Way, Paso Robles (93446-3620)
PHONE.................................805 238-2840
Mark Thek, *Genl Mgr*
Mike Ritter, *Dir Opers*
Kirsten Park, *VP*
EMP: 500 **EST:** 1997
SQ FT: 80,000
SALES (est): 21.45MM **Privately Held**
Web:
joslyn-sunbank-company-llc-in-paso-robles-ca.cityfos.com
SIC: 3678 3643 5065 Electronic connectors; Connectors and terminals for electrical devices; Connectors, electronic
HQ: Eaton Corporation
    1000 Eaton Blvd
    Cleveland OH 44122
    440 523-5000

(P-6954)
L & M MACHINING CORPORATION
550 S Melrose St, Placentia (92870-6327)
PHONE.................................714 414-0923
Mike Mai, *Pr*
EMP: 70 **EST:** 1985
SQ FT: 31,000
SALES (est): 8.47MM **Privately Held**
Web: www.lmcnc.com
SIC: 3678 Electronic connectors

(P-6955)
MIN-E-CON LLC
17312 Eastman, Irvine (92614-5522)
PHONE.................................949 250-0087
Wendell Jacob, *Managing Member*
John M Brown, *
Wendell P Jacob, *
▼ **EMP:** 60 **EST:** 1974
SALES (est): 9.99MM **Privately Held**
Web: www.min-e-con.com
SIC: 3678 Electronic connectors

(P-6956)
NEA ELECTRONICS INC
14370 White Sage Rd, Moorpark (93021-8720)
PHONE.................................805 292-4010
Steven Perkins, *Pr*
EMP: 24 **EST:** 1995
SQ FT: 20,000
SALES (est): 5.76MM
SALES (corp-wide): 696.33MM **Privately Held**
Web: www.ebad.com
SIC: 3678 3629 3592 Electronic connectors; Battery chargers, rectifying or nonrotating; Valves
HQ: Ensign-Bickford Aerospace & Defense Co
    640 Hopmeadow St
    Simsbury CT 06070
    860 843-2289

(P-6957)
R KERN ENGINEERING & MFG CORP
Also Called: Kern Engineering
13912 Mountain Ave, Chino (91710-9018)
PHONE.................................909 664-2440
Richard Kern, *CEO*
Roland A Kern, *
Helga Kern, *
Jose Nunez, *
▲ **EMP:** 54 **EST:** 1966
SQ FT: 34,000
SALES (est): 9.06MM **Privately Held**
Web: www.kerneng.com
SIC: 3678 3599 Electronic connectors; Machine shop, jobbing and repair

(P-6958)
RF INDUSTRIES LTD (PA)
Also Called: Comppro
16868 Via Del Campo Ct Ste 200, San Diego (92127-1772)
PHONE.................................858 549-6340
Robert Dawson, *CEO*
Mark K Holdsworth, *
Peter Yin, *CFO*
Ray Bibisi, *Pr*
EMP: 89 **EST:** 1979
SALES (est): 72.17MM
SALES (corp-wide): 72.17MM **Publicly Held**
Web: www.rfindustries.com
SIC: 3678 3643 3663 Electronic connectors; Electric connectors; Transmitter-receivers, radio

(P-6959)
SABRITEC
1550 Scenic Ave Ste 150, Costa Mesa (92626-1465)
PHONE.................................714 371-1100
EMP: 300
SIC: 3678 Electronic connectors

(P-6960)
TE CONNECTIVITY CORPORATION
Deutsch Engnred Intrcnnect Slt
3390 Alex Rd, Oceanside (92058-1319)
PHONE.................................760 757-7500
Ken Watkins, *Brnch Mgr*
EMP: 81
SALES (corp-wide): 9.17B **Privately Held**
Web: www.te.com
SIC: 3678 Electronic connectors
HQ: Te Connectivity Corporation
    1050 Westlakes Dr
    Berwyn PA 19312
    610 893-9800

(P-6961)
WINCHSTER INTRCNNECT MICRO LLC
1872 N Case St, Orange (92865-4233)
PHONE.................................714 637-7099
Ross Sealfon, *Pr*
Bruce I Billington, *
Thierry Pombart, *
Frank Malczyk Global, *Sls Mgr*
▲ **EMP:** 113 **EST:** 1977
SQ FT: 11,000
SALES (est): 23.35MM **Privately Held**
Web: www.winconn.com
SIC: 3678 Electronic connectors
HQ: Winchester Interconnect Corporation
    185 Plains Rd
    Milford CT 06461

3679 Electronic Components, Nec

(P-6962)
ACCRATRONICS SEALS LLC
Also Called: A T S
2211 Kenmere Ave, Burbank (91504-3493)
PHONE..............................818 843-1500
William Fisch, *CEO*
Corby Jones, *
Delbert Jones, *
Deken Jones, *
EMP: 72 **EST:** 1960
SQ FT: 10,000
SALES (est): 11.46MM
SALES (corp-wide): 696.33MM **Privately Held**
Web: www.accratronics.com
SIC: 3679 Hermetic seals, for electronic equipment
PA: Ensign-Bickford Industries, Inc.
999 17th St Ste 900
860 843-2000

(P-6963)
ADVANCED WAVEGUIDE TECH
29 Musick, Irvine (92618-1638)
PHONE..............................949 297-3564
Garrett Biele, *Owner*
Garrett Biele, *CEO*
EMP: 30 **EST:** 2013
SALES (est): 4.05MM **Privately Held**
SIC: 3679 Waveguides and fittings

(P-6964)
ALYN INDUSTRIES INC
Also Called: Electronic Source Company
16028 Arminta St, Van Nuys (91406-1808)
PHONE..............................818 988-7696
Scott J Alyn, *CEO*
▼ **EMP:** 100 **EST:** 1994
SALES (est): 27.93MM **Privately Held**
Web: www.electronic-source.com
SIC: 3679 Electronic circuits

(P-6965)
AMERICAN AUDIO COMPONENT INC
Also Called: AAC
20 Fairbanks Ste 198, Irvine (92618-1673)
PHONE..............................909 596-3788
David Plekenpol, *CEO*
Richard Monk, *
Willie Maglonso, *
▲ **EMP:** 26 **EST:** 1996
SALES (est): 5.11MM **Privately Held**
SIC: 3679 Transducers, electrical
HQ: Aac Acoustic Technologies
(Shenzhen) Co., Ltd.
Block A, Nanjing University Research
Center Shenzhen Branch, No.
Shenzhen GD 51805

(P-6966)
AMSCO US INC
15341 Texaco Ave, Paramount
(90723-3946)
PHONE..............................562 630-0333
Mike Yazdi, *Pr*
EMP: 110 **EST:** 1998
SALES (est): 4.23MM **Privately Held**
Web: www.amscous.com
SIC: 3679 Harness assemblies, for electronic use: wire or cable

(P-6967)
APEM INC
Also Called: Ch Products

970 Park Center Dr, Vista (92081-8301)
PHONE..............................760 598-2518
Peter Brouillette, *Pr*
EMP: 81
Web: www.chproducts.com
SIC: 3679 3577 Electronic switches;
Computer peripheral equipment, nec
HQ: Apem, Inc.
970 Park Center Dr
Vista CA 92081

(P-6968)
ASTRO SEAL INC
827 Palmyrita Ave Ste B, Riverside
(92507-1820)
PHONE..............................951 787-6670
Michael Hammer, *Pr*
Roger Hammer, *
Karen Upfold, *
▲ **EMP:** 34 **EST:** 1964
SQ FT: 42,000
SALES (est): 4.75MM **Privately Held**
Web: www.astroseal.com
SIC: 3679 3678 Hermetic seals, for electronic equipment; Electronic connectors

(P-6969)
AVR GLOBAL TECHNOLOGIES INC (PA)
Also Called: Avr Global Tech
500 La Terraza Blvd Ste 150, Escondido
(92025-3876)
P.O. Box 3814 (92629-8814)
PHONE..............................949 391-1180
Andy Bowman, *CEO*
Andy Bowman, *Pr*
Val Pontes, *Treas*
EMP: 197 **EST:** 2016
SALES (est): 5.3MM
SALES (corp-wide): 5.3MM **Privately Held**
Web: www.avrglobaltech.com
SIC: 3679 3714 5065 5063 Harness assemblies, for electronic use: wire or cable ; Automotive wiring harness sets; Electronic parts and equipment, nec; Wire and cable

(P-6970)
AZ DISPLAYS INC
2410 Birch St, Vista (92081-8472)
PHONE..............................949 831-5000
Reiner Moegling, *Pr*
▲ **EMP:** 50 **EST:** 1996
SALES (est): 1.15MM **Privately Held**
Web: www.azdisplays.com
SIC: 3679 Liquid crystal displays (LCD)
HQ: American Zettler Inc.
2410 Birch St
Vista CA 92081
949 831-5000

(P-6971)
BASIC ELECTRONICS INC
11371 Monarch St, Garden Grove
(92841-1406)
PHONE..............................714 530-2400
Nancy Balzano, *Pr*
Al Balzano, *
EMP: 27 **EST:** 1967
SQ FT: 20,000
SALES (est): 4.3MM **Privately Held**
Web: www.basicelectronicsinc.com
SIC: 3679 3672 3613 Electronic circuits;
Printed circuit boards; Switchgear and switchboard apparatus

(P-6972)
BI TECHNOLOGIES CORPORATION (HQ)
Also Called: TT Electronics
120 S State College Blvd Ste 175, Brea
(92821-5852)

PHONE..............................714 447-2300
▲ **EMP:** 260 **EST:** 1984
SALES (est): 64MM
SALES (corp-wide): 765.19MM **Privately Held**
Web: www.bitechnologies.com
SIC: 3679 5065 8711 Electronic circuits;
Electronic parts and equipment, nec;
Engineering services
PA: Tt Electronics Plc
4th Floor St. Andrews House
193 282-5300

(P-6973)
BI-SEARCH INTERNATIONAL INC
17550 Gillette Ave, Irvine (92614-5610)
PHONE..............................714 258-4500
Kevin Kim, *Pr*
◆ **EMP:** 40 **EST:** 1996
SQ FT: 45,000
SALES (est): 68.34MM **Privately Held**
Web: www.bisearch.com
SIC: 3679 Liquid crystal displays (LCD)

(P-6974)
BIVAR INC
Also Called: Bivar
4 Thomas, Irvine (92618-2593)
PHONE..............................949 951-8808
Thomas Silber, *CEO*
▲ **EMP:** 40 **EST:** 1965
SQ FT: 26,040
SALES (est): 6.78MM **Privately Held**
Web: www.bivar.com
SIC: 3679 Electronic circuits

(P-6975)
BREE ENGINEERING CORP
1750 Marilyn Ln, San Marcos (92069-9780)
PHONE..............................760 510-4950
Dan Bree, *Pr*
EMP: 30 **EST:** 1999
SALES (est): 2.51MM **Privately Held**
Web: www.breeeng.com
SIC: 3679 Electronic circuits

(P-6976)
CAES MISSION SYSTEMS LLC
4820 Eastgate Mall Ste 200, San Diego
(92121-1993)
PHONE..............................858 812-7300
EMP: 29
SALES (corp-wide): 4.59B **Privately Held**
Web: www.caes.com
SIC: 3679 Microwave components
HQ: Caes Mission Systems Llc
3061 Industry Dr
Lancaster PA 17603
717 397-2777

(P-6977)
CAL SOUTHERN BRAIDING INC
Also Called: Scb Division
7450 Scout Ave, Bell Gardens
(90201-4932)
PHONE..............................562 927-5531
Neal Castleman, *Pr*
EMP: 60 **EST:** 1976
SQ FT: 38,000
SALES (est): 5.41MM
SALES (corp-wide): 112.69MM **Privately Held**
SIC: 3679 Harness assemblies, for electronic use: wire or cable
PA: Dcx-Chol Enterprises, Inc.
12831 S Figueroa St
310 516-1692

(P-6978)
CALI RESOURCES INC
Also Called: Brimes International
2310 Michael Faraday Dr, San Diego
(92154-7900)
PHONE..............................619 661-5741
Carlos Kelvin, *CEO*
◆ **EMP:** 45 **EST:** 1995
SQ FT: 30,000
SALES (est): 7.29MM **Privately Held**
Web: www.caliresources.com
SIC: 3679 Electronic circuits

(P-6979)
CARROS SENSORS AMERICAS LLC
Also Called: Carros Americas, Inc.
2945 Townsgate Rd Ste 200, Westlake
Village (91361-5866)
PHONE..............................805 267-7176
Eric Pilaud, *Pr*
Ben Watt, *
EMP: 150 **EST:** 2015
SALES (est): 6.96MM
SALES (corp-wide): 675.45K **Privately Held**
Web: www.crouzet.com
SIC: 3679 3577 Electronic circuits;
Encoders, computer peripheral equipment
HQ: Lbo France Gestion
148 Rue De L Universite
Paris IDF 75007

(P-6980)
CCM ASSEMBLY & MFG INC (PA)
2275 Michael Faraday Dr Ste 6, San Diego
(92154-7927)
PHONE..............................760 560-1310
Erika Marcela Murillo, *CEO*
Sergio Murillo, *Pr*
John Savage, *VP*
▲ **EMP:** 28 **EST:** 1997
SQ FT: 10,000
SALES (est): 9.39MM
SALES (corp-wide): 9.39MM **Privately Held**
Web: www.ccmassembly.com
SIC: 3679 3441 Harness assemblies, for electronic use: wire or cable; Fabricated structural metal

(P-6981)
CIAO WIRELESS INC
Also Called: Ciao
4000 Via Pescador, Camarillo
(93012-5044)
PHONE..............................805 389-3224
Glen Wasylewski; *Pr*
▼ **EMP:** 70 **EST:** 2003
SQ FT: 42,000
SALES (est): 9.85MM **Privately Held**
Web: www.ciaowireless.com
SIC: 3679 3699 Microwave components;
Pulse amplifiers

(P-6982)
CICON ENGINEERING INC (PA)
6633 Odessa Ave, Van Nuys (91406-5746)
PHONE..............................818 909-6060
Ali Kolahi, *Pr*
Laurie Kertenian, *
Hamid Kolahi, *Stockholder* *
Farah Kolahi, *Stockholder* *
Abdi Kolahi, *
EMP: 169 **EST:** 1990
SQ FT: 50,000
SALES (est): 20.17MM
SALES (corp-wide): 20.17MM **Privately Held**
Web: www.cicon.com

SIC: **3679** Harness assemblies, for electronic use: wire or cable

(P-6983)
CKS SOLUTION INCORPORATED
556 Vanguard Way Ste C, Brea (92821-3929)
PHONE...............................714 292-6307
Patrick Park, *Mgr*
EMP: 34
SALES (corp-wide): 5.49MM **Privately Held**
Web: www.ckssolution.com
SIC: **3679** Liquid crystal displays (LCD)
PA: Cks Solution Incorporated
4293 Muhlhauser Rd
513 947-1277

(P-6984)
CLARY CORPORATION
150 E Huntington Dr, Monrovia (91016-3415)
PHONE...............................626 359-4486
John G Clary, *Ch Bd*
Donald G Ash, *
EMP: 40 **EST:** 1939
SQ FT: 26,000
SALES (est): 9.96MM **Privately Held**
Web: www.clary.com
SIC: **3679** 3612 Electronic loads and power supplies; Transformers, except electric

(P-6985)
COOPER INTERCONNECT INC
13039 Crossroads Pkwy S, City Of Industry (91746-3406)
PHONE...............................617 389-7080
Preston Shultz, *CEO*
EMP: 80
SIC: **3679** 3643 3812 3672 Harness assemblies, for electronic use: wire or cable ; Current-carrying wiring services; Search and navigation equipment; Printed circuit boards
HQ: Cooper Interconnect, Inc.
750 W Ventura Blvd
Camarillo CA 93010
805 484-0543

(P-6986)
CORELIS INC
13100 Alondra Blvd Ste 102, Cerritos (90703-2262)
PHONE...............................562 926-6727
George Lafever, *CEO*
EMP: 25 **EST:** 1991
SQ FT: 15,000
SALES (est): 6.72MM **Privately Held**
Web: www.corelis.com
SIC: **3679** Electronic circuits
HQ: Electronic Warfare Associates, Inc.
13873 Pk Ctr Rd Ste 500s
Herndon VA 20171
703 904-5700

(P-6987)
CUSTOM SENSORS & TECH INC
2475 Paseo De Las Americas, San Diego (92154-7255)
PHONE...............................805 716-0322
Carlos Borboa, *Supervisor*
EMP: 293
SALES (corp-wide): 4.05B **Privately Held**
Web: www.cstsensors.com
SIC: **3679** Electronic circuits
HQ: Custom Sensors & Technologies, Inc.
1461 Lawrence Dr
Thousand Oaks CA 91320
805 716-0322

(P-6988)
CUSTOM SENSORS & TECH INC (HQ)
Also Called: C S T
1461 Lawrence Dr, Thousand Oaks (91320-1303)
PHONE...............................805 716-0322
Martha Sullivan, *CEO*
▲ **EMP:** 801 **EST:** 1997
SALES (est): 470.66MM
SALES (corp-wide): 4.05B **Privately Held**
Web: www.cstsensors.com
SIC: **3679** Electronic circuits
PA: Sensata Technologies Holding Plc
Interface House
179 325-0031

(P-6989)
DAICO INDUSTRIES INC
1070 E 233rd St, Carson (90745-6205)
PHONE...............................310 507-3242
EMP: 90 **EST:** 1965
SALES (est): 15.1MM **Privately Held**
Web: www.daico.com
SIC: **3679** 3674 Microwave components; Semiconductors and related devices

(P-6990)
DCX-CHOL ENTERPRISES INC (PA)
12831 S Figueroa St, Los Angeles (90061-1157)
PHONE...............................310 516-1692
Neal Castleman, *Pr*
Brian Gamberg, *
Garret Hoffman, *
▲ **EMP:** 80 **EST:** 1997
SQ FT: 50,000
SALES (est): 112.69MM
SALES (corp-wide): 112.69MM **Privately Held**
Web: www.dcxchol.com
SIC: **3679** Electronic circuits

(P-6991)
DELTA GROUP ELECTRONICS INC
Also Called: Delta Group Electronics
10180 Scripps Ranch Blvd, San Diego (92131-1234)
PHONE...............................858 569-1681
Bill West, *Genl Mgr*
EMP: 55
SALES (corp-wide): 81.36MM **Privately Held**
Web: www.deltagroupinc.com
SIC: **3679** 3577 3672 Electronic circuits; Computer peripheral equipment, nec; Printed circuit boards
PA: Delta Group Electronics, Inc.
4521a Osuna Rd Ne
505 883-7674

(P-6992)
DELTA MICROWAVE LLC
300 Del Norte Blvd, Oxnard (93030-7217)
PHONE...............................805 751-1100
▼ **EMP:** 66
Web: www.mrcy.com
SIC: **3679** Microwave components

(P-6993)
DYTRAN INSTRUMENTS INC
21592 Marilla St, Chatsworth (91311-4137)
PHONE...............................818 700-7818
Benjamin Bryson, *CEO*
Anne Hackney, *
David Cianciosi, *
EMP: 194 **EST:** 1980

SQ FT: 8,000
SALES (est): 38.19MM
SALES (corp-wide): 1.81B **Privately Held**
Web: www.dytran.com
SIC: **3679** 3829 Transducers, electrical; Measuring and controlling devices, nec
HQ: Spectris Inc.
117 Flanders Rd
Westborough MA 01581
508 768-6400

(P-6994)
ELECTRO-TECH PRODUCTS INC
Also Called: Electro-Tech Products
2001 E Gladstone St Ste A, Glendora (91740-5381)
PHONE...............................909 592-1434
Ramzi Bader, *Pr*
▲ **EMP:** 30 **EST:** 1984
SQ FT: 11,000
SALES (est): 2.79MM **Privately Held**
Web: www.etp-inc.com
SIC: **3679** Electronic circuits

(P-6995)
ELECTROCUBE INC (PA)
Also Called: Southern Electronics
3366 Pomona Blvd, Pomona (91768-3234)
PHONE...............................909 595-1821
Langdon Clay Parrill, *Pr*
Donald Duquette, *
Scott Wieland, *
◆ **EMP:** 47 **EST:** 1961
SQ FT: 27,000
SALES (est): 9.95MM
SALES (corp-wide): 9.95MM **Privately Held**
Web: www.electrocube.com
SIC: **3679** 3675 Electronic circuits; Electronic capacitors

(P-6996)
EXPRESS MANUFACTURING INC (PA)
3519 W Warner Ave, Santa Ana (92704-5214)
PHONE...............................714 979-2228
Chauk Pan Chin, *Pr*
Tony Chin, *
Catherine Lee Chin, *
C M Chin, *
▲ **EMP:** 320 **EST:** 1982
SQ FT: 96,000
SALES (est): 96.84MM
SALES (corp-wide): 96.84MM **Privately Held**
Web: www.eminc.com
SIC: **3679** 3672 Electronic circuits; Printed circuit boards

(P-6997)
FEMA ELECTRONICS CORPORATION
22 Corporate Park, Irvine (92606-3112)
PHONE...............................714 825-0140
Bob Cheng, *CEO*
Chinyun Cheng, *
▲ **EMP:** 30 **EST:** 2010
SQ FT: 3,000
SALES (est): 7.18MM **Privately Held**
Web: www.femacorp.com
SIC: **3679** Electronic crystals

(P-6998)
FOX ENTERPRISES LLC (HQ)
Also Called: Fox Electronics
24422 Avenida De La Carlota Ste 290, Laguna Hills (92653-3648)

PHONE...............................239 693-0099
Eugene Trefethen, *Pr*
EMP: 24 **EST:** 1979
SALES (est): 3.72MM **Privately Held**
SIC: **3679** 5065 Quartz crystals, for electronic application; Electronic parts
PA: Abracon, Llc
5101 Hidden Creek Ln

(P-6999)
GAR ENTERPRISES
Also Called: K.G.S.electronics
1396 W 9th St, Upland (91786-5724)
PHONE...............................909 985-4575
Alex Morales, *Mgr*
EMP: 28
SALES (corp-wide): 23.35MM **Privately Held**
Web: www.kgselectronics.com
SIC: **3679** 3621 3577 Electronic loads and power supplies; Motors and generators; Computer peripheral equipment, nec
PA: Gar Enterprises
418 E Live Oak Ave
626 574-1175

(P-7000)
GENERAL POWER SYSTEMS INC
Also Called: General Power Systems
955 E Ball Rd, Anaheim (92805-5916)
PHONE...............................714 956-9321
David Noyes, *Pr*
Frank Castle, *
David Noyes, *Ex VP*
EMP: 30 **EST:** 1984
SQ FT: 30,000
SALES (est): 1.23MM
SALES (corp-wide): 46.24MM **Privately Held**
SIC: **3679** Power supplies, all types: static
PA: Components Corporation Of America
5950 Berkshire Ln # 1500
214 969-0166

(P-7001)
GTRAN INC (PA)
829 Flynn Rd, Camarillo (93012-8702)
PHONE...............................805 445-4500
Ray Yu, *Pr*
Deepak Mehrotra, *
Douglas Holmes, *
▲ **EMP:** 46 **EST:** 1999
SQ FT: 226,000
SALES (est): 2.62MM
SALES (corp-wide): 2.62MM **Privately Held**
Web: www.gtran.net
SIC: **3679** Electronic circuits

(P-7002)
GUNJOY INC
22895 Eastpark Dr, Yorba Linda (92887-4653)
PHONE...............................714 289-0055
▲ **EMP:** 26
SIC: **3679** Power supplies, all types: static

(P-7003)
HANNSPREE NORTH AMERICA INC
13223 Black Mountain Rd, San Diego (92129-2698)
PHONE...............................909 992-5025
▲ **EMP:** 60
SIC: **3679** Liquid crystal displays (LCD)

PRODUCTS & SVCS

(P-7004)

HARWIL PRECISION PRODUCTS

Also Called: Harwil
541 Kinetic Dr, Oxnard (93030-7923)
PHONE.............................805 988-6800
Geoffrey Strand, *Pr*
Cynthia Strand, *
Teresa Bowmar, *
EMP: 35 **EST:** 1957
SQ FT: 33,000
SALES (est): 4.46MM **Privately Held**
Web: www.harwil.com
SIC: 3679 3625 3823 Electronic circuits;
Flow actuated electrical switches; Process
control instruments

(P-7005)

HERMETIC SEAL CORPORATION (DH)

Also Called: Ametek HCC
4232 Temple City Blvd, Rosemead
(91770-1592)
PHONE.............................626 443-8931
Andrew Goldfarb, *Pr*
EMP: 200 **EST:** 1945
SQ FT: 36,000
SALES (est): 28.03MM
SALES (corp-wide): 6.6B **Publicly Held**
Web: www.ametekinterconnect.com
SIC: 3679 3469 Hermetic seals, for
electronic equipment; Metal stampings, nec
HQ: Hcc Industries Leasing, Inc.
4232 Temple City Blvd
Rosemead CA 91770
626 443-8933

(P-7006)

IJ RESEARCH INC

Also Called: Hermetics Material Solutions
2919 S Tech Center Dr, Santa Ana
(92705-5657)
PHONE.............................714 546-8522
Rick Yoon, *Pr*
◆ **EMP:** 35 **EST:** 1988
SQ FT: 12,500
SALES (est): 3.53MM
SALES (corp-wide): 3.27B **Publicly Held**
Web: www.ijresearch.com
SIC: 3679 Hermetic seals, for electronic
equipment
HQ: Superior Technical Ceramics
Corporation
600 Industrial Park Rd
Saint Albans VT 05478
802 527-7726

(P-7007)

IMPACT LLC

7121 Magnolia Ave, Riverside
(92504-3805)
PHONE.............................714 546-6000
EMP: 28 **EST:** 1998
SALES (est): 2.66MM **Privately Held**
Web: www.capitolimpact.org
SIC: 3679 3829 Electronic circuits;
Measuring and controlling devices, nec

(P-7008)

INFINITE ELECTRONICS INC (HQ)

Also Called: L-Com
17792 Fitch, Irvine (92614-6020)
PHONE.............................949 261-1920
Penny Cotner, *Pr*
David Quinn, *CRO*
Emily Campbell, *CMO*
David Collier, *COO*
Alexander Arrieta, *Chief Human Resource
Officer*
EMP: 47 **EST:** 2007

SQ FT: 40,000
SALES (est): 369.37MM
SALES (corp-wide): 1.84B **Privately Held**
Web: www.infiniteelectronics.com
SIC: 3679 Electronic circuits
PA: Warburg Pincus Llc
450 Lexington Ave
212 878-0600

(P-7009)

INTEGRATED MICROWAVE CORP

Also Called: Imcsd
11353 Sorrento Valley Rd, San Diego
(92121-1303)
PHONE.............................858 259-2600
John F Anderson, *Pr*
Steven Porter, *CFO*
Robert J Pema, *Sec*
◆ **EMP:** 85 **EST:** 1982
SQ FT: 24,142
SALES (est): 20.77MM
SALES (corp-wide): 707.6MM **Publicly Held**
Web: www.knowlescapacitors.com
SIC: 3679 Microwave components
HQ: Knowles Electronics, Llc
1151 Maplewood Dr
Itasca IL 60143
630 250-5100

(P-7010)

INTERCONNECT SOLUTIONS CO LLC

Also Called: Tri-Tek Electronics
25358 Avenue Stanford, Valencia
(91355-1214)
PHONE.............................661 295-0020
Tony Lopez, *Brnch Mgr*
EMP: 66
SALES (corp-wide): 49.73MM **Privately Held**
Web: www.interconnectsolutions.com
SIC: 3679 Harness assemblies, for
electronic use: wire or cable
PA: Interconnect Solutions Company, Llc
17595 Mt Herrmann St
714 556-7007

(P-7011)

INTERCTIVE DSPLAY SLUTIONS INC

Also Called: Interactive Display Solutions
490 Wald, Irvine (92618-4638)
PHONE.............................949 727-1959
Brian Chung, *Pr*
Paul Kitzerow Senior V Press, *Prin*
Son Park V Press, *Prin*
Danny Lee, *
▲ **EMP:** 26 **EST:** 2004
SALES (est): 5.4MM **Privately Held**
Web: www.idsdisplay.com
SIC: 3679 Liquid crystal displays (LCD)

(P-7012)

IQD FREQUENCY PRODUCTS INC

592 N Tercero Cir, Palm Springs
(92262-6243)
PHONE.............................408 250-1435
Neil Floodgate, *Pr*
EMP: 43 **EST:** 2010
SALES (est): 1.03MM
SALES (corp-wide): 22.17B **Privately Held**
Web: www.iqdfrequencyproducts.com
SIC: 3679 Microwave components
HQ: Iqd Frequency Products Limited
Station Road
Crewkerne TA18
146 027-0200

(P-7013)

J L COOPER ELECTRONICS INC

Also Called: Jlcooper
142 Arena St, El Segundo (90245-3901)
PHONE.............................310 322-9990
James Loren Cooper, *Pr*
▲ **EMP:** 34 **EST:** 1981
SALES (est): 6.22MM **Privately Held**
SIC: 3679 Recording and playback
apparatus, including phonograph

(P-7014)

JANCO CORPORATION

Also Called: Esterline Mason
13955 Balboa Blvd, Rancho Cascades
(91342-1084)
P.O. Box 3038 (91508-3038)
PHONE.............................818 361-3366
▼ **EMP:** 120 **EST:** 1947
SALES (est): 24.75MM
SALES (corp-wide): 7.94B **Publicly Held**
Web: www.esterline.com
SIC: 3679 3825 3643 5088 Electronic
switches; Shunts, electrical; Bus bars
(electrical conductors); Aircraft and parts,
nec
HQ: Esterline Technologies Corp
1350 Euclid Ave Ste 1600
Cleveland OH 44114
216 706-2960

(P-7015)

JASPER ELECTRONICS

1580 N Kellogg Dr, Anaheim (92807-1902)
PHONE.............................714 917-0749
Robert Nishimoto, *CEO*
Hiroshi Tango, *
◆ **EMP:** 30 **EST:** 1995
SQ FT: 17,000
SALES (est): 4.62MM **Privately Held**
Web: www.jasperelectronics.com
SIC: 3679 Electronic loads and power
supplies

(P-7016)

JAXX MANUFACTURING INC

Also Called: Craig Kackert Design Tech
1912 Angus Ave, Simi Valley (93063-3494)
PHONE.............................805 526-4979
Greg Liu, *Pr*
Veronica Liu, *
EMP: 45 **EST:** 2001
SALES (est): 3.39MM **Privately Held**
Web: www.jaxxmfg.com
SIC: 3679 Electronic circuits

(P-7017)

JAYCO/MMI INC

1351 Pico St, Corona (92881-3373)
PHONE.............................951 738-2000
Shaila Mistry, *Pr*
Hemant Mistry, *
EMP: 42 **EST:** 1992
SQ FT: 24,000
SALES (est): 1.14MM **Privately Held**
Web: www.jaycopanels.com
SIC: 3679 5065 3577 2759 Electronic circuits
; Electronic parts and equipment, nec;
Computer peripheral equipment, nec;
Commercial printing, nec

(P-7018)

KAVLICO CORPORATION (DH)

1461 Lawrence Dr, Thousand Oaks
(91320-1303)
PHONE.............................805 523-2000
Jeffrey J Cote, *CEO*
Martha Sullivan, *Pr*
▼ **EMP:** 1390 **EST:** 1962
SALES (est): 71.54MM

SALES (corp-wide): 4.05B **Privately Held**
Web: www.sensata.com
SIC: 3679 Transducers, electrical
HQ: Custom Sensors & Technologies, Inc.
1461 Lawrence Dr
Thousand Oaks CA 91320
805 716-0322

(P-7019)

LANDMARK ELECTRONICS INC

990 N Amelia Ave, San Dimas
(91773-1401)
PHONE.............................626 967-2857
▲ **EMP:** 23
Web: www.landmarkelectronics.com
SIC: 3679 7699 5088 Static power supply
converters for electronic applications;
Aircraft flight instrument repair; Aircraft and
space vehicle supplies and parts

(P-7020)

LHV POWER CORPORATION (PA)

10221 Buena Vista Ave Ste A, Santee
(92071-4484)
PHONE.............................619 258-7700
James Gevarges, *Pr*
▲ **EMP:** 25 **EST:** 1991
SQ FT: 20,000
SALES (est): 4.8MM **Privately Held**
Web: www.lhvpower.com
SIC: 3679 Power supplies, all types: static

(P-7021)

LUCIX CORPORATION (HQ)

Also Called: Lucix
800 Avenida Acaso Ste E, Camarillo
(93012-8758)
PHONE.............................805 987-6645
Mark Shahriary, *Pr*
Cheryl Johnson, *
D Ick Fanucchi, *
▲ **EMP:** 83 **EST:** 1999
SQ FT: 48,000
SALES (est): 48.27MM **Publicly Held**
Web: www.lucix.com
SIC: 3679 8731 Microwave components;
Commercial physical research
PA: Heico Corporation
3000 Taft St

(P-7022)

MAGNETIC SENSORS CORPORATION

1365 N Mccan St, Anaheim (92806-1316)
PHONE.............................714 630-8380
Charles Boudakian, *Pr*
Don Payne, *
EMP: 43 **EST:** 1983
SQ FT: 15,000
SALES (est): 8.88MM **Privately Held**
Web: www.magsensors.com
SIC: 3679 3677 Transducers, electrical; Coil
windings, electronic

(P-7023)

MAPLE IMAGING LLC (HQ)

1049 Camino Dos Rios, Thousand Oaks
(91360-2362)
PHONE.............................805 373-4545
Aldo Pichelli, *Pr*
EMP: 28 **EST:** 2019
SALES (est): 1.55MM
SALES (corp-wide): 5.64B **Publicly Held**
SIC: 3679 Electronic circuits
PA: Teledyne Technologies Inc
1049 Camino Dos Rios
805 373-4545

(P-7024)

MERCURY LLC - RF INTEGRATED SOLUTIONS

1000 Avenida Acaso, Camarillo
(93012-8712)
PHONE.....................805 388-1345
▲ EMP: 110
SIC: 3679 3663 Microwave components;
Amplifiers, RF power and IF

(P-7025)

MICROFABRICA INC

7911 Haskell Ave, Van Nuys (91406-1909)
PHONE.....................888 964-2763
Eric Miller, *Prin*
Michael Lockard, *Prin*
Uri Frodis, *
Richard Chen, *
Greg Schmitz, *
EMP: 50 EST: 1999
SQ FT: 39,000
SALES (est): 23.8MM **Privately Held**
Web: www.microfabrica.com
SIC: 3679 Electronic circuits

(P-7026)

MICROMETALS INC (PA)

5615 E La Palma Ave, Anaheim
(92807-2109)
PHONE.....................714 970-9400
Richard H Barden, *CEO*
◆ EMP: 159 EST: 1951
SQ FT: 50,000
SALES (est): 27MM
SALES (corp-wide): 27MM **Privately Held**
Web: www.micrometals.com
SIC: 3679 Cores, magnetic

(P-7027)

MITSUBSHI ELC VSUAL SLTONS AME

Also Called: Mevsa
10833 Valley View St Ste 300, Cypress
(90630-5051)
PHONE.....................800 553-7278
Kenichiro Yamanishi, *Ch*
Tadashi Hiraoka, *
Perry Pappous, *
◆ EMP: 150 EST: 2011
SALES (est): 24.07MM **Privately Held**
Web: www.me-vis.com
SIC: 3679 Liquid crystal displays (LCD)
PA: Mitsubishi Electric Corporation
2-7-3, Marunouchi

(P-7028)

MUNEKATA AMERICA INC

2320 Paseo De Las Americas Ste 112, San
Diego (92154-7281)
P.O. Box 15929 (92175-5929)
PHONE.....................619 661-8080
Nobumitsu Endo, *CEO*
Masayuki Sato, *
Naoharu Munekata, *
Koji Yanagida, *
▲ EMP: 500 EST: 1987
SQ FT: 700
SALES (est): 4.18MM **Privately Held**
Web: www.munekata.co.jp
SIC: 3679 Electronic circuits
PA: Munekata Co.,Ltd.
1-11-1, Horaicho

(P-7029)

NATEL ENGINEERING COMPANY LLC (PA)

Also Called: Neo Tech
9340 Owensmouth Ave, Chatsworth
(91311-6915)
PHONE.....................818 495-8617
Kunal Sharma, *
Laura Siegal, *
Victor Yamauchi, *
John Lowrey, *
▲ EMP: 210 EST: 1975
SQ FT: 200,000
SALES (est): 1.43B
SALES (corp-wide): 1.43B **Privately Held**
Web: www.neotech.com
SIC: 3679 3674 Antennas, receiving;
Semiconductors and related devices

(P-7030)

NEWVAC LLC

American Def Interconnect Div
9330 De Soto Ave, Chatsworth
(91311-4926)
PHONE.....................747 202-7333
Garrett Hoffman, *General Vice President*
EMP: 26
SALES (corp-wide): 96.54MM **Privately Held**
Web: www.newvac-llc.com
SIC: 3679 Harness assemblies, for
electronic use: wire or cable
HQ: Newvac, Llc
9330 De Soto Ave
Chatsworth CA 91311
310 525-1205

(P-7031)

OCM PE HOLDINGS LP

333 S Grand Ave Fl 28, Los Angeles
(90071-1530)
PHONE.....................213 830-6213
Mark C J Twaalfhoven, *CEO*
EMP: 10000 EST: 2012
SALES (est): 5.53MM **Privately Held**
SIC: 3679 3612 3663 Electronic circuits;
Transformers, except electric; Antennas,
transmitting and communications

(P-7032)

OMNI CONNECTION INTL INC

126 Via Trevizio, Corona (92879-1772)
PHONE.....................951 898-6232
Henry Cheng, *Pr*
Phyllis Ting, *VP*
▲ EMP: 410 EST: 1992
SQ FT: 65,000
SALES (est): 17.1MM
SALES (corp-wide): 6.55B **Privately Held**
Web: www.omni-conn.com
SIC: 3679 Harness assemblies, for
electronic use: wire or cable
HQ: Electrical Components International,
Inc.
1 City Pl Dr Ste 450
Saint Louis MO 63141

(P-7033)

ONSHORE TECHNOLOGIES INC

2771 Plaza Del Amo Ste 802-803, Torrance
(90503-9308)
PHONE.....................310 533-4888
Max Van Orden, *Pr*
Mark Wilkinson, *Prin*
EMP: 25 EST: 1992
SALES (est): 8.34MM **Privately Held**
Web: www.onshoretechnologies.com
SIC: 3679 Harness assemblies, for
electronic use: wire or cable

(P-7034)

OPTO 22

43044 Business Park Dr, Temecula
(92590-3614)
PHONE.....................951 695-3000
Mark Engman, *Pr*

Benson Hougland, *
Bob Sheffres, *
Kathleen Roe, *
◆ EMP: 200 EST: 1974
SQ FT: 135,000
SALES (est): 19.68MM **Privately Held**
Web: www.opto22.com
SIC: 3679 3823 3625 Electronic switches;
Process control instruments; Relays and
industrial controls

(P-7035)

PACMAG INC

Also Called: Pacific Magnetics
87 Georgina St, Chula Vista (91910-6121)
PHONE.....................619 872-0343
Mary Hill, *Pr*
▲ EMP: 29 EST: 1978
SALES (est): 1.42MM
SALES (corp-wide): 23.52MM **Privately Held**
SIC: 3679 Electronic circuits
PA: Careen, Inc.
15 Somsen St
800 795-8533

(P-7036)

PIONEER MAGNETICS INC

1745 Berkeley St, Santa Monica
(90404-4104)
PHONE.....................310 829-6751
EMP: 110
Web: www.pioneermagnetics.com
SIC: 3679 Power supplies, all types: static

(P-7037)

PPST INC (PA)

17692 Fitch, Irvine (92614-6022)
PHONE.....................800 421-1921
Kevin J Voelcker, *Pr*
▲ EMP: 35 EST: 2003
SALES (est): 25.52MM
SALES (corp-wide): 25.52MM **Privately Held**
Web: www.pacificpower.com
SIC: 3679 Power supplies, all types: static

(P-7038)

PRECISION HERMETIC TECH INC

Also Called: Precision Hermetic
1940 W Park Ave, Redlands (92373-8042)
PHONE.....................909 381-6011
Daniel B Schachtel, *Pr*
Sari Schachtel, *
EMP: 85 EST: 1989
SQ FT: 50,000
SALES (est): 13.87MM **Privately Held**
Web: www.precisionhermetic.com
SIC: 3679 Hermetic seals, for electronic
equipment

(P-7039)

PRED TECHNOLOGIES USA INC

Also Called: Pred
4901 Morena Blvd, San Diego
(92117-3423)
PHONE.....................858 999-2114
Charles Speidel, *CEO*
EMP: 70 EST: 2016
SALES (est): 2.92MM **Privately Held**
Web: www.tokktech.com
SIC: 3679 Headphones, radio

(P-7040)

PTB SALES INC (PA)

Also Called: Ptb
1361 Mountain View Cir, Azusa
(91702-1649)
PHONE.....................626 334-0500

Patrick T Blackwell, *CEO*
Brendan Riley, *
Dean Scarborough, *
Carmen Williams, *
▲ EMP: 28 EST: 1995
SQ FT: 16,000
SALES (est): 12.41MM
SALES (corp-wide): 12.41MM **Privately Held**
Web: www.ptbsales.com
SIC: 3679 3563 Power supplies, all types:
static; Air and gas compressors including
vacuum pumps

(P-7041)

PULSE ELECTRONICS CORPORATION (HQ)

Also Called: Pulse A Yageo Company
15255 Innovation Dr Ste 100, San Diego
(92128-3410)
PHONE.....................858 674-8100
Mark C J Twaalfhoven, *CEO*
▲ EMP: 45 EST: 1947
SQ FT: 50,000
SALES (est): 37.31MM **Privately Held**
Web: www.pulseelectronics.com
SIC: 3679 3612 3663 Electronic circuits;
Transformers, except electric; Antennas,
transmitting and communications
PA: Yageo Corporation
3f, No.233-1, Pao Chiao Rd.,

(P-7042)

Q MICROWAVE INC

1591 Pioneer Way, El Cajon (92020-1637)
PHONE.....................619 258-7322
Eric Maat, *CEO*
Craig Higginson, *
Craig Shauan, *
EMP: 84 EST: 1998
SQ FT: 18,000
SALES (est): 14.9MM
SALES (corp-wide): 12.55B **Publicly Held**
Web: www.qmicrowave.com
SIC: 3679 5065 Microwave components;
Electronic parts and equipment, nec
PA: Amphenol Corporation
358 Hall Ave
203 265-8900

(P-7043)

QORVO CALIFORNIA INC

Also Called: Qorvo US
950 Lawrence Dr, Newbury Park
(91320-1522)
PHONE.....................805 480-5050
Charles J Abronson, *Ch Bd*
Ralph O Quinsey, *
Paul O Daughenbaugh, *
Mark Lampenfeld, *
Susan Liles, *
EMP: 49 EST: 1996
SQ FT: 11,000
SALES (est): 8.15MM
SALES (corp-wide): 3.77B **Publicly Held**
Web: www.qorvo.com
SIC: 3679 Electronic circuits
HQ: Qorvo Us, Inc.
2300 Ne Brookwood Pkwy
Hillsboro OR 97124
503 615-9000

(P-7044)

REEDEX INC

15526 Commerce Ln, Huntington Beach
(92649-1602)
PHONE.....................714 894-0311
Dan Reed, *Pr*
Ted Reed, *
▲ EMP: 49 EST: 1972

PRODUCTS & SVCS

SALES (est): 4.41MM **Privately Held**
Web: www.reedex.com
SIC: **3679** Harness assemblies, for
electronic use: wire or cable

(P-7045)
ROCKER SOLENOID COMPANY
Also Called: Rocker Industries
5492 Bolsa Ave, Huntington Beach
(92649-1021)
PHONE.....................310 534-5660
John W Perry, *Pr*
Francis E Goodyear, *
Raymond Hatashita, *
Milton A Mather, *
▼ EMP: 88 EST: 1954
SQ FT: 23,000
SALES (est): 18.01MM **Privately Held**
Web: www.rockerindustries.com
SIC: **3679** 3672 Solenoids for electronic
applications; Printed circuit boards

(P-7046)
ROGAR MANUFACTURING INC
Also Called: Ro Gar Mfg
866 E Ross Ave, El Centro (92243-9652)
PHONE.....................760 335-3700
Pat Lewis, *Prin*
EMP: 126
SALES (corp-wide): 20.67MM **Privately
Held**
Web: www.rogarmfg.com
SIC: **3679** Electronic circuits
PA: Rogar Manufacturing Incorporated
866 E Ross Ave
760 335-3700

(P-7047)
SANDBERG INDUSTRIES INC
(PA)
Also Called: E M S
2921 Daimler St, Santa Ana (92705-5810)
PHONE.....................949 660-9473
J Sandberg, *CEO*
Steve Walker, *
Leo Boarts, *
John T Sandberg, *
Becky Tamblyn, *
EMP: 52 EST: 1978
SQ FT: 30,000
SALES (est): 3.14MM
SALES (corp-wide): 3.14MM **Privately
Held**
Web: www.unitindustriesgroup.com
SIC: **3679** 3825 3672 3643 Electronic circuits
; Test equipment for electronic and
electrical circuits; Printed circuit boards;
Current-carrying wiring services

(P-7048)
SAS MANUFACTURING INC
405 N Smith Ave, Corona (92878-4305)
PHONE.....................951 734-1808
Theo F Smit Junior, *CEO*
Sharon Smit, *
EMP: 45 EST: 1990
SQ FT: 24,000
SALES (est): 9.86MM **Privately Held**
Web: www.sasmanufacturing.com
SIC: **3679** Harness assemblies, for
electronic use: wire or cable

(P-7049)
SCEPTRE INC
Also Called: E-Scepter
16800 Gale Ave, City Of Industry
(91745-1804)
PHONE.....................626 369-3698
Stephen Liu, *CEO*
Cathy Liu, *

▲ EMP: 50 EST: 1984
SALES (est): 9.83MM **Privately Held**
Web: www.sceptre.com
SIC: **3679** Liquid crystal displays (LCD)

(P-7050)
SMITHS INTERCONNECT INC
375 Conejo Ridge Ave, Thousand Oaks
(91361-4928)
PHONE.....................805 267-0100
Dave Moorehouse, *Pr*
EMP: 68
SALES (corp-wide): 3.97B **Privately Held**
Web: www.smithsinterconnect.com
SIC: **3679** Microwave components
HQ: Smiths Interconnect, Inc.
4726 Eisenhower Blvd
Tampa FL 33634
813 901-7200

(P-7051)
SMITHS INTRCNNECT
AMERICAS INC
1231 E Dyer Rd Ste 235, Santa Ana
(92705-5665)
PHONE.....................714 371-1100
Dom Matos, *Pr*
EMP: 300
SALES (corp-wide): 3.97B **Privately Held**
Web: www.smithsinterconnect.com
SIC: **3679** Microwave components
HQ: Smiths Interconnect Americas, Inc.
2001 Ne 46th St Ste 188
Kansas City MO 64116
913 342-5544

(P-7052)
SPECTROLAB INC
12500 Gladstone Ave, Sylmar
(91342-5373)
P.O. Box 9209 (91392-9209)
PHONE.....................818 365-4611
David Lillington, *Pr*
Edward Ringo, *
Jeff Peacock, *
Nasser Karam, *
Paul Ballew, *
EMP: 400 EST: 1956
SQ FT: 50,000
SALES (est): 36.72MM
SALES (corp-wide): 77.79B **Publicly Held**
Web: www.spectrolab.com
SIC: **3679** 3674 Power supplies, all types:
static; Solar cells
HQ: Boeing Satellite Systems, Inc.
900 N Pacific Coast Hwy
El Segundo CA 90245

(P-7053)
STATEK CORPORATION
1449 W Orange Grove Ave, Orange
(92868-1120)
PHONE.....................714 639-7810
EMP: 121
SALES (corp-wide): 54.21MM **Privately
Held**
Web: www.statek.com
SIC: **3679** Electronic circuits
HQ: Statek Corporation
512 N Main St
Orange CA 92868
714 639-7810

(P-7054)
STATEK CORPORATION (HQ)
Also Called: Statek
512 N Main St, Orange (92868-1182)
PHONE.....................714 639-7810
Michael Dastmalchian, *
Margaritha W Werren, *

▲ EMP: 129 EST: 1970
SQ FT: 71,000
SALES (est): 16.06MM
SALES (corp-wide): 54.21MM **Privately
Held**
Web: www.statek.com
SIC: **3679** Electronic circuits
PA: Technicorp International Ii, Inc.
512 N Main St
714 639-7810

(P-7055)
STRIKE TECHNOLOGY INC
Also Called: Wilorco
24311 Wilmington Ave, Carson
(90745-6139)
PHONE.....................562 437-3428
Robert Kunesh, *Ch Bd*
EMP: 25 EST: 2001
SQ FT: 9,800
SALES (est): 4.52MM **Privately Held**
Web: www.wilorco.com
SIC: **3679** Electronic circuits

(P-7056)
TDK ELECTRONICS INC
8787 Complex Dr Ste 200, San Diego
(92123-1451)
PHONE.....................858 715-4200
Wolfgang Till, *Prin*
EMP: 105
Web: tdk-electronics.tdk.com
SIC: **3679** 5065 3546 Electronic crystals;
Diskettes, computer; Power-driven
handtools
HQ: Tdk Electronics Inc.
10 Wodbrdge Ctr Dr Ste 13
Woodbridge NJ 07095
732 906-4300

(P-7057)
TECHNICAL CABLE CONCEPTS
INC
350 Lear Ave, Costa Mesa (92626-6015)
PHONE.....................714 835-1081
▲ EMP: 50 EST: 1989
SALES (est): 7.8MM **Privately Held**
Web: www.techcable.com
SIC: **3679** 3229 Harness assemblies, for
electronic use: wire or cable; Fiber optics
strands

(P-7058)
TELEDYNE TECHNOLOGIES INC
(PA)
Also Called: Teledyne Technologies
1049 Camino Dos Rios, Thousand Oaks
(91360-2362)
PHONE.....................805 373-4545
Edwin Roks, *CEO*
Robert Mehrabian, *
Jason Vanwees, *Vice Chairman*
George C Bobb Iii, *Pr*
Melanie S Cibik, *CCO*
EMP: 250 EST: 1960
SALES (est): 5.64B
SALES (corp-wide): 5.64B **Publicly Held**
Web: www.teledyne.com
SIC: **3679** 3761 3519 3724 Electronic circuits
; Guided missiles and space vehicles;
Internal combustion engines, nec; Aircraft
engines and engine parts

(P-7059)
TELEDYNE TECHNOLOGIES INC
Also Called: Teledyne Controls
501 Continental Blvd, El Segundo
(90245-5036)
P.O. Box 1026 (90245-1026)
PHONE.....................310 765-3600

Masood Hassan, *Brnch Mgr*
EMP: 300
SALES (corp-wide): 5.64B **Publicly Held**
Web: www.teledyne.com
SIC: **3679** 8731 3812 3519 Electronic circuits
; Commercial physical research; Search
and navigation equipment; Internal
combustion engines, nec
PA: Teledyne Technologies Inc
1049 Camino Dos Rios
805 373-4545

(P-7060)
TELEDYNE TECHNOLOGIES INC
Also Called: Teledyne
12964 Panama St, Los Angeles
(90066-6534)
PHONE.....................310 822-8229
Bruce Gecks, *Mgr*
EMP: 360
SALES (corp-wide): 5.64B **Publicly Held**
Web: www.teledyne.com
SIC: **3679** Electronic circuits
PA: Teledyne Technologies Inc
1049 Camino Dos Rios
805 373-4545

(P-7061)
TERADYNE INC
30701 Agoura Rd, Agoura Hills
(91301-5928)
PHONE.....................818 991-2900
Greg Beecher, *Mgr*
EMP: 92
SALES (corp-wide): 2.68B **Publicly Held**
Web: www.teradyne.com
SIC: **3679** Electronic circuits
PA: Teradyne, Inc.
600 Riverpark Dr
978 370-2700

(P-7062)
TRANSICO INC
Also Called: Eeco Switch
1240 Pioneer St Ste A, Brea (92821-3740)
PHONE.....................714 835-6000
▲ EMP: 24 EST: 1992
SALES (est): 1MM **Privately Held**
Web: www.eecoswitch.com
SIC: **3679** 3672 3643 3577 Electronic
switches; Printed circuit boards; Current-
carrying wiring services; Computer
peripheral equipment, nec

(P-7063)
TT ELCTRNICS PWR SLTONS
US INC
1330 E Cypress St, Covina (91724-2103)
PHONE.....................626 967-6021
Michael Joseph Leahan, *CEO*
Matthew Alexander Sweaney, *Sec*
Kumen Rey Call, *CFO*
EMP: 120 EST: 2019
SALES (est): 24.32MM
SALES (corp-wide): 765.19MM **Privately
Held**
Web: www.ttelectronics.com
SIC: **3679** Electronic circuits
PA: Tt Electronics Plc
4th Floor St. Andrews House
193 282-5300

(P-7064)
U S CIRCUIT INC
2071 Wineridge Pl, Escondido
(92029-1931)
PHONE.....................760 489-1413
Michael Fariba, *Pr*
T J Sojitra, *Sr VP*
Mukesh Patel, *VP*

▲ = Import ▼ = Export
◆ = Import/Export

EMP: 80 **EST:** 1985
SQ FT: 40,000
SALES (est): 9.83MM
SALES (corp-wide): 13.47MM **Privately Held**
Web: www.uscircuit.com
SIC: 3679 3672 Electronic circuits; Printed circuit boards
PA: Ampel Incorporated
925 Estes Ave
847 952-1900

(P-7065)
VAS ENGINEERING INC
4750 Viewridge Ave, San Diego (92123-1640)
PHONE....................858 569-1601
Rohak Vora, *CEO*
Greg Atzmiller, *
T J Sojitra, *Stockholder*
▲ **EMP:** 50 **EST:** 1979
SQ FT: 19,200
SALES (est): 10.2MM **Privately Held**
Web: www.vasengineering.com
SIC: 3679 3823 Electronic circuits; Temperature measurement instruments, industrial

(P-7066)
VERTEX LCD INC
600 S Jefferson St Ste K, Placentia (92870-6634)
P.O. Box 206 (92871-0206)
PHONE....................714 223-7111
EMP: 35 **EST:** 1999
SALES (est): 893.6K **Privately Held**
Web: www.vertexlcd.com
SIC: 3679 Liquid crystal displays (LCD)

(P-7067)
VISUAL COMMUNICATIONS COMPANY LLC
Also Called: Vcc
2173 Salk Ave Ste 175, Carlsbad (92008-7836)
PHONE....................800 522-5546
EMP: 205 **EST:** 1976
SALES (est): 13.53MM **Privately Held**
Web: www.vcclite.com
SIC: 3679 Electronic circuits

(P-7068)
WAVESTREAM CORPORATION (HQ)
545 W Terrace Dr, San Dimas (91773-2915)
PHONE....................909 599-9080
Robert Huffman, *CEO*
Nimrod Itach, *
Lanis Bell, *
James Rosenberg, *
EMP: 103 **EST:** 2006
SQ FT: 33,000
SALES (est): 22.05MM **Privately Held**
Web: www.wavestream.com
SIC: 3679 8731 Microwave components; Commercial physical research
PA: Gilat Satellite Networks Ltd.
21 Yegia Kapaim

(P-7069)
WESTERN DIGITAL
19600 S Western Ave, Torrance (90501-1117)
P.O. Box 5084 (92609-8584)
PHONE....................510 557-7553
EMP: 97 **EST:** 2019
SALES (est): 5.55MM **Privately Held**
Web: www.westerndigital.com

SIC: 3679 Electronic components, nec

(P-7070)
WYVERN TECHNOLOGIES
1205 E Warner Ave, Santa Ana (92705-5431)
PHONE....................714 966-0710
James J Weber, *Pr*
EMP: 30 **EST:** 1984
SQ FT: 10,000
SALES (est): 1.74MM **Privately Held**
Web: www.wyverncorp.com
SIC: 3679 Microwave components

(P-7071)
XP POWER INC
Also Called: Switching Systems
1590 S Sinclair St, Anaheim (92806-5933)
PHONE....................714 712-2642
Fred Mckirigan, *VP*
EMP: 64
Web: www.xppower.com
SIC: 3679 Power supplies, all types: static
HQ: Xp Power Inc.
305 Foster St Ste 4
Littleton MA 01460
800 253-0490

3691 Storage Batteries

(P-7072)
BATTERY TECHNOLOGY INC (PA)
Also Called: B T I
16651 E Johnson Dr, City Of Industry (91745-2413)
PHONE....................626 336-6878
Christopher Chu, *Pr*
Andy Tong, *VP*
▲ **EMP:** 53 **EST:** 1992
SQ FT: 20,000
SALES (est): 3.88MM **Privately Held**
Web: www.batterytech.com
SIC: 3691 Storage batteries

(P-7073)
ENERGY VAULT INC (HQ)
4360 Park Terrace Dr Ste 100, Westlake Village (91361-4627)
PHONE....................805 852-0000
Robert Piconi, *CEO*
Andrea Wuttke, *
EMP: 38 **EST:** 2017
SQ FT: 15,767
SALES (est): 24.95MM
SALES (corp-wide): 341.54MM **Publicly Held**
Web: www.energyvault.com
SIC: 3691 Storage batteries
PA: Energy Vault Holdings, Inc.
4360 Park Ter Dr Ste 100
805 852-0000

(P-7074)
ENERSYS
5580 Edison Ave, Chino (91710-6936)
PHONE....................909 464-8251
Ken Hill, *Brnch Mgr*
EMP: 25
SALES (corp-wide): 3.58B **Publicly Held**
Web: www.enersys.com
SIC: 3691 Lead acid batteries (storage batteries)
PA: Enersys
2366 Bernville Rd
610 208-1991

(P-7075)
ENEVATE CORPORATION
Also Called: Enevate
101 Theory Ste 200, Irvine (92617-3089)
PHONE....................949 243-0399
Bob Kruse, *Pr*
Kirk Shockley, *
Doctor Benjamin Park, *Prin*
Jarvis Tou, *
Doug A Morris, *Quality Vice President*
▲ **EMP:** 62 **EST:** 2005
SQ FT: 17,000
SALES (est): 9.44MM **Privately Held**
Web: www.enevate.com
SIC: 3691 Storage batteries

(P-7076)
EREPLACEMENTS LLC
16885 W Bernardo Dr Ste 370, San Diego (92127-1660)
PHONE....................714 361-2652
Thomas M Peck, *Brnch Mgr*
EMP: 30
Web: www.ereplacements.com
SIC: 3691 Storage batteries
PA: Ereplacements, Llc
1300 Mnters Chpel Rd Ste

(P-7077)
FLUX POWER HOLDINGS INC (PA)
2685 S Melrose Dr, Vista (92081-8783)
PHONE....................877 505-3589
Ronald F Dutt, *Ch Bd*
Charles A Scheiwe, *Sec*
Jeffrey Mason, *VP Opers*
Kevin Royal, *CFO*
▲ **EMP:** 123 **EST:** 1998
SQ FT: 63,200
SALES (est): 66.34MM **Publicly Held**
Web: www.fluxpower.com
SIC: 3691 5063 Storage batteries; Storage batteries, industrial

(P-7078)
GOLD PEAK INDUSTRIES (NORTH AMERICA) INC
Also Called: GP Batteries
11245 W Bernardo Ct Ste 104, San Diego (92127-1676)
PHONE....................858 674-6099
▲ **EMP:** 40
Web: www.gpina.com
SIC: 3691 Batteries, rechargeable

(P-7079)
PALOS VERDES BUILDING CORP (PA)
Also Called: U.S. Battery Mfg Co
1675 Sampson Ave, Corona (02870-1880)
PHONE....................951 371-8090
◆ **EMP:** 115 **EST:** 1949
SALES (est): 57.03MM
SALES (corp-wide): 57.03MM **Privately Held**
Web: www.usbattery.com
SIC: 3691 Storage batteries

(P-7080)
SIMPLIPHI POWER INC
3100 Camino Del Sol, Oxnard (93030-7257)
PHONE....................805 640-6700
Stephen P Andrews, *CEO*
Mark A Schwertfeger, *
▲ **EMP:** 34 **EST:** 2001
SQ FT: 5,300
SALES (est): 15.72MM
SALES (corp-wide): 2.04B **Privately Held**

Web: energy.briggsandstratton.com
SIC: 3691 Storage batteries
HQ: Briggs & Stratton, Llc
12301 W Wirth St
Wauwatosa WI 53222
414 259-5333

(P-7081)
SUNFUSION ENERGY SYSTEMS INC
9020 Kenamar Dr Ste 204, San Diego (92121-2431)
PHONE....................800 544-0282
Walter Ellard, *Pr*
EMP: 24 **EST:** 2019
SQ FT: 6,000
SALES (est): 1.33MM **Privately Held**
Web: www.sunfusioness.com
SIC: 3691 Storage batteries

(P-7082)
TELEDYNE TECHNOLOGIES INC
Also Called: Teledyne Battery Products
840 W Brockton Ave, Redlands (92374-2902)
P.O. Box 7950 (92375-1150)
PHONE....................909 793-3131
Greg Donahey, *Brnch Mgr*
EMP: 58
SALES (corp-wide): 5.64B **Publicly Held**
Web: www.teledyne.com
SIC: 3691 3692 Storage batteries; Primary batteries, dry and wet
PA: Teledyne Technologies Inc
1049 Camino Dos Rios
805 373-4545

(P-7083)
TROJAN BATTERY HOLDINGS LLC
12380 Clark St, Santa Fe Springs (90670-3804)
PHONE....................800 423-6569
EMP: 73 **EST:** 2013
SALES (est): 4.65MM
SALES (corp-wide): 3.44B **Privately Held**
Web: www.trojanbattery.com
SIC: 3691 3692 Lead acid batteries (storage batteries); Primary batteries, dry and wet
HQ: Trojan Battery Company, Llc
12380 Clark St
Santa Fe Springs CA 90670
562 236-3000

3692 Primary Batteries, Dry And Wet

(P-7084)
ASSA ABLOY AB
Also Called: Hhi
19701 Da Vinci, Lake Forest (92610-2622)
PHONE....................949 672-4003
Lucas Boselli, *Division Head*
EMP: 700
SQ FT: 150,000
Web: www.assaabloy.com
SIC: 3692 Primary batteries, dry and wet
PA: Assa Abloy Ab
Klarabergsviadukten 90
850648500

(P-7085)
QUALLION LLC
12744 San Fernando Rd Ste 100, Sylmar (91342-3854)
PHONE....................818 833-2000
Jackie York, *
▲ **EMP:** 155 **EST:** 1998

SALES (est): 20.01MM
SALES (corp-wide): 3.58B **Publicly Held**
Web: www.enersys.com
SIC: **3692** Primary batteries, dry and wet
PA: Enersys
2366 Bernville Rd
610 208-1991

(P-7086)
TROJAN BATTERY COMPANY LLC (DH)
12380 Clark St, Santa Fe Springs (90670-3804)
PHONE...................562 236-3000
TOLL FREE: 800
Richard A Heller, *CEO*
Alex Dimitrijevic, *CFO*
◆ EMP: 182 EST: 2013
SALES (est): 658.32MM
SALES (corp-wide): 3.44B **Privately Held**
Web: www.trojanbattery.com
SIC: **3692** 3691 Primary batteries, dry and wet; Lead acid batteries (storage batteries)
HQ: C&D Technologies, Inc.
200 Precision Rd
Horsham PA 19044
215 619-2700

3694 Engine Electrical Equipment

(P-7087)
AMERICAN INDUSTRIAL MANUFACTURING SERVICES INC
41673 Corning Pl, Murrieta (92562-7023)
PHONE...................951 698-3379
▼ EMP: 107
SIC: **3694** Engine electrical equipment

(P-7088)
ARRIVER HOLDCO INC
5775 Morehouse Dr, San Diego (92121-1714)
PHONE...................858 587-1121
Jacob Svanberg, *CEO*
EMP: 7543 EST: 2017
SALES (est): 1.66B
SALES (corp-wide): 38.96B **Publicly Held**
Web: www.veoneer.com
SIC: **3694** 3714 Automotive electrical equipment, nec; Motor vehicle parts and accessories
PA: Qualcomm Incorporated
5775 Morehouse Dr
858 587-1121

(P-7089)
BATTERY-BIZ INC
Also Called: Ebatts.com
1380 Flynn Rd, Camarillo (93012-8016)
PHONE...................800 848-6782
Ophir Marish, *CEO*
Yossi Jakubovits, *
▲ EMP: 63 EST: 1988
SALES (est): 9.47MM **Privately Held**
Web: www.battery-biz.com
SIC: **3694** Battery charging generators, automobile and aircraft

(P-7090)
DSM&T CO INC
10609 Business Dr, Fontana (92337-8212)
PHONE...................909 357-7960
Sergio Corona, *CEO*
▲ EMP: 170 EST: 1982
SQ FT: 41,000
SALES (est): 24.97MM **Privately Held**

Web: www.dsmt.com
SIC: **3694** 3357 3634 3643 Harness wiring sets, internal combustion engines; Nonferrous wiredrawing and insulating; Heating pads, electric; Cord connectors, electric

(P-7091)
ELECTRICAL REBUILDERS SLS INC
Also Called: Vapex-Genex-Precision
7603 Willow Glen Rd, Los Angeles (90046-1608)
PHONE...................323 249-7545
Mike Klapper, *Pr*
David Klapper, *
Mary Ann Klapper, *
▲ EMP: 100 EST: 1966
SALES (est): 3.25MM **Privately Held**
SIC: **3694** 3592 3714 Distributors, motor vehicle engine; Carburetors; Motor vehicle brake systems and parts

(P-7092)
EV CHARGING SOLUTIONS INC
11800 Clark St, Arcadia (91006-6000)
PHONE...................866 300-3827
Gustavo Fabian Occhiuzzo, *CEO*
EMP: 56 EST: 2018
SALES (est): 5.55MM **Privately Held**
Web: www.evconnect.com
SIC: **3694** Battery charging alternators and generators

(P-7093)
LOOP INC
115 Eucalyptus Dr, El Segundo (90245-3839)
PHONE...................888 385-6674
Dustin Cavanaugh, *CEO*
EMP: 30 EST: 2019
SALES (est): 6.08MM **Privately Held**
Web: www.evloop.io
SIC: **3694** Battery charging generators, automobile and aircraft

(P-7094)
LOW COST INTERLOCK INC
2038 W Park Ave, Redlands (92373-6260)
P.O. Box 365 (92373-0121)
PHONE...................844 387-0326
Michael E Lyon, *CEO*
EMP: 39 EST: 2010
SALES (est): 2.42MM **Privately Held**
Web: www.lowcostinterlock.com
SIC: **3694** Ignition apparatus and distributors

(P-7095)
M & H ELECTRIC FABRICATORS INC
13537 Alondra Blvd, Santa Fe Springs (90670-5602)
PHONE...................562 926-9552
▲ EMP: 30 EST: 1985
SALES (est): 4.69MM **Privately Held**
Web: www.wiringharness.com
SIC: **3694** Automotive electrical equipment, nec

(P-7096)
MAXWELL TECHNOLOGIES INC (HQ)
Also Called: Maxwell
6155 Cornerstone Ct E Ste 210, San Diego (92121-4737)
PHONE...................858 503-3300
Franz Fink, *Pr*
David Lyle, *
Emily Lough, *

▲ EMP: 94 EST: 1965
SQ FT: 30,500
SALES (est): 55.86MM
SALES (corp-wide): 96.77B **Publicly Held**
Web: www.maxwell.com
SIC: **3694** 3629 Engine electrical equipment; Capacitors and condensers
PA: Tesla, Inc.
1 Tesla Rd
512 516-8177

(P-7097)
MYOTEK INDUSTRIES INCORPORATED (DH)
1278 Glenneyre St Ste 431, Laguna Beach (92651-3103)
PHONE...................949 502-3776
Robert Harrington, *Pr*
▲ EMP: 90 EST: 1998
SQ FT: 1,800
SALES (est): 28.81MM
SALES (corp-wide): 110.61MM **Privately Held**
Web: www.fordledfog.com
SIC: **3694** 5013 Automotive electrical equipment, nec; Automotive servicing equipment
HQ: Myotek Holdings, Inc.
1176 Main St Ste B
Irvine CA 92614
949 502-3776

(P-7098)
PERTRONIX INC
Also Called: Patriot Products
15601 Cypress Ave Unit B, Irwindale (91706-2120)
PHONE...................909 599-5955
Jack Porter, *Mgr*
EMP: 26
SALES (corp-wide): 13.89MM **Privately Held**
Web: www.pertronixbrands.com
SIC: **3694** 5013 Ignition apparatus, internal combustion engines; Automotive supplies and parts
PA: Pertronix, Llc
10955 Mill Creek Rd
909 599-5955

(P-7099)
POLAR POWER INC
Also Called: Polar Power
249 E Gardena Blvd, Gardena (90248-2813)
PHONE...................310 830-9153
EMP: 87 EST: 1979
SALES (est): 15.29MM **Privately Held**
Web: www.polarpower.com
SIC: **3694** Engine electrical equipment

(P-7100)
STABLE AUTO CORPORATION
124 Jupiter St, Encinitas (92024-1449)
PHONE...................415 967-2719
Rohan Puri, *CEO*
EMP: 30 EST: 2019
SALES (est): 3.09MM **Privately Held**
Web: www.stable.auto
SIC: **3694** Battery charging generators, automobile and aircraft

(P-7101)
TRADEMARK CONSTRUCTION CO INC (PA)
Also Called: Jmw Truss and Components
15916 Bernardo Center Dr, San Diego (92127-1828)
PHONE...................760 489-5647
Richard D Wilson, *Pr*

John Cao, *
Nancy Wilson, *
EMP: 60 EST: 1978
SQ FT: 12,000
SALES (est): 21.52MM
SALES (corp-wide): 21.52MM **Privately Held**
Web: www.jmwtruss.com
SIC: **3694** Engine electrical equipment

(P-7102)
VANTAGE VEHICLE INTL INC
Also Called: Vantage Vehicle Group
1740 N Delilah St, Corona (92879-1893)
PHONE...................951 735-1200
Michael Pak, *Pr*
◆ EMP: 30 EST: 2002
SQ FT: 50,000
SALES (est): 4.83MM **Privately Held**
Web: www.vantagevehicle.com
SIC: **3694** Distributors, motor vehicle engine

3695 Magnetic And Optical Recording Media

(P-7103)
CD VIDEO MANUFACTURING INC
Also Called: C D Video
12650 Westminster Ave, Santa Ana (92706-2139)
PHONE...................714 265-0770
Minh T Nguyen, *Pr*
▲ EMP: 60 EST: 1995
SQ FT: 11,000
SALES (est): 11.02MM **Privately Held**
Web: www.cdvideomfg.com
SIC: **3695** 3652 7819 Video recording tape, blank; Compact laser discs, prerecorded; Services allied to motion pictures

(P-7104)
FARSTONE TECHNOLOGY INC
184 Technology Dr Ste 205, Irvine (92618-2435)
PHONE...................949 336-4321
EMP: 110
SALES (est): 3.1MM **Privately Held**
Web: www.farstone.com
SIC: **3695** Computer software tape and disks: blank, rigid, and floppy

(P-7105)
NORDSON CALIFORNIA INC
Also Called: Nordson Asymtek
2747 Loker Ave W, Carlsbad (92010-6601)
PHONE...................760 918-8490
◆ EMP: 94
SIC: **3695** 3561 Computer software tape and disks: blank, rigid, and floppy; Pump jacks and other pumping equipment

(P-7106)
TARGET TECHNOLOGY COMPANY LLC
3420 Bristol St, Costa Mesa (92626-7170)
PHONE...................949 788-0909
EMP: 50 EST: 1998
SALES (est): 1.6MM **Privately Held**
Web: www.targettechnology.com
SIC: **3695** Magnetic and optical recording media

(P-7107)
TECHNICOLOR DISC SERVICES CORP (HQ)
3601 Calle Tecate Ste 120, Camarillo (93012-5097)

PHONE.................805 445-1122
Mary Fialkowski, *Pr*
O F Raimondo, ,*
▲ **EMP: 200 EST:** 1996
SALES (est): 1.36MM Privately Held
SIC: 3695 7361 Computer software tape and disks: blank, rigid, and floppy; Employment agencies
PA: Vantiva
10 Boulevard De Grenelle

3699 Electrical Equipment And Supplies, Nec

(P-7108)
AGENTS WEST INC
Also Called: Electrical Products Rep
6 Hughes Ste 210, Irvine (92618-2063)
PHONE.................949 614-0293
Aldo Pellicciotti, *Pr*
Stephen Benshoof, *VP*
Clyde Collins, *Treas*
Robert Rathburn, *Sec*
EMP: 38 EST: 1978
SQ FT: 30,000
SALES (est): 4.52MM Privately Held
Web: www.agentswest.com
SIC: 3699 5063 Electrical equipment and supplies, nec; Electrical apparatus and equipment

(P-7109)
AITECH DEFENSE SYSTEMS INC
19756 Prairie St, Chatsworth (91311-6531)
PHONE.................818 700-2000
Moshe Tal, *CEO*
Erez Konfino, *CFO*
◆ **EMP: 55 EST:** 1990
SQ FT: 22,000
SALES (est): 22.56MM Privately Held
Web: www.aitechsystems.com
SIC: 3699 Electrical equipment and supplies, nec
PA: Aitech Rugged Group, Inc.
19756 Prairie St

(P-7110)
AITECH RUGGED GROUP INC (PA)
19756 Prairie St, Chatsworth (91311-6531)
PHONE.................818 700-2000
Moshe Tal, *CEO*
Erez Konfino, *
EMP: 50 EST: 2008
SALES (est): 29.92MM Privately Held
Web: www.aitechsystems.com
SIC: 3699 Electrical equipment and supplies, nec

(P-7111)
BLISSLIGHTS INC
2449 Cades Way, Vista (92081-7873)
PHONE.................888 868-4603
Alan Lee, *Pr*
▲ **EMP: 24 EST:** 2007
SALES (est): 4.78MM Privately Held
Web: www.blisslights.com
SIC: 3699 Laser systems and equipment

(P-7112)
CARTTRONICS LLC (HQ)
90 Icon, Foothill Ranch (92610-3000)
PHONE.................888 696-2278
◆ **EMP: 27 EST:** 1997
SALES (est): 4.87MM
SALES (corp-wide): 40.85MM Privately Held
Web: www.gatekeepersystems.com

SIC: **3699** 7382 5065 Security devices; Security systems services; Security control equipment and systems
PA: Gatekeeper Systems, Inc.
90 Icon
888 808-9433

(P-7113)
COAST WIRE & PLASTIC TECH LLC
1048 E Burgrove St, Carson (90746-3514)
PHONE.................310 639-9473
George Lopez, *Co-Managing Member*
George Lopez, *Managing Member*
Mark Vanderwoude, *
David Ibanez, *
EMP: 750 EST: 1993
SQ FT: 60,000
SALES (est): 4.65MM
SALES (corp-wide): 2.51B Publicly Held
SIC: 3699 3357 Electrical equipment and supplies, nec; Communication wire
PA: Belden Inc.
1 N Brentwood Blvd Fl 15
314 854-8000

(P-7114)
COOPER CROUSE-HINDS LLC
Also Called: Cooper Interconnect
3350 Enterprise Dr, Bloomington (92316-3538)
PHONE.................951 241-8766
Morris Townsend, *Brnch Mgr*
EMP: 37
Web: www.coopercrouse-hinds.com
SIC: 3699 Fire control or bombing equipment, electronic
HQ: Cooper Crouse-Hinds, Llc
1201 Wolf St
Syracuse NY 13208
315 477-7000

(P-7115)
CUBIC DEFENSE APPLICATIONS INC (DH)
Also Called: Cubic Ground Training
9233 Balboa Ave, San Diego (92123-1513)
P.O. Box 85587 (92186)
PHONE.................858 776-5664
Steven Slijepcevic, *CEO*
John D Thomas, *
James R Edwards, *
Mark A Harrison, *
Norman R Bishop, *
▼ **EMP: 589 EST:** 1987
SQ FT: 130,000
SALES (est): 497.76MM
SALES (corp-wide): 1.48B Privately Held
Web: www.cubic.com
SIC: 3699 3663 3812 Flight simulators (training aids), electronic; Radio and t.v. communications equipment; Aircraft/aerospace flight instruments and guidance systems
HQ: Cubic Corporation
9233 Balboa Ave
San Diego CA 92123
858 277-6780

(P-7116)
CUBIC DEFENSE APPLICATIONS INC
4285 Ponderosa Ave, San Diego (92123-1525)
PHONE.................858 277-6780
EMP: 1039
SALES (corp-wide): 1.48B Privately Held
Web: www.cubic.com
SIC: 3699 Flight simulators (training aids), electronic

HQ: Cubic Defense Applications, Inc.
9233 Balboa Ave
San Diego CA 92123
858 776-5664

(P-7117)
CUBIC DEFENSE APPLICATIONS INC
CMS Secure Comms
9233 Balboa Ave, San Diego (92123-1513)
PHONE.................858 505-2870
Jerry Madigan, *VP*
EMP: 200
SALES (corp-wide): 1.48B Privately Held
Web: www.cubic.com
SIC: 3699 7382 Security devices; Security systems services
HQ: Cubic Defense Applications, Inc.
9233 Balboa Ave
San Diego CA 92123
858 776-5664

(P-7118)
CYMER LLC (HQ)
17075 Thornmint Ct, San Diego (92127-2413)
PHONE.................858 385-7300
▲ **EMP: 555 EST:** 1996
SQ FT: 135,000
SALES (est): 659.74MM
SALES (corp-wide): 29.96B Privately Held
Web: www.cymer.com
SIC: 3699 3827 Laser systems and equipment; Lens mounts
PA: Asml Holding N.V.
De Run 6501
402683000

(P-7119)
DISTRIBUTION ELECTRNICS VLUED
Also Called: Deva
2651 Dow Ave, Tustin (92780-7207)
PHONE.................714 368-1717
Rodger Dale Baker, *CEO*
Ken Plock, *
◆ **EMP: 23 EST:** 1974
SQ FT: 13,800
SALES (est): 8.14MM Privately Held
Web: www.devainc.com
SIC: 3699 5065 Electrical equipment and supplies, nec; Electronic parts and equipment, nec
HQ: Deva, Inc.
555 Madison Ave Ste 1100
New York NY 10022
212 223-2466

(P-7120)
DOORKING INC (PA)
Also Called: Doorking
120 S Glasgow Ave, Inglewood (90301-1502)
PHONE.................310 645-0023
Thomas Richmond, *Pr*
Pat Kochie, *
Susan Richmond, *
◆ **EMP: 185 EST:** 1948
SQ FT: 16,000
SALES (est): 32.06MM
SALES (corp-wide): 32.06MM Privately Held
Web: www.doorking.com
SIC: 3699 5065 3829 Security control equipment and systems; Security control equipment and systems; Measuring and controlling devices, nec

(P-7121)
DUTEK INCORPORATED
2228 Oak Ridge Way, Vista (92081-8341)
PHONE.................760 566-8888
David Du, *CEO*
Bill Marsh, *
EMP: 50 EST: 2000
SQ FT: 4,500
SALES (est): 20.57MM
SALES (corp-wide): 30.55MM Privately Held
Web: www.dutek.com
SIC: 3699 3629 3643 Electrical equipment and supplies, nec; Electronic generation equipment; Current-carrying wiring services
PA: Ddh Enterprise, Inc.
2220 Oak Ridge Way
760 599-0171

(P-7122)
ELECTRIC GATE STORE INC
15342 Chatsworth St, Mission Hills (91345-2041)
PHONE.................818 504-2300
Jorge Nunez, *Pr*
Karla Nunez, *
▲ **EMP: 150 EST:** 2001
SALES (est): 1.46MM Privately Held
Web: www.gatestore.com
SIC: 3699 Security devices

(P-7123)
FREEDOM PHOTONICS LLC
41 Aero Camino, Santa Barbara (93117-3104)
PHONE.................805 967-4900
Leif Johansson, *
EMP: 50 EST: 2005
SQ FT: 14,500
SALES (est): 11.28MM
SALES (corp-wide): 69.78MM Publicly Held
Web: www.freedomphotonics.com
SIC: 3699 3827 3674 Laser systems and equipment; Optical test and inspection equipment; Light sensitive devices
PA: Luminar Technologies, Inc.
2603 Discovery Dr Ste 100
800 532-2417

(P-7124)
GATEKEEPER SYSTEMS INC (PA)
90 Icon, Foothill Ranch (92610-3000)
PHONE.................888 808-9433
Robert Harling, *CEO*
Jason Crowl, *
Keith Kato, *
Greg Meisenzahl, *
Robert Newbold, *
▲ **EMP: 63 EST:** 1998
SQ FT: 15,000
SALES (est): 40.85MM
SALES (corp-wide): 40.85MM Privately Held
Web: www.gatekeepersystems.com
SIC: 3699 Security devices

(P-7125)
HC WEST LLC
7130 Convoy Ct, San Diego (92111-1019)
PHONE.................858 277-3473
Robert Hunter, *Managing Member*
EMP: 300 EST: 2020
SALES (est): 20.19MM Privately Held
SIC: 3699 Security control equipment and systems

(P-7126)
INSTRUMENTS INCORPORATED
7263 Engineer Rd Ste G, San Diego
(92111-1493)
PHONE...........................858 571-1111
EMP: 28 EST: 1941
SALES (est): 5.32MM Privately Held
Web: www.instrumentsinc.com
SIC: 3699 Electrical equipment and supplies,
nec

(P-7127)
IRONWOOD ELECTRIC INC
13 Ashton, Mission Viejo (92692-4731)
PHONE...........................714 630-2350
Raymond Chafe, Prin
EMP: 28 EST: 2011
SALES (est): 4.96MM Privately Held
Web: www.albdinc.com
SIC: 3699 1731 Electrical equipment and
supplies, nec; Electrical work

(P-7128)
ISC8 INC
Also Called: Irvine Sensors
151 Kalmus Dr Ste A203, Costa Mesa
(92626-5999)
PHONE...........................714 549-8211
EMP: 38
Web: www.isc8.com
SIC: 3699 3674 8731 Security control
equipment and systems; Semiconductors
and related devices; Electronic research

(P-7129)
IWERKS ENTERTAINMENT INC
Also Called: Simex-Iwerks
25040 Avenue Tibbitts Ste F, Valencia
(91355-3946)
PHONE...........................661 678-1800
Gary Matus, CEO
Jeff Dahl, *
Mark Cornell, *
Donald Stults, *
EMP: 75 EST: 1986
SALES (est): 6.79MM Privately Held
Web: www.simex-iwerks.com
SIC: 3699 7819 Electrical equipment and
supplies, nec; Developing and printing of
commercial motion picture film

(P-7130)
KANEX
9377 Haven Ave, Rancho Cucamonga
(91730-5340)
PHONE...........................714 332-1681
Kelvin Yan, CEO
▲ EMP: 25 EST: 1987
SALES (est): 1.9MM Privately Held
Web: www.kanex.com
SIC: 3699 5065 Electrical equipment and
supplies, nec; Electronic parts and
equipment, nec

(P-7131)
KULICKE SFFA WEDGE
BONDING INC
Also Called: Kulicke & Soffa Industries
1821 E Dyer Rd Ste 200, Santa Ana
(92705-5700)
PHONE...........................949 660-0440
Scott Kulicke, Pr
▲ EMP: 200 EST: 2008
SALES (est): 15.85MM
SALES (corp-wide): 706.23MM Publicly
Held
Web: www.kns.com
SIC: 3699 Electrical equipment and supplies,
nec
PA: Kulicke And Soffa Industries, Inc.
1005 Virginia Dr

215 784-6000

(P-7132)
KYOCERA SLD LASER INC
111 Castilian Dr, Goleta (93117-3025)
PHONE...........................310 808-4542
EMP: 31
Web: www.kyocera-sldlaser.com
SIC: 3699 Laser systems and equipment
HQ: Kyocera Sld Laser, Inc.
485 Pine Ave
Goleta CA 93117
805 696-6999

(P-7133)
MEGGITT SAFETY SYSTEMS
INC
11661 Sorrento Valley Rd, San Diego
(92121-1010)
PHONE...........................442 792-3217
EMP: 97
SALES (corp-wide): 19.93B Publicly Held
Web: www.meggitt.com
SIC: 3699 Betatrons
HQ: Meggitt Safety Systems, Inc.
1785 Voyager Ave
Simi Valley CA 93063
805 584-4100

(P-7134)
MEGGITT SAFETY SYSTEMS
INC (DH)
Also Called: Parker Meggitt
1785 Voyager Ave, Simi Valley
(93063-3363)
PHONE...........................805 584-4100
Michael Macgillis, CEO
Patrick Scott, *
Guy C Fabe, *
Daniel J Whitman, *
▲ EMP: 210 EST: 1999
SQ FT: 180,000
SALES (est): 118.2MM
SALES (corp-wide): 19.93B Publicly Held
Web: www.meggitt.com
SIC: 3699 3724 3728 7389 Betatrons;
Exhaust systems, aircraft; Aircraft parts and
equipment, nec; Fire protection service
other than forestry or public
HQ: Meggitt Limited
Ansty Bus.
Coventry W MIDLANDS CV7 9
247 682-6900

(P-7135)
MYE TECHNOLOGIES INC
25060 Avenue Stanford, Valencia
(91355-3411)
PHONE...........................661 964-0217
Anthony Garcia, Pr
▲ EMP: 45 EST: 2006
SALES (est): 4.83MM Privately Held
Web: www.myeinc.com
SIC: 3699 Electric sound equipment

(P-7136)
NUPHOTON TECHNOLOGIES
INC
41610 Corning Pl, Murrieta (92562-7023)
PHONE...........................951 696-8366
Ramadas Pillai, CEO
Sindu Pillai, VP
Vish Govindan, CFO
Dan Vera, COO
EMP: 25 EST: 1996
SQ FT: 12,000
SALES (est): 13.25MM Privately Held
Web: www.nuphoton.com

SIC: 3699 Laser systems and equipment

(P-7137)
O & S CALIFORNIA INC
Also Called: Osca-Arcosa
9731 Siempre Viva Rd Ste E, San Diego
(92154-7217)
PHONE...........................619 661-1800
Kazuo Murata, Pr
Jos Luis Furlong, *
▲ EMP: 400 EST: 1986
SQ FT: 4,676
SALES (est): 48.08MM Privately Held
Web: www.osca-arcosa.com
SIC: 3699 Electrical equipment and supplies,
nec
PA: Onamba Co.,Ltd.
4-1-2, Minamikyuhojimachi, Chuo-Ku

(P-7138)
OBRYANT ELECTRIC INC
3 Banting, Irvine (92618-3601)
PHONE...........................949 341-0025
EMP: 40
SALES (corp-wide): 21.3MM Privately
Held
Web: www.obryantelectric.com
SIC: 3699 1731 Electrical equipment and
supplies, nec; Electrical work
PA: O'bryant Electric, Inc.
9314 Eton Ave
818 407-1986

(P-7139)
ONESOURCE DISTRIBUTORS
LLC (DH)
3951 Oceanic Dr, Oceanside (92056-5846)
PHONE...........................760 966-4500
◆ EMP: 45 EST: 1983
SQ FT: 50,000
SALES (est): 492.79MM
SALES (corp-wide): 16.09MM Privately
Held
Web: www.1sourcedist.com
SIC: 3699 5063 5085 5084 Electrical
equipment and supplies, nec; Electrical
supplies, nec; Industrial supplies; Industrial
machinery and equipment
HQ: Sonepar Management Us, Inc.
4400 Leeds Ave Ste 500
Charleston SC 29405
843 872-3500

(P-7140)
ORTHODYNE ELECTRONICS
CORPORATION (HQ)
16700 Red Hill Ave, Irvine (92606-4802)
PHONE...........................949 660-0440
▲ EMP: 249 EST: 1960
SALES (est): 10.44MM
SALES (corp-wide): 706.23MM Publicly
Held
Web: www.orthodyneelectronics.com
SIC: 3699 Electrical equipment and supplies,
nec
PA: Kulicke And Soffa Industries, Inc.
1005 Virginia Dr
215 784-6000

(P-7141)
PALOMAR TECH COMPANIES
(PA)
6305 El Camino Real, Carlsbad
(92009-1606)
PHONE...........................760 931-3600
Gary E Gist, CEO
Bruce W Hurners, Pr
Dan Evans, Corporate Secretary
EMP: 59 EST: 1995

SALES (est): 2.57MM Privately Held
Web: www.palomartechnologies.com
SIC: 3699 6512 Electrical equipment and
supplies, nec; Nonresidential building
operators

(P-7142)
PHILATRON INTERNATIONAL
(PA)
Also Called: Santa Fe Supply Company
15315 Cornet St, Santa Fe Springs
(90670-5531)
PHONE...........................562 802-0452
Phillip M Ramos Junior, CEO
Phillip M Ramos Senior, Ex VP
EMP: 99 EST: 1978
SQ FT: 100,000
SALES (est): 24.17MM
SALES (corp-wide): 24.17MM Privately
Held
Web: www.philatron.com
SIC: 3699 3694 3357 Electrical equipment
and supplies, nec; Engine electrical
equipment; Communication wire

(P-7143)
PROTOTYPE EXPRESS LLC
3506 W Lake Center Dr Ste D, Santa Ana
(92704-6985)
PHONE...........................714 751-3533
Bob Tavi, Managing Member
EMP: 25 EST: 1995
SQ FT: 7,000
SALES (est): 3.75MM Privately Held
Web: www.prototypexpress.com
SIC: 3699 Electrical equipment and supplies,
nec

(P-7144)
PXISE ENERGY SOLUTIONS
LLC
1455 Frazee Rd Ste 150, San Diego
(92108-4436)
PHONE...........................619 696-2944
Patrick Lee, CEO
EMP: 36 EST: 2017
SALES (est): 4.2MM Privately Held
Web: www.pxise.com
SIC: 3699 Grids, electric
PA: Yokogawa Electric Corporation
2-9-32, Nakacho

(P-7145)
RAYTHEON COMPANY
Raytheon
6380 Hollister Ave, Goleta (93117-3114)
PHONE...........................805 967-5511
Jack Gressingh, Genl Mgr
EMP: 200
SQ FT: 102,570
SALES (corp-wide): 68.92B Publicly Held
Web: www.rtx.com
SIC: 3699 3812 Countermeasure simulators,
electric; Search and navigation equipment
HQ: Raytheon Company
870 Winter St
Waltham MA 02451
781 522-3000

(P-7146)
RIOT GLASS INC
17941 Brookshire Ln, Huntington Beach
(92647-7132)
PHONE...........................800 580-2303
Brad Campbell, CEO
Pat Glass, *
EMP: 30 EST: 2017
SALES (est): 4.64MM Privately Held
Web: www.riotglass.com
SIC: 3699 Security devices

▲ = Import ▼ = Export
◆ = Import/Export

(P-7147)
ROSEMEAD ELECTRICAL SUPPLY
9150 Dice Rd, Santa Fe Springs (90670-2522)
PHONE.....................562 298-4190
Rony Perez, *CEO*
EMP: 50 **EST:** 2019
SALES (est): 2.8MM **Privately Held**
Web:
www.rosemeadelectricalsupply.com
SIC: 3699 High-energy particle physics equipment

(P-7148)
SCHNEIDER ELC BUILDINGS LLC
Also Called: Invensys Climate Controls
100 W Victoria St, Long Beach (90805-2147)
PHONE.....................310 900-2385
Michael Utzman, *Prin*
EMP: 109
SALES (corp-wide): 1.09K **Privately Held**
SIC: 3699 Electrical equipment and supplies, nec
HQ: Schneider Electric Buildings, Llc
839 N Perryville Rd
Rockford IL 61107
815 381-5000

(P-7149)
SCHNEIDER ELECTRIC
1660 Scenic Ave, Costa Mesa (92626-1410)
PHONE.....................949 713-9200
EMP: 27
SALES (est): 5.06MM **Privately Held**
Web: www.se.com
SIC: 3699 Electrical equipment and supplies, nec

(P-7150)
SERRA LASER AND WATERJET INC
1740 N Orangethorpe Park, Anaheim (92801-1138)
PHONE.....................714 680-6211
Glenn Kline, *CEO*
EMP: 30 **EST:** 2012
SALES (est): 6.3MM **Privately Held**
Web: www.serralaser.com
SIC: 3699 Laser welding, drilling, and cutting equipment

(P-7151)
SERVEXO
Also Called: Servexo Protective Service
1411 W 190th St Ste 475, Gardena (90248-4323)
P.O. Box 9017 (90734)
PHONE.....................323 527-9994
John Palmer, *Pr*
John Palmer, *CEO*
EMP: 200 **EST:** 2012
SALES (est): 8.68MM **Privately Held**
Web: www.servexousa.com
SIC: 3699 8744 7382 4813 Security control equipment and systems; Facilities support services; Security systems services; Telephone communication, except radio

(P-7152)
SONNET TECHNOLOGIES INC
Also Called: Manufacturer
25 Empire Dr Ste 200, Lake Forest (92630-8539)
PHONE.....................949 587-3500
Robert Farnsworth, *CEO*

Robert Farnsworth, *Pr*
Robert Rich, *
Angelia Farnsworth Magill, *
▲ **EMP:** 30 **EST:** 1986
SQ FT: 17,000
SALES (est): 7.87MM **Privately Held**
Web: www.sonnettech.com
SIC: 3699 Electrical equipment and supplies, nec

(P-7153)
SOUNDCRAFT INC
Also Called: Secura Key
20301 Nordhoff St, Chatsworth (91311-6128)
PHONE.....................818 882-0020
Joel Smulson, *Pr*
Martin Casden, *
▲ **EMP:** 35 **EST:** 1971
SQ FT: 12,000
SALES (est): 6.87MM **Privately Held**
Web: www.securakey.com
SIC: 3699 1731 3829 Security control equipment and systems; Safety and security specialization; Measuring and controlling devices, nec

(P-7154)
SUSS MCRTEC PHTNIC SYSTEMS INC
2520 Palisades Dr, Corona (92882-0632)
PHONE.....................951 817-3700
Courtney T Sheets, *CEO*
Debora Blanchard, *
Debbie Brown, *
EMP: 90 **EST:** 1966
SALES (est): 5.64MM
SALES (corp-wide): 330.72MM **Privately Held**
Web: www.suss.com
SIC: 3699 7389 Electrical equipment and supplies, nec; Business Activities at Non-Commercial Site
PA: Suss Microtec Se
SchleiBheimer Str. 90
89320070

(P-7155)
ULTRA-STEREO LABS INC
Also Called: U S L
181 Bonetti Dr, San Luis Obispo (93401-7310)
PHONE.....................805 549-0161
James A Cashin, *Pr*
Jack Cashin, *Pr*
▲ **EMP:** 25 **EST:** 2016
SQ FT: 15,000
SALES (est): 6.45MM
SALES (corp-wide): 101.64MM **Privately Held**
SIC: 3699 Electric sound equipment
PA: Usc, Llc
1675 Mcarthur Blvd
800 854-4079

(P-7156)
UNDERSEA SYSTEMS INTL INC
Also Called: Ocean Technology Systems
3133 W Harvard St, Santa Ana (92704-3912)
PHONE.....................714 754-7848
Michael R Pelissier, *Pr*
Jerry Peck, *
▲ **EMP:** 62 **EST:** 1987
SQ FT: 18,000
SALES (est): 9.58MM **Privately Held**
Web:
www.oceantechnologysystems.com
SIC: 3699 8711 Underwater sound equipment; Acoustical engineering

(P-7157)
UNITED SECURITY PRODUCTS INC
Also Called: Amtek
12675 Danielson Ct Ste 405, Poway (92064-6835)
P.O. Box 785 (92074-0785)
PHONE.....................800 227-1592
Ted R Greene, *Pr*
▲ **EMP:** 32 **EST:** 1972
SALES (est): 4.58MM **Privately Held**
Web: www.unitedsecurity.com
SIC: 3699 5999 Security devices; Alarm signal systems

(P-7158)
UNIVERSAL SURVEILLANCE SYSTEMS LLC
Also Called: Universal Surveillance Systems
11172 Elm Ave, Rancho Cucamonga (91730-7670)
PHONE.....................909 484-7870
▲ **EMP:** 80
SIC: 3699 Security control equipment and systems

(P-7159)
USA VISION SYSTEMS INC (HQ)
9301 Irvine Blvd, Irvine (92618-1669)
PHONE.....................949 583-1519
Kuang Cheng Tai, *Pr*
▲ **EMP:** 40 **EST:** 2003
SALES (est): 5.54MM **Privately Held**
Web: www.geovision.com.tw
SIC: 3699 Security control equipment and systems
PA: Geovision, Inc.
9f, No. 246, Sec. 1, Neihu Rd.

(P-7160)
VTI INSTRUMENTS CORPORATION (HQ)
2031 Main St, Irvine (92614-6509)
PHONE.....................949 955-1894
Paul Dhillon, *CEO*
Jasdeep Dhillon, *
▲ **EMP:** 30 **EST:** 1990
SQ FT: 11,500
SALES (est): 8.09MM
SALES (corp-wide): 6.6B **Publicly Held**
Web: www.vtiinstruments.com
SIC: 3699 Electrical equipment and supplies, nec
PA: Ametek, Inc.
1100 Cassatt Rd
610 647-2121

(P-7161)
WEST COAST CHAIN MFG CO
Also Called: Key-Bak
4245 Pacific Privado, Ontario (91761-1588)
P.O. Box 9088 (91762-9088)
PHONE.....................909 923-7800
Boake Paugh, *Pr*
Mike Winegar, *
▲ **EMP:** 50 **EST:** 1948
SQ FT: 31,000
SALES (est): 9.51MM **Privately Held**
Web: www.keybak.com
SIC: 3699 Security devices

(P-7162)
WESTGATE MFG INC
Also Called: Westgate Manufacturing
2462 E 28th St, Vernon (90058-1402)
PHONE.....................323 826-9490
Isaac Hadjyan, *CEO*
Eryeh Hadjyan, *
Ebrahim Hadjyan, *

▲ **EMP:** 74 **EST:** 2008
SALES (est): 9.94MM **Privately Held**
Web: www.westgatemfg.com
SIC: 3699 5063 Electrical equipment and supplies, nec; Lighting fixtures

(P-7163)
XIRGO TECHNOLOGIES LLC
188 Camino Ruiz Fl 2, Camarillo (93012-6700)
PHONE.....................805 319-4079
Roberto Piolanti, *CEO*
Mark Grout, *
Shawn Aleman, *CMO**
Rich Farruggia, *Chief Human Resources Officer**
EMP: 62 **EST:** 2006
SALES (est): 14.96MM
SALES (corp-wide): 4.05B **Privately Held**
Web: www.sensatainsights.com
SIC: 3699 Electronic training devices
HQ: Sensata Technologies Holding Company U.K.
Cannon Place
London EC4N

3711 Motor Vehicles And Car Bodies

(P-7164)
ALAN JOHNSON PRFMCE ENGRG INC
Also Called: Johnson Racing
1097 Foxen Canyon Rd, Santa Maria (93454-9146)
PHONE.....................805 922-1202
Alan P Johnson, *Pr*
▲ **EMP:** 24 **EST:** 1985
SQ FT: 25,000
SALES (est): 2.56MM **Privately Held**
Web: www.alanjohnsonperformance.com
SIC: 3711 Motor vehicles and car bodies

(P-7165)
ALLIANZ SWEEPER COMPANY
5405 Industrial Pkwy, San Bernardino (92407-1803)
▼ **EMP:** 180
SIC: 3711 Street sprinklers and sweepers (motor vehicles), assembly of

(P-7166)
AMERICAN HX AUTO TRADE INC
Also Called: U.S. Specialty Vehicles
4845 Via Del Cerro, Yorba Linda (92887-2641)
PHONE.....................909 484-1010
▲ **EMP:** 72 **EST:** 2010
SALES (est): 4.63MM **Privately Held**
SIC: 3711 Automobile bodies, passenger car, not including engine, etc.

(P-7167)
ARTISAN VEHICLE SYSTEMS INC
742 Pancho Rd, Camarillo (93012-8576)
PHONE.....................805 402-6856
Michael Kasaba, *Pr*
EMP: 60 **EST:** 2010
SALES (est): 18.94MM
SALES (corp-wide): 12.03B **Privately Held**
Web: www.rocktechnology.sandvik
SIC: 3711 Personnel carriers (motor vehicles), assembly of
PA: Sandvik Ab
Spangvagen 10
26260000

(P-7168)
AZAA INVESTMENTS INC (PA)
6602 Convoy Ct Ste 200, San Diego
(92111-1000)
P.O. Box 2198 (38101-2198)
PHONE..................................858 569-8111
William C Rhodes Iii, *Pr*
David Klein, *COO*
Jamere Jackson, *Sec*
Brian L Campbell, *Treas*
▼ EMP: 36 EST: 2012
SALES (est): 24.84MM
SALES (corp-wide): 24.84MM **Privately
Held**
Web: www.americantrucks.com
SIC: 3711 Motor vehicles and car bodies

(P-7169)
BAATZ ENTERPRISES INC
Also Called: Tow Industries
2223 W San Bernardino Rd, West Covina
(91790-1008)
PHONE..................................323 660-4866
Mark Ormonde Baatz, *CEO*
John O Baatz, *
Helen Baatz, *
▼ EMP: 38 EST: 1988
SALES (est): 4.59MM **Privately Held**
Web: www.towindustries.com
SIC: 3711 5013 7538 Motor vehicles and car
bodies; Truck parts and accessories; Truck
engine repair, except industrial

(P-7170)
BECKER AUTOMOTIVE
DESIGNS INC
Also Called: Becker Automotive Design USA
1711 Ives Ave, Oxnard (93033-1866)
PHONE..................................805 487-5227
Howard Bernard Becker, *CEO*
Debra Becker, *
▲ EMP: 33 EST: 1996
SQ FT: 35,000
SALES (est): 7.35MM **Privately Held**
Web: www.beckerautodesign.com
SIC: 3711 Cars, armored, assembly of

(P-7171)
CAMBER OPERATING
COMPANY INC
393 Cheryl Ln, City Of Industry
(91789-3003)
PHONE..................................864 438-0000
EMP: 293
SALES (corp-wide): 309.36MM **Publicly
Held**
Web: www.proterra.com
SIC: 3711 Automobile assembly, including
specialty automobiles
HQ: Camber Operating Company, Inc.
3350 Virginia St Fl 2
Miami FL 33133

(P-7172)
CZV INC
Also Called: Czinger Vehicles
19601 Hamilton Ave, Torrance
(90502-1309)
PHONE..................................424 603-1450
Kevin Czinger, *CEO*
Jens Sverdrup, *
EMP: 77 EST: 2010
SALES (est): 1.64MM **Privately Held**
Web: www.czvinc.com
SIC: 3711 Automobile assembly, including
specialty automobiles

(P-7173)
ELDORADO NATIONAL CAL INC
(HQ)
Also Called: Enc
9670 Galena St, Riverside (92509-3089)
PHONE..................................909 591-9557
Peter Orthwein, *CEO*
◆ EMP: 34 EST: 1991
SQ FT: 62,000
SALES (est): 20.67MM
SALES (corp-wide): 64.66MM **Privately
Held**
Web: www.eldorado-ca.com
SIC: 3711 Buses, all types, assembly of
PA: Rivaz, Inc.
301 N Lake Ave Ste 1000

(P-7174)
FISKER AUTOMOTIVE INC
3080 Airway Ave, Costa Mesa
(92626-6034)
▲ EMP: 53
SIC: 3711 7539 Motor vehicles and car
bodies; Automotive repair shops, nec

(P-7175)
FISKER INC (PA)
Also Called: Fisker
14 Centerpointe Dr, La Palma
(90623-1028)
PHONE..................................833 434-7537
Henrik Fisker, *Ch Bd*
Geeta Gupta Fisker, *CFO*
Angel Salinas, *CAO*
EMP: 27 EST: 2016
SALES (est): 272.88MM
SALES (corp-wide): 272.88MM **Publicly
Held**
Web: www.fiskerinc.com
SIC: 3711 Motor vehicles and car bodies

(P-7176)
FLYER DEFENSE LLC
151 W 135th St, Los Angeles (90061-1645)
PHONE..................................310 324-5650
Oded Nechushtan, *CEO*
Steven Markowitz, *
▲ EMP: 75 EST: 2000
SALES (est): 12.4MM **Privately Held**
Web: www.flyerdefense.com
SIC: 3711 3714 Military motor vehicle
assembly; Motor vehicle parts and
accessories

(P-7177)
GLOBAL ENVIRONMENTAL
PDTS INC
Also Called: Global Sweeping Solutions
5405 Industrial Pkwy, San Bernardino
(92407-1803)
PHONE..................................909 713-1600
Walter Pusic, *Prin*
Walter Pusic, *Pr*
Jason Condon, *Prin*
Sebastian Mentelski, *
▲ EMP: 67 EST: 2011
SQ FT: 104,000
SALES (est): 8.7MM **Privately Held**
Web: www.globalsweeper.com
SIC: 3711 Street sprinklers and sweepers
(motor vehicles), assembly of

(P-7178)
GREENPOWER MOTOR
COMPANY INC
8885 Haven Ave Ste 200, Rancho
Cucamonga (91730-5199)
PHONE..................................909 308-0960
Fraser Atkinson, *CEO*

EMP: 56 EST: 2013
SALES (est): 9.29MM
SALES (corp-wide): 39.27MM **Privately
Held**
Web: www.greenpowermotor.com
SIC: 3711 Motor vehicles and car bodies
PA: Greenpower Motor Company Inc
240-209 Carrall St
604 563-4144

(P-7179)
HALCORE GROUP INC
Leader Industries
10941 Weaver Ave, South El Monte
(91733-2752)
PHONE..................................626 575-0880
Gary Hunter, *Mgr*
EMP: 36
Web: www.hortonambulance.com
SIC: 3711 Motor vehicles and car bodies
HQ: Halcore Group, Inc.
3800 Mcdowell Rd
Grove City OH 43123
614 539-8181

(P-7180)
HARBINGER MOTORS INC
12821 Knott St Ste A, Garden Grove
(92841-3941)
PHONE..................................714 684-1067
John Harris, *CEO*
Phillip Weicker, *
Will Eberts, *
Gilbert Passin, *CPO*
Benjamin Dusastre, *
EMP: 150 EST: 2021
SALES (est): 28.17MM **Privately Held**
Web: www.harbingermotors.com
SIC: 3711 Chassis, motor vehicle

(P-7181)
KARMA AUTOMOTIVE INC
Also Called: Karma Automotive LLC
9950 Jeronimo Rd, Irvine (92618-2014)
PHONE..................................855 565-2762
Marques Mccammon, *Pr*
Liang Zhou, *
John Maloney, *CRO*
Ashoka Achuthan, *
EMP: 896 EST: 2014
SQ FT: 262,463
SALES (est): 99.62MM **Privately Held**
Web: www.karmaautomotive.com
SIC: 3711 Automobile bodies, passenger
car, not including engine, etc.
HQ: Wanxiang America Corporation
88 Airport Rd
Elgin IL 60123

(P-7182)
KOVATCH MOBILE EQUIPMENT
CORP
Also Called: Kme Fire
14562 Manzanita Dr, Fontana
(92335-5377)
PHONE..................................951 685-1224
Ken Creese, *Brnch Mgr*
EMP: 33
SIC: 3711 Motor vehicles and car bodies
HQ: Kovatch Mobile Equipment Corp.
1 Industrial Complex
Nesquehoning PA 18240
570 669-9461

(P-7183)
MARVIN LAND SYSTEMS INC
Also Called: Marvin Group The
261 W Beach Ave, Inglewood (90302-2904)
PHONE..................................310 674-5030
Gerald M Friedman, *Pr*

Leon Tsimmerman, *
▲ EMP: 44 EST: 1995
SQ FT: 200,000
SALES (est): 23.87MM
SALES (corp-wide): 149.54MM **Privately
Held**
Web: www.marvingroup.com
SIC: 3711 Military motor vehicle assembly
PA: Marvin Engineering Co., Inc.
261 W Beach Ave
310 674-5030

(P-7184)
MAZDA MOTOR OF AMERICA
INC (HQ)
Also Called: Mazda North Amercn Operations
200 Spectrum Center Dr Ste 100, Irvine
(92618-5004)
P.O. Box 19734 (92623)
PHONE..................................949 727-1990
◆ EMP: 400 EST: 1970
SALES (est): 406.92MM **Privately Held**
Web: www.mazdausa.com
SIC: 3711 Motor vehicles and car bodies
PA: Mazda Motor Corporation
3-1, Shinchi, Fuchucho

(P-7185)
MILLENWORKS
1361 Valencia Ave, Tustin (92780-6459)
PHONE..................................714 426-5500
▲ EMP: 75
SIC: 3711 5012 7549 8731 Military motor
vehicle assembly; Commercial vehicles;
Automotive customizing services,
nonfactory basis; Electronic research

(P-7186)
MULLEN TECHNOLOGIES INC
(PA)
Also Called: Mullen Auto Sales
1405 Pioneer St, Brea (92821-3721)
PHONE..................................714 613-1900
David Michery, *CEO*
Jerry Alban, *
William Johnston, *
EMP: 40 EST: 2014
SQ FT: 24,730
SALES (est): 10.3MM
SALES (corp-wide): 10.3MM **Privately
Held**
Web: www.mullenusa.com
SIC: 3711 5013 Motor vehicles and car
bodies; Motor vehicle supplies and new
parts

(P-7187)
NEW FLYER OF AMERICA INC
2880 Jurupa St, Ontario (91761-2903)
P.O. Box 1464 (91743-1464)
PHONE..................................909 456-3566
EMP: 91
SALES (corp-wide): 2.05B **Privately Held**
Web: www.newflyer.com
SIC: 3711 Motor vehicles and car bodies
HQ: New Flyer Of America Inc.
6200 Glenn Carlson Dr
Saint Cloud MN 56301

(P-7188)
PHOENIX CARS LLC
Also Called: Phoenix Motorcars
1500 Lakeview Loop, Anaheim
(92807-1819)
PHONE..................................909 987-0815
Joseph Mitchell, *CEO*
Yasmin Fallah, *
▲ EMP: 39 EST: 2009
SQ FT: 40,000
SALES (est): 10.36MM **Publicly Held**

Web: www.spigroups.com
SIC: 3711 Cars, electric, assembly of
HQ: Edisonfuture Inc.
4677 Old Ironsides Dr # 1
Santa Clara CA 95054
408 919-8000

(P-7189)
RIVIAN AUTOMOTIVE INC (PA)
Also Called: Rivian
14600 Myford Rd, Irvine (92606-1005)
PHONE...................888 748-4261
Robert J Scaringe, *Ch Bd*
Claire Mcdonough, *CFO*
Dagan Mishoulam, *CCO*
EMP: 496 EST: 2009
SALES (est): 4.43B
SALES (corp-wide): 4.43B **Publicly Held**
Web: www.rivian.com
SIC: 3711 Motor vehicles and car bodies

(P-7190)
RIVIAN AUTOMOTIVE LLC
14451 Myford Rd, Tustin (92780-7023)
PHONE...................888 748-4261
EMP: 97
SALES (corp-wide): 4.43B **Publicly Held**
Web: www.rivian.com
SIC: 3711 Motor vehicles and car bodies
HQ: Rivian Automotive, Llc
13250 Haggerty Rd
Plymouth MI 48170
888 748-4261

(P-7191)
RIVIAN AUTOMOTIVE LLC
1648 Ashley Way, Colton (92324-4000)
PHONE...................309 249-8777
EMP: 97
SALES (corp-wide): 4.43B **Publicly Held**
Web: www.rivian.com
SIC: 3711 3714 Motor vehicles and car
bodies; Motor vehicle parts and accessories
HQ: Rivian Automotive, Llc
13250 Haggerty Rd
Plymouth MI 48170
888 748-4261

(P-7192)
SALEEN INCORPORATED (PA)
2735 Wardlow Rd, Corona (92882-2869)
PHONE...................714 400-2121
Paul Wilbur, *Pr*
Stephen Saleen, *
Brian Walsh, *
Michael Simmons, *Chief Marketing*
◆ EMP: 200 EST: 1984
SALES (est): 6.36MM **Privately Held**
Web: www.saleen.com
SIC: 3711 Automobile assembly, including
specialty automobiles

(P-7193)
SHYFT GROUP INC
1130 S Vail Ave, Montebello (90640-6021)
PHONE...................323 276-1933
EMP: 72
SALES (corp-wide): 872.2MM **Publicly
Held**
Web: www.utilimaster.com
SIC: 3711 Motor vehicles and car bodies
PA: The Shyft Group Inc
41280 Bridge St
517 543-6400

(P-7194)
TCI ENGINEERING INC
Also Called: Total Cost Involved
1416 Brooks St, Ontario (91762-3613)
PHONE...................909 984-1773

Edward Moss, *Pr*
Edward Moss, *Pr*
Sherly Prakarsa, *
EMP: 54 EST: 1974
SQ FT: 25,000
SALES (est): 8.82MM **Privately Held**
Web: www.totalcostinvolved.com
SIC: 3711 5531 3714 Chassis, motor vehicle
; Auto and home supply stores; Motor
vehicle parts and accessories

(P-7195)
WARLOCK INDUSTRIES
Also Called: Tiffany Coach Builders
23129 Cajalco Rd Ste A, Perris
(92570-7298)
PHONE...................951 657-2680
▼ EMP: 46 EST: 2009
SALES (est): 898.28K **Privately Held**
SIC: 3711 Motor vehicles and car bodies

(P-7196)
XOS FLEET INC (HQ)
Also Called: Xos Trucks
3550 Tyburn St Ste 100, Los Angeles
(90065-1427)
PHONE...................818 316-1890
Dakota Semler, *CEO*
Giordano Sordoni, *
Liana Pogosyan, *
EMP: 50 EST: 2015
SALES (est): 34.17MM
SALES (corp-wide): 44.52MM **Publicly
Held**
Web: www.xostrucks.com
SIC: 3711 3713 Truck and tractor truck
assembly; Truck bodies and parts
PA: Xos, Inc.
3550 Tyburn St Ste 100
818 316-1890

3713 Truck And Bus Bodies

(P-7197)
**COMMERCIAL TRUCK EQP CO
LLC**
Also Called: Commercial Truck Equipment Co
12351 Bellflower Blvd, Downey
(90242-2894)
PHONE...................562 803-4466
James E Anderson, *Pr*
Lorena Anderson, *
EMP: 56 EST: 2008
SALES (est): 3.92MM **Privately Held**
Web: www.ctec-truckbody.com
SIC: 3713 Truck bodies (motor vehicles)

(P-7198)
**COMPLETE TRUCK BODY
REPAIR INC**
1217 N Alameda St, Compton
(90222-4102)
P.O. Box 1792 (90723-1792)
PHONE...................323 445-2675
Rodrigo Robles, *CEO*
EMP: 23 EST: 2012
SQ FT: 10,225
SALES (est): 2.45MM **Privately Held**
Web: www.completetruckbody.com
SIC: 3713 Truck bodies and parts

(P-7199)
CTBLA INC
1740 Albion St, Los Angeles (90031-2520)
PHONE...................323 276-1933
Kam C Law, *Pr*
Peter Lee, *
◆ EMP: 99 EST: 1995
SALES (est): 4.19MM **Privately Held**

SIC: 3713 Truck bodies (motor vehicles)

(P-7200)
**CUSTOM TRUCK ONE SOURCE
LP**
4500 State Rd, Bakersfield (93308-4544)
PHONE...................316 627-2608
EMP: 39
SALES (corp-wide): 1.57B **Publicly Held**
Web: www.customtruck.com
SIC: 3713 Truck and bus bodies
HQ: Custom Truck One Source, L.P.
7701 E 24 Hwy
Kansas City MO 64125
855 931-1852

(P-7201)
DOUGLASS TRUCK BODIES INC
231 21st St, Bakersfield (93301-4138)
PHONE...................661 327-0258
TOLL FREE: 800
Rick Douglass, *Pr*
Deborah Douglass, *
Jean Raley, *
EMP: 24 EST: 1959
SQ FT: 5,000
SALES (est): 4.99MM **Privately Held**
Web: www.douglasstruckbodies.com
SIC: 3713 Truck bodies (motor vehicles)

(P-7202)
DYNAFLEX PRODUCTS (PA)
Also Called: Exhaust Tech
6466 Gayhart St, Commerce (90040-2506)
PHONE...................323 724-1555
Robert L Mcgovern, *Pr*
Denise Pehrsson, *CEO*
Robert L Mcgovern, *Prin*
Gil Contreras, *
EMP: 75 EST: 1971
SQ FT: 64,000
SALES (est): 16.78MM
SALES (corp-wide): 16.78MM **Privately
Held**
Web: www.dynaflexproducts.com
SIC: 3713 3498 3714 Truck and bus bodies;
Fabricated pipe and fittings; Exhaust
systems and parts, motor vehicle

(P-7203)
FLEMING METAL FABRICATORS
874 Camino De Los Mares, San Clemente
(92673-3122)
PHONE...................323 723-8203
Wade M Fleming, *Pr*
Marc Fleming, *
EMP: 30 EST: 1918
SALES (est): 3.98MM **Privately Held**
Web: www.flemingmetal.com
SIC: 3713 3441 3714 3577 Truck bodies and
parts; Fabricated structural metal; Motor
vehicle parts and accessories; Computer
peripheral equipment, nec

(P-7204)
HARBOR TRUCK BODIES INC
Also Called: Harbor Truck Body
255 Voyager Ave, Brea (92821-6223)
PHONE...................714 996-0411
Ken Lindt, *Pr*
EMP: 79 EST: 1973
SQ FT: 50,000
SALES (est): 8.69MM **Privately Held**
Web: www.harbortruckandvan.com
SIC: 3713 7532 Truck bodies (motor
vehicles); Body shop, automotive

(P-7205)
KRYSTAL INFINITY LLC
Also Called: Krystal Enterprises
6915 Arlington Ave, Riverside
(92504-1905)
EMP: 500
SIC: 3713 3711 Truck and bus bodies;
Automobile assembly, including specialty
automobiles

(P-7206)
LIMOS BY TIFFANY INC
Also Called: Tiffany Coachworks
23129 Cajalco Rd, Perris (92570-7298)
P.O. Box 46 (92572-0046)
PHONE...................951 657-2680
EMP: 35 EST: 2001
SALES (est): 1.29MM **Privately Held**
SIC: 3713 Specialty motor vehicle bodies

(P-7207)
MCNEILUS TRUCK AND MFG INC
401 N Pepper Ave, Colton (92324-1817)
P.O. Box 1588 (92324-0849)
PHONE...................909 370-2100
Liza Langley, *Brnch Mgr*
EMP: 33
SALES (corp-wide): 9.66B **Publicly Held**
Web: www.mcneilusgarbagetrucks.com
SIC: 3713 5511 3711 3531 Cement mixer
bodies; Pickups, new and used; Truck and
tractor truck assembly; Construction
machinery
HQ: Mcneilus Truck And Manufacturing, Inc.
524 E Highway St
Dodge Center MN 55927
507 374-6321

(P-7208)
PHENIX ENTERPRISES INC (PA)
Also Called: Phenix Truck Bodies and Eqp
1785 Mount Vernon Ave, Pomona
(91768-3330)
PHONE...................909 469-0411
Rick Albertini, *CEO*
Benjamin Albertini, *
Norma E Albertini, *
Paul Albertini, *
EMP: 39 EST: 1978
SQ FT: 100,000
SALES (est): 13.85MM
SALES (corp-wide): 13.85MM **Privately
Held**
Web: www.phenixent.com
SIC: 3713 3711 Truck bodies (motor
vehicles); Motor vehicles and car bodies

(P-7209)
REALTRUCK ENTERPRISE INC
Also Called: Realtruck
1747 W Lincoln Ave Ste K, Anaheim
(92801-6770)
PHONE...................956 324-5337
Carl-martin Lindahl, *Pr*
EMP: 40
SALES (corp-wide): 829.18MM **Privately
Held**
Web: www.realtruck.com
SIC: 3713 Truck bodies and parts
HQ: Realtruck Enterprise, Inc.
5400 Data Ct
Ann Arbor MI 48108
734 205-9093

(P-7210)
**SPARTAN TRUCK COMPANY
INC**
12266 Branford St, Sun Valley
(91352-1009)
PHONE...................818 899-1111

Myan Spaccarelli, *Pr*
EMP: 35 **EST:** 1972
SQ FT: 25,000
SALES (est): 9.62MM **Privately Held**
Web: www.spartantruck.com
SIC: 3713 7532 3537 Garbage, refuse truck bodies; Top and body repair and paint shops ; Industrial trucks and tractors

(P-7211)
SUPREME TRUCK BODIES CAL INC
Also Called: Wabash
22135 Alessandro Blvd, Moreno Valley (92553-8215)
PHONE..............................800 827-0753
Mark D Weber, *Pr*
EMP: 35 **EST:** 2013
SALES (est): 3.73MM
SALES (corp-wide): 2.54B **Publicly Held**
SIC: 3713 Truck bodies (motor vehicles)
HQ: Supreme Industries, Inc.
   2581 Kercher Rd
   Goshen IN 46528
   574 642-3070

(P-7212)
TABC INC (DH)
6375 N Paramount Blvd, Long Beach (90805-3301)
PHONE..............................562 984-3305
Michael Bafan, *CEO*
Yoshiaki Nishino, *
◆ **EMP:** 215 **EST:** 1974
SQ FT: 8,820
SALES (est): 59MM **Privately Held**
SIC: 3713 3469 3714 Truck beds; Metal stampings, nec; Motor vehicle parts and accessories
HQ: Toyota Motor Engineering & Manufacturing North America, Inc.
   6565 Hdqtr Dr W1-3c
   Plano TX 75024

(P-7213)
VAHE ENTERPRISES INC
Also Called: Aa Leasing
750 E Slauson Ave, Los Angeles (90011-5236)
PHONE..............................323 235-6657
Vahe Karapetian, *CEO*
▲ **EMP:** 90 **EST:** 1976
SQ FT: 60,000
SALES (est): 9.89MM **Privately Held**
Web: www.aacatertruck.com
SIC: 3713 7513 Truck bodies (motor vehicles); Truck leasing, without drivers

---

3714 Motor Vehicle Parts And Accessories

(P-7214)
89908 INC
Also Called: AMP Research
15651 Mosher Ave, Tustin (92780-6426)
PHONE..............................949 221-0023
EMP: 35
Web: www.realtruck.com
SIC: 3714 Motor vehicle parts and accessories

(P-7215)
ACHATES POWER INC
4060 Sorrento Valley Blvd Ste A, San Diego (92121-1428)
PHONE..............................858 535-9920
David Crompton, *Pr*
David Johnson, *CEO*
John Koszewnik, *Prin*

Jerome Paye, *Dir Opers*
Carol Mottershead, *Finance*
EMP: 95 **EST:** 2003
SALES (est): 24.96MM **Privately Held**
Web: www.achatespower.com
SIC: 3714 8711 Motor vehicle engines and parts; Mechanical engineering

(P-7216)
ACME HEADLINING CO
Also Called: Acme Auto Headlining
550 W 16th St, Long Beach (90813-1510)
P.O. Box 847 (90801-0847)
PHONE..............................562 432-0281
Bob Westmoreland, *VP*
Don Young, *
▲ **EMP:** 75 **EST:** 1948
SQ FT: 18,000
SALES (est): 4.99MM **Privately Held**
Web: www.acmeautoheadlining.com
SIC: 3714 Tops, motor vehicle

(P-7217)
ADVANCE ADAPTERS INC
4320 Aerotech Center Way, Paso Robles (93446-8529)
P.O. Box 247 (93447-0247)
PHONE..............................805 238-7000
Mike Partridge, *Pr*
John Partridge, *
Angela Partridge, *Ofcr*
Randy Cronkright, *Pur Mgr*
▲ **EMP:** 44 **EST:** 1971
SQ FT: 44,000
SALES (est): 4.72MM **Privately Held**
Web: www.advanceadapters.com
SIC: 3714 Transmission housings or parts, motor vehicle

(P-7218)
ADVANCE ADAPTERS LLC
4320 Aerotech Center Way, Paso Robles (93446-8529)
PHONE..............................805 238-7000
John Upshur, *Prin*
EMP: 45 **EST:** 2017
SALES (est): 3.86MM **Privately Held**
Web: www.advanceadapters.com
SIC: 3714 Motor vehicle parts and accessories

(P-7219)
ADVANCED CLUTCH TECHNOLOGY INC
206 E Avenue K4, Lancaster (93535-4685)
PHONE..............................661 940-7555
Tracy Nunez, *CEO*
Dirk Starksen, *
Danette Starksen, *
▲ **EMP:** 30 **EST:** 1994
SQ FT: 18,000
SALES (est): 5.08MM **Privately Held**
Web: www.advancedclutch.com
SIC: 3714 Clutches, motor vehicle

(P-7220)
ADVANCED FLOW ENGINEERING INC (PA)
Also Called: Afe Power
252 Granite St, Corona (92879-1283)
PHONE..............................951 493-7155
Shahriar Nick Niakan; *Pr*
Stuart Miyagishima, *
David Howey, *
Eric Griffith, *
Chris Barron, *
▲ **EMP:** 44 **EST:** 1999
SQ FT: 60,000
SALES (est): 21.62MM
SALES (corp-wide): 21.62MM **Privately Held**

Web: www.afepower.com
SIC: 3714 Motor vehicle engines and parts

(P-7221)
AIR FLOW RESEARCH HEADS INC
Also Called: Air Flow Research
28611 Industry Dr, Valencia (91355-5413)
PHONE..............................661 257-8124
Rick Sperling, *Pr*
▲ **EMP:** 40 **EST:** 1970
SQ FT: 14,000
SALES (est): 6.37MM **Privately Held**
Web: www.airflowresearch.com
SIC: 3714 Cylinder heads, motor vehicle

(P-7222)
AITA CLUTCH INC
960 S Santa Fe Ave, Compton (90221-4333)
PHONE..............................323 585-4140
Guillermo Rios, *Pr*
Fred Rios, *
Albert Rios, *
EMP: 23 **EST:** 1982
SALES (est): 2.02MM **Privately Held**
SIC: 3714 5013 Clutches, motor vehicle; Automotive supplies and parts

(P-7223)
ALLIED WHEEL COMPONENTS INC
Also Called: Raceline Wheels
12300 Edison Way, Garden Grove (92841-2810)
P.O. Box 5667 (92846-0667)
PHONE..............................800 529-4335
Bruce Higginson, *CEO*
◆ **EMP:** 38 **EST:** 1996
SQ FT: 91,000
SALES (est): 15.44MM **Privately Held**
Web: www.alliedwheel.com
SIC: 3714 5531 Wheels, motor vehicle; Automotive tires

(P-7224)
AMCOR INDUSTRIES INC
Also Called: Gorilla Automotive Products
6131 Knott Ave, Buena Park (90620-1031)
PHONE..............................323 585-2852
Peter J Schermer, *Pr*
▲ **EMP:** 25 **EST:** 1983
SQ FT: 30,000
SALES (est): 5.31MM
SALES (corp-wide): 731.01MM **Privately Held**
Web: www.gorilla-auto.com
SIC: 3714 3429 Motor vehicle wheels and parts; Hardware, nec
HQ: Wheel Pros, Llc
   5347 S Vlntia Way Ste 200
   Greenwood Village CO 80111

(P-7225)
AMERICAN FABRICATION CORP (PA)
Also Called: American Best Car Parts
2891 E Via Martens, Anaheim (92806-1751)
PHONE..............................714 632-1709
Greg Knox, *Pr*
Jodee Jensen Smith, *
▲ **EMP:** 70 **EST:** 1974
SALES (est): 2.34MM
SALES (corp-wide): 2.34MM **Privately Held**
Web: www.teamxenon.com
SIC: 3714 Motor vehicle parts and accessories

(P-7226)
AMERICAN RIM SUPPLY INC
1955 Kellogg Ave, Carlsbad (92008-6582)
PHONE..............................760 431-3666
Robert D Ward, *Pr*
▼ **EMP:** 40 **EST:** 1991
SQ FT: 20,000
SALES (est): 5.52MM **Privately Held**
Web: www.americanrim.com
SIC: 3714 Wheel rims, motor vehicle

(P-7227)
APEX PRECISION TECHNOLOGIES INC
23622 Calabasas Rd Ste 323, Calabasas (91302-1594)
PHONE..............................317 821-1000
EMP: 45 **EST:** 1951
SALES (est): 1.5MM **Privately Held**
SIC: 3714 3586 3498 3462 Motor vehicle parts and accessories; Measuring and dispensing pumps; Fabricated pipe and fittings; Iron and steel forgings

(P-7228)
APTIV SERVICES US LLC
5137 Clareton Dr Ste 220, Agoura Hills (91301-6311)
PHONE..............................818 661-6667
EMP: 288
Web: www.aptiv.com
SIC: 3714 Motor vehicle engines and parts
HQ: Aptiv Services Us, Llc
   5725 Innovation Dr
   Troy MI 48098

(P-7229)
AUTO MOTIVE POWER INC
11643 Telegraph Rd, Santa Fe Springs (90670-3656)
PHONE..............................800 894-7104
Anil Paryani, *Pr*
Lionel Selwood, *
Michael Rice, *CSO*
EMP: 120 **EST:** 2020
SALES (est): 16.43MM
SALES (corp-wide): 176.19B **Publicly Held**
Web: www.amp.tech
SIC: 3714 Motor vehicle electrical equipment
PA: Ford Motor Company
   1 American Rd
   313 322-3000

(P-7230)
AUTOMAX STYLING INC
16833 Krameria Ave, Riverside (92504-6118)
PHONE..............................951 530-1876
Guoxiang Zhou, *CEO*
EMP: 40 **EST:** 2005
SQ FT: 100,000
SALES (est): 944.86K **Privately Held**
Web: www.automaxstyling.com
SIC: 3714 Motor vehicle parts and accessories

(P-7231)
BUNKER CORP (PA)
Also Called: Energy Suspension
1131 Via Callejon, San Clemente (92673-6230)
PHONE..............................949 361-3935
Donald Bunker, *CEO*
Boni Cambel, *
▼ **EMP:** 100 **EST:** 1985
SQ FT: 78,000
SALES (est): 8.95MM
SALES (corp-wide): 8.95MM **Privately Held**

Web: www.teamenergysuspension.com
SIC: 3714 Motor vehicle body components
and frame

(P-7232)
BYD MOTORS LLC (DH)
888 E Walnut St Fl 2, Pasadena
(91101-1897)
PHONE...............................213 748-3980
Stella Li, *CEO*
Ke Li, *Pr*
▲ EMP: 39 EST: 2010
SALES (est): 29.53MM **Privately Held**
Web: en.byd.com
SIC: 3714 Motor vehicle electrical equipment
HQ: Byd Us Holding Inc.
1800 S Figueroa St
Los Angeles CA 90015
213 748-3980

(P-7233)
C R LAURENCE CO INC (HQ)
Also Called: Crl
2503 E Vernon Ave, Los Angeles
(90058-1826)
PHONE...............................323 588-1281
Michael Marcely, *CEO*
Barbara Haaksma, *
Shirin Khosravi, *
Jacque Maples, *
Steve Whitcomb, *
◆ EMP: 380 EST: 1963
SQ FT: 170,000
SALES (est): 483.56MM
SALES (corp-wide): 34.95B **Privately Held**
Web: azure.crlaurence.com
SIC: 3714 5072 5039 Sun roofs, motor
vehicle; Hand tools; Glass construction
materials
PA: Crh Public Limited Company
Stonemason S Way
14041000

(P-7234)
CANOO INC (PA)
Also Called: Canoo
19951 Mariner Ave, Torrance (90503-1672)
PHONE...............................424 271-2144
Tony Aquila, *Ex Ch Bd*
Josette Sheeran, *Pr*
Greg Ethridge, *CFO*
Ramesh Murthy, *CAO*
Hector Ruiz, *Corporate Secretary*
EMP: 45 EST: 2017
SALES (est): 886K
SALES (corp-wide): 886K **Publicly Held**
Web: www.canoo.com
SIC: 3714 Motor vehicle parts and
accessories

(P-7235)
**CAR SOUND EXHAUST
SYSTEM INC**
Also Called: Magnaslow
30142 Avenida De Las Bandera, Rcho Sta
Marg (92688-2116)
PHONE...............................949 858-5900
Don Billings, *Mgr*
EMP: 43
SALES (corp-wide): 89.19MM **Privately
Held**
Web: www.magnaflow.com
SIC: 3714 Exhaust systems and parts, motor
vehicle
PA: Car Sound Exhaust System, Inc.
1901 Corporate Centre
949 858-5900

(P-7236)
**CAR SOUND EXHAUST
SYSTEM INC**
23201 Antonio Pkwy, Rcho Sta Marg
(92688-2653)
PHONE...............................949 858-5900
Jerry Paolone, *Brnch Mgr*
EMP: 29
SALES (corp-wide): 89.19MM **Privately
Held**
Web: www.magnaflow.com
SIC: 3714 Exhaust systems and parts, motor
vehicle
PA: Car Sound Exhaust System, Inc.
1901 Corporate Centre
949 858-5900

(P-7237)
CARLSTAR GROUP LLC
10730 Production Ave, Fontana
(92337-8008)
PHONE...............................909 829-1703
EMP: 98
SALES (corp-wide): 1.82B **Publicly Held**
Web: www.carlstargroup.com
SIC: 3714 Motor vehicle parts and
accessories
HQ: The Carlstar Group Llc
725 Cool Sprng Blvd Ste 5
Franklin TN 37067

(P-7238)
COAST AUTONOMOUS INC (PA)
23 E Colorado Blvd Ste 203, Pasadena
(91105-3747)
PHONE...............................626 838-2469
David M Hickey, *CEO*
Adrian Sussman, *
EMP: 23 EST: 2017
SALES (est): 8.19MM
SALES (corp-wide): 8.19MM **Privately
Held**
Web: www.coastautonomous.com
SIC: 3714 Motor vehicle electrical equipment

(P-7239)
**CRAIG MANUFACTURING
COMPANY (PA)**
8129 Slauson Ave, Montebello
(90640-6621)
PHONE...............................323 726-7355
Craig Taslitt, *Pr*
Julie Taslitt Gross, *
EMP: 60 EST: 1976
SQ FT: 16,000
SALES (est): 4.73MM
SALES (corp-wide): 4.73MM **Privately
Held**
Web: www.craigattachments.com
SIC: 3714 Radiators and radiator shells and
cores, motor vehicle

(P-7240)
CROWER ENGRG & SLS CO INC
Also Called: Crower Cams
6180 Business Center Ct, San Diego
(92154-5604)
PHONE...............................619 661-6477
Barbara Crower, *Pr*
Loren Harris, *
Peter Harris, *
Donald Cave, *
Brett Cave, *
▲ EMP: 88 EST: 1955
SQ FT: 40,000
SALES (est): 7.13MM **Privately Held**
Web: www.crower.com
SIC: 3714 Camshafts, motor vehicle

(P-7241)
CURRIE ENTERPRISES
382 N Smith Ave, Corona (92878-4371)
PHONE...............................714 528-6957
Raymond Currie, *Pr*
Raymond Currie, *Pr*
Charles Currie, *
John Currie, *
◆ EMP: 60 EST: 1960
SQ FT: 13,000
SALES (est): 11.01MM **Privately Held**
Web: www.currieenterprises.com
SIC: 3714 3599 Differentials and parts,
motor vehicle; Machine shop, jobbing and
repair

(P-7242)
**DANCHUK MANUFACTURING
INC**
3211 Halladay St, Santa Ana (92705-5628)
PHONE...............................714 540-4363
Arthur Danchuk, *Pr*
Daniel Danchuk, *
▲ EMP: 71 EST: 1967
SALES (est): 2.91MM **Privately Held**
Web: www.danchuk.com
SIC: 3714 3465 Motor vehicle parts and
accessories; Automotive stampings

(P-7243)
DEE ENGINEERING INC
6918 Ed Perkic St, Riverside (92504-1001)
PHONE...............................909 947-5616
Gary Fulton, *VP*
EMP: 25
SALES (corp-wide): 4.52MM **Privately
Held**
Web: www.prothane.com
SIC: 3714 Mufflers (exhaust), motor vehicle
PA: Dee Engineering, Inc.
1284 E 10 S
714 979-4990

(P-7244)
**DEL WEST ENGINEERING INC
(PA)**
Also Called: Del West USA
28128 Livingston Ave, Valencia
(91355-4115)
PHONE...............................661 295-5700
Al Sommer, *Ch*
Mark Sommer, *
Rosemarie Chegwin, *
Guido Keijzers, *
EMP: 120 EST: 1973
SQ FT: 50,000
SALES (est): 20.98MM
SALES (corp-wide): 20.98MM **Privately
Held**
Web: www.delwestengineering.com
SIC: 3714 Motor vehicle parts and
accessories

(P-7245)
**DENSO PDTS & SVCS
AMERICAS INC**
41673 Corning Pl, Murrieta (92562-7023)
PHONE...............................951 698-3379
Yoshihiko Yamada, *Pr*
EMP: 150
Web: www.densorobotics.com
SIC: 3714 Motor vehicle parts and
accessories
HQ: Denso Products And Services
Americas, Inc.
3900 Via Oro Ave
Long Beach CA 90810
310 834-6352

(P-7246)
DONALDSON COMPANY INC
26235 Technology Dr, Valencia
(91355-1147)
PHONE...............................661 295-0800
Paul Akian, *Pr*
EMP: 35
SALES (corp-wide): 3.59B **Publicly Held**
Web: www.donaldson.com
SIC: 3714 Mufflers (exhaust), motor vehicle
PA: Donaldson Company, Inc.
1400 W 94th St
952 887-3131

(P-7247)
**DOUGLAS TECHNOLOGIES
GROUP INC**
Also Called: Douglas Wheel
42092 Winchester Rd Ste B, Temecula
(92590-4805)
PHONE...............................760 758-5560
Johnny Leach, *Pr*
◆ EMP: 40 EST: 1982
SQ FT: 60,000
SALES (est): 4.29MM **Privately Held**
Web: www.dwtracing.com
SIC: 3714 Wheel rims, motor vehicle

(P-7248)
DRIVESHAFTPRO
7532 Anthony Ave, Garden Grove
(92841-4006)
PHONE...............................714 893-4585
Ronald Hart, *Pr*
EMP: 32 EST: 2016
SALES (est): 838.82K **Privately Held**
Web: www.driveshaftpro.com
SIC: 3714 Motor vehicle parts and
accessories

(P-7249)
DYNATRAC PRODUCTS LLC
7392 Count Cir, Huntington Beach
(92647-4551)
PHONE...............................714 596-4461
Jim Mcgean, *Pr*
EMP: 27 EST: 2021
SALES (est): 2.55MM **Privately Held**
Web: www.dynatrac.com
SIC: 3714 5013 5531 Motor vehicle
transmissions, drive assemblies, and parts;
Motor vehicle supplies and new parts;
Truck equipment and parts

(P-7250)
EDELBROCK LLC
501 Amapola Ave, Torrance (90501-1466)
PHONE...............................310 781-2290
EMP: 30
Web: www.edelbrock.com
SIC: 3714 Motor vehicle parts and
accessories
HQ: Edelbrock, Llc
8649 Hacks Cross Rd
Olive Branch MS 38654
310 781-2222

(P-7251)
EGR INCORPORATED (DH)
4000 Greystone Dr, Ontario (91761-3101)
PHONE...............................800 757-7075
Rod Horwill, *CEO*
Simon Mclellan, *CFO*
John Whitten, *
▲ EMP: 26 EST: 1993
SQ FT: 70,000
SALES (est): 24.8MM **Privately Held**
Web: www.egrusa.com

SIC: 3714 Motor vehicle parts and accessories
HQ: Oakmoore Pty. Ltd.
84 Evans Rd
Salisbury QLD 4107

(P-7252)
FOOTE AXLE & FORGE LLC
250 W Duarte Rd Ste A, Monrovia (91016-7460)
PHONE..............................323 268-4151
Michael F Denton Senior, *Managing Member*
Merrie N Denton, *
▲ **EMP:** 32 **EST:** 1937
SALES (est): 924.09K **Privately Held**
Web: www.footeaxle.com
SIC: 3714 Differentials and parts, motor vehicle

(P-7253)
FORGIATO INC
Also Called: Forgiato
11915 Wicks St, Sun Valley (91352-1908)
PHONE..............................818 771-9779
Norman Celik, *CEO*
Nisan G Celik, *
▲ **EMP:** 62 **EST:** 2006
SQ FT: 60,000
SALES (est): 5.19MM **Privately Held**
Web: www.forgiato.com
SIC: 3714 Motor vehicle wheels and parts

(P-7254)
GARRISON MANUFACTURING INC
3320 S Yale St, Santa Ana (92704-6447)
PHONE..............................714 549-4880
Venu Shan, *Pr*
Jake Ralli, *
EMP: 30 **EST:** 1939
SQ FT: 26,000
SALES (est): 2.73MM **Privately Held**
Web: www.garrisonmfg.com
SIC: 3714 7699 5084 3593 Steering mechanisms, motor vehicle; Industrial machinery and equipment repair; Hydraulic systems equipment and supplies; Fluid power cylinders and actuators

(P-7255)
GEAR VENDORS INC
Also Called: Gear Vendors
1717 N Magnolia Ave, El Cajon (92020-1243)
PHONE..............................619 562-0060
Ken R Johnson, *CEO*
Rick Johnson, *
▲ **EMP:** 35 **EST:** 1981
SQ FT: 35,000
SALES (est): 3.09MM **Privately Held**
Web: www.gearvendors.com
SIC: 3714 Transmissions, motor vehicle

(P-7256)
GERHARDT GEAR CO INC
133 E Santa Anita Ave, Burbank (91502-1926)
PHONE..............................818 842-6700
Ronald J Gerhardt, *CEO*
Mitch Gerhardt, *
John Kim, *
Kurht Gerhardt, *
EMP: 46 **EST:** 1937
SQ FT: 30,000
SALES (est): 8.14MM **Privately Held**
Web: www.gerhardtgear.com

SIC: 3714 3728 3769 3462 Gears, motor vehicle; Gears, aircraft power transmission; Space vehicle equipment, nec; Iron and steel forgings

(P-7257)
GIBSON PERFORMANCE CORPORATION
Also Called: Gibson Exhaust Systems
1270 Webb Cir, Corona (92879-5760)
PHONE..............................951 372-1220
Ronald Gibson, *Pr*
Julie Gibson, *
▲ **EMP:** 75 **EST:** 1990
SQ FT: 50,000
SALES (est): 4.81MM **Privately Held**
Web: www.gibsonperformance.com
SIC: 3714 5013 Exhaust systems and parts, motor vehicle; Motor vehicle supplies and new parts

(P-7258)
GRANATELLI MOTOR SPORTS INC
1000 Yarnell Pl, Oxnard (93033-2454)
PHONE..............................805 486-6644
Joseph R Granatelli, *CEO*
▲ **EMP:** 31 **EST:** 1998
SQ FT: 49,000
SALES (est): 2.14MM **Privately Held**
Web: www.granatellimotorsports.com
SIC: 3714 Fuel systems and parts, motor vehicle

(P-7259)
GROVER PRODUCTS CO
3424 E Olympic Blvd, Los Angeles (90023-3000)
P.O. Box 23966 (90023-0966)
PHONE..............................323 263-9981
John A Roesch, *CEO*
▲ **EMP:** 100 **EST:** 1932
SQ FT: 60,000
SALES (est): 4.7MM **Privately Held**
Web: www.airhorns.com
SIC: 3714 3494 5999 Motor vehicle brake systems and parts; Valves and pipe fittings, nec; Plumbing and heating supplies

(P-7260)
HEDMAN MANUFACTURING (PA)
Also Called: Hedman Hedders
12438 Putnam St, Whittier (90602-1002)
PHONE..............................562 204-1031
Robert Bandergriff, *Pr*
Ron Funfar, *
▲ **EMP:** 45 **EST:** 1978
SALES (est): 6.06MM
SALES (corp-wide): 6.06MM **Privately Held**
Web: www.hedman.com
SIC: 3714 Exhaust systems and parts, motor vehicle

(P-7261)
HITACHI ASTEMO AMERICAS INC
1235 Graphite Dr, Corona (92881-7252)
PHONE..............................951 340-0702
Satoru Panno, *Brnch Mgr*
EMP: 193
Web: www.amshowa.com
SIC: 3714 Motor vehicle parts and accessories
HQ: Hitachi Astemo Americas, Inc.
955 Warwick Rd
Harrodsburg KY 40330
859 734-9451

(P-7262)
IMPCO TECHNOLOGIES INC (HQ)
Also Called: Impco
3030 S Susan St, Santa Ana (92704-6435)
PHONE..............................714 656-1200
Massimo Fracchia, *Genl Mgr*
Peter Chase, *
◆ **EMP:** 160 **EST:** 1958
SQ FT: 108,000
SALES (est): 29.5MM
SALES (corp-wide): 331.8MM **Privately Held**
Web: www.impcotechnologies.com
SIC: 3714 3592 7363 Fuel systems and parts, motor vehicle; Carburetors; Engineering help service
PA: Westport Fuel Systems Inc
1691 75th Ave W
604 718-2000

(P-7263)
INNOVA ELECTRONICS CORPORATION
Also Called: Equipment & Tool Institute
17352 Von Karman Ave, Irvine (92614-6204)
PHONE..............................714 241-6800
Ieon C Chenn, *Pr*
EMP: 29 **EST:** 1990
SQ FT: 12,000
SALES (est): 15.88MM **Privately Held**
Web: www.innova.com
SIC: 3714 Motor vehicle electrical equipment

(P-7264)
KING SHOCK TECHNOLOGY INC
12472 Edison Way, Garden Grove (92841-2821)
PHONE..............................719 394-3754
Brett King, *CEO*
Brett King, *Pr*
Ross King, *
Lance King, *
Sharon King, *
◆ **EMP:** 99 **EST:** 2001
SQ FT: 18,000
SALES (est): 17.87MM **Privately Held**
Web: www.kingshocks.com
SIC: 3714 Motor vehicle body components and frame

(P-7265)
LLOYD DESIGN CORPORATION
Also Called: Lloyd Mats
19731 Nordhoff St, Northridge (91324-3330)
PHONE..............................818 768-6001
Lloyd S Levine, *CEO*
Brendan Dooley, *
▲ **EMP:** 55 **EST:** 1974
SALES (est): 4.9MM **Privately Held**
Web: www.lloydmats.com
SIC: 3714 Motor vehicle parts and accessories

(P-7266)
LOS ANGELES SLEEVE CO INC
Also Called: L.A. Sleeve
12051 Rivera Rd, Santa Fe Springs (90670-2211)
PHONE..............................562 945-7578
Nick G Metchkoff, *Pr*
David Metchkoff, *
James G Metchkoff, *
Sarah Metchkoff, *
▲ **EMP:** 29 **EST:** 1975
SQ FT: 33,000
SALES (est): 4.5MM **Privately Held**
Web: www.lasleeve.com

SIC: 3714 Exhaust systems and parts, motor vehicle

(P-7267)
LUND MOTION PRODUCTS INC
Also Called: AMP Research
3172 Nasa St, Brea (92821-6234)
PHONE..............................888 983-2204
Mitch Fogle, *Pr*
EMP: 35
SALES (corp-wide): 829.18MM **Privately Held**
Web: www.realtruck.com
SIC: 3714 Motor vehicle parts and accessories
HQ: Lund Motion Products, Inc.
4325 Hamilton Mill Rd # 4
Buford GA 30518
678 804-3767

(P-7268)
M E D INC
14001 Marquardt Ave, Santa Fe Springs (90670-5088)
PHONE..............................562 921-0464
Steven Moore, *CEO*
Susan Lowe, *CFO*
EMP: 70 **EST:** 1974
SQ FT: 40,000
SALES (est): 9.37MM **Privately Held**
Web: www.dme-mfg.com
SIC: 3714 3429 Exhaust systems and parts, motor vehicle; Clamps, couplings, nozzles, and other metal hose fittings

(P-7269)
MAGNUSON PRODUCTS LLC
Also Called: Magnuson Superchargers
1990 Knoll Dr Ste A, Ventura (93003-7309)
PHONE..............................805 642-8833
Kim Pendergast, *CEO*
Tim Krauskopf, *
EMP: 49 **EST:** 1970
SQ FT: 45,600
SALES (est): 12.41MM **Privately Held**
Web: www.magnusonsuperchargers.com
SIC: 3714 Motor vehicle parts and accessories

(P-7270)
MAXON INDUSTRIES INC
11921 Slauson Ave, Santa Fe Springs (90670-2221)
P.O. Box 3434 (90051)
PHONE..............................562 464-0099
Murray Lugash, *Pr*
Larry Lugash, *
Brenda Leung, *
EMP: 75 **EST:** 1957
SQ FT: 250,000
SALES (est): 10.67MM **Privately Held**
Web: www.maxonlift.com
SIC: 3714 Motor vehicle parts and accessories

(P-7271)
MID-WEST FABRICATING CO
Also Called: West Bent Bolt Division
8623 Dice Rd, Santa Fe Springs (90670-2511)
PHONE..............................562 698-9615
Steve Petersen, *Mgr*
EMP: 46
SQ FT: 40,000
SALES (corp-wide): 28.07MM **Privately Held**
Web: www.midwestfab.com

SIC: 3714 3452 3316 3312 Tie rods, motor vehicle; Bolts, nuts, rivets, and washers; Cold finishing of steel shapes; Wire products, steel or iron
PA: Mid-West Fabricating Co.
313 N Johns St
740 969-4411

(P-7272)
MILODON INCORPORATED
2250 Agate Ct, Simi Valley (93065-1842)
PHONE....................................805 577-5950
Steve Morrison, Pr
▲ EMP: 40 EST: 1957
SQ FT: 32,000
SALES (est): 5.14MM Privately Held
Web: www.milodon.com
SIC: 3714 Motor vehicle engines and parts

(P-7273)
MOGUL
10106 Sunbrook Dr, Beverly Hills (90210-2032)
PHONE....................................424 245-4331
Deborah Harpur, Prin
EMP: 40 EST: 2011
SALES (est): 175.39K Privately Held
Web: www.mogul-inc.com
SIC: 3714 Motor vehicle parts and accessories

(P-7274)
MOTORCAR PARTS OF AMERICA INC (PA)
Also Called: MPA
2929 California St, Torrance (90503-3914)
PHONE....................................310 212-7910
Selwyn Joffe, Ch Bd
David Lee, CFO
Kamlesh Shah, CAO
Douglas Schooner, CMO
Richard Mochulsky, S&M/VP
◆ EMP: 768 EST: 1968
SQ FT: 231,000
SALES (est): 717.68MM
SALES (corp-wide): 717.68MM Publicly Held
Web: www.motorcarparts.com
SIC: 3714 3694 3625 Motor vehicle parts and accessories; Alternators, automotive; Starter, electric motor

(P-7275)
MYGRANT GLASS COMPANY INC
10220 Camino Santa Fe, San Diego (92121-3105)
PHONE....................................858 455-8022
Tom Andia, Pr
EMP: 25
SQ FT: 32,185
SALES (corp-wide): 168.98MM Privately Held
Web: www.mygrantglass.com
SIC: 3714 5013 Motor vehicle parts and accessories; Motor vehicle supplies and new parts
PA: Mygrant Glass Company, Inc.
3271 Arden Rd
510 785-4360

(P-7276)
NEW CENTURY INDUSTRIES INC
7231 Rosecrans Ave, Paramount (90723-2501)
P.O. Box 1845 (90723-1845)
PHONE....................................562 634-9551
Michael Mason, CEO

EMP: 50 EST: 1991
SQ FT: 32,000
SALES (est): 9.57MM Privately Held
SIC: 3714 3465 3469 Wheels, motor vehicle; Automotive stampings; Stamping metal for the trade

(P-7277)
NMSP INC (DH)
Also Called: A E M
2205 W 126th St Ste A, Hawthorne (90250-3367)
PHONE....................................310 484-2322
Gregory Neuwirth, Pr
Peter Neuwirth, *
◆ EMP: 54 EST: 1997
SQ FT: 78,000
SALES (est): 25.47MM
SALES (corp-wide): 659.7MM Publicly Held
SIC: 3714 Motor vehicle engines and parts
HQ: Holley Performance Products Inc.
2445 Nashville Rd
Bowling Green KY 42101
270 782-2900

(P-7278)
NMSP INC
1451 E 6th St, Corona (92879-1715)
PHONE....................................951 734-2453
Darrell Contreras, Mgr
EMP: 46
SALES (corp-wide): 659.7MM Publicly Held
SIC: 3714 Motor vehicle engines and parts
HQ: Nmsp, Inc.
2205 126th St Unit A
Hawthorne CA 90250
310 484-2322

(P-7279)
NORTHROP GRMMN SPCE & MSSN SYS
2501 Santa Fe Ave, Redondo Beach (90278-1117)
PHONE....................................310 812-4321
EMP: 334
SIC: 3714 7373 3663 3661 Motor vehicle parts and accessories; Computer integrated systems design; Radio and t.v. communications equipment; Telephone and telegraph apparatus
HQ: Northrop Grumman Space & Mission Systems Corp.
6379 San Ignacio Ave
San Jose CA 95119
703 280-2900

(P-7280)
NRG MOTORSPORTS INC
Also Called: Boyd Coddington Wheels
861 E Lambert Rd, La Habra (90631-6143)
PHONE....................................714 541-1173
Boyd Coddington, Pr
▲ EMP: 55 EST: 1998
SALES (est): 872.19K Privately Held
Web: www.nrgmotorsports.net
SIC: 3714 Wheels, motor vehicle

(P-7281)
PANKL ENGINE SYSTEMS INC
Also Called: Sp Crankshaft
1902 Mcgaw Ave, Irvine (92614-0910)
PHONE....................................949 428-8788
▲ EMP: 31
Web: www.pankl.com
SIC: 3714 Crankshaft assemblies, motor vehicle

(P-7282)
PHOENIX MOTOR INC (DH)
Also Called: Phoenix Motorcars
1500 Lakeview Loop, Anaheim (92807-1819)
PHONE....................................909 987-0815
Xiaofeng Denton Peng, Ch Bd
Wenbing Chris Wang, CFO
Tarek Helou, COO
Michael Yung, CFO
EMP: 29 EST: 2020
SALES (est): 3.12MM Publicly Held
Web: www.spigroups.com
SIC: 3714 Motor vehicle electrical equipment
HQ: Edisonfuture Inc.
4677 Old Ironsides Dr # 1
Santa Clara CA 95054
408 919-8000

(P-7283)
PRIME WHEEL CORPORATION (PA)
17705 S Main St, Gardena (90248-3516)
PHONE....................................310 516-9126
Philip Chen, CEO
Henry Chen, *
Mitchell M Tung, *
Albert Huang, *
Webb Carter, Vice Chairman*
◆ EMP: 600 EST: 1989
SQ FT: 320,000
SALES (est): 315.67MM
SALES (corp-wide): 315.67MM Privately Held
Web: www.primewheel.com
SIC: 3714 Wheels, motor vehicle

(P-7284)
PRIME WHEEL CORPORATION
23920 Vermont Ave, Harbor City (90710-1602)
PHONE....................................310 326-5080
Eddie Chen, Mgr
EMP: 453
SQ FT: 200,000
SALES (corp-wide): 315.67MM Privately Held
Web: www.primewheel.com
SIC: 3714 3471 5013 Motor vehicle wheels and parts; Plating and polishing; Automotive supplies and parts
PA: Prime Wheel Corporation
17705 S Main St
310 516-9126

(P-7285)
PRIME WHEEL CORPORATION
Also Called: Prime Wheel of Figueroa
17680 S Figueroa St, Gardena (90248-3419)
PHONE....................................310 810-1123
Peter Liang, Brnch Mgr
EMP: 25
SALES (corp-wide): 315.67MM Privately Held
Web: www.primewheel.com
SIC: 3714 Wheels, motor vehicle
PA: Prime Wheel Corporation
17705 S Main St
310 516-9126

(P-7286)
QF LIQUIDATION INC (PA)
Also Called: Quantum Technologies
25242 Arctic Ocean Dr, Lake Forest (92630-8821)
PHONE....................................949 930-3400
W Brian Olson, Pr
Bradley J Timon, CFO
Kenneth R Lombardo, Corporate Secretary

Mark Arold, VP Opers
David M Mazaika, Development
◆ EMP: 140 EST: 2000
SQ FT: 156,000
SALES (est): 28.07MM Privately Held
Web: www.qtww.com
SIC: 3714 3764 8711 Motor vehicle parts and accessories; Space propulsion units and parts; Engineering services

(P-7287)
R A PHILLIPS INDUSTRIES INC (PA)
Also Called: Phillips Industries
12012 Burke St, Santa Fe Springs (90670-2676)
PHONE....................................562 781-2121
◆ EMP: 35 EST: 1969
SALES (est): 71.29MM
SALES (corp-wide): 71.29MM Privately Held
Web: www.phillipsind.com
SIC: 3714 5531 Motor vehicle body components and frame; Truck equipment and parts

(P-7288)
RACEPAK LLC
30402 Esperanza, Rcho Sta Marg (92688-2144)
PHONE....................................949 709-5555
Tom Tomlinson, Pr
EMP: 28 EST: 2014
SALES (est): 2.84MM
SALES (corp-wide): 659.7MM Publicly Held
Web: www.holley.com
SIC: 3714 Motor vehicle parts and accessories
HQ: Holley Performance Products Inc.
2445 Nashville Rd
Bowling Green KY 42101
270 782-2900

(P-7289)
ROLL ALONG VANS INC
1350 E Yorba Linda Blvd, Placentia (92870-3833)
PHONE....................................714 528-9600
Dan Williams, Mgr
EMP: 34 EST: 1976
SQ FT: 40,400
SALES (est): 1.22MM Privately Held
Web: www.rollalongvans.com
SIC: 3714 Motor vehicle parts and accessories

(P-7290)
S C I INDUSTRIES INC
Also Called: SCI
1433 Adelia Ave, South El Monte (91733-3002)
EMP: 25 EST: 1950
SALES (est): 630.34K Privately Held
SIC: 3714 3599 Motor vehicle brake systems and parts; Machine shop, jobbing and repair

(P-7291)
S&B FILTERS INC (PA)
15461 Slover Ave Ste A, Fontana (92337-1306)
PHONE....................................909 947-0015
Berry Carter, Pr
▲ EMP: 47 EST: 1981
SALES (est): 11.01MM
SALES (corp-wide): 11.01MM Privately Held
Web: www.sandbfilters.com

PRODUCTS & SVCS

SIC: 3714 3564 Filters: oil, fuel, and air, motor vehicle; Filters, air: furnaces, air conditioning equipment, etc.

(P-7292)
SANDRA GRUCA
Also Called: Ding Sticks
16993 Bluewater Ln, Huntington Beach (92649-2928)
PHONE..............................714 661-6464
Sandra Gruca, *Owner*
Jim Gruca, *Pr*
EMP: 41 EST: 2014
SALES (est): 800K **Privately Held**
SIC: 3714 Shock absorbers, motor vehicle

(P-7293)
SHEPARD-THOMASON COMPANY
901 S Leslie St, La Habra (90631-6841)
PHONE..............................714 773-5539
Thomas A Ruhe, *Pr*
Connie Ruhe, *
EMP: 74 EST: 1913
SQ FT: 25,000
SALES (est): 1.36MM **Privately Held**
SIC: 3714 Clutches, motor vehicle
PA: Ruhe Corporation
901 S Leslie St

(P-7294)
SPECIAL DEVICES INCORPORATED
Also Called: Sdi
2655 1st St Ste 125, Simi Valley (93065-1548)
PHONE..............................805 387-1000
Yasuhiro Sakaki, *CEO*
Kenichi Tanaka, *
Kenichi Yamada, *
Harry Rector, *
Nicholas J Bruge, *CCO*
▲ EMP: 600 EST: 1959
SALES (est): 46.65MM **Privately Held**
Web: www.daicelssa.com
SIC: 3714 Motor vehicle parts and accessories
PA: Daicel Corporation
3-1, Ofukacho, Kita-Ku

(P-7295)
SWAY-A-WAY INC
8031 Remmet Ave, Canoga Park (91304-4128)
PHONE..............................818 700-9712
▲ EMP: 31 EST: 1988
SALES (est): 2.57MM **Privately Held**
Web: www.swayaway.com
SIC: 3714 Motor vehicle parts and accessories

(P-7296)
THERMAL SOLUTIONS MFG INC
1390 S Tippecanoe Ave Ste B, San Bernardino (92408-2998)
PHONE..............................909 796-0754
Maureen Baker, *Brnch Mgr*
EMP: 33
SALES (corp-wide): 47.17MM **Privately Held**
Web: www.thermalsolutionsmfg.com
SIC: 3714 Radiators and radiator shells and cores, motor vehicle
PA: Thermal Solutions Manufacturing, Inc.
25 Century Blvd Ste 210
800 359-9186

(P-7297)
THMX HOLDINGS LLC
Also Called: Thermal Dynamics
4850 E Airport Dr, Ontario (91761-7818)
PHONE..............................909 390-3944
▲ EMP: 187
SIC: 3714 Motor vehicle parts and accessories

(P-7298)
THYSSENKRUPP BILSTEIN AMER INC
13225 Danielson St # 100, Poway (92064-6843)
PHONE..............................858 386-5900
Doug Robertson, *VP*
EMP: 42
SALES (corp-wide): 39.13B **Privately Held**
Web: www.bilstein.com
SIC: 3714 5013 Motor vehicle parts and accessories; Motor vehicle supplies and new parts
HQ: Thyssenkrupp Bilstein Of America, Inc.
8685 Bilstein Blvd
Hamilton OH 45015
513 881-7600

(P-7299)
TILTON ENGINEERING INC
25 Easy St, Buellton (93427-9566)
P.O. Box 1787 (93427-1787)
PHONE..............................805 688-2353
Jason Wahl, *Pr*
Todd Cooper, *
▲ EMP: 50 EST: 1972
SQ FT: 15,000
SALES (est): 6.35MM **Privately Held**
Web: www.tiltonracing.com
SIC: 3714 Motor vehicle parts and accessories

(P-7300)
TMI PRODUCTS INC
Also Called: TMI Visualogic
1493 E Bentley Dr Ste 102, Corona (92879-5102)
PHONE..............................951 272-1996
▲ EMP: 150 EST: 1982
SALES (est): 20.8MM **Privately Held**
Web: www.tmiproducts.com
SIC: 3714 2399 Motor vehicle parts and accessories; Seat covers, automobile

(P-7301)
TRANS-DAPT CALIFORNIA INC
12438 Putnam St, Whittier (90602-1002)
PHONE..............................562 921-0404
Robert Vandergriff, *Pr*
Ron Funfar, *General Vice President*
Jan Garner, *
EMP: 40 EST: 1959
SQ FT: 37,000
SALES (est): 1.45MM **Privately Held**
Web: www.hedman.com
SIC: 3714 Motor vehicle parts and accessories

(P-7302)
TRANSPORTATION POWER LLC
Also Called: Transpower
2057 Aldergrove Ave, Escondido (92029-1902)
PHONE..............................858 248-4255
Michael C Simon, *Pr*
Paul Scott, *
James Burns, *
EMP: 45 EST: 2010
SALES (est): 12.77MM
SALES (corp-wide): 34.06B **Publicly Held**
Web: www.transpowerusa.com

SIC: 3714 Motor vehicle parts and accessories
HQ: Meritor, Inc.
2135 W Maple Rd
Troy MI 48084

(P-7303)
TUBE TECHNOLOGIES INC
Also Called: TTI Performance Exhaust
1555 Consumer Cir, Corona (92878-3226)
PHONE..............................951 371-4878
Sam Davis, *Pr*
Raul Rodriguez, *
Tom Nakawatase, *
Trini Respico, *
▲ EMP: 30 EST: 1988
SQ FT: 18,400
SALES (est): 2.69MM **Privately Held**
Web: www.ttiexhaust.com
SIC: 3714 3498 Exhaust systems and parts, motor vehicle; Tube fabricating (contract bending and shaping)
PA: Jindal Saw Limited
Jindal Centre, 12 Bhikaiji

(P-7304)
ULTRA WHEEL COMPANY
Also Called: Platinum
586 N Gilbert St, Fullerton (92833-2549)
PHONE..............................714 449-7100
Sharon A Wood, *Pr*
Fred Dobler, *
James Smith, *Stockholder*
Jim Smith, *
▼ EMP: 25 EST: 1984
SQ FT: 65,000
SALES (est): 4.65MM **Privately Held**
Web: www.ultrawheel.com
SIC: 3714 Motor vehicle parts and accessories

(P-7305)
US MOTOR WORKS LLC (PA)
14722 Anson Ave, Santa Fe Springs (90670-5306)
PHONE..............................562 404-0488
Gil Benjamin, *Pr*
Doron Goren, *
◆ EMP: 43 EST: 1995
SQ FT: 37,000
SALES (est): 25.02MM **Privately Held**
Web: www.usmotorworks.com
SIC: 3714 Water pump, motor vehicle

(P-7306)
US RADIATOR CORPORATION (PA)
4423 District Blvd, Vernon (90058-3111)
P.O. Box 5486 (90255-9486)
PHONE..............................323 826-0965
Donald Armstrong, *Pr*
Tim Armstrong, *
William Zimmerman, *
▲ EMP: 29 EST: 1956
SQ FT: 35,000
SALES (est): 1.35MM
SALES (corp-wide): 1.35MM **Privately Held**
Web: www.usradiator.com
SIC: 3714 Radiators and radiator shells and cores, motor vehicle

(P-7307)
VETRONIX CORPORATION
2030 Alameda Padre Serra, Santa Barbara (93103-1716)
PHONE..............................805 966-2000
EMP: 152

SIC: 3714 3829 Motor vehicle parts and accessories; Aircraft and motor vehicle measurement equipment

(P-7308)
WALKER PRODUCTS
Also Called: WALKER PRODUCTS
14291 Commerce Dr, Garden Grove (92843-4944)
PHONE..............................714 554-5151
Chris Weaver, *Genl Mgr*
EMP: 50
SALES (corp-wide): 49.38MM **Privately Held**
Web: www.walkerproducts.com
SIC: 3714 Motor vehicle parts and accessories
PA: Walker Products, Inc.
525 W Congress St
636 257-2400

(P-7309)
WILWOOD ENGINEERING (PA)
4700 Calle Bolero, Camarillo (93012-8561)
PHONE..............................805 388-1188
William H Wood, *Pr*
▲ EMP: 108 EST: 1977
SALES (est): 15.01MM
SALES (corp-wide): 15.01MM **Privately Held**
Web: www.wilwood.com
SIC: 3714 Motor vehicle parts and accessories

(P-7310)
WSW CORP (PA)
Also Called: Waag
16000 Strathern St, Van Nuys (91406-1316)
PHONE..............................818 989-5008
Gary Waagenaar, *CEO*
Mike Calka, *
Jennifer Waagenaar, *
▲ EMP: 45 EST: 1978
SQ FT: 55,000
SALES (est): 5.23MM
SALES (corp-wide): 5.23MM **Privately Held**
Web: www.waag.com
SIC: 3714 5712 Motor vehicle parts and accessories; Beds and accessories

(P-7311)
XOS INC (PA)
Also Called: Xos
3550 Tyburn St Ste 100, Los Angeles (90065-1427)
PHONE..............................818 316-1890
Dakota Semler, *Ch Bd*
Giordano Sordoni, *COO*
Liana Pogosyan, *VP Fin*
EMP: 25 EST: 2020
SQ FT: 85,142
SALES (est): 44.52MM
SALES (corp-wide): 44.52MM **Publicly Held**
Web: www.xostrucks.com
SIC: 3714 3694 Motor vehicle engines and parts; Automotive electrical equipment, nec

(P-7312)
YINLUN TDI LLC (HQ)
10668 N Trademark Pkwy, Rancho Cucamonga (91730-5934)
PHONE..............................909 390-3944
Zack Yang, *Pr*
EMP: 24 EST: 2012
SQ FT: 85,000
SALES (est): 29.58MM
SALES (corp-wide): 1.54B **Privately Held**

Web: www.yinluntdi.com
SIC: 3714 Motor vehicle engines and parts
PA: Zhejiang Yinlun Machinery Co.,Ltd.
No.8, Shifeng East Rd., Fuxi Street,
Tiantai County
57683938250

3715 Truck Trailers

(P-7313)
ANDERSEN INDUSTRIES INC
17079 Muskrat Ave, Adelanto (92301-2259)
PHONE..........................760 246-8766
Steven Andersen, *CEO*
Wayne Andersen, *
Neil Andersen, *
EMP: 25 EST: 1980
SQ FT: 110,000
SALES (est): 4.88MM **Privately Held**
Web: www.andersenmp.com
SIC: 3715 3441 3444 Truck trailers;
Fabricated structural metal; Hoppers, sheet
metal

(P-7314)
CIMC INTERMODAL
EQUIPMENT LLC (HQ)
Also Called: Cimc Intermodal Equipment
10530 Sessler St, South Gate
(90280-7252)
PHONE..........................562 904-8600
Frank Sonzala, *CEO*
Trevor Ash, *
▲ EMP: 70 EST: 2007
SALES (est): 24.91MM **Privately Held**
Web: www.ciemanufacturing.com
SIC: 3715 7539 Truck trailer chassis; Trailer
repair
PA: China International Marine Containers
(Group) Co.,Ltd.
Floor 8, Zhongji Group Yanfa Center,
No.2, Shekou Gangwan Avenue

(P-7315)
DEXTER AXLE COMPANY
Also Called: Unique Functional Products
135 Sunshine Ln, San Marcos
(92069-1733)
PHONE..........................760 744-1610
Steve Moore, *Dir*
EMP: 45
SALES (corp-wide): 1.41B **Privately Held**
Web: www.dexteraxle.com
SIC: 3715 3714 Trailer bodies; Motor vehicle
parts and accessories
HQ: Dexter Axle Company Llc
2900 Industrial Pkwy E
Elkhart IN 46516

(P-7316)
OWEN TRAILERS INC
9020 Jurupa Rd, Riverside (92509-3106)
P.O. Box 36 (90633-0036)
PHONE..........................951 361-4557
Loren Owen Junior, *Pr*
Angela P Owen, *
EMP: 25 EST: 1946
SQ FT: 34,000
SALES (est): 2.43MM **Privately Held**
Web: www.owentrailers.com
SIC: 3715 Truck trailers

(P-7317)
REFRIGRATED TRCK
SOLUTIONS LLC
1115 E Dominguez St, Carson
(90746-3517)
PHONE..........................323 594-4500
Frederick Lukken, *Pr*

EMP: 26 EST: 2015
SALES (est): 1.89MM **Privately Held**
Web: www.truckreefer.com
SIC: 3715 Truck trailers

(P-7318)
UNIQUE FUNCTIONAL
PRODUCTS
Also Called: U F P
135 Sunshine Ln, San Marcos
(92069-1733)
PHONE..........................760 744-1610
▲ EMP: 125
Web: www.dexteraxle.com
SIC: 3715 3714 Trailer bodies; Motor vehicle
parts and accessories

(P-7319)
UNITED STATES LOGISTICS
GROUP
Also Called: US Logistics
2700 Rose Ave Ste A, Signal Hill
(90755-1929)
P.O. Box 10129 (91209-3129)
PHONE..........................562 989-9555
Khachatur Khudikyan, *CEO*
EMP: 32 EST: 2009
SALES (est): 2.65MM **Privately Held**
Web: www.uslginc.com
SIC: 3715 Truck trailers

(P-7320)
UTILITY TRAILER
MANUFACTURING (PA)
17295 Railroad St Ste A, City Of Industry
(91748-1043)
PHONE..........................626 965-1514
Paul F Bennett, *CEO*
Harold C Bennett, *
Craig M Bennett, *
Jeffrey J Bennett, *
Stephen F Bennett, *
◆ EMP: 300 EST: 1914
SQ FT: 50,000
SALES (est): 897.7MM
SALES (corp-wide): 897.7MM **Privately
Held**
Web: www.utilitytrailer.com
SIC: 3715 Truck trailers

(P-7321)
UTILITY TRAILER MFG CO
Also Called: Utility Trlr Sls Southern Cal
15567 Valley Blvd, Fontana (92335-6351)
PHONE..........................909 428-8300
TOLL FREE: 800
Thayne Stanger, *Brnch Mgr*
EMP: 172
SALES (corp-wide): 897.7MM **Privately
Held**
Web: www.utilitytrailer.com
SIC: 3715 Semitrailers for truck tractors
PA: Utility Trailer Manufacturing Company,
Llc
17295 E Railroad St
626 965-1514

(P-7322)
UTILITY TRAILER MFG CO
Tautliner Division
17295 Railroad St Ste A, City Of Industry
(91748-1043)
PHONE..........................909 594-6026
Linda Baker, *Mgr*
EMP: 148
SALES (corp-wide): 897.7MM **Privately
Held**
Web: www.utilitytrailer.com

SIC: 3715 5199 Truck trailers; Tarpaulins
PA: Utility Trailer Manufacturing Company,
Llc
17295 E Railroad St
626 965-1514

3716 Motor Homes

(P-7323)
REXHALL INDUSTRIES INC
26857 Tannahill Ave, Canyon Country
(91387-3969)
PHONE..........................661 726-5470
William Jonathan Rex, *Ch Bd*
Cheryl Rex, *Corporate Secretary*
James C Rex, *General Vice President*
▲ EMP: 46 EST: 1986
SQ FT: 120,000
SALES (est): 4.99MM **Privately Held**
Web: www.rexhall.com
SIC: 3716 Motor homes

3721 Aircraft

(P-7324)
AEROVIRONMENT INC
825 S Myrtle Ave, Monrovia (91016-3424)
PHONE..........................626 357-9983
Stewart Hindle, *Mgr*
EMP: 42
SALES (corp-wide): 716.72MM **Publicly
Held**
Web: www.avinc.com
SIC: 3721 Aircraft
PA: Aerovironment, Inc.
241 18th St S Ste 415
805 520-8350

(P-7325)
AEROVIRONMENT INC
1610 S Magnolia Ave, Monrovia
(91016-4547)
PHONE..........................626 357-9983
EMP: 37
SALES (corp-wide): 716.72MM **Publicly
Held**
Web: www.avinc.com
SIC: 3721 Aircraft
PA: Aerovironment, Inc.
241 18th St S Ste 415
805 520-8350

(P-7326)
AEROVIRONMENT INC
222 E Huntington Dr Ste 118, Monrovia
(91016-8014)
P.O. Box 5130 (93062-5130)
PHONE..........................626 357-9983
EMP: 37
SALES (corp-wide): 716.72MM **Publicly
Held**
Web: www.avinc.com
SIC: 3721 Aircraft
PA: Aerovironment, Inc.
241 18th St S Ste 415
805 520-8350

(P-7327)
AEROVIRONMENT INC
900 Innovators Way, Simi Valley
(93065-2072)
PHONE..........................805 520-8350
Wahid Nawabi, *Pr*
EMP: 51
SALES (corp-wide): 716.72MM **Publicly
Held**
Web: www.avinc.com
SIC: 3721 Gliders (aircraft)

PA: Aerovironment, Inc.
241 18th St S Ste 415
805 520-8350

(P-7328)
ALLCLEAR INC
200 N Pacific Coast Hwy Ste 1350, El
Segundo (90245-5680)
PHONE..........................424 316-1596
Darryl Mayhorn, *CEO*
EMP: 32 EST: 2020
SALES (est): 2.39MM **Privately Held**
Web: www.goallclear.com
SIC: 3721 Aircraft

(P-7329)
AMERICAN SCENCE TECH AS T
CORP
2372 Morse Ave Ste 571, Irvine
(92614-6234)
PHONE..........................310 773-1978
Kinda Assouad, *Brnch Mgr*
EMP: 85
SALES (corp-wide): 4.06MM **Privately
Held**
Web: www.ast-d.com
SIC: 3721 3724 3761 3764 Aircraft; Aircraft
engines and engine parts; Guided missiles
and space vehicles; Space propulsion units
and parts
PA: American Science & Technology
(As&T) Corporation
50 California St Fl 21
415 251-2800

(P-7330)
APM MANUFACTURING
341 W Blueridge Ave, Orange
(92865-4201)
PHONE..........................714 453-0100
Gilles Madelmont, *Contrlr*
EMP: 128
SALES (corp-wide): 43.53MM **Privately
Held**
Web: www.anaheimprecision.com
SIC: 3721 Aircraft
HQ: Apm Manufacturing
1738 N Neville St
Orange CA 92865
714 453-0100

(P-7331)
BOEING COMPANY
Also Called: Boeing
4000 N Lakewood Blvd, Long Beach
(90808-1700)
PHONE..........................562 496-1000
Nan Bouchard, *VP*
EMP: 2000
SALES (corp-wide): 77.79B **Publicly Held**
Web: www.boeing.com
SIC: 3721 Airplanes, fixed or rotary wing
PA: The Boeing Company
929 Long Bridge Dr
703 465-3500

(P-7332)
BOEING COMPANY
Also Called: Boeing
2220 E Carson St, Carson (90810-1226)
PHONE..........................310 522-2809
Jim Brown, *Mgr*
EMP: 125
SQ FT: 71,912
SALES (corp-wide): 77.79B **Publicly Held**
Web: www.boeing.com
SIC: 3721 Aircraft
PA: The Boeing Company
929 Long Bridge Dr
703 465-3500

(P-7333)

BOEING COMPANY

Also Called: Boeing
4060 N Lakewood Blvd, Long Beach
(90808-1700)
P.O. Box 200 (90801-0200)
PHONE.............................562 593-5511
Linda Van Reeden, *Mgr*
EMP: 1400
SALES (corp-wide): 77.79B **Publicly Held**
Web: www.boeing.com
SIC: 3721 Airplanes, fixed or rotary wing
PA: The Boeing Company
929 Long Bridge Dr
703 465-3500

(P-7334)

BOEING COMPANY

Also Called: Boeing
Bldg-1454 Receiving, San Diego (92135)
PHONE.............................619 545-8382
EMP: 996
SALES (corp-wide): 77.79B **Publicly Held**
Web: www.boeing.com
SIC: 3721 Airplanes, fixed or rotary wing
PA: The Boeing Company
929 Long Bridge Dr
703 465-3500

(P-7335)

BOEING INTLLCTUAL PRPRTY LCNSI

14441 Astronautics Ln, Huntington Beach
(92647-2080)
PHONE.............................562 797-2020
EMP: 245 **EST:** 2011
SALES (est): 12.76MM
SALES (corp-wide): 77.79B **Publicly Held**
Web: www.boeing.com
SIC: 3721 Airplanes, fixed or rotary wing
PA: The Boeing Company
929 Long Bridge Dr
703 465-3500

(P-7336)

BOEING SATELLITE SYSTEMS INC

Also Called: Boeing
2300 E Imperial Hwy, El Segundo
(90245-2813)
P.O. Box 92919 (90009-2919)
PHONE.............................310 568-2735
Steve Tsukamoto, *Mgr*
EMP: 4729
SALES (corp-wide): 77.79B **Publicly Held**
Web: www.boeing.com
SIC: 3721 Aircraft
HQ: Boeing Satellite Systems, Inc.
900 N Pacific Coast Hwy
El Segundo CA 90245

(P-7337)

CHIPTON-ROSS INC

420 Culver Blvd, Playa Del Rey
(90293-7706)
PHONE.............................310 414-7800
Judith Hinkley, *Pr*
EMP: 100 **EST:** 1983
SQ FT: 6,000
SALES (est): 9.01MM **Privately Held**
Web: www.chiptonross.com
SIC: 3721 3731 8731 7363 Motorized aircraft
; Military ships, building and repairing;
Commercial physical research; Temporary
help service

(P-7338)

COMAC AMERICA CORPORATION

4350 Von Karman Ave Ste 400, Newport
Beach (92660-2007)
PHONE.............................760 616-9614
Wei Ye, *CEO*
EMP: 31 **EST:** 2013
SALES (est): 4.31MM **Privately Held**
Web: www.comacamerica.com
SIC: 3721 Aircraft
PA: Commercial Aircraft Corporation Of
China,Ltd.
No.1919, Shibo Avenue, Pudong New
District

(P-7339)

EMPIRICAL SYSTEMS AROSPC INC (PA)

Also Called: Esaero
3580 Sueldo St, San Luis Obispo
(93401-7338)
P.O. Box 595 (93448-0595)
PHONE.............................805 474-5900
Andrew Gibson, *Pr*
Benjamin Schiltgen, *
EMP: 124 **EST:** 2003
SQ FT: 1,000
SALES (est): 22.49MM
SALES (corp-wide): 22.49MM **Privately
Held**
Web: www.esaero.com
SIC: 3721 Aircraft

(P-7340)

FASTENER DIST HOLDINGS LLC

Also Called: Fdh Aero
5200 Sheila St, Commerce (90040-3906)
PHONE.............................213 620-9950
EMP: 26
SALES (corp-wide): 512.41MM **Privately
Held**
Web: www.aircraftfast.com
SIC: 3721 Aircraft
HQ: Fastener Distribution Holdings, Llc
5200 Sheila St
Commerce CA 90040
213 620-9950

(P-7341)

GENERAL ATMICS ARNTCAL SYSTEMS

11906 Tech Center Ct, Poway
(92064-7139)
PHONE.............................858 455-3358
EMP: 62
Web: www.ga-asi.com
SIC: 3721 Aircraft
HQ: General Atomics Aeronautical
Systems, Inc.
14200 Kirkham Way
Poway CA 92064

(P-7342)

GENERAL ATMICS ARNTCAL SYSTEMS

13330 Evening Creek Dr N, San Diego
(92128-4110)
PHONE.............................858 964-6700
Neal Blue, *Pr*
EMP: 332
Web: www.ga-asi.com
SIC: 3721 Aircraft
HQ: General Atomics Aeronautical
Systems, Inc.
14200 Kirkham Way
Poway CA 92064

(P-7343)

GENERAL ATMICS ARNTCAL SYSTEMS

13550 Stowe Dr, Poway (92064-6858)

PHONE.............................858 312-4247
EMP: 293
Web: www.ga-asi.com
SIC: 3721 Aircraft
HQ: General Atomics Aeronautical
Systems, Inc.
14200 Kirkham Way
Poway CA 92064

(P-7344)

GENERAL ATMICS ARNTCAL SYSTEMS

12220 Parkway Centre Dr, Poway
(92064-6867)
PHONE.............................858 455-3000
Eric Jones, *Brnch Mgr*
EMP: 268
Web: www.ga-asi.com
SIC: 3721 Aircraft
HQ: General Atomics Aeronautical
Systems, Inc.
14200 Kirkham Way
Poway CA 92064

(P-7345)

GENERAL ATMICS ARNTCAL SYSTEMS

16761 Via Del Campo Ct, San Diego
(92127-1713)
PHONE.............................858 762-6700
EMP: 542
Web: www.ga-asi.com
SIC: 3721 Aircraft
HQ: General Atomics Aeronautical
Systems, Inc.
14200 Kirkham Way
Poway CA 92064

(P-7346)

GENERAL ATMICS ARNTCAL SYSTEMS

14102 Stowe Dr Ste A47, Poway
(92064-7147)
PHONE.............................858 312-2810
EMP: 93
Web: www.ga-asi.com
SIC: 3721 Aircraft
HQ: General Atomics Aeronautical
Systems, Inc.
14200 Kirkham Way
Poway CA 92064

(P-7347)

GENERAL ATMICS ARNTCAL SYSTEMS

Also Called: General Atomics
3550 General Atomics Ct, San Diego
(92121-1122)
PHONE.............................858 455-2810
EMP: 500
Web: www.ga-asi.com
SIC: 3721 Aircraft
HQ: General Atomics Aeronautical
Systems, Inc.
14200 Kirkham Way
Poway CA 92064

(P-7348)

GENERAL ATMICS ARNTCAL SYSTEMS

12365 Crosthwaite Cir, Poway
(92064-6817)
PHONE.............................858 762-6700
Cyndra Flanagen, *Dir*
EMP: 500
Web: www.ga-asi.com
SIC: 3721 Aircraft

HQ: General Atomics Aeronautical
Systems, Inc.
14200 Kirkham Way
Poway CA 92064

(P-7349)

GENERAL ATMICS ARNTCAL SYSTEMS (DH)

Also Called: Ga-Asi
14200 Kirkham Way, Poway (92064-7103)
PHONE.............................858 312-2810
Neal Blue, *Pr*
Brad Clark, *
Stacy Jakuttis, *
Tony Navarra, *
◆ **EMP:** 500 **EST:** 1992
SQ FT: 900,000
SALES (est): 1.59B **Privately Held**
Web: www.ga-asi.com
SIC: 3721 Aircraft
HQ: Aeronautical Systems Inc
16761 Via Del Campo Ct
San Diego CA 92127

(P-7350)

GENERAL ATOMIC AERON

Also Called: General Atomics
73 El Mirage Airport Rd Ste B, Adelanto
(92301-9540)
PHONE.............................760 388-8208
Gary Bener, *Brnch Mgr*
EMP: 200
SQ FT: 34,425
Web: www.ga-asi.com
SIC: 3721 Aircraft
HQ: General Atomics Aeronautical
Systems, Inc.
14200 Kirkham Way
Poway CA 92064

(P-7351)

GENERAL ATOMIC AERON

14040 Danielson St, Poway (92064-6857)
PHONE.............................858 455-4560
EMP: 185
Web: www.ga-asi.com
SIC: 3721 Aircraft
HQ: General Atomics Aeronautical
Systems, Inc.
14200 Kirkham Way
Poway CA 92064

(P-7352)

GENERAL ATOMIC AERON

13950 Stowe Dr, Poway (92064-8803)
PHONE.............................858 312-3428
James N Blue, *Brnch Mgr*
EMP: 267
Web: www.ga-asi.com
SIC: 3721 Aircraft
HQ: General Atomics Aeronautical
Systems, Inc.
14200 Kirkham Way
Poway CA 92064

(P-7353)

GENERAL ATOMIC AERON

14115 Stowe Dr, Poway (92064-7145)
PHONE.............................858 312-2543
EMP: 500
Web: www.ga-asi.com
SIC: 3721 Aircraft
HQ: General Atomics Aeronautical
Systems, Inc.
14200 Kirkham Way
Poway CA 92064

▲ = Import ▼ = Export
◆ = Import/Export

(P-7354)

GENERAL ELECTRIC COMPANY
Also Called: G E Aviation
18000 Phantom St, Victorville (92394-7913)
PHONE..............................760 530-5200
John Hardell, *Prin*
EMP: 50
SALES (corp-wide): 67.95B **Publicly Held**
Web: www.ge.com
SIC: 3721 Aircraft
PA: General Electric Company
1 Neumann Way
617 443-3000

(P-7355)

GKN AEROSPACE
12122 Western Ave, Garden Grove
(92841-2915)
PHONE..............................714 653-7531
Peter Dilnot, *CEO*
Matthew Gregory, *CFO*
Warren Fernandez, *Sec*
EMP: 103 **EST:** 2016
SALES (est): 10.29MM **Privately Held**
Web: www.gknaerospace.com
SIC: 3721 Aircraft

(P-7356)

GULFSTREAM AEROSPACE CORP GA
9818 Mina Ave, Whittier (90605-3035)
PHONE..............................562 907-9300
EMP: 215
SALES (corp-wide): 42.27B **Publicly Held**
SIC: 3721 Airplanes, fixed or rotary wing
HQ: Gulfstream Aerospace Corporation
(Georgia)
500 Gulfstream Rd
Savannah GA 31408
912 965-3000

(P-7357)

GULFSTREAM AEROSPACE CORP GA
Also Called: Gulfstream
16644 Roscoe Blvd, Van Nuys
(91406-1103)
PHONE..............................805 236-5755
EMP: 429
SALES (corp-wide): 42.27B **Publicly Held**
SIC: 3721 Aircraft
HQ: Gulfstream Aerospace Corporation
(Georgia)
500 Gulfstream Rd
Savannah GA 31408
912 965-3000

(P-7358)

GULFSTREAM AEROSPACE CORP GA
4150 E Donald Douglas Dr, Long Beach
(90808-1725)
PHONE..............................562 420-1818
Barry Russell, *Brnch Mgr*
EMP: 1073
SALES (corp-wide): 42.27B **Publicly Held**
SIC: 3721 Aircraft
HQ: Gulfstream Aerospace Corporation
(Georgia)
500 Gulfstream Rd
Savannah GA 31408
912 965-3000

(P-7359)

JETZERO INC (PA)
4150 E Donald Douglas Dr, Long Beach
(90808-1725)
PHONE..............................949 474-8222
Thomas O'leary, *CEO*

EMP: 36 **EST:** 2021
SALES (est): 1.67MM
SALES (corp-wide): 1.67MM **Privately Held**
Web: www.jetzero.aero
SIC: 3721 Aircraft

(P-7360)

JVR SHEETMETAL FABRICATION INC
Also Called: Talsco
7101 Patterson Dr, Garden Grove
(92841-1415)
PHONE..............................714 841-2464
Jose Castaneda, *CEO*
EMP: 33 **EST:** 2003
SQ FT: 1,000
SALES (est): 4.58MM **Privately Held**
Web: www.talsco.com
SIC: 3721 Aircraft

(P-7361)

LEARJET INC
16750 Schoenborn St, North Hills
(91343-6108)
PHONE..............................818 894-8241
Tonya Sudduth, *Brnch Mgr*
EMP: 28
SALES (corp-wide): 8.05B **Privately Held**
Web: www.bombardier.com
SIC: 3721 Aircraft
HQ: Learjet Inc.
1 Learjet Way
Wichita KS 67209
316 946-2000

(P-7362)

LIGHT COMPOSITES INC
12170 Paine Pl, Poway (92064-7153)
PHONE..............................619 339-0638
Ryan Hosmer, *CEO*
EMP: 35 **EST:** 2016
SALES (est): 5.5MM **Privately Held**
Web: www.lightcomposites.net
SIC: 3721 3841 3624 Aircraft; Surgical and
medical instruments; Carbon and graphite
products

(P-7363)

MADN AIRCRAFT HINGE
26911 Ruether Ave Ste Q, Santa Clarita
(91351-6513)
PHONE..............................661 257-3430
Aroosh Shahbazian, *CEO*
EMP: 45 **EST:** 2020
SALES (est): 554.47K **Privately Held**
Web: www.madnaircrafthinge.com
SIC: 3721 3720 Aircraft; Aircraft parts and
equipment, nec

(P-7364)

NORTHROP GRUMMAN SYSTEMS CORP
Northrop Grumman
1 Space Park Blvd # D1 1024, Redondo
Beach (90278-1001)
PHONE..............................310 812-4321
Bruce Gaines, *Prin*
EMP: 305
Web: www.northropgrumman.com
SIC: 3721 3761 3728 Airplanes, fixed or
rotary wing; Guided missiles, complete;
Fuselage assembly, aircraft
HQ: Northrop Grumman Systems
Corporation
2980 Fairview Park Dr
Falls Church VA 22042
703 280-2900

(P-7365)

NORTHROP GRUMMAN SYSTEMS CORP
Also Called: Air Combat Systems
3520 E Avenue M, Palmdale (93550-7401)
PHONE..............................661 272-7000
David G Hogarth, *Mgr*
EMP: 300
Web: www.northropgrumman.com
SIC: 3721 3812 3761 Aircraft; Search and
navigation equipment; Guided missiles and
space vehicles
HQ: Northrop Grumman Systems
Corporation
2980 Fairview Park Dr
Falls Church VA 22042
703 280-2900

(P-7366)

NORTHROP GRUMMAN SYSTEMS CORP
Also Called: Aerospace Systems
1 Space Park Blvd, Redondo Beach
(90278-1071)
PHONE..............................310 812-1089
Gary Ervin, *Brnch Mgr*
EMP: 305
Web: www.northropgrumman.com
SIC: 3721 3761 3728 3812 Airplanes, fixed
or rotary wing; Guided missiles, complete;
Fuselage assembly, aircraft; Inertial
guidance systems
HQ: Northrop Grumman Systems
Corporation
2980 Fairview Park Dr
Falls Church VA 22042
703 280-2900

(P-7367)

OVERAIR INC
3001 S Susan St, Santa Ana (92704-6434)
PHONE..............................949 503-7503
Benjamin Tigner, *CEO*
Valerie Manning, *CCO**
EMP: 30 **EST:** 2019
SALES (est): 11.28MM **Privately Held**
Web: www.overair.com
SIC: 3721 Research and development on
aircraft by the manufacturer

(P-7368)

QUALITY TECH MFG INC
170 W Mindanao St, Bloomington
(92316-2946)
PHONE..............................909 465-9565
Rudolph A Gutierrez, *Pr*
Camilio Gutierrez, *
EMP: 37 **EST:** 1996
SQ FT: 18,000
SALES (est): 4.63MM **Privately Held**
Web: www.qualitytechmfg.com
SIC: 3721 Aircraft

(P-7369)

SCALED COMPOSITES LLC
1624 Flight Line, Mojave (93501-1663)
PHONE..............................661 824-4541
Greg Morris, *Pr*
Mark Taylor, *VP*
Jennifer Santiago, *Ex VP*
Ben Diachun, *VP*
Jason Kelley, *VP*
EMP: 500 **EST:** 2000
SQ FT: 160,000
SALES (est): 98.52MM **Publicly Held**
Web: www.scaled.com
SIC: 3721 3999 8711 Aircraft; Models,
except toy; Aviation and/or aeronautical
engineering

HQ: Northrop Grumman Systems
Corporation
2980 Fairview Park Dr
Falls Church VA 22042
703 280-2900

(P-7370)

SHIELD AI INC (PA)
600 W Broadway Ste 250, San Diego
(92101-3357)
PHONE..............................619 719-5740
Brandon Tseng, *Ch Bd*
Ryan Tseng, *CEO*
Jim Carlson, *Sec*
Kingsley Afemikhe, *CFO*
Thomas Tull, *Dir*
EMP: 601 **EST:** 2015
SQ FT: 20,000
SALES (est): 90.64MM
SALES (corp-wide): 90.64MM **Privately
Held**
Web: www.shield.ai
SIC: 3721 Aircraft

(P-7371)

SOARING AMERICA CORPORATION
Also Called: Mooney International
8354 Kimball Ave # F360, Chino
(91708-9267)
PHONE..............................909 270-2628
Cheng-yuan Jerry Chen, *CEO*
Albert Li, *CFO*
EMP: 45 **EST:** 2012
SALES (est): 2.14MM **Privately Held**
SIC: 3721 3728 Research and development
on aircraft by the manufacturer; R and D by
manuf., aircraft parts and auxiliary
equipment

(P-7372)

SPACE EXPLORATION TECH CORP
731 Kelp Rd Slc-4, Vandenberg Afb
(93437)
PHONE..............................310 848-4410
EMP: 157
SALES (corp-wide): 2.07B **Privately Held**
Web: www.spacex.com
SIC: 3721 Aircraft
PA: Space Exploration Technologies Corp.
1 Rocket Rd
310 363-6000

(P-7373)

SWIFT AUTONOMY INC
1141a Via Callejon, San Clemente
(92673-6230)
PHONE..............................800 547-9438
Richard Heise, *CEO*
EMP: 25 **EST:** 2019
SALES (est): 2.13MM **Privately Held**
Web: www.swiftautonomy.com
SIC: 3721 Aircraft

(P-7374)

TRI MODELS INC
5191 Oceanus Dr, Huntington Beach
(92649-1026)
PHONE..............................714 896-0823
Prince A Herzog Senior, *CEO*
Jeff Herzog, *
▲ **EMP:** 82 **EST:** 1972
SALES (est): 14.85MM **Privately Held**
Web: www.trimodels.com
SIC: 3721 Airplanes, fixed or rotary wing

PRODUCTS & SVCS

(P-7375)
WORLDWIDE AEROS CORP
3971 Fredonia Dr, Los Angeles
(90068-1213)
PHONE..............................818 344-3999
Igor Pasternak, *CEO*
▲ **EMP: 82 EST:** 1987
SALES (est): 5.27MM **Privately Held**
Web: www.aeroscraft.com
SIC: 3721 8711 Airships; Aviation and/or
aeronautical engineering

3724 Aircraft Engines And Engine Parts

(P-7376)
AC&A ENTERPRISES LLC (HQ)
25671 Commercentre Dr, Lake Forest
(92630-8801)
PHONE..............................949 716-3511
Justin Uchida, *CEO*
Justin Schultz, *
▲ **EMP: 34 EST:** 2004
SALES (est): 25.48MM
SALES (corp-wide): 189.21MM **Privately
Held**
Web: www.acamfg.com
SIC: 3724 3511 Aircraft engines and engine
parts; Turbines and turbine generator sets
PA: Applied Composites Holdings, Llc
25692 Atlantic Ocean Dr
949 716-3511

(P-7377)
ACCURATE GRINDING AND MFG CORP
807 E Parkridge Ave, Corona (92879-6609)
PHONE..............................951 479-0909
Douglas Nilsen, *CEO*
Hans J Nilsen, *
David Nilsen, *
▲ **EMP: 35 EST:** 1950
SQ FT: 15,000
SALES (est): 4.76MM **Privately Held**
Web: www.accuratefishing.com
SIC: 3724 3812 Aircraft engines and engine
parts; Search and navigation equipment

(P-7378)
ADVANCED GRUND SYSTEMS ENGRG L (HQ)
Also Called: Agse
10805 Painter Ave, Santa Fe Springs
(90670-4502)
PHONE..............................562 906-9300
Diane Henderson, *CEO*
David Chetwood, *
▲ **EMP: 40 EST:** 1973
SALES (est): 23.69MM
SALES (corp-wide): 25.56MM **Privately
Held**
Web: www.agsecorp.com
SIC: 3724 Aircraft engines and engine parts
PA: Westmont Industries Llc
10805 Painter Ave Uppr
562 944-6137

(P-7379)
AEROJET ROCKETDYNE DE INC
6633 Canoga Ave, Canoga Park
(91303-2703)
P.O. Box 7922 (91309-7922)
PHONE..............................818 586-1000
Jerry Jackson, *Brnch Mgr*
EMP: 355
SALES (corp-wide): 19.42B **Publicly Held**
Web: www.l3harris.com

SIC: 3724 Aircraft engines and engine parts
HQ: Inc Aerojet Rocketdyne Of De
8900 De Soto Ave
Canoga Park CA 91304
818 586-1000

(P-7380)
AMERICAN MTAL MFG RESOURCE INC
Also Called: American Metal
1989 W Holt Ave, Pomona (91768-3352)
PHONE..............................909 620-4500
Vikas Sharma, *Pr*
EMP: 25 EST: 2007
SQ FT: 6,000
SALES (est): 2.38MM **Privately Held**
Web: www.ammrinc.com
SIC: 3724 3999 Aircraft engines and engine
parts; Barber and beauty shop equipment

(P-7381)
CHROMALLOY COMPONENT SVCS INC
Precision Component Tech
7007 Consolidated Way, San Diego
(92121-2604)
PHONE..............................858 877-2800
Nat Love, *Genl Mgr*
EMP: 45
SALES (corp-wide): 517.74MM **Privately
Held**
Web: www.chromalloy.com
SIC: 3724 Aircraft engines and engine parts
HQ: Chromalloy Component Services, Inc.
303 Industrial Park Rd
San Antonio TX 78226
210 331-2300

(P-7382)
CHROMALLOY GAS TURBINE LLC
Also Called: Chromalloy Southwest
1749 Stergios Rd Ste 2, Calexico
(92231-9657)
PHONE..............................760 768-3723
EMP: 88
SALES (corp-wide): 517.74MM **Privately
Held**
Web: www.chromalloy.com
SIC: 3724 Aircraft engines and engine parts
HQ: Chromalloy Gas Turbine Llc
4100 Rca Blvd
Palm Beach Gardens FL 33410
561 935-3571

(P-7383)
DUCOMMUN AEROSTRUCTURES INC (HQ)
600 Anton Blvd Ste 1100, Costa Mesa
(92626-7100)
PHONE..............................310 380-5390
Anthony Reardon, *CEO*
◆ **EMP: 450 EST:** 1949
SQ FT: 300,000
SALES (est): 434.48MM
SALES (corp-wide): 756.99MM **Publicly
Held**
Web: www.ducommun.com
SIC: 3724 3812 3728 Aircraft engines and
engine parts; Search and navigation
equipment; Aircraft parts and equipment,
nec
PA: Ducommun Incorporated
600 Anton Blvd Ste 1100
657 335-3665

(P-7384)
DUCOMMUN AEROSTRUCTURES INC

1885 N Batavia St, Orange (92865-4105)
PHONE..............................714 637-4401
Kent T Christensen, *Brnch Mgr*
EMP: 109
SALES (corp-wide): 756.99MM **Publicly
Held**
Web: www.ducommun.com
SIC: 3724 3812 3728 Aircraft engines and
engine parts; Search and navigation
equipment; Aircraft parts and equipment,
nec
HQ: Ducommun Aerostructures, Inc.
600 Anton Blvd Ste 1100
Costa Mesa CA 92626
310 380-5390

(P-7385)
GARRETT TRANSPORTATION I INC (HQ)
2525 W 190th St, Torrance (90504-6002)
PHONE..............................973 455-2000
Darius Adamczyk, *CEO*
EMP: 26 EST: 2018
SALES (est): 11.76MM
SALES (corp-wide): 3.89B **Privately Held**
Web: www.garrettmotion.com
SIC: 3724 Aircraft engines and engine parts
PA: Garrett Motion Inc.
47548 Halyard Dr
734 392-5500

(P-7386)
GKN AEROSPACE CHEM-TRONICS INC (DH)
Also Called: Chem-Tronics
1150 W Bradley Ave, El Cajon
(92020-1504)
P.O. Box 1604 (92020)
PHONE..............................619 258-5000
James Wilson, *CEO*
Mark Fowler, *CFO*
Warren Fernandez, *Sec*
▲ **EMP: 648 EST:** 1953
SQ FT: 400,000
SALES (est): 194.63MM
SALES (corp-wide): 4.18B **Privately Held**
Web: www.gknaerospace.com
SIC: 3724 7699 Aircraft engines and engine
parts; Aircraft and heavy equipment repair
services
HQ: Gkn Limited
11th Floor, The Colmore Building
Birmingham W MIDLANDS B4 6A
121 210-9800

(P-7387)
HONEYWELL INTERNATIONAL INC
Also Called: Honeywell
2525 W 190th St, Torrance (90504-6002)
PHONE..............................310 323-9500
Ken Defusco, *Brnch Mgr*
EMP: 1000
SALES (corp-wide): 36.66B **Publicly Held**
Web: www.honeywell.com
SIC: 3724 Aircraft engines and engine parts
PA: Honeywell International Inc.
855 S Mint St
704 627-6200

(P-7388)
HONEYWELL SAFETY PDTS USA INC
7828 Waterville Rd, San Diego
(92154-8205)
PHONE..............................619 661-8383
Dave M Cote, *CEO*
EMP: 110
SALES (corp-wide): 36.66B **Publicly Held**
Web: www.honeywell.com

SIC: 3724 Aircraft engines and engine parts
HQ: Honeywell Safety Products Usa, Inc.
855 S Mint St
Charlotte NC 28202
800 430-5490

(P-7389)
INTERNATIONAL WIND INC (PA)
137 N Joy St, Corona (92879-1321)
PHONE..............................562 240-3963
Cory Arendt, *Pr*
EMP: 49 EST: 2013
SALES (est): 7.67MM
SALES (corp-wide): 7.67MM **Privately
Held**
Web: www.international-wind.com
SIC: 3724 8711 8742 Turbines, aircraft type;
Engineering services; Management
consulting services

(P-7390)
IRISH INTERNATIONAL
5511 Skylab Rd, Huntington Beach
(92647-2068)
PHONE..............................949 559-0930
Tom Mcfarland, *CEO*
Antonio Perez, *Corporate Secretary*
Jude Dozor, *
Mike Melancon, *
▲ **EMP: 250 EST:** 2015
SQ FT: 80,000
SALES (est): 9.35MM **Privately Held**
Web: www.encoregroup.aero
SIC: 3724 Aircraft engines and engine parts

(P-7391)
LOGISTICAL SUPPORT LLC
Also Called: RTC Aerospace
20409 Prairie St, Chatsworth (91311-6029)
PHONE..............................818 341-3344
EMP: 125 EST: 1997
SQ FT: 14,600
SALES (est): 1.83MM **Privately Held**
Web: www.rtcaerospace.com
SIC: 3724 Aircraft engines and engine parts

(P-7392)
MARTON PRECISION MFG LLC
1365 S Acacia Ave, Fullerton (92831-5315)
PHONE..............................714 808-6523
Daniel J Marton, *Pr*
Mary Marton, *
EMP: 47 EST: 1986
SQ FT: 20,000
SALES (est): 13.8MM **Privately Held**
Web: www.martoninc.com
SIC: 3724 3599 3827 Aircraft engines and
engine parts; Machine and other job shop
work; Optical instruments and apparatus

(P-7393)
PARKER-HANNIFIN CORPORATION
Fluid Systems Division
16666 Von Karman Ave, Irvine
(92606-4997)
PHONE..............................949 833-3000
Matthew Stafford, *Mgr*
EMP: 246
SALES (corp-wide): 19.93B **Publicly Held**
Web: www.parker.com
SIC: 3724 3728 Aircraft engines and engine
parts; Aircraft parts and equipment, nec
PA: Parker-Hannifin Corporation
6035 Parkland Blvd
216 896-3000

(P-7394)
PRATT & WHITNEY ENG SVCS INC
Also Called: Pratt Whitney Engine Services
11190 Valley View St, Cypress
(90630-5231)
PHONE.............................714 373-0110
Oliver Ho, *Mgr*
EMP: 1753
SALES (corp-wide): 68.92B **Publicly Held**
Web: www.prattwhitney.com
SIC: 3724 Aircraft engines and engine parts
HQ: Pratt & Whitney Engine Services, Inc.
    1525 Midway Park Rd
    Bridgeport WV 26330
    304 842-5421

(P-7395)
SAFRAN PWR UNITS SAN DIEGO LLC
Also Called: Safran Power Units
4255 Ruffin Rd Ste 100, San Diego
(92123-1247)
PHONE.............................858 223-2228
EMP: 70 **EST:** 2015
SQ FT: 22,000
SALES (est): 9.29MM
SALES (corp-wide): 940.23MM **Privately Held**
Web: www.melomano.us
SIC: 3724 Research and development on aircraft engines and parts
HQ: Safran Power Units
    8 Che Du Pont De Rupe
    Toulouse OCC 31200
    561375500

(P-7396)
THERMAL STRUCTURES INC (DH)
2362 Railroad St, Corona (92878-5421)
PHONE.............................951 736-9911
Vaughn Barnes, *Pr*
▲ **EMP:** 270 **EST:** 1952
SQ FT: 175,000
SALES (est): 31.98MM **Publicly Held**
Web: www.thermalstructures.com
SIC: 3724 Aircraft engines and engine parts
HQ: Heico Aerospace Holdings Corp.
    3000 Taft St
    Hollywood FL 33021
    954 987-4000

3728 Aircraft Parts And Equipment, Nec

(P-7397)
A-INFO INC
60 Tesla, Irvine (92618-4603)
PHONE.............................949 346-7326
Linda Williams, *Asst Mgr*
EMP: 35 **EST:** 2017
SALES (est): 2.5MM **Privately Held**
Web: www.ainfoinc.com
SIC: 3728 3812 5049 Aircraft parts and equipment, nec; Antennas, radar or communications; Analytical instruments

(P-7398)
ACE CLEARWATER ENTERPRISES INC (PA)
19815 Magellan Dr, Torrance (90502-1107)
PHONE.............................310 323-2140
James D Dodson, *Pr*
Kellie Johnson, *
EMP: 100 **EST:** 1961
SALES (est): 19.32MM
SALES (corp-wide): 19.32MM **Privately Held**

Web: www.aceclearwater.com
SIC: 3728 3544 7692 3812 Aircraft parts and equipment, nec; Special dies, tools, jigs, and fixtures; Welding repair; Search and navigation equipment

(P-7399)
ACROMIL LLC
1168 Sherborn St, Corona (92879-2089)
PHONE.............................951 808-9929
David Nguyen, *Pr*
EMP: 60
SALES (corp-wide): 44.93MM **Privately Held**
Web: www.acromil.com
SIC: 3728 Aircraft body and wing assemblies and parts
HQ: Acromil, Llc
    18421 Railroad St
    City Of Industry CA 91748
    626 964-2522

(P-7400)
ACROMIL LLC (HQ)
18421 Railroad St, City Of Industry
(91748-1281)
PHONE.............................626 964-2522
Gerald A Niznick, *
Jon Konheim, *
EMP: 144 **EST:** 2015
SQ FT: 96,000
SALES (est): 44.93MM
SALES (corp-wide): 44.93MM **Privately Held**
Web: www.acromil.com
SIC: 3728 Aircraft body and wing assemblies and parts
PA: Acromil Corporation
    18421 Railroad St
    626 964-2522

(P-7401)
ACROMIL CORPORATION (PA)
18421 Railroad St, City Of Industry
(91748-1281)
PHONE.............................626 964-2522
Gerald A Niznick, *Pr*
Jeanne Aguilera, *CFO*
Jon Konheim, *COO*
◆ **EMP:** 104 **EST:** 1961
SQ FT: 100,000
SALES (est): 44.93MM
SALES (corp-wide): 44.93MM **Privately Held**
Web: www.acromil.com
SIC: 3728 Aircraft body and wing assemblies and parts

(P-7402)
ACUFAST AIRCRAFT PRODUCTS INC
12445 Gladstone Ave, Sylmar
(91342-5321)
PHONE.............................818 365-7077
Art Dovlatian, *Pr*
Jaime Salazar, *
EMP: 40 **EST:** 2006
SALES (est): 9.4MM **Privately Held**
Web: www.acufastap.com
SIC: 3728 Aircraft parts and equipment, nec

(P-7403)
ADAMS RITE AEROSPACE INC (DH)
4141 N Palm St, Fullerton (92835-1025)
PHONE.............................714 278-6500
John Schaefer, *Pr*
EMP: 71 **EST:** 1973
SQ FT: 100,000
SALES (est): 41.7MM

SALES (corp-wide): 7.94B **Publicly Held**
Web: www.araero.com
SIC: 3728 Aircraft parts and equipment, nec
HQ: Transdigm, Inc.
    1350 Euclid Ave
    Cleveland OH 44115

(P-7404)
ADAPTIVE AEROSPACE CORPORATION
501 Bailey Ave, Tehachapi (93561-9012)
PHONE.............................661 300-0616
Bill Mccune, *CEO*
EMP: 25 **EST:** 2001
SALES (est): 3.45MM **Privately Held**
Web: www.adapt.aero
SIC: 3728 Aircraft parts and equipment, nec

(P-7405)
ADEPT FASTENERS INC (PA)
27949 Hancock Pkwy, Valencia
(91355-4116)
P.O. Box 579 (91310)
PHONE.............................661 257-6600
Gary Young, *Pr*
Don List, *
EMP: 106 **EST:** 2001
SQ FT: 40,000
SALES (est): 35.47MM
SALES (corp-wide): 35.47MM **Privately Held**
Web: www.adeptfasteners.com
SIC: 3728 Aircraft parts and equipment, nec

(P-7406)
ADVANCED DIGITAL MFG LLC
Also Called: ADM Works
1343 E Wilshire Ave, Santa Ana
(92705-4420)
PHONE.............................714 245-0536
Javier Valdiveso, *Pr*
Javier J Valdiveso, *
Jimmy Garcia, *
EMP: 27 **EST:** 2003
SALES (est): 2.56MM **Privately Held**
Web: www.adm-works.com
SIC: 3728 R and D by manuf., aircraft parts and auxiliary equipment

(P-7407)
ADVANCED MTLS JOINING CORP (PA)
Also Called: Advanced Technology Co
2858 E Walnut St, Pasadena (91107-3755)
PHONE.............................626 449-2696
Jean L De Silvestri, *Pr*
Mohammed Islam, *
EMP: 41 **EST:** 1971
SQ FT: 23,000
SALES (est): 11.55MM
SALES (corp-wide): 11.55MM **Privately Held**
Web: www.at-co.com
SIC: 3728 3724 Aircraft parts and equipment, nec; Aircraft engines and engine parts

(P-7408)
AERO ENGINEERING & MFG CO LLC
Also Called: Aero Engineering
28217 Avenue Crocker, Valencia
(91355-1249)
PHONE.............................661 295-0875
Dennis L Junker, *CEO*
Lance R Junker, *
Richard Jucksch, *
▼ **EMP:** 55 **EST:** 1948
SQ FT: 21,000

SALES (est): 9.59MM **Privately Held**
Web: www.aeroeng.com
SIC: 3728 5088 Aircraft assemblies, subassemblies, and parts, nec; Aircraft and parts, nec

(P-7409)
AERO PACIFIC CORPORATION
Also Called: Merco Manufacturing Co
20445 E Walnut Dr N, Walnut (91789-2918)
PHONE.............................714 961-9200
Mark Heasley, *Pr*
EMP: 130 **EST:** 1961
SALES (est): 8.96MM **Privately Held**
Web: www.alignprecision.com
SIC: 3728 Aircraft parts and equipment, nec

(P-7410)
AERO-CRAFT HYDRAULICS INC
392 N Smith Ave, Corona (92878-4371)
PHONE.............................951 736-4690
Rod Guzman Senior, *Pr*
Brad Davidson, *
Cathy Norris, *
Suzane Treneer, *
EMP: 43 **EST:** 1963
SQ FT: 16,500
SALES (est): 6.83MM **Privately Held**
Web: www.aero-craft.com
SIC: 3728 5084 7699 Aircraft body and wing assemblies and parts; Hydraulic systems equipment and supplies; Aircraft and heavy equipment repair services

(P-7411)
AEROSHEAR AVIATION SVCS INC (PA)
7701 Woodley Ave 200, Van Nuys
(91406-1732)
PHONE.............................818 779-1650
Lonnie Paschal, *CEO*
Christine Paschal, *
Ryan Hogan, *
EMP: 32 **EST:** 1996
SQ FT: 42,000
SALES (est): 4.92MM
SALES (corp-wide): 4.92MM **Privately Held**
Web: www.aeroshearaviation.com
SIC: 3728 3599 1799 Aircraft parts and equipment, nec; Machine shop, jobbing and repair; Welding on site

(P-7412)
AEROSPACE DYNAMICS INTL INC
25575 Rye Canyon Rd, Santa Clarita
(91355-1108)
PHONE.............................661 310-6986
EMP: 279
SALES (corp-wide): 364.48B **Publicly Held**
Web: www.pccaero.com
SIC: 3728 Aircraft parts and equipment, nec
HQ: Aerospace Dynamics International, Inc.
    25540 Rye Canyon Rd
    Valencia CA 91355

(P-7413)
AEROSPACE DYNAMICS INTL INC (DH)
Also Called: ADI
25540 Rye Canyon Rd, Valencia
(91355-1169)
PHONE.............................661 257-3535
Joseph I Snowden, *CEO*
◆ **EMP:** 171 **EST:** 1989
SQ FT: 250,000
SALES (est): 97.53MM

PRODUCTS & SVCS

SALES (corp-wide): 364.48B **Publicly Held**
Web: www.pccaero.com
SIC: 3728 Aircraft parts and equipment, nec
HQ: Precision Castparts Corp.
　　5885 Meadows Rd Ste 620
　　Lake Oswego OR 97035
　　503 946-4800

(P-7414)
AEROSPACE ENGINEERING LLC
2141 S Standard Ave, Santa Ana
(92707-3034)
PHONE..............................714 641-5884
EMP: 31
Web: www.karman-sd.com
SIC: 3728 Aircraft parts and equipment, nec
PA: Aerospace Engineering, Llc
　　2632 Saturn St

(P-7415)
AEROSPACE ENGINEERING LLC (PA)
Also Called: AEC
2632 Saturn St, Brea (92821-6701)
PHONE..............................714 996-8178
Mohammad Mahboubi, *Pr*
EMP: 89 **EST:** 2008
SALES (est): 27.29MM **Privately Held**
Web: www.karman-sd.com
SIC: 3728 3541 3599 Aircraft parts and equipment, nec; Numerically controlled metal cutting machine tools; Machine and other job shop work

(P-7416)
AEROSPACE ENGRG SUPPORT CORP
Also Called: J and L Industries
645 Hawaii St, El Segundo (90245-4814)
P.O. Box 999 (90245-0999)
PHONE..............................310 297-4050
Asher Bartov, *CEO*
Abraham Wacht, *
EMP: 27 **EST:** 1987
SQ FT: 30,000
SALES (est): 3.83MM
SALES (corp-wide): 1.3B **Privately Held**
Web: www.aerospace.org
SIC: 3728 Aircraft parts and equipment, nec
PA: The Aerospace Corporation
　　14745 Lee Rd
　　310 336-5000

(P-7417)
AEROSPACE PARTS HOLDINGS INC
Also Called: Cadence Aerospace
3150 E Miraloma Ave, Anaheim
(92806-1906)
PHONE..............................949 877-3630
Olivier Jarrault, *CEO*
Ron Case, *
Don Devore, *
Mike Coburn, *
EMP: 1175 **EST:** 2012
SALES (est): 5.23MM **Privately Held**
Web: www.verusaerospace.com
SIC: 3728 Aircraft parts and equipment, nec

(P-7418)
AHF-DUCOMMUN INCORPORATED (HQ)
Also Called: Ducommun Arostructures-Gardena
268 E Gardena Blvd, Gardena
(90248-2814)
PHONE..............................310 380-5390

Joseph C Berenato, *Prin*
Eugene P Conese, *Prin*
Ralph D Crosby, *Prin*
Jay L Haberland, *Prin*
Robert D Paulson, *Prin*
◆ **EMP:** 250 **EST:** 1950
SQ FT: 105,000
SALES (est): 434.48MM
SALES (corp-wide): 756.99MM **Publicly Held**
Web: www.ducommun.com
SIC: 3728 3812 3769 3469 Aircraft body and wing assemblies and parts; Search and navigation equipment; Space vehicle equipment, nec; Metal stampings, nec
PA: Ducommun Incorporated
　　600 Anton Blvd Ste 1100
　　657 335-3665

(P-7419)
AIR CABIN ENGINEERING INC
231 W Blueridge Ave, Orange
(92865-4226)
PHONE..............................714 637-4111
EMP: 25 **EST:** 1981
SALES (est): 4.32MM **Privately Held**
Web: www.aircabin.com
SIC: 3728 Aircraft parts and equipment, nec

(P-7420)
AIRBORNE TECHNOLOGIES INC
Also Called: Airborne Technologies
999 Avenida Acaso, Camarillo
(93012-8700)
P.O. Box 2210 (93011-2210)
PHONE..............................805 389-3700
Greg Beason, *CEO*
Christopher Celtruda, *
Richard Drinkward, *
EMP: 232 **EST:** 1980
SQ FT: 40,000
SALES (est): 25.5MM
SALES (corp-wide): 75.91MM **Privately Held**
Web: www.goallclear.com
SIC: 3728 5088 7699 3812 Aircraft parts and equipment, nec; Aircraft equipment and supplies, nec; Aircraft and heavy equipment repair services; Search and navigation equipment
PA: Kellstrom Holding Corporation
　　100 N Pcf Cast Hwy Ste 19
　　561 222-7455

(P-7421)
AIRTECH INTERNATIONAL INC (PA)
Also Called: Airtech Advanced Mtls Group
5700 Skylab Rd, Huntington Beach
(92647-2055)
PHONE..............................714 899-8100
William Dahlgren, *CEO*
Jeffrey Dahlgren, *CFO*
Audrey Dahlgren, *Sec*
Darren Carson, *Dir*
August Fester, *Dir*
◆ **EMP:** 130 **EST:** 1973
SQ FT: 150,000
SALES (est): 57.3MM
SALES (corp-wide): 57.3MM **Privately Held**
Web: www.airtechintl.com
SIC: 3728 3081 5088 2673 Aircraft parts and equipment, nec; Unsupported plastics film and sheet; Aeronautical equipment and supplies; Bags: plastic, laminated, and coated

(P-7422)
ALATUS AEROSYSTEMS
9301 Mason Ave, Chatsworth (91311-5202)
PHONE..............................626 498-7376
Richard Oak, *Mgr*
EMP: 80
SALES (corp-wide): 11.4MM **Privately Held**
Web: www.alatusaero.com
SIC: 3728 3489 Aircraft parts and equipment, nec; Artillery or artillery parts, over 30 mm.
PA: Alatus Aerosystems
　　9301 Mason Ave
　　610 965-1630

(P-7423)
ALATUS AEROSYSTEMS
Also Called: Triumph Structures - Brea
9301 Mason Ave, Chatsworth (91311-5202)
PHONE..............................714 732-0559
Manny Chacon, *Mgr*
EMP: 87
SALES (corp-wide): 11.4MM **Privately Held**
Web: www.alatusaero.com
SIC: 3728 3489 Aircraft parts and equipment, nec; Artillery or artillery parts, over 30 mm.
PA: Alatus Aerosystems
　　9301 Mason Ave
　　610 965-1630

(P-7424)
ALIGN AEROSPACE LLC (PA)
9401 De Soto Ave, Chatsworth
(91311-4920)
PHONE..............................818 727-7800
EMP: 287 **EST:** 2011
SQ FT: 73,000
SALES (est): 98.89MM **Privately Held**
Web: www.alignaero.com
SIC: 3728 Aircraft parts and equipment, nec

(P-7425)
ALIGN PRECISION - ANAHEIM INC (DH)
7100 Belgrave Ave, Garden Grove
(92841-2809)
PHONE..............................714 961-9200
Mark Cherry, *CEO*
EMP: 80 **EST:** 2010
SALES (est): 27.6MM
SALES (corp-wide): 1.89B **Privately Held**
Web: www.alignprecision.com
SIC: 3728 Aircraft parts and equipment, nec
HQ: Align Precision Corp.
　　730 W 22nd St
　　Tempe AZ 85282
　　480 968-1778

(P-7426)
ALL POWER MANUFACTURING CO
13141 Molette St, Santa Fe Springs
(90670-5500)
PHONE..............................562 802-2640
Michael J Hartnett, *CEO*
▲ **EMP:** 130 **EST:** 1948
SALES (est): 14.71MM
SALES (corp-wide): 1.56B **Publicly Held**
Web: www.rbcbearings.com
SIC: 3728 2899 Aircraft assemblies, subassemblies, and parts, nec; Chemical preparations, nec
PA: Rbc Bearings Incorporated
　　1 Tribology Ctr
　　203 267-7001

(P-7427)
ALLCLEAR AEROSPACE & DEF INC
Also Called: Williams Aerospace and Mfg
757 Main St # 102, Chula Vista
(91911-6168)
PHONE..............................619 660-6220
EMP: 45
SALES (corp-wide): 156.2MM **Privately Held**
Web: www.kellstromdefense.com
SIC: 3728 Aircraft parts and equipment, nec
HQ: Allclear Aerospace & Defense, Inc.
　　15501 Sw 29th St Ste 101
　　Miramar FL 33027
　　954 239-7844

(P-7428)
ALLCLEAR AEROSPACE & DEF INC
1283 Flynn Rd, Camarillo (93012-8013)
PHONE..............................805 446-2700
EMP: 54
SALES (corp-wide): 156.2MM **Privately Held**
Web: www.kellstromdefense.com
SIC: 3728 Aircraft parts and equipment, nec
HQ: Allclear Aerospace & Defense, Inc.
　　15501 Sw 29th St Ste 101
　　Miramar FL 33027
　　954 239-7844

(P-7429)
ALVA MANUFACTURING INC
236 E Orangethorpe Ave, Placentia
(92870-6442)
PHONE..............................714 237-0925
Tam V Nguyen, *CEO*
Tam V Nguyen, *Pr*
EMP: 44 **EST:** 2011
SQ FT: 15,000
SALES (est): 4.48MM **Privately Held**
Web: www.alvamanufacturing.com
SIC: 3728 3599 Aircraft parts and equipment, nec; Machine and other job shop work

(P-7430)
AMRO FABRICATING CORPORATION (PA)
Also Called: Karman Missile & Space Systems
1430 Amro Way, South El Monte
(91733-3046)
PHONE..............................626 579-2200
John Hammond, *Pr*
Michael Riley, *
EMP: 238 **EST:** 1977
SQ FT: 150,000
SALES (est): 45.24MM
SALES (corp-wide): 45.24MM **Privately Held**
Web: www.karman-sd.com
SIC: 3728 3769 3544 5088 Aircraft parts and equipment, nec; Space vehicle equipment, nec; Special dies, tools, jigs, and fixtures; Aircraft and space vehicle supplies and parts

(P-7431)
APPLIED CMPSITE STRUCTURES INC (HQ)
1195 Columbia St, Brea (92821-2922)
PHONE..............................714 990-6300
David Horner, *CEO*
Jorge Garcia, *
Justin Uchida, *
EMP: 87 **EST:** 1975
SQ FT: 100,000

SALES (est): 50.87MM
SALES (corp-wide): 189.21MM **Privately Held**
Web: www.appliedcomposites.com
SIC: **3728** Aircraft parts and equipment, nec
PA: Applied Composites Holdings, Llc
25692 Atlantic Ocean Dr
949 716-3511

(P-7432)

APPROVED AERONAUTICS LLC
Also Called: Manufacturer and Distributor
9130 Pulsar Ct, Corona (92883-4630)
PHONE....................................951 200-3730
Anthony Janes, *CEO*
EMP: 42 EST: 1999
SALES (est): 5.04MM **Privately Held**
Web: www.approvedaeronautics.com
SIC: **3728** Aircraft parts and equipment, nec

(P-7433)

ARDEN ENGINEERING INC
1878 N Main St, Orange (92865-4117)
Rural Route 3130 (92806)
PHONE....................................714 998-6410
Thorin Southworth, *of Corp*
EMP: 197
SALES (corp-wide): 666.39MM **Privately Held**
Web: www.arden-engr.com
SIC: **3728** Aircraft body assemblies and parts
HQ: Arden Engineering, Inc.
3130 E Miraloma Ave
Anaheim CA 92806
949 877-3642

(P-7434)

ARROWHEAD PRODUCTS CORPORATION
Also Called: Arrowhead Products
4411 Katella Ave, Los Alamitos
(90720-3599)
PHONE....................................714 822-2513
Andrew Whelan, *Pr*
Bill Gardner, *
Erick Reinhold, *
Pete Kraft, *
▲ EMP: 640 EST: 1968
SQ FT: 250,000
SALES (est): 67.49MM
SALES (corp-wide): 459.42MM **Privately Held**
Web: www.arrowheadproducts.net
SIC: **3728** Accumulators, aircraft propeller
HQ: Industrial Manufacturing Company Llc
8223 Brcksvlle Rd Ste 100
Brecksville OH 44141
440 838-4700

(P-7435)

ASTOR MANUFACTURING
779 Anita St Ste B, Chula Vista
(91911-3937)
PHONE....................................661 645-5585
Erick Muschenheim, *Pr*
EMP: 25 EST: 2016
SQ FT: 3,500
SALES (est): 4.42MM **Privately Held**
Web: www.astormanufacturing.com
SIC: **3728** Aircraft body assemblies and parts

(P-7436)

ASTRO SPAR INC
3130 E Miraloma Ave, Anaheim
(92806-1906)
PHONE....................................626 839-7858
▲ EMP: 42
Web: www.astrospar.com
SIC: **3728** Aircraft assemblies,
subassemblies, and parts, nec

(P-7437)

ASTURIES MANUFACTURING CO INC
310 Cessna Cir, Corona (92878-5009)
PHONE....................................951 270-1766
Manuel Perez, *Pr*
Luis Perez, *
EMP: 25 EST: 1979
SQ FT: 50,850
SALES (est): 6.76MM **Privately Held**
SIC: **3728** 3559 Aircraft parts and
equipment, nec; Semiconductor
manufacturing machinery

(P-7438)

AVANTUS AEROSPACE INC (DH)
29101 The Old Rd, Valencia (91355-1014)
PHONE....................................661 295-8620
Brian Williams, *CEO*
Dennis Suedkamp, *
Scott Wilkinson, *
EMP: 125 EST: 2015
SQ FT: 75,000
SALES (est): 57.2MM
SALES (corp-wide): 145.58MM **Privately Held**
Web: www.avantusaerospace.com
SIC: **3728** Aircraft parts and equipment, nec
HQ: Avantus Aerospace Limited
Unit 7 Millington Road
Hayes MIDDX UB3 4

(P-7439)

AVIATION DESIGN GROUP INC
Also Called: Gst Industries, Inc.
9060 Winnetka Ave, Northridge
(91324-3235)
PHONE....................................818 350-1900
Michael Saville, *Pr*
EMP: 24 EST: 2005
SQ FT: 9,700
SALES (est): 974.46K
SALES (corp-wide): 9.05MM **Privately Held**
SIC: **3728** Aircraft assemblies,
subassemblies, and parts, nec
PA: Infinity Aerospace, Inc.
9060 Winnetka Ave
818 998-9811

(P-7440)

AVIBANK MFG INC (DH)
Also Called: Avibank
11500 Sherman Way, North Hollywood
(91605-5827)
P.O. Box 9909 (91609-1909)
PHONE....................................818 392-2100
Dan Woltor, *Pr*
John Duran, *
▲ EMP: 115 EST: 1945
SALES (est): 90.28MM
SALES (corp-wide): 364.48B **Publicly Held**
Web: www.avibank.com
SIC: **3728** Aircraft parts and equipment, nec
HQ: Sps Technologies, Llc
301 Highland Ave
Jenkintown PA 19046
215 572-3000

(P-7441)

B & E MANUFACTURING CO INC
12151 Monarch St, Garden Grove
(92841-2927)
PHONE....................................714 898-2269
Emmanuel Neildez, *Pr*
Jerome Guilloteau, *Sec*
EMP: 45 EST: 1981
SQ FT: 26,000
SALES (est): 10.02MM

SALES (corp-wide): 2.67MM **Privately Held**
Web: www.bandmfg.com
SIC: **3728** Aircraft parts and equipment, nec
HQ: Lisi
6 Rue Juvenal Viellard
Grandvillars BFC 90600
384573000

(P-7442)

B/E AEROSPACE INC
7155 Fenwick Ln, Westminster
(92683-5218)
PHONE....................................714 896-9001
Jim Melrose, *Mgr*
EMP: 136
SALES (corp-wide): 68.92B **Publicly Held**
Web: www.collinsaerospace.com
SIC: **3728** 3647 Aircraft parts and
equipment, nec; Aircraft lighting fixtures
HQ: B/E Aerospace, Inc.
2730 West Tyvola Rd
Charlotte NC 28217
704 423-7000

(P-7443)

B/E AEROSPACE MACROLINK
1500 N Kellogg Dr, Anaheim (92807-1902)
PHONE....................................714 777-8800
Mark Cordivari, *Pr*
EMP: 32 EST: 2015
SALES (est): 3.06MM **Privately Held**
SIC: **3728** Aircraft parts and equipment, nec

(P-7444)

BANDY MANUFACTURING LLC
3420 N San Fernando Blvd, Burbank
(91504-2532)
P.O. Box 7716 (91510-7716)
PHONE....................................818 846-9020
Tom Fulton, *Pr*
Kevin L Cummings, *
EMP: 93 EST: 1952
SQ FT: 60,000
SALES (est): 10.85MM **Privately Held**
Web: www.bandymanufacturing.com
SIC: **3728** Aircraft parts and equipment, nec

(P-7445)

BISH INC
2820 Via Orange Way Ste G, Spring Valley
(91978-1742)
PHONE....................................619 660-6220
William L Cary, *Pr*
Shane Nonthavet, *VP*
EMP: 23 EST: 1997
SQ FT: 16,000
SALES (est): 1.05MM **Privately Held**
SIC: **3728** Aircraft parts and equipment, nec

(P-7446)

C&D ZODIAC AEROSPACE
7330 Lincoln Way, Garden Grove
(92841-1427)
PHONE....................................714 891-0683
▲ EMP: 26 EST: 2015
SALES (est): 944.67K **Privately Held**
Web: www.zodiacaerospace.com
SIC: **3728** Aircraft parts and equipment, nec

(P-7447)

CAL TECH PRECISION INC
1830 N Lemon St, Anaheim (92801-1000)
PHONE....................................714 992-4130
Guy Haarlammert, *Pr*
▲ EMP: 99 EST: 1989
SALES (est): 10.99MM **Privately Held**
Web: www.caltechprecision.com
SIC: **3728** Aircraft parts and equipment, nec

(P-7448)

CANYON COMPOSITES INCORPORATED
1548 N Gemini Pl, Anaheim (92801-1152)
PHONE....................................714 991-8181
Bj Rutkoski, *Pr*
Robert Gray, *
Eric Collins, *
EMP: 40 EST: 1996
SQ FT: 31,500
SALES (est): 8.17MM **Privately Held**
Web: www.canyoncomposites.com
SIC: **3728** 8711 Aircraft parts and
equipment, nec; Engineering services

(P-7449)

CANYON ENGINEERING PDTS INC
28909 Avenue Williams, Valencia
(91355-4183)
PHONE....................................661 294-0084
Todd Strickland, *Pr*
Paul Knerr, *
EMP: 88 EST: 1979
SQ FT: 70,000
SALES (est): 6.86MM **Publicly Held**
Web: www.crissair.com
SIC: **3728** Aircraft assemblies,
subassemblies, and parts, nec
PA: Esco Technologies Inc.
9900 A Clayton Rd

(P-7450)

CARBON BY DESIGN LLC
1491 Poinsettia Ave Ste 136, Vista
(92081-8541)
PHONE....................................760 643-1300
EMP: 75 EST: 2003
SQ FT: 65,000
SALES (est): 8.83MM **Publicly Held**
Web: www.carbonbydesign.com
SIC: **3728** 3761 Airframe assemblies, except
for guided missiles; Guided missiles and
space vehicles
HQ: Heico Flight Support Corp.
3000 Taft St
Hollywood FL 33021
954 987-4000

(P-7451)

CARDONA MANUFACTURING CORP
1869 N Victory Pl, Burbank (91504-3476)
PHONE....................................818 841-8358
Louis Cardona, *Pr*
Jo Ann Cardona, *
EMP: 26 EST: 1971
SQ FT: 10,000
SALES (est): 2.48MM **Privately Held**
Web: www.cardonamfg.com
SIC: **3728** 3812 Aircraft parts and
equipment, nec; Search and navigation
equipment

(P-7452)

CAVOTEC DABICO US INC
5665 Corporate Ave, Cypress
(90630-4727)
PHONE....................................714 947-0005
Gary Matthews, *Pr*
Christian Bernadotte, *
Dorothy Chen, *
▲ EMP: 36 EST: 2008
SALES (est): 5.21MM **Privately Held**
Web: www.cavotec.com
SIC: **3728** Aircraft parts and equipment, nec

(P-7453)
COAST COMPOSITES LLC (PA)
5 Burroughs, Irvine (92618-2804)
PHONE..............................949 455-0665
Daniel Nowicki, *CFO*
◆ **EMP:** 80 **EST:** 1988
SQ FT: 60,000
SALES (est): 7.68MM
SALES (corp-wide): 7.68MM **Privately Held**
Web: www.ascentaerospace.com
SIC: 3728 3544 3599 Aircraft parts and equipment, nec; Special dies, tools, jigs, and fixtures; Machine shop, jobbing and repair

(P-7454)
COI CERAMICS INC
Also Called: Coic
7130 Miramar Rd Ste 100b, San Diego (92121-2340)
PHONE..............................858 621-5700
David A Shanahan, *CEO*
Steve Atmur, *
Andy Szweda, *
EMP: 41 **EST:** 1999
SQ FT: 3,000
SALES (est): 1.12MM **Publicly Held**
Web: www.coiceramics.com
SIC: 3728 Aircraft parts and equipment, nec
HQ: Northrop Grumman Innovation Systems, Inc.
      2980 Fairview Park Dr
      Falls Church VA 22042

(P-7455)
COMPUCRAFT INDUSTRIES INC
Also Called: Cii
8787 Olive Ln, Santee (92071-4137)
P.O. Box 712529 (92072-2529)
PHONE..............................619 448-0787
Maurice Brear, *Pr*
Margarita Brear, *
EMP: 50 **EST:** 1972
SQ FT: 85,000
SALES (est): 4.88MM **Privately Held**
Web: www.ccind.com
SIC: 3728 Aircraft assemblies, subassemblies, and parts, nec

(P-7456)
CORONADO MANUFACTURING LLC
8991 Glenoaks Blvd, Sun Valley (91352-2038)
PHONE..............................818 768-5010
Allen F Gowing, *Pr*
Phillip Belmonte, *
▼ **EMP:** 50 **EST:** 1959
SQ FT: 19,000
SALES (est): 7.12MM **Privately Held**
Web: www.coronadomfg.com
SIC: 3728 5084 Military aircraft equipment and armament; Industrial machine parts

(P-7457)
CRANE AEROSPACE INC
Crane Aerospace & Electronics
3000 Winona Ave, Burbank (91504-2540)
PHONE..............................818 526-2600
Brendan Curran, *AERO GROUP*
EMP: 59
SALES (corp-wide): 2.09B **Publicly Held**
Web: www.craneae.com
SIC: 3728 Aircraft parts and equipment, nec
HQ: Crane Aerospace, Inc.
      100 First Stamford Pl
      Stamford CT 06902

(P-7458)
CURTISS-WRIGHT CONTROLS INC
6940 Farmdale Ave, North Hollywood (91605-6210)
PHONE..............................818 503-0998
EMP: 28
SALES (corp-wide): 2.85B **Publicly Held**
Web: www.curtisswright.com
SIC: 3728 Aircraft assemblies, subassemblies, and parts, nec
HQ: Curtiss-Wright Controls, Inc.
      15801 Brixham Hill Ave # 200
      Charlotte NC 28277
      704 869-4600

(P-7459)
D & D GEAR INCORPORATED
Also Called: Absolute Technologies
4890 E La Palma Ave, Anaheim (92807-1911)
PHONE..............................714 692-6570
Bill Beverage, *Pr*
▲ **EMP:** 210 **EST:** 1969
SQ FT: 82,500
SALES (est): 19.04MM **Privately Held**
Web: www.absolutetechnologies.com
SIC: 3728 Aircraft parts and equipment, nec

(P-7460)
DASCO ENGINEERING CORP
24747 Crenshaw Blvd, Torrance (90505-5308)
PHONE..............................310 326-2277
Ward Olson, *Pr*
Glen Olson, *
John Karle, *
◆ **EMP:** 110 **EST:** 1964
SQ FT: 50,000
SALES (est): 19.53MM **Privately Held**
Web: www.dascoeng.com
SIC: 3728 Aircraft body and wing assemblies and parts

(P-7461)
DATRON ADVANCED TECH INC
200 W Los Angeles Ave, Simi Valley (93065-1650)
PHONE..............................805 579-2966
Mellon C Baird, *CEO*
EMP: 120 **EST:** 1990
SALES (est): 3.19MM **Privately Held**
SIC: 3728 3663 1799 R and D by manuf., aircraft parts and auxiliary equipment; Satellites, communications; Antenna installation

(P-7462)
DESIGNED METAL CONNECTIONS INC (DH)
Also Called: Permaswage USA
14800 S Figueroa St, Gardena (90248-1719)
PHONE..............................310 323-6200
Thomas Mcdonnell, *VP*
▲ **EMP:** 500 **EST:** 2004
SQ FT: 175,000
SALES (est): 84.78MM
SALES (corp-wide): 364.48B **Publicly Held**
Web: www.pccfluidfittings.com
SIC: 3728 Aircraft parts and equipment, nec
HQ: Precision Castparts Corp.
      5885 Meadows Rd Ste 620
      Lake Oswego OR 97035
      503 946-4800

(P-7463)
DPI LABS INC
1350 Arrow Hwy, La Verne (91750-5218)
PHONE..............................909 392-5777
Vicki Brown, *CEO*
Al Snow, *
Greg Desmet, *
Pam Archibald, *
EMP: 35 **EST:** 1984
SALES (est): 5.04MM **Privately Held**
Web: www.dpilabs.com
SIC: 3728 Aircraft parts and equipment, nec

(P-7464)
DUCOMMUN AEROSTRUCTURES INC
801 Royal Oaks Dr, Monrovia (91016-3630)
PHONE..............................626 358-3211
Maurice Harris, *Genl Mgr*
EMP: 30
SALES (corp-wide): 756.99MM **Publicly Held**
Web: www.ducommun.com
SIC: 3728 Aircraft parts and equipment, nec
HQ: Ducommun Aerostructures, Inc.
      600 Anton Blvd Ste 1100
      Costa Mesa CA 92626
      310 380-5390

(P-7465)
DUCOMMUN AEROSTRUCTURES INC
23301 Wilmington Ave, Carson (90745-6209)
PHONE..............................310 513-7200
Eugene Conese Junior, *Dir*
EMP: 93
SALES (corp-wide): 756.99MM **Publicly Held**
Web: www.ducommun.com
SIC: 3728 Aircraft parts and equipment, nec
HQ: Ducommun Aerostructures, Inc.
      600 Anton Blvd Ste 1100
      Costa Mesa CA 92626
      310 380-5390

(P-7466)
DUCOMMUN AEROSTRUCTURES INC
4001 El Mirage Rd, Adelanto (92301-9489)
PHONE..............................760 246-4191
Art Mcfarlan, *Mgr*
EMP: 47
SQ FT: 1,152
SALES (corp-wide): 756.99MM **Publicly Held**
Web: www.ducommun.com
SIC: 3728 Aircraft parts and equipment, nec
HQ: Ducommun Aerostructures, Inc.
      600 Anton Blvd Ste 1100
      Costa Mesa CA 92626
      310 380-5390

(P-7467)
DUCOMMUN INCORPORATED (PA)
Also Called: DUCOMMUN
600 Anton Blvd Ste 1100, Costa Mesa (92626-7100)
PHONE..............................657 335-3665
Stephen G Oswald, *Ch Bd*
Suman Mookerjim, *CFO*
Christopher D Wampler, *CFO*
Laureen S Gonzalez, *Chief Human Resource Officer*
▲ **EMP:** 216 **EST:** 1849
SALES (est): 756.99MM
SALES (corp-wide): 756.99MM **Publicly Held**

Web: www.ducommun.com
SIC: 3728 3679 Aircraft body and wing assemblies and parts; Microwave components

(P-7468)
DUCOMMUN INCORPORATED
801 Royal Oaks Dr, Monrovia (91016-3630)
PHONE..............................626 358-3211
Bradley W Spahr, *CEO*
EMP: 27
SALES (corp-wide): 712.54MM **Publicly Held**
Web: www.ducommun.com
SIC: 3728 Aircraft parts and equipment, nec
PA: Ducommun Incorporated
      600 Anton Blvd Ste 1100
      657 335-3665

(P-7469)
DUCOMMUN LABARGE TECH INC (HQ)
Also Called: American Electronics
23301 Wilmington Ave, Carson (90745-6209)
PHONE..............................310 513-7200
Stephen G Oswald, *Pr*
Christopher Wampler, *VP*
Jerry Redondo, *VP*
Michelle Stein, *VP*
Rajiv Tata, *Sec*
▲ **EMP:** 180 **EST:** 1958
SQ FT: 117,000
SALES (est): 85.22MM
SALES (corp-wide): 756.99MM **Publicly Held**
Web: www.ducommun.com
SIC: 3728 3769 5065 3812 Aircraft parts and equipment, nec; Space vehicle equipment, nec; Electronic parts and equipment, nec; Search and navigation equipment
PA: Ducommun Incorporated
      600 Anton Blvd Ste 1100
      657 335-3665

(P-7470)
DYNAMIC FABRICATION INC
890 Mariner St, Brea (92821-3831)
PHONE..............................714 662-2440
Andrew Crook, *Pr*
Olga Garcia Crook, *
EMP: 25 **EST:** 1991
SQ FT: 22,000
SALES (est): 7.54MM **Privately Held**
Web: www.dynamicfab.com
SIC: 3728 3764 3761 3812 Aircraft parts and equipment, nec; Engines and engine parts, guided missile; Guided missiles and space vehicles; Defense systems and equipment

(P-7471)
ENCORE SEATS INC
Also Called: Lift By Encore
5511 Skylab Rd, Huntington Beach (92647-2068)
PHONE..............................949 559-0930
Thomas Mcfarland, *CEO*
Mike Melancon, *
Aram Krikorian, *
EMP: 46 **EST:** 2015
SQ FT: 80,000
SALES (est): 824.44K **Privately Held**
Web: www.encoregroup.aero
SIC: 3728 Aircraft assemblies, subassemblies, and parts, nec.

(P-7472)
ENGINEERING JK AEROSPACE & DEF
Also Called: Nytron Aerospace - Mfg Systems

23231 La Palma Ave, Yorba Linda
(92887-4768)
PHONE.....................714 499-9092
Jonathan Crisan, *Pr*
EMP: 25 **EST:** 2012
SALES (est): 6.82MM **Privately Held**
Web: mfg.nytron.aero
SIC: 3728 3724 Aircraft parts and
    equipment, nec; Aircraft engines and
    engine parts

(P-7473)
FERRA AEROSPACE INC
940 E Orangethorpe Ave Ste A, Anaheim
(92801-1129)
PHONE.....................918 787-2220
EMP: 46
SALES (corp-wide): 23.49MM **Privately
Held**
Web: www.ferra-group.com
SIC: 3728 Aircraft parts and equipment, nec
PA: Ferra Aerospace, Inc.
    64353 E 290 Rd
    918 787-2220

(P-7474)
FLARE GROUP
Also Called: Aviation Equipment Processing
1571 Macarthur Blvd, Costa Mesa
(92626-1407)
PHONE.....................714 850-2080
Dennis Heider, *Pr*
Steve Osorio, *
Daryl Silva, *
Jim Vinyard, *
Eric Trainor, *
EMP: 25 **EST:** 2010
SALES (est): 4.42MM **Privately Held**
Web: www.aveprocessing.com
SIC: 3728 Aircraft parts and equipment, nec

(P-7475)
FLEXCO INC
6855 Suva St, Bell Gardens (90201-1999)
PHONE.....................562 927-2525
Erik Moller, *Pr*
EMP: 36 **EST:** 1966
SQ FT: 14,000
SALES (est): 4.15MM **Privately Held**
Web: www.flexcoinc.com
SIC: 3728 3496 Aircraft parts and
    equipment, nec; Miscellaneous fabricated
    wire products

(P-7476)
FLIGHT ENVIRONMENTS INC
570 Linne Rd Ste 100, Paso Robles
(93446-9460)
P.O. Box 3169 (93447-3169)
EMP: 25 **EST:** 1998
SALES (est): 2.25MM **Privately Held**
Web: www.luminary.aero
SIC: 3728 Aircraft parts and equipment, nec

(P-7477)
FLIGHT LINE PRODUCTS INC
Also Called: Flightways Manufacturing
28732 Witherspoon Pkwy, Valencia
(91355-5425)
PHONE.....................661 775-8366
▲ **EMP:** 40
SIC: 3728 5599 Aircraft parts and
    equipment, nec; Aircraft, self-propelled

(P-7478)
FMH AEROSPACE CORP
Also Called: F M H
17072 Daimler St, Irvine (92614-5548)
PHONE.....................714 751-1000
Rick Busch, *CEO*

David Difranco, *
Valerie Gorman, *
▲ **EMP:** 100 **EST:** 1991
SQ FT: 15,000
SALES (est): 41.21MM
SALES (corp-wide): 6.6B **Publicly Held**
Web: www.fmhaerospace.com
SIC: 3728 Aircraft parts and equipment, nec
PA: Ametek, Inc.
    1100 Cassatt Rd
    610 647-2121

(P-7479)
FORREST MACHINING LLC
Also Called: Forrestmachining
27756 Avenue Mentry, Valencia
(91355-3453)
PHONE.....................661 257-0231
Tim Mickael, *CEO*
▲ **EMP:** 240 **EST:** 1979
SALES (est): 47.57MM
SALES (corp-wide): 47.57MM **Privately
Held**
Web: www.fmiaerostructures.com
SIC: 3728 Aircraft parts and equipment, nec
PA: Dvsm, L.L.C.
    760 Sw 9th Ave Ste 2300
    503 223-2721

(P-7480)
FRAZIER AVIATION INC
445 N Fox St, San Fernando (91340-2501)
PHONE.....................818 898-1998
Robert L Frazier, *CEO*
Robert Frazier Iii, *Pr*
Charles E Ricard, *
Robert Frazier Iv, *Ex VP*
EMP: 44 **EST:** 1956
SQ FT: 44,000
SALES (est): 5.37MM **Privately Held**
Web: www.frazieraviation.com
SIC: 3728 5088 Aircraft body assemblies
    and parts; Transportation equipment and
    supplies

(P-7481)
GEAR MANUFACTURING INC
Also Called: G M I
3701 E Miraloma Ave, Anaheim
(92806-2123)
PHONE.....................714 792-2895
Gary M Smith, *CEO*
EMP: 50 **EST:** 1989
SQ FT: 26,500
SALES (est): 9.63MM **Privately Held**
Web: www.gearmfg.com
SIC: 3728 3714 3566 3568 Gears, aircraft
    power transmission; Bearings, motor vehicle
    ; Speed changers, drives, and gears;
    Power transmission equipment, nec

(P-7482)
GENERAL DYNAMICS OTS CAL
INC
Also Called: GENERAL DYNAMICS OTS
(CALIFORNIA), INC.
7603 Saint Andrews Ave Ste H, San Diego
(92154-8217)
PHONE.....................619 671-5411
EMP: 121
SALES (corp-wide): 42.27B **Publicly Held**
Web: www.gd-ots.com
SIC: 3728 Military aircraft equipment and
    armament
HQ: General Dynamics-Ots, Inc.
    100 Carillon Pkwy Ste 100
    Saint Petersburg FL 33716
    727 578-8100

(P-7483)
GIDDENS INDUSTRIES INC (DH)
3130 E Miraloma Ave, Anaheim
(92806-1906)
EMP: 150 **EST:** 1974
SALES (est): 8.75MM
SALES (corp-wide): 666.39MM **Privately
Held**
Web: www.giddens.com
SIC: 3728 Aircraft parts and equipment, nec
HQ: Giddens Holdings, Inc.
    2600 94th St Sw Ste 150
    Everett WA 98204
    425 353-0405

(P-7484)
GLEDHILL/LYONS INC
Also Called: Accurate Technology
2511 Termino Ave, Long Beach
(90815-1726)
PHONE.....................714 502-0274
David M Lyons, *Pr*
EMP: 43 **EST:** 2000
SALES (est): 1.29MM **Privately Held**
Web: www.accuratetechnology.net
SIC: 3728 Aircraft parts and equipment, nec

(P-7485)
GOODRICH CORPORATION
Goodrich Wheel and Brake Svcs
9920 Freeman Ave, Santa Fe Springs
(90670-3421)
PHONE.....................562 944-4441
Hosrow Bordbar, *Mgr*
EMP: 87
SALES (corp-wide): 68.92B **Publicly Held**
Web: www.collinsaerospace.com
SIC: 3728 Aircraft parts and equipment, nec
HQ: Goodrich Corporation
    2730 W Tyvola Rd
    Charlotte NC 28217
    704 423-7000

(P-7486)
GOODRICH CORPORATION
3355 E La Palma Ave, Anaheim
(92806-2815)
PHONE.....................714 984-1461
Rob Gibbs, *Genl Mgr*
EMP: 140
SALES (corp-wide): 68.92B **Publicly Held**
Web: www.collinsaerospace.com
SIC: 3728 Aircraft parts and equipment, nec
HQ: Goodrich Corporation
    2730 W Tyvola Rd
    Charlotte NC 28217
    704 423-7000

(P-7487)
HANSEN ENGINEERING CO
Also Called: Plant 2
24050 Frampton Ave, Harbor City
(90710-2197)
PHONE.....................310 534-3870
EMP: 28 **EST:** 2019
SALES (est): 4.96MM **Privately Held**
Web: www.hansenengineering.com
SIC: 3728 Aircraft parts and equipment, nec

(P-7488)
HELICOPTER TECH CO LTD
PARTNR
Also Called: Helicopter Technology Company
12902 S Broadway, Los Angeles
(90061-1118)
PHONE.....................310 523-2750
Frank Palminteri, *Pr*
Gary Burdorf, *
◆ **EMP:** 24 **EST:** 1995
SQ FT: 197,000

SALES (est): 4.26MM **Privately Held**
Web: www.helicoptertech.com
SIC: 3728 3721 Aircraft parts and
    equipment, nec; Helicopters

(P-7489)
HORNET ACQUISITIONCO LLC
✪
Also Called: Onboard Systems Hoist & Winch
3355 E La Palma Ave, Anaheim
(92806-2815)
PHONE.....................714 984-1461
Norman D Jordan, *CEO*
EMP: 191 **EST:** 2024
SALES (est): 5.06MM
SALES (corp-wide): 15.01MM **Privately
Held**
SIC: 3728 3537 3531 Aircraft body and wing
    assemblies and parts; Aircraft loading hoists
    ; Winches
PA: Signia Aerospace Holdings, Inc.
    1575 W 124th Ave

(P-7490)
HUTCHINSON AROSPC &
INDUST INC
Also Called: ARS
4510 W Vanowen St, Burbank
(91505-1135)
PHONE.....................818 843-1000
Shano Cristilli, *Brnch Mgr*
EMP: 165
SALES (corp-wide): 7.88B **Privately Held**
Web: www.hutchinsonai.com
SIC: 3728 Aircraft parts and equipment, nec
HQ: Hutchinson Aerospace & Industry, Inc.
    82 South St
    Hopkinton MA 01748
    508 417-7000

(P-7491)
HYDRAFLOW
Also Called: Hydraflow
1881 W Malvern Ave, Fullerton
(92833-2403)
PHONE.....................714 773-2600
EMP: 255 **EST:** 1961
SALES (est): 29.15MM **Privately Held**
Web: www.hydraflow.com
SIC: 3728 3492 Aircraft parts and
    equipment, nec; Fluid power valves for
    aircraft

(P-7492)
HYDRAULICS INTERNATIONAL
INC (PA)
20961 Knapp St, Chatsworth (91311-5926)
PHONE.....................818 998-1231
Nicky Ghaemmaghami, *CEO*
Shah Banifazl, *
◆ **EMP:** 356 **EST:** 1976
SQ FT: 78,000
SALES (est): 107.64MM
SALES (corp-wide): 107.64MM **Privately
Held**
Web: www.hiigroup.com
SIC: 3728 Aircraft parts and equipment, nec

(P-7493)
HYDRO-AIRE INC (HQ)
3000 Winona Ave, Burbank (91504-2572)
PHONE.....................818 526-2600
Brendan J Curran, *CEO*
Tazewell Rowe, *
▲ **EMP:** 97 **EST:** 1996
SQ FT: 173,000
SALES (est): 184.7MM
SALES (corp-wide): 2.09B **Publicly Held**
Web: www.craneae.com

P R O D U C T S   &   S V C S

SIC: 3728 Aircraft parts and equipment, nec
PA: Crane Company
100 1st Stmford Pl Ste 40
203 363-7300

(P-7494)
HYDRO-AIRE AEROSPACE CORP
3000 Winona Ave, Burbank (91504-2572)
PHONE..................818 526-2600
Jay Higgs, *Pr*
EMP: 200
SALES (corp-wide): 2.09B Publicly Held
SIC: 3728 Aircraft parts and equipment, nec
HQ: Hydro-Aire Aerospace Corp.
249 Abbe Rd S
Elyria OH 44035
440 323-3211

(P-7495)
HYDROFORM USA INCORPORATED
2848 E 208th St, Carson (90810-1101)
PHONE..................310 632-6353
Chester K Jablonski, *CEO*
Mauricio Salazar, *
Jeffrey Lake, *Corporate Counsel*
▼ EMP: 154 EST: 1982
SQ FT: 95,000
SALES (est): 23.87MM Privately Held
Web: www.hydroformusa.com
SIC: 3728 Aircraft parts and equipment, nec

(P-7496)
ICE MANAGEMENT SYSTEMS INC
Also Called: IMS-Ess
27449 Colt Ct, Temecula (92590-3674)
PHONE..................951 676-2751
EMP: 28
SIC: 3728 3694 3357 Deicing equipment, aircraft; Harness wiring sets, internal combustion engines; Aircraft wire and cable, nonferrous

(P-7497)
IKHANA GROUP LLC
Also Called: Ikhana Aircraft Services
37260 Sky Canyon Dr Hngr 20, Murrieta (92563-2680)
PHONE..................951 600-0009
Brian Raduenz, *CEO*
▲ EMP: 120 EST: 2007
SALES (est): 24.83MM Privately Held
Web: www.ikhanagroup.com
SIC: 3728 Flaps, aircraft wing
PA: Aevex Aerospace, Llc
440 Stevens Ave Ste 150

(P-7498)
IMPRESA AEROSPACE LLC
344 W 157th St, Gardena (90248-2135)
PHONE..................310 354-1200
Steve Loye, *
Dennis Fitzgerald, *
Marco Barrantes, *
EMP: 169 EST: 1987
SQ FT: 26,000
SALES (est): 42MM
SALES (corp-wide): 42.24MM Privately Held
Web: www.impresaaerospace.com
SIC: 3728 3444 Aircraft parts and equipment, nec; Sheet metalwork
HQ: Impresa Acquisition Corporation
344 W 157th St
Gardena CA

(P-7499)
INET AIRPORT SYSTEMS INC
Also Called: Inet
5665 Corporate Ave, Cypress (90630-4727)
PHONE..................714 888-2700
EMP: 50
SIC: 3728 4581 5088 Aircraft parts and equipment, nec; Aircraft servicing and repairing; Aircraft and parts, nec

(P-7500)
INFINITY AEROSPACE INC (PA)
9060 Winnetka Ave, Northridge (91324-3235)
PHONE..................818 998-9811
Chet Huffman, *CEO*
R Lloyd Huffman, *
Steve Lonngren, *
EMP: 50 EST: 1958
SQ FT: 30,000
SALES (est): 9.05MM
SALES (corp-wide): 9.05MM Privately Held
SIC: 3728 Aircraft parts and equipment, nec

(P-7501)
INTEGRAL AEROSPACE LLC
Also Called: Pcx Aerosystems - Santa Ana
2040 E Dyer Rd, Santa Ana (92705-5710)
PHONE..................949 250-3123
Thomas Holzthum, *CEO*
John Kutler, *
Bryan Mclean, *VP*
Alan Guzik, *
EMP: 190 EST: 2016
SQ FT: 270,000
SALES (est): 50MM
SALES (corp-wide): 151.59MM Privately Held
Web: www.integralaerospace.com
SIC: 3728 Aircraft parts and equipment, nec
PA: Pcx Aerostructures, Llc
300 Fenn Rd
860 666-2471

(P-7502)
IRISH INTERIORS INC
5511 Skylab Rd Ste 101, Huntington Beach (92647-2071)
PHONE..................562 344-1700
Karl Jonson, *VP*
EMP: 200
SALES (corp-wide): 77.79B Publicly Held
Web: www.encoreaerospace.com
SIC: 3728 Aircraft parts and equipment, nec
HQ: Irish Interiors, Inc.
5511 Skylab Rd Ste 101
Huntington Beach CA 92647
949 559-0930

(P-7503)
IRISH INTERIORS INC (HQ)
Also Called: Lift By Encore
5511 Skylab Rd Ste 101, Huntington Beach (92647-2071)
PHONE..................949 559-0930
Thomas Mcfarland, *Pr*
Micheal Melancon, *
Karl Jonson, *
▲ EMP: 130 EST: 1972
SQ FT: 42,000
SALES (est): 34.99MM
SALES (corp-wide): 77.79B Publicly Held
Web: www.encoreaerospace.com
SIC: 3728 1799 Aircraft parts and equipment, nec; Renovation of aircraft interiors
PA: The Boeing Company
929 Long Bridge Dr

703 465-3500

(P-7504)
IRWIN AVIATION INC
Also Called: Aero Performance
225 Airport Cir, Corona (92878-5027)
PHONE..................951 372-9555
James Irwin, *CEO*
Nanci Irwin, *
EMP: 30 EST: 2014
SALES (est): 4.75MM Privately Held
Web: www.aeroperformance.com
SIC: 3728 Aircraft parts and equipment, nec

(P-7505)
ITT AEROSPACE CONTROLS LLC (HQ)
28150 Industry Dr, Valencia (91355-4101)
PHONE..................315 568-7258
Steven Giuliano, *
▲ EMP: 78 EST: 2011
SALES (est): 19.26MM
SALES (corp-wide): 3.28B Publicly Held
Web: www.ittaerospace.com
SIC: 3728 Aircraft parts and equipment, nec
PA: Itt Inc.
100 Washington Blvd Fl 6
914 641-2000

(P-7506)
ITT AEROSPACE CONTROLS LLC
ITT Aerospace Controls Unit S
28150 Industry Dr, Valencia (91355-4101)
PHONE..................661 295-4000
Robert Briggs, *Mgr*
EMP: 300
SALES (corp-wide): 3.28B Publicly Held
Web: www.ittaerospace.com
SIC: 3728 Aircraft parts and equipment, nec
HQ: Itt Aerospace Controls Llc
28150 Industry Dr
Valencia CA 91355
315 568-7258

(P-7507)
JET AIR FBO LLC
681 Kenney St, El Cajon (92020-1278)
PHONE..................619 448-5991
EMP: 30 EST: 2005
SQ FT: 250,000
SALES (est): 1.46MM Privately Held
Web: www.circleag.com
SIC: 3728 Refueling equipment for use in flight, airplane

(P-7508)
JOHNSON CALDRAUL INC
Also Called: Cal-Draulics
220 N Delilah St Ste 101, Corona (92879-1883)
PHONE..................951 340-1067
Douglas Johnson, *Pr*
Kenneth W Johnson, *
EMP: 30 EST: 1992
SQ FT: 12,000
SALES (est): 5.33MM Privately Held
Web: www.caldraulics.com
SIC: 3728 3593 Aircraft parts and equipment, nec; Fluid power cylinders and actuators

(P-7509)
KAREM AIRCRAFT INC
1 Capital Dr, Lake Forest (92630-2203)
PHONE..................949 859-4444
EMP: 48 EST: 2004
SALES (est): 11.02MM Privately Held
Web: www.karemaircraft.com

SIC: 3728 Aircraft parts and equipment, nec

(P-7510)
KIRKHILL INC (HQ)
Also Called: Sfs
300 E Cypress St, Brea (92821-4097)
PHONE..................714 529-4901
Kevin Stein, *Pr*
EMP: 98 EST: 2018
SALES (est): 46.44MM
SALES (corp-wide): 7.94B Publicly Held
Web: www.kirkhill.com
SIC: 3728 Aircraft parts and equipment, nec
PA: Transdigm Group Incorporated
1350 Euclid Ave Ste 1600
216 706-2960

(P-7511)
KLUNE INDUSTRIES INC (DH)
Also Called: PCC Aerostructures
7323 Coldwater Canyon Ave, North Hollywood (91605-4206)
PHONE..................818 503-8100
Joseph I Snowden, *CEO*
Kenneth Ward, *
▲ EMP: 358 EST: 1972
SQ FT: 125,000
SALES (est): 131.11MM
SALES (corp-wide): 364.48B Publicly Held
Web: www.pccaero.com
SIC: 3728 Aircraft parts and equipment, nec
HQ: Klune Holdings, Inc.
7323 Coldwater Canyon Ave
North Hollywood CA 91605

(P-7512)
LANIC ENGINEERING INC (PA)
Also Called: Lanic Aerospace
12144 6th St, Rancho Cucamonga (91730-6111)
PHONE..................877 763-0411
S Robert Leaming, *CEO*
Shaun Arnold, *
Jason Arnold, *Prin*
EMP: 35 EST: 1984
SQ FT: 30,000
SALES (est): 17.35MM
SALES (corp-wide): 17.35MM Privately Held
Web: www.lanicaerospace.com
SIC: 3728 3721 Aircraft parts and equipment, nec; Aircraft

(P-7513)
LEACH INTERNATIONAL CORP (DH)
6900 Orangethorpe Ave, Buena Park (90620-1390)
P.O. Box 5032 (90622-5032)
PHONE..................714 736-7537
Richard Brad Lawrence, *CEO*
Mark Thek, *
Alain Durand, *
Carsten Muller, *
EMP: 500 EST: 1919
SALES (est): 94.17MM
SALES (corp-wide): 7.94B Publicly Held
Web: www.leachcorp.com
SIC: 3728 Aircraft parts and equipment, nec
HQ: Esterline Technologies Corp
1350 Euclid Ave Ste 1600
Cleveland OH 44114
216 706-2960

(P-7514)
LEFIELL MANUFACTURING COMPANY
Also Called: Lefiell
13700 Firestone Blvd, Santa Fe Springs (90670-5652)

PHONE.............................562 921-3411
▲ **EMP: 150 EST:** 1930
SALES (est): 26.8MM **Privately Held**
Web: www.lefiell.com
SIC: 3728 3599 3724 Aircraft assemblies,
subassemblies, and parts, nec; Machine
shop, jobbing and repair; Aircraft engines
and engine parts

(P-7515)
LLAMAS PLASTICS INC
12970 Bradley Ave, Sylmar (91342-3851)
PHONE..............................818 362-0371
James Lee, *Pr*
Ricardo M Llamas, *
Jeff Mabry, *
Robert Young, *
Oswald Llamas, *
EMP: 105 EST: 1977
SQ FT: 37,000
SALES (est): 19.45MM **Privately Held**
Web: www.llamasplastics.com
SIC: 3728 3089 3083 Aircraft parts and
equipment, nec; Plastics containers, except
foam; Laminated plastics plate and sheet

(P-7516)
LUXFER INC (DH)
Also Called: Luxfer Gas Cylinder
3016 Kansas Ave Bldg 1, Riverside
(92507-3445)
PHONE..............................951 684-5110
John Rhodes, *Pr*
◆ **EMP: 70 EST:** 1973
SQ FT: 120,000
SALES (est): 64.36MM
SALES (corp-wide): 405MM **Privately
Held**
Web: www.luxfercylinders.com
SIC: 3728 3354 Aircraft parts and
equipment, nec; Shapes, extruded
aluminum, nec
HQ: Ba Holdings, Inc.
3016 Kansas Ave Bldg 1
Riverside CA 92507

(P-7517)
MANEY AIRCRAFT INC
Also Called: Maney Aircraft
1305 S Wanamaker Ave, Ontario
(91761-2237)
PHONE..............................909 390-2500
Martin T Bright, *CEO*
David A Ederer, *
Michael Neely, *
EMP: 30 EST: 1955
SQ FT: 14,700
SALES (est): 4.02MM **Privately Held**
Web: www.maneyaircraft.com
SIC: 3728 5088 3829 3812 Aircraft
assemblies, subassemblies, and parts, nec;
Aircraft and parts, nec; Aircraft and motor
vehicle measurement equipment; Search
and navigation equipment

(P-7518)
MARINO ENTERPRISES INC
Also Called: Gear Technology
10671 Civic Center Dr, Rancho Cucamonga
(91730-3804)
PHONE..............................909 476-0343
Thomas Marino, *Pr*
EMP: 35 EST: 1986
SQ FT: 16,320
SALES (est): 4.11MM **Privately Held**
Web: www.intra-aerospace.com
SIC: 3728 3769 Gears, aircraft power
transmission; Space vehicle equipment, nec

(P-7519)
MASON ELECTRIC CO
13955 Balboa Blvd, Rancho Cascades
(91342-1084)
PHONE..............................818 361-3366
Steven Brune, *Pr*
EMP: 350 EST: 1968
SQ FT: 105,000
SALES (est): 35.46MM
SALES (corp-wide): 7.94B **Publicly Held**
Web: www.masoncontrols.com
SIC: 3728 Aircraft parts and equipment, nec
HQ: Esterline Technologies Corp
1350 Euclid Ave Ste 1600
Cleveland OH 44114
216 706-2960

(P-7520)
MASTER RESEARCH & MFG INC
13528 Pumice St, Norwalk (90650-5249)
PHONE..............................562 483-8789
Enrique Viano, *VP*
EMP: 52 EST: 1977
SQ FT: 31,200
SALES (est): 4.56MM **Privately Held**
SIC: 3728 Aircraft body assemblies and parts

(P-7521)
MAVERICK AEROSPACE LLC
3718 Capitol Ave, City Of Industry
(90601-1731)
PHONE..............................714 578-1700
Steve Crisanti, *CEO*
Steve Crisanti, *Managing Member*
George Ono, *
Val Darie, *
Scott Curry, *
EMP: 100 EST: 2017
SQ FT: 40,000
SALES (est): 10.93MM **Privately Held**
Web: www.mavaero.com
SIC: 3728 3544 3761 3441 Aircraft parts and
equipment, nec; Special dies, tools, jigs,
and fixtures; Guided missiles and space
vehicles; Fabricated structural metal

(P-7522)
MEGGITT (SAN DIEGO) INC (HQ)
Also Called: Meggitt Polymers & Composites
6650 Top Gun St, San Diego (92121-4112)
PHONE..............................858 824-8976
Pablo Florin, *Genl Mgr*
EMP: 120 EST: 2008
SQ FT: 120,000
SALES (est): 39.97MM
SALES (corp-wide): 19.93B **Publicly Held**
Web: www.mcggitt.com
SIC: 3728 Roto-blades for helicopters
PA: Parker-Hannifin Corporation
6035 Parkland Blvd
216 896-3000

(P-7523)
MEGGITT DEFENSE SYSTEMS INC
9801 Muirlands Blvd, Irvine (92618-2521)
PHONE..............................949 465-7700
Roger Brum, *Pr*
Greg Brostek, *
Bob Bettwy, *
EMP: 353 EST: 1998
SQ FT: 153,000
SALES (est): 64.83MM
SALES (corp-wide): 19.93B **Publicly Held**
Web: www.meggittdefense.com
SIC: 3728 Military aircraft equipment and
armament
HQ: Meggitt Limited
Ansty Bus.

Coventry W MIDLANDS CV7 9
247 682-6900

(P-7524)
MEGGITT NORTH HOLLYWOOD INC
10092 Foxrun Rd, Santa Ana (92705-1407)
PHONE..............................818 691-6258
Jen Larsen, *Brnch Mgr*
EMP: 23
SALES (corp-wide): 19.93B **Publicly Held**
Web: www.meggitt.com
SIC: 3728 Aircraft parts and equipment, nec
HQ: Meggitt (North Hollywood), Inc.
12838 Saticoy St
North Hollywood CA 91605

(P-7525)
MEGGITT NORTH HOLLYWOOD INC (DH)
Also Called: Meggitt Control Systems
12838 Saticoy St, North Hollywood
(91605-3505)
PHONE..............................818 765-8160
Dennis Hutton, *CEO*
▲ **EMP: 230 EST:** 1969
SQ FT: 10,000
SALES (est): 46.77MM
SALES (corp-wide): 19.93B **Publicly Held**
Web: www.meggitt.com
SIC: 3728 Aircraft parts and equipment, nec
HQ: Meggitt Limited
Ansty Bus.
Coventry W MIDLANDS CV7 9
247 682-6900

(P-7526)
MEGGITT SAFETY SYSTEMS INC
Also Called: Htl Manufacturing Div
1785 Voyager Ave, Simi Valley
(93063-3363)
PHONE..............................805 584-4100
Dennis Hutton, *Pr*
EMP: 97
SALES (corp-wide): 19.93B **Publicly Held**
Web: www.meggitt.com
SIC: 3728 Aircraft parts and equipment, nec
HQ: Meggitt Safety Systems, Inc.
1785 Voyager Ave
Simi Valley CA 93063
805 584-4100

(P-7527)
MEGGITT-USA INC (DH)
Also Called: Meggitt Polymers & Composites
1955 Surveyor Ave, Simi Valley
(93063-3369)
PHONE..............................805 526-5700
Eric Lardiere, *Sr VP*
Robert W Soukup, *
Greg Brostek, *
▲ **EMP: 310 EST:** 1980
SQ FT: 3,000
SALES (est): 317.2MM
SALES (corp-wide): 19.93B **Publicly Held**
Web: www.meggitt.com
SIC: 3728 3829 3679 Aircraft parts and
equipment, nec; Vibration meters,
analyzers, and calibrators; Electronic
switches
HQ: Meggitt Limited
Ansty Bus.
Coventry W MIDLANDS CV7 9
247 682-6900

(P-7528)
MULGREW ARCFT COMPONENTS INC

1810 S Shamrock Ave, Monrovia
(91016-4251)
PHONE..............................626 256-1375
Mike Houshiar, *CEO*
EMP: 58 EST: 1979
SQ FT: 45,000
SALES (est): 8.89MM **Privately Held**
Web: www.mulgrewaircraft.com
SIC: 3728 Aircraft assemblies,
subassemblies, and parts, nec

(P-7529)
NASCO AIRCRAFT BRAKE INC
Also Called: Meggitt Arcft Braking Systems
13300 Estrella Ave, Gardena (90248-1519)
PHONE..............................310 532-4430
Daniel Aron, *CEO*
Phil Friedman, *
EMP: 100 EST: 1981
SQ FT: 25,000
SALES (est): 8.02MM
SALES (corp-wide): 19.93B **Publicly Held**
Web: www.nascoaircraft.com
SIC: 3728 Brakes, aircraft
HQ: Meggitt Aircraft Braking Systems
Corporation
1204 Massillon Rd
Akron OH 44306
330 796-4400

(P-7530)
NEILL AIRCRAFT CO
1260 W 15th St, Long Beach (90813-1390)
PHONE..............................562 432-7981
Judith L Carpenter, *Pr*
EMP: 275 EST: 1956
SQ FT: 150,000
SALES (est): 26.73MM **Privately Held**
Web: www.neillaircraft.com
SIC: 3728 Aircraft body and wing assemblies
and parts

(P-7531)
OTTO INSTRUMENT SERVICE INC (PA)
1441 Valencia Pl, Ontario (91761-7639)
PHONE..............................909 930-5800
William R Otto Junior, *Pr*
Lynne Amber Otto-miller, *BORN 1979 1999*
EMP: 45 EST: 1946
SQ FT: 36,800
SALES (est): 29.55MM
SALES (corp-wide): 29.55MM **Privately
Held**
Web: www.ottoinstrument.com
SIC: 3728 5088 7699 Aircraft parts and
equipment, nec; Aircraft equipment and
supplies, nec; Aircraft flight instrument
repair

(P-7532)
PACIFIC CONTOURS CORPORATION
5340 E Hunter Ave, Anaheim (92807-2053)
PHONE..............................714 693-1260
Tom Rapacz, *Pr*
Tim Anderson, *
Jon Stannard, *
EMP: 60 EST: 1997
SQ FT: 36,000
SALES (est): 11.75MM **Privately Held**
Web: www.pacificcontours.com
SIC: 3728 5088 Aircraft assemblies,
subassemblies, and parts, nec; Aircraft and
parts, nec

(P-7533)
PACIFIC PRECISION PRODUCTS MFG INC

Also Called: Pacific Precision Products
9671 Irvine Ctr Dr Koll Ctr Ii Bldg 6, Irvine
(92618)
PHONE..............................949 727-3844
EMP: 40 EST: 1973
SALES (est): 3.43MM Privately Held
SIC: 3728 3812 Oxygen systems, aircraft;
Search and navigation equipment

(P-7534)
PACIFIC SKY SUPPLY INC
8230 San Fernando Rd, Sun Valley
(91352-3218)
PHONE..............................818 768-3700
Emilio B Perez, CEO
Emilio Perez, *
Kelly Anderson, *
EMP: 59 EST: 1954
SQ FT: 27,000
SALES (est): 9.14MM Privately Held
Web: www.pacsky.com
SIC: 3728 3724 5088 Aircraft parts and
equipment, nec; Aircraft engines and
engine parts; Transportation equipment and
supplies

(P-7535)
PARKER-HANNIFIN CORPORATION
Also Called: Parker Aerospace
14300 Alton Pkwy, Irvine (92618-1898)
PHONE..............................949 833-3000
Robert Bond, Brnch Mgr
EMP: 169
SQ FT: 180,000
SALES (corp-wide): 19.93B Publicly Held
Web: www.parker.com
SIC: 3728 Aircraft assemblies,
subassemblies, and parts, nec
PA: Parker-Hannifin Corporation
6035 Parkland Blvd
216 896-3000

(P-7536)
PARKER-HANNIFIN CORPORATION
Also Called: Stratoflex Product Division
3800 Calle Tecate, Camarillo (93012-5070)
PHONE..............................805 484-8533
William Cartmill, Brnch Mgr
EMP: 46
SALES (corp-wide): 19.93B Publicly Held
Web: www.parker.com
SIC: 3728 3769 3568 Aircraft parts and
equipment, nec; Space vehicle equipment,
nec; Power transmission equipment, nec
PA: Parker-Hannifin Corporation
6035 Parkland Blvd
216 896-3000

(P-7537)
PCA AEROSPACE INC
15282 Newsboy Cir, Huntington Beach
(92649-1202)
PHONE..............................714 901-5209
Ron Brandenburg, Pr
EMP: 26
SALES (corp-wide): 6.54MM Privately
Held
Web: www.lanicaerospace.com
SIC: 3728 Aircraft parts and equipment, nec
PA: Pca Aerospace, Inc.
17800 Gothard St
714 841-1750

(P-7538)
PCA AEROSPACE INC (PA)
17800 Gothard St, Huntington Beach
(92647-6217)
PHONE..............................714 841-1750

Brian Murray, CEO
Gregory Ruffalo, *
▲ EMP: 71 EST: 1963
SQ FT: 58,000
SALES (est): 6.54MM
SALES (corp-wide): 6.54MM Privately
Held
Web: www.lanicaerospace.com
SIC: 3728 3599 Aircraft parts and
equipment, nec; Machine shop, jobbing and
repair

(P-7539)
PERFORMANCE PLASTICS INC
7919 Saint Andrews Ave, San Diego
(92154-8224)
PHONE..............................714 343-3928
Jim Renaud, Pr
EMP: 99 EST: 1977
SQ FT: 50,000
SALES (est): 22.56MM Privately Held
Web: www.perf-plastics.com
SIC: 3728 Aircraft parts and equipment, nec
PA: Rock West Composites, Inc.
7625 Panasonic Way

(P-7540)
PMC INC (HQ)
12243 Branford St, Sun Valley
(91352-1010)
PHONE..............................818 896-1101
Christopher Lette, Pr
EMP: 88 EST: 1962
SALES (est): 541.32MM
SALES (corp-wide): 1.71B Privately Held
Web: www.pmcglobalinc.com
SIC: 3728 3724 Bodies, aircraft; Engine
mount parts, aircraft
PA: Pmc Global, Inc.
12243 Branford St
818 896-1101

(P-7541)
PRECISION AEROSPACE CORP
11155 Jersey Blvd Ste A, Rancho
Cucamonga (91730-5148)
PHONE..............................909 945-9604
Jim Hudson, Pr
EMP: 70 EST: 1989
SQ FT: 50,000
SALES (est): 9.42MM Privately Held
Web: www.pac.cc
SIC: 3728 Aircraft assemblies,
subassemblies, and parts, nec

(P-7542)
PRECISION TUBE BENDING
13626 Talc St, Santa Fe Springs
(90670-5173)
PHONE..............................562 921-6723
Diane M Williams, CEO
EMP: 98 EST: 1957
SQ FT: 60,000
SALES (est): 18.84MM Privately Held
Web: www.precision-tube-bending.com
SIC: 3728 3498 Aircraft parts and
equipment, nec; Tube fabricating (contract
bending and shaping)

(P-7543)
PTI TECHNOLOGIES INC (DH)
501 Del Norte Blvd, Oxnard (93030-7983)
PHONE..............................805 604-3700
Rowland Ellis, Pr
Beth Kozlowski, *
▲ EMP: 212 EST: 1979
SQ FT: 225,000
SALES (est): 38.12MM Publicly Held
Web: www.ptitechnologies.com

SIC: 3728 Aircraft parts and equipment, nec
HQ: Esco Technologies Holding Llc
9900a Clayton Rd
Saint Louis MO 63124
314 213-7200

(P-7544)
QUALITY FORMING LLC
Also Called: Qfi Prv Aerospace
22906 Frampton Ave, Torrance
(90501-5035)
PHONE..............................310 539-2855
Mark Severns, Pr
▲ EMP: 100 EST: 1972
SALES (est): 9.86MM
SALES (corp-wide): 666.39MM Privately
Held
Web: www.verusaerospace.com
SIC: 3728 Aircraft assemblies,
subassemblies, and parts, nec
HQ: Qpi Holdings, Inc.
22906 Frampton Ave
Torrance CA 90501
310 539-2855

(P-7545)
QUATRO COMPOSITES LLC
Also Called: Quatro Composites
13250 Gregg St Ste A1, Poway
(92064-7164)
PHONE..............................712 707-9200
Karash Quepin, Mgr
EMP: 160
Web: www.sekisuiaerospace.com
SIC: 3728 Aircraft parts and equipment, nec
HQ: Quatro Composites, L.L.C.
403 14th St Se
Orange City IA 51041
712 707-9200

(P-7546)
ROBINSON HELICOPTER CO INC (PA)
2901 Airport Dr, Torrance (90505-6115)
PHONE..............................310 539-0508
David Smith, Pr
Frank Robinson, Pr
Tim Goetz, CFO
P Wayne Walden, VP Mfg
◆ EMP: 460 EST: 1973
SQ FT: 260,000
SALES (est): 98.78MM
SALES (corp-wide): 98.78MM Privately
Held
Web: shop.robinsonheli.com
SIC: 3728 Aircraft parts and equipment, nec

(P-7547)
ROCKWELL COLLINS INC
1757 Carr Rd Ste 100, Calexico
(92231-9781)
PHONE..............................760 768-4732
Nicolas Pineda, Mgr
EMP: 25
SALES (corp-wide): 68.92B Publicly Held
Web: www.rockwellcollins.com
SIC: 3728 Aircraft parts and equipment, nec
HQ: Rockwell Collins, Inc.
400 Collins Rd Ne
Cedar Rapids IA 52498

(P-7548)
ROHR INC (HQ)
Also Called: Collins Aerospace
850 Lagoon Dr, Chula Vista (91910-2098)
PHONE..............................619 691-4111
Greg Peters, Pr
Curtis Reusser, *
Kenneth Wood, *
Robert A Gustafson, General Vice
President*

Brian Broderick, *
▲ EMP: 2100 EST: 1969
SQ FT: 2,770,000
SALES (est): 1.06B
SALES (corp-wide): 68.92B Publicly Held
Web: www.roehrs-timm.de
SIC: 3728 Nacelles, aircraft
PA: Rtx Corporation
1000 Wilson Blvd
781 522-3000

(P-7549)
RSA ENGINEERED PRODUCTS LLC
Also Called: Trimas Aerospace
110 W Cochran St Ste A, Simi Valley
(93065-6228)
PHONE..............................805 584-4150
Ray Scarcello, CEO
◆ EMP: 90 EST: 2012
SQ FT: 43,000
SALES (est): 27.89MM
SALES (corp-wide): 893.55MM Publicly
Held
Web: www.rsaeng.com
SIC: 3728 Aircraft parts and equipment, nec
PA: Trimas Corporation
38505 Wodward Ave Ste 200
248 631-5450

(P-7550)
SAFRAN CABIN GALLEYS US INC (HQ)
17311 Nichols Ln, Huntington Beach
(92647-5721)
PHONE..............................714 861-7300
Matthew Stafford, CEO
Vincent Kozar, CFO
◆ EMP: 717 EST: 1986
SQ FT: 90,000
SALES (est): 57.57MM
SALES (corp-wide): 940.23MM Privately
Held
SIC: 3728 Aircraft parts and equipment, nec
PA: Safran
2 Boulevard Du General Martial Valin

(P-7551)
SAFRAN CABIN INC (HQ)
5701 Bolsa Ave, Huntington Beach
(92647-2063)
PHONE..............................714 934-0000
Jorge Ortega, CEO
Norman Jordan, *
Scott Savian, *
Daniel Edmundson, *
Arnault Dumont Lauret, *
▲ EMP: 500 EST: 1972
SQ FT: 150,000
SALES (est): 493.55MM
SALES (corp-wide): 940.23MM Privately
Held
Web: www.safran-group.com
SIC: 3728 Aircraft assemblies,
subassemblies, and parts, nec
PA: Safran
2 Boulevard Du General Martial Valin

(P-7552)
SAFRAN CABIN INC
12472 Industry St, Garden Grove
(92841-2819)
PHONE..............................714 901-2672
Mike Boyd, Brnch Mgr
EMP: 137
SALES (corp-wide): 940.23MM Privately
Held
Web: www.safran-group.com
SIC: 3728 Aircraft parts and equipment, nec
HQ: Safran Cabin Inc.
5701 Bolsa Ave

Huntington Beach CA 92647
714 934-0000

(P-7553)
SAFRAN CABIN INC
Also Called: Safran Cabin - Cypress
12240 Warland Dr, Cypress (90630)
PHONE.................................562 344-4780
Gary Reese, *Brnch Mgr*
EMP: 248
SALES (corp-wide): 940.23MM **Privately Held**
Web: www.safran-group.com
SIC: 3728 Aircraft assemblies, subassemblies, and parts, nec
HQ: Safran Cabin Inc.
5701 Bolsa Ave
Huntington Beach CA 92647
714 934-0000

(P-7554)
SAFRAN CABIN INC
Also Called: C & D Aerospace
7330 Lincoln Way, Garden Grove (92841-1427)
PHONE.................................714 891-1906
Alec Azarian, *Brnch Mgr*
EMP: 140
SALES (corp-wide): 940.23MM **Privately Held**
Web: www.zodiacaerospace.com
SIC: 3728 3443 Aircraft assemblies, subassemblies, and parts, nec; Fabricated plate work (boiler shop)
HQ: Safran Cabin Inc.
5701 Bolsa Ave
Huntington Beach CA 92647
714 934-0000

(P-7555)
SAFRAN CABIN INC
Also Called: Safran Cabin Tijuana S.a De Cv
2695 Customhouse Ct Ste 111, San Diego (92154-7645)
PHONE.................................619 661-6292
EMP: 173
SALES (corp-wide): 940.23MM **Privately Held**
Web: www.safran-group.com
SIC: 3728 Aircraft assemblies, subassemblies, and parts, nec
HQ: Safran Cabin Inc.
5701 Bolsa Ave
Huntington Beach CA 92647
714 934-0000

(P-7556)
SAFRAN CABIN INC
Also Called: C&D Aerodesign
6754 Calle De Linea Ste 111, San Diego (92154-8021)
PHONE.................................619 671-0430
Jose Martinez, *Mgr*
EMP: 223
SALES (corp-wide): 940.23MM **Privately Held**
Web: www.safran-group.com
SIC: 3728 Aircraft parts and equipment, nec
HQ: Safran Cabin Inc.
5701 Bolsa Ave
Huntington Beach CA 92647
714 934-0000

(P-7557)
SAFRAN CABIN INC
2850 Skyway Dr, Santa Maria (93455-1410)
PHONE.................................805 922-3013
Jude F Dozor, *Brnch Mgr*
EMP: 140

SALES (corp-wide): 940.23MM **Privately Held**
Web: www.safran-group.com
SIC: 3728 Aircraft parts and equipment, nec
HQ: Safran Cabin Inc.
5701 Bolsa Ave
Huntington Beach CA 92647
714 934-0000

(P-7558)
SAFRAN CABIN INC
Also Called: 4 Flight
8595 Milliken Ave Ste 101, Rancho Cucamonga (91730-4942)
PHONE.................................909 652-9700
Tom Mcfarland, *CEO*
EMP: 158
SALES (corp-wide): 940.23MM **Privately Held**
Web: www.zodiacaerospace.com
SIC: 3728 Aircraft parts and equipment, nec
HQ: Safran Cabin Inc.
5701 Bolsa Ave
Huntington Beach CA 92647
714 934-0000

(P-7559)
SAFRAN CABIN INC
1500 Glenn Curtiss St, Carson (90746-4012)
PHONE.................................714 934-0000
EMP: 96
SALES (corp-wide): 940.23MM **Privately Held**
Web: www.safran-group.com
SIC: 3728 Aircraft assemblies, subassemblies, and parts, nec
HQ: Safran Cabin Inc.
5701 Bolsa Ave
Huntington Beach CA 92647
714 934-0000

(P-7560)
SAFRAN SEATS SANTA MARIA LLC
2641 Airpark Dr, Santa Maria (93455-1415)
PHONE.................................805 922-5995
▲ **EMP:** 638 **EST:** 2012
SALES (est): 48.96MM
SALES (corp-wide): 940.23MM **Privately Held**
Web: weber.zodiac.com
SIC: 3728 Aircraft parts and equipment, nec
HQ: Safran Seats Usa Llc
2000 Weber Dr
Gainesville TX 76240
940 668-4825

(P-7561)
SANDERS COMPOSITES INC (HQ)
Also Called: Sanders Composites Industries
3701 E Conant St, Long Beach (90808-1783)
PHONE.................................562 354-2800
Larry O'toole, *CEO*
EMP: 49 **EST:** 1988
SQ FT: 44,400
SALES (est): 4.54MM
SALES (corp-wide): 150.17MM **Privately Held**
Web: www.sanderscomposites.com
SIC: 3728 Aircraft assemblies, subassemblies, and parts, nec
PA: Sanders Industries Holdings, Inc.
3701 E Conant St
562 354-2920

(P-7562)
SENIOR OPERATIONS LLC
Senior Aerospace SSP
2980 N San Fernando Blvd, Burbank (91504-2522)
PHONE.................................818 260-2900
Launie Flemning, *Mgr*
EMP: 380
SALES (corp-wide): 1.2B **Privately Held**
Web: www.seniorssp.com
SIC: 3728 3599 Aircraft parts and equipment, nec; Bellows, industrial: metal
HQ: Senior Operations Llc
300 E Devon Ave
Bartlett IL 60103
630 372-3500

(P-7563)
SKYLOCK INDUSTRIES LLC
1290 W Optical Dr, Azusa (91702-3249)
PHONE.................................626 334-2391
Jeff Creoiserat, *Ch Bd*
Jim Pease, *
EMP: 70 **EST:** 1973
SQ FT: 14,000
SALES (est): 19.69MM **Privately Held**
Web: www.skylock.com
SIC: 3728 Aircraft parts and equipment, nec

(P-7564)
SOUTHWEST MACHINE & PLASTIC CO
Also Called: Southwest Plastics Co
620 W Foothill Blvd, Glendora (91741-2403)
PHONE.................................626 963-6919
W Thomas Jorgensen, *Pr*
Alfred D Jorgensen, *
▲ **EMP:** 30 **EST:** 1937
SALES (est): 5.53MM **Privately Held**
Web: www.southwestplastics.com
SIC: 3728 3089 3544 Aircraft parts and equipment, nec; Injection molding of plastics ; Special dies, tools, jigs, and fixtures

(P-7565)
SPACE-LOK INC
13306 Halldale Ave, Gardena (90249-2204)
P.O. Box 2919 (90247-1119)
PHONE.................................310 527-6150
Scott F Wade, *Pr*
Jeffrey Wade, *
EMP: 138 **EST:** 1962
SALES (est): 23.96MM
SALES (corp-wide): 218.18MM **Privately Held**
Web: space-lok.herokuapp.com
SIC: 3728 3542 3812 3452 Aircraft assemblies, subassemblies, and parts, nec; Machine tools, metal forming type; Search and navigation equipment; Bolts, nuts, rivets, and washers
HQ: Novaria Fastening Systems, Llc
6300 Ridglea Pl Ste 800
Fort Worth TX 76116
817 381-3810

(P-7566)
SPEC TOOL COMPANY
Also Called: Alice G Fink-Painter
11805 Wakeman St, Santa Fe Springs (90670-2130)
P.O. Box 1056 (90660-1056)
PHONE.................................323 723-9533
Alice G Fink-painter, *Pr*
D B Fink, *
Albert G Fink Junior, *VP*
EMP: 50 **EST:** 1954
SALES (est): 5.78MM **Privately Held**
Web: www.spectoolgse.com

SIC: 3728 Aircraft parts and equipment, nec

(P-7567)
SPS TECHNOLOGIES LLC
Air Industries
12570 Knott St, Garden Grove (92841-3932)
PHONE.................................714 892-5571
Michael Wu, *Contrlr*
EMP: 50
SALES (corp-wide): 364.48B **Publicly Held**
Web: www.pccfasteners.com
SIC: 3728 Aircraft parts and equipment, nec
HQ: Sps Technologies, Llc
301 Highland Ave
Jenkintown PA 19046
215 572-3000

(P-7568)
SUMMIT MACHINE LLC
2880 E Philadelphia St, Ontario (91761-8523)
PHONE.................................909 923-2744
▼ **EMP:** 120 **EST:** 2003
SQ FT: 103,000
SALES (est): 22.83MM
SALES (corp-wide): 364.48B **Publicly Held**
Web: www.summitmachining.com
SIC: 3728 3599 Aircraft parts and equipment, nec; Machine shop, jobbing and repair
HQ: Precision Castparts Corp.
5885 Meadows Rd Ste 620
Lake Oswego OR 97035
503 946-4800

(P-7569)
SUNGEAR INC
8535 Arjons Dr Ste G, San Diego (92126-4360)
PHONE.................................858 549-3166
Lee Miramontes, *Managing Member*
Glenn Wilcox, *Mfg Mgr*
Paul Scott, *QA*
EMP: 42 **EST:** 1982
SQ FT: 16,000
SALES (est): 11.23MM
SALES (corp-wide): 93.1MM **Privately Held**
Web: www.sungearinc.com
SIC: 3728 Gears, aircraft power transmission
PA: H-D Advanced Manufacturing Company
2418 Greens Rd
346 219-0320

(P-7570)
SUNVAIR INC (HQ)
Also Called: Sunvair
29145 The Old Rd, Valencia (91355-1015)
PHONE.................................661 294-3777
Robert Dann, *Pr*
Edward Waschak, *
Melba Waschak, *
EMP: 32 **EST:** 1956
SQ FT: 26,000
SALES (est): 17.73MM
SALES (corp-wide): 30.17MM **Privately Held**
Web: www.sunvair.com
SIC: 3728 7699 Aircraft landing assemblies and brakes; Aircraft and heavy equipment repair services
PA: Sunvair Aerospace Group, Inc.
29145 The Old Rd
661 294-3777

PRODUCTS & SVCS

(P-7571)
SWIFT ENGINEERING INC
Also Called: Swift Engineering
1141a Via Callejon, San Clemente
(92673-6230)
PHONE..................949 492-6608
▲ EMP: 83 EST: 1982
SALES (est): 10.86MM Privately Held
Web: www.swiftengineering.com
SIC: 3728 3714 3624 Aircraft body and wing assemblies and parts; Motor vehicle parts and accessories; Fibers, carbon and graphite
PA: Matsushita International Corp
    1141 Via Callejon

(P-7572)
SYMBOLIC DISPLAYS INC
1917 E Saint Andrew Pl, Santa Ana
(92705-5143)
PHONE..................714 258-2811
Candy Suits, CEO
▼ EMP: 76 EST: 1964
SQ FT: 15,860
SALES (est): 9.75MM Privately Held
Web: www.symbolicdisplays.com
SIC: 3728 3812 3577 Aircraft parts and equipment, nec; Search and navigation equipment; Computer peripheral equipment, nec

(P-7573)
SYNERGETIC TECH GROUP INC
1712 Earhart, La Verne (91750-5826)
PHONE..................909 305-4711
Tony Espinoza, CEO
EMP: 27 EST: 1997
SQ FT: 2,400
SALES (est): 6.8MM Privately Held
Web: www.synergetic-us.com
SIC: 3728 Aircraft parts and equipment, nec

(P-7574)
TALSCO INC
7101 Patterson Dr, Garden Grove
(92841-1415)
PHONE..................714 841-2464
EMP: 36
SIC: 3728 Aircraft assemblies, subassemblies, and parts, nec

(P-7575)
THALES AVIONICS INC
48 Discovery, Irvine (92618-3151)
PHONE..................949 381-3033
Dominique Giannoni, Owner
EMP: 39
SALES (corp-wide): 269.57MM Privately Held
Web: www.thalesgroup.com
SIC: 3728 Aircraft parts and equipment, nec
HQ: Thales Avionics, Inc.
    7415 Emrald Dnes Dr Ste 2
    Orlando FL 32822
    407 812-2600

(P-7576)
THALES AVIONICS INC
Also Called: Inflight Entrmt & Connectivity
51 Discovery Ste 100, Irvine (92618-3120)
PHONE..................949 790-2500
Brad Foreman, Mgr
EMP: 39
SALES (corp-wide): 269.57MM Privately Held
Web: www.thalesgroup.com
SIC: 3728 3663 Aircraft parts and equipment, nec; Radio and t.v. communications equipment
HQ: Thales Avionics, Inc.
    7415 Emrald Dnes Dr Ste 2

Orlando FL 32822
407 812-2600

(P-7577)
THALES AVIONICS INC
9975 Toledo Way, Irvine (92618-1826)
PHONE..................949 829-5808
EMP: 39
SALES (corp-wide): 269.57MM Privately Held
Web: www.thalesgroup.com
SIC: 3728 Aircraft parts and equipment, nec
HQ: Thales Avionics, Inc.
    7415 Emrald Dnes Dr Ste 2
    Orlando FL 32822
    407 812-2600

(P-7578)
THOMPSON INDUSTRIES LTD
Also Called: Thompson ADB Industries
7155 Fenwick Ln, Westminster
(92683-5218)
PHONE..................310 679-9193
EMP: 109
SALES (est): 8.33MM Privately Held
SIC: 3728 Aircraft parts and equipment, nec

(P-7579)
TJ AEROSPACE INC
Also Called: Tj Aerospace
12601 Monarch St, Garden Grove
(92841-3918)
PHONE..................714 891-3564
Tien Dang, CEO
Tien N Dang, CEO
EMP: 23 EST: 2007
SQ FT: 6,000
SALES (est): 8.06MM Privately Held
Web: www.tjaerospace.com
SIC: 3728 3541 Aircraft parts and equipment, nec; Machine tools, metal cutting type

(P-7580)
TMW CORPORATION (PA)
Also Called: Crown Discount Tools
15148 Bledsoe St, Sylmar (91342-3807)
PHONE..................818 362-5665
William Windette, Pr
Gary Berger, *
EMP: 110 EST: 1973
SQ FT: 115,000
SALES (est): 4.96MM
SALES (corp-wide): 4.96MM Privately Held
SIC: 3728 Aircraft landing assemblies and brakes

(P-7581)
TRANSDIGM INC
Adel Wggins Grp-Commercial Div
5000 Triggs St, Commerce (90022-4833)
P.O. Box 22228 (90022-0228)
PHONE..................323 269-9181
Cindy Terakawa, Brnch Mgr
EMP: 76
SALES (corp-wide): 7.94B Publicly Held
Web: www.transdigm.com
SIC: 3728 3365 Aircraft parts and equipment, nec; Aerospace castings, aluminum
HQ: Transdigm, Inc.
    1350 Euclid Ave
    Cleveland OH 44115

(P-7582)
TRIO MANUFACTURING INC
Also Called: Trio Manufacturing
601 Lairport St, El Segundo (90245-5005)
PHONE..................310 640-6123

Michael Hunkins, Pr
Michael Hunkins, Pr
Brian Hunkins, *
▲ EMP: 125 EST: 1943
SALES (est): 24.47MM Privately Held
Web: www.triomfg.com
SIC: 3728 3829 3812 3663 Aircraft parts and equipment, nec; Measuring and controlling devices, nec; Search and navigation equipment; Radio and t.v. communications equipment

(P-7583)
TRIUMPH ACTTION SYSTEMS - VLNC
Also Called: Triumph Group
28150 Harrison Pkwy, Valencia
(91355-4109)
PHONE..................661 702-7537
Daniel J Crowley, Pr
Jim Mccabe, Sr VP
Dan Ostrosky, VP
Gary Tenison, *
John B Wright Ii, Sr VP
EMP: 250 EST: 2001
SALES (est): 37.55MM Publicly Held
SIC: 3728 Aircraft parts and equipment, nec
PA: Triumph Group, Inc.
    555 E Lncster Ave Ste 400

(P-7584)
TRIUMPH INSULATION SYSTEMS LLC
Also Called: Triumph Group
1754 Carr Rd Ste 103, Calexico
(92231-9509)
PHONE..................760 618-7543
▲ EMP: 900 EST: 1976
SALES (est): 35.91MM Publicly Held
SIC: 3728 Aircraft parts and equipment, nec
HQ: Triumph Aerospace Systems Group, Llc
    899 Cassatt Rd Ste 210
    Berwyn PA 19312

(P-7585)
TRIUMPH STRUCTURES - EVERETT INC
Also Called: Triumph Structures
17055 Gale Ave, City Of Industry
(91745-1808)
PHONE..................425 348-4100
▲ EMP: 202
SIC: 3728 Aircraft parts and equipment, nec

(P-7586)
VANGUARD SPACE TECH INC
Also Called: Alliance Spacesystems
4398 Corporate Center Dr, Los Alamitos
(90720-2537)
PHONE..................858 587-4210
Frank Belknap, CEO
Ronald Miller, *
John Richer, *
EMP: 101 EST: 1994
SQ FT: 50,000
SALES (est): 18.85MM
SALES (corp-wide): 244.59MM Publicly Held
Web: www.appliedcomposites.com
SIC: 3728 Aircraft parts and equipment, nec
HQ: Solaero Technologies Corp.
    10420 Res Rd Se Bldg 1
    Albuquerque NM 87123
    505 332-5000

(P-7587)
VANTAGE ASSOCIATES INC
Also Called: Vantage Master Machine Company

1565 Macarthur Blvd, Costa Mesa
(92626-1407)
PHONE..................562 968-1400
Paul Roy, Brnch Mgr
EMP: 40
SALES (corp-wide): 24.86MM Privately Held
Web: www.vantageassoc.com
SIC: 3728 Aircraft assemblies, subassemblies, and parts, nec
PA: Vantage Associates Inc.
    1565 Macarthur Blvd
    619 477-6940

(P-7588)
VERUS AEROSPACE LLC (HQ)
Also Called: Cadence Aerospace, LLC
3150 E Miraloma Ave, Anaheim
(92806-1906)
PHONE..................949 877-3630
Olivier Jarrault, CEO
EMP: 94 EST: 2010
SQ FT: 5,000
SALES (est): 256.2MM
SALES (corp-wide): 666.39MM Privately Held
Web: www.verusaerospace.com
SIC: 3728 Aircraft body assemblies and parts
PA: Arlington Capital Partners Iv, L.P.
    5425 Wsconsin Ave Ste 200
    202 337-7500

(P-7589)
VISION AEROSPACE LLC
Also Called: Romakk Engineering
19863 Nordhoff St, Northridge
(91324-3331)
PHONE..................818 700-1035
EMP: 24 EST: 2018
SALES (est): 3.13MM Privately Held
SIC: 3728 Aircraft parts and equipment, nec

(P-7590)
WESANCO INC
14870 Desman Rd, La Mirada
(90638-5746)
PHONE..................714 739-4989
Brain Szymanski, CFO
▲ EMP: 30 EST: 1973
SQ FT: 30,000
SALES (est): 2.11MM
SALES (corp-wide): 242.37MM Privately Held
Web: www.wesanco.com
SIC: 3728 Oleo struts, aircraft
HQ: Zsi-Foster, Inc.
    1751 Summit Dr
    Auburn Hills MI 48326

(P-7591)
WESTERN METHODS MACHINERY CORPORATION
Also Called: Western Methods
2344 Pullman St, Santa Ana (92705-5507)
PHONE..................949 252-6600
EMP: 120 EST: 1977
SALES (est): 1.57MM Privately Held
SIC: 3728 3769 Aircraft parts and equipment, nec; Space vehicle equipment, nec

(P-7592)
WHITTAKER CORPORATION
1955 Surveyor Ave Fl 2, Simi Valley
(93063-3369)
PHONE..................805 526-5700
Erick Lardiere, Pr
▲ EMP: 40 EST: 1942
SQ FT: 276,000
SALES (est): 8.25MM

SALES (corp-wide): 19.93B Publicly Held
Web: www.whittakercorp.com
SIC: 3728 3669 7373 Aircraft parts and
equipment, nec; Fire detection systems,
electric; Systems integration services
HQ: Meggitt Limited
Ansty Bus.
Coventry W MIDLANDS CV7 9
247 682-6900

(P-7593)
WOODWARD HRT INC
Also Called: Woodward Duarte
1700 Business Center Dr, Duarte
(91010-2859)
PHONE..............................626 359-9211
Don Grimes, Mgr
EMP: 250
SALES (corp-wide): 3.32B Publicly Held
SIC: 3728 5084 Aircraft parts and
equipment, nec; Hydraulic systems
equipment and supplies
HQ: Woodward Hrt, Inc.
25200 Rye Canyon Rd
Santa Clarita CA 91355
661 294-6000

(P-7594)
ZENITH MANUFACTURING INC
Also Called: Zipco
3087 12th St, Riverside (92507-4904)
PHONE..............................818 767-2106
James Phoung, Pr
EMP: 25 EST: 2006
SQ FT: 47,000
SALES (est): 2.01MM Privately Held
SIC: 3728 Aircraft parts and equipment, nec

(P-7595)
ZODIAC WTR WASTE AERO SYSTEMS
Also Called: Monogram Systems
1500 Glenn Curtiss St, Carson
(90746-4012)
PHONE..............................310 884-7000
EMP: 83 EST: 1958
SALES (est): 15.32MM
SALES (corp-wide): 650.78MM Privately
Held
SIC: 3728 Aircraft parts and equipment, nec
PA: Safran
2 Bd Du General Martial Valin

3731 Shipbuilding And Repairing

(P-7596)
APR ENGINEERING INC
Also Called: Oceanwide Repairs
1812 W 9th St, Long Beach (00813-2614)
P.O. Box 9100 (90810-0100)
PHONE..............................562 983-3800
Roy Herington, Pr
Trina Young, *
▲ EMP: 33 EST: 1997
SALES (est): 2.02MM Privately Held
Web: www.oceanwiderepair.com
SIC: 3731 Shipbuilding and repairing

(P-7597)
BAE SYSTEMS SAN DEGO SHIP REPR
2205 Belt St, San Diego (92113-3634)
P.O. Box 13308 (92170)
PHONE..............................619 238-1000
Eric Icke, Pr
James M Blue, *
Alice M Eldridge, *

◆ EMP: 732 EST: 1976
SALES (est): 28.01MM
SALES (corp-wide): 28.77B Privately Held
SIC: 3731 Shipbuilding and repairing
HQ: Bae Systems Ship Repair Inc.
750 W Berkley Ave
Norfolk VA 23523
757 494-4000

(P-7598)
COLONNAS SHIPYARD WEST LLC
2890 Faivre St Ste 150, Chula Vista
(91911-4983)
PHONE..............................757 545-2414
Robert Boyd, Prin
Ana Nowland, Ofcr
EMP: 30 EST: 2017
SALES (est): 2.39MM Privately Held
Web: www.colonnaship.com
SIC: 3731 Shipbuilding and repairing

(P-7599)
CONTINENTAL MARITIME INDS INC
1995 Bay Front St, San Diego
(92113-2122)
PHONE..............................619 234-8851
David H Mc Queary, Pr
Lee E Wilson, *
EMP: 429 EST: 1990
SQ FT: 90,000
SALES (est): 8.1MM Publicly Held
Web: www.cmsd-msr.com
SIC: 3731 Shipbuilding and repairing
PA: Huntington Ingalls Industries, Inc.
4101 Washington Ave

(P-7600)
CRAFT LABOR & SUPPORT SVCS LLC
1545 Tidelands Ave Ste C, National City
(91950-4240)
PHONE..............................619 336-9977
Michael Greene, Brnch Mgr
EMP: 169
SALES (corp-wide): 8.27MM Privately
Held
Web: www.craftlabor.com
SIC: 3731 Shipbuilding and repairing
PA: Craft Labor And Support Services, Llc
7636 230th St Sw Apt B
206 304-4543

(P-7601)
HII SAN DIEGO SHIPYARD INC
1995 Bay Front St, San Diego
(92101-1951)
PHONE..............................619 234-8851
Christopher Joseph Miner, CEO
Ronald Sugar, *
EMP: 325 EST: 1981
SQ FT: 90,000
SALES (est): 16.28MM Publicly Held
Web: www.cmsd-msr.com
SIC: 3731 Military ships, building and
repairing
PA: Huntington Ingalls Industries, Inc.
4101 Washington Ave

(P-7602)
INTEGRATED MARINE SERVICES INC
Also Called: IMS
2320 Main St, Chula Vista (91911-4610)
PHONE..............................619 429-0300
Larry Samano, Pr
EMP: 55 EST: 2003
SALES (est): 9.4MM Privately Held

Web: www.imships.com
SIC: 3731 Shipbuilding and repairing

(P-7603)
LARSON AL BOAT SHOP
1046 S Seaside Ave, San Pedro
(90731-7392)
PHONE..............................310 514-4100
Jack Wall, CEO
Gloria Wall, *
George Wall, *
▲ EMP: 70 EST: 1903
SQ FT: 65,000
SALES (est): 7.2MM Privately Held
Web: www.larsonboat.com
SIC: 3731 4493 Military ships, building and
repairing; Marinas

(P-7604)
MILLER MARINE
2275 Manya St, San Diego (92154-4713)
PHONE..............................619 791-1500
Pauline Senter, CEO
Edward Senter, *
Miller Marine, *
EMP: 45 EST: 1989
SQ FT: 13,500
SALES (est): 9.51MM Privately Held
Web: www.millermarine.us
SIC: 3731 7389 Shipbuilding and repairing;
Grinding, precision: commercial or industrial

(P-7605)
NASSCO
7470 Mission Valley Rd, San Diego
(92108-4406)
PHONE..............................619 929-3019
EMP: 35 EST: 2018
SALES (est): 474K Privately Held
Web: www.nassco.com
SIC: 3731 Shipbuilding and repairing

(P-7606)
NATIONAL STL & SHIPBUILDING CO (HQ)
2798 Harbor Dr, San Diego (92113-3650)
P.O. Box 85278 (92186-5278)
PHONE..............................619 544-3400
Michael Toner, Ch Bd
David Carver, *
Phebe Novakoviz, *
Blaise Brennan, *
Andrew Chen, *
◆ EMP: 477 EST: 1892
SQ FT: 100,000
SALES (est): 153.93MM
SALES (corp-wide): 42.27B Publicly Held
Web: www.nassco.com
SIC: 3731 Military ships, building and
repairing
PA: General Dynamics Corporation
11011 Sunset Hills Rd
703 876-3000

(P-7607)
PACIFIC SHIP REPR FBRCTION INC (PA)
1625 Rigel St, San Diego (92113-3887)
P.O. Box 13428 (92170-3428)
PHONE..............................619 232-3200
David J Moore, CEO
Gary N Thomas, Contracts Director*
EMP: 287 EST: 1969
SQ FT: 136,000
SALES (est): 46.49MM
SALES (corp-wide): 46.49MM Privately
Held
Web: www.pacship.com
SIC: 3731 3444 Combat vessels, building
and repairing; Sheet metalwork

(P-7608)
PYR PRESERVATION SERVICES
Also Called: Pyr
2393 Newton Ave Ste B, San Diego
(92113-3666)
PHONE..............................619 338-8395
Daniel R Cummins, CEO
▲ EMP: 30 EST: 1997
SQ FT: 12,500
SALES (est): 2.5MM Privately Held
Web: www.pyrsd.com
SIC: 3731 3589 3479 2851 Commercial
cargo ships, building and repairing;
Sandblasting equipment; Etching and
engraving; Epoxy coatings

(P-7609)
TRIDENT MARITIME SYSTEMS INC
651 Drucker Ln, San Diego (92154)
PHONE..............................619 346-3800
EMP: 54
SALES (corp-wide): 449.31MM Privately
Held
Web: www.tridentllc.com
SIC: 3731 Shipbuilding and repairing
HQ: Trident Maritime Systems, Inc.
2011 Crystal Dr Ste 1102
Arlington VA 22202
703 236-1590

(P-7610)
UNITED STATES DEPT OF NAVY
Also Called: Supervision of Shipbuilding
32nd St Naval Sta, San Diego
(92136-0001)
P.O. Box 368119 (92136-0001)
PHONE..............................619 556-6033
Ron Craig, Brnch Mgr
EMP: 712
Web: www.navy.mil
SIC: 3731 9711 Shipbuilding and repairing;
Navy
HQ: United States Department Of The Navy
1200 Navy Pentagon
Washington DC 20350

(P-7611)
VALIANT TECHNICAL SERVICES INC
1785 Utah Ave, Lompoc (93437-6020)
PHONE..............................757 628-9500
Danny Schanick, Mgr
EMP: 57
SQ FT: 5,734
SALES (corp-wide): 560.35MM Privately
Held
Web: www.onevaliant.com
SIC: 3731 Shipbuilding and repairing
HQ: Valiant Technical Services Inc.
4465 Guthrie Hwy
Clarksville TN 37040

(P-7612)
VIGOR MARINE LLC
1636 Wilson Ave, National City
(91950-4449)
PHONE..............................619 474-4352
Shelton Smith, Brnch Mgr
EMP: 73
SALES (corp-wide): 1.05B Privately Held
Web: www.vigor.net
SIC: 3731 Shipbuilding and repairing
HQ: Vigor Marine Llc
5555 N Channel Ave
Portland OR 97217

(P-7613)
WALASHEK INDUSTRIAL & MAR INC
1428 Mckinley Ave, National City (91950-4217)
PHONE.....................619 498-1711
Frank Walashek, *Mgr*
EMP: 42
SALES (corp-wide): 30.82MM **Privately Held**
Web: www.walashek.com
SIC: 3731 Shipbuilding and repairing
HQ: Walashek Industrial & Marine, Inc.
3411 Amherst St
Norfolk VA 23513

(P-7614)
WALKER DESIGN INC
Also Called: Walker Engineering Enterprises
9255 San Fernando Rd, Sun Valley (91352-1416)
PHONE.....................818 252-7788
Robert A Walker Junior, *CEO*
Shari Goodgame, *
Michael Delillo, *
▲ **EMP:** 33 **EST:** 1976
SQ FT: 29,800
SALES (est): 5.83MM **Privately Held**
Web: www.walkerengineering.co
SIC: 3731 Lighters, marine: building and repairing

3732 Boatbuilding And Repairing

(P-7615)
ADEPT PROCESS SERVICES INC
Also Called: APS Marine
609 Anita St, Chula Vista (91911-4619)
P.O. Box 2130 (91933-2130)
PHONE.....................619 434-3194
Gary Southerland, *Pr*
EMP: 34 **EST:** 2005
SALES (est): 2.33MM **Privately Held**
Web: www.adeptworks.net
SIC: 3732 4493 7699 Boatbuilding and repairing; Boat yards, storage and incidental repair; Boat repair

(P-7616)
AIR & GAS TECH INC
Also Called: Cem
11433 Woodside Ave, Santee (92071-4725)
PHONE.....................619 955-5980
Anthony Greenwell, *Pr*
Berenice Cossio, *
Jacob Meek, *
EMP: 25 **EST:** 1979
SQ FT: 18,000
SALES (est): 4.86MM **Privately Held**
Web: www.cemcorp.net
SIC: 3732 Boatbuilding and repairing

(P-7617)
BASIN MARINE INC
Also Called: Basin Marine Shipyard
829 Harbor Island Dr Ste A, Newport Beach (92660-7235)
PHONE.....................949 673-0360
Paul Smith, *Pr*
▲ **EMP:** 28 **EST:** 1956
SQ FT: 44,000
SALES (est): 2.77MM **Privately Held**
Web: www.basinmarine.com
SIC: 3732 5551 Boatbuilding and repairing; Marine supplies, nec

(P-7618)
CATALINA YACHTS INC (PA)
Also Called: Morgan Marine
2259 Ward Ave, Simi Valley (93065-1880)
PHONE.....................818 884-7700
Frank W Butler, *Pr*
Sharon Day, *
◆ **EMP:** 50 **EST:** 1968
SALES (est): 16.95MM
SALES (corp-wide): 16.95MM **Privately Held**
Web: www.catalinayachts.com
SIC: 3732 5551 Sailboats, building and repairing; Boat dealers

(P-7619)
DRISCOLL INC
Also Called: Driscoll Boat Works
2500 Shelter Island Dr, San Diego (92106-3114)
PHONE.....................619 226-2500
Thomas Driscoll, *Pr*
John Gerald Driscoll, *
Joseph E Driscoll, *
Mary-carol Driscoll, *Sec*
▲ **EMP:** 50 **EST:** 1947
SQ FT: 2,400
SALES (est): 3.79MM **Privately Held**
Web: www.driscollinc.com
SIC: 3732 Boatbuilding and repairing

(P-7620)
GAMBOL INDUSTRIES INC
1880 Century Park E Ste 950, Los Angeles (90067-1612)
PHONE.....................562 901-2470
Robert A Stein, *Pr*
John Bridwell, *
▲ **EMP:** 45 **EST:** 1992
SALES (est): 4.16MM **Privately Held**
Web: www.gambolindustries.com
SIC: 3732 7699 4493 Yachts, building and repairing; Boat repair; Boat yards, storage and incidental repair

(P-7621)
HOBIE CAT COMPANY (PA)
4925 Oceanside Blvd, Oceanside (92056-3099)
PHONE.....................760 758-9100
Richard Rogers, *CEO*
Doug Skidmore, *
Bill Baldwin, *
◆ **EMP:** 140 **EST:** 1995
SQ FT: 60,000
SALES (est): 35.3MM
SALES (corp-wide): 35.3MM **Privately Held**
Web: www.hobie.com
SIC: 3732 Sailboats, building and repairing

(P-7622)
INDEL ENGINEERING INC
Also Called: Marina Shipyard
6400 E Marina Dr, Long Beach (90803-4618)
PHONE.....................562 594-0995
D E Bud Tretter, *Pr*
Jerry Tretter, *
Kurt Tretter, *
EMP: 35 **EST:** 1964
SQ FT: 3,000
SALES (est): 2.61MM **Privately Held**
Web: www.marinashipyard.com
SIC: 3732 Houseboats, building and repairing

(P-7623)
OCEAN PROTECTA INCORPORATED
14708 Biola Ave, La Mirada (90638-4450)

PHONE.....................714 891-2628
Edgar Chong Tan, *CEO*
Myron Reyes, *
EMP: 50 **EST:** 2014
SALES (est): 455.98K **Privately Held**
Web: www.oceanprotecta.com
SIC: 3732 Boatbuilding and repairing

(P-7624)
VENTURA HARBOR BOATYARD INC
1415 Spinnaker Dr, Ventura (93001-4339)
PHONE.....................805 654-1433
Robert Bartosh, *Pr*
Stephen James, *
Kim Morris, *
Dale Morris, *
EMP: 35 **EST:** 1986
SQ FT: 2,000
SALES (est): 4.57MM **Privately Held**
Web: www.vhby.com
SIC: 3732 4493 Boatbuilding and repairing; Boat yards, storage and incidental repair

(P-7625)
W D SCHOCK CORP
1232 E Pomona St, Santa Ana (92707-2404)
P.O. Box 79184 (92877-0172)
PHONE.....................951 277-3377
Alexander Vucelic, *Pr*
▼ **EMP:** 30 **EST:** 1946
SQ FT: 30,000
SALES (est): 446.01K **Privately Held**
Web: www.wdschockcorp.com
SIC: 3732 Sailboats, building and repairing

(P-7626)
WILLARD MARINE INC
4602 North Ave, Oceanside (92056-3509)
PHONE.....................714 666-2150
Jordan Angle, *CEO*
Joseph Nangle, *
Justin Law, *
▲ **EMP:** 55 **EST:** 1957
SALES (est): 9.32MM **Privately Held**
Web: www.willardmarine.com
SIC: 3732 Boats, fiberglass: building and repairing

3743 Railroad Equipment

(P-7627)
KINKISHARYO (USA) INC
300 Continental Blvd Ste 300, El Segundo (90245-5043)
PHONE.....................424 276-1803
▲ **EMP:** 146
Web: www.kinkisharyo.com
SIC: 3743 Train cars and equipment, freight or passenger

3751 Motorcycles, Bicycles, And Parts

(P-7628)
ALL AMERICAN RACERS INC
Also Called: Dan Gurneys All Amercn Racers
2334 S Broadway, Santa Ana (92707-3250)
P.O. Box 2186 (92707-0186)
PHONE.....................714 540-1771
Daniel S Gurney, *CEO*
Justin B Gurney, *
Kathy Weida, *
EMP: 162 **EST:** 1962
SQ FT: 25,000
SALES (est): 24.03MM **Privately Held**
Web: www.allamericanracers.com

SIC: 3751 Motorcycles and related parts

(P-7629)
BARNETT TOOL & ENGINEERING
Also Called: Barnett Performance Products
2238 Palma Dr, Ventura (93003-8068)
PHONE.....................805 642-9435
Michael Taylor, *Pr*
Colleen Taylor, *
EMP: 60 **EST:** 1948
SQ FT: 43,000
SALES (est): 4.58MM **Privately Held**
Web: www.barnettclutches.com
SIC: 3751 Motorcycle accessories

(P-7630)
FMF RACING
Also Called: Flying Machine Factory
18033 S Santa Fe Ave, Compton (90221-5514)
PHONE.....................310 631-4363
Don Emler, *CEO*
▲ **EMP:** 150 **EST:** 1985
SALES (est): 24.53MM **Privately Held**
Web: www.fmfracing.com
SIC: 3751 5571 Motorcycle accessories; Motorcycle parts and accessories

(P-7631)
K & N ENGINEERING INC (PA)
Also Called: K&N
1455 Citrus St, Riverside (92507-1603)
P.O. Box 1329 (92502-1329)
PHONE.....................951 826-4000
Craige Scanlon, *CEO*
Chance Miller, *
Steve Williams, *
◆ **EMP:** 565 **EST:** 1964
SQ FT: 270,000
SALES (est): 140.52MM
SALES (corp-wide): 140.52MM **Privately Held**
Web: www.knfilters.com
SIC: 3751 3599 3714 Handle bars, motorcycle and bicycle; Air intake filters, internal combustion engine, except auto; Filters: oil, fuel, and air, motor vehicle

(P-7632)
MARKLAND INDUSTRIES INC (PA)
21 Merano, Laguna Niguel (92677-8606)
PHONE.....................714 245-2850
Donald R Markland, *Pr*
▲ **EMP:** 44 **EST:** 1978
SALES (est): 4.28MM
SALES (corp-wide): 4.28MM **Privately Held**
Web: www.marklandindustries.com
SIC: 3751 Motorcycle accessories

(P-7633)
PERFORMANCE MACHINE INC
Also Called: Performance Machine
6892 Marlin Cir, La Palma (90623-1017)
PHONE.....................714 523-3000
▲ **EMP:** 200
SIC: 3751 3714 Motorcycle accessories; Brake drums, motor vehicle

(P-7634)
RAZOR USA LLC (PA)
Also Called: Razor
12723 166th St, Cerritos (90703-2102)
P.O. Box 3610 (90703-3610)
PHONE.....................562 345-6000
Carlton Calvin, *Managing Member*
Robert Chen, *Managing Member*

◆ **EMP:** 60 **EST:** 2000
SQ FT: 50,000
SALES (est): 61.89MM **Privately Held**
Web: www.razor.com
SIC: 3751 Motor scooters and parts

(P-7635)
SEGWAY INC
405 E Santa Clara St Ste 100, Arcadia
(91006-7219)
PHONE..................603 222-6000
Luke Gao, *CEO*
Chen Huang, *
Ye Wang, *
◆ **EMP:** 120 **EST:** 2000
SALES (est): 3.03MM
SALES (corp-wide): 5.08MM **Privately Held**
Web: www.segway.com
SIC: 3751 Motor scooters and parts
HQ: Nunn Bo (Tianjin) Technology Co., Ltd.
No.3, Tianrui Road, Qiche Industries
Park, Wu Qing District
Tianjin TJ 30170

(P-7636)
SPINERGY INC
1709 La Costa Meadows Dr, San Marcos
(92078-5105)
PHONE..................760 496-2121
Martin Connolly, *Pr*
▲ **EMP:** 80 **EST:** 1977
SQ FT: 63,000
SALES (est): 7.82MM **Privately Held**
Web: www.spinergy.com
SIC: 3751 3949 7389 Bicycles and related
parts; Exercise equipment; Design services

(P-7637)
SUPER73 INC (PA)
2722 Michelson Dr Ste 125, Irvine
(92612-8907)
PHONE..................949 258-9245
Legrand Crewse, *CEO*
▼ **EMP:** 23 **EST:** 2018
SALES (est): 5.03MM
SALES (corp-wide): 5.03MM **Privately Held**
Web: www.super73.com
SIC: 3751 5012 Motorcycles and related
parts; Motorcycles

(P-7638)
V&H PERFORMANCE LLC
Also Called: Vance & Hines
13861 Rosecrans Ave, Santa Fe Springs
(90670-5207)
PHONE..................562 921-7461
Andrew Graves, *CEO*
Mike Kennedy, *
Terry Vance, *
Byron Hines, *Stockholder*
▼ **EMP:** 65 **EST:** 2010
SQ FT: 12,000
SALES (est): 23.75MM
SALES (corp-wide): 251.1MM **Privately Held**
Web: www.vanceandhines.com
SIC: 3751 5013 Motorcycles, bicycles and
parts; Motorcycle parts
PA: Motorsport Aftermarket Group, Inc.
13861 Rosecrans Ave
917 838-4002

(P-7639)
WESTERN MFG & DISTRG LLC
Also Called: I.V. League Medical
835 Flynn Rd, Camarillo (93012-8702)
P.O. Box 7192 (92067-7192)
PHONE..................805 988-1010

EMP: 40 **EST:** 1970
SQ FT: 25,000
SALES (est): 1.79MM **Privately Held**
Web:
www.westernmanufacturinganddistributing.com
SIC: 3751 3841 3599 Motorcycles and
related parts; Surgical and medical
instruments; Machine shop, jobbing and
repair

3761 Guided Missiles And Space Vehicles

(P-7640)
ABL SPACE SYSTEMS COMPANY
224 Oregon St, El Segundo (90245-4214)
P.O. Box 1608 (90245-6608)
PHONE..................424 321-6060
Harrison Fagan O'hanley, *CEO*
Daniel George Piemont, *
EMP: 60 **EST:** 2017
SALES (est): 22.47MM **Privately Held**
Web: www.ablspacesystems.com
SIC: 3761 Guided missiles and space
vehicles

(P-7641)
ASTROBOTIC TECHNOLOGY INC
1570 Sabovich St, Mojave (93501-1681)
PHONE..................888 488-8455
David Masten, *Engr*
EMP: 92
SALES (corp-wide): 44.28MM **Privately Held**
Web: www.astrobotic.com
SIC: 3761 Guided missiles and space
vehicles
PA: Astrobotic Technology, Inc.
1016 N Lincoln Ave
412 682-3282

(P-7642)
BOEING COMPANY
Also Called: Boeing
14441 Astronautics Ln, Huntington Beach
(92647-2080)
PHONE..................714 896-3311
James Mcnerney, *Brnch Mgr*
EMP: 368
SQ FT: 2,200,000
SALES (corp-wide): 77.79B **Publicly Held**
Web: www.boeing.com
SIC: 3761 3769 Guided missiles and space
vehicles; Space vehicle equipment, nec
PA: The Boeing Company
929 Long Bridge Dr
703 465-3500

(P-7643)
EDGE AUTONOMY BEND LLC (HQ)
831 Buckley Rd, San Luis Obispo
(93401-8130)
PHONE..................541 678-0515
John Purvis, *CEO*
Josh Brungardt, *COO*
EMP: 24 **EST:** 2009
SQ FT: 200
SALES (est): 10.38MM
SALES (corp-wide): 1.05B **Privately Held**
Web: www.edgeautonomy.io
SIC: 3761 Guided missiles and space
vehicles, research and development
PA: Ae Industrial Partners, Lp
6700 Broken Sound Pkwy Nw
561 372-7820

(P-7644)
IMPULSE SPACE INC
2651 Manhattan Beach Blvd, Redondo
Beach (90278-1604)
PHONE..................949 315-5540
Thomas Mueller, *CEO*
EMP: 25 **EST:** 2021
SALES (est): 16.72MM **Privately Held**
Web: www.impulsespace.com
SIC: 3761 Guided missiles and space
vehicles

(P-7645)
K2 SPACE CORPORATION
960 Knox St Bldg A, Torrance (90502-1086)
PHONE..................312 307-8930
Karan Kunjur, *CEO*
Neel Kunjur, *
EMP: 81 **EST:** 2022
SALES (est): 1.56MM **Privately Held**
Web: www.k2space.com
SIC: 3761 3764 Guided missiles and space
vehicles; Engines and engine parts, guided
missile

(P-7646)
KRATOS DEF & SEC SOLUTIONS INC (PA)
Also Called: KRATOS
10680 Treena St Ste 600, San Diego
(92131-2440)
PHONE..................858 812-7300
Eric Demarco, *Pr*
William Hoglund, *
Deanna Lund, *
Marie Mendoza, *Sr VP*
Benjamin Goodwin, *Senior Vice President
Corporate Development*
EMP: 166 **EST:** 1995
SALES (est): 1.04B **Publicly Held**
Web: www.kratosdefense.com
SIC: 3761 3663 7382 8711 Guided missiles
and space vehicles; Microwave
communication equipment; Security
systems services; Engineering services

(P-7647)
MASTEN SPACE SYSTEMS INC
Also Called: Masten Space
1570 Sabovich St 25, Mojave (93501-1681)
PHONE..................888 488-8455
EMP: 38 **EST:** 2004
SQ FT: 6,000
SALES (est): 5.11MM **Privately Held**
Web: www.masten.aero
SIC: 3761 Guided missiles and space
vehicles

(P-7648)
ROCKET LAB USA INC
4022 E Conant St, Long Beach
(90808-1777)
PHONE..................714 465-5737
EMP: 32
SALES (corp-wide): 244.59MM **Publicly Held**
Web: www.rocketlabusa.com
SIC: 3761 Guided missiles and space
vehicles, research and development
PA: Rocket Lab Usa, Inc.
3881 Mcgowen St
714 465-5737

(P-7649)
ROCKET LAB USA INC (PA)
3881 Mcgowen St, Long Beach
(90808-1702)
PHONE..................714 465-5737
Peter Beck, *Ch Bd*
Adam Spice, *CFO*

Shaun O'donnell, *Executive Global
Operations Vice President*
Arjun Kampani, *Corporate Secretary*
Frank Klein, *COO*
EMP: 50 **EST:** 2006
SALES (est): 244.59MM
SALES (corp-wide): 244.59MM **Publicly Held**
Web: www.rocketlabusa.com
SIC: 3761 Guided missiles and space
vehicles

(P-7650)
SPACE EXPLORATION TECH CORP (PA)
Also Called: Spacex
1 Rocket Rd, Hawthorne (90250-6844)
PHONE..................310 363-6000
Elon Musk, *CEO*
Gwynne Shotwell, *
Bret Johnsen, *
◆ **EMP:** 340 **EST:** 2002
SQ FT: 964,000
SALES (est): 2.07B
SALES (corp-wide): 2.07B **Privately Held**
Web: www.spacex.com
SIC: 3761 Rockets, space and military,
complete

(P-7651)
SPACE EXPLORATION TECH CORP
Also Called: Spacex
2980 Nimitz Rd, Long Beach (90802-1048)
PHONE..................310 363-6289
EMP: 157
SALES (corp-wide): 2.07B **Privately Held**
Web: www.spacex.com
SIC: 3761 Guided missiles and space
vehicles
PA: Space Exploration Technologies Corp.
1 Rocket Rd
310 363-6000

(P-7652)
SPACE EXPLORATION TECH CORP
Also Called: Spacex
2700 Miner St, San Pedro (90731)
PHONE..................714 330-8668
EMP: 157
SALES (corp-wide): 2.07B **Privately Held**
Web: www.spacex.com
SIC: 3761 Rockets, space and military,
complete
PA: Space Exploration Technologies Corp.
1 Rocket Rd
310 363-6000

(P-7653)
SPACE EXPLORATION TECH CORP
Also Called: Spacex Wilkie
12520 Wilkie Ave, Gardena (90249)
PHONE..................323 754-1285
EMP: 157
SALES (corp-wide): 2.07B **Privately Held**
Web: www.spacex.com
SIC: 3761 Rockets, space and military,
complete
PA: Space Exploration Technologies Corp.
1 Rocket Rd
310 363-6000

(P-7654)
SPACE EXPLORATION TECH CORP
Also Called: Spacex
3976 Jack Northrop Ave, Hawthorne
(90250-4441)

PRODUCTS & SVCS

PHONE..................310 889-4968
EMP: 236
SALES (corp-wide): 2.07B **Privately Held**
Web: www.spacex.com
SIC: 3761 Rockets, space and military, complete
PA: Space Exploration Technologies Corp.
1 Rocket Rd
310 363-6000

(P-7655)
SPACEX LLC
12533 Crenshaw Blvd, Hawthorne (90250-3302)
PHONE..................310 970-5845
EMP: 1417 **EST:** 2004
SALES (est): 8.48MM
SALES (corp-wide): 2.07B **Privately Held**
Web: www.spacex.com
SIC: 3761 Guided missiles and space vehicles
PA: Space Exploration Technologies Corp.
1 Rocket Rd
310 363-6000

(P-7656)
STELLAR EXPLORATION INC
835 Airport Dr, San Luis Obispo (93401-8370)
PHONE..................805 459-1425
Tomas Svitek, *Pr*
Tomas Svitek, *Pr*
Iva Svitek, *
EMP: 24 **EST:** 2001
SQ FT: 3,000
SALES (est): 3.17MM **Privately Held**
Web: www.stellar-exploration.com
SIC: 3761 Space vehicles, complete

(P-7657)
TAYCO ENGINEERING INC
10874 Hope St, Cypress (90630-5214)
P.O. Box 6034 (90630-0034)
PHONE..................714 952-2240
Jay Chung, *Pr*
Ann Taylor, *
Sheri T Nikolakopulos, *
EMP: 130 **EST:** 1971
SQ FT: 55,600
SALES (est): 15.87MM **Privately Held**
Web: www.taycoeng.com
SIC: 3761 Guided missiles and space vehicles

(P-7658)
TYVAK NN-SATELLITE SYSTEMS INC (DH)
15330 Barranca Pkwy, Irvine (92618-2215)
PHONE..................949 753-1020
Marc Bell, *Pr*
Roger Teague, *
James Black, *
Gary Hobart, *
EMP: 35 **EST:** 2011
SALES (est): 22.29MM
SALES (corp-wide): 135.91MM **Privately Held**
Web: www.terranorbital.com
SIC: 3761 3764 Space vehicles, complete; Space propulsion units and parts
HQ: Terran Orbital Operating Corporation
6800 Brken Sund Pkwy Nw S
Boca Raton FL 33487
561 988-1704

(P-7659)
UNITED LAUNCH ALLIANCE LLC
1579 Utah Ave, Bldg. 7525, Vandenberg Afb (93437)

PHONE..................303 269-5876
Deborah Settit, *Prin*
EMP: 440
Web: www.ulalaunch.com
SIC: 3761 Guided missiles and space vehicles
PA: United Launch Alliance, L.L.C.
9501 E Panorama Cir

(P-7660)
VARDA SPACE INDUSTRIES INC
225 S Aviation Blvd, El Segundo (90245-4604)
PHONE..................833 707-0020
Delian Asparouhov, *Pr*
EMP: 70 **EST:** 2020
SALES (est): 10.15MM **Privately Held**
Web: www.varda.com
SIC: 3761 Space vehicles, complete

(P-7661)
VIRGIN GALACTIC HOLDINGS INC (PA)
Also Called: VIRGIN GALACTIC
1700 Flight Way Ste 400, Tustin (92782-1854)
PHONE..................949 774-7640
Michael Colglazier, *Pr*
Raymond Mabus Junior, *Ch Bd*
Doug Ahrens, *CFO*
Aparna Chitale, *CPO*
Sarah Kim, *CLO*
EMP: 36 **EST:** 2017
SALES (est): 6.8MM
SALES (corp-wide): 6.8MM **Publicly Held**
Web: www.virgingalactic.com
SIC: 3761 3812 Space vehicles, complete; Space vehicle guidance systems and equipment

(P-7662)
XCOR AEROSPACE INC
Also Called: Xcor
1314 Flight Line, Mojave (93501-1665)
P.O. Box 61310 (93501)
PHONE..................661 824-4714
▲ **EMP:** 87
Web: www.xcor.com
SIC: 3761 Guided missiles and space vehicles, research and development

3764 Space Propulsion Units And Parts

(P-7663)
MICROCOSM INC
3111 Lomita Blvd, Torrance (90505-5108)
PHONE..................310 539-2306
James Wertz, *Pr*
Alice Wertz, *
Robert E Conger, *
EMP: 40 **EST:** 1984
SQ FT: 50,000
SALES (est): 3.5MM **Privately Held**
Web: www.smad.com
SIC: 3764 2731 3769 Space propulsion units and parts; Book publishing; Space vehicle equipment, nec

(P-7664)
RELATIVITY SPACE INC (PA)
3500 E Burnett St, Long Beach (90815-1730)
PHONE..................424 393-4309
Timothy Ellis, *CEO*
Jordan Noone, *
Alexander Kwan, *
Muhammad Shahzad, *
Roxanne Fung, *Corporate Controller*

EMP: 337 **EST:** 2015
SQ FT: 10,000
SALES (est): 135.25MM
SALES (corp-wide): 135.25MM **Privately Held**
Web: www.relativityspace.com
SIC: 3764 Space propulsion units and parts

(P-7665)
SPINLAUNCH INC
3816 Stineman Ct, Long Beach (90808-2572)
PHONE..................650 516-7746
Jonathan Yaney, *Pr*
Domhnal Slattery, *
EMP: 166 **EST:** 2015
SALES (est): 7.8MM **Privately Held**
Web: www.spinlaunch.com
SIC: 3764 Propulsion units for guided missiles and space vehicles

3769 Space Vehicle Equipment, Nec

(P-7666)
AMERICAN AUTOMATED ENGRG INC
Also Called: A A E Aerospace & Coml Tech
5382 Argosy Ave, Huntington Beach (92649-1037)
PHONE..................714 898-9951
Kenneth Christensen, *Pr*
EMP: 215 **EST:** 1967
SQ FT: 48,000
SALES (est): 8.78MM **Privately Held**
SIC: 3769 Space vehicle equipment, nec

(P-7667)
CLIFFDALE MANUFACTURING LLC
Also Called: RTC Aerospace
20409 Prairie St, Chatsworth (91311-6029)
PHONE..................818 341-3344
Brad Hart, *CEO*
EMP: 200 **EST:** 1943
SQ FT: 42,000
SALES (est): 9.9MM **Privately Held**
Web: www.rtcaerospace.com
SIC: 3769 3599 Space vehicle equipment, nec; Machine shop, jobbing and repair

(P-7668)
COMPOSITE OPTICS INCORPORATED
Also Called: Atk
7130 Miramar Rd Ste 100b, San Diego (92121-2340)
PHONE..................937 490-4145
EMP: 800
SIC: 3769 Space vehicle equipment, nec

(P-7669)
DW AND BB CONSULTING INC
11381 Bradley Ave, Pacoima (91331-2358)
PHONE..................818 896-9899
David Wyckoff, *Pr*
Lee Brown, *
Ben Bensal, *
EMP: 70 **EST:** 1989
SQ FT: 10,000
SALES (est): 3.87MM **Privately Held**
Web: www.kdlprecision.com
SIC: 3769 2822 3061 Space vehicle equipment, nec; Silicone rubbers; Oil and gas field machinery rubber goods (mechanical)

(P-7670)
HYDROMACH INC
20400 Prairie St, Chatsworth (91311-8129)
PHONE..................818 341-0915
Norberto A Cusinato, *CEO*
Jose Nicosia, *
Anna M Cusinato, *
EMP: 40 **EST:** 1976
SQ FT: 23,000
SALES (est): 5.61MM **Privately Held**
Web: www.hydromach.com
SIC: 3769 3599 Space vehicle equipment, nec; Machine shop, jobbing and repair

(P-7671)
LEDA CORPORATION
7080 Kearny Dr, Huntington Beach (92648-6254)
PHONE..................714 841-7821
Joseph K Tung, *Pr*
Dorothy Tung, *
David Tung, *
EMP: 30 **EST:** 1985
SQ FT: 15,000
SALES (est): 5.58MM **Privately Held**
Web: www.ledacorp.net
SIC: 3769 Guided missile and space vehicle parts and aux. equip., R&D

(P-7672)
MICRO STEEL INC
7850 Alabama Ave, Canoga Park (91304-4905)
PHONE..................818 348-8701
Lazar Hersko, *Pr*
Claudia Sceelo, *
Tova Hersko, *
EMP: 25 **EST:** 1986
SQ FT: 14,500
SALES (est): 3.5MM **Privately Held**
Web: www.microsteel.net
SIC: 3769 Space vehicle equipment, nec.

(P-7673)
STANFORD MU CORPORATION
Also Called: Airborne Components
20725 Annalee Ave, Carson (90746-3503)
PHONE..................310 605-2888
Stanford Mu, *Pr*
Lynn Price, *
Robert Friend, *
EMP: 40 **EST:** 1992
SALES (est): 4.04MM **Privately Held**
Web: www.stanfordmu.com
SIC: 3769 3764 7699 Space vehicle equipment, nec; Space propulsion units and parts; Aircraft and heavy equipment repair services

(P-7674)
VANTAGE ASSOCIATES INC (PA)
1565 Macarthur Blvd, Costa Mesa (92626-1407)
PHONE..................619 477-6940
Mary Normand, *CEO*
Eric Clack, *
Andrea Alpinieri Glover, *
EMP: 35 **EST:** 1980
SALES (est): 24.86MM
SALES (corp-wide): 24.86MM **Privately Held**
Web: www.vantageassoc.com
SIC: 3769 2821 3728 3083 Space vehicle equipment, nec; Plastics materials and resins; Aircraft parts and equipment, nec; Laminated plastics plate and sheet

▲ = Import ▼ = Export
◆ = Import/Export

3792 Travel Trailers And Campers

(P-7675)
CUSTOM FIBREGLASS MFG CO
Also Called: Custom Hardtops
1711 Harbor Ave, Long Beach
(90813-1300)
PHONE.....................562 432-5454
Hartmut W Schroeder, *Pr*
Joel Thiefburg, *
Robert L Edwards, *
◆ **EMP:** 165 **EST:** 1966
SQ FT: 135,000
SALES (est): 10.43MM
SALES (corp-wide): 1.62B **Privately Held**
Web: www.snugtop.com
SIC: 3792 Pickup covers, canopies or caps
HQ: Truck Accessories Group, Llc
28858 Ventura Dr
Elkhart IN 46517
574 522-5337

(P-7676)
FLEETWOOD TRAVEL TRLRS IND INC (DH)
3125 Myers St, Riverside (92503-5527)
P.O. Box 7638 (92513-7638)
PHONE.....................951 354-3000
Edward B Caudill, *Pr*
Edward B Caudill, *Pr*
Boyd R Plowman, *Ex VP*
Forrest D Theobald, *Sr VP*
Lyle N Larkin, *VP*
EMP: 143 **EST:** 1971
SQ FT: 262,900
SALES (est): 8.5MM **Privately Held**
SIC: 3792 Travel trailers and campers
HQ: Fleetwood Enterprises, Inc.
1351 Pomona Rd Ste 230
Corona CA 92882
951 354-3000

(P-7677)
PACIFIC COACHWORKS INC
3411 N Perris Blvd Bldg 1, Perris
(92571-3100)
PHONE.....................951 686-7294
Brett Bashaw, *CEO*
Michael Rhodes, *
EMP: 155 **EST:** 2006
SALES (est): 15.62MM **Privately Held**
Web: www.pacificcoachworks.com
SIC: 3792 Travel trailers and campers

(P-7678)
PROTO HOMES LLC
11301 W Olympic Blvd, Los Angeles
(90064-1653)
PHONE.....................310 271 7644
EMP: 40 **EST:** 2009
SALES (est): 5.15MM **Privately Held**
Web: www.protohomes.com
SIC: 3792 House trailers, except as
permanent dwellings

3795 Tanks And Tank Components

(P-7679)
DN TANKS INC
Also Called: Dyk
351 Cypress Ln, El Cajon (92020-1603)
P.O. Box 696 (92022-0696)
PHONE.....................619 440-8181
EMP: 142
Web: www.dntanks.com

SIC: 3795 Tanks and tank components
PA: Dn Tanks, Inc.
11 Teal Rd

(P-7680)
DYK INCORPORATED (HQ)
Also Called: Dyk Prestressed Tanks
351 Cypress Ln, El Cajon (92020-1603)
P.O. Box 696 (92022-0696)
PHONE.....................619 440-8181
Charles Crowley, *CEO*
Max R Dykmans, *
Bill Hendrickson, *
Bill Crowley, *
David Gourley, *
◆ **EMP:** 24 **EST:** 1989
SALES (est): 3.99MM **Privately Held**
Web: www.dntanks.com
SIC: 3795 8711 1542 Tanks and tank
components; Engineering services;
Nonresidential construction, nec
PA: Dn Tanks, Inc.
11 Teal Rd

(P-7681)
TIGER TANKS INC
3397 Edison Hwy, Bakersfield
(93307-2234)
P.O. Box 21041 (93390-1041)
PHONE.....................661 363-8335
TOLL FREE: 888
Robert E Bimat, *Ch Bd*
Darryck Selk, *
Bryan Lewis, *
Carol Bimat, *
Roger Burns, *
EMP: 30 **EST:** 1997
SQ FT: 55,000
SALES (est): 4.78MM **Privately Held**
Web: www.tigertanksinc.com
SIC: 3795 3443 Tanks and tank components
; Fabricated plate work (boiler shop)

3799 Transportation Equipment, Nec

(P-7682)
DG PERFORMANCE SPC INC
4100 E La Palma Ave, Anaheim
(92807-1814)
PHONE.....................714 961-8850
Mark W Dooley, *Pr*
William J Dooley, *
Joan K Dooley, *
EMP: 100 **EST:** 1972
SQ FT: 25,000
SALES (est): 1.83MM **Privately Held**
Web: www.dgperformance.com
SIC: 3799 3751 5012 5961 Recreational
vehicles; Motorcycles and related parts;
Recreation vehicles, all-terrain; Fitness and
sporting goods, mail order

(P-7683)
NATIONAL SIGNAL LLC
14489 Industry Cir, La Mirada (90638-5812)
PHONE.....................714 441-7707
Alex Henderson, *
James M Welch, *
EMP: 99 **EST:** 2022
SALES (est): 26.66MM
SALES (corp-wide): 1.03B **Privately Held**
SIC: 3799 3669 Trailers and trailer
equipment; Highway signals, electric
PA: Hill & Smith Plc
Westhaven House
121 704-7430

3812 Search And Navigation Equipment

(P-7684)
ACCUTURN CORPORATION
7189 Old 215 Frontage Rd Ste 101,
Moreno Valley (92553-7903)
PHONE.....................951 656-6621
Ignatius C Araujo, *CEO*
Iggy Araujo, *
Mark Sayegh, *Stockholder*
Henri Rahmon, *Stockholder*
EMP: 26 **EST:** 1974
SQ FT: 15,000
SALES (est): 4.82MM **Privately Held**
Web: www.accuturninc.com
SIC: 3812 3089 3599 Acceleration indicators
and systems components, aerospace;
Automotive parts, plastic; Machine shop,
jobbing and repair

(P-7685)
AEROANTENNA TECHNOLOGY INC
20732 Lassen St, Chatsworth (91311-4507)
PHONE.....................818 993-3842
Yosef Klein, *Pr*
Joe Klein, *
Carmela Klein, *
▲ **EMP:** 140 **EST:** 1991
SALES (est): 22.32MM **Publicly Held**
Web: www.aeroantenna.com
SIC: 3812 3663 Antennas, radar or
communications; Antennas, transmitting
and communications
HQ: Heico Electronic Technologies Corp.
3000 Taft St
Hollywood FL 33021
954 987-6101

(P-7686)
AEROJET RCKETDYNE HOLDINGS INC (HQ)
222 N Pacific Coast Hwy Ste 500, El
Segundo (90245-5603)
P.O. Box 537012 (95853-7012)
PHONE.....................310 252-8100
Ross Niebergall, *Pr*
Joseph Chontos, *VP*
EMP: 75 **EST:** 1915
SALES (est): 2.24B
SALES (corp-wide): 19.42B **Publicly Held**
Web: www.l3harris.com
SIC: 3812 3764 3769 6552 Defense systems
and equipment; Propulsion units for guided
missiles and space vehicles; Space vehicle
equipment, nec; Subdividers and
developers, nec
PA: L3harris Technologies, Inc.
1025 W Nasa Blvd
321 727-9100

(P-7687)
AEROJET ROCKETDYNE DE INC
222 N Pacific Coast Hwy Ste 50, El
Segundo (90245-5648)
PHONE.....................310 414-0110
EMP: 644
SALES (corp-wide): 19.42B **Publicly Held**
Web: www.l3harris.com
SIC: 3812 Defense systems and equipment
HQ: Inc Aerojet Rocketdyne Of De
8900 De Soto Ave
Canoga Park CA 91304
818 586-1000

(P-7688)
ALLIANT TCHSYSTEMS OPRTONS LLC
9401 Corbin Ave, Northridge (91324-2400)
PHONE.....................818 887-8195
Albert Calabrese, *Pr*
EMP: 27
Web: www.northropgrumman.com
SIC: 3812 Search and navigation equipment
HQ: Alliant Techsystems Operations Llc
2980 Fairview Park Dr
Falls Church VA 22042

(P-7689)
ALLIANT TCHSYSTEMS OPRTONS LLC
9401 Corbin Ave, Northridge (91324-2400)
PHONE.....................818 887-8195
Ronald Hill, *Prin*
EMP: 400 **EST:** 2002
SALES (est): 15.53MM **Publicly Held**
SIC: 3812 Search and navigation equipment
HQ: Northrop Grumman Innovation
Systems, Inc.
2980 Fairview Park Dr
Falls Church VA 22042

(P-7690)
ANDURIL INDUSTRIES INC
2910 S Tech Center Dr, Santa Ana
(92705-5657)
PHONE.....................949 891-1607
EMP: 43
SALES (corp-wide): 457.43MM **Privately
Held**
Web: www.anduril.com
SIC: 3812 Search and navigation equipment
PA: Anduril Industries, Inc.
1400 Anduril
949 891-1607

(P-7691)
ANDURIL INDUSTRIES INC (PA)
1400 Anduril, Costa Mesa (92626-1548)
PHONE.....................949 891-1607
Brian Schimpf, *CEO*
Matthew Grimm, *
EMP: 596 **EST:** 2017
SQ FT: 155,000
SALES (est): 457.43MM
SALES (corp-wide): 457.43MM **Privately
Held**
Web: www.anduril.com
SIC: 3812 Search and navigation equipment

(P-7692)
APEX TECHNOLOGY HOLDINGS INC
Also Called: Apex Design Technology
2050 E Coronado St, Anaheim
(92806-2503)
PHONE.....................321 270-3630
Lance Schroeder, *Pr*
EMP: 513 **EST:** 2005
SQ FT: 80,000
SALES (est): 3.75MM **Privately Held**
Web: www.apexdt.com
SIC: 3812 Acceleration indicators and
systems components, aerospace

(P-7693)
ARETE ASSOCIATES (PA)
Also Called: Arete Associates
9301 Corbin Ave Ste 2000, Northridge
(91324-2508)
PHONE.....................818 885-2200
David Campion, *Pr*
Doug Deprospo, *CSO*
Christopher Choi, *

PRODUCTS & SVCS

Sallie Di Vincenzo, *CAO**
EMP: 125 **EST:** 1975
SQ FT: 170,000
SALES (est): 100MM
SALES (corp-wide): 100MM **Privately Held**
Web: www.arete.com
SIC: 3812 3827 Aircraft/aerospace flight instruments and guidance systems; Sighting and fire control equipment, optical

(P-7694)
ARGON ST INC
6696 Mesa Ridge Rd Ste A, San Diego (92121-2950)
PHONE....................703 270-6927
Matthew Hoff, *Brnch Mgr*
EMP: 66
SALES (corp-wide): 77.79B **Publicly Held**
Web: www.argonst.com
SIC: 3812 Search and navigation equipment
HQ: Argon St, Inc.
　12701 Fair Lkes Cir Ste 8
　Fairfax VA 22033
　703 322-0881

(P-7695)
ASCENT AEROSPACE
1395 S Lyon St, Santa Ana (92705-4608)
PHONE....................586 726-0500
EMP: 64 **EST:** 2020
SALES (est): 8.66MM **Privately Held**
Web: www.ascentaerospace.com
SIC: 3812 Search and navigation equipment

(P-7696)
ATK LAUNCH SYSTEMS LLC
16707 Via Del Campo Ct, San Diego (92127-1713)
PHONE....................858 592-2509
Audrey Clarck, *Brnch Mgr*
EMP: 464
Web: www.northropgrumman.com
SIC: 3812 Search and navigation equipment
HQ: Atk Launch Systems Llc
　9160 N Highway 83
　Corinne UT 84307
　801 251-2512

(P-7697)
ATK SPACE SYSTEMS LLC
Also Called: Atk Arspace Strctres Test Fclt
16707 Via Del Campo Ct, San Diego (92127-1713)
PHONE....................858 487-0970
Brian Welge, *Mgr*
EMP: 96
Web: www.psi-pci.com
SIC: 3812 Search and navigation equipment
HQ: Atk Space Systems Llc
　6033 Bandini Blvd
　Commerce CA 90040
　323 722-0222

(P-7698)
ATK SPACE SYSTEMS LLC
Space Components Business Unit
7130 Miramar Rd Ste 100b, San Diego (92121-2340)
PHONE....................858 530-3047
EMP: 112
Web: www.psi-pci.com
SIC: 3812 Search and navigation equipment
HQ: Atk Space Systems Llc
　6033 Bandini Blvd
　Commerce CA 90040
　323 722-0222

(P-7699)
ATK SPACE SYSTEMS LLC
Also Called: Space Components Division
7130 Miramar Rd Ste 100b, San Diego (92121-2340)
PHONE....................858 621-5700
EMP: 96
Web: www.psi-pci.com
SIC: 3812 Search and navigation equipment
HQ: Atk Space Systems Llc
　6033 Bandini Blvd
　Commerce CA 90040
　323 722-0222

(P-7700)
ATK SPACE SYSTEMS LLC
600 Pine Ave, Goleta (93117-3803)
PHONE....................805 685-2262
Blake Larson, *CEO*
EMP: 96
Web: www.psi-pci.com
SIC: 3812 Search and navigation equipment
HQ: Atk Space Systems Llc
　6033 Bandini Blvd
　Commerce CA 90040
　323 722-0222

(P-7701)
ATK SPACE SYSTEMS LLC (DH)
Also Called: Space Components
6033 Bandini Blvd, Commerce (90040-2968)
PHONE....................323 722-0222
Blake Larson, *Pr*
Daniel J Murphy, *
Ronald D Dittemore, *
James Armor, *
Thomas R Wilson, *
◆ **EMP:** 50 **EST:** 1963
SQ FT: 104,000
SALES (est): 76.83MM **Publicly Held**
Web: www.psi-pci.com
SIC: 3812 Search and navigation equipment
HQ: Northrop Grumman Innovation Systems, Inc.
　2980 Fairview Park Dr
　Falls Church VA 22042

(P-7702)
ATK SPACE SYSTEMS LLC
1960 E Grand Ave Ste 1150, El Segundo (90245-5166)
PHONE....................310 343-3799
Dale Woolheater, *Brnch Mgr*
EMP: 64
Web: www.psi-pci.com
SIC: 3812 Search and navigation equipment
HQ: Atk Space Systems Llc
　6033 Bandini Blvd
　Commerce CA 90040
　323 722-0222

(P-7703)
ATK SPACE SYSTEMS LLC
370 N Halstead St, Pasadena (91107-3122)
PHONE....................626 351-0205
Joe Tellegrino, *Mgr*
EMP: 96
Web: www.psi-pci.com
SIC: 3812 3826 8711 Search and navigation equipment; Instruments measuring thermal properties; Engineering services
HQ: Atk Space Systems Llc
　6033 Bandini Blvd
　Commerce CA 90040
　323 722-0222

(P-7704)
BAE SYSTEMS LAND ARMAMENTS LP
1650 Industrial Blvd, Chula Vista (91911-3922)
PHONE....................619 455-0213
Todd Eden, *Brnch Mgr*
EMP: 37
SALES (corp-wide): 28.77B **Privately Held**
Web: www.baesystems.com
SIC: 3812 Search and navigation equipment
HQ: Bae Systems Land & Armaments L.P.
　2941 Frview Pk Dr Ste 100
　Falls Church VA 22042
　571 461-6000

(P-7705)
BAE SYSTEMS TECH SLTONS SVCS I
9650 Chesapeake Dr, San Diego (92123-1307)
PHONE....................858 278-3042
David Davis, *Brnch Mgr*
EMP: 53
SALES (corp-wide): 28.77B **Privately Held**
SIC: 3812 Navigational systems and instruments
HQ: Bae Systems Technology Solutions & Services Inc.
　520 Gaither Rd
　Rockville MD 20850
　703 847-5820

(P-7706)
CAES SYSTEMS LLC
9404 Chesapeake Dr, San Diego (92123-1303)
PHONE....................858 560-1301
Dave Young, *Brnch Mgr*
EMP: 208
SALES (corp-wide): 4.59B **Privately Held**
Web: www.caes.com
SIC: 3812 Search and navigation equipment
HQ: Caes Systems Llc
　305 Richardson Rd
　Lansdale PA 19446

(P-7707)
CHANNEL TECHNOLOGIES GROUP LLC
Also Called: Ctg
879 Ward Dr, Santa Barbara (93111-2920)
EMP: 1356 **EST:** 2012
SALES (est): 2.6MM **Privately Held**
SIC: 3812 Search and navigation equipment

(P-7708)
COHERENT AEROSPACE & DEFENSE INC (HQ)
Also Called: Ii-VI Aerospace & Defense Inc
36570 Briggs Rd, Murrieta (92563-2387)
PHONE....................951 926-2994
EMP: 121 **EST:** 1961
SALES (est): 60.26MM
SALES (corp-wide): 4.71B **Publicly Held**
Web: www.iiviad.com
SIC: 3812 3827 Infrared object detection equipment; Optical instruments and apparatus
PA: Coherent Corp.
　375 Saxonburg Blvd
　724 352-4455

(P-7709)
CONSOLIDATED AEROSPACE MFG LLC (HQ)
Also Called: CAM
1425 S Acacia Ave, Fullerton (92831-5317)
PHONE....................714 989-2797
Dave Werner, *Managing Member*
EMP: 46 **EST:** 2012
SALES (est): 434.9MM

SALES (corp-wide): 15.78B **Publicly Held**
Web: www.stanleyblackanddecker.com
SIC: 3812 Search and navigation equipment
PA: Stanley Black & Decker, Inc.
　1000 Stanley Dr
　860 225-5111

(P-7710)
CUBIC CORPORATION (HQ)
Also Called: Cubic
9233 Balboa Ave, San Diego (92123-1513)
PHONE....................858 277-6780
Stevan Slijepcevic, *Pr*
Anshooman Aga, *Ex VP*
Mark A Harrison, *CAO*
Grace G Lee, *Chief Human Resources Officer*
Hilary L Hageman, *Corporate Secretary*
EMP: 1243 **EST:** 1951
SQ FT: 265,000
SALES (est): 1.48B
SALES (corp-wide): 1.48B **Privately Held**
Web: www.cubic.com
SIC: 3812 3699 7372 3724 Defense systems and equipment; Flight simulators (training aids), electronic; Application computer software; Aircraft engines and engine parts
PA: Atlas Cc Acquisition Corp.
　850 New Burton Rd Ste 201
　858 277-6780

(P-7711)
CUMMINS AEROSPACE LLC (PA)
Also Called: Cummins Aerospace
2320 E Orangethorpe Ave, Anaheim (92806-1223)
PHONE....................714 879-2800
Sean Beriah Cummins, *CEO*
William Beriah Cummins, *
Tina Marie Cummins, *
Mary Ellen Cummins, *
Sean Beriah Cummins, *Dir*
EMP: 30 **EST:** 1978
SQ FT: 35,000
SALES (est): 11.98MM
SALES (corp-wide): 11.98MM **Privately Held**
Web: www.cumminsaerospace.com
SIC: 3812 3519 3728 Search and navigation equipment; Internal combustion engines, nec; Aircraft parts and equipment, nec

(P-7712)
DECA INTERNATIONAL CORP
Also Called: Golf Buddy
10700 Norwalk Blvd, Santa Fe Springs (90670-3824)
PHONE....................714 367-5900
Seung Wook Jung, *CEO*
▲ **EMP:** 28 **EST:** 2005
SQ FT: 3,000
SALES (est): 4.96MM **Privately Held**
SIC: 3812 Navigational systems and instruments

(P-7713)
DECATUR ELECTRONICS INC (DH)
15890 Bernardo Center Dr, San Diego (92127-2320)
PHONE....................888 428-4315
Brian Brown, *CEO*.
Luisa Nechodom, *
◆ **EMP:** 70 **EST:** 1955
SQ FT: 10,000
SALES (est): 7.22MM
SALES (corp-wide): 179.22MM **Privately Held**
Web: www.decaturelectronics.com

SIC: **3812** Radar systems and equipment
HQ: D & K Engineering
16990 Goldentop Rd
San Diego CA 92127

(P-7714)
EATON AEROSPACE LLC
Also Called: Eaton
9650 Jeronimo Rd, Irvine (92618-2024)
PHONE.............................949 452-9500
Lily Bridenbaker, *Mgr*
EMP: 25
SIC: **3812** 3365 Acceleration indicators and
systems components, aerospace;
Aerospace castings, aluminum
HQ: Eaton Aerospace Llc
1000 Eaton Blvd
Cleveland OH 44114
818 409-0200

(P-7715)
EDGE AUTONOMY SLO LLC
831 Buckley Rd, San Luis Obispo
(93401-8130)
PHONE.............................805 544-0932
John Purvis, *CEO*
Gordon Jennings, *
EMP: 41 EST: 1989
SQ FT: 19,000
SALES (est): 10.38MM
SALES (corp-wide): 1.05B **Privately Held**
Web: www.edgeautonomy.io
SIC: **3812** 7371 3721 Electronic detection
systems (aeronautical); Computer software
development and applications; Aircraft
HQ: Edge Autonomy Bend, Llc
831 Buckley Rd
San Luis Obispo CA 93401
541 678-0515

(P-7716)
EDO COMMUNICATIONS AND COUNTERMEASURES SYSTEMS INC
Also Called: Force Protection Systems
7821 Orion Ave, Van Nuys (91406-2029)
PHONE.............................818 464-2475
EMP: 60
SIC: **3812** 3663 3612 7371 Search and
navigation equipment; Radio and t.v.
communications equipment; Signaling
transformers, electric; Custom computer
programming services

(P-7717)
EMPLOYER DEFENSE GROUP
2390 E Orangewood Ave Ste 520, Anaheim
(92806-6178)
PHONE.............................949 200-0137
Michelle Oelhafen, *Prin*
EMP: 24 EST: 2017
SALES (est): 1.95MM **Privately Held**
Web: www.edglaw.com
SIC: **3812** Defense systems and equipment

(P-7718)
ENSIGN-BICKFORD AROSPC DEF CO
14370 White Sage Rd, Moorpark
(93021-8720)
P.O. Box 429 (93020-0429)
PHONE.............................805 292-4000
Brendan Walsh, *General Vice President*
EMP: 119
SALES (corp-wide): 696.33MM **Privately Held**
Web: www.ensign-bickfordind.com
SIC: **3812** Search and navigation equipment

HQ: Ensign-Bickford Aerospace & Defense
Co
640 Hopmeadow St
Simsbury CT 06070
860 843-2289

(P-7719)
FIRAN TECH GROUP USA CORP (HQ)
20750 Marilla St, Chatsworth (91311-4407)
PHONE.............................818 407-4024
Brad Bourne, *Pr*
EMP: 65 EST: 2004
SALES (est): 98.57MM
SALES (corp-wide): 98.06MM **Privately Held**
Web: www.ftgcorp.com
SIC: **3812** Aircraft control systems, electronic
PA: Firan Technology Group Corporation
250 Finchdene Sq
416 299-4000

(P-7720)
GARMIN INTERNATIONAL INC
135 S State College Blvd Ste 110, Brea
(92821-5819)
PHONE.............................909 444-5000
EMP: 491
Web: www.garmin.com
SIC: **3812** Navigational systems and
instruments
HQ: Garmin International, Inc.
1200 E 151st St
Olathe KS 66062

(P-7721)
GENERAL FORMING CORPORATION
640 Alaska Ave, Torrance (90503-5100)
PHONE.............................310 326-0624
Ward Olson, *CEO*
EMP: 43 EST: 1956
SALES (est): 3.66MM **Privately Held**
Web: www.generalformingcorporation.com
SIC: **3812** 3769 3444 3728 Search and
navigation equipment; Space vehicle
equipment, nec; Sheet metal specialties,
not stamped; Aircraft parts and equipment,
nec

(P-7722)
GLOBAL A LGISTICS TRAINING INC
Also Called: Galt
3860 Calle Fortunada Ste 100, San Diego
(92123-4802)
PHONE.............................760 688-0365
John Kohut, *CEO*
Lili Topchev, *CFO*
David Helsi, *CSO*
Mark Kempf, *COO*
EMP: 47 EST: 2015
SQ FT: 18,000
SALES (est): 22.43MM **Privately Held**
Web: www.galt.aero
SIC: **3812** 3721 3728 8711 Aircraft/
aerospace flight instruments and guidance
systems; Research and development on
aircraft by the manufacturer; Military aircraft
equipment and armament; Engineering
services

(P-7723)
GOLDAK INC
15835 Monte St Ste 104, Sylmar
(91342-7674)
P.O. Box 1988 (91209-1988)
PHONE.............................818 240-2666
Dan Mulcahey, *Pr*

Dan Mulcahey, *Pr*
Butch Mulcahey, *
Thomas Mulcahey, *
Jeanie Mulcahey, *
EMP: 25 EST: 1970
SQ FT: 3,000
SALES (est): 2.29MM **Privately Held**
Web: www.goldak.com
SIC: **3812** Detection apparatus: electronic/
magnetic field, light/heat

(P-7724)
INTELLISENSE SYSTEMS INC
21041 S Western Ave, Torrance
(90501-1727)
PHONE.............................310 320-1827
Robert Waldo, *CEO*
Robert Waldo, *Pr*
Selvy Utama, *VP*
EMP: 146 EST: 2017
SQ FT: 43,000
SALES (est): 62.11MM **Privately Held**
Web: www.intellisenseinc.com
SIC: **3812** Search and navigation equipment

(P-7725)
INTEROCEAN INDUSTRIES INC
Also Called: Interocean Systems
9201 Isaac St Ste C, Santee (92071-5627)
PHONE.............................858 292-0808
Michael Pearlman, *CEO*
Stephen Pearlman, *
▼ EMP: 31 EST: 1945
SALES (est): 4.48MM **Privately Held**
Web: www.interoceansystems.com
SIC: **3812** 3699 3826 3531 Search and
navigation equipment; Underwater sound
equipment; Environmental testing
equipment; Marine related equipment

(P-7726)
INTEROCEAN SYSTEMS LLC
9201 Isaac St Ste C, Santee (92071-5627)
PHONE.............................858 565-8400
Michael D Pearlman, *Pr*
EMP: 35 EST: 2005
SALES (est): 3.94MM
SALES (corp-wide): 19.66MM **Privately Held**
Web: www.interoceansystems.com
SIC: **3812** 3699 Search and navigation
equipment; Underwater sound equipment
PA: Delmar Systems, Inc.
8114 Highway 90 E
337 365-0180

(P-7727)
JARIET TECHNOLOGIES INC
103 W Torrance Blvd, Redondo Beach
(90277-3633)
PHONE.............................310 698-1000
Charles Harper, *CEO*
David Clark, *
Monica Gilbert, *
Matthew Hoppe, *
Craig Hornbuckle, *
EMP: 35 EST: 2015
SQ FT: 20,000
SALES (est): 12.51MM **Privately Held**
Web: www.jariettech.com
SIC: **3812** Search and navigation equipment

(P-7728)
L3 TECHNOLOGIES INC
901 E Ball Rd, Anaheim (92805-5916)
PHONE.............................714 956-9200
EMP: 30
SALES (corp-wide): 19.42B **Publicly Held**
Web: www.l3harris.com

SIC: **3812** Search and navigation equipment
HQ: L3 Technologies, Inc.
600 3rd Ave Fl 34
New York NY 10016
321 727-9100

(P-7729)
L3 TECHNOLOGIES INC
Also Called: Photonics Division
5957 Landau Ct, Carlsbad (92008-8803)
PHONE.............................760 431-6800
Tim Call, *VP*
EMP: 131
SALES (corp-wide): 19.42B **Publicly Held**
Web: www.l3harris.com
SIC: **3812** Search and navigation equipment
HQ: L3 Technologies, Inc.
600 3rd Ave Fl 34
New York NY 10016
321 727-9100

(P-7730)
L3 TECHNOLOGIES INC
Datron Advanced Tech Div
200 W Los Angeles Ave, Simi Valley
(93065-1650)
PHONE.............................805 584-1717
John Digioia, *Brnch Mgr*
EMP: 100
SALES (corp-wide): 19.42B **Publicly Held**
Web: www.l3harris.com
SIC: **3812** Search and navigation equipment
HQ: L3 Technologies, Inc.
600 3rd Ave Fl 34
New York NY 10016
321 727-9100

(P-7731)
L3 TECHNOLOGIES INC
Ocean Systems Division
28022 Industry Dr, Valencia (91355-4191)
PHONE.............................818 367-0111
David Defranco, *Brnch Mgr*
EMP: 200
SALES (corp-wide): 19.42B **Publicly Held**
Web: www.l3harris.com
SIC: **3812** Search and navigation equipment
HQ: L3 Technologies, Inc.
600 3rd Ave Fl 34
New York NY 10016
321 727-9100

(P-7732)
L3HARRIS TECHNOLOGIES INC
Also Called: Harris
7821 Orion Ave, Van Nuys (91406-2029)
P.O. Box 7713 (91409-7713)
PHONE.............................818 901-2523
EMP: 350
SALES (corp-wide): 19.42B **Publicly Held**
Web: www.l3harris.com
SIC: **3812** Search and navigation equipment
PA: L3harris Technologies, Inc.
1025 W Nasa Blvd
321 727-9100

(P-7733)
L3HARRIS TECHNOLOGIES INC
Also Called: Harris
12121 Wilshire Blvd Ste 910, Los Angeles
(90025-1166)
PHONE.............................310 481-6000
EMP: 42
SALES (corp-wide): 19.42B **Publicly Held**
Web: www.l3harris.com
SIC: **3812** 7371 Search and navigation
equipment; Computer software development
PA: L3harris Technologies, Inc.
1025 W Nasa Blvd
321 727-9100

(P-7734)
L3HARRIS TECHNOLOGIES INC
1400 S Shamrock Ave, Monrovia
(91016-4267)
PHONE..................626 305-6230
Pat Carr, *Brnch Mgr*
EMP: 134
SALES (corp-wide): 19.42B **Publicly Held**
Web: www.l3harris.com
SIC: 3812 Search and navigation equipment
PA: L3harris Technologies, Inc.
1025 W Nasa Blvd
321 727-9100

(P-7735)
LAIRD R & F PRODUCTS INC (DH)
2091 Rutherford Rd, Carlsbad
(92008-7316)
PHONE..................760 916-9410
Scott Griffiths, *Pr*
▲ **EMP:** 49 **EST:** 1996
SQ FT: 62,000
SALES (est): 21.48MM
SALES (corp-wide): 2.93B **Publicly Held**
SIC: 3812 Radar systems and equipment
HQ: Laird Technologies, Inc.
16401 Swingley Ridge Rd
Chesterfield MO 63017
636 898-6000

(P-7736)
LOCKHEED MARTIN CORPORATION
Santa Barbara Focal Plane
346 Bollay Dr, Goleta (93117-5550)
PHONE..................805 571-2346
Bryan Butler, *Mgr*
EMP: 25
SQ FT: 8,500
Web: www.lockheedmartin.com
SIC: 3812 Search and navigation equipment
PA: Lockheed Martin Corporation
6801 Rockledge Dr

(P-7737)
LOCKHEED MARTIN CORPORATION
Also Called: Lockheed Martin
Nas North Island, Coronado (92118)
PHONE..................619 437-7230
EMP: 232
Web: www.lockheedmartin.com
SIC: 3812 Search and navigation equipment
PA: Lockheed Martin Corporation
6801 Rockledge Dr

(P-7738)
LOCKHEED MARTIN CORPORATION
Also Called: Helendale Lckheed Plant Prtcti
17452 Wheeler Rd, Helendale
(92342-9677)
PHONE..................760 952-4200
EMP: 51
Web: www.lockheedmartin.com
SIC: 3812 Search and navigation equipment
PA: Lockheed Martin Corporation
6801 Rockledge Dr

(P-7739)
LOCKHEED MARTIN CORPORATION
Also Called: Lockheed Martin Aeronautics Co
1011 Lockheed Way, Palmdale
(93599-0001)
PHONE..................661 572-7428
Rick Baker, *VP*

EMP: 4000
Web: www.lockheedmartin.com
SIC: 3812 Search and navigation equipment
PA: Lockheed Martin Corporation
6801 Rockledge Dr

(P-7740)
LOCKHEED MARTIN ORINCON CORP (HQ)
10325 Meanley Dr, San Diego
(92131-3011)
PHONE..................858 455-5530
Daniel Alspach, *Ch Bd*
EMP: 200 **EST:** 1973
SQ FT: 41,000
SALES (est): 12.35MM **Publicly Held**
SIC: 3812 Search and navigation equipment
PA: Lockheed Martin Corporation
6801 Rockledge Dr

(P-7741)
LYTX INC (PA)
9785 Towne Centre Dr, San Diego
(92121-1968)
PHONE..................858 430-4000
Brandon Nixon, *CEO*
Paul J Pucino, *CFO*
Tom Fisher, *VP*
Drew Martin, *Ex VP*
David Riordan, *Ex VP*
EMP: 300 **EST:** 1998
SQ FT: 100,000
SALES (est): 123.43MM
SALES (corp-wide): 123.43MM **Privately Held**
Web: www.lytx.com
SIC: 3812 Search and detection systems and instruments

(P-7742)
MAPQUEST HOLDINGS LLC
4235 Redwood Ave, Los Angeles
(90066-5605)
PHONE..................310 256-4882
Michael Blend, *CEO*
EMP: 400 **EST:** 2019
SALES (est): 1.32MM
SALES (corp-wide): 401.97MM **Publicly Held**
Web: www.mapquest.com
SIC: 3812 Navigational systems and instruments
PA: System1, Inc.
4235 Redwood Ave
310 924-6037

(P-7743)
MOOG INC
21339 Nordhoff St, Chatsworth
(91311-5819)
PHONE..................818 341-5156
Ruben Nalbandian, *Sls Mgr*
EMP: 150
SALES (corp-wide): 3.32B **Publicly Held**
Web: www.moog.com
SIC: 3812 Aircraft control systems, electronic
PA: Moog Inc.
400 Jamison Rd
716 652-2000

(P-7744)
MOOG INC
Also Called: Moog Aircraft Group
20263 S Western Ave, Torrance
(90501-1310)
PHONE..................310 533-1178
Alberto Bilalon, *Mgr*
EMP: 450
SALES (corp-wide): 3.32B **Publicly Held**
Web: www.moog.com

SIC: 3812 Search and navigation equipment
PA: Moog Inc.
400 Jamison Rd
716 652-2000

(P-7745)
MOOG INC
7406 Hollister Ave, Goleta (93117-2583)
PHONE..................805 618-3900
Robert W Urban, *Genl Mgr*
EMP: 300
SALES (corp-wide): 3.32B **Publicly Held**
Web: www.moog.com
SIC: 3812 3492 3625 3769 Aircraft control systems, electronic; Electrohydraulic servo valves, metal; Relays and industrial controls ; Space vehicle equipment, nec
PA: Moog Inc.
400 Jamison Rd
716 652-2000

(P-7746)
MTI DE BAJA INC
915 Industrial Way, San Jacinto
(92582-3890)
PHONE..................951 654-2333
Monty Merkin, *CEO*
EMP: 24 **EST:** 2009
SALES (est): 999.25K **Privately Held**
Web: www.mtibaja.com
SIC: 3812 Acceleration indicators and systems components, aerospace

(P-7747)
NIGHTHAWK FLIGHT SYSTEMS INC
1370 Decision St Ste D, Vista (92081-8551)
PHONE..................760 727-4900
Paul Martin, *CEO*
Richard Lanning, *
EMP: 25 **EST:** 2022
SALES (est): 3.94MM **Privately Held**
Web: www.nighthawkfs.com
SIC: 3812 Navigational systems and instruments

(P-7748)
NORTHROP GRMMAN INNVTION SYSTE
Also Called: Ca75 Atk
9617 Distribution Ave, San Diego
(92121-2307)
PHONE..................858 621-5700
David W Thompson, *Pr*
EMP: 300
Web: www.northropgrumman.com
SIC: 3812 Search and navigation equipment
HQ: Northrop Grumman Innovation Systems, Inc.
2980 Fairview Park Dr
Falls Church VA 22042

(P-7749)
NORTHROP GRMMAN INNVTION SYSTE
9401 Corbin Ave, Northridge (91324-2400)
PHONE..................818 887-8100
EMP: 100
Web: www.northropgrumman.com
SIC: 3812 Search and navigation equipment
HQ: Northrop Grumman Innovation Systems, Inc.
2980 Fairview Park Dr
Falls Church VA 22042

(P-7750)
NORTHROP GRUMMAN CORPORATION
500 N Douglas St, El Segundo (90245)

PHONE..................310 332-0461
EMP: 54 **EST:** 2011
SALES (est): 6.38MM **Privately Held**
Web: www.northropgrumman.com
SIC: 3812 Search and navigation equipment

(P-7751)
NORTHROP GRUMMAN CORPORATION
Northrop Grumman Aviation
1 Hornet Way, El Segundo (90245-2804)
PHONE..................310 332-1000
Ray Pollok, *Mgr*
EMP: 200
Web: www.northropgrumman.com
SIC: 3812 Search and navigation equipment
PA: Northrop Grumman Corporation
2980 Fairview Park Dr

(P-7752)
NORTHROP GRUMMAN CORPORATION
Also Called: Northrop Grmman Arospc Systems
3520 E Avenue M, Palmdale (93550-7401)
PHONE..................661 272-7334
EMP: 44
Web: www.northropgrumman.com
SIC: 3812 Search and navigation equipment
PA: Northrop Grumman Corporation
2980 Fairview Park Dr

(P-7753)
NORTHROP GRUMMAN CORPORATION
19782 Macarthur Blvd, Irvine (92612-2452)
PHONE..................949 260-9800
Jeffrey Smith, *Mgr*
EMP: 46
Web: www.northropgrumman.com
SIC: 3812 Search and navigation equipment
PA: Northrop Grumman Corporation
2980 Fairview Park Dr

(P-7754)
NORTHROP GRUMMAN CORPORATION
18701 Caminito Pasadero, San Diego
(92128-6162)
PHONE..................858 967-1221
Dagnall Barry, *Brnch Mgr*
EMP: 735
Web: www.northropgrumman.com
SIC: 3812 Search and detection systems and instruments
PA: Northrop Grumman Corporation
2980 Fairview Park Dr

(P-7755)
NORTHROP GRUMMAN CORPORATION
198 Willow Grove Pl, Escondido
(92027-5348)
PHONE..................310 864-7342
EMP: 37
Web: www.northropgrumman.com
SIC: 3812 Search and navigation equipment
PA: Northrop Grumman Corporation
2980 Fairview Park Dr

(P-7756)
NORTHROP GRUMMAN SYSTEMS CORP
9326 Spectrum Center Blvd, San Diego
(92123-1443)
PHONE..................858 514-9020
EMP: 92
Web: www.northropgrumman.com

SIC: **3812** Search and navigation equipment
HQ: Northrop Grumman Systems
Corporation
2980 Fairview Park Dr
Falls Church VA 22042
703 280-2900

(P-7757)
NORTHROP GRUMMAN
SYSTEMS CORP

7130 Miramar Rd Ste 100b, San Diego
(92121-2340)
PHONE.................................858 621-7395
EMP: 92
Web: www.northropgrumman.com
SIC: **3812** Aircraft/aerospace flight
instruments and guidance systems
HQ: Northrop Grumman Systems
Corporation
2980 Fairview Park Dr
Falls Church VA 22042
703 280-2900

(P-7758)
NORTHROP GRUMMAN
SYSTEMS CORP

Also Called: Northrop Grumman Space
9326 Spectrum Center Blvd, San Diego
(92123-1443)
PHONE.................................858 514-9000
Mike Twyman, *Brnch Mgr*
EMP: 92
Web: www.northropgrumman.com
SIC: **3812** Search and navigation equipment
HQ: Northrop Grumman Systems
Corporation
2980 Fairview Park Dr
Falls Church VA 22042
703 280-2900

(P-7759)
NORTHROP GRUMMAN
SYSTEMS CORP

2601 Camino Del Sol, Oxnard
(93030-7996)
PHONE.................................805 684-6641
Kathy Warden, *CEO*
Richard Nelson, *
Alice Reed, *
EMP: 110 **EST**: 1999
SQ FT: 70,000
SALES (est): 35.8MM **Publicly Held**
Web: www.northropgrumman.com
SIC: **3812** Search and navigation equipment
HQ: Northrop Grumman Systems
Corporation
2980 Fairview Park Dr
Falls Church VA 22042
703 280-2900

(P-7760)
NORTHROP GRUMMAN
SYSTEMS CORP

Building 806, Fort Irwin (92310)
PHONE.................................760 380-4268
EMP: 73
Web: www.northropgrumman.com
SIC: **3812** Search and navigation equipment
HQ: Northrop Grumman Systems
Corporation
2980 Fairview Park Dr
Falls Church VA 22042
703 280-2900

(P-7761)
NORTHROP GRUMMAN
SYSTEMS CORP

Also Called: Technical Services
862 E Hospitality Ln, San Bernardino
(92408-3530)

PHONE.................................703 713-4096
Ben Overall, *Mgr*
EMP: 55
Web: www.northropgrumman.com
SIC: **3812** Search and navigation equipment
HQ: Northrop Grumman Systems
Corporation
2980 Fairview Park Dr
Falls Church VA 22042
703 280-2900

(P-7762)
NORTHROP GRUMMAN
SYSTEMS CORP

600 Pine Ave, Goleta (93117-3803)
PHONE.................................714 240-6521
EMP: 92
Web: www.northropgrumman.com
SIC: **3812** Aircraft/aerospace flight
instruments and guidance systems
HQ: Northrop Grumman Systems
Corporation
2980 Fairview Park Dr
Falls Church VA 22042
703 280-2900

(P-7763)
NORTHROP GRUMMAN
SYSTEMS CORP

Strategic Deterrent Systems
1467 Fairway Dr, Santa Maria
(93455-1404)
PHONE.................................805 315-5728
EMP: 55
Web: www.northropgrumman.com
SIC: **3812** Search and navigation equipment
HQ: Northrop Grumman Systems
Corporation
2980 Fairview Park Dr
Falls Church VA 22042
703 280-2900

(P-7764)
NORTHROP GRUMMAN
SYSTEMS CORP

2700 Camino Del Sol, Oxnard
(93030-7967)
PHONE.................................805 278-2074
Pierre Courduroux, *Brnch Mgr*
EMP: 73
Web: www.northropgrumman.com
SIC: **3812** Aircraft/aerospace flight
instruments and guidance systems
HQ: Northrop Grumman Systems
Corporation
2980 Fairview Park Dr
Falls Church VA 22042
703 280-2900

(P-7765)
NORTHROP GRUMMAN
SYSTEMS CORP

760 Paseo Camarillo Ste 200, Camarillo
(93010-6002)
PHONE.................................805 987-8831
Steve Crans, *Mgr*
EMP: 170
Web: www.northropgrumman.com
SIC: **3812** Search and navigation equipment
HQ: Northrop Grumman Systems
Corporation
2980 Fairview Park Dr
Falls Church VA 22042
703 280-2900

(P-7766)
NORTHROP GRUMMAN
SYSTEMS CORP

5161 Verdugo Way, Camarillo
(93012-8603)

PHONE.................................805 987-9739
Jim Lueck, *Brnch Mgr*
EMP: 55
Web: www.northropgrumman.com
SIC: **3812** 8731 8711 7371 Search and
navigation equipment; Commercial physical
research; Engineering services; Custom
computer programming services
HQ: Northrop Grumman Systems
Corporation
2980 Fairview Park Dr
Falls Church VA 22042
703 280-2900

(P-7767)
NORTHROP GRUMMAN
SYSTEMS CORP

6411 W Imperial Hwy, Los Angeles
(90045-6307)
PHONE.................................310 556-4911
Shea Mark, *Prin*
EMP: 303
Web: www.northropgrumman.com
SIC: **3812** Search and navigation equipment
HQ: Northrop Grumman Systems
Corporation
2980 Fairview Park Dr
Falls Church VA 22042
703 280-2900

(P-7768)
NORTHROP GRUMMAN
SYSTEMS CORP

Litton Navigation Systems Div
21240 Burbank Blvd Ms 29, Woodland Hills
(91367-6680)
PHONE.................................818 715-4040
Bill Allison, *Div Pres*
EMP: 1000
Web: www.northropgrumman.com
SIC: **3812** Search and navigation equipment
HQ: Northrop Grumman Systems
Corporation
2980 Fairview Park Dr
Falls Church VA 22042
703 280-2900

(P-7769)
NORTHROP GRUMMAN
SYSTEMS CORP

Also Called: Northrop Grumman CMS
21240 Burbank Blvd, Woodland Hills
(91367-6680)
PHONE.................................818 715-4854
Roy Medland, *Brnch Mgr*
EMP: 386
Web: www.northropgrumman.com
SIC: **3812** Search and navigation equipment
HQ: Northrop Grumman Systems
Corporation
2980 Fairview Park Dr
Falls Church VA 22042
703 280-2900

(P-7770)
NORTHROP GRUMMAN
SYSTEMS CORP

California Microwave Systems
21200 Burbank Blvd, Woodland Hills
(91367-6675)
PHONE.................................818 715-2597
Roy Medlin, *Brnch Mgr*
EMP: 239
Web: www.northropgrumman.com
SIC: **3812** Search and navigation equipment
HQ: Northrop Grumman Systems
Corporation
2980 Fairview Park Dr
Falls Church VA 22042
703 280-2900

(P-7771)
NORTHROP GRUMMAN
SYSTEMS CORP

Also Called: Weapons System Division
9401 Corbin Ave, Northridge (91324-2400)
PHONE.................................818 887-8110
Richard Nolan, *Brnch Mgr*
EMP: 441
Web: www.northropgrumman.com
SIC: **3812** Search and navigation equipment
HQ: Northrop Grumman Systems
Corporation
2980 Fairview Park Dr
Falls Church VA 22042
703 280-2900

(P-7772)
NORTHROP GRUMMAN
SYSTEMS CORP

6033 Bandini Blvd, Commerce
(90040-2968)
PHONE.................................714 240-6521
EMP: 202
Web: www.northropgrumman.com
SIC: **3812** Aircraft/aerospace flight
instruments and guidance systems
HQ: Northrop Grumman Systems
Corporation
2980 Fairview Park Dr
Falls Church VA 22042
703 280-2900

(P-7773)
NORTHROP GRUMMAN
SYSTEMS CORP

400 Continental Blvd, El Segundo
(90245-5076)
PHONE.................................480 355-7716
EMP: 73
Web: www.northropgrumman.com
SIC: **3812** Aircraft/aerospace flight
instruments and guidance systems
HQ: Northrop Grumman Systems
Corporation
2980 Fairview Park Dr
Falls Church VA 22042
703 280-2900

(P-7774)
NORTHROP GRUMMAN
SYSTEMS CORP

2550 Honolulu Ave, Montrose
(91020-1858)
PHONE.................................818 249-5252
Arthur F Brown, *Mgr*
EMP: 92
Web: www.northropgrumman.com
SIC: **3812** Search and navigation equipment
HQ: Northrop Grumman Systems
Corporation
2980 Fairview Park Dr
Falls Church VA 22042
703 280-2900

(P-7775)
NORTHROP GRUMMAN
SYSTEMS CORP

Also Called: Northrop Grmman Elctrnic Syste
1100 W Hollyvale St, Azusa (91702-3305)
P.O. Box 296 (91702-0296)
PHONE.................................626 812-1000
Carl Fischer, *Mgr*
EMP: 4866
Web: www.northropgrumman.com
SIC: **3812** Search and navigation equipment
HQ: Northrop Grumman Systems
Corporation
2980 Fairview Park Dr
Falls Church VA 22042
703 280-2900

(P-7776)
NORTHROP GRUMMAN SYSTEMS CORP
Western Region
3520 E Avenue M, Palmdale (93550-7401)
PHONE..............................661 540-0446
Jim Pace, *Brnch Mgr*
EMP: 73
Web: www.northropgrumman.com
SIC: 3812 Search and navigation equipment
HQ: Northrop Grumman Systems
  Corporation
  2980 Fairview Park Dr
  Falls Church VA 22042
  703 280-2900

(P-7777)
NORTHROP GRUMMAN SYSTEMS CORP
Defense Systems Sector
1 Space Park Blvd, Redondo Beach
(90278-1071)
PHONE..............................855 737-8364
Jack Distaso, *Brnch Mgr*
EMP: 140
SQ FT: 500,000
Web: www.northropgrumman.com
SIC: 3812 Search and navigation equipment
HQ: Northrop Grumman Systems
  Corporation
  2980 Fairview Park Dr
  Falls Church VA 22042
  703 280-2900

(P-7778)
NORTHROP GRUMMAN SYSTEMS CORP
2477 Manhattan Beach Blvd, Redondo
Beach (90278-1544)
PHONE..............................310 812-4321
Bruce R Gerding, *VP*
EMP: 73
Web: www.northropgrumman.com
SIC: 3812 Search and navigation equipment
HQ: Northrop Grumman Systems
  Corporation
  2980 Fairview Park Dr
  Falls Church VA 22042
  703 280-2900

(P-7779)
NORTHROP GRUMMAN SYSTEMS CORP
1111 W 3rd St, Azusa (91702-3328)
PHONE..............................626 812-1464
Michael Clayton, *Mgr*
EMP: 790
Web: www.northropgrumman.com
SIC: 3812 Search and navigation equipment
HQ: Northrop Grumman Systems
  Corporation
  2980 Fairview Park Dr
  Falls Church VA 22042
  703 280-2900

(P-7780)
NORTHROP GRUMMAN SYSTEMS CORP
1 Hornet Way, El Segundo (90245-2804)
PHONE..............................310 332-1000
Kevin Witherell, *Prin*
EMP: 514
Web: www.northropgrumman.com
SIC: 3812 Search and navigation equipment
HQ: Northrop Grumman Systems
  Corporation
  2980 Fairview Park Dr
  Falls Church VA 22042
  703 280-2900

(P-7781)
NORTHROP GRUMMAN SYSTEMS CORP
Also Called: Northrop Grmman Def Mssion Sys
9326 Spectrum Center Blvd, San Diego
(92123-1443)
PHONE..............................410 765-5589
Steve Appel, *Brnch Mgr*
EMP: 2883
Web: www.northropgrumman.com
SIC: 3812 7379 Search and navigation
  equipment; Computer related consulting
  services
HQ: Northrop Grumman Systems
  Corporation
  2980 Fairview Park Dr
  Falls Church VA 22042
  703 280-2900

(P-7782)
NORTHROP GRUMMAN SYSTEMS CORP
15120 Innovation Dr, San Diego
(92128-3402)
PHONE..............................858 592-4518
Chris Willenborg, *Brnch Mgr*
EMP: 477
SQ FT: 211,000
Web: www.northropgrumman.com
SIC: 3812 8711 7373 Search and navigation
  equipment; Engineering services;
  Computer integrated systems design
HQ: Northrop Grumman Systems
  Corporation
  2980 Fairview Park Dr
  Falls Church VA 22042
  703 280-2900

(P-7783)
NORTHROP GRUMMAN SYSTEMS CORP
17066 Goldentop Rd, San Diego
(92127-2412)
PHONE..............................858 618-4349
Gerald Dufresne, *Mgr*
EMP: 294
Web: www.northropgrumman.com
SIC: 3812 3761 7373 3721 Search and
  detection systems and instruments; Guided
  missiles, complete; Computer integrated
  systems design; Airplanes, fixed or rotary
  wing
HQ: Northrop Grumman Systems
  Corporation
  2980 Fairview Park Dr
  Falls Church VA 22042
  703 280-2900

(P-7784)
ONE STEP GPS LLC
675 Glenoaks Blvd Unit C, San Fernando
(91340-4803)
PHONE..............................818 659-2031
Kevin Kenneth Dale, *
EMP: 52 **EST:** 2017
SALES (est): 5.44MM **Privately Held**
Web: www.onestepgps.com
SIC: 3812 Search and navigation equipment

(P-7785)
ORBITAL SCIENCES LLC
1151 W Reeves Ave, Ridgecrest
(93555-2313)
PHONE..............................818 887-8345
David Rocca, *Brnch Mgr*
EMP: 230
Web: www.orbitalsciencesllc.com

SIC: 3812 Search and navigation equipment
HQ: Orbital Sciences Llc
  2980 Fairview Park Dr
  Falls Church VA 22042
  703 552-8203

(P-7786)
ORBITAL SCIENCES LLC
Also Called: Space Systems Division
2401 E El Segundo Blvd Ste 200, El
Segundo (90245-4656)
PHONE..............................703 406-5000
Antonio Elias, *Ex VP*
EMP: 230
Web: www.orbitalsciencesllc.com
SIC: 3812 Search and navigation equipment
HQ: Orbital Sciences Llc
  2980 Fairview Park Dr
  Falls Church VA 22042
  703 552-8203

(P-7787)
ORBITAL SCIENCES LLC
Talo Rd Bldg 1555, Lompoc (93437)
P.O. Box 5159 (93437-0159)
PHONE..............................805 734-5400
Eric Denbrook, *Mgr*
EMP: 421
Web: www.orbitalsciencesllc.com
SIC: 3812 Search and navigation equipment
HQ: Orbital Sciences Llc
  2980 Fairview Park Dr
  Falls Church VA 22042
  703 552-8203

(P-7788)
ORBITAL SCIENCES LLC
16707 Via Del Campo Ct, San Diego
(92127-1713)
PHONE..............................858 618-1847
Brian Welge, *Brnch Mgr*
EMP: 230
Web: www.orbitalsciencesllc.com
SIC: 3812 Search and navigation equipment
HQ: Orbital Sciences Llc
  2980 Fairview Park Dr
  Falls Church VA 22042
  703 552-8203

(P-7789)
PACIFIC DEFENSE STRATEGIES INC (PA)
Also Called: Pacific Defense
400 Continental Blvd Ste 100, El Segundo
(90245-5062)
PHONE..............................310 722-6050
Travis Slocumb, *CEO*
Scott Hoffman, *CFO*
Kent Mader, *COO*
EMP: 33 **EST:** 2020
SALES (est): 61MM
SALES (corp-wide): 61MM **Privately Held**
Web: www.pacific-defense.com
SIC: 3812 3731 Defense systems and
  equipment; Military ships, building and
  repairing

(P-7790)
PACIFIC SCIENTIFIC COMPANY (DH)
Also Called: Electro Kinetics Division
1785 Voyager Ave, Simi Valley
(93063-3363)
PHONE..............................805 526-5700
James Simpkins, *Prin*
David Penner, *
James Healey, *
◆ **EMP:** 23 **EST:** 1998
SALES (est): 68.11MM
SALES (corp-wide): 19.93B **Publicly Held**

Web: www.hachultra.com
SIC: 3812 3669 3621 3694 Aircraft control
  systems, electronic; Fire detection systems,
  electric; Generators and sets, electric;
  Alternators, automotive
HQ: Meggitt-Usa, Inc.
  1955 Surveyor Ave
  Simi Valley CA 93063
  805 526-5700

(P-7791)
PNEUDRAULICS INC
8575 Helms Ave, Rancho Cucamonga
(91730-4591)
PHONE..............................909 980-5366
Michael Saville, *CEO*
Dain Miller, *
▼ **EMP:** 275 **EST:** 1956
SQ FT: 48,000
SALES (est): 25.53MM
SALES (corp-wide): 7.94B **Publicly Held**
Web: www.pneudraulics.com
SIC: 3812 Acceleration indicators and
  systems components, aerospace
PA: Transdigm Group Incorporated
  1350 Euclid Ave Ste 1600
  216 706-2960

(P-7792)
RANTEC MICROWAVE SYSTEMS INC (PA)
31186 La Baya Dr, Westlake Village
(91362-4003)
PHONE..............................818 223-5000
Carl Grindle, *CEO*
Carl E Grindle, *
Graham R Wilson, *
Steven B Chegwin, *
Steven Chegwin, *
EMP: 55 **EST:** 2000
SQ FT: 35,000
SALES (est): 12.58MM
SALES (corp-wide): 12.58MM **Privately Held**
Web: www.rantecantennas.com
SIC: 3812 Antennas, radar or
  communications

(P-7793)
RAYTHEON COMPANY
Also Called: Raytheon
8650 Balboa Ave, San Diego (92123-1502)
PHONE..............................858 571-6598
EMP: 54
SALES (corp-wide): 68.92B **Publicly Held**
Web: www.rtx.com
SIC: 3812 Sonar systems and equipment
HQ: Raytheon Company
  870 Winter St
  Waltham MA 02451
  781 522-3000

(P-7794)
RAYTHEON COMPANY
Also Called: Raytheon
2000 E El Segundo Blvd, El Segundo
(90245-4501)
PHONE..............................310 647-1000
John Jones, *Mgr*
EMP: 500
SALES (corp-wide): 68.92B **Publicly Held**
Web: www.rtx.com
SIC: 3812 Defense systems and equipment
HQ: Raytheon Company
  870 Winter St
  Waltham MA 02451
  781 522-3000

(P-7795)
RAYTHEON COMPANY
Also Called: Raytheon
2000 E El Segundo Blvd, El Segundo
(90245-4501)
P.O. Box 925 (90245-0925)
PHONE..............................310 647-9438
EMP: 50
SALES (corp-wide): 68.92B **Publicly Held**
Web: www.rtx.com
SIC: **3812** Aircraft/aerospace flight
instruments and guidance systems
HQ: Raytheon Company
870 Winter St
Waltham MA 02451
781 522-3000

(P-7796)
RAYTHEON COMPANY
Also Called: Raytheon
2000 E El Segundo Blvd, El Segundo
(90245-4501)
P.O. Box 902 (90245-0902)
PHONE..............................310 647-9438
Rick Yuse, *Brnch Mgr*
EMP: 10000
SALES (corp-wide): 68.92B **Publicly Held**
Web: www.rtx.com
SIC: **3812** Defense systems and equipment
HQ: Raytheon Company
870 Winter St
Waltham MA 02451
781 522-3000

(P-7797)
RAYTHEON COMPANY
Also Called: Raytheon
75 Coromar Dr, Goleta (93117-3023)
PHONE..............................805 562-4611
Mike E Allgeier, *Brnch Mgr*
EMP: 171
SALES (corp-wide): 68.92B **Publicly Held**
Web: www.rtx.com
SIC: **3812** 8731 3845 3825 Sonar systems
and equipment; Commercial research
laboratory; Electromedical equipment;
Instruments to measure electricity
HQ: Raytheon Company
870 Winter St
Waltham MA 02451
781 522-3000

(P-7798)
RAYTHEON COMPANY
Also Called: Raytheon
1921 E Mariposa Ave, El Segundo
(90245-3445)
PHONE..............................310 647-1000
David Wajsgras, *Brnch Mgr*
EMP: 100
SALES (corp-wide): 68.92B **Publicly Held**
Web: www.rtx.com
SIC: **3812** 4899 Sonar systems and
equipment; Satellite earth stations
HQ: Raytheon Company
870 Winter St
Waltham MA 02451
781 522-3000

(P-7799)
RAYTHEON COMPANY
Raytheon
1801 Hughes Dr, Fullerton (92833-2200)
P.O. Box 3310 (92834-3310)
PHONE..............................714 732-0119
EMP: 89
SALES (corp-wide): 68.92B **Publicly Held**
Web: www.rtx.com

SIC: **3812** 7371 Sonar systems and
equipment; Computer software
development and applications
HQ: Raytheon Company
870 Winter St
Waltham MA 02451
781 522-3000

(P-7800)
**RAYTHEON DGITAL FORCE
TECH LLC (DH)**
Also Called: Digital Force Technologies
6779 Mesa Ridge Rd Ste 150, San Diego
(92121-2932)
PHONE..............................858 546-1244
EMP: 38 EST: 2000
SQ FT: 14,500
SALES (est): 11.85MM
SALES (corp-wide): 68.92B **Publicly Held**
Web: www.digitalforcetech.com
SIC: **3812** 8711 Defense systems and
equipment; Engineering services
HQ: Raytheon Bbn Technologies Corp.
10 Moulton St
Cambridge MA 02138
617 873-8000

(P-7801)
REMEC DEFENSE & SPACE INC
Also Called: Cobham
9404 Chesapeake Dr, San Diego
(92123-1388)
PHONE..............................858 560-1301
EMP: 1000
Web: www.caes.com
SIC: **3812** Search and navigation equipment

(P-7802)
ROCKWELL COLLINS INC
1733 Alton Pkwy, Irvine (92606-4901)
PHONE..............................714 929-3000
EMP: 51
SALES (corp-wide): 68.92B **Publicly Held**
Web: www.rtx.com
SIC: **3812** Search and navigation equipment
HQ: Rockwell Collins, Inc.
400 Collins Rd Ne
Cedar Rapids IA 52498

(P-7803)
ROCKWELL COLLINS INC
1733 Alton Pkwy, Irvine (92606-4901)
PHONE..............................714 929-3000
EMP: 26
SALES (corp-wide): 68.92B **Publicly Held**
Web: www.rockwellcollins.com
SIC: **3812** Search and navigation equipment
HQ: Rockwell Collins, Inc.
400 Collins Rd Ne
Cedar Rapids IA 52498

(P-7804)
**ROGERSON AIRCRAFT
CORPORATION (PA)**
16940 Von Karman Ave, Irvine
(92606-4923)
PHONE..............................949 660-0666
Michael J Rogerson, *Pr*
Milton R Pizinger, *
Jonathan C Smith, *
EMP: 80 EST: 1975
SALES (est): 24.72MM
SALES (corp-wide): 24.72MM **Privately
Held**
Web: www.rogerson.com
SIC: **3812** 3545 3492 3728 Aircraft flight
instruments; Machine tool accessories;
Fluid power valves and hose fittings; Fuel
tanks, aircraft

(P-7805)
ROGERSON KRATOS
403 S Raymond Ave, Pasadena
(91105-2609)
PHONE..............................626 449-3090
Lawrence Smith, *CEO*
Michael Rogerson, *
Milton R Pizinger, *
Cannon Mathews, *
Alice Williams Cstr Srv, *Prin*
EMP: 160 EST: 1981
SQ FT: 28,000
SALES (est): 9.99MM
SALES (corp-wide): 24.72MM **Privately
Held**
Web: www.rogersonkratos.com
SIC: **3812** 3825 3699 Aircraft flight
instruments; Instruments to measure
electricity; Electrical equipment and
supplies, nec
PA: Rogerson Aircraft Corporation
16940 Von Karman Ave
949 660-0666

(P-7806)
SANDEL AVIONICS INC (PA)
Also Called: Sandel
1370 Decision St Ste D, Vista (92081-8551)
PHONE..............................760 727-4900
Steven Jeppson, *Pr*
Grant Miller, *
EMP: 31 EST: 1997
SALES (est): 22.51MM
SALES (corp-wide): 22.51MM **Privately
Held**
Web: www.sandel.com
SIC: **3812** Aircraft control instruments

(P-7807)
SANDEL AVIONICS INC
Also Called: Sandel Avionics
2405 Dogwood Way, Vista (92081-8409)
PHONE..............................760 727-4900
Gerald Block, *Brnch Mgr*
EMP: 169
SALES (corp-wide): 22.51MM **Privately
Held**
Web: www.sandel.com
SIC: **3812** Aircraft control instruments
PA: Sandel Avionics, Inc.
1370 Decision St Ste D
760 727-4900

(P-7808)
**SANTA BARBARA INFRARED
INC (DH)**
Also Called: Sbir
30 S Calle Cesar Chavez Ste D, Santa
Barbara (93103-5652)
PHONE..............................805 965-3669
EMP: 90 EST: 1086
SALES (est): 15.79MM **Publicly Held**
Web: www.sbir.com
SIC: **3812** Infrared object detection
equipment
HQ: Heico Electronic Technologies Corp.
3000 Taft St
Hollywood FL 33021
954 987-6101

(P-7809)
SCIENTIFIC-ATLANTA LLC
Scientific Atlanta
13112 Evening Creek Dr S, San Diego
(92128-4108)
PHONE..............................619 679-6000
Richard Lapointe, *Contrlr*
EMP: 25
SALES (corp-wide): 53.8B **Publicly Held**

SIC: **3812** Navigational systems and
instruments
HQ: Scientific-Atlanta, Llc
5030 Sugarloaf Pkwy # 1
Lawrenceville GA 30044
678 277-1000

(P-7810)
SENSOR SYSTEMS INC
8929 Fullbright Ave, Chatsworth
(91311-6179)
PHONE..............................818 341-5366
Mary E Bazar, *CEO*
Si Robin, *
Dennis E Bazar, *
EMP: 258 EST: 1961
SQ FT: 60,000
SALES (est): 22.44MM **Publicly Held**
Web: www.sensorantennas.com
SIC: **3812** Aircraft flight instruments
HQ: Heico Electronic Technologies Corp.
3000 Taft St
Hollywood FL 33021
954 987-6101

(P-7811)
**SIMULATOR PDT SOLUTIONS
LLC**
Also Called: Panel Products
21818 S Wilmington Ave Ste 411, Long
Beach (90810-1642)
PHONE..............................310 830-3331
Nabil Abdou, *Pr*
EMP: 26 EST: 2021
SQ FT: 5,200
SALES (est): 10.54MM
SALES (corp-wide): 35.49MM **Publicly
Held**
SIC: **3812** Aircraft control instruments
PA: Orbit International Corp.
80 Cabot Ct
631 435-8300

(P-7812)
SPACE VECTOR CORPORATION
20520 Nordhoff St, Chatsworth
(91311-6113)
PHONE..............................818 734-2600
EMP: 37 EST: 1969
SALES (est): 7.45MM **Privately Held**
SIC: **3812** 3691 3663 3761 Defense systems
and equipment; Batteries, rechargeable;
Global positioning systems (GPS)
equipment; Guided missiles and space
vehicles

(P-7813)
STELLANT SYSTEMS INC (DH)
Also Called: Electron Devices
3100 Lomita Blvd, Torrance (90505-5104)
P.O. Box 2999 (90509)
PHONE..............................310 517-6000
Keith Barclay, *CEO*
Steve Shpock, *
Todd Hansen, *WILLIAMSPORT*
Mansoor Mosallaie, *
▲ EMP: 508 EST: 2000
SALES (est): 181.58MM
SALES (corp-wide): 296.08MM **Privately
Held**
Web: www.stellantsystems.com
SIC: **3812** 3764 3671 Navigational systems
and instruments; Space propulsion units
and parts; Traveling wave tubes
HQ: Stellant Midco, Llc
Torrance CA

(P-7814)
TECHNOVATIVE APPLICATIONS
3160 Enterprise St Ste A, Brea
(92821-6288)

PHONE..................714 996-0104
EMP: 61 **EST:** 1987
SALES (est): 10.92MM **Privately Held**
Web: www.tnov.com
SIC: 3812 Radar systems and equipment

(P-7815)
TELEDYNE CONTROLS LLC
501 Continental Blvd, El Segundo
(90245-5036)
P.O. Box 1026 (90245-1026)
PHONE..................310 765-3600
George C Bobb Iii, *CEO*
Robert Mehrabian, *
Masood Hassan, *
Susan L Main, *
Melanie S Cibik, *
EMP: 616 **EST:** 2015
SALES (est): 123.25MM
SALES (corp-wide): 5.64B **Publicly Held**
Web: www.teledynecontrols.com
SIC: 3812 Search and navigation equipment
PA: Teledyne Technologies Inc
     1049 Camino Dos Rios
     805 373-4545

(P-7816)
TELEDYNE FLIR LLC
6769 Hollister Ave, Goleta (93117-3001)
PHONE..................805 964-9797
James Woolaway, *CEO*
EMP: 110
SALES (corp-wide): 5.64B **Publicly Held**
Web: www.flir.com
SIC: 3812 Aircraft/aerospace flight
instruments and guidance systems
HQ: Teledyne Flir, Llc
     27700 Sw Parkway Ave
     Wilsonville OR 97070
     503 498-3547

(P-7817)
TELEDYNE INSTRUMENTS INC
Also Called: Teledyne Rd Instruments
14020 Stowe Dr, Poway (92064-6846)
PHONE..................858 842-2600
Dennis Klahn, *Brnch Mgr*
EMP: 140
SALES (corp-wide): 5.64B **Publicly Held**
Web: www.teledynemarine.com
SIC: 3812 3829 Search and navigation
equipment; Measuring and controlling
devices, nec
HQ: Teledyne Instruments, Inc.
     16830 Chestnut St
     City Of Industry CA 91748
     626 934-1500

(P-7818)
TELEDYNE RD INSTRUMENTS INC
14020 Stowe Dr, Poway (92064-6846)
PHONE..................858 842-2600
EMP: 200
SIC: 3812 3829 Search and navigation
equipment; Measuring and controlling
devices, nec

(P-7819)
TINKER & RASOR
791 S Waterman Ave, San Bernardino
(92408-2331)
P.O. Box 1667 (92402-1667)
PHONE..................909 890-0700
Theodore Byerley, *Pr*
Denise Byerley, *
Mary Butcher, *
▲ **EMP:** 23 **EST:** 1948
SQ FT: 15,000
SALES (est): 2.41MM **Privately Held**

Web: www.tinker-rasor.com
SIC: 3812 3829 Detection apparatus:
electronic/magnetic field, light/heat;
Measuring and controlling devices, nec

(P-7820)
TOWER MECHANICAL PRODUCTS INC
Also Called: Allied Mechanical Products
1720 S Bon View Ave, Ontario
(91761-4411)
PHONE..................714 947-2723
Richard B Slater, *Pr*
James W Longcrier, *
Susan J Hardy, *
EMP: 126 **EST:** 1953
SQ FT: 148,000
SALES (est): 20.52MM
SALES (corp-wide): 28.17MM **Privately Held**
Web: www.alliedmech.com
SIC: 3812 Acceleration indicators and
systems components, aerospace
PA: Tower Industries, Inc.
     1518 N Endeavor Ln Ste C

(P-7821)
TUFFER MANUFACTURING CO INC
163 E Liberty Ave, Anaheim (92801-1012)
PHONE..................714 526-3077
Cathy Kim, *Pr*
Ken Kim, *
EMP: 39 **EST:** 1977
SQ FT: 12,000
SALES (est): 4.93MM **Privately Held**
Web: www.tuffermfg.com
SIC: 3812 3599 Search and navigation
equipment; Machine shop, jobbing and
repair

(P-7822)
VOTAW PRECISION TECHNOLOGIES
Also Called: Votaw
13153 Lakeland Rd, Santa Fe Springs
(90670-4542)
P.O. Box 314 (90740-0314)
PHONE..................562 944-0661
Steve Lamb, *CEO*
David Takes, *Pr*
Jonathan Miller, *CFO*
▲ **EMP:** 140 **EST:** 1964
SQ FT: 240,000
SALES (est): 23.48MM **Privately Held**
Web: www.votaw.com
SIC: 3812 Acceleration indicators and
systems components, aerospace

3821 Laboratory Apparatus And Furniture

(P-7823)
CHEMAT TECHNOLOGY INC
Also Called: Chemat Vision
9036 Winnetka Ave, Northridge
(91324-3235)
PHONE..................818 727-9786
Haixing Zheng, *CEO*
▲ **EMP:** 32 **EST:** 1990
SQ FT: 30,000
SALES (est): 5MM **Privately Held**
Web: www.chemat.com
SIC: 3821 3827 Chemical laboratory
apparatus, nec; Optical test and inspection
equipment

(P-7824)
CLEATECH LLC
Also Called: GLOBAL LAB SUPPLY
2106 N Glassell St, Orange (92865-3308)
PHONE..................714 754-6668
Sam Kashanchi, *CEO*
EMP: 45 **EST:** 2010
SALES (est): 8.22MM **Privately Held**
Web: www.cleatech.com
SIC: 3821 Laboratory apparatus and furniture

(P-7825)
EVERGREEN INDUSTRIES INC (DH)
Also Called: Evergreen Scientific
2254 E 49th St, Vernon (90058-2823)
PHONE..................323 583-1331
◆ **EMP:** 73 **EST:** 1969
SALES (est): 2.82MM
SALES (corp-wide): 2.26B **Privately Held**
Web: www.evergreensci.com
SIC: 3821 Laboratory equipment: fume
hoods, distillation racks, etc.
HQ: Caplugs, Inc.
     2150 Elmwood Ave
     Buffalo NY 14207
     716 876-9855

(P-7826)
GENETRONICS INC
11494 Sorrento Valley Rd Ste A, San Diego
(92121-1318)
PHONE..................858 597-6006
James Heppell, *Ch*
Avtar Dhillon, *
Peter Kies, *
Douglas Murdock, *
EMP: 26 **EST:** 1983
SQ FT: 25,000
SALES (est): 177.31K **Publicly Held**
SIC: 3821 8731 3826 Laboratory apparatus,
except heating and measuring; Biotechnical
research, commercial; Analytical
instruments
PA: Inovio Pharmaceuticals, Inc.
     660 W Grmntown Pike Ste 1

(P-7827)
HANSON LAB SOLUTIONS LLC
747 Calle Plano, Camarillo (93012-8556)
PHONE..................805 498-3121
Reid Hanson, *Pr*
Joe Matta, *
Joseph F Matta, *
▲ **EMP:** 30 **EST:** 1971
SQ FT: 40,000
SALES (est): 7.02MM **Privately Held**
Web: www.hansonlab.com
SIC: 3821 Laboratory furniture

(P-7828)
ISEC INCORPORATED
5735 Kearny Villa Rd Ste 105, San Diego
(92123-1138)
PHONE..................858 279-9085
Don Shaw, *Pr*
EMP: 103
SALES (corp-wide): 317.22MM **Privately Held**
Web: www.isecinc.com
SIC: 3821 Laboratory apparatus and furniture
PA: Isec, Incorporated
     6000 Grnwood Plz Blvd Ste
     303 790-1444

(P-7829)
NEWPORT CORPORATION (HQ)
Also Called: Newport
1791 Deere Ave, Irvine (92606-4814)
P.O. Box 19607 (92623-9607)

PHONE..................949 863-3144
Seth Bagshaw, *Pr*
Kathleen Burke, *
Derek D'antilio, *Treas*
◆ **EMP:** 467 **EST:** 1938
SALES (est): 355.83MM
SALES (corp-wide): 3.62B **Publicly Held**
Web: www.newport.com
SIC: 3821 3699 3827 3826 Worktables,
laboratory; Laser systems and equipment;
Optical instruments and lenses; Analytical
optical instruments
PA: Mks Instruments, Inc.
     2 Tech Dr Ste 201
     978 645-5500

(P-7830)
PROCISEDX INC
9449 Carroll Park Dr, San Diego
(92121-5202)
PHONE..................858 382-4598
Peter Westlake, *Pr*
Larry Mimms, *
EMP: 30 **EST:** 2019
SALES (est): 4.62MM **Privately Held**
Web: www.procisedx.com
SIC: 3821 Balances, laboratory

(P-7831)
ROMAR INNOVATIONS INC
Also Called: Romar Innovations
38429 Innovation Ct, Murrieta
(92563-2570)
PHONE..................951 296-3480
EMP: 100 **EST:** 1998
SALES (est): 9.27MM **Privately Held**
Web: www.aquaultraviolet.com
SIC: 3821 Sterilizers

(P-7832)
THERMAL EQUIPMENT CORPORATION
Also Called: TEC
2146 E Gladwick St, Rancho Dominguez
(90220-6203)
PHONE..................310 328-6600
Nancy Huffman, *CEO*
Nancy Huffman, *Pr*
▼ **EMP:** 45 **EST:** 1969
SALES (est): 6.51MM **Privately Held**
Web: www.thermalequipment.com
SIC: 3821 2842 3443 Laboratory apparatus
and furniture; Polishes and sanitation goods
; Autoclaves, industrial
PA: Km3 Holdings, Inc.
     2030 E University Dr

3822 Environmental Controls

(P-7833)
CATALYTIC SOLUTIONS INC (HQ)
1700 Fiske Pl, Oxnard (93033-1863)
PHONE..................805 486-4649
David Gann, *CEO*
Charlie Karl, *CEO*
Kevin Mcdonnell, *CFO*
Dan Mcguire, *VP*
▲ **EMP:** 24 **EST:** 1996
SQ FT: 75,000
SALES (est): 6.28MM **Privately Held**
Web: www.cdti.com
SIC: 3822 Environmental controls
PA: Cdti Advanced Materials, Inc.
     1641 Fiske Pl

(P-7834)
CHRONOMITE LABORATORIES INC

17451 Hurley St, City Of Industry
(91744-5106)
P.O. Box 3527 (91744-0527)
PHONE...............................310 534-2300
Donald E Morris, *CEO*
▲ **EMP:** 34 **EST:** 1967
SALES (est): 6.52MM
SALES (corp-wide): 99.75MM **Privately Held**
Web: www.chronomite.com
SIC: 3822 8731 3432 Water heater controls; Commercial physical research; Plumbing fixture fittings and trim
PA: Acorn Engineering Company
15125 E Proctor Ave
800 488-8999

(P-7835)
ELECTRASEM CORP
372 Elizabeth Ln, Corona (92878-5028)
PHONE...............................951 371-6140
Don S Edwards, *Pr*
▲ **EMP:** 84 **EST:** 1980
SALES (est): 3.73MM
SALES (corp-wide): 1.79B **Publicly Held**
SIC: 3822 Electric heat proportioning controls, modulating controls
HQ: General Monitors, Inc.
16782 Von Krman Ave Ste 1
Irvine CA 92606
949 581-4464

(P-7836)
HONEYWELL INTERNATIONAL INC
Also Called: Honeywell
2055 Dublin Dr, San Diego (92154-8203)
PHONE...............................619 671-5612
Virgel Mccormick, *Mgr*
EMP: 110
SALES (corp-wide): 36.66B **Publicly Held**
Web: www.honeywell.com
SIC: 3822 3494 Environmental controls; Valves and pipe fittings, nec
PA: Honeywell International Inc.
855 S Mint St
704 627-6200

(P-7837)
MEGGITT WESTERN DESIGN INC
Also Called: Western Design
9801 Muirlands Blvd, Irvine (92618-2521)
PHONE...............................949 465-7700
▲ **EMP:** 104
SIC: 3822 3483 Environmental controls; Ammunition components

(P-7838)
PERTRONIX LLC
Also Called: Pertronix Performance Brands
440 E Arrow Hwy, San Dimas (91773-3340)
PHONE...............................909 599-5955
EMP: 26
SALES (corp-wide): 13.89MM **Privately Held**
Web: www.pertronixbrands.com
SIC: 3822 3694 Environmental controls; Ignition apparatus, internal combustion engines
PA: Pertronix, Llc
10955 Mill Creek Rd
909 599-5955

(P-7839)
RANGE WD 2 LLC
1751 3rd St Ste 102, Norco (92860-2670)
PHONE...............................951 893-6233
Jeff From, *Brnch Mgr*
EMP: 46
Web: www.robertshaw.com

SIC: 3822 Environmental controls
HQ: Range Wd 2 Llc
1222 Hamilton Pkwy
Itasca IL 60143

(P-7840)
TELLKAMP SYSTEMS INC (PA)
15523 Carmenita Rd, Santa Fe Springs
(90670-5609)
PHONE...............................562 802-1621
◆ **EMP:** 49 **EST:** 1971
SALES (est): 793.73K
SALES (corp-wide): 793.73K **Privately Held**
Web: www.tellkamp.com
SIC: 3822 3564 Environmental controls; Air purification equipment

(P-7841)
TRUE FRESH HPP LLC
6535 Caballero Blvd Unit B, Buena Park
(90620-8106)
PHONE...............................949 922-8801
EMP: 35 **EST:** 2015
SALES (est): 5.92MM **Privately Held**
Web: www.truefreshhpp.com
SIC: 3822 Refrigeration controls (pressure)

(P-7842)
WESTERN ENVIRONMENTAL INC
62150 Gene Welmas Way, Mecca
(92254-6550)
PHONE...............................760 396-0222
Ed Kennon, *Pt*
EMP: 30 **EST:** 2002
SALES (est): 602.52K **Privately Held**
Web: www.wei-mecca.com
SIC: 3822 Environmental controls

(P-7843)
XPOWER MANUFACTURE INC
668 S 6th Ave, City Of Industry
(91746-3025)
PHONE...............................626 285-3301
Keidy Gu, *CEO*
Guogen Cui, *
▲ **EMP:** 40 **EST:** 2011
SALES (est): 3.43MM **Privately Held**
Web: www.xpower.com
SIC: 3822 3999 3564 Air flow controllers, air conditioning and refrigeration; Pet supplies; Blowing fans: industrial or commercial
PA: Xinshengyuan Electrical Appliances Co., Ltd.
No.3, East Area No.3 Road, Xiantang Industrial Zone, Longjiang T

3823 Process Control Instruments

(P-7844)
3D INSTRUMENTS LLC
Also Called: Sierra Precision
4990 E Hunter Ave, Anaheim (92807-2057)
PHONE...............................714 399-9200
EMP: 100
Web: www.wika.com
SIC: 3823 Pressure gauges, dial and digital

(P-7845)
ADVANCED ELECTROMAGNETICS INC
Also Called: Aemi
1320 Air Wing Rd Ste 101, San Diego
(92154-7707)
PHONE...............................619 449-9492
Per Iversen, *Pr*
Andrew Mcfadden, *Prin*

◆ **EMP:** 37 **EST:** 1980
SQ FT: 16,000
SALES (est): 9.95MM
SALES (corp-wide): 14.04MM **Privately Held**
Web: www.mvg-world.com
SIC: 3823 3825 Absorption analyzers: infrared, x-ray, etc.: industrial; Instruments to measure electricity
HQ: Orbit/Fr, Inc.
650 Louis Dr Ste 100
Warminster PA 18974

(P-7846)
ALPHA TECHNICS INC
24024 Humphries Rd, Tecate (91980-4008)
PHONE...............................949 250-6578
Lisa Marie Ryan, *Pr*
Dan Obrien, *
EMP: 200 **EST:** 2011
SALES (est): 6.36MM
SALES (corp-wide): 9.17B **Privately Held**
SIC: 3823 Process control instruments
PA: Te Connectivity Inc.
601 13th St Nw Ste 850s
800 522-6752

(P-7847)
AMETEK AMERON LLC (HQ)
Also Called: Mass Systems
4750 Littlejohn St, Baldwin Park
(91706-2274)
PHONE...............................626 856-0101
Keith Marsicola, *Managing Member*
Steve Tanner, *Managing Member*
EMP: 55 **EST:** 1988
SQ FT: 2,600
SALES (est): 25.88MM
SALES (corp-wide): 6.6B **Publicly Held**
Web: www.ameronglobal.com
SIC: 3823 3999 3728 8711 Pressure gauges, dial and digital; Fire extinguishers, portable; Aircraft parts and equipment, nec; Industrial engineers
PA: Ametek, Inc.
1100 Cassatt Rd
610 647-2121

(P-7848)
ANALYTICAL INDUSTRIES INC
Also Called: Advanced Instruments
2855 Metropolitan Pl, Pomona
(91767-1853)
PHONE...............................909 392-6900
Frank S Gregus, *Pr*
Patrick J Prindible, *
Mohammad Razaq, *
EMP: 45 **EST:** 1994
SQ FT: 15,000
SALES (est): 9.3MM **Privately Held**
Web: www.aii1.com
SIC: 3823 Process control instruments

(P-7849)
BIODOT INC (HQ)
2852 Alton Pkwy, Irvine (92606-5104)
PHONE...............................949 440-3685
Anthony Lemmo, *CEO*
EMP: 93 **EST:** 1994
SQ FT: 24,000
SALES (est): 21.44MM
SALES (corp-wide): 2.24B **Privately Held**
Web: www.biodot.com
SIC: 3823 3826 Process control instruments; Analytical instruments
PA: Ats Corporation
730 Fountain St N Bldg 3
604 332-2666

(P-7850)
CALIFRNIA ANLYTICAL INSTRS INC
Also Called: Cai
1312 W Grove Ave, Orange (92865-4136)
PHONE...............................714 974-5560
R Pete Furton, *Ch*
Harold J Peper, *
Loren T Mathews, *
EMP: 61 **EST:** 1992
SQ FT: 26,400
SALES (est): 11.34MM **Privately Held**
Web: www.gasanalyzers.com
SIC: 3823 Process control instruments

(P-7851)
CAMERON TECHNOLOGIES US LLC
Also Called: Cameron's Measurement Systems
4040 Capitol Ave, Whittier (90601-1735)
PHONE...............................562 222-8440
Victor Hart, *Manager*
EMP: 26
SIC: 3823 Industrial flow and liquid measuring instruments
HQ: Cameron Technologies Us, Llc
1000 Mcclaren Woods Dr
Coraopolis PA 15108

(P-7852)
COMPUTATIONAL SYSTEMS INC
4301 Resnik Ct, Bakersfield (93313-4852)
PHONE...............................661 832-5306
Shannon Romine, *Brnch Mgr*
EMP: 85
SALES (corp-wide): 17.49B **Publicly Held**
Web: www.emerson.com
SIC: 3823 Process control instruments
HQ: Computational Systems, Incorporated
8000 West Florissant Ave
Saint Louis MO 63136
314 553-2000

(P-7853)
CONTINENTAL CONTROLS CORP
Also Called: Manufacturing
7710 Kenamar Ct, San Diego (92121-2425)
PHONE...............................858 453-9880
David Fisher, *Pr*
David Fisher, *Pr*
Richard Fisher, *
Judith Fisher, *
Ross Fisher, *
▲ **EMP:** 28 **EST:** 1989
SQ FT: 17,000
SALES (est): 4.38MM **Privately Held**
Web: www.continentalcontrols.com
SIC: 3823 3533 Process control instruments; Oil and gas field machinery

(P-7854)
CRYSTAL ENGINEERING CORP
708 Fiero Ln Ste 9, San Luis Obispo
(93401-7945)
P.O. Box 3033 (93403-3033)
PHONE...............................805 595-5477
David Porter, *Pr*
▲ **EMP:** 38 **EST:** 1981
SALES (est): 12.29MM
SALES (corp-wide): 6.6B **Publicly Held**
Web: www.crystalengineering.net
SIC: 3823 Pressure gauges, dial and digital
PA: Ametek, Inc.
1100 Cassatt Rd
610 647-2121

P
R
O
D
U
C
T
S

& S
V
C
S

(P-7855)
E D Q INC
2920 Halladay St, Santa Ana (92705-5623)
PHONE...................714 546-6010
Erik K Moller, *CEO*
Randy Heartfield, *
Mary C Heartfield, *
▲ **EMP:** 39 **EST:** 1960
SQ FT: 14,000
SALES (est): 5.3MM **Privately Held**
Web: www.qedaero.com
SIC: 3823 3829 3812 Pressure gauges, dial
and digital; Accelerometers; Aircraft/
aerospace flight instruments and guidance
systems

(P-7856)
EMBEDDED DESIGNS INC
Also Called: K I C
16120 W Bernardo Dr Ste A, San Diego
(92127-1875)
PHONE...................858 673-6050
Casey Kazmierowicz, *Ch*
Bjorn Dahle, *
Henryk J Kazmier, *
Miles Moreau, *
Phil Kazmierowicz, *
EMP: 32 **EST:** 1984
SQ FT: 9,500
SALES (est): 6.05MM **Privately Held**
Web: www.kicthermal.com
SIC: 3823 Temperature measurement
instruments, industrial

(P-7857)
ETI SYSTEMS
Also Called: Polaris Music
1800 Century Park E Ste 600, Los Angeles
(90067-1508)
PHONE...................310 684-3664
Bill Tice, *Pr*
Gayle Tice, *
EMP: 60 **EST:** 1962
SQ FT: 8,200
SALES (est): 1.8MM **Privately Held**
Web: www.etisystems.com
SIC: 3823 Potentiometric self-balancing
inst., except X-Y plotters

(P-7858)
FUNDAMENTAL TECH INTL INC
Also Called: F T I
2900 E 29th St, Long Beach (90806-2315)
PHONE...................562 595-0661
Maarten Propper, *CEO*
John Jacobson, *
▼ **EMP:** 24 **EST:** 1996
SQ FT: 20,000
SALES (est): 1.14MM **Privately Held**
SIC: 3823 Liquid analysis instruments,
industrial process type

(P-7859)
FUTEK ADVANCED SENSOR TECH INC
Also Called: Futek Advanced Sensor Tech
10 Thomas, Irvine (92618-2702)
PHONE...................949 465-0900
Javad Mokhberi, *CEO*
Javad Mokhbery, *
▼ **EMP:** 140 **EST:** 1988
SQ FT: 23,000
SALES (est): 17.89MM **Privately Held**
Web: www.futek.com
SIC: 3823 8711 Process control instruments;
Engineering services

(P-7860)
GEORG FISCHER SIGNET LLC
5462 Irwindale Ave Ste A, Baldwin Park
(91706-2074)
PHONE...................626 571-2770
Charlotte Hill, *Managing Member*
James Jackson, *Prin*
John Pregenzer, *Prin*
▲ **EMP:** 90 **EST:** 1953
SALES (est): 20.69MM **Privately Held**
Web: www.gfsignet.com
SIC: 3823 Process control instruments
HQ: Georg Fischer Spa
Via Eugenio Villoresi 2/4
Agrate Brianza MB 20864

(P-7861)
GRAPHTEC AMERICA INC (DH)
Also Called: Graphtec
17462 Armstrong Ave, Irvine (92614-5724)
PHONE...................949 770-6010
Yasutaka Arakawa, *CEO*
◆ **EMP:** 49 **EST:** 1949
SQ FT: 35,000
SALES (est): 16.5MM **Privately Held**
Web: www.graphtecamerica.com
SIC: 3823 5064 Process control instruments;
Video cassette recorders and accessories
HQ: Graphtec Corp.
503-10, Shinanocho, Totsuka-Ku
Yokohama KNG 244-0

(P-7862)
HARDY PROCESS SOLUTIONS
Also Called: Hardy Process Solutions
10075 Mesa Rim Rd, San Diego
(92121-2913)
PHONE...................858 278-2900
Eric Schellenberger, *Pr*
Steve Hanes, *
◆ **EMP:** 50 **EST:** 1980
SALES (est): 19.57MM
SALES (corp-wide): 6.18B **Publicly Held**
Web: www.hardysolutions.com
SIC: 3823 3829 3596 Process control
instruments; Measuring and controlling
devices, nec; Scales and balances, except
laboratory
HQ: Dynamic Instruments, Inc.
10737 Lexington Dr
Knoxville TN 37932
858 278-4900

(P-7863)
INNOVATIVE INTEGRATION INC
741 Flynn Rd, Camarillo (93012-8056)
PHONE...................805 520-3300
Jim Henderson, *Pr*
Dan Mclane, *VP*
▲ **EMP:** 30 **EST:** 1988
SQ FT: 11,000
SALES (est): 2.05MM **Privately Held**
Web: www.isipkg.com
SIC: 3823 3571 Process control instruments;
Electronic computers

(P-7864)
KING INSTRUMENT COMPANY INC
12700 Pala Dr, Garden Grove
(92841-3924)
PHONE...................714 891-0008
Clyde F King, *Pr*
EMP: 50 **EST:** 1983
SQ FT: 46,000
SALES (est): 10.2MM **Privately Held**
Web: www.kinginstrumentco.com
SIC: 3823 Flow instruments, industrial
process type

(P-7865)
KING NUTRONICS LLC
Also Called: King Nutronics Corporation
6421 Independence Ave, Woodland Hills
(91367-2608)
PHONE...................818 887-5460
Robert Welther, *Pr*
EMP: 34 **EST:** 1960
SQ FT: 21,000
SALES (est): 6.62MM
SALES (corp-wide): 17.9MM **Privately Held**
Web: www.raptor-scientific.com
SIC: 3823 3825 Pressure measurement
instruments, industrial; Instruments to
measure electricity
PA: Raptor Scientific
81 Fuller Way
860 829-0001

(P-7866)
MCCROMETER INC (HQ)
3255 W Stetson Ave, Hemet (92545-7763)
PHONE...................951 652-6811
David Oveson, *CEO*
Sameer Ralhan, *
Jonathan Hinkemeyer, *
Michael Vagnini, *
◆ **EMP:** 214 **EST:** 1996
SQ FT: 9,090
SALES (est): 39.7MM
SALES (corp-wide): 5.02B **Publicly Held**
Web: www.mccrometer.com
SIC: 3823 Process control instruments
PA: Veralto Corporation
225 Wyman St Ste 250
781 755-3655

(P-7867)
MOORE INDUSTRIES-INTERNATIONAL INC (PA)
Also Called: Moore Industries
16650 Schoenborn St, North Hills
(91343-6106)
PHONE...................818 894-7111
▲ **EMP:** 200 **EST:** 1965
SALES (est): 39.36MM
SALES (corp-wide): 39.36MM **Privately Held**
Web: www.miinet.com
SIC: 3823 5084 Process control instruments;
Industrial machinery and equipment

(P-7868)
MYRON L COMPANY
2450 Impala Dr, Carlsbad (92010-7226)
PHONE...................760 438-2021
Gary O Robinson, *Pr*
Jerry Adams, *
◆ **EMP:** 80 **EST:** 1957
SQ FT: 43,000
SALES (est): 23.98MM **Privately Held**
Web: www.myronl.com
SIC: 3823 3825 3613 Electrodes used in
industrial process measurement;
Instruments to measure electricity;
Switchgear and switchboard apparatus

(P-7869)
NORDSON ASYMTEK INC
Also Called: Nordson Asymtek
2747 Loker Ave W, Carlsbad (92010-6601)
PHONE...................760 431-1919
▲ **EMP:** 250
Web: www.nordson.com
SIC: 3823 Industrial flow and liquid
measuring instruments

(P-7870)
NUMATIC ENGINEERING INC
7915 Ajay Dr, Sun Valley (91352-5315)
P.O. Box 1477 (35201-1477)
PHONE...................818 768-1200
▲ **EMP:** 38
SIC: 3823 Process control instruments

(P-7871)
OLEUMTECH CORPORATION
19762 Pauling, Foothill Ranch
(92610-2611)
PHONE...................949 305-9009
Paul Gregory, *CEO*
Vrej Isa, *COO*
EMP: 57 **EST:** 2002
SQ FT: 55,000
SALES (est): 9.59MM **Privately Held**
Web: www.oleumtech.com
SIC: 3823 Process control instruments

(P-7872)
PRIMORDIAL DIAGNOSTICS INC
Also Called: Pulse Instruments
3233 Mission Oaks Blvd Ste P, Camarillo
(93012-5134)
PHONE...................800 462-1926
Karan Khurana, *Pr*
Mridula Khurana, *
EMP: 25 **EST:** 1985
SALES (est): 2.69MM **Privately Held**
SIC: 3823 5063 5074 Water quality
monitoring and control systems; Electrical
apparatus and equipment; Water
purification equipment

(P-7873)
PROCESS INSGHTS - GDED WAVE IN
2121 Aviation Dr, Upland (91786-2195)
PHONE...................919 264-9651
Mark Morano, *Mgr*
EMP: 25
SALES (corp-wide): 45.56MM **Privately Held**
Web: www.process-insights.com
SIC: 3823 Process control instruments
HQ: Process Insights - Guided Wave, Inc.
3033 Gold Canal Dr
Rancho Cordova CA 95670
916 638-4944

(P-7874)
REOTEMP INSTRUMENT CORPORATION (PA)
10656 Roselle St, San Diego (92121-1524)
PHONE...................858 784-0710
▲ **EMP:** 55 **EST:** 1965
SALES (est): 14.45MM
SALES (corp-wide): 14.45MM **Privately Held**
Web: www.reotemp.com
SIC: 3823 3829 3585 Thermometers, filled
system: industrial process type;
Thermometers and temperature sensors;
Heating equipment, complete

(P-7875)
ROHRBACK COSASCO SYSTEMS INC (DH)
11841 Smith Ave, Santa Fe Springs
(90670-3226)
PHONE...................562 949-0123
Bryan Sanderlin, *CEO*
▼ **EMP:** 71 **EST:** 1977
SQ FT: 37,000
SALES (est): 17.49MM
SALES (corp-wide): 2.58B **Privately Held**
Web: www.rohrbackcosasco.com

▲ = Import ▼ = Export
◆ = Import/Export

SIC: **3823** 8742 Process control instruments;
Industry specialist consultants
HQ: Halma Investment Holdings Limited
Misbourne Court Rectory Way
Amersham BUCKS HP7 0

(P-7876)
RONAN ENGINEERING COMPANY (PA)
Also Called: Ronan Engnrng/Rnan Msrment
Div
28209 Avenue Stanford, Valencia
(91355-3984)
P.O. Box 129 (91310-0129)
PHONE..................................661 702-1344
John A Hewitson, *CEO*
▼ **EMP:** 56 **EST:** 1962
SQ FT: 50,000
SALES (est): 9.69MM
SALES (corp-wide): 9.69MM **Privately Held**
Web: www.ronan.com
SIC: **3823** 3825 Process control instruments;
Measuring instruments and meters, electric

(P-7877)
SABIA INCORPORATED (PA)
Also Called: Sabia
10919 Technology Pl Ste A, San Diego
(92127-1882)
PHONE..................................858 217-2200
Steve Foster, *CEO*
Clinton L Lingren, *
James Miller, *
Craig Belnap, *
Edward Nunn, *
EMP: 24 **EST:** 2000
SALES (est): 7.64MM
SALES (corp-wide): 7.64MM **Privately Held**
Web: www.sabiainc.com
SIC: **3823** Process control instruments

(P-7878)
SENSOREX CORPORATION
11751 Markon Dr, Garden Grove
(92841-1812)
PHONE..................................714 895-4344
▲ **EMP:** 62 **EST:** 1972
SALES (est): 14.59MM
SALES (corp-wide): 2.58B **Privately Held**
Web: www.sensorex.com
SIC: **3823** 3826 Process control instruments;
PH meters, except industrial process type
HQ: Halma Holdings Inc.
535 Sprngfeld Ave Ste 110
Summit NJ 07901
513 772-5501

(P-7879)
SENSOSCIENTIFIC LLC
685 Cochran St Ste 200, Simi Valley
(93065-1921)
PHONE..................................800 279-3101
Masoud Zarei, *Pr*
Ramin Rostami, *
Mike Zarei, *
▲ **EMP:** 43 **EST:** 2005
SQ FT: 4,000
SALES (est): 10.31MM
SALES (corp-wide): 231.49MM **Privately Held**
Web: www.sensoscientific.com
SIC: **3823** Process control instruments
HQ: Process Sensing Technologies Corp.
135 Engineers Rd Ste 150
Hauppauge NY 11788
631 427-3898

(P-7880)
SOFFA ELECTRIC INC
5901 Corvette St, Commerce (90040-1690)
PHONE..................................323 728-0230
EMP: 48 **EST:** 1971
SALES (est): 24.57MM **Privately Held**
Web: www.soffaelectric.com
SIC: **3823** 1731 8711 8742 Process control
instruments; General electrical contractor;
Engineering services; Automation and
robotics consultant

(P-7881)
TERN DESIGN LTD
Also Called: Oceanscience
14020 Stowe Dr, Poway (92064-6846)
PHONE..................................760 754-2400
Ronald George, *Pr*
EMP: 25 **EST:** 1995
SQ FT: 4,800
SALES (est): 1.98MM **Privately Held**
Web: www.teledynemarine.com
SIC: **3823** Buoyancy instruments, industrial
process type

(P-7882)
TRANSLOGIC INCORPORATED
5641 Engineer Dr, Huntington Beach
(92649-1123)
PHONE..................................714 890-0058
Donald Ross, *CEO*
Gregory Ross, *
EMP: 41 **EST:** 1979
SALES (est): 4.23MM **Privately Held**
Web: www.translogicinc.com
SIC: **3823** 3829 Temperature instruments:
industrial process type; Measuring and
controlling devices, nec

(P-7883)
VERTIV CORPORATION
Also Called: Vertiv
35 Parker, Irvine (92618-1605)
PHONE..................................949 457-3600
Anita Golden, *Brnch Mgr*
EMP: 52
SALES (corp-wide): 6.86B **Publicly Held**
Web: www.vertiv.com
SIC: **3823** Process control instruments
HQ: Vertiv Corporation
505 N Cleveland Ave
Westerville OH 43082
614 888-0246

(P-7884)
WORLD WATER INC
9848 Everest St, Downey (90242-3114)
P.O. Box 2331 (90662-2331)
PHONE..................................562 940-1964
Fernando Guerrero, *CEO*
EMP: 40 **EST:** 2006
SQ FT: 1,000
SALES (est): 2.21MM **Privately Held**
Web: www.worldwaterinc.com
SIC: **3823** Water quality monitoring and
control systems

(P-7885)
WORLDWIDE ENVMTL PDTS INC (PA)
Also Called: Imperials Sand Dunes
1100 Beacon St, Brea (92821-2936)
PHONE..................................714 990-2700
William Oscar Delaney, *CEO*
EMP: 90 **EST:** 1991
SQ FT: 23,000
SALES (est): 20.12MM **Privately Held**
Web: www.wep-inc.com

SIC: **3823** 3694 Process control instruments;
Automotive electrical equipment, nec

(P-7886)
XIRRUS INC
2545 W Hillcrest Dr Ste 220, Newbury Park
(91320-2217)
PHONE..................................805 262-1600
Shane Buckley, *CEO*
Dirk Gates, *Ofcr*
Patrick Parker, *CDO*
Sam Bass, *VP*
◆ **EMP:** 24 **EST:** 2004
SALES (est): 5.09MM **Privately Held**
Web: www.xirrus.com
SIC: **3823** Computer interface equipment, for
industrial process control

3824 Fluid Meters And Counting Devices

(P-7887)
BLUE-WHITE INDUSTRIES LTD (PA)
5300 Business Dr, Huntington Beach
(92649-1224)
PHONE..................................714 893-8529
Robert E Gledhill, *Pr*
Robert E Gledhill Iii, *VP*
Jeanne Hendrickson, *
Cindy Henderson, *
▲ **EMP:** 69 **EST:** 1957
SQ FT: 48,000
SALES (est): 19.72MM
SALES (corp-wide): 19.72MM **Privately Held**
Web: www.blue-white.com
SIC: **3824** 3561 3589 Water meters;
Industrial pumps and parts; Sewage and
water treatment equipment

(P-7888)
D & K ENGINEERING (HQ)
16990 Goldentop Rd, San Diego
(92127-2415)
PHONE..................................760 840-2214
Jeffrey Moss, *CEO*
Alex Kunczynski, *
Diane Law, *
Bill Suttner, *
Peter Ma, *VP*
▲ **EMP:** 84 **EST:** 2000
SQ FT: 60,000
SALES (est): 97.11MM
SALES (corp-wide): 179.22MM **Privately Held**
Web: www.ascentialtech.com
SIC: **3824** 8711 Mechanical and
electromechanical counters and devices;
Acoustical engineering
PA: Burke E. Porter Machinery Company
730 Plymouth Ave Ne
616 234-1200

(P-7889)
EMCOR FACILITIES SERVICES INC
2 Cromwell, Irvine (92618-1816)
PHONE..................................949 475-6020
EMP: 220
SALES (corp-wide): 12.58B **Publicly Held**
Web: www.emcorfacilities.com
SIC: **3824** Fluid meters and counting devices
HQ: Emcor Facilities Services, Inc.
9655 Reading Rd
Cincinnati OH 45215
888 846-9462

(P-7890)
INTERSCAN CORPORATION
4590 Ish Dr Ste 110, Simi Valley
(93063-7682)
PHONE..................................805 823-8301
Richard Shaw, *Pr*
Michael Shaw, *VP*
Lorienne Shaw, *VP*
EMP: 23 **EST:** 1975
SQ FT: 10,000
SALES (est): 2.36MM **Privately Held**
Web: www.gasdetection.com
SIC: **3824** 3829 Gasmeters, domestic and
large capacity: industrial; Measuring and
controlling devices, nec
PA: Chen Instrument Design Inc.
1554 Ne 3rd Ave

(P-7891)
IPS GROUP INC (PA)
7737 Kenamar Ct, San Diego (92121-2425)
PHONE..................................858 404-0607
David W King, *CEO*
Amir Sedadi, *VP*
Dario Paduano, *CFO*
Chad Randall, *COO*
▲ **EMP:** 36 **EST:** 2000
SALES (est): 58.9MM
SALES (corp-wide): 58.9MM **Privately Held**
Web: www.ipsgroupinc.com
SIC: **3824** 4899 Parking meters;
Communication signal enhancement
network services

(P-7892)
MINDRUM PRECISION INC
Also Called: Mindrum Precision Products
10000 4th St, Rancho Cucamonga
(91730-5793)
PHONE..................................909 989-1728
Diane Mindrum, *CEO*
Daniel Mindrum, *
Matt Wade, *
EMP: 49 **EST:** 1956
SQ FT: 30,000
SALES (est): 9.77MM **Privately Held**
Web: www.mindrum.com
SIC: **3824** 3827 3823 3264 Fluid meters and
counting devices; Optical instruments and
lenses; Process control instruments;
Porcelain electrical supplies

(P-7893)
SPARLING INSTRUMENTS LLC
4097 Temple City Blvd, El Monte
(91731-1089)
PHONE..................................626 444-0571
Yosufi Tyebkhan, *Managing Member*
▲ **EMP:** 25 **EST:** 1996
SQ FT: 56,000
SALES (est): 4.8MM **Privately Held**
Web: www.sparlinginstruments.com
SIC: **3824** 3823 5084 Fluid meters and
counting devices; Process control
instruments; Industrial machinery and
equipment

3825 Instruments To Measure Electricity

(P-7894)
AGILENT TECHNOLOGIES INC
11011 N Torrey Pines Rd, La Jolla
(92037-1007)
PHONE..................................858 373-6300
Janet King, *Prin*
EMP: 42
SALES (corp-wide): 6.83B **Publicly Held**

PRODUCTS & SVCS

Web: www.agilent.com
SIC: 3825 Instruments to measure electricity
PA: Agilent Technologies, Inc.
5301 Stevens Creek Blvd
800 227-9770

(P-7895)
AGILENT TECHNOLOGIES INC
1170 Mark Ave, Carpinteria (93013-2918)
PHONE..................................805 566-6655
Britt Meelby Jensen, *Genl Mgr*
EMP: 46
SALES (corp-wide): 6.83B Publicly Held
Web: www.agilent.com
SIC: 3825 Instruments to measure electricity
PA: Agilent Technologies, Inc.
5301 Stevens Creek Blvd
800 227-9770

(P-7896)
AGILENT TECHNOLOGIES INC
Also Called: Agilent Technologies
6392 Via Real, Carpinteria (93013-2921)
PHONE..................................805 566-1405
EMP: 44
SALES (corp-wide): 6.83B Publicly Held
Web: www.agilent.com
SIC: 3825 Instruments to measure electricity
PA: Agilent Technologies, Inc.
5301 Stevens Creek Blvd
800 227-9770

(P-7897)
AMETEK PROGRAMMABLE POWER INC (HQ)
Also Called: Ametek Programmable Power
9250 Brown Deer Rd, San Diego
(92121-2267)
PHONE..................................858 450-0085
Matthew Mannell, *CEO*
Dalip Puri, *CFO*
▲ EMP: 350 EST: 2006
SQ FT: 110,000
SALES (est): 114.65MM
SALES (corp-wide): 6.6B Publicly Held
Web: www.programmablepower.com
SIC: 3825 Instruments to measure electricity
PA: Ametek, Inc.
1100 Cassatt Rd
610 647-2121

(P-7898)
ARBITER SYSTEMS INCORPORATED (PA)
1324 Vendels Cir Ste 121, Paso Robles
(93446-3806)
PHONE..................................805 237-3831
Craig Armstrong, *Pr*
Bruce Roeder, *
EMP: 30 EST: 1973
SQ FT: 15,000
SALES (est): 6.05MM
SALES (corp-wide): 6.05MM Privately Held
Web: www.arbiter.com
SIC: 3825 3829 3663 Test equipment for
electronic and electric measurement;
Measuring and controlling devices, nec;
Radio and t.v. communications equipment

(P-7899)
ASTRONICS TEST SYSTEMS INC (HQ)
2652 Mcgaw Ave, Irvine (92614-5840)
PHONE..................................800 722-2528
James Mulato, *Pr*
David Burney, *
Brian Price, *
◆ EMP: 130 EST: 2014

SQ FT: 98,600
SALES (est): 73.5MM
SALES (corp-wide): 689.21MM Publicly
Held
Web: www.astronics.com
SIC: 3825 Test equipment for electronic and
electric measurement
PA: Astronics Corporation
130 Commerce Way
716 805-1599

(P-7900)
BAE SYSTEMS INFO ELCTRNIC SYST
Also Called: Bae Systems
10920 Technology Pl, San Diego
(92127-1874)
PHONE..................................858 592-5000
Mark Gist, *Brnch Mgr*
EMP: 719
SALES (corp-wide): 28.77B Privately Held
Web: www.baesystems.com
SIC: 3825 7373 3812 Test equipment for
electronic and electric measurement;
Computer integrated systems design;
Search and navigation equipment
HQ: Bae Systems Information And
Electronic Systems Integration Inc.
65 Spit Brook Rd
Nashua NH 03060
603 885-4321

(P-7901)
BAE SYSTEMS NATIONAL SECURITY SOLUTIONS INC
10920 Technology Pl, San Diego
(92127-1874)
P.O. Box 509008 (92150-9008)
PHONE..................................858 592-5000
▲ EMP: 2200
SIC: 3825 7373 3812 Test equipment for
electronic and electric measurement;
Computer integrated systems design;
Search and navigation equipment

(P-7902)
BOURNS INC
Bourns Sensor Controls
1200 Columbia Ave, Riverside
(92507-2129)
PHONE..................................951 781-5690
James Davis, *Pr*
EMP: 29
SALES (corp-wide): 459.73MM Privately
Held
Web: www.bourns.com
SIC: 3825 Instruments to measure electricity
PA: Bourns, Inc.
1200 Columbia Ave
951 781-5500

(P-7903)
CHILICON POWER LLC (PA)
15415 W Sunset Blvd Ste 102, Pacific
Palisades (90272-3551)
PHONE..................................310 800-1396
▲ EMP: 24 EST: 2011
SALES (est): 2.59MM
SALES (corp-wide): 2.59MM Privately
Held
Web: www.chiliconpower.com
SIC: 3825 Power measuring equipment,
electrical

(P-7904)
CHROMA SYSTEMS SOLUTIONS INC
25612 Commercentre Dr, Lake Forest
(92630-8813)

PHONE..................................949 600-6400
EMP: 27
Web: www.chromausa.com
SIC: 3825 Measuring instruments and
meters, electric
HQ: Chroma Systems Solutions, Inc.
19772 Pauling
Foothill Ranch CA 92610
949 297-4848

(P-7905)
COHU INC (PA)
Also Called: Cohu
12367 Crosthwaite Cir, Poway
(92064-6817)
PHONE..................................858 848-8100
Luis A Muller, *Pr*
James A Donahue, *Non-Executive
Chairman of the Board*
Christopher G Bohrson, *CCO*
Ian P Lawee, *Sr VP*
Jeffrey D Jones, *VP Fin*
▲ EMP: 220 EST: 1947
SQ FT: 147,000
SALES (est): 636.32MM
SALES (corp-wide): 636.32MM Publicly
Held
Web: www.cohu.com
SIC: 3825 Semiconductor test equipment

(P-7906)
COHU INTERFACE SOLUTIONS LLC (HQ)
Also Called: Factron Test Fixtures
12367 Crosthwaite Cir, Poway
(92064-6817)
PHONE..................................858 848-8000
Luis Muller, *CEO*
▲ EMP: 75 EST: 1965
SALES (est): 25.01MM
SALES (corp-wide): 636.32MM Publicly
Held
Web: www.cohu.com
SIC: 3825 3678 Test equipment for
electronic and electrical circuits; Electronic
connectors
PA: Cohu, Inc.
12367 Crosthwaite Cir
858 848-8100

(P-7907)
CONCISYS
5452 Oberlin Dr, San Diego (92121-1715)
PHONE..................................858 292-5888
Giao Huu Nguyen, *Managing Member*
Vu Wing, *
▲ EMP: 40 EST: 2000
SALES (est): 17.55MM Privately Held
Web: www.concisys.com
SIC: 3825 Digital test equipment, electronic
and electrical circuits

(P-7908)
DELTA DESIGN (LITTLETON) INC
12367 Crosthwaite Cir, Poway
(92064-6817)
PHONE..................................858 848-8100
Charles A Schwan, *Ch Bd*
Nicholas J Cedrone, *
▲ EMP: 570 EST: 1994
SQ FT: 102,000
SALES (est): 3.6MM
SALES (corp-wide): 636.32MM Publicly
Held
SIC: 3825 Test equipment for electronic and
electrical circuits
PA: Cohu, Inc.
12367 Crosthwaite Cir
858 848-8100

(P-7909)
DIVERSFIED TCHNCAL SYSTEMS INC (HQ)
1720 Apollo Ct, Seal Beach (90740-5617)
PHONE..................................562 493-0158
Stephen D Pruitt, *CEO*
Steve Pruitt, *
George M Beckage, *
Tim Kippen, *
Kirsten Larsen, *
▲ EMP: 29 EST: 1990
SQ FT: 55,000
SALES (est): 11.58MM
SALES (corp-wide): 355.05MM Publicly
Held
Web: www.dtsweb.com
SIC: 3825 3679 3495 8731 Instruments to
measure electricity; Electronic circuits;
Clock springs, precision; Commercial
physical research
PA: Vishay Precision Group, Inc.
3 Great Vly Pkwy Ste 150
484 321-5300

(P-7910)
EQUUS PRODUCTS INC
17352 Von Karman Ave, Irvine
(92614-6204)
PHONE..................................714 424-6779
Ieon C Chen, *CEO*
Cynthia H Tsai, *
Duke Chen Skthldr, *Prin*
Michael Chen Skthldr, *Prin*
◆ EMP: 31 EST: 1982
SQ FT: 36,000
SALES (est): 1.91MM Privately Held
Web: www.equsus.com
SIC: 3825 3545 3714 Electrical power
measuring equipment; Machine tool
accessories; Motor vehicle parts and
accessories

(P-7911)
FIELDPIECE INSTRUMENTS INC (PA)
Also Called: Fieldpiece
1636 W Collins Ave, Orange (92867-5421)
PHONE..................................714 634-1844
Cameron Rouns, *CEO*
Tim J Way, *
▲ EMP: 38 EST: 1990
SQ FT: 4,000
SALES (est): 9.21MM Privately Held
Web: www.fieldpiece.com
SIC: 3825 3829 3826 3823 Instruments for
measuring electrical quantities; Measuring
and controlling devices, nec; Analytical
instruments; Process control instruments

(P-7912)
FIRST LEGAL NETWORK
1517 Beverly Blvd, Los Angeles
(90026-5704)
PHONE..................................213 250-1111
Alex Martinez, *CEO*
EMP: 154 EST: 2015
SALES (est): 5.39MM Privately Held
Web: www.firstlegalnetwork.com
SIC: 3825 4899 Network analyzers;
Communication signal enhancement
network services

(P-7913)
GOULD & BASS COMPANY INC
1431 W 2nd St, Pomona (91766-1299)
PHONE..................................909 623-6793
John S Bass, *CEO*
EMP: 32 EST: 1971
SQ FT: 66,000
SALES (est): 6.3MM Privately Held

▲ = Import ▼ = Export
◆ = Import/Export

Web: www.gould-bass.net

SIC: 3825 3535 3556 Test equipment for electronic and electric measurement; Belt conveyor systems, general industrial use; Packing house machinery

(P-7914)
HEXAGON MFG INTELLIGENCE INC

Romer Cimcore
3536 Seagate Way Ste 100, Oceanside (92056-2672)
PHONE......................760 994-1401
Steve Ilmrud, *Genl Mgr*
EMP: 60
SALES (corp-wide): 2.5MM **Privately Held**
Web: www.hexagon.com
SIC: 3825 Instruments to measure electricity
HQ: Hexagon Manufacturing Intelligence, Inc.
250 Circuit Dr
North Kingstown RI 02852
401 886-2000

(P-7915)
HID GLOBAL CORPORATION

15370 Barranca Pkwy, Irvine (92618-2215)
PHONE......................949 732-2000
EMP: 56
Web: www.hidglobal.com
SIC: 3825 Instruments to measure electricity
HQ: Hid Global Corporation
611 Center Ridge Dr
Austin TX 78753

(P-7916)
INTELLIGENT CMPT SOLUTIONS INC (PA)

8968 Fullbright Ave, Chatsworth (91311-6123)
PHONE......................818 998-5805
Uzi Kohavi, *Pr*
Gonen Ravid, *
▲ **EMP:** 25 **EST:** 1989
SQ FT: 21,000
SALES (est): 3.32MM **Privately Held**
Web: www.icsiq.com
SIC: 3825 3577 3572 Test equipment for electronic and electrical circuits; Computer peripheral equipment, nec; Computer storage devices

(P-7917)
INTERNATIONAL TRANDUCER CORP

Also Called: Channel Technologies Group
869 Ward Dr, Santa Barbara (93111-2959)
PHONE......................805 683-2575
Robert F Carlson, *
Kevin Ruelas, *
Brian Dolan, *
EMP: 160 **EST:** 1966
SALES (est): 7.53MM
SALES (corp-wide): 40.31MM **Privately Held**
SIC: 3825 3812 Transducers for volts, amperes, watts, vars, frequency, etc.; Search and navigation equipment
PA: Gavial Holdings, Inc.
1435 W Mccoy Ln
805 614-0060

(P-7918)
IXIA (HQ)

26601 Agoura Rd, Calabasas (91302-1959)
PHONE......................818 871-1800
Neil Dougherty, *Pr*
Jeffrey Li, *VP*
Jason Kary, *

Matthew S Alexander, *Corporate Secrotary*
Stephen Williams, *
EMP: 231 **EST:** 1997
SQ FT: 116,000
SALES (est): 51.28MM
SALES (corp-wide): 5.46B **Publicly Held**
Web: support.ixiacom.com
SIC: 3825 7371 Network analyzers; Custom computer programming services
PA: Keysight Technologies, Inc.
1400 Fountaingrove Pkwy
800 829-4444

(P-7919)
IXIA

Also Called: Ixia Communications
26701 Agoura Rd, Calabasas (91302-1960)
PHONE......................818 871-1800
EMP: 37
SALES (corp-wide): 5.46B **Publicly Held**
Web: www.keysight.com
SIC: 3825 Network analyzers
HQ: Ixia
26601 Agoura Rd
Calabasas CA 91302
818 871-1800

(P-7920)
J2M TEST SOLUTIONS INC

13225 Gregg St, Poway (92064-7120)
PHONE......................571 333-0291
John Ronk, *Pr*
EMP: 80 **EST:** 2005
SALES (est): 1.48MM **Privately Held**
SIC: 3825 Instruments to measure electricity

(P-7921)
L3HARRIS INTERSTATE ELEC CORP

3033 Science Park Rd, San Diego (92121-1167)
PHONE......................858 552-9500
Andrew Leuthe, *Prin*
EMP: 70
SALES (corp-wide): 19.42B **Publicly Held**
Web: www.l3harris.com
SIC: 3825 7379 5045 Test equipment for electronic and electric measurement; Computer related consulting services; Computer software
HQ: L3harris Interstate Electronics Corporation
602 E Vermont Ave
Anaheim CA 92805
714 758-0500

(P-7922)
L3HARRIS INTERSTATE ELEC CORP

Also Called: Human Resources
700 E Vermont Ave, Anaheim (92805-5811)
PHONE......................714 758-0500
EMP: 70
SALES (corp-wide): 19.42B **Publicly Held**
Web: www.l3harris.com
SIC: 3825 Test equipment for electronic and electric measurement
HQ: L3harris Interstate Electronics Corporation
602 E Vermont Ave
Anaheim CA 92805
714 758-0500

(P-7923)
L3HARRIS INTERSTATE ELEC CORP

Also Called: Integrated Technical Services
600 E Vermont Ave, Anaheim (92805-5607)
PHONE......................714 758-0500

Robert Schembre, *Brnch Mgr*
EMP: 70
SALES (corp-wide): 19.42B **Publicly Held**
Web: www.l3harris.com
SIC: 3825 Instruments to measure electricity
HQ: L3harris Interstate Electronics Corporation
602 E Vermont Ave
Anaheim CA 92805
714 758-0500

(P-7924)
L3HARRIS INTERSTATE ELEC CORP (DH)

Also Called: L-3 Interstate Electronics
602 E Vermont Ave, Anaheim (92805-5607)
P.O. Box 3117 (92803-3117)
PHONE......................714 758-0500
Christopher E Kubasik, *CEO*
Arthur H Lim, *Treas*
Scott T Mikuen, *Dir*
Kristene E Schumacher, *Dir*
EMP: 275 **EST:** 1955
SQ FT: 235,700
SALES (est): 65.62MM
SALES (corp-wide): 19.42B **Publicly Held**
Web: www.l3harris.com
SIC: 3825 3812 3679 Test equipment for electronic and electric measurement; Navigational systems and instruments; Liquid crystal displays (LCD)
HQ: L3 Technologies, Inc.
600 3rd Ave Fl 34
New York NY 10016
321 727-9100

(P-7925)
MAGNEBIT HOLDING CORP

9474 La Cuesta Dr, La Mesa (91941-5634)
PHONE......................858 573-0727
Catherine Jacobson, *Pr*
Peter Jacobson, *
EMP: 25 **EST:** 1981
SALES (est): 736.4K **Privately Held**
Web: www.magnebit.com
SIC: 3825 3471 Instruments to measure electricity; Plating and polishing

(P-7926)
MARVIN TEST SOLUTIONS INC

1770 Kettering, Irvine (92614-5616)
PHONE......................949 263-2222
Loofie Gutterman, *Pr*
Leon Tsimmerman, *
Gerald Friedman, *
EMP: 96 **EST:** 1987
SQ FT: 31,000
SALES (est): 17.55MM
SALES (corp-wide): 149.54MM **Privately Held**
Web: www.marvintest.com
SIC: 3825 Instruments to measure electricity
PA: Marvin Engineering Co., Inc.
261 W Beach Ave
310 674-5030

(P-7927)
N H RESEARCH LLC (DH)

Also Called: Nhr
16601 Hale Ave, Irvine (92606-5049)
PHONE......................949 474-3900
Eric H Starkloff, *Pr*
▲ **EMP:** 65 **EST:** 1965
SALES (est): 24.81MM
SALES (corp-wide): 17.49B **Publicly Held**
Web: www.nhresearch.com
SIC: 3825 3829 Test equipment for electronic and electrical circuits; Measuring and controlling devices, nec
HQ: National Instruments Corporation
11500 N Mopac Expy

Austin TX 78759
512 683-0100

(P-7928)
NEARFIELD SYSTEMS INC

19730 Magellan Dr, Torrance (90502-1104)
PHONE......................310 525-7000
Greg Hindman, *Pr*
Dan Slater, *
Rod Douglass, *
▼ **EMP:** 62 **EST:** 1988
SALES (est): 4.95MM
SALES (corp-wide): 6.6B **Publicly Held**
Web: www.nearfield.com
SIC: 3825 3829 Test equipment for electronic and electric measurement; Measuring and controlling devices, nec
HQ: Nsi-Mi Technologies Inc.
1125 Stllite Blvd Nw Ste
Suwanee GA 30024
678 475-8300

(P-7929)
NEOLOGY INC (PA)

Also Called: Neology
1917 Palomar Oaks Way Ste 110, Carlsbad (92008-5513)
PHONE......................858 391-0260
Bradley Feldmann, *CEO*
Aaron Moser, *CFO*
◆ **EMP:** 118 **EST:** 1986
SALES (est): 28.19MM
SALES (corp-wide): 28.19MM **Privately Held**
Web: www.neology.net
SIC: 3825 Integrated circuit testers

(P-7930)
PULSE INSTRUMENTS

22301 S Western Ave Ste 107, Torrance (90501-4155)
PHONE......................310 515-5330
Sylvia Kan, *Pr*
David Kan, *
EMP: 23 **EST:** 1975
SALES (est): 4.75MM **Privately Held**
Web: www.pulseinstruments.com
SIC: 3825 3823 Pulse (signal) generators; Process control instruments

(P-7931)
SURFACE OPTICS CORPORATION

11555 Rancho Bernardo Rd, San Diego (92127-1441)
PHONE......................858 675-7404
Jonathan Dummer, *CEO*
James C Jafolla, *
Mark Dombrowski, *
Marian Geremia, *
James Jafolla, *
EMP: 50 **EST:** 1977
SQ FT: 18,000
SALES (est): 12.16MM **Privately Held**
Web: www.surfaceoptics.com
SIC: 3825 8748 3829 8731 Instruments to measure electricity; Business consulting, nec; Measuring and controlling devices, nec ; Commercial physical research

(P-7932)
TELEDYNE LECROY INC

1049 Camino Dos Rios, Thousand Oaks (91360-2362)
PHONE......................434 984-4500
EMP: 34
SALES (corp-wide): 5.64B **Publicly Held**
Web: www.teledynelecroy.com
SIC: 3825 Oscillographs and oscilloscopes
HQ: Teledyne Lecroy, Inc.
700 Chestnut Ridge Rd

PRODUCTS & SVCS

Chestnut Ridge NY 10977
845 425-2000

(P-7933)
TESCO CONTROLS INC
Also Called: TESCO CONTROLS, INC.
42015 Remington Ave Ste 102, Temecula
(92590-2563)
PHONE.....................916 395-8800
Tracy Adams, *Pr*
EMP: 91
SALES (corp-wide): 100MM **Privately Held**
Web: www.tescocontrols.com
SIC: 3825 3571 3625 Meters: electric, pocket, portable, panelboard, etc.; Minicomputers; Relays and industrial controls
PA: Tesco Controls, Llc
8440 Florin Rd
916 395-8800

(P-7934)
VELHER LLC
350 10th Ave Ste 1000, San Diego
(92101-8705)
PHONE.....................619 494-6310
Luis Velazquez, *Managing Member*
EMP: 50 **EST:** 2019
SALES (est): 2.34MM **Privately Held**
Web: www.velher.net
SIC: 3825 Energy measuring equipment, electrical

(P-7935)
VITREK LLC (PA)
Also Called: Xitron Technologies
12169 Kirkham Rd Ste C, Poway
(92064-8835)
PHONE.....................858 689-2755
Kevin Clark, *CEO*
Don Millstein, *
▲ **EMP:** 27 **EST:** 1990
SQ FT: 4,000
SALES (est): 22.23MM **Privately Held**
Web: www.vitrek.com
SIC: 3825 Test equipment for electronic and electric measurement

3826 Analytical Instruments

(P-7936)
AFFYMETRIX INC
5893 Oberlin Dr, San Diego (92121-3773)
PHONE.....................858 642-2058
EMP: 54
SALES (corp-wide): 42.86B **Publicly Held**
Web: www.affymetrix.com
SIC: 3826 Analytical instruments
HQ: Affymetrix, Inc.
428 Oakmead Pkwy
Sunnyvale CA 94085

(P-7937)
APPLIED INSTRUMENT TECH INC
2121 Aviation Dr, Upland (91786-2195)
PHONE.....................909 204-3700
Joseph Laconte, *Pr*
EMP: 40 **EST:** 2010
SALES (est): 3.57MM
SALES (corp-wide): 1.09K **Privately Held**
SIC: 3826 Analytical instruments
HQ: Schneider Electric Usa, Inc.
One Boston Pl Ste 2700
Boston MA 02108
978 975-9600

(P-7938)
AUTONOMOUS MEDICAL DEVICES INC (PA)
3511 W Sunflower Ave, Santa Ana
(92704-6944)
P.O. Box 28404 (92799)
PHONE.....................657 660-6800
David Okrongly, *CEO*
Christopher Bissell, *CFO*
EMP: 28 **EST:** 2013
SQ FT: 3,750
SALES (est): 11.04MM
SALES (corp-wide): 11.04MM **Privately Held**
Web: www.amdilabs.com
SIC: 3826 Analytical instruments

(P-7939)
AUTONOMOUS MEDICAL DEVICES INC
10524 S La Cienega Blvd, Inglewood
(90304-1116)
PHONE.....................310 641-2700
EMP: 43
SALES (corp-wide): 11.04MM **Privately Held**
Web: www.amdilabs.com
SIC: 3826 Analytical instruments
PA: Autonomous Medical Devices Incorporated
3511 W Sunflower Ave
657 660-6800

(P-7940)
BECKMAN COULTER INC
2470 Faraday Ave, Carlsbad (92010-7224)
PHONE.....................760 438-9151
Claire O'donadan, *Mgr*
EMP: 125
SALES (corp-wide): 23.89B **Publicly Held**
Web: www.beckmancoulter.com
SIC: 3826 Analytical instruments
HQ: Beckman Coulter, Inc.
250 S Kraemer Blvd
Brea CA 92821
714 993-5321

(P-7941)
BECKMAN COULTER INC (HQ)
250 S Kraemer Blvd, Brea (92821-6232)
P.O. Box 2268 (92822-2268)
PHONE.....................714 993-5321
◆ **EMP:** 1200 **EST:** 1935
SALES (est): 274.59K
SALES (corp-wide): 23.89B **Publicly Held**
Web: www.beckmancoulter.com
SIC: 3826 3841 3821 Analytical instruments; Diagnostic apparatus, medical; Chemical laboratory apparatus, nec
PA: Danaher Corporation
2200 Pa Ave Nw Ste 800w
202 828-0850

(P-7942)
BECKMAN INSTRUMENTS INC
8733 Scott St, Rosemead (91770-1363)
PHONE.....................626 309-0110
J Cendejas, *Pr*
EMP: 86 **EST:** 2003
SALES (est): 2.73MM **Privately Held**
Web: www.beckman.com
SIC: 3826 Analytical instruments

(P-7943)
BECTON DICKINSON AND COMPANY
Also Called: Bdc Distribution Center
2200 W San Bernardino Ave, Redlands
(92374-5008)

PHONE.....................909 748-7300
Ricardo Frias, *Brnch Mgr*
EMP: 59
SALES (corp-wide): 20.18B **Publicly Held**
Web: www.bd.com
SIC: 3826 Elemental analyzers
PA: Becton, Dickinson And Company
1 Becton Dr
201 847-6800

(P-7944)
BEMCO INC (PA)
2255 Union Pl, Simi Valley (93065-1661)
PHONE.....................805 583-4970
Randy Jean Bruskrud, *Pr*
Brian Bruskrud, *
EMP: 24 **EST:** 1951
SQ FT: 50,000
SALES (est): 6.35MM
SALES (corp-wide): 6.35MM **Privately Held**
Web: www.bemcoinc.com
SIC: 3826 Environmental testing equipment

(P-7945)
BIONANO GENOMICS INC (PA)
Also Called: Bionano Genomics
9540 Towne Centre Dr Ste 100, San Diego
(92121-1989)
PHONE.....................858 888-7600
R Erik Holmlin, *Pr*
David L Barker, *Ch Bd*
Mark Oldakowski, *COO*
Gulsen Kama, *CFO*
Alka Chaubey, *CMO*
EMP: 56 **EST:** 2003
SQ FT: 41,101
SALES (est): 36.12MM
SALES (corp-wide): 36.12MM **Publicly Held**
Web: www.bionano.com
SIC: 3826 Analytical instruments

(P-7946)
BIOPAC SYSTEMS INC
42 Aero Camino, Goleta (93117-3105)
PHONE.....................805 685-0066
Alan Macy, *CEO*
William Mcmullen, *VP*
Marc Wester, *
EMP: 40 **EST:** 1986
SQ FT: 16,000
SALES (est): 9.16MM **Privately Held**
Web: www.biopac.com
SIC: 3826 Analytical instruments

(P-7947)
BROADLEY-JAMES CORPORATION (PA)
19 Thomas, Irvine (92618-2704)
PHONE.....................949 829-5555
Scott Broadley, *Pr*
Leighton S Broadley, *
Scott T Broadley, *Prin*
Catherine A Broadley, *
EMP: 79 **EST:** 1967
SQ FT: 24,000
SALES (est): 16.17MM
SALES (corp-wide): 16.17MM **Privately Held**
Web: www.broadleyjames.com
SIC: 3826 3823 Analytical instruments; Industrial process measurement equipment

(P-7948)
CAPILLARY BIOMEDICAL INC
2 Wrigley Ste 101, Irvine (92618-2759)
PHONE.....................949 317-1701
Paul Strasma, *Pr*
EMP: 28 **EST:** 2014

SALES (est): 2.41MM **Publicly Held**
Web: www.capillarybio.com
SIC: 3826 3841 Analytical instruments; Surgical and medical instruments
PA: Tandem Diabetes Care, Inc.
12400 High Bluff Dr

(P-7949)
CITY OF SAN DIEGO
Also Called: Public Utilites Emts
2392 Kincaid Rd, San Diego (92101-0811)
PHONE.....................619 758-2310
Steve Meyer, *Mgr*
EMP: 158
SQ FT: 92,782
SALES (corp-wide): 2.9B **Privately Held**
Web: www.sandiego.gov
SIC: 3826 Sewage testing apparatus
PA: City Of San Diego
202 C St
619 236-6330

(P-7950)
DOE & INGALLS CAL OPER LLC
1060 Citrus St, Riverside (92507-1730)
PHONE.....................951 801-7175
John Hollenbach, *Managing Member*
EMP: 36 **EST:** 2008
SQ FT: 43,000
SALES (est): 3.63MM
SALES (corp-wide): 42.86B **Publicly Held**
SIC: 3826 Analytical instruments
HQ: Doe & Ingalls Management, Llc
4813 Emperor Blvd Ste 300
Durham NC 27703

(P-7951)
EMD MILLIPORE CORPORATION
28835 Single Oak Dr, Temecula
(92590-5501)
PHONE.....................951 676-8080
Patrick Schneider, *Mgr*
EMP: 56
SALES (corp-wide): 22.82B **Privately Held**
Web: www.emdmillipore.com
SIC: 3826 Analytical instruments
HQ: Emd Millipore Corporation
400 Summit Dr
Burlington MA 01803
800 645-5476

(P-7952)
EMD MILLIPORE CORPORATION
26578 Old Julian Hwy, Ramona
(92065-6733)
PHONE.....................760 788-9692
Haizhen Liu, *Mgr*
EMP: 36
SQ FT: 9,694
SALES (corp-wide): 22.82B **Privately Held**
Web: www.emdmillipore.com
SIC: 3826 Analytical instruments
HQ: Emd Millipore Corporation
400 Summit Dr
Burlington MA 01803
800 645-5476

(P-7953)
ENDRESS & HAUSER CONDUCTA INC
Also Called: Endresshauser Conducta
4123 E La Palma Ave St200, Anaheim
(92807-1867)
PHONE.....................800 835-5474
Manfred A Jagiella, *CEO*
Claude Genswein, *
EMP: 50 **EST:** 1976
SQ FT: 31,000
SALES (est): 12.5MM **Privately Held**
Web: www.analysis-oem.com

SIC: 3826 3823 Water testing apparatus; Process control instruments
HQ: Endress+Hauser Conducta Gmbh+Co. Kg
Dieselstr. 24
Gerlingen BW 70839
71562090

(P-7954)
ENDRESS+HSER OPTCAL ANALIS INC
11027 Arrow Rte, Rancho Cucamonga (91730-4866)
PHONE..............................909 477-2329
EMP: 32 EST: 2001
SALES (est): 1.81MM **Privately Held**
SIC: 3826 Analytical instruments
PA: Endress+Hauser Ag
Kagenstrasse 2

(P-7955)
ENTECH INSTRUMENTS INC
2207 Agate Ct, Simi Valley (93065-1839)
PHONE..............................805 527-5939
Daniel B Cardin, CEO
▲ EMP: 55 EST: 1989
SQ FT: 25,000
SALES (est): 9.34MM **Privately Held**
Web: www.entechinst.com
SIC: 3826 Environmental testing equipment

(P-7956)
HAMILTON SUNDSTRAND CORP
Collins Aerospace
960 Overland Ct, San Dimas (91773-1742)
P.O. Box 2801 (91769-2801)
PHONE..............................909 593-5300
Bob Hertel, Brnch Mgr
EMP: 240
SALES (corp-wide): 68.92B **Publicly Held**
Web: www.collinsaerospace.com
SIC: 3826 3861 3812 Spectrometers; Cameras, still and motion picture (all types); Search and navigation equipment
HQ: Hamilton Sundstrand Corporation
1 Hamilton Rd
Windsor Locks CT 06096
619 714-9442

(P-7957)
HORIBA AMERICAS HOLDING INC (HQ)
9755 Research Dr, Irvine (92618-4626)
PHONE..............................949 250-4811
Juichi Saito, CEO
EMP: 1055 EST: 2017
SALES (est): 438.93MM **Privately Held**
Web: www.horiba.com
SIC: 3826 Analytical instruments
PA: Horiba, Ltd.
2, Kisshoinmiyanohigashicho, Minami Ku

(P-7958)
HORIBA INSTRUMENTS INC (DH)
Also Called: Horiba Automotive Test Systems
9755 Research Dr, Irvine (92618-4626)
PHONE..............................949 250-4811
Jai Hakhu, Ch Bd
▲ EMP: 195 EST: 1998
SQ FT: 80,000
SALES (est): 194.11MM **Privately Held**
Web: www.horiba.com
SIC: 3826 3829 3511 3825 Analytical instruments; Measuring and controlling devices, nec; Turbines and turbine generator set units, complete; Instruments to measure electricity
HQ: Horiba Americas Holding Incorporated
9755 Research Dr

Irvine CA 92618
949 250-4811

(P-7959)
ILLUMINA INC
9885 Towne Centre Dr, San Diego (92121-1975)
PHONE..............................800 809-4566
William Rastetter, Ch
EMP: 25
SALES (corp-wide): 4.5B **Publicly Held**
Web: www.illumina.com
SIC: 3826 Analytical instruments
PA: Illumina, Inc.
5200 Illumina Way
858 202-4500

(P-7960)
ILLUMINA INC (PA)
Also Called: Illumina
5200 Illumina Way, San Diego (92122-4616)
PHONE..............................858 202-4500
Jacob Thaysen, CEO
Stephen P Macmillan, *
Kevin Pegels, OF GLOBAL Operations
Charles Dadswell, Ch Bd
▲ EMP: 483 EST: 1998
SQ FT: 859,000
SALES (est): 4.5B
SALES (corp-wide): 4.5B **Publicly Held**
Web: www.illumina.com
SIC: 3826 3821 Analytical instruments; Clinical laboratory instruments, except medical and dental

(P-7961)
INTERGLOBAL WASTE MGT INC
820 Calle Plano, Camarillo (93012-8557)
PHONE..............................805 388-1588
Harold Katersky, Ch Bd
Thomas Williams, Stockholder*
EMP: 80 EST: 2000
SALES (est): 1.28MM **Privately Held**
SIC: 3826 Analytical instruments

(P-7962)
INVITROGEN IP HOLDINGS INC
5791 Van Allen Way, Carlsbad (92008-7321)
PHONE..............................760 603-7200
Stuart Hepburn, Pr
EMP: 97 EST: 2003
SALES (est): 15.46MM
SALES (corp-wide): 42.86B **Publicly Held**
SIC: 3826 Analytical instruments
HQ: Life Technologies Corporation
5781 Van Allen Way
Carlsbad CA 92008
760 603-7200

(P-7963)
LAMBDA RESEARCH OPTICS INC
1695 Macarthur Blvd, Costa Mesa (92626-1440)
PHONE..............................714 327-0600
Mark Youn, Pr
▲ EMP: 65 EST: 1991
SQ FT: 3,500
SALES (est): 8.77MM **Privately Held**
Web: www.lambda.cc
SIC: 3826 3827 3229 Laser scientific and engineering instruments; Optical instruments and lenses; Pressed and blown glass, nec

(P-7964)
LEICA BIOSYSTEMS IMAGING INC (HQ)
Also Called: Aperio
1360 Park Center Dr, Vista (92081-8300)
PHONE..............................760 539-1100
James F O'reilly, VP
Dirk G Soenksen, Pr
Greg Crandall, VP Engg
Jared N Schwartz, Chief Medical Officer
Keith B Hagen, COO
EMP: 106 EST: 2011
SQ FT: 37,000
SALES (est): 51.62MM
SALES (corp-wide): 23.89B **Publicly Held**
Web: www.leicabiosystems.com
SIC: 3826 Analytical instruments
PA: Danaher Corporation
2200 Pa Ave Nw Ste 800w
202 828-0850

(P-7965)
LIFE TECHNOLOGIES CORPORATION
Also Called: Life Technologies
5791 Van Allen Way, Carlsbad (92008-7321)
PHONE..............................760 918-0135
EMP: 369
SALES (corp-wide): 42.86B **Publicly Held**
Web: www.thermofisher.com
SIC: 3826 Analytical instruments
HQ: Life Technologies Corporation
5781 Van Allen Way
Carlsbad CA 92008
760 603-7200

(P-7966)
LIFE TECHNOLOGIES CORPORATION
Also Called: Supplier Diversity Program
5791 Van Allen Way, Carlsbad (92008-7321)
PHONE..............................760 918-4259
EMP: 28
SALES (corp-wide): 42.86B **Publicly Held**
Web: www.thermofisher.com
SIC: 3826 Analytical instruments
HQ: Life Technologies Corporation
5781 Van Allen Way
Carlsbad CA 92008
760 603-7200

(P-7967)
MEANS ENGINEERING INC
5927 Geiger Ct, Carlsbad (92008-7305)
PHONE..............................760 931 0462
David William Means, CEO
Lisa Means, *
EMP: 70 EST: 1996
SQ FT: 34,000
SALES (est): 16.4MM **Privately Held**
Web: www.meanseng.com
SIC: 3826 3699 3559 Analytical instruments; Electrical equipment and supplies, nec; Semiconductor manufacturing machinery

(P-7968)
MOLECULAR BIOPRODUCTS INC (DH)
9389 Waples St, San Diego (92121-3903)
PHONE..............................858 453-7551
Seth H Hoogasian, CEO
Gary J Marmontello, *
R Jeffrey Harris, *
Michael K Bresson, *
John Buono, *
◆ EMP: 110 EST: 1978
SQ FT: 45,000

SALES (est): 89.79MM
SALES (corp-wide): 42.86B **Publicly Held**
Web: www.thermofisher.com
SIC: 3826 Analytical instruments
HQ: Fisher Scientific International Llc
81 Wyman St
Waltham MA 02451

(P-7969)
MOTIONLOFT INC
13681 Newport Ave Ste 8, Tustin (92780-7815)
PHONE..............................415 580-7671
Joyce Reitman, CEO
Chris Garrison, *
EMP: 39 EST: 2010
SALES (est): 2.62MM **Privately Held**
Web: www.motionloft.com
SIC: 3826 7372 Analytical instruments; Application computer software

(P-7970)
OXFORD INSTRS ASYLUM RES INC (HQ)
Also Called: Asylum Research
7416 Hollister Ave, Santa Barbara (93117-2583)
PHONE..............................805 696-6466
Jason Cleveland, CEO
Roger Proksch, *
John Green, *
Richard Clark, *
Dick Clark, *
EMP: 55 EST: 2012
SALES (est): 11.73MM
SALES (corp-wide): 596.99MM **Privately Held**
Web: www.oxinst.com
SIC: 3826 Analytical instruments
PA: Oxford Instruments Plc
Magnetic Resonance
186 539-3200

(P-7971)
OXFORD NANOIMAGING INC
11045 Roselle St Ste 3, San Diego (92121-1218)
PHONE..............................858 999-8860
Paul Scagnetti, CEO
Feyo Sickinghe, *
James Smobry, *
Nick Dobbs, *
EMP: 95 EST: 2019
SALES (est): 4.06MM **Privately Held**
Web: www.oni.bio
SIC: 3826 Microscopes, electron and proton

(P-7972)
PHENOMENEX INC (HQ)
411 Madrid Ave, Torrance (90501-1430)
PHONE..............................310 212-0555
Farshad Mahjoor, Pr
James F O Reilly, *
Frank T Mcfaden, CFO
Kaveh Kahen, *
▲ EMP: 250 EST: 1982
SQ FT: 100,000
SALES (est): 132.13MM
SALES (corp-wide): 23.89B **Publicly Held**
Web: www.phenomenex.com
SIC: 3826 Analytical instruments
PA: Danaher Corporation
2200 Pa Ave Nw Ste 800w
202 828-0850

(P-7973)
QUANTUM DESIGN INC (PA)
Also Called: Quantum Design International
10307 Pacific Center Ct, San Diego (92121-4340)

PRODUCTS & SVCS

PHONE...............................858 481-4400
Greg Degeller, *Pr*
Michael B Simmonds, *
David Schultz, *
Martin Kugler, *
▲ **EMP:** 217 **EST:** 1982
SQ FT: 118,000
SALES (est): 35.39MM
SALES (corp-wide): 35.39MM **Privately Held**
Web: www.qdusa.com
SIC: 3826 Laser scientific and engineering instruments

(P-7974)
QUANTUM MAGNETICS LLC
1251 E Dyer Rd Ste 140, Santa Ana (92705-5677)
PHONE...............................714 258-4400
EMP: 609
SIC: 3826 3812 Magnetic resonance imaging apparatus; Search and navigation equipment

(P-7975)
SAFEGUARD ENVIROGROUP INC
153 Lowell Ave, Glendora (91741-2449)
PHONE...............................626 512-7585
EMP: 24
SALES (est): 2.77MM **Privately Held**
Web: www.safeguardenviro.com
SIC: 3826 Moisture analyzers

(P-7976)
SCREENING SYSTEMS INC (PA)
36 Blackbird Ln, Aliso Viejo (92656-1765)
P.O. Box 1357 (78646-1357)
PHONE...............................949 855-1751
Susan L Baker, *Pr*
Susan Baker, *
EMP: 25 **EST:** 1979
SQ FT: 34,000
SALES (est): 823.63K
SALES (corp-wide): 823.63K **Privately Held**
Web: www.scrsys.com
SIC: 3826 3829 Environmental testing equipment; Measuring and controlling devices, nec

(P-7977)
SHORE WESTERN MANUFACTURING
19888 Quiroz Ct, Walnut (91789-2828)
PHONE...............................626 357-3251
Donald Schroeder, *Pr*
Alice Schroeder, *
▲ **EMP:** 34 **EST:** 1967
SALES (est): 1.67MM **Privately Held**
SIC: 3826 Environmental testing equipment

(P-7978)
SINGULAR GENOMICS SYSTEMS INC (PA)
Also Called: Singular Genomics
3010 Science Park Rd, San Diego (92121-1102)
PHONE...............................858 333-7830
Andrew Spaventa, *Ch Bd*
Jyotsna Ghai, *COO*
Dalen Meeter, *CFO*
Eli Glezer, *CSO*
Jorge Velarde, *Chief Business Officer*
EMP: 166 **EST:** 2016
SQ FT: 135,000
SALES (est): 2.91MM
SALES (corp-wide): 2.91MM **Publicly Held**

Web: www.singulargenomics.com
SIC: 3826 Analytical instruments

(P-7979)
SINGULAR GENOMICS SYSTEMS INC
10010 Mesa Rim Rd, San Diego (92121-2912)
PHONE...............................619 703-8135
EMP: 99
SALES (corp-wide): 2.91MM **Publicly Held**
Web: www.singulargenomics.com
SIC: 3826 Analytical instruments
PA: Singular Genomics Systems, Inc.
3010 Science Park Rd
858 333-7830

(P-7980)
TELEDYNE FLIR COML SYSTEMS INC (DH)
6769 Hollister Ave, Goleta (93117-3001)
PHONE...............................805 964-9797
Robert Mehrabian, *CEO*
Todd Booth, *
Melanie S Cibik, *
▲ **EMP:** 350 **EST:** 1996
SALES (est): 99.7MM
SALES (corp-wide): 5.64B **Publicly Held**
Web: www.flir.com
SIC: 3826 Analytical instruments
HQ: Teledyne Flir, Llc
27700 Sw Parkway Ave
Wilsonville OR 97070
503 498-3547

(P-7981)
TELEDYNE HANSON RESEARCH INC
9810 Variel Ave, Chatsworth (91311-4316)
PHONE...............................818 882-7266
▲ **EMP:** 31
SIC: 3826 Analytical instruments

(P-7982)
TELEDYNE INSTRUMENTS INC
Teledyne Hanson Research
9810 Variel Ave, Chatsworth (91311-4316)
PHONE...............................818 882-7266
Thomas Reslewic, *Mgr*
EMP: 31
SALES (corp-wide): 5.64B **Publicly Held**
Web: www.teledynelabs.com
SIC: 3826 Analytical instruments
HQ: Teledyne Instruments, Inc.
16830 Chestnut St
City Of Industry CA 91748
626 934-1500

(P-7983)
TELESIS BIO INC (PA)
Also Called: Bioxp
10421 Wateridge Cir Ste 200, San Diego (92121-5787)
PHONE...............................858 228-4115
Eric Esser, *Pr*
Franklin R Witney, *Non-Executive Chairman of the Board*
William Kullback, *CFO*
Robert H Cutler, *CLO*
EMP: 37 **EST:** 2011
SALES (est): 27.51MM
SALES (corp-wide): 27.51MM **Publicly Held**
Web: www.codexdna.com
SIC: 3826 Analytical instruments

(P-7984)
TERUMO AMERICAS HOLDING INC
Also Called: Cardiovascular Systems
1311 Valencia Ave, Tustin (92780-6447)
PHONE...............................714 258-8001
Kevin Hoffman, *Brnch Mgr*
EMP: 28
Web: www.terumo.com
SIC: 3826 Hemoglobinometers
HQ: Terumo Americas Holding, Inc.
265 Davidson Ave Ste 320
Somerset NJ 08873
732 302-4900

(P-7985)
TETRA TECH EC INC
17885 Von Karman Ave Ste 500, Irvine (92614-5227)
PHONE...............................949 809-5000
Andrew Brack, *Brnch Mgr*
EMP: 39
SALES (corp-wide): 4.52B **Publicly Held**
SIC: 3826 Environmental testing equipment
HQ: Tetra Tech Ec, Inc.
6 Century Dr Ste 3
Parsippany NJ 07054
973 630-8000

(P-7986)
THERMO FISHER SCIENTIFIC INC
5823 Newton Dr, Carlsbad (92008-7361)
PHONE...............................781 622-1000
EMP: 32
SALES (corp-wide): 42.86B **Publicly Held**
Web: www.thermofisher.com
SIC: 3826 Analytical instruments
PA: Thermo Fisher Scientific Inc.
168 3rd Ave
781 622-1000

(P-7987)
THERMO FISHER SCIENTIFIC INC
Also Called: Molecular Bio Products
9389 Waples St, San Diego (92121-3903)
PHONE...............................858 453-7551
Cesar Ramirez, *Brnch Mgr*
EMP: 70
SALES (corp-wide): 42.86B **Publicly Held**
Web: www.thermofisher.com
SIC: 3826 Analytical instruments
PA: Thermo Fisher Scientific Inc.
168 3rd Ave
781 622-1000

(P-7988)
THERMO FISHER SCIENTIFIC INC
5791 Van Allen Way, Carlsbad (92008-7321)
PHONE...............................760 603-7200
EMP: 51
SALES (corp-wide): 42.86B **Publicly Held**
Web: www.thermofisher.com
SIC: 3826 Analytical instruments
PA: Thermo Fisher Scientific Inc.
168 3rd Ave
781 622-1000

(P-7989)
THERMO FSHER SCNTIFIC PSG CORP (HQ)
5791 Van Allen Way, Carlsbad (92008-7321)
PHONE...............................760 603-7200
Marc N Casper, *Pr*

EMP: 214 **EST:** 2020
SALES (est): 22.3MM
SALES (corp-wide): 42.86B **Publicly Held**
SIC: 3826 Analytical instruments
PA: Thermo Fisher Scientific Inc.
168 3rd Ave
781 622-1000

(P-7990)
VEECO PROCESS EQUIPMENT INC
Digital Instruments Div
112 Robin Hill Rd, Goleta (93117-3107)
PHONE...............................805 967-1400
Don Kenia, *CEO*
EMP: 96
Web: www.veeco.com
SIC: 3826 3827 Microscopes, electron and proton; Optical instruments and lenses
HQ: Veeco Process Equipment Inc.
1 Terminal Dr
Plainview NY 11803

(P-7991)
WYATT TECHNOLOGY LLC (HQ)
Also Called: Wyatt Technology
6330 Hollister Ave, Goleta (93117-3115)
PHONE...............................805 681-9009
Philip J Wyatt, *CEO*
Geofrey K Wyatt, *
Clifford D Wyatt, *
Carolyn Walton, *
EMP: 118 **EST:** 1982
SQ FT: 30,000
SALES (est): 20.69MM **Publicly Held**
Web: www.wyatt.com
SIC: 3826 Laser scientific and engineering instruments
PA: Waters Corporation
34 Maple St

(P-7992)
YSI INCORPORATED
Also Called: Yellow Springs Instruments
9940 Summers Ridge Rd, San Diego (92121-2997)
PHONE...............................858 546-8327
Chris Ward, *Brnch Mgr*
EMP: 37
Web: www.ysi.com
SIC: 3826 3823 3841 Water testing apparatus; Process control instruments; Diagnostic apparatus, medical
HQ: Ysi Incorporated
1700 Brannum Ln 1725
Yellow Springs OH 45387
937 767-7241

3827 Optical Instruments And Lenses

(P-7993)
AAREN SCIENTIFIC INC (DH)
Also Called: Carl Zeiss Meditec,
9010 Hellman Ave, Rancho Cucamonga (91730-4425)
PHONE...............................909 937-1033
Hans-joachim Miesner, *Pr*
Stevens Chevillotte, *
James Thornton, *
Victor Garcia, *
Jan Willem De Cler, *
▲ **EMP:** 83 **EST:** 2008
SALES (est): 9.28MM **Privately Held**
Web: www.aareninc.com
SIC: 3827 3851 Optical instruments and lenses; Ophthalmic goods
HQ: Carl Zeiss Meditec, Inc.
5300 Central Pkwy

Dublin CA 94568
925 557-4100

(P-7994)
ABRISA INDUSTRIAL GLASS INC (HQ)
200 Hallock Dr, Santa Paula (93060-9646)
P.O. Box 85055 (60680-0851)
PHONE.............................805 525-4902
Rajiv Ahuja, *CEO*
▲ **EMP:** 90 **EST:** 1980
SQ FT: 93,000
SALES (est): 18.09MM **Privately Held**
Web: www.abrisatechnologies.com
SIC: 3827 Optical instruments and lenses
PA: Graham Partners, Inc.
   3811 W Chster Pike Bldg 2

(P-7995)
ABRISA TECHNOLOGIES
200 Hallock Dr, Santa Paula (93060-9646)
P.O. Box 489 (93061-0489)
PHONE.............................805 525-4902
Blake Fennell, *CEO*
Maartin Ostendorp, *CFO*
EMP: 46 **EST:** 2013
SALES (est): 9.75MM **Privately Held**
Web: www.abrisatechnologies.com
SIC: 3827 Optical instruments and lenses

(P-7996)
BUK OPTICS INC
Also Called: Precision Glass & Optics
3600 W Moore Ave, Santa Ana
(92704-6835)
PHONE.............................714 384-9620
Daniel S Bukaty, *CEO*
Daniel Bukaty Junior, *Pr*
▲ **EMP:** 42 **EST:** 1985
SQ FT: 25,000
SALES (est): 5.1MM **Privately Held**
Web: www.pgo.com
SIC: 3827 Optical instruments and apparatus

(P-7997)
CARL ZEISS MEDITEC PROD LLC
1040 S Vintage Ave Ste A, Ontario
(91761-3631)
PHONE.............................877 644-4657
Hans-joachim Miesner, *Pr*
James Thornton, *
Paul Yun, *
Min Qu, *
EMP: 99 **EST:** 2017
SQ FT: 67,000
SALES (est): 10.08MM **Privately Held**
Web: www.zeiss.com
SIC: 3827 Optical instruments and lenses
HQ: Carl Zeiss Meditec, Inc.
   5300 Central Pkwy
   Dublin CA 94568
   925 557-4100

(P-7998)
COHERENT AEROSPACE & DEF INC
14192 Chambers Rd, Tustin (92780-6908)
PHONE.............................714 247-7100
Mark Maiberger, *Genl Mgr*
EMP: 60
SALES (corp-wide): 4.71B **Publicly Held**
Web: www.iiviad.com
SIC: 3827 7389 8748 Optical instruments
and apparatus; Design services; Business
consulting, nec
HQ: Coherent Aerospace & Defense, Inc.
   36570 Briggs Rd
   Murrieta CA 92563
   951 926-2994

(P-7999)
DELTRONIC CORPORATION
Also Called: Hi-Precision Grinding
3900 W Segerstrom Ave, Santa Ana
(92704-6312)
PHONE.............................714 545-5800
Robert C Larzelere, *Pr*
Diane Larzelere, *
Sterling Sander, *
▼ **EMP:** 73 **EST:** 1955
SQ FT: 40,000
SALES (est): 9.15MM **Privately Held**
Web: www.deltronic.com
SIC: 3827 3545 Optical comparators;
Gauges (machine tool accessories)

(P-8000)
ENHANCED VISION SYSTEMS INC (HQ)
15301 Springdale St, Huntington Beach
(92649-1140)
PHONE.............................800 440-9476
Tom Tiernan, *CEO*
Rose Mayer, *
◆ **EMP:** 65 **EST:** 1996
SALES (est): 21.72MM
SALES (corp-wide): 26.74MM **Privately Held**
Web: www.enhancedvision.com
SIC: 3827 Optical instruments and lenses
PA: Freedom Scientific Blv Group, Llc
   17757 Us Highway 19 N # 200
   727 803-8000

(P-8001)
GMTO CORPORATION
Also Called: Giant Mgllan Tlscope Orgnztion
300 N Lake Ave Fl 14, Pasadena
(91101-4164)
PHONE.............................626 204-0500
Robert Shelton, *Pr*
Alan Gordon, *
Amy Honbo, *
Doctor Robert N Shelton, *Pr*
Sara Lee Keller, *
▲ **EMP:** 70 **EST:** 2007
SALES (est): 8.77MM **Privately Held**
Web: www.giantmagellan.org
SIC: 3827 8733 Telescopes: elbow,
panoramic, sighting, fire control, etc.;
Noncommercial research organizations

(P-8002)
GOOCH AND HOUSEGO CAL LLC
5390 Kazuko Ct, Moorpark (93021-1790)
PHONE.............................805 529-3324
Kenneth Neczypor, *Managing Member*
EMP: 80 **EST:** 2008
SALES (est): 9.47MM
SALES (corp-wide): 107.30MM **Privately Held**
Web: www.gandh.com
SIC: 3827 3823 Optical instruments and
lenses; Process control instruments
PA: Gooch & Housego Plc
   Dowlish Ford
   146 025-6440

(P-8003)
HOYA CORPORATION
Also Called: Hoya San Diego
4255 Ruffin Rd, San Diego (92123-1232)
PHONE.............................858 309-6050
Charlie Pendrell, *Prin*
EMP: 30
Web: www.hoya.com
SIC: 3827 Optical instruments and lenses
HQ: Hoya Corporation
   651 E Corporate Dr

Lewisville TX 75057
972 221-4141

(P-8004)
HOYA HOLDINGS INC
Hoya Corporation USA
425 E Huntington Dr, Monrovia
(91016-3632)
PHONE.............................626 739-5200
Al Benzoni, *VP*
EMP: 151
Web: www.hoyaoptics.com
SIC: 3827 Optical instruments and lenses
HQ: Hoya Holdings, Inc.
   820 N Mccarthy Blvd
   Milpitas CA 95035

(P-8005)
I-COAT COMPANY LLC
12020 Mora Dr Ste 2, Santa Fe Springs
(90670-6082)
PHONE.............................562 941-9989
Arman Bernardi, *CEO*
▲ **EMP:** 50 **EST:** 2003
SQ FT: 6,000
SALES (est): 6.27MM
SALES (corp-wide): 7.66MM **Privately Held**
Web: www.icoatcompany.com
SIC: 3827 Optical instruments and lenses
HQ: Essilor Of America, Inc.
   13555 N Stemmons Fwy
   Dallas TX 75234

(P-8006)
IDEX HEALTH & SCIENCE LLC
2051 Palomar Airport Rd Ste 200, Carlsbad
(92011-1462)
PHONE.............................760 438-2131
Blake Fennell, *Brnch Mgr*
EMP: 99
SALES (corp-wide): 3.27B **Publicly Held**
Web: www.idex-hs.com
SIC: 3827 3699 Optical instruments and
lenses; Laser systems and equipment
HQ: Idex Health & Science Llc
   600 Park Ct
   Rohnert Park CA 94928
   707 588-2000

(P-8007)
INFINITE OPTICS INC
1712 Newport Cir Ste F, Santa Ana
(92705-5118)
PHONE.............................714 557-2299
Geza Keller, *Pr*
Daniel Houston, *
Joooph Coodhand, *
Steven Crawford, *
Denise Banionis, *
EMP: 24 **EST:** 2003
SQ FT: 12,860
SALES (est): 4.21MM **Privately Held**
Web: www.infiniteoptics.com
SIC: 3827 Lens coating and grinding
equipment

(P-8008)
LIGHTWORKS OPTICS INC
14192 Chambers Rd, Tustin (92780-6908)
PHONE.............................714 247-7100
EMP: 60
Web: www.iiviad.com
SIC: 3827 7389 8748 Optical instruments
and apparatus; Design services; Business
consulting, nec

(P-8009)
LUMINIT LLC
1850 W 205th St, Torrance (90501-1526)

PHONE.............................310 320-1066
Engin Arik, *Managing Member*
Linh Whitaker, *
Jonathan Waldern, *
▲ **EMP:** 42 **EST:** 2005
SALES (est): 9.76MM **Privately Held**
Web: www.luminitco.com
SIC: 3827 Optical instruments and lenses

(P-8010)
MACHINE VISION PRODUCTS INC (PA)
3270 Corporate Vw Ste D, Vista
(92081-8570)
PHONE.............................760 438-1138
George T Ayoub, *CEO*
▲ **EMP:** 36 **EST:** 1993
SQ FT: 60,000
SALES (est): 10.51MM **Privately Held**
Web: www.visionpro.com
SIC: 3827 7371 3229 Optical instruments
and lenses; Custom computer
programming services; Pressed and blown
glass, nec

(P-8011)
MELLES GRIOT INC
2051 Palomar Airport Rd, Carlsbad
(92011-1461)
PHONE.............................760 438-2254
EMP: 85
Web: www.idex-hs.com
SIC: 3827 3699 Optical instruments and
lenses; Laser systems and equipment

(P-8012)
NIPRO OPTICS INC
7 Marconi, Irvine (92618-2701)
PHONE.............................949 215-1151
Tom Gross, *Pr*
EMP: 30 **EST:** 2005
SQ FT: 3,500
SALES (est): 2.73MM **Privately Held**
Web: www.niprooptics.com
SIC: 3827 Reflectors, optical

(P-8013)
OPTICAL CORPORATION (DH)
9731 Topanga Canyon Pl, Chatsworth
(91311-4135)
PHONE.............................818 725-9750
Francis Dominic, *Pr*
EMP: 23 **EST:** 1932
SQ FT: 14,000
SALES (est): 2.74MM **Publicly Held**
Web: www.theopticalco.com
SIC: 3827 Optical instruments and lenses
HQ: Excel Technology, Inc.
   125 Middlesex Tpke
   Bedford MA 01730
   781 266-5700

(P-8014)
OPTOSIGMA CORPORATION
1540 Scenic Ave, Costa Mesa
(92626-1408)
PHONE.............................949 851-5881
Scott Rudder, *Pr*
Guy Ear, *
Roger Matsunaga, *
Steve Mcnamee, *VP*
EMP: 25 **EST:** 1995
SQ FT: 13,000
SALES (est): 10.33MM **Privately Held**
Web: www.optosigma.com
SIC: 3827 Optical instruments and lenses
PA: Sigma Koki Co.,Ltd.
   1-19-9, Midori

PRODUCTS & SVCS

(P-8015)
PHOTO RESEARCH INC
Also Called: Photo Research
9731 Topanga Canyon Pl, Chatsworth
(91311-4135)
PHONE.................................818 341-5151
EMP: 24
SIC: 3827 Optical instruments and lenses

(P-8016)
PVP ADVANCED EO SYSTEMS INC (DH)
14312 Franklin Ave Ste 100, Tustin
(92780-7066)
PHONE.................................714 508-2740
Bruce E Ferguson, *CEO*
John Le Blanc, *
▲ **EMP:** 48 **EST:** 1997
SQ FT: 21,000
SALES (est): 14.7MM **Privately Held**
Web: www.advancedeo.systems
SIC: 3827 Optical instruments and apparatus
HQ: Rafael U.S.A., Inc.
　6903 Rockledge Dr Ste 850
　Bethesda MD 20817

(P-8017)
REYNARD CORPORATION
1020 Calle Sombra, San Clemente
(92673-6227)
PHONE.................................949 366-8866
Forrest Reynard, *Pr*
Jean Reynard, *
Randy Reynard, *
EMP: 32 **EST:** 1984
SQ FT: 28,000
SALES (est): 4.72MM **Privately Held**
Web: www.reynardcorp.com
SIC: 3827 Mirrors, optical

(P-8018)
SAFRAN DEFENSE & SPACE INC
2960 Airway Ave Ste A103, Costa Mesa
(92626-6001)
PHONE.................................603 296-0469
EMP: 74
SALES (corp-wide): 940.23MM **Privately Held**
Web: www.optics1.com
SIC: 3827 Optical instruments and lenses
HQ: Safran Defense & Space, Inc.
　2 Cooper Ln
　Bedford NH 03110
　603 296-0469

(P-8019)
SAFRAN DEFENSE & SPACE INC
2665 Park Center Dr Ste A, Simi Valley
(93065-6200)
PHONE.................................805 373-9340
Garrick Matheson, *COO*
EMP: 80
SALES (corp-wide): 940.23MM **Privately Held**
Web: www.optics1.com
SIC: 3827 Optical instruments and lenses
HQ: Safran Defense & Space, Inc.
　2 Cooper Ln
　Bedford NH 03110
　603 296-0469

(P-8020)
SCOPE CITY (PA)
2978 Topaz Ave, Simi Valley (93063-2168)
P.O. Box 1630 (93062-1630)
PHONE.................................805 522-6646
Maurice Sweiss, *CEO*

▲ **EMP:** 35 **EST:** 1980
SQ FT: 35,000
SALES (est): 1.11MM
SALES (corp-wide): 1.11MM **Privately Held**
Web: www.scope.city
SIC: 3827 Optical instruments and lenses

(P-8021)
SELLERS OPTICAL INC
Also Called: Precision Optical
320 Kalmus Dr, Costa Mesa (92626-6013)
PHONE.................................949 631-6800
Alan Mixon Lambert, *Ch Bd*
Paul Dimeck, *
Rod Randolph, *
Janice Lambert, *
Alan Lambert Junior, *VP*
EMP: 57 **EST:** 1981
SQ FT: 17,000
SALES (est): 10.12MM **Privately Held**
Web: www.precisionoptical.com
SIC: 3827 Optical instruments and apparatus

(P-8022)
SPECTRUM SCIENTIFIC INC
16692 Hale Ave Ste A, Irvine (92606-5052)
PHONE.................................949 260-9900
Daphnie Chakran, *Pr*
EMP: 27 **EST:** 2004
SALES (est): 2.4MM **Privately Held**
Web: www.ssioptics.com
SIC: 3827 Optical instruments and lenses

(P-8023)
SYNERGEYES INC (HQ)
Also Called: Synergeyes
2236 Rutherford Rd Ste 115, Carlsbad
(92008-8836)
PHONE.................................760 476-9410
James K Kirchner, *Pr*
Thomas M Crews, *
David Voris, *
James Gorechner, *
David Fancher, *
▲ **EMP:** 98 **EST:** 2005
SALES (est): 24.15MM
SALES (corp-wide): 3.9B **Publicly Held**
Web: www.synergeyes.com
SIC: 3827 Optical instruments and lenses
PA: The Cooper Companies Inc
　6101 Bllnger Cyn Rd Ste 5
　925 460-3600

(P-8024)
TELEDYNE SCENTIFIC IMAGING LLC
Also Called: Teledyne Optmum Optcal Systems
4153 Calle Tesoro, Camarillo (93012-8760)
EMP: 48
SALES (corp-wide): 5.64B **Publicly Held**
Web: www.teledyne-si.com
SIC: 3827 Optical instruments and lenses
HQ: Teledyne Scientific & Imaging, Llc
　1049 Camino Dos Rios
　Thousand Oaks CA 91360

(P-8025)
TFD INCORPORATED
Also Called: Thin Film Devices
39 Heritage, Irvine (92604-1957)
PHONE.................................714 630-7127
Saleem Shaikh, *CEO*
Joy Shaikh, *
▲ **EMP:** 25 **EST:** 1984
SALES (est): 4.95MM **Privately Held**
Web: www.tfdinc.com
SIC: 3827 Optical instruments and lenses

(P-8026)
TOUCH INTERNATIONAL DISPLAY ENHANCEMENTS CORP
11231 Jola Ln, Garden Grove (92843-3515)
PHONE.................................512 646-0310
EMP: 28
SIC: 3827 Optical instruments and lenses

(P-8027)
UNITED SCOPE LLC (HQ)
Also Called: Amscope
3210 El Camino Real, Irvine (92602-1365)
PHONE.................................714 942-3202
Frank Dai, *CEO*
Andrew Wu, *VP*
Mandy J Liu, *CFO*
Nathaniel Fasnacht, *CFO*
▲ **EMP:** 24 **EST:** 2013
SALES (est): 11.57MM
SALES (corp-wide): 333.76MM **Privately Held**
Web: www.unitedscope.com
SIC: 3827 5049 Optical instruments and lenses; Optical goods
PA: L Squared Capital Partners Llc
　3434 Via Lido Ste 300
　949 398-0168

(P-8028)
WINTRISS ENGINEERING CORP
9010 Kenamar Dr Ste 101, San Diego
(92121-3437)
PHONE.................................858 550-7300
Andrew W Ash, *CEO*
Vic Wintriss, *Pr*
Pete Burggren, *Sls Dir*
▲ **EMP:** 23 **EST:** 1986
SQ FT: 11,576
SALES (est): 11.41MM **Privately Held**
Web: www.weco.com
SIC: 3827 Optical test and inspection equipment

(P-8029)
Z C & R COATING FOR OPTICS INC
1401 Abalone Ave, Torrance (90501-2889)
PHONE.................................310 381-3060
Rajiv Ahuja, *CEO*
EMP: 43 **EST:** 1979
SQ FT: 21,781
SALES (est): 3.93MM **Privately Held**
Web: www.abrisatechnologies.com
SIC: 3827 Lens coating equipment
HQ: Abrisa Industrial Glass, Inc.
　200 Hallock Dr
　Santa Paula CA 93060
　805 525-4902

3829 Measuring And Controlling Devices, Nec

(P-8030)
ADVANCED MICRO INSTRUMENTS INC
Also Called: AMI
225 Paularino Ave, Costa Mesa
(92626-3313)
PHONE.................................714 848-5533
Kenneth Biele, *CEO*
EMP: 23 **EST:** 1999
SQ FT: 2,500
SALES (est): 12.38MM
SALES (corp-wide): 1.06B **Publicly Held**
Web: www.amio2.com
SIC: 3829 Measuring and controlling devices, nec

PA: Enpro Inc.
　5605 Crnegie Blvd Ste 500
　704 731-1500

(P-8031)
ALVARADO MANUFACTURING CO INC
12660 Colony Ct, Chino (91710-2975)
PHONE.................................909 591-8431
Bret Armatas, *CEO*
◆ **EMP:** 108 **EST:** 1955
SQ FT: 69,000
SALES (est): 23.33MM **Privately Held**
Web: www.alvaradomfg.com
SIC: 3829 Turnstiles, equipped with counting mechanisms

(P-8032)
APPLIED TECHNOLOGIES ASSOC INC (HQ)
Also Called: A T A
3025 Buena Vista Dr, Paso Robles
(93446-8555)
PHONE.................................805 239-9100
William B Wade, *Pr*
William B Wade, *Pr*
George Walker, *
▲ **EMP:** 127 **EST:** 1981
SALES (est): 24.2MM
SALES (corp-wide): 400.64MM **Privately Held**
Web: www.ata-sd.com
SIC: 3829 1381 Surveying instruments and accessories; Drilling oil and gas wells
PA: Scientific Drilling International, Inc.
　1450 Lk Rbbins Dr Ste 200
　281 443-3300

(P-8033)
BARKSDALE INC (DH)
3211 Fruitland Ave, Los Angeles
(90058-3757)
P.O. Box 58843 (90058-0843)
PHONE.................................323 583-6243
Subramanya Prasad, *Pr*
▲ **EMP:** 100 **EST:** 1946
SQ FT: 115,000
SALES (est): 65.75MM
SALES (corp-wide): 2.09B **Publicly Held**
Web: www.barksdale.com
SIC: 3829 3491 3823 3643 Measuring and controlling devices, nec; Industrial valves; Process control instruments; Current-carrying wiring services
HQ: Crane Controls, Inc.
　100 Stamford Pl
　Stamford CT 06902

(P-8034)
BEI NORTH AMERICA LLC (DH)
1461 Lawrence Dr, Thousand Oaks
(91320-1303)
PHONE.................................805 716-0642
Martha Sullivan, *Pr*
Jeffrey Cote, *VP*
Alison Roelke, *VP*
EMP: 103 **EST:** 2015
SALES (est): 19.1MM
SALES (corp-wide): 4.05B **Privately Held**
SIC: 3829 Measuring and controlling devices, nec
HQ: Custom Sensors & Technologies, Inc.
　1461 Lawrence Dr
　Thousand Oaks CA 91320
　805 716-0322

(P-8035)
BRENNER-FIEDLER & ASSOC INC (PA)

Also Called: B F
4059 Flat Rock Dr, Riverside (92505-5859)
P.O. Box 7938 (92513-7938)
PHONE...............................562 404-2721
James Kloman, *CEO*
EMP: 39 **EST:** 1957
SQ FT: 28,669
SALES (est): 12.74MM
SALES (corp-wide): 12.74MM **Privately Held**
Web: www.brenner-fiedler.com
SIC: 3829 5085 Accelerometers; Hydraulic and pneumatic pistons and valves

(P-8036)
CALIFORNIA DYNAMICS CORP (PA)
Also Called: Caldyn
20500 Prairie St, Chatsworth (91311-6006)
PHONE...............................323 223-3882
Donald Benkert, *Pr*
Adell Benkert, *VP*
▲ **EMP:** 24 **EST:** 1966
SALES (est): 9.15MM
SALES (corp-wide): 9.15MM **Privately Held**
Web: www.caldyn.com
SIC: 3829 Vibration meters, analyzers, and calibrators

(P-8037)
CALIFORNIA SENSOR CORPORATION
Also Called: Calsense
2075 Corte Del Nogal Ste P, Carlsbad (92011-1415)
PHONE...............................760 438-0525
Adrianus Van De Ven, *CEO*
Ralph Miller, *
David L Byma, *
Robert Destremps, *
Richard Wilkinson, *
EMP: 38 **EST:** 1986
SQ FT: 6,000
SALES (est): 4.96MM **Privately Held**
Web: www.calsense.com
SIC: 3829 5083 Measuring and controlling devices, nec; Irrigation equipment

(P-8038)
CARROS SENSORS SYSTEMS CO LLC (DH)
Also Called: BEI Industrial Encoders
1461 Lawrence Dr, Thousand Oaks (91320-1303)
PHONE...............................805 968-0782
Eric Pilaud, *CEO*
Jean-yves Mouttet, *Treas*
Victor Copeland, *
▲ **EMP:** 125 **EST:** 1990
SALES (est): 15.94MM
SALES (corp-wide): 4.05B **Privately Held**
SIC: 3829 Measuring and controlling devices, nec
HQ: Sensata Technologies, Inc.
529 Pleasant St
Attleboro MA 02703

(P-8039)
ECKERT ZEGLER ISOTOPE PDTS INC (HQ)
Also Called: Isotope Products Lab
24937 Avenue Tibbitts, Valencia (91355-3427)
PHONE...............................661 309-1010
Frank Yeager, *CEO*
Joe Hathcock, *
Karen Haskins, *
EMP: 45 **EST:** 1967

SQ FT: 40,000
SALES (est): 67.75MM
SALES (corp-wide): 267.49MM **Privately Held**
Web: www.isotopeproducts.com
SIC: 3829 Nuclear radiation and testing apparatus
PA: Eckert & Ziegler Se
Robert-Rossle-Str. 10
309410840

(P-8040)
ECKERT ZEGLER ISOTOPE PDTS INC
1800 N Keystone St, Burbank (91504-3417)
PHONE...............................661 309-1010
Karl Amlauer, *Brnch Mgr*
EMP: 33
SALES (corp-wide): 267.49MM **Privately Held**
Web: sales.isotopeproducts.com
SIC: 3829 Nuclear radiation and testing apparatus
HQ: Eckert & Ziegler Isotope Products, Inc.
24937 Avenue Tibbitts
Valencia CA 91355
661 309-1010

(P-8041)
FITBIT LLC
15255 Innovation Dr Ste 200, San Diego (92128-3410)
PHONE...............................415 513-1000
EMP: 209
SALES (corp-wide): 307.39B **Publicly Held**
Web: www.fitbit.com
SIC: 3829 Measuring and controlling devices, nec
HQ: Fitbit Llc
199 Fremont St Fl 14
San Francisco CA 94105

(P-8042)
FLOWLINE INC
Also Called: Flowline Liquid Intelligence
10500 Humbolt St, Los Alamitos (90720-2439)
PHONE...............................562 598-3015
Stephen E Olson, *Ch Bd*
Scott Olson, *
EMP: 25 **EST:** 1990
SQ FT: 8,000
SALES (est): 3.25MM **Privately Held**
Web: www.flowline.com
SIC: 3829 5084 Measuring and controlling devices, nec; Industrial machinery and equipment

(P-8043)
GAMMA SCIENTIFIC INC
Also Called: Road Vista
9925 Carroll Canyon Rd, San Diego (92131-1105)
PHONE...............................858 635-9008
Kong G Loh, *CEO*
▲ **EMP:** 48 **EST:** 1961
SQ FT: 20,000
SALES (est): 8.45MM **Privately Held**
Web: www.gamma-sci.com
SIC: 3829 3648 3821 Measuring and controlling devices, nec; Reflectors, for lighting equipment: metal; Calibration tapes, for physical testing machines

(P-8044)
GANTNER INSTRUMENTS INC
402 W Broadway Ste 400, San Diego (92101-3554)

PHONE...............................888 512-5788
Ravi Shukla, *CEO*
EMP: 50 **EST:** 2010
SALES (est): 2.11MM
SALES (corp-wide): 22.73MM **Privately Held**
Web: www.gantner-instruments.com
SIC: 3829 Measuring and controlling devices, nec
PA: Gantner Instruments Gmbh
Montafoner StraBe 4
555 677-4630

(P-8045)
HAMILTON SUNDSTRAND SPC SYSTMS
Also Called: Hsssi
960 Overland Ct, San Dimas (91773-1742)
PHONE...............................909 288-5300
Edward Francis, *Ex Dir*
Lawrence R Mcnamara, *Pr*
Daniel C Lee, *
Clinton Gardiner, *
Eugene Dougherty, *
EMP: 76 **EST:** 2002
SQ FT: 134,000
SALES (est): 20.27MM
SALES (corp-wide): 68.92B **Publicly Held**
Web: www.collinsaerospace.com
SIC: 3829 Measuring and controlling devices, nec
HQ: Goodrich Corporation
2730 W Tyvola Rd
Charlotte NC 28217
704 423-7000

(P-8046)
HORIBA INTERNATIONAL CORP
9755 Research Dr, Irvine (92618-4626)
PHONE...............................949 250-4811
▲ **EMP:** 930
SIC: 3829 Measuring and controlling devices, nec

(P-8047)
INTELLIGUARD GROUP LLC
Also Called: Intellgard Inventory Solutions
12220 World Trade Dr Ste 210, San Diego (92128-3900)
P.O. Box 10481 (83001)
PHONE...............................760 448-9500
Bob Howard, *CEO*
Jennifer Bees Ctrl, *Prin*
Rob Sobie, *Chief Product Officer*
EMP: 50 **EST:** 2000
SALES (est): 8.02MM **Privately Held**
Web: www.ig.solutions
SIC: 3829 Accelerometers

(P-8048)
J L SHEPHERD AND ASSOC INC
1010 Arroyo St, San Fernando (91340-1822)
PHONE...............................818 898-2361
Dorothy Shepherd, *Pr*
Joseph L Shepherd, *
Diana Shepherd, *
Mary Shepherd, *
Dorothy Shepherd, *Sec*
▲ **EMP:** 27 **EST:** 1967
SQ FT: 15,000
SALES (est): 2.71MM **Privately Held**
Web: www.jlshepherd.com
SIC: 3829 3844 Nuclear radiation and testing apparatus; Irradiation equipment, nec

(P-8049)
KAP MEDICAL
1395 Pico St, Corona (92881-3373)

PHONE...............................951 340-4360
Raj K Gowda, *Pr*
Dave Lewis, *
Dan Rosenmayer, *
◆ **EMP:** 35 **EST:** 1999
SQ FT: 20,000
SALES (est): 7.42MM **Privately Held**
Web: www.kapmedical.com
SIC: 3829 8711 Medical diagnostic systems, nuclear; Consulting engineer

(P-8050)
KARL STORZ IMAGING INC (HQ)
Also Called: Optronics
1 S Los Carneros Rd, Goleta (93117-5506)
PHONE...............................805 968-5563
Miles Hartfield, *Genl Mgr*
EMP: 344 **EST:** 1984
SQ FT: 105,000
SALES (est): 95.1MM
SALES (corp-wide): 2.14B **Privately Held**
Web: www.karlstorz.com
SIC: 3829 3841 Measuring and controlling devices, nec; Surgical and medical instruments
PA: Karl Storz Se & Co. Kg
Dr.-Karl-Storz-Str. 34
74617080

(P-8051)
MEASURE UAS INC
Also Called: Pilatus Unmanned
5862 Bolsa Ave Ste 104, Huntington Beach (92649-1169)
PHONE...............................714 916-6166
Josh Kornoff, *Mgr*
EMP: 25
SALES (corp-wide): 5.56MM **Privately Held**
Web: www.ageagle.com
SIC: 3829 Surveying instruments and accessories
PA: Measure Uas, Inc.
1701 Rhode Island Ave Nw
202 793-3052

(P-8052)
MEASUREMENT SPECIALTIES INC
9131 Oakdale Ave Ste 170, Chatsworth (91311-6502)
PHONE...............................818 701-2750
Robert Simon, *Brnch Mgr*
EMP: 187
SALES (corp-wide): 400.61MM **Privately Held**
Web: www.te.com
SIC: 3829 Measuring and controlling devices, nec
PA: Measurement Specialties, Inc.
1000 Lucas Way
757 766-1500

(P-8053)
MEGGITT (ORANGE COUNTY) INC (DH)
Also Called: Meggitt Sensing Systems
4 Marconi, Irvine (92618-2525)
PHONE...............................949 493-8181
▲ **EMP:** 230 **EST:** 1947
SALES (est): 35.88MM
SALES (corp-wide): 19.93B **Publicly Held**
Web: www.reflection-dental.com
SIC: 3829 Vibration meters, analyzers, and calibrators
HQ: Meggitt Limited
Ansty Bus.
Coventry W MIDLANDS CV7 9
247 682-6900

(P-8054)
MINUS K TECHNOLOGY INC
460 Hindry Ave Ste C, Inglewood
(90301-2044)
PHONE..............................310 348-9656
David L Platus, *Pr*
Nancee Schwartz, *
EMP: 110 **EST:** 1991
SQ FT: 2,500
SALES (est): 5.25MM **Privately Held**
Web: www.minusk.com
SIC: 3829 Measuring and controlling
devices, nec

(P-8055)
NDC TECHNOLOGIES INC
5314 Irwindale Ave, Irwindale (91706-2086)
PHONE..............................626 960-3300
▲ **EMP:** 53
SALES (corp-wide): 2.69B **Publicly Held**
Web: www.ndc.com
SIC: 3829 Measuring and controlling
devices, nec
HQ: Ndc Technologies, Inc.
8001 Technology Blvd
Dayton OH 45424
937 233-9935

(P-8056)
**OMNI OPTICAL PRODUCTS INC
(PA)**
17282 Eastman, Irvine (92614-5522)
PHONE..............................714 634-5700
Ken Panique, *Pr*
▲ **EMP:** 25 **EST:** 1986
SALES (est): 1.9MM
SALES (corp-wide): 1.9MM **Privately Held**
SIC: 3829 Surveying instruments and
accessories

(P-8057)
**OPTIVUS PROTON THERAPY
INC (PA)**
1475 Victoria Ct, San Bernardino
(92408-2831)
P.O. Box 608 (92354-0608)
PHONE..............................909 799-8300
Jon W Slater, *CEO*
Daryl L Anderson, *CFO*
EMP: 51 **EST:** 1992
SQ FT: 35,000
SALES (est): 10.22MM **Privately Held**
Web: www.optivus.com
SIC: 3829 7371 8742 3699 Nuclear radiation
and testing apparatus; Custom computer
programming services; Maintenance
management consultant; Electrical
equipment and supplies, nec

(P-8058)
**PACIFIC DIVERSIFIED CAPITAL
CO**
101 Ash St, San Diego (92101-3017)
PHONE..............................619 696-2000
Steve Baum, *Ch Bd*
Thomas Page, *
Henry Huta, *
Michael Lowell, *
EMP: 39 **EST:** 1983
SALES (est): 4.94MM
SALES (corp-wide): 16.72B **Publicly Held**
SIC: 3829 Measuring and controlling
devices, nec
HQ: San Diego Gas & Electric Company
8330 Century Park Ct
San Diego CA 92123
619 696-2000

(P-8059)
**PROPRIETARY CONTROLS
SYSTEMS**
Also Called: P C S C
3830 Del Amo Blvd # 102, Torrance
(90503-2119)
PHONE..............................310 303-3600
Masami Kosaka, *Pr*
Robert K Takahashi, *
▲ **EMP:** 45 **EST:** 1983
SALES (est): 5.21MM
SALES (corp-wide): 9.94MM **Privately
Held**
Web: www.pcscsecurity.com
SIC: 3829 3669 Measuring and controlling
devices, nec; Burglar alarm apparatus,
electric
PA: Ttik, Inc.
3541 Challenger St
310 303-3600

(P-8060)
RADCAL CORPORATION
Also Called: Mdh
426 W Duarte Rd, Monrovia (91016-4591)
PHONE..............................626 357-7921
Margarita Blinchik, *CEO*
Curt Harkless, *
▲ **EMP:** 35 **EST:** 1973
SQ FT: 10,000
SALES (est): 8.19MM
SALES (corp-wide): 339.04MM **Privately
Held**
Web: www.radcal.com
SIC: 3829 Nuclear radiation and testing
apparatus
PA: Ion Beam Applications
Chemin Du Cyclotron 3
10475811

(P-8061)
REDLINE DETECTION LLC (PA)
828 W Taft Ave, Orange (92865-4232)
PHONE..............................714 579-6961
Zachary Parker, *CEO*
▲ **EMP:** 23 **EST:** 2004
SQ FT: 21,000
SALES (est): 14.62MM
SALES (corp-wide): 14.62MM **Privately
Held**
Web: www.redlinedetection.com
SIC: 3829 Liquid leak detection equipment

(P-8062)
SEMCO
1495 S Gage St, San Bernardino
(92408-2835)
PHONE..............................909 799-9666
Shawn Martin, *Owner*
▲ **EMP:** 25 **EST:** 1994
SQ FT: 5,400
SALES (est): 2.35MM **Privately Held**
Web: www.semco.com
SIC: 3829 3599 Physical property testing
equipment; Machine shop, jobbing and
repair

(P-8063)
**SKF CONDITION MONITORING
INC (DH)**
Also Called: SKF Aptitude Exchange
9444 Balboa Ave Ste 150, San Diego
(92123-4377)
PHONE..............................858 496-3400
Mark Mcginn, *CEO*
EMP: 120 **EST:** 1983
SQ FT: 31,000
SALES (est): 4.98MM
SALES (corp-wide): 740.17MM **Privately
Held**

SIC: 3829 Vibration meters, analyzers, and
calibrators
HQ: Skf Usa Inc.
801 Lakeview Dr Ste 120
Blue Bell PA 19422
267 436-6000

(P-8064)
**SOILMOISTURE EQUIPMENT
CORP**
601 Pine Ave Ste A, Goleta (93117-3886)
P.O. Box 30025 (93130-0025)
PHONE..............................805 964-3525
Whitney Skaling, *CEO*
Percy E Skaling, *
Jan Skaling, *
Kenneth Macaulay, *
▲ **EMP:** 23 **EST:** 1950
SQ FT: 14,000
SALES (est): 4.86MM **Privately Held**
Web: www.soilmoisture.com
SIC: 3829 Measuring and controlling
devices, nec
PA: Stevens Water Monitoring Systems,
Inc.
12067 Ne Glenn Wding Dr S

(P-8065)
**STRUCTURAL DIAGNOSTICS
INC**
Also Called: S D I
650 Via Alondra, Camarillo (93012-8733)
PHONE..............................805 987-7755
Paul R Teagle, *Pr*
EMP: 33 **EST:** 1994
SQ FT: 30,000
SALES (est): 4MM **Privately Held**
Web: www.sdindt.com
SIC: 3829 Measuring and controlling
devices, nec

(P-8066)
TELEDYNE INSTRUMENTS INC
Also Called: Teledyne API
9970 Carroll Canyon Rd Ste A, San Diego
(92131-1106)
PHONE..............................619 239-5959
Jeff Franks, *Brnch Mgr*
EMP: 100
SALES (corp-wide): 5.64B **Publicly Held**
Web: www.teledyne-api.com
SIC: 3829 3823 Measuring and controlling
devices, nec; Process control instruments
HQ: Teledyne Instruments, Inc.
16830 Chestnut St
City Of Industry CA 91748
626 934-1500

(P-8067)
TELEDYNE INSTRUMENTS INC
Teledyne Advnced Plltion Instr
9970 Carroll Canyon Rd, San Diego
(92131-1106)
PHONE..............................858 657-9800
Robert Mehrabian, *CEO*
EMP: 49
SALES (corp-wide): 5.64B **Publicly Held**
Web: www.teledyne-api.com
SIC: 3829 Measuring and controlling
devices, nec
HQ: Teledyne Instruments, Inc.
16830 Chestnut St
City Of Industry CA 91748
626 934-1500

(P-8068)
TELEDYNE INSTRUMENTS INC
Also Called: Teledyne Analytical Instrs
16830 Chestnut St, City Of Industry
(91748-1017)

PHONE..............................626 934-1500
Tom Compas, *Brnch Mgr*
EMP: 170
SQ FT: 70,000
SALES (corp-wide): 5.64B **Publicly Held**
Web: www.teledyne-ai.com
SIC: 3829 Measuring and controlling
devices, nec
HQ: Teledyne Instruments, Inc.
16830 Chestnut St
City Of Industry CA 91748
626 934-1500

(P-8069)
TEMPTRON ENGINEERING INC
7823 Deering Ave, Canoga Park
(91304-5006)
PHONE..............................818 346-4900
Edward Skei, *Pr*
Beverly Skei, *
EMP: 35 **EST:** 1971
SQ FT: 13,000
SALES (est): 6.85MM **Privately Held**
Web: www.temptronengineeringinc.com
SIC: 3829 3769 3823 Measuring and
controlling devices, nec; Space vehicle
equipment, nec; Temperature instruments:
industrial process type

(P-8070)
**TRANSDUCER TECHNIQUES
LLC**
42480 Rio Nedo, Temecula (92590-3734)
PHONE..............................951 719-3965
Randy A Baker, *Managing Member*
EMP: 37 **EST:** 1978
SQ FT: 27,000
SALES (est): 3.78MM **Privately Held**
Web: www.transducertechniques.com
SIC: 3829 Measuring and controlling
devices, nec

3841 Surgical And Medical Instruments

(P-8071)
AALTO SCIENTIFIC LTD
1959 Kellogg Ave, Carlsbad (92008-6582)
PHONE..............................800 748-6674
R Reynolds, *Director of Information*
EMP: 25 **EST:** 2018
SALES (est): 1.19MM **Privately Held**
Web: www.aaltoscientific.com
SIC: 3841 Surgical and medical instruments

(P-8072)
ABBOTT VASCULAR INC
42301 Zevo Dr Ste D, Temecula
(92590-3731)
PHONE..............................951 914-2400
Rhonda Reddick, *Mgr*
EMP: 665
SALES (corp-wide): 40.11B **Publicly Held**
Web: www.cardiovascular.abbott
SIC: 3841 Catheters
HQ: Abbott Vascular Inc.
3200 Lakeside Dr
Santa Clara CA 95054
408 845-3000

(P-8073)
ABBOTT VASCULAR INC
Also Called: Abbott Vascular
30590 Cochise Cir, Murrieta (92563-2501)
P.O. Box 3020 (60064-9320)
PHONE..............................408 845-3186
EMP: 568
SALES (corp-wide): 40.11B **Publicly Held**
Web: www.abbott.com

SIC: 3841 Surgical instruments and apparatus
HQ: Abbott Vascular Inc.
3200 Lakeside Dr
Santa Clara CA 95054
408 845-3000

(P-8074)
ACCLARENT INC
31 Technology Dr Ste 200, Irvine (92618-2302)
PHONE..................650 687-5888
David Shepherd, *Pr*
Cristina Todasco, *
EMP: 400 EST: 2004
SALES (est): 28.1MM **Publicly Held**
Web: www.acclarent.com
SIC: 3841 Surgical and medical instruments
PA: Integra Lifesciences Holdings Corporation
1100 Campus Rd

(P-8075)
ACCRIVA DGNOSTICS HOLDINGS INC (DH)
Also Called: Itc Nexus Holding Company
6260 Sequence Dr, San Diego (92121-4358)
PHONE..................858 404-8203
Scott Cramer, *CEO*
Greg Tibbitts, *CFO*
Tom Whalen, *CSO*
EMP: 350 EST: 2010
SALES (est): 55.46MM **Privately Held**
Web: www.werfen.com
SIC: 3841 2835 6719 Diagnostic apparatus, medical; Blood derivative diagnostic agents; Investment holding companies, except banks
HQ: Instrumentation Laboratory Company
180 Hartwell Rd
Bedford MA 01730

(P-8076)
ACI MEDICAL LLC
1857 Diamond St Ste A, San Marcos (92078-5129)
PHONE..................760 744-4400
EMP: 47 EST: 1984
SALES (est): 4.27MM **Privately Held**
Web: www.acimedical.com
SIC: 3841 Diagnostic apparatus, medical

(P-8077)
ACUTUS MEDICAL INC
Also Called: Acutus Medical
2210 Faraday Ave Ste 100, Carlsbad (92008-7225)
PHONE..................442 232-6080
David Roman, *Pr*
R Scott Huennekens, *
Takeo Mukai, *Sr VP*
Steven Mcquillan, *Sr VP*
EMP: 160 EST: 2011
SQ FT: 50,800
SALES (est): 7.16MM **Privately Held**
Web: www.acutusmedical.com
SIC: 3841 Surgical and medical instruments

(P-8078)
ADVANCED STERLIZATION (HQ)
Also Called: A S P
33 Technology Dr, Irvine (92618-2346)
PHONE..................800 595-0200
Bernard Zovighian, *CEO*
EMP: 146 EST: 1991
SALES (est): 6.64MM
SALES (corp-wide): 6.07B **Publicly Held**
Web: www.asp.com

SIC: 3841 Surgical and medical instruments
PA: Fortive Corporation
6920 Seaway Blvd
425 446-5000

(P-8079)
AJINOMOTO ALTHEA INC (HQ)
Also Called: Ajinomoto Bio-Pharma Services
11040 Roselle St, San Diego (92121-1205)
PHONE..................858 882-0123
David Enloe Junior, *Pr*
Martha J Demski, *
Chris Duffy, *
Ej Brandreth, *Regional*
Jack Wright, *
EMP: 25 EST: 1997
SALES (est): 81.4MM **Privately Held**
Web: www.ajibio-pharma.com
SIC: 3841 2836 Hypodermic needles and syringes; Coagulation products
PA: Ajinomoto Co., Inc.
1-15-1, Kyobashi

(P-8080)
ALCON LENSX INC (DH)
Also Called: Alcon
15800 Alton Pkwy, Irvine (92618-3818)
PHONE..................949 753-1393
Kevin J Buehler, *CEO*
Elaine Whitbeck, *CLO*
EMP: 99 EST: 2006
SQ FT: 20,000
SALES (est): 15.8MM **Privately Held**
Web: www.myalcon.com
SIC: 3841 Surgical lasers
HQ: Alcon, Inc.
1132 Ferris Rd
Amelia OH 45102
513 722-1037

(P-8081)
ALCON RESEARCH LTD
Also Called: ALCON RESEARCH, LTD.
15800 Alton Pkwy, Irvine (92618-3818)
PHONE..................949 387-2142
Ed Richards, *Owner*
EMP: 55
Web: www.alcon.com
SIC: 3841 Surgical instruments and apparatus
HQ: Alcon Research, Llc
6201 S Fwy
Fort Worth TX 76134
817 551-4555

(P-8082)
ALCON VISION LLC
24514 Sunshine Dr, Laguna Niguel (92677-7826)
PHONE..................949 753-6218
EMP: 340
Web: www.alcon.com
SIC: 3841 Surgical and medical instruments
HQ: Alcon Vision, Llc
6201 South Fwy
Fort Worth TX 76134
817 293-0450

(P-8083)
ALCON VISION LLC
Also Called: Alcon Surgical
15800 Alton Pkwy, Irvine (92618-3818)
P.O. Box 19587 (92623-9587)
PHONE..................949 753-6488
Kenneth Lickel, *Mgr*
EMP: 600
SQ FT: 32,000
Web: www.alcon.com

SIC: 3841 3851 5049 Surgical and medical instruments; Ophthalmic goods; Optical goods
HQ: Alcon Vision, Llc
6201 South Fwy
Fort Worth TX 76134
817 293-0450

(P-8084)
ALL MANUFACTURERS INC
Also Called: Allied Harbor Aerospace Fas
1831 Commerce St Ste 101, Corona (92878-5026)
PHONE..................951 280-4200
Jon R Gerwin, *CEO*
Ron Gerwin, *
EMP: 197 EST: 1993
SALES (est): 8.04MM **Privately Held**
Web: www.allied1.com
SIC: 3841 3694 Surgical and medical instruments; Motors, starting: automotive and aircraft

(P-8085)
ALLIANCE MEDICAL PRODUCTS INC (DH)
Also Called: Siegfried Irvine
9342 Jeronimo Rd, Irvine (92618-1903)
PHONE..................949 768-4690
Robert Hughes, *CEO*
Brian Jones, *
Frank Pham, *
▲ EMP: 41 EST: 2001
SQ FT: 55,000
SALES (est): 49.25MM **Privately Held**
Web: www.siegfried.ch
SIC: 3841 7819 Medical instruments and equipment, blood and bone work; Laboratory service, motion picture
HQ: Siegfried Usa Holding , Inc.
33 Industrial Park Rd
Pennsville NJ 08070
856 678-3601

(P-8086)
ALLIANCE MEDICAL PRODUCTS INC
Also Called: Siegfried Irvine
9292 Jeronimo Rd, Irvine (92618-1905)
PHONE..................949 664-9616
EMP: 45
Web: www.siegfried.ch
SIC: 3841 Medical instruments and equipment, blood and bone work
HQ: Alliance Medical Products, Inc.
9342 Jeronimo Rd
Irvine CA 92618
949 700-4090

(P-8087)
ALPHATEC HOLDINGS INC (PA)
Also Called: Alphatec
1950 Camino Vida Roble, Carlsbad (92008-6505)
PHONE..................760 431-9286
Patrick S Miles, *Pr*
Scott Lish, *COO*
J Todd Koning, *Ex VP*
Tyson Marshall, *Corporate Secretary*
EMP: 428 EST: 1990
SQ FT: 121,541
SALES (est): 482.26MM **Publicly Held**
Web: www.atecspine.com
SIC: 3841 Surgical and medical instruments

(P-8088)
AMADA WELD TECH INC
245 E El Norte St, Monrovia (91016-4828)
PHONE..................626 303-5676
Susan Gu, *Mgr*

EMP: 30
Web: www.amadaweldtech.com
SIC: 3841 Surgical and medical instruments
HQ: Amada Weld Tech Inc.
1820 S Myrtle Ave
Monrovia CA 91016

(P-8089)
AMEDITECH INC
9940 Mesa Rim Rd, San Diego (92121-2910)
PHONE..................858 535-1968
Robert Joel, *Prin*
▲ EMP: 118 EST: 1999
SQ FT: 47,000
SALES (est): 11.92MM
SALES (corp-wide): 40.11B **Publicly Held**
SIC: 3841 Medical instruments and equipment, blood and bone work
HQ: Alere Inc.
51 Sawyer Rd Ste 200
Waltham MA 02453
781 647-3900

(P-8090)
AMO USA INC
1700 E Saint Andrew Pl, Santa Ana (92705-4933)
PHONE..................714 247-8200
Tom Frinzi, *Pr*
EMP: 200 EST: 2002
SQ FT: 100,000
SALES (est): 4.22MM
SALES (corp-wide): 85.16B **Publicly Held**
SIC: 3841 3845 Surgical and medical instruments; Laser systems and equipment, medical
HQ: Johnson & Johnson Surgical Vision, Inc.
31 Technology Dr Bldg 29a
Irvine CA 92618
949 581-5799

(P-8091)
APPLIED CARDIAC SYSTEMS INC
1 Hughes Ste A, Irvine (92618-2021)
PHONE..................949 855-9366
Loren A Manera, *CEO*
Tricia Meads, *
Susan Marcus, *
Robert Wilks, *
▲ EMP: 64 EST: 1981
SQ FT: 18,000
SALES (est): 4.34MM **Privately Held**
Web: www.cardiacmonitoring.com
SIC: 3841 Diagnostic apparatus, medical

(P-8092)
APPLIED MANUFACTURING LLC
22872 Avenida Empresa, Rancho Santa Margari (92688-2650)
PHONE..................949 713-8000
Tom Wachli, *Pr*
EMP: 1200 EST: 2017
SALES (est): 21.23MM
SALES (corp-wide): 699.84MM **Privately Held**
Web: www.appliedmed.com
SIC: 3841 Surgical and medical instruments
HQ: Applied Medical Resources Corporation
22872 Avenida Empresa
Rancho Santa Margari CA 92688
949 713-8000

(P-8093)
APPLIED MEDICAL CORPORATION (PA)
Also Called: Applied Medical Resources

22872 Avenida Empresa, Rancho Santa
Margari (92688-2650)
PHONE...................................949 713-8000
Said Hilal, CEO
EMP: 225 EST: 1987
SALES (est): 699.84MM
SALES (corp-wide): 699.84MM Privately
Held
Web: www.appliedmedical.com
SIC: 3841 Surgical and medical instruments

(P-8094)
APPLIED MEDICAL DIST CORP
22872 Avenida Empresa, Rcho Sta Marg
(92688-2650)
PHONE...................................949 713-8000
Said Hilal, CEO
Stephen Stanley, *
EMP: 700 EST: 1998
SALES (est): 4.05MM
SALES (corp-wide): 699.84MM Privately
Held
Web: www.appliedmedical.com
SIC: 3841 Surgical and medical instruments
HQ: Applied Medical Resources
    Corporation
    22872 Avenida Empresa
    Rancho Santa Margari CA 92688
    949 713-8000

(P-8095)
APPLIED MEDICAL RESOURCES
30152 Esperanza, Rcho Sta Marg
(92688-2120)
PHONE...................................949 459-1042
EMP: 37 EST: 2013
SALES (est): 3MM Privately Held
Web: www.appliedmedical.com
SIC: 3841 Surgical and medical instruments

(P-8096)
APPLIED MEDICAL RESOURCES CORP (HQ)
Also Called: Applied Medical Distribution
22872 Avenida Empresa, Rancho Santa
Margari (92688-2650)
PHONE...................................949 713-8000
Said S Hilal, Pr
Stephen E Stanley, Group President*
Nabil Hilal, Group President*
Samir Tall, *
Gary Johnson, Group President*
▲ EMP: 50 EST: 1987
SQ FT: 800,000
SALES (est): 649.89MM
SALES (corp-wide): 699.84MM Privately
Held
Web: www.appliedmedical.com
SIC: 3841 Surgical and medical instruments
PA: Applied Medical Corporation
    22872 Avenida Empresa
    949 713-8000

(P-8097)
ARCH MED SLTONS - ESCNDIDO LLC
950 Borra Pl, Escondido (92029-2011)
PHONE...................................760 432-9785
Eli Crotzer, CEO
EMP: 193 EST: 2020
SALES (est): 6.35MM
SALES (corp-wide): 22.33MM Privately
Held
SIC: 3841 Surgical and medical instruments
PA: Arch Cutting Tools, Llc
    2600 S Telg Rd Ste 180
    734 266-6900

(P-8098)
ASPEN MEDICAL PRODUCTS LLC
6481 Oak Cyn, Irvine (92618-5202)
P.O. Box 22116 (91185-0001)
PHONE...................................949 681-0200
Jim Cloar, Pr
▲ EMP: 70 EST: 1993
SQ FT: 52,000
SALES (est): 14.85MM
SALES (corp-wide): 174.71MM Privately
Held
Web: www.aspenmp.com
SIC: 3841 Surgical and medical instruments
PA: Cogr, Inc.
    140 E 45th St 43rd Fl
    212 370-5600

(P-8099)
AXIOM MEDICAL INCORPORATED
19320 Van Ness Ave, Torrance
(90501-1103)
PHONE...................................310 533-9020
EMP: 40 EST: 1976
SALES (est): 4.37MM Privately Held
Web: www.axiommed.com
SIC: 3841 3842 Surgical and medical
    instruments; Surgical appliances and
    supplies

(P-8100)
B BRAUN MEDICAL INC
1151 Mildred St Ste B, Ontario
(91761-3504)
PHONE...................................909 906-7575
EMP: 58
SALES (corp-wide): 972.41MM Privately
Held
Web: www.bbraunusa.com
SIC: 3841 Surgical and medical instruments
HQ: B. Braun Medical Inc.
    824 12th Ave
    Bethlehem PA 18018
    610 691-5400

(P-8101)
B BRAUN US PHRM MFG LLC
2525 Mcgaw Ave, Irvine (92614-5841)
P.O. Box 19791 (92623-9791)
PHONE...................................610 691-5400
Keith Klaes, Brnch Mgr
EMP: 1300
SALES (corp-wide): 972.41MM Privately
Held
Web: www.bbraunusa.com
SIC: 3841 Catheters
HQ: B. Braun Us Pharmaceutical
    Manufacturing Llc
    211 E 7th St Ste 620
    Austin TX

(P-8102)
BAXALTA US INC
1700 Rancho Conejo Blvd, Thousand Oaks
(91320-1424)
PHONE...................................805 498-8664
Paul Marshall, Brnch Mgr
EMP: 520
SIC: 3841 2835 2389 3842 Surgical and
    medical instruments; Blood derivative
    diagnostic agents; Hospital gowns; Surgical
    appliances and supplies
HQ: Baxalta Us Inc.
    1200 Lakeside Dr
    Bannockburn IL

(P-8103)
BAXTER HEALTHCARE CORPORATION
Also Called: Baxter Medication Delivery
17511 Armstrong Ave, Irvine (92614-5725)
PHONE...................................949 474-6301
Michael Mussallem, Mgr
EMP: 250
SALES (corp-wide): 14.81B Publicly Held
Web: www.baxter.com
SIC: 3841 Surgical and medical instruments
HQ: Baxter Healthcare Corporation
    1 Baxter Pkwy
    Deerfield IL 60015
    224 948-2000

(P-8104)
BEAUTY HEALTH COMPANY (PA)
2165 E Spring St, Long Beach
(90806-2114)
PHONE...................................800 603-4996
Marla Beck, Pr
Brenton L Saunders, *
Michael Monahan, CFO
Ron Menezes, CRO
Carrie Caulkins, CMO
EMP: 350 EST: 1997
SQ FT: 23,000
SALES (est): 397.99MM
SALES (corp-wide): 397.99MM Publicly
Held
SIC: 3841 Surgical and medical instruments

(P-8105)
BECKMAN COULTER INC
Beckman Coulter Diagnostics
250 S Kraemer Blvd, Brea (92821-6232)
P.O. Box 8000 (92822-8000)
PHONE...................................818 970-2161
Albert Ziegler, Mgr
EMP: 200
SALES (corp-wide): 23.89B Publicly Held
Web: www.beckmancoulter.com
SIC: 3841 3821 Surgical and medical
    instruments; Clinical laboratory instruments,
    except medical and dental
HQ: Beckman Coulter, Inc.
    250 S Kraemer Blvd
    Brea CA 92821
    714 993-5321

(P-8106)
BECTON DICKINSON AND COMPANY
Also Called: Care Fusion Products
3750 Torrey View Ct, San Diego
(92130-2622)
PHONE...................................888 876-4287
EMP: 56
SALES (corp-wide): 20.18B Publicly Held
Web: www.bd.com
SIC: 3841 Medical instruments and
    equipment, blood and bone work
PA: Becton, Dickinson And Company
    1 Becton Dr
    201 847-6800

(P-8107)
BECTON DICKINSON AND COMPANY
3750 Torrey View Ct, San Diego
(92130-2622)
PHONE...................................858 617-2000
EMP: 24
SALES (corp-wide): 20.18B Publicly Held
Web: www.bd.com
SIC: 3841 Surgical and medical instruments
PA: Becton, Dickinson And Company
    1 Becton Dr

201 847-6800

(P-8108)
BIO-MEDICAL DEVICES INC
Also Called: Maxair Systems
17171 Daimler St, Irvine (92614-5508)
PHONE...................................949 752-9642
Nick Herbert, Pr
Alan Davidner, Stockholder*
Harry N Herbert, *
▲ EMP: 37 EST: 1988
SQ FT: 40,000
SALES (est): 9.49MM Privately Held
Web: www.maxair-systems.com
SIC: 3841 2353 Surgical and medical
    instruments; Hats, caps, and millinery

(P-8109)
BIO-MEDICAL DEVICES INTL INC
17171 Daimler St, Irvine (92614-5508)
PHONE...................................949 752-9642
Nicholas Herbert, Pr
Allan Schultz, *
EMP: 23 EST: 1998
SALES (est): 4.32MM Privately Held
Web: www.maxair-systems.com
SIC: 3841 2353 Surgical and medical
    instruments; Hats, caps, and millinery

(P-8110)
BIOFILM INC
3225 Executive Rdg, Vista (92081-8527)
PHONE...................................760 727-9030
Lisa A O'carroll, CEO
Daniel Wray, *
Mike Adams, *
Lois Wray, *
Natalie Garcia, *
EMP: 54 EST: 1991
SQ FT: 61,000
SALES (est): 13.28MM Privately Held
Web: www.biofilm.com
SIC: 3841 Surgical and medical instruments

(P-8111)
BIOGENERAL INC
9925 Mesa Rim Rd, San Diego
(92121-2911)
PHONE...................................858 453-4451
Victor Wild, Pr
▲ EMP: 30 EST: 1986
SALES (est): 5.6MM Privately Held
Web: www.biogeneral.com
SIC: 3841 Surgical and medical instruments

(P-8112)
BIOSEAL
167 W Orangethorpe Ave, Placentia
(92870-6922)
PHONE...................................714 528-4695
Bill Runion, Pr
Robert C Kopple, *
Jeff Myers, *
▲ EMP: 40 EST: 1988
SQ FT: 8,500
SALES (est): 13.71MM Privately Held
Web: www.biosealnet.com
SIC: 3841 5047 Surgical and medical
    instruments; Hospital equipment and
    furniture

(P-8113)
BOLT MEDICAL INC
2131 Faraday Ave, Carlsbad (92008-7252)
PHONE...................................949 287-3207
Keegan Harper, CEO
Scott Murano, *
EMP: 58 EST: 2019
SALES (est): 10.29MM Privately Held

SIC: 3841 8731 Surgical and medical instruments; Biological research

(P-8114)
BOSTON SCIENTIFIC CORPORATION
Also Called: Boston Scientific - Valencia
25155 Rye Canyon Loop, Valencia
(91355-5004)
PHONE..............................800 678-2575
Phill Tarves, *Mgr*
EMP: 45
SALES (corp-wide): 12.68B **Publicly Held**
Web: www.bostonscientific.com
SIC: 3841 Surgical and medical instruments
PA: Boston Scientific Corporation
300 Boston Scientific Way
508 683-4000

(P-8115)
BRANAN MEDICAL CORPORATION (PA)
9940 Mesa Rim Rd, San Diego
(92121-2910)
PHONE..............................949 598-7166
Cindy Horton, *CEO*
Raphael Wong, *
Beckie Chien, *
▲ **EMP:** 32 **EST:** 1998
SQ FT: 8,400
SALES (est): 4.07MM
SALES (corp-wide): 4.07MM **Privately Held**
SIC: 3841 Diagnostic apparatus, medical

(P-8116)
BREG INC (HQ)
2382 Faraday Ave Ste 300, Carlsbad
(92008-7220)
PHONE..............................760 599-3000
Dave Mowry, *CEO*
Brad Lee, *
Stuart M Essig, *
Aaron Heisler, *
Tom Sohn, *
◆ **EMP:** 171 **EST:** 1989
SALES (est): 24K **Privately Held**
Web: www.breg.com
SIC: 3841 Surgical and medical instruments
PA: Water Street Healthcare Partners Llc
444 W Lake St Ste 1800

(P-8117)
CALBIOTECH EXPORT INC
1935 Cordell Ct, El Cajon (92020-0911)
PHONE..............................619 660-6162
Noori Barka, *Pr*
▼ **EMP:** 38 **EST:** 1998
SQ FT: 22,500
SALES (est): 9.43MM **Privately Held**
Web: www.calbiotech.com
SIC: 3841 8731 8071 Diagnostic apparatus, medical; Medical research, commercial; Medical laboratories
HQ: Erba Diagnostics Mannheim Gmbh
Mallaustr. 69-73
Mannheim BW 68219

(P-8118)
CALDERA MEDICAL INC (PA)
4360 Park Terrace Dr Ste 140, Westlake Village (91361-4634)
PHONE..............................818 879-6555
Bryon L Merade, *Pr*
Jeff Hubauer, *COO*
John Pitstick, *CFO*
EMP: 70 **EST:** 2002
SQ FT: 25,000
SALES (est): 20.41MM
SALES (corp-wide): 20.41MM **Privately Held**

Web: www.calderamedical.com
SIC: 3841 Surgical and medical instruments

(P-8119)
CANARY MEDICAL USA LLC
2710 Loker Ave W Ste 350, Carlsbad
(92010-6645)
PHONE..............................760 448-5066
William Hunter, *CEO*
Jeffrey M Gross, *
EMP: 100 **EST:** 2018
SALES (est): 9.17MM **Privately Held**
Web: www.canarymedical.com
SIC: 3841 Surgical and medical instruments

(P-8120)
CAREFUSION 207 INC
1100 Bird Center Dr, Palm Springs
(92262-8000)
PHONE..............................760 778-7200
Edward Borkowski, *CFO*
Carol Zilm, *INFUS & RESP*
Cathy Cooney, *
Neil Ryding, *GLOBAL MFG SUPPLY*
Joan Stafslien, *
▲ **EMP:** 327 **EST:** 2005
SALES (est): 4.81MM
SALES (corp-wide): 1.73B **Privately Held**
SIC: 3841 8741 Surgical and medical instruments; Nursing and personal care facility management
PA: Vyaire Holding Company
26125 N Riverwoods Blvd
872 757-0114

(P-8121)
CAREFUSION 213 LLC (DH)
3750 Torrey View Ct, San Diego
(92130-2622)
PHONE..............................800 523-0502
David L Schlotterbeck, *CEO*
Edward Borkowski, *
Dwight Windstead, *
◆ **EMP:** 450 **EST:** 2008
SALES (est): 29.12MM
SALES (corp-wide): 20.18B **Publicly Held**
Web: www.bd.com
SIC: 3841 Surgical and medical instruments
HQ: Carefusion Corporation
3750 Torrey View Ct
San Diego CA 92130

(P-8122)
CAREFUSION CORPORATION
10020 Pacific Mesa Blvd Bldg A, San Diego
(92121-4386)
PHONE..............................858 617-4271
EMP: 52
SALES (corp-wide): 20.18B **Publicly Held**
Web: www.bd.com
SIC: 3841 Surgical and medical instruments
HQ: Carefusion Corporation
3750 Torrey View Ct
San Diego CA 92130

(P-8123)
CAREFUSION CORPORATION
1100 Bird Center Dr, Palm Springs
(92262-8000)
PHONE..............................760 778-7200
Carol Zilm, *Pr*
EMP: 46
SALES (corp-wide): 20.18B **Publicly Held**
Web: www.bd.com
SIC: 3841 Surgical and medical instruments
HQ: Carefusion Corporation
3750 Torrey View Ct
San Diego CA 92130

(P-8124)
CAREFUSION CORPORATION
22745 Savi Ranch Pkwy, Yorba Linda
(92887-4668)
PHONE..............................800 231-2466
Bill Ross, *Brnch Mgr*
EMP: 73
SALES (corp-wide): 20.18B **Publicly Held**
Web: www.bd.com
SIC: 3841 Surgical and medical instruments
HQ: Carefusion Corporation
3750 Torrey View Ct
San Diego CA 92130

(P-8125)
CAREFUSION SOLUTIONS LLC (DH)
3750 Torrey View Ct, San Diego
(92130-2622)
PHONE..............................858 617-2100
Keiran Gallahue, *CEO*
Tom Leonard, *
James Hinrichs, *CFO*
Don Abbey, *Ex VP*
Scott Bostick, *Sr VP*
EMP: 600 **EST:** 2007
SALES (est): 18.82MM
SALES (corp-wide): 20.18B **Publicly Held**
Web: www.bd.com
SIC: 3841 Surgical and medical instruments
HQ: Carefusion Corporation
3750 Torrey View Ct
San Diego CA 92130

(P-8126)
CAROL COLE COMPANY
Also Called: Nuface
1325 Sycamore Ave Ste A, Vista
(92081-7889)
PHONE..............................888 360-9171
Carol Cole, *CEO*
Ted Schwarz, *
EMP: 123 **EST:** 1989
SQ FT: 3,000
SALES (est): 23.37MM **Privately Held**
Web: www.mynuface.com
SIC: 3841 Skin grafting equipment

(P-8127)
CAROLINA LQUID CHMISTRIES CORP
510 W Central Ave Ste C, Brea
(92821-3032)
P.O. Box 92249 (92822)
PHONE..............................336 722-8910
Phil Shugart, *Brnch Mgr*
EMP: 25
Web: www.carolinachemistries.com
SIC: 3841 Surgical and medical instruments
PA: Carolina Liquid Chemistries Corporation
313 Gallimore Dairy Rd

(P-8128)
CAS MEDICAL SYSTEMS INC (HQ)
1 Edwards Way, Irvine (92614-5688)
PHONE..............................203 488-6056
Thomas Patton, *Pr*
Jeffery Baird, *
Paul Benni, *CSO*
EMP: 53 **EST:** 2018
SALES (est): 21.92MM
SALES (corp-wide): 6B **Publicly Held**
Web: www.edwards.com
SIC: 3841 Diagnostic apparatus, medical
PA: Edwards Lifesciences Corp
1 Edwards Way
949 250-2500

(P-8129)
CHART SEQUAL TECHNOLOGIES INC
12230 World Trade Dr Ste 100, San Diego
(92128-3796)
PHONE..............................858 202-3100
▲ **EMP:** 90
Web: www.caireinc.com
SIC: 3841 Diagnostic apparatus, medical

(P-8130)
CHEN-TECH INDUSTRIES INC (DH)
Also Called: ATI Forged Products
9 Wrigley, Irvine (92618-2711)
PHONE..............................949 855-6716
Richard Harshman, *CEO*
Shannon Ko, *
EMP: 38 **EST:** 1979
SQ FT: 18,000
SALES (est): 12.39MM **Publicly Held**
Web: www.atimaterials.com
SIC: 3841 3769 3724 3463 Surgical and medical instruments; Space vehicle equipment, nec; Aircraft engines and engine parts; Aluminum forgings
HQ: Ati Ladish Llc
5481 S Packard Ave
Cudahy WI 53110
414 747-2611

(P-8131)
CHROMOLOGIC LLC
Also Called: Chromologic
1225 S Shamrock Ave, Monrovia
(91016-4244)
PHONE..............................626 381-9974
Naresh Menon, *Managing Member*
EMP: 28 **EST:** 2008
SALES (est): 5.12MM **Privately Held**
Web: www.chromologic.com
SIC: 3841 Diagnostic apparatus, medical

(P-8132)
CLEARPOINT NEURO INC (PA)
Also Called: Clearpoint Neuro
120 S Sierra Ave Ste 100, Solana Beach
(92075-1874)
PHONE..............................888 287-9109
Joseph M Burnett, *Pr*
R John Fletcher, *Ch Bd*
Danilo D' Alessandro, *CFO*
Mazin Sabra, *COO*
Jeremy L Stigall, *Chief Business Officer*
EMP: 91 **EST:** 1998
SQ FT: 7,500
SALES (est): 23.95MM **Publicly Held**
Web: www.clearpointneuro.com
SIC: 3841 Surgical and medical instruments

(P-8133)
COMPANION MEDICAL INC
11011 Via Frontera Ste D, San Diego
(92127-1752)
PHONE..............................858 522-0252
Sean Saint, *CEO*
Michael Mensinger, *
EMP: 58 **EST:** 2015
SALES (est): 7.1MM **Privately Held**
Web: www.medtronicdiabetes.com
SIC: 3841 Surgical and medical instruments
PA: Medtronic Public Limited Company
20 Hatch Street Lower

(P-8134)
COMPOSITE MANUFACTURING INC
Also Called: CMI
970 Calle Amanecer Ste D, San Clemente
(92673-6250)

PRODUCTS & SVCS

PHONE..................949 361-7580
Roger Malcolm, *Pr*
Tim Salter, *
EMP: 36 **EST:** 1995
SQ FT: 16,000
SALES (est): 5.36MM **Privately Held**
Web: www.carbonfiber.com
SIC: 3841 3624 Operating tables; Carbon and graphite products

(P-8135)
CONFLUENT MEDICAL TECH INC
Also Called: Interface Associates
27752 El Lazo, Laguna Niguel
(92677-3914)
PHONE..................949 448-7056
Gary D Curtis, *Brnch Mgr*
EMP: 103
Web: www.confluentmedical.com
SIC: 3841 Catheters
PA: Confluent Medical Technologies, Inc.
6263 N Scttsdale Rd Ste 2

(P-8136)
CONFLUENT MEDICAL TECH INC
27721 La Paz Rd, Laguna Niguel
(92677-3948)
PHONE..................949 448-7056
EMP: 54
Web: www.confluentmedical.com
SIC: 3841 5047 Surgical and medical instruments; Medical and hospital equipment
PA: Confluent Medical Technologies, Inc.
6263 N Scttsdale Rd Ste 2

(P-8137)
COVIDIEN HOLDING INC
2101 Faraday Ave, Carlsbad (92008-7205)
PHONE..................760 603-5020
EMP: 177
Web: www.medtronic.com
SIC: 3841 Surgical and medical instruments
HQ: Covidien Holding Inc.
710 Medtronic Pkwy
Minneapolis MN 55432

(P-8138)
COVIDIEN HOLDING INC
Also Called: Covidien Kenmex
2475 Paseo De Las Americas Ste A, San Diego (92154-7255)
PHONE..................619 690-8500
Javira Gonzales, *Mgr*
EMP: 177
Web: www.medtronic.com
SIC: 3841 Surgical and medical instruments
HQ: Covidien Holding Inc.
710 Medtronic Pkwy
Minneapolis MN 55432

(P-8139)
COVIDIEN LP
Also Called: Vascular Therapies
9775 Toledo Way, Irvine (92618-1811)
PHONE..................949 837-3700
Hal Hurwitz, *CFO*
EMP: 174
Web: global.medtronic.com
SIC: 3841 Surgical and medical instruments
HQ: Covidien Lp
15 Hampshire St
Mansfield MA 02048
763 514-4000

(P-8140)
DAVID KOPF INSTRUMENTS
7324 Elmo St, Tujunga (91042-2205)
P.O. Box 636 (91043-0636)
PHONE..................818 352-3274

Carl Koph, *CEO*
J David Kopf, *
Carol Kopf, *
EMP: 28 **EST:** 1959
SQ FT: 13,836
SALES (est): 3.86MM **Privately Held**
Web: www.kopfinstruments.com
SIC: 3841 Veterinarians' instruments and apparatus

(P-8141)
DEVAX INC
13900 Alton Pkwy Ste 125, Irvine
(92618-1621)
PHONE..................949 461-0450
Jeff Theil, *CEO*
EMP: 32 **EST:** 1999
SQ FT: 5,000
SALES (est): 2.43MM **Privately Held**
SIC: 3841 Surgical and medical instruments

(P-8142)
DEXCOM INC (PA)
Also Called: Dexcom
6340 Sequence Dr, San Diego
(92121-4356)
PHONE..................858 200-0200
Kevin R Sayer, *Ch Bd*
Jereme M Sylvain, *CAO*
Jacob S Leach, *Ex VP*
Michael Brown, *CLO*
Girish Naganathan, *Ex VP*
EMP: 568 **EST:** 1999
SALES (est): 3.62B
SALES (corp-wide): 3.62B **Publicly Held**
Web: www.dexcom.com
SIC: 3841 Surgical and medical instruments

(P-8143)
DIALITY INC
181 Technology Dr Ste 150, Irvine
(92618-2484)
PHONE..................949 916-5851
Osman Khawar, *CEO*
Aaron Mishkin, *Sec*
Ather Khan, *CFO*
EMP: 81 **EST:** 2015
SALES (est): 9.85MM **Privately Held**
Web: www.diality.com
SIC: 3841 Hemodialysis apparatus

(P-8144)
DIGITAL SURGERY SYSTEMS INC
Also Called: True Digital Surgery
125 Cremona Dr Pmb 110, Goleta
(93117-3083)
PHONE..................805 978-5400
Aidan Foley, *Pr*
Arthur Rice, *
Simon Raab, *
Kevin Foley, *
J Flagg Flanagan, *
EMP: 34 **EST:** 2018
SALES (est): 9.45MM **Privately Held**
Web: www.truedigitalsurgery.com
SIC: 3841 Surgical and medical instruments

(P-8145)
DUPACO INC
4144 Avenida De La Plata Ste B, Oceanside
(92056-6038)
PHONE..................760 758-4550
Gregory Jordan, *Pr*
EMP: 43 **EST:** 1962
SQ FT: 30,000
SALES (est): 4.35MM **Privately Held**
Web: www.dupacoinc.com

SIC: 3841 3845 Medical instruments and equipment, blood and bone work; Electromedical equipment

(P-8146)
EAGLE LABS LLC
Also Called: Eagle Labs
10201a Trademark St Ste A, Rancho
Cucamonga (91730-5849)
PHONE..................909 481-0011
Richard J De Camp, *Pr*
EMP: 65 **EST:** 1988
SQ FT: 30,000
SALES (est): 7.53MM
SALES (corp-wide): 17.47MM **Privately Held**
Web: www.eaglelabs.com
SIC: 3841 Surgical and medical instruments
HQ: Summit Medical, Llc
815 Northwest Pkwy # 100
Saint Paul MN 55121
651 789-3939

(P-8147)
ELECTRONIC WAVEFORM LAB INC
5702 Bolsa Ave, Huntington Beach
(92649-1128)
PHONE..................714 843-0463
Ryan Haney, *Pr*
William Jim Heaney, *Pr*
Patricia Heaney, *
Ryan Haney, *Pr*
EMP: 25 **EST:** 1981
SALES (est): 4.91MM **Privately Held**
Web: www.h-wave.com
SIC: 3841 Anesthesia apparatus

(P-8148)
ENCHANNEL MEDICAL LTD
555 Corporate Dr Ste 165, Ladera Ranch
(92694-2170)
PHONE..................949 694-6802
Jun Feng, *CEO*
EMP: 25 **EST:** 2021
SALES (est): 5.47MM **Privately Held**
SIC: 3841 Diagnostic apparatus, medical

(P-8149)
ENDOLOGIX INC (PA)
Also Called: Endologix
2 Musick, Irvine (92618-1631)
PHONE..................949 595-7200
John Onopchenko, *CEO*
Daniel Lemaitre, *
Matthew Thompson, *CMO*
Jeff Fecho Cqo, *Prin*
Cindy Pinto, *Interim Vice President*
▲ **EMP:** 108 **EST:** 1992
SQ FT: 129,000
SALES (est): 143.37MM **Privately Held**
Web: www.endologix.com
SIC: 3841 Surgical and medical instruments

(P-8150)
ENDOLOGIX CANADA LLC
2 Musick, Irvine (92618-1631)
PHONE..................949 595-7200
EMP: 79 **EST:** 2014
SALES (est): 4.23MM **Privately Held**
Web: www.endologix.com
SIC: 3841 Catheters
HQ: Trivascular, Inc.
2 Musick
Irvine CA 92618

(P-8151)
ENVVENO MEDICAL CORPORATION

Also Called: Nvno
70 Doppler, Irvine (92618-4306)
PHONE..................949 261-2900
Robert A Berman, *CEO*
Craig Glynn, *CFO*
Hamed Alavi, *Sr VP*
Marc H Glickman, *CMO*
EMP: 31 **EST:** 1999
SQ FT: 14,507
SALES (est): 5.99MM **Privately Held**
Web: www.envveno.com
SIC: 3841 Surgical and medical instruments

(P-8152)
EPICA MEDICAL INNOVATIONS LLC
901 Calle Amanecer Ste 150, San Clemente
(92673-4219)
PHONE..................949 238-6323
▲ **EMP:** 24 **EST:** 2012
SQ FT: 4,441
SALES (est): 2.69MM
SALES (corp-wide): 9.24MM **Privately Held**
Web: www.epicaanimalhealth.com
SIC: 3841 5047 Surgical and medical instruments; Medical equipment and supplies
PA: Epica International, Inc.
901 Calle Amanecer # 150
949 238-6323

(P-8153)
FLUID LINE TECHNOLOGY CORP
4590 Ish Dr, Simi Valley (93063-7678)
P.O. Box 3116 (91313-3116)
PHONE..................818 998-8848
Joseph Marcilese, *Pr*
Phillip Jaramilla, *
▼ **EMP:** 25 **EST:** 1989
SALES (est): 5.59MM **Privately Held**
Web: www.fluidlinetech.com
SIC: 3841 2833 Surgical and medical instruments; Medicinals and botanicals

(P-8154)
FREUDENBERG MEDICAL LLC
5050 Rivergrade Rd, Baldwin Park
(91706-1405)
PHONE..................626 814-9684
Coburn Pharr, *Brnch Mgr*
EMP: 149
SALES (corp-wide): 12.96B **Privately Held**
Web: www.inhealth.com
SIC: 3841 Surgical and medical instruments
HQ: Freudenberg Medical, Llc
1110 Mark Ave
Carpinteria CA 93013
805 684-3304

(P-8155)
FUSION BIOTEC LLC
160 S Cypress St Ste 400, Orange
(92866-1314)
PHONE..................949 264-3437
Bruce Alan Sargeant, *CEO*
EMP: 27 **EST:** 2016
SQ FT: 3,000
SALES (est): 4.26MM **Privately Held**
Web: www.fusion-biotec.com
SIC: 3841 Surgical and medical instruments

(P-8156)
FZIOMED INC (PA)
231 Bonetti Dr, San Luis Obispo
(93401-7376)
PHONE..................805 546-0610
Paul Mraz, *Pr*
Ronald F Haynes, *
EMP: 39 **EST:** 1996

SQ FT: 36,000
SALES (est): 4.83MM **Privately Held**
Web: www.fziomed.com
SIC: 3841 Surgical and medical instruments

(P-8157)
GENBODY AMERICA LLC
3420 De Forest Cir, Jurupa Valley
(91752-1169)
PHONE.................949 561-0664
David Yoo, *CEO*
EMP: 34 **EST:** 2020
SALES (est): 2.32MM **Privately Held**
Web: www.genbodyamerica.com
SIC: 3841 5047 2835 Diagnostic apparatus,
medical; Medical equipment and supplies;
Microbiology and virology diagnostic
products

(P-8158)
GENMARK DIAGNOSTICS INC
(DH)
Also Called: Genmark
5964 La Place Ct Ste 100, Carlsbad
(92008-8829)
PHONE.................760 448-4300
Scott Mendel, *Pr*
Johnny Ek, *CFO*
Brian Mitchell, *VP Opers*
Eric Stier, *Sr VP*
Hollis Winkler, *Pers/VP*
EMP: 583 **EST:** 2020
SALES (est): 171.55MM **Privately Held**
Web: diagnostics.roche.com
SIC: 3841 Surgical and medical instruments
HQ: Roche Holdings, Inc.
1 Dna Way
South San Francisco CA 94080
650 225-1000

(P-8159)
GLAUKOS CORPORATION (PA)
1 Glaukos Way, Aliso Viejo (92656-2704)
PHONE.................949 367-9600
Thomas W Burns, *Ch Bd*
Joseph E Gilliam, *Pr*
Tomas Navratil, *CDO*
Alex R Thurman, *Sr VP*
EMP: 208 **EST:** 1998
SQ FT: 160,000
SALES (est): 314.71MM
SALES (corp-wide): 314.71MM **Publicly
Held**
Web: www.glaukos.com
SIC: 3841 Eye examining instruments and
apparatus

(P-8160)
GLYSENS INCORPORATED
3931 Sorrento Valley Blvd Ste 110, San
Diego (92121-1402)
PHONE.................858 638-7708
Bill Markle, *CEO*
Timothy Routh, *
EMP: 30 **EST:** 1997
SALES (est): 5.27MM **Privately Held**
Web: www.glysens.com
SIC: 3841 Surgical and medical instruments

(P-8161)
HAEMONETICS
MANUFACTURING INC (HQ)
1630 W Industrial Park St, Covina
(91722-3419)
PHONE.................626 339-7388
Neil Ryding, *CEO*
◆ **EMP:** 43 **EST:** 2012
SQ FT: 61,313
SALES (est): 26.96MM
SALES (corp-wide): 1.17B **Publicly Held**

Web: www.haemonetics.com
SIC: 3841 Surgical and medical instruments
PA: Haemonetics Corporation
125 Summer St
781 848-7100

(P-8162)
HYCOR BIOMEDICAL LLC
Also Called: Hycor
7272 Chapman Ave Ste A, Garden Grove
(92841-2129)
PHONE.................714 933-3000
Dick Aderman, *Pr*
Richard Hockins, *
Phil Crusco, *
Mark Van Cleve, *
Eric Whitters, *
▲ **EMP:** 120 **EST:** 1985
SQ FT: 76,000
SALES (est): 24.7MM
SALES (corp-wide): 91.99MM **Privately
Held**
Web: www.hycorbiomedical.com
SIC: 3841 2835 Surgical and medical
instruments; Diagnostic substances
PA: Linden, Llc
111 S Wacker Dr Ste 3350
312 506-5657

(P-8163)
HYDRAFACIAL LLC (HQ)
Also Called: Hydrafacial Company, The
3600 E Burnett St, Long Beach
(90815-1749)
PHONE.................800 603-4996
Clint Carnell, *CEO*
Jeff Nardoci, *
Randy Sieve, *
Paul Bokota, *
Michael Monahan, *
▲ **EMP:** 102 **EST:** 2012
SQ FT: 22,515
SALES (est): 20.9MM
SALES (corp-wide): 397.99MM **Publicly
Held**
Web: www.hydrafacial.com
SIC: 3841 Surgical and medical instruments
PA: The Beauty Health Company
2165 Spring St
800 603-4996

(P-8164)
HYDRAFACIAL LLC
Also Called: Edge Systems
3600 E Burnett St, Long Beach
(90815-1749)
PHONE.................562 391-2052
Evan Hoover, *Brnch Mgr*
EMP: 30
SALES (corp-wide): 397.99MM **Publicly
Held**
Web: www.hydrafacial.com
SIC: 3841 Surgical and medical instruments
HQ: Hydrafacial Llc
3600 E Burnett St
Long Beach CA 90815
800 603-4996

(P-8165)
I-FLOW LLC
43 Discovery Ste 100, Irvine (92618-3773)
PHONE.................800 448-3569
Donald Earhart, *Pr*
James J Dal Porto, *
James R Talevich, *
EMP: 1100 **EST:** 1985
SQ FT: 66,675
SALES (est): 17.42MM
SALES (corp-wide): 20.43B **Publicly Held**
Web: www.iflo.com

SIC: 3841 Surgical instruments and
apparatus
PA: Kimberly-Clark Corporation
351 Phelps Dr
972 281-1200

(P-8166)
ICU MEDICAL INC (PA)
Also Called: Clave
951 Calle Amanecer, San Clemente
(92673-6212)
PHONE.................949 366-2183
Vivek Jain, *Ch Bd*
Brian Bonnell, *CFO*
Christian B Voigtlander, *COO*
Daniel Woolson, *Corporate Vice President*
Virginia Sanzone, *Corporate Vice President*
▲ **EMP:** 503 **EST:** 1984
SQ FT: 19,958
SALES (est): 2.26B
SALES (corp-wide): 2.26B **Publicly Held**
Web: www.icumed.com
SIC: 3841 3845 IV transfusion apparatus;
Pacemaker, cardiac

(P-8167)
IGENOMIX USA INC
Also Called: Ivigen
383 Van Ness Ave Ste 1605, Torrance
(90501-7225)
PHONE.................818 919-1657
Refik Kayali, *Mgr*
EMP: 37
SALES (corp-wide): 4.47MM **Privately
Held**
Web: www.igenomix.com
SIC: 3841 8071 Biopsy instruments and
equipment; Medical laboratories
HQ: Igenomix Usa, Inc.
5201 Waterford Dst Dr
Miami FL 33126
305 501-4948

(P-8168)
INARI MEDICAL INC (PA)
Also Called: Inari Medical
6001 Oak Cyn Ste 100, Irvine (92618-5200)
PHONE.................877 923-4747
Andrew Hykes, *Pr*
Donald Milder, *Ch Bd*
Kevin Strange, *CFO*
Thomas Tu, *CMO*
EMP: 1203 **EST:** 2011
SQ FT: 130,000
SALES (est): 493.63MM
SALES (corp-wide): 493.63MM **Publicly
Held**
Web: www.inarimedical.com
SIC: 3841 Surgical and medical instruments

(P-8169)
INOGEN INC (PA)
Also Called: Inogen
859 Ward Dr Ste 200, Goleta (93111-2920)
PHONE.................805 562-0500
Kevin Rm Smith, *Pr*
Elizabeth Mora, *
Michael K Sergesketter, *Corporate
Treasurer*
Gregoire Ramade, *CCO*
Kevin P Smith, *Corporate Secretary*
◆ **EMP:** 208 **EST:** 2001
SQ FT: 18,000
SALES (est): 315.66MM
SALES (corp-wide): 315.66MM **Publicly
Held**
Web: www.inogen.com
SIC: 3841 3842 7352 Surgical and medical
instruments; Surgical appliances and
supplies; Medical equipment rental

(P-8170)
INOVA LABS INC
9001 Spectrum Center Blvd Ste 200, San
Diego (92123-1438)
P.O. Box 18536 (78760-8536)
PHONE.................866 647-0691
Brooke Harding, *CEO*
John B Rush, *
Phil Martin, *
Randy Williams, *
Dragan Nebrigic, *
▲ **EMP:** 55 **EST:** 2008
SALES (est): 4.23MM **Publicly Held**
Web: www.ariahealth.com
SIC: 3841 Surgical and medical instruments
PA: Resmed Inc.
9001 Spectrum Center Blvd

(P-8171)
INTEGER HOLDINGS
CORPORATION
Also Called: Greatbatch Medical
8830 Siempre Viva Rd Ste 100, San Diego
(92101)
PHONE.................619 498-9448
Raul Mata, *Brnch Mgr*
EMP: 24
SALES (corp-wide): 1.6B **Publicly Held**
Web: www.integer.net
SIC: 3841 Surgical and medical instruments
PA: Integer Holdings Corporation
5830 Gran Pkwy Ste 1150
214 618-5243

(P-8172)
INTEGRA LFSCNCES HOLDINGS
CORP
5955 Pacific Center Blvd, San Diego
(92121-4309)
PHONE.................609 529-9748
Peter Arduini, *CEO*
EMP: 25
Web: marketing.integralife.com
SIC: 3841 3845 Surgical and medical
instruments; Electromedical equipment
PA: Integra Lifesciences Holdings
Corporation
1100 Campus Rd

(P-8173)
INTERFACE ASSOCIATES INC
Also Called: Interface Catheter Solutions
27721 La Paz Rd, Laguna Niguel
(92677-3948)
PHONE.................949 448-7056
EMP: 175
Web: www.interfaceusa.com
SIC: 3841 5047 Surgical and medical
instruments; Hospital equipment and
furniture

(P-8174)
INTERNATIONAL TECHNIDYNE
CORP (DH)
Also Called: Itc
6260 Sequence Dr, San Diego
(92121-4358)
PHONE.................858 263-2300
Scott Cramer, *Pr*
Greg Tibbitts, *
Tom Whalen, *
Matt Bastardi, *
Kimberly Ballard, *
EMP: 250 **EST:** 1969
SQ FT: 130,000
SALES (est): 32.68MM **Privately Held**
Web: www.werfen.com

PRODUCTS & SVCS

SIC: **3841** 3829 Diagnostic apparatus, medical; Medical diagnostic systems, nuclear
HQ: Accriva Diagnostics Holdings, Inc.
6260 Sequence Dr
San Diego CA 92121
858 404-8203

(P-8175)
IRVINE BIOMEDICAL INC
2375 Morse Ave, Irvine (92614-6233)
PHONE..............................949 851-3053
EMP: 200
SIC: **3841** Catheters

(P-8176)
ISSAC MEDICAL INC
2761 Walnut Ave, Tustin (92780-7051)
PHONE..............................805 239-4284
EMP: 320
SIC: **3841** 2822 2821 Surgical and medical instruments; Synthetic rubber; Plastics materials and resins

(P-8177)
JIT MANUFACTURING INC
1610 Commerce Way, Paso Robles (93446-3699)
PHONE..............................805 238-5000
Sharon Smith, *CEO*
EMP: 50
SALES (est): 4.69MM **Privately Held**
Web: www.jitmfginc.com
SIC: **3841** Medical instruments and equipment, blood and bone work

(P-8178)
JOIMAX INC
140 Technology Dr Ste 150, Irvine (92618-2453)
PHONE..............................949 859-3472
Maximilian Ries, *Genl Mgr*
EMP: 38 **EST:** 2005
SALES (est): 4.64MM **Privately Held**
Web: www.joimax.com
SIC: **3841** Surgical and medical instruments

(P-8179)
KARL STORZ ENDSCPY-AMERICA INC (HQ)
Also Called: Karl Storz Intgrated Solutions
2151 E Grand Ave, El Segundo (90245-5017)
PHONE..............................424 218-8100
Charles Wilhelm, *CEO*
Mark Green, *
Sken Huang, *
Sonal Matai, *
▲ **EMP:** 220 **EST:** 1971
SQ FT: 90,000
SALES (est): 280.88MM
SALES (corp-wide): 2.14B **Privately Held**
Web: www.karlstorz.com
SIC: **3841** 5047 Surgical and medical instruments; Medical equipment and supplies
PA: Karl Storz Se & Co. Kg
Dr.-Karl-Storz-Str. 34
74617080

(P-8180)
KARL STORZ ENDSCPY-AMERICA INC
1 N Los Carneros Dr, Goleta (93117)
PHONE..............................800 964-5563
EMP: 65
SALES (corp-wide): 2.14B **Privately Held**
Web: www.karlstorz.com

SIC: **3841** 3845 Suction therapy apparatus; Endoscopic equipment, electromedical, nec
HQ: Karl Storz Endoscopy-America, Inc.
2151 Grand Ave
El Segundo CA 90245
424 218-8100

(P-8181)
KARL STORZ IMAGING INC
32 Aero Camino, Goleta (93117-3105)
PHONE..............................805 968-5563
EMP: 28
SALES (corp-wide): 2.14B **Privately Held**
Web: www.karlstorz.com
SIC: **3841** Surgical and medical instruments
HQ: Karl Storz Imaging, Inc.
1 S Los Carneros Rd
Goleta CA 93117

(P-8182)
KONIGSBERG INSTRUMENTS INC
1017 S Mountain Ave, Monrovia (91016-3642)
PHONE..............................626 775-6500
▼ **EMP:** 35
SIC: **3841** Surgical and medical instruments

(P-8183)
KOROS USA INC
610 Flinn Ave, Moorpark (93021-2008)
PHONE..............................805 529-0825
Tibor Koros, *Pr*
▲ **EMP:** 25 **EST:** 1974
SQ FT: 12,000
SALES (est): 4.56MM **Privately Held**
Web: www.korosusa.com
SIC: **3841** Diagnostic apparatus, medical

(P-8184)
LIFE SCIENCE OUTSOURCING INC
Also Called: Medical Device Manufacturing
830 Challenger St, Brea (92821-2946)
PHONE..............................714 672-1090
Barry Kazemi, *Pr*
Charlie Ricci, *
Neil A Goldman, *
◆ **EMP:** 80 **EST:** 1997
SQ FT: 56,000
SALES (est): 21.53MM **Privately Held**
Web: www.lso-inc.com
SIC: **3841** Surgical instruments and apparatus

(P-8185)
LISI AEROSPACE
2600 Skypark Dr, Torrance (90505-5314)
PHONE..............................310 326-8110
EMP: 30 **EST:** 2019
SALES (est): 13.84MM **Privately Held**
Web: www.lisi-medical.com
SIC: **3841** Surgical and medical instruments

(P-8186)
MARLEE MANUFACTURING INC
4711 E Guasti Rd, Ontario (91761-8106)
PHONE..............................909 390-3222
Russell Wells, *Pr*
Patricia Wells, *
Shawn Cory, *
EMP: 39 **EST:** 1984
SQ FT: 41,000
SALES (est): 3.3MM **Privately Held**
Web: www.marleemanufacturing.com
SIC: **3841** 3599 Surgical and medical instruments; Machine shop, jobbing and repair

(P-8187)
MASIMO AMERICAS INC
52 Discovery, Irvine (92618-3105)
PHONE..............................949 297-7000
Rick Fishel, *CEO*
EMP: 26 **EST:** 2004
SALES (est): 6.81MM **Publicly Held**
Web: www.masimo.com
SIC: **3841** Surgical and medical instruments
PA: Masimo Corporation
52 Discovery

(P-8188)
MAST BIOSURGERY USA INC
Also Called: Mast Biosurgery
6749 Top Gun St Ste 108, San Diego (92121-4151)
PHONE..............................858 550-8050
Thomas Brooas, *Pr*
Thoms Brooas, *
EMP: 30 **EST:** 2004
SQ FT: 10,000
SALES (est): 5.29MM **Privately Held**
Web: www.mastbio.com
SIC: **3841** Surgical and medical instruments

(P-8189)
MEDICAL DEPOT INC
Also Called: Drive Devilbiss Healthcare
548 W Merrill Ave, Rialto (92376-9101)
PHONE..............................877 224-0946
EMP: 81
SALES (corp-wide): 409.99MM **Privately Held**
Web: www.drivemedical.com
SIC: **3841** Surgical and medical instruments
HQ: Medical Depot, Inc.
99 Seaview Blvd
Port Washington NY 11050

(P-8190)
MEDTRONIC INC
Also Called: Medtronic
1659 Gailes Blvd, San Diego (92154-8230)
PHONE..............................949 798-3934
Araceli Rodriguez, *Brnch Mgr*
EMP: 27
Web: www.medtronic.com
SIC: **3841** Surgical and medical instruments
HQ: Medtronic, Inc.
710 Medtronic Pkwy
Minneapolis MN 55432
763 514-4000

(P-8191)
MEDTRONIC INC
Also Called: Medtronic
2101 Faraday Ave, Carlsbad (92008-7205)
PHONE..............................760 214-3009
EMP: 25
Web: medtronic.dejobs.org
SIC: **3841** Surgical and medical instruments
HQ: Medtronic, Inc.
710 Medtronic Pkwy
Minneapolis MN 55432
763 514-4000

(P-8192)
MEDTRONIC INC
Also Called: Medtronic
9775 Toledo Way, Irvine (92618-1811)
PHONE..............................949 837-3700
Geoff Martha, *Ch Bd*
EMP: 200
Web: www.medtronic.com
SIC: **3841** Surgical and medical instruments
HQ: Medtronic, Inc.
710 Medtronic Pkwy
Minneapolis MN 55432
763 514-4000

(P-8193)
MEDTRONIC INC
Medtronic
1851 E Deere Ave, Santa Ana (92705-5720)
PHONE..............................949 474-3943
Walter Cuevas, *Mgr*
EMP: 518
SQ FT: 47,000
Web: www.medtronic.com
SIC: **3841** Surgical and medical instruments
HQ: Medtronic, Inc.
710 Medtronic Pkwy
Minneapolis MN 55432
763 514-4000

(P-8194)
MEDTRONIC ATS MEDICAL INC
1851 E Deere Ave, Santa Ana (92705-5720)
PHONE..............................949 380-9333
Walter Cuevas, *Brnch Mgr*
EMP: 133
Web: www.medtronic.com
SIC: **3841** Surgical instruments and apparatus
HQ: Medtronic Ats Medical, Inc.
710 Medtronic Pkwy
Minneapolis MN 55432
763 553-7736

(P-8195)
MEDTRONIC MINIMED INC (DH)
Also Called: Medtronic
18000 Devonshire St, Northridge (91325-1219)
PHONE..............................800 646-4633
Sean Salmon, *Pr*
Que Dallara, *
Austin Domenici, *
Eric P Geismar, *
George J Montague, *
▲ **EMP:** 1200 **EST:** 1993
SQ FT: 250,000
SALES (est): 443.05MM **Privately Held**
Web: www.medtronicdiabetes.com
SIC: **3841** Surgical and medical instruments
HQ: Medtronic, Inc.
710 Medtronic Pkwy
Minneapolis MN 55432
763 514-4000

(P-8196)
MEDTRONIC PS MEDICAL INC (DH)
Also Called: Medtronic
5290 California Ave # 100, Irvine (92617-3229)
PHONE..............................805 571-3769
◆ **EMP:** 200 **EST:** 1978
SALES (est): 102.71MM **Privately Held**
Web: www.medtronic.com
SIC: **3841** Surgical and medical instruments
HQ: Medtronic, Inc.
710 Medtronic Pkwy
Minneapolis MN 55432
763 514-4000

(P-8197)
MERIT CABLES INCORPORATED
830 N Poinsettia St, Santa Ana (92701-3853)
PHONE..............................714 918-1932
Ted Hendrickson, *CEO*
David Greenwald, *
Ruben Mauricio, *
Rich Mchugh, *Dir*
▼ **EMP:** 25 **EST:** 1986
SQ FT: 8,000
SALES (est): 2.59MM

▲ = Import ▼ = Export
◆ = Import/Export

SALES (corp-wide): 130.59MM **Privately Held**
Web: www.meritcables.com
SIC: 3841 Surgical and medical instruments
PA: Addvise Group Ab (Publ)
Grev Turegatan 30, 2 Tr
856485180

(P-8198)
METTLER ELECTRONICS CORP
1333 S Claudina St, Anaheim (92805-6266)
PHONE..................714 533-2221
Stephen C Mettler, *CEO*
Mark Mettler, *
Donna Mettler, *
Matthew Ferrari, *
▲ **EMP:** 42 **EST:** 1957
SQ FT: 22,500
SALES (est): 3.56MM **Privately Held**
Web: www.mettlerelectronics.com
SIC: 3841 Surgical and medical instruments

(P-8199)
MICRO THERAPEUTICS INC (HQ)
Also Called: Ev3 Neurovascular
9775 Toledo Way, Irvine (92618-1811)
PHONE..................949 837-3700
Thomas C Wilder Iii, *Pr*
Thomas Berryman, *CFO*
EMP: 29 **EST:** 1993
SQ FT: 43,000
SALES (est): 4.46MM **Privately Held**
Web: www.medtronic.com
SIC: 3841 Surgical and medical instruments
PA: Medtronic Public Limited Company
20 Hatch Street Lower

(P-8200)
MICROVENTION INC (DH)
Also Called: Microvention Terumo
35 Enterprise, Aliso Viejo (92656-2601)
PHONE..................714 258-8000
Carsten Schroeder, *Pr*
Kazuaki Kitabatake, *
Bruce Canter, *
Thierry De Bosson, *
Jacques Dion, *
▲ **EMP:** 190 **EST:** 1997
SQ FT: 35,000
SALES (est): 222.49MM **Privately Held**
Web: www.microvention.com
SIC: 3841 Surgical and medical instruments
HQ: Terumo Americas Holding, Inc.
265 Davidson Ave Ste 320
Somerset NJ 08873
732 302-4900

(P-8201)
MONOBIND SALES INC (PA)
100 N Pointe Dr, Lake Forest (92630-2270)
PHONE..................949 951-2665
Frederick Jerome, *Pr*
Doctor Jay Singh, *VP*
▲ **EMP:** 25 **EST:** 1977
SQ FT: 18,000
SALES (est): 8.27MM
SALES (corp-wide): 8.27MM **Privately Held**
Web: www.monobind.com
SIC: 3841 Diagnostic apparatus, medical

(P-8202)
MPS MEDICAL INC
785 Challenger St, Brea (92821-2948)
PHONE..................714 672-1090
Barry A Kazemi, *CEO*
EMP: 37 **EST:** 2014
SALES (est): 4.35MM
SALES (corp-wide): 46.95MM **Privately Held**

Web: www.mpsmedical-inc.com
SIC: 3841 Surgical and medical instruments
PA: Innova Medical Group, Inc.
800 E Colo Blvd Ste 288
760 330-6123

(P-8203)
NELLIX INC
2 Musick, Irvine (92618-1631)
PHONE..................650 213-8700
Robert D Mitchell, *Pr*
Doug Hughes, *
EMP: 29 **EST:** 2001
SQ FT: 7,500
SALES (est): 1.24MM **Privately Held**
SIC: 3841 Surgical and medical instruments
PA: Endologix, Inc.
2 Musick

(P-8204)
NEOMEND INC
60 Technology Dr, Irvine (92618-2301)
PHONE..................949 783-3300
David Renzi, *Pr*
Kevin Cousins, *
David Hanson, *
Pete Davis, *
▼ **EMP:** 90 **EST:** 1999
SQ FT: 21,000
SALES (est): 23.51MM
SALES (corp-wide): 20.18B **Publicly Held**
SIC: 3841 Surgical and medical instruments
HQ: C. R. Bard, Inc.
1 Becton Dr
Franklin Lakes NJ 07417
201 847-6800

(P-8205)
NEUROPTICS INC
9223 Research Dr, Irvine (92618-4286)
PHONE..................949 250-9792
William Worthen, *CEO*
Kamran Siminou, *
William Worthen, *Pr*
Deborah Fineberg, *Global Vice President*
▲ **EMP:** 45 **EST:** 1995
SALES (est): 7.57MM **Privately Held**
Web: www.neuroptics.com
SIC: 3841 Surgical and medical instruments

(P-8206)
NEXUS DX INC
6759 Mesa Ridge Rd, San Diego (92121-4902)
PHONE..................858 410-4600
Nam Shin, *CEO*
▼ **EMP:** 34 **EST:** 2009
SQ FT: 39,000
SALES (est): 8.02MM
SALES (corp-wide): 310.54K **Privately Held**
Web: www.nexus-dx.com
SIC: 3841 Diagnostic apparatus, medical
HQ: Polaris Medinet, Llc
13571 Zinnia Hills Pl
San Diego CA 92130
858 410-4600

(P-8207)
NOBLES MEDICAL TECH INC
17080 Newhope St, Fountain Valley (92708-4206)
PHONE..................714 427-0398
Anthony A Nobles, *Prin*
EMP: 42 **EST:** 2009
SALES (est): 1.86MM **Privately Held**
SIC: 3841 Medical instruments and equipment, blood and bone work

(P-8208)
NORDSON MEDICAL (CA) LLC
7612 Woodwind Dr, Huntington Beach (92647-7164)
PHONE..................657 215-4200
David Zgonc, *Managing Member*
EMP: 51 **EST:** 1991
SQ FT: 40,000
SALES (est): 11.23MM
SALES (corp-wide): 2.69B **Publicly Held**
Web: www.nordson.com
SIC: 3841 Surgical and medical instruments
PA: Nordson Corporation
28601 Clemens Rd
440 892-1580

(P-8209)
NU-HOPE LABORATORIES INC
12640 Branford St, Pacoima (91331-3451)
P.O. Box 331150 (91333-1150)
PHONE..................818 899-7711
Bradley Johnson Galindo, *CEO*
Estelle Galindo, *
▲ **EMP:** 38 **EST:** 1959
SQ FT: 25,000
SALES (est): 2.62MM **Privately Held**
Web: www.nu-hope.com
SIC: 3841 Surgical and medical instruments

(P-8210)
NUVASIVE INC (HQ)
7475 Lusk Blvd, San Diego (92121-5707)
PHONE..................858 909-1800
J Christopher Barry, *CEO*
Daniel J Wolterman, *
Rajesh J Asarpota, *CAO*
Carol A Cox, *External Affairs Vice President*
Joan B Stafslien, *Corporate Secretary*
▲ **EMP:** 75 **EST:** 1997
SQ FT: 152,000
SALES (est): 406.33MM
SALES (corp-wide): 1.57B **Publicly Held**
Web: www.nuvasive.com
SIC: 3841 Surgical and medical instruments
PA: Globus Medical, Inc.
2560 Gen Armistead Ave
610 930-1800

(P-8211)
ORCHID MPS
3233 W Harvard St, Santa Ana (92704-3917)
PHONE..................714 549-9203
Mark Deischter, *VP*
EMP: 100 **EST:** 2005
SALES (est): 4.82MM **Privately Held**
Web: www.orchid-ortho.com
SIC: 3841 Surgical and medical instruments

(P-8212)
PACIFIC INTEGRATED MFG INC
4364 Bonita Rd Ste 454, Bonita (91902-1421)
PHONE..................619 921-3464
Stephen F Keane, *CEO*
Charles Peinado, *
EMP: 200 **EST:** 2000
SALES (est): 10.9MM **Privately Held**
Web: www.pacific-im.com
SIC: 3841 Diagnostic apparatus, medical

(P-8213)
PETER BRASSELER HOLDINGS LLC
4837 Mcgrath St, Ventura (93003-6442)
PHONE..................805 658-2643
Laura Kriese, *Brnch Mgr*
EMP: 74
SALES (corp-wide): 22.1MM **Privately Held**

Web: www.brasselerusa.com
SIC: 3841 Surgical and medical instruments
PA: Peter Brasseler Holdings, Llc
1 Brasseler Blvd
912 925-8525

(P-8214)
PHARMACO-KINESIS CORPORATION
10604 S La Cienega Blvd, Inglewood (90304-1115)
PHONE..................310 641-2700
Frank Adell, *Prin*
Thomas Chen, *
Peter Hirshfield, *
John Muthew, *
EMP: 26 **EST:** 2006
SALES (est): 4.94MM **Privately Held**
Web: www.pharmaco-kinesis.com
SIC: 3841 Surgical and medical instruments

(P-8215)
PHILLPS-MDISIZE COSTA MESA LLC
3545 Harbor Blvd, Costa Mesa (92626-1406)
PHONE..................949 477-9495
Bob Frank, *Genl Mgr*
EMP: 240 **EST:** 1997
SQ FT: 45,000
SALES (est): 31.09MM
SALES (corp-wide): 64.37B **Privately Held**
Web: www.phillipsmedisize.com
SIC: 3841 Surgical and medical instruments
HQ: Molex, Llc
2222 Wellington Ct
Lisle IL 60532
630 969-4550

(P-8216)
PLANET INNOVATION INC
2720 Loker Ave W Ste P, Carlsbad (92010-6606)
PHONE..................949 238-1200
Anthony White, *Pr*
EMP: 30 **EST:** 2013
SALES (est): 22.93MM **Privately Held**
Web: www.planetinnovation.com
SIC: 3841 Surgical and medical instruments
PA: Planet Innovation Holdings Ltd
436 Elgar Rd

(P-8217)
PRO-DEX INC (PA)
Also Called: Pro-Dex
2361 Mcgaw Ave, Irvine (92614-5831)
PHONE..................949 769 3200
Richard L Van Kirk, *Pr*
Nicholas J Swenson, *
Alisha K Charlton, *CFO*
EMP: 120 **EST:** 1978
SQ FT: 28,000
SALES (est): 53.84MM **Publicly Held**
Web: www.pro-dex.com
SIC: 3841 3843 7372 3594 Surgical and medical instruments; Dental equipment; Business oriented computer software; Motors, pneumatic

(P-8218)
PROVIDIEN LLC (HQ)
6740 Nancy Ridge Dr, San Diego (92121-2230)
PHONE..................480 344-5000
Jeffrey S Goble, *CEO*
Paul Jazwin, *CFO*
Charles Stroupe, *Ch Bd*
EMP: 71 **EST:** 2011
SALES (est): 46.89MM
SALES (corp-wide): 4.59B **Publicly Held**

Web: www.providienmedical.com
SIC: 3841 Surgical and medical instruments
PA: Carlisle Companies Incorporated
16430 N Scttsdale Rd Ste
480 781-5000

(P-8219)
PROVIDIEN MACHINING & METALS LLC
Also Called: Providien Machining Mtls Corp
12840 Bradley Ave, Sylmar (91342-3827)
PHONE..................................818 367-3161
◆ EMP: 70 EST: 1987
SALES (est): 8.39MM
SALES (corp-wide): 4.59B **Publicly Held**
Web: resource.dynaroll.com
SIC: 3841 Surgical and medical instruments
HQ: Providien, Llc
6740 Nancy Ridge Dr
San Diego CA 92121

(P-8220)
PRYOR PRODUCTS
1819 Peacock Blvd, Oceanside
(92056-3578)
PHONE..................................760 724-8244
Jeffrey Pryor, CEO
Paul Pryor, *
▲ EMP: 50 EST: 1971
SQ FT: 29,000
SALES (est): 8.96MM **Privately Held**
Web: www.pryorproducts.com
SIC: 3841 IV transfusion apparatus

(P-8221)
RADIOLOGY SUPPORT DEVICES INC
1501 W 178th St, Gardena (90248-3203)
P.O. Box 7490 (90504-8890)
PHONE..................................310 518-0527
Matthew Alderson, CEO
EMP: 29 EST: 1989
SQ FT: 16,000
SALES (est): 2.49MM **Privately Held**
Web: www.rsdphantoms.com
SIC: 3841 3844 Diagnostic apparatus,
medical; X-ray apparatus and tubes

(P-8222)
REBOUND THERAPEUTICS CORP
13900 Alton Pkwy Ste 120, Irvine
(92618-1621)
PHONE..................................949 305-8111
Jeffrey Valko, CEO
EMP: 26 EST: 2015
SALES (est): 2.38MM **Publicly Held**
SIC: 3841 Surgical and medical instruments
PA: Integra Lifesciences Holdings
Corporation
1100 Campus Rd

(P-8223)
RESMED INC (PA)
Also Called: Resmed
9001 Spectrum Center Blvd, San Diego
(92123-1438)
PHONE..................................858 836-5000
Michael Farrell, Ch Bd
Rob Douglas, Pr
Brett Sandercock, CFO
EMP: 702 EST: 1989
SQ FT: 230,000
SALES (est): 4.69B **Publicly Held**
Web: www.resmed.com
SIC: 3841 7372 Diagnostic apparatus,
medical; Application computer software

(P-8224)
REVERSE MEDICAL CORPORATION
Also Called: Reverse Medical
13700 Alton Pkwy Ste 167, Irvine
(92618-1618)
PHONE..................................949 215-0660
Jeffrey Valko, Pr
EMP: 47 EST: 2007
SALES (est): 5.43MM **Privately Held**
Web: www.reversemed.com
SIC: 3841 Surgical and medical instruments
HQ: Covidien Limited
20 Lower Hatch Street
Dublin D02 H

(P-8225)
RF SURGICAL SYSTEMS LLC
5927 Landau Ct, Carlsbad (92008-8803)
PHONE..................................855 522-7027
John Buhler, Pr
Ron Wangerin, CFO
▲ EMP: 55 EST: 2008
SQ FT: 24,000
SALES (est): 2.3MM **Privately Held**
SIC: 3841 Surgical and medical instruments
HQ: Medtronic, Inc.
710 Medtronic Pkwy
Minneapolis MN 55432
763 514-4000

(P-8226)
SECHRIST INDUSTRIES INC
4225 E La Palma Ave, Anaheim
(92807-1844)
PHONE..................................714 579-8400
Edward Pulwer, CEO
John Razzano, *
◆ EMP: 1254 EST: 1973
SQ FT: 74,000
SALES (est): 9.72MM
SALES (corp-wide): 85.84MM **Privately Held**
Web: www.sechristusa.com
SIC: 3841 Surgical and medical instruments
HQ: Wound Care Holdings, Llc
5220 Belfort Rd Ste 130
Jacksonville FL 32256
800 379-9774

(P-8227)
SEQUENT MEDICAL INC
35 Enterprise, Aliso Viejo (92656-2601)
PHONE..................................949 830-9600
Thomas C Wilder, Pr
Kevin J Cousins, *
EMP: 65 EST: 2006
SALES (est): 5.9MM **Privately Held**
Web: www.microvention.com
SIC: 3841 Surgical and medical instruments
HQ: Microvention, Inc.
35 Enterprise
Aliso Viejo CA 92656
714 258-8000

(P-8228)
SOURCE SCIENTIFIC LLC
2144 Michelson Dr, Irvine (92612-1304)
PHONE..................................949 231-5096
▲ EMP: 39
Web: www.bit-group.com
SIC: 3841 8711 Surgical and medical
instruments; Engineering services

(P-8229)
SPECTRUM INC
Also Called: Spectrum Laboratories
18617 S Broadwick St, Rancho Dominguez
(90220-6435)
P.O. Box 512939 (90051-0939)

PHONE..................................310 885-4600
▲ EMP: 200
SIC: 3841 3821 3842 Surgical and medical
instruments; Laboratory apparatus and
furniture; Surgical appliances and supplies

(P-8230)
SPINAL ELEMENTS HOLDINGS INC
Also Called: Spinal Elements
3115 Melrose Dr Ste 200, Carlsbad
(92010-6690)
PHONE..................................877 774-6255
Ronald Lloyd, Pr
Steven J Healy, *
Steve Mcgowan, CFO
Ricardo J Simmons, CMO
Paul Graveline, Ex VP
EMP: 120 EST: 2016
SQ FT: 42,000
SALES (est): 95.92MM **Privately Held**
Web: www.spinalelements.com
SIC: 3841 Surgical and medical instruments

(P-8231)
SURGISTAR INC (PA)
Also Called: Sabel
2310 La Mirada Dr, Vista (92081-7862)
PHONE..................................760 598-2480
Jonathan Woodward, Pr
Hema Chaudhary, *
◆ EMP: 35 EST: 1992
SQ FT: 12,000
SALES (est): 5.02MM **Privately Held**
Web: www.surgistar.com
SIC: 3841 Surgical and medical instruments

(P-8232)
SWEDEN & MARTINA INC
600 Anton Blvd Ste 1134, Costa Mesa
(92626-7221)
PHONE..................................844 862-7846
Elisabetta Martina, Pr
EMP: 33 EST: 2014
SALES (est): 735.91K **Privately Held**
SIC: 3841 Medical instruments and
equipment, blood and bone work

(P-8233)
SYNERGY HEALTH AST LLC (DH)
Also Called: Americas Regional Division
9020 Activity Rd Ste D, San Diego
(92126-4454)
PHONE..................................858 586-1166
▲ EMP: 54 EST: 2004
SALES (est): 8.68MM **Privately Held**
SIC: 3841 Surgical and medical instruments
HQ: Steris Corporation
5960 Heisley Rd
Mentor OH 44060
440 354-2600

(P-8234)
TANDEM DIABETES CARE INC (PA)
Also Called: TANDEM DIABETES CARE
12400 High Bluff Dr, San Diego
(92130-3077)
PHONE..................................858 366-6900
John Sheridan, Pr
Jean-claude Kyrillos, Ex VP
Leigh Vosseller, Ex VP
Mark Novara, CCO
Elizabeth Gasser, CSO CPO
EMP: 2343 EST: 2006
SQ FT: 181,949
SALES (est): 747.72MM **Publicly Held**
Web: www.tandemdiabetes.com

SIC: 3841 2833 Surgical and medical
instruments; Insulin: bulk, uncompounded

(P-8235)
TEARLAB CORPORATION
42309 Winchester Rd Ste I, Temecula
(92590-4859)
PHONE..................................858 455-6006
Kelley Hall, Brnch Mgr
EMP: 25
SALES (corp-wide): 8.76B **Privately Held**
Web: www.trukera.com
SIC: 3841 3851 Eye examining instruments
and apparatus; Ophthalmic goods
HQ: Tearlab Corporation
940 S Kimball Ave
Southlake TX 76092
855 832-7522

(P-8236)
TECOMET INC
Also Called: Tecomet
503 S Vincent Ave, Azusa (91702-5131)
PHONE..................................626 334-1519
EMP: 575
SALES (corp-wide): 832.81MM **Privately Held**
Web: www.tecometetch.com
SIC: 3841 3444 Diagnostic apparatus,
medical; Sheet metalwork
HQ: Tecomet Inc.
18 Commerce Way Ste 4800
Woburn MA 01801
978 642-2400

(P-8237)
TENEX HEALTH INC
26902 Vista Ter, Lake Forest (92630-8123)
PHONE..................................949 454-7500
William Maya, Pr
Bernard Morrey, Chief Medical Officer*
Ivan Mijatovic, *
Jagi Gill, *
▲ EMP: 70 EST: 2011
SQ FT: 15,000
SALES (est): 9.22MM **Privately Held**
Web: www.tenexhealth.com
SIC: 3841 Surgical and medical instruments

(P-8238)
THI INC
1525 E Edinger Ave, Santa Ana
(92705-4907)
PHONE..................................714 444-4643
Jim Willett, CEO
▲ EMP: 100 EST: 2000
SQ FT: 35,000
SALES (est): 4.67MM **Privately Held**
Web: www.tenacore.com
SIC: 3841 7699 Surgical instruments and
apparatus; Surgical instrument repair

(P-8239)
TMJ SOLUTIONS LLC
Also Called: TMJ Concepts
6059 King Dr, Ventura (93003-7607)
PHONE..................................805 650-3391
Heather Wise, Pr
EMP: 54 EST: 1989
SQ FT: 7,280
SALES (est): 5.11MM
SALES (corp-wide): 20.5B **Publicly Held**
SIC: 3841 Surgical and medical instruments
PA: Stryker Corporation
1941 Stryker Way
269 385-2600

(P-8240)
TRELLBORG SLING SLTIONS US INC (DH)

Also Called: Issac
2761 Walnut Ave, Tustin (92780-7051)
PHONE..............................714 415-0280
William Reising, *CEO*
Tom Mazelin, *
Ron Fraleigh, *
Kevin Beatty, *
Fiona Guo, *
EMP: 150 **EST:** 1993
SQ FT: 1,600
SALES (est): 43.74MM
SALES (corp-wide): 60.4MM **Privately Held**
SIC: 3841 Surgical and medical instruments
HQ: Trelleborg Corporation
200 Veterans Blvd Ste 3
South Haven MI 49090
269 639-9891

(P-8241)
TRELLEBORG SEALING SOLUTIONS
Also Called: TRELLEBORG SEALING SOLUTIONS TUSTIN, INC.
3034 Propeller Dr, Paso Robles (93446-9519)
PHONE..............................805 239-4284
William E Reising, *Brnch Mgr*
EMP: 85
SALES (corp-wide): 60.4MM **Privately Held**
SIC: 3841 Surgical and medical instruments
HQ: Trelleborg Sealing Solutions Us, Inc.
2761 Walnut Ave
Tustin CA 92780

(P-8242)
TRIVASCULAR INC (DH)
2 Musick, Irvine (92618-1631)
PHONE..............................707 543-8800
John Onopchenko, *CEO*
EMP: 36 **EST:** 1998
SALES (est): 10.47MM **Privately Held**
Web: www.endologix.com
SIC: 3841 Surgical and medical instruments
HQ: Trivascular Technologies, Inc.
2 Musik
Irvine CA 92618
707 543-8800

(P-8243)
TRIVASCULAR TECHNOLOGIES INC (HQ)
2 Musick, Irvine (92618-1631)
PHONE..............................707 543-8800
John Onopchenko, *CEO*
Christopher G Chavez, *Pr*
Michael R Kramer, *CFO*
EMP: 188 **EST:** 2008
SQ FT: 110,000
SALES (est): 19.97MM **Privately Held**
Web: www.endologix.com
SIC: 3841 Surgical and medical instruments
PA: Endologix, Inc.
2 Musick

(P-8244)
TRUEVISION SYSTEMS INC
Also Called: Truevision 3d Surgical
315 Bollay Dr Ste 101, Goleta (93117-2948)
PHONE..............................805 963-9700
A Burton Tripathi, *CEO*
Robert Reali, *
▲ **EMP:** 43 **EST:** 2003
SQ FT: 10,549
SALES (est): 4.74MM **Privately Held**
Web: www.myalcon.com
SIC: 3841 Surgical and medical instruments
HQ: Alcon, Inc.
1132 Ferris Rd

Amelia OH 45102
513 722-1037

(P-8245)
U S MEDICAL INSTRUMENTS INC (PA)
888 Prospect St Ste 100, La Jolla (92037-8200)
P.O. Box 928439 (92192-8439)
PHONE..............................619 661-5500
Matthew Mazur, *Ch*
George A Schapiro, *Sec*
Carlos H Manjarrez, *VP Opers*
Eldridge Fridge, *Dir*
A R Moosa, *Dir*
EMP: 33 **EST:** 1991
SQ FT: 60,000
SALES (est): 1.63MM **Privately Held**
SIC: 3841 Surgical and medical instruments

(P-8246)
V-WAVE INC
29219 Canwood St Ste 100, Agoura Hills (91301-1582)
PHONE..............................818 629-2164
Neal L Eigler, *Admn*
EMP: 23 **EST:** 2015
SALES (est): 2.07MM **Privately Held**
Web: www.vwavemedical.com
SIC: 3841 Surgical and medical instruments

(P-8247)
VERTIFLEX INC
25155 Rye Canyon Loop, Valencia (91355-5004)
PHONE..............................442 325-5900
Earl Fender, *CEO*
EMP: 40 **EST:** 2004
SALES (est): 4.56MM
SALES (corp-wide): 12.68B **Publicly Held**
Web: www.bostonscientific.com
SIC: 3841 Surgical and medical instruments
PA: Boston Scientific Corporation
300 Boston Scientific Way
508 683-4000

(P-8248)
VERTOS MEDICAL INC LLC
95 Enterprise Ste 325, Aliso Viejo (92656-2612)
PHONE..............................949 349-0008
James M Corbett, *CEO*
Rebecca Colbert, *CFO*
Stephen E Paul, *Chief Commercial Officer*
EMP: 62 **EST:** 2005
SQ FT: 25,000
SALES (est): 9.06MM **Privately Held**
Web: www.vertosmed.com
SIC: 3841 3842 Medical instruments and equipment, blood and bone work; Surgical appliances and supplies

---

3842 Surgical Appliances And Supplies

(P-8249)
ADVANCED BIONICS LLC (HQ)
Also Called: A B
12740 San Fernando Rd, Sylmar (91342-3700)
PHONE..............................661 362-1400
Rainer Platz, *CEO*
EMP: 450 **EST:** 1997
SALES (est): 23.32MM **Privately Held**
Web: www.advancedbionics.com
SIC: 3842 Hearing aids
PA: Sonova Holding Ag
Laubisrutistrasse 28

(P-8250)
ADVANCED BIONICS CORPORATION (HQ)
28515 Westinghouse Pl, Valencia (91355-4833)
PHONE..............................661 362-1400
Rainer Platz, *CEO*
Alfred Mann, *
Jeffrey Goldberg, *
▲ **EMP:** 158 **EST:** 2007
SALES (est): 108.47MM **Privately Held**
Web: www.advancedbionics.com
SIC: 3842 Hearing aids
PA: Sonova Holding Ag
Laubisrutistrasse 28

(P-8251)
ALPHATEC SPINE INC (HQ)
Also Called: Atec Spine
1950 Camino Vida Roble, Carlsbad (92008-6505)
PHONE..............................760 431-9286
James M Corbett, *CEO*
Patrick Ryan, *
Thomas Mcleer, *Sr VP*
Ebun S Garner, *
Michael O'neill, *CFO*
▲ **EMP:** 250 **EST:** 1990
SALES (est): 93.43MM **Publicly Held**
Web: www.atecspine.com
SIC: 3842 8711 5047 Surgical appliances and supplies; Engineering services; Medical equipment and supplies
PA: Alphatec Holdings, Inc.
1950 Camino Vida Roble

(P-8252)
AMERICH CORPORATION (PA)
13222 Saticoy St, North Hollywood (91605-3404)
PHONE..............................818 982-1711
Edward Richmond, *Pr*
Dino Pacifici, *
Greg Richmond, *
▲ **EMP:** 120 **EST:** 1982
SALES (est): 23.68MM
SALES (corp-wide): 23.68MM **Privately Held**
Web: www.americh.com
SIC: 3842 3432 3431 3261 Whirlpool baths, hydrotherapy equipment; Plumbing fixture fittings and trim; Metal sanitary ware; Vitreous plumbing fixtures

(P-8253)
ANSELL SNDEL MED SOLUTIONS LLC
9301 Oakdale Ave Ste 300, Chatsworth (91311-6539)
PHONE..............................818 534-2500
Anthony B Lopez, *Pr*
Wendell Franke, *Associate Director Global Training*
Stephanie Barth, *
◆ **EMP:** 32 **EST:** 2002
SQ FT: 14,600
SALES (est): 6.94MM **Privately Held**
Web: www.ansell.com
SIC: 3842 Surgical appliances and supplies
PA: Ansell Limited
678 Victoria St

(P-8254)
BIOMET INC
181 Technology Dr, Irvine (92618-2484)
PHONE..............................949 453-3200
EMP: 29
SALES (corp-wide): 7.39B **Publicly Held**
Web: www.zimmerbiomet.com

SIC: 3842 Orthopedic appliances
HQ: Biomet, Inc.
345 East Main St
Warsaw IN 46580
800 613-6131

(P-8255)
BOSTON SCNTFIC NRMDLATION CORP (HQ)
25155 Rye Canyon Loop, Valencia (91355-5004)
PHONE..............................661 949-4310
Michael F Mahoney, *CEO*
Kevin Ballinger, *
Wendy Carruthers, *
Supratim Bose, *
Jeffrey D Capello, *
▲ **EMP:** 450 **EST:** 1993
SQ FT: 26,000
SALES (est): 32.14MM
SALES (corp-wide): 12.68B **Publicly Held**
Web: www.bostonscientific.com
SIC: 3842 3841 5047 Hearing aids; Surgical and medical instruments; Medical and hospital equipment
PA: Boston Scientific Corporation
300 Boston Scientific Way
508 683-4000

(P-8256)
BOYD CHATSWORTH INC
9959 Canoga Ave, Chatsworth (91311-3002)
PHONE..............................818 998-1477
Douglas Britt, *CEO*
Jeremiah Shives, *
Kelly Weber, *
▲ **EMP:** 59 **EST:** 1972
SQ FT: 14,000
SALES (est): 2.26MM **Privately Held**
Web: www.boydcorp.com
SIC: 3842 Adhesive tape and plasters, medicated or non-medicated
HQ: Boyd Corporation
5960 Inglewood Dr Ste 125
Pleasanton CA 94588
209 236-1111

(P-8257)
BREATHE TECHNOLOGIES INC
15091 Bake Pkwy, Irvine (92618-2501)
PHONE..............................949 988-7700
Lawrence A Mastrovich, *Pr*
Paul J Lytle, *
John L Miclot, *
Rebecca Mabry, *
Gary Berman, *Chief Business Officer*
EMP: 30 **EST:** 2005
SALES (est): 9.84MM
SALES (corp-wide): 14.81B **Publicly Held**
Web: www.hillrom.com
SIC: 3842 Respirators
HQ: Hill-Rom, Inc.
1069 State Rte 46 E
Batesville IN 47006
812 934-7777

(P-8258)
CURTISS-WRGHT CNTRLS INTGRTED
Also Called: Penny & Giles Drive Technology
210 Ranger Ave, Brea (92821-6215)
PHONE..............................714 982-1860
John Camp, *Pr*
EMP: 61
SALES (corp-wide): 2.85B **Publicly Held**
Web: www.curtisswright.com
SIC: 3842 Braces, elastic

PRODUCTS & SVCS

HQ: Curtiss-Wright Controls Integrated
   Sensing, Inc.
   28965 Avenue Penn
   Valencia CA 91355
   661 257-4430

(P-8259)
DJO LLC (HQ)
5919 Sea Otter Pl Ste 200, Carlsbad
(92010-6750)
PHONE....................800 321-9549
Brady Shirley, *CEO*
Gordon Briscoe, *
Bradley Tandy, *
Susan Crawford, *Managing Member**
Thomas A Capizzi, *
◆ EMP: 80 EST: 1999
SALES (est): 98.62MM
SALES (corp-wide): 1.71B **Publicly Held**
Web: www.djoglobal.com
SIC: 3842 Surgical appliances and supplies
PA: Enovis Corporation
   2711 Cntrville Rd Ste 400
   301 252-9160

(P-8260)
**DYNAMICS ORTHTICS
PRSTHTICS IN**
Also Called: Dynamics O&P
1830 W Olympic Blvd Ste 123, Los Angeles
   (90006-3734)
PHONE....................213 383-9212
Peter J Sean, *CEO*
EMP: 27 EST: 1988
SQ FT: 20,662
SALES (est): 4.39MM **Privately Held**
Web: www.walkagain.com
SIC: 3842 Orthopedic appliances

(P-8261)
EDWARDS LIFESCIENCES CORP
Also Called: Edwards Life Sciences Cardio V
17221 Red Hill Ave, Irvine (92614-5628)
PHONE....................949 250-2500
EMP: 100
SALES (corp-wide): 6B **Publicly Held**
Web: www.edwards.com
SIC: 3842 Surgical appliances and supplies
PA: Edwards Lifesciences Corp
   1 Edwards Way
   949 250-2500

(P-8262)
EDWARDS LIFESCIENCES CORP
1212 Alton Pkwy, Irvine (92606-4837)
PHONE....................949 553-0611
Rita Hernandez, *Brnch Mgr*
EMP: 30
SALES (corp-wide): 6B **Publicly Held**
Web: www.edwards.com
SIC: 3842 Surgical appliances and supplies
PA: Edwards Lifesciences Corp
   1 Edwards Way
   949 250-2500

(P-8263)
**EDWARDS LIFESCIENCES
CORP (PA)**
Also Called: Edwards
   1 Edwards Way, Irvine (92614-5688)
PHONE....................949 250-2500
Bernard J Zovighian, *CEO*
Nicholas J Valeriani, *
Andrew M Dahl, *CAO*
Scott B Ullem, *Corporate Vice President*
Donald E Bobo Junior, *Corporate Vice
President*
EMP: 1379 EST: 1958
SALES (est): 6B
SALES (corp-wide): 6B **Publicly Held**

Web: www.edwards.com
SIC: 3842 Surgical appliances and supplies

(P-8264)
EMERGENT GROUP INC (DH)
10939 Pendleton St, Sun Valley
(91352-1522)
PHONE....................818 394-2800
Bruce J Haber, *CEO*
Louis Buther, *Pr*
William M Mckay, *CFO*
EMP: 55 EST: 1996
SQ FT: 13,000
SALES (est): 1.01MM
SALES (corp-wide): 1.23B **Privately Held**
Web: sun-valley-e-wire.sitey.me
SIC: 3842 7352 Surgical appliances and
   supplies; Medical equipment rental
HQ: Agiliti Health, Inc.
   6625 W 78th St Ste 300
   Minneapolis MN 55439
   952 893-3200

(P-8265)
ETHICON INC
33 Technology Dr, Irvine (92618-2346)
PHONE....................949 581-5799
Charles Austin, *Brnch Mgr*
EMP: 300
SALES (corp-wide): 85.16B **Publicly Held**
Web: www.jnj.com
SIC: 3842 Sutures, absorbable and non-
   absorbable
HQ: Ethicon Inc.
   1000 Route 202
   Raritan NJ 08869
   800 384-4266

(P-8266)
FERRACO INC (HQ)
Also Called: Human Dsgns Prsthic Orthtic L
2933 Long Beach Blvd, Long Beach
(90806-1517)
PHONE....................562 988-2414
Natalie Rose Cronin, *CEO*
Eric Ferraco, *
Brian Cronin, *
EMP: 23 EST: 1991
SALES (est): 9.13MM
SALES (corp-wide): 10.71MM **Privately
Held**
Web: www.humandesigns.com
SIC: 3842 Surgical appliances and supplies
PA: Arc-V, Inc.
   1639 N Hollywood Way
   626 445-7797

(P-8267)
FINEST HOUR HOLDINGS INC
Also Called: Aos
3203 Kashiwa St, Torrance (90505-4020)
PHONE....................310 533-9966
Gary Sohngen, *CEO*
Paul Doner, *
Barry Hubbard, *
Michael Payne, *
EMP: 34 EST: 2001
SALES (est): 4.4MM **Privately Held**
Web: www.aosortho.com
SIC: 3842 Implants, surgical

(P-8268)
FREEDOM DESIGNS INC
2241 N Madera Rd, Simi Valley
(93065-1762)
PHONE....................805 582-0077
Kathleen Leneghan, *Pr*
▲ EMP: 120 EST: 1981
SQ FT: 40,000
SALES (est): 8.3MM

SALES (corp-wide): 741.73MM **Privately
Held**
Web: www.freedomdesigns.com
SIC: 3842 Wheelchairs
PA: Invacare Corporation
   1 Invacare Way
   440 329-6000

(P-8269)
FREUDENBERG MEDICAL LLC
6385 Rose Ln Ste A, Carpinteria
(93013-2941)
PHONE....................805 576-5308
Belinda Jackson, *Mgr*
EMP: 66
SALES (corp-wide): 12.96B **Privately Held**
Web: www.freudenbergmedical.com
SIC: 3842 Prosthetic appliances
HQ: Freudenberg Medical, Llc
   1110 Mark Ave
   Carpinteria CA 93013
   805 684-3304

(P-8270)
FREUDENBERG MEDICAL LLC
1009 Cindy Ln, Carpinteria (93013-2905)
PHONE....................805 684-3304
Lorena Lundeen, *Mgr*
EMP: 49
SALES (corp-wide): 12.96B **Privately Held**
Web: www.freudenbergmedical.com
SIC: 3842 Prosthetic appliances
HQ: Freudenberg Medical, Llc
   1110 Mark Ave
   Carpinteria CA 93013
   805 684-3304

(P-8271)
**FREUDENBERG MEDICAL LLC
(DH)**
Also Called: Helix Medical
1110 Mark Ave, Carpinteria (93013-2918)
PHONE....................805 684-3304
Jorg Schneewind, *CEO*
Thomas Vassalo, *
▲ EMP: 177 EST: 1984
SQ FT: 66,000
SALES (est): 89.6MM
SALES (corp-wide): 12.96B **Privately Held**
Web: www.freudenbergmedical.com
SIC: 3842 Prosthetic appliances
HQ: Freudenberg North America Limited
   Partnership
   47774 W Anchor Ct
   Plymouth MI 48170

(P-8272)
**HANGER PRSTHTICS ORTHTICS
W IN**
1127 Wilshire Blvd Ste 310, Los Angeles
(90017-3913)
PHONE....................213 250-7850
Rafael Bibbens, *Mgr*
EMP: 60
SALES (corp-wide): 1.12B **Privately Held**
SIC: 3842 5999 Orthopedic appliances;
   Orthopedic and prosthesis applications
HQ: Hanger Prosthetics & Orthotics West,
   Inc.
   4155 E La Palma Ave B4
   Anaheim CA 92807
   714 961-2112

(P-8273)
HOWMEDICA OSTEONICS CORP
6885 Flanders Dr Ste G, San Diego
(92121-2933)
PHONE....................800 621-6104
EMP: 107
SALES (corp-wide): 20.5B **Publicly Held**

Web: www.patientwebsitecontent.com
SIC: 3842 Surgical appliances and supplies
HQ: Howmedica Osteonics Corp.
   325 Corporate Dr
   Mahwah NJ 07430
   201 831-5000

(P-8274)
IMPLANTECH ASSOCIATES INC
Also Called: Allied Bio Medical
6025 Nicolle St Ste B, Ventura
(93003-7602)
P.O. Box 392 (93002-0392)
PHONE....................805 289-1665
William Binder, *Pr*
EMP: 30 EST: 1989
SQ FT: 11,000
SALES (est): 7.19MM **Privately Held**
Web: www.implantech.com
SIC: 3842 Implants, surgical

(P-8275)
INFAB LLC
1040 Avenida Acaso, Camarillo
(93012-8712)
PHONE....................805 987-5255
Brittany Lepley, *CEO*
Donald J Cusick, *
Justine Peterson, *
Daren Dickerson, *
◆ EMP: 57 EST: 1980
SQ FT: 40,000
SALES (est): 19.05MM **Privately Held**
Web: www.infabcorp.com
SIC: 3842 Radiation shielding aprons,
   gloves, sheeting, etc.

(P-8276)
**INTERPORE CROSS INTL INC
(DH)**
181 Technology Dr, Irvine (92618-2484)
PHONE....................949 453-3200
Dan Hann, *Pr*
Greg Hartman, *CFO*
▲ EMP: 58 EST: 1975
SALES (est): 4.96MM
SALES (corp-wide): 7.39B **Publicly Held**
Web: www.interpore.org
SIC: 3842 3843 Orthopedic appliances;
   Dental equipment and supplies
HQ: Biomet, Inc.
   345 East Main St
   Warsaw IN 46580
   800 613-6131

(P-8277)
ISOMEDIX OPERATIONS INC
Also Called: Steris Isomedix
43425 Business Park Dr, Temecula
(92590-3647)
PHONE....................951 694-9340
Chris Bares, *Mgr*
EMP: 57
Web: www.steris.com
SIC: 3842 Surgical appliances and supplies
HQ: Isomedix Operations Inc.
   5960 Heisley Rd
   Mentor OH 44060

(P-8278)
ISOMEDIX OPERATIONS INC
Also Called: A Steris Company
1000 Sarah Pl, Ontario (91761-8621)
PHONE....................909 390-9942
Michael Au, *Brnch Mgr*
EMP: 40
Web: www.steris.com
SIC: 3842 Surgical appliances and supplies
HQ: Isomedix Operations Inc.
   5960 Heisley Rd

Mentor OH 44060

(P-8279)

JOHNSON & JOHNSON

15715 Arrow Hwy, Irwindale (91706-2006)
PHONE.................................909 839-8650
Cathy Somalis, *Mgr*
EMP: 300
SALES (corp-wide): 85.16B **Publicly Held**
Web: www.jnj.com
SIC: 3842 Dressings, surgical
PA: Johnson & Johnson
   1 Johnson & Johnson Plz
   732 524-0400

(P-8280)

JOHNSON WILSHIRE INC

17343 Freedom Way, City Of Industry
(91748-1001)
PHONE.................................562 777-0088
David W Pang, *Pr*
EMP: 25 **EST:** 2007
SQ FT: 120,000
SALES (est): 1.23MM **Privately Held**
Web: www.johnsonwilshire.com
SIC: 3842 Personal safety equipment

(P-8281)

KINAMED INC

820 Flynn Rd, Camarillo (93012-8701)
PHONE.................................805 384-2748
Clyde R Pratt, *Pr*
Vineet Sarin, *
Bob Bruce, *
EMP: 26 **EST:** 1987
SQ FT: 28,828
SALES (est): 8.41MM **Privately Held**
Web: www.kinamed.com
SIC: 3842 Implants, surgical
PA: Vme Acquisition Corp.
   820 Flynn Rd

(P-8282)

KYOCERA MEDICAL TECH INC

1289 Bryn Mawr Ave Ste A, Redlands
(92374-0106)
PHONE.................................909 557-2360
Ken Kaneko, *Pr*
Takahiro Kobayashi, *
EMP: 50 **EST:** 2019
SALES (est): 5.68MM **Privately Held**
Web: www.kyocera-medical.com
SIC: 3842 Prosthetic appliances

(P-8283)

MEDICAL DEVICE BUS SVCS INC

Also Called: Depuy
5644 Kearny Mesa Rd Ste I, San Diego
(92111-1311)
PHONE.................................858 560-4165
Jim Lent, *Pr*
EMP: 26
SALES (corp-wide): 85.16B **Publicly Held**
SIC: 3842 Surgical appliances and supplies
HQ: Medical Device Business Services, Inc.
   700 Orthopaedic Dr
   Warsaw IN 46582

(P-8284)

MEDICAL PACKAGING CORPORATION

Also Called: Hygenia
941 Avenida Acaso, Camarillo
(93012-8700)
PHONE.................................805 388-2383
Frederic L Nason, *Pr*
Susan J Nason, *
EMP: 100 **EST:** 1974
SQ FT: 45,000
SALES (est): 4.91MM **Privately Held**

Web: www.medicalpackaging.com
SIC: 3842 2835 Surgical appliances and
   supplies; Diagnostic substances

(P-8285)

MEDLINE INDUSTRIES LP

42500 Winchester Rd, Temecula
(92590-2570)
PHONE.................................951 296-2600
EMP: 25
SALES (corp-wide): 7.75B **Privately Held**
Web: www.medline.com
SIC: 3842 Surgical appliances and supplies
PA: Medline Industries, Lp
   3 Lakes Dr
   800 633-5463

(P-8286)

MEGIDDO GLOBAL LLC

17101 Central Ave Ste 1c, Carson
(90746-1360)
PHONE.................................844 477-7007
EMP: 25 **EST:** 2017
SALES (est): 3.38MM **Privately Held**
Web: www.megiddo-global.com
SIC: 3842 2393 2329 3728 Bulletproof vests;
   Textile bags; Field jackets, military; Military
   aircraft equipment and armament

(P-8287)

MENTOR WORLDWIDE LLC (DH)

31 Technology Dr Ste 200, Irvine
(92618-2302)
PHONE.................................800 636-8678
David Shepherd, *Pr*
Joshua H Levine, *Managing Member*
Flavia Pease, *
▲ **EMP:** 250 **EST:** 1969
SALES (est): 455.62MM
SALES (corp-wide): 85.16B **Publicly Held**
Web: www.mentordirect.com
SIC: 3842 3845 3841 Surgical appliances
   and supplies; Ultrasonic medical
   equipment, except cleaning; Medical
   instruments and equipment, blood and
   bone work
HQ: Ethicon Inc.
   1000 Route 202
   Raritan NJ 08869
   800 384-4266

(P-8288)

MIST INC

Also Called: Miradry
3333 Michelson Dr Ste 650, Irvine
(92612-0681)
PHONE.................................408 940-8700
Ronald Menezes, *Pr*
Ron Menezes, *
Brigid A Makes, *
Steven W Kim, *
EMP: 102 **EST:** 2006
SALES (est): 22.19MM
SALES (corp-wide): 38.75MM **Privately Held**
Web: www.miradryhcp.com
SIC: 3842 Surgical appliances and supplies
PA: 1315 Capital Llc
   2929 Walnut St Ste 1240
   215 662-1315

(P-8289)

MOLDEX-METRIC INC

Also Called: Moldex
10111 Jefferson Blvd, Culver City
(90232-3509)
PHONE.................................310 837-6300
Mark Magidson, *CEO*
Debra Magidson, *
◆ **EMP:** 500 **EST:** 1960

SQ FT: 80,000
SALES (est): 24.17MM **Privately Held**
Web: www.moldex.com
SIC: 3842 Personal safety equipment

(P-8290)

MPS ANZON LLC

Also Called: Orchid Orthopedis
11911 Clark St, Arcadia (91006-6026)
PHONE.................................626 471-3553
EMP: 112
SALES (est): 613.6K
SALES (corp-wide): 496.98MM **Privately
Held**
SIC: 3842 Orthopedic appliances
PA: Tulip Us Holdings, Inc.
   1365 N Cedar Rd
   517 694-2300

(P-8291)

OSSUR AMERICAS INC

19762 Pauling, Foothill Ranch
(92610-2611)
PHONE.................................949 382-3883
Edward Castillo, *Brnch Mgr*
EMP: 110
SALES (corp-wide): 787.61MM **Privately
Held**
SIC: 3842 Prosthetic appliances
HQ: Ossur Americas, Inc.
   200 Spctrum Ctr Dr Ste 70
   Irvine CA 92618
   800 233-6263

(P-8292)

OSSUR AMERICAS INC (HQ)

200 Spectrum Center Dr Ste 700, Irvine
(92618-5005)
PHONE.................................800 233-6263
Sveinn Solvason, *CEO*
◆ **EMP:** 55 **EST:** 1984
SALES (est): 98.04MM
SALES (corp-wide): 787.61MM **Privately
Held**
SIC: 3842 Braces, orthopedic
PA: Embla Medical Hf.
   Grjothalsi 5
   4253400

(P-8293)

PASSY-MUIR INC (PA)

17992 Mitchell S Ste 200, Irvine
(92614-6813)
PHONE.................................949 833-8255
Cameron Jolly, *Pr*
EMP: 30 **EST:** 1985
SQ FT: 1,200
SALES (est): 6.69MM
SALES (corp-wide): 6.69MM **Privately Held**
Web: www.passy-muir.com
SIC: 3842 Orthopedic appliances

(P-8294)

PATIENT SAFETY TECHNOLOGIES INC

15440 Laguna Canyon Rd Ste 150, Irvine
(92618-2143)
PHONE.................................949 387-2277
EMP: 25
Web: www.safeor.com
SIC: 3842 Surgical appliances and supplies

(P-8295)

PAULSON MANUFACTURING CORP (PA)

46752 Rainbow Canyon Rd, Temecula
(92592-5984)
PHONE.................................951 676-2451

Roy Paulson, *Pr*
Thomas V Paulson, *
Joyce Paulson, *
▲ **EMP:** 95 **EST:** 1947
SQ FT: 42,000
SALES (est): 24.76MM
SALES (corp-wide): 24.76MM **Privately
Held**
Web: www.paulsonmfg.com
SIC: 3842 Personal safety equipment

(P-8296)

REVA MEDICAL INC (PA)

5751 Copley Dr Ste B, San Diego
(92111-7912)
PHONE.................................858 966-3000
Jeffrey Anderson, *CEO*
Jeff Anderson, *Pr*
C Raymond Larkin Junior, *Ch Bd*
Leigh F Elkolli, *Corporate Secretary*
EMP: 41 **EST:** 1998
SQ FT: 37,000
SALES (est): 7.88MM
SALES (corp-wide): 7.88MM **Privately
Held**
Web: www.revamedical.com
SIC: 3842 Surgical appliances and supplies

(P-8297)

RIZZO INC

Also Called: Om Tactical
7720 Airport Business Pkwy, Van Nuys
(91406-1720)
PHONE.................................818 781-6891
▲ **EMP:** 23
Web: www.omtactical.com
SIC: 3842 Personal safety equipment

(P-8298)

SAFARILAND LLC

4700 E Airport Dr, Ontario (91761-7875)
PHONE.................................909 923-7300
Warren B Kanders, *Brnch Mgr*
EMP: 354
SALES (corp-wide): 482.53MM **Publicly
Held**
Web: www.safariland.com
SIC: 3842 Bulletproof vests
HQ: Safariland, Llc
   13386 International Pkwy
   Jacksonville FL 32218
   904 741-5400

(P-8299)

SAS SAFETY CORPORATION

Also Called: Sas Safety
17785 Center Court Dr N, Cerritos
(90703-0573)
PHONE.................................562 427-2775
James Anthony Mccool, *Pr*
Daniel M Deambrosio, *
Daniel J Lett, *
Anh Phuong Katy Vu, *Treas*
◆ **EMP:** 60 **EST:** 1983
SALES (est): 8.37MM **Privately Held**
Web: www.sassafety.com
SIC: 3842 Personal safety equipment

(P-8300)

SEASPINE INC

Also Called: Integra Lifesciences
5770 Armada Dr, Carlsbad (92008-4608)
PHONE.................................760 727-8399
Keith Valentine, *CEO*
EMP: 80 **EST:** 2002
SQ FT: 22,000
SALES (est): 16.03MM
SALES (corp-wide): 746.64MM **Privately
Held**
Web: www.seaspine.com

(PA)=Parent Co (HQ)=Headquarters
✪ = New Business established in last 2 years   2025 Southern California
Business Directory and Buyers Guide   417

SIC: 3842 5999 Orthopedic appliances;
Orthopedic and prosthesis applications
HQ: Seaspine Orthopedics Corporation
5770 Armada Dr
Carlsbad CA 92008
866 942-8698

(P-8301)
SIENTRA INC (HQ)
Also Called: Sientra
3333 Michelson Dr Ste 650, Irvine
(92612-0681)
PHONE..................805 562-3500
Ronald Menezes, *Pr*
Caroline Van Hove, *
Andy Schmidt, *Sr VP*
Oliver Bennett, *Legal CCDO*
EMP: 29 EST: 2003
SQ FT: 14,000
SALES (est): 46.66MM
SALES (corp-wide): 89.45MM **Publicly Held**
Web: www.sientra.com
SIC: 3842 Surgical appliances and supplies
PA: Tiger Aesthetics Medical Llc
9630 S 54th St
888 694-6694

(P-8302)
STERIS CORPORATION
Also Called: Steris
9020 Activity Rd Ste D, San Diego
(92126-4454)
PHONE..................858 586-1166
Walt Rosebrough, *Mgr*
EMP: 25
Web: www.steris.com
SIC: 3842 Surgical appliances and supplies
HQ: Steris Corporation
5960 Heisley Rd
Mentor OH 44060
440 354-2600

(P-8303)
SUREFIRE LLC
17680 Newhope St Ste B, Fountain Valley
(92708-4220)
PHONE..................714 545-9444
Daniel Fischer, *Pdt Mgr*
EMP: 45
SALES (corp-wide): 97.06MM **Privately Held**
Web: www.surefire.com
SIC: 3842 3484 3648 Ear plugs; Guns
(firearms) or gun parts, 30 mm. and below;
Flashlights
PA: Surefire, Llc
18300 Mount Baldy Cir
714 545-9444

(P-8304)
SUREFIRE LLC
17760 Newhope St Ste A, Fountain Valley
(92708-5401)
PHONE..................714 545-9444
Daniel Fischer, *Pdt Mgr*
EMP: 45
SALES (corp-wide): 97.06MM **Privately Held**
Web: www.surefire.com
SIC: 3842 3484 3648 Ear plugs; Guns
(firearms) or gun parts, 30 mm. and below;
Flashlights
PA: Surefire, Llc
18300 Mount Baldy Cir
714 545-9444

(P-8305)
SUREFIRE LLC
2110 S Anne St, Santa Ana (92704-4409)

PHONE..................714 641-0483
Gustav Bonse, *Mfg Mgr*
EMP: 45
SALES (corp-wide): 97.06MM **Privately Held**
Web: www.surefire.com
SIC: 3842 3484 3648 Ear plugs; Guns
(firearms) or gun parts, 30 mm. and below;
Flashlights
PA: Surefire, Llc
18300 Mount Baldy Cir
714 545-9444

(P-8306)
SUREFIRE LLC
18300 Mount Baldy Cir, Fountain Valley
(92708-6122)
PHONE..................714 545-9444
Joel Smith, *Brnch Mgr*
EMP: 45
SALES (corp-wide): 97.06MM **Privately Held**
Web: www.surefire.com
SIC: 3842 Surgical appliances and supplies
PA: Surefire, Llc
18300 Mount Baldy Cir
714 545-9444

(P-8307)
SUREFIRE LLC
2121 S Yale St, Santa Ana (92704-4437)
PHONE..................714 545-9444
John D Matthews, *Brnch Mgr*
EMP: 45
SALES (corp-wide): 97.06MM **Privately Held**
Web: www.surefire.com
SIC: 3842 Ear plugs
PA: Surefire, Llc
18300 Mount Baldy Cir
714 545-9444

(P-8308)
SUREFIRE LLC
2300 S Yale St, Santa Ana (92704-5330)
PHONE..................714 641-0483
Gustav Bonse, *Mgr*
EMP: 45
SALES (corp-wide): 158.99MM **Privately Held**
Web: www.surefire.com
SIC: 3842 3484 3648 Ear plugs; Guns
(firearms) or gun parts, 30 mm. and below;
Flashlights
PA: Surefire, Llc
18300 Mount Baldy Cir
714 545-9444

(P-8309)
TOTAL RESOURCES INTL INC (PA)
420 S Lemon Ave, Walnut (91789-2956)
PHONE..................909 594-1220
George Rivera, *CEO*
Gregg Rivera, *
Merlyn Rivera, *
▲ EMP: 49 EST: 1993
SQ FT: 115,000
SALES (est): 12.4MM **Privately Held**
Web: www.trikits.com
SIC: 3842 First aid, snake bite, and burn kits

(P-8310)
TOWNSEND INDUSTRIES INC
4401 Stine Rd, Bakersfield (93313-2306)
PHONE..................661 837-1795
EMP: 65
SALES (corp-wide): 1.25MM **Privately Held**
Web: www.townsenddesign.com

SIC: 3842 Braces, orthopedic
HQ: Townsend Industries, Inc.
4615 Shepard St
Bakersfield CA 93313
661 837-1795

(P-8311)
TOWNSEND INDUSTRIES INC
4833 N Hills Dr, Bakersfield (93308-1186)
PHONE..................661 837-1795
Rick Riley, *Brnch Mgr*
EMP: 65
SALES (corp-wide): 1.25MM **Privately Held**
Web: www.thuasneusa.com
SIC: 3842 Braces, orthopedic
HQ: Townsend Industries, Inc.
4615 Shepard St
Bakersfield CA 93313
661 837-1795

(P-8312)
TOWNSEND INDUSTRIES INC (DH)
Also Called: Townsend Design
4615 Shepard St, Bakersfield (93313-2339)
PHONE..................661 837-1795
EMP: 130 EST: 1984
SALES (est): 31.67MM
SALES (corp-wide): 1.25MM **Privately Held**
Web: www.townsenddesign.com
SIC: 3842 Braces, orthopedic
HQ: Thuasne North America Inc.
4615 Shepard St
Bakersfield CA 93313
800 432-3466

(P-8313)
ULTIMATE EARS CONSUMER LLC
3 Jenner Ste 180, Irvine (92618-3835)
PHONE..................949 502-8340
Mindy Harvey, *Owner*
▲ EMP: 229 EST: 2004
SALES (est): 2.02MM **Privately Held**
Web: www.ultimateears.com
SIC: 3842 Hearing aids
HQ: Logitech Inc.
3930 N 1st St
San Jose CA 95134
510 795-8500

(P-8314)
UNITED BIOLOGICS INC
1642 Kaiser Ave, Irvine (92614-5700)
PHONE..................949 345-7490
Craig Johnson, *CEO*
John Barnhill, *
EMP: 37 EST: 2002
SALES (est): 4.88MM **Privately Held**
Web: www.unitedbiologics.com
SIC: 3842 Models, anatomical

(P-8315)
US ARMOR CORPORATION
10715 Bloomfield Ave, Santa Fe Springs
(90670-3913)
PHONE..................562 207-4240
Stephen Armellino, *Pr*
Susan L Armellino, *
Jana Armellino, *CFO*
▲ EMP: 45 EST: 1986
SQ FT: 14,000
SALES (est): 8.14MM **Privately Held**
Web: www.usarmor.com
SIC: 3842 2326 5999 Bulletproof vests;
Men's and boy's work clothing; Safety
supplies and equipment

(P-8316)
VALEDA COMPANY LLC
Also Called: Safe Haven
13571 Vaughn St Unit E, San Fernando
(91340-3006)
PHONE..................800 421-8700
EMP: 47
SALES (corp-wide): 13.9MM **Privately Held**
Web: www.qstraint.com
SIC: 3842 Wheelchairs
PA: Valeda Company, Llc
4031 Ne 12th Ter
954 986-6665

(P-8317)
VCP MOBILITY HOLDINGS INC
Also Called: Sunrise Med HM Hlth Care Group
745 Design Ct Ste 602, Chula Vista
(91911-6165)
PHONE..................619 213-6500
Steve Winston, *Mgr*
EMP: 25
SALES (corp-wide): 463.03MM **Privately Held**
SIC: 3842 Wheelchairs
HQ: Vcp Mobility Holdings, Inc.
7477 Dry Creek Pkwy
Niwot CO 80503
303 218-4600

(P-8318)
VISION QUEST INDUSTRIES INC
Also Called: V Q Orthocare
1390 Decision St Ste A, Vista (92081-8578)
PHONE..................949 261-6382
James W Knape, *CEO*
Kevin Lunau, *
Bob Blachford, *
▲ EMP: 175 EST: 1989
SALES (est): 26.04MM **Privately Held**
Web: www.vqorthocare.com
SIC: 3842 5999 Braces, orthopedic; Medical
apparatus and supplies

(P-8319)
WEBER ORTHOPEDIC LP (PA)
Also Called: Hely & Weber Orthopedic
1185 E Main St, Santa Paula (93060-2954)
P.O. Box 832 (93061-0832)
PHONE..................800 221-5465
Jim Weber, *Pt*
Jim Weber, *Pr*
John P Hely, *
▲ EMP: 62 EST: 1982
SQ FT: 28,000
SALES (est): 4.38MM
SALES (corp-wide): 4.38MM **Privately Held**
Web: www.hely-weber.com
SIC: 3842 5047 Braces, orthopedic;
Orthopedic equipment and supplies

(P-8320)
XR LLC
15251 Pipeline Ln, Huntington Beach
(92649-1135)
PHONE..................714 847-9292
Ari Suss, *Managing Member*
Kelly Eberhard Allen, *
▲ EMP: 27 EST: 2002
SQ FT: 68,000
SALES (est): 5.04MM **Privately Held**
Web: www.xrllc.com
SIC: 3842 Personal safety equipment

(P-8321)
ZIMMER DENTAL INC
1900 Aston Ave, Carlsbad (92008-7308)

PHONE..................800 854-7019
EMP: 440 **EST:** 1981
SALES (est): 4.92MM
SALES (corp-wide): 7.39B **Publicly Held**
Web: www.zimvie.com
SIC: 3842 8021 3843 Implants, surgical; Offices and clinics of dentists; Dental equipment and supplies
HQ: Zimmer, Inc.
1800 W Center St
Warsaw IN 46580
800 348-9500

(P-8322)
ZIMMER MELIA & ASSOCIATES INC (PA)
6832 Presidio Dr, Huntington Beach (92648-3025)
PHONE..................615 377-0118
K Michael Melia, *Pr*
EMP: 25 **EST:** 2005
SALES (est): 1.48MM **Privately Held**
Web: www.zimmerbiomet.com
SIC: 3842 Orthopedic appliances

3843 Dental Equipment And Supplies

(P-8323)
3M COMPANY
3M
2111 Mcgaw Ave, Irvine (92614-0913)
PHONE..................949 863-1360
David Goldinger, *Brnch Mgr*
EMP: 274
SQ FT: 77,656
SALES (corp-wide): 32.68B **Publicly Held**
Web: www.3m.com
SIC: 3843 5047 Dental equipment and supplies; Dental equipment and supplies
PA: 3m Company
3m Center
651 733-1110

(P-8324)
3M UNITEK CORPORATION
Also Called: 3M Unitek
2724 Peck Rd, Monrovia (91016-5097)
PHONE..................626 445-7960
Mary Jo Abler, *CEO*
Fred Palensky, *
▲ **EMP:** 480 **EST:** 1948
SQ FT: 249,000
SALES (est): 32.23MM
SALES (corp-wide): 32.68B **Publicly Held**
SIC: 3843 Orthodontic appliances
PA: 3m Company
3m Center
651 733-1110

(P-8325)
ALPHA DENTAL OF UTAH INC
12898 Towne Center Dr, Cerritos (90703-8546)
PHONE..................562 467-7759
Anthony S Barth, *Prin*
EMP: 27 **EST:** 2010
SALES (est): 3.55MM **Privately Held**
Web: www.delta.org
SIC: 3843 Dental equipment and supplies

(P-8326)
AURIDENT INCORPORATED
610 S State College Blvd, Fullerton (92831-5138)
P.O. Box 7200 (92834-7200)
PHONE..................714 870-1851
Howard M Hoffman, *Pr*
David H Fell, *

Fredelle G Hoffman, *
EMP: 30 **EST:** 1974
SQ FT: 2,700
SALES (est): 2.55MM **Privately Held**
Web: www.aurident.com
SIC: 3843 Dental alloys for amalgams

(P-8327)
BIEN AIR USA INC
Also Called: Bien Air
8861 Research Dr Ste 100, Irvine (92618-4255)
PHONE..................949 477-6050
Arhur Mateen, *Pr*
Jean Claude Maeier, *
Arthur Mateen, *
EMP: 65 **EST:** 1959
SALES (est): 39.95MM **Privately Held**
Web: dental.bienair.com
SIC: 3843 7699 5047 Dental equipment; Dental instrument repair; Hospital equipment and furniture
HQ: Bien-Air Dental Sa
Langgasse 60
Biel-Bienne BE 2504

(P-8328)
BIOLASE INC (PA)
Also Called: Biolase
27042 Towne Centre Dr Ste 270, Lake Forest (92610-2811)
EMP: 62 **EST:** 1984
SALES (est): 49.16MM
SALES (corp-wide): 49.16MM **Publicly Held**
Web: www.biolase.com
SIC: 3843 3841 Dental equipment and supplies; Surgical lasers

(P-8329)
BIOLASE INC
4225 Prado Rd Ste 102, Corona (92880)
PHONE..................949 361-1200
Richard Whitt, *Brnch Mgr*
EMP: 75
SALES (corp-wide): 49.16MM **Publicly Held**
Web: www.biolase.com
SIC: 3843 Dental equipment and supplies
PA: Biolase, Inc.
27042 Twne Cntre Dr Ste 2

(P-8330)
CONAMCO SA DE CV
3008 Palm Hill Dr, Vista (92084-6555)
PHONE..................760 586-4356
Jane Mitchell, *VP*
Herman Mitchell, *VP*
Alfredo Mobarak, *Ch Bd*
EMP: 75 **EST:** 2017
SQ FT: 20,000
SALES (est): 1.02MM **Privately Held**
SIC: 3843 Cement, dental

(P-8331)
CYBER MEDICAL IMAGING INC
Also Called: Xdr Radiology
11300 W Olympic Blvd Ste 710, Los Angeles (90064-1643)
PHONE..................888 937-9729
Douglas Yoon, *CEO*
Adam Chen, *
Joel Karafin, *
EMP: 25 **EST:** 2003
SQ FT: 2,800
SALES (est): 2.34MM **Privately Held**
Web: www.xdrradiology.com
SIC: 3843 Dental equipment and supplies

(P-8332)
DANSEREAU HEALTH PRODUCTS
1581 Commerce St, Corona (92878-3230)
PHONE..................951 549-1400
▲ **EMP:** 36 **EST:** 1957
SALES (est): 3.5MM **Privately Held**
Web: www.dhpdental.com
SIC: 3843 Dental equipment and supplies

(P-8333)
DCII NORTH AMERICA LLC (HQ)
200 S Kraemer Blvd Bldg E, Brea (92821-6208)
PHONE..................714 817-7000
John Bedford, *VP*
EMP: 56 **EST:** 2018
SALES (est): 1.27MM
SALES (corp-wide): 2.57B **Publicly Held**
SIC: 3843 Dental equipment and supplies
PA: Envista Holdings Corporation
200 S Kraemer Blvd Bldg E
714 817-7000

(P-8334)
DUX INDUSTRIES INC
Also Called: Dux Dental Products
1717 W Collins Ave, Orange (92867-5422)
P.O. Box 14247 (92863-1447)
PHONE..................805 488-1122
▲ **EMP:** 65
Web: www.duxdental.com
SIC: 3843 Dental equipment and supplies

(P-8335)
ENVISTA HOLDINGS CORPORATION (PA)
Also Called: Envista
200 S Kraemer Blvd Bldg E, Brea (92821-6208)
PHONE..................714 817-7000
Paul Keel, *Pr*
Scott Huennekens, *Ch Bd*
Mark E Nance, *Sr VP*
Mischa M Reis Senior, *Strategy Vice President*
Eric Hammes, *CFO*
EMP: 51 **EST:** 2018
SALES (est): 2.57B
SALES (corp-wide): 2.57B **Publicly Held**
Web: www.envistaco.com
SIC: 3843 Dental equipment and supplies

(P-8336)
HANDPIECE PARTS & PRODUCTS INC
707 W Angus Ave, Orange (92868-1305)
PHONE..................714 997-4331
Steve Bowen, *Pr*
Lyla Bowen, *
EMP: 30 **EST:** 1992
SQ FT: 18,000
SALES (est): 2.22MM **Privately Held**
Web: www.handpieceparts.com
SIC: 3843 Dental materials

(P-8337)
IMPLANT DIRECT SYBRON INTL LLC (HQ)
3050 E Hillcrest Dr Ste 100, Westlake Village (91362-3195)
PHONE..................818 444-3000
EMP: 52 **EST:** 2010
SALES (est): 5.38MM
SALES (corp-wide): 23.89B **Publicly Held**
Web: www.implantdirect.com
SIC: 3843 Dental equipment and supplies
PA: Danaher Corporation
2200 Pa Ave Nw Ste 800w

202 828-0850

(P-8338)
IMPLANT DIRECT SYBRON MFG LLC
Also Called: Implant Direct
3050 E Hillcrest Dr, Thousand Oaks (91362-3171)
PHONE..................818 444-3300
Gerald A Niznick, *Managing Member*
Philip Davis, *
EMP: 200 **EST:** 2010
SQ FT: 45,622
SALES (est): 41.85MM
SALES (corp-wide): 23.89B **Publicly Held**
Web: www.implantdirect.com
SIC: 3843 Dental equipment and supplies
PA: Danaher Corporation
2200 Pa Ave Nw Ste 800w
202 828-0850

(P-8339)
JENERIC/PENTRON INCORPORATED (HQ)
1717 W Collins Ave, Orange (92867-5422)
PHONE..................203 265-7397
Gordon Cohen, *Pr*
Martin Schulman, *
EMP: 200 **EST:** 1977
SQ FT: 46,000
SALES (est): 3.35MM
SALES (corp-wide): 7.1MM **Privately Held**
SIC: 3843 Dental equipment
PA: Pentron Corporation
53 N Plains Industrial Rd
203 265-7397

(P-8340)
KERR CORPORATION (HQ)
1717 W Collins Ave, Orange (92867-5422)
P.O. Box 14247 (92863-1447)
PHONE..................714 516-7400
Damien Mcdonald, *CEO*
Steve Semmelmayer, *
Steve Dunkerken, *
Leo Pranitis, *
◆ **EMP:** 218 **EST:** 1891
SQ FT: 105,000
SALES (est): 44.87MM **Privately Held**
Web: www.kerrdental.com
SIC: 3843 Dental materials
PA: Sybron Dental Specialties, Inc.
1717 W Collins Ave

(P-8341)
KETTENBACH LP
16052 Beach Blvd Ste 221, Huntington Beach (92647-3855)
PHONE..................877 532-2123
Daniel Parrilli, *Dir*
EMP: 44 **EST:** 2007
SALES (est): 2.52MM **Privately Held**
Web: www.kettenbach-dental.us
SIC: 3843 5047 Dental equipment and supplies; Dental equipment and supplies

(P-8342)
KEYSTONE DENTAL INC
5 Holland Ste 209, Irvine (92618-2576)
PHONE..................781 328-3324
Michael Nealon, *Owner*
EMP: 37
Web: www.keystonedental.com
SIC: 3843 Dental equipment and supplies
PA: Keystone Dental, Inc.
154 Middlesex Tpke Ste 2

P R O D U C T S & S V C S

(P-8343)
KEYSTONE DENTAL INC
13645 Alton Pkwy Ste A, Irvine
(92618-1693)
PHONE..............................781 328-3382
Michael Nealon, *Brnch Mgr*
EMP: 37
Web: www.keystonedental.com
SIC: 3843 Enamels, dentists'
PA: Keystone Dental, Inc.
    154 Middlesex Tpke Ste 2

(P-8344)
LACLEDE INC
Also Called: Laclede Research Center
2103 E University Dr, Rancho Dominguez
(90220-6413)
PHONE..............................310 605-4280
Michael Pellico, *Pr*
Stephen Pellico, *
◆ EMP: 35 EST: 1978
SQ FT: 25,000
SALES (est): 9.1MM **Privately Held**
Web: www.laclede.com
SIC: 3843 Dental equipment

(P-8345)
ORMCO CORPORATION
200 S Kraemer Blvd, Brea (92821-6208)
PHONE..............................909 962-5705
EMP: 41
SALES (corp-wide): 2.57B **Publicly Held**
Web: www.ormco.com
SIC: 3843 Orthodontic appliances
HQ: Ormco Corporation
    1717 W Collins Ave
    Orange CA 92867
    714 516-7400

(P-8346)
ORMCO CORPORATION (HQ)
Also Called: Sybron Endo
1717 W Collins Ave, Orange (92867-5422)
PHONE..............................714 516-7400
Patrik Eriksson, *CEO*
Jason R Davis, *VP*
◆ EMP: 100 EST: 1975
SQ FT: 104,000
SALES (est): 85.59MM
SALES (corp-wide): 2.57B **Publicly Held**
Web: www.ormco.com
SIC: 3843 Orthodontic appliances
PA: Envista Holdings Corporation
    200 S Kraemer Blvd Bldg E
    714 817-7000

(P-8347)
ORTHO ORGANIZERS INC
Also Called: Henry Schein Orthodontics
1822 Aston Ave, Carlsbad (92008-7306)
PHONE..............................760 448-8600
David Parker, *Ch*
Russell J Bonafede, *
Robert Riley, *
Ted Dreifuss, *
Alison Weber, *
▲ EMP: 226 EST: 1975
SQ FT: 65,000
SALES (est): 22.93MM
SALES (corp-wide): 12.34B **Publicly Held**
Web: www.henryscheinortho.com
SIC: 3843 5047 Orthodontic appliances;
    Dental equipment and supplies
PA: Henry Schein, Inc.
    135 Duryea Rd
    631 843-5500

(P-8348)
ORTHODENTAL INTERNATIONAL INC

280 Campillo St Ste J, Calexico
(92231-3200)
PHONE..............................760 357-8070
Armando Lozano, *Pr*
▲ EMP: 57 EST: 1994
SALES (est): 2.19MM
SALES (corp-wide): 3.96B **Publicly Held**
SIC: 3843 Orthodontic appliances
PA: Dentsply Sirona Inc.
    13320 Ballantyne Corp Pl
    844 848-0137

(P-8349)
PAC-DENT INC
670 Endeavor Cir, Brea (92821-2949)
PHONE..............................909 839-0888
Daniel Wang, *CEO*
EMP: 49 EST: 2003
SALES (est): 2.67MM **Privately Held**
Web: www.pac-dent.com
SIC: 3843 Dental equipment and supplies

(P-8350)
PDMA VENTURES INC
Also Called: Zet-Tek Precision Machining
22951 La Palma Ave, Yorba Linda
(92887-6701)
PHONE..............................714 777-8770
Charles Platt, *Pr*
Mark Deischter, *
EMP: 35 EST: 2016
SALES (est): 2.35MM **Privately Held**
SIC: 3843 3842 3841 Dental equipment and
    supplies; Surgical appliances and supplies;
    Surgical and medical instruments

(P-8351)
PRECISION ONE MEDICAL INC
3923 Oceanic Dr Ste 200, Oceanside
(92056-5866)
PHONE..............................760 945-7966
J Todd Strong, *CEO*
David P Dutil, *
Mike Mills, *
EMP: 80 EST: 2009
SQ FT: 10,000
SALES (est): 8.66MM **Privately Held**
Web: www.precisiononemedical.com
SIC: 3843 Dental equipment and supplies

(P-8352)
PROMA INC
730 Kingshill Pl, Carson (90746-1219)
PHONE..............................310 327-0035
Raymond Tai, *CEO*
Harold Tai, *
▲ EMP: 40 EST: 1967
SQ FT: 37,000
SALES (est): 4.55MM **Privately Held**
Web: www.proma.us
SIC: 3843 Dental equipment and supplies

(P-8353)
REPLACEMENT PARTS INDS INC
Also Called: RPI
625 Cochran St, Simi Valley (93065-1939)
P.O. Box 713198 (60677-0398)
PHONE..............................818 882-8611
Ira Lapides, *Pr*
Albert M Lapides, *
Sherry Lapides, *
◆ EMP: 25 EST: 1972
SQ FT: 15,000
SALES (est): 6.32MM **Privately Held**
Web: www.rpiparts.com
SIC: 3843 3841 3821 Dental equipment;
    Surgical and medical instruments;
    Laboratory apparatus, except heating and
    measuring

(P-8354)
SCIENTIFIC PHARMACEUTICALS INC
Also Called: SCI-Pharm
3221 Producer Way, Pomona (91768-3916)
PHONE..............................909 595-9922
▲ EMP: 40 EST: 1979
SALES (est): 5.54MM **Privately Held**
Web: www.scipharm.com
SIC: 3843 2891 Dental materials; Adhesives
    and sealants

(P-8355)
SELANE PRODUCTS INC (PA)
Also Called: Sml Space Maintainers Labs
9129 Lurline Ave, Chatsworth (91311-5922)
P.O. Box 2101 (91313-2101)
PHONE..............................818 998-7460
Rob Veis, *CEO*
▲ EMP: 60 EST: 1957
SQ FT: 12,000
SALES (est): 9.83MM
SALES (corp-wide): 9.83MM **Privately
Held**
Web: www.smlglobal.com
SIC: 3843 8072 Orthodontic appliances;
    Dental laboratories

(P-8356)
SONENDO INC (PA)
Also Called: SONENDO
26061 Merit Cir Ste 102, Laguna Hills
(92653-7010)
PHONE..............................949 766-3636
Bjarne Bergheim, *Pr*
Anthony P Bihl Iii, *Ch Bd*
John P Mcgaugh, *VP Opers*
Chris Guo, *CORP CTRL*
John Bostjancic, *CFO*
EMP: 214 EST: 2006
SQ FT: 59,000
SALES (est): 43.87MM **Publicly Held**
Web: www.sonendo.com
SIC: 3843 Dental equipment and supplies

(P-8357)
SPRINTRAY INC (PA)
2710 Media Center Dr, Los Angeles
(90065-1746)
PHONE..............................800 914-8004
Amir Mansouri, *CEO*
Jing Zhang, *
Erich Kreidler, *
Arun Subramony, *
Jessie Zhang, *
EMP: 51 EST: 2017
SALES (est): 31.98MM
SALES (corp-wide): 31.98MM **Privately
Held**
Web: www.sprintray.com
SIC: 3843 Dental equipment and supplies

(P-8358)
SYBRON DENTAL SPECIALTIES INC (PA)
Also Called: Analytic Endodontics
1717 W Collins Ave, Orange (92867-5422)
PHONE..............................714 516-7400
Damien Mcdonald, *CEO*
◆ EMP: 250 EST: 1993
SQ FT: 16,000
SALES (est): 375.07MM **Privately Held**
Web: www.kavokerr.com
SIC: 3843 2834 Dental laboratory equipment
    ; Pharmaceutical preparations

(P-8359)
SYBRON DENTAL SPECIALTIES INC

1332 S Lone Hill Ave, Glendora
(91740-5339)
PHONE..............................909 596-0276
Andy Astadurian, *Brnch Mgr*
EMP: 47
Web: www.peakdentalspecialists.com
SIC: 3843 Dental equipment and supplies
PA: Sybron Dental Specialties, Inc.
    1717 W Collins Ave

(P-8360)
TALLADIUM INC (PA)
27360 Muirfield Ln, Valencia (91355-1010)
PHONE..............................661 295-0900
Eddie Harms, *CEO*
Geoff Harms, *
◆ EMP: 26 EST: 1980
SQ FT: 9,000
SALES (est): 7.46MM
SALES (corp-wide): 7.46MM **Privately
Held**
Web: www.talladium.com
SIC: 3843 3541 5047 Investment material,
    dental; Milling machines; Dental equipment
    and supplies

(P-8361)
WESTSIDE RESOURCES INC
Also Called: Crystal Tip
8850 Research Dr, Irvine (92618-4223)
PHONE..............................800 944-3939
Donovan Berkely, *CEO*
Derek Jenkins, *
▲ EMP: 40 EST: 2000
SQ FT: 18,000
SALES (est): 3.66MM **Privately Held**
Web: www.naturestip.com
SIC: 3843 5047 Dental equipment and
    supplies; Medical and hospital equipment

(P-8362)
ZYRIS INC
6868 Cortona Dr Ste A, Santa Barbara
(93117-1362)
PHONE..............................805 560-9888
Sandra Hirsch, *CEO*
Sandra Y Hirsch, *
James Hirsch, *
Rolando Mia, *
Catherine Gloster Vv, *Pr*
▲ EMP: 50 EST: 2001
SQ FT: 10,200
SALES (est): 8.97MM **Privately Held**
Web: www.zyris.com
SIC: 3843 5047 Dental equipment; Dental
    equipment and supplies

3844 X-ray Apparatus And Tubes

(P-8363)
ASHTEL STUDIOS INC
Also Called: Ashtel Dental
1610 E Philadelphia St, Ontario
(91761-5759)
PHONE..............................909 434-0911
Anish Patel, *CEO*
◆ EMP: 50 EST: 2006
SQ FT: 40,000
SALES (est): 1.58MM **Privately Held**
Web: www.ashtelstudios.com
SIC: 3844 3991 5122 X-ray apparatus and
    tubes; Toothbrushes, except electric;
    Toothbrushes, except electric

(P-8364)
ASTROPHYSICS INC (PA)
21481 Ferrero, City Of Industry
(91789-5233)

PHONE..................909 598-5488
Francois Zayek, *CEO*
Francois Zayek, *Pr*
John Pan, *
▼ **EMP:** 129 **EST:** 2002
SQ FT: 65,376
SALES (est): 59.64MM
SALES (corp-wide): 59.64MM **Privately Held**
Web: www.astrophysicsinc.com
SIC: 3844 X-ray apparatus and tubes

(P-8365)
CARR CORPORATION (PA)
1547 11th St, Santa Monica (90401-2999)
PHONE..................310 587-1113
John Carr, *Pr*
Paul Carr, *
Reese Carr, *
EMP: 25 **EST:** 1946
SQ FT: 25,000
SALES (est): 2.48MM
SALES (corp-wide): 2.48MM **Privately Held**
Web: www.carrcorporation.com
SIC: 3844 3861 3842 X-ray apparatus and tubes; Processing equipment, photographic; Surgical appliances and supplies

(P-8366)
NORDSON DAGE INC
Also Called: Nordson
2762 Loker Ave W, Carlsbad (92010-6603)
PHONE..................440 985-4496
John J Keane, *CEO*
Robert E Veillette, *
Phil Vere, *
▲ **EMP:** 30 **EST:** 1977
SALES (est): 9.76MM
SALES (corp-wide): 2.69B **Publicly Held**
Web: www.nordson.com
SIC: 3844 3544 5065 3823 X-ray apparatus and tubes; Special dies, tools, jigs, and fixtures; Electronic parts; Process control instruments
PA: Nordson Corporation
28601 Clemens Rd
440 892-1580

(P-8367)
RAPISCAN SYSTEMS INC (HQ)
2805 Columbia St, Torrance (90503-3804)
PHONE..................310 978-1457
Deepak Chopra, *CEO*
Ajay Mehra, *
Eric Luiz, *
Andy Kotowski, *
◆ **EMP:** 114 **EST:** 1993
SQ FT: 93,000
SALES (est): 45.51MM
SALES (corp-wide): 1.54B **Publicly Held**
Web: www.rapiscansystems.com
SIC: 3844 X-ray apparatus and tubes
PA: Osi Systems, Inc.
12525 Chadron Ave
310 978-0516

3845 Electromedical Equipment

(P-8368)
AMPRONIX LLC
15 Whatney, Irvine (92618-2808)
PHONE..................949 273-8000
Burton Tripathi, *Managing Member*
◆ **EMP:** 62 **EST:** 1982
SQ FT: 58,000
SALES (est): 8.86MM **Privately Held**
Web: www.ampronix.com

SIC: 3845 5047 Electrotherapeutic apparatus; Diagnostic equipment, medical

(P-8369)
AXELGAARD MANUFACTURING CO (PA)
Also Called: Axelgaard
520 Industrial Way, Fallbrook (92028-2244)
PHONE..................760 723-7554
Jens Axelgaard, *CSO*
Dan Jeffery, *
▲ **EMP:** 92 **EST:** 1985
SQ FT: 33,000
SALES (est): 24.9MM
SALES (corp-wide): 24.9MM **Privately Held**
Web: www.axelgaard.com
SIC: 3845 Electromedical equipment

(P-8370)
AXELGAARD MANUFACTURING CO
Also Called: Axelgaard Manufacturing
329 W Aviation Rd, Fallbrook (92028-3201)
PHONE..................760 723-7554
Yen Axelgaard, *Mgr*
EMP: 23
SALES (corp-wide): 24.9MM **Privately Held**
Web: www.axelgaard.com
SIC: 3845 Electromedical equipment
PA: Axelgaard Manufacturing Co., Ltd
520 Industrial Way
760 723-7554

(P-8371)
BETA BIONICS INC
11 Hughes, Irvine (92618-1902)
PHONE..................949 297-6635
Edward Damiano, *Brnch Mgr*
EMP: 24
SALES (corp-wide): 17.41MM **Privately Held**
Web: www.betabionics.com
SIC: 3845 Patient monitoring apparatus, nec
PA: Beta Bionics, Inc.
300 Baker Ave Ste 301
855 745-3800

(P-8372)
BIONESS INC
25103 Rye Canyon Loop, Valencia (91355-5004)
PHONE..................661 362-4850
Todd Cushman, *Pr*
Alfred E Mann, *Ch*
Jim Mchargue, *COO*
Dan Lutz, *Sr VP*
Perry Payne, *VP Opers*
▲ **EMP:** 190 **EST:** 2004
SQ FT: 20,000
SALES (est): 47.00MM
SALES (corp-wide): 512.35MM **Publicly Held**
Web: www.bionessrehab.com
SIC: 3845 5047 Transcutaneous electrical nerve stimulators (TENS); Medical and hospital equipment
PA: Bioventus Inc.
4721 Emperor Blvd Ste 100
919 474-6700

(P-8373)
BIOSENSE WEBSTER INC (HQ)
31 Technology Dr Ste 200, Irvine (92618-2302)
PHONE..................909 839-8500
Uri Yaron, *CEO*
Jasmina Brooks, *
Kevin Robert Costello, *

Gerianne T Sarte, *
▲ **EMP:** 150 **EST:** 1980
SALES (est): 146.03MM
SALES (corp-wide): 85.16B **Publicly Held**
Web: www.jnj.com
SIC: 3845 3841 Electromedical apparatus; Surgical and medical instruments
PA: Johnson & Johnson
1 Johnson & Johnson Plz
732 524-0400

(P-8374)
CAREFUSION CORPORATION (HQ)
Also Called: Bd Carefusion
3750 Torrey View Ct, San Diego (92130-2622)
PHONE..................858 617-2000
Thomas E Polen Junior, *Pr*
Christopher R Reidy, *
▲ **EMP:** 474 **EST:** 2009
SALES (est): 2.32B
SALES (corp-wide): 20.18B **Publicly Held**
Web: www.bd.com
SIC: 3845 8742 3841 Electromedical equipment; Hospital and health services consultant; Surgical instruments and apparatus
PA: Becton, Dickinson And Company
1 Becton Dr
201 847-6800

(P-8375)
COASTLINE INTERNATIONAL
1207 Bangor St, San Diego (92106-2407)
PHONE..................888 748-7177
Larry Angione, *CEO*
▲ **EMP:** 250 **EST:** 1982
SQ FT: 32,000
SALES (est): 1.61MM **Privately Held**
Web: www.coastlineintl.com
SIC: 3845 3841 Electromedical equipment; Surgical and medical instruments

(P-8376)
DAYLIGHT DEFENSE LLC
Also Called: Drs Daylight Defense
16465 Via Esprillo Ste 100, San Diego (92127-1701)
PHONE..................858 432-7500
EMP: 175 **EST:** 2009
SALES (est): 9.83MM
SALES (corp-wide): 16.62B **Publicly Held**
Web: www.daylightsolutions.com
SIC: 3845 Laser systems and equipment, medical
HQ: Daylight Solutions, Inc.
16465 Via Esprillo # 100
San Diego CA 92127
858 432-7500

(P-8377)
DOLPHIN MEDICAL INC (HQ)
12525 Chadron Ave, Hawthorne (90250-4807)
PHONE..................800 448-6506
Deepak Chopra, *Pr*
Thomas Scharf, *
▲ **EMP:** 100 **EST:** 2001
SALES (est): 6.62MM
SALES (corp-wide): 1.54B **Publicly Held**
SIC: 3845 Ultrasonic medical equipment, except cleaning
PA: Osi Systems, Inc.
12525 Chadron Ave
310 978-0516

(P-8378)
EDWARDS LIFESCIENCES US INC (HQ)

Also Called: Edwards
1 Edwards Way, Irvine (92614-5688)
PHONE..................949 250-2500
Michael A Mussallem, *Ch*
Dirksen J Lehman, *VP*
Christine Z Mccauley, *VP*
Stanton J Rowe, *VP*
Scott B Ullem, *VP*
EMP: 80 **EST:** 2011
SALES (est): 6.89MM
SALES (corp-wide): 6B **Publicly Held**
Web: www.edwards.com
SIC: 3845 Patient monitoring apparatus, nec
PA: Edwards Lifesciences Corp
1 Edwards Way
949 250-2500

(P-8379)
FLEXICARE INCORPORATED
15281 Barranca Pkwy Ste D, Irvine (92618-2202)
PHONE..................949 450-9999
Ghassem Poormand, *Pr*
▲ **EMP:** 40 **EST:** 2006
SALES (est): 8.29MM **Privately Held**
Web: www.flexicare.com
SIC: 3845 Electromedical equipment

(P-8380)
GEN-PROBE SALES & SERVICE INC
10210 Genetic Center Dr, San Diego (92121-4362)
PHONE..................858 410-8000
Carl Hull, *Pr*
EMP: 54 **EST:** 2010
SALES (est): 5.59MM
SALES (corp-wide): 4.03B **Publicly Held**
Web: www.hologic.com
SIC: 3845 Electromedical equipment
PA: Hologic, Inc.
250 Campus Dr
508 263-2900

(P-8381)
GIVEN IMAGING LOS ANGELES LLC
5860 Uplander Way, Culver City (90230-6608)
PHONE..................310 641-8492
Ron Mcintyre, *Business Operations Vice President*
Eric Finkelman, *ENGG**
Jeffrey Sawyer, *Global Marketing Director**
◆ **EMP:** 175 **EST:** 2003
SALES (est): 5.41MM **Privately Held**
SIC: 3845 Electromedical equipment
HQ: Given Imaging Ltd.
2 Hacarmel
Yokneam Illit

(P-8382)
HOLOGIC INC
9393 Waples St, San Diego (92121-3907)
PHONE..................858 410-8792
EMP: 23 **EST:** 1995
SALES (est): 2.38MM **Privately Held**
Web: www.hologic.com
SIC: 3845 Electromedical equipment

(P-8383)
HOLOGIC INC
10210 Genetic Center Dr, San Diego (92121-4362)
PHONE..................858 410-8000
Gonzalo Martinez, *Brnch Mgr*
EMP: 286
SALES (corp-wide): 4.03B **Publicly Held**
Web: www.hologic.com

SIC: 3845 Ultrasonic medical equipment,
except cleaning
PA: Hologic, Inc.
250 Campus Dr
508 263-2900

(P-8384)
HYGEIA II MEDICAL GROUP INC
Also Called: A Breast Pump and More
6241 Yarrow Dr Ste A, Carlsbad
(92011-1541)
PHONE.....................714 515-7571
Brett Nakfoor, *CEO*
Mark Engler, *
Brett Nakfoor, *Pr*
▲ EMP: 40 EST: 2007
SALES (est): 5.01MM **Privately Held**
Web: www.hygeiahealth.com
SIC: 3845 Electromedical equipment

(P-8385)
HYPERBARIC TECHNOLOGIES
INC
3224 Hoover Ave, National City
(91950-7224)
PHONE.....................619 336-2022
W T Gurnee, *Pr*
EMP: 80 EST: 1992
SQ FT: 15,000
SALES (est): 1.57MM **Privately Held**
SIC: 3845 3841 7352 3443 Electromedical
equipment; Medical instruments and
equipment, blood and bone work; Medical
equipment rental; Fabricated plate work
(boiler shop)

(P-8386)
JOHNSON JHNSON SRGCAL
VSION IN (HQ)
Also Called: Johnson & Johnson Vision
31 Technology Dr Bldg 29a, Irvine
(92618-2302)
P.O. Box 25929 (92799)
PHONE.....................949 581-5799
Warren C Foust, *CEO*
Craig S Virgil, *
Christian A Cuzick, *
▲ EMP: 300 EST: 2001
SALES (est): 371.04MM
SALES (corp-wide): 85.16B **Publicly Held**
Web: www.jnjvisionpro.com
SIC: 3845 3841 Laser systems and
equipment, medical; Ophthalmic
instruments and apparatus
PA: Johnson & Johnson
1 Johnson & Johnson Plz
732 524-0400

(P-8387)
MASIMO CORPORATION
40 Parker, Irvine (92618-1604)
PHONE.....................949 297-7000
EMP: 50
Web: www.masimo.com
SIC: 3845 Electromedical equipment
PA: Masimo Corporation
52 Discovery

(P-8388)
MASIMO CORPORATION
9600 Jeronimo Rd, Irvine (92618-2024)
PHONE.....................949 297-7000
EMP: 50
Web: www.masimo.com
SIC: 3845 Electromedical equipment
PA: Masimo Corporation
52 Discovery

(P-8389)
MASIMO CORPORATION (PA)
Also Called: Masimo
52 Discovery, Irvine (92618-3105)
PHONE.....................949 297-7000
Michelle Brennan, *Interim Chief Executive
Officer*
Micah Young, *Ex VP*
Tao Levy, *Ex VP*
Tom Mcclenahan, *Corporate Secretary*
▲ EMP: 350 EST: 1989
SQ FT: 314,400
SALES (est): 2.05B **Publicly Held**
Web: www.masimo.com
SIC: 3845 Electromedical equipment

(P-8390)
NATUS MEDICAL
INCORPORATED
5955 Pacific Center Blvd, San Diego
(92121-4309)
PHONE.....................858 260-2590
Stephen Dirocco, *Dir Opers*
EMP: 71
SALES (corp-wide): 28.49MM **Privately
Held**
Web: www.natus.com
SIC: 3845 3841 Electromedical equipment;
Surgical instruments and apparatus
HQ: Natus Medical Incorporated
6701 Koll Center Pkwy # 12
Pleasanton CA 94566
925 223-6700

(P-8391)
NEURASIGNAL INC
Also Called: Novasignal
1109 Westwood Blvd, Los Angeles
(90024-3411)
PHONE.....................877 638-7251
Robert Hamilton, *CEO*
EMP: 35
SALES (est): 7.28MM **Privately Held**
Web: www.novasignal.com
SIC: 3845 Electromedical equipment

(P-8392)
PACESETTER INC
13150 Telfair Ave, Sylmar (91342-3573)
PHONE.....................818 493-2715
Ignacio Machuca, *Brnch Mgr*
▲ EMP: 270
SALES (corp-wide): 40.11B **Publicly Held**
SIC: 3845 Defibrillator
HQ: Pacesetter, Inc.
15900 Valley View Ct
Sylmar CA 91342

(P-8393)
PACESETTER INC
4946 Florence Ave, Bell (90201-4319)
PHONE.....................323 773-0591
Rosa Martinez, *Brnch Mgr*
EMP: 268
SALES (corp-wide): 40.11B **Publicly Held**
SIC: 3845 Electromedical equipment
HQ: Pacesetter, Inc.
15900 Valley View Ct
Sylmar CA 91342

(P-8394)
PACESETTER INC (DH)
Also Called: Ventritex
15900 Valley View Ct, Sylmar (91342-3585)
P.O. Box 9221 (91392-9221)
PHONE.....................818 362-6822
Eric S Fain, *CEO*
Ronald A Matricaria, *
▲ EMP: 725 EST: 1994
SALES (est): 113.43MM

SALES (corp-wide): 40.11B **Publicly Held**
SIC: 3845 Defibrillator
HQ: St. Jude Medical, Llc
1 Saint Jude Medical Dr
Saint Paul MN 55117
651 756-2000

(P-8395)
PALYON MEDICAL
CORPORATION
28432 Constellation Rd, Valencia
(91355-5081)
P.O. Box 2091 (85646-2091)
EMP: 25 EST: 2009
SALES (est): 3.95MM **Privately Held**
Web: www.palyonmedical.com
SIC: 3845 Ultrasonic scanning devices,
medical

(P-8396)
PHILIPS IMAGE GDED THRAPY
CORP (DH)
Also Called: Volcano
3721 Valley Centre Dr Ste 500, San Diego
(92130-3328)
PHONE.....................800 228-4728
Ronald A Matricaria, *Ch Bd*
R Scott Huennekens, *
John T Dahldorf, *
Darin M Lippoldt, *Chief Compliance Officer*
John Onopchenko, *Executive Strategy Vice
President*
▲ EMP: 300 EST: 2000
SQ FT: 92,602
SALES (est): 47.32MM
SALES (corp-wide): 18.51B **Publicly Held**
SIC: 3845 Ultrasonic medical equipment,
except cleaning
HQ: Philips Holding U.S.A., Inc.
222 Jacobs St
Cambridge MA 02141

(P-8397)
RESMED CORP (HQ)
9001 Spectrum Center Blvd, San Diego
(92123-1438)
PHONE.....................858 836-5000
Michael Farrell, *CEO*
Robert Douglas, *COO*
Brett Sandercock, *CFO*
David Pendarvis, *CAO*
Hemanth Reddy, *CSO*
EMP: 58 EST: 2016
SALES (est): 34.42MM **Publicly Held**
Web: www.resmedfoundation.org
SIC: 3845 Ultrasonic scanning devices,
medical
PA: Resmed Inc.
9001 Spectrum Center Blvd

(P-8398)
SOTERA WIRELESS INC
5841 Edison Pl Ste 140, Carlsbad
(92008-6500)
PHONE.....................858 427-4620
Tom Watlington, *CEO*
Benjamin Kanter, *CMO*
Mark Spring, *CFO*
Jim Welch, *Ex VP*
EMP: 104 EST: 2002
SALES (est): 19.07MM **Privately Held**
Web: www.soteradigitalhealth.com
SIC: 3845 Electromedical equipment

(P-8399)
SYNERON INC (DH)
Also Called: Syneron Candela
3 Goodyear Ste A, Irvine (92618-2050)
PHONE.....................866 259-6661
Doctor Shimon Eckhouse, *Ch Bd*

Shimon Eckhouse, *
Doctor Opher Shapira, *VP*
Doron Gerstel, *
Leslie Rigali, *
EMP: 87 EST: 2000
SALES (est): 102.55MM **Privately Held**
Web: www.candelamedical.com
SIC: 3845 Laser systems and equipment,
medical
HQ: Syneron Medical Ltd
26 Hakidma
Yokneam Illit 20667

(P-8400)
TEK84 INC
13495 Gregg St, Poway (92064-7135)
PHONE.....................858 676-5382
Steven Smith, *CEO*
Kevin Russeth, *
Richard Wagner, *
Eduardo Parodi, *
Jonathan Shultz, *
EMP: 51 EST: 2009
SALES (est): 11.28MM **Privately Held**
Web: www.tek84.com
SIC: 3845 Electromedical apparatus

(P-8401)
TENSYS MEDICAL INC
12625 High Bluff Dr Ste 213, San Diego
(92130-2054)
PHONE.....................858 552-1941
Stuart Gallant, *CEO*
EMP: 32 EST: 1995
SQ FT: 25,370
SALES (est): 1.9MM **Privately Held**
Web: www.tensysmedical.com
SIC: 3845 3841 Ultrasonic scanning devices,
medical; Surgical and medical instruments

(P-8402)
VIVOMETRICS INC
16030 Ventura Blvd Ste 470, Encino
(91436-4493)
PHONE.....................805 667-2225
Howard R Baker, *Pr*
EMP: 24 EST: 1999
SQ FT: 8,220
SALES (est): 562.08K **Privately Held**
SIC: 3845 3842 Patient monitoring
apparatus, nec; Surgical appliances and
supplies

3851 Ophthalmic Goods

(P-8403)
ADVANCED VISION SCIENCE
INC
5743 Thornwood Dr, Goleta (93117-3801)
PHONE.....................805 683-3851
Cynthia Bentley, *Pr*
EMP: 40 EST: 1976
SQ FT: 30,000
SALES (est): 8.67MM **Privately Held**
Web: www.santen.com
SIC: 3851 3841 8011 Intraocular lenses;
Surgical and medical instruments; Offices
and clinics of medical doctors
PA: Santen Pharmaceutical Co., Ltd.
4-20, Ofukacho, Kita-Ku

(P-8404)
BARTON PERREIRA LLC
459 Wald, Irvine (92618-4639)
PHONE.....................949 305-5360
Patty Jo L Perreira, *
▲ EMP: 25 EST: 2006
SALES (est): 4.24MM **Privately Held**
Web: www.bartonperreira.com

▲ = Import ▼ = Export
◆ = Import/Export

SIC: 3851 Protective eyeware

(P-8405)

BLENDERS EYEWEAR LLC

Also Called: Blenders Eyewear
4683 Cass St, San Diego (92109-2808)
PHONE.............................858 490-2178
Chase Fisher, *CEO*
EMP: 75 EST: 2012
SALES (est): 8.99MM **Privately Held**
Web: www.blenderseyewear.com
SIC: 3851 Glasses, sun or glare
HQ: Safilo America, Inc.
   300 Lighting Way Ste 400
   Secaucus NJ 07094

(P-8406)

ELECTRIC VISUAL EVOLUTION LLC (PA)

Also Called: Electric
950 Calle Amanecer Ste 101, San Clemente
(92673-4231)
PHONE.............................949 940-9125
◆ **EMP: 28 EST:** 1999
SQ FT: 2,000
SALES (est): 8.57MM
SALES (corp-wide): 8.57MM **Privately Held**
Web: www.electriccalifornia.com
SIC: 3851 5094 5136 Glasses, sun or glare;
   Watchcases; Apparel belts, men's and boys'

(P-8407)

EYEONICS INC

Also Called: Bausch & Lomb Surgical Div
32 Discovery, Irvine (92618-3158)
PHONE.............................949 788-6000
Joseph F Gordon, *CEO*
EMP: 50 **EST:** 1998
SALES (est): 3.74MM
SALES (corp-wide): 8.76B **Privately Held**
SIC: 3851 Ophthalmic goods
HQ: Bausch & Lomb Incorporated
   400 Somerset Corp Blvd
   Bridgewater NJ 08807
   866 246-8245

(P-8408)

MARCH VISION CARE INC

6701 Center Dr W Ste 790, Los Angeles
(90045-1563)
PHONE.............................310 665-0975
EMP: 42 **EST:** 2005
SALES (est): 3.58MM
SALES (corp-wide): 371.62B **Publicly Held**
Web: www.marchvisioncare.com
SIC: 3851 Frames, lenses, and parts,
   eyeglass and spectacle
HQ: March Holdings, Inc.
   6701 Center Dr W Ste 790
   Los Angeles CA 90045

(P-8409)

MEDENNIUM INC (PA)

9 Parker Ste 150, Irvine (92618-1691)
PHONE.............................949 789-9000
Jacob Feldman, *Pr*
James R Zullo, *
EMP: 40 **EST:** 1998
SQ FT: 20,000
SALES (est): 4.77MM
SALES (corp-wide): 4.77MM **Privately Held**
Web: www.medennium.com
SIC: 3851 Intraocular lenses

(P-8410)

OAKLEY INC (DH)

1 Icon, Foothill Ranch (92610-3000)
PHONE.............................949 951-0991
Colin Baden, *Pr*
D Scott Olivet, *
Jim Jannard, *
Gianluca Tagliabue, *
Jon Krause, *
◆ **EMP:** 900 **EST:** 1994
SQ FT: 550,000
SALES (est): 984.07MM
SALES (corp-wide): 7.66MM **Privately Held**
Web: www.oakley.com
SIC: 3851 2339 3873 3143 Ophthalmic
   goods; Women's and misses' outerwear,
   nec; Watches, clocks, watchcases, and
   parts; Men's footwear, except athletic
HQ: Luxottica Of America Inc.
   4000 Luxottica Pl
   Mason OH 45040

(P-8411)

OASIS MEDICAL INC (PA)

510-528 S Vermont Ave, Glendora (91741)
P.O. Box 1137 (91740-1137)
PHONE.............................909 305-5400
Norman Delgado, *Ch Bd*
Craig Delgado, *
Arlene Delgado, *
◆ **EMP:** 55 **EST:** 1987
SQ FT: 14,000
SALES (est): 18.37MM
SALES (corp-wide): 18.37MM **Privately Held**
Web: www.oasismedical.com
SIC: 3851 5048 Ophthalmic goods;
   Ophthalmic goods

(P-8412)

OPHTHONIX INC

900 Glenneyre St, Laguna Beach
(92651-2707)
PHONE.............................760 842-5600
▲ **EMP:** 25 **EST:** 2000
SQ FT: 50,000
SALES (est): 2.21MM **Privately Held**
Web: www.ophthonix.com
SIC: 3851 Eyes, glass and plastic

(P-8413)

PRESBIBIO LLC

Also Called: Presbia
36 Plateau, Aliso Viejo (92656-8026)
PHONE.............................949 502-7010
Vladimir Feingold, *
EMP: 16 **EST:** 2008
SALES (est): 4.68MM **Privately Held**
SIC: 3851 Frames, lenses, and parts,
   eyeglass and spectacle

(P-8414)

RXSIGHT INC (PA)

Also Called: RXSIGHT
100 Columbia Ste 120, Aliso Viejo
(92656-4114)
PHONE.............................949 521-7830
Ron Kurtz, *Pr*
J Andy Corley, *Ch Bd*
Shelley Thunen, *CFO*
Ilya Goldshleger, *COO*
Eric Weinberg, *CCO*
▼ **EMP:** 100 **EST:** 1997
SQ FT: 109,822
SALES (est): 89.08MM
SALES (corp-wide): 89.08MM **Publicly Held**
Web: www.rxsight.com

SIC: 3851 Ophthalmic goods

(P-8415)

SIGNET ARMORLITE INC (DH)

5803 Newton Dr Ste A, Carlsbad
(92008-7380)
P.O. Box 3309 (60132-3309)
PHONE.............................760 744-4000
Brad Staley, *Pr*
Bruno Salvadori, *
Andrea Moscatelli, *
M Kathryn Bernard, *
John Hingey, *
▲ **EMP:** 400 **EST:** 1969
SQ FT: 138,000
SALES (est): 19.2MM
SALES (corp-wide): 7.66MM **Privately Held**
Web: www.signetarmorlite.com
SIC: 3851 Ophthalmic goods
HQ: Essilor Of America, Inc.
   13555 N Stemmons Fwy
   Dallas TX 75234

(P-8416)

SPY INC (PA)

1896 Rutherford Rd, Carlsbad
(92008-7326)
PHONE.............................760 804-8420
Seth Hamot, *Interim Chief Executive Officer*
James Mcginty, *CFO*
Jim Sepanek, *Ex VP*
▲ **EMP:** 69 **EST:** 1994
SQ FT: 32,551
SALES (est): 1.93MM **Privately Held**
Web: www.spyoptic.com
SIC: 3851 5099 Glasses, sun or glare;
   Sunglasses

(P-8417)

STAAR SURGICAL COMPANY (PA)

Also Called: Staar
25510 Commercentre Dr, Lake Forest
(92630-8855)
PHONE.............................626 303-7902
Thomas G Frinzi, *Ch Bd*
Scott Barnes, *CMO*
Warren Foust, *COO*
Patrick F Williams, *CFO*
▲ **EMP:** 874 **EST:** 1982
SALES (est): 322.42MM
SALES (corp-wide): 322.42MM **Publicly Held**
Web: www.staar.com
SIC: 3851 Ophthalmic goods

(P 8418)

VISIONARY CONTACT LENS INC

2940 E Miraloma Ave, Anaheim
(02806-1811)
PHONE.............................714 237-1900
Richard Belliveau, *Pr*
Cindy Belliveau, *Treas*
EMP: 23 **EST:** 1992
SQ FT: 16,000
SALES (est): 3.75MM **Privately Held**
Web: www.visionarylens.com
SIC: 3851 5048 Contact lenses; Contact
   lenses

(P-8419)

YOUNGER MFG CO (PA)

Also Called: Younger Optics
2925 California St, Torrance (90503-3914)
PHONE.............................310 783-1533
Joseph David Rips, *CEO*
Tom Balch, *
Roshan Seresinhe, *
◆ **EMP:** 280 **EST:** 1955

SQ FT: 130,000
SALES (est): 44.68MM
SALES (corp-wide): 44.68MM **Privately Held**
Web: www.youngeroptics.com
SIC: 3851 Lens coating, ophthalmic

3861 Photographic Equipment And Supplies

(P-8420)

ANSCHUTZ FILM GROUP LLC (HQ)

10201 W Pico Blvd # 52, Los Angeles
(90064-2606)
PHONE.............................310 887-1000
Michael Bostick, *CEO*
▲ **EMP:** 30 **EST:** 2004
SALES (est): 845.86K **Privately Held**
Web: www.walden.com
SIC: 3861 Motion picture film
PA: The Anschutz Corporation
   555 17th St Ste 2400

(P-8421)

AVID TECHNOLOGY INC

Also Called: Avid
101 S 1st St Ste 200, Burbank
(91502-1938)
PHONE.............................818 557-2520
Kristin Bedient, *Mgr*
EMP: 60
SALES (corp-wide): 447.28MM **Privately Held**
Web: www.avid.com
SIC: 3861 Editing equipment, motion picture:
   viewers, splicers, etc.
HQ: Avid Technology, Inc.
   75 Blue Sky Dr
   Burlington MA 01803
   978 640-3000

(P-8422)

CAROLENSE ENTRMT GROUP LLC

506 S Spring St, Los Angeles (90013-3200)
PHONE.............................405 493-1120
Danesha Barber, *Managing Member*
EMP: 60 **EST:** 2022
SALES (est): 2.94MM **Privately Held**
SIC: 3861 7389 Film, sensitized motion
   picture, X-ray, still camera, etc.; Business
   Activities at Non-Commercial Site

(P-8423)

CHRISTIE DIGITAL SYSTEMS INC (HQ)

10550 Camden Dr, Cypress (90630-4600)
PHONE.............................714 236-8610
Hideaki Onishi, *CEO*
Michael Phipps, *
EMP: 83 **EST:** 1999
SALES (est): 99.79MM **Privately Held**
Web: www.christiedigital.com
SIC: 3861 6719 Projectors, still or motion
   picture, silent or sound; Investment holding
   companies, except banks
PA: Ushio Inc.
   1-6-5, Marunouchi

(P-8424)

CLOVER ENVMTL SOLUTIONS LLC

Also Called: Clover Imaging
315 Weakley St Bldg 3, Calexico
(92231-9659)
PHONE.............................760 357-9277
Jim Cerkleski, *Ofcr*

EMP: 50
SALES (corp-wide): 173.68MM **Privately Held**
Web: www.cloverimaging.com
SIC: **3861** Printing equipment, photographic
PA: Clover Environmental Solutions Llc
4200 Columbus St
866 734-6548

(P-8425)
DJI TECHNOLOGY INC
17301 Edwards Rd, Cerritos (90703-2427)
PHONE..............................818 235-0789
Jie Shen, *CEO*
EMP: 104 EST: 2015
SALES (est): 5.18MM **Privately Held**
SIC: **3861** Aerial cameras

(P-8426)
ELITE SCREENS INC
12282 Knott St, Garden Grove
(92841-2825)
PHONE..............................877 511-1211
Jeff Chen, *Pr*
Henry Yoh, *
◆ EMP: 30 EST: 2004
SALES (est): 6.64MM **Privately Held**
Web: www.elitescreens.com
SIC: **3861** Photographic equipment and
supplies

(P-8427)
**FASTEC IMAGING
CORPORATION**
17150 Via Del Campo Ste 301, San Diego
(92127-2139)
PHONE..............................858 592-2342
Stephen W Ferrell, *Pr*
Charles Mrdjenovich, *
EMP: 25 EST: 2003
SALES (est): 3.79MM **Privately Held**
Web: www.fastecimaging.com
SIC: **3861** Cameras and related equipment

(P-8428)
FPC INC
1017 N Las Palmas Ave, Los Angeles
(90038-2400)
PHONE..............................323 468-5778
◆ EMP: 40
SIC: **3861** 7829 Photographic equipment
and supplies; Motion picture distribution
services

(P-8429)
**FUJIFILM RCRDING MEDIA USA
INC**
6200 Phyllis Dr, Cypress (90630-5239)
PHONE..............................310 536-0800
EMP: 88
Web: www.fujifilm-ffem.com
SIC: **3861** Photographic equipment and
supplies
HQ: Fujifilm Recording Media U.S.A., Inc.
45 Crosby Dr
Bedford MA 01730

(P-8430)
HF GROUP INC (PA)
Also Called: Houston Fearless 76
203 W Artesia Blvd, Compton (90220-5517)
PHONE..............................310 605-0755
Myung S Lee, *Ch Bd*
James H Lee, *
Scott Mccormack, *VP Fin*
Virginia C Clark, *
EMP: 28 EST: 1929
SQ FT: 45,000
SALES (est): 7.95MM

SALES (corp-wide): 7.95MM **Privately Held**
Web: www.hf76.com
SIC: **3861** Processing equipment,
photographic

(P-8431)
JONDO LTD (HQ)
22700 Savi Ranch Pkwy, Yorba Linda
(92887-4608)
PHONE..............................714 279-2300
John Stuart Doe, *CEO*
EMP: 60 EST: 1989
SQ FT: 50,000
SALES (est): 8MM
SALES (corp-wide): 496.73MM **Privately Held**
Web: www.jondo.com
SIC: **3861** Photographic equipment and
supplies
PA: Circle Graphics, Inc.
120 9th Ave
303 532-2370

(P-8432)
**LASER TECHNOLOGIES &
SERVICES LLC**
Also Called: Laser Technologies
1175 Aviation Pl, San Fernando
(91340-1460)
▲ EMP: 100
SIC: **3861** 5999 Reproduction machines and
equipment; Telephone and communication
equipment

(P-8433)
**MATTHEWS STUDIO
EQUIPMENT INC**
Also Called: M S E
4520 W Valerio St, Burbank (91505-1046)
PHONE..............................818 843-6715
Edward Phillips Iii, *Pr*
▲ EMP: 29 EST: 1970
SALES (est): 3.49MM **Privately Held**
Web: www.msegrip.com
SIC: **3861** Motion picture apparatus and
equipment

(P-8434)
**MOVING IMAGE
TECHNOLOGIES LLC**
17760 Newhope St Ste B, Fountain Valley
(92708-5442)
PHONE..............................714 751-7998
Glenn Sherman, *Managing Member*
Bevan Wright, *
Joe Delgado, *
Phil Rassnon, *
David Richards, *
▲ EMP: 32 EST: 2003
SQ FT: 18,000
SALES (est): 5.71MM
SALES (corp-wide): 20.14MM **Publicly Held**
Web: www.movingimagetech.com
SIC: **3861** Motion picture apparatus and
equipment
PA: Moving Image Technologies, Inc.
17760 Newhope St
714 751-7998

(P-8435)
MPO VIDEOTRONICS INC (PA)
5069 Maureen Ln, Moorpark (93021-7148)
PHONE..............................805 499-8513
Larry Kaiser, *Pr*
Julius Barron, *
Don Gaston, *
EMP: 75 EST: 1947

SALES (est): 1.66MM
SALES (corp-wide): 1.66MM **Privately Held**
Web: www.mpo-video.com
SIC: **3861** 5065 7819 3823 Motion picture
apparatus and equipment; Video
equipment, electronic; Equipment rental,
motion picture; Process control instruments

(P-8436)
PANAVISION INC
Also Called: Panavision Hollywood
6735 Selma Ave, Los Angeles
(90028-6134)
PHONE..............................323 464-3800
Lisa Harp, *VP*
EMP: 29
Web: www.panavision.com
SIC: **3861** Photographic equipment and
supplies
PA: Panavision Inc.
6101 Variel Ave

(P-8437)
**PANAVISION INTERNATIONAL
LP (HQ)**
6101 Variel Ave, Woodland Hills
(91367-3722)
P.O. Box 4360 (91365-4360)
PHONE..............................818 316-1080
Robert Beitcher, *Pr*
Ross Landfbuam, *
▲ EMP: 380 EST: 1991
SQ FT: 150,000
SALES (est): 47.23MM **Privately Held**
Web: www.panavision.com
SIC: **3861** Cameras and related equipment
PA: Panavision Inc.
6101 Variel Ave

(P-8438)
PHOTO-SONICS INC (PA)
9131 Independence Ave, Chatsworth
(91311-5903)
PHONE..............................818 842-2141
EMP: 33 EST: 1928
SALES (est): 14.13MM
SALES (corp-wide): 14.13MM **Privately Held**
Web: www.photosonics.com
SIC: **3861** 3827 3663 7819 Photographic
equipment and supplies; Lenses, optical: all
types except ophthalmic;
Phototransmission equipment; Equipment
rental, motion picture

(P-8439)
PHOTRONICS INC (DH)
Also Called: Photronics California
2428 N Ontario St, Burbank (91504-3119)
PHONE..............................203 740-5653
James Mac Donald Junior, *Ch Bd*
Constantine Maristos, *
EMP: 280 EST: 1970
SQ FT: 30,000
SALES (est): 5MM
SALES (corp-wide): 866.95MM **Publicly Held**
Web: photronicsinc.gcs-web.com
SIC: **3861** Photographic equipment and
supplies
HQ: Align-Rite International Limited
1 Technology Dr
Bridgend M GLAM

(P-8440)
PHOTRONICS INC
1760 Arroyo Gln, Escondido (92026-1859)
PHONE..............................760 294-1896
Bob Rhodes, *Mgr*

EMP: 160
SALES (corp-wide): 866.95MM **Publicly Held**
Web: www.photronics.com
SIC: **3861** Photographic equipment and
supplies
HQ: Photronics Inc
2428 N Ontario St
Burbank CA 91504
203 740-5653

(P-8441)
REDCOM LLC
Also Called: Red Digital Cinema Camera Co
94 Icon, Foothill Ranch (92610-3000)
PHONE..............................949 404-4084
James H Jannard, *CEO*
Mike D Executive, *
Vince Hassel, *
Greg Weeks, *
Scott Olivet, *
▲ EMP: 498 EST: 1999
SALES (est): 17.97MM **Privately Held**
Web: www.red.com
SIC: **3861** Motion picture apparatus and
equipment
PA: Nikon Corporation
1-5-20, Nishioi

(P-8442)
RICOH ELECTRONICS INC
2310 Redhill Ave, Santa Ana (92705-5538)
PHONE..............................714 566-6079
EMP: 250
Web: rei.ricoh.com
SIC: **3861** 3695 Photocopy machines;
Magnetic and optical recording media
HQ: Ricoh Electronics, Inc.
1125 Hurricane Shoals Rd
Lawrenceville GA 30043
714 566-2500

(P-8443)
**SANTA BARBARA INSTRUMENT
GP INC**
Also Called: Sbig Astronomical Instruments
150 Castilian Dr, Goleta (93117-3028)
PHONE..............................925 463-3410
EMP: 23 EST: 1991
SALES (est): 2.11MM **Privately Held**
Web: www.diffractionlimited.com
SIC: **3861** Cameras and related equipment

(P-8444)
**STEWART FILMSCREEN CORP
(PA)**
1161 Sepulveda Blvd, Torrance
(90502-2797)
PHONE..............................310 784-5300
Donald R Stewart, *Ex VP*
Thomas E Stewart, *
Adrian Silva, *
◆ EMP: 160 EST: 1947
SQ FT: 43,000
SALES (est): 24.61MM
SALES (corp-wide): 24.61MM **Privately Held**
Web: www.stewartfilmscreen.com
SIC: **3861** Screens, projection

(P-8445)
THERMAPRINT CORPORATION
11 Autry Ste B, Irvine (92618-2766)
PHONE..............................949 583-0800
Natalie J Hochner, *Pr*
Gary Larsen, *
▲ EMP: 25 EST: 1985
SQ FT: 14,500
SALES (est): 2.38MM **Privately Held**
Web: www.thermaprint.com

SIC: 3861 3443 3585 2759 Graphic arts plates, sensitized; Fabricated plate work (boiler shop); Parts for heating, cooling, and refrigerating equipment; Screen printing

(P-8446)
WBI INC
8201 Woodley Ave, Van Nuys (91406-1231)
PHONE..................................800 673-4968
◆ EMP: 600
SIC: 3861 Toners, prepared photographic (not made in chemical plants)

3873 Watches, Clocks, Watchcases, And Parts

(P-8447)
MOD-ELECTRONICS INC
Also Called: Ese
142 Sierra St, El Segundo (90245-4117)
PHONE..................................310 322-2136
William Kaiser, Pr
Brian Way, *
▲ EMP: 26 EST: 1971
SQ FT: 7,500
SALES (est): 3.13MM Privately Held
Web: www.ese-web.com
SIC: 3873 3663 3651 3625 Clocks, assembly of; Radio and t.v. communications equipment; Household audio and video equipment; Relays and industrial controls

---

3911 Jewelry, Precious Metal

(P-8448)
ALLISON-KAUFMAN CO
7640 Haskell Ave, Van Nuys (91406-2005)
PHONE..................................818 373-5100
Bart Kaufman, CEO
Jay A Kaufman, *
▲ EMP: 75 EST: 1946
SQ FT: 21,000
SALES (est): 2.44MM Privately Held
Web: www.allisonkaufman.com
SIC: 3911 Jewel settings and mountings, precious metal

(P-8449)
ALOR INTERNATIONAL LTD
Also Called: Philippe Charriol USA
11722 Sorrento Valley Rd, San Diego (92121-1021)
PHONE..................................858 454-0011
Jack Zemer, CEO
Sandy Zemer, *
Ori Zemer, *
Tal Zemer, *
▲ EMP: 45 EST: 1975
SALES (est): 5.49MM Privately Held
Web: www.alor.com
SIC: 3911 3172 3915 Vanity cases, precious metal; Personal leather goods, nec; Jewel preparing: instruments, tools, watches, and jewelry

(P-8450)
AMERICAS GOLD INC
Also Called: Americas Gold - Amrcas Damonds
650 S Hill St Ste 224, Los Angeles (90014-1769)
PHONE..................................213 688-4904
Rafi M Siddiqui, Pr
Samina Siddiqui, *
EMP: 30 EST: 1999
SQ FT: 4,500

SALES (est): 1.45MM Privately Held
Web: www.americasgold.com
SIC: 3911 Jewelry, precious metal

(P-8451)
AMINCO INTERNATIONAL USA INC
Also Called: California Premium Incentives
20571 Crescent Bay Dr, Lake Forest (92630-8825)
PHONE..................................949 457-3261
Ann Wu, Ex Dir
William Wu, *
Ann Wu, Treas
▲ EMP: 62 EST: 1978
SQ FT: 35,000
SALES (est): 9.62MM Privately Held
Web: www.amincousa.com
SIC: 3911 5099 Jewelry, precious metal; Brass goods

(P-8452)
ARTS ELEGANCE INC
154 W Bellevue Dr, Pasadena (91105-2504)
PHONE..................................626 793-4794
Arutiun Mikaelian, Pr
EMP: 45
SALES (corp-wide): 4.63MM Privately Held
SIC: 3911 Jewelry, precious metal
PA: Art's Elegance, Inc.
739 E Walnut St Ste 200
626 405-1522

(P-8453)
CRISLU CORP
20916 Higgins Ct, Torrance (90501-1722)
PHONE..................................310 322-3444
◆ EMP: 30 EST: 1961
SALES (est): 3MM Privately Held
Web: www.crislu.com
SIC: 3911 Jewel settings and mountings, precious metal

(P-8454)
GIVING KEYS INC
836 Traction Ave, Los Angeles (90013-1816)
PHONE..................................213 935-8791
Caitlin Crosby, CEO
Brit Gilmore, *
▲ EMP: 25 EST: 2012
SQ FT: 8,000
SALES (est): 759.78K Privately Held
Web: www.thegivingkeys.com
SIC: 3911 Jewelry, precious metal

(P-8455)
KRYSTAL VENTURES LLC
Also Called: Gracek Jewelry
17 Shell Bch, Newport Coast (92657-2151)
PHONE..................................213 507-2215
Daniel Kang, Managing Member
Krystal Kang, *
EMP: 30 EST: 2016
SALES (est): 2.12MM Privately Held
SIC: 3911 4813 5734 Jewelry, precious metal; Online service providers; Software, business and non-game

(P-8456)
L SPARK
1140 Kendall Rd Ste A, San Luis Obispo (93401-8047)
PHONE..................................805 626-0511
Courtney Bonzi, CEO
EMP: 40 EST: 2016
SALES (est): 2.3MM Privately Held
Web: www.sparklbands.com

SIC: 3911 Jewelry apparel

(P-8457)
LA GEM AND JEWELRY DESIGN (PA)
Also Called: La Rocks
659 S Broadway Fl 7, Los Angeles (90014-2291)
PHONE..................................213 488-1290
Ashish Arora, CEO
Elsa Behney, Sec
▲ EMP: 37 EST: 2002
SALES (est): 9.6MM
SALES (corp-wide): 9.6MM Privately Held
Web: www.la-rocks.com
SIC: 3911 5094 Jewelry, precious metal; Jewelry

(P-8458)
LA GEM AND JEWELRY DESIGN
3232 E Washington Blvd, Los Angeles (90058-8022)
PHONE..................................213 488-1290
Joseph W Behney, CEO
EMP: 63
SALES (corp-wide): 9.6MM Privately Held
Web: www.la-rocks.com
SIC: 3911 Jewelry, precious metal
PA: L.A. Gem And Jewelry Design, Inc
659 S Broadway Fl 7
213 488-1290

(P-8459)
LEONARD CRAFT CO LLC
1815 Ritchey St Ste B, Santa Ana (92705-5124)
PHONE..................................714 549-0678
Stephen D Leonard, CEO
Stephen D Leonard, Managing Member
EMP: 95 EST: 2017
SALES (est): 4.64MM Privately Held
SIC: 3911 5947 Jewelry, precious metal; Gift shop

(P-8460)
RASTACLAT LLC
100 W Broadway Ste 3000, Long Beach (90802-4467)
PHONE..................................424 287-0902
EMP: 36 EST: 2010
SALES (est): 4.18MM Privately Held
Web: www.rastaclat.com
SIC: 3911 Bracelets, precious metal

(P-8461)
SAGE GODDESS INC
21010 Figueroa St, Carson (90745-1937)
PHONE..................................650 733-6639
Athena I Perrakis, CEO
David Maeizlik, *
EMP: 42 EST: 2013
SALES (est): 2.51MM Privately Held
Web: www.sagegoddess.com
SIC: 3911 5944 5999 Jewelry apparel; Jewelry, precious stones and precious metals; Perfumes and colognes

(P-8462)
TEMPLE CUSTOM JEWELERS LLC
1640 Camino Del Rio N Ste 220, San Diego (92108-1506)
PHONE..................................800 988-3844
Anthony Temple, CEO
EMP: 50 EST: 2016
SALES (est): 2.5MM Privately Held
SIC: 3911 5094 Jewelry mountings and trimmings; Jewelry and precious stones

---

3914 Silverware And Plated Ware

(P-8463)
CAL SIMBA INC (PA)
1283 Flynn Rd, Camarillo (93012-8013)
PHONE..................................805 240-1177
Jay Schechter, CEO
Stuart Seeler, *
John Stout, *
▲ EMP: 38 EST: 1974
SALES (est): 9.17MM
SALES (corp-wide): 9.17MM Privately Held
Web: www.simbaline.com
SIC: 3914 2672 3452 2821 Trophies, plated (all metals); Labels (unprinted), gummed: made from purchased materials; Pins; Polyurethane resins

---

3915 Jewelers' Materials And Lapidary Work

(P-8464)
CGM INC
Also Called: Cgm Findings
19611 Ventura Blvd Ste 211, Tarzana (91356-2907)
PHONE..................................818 609-7088
TOLL FREE: 800
Devinder Bindra, CEO
▲ EMP: 25 EST: 1984
SQ FT: 12,000
SALES (est): 1.22MM Privately Held
Web: www.cgmfindings.com
SIC: 3915 5094 Jewelers' materials and lapidary work; Precious metals

(P-8465)
LUCENT DIAMONDS INC
6303 Owensmouth Ave Fl 10, Woodland Hills (91367-2262)
PHONE..................................424 781-7127
Alex Grizenko, *
EMP: 31 EST: 2015
SALES (est): 850.83K Privately Held
Web: www.lucentdiamonds.com
SIC: 3915 5094 5999 Diamond cutting and polishing; Diamonds (gems); Gems and precious stones

---

3931 Musical Instruments

(P-8466)
DUNCAN CARTER CORPORATION (PA)
Also Called: Seymour Duncan
5427 Hollister Ave, Santa Barbara (93111-2307)
PHONE..................................805 964-9749
Seymour Duncan, Ch
Cathy Carter Duncan, *
▲ EMP: 99 EST: 1976
SQ FT: 20,000
SALES (est): 21.03MM
SALES (corp-wide): 21.03MM Privately Held
Web: www.seymourduncan.com
SIC: 3931 5736 3674 3651 Guitars and parts, electric and nonelectric; Musical instrument stores; Semiconductors and related devices; Household audio and video equipment

PRODUCTS & SVCS

(P-8467)

ERNIE BALL INC (PA)

Also Called: Ernie Ball
4117 Earthwood Ln, San Luis Obispo (93401-7541)
PHONE................................805 544-7726
Brian Ball, *CEO*
Sterling C Ball, *VP*
▲ **EMP:** 29 **EST:** 1965
SQ FT: 50,000
SALES (est): 23.36MM
SALES (corp-wide): 23.36MM **Privately Held**
Web: www.ernieball.com
SIC: 3931 Guitars and parts, electric and nonelectric

(P-8468)

FENDER MUSICAL INSTRS CORP

311 Cessna Cir, Corona (92878-5021)
PHONE................................480 596-9690
EMP: 800
SALES (corp-wide): 1.87B **Privately Held**
Web: www.fender.com
SIC: 3931 3651 Musical instruments; Amplifiers: radio, public address, or musical instrument
HQ: Fender Musical Instruments Corporation
17600 N Perimeter Dr # 100
Scottsdale AZ 85255
480 596-9690

(P-8469)

KANSTUL MUSICAL INSTRS INC

Also Called: K M I
23772 Perth Bay, Dana Point (92629-4203)
PHONE................................714 563-1000
Zigmant J Kanstul, *Pr*
EMP: 42 **EST:** 1982
SALES (est): 676.06K **Privately Held**
Web: www.kanstul.com
SIC: 3931 Brass instruments and parts

(P-8470)

PALADAR MFG INC

53973 Polk St, Coachella (92236-3816)
P.O. Box 4117 (93403-4117)
PHONE................................760 775-4222
Sterling C Ball, *Pr*
Roland S Ball, *
▲ **EMP:** 52 **EST:** 1979
SQ FT: 6,000
SALES (est): 6.65MM **Privately Held**
Web: www.bigpoppasmokers.com
SIC: 3931 Strings, musical instrument

(P-8471)

REMO INC (PA)

28101 Industry Dr, Valencia (91355-4113)
PHONE................................661 294-5600
Remo D Belli, *Pr*
Fredy Shen, *
Douglas Sink, *
◆ **EMP:** 300 **EST:** 1957
SQ FT: 216,000
SALES (est): 44.59MM
SALES (corp-wide): 44.59MM **Privately Held**
Web: www.remo.com
SIC: 3931 Heads, drum

(P-8472)

RICKENBACKER INTERNATIONAL CORPORATION

Also Called: Ric
3895 S Main St, Santa Ana (92707-5774)
PHONE................................714 545-5574
EMP: 75 **EST:** 1931
SALES (est): 4.55MM **Privately Held**
Web: www.rickenbacker.com
SIC: 3931 Guitars and parts, electric and nonelectric

(P-8473)

SCHECTER GUITAR RESEARCH INC

10953 Pendleton St, Sun Valley (91352-1522)
PHONE................................818 767-1029
Michael Ciravolo, *Pr*
◆ **EMP:** 43 **EST:** 1987
SQ FT: 11,000
SALES (est): 6.37MM **Privately Held**
Web: www.schecterguitars.com
SIC: 3931 Musical instruments

(P-8474)

YAMAHA GUITAR GROUP INC

26664 Agoura Rd, Calabasas (91302-1954)
PHONE................................818 575-3900
Paul Foeckler, *Pr*
EMP: 38
Web: www.line6.com
SIC: 3931 Musical instruments
HQ: Yamaha Guitar Group, Inc.
26580 Agoura Rd
Calabasas CA 91302
818 575-3600

(P-8475)

YAMAHA GUITAR GROUP INC (HQ)

26580 Agoura Rd, Calabasas (91302-1921)
PHONE................................818 575-3600
Joe Bentivegna, *Pr*
Christine Hagemann, *
◆ **EMP:** 120 **EST:** 1988
SQ FT: 20,000
SALES (est): 45.84MM **Privately Held**
Web: www.yamahaguitargroup.com
SIC: 3931 Musical instruments
PA: Yamaha Corporation
10-1, Nakazawacho, Chuo-Ku

3942 Dolls And Stuffed Toys

(P-8476)

MAHAR MANUFACTURING CORP (PA)

Also Called: Fiesta Concession
2834 E 46th St, Vernon (90058-2404)
PHONE................................323 581-9988
Donald Mcintyre, *CEO*
Carol Reynolds, *
David Foster, *
◆ **EMP:** 39 **EST:** 1971
SQ FT: 100,000
SALES (est): 5.25MM
SALES (corp-wide): 5.25MM **Privately Held**
Web: www.fiestatoy.com
SIC: 3942 Stuffed toys, including animals

(P-8477)

MATTEL INC (PA)

Also Called: Mattel
333 Continental Blvd, El Segundo (90245-5012)
PHONE................................310 252-2000
Ynon Kreiz, *Ch Bd*
Steve Totzke, *CCO*
Anthony Disilvestro, *CFO*
Jonathan Anschell, *CLO*
Yoon Hugh, *CAO*
◆ **EMP:** 1700 **EST:** 1945
SQ FT: 360,000
SALES (est): 5.44B
SALES (corp-wide): 5.44B **Publicly Held**
Web: about.mattel.com
SIC: 3942 3944 Dolls and stuffed toys; Games, toys, and children's vehicles

(P-8478)

MOOSE TOYS LLC

Also Called: Moose
737 Campus Sq W, El Segundo (90245-2567)
PHONE................................310 341-4642
Manny Stul, *Ch*
EMP: 95 **EST:** 2018
SALES (est): 2.01MM **Privately Held**
Web: www.moosetoys.com
SIC: 3942 3944 5092 7389 Dolls and stuffed toys; Electronic games and toys; Toys and hobby goods and supplies; Business Activities at Non-Commercial Site
HQ: Mtha Pty Ltd
29 Grange Rd
Cheltenham VIC

(P-8479)

STROTTMAN INTERNATIONAL INC (PA)

Also Called: Strottman
28 Executive Park Ste 200, Irvine (92614-4741)
PHONE................................949 623-7900
◆ **EMP:** 25 **EST:** 1983
SALES (est): 12.5MM
SALES (corp-wide): 12.5MM **Privately Held**
Web: www.strottman.com
SIC: 3942 5092 5145 Dolls and stuffed toys; Toy novelties and amusements; Confectionery

(P-8480)

UPD INC

Also Called: United Pacific Designs
4507 S Maywood Ave, Vernon (90058-2610)
PHONE................................323 588-8811
Shahin Dardashty, *Pr*
Fred Dardashty, *
Ben Hooshim, *
◆ **EMP:** 60 **EST:** 1990
SQ FT: 140,000
SALES (est): 9.88MM **Privately Held**
Web: www.updinc.net
SIC: 3942 5112 3944 Dolls and stuffed toys; Pens and/or pencils; Puzzles

3944 Games, Toys, And Children's Vehicles

(P-8481)

ALIQUANTUM INTERNATIONAL INC

Also Called: Aqi
1131 W 6th St Ste 260b, Ontario (91762-1121)
PHONE................................909 773-0880
David Ringer, *CEO*
Wayne Lin, *
▲ **EMP:** 40 **EST:** 2010
SQ FT: 15,000
SALES (est): 7.14MM **Privately Held**
Web: www.aqi-intl.com
SIC: 3944 Games, toys, and children's vehicles

(P-8482)

BANDAI NMCO TOYS CLLCTBLES AME (DH)

23 Odyssey, Irvine (92618-3144)
PHONE................................949 271-6000
Shusuke Takahara, *CEO*
Atsushi Takeuchi, *
Katsushi Murakami, *
Takeshi Nojima, *
Brian Goldner, *
▲ **EMP:** 53 **EST:** 1978
SQ FT: 75,000
SALES (est): 16.9MM **Privately Held**
Web: www.bandai.com
SIC: 3944 Games, toys, and children's vehicles
HQ: Bandai Namco Holdings Usa Inc.
2120 Park Pl Ste 120
El Segundo CA 90245

(P-8483)

DREAMGEAR LLC

Also Called: Isound
20001 S Western Ave, Torrance (90501-1306)
P.O. Box 478 (90508-0478)
PHONE................................310 222-5522
Yahya Ahdout, *CEO*
Richard Weston, *
◆ **EMP:** 49 **EST:** 2002
SQ FT: 60,000
SALES (est): 17.32MM **Privately Held**
Web: www.dreamgear.com
SIC: 3944 Electronic games and toys

(P-8484)

DT MATTSON ENTERPRISES INC

Also Called: Protoform
201 W Lincoln St, Banning (92220-4933)
P.O. Box 456 (92223-0456)
PHONE................................951 849-9781
Todd Mattson, *CEO*
▲ **EMP:** 40 **EST:** 1983
SQ FT: 20,000
SALES (est): 4.87MM **Privately Held**
Web: www.prolineracing.com
SIC: 3944 5521 Games, toys, and children's vehicles; Trucks, tractors, and trailers: used

(P-8485)

EXPLODING KITTENS LLC

101 S La Brea Ave Ste A, Los Angeles (90036-2998)
PHONE................................310 788-8699
Matthew Inman, *
EMP: 29 **EST:** 2015
SALES (est): 5.26MM **Privately Held**
Web: www.explodingkittens.com
SIC: 3944 7371 Board games, children's and adults'; Computer software development and applications
PA: Asmodee Group
Quartier Villaroy

(P-8486)

IMPERIAL TOY LLC (PA)

16641 Roscoe Pl, North Hills (91343-6104)
PHONE................................818 536-6500
Peter Tiger, *Managing Member*
Arthur Hirsch, *
◆ **EMP:** 115 **EST:** 1969
SQ FT: 400,000
SALES (est): 14.6MM
SALES (corp-wide): 14.6MM **Privately Held**
Web: www.jaru.com
SIC: 3944 Games, toys, and children's vehicles

(P-8487)

INSOMNIAC GAMES INC (PA)

2255 N Ontario St Ste 550, Burbank (91504-3197)

PHONE..............................818 729-2400
Theodore C Price, *Pr*
Alex Hastings, *VP*
Brian Hastings, *Sec*
EMP: 74 **EST:** 1994
SALES (est): 25.66MM
SALES (corp-wide): 25.66MM **Privately Held**
Web: www.insomniac.games
SIC: 3944 Electronic games and toys

(P-8488)
JADA GROUP INC
Also Called: Jada Toys
18521 Railroad St, City Of Industry (91748-1316)
PHONE..............................626 810-8382
William Anthony Simons, *CEO*
Wai Han Ko, *
Manfred Duschl, *
◆ **EMP:** 70 **EST:** 1999
SALES (est): 23.52MM
SALES (corp-wide): 207.43MM **Privately Held**
Web: www.jadatoys.com
SIC: 3944 Games, toys, and children's vehicles
HQ: Simba-Dickie-Group Gmbh
   Werkstr. 1
   Furth BY 90765
   911976501

(P-8489)
JAKKS PACIFIC INC (PA)
Also Called: Jakks
2951 28th St, Santa Monica (90405-2961)
PHONE..............................424 268-9444
Stephen G Berman, *Ch Bd*
Stephen G Berman, *Ch Bd*
John L Kimble, *Ex VP*
John J Mcgrath, *COO*
EMP: 66 **EST:** 1995
SQ FT: 65,858
SALES (est): 711.56MM **Publicly Held**
Web: www.jakks.com
SIC: 3944 Games, toys, and children's vehicles

(P-8490)
JAKKS PACIFIC INC
Also Called: Flying Colors
21749 Baker Pkwy, Walnut (91789-5234)
PHONE..............................909 594-7771
Michelle Tromp, *Bmch Mgr*
EMP: 30
Web: www.jakks.com
SIC: 3944 5092 Games, toys, and children's vehicles; Toys, nec
PA: Jakks Pacific, Inc.
   2951 28th St

(P-8491)
MATTEL DIRECT IMPORT INC (HQ)
Also Called: Mattel
333 Continental Blvd, El Segundo (90245-5032)
PHONE..............................310 252-2000
Kevin Farr, *CEO*
Bryan G Stockton, *Pr*
EMP: 48 **EST:** 2007
SALES (est): 3.96MM
SALES (corp-wide): 5.44B **Publicly Held**
SIC: 3944 3942 3949 Games, toys, and children's vehicles; Dolls, except stuffed toy animals; Sporting and athletic goods, nec
PA: Mattel, Inc.
   333 Continental Blvd
   310 252-2000

(P-8492)
MEGA BRANDS AMERICA INC (DH)
Also Called: Rose Art Industries
333 Continental Blvd, El Segundo (90245-5032)
PHONE..............................949 727-9009
Marc Bertrand, *CEO*
Vic Bertrand, *
◆ **EMP:** 80 **EST:** 1923
SALES (est): 37.73MM
SALES (corp-wide): 5.44B **Publicly Held**
Web: support.megabrands.com
SIC: 3944 Blocks, toy
HQ: Mega Brands Inc.
   4505 Rue Hickmore
   Saint-Laurent QC H4T 1
   514 333-5555

(P-8493)
NINJA JUMP INC
3221 N San Fernando Rd, Los Angeles (90065-1414)
PHONE..............................323 255-5418
Rouben Gourchounian, *Pr*
◆ **EMP:** 75 **EST:** 1984
SQ FT: 35,000
SALES (est): 789.41K **Privately Held**
Web: www.ninjajump.com
SIC: 3944 Games, toys, and children's vehicles

(P-8494)
ROAD CHAMPS INC
22619 Pacific Coast Hwy Ste 250, Malibu (90265-5080)
PHONE..............................310 456-7799
Stephen Berman, *Pr*
EMP: 150 **EST:** 1960
SQ FT: 51,000
SALES (est): 471.75K **Publicly Held**
SIC: 3944 Automobiles and trucks, toy
PA: Jakks Pacific, Inc.
   2951 28th St

(P-8495)
SHELCORE INC (PA)
Also Called: Shelcore Toys
7811 Lemona Ave, Van Nuys (91405-1139)
PHONE..............................818 883-2400
Arnold Rubin, *Pr*
◆ **EMP:** 29 **EST:** 1975
SQ FT: 20,000
SALES (est): 61.17MM
SALES (corp-wide): 61.17MM **Privately Held**
Web: www.funrise.com
SIC: 3944 Blocks, toy

(P-8496)
TOYMAX INTERNATIONAL INC (HQ)
22619 Pacific Coast Hwy, Malibu (90265-5054)
PHONE..............................310 456-7799
Jack Friedman, *CEO*
Stephen G Berman, *
Joel M Bennett, *CFO*
◆ **EMP:** 56 **EST:** 1990
SQ FT: 30,000
SALES (est): 1.25MM **Publicly Held**
Web: jadehomeremodeling.website2.me
SIC: 3944 5092 Games, toys, and children's vehicles; Toys and games
PA: Jakks Pacific, Inc.
   2951 28th St

(P-8497)
USAOPOLY INC
Also Called: Op Games, The
5999 Avenida Encinas Ste 150, Carlsbad (92008-4443)
PHONE..............................760 431-5910
Dane S Chapin, *CEO*
Tom Nirschel, *
▲ **EMP:** 94 **EST:** 1994
SQ FT: 10,000
SALES (est): 17.94MM **Privately Held**
Web: www.theop.games
SIC: 3944 Board games, puzzles, and models, except electronic

---

3949 Sporting And Athletic Goods, Nec

(P-8498)
ACUSHNET COMPANY
Also Called: Titleist
2819 Loker Ave E, Carlsbad (92010-6626)
PHONE..............................760 804-6500
John Worster, *Bmch Mgr*
EMP: 300
Web: www.titleist.com
SIC: 3949 Shafts, golf club
HQ: Acushnet Company
   333 Bridge St
   Fairhaven MA 02719
   508 979-2000

(P-8499)
ALDILA GOLF CORP
13450 Stowe Dr, Poway (92064-6860)
PHONE..............................858 513-1801
EMP: 104
Web: www.aldila.com
SIC: 3949 Shafts, golf club
HQ: Aldila Golf Corp.
   1945 Kellogg Ave
   Carlsbad CA 92008

(P-8500)
ALDILA GOLF CORP (DH)
1945 Kellogg Ave, Carlsbad (92008-6582)
PHONE..............................858 513-1801
Peter R Mathewson, *CEO*
Scott Bier, *
Sue-wei Yeh, *Contrlr*
▲ **EMP:** 78 **EST:** 1991
SQ FT: 52,156
SALES (est): 3.17MM **Privately Held**
Web: www.aldila.com
SIC: 3949 Shafts, golf club
HQ: Aldila, Inc.
   1945 Kellogg Ave
   Carlsbad CA 92008
   858 513-1801

(P-8501)
AMRON INTERNATIONAL INC (PA)
Also Called: Amron
1380 Aspen Way, Vista (92081-8349)
PHONE..............................760 208-6500
Debra L Ritchie, *CEO*
◆ **EMP:** 69 **EST:** 1979
SQ FT: 40,000
SALES (est): 10.62MM
SALES (corp-wide): 10.62MM **Privately Held**
Web: www.amronintl.com
SIC: 3949 5091 Skin diving equipment, scuba type; Diving equipment and supplies

(P-8502)
ASPHALT FABRIC AND ENGRG INC
2683 Lime Ave, Signal Hill (90755-2709)
PHONE..............................562 997-4129
Bill Goldsmith, *Pr*
Doug Coulter, *
Joe Salamone, *
EMP: 90 **EST:** 1998
SQ FT: 5,000
SALES (est): 1.29MM **Privately Held**
Web: www.afesports.com
SIC: 3949 Sporting and athletic goods, nec

(P-8503)
AZA INDUSTRIES INC (PA)
1410 Vantage Ct, Vista (92081-8509)
PHONE..............................760 560-0440
David H Brown, *Pr*
Jim Passamonte, *
Bill Pierce, *
▲ **EMP:** 40 **EST:** 1977
SQ FT: 27,000
SALES (est): 600.58K **Privately Held**
Web: www.ca-tf.com
SIC: 3949 Skateboards

(P-8504)
BELL FOUNDRY CO (PA)
5310 Southern Ave, South Gate (90280-3690)
P.O. Box 1070 (90280-1070)
PHONE..............................323 564-5701
Cesar Capallini, *Pr*
Wanda De Wald, *
Dimitry Rabyy, *
▲ **EMP:** 50 **EST:** 1924
SQ FT: 140,000
SALES (est): 4.18MM
SALES (corp-wide): 4.18MM **Privately Held**
Web: www.bfco.com
SIC: 3949 3321 Dumbbells and other weightlifting equipment; Gray and ductile iron foundries

(P-8505)
BELL SPORTS INC (HQ)
Also Called: Easton Bell Sports
16752 Armstrong Ave, Irvine (92606-4912)
PHONE..............................469 417-6600
Andrew Keegan, *CEO*
Jung Choi, *
◆ **EMP:** 75 **EST:** 1952
SQ FT: 27,197
SALES (est): 21.93MM
SALES (corp-wide): 2.75B **Publicly Held**
Web: www.bellhelmets.com
SIC: 3949 3751 Helmets, athletic; Bicycles and related parts
PA: Vista Outdoor Inc.
   1 Vista Way
   763 433-1000

(P-8506)
BLACK BOX DISTRIBUTION LLC
371 2nd St Ste 1, Encinitas (92024-3524)
PHONE..............................760 268-1174
James Thomas, *
Michelle Wenner, *
◆ **EMP:** 70 **EST:** 2009
SALES (est): 2.48MM **Privately Held**
SIC: 3949 Skateboards

(P-8507)
BRAVO HIGHLINE LLC ✪
3101 Ocean Park Blvd Ste 100, Santa Monica (90405-3029)
PHONE..............................562 484-5100
Bart Thielen, *CEO*

Nicholas Schultz, *Managing Member**
Dinesh Mirchandani, *
EMP: 25 **EST:** 2023
SALES (est): 2.87MM **Privately Held**
SIC: 3949 3944 Skateboards; Scooters, children's

(P-8508)
BRAVO SPORTS
Also Called: Sector9
4370 Jutland Dr, San Diego (92117-3642)
PHONE..............................858 408-0083
Derek Oneill, *CEO*
EMP: 23
SALES (corp-wide): 28.11MM **Privately Held**
Web: www.bravosportscorp.com
SIC: 3949 Skateboards
HQ: Bravo Sports
12801 Carmenita Rd
Santa Fe Springs CA 90670
562 484-5100

(P-8509)
BRAVO SPORTS
9043 Siempre Viva Rd, San Diego (92154-7662)
PHONE..............................562 457-8916
EMP: 23
SALES (corp-wide): 28.11MM **Privately Held**
Web: www.bravosportscorp.com
SIC: 3949 Sporting and athletic goods, nec
HQ: Bravo Sports
12801 Carmenita Rd
Santa Fe Springs CA 90670
562 484-5100

(P-8510)
BRAVO SPORTS (HQ)
12801 Carmenita Rd, Santa Fe Springs (90670-4805)
P.O. Box 2967 (90670)
PHONE..............................562 484-5100
Nicholas R Schultz, *Pr*
◆ **EMP:** 80 **EST:** 1987
SQ FT: 100,000
SALES (est): 27.31MM
SALES (corp-wide): 28.11MM **Privately Held**
Web: www.bravosportscorp.com
SIC: 3949 Sporting and athletic goods, nec
PA: Transom Bravo Holdings Corp.
12801 Carmenita Rd
562 484-5100

(P-8511)
CASA DE HERMANDAD (PA)
Also Called: West Area Opportunity Center
1639 11th St, Santa Monica (90404-3727)
PHONE..............................310 477-8272
David Abelar, *Pr*
EMP: 25 **EST:** 1970
SALES (est): 80.05K
SALES (corp-wide): 80.05K **Privately Held**
SIC: 3949 Driving ranges, golf, electronic

(P-8512)
CONDOR OUTDOOR PRODUCTS INC (PA)
Also Called: Condor
5268 Rivergrade Rd, Baldwin Park (91706-1336)
PHONE..............................626 358-3270
Spencer Tien, *Pr*
Neil Chen, *
◆ **EMP:** 38 **EST:** 1994
SQ FT: 11,000
SALES (est): 8.26MM
SALES (corp-wide): 8.26MM **Privately Held**

Web: www.condoroutdoor.com
SIC: 3949 Sporting and athletic goods, nec

(P-8513)
CRAZY INDUSTRIES
Also Called: Savi Customs
8675 Avenida Costa Norte, San Diego (92154-6253)
PHONE..............................619 270-9090
Jane Roe, *CEO*
Don Roe, *CFO*
EMP: 45 **EST:** 2018
SALES (est): 4.49MM **Privately Held**
Web: www.submfg.com
SIC: 3949 2339 2329 Sporting and athletic goods, nec; Sportswear, women's; Men's and boys' sportswear and athletic clothing

(P-8514)
DIAMOND BASEBALL COMPANY INC
Also Called: Diamond Sports
121 Waterworks Way Ste 150, Irvine (92618-7720)
P.O. Box 55090 (92619-5090)
PHONE..............................949 409-9300
Jay Hicks, *CEO*
Andrea Gordon, *
Robert W Ezell, *
◆ **EMP:** 23 **EST:** 1977
SQ FT: 120,000
SALES (est): 3.03MM **Privately Held**
Web: www.diamond-sports.com
SIC: 3949 5091 Baseball equipment and supplies, general; Athletic goods

(P-8515)
DIVING UNLIMITED INTL INC
Also Called: Diving Unlimited Int.
1148 Delevan Dr, San Diego (92102-2499)
PHONE..............................619 236-1203
Susan Long, *CEO*
Richard Long, *
◆ **EMP:** 75 **EST:** 1963
SQ FT: 14,500
SALES (est): 3.62MM **Privately Held**
Web: www.divedui.com
SIC: 3949 Skin diving equipment, scuba type

(P-8516)
EASTON HOCKEY INC
Also Called: Eastern Sports
3500 Willow Ln, Thousand Oaks (91361-4921)
PHONE..............................818 782-6445
◆ **EMP:** 1500
Web: www.eastonhockey.com
SIC: 3949 Sporting and athletic goods, nec

(P-8517)
FITNESS WAREHOUSE LLC (PA)
Also Called: Hoist Fitness Systems
9990 Alesmith Ct Ste 130, San Diego (92126-4200)
PHONE..............................858 578-7676
Jeffrey Partrick, *Pt*
◆ **EMP:** 30 **EST:** 1999
SALES (est): 4.65MM
SALES (corp-wide): 4.65MM **Privately Held**
Web: www.fitnesswarehouseusa.com
SIC: 3949 Sporting and athletic goods, nec

(P-8518)
GOLF SALES WEST INC
Also Called: Golf Sales West
1901 Eastman Ave, Oxnard (93030-5171)
PHONE..............................805 988-3363
▲ **EMP:** 50 **EST:** 1988
SALES (est): 796.18K **Privately Held**

Web: www.golfsaleswest.com
SIC: 3949 Bags, golf

(P-8519)
GOLF SUPPLY HOUSE USA INC
Also Called: Eagle One Golf Products
1340 N Jefferson St, Anaheim (92807-1614)
PHONE..............................714 983-0050
◆ **EMP:** 70
SIC: 3949 5941 Golf equipment; Golf goods and equipment

(P-8520)
HEART RATE INC
Also Called: Versaclimber
2619 Oak St, Santa Ana (92707-3720)
PHONE..............................714 850-9716
Richard D Charnitski, *Pr*
Dan Charnitski, *
▲ **EMP:** 38 **EST:** 1978
SQ FT: 18,000
SALES (est): 75.04K **Privately Held**
Web: www.versaclimber.com
SIC: 3949 Exercise equipment

(P-8521)
HOBIE CAT COMPANY II LLC
4925 Oceanside Blvd, Oceanside (92056-3099)
PHONE..............................760 758-9100
EMP: 200 **EST:** 2021
SALES (est): 17.31MM **Privately Held**
Web: www.hobie.com
SIC: 3949 Water sports equipment

(P-8522)
HOIST FITNESS SYSTEMS INC
Also Called: Hoist Fitness
11900 Community Rd, Poway (92064-7143)
PHONE..............................858 578-7676
Jeffrey Partrick, *CEO*
Billy Kim, *
◆ **EMP:** 81 **EST:** 1977
SQ FT: 105,000
SALES (est): 8.36MM **Privately Held**
Web: www.hoistfitness.com
SIC: 3949 5941 Exercise equipment; Exercise equipment

(P-8523)
HYPER ICE INC (PA)
Also Called: Hyperice
525 Technology Dr Ste 100, Irvine (92618-1389)
PHONE..............................949 565-4994
Jim Huether, *CEO*
Robert Marton, *
▲ **EMP:** 44 **EST:** 2010
SALES (est): 13.68MM
SALES (corp-wide): 13.68MM **Privately Held**
Web: www.hyperice.com
SIC: 3949 5136 5621 5699 Sporting and athletic goods, nec; Sportswear, men's and boys'; Women's sportswear; Sports apparel

(P-8524)
HYPERFLY INC
8390 Miramar Pl Ste D, San Diego (92121-2104)
PHONE..............................760 300-0909
Pascal Jean Pakter, *CEO*
Kerstin Pakter, *
Pascal Pakter, *
EMP: 25 **EST:** 2019
SALES (est): 832K **Privately Held**
Web: www.hyperfly.com

SIC: 3949 Sporting and athletic goods, nec

(P-8525)
IFIT INC
2220 Almond Ave, Redlands (92374-2073)
PHONE..............................909 335-2888
EMP: 1333
SALES (corp-wide): 1.75B **Privately Held**
Web: company.ifit.com
SIC: 3949 Treadmills
HQ: Ifit Inc.
1500 S 1000 W
Logan UT 84321
435 750-5000

(P-8526)
ILLAH SPORTS INC
Also Called: Belding Golf Bag Company, The
1610 Fiske Pl, Oxnard (93033-1849)
PHONE..............................805 240-7790
Brien Patermo, *CEO*
Steve Perrin, *
Jackie Perrin, *
▲ **EMP:** 50 **EST:** 2003
SALES (est): 934.49K **Privately Held**
SIC: 3949 Sporting and athletic goods, nec

(P-8527)
INDIAN INDUSTRIES INC
Also Called: Escalade Sports
7756 Saint Andrews Ave Ste 115, San Diego (92154-8210)
P.O. Box 530960 (92153-0960)
PHONE..............................800 467-1421
Daniel A Messmer, *Prin*
EMP: 29
SALES (corp-wide): 263.57MM **Publicly Held**
Web: www.escaladesports.com
SIC: 3949 Ping-pong tables
HQ: Indian Industries Inc
817 Maxwell Ave
Evansville IN 47711
812 467-1200

(P-8528)
IRON GRIP BARBELL COMPANY INC
11377 Markon Dr, Garden Grove (92841-1402)
PHONE..............................714 850-6900
Scott Frasco, *CEO*
Michael Rojas, *
Donna Lins, *Prin*
▼ **EMP:** 85 **EST:** 1993
SALES (est): 10.34MM **Privately Held**
Web: www.irongrip.com
SIC: 3949 Exercise equipment

(P-8529)
JOHNSON OUTDOORS INC
Scuba Pro
1166 Fesler St Ste A, El Cajon (92020-1813)
PHONE..............................619 402-1023
Joe Stella, *Brnch Mgr*
EMP: 96
SALES (corp-wide): 592.85MM **Publicly Held**
Web: scubapro.johnsonoutdoors.com
SIC: 3949 5091 Skin diving equipment, scuba type; Diving equipment and supplies
PA: Johnson Outdoors Inc.
555 Main St
262 631-6600

(P-8530)
LUCITE INTL PRTNR HOLDINGS INC

MRC Composite Product
5441 Avenida Encinas Ste B, Carlsbad
(92008-4412)
PHONE..................760 929-0001
Hikaro Shikashi, *VP*
EMP: 99
SIC: 3949 Golf equipment
PA: Lucite International Partnership
Holdings, Inc.
1403 Foulk Rd

(P-8531)
MALBON GOLF LLC
1740 Stanford St, Santa Monica
(90404-4116)
PHONE..................323 433-4028
Stephen Malbon, *Pr*
EMP: 40 **EST:** 2016
SALES (est): 867.81K **Privately Held**
Web: www.malbongolf.com
SIC: 3949 Golf equipment

(P-8532)
MELIN LLC
10 Faraday, Irvine (92618-2714)
PHONE..................323 489-3274
Hoang Tu, *Prin*
EMP: 47 **EST:** 2019
SALES (est): 1.79MM **Privately Held**
Web: www.melin.com
SIC: 3949 Sporting and athletic goods, nec

(P-8533)
ORCA ARMS LLC
Also Called: Orca Arms
26500 Agoura Rd, Calabasas (91302-1952)
PHONE..................858 586-0503
Hamid R Ray Akhavan, *Managing Member*
Ardeshir Akhavan, *
▲ **EMP:** 68 **EST:** 2012
SQ FT: 5,500
SALES (est): 380.42K **Privately Held**
Web: www.orcaarms.com
SIC: 3949 5099 Sporting and athletic goods,
nec; Firearms and ammunition, except
sporting

(P-8534)
RIP CURL INC
193 Avenida La Pata, San Clemente
(92673-6307)
PHONE..................714 422-3617
EMP: 25
Web: www.ripcurl.com
SIC: 3949 Surfboards
HQ: Rip Curl, Inc.
3030 Ariway Ave
Costa Mesa CA 92626

(P-8535)
RIP CURL INC (DH)
Also Called: Rip Curl USA
3030 Airway Ave, Costa Mesa
(92626-6036)
PHONE..................714 422-3600
Kelly Gibson, *CEO*
Matt Szot, *
◆ **EMP:** 60 **EST:** 1992
SALES (est): 20.77MM **Privately Held**
Web: www.ripcurl.com
SIC: 3949 Surfboards
HQ: Rip Curl International Pty Ltd
101 Surf Coast Hwy
Torquay VIC 3228

(P-8536)
ROSEN & ROSEN INDUSTRIES INC
Also Called: R & R Industries
204 Avenida Fabricante, San Clemente
(92672-7538)
PHONE..................949 361-9238
Richard Rosen, *Pr*
Daniel Rosen, *
▲ **EMP:** 80 **EST:** 1979
SQ FT: 22,500
SALES (est): 4.15MM **Privately Held**
Web: www.rrind.com
SIC: 3949 7389 Sporting and athletic goods,
nec; Embroidery advertising

(P-8537)
RPSZ CONSTRUCTION LLC
1201 W 5th St Ste T340, Los Angeles
(90017-1489)
PHONE..................314 677-5831
Rick Platt, *Managing Member*
EMP: 94 **EST:** 2008
SQ FT: 3,500
SALES (est): 233.68K
SALES (corp-wide): 5.6MM **Privately Held**
SIC: 3949 Trampolines and equipment
PA: Sky Zone, Llc
1201 W 5th St T-340
310 734-0300

(P-8538)
SAFER SPORTS INC
Also Called: Light Helmets
5670 El Camino Real Ste B, Carlsbad
(92008-7125)
PHONE..................760 444-0082
Nick Esayian, *CEO*
Justin Bert, *
EMP: 30 **EST:** 2017
SALES (est): 2.07MM **Privately Held**
Web: www.lighthelmets.com
SIC: 3949 Helmets, athletic

(P-8539)
SAINT NINE AMERICA INC
10700 Norwalk Blvd, Santa Fe Springs
(90670-3824)
PHONE..................562 921-5300
Timothy Chae, *CEO*
Terry Kim, *
Max Kim, *
EMP: 40 **EST:** 2018
SALES (est): 619.71K **Privately Held**
Web: www.saintnineamerica.com
SIC: 3949 Team sports equipment

(P-8540)
SEIRUS INNOVATIVE ACC INC
Also Called: Seirus Innovation
13975 Danielson St, Poway (92064-6889)
PHONE..................858 513-1212
Michael Carey, *Pr*
Joseph H Edwards, *
Wendy Carey, *
Robert Murphy, *
▲ **EMP:** 65 **EST:** 1984
SQ FT: 11,000
SALES (est): 8.53MM **Privately Held**
Web: www.seirus.com
SIC: 3949 Sporting and athletic goods, nec

(P-8541)
SHOCK DOCTOR INC (PA)
Also Called: Shock Doctor Sports
11488 Slater Ave, Fountain Valley
(92708-5440)
PHONE..................800 233-6956
Philip Gyori, *CEO*
Kevin Johnson, *CFO*
▲ **EMP:** 82 **EST:** 2008
SALES (est): 74.86MM **Privately Held**
Web: www.shockdoctor.com
SIC: 3949 Protective sporting equipment

(P-8542)
SHOCK DOCTOR INC
Also Called: United Sports Brands
11488 Slater Ave, Fountain Valley
(92708-5440)
PHONE..................657 383-4400
EMP: 40
Web: www.shockdoctor.com
SIC: 3949 Sporting and athletic goods, nec
PA: Doctor Shock Inc
11488 Slater Ave

(P-8543)
SKATE ONE CORP
Also Called: Roller Bones
6860 Cortona Dr Ste B, Goleta
(93117-5568)
PHONE..................805 964-1330
George Powell, *Pr*
▲ **EMP:** 80 **EST:** 1976
SALES (est): 9.17MM **Privately Held**
Web: www.skateone.com
SIC: 3949 Skateboards

(P-8544)
STANDARD SALES LLC (PA)
Also Called: Stansport
2801 E 12th St, Los Angeles (90023-3600)
PHONE..................323 269-0510
Max Wartnik, *Ch*
Victor Preisler, *
Eva Wartnik, *
◆ **EMP:** 35 **EST:** 1964
SQ FT: 100,000
SALES (est): 7.75MM
SALES (corp-wide): 7.75MM **Privately Held**
Web: www.stansport.com
SIC: 3949 Camping equipment and supplies

(P-8545)
STAR TRAC STRENGTH INC
Also Called: Star Trac Fitness
14410 Myford Rd, Irvine (92606-1001)
Rural Route 300 (98662)
PHONE..................714 669-1660
▲ **EMP:** 405
SIC: 3949 5091 Exercise equipment;
Exercise equipment

(P-8546)
SURE GRIP INTERNATIONAL
5519 Rawlings Ave, South Gate
(90280-7495)
PHONE..................562 923-0724
James Ball, *VP*
Ione L Ball, *
▲ **EMP:** 60 **EST:** 1937
SQ FT: 30,000
SALES (est): 4.61MM **Privately Held**
Web: www.suregrip.com
SIC: 3949 Skates and parts, roller

(P-8547)
THOUSAND LLC
915 Mateo St Ste 302, Los Angeles
(90021-1786)
PHONE..................310 745-0110
EMP: 38 **EST:** 2016
SALES (est): 4.8MM **Privately Held**
Web: www.explorethousand.com
SIC: 3949 Sporting and athletic goods, nec

(P-8548)
TOPGOLF CALLAWAY BRANDS CORP (PA)
2180 Rutherford Rd, Carlsbad
(92008-7328)
PHONE..................760 931-1771
Oliver G Brewer Iii, *Pr*
John F Lundgren, *
Erik J Anderson, *
Rebecca Fine, *CPO*
Brian P Lynch, *CLO*
◆ **EMP:** 349 **EST:** 1982
SALES (est): 4.28B
SALES (corp-wide): 4.28B **Publicly Held**
Web: prodpwa.callawaygolf.com
SIC: 3949 2329 2339 6794 Golf equipment;
Men's and boys' sportswear and athletic
clothing; Women's and misses' athletic
clothing and sportswear; Patent buying,
licensing, leasing

(P-8549)
TUFFSTUFF FITNESS INTL INC
155 N Riverview Dr, Anaheim (92808-1225)
PHONE..................909 629-1600
Richard M Reyes Junior, *Ch Bd*
Cammie Grider, *
◆ **EMP:** 66 **EST:** 1992
SALES (est): 12.82MM
SALES (corp-wide): 12.82MM **Privately Held**
Web: www.tuffstuffitness.com
SIC: 3949 Exercise equipment
PA: Brooks Industrial Marketplace
23401 Mount Ashland Ct
714 269-1689

(P-8550)
TWIN PEAK INDUSTRIES INC
Also Called: Jungle Jumps
12420 Montague St Ste E, Pacoima
(91331-2140)
PHONE..................800 259-5906
Edmond K Keshishian, *Pr*
Raffi Sepanian, *
EMP: 32 **EST:** 2008
SALES (est): 1.76MM **Privately Held**
SIC: 3949 3069 Playground equipment; Air-
supported rubber structures

(P-8551)
UKE CORPORATION
Also Called: Underwater Kinetics
13400 Danielson St, Poway (92064-8830)
PHONE..................858 513-9100
◆ **EMP:** 95 **EST:** 1971
SALES (est): 2.07MM **Privately Held**
Web: www.uwk.com
SIC: 3949 3648 3646 3161 Water sports
equipment; Flashlights; Commercial lighting
fixtures; Luggage

(P-8552)
WEST COAST TRENDS INC
Also Called: Train Reaction
17811 Jamestown Ln, Huntington Beach
(92647-7136)
PHONE..................714 843-9288
Jeffrey C Herold, *CEO*
Vivienne Herold, *
▲ **EMP:** 50 **EST:** 1990
SQ FT: 26,000
SALES (est): 5.75MM **Privately Held**
Web: www.scheyden.com
SIC: 3949 Golf equipment

(P-8553)
WESTERN GOLF CAR MFG INC
Also Called: Western Golf Car Sales Co
69391 Dillon Rd, Desert Hot Springs
(92241-8433)
PHONE..................760 671-6691
Scott Stevens, *Pr*
Robert W Thomas, *
EMP: 55 **EST:** 1981
SQ FT: 60,000

SALES (est): 1.7MM **Privately Held**
SIC: 3949 3799 Sporting and athletic goods, nec; Golf carts, powered

(P-8554)
**WORLD CLASS
CHEERLEADING INC**
20212 Hart St, Winnetka (91306-3520)
PHONE....................877 923-2645
Akram Hemaidan, *CEO*
EMP: 33 EST: 2009
SALES (est): 409.75K **Privately Held**
Web: www.worldclasscheerleading.com
SIC: 3949 Sporting and athletic goods, nec

(P-8555)
XS SCUBA INC (PA)
Also Called: Atlantic Diving Equipment
4040 W Chandler Ave, Santa Ana
(92704-5202)
PHONE....................714 424-0434
Daniel F Babcock, *Pr*
◆ **EMP: 24 EST: 2002**
SALES (est): 5.47MM
SALES (corp-wide): 5.47MM **Privately
Held**
Web: www.xsscuba.com
SIC: 3949 5091 Skin diving equipment, scuba type; Diving equipment and supplies

(P-8556)
ZONSON COMPANY INC
3197 Lionshead Ave, Carlsbad
(92010-4702)
PHONE....................760 597-0338
Jeff Yearours, *VP*
▲ **EMP: 26 EST: 2001**
SALES (est): 1.96MM **Privately Held**
Web: www.zonson.com
SIC: 3949 Bags, golf

3952 Lead Pencils And Art Goods

(P-8557)
**AARDVARK CLAY & SUPPLIES
INC (PA)**
1400 E Pomona St, Santa Ana
(92705-4858)
PHONE....................714 541-4157
George Johnston, *Pr*
Daniel T Carreon, *
Richard Mac Pherson, *General Vice
President*
K Douglas Pherson Mac, *Sec*
▲ **EMP: 30 EST: 1972**
SQ FT: 25,000
SALES (est): 5.34MM
SALES (corp-wide): 5.34MM **Privately
Held**
Web: www.aardvarkclay.com
SIC: 3952 5945 Modeling clay; Arts and crafts supplies

(P-8558)
**CONVERSION TECHNOLOGY
CO INC (PA)**
5360 N Commerce Ave, Moorpark
(93021-1762)
PHONE....................805 378-0033
Jim Newkirk, *Pr*
Russell Greenhouse, *
▲ **EMP: 50 EST: 1994**
SQ FT: 28,000
SALES (est): 3.01MM **Privately Held**
SIC: 3952 2893 2899 Ink, drawing: black and colored; Printing ink; Ink or writing fluids

(P-8559)
SALIS INTERNATIONAL INC
3921 Oceanic Dr Ste 802, Oceanside
(92056-5857)
PHONE....................303 384-3588
Lawrence R Salis, *Pr*
◆ **EMP: 38 EST: 1934**
SQ FT: 10,000
SALES (est): 2.22MM **Privately Held**
Web: www.docmartins.com
SIC: 3952 Water colors, artists'

(P-8560)
WESTECH PRODUCTS INC (PA)
Also Called: Westech Wax Products
1242 Enterprise Ct, Corona (92882-7125)
PHONE....................951 279-4496
Lawrence Dahlin, *Pr*
Erik Dahlin, *
Barry Dahlin, *
▲ **EMP: 24 EST: 1980**
SQ FT: 31,000
SALES (est): 7.33MM
SALES (corp-wide): 7.33MM **Privately
Held**
Web: www.westechwax.com
SIC: 3952 5169 Crayons: chalk, gypsum, charcoal, fusains, pastel, wax, etc.; Waxes, except petroleum

3955 Carbon Paper And Inked Ribbons

(P-8561)
**CALIFORNIA RIBBON CARBN
CO INC**
8420 Quinn St, Downey (90241-2624)
PHONE....................323 724-9100
Robert J Picou, *CEO*
Robert J Picou, *Pr*
Clara Picou, *
Louis Titus, *
▲ **EMP: 100 EST: 1939**
SALES (est): 1.63MM **Privately Held**
SIC: 3955 Ribbons, inked: typewriter, adding machine, register, etc.

(P-8562)
ECMM SERVICES INC
1320 Valley Vista Dr # 204, Diamond Bar
(91765-3956)
PHONE....................714 988-9388
Vincent Yang, *Pr*
Donald Sung, *
EMP: 250 EST: 2010
SALES (est): 5.1MM **Privately Held**
SIC: 3955 5045 Print cartridges for laser and other computer printers; Printers, computer
PA: Hon Hai Precision Industry Co., Ltd.
No. 2, Ziyou St.

(P-8563)
GENERAL RIBBON CORP
Also Called: G R C
5775 E Los Angeles Ave Ste 230,
Chatsworth (91311)
PHONE....................818 709-1234
Stephen R Morgan, *Pr*
Robert W Daggs, *
▲ **EMP: 500 EST: 1946**
SQ FT: 110,000
SALES (est): 993.96K **Privately Held**
Web: www.printgrc.com
SIC: 3955 3861 Ribbons, inked: typewriter, adding machine, register, etc.; Photographic equipment and supplies

(P-8564)
**LASERCARE TECHNOLOGIES
INC (PA)**
Also Called: Lasercare
14370 Myford Rd Ste 100, Irvine
(92606-1015)
PHONE....................310 202-4200
TOLL FREE: 800
Paul Wilhelm, *Pr*
EMP: 34 EST: 1993
SALES (est): 2.06MM
SALES (corp-wide): 2.06MM **Privately
Held**
Web: www.lasercare.com
SIC: 3955 7378 5734 Print cartridges for laser and other computer printers; Computer peripheral equipment repair and maintenance; Printers and plotters: computers

(P-8565)
**PLANET GREEN CARTRIDGES
INC**
Also Called: Planet Green
20724 Lassen St, Chatsworth (91311-4507)
PHONE....................818 725-2596
Sean Levi, *Pr*
Natalya Levi, *
◆ **EMP: 84 EST: 2000**
SQ FT: 29,699
SALES (est): 8.94MM **Privately Held**
Web: www.pginkjets.com
SIC: 3955 5093 Print cartridges for laser and other computer printers; Plastics scrap

(P-8566)
RAYZIST PHOTOMASK INC (PA)
Also Called: Honor Life
955 Park Center Dr, Vista (92081-8312)
PHONE....................760 727-8561
Randy S Willis, *CEO*
▲ **EMP: 54 EST: 1984**
SQ FT: 28,000
SALES (est): 9.76MM
SALES (corp-wide): 9.76MM **Privately
Held**
Web: www.rayzist.com
SIC: 3955 3281 3589 Stencil paper, gelatin or spirit process; Cut stone and stone products; Sandblasting equipment

(P-8567)
SERCOMP LLC (PA)
5401 Tech Cir Ste 200, Moorpark
(93021-1713)
P.O. Box 92728 (91715-2728)
PHONE....................805 299-0020
EMP: 89 EST: 2003
SQ FT: 67,000
SALES (est): 480.06K
SALES (corp-wide): 480.06K **Privately
Held**
Web: www.sercomp.com
SIC: 3955 3577 Print cartridges for laser and other computer printers; Computer peripheral equipment, nec

(P-8568)
VISION IMAGING SUPPLIES INC
9540 Cozycroft Ave, Chatsworth
(91311-5101)
PHONE....................818 885-4515
Bernard Khachi, *CEO*
Raymond Khachi, *
▲ **EMP: 40 EST: 2004**
SALES (est): 1.22MM **Privately Held**
Web: www.vis-llc.com
SIC: 3955 Print cartridges for laser and other computer printers

3961 Costume Jewelry

(P-8569)
BOB SIEMON DESIGNS INC
3501 W Segerstrom Ave, Santa Ana
(92704-6449)
PHONE....................714 549-0678
▲ **EMP: 95**
Web: www.bobsiemon.com
SIC: 3961 3911 Costume jewelry, ex. precious metal and semiprecious stones; Jewelry, precious metal

(P-8570)
LOUNGEFLY LLC
Also Called: Lounge Fly
108 S Mayo Ave, Walnut (91789-3090)
PHONE....................818 718-5600
Dale Schultz, *
▲ **EMP: 25 EST: 1998**
SALES (est): 4.97MM
SALES (corp-wide): 1.1B **Publicly Held**
Web: www.loungefly.com
SIC: 3961 Costume jewelry
PA: Funko, Inc.
2802 Wetmore Ave
425 783-3616

(P-8571)
PINCRAFT INC
Also Called: Pin Concepts
7933 Ajay Dr, Sun Valley (91352-5315)
PHONE....................818 248-0077
Vahe Asatourian, *Pr*
▲ **EMP: 27 EST: 1999**
SALES (est): 2.37MM **Privately Held**
Web: www.pincraft.com
SIC: 3961 Pins (jewelry), except precious metal

3965 Fasteners, Buttons, Needles, And Pins

(P-8572)
LABELTEX MILLS INC (PA)
5301 S Santa Fe Ave, Vernon
(90058-3519)
PHONE....................323 582-0228
Torag Pourshamtobi, *CEO*
Shahrokh Shamtobi, *
Ben Younessi, *
Babak Younessi, *
◆ **EMP: 200 EST: 1994**
SALES (est): 7.37MM **Privately Held**
Web: www.labeltexusa.com
SIC: 3965 2253 2241 Fasteners; buttons, needles, and pins; Collar and cuff sets, knit; Labels, woven

(P-8573)
MATTHEW WARREN INC
Also Called: Mw Compnnts - Anheim Ideal
Fas
3850 E Miraloma Ave, Anaheim
(92806-2108)
PHONE....................714 630-7840
Simon Newman, *CEO*
EMP: 50 EST: 2021
SALES (est): 467.08K **Privately Held**
SIC: 3965 Fasteners, buttons, needles, and pins

(P-8574)
MORTON GRINDING INC
Also Called: Morton Manufacturing
201 E Avenue K15, Lancaster
(93535-4572)
PHONE....................661 298-0895

Yolanda A Morton, *Ch Bd*
Wallace Morton, *
John Morton, *
Patrick Dansby, *
EMP: 110 **EST:** 1967
SQ FT: 45,000
SALES (est): 15.62MM **Privately Held**
Web: www.mortonmanufacturing.com
SIC: 3965 3769 3452 Fasteners; Space
vehicle equipment, nec; Bolts, nuts, rivets,
and washers

(P-8575)
ROSE LILLA INC
1050 S Cypress St, La Habra (90631-6862)
PHONE..............................888 519-8889
EMP: 29 **EST:** 2015
SALES (est): 796.15K **Privately Held**
Web: www.lillarose.com
SIC: 3965 Hairpins, except rubber

(P-8576)
SPS TECHNOLOGIES LLC
Also Called: Aerospace Fasteners Group
1224 E Warner Ave, Santa Ana
(92705-5414)
PHONE..............................714 545-9311
Mike Kleene, *Brnch Mgr*
EMP: 500
SQ FT: 40,000
SALES (corp-wide): 364.48B **Publicly
Held**
Web: www.pccfasteners.com
SIC: 3965 3728 3452 3714 Fasteners;
Aircraft parts and equipment, nec; Bolts,
nuts, rivets, and washers; Motor vehicle
parts and accessories
HQ: Sps Technologies, Llc
301 Highland Ave
Jenkintown PA 19046
215 572-3000

(P-8577)
SPS TECHNOLOGIES LLC
Cherry Aerospace Div
1224 E Warner Ave, Santa Ana
(92705-5414)
PHONE..............................714 371-1925
Michael Harhen, *Brnch Mgr*
EMP: 500
SALES (corp-wide): 364.48B **Publicly
Held**
Web: www.pccfasteners.com
SIC: 3965 3452 Fasteners; Bolts, nuts,
rivets, and washers
HQ: Sps Technologies, Llc
301 Highland Ave
Jenkintown PA 19046
215 572-3000

(P-8578)
**TOLEETO FASTENER
INTERNATIONAL**
1580 Jayken Way, Chula Vista
(91911-4644)
PHONE..............................619 662-1355
David Deavenport, *Pr*
Tom V Oss, *
Sara Davenport, *
EMP: 26 **EST:** 1985
SQ FT: 10,000
SALES (est): 761.4K **Privately Held**
Web: www.tfifab.com
SIC: 3965 Fasteners

(P-8579)
TWO LADS INC (PA)
5001 Hampton St, Vernon (90058-2133)
P.O. Box 58572 (90058-0572)
PHONE..............................323 584-0064

Lee R Adams, *Pr*
David Scharf, *
▼ **EMP:** 30 **EST:** 1991
SQ FT: 6,300
SALES (est): 1.01MM **Privately Held**
Web: www.2lads.com
SIC: 3965 5131 2241 Buttons and parts;
Buttons; Narrow fabric mills

(P-8580)
WCBM COMPANY (PA)
Also Called: West Coast Button Mfg Co
1812 W 135th St, Gardena (90249-2520)
PHONE..............................323 262-3274
Keith Tanabe, *CEO*
Grace Kadoya, *
▲ **EMP:** 32 **EST:** 1976
SQ FT: 19,000
SALES (est): 471.86K
SALES (corp-wide): 471.86K **Privately
Held**
SIC: 3965 Buttons and parts

(P-8581)
**WEST COAST AEROSPACE INC
(PA)**
220 W E St, Wilmington (90744-5502)
PHONE..............................310 518-3167
Kenneth L Wagner Junior, *Pr*
Thomas Lieb, *
▲ **EMP:** 90 **EST:** 1977
SQ FT: 7,200
SALES (est): 9.77MM
SALES (corp-wide): 9.77MM **Privately
Held**
Web: www.westcoastaerospace.com
SIC: 3965 3452 Fasteners; Bolts, nuts,
rivets, and washers

(P-8582)
YKK (USA) INC
Also Called: Y K K U S A
5001 E La Palma Ave, Anaheim
(92807-1926)
PHONE..............................714 701-1200
Mike Blunt, *Mgr*
EMP: 27
Web: www.ykkamericas.com
SIC: 3965 5131 Fasteners; Zippers
HQ: Ykk (U.S.A.) Inc.
1300 Cobb Industrial Dr
Marietta GA 30066
770 427-5521

3991 Brooms And Brushes

(P-8583)
**AMERICAN ROTARY BROOM CO
INC**
088 New York Dr, Pomona (91768-3311)
PHONE..............................909 629-9117
Joe Baeskens, *Brnch Mgr*
EMP: 23
SALES (corp-wide): 2.27MM **Privately
Held**
Web: www.united-rotary.com
SIC: 3991 3711 4959 Brooms; Motor
vehicles and car bodies; Sweeping service:
road, airport, parking lot, etc.
PA: American Rotary Broom Co., Inc.
181 Pawnee St Ste B
760 591-4025

(P-8584)
BRUSH RESEARCH MFG CO INC
Also Called: Brm Manufacturing
4642 Floral Dr, Los Angeles (90022-1288)
PHONE..............................323 261-2193
Tara L Rands, *CEO*

Robert Fowlie, *
Grant Fowlie, *
Heather Jones, *
▲ **EMP:** 130 **EST:** 1962
SALES (est): 21.15MM **Privately Held**
Web: www.brushresearch.com
SIC: 3991 Brushes, household or industrial

(P-8585)
BUTLER HOME PRODUCTS LLC
9409 Buffalo Ave, Rancho Cucamonga
(91730-6012)
PHONE..............................909 476-3884
Paul Anton, *Brnch Mgr*
EMP: 176
SALES (corp-wide): 642.04MM **Privately
Held**
Web: www.cleanerhomeliving.com
SIC: 3991 2392 Brooms; Mops, floor and
dust
HQ: Butler Home Products, Llc
2 Cabot Rd Ste 102
Hudson MA 01749
508 597-8000

(P-8586)
EASY REACH SUPPLY LLC
3737 Capitol Ave, City Of Industry
(90601-1732)
PHONE..............................601 582-7866
EMP: 26
SALES (corp-wide): 14.37MM **Privately
Held**
Web: www.easyreachinc.com
SIC: 3991 Brooms and brushes
HQ: Easy Reach Supply, Llc
32 Raspberry Ln
Hattiesburg MS 39402
601 582-7866

(P-8587)
FOAMPRO MFG INC
Also Called: Foampro Manufacturing
1438 Ritchey St, Santa Ana (92705-4729)
P.O. Box 18888 (92623-8888)
PHONE..............................949 252-0112
Gregory Isaac, *Ch Bd*
Chad Coil, *
▲ **EMP:** 80 **EST:** 1952
SQ FT: 25,000
SALES (est): 5.81MM **Privately Held**
Web: www.foampromfg.com
SIC: 3991 Paint rollers

3993 Signs And Advertising Specialties

(P-8588)
3S SIGN SERVICES INC
Also Called: P.S. Services
1320 N Red Gum St, Anaheim
(92806-1317)
PHONE..............................714 683-1120
Michael W Schmidt, *CEO*
EMP: 25 **EST:** 2018
SALES (est): 361.29K **Privately Held**
Web: www.psserv.com
SIC: 3993 Signs and advertising specialties

(P-8589)
**AMERICAN FLEET & RET
GRAPHICS**
Also Called: Amgraph
2091 Del Rio Way, Ontario (91761-8038)
PHONE..............................909 937-7570
Kristin Stewart, *CEO*
Brian Stewart, *
EMP: 37 **EST:** 2006
SALES (est): 5.7MM **Privately Held**

Web: www.theamgraphgroup.com
SIC: 3993 Signs and advertising specialties

(P-8590)
**ARCHITECTURAL DESIGN
SIGNS INC (PA)**
Also Called: Ad/S Companies
1160 Railroad St, Corona (92882-1835)
PHONE..............................951 278-0680
Sean L Solomon, *Pr*
Roberto Soltero Iii, *VP*
EMP: 95 **EST:** 1995
SQ FT: 630,000
SALES (est): 23.4MM **Privately Held**
Web: www.ad-s.com
SIC: 3993 Signs and advertising specialties

(P-8591)
CALIFORNIA NEON PRODUCTS
Also Called: C N P Signs & Graphics
9944 Blossom Valley Rd, El Cajon
(92021-2203)
PHONE..............................619 283-2191
Peter Mccarter, *CEO*
Robert Mccarter, *VP*
Richard Mccarter, *Sec*
EMP: 70 **EST:** 1939
SALES (est): 4.07MM **Privately Held**
Web: www.cnpsigns.com
SIC: 3993 1799 Electric signs; Sign
installation and maintenance

(P-8592)
CALIFORNIA SIGNS INC
Also Called: CA Signs
10280 Glenoaks Blvd, Pacoima
(91331-1604)
PHONE..............................818 899-1888
Matthew Miller, *Pr*
Yvette Miller, *
EMP: 35 **EST:** 1962
SQ FT: 21,000
SALES (est): 5.03MM **Privately Held**
Web: www.casigns.com
SIC: 3993 Signs, not made in custom sign
painting shops

(P-8593)
CLEGG INDUSTRIES INC
Also Called: Clegg Promo
19032 S Vermont Ave, Gardena
(90248-4412)
PHONE..............................310 225-3800
Timothy P Clegg, *CEO*
Kevin Clegg, *
Michael Bistocchi, *
Michael Amar, *
Los Angeles, *
▲ **EMP:** 175 **EST:** 1987
SQ FT: 31,000
SALES (est): 7.46MM **Privately Held**
SIC: 3993 3648 2542 Advertising novelties;
Lighting equipment, nec; Partitions and
fixtures, except wood

(P-8594)
COAST SIGN INCORPORATED
Also Called: Coast Sign Display
1500 W Embassy St, Anaheim
(92802-1016)
PHONE..............................714 520-9144
Afshan Alemi, *CEO*
S Charlie Alemi, *
Bonnie Metz, *
▲ **EMP:** 250 **EST:** 1964
SQ FT: 130,000
SALES (est): 27.64MM **Privately Held**
Web: www.coastsign.com
SIC: 3993 Signs, not made in custom sign
painting shops

(P-8595)

CORNERSTONE DISPLAY GROUP INC

Also Called: Cornerstone
28340 Avenue Crocker, Valencia (91355-1238)
PHONE..............................661 705-1700
Tom Hester, *Prin*
▲ EMP: 45 EST: 1995
SQ FT: 20,000
SALES (est): 9.57MM **Privately Held**
Web: www.cornerstonedisplay.com
SIC: 3993 Advertising artwork

(P-8596)

COWBOY DIRECT RESPONSE

Also Called: Synergy Direct Response
130 E Alton Ave, Santa Ana (92707-4415)
PHONE..............................714 824-3780
Cynthia Rogers, *CEO*
John T Rogers, *
Cynthia Rogers, *Pr*
EMP: 35 EST: 2004
SQ FT: 10,000
SALES (est): 4.53MM **Privately Held**
Web: www.synergydr.com
SIC: 3993 8999 2759 Advertising artwork;
Advertising copy writing; Promotional printing

(P-8597)

CUMMINGS RESOURCES LLC

1495 Columbia Ave, Riverside (92507-2021)
PHONE..............................951 248-1130
Jim Mole, *Manager*
EMP: 39
SQ FT: 50,000
SALES (corp-wide): 691.84MM **Privately Held**
Web: www.cummingssigns.com
SIC: 3993 Signs and advertising specialties
HQ: Cummings Resources Llc
15 Century Blvd Ste 200
Nashville TN 37214

(P-8598)

CUMMINGS RESOURCES LLC

330 W Citrus St, Colton (92324-1417)
PHONE..............................951 248-1130
EMP: 39
SALES (corp-wide): 691.84MM **Privately Held**
Web: www.cummingssigns.com
SIC: 3993 Signs and advertising specialties
HQ: Cummings Resources Llc
15 Century Blvd Ste 200
Nashville TN 37214

(P-8599)

DG-DISPLAYS LLC

355 Parkside Dr, San Fernando (91340-3036)
PHONE..............................877 358-5976
Zachary Blumenfeld, *
EMP: 30 EST: 2016
SQ FT: 25,000
SALES (est): 378.76K **Privately Held**
Web: shop.abex.com
SIC: 3993 Signs and advertising specialties

(P-8600)

ENCORE IMAGE INC

303 W Main St, Ontario (91762-3843)
P.O. Box 9297 (91762-9297)
PHONE..............................909 986-4632
Terry Wilkins, *CEO*
EMP: 27 EST: 2006
SQ FT: 30,000
SALES (est): 4.14MM

SALES (corp-wide): 9.86MM **Privately Held**
Web: www.encoreimage.com
SIC: 3993 1799 Electric signs; Sign installation and maintenance
PA: Encore Image Group, Inc.
1445 W Sepulveda Blvd
310 534-7500

(P-8601)

ENCORE IMAGE GROUP INC (PA)

Also Called: Encore Image
1445 Sepulveda Blvd, Torrance (90501-5004)
PHONE..............................310 534-7500
Kozell Boren, *Ch Bd*
Tom Johnson, *
Tommy K Boren, *Prin*
▲ EMP: 90 EST: 1959
SQ FT: 70,000
SALES (est): 9.86MM
SALES (corp-wide): 9.86MM **Privately Held**
Web: www.encoreimagegroup.com
SIC: 3993 Electric signs

(P-8602)

EVANS MANUFACTURING LLC (HQ)

Also Called: Evans Manufacturing, Inc.
7422 Chapman Ave, Garden Grove (92841-2106)
P.O. Box 5669 (92846-0669)
PHONE..............................714 379-6100
Alan Vaught, *CEO*
▲ EMP: 185 EST: 1990
SQ FT: 17,000
SALES (est): 49.63MM
SALES (corp-wide): 94.31MM **Privately Held**
Web: www.evans-mfg.com
SIC: 3993 3089 Signs and advertising specialties; Injection molding of plastics
PA: Hub Pen Company, Llc
1525 Washington St Ste 1
781 535-5500

(P-8603)

EXITON INC

Also Called: Loren Electric Sign & Lighting
12226 Coast Dr, Whittier (90601-1607)
PHONE..............................562 699-1122
Daniel Marc Lorenzon, *CEO*
Michelle Lornezon, *
EMP: 45 EST: 1996
SQ FT: 8,000
SALES (est): 6.78MM **Privately Held**
Web: www.lorenindustries.com
SIC: 3993 3648 1799 Electric signs; Outdoor lighting equipment; Sign installation and maintenance

(P-8604)

FEDERAL HEATH SIGN COMPANY LLC

3609 Ocean Ranch Blvd Ste 204, Oceanside (92056-8601)
PHONE..............................760 941-0715
Tim O'donald, *Brnch Mgr*
EMP: 120
Web: www.federalheath.com
SIC: 3993 Neon signs
HQ: Federal Heath Sign Company, Llc
1845 Prcnct Line Rd Ste 1
Hurst TX 76054

(P-8605)

FOVELL ENTERPRISES INC

Also Called: Southwest Sign Company
1852 Pomona Rd, Corona (92878-3277)
P.O. Box 6376 (92878-6376)
PHONE..............................951 734-6275
Jack Fovell, *CEO*
▲ EMP: 26 EST: 1991
SQ FT: 12,500
SALES (est): 3.59MM **Privately Held**
Web: www.southwestsign.com
SIC: 3993 Electric signs

(P-8606)

FUSION SIGN & DESIGN INC

12226 Coast Dr, Whittier (90601-1607)
PHONE..............................562 946-7545
EMP: 26
Web: www.fusionsign.com
SIC: 3993 Electric signs
PA: Fusion Sign & Design, Inc.
680 Columbia Ave

(P-8607)

GEORGE P JOHNSON COMPANY

18500 Crenshaw Blvd, Torrance (90504-5055)
PHONE..............................310 965-4300
Chris Meyer, *CEO*
EMP: 38
SALES (corp-wide): 281.93MM **Privately Held**
Web: www.gpj.com
SIC: 3993 Signs and advertising specialties
HQ: George P. Johnson Company
1914 Taylor Point Rd
Auburn Hills MI 48326
248 475-2500

(P-8608)

INFINITY WATCH CORPORATION

Also Called: Iwcus
21078 Commerce Point Dr, Walnut (91789-3051)
PHONE..............................626 289-9878
Patrick Tam, *Pr*
Brenda Tam, *
▲ EMP: 25 EST: 1990
SQ FT: 12,000
SALES (est): 792.51K **Privately Held**
Web: www.infinitywatch.com
SIC: 3993 Signs and advertising specialties

(P-8609)

INTEGRTED SIGN ASSOC A CAL COR

Also Called: Integrated Sign Associates
1160 Pioneer Way Ste M, El Cajon (92020-1944)
PHONE..............................619 579-2229
Aaron Coippinger, *Pr*
EMP: 30 EST: 1982
SQ FT: 15,000
SALES (est): 2.57MM **Privately Held**
Web: www.isasign.com
SIC: 3993 Neon signs

(P-8610)

JOHN BISHOP DESIGN INC

Also Called: J B3d
731 N Main St, Orange (92868-1105)
PHONE..............................714 744-2300
John Bishop, *Pr*
Lisa Bishop, *
EMP: 38 EST: 1989
SQ FT: 1,000
SALES (est): 3.33MM **Privately Held**
Web: www.jb3d.com

SIC: 3993 Signs and advertising specialties

(P-8611)

JONES SIGN CO INC

Also Called: Ultrasigns Electrical Advg
9474 Chesapeake Dr Ste 902, San Diego (92123-1027)
PHONE..............................858 569-1400
John Mortensen, *Pr*
EMP: 130
SALES (corp-wide): 63.86MM **Privately Held**
Web: www.jonessign.com
SIC: 3993 Signs and advertising specialties
PA: Jones Sign Co., Inc.
1711 Scheuring Rd
920 983-6700

(P-8612)

K S DESIGNS INC

Also Called: Cal West Designs
901 S Cypress St, La Habra (90631-6833)
PHONE..............................562 929-3973
Robin Shelton, *Pr*
EMP: 32 EST: 1979
SALES (est): 2.96MM **Privately Held**
SIC: 3993 Displays and cutouts, window and lobby

(P-8613)

MANERI SIGN CO INC

2722 S Fairview St, Santa Ana (92704-5947)
PHONE..............................310 327-6261
Don Nicholas, *Pr*
EMP: 35 EST: 1980
SALES (est): 3.25MM
SALES (corp-wide): 48.27MM **Privately Held**
Web: www.statewidess.com
SIC: 3993 Signs and advertising specialties
PA: Traffic Solutions Corporation
4244 Mount Pleasant St Nw
949 553-8272

(P-8614)

MAXWELL ALARM SCREEN MFG INC

Also Called: Maxwell Sign and Decal Div
20327 Nordhoff St, Chatsworth (91311-6128)
PHONE..............................818 773-5533
Michael A Kagen, *CEO*
Patty Kagen, *
EMP: 28 EST: 1977
SQ FT: 28,000
SALES (est): 3.58MM **Privately Held**
Web: www.maxwellmfg.com
SIC: 3993 3442 Signs and advertising specialties; Screens, window, metal

(P-8615)

MEDIA NATION ENTERPRISES LLC (PA)

Also Called: Media Nation USA
15271 Barranca Pkwy, Irvine (92618-2201)
PHONE..............................888 502-8222
Navin D Narang, *Managing Member*
EMP: 24 EST: 2009
SALES (est): 968.46K
SALES (corp-wide): 968.46K **Privately Held**
Web: www.medianationoutdoor.com
SIC: 3993 5699 7371 Signs and advertising specialties; Customized clothing and apparel; Software programming applications

▲ = Import ▼ = Export
◆ = Import/Export

(P-8616)

METAL ART OF CALIFORNIA INC (PA)

Also Called: Sign Mart
640 N Cypress St, Orange (92867-6604)
PHONE...............................714 532-7100
Gene S Sobel, *Pr*
Calvin Larson, *
◆ **EMP: 91 EST: 1974**
SQ FT: 22,000
SALES (est): 9.16MM
SALES (corp-wide): 9.16MM Privately Held
Web: www.sign-mart.com
SIC: 3993 Signs and advertising specialties

(P-8617)

MMXVIII HOLDINGS INC

20251 Sw Acacia St Ste 120, Newport Beach (92660-1716)
PHONE...............................800 672-3974
EMP: 24 EST: 2016
SQ FT: 7,500
SALES (est): 984.42K Privately Held
SIC: 3993 Signs and advertising specialties

(P-8618)

MYERS & SONS HI-WAY SAFETY INC (PA)

Also Called: Hi-Way Safety
13310 5th St, Chino (91710-5125)
P.O. Box 1030 (91708-1030)
PHONE...............................909 591-1781
TOLL FREE: 800
Michael Rodgers, *CEO*
Brandon Myer, *
▲ **EMP: 80 EST: 1970**
SQ FT: 36,400
SALES (est): 27.34MM
SALES (corp-wide): 27.34MM Privately Held
SIC: 3993 Signs, not made in custom sign painting shops

(P-8619)

NATIONAL SIGN & MARKETING CORP

Also Called: Visual Information Systems Co
13580 5th St, Chino (91710-5113)
P.O. Box 2409 (91710)
PHONE...............................909 591-4742
John J Kane, *Pr*
Jeffrey Fredrickson, *
EMP: 70 EST: 1997
SQ FT: 46,000
SALES (est): 9.42MM Privately Held
Web: www.nsmc.com
SIC: 3993 Neon signs

(P-8620)

NEIMAN/HOELLER INC

Also Called: Neiman & Company
6842 Valjean Ave, Van Nuys (91406-4712)
PHONE...............................818 781-8600
Harry J Neiman, *CEO*
Robert R Hoeller Iii, *Pr*
EMP: 56 EST: 1965
SQ FT: 17,000
SALES (est): 6.06MM Privately Held
Web: www.neimanandco.com
SIC: 3993 3646 Electric signs; Ornamental lighting fixtures, commercial

(P-8621)

OPTEC DISPLAYS INC

1700 S De Soto Pl Ste A, Ontario (91761-8060)
PHONE...............................866 924-5239
Jerry Luan, *CEO*

Shu-hwa Wu, *Sec*
◆ **EMP: 64 EST: 1996**
SALES (est): 21.51MM Privately Held
Web: www.optec.com
SIC: 3993 Signs and advertising specialties

(P-8622)

ORANGE CNTY NAME PLATE CO INC

13201 Arctic Cir, Santa Fe Springs (90670-5572)
P.O. Box 2764 (90670-0764)
PHONE...............................714 522-7693
Elias Rodriguez, *Pr*
Ben L Rodriguez, *
Sam Rodriguez, *
EMP: 85 EST: 1965
SQ FT: 31,000
SALES (est): 3.95MM Privately Held
Web: www.ocnameplates.com
SIC: 3993 Name plates: except engraved, etched, etc.: metal

(P-8623)

PD GROUP

Also Called: Sign-A-Rama
41945 Boardwalk Ste L, Palm Desert (92211-9099)
PHONE...............................760 674-3028
Jeff Gracy, *Pr*
Terrance Flannagan, *
EMP: 28 EST: 1995
SQ FT: 11,500
SALES (est): 2.95MM Privately Held
Web: www.pdsignarama.com
SIC: 3993 7389 5999 Signs and advertising specialties; Sign painting and lettering shop ; Banners

(P-8624)

PRIMUS INC

Also Called: Western Highway Products
17901 Jamestown Ln, Huntington Beach (92647-7138)
P.O. Box 534 (92648-0534)
PHONE...............................714 527-2261
Steve Ellsworth, *Pr*
Timothy M Riordan, *
▲ **EMP: 80 EST: 1926**
SQ FT: 120,000
SALES (est): 1.78MM Privately Held
Web: www.primus.us
SIC: 3993 Signs, not made in custom sign painting shops

(P-8625)

QUIEL BROS ELC SIGN SVC CO INC

272 S I St, San Bernardino (92410-2408)
PHONE...............................909 885-4476
Larry R Quiel, *Pr*
Raymond Quiel, *
Jerry Quiel, *
Gary Quiel, *
▲ **EMP: 40 EST: 1962**
SQ FT: 8,000
SALES (est): 470.21K Privately Held
Web: www.quielsigns.com
SIC: 3993 7353 1731 7629 Electric signs; Cranes and aerial lift equipment, rental or leasing; General electrical contractor; Electrical equipment repair, high voltage

(P-8626)

RICHARDS NEON SHOP INC

Also Called: RNS Channel Letters
4375 Prado Rd Ste 102, Corona (92878-7444)
PHONE...............................951 279-6767
Richard Pando, *Pr*

EMP: 24 EST: 1991
SALES (est): 3.08MM Privately Held
Web: www.rnsletters.com
SIC: 3993 Electric signs

(P-8627)

ROSS NAME PLATE COMPANY

2 Red Plum Cir, Monterey Park (91755-7486)
PHONE...............................323 725-6812
Michael Ross, *Pr*
EMP: 37 EST: 1957
SQ FT: 25,000
SALES (est): 3.43MM Privately Held
Web: www.rossnameplate.com
SIC: 3993 2754 Name plates: except engraved, etched, etc.: metal; Labels: gravure printing

(P-8628)

S2K GRAPHICS INC

Also Called: S 2 K
4686 Industrial St, Simi Valley (93063-3413)
PHONE...............................818 885-3900
Dan C Pulos, *CEO*
Jack Wilson, *Ch Bd*
Dana Rosellini, *Sec*
EMP: 35 EST: 1989
SALES (est): 3.3MM Privately Held
Web: www.s2kgraphics.com
SIC: 3993 7532 2759 Signs and advertising specialties; Truck painting and lettering; Screen printing
HQ: Franke Usa Holding, Inc.
   800 Aviation Pkwy
   Smyrna TN 37167

(P-8629)

SAFEWAY SIGN COMPANY

9875 Yucca Rd, Adelanto (92301-2282)
PHONE...............................760 246-7070
Michael F Moore, *Pr*
David C Moore, *
Andrea M Gutierrez, *
EMP: 49 EST: 1948
SQ FT: 60,000
SALES (est): 6.04MM Privately Held
Web: www.safewaysign.com
SIC: 3993 Signs, not made in custom sign painting shops

(P-8630)

SANTA CLARITA SIGNS

26330 Diamond Pl, Santa Clarita (91350-5822)
PHONE...............................661 291-1188
EMP: 23 EST: 2009
SALES (est): 302.69K Privately Held
Web: www.signalscv.com
SIC: 3993 Signs and advertising specialties

(P-8631)

SHYE WEST INC (PA)

Also Called: Imagine This
43 Corporate Park Ste 102, Irvine (92606-5137)
PHONE...............................949 486-4598
Patrick Papaccio, *Pr*
Shawn Keep, *
▲ **EMP: 27 EST: 1999**
SQ FT: 6,000
SALES (est): 2.32MM
SALES (corp-wide): 2.32MM Privately Held
Web: www.imaginethis.com
SIC: 3993 5099 Advertising novelties; Novelties, durable

(P-8632)

SIGN INDUSTRIES INC

2101 Carrillo Privado, Ontario (91761-7600)
PHONE...............................909 930-0303
Maria Saavedra, *Pr*
Enrique Saavedra, *
▲ **EMP: 30 EST: 1994**
SQ FT: 4,500
SALES (est): 6.46MM Privately Held
Web: www.signindustries.tv
SIC: 3993 Neon signs

(P-8633)

SIGNAGE SOLUTIONS CORPORATION

2231 S Dupont Dr, Anaheim (92806-6105)
PHONE...............................714 491-0299
Chris Deruyter, *CEO*
Jim Gledhill, *
EMP: 30 EST: 1990
SQ FT: 14,000
SALES (est): 4.2MM Privately Held
Web: www.signage-solutions.com
SIC: 3993 7389 Signs and advertising specialties; Sign painting and lettering shop

(P-8634)

SIGNRESOURCE LLC

6135 District Blvd, Maywood (90270-3449)
PHONE...............................323 771-2098
EMP: 162
Web: www.signresource.com
SIC: 3993 Signs and advertising specialties
HQ: Signresource, Llc
   242 Industrial Pkwy
   Jacksboro TN 37757
   323 771-2098

(P-8635)

SIGNS AND SERVICES COMPANY

10980 Boatman Ave, Stanton (90680-2602)
PHONE...............................714 761-8200
Jacob Deryuyter, *CEO*
Matt De Ruyter, *
EMP: 33 EST: 1986
SQ FT: 16,000
SALES (est): 4.61MM Privately Held
Web: www.signsandservicesco.com
SIC: 3993 Signs, not made in custom sign painting shops

(P-8636)

SIGNTECH ELECTRICAL ADVG INC

Also Called: Signtech
4444 Federal Blvd, San Diego (92102-2505)
PHONE...............................619 527-6100
Harold E Schauer Junior, *CEO*
David E Schauer, *
Kimra Schauer, *
Art Navarro, *
Patty Soria, *
EMP: 120 EST: 1984
SQ FT: 25,000
SALES (est): 19.82MM Privately Held
Web: www.signtech.com
SIC: 3993 1799 Electric signs; Sign installation and maintenance

(P-8637)

SIGNTRONIX INC

Also Called: Gulf Development
1445 Sepulveda Blvd, Torrance (90501-5004)
PHONE...............................310 534-7500
▲ **EMP: 100**

Web: www.signtronix.com
SIC: 3993 Signs and advertising specialties

(P-8638)
STANDARDVISION LLC
3370 N San Fernando Rd Ste 206, Los
Angeles (90065-1437)
PHONE..................................323 222-3630
Alberto Garcia, *Prin*
Kevin Bartanian, *Prin*
Hs Moon, *Prin*
▲ EMP: 34 EST: 2007
SQ FT: 25,000
SALES (est): 11.09MM **Privately Held**
Web: www.standardvision.com
SIC: 3993 7336 Signs and advertising
specialties; Commercial art and graphic
design

(P-8639)
**STANFORD SIGN & AWNING INC
(PA)**
2556 Faivre St, Chula Vista (91911-4604)
PHONE..................................619 423-6200
David Lesage, *Pr*
EMP: 50 EST: 1974
SQ FT: 35,000
SALES (est): 5.09MM
SALES (corp-wide): 5.09MM **Privately
Held**
Web: www.stanfordsign.com
SIC: 3993 2394 Electric signs; Canvas
awnings and canopies

(P-8640)
**STATEWIDE TRFFIC SFETY
SGNS IN**
2722 S Fairview St, Santa Ana
(92704-5947)
PHONE..................................714 468-1919
Don Nicholas, *Owner*
EMP: 26
SALES (corp-wide): 539.72MM **Privately
Held**
Web: www.statewidess.com
SIC: 3993 Signs and advertising specialties
HQ: Statewide Traffic Safety And Signs, Inc.
2722 S Fairview St Fl 2
Santa Ana CA 92704
949 553-8272

(P-8641)
**STATEWIDE TRFFIC SFETY
SGNS IN**
1100 Main St Ste 100, Irvine (92614-6737)
P.O. Box 5299 (92616-5299)
PHONE..................................949 553-8272
EMP: 26
SALES (corp-wide): 539.72MM **Privately
Held**
Web: www.statewidess.com
SIC: 3993 Signs and advertising specialties
HQ: Statewide Traffic Safety And Signs, Inc.
2722 S Fairview St Fl 2
Santa Ana CA 92704
949 553-8272

(P-8642)
**SUNSET SIGNS AND PRINTING
INC**
Also Called: Contractor
2906 E Coronado St, Anaheim
(92806-2501)
PHONE..................................714 255-9104
Tracy Eschenbrenner, *CEO*
EMP: 50 EST: 1992
SALES (est): 9.44MM **Privately Held**
Web: www.sunsetsignsoc.com

SIC: 3993 Signs and advertising specialties

(P-8643)
**SUPERIOR SIGNS &
INSTALLATION (PA)**
1700 W Anaheim St, Long Beach
(90813-1195)
PHONE..................................562 495-3808
Jim Sterk, *CEO*
Patti Skoglundadams, *
Doug Tokeshi, *
Stan Janocha, *
▲ EMP: 85 EST: 1962
SQ FT: 100,000
SALES (est): 24.66MM
SALES (corp-wide): 24.66MM **Privately
Held**
Web: www.superiorsigns.com
SIC: 3993 7629 Electric signs; Electrical
equipment repair services

(P-8644)
TDI SIGNS
13158 Arctic Cir, Santa Fe Springs
(90670-5508)
PHONE..................................562 436-5188
Arthur Rivas, *Pr*
EMP: 25 EST: 2003
SALES (est): 5.21MM **Privately Held**
Web: www.tdisigns.com
SIC: 3993 Electric signs

(P-8645)
**TFN ARCHITECTURAL SIGNAGE
INC (PA)**
Also Called: Third Floor North Company
527 Fee Ana St, Placentia (92870-6702)
PHONE..................................714 556-0990
Brian L Burnett, *Pr*
Ellen Vaughn, *
Teresa Burnett, *
Catherine Burnett, *Stockholder*
Jeff Burnett, *Stockholder*
EMP: 44 EST: 1980
SALES (est): 4.28MM
SALES (corp-wide): 4.28MM **Privately
Held**
Web: www.thirdfloornorth.com
SIC: 3993 Signs, not made in custom sign
painting shops

(P-8646)
TRADENET ENTERPRISE INC
Also Called: Vantage Led
1580 Magnolia Ave, Corona (92879-2073)
PHONE..................................888 595-3956
Chris Ma, *CEO*
▲ EMP: 60 EST: 1997
SALES (est): 9.89MM **Privately Held**
Web: www.vantageled.com
SIC: 3993 Electric signs

(P-8647)
**TRAFFIC CONTROL & SAFETY
CORP**
13755 Blaisdell Pl, Poway (92064-6837)
PHONE..................................858 679-7292
David Nicholas, *Brnch Mgr*
EMP: 42
Web: www.statewidess.com
SIC: 3993 5088 7359 5082 Signs, not made
in custom sign painting shops;
Transportation equipment and supplies;
Work zone traffic equipment (flags, cones,
barrels, etc.); Contractor's materials
PA: Traffic Control And Safety Corporation
1100 Main St

(P-8648)
VALLEY ENERPRISES INC
18600 Van Buren Blvd, Riverside
(92508-9111)
PHONE..................................951 789-0843
EMP: 25 EST: 2011
SALES (est): 127.59K **Privately Held**
Web: www.vesigns.com
SIC: 3993 Signs and advertising specialties

(P-8649)
**WESTERN ELECTRICAL ADVG
CO**
Also Called: Southwest Sign Systems
853 S Dogwood Rd, El Centro
(92243-4606)
P.O. Box 587 (92244-0587)
PHONE..................................760 352-0471
Dennis Berg, *Pr*
Vernon I Berg, *
Glenna L Berg, *
EMP: 25 EST: 1947
SALES (est): 635.31K **Privately Held**
SIC: 3993 1731 Electric signs; General
electrical contractor

(P-8650)
WESTERN SIGN SYSTEMS INC
Also Called: Western Sign Systems
261 S Pacific St, San Marcos (92078-2429)
PHONE..................................760 736-6070
David Lesage, *Pr*
EMP: 25 EST: 1993
SQ FT: 6,000
SALES (est): 2.21MM **Privately Held**
Web: www.western-sign.com
SIC: 3993 Signs and advertising specialties

(P-8651)
WOLFPACK INC
Also Called: Wolfpack Sign Group
2440 Grand Ave Ste B, Vista (92081-7829)
P.O. Box 3620 (92085-3620)
PHONE..................................760 736-4500
Carolyn Wolf, *CEO*
Ryan Meyer, *VP*
Peter Wolf, *Sec*
EMP: 24 EST: 1995
SQ FT: 15,000
SALES (est): 2.86MM **Privately Held**
Web: www.wolfpackllc.com
SIC: 3993 Signs, not made in custom sign
painting shops

(P-8652)
**YOUNG ELECTRIC SIGN
COMPANY**
Also Called: Yesco
10235 Bellegrave Ave, Jurupa Valley
(91752-1919)
PHONE..................................909 923-7668
Duane Wardle, *Brnch Mgr*
EMP: 197
SQ FT: 8,500
SALES (corp-wide): 498.12MM **Privately
Held**
Web: www.yesco.com
SIC: 3993 1799 Electric signs; Sign
installation and maintenance
PA: Young Electric Sign Company Inc
2401 Foothill Dr
801 464-4000

3996 Hard Surface Floor
Coverings, Nec

(P-8653)
ALTRO USA INC
Also Called: Compass Flooring
12648 Clark St, Santa Fe Springs
(90670-3950)
PHONE..................................562 944-8292
Al Boegh, *Prin*
EMP: 73
SALES (corp-wide): 216.3MM **Privately
Held**
Web: www.altro.com
SIC: 3996 5023 Hard surface floor
coverings, nec; Resilient floor coverings:
tile or sheet
HQ: Altro Usa, Inc.
80 Industrial Way Suite 1
Wilmington MA 01887
800 377-5597

(P-8654)
RAM BOARD INC
27460 Avenue Scott Unit A, Valencia
(91355-3472)
PHONE..................................818 848-0400
◆ EMP: 30 EST: 2008
SALES (est): 5.19MM **Privately Held**
Web: www.ramboard.com
SIC: 3996 5023 Hard surface floor
coverings, nec; Floor coverings

3999 Manufacturing
Industries, Nec

(P-8655)
**ABOVE & BEYOND BALLOONS
INC**
Also Called: Above and Beyond
1 Wrigley Unit A, Irvine (92618-2711)
PHONE..................................949 586-8470
Michael Chaklos, *CEO*
Karen Chaklos, *
▲ EMP: 44 EST: 2002
SALES (est): 4.31MM **Privately Held**
Web: www.advertisingballoons.com
SIC: 3999 Advertising display products

(P-8656)
**ADVANCED COSMETIC RES
LABS INC**
Also Called: Acrl
20550 Prairie St, Chatsworth (91311-6006)
PHONE..................................818 709-9945
Kitty Hunter, *Pr*
▲ EMP: 50 EST: 1994
SQ FT: 48,000
SALES (est): 10.05MM **Privately Held**
Web:
www.advancedcosmeticresearchlaboratories.
com
SIC: 3999 2844 Barber and beauty shop
equipment; Perfumes, cosmetics and other
toilet preparations

(P-8657)
**AMGEN MANUFACTURING
LIMITED**
1 Amgen Center Dr, Newbury Park
(91320-1799)
PHONE..................................787 656-2000
Victoria H Blatter, *Prin*
EMP: 34 EST: 2008
SALES (est): 10.71MM
SALES (corp-wide): 28.19B **Publicly Held**
Web: www.amgen.com

▲ = Import ▼ = Export
◆ = Import/Export

SIC: **3999** Atomizers, toiletry
PA: Amgen Inc.
1 Amgen Center Dr
805 447-1000

(P-8658)
ARMINAK SOLUTIONS LLC
475 N Sheridan St, Corona (92878-4021)
PHONE..............................626 802-7332
Helga Arminak, *Pr*
EMP: 35 EST: 2019
SALES (est): 1.63MM **Privately Held**
SIC: **3999** Manufacturing industries, nec

(P-8659)
ARTBOXX FRAMING INC
Also Called: Intercontinental Art
555 W Victoria St, Compton (90220-5513)
PHONE..............................310 604-6933
EMP: 26
SIC: **3999** 5999 Framed artwork; Art, picture frames, and decorations

(P-8660)
ARTIFICIAL GRASS LIQUIDATORS
Also Called: Agl
42505 Rio Nedo, Temecula (92590-3726)
PHONE..............................951 677-3377
Dillon Georgian, *Pr*
Vicky Hernandez, *Prin*
EMP: 30 EST: 2015
SALES (est): 473.22K **Privately Held**
Web: www.artificialgrassliquidators.com
SIC: **3999** Grasses, artificial and preserved

(P-8661)
BEACH HOUSE GROUP LLC
Also Called: Beach House Group
222 N Pacific Coast Hwy Fl 10, El Segundo (90245-5615)
PHONE..............................310 356-6180
Paul James Brice, *Managing Member*
Lance Kalish, *
Shaun Neff, *
Ido Leffler, *
Sachin Harneja, *
EMP: 54 EST: 2014
SALES (est): 6.29MM **Privately Held**
Web: www.beachhousegrp.com
SIC: **3999** Advertising display products

(P-8662)
BEAUTY TENT INC
1131 N Kenmore Ave Apt 6, Los Angeles (90029-1525)
PHONE..............................323 717-7131
Naira Harutyunyan, *Pr*
EMP: 25 EST: 2019
SALES (est): 735.9K **Privately Held**
Web: www.beautytent.com
SIC: **3999** Hair curlers, designed for beauty parlors

(P-8663)
BLOOMIOS INC
201 W Montecito St, Santa Barbara (93101-3824)
PHONE..............................805 222-6330
EMP: 30 EST: 2001
SALES (est): 6.08MM **Privately Held**
Web: www.bloomios.com
SIC: **3999** 5159

(P-8664)
BRIGHT GLOW CANDLE COMPANY INC (PA)
Also Called: Bright Glow
20591 E Via Verde St, Covina (91724-3715)

PHONE..............................909 469-4733
Richard Alcedo, *Pr*
◆ EMP: 24 EST: 1990
SALES (est): 5.11MM
SALES (corp-wide): 5.11MM **Privately Held**
Web: www.brightglowcandle.com
SIC: **3999** Candles

(P-8665)
CALIFORNIA EXOTIC NOVLT LLC
1455 E Francis St, Ontario (91761-8329)
P.O. Box 50400 (91761-1078)
PHONE..............................909 606-1950
Susan Colvin, *Managing Member*
Jackie White, *
▲ EMP: 88 EST: 1994
SQ FT: 66,000
SALES (est): 9.47MM **Privately Held**
Web: www.calexotics.com
SIC: **3999** 5947 Novelties, bric-a-brac, and hobby kits; Novelties

(P-8666)
CAMBRO MANUFACTURING COMPANY
21558 Ferrero, City Of Industry (91789-5216)
PHONE..............................909 354-8962
EMP: 108
SALES (corp-wide): 307.89MM **Privately Held**
Web: www.cambro.com
SIC: **3999** Barber and beauty shop equipment
PA: Cambro Manufacturing Company Inc
5801 Skylab Rd
714 848-1555

(P-8667)
CARBERRY LLC
3645 Long Beach Blvd, Long Beach (90807-4018)
PHONE..............................562 264-5078
EMP: 24
SALES (corp-wide): 2.19MM **Privately Held**
SIC: **3999** 2064
; Chewing candy, not chewing gum
HQ: Carberry Llc
17130 Muskrat Ave Ste B
Adelanto CA 92301
800 564-0842

(P-8668)
CARBERRY LLC (HQ)
Also Called: Plus Products
17130 Muskrat Ave Ste B, Adelanto (92301-2473)
PHONE..............................800 564-0842
EMP: 24 EST: 2017
SQ FT: 12,000
SALES (est): 2.19MM
SALES (corp-wide): 2.19MM **Privately Held**
SIC: **3999** 2064
; Chewing candy, not chewing gum
PA: Plus Products Holdings Inc.
340 S Lemon Ave Ste 9392
800 564-0842

(P-8669)
CBD LIVING WATER
1343 Versante Cir, Corona (92881-4192)
PHONE..............................800 940-3660
EMP: 25 EST: 2016
SALES (est): 1.66MM **Privately Held**
Web: www.cbdliving.com
SIC: **3999**

(P-8670)
CDM COMPANY INC
Also Called: CDM
12 Corporate Plaza Dr Ste 200, Newport Beach (92660-7986)
PHONE..............................949 644-2820
Mitchell Jankins, *CEO*
▲ EMP: 23 EST: 1990
SQ FT: 7,000
SALES (est): 2.37MM **Privately Held**
Web: www.thecdmco.com
SIC: **3999** 3944 8742 5112 Novelties, bric-a-brac, and hobby kits; Games, toys, and children's vehicles; Marketing consulting services; Pens and/or pencils

(P-8671)
CHRIS PUTRIMAS
1930 E Carson St Ste 102, Carson (90810-1246)
PHONE..............................877 434-1666
Chris Putrimas, *Owner*
EMP: 50
SALES (est): 575.93K **Privately Held**
SIC: **3999** Manufacturing industries, nec

(P-8672)
CJ FOODS MFG BEAUMONT LLC
415 Nicholas Rd, Beaumont (92223-2612)
PHONE..............................951 916-9300
Geon Il Lee, *CEO*
EMP: 71 EST: 2018
SALES (est): 20.76MM **Privately Held**
SIC: **3999** Chairs, hydraulic, barber and beauty shop
PA: Cj Cheiljedang Corporation
330 Dongho-Ro, Jung-Gu

(P-8673)
COMMERCE ON DEMAND LLC
Also Called: Good Tree
7121 Telegraph Rd, Montebello (90640-6511)
PHONE..............................562 360-4819
Rashaan Everett, *Managing Member*
EMP: 60 EST: 2020
SALES (est): 10MM **Privately Held**
SIC: **3999** Manufacturing industries, nec

(P-8674)
DEVELOPLUS INC
1575 Magnolia Ave, Corona (92879-2073)
PHONE..............................951 738-8595
Jeanne Nicodemus, *CEO*
Kiran Agrey, *
▲ EMP: 140 EST: 1990
SQ FT: 40,000
SALES (est): 24.5MM **Privately Held**
Web: www.developlus.com
SIC: **3999** 5087 Hair and hair-based products
, Beauty parlor equipment and supplies

(P-8675)
DMA ENTERPRISES INC (PA)
Also Called: Thermasol Steam Bath
2255 Union Pl, Simi Valley (93065-1661)
PHONE..............................805 520-2468
▲ EMP: 30 EST: 1989
SALES (est): 2.71MM **Privately Held**
SIC: **3999** 3431 Hot tubs; Bathroom fixtures, including sinks

(P-8676)
FLAME AND WAX INC
Also Called: Voluspa
2900 Mccabe Way, Irvine (92614-6239)
PHONE..............................949 752-4000
Troy C Arntsen, *CEO*
Troy C Arntsen, *CEO*

Traci Arntsen, *
▲ EMP: 134 EST: 2001
SALES (est): 18.59MM **Privately Held**
Web: www.voluspa.com
SIC: **3999** 2844 Candles; Perfumes, cosmetics and other toilet preparations

(P-8677)
FLORA GOLD CORPORATION (PA) ✪
3165 Red Hill Ave Ste 201, Costa Mesa (92626-3417)
PHONE..............................949 252-1908
Laurie Holcomb, *CEO*
Marshall Minor, *CFO*
Judith Schvimmer, *Sec*
EMP: 586 EST: 2023
SALES (est): 90.96MM
SALES (corp-wide): 90.96MM **Privately Held**
SIC: **3999**

(P-8678)
GENERAL WAX CO INC (PA)
Also Called: General Wax & Candle Co
6863 Beck Ave, North Hollywood (91605-6206)
P.O. Box 9398 (91609-1398)
PHONE..............................818 765-5800
Carol Lazar, *CEO*
Mike Tapp, *
Colton Lazar, *
Keith Tapp, *
J C Edmond, *
◆ EMP: 85 EST: 1949
SQ FT: 120,000
SALES (est): 11.31MM
SALES (corp-wide): 11.31MM **Privately Held**
Web: www.generalwax.com
SIC: **3999** Candles

(P-8679)
GOLDEN SUPREME INC
12304 Mccann Dr, Santa Fe Springs (90670-3333)
PHONE..............................562 903-1063
Ross Stillwagon, *Pr*
Fernando Fischbach, *
Ricardo J Fischbach, *
▲ EMP: 30 EST: 1990
SQ FT: 13,000
SALES (est): 956.66K **Privately Held**
Web: www.goldensupreme.com
SIC: **3999** 5087 Hair curlers, designed for beauty parlors; Beauty parlor equipment and supplies

(P-8680)
H & H SPECIALTIES INC
14850 Don Julian Rd Ste B, City Of Industry (91746-3122)
PHONE..............................626 575-0776
Reid Neslage, *Owner*
Mary Louise Higgins, *
EMP: 31 EST: 1967
SQ FT: 30,000
SALES (est): 3.55MM **Privately Held**
Web: www.hhspecialties.com
SIC: **3999** 3625 Stage hardware and equipment, except lighting; Relays and industrial controls

(P-8681)
HEMP INDUSTRIES
3717 El Cajon Blvd, San Diego (92105-1004)
PHONE..............................619 458-9090
Brian S Gallagher, *Owner*
EMP: 25 EST: 2017

PRODUCTS & SVCS

SALES (est): 236.26K **Privately Held**
Web: www.thehia.org
SIC: 3999 Manufacturing industries, nec

(P-8682)
HEXODEN HOLDINGS INC (PA)
1219 Linda Vista Dr, San Marcos
(92078-3809)
PHONE..............................858 201-3412
Donna Razzoli, *Pr*
EMP: 89 **EST:** 2017
SALES (est): 299.72K
SALES (corp-wide): 299.72K **Privately Held**
SIC: 3999 Manufacturing industries, nec

(P-8683)
HOLIDAY FOLIAGE INC
Also Called: Holiday Foliage
2592 Otay Center Dr, San Diego
(92154-7611)
PHONE..............................619 661-9094
Kristine Vanzutphen, *CEO*
Juanita Keller, *VP*
William Vanzutphen Junior, *CFO*
▲ **EMP:** 38 **EST:** 1994
SQ FT: 18,000
SALES (est): 9.46MM **Privately Held**
Web: www.holidayfoliage.com
SIC: 3999 Artificial trees and flowers

(P-8684)
HUNTINGTON INGALLS INDUSTRIES
9444 Balboa Ave Ste 400, San Diego
(92123-4378)
PHONE..............................858 522-6000
EMP: 24 **EST:** 2011
SALES (est): 1.01MM **Privately Held**
Web: www.hii.com
SIC: 3999 Manufacturing industries, nec

(P-8685)
INNOVATIVE CASEWORK MFG INC
12261 Industry St, Garden Grove
(92841-2815)
PHONE..............................714 890-9100
Valerie Perez, *Prin*
EMP: 25 **EST:** 2017
SALES (est): 217.84K **Privately Held**
SIC: 3999 Manufacturing industries, nec

(P-8686)
INTEGRATED MFG SOLUTIONS LLC
2590 Pioneer Ave Ste C, Vista
(92081-8427)
PHONE..............................760 599-4300
Baophuong Nguyen, *Pr*
EMP: 24 **EST:** 2007
SQ FT: 2,000
SALES (est): 1.37MM **Privately Held**
Web: www.integratedmfg.net
SIC: 3999 Chairs, hydraulic, barber and beauty shop

(P-8687)
JACUZZI BRANDS LLC
Also Called: Sundance Spas
14525 Monte Vista Ave, Chino
(91710-5721)
P.O. Box 2900 (91708-2900)
PHONE..............................909 606-1416
Diana Fox, *Mgr*
EMP: 41
SALES (corp-wide): 430.34K **Privately Held**
Web: www.jacuzzi.com

SIC: 3999 Hot tubs
HQ: Jacuzzi Brands Llc
17872 Gllette Ave Ste 300
Irvine CA 92614
909 606-1416

(P-8688)
JOE BLASCO ENTERPRISES INC
Also Called: Joe Blasco Cosmetics
1285 N Valdivia Way # A, Palm Springs
(92262-5428)
PHONE..............................323 467-4949
Joseph D Blasco, *Pr*
▲ **EMP:** 38 **EST:** 1986
SQ FT: 13,788
SALES (est): 346.06K
SALES (corp-wide): 787.09K **Privately Held**
Web: www.joeblasco.com
SIC: 3999 7231 2844 Barber and beauty shop equipment; Cosmetology school; Perfumes, cosmetics and other toilet preparations
PA: Joe Blasco Make-Up Center West, Inc.
1285 N Valdivia Way # A
323 467-4949

(P-8689)
K31 ROAD ENGINEERING LLC
Also Called: K31
1968 S Coast Hwy Pmb 593, Laguna Beach
(92651-3681)
PHONE..............................305 928-1968
Rainer Piel, *CEO*
EMP: 35 **EST:** 2014
SALES (est): 212.55K **Privately Held**
Web: www.k31.org
SIC: 3999 5039 Manufacturing industries, nec; Construction materials, nec

(P-8690)
KURZ TRANSFER PRODUCTS LP
415 N Smith Ave, Corona (92878-4305)
PHONE..............................951 738-9521
Hastings Kurz, *Prin*
EMP: 65
SALES (corp-wide): 1B **Privately Held**
Web: www.kurzusa.com
SIC: 3999 Atomizers, toiletry
HQ: Kurz Transfer Products, Lp
11836 Patterson Rd
Huntersville NC 28078
704 927-3700

(P-8691)
LA SPAS INC
1325 N Blue Gum St, Anaheim
(92806-1750)
PHONE..............................714 630-1150
▲ **EMP:** 130
Web: www.maaxspas.com
SIC: 3999 5091 Hot tubs; Fitness equipment and supplies

(P-8692)
LEOBEN COMPANY
16692 Burke Ln, Huntington Beach
(92647-4536)
PHONE..............................951 284-9653
Samir Tabikha, *Pr*
EMP: 26 **EST:** 2017
SALES (est): 3.65MM **Privately Held**
Web: www.leobenco.com
SIC: 3999 Barber and beauty shop equipment

(P-8693)
LEXOR INC
7400 Hazard Ave, Westminster
(92683-5031)
PHONE..............................714 444-4144
Marianna Magos, *CEO*
Christopher L Long, *
▲ **EMP:** 90 **EST:** 2007
SALES (est): 5.28MM **Privately Held**
Web: www.lexor.com
SIC: 3999 Chairs, hydraulic, barber and beauty shop

(P-8694)
LMS
1462 E 9th St, Pomona (91766-3833)
PHONE..............................909 623-8781
George R Phillips Junior, *Admn*
EMP: 26 **EST:** 2016
SALES (est): 6.34MM **Privately Held**
SIC: 3999 Manufacturing industries, nec

(P-8695)
MACS LIFT GATE INC (PA)
2801 E South St, Long Beach
(90805-3736)
PHONE..............................562 529-3465
Michael Macdonald, *CEO*
Richard Mac Donald, *
Lawrence Mac Donald, *
Gerald J Donald Mac, *VP*
EMP: 24 **EST:** 1957
SALES (est): 4.96MM
SALES (corp-wide): 4.96MM **Privately Held**
Web: www.macsliftgate.com
SIC: 3999 5013 Wheelchair lifts; Motor vehicle supplies and new parts

(P-8696)
MADE IN LOVE DGGY CTURE THRAPY
3946 Ceanothus Pl, Calabasas
(91302-2909)
PHONE..............................805 410-0774
Alison Ungaro, *CEO*
James Pugliese, *
Gwenyth Ungaro Ad, *Sec*
EMP: 60 **EST:** 2021
SALES (est): 1.36MM **Privately Held**
SIC: 3999 Pet supplies

(P-8697)
MANUFACTURED SOLUTIONS LLC
9601 Janice Cir, Villa Park (92861-2705)
PHONE..............................714 548-6915
Marcela Cortes, *Pr*
EMP: 40 **EST:** 2020
SALES (est): 2.21MM **Privately Held**
SIC: 3999 3444 Manufacturing industries, nec; Sheet metalwork

(P-8698)
MARCH PRODUCTS INC
Also Called: Astella
4645 Troy Ct, Jurupa Valley (92509-2003)
PHONE..............................909 622-4800
Yungcheng Ma, *Pr*
◆ **EMP:** 72 **EST:** 2001
SQ FT: 70,000
SALES (est): 17.5MM **Privately Held**
Web: www.californiaumbrella.com
SIC: 3999 2211 Umbrellas, garden or wagon ; Umbrella cloth, cotton

(P-8699)
MEDICAL BRKTHRUGH MSSAGE CHIRS

Also Called: Alicorns
24971 Avenue Stanford, Valencia
(91355-1278)
PHONE..............................408 677-7702
Max Lun, *CEO*
EMP: 24 **EST:** 2016
SALES (est): 6.01MM **Privately Held**
Web: www.medicalbreakthrough.org
SIC: 3999 Massage machines, electric: barber and beauty shops

(P-8700)
MERCADO LATINO INC
Continental Candle Company
1420 W Walnut St, Compton (90220-5013)
PHONE..............................310 537-1062
EMP: 63
SALES (corp-wide): 32.57MM **Privately Held**
Web: www.continentalcandle.com
SIC: 3999 3641 7699 3645 Candles; Electric lamps; Restaurant equipment repair; Residential lighting fixtures
PA: Mercado Latino, Inc.
245 Baldwin Park Blvd
626 333-6862

(P-8701)
MGR DESIGN INTERNATIONAL INC
1950 Williams Dr, Oxnard (93036-2630)
PHONE..............................805 981-6400
Rony Haviv, *CEO*
◆ **EMP:** 200 **EST:** 2001
SQ FT: 80,000
SALES (est): 8.77MM **Privately Held**
Web: www.mgrdesign.com
SIC: 3999 Potpourri

(P-8702)
NANO FILTER INC
22310 Bonita St, Carson (90745-4103)
PHONE..............................949 316-8866
Bennett Koo, *Pr*
EMP: 60 **EST:** 2020
SALES (est): 394.96K **Privately Held**
SIC: 3999 Manufacturing industries, nec

(P-8703)
NEIGHBRHOOD BUS ADVRTSMENT LTD
14752 Crenshaw Blvd, Gardena
(90249-3602)
PHONE..............................442 300-1803
EMP: 26 **EST:** 2022
SALES (est): 437.13K **Privately Held**
SIC: 3999 Advertising display products

(P-8704)
NEW DIMENSION ONE SPAS INC (DH)
1819 Aston Ave Ste 105, Carlsbad
(92008-7338)
P.O. Box 2600 (92051-2600)
PHONE..............................800 345-7727
Robert Hallam, *Pr*
Linda Hallam, *
Chris Theriot, *CIO**
Phil Sandner, *PROC**
Terry Hauser, *
◆ **EMP:** 160 **EST:** 1977
SQ FT: 125,000
SALES (est): 9.59MM
SALES (corp-wide): 430.34K **Privately Held**
Web: www.d1spas.com
SIC: 3999 3088 Hot tubs; Plastics plumbing fixtures
HQ: Jacuzzi Brands Llc
17872 Gllette Ave Ste 300

▲ = Import ▼ = Export
◆ = Import/Export

Irvine CA 92614
909 606-1416

(P-8705)
NORLAINE INC
Also Called: Patina V
1449 W Industrial Park St, Covina
(91722-3414)
PHONE..............................626 961-2471
◆ **EMP:** 200
Web: www.cnl-patina-v.com
SIC: 3999 Mannequins

(P-8706)
ON PREMISE PRODUCTS INC
8021 Wing Ave, El Cajon (92020-1245)
PHONE..............................619 562-1486
Michael Barnhill, *Pr*
EMP: 30 **EST:** 2018
SALES (est): 814.64K **Privately Held**
Web: www.onpremiseproducts.com
SIC: 3999 Manufacturing industries, nec

(P-8707)
ORIGIN LLC
119 E Graham Pl, Burbank (91502-2028)
PHONE..............................818 848-1648
▲ **EMP:** 35
SIC: 3999 Advertising display products

(P-8708)
PACIFICA BEAUTY LLC
Also Called: Pacifica International
1090 Eugenia Pl Ste 200, Carpinteria
(93013-2011)
PHONE..............................844 332-8440
Brook Harvey Taylor, *CEO*
▲ **EMP:** 100 **EST:** 1997
SQ FT: 58,000
SALES (est): 9.74MM **Privately Held**
Web: www.pacificabeauty.com
SIC: 3999 2844 Candles; Perfumes,
cosmetics and other toilet preparations

(P-8709)
PACMIN INCORPORATED (PA)
Also Called: Pacific Miniatures
2021 Raymer Ave, Fullerton (92833-2664)
PHONE..............................714 447-4478
Frederick Ouweleen Junior, *Pr*
Flora Ouweleen, *
Daniel Ouweleen, *
▲ **EMP:** 91 **EST:** 1981
SQ FT: 35,400
SALES (est): 10.66MM
SALES (corp-wide): 10.66MM **Privately
Held**
Web: www.pacmin.com
SIC: 3999 Models, general, except toy

(P-8710)
PAUL FERRANTE INC
Also Called: Ferrante Paul Cstm Lmps & Shds
8464 Melrose Pl, West Hollywood
(90069-5388)
PHONE..............................310 854-4412
Thomas Raynor, *Pr*
▲ **EMP:** 40 **EST:** 1962
SQ FT: 2,000
SALES (est): 2.48MM **Privately Held**
Web: www.paulferrante.com
SIC: 3999 5099 3645 Shades, lamp or
candle; Antiques; Residential lighting
fixtures

(P-8711)
PCI INDUSTRIES INC
700 S Vail Ave, Montebello (90640-4954)
PHONE..............................323 889-6770

Jack Scilley, *Owner*
EMP: 27
SALES (corp-wide): 45.1MM **Privately
Held**
Web: www.pottorff.com
SIC: 3999 Atomizers, toiletry
PA: Pci Industries, Inc.
5101 Blue Mound Rd
817 509-2300

(P-8712)
PCI INDUSTRIES INC
6490 Fleet St, Commerce (90040-1710)
PHONE..............................323 728-0004
Jim Turner, *Mgr*
EMP: 27
SALES (corp-wide): 45.1MM **Privately
Held**
Web: www.pottorff.com
SIC: 3999 Atomizers, toiletry
PA: Pci Industries, Inc.
5101 Blue Mound Rd
817 509-2300

(P-8713)
PERFECT CHOICE MFRS INC
Also Called: West Coast Metal Stamping
17819 Gillette Ave, Irvine (92614-6501)
PHONE..............................714 792-0322
Kevin Price, *CEO*
EMP: 42 **EST:** 2021
SALES (est): 2.85MM **Privately Held**
SIC: 3999 Manufacturing industries, nec

(P-8714)
PET PARTNERS INC (PA)
Also Called: North American Pet Products
450 N Sheridan St, Corona (92878-4020)
PHONE..............................951 279-9888
Keith Bonner, *CEO*
Ronald Bonner, *
Gordan Thulemeyer, *
Gloria Bonner, *
▲ **EMP:** 170 **EST:** 1995
SQ FT: 120,000
SALES (est): 22.46MM **Privately Held**
Web: www.petpartners.org
SIC: 3999 Pet supplies

(P-8715)
PHIARO INCORPORATED
9016 Research Dr, Irvine (92618-4215)
PHONE..............................949 727-1261
Takeichiro Iwasaki, *Pr*
▲ **EMP:** 32 **EST:** 1988
SQ FT: 35,000
SALES (est): 7.97MM **Privately Held**
Web: www.phiaro.jp
SIC: 3999 Models, general, except toy
PA: Phiaro Corporation, Inc.
8-2-3, Nohitome

(P-8716)
PICNIC TIME INC
Also Called: Beach State
5131 Maureen Ln, Moorpark (93021-1783)
PHONE..............................805 529-7400
Paul Cosaro, *CEO*
Gustavo Cosaro, *
◆ **EMP:** 77 **EST:** 1982
SQ FT: 20,000
SALES (est): 9.93MM **Privately Held**
Web: www.picnictime.com
SIC: 3999 5199 Handles, handbag and
luggage; Bags, baskets, and cases

(P-8717)
POMMES FRITES CANDLE CO
Also Called: Pf Candle Co
7300 E Slauson Ave, Commerce
(90040-3627)

PHONE..............................213 488-2016
Kristen Pumphrey, *CEO*
Thomas Neuberger, *
EMP: 30 **EST:** 2014
SALES (est): 4.79MM **Privately Held**
Web: www.pfcandleco.com
SIC: 3999 5149 5199 5999 Candles;
Flavorings and fragrances; Candles;
Candle shops

(P-8718)
PRESERVED TREESCAPES
INTERNATIONAL INC
Also Called: Preserved Treescapes Intl
180 Vallecitos De Oro, San Marcos
(92069-1435)
PHONE..............................760 631-6789
◆ **EMP:** 75
Web: www.treescapes.com
SIC: 3999 Artificial trees and flowers

(P-8719)
REEL EFX INC
5539 Riverton Ave, North Hollywood
(91601-2816)
PHONE..............................818 762-1710
Jim Gill, *Pr*
Susan Gill, *
Rosy Romano, *
Susan Milliken, *
EMP: 25 **EST:** 1982
SQ FT: 34,000
SALES (est): 5.39MM **Privately Held**
Web: www.reelefx.com
SIC: 3999 Stage hardware and equipment,
except lighting

(P-8720)
RICON CORPORATION
1135 Aviation Pl, San Fernando
(91340-1460)
PHONE..............................818 267-3000
William Baldwin, *Pr*
◆ **EMP:** 135 **EST:** 1971
SQ FT: 225,000
SALES (est): 22.28MM **Publicly Held**
Web: www.riconcorp.com
SIC: 3999 Wheelchair lifts
PA: Westinghouse Air Brake Technologies
Corporation
30 Isabella St

(P-8721)
SCRIPTO-TOKAI CORPORATION
(HQ)
2055 S Haven Ave, Ontario (91761-0736)
PHONE..............................909 930-5000
Tomoyuki Kurata, *Pr*
Tokiharu Murofushi, *
Fred Ashley, *
▲ **EMP:** 80 **EST:** 1923
SQ FT: 120,000
SALES (est): 3.88MM **Privately Held**
Web: www.calicobrands.com
SIC: 3999 3951 Cigarette lighters, except
precious metal; Ball point pens and parts
PA: Tokai Corporation
6-21-1, Nishishinjuku

(P-8722)
SEGA HOLDINGS USA INC
9737 Lurline Ave, Chatsworth (91311-4404)
PHONE..............................415 701-6000
◆ **EMP:** 1880
SIC: 3999 5045 Coin-operated amusement
machines; Computers and accessories,
personal and home entertainment

(P-8723)
SGPS INC
Also Called: Show Group Production Services
15823 S Main St, Gardena (90248-2548)
PHONE..............................310 538-4175
Barrie Owen, *CEO*
Katy Marx, *
EMP: 85 **EST:** 1991
SQ FT: 40,000
SALES (est): 8.99MM **Privately Held**
Web: www.sgpsshowrig.com
SIC: 3999 Theatrical scenery

(P-8724)
SHAPELL INDUSTRIES
1990 S Bundy Dr Ste 500, Los Angeles
(90025-5245)
PHONE..............................323 655-7330
EMP: 86 **EST:** 2018
SALES (est): 1.82MM **Privately Held**
Web: www.shapell.com
SIC: 3999 Manufacturing industries, nec

(P-8725)
SILVESTRI STUDIO INC (PA)
Also Called: Silvester California
8125 Beach St, Los Angeles (90001-3426)
P.O. Box P.O. Box 512198 (90061)
PHONE..............................323 277-4420
E Alain Levi, *CEO*
▲ **EMP:** 80 **EST:** 1934
SQ FT: 130,000
SALES (est): 4.61MM
SALES (corp-wide): 4.61MM **Privately
Held**
Web: www.silvestricalifornia.com
SIC: 3999 2542 3993 Mannequins; Office
and store showcases and display fixtures;
Signs and advertising specialties

(P-8726)
SOFTUB INC (PA)
24700 Avenue Rockefeller, Valencia
(91355-3465)
PHONE..............................858 602-1920
Randal Sheldon, *CEO*
Tom Thornbury, *
▲ **EMP:** 85 **EST:** 1983
SALES (est): 27.1MM
SALES (corp-wide): 27.1MM **Privately
Held**
Web: www.softub.com
SIC: 3999 Hot tubs

(P-8727)
SPARKS EXHBITS
ENVRNMENTS CORP
Also Called: Sparks Los Angeles
3143 S La Cienega Blvd, Los Angeles
(90016-3110)
PHONE..............................562 941-0101
EMP: 42
SALES (corp-wide): 1.56B **Privately Held**
Web: www.wearesparks.com
SIC: 3999 Advertising display products
HQ: Sparks Exhibits & Environments Pa Llc
2828 Charter Rd
Philadelphia PA 19154
215 676-1100

(P-8728)
STEELDECK INC
13147 S Western Ave, Gardena
(90249-1921)
PHONE..............................323 290-2100
Phil Parsons, *Pr*
Adrian Funnell, *
▲ **EMP:** 25 **EST:** 1993
SALES (est): 2.54MM **Privately Held**
Web: www.steeldeck.com

P
R
O
D
U
C
T
S
&
S
V
C
S

SIC: 3999 2541 2531 Stage hardware and equipment, except lighting; Partitions for floor attachment, prefabricated: wood; Theater furniture

(P-8729)
SUN BADGE CO
2248 S Baker Ave, Ontario (91761-7710)
PHONE....................909 930-1444
Rick Hamilton, *Pr*
Chris Hamilton, *
▲ EMP: 35 EST: 1957
SQ FT: 24,000
SALES (est): 2.33MM **Privately Held**
Web: www.sunbadgeorders.com
SIC: 3999 Badges, metal: policemen, firemen, etc.

(P-8730)
SUNDANCE SPAS INC (DH)
Also Called: Sundance Spas
17872 Gillette Ave Ste 300, Irvine (92614-6573)
PHONE....................909 606-7733
David Jackson, *CEO*
Rich Strong, *
Jason Weintraub, *
◆ EMP: 73 EST: 1998
SALES (est): 18.65MM
SALES (corp-wide): 430.34K **Privately Held**
Web: www.sundancespas.com
SIC: 3999 1799 5999 Hot tubs; Swimming pool construction; Spas and hot tubs
HQ: Jacuzzi Brands Llc
17872 Gllette Ave Ste 300
Irvine CA 92614
909 606-1416

(P-8731)
SUNSTAR SPA COVERS INC (HQ)
26074 Avenue Hall Ste 13, Valencia (91355-3445)
PHONE....................858 602-1950
Tom Thornbury, *Ch Bd*
Edward Mcgarry, *Pr*
▲ EMP: 40 EST: 2000
SALES (est): 2.48MM
SALES (corp-wide): 27.1MM **Privately Held**
SIC: 3999 Hot tub and spa covers
PA: Softub, Inc.
24700 Ave Rockefeller
858 602-1920

(P-8732)
TAG TOYS INC
1810 S Acacia Ave, Compton (90220-4927)
PHONE....................310 639-4566
Lawrence Mestyanek, *CEO*
Judy Mestyanek, *
EMP: 65 EST: 1976
SQ FT: 60,000
SALES (est): 4.71MM **Privately Held**
Web: www.tagtoys.com
SIC: 3999 8351 3944 Education aids, devices and supplies; Child day care services; Games, toys, and children's vehicles

(P-8733)
TANDEM DESIGN INC
Also Called: Tandem Exhibit
1916 W 144th St, Gardena (90249-2928)
PHONE....................714 978-7272
Maury Bonas, *Pr*
Susan Bonas, *VP*
EMP: 23 EST: 1975
SALES (est): 1.41MM **Privately Held**

Web: www.presentationmedia.com
SIC: 3999 Preparation of slides and exhibits

(P-8734)
TECHNICAL MANUFACTURING W LLC
24820 Avenue Tibbitts, Valencia (91355-3404)
PHONE....................661 295-7226
EMP: 28 EST: 2010
SALES (est): 3.64MM **Privately Held**
Web: www.tmwmedical.com
SIC: 3999 Barber and beauty shop equipment

(P-8735)
TOWER 26 INC
8826 Bradley Ave Ste B, Sun Valley (91352-2703)
PHONE....................347 366-2706
Alexey Shkavrov, *CEO*
Eric Gersh, *
EMP: 30 EST: 2016
SALES (est): 741.78K **Privately Held**
Web: tower26official.com
SIC: 3999

(P-8736)
TRAXX CORPORATION
1201 E Lexington Ave, Pomona (91766-5520)
PHONE....................909 623-8032
Craig Silvers, *CEO*
Jon Hall, *
▲ EMP: 100 EST: 2007
SQ FT: 52,000
SALES (est): 2.78MM **Privately Held**
Web: www.traxxcorp.com
SIC: 3999 Carpet tackles

(P-8737)
TRNLWB LLC
Also Called: Trinity Lighweight
17410 Lockwood Valley Rd, Frazier Park (93225-9318)
PHONE....................661 245-3736
EMP: 4900
SALES (corp-wide): 21.91MM **Privately Held**
Web: www.trinityesc.com
SIC: 3999 Barber and beauty shop equipment
PA: Trnlwb, Llc
1112 E Cpeland Rd Ste 500
800 581-3117

(P-8738)
VAL USA MANUFACTURER INC
1050 W Central Ave Ste A, Brea (92821-2200)
PHONE....................626 839-8069
Lijuan Zhen, *Mgr*
▲ EMP: 30 EST: 2014
SALES (est): 1.84MM **Privately Held**
Web: www.valcosmetics.com
SIC: 3999 Manufacturing industries, nec

(P-8739)
WALLY & PAT ENTERPRISES
Also Called: Complete Aquatic Systems
13530 S Budlong Ave, Gardena (90247-2030)
PHONE....................310 532-2031
Shareen King, *Pr*
EMP: 48 EST: 2000
SALES (est): 4.72MM **Privately Held**
Web: www.completeaquaticsystems.com
SIC: 3999 Barber and beauty shop equipment

(P-8740)
WATKINS MANUFACTURING CORP (HQ)
Also Called: Watkins Wellness
1280 Park Center Dr, Vista (92081-8398)
PHONE....................760 598-6464
Vijaikrishna Teenarsipur, *CEO*
Christopher Peavey, *
◆ EMP: 127 EST: 1977
SQ FT: 430,000
SALES (est): 164.33MM
SALES (corp-wide): 7.97B **Publicly Held**
Web: www.hotspring.com
SIC: 3999 Hot tubs
PA: Masco Corporation
17450 College Pkwy
313 274-7400

(P-8741)
WBT GROUP LLC
Also Called: Wbt Industries
1401 S Shamrock Ave, Monrovia (91016-4246)
PHONE....................323 735-1201
▲ EMP: 40 EST: 2009
SALES (est): 4.44MM **Privately Held**
Web: www.wbtindustries.com
SIC: 3999 Buttons: Red Cross, union, identification

(P-8742)
WOOD CANDLE WICK TECH INC
Also Called: Makesy
9750 Irvine Blvd Ste 106, Irvine (92618-1676)
PHONE....................310 488-5885
Dayna Marie Decker, *CEO*
EMP: 31 EST: 2015
SALES (est): 6.38MM **Privately Held**
SIC: 3999 Candles

(P-8743)
ZOO MED LABORATORIES INC
3650 Sacramento Dr, San Luis Obispo (93401-7113)
PHONE....................805 542-9988
▲ EMP: 133 EST: 1977
SALES (est): 11.15MM **Privately Held**
Web: www.zoomed.com
SIC: 3999 5199 Pet supplies; Pets and pet supplies

4011 Railroads, Line-haul Operating

(P-8744)
TRONA RAILWAY COMPANY
13068 Main St, Trona (93562-1911)
PHONE....................760 372-2312
EMP: 365 EST: 1913
SQ FT: 30,000
SALES (est): 2.49MM **Privately Held**
SIC: 4011 Railroads, line-haul operating
HQ: Searles Valley Minerals Inc.
9401 Indian Creek Pkwy
Overland Park KS 66210

(P-8745)
UNION PACIFIC RAILROAD COMPANY
Also Called: Union Pacific Lines
2401 E Sepulveda Blvd, Long Beach (90810-1945)
PHONE....................562 490-7000
Herman Madden, *Superintnt*
EMP: 300
SALES (corp-wide): 24.12B **Publicly Held**
Web: www.up.com

SIC: 4011 Railroads, line-haul operating
HQ: Union Pacific Railroad Company Inc
1400 Douglas St
Omaha NE 68179
402 544-5000

4111 Local And Suburban Transit

(P-8746)
ACCESS SERVICES
Also Called: ACCESS PARATRANSIT
3449 Santa Anita Ave, El Monte (91731-2424)
P.O. Box 5728 (91734-1728)
PHONE....................213 270-6000
Doran J Barnes, *CEO*
Shelly Verrinder, *
EMP: 80 EST: 1994
SALES (est): 176.28MM **Privately Held**
Web: www.accessla.org
SIC: 4111 Local and suburban transit

(P-8747)
AIRPORT CONNECTION INC
Also Called: Roadrunner Shuttle
95 Dawson Dr, Camarillo (93012-8001)
PHONE....................805 389-8196
Sumaia Sandlin, *CEO*
Desmond P Sandlin, *
EMP: 180 EST: 1991
SQ FT: 3,500
SALES (est): 4.31MM **Privately Held**
SIC: 4111 4119 Airport transportation; Limousine rental, with driver

(P-8748)
CALIFORNIA TRANSIT INC
1900 S Alameda St, Vernon (90058-1014)
PHONE....................323 234-8750
Timmy Mardirossian, *Pr*
Eda Aghajanian, *
Carol Story, *
Sedik Mardirossian, *
EMP: 71 EST: 2008
SALES (est): 2.12MM
SALES (corp-wide): 15.23MM **Privately Held**
SIC: 4111 Bus line operations
PA: San Gabriel Transit, Inc.
3650 Rockwell Ave
626 258-1310

(P-8749)
FIRST TRANSIT INC
4337 Rowland Ave, El Monte (91731-1119)
PHONE....................626 307-7842
Kenneth Beard, *Mgr*
EMP: 98
SALES (corp-wide): 4.23MM **Privately Held**
Web: www.transdevna.com
SIC: 4111 Local and suburban transit
HQ: First Transit, Inc.
720 E Bttrfeld Rd Ste 300
Lombard IL 60148
800 225-8880

(P-8750)
FIRST TRANSIT INC
Also Called: First Group
1213 W Arbor Vitae St, Inglewood (90301-2903)
PHONE....................310 216-9584
EMP: 98
SALES (corp-wide): 4.23MM **Privately Held**
Web: www.firststudentinc.com

▲ = Import ▼ = Export
◆ = Import/Export

SIC: 4111 Local and suburban transit
HQ: First Transit, Inc.
720 E Bttrfeld Rd Ste 300
Lombard IL 60148
800 225-8880

(P-8751)
FIRST TRANSIT INC
15730 S Figueroa St, Gardena
(90248-2429)
P.O. Box Figueroa (90248)
PHONE...............................323 222-0010
John Britt, *Brnch Mgr*
EMP: 98
SALES (corp-wide): 4.23MM **Privately Held**
Web: www.transdevna.com
SIC: 4111 Local and suburban transit
HQ: First Transit, Inc.
720 E Bttrfeld Rd Ste 300
Lombard IL 60148
800 225-8880

(P-8752)
FIRST TRANSIT INC
29 Prado Rd, San Luis Obispo
(93401-7314)
PHONE...............................805 544-2730
Kim Blakeman, *Mgr*
EMP: 180
SALES (corp-wide): 4.23MM **Privately Held**
Web: www.transdevna.com
SIC: 4111 Bus transportation
HQ: First Transit, Inc.
720 E Bttrfeld Rd Ste 300
Lombard IL 60148
800 225-8880.

(P-8753)
FIRST TRANSIT INC
9421 Feron Blvd Ste 101, Rancho
Cucamonga (91730-4575)
PHONE...............................909 948-3474
EMP: 82
SALES (corp-wide): 4.23MM **Privately Held**
Web: www.transdevna.com
SIC: 4111 Local and suburban transit
HQ: First Transit, Inc.
720 E Bttrfeld Rd Ste 300
Lombard IL 60148
800 225-8880

(P-8754)
FIRST TRANSIT INC
1717 E Via Burton, Anaheim (92806-1212)
PHONE...............................714 644-9828
EMP: 82
SALES (corp-wide): 4.23MM **Privately Held**
Web: www.transdevna.com
SIC: 4111 Local and suburban transit
HQ: First Transit, Inc.
720 E Bttrfeld Rd Ste 300
Lombard IL 60148
800 225-8880

(P-8755)
FORREST GROUP LLC (PA)
Also Called: Fly On My Jet
1422 N Curson Ave Apt 9, Los Angeles
(90046-4037)
PHONE...............................619 808-9798
Allen Forrest, *CEO*
EMP: 64 EST: 2016
SALES (est): 2.66MM
SALES (corp-wide): 2.66MM **Privately Held**
Web: www.tfgla.com

SIC: 4111 8742 7319 3532 Airport
transportation; Food and beverage
consultant; Display advertising service;
Shuttle cars, underground

(P-8756)
GOLDEN EMPIRE TRANSIT DISTRICT (PA)
Also Called: Get-A-Lift Handicap Bus Trnsp
1830 Golden State Ave, Bakersfield
(93301-1012)
PHONE...............................661 869-2438
Steven Woods, *CEO*
Karen King, *
EMP: 232 EST: 1973
SALES (est): 14.76MM
SALES (corp-wide): 14.76MM **Privately Held**
Web: www.getbus.org
SIC: 4111 Bus line operations

(P-8757)
KEOLIS TRANSIT AMERICA INC
14663 Keswick St, Van Nuys (91405-1204)
PHONE...............................818 616-5254
Steve Shaw, *Pr*
EMP: 175
SALES (corp-wide): 4.23MM **Privately Held**
Web: www.keolistransit.com
SIC: 4111 Local and suburban transit
HQ: Keolis Transit America, Inc.
53 State St Fl 11
Boston MA 02109

(P-8758)
KEOLIS TRANSIT AMERICA INC
660 W Avenue L, Lancaster (93534-7117)
PHONE...............................661 341-3910
Steve Shaw, *Pr*
EMP: 90
SALES (corp-wide): 4.23MM **Privately Held**
Web: www.keolistransit.com
SIC: 4111 Local and suburban transit
HQ: Keolis Transit America, Inc.
53 State St Fl 11
Boston MA 02109

(P-8759)
LONG BEACH PUBLIC TRNSP CO
1300 Gardenia Ave, Long Beach
(90804-3220)
PHONE...............................562 591-2301
Laurence Jackson, *Brnch Mgr*
EMP: 80
SALES (corp-wide): 43.28MM **Privately Held**
Web: www.ridelbt.com
SIC: 4111 Bus line operations
PA: Long Beach Public Transportation Co
Inc
1963 E Anaheim St
562 599-8571

(P-8760)
LONG BEACH PUBLIC TRNSP CO (PA)
Also Called: Long Beach Transit
1963 E Anaheim St, Long Beach
(90813-3907)
PHONE...............................562 599-8571
Kenneth A Mcdonald, *CEO*
Kenneth A Mcdonald, *CEO*
Laurence W Jackson, *
EMP: 570 EST: 1963
SQ FT: 10,000
SALES (est): 57.81MM

SALES (corp-wide): 57.81MM **Privately Held**
Web: www.ridelbt.com
SIC: 4111 Local and suburban transit

(P-8761)
LOS ANGLES CNTY MTRO TRNSP AUT (PA)
Also Called: Metro
1 Gateway Plz Fl 25, Los Angeles
(90012-3745)
P.O. Box 512296 (90051-0296)
PHONE...............................323 466-3876
Stephanie Wiggins, *CEO*
Rick Thorpe, *
Nalini Ahuja, *
Brian Boudreau, *
Greg Kildare, *
EMP: 900 EST: 1964
SALES (est): 461.7MM
SALES (corp-wide): 461.7MM **Privately Held**
Web: www.metro.net
SIC: 4111 Local and suburban transit

(P-8762)
LOS ANGLES CNTY MTRO TRNSP AUT
Also Called: Green Line Rail Eqp Maint
14724 Aviation Blvd, Lawndale
(90260-1122)
PHONE...............................310 643-3804
Ed Smith, *Mgr*
EMP: 362
SALES (corp-wide): 461.7MM **Privately Held**
Web: www.metro.net
SIC: 4111 Local and suburban transit
PA: Los Angeles County Metropolitan
Transportation Authority
1 Gateway Plz Fl 25
323 466-3876

(P-8763)
LOS ANGLES CNTY MTRO TRNSP AUT
9201 Canoga Ave, Chatsworth
(91311-5839)
PHONE...............................213 922-6308
Pat Orr, *Mgr*
EMP: 724
SALES (corp-wide): 461.7MM **Privately Held**
Web: www.metro.net
SIC: 4111 Bus line operations
PA: Los Angeles County Metropolitan
Transportation Authority
1 Gateway Plz Fl 25
323 466-3876

(P-8764)
LOS ANGLES CNTY MTRO TRNSP AUT
900 Lyon St, Los Angeles (90012-2913)
PHONE...............................213 922-5887
John Drayton, *Mgr*
EMP: 362
SALES (corp-wide): 461.7MM **Privately Held**
Web: www.metro.net
SIC: 4111 Bus line operations
PA: Los Angeles County Metropolitan
Transportation Authority
1 Gateway Plz Fl 25
323 466-3876

(P-8765)
LOS ANGLES CNTY MTRO TRNSP AUT

Also Called: Division 1
1130 E 6th St, Los Angeles (90021-1108)
PHONE...............................213 922-6301
Ron Reedy, *Brnch Mgr*
EMP: 363
SALES (corp-wide): 461.7MM **Privately Held**
Web: www.metro.net
SIC: 4111 Bus line operations
PA: Los Angeles County Metropolitan
Transportation Authority
1 Gateway Plz Fl 25
323 466-3876

(P-8766)
LOS ANGLES CNTY MTRO TRNSP AUT
630 W Avenue 28, Los Angeles
(90065-1502)
PHONE...............................213 922-6203
Cheryl Brown, *Mgr*
EMP: 363
SALES (corp-wide): 461.7MM **Privately Held**
Web: www.metro.net
SIC: 4111 Bus line operations
PA: Los Angeles County Metropolitan
Transportation Authority
1 Gateway Plz Fl 25
323 466-3876

(P-8767)
LOS ANGLES CNTY MTRO TRNSP AUT
1 Gateway Plz, Los Angeles (90012-3745)
PHONE...............................213 922-6202
Maria Japardi, *Brnch Mgr*
EMP: 544
SALES (corp-wide): 461.7MM **Privately Held**
Web: www.metro.net
SIC: 4111 Bus line operations
PA: Los Angeles County Metropolitan
Transportation Authority
1 Gateway Plz Fl 25
323 466-3876

(P-8768)
LOS ANGLES CNTY MTRO TRNSP AUT
8800 Santa Monica Blvd, Los Angeles
(90069-4536)
PHONE...............................213 922-6207
Grant Myers, *Mgr*
EMP: 363
SALES (corp-wide): 461.7MM **Privately Held**
Web: www.metro.net
SIC: 4111 Bus line operations
PA: Los Angeles County Metropolitan
Transportation Authority
1 Gateway Plz Fl 25
323 466-3876

(P-8769)
LOS ANGLES CNTY MTRO TRNSP AUT
Also Called: Metro
11900 Branford St, Sun Valley
(91352-1003)
PHONE...............................213 922-6215
Gary Stivack, *Mgr*
EMP: 906
SALES (corp-wide): 461.7MM **Privately Held**
Web: www.metro.net
SIC: 4111 Bus line operations
PA: Los Angeles County Metropolitan
Transportation Authority
1 Gateway Plz Fl 25

323 466-3876

(P-8770)
LOS ANGLES CNTY MTRO
TRNSP AUT
Also Called: Metro
720 E 15th St, Los Angeles (90021-2122)
PHONE...................213 533-1506
Carla Aleman, *Brnch Mgr*
EMP: 544
SALES (corp-wide): 461.7MM **Privately Held**
Web: www.metro.net
SIC: 4111 Bus line operations
PA: Los Angeles County Metropolitan
    Transportation Authority
    1 Gateway Plz Fl 25
    323 466-3876

(P-8771)
LOS ANGLES CNTY MTRO
TRNSP AUT
Also Called: Lacmta
470 Bauchet St, Los Angeles (90012-2907)
PHONE...................213 922-5012
Jim Montoya, *Brnch Mgr*
EMP: 1994
SALES (corp-wide): 461.7MM **Privately Held**
Web: www.metro.net
SIC: 4111 Bus transportation
PA: Los Angeles County Metropolitan
    Transportation Authority
    1 Gateway Plz Fl 25
    323 466-3876

(P-8772)
LOS ANGLES CNTY MTRO
TRNSP AUT
Also Called: Division 7
100 Sunset Ave, Venice (90291-2517)
PHONE...................310 392-8636
John Adams, *Mgr*
EMP: 363
SALES (corp-wide): 461.7MM **Privately Held**
Web: www.metro.net
SIC: 4111 Bus transportation
PA: Los Angeles County Metropolitan
    Transportation Authority
    1 Gateway Plz Fl 25
    323 466-3876

(P-8773)
LOS ANGLES CNTY MTRO
TRNSP AUT
Also Called: Office of Inspector General
818 W 7th St Ste 500, Los Angeles
(90017-3463)
PHONE...................213 244-6783
Arthur Sinai, *Mgr*
EMP: 363
SALES (corp-wide): 461.7MM **Privately Held**
Web: www.metro.net
SIC: 4111 Bus line operations
PA: Los Angeles County Metropolitan
    Transportation Authority
    1 Gateway Plz Fl 25
    323 466-3876

(P-8774)
LOS ANGLES CNTY MTRO
TRNSP AUT
1600 S California Ave, Monrovia
(91016-4622)
PHONE...................626 471-7855
EMP: 906
SALES (corp-wide): 461.7MM **Privately Held**

SIC: 4111 Local and suburban transit
PA: Los Angeles County Metropolitan
    Transportation Authority
    1 Gateway Plz Fl 25
    323 466-3876

(P-8775)
LOS ANGLES CNTY MTRO
TRNSP AUT
320 S Santa Fe Ave, Los Angeles
(90013-1812)
P.O. Box 194 (90078-0194)
PHONE...................213 626-4455
Julian Burke, *CEO*
EMP: 725
SALES (corp-wide): 461.7MM **Privately Held**
Web: www.metro.net
SIC: 4111 Bus line operations
PA: Los Angeles County Metropolitan
    Transportation Authority
    1 Gateway Plz Fl 25
    323 466-3876

(P-8776)
MV TRANSPORTATION INC
1242 Los Angeles St, Glendale
(91204-2404)
PHONE...................818 409-3387
Jesse Saavedra, *Brnch Mgr*
EMP: 282
SALES (corp-wide): 437.28MM **Privately Held**
Web: www.mvtransit.com
SIC: 4111 Local and suburban transit
PA: Mv Transportation, Inc.
    2711 N Hskell Ave Ste 150
    972 391-4600

(P-8777)
MV TRANSPORTATION INC
15677 Phoebe Ave, La Mirada
(90638-5214)
PHONE...................562 943-6776
EMP: 211
SALES (corp-wide): 437.28MM **Privately Held**
Web: www.mvtransit.com
SIC: 4111 Local and suburban transit
PA: Mv Transportation, Inc.
    2711 N Hskell Ave Ste 150
    972 391-4600

(P-8778)
MV TRANSPORTATION INC
5420 W Jefferson Blvd, Los Angeles
(90016-3716)
PHONE...................323 936-9783
EMP: 282
SALES (corp-wide): 437.28MM **Privately Held**
Web: www.mvtransit.com
SIC: 4111 Local and suburban transit
PA: Mv Transportation, Inc.
    2711 N Hskell Ave Ste 150
    972 391-4600

(P-8779)
MV TRANSPORTATION INC
14011 S Central Ave, Los Angeles
(90059-3622)
PHONE...................310 638-0556
EMP: 282
SALES (corp-wide): 437.28MM **Privately Held**
Web: www.mvtransit.com
SIC: 4111 Local and suburban transit
PA: Mv Transportation, Inc.
    2711 N Hskell Ave Ste 150
    972 391-4600

(P-8780)
MV TRANSPORTATION INC
16738 Stagg St, Van Nuys (91406-1635)
PHONE...................818 374-9145
Judy Smith, *Mgr*
EMP: 246
SALES (corp-wide): 437.28MM **Privately Held**
Web: www.mvtransit.com
SIC: 4111 Local and suburban transit
PA: Mv Transportation, Inc.
    2711 N Hskell Ave Ste 150
    972 391-4600

(P-8781)
MV TRANSPORTATION INC
13690 Vaughn St, San Fernando
(91340-3017)
PHONE...................323 666-0856
EMP: 247
SALES (corp-wide): 437.28MM **Privately Held**
Web: www.mvtransit.com
SIC: 4111 Local and suburban transit
PA: Mv Transportation, Inc.
    2711 N Hskell Ave Ste 150
    972 391-4600

(P-8782)
MV TRANSPORTATION INC
7231 Rosecrans Ave, Paramount
(90723-2501)
PHONE...................562 259-9911
EMP: 75
SALES (corp-wide): 437.28MM **Privately Held**
Web: www.mvtransit.com
SIC: 4111 Local and suburban transit
PA: Mv Transportation, Inc.
    2711 N Hskell Ave Ste 150
    972 391-4600

(P-8783)
MV TRANSPORTATION INC
265 S Rancho Rd, Thousand Oaks
(91361-5222)
PHONE...................805 557-7372
Cheryl Seafert, *Brnch Mgr*
EMP: 246
SALES (corp-wide): 437.28MM **Privately Held**
Web: www.mvtransit.com
SIC: 4111 Local and suburban transit
PA: Mv Transportation, Inc.
    2711 N Hskell Ave Ste 150
    972 391-4600

(P-8784)
MV TRANSPORTATION INC
Also Called: Mv Transportation
670 Lawrence Dr, Newbury Park
(91320-2205)
PHONE...................805 375-5467
EMP: 211
SALES (corp-wide): 437.28MM **Privately Held**
Web: www.mvtransit.com
SIC: 4111 Local and suburban transit
PA: Mv Transportation, Inc.
    2711 N Hskell Ave Ste 150
    972 391-4600

(P-8785)
MV TRANSPORTATION INC
1612 State St, Barstow (92311-4107)
PHONE...................760 255-3330
Tom Conlon, *Mgr*
EMP: 211
SALES (corp-wide): 437.28MM **Privately Held**

Web: www.mvtransit.com
SIC: 4111 Local and suburban transit
PA: Mv Transportation, Inc.
    2711 N Hskell Ave Ste 150
    972 391-4600

(P-8786)
MV TRANSPORTATION INC
303 Via Del Norte, Oceanside
(92058-1231)
PHONE...................760 400-0300
EMP: 282
SALES (corp-wide): 437.28MM **Privately Held**
Web: www.mvtransit.com
SIC: 4111 Local and suburban transit
PA: Mv Transportation, Inc.
    2711 N Hskell Ave Ste 150
    972 391-4600

(P-8787)
MV TRANSPORTATION INC
755 Norlak Ave, Escondido (92025-2514)
PHONE...................760 520-0118
EMP: 211
SALES (corp-wide): 437.28MM **Privately Held**
Web: www.mvtransit.com
SIC: 4111 Local and suburban transit
PA: Mv Transportation, Inc.
    2711 N Hskell Ave Ste 150
    972 391-4600

(P-8788)
OMNITRANS
Also Called: Omnitrans Access
234 S I St, San Bernardino (92410-2408)
PHONE...................909 383-1680
Brian Niemann, *Prin*
EMP: 219
SALES (corp-wide): 8.29MM **Privately Held**
Web: www.omnitrans.org
SIC: 4111 Local and suburban transit
PA: Omnitrans
    1700 W 5th St
    909 379-7100

(P-8789)
OMNITRANS
4748 Arrow Hwy, Montclair (91763-1208)
PHONE...................909 379-7100
John Steffon, *Brnch Mgr*
EMP: 219
SALES (corp-wide): 8.29MM **Privately Held**
Web: www.omnitrans.org
SIC: 4111 Bus line operations
PA: Omnitrans
    1700 W 5th St
    909 379-7100

(P-8790)
OMNITRANS (PA)
1700 W 5th St, San Bernardino
(92411-2499)
PHONE...................909 379-7100
TOLL FREE: 800
EMP: 212 EST: 1976
SALES (est): 8.48MM
SALES (corp-wide): 8.48MM **Privately Held**
Web: www.omnitrans.org
SIC: 4111 Bus line operations

(P-8791)
ORANGE CNTY TRNSP AUTH
SCHLRSH (PA)
Also Called: Orange County Tmsp Auth
550 S Main St, Orange (92868-4506)

P.O. Box 14184 (92863-1584)
PHONE..............................714 636-7433
Darrell Johnson, *CEO*
Don Hansen, *
John Dunning Junior, *COO*
Amy Wu, *
EMP: 350 **EST:** 1972
SQ FT: 77,000
SALES (est): 869MM
SALES (corp-wide): 869MM **Privately Held**
Web: www.octa.net
SIC: 4111 8711 Bus line operations; Construction and civil engineering

(P-8792)
ORANGE CNTY TRNSP AUTH SCHLRSH
Also Called: Octa
600 S Main St Ste 910, Orange (92868-4689)
PHONE..............................714 999-1726
Oscar Moreno, *Brnch Mgr*
EMP: 600
SALES (corp-wide): 869MM **Privately Held**
Web: www.octa.net
SIC: 4111 Bus line operations
PA: Orange County Transportation Authority Scholarship Foundation, Inc.
550 S Main St
714 636-7433

(P-8793)
ORANGE CNTY TRNSP AUTH SCHLRSH
11790 Cardinal Cir, Garden Grove (92843-3839)
P.O. Box 14184 (92863-1584)
PHONE..............................714 560-6282
Arthur Leahy, *CEO*
EMP: 83
SALES (corp-wide): 869MM **Privately Held**
Web: www.orangeautotransport.com
SIC: 4111 Bus line operations
PA: Orange County Transportation Authority Scholarship Foundation, Inc.
550 S Main St
714 636-7433

(P-8794)
PRIVATE SUITE LAX LLC
Also Called: PS
6871 W Imperial Hwy, Los Angeles (90045-6311)
PHONE..............................310 907-9950
Amina Belouizdad, *CEO*
Joshua Gausman, *Managing Member**
Amina Belouizdad, *Managing Member*
Jordi Mena, *
EMP: 200 **EST:** 2017
SQ FT: 57,590
SALES (est): 6.19MM **Privately Held**
Web: www.reserveps.com
SIC: 4111 Airport transportation

(P-8795)
RIVERSIDE TRANSIT AGENCY (PA)
Also Called: R T A
1825 3rd St, Riverside (92507-3484)
P.O. Box 59968 (92517-1968)
PHONE..............................951 565-5000
Larry Rubio, *CEO*
EMP: 350 **EST:** 1977
SQ FT: 10,400
SALES (est): 3.22MM
SALES (corp-wide): 3.22MM **Privately Held**

Web: www.riversidetransit.com
SIC: 4111 Bus transportation

(P-8796)
SAN BERNARDINO CNTY TRNSP AUTH
Also Called: SANBAG
1170 W 3rd St Fl 2, San Bernardino (92410-1724)
PHONE..............................909 884-8276
Raymond Wolfe, *Ex Dir*
EMP: 125 **EST:** 1973
SALES (est): 630.02MM **Privately Held**
Web: www.gosbcta.com
SIC: 4111 Local and suburban transit

(P-8797)
SAN DIEGO METRO TRNST SYS
1255 Imperial Ave Ste 1000, San Diego (92101-7490)
PHONE..............................619 231-1466
Sharon Cooney, *CEO*
Paul Jadlonski, *
Stan Abrams, *
EMP: 1600 **EST:** 1976
SQ FT: 40,000
SALES (est): 112.66MM **Privately Held**
Web: www.sandiego.com
SIC: 4111 Bus line operations

(P-8798)
SAN DIEGO TRANSIT CORPORATION (PA)
Also Called: San Diego Metro Trnst Sys
100 16th St, San Diego (92101-7694)
PHONE..............................619 238-0100
Langley Powell, *Ex Dir*
EMP: 650 **EST:** 1967
SQ FT: 20,000
SALES (est): 87.04MM
SALES (corp-wide): 87.04MM **Privately Held**
Web: www.sdmts.com
SIC: 4111 Commuter bus operation

(P-8799)
SAN DIEGO TROLLEY INC
Also Called: SAN DIEGO TROLLEY INC
1341 Commercial St, San Diego (92113-1021)
PHONE..............................619 595-4933
Bill Brown, *Brnch Mgr*
EMP: 483
SALES (corp-wide): 73.42MM **Privately Held**
Web: www.sdmts.com
SIC: 4111 Trolley operation
HQ: San Diego Trolley, Inc.
1255 Imperial Ave Ste 900
San Diego CA 92101
619 595-4949

(P-8800)
SAN GABRIEL TRANSIT INC (PA)
Also Called: San Gabriel Valley Cab Co
3650 Rockwell Ave, El Monte (91731-2322)
PHONE..............................626 258-1310
Timmy Mardirossian, *Pr*
Sedik Mardirossian, *
Eda Aghajanian, *
EMP: 220 **EST:** 1953
SQ FT: 8,000
SALES (est): 15.23MM
SALES (corp-wide): 15.23MM **Privately Held**
Web: www.sgtransit.com
SIC: 4111 Local and suburban transit

(P-8801)
SAN LUIS OBSPO RGNAL TRNST AUT
Also Called: Slorta
253 Elks Ln, San Luis Obispo (93401-5410)
PHONE..............................805 781-4465
Omar Mcpherson, *Prin*
Geoff Straw, *
Tania Arnold, *
EMP: 90 **EST:** 1989
SALES (est): 6.26MM **Privately Held**
Web: www.slorta.org
SIC: 4111 Local and suburban transit

(P-8802)
SANTA BARBARA METRO TRNST DST (PA)
Also Called: M T D
550 Olive St, Santa Barbara (93101-1610)
PHONE..............................805 963-3364
David Davis, *Ch*
John Britton, *
Chuck Mcquary, *Vice Chairman*
Bill Shelor, *
Roger Aceves, *
EMP: 85 **EST:** 1967
SQ FT: 8,500
SALES (est): 8.4MM
SALES (corp-wide): 8.4MM **Privately Held**
Web: www.sbmtd.gov
SIC: 4111 Bus line operations

(P-8803)
SHUTTLE SMART INC
6150 W 96th St, Los Angeles (90045-5218)
PHONE..............................310 338-9466
Brian Clark, *Brnch Mgr*
EMP: 130
SALES (corp-wide): 2.99MM **Privately Held**
Web: www.shuttlesmart.net
SIC: 4111 Airport transportation
PA: Shuttle Smart, Inc.
25923 Washington Blvd Ne
303 757-4870

(P-8804)
SMS TRANSPORTATION SVCS INC
865 S Figueroa St Ste 2750, Los Angeles (90017-2627)
PHONE..............................213 489-5367
John Harris, *CEO*
Delilah Lanoix, *
Danielle Wiltz, *
Jennifer Wiltz, *
EMP: 150 **EST:** 1004
SQ FT: 3,000
SALES (est): 1.42MM **Privately Held**
Web: www.smstransportation.net
SIC: 4111 Airport transportation

(P-8805)
SOUTHERN CAL RGIONAL RAIL AUTH
Also Called: Metrolink Doc
2704 N Garey Ave, Pomona (91767-1810)
PHONE..............................213 808-7043
EMP: 143
Web: www.metrolinktrains.com
SIC: 4111 Commuter rail passenger operation
PA: Southern California Regional Rail Authority
900 Wlshire Blvd Ste 1500

(P-8806)
SOUTHERN CAL RGIONAL RAIL AUTH (PA)
Also Called: Metrolink
900 Wilshire Blvd Ste 1500, Los Angeles (90017-4791)
P.O. Box 812060 (90081-0018)
PHONE..............................213 452-0200
Darren M Kettle, *CEO*
Stephanie Wiggins, *
Elissa Konove, *
Gary Lettengarver, *
Ronnie Campbell, *
EMP: 128 **EST:** 1991
SALES (est): 93.97MM **Privately Held**
Web: www.metrolinktrains.com
SIC: 4111 Commuter rail passenger operation

(P-8807)
SUNLINE TRANSIT AGENCY (PA)
Also Called: STA
32505 Harry Oliver Trl, Thousand Palms (92276-3501)
PHONE..............................760 343-3456
Glenn Miller, *Ch*
Caroline Rude, *
Greg Pettis, *
EMP: 160 **EST:** 1977
SQ FT: 19,006
SALES (est): 15.86MM
SALES (corp-wide): 15.86MM **Privately Held**
Web: www.sunline.org
SIC: 4111 Local and suburban transit

(P-8808)
TRANSITAMERICA SERVICES INC
1 Coaster Way, Camp Pendleton (92055)
P.O. Box 555 (64502-0555)
PHONE..............................760 430-0770
Robert J Smith, *Pr*
EMP: 84 **EST:** 2006
SALES (est): 2.19MM **Privately Held**
Web: www.herzog.com
SIC: 4111 Local and suburban transit

4119 Local Passenger Transportation, Nec

(P-8809)
AMBULNZ HEALTH LLC
12531 Vanowen St, North Hollywood (91605-5321)
PHONE..............................877 311-5555
EMP: 261
SALES (corp-wide): 4.79MM **Privately Held**
Web: www.docgo.com
SIC: 4119 Ambulance service
PA: Ambulnz Health, Llc
3550 N Academy Blvd
877 311-5555

(P-8810)
AMERICAN MED RSPNSE INLAND EMP (HQ)
879 Marlborough Ave, Riverside (92507-2133)
PHONE..............................951 782-5200
Bill Fanger, *Pr*
EMP: 80 **EST:** 1962
SALES (est): 2.74MM **Privately Held**
SIC: 4119 Ambulance service
PA: Global Medical Response, Inc.
4400 State Hwy 121

PRODUCTS & SVCS

(P-8811)
AMERICAN MEDICAL RESPONSE INC
Also Called: American Medical Response
1111 Montalvo Way, Palm Springs
(92262-5440)
PHONE...............................760 883-5000
Wayne Dennis, *Prin*
EMP: 160
Web: www.amr.net
SIC: 4119 8099 Ambulance service; Medical rescue squad
HQ: American Medical Response, Inc.
6501 S Fiddlers Green Cir
Greenwood Village CO 80111

(P-8812)
AMERICAN PROF AMBULANCE CORP
16945 Sherman Way, Van Nuys
(91406-3614)
P.O. Box 7263 (91409-7263)
PHONE...............................818 996-2200
Lyubov Popok, *Pr*
EMP: 83 EST: 2002
SALES (est): 1.7MM **Privately Held**
Web: www.apa-ems.com
SIC: 4119 Ambulance service

(P-8813)
ATLANTIC EXPRESS TRNSP
Also Called: Atlantic Express of California
2450 Long Beach Blvd, Long Beach
(90806-3125)
PHONE...............................562 997-6868
Darinda Garnett, *Mgr*
EMP: 266
SALES (corp-wide): 25.76MM **Privately Held**
SIC: 4119 8748 4151 Local passenger transportation, nec; Traffic consultant; School buses
HQ: Atlantic Express Transportation Corp
7 N St
Staten Island NY 10302
718 442-7000

(P-8814)
BLS LMSINE SVC LOS ANGELES INC
Also Called: B L S Limousine Service
2860 Fletcher Dr, Los Angeles
(90039-2452)
PHONE...............................323 644-7166
Jay D Okon, *Pr*
Phyllis Okon, *
EMP: 350 EST: 1988
SQ FT: 20,000
SALES (est): 2.32MM **Privately Held**
Web: www.blsco.com
SIC: 4119 Limousine rental, with driver

(P-8815)
CALIFORNIA MED RESPONSE INC
Also Called: Cal-Med Ambulance
1557 Santa Anita Ave, South El Monte
(91733-3313)
PHONE...............................562 968-1818
Ronald A Marks, *Pr*
Ronald A Marks, *Pr*
Linda Marks, *
EMP: 80 EST: 2009
SALES (est): 4.94MM **Privately Held**
Web: www.calmedambulance.com
SIC: 4119 Ambulance service

(P-8816)
CALL-THE-CAR
2589 E Washington Blvd, Pasadena
(91107-1446)
P.O. Box 4114 (90640-9302)
PHONE...............................855 282-6968
Michelle Tyson, *CEO*
EMP: 104 EST: 2012
SALES (est): 14.63MM **Privately Held**
Web: www.callthecar.com
SIC: 4119 Local passenger transportation, nec

(P-8817)
CARE MEDICAL TRNSP INC
Also Called: Care Ambulance
1801 Orange Tree Ln Ste 100, Redlands
(92374-4588)
PHONE...............................858 653-4520
Kelvin Carlisle, *Pr*
EMP: 190 EST: 1995
SALES (est): 4.37MM **Privately Held**
SIC: 4119 Ambulance service

(P-8818)
CAV INC
Also Called: Care A Van Transport
5931 Sea Lion Pl Ste 110, Carlsbad
(92010-6622)
PHONE...............................760 729-5199
Richard Dripps, *Pr*
Robert Sneedon, *
Robert Newkirk, *Operations**
Deana Mason, *Marketing MNG**
EMP: 75 EST: 1993
SQ FT: 1,200
SALES (est): 4.41MM **Privately Held**
SIC: 4119 Ambulance service

(P-8819)
CLS TRNSPRTTION LOS ANGLES LLC (HQ)
Also Called: Empire Cls Wrldwide Chffred Sv
600 S Allied Way, El Segundo
(90245-4727)
PHONE...............................310 414-8189
David Singler, *Managing Member*
William Minich, *
EMP: 150 EST: 1987
SALES (est): 939.9K **Privately Held**
Web: www.empirecls.com
SIC: 4119 Limousine rental, with driver
PA: Gts Holdings, Inc.
225 Meadowlands Pkwy

(P-8820)
EASTWESTPROTO INC
Also Called: Lifeline Ambulance
6605 E Washington Blvd, Commerce
(90040-1813)
PHONE...............................888 535-5728
Genady Gorin, *CEO*
Genia Gorin, *
EMP: 275 EST: 2002
SQ FT: 10,000
SALES (est): 23.85MM **Privately Held**
Web: www.lifeline-ems.com
SIC: 4119 Ambulance service

(P-8821)
EMERGENCY AMBULANCE SVC INC
3200 E Birch St Ste A, Brea (92821-6287)
PHONE...............................714 990-1331
Phillip E Davis, *Pr*
EMP: 80 EST: 1977
SALES (est): 15.3MM **Privately Held**
Web: www.emergencyambulance.com

SIC: 4119 Ambulance service

(P-8822)
EXECUTIVE NETWORK ENTPS INC (PA)
Also Called: Malibu Limousine Service
13440 Beach Ave, Marina Del Rey
(90292-5624)
PHONE...............................310 447-2759
Patricia Stephenson, *Pr*
Stori Stephenson, *
Trish Rudd, *
EMP: 80 EST: 2003
SQ FT: 5,000
SALES (est): 5.02MM **Privately Held**
SIC: 4119 Limousine rental, with driver

(P-8823)
EXECUTIVE NETWORK ENTPS INC
1224 21st St Apt E, Santa Monica
(90404-1390)
PHONE...............................310 457-8822
Patricia Stephenson, *Mgr*
EMP: 520
SIC: 4119 Limousine rental, with driver
PA: Executive Network Enterprises, Inc.
13440 Beach Ave

(P-8824)
FALCK MOBILE HEALTH CORP
212 S Atlantic Blvd Ste 102, Los Angeles
(90022-1775)
PHONE...............................323 720-1578
EMP: 444
SALES (corp-wide): 5.35B **Privately Held**
Web: www.falck.us
SIC: 4119 Ambulance service
HQ: Falck Mobile Health Corp.
1517 W Braden Ct
Orange CA 92868
714 288-3800

(P-8825)
FALCK MOBILE HEALTH CORP
8932 Katella Ave Ste 201, Anaheim
(92804-6299)
PHONE...............................714 828-7750
Dan Richardson, *Prin*
EMP: 444
SALES (corp-wide): 5.35B **Privately Held**
Web: www.falck.us
SIC: 4119 Ambulance service
HQ: Falck Mobile Health Corp.
1517 W Braden Ct
Orange CA 92868
714 288-3800

(P-8826)
FILYN CORPORATION
Also Called: Lynch Ambulance Service
2950 E La Jolla St, Anaheim (92806-1307)
PHONE...............................714 632-0225
Walter John Lynch, *CEO*
Nancy Lynch, *
EMP: 200 EST: 1986
SALES (est): 4.42MM **Privately Held**
Web: www.lynchambulance.com
SIC: 4119 Ambulance service

(P-8827)
FLIXBUS INC
12575 Beatrice St, Los Angeles
(90066-7001)
PHONE...............................925 577-4164
Pierre Gourdain, *CEO*
EMP: 104 EST: 2017
SALES (est): 1.85MM
SALES (corp-wide): 1.59B **Privately Held**

Web: www.flixbus.com
SIC: 4119 Local rental transportation
HQ: Flix North America Inc.
315 Continental Ave
Dallas TX 75207
214 564-8215

(P-8828)
GARY CARDIFF ENTERPRISES INC
Also Called: Cardiff Transportation
75255 Sheryl Ave, Palm Desert
(92211-5129)
PHONE...............................760 568-1403
Gary Cardiff, *CEO*
Sharon Cardiff, *
EMP: 89 EST: 1990
SQ FT: 10,000
SALES (est): 8.46MM **Privately Held**
Web: www.cardifflimo.com
SIC: 4119 Limousine rental, with driver

(P-8829)
GLOBAL PARATRANSIT INC
400 W Compton Blvd, Gardena
(90248-1700)
PHONE...............................310 715-7550
Reza Nasrollahy, *Pr*
EMP: 300 EST: 2000
SQ FT: 17,000
SALES (est): 9.51MM **Privately Held**
Web: www.global-paratransit.com
SIC: 4119 Ambulance service

(P-8830)
HALL AMBULANCE SERVICE INC
2001 O St # O, Bakersfield (93301-4724)
PHONE...............................661 322-8741
Harvy Hall, *Pr*
EMP: 72
SALES (corp-wide): 15.79MM **Privately Held**
Web: www.hallamb.com
SIC: 4119 Ambulance service
PA: Hall Ambulance Service, Inc.
1001 21st St
661 322-8741

(P-8831)
LANDJET (PA)
1090 Hall Ave, Jurupa Valley (92509-1800)
PHONE...............................909 873-4636
Kevin Sacalas, *CEO*
EMP: 131 EST: 2018
SALES (est): 6.31MM
SALES (corp-wide): 6.31MM **Privately Held**
Web: www.landjet-inc.com
SIC: 4119 Local rental transportation

(P-8832)
LEADER INDUSTRIES INC
Also Called: Leader Emergency Vehicles
10941 Weaver Ave, South El Monte
(91733-2752)
PHONE...............................626 575-0880
Gary Hunter, *Prin*
EMP: 160 EST: 2001
SALES (est): 16.12MM **Privately Held**
Web: www.leaderambulance.com
SIC: 4119 5046 3711 Ambulance service; Commercial equipment, nec; Motor vehicles and car bodies

(P-8833)
LIBERTY AMBULANCE LLC
9770 Candida St, San Diego (92126-4536)
PHONE...............................562 741-6230

EMP: 199 **EST:** 2008
SALES (est): 11.35MM **Privately Held**
Web: www.libertyambulance.com
SIC: 4119 Ambulance service

(P-8834)
LIFESTAR RESPONSE OF ALABAMA
Also Called: Care Ambulance
1517 W Braden Ct, Orange (92868-1125)
P.O. Box 241468 (36124-1468)
PHONE..............................800 449-4911
Charles Maymon, *CEO*
Michael Arguelles, *COO*
EMP: 117 **EST:** 2007
SALES (est): 3.07MM **Privately Held**
Web: www.care-ambulance.com
SIC: 4119 Ambulance service

(P-8835)
MEDIC-1 AMBULANCE SERVICE INC
1305 W Arrow Hwy Ste 206, San Dimas (91773-2338)
PHONE..............................909 592-8840
Gordon Shipp, *Pr*
Todd Duprey, *
Gary Sylvester, *
EMP: 92 **EST:** 2001
SALES (est): 535.66K **Privately Held**
SIC: 4119 Ambulance service

(P-8836)
MEDIX AMBULANCE SERVICE INC (PA)
26021 Pala, Mission Viejo (92691-2718)
P.O. Box 1000 (92609-1000)
PHONE..............................949 470-8915
EMP: 157 **EST:** 1978
SALES (est): 1.99MM
SALES (corp-wide): 1.99MM **Privately Held**
SIC: 4119 Ambulance service

(P-8837)
MEDRESPONSE (PA)
7040 Hayvenhurst Ave, Van Nuys (91406-3801)
P.O. Box 8379 (91409-8379)
PHONE..............................818 442-9222
Andrew Stepansky, *CEO*
EMP: 113 **EST:** 2002
SALES (est): 1.6MM
SALES (corp-wide): 1.6MM **Privately Held**
Web: www.mr-ems.com
SIC: 4119 Ambulance service

(P-8838)
MEDRESPONSE LLC
9961 Baldwin Pl, El Monte (91731-2203)
PHONE..............................877 311-5555
Vince Pinsky, *CEO*
EMP: 75 **EST:** 2019
SALES (est): 1.69MM **Privately Held**
Web: www.mr-ems.com
SIC: 4119 Ambulance service

(P-8839)
MEDTRANS INC
Also Called: Medtrans Inc
345 S Woods Ave, Los Angeles (90022-1941)
PHONE..............................323 780-9500
Avetis Avetisyan, *CEO*
EMP: 75 **EST:** 2008
SALES (est): 2.21MM **Privately Held**
Web: www.medtrans.ai
SIC: 4119 Ambulance service

(P-8840)
MERCY MEDICAL TRNSP INC
Also Called: Mercy Ambulance
27350 Valley Center Rd Ste A, Valley Center (92082-7220)
P.O. Box 530 (92082)
PHONE..............................760 739-8026
Richard Roesch, *Pr*
EMP: 188 **EST:** 1993
SALES (est): 2.49MM **Privately Held**
Web: www.mercymedtrans.com
SIC: 4119 8062 Ambulance service; General medical and surgical hospitals

(P-8841)
MISSION AMBULANCE INC
400 Ramona Ave, Corona (92879-1440)
P.O. Box 3111 (92878-3111)
PHONE..............................951 272-2300
Daniel Gold, *Pr*
EMP: 81 **EST:** 1999
SALES (est): 4.03MM **Privately Held**
Web: www.missionsafetyservices.com
SIC: 4119 Ambulance service

(P-8842)
MUSIC EXPRESS INC (PA)
2601 W Empire Ave, Burbank (91504-3225)
PHONE..............................818 845-1502
EMP: 171 **EST:** 1973
SALES (est): 4.84MM
SALES (corp-wide): 4.84MM **Privately Held**
Web: www.musicexpress.com
SIC: 4119 Limousine rental, with driver

(P-8843)
PREMIER MEDICAL TRANSPORT INC
Also Called: Premier Ambulance
260 N Palm St # 200, Brea (92821-2870)
PHONE..............................805 340-5191
Adrian Dehghanmanesh, *CEO*
Paul Scarborough, *
EMP: 650 **EST:** 2007
SQ FT: 40,825
SALES (est): 47.98MM **Privately Held**
Web: www.premieramb.com
SIC: 4119 Ambulance service

(P-8844)
PRIORITY ONE MED TRNSPT INC (PA)
9327 Fairway View Pl Ste 300, Rancho Cucamonga (91730-0970)
PHONE..............................909 948 1400
Michael Parker, *Pr*
EMP: 70 **EST:** 1996
SQ FT: 7,000
SALES (est): 870.05K
SALES (corp-wide): 870.05K **Privately Held**
Web: www.priorityonemedical.com
SIC: 4119 Ambulance service

(P-8845)
PRN AMBULANCE LLC
8928 Sepulveda Blvd, North Hills (91343-4306)
PHONE..............................818 810-3600
Mike Sechrist, *CEO*
Avo Avetisyan, *Pr*
Elena Whorton, *Pr*
Kevin Gorman, *CFO*
Michael Gorman, *COO*
EMP: 300 **EST:** 2001
SQ FT: 3,000
SALES (est): 5.15MM

SALES (corp-wide): 69.26MM **Privately Held**
Web: www.prnambulance.com
SIC: 4119 Ambulance service
PA: Pt-1 Holdings, Llc
720 Portal St
707 665-4295

(P-8846)
RYANS EXPRESS TRNSP SVCS INC (PA)
Also Called: Ryan's Express
19500 Mariner Ave, Torrance (90503-1644)
PHONE..............................310 219-2960
John Busskohl, *CEO*
Chris Sanchez, *
George Cohen, *
Alexander E Hansen, *
Daniel Azar, *
EMP: 80 **EST:** 1999
SQ FT: 20,000
SALES (est): 1.54MM
SALES (corp-wide): 1.54MM **Privately Held**
Web: www.ryanstransportation.com
SIC: 4119 Limousine rental, with driver

(P-8847)
SAN LUIS AMBULANCE SERVICE INC
3546 S Higuera St, San Luis Obispo (93401-7304)
P.O. Box 954 (93406-0954)
PHONE..............................805 543-2626
Frank I Kelton, *Pr*
Betsy Kelton, *
EMP: 124 **EST:** 1967
SQ FT: 7,500
SALES (est): 8.98MM **Privately Held**
Web: www.sanluisambulance.info
SIC: 4119 Ambulance service

(P-8848)
SCHAEFER AMBULANCE SERVICE INC
Also Called: Gold Cross Ambulance
4627 Beverly Blvd, Los Angeles (90004-3101)
P.O. Box 74609 (90004-0609)
PHONE..............................323 468-1642
TOLL FREE: 800
EMP: 463
Web: www.schaeferamb.com
SIC: 4119 Ambulance service

(P-8849)
SUNI INF TRANSIT AGENCY
790 Vine Ave, Coachella (92236-1736)
PHONE..............................760 972-4059
EMP: 119
SALES (corp-wide): 15.86MM **Privately Held**
Web: www.sunline.org
SIC: 4119 Local passenger transportation, nec
PA: Sunline Transit Agency
32505 Harry Oliver Trl
760 343-3456

(P-8850)
TRANSDEV SERVICES INC
544 Vernon Way, El Cajon (92020-1935)
PHONE..............................619 401-4503
EMP: 342
SALES (corp-wide): 4.23MM **Privately Held**
Web: www.ryanstransportation.com
SIC: 4119 Local passenger transportation, nec

HQ: Transdev Services, Inc.
720 E Bttrfeld Rd Ste 300
Lombard IL 60148
630 571-7070

(P-8851)
TRANSDEV SERVICES INC
5640 Peck Rd, Arcadia (91006-5850)
PHONE..............................626 357-7912
EMP: 770
SALES (corp-wide): 4.23MM **Privately Held**
Web: www.transdevna.com
SIC: 4119 4121 Local passenger transportation, nec; Taxicabs
HQ: Transdev Services, Inc.
720 E Bttrfeld Rd Ste 300
Lombard IL 60148
630 571-7070

(P-8852)
TRIPLE R TRANSPORTATION INC
978 Rd 192, Delano (93215)
P.O. Box 38 (93216-0038)
PHONE..............................661 725-6494
Joe Rodriguez, *Pr*
EMP: 80 **EST:** 2008
SALES (est): 3.28MM **Privately Held**
SIC: 4119 Local rental transportation

(P-8853)
VIRGIN FISH INC (PA)
Also Called: Avalon Transportation Co
1000 Corporate Pointe Ste 150, Culver City (90230-7690)
PHONE..............................310 391-6161
Jeff Brush, *Pr*
David Dinwiddie, *VP*
EMP: 150 **EST:** 1990
SQ FT: 3,000
SALES (est): 23.41MM **Privately Held**
Web: www.avalontrans.com
SIC: 4119 Limousine rental, with driver

(P-8854)
WESTMED AMBULANCE INC
Also Called: WESTMED AMBULANCE, INC
2537 Old San Pasqual Rd, Escondido (92027-4753)
PHONE..............................310 219-1779
Allen Cress, *Prin*
EMP: 103
Web: www.westmedambulance.com
SIC: 4119 Ambulance service
PA: Westmed Ambulance, Inc.
13933 Crenshaw Blvd

(P-8855)
WESTMED AMBULANCE INC
Also Called: McCormick Ambulance
2020 S Central Ave, Compton (90220-5302)
P.O. Box 5004 (95338-5004)
PHONE..............................310 837-0102
EMP: 103
Web: www.westmedambulance.com
SIC: 4119 Ambulance service
PA: Westmed Ambulance, Inc.
13933 Crenshaw Blvd

(P-8856)
WESTMED AMBULANCE INC
Also Called: WESTMED AMBULANCE, INC
3872 Las Flores Canyon Rd, Malibu (90265-5264)
PHONE..............................310 456-3830
EMP: 103
Web: www.westmedambulance.com

SIC: 4119 Ambulance service
PA: Westmed Ambulance, Inc.
13933 Crenshaw Blvd

4121 Taxicabs

(P-8857)
ADMINISTRATIVE SVCS COOP INC
2129 W Rosecrans Ave, Gardena (90249-2933)
PHONE.....................310 715-1968
Martiros Manukyan, CEO
Raymond Mcgreevy, Pr
EMP: 200 EST: 1992
SALES (est): 4.88MM Privately Held
Web: www.layellowcab.com
SIC: 4121 Taxicabs

4131 Intercity And Rural Bus Transportation

(P-8858)
GREYHOUND LINES INC
1716 E 7th St, Los Angeles (90021-1202)
PHONE.....................213 629-8400
Mark Jacobson, Prin
EMP: 80
SQ FT: 100,000
SALES (corp-wide): 1.59B Privately Held
Web: www.greyhound.com
SIC: 4131 Intercity and rural bus transportation
HQ: Greyhound Lines, Inc.
350 N Saint Paul St
Dallas TX 75201
214 849-8000

(P-8859)
SANTA BARBARA TRNSP CORP
Also Called: Student Transportation America
26501 Ruether Ave, Santa Clarita (91350-2600)
PHONE.....................661 259-7285
Richard Varner, Dir
EMP: 100
SALES (corp-wide): 110.06MM Privately Held
SIC: 4131 4151 Intercity and rural bus transportation; School buses
HQ: Santa Barbara Transportation Corporation
3349 Hwy 138 Ste C
Wall Township NJ 07719
732 280-4200

(P-8860)
SANTA MONICA CITY OF
Santa Monica Big Blue Bus
1685 Main St, Santa Monica (90401-3248)
PHONE.....................310 458-1975
Edward King, Mgr
EMP: 220
SALES (corp-wide): 546.23MM Privately Held
Web: www.santamonica.gov
SIC: 4131 Intercity and rural bus transportation
PA: City Of Santa Monica
1685 Main St
310 458-8411

4141 Local Bus Charter Service

(P-8861)
EMPIRE TRANSPORTATION INC
8800 Park St, Bellflower (90706-5529)
PHONE.....................562 529-2676
Miguel Oliver, CEO
Bertha Aguirre, *
Monica Escorza Oliver, *
EMP: 425 EST: 2005
SQ FT: 25,000
SALES (est): 2.31MM Privately Held
Web: www.emptransportation.com
SIC: 4141 7521 4111 Local bus charter service; Indoor parking services; Bus transportation

4142 Bus Charter Service, Except Local

(P-8862)
CERTIFIED TRNSP SVCS INC
Also Called: Certified Transportation
1038 N Custer St, Santa Ana (92701-3915)
PHONE.....................714 835-8676
David Gregory, CEO
EMP: 70 EST: 1990
SQ FT: 3,000
SALES (est): 8.22MM Privately Held
Web: www.ctsbus.com
SIC: 4142 Bus charter service, except local

(P-8863)
COACH USA INC
Also Called: Foothill Transit West Covina
5640 Peck Rd, Arcadia (91006-5850)
PHONE.....................626 357-7912
Keith Whalen, Brnch Mgr
EMP: 100
Web: www.coachusa.com
SIC: 4142 Bus charter service, except local
HQ: Coach Usa, Inc.
160 S State Rt 17
Paramus NJ 07652

(P-8864)
HOT DOGGER TOURS INC
Also Called: Gold Coast Tours
105 Gemini Ave, Brea (92821-3702)
PHONE.....................714 449-6888
TOLL FREE: 800
John Hartley, Pr
Mark Wilkerson, *
EMP: 120 EST: 1976
SQ FT: 955
SALES (est): 6.59MM Privately Held
Web: www.goldcoasttours.com
SIC: 4142 4725 4141 Bus charter service, except local; Tours, conducted; Local bus charter service

(P-8865)
SURERIDE CHARTER INC
Also Called: Sun Diego Charter
522 W 8th St, National City (91950-1004)
PHONE.....................619 336-9200
Richard Illes, Pr
EMP: 120 EST: 1994
SQ FT: 60,000
SALES (est): 3.2MM Privately Held
Web: www.sundiegocharter.com
SIC: 4142 Bus charter service, except local

4151 School Buses

(P-8866)
ANTELOPE VLY SCHL TRNSP AGCY
670 W Avenue L8, Lancaster (93534-7100)
PHONE.....................661 952-3106
Morris Fuselier Iii, CEO
Gary Russell, *
Joanne Downen, *
EMP: 206 EST: 1980
SALES (est): 4.09MM Privately Held
Web: www.avsta.com
SIC: 4151 School buses

(P-8867)
COUNTY OF LOS ANGELES
Also Called: Pupil Transportation
9402 Greenleaf Ave, Whittier (90605-2700)
PHONE.....................562 945-2581
Dan Ibarra, Dir
EMP: 233
Web: www.lacounty.gov
SIC: 4151 9621 School buses; Regulation, administration of transportation
PA: County Of Los Angeles
500 W Temple St Ste 437
213 974-1101

(P-8868)
DURHAM SCHOOL SERVICES L P
4029 Las Virgenes Rd, Calabasas (91302-3505)
PHONE.....................818 880-4257
Nanette Nanzini, Genl Mgr
EMP: 170
Web: www.durhamschoolservices.com
SIC: 4151 School buses
HQ: Durham School Services, L. P.
2601 Navistar Dr
Lisle IL 60532
630 836-0292

(P-8869)
DURHAM SCHOOL SERVICES L P
723 S Alameda St, Compton (90220-3809)
PHONE.....................310 767-5820
Raphael Balonos, Mgr
EMP: 198
Web: www.durhamschoolservices.com
SIC: 4151 School buses
HQ: Durham School Services, L. P.
2601 Navistar Dr
Lisle IL 60532
630 836-0292

(P-8870)
DURHAM SCHOOL SERVICES L P
8555 Flower Ave, Paramount (90723-5602)
PHONE.....................562 408-1206
Paul Wiggins, Genl Mgr
EMP: 113
Web: www.durhamschoolservices.com
SIC: 4151 School buses
HQ: Durham School Services, L. P.
2601 Navistar Dr
Lisle IL 60532
630 836-0292

(P-8871)
DURHAM SCHOOL SERVICES L P
2713 River Ave, Rosemead (91770-3303)
PHONE.....................626 573-3769

David Gonzales, Genl Mgr
EMP: 821
Web: www.durhamschoolservices.com
SIC: 4151 School buses
HQ: Durham School Services, L. P.
2601 Navistar Dr
Lisle IL 60532
630 836-0292

(P-8872)
DURHAM SCHOOL SERVICES L P
Also Called: Lidlaw Educational Services
12999 Victoria St, Rancho Cucamonga (91739-9532)
PHONE.....................909 899-1809
Laura Randals, Mgr
EMP: 113
Web: www.durhamschoolservices.com
SIC: 4151 School buses
HQ: Durham School Services, L. P.
2601 Navistar Dr
Lisle IL 60532
630 836-0292

(P-8873)
DURHAM SCHOOL SERVICES L P
3151 W 5th St Ste A, Oxnard (93030-6415)
PHONE.....................805 483-6076
Lee Philips, Genl Mgr
EMP: 198
Web: www.durhamschoolservices.com
SIC: 4151 School buses
HQ: Durham School Services, L. P.
2601 Navistar Dr
Lisle IL 60532
630 836-0292

(P-8874)
DURHAM SCHOOL SERVICES L P
2003 Laguna Canyon Rd, Laguna Beach (92651-1123)
PHONE.....................949 376-0376
Kathie Lee, Mgr
EMP: 113
Web: www.durhamschoolservices.com
SIC: 4151 School buses
HQ: Durham School Services, L. P.
2601 Navistar Dr
Lisle IL 60532
630 836-0292

(P-8875)
DURHAM SCHOOL SERVICES L P
2818 W 5th St, Santa Ana (92703-1824)
PHONE.....................714 542-8989
Debbie Williams, Mgr
EMP: 283
SQ FT: 4,843
Web: www.durhamschoolservices.com
SIC: 4151 School buses
HQ: Durham School Services, L. P.
2601 Navistar Dr
Lisle IL 60532
630 836-0292

(P-8876)
FIRST STUDENT INC
16332 Construction Cir W, Irvine (92606-4415)
PHONE.....................855 870-8747
EMP: 80
Web: www.firststudentinc.com
SIC: 4151 School buses
PA: First Student, Inc.
191 Rosa Parks St Ste 800

(P-8877)
FIRST STUDENT INC
234 S I St, San Bernardino (92410-2408)
PHONE....................909 383-1640
Cheryl Seifert, *Mgr*
EMP: 116
Web: www.firststudentinc.com
SIC: 4151 School buses
PA: First Student, Inc.
191 Rosa Parks St Ste 800

(P-8878)
FIRST STUDENT INC
300 S Buena Vista Ave, Corona
(92882-1937)
PHONE....................951 736-3234
Jackie Mansperger, *Mgr*
EMP: 95
Web: www.firststudentinc.com
SIC: 4151 School buses
PA: First Student, Inc.
191 Rosa Parks St Ste 800

(P-8879)
FIRST STUDENT INC
Also Called: First Student
5127 Heintz St, Baldwin Park (91706-1820)
PHONE....................855 870-8747
EMP: 112
Web: www.firststudentinc.com
SIC: 4151 School buses
PA: First Student, Inc.
191 Rosa Parks St Ste 800

(P-8880)
FIRST STUDENT INC
Also Called: Cardinal Transportation
14800 S Avalon Blvd, Gardena
(90248-2012)
PHONE....................310 769-2400
Ray Borales, *Pr*
Roy J Weber, *
▲ **EMP:** 3196 **EST:** 1987
SQ FT: 18,000
SALES (est): 872.36K
SALES (corp-wide): 5.98B **Privately Held**
Web: www.firststudentinc.com
SIC: 4151 School buses
HQ: Firstgroup America, Inc.
191 Rosa Parks St
Cincinnati OH 45202
513 241-2200

(P-8881)
LONG BEACH UNIFIED SCHOOL DST
Also Called: Transportation Department
2700 Pine Ave, Long Beach (90806-2617)
PHONE....................562 426-6176
Paul Bailey, *Dir*
EMP: 1/2
SALES (corp-wide): 375.96MM **Privately Held**
Web: www.lbschools.net
SIC: 4151 School buses
PA: Long Beach Unified School District
1515 Hughes Way
562 997-8000

(P-8882)
RIM OF WORLD UNIFIED SCHL DST
Also Called: Transportation
27614 Hwy 18 Across Building I, Lake
Arrowhead (92352)
P.O. Box 430 (92352-0430)
PHONE....................909 336-0330
Susie Hubbard, *Dir*
EMP: 76

SALES (corp-wide): 59.02MM **Privately Held**
Web: www.rimsd.k12.ca.us
SIC: 4151 School buses
PA: Rim Of The World Unified School District
24740 San Moritz Way
909 336-4100

(P-8883)
SANTA BARBARA TRNSP CORP
Also Called: Student Transportation America
520 Gannon Pl, Escondido (92025-2513)
PHONE....................760 746-0850
Jane Hyman, *Dir*
EMP: 216
SALES (corp-wide): 110.06MM **Privately Held**
SIC: 4151 School buses
HQ: Santa Barbara Transportation
Corporation
3349 Hwy 138 Ste C
Wall Township NJ 07719
732 280-4200

(P-8884)
SANTA BARBARA TRNSP CORP
42138 7th St W, Lancaster (93534-7145)
PHONE....................661 510-0566
EMP: 123
SALES (corp-wide): 110.06MM **Privately Held**
SIC: 4151 School buses
HQ: Santa Barbara Transportation
Corporation
3349 Hwy 138 Ste C
Wall Township NJ 07719
732 280-4200

(P-8885)
SANTA BARBARA TRNSP CORP
Also Called: Student Transportation America
7394 Calle Real Ste A, Goleta
(93117-1244)
PHONE....................805 928-0402
Paula Sauvadon, *VP*
EMP: 185
SALES (corp-wide): 110.06MM **Privately Held**
SIC: 4151 4121 School buses; Taxicabs
HQ: Santa Barbara Transportation
Corporation
3349 Hwy 138 Ste C
Wall Township NJ 07719
732 280-4200

4212 Local Trucking, Without Storage

(P-8886)
365 DELIVERY INC
440 E Huntington Dr Ste 300, Arcadia
(91006-3775)
PHONE....................818 815-5005
Bernardo Anders, *Pr*
Ariana Barrera, *
EMP: 100 **EST:** 2017
SALES (est): 2.52MM **Privately Held**
SIC: 4212 Delivery service, vehicular

(P-8887)
A G HACIENDA INCORPORATED
32794 Sherwood Ave, Mc Farland
(93250-9626)
P.O. Box 367 (93250-0367)
PHONE....................661 792-2418
Xochilht Gonzalez, *Pr*
EMP: 400 **EST:** 1997
SALES (est): 4.51MM **Privately Held**

SIC: 4212 0761 4214 Local trucking, without storage; Farm labor contractors; Local trucking with storage

(P-8888)
A-1 DELIVERY CO
1777 S Vintage Ave, Ontario (91761-3659)
P.O. Box 4210 (91761-8910)
PHONE....................909 444-1220
Joe Romine, *Pr*
Johnny Romine, *
William Turner, *
EMP: 75 **EST:** 1976
SQ FT: 10,000
SALES (est): 7.16MM **Privately Held**
Web: www.a1deliveryco.com
SIC: 4212 Delivery service, vehicular

(P-8889)
A-TEAM DELIVERS LLC
12127 Mall Blvd Ste A322, Victorville
(92392-7665)
PHONE....................858 254-8401
Steve Ford, *CEO*
EMP: 80 **EST:** 2020
SALES (est): 2.55MM **Privately Held**
SIC: 4212 Delivery service, vehicular

(P-8890)
ADVANCED CHEMICAL TRNSPT INC
600 Iowa St, Redlands (92373-8047)
PHONE....................951 790-7989
EMP: 196
SALES (corp-wide): 95.12MM **Privately Held**
Web: www.actenviro.com
SIC: 4212 Hazardous waste transport
PA: Advanced Chemical Transport, Inc.
967 Mabury Rd
408 548-5050

(P-8891)
AILO LOGISTICS
435 E Weber Ave, Compton (90222-1424)
PHONE....................310 707-1120
Hakop Khudikyan, *CEO*
Khachatur Khudikyan, *
Armen Baibourtian, *
EMP: 520 **EST:** 1990
SQ FT: 10,000
SALES (est): 34.57MM **Privately Held**
Web: www.ajrtrucking.com
SIC: 4212 Mail carriers, contract

(P-8892)
ANCON MARINE LLC
Also Called: Ancon Services
2735 Rose Ave, Signal Hill (90755-1927)
PHONE....................562 326-5900
EMP: 116
SALES (corp-wide): 102.92MM **Privately Held**
Web: www.anconservices.com
SIC: 4212 Local trucking, without storage
PA: Ancon Marine, Llc
10571 Los Alamitos Blvd
707 756-0286

(P-8893)
APEX BULK COMMODITIES INC (PA)
Also Called: Apex Bulk Commodities
12531 Violet Rd Ste A, Adelanto
(92301-2731)
PHONE....................760 246-6077
EMP: 200 **EST:** 1967
SALES (est): 41.54MM
SALES (corp-wide): 41.54MM **Privately Held**

Web: www.apexbulk.com
SIC: 4212 4213 Liquid haulage, local; Trucking, except local

(P-8894)
ARAKELIAN ENTERPRISES INC
Also Called: Athens Services
11121 Pendleton St, Sun Valley
(91352-1513)
PHONE....................818 768-2644
Ron Arakelian Junior, *CEO*
EMP: 164
SALES (corp-wide): 199.65MM **Privately Held**
Web: www.athensservices.com
SIC: 4212 Garbage collection and transport, no disposal
PA: Arakelian Enterprises, Inc.
14048 Valley Blvd
626 336-3636

(P-8895)
ASBURY ENVIRONMENTAL SERVICES (PA)
Also Called: World Oil Environmental Svcs
1300 S Santa Fe Ave, Compton
(90221-4916)
PHONE....................310 886-3400
Steve Kerdoon, *CEO*
Bruce De Menno, *
Chris Mahoney, *
Anne Asbury, *
EMP: 75 **EST:** 1936
SQ FT: 22,000
SALES (est): 41.47MM
SALES (corp-wide): 41.47MM **Privately Held**
Web: www.asburyenv.com
SIC: 4212 Local trucking, without storage

(P-8896)
BELSHIRE TRNSP SVCS INC
Also Called: Belshire
25971 Towne Centre Dr, Foothill Ranch
(92610-2462)
PHONE....................949 460-5200
Karen Cass, *Pr*
EMP: 125 **EST:** 2002
SALES (est): 5.97MM **Privately Held**
Web: www.belshire.com
SIC: 4212 Hazardous waste transport

(P-8897)
BURNS AND SONS TRUCKING INC
Also Called: Dependable Disposal and Recycl
9210 Olive Dr, Spring Valley (91977-2305)
P.O. Box 1640 (91979-1640)
PHONE....................619 460-5394
TOLL FREE: 800
Eva N Burns, *CEO*
Jack Burns Senior, *Pr*
Tom Mcfarlane, *Genl Mgr*
Jim Burns, *
Jack Burns Junior, *VP*
EMP: 85 **EST:** 1977
SQ FT: 6,000
SALES (est): 4.77MM **Privately Held**
Web: www.burnsandsons.com
SIC: 4212 4214 Local trucking, without storage; Local trucking with storage

(P-8898)
C P S EXPRESS
4375 E Lowell St Ste G, Ontario
(91761-2227)
P.O. Box 248 (91752-0248)
PHONE....................951 685-1041
Kurt Allen, *CEO*
Timothy Pollock, *

P R O D U C T S & S V C S

Paul Anderson, *
EMP: 115 **EST:** 1980
SQ FT: 7,000
SALES (est): 23.73MM
SALES (corp-wide): 23.73MM **Privately Held**
Web: www.cpsexpress.com
SIC: 4212 4213 4214 Local trucking, without storage; Trucking, except local; Local trucking with storage
PA: Haddy, J G Sales Co, Inc
4375 E Lowell St Ste G
951 685-4100

(P-8899)
CARGO SOLUTION BROKERAGE LLC
14769 San Bernardino Ave, Fontana (92335-2554)
PHONE.........................909 350-1644
Bobby Kang, *CEO*
Baldev Kang, *
EMP: 200 **EST:** 2004
SALES (est): 14.05MM **Privately Held**
Web: www.cargosolutionexpress.com
SIC: 4212 Local trucking, without storage

(P-8900)
CENTRAL STATES LOGISTICS INC
Also Called: Diligent Delivery Systems
28338 Constellation Rd Ste 940, Valencia (91355-5800)
PHONE.........................661 295-7222
Larry Browne, *Brnch Mgr*
EMP: 86
SALES (corp-wide): 36.79MM **Privately Held**
Web: www.diligentusa.com
SIC: 4212 Delivery service, vehicular
PA: Central States Logistics, Inc.
9200 Derrington Rd # 100
888 374-3354

(P-8901)
CJ LOGISTICS AMERICA LLC
12350 Philadelphia Ave, Eastvale (91752-3228)
PHONE.........................909 605-7233
Adrian Potgieter, *Mgr*
EMP: 168
Web: america.cjlogistics.com
SIC: 4212 4213 4225 4731 Local trucking, without storage; Trucking, except local; General warehousing and storage; Freight consolidation
HQ: Cj Logistics America, Llc
1750 S Wolf Rd
Des Plaines IL 60018

(P-8902)
CNET EXPRESS
15134 Indiana Ave Apt 38, Paramount (90723-3582)
PHONE.........................949 357-5475
Diana Diaz Vargas, *CEO*
Tamara Lupoe, *Prin*
Allen E Lupoe Junior, *Prin*
EMP: 102 **EST:** 2018
SALES (est): 866.62K **Privately Held**
SIC: 4212 Delivery service, vehicular

(P-8903)
DELIVERY SOLUTIONS INC
Also Called: D S I
595 Tamarack Ave Ste D, Brea (92821-3125)
PHONE.........................800 335-6557
▲ **EMP:** 75
Web: www.deliverysolutions.co

SIC: **4212** Delivery service, vehicular

(P-8904)
DLF LOGISTICS LLC
Also Called: Dlf Logistics
1019 S Rimpau Blvd, Los Angeles (90019-1810)
P.O. Box 1929 (90801-1929)
PHONE.........................626 387-3797
Durran Felton, *Managing Member*
EMP: 81 **EST:** 2019
SALES (est): 5.35MM **Privately Held**
Web: www.dflogistics.com
SIC: 4212 Local trucking, without storage

(P-8905)
FOX TRANSPORTATION INC (PA)
8610 Helms Ave, Rancho Cucamonga (91730-4520)
P.O. Box 3119 (91730)
PHONE.........................909 291-4646
Michael K Fox, *CEO*
David Langrehr, *Sr VP*
David Burns, *VP*
Joey Ramirez, *Dir*
Mary Anne Fox, *Stockholder*
EMP: 73 **EST:** 2003
SALES (est): 24.7MM **Privately Held**
Web: www.foxtransportationinc.com
SIC: 4212 Local trucking, without storage

(P-8906)
FRESGO LLC
Also Called: Kitchen United
55 S Madison Ave, Pasadena (91101-2029)
PHONE.........................626 389-3500
James Collins, *Managing Member*
EMP: 77 **EST:** 2019
SALES (est): 4.88MM **Privately Held**
SIC: 4212 Delivery service, vehicular

(P-8907)
GALE/TRIANGLE INC (PA)
Also Called: Triangle West
12816 Shoemaker Ave, Santa Fe Springs (90670-6346)
PHONE.........................562 741-1300
Michael Kaplan, *CEO*
Bob Kaplan, *Pr*
Craig Kaplan, *CEO*
▲ **EMP:** 94 **EST:** 1994
SQ FT: 40,000
SALES (est): 4.82MM **Privately Held**
SIC: 4212 4214 Local trucking, without storage; Local trucking with storage

(P-8908)
GATEWAY LOGISTICS TECH LLC
11400 W Olympic Blvd, Los Angeles (90064-1550)
PHONE.........................732 750-9000
Jim Deveau, *CEO*
EMP: 218 **EST:** 2020
SALES (est): 4.21MM
SALES (corp-wide): 26.36MM **Privately Held**
SIC: 4212 4213 Local trucking, without storage; Trucking, except local
PA: Taylored Services Parent Co. Inc.
1495 E Locust St
909 510-4800

(P-8909)
GAZELLE TRANSPORTATION LLC
34915 Gazelle Ct, Bakersfield (93308-9618)
PHONE.........................661 322-8868

EMP: 193 **EST:** 1992
SALES (est): 20.08MM **Privately Held**
Web: www.gazelletrans.com
SIC: 4212 Local trucking, without storage

(P-8910)
GENERAL LGSTICS SYSTEMS US INC
12300 Bell Ranch Dr, Santa Fe Springs (90670-3356)
PHONE.........................562 577-6037
EMP: 223
SALES (corp-wide): 16.09B **Privately Held**
Web: www.gls-us.com
SIC: 4212 Delivery service, vehicular
HQ: General Logistics Systems Us, Inc.
4000 Exec Pkwy Ste 295
San Ramon CA 94583

(P-8911)
GENERAL LGSTICS SYSTEMS US INC
24305 Prielipp Rd, Wildomar (92595-7425)
PHONE.........................951 677-3972
EMP: 111
SALES (corp-wide): 16.09B **Privately Held**
Web: www.gls-us.com
SIC: 4212 Delivery service, vehicular
HQ: General Logistics Systems Us, Inc.
4000 Exec Pkwy Ste 295
San Ramon CA 94583

(P-8912)
GRIMMWAY ENTERPRISES INC
11646 Malaga Rd, Arvin (93203-9641)
PHONE.........................307 302-0090
EMP: 70
SALES (corp-wide): 577.4MM **Privately Held**
Web: www.grimmway.com
SIC: 4212 Farm to market haulage, local
PA: Grimmway Enterprises, Inc.
12064 Buena Vista Blvd
800 301-3101

(P-8913)
HANKS INC
Also Called: Sun Express
13866 Slover Ave, Fontana (92337-7037)
PHONE.........................909 350-8365
Brenda Cash, *Pr*
Shirley Bachar, *
▲ **EMP:** 74 **EST:** 1961
SQ FT: 24,000
SALES (est): 5.02MM
SALES (corp-wide): 20.76B **Publicly Held**
Web: www.shipsun.com
SIC: 4212 4213 Local trucking, without storage; Trucking, except local
PA: Jones Lang Lasalle Incorporated
200 E Rndolph St Fl 43-48
312 782-5800

(P-8914)
HARTWICK & HAND INC (PA)
Also Called: H & H Truck Terminal
16953 N D St, Victorville (92394-1417)
P.O. Box 1595 (92393-1595)
PHONE.........................760 245-1666
Stacy L Hand, *CEO*
Edward Perreria, *
EMP: 73 **EST:** 1961
SQ FT: 8,800
SALES (est): 1.85MM
SALES (corp-wide): 1.85MM **Privately Held**
SIC: 4212 Local trucking, without storage

(P-8915)
HEAVY LOAD TRANSFER LLC
4811 Airport Plaza Dr, Long Beach (90815-1371)
PHONE.........................310 816-0260
EMP: 75 **EST:** 2016
SALES (est): 2.36MM **Privately Held**
Web: www.ttsi.com
SIC: 4212 Local trucking, without storage

(P-8916)
HF COX INC
Also Called: Cox Petroleum Transport
8330 Atlantic Ave, Cudahy (90201-5808)
PHONE.........................323 587-2359
Diane Judge, *Brnch Mgr*
EMP: 290
SALES (corp-wide): 683.25K **Privately Held**
Web: www.coxpetroleum.com
SIC: 4212 Petroleum haulage, local
PA: H.F. Cox, Inc.
118 Cox Transport Way
661 366-3236

(P-8917)
HIGH PERFORMANCE LOGISTICS LLC
7227 Central Ave, Riverside (92504-1432)
PHONE.........................702 300-4880
Michael Waters, *Managing Member*
EMP: 75 **EST:** 2018
SALES (est): 2.39MM **Privately Held**
SIC: 4212 Local trucking, without storage

(P-8918)
HUB GROUP TRUCKING INC
13867 Valley Blvd, Fontana (92335-5230)
PHONE.........................909 770-8950
Roy Sheredon, *Brnch Mgr*
EMP: 500
SALES (corp-wide): 4.2B **Publicly Held**
Web: www.hubgroup.com
SIC: 4212 Local trucking, without storage
HQ: Hub Group Trucking, Inc.
2001 Hub Group Way
Oak Brook IL 60523
630 271-3600

(P-8919)
M-G DISPOSAL SERVICE INC
Also Called: M G Disposal
1131 N Blue Gum St, Anaheim (92806-2408)
PHONE.........................714 238-3300
TOLL FREE: 866
Tom Vogt, *Pr*
EMP: 70 **EST:** 1957
SALES (est): 4.61MM
SALES (corp-wide): 14.96B **Publicly Held**
SIC: 4212 Garbage collection and transport, no disposal
PA: Republic Services, Inc.
18500 N Allied Way
480 627-2700

(P-8920)
MULECHAIN INC
2901 W Coast Hwy Ste 200, Newport Beach (92663-4045)
PHONE.........................888 456-8881
Ralph Liu, *CEO*
EMP: 56 **EST:** 2017
SALES (est): 768.35K **Privately Held**
Web: www.mulechain.com
SIC: 4212 7372 Delivery service, vehicular; Application computer software

▲ = Import ▼ = Export
◆ = Import/Export

(P-8921)
NIPPON EX NEC LGSTICS AMER INC
Also Called: Nec Logistics America
18615 S Ferris Pl, Rancho Dominguez
(90220-6452)
PHONE..............................310 604-6100
Kazuhiko Takahashi, *CEO*
Hidehito Tachikawa, *
▲ **EMP:** 75 **EST:** 1990
SQ FT: 353,000
SALES (est): 24.92MM **Privately Held**
SIC: 4212 4213 4225 Local trucking, without storage; Trucking, except local; General warehousing and storage
HQ: Nec Corporation Of America
5205 N O Cnnor Blvd Ste 4
Irving TX 75039
214 262-6000

(P-8922)
ROY MILLER FREIGHT LINES LLC (PA)
3165 E Coronado St, Anaheim
(92806-1915)
P.O. Box 18419 (92817-8419)
PHONE..............................714 632-5511
Danny Miller, *Mng*
Danny Miller, *CEO*
Wiley R Miller Junior, *Managing Member*
EMP: 100 **EST:** 1942
SALES (est): 19.14MM
SALES (corp-wide): 19.14MM **Privately Held**
Web: www.roymiller.com
SIC: 4212 Local trucking, without storage

(P-8923)
SOUTH COAST TRNSP & DIST INC
Western Regional Delivery
1424 S Raymond Ave, Fullerton
(92831-5235)
PHONE..............................310 816-0280
Elias Youkhehpaz, *Pr*
EMP: 73
Web: www.wrds.com
SIC: 4212 Local trucking, without storage
PA: South Coast Transportation & Distribution, Inc.
1424 S Raymond Ave

(P-8924)
SOUTHERN COUNTIES TERMINALS
Also Called: Griley Air Freight
5341 W 104th St, Loo Angoloo
(90045-6009)
P.O. Box 92940 (90009-2940)
PHONE..............................310 642-0462
EMP: 90 **EST:** 1973
SALES (est): 10.55MM **Privately Held**
Web: www.grileyair.com
SIC: 4212 Local trucking, without storage

(P-8925)
TRAIL LINES INC
9415 Sorensen Ave, Santa Fe Springs
(90670-2648)
P.O. Box 3567 (90670-1567)
PHONE..............................562 758-6980
Ofer Shitrit, *CEO*
Reuven Spivak, *
EMP: 75 **EST:** 1994
SALES (est): 9.58MM **Privately Held**
Web: www.traillines.com
SIC: 4212 4789 Local trucking, without storage; Pipeline terminal facilities, independently operated

(P-8926)
TRANSPRTTION BRKG SPCLISTS INC
Also Called: Tbs
3151 Airway Ave Ste F208, Costa Mesa
(92626-4621)
PHONE..............................714 754-4236
Ben Haeri, *CEO*
Steve Kennedy, *
Mike Owens, *
Lee Mayer, *
Fred Khac, *
EMP: 450 **EST:** 2016
SALES (est): 2.92MM **Privately Held**
SIC: 4212 Local trucking, without storage

(P-8927)
TT TRUCKING SERVICES LLC
Also Called: TT Trucking Services
12745 Jade Rd, Victorville (92392-6256)
P.O. Box 6216 (92554)
PHONE..............................323 790-3408
Tiffany Taylor, *Managing Member*
Terry Taylor, *Managing Member*
EMP: 76 **EST:** 2019
SALES (est): 888.02K **Privately Held**
SIC: 4212 4215 Delivery service, vehicular; Courier services, except by air

(P-8928)
ULS EXPRESS INC
2850 E Del Amo Blvd, Compton
(90221-6007)
P.O. Box 7547 (90807-0547)
PHONE..............................310 631-0800
EMP: 157 **EST:** 1987
SQ FT: 220,000
SALES (est): 4.62MM **Privately Held**
Web: www.uwc-net.com
SIC: 4212 Local trucking, without storage
HQ: Universal Logistics System, Inc.
2850 Del Amo Blvd
Carson CA 90810
310 631-0800

(P-8929)
UNITED PUMPING SERVICE INC
14000 Valley Blvd, City Of Industry
(91746-2801)
PHONE..............................626 961-9326
Eduardo T Perry Senior, *Pr*
Daniel C Perry, *
Margaret Perry, *
Eduardo Perry Junior, *Sec*
EMP: 95 **EST:** 1970
SQ FT: 25,000
SALES (est): 21.71MM **Privately Held**
Web: www.unitedpumping.com
SIC: 4212 Hazardous waste transport

(P 8030)
WETZEL & SONS MVG & STOR INC
Also Called: Wetzel Trucking
12400 Osborne St, Pacoima (91331-2002)
PHONE..............................818 890-0992
Donald C Wetzel, *Pr*
Daniel S Wetzel, *
EMP: 70 **EST:** 1976
SQ FT: 146,000
SALES (est): 4.48MM **Privately Held**
Web: www.wetzelmovingandstorage.com
SIC: 4212 Moving services

(P-8931)
XPO CARTAGE INC
Also Called: Pacer
5800 Sheila St, Commerce (90040-2322)
PHONE..............................800 837-7584

EMP: 83
SIC: 4212 Local trucking, without storage

4213 Trucking, Except Local

(P-8932)
ARDWIN INC
Also Called: Ardwin Freight
2940 N Hollywood Way, Burbank
(91505-1024)
P.O. Box 1609 (91507-1609)
PHONE..............................818 767-7777
Edwin Sahakian, *Pr*
EMP: 130 **EST:** 1988
SQ FT: 10,000
SALES (est): 8.49MM **Privately Held**
Web: www.ardwin.com
SIC: 4213 Contract haulers

(P-8933)
BEST OVERNITE EXPRESS INC (PA)
Also Called: Best Overnight Express
406 Live Oak Ave, Irwindale (91706-1314)
P.O. Box 90816 (91715-0816)
PHONE..............................626 256-6340
William K Applebee, *Pr*
Mike White, *
Micah Applebee, *
EMP: 100 **EST:** 1988
SQ FT: 25,000
SALES (est): 27.6MM **Privately Held**
Web: www.bestovernite.com
SIC: 4213 Trucking, except local

(P-8934)
CARGO SOLUTION EXPRESS INC (PA)
14587 Valley Blvd # 89, Fontana
(92335-6248)
PHONE..............................800 582-5104
Balwinder Kaur Kang, *Pr*
Sammy Kang, *
EMP: 250 **EST:** 2002
SQ FT: 10,000
SALES (est): 99.94MM
SALES (corp-wide): 99.94MM **Privately Held**
Web: www.cargosolutionexpress.com
SIC: 4213 Trucking, except local

(P-8935)
CERTIFIED FRT LOGISTICS INC (PA)
1344 White Ct, Santa Maria (93458-3732)
P.O. Box 5668 (93456-5668)
PHONE..............................800 592-5906
James O Nelson, *Pr*
Edwin F Nelson Junior, *VP*
Jon Cramer, *
Scott Cramer, *
EMP: 120 **EST:** 1963
SQ FT: 40,000
SALES (est): 42.02MM
SALES (corp-wide): 42.02MM **Privately Held**
Web: www.certifiedfreightlogistics.com
SIC: 4213 Refrigerated products transport

(P-8936)
CJ LOGISTICS AMERICA LLC
1895 Marigold Ave, Redlands (92374-5028)
PHONE..............................909 363-4354
Greg Hart, *Genl Pt*
EMP: 89
Web: america.cjlogistics.com
SIC: 4213 4212 Trucking, except local; Local trucking, without storage
HQ: Cj Logistics America, Llc
1750 S Wolf Rd

Des Plaines IL 60018

(P-8937)
COMPLETE LOGISTICS COMPANY
1207 Air Wing Rd, San Diego (92154-7713)
PHONE..............................619 661-9610
Roseles Ray, *Mgr*
EMP: 73
SALES (corp-wide): 24.29MM **Privately Held**
Web: www.logisticsinc.com
SIC: 4213 Trucking, except local
PA: The Complete Logistics Company
15895 Valley Blvd 200
909 544-5040

(P-8938)
CONTRACTORS CARGO COMPANY (PA)
Also Called: Contractors Rigging & Erectors
7233 Alondra Blvd, Paramount
(90723-3901)
P.O. Box 5290 (90224-5290)
PHONE..............................310 609-1957
Carla Ann Wheeler, *CEO*
Gerald D Wheeler, *
Kimberly Dorio, *
◆ **EMP:** 80 **EST:** 1959
SALES (est): 24.28MM
SALES (corp-wide): 24.28MM **Privately Held**
Web: www.contractorscargo.com
SIC: 4213 4731 1623 4741 Contract haulers; Freight transportation arrangement; Water, sewer, and utility lines; Rental of railroad cars

(P-8939)
COVENANT TRANSPORT INC
Also Called: Covenant Transport
1300 E Franklin Ave, Pomona
(91766-5416)
PHONE..............................909 469-0130
Bill Furgess, *Mgr*
EMP: 719
Web: www.covenantlogistics.com
SIC: 4213 Contract haulers
HQ: Covenant Transport, Inc.
400 Birmingham Hwy
Chattanooga TN 37419
423 821-1212

(P-8940)
CRST EXPEDITED INC
Also Called: Gardner Logistics
9032 Merrill Ave, Chino (91708)
P.O. Box 747 (91708-0747)
PHONE..............................909 563-5606
EMP: 259
SALES (corp-wide): 980.15MM **Privately Held**
Web: www.crst.com
SIC: 4213 Contract haulers
HQ: Crst Expedited, Inc.
201 1st St Se
Cedar Rapids IA 52401
800 443-0940

(P-8941)
CRST EXPEDITED INC
1219 E Elm St, Ontario (91761-4585)
PHONE..............................909 563-5606
John Smith, *Brnch Mgr*
EMP: 500
SALES (corp-wide): 980.15MM **Privately Held**
Web: www.crst.com
SIC: 4213 4212 Trucking, except local; Local trucking, without storage

HQ: Crst Expedited, Inc.
201 1st St Se
Cedar Rapids IA 52401
800 443-0940

(P-8942)
D C SHOWER DOORS INC
Also Called: Image Transfer
26121 Avenue Hall, Valencia (91355-3490)
PHONE...............................661 257-1177
Jason Shepard, *Pr*
EMP: 133 **EST:** 1996
SQ FT: 125,000
SALES (est): 1MM
SALES (corp-wide): 81.02MM **Privately Held**
Web: www.cwdoors.com
SIC: 4213 Trucking, except local
PA: Contractors Wardrobe, Inc.
26121 Ave Hall
661 257-1177

(P-8943)
DEPENDABLE COMPANIES
2555 E Olympic Blvd, Los Angeles
(90023-2656)
PHONE...............................800 548-8608
Ron Massman, *CEO*
EMP: 185 **EST:** 2015
SALES (est): 9.37MM **Privately Held**
Web: www.godependable.com
SIC: 4213 Trucking, except local

(P-8944)
DEPENDABLE HIGHWAY EXPRESS INC (PA)
Also Called: Dependable Supply Chain Svcs
2555 E Olympic Blvd, Los Angeles
(90023-2656)
P.O. Box 58047 (90058-0047)
PHONE...............................323 526-2200
Ronald Massman, *Pr*
Robert Massman, *
Michael Dougan, *
◆ **EMP:** 300 **EST:** 1984
SQ FT: 1,680,000
SALES (est): 206.32MM
SALES (corp-wide): 206.32MM **Privately Held**
Web: www.godependable.com
SIC: 4213 4225 Contract haulers; General warehousing and storage

(P-8945)
DEPENDABLE HIGHWAY EXPRESS INC
800 E 230th St, Carson (90745-5002)
PHONE...............................310 522-4111
Keith Norris, *Mgr*
EMP: 139
SALES (corp-wide): 206.32MM **Privately Held**
Web: www.godependable.com
SIC: 4213 4225 Contract haulers; General warehousing and storage
PA: Dependable Highway Express, Inc.
2555 E Olympic Blvd
323 526-2200

(P-8946)
DEPENDABLE HIGHWAY EXPRESS INC
Also Called: Dhe
1351 S Campus Ave, Ontario (91761-4352)
PHONE...............................909 923-0065
Bob Bianchi, *Brnch Mgr*
EMP: 119
SALES (corp-wide): 206.32MM **Privately Held**

Web: www.godependable.com
SIC: 4213 Trucking, except local
PA: Dependable Highway Express, Inc.
2555 E Olympic Blvd
323 526-2200

(P-8947)
DOUBLE EAGLE TRNSP CORP
12135 Scarbrough Ct, Oak Hills
(92344-9200)
PHONE...............................760 956-3770
Gerald E Butcher, *Pr*
EMP: 140 **EST:** 1992
SQ FT: 10,125
SALES (est): 5.32MM **Privately Held**
Web:
www.doubleeagletransportation.com
SIC: 4213 4212 Contract haulers; Local trucking, without storage

(P-8948)
ESPARZA ENTERPRISES INC
500 Workman St, Bakersfield (93307-6871)
PHONE...............................661 631-0347
EMP: 792
SALES (corp-wide): 135MM **Privately Held**
Web: www.esparzainc.com
SIC: 4213 Trucking, except local
PA: Esparza Enterprises, Inc.
3851 Fruitvale Ave
661 831-0002

(P-8949)
ESTES EXPRESS LINES
Also Called: Estes
13327 Temple Ave, City Of Industry
(91746-1513)
PHONE...............................626 333-9090
Kieran O'carroll, *Mgr*
EMP: 103
SQ FT: 6,156
SALES (corp-wide): 3.56B **Privately Held**
Web: www.estes-express.com
SIC: 4213 4212 Less-than-truckload (LTL); Local trucking, without storage
PA: Estes Express Lines
3901 W Broad St
804 353-1900

(P-8950)
ESTES EXPRESS LINES
10736 Cherry Ave, Fontana (92337-7196)
PHONE...............................909 427-9850
Mark Brown, *Mgr*
EMP: 116
SALES (corp-wide): 3.56B **Privately Held**
Web: www.estes-express.com
SIC: 4213 4212 Less-than-truckload (LTL); Local trucking, without storage
PA: Estes Express Lines
3901 W Broad St
804 353-1900

(P-8951)
ESTES EXPRESS LINES
120 Press Ln, Chula Vista (91910-1012)
PHONE...............................619 425-4040
Craig Buker, *Brnch Mgr*
EMP: 90
SALES (corp-wide): 3.56B **Privately Held**
Web: www.estes-express.com
SIC: 4213 Contract haulers
PA: Estes Express Lines
3901 W Broad St
804 353-1900

(P-8952)
FRIENDS GROUP EXPRESS INC
14520 Village Dr Apt 1013, Fontana
(92337-2501)

P.O. Box 310488 (92331-0488)
PHONE...............................909 346-6814
Parmjit Singh Grewal, *Prin*
EMP: 78 **EST:** 2014
SQ FT: 700
SALES (est): 5.24MM **Privately Held**
SIC: 4213 4212 Trucking, except local; Local trucking, without storage

(P-8953)
H RAUVEL INC
Also Called: Nova Transportation Services
501 W Walnut St, Compton (90220-5221)
PHONE...............................562 989-3333
Hector Velasco, *Mgr*
EMP: 180
SALES (corp-wide): 2.79MM **Privately Held**
Web: www.novafreight.net
SIC: 4213 Trucking, except local
PA: H. Rauvel, Inc.
1710 E Sepulveda Blvd
310 604-0060

(P-8954)
HEARTLAND EXPRESS INC IOWA
Also Called: Heartland Express
10131 Redwood Ave, Fontana
(92335-6236)
PHONE...............................319 626-3600
Matthew Gonzalez, *Supervisor*
EMP: 541
SALES (corp-wide): 1.21B **Publicly Held**
Web: www.heartlandexpress.com
SIC: 4213 Contract haulers
HQ: Heartland Express, Inc. Of Iowa
901 Heartland Way
North Liberty IA 52317
319 626-3600

(P-8955)
HI PRO INC
57019 Yucca Trl Ste D, Yucca Valley
(92284-7909)
P.O. Box 148 (92277-0148)
PHONE...............................442 205-0063
Joshua Stoneback, *CEO*
EMP: 200 **EST:** 2012
SALES (est): 10.27MM **Privately Held**
Web: www.hiproinc.com
SIC: 4213 7389 4212 Trucking, except local; Brokers, contract services; Delivery service, vehicular

(P-8956)
IMC LOGISTICS LLC
550 W Artesia Blvd, Compton (90220-5524)
PHONE...............................844 903-4737
EMP: 101
SALES (corp-wide): 1.58B **Privately Held**
Web: www.imcc.com
SIC: 4213 Trucking, except local
HQ: Imc Logistics, Llc
1305 Schilling Blvd W
Collierville TN 38017
833 334-4622

(P-8957)
JACK JONES TRUCKING INC
1090 E Belmont St, Ontario (91761-4501)
PHONE...............................909 456-2500
Valerie Liese, *Pr*
Erin Craig, *
Bob Liese, *
Kristy Richardson, *
Robert Liese, *
EMP: 100 **EST:** 1971
SQ FT: 3,000
SALES (est): 6.22MM **Privately Held**

Web: www.jjtinc.com
SIC: 4213 Trucking, except local

(P-8958)
KLLM TRANSPORT SERVICES LLC
5361 Santa Ana St, Ontario (91761-8624)
PHONE...............................909 350-9600
EMP: 76
SALES (corp-wide): 495.07MM **Privately Held**
Web: www.kllm.com
SIC: 4213 Trucking, except local
PA: Kllm Transport Services, Llc
135 Riverview Dr
800 925-1000

(P-8959)
LANDFORCE CORPORATION
17201 N D St, Victorville (92394-1401)
PHONE...............................760 843-7839
Rajinder Bhangu, *CEO*
EMP: 120 **EST:** 2000
SALES (est): 9.51MM **Privately Held**
Web: www.landforcecorp.com
SIC: 4213 Trucking, except local

(P-8960)
LANDSTAR GLOBAL LOGISTICS INC
2313 E Philadelphia St Ste D, Ontario
(91761-8048)
PHONE...............................909 266-0096
EMP: 91
Web: www.landstar.com
SIC: 4213 Trucking, except local
HQ: Landstar Global Logistics, Inc.
13410 Sutton Pk Dr S
Jacksonville FL 32224

(P-8961)
LAS VEGAS / LA EXPRESS INC (PA)
1000 S Cucamonga Ave, Ontario
(91761-3461)
PHONE...............................909 972-3100
Ronald Cain Junior, *CEO*
Beverly A Adley, *
Michael P Adley, *
EMP: 170 **EST:** 1988
SQ FT: 163,000
SALES (est): 9.78MM **Privately Held**
Web: www.vegasexpress.com
SIC: 4213 Trucking, except local

(P-8962)
LOAD DELIVERED LOGISTICS LLC
214 Main St, Venice (90291-2522)
PHONE...............................310 822-0215
Michael Cherney, *Mgr*
EMP: 141
SALES (corp-wide): 609.82MM **Privately Held**
Web: www.capstonelogistics.com
SIC: 4213 Trucking, except local
HQ: Load Delivered Logistics Llc
640 N Lasalle Ste 555
Chicago IL 60654
877 930-5623

(P-8963)
LTL PROS INC
13610 S Archibald Ave, Ontario
(91761-7930)
PHONE...............................909 350-1600
Manuel Vargas, *Pr*
EMP: 80 **EST:** 2017
SALES (est): 2.78MM **Privately Held**

▲ = Import ▼ = Export
◆ = Import/Export

Web: www.ltlpros.com
SIC: 4213 Trucking, except local

(P-8964)
MARK CLEMONS
Also Called: Mtc Transportation
4584 Adobe Rd, Twentynine Palms
(92277-1671)
P.O. Box 148 (92277-0148)
PHONE..............................760 361-1531
Mark Clemons, *Owner*
Genevieve Clemons, *Mgr*
EMP: 200 **EST:** 1978
SALES (est): 7.35MM **Privately Held**
SIC: 4213 4212 4513 4522 Heavy
machinery transport; Local trucking, without
storage; Air courier services; Air
transportation, nonscheduled

(P-8965)
MASHBURN TRNSP SVCS INC
22140 Rosedale Hwy, Bakersfield
(93314-9704)
P.O. Box 66 (93268-8066)
PHONE..............................661 763-5724
Denise Mashburn, *Pr*
Michael Mashburn, *
EMP: 120 **EST:** 1987
SQ FT: 2,000
SALES (est): 16.63MM **Privately Held**
Web: www.mashburntransportation.com
SIC: 4213 4212 Contract haulers; Local
trucking, without storage

(P-8966)
NATIONAL RETAIL TRNSP INC
400 Harley Knox Blvd, Perris (92571-7566)
PHONE..............................951 243-6110
EMP: 77
SALES (corp-wide): 353.52MM **Privately
Held**
Web: www.nrs3pl.com
SIC: 4213 Trucking, except local
HQ: National Retail Transportation, Inc.
2820 16th St
North Bergen NJ 07047
201 866-0462

(P-8967)
NEW LEGEND INC
8613 Etiwanda Ave, Rancho Cucamonga
(91739-9611)
PHONE..............................855 210-2300
EMP: 226
Web: www.newlegendinc.com
SIC: 4213 4212 Trucking, except local; Local
trucking, without storage
PA: New Legend, Inc.
811 S 59th Ave

(P-8968)
NEXT FREIGHT SOLUTIONS INC
2383 Utah Ave Ste 100, El Segundo
(90245-4845)
PHONE..............................442 291-9220
Hanbing Yan, *CEO*
EMP: 77 **EST:** 2020
SALES (est): 8.03MM **Privately Held**
Web: www.nexttrucking.com
SIC: 4213 Trucking, except local

(P-8969)
PACIFIC DRAYAGE SERVICES LLC
Also Called: Pds
550 W Artesia Blvd, Compton (90220-5524)
PHONE..............................833 334-4622
Mark George, *Managing Member*
EMP: 210 **EST:** 2019
SALES (est): 8.4MM

SALES (corp-wide): 1.58B **Privately Held**
Web: www.imcc.com
SIC: 4213 Trucking, except local
HQ: Imc Companies - National Accounts,
Llc
1305 Schilling Blvd W
Collierville TN 38017
901 746-3700

(P-8970)
PAN PACIFIC PETROLEUM CO INC (PA)
9302 Garfield Ave, South Gate
(90280-3805)
P.O. Box 1966 (90280-1966)
PHONE..............................562 928-0100
Robert Roth, *CEO*
Dale Snyder, *
Steven Roth, *
EMP: 100 **EST:** 1962
SQ FT: 600
SALES (est): 5.85K
SALES (corp-wide): 5.85K **Privately Held**
SIC: 4213 5172 Liquid petroleum transport,
non-local; Petroleum brokers

(P-8971)
POINTDIRECT TRANSPORT INC
19083 Mermack Ave, Lake Elsinore
(92532-2256)
PHONE..............................909 371-0837
Adolfo De La Herran, *Pr*
EMP: 100 **EST:** 2014
SALES (est): 3.28MM **Privately Held**
Web: www.point-direct.com
SIC: 4213 Trucking, except local

(P-8972)
PROGRESSIVE TRANSPORTATION INC
Also Called: PROGRESSIVE
TRANSPORTATION, INC.
1210 E 223rd St Ste 328, Carson
(90745-4254)
PHONE..............................310 684-2100
Kevin Dukesherer, *Prin*
EMP: 71
Web: www.progressivetransportation.com
SIC: 4213 Contract haulers
HQ: Progressive Transportation, Llc
156535 E Wausau Ave
Wausau WI 54403

(P-8973)
RPM TRANSPORTATION INC (DH)
11660 Arroyo Ave, Santa Ana
(92705-3057)
PHONE..............................714 388-3500
Shawn Duke, *Pr*
Andrew Lewes, *
▲ **EMP:** 110 **EST:** 1985
SQ FT: 175,000
SALES (est): 16.25MM
SALES (corp-wide): 1.16B **Privately Held**
Web: www.odysseylogistics.com
SIC: 4213 4225 4214 Trailer or container on
flat car (TOFC/COFC); General
warehousing; Local trucking with storage
HQ: Rpm Consolidated Services, Inc.
1901 Raymer Ave
Fullerton CA 92833
714 388-3500

(P-8974)
STANLEY G ALEXANDER INC (PA)
Also Called: Alexander's Moving & Storage
2942 Dow Ave, Tustin (92780-7220)

PHONE..............................714 731-1658
EMP: 130 **EST:** 1953
SALES (est): 72.94MM
SALES (corp-wide): 72.94MM **Privately
Held**
Web: www.alexanders.net
SIC: 4213 Trucking, except local

(P-8975)
STEVENS TRANSPORTATION INC
Also Called: Stevens Trucking
7100 E Brundage Ln, Bakersfield
(93307-3060)
PHONE..............................661 366-3286
EMP: 150 **EST:** 1984
SALES (est): 23.69MM **Privately Held**
Web: www.stibk.com
SIC: 4213 Refrigerated products transport

(P-8976)
SWIFT LEASING CO LLC
14392 Valley Blvd, Fontana (92335-5240)
PHONE..............................909 347-0500
EMP: 289
Web: www.swifttrans.com
SIC: 4213 Contract haulers
HQ: Swift Leasing Co., Llc
2200 S 75th Ave
Phoenix AZ 85043
602 269-9700

(P-8977)
TCI TRANSPORTATION SERVICES
14561 Merrill Ave Bldg B, Fontana
(92335-4219)
PHONE..............................909 355-8545
EMP: 194
SALES (corp-wide): 23.05MM **Privately
Held**
Web: www.tcitransportation.com
SIC: 4213 Trucking, except local
PA: Tci Transportation Services
4950 Triggs St
323 269-3033

(P-8978)
TOTAL TRNSP LOGISTICS INC
Also Called: Total Transportation Logistics
10 Longitude Way, Corona (92881-4911)
PHONE..............................951 360-9521
Douglas Shockley, *Pr*
Robert L Hicks, *
▲ **EMP:** 75 **EST:** 2000
SALES (est): 22.2MM **Privately Held**
Web: www.ttllogistics.com
SIC: 4213 Contract haulers

(P-8979)
U C L INCORPORATED (PA)
Also Called: United Cargo Logistics
620 S Hacienda Blvd, City Of Industry
(91745-1126)
PHONE..............................323 235-0099
Byung Y Chang, *CEO*
Chris Chang, *
Yong Ku, *
EMP: 100 **EST:** 1998
SQ FT: 16,000
SALES (est): 27.76MM
SALES (corp-wide): 27.76MM **Privately
Held**
Web: www.uclinc.com
SIC: 4213 Trucking, except local

(P-8980)
U S XPRESS INC
363 Nina Lee Rd, Calexico (92231-9527)

PHONE..............................760 768-6707
EMP: 265
Web: www.usxpress.com
SIC: 4213 Contract haulers
HQ: U. S. Xpress, Inc.
4080 Jenkins Rd
Chattanooga TN 37421
866 266-7270

(P-8981)
VALLEY BULK INC
17649 Turner Rd, Victorville (92394-8716)
P.O. Box 1100 (92393-1100)
PHONE..............................760 843-0574
Jeff W Golson, *Pr*
EMP: 85 **EST:** 1995
SALES (est): 7.83MM **Privately Held**
Web: www.valleybulkinc.com
SIC: 4213 Contract haulers

(P-8982)
VAN KING & STORAGE INC
Also Called: King Relocation Services
13535 Larwin Cir, Santa Fe Springs
(90670-5032)
PHONE..............................562 921-0555
TOLL FREE: 800
Steve Komorous, *Pr*
Edwin Nabal, *
Keith Hindsley, *
EMP: 75 **EST:** 1955
SQ FT: 60,000
SALES (est): 23.33MM **Privately Held**
Web: www.kingvanstorage.com
SIC: 4213 4225 Trucking, except local;
General warehousing and storage

(P-8983)
VENTURA TRANSFER COMPANY (PA)
2418 E 223rd St, Long Beach (90810-1697)
PHONE..............................310 549-1660
Randall J Clifford, *CEO*
Greg Clifford, *
Galen Clifford, *
Phyllis E Batchelor, *
Steven F Clifford, *
▲ **EMP:** 75 **EST:** 1927
SQ FT: 10,000
SALES (est): 20.11MM
SALES (corp-wide): 20.11MM **Privately
Held**
Web: www.venturatransfercompany.com
SIC: 4213 4212 4214 Contract haulers;
Local trucking, without storage; Local
trucking with storage

(P-8984)
XPO LOGISTICS FREIGHT INC
2102 N Batavia St, Orange (92865-3104)
PHONE..............................714 282-7777
Tim Worner, *Mgr*
EMP: 87
SALES (corp-wide): 7.74B **Publicly Held**
Web: www.xpo.com
SIC: 4213 Contract haulers
HQ: Xpo Logistics Freight, Inc.
2211 Old Erhart Rd Ste 10
Ann Arbor MI 48105
800 755-2728

(P-8985)
XPO LOGISTICS FREIGHT INC
13364 Marlay Ave, Fontana (92337-6919)
PHONE..............................951 685-1244
Mark Logan, *Genl Mgr*
EMP: 128
SALES (corp-wide): 7.74B **Publicly Held**
Web: www.xpo.com
SIC: 4213 Contract haulers

HQ: Xpo Logistics Freight, Inc.
2211 Old Erhart Rd Ste 10
Ann Arbor MI 48105
800 755-2728

(P-8986)
XPO LOGISTICS FREIGHT INC
1955 E Washington Blvd, Los Angeles
(90021-3206)
PHONE..................213 744-0664
Todd Liverman, *Brnch Mgr*
EMP: 139
SQ FT: 39,842
SALES (corp-wide): 7.74B **Publicly Held**
Web: www.xpo.com
SIC: 4213 4212 4731 Contract haulers;
Local trucking, without storage; Freight
forwarding
HQ: Xpo Logistics Freight, Inc.
2211 Old Erhart Rd Ste 10
Ann Arbor MI 48105
800 755-2728

(P-8987)
XPO LOGISTICS FREIGHT INC
12903 Lakeland Rd, Santa Fe Springs
(90670-4516)
PHONE..................562 946-8331
Jim Lutze, *Mgr*
EMP: 94
SALES (corp-wide): 7.74B **Publicly Held**
Web: www.xpo.com
SIC: 4213 Contract haulers
HQ: Xpo Logistics Freight, Inc.
2211 Old Erhart Rd Ste 10
Ann Arbor MI 48105
800 755-2728

4214 Local Trucking With Storage

(P-8988)
ALL CARTAGE TRANSPORTATION INC (PA)
Also Called: A C T
12621 Chadron Ave, Hawthorne
(90250-4809)
P.O. Box 90521 (90009-0521)
PHONE..................310 970-0600
George Aiello, *Pr*
Jeff De Seire, *
EMP: 77 EST: 1979
SQ FT: 24,000
SALES (est): 9.56MM
SALES (corp-wide): 9.56MM **Privately Held**
Web: www.allcartage.com
SIC: 4214 4449 Local trucking with storage;
Transportation (freight) on bays and sounds
of the ocean

(P-8989)
COROVAN CORPORATION (PA)
12302 Kerran St, Poway (92064-6884)
PHONE..................858 762-8100
Richard R Schmitz, *CEO*
Robert J Schmitz, *
Thomas A Schmitz, *
EMP: 175 EST: 1994
SQ FT: 80,000
SALES (est): 98.92MM **Privately Held**
Web: www.corovan.com
SIC: 4214 Local trucking with storage

(P-8990)
COROVAN MOVING & STORAGE CO (HQ)
12302 Kerran St, Poway (92064-6884)

PHONE..................858 748-1100
Kim Kamencik, *Pr*
Robert J Schmitz, *
Thomas A Schmitz, *
Jerry P Brothers, *
▲ EMP: 100 EST: 1948
SQ FT: 600,000
SALES (est): 23.11MM **Privately Held**
Web: www.corovan.com
SIC: 4214 4213 Household goods moving
and storage, local; Household goods
transport
PA: Corovan Corporation
12302 Kerran St

(P-8991)
FN LOGISTICS LLC
12588 Florence Ave, Santa Fe Springs
(90670-3919)
PHONE..................213 625-5900
Richard Saghian, *Pr*
EMP: 851
SIC: 4214 Local trucking with storage
HQ: Fn Logistics, Llc.
2801 E 46th St
Vernon CA 90058
213 625-5900

(P-8992)
FOX TRANSPORTATION INC
18408 S Laurel Park Rd, Compton
(90220-6015)
PHONE..................310 971-0867
Luke Shire, *Mgr*
EMP: 227
Web: www.foxtransportationinc.com
SIC: 4214 4225 Local trucking with storage;
General warehousing and storage
PA: Fox Transportation, Inc.
8610 Helms Ave

(P-8993)
GREAT AMRCN LOGISTICS DIST INC
13565 Larwin Cir, Santa Fe Springs
(90670-5032)
PHONE..................562 229-3601
TOLL FREE: 800
James Hooper, *Pr*
Lisa Moran, *
Soshie Young, *
EMP: 85 EST: 1993
SQ FT: 120,000
SALES (est): 13.49MM **Privately Held**
Web: www.greatamerican-logistics.com
SIC: 4214 4212 4213 6719 Household
goods moving and storage, local; Moving
services; Trucking, except local; Investment
holding companies, except banks

(P-8994)
SAMUEL J PIAZZA & SON INC (PA)
Also Called: Piazza Trucking
9001 Rayo Ave, South Gate (90280-3606)
PHONE..................323 357-1999
Michael Piazza, *CEO*
Robert Piazza, *
William Piazza, *
EMP: 70 EST: 1970
SQ FT: 20,000
SALES (est): 18.83MM
SALES (corp-wide): 18.83MM **Privately Held**
Web: www.piazzatrucking.com
SIC: 4214 4213 Local trucking with storage;
Trucking, except local

(P-8995)
SCHICK MOVING & STORAGE CO (PA)
2721 Michelle Dr, Tustin (92780-7018)
P.O. Box 3627 (92781-3627)
PHONE..................714 731-5500
TOLL FREE: 800
Gordon C Schick, *Pr*
Arthur C Schick Junior, *VP*
Beverly C Schick, *
Gordon Schick, *
Lynne M Larson, *
EMP: 100 EST: 1956
SQ FT: 113,000
SALES (est): 6.75MM
SALES (corp-wide): 6.75MM **Privately Held**
Web: www.schickusa.com
SIC: 4214 Household goods moving and
storage, local

(P-8996)
VAN TORRANCE & STORAGE COMPANY (PA)
Also Called: S & M Moving Systems
12128 Burke St, Santa Fe Springs
(90670-2678)
PHONE..................562 567-2101
TOLL FREE: 800
Steven Todare, *Pr*
Martin Stadler, *
◆ EMP: 100 EST: 1918
SQ FT: 95,000
SALES (est): 49.58MM
SALES (corp-wide): 49.58MM **Privately Held**
Web: www.unitedvanlines.com
SIC: 4214 4213 Local trucking with storage;
Trucking, except local

(P-8997)
VERNON CENTRAL WAREHOUSE INC
Also Called: Vernon Warehouse Co
2050 E 38th St, Vernon (90058-1615)
P.O. Box 58426 (90058-0426)
PHONE..................323 234-2200
Joseph E Tack, *CEO*
Robert L Shipp, *
Joe Tack, *
Jim Boltinghouse, *
Steve Shanklin, *
EMP: 125 EST: 1933
SQ FT: 100,000
SALES (est): 20.6MM **Privately Held**
Web: www.sweetenerproducts.com
SIC: 4214 5149 Local trucking with storage;
Natural and organic foods

4215 Courier Services, Except By Air

(P-8998)
ALL COUNTIES COURIER INC
1900 S State College Blvd Ste 450,
Anaheim (92806-6163)
PHONE..................714 599-9300
Patricia Cochran, *Pr*
EMP: 200 EST: 1984
SALES (est): 9.79MM **Privately Held**
Web: www.accdelivers.com
SIC: 4215 Package delivery, vehicular

(P-8999)
BATTLE-TESTED STRATEGIES LLC
650 Commerce Ave Ste E, Palmdale
(93551-3884)

PHONE..................661 802-6509
Johnathon Ervin, *CEO*
EMP: 90 EST: 2018
SALES (est): 3.48MM **Privately Held**
SIC: 4215 7379 Package delivery, vehicular;
Computer related services, nec

(P-9000)
DHB DELIVERY LLC
1134 N Chestnut Ln, Azusa (91702-6867)
PHONE..................626 588-7562
Daniel R Bourgault, *Managing Member*
EMP: 84 EST: 2019
SALES (est): 2.73MM **Privately Held**
SIC: 4215 Package delivery, vehicular

(P-9001)
DI OVERNITE LLC
Also Called: Deliver-It
1900 S State College Blvd Ste 450,
Anaheim (92806-6163)
PHONE..................877 997-7447
EMP: 98 EST: 2013
SALES (est): 12.11MM **Privately Held**
Web: www.deliver-it.com
SIC: 4215 Package delivery, vehicular

(P-9002)
EXPRESS GROUP INCORPORATED (PA)
Also Called: Westwood Express Messenger
Svc
10801 National Blvd Ste 104, Los Angeles
(90064-4140)
PHONE..................310 474-5999
David F Davoodian, *Pr*
Malek Neman, *
EMP: 74 EST: 1980
SQ FT: 4,000
SALES (est): 3.19MM
SALES (corp-wide): 3.19MM **Privately Held**
Web: www.deliverla.com
SIC: 4215 Courier services, except by air

(P-9003)
FUNNELCLOUDSALES
21758 Placeritos Blvd, Santa Clarita
(91321-1830)
PHONE..................661 284-6032
Timothy Kane, *Pr*
EMP: 90
SALES (est): 3.76MM **Privately Held**
SIC: 4215 7389 Package delivery, vehicular;
Business services, nec

(P-9004)
INTEGRATED PARCEL NETWORK
Also Called: Pacific Couriers
11135 Rush St Ste A, South El Monte
(91733-3520)
PHONE..................714 278-6100
Nadia Youssef, *CEO*
EMP: 275 EST: 1985
SALES (est): 1.84MM **Privately Held**
Web: www.iparcelnetwork.com
SIC: 4215 4214 7389 Package delivery,
vehicular; Local trucking with storage;
Courier or messenger service

(P-9005)
JET DELIVERY INC (PA)
2169 Wright Ave, La Verne (91750-5835)
PHONE..................800 716-7177
Michael Barbata, *Pr*
Jason Barbata, *CIO**
Mark Sur, *
EMP: 90 EST: 1950

SQ FT: 34,000
SALES (est): 24.72MM
SALES (corp-wide): 24.72MM **Privately Held**
Web: www.jetdelivery.com
SIC: 4215 4231 4212 4213 Package delivery, vehicular; Trucking terminal facilities; Local trucking, without storage; Trucking, except local

(P-9006)
KXP CARRIER SERVICES LLC
Also Called: Expak Logistics
11777 San Vicente Blvd, Los Angeles (90049-5011)
PHONE................................424 320-5300
Michael S Kraus, *CEO*
EMP: 140 **EST:** 2014
SQ FT: 1,500
SALES (est): 690.35K
SALES (corp-wide): 24.03MM **Privately Held**
Web: www.expak.com
SIC: 4215 Parcel delivery, vehicular
PA: Kxp Advantage Services, Llc
    11777 San Vicente Blvd # 747
    424 320-5300

(P-9007)
MESSENGER EXPRESS (PA)
5435 Cahuenga Blvd Ste C, North Hollywood (91601-2948)
PHONE................................213 614-0475
Gilbert Kort, *Pr*
EMP: 143 **EST:** 1976
SALES (est): 1.04MM
SALES (corp-wide): 1.04MM **Privately Held**
Web:
www.lightningmessengerexpress.com
SIC: 4215 7389 4212 Package delivery, vehicular; Courier or messenger service; Delivery service, vehicular

(P-9008)
ONTRAC LOGISTICS INC
Ontrac
11085 Olinda St, Sun Valley (91352-3302)
PHONE................................818 504-9043
EMP: 73
SALES (corp-wide): 735.78MM **Privately Held**
Web: www.ontrac.com
SIC: 4215 Courier services, except by air
HQ: Ontrac Logistics, Inc.
    8401 Greensboro Dr Fl 7
    Mc Lean VA 22102

(P-9009)
ONTRAC LOGISTICS INC
Ontrac
9774 Calabash Ave, Fontana (92335-5204)
PHONE................................804 334-5000
EMP: 98
SALES (corp-wide): 735.78MM **Privately Held**
Web: www.ontrac.com
SIC: 4215 Package delivery, vehicular
HQ: Ontrac Logistics, Inc.
    8401 Greensboro Dr Fl 7
    Mc Lean VA 22102

(P-9010)
PEACH INC
Also Called: Action Messenger Service
1311 N Highland Ave, Los Angeles (90028-7608)
P.O. Box 69763 (90069-0763)
PHONE................................323 654-2333
Arthur P Ruben, *Pr*

EMP: 125 **EST:** 1990
SQ FT: 3,500
SALES (est): 8.34MM **Privately Held**
Web: www.actionmessenger.com
SIC: 4215 7389 Courier services, except by air; Courier or messenger service

(P-9011)
SABSAF LLC
Also Called: Sabsaf Logistics
17192 Murphy Ave Unit 18641, Irvine (92623-0519)
PHONE................................951 266-6676
Saba Safiari, *Managing Member*
EMP: 75 **EST:** 2019
SALES (est): 5.72MM **Privately Held**
Web: www.sabsaf.com
SIC: 4215 Package delivery, vehicular

(P-9012)
SPEEDY EXPRESS LLC
4401 W Slauson Ave Ste A, Los Angeles (90043-2717)
PHONE................................818 300-7785
Kentrice Jones, *Prin*
EMP: 96 **EST:** 2020
SALES (est): 997.66K **Privately Held**
SIC: 4215 Courier services, except by air

(P-9013)
UNITED PARCEL SERVICE INC
Also Called: UPS
290 W Avenue L, Lancaster (93534-7109)
PHONE................................800 828-8264
James Adams, *Prin*
EMP: 89
SALES (corp-wide): 90.96B **Publicly Held**
Web: www.ups.com
SIC: 4215 Parcel delivery, vehicular
HQ: United Parcel Service, Inc.
    55 Glenlake Pkwy
    Atlanta GA 30328
    404 828-6000

(P-9014)
UNITED PARCEL SERVICE INC
Also Called: UPS
16000 Arminta St, Van Nuys (91406-1895)
PHONE................................404 828-6000
EMP: 314
SALES (corp-wide): 90.96B **Publicly Held**
Web: www.ups.com
SIC: 4215 Parcel delivery, vehicular
HQ: United Parcel Service, Inc.
    55 Glenlake Pkwy
    Atlanta GA 30328
    404 828-6000

(P-9015)
UNITED PARCEL SERVICE INC
Also Called: UPS
1522 Sabovich St, Mojave (93501-1681)
PHONE................................661 824-9391
Bobby Pastrole, *Mgr*
EMP: 76
SALES (corp-wide): 90.96B **Publicly Held**
Web: www.ups.com
SIC: 4215 Parcel delivery, vehicular
HQ: United Parcel Service, Inc.
    55 Glenlake Pkwy
    Atlanta GA 30328
    404 828-6000

(P-9016)
UNITED PARCEL SERVICE INC
Also Called: UPS
2800 W 227th St, Torrance (90505-2912)
PHONE................................800 742-5877
EMP: 76
SALES (corp-wide): 90.96B **Publicly Held**

Web: www.ups.com
SIC: 4215 Package delivery, vehicular
HQ: United Parcel Service, Inc.
    55 Glenlake Pkwy
    Atlanta GA 30328
    404 828-6000

(P-9017)
UNITED PARCEL SERVICE INC
Also Called: UPS
17115 S Western Ave, Gardena (90247-5299)
PHONE................................310 217-2646
Randy Hulhellt, *Mgr*
EMP: 101
SALES (corp-wide): 90.96B **Publicly Held**
Web: www.ups.com
SIC: 4215 4513 Parcel delivery, vehicular; Air courier services
HQ: United Parcel Service, Inc.
    55 Glenlake Pkwy
    Atlanta GA 30328
    404 828-6000

(P-9018)
UNITED PARCEL SERVICE INC
Also Called: UPS
16301 Trojan Way, La Mirada (90638-5626)
PHONE................................800 742-5877
EMP: 101
SALES (corp-wide): 90.96B **Publicly Held**
Web: www.ups.com
SIC: 4215 Package delivery, vehicular
HQ: United Parcel Service, Inc.
    55 Glenlake Pkwy
    Atlanta GA 30328
    404 828-6000

(P-9019)
UNITED PARCEL SERVICE INC
Also Called: UPS
13233 Moore St, Cerritos (90703-2276)
PHONE................................562 404-3236
Gary Mieredos, *Mgr*
EMP: 253
SALES (corp-wide): 90.96B **Publicly Held**
Web: www.ups.com
SIC: 4215 Parcel delivery, vehicular
HQ: United Parcel Service, Inc.
    55 Glenlake Pkwy
    Atlanta GA 30328
    404 828-6000

(P-9020)
UNITED PARCEL SERVICE INC
Also Called: UPS
1100 Baldwin Park Blvd, Baldwin Park (91700-5095)
PHONE................................626 814-6216
Lero Stamply, *Mgr*
EMP: 418
SALES (corp-wide): 90.96B **Publicly Held**
Web: www.ups.com
SIC: 4215 4513 Parcel delivery, vehicular; Air courier services
HQ: United Parcel Service, Inc.
    55 Glenlake Pkwy
    Atlanta GA 30328
    404 828-6000

(P-9021)
UNITED PARCEL SERVICE INC
Also Called: UPS
3140 Jurupa St, Ontario (91761-2902)
PHONE................................909 974-7212
EMP: 753
SALES (corp-wide): 90.96B **Publicly Held**
Web: www.ups.com
SIC: 4215 Parcel delivery, vehicular
HQ: United Parcel Service, Inc.
    55 Glenlake Pkwy

Atlanta GA 30328
    404 828-6000

(P-9022)
UNITED PARCEL SERVICE INC
Also Called: UPS
3221 E Jurupa, Ontario (91764)
PHONE................................909 974-7250
Richard Ricardo, *Genl Mgr*
EMP: 127
SALES (corp-wide): 90.96B **Publicly Held**
Web: www.ups.com
SIC: 4215 Parcel delivery, vehicular
HQ: United Parcel Service, Inc.
    55 Glenlake Pkwy
    Atlanta GA 30328
    404 828-6000

(P-9023)
UNITED PARCEL SERVICE INC
Also Called: UPS
650 N Commercial Rd, Palm Springs (92262-6299)
PHONE................................760 325-1762
Doug Nelson, *Mgr*
EMP: 89
SALES (corp-wide): 90.96B **Publicly Held**
Web: www.ups.com
SIC: 4215 4513 Parcel delivery, vehicular; Air courier services
HQ: United Parcel Service, Inc.
    55 Glenlake Pkwy
    Atlanta GA 30328
    404 828-6000

(P-9024)
UNITED PARCEL SERVICE INC
Also Called: UPS
11811 Landon Dr, Eastvale (91752-4002)
PHONE................................951 749-3400
Paul Slater, *Prin*
EMP: 89
SALES (corp-wide): 90.96B **Publicly Held**
Web: www.ups.com
SIC: 4215 Parcel delivery, vehicular
HQ: United Parcel Service, Inc.
    55 Glenlake Pkwy
    Atlanta GA 30328
    404 828-6000

(P-9025)
UNITED PARCEL SERVICE INC
Also Called: UPS
2300 Boswell Ct, Chula Vista (91914-3520)
PHONE................................619 482-8119
EMP: 215
SALES (corp-wide): 90.96B **Publicly Held**
Web: www.ups.com
SIC: 4215 Parcel delivery, vehicular
HQ: United Parcel Service, Inc.
    55 Glenlake Pkwy
    Atlanta GA 30328
    404 828-6000

(P-9026)
UNITED PARCEL SERVICE INC
Also Called: UPS
6060 Cornerstone Ct W, San Diego (92121-3712)
PHONE................................858 455-8800
EMP: 114
SALES (corp-wide): 90.96B **Publicly Held**
Web: www.ups.com
SIC: 4215 Parcel delivery, vehicular
HQ: United Parcel Service, Inc.
    55 Glenlake Pkwy
    Atlanta GA 30328
    404 828-6000

PRODUCTS & SVCS

(P-9027)

UNITED PARCEL SERVICE INC

Also Called: UPS

7925 Ronson Rd, San Diego (92111-1997)

PHONE..............................909 279-5111

EMP: 367

SALES (corp-wide): 90.96B **Publicly Held**

Web: www.ups.com

SIC: 4215 Parcel delivery, vehicular

HQ: United Parcel Service, Inc.

   55 Glenlake Pkwy

   Atlanta GA 30328

   404 828-6000

(P-9028)

UNITED PARCEL SERVICE INC

Also Called: UPS

3601 Sacramento Dr, San Luis Obispo

(93401-7115)

PHONE..............................801 973-3400

EMP: 114

SALES (corp-wide): 90.96B **Publicly Held**

Web: www.ups.com

SIC: 4215 Parcel delivery, vehicular

HQ: United Parcel Service, Inc.

   55 Glenlake Pkwy

   Atlanta GA 30328

   404 828-6000

(P-9029)

UNITED PARCEL SERVICE INC

Also Called: UPS

505 Pine Ave, Goleta (93117-3707)

PHONE..............................805 964-7848

Jason Chang, *Mgr*

EMP: 76

SALES (corp-wide): 90.96B **Publicly Held**

Web: www.ups.com

SIC: 4215 Parcel delivery, vehicular

HQ: United Parcel Service, Inc.

   55 Glenlake Pkwy

   Atlanta GA 30328

   404 828-6000

(P-9030)

UNITED PARCEL SERVICE INC

Also Called: UPS

309 Cooley Ln, Santa Maria (93455-1218)

PHONE..............................805 922-7851

Michael King, *Mgr*

EMP: 139

SALES (corp-wide): 90.96B **Publicly Held**

Web: www.ups.com

SIC: 4215 Parcel delivery, vehicular

HQ: United Parcel Service, Inc.

   55 Glenlake Pkwy

   Atlanta GA 30328

   404 828-6000

(P-9031)

UNITED PARCEL SERVICE INC

Also Called: UPS

22 Brookline, Aliso Viejo (92656-1461)

PHONE..............................949 643-6634

EMP: 565

SALES (corp-wide): 90.96B **Publicly Held**

Web: www.ups.com

SIC: 4215 Parcel delivery, vehicular

HQ: United Parcel Service, Inc.

   55 Glenlake Pkwy

   Atlanta GA 30328

   404 828-6000

(P-9032)

UNITY COURIER SERVICE INC
(DH)

3231 Fletcher Dr, Los Angeles

(90065-2919)

P.O. Box 10909 (91510-0909)

PHONE..............................323 255-9800

Ali Sharifi, *CEO*

Larry Lum, *

EMP: 200 EST: 1984

SQ FT: 11,000

SALES (est): 21.45MM

SALES (corp-wide): 8.81B **Privately Held**

Web: www.unitycourier.com

SIC: 4215 Package delivery, vehicular

HQ: Tforce Tl Holdings Usa, Inc.

   4701 E 32nd St

   Joplin MO 64804

   877 396-2639

4221 Farm Product Warehousing And Storage

(P-9033)

HONEYVILLE INC

11600 Dayton Dr, Rancho Cucamonga

(91730-5525)

PHONE..............................909 980-9500

David Brown, *CEO*

EMP: 85

SALES (corp-wide): 188.43MM **Privately Held**

Web: www.honeyville.com

SIC: 4221 5153 2045 2041 Grain elevator, storage only; Grains; Prepared flour mixes and doughs; Flour and other grain mill products

PA: Honeyville, Inc.

   1040 W 600 N

   435 494-4193

4222 Refrigerated Warehousing And Storage

(P-9034)

AMERICOLD LOGISTICS LLC

5401 Santa Ana St, Ontario (91761-8626)

PHONE..............................909 937-2200

Chris Mckeon, *Brnch Mgr*

EMP: 112

SALES (corp-wide): 2.67B **Publicly Held**

Web: www.americold.com

SIC: 4222 Warehousing, cold storage or refrigerated

HQ: Americold Logistics, Llc

   10 Glenlake Pkwy Ste 600

   Atlanta GA 30328

   678 441-1400

(P-9035)

AMERICOLD LOGISTICS LLC

Also Called: Americold Realty

700 Malaga St, Ontario (91761-8627)

P.O. Box 3967 (91761-0989)

PHONE..............................909 390-4950

Jeff Canfield, *Mgr*

EMP: 91

SALES (corp-wide): 2.67B **Publicly Held**

Web: www.americold.com

SIC: 4222 Warehousing, cold storage or refrigerated

HQ: Americold Logistics, Llc

   10 Glenlake Pkwy Ste 600

   Atlanta GA 30328

   678 441-1400

(P-9036)

EXETER PACKERS INC

Also Called: Sun Pacific Cold Storage

33374 Lerdo Hwy, Bakersfield

(93308-9782)

PHONE..............................661 399-0416

Richard Peters, *Mgr*

EMP: 118

SALES (corp-wide): 42.6MM **Privately Held**

Web: www.sunpacific.com

SIC: 4222 0172 Warehousing, cold storage or refrigerated; Grapes

PA: Exeter Packers, Inc.

   1250 E Myer Ave

   559 592-5168

(P-9037)

MIKE CAMPBELL & ASSOCIATES LTD

Also Called: Mike Campbell Assoc Logistics

10907 Downey Ave Ste 203, Downey

(90241-3737)

PHONE..............................626 369-3981

Vickie J Campbell, *CEO*

James Heermans, *

Paul Trump, *

EMP: 1000 EST: 1983

SALES (est): 32.4MM **Privately Held**

SIC: 4222 4225 4214 4213 Storage, frozen or refrigerated goods; General warehousing and storage; Local trucking with storage; Trucking, except local

(P-9038)

MOUNTAIN WATER ICE COMPANY

2843 Benet Rd, Oceanside (92058-1245)

PHONE..............................760 722-7611

Steven Gabriel, *Pr*

EMP: 26

SALES (corp-wide): 4.83MM **Privately Held**

Web: www.arcticglacier.com

SIC: 4222 2097 5999 Warehousing, cold storage or refrigerated; Block ice; Ice

PA: Mountain Water Ice Company Inc

   17011 Central Ave

   310 638-0321

(P-9039)

POWERED BY FULFILLMENT INC

20880 Krameria Ave, Riverside

(92518-1512)

PHONE..............................626 825-9841

Caleb Alexander Lee, *CEO*

EMP: 100 EST: 2020

SALES (est): 6.66MM **Privately Held**

Web: www.poweredbyfulfillment.com

SIC: 4222 Warehousing, cold storage or refrigerated

(P-9040)

PREFERRED FRZR SVCS - LBF LLC

4901 Bandini Blvd, Vernon (90058-5400)

PHONE..............................323 263-8811

Brian Beattie, *CEO*

▲ EMP: 100 EST: 2013

SALES (est): 3.86MM **Privately Held**

SIC: 4222 Warehousing, cold storage or refrigerated

(P-9041)

PREMIER COLD STORAGE & PKG LLC

1071 E 233rd St, Carson (90745-6206)

PHONE..............................949 444-8859

Steve Karo, *Pr*

EMP: 205 EST: 2022

SALES (est): 9.55MM **Privately Held**

SIC: 4222 3053 Warehousing, cold storage or refrigerated; Packing materials

(P-9042)

STANDARD-SOUTHERN CORPORATION

Also Called: Los Angeles Cold Storage

715 E 4th St, Los Angeles (90013-1727)

PHONE..............................213 624-1831

Thom Thomas, *Brnch Mgr*

EMP: 185

SALES (corp-wide): 14.86MM **Privately Held**

Web: www.standardsouthern.com

SIC: 4222 Warehousing, cold storage or refrigerated

PA: Standard-Southern Corporation

   400 S Central Ave

   213 624-1831

(P-9043)

STANDARD-SOUTHERN CORPORATION

Also Called: L.A. Cold Storage

440 S Central Ave, Los Angeles

(90013-1712)

PHONE..............................213 624-1831

Larry Rauch, *Pr*

EMP: 185

SALES (corp-wide): 14.86MM **Privately Held**

Web: www.standardsouthern.com

SIC: 4222 Warehousing, cold storage or refrigerated

PA: Standard-Southern Corporation

   400 S Central Ave

   213 624-1831

(P-9044)

UNITED STATES COLD STORAGE INC

Also Called: United States Cold Storage Cal

6501 District Blvd, Bakersfield

(93313-2000)

P.O. Box 45001 (93384-5001)

PHONE..............................661 832-2653

Randall Dorrell, *Mgr*

EMP: 77

SALES (corp-wide): 18.29B **Privately Held**

Web: www.uscold.com

SIC: 4222 Warehousing, cold storage or refrigerated

HQ: United States Cold Storage, Inc.

   2 Aquarium Dr Ste 400

   Camden NJ 08103

   856 354-8181

4225 General Warehousing And Storage

(P-9045)

ACT FULFILLMENT INC (PA)

3155 Universe Dr, Mira Loma (91752-3252)

PHONE..............................909 930-9083

Randolph Cox, *CEO*

Randolph Cox, *Pr*

Lydiann Cox, *

▲ EMP: 220 EST: 2004

SALES (est): 28.14MM **Privately Held**

Web: www.actfulfillment.com

SIC: 4225 General warehousing

(P-9046)

ADVANCED STRLZTION PDTS SVCS I

Also Called: Advanced Strlztion Pdts Lgstic

13135 Napa St, Fontana (92335-2961)

PHONE..............................909 350-6987

EMP: 88

SALES (corp-wide): 6.07B **Publicly Held**

Web: www.asp.com

SIC: 4225 General warehousing and storage

HQ: Advanced Sterlization Products

   Services Inc.

   33 Technology Dr

   Irvine CA 92618

(P-9047)

ADVANTAGE MEDIA SERVICES INC

Also Called: AMS Fulfillment
28220 Industry Dr, Valencia (91355-4105)
PHONE...............................661 705-7588
John Bevacqua, *VP*
EMP: 140
SALES (corp-wide): 56.03MM **Privately Held**
Web: www.amsfulfillment.com
SIC: 4225 General warehousing
PA: Advantage Media Services, Inc.
29010 Commerce Center Dr
661 775-0611

(P-9048)

ALBERTSONS LLC

Also Called: Albertson's Distribution Ctr
9300 Toledo Way, Irvine (92618-1802)
PHONE...............................949 855-2465
Jim Rollins, *Genl Mgr*
EMP: 86
SALES (corp-wide): 79.24B **Publicly Held**
Web: www.albertsons.com
SIC: 4225 General warehousing and storage
HQ: Albertson's Llc
250 E Parkcenter Blvd
Boise ID 83706
208 395-6200

(P-9049)

ARMLOGI HOLDING CORP (PA)

20301 E Walnut Dr N, Walnut (91789-2916)
PHONE...............................888 691-2911
Aidy Chou, *Ch Bd*
Zhiliang Zhou, *CFO*
Tong Wu, *Sec*
EMP: 200 **EST:** 2020
SQ FT: 350,000
SALES (est): 166.98MM
SALES (corp-wide): 166.98MM **Publicly Held**
Web: www.armlg.com
SIC: 4225 General warehousing and storage

(P-9050)

ASHLEY FURNITURE INDS LLC

Also Called: Ashley Furniture
2250 W Lugonia Ave, Redlands
(92374-5050)
PHONE...............................909 825-4900
EMP: 470
SALES (corp-wide): 4.17B **Privately Held**
Web: www.ashleyfurniture.com
SIC: 4225 5021 General warehousing; Furniture
PA: Ashley Furniture Industries, Llc
1 Ashley Way
608 323-3377

(P-9051)

C & B DELIVERY SERVICE

Also Called: Temco
1405 E Franklin Ave, Pomona
(91766-5453)
PHONE...............................909 623-4708
Virginia Templeton, *Pr*
EMP: 85 **EST:** 1967
SQ FT: 91,000
SALES (est): 4.69MM **Privately Held**
Web: www.temcologistics.com
SIC: 4225 General warehousing

(P-9052)

CARROLL SHELBY LICENSING INC

7927 Garden Grove Blvd, Garden Grove
(92841-4225)

PHONE...............................310 914-1843
Tracey Smith, *Pr*
EMP: 78 **EST:** 2001
SALES (est): 1.67MM **Privately Held**
SIC: 4225 General warehousing
PA: Shelby Carroll International Inc
7927 Garden Grove Blvd

(P-9053)

CJ LOGISTICS AMERICA LLC

17789 Harvill Ave, Perris (92570-9595)
PHONE...............................951 436-7131
EMP: 98
Web: america.cjlogistics.com
SIC: 4225 General warehousing and storage
HQ: Cj Logistics America, Llc
1750 S Wolf Rd
Des Plaines IL 60018

(P-9054)

COASTAL PACIFIC FD DISTRS INC

Also Called: Coastal Pacific Foods
1520 E Mission Blvd Ste B, Ontario
(91761-2124)
PHONE...............................909 947-2066
David Jared, *Pr*
EMP: 78
SALES (corp-wide): 493.57MM **Privately Held**
Web: www.cpfd.com
SIC: 4225 General warehousing and storage
PA: Coastal Pacific Food Distributors, Inc.
1015 Performance Dr
909 947-2066

(P-9055)

COSTCO WHOLESALE CORPORATION

Also Called: Mira Loma Dry Depot
11600 Riverside Dr Ste A, Jurupa Valley
(91752-3700)
PHONE...............................951 361-3606
Rachell Aguire, *Brnch Mgr*
EMP: 613
SALES (corp-wide): 254.45B **Publicly Held**
Web: www.costco.com
SIC: 4225 General warehousing and storage
PA: Costco Wholesale Corporation
999 Lake Dr
425 313-8100

(P-9056)

COUNTY OF LOS ANGELES

Also Called: Public Works, Dept of
1537 Alcazar St, Los Angeles (90033-1001)
PHONE...............................626 458-1707
Shirely Gist, *Mgr*
EMP: 81
Web: www.lacounty.gov
SIC: 4225 9511 General warehousing and storage; Air, water, and solid waste management
PA: County Of Los Angeles
500 W Temple St Ste 437
213 974-1101

(P-9057)

CUSTOM GOODS LLC

809 E 236th St, Carson (90745-6232)
PHONE...............................310 241-6700
EMP: 71
Web: www.custom-goods.com
SIC: 4225 General warehousing
PA: Custom Goods, Llc
1035 E Watson Center Rd

(P-9058)

CUSTOM GOODS LLC

907 E 236th St, Carson (90745-6234)
PHONE...............................310 241-6700
EMP: 71
Web: www.custom-goods.com
SIC: 4225 General warehousing
PA: Custom Goods, Llc
1035 E Watson Center Rd

(P-9059)

DALTON TRUCKING INC (PA)

13560 Whittram Ave, Fontana
(92335-2951)
P.O. Box 5025 (92334-5025)
PHONE...............................909 823-0663
Terry Klenske, *CEO*
Mathew Klenske, *
Eleanor Klenske, *
Roszetta Bautista, *
EMP: 102 **EST:** 1970
SQ FT: 11,000
SALES (est): 25.16MM
SALES (corp-wide): 25.16MM **Privately Held**
Web: www.daltontrucking.com
SIC: 4225 General warehousing and storage

(P-9060)

DART INTERNATIONAL A CORP (HQ)

Also Called: Dart Entities
1430 S Eastman Ave, Commerce
(90023-4006)
P.O. Box 23944 (90023-0944)
PHONE...............................323 264-8746
Terence Dedeaux, *CEO*
Paul Martin, *
William J Smollen, *
EMP: 110 **EST:** 1979
SQ FT: 50,000
SALES (est): 9.29MM
SALES (corp-wide): 61.62MM **Privately Held**
Web: www.dartentities.com
SIC: 4225 General warehousing
PA: Dart Transportation Service, A Corporation
1430 S Eastman Ave Ste 1
323 981-8205

(P-9061)

DART WAREHOUSE CORPORATION (HQ)

1430 S Eastman Ave, Commerce
(90023-4091)
PHONE...............................323 264-1011
Robert Anthony Santich, *CEO*
Raoul Dedeaux, *
Eileen Takahashi, *
Ashok Agarwal, *
Don Brown, *
▲ **EMP:** 255 **EST:** 1938
SALES (est): 43.41MM
SALES (corp-wide): 61.62MM **Privately Held**
Web: www.dartentities.com
SIC: 4225 General warehousing
PA: Dart Transportation Service, A Corporation
1430 S Eastman Ave Ste 1
323 981-8205

(P-9062)

DISTRIBUTION ALTERNATIVES INC

10621 6th St, Rancho Cucamonga
(91730-5900)
PHONE...............................909 746-5600

EMP: 85
SALES (corp-wide): 38.56MM **Privately Held**
Web: www.daserv.com
SIC: 4225 General warehousing
PA: Distribution Alternatives, Inc.
6870 21st Ave S
651 636-9167

(P-9063)

EDMUND A GRAY CO

1901 Imperial St, Los Angeles
(90021-2830)
PHONE...............................213 625-2725
Lawrence Gray Junior, *Brnch Mgr*
EMP: 35
SALES (corp-wide): 13.68MM **Privately Held**
Web: www.eagray.com
SIC: 4225 3498 General warehousing and storage; Pipe fittings, fabricated from purchased pipe
PA: Edmund A. Gray Co.
2277 E 15th St
213 625-0376

(P-9064)

F R T INTERNATIONAL INC

Also Called: Frontier Logistics Services
14439 S Avalon Blvd, Gardena
(90248-2005)
PHONE...............................310 329-5700
Daniel Park, *Brnch Mgr*
EMP: 73
SALES (corp-wide): 25.45MM **Privately Held**
Web: www.frontier-logistics.com
SIC: 4225 4731 4412 4214 General warehousing; Customhouse brokers; Deep sea foreign transportation of freight; Local trucking with storage
PA: F. R. T. International, Inc.
1700 N Alameda St
310 604-8208

(P-9065)

F R T INTERNATIONAL INC (PA)

Also Called: Frontier Logistics Services
1700 N Alameda St, Compton
(90222-4128)
PHONE...............................310 604-8208
Brian Chung, *CEO*
Joyce Chung, *
◆ **EMP:** 80 **EST:** 1983
SQ FT: 200,000
SALES (est): 25.45MM
SALES (corp-wide): 25.45MM **Privately Held**
Web: www.frontier-logistics.com
SIC: 4225 4731 4412 4214 General warehousing; Customhouse brokers; Deep sea foreign transportation of freight; Local trucking with storage

(P-9066)

FASHION LOGISTICS INC

20550 Denker Ave, Torrance (90501-1645)
PHONE...............................424 201-4100
EMP: 130
SALES (corp-wide): 22.46MM **Privately Held**
Web: www.fashionlogistics.com
SIC: 4225 General warehousing
PA: Fashion Logistics, Inc.
621 Us Hwy 46 W
201 596-0040

(P-9067)

FOAMEX LP

Foamex

19201 S Reyes Ave, Compton
(90221-5807)
PHONE.............................323 774-5600
Dean Offerman, *Brnch Mgr*
EMP: 150
Web: www.fxi.com
SIC: 4225 General warehousing and storage
PA: Foamex L.P.
   100 W Matsonford Rd # 5

(P-9068)
FTDI WEST INC
3375 Enterprise Dr, Bloomington
(92316-3539)
PHONE.............................909 473-1111
Alan Baum, *Pr*
Steve Rocha, *
EMP: 80 **EST:** 2008
SALES (est): 19.26MM **Privately Held**
Web: www.ftdicorp.com
SIC: 4225 Warehousing, self storage

(P-9069)
FULGENT GENETICS INC
Also Called: Fulgent Receiving
4373 Santa Anita Ave, El Monte
(91731-1690)
PHONE.............................626 350-0537
EMP: 1037
SALES (corp-wide): 289.21MM **Publicly Held**
SIC: 4225 General warehousing and storage
PA: Fulgent Genetics, Inc.
   4399 Santa Anita Ave
   626 350-0537

(P-9070)
GENERATIONAL PROPERTIES INC
3141 E 44th St, Vernon (90058-2405)
PHONE.............................323 583-3163
Angelo V Antoci, *Prin*
Angelo V Antoci, *Prin*
Sam Perricone, *
EMP: 291 **EST:** 1950
SQ FT: 4,000
SALES (est): 22.29MM **Privately Held**
SIC: 4225 General warehousing and storage

(P-9071)
GXO LOGISTICS SUPPLY CHAIN INC
3520 S Cactus Ave, Bloomington
(92316-3816)
PHONE.............................336 309-6201
Christopher Cotto, *Mgr*
EMP: 1000
SALES (corp-wide): 9.78B **Publicly Held**
Web: www.gxo.com
SIC: 4225 General warehousing and storage
HQ: Gxo Logistics Supply Chain, Inc.
   4043 Piedmont Pkwy
   High Point NC 27265
   336 232-4100

(P-9072)
GXO LOGISTICS SUPPLY CHAIN INC
2163 S Riverside Ave, Colton (92324-3355)
PHONE.............................951 512-1201
Miguel Moreno, *Brnch Mgr*
EMP: 100
SALES (corp-wide): 9.78B **Publicly Held**
Web: www.gxo.com
SIC: 4225 General warehousing
HQ: Gxo Logistics Supply Chain, Inc.
   4043 Piedmont Pkwy
   High Point NC 27265
   336 232-4100

(P-9073)
H RAUVEL INC (PA)
Also Called: Nova Container Freight Station
1710 E Sepulveda Blvd, Carson
(90745-6142)
PHONE.............................310 604-0060
Hector R Velasco, *Pr*
▼ **EMP:** 70 **EST:** 1978
SQ FT: 258,000
SALES (est): 2.79MM
SALES (corp-wide): 2.79MM **Privately Held**
Web: www.novafreight.net
SIC: 4225 4731 General warehousing;
   Agents, shipping

(P-9074)
HAULAWAY STORAGE CNTRS INC
11292 Western Ave, Stanton (90680-2912)
P.O. Box 125 (90680-0125)
PHONE.............................800 826-9040
Clifford Robert Ronnenberg, *CEO*
Daniel Letto, *
Joyce Amato, *
EMP: 654 **EST:** 2000
SALES (est): 6.78MM
SALES (corp-wide): 450.25MM **Privately Held**
Web: www.haulaway.com
SIC: 4225 General warehousing and storage
PA: Cr&R Incorporated
   11292 Western Ave
   714 826-9049

(P-9075)
HOME DEPOT USA INC
Also Called: Home Depot, The
14659 Alondra Blvd Ste B, La Mirada
(90638-5629)
PHONE.............................714 522-8651
Maurice Martinez, *Mgr*
EMP: 108
SALES (corp-wide): 152.67B **Publicly Held**
Web: www.homedepot.com
SIC: 4225 General warehousing and storage
HQ: Home Depot U.S.A., Inc.
   2455 Paces Ferry Rd
   Atlanta GA 30339

(P-9076)
HOME DEPOT USA INC
Also Called: Home Depot, The
8535 Oakwood Pl Ste B, Rancho
Cucamonga (91730-4864)
PHONE.............................909 483-8115
Rose Navares, *Mgr*
EMP: 104
SALES (corp-wide): 152.67B **Publicly Held**
Web: www.homedepot.com
SIC: 4225 General warehousing and storage
HQ: Home Depot U.S.A., Inc.
   2455 Paces Ferry Rd
   Atlanta GA 30339

(P-9077)
HOME DEPOT USA INC
Also Called: Home Depot, The
11650 Venture Dr, Mira Loma (91752-3209)
PHONE.............................951 361-1235
John Lawson, *Brnch Mgr*
EMP: 119
SALES (corp-wide): 152.67B **Publicly Held**
Web: www.homedepot.com
SIC: 4225 General warehousing and storage
HQ: Home Depot U.S.A., Inc.
   2455 Paces Ferry Rd

Atlanta GA 30339

(P-9078)
HOME DEPOT USA INC
Also Called: Home Depot, The
13250 Gregg St Ste A2, Poway
(92064-7164)
PHONE.............................858 859-4143
Greg Williams, *Prin*
EMP: 77
SALES (corp-wide): 152.67B **Publicly Held**
Web: www.homedepot.com
SIC: 4225 General warehousing and storage
HQ: Home Depot U.S.A., Inc.
   2455 Paces Ferry Rd
   Atlanta GA 30339

(P-9079)
KAIR HARBOR EXPRESS LLC (PA)
2200 Technology Pl, Long Beach
(90810-3801)
PHONE.............................562 432-6800
Peter Wu, *Managing Member*
EMP: 80 **EST:** 2015
SQ FT: 50,000
SALES (est): 21.96MM
SALES (corp-wide): 21.96MM **Privately Held**
Web: www.kairharborexpress.com
SIC: 4225 4214 General warehousing and
   storage; Local trucking with storage

(P-9080)
KENCO GROUP INC
Also Called: KENCO GROUP, INC.
6509 Kimball Ave, Chino (91708-9130)
PHONE.............................800 758-3289
Paul Waibel, *Prin*
EMP: 102
SALES (corp-wide): 494.7MM **Privately Held**
Web: www.kencogroup.com
SIC: 4225 General warehousing
PA: Rivermill Group, Inc.
   2001 Riverside Dr Ste 3100
   800 758-3289

(P-9081)
KKW TRUCKING INC (PA)
3100 Pomona Blvd, Pomona (91768-3230)
P.O. Box 2960 (91769)
PHONE.............................909 869-1200
Dennis W Firestone, *CEO*
Lynnette Brown, *
EMP: 550 **EST:** 1962
SQ FT: 150,000
SALES (est): 40.69MM
SALES (corp-wide): 40.69MM **Privately Held**
Web: www.kkwtrucks.com
SIC: 4225 4231 4226 4214 General
   warehousing and storage; Trucking
   terminal facilities; Special warehousing and
   storage, nec; Local trucking with storage

(P-9082)
KROGER CO
Also Called: Ralphs
2201 S Wilmington Ave, Compton
(90220-5448)
PHONE.............................859 630-6959
Lisa Allen, *Brnch Mgr*
EMP: 500
SALES (corp-wide): 150.04B **Publicly Held**
Web: www.thekrogerco.com
SIC: 4225 General warehousing and storage
PA: The Kroger Co
   1014 Vine St

513 762-4000

(P-9083)
LAVA SCS LLC
218 Machlin Ct, Walnut (91789-3048)
PHONE.............................909 437-7881
Chris Deman, *Brnch Mgr*
EMP: 79
Web: www.lavascs.com
SIC: 4225 4731 General warehousing and
   storage; Truck transportation brokers
PA: Lava Scs, Llc
   801 River Dr

(P-9084)
LOCKHEED MARTIN CORPORATION
Also Called: Rotary and Miission Systems
Bldg 821 South Loop, Fort Irwin (92310)
PHONE.............................760 386-2572
Kurt Pinkerton, *Mgr*
EMP: 142
Web: www.lockheedmartin.com
SIC: 4225 General warehousing and storage
PA: Lockheed Martin Corporation
   6801 Rockledge Dr

(P-9085)
LOWES HOME CENTERS LLC
Also Called: Lowe's
3984 Indian Ave, Perris (92571-3154)
PHONE.............................951 443-2500
Thomas Tucker, *Brnch Mgr*
EMP: 279
SALES (corp-wide): 86.38B **Publicly Held**
Web: www.lowes.com
SIC: 4225 General warehousing and storage
HQ: Lowe's Home Centers, Llc
   1000 Lowes Blvd
   Mooresville NC 28117
   336 658-4000

(P-9086)
MAGNELL ASSOCIATE INC
Also Called: ABS Computer Technologies
9997 Rose Hills Rd, Whittier (90601-1701)
PHONE.............................626 271-1420
Brian Cheng, *Brnch Mgr*
EMP: 256
SALES (corp-wide): 2.38B **Publicly Held**
Web: www.absgamingpc.com
SIC: 4225 General warehousing
HQ: Magnell Associate, Inc.
   21688 Gtwy Ctr Dr Ste 300
   Diamond Bar CA 91765

(P-9087)
MAKESPACE LABS INC
3526 Hayden Ave, Culver City
(90232-2413)
PHONE.............................800 920-9440
Rahul Gandhi, *CEO*
Chang Paik, *
EMP: 200 **EST:** 2013
SALES (est): 9.49MM **Privately Held**
Web: www.clutter.com
SIC: 4225 General warehousing and storage

(P-9088)
MCR PRINTING AND PACKG CORP
8830 Siempre Viva Rd, San Diego
(92154-6278)
PHONE.............................619 488-3012
EMP: 170
SALES (corp-wide): 12.73MM **Privately Held**
Web:
www.mcrprintingandpackaging.com

SIC: **4225** General warehousing
PA: Mcr Printing And Packaging, Corp.
113 W G St Pmb 438
619 488-3169

(P-9089)
MIDAS EXPRESS LOS ANGELES INC

11854 Alameda St, Lynwood (90262-4019)
PHONE..............................310 609-0366
Jack Wu, *Pr*
Jacky Strong, *Stockholder*
▲ **EMP:** 200 **EST:** 1995
SQ FT: 90,000
SALES (est): 11.84MM **Privately Held**
Web: www.midasexpress.com
SIC: **4225** 4731 4226 General warehousing
and storage; Freight forwarding; Textile
warehousing

(P-9090)
MOULTON LOGISTICS MANAGEMENT

7855 Hayvenhurst Ave, Van Nuys
(91406-1712)
P.O. Box 8191 (91409-8191)
PHONE..............................818 997-1800
◆ **EMP:** 175
Web: www.moultonlogistics.com
SIC: **4225** 4822 General warehousing and
storage; Electronic mail

(P-9091)
MSBLOUS LLC

11671 Dayton Dr, Rancho Cucamonga
(91730-5526)
PHONE..............................909 929-9689
Jiayi Cu, *Mgr*
EMP: 84
SALES (corp-wide): 224.86K **Privately Held**
SIC: **4225** General warehousing and storage
PA: Msblous Llc
8 The Grn Ste 7360
909 908-1889

(P-9092)
MULHOLLAND BROTHERS

11840 Dorothy St Apt 301, Los Angeles
(90049-7902)
PHONE..............................510 280-5485
John Holland, *Prin*
EMP: 49
SALES (corp-wide): 3.7MM **Privately Held**
Web: www.shopmulholland.com
SIC: **4225** 3161 2512 General warehousing;
Luggage; Upholstered household furniture
PA: Mulholland Brothers
1710 4th St
415 824-5995

(P-9093)
NAVY EXCHANGE SERVICE COMMAND

4250 Eucalyptus Ave, Chino (91710-9704)
PHONE..............................909 517-2640
Ron Patel, *Mgr*
EMP: 75
Web: www.mynavyexchange.com
SIC: **4225** 9711 General warehousing and
storage; Navy
HQ: Navy Exchange Service Command
3280 Virginia Beach Blvd
Virginia Beach VA 23452
757 463-6200

(P-9094)
NBCUNIVERSAL LLC

Also Called: NBC Asset Warehouse

11625 Hart St, North Hollywood
(91605-5802)
PHONE..............................310 989-8771
EMP: 126
SALES (corp-wide): 121.57B **Publicly
Held**
Web: www.nbcuniversal.com
SIC: **4225** General warehousing and storage
HQ: Nbcuniversal, Llc
100 Universal City Plz
Universal City CA 91608

(P-9095)
NEOVIA LOGISTICS DIST LP

5750 E Francis St, Ontario (91761-3607)
PHONE..............................909 657-4900
EMP: 96
SALES (corp-wide): 461.1MM **Privately
Held**
Web: www.neovialogistics.com
SIC: **4225** General warehousing and storage
HQ: Neovia Logistics Distribution, Lp
8840 Cypress Wters Blvd S
Coppell TX 75019

(P-9096)
NORDSTROM INC

Also Called: Nordstrom
1600 S Milliken Ave, Ontario (91761-2301)
PHONE..............................909 390-1040
Pat Smith, *Mgr*
EMP: 300
SALES (corp-wide): 14.69B **Publicly Held**
Web: www.nordstrom.com
SIC: **4225** 4226 General warehousing and
storage; Special warehousing and storage,
nec
PA: Nordstrom, Inc.
1617 6th Ave
206 628-2111

(P-9097)
OSRAM SYLVANIA INC

1651 S Archibald Ave, Ontario
(91761-7651)
PHONE..............................909 923-3003
Wayne Cansford, *Brnch Mgr*
EMP: 88
SALES (corp-wide): 3.9B **Privately Held**
Web: www.sylvania-automotive.com
SIC: **4225** Warehousing, self storage
HQ: Osram Sylvania Inc.
200 Ballardvale St Bldg 2
Wilmington MA 01887
978 570-3000

(P-9098)
PENNEY OPCO LLC

Also Called: JC Penney
5959 Palm Ave, San Bernardino
(92407-1844)
PHONE..............................972 431-2618
EMP: 75
SALES (corp-wide): 1.93B **Privately Held**
SIC: **4225** General warehousing and storage
HQ: Penney Opco Llc
6501 Legacy Dr
Plano TX 75024
972 431-4746

(P-9099)
PEPSICO BEVERAGE SALES LLC

1200 Arroyo St, San Fernando
(91340-1545)
PHONE..............................818 361-0685
EMP: 284
SALES (corp-wide): 86.39B **Publicly Held**
SIC: **4225** General warehousing and storage
HQ: Pepsico Beverage Sales, Llc
700 Anderson Hill Rd

Purchase NY 10577
914 767-6000

(P-9100)
PEPSICO BEVERAGE SALES LLC

27717 Aliso Creek Rd, Aliso Viejo
(92656-3804)
PHONE..............................949 362-2860
EMP: 152
SALES (corp-wide): 86.39B **Publicly Held**
SIC: **4225** General warehousing and storage
HQ: Pepsico Beverage Sales, Llc
700 Anderson Hill Rd
Purchase NY 10577
914 767-6000

(P-9101)
PEPSICO BEVERAGE SALES LLC

6261 Caballero Blvd, Buena Park
(90620-1123)
PHONE..............................714 228-9719
EMP: 435
SALES (corp-wide): 86.39B **Publicly Held**
SIC: **4225** General warehousing and storage
HQ: Pepsico Beverage Sales, Llc
700 Anderson Hill Rd
Purchase NY 10577
914 767-6000

(P-9102)
QUICK BOX LLC

13838 S Figueroa St, Los Angeles
(90061-1026)
PHONE..............................310 436-6444
EMP: 130
SALES (corp-wide): 49.8MM **Privately
Held**
Web: www.quickbox.com
SIC: **4225** General warehousing and storage
PA: Quick Box, Llc
11551 E 45th Ave Unit B-C
303 757-6500

(P-9103)
QUILL LLC

Also Called: Quill Distribution Center
1500 S Dupont Ave, Ontario (91761-1406)
PHONE..............................909 390-0600
Rocky Velasquez, *Mgr*
EMP: 276
Web: www.quill.com
SIC: **4225** General warehousing and storage
HQ: Quill Llc
300 Tri State Intl Dr Ste
Lincolnshire IL 60069
800 982-3400

(P-9104)
RADIAL SOUTH LP

Also Called: Radial
2225 Alder Ave, Rialto (92377-8513)
PHONE..............................610 491-7000
EMP: 502
SALES (corp-wide): 2.55B **Privately Held**
Web: www.radial.com
SIC: **4225** General warehousing
HQ: Radial South, L.P.
935 1st Ave
King Of Prussia PA 19406
610 491-7000

(P-9105)
ROADEX AMERICA INC

2132 E Dominguez St Ste B, Long Beach
(90810-1026)
PHONE..............................310 878-9800
Nicholas Sim, *Pr*

Russle Loh, *
Johnny Kwan, *
▲ **EMP:** 100 **EST:** 2001
SALES (est): 24.54MM **Privately Held**
Web: www.roadexamerica.com
SIC: **4225** 5113 4789 General warehousing
and storage; Industrial and personal service
paper; Cargo loading and unloading
services

(P-9106)
RPM CONSOLIDATED SERVICES INC (HQ)

1901 Raymer Ave, Fullerton (92833-2512)
PHONE..............................714 388-3500
Shawn K Duke, *CEO*
Dan Laporte, *
▲ **EMP:** 100 **EST:** 2002
SQ FT: 15,000
SALES (est): 82.15MM
SALES (corp-wide): 1.16B **Privately Held**
Web: www.odysseylogistics.com
SIC: **4225** 4214 General warehousing and
storage; Local trucking with storage
PA: Odyssey Logistics & Technology
Corporation
39 Old Ridgebury Rd
203 448-3900

(P-9107)
SAN DIEGO GAS & ELECTRIC CO

Mirimar Storage
6875c Consolidated Way, San Diego
(92121-2602)
PHONE..............................858 547-2086
EMP: 112
SALES (corp-wide): 16.72B **Publicly Held**
Web: www.sdge.com
SIC: **4225** 4932 4924 4911 General
warehousing and storage; Gas and other
services combined; Natural gas distribution;
Electric services
HQ: San Diego Gas & Electric Company
8330 Century Park Ct
San Diego CA 92123
619 696-2000

(P-9108)
SCHNEIDER ELECTRIC USA INC

Also Called: Pelco By Schneider Electric
14725 Monte Vista Ave, Chino
(91710-5732)
PHONE..............................909 438-2295
Jessie Ortega, *Mng Dir*
EMP: 100
SALES (corp-wide): 1.09K **Privately Held**
Web: www.se.com
SIC: **4225** General warehousing and storage
HQ: Schneider Electric Usa, Inc.
One Boston Pl Ste 2700
Boston MA 02108
978 975-9600

(P-9109)
SMART & FINAL STORES LLC

5500 Sheila St, Commerce (90040-1425)
PHONE..............................323 725-0791
Tom Bullici, *Mgr*
EMP: 253
Web: www.smartandfinal.com
SIC: **4225** General warehousing and storage
HQ: Smart & Final Stores Llc
600 Citadel Dr
Los Angeles CA 90040

(P-9110)
SPROUTS FARMERS MARKET INC

PRODUCTS & SVCS

280 De Berry St, Colton (92324-4404)
PHONE...............................888 577-7688
EMP: 190
SALES (corp-wide): 6.84B **Publicly Held**
Web: www.sprouts.com
SIC: 4225 5411 General warehousing and storage; Grocery stores
PA: Sprouts Farmers Market, Inc.
   5455 E High St Ste 111
   480 814-8016

(P-9111)
SST IV 8020 LAS VGAS BLVD S LL
Also Called: Smartstop Self Storage
10 Terrace Rd, Ladera Ranch (92694-1182)
PHONE...............................949 429-6600
H Michael Schwartz, *Managing Member*
Paula Mathews, *
Wayne Johnson, *
Michael Terjung, *
EMP: 99 **EST:** 2018
SALES (est): 2.3MM **Privately Held**
Web: www.smartstopselfstorage.com
SIC: 4225 Warehousing, self storage

(P-9112)
STATES LOGISTICS SERVICES INC
7151 Cate Dr, Buena Park (90621-1881)
PHONE...............................714 523-1276
EMP: 83
Web: www.stateslogistics.com
SIC: 4225 General warehousing
PA: States Logistics Services, Inc.
   5650 Dolly Avenue

(P-9113)
TAKANE USA INC
2055 S Haven Ave, Ontario (91761-0736)
PHONE...............................909 923-5511
Masahiko Yamada, *Manager*
EMP: 129
Web: www.calicobrands.com
SIC: 4225 General warehousing and storage
HQ: Takane U.S.A., Inc.
   369 Van Ness Way Ste 715
   Torrance CA 90501
   310 212-1411

(P-9114)
TANIMURA ANTLE FRESH FOODS INC
761 Commercial Ave, Oxnard (93030-7233)
PHONE...............................805 483-2358
Sergio Romero, *Mgr*
EMP: 281
SALES (corp-wide): 321.47MM **Privately Held**
Web: www.taproduce.com
SIC: 4225 Warehousing, self storage
PA: Tanimura & Antle Fresh Foods, Inc.
   1 Harris Rd
   831 455-2950

(P-9115)
TARGET CORPORATION
Also Called: T.com Ontario Fc T-9479
1505 S Haven Ave, Ontario (91761-2928)
PHONE...............................909 937-5500
Jacqueline Yee, *Brnch Mgr*
EMP: 177
SALES (corp-wide): 107.41B **Publicly Held**
Web: www.target.com
SIC: 4225 General warehousing and storage
PA: Target Corporation
   1000 Nicollet Mall
   612 304-6073

(P-9116)
TARGET CORPORATION
Also Called: Target
14750 Miller Ave, Fontana (92336-1685)
PHONE...............................909 355-6000
George Spreiser, *Genl Mgr*
EMP: 72
SALES (corp-wide): 107.41B **Publicly Held**
Web: www.target.com
SIC: 4225 General warehousing and storage
PA: Target Corporation
   1000 Nicollet Mall
   612 304-6073

(P-9117)
TAYLORED FMI LLC
1495 E Locust St, Ontario (91761-4570)
PHONE...............................909 510-4800
Jim Deveau, *CEO*
EMP: 109 **EST:** 2020
SALES (est): 4.47MM
SALES (corp-wide): 26.36MM **Privately Held**
Web: www.tayloredservices.com
SIC: 4225 General warehousing
PA: Taylored Services Parent Co. Inc.
   1495 E Locust St
   909 510-4800

(P-9118)
TAYLORED SERVICES LLC (DH)
Also Called: Taylored Services
1495 E Locust St, Ontario (91761-4570)
PHONE...............................909 510-4800
Jim Deveau, *CEO*
▲ **EMP:** 80 **EST:** 1992
SQ FT: 330,000
SALES (est): 117.01MM **Privately Held**
Web: www.tayloredservices.com
SIC: 4225 4731 General warehousing and storage; Agents, shipping
HQ: Taylored Services Holdings, Llc
   1495 E Locust St
   Ontario CA 91761
   909 510-4800

(P-9119)
TAYLORED SERVICES HOLDINGS LLC (DH)
Also Called: Taylored Services
1495 E Locust St, Ontario (91761-4570)
PHONE...............................909 510-4800
Mikhail Kholyavenko, *CEO*
EMP: 80 **EST:** 2008
SQ FT: 330,000
SALES (est): 118.57MM **Privately Held**
Web: www.tayloredservices.com
SIC: 4225 General warehousing and storage
HQ: Yusen Logistics (Americas) Inc.
   300 Lighting Way Ste 100
   Secaucus NJ 07094
   201 553-3800

(P-9120)
TOTAL WAREHOUSE INC
Also Called: Total Warehouse
2895 E Miraloma Ave, Anaheim (92806-1804)
PHONE...............................714 332-3082
Boyd Kiefus, *CEO*
Dawn Koopmann, *
EMP: 119 **EST:** 2017
SALES (est): 2.23MM **Privately Held**
Web: www.totalwarehouse.com
SIC: 4225 7699 3537 5046 Miniwarehouse, warehousing; Industrial equipment services ; Forklift trucks; Commercial equipment, nec

(P-9121)
TRI-MODAL DIST SVCS INC
22560 Lucerne St, Carson (90745-4303)
PHONE...............................310 522-1844
Gregory Owen, *Prin*
▲ **EMP:** 91
SALES (corp-wide): 21.22MM **Privately Held**
Web: www.abilitytrimodal.com
SIC: 4225 General warehousing and storage
PA: Tri-Modal Distribution Services, Inc.
   2011 E Carson St
   310 522-5506

(P-9122)
TROPICANA MANUFACTURING CO INC
Also Called: St George Logistics
1650 S Central Ave, Compton (90220-5317)
PHONE...............................310 764-4395
EMP: 73
SALES (corp-wide): 18.75MM **Privately Held**
Web: www.stgusa.com
SIC: 4225 General warehousing
PA: Patina Freight, Inc.
   20405 E Business Pkwy
   909 594-0349

(P-9123)
UNIFIED GROCERS INC
Also Called: U W G Southern California Div
457 E Martin Luther King Jr Blvd, Los Angeles (90011-5650)
PHONE...............................323 232-6124
Maurice Ochua, *Brnch Mgr*
EMP: 105
Web: www.unfi.com
SIC: 4225 8742 2051 General warehousing and storage; Marketing consulting services; Bread, cake, and related products
HQ: Unfi Grocers Distribution, Inc.
   2500 S Atlantic Blvd
   Commerce CA 90040
   323 264-5200

(P-9124)
UNIS LLC
19914 S Via Baron, Rancho Dominguez (90220-6104)
PHONE...............................310 747-7388
Omar Garcia, *Brnch Mgr*
EMP: 90
SALES (corp-wide): 194.54MM **Privately Held**
Web: www.unisco.com
SIC: 4225 General warehousing and storage
PA: Unis, Llc
   218 Machlin Ct
   909 839-2600

(P-9125)
UNIVERSAL PACKG SYSTEMS INC
Also Called: Paklab
14570 Monte Vista Ave, Chino (91710-5743)
PHONE...............................909 517-2442
EMP: 125
SALES (corp-wide): 359.71MM **Privately Held**
SIC: 4225 General warehousing
PA: Universal Packaging Systems, Inc.
   380 Townline Rd Ste 130
   631 543-2277

(P-9126)
US ELOGISTICS SERVICE CORP
1420 Tamarind Ave, Rialto (92376-3007)
PHONE...............................909 927-7483
Maggie Lu, *Mgr*
EMP: 200
SALES (corp-wide): 26MM **Privately Held**
Web: www.cirroglobal.com
SIC: 4225 General warehousing and storage
PA: Us Elogistics Service Corp
   1100 Cranbury S River Rd
   732 881-6606

(P-9127)
WALMART INC
Also Called: Walmart
1001 Columbia Ave, Riverside (92507-2135)
PHONE...............................951 320-5722
EMP: 120
SALES (corp-wide): 648.13B **Publicly Held**
Web: corporate.walmart.com
SIC: 4225 General warehousing and storage
PA: Walmart Inc.
   702 Sw 8th St
   479 273-4000

(P-9128)
WEBER DISTRIBUTION LLC
Also Called: Weber Distribution
15301 Shoemaker Ave, Norwalk (90650-6859)
PHONE...............................562 404-9996
John Nutt, *VP*
EMP: 86
Web: www.weberlogistics.com
SIC: 4225 4214 General warehousing; Local trucking with storage
PA: Weber Distribution, Llc
   13530 Rosecrans Ave

(P-9129)
WILSONART LLC
Also Called: Ralph Wilson Plastics
13911 Gannet St, Santa Fe Springs (90670-5326)
P.O. Box 2336 (90670-0336)
PHONE...............................562 921-7426
Carl Stephens, *Mgr*
EMP: 32
SQ FT: 72,000
SALES (corp-wide): 982.77MM **Privately Held**
Web: www.wilsonart.com
SIC: 4225 5162 3083 2891 General warehousing and storage; Plastics materials and basic shapes; Laminated plastics plate and sheet; Adhesives and sealants
HQ: Wilsonart Llc
   2501 Wilsonart Dr
   Temple TX 76504
   254 207-7000

(P-9130)
WORLD CLASS DISTRIBUTION INC
800 S Shamrock Ave, Monrovia (91016-6346)
PHONE...............................909 574-4140
Charles Pilliter, *Pr*
EMP: 90
SALES (corp-wide): 355.83K **Privately Held**
SIC: 4225 General warehousing and storage
HQ: World Class Distribution Inc.
   10288 Calabash Ave
   Fontana CA 92335

▲ = Import ▼ = Export
◆ = Import/Export

(P-9131)
XPDEL INC
13012 Molette St, Santa Fe Springs
(90670-5522)
PHONE..............................805 267-1214
Manish Kapoor, *CEO*
EMP: 290
SALES (corp-wide): 23.97MM **Privately Held**
SIC: 4225 General warehousing and storage
PA: Xpdel, Inc.
2625 Townsgate Rd Ste 330
516 530-9108

4226 Special Warehousing And Storage, Nec

(P-9132)
ACCESS INFO HOLDINGS LLC
12135 Davis St, Moreno Valley
(92557-6369)
PHONE..............................909 459-1417
EMP: 727
SALES (corp-wide): 18.11MM **Privately Held**
Web: www.accesscorp.com
SIC: 4226 Document and office records storage
PA: Access Information Holdings, Llc
500 Unicorn Pk Dr Ste 503
925 583-0100

(P-9133)
DSV SOLUTIONS LLC
6681 River Run, Riverside (92507-7128)
PHONE..............................732 850-8000
Michael Marlow, *Pr*
EMP: 90
SALES (corp-wide): 21.99B **Privately Held**
Web: www.go2uti.com
SIC: 4226 Special warehousing and storage, nec
HQ: Dsv Solutions, Llc
200 S Wood Ave Fl 3
Iselin NJ 08830
732 850-8000

(P-9134)
EXPRESS IMAGING SERVICES INC
1805 W 208th St Ste 202, Torrance
(90501-1808)
PHONE..............................888 846-8804
Paul Terry, *Pr*
Kenny Ly, *
Tan Ly, *CIO*
Anni Ly, *Leasing Manager*
EMP: 100 **EST:** 2004
SQ FT: 10,000
SALES (est): 14.62MM **Privately Held**
Web: www.eiscallcenter.com
SIC: 4226 Document and office records storage

(P-9135)
PACIFIC CHEMICAL DIST CORP (HQ)
Also Called: Pacific Chemical
6250 Caballero Blvd, Buena Park
(90620-1124)
PHONE..............................714 521-7161
James N Tausz, *Pr*
James Banister, *
Rhonda Tausz, *
◆ **EMP:** 100 **EST:** 1978
SQ FT: 144,000
SALES (est): 3.71MM
SALES (corp-wide): 552.56MM **Privately Held**

Web: www.pacchem.com
SIC: 4226 Special warehousing and storage, nec
PA: Quantix Scs, Llc
24 Waterway Ave Ste 450
800 542-8058

4424 Deep Sea Domestic Transportation Of Freight

(P-9136)
POLAR TANKERS INC (DH)
300 Oceangate, Long Beach (90802-6801)
PHONE..............................562 388-1400
John R Hennon, *Pr*
John L Sullivan, *
George Mcshea, *VP Opers*
▲ **EMP:** 75 **EST:** 1956
SALES (est): 19.98MM
SALES (corp-wide): 58.57B **Publicly Held**
Web: polartankers.conocophillips.com
SIC: 4424 4412 Deep sea domestic transportation of freight; Deep sea foreign transportation of freight
HQ: Conocophillips Company
925 N Eldridge Pkwy
Houston TX 77079
281 293-1000

(P-9137)
POLAR TANKERS INC
60 Berth, San Pedro (90731-7252)
PHONE..............................310 519-8260
Chris Adams, *Brnch Mgr*
EMP: 210
SALES (corp-wide): 58.57B **Publicly Held**
Web: polartankers.conocophillips.com
SIC: 4424 Deep sea domestic transportation of freight
HQ: Polar Tankers, Inc.
300 Oceangate
Long Beach CA 90802
562 388-1400

4481 Deep Sea Passenger Transportation, Except Ferry

(P-9138)
PRINCESS CRUISE LINES LTD (HQ)
Also Called: Princess Cruises
24305 Town Center Dr, Santa Clarita
(91355-4999)
P.O. Box 959 (91380)
PHONE..............................661 753-0000
Jan Swartz, *CEO*
Gus Antorcha, *
Natalya Leahy, *
Jim Berra, *CMO*
◆ **EMP:** 2000 **EST:** 1965
SALES (est): 275.91MM
SALES (corp-wide): 7.98B **Privately Held**
Web: www.princess.com
SIC: 4481 4725 7011 Deep sea passenger transportation, except ferry; Tour operators; Hotels
PA: Carnival Plc
Carnival House
238 065-6666

4489 Water Passenger Transportation

(P-9139)
CATALINA CHANNEL EXPRESS INC (HQ)

Also Called: Catalina Express Cruises
385 E Swinford St, San Pedro
(90731-1002)
PHONE..............................310 519-7971
Greg Bombard, *Pr*
Douglas Bombard, *
EMP: 200 **EST:** 1981
SQ FT: 20,000
SALES (est): 28.14MM
SALES (corp-wide): 43.85MM **Privately Held**
Web: www.catalinaexpress.com
SIC: 4489 Excursion boat operators
PA: Bombard Marine & Resort Management Services, Inc.
95 Berth
310 519-7971

(P-9140)
SO CAL SHIP SERVICES
Also Called: Ship Services
971 S Seaside Ave, San Pedro
(90731-7331)
PHONE..............................310 519-8411
Michael A Lanham, *Pr*
EMP: 85 **EST:** 1982
SQ FT: 10,000
SALES (est): 12.25MM **Privately Held**
Web: www.ship-services.com
SIC: 4489 Water taxis

4491 Marine Cargo Handling

(P-9141)
INTERNATIONAL TRNSP SVC LLC (PA)
1281 Pier G Way, Long Beach
(90802-6353)
P.O. Box 22704 (90801-5704)
PHONE..............................562 435-7781
Kim Holtermand, *CEO*
Sean Lindsay, *COO*
Louis Paul, *Bd of Dir*
Richard Nicholson, *Bd of Dir*
▲ **EMP:** 114 **EST:** 1971
SQ FT: 10,000
SALES (est): 22.84MM
SALES (corp-wide): 22.84MM **Privately Held**
Web: www.itslb.com
SIC: 4491 Marine loading and unloading services

(P-9142)
LBCT LLC
1171 Pier F Ave, Long Beach (90802-6252)
PHONE..............................562 951-6000
Anthony Otto, *Mgr*
EMP: 90 **EST:** 1980
SALES (est): 7.55MM **Privately Held**
Web: www.lbct.com
SIC: 4491 Marine terminals

(P-9143)
MARINE TERMINALS CORPORATION
389 Terminal Way, San Pedro
(90731-7430)
PHONE..............................310 519-2300
◆ **EMP:** 300 **EST:** 1931
SALES (est): 3.45MM
SALES (corp-wide): 251B **Privately Held**
Web: www.portsamerica.com
SIC: 4491 Stevedoring
HQ: Mtc Holdings
3 Embarcadero Ctr Ste 550
San Francisco CA 94111
912 651-4000

(P-9144)
PORT OF LONG BEACH
415 W Ocean Blvd, Long Beach
(90802-4511)
P.O. Box 570 (90801-0570)
PHONE..............................562 283-7000
Paula Grond, *Sec*
EMP: 544 **EST:** 2014
SALES (est): 36.82MM **Privately Held**
Web: www.polb.com
SIC: 4491 Docks, piers and terminals
PA: City Of Long Beach
1800 E Wardlow Rd
562 570-6450

(P-9145)
PORT OF LOS ANGELES
425 S Palos Verdes St, San Pedro
(90731-3309)
PHONE..............................310 732-3508
Gene Seroka, *Ex Dir*
EMP: 204 **EST:** 2017
SALES (est): 656.4MM **Privately Held**
Web: www.portoflosangeles.org
SIC: 4491 Waterfront terminal operation

(P-9146)
SAN DIEGO UNIFIED PORT DST (PA)
Also Called: Port of San Diego
3165 Pacific Hwy, San Diego (92101-1128)
P.O. Box 120488 (92112-0488)
PHONE..............................619 686-6200
John Bolduc, *CEO*
Robert Deangelis, *
Karen Porteous, *
Randa Coniglio, *
Thomas Russell, *
EMP: 240 **EST:** 1962
SQ FT: 120,000
SALES (est): 202.99MM
SALES (corp-wide): 202.99MM **Privately Held**
Web: www.portofsandiego.org
SIC: 4491 Marine cargo handling

(P-9147)
SAN DIEGO UNIFIED PORT DST
1400 Tidelands Ave, National City
(91950-4224)
PHONE..............................619 686-6200
EMP: 129
SALES (corp-wide): 202.99MM **Privately Held**
Web: www.portofsandiego.org
SIC: 4491 Marine cargo handling
PA: San Diego Unified Port District
3165 Pacific Hwy
619 686-6200

(P-9148)
SUDERMAN CONTG STEVEDORES INC (PA)
Also Called: Metro Ports
3806 Worsham Ave, Long Beach
(90808-1896)
PHONE..............................409 762-8131
Robert Dickey, *Pr*
Robert Willett, *
Walter W Hansel, *
EMP: 100 **EST:** 1987
SQ FT: 4,500
SALES (est): 4.26MM **Privately Held**
Web: www.metroports.com
SIC: 4491 Stevedoring

(P-9149)
TOTAL INTERMODAL SERVICES INC (PA)

7101 Jackson St, Paramount (90723-4836)
PHONE..................................562 427-6300
Amador Sanchez Junior, *Pr*
▲ **EMP:** 50 **EST:** 1991
SALES (est): 18.62MM **Privately Held**
Web: www.totalintermodal.com
SIC: 4491 4213 7534 4731 Marine cargo
handling; Trucking, except local; Tire
retreading and repair shops; Freight
forwarding

4492 Towing And Tugboat Service

(P-9150)
BRUSCO TUG & BARGE INC
170 E Port Hueneme Rd, Port Hueneme
(93041-3213)
PHONE..................................805 986-1600
David Brusco, *Brnch Mgr*
EMP: 125
SALES (corp-wide): 33.82MM **Privately Held**
Web: www.bruscotug.com
SIC: 4492 Tugboat service
PA: Brusco Tug & Barge, Inc.
548 14th Ave
360 423-9856

(P-9151)
PACIFIC MARITIME GROUP INC
1512 Pier C St, Long Beach (90813-4043)
PHONE..................................562 590-8188
EMP: 95
SALES (corp-wide): 41.59MM **Privately Held**
Web: www.pacificmaritimegroup.com
SIC: 4492 Tugboat service
PA: Pacific Maritime Group, Inc.
1444 Cesar E Chavez Pkwy
619 533-7932

4493 Marinas

(P-9152)
SHELTER POINTE LLC
Also Called: Shelter Pointe Hotel & Marina
1551 Shelter Island Dr, San Diego
(92106-3102)
PHONE..................................619 221-8000
Jeff Foster, *Managing Member*
EMP: 242 **EST:** 1993
SALES (est): 4.49MM
SALES (corp-wide): 98.27MM **Privately Held**
Web: www.resortkonakai.com
SIC: 4493 7011 7997 5812 Marinas; Resort
hotel; Country club, membership; American
restaurant
HQ: Pacifica Hotel Company
39 Argonaut
Aliso Viejo CA 92656
805 957-0095

4499 Water Transportation Services, Nec

(P-9153)
BLUE OCEAN MARINE LLC
2060 Knoll Dr Ste 100, Ventura
(93003-7391)
PHONE..................................805 658-2628
EMP: 30 **EST:** 2010
SALES (est): 512.99K **Privately Held**
SIC: 4499 1389 7359 Boat rental,
commercial; Oil field services, nec;
Equipment rental and leasing, nec

(P-9154)
HANJIN SHIPPING CO LTD
301 Hanjin Rd, Long Beach (90802)
PHONE..................................201 291-4600
Taisoo Suk, *Ex Dir*
◆ **EMP:** 691 **EST:** 1994
SALES (est): 3.94MM **Privately Held**
SIC: 4499 Steamship leasing

4512 Air Transportation, Scheduled

(P-9155)
AEROTRANSPORTE DE CARGE UNION
Also Called: Aerounion
5625 W Imperial Hwy, Los Angeles
(90045-6323)
PHONE..................................310 649-0069
Luis Ramo, *Pr*
Steven Connolly, *VP*
EMP: 400 **EST:** 2006
SALES (est): 9.64MM **Privately Held**
Web: pcola.gulf.net
SIC: 4512 Air cargo carrier, scheduled

(P-9156)
AIR NEW ZEALAND LIMITED
222 N Pacific Coast Hwy Ste 900, El
Segundo (90245-5670)
PHONE..................................310 648-7000
Roger Poulton, *VP*
EMP: 100
Web: www.airnewzealand.com
SIC: 4512 Air passenger carrier, scheduled
PA: Air New Zealand Limited
185 Fanshawe St

(P-9157)
AMERICAN AIRLINES INC
400 World Way Ste F, Los Angeles
(90045-5863)
P.O. Box 92246 (90009-2246)
PHONE..................................310 646-4553
Sally Rabideau, *Owner*
EMP: 219
SALES (corp-wide): 52.79B **Publicly Held**
Web: www.aacreditunion.org
SIC: 4512 Air passenger carrier, scheduled
HQ: American Airlines, Inc.
1 Skyview Dr
Fort Worth TX 76155
682 278-9000

(P-9158)
AMERIFLIGHT LLC
4700 W Empire Ave, Burbank
(91505-1098)
PHONE..................................818 847-0000
EMP: 75
SALES (corp-wide): 32.05MM **Privately Held**
Web: www.ameriflight.com
SIC: 4512 Air cargo carrier, scheduled
PA: Ameriflight, Llc
1515 W 20th St
800 800-4538

(P-9159)
KOREAN AIR LINES CO LTD
Also Called: Korean Air
380 World Way Ste S4, Los Angeles
(90045-5847)
PHONE..................................310 646-4866
EMP: 175
Web: www.koreanair.com
SIC: 4512 Air passenger carrier, scheduled
PA: Korean Airlines Co., Ltd.
260 Haneul-Gil, Gangseo-Gu

(P-9160)
KOREAN AIRLINES CO LTD
Also Called: Korean Arln Crgo Reservations
6101 W Imperial Hwy, Los Angeles
(90045-6330)
PHONE..................................310 410-2000
Jinkul Lee, *Pr*
EMP: 250
Web: www.koreanair.com
SIC: 4512 4513 Air passenger carrier,
scheduled; Package delivery, private air
PA: Korean Airlines Co., Ltd.
260 Haneul-Gil, Gangseo-Gu

(P-9161)
L A AIR INC
5933 W Century Blvd # 500, Los Angeles
(90045-5471)
PHONE..................................310 215-8245
Dennis W Altbrandt, *CEO*
Wayne Schoenfeld, *
Tim Clary, *MARKET PLANNING**
William J Wolf, *
EMP: 134 **EST:** 1980
SQ FT: 6,119
SALES (est): 450.75K **Privately Held**
SIC: 4512 Air passenger carrier, scheduled

(P-9162)
PACIFIC AVIATION LLC (PA)
201 Continental Blvd Ste 220, El Segundo
(90245-4507)
PHONE..................................310 322-6290
Evan Gobdel, *CEO*
Phil Shaw, *
Robert Steinberger, *
EMP: 1524 **EST:** 2015
SALES (est): 20MM
SALES (corp-wide): 20MM **Privately Held**
SIC: 4512 Air passenger carrier, scheduled

(P-9163)
PIEDMONT AIRLINES INC
Also Called: American Airlines/Eagle
4100 E Donald Douglas Dr, Long Beach
(90808-1754)
PHONE..................................562 421-1806
Sean Lucas, *Mgr*
EMP: 133
SALES (corp-wide): 52.79B **Publicly Held**
Web: www.piedmont-airlines.com
SIC: 4512 Air passenger carrier, scheduled
HQ: Piedmont Airlines, Inc.
5443 Airport Terminal Rd
Salisbury MD 21804
410 572-5100

(P-9164)
POLAR AIR CARGO LP
100 Oceangate Fl 15, Long Beach
(90802-4347)
PHONE..................................310 568-4551
FAX: 562 436-9333
EMP: 480
SALES (est): 13.37MM
SALES (corp-wide): 1.84B **Publicly Held**
SIC: 4512 Air cargo carrier, scheduled
PA: Atlas Air Worldwide Holdings, Inc.
2000 Westchester Ave
914 701-8000

(P-9165)
SINGAPORE AIRLINES LIMITED
222 N Pacific Coast Hwy Ste 1600, El
Segundo (90245-5615)
PHONE..................................310 647-1922
Tee Hooi Teoh, *Mgr*
EMP: 135
Web: www.singaporeair.com

SIC: 4512 Air passenger carrier, scheduled
PA: Singapore Airlines Limited
25 Airline Road

(P-9166)
SOUTHWEST AIRLINES CO
Also Called: Southwest Airlines
18601 Airport Way Ste 237, Santa Ana
(92707-5257)
PHONE..................................949 252-5200
Larry Pits, *Mgr*
EMP: 80
SALES (corp-wide): 26.09B **Publicly Held**
Web: www.southwest.com
SIC: 4512 Air passenger carrier, scheduled
PA: Southwest Airlines Co.
2702 Love Field Dr
214 792-4000

(P-9167)
SPIRIT AIRLINES INC
San Diego Intl Airport Terminal 2 E, San
Diego (92101)
PHONE..................................800 772-7117
EMP: 195
SALES (corp-wide): 5.36B **Privately Held**
Web: www.spirit.com
SIC: 4512 Air transportation, scheduled
PA: Spirit Airlines, Inc.
1731 Radiant Dr
954 447-7920

(P-9168)
UNITED AIRLINES INC
Also Called: Continental Airlines
7300 World Way W Rm 144, Los Angeles
(90045-5829)
PHONE..................................310 258-3319
Ken Jaminson, *Mgr*
EMP: 89
SALES (corp-wide): 53.72B **Publicly Held**
Web: jetstream.united.com
SIC: 4512 Air passenger carrier, scheduled
HQ: United Airlines, Inc.
233 S Wacker Dr
Chicago IL 60606
872 825-4000

(P-9169)
UNITED COURIERS INC (DH)
Also Called: U C I Distribution Plus
3280 E Foothill Blvd, Pasadena
(91107-3103)
PHONE..................................213 383-3611
Stephan Cretier, *CEO*
Richard R Irvin, *
Robert G Irvin, *
EMP: 200 **EST:** 1957
SQ FT: 25,000
SALES (est): 6.44MM
SALES (corp-wide): 170.74MM **Privately Held**
SIC: 4512 4215 4212 7381 Air cargo carrier,
scheduled; Courier services, except by air;
Local trucking, without storage; Armored
car services
HQ: Ati Systems International, Inc.
2000 Nw Corp Blvd Ste 101
Boca Raton FL 33431
561 939-7000

(P-9170)
UNITED PARCEL SERVICE INC
Also Called: UPS
2925 Jurupa St, Ontario (91761-2915)
PHONE..................................909 906-5700
EMP: 76
SALES (corp-wide): 90.96B **Publicly Held**
Web: www.ups.com

SIC: 4512 Air cargo carrier, scheduled
HQ: United Parcel Service, Inc.
55 Glenlake Pkwy
Atlanta GA 30328
404 828-6000

(P-9171)
UNITED PARCEL SERVICE INC
Also Called: UPS
1457 E Victoria Ave, San Bernardino
(92408-2923)
PHONE..............................800 742-5877
EMP: 177
SALES (corp-wide): 90.96B **Publicly Held**
Web: www.ups.com
SIC: 4512 Air cargo carrier, scheduled
HQ: United Parcel Service, Inc.
55 Glenlake Pkwy
Atlanta GA 30328
404 828-6000

(P-9172)
UNITED PARCEL SERVICE INC
Also Called: UPS
10760 Tamarind Ave, Bloomington
(92316-2546)
PHONE..............................909 349-4343
EMP: 89
SALES (corp-wide): 90.96B **Publicly Held**
Web: www.ups.com
SIC: 4512 Air cargo carrier, scheduled
HQ: United Parcel Service, Inc.
55 Glenlake Pkwy
Atlanta GA 30328
404 828-6000

(P-9173)
UNITED PARCEL SERVICE INC
Also Called: UPS
3110 Jurupa St, Ontario (91761-2902)
PHONE..............................909 605-7740
EMP: 177
SALES (corp-wide): 90.96B **Publicly Held**
Web: www.ups.com
SIC: 4512 Air cargo carrier, scheduled
HQ: United Parcel Service, Inc.
55 Glenlake Pkwy
Atlanta GA 30328
404 828-6000

4513 Air Courier Services

(P-9174)
FEDERAL EXPRESS CORPORATION
Also Called: Fedex
3333 S Grand Ave, Los Angeles
(90007-4116)
PHONE..............................800 463-3339
EMP: 100
SALES (corp-wide): 87.69B **Publicly Held**
Web: www.fedex.com
SIC: 4513 Package delivery, private air
HQ: Federal Express Corporation
3610 Hacks Cross Rd
Memphis TN 38125
901 369-3600

(P-9175)
MEJICO EXPRESS INC (PA)
Also Called: Grupoex
14849 Firestone Blvd Fl 1, La Mirada
(90638)
PHONE..............................714 690-8300
Jose Leon, *Pr*
EMP: 150 **EST:** 1988
SALES (est): 614.08K **Privately Held**
SIC: 4513 Letter delivery, private air

(P-9176)
UNITED PARCEL SERVICE INC
Also Called: UPS
3333 S Downey Rd, Los Angeles (90023)
PHONE..............................323 260-8957
Tony Peralta, *Mgr*
EMP: 203
SALES (corp-wide): 90.96B **Publicly Held**
Web: www.ups.com
SIC: 4513 4215 Air courier services; Courier
services, except by air
HQ: United Parcel Service, Inc.
55 Glenlake Pkwy
Atlanta GA 30328
404 828-6000

(P-9177)
UNITED PARCEL SERVICE INC
Also Called: UPS
25283 Sherman Rd, Sun City (92585-9352)
PHONE..............................951 928-5221
Sean Nichols, *Brnch Mgr*
EMP: 89
SALES (corp-wide): 90.96B **Publicly Held**
Web: www.ups.com
SIC: 4513 Parcel delivery, private air
HQ: United Parcel Service, Inc.
55 Glenlake Pkwy
Atlanta GA 30328
404 828-6000

4522 Air Transportation, Nonscheduled

(P-9178)
ADVANCED AIR LLC
Also Called: Advanced Air
12101 Crenshaw Blvd Ste 100, Hawthorne
(90250-3444)
PHONE..............................310 644-3344
Levi Stockton, *Pr*
EMP: 150 **EST:** 2005
SQ FT: 2,500
SALES (est): 1.38MM **Privately Held**
Web: www.advancedairlines.com
SIC: 4522 4512 Air transportation,
nonscheduled; Air transportation, scheduled

(P-9179)
AERO TECHNOLOGIES INC (PA)
16233 Vanowen St, Van Nuys
(91406-4700)
Rural Route 16233 Vanowen St (91406)
PHONE..............................323 745-2376
Benjamin Klein, *CEO*
Garrett Camp, *Ch*
EMP: 118 **EST:** 2013
SALES (est): 7.04MM
SALES (corp-wide): 7.04MM **Privately Hold**
Web: www.aero.com
SIC: 4522 Air transportation, nonscheduled

(P-9180)
AVJET CORPORATION (DH)
4301 W Empire Ave, Burbank (91505-1109)
PHONE..............................818 841-6190
EMP: 80 **EST:** 1979
SALES (est): 8.77MM
SALES (corp-wide): 42.27B **Publicly Held**
Web: www.avjet.com
SIC: 4522 5599 4581 Flying charter service;
Aircraft, self-propelled; Aircraft cleaning and
janitorial service
HQ: Jet Aviation Of America, Inc.
112 Chrles A Lndbrgh Dr T
Teterboro NJ 07608
201 288-8400

(P-9181)
NAVAJO INVESTMENTS INC (PA)
17962 Cowan, Irvine (92614-6026)
PHONE..............................949 863-9200
William Langston, *Pr*
EMP: 98 **EST:** 1985
SQ FT: 17,000
SALES (est): 1.82MM
SALES (corp-wide): 1.82MM **Privately Held**
Web: www.snyderlangston.com
SIC: 4522 Air transportation, nonscheduled

(P-9182)
PEGASUS ELITE AVIATION INC
7943 Woodley Ave, Van Nuys
(91406-1232)
PHONE..............................818 742-6666
Lina Tullberg, *Pr*
Wing Ki Hui, *Sec*
Allen Chen, *Treas*
Charles Huang, *Dir*
Gentry Long, *Dir*
EMP: 162 **EST:** 2007
SALES (est): 5.59MM
SALES (corp-wide): 5.59MM **Privately Held**
Web: www.pegjet.com
SIC: 4522 Flying charter service
PA: Prima Air Group Llc
800 E Colo Blvd Ste 888

(P-9183)
SUN AIR JETS LLC
855 Aviation Dr Ste 200, Camarillo
(93010-8850)
PHONE..............................805 389-9301
Brian Counsil, *Pr*
Steve Maloney, *
Rob Cox, *OF Maintenance**
Ed Fares, *
EMP: 114 **EST:** 1999
SQ FT: 10,000
SALES (est): 22.14MM **Privately Held**
Web: www.sunairjets.com
SIC: 4522 4581 Flying charter service;
Aircraft servicing and repairing

4581 Airports, Flying Fields, And Services

(P-9184)
ADIENT AEROSPACE LLC (PA)
2850 Skyway Dr, Santa Maria
(93455-1410)
PHONE..............................949 514-1851
Tony Guy, *CEO*
Michael Rowen, *COO*
EMP: 122 **EST:** 2018
SALES (est): 85MM
SALES (corp-wide): 85MM **Privately Held**
SIC: 4581 Aircraft servicing and repairing

(P-9185)
AGI CARGO LLC
6181 W Imperial Hwy, Los Angeles
(90045-6305)
PHONE..............................310 646-2446
EMP: 1810
SALES (corp-wide): 266.32MM **Privately Held**
Web: www.allianceground.com
SIC: 4581 Airfreight loading and unloading
services
HQ: Agi Cargo, Llc
9130 S Ddland Blvd Ste 18
Miami FL 33156
305 740-3252

(P-9186)
AGI CARGO LLC
6851 W Imperial Hwy, Los Angeles
(90045-6311)
PHONE..............................310 342-0136
EMP: 1013
SALES (corp-wide): 266.32MM **Privately Held**
Web: www.agi.aero
SIC: 4581 Airfreight loading and unloading
services
HQ: Agi Cargo, Llc
9130 S Ddland Blvd Ste 18
Miami FL 33156
305 740-3252

(P-9187)
AGI GROUND INC
Also Called: Airport Terminal Services
300 World Way, Los Angeles (90045-5856)
P.O. Box 881359 (90009-7359)
PHONE..............................310 215-4902
Don Tippin, *Brnch Mgr*
EMP: 97
SALES (corp-wide): 38.08MM **Privately Held**
Web: www.agi.aero
SIC: 4581 Airports, flying fields, and services
PA: Agi Ground, Inc.
9130 S Dadeland Blvd
314 739-1900

(P-9188)
AIR 88 INC
Also Called: Crownair Aviation
3753 John J Montgomery Dr, San Diego
(92123-1732)
PHONE..............................858 277-1453
David Ryan, *Pr*
Laura Cagliero, *
EMP: 32 **EST:** 1951
SQ FT: 53,600
SALES (est): 2.54MM **Privately Held**
Web: www.crownairaviation.com
SIC: 4581 3829 Aircraft maintenance and
repair services; Fuel system instruments,
aircraft

(P-9189)
AIRPORT TERMINAL MGT INC
6851 W Imperial Hwy, Los Angeles
(90045-6311)
PHONE..............................310 988-1492
EMP: 325
SALES (corp-wide): 7.78MM **Privately Held**
Web: www.atmlax.com
SIC: 4581 Airport terminal services
PA: Airport Terminal Management, Inc.
216 W Florence Ave
310 590-1650

(P-9190)
AVIATION & DEFENSE INC
Also Called: ADI
255 S Leland Norton Way, San Bernardino
(92408-0103)
PHONE..............................909 382-3487
Daniel M Scanlon, *CEO*
Mike Scanlon, *Pr*
Dan Scanlon, *VP*
Kathy Meza, *Contrlr*
Jim Anderson, *Sls Dir*
EMP: 180 **EST:** 2011
SQ FT: 180,000
SALES (est): 2.04MM **Privately Held**
Web: www.adi.aero
SIC: 4581 Aircraft maintenance and repair
services

(P-9191)
AVIATION CONSULTANTS INC
Also Called: Aci Jet
19301 Campus Dr, Santa Ana
(92707-5246)
PHONE..........................949 201-2550
William Borgsmiller, *Brnch Mgr*
EMP: 83
SALES (corp-wide): 43.44MM **Privately Held**
Web: www.acijet.com
SIC: **4581** Aircraft storage at airports
PA: Aviation Consultants, Inc.
4751 Aviadores Way
805 782-9722

(P-9192)
AVIATION CONSULTANTS INC
4900 Wing Way, Paso Robles
(93446-8522)
PHONE..........................805 596-0212
William Borgsmiller, *Brnch Mgr*
EMP: 83
SALES (corp-wide): 43.44MM **Privately Held**
Web: www.acijet.com
SIC: **4581** Airports, flying fields, and services
PA: Aviation Consultants, Inc.
4751 Aviadores Way
805 782-9722

(P-9193)
AVIATION MAINTENANCE GROUP INC
8352 Kimball Ave Hngr 3, Chino
(91708-9267)
PHONE..........................714 469-0515
Jeremy G Schuster, *Pr*
Doug Crowther, *
EMP: 85 EST: 1995
SALES (est): 2.35MM **Privately Held**
Web: www.amgassociates.com
SIC: **4581** Aircraft maintenance and repair services

(P-9194)
CERTIFIED AVIATION SVCS LLC (PA)
Also Called: C A S
3237 E Guasti Rd Ste 120, Ontario
(91761-1242)
PHONE..........................909 605-0380
Brad Caban, *Managing Member*
Mark Lee, *
Brad Caban, *Pr*
EMP: 91 EST: 1990
SQ FT: 3,300
SALES (est): 24.03MM **Privately Held**
Web: www.certifiedaviation.com
SIC: **4581** Aircraft maintenance and repair services

(P-9195)
CLAY LACY AVIATION INC (PA)
Also Called: C L A
7435 Valjean Ave, Van Nuys (91406-2977)
PHONE..........................818 989-2900
TOLL FREE: 800
Brian Kirkdoffer, *Pr*
Hershel Clay Lacy, *
EMP: 317 EST: 1969
SQ FT: 18,000
SALES (est): 86.63MM
SALES (corp-wide): 86.63MM **Privately Held**
Web: www.claylacy.com
SIC: **4581** Airport terminal services

(P-9196)
COMAV LLC
Also Called: Comav Aviation
18260 Phantom W, Victorville (92394-7971)
PHONE..........................760 523-5100
EMP: 108
SALES (corp-wide): 43.18MM **Privately Held**
Web: www.comav.com
SIC: **4581** Aircraft maintenance and repair services
PA: Comav, Llc
18499 Phantom St Ste 17
760 523-5100

(P-9197)
COMAV TECHNICAL SERVICES LLC
Also Called: S C A
18438 Readiness St, Victorville
(92394-7945)
PHONE..........................760 530-2400
Craig Garrick, *CEO*
Jon Day, *
▲ EMP: 223 EST: 1999
SQ FT: 47,625
SALES (est): 12.86MM
SALES (corp-wide): 43.18MM **Privately Held**
Web: www.comav.com
SIC: **4581** Aircraft maintenance and repair services
PA: Comav, Llc
18499 Phantom St Ste 17
760 523-5100

(P-9198)
COUNTY OF ORANGE
Also Called: John Wayne Airport
3160 Airway Ave, Costa Mesa
(92626-4608)
PHONE..........................949 252-5006
Loan Leblow, *Brnch Mgr*
EMP: 135
SALES (corp-wide): 5.63B **Privately Held**
Web: www.ocgov.com
SIC: **4581 9621** Airport; Aircraft regulating agencies
PA: County Of Orange
400 W. Civic Center Dr
714 834-6200

(P-9199)
DEPARTMENT OF ARPRTS OF THE CY
1 World Way, Los Angeles (90045-5803)
PHONE..........................855 463-5252
EMP: 810
SALES (est): 1.64MM
SALES (corp-wide): 1.38B **Privately Held**
Web: www.lawa.org
SIC: **4581** Airport
PA: Los Angeles World Airports
1 World Way
855 463-5252

(P-9200)
DSD TRUCKING INC
2411 Santa Fe Ave, Redondo Beach
(90278-1125)
PHONE..........................310 338-3395
Dan Cuevas, *Pr*
EMP: 100 EST: 1984
SQ FT: 300,000
SALES (est): 9.85MM **Privately Held**
Web: www.dsdcompanies.com
SIC: **4581** Air freight handling at airports

(P-9201)
F & E ARCFT MINT LOS ANGLES LL
531 Main St Ste 672, El Segundo
(90245-3006)
PHONE..........................310 338-0063
EMP: 350 EST: 1992
SALES (est): 17.58MM **Privately Held**
Web: www.feairmaintenance.com
SIC: **4581 7699** Aircraft servicing and repairing; Aircraft and heavy equipment repair services

(P-9202)
LOS ANGELES WORLD AIRPORTS (PA)
1 World Way, Los Angeles (90045-5803)
P.O. Box P.O. Box 92216 (90045)
PHONE..........................855 463-5252
Justin Erbacci, *CEO*
Michael Cummings, *
Robert L Gilbert, *Chief Development Officer*
Arif Alikhan, *
EMP: 222 EST: 2010
SALES (est): 1.38B
SALES (corp-wide): 1.38B **Privately Held**
Web: www.lawa.org
SIC: **4581** Airport

(P-9203)
LOS ANGELES WORLD AIRPORTS
Also Called: Human Resources Services
7301 World Way W Fl 5, Los Angeles
(90045-5828)
PHONE..........................424 646-5900
EMP: 694
SALES (corp-wide): 1.38B **Privately Held**
Web: www.lawa.org
SIC: **4581** Airport
PA: Los Angeles World Airports
1 World Way
855 463-5252

(P-9204)
LOS ANGELES WORLD AIRPORTS
5312 W 99th Pl, Los Angeles (90045-5722)
PHONE..........................424 646-9118
Joseph Ricksecker, *Brnch Mgr*
EMP: 347
SALES (corp-wide): 1.38B **Privately Held**
Web: www.lawa.org
SIC: **4581** Airport
PA: Los Angeles World Airports
1 World Way
855 463-5252

(P-9205)
PACIFIC AVIATION CORPORATION (HQ)
201 Continental Blvd Ste 220, El Segundo
(90245-4507)
PHONE..........................310 646-4015
Evan Gobdel, *CEO*
Scott White, *
Robert Steinberger, *
EMP: 200 EST: 1995
SALES (est): 9.32MM
SALES (corp-wide): 20MM **Privately Held**
Web: www.pacificaviation.com
SIC: **4581** Airport terminal services
PA: Pacific Aviation Llc
201 Continental Blvd # 220
310 322-6290

(P-9206)
PHS / MWA
Also Called: Phs/Mwa Aviation Services
42374 Avenida Alvarado # A, Temecula
(92590-3445)
PHONE..........................951 695-1008
Mary Bale, *CEO*
Bill Voetsch, *
EMP: 147 EST: 2003
SALES (est): 20.82MM **Publicly Held**
Web: www.wencor.com
SIC: **4581 3492 7629** Aircraft servicing and repairing; Control valves, aircraft: hydraulic and pneumatic; Electrical repair shops
HQ: Wencor Group, Llc
416 Dividend Dr
Peachtree City GA 30269
678 490-0140

(P-9207)
REPAIRTECH INTERNATIONAL INC
Also Called: Repair Tech International
7850 Gloria Ave, Van Nuys (91406-1821)
PHONE..........................818 989-2681
Stanley H Bennett, *Pr*
Patricia J Bennett, *
EMP: 30 EST: 1978
SALES (est): 2.05MM **Privately Held**
Web: www.repairtechinternational.com
SIC: **4581 3721 3999** Aircraft servicing and repairing; Aircraft; Atomizers, toiletry

(P-9208)
SAN DEGO CNTY RGNAL ARPRT AUTH (PA)
Also Called: Sdcraa
3225 N Harbor Dr Fl 3, San Diego
(92101-1045)
P.O. Box 82776 (92138-2776)
PHONE..........................619 400-2400
Thella F Bowens, *CEO*
EMP: 229 EST: 2003
SALES (est): 215.94MM
SALES (corp-wide): 215.94MM **Privately Held**
Web: www.san.org
SIC: **4581** Airport

(P-9209)
SUPERIOR AIRCRAFT SERVICES INC (HQ)
201 Continental Blvd Ste 220, El Segundo
(90245-4507)
PHONE..........................636 778-2300
Danny Pyne, *Pr*
Scott White Ctrl, *Prin*
EMP: 90 EST: 1999
SALES (est): 5.17MM
SALES (corp-wide): 20MM **Privately Held**
Web: www.pacificaviation.com
SIC: **4581** Aircraft servicing and repairing
PA: Pacific Aviation Llc
201 Continental Blvd # 220
310 322-6290

(P-9210)
SWISSPORT CARGO SERVICES LP
Also Called: Cargo Service Center
11001 Aviation Blvd, Los Angeles
(90045-6123)
PHONE..........................310 910-9541
Mark Wood, *Genl Mgr*
EMP: 81
SALES (corp-wide): 2.67MM **Privately Held**
Web: www.swissport.com

SIC: **4581** Airport terminal services
HQ: Swissport Cargo Services, L.P.
23723 Air Frt Ln Bldg 5
Dulles VA 20166
703 742-4300

(P-9211)
SWISSPORT USA INC
Also Called: Employment Intake Training Ctr
7025 W Imperial Hwy, Los Angeles
(90045-6313)
PHONE...................310 345-1986
Jerry Harris, *Genl Mgr*
EMP: 99
SALES (corp-wide): 2.67MM **Privately
Held**
Web: www.swissport.com
SIC: **4581** Air freight handling at airports
HQ: Swissport Usa, Inc.
227 Fyttville St Fl 9 Ste
Raleigh NC 27601

(P-9212)
SWISSPORT USA INC
11001 Aviation Blvd, Los Angeles
(90045-6123)
PHONE...................310 910-9560
EMP: 85
SALES (corp-wide): 2.67MM **Privately
Held**
Web: www.swissport.com
SIC: **4581** Airport terminal services
HQ: Swissport Usa, Inc.
227 Fyttville St Fl 9 Ste
Raleigh NC 27601

(P-9213)
WORLD SVC WST/LA INFLGHT SVC L
Also Called: L.A. Inflight Service Company
1812 W 135th St, Gardena (90249-2520)
PHONE...................310 538-7000
Steven H Yoon, *Managing Member*
◆ **EMP:** 170 **EST:** 1988
SQ FT: 13,572
SALES (est): 2.43MM **Privately Held**
SIC: **4581** Aircraft cleaning and janitorial
service

4613 Refined Petroleum Pipelines

(P-9214)
SFPP LP (DH)
1100 W Town And Country Rd Ste 600,
Orange (92868-4647)
PHONE...................714 560-4400
Park Shaper, *Genl Pt*
Richard D Kinder, *Genl Pt*
EMP: 150 **EST:** 1998
SQ FT: 75,000
SALES (est): 319.91MM **Publicly Held**
Web: www.kindermorgan.com
SIC: **4613** Gasoline pipelines (common
carriers)
HQ: Kinder Morgan Energy Partners, L.P.
1001 La St Ste 1000
Houston TX 77002
713 369-9000

4619 Pipelines, Nec

(P-9215)
KINDER MRGAN ENRGY PARTNERS LP
Also Called: Santa Fe Pacific Pipeline
2319 S Riverside Ave, Bloomington
(92316-2931)

PHONE...................909 873-5100
Ron Moranes, *Mgr*
EMP: 77
Web: www.kindermorgan.com
SIC: **4619** 1623 Coal pipeline operation;
Pipeline construction, nsk
HQ: Kinder Morgan Energy Partners, L.P.
1001 La St Ste 1000
Houston TX 77002
713 369-9000

4724 Travel Agencies

(P-9216)
ALTOUR INTERNATIONAL INC (PA)
12100 W Olympic Blvd Ste 300, Los
Angeles (90064-1051)
PHONE...................310 571-6000
Alexander Chemla, *Pr*
David Sefton, *
EMP: 80 **EST:** 1995
SQ FT: 8,000
SALES (est): 2.04MM **Privately Held**
Web: www.altour.com
SIC: **4724** Tourist agency arranging
transport, lodging and car rental

(P-9217)
ALTOUR INTERNATIONAL INC
21800 Burbank Blvd Ste 120, Woodland
Hills (91367-7474)
PHONE...................818 464-9200
Karleen Moussa, *Mgr*
EMP: 82
Web: www.altour.com
SIC: **4724** Tourist agency arranging
transport, lodging and car rental
PA: Altour International, Inc.
1270 Ave Of The Amrcas Fl

(P-9218)
ALTOUR INTERNATIONAL INC
Also Called: Altour Travel Master
10635 Santa Monica Blvd Ste 200, Los
Angeles (90025-8307)
PHONE...................310 571-6000
Julie Valentine, *Brnch Mgr*
EMP: 294
Web: www.altour.com
SIC: **4724** Tourist agency arranging
transport, lodging and car rental
PA: Altour International, Inc.
1270 Ave Of The Amrcas Fl

(P-9219)
AMAWATERWAYS LLC (PA)
4500 Park Granada Ste 200, Calabasas
(91302-1677)
PHONE...................800 020-0120
Rudi Schreiner, *Managing Member*
Janet Bava, *CMO*
EMP: 242 **EST:** 2008
SALES (est): 42.61MM **Privately Held**
Web: www.amawaterways.com
SIC: **4724** Travel agencies

(P-9220)
AMERICANTOURS INTL LLC (HQ)
6053 W Century Blvd Ste 700, Los Angeles
(90045-6411)
PHONE...................310 641-9953
Michael Fitzpatrick, *
EMP: 105 **EST:** 2003
SQ FT: 20,000
SALES (est): 4.82MM
SALES (corp-wide): 24.7MM **Privately
Held**

Web: www.americantours.com
SIC: **4724** 4725 Travel agencies; Tour
operators
PA: Americantours International Inc.
6053 W Century Blvd # 70
310 641-9953

(P-9221)
C & H TRAVEL & TOURS INC (HQ)
Also Called: C and H International
4751 Wilshire Blvd Ste 201, Los Angeles
(90010-3860)
PHONE...................323 933-2288
Patsy Ho, *CEO*
Dorothy Chan, *
Cho Tai, *
◆ **EMP:** 124 **EST:** 1980
SQ FT: 11,000
SALES (est): 7.15MM
SALES (corp-wide): 223.32MM **Publicly
Held**
Web: www.cnhintl.com
SIC: **4724** Travel agencies
PA: Mondee Holdings, Inc.
10800 Pcan Pk Blvd Ste 40
866 855-9630

(P-9222)
GLOBAL TRAVEL COLLECTION LLC
345 N Maple Dr, Beverly Hills (90210-3869)
PHONE...................310 271-9566
Sara Sessa, *Brnch Mgr*
EMP: 100
SALES (corp-wide): 900MM **Privately
Held**
Web: www.protravelinc.com
SIC: **4724** Travel agencies
HQ: Global Travel Collection, Llc
1633 Broadway Fl 35
New York NY 10019
212 755-4550

(P-9223)
HELLOWORLD TRAVEL SVCS USA INC
Also Called: Qantas Vctons Nwmans
Vacations
6171 W Century Blvd Ste 160, Los Angeles
(90045-5335)
PHONE...................310 535-1005
Ross Webster, *Pr*
Gary Goeldner, *
EMP: 100 **EST:** 1985
SALES (est): 1.43MM **Privately Held**
Web: www.qantasvacations.com
SIC: **4724** Tourist agency arranging
transport, lodging and car rental
PA: Helloworld Travel Limited
179 Normanby Rd

(P-9224)
HORNBLOWER YACHTS LLC
13755 Fiji Way, Marina Del Rey
(90292-9328)
PHONE...................310 301-9900
EMP: 148
SALES (corp-wide): 601.01MM **Privately
Held**
Web: www.cityexperiences.com
SIC: **4724** Travel agencies
PA: Hornblower Yachts, Llc
Pier 3 The Embarcadero

(P-9225)
IDS INC
Also Called: IDS Technology
20300 Ventura Blvd Ste 200, Woodland Hills
(91364-0959)

PHONE...................866 297-5757
Nathan Morad, *CEO*
Alberto Gamez, *CMO*
John Ledo, *
Gary Kurtz, *Legal Counsel*
EMP: 97 **EST:** 2009
SQ FT: 9,000
SALES (est): 460.78K **Privately Held**
Web: www.idscontrols.com
SIC: **4724** 7372 Travel agencies; Business
oriented computer software

(P-9226)
JTB AMERICAS LTD (HQ)
3625 Del Amo Blvd Ste 260, Torrance
(90503-1688)
PHONE...................310 406-3121
Tsuneo Irita, *Pr*
Benny Harrell, *
EMP: 100 **EST:** 1963
SALES (est): 196.64MM **Privately Held**
Web: www.jtbamericas.com
SIC: **4724** Travel agencies
PA: Jtb Corp.
2-3-11, Higashishinagawa

(P-9227)
LBF TRAVEL INC
Also Called: Travelerhelpdesk.com
4545 Murphy Canyon Rd Ste 210, San
Diego (92123-4363)
PHONE...................858 429-7599
Michael H Thomas, *CEO*
Adrian Myram, *
EMP: 300 **EST:** 2010
SALES (est): 3.84MM **Privately Held**
Web: www.lbftravel.com
SIC: **4724** Tourist agency arranging
transport, lodging and car rental

(P-9228)
MAGICAL CRUISE COMPANY LIMITED
500 S Buena Vista St, Burbank
(91521-0001)
PHONE...................800 742-8939
EMP: 79
SALES (corp-wide): 245.4K **Privately Held**
Web: disneycruise.disney.go.com
SIC: **4724** Tourist agency arranging
transport, lodging and car rental
HQ: Magical Cruise Company, Limited
3 Queen Caroline Street
London W6 9P

(P-9229)
NIPPON TRAVEL AGENCY AMER INC
Also Called: Nta America
1411 W 190th St Ste 650, Gardena
(90248-4369)
PHONE...................310 768-1817
Tadashi Wakayama, *Pr*
EMP: 70 **EST:** 1999
SQ FT: 8,000
SALES (est): 1.34MM **Privately Held**
Web: www.ntaamerica.com
SIC: **4724** Tourist agency arranging
transport, lodging and car rental

(P-9230)
NIPPON TRAVEL AGENCY PCF INC (DH)
Also Called: Nta Pacific
1411 W 190th St Ste 650, Gardena
(90248-4369)
PHONE...................310 768-0017
Tadashi Wakayama, *Pr*
Akio Tsuna, *

▲ **EMP:** 80 **EST:** 1973
SQ FT: 20,000
SALES (est): 3.28MM **Privately Held**
Web: www.ntaamerica.com
SIC: 4724 Tourist agency arranging
transport, lodging and car rental
HQ: Nippon Travel Agency Co., Ltd.
1-19-1, Nihombashi
Chuo-Ku TKY 103-0

(P-9231)
PINNACLE TRAVEL SERVICES LLC
390 N Pacific Coast Hwy, El Segundo
(90245-4475)
PHONE..........................310 414-1787
Robert G Singh, *CEO*
EMP: 151 **EST:** 1999
SQ FT: 15,000
SALES (est): 839.34K **Privately Held**
Web: www.ptsla.com
SIC: 4724 Tourist agency arranging
transport, lodging and car rental

(P-9232)
PLEASANT HOLIDAYS LLC (HQ)
Also Called: Pleasant Hawaiian Holiday
2404 Townsgate Rd, Westlake Village
(91361-2505)
PHONE..........................818 991-3390
Jack E Richards, *CEO*
Duke Ah Moo, *
Bruce Rosenberg, *
EMP: 300 **EST:** 1998
SQ FT: 55,000
SALES (est): 55.55MM
SALES (corp-wide): 1.08B **Privately Held**
Web: beta.pleasantholidays.com
SIC: 4724 Tourist agency arranging
transport, lodging and car rental
PA: Automobile Club Of Southern California
2601 S Figueroa St
213 741-3686

(P-9233)
PRINCESS CRUISE LINES LTD
1242 E 25th St, Los Angeles (90011-1708)
PHONE..........................213 745-0314
Delcino Fernandez, *Brnch Mgr*
EMP: 210
SALES (corp-wide): 7.98B **Privately Held**
Web: www.princess.com
SIC: 4724 Tourist agency arranging
transport, lodging and car rental
HQ: Princess Cruise Lines, Ltd.
24305 Town Ctr Dr
Santa Clarita CA 91355
661 753-0000

(P-9234)
PRINCESS CRUISE LINES LTD
Also Called: Princess Cruises
24833 Anza Dr, Santa Clarita (91380)
P.O. Box 966 (91380-9066)
PHONE..........................661 753-2197
Princess Cruise, *Prin*
EMP: 1114
SALES (corp-wide): 7.98B **Privately Held**
Web: www.princess.com
SIC: 4724 Tourist agency arranging
transport, lodging and car rental
HQ: Princess Cruise Lines, Ltd.
24305 Town Ctr Dr
Santa Clarita CA 91355
661 753-0000

(P-9235)
SEAT PLANNERS LLC
311 4th Ave Apt 509, San Diego
(92101-6973)

PHONE..........................619 237-9434
Veronica Sosa, *Prin*
Antonio Sosa, *
EMP: 75 **EST:** 2019
SALES (est): 824.15K **Privately Held**
Web: www.seatplanners.com
SIC: 4724 Travel agencies

(P-9236)
TRAVEL CORPORATION
5551 Katella Ave, Cypress (90630-5002)
PHONE..........................714 385-8401
Richard Launder, *Pr*
EMP: 102 **EST:** 2010
SALES (est): 1.99MM **Privately Held**
Web: www.ttc.com
SIC: 4724 Travel agencies

(P-9237)
TRAVEL STORE (PA)
Also Called: Travelstore
11601 Wilshire Blvd Ste 300, Los Angeles
(90025-0509)
P.O. Box 6576 (90734-6576)
PHONE..........................310 575-5540
Wido Schaefer, *Pr*
Osvaldo Ramos, *
Dan Ilves, *
EMP: 70 **EST:** 1975
SQ FT: 7,000
SALES (est): 11.45MM
SALES (corp-wide): 11.45MM **Privately Held**
Web: www.travelstore.com
SIC: 4724 Tourist agency arranging
transport, lodging and car rental

4725 Tour Operators

(P-9238)
ANTENNA AUDIO INC (PA)
Also Called: Antenna International
555 W 5th St Ste 3725, Los Angeles
(90013-2670)
PHONE..........................203 523-0320
Janet Matricciani, *CEO*
Ira Morgenstern, *
▲ **EMP:** 796 **EST:** 1997
SALES (est): 936.48K
SALES (corp-wide): 936.48K **Privately Held**
Web: www.homeantenna.com
SIC: 4725 Tour operators

(P-9239)
PRINCESS CRUISE LINES LTD
24200 Magic Mountain Pkwy, Santa Clarita
(91355-4890)
PHONE..........................661 753-0000
Barbara Potter, *Brnch Mgr*
EMP: 11408
SALES (corp-wide): 7.98B **Privately Held**
Web: www.princess.com
SIC: 4725 7011 4481 Tours, conducted;
Hotels; Deep sea passenger transportation,
except ferry
HQ: Princess Cruise Lines, Ltd.
24305 Town Ctr Dr
Santa Clarita CA 91355
661 753-0000

(P-9240)
SANTA CATALINA ISLAND COMPANY (PA)
Also Called: Scico
4 Park Plz Ste 420, Irvine (92614-5259)
P.O. Box 737 (90704-0737)
PHONE..........................310 510-2000
Randall Herrel Senior, *CEO*

Paxson H Offield, *
John T Dravinski, *
Ronald C Doutt, *
EMP: 98 **EST:** 1959
SALES (est): 75.32MM
SALES (corp-wide): 75.32MM **Privately Held**
Web: www.visitcatalinaisland.com
SIC: 4725 Sightseeing tour companies

(P-9241)
SCREAMLINE INVESTMENT CORP
Also Called: Tourcoach Transportation
2130 S Tubeway Ave, Commerce
(90040-1614)
PHONE..........................323 201-0114
Kamrouz Farhadi, *CEO*
Vahid Sapir, *
Farima Akopians, *
Shoeleh Sapir, *
▲ **EMP:** 120 **EST:** 1992
SQ FT: 8,000
SALES (est): 24.5MM **Privately Held**
Web: www.tourcoach.com
SIC: 4725 Sightseeing tour companies

(P-9242)
VIP TOURS OF CALIFORNIA INC
1419 E Maple Ave, El Segundo
(90245-3302)
PHONE..........................310 216-7507
Marco Khorasani, *Pr*
Nicole J Khorasani, *
EMP: 70 **EST:** 2002
SALES (est): 3.87MM **Privately Held**
Web: www.viptoursofcalifornia.com
SIC: 4725 Tours, conducted

4729 Passenger Transportation Arrangement

(P-9243)
KOREAN AIRLINES CO LTD
Also Called: Korean Air
900 Wilshire Blvd Ste 1100, Los Angeles
(90017-4789)
PHONE..........................213 484-5700
Kitaek Kang, *Genl Mgr*
EMP: 489
Web: www.koreanair.com
SIC: 4729 Airline ticket offices
PA: Korean Airlines Co., Ltd.
260 Haneul-Gil, Gangseo-Gu

(P-9244)
MATRIX AVIATION SERVICES INC
6171 W Century Blvd Ste 100, Los Angeles
(90045-5343)
PHONE..........................310 337-3037
Ramez Reno, *CEO*
Borseen Oushana, *
EMP: 175 **EST:** 2008
SQ FT: 3,000
SALES (est): 3.1MM **Privately Held**
Web: www.matrix-aviation.com
SIC: 4729 Airline ticket offices

4731 Freight Transportation Arrangement

(P-9245)
ABLE FREIGHT SERVICES LLC
5140 W 104th St, Inglewood (90304-1128)
PHONE..........................310 568-8883
EMP: 100

Web: www.ablefreight.com
SIC: 4731 Freight forwarding
PA: Able Freight Services, Llc
5340 W 104th St

(P-9246)
ABLE FREIGHT SERVICES LLC (PA)
5340 W 104th St, Los Angeles
(90045-6010)
PHONE..........................310 568-8883
◆ **EMP:** 90 **EST:** 1992
SALES (est): 30.82MM **Privately Held**
Web: www.ablefreight.com
SIC: 4731 Freight forwarding

(P-9247)
AERONET WORLDWIDE INC
850 W Artesia Blvd, Compton (90220-5104)
PHONE..........................310 787-6960
Mark Pereira, *Mgr*
EMP: 210
SALES (corp-wide): 236.68MM **Privately Held**
SIC: 4731 Freight transportation arrangement
PA: Aeronet Worldwide, Inc.
42 Corporate Park Ste 100
949 474-3000

(P-9248)
AGILITY HOLDINGS INC (DH)
Also Called: Agility Logistics
310 Commerce Ste 250, Irvine
(92602-1399)
PHONE..........................714 617-6300
Essa Al-saleh, *Pr*
Bassam Fawaz, *CIO*
Nicholas Franck, *
John Kao, *Sec*
James Fredholm, *
◆ **EMP:** 80 **EST:** 1996
SALES (est): 1.01B
SALES (corp-wide): 21.99B **Privately Held**
Web: www.agility.com
SIC: 4731 4213 4214 Domestic freight
forwarding; Household goods transport;
Household goods moving and storage, local
HQ: Agility Logistics International B.V.
Incheonweg 17
Rozenburg Nh NH 1437
884360105

(P-9249)
AGILITY LOGISTICS CORP (DH)
Also Called: Global Integrated Logistics
310 Commerce Ste 250, Irvine
(92602-1399)
PHONE..........................714 617-6300
◆ **EMP:** 90 **EST:** 1973
SALES (est): 426.24MM
SALES (corp-wide): 21.99B **Privately Held**
Web: www.agility.com
SIC: 4731 7372 1381 Freight transportation
arrangement; Prepackaged software;
Drilling oil and gas wells
HQ: Agility Holdings, Inc.
310 Commerce Ste 250
Irvine CA 92602

(P-9250)
AIR GROUP LEASING INC
1111 E Watson Center Rd Ste C, Carson
(90745-4217)
PHONE..........................310 684-4095
Victor Leigh, *Pr*
Thomas Bowling, *
▲ **EMP:** 365 **EST:** 1992
SQ FT: 2,900
SALES (est): 988.54K
SALES (corp-wide): 10.43B **Publicly Held**

SIC: **4731** 4513 Freight forwarding; Package delivery, private air
PA: Alaska Air Group, Inc
19300 International Blvd
206 392-5040

(P-9251)
ALLEN LUND COMPANY LLC (HQ)
4529 Angeles Crest Hwy, La Canada Flintridge (91011-3299)
P.O. Box 1369 (91012)
PHONE..............................800 777-6142
Eddie Lund, *CEO*
David Lund, *
Kathleen M Lund, *
Edward V Lund, *
Steve Doerfler, *
EMP: 70 **EST:** 1978
SQ FT: 16,000
SALES (est): 201.71MM **Privately Held**
Web: www.allenlund.com
SIC: **4731** Truck transportation brokers
PA: Allen Lund Corporation
4529 Angles Crest Hwy Ste

(P-9252)
APEX LOGISTICS INTL INC (DH)
Also Called: Apex USA
18554 S Susana Rd, East Rancho Domingue (90221-5620)
PHONE..............................310 665-0288
Elsie Qian, *CEO*
Hui Qian, *
▲ **EMP:** 227 **EST:** 2003
SALES (est): 2.72B **Privately Held**
Web: www.apexglobe.com
SIC: **4731** Freight forwarding
HQ: Kuehne + Nagel Inc.
10 Exchange Pl Fl 19-20
Jersey City NJ 07302
201 413-5500

(P-9253)
APM TERMINALS PACIFIC LLC
Also Called: Mearsk
2500 Navy Way Pier 400, San Pedro (90731-7554)
PHONE..............................310 221-4000
Milan D.o.s., *Brnch Mgr*
EMP: 401
SALES (corp-wide): 2.41MM **Privately Held**
Web: www.apmterminals.com
SIC: **4731** Agents, shipping
HQ: Apm Terminals Pacific Llc
9300 Arrowpoint Blvd
Charlotte NC 28273

(P-9254)
BINEX LINE CORP (PA)
Also Called: Binex
19515 S Vermont Ave, Torrance (90502-1121)
PHONE..............................310 416-8600
David Paek, *Pr*
Tim Park, *
Hyun K Cho, *
◆ **EMP:** 70 **EST:** 1995
SQ FT: 32,000
SALES (est): 271.3MM **Privately Held**
Web: www.binexline.com
SIC: **4731** Freight transportation arrangement

(P-9255)
BLACKROCK LOGISTICS INC
Also Called: Blackrock Logistics
14601 Slover Ave, Fontana (92337-7163)
PHONE..............................909 259-5357
Larry T James, *Pr*

EMP: 114
SALES (corp-wide): 22.96MM **Privately Held**
Web: www.blackrock-logistics.net
SIC: **4731** Freight forwarding
PA: Blackrock Logistics Inc.
7031 Koll Center Pkwy # 250
925 523-3878

(P-9256)
CAPABLE TRANSPORT INC
3528 Torrance Blvd Ste 220, Torrance (90503-4826)
PHONE..............................310 697-0198
Steven Troyer, *Pr*
EMP: 70 **EST:** 2004
SALES (est): 4.7MM **Privately Held**
SIC: **4731** Truck transportation brokers

(P-9257)
CARGOMATIC INC (PA)
211 E Ocean Blvd Ste 350, Long Beach (90802-8837)
PHONE..............................866 513-2343
Richard Gerstein, *CEO*
Andrew Straub, *
Matt Hogan, *
Steve Jackson, *CAO**
EMP: 155 **EST:** 2013
SALES (est): 96.31MM
SALES (corp-wide): 96.31MM **Privately Held**
Web: www.cargomatic.com
SIC: **4731** Transportation agents and brokers

(P-9258)
CARMICHAEL INTERNATIONAL SVC (DH)
Also Called: C I Container Line
1200 Corporate Center Dr Ste 200, Monterey Park (91754-7681)
PHONE..............................213 353-0800
John Salvo, *Pr*
Vince Salvo, *
Jim Ryan, *
◆ **EMP:** 100 **EST:** 1961
SQ FT: 19,000
SALES (est): 40.43MM **Privately Held**
Web: www.carmnet.com
SIC: **4731** Customhouse brokers
HQ: Kintetsu World Express, Inc.
2-15-1, Konan
Minato-Ku TKY 108-6

(P-9259)
CARROLL FULMER LOGISTICS CORP
13773 Algranti Ave, Sylmar (91342-2607)
PHONE..............................626 435-9940
Josh Quijano, *Brnch Mgr*
EMP: 230
SALES (corp-wide): 133.37MM **Privately Held**
Web: www.cfulmer.com
SIC: **4731** Truck transportation brokers
HQ: Carroll Fulmer Logistics Corporation
8340 American Way
Groveland FL 34736
352 429-5000

(P-9260)
CEVA FREIGHT LLC
Also Called: Ceva Ocean Line
19600 S Western Ave, Torrance (90501-1117)
PHONE..............................310 972-5500
Randy Mondello, *VP*
EMP: 110
SALES (corp-wide): 31.16K **Privately Held**
Web: www.cevalogistics.com

SIC: **4731** Freight forwarding
HQ: Ceva Freight, Llc
15350 Vickery Dr
Houston TX 77032

(P-9261)
CEVA LOGISTICS LLC
19600 S Western Ave, Torrance (90501-1117)
PHONE..............................310 223-6500
Marvin O Schlanger, *Mgr*
EMP: 300
SALES (corp-wide): 31.16K **Privately Held**
Web: www.cevalogistics.com
SIC: **4731** Domestic freight forwarding
HQ: Ceva Logistics, Llc
15350 Vickery Dr
Houston TX 77032
281 618-3100

(P-9262)
CFR RINKENS LLC (DH)
Also Called: Cfr Rinknes
444 W Ocean Blvd Ste 1200, Long Beach (90802-8128)
PHONE..............................310 639-7725
Christoph Seitz, *CEO*
▼ **EMP:** 75 **EST:** 1994
SALES (est): 22.28MM **Privately Held**
Web: www.cfrrinkens.com
SIC: **4731** Freight forwarding
HQ: Dp World Limited
5th Floor, Jafza 17, Jebel Ali Free Zone Area, Sheikh Zayed Road
Dubai DU

(P-9263)
CJ LOGISTICS AMERICA LLC
5690 Industrial Pkwy, San Bernardino (92407-1885)
PHONE..............................540 377-2302
EMP: 140
Web: america.cjlogistics.com
SIC: **4731** Freight forwarding
HQ: Cj Logistics America, Llc
1750 S Wolf Rd
Des Plaines IL 60018

(P-9264)
CNC WORLDWIDE INC (PA)
2805 E Ana St, Compton (90221-5601)
PHONE..............................310 670-7121
Henry Kim, *Pr*
▲ **EMP:** 93 **EST:** 2001
SALES (est): 5.91MM
SALES (corp-wide): 5.91MM **Privately Held**
Web: www.oneworldwide.com
SIC: **4731** Transportation agents and brokers

(P-9265)
COMMODITY FORWARDERS INC (DH)
Also Called: C F I
11101 S La Cienega Blvd, Los Angeles (90045-6111)
P.O. Box 894925 (90189-4925)
PHONE..............................310 348-8855
◆ **EMP:** 150 **EST:** 1974
SALES (est): 97.5MM **Privately Held**
Web: www.cfiperishables.com
SIC: **4731** Foreign freight forwarding
HQ: Kuhne + Nagel International Ag
Dorfstrasse 50
Schindellegi SZ 8834

(P-9266)
CROWLEY MARINE SERVICES INC

86 Berth 300 S Harbor Blvd, San Pedro (90731-3353)
PHONE..............................310 732-6500
Andrew Gauphier, *Mgr*
EMP: 431
Web: www.crowley.com
SIC: **4731** Freight transportation arrangement
HQ: Crowley Marine Services, Inc.
9487 Regency Square Blvd
Jacksonville FL 32225

(P-9267)
DCW DCW INC
20500 Denker Ave, Torrance (90501-1645)
PHONE..............................310 324-3147
Henry Mandil, *CEO*
EMP: 100 **EST:** 2020
SALES (est): 10MM **Privately Held**
SIC: **4731** 4225 Freight transportation arrangement; General warehousing and storage

(P-9268)
DE WELL CONTAINER SHIPPING INC
Also Called: Logistics
5553 Bandini Blvd Unit A, Bell (90201-6421)
PHONE..............................310 735-8600
Yang Shi, *CEO*
▲ **EMP:** 90 **EST:** 2004
SALES (est): 46.58MM **Privately Held**
Web: www.de-well.com
SIC: **4731** Freight forwarding
PA: De Well Container Shipping Corp.
No.1568, Gangcheng Road, Pudong New District

(P-9269)
DEPENDABLE GLOBAL EXPRESS INC (PA)
Also Called: D G X
19201 S Susana Rd, E Rncho Dmngz (90221-5710)
P.O. Box 513370 (90051-3370)
PHONE..............................310 537-2000
Ronald Massman, *CEO*
Bradley Dechter, *
Tim Rice, *
◆ **EMP:** 144 **EST:** 2004
SALES (est): 24.8MM **Privately Held**
Web: www.dgxglobal.com
SIC: **4731** Freight forwarding

(P-9270)
DFDS INTERNATIONAL CORPORATION
Also Called: Dfds Transport US
898 N Pacific Coast Hwy 6th Fl, El Segundo (90245-2705)
PHONE..............................310 414-1516
Tina Larsen, *Genl Mgr*
EMP: 80
SALES (corp-wide): 3.98B **Privately Held**
Web: www.dfds.com
SIC: **4731** Foreign freight forwarding
HQ: Dfds International Corporation
100 Walnut Ave Ste 405
Clark NJ 07066

(P-9271)
DHX-DEPENDABLE HAWAIIAN EX INC (PA)
19201 S Susana Rd, Compton (90221-5710)
PHONE..............................310 537-2000
Ronald Massman, *Ch*
Annette Massman, *
Bradley Dechter, *

◆ **EMP:** 150 **EST:** 1980
SQ FT: 106,000
SALES (est): 53.75MM
SALES (corp-wide): 53.75MM **Privately Held**
Web: www.dhx.com
SIC: 4731 Foreign freight forwarding

(P-9272)
DISPATCH TRUCKING LLC (PA)
14032 Santa Ana Ave, Fontana
(92337-7035)
PHONE...................909 355-5531
Bruce L Degler, *CEO*
Jalayne Pugmire, *
EMP: 70 **EST:** 1991
SQ FT: 600
SALES (est): 9.59MM
SALES (corp-wide): 9.59MM **Privately Held**
SIC: 4731 Truck transportation brokers

(P-9273)
DSV SOLUTIONS LLC
Also Called: Corp., R.g Barry
13230 San Bernardino Ave, Fontana
(92335-5229)
PHONE...................909 349-6100
EMP: 102
SALES (corp-wide): 21.99B **Privately Held**
Web: www.go2uti.com
SIC: 4731 Freight forwarding
HQ: Dsv Solutions, Llc
200 S Wood Ave Fl 3
Iselin NJ 08830
732 850-8000

(P-9274)
DSV SOLUTIONS LLC
1670 Etiwanda Ave Ste A, Ontario
(91761-3641)
PHONE...................909 390-4563
Bob Mccullough, *Mgr*
EMP: 88
SQ FT: 400,000
SALES (corp-wide): 21.99B **Privately Held**
Web: www.go2uti.com
SIC: 4731 Freight forwarding
HQ: Dsv Solutions, Llc
200 S Wood Ave Fl 3
Iselin NJ 08830
732 850-8000

(P-9275)
DSV SOLUTIONS LLC
Also Called: DSV
13032 Slover Ave Ste 200, Fontana
(92337-6901)
PHONE...................909 829-5804
EMP: 90
SALES (corp-wide): 21.99B **Privately Held**
Web: www.go2uti.com
SIC: 4731 Freight forwarding
HQ: Dsv Solutions, Llc
200 S Wood Ave Fl 3
Iselin NJ 08830
732 850-8000

(P-9276)
DSV SOLUTIONS LLC
3454 E Miraloma Ave, Anaheim
(92806-2101)
PHONE...................714 630-0110
EMP: 77
SALES (corp-wide): 21.99B **Privately Held**
Web: www.go2uti.com
SIC: 4731 Freight forwarding
HQ: Dsv Solutions, Llc
200 S Wood Ave Fl 3
Iselin NJ 08830
732 850-8000

(P-9277)
EMPIRE MED TRANSPORTATIONS LLC
Also Called: Unicare Medical Transportation
1433 W Linden St Ste M, Riverside
(92507-6816)
PHONE...................877 473-6029
EMP: 83 **EST:** 2017
SALES (est): 800K **Privately Held**
SIC: 4731 Freight forwarding

(P-9278)
EXPEDITORS INTL OCEAN INC
5200 W Century Blvd Fl 6, Los Angeles
(90045-5939)
PHONE...................310 343-6200
Gene Alger, *Brnch Mgr*
EMP: 74
SALES (corp-wide): 9.3B **Publicly Held**
SIC: 4731 Freight forwarding
HQ: Expeditors International Ocean, Inc.
1015 3rd Ave Ste 1200
Seattle WA 98104

(P-9279)
EXPEDITORS INTL WASH INC
Also Called: Expeditors International
12200 Wilkie Ave # 100, Hawthorne
(90250-1838)
PHONE...................310 343-6200
EMP: 96
SALES (corp-wide): 9.3B **Publicly Held**
Web: www.expeditors.com
SIC: 4731 Foreign freight forwarding
PA: Expeditors International Of
Washington, Inc.
3545 Fctoria Blvd Se Fl 3
206 674-3400

(P-9280)
EXPEDITORS INTL WASH INC
19701 Hamilton Ave, Torrance
(90502-1352)
PHONE...................310 343-6200
Eric Mooney, *Brnch Mgr*
EMP: 300
SALES (corp-wide): 9.3B **Publicly Held**
Web: www.expeditors.com
SIC: 4731 Freight forwarding
PA: Expeditors International Of
Washington, Inc.
3545 Fctoria Blvd Se Fl 3
206 674-3400

(P-9281)
F R T INTERNATIONAL INC
Also Called: Frontier Logistics Services
5750 E Francis St, Ontario (91761-3607)
PHONE...................909 390-4892
Steven Hall, *Brnch Mgr*
EMP: 74
SALES (corp-wide): 25.45MM **Privately Held**
Web: www.frontier-logistics.com
SIC: 4731 Freight forwarding
PA: F. R. T. International, Inc.
1700 N Alameda St
310 604-8208

(P-9282)
FLOCK FREIGHT INC
Also Called: Auptix and Flock Freight
701 S Coast Highway 101, Encinitas
(92024-4441)
PHONE...................855 744-7585
Oren Zaslansky, *CEO*
Pete Price, *
Luis Saenz, *
EMP: 120 **EST:** 2015
SALES (est): 132.25MM **Privately Held**
Web: www.flockfreight.com
SIC: 4731 Freight forwarding

(P-9283)
FNS INC (PA)
Also Called: FNS
1545 Francisco St, Torrance (90501-1330)
PHONE...................661 615-2300
Young Bin Kim, *CEO*
Dong Eon Kim, *
◆ **EMP:** 100 **EST:** 1995
SQ FT: 100,000
SALES (est): 244.23MM **Privately Held**
Web: www.fnsusa.com
SIC: 4731 Freight forwarding

(P-9284)
GLOBAL MAIL INC
921 W Artesia Blvd, Compton (90220-5105)
PHONE...................310 735-0800
Eric Ricardo, *Brnch Mgr*
EMP: 217
SALES (corp-wide): 88.87B **Privately Held**
SIC: 4731 Freight transportation arrangement
HQ: Global Mail, Inc.
2700 S Comm Pkwy Ste 300
Weston FL 33331
800 805-9306

(P-9285)
GLOVIS AMERICA INC (HQ)
18191 Von Karman Ave Ste 500, Irvine
(92612-7108)
PHONE...................714 427-0944
Bong Jeong Ko, *CEO*
Scott Cornell, *
◆ **EMP:** 185 **EST:** 2002
SQ FT: 34,700
SALES (est): 532.36MM **Privately Held**
Web: www.glovisusa.com
SIC: 4731 Freight forwarding
PA: Hyundai Glovis Co.,Ltd
83-21 Wangsimni-Ro, Seongdong-Gu

(P-9286)
GOLDEN HOUR DATA SYSTEMS INC
10052 Mesa Ridge Ct Ste 200, San Diego
(92121-2971)
P.O. Box 19786 (92159-0786)
PHONE...................858 768-2500
Kevin Hutton, *Pr*
Charles Haczewski, *
Peter Goutmann, *
Bill Dow, *
Eric Fleming, *CSO*
EMP: 120 **EST:** 1997
SQ FT: 14,000
SALES (est): 12.93MM **Privately Held**
Web: www.goldenhour.com
SIC: 4731 Transportation agents and brokers
HQ: Zoll Medical Corporation
269 Mill Rd
Chelmsford MA 01824
978 421-9655

(P-9287)
GREATWIDE LOGISTICS SVCS LLC
Also Called: Greatwide Dedicated Transport
4310 Bandini Blvd, Vernon (90058-4308)
PHONE...................323 268-7100
Angela Remling, *Brnch Mgr*
EMP: 94
SALES (corp-wide): 11.78B **Publicly Held**
Web: www.greatwide-tm.com
SIC: 4731 Truck transportation brokers
HQ: Greatwide Logistics Services, Llc.
12404 Pk Cntl Dr Ste 300
Dallas TX 75251

(P-9288)
GXO LOGISTICS SUPPLY CHAIN INC
7140 Cajon Blvd, San Bernardino
(92407-1898)
PHONE...................909 838-5631
Luis Gonzales, *Mgr*
EMP: 100
SALES (corp-wide): 9.78B **Publicly Held**
Web: www.gxo.com
SIC: 4731 Freight forwarding
HQ: Gxo Logistics Supply Chain, Inc.
4043 Piedmont Pkwy
High Point NC 27265
336 232-4100

(P-9289)
GXO LOGISTICS SUPPLY CHAIN INC
2615 E 3rd St, San Bernardino
(92415-0001)
PHONE...................909 253-5356
Sonja Lawson, *Mgr*
EMP: 70
SALES (corp-wide): 9.78B **Publicly Held**
Web: www.gxo.com
SIC: 4731 Freight forwarding
HQ: Gxo Logistics Supply Chain, Inc.
4043 Piedmont Pkwy
High Point NC 27265
336 232-4100

(P-9290)
GXO LOGISTICS SUPPLY CHAIN INC
2401 Chain Dr, Simi Valley (93065-7560)
PHONE...................336 989-0537
Jim Testerman, *Brnch Mgr*
EMP: 150
SALES (corp-wide): 9.78B **Publicly Held**
Web: www.gxo.com
SIC: 4731 Freight forwarding
HQ: Gxo Logistics Supply Chain, Inc.
4043 Piedmont Pkwy
High Point NC 27265
336 232-4100

(P-9291)
HANJIN TRANSPORTATION CO LTD
Also Called: Hanjin Global Logistics
15913 S Main St, Gardena (90248-2550)
PHONE...................310 522-5030
Bryce Dalziel, *Pr*
J B Park, *
EMP: 90 **EST:** 1996
SALES (est): 16.11MM **Privately Held**
Web: www.hanjinusa.com
SIC: 4731 Transportation agents and brokers

(P-9292)
HITACHI TRANSPORT SYSTEM (AMERICA) LTD
21061 S Western Ave Ste 300, Torrance
(90501-1735)
P.O. Box 512046 (90051-0046)
PHONE...................310 787-3420
▲ **EMP:** 283
SIC: 4731 Freight forwarding

(P-9293)
HOME EXPRESS DELIVERY SVC LLC
Also Called: Temco Logistics
1405 E Franklin Ave, Pomona
(91766-5453)
PHONE...................949 715-9844
EMP: 1000 **EST:** 2013

SALES (est): 3.17MM **Privately Held**
Web: www.temcologistics.com
SIC: **4731** Freight transportation arrangement

(P-9294)
HUB GROUP LOS ANGELES LLC
Also Called: Hub City
1400 N Harbor Blvd Ste 300, Fullerton
(92835-4145)
P.O. Box 71357 (60694-1357)
PHONE...............................714 449-6300
▲ EMP: 85
SIC: **4731** Agents, shipping

(P-9295)
INLOG INC
6765 Westminster Blvd Ste 424,
Westminster (92683-3769)
PHONE...............................949 212-3867
EMP: 85
SALES (corp-wide): 2.44MM **Privately Held**
SIC: **4731** Freight transportation arrangement
PA: Inlog, Inc.
4760 Preston Rd
949 212-5241

(P-9296)
INNOVEL SOLUTIONS INC
Also Called: Sears
960 Sherman St, San Diego (92110-4013)
PHONE...............................619 497-1123
Steve Tiger, *Mgr*
EMP: 642
SALES (corp-wide): 254.45B **Publicly Held**
Web: www.searshomeservices.com
SIC: **4731** Agents, shipping
HQ: Innovel Solutions, Inc.
3333 Beverly Rd
Hoffman Estates IL 60179
847 286-2500

(P-9297)
IRON MOUNTAIN INFO MGT LLC
441 N Oak St, Inglewood (90302-3314)
PHONE...............................818 848-9766
Jesse Ascencio, *Mgr*
EMP: 85
Web: www.bondednj.com
SIC: **4731** Freight forwarding
HQ: Iron Mountain Information
Management, Llc
3205 Burton Ave
Burbank CA 91504

(P-9298)
JW FULFILLMENT LAX INC
4039 State St, Montclair (91763-6026)
PHONE...............................909 578-9228
Yu Guo, *Pr*
EMP: 100 EST: 2020
SALES (est): 800.02K **Privately Held**
SIC: **4731** Freight forwarding

(P-9299)
KUEHNE + NAGEL INC
9425 Nevada St, Redlands (92374-5106)
PHONE...............................909 574-2300
Paul Schmidt, *Brnch Mgr*
EMP: 102
Web: home.kuehne-nagel.com
SIC: **4731** Freight forwarding
HQ: Kuehne + Nagel Inc.
10 Exchange Pl Fl 19-20
Jersey City NJ 07302
201 413-5500

(P-9300)
KUEHNE + NAGEL INC
20000 S Western Ave, Torrance
(90501-1305)
PHONE...............................310 641-5500
Horst Gerjets, *Mgr*
EMP: 311
Web: home.kuehne-nagel.com
SIC: **4731** Freight forwarding
HQ: Kuehne + Nagel Inc.
10 Exchange Pl Fl 19-20
Jersey City NJ 07302
201 413-5500

(P-9301)
KW INTERNATIONAL INC
1457 Glenn Curtiss St, Carson
(90746-4036)
PHONE...............................310 354-6944
Dj Kim, *Brnch Mgr*
EMP: 79
Web: www.kwinternational.com
SIC: **4731** Freight forwarding
PA: Kw International, Inc.
1650 Glenn Curtiss St

(P-9302)
KW INTERNATIONAL INC
18511 S Broadwick St, Rancho Dominguez
(90220-6440)
PHONE...............................310 747-1380
Dj Kim, *Mgr*
EMP: 70
Web: www.kwinternational.com
SIC: **4731** Freight forwarding
PA: Kw International, Inc.
1650 Glenn Curtiss St

(P-9303)
L E COPPERSMITH INC (HQ)
Also Called: Coppersmith Global Logistics
525 S Douglas St Ste 100, El Segundo
(90245-4828)
PHONE...............................310 607-8000
Jeffrey Craig Coppersmith, *Pr*
Lew E Coppersmith Ii, *Sec*
Douglas S Walkley, *
Jim Rowley, *
◆ EMP: 80 EST: 1948
SQ FT: 40,000
SALES (est): 286.05MM
SALES (corp-wide): 25.84MM **Privately Held**
Web: www.coppersmith.com
SIC: **4731** **4789** Customhouse brokers;
Cargo loading and unloading services
PA: Honour Lane Logistics (Usa), Inc.
17070 Castleton St Ste 328
626 363-4475

(P-9304)
LECANGS LLC (PA)
728 W Rider St, Perris (92571-3500)
PHONE...............................925 968-5094
Yi Jiang, *CEO*
EMP: 251 EST: 2020
SQ FT: 1,200,000
SALES (est): 11.54MM
SALES (corp-wide): 11.54MM **Privately Held**
Web: us.lecangs.com
SIC: **4731** Transportation agents and brokers

(P-9305)
LOGISTEED AMERICA INC
Also Called: Logisteed Monterey Park
1000 Corporate Center Dr Ste 400,
Monterey Park (91754-7686)
PHONE...............................323 263-8100
Tomoyuki Miyazaki, *Pr*

EMP: 100
Web: www.hitachi-vht.com
SIC: **4731** Customhouse brokers
HQ: Logisteed America, Inc.
21061 S Wstn Ave Ste 300
Torrance CA 90501
310 787-3420

(P-9306)
LOMA LINDA UNIVERSITY MED CTR
Also Called: Warehouse and Receiving
Center
1269 E San Bernardino Ave, San
Bernardino (92408-2943)
P.O. Box 2000 (92354-0200)
PHONE...............................909 558-4000
Al Mendoza, *Dir*
EMP: 80
SALES (corp-wide): 379.88MM **Privately Held**
Web: www.llu.edu
SIC: **4731** Freight transportation arrangement
HQ: Loma Linda University Medical Center
11234 Anderson St
Loma Linda CA 92354
909 558-4000

(P-9307)
M-7 CONSOLIDATION INC
475 W Apra St, Compton (90220-5527)
PHONE...............................310 898-3456
John J Brown, *Pr*
Harald Niehenke, *
John Brown, *
Kathleen Hogan, *
Harvey Turner, *
▼ EMP: 140 EST: 1994
SQ FT: 2,000
SALES (est): 1.69MM **Privately Held**
SIC: **4731** Foreign freight forwarding

(P-9308)
MAERSK WHSNG DIST SVCS USA LLC
Also Called: Performance Team Freight
12920 Imperial Hwy, Santa Fe Springs
(90670-4716)
PHONE...............................562 977-1820
EMP: 74
SALES (corp-wide): 2.41MM **Privately Held**
Web: www.ptgt.net
SIC: **4731** Freight forwarding
HQ: Maersk Warehousing & Distribution
Services Usa Llc
2240 E Maple Ave
El Segundo CA 90245
562 345-2200

(P-9309)
MAERSK WHSNG DIST SVCS USA LLC
1651 California St Ste A, Redlands
(92374-2904)
PHONE...............................801 301-1732
EMP: 147
SALES (corp-wide): 2.41MM **Privately Held**
Web: www.ptgt.net
SIC: **4731** Freight forwarding
HQ: Maersk Warehousing & Distribution
Services Usa Llc
2240 E Maple Ave
El Segundo CA 90245
562 345-2200

(P-9310)
MAERSK WHSNG DIST SVCS USA LLC (DH)
Also Called: Performance Team
2240 E Maple Ave, El Segundo
(90245-6507)
PHONE...............................562 345-2200
Cliff Katab, *
Michael B Kaplan, *
Tracy Kaplan, *
Linda Kaplan, *
◆ EMP: 200 EST: 1987
SALES (est): 507.16MM
SALES (corp-wide): 2.41MM **Privately Held**
Web: www.ptgt.net
SIC: **4731** **4225** **4213** Freight forwarding;
General warehousing and storage;
Trucking, except local
HQ: A.P. Moller - Marsk A/S
Esplanaden 50
Kobenhavn K 1263
33142990

(P-9311)
MAPCARGO GLOBAL LOGISTICS (PA)
2501 Santa Fe Ave, Redondo Beach
(90278-1117)
PHONE...............................310 297-8300
Marek Adam Panasewicz, *Pr*
◆ EMP: 74 EST: 1990
SQ FT: 20,000
SALES (est): 28.38MM **Privately Held**
Web: www.mapcargo.com
SIC: **4731** **2448** Domestic freight forwarding;
Cargo containers, wood and wood with
metal

(P-9312)
MARINE CORPS UNITED STATES
Traffic Management Office, Camp
Pendleton (92055)
P.O. Box 555004 (92055-5004)
PHONE...............................760 725-3092
EMP: 72
Web: www.marines.mil
SIC: **4731** **9711** Transport clearinghouse;
Marine Corps
HQ: United States Marine Corps
Branch Hlth Clnic Bldg #5
Beaufort SC 29904

(P-9313)
MIRAMAR TRANSPORTATION INC
Also Called: Pilot Freight Services
9340 Cabot Dr Ste I, San Diego
(92126-4397)
P.O. Box 502850 (92150-2850)
PHONE...............................858 693-0071
Richard Evan Fore, *Pr*
Richard Evan Fore, *Pr*
Bob Mirinda, *
Carrie Jones, *
EMP: 100 EST: 1993
SALES (est): 8.42MM **Privately Held**
Web: www.miramartrans.com
SIC: **4731** Freight forwarding

(P-9314)
MODIVCARE SOLUTIONS LLC
770 The City Dr S, Orange (92868-4900)
PHONE...............................714 503-6871
Kymblyn Brown, *Prin*
EMP: 124
SALES (corp-wide): 2.76B **Publicly Held**
Web: www.modivcare.com

SIC: 4731 Freight transportation arrangement
HQ: Modivcare Solutions, Llc
6900 Layton Ave Ste 1200
Denver CO 80237

(P-9315)
NATIONWIDE TRANS INC (PA)
11727 Eastend Ave, Chino (91710-1560)
P.O. Box 2558 (91708-2558)
PHONE.....................909 355-3211
Kong Lee, *Pr*
Chris Bendigo, *
Max Paul, *
EMP: 100 EST: 2006
SALES (est): 3.2MM
SALES (corp-wide): 3.2MM **Privately Held**
SIC: 4731 Freight transportation arrangement

(P-9316)
NEOVIA LOGISTICS DIST LP
2289 E Orangethorpe Ave, Fullerton
(92831-5329)
PHONE.....................815 552-5900
John Goelitz, *Brnch Mgr*
EMP: 96
SALES (corp-wide): 461.1MM **Privately Held**
Web: www.neovialogistics.com
SIC: 4731 Freight transportation arrangement
HQ: Neovia Logistics Distribution, Lp
8840 Cypress Wters Blvd S
Coppell TX 75019

(P-9317)
NEX GROUP LLC
9018 Rancho Viejo Dr, Bakersfield
(93314-8547)
PHONE.....................209 317-6677
Harpinder Sekhon, *Managing Member*
EMP: 70 EST: 2019
SALES (est): 5.51MM **Privately Held**
SIC: 4731 Freight forwarding

(P-9318)
NIPPON EXPRESS
Also Called: Co Ltd, All Nippon Airways
21250 Hawthorne Blvd Fl 2, Torrance
(90503-5513)
PHONE.....................310 782-3000
EMP: 100 EST: 2011
SALES (est): 9.98MM **Privately Held**
Web: www.nipponexpress.com
SIC: 4731 Freight forwarding

(P-9319)
NIPPON EXPRESS USA INC
19500 S Vermont Ave, Torrance
(90502-1120)
PHONE.....................310 527-4237
Masashi Hachimoto, *Prin*
EMP: 70
Web: www.nipponexpress.com
SIC: 4731 Freight forwarding
HQ: Nippon Express U.S.A., Inc.
800 N Il Route 83
Wood Dale IL 60191
708 304-9800

(P-9320)
NRI USA LLC (PA)
Also Called: Nri Distribution
13200 S Broadway, Los Angeles
(90061-1124)
PHONE.....................323 345-6456
▲ EMP: 100 EST: 2011
SQ FT: 65,000
SALES (est): 71.28MM
SALES (corp-wide): 71.28MM **Privately Held**
Web: www.careers-nri3pl.com

SIC: 4731 Freight forwarding

(P-9321)
PACIFIC LOGISTICS CORP (PA)
Also Called: Paclo
7255 Rosemead Blvd, Pico Rivera
(90660-4047)
PHONE.....................562 478-4700
Douglas E Hockersmith, *Pr*
Timothy K Hewey, *
Diane J Hockersmith, *
▲ EMP: 208 EST: 1999
SQ FT: 206,000
SALES (est): 67.51MM
SALES (corp-wide): 67.51MM **Privately Held**
Web: www.pacific-logistics.com
SIC: 4731 Freight forwarding

(P-9322)
PACTRACK INC
11135 Rush St Ste A, South El Monte
(91733-3520)
PHONE.....................213 201-5856
Nabeil Hazu, *CEO*
Michael Vega, *
Nabeil Hazu, *VP*
EMP: 75 EST: 2014
SALES (est): 9.23MM **Privately Held**
Web: www.pactrack.com
SIC: 4731 7389 Freight transportation
arrangement; Courier or messenger service

(P-9323)
PATRIOT BROKERAGE INC
7840 Foothill Blvd Ste H, Sunland
(91040-2907)
PHONE.....................910 227-4142
Ross Tsarukyan, *Managing Member*
Liyan Tsarukyan, *
EMP: 84 EST: 2014
SQ FT: 13,000
SALES (est): 4.94MM **Privately Held**
SIC: 4731 Freight forwarding

(P-9324)
PEGASUS MARITIME INC
505 N Brand Blvd Ste 210, Glendale
(91203-2877)
PHONE.....................714 728-8565
Khurram Mahmood, *Pr*
Moazam Mahmood, *
Mookie Mahmood, *
Syed M Ali, *
EMP: 75 EST: 2000
SALES (est): 8.79MM **Privately Held**
Web: www.pegasusmaritime.com
SIC: 4731 Freight forwarding

(P-9325)
PORT LOGISTICS GROUP INC
Also Called: PORT LOGISTICS GROUP, INC.
19801 S Santa Fe Ave, Compton
(90221-5915)
PHONE.....................310 669-2551
Timothy Page, *Prin*
EMP: 201
SALES (corp-wide): 11.78B **Publicly Held**
Web: www.portlogisticsgroup.com
SIC: 4731 Freight transportation arrangement
HQ: Port Logistics Group, Llc
288 S Mayo Ave
City Of Industry CA 91789

(P-9326)
PORT PRIORITY CORP
855 W Valley Blvd, Bloomington
(92316-2216)
PHONE.....................845 746-4300
Joseph Waldman, *CEO*

EMP: 180 EST: 2015
SALES (est): 9.28MM **Privately Held**
Web: www.portpriority.com
SIC: 4731 Freight forwarding

(P-9327)
PREMIERE CUSTOMS BROKERS INC
5951 Skylab Rd, Huntington Beach
(92647-2062)
PHONE.....................310 410-6825
Richard K Lowery, *CEO*
EMP: 708 EST: 1994
SALES (est): 2.95MM
SALES (corp-wide): 1.17B **Publicly Held**
Web: www.pcbfs.com
SIC: 4731 Freight forwarding
HQ: Smart Modular Technologies Inc.
39870 Eureka Dr
Newark CA 94560

(P-9328)
PRO LOADERS INC
14032 Santa Ana Ave, Fontana
(92337-7035)
PHONE.....................909 355-5531
Bruce Degler, *Pr*
Kim Pugmire, *
Christopher Ebert, *
EMP: 200 EST: 1981
SQ FT: 600
SALES (est): 3.68MM **Privately Held**
SIC: 4731 1629 7359 7519 Truck
transportation brokers; Earthmoving
contractor; Equipment rental and leasing,
nec; Trailer rental

(P-9329)
QUIK PICK EXPRESS LLC
23610 Banning Blvd, Carson (90745-6220)
PHONE.....................310 763-3000
Tom Boyle, *Managing Member*
EMP: 193
SALES (corp-wide): 45.27MM **Privately Held**
Web: www.quikpickexpress.com
SIC: 4731 Freight transportation arrangement
PA: Quik Pick Express Llc
1021 E 233rd St
310 763-3000

(P-9330)
R L JONES-SAN DIEGO INC (PA)
1778 Zinetta Rd Ste A, Calexico
(92231-9511)
P.O. Box 472 (92232-0472)
PHONE.....................760 357-3177
Russell L Jones, *Pr*
Earl Roberts, *
▲ EMP: 100 EST: 1952
SALES (est): 46.48MM
SALES (corp-wide): 46.48MM **Privately Held**
Web: www.rljones.com
SIC: 4731 4225 Customhouse brokers;
General warehousing and storage

(P-9331)
RED ROCK PALLET COMPANY
81153 Red Rock Rd, La Quinta
(92253-9334)
P.O. Box 1231 (95763-1231)
PHONE.....................530 852-7744
Mark John Allen, *CEO*
EMP: 41 EST: 2008
SQ FT: 2,000
SALES (est): 950.46K **Privately Held**
Web: www.redrockcompany.com
SIC: 4731 2448 Freight transportation
arrangement; Pallets, wood

(P-9332)
RUNBUGGY OMI INC
1377 Kettering Dr, Ontario (91761-2217)
PHONE.....................888 872-8449
EMP: 140 EST: 2018
SALES (est): 3.74MM **Privately Held**
Web: www.runbuggy.com
SIC: 4731 Shipping documents preparation

(P-9333)
SALSON LOGISTICS INC
1331 Torrance Blvd, Torrance (90501-2351)
PHONE.....................973 986-0200
Brian Howver, *Brnch Mgr*
EMP: 158
Web: www.salson.com
SIC: 4731 Freight forwarding
HQ: Salson Logistics, Inc.
888 Doremus Ave
Newark NJ 07114
973 986-0200

(P-9334)
SEAWORLD GLOBAL LOGISTICS
3743 Legato Ct, Pomona (91766-0984)
PHONE.....................310 742-3882
Dhakshitha Gabriel, *CEO*
EMP: 385 EST: 2017
SALES (est): 5.18MM **Privately Held**
Web: www.seaworldglobal.com
SIC: 4731 Foreign freight forwarding

(P-9335)
SELECT AIRCARGO SERVICES INC
12801 S Figueroa St, Los Angeles
(90061-1157)
PHONE.....................310 851-8500
◆ EMP: 80
SIC: 4731 Foreign freight forwarding

(P-9336)
SILVER HAWK FREIGHT INC
Also Called: Titan Wolrdwide
16410 Bloomfield Ave, Cerritos
(90703-2144)
PHONE.....................562 404-0226
Amar Durrani, *CEO*
EMP: 96 EST: 2011
SALES (est): 16.3MM **Privately Held**
Web: www.titan-worldwide.com
SIC: 4731 Freight forwarding

(P-9337)
STATES LOGISTICS SERVICES INC (PA)
5650 Dolly Ave, Buena Park (90621-1872)
PHONE.....................714 521-6520
Daniel Monson, *CEO*
William Donovan, *
Kirk Hellofs, *
Jennifer Monson, *
▲ EMP: 140 EST: 1958
SQ FT: 900,000
SALES (est): 138.74MM **Privately Held**
Web: www.stateslogistics.com
SIC: 4731 Freight transportation arrangement

(P-9338)
STEVENS GLOBAL LOGISTICS INC (PA)
Also Called: Steven Global Freight Services
3700 Redondo Beach Ave, Redondo Beach
(90278-1108)
P.O. Box 729 (90260-0729)
PHONE.....................800 229-7284
Thomas J Petrizzio, *CEO*
Karl Chambers, *

Gary Hooper, *
◆ **EMP:** 95 **EST:** 1985
SQ FT: 48,000
SALES (est): 69.68MM
SALES (corp-wide): 69.68MM **Privately Held**
Web: www.stevensglobal.com
SIC: 4731 Freight forwarding

(P-9339)

STRAIGHT FORWARDING INC

Also Called: Meow Logistics
20275 Business Pkwy, Walnut
(91789-2950)
PHONE................................909 594-3400
Yihsiang Wu, *CEO*
EMP: 100 **EST:** 2011
SALES (est): 78.88MM **Privately Held**
Web: www.sfi.com
SIC: 4731 Foreign freight forwarding

(P-9340)

SUPRA NATIONAL EXPRESS INC

1421 Charles Willard St, Carson
(90746-4025)
PHONE................................310 549-7105
Daniel Linares, *CEO*
EMP: 125 **EST:** 2014
SALES (est): 5.31MM **Privately Held**
Web: www.snecorp.com
SIC: 4731 Truck transportation brokers

(P-9341)

TAYLORED SVCS PARENT CO INC (PA)

1495 E Locust St, Ontario (91761-4570)
PHONE................................909 510-4800
Bill Butler, *CEO*
Michael Yusko, *
EMP: 80 **EST:** 2012
SQ FT: 330,000
SALES (est): 26.36MM
SALES (corp-wide): 26.36MM **Privately Held**
Web: www.tayloredservices.com
SIC: 4731 Agents, shipping

(P-9342)

THUNDER INTERNATIONAL GROUP (PA)

19485 E Walnut Dr N, City Of Industry
(91748)
PHONE................................626 723-3715
Feng Ye, *CEO*
Mingming Wang, *
EMP: 99 **EST:** 2019
SALES (est): 12.45MM
SALES (corp-wide): 12.45MM **Privately Held**
SIC: 4731 Freight transportation arrangement

(P-9343)

TOLL GLOBAL FWDG SCS USA INC

Also Called: TOLL GLOBAL FORWARDING SCS (USA) INC.
3355 Dulles Dr, Jurupa Valley (91752-3244)
PHONE................................951 360-8310
Bryan Howber, *Sr VP*
EMP: 100
SIC: 4731 Freight forwarding
HQ: Toll Global Forwarding Scs (Usa) Inc.
800 Federal Blvd Ste 2
Carteret NJ 07008
732 750-9000

(P-9344)

TOLL GLOBAL FWDG SCS USA INC

Also Called: FMI International West 2
400 Westmont Dr 450, San Pedro
(90731-1010)
PHONE................................732 750-9000
Gary Hecht, *Mgr*
EMP: 105
SIC: 4731 Freight forwarding
HQ: Toll Global Forwarding Scs (Usa) Inc.
800 Federal Blvd Ste 2
Carteret NJ 07008
732 750-9000

(P-9345)

TOTAL LOGISTICS ONLINE LLC

628 N Gilbert St, Fullerton (92833-2555)
PHONE................................714 526-3559
Ed Mock, *Brnch Mgr*
EMP: 78
SALES (corp-wide): 11.78B **Publicly Held**
Web: www.ryder.com
SIC: 4731 Freight transportation arrangement
HQ: Total Logistics Online L.L.C.
4432 S Bttrmilk Ct Ste 10
Hudsonville MI 49426

(P-9346)

TRANSIT AIR CARGO INC

2204 E 4th St, Santa Ana (92705-3868)
P.O. Box 10053 (92711-0053)
PHONE................................714 571-0393
Gulnawaz Khodayar, *CEO*
Christy Colton, *
Michelle Nguyen, *
◆ **EMP:** 87 **EST:** 1989
SQ FT: 10,000
SALES (est): 10.13MM **Privately Held**
Web: www.transitair.com
SIC: 4731 Foreign freight forwarding

(P-9347)

TRI-TECH LOGISTICS LLC

1370 Brea Blvd Ste 200, Fullerton
(92835-4128)
PHONE................................855 373-7049
Gurdeep Singh Dhaliwal, *
Jeremy Engstrom, *
EMP: 210 **EST:** 2014
SALES (est): 10MM
SALES (corp-wide): 6.55MM **Privately Held**
Web: www.tritechlogistics.com
SIC: 4731 Freight forwarding
PA: Tri-Tech Logistics Ltd
208-17660 65a Ave
604 415-9898

(P-9348)

US LINES LLC (DH)

Also Called: US Lines
3501 Jamboree Rd Ste 300, Newport Beach
(92660-2936)
PHONE................................714 751-3333
◆ **EMP:** 75 **EST:** 2004
SALES (est): 5.14MM
SALES (corp-wide): 31.16K **Privately Held**
SIC: 4731 Freight forwarding
HQ: Cma Cgm
4 Boulevard Saade - Quai Arenc
Marseille PAC 13002
488919000

(P-9349)

VANGUARD LGISTICS SVCS USA INC (HQ)

Also Called: Brennan International Trnspt
5000 Airport Plaza Dr Ste 200, Long Beach
(90815-1367)

PHONE................................310 847-3000
Charles Brennan, *Ch*
J Thurso Barendse, *VP*
Therese Groff, *VP*
Derek Moore, *TAX*
Ank Deroos, *Dir*
◆ **EMP:** 100 **EST:** 1978
SALES (est): 227.78MM
SALES (corp-wide): 549.33MM **Privately Held**
Web: www.vanguardlogistics.com
SIC: 4731 Freight consolidation
PA: Naca Holdings, Inc.
5000 Arprt Plz Dr Ste 200
310 847-3000

(P-9350)

VEG FRESH LOGISTICS LLC

1400 W Rincon St, Corona (92878-9205)
PHONE................................714 446-8800
EMP: 220 **EST:** 2022
SALES (est): 10.21MM **Privately Held**
Web: www.vegfresh.com
SIC: 4731 Transportation agents and brokers
PA: Veg-Fresh Farms, Llc
1400 W Rincon St

(P-9351)

XPO LOGISTICS SUPPLY CHAIN INC

5200b E Airport Dr, Ontario (91761-8601)
PHONE................................909 390-9799
FAX: 909 937-6089
EMP: 156
SALES (corp-wide): 14.62B **Publicly Held**
SIC: 4731 Freight transportation arrangement
HQ: Xpo Logistics Supply Chain, Inc.
4035 Piedmont Pkwy
High Point NC 27265
336 232-4100

4783 Packing And Crating

(P-9352)

ADVANTAGE MEDIA SERVICES INC (PA)

Also Called: AMS Fulfillment
29010 Commerce Center Dr, Valencia
(91355-4188)
PHONE................................661 775-0611
Jay Catlin, *Pr*
Ken Wiseman, *CEO*
David Catlin, *Dir*
Louise Aldrich, *Prin*
▲ **EMP:** 76 **EST:** 2002
SQ FT: 142,000
SALES (est): 56.03MM
SALES (corp-wide): 56.03MM **Privately Held**
Web: www.amsfulfillment.com
SIC: 4783 4731 Packing goods for shipping;
Agents, shipping

(P-9353)

CHANDLER PACKAGING A TRANSPAK COMPANY

Also Called: Fragile Handle With Care
7595 Raytheon Rd, San Diego
(92111-1506)
P.O. Box 421110 (92142-1110)
PHONE................................858 292-5674
EMP: 64
Web: www.chanpack.com
SIC: 4783 2449 3081 3086 Packing and
crating; Wood containers, nec; Packing
materials, plastics sheet; Packaging and
shipping materials, foamed plastics

(P-9354)

MEK ENTERPRISES INC

3517 Camino Del Rio S Ste 215, San Diego
(92108-4098)
PHONE................................619 527-0957
Marc Kranz, *CEO*
EMP: 100 **EST:** 2012
SALES (est): 8.53MM **Privately Held**
Web: www.4mek.com
SIC: 4783 4214 Packing and crating;
Furniture moving and storage, local

(P-9355)

WHALING PACKAGING CO

21020 S Wilmington Ave, Carson
(90810-1232)
P.O. Box 4547 (90749-4547)
PHONE................................310 518-6021
Thomas Whaling, *Pr*
Michelle Whaling, *
EMP: 27 **EST:** 1978
SQ FT: 12,973
SALES (est): 4.61MM **Privately Held**
Web: www.whalingpackaging.com
SIC: 4783 2653 2441 Packing and crating;
Corrugated and solid fiber boxes; Nailed
wood boxes and shook

4785 Inspection And Fixed Facilities

(P-9356)

PACIFIC TOLL PROCESSING INC

Also Called: P T P
24724 Wilmington Ave, Carson
(90745-6127)
PHONE................................310 952-4992
Anthony Camasta, *Pr*
Anthony J Camasta, *
Mark Proner, *
EMP: 30 **EST:** 1999
SQ FT: 101,000
SALES (est): 5.3MM **Privately Held**
Web: www.pacifictoll.com
SIC: 4785 3547 5051 Toll road operation;
Steel rolling machinery; Steel

4789 Transportation Services, Nec

(P-9357)

ADVANCED MULTIMODAL DIST INC

Also Called: Preferred Carrier California
14822 Central Ave, Chino (91710-9509)
PHONE................................800 838-3058
Fredy Salvador Funes, *CEO*
EMP: 150 **EST:** 2017
SALES (est): 8.36MM **Privately Held**
SIC: 4789 4731 Cargo loading and
unloading services; Freight forwarding

(P-9358)

AMBIANCE TRANSPORTATION LLC

6901 San Fernando Rd, Glendale
(91201-1608)
PHONE................................818 955-5757
EMP: 90 **EST:** 2018
SALES (est): 8.62MM **Privately Held**
Web: www.ambiancetrans.com
SIC: 4789 Transportation services, nec

(P-9359)
AMERICAN TRANSPORTATION CO LLC
635 W Colorado St Ste 108a, Glendale (91204-1178)
PHONE..............................818 660-2343
Isaac Albekyan, *Prin*
EMP: 88 EST: 2012
SALES (est): 327.94K **Privately Held**
SIC: 4789 Transportation services, nec

(P-9360)
CAPSTONE LOGISTICS LLC
Also Called: Capstone Logistics
12661 Aldi Pl, Moreno Valley (92555-6703)
PHONE..............................770 414-1929
EMP: 225
SALES (corp-wide): 609.82MM **Privately Held**
Web: www.capstonelogistics.com
SIC: 4789 Cargo loading and unloading services
PA: Capstone Logistics, Llc
　　30 Technlogy Pkwy S Ste 2
　　770 414-1929

(P-9361)
COMPREHENSIVE DIST SVCS INC
18726 S Western Ave Ste 300, Gardena (90248-3861)
PHONE..............................310 523-1546
Sam Lee, *Pr*
EMP: 150 EST: 2010
SALES (est): 4.05MM **Privately Held**
Web: www.cdsintro.com
SIC: 4789 Freight car loading and unloading

(P-9362)
DREAMTEAM LOGISTICS LLC
8605 Santa Monica Blvd, West Hollywood (90069-4109)
PHONE..............................818 300-7785
EMP: 75 EST: 2020
SALES (est): 1.8MM **Privately Held**
SIC: 4789 Transportation services, nec

(P-9363)
FLUOR FLTRON BLFOUR BTTY DRGDO
5901 W Century Blvd, Los Angeles (90045-5411)
PHONE..............................949 420-5000
Kenneth Isett, *Prin*
Terry Gohde, *Prin*
EMP: 99 EST: 2018
SALES (est): 4.05MM **Privately Held**
Web: www.lalinxs.com
SIC: 4789 Transportation services, nec

(P-9364)
FULL SCALE LOGISTICS LLC
2722 Rocky Point Ct, Thousand Oaks (91362-4943)
PHONE..............................805 279-6799
Kristen Infeld, *CEO*
EMP: 85 EST: 2020
SALES (est): 16.05MM **Privately Held**
SIC: 4789 Transportation services, nec

(P-9365)
GUNDERSON RAIL SERVICES LLC
Also Called: Greenbrier Rail Services
1475 Cooley Ct, San Bernardino (92408-2830)
P.O. Box 1715 (92402-1715)
PHONE..............................909 478-0541

Kevin Johnson, *Contrlr*
EMP: 117
SQ FT: 64,248
SALES (corp-wide): 3.54B **Publicly Held**
Web: www.gbrx.com
SIC: 4789 Railroad car repair
HQ: Gunderson Rail Services Llc
　　One Cntrpointe Dr Ste 200
　　Lake Oswego OR 97035
　　503 684-7000

(P-9366)
HARRIS & HURI TRNSP SVCS LLC ✪
9520 Palo Alto St, Rancho Cucamonga (91730-1340)
PHONE..............................909 791-0531
Aris Karabit, *Pr*
EMP: 71 EST: 2023
SALES (est): 400.96K **Privately Held**
SIC: 4789 Transportation services, nec

(P-9367)
KAYDAN LOGISTICS LLC
45562 Ponderosa Ct, Temecula (92592-2829)
PHONE..............................951 961-9000
Kirk Morrison, *CEO*
EMP: 91 EST: 2020
SALES (est): 3.04MM **Privately Held**
SIC: 4789 Transportation services, nec

(P-9368)
LANDMARK DISTRIBUTION LLC
34 E Sola St, Santa Barbara (93101-2506)
PHONE..............................805 965-3058
EMP: 75
Web: www.landmarkglobal.com
SIC: 4789 4731 Cargo loading and unloading services; Foreign freight forwarding

(P-9369)
LEADING EDGE LOGISTIX LLC
29436 Tremont Dr, Menifee (92584-6951)
PHONE..............................951 870-6801
Sean C Redwine, *Mgr*
EMP: 107 EST: 2021
SALES (est): 3.24MM **Privately Held**
SIC: 4789 Transportation services, nec

(P-9370)
MERIDIAN RAIL ACQUISITION
Also Called: Greenbrier Rail
1475 Cooley Ct, San Bernardino (92408-2830)
P.O. Box 1715 (92402-1715)
PHONE..............................909 478-0541
EMP: 102
SALES (corp-wide): 3.54B **Publicly Held**
Web: www.gbrx.com
SIC: 4789 Railroad car repair
HQ: Meridian Rail Acquisition Corp
　　1 Centerpointe Dr Ste 200
　　Lake Oswego OR 97035
　　503 684-7000

(P-9371)
NERYS LOGISTICS INC
9925 Airway Rd, San Diego (92154-7932)
PHONE..............................619 616-2124
EMP: 124
SALES (corp-wide): 3.63MM **Privately Held**
SIC: 4789 Cargo loading and unloading services
PA: Nery's Logistics, Inc.
　　774 Mays Blvd
　　775 338-7060

(P-9372)
ODW LOGISTICS ✪
2600 Stanford Ave, Ontario (91761-3102)
PHONE..............................614 549-5000
Grant Baker, *Contrlr*
EMP: 80 EST: 2023
SALES (est): 2.71MM **Privately Held**
Web: www.odwlogistics.com
SIC: 4789 Transportation services, nec

(P-9373)
PATRIOT LOGISTICS SERVICES LLC
1520 Independence Way, Vista (92084-3616)
PHONE..............................443 994-9660
Joshua Schraeder, *Prin*
Kenneth Dinsmore, *
EMP: 80 EST: 2020
SALES (est): 3.23MM **Privately Held**
SIC: 4789 Transportation services, nec

(P-9374)
PROPAK LOGISTICS INC
Also Called: PROPAK LOGISTICS, INC.
11555 Iberia St, Jurupa Valley (91752-3288)
PHONE..............................951 934-7160
Brian Harris, *Brnch Mgr*
EMP: 72
Web: www.propak.com
SIC: 4789 Cargo loading and unloading services
PA: Propak Logistics, Llc
　　1100 Garrison Ave

(P-9375)
RIOLO TRANSPORTATION INC
2725 Jefferson St Ste 2d, Carlsbad (92008-1705)
PHONE..............................760 729-4405
Gail Phipps, *Brnch Mgr*
EMP: 378
Web: www.riolo.com
SIC: 4789 Pipeline terminal facilities, independently operated
PA: Riolo Transportation, Inc.
　　759 N Vulcan Ave

(P-9376)
TAYLORED TRANSLOAD LLC
1495 E Locust St, Ontario (91761-4570)
PHONE..............................909 510-4800
Jim Deveau, *Prin*
EMP: 109 EST: 2020
SALES (est): 1.02MM
SALES (corp-wide): 26.36MM **Privately Held**
Web: www.tayloredservices.com
SIC: 4789 Cargo loading and unloading services
PA: Taylored Services Parent Co. Inc.
　　1495 E Locust St
　　909 510-4800

(P-9377)
TW SERVICES INC
1801 W Romneya Dr Ste 601, Anaheim (92801-1828)
PHONE..............................714 441-2400
Charles An, *Pr*
Thomas Hwang, *
EMP: 300 EST: 2009
SALES (est): 17.45MM **Privately Held**
Web: www.twserviceinc.com
SIC: 4789 Freight car loading and unloading

(P-9378)
VX LOGISTICS LLC
10089 Willow Creek Rd Ste 200, San Diego (92131-1699)
PHONE..............................858 868-1885
Ian Lucas, *Managing Member*
EMP: 80 EST: 2020
SALES (est): 4.18MM **Privately Held**
SIC: 4789 Transportation services, nec

4812 Radiotelephone Communication

(P-9379)
20/20 MOBILE CORP
3380 La Sierra Ave, Riverside (92503-5271)
PHONE..............................909 587-2973
EMP: 83
SALES (corp-wide): 2.62MM **Privately Held**
SIC: 4812 Cellular telephone services
PA: 20/20 Mobile Corp
　　10050 Magnolia Ave
　　951 354-8100

(P-9380)
3H COMMUNICATION SYSTEMS INC
3 Winterbranch, Irvine (92604-4604)
PHONE..............................949 529-1583
Purna Subedi, *CEO*
Michael Giarratano, *
EMP: 47 EST: 2014
SALES (est): 2.19MM **Privately Held**
Web: www.3hcommunicationsystems.com
SIC: 4812 3663 3761 3812 Radiotelephone communication; Radio and t.v. communications equipment; Rockets, space and military, complete; Search and navigation equipment

(P-9381)
4G WIRELESS INC (PA)
Also Called: Verizon Wireless
775 Laguna Canyon Rd, Laguna Beach (92651-1838)
PHONE..............................949 748-6100
Mohammad Honarkar, *Pr*
EMP: 79 EST: 2005
SALES (est): 20.95MM **Privately Held**
Web: www.4g-ventures.com
SIC: 4812 Cellular telephone services

(P-9382)
AT&T ENTERPRISES LLC
24321 Avenida De La Carlota Ste H3, Laguna Hills (92653-3681)
PHONE..............................949 581-1600
EMP: 97
SALES (corp-wide): 122.43B **Publicly Held**
Web: www.att.com
SIC: 4812 Cellular telephone services
HQ: At&T Enterprises, Llc
　　208 S Akard St
　　Dallas TX 75202
　　800 403-3302

(P-9383)
AT&T ENTERPRISES LLC
Rm 620, Anaheim (92805)
PHONE..............................714 284-2878
EMP: 311
SALES (corp-wide): 122.43B **Publicly Held**
Web: www.att.com

SIC: 4812 Cellular telephone services
HQ: At&t Enterprises, Llc
208 S Akard St
Dallas TX 75202
800 403-3302

(P-9384)
AT&T ENTERPRISES LLC
2400 E Katella Ave, Anaheim (92806-5945)
PHONE...............................714 940-9976
EMP: 107
SALES (corp-wide): 122.43B **Publicly Held**
Web: www.att.com
SIC: 4812 Cellular telephone services
HQ: At&t Enterprises, Llc
208 S Akard St
Dallas TX 75202
800 403-3302

(P-9385)
AT&T MOBILITY LLC
Also Called: Cingular Wireless
12900 Park Plaza Dr, Cerritos
(90703-9329)
PHONE...............................562 468-6142
EMP: 350
SALES (corp-wide): 122.43B **Publicly Held**
Web: www.att.com
SIC: 4812 Cellular telephone services
HQ: At&t Mobility Llc
1025 Lenox Park Blvd Ne
Atlanta GA 30319
800 331-0500

(P-9386)
BLACK DOT WIRELESS LLC
23456 Madero Ste 210, Mission Viejo
(92691-2783)
PHONE...............................949 502-3800
Marc Anthony, *Managing Member*
Gary Arnett, *
EMP: 85 EST: 2004
SALES (est): 3.34MM **Privately Held**
Web: www.blackdotwireless.com
SIC: 4812 Cellular telephone services

(P-9387)
CELLCO PARTNERSHIP
Also Called: Verizon Wireless
20 City Blvd W, Orange (92868-3100)
PHONE...............................951 205-4170
Cvc Cellular, *Prin*
EMP: 71
SALES (corp-wide): 133.97B **Publicly Held**
Web: www.verizonwireless.com
SIC: 4812 Cellular telephone services
HQ: Cellco Partnership
1 Verizon Way
Basking Ridge NJ 07920

(P-9388)
CELLCO PARTNERSHIP
Also Called: Verizon Wireless
23718 El Toro Rd Ste A, Lake Forest
(92630-8908)
PHONE...............................949 472-0700
Tracie Kemper, *Brnch Mgr*
EMP: 71
SALES (corp-wide): 133.97B **Publicly Held**
Web: www.verizon.com
SIC: 4812 Cellular telephone services
HQ: Cellco Partnership
1 Verizon Way
Basking Ridge NJ 07920

(P-9389)
CELLCO PARTNERSHIP
Also Called: Verizon Wireless
2687 Park Ave, Tustin (92782-2707)
PHONE...............................714 258-8870
EMP: 71
SALES (corp-wide): 133.97B **Publicly Held**
Web: www.verizon.com
SIC: 4812 Cellular telephone services
HQ: Cellco Partnership
1 Verizon Way
Basking Ridge NJ 07920

(P-9390)
CELLCO PARTNERSHIP
Also Called: Verizon Wireless
691 S Main St Ste 80, Orange
(92868-5619)
PHONE...............................714 564-0050
EMP: 71
SALES (corp-wide): 133.97B **Publicly Held**
Web: www.verizon.com
SIC: 4812 Cellular telephone services
HQ: Cellco Partnership
1 Verizon Way
Basking Ridge NJ 07920

(P-9391)
CELLCO PARTNERSHIP
Also Called: Verizon Wireless
237 E Compton Blvd, Compton
(90220-2412)
PHONE...............................310 603-0101
EMP: 71
SALES (corp-wide): 133.97B **Publicly Held**
Web: www.verizonwireless.com
SIC: 4812 Cellular telephone services
HQ: Cellco Partnership
1 Verizon Way
Basking Ridge NJ 07920

(P-9392)
CELLCO PARTNERSHIP
Also Called: Verizon Wireless
26445 Bouquet Canyon Rd, Santa Clarita
(91350-2396)
PHONE...............................661 296-7585
Yesenia Alapisco, *Brnch Mgr*
EMP: 71
SALES (corp-wide): 133.97B **Publicly Held**
Web: www.verizonwireless.com
SIC: 4812 Cellular telephone services
HQ: Cellco Partnership
1 Verizon Way
Basking Ridge NJ 07920

(P-9393)
CELLCO PARTNERSHIP
Also Called: Verizon Wireless
2921 Los Feliz Blvd, Los Angeles
(90039-1539)
PHONE...............................323 662-0009
Fernando Lara, *Prin*
EMP: 71
SALES (corp-wide): 133.97B **Publicly Held**
Web: www.wirelessplus.com
SIC: 4812 Cellular telephone services
HQ: Cellco Partnership
1 Verizon Way
Basking Ridge NJ 07920

(P-9394)
CELLCO PARTNERSHIP
Also Called: Verizon Wireless
11902 Gem St, Norwalk (90650-2448)

PHONE...............................562 244-8814
Jorge A Molina, *Prin*
EMP: 74
SALES (corp-wide): 136.84B **Publicly Held**
Web: www.verizonwireless.com
SIC: 4812 Cellular telephone services
HQ: Cellco Partnership
1 Verizon Way
Basking Ridge NJ 07920

(P-9395)
CELLCO PARTNERSHIP
Also Called: Verizon Wireless
407 Kern St, Taft (93268-2812)
PHONE...............................661 765-5397
EMP: 71
SALES (corp-wide): 133.97B **Publicly Held**
Web: www.verizonwireless.com
SIC: 4812 Cellular telephone services
HQ: Cellco Partnership
1 Verizon Way
Basking Ridge NJ 07920

(P-9396)
CELLCO PARTNERSHIP
Also Called: Verizon Wireless
71800 Highway 111 Ste A110, Rancho
Mirage (92270-4493)
PHONE...............................760 568-5542
Hicks Duana, *Prin*
EMP: 71
SALES (corp-wide): 133.97B **Publicly Held**
Web: www.verizonwireless.com
SIC: 4812 Cellular telephone services
HQ: Cellco Partnership
1 Verizon Way
Basking Ridge NJ 07920

(P-9397)
CELLCO PARTNERSHIP
Also Called: Verizon Wireless
258 N El Camino Real Ste A, Encinitas
(92024-2851)
PHONE...............................760 642-0430
EMP: 71
SALES (corp-wide): 133.97B **Publicly Held**
Web: www.verizonwireless.com
SIC: 4812 Cellular telephone services
HQ: Cellco Partnership
1 Verizon Way
Basking Ridge NJ 07920

(P-9398)
CELLCO PARTNERSHIP
Also Called: Verizon Wireless
3825 Grand Ave, Chino (91710-5448)
PHONE...............................909 591-9740
EMP: 71
SALES (corp-wide): 133.97B **Publicly Held**
Web: www.verizonwireless.com
SIC: 4812 Cellular telephone services
HQ: Cellco Partnership
1 Verizon Way
Basking Ridge NJ 07920

(P-9399)
CUBIC SECURE COMMUNICATIONS I
9233 Balboa Ave, San Diego (92123-1513)
PHONE...............................858 505-2000
Steve Slijepcevic, *Managing Member*
EMP: 275
SALES (est): 692.31K **Privately Held**
Web: www.cubic.com

SIC: 4812 Radiotelephone communication

(P-9400)
DIRECTV GROUP HOLDINGS LLC (HQ)
Also Called: Directv
2260 E Imperial Hwy, El Segundo
(90245-3501)
PHONE...............................424 432-5554
Michael White, *CEO*
Patrick Doyle, *VP*
Larry Hunter, *Ex VP*
Joseph Bosch, *Chief Human Resources Officer*
Steven Adams, *Sr VP*
▲ EMP: 170 EST: 1977
SALES (est): 2.54B
SALES (corp-wide): 122.43B **Publicly Held**
SIC: 4812 Cellular telephone services
PA: At&t Inc.
208 S Akard St
210 821-4105

(P-9401)
ESCHAT ✪
3450 Broad St Ste 106, San Luis Obispo
(93401-7214)
PHONE...............................805 541-5044
EMP: 100 EST: 2023
SALES (est): 1.62MM **Privately Held**
Web: www.eschat.com
SIC: 4812 Radiotelephone communication

(P-9402)
GOLDEN STATE PHONE & WIRELESS
Also Called: Phone & Wireless
138 W Branch St Ste B, Arroyo Grande
(93420-2612)
P.O. Box 1955 (93448-1955)
PHONE...............................805 545-5400
G W Peterson, *Ch Bd*
Bill Peterson, *
Merikay Guhring, *
EMP: 70 EST: 1980
SQ FT: 1,600
SALES (est): 1.13MM **Privately Held**
Web: www.verizon.com
SIC: 4812 Cellular telephone services

(P-9403)
IMOBILE LLC
Also Called: Imobile
875 W Arrow Hwy, San Dimas
(91773-2406)
PHONE...............................909 599-8822
Nahrain Simonov, *Brnch Mgr*
EMP: 102
Web: www.imobileus.com
SIC: 4812 Cellular telephone services
PA: Imobile Llc
111 Express St

(P-9404)
MBIT WIRELESS INC (PA)
4340 Von Karman Ave Ste 140, Newport
Beach (92660-1201)
PHONE...............................949 205-4559
Bhasker Patel, *Pr*
Mw Sohn, *
EMP: 130 EST: 2005
SALES (est): 9.98MM **Privately Held**
Web: www.mbitwireless.com
SIC: 4812 Cellular telephone services

(P-9405)
NEW CINGULAR WIRELESS SVCS INC

PRODUCTS & SVCS

Also Called: AT&T
252 Broadway, San Diego (92101-5004)
PHONE..............................619 238-3638
Jason Cid, *Brnch Mgr*
EMP: 79
SALES (corp-wide): 122.43B **Publicly Held**
Web: www.att.com
SIC: 4812 5999 Cellular telephone services; Mobile telephones and equipment
HQ: New Cingular Wireless Services, Inc.
7277 164th Ave Ne
Redmond WA 98052
425 827-4500

(P-9406)
NEXTEL COMMUNICATIONS INC
Also Called: Nextel
330 Commerce, Irvine (92602-1398)
PHONE..............................714 368-4509
Don Girkis, *VP*
EMP: 150
SALES (corp-wide): 78.56B **Publicly Held**
Web: www.sprint.com
SIC: 4812 Cellular telephone services
HQ: Nextel Communications, Inc.
12502 Sunrise Valley Dr
Reston VA 20191
833 639-8353

(P-9407)
PACIFIC BELL TELEPHONE COMPANY
3847 Cardiff Ave, Culver City (90232-2613)
PHONE..............................310 515-2898
EMP: 4444
SALES (corp-wide): 122.43B **Publicly Held**
Web: www.att.com
SIC: 4812 Cellular telephone services
HQ: Pacific Bell Telephone Company
430 Bush St Fl 3
San Francisco CA 94108
415 542-9000

(P-9408)
RED POCKET INC
Also Called: Red Pocket Mobile
2060d E Avenida De Los Arboles Ste 288, Thousand Oaks (91362-1376)
PHONE..............................888 993-3888
Joshua Gordon, *Pr*
Steve Bowman, ***
EMP: 75 **EST:** 2005
SALES (est): 6.87MM **Privately Held**
Web: www.redpocket.com
SIC: 4812 Cellular telephone services

(P-9409)
SPRINT COMMUNICATIONS CO LP
15582 Whittwood Ln, Whittier (90603-2355)
PHONE..............................562 943-8907
EMP: 152
SALES (corp-wide): 78.56B **Publicly Held**
SIC: 4812 Cellular telephone services
HQ: Sprint Communications Company L.P.
6391 Sprint Pkwy
Overland Park KS 66251
800 829-0965

(P-9410)
SPRINT COMMUNICATIONS CO LP
5381 W Centinela Ave, Los Angeles (90045-2003)
PHONE..............................310 216-9093
EMP: 228
SALES (corp-wide): 78.56B **Publicly Held**

SIC: 4812 4813 Cellular telephone services; Local and long distance telephone communications
HQ: Sprint Communications Company L.P.
6391 Sprint Pkwy
Overland Park KS 66251
800 829-0965

(P-9411)
SPRINT COMMUNICATIONS CO LP
44416 Valley Central Way, Lancaster (93536-6528)
PHONE..............................661 951-8927
EMP: 228
SALES (corp-wide): 78.56B **Publicly Held**
SIC: 4812 Cellular telephone services
HQ: Sprint Communications Company L.P.
6391 Sprint Pkwy
Overland Park KS 66251
800 829-0965

(P-9412)
SPRINT COMMUNICATIONS CO LP
1270 W Redondo Beach Blvd, Gardena (90247-3411)
PHONE..............................310 515-0293
EMP: 152
SALES (corp-wide): 78.56B **Publicly Held**
SIC: 4812 Cellular telephone services
HQ: Sprint Communications Company L.P.
6391 Sprint Pkwy
Overland Park KS 66251
800 829-0965

(P-9413)
SPRINT COMMUNICATIONS CO LP
4225 Oceanside Blvd, Oceanside (92056-3472)
PHONE..............................760 941-4535
EMP: 228
SALES (corp-wide): 78.56B **Publicly Held**
SIC: 4812 Cellular telephone services
HQ: Sprint Communications Company L.P.
6391 Sprint Pkwy
Overland Park KS 66251
800 829-0965

(P-9414)
SPRINT COMMUNICATIONS CO LP
Also Called: Sprint
31754 Temecula Pkwy Ste A, Temecula (92592-6805)
PHONE..............................951 303-8501
EMP: 152
SALES (corp-wide): 78.56B **Publicly Held**
SIC: 4812 5065 4813 Cellular telephone services; Telephone and telegraphic equipment; Local and long distance telephone communications
HQ: Sprint Communications Company L.P.
6391 Sprint Pkwy
Overland Park KS 66251
800 829-0965

(P-9415)
SPRINT COMMUNICATIONS CO LP
23865 Clinton Keith Rd, Wildomar (92595-9829)
PHONE..............................951 461-9786
EMP: 152
SALES (corp-wide): 78.56B **Publicly Held**
SIC: 4812 Cellular telephone services
HQ: Sprint Communications Company L.P.
6391 Sprint Pkwy

Overland Park KS 66251
800 829-0965

(P-9416)
SPRINT COMMUNICATIONS CO LP
3580 Grand Oaks, Corona (92881-4656)
PHONE..............................951 340-1924
EMP: 152
SALES (corp-wide): 78.56B **Publicly Held**
SIC: 4812 4813 Cellular telephone services; Local and long distance telephone communications
HQ: Sprint Communications Company L.P.
6391 Sprint Pkwy
Overland Park KS 66251
800 829-0965

(P-9417)
SPRINT CORPORATION
Also Called: Sprint
432 S Broadway, Los Angeles (90013-1103)
PHONE..............................213 613-4200
EMP: 172
SALES (corp-wide): 78.56B **Publicly Held**
Web: www.sprint.com
SIC: 4812 Cellular telephone services
HQ: Sprint Llc
6200 Sprint Pkwy
Overland Park KS 66251
913 794-1091

(P-9418)
SPRINT CORPORATION
Also Called: Sprint
4707 Firestone Blvd, South Gate (90280-3403)
PHONE..............................323 357-0797
EMP: 172
SALES (corp-wide): 78.56B **Publicly Held**
Web: www.sprint.com
SIC: 4812 Cellular telephone services
HQ: Sprint Llc
6200 Sprint Pkwy
Overland Park KS 66251
913 794-1091

(P-9419)
SPRINT CORPORATION
Also Called: Sprint
6591 Irvine Center Dr Ste 100, Irvine (92618-2130)
PHONE..............................949 748-3353
Mohammed Nasser, *Ex Dir*
EMP: 86
SALES (corp-wide): 78.56B **Publicly Held**
Web: www.sprint.com
SIC: 4812 Cellular telephone services
HQ: Sprint Llc
6200 Sprint Pkwy
Overland Park KS 66251
913 794-1091

(P-9420)
TRELLISWARE TECHNOLOGIES INC (HQ)
10641 Scripps Summit Ct Ste 100, San Diego (92131-3939)
PHONE..............................858 753-1600
Metin Bayram, *Pr*
Steve Fisher, *CFO*
Paul Konopka, *CCO*
Anna Kochka, *Pers/VP*
Matt Fallows, *Vice-President Global Business Development*
EMP: 115 **EST:** 2000
SQ FT: 46,000
SALES (est): 51.69MM
SALES (corp-wide): 4.28B **Publicly Held**

Overland Park KS 66251
800 829-0965

Web: www.trellisware.com
SIC: 4812 4813 3663 Radiotelephone communication; Local and long distance telephone communications; Airborne radio communications equipment
PA: Viasat, Inc.
6155 El Camino Real
760 476-2200

(P-9421)
VERIZON MEDIA INC (DH)
11995 Bluff Creek Dr, Los Angeles (90094-2929)
PHONE..............................310 907-3016
Guru Gowrappan, *CEO*
EMP: 78 **EST:** 2020
SALES (est): 9.86MM
SALES (corp-wide): 32.64B **Publicly Held**
Web: www.yahooinc.com
SIC: 4812 Cellular telephone services
HQ: Apollo Asset Management, Inc.
9 W 57th St Fl 42
New York NY 10019

(P-9422)
VERIZON NEW YORK INC
Also Called: Verizon
961 N Milliken Ave Ste 101, Ontario (91764-5022)
PHONE..............................909 481-7897
Terry L Lukens, *Principal B*
EMP: 100
SALES (corp-wide): 133.97B **Publicly Held**
Web: www.victra.com
SIC: 4812 Cellular telephone services
HQ: Verizon New York Inc.
140 West St
New York NY 10007
212 395-1000

(P-9423)
VERIZON SERVICES CORP
Also Called: Verizon
2530 Wilshire Blvd Fl 1, Santa Monica (90403-4664)
PHONE..............................310 315-1100
EMP: 346
SALES (corp-wide): 133.97B **Publicly Held**
Web: www.verizoninternet.com
SIC: 4812 Cellular telephone services
HQ: Verizon Services Corp.
22001 Loudoun County Pkwy
Ashburn VA 20147
703 729-5931

(P-9424)
VERIZON SOUTH INC
Also Called: Verizon
424 S Patterson Ave, Goleta (93111-2404)
PHONE..............................805 681-8527
Dennis Candini, *Mgr*
EMP: 229
SALES (corp-wide): 133.97B **Publicly Held**
Web: www.verizon.com
SIC: 4812 Cellular telephone services
HQ: Verizon South Inc.
600 Hidden Rdg
Irving TX 75038
972 718-5600

4813 Telephone Communication, Except Radio

(P-9425)
AB CELLULAR HOLDING LLC

Also Called: At & T Wireless Service
1452 Edinger Ave, Tustin (92780-6246)
PHONE.................................562 468-6846
EMP: 2100
SIC: 4813 Local and long distance telephone communications

(P-9426)
ADICIO INC
5857 Owens Ave Ste 300, Carlsbad (92008-5507)
PHONE.................................760 602-9502
Richard Miller, *Pr*
Richette Lock, *
Mike Cavallo, *
EMP: 90 **EST:** 1997
SALES (est): 3.57MM **Privately Held**
Web: www.adicio.com
SIC: 4813 Internet host services

(P-9427)
BOLDYN NETWRKS US SERVICES LL
Also Called: Mobilitie Services, LLC
121 Innovation Dr Ste 200, Irvine (92617-3094)
PHONE.................................877 999-7070
Gary Jabara, *Ch*
Christos Karmis, *
Dissy Sarabosing, *
Dana Tardelli, *
EMP: 350 **EST:** 2015
SALES (est): 5.83MM
SALES (corp-wide): 20.49MM **Privately Held**
Web: www.boldyn.com
SIC: 4813 Local telephone communications
PA: Boardwalk Ig Management, Llc
1945 Placentia Ave Ste D

(P-9428)
BOLDYN NTWRKS US OPRATIONS LLC
121 Innovation Dr Ste 200, Irvine (92617-3094)
PHONE.................................949 515-1500
EMP: 145 **EST:** 2021
SALES (est): 7.49MM **Privately Held**
Web: www.boldyn.com
SIC: 4813 Online service providers

(P-9429)
BROADVIEW NETWORKS INC
7731 Hayvenhurst Ave, Van Nuys (91406-1735)
PHONE.................................818 939-0015
EMP: 121
SALES (corp-wide): 6.57B **Privately Held**
SIC: 4813 Local and long distance telephone communications
HQ: Broadview Networks, Inc.
4001 N Rodney Parham Rd
Little Rock AR 72212

(P-9430)
CALIFORNIA INTERNET LP (PA)
Also Called: Geolinks
251 Camarillo Ranch Rd, Camarillo (93012-5082)
PHONE.................................805 225-4638
Skyler Ditchfield, *Pt*
Ryan Adams, *
Phil Oseas, *
Ryan Hauf, *
EMP: 164 **EST:** 2011
SALES (est): 46.21MM
SALES (corp-wide): 46.21MM **Privately Held**
Web: www.geolinks.com

SIC: 4813 Internet connectivity services

(P-9431)
CONNEXITY INC (DH)
Also Called: Shopzilla.com
2120 Colorado Ave Ste 400, Santa Monica (90404-3563)
PHONE.................................310 571-1235
William Glass, *CEO*
Aaron Young, *CFO*
Blythe Holden, *Sr VP*
EMP: 203 **EST:** 2012
SALES (est): 44.7MM
SALES (corp-wide): 85.63MM **Privately Held**
Web: www.connexity.com
SIC: 4813 7383 7331 Online service providers; News syndicates; Direct mail advertising services
HQ: Taboola, Inc.
16 Madison Sq West 7th Fl
New York NY 10010

(P-9432)
DIGITALMOJO INC
3111 Camino Del Rio N Ste 400, San Diego (92108-5724)
PHONE.................................800 413-5916
Martin Smith, *CEO*
Jerry Papazian, *
Martin Caverly, *
Michael Hart, *
Mary Khoury, *
EMP: 75 **EST:** 2005
SQ FT: 800
SALES (est): 2.92MM **Privately Held**
Web: www.digitalmojo.com
SIC: 4813 8742 Internet connectivity services; Marketing consulting services

(P-9433)
FORTITUDE TECHNOLOGY INC
Also Called: Carinet
8929 Complex Dr Ste A, San Diego (92123-1454)
PHONE.................................858 974-5060
Tim Caulfield, *CEO*
Joe Mcmillen, *Prin*
Michael C Robert, *
EMP: 85 **EST:** 1997
SQ FT: 40,000
SALES (est): 898.93K **Privately Held**
Web: www.fortitudetechnology.com
SIC: 4813 Internet connectivity services

(P-9434)
FOX INTERACTIVE MEDIA INC
6100 Center Dr Ste 000, Los Angeles (90045-9201)
PHONE.................................310 969-7000
EMP: 128
SIC: 4813 Online service providers

(P-9435)
FREE CONFERENCING CORPORATION
Also Called: Freeconferencecall.com
4300 E Pacific Coast Hwy, Long Beach (90804-2114)
P.O. Box 41069 (90853-1069)
PHONE.................................562 437-1411
David Erickson, *CEO*
Jeff Erickson, *
Robert Wise, *
Scott Southron, *
Josh Lowenthal, *
EMP: 116 **EST:** 2004
SQ FT: 10,000
SALES (est): 4.44MM **Privately Held**
Web: www.freeconferencecall.com

SIC: 4813 7389 Voice telephone communications

(P-9436)
FRONTIER CALIFORNIA INC
Also Called: Verizon
510 Park Ave, San Fernando (91340-2527)
PHONE.................................818 365-0542
Gloria Caudill, *Brnch Mgr*
EMP: 348
SALES (corp-wide): 5.75B **Publicly Held**
SIC: 4813 Telephone communication, except radio
HQ: Frontier California Inc.
401 Merritt 7
Norwalk CT 06851
203 614-5600

(P-9437)
FRONTIER CALIFORNIA INC
Also Called: Verizon
83793 Doctor Carreon Blvd, Indio (92201-7035)
PHONE.................................760 342-0500
EMP: 309
SALES (corp-wide): 5.75B **Publicly Held**
SIC: 4813 Local and long distance telephone communications
HQ: Frontier California Inc.
401 Merritt 7
Norwalk CT 06851
203 614-5600

(P-9438)
FRONTIER CALIFORNIA INC
Also Called: Verizon
1 Wellpoint Way, Westlake Village (91362-3893)
PHONE.................................805 372-6000
Alex Stadler, *Prin*
EMP: 271
SALES (corp-wide): 5.75B **Publicly Held**
SIC: 4813 Telephone communication, except radio
HQ: Frontier California Inc.
401 Merritt 7
Norwalk CT 06851
203 614-5600

(P-9439)
FRONTIER CALIFORNIA INC
Also Called: Verizon
200 W Church St, Santa Maria (93458-5005)
PHONE.................................805 925-0000
Carrie Ramsey, *Mgr*
EMP: 309
SALES (corp-wide): 5.75B **Publicly Held**
SIC: 4813 Long distance telephone communications
HQ: Frontier California Inc.
401 Merritt 7
Norwalk CT 06851
203 614-5600

(P-9440)
FRONTIER CALIFORNIA INC
Also Called: Verizon
7352 Slater Ave, Huntington Beach (92647-6227)
PHONE.................................714 375-6713
Patrick Dillon, *Mgr*
EMP: 348
SALES (corp-wide): 5.75B **Publicly Held**
SIC: 4813 8721 5065 8711 Local and long distance telephone communications; Billing and bookkeeping service; Telephone and telegraphic equipment; Electrical or electronic engineering
HQ: Frontier California Inc.
401 Merritt 7

Norwalk CT 06851
203 614-5600

(P-9441)
GOOGLE INTERNATIONAL LLC (DH)
35018 Avenue D, Yucaipa (92399-4407)
PHONE.................................650 253-0000
Eric Schmidt, *Ch Bd*
Larry Page, *CEO*
David C Drummond, *Sr VP*
▼ **EMP:** 83 **EST:** 2014
SALES (est): 24.55MM
SALES (corp-wide): 307.39B **Publicly Held**
Web: www.google.com
SIC: 4813 7375 Internet connectivity services; Information retrieval services
HQ: Google Llc
1600 Amphitheatre Pkwy
Mountain View CA 94043
650 253-0000

(P-9442)
HULU LLC (HQ)
2500 Broadway Ste 200, Santa Monica (90404-3071)
PHONE.................................310 571-4700
Randy Freer, *CEO*
Joe Earley, *Pr*
EMP: 250 **EST:** 2007
SALES (est): 352.48MM
SALES (corp-wide): 91.36B **Publicly Held**
Web: www.hulu.com
SIC: 4813 4833 Internet host services; Television translator station
PA: The Walt Disney Company
500 S Buena Vista St
818 560-1000

(P-9443)
HULU LLC
12312 W Olympic Blvd, Los Angeles (90064-1033)
PHONE.................................888 631-4858
Mike Hopkins, *CEO*
EMP: 748
SALES (corp-wide): 91.36B **Publicly Held**
Web: www.hulu.com
SIC: 4813 4833 Internet host services; Television translator station
HQ: Hulu, Llc
2500 Broadway Ste 200
Santa Monica CA 90404

(P-9444)
INCOMNET COMMUNICATIONS CORP
2801 Main St, Irvine (92614-5027)
PHONE.................................949 251-8000
George P Blanco, *Pr*
John Hill, *Ch Bd*
Stephen A Garcia, *CFO*
Andrew Kalinowski, *VP Mktg*
EMP: 80 **EST:** 1983
SQ FT: 68,000
SALES (est): 385.67K **Privately Held**
SIC: 4813 Long distance telephone communications

(P-9445)
INFONET SERVICES CORPORATION (DH)
Also Called: BT Infonet
2160 E Grand Ave, El Segundo (90245-5024)
PHONE.................................310 335-2600
David Andrew, *CEO*
Jose A Collazo, *

P R O D U C T S & S V C S

Paul Galleberg, *
Akbar H Firdosy, *
John C Hoffman, *
▲ **EMP:** 600 **EST:** 1988
SQ FT: 150,000
SALES (est): 34.84MM
SALES (corp-wide): 26.39B **Privately Held**
Web: www.infonet.com
SIC: 4813 7373 7375 Data telephone communications; Computer integrated systems design; Information retrieval services
HQ: British Telecommunications Public Limited Company
One Braham
London E1 8E
800 917-1017

(P-9446)
JUSTANSWER LLC
440 N Barranca Ave # 7508, Covina (91723-1722)
PHONE..................................800 785-2305
Jeremy Liegl, *CLO**
EMP: 126 **EST:** 2011
SALES (est): 7.61MM **Privately Held**
Web: www.justanswer.com
SIC: 4813 Online service providers

(P-9447)
MEDIA TEMPLE INC
12655 W Jefferson Blvd # 400, Los Angeles (90066-7008)
PHONE..................................877 578-4000
Russell P Reeder, *CEO*
Marc Dumont, *
John Carey, *
Albert Lopez, *
Rod Stoddard, *
EMP: 203 **EST:** 1998
SALES (est): 8.63MM
SALES (corp-wide): 4.25B **Publicly Held**
Web: www.mediatemple.net
SIC: 4813 7371 Internet host services; Computer software development and applications
HQ: Godaddy.Com, Llc
100 S Mill Ave
Tempe AZ 85281

(P-9448)
MIS SCIENCES CORP
2550 N Hollywood Way Ste 404, Burbank (91505-5046)
PHONE..................................818 847-0213
Lauren Ross, *Pr*
Jeff Willis, *
EMP: 125 **EST:** 1996
SQ FT: 7,500
SALES (est): 4.65MM **Privately Held**
Web: www.mis-sciences.com
SIC: 4813 8748 7376 8742 Internet connectivity services; Systems engineering consultant, ex. computer or professional; Computer facilities management; Management information systems consultant

(P-9449)
MPOWER HOLDING CORPORATION (HQ)
Also Called: Tpx Communications
515 S Flower St Fl 36, Los Angeles (90071-2221)
PHONE..................................866 699-8242
Richard A Jalkut, *CEO*
Richard A Jalkut, *Ch Bd*
Timothy J Medina, *
EMP: 89 **EST:** 1996
SALES (est): 102.29MM **Privately Held**

SIC: 4813 Internet connectivity services
PA: U.S. Telepacific Holdings Corp.
515 S Flower St Fl 47

(P-9450)
NEW DREAM NETWORK LLC
Also Called: Dreamhost
707 Wilshire Blvd Ste 5050, Los Angeles (90017-3607)
PHONE..................................323 375-3842
Art Elivarov, *Mgr*
EMP: 74
SALES (corp-wide): 8.55MM **Privately Held**
Web: www.dreamhost.com
SIC: 4813 Internet host services
PA: New Dream Network, Llc
417 Assod Rd Pmb 257 257 Pmb
626 644-9466

(P-9451)
NEXTPOINT INC (PA)
Also Called: Break Media
8750 Wilshire Blvd Ste 200, Beverly Hills (90211-2707)
PHONE..................................310 360-5904
Keith Richman, *Pr*
Andrew Doyle, *
David Subar, *
EMP: 80 **EST:** 2005
SALES (est): 3.2MM **Privately Held**
Web: www.breakmedia.com
SIC: 4813 Internet connectivity services

(P-9452)
NUERA COMMUNICATIONS INC (DH)
9890 Towne Centre Dr Ste 150, San Diego (92121-1999)
PHONE..................................858 625-2400
William Ingram, *Pr*
Steven Morley, *
Michael R Rinehart, *
Craig Lee, *
Bob Gersten, *
EMP: 75 **EST:** 1997
SQ FT: 48,709
SALES (est): 2.24MM **Privately Held**
Web: www.nuera.com
SIC: 4813 Telephone communication, except radio
HQ: Audiocodes, Inc.
80 Kingsbridge Rd Ste 1
Piscataway NJ 08854
732 469-0880

(P-9453)
PAYCHEX BENEFIT TECH INC
Also Called: Benetrac
2385 Northside Dr Ste 100, San Diego (92108-2716)
PHONE..................................800 322-7292
Martin Mucci, *CEO*
B Thomas Golisano, *
Jan Hawthorne, *
Susan Short, *
John B Gibson, *
EMP: 110 **EST:** 1986
SALES (est): 17.2MM
SALES (corp-wide): 5.01B **Publicly Held**
Web: www.benetrac.com
SIC: 4813 Online service providers
PA: Paychex, Inc.
911 Panorama Trail S
585 385-6666

(P-9454)
PCS MOBILE SOLUTIONS LLC
3534 Tweedy Blvd, South Gate (90280-6026)

PHONE..................................323 567-2490
EMP: 80
SALES (corp-wide): 6.22MM **Privately Held**
Web: www.pcsmobilesolutions.com
SIC: 4813 4812 Local and long distance telephone communications; Cellular telephone services
PA: Pcs Mobile Solutions, Llc
32000 Northwestern Hwy # 279
248 539-2221

(P-9455)
PUBLIC COMMUNICATIONS SVCS INC
Also Called: Gtl
11859 Wilshire Blvd Ste 600, Los Angeles (90025-6621)
P.O. Box 2868 (36652-2868)
PHONE..................................310 231-1000
Paul Jennings, *CEO*
Tommie Joe, *
Dennis Komai, *
EMP: 150 **EST:** 1987
SQ FT: 15,000
SALES (est): 1.7MM **Privately Held**
SIC: 4813 Local and long distance telephone communications

(P-9456)
QWEST CYBERSOLUTIONS LLC
Also Called: Qwest
3015 Winona Ave, Burbank (91504-2541)
PHONE..................................818 729-2100
Gino Roa, *Dir*
EMP: 154
SALES (corp-wide): 14.56MM **Publicly Held**
Web: www.centurylink.com
SIC: 4813 Telephone communication, except radio
HQ: Qwest Cyber.Solutions Llc
931 14th St
Denver CO 80202
303 296-2787

(P-9457)
SCALEFAST INC (PA)
Also Called: Pepitastore
2100 E Grand Ave, El Segundo (90245-5055)
PHONE..................................310 595-4040
Nicolas Stehle, *CEO*
Yanick Turgeon, *
Olivier Schott, *
EMP: 103 **EST:** 2014
SALES (est): 24.98MM
SALES (corp-wide): 24.98MM **Privately Held**
Web: www.esw.com
SIC: 4813 Proprietary online service networks

(P-9458)
SPOKEO INC
556 S Fair Oaks Ave Ste 1, Pasadena (91105-2656)
PHONE..................................877 913-3088
EMP: 248
Web: www.spokeo.com
SIC: 4813 Internet host services
PA: Spokeo, Inc.
199 S Los Robles Ave # 711

(P-9459)
SPRINT COMMUNICATIONS CO LP
111 Universal Hollywood Dr, Universal City (91608-1054)
PHONE..................................818 755-7100

Bill Henry, *Mgr*
EMP: 152
SALES (corp-wide): 78.56B **Publicly Held**
SIC: 4813 4812 Long distance telephone communications; Radiotelephone communication
HQ: Sprint Communications Company L.P.
6391 Sprint Pkwy
Overland Park KS 66251
800 829-0965

(P-9460)
SPRINT COMMUNICATIONS CO LP
1316 N Azusa Ave, Covina (91722-1259)
PHONE..................................626 339-0430
EMP: 152
SALES (corp-wide): 78.56B **Publicly Held**
SIC: 4813 4812 Local and long distance telephone communications; Cellular telephone services
HQ: Sprint Communications Company L.P.
6391 Sprint Pkwy
Overland Park KS 66251
800 829-0965

(P-9461)
SPRINT COMMUNICATIONS CO LP
Also Called: Sprint
12913 Harbor Blvd Ste Q4, Garden Grove (92840-5856)
PHONE..................................714 534-2107
EMP: 247
SALES (corp-wide): 78.56B **Publicly Held**
SIC: 4813 4812 Local and long distance telephone communications; Cellular telephone services
HQ: Sprint Communications Company L.P.
6391 Sprint Pkwy
Overland Park KS 66251
800 829-0965

(P-9462)
SPRINT COMMUNICATIONS CO LP
1505 E Enterprise Dr, San Bernardino (92408-0159)
PHONE..................................909 382-6030
Bill Neece, *Mgr*
EMP: 152
SALES (corp-wide): 78.56B **Publicly Held**
SIC: 4813 4812 Long distance telephone communications; Radiotelephone communication
HQ: Sprint Communications Company L.P.
6391 Sprint Pkwy
Overland Park KS 66251
800 829-0965

(P-9463)
SYDATA INC
6494 Weathers Pl Ste 100, San Diego (92121-2938)
PHONE..................................760 444-4368
Sindhura Thummalasetty, *CEO*
EMP: 125 **EST:** 2018
SALES (est): 2.15MM **Privately Held**
Web: www.sydatainc.com
SIC: 4813 7371 Internet connectivity services ; Custom computer programming services

(P-9464)
TEKWORKS INC
12742 Knott St, Garden Grove (92841-3904)
PHONE..................................877 835-9675
William E Bourgeois, *CEO*
EMP: 70

SALES (corp-wide): 13.15MM **Privately Held**
Web: www.paladintechnologies.com
SIC: **4813** 1731 Telephone communication, except radio; Communications specialization
PA: Paladin Technologies Inc
1350-355 Burrard St
604 676-0136

(P-9465)
TELISIMO INTERNATIONAL CORP
2330 Shelter Island Dr Ste 210a, San Diego (92106-3128)
PHONE..............................619 325-1593
Linda G Noda Hobbs, *Pr*
Mark D Wooster, *
▲ **EMP:** 400 **EST:** 1990
SQ FT: 15,000
SALES (est): 3.39MM **Privately Held**
Web: www.wirelessweb.com
SIC: **4813** Telephone communication, except radio

(P-9466)
TEMPO COMMUNICATIONS INC (PA)
1390 Aspen Way, Vista (92081-8349)
PHONE..............................800 642-2155
Jason Edward Butchko, *CEO*
John Parizek, *CFO*
David Collmann, *Prin*
EMP: 85 **EST:** 2019
SALES (est): 29.18MM
SALES (corp-wide): 29.18MM **Privately Held**
Web: www.tempocom.com
SIC: **4813** 3823 Telephone communication, except radio; Absorption analyzers: infrared, x-ray, etc.: industrial

(P-9467)
TRUCONNECT COMMUNICATIONS INC (PA)
Also Called: Telescape
1149 S Hill St Ste 400, Los Angeles (90015-2894)
PHONE..............................512 919-2641
Mathew Johnson, *CEO*
Robert A Yap, *
Nathan Johnson, *
EMP: 201 **EST:** 2001
SALES (est): 22.59MM
SALES (corp-wide): 22.59MM **Privately Held**
Web: www.truconnect.com
SIC: **4813** Internet host services

(P-9468)
ULTRA COMMUNICATIONS INC
990 Park Center Dr Ste H, Vista (92081-8352)
PHONE..............................760 652-0011
Charles Kuznia, *Pr*
EMP: 44 **EST:** 2004
SALES (est): 10.27MM
SALES (corp-wide): 769.22MM **Privately Held**
Web: www.ultracomm-inc.com
SIC: **4813** 2653 Telephone communication, except radio; Corrugated and solid fiber boxes
PA: Samtec Inc
520 Park E Blvd
812 944-6733

(P-9469)
UVNV INC
Also Called: Ultra Mobile
1550 Scenic Ave, Costa Mesa (92626-1420)
PHONE..............................888 777-0446
David Glickman, *CEO*
Tyler R Leshney, *Pr*
Chris Furlong, *Ex VP*
Rizwan Kassim, *Ex VP*
Chuck Harvey, *CIO*
EMP: 115 **EST:** 2012
SQ FT: 8,600
SALES (est): 190.25MM
SALES (corp-wide): 78.56B **Publicly Held**
Web: www.ultramobile.com
SIC: **4813** Telephone communication, except radio
PA: T-Mobile Us, Inc.
12920 Se 38th St
425 378-4000

(P-9470)
VERVE CLOUD INC
10967 Via Frontera, San Diego (92127-1703)
PHONE..............................888 590-4888
Derek Gietzen, *CEO*
EMP: 85
SALES (est): 1.57MM **Privately Held**
SIC: **4813** Data telephone communications

(P-9471)
VIACOM BROADBAND INC
802 Groveton Ave, Glendora (91740-4624)
PHONE..............................909 592-3335
Russ Johnson, *Pr*
EMP: 125 **EST:** 2009
SQ FT: 1,600
SALES (est): 1.31MM **Privately Held**
SIC: **4813** Internet connectivity services

(P-9472)
YTEL INC
26632 Towne Centre Dr Ste 300, Lake Forest (92610-2814)
PHONE..............................800 382-4913
Nick Newsom, *CEO*
EMP: 100 **EST:** 2012
SALES (est): 8.4MM **Privately Held**
Web: www.ytel.com
SIC: **4813** Internet host services

(P-9473)
ZYXEL COMMUNICATIONS INC
Also Called: Zyxel
1130 N Miller St, Anaheim (92806-2001)
PHONE..............................714 632-0882
Howie Chu, *Pr*
◆ **EMP:** 80 **EST:** 1989
SQ FT: 32,000
SALES (est): 10.07MM **Privately Held**
Web: www.zyxel.com
SIC: **4813** Internet host services
HQ: Zyxel Communications Corporation
No. 2, Gongye E. 9th Rd.,
Baoshan Township HSI 30009

4832 Radio Broadcasting Stations

(P-9474)
ABC CABLE NETWORKS GROUP (HQ)
Also Called: ABC
500 S Buena Vista St, Burbank (91521-0007)
PHONE..............................818 460-7477

Gary K Marsh, *CEO*
Anne M Sweeney, *
Patrick Lopker, *
▲ **EMP:** 200 **EST:** 1969
SALES (est): 94.42MM
SALES (corp-wide): 91.36B **Publicly Held**
Web: www.abc.com
SIC: **4832** 4833 Radio broadcasting stations; Television broadcasting stations
PA: The Walt Disney Company
500 S Buena Vista St
818 560-1000

(P-9475)
AGM CALIFORNIA INC
1400 Easton Dr Ste 144, Bakersfield (93309-9404)
P.O. Box 2700 (93303-2700)
PHONE..............................661 328-0118
Lawrence Rogers Brandon, *Pr*
EMP: 126 **EST:** 2010
SALES (est): 1.51MM **Privately Held**
Web: www.americangeneralmedia.com
SIC: **4832** Radio broadcasting stations

(P-9476)
AUDACY INC
5670 Wilshire Blvd Ste 200, Los Angeles (90036-5657)
PHONE..............................323 569-1070
EMP: 169
SALES (corp-wide): 1.17B **Publicly Held**
Web: www.audacyinc.com
SIC: **4832** Radio broadcasting stations
PA: Audacy, Inc.
2400 Market St Fl 4
610 660-5610

(P-9477)
DISNEY ENTERPRISES INC (DH)
Also Called: Disney
500 S Buena Vista St, Burbank (91521-0001)
P.O. Box 3232 (92803-3232)
PHONE..............................818 560-1000
Christine M Mccarthy, *Pr*
◆ **EMP:** 532 **EST:** 1986
SALES (est): 40.66B
SALES (corp-wide): 91.36B **Publicly Held**
Web: en.disneyme.com
SIC: **4832** 6794 5331 7996 Radio broadcasting stations; Copyright buying and licensing; Variety stores; Theme park, amusement
HQ: Twdc Enterprises 18 Corp.
500 S Buena Vista St
Burbank CA 91521

(P-9478)
KIFM SMOOTH JAZZ 981 INC
1615 Murray Canyon Rd, San Diego (92108-4314)
PHONE..............................619 297-3698
Mike Stafford, *Pr*
EMP: 110 **EST:** 1999
SQ FT: 12,000
SALES (est): 952.84K
SALES (corp-wide): 1.17B **Publicly Held**
SIC: **4832** Radio broadcasting stations
HQ: Abe Entercom Holdings Llc
401 E City Ave Ste 809
Bala Cynwyd PA 19004
404 239-7211

(P-9479)
KRCA LICENSE LLC
1845 W Empire Ave, Burbank (91504-3402)
PHONE..............................818 840-1400
EMP: 105 **EST:** 2001

SALES (est): 1.31MM
SALES (corp-wide): 86.99MM **Privately Held**
SIC: **4832** Radio broadcasting stations
HQ: Krca Television Llc
1 Estrella Way
Burbank CA 91504

(P-9480)
LBI MEDIA HOLDINGS INC (HQ)
1845 W Empire Ave, Burbank (91504-3402)
PHONE..............................818 563-5722
Brian Kei, *Prin*
Lenard Liberman, *Pr*
Blima Tuller, *CFO*
Winter Horton, *COO*
EMP: 103 **EST:** 2003
SALES (est): 70.51MM
SALES (corp-wide): 86.99MM **Privately Held**
SIC: **4832** Radio broadcasting stations
PA: Liberman Broadcasting, Inc.
1845 Empire Ave
818 729-5300

(P-9481)
LBI RADIO LICENSE LLC
1845 W Empire Ave, Burbank (91504-3402)
PHONE..............................818 563-5722
EMP: 110
SALES (est): 877.88K
SALES (corp-wide): 86.99MM **Privately Held**
SIC: **4832** Radio broadcasting stations
HQ: Liberman Broadcasting Of California Llc
1 Estrella Way
Burbank CA

(P-9482)
LIBERMAN BROADCASTING INC (PA)
1845 W Empire Ave, Burbank (91504-3402)
PHONE..............................818 729-5300
Lenard D Liberman, *CEO*
Jose Liberman, *
Frederic T Boyer, *
Eduardo Leon, *
Winter Horton, *
EMP: 83 **EST:** 2004
SALES (est): 86.99MM
SALES (corp-wide): 86.99MM **Privately Held**
Web: tv-broadcasting companies.omae.wo
SIC: **4832** Radio broadcasting stations

(P-9483)
LOCAL MEDIA SAN DIEGO LLC
Also Called: Magic 92.5
6160 Cornerstone Ct E Ste 150, San Diego (92121-3720)
PHONE..............................858 888-7000
Norman Mckee, *CFO*
EMP: 100 **EST:** 2009
SALES (est): 6.91MM **Privately Held**
Web: www.magic925.com
SIC: **4832** Radio broadcasting stations, music format

(P-9484)
MULTICULTURAL RDO BRDCSTG INC
747 E Green St, Pasadena (91101-2145)
PHONE..............................626 844-8882
EMP: 113
SALES (corp-wide): 19.92MM **Privately Held**

P R O D U C T S & S V C S

Web: www.wpat930am.com
SIC: 4832 Radio broadcasting stations,
music format
PA: Multicultural Radio Broadcasting, Inc.
207 William St Fl 11
212 966-1059

(P-9485)
NBCUNIVERSAL MEDIA LLC
Also Called: Universal Pictures Intl
100 Universal City Plz Bldg 2160, Universal
City (91608-1002)
PHONE...................818 777-1000
Max Liles, *Brnch Mgr*
EMP: 1614
SALES (corp-wide): 121.57B **Publicly
Held**
Web: www.nbcuniversal.com
SIC: 4832 7812 Radio broadcasting stations;
Motion picture production and distribution
HQ: Nbcuniversal Media, Llc
30 Rockefeller Plz
New York NY 10112

(P-9486)
NEW INSPIRATION BRDCSTG CO INC (HQ)
4880 Santa Rosa Rd, Camarillo
(93012-5190)
PHONE...................805 987-0400
Edward G Atsinger Iii, *CEO*
Stuart Epperson, *Ch Bd*
Evan Masyr, *VP*
Christopher Henderson, *VP*
David Evans, *NEW Business Development*
EMP: 30 **EST:** 1982
SQ FT: 40,000
SALES (est): 4.36MM
SALES (corp-wide): 266.97MM **Publicly
Held**
SIC: 4832 2731 Radio broadcasting stations;
Book publishing
PA: Salem Media Group, Inc.
6400 N Belt Line Rd
805 987-0400

(P-9487)
PANDORA MEDIA LLC
3000 Ocean Park Blvd Ste 3050, Santa
Monica (90405-3052)
PHONE...................424 653-6803
EMP: 258
SALES (corp-wide): 8.95B **Publicly Held**
Web: www.pandora.com
SIC: 4832 Radio broadcasting stations
HQ: Pandora Media, Llc
2100 Franklin St Ste 700
Oakland CA 94612
510 451-4100

(P-9488)
SAN BRNRDINO CMNTY COLLEGE DST
Also Called: Kvcr, TV & FM
701 S Mount Vernon Ave, San Bernardino
(92410-2798)
PHONE...................909 384-4444
Larry Ciecalone, *Pr*
EMP: 98
SALES (corp-wide): 46.53MM **Privately
Held**
Web: www.sbccd.cc.ca.us
SIC: 4832 4833 Radio broadcasting stations;
Television broadcasting stations
PA: San Bernardino Community College
District
550 E Hsptlity Ln Ste 200
909 382-4000

(P-9489)
SPANISH BRDCSTG SYS OF CAL
Also Called: Klax Radio Station
7007 Nw 77th Ave, Los Angeles (90064)
PHONE...................310 203-0900
Raul Alarcon Senior, *Ch Bd*
Joseph Garcia, *
EMP: 70 **EST:** 1984
SALES (est): 973.42K
SALES (corp-wide): 102.08MM **Privately
Held**
Web: www.spanishbroadcasting.com
SIC: 4832 7313 Radio broadcasting stations;
Radio advertising representative
HQ: Spanish Broadcasting System Of
Greater Miami, Inc.
7007 Nw 77th Ave
Medley FL 33166
305 644-4800

(P-9490)
TRITON MEDIA GROUP LLC
Also Called: Dial Global Digital
8935 Lindblade St, Culver City
(90232-2438)
PHONE...................661 294-9000
Phil Barry, *Brnch Mgr*
EMP: 146
Web: www.tritondigital.com
SIC: 4832 Radio broadcasting stations,
music format
PA: Triton Media Group, Llc
1350 Broadway

4833 Television Broadcasting Stations

(P-9491)
ABC SIGNATURE STUDIOS INC
500 S Buena Vista St, Burbank
(91521-0001)
PHONE...................818 560-1000
Linda A Bagley, *CEO*
EMP: 86 **EST:** 1989
SALES (est): 3.66MM
SALES (corp-wide): 91.36B **Publicly Held**
SIC: 4833 Television broadcasting stations
PA: The Walt Disney Company
500 S Buena Vista St
818 560-1000

(P-9492)
AMERICAN MULTIMEDIA TV USA
Also Called: Amtv USA
530 S Lake Ave Unit 368, Pasadena
(91101-3515)
PHONE...................626 466-1038
Jason Quin, *Pr*
EMP: 67 **EST:** 2004
SALES (est): 326.55K **Privately Held**
Web: www.amtvusa.tv
SIC: 4833 7372 Television broadcasting
stations; Application computer software

(P-9493)
BAY CITY TELEVISION INC (PA)
8253 Ronson Rd, San Diego (92111-2004)
P.O. Box 880083 (92168-0083)
PHONE...................858 279-6666
Jose Antonio Baston Patino, *CEO*
Robert Taylor, *
EMP: 100 **EST:** 1953
SQ FT: 12,000
SALES (est): 6.48MM
SALES (corp-wide): 6.48MM **Privately
Held**
Web: www.mystparties.com
SIC: 4833 7311 Television broadcasting
stations; Advertising agencies

(P-9494)
CBS BROADCASTING INC
Also Called: CBS
4024 Radford Ave Bldg 4, Studio City
(91604-2101)
PHONE...................818 655-8500
Michael Klausman, *Pr*
EMP: 73
SALES (corp-wide): 29.65B **Publicly Held**
Web: www.cbsnews.com
SIC: 4833 Television broadcasting stations
HQ: Cbs Broadcasting Inc.
524 W 57th St
New York NY 10019
212 975-4321

(P-9495)
CBS STUDIOS INC
Also Called: Csi Vegas
27420 Avenue Scott Ste A, Santa Clarita
(91355-3450)
PHONE...................661 964-6020
EMP: 469
SALES (corp-wide): 29.65B **Publicly Held**
Web: www.paramount.com
SIC: 4833 Television broadcasting stations
HQ: Cbs Studios Inc.
6100 Wlshire Blvd Ste 818
Los Angeles CA 90048

(P-9496)
CW NETWORK LLC (HQ)
Also Called: Cwtv
3300 W Olive Ave Fl 3, Burbank
(91505-4640)
PHONE...................818 977-2500
Dennis Miller, *Pr*
John Maatta, *
Mitchell Nedick, *
Tom Martin, *
Ashley Hovey, *Chief Digital Officer*
EMP: 210 **EST:** 2006
SALES (est): 98.35MM
SALES (corp-wide): 4.93B **Publicly Held**
Web: www.cwtv.com
SIC: 4833 Television broadcasting stations
PA: Nexstar Media Group, Inc.
545 E John Crptr Fwy Ste
972 373-8800

(P-9497)
DISNEY NETWORKS GROUP LLC (DH)
Also Called: Fox Network Center
10201 W Pico Blvd Bldg 101, Los Angeles
(90064-2606)
P.O. Box 900 (90213-0900)
PHONE...................310 369-1000
Brian Sullivan, *Pr*
EMP: 94 **EST:** 1996
SALES (est): 15.66MM
SALES (corp-wide): 91.36B **Publicly Held**
SIC: 4833 Television broadcasting stations
HQ: Fox Entertainment Group, Llc
1211 Ave Of The Americas
New York NY 10036
212 852-7000

(P-9498)
ENTRAVSION COMMUNICATIONS CORP (PA)
2425 Olympic Blvd Ste 6000w, Santa
Monica (90404-4056)
PHONE...................310 447-3870
Michael Christenson, *CEO*
Paul Anton Zevnik, *
Jeffery Liberman, *Pr*
Mark Boelke, *CFO*
EMP: 118 **EST:** 1996
SQ FT: 38,000

SALES (est): 1.11B **Publicly Held**
Web: www.entravision.com
SIC: 4833 4832 Television broadcasting
stations; Radio broadcasting stations

(P-9499)
ENTRAVSION COMMUNICATIONS CORP
Also Called: K S S C - F M
5700 Wilshire Blvd Ste 250, Los Angeles
(90036-3647)
PHONE...................323 900-6100
Jeff Liberman, *Pr*
EMP: 100
Web: www.entravision.com
SIC: 4833 4832 Television broadcasting
stations; Radio broadcasting stations
PA: Entravision Communications
Corporation
2425 Olympic Blvd Ste 600

(P-9500)
EW SCRIPPS COMPANY
Also Called: Kgtv
4600 Air Way, San Diego (92102-2528)
PHONE...................619 237-1010
Derek Dalton, *VP*
EMP: 709
SALES (corp-wide): 2.29B **Publicly Held**
Web: www.10news.com
SIC: 4833 Television broadcasting stations
PA: The E W Scripps Company
312 Walnut St
513 977-3000

(P-9501)
FOX INC (DH)
Also Called: Home Entertainment Div
10201 W Pico Blvd, Los Angeles
(90064-2606)
P.O. Box 900 (90213)
PHONE...................310 369-1000
K Rupert Murdoch, *Ch Bd*
Mike Dunn, *
Jay Itzkowitz, *
▲ **EMP:** 2000 **EST:** 1984
SQ FT: 25,000
SALES (est): 1.78MM
SALES (corp-wide): 91.36B **Publicly Held**
Web: www.foxstudiolot.com
SIC: 4833 7812 Television broadcasting
stations; Motion picture production and
distribution
HQ: News America Incorporated
1211 Ave Of The Americas
New York NY 10036
212 852-7000

(P-9502)
FOX BROADCASTING COMPANY LLC (HQ)
10201 W Pico Blvd Bldg 1003220, Los
Angeles (90064-2606)
P.O. Box 900 (90213-0900)
PHONE...................310 369-1000
David F Devoe Junior, *CEO*
Nancy Utley, *
Sang Gong, *
Del Mayberry, *
Joe Earley, *
EMP: 200 **EST:** 1986
SQ FT: 41,000
SALES (est): 30.48MM
SALES (corp-wide): 13.98B **Publicly Held**
Web: www.fox.com
SIC: 4833 Television broadcasting stations
PA: Fox Corporation
1211 Ave Of The Americas
212 852-7000

(P-9503)
FOX SPORTS INC (DH)
Also Called: F O X
10201 W Pico Blvd, Los Angeles (90035)
PHONE...............310 369-1000
Randy Freer, *CEO*
Eric Shanks, *
EMP: 131 EST: 1995
SALES (est): 85.22MM
SALES (corp-wide): 91.36B **Publicly Held**
Web: www.foxsports.com
SIC: 4833 Television broadcasting stations
HQ: Fox Entertainment Group, Llc
1211 Ave Of The Americas
New York NY 10036
212 852-7000

(P-9504)
FOX TELEVISION STATIONS INC (HQ)
Also Called: Fox Television Center
1999 S Bundy Dr, Los Angeles
(90025-5203)
PHONE...............310 584-2000
Roger Ailes, *Ch Bd*
Murdock Lachlan, *
Bill Lamb, *
Amy Carney, *
Dick Slenker, *Operations*
▲ EMP: 300 EST: 1998
SALES (est): 195.59MM
SALES (corp-wide): 13.98B **Publicly Held**
Web: www.myfoxorlando.com
SIC: 4833 7313 Television broadcasting
stations; Radio, television, publisher
representatives
PA: Fox Corporation
1211 Ave Of The Americas
212 852-7000

(P-9505)
FOX US PRODUCTIONS 27 INC
1600 Rosecrans Ave Bldg 5a, Manhattan
Beach (90266-3708)
PHONE...............310 727-2550
EMP: 1036
SALES (est): 1.11MM
SALES (corp-wide): 91.36B **Publicly Held**
SIC: 4833 Television broadcasting stations
HQ: Fox Entertainment Group, Llc
1211 Ave Of The Americas
New York NY 10036
212 852-7000

(P-9506)
HALLMARK MEDIA US LLC (DH)
Also Called: Hallmark Channel
12700 Ventura Blvd Ste 100, Studio City
(91604-2469)
PHONE...............818 755-2400
EMP: 95 EST: 1995
SALES (est): 24.09MM
SALES (corp-wide): 2.72B **Privately Held**
Web: www.hallmark.com
SIC: 4833 Television broadcasting stations
HQ: Crown Media Holdings, Inc.
12700 Vntura Blvd Ste 200
Studio City CA 91604
888 390-7474

(P-9507)
HERRING NETWORKS INC
Also Called: Awe
4757 Morena Blvd, San Diego
(92117-3462)
PHONE...............858 270-6900
Charles P Herring, *Pr*
EMP: 130 EST: 2003
SALES (est): 5.42MM **Privately Held**
Web: www.awetv.com

SIC: 4833 Television broadcasting stations

(P-9508)
HUB TELEVISION NETWORKS LLC
2950 N Hollywood Way Ste 100, Burbank
(91505-1069)
PHONE...............818 531-3600
EMP: 70
Web: www.hubworld.com
SIC: 4833 Television broadcasting stations

(P-9509)
KSBY COMMUNICATIONS LLC
1772 Calle Joaquin, San Luis Obispo
(93405-7210)
PHONE...............805 541-6666
Kathleen Choal, *Pr*
EMP: 78 EST: 2005
SALES (est): 2.28MM
SALES (corp-wide): 2.29B **Publicly Held**
Web: www.ksby.com
SIC: 4833 Television broadcasting stations
PA: The E W Scripps Company
312 Walnut St
513 977-3000

(P-9510)
LIFETIME ENTRMT SVCS LLC
Also Called: Lifetime TV Network
2049 Century Park E Ste 840, Los Angeles
(90067-3110)
PHONE...............310 556-7500
Maryann Harris, *Genl Mgr*
EMP: 300
SALES (corp-wide): 91.36B **Publicly Held**
Web: www.mylifetime.com
SIC: 4833 5942 Television broadcasting
stations; Book stores
HQ: Lifetime Entertainment Services, Llc
235 E 45th St
New York NY 10017
212 424-7000

(P-9511)
MCKINNON PUBLISHING COMPANY
4575 Viewridge Ave, San Diego
(92123-1623)
PHONE...............858 571-5151
Michael Mckinnon, *Pr*
EMP: 599 EST: 1993
SALES (est): 612.36K **Privately Held**
Web: www.fox5sandiego.com
SIC: 4833 Television broadcasting stations
HQ: Mckinnon Broadcasting Company
565 Gage Ln
San Diego CA 92106
858 571-5151

(P-9512)
NBC SUBSIDIARY (KNBC-TV) LLC
Also Called: NBC
100 Universal City Plz Bldg 2120, Universal
City (91608-1002)
P.O. Box 66132 (90066-0132)
PHONE...............818 684-5746
Todd Mokhtari, *Pr*
Jenik Badalian, *
EMP: 250 EST: 2009
SALES (est): 9.1MM
SALES (corp-wide): 121.57B **Publicly Held**
Web: www.nbcuniversal.com
SIC: 4833 Television broadcasting stations
PA: Comcast Corporation
1 Comcast Ctr
215 286-1700

(P-9513)
NEWPORT TELEVISION LLC
Kget-TV
2120 L St, Bakersfield (93301-2331)
PHONE...............661 283-1700
Sandy Dipasquale, *Pr*
EMP: 653
SALES (corp-wide): 9.6MM **Privately Held**
Web: www.kget.com
SIC: 4833 Television translator station
PA: Newport Television Llc
460 Nichols Rd Ste 250
816 751-0200

(P-9514)
PUBLIC MDIA GROUP SOUTHERN CAL (PA)
Also Called: Community TV Southern Cal
2900 W Alameda Ave Unit 600, Burbank
(91505-4267)
PHONE...............714 241-4100
Andrew Russell, *Pr*
Jamie Myers, *
Paul Nelson, *
Dawn Ariza, *
EMP: 100 EST: 1960
SQ FT: 50,000
SALES (est): 37.06MM
SALES (corp-wide): 37.06MM **Privately Held**
Web: www.pbssocal.org
SIC: 4833 Television broadcasting stations

(P-9515)
REVOLT MEDIA AND TV LLC
Also Called: Revolt
3336 S La Cienega Blvd, Los Angeles
(90016-3115)
PHONE...............323 645-3000
Detavio Samuels, *CEO*
Keith Clinkscales, *
EMP: 120 EST: 2010
SALES (est): 21.93MM **Privately Held**
Web: www.revolt.tv
SIC: 4833 Television broadcasting stations

(P-9516)
SF BROADCASTING WISCONSIN INC
2425 Olympic Blvd, Santa Monica
(90404-4030)
PHONE...............310 586-2410
EMP: 151 EST: 1994
SALES (est): 1.57MM
SALES (corp-wide): 3.36B **Publicly Held**
SIC: 4833 Television broadcasting stations
PA: Match Group, Inc
8750 N Cntl Expy Ste 1400
214 576-9352

(P-9517)
SMITH BROADCASTING GROUP INC
Also Called: Keyt Television
730 Miramonte Dr, Santa Barbara
(93109-1417)
P.O. Box 729 (93102-0729)
PHONE...............805 882-3933
Michael Granados, *Genl Mgr*
EMP: 332
SALES (corp-wide): 4.14MM **Privately Held**
Web: www.keyt.com
SIC: 4833 7313 Television broadcasting
stations; Television and radio time sales
PA: Smith Broadcasting Group, Inc
2315 Red Rose Way
805 965-0400

(P-9518)
STATION VENTURE OPERATIONS LP
Also Called: NBC 7/Channel 39
9680 Granite Ridge Dr, San Diego
(92123-2673)
PHONE...............619 231-3939
Dick Kelley, *Genl Mgr*
Jackie Bradford, *Genl Mgr*
▲ EMP: 76 EST: 1967
SQ FT: 23,000
SALES (est): 3.66MM
SALES (corp-wide): 121.57B **Publicly Held**
Web: www.nbcsandiego.com
SIC: 4833 Television broadcasting stations
HQ: Nbcuniversal, Llc
1221 Ave Of The Amrcas St
New York NY 10020
212 664-4444

(P-9519)
TRINITY BRDCSTG NETWRK INC
Also Called: Trinity Christn Ctr Santa Ana
2442 Michelle Dr, Tustin (92780-7091)
PHONE...............714 665-3619
Paul F Crouch, *Pr*
EMP: 150 EST: 1987
SALES (est): 6.36MM
SALES (corp-wide): 73.53MM **Privately Held**
Web: www.tbn.org
SIC: 4833 Television broadcasting stations
PA: Trinity Christian Center Of Santa Ana,
Inc.
13600 Heritage Pkwy
714 665-3619

(P-9520)
TWDC ENTERPRISES 18 CORP (HQ)
Also Called: Disney Financial Services
500 S Buena Vista St, Burbank
(91521-0001)
PHONE...............818 560-1000
Robert Iger, *CEO*
Christine M Mccarthy, *V*
Alan N Braverman, *
Kevin A Mayer, *CSO*
M Jayne Parker, *Chief Human Resources
Officer*
◆ EMP: 521 EST: 1925
SALES (est): 46.53B
SALES (corp-wide): 91.36B **Publicly Held**
Web: www.thewaltdisneycompany.com
SIC: 4833 4841 7011 7996 Television
broadcasting stations; Cable television
services; Resort hotel; Amusement parks
PA: The Walt Disney Company
500 S Buena Vista St
818 560 1000

(P-9521)
TWENTETH CNTURY FOX INTL TV IN
10201 W Pico Blvd, Los Angeles
(90064-2606)
PHONE...............310 369-1000
Peter Chernin, *Ch Bd*
EMP: 1036 EST: 1996
SALES (est): 2.84MM
SALES (corp-wide): 91.36B **Publicly Held**
SIC: 4833 Television broadcasting stations
HQ: Fox Entertainment Group, Llc
1211 Ave Of The Americas
New York NY 10036
212 852-7000

PRODUCTS & SVCS

(P-9522)
VALLEYCREST PRODUCTIONS LTD
500 S Buena Vista St, Burbank
(91521-0001)
PHONE..............................818 560-5391
Joseph Santaniello, *CEO*
EMP: 100 EST: 1999
SALES (est): 2.17MM
SALES (corp-wide): 91.36B **Publicly Held**
SIC: **4833** Television broadcasting stations
HQ: Twdc Enterprises 18 Corp.
  500 S Buena Vista St
  Burbank CA 91521

4841 Cable And Other Pay Television Services

(P-9523)
AMC NETWORKS INC
2425 Olympic Blvd Ste 5050w, Santa
Monica (90404-4096)
PHONE..............................310 998-9300
David Ryan, *Prin*
EMP: 84
SALES (corp-wide): 2.71B **Publicly Held**
Web: www.amcnetworks.com
SIC: **4841** Subscription television services
PA: Amc Networks Inc.
  11 Penn Plz
  212 324-8500

(P-9524)
BDR INDUSTRIES INC (PA)
Also Called: R N D Enterprises
820 E Avenue L12, Lancaster
(93535-5403)
PHONE..............................661 940-8554
Scott Riddle, *Pr*
Edward Donovan, *
▲ EMP: 95 EST: 1984
SQ FT: 30,000
SALES (est): 24.38MM
SALES (corp-wide): 24.38MM **Privately Held**
Web: www.rndcable.com
SIC: **4841** Cable television services

(P-9525)
CCO HOLDINGS LLC
2684 N Tustin St, Orange (92865-2438)
PHONE..............................714 509-5861
EMP: 151
SALES (corp-wide): 54.61B **Publicly Held**
SIC: **4841 3663 3651** Cable television
  services; Radio and t.v. communications
  equipment; Household audio and video
  equipment
HQ: Cco Holdings, Llc
  400 Atlantic St
  Stamford CT 06901
  203 905-7801

(P-9526)
CCO HOLDINGS LLC
3106 San Gabriel Blvd, Rosemead
(91770-2579)
PHONE..............................626 500-1214
Steve Stannard, *Brnch Mgr*
EMP: 151
SALES (corp-wide): 54.61B **Publicly Held**
SIC: **4841** Cable television services
HQ: Cco Holdings, Llc
  400 Atlantic St
  Stamford CT 06901
  203 905-7801

(P-9527)
CCO HOLDINGS LLC
23841 Malibu Rd, Malibu (90265-4644)
PHONE..............................310 589-3008
EMP: 151
SALES (corp-wide): 54.61B **Publicly Held**
SIC: **4841** Cable television services
HQ: Cco Holdings, Llc
  400 Atlantic St
  Stamford CT 06901
  203 905-7801

(P-9528)
CCO HOLDINGS LLC
12319 Norwalk Blvd, Norwalk (90650-2039)
PHONE..............................562 239-2761
EMP: 155
SALES (corp-wide): 54.61B **Publicly Held**
SIC: **4841** Cable television services
HQ: Cco Holdings, Llc
  400 Atlantic St
  Stamford CT 06901
  203 905-7801

(P-9529)
CCO HOLDINGS LLC
1151 N Azusa Ave, Azusa (91702-2005)
PHONE..............................626 513-0204
EMP: 155
SALES (corp-wide): 54.61B **Publicly Held**
SIC: **4841** Cable television services
HQ: Cco Holdings, Llc
  400 Atlantic St
  Stamford CT 06901
  203 905-7801

(P-9530)
CCO HOLDINGS LLC
Also Called: Charter Communications
2310 N Bellflower Blvd, Long Beach
(90815-2019)
PHONE..............................562 228-1262
EMP: 151
SALES (corp-wide): 54.61B **Publicly Held**
SIC: **4841** Cable television services
HQ: Cco Holdings, Llc
  400 Atlantic St
  Stamford CT 06901
  203 905-7801

(P-9531)
CCO HOLDINGS LLC
21898 Us Highway 18, Apple Valley
(92307-3916)
PHONE..............................760 810-4076
EMP: 201
SALES (corp-wide): 54.61B **Publicly Held**
SIC: **4841** Cable television services
HQ: Cco Holdings, Llc
  400 Atlantic St
  Stamford CT 06901
  203 905-7801

(P-9532)
CCO HOLDINGS LLC
26827 Baseline St, Highland (92346-3059)
PHONE..............................909 742-8273
EMP: 151
SALES (corp-wide): 54.61B **Publicly Held**
SIC: **4841 3663 3651** Cable television
  services; Radio and t.v. communications
  equipment; Household audio and video
  equipment
HQ: Cco Holdings, Llc
  400 Atlantic St
  Stamford CT 06901
  203 905-7801

(P-9533)
CCO HOLDINGS LLC
1128 W Branch St, Arroyo Grande
(93420-1906)
PHONE..............................805 904-1047
EMP: 151
SALES (corp-wide): 54.61B **Publicly Held**
SIC: **4841** Cable television services
HQ: Cco Holdings, Llc
  400 Atlantic St
  Stamford CT 06901
  203 905-7801

(P-9534)
CCO HOLDINGS LLC
1131 Creston Rd, Paso Robles
(93446-3031)
PHONE..............................805 400-1002
EMP: 155
SALES (corp-wide): 54.61B **Publicly Held**
SIC: **4841** Cable television services
HQ: Cco Holdings, Llc
  400 Atlantic St
  Stamford CT 06901
  203 905-7801

(P-9535)
CCO HOLDINGS LLC
Also Called: Charter Communications
51 W Main St Ste F, Ventura (93001-2566)
PHONE..............................805 232-5887
EMP: 151
SALES (corp-wide): 54.61B **Publicly Held**
SIC: **4841** Cable television services
HQ: Cco Holdings, Llc
  400 Atlantic St
  Stamford CT 06901
  203 905-7801

(P-9536)
COMCAST CORPORATION
Also Called: Comcast
1205 S Dupont Ave, Ontario (91761-1536)
PHONE..............................909 890-0886
Mike Shanter, *Brnch Mgr*
EMP: 100
SQ FT: 23,318
SALES (corp-wide): 121.57B **Publicly
Held**
Web: corporate.comcast.com
SIC: **4841** Cable television services
PA: Comcast Corporation
  1 Comcast Ctr
  215 286-1700

(P-9537)
COX COMMUNICATIONS INC
Also Called: Cox Communications
1535 Euclid Ave, San Diego (92105-5426)
PHONE..............................858 715-4500
Deborah Lawrence, *Dir*
EMP: 302
SALES (corp-wide): 16.61B **Privately Held**
Web: www.cox.com
SIC: **4841 4812 1731** Cable television
  services; Radiotelephone communication;
  Electrical work
HQ: Cox Communications, Inc.
  6205 B Pchtree Dnwody Rd
  Atlanta GA 30328

(P-9538)
COX COMMUNICATIONS INC
Also Called: Cox Communications
1985 Gillespie Way, El Cajon (92020-1097)
PHONE..............................619 592-4011
EMP: 70
SALES (corp-wide): 16.61B **Privately Held**
Web: www.cox.com

SIC: **4841** Cable television services
HQ: Cox Communications, Inc.
  6205 B Pchtree Dnwody Rd
  Atlanta GA 30328

(P-9539)
COX COMMUNICATIONS INC
Also Called: Cox Communications
20 Icon, Foothill Ranch (92610-3000)
PHONE..............................949 216-9765
Danny Flores, *Brnch Mgr*
EMP: 1026
SALES (corp-wide): 16.61B **Privately Held**
Web: www.cox.com
SIC: **4841** Cable television services
HQ: Cox Communications, Inc.
  6205 B Pchtree Dnwody Rd
  Atlanta GA 30328

(P-9540)
COX COMMUNICATIONS CAL LLC
5159 Federal Blvd, San Diego
(92105-5428)
PHONE..............................619 262-1122
James Robbins, *CEO*
EMP: 380
SALES (corp-wide): 16.61B **Privately Held**
Web: www.cox.com
SIC: **4841** Cable television services
HQ: Cox Communications California, Llc
  6205 Pachtree Dunwoody Rd
  Atlanta GA 30328
  404 843-5000

(P-9541)
DIRECTV INC
2260 E Imperial Hwy, El Segundo
(90245-3501)
P.O. Box 105249 (30348-5249)
PHONE..............................888 388-4249
EMP: 476 EST: 2015
SALES (est): 24.13MM **Privately Held**
Web: www.directv.com
SIC: **4841** Cable and other pay television
  services

(P-9542)
DIRECTV ENTERPRISES LLC
2230 E Imperial Hwy, El Segundo
(90245-3504)
P.O. Box 956 (90245-0956)
PHONE..............................310 535-5000
Eddy W Hartenstein, *
Odie C Donald, *
R L Myers, *
EMP: 16229 EST: 1995
SQ FT: 75,000
SALES (est): 7.25MM
SALES (corp-wide): 122.43B **Publicly
Held**
SIC: **4841** Direct broadcast satellite services
  (DBS)
HQ: Directv Holdings Llc
  2230 E Imperial Hwy
  El Segundo CA 90245
  310 964-5000

(P-9543)
DIRECTV GROUP HOLDINGS LLC
715 E Avenue L8 Ste 101, Lancaster
(93535-5405)
PHONE..............................661 632-6562
EMP: 890
SALES (corp-wide): 122.43B **Publicly
Held**
SIC: **4841** Direct broadcast satellite services
  (DBS)
HQ: Directv Group Holdings, Llc
  2260 E Imperial Hwy

El Segundo CA 90245

(P-9544)
DIRECTV GROUP HOLDINGS LLC
140 Station Ave, Ridgecrest (93555-3838)
PHONE..........................760 375-8300
EMP: 890
SALES (corp-wide): 122.43B **Publicly Held**
SIC: 4841 Cable and other pay television services
HQ: Directv Group Holdings, Llc
2260 E Imperial Hwy
El Segundo CA 90245

(P-9545)
DIRECTV GROUP HOLDINGS LLC
360 Cortez Cir, Camarillo (93012-8630)
PHONE..........................805 207-6675
EMP: 890
SALES (corp-wide): 122.43B **Publicly Held**
SIC: 4841 Cable television services
HQ: Directv Group Holdings, Llc
2260 E Imperial Hwy
El Segundo CA 90245

(P-9546)
DIRECTV GROUP INC (DH)
Also Called: Directv
2260 E Imperial Hwy, El Segundo (90245-3501)
PHONE..........................310 964-5000
Michael White, *CEO*
Patrick T Doyle, *
Romulo Pontual, *
John F Murphy, *CAO**
J William Little, *
▲ **EMP:** 128 **EST:** 1977
SALES (est): 168.3MM
SALES (corp-wide): 122.43B **Publicly Held**
Web: www.directv.com
SIC: 4841 6794 Direct broadcast satellite services (DBS); Franchises, selling or licensing
HQ: Directv Group Holdings, Llc
2260 E Imperial Hwy
El Segundo CA 90245

(P-9547)
DIRECTV HOLDINGS LLC (DH)
2230 E Imperial Hwy, El Segundo (90245-3504)
PHONE..........................310 964-5000
Michael D White, *Pr*
Larry D Hunter, *Ex VP*
Patrick T Doyle, *Ex VP*
John F Murphy, *CAO*
◆ **EMP:** 71 **EST:** 2002
SALES (est): 73.92MM
SALES (corp-wide): 122.43B **Publicly Held**
SIC: 4841 Direct broadcast satellite services (DBS)
HQ: The Directv Group Inc
2260 E Imperial Hwy
El Segundo CA 90245
310 964-5000

(P-9548)
DIRECTV INTERNATIONAL INC
2230 E Imperial Hwy Fl 10, El Segundo (90245-3504)
PHONE..........................310 964-6460
Kevin Mcgrath, *Pr*
Celso Azevedo, *
EMP: 700 **EST:** 1996

SALES (est): 1.18MM
SALES (corp-wide): 122.43B **Publicly Held**
SIC: 4841 Cable and other pay television services
HQ: The Directv Group Inc
2260 E Imperial Hwy
El Segundo CA 90245
310 964-5000

(P-9549)
E ENTERTAINMENT TELEVISION INC
Also Called: Style Network
5750 Wilshire Blvd Ste 500, Los Angeles (90036-3635)
PHONE..........................323 954-2400
EMP: 900
Web: www.eonline.com
SIC: 4841 4833 Cable television services; Television broadcasting stations

(P-9550)
FX NETWORKS LLC
10201 W Pico Blvd Bldg 103, Los Angeles (90064-2606)
P.O. Box 900 (90213-0900)
PHONE..........................310 369-1000
John Landgraf, *Managing Member*
Stephanie Gibbons, *
EMP: 150 **EST:** 1997
SALES (est): 6.92MM
SALES (corp-wide): 91.36B **Publicly Held**
Web: www.fxnetworkspressroom.com
SIC: 4841 Cable television services
HQ: Fox Entertainment Group, Llc
1211 Ave Of The Americas
New York NY 10036
212 852-7000

(P-9551)
GAME SHOW NETWORK MUSIC LLC (DH)
Also Called: G S N
2150 Colorado Ave Ste 100, Santa Monica (90404-5514)
PHONE..........................310 255-6800
Mark Seldman, *Managing Member*
EMP: 187 **EST:** 1992
SALES (est): 11.48MM **Privately Held**
Web: www.gsn.com
SIC: 4841 Cable television services
HQ: Sony Pictures Entertainment, Inc.
10202 W Washington Blvd
Culver City CA 90232
310 244-4000

(P-9552)
GLOBECAST AMERICA INCORPORATED
2 Dole Dr, Westlake Village (91362-7300)
PHONE..........................310 845-3900
Lisa Coelho, *Brnch Mgr*
EMP: 205
SALES (corp-wide): 24.27B **Privately Held**
Web: www.globecast.com
SIC: 4841 Satellite master antenna systems services (SMATV)
HQ: Globecast America Incorporated
2 Dole Dr
Westlake Village CA 91362
310 845-3900

(P-9553)
INTERNATIONAL FMLY ENTRMT INC (DH)
Also Called: Fox Family Channel
3800 W Alameda Ave, Burbank (91505-4300)

PHONE..........................818 560-1000
Mel Woods, *Pr*
EMP: 144 **EST:** 1990
SALES (est): 5.92MM
SALES (corp-wide): 91.36B **Publicly Held**
SIC: 4841 7812 7922 7999 Cable television services; Television film production; Theatrical producers; Recreation services
HQ: Abc Family Worldwide, Inc.
500 S Buena Vista
Burbank CA 91521
818 560-1000

(P-9554)
NDS AMERICAS INC (DH)
3500 Hyland Ave, Costa Mesa (92626-1459)
PHONE..........................714 434-2100
Abe Peled, *Pr*
Dov Rubin, *
Alex Gersh, *
EMP: 90 **EST:** 1992
SALES (est): 4.16MM
SALES (corp-wide): 53.8B **Publicly Held**
Web: www.synamedia.com
SIC: 4841 Cable television services
HQ: Nds Group Limited
9-11 New Square
Feltham MIDDX TW14

(P-9555)
OWN LLC
Also Called: Oprah Winfrey Network
4000 Warner Blvd, Burbank (91522-0001)
PHONE..........................323 602-5500
Oprah Winfrey, *CRO*
Oprah Winfrey, *Chief Creative Officer*
Erik Logan, *
Sheri Salata, *
EMP: 140 **EST:** 2008
SALES (est): 9.38MM
SALES (corp-wide): 97.31MM **Privately Held**
Web: www.oprah.com
SIC: 4841 Cable television services
PA: Discovery Communications, Inc.
10100 Santa Monica Blvd
310 975-5906

(P-9556)
SPECTRUM MGT HOLDG CO LLC
Also Called: Time Warner
5865 Friars Rd, San Diego (92110-6009)
PHONE..........................619 684-6106
EMP: 86
SALES (corp-wide): 54.61B **Publicly Held**
Web: www.spectrum.com
SIC: 4841 Cable television services
HQ: Spectrum Management Holding Company, Llc
400 Atlantic St
Stamford CT 06901
203 905-7801

(P-9557)
SPECTRUM MGT HOLDG CO LLC
Also Called: Time Warner
3550 Wilshire Blvd, Los Angeles (90010-2401)
PHONE..........................323 657-0899
EMP: 84
SALES (corp-wide): 54.61B **Publicly Held**
Web: www.spectrum.com
SIC: 4841 Cable television services
HQ: Spectrum Management Holding Company, Llc
400 Atlantic St
Stamford CT 06901
203 905-7801

(P-9558)
TIME WARNER CABLE ENTPS LLC
Also Called: Time Warner
4000 Warner Blvd, Burbank (91526-0001)
PHONE..........................818 977-7840
Mark Pincus, *Brnch Mgr*
EMP: 138
SALES (corp-wide): 54.61B **Publicly Held**
Web: www.wbd.com
SIC: 4841 Cable television services
HQ: Time Warner Cable Enterprises Llc
400 Atlantic St Ste 6
Stamford CT 06901

(P-9559)
VIDEO VICE DATA COMMUNICATIONS (PA)
Also Called: Vvd Communications
7391 Lincoln Way, Garden Grove (92841-1428)
P.O. Box 91421 (90809)
PHONE..........................714 897-6300
Bantofin Montoya, *Pr*
Annie Yonemura, *
EMP: 201 **EST:** 2002
SQ FT: 30,000
SALES (est): 39.3MM
SALES (corp-wide): 39.3MM **Privately Held**
Web: www.vvdservices.com
SIC: 4841 1731 Cable and other pay television services; Electrical work

(P-9560)
VUBIQUITY HOLDINGS INC (DH)
Also Called: Vubiquity
15301 Ventura Blvd Ste 3000, Sherman Oaks (91403-5837)
PHONE..........................818 526-5000
Darcy Antonellis, *CEO*
Doug Sylvester, *
William G Arendt, *
James P Riley, *
Stephen Holsten, *
EMP: 185 **EST:** 2006
SALES (est): 74.66MM
SALES (corp-wide): 4.89B **Privately Held**
Web: www.amdocs.com
SIC: 4841 Cable and other pay television services
HQ: Amdocs, Inc.
625 Mryvlle Cntre Dr Ste
Saint Louis MO 63141
314 212-7000

4099 Communication Services, Nec

(P-9561)
COMMUNICATIONS SUPPLY CORP
6251 Knott Ave, Buena Park (90620-1010)
PHONE..........................714 670-7711
Michael Davis, *Genl Mgr*
EMP: 70
Web: www.wesco.com
SIC: 4899 1731 3577 3357 Data communication services; Communications specialization; Computer peripheral equipment, nec; Nonferrous wiredrawing and insulating
HQ: Communications Supply Corp
225 W Stn Sq Dr Ste 700
Pittsburgh PA 15219
630 221-6400

P
R
O
D
U
C
T
S
&
S
V
C
S

(P-9562)
CTEK INC
2425 Golden Hill Rd Ste 106, Paso Robles
(93446-7039)
PHONE...................310 241-2973
Phil Sutter, *Pr*
EMP: 25 **EST:** 2003
SALES (est): 1.88MM
SALES (corp-wide): 424.05MM **Publicly
Held**
Web: www.ctekproducts.com
SIC: 4899 3661 Communication signal
enhancement network services; Fiber
optics communications equipment
PA: Digi International Inc.
9350 Exclsior Blvd Ste 70
952 912-3444

(P-9563)
**DISCOVERY COMMUNICATIONS
INC (PA)**
10100 Santa Monica Blvd Ste 1500, Los
Angeles (90067-4117)
PHONE...................310 975-5906
David Zazlov, *CEO*
EMP: 260 **EST:** 2014
SALES (est): 97.31MM
SALES (corp-wide): 97.31MM **Privately
Held**
Web: www.discovery.com
SIC: 4899 Data communication services

(P-9564)
EEG GLIDER INC (HQ)
Also Called: Global Eagle
1561 E Orangethorpe Ave, Fullerton
(92831-5217)
PHONE...................310 437-6000
Jeffrey A Leddy, *CEO*
Per Noren, *Pr*
Sarlina See, *CAO*
Christian Mezger, *Ex VP*
Stephen Ballas, *Corporate Secretary*
EMP: 120 **EST:** 2011
SALES (est): 656.88MM
SALES (corp-wide): 656.88MM **Privately
Held**
Web: www.anuvu.com
SIC: 4899 7371 4813 Data communication
services; Custom computer programming
services; Internet connectivity services
PA: Anuvu Operations Llc
1561 E Orangethorpe Ave
310 437-6000

(P-9565)
**HORIZON COMMUNICATION
TECH INC**
Also Called: Horizon Communication
13700 Alton Pkwy Ste 154-278, Irvine
(92618-1617)
PHONE...................714 982-3900
Nicolle Degraw, *CEO*
Micheal Degraw, *
Anthony Turrentine, *
Alex Hisa, *
EMP: 80 **EST:** 1998
SALES (est): 8.18MM **Privately Held**
SIC: 4899 Data communication services

(P-9566)
INTELSAT US LLC
Also Called: Intell Set
1600 Forbes Way, Long Beach
(90810-1830)
PHONE...................310 525-5500
Tom Nassis, *Brnch Mgr*
EMP: 145
SALES (corp-wide): 620.69MM **Privately
Held**

Web: www.intelsat.com
SIC: 4899 Satellite earth stations
HQ: Intelsat Us Llc
7900 Tysons One Pl
Mclean VA 22102

(P-9567)
MADE MEDIA LLC
Also Called: Made Merch
2337 Roscomare Rd Ste 2302, Los Angeles
(90077-1854)
PHONE...................866 263-6233
Leamon Keishan Moseley, *CEO*
EMP: 25 **EST:** 2021
SALES (est): 415.74K **Privately Held**
SIC: 4899 2741 2211 2389 Communication
services, nec; Art copy: publishing and
printing; Apparel and outerwear fabrics,
cotton; Apparel and accessories, nec

(P-9568)
NEXUS IS INC
27202 Turnberry Ln Ste 100, Valencia
(91355-1023)
PHONE...................704 969-2200
EMP: 340
Web: www.ktscnow.com
SIC: 4899 Data communication services

(P-9569)
**PROSOFT TECHNOLOGY INC
(HQ)**
9201 Camino Media Ste 200, Bakersfield
(93311-1362)
PHONE...................661 716-5100
Thomas Crone, *Pr*
EMP: 94 **EST:** 1990
SALES (est): 22.51MM
SALES (corp-wide): 2.51B **Publicly Held**
Web: www.prosoft-tested.com
SIC: 4899 Data communication services
PA: Belden Inc.
1 N Brentwood Blvd Fl 15
314 854-8000

(P-9570)
THINKOM SOLUTIONS INC
4881 W 145th St, Hawthorne (90250-6701)
PHONE...................310 371-5486
Mark Silk, *CEO*
William W Milroy, *
Michael Burke, *
Stuart Coppedge, *
Matthew Turk, *
EMP: 116 **EST:** 2000
SQ FT: 74,000
SALES (est): 26.05MM **Privately Held**
Web: www.thinkom.com
SIC: 4899 Satellite earth stations

(P-9571)
UNITED THERAPEUTICS CORP
10578 Science Center Dr Ste 215, San
Diego (92121-1144)
PHONE...................858 754-2970
EMP: 94
Web: www.unither.com
SIC: 4899 Satellite earth stations
PA: United Therapeutics Corporation
1000 Spring St

(P-9572)
WOVEXX HOLDINGS INC (DH)
Also Called: Redwood
10381 Jefferson Blvd, Culver City
(90232-3511)
PHONE...................310 424-2080
Benjamin Blank, *CCO*
EMP: 90 **EST:** 2010
SQ FT: 12,000

SALES (est): 46.91MM **Publicly Held**
SIC: 4899 7929 Data communication
services; Entertainment service
HQ: Warner Music Group Corp.
1633 Broadway
New York NY 10019
212 275-2000

4911 Electric Services

(P-9573)
AES ALAMITOS LLC
Also Called: AES
690 N Studebaker Rd, Long Beach
(90803-2221)
PHONE...................562 493-7891
Weikko Wirta, *Managing Member*
EMP: 90 **EST:** 1997
SALES (est): 22.25MM
SALES (corp-wide): 12.67B **Publicly Held**
Web: www.aes.com
SIC: 4911 Generation, electric power
PA: The Aes Corporation
4300 Wilson Blvd Ste 1100
703 522-1315

(P-9574)
CITY OF GLENDALE
Also Called: Power Plant
634 Bekins Way, Glendale (91201-3013)
PHONE...................818 548-3980
Larry Moorehouse, *Superintnt*
EMP: 84
SALES (corp-wide): 390.24MM **Privately
Held**
Web: www.glendaleca.gov
SIC: 4911 Generation, electric power
PA: City Of Glendale
141 N Glendale Ave Fl 2
818 548-2085

(P-9575)
COMBUSTION ASSOCIATES INC
Also Called: Cai
555 Monica Cir, Corona (92878-5447)
PHONE...................951 272-6999
Mukund Kavia, *Pr*
Kusum Kavia, *
Prajesh Kavia, *
▼ **EMP:** 50 **EST:** 1991
SQ FT: 40,000
SALES (est): 48.76MM **Privately Held**
Web: www.cai3.com
SIC: 4911 3443 Fossil fuel electric power
generation; Boiler and boiler shop work

(P-9576)
**CYPRESS CREEK HOLDINGS
LLC**
3402 Pico Blvd Ste 215, Santa Monica
(90405-2091)
PHONE...................310 581-6299
Ben Van De Bunt, *Ch*
Matthew Mcgovern, *CEO*
Michael Cohen, *
EMP: 100 **EST:** 2014
SALES (est): 4.6MM **Privately Held**
Web: www.ccrenew.com
SIC: 4911

(P-9577)
**CYPRESS CREEK RNWBLES
HLDNGS L (HQ)**
3402 Pico Blvd, Santa Monica
(90405-2025)
PHONE...................310 581-6299
Sarah Slusser, *CEO*
EMP: 320 **EST:** 2017
SALES (est): 278.39MM

SALES (corp-wide): 187MM **Publicly Held**
Web: www.ccrenew.com
SIC: 4911 6719
; Investment holding companies, except
banks
PA: Eqt Ab
Regeringsgatan 25
850655300

(P-9578)
EDF RENEWABLES INC (PA)
15445 Innovation Dr, San Diego
(92128-3432)
P.O. Box 504080 (92150)
PHONE...................858 521-3300
Tristan Grimbert, *Pr*
Luis Silva, *
▲ **EMP:** 225 **EST:** 1987
SALES (est): 678.73MM **Privately Held**
Web: www.edf-re.com
SIC: 4911 Electric services

(P-9579)
EDISON CAPITAL
18101 Von Karman Ave Ste 1700, Irvine
(92612-0181)
PHONE...................909 594-3789
Thomas Mc Daniel, *Pr*
Larry Mount, *
Jim Phillipsen, *
Richard E Lucey, *
Phillip Dandridge, *
EMP: 103 **EST:** 1987
SQ FT: 12,000
SALES (est): 5.78MM
SALES (corp-wide): 16.34B **Publicly Held**
SIC: 4911 Electric services
HQ: Edison Mission Group Inc.
2244 Walnut Grove Ave
Rosemead CA 91770
626 302-2222

(P-9580)
EDISON ENERGY LLC
18500 Von Karman Ave Ste 260, Irvine
(92612-0545)
PHONE...................949 491-1633
EMP: 147 **EST:** 2012
SALES (est): 10.66MM **Privately Held**
Web: www.edisonenergy.com
SIC: 4911 Electric services

(P-9581)
EDISON INTERNATIONAL (PA)
2244 Walnut Grove Ave, Rosemead
(91770-3714)
P.O. Box 976 (91770-0976)
PHONE...................626 302-2222
Pedro J Pizarro, *Pr*
Maria Rigatti, *Ex VP*
Adam S Umanoff, *Corporate Secretary*
Caroline Choi Senior, *Corporate Affairs
Vice President*
Natalie K Schilling, *Senior Vice President
Human Resources*
EMP: 922 **EST:** 1987
SALES (est): 16.34B
SALES (corp-wide): 16.34B **Publicly Held**
Web: www.edison.com
SIC: 4911 Electric services

(P-9582)
EDISON MISSION ENERGY (PA)
Also Called: Edison Mission
2244 Walnut Grove Ave, Rosemead
(91770-3714)
PHONE...................626 302-5778
Theodore F Craver Junior, *Dir*
Raymond W Vickers, *Dir*
John P Finneran Junior, *Dir*

Paul Jacob, *Dir*
W James Scilacci, *Dir*
▲ **EMP:** 95 **EST:** 2001
SQ FT: 71,000
SALES (est): 111.26MM
SALES (corp-wide): 111.26MM **Privately Held**
Web: www.edison.com
SIC: 4911 Electric services

(P-9583)
EDISON MSSION MIDWEST HOLDINGS
2244 Walnut Grove Ave, Rosemead (91770-3714)
PHONE..........................626 302-2222
Guy F Gorney, *Pr*
EMP: 820 **EST:** 1999
SALES (est): 4.13MM
SALES (corp-wide): 16.34B **Publicly Held**
Web: www.edison.com
SIC: 4911 Generation, electric power
HQ: Edison Mission Group Inc.
2244 Walnut Grove Ave
Rosemead CA 91770
626 302-2222

(P-9584)
ENRON WIND CORP
13000 Jameson Rd, Tehachapi (93561-8157)
P.O. Box 1910 (93581-5910)
PHONE..........................661 822-6835
Kenneth C Karas, *Pr*
Kenneth C Karas, *Pr*
Michael Westbeld, *
Adam Umanoff, *
Robert H Gage, *Executive Business Development Vice President*
EMP: 1345 **EST:** 1997
SQ FT: 60,000
SALES (est): 2.43MM **Privately Held**
SIC: 4911 Electric services

(P-9585)
ENRON WIND SYSTEMS
13000 Jameson Rd, Tehachapi (93561-8157)
P.O. Box 1910 (93581-5910)
PHONE..........................661 822-6835
Adam S Umanoff, *Pr*
Robert H Gates, *Sr VP*
Michael Westbeld, *VP*
EMP: 650 **EST:** 1980
SQ FT: 30,000
SALES (est): 2.34MM **Privately Held**
SIC: 4911 Generation, electric power

(P-9586)
GENON HOLDINGS LLC
Also Called: NRG
393 Harbor Blvd, Oxnard (93035-1108)
PHONE..........................805 984-5215
Tom Diciolli, *Prin*
EMP: 76
SALES (corp-wide): 152.15MM **Privately Held**
Web: www.genon.com
SIC: 4911 Electric services
PA: Genon Holdings, Llc
1360 Post Oak Blvd # 2000
832 910-9140

(P-9587)
HANWHA Q CELLS USA CORP
300 Spectrum Center Dr Ste 1250, Irvine (92618-3009)
PHONE..........................949 748-5996
Jae Kyu Lee, *Pr*
EMP: 95 **EST:** 2000

SALES (est): 12.87MM **Privately Held**
Web: us.qcells.com
SIC: 4911
HQ: Hanwha Q Cells Americas Holdings Corp.
300 Spctrum Ctr Dr Ste 12
Irvine CA 92618
949 748-5996

(P-9588)
IMPERIAL IRRIGATION DISTRICT (PA)
Also Called: I I D
333 E Barioni Blvd, Imperial (92251-1773)
P.O. Box 937 (92251-0937)
PHONE..........................800 303-7756
Stephen Benson, *Pr*
Anthony Sanchez, *
Stella Mendoza, *
Mike Abatti, *
Keven Kelly, *
▲ **EMP:** 700 **EST:** 1911
SQ FT: 10,000
SALES (est): 890.06MM
SALES (corp-wide): 890.06MM **Privately Held**
Web: www.iid.com
SIC: 4911 4971 4931 Hydro electric power generation; Water distribution or supply systems for irrigation; Electric and other services combined

(P-9589)
INSPIRE ENERGY HOLDINGS LLC
Also Called: Inspire Energy
3402 Pico Blvd Ste 300, Santa Monica (90405-2091)
PHONE..........................866 403-2620
Patrick Maloney, *CEO*
EMP: 138 **EST:** 2013
SALES (est): 43.81MM
SALES (corp-wide): 316.62B **Privately Held**
Web: www.inspirecleanenergy.com
SIC: 4911 Distribution, electric power
PA: Shell Plc
Shell Centre
207 934-3363

(P-9590)
JTI ELCTRCAL INSTRMNTATION LLC
3901 Fanucchi Way Unit 201, Shafter (93263-9590)
PHONE..........................661 393-5535
EMP: 100 **EST:** 2013
SALES (est): 4.66MM **Privately Held**
Web: www.jtielectric.com
SIC: 4911 Electric services

(P-9591)
MT POSO CGNRTION A CAL LTD PR
10000 Stockdale Hwy Ste 100, Bakersfield (93311-3602)
PHONE..........................661 663-3155
Roger C Allred, *Genl Mgr*
EMP: 28 **EST:** 1986
SQ FT: 2,500
SALES (est): 9.65MM **Privately Held**
SIC: 4911 1311 Generation, electric power; Crude petroleum production
HQ: Northern Star Generation Services, Llc
2929 Allen Pkwy
Houston TX 77019
713 580-6300

(P-9592)
ORMAT NEVADA INC
Also Called: ORMAT NEVADA, INC.
947 Dogwood Rd, Heber (92249-9762)
PHONE..........................760 353-8200
Celia Velasco, *Admn Mgr*
EMP: 115
Web: www.ormat.com
SIC: 4911 Generation, electric power
HQ: Ormat Nevada Inc.
6884 Sierra Center Pkwy
Reno NV 89511

(P-9593)
ORMAT TECHNOLOGIES INC
855 Dogwood Rd, Heber (92249-9758)
PHONE..........................760 337-8872
Miki Juarez, *Brnch Mgr*
EMP: 44
Web: www.ormat.com
SIC: 4911 3621 3691 Electric services; Power generators; Alkaline cell storage batteries
PA: Ormat Technologies, Inc.
6140 Plumas St

(P-9594)
OUTSOURCE UTILITY CONTR LLC
970 W 190th St, Torrance (90502-1000)
PHONE..........................714 238-9263
Mathew Bates, *CEO*
Heather Morgan, *
Joe Morgan, *
Josh Stewart, *
EMP: 515 **EST:** 2010
SALES (est): 24.38MM **Privately Held**
Web: www.outsourceucc.com
SIC: 4911 Distribution, electric power

(P-9595)
PACIFIC GAS AND ELECTRIC CO
Also Called: PG&e
145453 National Trails Hway, Needles (92363)
P.O. Box 337 (92363-0337)
PHONE..........................760 326-2615
Felix Vasquez, *Mgr*
EMP: 156
Web: www.pge.com
SIC: 4911 Transmission, electric power
HQ: Pacific Gas And Electric Company
300 Lakeside Dr
Oakland CA 94612
415 973-7000

(P-9596)
PACIFIC GAS AND ELECTRIC CO
Also Called: PG&e
35863 Fairview Rd, Hinkley (92347-9710)
PHONE..........................760 253-2925
Dan Lytle, *Mgr*
EMP: 134
Web: www.pge.com
SIC: 4911 Transmission, electric power
HQ: Pacific Gas And Electric Company
300 Lakeside Dr
Oakland CA 94612
415 973-7000

(P-9597)
PACIFIC GAS AND ELECTRIC CO
Also Called: PG&e
4340 Old Santa Fe Rd, San Luis Obispo (93401-8160)
PHONE..........................805 545-4562
Del Richie, *Mgr*
EMP: 279
Web: www.pge.com

SIC: 4911 Transmission, electric power
HQ: Pacific Gas And Electric Company
300 Lakeside Dr
Oakland CA 94612
415 973-7000

(P-9598)
PACIFIC GAS AND ELECTRIC CO
Also Called: PG&e
9 Mi Nw Of Avila Bch, Avila Beach (93424)
P.O. Box 56 (93424-0056)
PHONE..........................805 506-5280
David Oatley, *Brnch Mgr*
EMP: 1400
Web: www.pge.com
SIC: 4911 Transmission, electric power
HQ: Pacific Gas And Electric Company
300 Lakeside Dr
Oakland CA 94612
415 973-7000

(P-9599)
PACIFIC GAS AND ELECTRIC CO
Also Called: PG&e
800 Price Canyon Rd, Pismo Beach (93449-2722)
PHONE..........................805 546-5267
Don Boatman, *Brnch Mgr*
EMP: 145
Web: www.pge.com
SIC: 4911 Transmission, electric power
HQ: Pacific Gas And Electric Company
300 Lakeside Dr
Oakland CA 94612
415 973-7000

(P-9600)
PACIFIC GAS AND ELECTRIC CO
Also Called: PG&e
160 Cow Meadow Pl, Templeton (93465)
PHONE..........................805 434-4418
Bob Burroughs, *Brnch Mgr*
EMP: 89
Web: www.pge.com
SIC: 4911 Transmission, electric power
HQ: Pacific Gas And Electric Company
300 Lakeside Dr
Oakland CA 94612
415 973-7000

(P-9601)
RESA SERVICE LLC
Also Called: Dymax Service
13842 Bettencourt St, Cerritos (90703-1010)
PHONE..........................562 567-6279
EMP: 107
SALES (corp-wide): 98.17MM **Privately Held**
Web: www.resapower.com
SIC: 4911 Electric services
PA: Resa Service, Llc
8723 Fallbrook Dr
832 900-8340

(P-9602)
SAN DIEGO GAS & ELECTRIC CO
Also Called: SDG&e
1801 S Atlantic Blvd, Monterey Park (91754-5207)
PHONE..........................619 696-2000
J Walker Martin, *CEO*
EMP: 191
SALES (corp-wide): 16.72B **Publicly Held**
Web: www.sdge.com
SIC: 4911 Distribution, electric power
HQ: San Diego Gas & Electric Company
8330 Century Park Ct
San Diego CA 92123
619 696-2000

(P-9603)

SAN DIEGO GAS & ELECTRIC CO

Also Called: SDG&e
2300 Harveson Pl, Escondido
(92029-1965)
PHONE.................................760 432-2508
Carl La Peter, *Prin*
EMP: 303
SALES (corp-wide): 16.72B **Publicly Held**
Web: www.sdge.com
SIC: 4911 Distribution, electric power
HQ: San Diego Gas & Electric Company
      8330 Century Park Ct
      San Diego CA 92123
      619 696-2000

(P-9604)

SAN DIEGO GAS & ELECTRIC CO

Also Called: SDG&e
5488 Overland Ave, San Diego
(92123-1205)
PHONE.................................858 654-6377
E Dimuzio, *Brnch Mgr*
EMP: 460
SALES (corp-wide): 16.72B **Publicly Held**
Web: www.sdge.com
SIC: 4911 Distribution, electric power
HQ: San Diego Gas & Electric Company
      8330 Century Park Ct
      San Diego CA 92123
      619 696-2000

(P-9605)

SAN DIEGO GAS & ELECTRIC CO

Project Construction Metro
701 33rd St, San Diego (92102-3341)
PHONE.................................619 699-1018
Scott Furgerson, *Mgr*
EMP: 202
SALES (corp-wide): 16.72B **Publicly Held**
Web: www.sdge.com
SIC: 4911 Distribution, electric power
HQ: San Diego Gas & Electric Company
      8330 Century Park Ct
      San Diego CA 92123
      619 696-2000

(P-9606)

SAN DIEGO GAS & ELECTRIC CO

Also Called: SDG&e
10975 Technology Pl, San Diego
(92127-1811)
PHONE.................................858 613-3216
EMP: 123
SALES (corp-wide): 16.72B **Publicly Held**
Web: www.sdge.com
SIC: 4911 Distribution, electric power
HQ: San Diego Gas & Electric Company
      8330 Century Park Ct
      San Diego CA 92123
      619 696-2000

(P-9607)

SAN DIEGO GAS & ELECTRIC CO

Also Called: SDG&e
8306 Century Park Ct # Cp42c, San Diego
(92123-1593)
PHONE.................................858 654-1289
Eric Llewellyn, *Brnch Mgr*
EMP: 90
SALES (corp-wide): 16.72B **Publicly Held**
Web: www.sdge.com
SIC: 4911 Distribution, electric power
HQ: San Diego Gas & Electric Company
      8330 Century Park Ct

San Diego CA 92123
619 696-2000

(P-9608)

SAN DIEGO GAS & ELECTRIC CO

Also Called: Eastern District Office
104 N Johnson Ave, El Cajon (92020-3181)
PHONE.................................619 441-3834
Allan Marchart, *Mgr*
EMP: 334
SALES (corp-wide): 16.72B **Publicly Held**
Web: www.sdge.com
SIC: 4911 Distribution, electric power
HQ: San Diego Gas & Electric Company
      8330 Century Park Ct
      San Diego CA 92123
      619 696-2000

(P-9609)

SAN DIEGO GAS & ELECTRIC CO

Also Called: SDG&ec
5488 Overland Ave, San Diego
(92123-1205)
P.O. Box 129007 (92112-9007)
PHONE.................................858 541-5920
Patrick Lee, *Mgr*
EMP: 185
SALES (corp-wide): 16.72B **Publicly Held**
Web: www.sdge.com
SIC: 4911 4924 Generation, electric power;
      Natural gas distribution
HQ: San Diego Gas & Electric Company
      8330 Century Park Ct
      San Diego CA 92123
      619 696-2000

(P-9610)

SEMPRA ENERGY

Also Called: Sempra Energy
9305 Lightwave Ave, San Diego
(92123-6463)
PHONE.................................619 696-2000
Scan Luko, *Brnch Mgr*
EMP: 1000
SALES (corp-wide): 16.72B **Publicly Held**
Web: www.sempra.com
SIC: 4911 4923 Distribution, electric power;
      Gas transmission and distribution
PA: Sempra
      488 8th Ave
      619 696-2000

(P-9611)

SEMPRA ENERGY GLOBAL ENTPS

101 Ash St, San Diego (92101-3017)
PHONE.................................619 696-2000
Mark Snell, *Pr*
Mark Fisher, *
Michael Allman, *
EMP: 1000 **EST:** 1997
SQ FT: 10,000
SALES (est): 499.4MM
SALES (corp-wide): 16.72B **Publicly Held**
Web: www.sempra.com
SIC: 4911 4924 Generation, electric power;
      Natural gas distribution
PA: Sempra
      488 8th Ave
      619 696-2000

(P-9612)

SEMPRA ENERGY INTERNATIONAL

Also Called: Sempra Energy Utilities
101 Ash St, San Diego (92101-3017)
PHONE.................................619 696-2000

Luis Eduardo Pawluszek, *CEO*
Donald E Felsinger, *
Mark A Snell, *
Javade Chaudhri, *
Randall L Clark, *
EMP: 1200 **EST:** 1998
SALES (est): 599.27MM
SALES (corp-wide): 16.72B **Publicly Held**
Web: www.sempra.com
SIC: 4911 Electric services
PA: Sempra
      488 8th Ave
      619 696-2000

(P-9613)

SOLARRESERVE INC

520 Broadway 6th Fl, Santa Monica
(90401-2420)
PHONE.................................310 315-2200
Kevin B Smith, *CEO*
Stephen Mullennix, *
EMP: 99 **EST:** 2008
SQ FT: 20,000
SALES (est): 2.7MM **Privately Held**
SIC: 4911 Distribution, electric power

(P-9614)

SOLV ENERGY LLC (HQ)

16680 W Bernardo Dr, San Diego
(92127-1900)
PHONE.................................858 251-4888
George Hershman, *CEO*
Ben Catalano, *CFO*
EMP: 159 **EST:** 2015
SALES (est): 30.23MM **Privately Held**
Web: www.solvenergy.com
SIC: 4911
PA: American Securities Llc
      590 Madison Ave Fl 38

(P-9615)

SOUTHERN CALIFORNIA EDISON CO

Also Called: Valley Substation
26125 Menifee Rd, Romoland
(92585-9441)
PHONE.................................800 336-2822
Henry Herrea, *Brnch Mgr*
EMP: 90
SALES (corp-wide): 16.34B **Publicly Held**
Web: www.sce.com
SIC: 4911 Generation, electric power
HQ: Southern California Edison Company
      2244 Walnut Grove Ave
      Rosemead CA 91770
      626 302-1212

(P-9616)

SOUTHERN CALIFORNIA EDISON CO

Also Called: Orange Coast Service Center
7333 Bolsa Ave, Westminster (92683-5294)
PHONE.................................714 895-0163
Jeff Lebow, *Brnch Mgr*
EMP: 152
SALES (corp-wide): 16.34B **Publicly Held**
Web: www.sce.com
SIC: 4911 Electric services
HQ: Southern California Edison Company
      2244 Walnut Grove Ave
      Rosemead CA 91770
      626 302-1212

(P-9617)

SOUTHERN CALIFORNIA EDISON CO

7400 Fenwick Ln, Westminster
(92683-5243)
PHONE.................................714 895-0119

EMP: 114
SALES (corp-wide): 16.34B **Publicly Held**
Web: www.sce.com
SIC: 4911 Electric services
HQ: Southern California Edison Company
      2244 Walnut Grove Ave
      Rosemead CA 91770
      626 302-1212

(P-9618)

SOUTHERN CALIFORNIA EDISON CO

Also Called: North Orange County Svc Ctr
1851 W Valencia Dr, Fullerton
(92833-3215)
PHONE.................................714 870-3225
David Kama, *Dist Mgr*
EMP: 423
SALES (corp-wide): 16.34B **Publicly Held**
Web: www.sce.com
SIC: 4911 Distribution, electric power
HQ: Southern California Edison Company
      2244 Walnut Grove Ave
      Rosemead CA 91770
      626 302-1212

(P-9619)

SOUTHERN CALIFORNIA EDISON CO

Also Called: Southeastern Westminster
7300 Fenwick Ln, Westminster
(92683-5288)
PHONE.................................714 895-0420
Dee Pak Nanda, *VP*
EMP: 1378
SALES (corp-wide): 16.34B **Publicly Held**
Web: www.sce.com
SIC: 4911 Electric services
HQ: Southern California Edison Company
      2244 Walnut Grove Ave
      Rosemead CA 91770
      626 302-1212

(P-9620)

SOUTHERN CALIFORNIA EDISON CO

Also Called: Saddleback Valley Service Ctr
14155 Bake Pkwy, Irvine (92618-1818)
PHONE.................................949 587-5416
Robert Torres, *Mgr*
EMP: 124
SALES (corp-wide): 16.34B **Publicly Held**
Web: www.sce.com
SIC: 4911 Electric services
HQ: Southern California Edison Company
      2244 Walnut Grove Ave
      Rosemead CA 91770
      626 302-1212

(P-9621)

SOUTHERN CALIFORNIA EDISON CO (HQ)

Also Called: SCE
2244 Walnut Grove Ave, Rosemead
(91770-3714)
P.O. Box 976 (91770-0800)
PHONE.................................626 302-1212
Kevin M Payne, *Pr*
Steven D Powell, *Ofcr*
William M Petmecky Iii, *Sr VP*
Caroline Choi Senior, *Corporate Affairs
Vice President*
Jacqueline Trapp, *Senior Vice President
Human Resources*
▲ **EMP:** 1200 **EST:** 1909
SALES (est): 16.27B
SALES (corp-wide): 16.34B **Publicly Held**
Web: www.sce.com
SIC: 4911 Generation, electric power
PA: Edison International
      2244 Walnut Grove Ave

626 302-2222

(P-9622)
SOUTHERN CALIFORNIA EDISON CO
2 Innovation Way Fl 1, Pomona (91768-2560)
PHONE.....................909 274-1925
EMP: 390
SALES (corp-wide): 16.34B **Publicly Held**
Web: www.sce.com
SIC: 4911 Electric services
HQ: Southern California Edison Company
 2244 Walnut Grove Ave
 Rosemead CA 91770
 626 302-1212

(P-9623)
SOUTHERN CALIFORNIA EDISON CO
265 Ne End Ave, Pomona (91767-5803)
PHONE.....................909 469-0251
John Risen, *Brnch Mgr*
EMP: 656
SALES (corp-wide): 16.34B **Publicly Held**
Web: www.sce.com
SIC: 4911 Electric services
HQ: Southern California Edison Company
 2244 Walnut Grove Ave
 Rosemead CA 91770
 626 302-1212

(P-9624)
SOUTHERN CALIFORNIA EDISON CO
8380 Klingerman St, Rosemead (91770-3609)
PHONE.....................626 302-5101
Arthur Guerra, *Prin*
EMP: 86
SALES (corp-wide): 16.34B **Publicly Held**
Web: www.sce.com
SIC: 4911 Generation, electric power
HQ: Southern California Edison Company
 2244 Walnut Grove Ave
 Rosemead CA 91770
 626 302-1212

(P-9625)
SOUTHERN CALIFORNIA EDISON CO
Also Called: Southern Cal Edson - Prvate Ch
2131 Walnut Grove Ave, Rosemead (91770-3769)
PHONE.....................626 302-1212
Grant Thomas, *Brnch Mgr*
EMP: 470
SALES (corp-wide): 16.34B **Publicly Held**
Web: www.sce.com
SIC: 4911 Distribution, electric power
HQ: Southern California Edison Company
 2244 Walnut Grove Ave
 Rosemead CA 91770
 626 302-1212

(P-9626)
SOUTHERN CALIFORNIA EDISON CO
Also Called: Compton Service Center
1924 E Cashdan St, Compton (90220-6403)
PHONE.....................310 608-5029
Floyd Rich, *Brnch Mgr*
EMP: 375
SALES (corp-wide): 16.34B **Publicly Held**
Web: www.sce.com
SIC: 4911 Electric services
HQ: Southern California Edison Company
 2244 Walnut Grove Ave

Rosemead CA 91770
626 302-1212

(P-9627)
SOUTHERN CALIFORNIA EDISON CO
Also Called: N Trans/Sub Regional Office
28250 Gateway Village Dr, Valencia (91355-1177)
PHONE.....................661 607-0207
EMP: 195
SALES (corp-wide): 16.34B **Publicly Held**
Web: www.sce.com
SIC: 4911 Electric services
HQ: Southern California Edison Company
 2244 Walnut Grove Ave
 Rosemead CA 91770
 626 302-1212

(P-9628)
SOUTHERN CALIFORNIA EDISON CO
6042 N Irwindale Ave Ste A, Irwindale (91702-3250)
PHONE.....................626 633-3070
Jami Mcdonald, *Brnch Mgr*
EMP: 71
SALES (corp-wide): 16.34B **Publicly Held**
Web: www.sce.com
SIC: 4911 Generation, electric power
HQ: Southern California Edison Company
 2244 Walnut Grove Ave
 Rosemead CA 91770
 626 302-1212

(P-9629)
SOUTHERN CALIFORNIA EDISON CO
Also Called: Lightthipe Substation
6900 Orange Ave, Long Beach (90805-1599)
PHONE.....................562 529-7301
Jim Hill, *Mgr*
EMP: 81
SQ FT: 38,928
SALES (corp-wide): 16.34B **Publicly Held**
Web: www.sce.com
SIC: 4911 Electric services
HQ: Southern California Edison Company
 2244 Walnut Grove Ave
 Rosemead CA 91770
 626 302-1212

(P-9630)
SOUTHERN CALIFORNIA EDISON CO
13025 Los Angeles St, Irwindale (91706-2241)
PHONE.....................626 814-4212
Ed Entillon, *Brnch Mgr*
EMP: 295
SQ FT: 21,000
SALES (corp-wide): 16.34B **Publicly Held**
Web: www.sce.com
SIC: 4911 Electric services
HQ: Southern California Edison Company
 2244 Walnut Grove Ave
 Rosemead CA 91770
 626 302-1212

(P-9631)
SOUTHERN CALIFORNIA EDISON CO
Also Called: Covina Service Center
800 W Cienega Ave, San Dimas (91773-2490)
PHONE.....................909 592-3757
Gary Martinez, *Brnch Mgr*
EMP: 200

SALES (corp-wide): 16.34B **Publicly Held**
Web: www.sce.com
SIC: 4911 Electric services
HQ: Southern California Edison Company
 2244 Walnut Grove Ave
 Rosemead CA 91770
 626 302-1212

(P-9632)
SOUTHERN CALIFORNIA EDISON CO
Also Called: Whittier Service Center
9901 Geary Ave, Santa Fe Springs (90670-3251)
PHONE.....................562 903-3191
Fred Swearingen, *Prin*
EMP: 385
SALES (corp-wide): 16.34B **Publicly Held**
Web: www.sce.com
SIC: 4911 Electric services
HQ: Southern California Edison Company
 2244 Walnut Grove Ave
 Rosemead CA 91770
 626 302-1212

(P-9633)
SOUTHERN CALIFORNIA EDISON CO
Also Called: Western Division Regional Off
125 Elm Ave, Long Beach (90802-4918)
PHONE.....................562 491-3803
Lorene Miller, *Mgr*
EMP: 266
SALES (corp-wide): 16.34B **Publicly Held**
Web: www.sce.com
SIC: 4911 Generation, electric power
HQ: Southern California Edison Company
 2244 Walnut Grove Ave
 Rosemead CA 91770
 626 302-1212

(P-9634)
SOUTHERN CALIFORNIA EDISON CO
Also Called: Ctac Research 60901
6090 N Irwindale Ave, Irwindale (91702-3207)
PHONE.....................626 812-7380
Diane Ronewko, *Mgr*
EMP: 257
SALES (corp-wide): 16.34B **Publicly Held**
Web: www.sce.com
SIC: 4911 Electric services
HQ: Southern California Edison Company
 2244 Walnut Grove Ave
 Rosemead CA 91770
 626 302-1212

(P-9635)
SOUTHERN CALIFORNIA EDISON CO
Alhambra Combined Facility
501 S Marengo Ave, Alhambra (91803-1640)
P.O. Box 700 (91770-0700)
PHONE.....................626 308-6193
Kevin M Payne, *CEO*
EMP: 551
SALES (corp-wide): 16.34B **Publicly Held**
Web: www.sce.com
SIC: 4911 Generation, electric power
HQ: Southern California Edison Company
 2244 Walnut Grove Ave
 Rosemead CA 91770
 626 302-1212

(P-9636)
SOUTHERN CALIFORNIA EDISON CO

Also Called: Ridgecrest Service Center
510 S China Lake Blvd, Ridgecrest (93555-5098)
PHONE.....................760 375-1821
Howell Applegrath, *Mgr*
EMP: 124
SALES (corp-wide): 16.34B **Publicly Held**
Web: www.sce.com
SIC: 4911 Electric services
HQ: Southern California Edison Company
 2244 Walnut Grove Ave
 Rosemead CA 91770
 626 302-1212

(P-9637)
SOUTHERN CALIFORNIA EDISON CO
4900 Rivergrade Rd Bldg 2b1, Irwindale (91706-1401)
PHONE.....................626 543-8081
Peter Quon, *Brnch Mgr*
EMP: 71
SALES (corp-wide): 16.34B **Publicly Held**
Web: www.sce.com
SIC: 4911 Generation, electric power
HQ: Southern California Edison Company
 2244 Walnut Grove Ave
 Rosemead CA 91770
 626 302-1212

(P-9638)
SOUTHERN CALIFORNIA EDISON CO
Also Called: Monrovia Service Center
1440 S California Ave, Monrovia (91016-4211)
PHONE.....................626 303-8480
Robert Robinson, *Prin*
EMP: 181
SQ FT: 31,603
SALES (corp-wide): 16.34B **Publicly Held**
Web: www.sce.com
SIC: 4911 Electric services
HQ: Southern California Edison Company
 2244 Walnut Grove Ave
 Rosemead CA 91770
 626 302-1212

(P-9639)
SOUTHERN CALIFORNIA EDISON CO
Also Called: Thousand Oaks Service Center
3589 Foothill Dr, Thousand Oaks (91361-2475)
PHONE.....................818 999-1880
Jerry Willaferd, *Brnch Mgr*
EMP: 90
SALES (corp-wide): 16.34B **Publicly Held**
Web: www.sce.com
SIC: 4911 8741 Electric services; Business management
HQ: Southern California Edison Company
 2244 Walnut Grove Ave
 Rosemead CA 91770
 626 302-1212

(P-9640)
SUNNOVA ENERGY CORPORATION
2211 Michelson Dr, Irvine (92612-1384)
PHONE.....................877 757-7697
EMP: 154
SALES (corp-wide): 720.65MM **Publicly Held**
Web: www.sunnova.com
SIC: 4911
HQ: Sunnova Energy Corporation
 20 Greenway Plz Ste 540
 Houston TX 77046
 281 985-9900

PRODUCTS & SVCS

(P-9641)
TWIN OAKS POWER LP (HQ)
101 Ash St Hq10b, San Diego
(92101-3017)
PHONE..............................619 696-2034
EMP: 100 EST: 2002
SALES (est): 74.91MM
SALES (corp-wide): 16.72B **Publicly Held**
SIC: 4911 4924 Generation, electric power;
 Natural gas distribution
PA: Sempra
 488 8th Ave
 619 696-2000

4922 Natural Gas Transmission

(P-9642)
SAN DIEGO GAS & ELECTRIC CO
Also Called: South Bay Power Plant
990 Bay Blvd, Chula Vista (91911-1651)
PHONE..............................800 411-7343
Carl Creelman, *Brnch Mgr*
EMP: 84
SALES (corp-wide): 16.72B **Publicly Held**
Web: www.sdge.com
SIC: 4922 4911 Natural gas transmission;
 Generation, electric power
HQ: San Diego Gas & Electric Company
 8330 Century Park Ct
 San Diego CA 92123
 619 696-2000

(P-9643)
SOUTHERN CALIFORNIA GAS CO
9400 Oakdale Ave, Chatsworth
(91311-6511)
P.O. Box 513249 (90051-1249)
PHONE..............................818 701-2592
Cathy Maguire, *Brnch Mgr*
EMP: 279
SALES (corp-wide): 16.72B **Publicly Held**
Web: www.socalgas.com
SIC: 4922 4923 Pipelines, natural gas; Gas
 transmission and distribution
HQ: Southern California Gas Company
 555 W 5th St Ste 14h1
 Los Angeles CA 90013
 213 244-1200

4924 Natural Gas Distribution

(P-9644)
CLEAN ENERGY
4675 Macarthur Ct Ste 800, Newport Beach
(92660-1895)
PHONE..............................949 437-1000
Andrew Littlefair, *Pr*
Mitchell Pratt, *Corporate Secretary**
Robert Vreeland, *
EMP: 832 EST: 1996
SALES (est): 96.18MM
SALES (corp-wide): 425.16MM **Publicly Held**
Web: www.cleanenergyfuels.com
SIC: 4924 Natural gas distribution
PA: Clean Energy Fuels Corp.
 4675 Macarthur Ct Ste 800
 949 437-1000

(P-9645)
SAN DIEGO GAS & ELECTRIC CO
Also Called: SDG&e
14601 Virginia St, Moreno Valley
(92555-8100)

PHONE..............................951 243-2241
John Garcia, *Mgr*
EMP: 269
SALES (corp-wide): 16.72B **Publicly Held**
Web: www.sdge.com
SIC: 4924 Natural gas distribution
HQ: San Diego Gas & Electric Company
 8330 Century Park Ct
 San Diego CA 92123
 619 696-2000

(P-9646)
SOUTHERN CALIFORNIA GAS CO
Also Called: Southern Cal Nursing Academy
73700 Dinah Shore Dr Ste 106, Palm
Desert (92211-0815)
PHONE..............................714 262-0091
Ryan Nuqui, *Brnch Mgr*
EMP: 86
SALES (corp-wide): 16.72B **Publicly Held**
Web: www.socalgas.com
SIC: 4924 Natural gas distribution
HQ: Southern California Gas Company
 555 W 5th St Ste 14h1
 Los Angeles CA 90013
 213 244-1200

(P-9647)
SOUTHERN CALIFORNIA GAS CO
25200 Trumble Rd, Romoland
(92585-9664)
PHONE..............................213 244-1200
EMP: 107
SALES (corp-wide): 16.72B **Publicly Held**
Web: www.socalgas.com
SIC: 4924 Natural gas distribution
HQ: Southern California Gas Company
 555 W 5th St Ste 14h1
 Los Angeles CA 90013
 213 244-1200

(P-9648)
SOUTHERN CALIFORNIA GAS CO
Also Called: Regional Office
1981 W Lugonia Ave, Redlands
(92374-9796)
P.O. Box 513249 (90051-1249)
PHONE..............................909 335-7802
James Boland, *Mgr*
EMP: 386
SALES (corp-wide): 16.72B **Publicly Held**
Web: www.socalgas.com
SIC: 4924 Natural gas distribution
HQ: Southern California Gas Company
 555 W 5th St Ste 14h1
 Los Angeles CA 90013
 213 244-1200

(P-9649)
SOUTHERN CALIFORNIA GAS CO
155 S G St, San Bernardino (92410-3317)
PHONE..............................909 335-7941
Al Garcia, *Brnch Mgr*
EMP: 129
SALES (corp-wide): 16.72B **Publicly Held**
Web: www.socalgas.com
SIC: 4924 Natural gas distribution
HQ: Southern California Gas Company
 555 W 5th St Ste 14h1
 Los Angeles CA 90013
 213 244-1200

(P-9650)
SOUTHERN CALIFORNIA GAS CO

1050 Overland Ct, San Dimas
(91773-1704)
P.O. Box 513249 (90051-1249)
PHONE..............................909 305-8297
Janet Yee, *Mgr*
EMP: 279
SQ FT: 39,344
SALES (corp-wide): 16.72B **Publicly Held**
Web: www.socalgas.com
SIC: 4924 Natural gas distribution
HQ: Southern California Gas Company
 555 W 5th St Ste 14h1
 Los Angeles CA 90013
 213 244-1200

(P-9651)
SOUTHERN CALIFORNIA GAS CO
Also Called: Southern California Gas
3318 Shadylawn Dr, Duarte (91010-1667)
PHONE..............................626 358-4700
Patrick Moore, *Prin*
EMP: 86
SALES (corp-wide): 16.72B **Publicly Held**
Web: www.socalgas.com
SIC: 4924 Natural gas distribution
HQ: Southern California Gas Company
 555 W 5th St Ste 14h1
 Los Angeles CA 90013
 213 244-1200

(P-9652)
SOUTHERN CALIFORNIA GAS CO
Also Called: Honor Rancho Station
23130 Valencia Blvd, Valencia
(91355-1716)
PHONE..............................800 427-2200
Dan Skope, *VP*
EMP: 129
SALES (corp-wide): 16.72B **Publicly Held**
Web: www.socalgas.com
SIC: 4924 Natural gas distribution
HQ: Southern California Gas Company
 555 W 5th St Ste 14h1
 Los Angeles CA 90013
 213 244-1200

(P-9653)
SOUTHERN CALIFORNIA GAS CO
333 E Main St Ste J, Alhambra
(91801-3914)
PHONE..............................323 881-3587
G H Chavez, *Brnch Mgr*
EMP: 107
SALES (corp-wide): 16.72B **Publicly Held**
Web: www.socalgas.com
SIC: 4924 Natural gas distribution
HQ: Southern California Gas Company
 555 W 5th St Ste 14h1
 Los Angeles CA 90013
 213 244-1200

(P-9654)
SOUTHERN CALIFORNIA GAS CO
6738 Bright Ave, Whittier (90601-4306)
PHONE..............................562 803-3341
Richard Duran, *Brnch Mgr*
EMP: 107
SALES (corp-wide): 16.72B **Publicly Held**
Web: www.socalgas.com
SIC: 4924 Natural gas distribution
HQ: Southern California Gas Company
 555 W 5th St Ste 14h1
 Los Angeles CA 90013
 213 244-1200

(P-9655)
SOUTHERN CALIFORNIA GAS CO
8141 Gulana Ave, Venice (90293-7930)
PHONE..............................310 823-7945
James Wine, *Mgr*
EMP: 407
SALES (corp-wide): 16.72B **Publicly Held**
Web: www.socalgas.com
SIC: 4924 Natural gas distribution
HQ: Southern California Gas Company
 555 W 5th St Ste 14h1
 Los Angeles CA 90013
 213 244-1200

(P-9656)
SOUTHERN CALIFORNIA GAS CO
1600 Corporate Center Dr, Monterey Park
(91754-7626)
P.O. Box C (91756-0001)
PHONE..............................213 244-1200
Joe M Rivera, *Rgnl Mgr*
EMP: 223
SALES (corp-wide): 16.72B **Publicly Held**
Web: www.socalgas.com
SIC: 4924 Natural gas distribution
HQ: Southern California Gas Company
 555 W 5th St Ste 14h1
 Los Angeles CA 90013
 213 244-1200

(P-9657)
SOUTHERN CALIFORNIA GAS CO
Also Called: Northern Reg. Sub Base
1510 N Chester Ave, Bakersfield
(93308-2559)
PHONE..............................661 399-4431
James Pina, *Mgr*
EMP: 129
SALES (corp-wide): 16.72B **Publicly Held**
Web: www.socalgas.com
SIC: 4924 Natural gas distribution
HQ: Southern California Gas Company
 555 W 5th St Ste 14h1
 Los Angeles CA 90013
 213 244-1200

(P-9658)
SOUTHERN CALIFORNIA GAS CO
Also Called: Socalgas
12801 Tampa Ave, Northridge
(91326-1045)
PHONE..............................818 363-8542
EMP: 386
SALES (corp-wide): 16.72B **Publicly Held**
Web: www.socalgas.com
SIC: 4924 Natural gas distribution
HQ: Southern California Gas Company
 555 W 5th St Ste 14h1
 Los Angeles CA 90013
 213 244-1200

(P-9659)
SOUTHERN CALIFORNIA GAS CO
Also Called: Gas Company, The
9240 Firestone Blvd, Downey (90241-5388)
PHONE..............................562 803-7500
EMP: 493
SALES (corp-wide): 16.72B **Publicly Held**
Web: www.socalgas.com
SIC: 4924 Natural gas distribution
HQ: Southern California Gas Company
 555 W 5th St Ste 14h1
 Los Angeles CA 90013
 213 244-1200

▲ = Import ▼ = Export
◆ = Import/Export

(P-9660)

SOUTHERN CALIFORNIA GAS CO

1801 S Atlantic Blvd, Monterey Park (91754-5298)
PHONE.................213 244-1200
W J Torres, *Brnch Mgr*
EMP: 1372
SALES (corp-wide): 16.72B **Publicly Held**
Web: www.socalgas.com
SIC: 4924 Natural gas distribution
HQ: Southern California Gas Company
555 W 5th St Ste 14h1
Los Angeles CA 90013
213 244-1200

(P-9661)

SOUTHERN CALIFORNIA GAS CO

Also Called: Industry Station
920 S Stimson Ave, City Of Industry (91745-1640)
PHONE.................213 244-1200
EMP: 86
SALES (corp-wide): 16.72B **Publicly Held**
Web: www.socalgas.com
SIC: 4924 Natural gas distribution
HQ: Southern California Gas Company
555 W 5th St Ste 14h1
Los Angeles CA 90013
213 244-1200

(P-9662)

SOUTHERN CALIFORNIA GAS CO

1 Liberty, Aliso Viejo (92656-3830)
PHONE.................714 634-7221
Bill Jameson, *Brnch Mgr*
EMP: 107
SALES (corp-wide): 16.72B **Publicly Held**
Web: www.socalgas.com
SIC: 4924 Natural gas distribution
HQ: Southern California Gas Company
555 W 5th St Ste 14h1
Los Angeles CA 90013
213 244-1200

(P-9663)

SOUTHERN CALIFORNIA GAS CO

Also Called: La Jolla Station
3050 E La Jolla St, Anaheim (92806-1312)
PHONE.................213 244-1200
EMP: 129
SALES (corp-wide): 16.72B **Publicly Held**
Web: www.socalgas.com
SIC: 4924 4922 4932 Natural gas distribution ; Natural gas transmission; Gas and other services combined
HQ: Southern California Gas Company
555 W 5th St Ste 14h1
Los Angeles CA 90013
213 244-1200

(P-9664)

SOUTHERN CALIFORNIA GAS CO (HQ)

Also Called: Gas Company, The
555 W 5th St Ste 14h1, Los Angeles (90013-1010)
PHONE.................213 244-1200
Debra L Reed, *Ch*
Scott D Drury, *CEO*
Maryam Sabbaghian Brown, *Pr*
Steven D Davis, *Ex VP*
Joseph A Householder, *Ex VP*
EMP: 667 EST: 1910
SALES (est): 8.29B
SALES (corp-wide): 16.72B **Publicly Held**

Web: www.socalgas.com
SIC: 4924 4922 4932 Natural gas distribution ; Natural gas transmission; Gas and other services combined
PA: Sempra
488 8th Ave
619 696-2000

(P-9665)

SOUTHERN CALIFORNIA GAS CO

1919 S State College Blvd, Anaheim (92806-6114)
PHONE.................714 634-3065
EMP: 150
SALES (corp-wide): 16.72B **Publicly Held**
Web: www.socalgas.com
SIC: 4924 Natural gas distribution
HQ: Southern California Gas Company
555 W 5th St Ste 14h1
Los Angeles CA 90013
213 244-1200

(P-9666)

SOUTHERN CALIFORNIA GAS TOWER

555 W 5th St, Los Angeles (90013-1011)
PHONE.................213 244-1200
Ed Guiles, *Pr*
EMP: 1000 EST: 1987
SALES (est): 17.47MM
SALES (corp-wide): 16.72B **Publicly Held**
SIC: 4924 Natural gas distribution
HQ: Southern California Gas Company
555 W 5th St Ste 14h1
Los Angeles CA 90013
213 244-1200

4931 Electric And Other Services Combined

(P-9667)

AMERICAN GREEN LIGHTS LLC

Also Called: American Green Lights
10755 Scripps Poway Pkwy Ste 419, San Diego (92131-3924)
PHONE.................858 547-8837
EMP: 25 EST: 2008
SQ FT: 25,000
SALES (est): 2.59MM **Privately Held**
Web: www.americangreenlights.com
SIC: 4931 3648 3646 Electric and other services combined; Outdoor lighting equipment; Commercial lighting fixtures

(P-9668)

CALPINE ENERGY SOLUTIONS LLC (DH)

401 W A St Ste 500, San Diego (92101-7991)
PHONE.................877 273-6772
Sean Fallmer, *Pr*
Jim Wood, *Pr*
EMP: 112 EST: 2006
SALES (est): 403.3MM
SALES (corp-wide): 10.07B **Privately Held**
Web: www.calpinesolutions.com
SIC: 4931 4932 Electric and other services combined; Gas and other services combined
HQ: Calpine Corporation
717 Texas St Ste 1000
Houston TX 77002
713 830-2000

(P-9669)

CITY OF BURBANK

Also Called: Burbank Water & Power

164 W Magnolia Blvd, Burbank (91502-1772)
PHONE.................818 238-3550
Ronald E Davis, *Brnch Mgr*
EMP: 315
SALES (corp-wide): 282.12MM **Privately Held**
Web: www.burbankwaterandpower.com
SIC: 4931 4941 4911 7389 Electric and other services combined; Water supply; Electric services; Interior design services
PA: City Of Burbank
275 E Olive Ave
818 238-5800

(P-9670)

CITY OF CORONADO

Also Called: Public Services
101 B Ave, Coronado (92118-1510)
PHONE.................619 522-7380
Scott Huth, *Dir*
EMP: 117
SALES (corp-wide): 90.79MM **Privately Held**
Web: www.coronado.ca.us
SIC: 4931 9111 Electric and other services combined; Mayors' office
PA: City Of Coronado
1825 Strand Way
619 522-7300

(P-9671)

SAN DIEGO GAS & ELECTRIC CO

Also Called: Supplier Diversity
8315 Century Park Ct Ste Cp-21d, San Diego (92123-1548)
PHONE.................866 616-5565
EMP: 146
SALES (corp-wide): 16.72B **Publicly Held**
Web: www.sdge.com
SIC: 4931 4911 Electric and other services combined; Generation, electric power
HQ: San Diego Gas & Electric Company
8330 Century Park Ct
San Diego CA 92123
619 696-2000

(P-9672)

SAN DIEGO GAS & ELECTRIC CO

Also Called: Orange County Service Center
662 Camino De Los Mares, San Clemente (92673-2827)
PHONE.................949 361-8090
James Valentine, *Brnch Mgr*
EMP: 118
SALES (corp-wide): 16.72B **Publicly Held**
Web: www.sdge.com
SIC: 4931 4911 Electric and other services combined; Electric services
HQ: San Diego Gas & Electric Company
8330 Century Park Ct
San Diego CA 92123
619 696-2000

(P-9673)

SAN DIEGO GAS & ELECTRIC CO (DH)

Also Called: SDG&E
8330 Century Park Ct, San Diego (92123-1530)
PHONE.................619 696-2000
TOLL FREE: 800
Caroline A Winn, *CEO*
Jessie J Knight Junior, *Ch Bd*
Scott D Drury, *
Steven D Davis, *
J Chris Baker, *Chief Information Technology Officer**

◆ EMP: 338 EST: 1905
SALES (est): 5.6B
SALES (corp-wide): 16.72B **Publicly Held**
Web: www.sdge.com
SIC: 4931 4911 4924 Electric and other services combined; Generation, electric power; Natural gas distribution
HQ: Enova Corporation
101 Ash St
San Diego CA 92101

4932 Gas And Other Services Combined

(P-9674)

CITY OF LONG BEACH

City of Long Beach Gas & Oil
2400 E Spring St, Long Beach (90806-2285)
PHONE.................562 570-2000
Christopher J Garner, *Mgr*
EMP: 75
Web: www.longbeach.gov
SIC: 4932 9111 4924 Gas and other services combined; Mayors' office; Natural gas distribution
PA: City Of Long Beach
1800 E Wardlow Rd
562 570-6450

(P-9675)

CLEAN ENERGY FUELS CORP (PA)

4675 Macarthur Ct Ste 800, Newport Beach (92660-1895)
PHONE.................949 437-1000
Stephen A Scully, *Ch Bd*
Andrew J Littlefair, *Pr*
Robert M Vreeland, *CFO*
Mitchell W Pratt, *Corporate Secretary*
Barclay F Corbus, *Senior Vice President Strategic Development*
▲ EMP: 77 EST: 2001
SQ FT: 48,000
SALES (est): 425.16MM
SALES (corp-wide): 425.16MM **Publicly Held**
Web: www.cleanenergyfuels.com
SIC: 4932 4924 4922 Gas and other services combined; Natural gas distribution; Natural gas transmission

(P-9676)

SEMPRA (PA)

488 8th Ave, San Diego (92101-7123)
PHONE.................619 696-2000
Jeffrey W Martin, *Ch Bd*
Karen L Sedgwick, *Ex VP*
Justin C Bird, *Ex VP*
Peter R Wall *Senior, Care Vice President*
Diana L Day, *CLO*
EMP: 229 EST: 1996
SALES (est): 16.72B
SALES (corp-wide): 16.72B **Publicly Held**
Web: www.sempra.com
SIC: 4932 4911 5172 4922 Gas and other services combined; Electric services; Petroleum products, nec; Natural gas transmission

4939 Combination Utilities, Nec

(P-9677)

AGILE SOURCING PARTNERS INC

Also Called: Agile

2385 Railroad St, Corona (92878-5411)
PHONE...............................951 279-4154
Matthew G Simmons, *CEO*
Maria Thompson, *
EMP: 225 EST: 2006
SQ FT: 2,300
SALES (est): 28.46MM Privately Held
Web: www.agilesourcingpartners.com
SIC: 4939 Combination utilities, nec

(P-9678)
IMPERIAL IRRIGATION DISTRICT
81600 58th Ave, La Quinta (92253-7663)
P.O. Box 1080 (92247-1080)
PHONE...............................760 398-5811
Charles Haskin, *Genl Mgr*
EMP: 130
SALES (corp-wide): 890.06MM Privately
Held
Web: www.iid.com
SIC: 4939 4911 Combination utilities, nec;
Electric services
PA: Imperial Irrigation District
333 E Barioni Blvd
800 303-7756

(P-9679)
LOS ANGELES DEPT WTR &
PWR
Also Called: Scattergood Generation Plant
12700 Vista Del Mar, Playa Del Rey
(90293-8502)
PHONE...............................310 524-8500
Nazih Batarseh, *Brnch Mgr*
EMP: 1112
SALES (corp-wide): 9.82B Privately Held
Web: www.ladwp.com
SIC: 4939 Combination utilities, nec
HQ: Los Angeles Department Of Water And
Power
111 N Hope St
Los Angeles CA 90012
213 367-1320

(P-9680)
SAN DIEGO GAS & ELECTRIC
CO
North Coast O & M Center
5016 Carlsbad Blvd, Carlsbad
(92008-4303)
PHONE...............................760 438-6200
Jim Boland, *Dir*
EMP: 213
SALES (corp-wide): 16.72B Publicly Held
Web: www.sdge.com
SIC: 4939 4924 4911 Combination utilities,
nec; Natural gas distribution; Electric
services
HQ: San Diego Gas & Electric Company
8330 Century Park Ct
San Diego CA 92123
619 696-2000

(P-9681)
SAN DIEGO GAS & ELECTRIC
CO
Also Called: SDG&e
436 H St, Chula Vista (91910-4308)
PHONE...............................858 654-1135
Charles Johnson, *Crdt Mgr*
EMP: 290
SALES (corp-wide): 16.72B Publicly Held
Web: www.sdge.com
SIC: 4939 Combination utilities, nec
HQ: San Diego Gas & Electric Company
8330 Century Park Ct
San Diego CA 92123
619 696-2000

4941 Water Supply

(P-9682)
AMERICAN STATES WATER
COMPANY (PA)
Also Called: Awr
630 E Foothill Blvd, San Dimas
(91773-1207)
PHONE...............................909 394-3600
Robert J Sprowls, *Pr*
Anne M Holloway, *
Eva G Tang, *Corporate Secretary*
EMP: 568 EST: 1929
SALES (est): 595.7MM
SALES (corp-wide): 595.7MM Publicly
Held
Web: www.aswater.com
SIC: 4941 4911 Water supply; Electric
services

(P-9683)
CITY OF AZUSA
Also Called: Azusa Lights & Water Dept
729 N Azusa Ave, Azusa (91702-2528)
PHONE...............................626 969-4408
Joseph Hsu, *Mgr*
EMP: 88
SQ FT: 2,515
SALES (corp-wide): 74.26MM Privately
Held
Web: www.azusaca.gov
SIC: 4941 Water supply
PA: City Of Azusa
213 E Foothill Blvd
626 812-5200

(P-9684)
CITY OF GLENDALE
Also Called: Public Service Yard
800 Air Way, Glendale (91201-3012)
PHONE...............................818 548-2011
Pat Reily, *Mgr*
EMP: 74
SALES (corp-wide): 390.24MM Privately
Held
Web: www.glendaleca.gov
SIC: 4941 Water supply
PA: City Of Glendale
141 N Glendale Ave Fl 2
818 548-2085

(P-9685)
COACHLLA VLY WTR DST PUB
FCLTI
75525 Hovley Ln E, Palm Desert (92260)
PHONE...............................760 398-2651
Steve Robins, *Brnch Mgr*
EMP: 172
SALES (corp-wide): 185.22MM Privately
Held
Web: www.cvwd.org
SIC: 4941 4952 4971 Water supply;
Sewerage systems; Irrigation systems
PA: Coachella Valley Water District Public
Facilities Corporation
75515 Hovley Ln E
760 398-2651

(P-9686)
COACHLLA VLY WTR DST PUB
FCLTI (PA)
Also Called: Coachella Valley Water Dst
75515 Hovley Ln E, Palm Desert
(92211-5104)
P.O. Box 1058 (92236-1058)
PHONE...............................760 398-2651
TOLL FREE: 888
James M Barrett, *Genl Mgr*
Steve Robbins, *Interim General Manager*

Amy Ammons, *Finance*
Jim Barrett, *
Isabel Luna, *
▲ EMP: 225 EST: 1918
SALES (est): 185.22MM
SALES (corp-wide): 185.22MM Privately
Held
Web: www.cvwd.org
SIC: 4941 4971 4952 7389 Water supply;
Water distribution or supply systems for
irrigation; Sewerage systems; Water
softener service

(P-9687)
COUNTY OF LOS ANGELES
Also Called: Water & Power Department
6801 E 2nd St, Long Beach (90803-4324)
PHONE...............................213 367-3176
Victor Barra, *Dir*
EMP: 81
Web: www.lacounty.gov
SIC: 4941 9511 9631 4939 Water supply;
Air, water, and solid waste management;
Regulation, administration of utilities;
Combination utilities, nec
PA: County Of Los Angeles
500 W Temple St Ste 437
213 974-1101

(P-9688)
COUNTY OF LOS ANGELES
Also Called: Department of Public Works
900 S Fremont Ave, Alhambra
(91803-1331)
P.O. Box 1460 (91802-2460)
PHONE...............................626 458-4000
Gail Farber, *Dir*
EMP: 300
Web: www.ladpw.org
SIC: 4941 9511 4971 Water supply; Air,
water, and solid waste management;
Irrigation systems
PA: County Of Los Angeles
500 W Temple St Ste 437
213 974-1101

(P-9689)
CUCAMONGA VALLEY WATER
DST
10440 Ashford St, Rancho Cucamonga
(91730-3057)
P.O. Box Po Box638 (91729-0638)
PHONE...............................909 987-2591
Martin Zvirbulis, *CEO*
Kathleen Tiegs, *
Oscar Gonzalez, *
EMP: 100 EST: 1955
SQ FT: 15,000
SALES (est): 95.95MM Privately Held
Web: www.cvwdwater.com
SIC: 4941 Water supply

(P-9690)
DESERT WATER AGENCY FING
CORP
Also Called: DWA
1200 S Gene Autry Trl, Palm Springs
(92264-3533)
P.O. Box 1710 (92263-1710)
PHONE...............................760 323-4971
Patricia G Oyga, *CEO*
Craig Ewing Undtermined, *Prin*
EMP: 88 EST: 2007
SQ FT: 38,000
SALES (est): 41.87MM Privately Held
Web: www.dwa.org
SIC: 4941 Water supply

(P-9691)
EASTERN MNCPL WTR DST
FCLTIES
2270 Trumble Rd, Perris (92572)
P.O. Box 8300 (92572-8300)
PHONE...............................951 928-3777
Paul D Jones Ii, *CEO*
EMP: 595 EST: 2007
SALES (est): 5.88MM Privately Held
Web: www.emwd.org
SIC: 4941 Water supply

(P-9692)
EASTERN MUNICIPAL WATER
DST
19750 Evans Rd, Perris (92571-7469)
PHONE...............................951 657-7469
Paul D Jones Ii, *Brnch Mgr*
EMP: 200
SALES (corp-wide): 292.09MM Privately
Held
Web: www.emwd.org
SIC: 4941 Water supply
PA: Eastern Municipal Water District
2270 Trumble Rd
951 928-3777

(P-9693)
EASTERN MUNICIPAL WATER
DST (PA)
2270 Trumble Rd, Perris (92572)
P.O. Box 8300 (92572-8300)
PHONE...............................951 928-3777
Paul D Jones Ii, *CEO*
▲ EMP: 420 EST: 1950
SQ FT: 160,000
SALES (est): 292.09MM
SALES (corp-wide): 292.09MM Privately
Held
Web: www.emwd.org
SIC: 4941 4952 Water supply; Sewerage
systems

(P-9694)
INLAND EMPIRE UTLTIES AGCY
A M (PA)
6075 Kimball Ave, Chino (91708-9174)
P.O. Box 9020 (91709-0902)
PHONE...............................909 993-1600
Shivaji Deshmukh, *CEO*
Kati Parker, *
John Anderson, *
Michael Camacho, *
Wyatt Troxel, *
EMP: 92 EST: 1950
SQ FT: 60,000
SALES (est): 150.66MM
SALES (corp-wide): 150.66MM Privately
Held
Web: www.ieua.org
SIC: 4941 Water supply

(P-9695)
IRVINE RANCH WATER
DISTRICT (PA)
15600 Sand Canyon Ave, Irvine
(92618-3102)
P.O. Box 57000 (92619-7000)
PHONE...............................949 453-5300
Paul Jones, *Genl Mgr*
Robert Jacobson, *
EMP: 110 EST: 1961
SQ FT: 52,000
SALES (est): 88.94MM
SALES (corp-wide): 88.94MM Privately
Held
Web: www.irwd.com
SIC: 4941 4952 Water supply; Sewerage
systems

▲ = Import ▼ = Export
◆ = Import/Export

(P-9696)

IRVINE RANCH WATER DISTRICT

3512 Michelson Dr, Irvine (92612-1799)
P.O. Box 14128 (92623-4128)
PHONE..............................949 453-5300
Carl Ballard, *Dir*
EMP: 205
SALES (corp-wide): 88.94MM **Privately Held**
Web: www.irwd.com
SIC: 4941 4952 Water supply; Sewerage systems
PA: Irvine Ranch Water District Inc
15600 Sand Canyon Ave
949 453-5300

(P-9697)

JURUPA COMMUNITY SERVICES DST

11201 Harrel St, Riverside (92509)
PHONE..............................951 685-7073
Carol Mcgreevy, *Mgr*
EMP: 89
SALES (corp-wide): 14.3MM **Privately Held**
Web: www.jcsd.us
SIC: 4941 4952 Water supply; Sewerage systems
PA: Jurupa Community Services District
11201 Harrel St
951 360-5770

(P-9698)

LAS VIRGENES MUNICIPAL WTR DST

4232 Las Virgenes Rd Lbby, Calabasas (91302-3594)
PHONE..............................818 251-2100
Glen Peterson, *Pr*
Charles Caspary, *
Lee Renger, *
Jay Lewitt, *
Leonard E Polan, *
EMP: 125 **EST:** 1958
SQ FT: 10,000
SALES (est): 67.09MM **Privately Held**
Web: www.lvmwd.com
SIC: 4941 Water supply

(P-9699)

LOS ANGELES DEPT WTR & PWR (HQ)

Also Called: Ladwp
111 N Hope St, Los Angeles (90012-2607)
P.O. Box 51111 (90051-5700)
PHONE..............................213 367-1320
Martin Adams, *Genl Mgr*
David H Wright, *
Joseph A Brajevich, *
▲ **EMP:** 897 **EST:** 1902
SALES (est): 1.06B
SALES (corp-wide): 9.82B **Privately Held**
Web: www.ladwp.com
SIC: 4941 4911 Water supply; Electric services
PA: City Of Los Angeles
200 N Spring St Ste 303
213 978-0600

(P-9700)

LOS ANGELES DEPT WTR & PWR

1141 W 2nd St Bldg D, Los Angeles (90012-2007)
PHONE..............................213 367-5706
Carol Tharp, *Brnch Mgr*
EMP: 1112
SALES (corp-wide): 9.82B **Privately Held**
Web: www.ladwp.com

SIC: 4941 Water supply
HQ: Los Angeles Department Of Water And Power
111 N Hope St
Los Angeles CA 90012
213 367-1320

(P-9701)

LOS ANGELES DEPT WTR & PWR

1630 N Main St, Los Angeles (90012-1936)
PHONE..............................213 367-4211
Paul Abram, *Mgr*
▲ **EMP:** 1112
SALES (corp-wide): 9.82B **Privately Held**
Web: www.ladwp.com
SIC: 4941 4911 Water supply; Electric services
HQ: Los Angeles Department Of Water And Power
111 N Hope St
Los Angeles CA 90012
213 367-1320

(P-9702)

LOS ANGELES DEPT WTR & PWR

4030 Crenshaw Blvd, Los Angeles (90008-2533)
P.O. Box 51211 (90051-5511)
PHONE..............................323 256-8079
EMP: 1589
SALES (corp-wide): 9.82B **Privately Held**
Web: www.ladwp.com
SIC: 4941 4911 Water supply; Electric services
HQ: Los Angeles Department Of Water And Power
111 N Hope St
Los Angeles CA 90012
213 367-1320

(P-9703)

LOS ANGELES DEPT WTR & PWR

11801 Sheldon St, Sun Valley (91352-1508)
PHONE..............................213 367-1342
Kirk Bergland, *Brnch Mgr*
EMP: 1112
SALES (corp-wide): 9.82B **Privately Held**
Web: www.ladwp.com
SIC: 4941 Water supply
HQ: Los Angeles Department Of Water And Power
111 N Hope St
Los Angeles CA 90012
213 367-1320

(P-9704)

METROPLTAN WTR DST OF STHERN C

Also Called: Metropolitan Water Lavern
700 Moreno Ave, La Verne (91750-3303)
P.O. Box 54153 (90054-0153)
PHONE..............................909 593-7474
Wendell Williams, *Brnch Mgr*
EMP: 370
SALES (corp-wide): 1.48B **Privately Held**
Web: www.mwdh2o.com
SIC: 4941 Water supply
PA: The Metropolitan Water District Of
Southern California
700 N Alameda St
213 217-6000

(P-9705)

METROPLTAN WTR DST OF STHERN C

Also Called: Robert B Diemer Trtmnt Plant
3972 Valley View Ave, Yorba Linda (92886-1828)
PHONE..............................714 577-5031
Trudi Loy, *Mgr*
EMP: 76
SALES (corp-wide): 1.48B **Privately Held**
Web: www.mwdh2o.com
SIC: 4941 Water supply
PA: The Metropolitan Water District Of
Southern California
700 N Alameda St
213 217-6000

(P-9706)

MOULTON NGUEL WTR DST PUB FCLT

Also Called: Moulton Niguel Water District
26161 Gordon Rd, Laguna Hills (92653-8224)
P.O. Box 30203 (92607)
PHONE..............................949 831-2500
Richard Fiore, *Pr*
David Cain, *
John V Foley, *
EMP: 97 **EST:** 1960
SALES (est): 70.63MM **Privately Held**
Web: www.mnwd.com
SIC: 4941 4959 Water supply; Sanitary services, nec

(P-9707)

OLIVENHAIN MUNICIPAL WATER DST

1966 Olivenhain Rd, Encinitas (92024-5699)
PHONE..............................760 753-6466
Edmund Sprague, *Pr*
Robert F Topolavac, *
Kimberly A Thorner, *
George Briest, *
Rainy Selamat, *
EMP: 79 **EST:** 1959
SQ FT: 11,000
SALES (est): 60.34MM **Privately Held**
Web: www.olivenhain.com
SIC: 4941 4971 Water supply; Impounding reservoir, irrigation

(P-9708)

ORANGE COUNTY WATER DISTRICT (PA)

Also Called: Ocwd
18700 Ward St, Fountain Valley (92708-6930)
P.O. Box 8300 (92728-8300)
PHONE..............................714 378-3200
EMP: 70 **EST:** 1933
SALES (est): 180.9MM
SALES (corp-wide): 180.9MM **Privately Held**
Web: www.ocwd.com
SIC: 4941 Water supply

(P-9709)

OTAY WATER DISTRICT

2554 Sweetwater Springs Blvd, Spring Valley (91978-2004)
PHONE..............................619 670-2222
Gary Croucher, *Pr*
Jose Lopez, *
Mark Watton, *
German Alvarez, *
Manny Magana, *
EMP: 170 **EST:** 1956
SQ FT: 6,000
SALES (est): 106.19MM **Privately Held**
Web: www.otaywater.gov
SIC: 4941 1623 Water supply; Water, sewer, and utility lines

(P-9710)

PALMDALE WATER DISTRICT (PA)

2029 E Avenue Q, Palmdale (93550-4050)
PHONE..............................661 947-4111
Michael Williams, *CFO*
Dennis Hoffmeyer, *CFO*
EMP: 71 **EST:** 1918
SALES (est): 34.57MM **Privately Held**
Web: www.palmdalewater.org
SIC: 4941 Water supply

(P-9711)

RANCHO CALIFORNIA WATER DST (PA)

Also Called: Rcwd
42135 Winchester Rd, Temecula (92590-4800)
P.O. Box 9017 (92589-9017)
PHONE..............................951 296-6900
William E Plummer, *Prin*
Bennet Drake, *
Stephen J Corona, *Pr*
Ralph Daily, *Pr*
John E Hoagland, *VP*
EMP: 143 **EST:** 1965
SQ FT: 71,000
SALES (est): 67.4MM
SALES (corp-wide): 67.4MM **Privately Held**
Web: www.ranchowater.com
SIC: 4941 Water supply

(P-9712)

SAN DIEGO COUNTY WATER AUTH

610 W 5th Ave, Escondido (92025-4093)
PHONE..............................760 480-1991
Brendan Sheehan, *Pr*
EMP: 184
SALES (corp-wide): 91.76MM **Privately Held**
Web: www.sdcwa.org
SIC: 4941 Water supply
PA: San Diego County Water Authority
4677 Overland Ave
858 522-6600

(P-9713)

SAN DIEGO COUNTY WATER AUTH (PA)

4677 Overland Ave, San Diego (92123-1233)
PHONE..............................858 522-6600
Maureen Stapleton, *Genl Mgr*
Dennis Cushman, *
Eric Sandler, *
Sandy Kerl, *
Mark Muir, *
▲ **EMP:** 90 **EST:** 1944
SQ FT: 26,000
SALES (est): 91.76MM
SALES (corp-wide): 91.76MM **Privately Held**
Web: www.sdcwa.org
SIC: 4941 Water supply

(P-9714)

SAN GABRIEL VALLEY WATER ASSN

725 N Azusa Ave, Azusa (91702-2528)
PHONE..............................626 815-1305
Carol Williams, *Ex Sec*
EMP: 100 **EST:** 1955
SALES (est): 244.87K **Privately Held**
Web: www.sgvwa.org
SIC: 4941 Water supply

PRODUCTS & SVCS

(P-9715)
SAN GABRIEL VALLEY WATER CO
8440 Nuevo Ave, Fontana (92335-3824)
P.O. Box 987 (92334-0987)
PHONE..............................909 822-2201
Mike Mcgraw, *Mgr*
EMP: 116
SQ FT: 2,727
SALES (corp-wide): 48.82MM **Privately Held**
Web: www.sgvwater.com
SIC: 4941 Water supply
PA: San Gabriel Valley Water Co.
11142 Garvey Ave
626 448-6183

(P-9716)
SAN GABRIEL VALLEY WATER CO (PA)
Also Called: Fontana Water Company
11142 Garvey Ave, El Monte (91733-2498)
P.O. Box 6010 (91734-2010)
PHONE..............................626 448-6183
R H Nicholson Junior, *Ch Bd*
Michael L Whitehead, *Pr*
David Batt, *VP*
Frank A Lo Guidice, *VP Opers*
T J Ryan, *Sec*
EMP: 125 **EST:** 1936
SQ FT: 30,000
SALES (est): 48.82MM
SALES (corp-wide): 48.82MM **Privately Held**
Web: www.sgvwater.com
SIC: 4941 Water supply

(P-9717)
SANTA CLARITA VALLEY WTR AGCY
Also Called: Santa Clarita Water Division
26521 Summit Cir, Santa Clarita (91350-3049)
PHONE..............................661 259-2737
Mauricio E Guardado Junior, *Prin*
EMP: 160
SALES (corp-wide): 83.27MM **Privately Held**
Web: www.yourscvwater.com
SIC: 4941 Water supply
PA: Santa Clarita Valley Water Agency
27234 Bouquet Canyon Rd
661 297-1600

(P-9718)
SANTA CLRITA VLY WTR AGCY FING
27234 Bouquet Canyon Rd, Santa Clarita (91350-2173)
PHONE..............................661 259-2737
Tom Campbell, *CEO*
Ronald J Kelly, *
April Jacobs, *
Dan Masnada, *
William Cooper, *
EMP: 120 **EST:** 1962
SQ FT: 1,000
SALES (est): 7.84MM **Privately Held**
Web: www.yourscvwater.com
SIC: 4941 Water supply

(P-9719)
SANTA MARGARITA WATER DISTRICT
26101 Antonio Pkwy, Rcho Sta Marg (92688-5505)
P.O. Box 7005 (92690-7005)
PHONE..............................949 459-6400
Daniel Ferns, *Brnch Mgr*

EMP: 135
SALES (corp-wide): 87.95MM **Privately Held**
Web: www.smwd.com
SIC: 4941 Water supply
PA: Santa Margarita Water District
26111 Antonio Pkwy
949 459-6400

(P-9720)
SANTA MARGARITA WATER DISTRICT (PA)
26111 Antonio Pkwy, Rcho Sta Marg (92688-5596)
PHONE..............................949 459-6400
Daniel R Ferons, *Managing Member*
EMP: 70 **EST:** 1964
SQ FT: 5,600
SALES (est): 55.73MM
SALES (corp-wide): 55.73MM **Privately Held**
Web: www.smwd.com
SIC: 4941 Water supply

(P-9721)
SWEETWTER AUTH EMPLYEES CMMTTE (PA)
505 Garrett Ave, Chula Vista (91910-5505)
P.O. Box 2328 (91912)
PHONE..............................619 420-1413
Mark Rogers, *Ex Dir*
James Smyth, *
Teresa Thomas, *
W D Pocklington, *
Margaret C Welsh, *
EMP: 112 **EST:** 2004
SALES (est): 55.39MM
SALES (corp-wide): 55.39MM **Privately Held**
Web: www.sweetwater.org
SIC: 4941 Water supply

(P-9722)
SWWC UTILITIES INC (DH)
1325 N Grand Ave Ste 100, Covina (91724-4044)
EMP: 173 **EST:** 2007
SQ FT: 32,000
SALES (est): 34.23MM **Privately Held**
Web: www.swwc.com
SIC: 4941 4952 Water supply; Sewerage systems
HQ: Southwest Water Company
1325 N Grand Ave Ste 100
Covina CA 91724
626 543-2500

(P-9723)
THE METROPOLITAN WATER DISTRICT OF SOUTHERN CALIFORNIA (PA)
Also Called: Mwd
700 N Alameda St, Los Angeles (90012-3352)
P.O. Box 54153 (90054-0153)
PHONE..............................213 217-6000
EMP: 850 **EST:** 1928
SALES (est): 1.48B
SALES (corp-wide): 1.48B **Privately Held**
Web: www.mwdh2o.com
SIC: 4941 Water supply

(P-9724)
VALLECITOS WATER DISTRICT FINANCING CORPORATION (HQ)
Also Called: Vallecitos Water District
201 Vallecitos De Oro, San Marcos (92069-1453)
PHONE..............................760 744-0460

EMP: 96 **EST:** 1955
SALES (est): 66.29MM **Privately Held**
Web: www.vwd.org
SIC: 4941 4952 Water supply; Sewerage systems
PA: Vallecitos Water District
201 Vallecitos De Oro

4952 Sewerage Systems

(P-9725)
HADRONEX INC (PA)
Also Called: Smartcover Systems
2110 Enterprise St, Escondido (92029-2000)
PHONE..............................760 291-1980
David Drake, *Pr*
Gregory Quist, *CEO*
EMP: 33 **EST:** 2006
SALES (est): 36.59MM **Privately Held**
Web: www.smartcoversystems.com
SIC: 4952 3594 Sewerage systems; Fluid power motors

4953 Refuse Systems

(P-9726)
AGRI SERVICE INC
2141 Oceanside Blvd, Oceanside (92054-4405)
PHONE..............................760 295-6255
Mary Matava, *Pr*
Francesca San Diego, *
EMP: 24 **EST:** 1979
SQ FT: 1,700
SALES (est): 2.36MM **Privately Held**
Web: www.agriserviceinc.com
SIC: 4953 2875 Recycling, waste materials; Potting soil, mixed

(P-9727)
ARACO ENTERPRISES LLC
Also Called: Athens Environmental Services
9189 De Garmo Ave, Sun Valley (91352-2609)
PHONE..............................818 767-0675
Michael R Arakelian, *
EMP: 400 **EST:** 2017
SALES (est): 8.2MM **Privately Held**
SIC: 4953 Garbage: collecting, destroying, and processing

(P-9728)
ARAKELIAN ENTERPRISES INC
Also Called: Athens Services
15045 Salt Lake Ave, City Of Industry (91746-3315)
PHONE..............................626 336-3636
Ron Arakelian Junior, *Owner*
EMP: 413
SALES (corp-wide): 199.65MM **Privately Held**
Web: www.athensservices.com
SIC: 4953 Rubbish collection and disposal
PA: Arakelian Enterprises, Inc.
14048 Valley Blvd
626 336-3636

(P-9729)
ARAKELIAN ENTERPRISES INC (PA)
Also Called: Athens Services
14048 Valley Blvd, City Of Industry (91746-2801)
P.O. Box 60009 (91716)
PHONE..............................626 336-3636
Ron Arakelian Junior, *CEO*
Michael Arakelian, *

Kevin Hanifin, *
Gary Clifford, *
Dennis Chiappetta, *
EMP: 244 **EST:** 1958
SQ FT: 10,000
SALES (est): 199.65MM
SALES (corp-wide): 199.65MM **Privately Held**
Web: www.athensservices.com
SIC: 4953 Recycling, waste materials

(P-9730)
ARAKELIAN ENTERPRISES INC
687 Iowa Ave, Riverside (92507-1610)
PHONE..............................951 342-3300
Sal Orozco, *Mgr*
EMP: 131
SALES (corp-wide): 199.65MM **Privately Held**
Web: www.athensservices.com
SIC: 4953 Recycling, waste materials
PA: Arakelian Enterprises, Inc.
14048 Valley Blvd
626 336-3636

(P-9731)
ATHENS DISPOSAL COMPANY INC (PA)
14048 Valley Blvd, La Puente (91746-2801)
P.O. Box 60009 (91716-0009)
PHONE..............................626 336-3636
Ron Arakelian Senior, *Pr*
Ron Arakelian Junior, *VP*
EMP: 350 **EST:** 1958
SALES (est): 22.27MM
SALES (corp-wide): 22.27MM **Privately Held**
Web: www.athensservices.com
SIC: 4953 Recycling, waste materials

(P-9732)
BEST WAY DISPOSAL CO INC
Also Called: Advance Disposal Company
17105 Mesa St, Hesperia (92345-5155)
P.O. Box 400997 (92340-0997)
PHONE..............................760 244-9773
Robert Bath, *Ch Bd*
Sheila Bath, *
EMP: 75 **EST:** 1965
SALES (est): 7.78MM **Privately Held**
Web: www.advancedisposal.com
SIC: 4953 Garbage: collecting, destroying, and processing

(P-9733)
BFI WASTE SYSTEMS N AMER INC
Also Called: Site 906
9200 Glenoaks Blvd, Sun Valley (91352-2613)
PHONE..............................323 321-1722
Doug Moore, *Mgr*
EMP: 73
SALES (corp-wide): 14.96B **Publicly Held**
SIC: 4953 Garbage: collecting, destroying, and processing
HQ: Bfi Waste Systems Of North America, Inc.
2394 E Camelback Rd
Phoenix AZ 85016

(P-9734)
BURRTEC WASTE INDUSTRIES INC (HQ)
Also Called: Burrtec
9890 Cherry Ave, Fontana (92335-5298)
PHONE..............................909 429-4200
Cole Burr, *Pr*
▲ **EMP:** 150 **EST:** 1978

▲ = Import ▼ = Export
◆ = Import/Export

SQ FT: 10,000
SALES (est): 307.49MM
SALES (corp-wide): 320.11MM **Privately Held**
Web: www.burrtec.com
SIC: 4953 4212 Rubbish collection and disposal; Local trucking, without storage
PA: Burrtec Waste Group, Inc.
9890 Cherry Ave
909 429-4200

(P-9735)
CALIFORNIA MARINE CLEANING INC (PA)
2049 Main St, San Diego (92113-2216)
P.O. Box 13653 (92170-3653)
PHONE.................................619 231-8788
Matthew R Carr, *Pr*
Hazel Carr, *
EMP: 110 **EST:** 1985
SQ FT: 10,000
SALES (est): 41.23MM
SALES (corp-wide): 41.23MM **Privately Held**
Web: www.marinecleaning.com
SIC: 4953 Hazardous waste collection and disposal

(P-9736)
CALIFORNIA WASTE SERVICES LLC
621 W 152nd St, Gardena (90247-2732)
PHONE.................................310 538-5998
Eric Casper, *Pr*
EMP: 120 **EST:** 1999
SQ FT: 20,000
SALES (est): 24.33MM **Privately Held**
Web: www.californiawasteservices.com
SIC: 4953 Refuse collection and disposal services

(P-9737)
CALMET INC (PA)
Also Called: Metropolitan Waste Disposal
7202 Petterson Ln, Paramount (90723-2022)
PHONE.................................323 721-8120
Thomas K Blackman, *Pr*
William Kalpakoff, *VP*
Kris Kazarian, *Sec*
Gary Kazarian, *Treas*
EMP: 180 **EST:** 1953
SQ FT: 38,000
SALES (est): 3.41MM
SALES (corp-wide): 3.41MM **Privately Held**
Web: www.calmet.com
SIC: 4953 4212 Rubbish collection and disposal; Local trucking, without storage

(P-9738)
CEDARWOOD-YOUNG COMPANY (PA)
Also Called: Allan Company
14620 Joanbridge St, Baldwin Park (91706-1750)
PHONE.................................626 962-4047
Jason Young, *Pr*
Stephen Young, *Ch*
Michael Ochniak, *CFO*
Richard Hubbard, *VP Opers*
Don Rogers, *VP Mktg*
◆ **EMP:** 175 **EST:** 1963
SQ FT: 4,350
SALES (est): 252.16MM
SALES (corp-wide): 252.16MM **Privately Held**
Web: www.allancompany.com
SIC: 4953 Recycling, waste materials

(P-9739)
COVANTA LONG BCH RNWBLE ENRGY
118 Pier S Ave, Long Beach (90802-1039)
PHONE.................................562 436-0636
▲ **EMP:** 82 **EST:** 2013
SALES (est): 5.25MM
SALES (corp-wide): 187MM **Publicly Held**
SIC: 4953 Recycling, waste materials
HQ: Reworld Waste, Llc
445 S St
Morristown NJ 07960
862 345-5000

(P-9740)
CR&R INCORPORATED
Also Called: Perris Disposal Company
1706 Goetz Rd, Perris (92570-6274)
P.O. Box 1208 (92572-1208)
PHONE.................................951 634-8079
TOLL FREE: 800
Ed Campos, *Brnch Mgr*
EMP: 170
SALES (corp-wide): 450.25MM **Privately Held**
Web: www.crrwasteservices.com
SIC: 4953 Recycling, waste materials
PA: Cr&R Incorporated
11292 Western Ave
714 826-9049

(P-9741)
DOWNTOWN DIVERSION INC
9081 Tujunga Ave, Sun Valley (91352-1516)
PHONE.................................818 252-0019
Mike Hammer, *Pr*
Myan Spaccarelli, *
EMP: 100 **EST:** 2003
SALES (est): 415.07K **Privately Held**
SIC: 4953 Recycling, waste materials

(P-9742)
E J HARRISON & SONS INC
Also Called: Harrison, E J & Sons Recycling
1589 Lirio Ave, Ventura (93004-3227)
PHONE.................................805 647-1414
TOLL FREE: 800
Ken Keys, *Genl Mgr*
EMP: 173
SALES (corp-wide): 24.61MM **Privately Held**
Web: www.ejharrison.com
SIC: 4953 2611 Rubbish collection and disposal; Pulp mills
PA: E. J. Harrison & Sons, Inc.
5275 Colt St
805 647-1414

(P-9743)
ECOBAT CALIFORNIA RE LLC
720 S 7th Ave, City Of Industry (91746-3124)
PHONE.................................626 937-3201
Thyson Jordan, *Managing Member*
Craig Clark, *
Brandon James Hunt, *
EMP: 300 **EST:** 1950
SALES (est): 2.07MM **Privately Held**
Web: www.ecobat.com
SIC: 4953 Recycling, waste materials

(P-9744)
ECOLOGY RECYCLING SERVICES LLC
785 E M St, Colton (92324-3911)
PHONE.................................909 370-1318
EMP: 177
SALES (corp-wide): 13.87B **Publicly Held**

Web: www.aim-recyclingca.com
SIC: 4953 Recycling, waste materials
HQ: Ecology Recycling Services, Llc
16700 Vly View Ave Ste 34
La Mirada CA 90638
855 212-9959

(P-9745)
EDCO DISPOSAL CORPORATION (PA)
Also Called: La Mesa Disposal
2755 California Ave, Signal Hill (90755-3304)
PHONE.................................619 287-7555
Steve South, *CEO*
Edward Burr, *
Sandra Burr, *
EMP: 250 **EST:** 1967
SQ FT: 8,000
SALES (est): 134.33MM
SALES (corp-wide): 134.33MM **Privately Held**
Web: www.edcodisposal.com
SIC: 4953 Rubbish collection and disposal

(P-9746)
IMS ELECTRONICS RECYCLING INC
Also Called: I M S Electonics Recycling
12455 Kerran St Ste 300, Poway (92064-8834)
PHONE.................................858 679-1555
▼ **EMP:** 102
SIC: 4953 Recycling, waste materials

(P-9747)
IMS RECYCLING SERVICES INC (PA)
Also Called: IMS Recycling Services
2697 Main St, San Diego (92113-3612)
P.O. Box 13666 (92170-3666)
PHONE.................................619 231-2521
Robert M Davis, *CEO*
Ruth Davis, *
Theodora Davis Inman, *
Deborah Odle, *
▼ **EMP:** 70 **EST:** 1954
SQ FT: 25,000
SALES (est): 81.98MM
SALES (corp-wide): 81.98MM **Privately Held**
Web: www.cpgrp.com
SIC: 4953 Recycling, waste materials

(P-9748)
LOONEY BINS INC (HQ)
12153 Montague St, Pacoima (91331-2210)
PHONE.................................818 485-8200
Myan Spaccarelli, *Pr*
Phyllis Shukiar, *
Jerry Lucera, *
EMP: 70 **EST:** 1995
SQ FT: 1,000
SALES (est): 26.87MM
SALES (corp-wide): 20.43B **Publicly Held**
SIC: 4953 Garbage: collecting, destroying, and processing
PA: Waste Management, Inc.
800 Capitol St Ste 3000
713 512-6200

(P-9749)
MARBORG INDUSTRIES (PA)
728 E Yanonali St, Santa Barbara (93103-3233)
P.O. Box 4127 (93140-4127)
PHONE.................................805 963-1852
Mario Borgatello Junior, *Pr*

David Borgatello, *
EMP: 250 **EST:** 1974
SALES (est): 48.23MM
SALES (corp-wide): 48.23MM **Privately Held**
Web: www.marborg.com
SIC: 4953 7359 7699 4212 Rubbish collection and disposal; Portable toilet rental ; Septic tank cleaning service; Local trucking, without storage

(P-9750)
MARBORG RECOVERY LP
14470 Calle Real, Goleta (93117-9732)
PHONE.................................805 963-1852
Brian Borgatello, *Pt*
EMP: 250 **EST:** 2016
SALES (est): 7.19MM
SALES (corp-wide): 48.23MM **Privately Held**
Web: www.marborg.com
SIC: 4953 Recycling, waste materials
PA: Marborg Industries
728 E Yanonali St
805 963-1852

(P-9751)
MP ENVIRONMENTAL SVCS INC (PA)
3400 Manor St, Bakersfield (93308-1451)
P.O. Box 80358 (93380)
PHONE.................................800 458-3036
Dawn Calderwood, *Pr*
▲ **EMP:** 117 **EST:** 1991
SQ FT: 8,000
SALES (est): 62.05MM **Privately Held**
Web: www.mpenviro.com
SIC: 4953 4213 8748 7699 Hazardous waste collection and disposal; Trucking, except local; Environmental consultant; Tank repair and cleaning services

(P-9752)
NORCAL WASTE SERVICES INC
3514 Emery St, Los Angeles (90023-3908)
PHONE.................................626 357-8666
John Harabedian, *Genl Mgr*
EMP: 100 **EST:** 1982
SALES (est): 1.33MM **Privately Held**
SIC: 4953 Rubbish collection and disposal

(P-9753)
ORANGE CNTY SNTTION DST FING C (PA)
10844 Ellis Ave, Fountain Valley (92708-7018)
P.O. Box 8127 (92728-8127)
PHONE.................................714 962-2411
James Herberg, *Genl Mgr*
James Ruth, *
▲ **EMP:** 300 **EST:** 1954
SALES (est): 315.43MM
SALES (corp-wide): 315.43MM **Privately Held**
Web: www.ocsan.gov
SIC: 4953 Waste materials, disposal at sea

(P-9754)
PALM SPRINGS DISPOSAL SERVICES
4690 E Mesquite Ave, Palm Springs (92264-3510)
P.O. Box 2711 (92263-2711)
PHONE.................................760 327-1351
Frederic Wade, *CEO*
James Cunningham, *
Ray Wade, *
Mike Jaycox, *
EMP: 82 **EST:** 1972

SQ FT: 2,000
SALES (est): 8.98MM **Privately Held**
Web: www.palmspringsdisposal.com
SIC: **4953** Recycling, waste materials

(P-9755)
PJBS HOLDINGS INC (PA)
Also Called: Benz - One Complete Operation
1401 Goodrick Dr, Tehachapi (93561-1532)
P.O. Box 1750 (93581-1750)
PHONE..............................661 822-5273
Paul Benz, *CEO*
Louis Visco, *
Joan Benz, *
EMP: 75 EST: 1975
SQ FT: 4,500
SALES (est): 4.93MM
SALES (corp-wide): 4.93MM **Privately
Held**
Web: www.benz.blue
SIC: **4953 4212** Refuse collection and
disposal services; Petroleum haulage, local

(P-9756)
**POTENTIAL INDUSTRIES INC
(PA)**
720 East E St, Wilmington (90744-6014)
P.O. Box 293 (90748-0293)
PHONE..............................310 549-5901
Anthony J Fan, *Pr*
Phillip C Chen, *Vice Chairman*
Daniel J Domonoske, *
Henry J Chen, *
Jessie Chen, *
◆ EMP: 149 EST: 1975
SQ FT: 45,000
SALES (est): 52.5MM
SALES (corp-wide): 52.5MM **Privately
Held**
Web: www.potentialindustries.com
SIC: **4953 5093** Recycling, waste materials;
Scrap and waste materials

(P-9757)
R PLANET EARTH LLC
3200 Fruitland Ave, Vernon (90058-3718)
PHONE..............................213 320-0601
EMP: 135 EST: 2013
SALES (est): 8.64MM **Privately Held**
Web: www.rplanetearth.com
SIC: **4953** 2611 Recycling, waste materials;
Pulp mills, mechanical and recycling
processing

(P-9758)
**RAINBOW DISPOSAL CO INC
(HQ)**
Also Called: Rainbow Refuse Recycling
17121 Nichols Ln, Huntington Beach
(92647-5719)
P.O. Box 1026 (92647-1026)
PHONE..............................714 847-3581
Jerry Moffatt, *CEO*
Stan Tkaczyck, *
EMP: 115 EST: 1956
SQ FT: 6,000
SALES (est): 10.12MM
SALES (corp-wide): 14.96B **Publicly Held**
SIC: **4953** Garbage: collecting, destroying,
and processing
PA: Republic Services, Inc.
18500 N Allied Way
480 627-2700

(P-9759)
RECOLOGY LOS ANGELES
Also Called: Recology
9189 De Garmo Ave, Sun Valley
(91352-2609)
PHONE..............................818 767-0675

EMP: 400 EST: 2006
SALES (est): 22.28MM **Privately Held**
SIC: **4953** Garbage: collecting, destroying,
and processing

(P-9760)
**RECYCLER CORE COMPANY
INC**
Also Called: Northwest Recycler Core
2727 Kansas Ave, Riverside (92507-2638)
PHONE..............................951 276-1687
Kenneth Meier, *Pr*
Gisela Meier, *
Ruth Harris, *
▲ EMP: 100 EST: 1984
SQ FT: 280,000
SALES (est): 16.01MM **Privately Held**
Web: www.rccauto.com
SIC: **4953** Recycling, waste materials

(P-9761)
SA RECYCLING LLC (PA)
Also Called: SA Recycling
2411 N Glassell St, Orange (92865-2717)
PHONE..............................714 632-2000
George Adams, *CEO*
George Adams, *Managing Member*
Mark Sweetman, *
◆ EMP: 160 EST: 2007
SQ FT: 40,000
SALES (est): 454.24MM **Privately Held**
Web: www.sarecycling.com
SIC: **4953** Recycling, waste materials

(P-9762)
SANITEC INDUSTRIES INC
10700 Sherman Way, Burbank
(91505-1042)
PHONE..............................818 523-1942
James Harkess, *Pr*
▲ EMP: 75 EST: 2003
SQ FT: 200,000
SALES (est): 677.46K **Privately Held**
Web: www.sanitecind.com
SIC: **4953** 5047 Medical waste disposal;
Medical and hospital equipment

(P-9763)
**SANITTION DSTRCTS LOS
ANGLES C**
1955 Workman Mill Rd, Whittier
(90601-1415)
P.O. Box 4998 (90607-4998)
PHONE..............................562 908-4288
Steve Mcguin, *Mgr*
Grace Robinson Chan, *Genl Mgr*
EMP: 1698 EST: 2007
SALES (est): 47.61MM
SALES (corp-wide): 423.61MM **Privately
Held**
Web: www.lacsd.org
SIC: **4953** Sanitary landfill operation
PA: Los Angeles County Sanitation Districts
1955 Workman Mill Rd
562 699-7411

(P-9764)
**SILICON PROCESSING AND
TRADING INC**
Also Called: SRS
322 N Aviador St, Camarillo (93010-8302)
PHONE..............................805 388-8683
▲ EMP: 72
SIC: **4953** Recycling, waste materials

(P-9765)
SMC GREASE SPECIALIST INC
1600 W Pellisier Rd, Colton (92324-3301)
P.O. Box 79200 (92877-0173)

PHONE..............................951 788-6042
Salvatore Coco, *Pr*
EMP: 27 EST: 2003
SQ FT: 2,500
SALES (est): 5.03MM **Privately Held**
Web: www.smcgrease.com
SIC: **4953** 2992 Recycling, waste materials;
Oils and greases, blending and
compounding

(P-9766)
SOLAG INCORPORATED
Also Called: Solag Disposal Co
31641 Ortega Hwy, San Juan Capistrano
(92675)
PHONE..............................949 728-1206
Clifford Ronnenberg, *Ch Bd*
Patricia Leyes, *
EMP: 122 EST: 1958
SALES (est): 2.75MM
SALES (corp-wide): 450.25MM **Privately
Held**
SIC: **4953 4212** Rubbish collection and
disposal; Local trucking, without storage
PA: Cr&R Incorporated
11292 Western Ave
714 826-9049

(P-9767)
**STAR SCRAP METAL COMPANY
INC**
1509 S Bluff Rd, Montebello (90640-6601)
PHONE..............................562 921-5045
Rose Starow Stein, *Pr*
Allen Stein, *
▼ EMP: 70 EST: 1974
SQ FT: 600
SALES (est): 1.78MM **Privately Held**
Web: www.starscrap.com
SIC: **4953** Recycling, waste materials

(P-9768)
TALCO PLASTICS INC (PA)
1000 W Rincon St, Corona (92878-9228)
PHONE..............................951 531-2000
John L Shedd Senior, *Ch*
John L Shedd Junior, *Pr*
Bob Shedd, *
Ron Petty, *
William O'grady, *VP*
EMP: 85 EST: 1972
SQ FT: 110,000
SALES (est): 23.05MM
SALES (corp-wide): 23.05MM **Privately
Held**
Web: www.talcoplastics.com
SIC: **4953** 2821 Recycling, waste materials;
Plastics materials and resins

(P-9769)
UNITED PACIFIC WASTE
6500 Stanford Ave, Los Angeles
(90001-1536)
P.O. Box 2924 (92628-2924)
PHONE..............................562 699-7600
Michael Kandilian, *Pr*
Mike Kandilian, *
Shawna Kandilian, *
EMP: 70 EST: 2001
SQ FT: 3,500
SALES (est): 5.12MM **Privately Held**
Web: www.crrwasteservices.com
SIC: **4953** 4213 Garbage: collecting,
destroying, and processing; Contract
haulers

(P-9770)
**USA WASTE OF CALIFORNIA
INC**
Also Called: Los Angeles City Hauling

9081 Tujunga Ave, Sun Valley
(91352-1516)
P.O. Box 541 (90078-0541)
PHONE..............................818 252-3112
Jim Fish, *CEO*
EMP: 100
SALES (corp-wide): 20.43B **Publicly Held**
SIC: **4953** Recycling, waste materials
HQ: Usa Waste Of California, Inc.
11931 Foundation Pl # 200
Gold River CA 95670
916 387-1400

(P-9771)
VARNER BROS INC
1808 Roberts Ln, Bakersfield (93308-2228)
P.O. Box 80427 (93380-0427)
PHONE..............................661 399-2944
Vernon Varner, *Sec*
Elvey L Varner, *
EMP: 70 EST: 1959
SQ FT: 12,000
SALES (est): 11.45MM **Privately Held**
Web: www.varnerbros.com
SIC: **4953** Garbage: collecting, destroying,
and processing

(P-9772)
VERDECO RECYCLING INC
8685 Bowers Ave, South Gate
(90280-3317)
PHONE..............................323 537-4617
Robert Bindner, *CEO*
Alexander Delnik, *
Carmen Chivu, *
◆ EMP: 25 EST: 2011
SALES (est): 23.51MM
SALES (corp-wide): 1.4MM **Privately Held**
Web: www.verdecorecycling.com
SIC: **4953** 3089 Recycling, waste materials;
Plastics containers, except foam
HQ: Verdeco Recycling Holdings Llc
8685 Bowers Ave
South Gate CA 90280
323 537-4617

(P-9773)
WARE DISPOSAL INC
1451 Manhattan Ave, Fullerton
(92831-5221)
PHONE..............................714 834-0234
Judith Helaine Ware, *CEO*
Ben Ware, *
Jay Ware, *
EMP: 120 EST: 1970
SQ FT: 48,900
SALES (est): 22.52MM **Privately Held**
Web: www.waredisposal.com
SIC: **4953** Refuse collection and disposal
services

(P-9774)
WASTE MANAGEMENT CAL INC
Also Called: Waste Management
1001 W Bradley Ave, El Cajon
(92020-1501)
PHONE..............................619 596-5100
TOLL FREE: 800
Rex Buck, *Prin*
EMP: 165
SQ FT: 2,000
SALES (corp-wide): 20.43B **Publicly Held**
SIC: **4953** Recycling, waste materials
HQ: Waste Management Of California, Inc.
9081 Tujunga Ave
Sun Valley CA 91352
877 836-6526

(P-9775)
WASTE MANAGEMENT CAL INC
Also Called: Waste Management
2141 Oceanside Blvd, Oceanside
(92054-4405)
PHONE..............................760 439-2824
John Lusignan, *Mgr*
EMP: 140
SQ FT: 4,500
SALES (corp-wide): 20.43B **Publicly Held**
SIC: 4953 4212 Garbage: collecting,
destroying, and processing; Local trucking,
without storage
HQ: Waste Management Of California, Inc.
9081 Tujunga Ave
Sun Valley CA 91352
877 836-6526

(P-9776)
WASTE MANAGEMENT CAL INC
Also Called: Waste Management
10910 Dawson Canyon Rd, Corona
(92883-5020)
PHONE..............................951 277-1740
Damon De Frates, *Brnch Mgr*
EMP: 127
SALES (corp-wide): 20.43B **Publicly Held**
SIC: 4953 Garbage: collecting, destroying,
and processing
HQ: Waste Management Of California, Inc.
9081 Tujunga Ave
Sun Valley CA 91352
877 836-6526

(P-9777)
WASTE MANAGEMENT CAL INC
Also Called: Waste Management
1200 W City Ranch Rd, Palmdale
(93551-4456)
PHONE..............................661 947-7197
Carl Mccarthy, *Mgr*
EMP: 127
SALES (corp-wide): 20.43B **Publicly Held**
SIC: 4953 Rubbish collection and disposal
HQ: Waste Management Of California, Inc.
9081 Tujunga Ave
Sun Valley CA 91352
877 836-6526

(P-9778)
WASTE MANAGEMENT CAL INC
Also Called: Waste Management
2801 N Madera Rd, Simi Valley
(93065-6208)
PHONE..............................805 522-7023
Scott Tignac, *Mgr*
EMP: 140
SALES (corp-wide): 20.43B **Publicly Held**
SIC: 4953 Recycling, waste materials
HQ: Waste Management Of California, Inc.
9081 Tujunga Ave
Sun Valley CA 91352
877 836-6526

(P-9779)
WASTE MANAGEMENT CAL INC (HQ)
Also Called: Waste Management
9081 Tujunga Ave, Sun Valley
(91352-1516)
PHONE..............................877 836-6526
EMP: 230 **EST:** 1953
SQ FT: 35,000
SALES (est): 404.08MM
SALES (corp-wide): 20.43B **Publicly Held**
SIC: 4953 Garbage: collecting, destroying,
and processing
PA: Waste Management, Inc.
800 Capitol St Ste 3000
713 512-6200

(P-9780)
WASTE MGT COLLECTN RECYCL INC
Also Called: Waste Management
16122 Construction Cir E, Irvine
(92606-4403)
PHONE..............................949 451-2600
Fidel Gutierrez, *Brnch Mgr*
EMP: 124
SALES (corp-wide): 20.43B **Publicly Held**
SIC: 4953 4212 Recycling, waste materials;
Garbage collection and transport, no
disposal
HQ: Waste Management Collection And
Recycling, Inc.
1001 Fannin St Ste 4000
Houston TX 77002

(P-9781)
WASTE MGT COLLECTN RECYCL INC
Also Called: Waste Management
13940 Live Oak Ave, Baldwin Park
(91706-1321)
PHONE..............................626 960-7551
Rick Decaiva, *Mgr*
EMP: 86
SALES (corp-wide): 20.43B **Publicly Held**
SIC: 4953 4212 Rubbish collection and
disposal; Local trucking, without storage
HQ: Waste Management Collection And
Recycling, Inc.
1001 Fannin St Ste 4000
Houston TX 77002

(P-9782)
WASTE MGT COLLECTN RECYCL INC
Also Called: Waste Management
1449 W Rosecrans Ave, Gardena
(90249-2639)
P.O. Box 1428 (90249-0428)
PHONE..............................310 532-6511
Dave Hauser, *Prin*
EMP: 121
SALES (corp-wide): 20.43B **Publicly Held**
SIC: 4953 5064 Garbage: collecting,
destroying, and processing; Garbage
disposals
HQ: Waste Management Collection And
Recycling, Inc.
1001 Fannin St Ste 4000
Houston TX 77002

(P-9783)
WASTE MGT COLLECTN RECYCL INC
Also Called: Waste Management
17700 Indian St, Moreno Valley
(92551-9511)
PHONE..............................951 242-0421
Scott Jenkins, *Mgr*
EMP: 121
SALES (corp-wide): 20.43B **Publicly Held**
SIC: 4953 Recycling, waste materials
HQ: Waste Management Collection And
Recycling, Inc.
1001 Fannin St Ste 4000
Houston TX 77002

(P-9784)
ZEREP MANAGEMENT CORPORATION (PA)
17445 Railroad St, City Of Industry
(91748-1026)
PHONE..............................626 855-5522
Manuel Perez, *CEO*
EMP: 245 **EST:** 1970
SQ FT: 4,000

SALES (est): 37.94MM
SALES (corp-wide): 37.94MM **Privately Held**
Web: www.valleyvistaservices.com
SIC: 4953 4212 Refuse collection and
disposal services; Local trucking, without
storage

4959 Sanitary Services, Nec

(P-9785)
AMPCO CONTRACTING INC
17991 Cowan, Irvine (92614-6025)
PHONE..............................949 955-2255
Andrew Pennor, *Ch*
Tim Vitta, *
Reggie Kama, *
Joe Ha, *
EMP: 220 **EST:** 2004
SALES (est): 33.35MM **Privately Held**
Web: www.ampcocontracting.com
SIC: 4959 1795 1794 Environmental cleanup
services; Wrecking and demolition work;
Excavation and grading, building
construction

(P-9786)
CLEANSTREET LLC
1918 W 169th St, Gardena (90247-5254)
PHONE..............................800 225-7316
TOLL FREE: 800
Christopher Valerian, *Pr*
EMP: 194 **EST:** 1965
SALES (est): 10.62MM
SALES (corp-wide): 536.39MM **Privately Held**
Web: www.sweepingcorp.com
SIC: 4959 Sweeping service: road, airport,
parking lot, etc.
HQ: Sca Of Ca, Llc
4141 Rockside Rd Ste 100
Seven Hills OH 44131
216 777-2750

(P-9787)
JONSET LLC
Also Called: Sunset Property Services
16251 Construction Cir W, Irvine
(92606-4412)
PHONE..............................949 551-5151
John Howhannesian, *Pr*
EMP: 96 **EST:** 1968
SQ FT: 6,000
SALES (est): 7.95MM
SALES (corp-wide): 536.39MM **Privately Held**
SIC: 4959 7349 Sweeping service: road,
airport, parking lot, etc.; Janitorial service,
contract basis
HQ: Sca Of Ca, Llc
4141 Rockside Rd Ste 100
Seven Hills OH 44131
216 777-2750

(P-9788)
LOS ANGLES CNTY SNTTION DSTRCT (PA)
Also Called: L.A.coO.
1955 Workman Mill Rd, Whittier
(90601-1415)
P.O. Box 4998 (90607)
PHONE..............................562 699-7411
Stephen Maguin, *Genl Mgr*
EMP: 850 **EST:** 1924
SALES (est): 423.61MM
SALES (corp-wide): 423.61MM **Privately Held**
Web: www.lasd.org

SIC: 4959 Sanitary services, nec

(P-9789)
SULLIVAN INTERNATIONAL GROUP INC
Also Called: Sullivan
2750 Womble Rd Ste 100, San Diego
(92106-6114)
PHONE..............................619 260-1432
EMP: 132
SIC: 4959 Toxic or hazardous waste cleanup

4971 Irrigation Systems

(P-9790)
CITY OF ANAHEIM
Anaheim City Utilities Div
201 S Anaheim Blvd, Anaheim
(92805-3826)
P.O. Box 3069 (92803-3069)
PHONE..............................714 254-0125
Ed Aghjayan, *Brnch Mgr*
EMP: 100
SALES (corp-wide): 782.72MM **Privately Held**
Web: www.anaheim.net
SIC: 4971 9111 Water distribution or supply
systems for irrigation; Mayors' office
PA: City Of Anaheim
200 S Anaheim Blvd
714 765-5162

(P-9791)
HUNTER INDUSTRIES INCORPORATED (PA)
Also Called: Hunter
1940 Diamond St, San Marcos
(92078-5190)
PHONE..............................760 744-5240
Gregory R Hunter, *CEO*
Stephanie C Brownell, *
◆ **EMP:** 193 **EST:** 1993
SQ FT: 450,000
SALES (est): 423.39MM **Privately Held**
Web: www.hunterindustries.com
SIC: 4971 3089 Irrigation systems; Fittings
for pipe, plastics

(P-9792)
OAK SPRINGS NURSERY INC
13761 Eldridge Ave, Sylmar (91342-1764)
P.O. Box 922906 (91392-2906)
PHONE..............................818 367-5832
Manuel Cacho, *Pr*
EMP: 90 **EST:** 1993
SALES (est): 9.37MM **Privately Held**
Web: www.oaksprings.com
SIC: 4971 0781 Irrigation systems;
Landscape services

(P-9793)
PALO VERDE IRRIGATION DISTRICT
180 W 14th Ave, Blythe (92225-2714)
PHONE..............................760 922-3144
Ed Smith, *Genl Mgr*
Janice Love, *CLLTR*
EMP: 85 **EST:** 1923
SQ FT: 8,125
SALES (est): 4.72MM **Privately Held**
Web: www.pvid.org
SIC: 4971 Water distribution or supply
systems for irrigation

(P-9794)
VISTA IRRIGATION DISTRICT
Also Called: Vid
1391 Engineer St, Vista (92083)

PHONE..............................760 597-3100
John Amodeo, *Genl Mgr*
Roy Coox, *
EMP: 99 **EST:** 1923
SQ FT: 2,500
SALES (est): 43.19MM **Privately Held**
Web: www.vidwater.org
SIC: 4971 Water distribution or supply
    systems for irrigation

5012 Automobiles And Other Motor Vehicles

(P-9795)
A-Z BUS SALES INC (PA)
Also Called: John Deere Authorized Dealer
1900 S Riverside Ave, Colton (92324-3344)
PHONE..............................951 781-7188
Edwin John Landherr, *CEO*
James Reynolds, *
▼ **EMP:** 90 **EST:** 1984
SQ FT: 20,000
SALES (est): 49.64MM
SALES (corp-wide): 49.64MM **Privately
Held**
Web: www.a-zbus.com
SIC: 5012 5082 Busses; Construction and
    mining machinery

(P-9796)
ABC BUS INC
1485 Dale Way, Costa Mesa (92626-3918)
PHONE..............................714 444-5888
Dane Cornell, *CEO*
EMP: 99
SALES (corp-wide): 84.36MM **Privately
Held**
Web: www.abc-companies.com
SIC: 5012 4173 Busses; Bus terminal and
    service facilities
HQ: Abc Bus, Inc.
    1506 30th St Nw
    Faribault MN 55021
    507 334-1871

(P-9797)
ADESA CORPORATION LLC
2175 Cactus Rd, San Diego (92154-8002)
PHONE..............................619 661-5565
Dale Mcilroy, *Mgr*
EMP: 102
Web: www.adesa.com
SIC: 5012 5521 Automobile auction; Used
    car dealers
HQ: Adesa Corporation, Llc
    11299 Illinois St
    Carmel IN 46032

(P-9798)
ALEXANDER DENNIS INCORPORATED
31566 Railroad Canyon Rd Ste 3, Canyon
Lake (92587-9446)
PHONE..............................951 244-9429
Colin Robertson, *CEO*
Stephen Walsh, *
▲ **EMP:** 2000 **EST:** 2004
SALES (est): 5.81MM
SALES (corp-wide): 2.05B **Privately Held**
Web: www.alexander-dennis.com
SIC: 5012 Busses
HQ: Alexander Dennis Limited
    9 Central Boulevard
    Larbert FK5 4

(P-9799)
AMERICAN HONDA MOTOR CO INC (HQ)
Also Called: American Honda
1919 Torrance Blvd, Torrance (90501-2746)
P.O. Box 2200 (90509-2200)
PHONE..............................310 783-2000
Noriya Kaihara, *CEO*
Lyle Shroyer, *VP*
Yuichi Shimizu, *Sec*
Mikio Himuro, *CFO*
◆ **EMP:** 2375 **EST:** 1959
SALES (est): 12.82B **Privately Held**
Web: www.honda.com
SIC: 5012 3732 Automobiles; Jet skis
PA: Honda Motor Co., Ltd.
    2-1-1, Minamiaoyama

(P-9800)
AQUIRECORPS NORWALK AUTO AUCTN
Also Called: Aquire
12405 Rosecrans Ave, Norwalk
(90650-5056)
PHONE..............................562 864-7464
Rj Romero, *Ch Bd*
Lou Rudich, *
Chuck Doskow, *
Steve Fleurant, *
EMP: 125 **EST:** 1979
SQ FT: 55,000
SALES (est): 7.05MM **Privately Held**
Web: www.norwalkautoauction.com
SIC: 5012 Automobile auction

(P-9801)
CALIFRNIA AUTO DALERS EXCH LLC
Also Called: Riverside Auto Auction
1320 N Tustin Ave, Anaheim (92807-1686)
PHONE..............................714 996-2400
Tim Van Dam, *Genl Mgr*
EMP: 400 **EST:** 1985
SALES (est): 17.09MM
SALES (corp-wide): 16.61B **Privately Held**
SIC: 5012 Automobile auction
HQ: Manheim Investments, Inc.
    6205 Pachtree Dunwoody Rd
    Atlanta GA 30328
    866 626-4346

(P-9802)
HYUNDAI MOTOR AMERICA (HQ)
10550 Talbert Ave, Fountain Valley
(92708-6032)
P.O. Box 20850 (92728-0850)
PHONE..............................714 965-3000
Randy Parker, *CEO*
Jerry Flannery, *Legal*
Brian Smith, *COO*
Youngil Ko, *CFO*
Michael Poirier, *VP*
◆ **EMP:** 454 **EST:** 1985
SQ FT: 469,000
SALES (est): 1.1B **Privately Held**
Web: www.hyundaiusa.com
SIC: 5012 5511 Automobiles and other
    motor vehicles; Automobiles, new and used
PA: Hyundai Motor Company
    12 Heolleung-Ro, Seocho-Gu

(P-9803)
INLAND KENWORTH INC (HQ)
9730 Cherry Ave, Fontana (92335-5257)
PHONE..............................909 823-9955
TOLL FREE: 800
Leigh Parker, *Ch*
William Currie, *
Les Ziegler, *
Jim Beidrwieden, *
▼ **EMP:** 105 **EST:** 1934
SQ FT: 60,000
SALES (est): 74.55MM

SALES (corp-wide): 1.1MM **Privately Held**
Web: www.inland-group.com
SIC: 5012 7538 5013 7513 Trucks,
    commercial; Diesel engine repair;
    automotive; Truck parts and accessories;
    Truck rental and leasing, no drivers
PA: Inland Industries Ltd
    2482 Douglas Rd
    604 291-6021

(P-9804)
LOS ANGELES TRUCK CENTERS LLC
Also Called: Los Angeles Freightliner
13800 Valley Blvd, Fontana (92335-5216)
PHONE..............................909 510-4000
Ricardo Flores, *Mgr*
EMP: 200
SALES (corp-wide): 233.56MM **Privately
Held**
Web: www.velocitytruckcenters.com
SIC: 5012 7538 5531 5511 Trucks,
    commercial; General automotive repair
    shops; Auto and home supply stores; New
    and used car dealers
PA: Los Angeles Truck Centers, Llc
    2429 Peck Rd
    562 447-1200

(P-9805)
MARATHON INDUSTRIES INC
Also Called: Marathon Truck Bodies
20950 Centre Pointe Pkwy, Santa Clarita
(91350-2975)
P.O. Box 800279 (91380-0279)
PHONE..............................661 286-1520
Chad Hess, *Pr*
Roger K Hess, *
Tom Garcia, *
EMP: 145 **EST:** 1993
SALES (est): 27.5MM **Privately Held**
Web: www.marathontruckbody.com
SIC: 5012 3713 Automobiles and other
    motor vehicles; Truck and bus bodies

(P-9806)
MIRAMAR FORD TRUCK SALES INC
Also Called: NationaLease
6066 Miramar Rd, San Diego (92121-2591)
PHONE..............................619 272-5340
Michael Buscher, *Pr*
Richard Harrigan, *
Michael Maury, *
EMP: 74 **EST:** 1982
SQ FT: 22,000
SALES (est): 3.66MM
SALES (corp-wide): 233.56MM **Privately
Held**
Web: www.miramartrkctr.com
SIC: 5012 5013 7513 Trucks, commercial;
    Truck parts and accessories; Truck rental
    and leasing, no drivers
PA: Los Angeles Truck Centers, Llc
    2429 Peck Rd
    562 447-1200

(P-9807)
NISSAN NORTH AMERICA INC
Nissan Division
1683 Sunflower Ave, Costa Mesa
(92626-1540)
P.O. Box 5555 (92628-5555)
PHONE..............................714 433-3700
FAX: 714 433-3746
EMP: 150
SALES (corp-wide): 103.12B **Privately
Held**
SIC: 5012 Automotive brokers
HQ: Nissan North America Inc
    1 Nissan Way

Franklin TN 37067
615 725-1000

(P-9808)
UTILITY TRAILER CALIFORNIA LLC (PA)
15567 Valley Blvd, Fontana (92335-6351)
PHONE..............................877 275-4887
Craig M Bennett, *
Stephen F Bennet, *
Harold C Bennett, *
Jeffrey J Bennett, *
EMP: 100 **EST:** 2007
SALES (est): 11.45MM **Privately Held**
Web: www.utilitytrailersales.com
SIC: 5012 5013 5531 5561 Trailers for
    passenger vehicles; Automotive supplies
    and parts; Auto and truck equipment and
    parts; Travel trailers; automobile, new and
    used

5013 Motor Vehicle Supplies And New Parts

(P-9809)
4 WHEEL PARTS WHOLESALERS LLC
400 W Artesia Blvd, Compton (90220-5501)
PHONE..............................310 900-7725
▼ **EMP:** 152 **EST:** 2010
SALES (est): 9.95MM **Privately Held**
Web: www.4wheelparts.com
SIC: 5013 Automotive supplies and parts

(P-9810)
AMPURE CHARGING SYSTEMS INC (PA)
1333 S Mayflower Ave Ste 100, Monrovia
(91016-5265)
PHONE..............................626 415-4000
John Thomas, *CEO*
Doug Mcelroy, *CFO*
EMP: 85 **EST:** 2018
SALES (est): 52.58MM
SALES (corp-wide): 52.58MM **Privately
Held**
Web: www.evsolutions.com
SIC: 5013 Automobile service station
    equipment

(P-9811)
APW KNOX-SEEMAN WAREHOUSE INC (HQ)
1073 E Artesia Blvd, Carson (90746-1601)
PHONE..............................310 604-4373
Tong Y Suhr, *CEO*
Susan Suhr, *
▲ **EMP:** 98 **EST:** 1972
SQ FT: 32,000
SALES (est): 23.09MM
SALES (corp-wide): 23.25MM **Privately
Held**
Web: www.apwks.com
SIC: 5013 5531 Automotive supplies and
    parts; Automotive parts
PA: Auto Parts Warehouse, Inc.
    16941 Keegan Ave
    800 913-6119

(P-9812)
ASIAN EUROPEAN PRODUCTS INC
Also Called: E P I
18071 Fitch Fl 250, Irvine (92614-6085)
P.O. Box 28989 (92799-8989)
PHONE..............................949 553-3900
▲ **EMP:** 150

SIC: 5013 Automotive supplies and parts

(P-9813)
AUTOMOTIVE AFTERMARKET INC
Also Called: Completes Plus
15912 Hawthorne Blvd, Lawndale
(90260-2644)
PHONE..................310 793-0046
Guy Cooper, *Brnch Mgr*
EMP: 72
SALES (corp-wide): 4.9MM Privately Held
Web: www.completesplus.com
SIC: 5013 Truck parts and accessories
PA: Automotive Aftermarket, Inc.
10425 S La Cienega Blvd
310 703-5700

(P-9814)
AZIMC INVESTMENTS INC
Also Called: IMC
8901 Canoga Ave, Canoga Park
(91304-1512)
PHONE..................818 678-1200
Kristen Wright, *Sec*
Thomas Kliman, *
William Giles, *
◆ EMP: 250 EST: 1962
SALES (est): 13.83MM
SALES (corp-wide): 745.08MM Privately Held
SIC: 5013 Automotive supplies and parts
HQ: Interamerican Motor, Llc
8901 Canoga Ave
Canoga Park CA 91304
800 874-8925

(P-9815)
BBK PERFORMANCE INC
Also Called: Gripp
27427 Bostik Ct, Temecula (92590-3698)
PHONE..................951 296-1771
Brian Murphy, *Pr*
Ken Murphy, *
EMP: 75 EST: 1988
SALES (est): 9.61MM Privately Held
Web: www.bbkperformance.com
SIC: 5013 5531 Automotive supplies and parts; Automotive parts

(P-9816)
BESTOP BAJA LLC
Also Called: Baja Designs
2950 Norman Strasse Rd, San Marcos
(92069-5946)
PHONE..................760 560-2252
John Larson, *Managing Member*
▲ EMP: 115 EST: 1992
SQ FT: 14,000
SALES (est): 14.27MM
SALES (corp wide): 61.0MM Privately Held
Web: www.bajadesigns.com
SIC: 5013 5571 3714 Motorcycle parts; Motorcycle parts and accessories; Motor vehicle electrical equipment
PA: Bestop, Inc.
333 Centennial Pkwy Ste B
303 464-2548

(P-9817)
BRAGG INVESTMENT COMPANY INC
Also Called: Coastline Equipment
1930 Lockwood St, Oxnard (93036-2679)
PHONE..................805 485-2106
Buck Baird, *Mgr*
EMP: 116
SQ FT: 17,900
SALES (corp-wide): 489.53MM Privately Held

Web: www.braggcompanies.com
SIC: 5013 7629 7359 5082 Trailer parts and accessories; Business machine repair, electric; Lawn and garden equipment rental ; Construction and mining machinery
PA: Bragg Investment Company, Inc.
6251 N Paramount Blvd
562 984-2400

(P-9818)
CAL-STATE AUTO PARTS INC (PA)
Also Called: Auto Pride
1361 N Red Gum St, Anaheim
(92806-1318)
PHONE..................714 630-5950
Richard J Deblasi, *CEO*
Steven Brooker, *
John Mcmillin, *CFO*
▲ EMP: 105 EST: 1971
SQ FT: 76,000
SALES (est): 44.73MM
SALES (corp-wide): 44.73MM Privately Held
Web: www.calstateautoparts.com
SIC: 5013 Automotive supplies and parts

(P-9819)
COMPETITION CLUTCH INC
1570 Lakeview Loop, Anaheim
(92807-1819)
P.O. Box 380 (30012-0380)
PHONE..................800 809-6598
Vaughn Christopher Jewell, *CEO*
Kimberly Mccool, *CFO*
Carla Oglesby, *Sec*
▲ EMP: 23 EST: 2003
SALES (est): 12.07MM
SALES (corp-wide): 12.07MM Privately Held
Web: www.competitionclutch.com
SIC: 5013 3568 Clutches; Clutches, except vehicular
PA: Wharton Automotive Group Inc.
2590 N San Miguel Dr

(P-9820)
CUSTOM CHROME MANUFACTURING
Also Called: Custom Chrome
9228 Rush St, South El Monte
(91733-2522)
PHONE..................408 825-5000
Dan Cook, *Prin*
Dan Cook, *CEO*
Bill Prescott, *
◆ EMP: 306 EST: 1990
SALES (est): 4.42MM Privately Held
Web: www.customchrome.com
SIC: 5013 Motorcycle parts
HQ: Dae-Il Usa, Inc.
112 Robert Young Blvd
Murray KY 42071

(P-9821)
DENSO PDTS & SVCS AMERICAS INC (DH)
Also Called: Dsca
3900 Via Oro Ave, Long Beach
(90810-1868)
PHONE..................310 834-6352
Yoshihiko Yamada, *CEO*
Hirokatsu Yamashita, *Pr*
Roy Nakaue, *Ex VP*
Peter Clotz, *VP Sls*
Eugene Stark, *VP Prd*
◆ EMP: 478 EST: 1971
SQ FT: 235,000
SALES (est): 221.87MM Privately Held
Web: www.densoautocare.com

SIC: 5013 7361 5075 3714 Automotive supplies and parts; Employment agencies; Warm air heating and air conditioning; Motor vehicle parts and accessories
HQ: Denso International America, Inc.
24777 Denso Dr
Southfield MI 48033
248 350-7500

(P-9822)
DNA SPECIALTY INC
200 W Artesia Blvd, Compton (90220-5500)
PHONE..................310 767-4070
James Choi, *CEO*
▲ EMP: 90 EST: 1984
SQ FT: 80,000
SALES (est): 24.13MM Privately Held
Web: www.dnaspecialty.com
SIC: 5013 3714 Wheels, motor vehicle; Wheels, motor vehicle

(P-9823)
EGGE MACHINE COMPANY INC (PA)
8403 Allport Ave, Santa Fe Springs
(90670-2109)
PHONE..................562 945-3419
Robert Egge, *Pr*
Kathy Weaver, *
Judy Egge, *
▲ EMP: 23 EST: 1915
SQ FT: 10,000
SALES (est): 5.16MM
SALES (corp-wide): 5.16MM Privately Held
Web: www.egge.com
SIC: 5013 3592 5531 Automotive supplies and parts; Valves; Automotive parts

(P-9824)
EMPI INC
Also Called: Euro Motorparts Group
301 E Orangethorpe Ave, Anaheim
(92801-1032)
PHONE..................714 446-9606
Peter Guile, *CEO*
Robert Keller, *
Todd Tyler, *
EMP: 89 EST: 2018
SQ FT: 127,000
SALES (est): 25.53MM Privately Held
Web: www.empius.com
SIC: 5013 3713 Automotive supplies and parts; Specialty motor vehicle bodies

(P-9825)
FIND IT PARTS INC
Also Called: Finditparts
11858 La Grange Ave, Los Angeles
(90025-5273)
PHONE..................888 312-8812
David Seewack, *CEO*
Scott Spiwak, *
Ron Hendrixson, *CPO*
Mohammad Wardak, *
EMP: 75 EST: 2002
SALES (est): 15.05MM Privately Held
Web: www.finditparts.com
SIC: 5013 Automotive supplies and parts

(P-9826)
G-GLOBAL INC (PA)
Also Called: G Global Alpha
2695 Customhouse Ct, San Diego
(92154-7645)
PHONE..................619 661-6292
Fidel J Gutierrez Junior, *CEO*
◆ EMP: 167 EST: 1985
SQ FT: 36,000
SALES (est): 13.2MM

SALES (corp-wide): 13.2MM Privately Held
Web: www.g-global.com
SIC: 5013 4731 Automotive supplies and parts; Truck transportation brokers

(P-9827)
HANSON DISTRIBUTING COMPANY (PA)
975 W 8th St, Azusa (91702-2246)
PHONE..................626 224-9800
Daniel Hanson, *CEO*
EMP: 115 EST: 1973
SQ FT: 160,000
SALES (est): 49.54MM
SALES (corp-wide): 49.54MM Privately Held
Web: www.hansondistributing.com
SIC: 5013 Automotive supplies and parts

(P-9828)
HIGHLINE AFTERMARKET LLC
Also Called: Atlantic Pacific Automotive
10385 San Sevaine Way Ste B, Jurupa Valley (91752-3274)
PHONE..................951 361-0331
Scott Hultman, *Mgr*
EMP: 57
SQ FT: 37,000
SALES (corp-wide): 741.18MM Privately Held
Web: www.highlinewarren.com
SIC: 5013 6512 2992 3519 Automotive supplies and parts; Commercial and industrial building operation; Lubricating oils ; Parts and accessories, internal combustion engines
HQ: Highline Aftermarket, Llc
4500 Malone Rd
Memphis TN 38118

(P-9829)
HINO MOTORS MFG USA INC
4550 Wineville Ave, Jurupa Valley
(91752-3723)
PHONE..................951 727-0286
Debra Martinas, *Brnch Mgr*
EMP: 93
Web: www.hmmusa.com
SIC: 5013 Truck parts and accessories
HQ: Hino Motors Manufacturing U.S.A., Inc.
45501 Twelve Mile Rd
Novi MI 48377

(P-9830)
IAP WEST INC
Also Called: Durago
20036 S Via Baron, Rancho Dominguez
(90220-6105)
PHONE..................310 667-9720
Michel Berg, *CEO*
Louis Berg, *Pr*
Sharon Berg, *Sec*
John Kelley, *CFO*
◆ EMP: 71 EST: 1981
SQ FT: 80,000
SALES (est): 11.82MM Privately Held
Web: www.iapperformance.com
SIC: 5013 Automotive engines and engine parts

(P-9831)
KEYSTONE AUTOMOTIVE WAREHOUSE
Also Called: KEYSTONE AUTOMOTIVE WAREHOUSE
15640 Cantu Galleano Ranch Rd, Eastvale
(91752-1404)
PHONE..................951 277-5237
Michael Decicco, *Prin*

EMP: 100
SALES (corp-wide): 13.87B **Publicly Held**
Web: www.keystoneautomotive.com
SIC: 5013 Radiators
HQ: Keystone Automotive Warehouse, Inc.
44 Tunkhannock Ave
Exeter PA 18643
570 655-4514

(P-9832)
MAXZONE VEHICLE LIGHTING CORP (HQ)
Also Called: Depo Auto Parts
15889 Slover Ave Unit A, Fontana
(92337-7299)
PHONE.....................909 822-3288
Polo Hsu, Pr
◆ EMP: 50 EST: 1997
SQ FT: 32,000
SALES (est): 32.22MM **Privately Held**
Web: www.maxzone.com
SIC: 5013 3714 Automotive supplies and
parts; Motor vehicle electrical equipment
PA: Depo Auto Parts Ind. Co., Ltd.
No. 20-3, Nanshi Ln.

(P-9833)
MERIDIAN RACK & PINION INC
Also Called: Meridian
9980 Huennekens St Ste 200, San Diego
(92121-2968)
PHONE.....................888 875-0026
Renee Thomas-jacobs, CEO
Dara Greaney, VP
Matt Glauber, Pr
Chris Struempler, CFO
▲ EMP: 130 EST: 1989
SALES (est): 9.97MM **Privately Held**
Web: www.buyautoparts.com
SIC: 5013 5961 Automotive supplies and
parts; Mail order house, order taking office
only

(P-9834)
METROPOLITAN AUTOMOTIVE WAREHOUSE
Also Called: Auto Value
535 Tennis Court Ln, San Bernardino
(92408-1615)
P.O. Box 1529 (92402-1529)
PHONE.....................909 885-2886
▼ EMP: 700
SIC: 5013 Automotive supplies and parts

(P-9835)
MOBIS PARTS AMERICA LLC (HQ)
Also Called: Mobis Ventures Sv
10550 Talbert Ave Fl 4, Fountain Valley
(92708-6031)
PHONE.....................786 515-1101
Jae Hee Kim, Pr
Chanmo Son, *
Gee Tae Jung, *
◆ EMP: 90 EST: 2003
SALES (est): 224.39MM **Privately Held**
Web: www.mobisusa.com
SIC: 5013 3714 Automotive supplies and
parts; Motor vehicle body components and
frame
PA: Hyundai Mobis Co., Ltd.
203 Teheran-Ro, Gangnam-Gu

(P-9836)
NSV INTERNATIONAL CORP
1250 E 29th St, Signal Hill (90755-1800)
P.O. Box 14660 (90853-4660)
PHONE.....................562 438-3836
Victor Harris, CEO

Stephan Humphries, *
Isabel Palafox, *
EMP: 100 EST: 2011
SQ FT: 1,200
SALES (est): 2.87MM **Privately Held**
Web: www.nsvauto.com
SIC: 5013 Automotive supplies

(P-9837)
PARTS AUTHORITY LLC
Also Called: Fast Undercar
4277 Transport St, Ventura (93003-5657)
PHONE.....................805 676-3410
Randy Buller, Pr
EMP: 110
SALES (corp-wide): 745.08MM **Privately Held**
Web: www.fastundercar.com
SIC: 5013 Automotive supplies and parts
PA: Parts Authority, Llc
3 Dakota Dr Ste 110
833 380-8511

(P-9838)
PHOENIX WHEEL COMPANY INC
Also Called: Hre Performance Wheels
2611 Commerce Way Ste D, Vista
(92081-8455)
PHONE.....................760 598-1960
Christian J Luhnow, CEO
Alan Peltier, *
Phillip Hillhouse, *
▲ EMP: 40 EST: 1993
SQ FT: 58,000
SALES (est): 17.47MM **Privately Held**
Web: www.hrewheels.com
SIC: 5013 3714 Wheels, motor vehicle;
Motor vehicle wheels and parts

(P-9839)
PREVOST CAR (US) INC
3384 De Forest Cir, Mira Loma
(91752-3253)
PHONE.....................951 360-2550
Tim Willmuth, Brnch Mgr
EMP: 57
SALES (corp-wide): 52.58B **Privately Held**
Web: www.prevostcar.com
SIC: 5013 4173 5012 3711 Automotive
supplies and parts; Maintenance facilities,
buses; Busses; Buses, all types, assembly
of
HQ: Prevost Car (Us) Inc.
7817 National Service Rd
Greensboro NC 27409
908 222-7211

(P-9840)
R1 CONCEPTS INC (PA)
Also Called: Zion Automotive Group
13140 Midway Pl, Cerritos (90703-2233)
PHONE.....................714 777-2323
Phouc Martin Trinh, Pr
Thang Trinh, COO
◆ EMP: 25 EST: 2004
SALES (est): 22.47MM
SALES (corp-wide): 22.47MM **Privately Held**
Web: www.r1concepts.com
SIC: 5013 3714 Automotive engines and
engine parts; Motor vehicle brake systems
and parts

(P-9841)
RALCO HOLDINGS INC (DH)
13861 Rosecrans Ave, Santa Fe Springs
(90670-5207)
PHONE.....................949 440-5094
Michael Moore, CEO
EMP: 159 EST: 2009

SALES (est): 28.73MM **Privately Held**
SIC: 5013 3751 Motorcycle parts;
Motorcycle accessories
HQ: Velocity Pooling Vehicle, Llc
651 Canyon Drive Ste 100
Coppell TX

(P-9842)
RALLY HOLDINGS LLC
17771 Mitchell N, Irvine (92614-6028)
PHONE.....................817 919-6833
EMP: 1151 EST: 2006
SALES (est): 3.08MM **Privately Held**
SIC: 5013 3751 Motorcycle parts;
Motorcycle accessories
HQ: Ralco Holdings, Inc.
13861 Rosecrans Ave
Santa Fe Springs CA 90670
949 440-5094

(P-9843)
RAMCAR BATTERIES INC
2700 Carrier Ave, Commerce (90040-2572)
PHONE.....................323 726-1212
Clifford J Crowe, CEO
Jaime Agustines, *
◆ EMP: 42 EST: 1919
SQ FT: 90,000
SALES (est): 2.31MM **Privately Held**
Web: www.ramcarbattery.com
SIC: 5013 3691 Automotive batteries; Lead
acid batteries (storage batteries)

(P-9844)
REELS INC
Also Called: Mr Bug
301 E Orangethorpe Ave, Anaheim
(92801-1032)
PHONE.....................714 446-9606
▲ EMP: 80 EST: 1971
SALES (est): 1.64MM **Privately Held**
Web: www.empius.com
SIC: 5013 3714 Automotive supplies and
parts; Motor vehicle parts and accessories

(P-9845)
RICHARD HUETTER INC
Also Called: Pacific Parts International
21050 Osborne St, Canoga Park
(91304-1744)
PHONE.....................818 700-8001
Richard Huetter, CEO
Maria L Huetter, *
▲ EMP: 70 EST: 1982
SQ FT: 30,000
SALES (est): 4.63MM **Privately Held**
Web: www.pacificparts.net
SIC: 5013 Automotive supplies and parts

(P-9846)
SADDLEMEN CORPORATION
Also Called: Saddlemen
17801 S Susana Rd, Compton
(90221-5411)
PHONE.....................310 638-1222
David Echert, CEO
▲ EMP: 140 EST: 1987
SQ FT: 20,000
SALES (est): 12.75MM **Privately Held**
Web: www.saddlemen.com
SIC: 5013 3751 Motorcycle parts;
Motorcycle accessories

(P-9847)
SCAT ENTERPRISES INC
1400 Kingsdale Ave Ste B, Redondo Beach
(90278-3983)
PHONE.....................310 370-5501
Philip T Lieb, Pr
Craig Schenasi, *

◆ EMP: 65 EST: 1967
SALES (est): 24.68MM **Privately Held**
Web: www.scatenterprises.com
SIC: 5013 3714 Automotive supplies and
parts; Motor vehicle parts and accessories

(P-9848)
SHRIN LLC
Also Called: Coverking
900 E Arlee Pl, Anaheim (92805-5645)
P.O. Box 9860 (92812)
PHONE.....................714 850-0303
Narendra Gupta, Managing Member
◆ EMP: 100 EST: 1986
SQ FT: 90,000
SALES (est): 23.09MM **Privately Held**
Web: www.coverking.com
SIC: 5013 3714 Automotive supplies and
parts; Motor vehicle parts and accessories

(P-9849)
SILLA AUTOMOTIVE LLC
Also Called: Silla Cooling Systems
1217 W Artesia Blvd, Compton
(90220-5305)
PHONE.....................800 624-1499
▲ EMP: 200
SIC: 5013 Radiators

(P-9850)
SPECIALTY INTERIOR MFG INC
Also Called: Sim Ideation
16751 Millikan Ave, Irvine (92606-5009)
PHONE.....................714 296-8618
Courtney Tassie, CEO
EMP: 35 EST: 2012
SQ FT: 4,500
SALES (est): 1.98MM **Privately Held**
SIC: 5013 2531 Automotive supplies and
parts; Seats, aircraft

(P-9851)
SUPERWINCH LLC
Also Called: Superwinch
320 W Covina Blvd, San Dimas
(91773-2907)
PHONE.....................800 323-2031
◆ EMP: 40 EST: 1970
SALES (est): 1.67MM **Privately Held**
Web: www.superwinch.com
SIC: 5013 3531 Automotive supplies;
Winches

(P-9852)
VGP HOLDINGS LLC
9520 John St, Santa Fe Springs
(90670-2904)
PHONE.....................562 906-6200
EMP: 288
SIC: 5013 Automotive engines and engine
parts
HQ: Vgp Holdings Llc
100 Valvoline Way Pmb 200
Lexington KY 40509
859 357-7777

(P-9853)
WABASH NATIONAL TRLR CTRS INC
16025 Slover Ave, Fontana (92337-7368)
PHONE.....................765 771-5300
Joe Newfield, Mgr
EMP: 46
SALES (corp-wide): 2.54B **Publicly Held**
Web: www.onewabash.com
SIC: 5013 5012 7539 3715 Motor vehicle
supplies and new parts; Automobiles and
other motor vehicles; Automotive repair
shops, nec; Truck trailers
HQ: Wabash National Trailer Centers, Inc.
1000 Sagamore Pkwy S

Lafayette IN 47905
765 771-5300

(P-9854)

YOSHIMURA RES & DEV AMER INC

5420 Daniels St Ste A, Chino (91710-9012)
PHONE.....................909 628-4722
Fujio Yoshimura, *Pr*
Suehiro Watanabe, *
Don Sakakura, *
▲ **EMP:** 100 **EST:** 1975
SQ FT: 12,000
SALES (est): 24.8MM **Privately Held**
Web: www.yoshimura-rd.com
SIC: 5013 Motorcycle parts

5014 Tires And Tubes

(P-9855)

FALKEN TIRE HOLDINGS INC

Also Called: Falken Tires
8656 Haven Ave, Rancho Cucamonga
(91730-9103)
PHONE.....................800 723-2553
Richard Smallwood, *Pr*
▲ **EMP:** 80 **EST:** 2006
SALES (est): 4.04MM **Privately Held**
SIC: 5014 Automobile tires and tubes
PA: Sumitomo Rubber Industries, Ltd.
3-6-9, Wakinohamacho, Chuo-Ku

(P-9856)

GREENBALL CORP (PA)

Also Called: Towmaster Tire & Wheel
222 S Harbor Blvd Ste 700, Anaheim
(92805-3730)
PHONE.....................714 782-3060
Chris S H Tsai, *CEO*
Jenny Tsai, *
◆ **EMP:** 50 **EST:** 1976
SALES (est): 55.96MM
SALES (corp-wide): 55.96MM **Privately Held**
Web: www.greenballtires.com
SIC: 5014 5013 3999 Automobile tires and tubes; Wheels, motor vehicle; Atomizers, toiletry

(P-9857)

ITD ARIZONA INC

6737 E Washington Blvd, Commerce
(90040-1801)
PHONE.....................323 722-8542
◆ **EMP:** 98
SIC: 5014 Tires and tubes

(P-9858)

LAKIN TIRE WEST INCORPORATED (PA)

Also Called: Lakin Tire of Calif
15305 Spring Ave, Santa Fe Springs
(90670-5645)
PHONE.....................562 802-2752
Robert Lakin, *CEO*
David Lakin, *
◆ **EMP:** 164 **EST:** 1973
SQ FT: 50,000
SALES (est): 43.62MM
SALES (corp-wide): 43.62MM **Privately Held**
Web: www.lakintire.com
SIC: 5014 5531 Tires, used; Auto and home supply stores

(P-9859)

PETES ROAD SERVICE INC (PA)

2230 E Orangethorpe Ave, Fullerton
(92831-5329)
PHONE.....................714 446-1207
▲ **EMP:** 55 **EST:** 1954
SALES (est): 51.31MM
SALES (corp-wide): 51.31MM **Privately Held**
Web: www.petesrs.com
SIC: 5014 7534 7539 Tires and tubes; Tire retreading and repair shops; Wheel alignment, automotive

(P-9860)

SUMITOMO RUBBER NORTH AMER INC (HQ)

Also Called: Falken Tire
8656 Haven Ave, Rancho Cucamonga
(91730-9103)
PHONE.....................909 466-1116
Richard Smallwood, *CEO*
Toby Beiner, *
◆ **EMP:** 120 **EST:** 1963
SQ FT: 190,000
SALES (est): 101.56MM **Privately Held**
Web: www.falkentire.com
SIC: 5014 Automobile tires and tubes
PA: Sumitomo Rubber Industries, Ltd.
3-6-9, Wakinohamacho, Chuo-Ku

(P-9861)

TIRECO INC (PA)

500 W 190th St Ste 600, Gardena
(90248-4269)
PHONE.....................310 767-7990
Robert W Liu, *Ch*
Justin R Liu, *
Mimi Liu, *
◆ **EMP:** 150 **EST:** 2000
SALES (est): 112.53MM
SALES (corp-wide): 112.53MM **Privately Held**
Web: www.tireco.com
SIC: 5014 5013 5051 Automobile tires and tubes; Wheels, motor vehicle; Tubing, metal

(P-9862)

TOYO TIRE USA CORP (DH)

Also Called: Nitto Tyres
5665 Plaza Dr Ste 300, Cypress
(90630-5066)
P.O. Box 6052 (90630-0052)
PHONE.....................714 236-2080
◆ **EMP:** 71 **EST:** 1966
SALES (est): 105.8MM **Privately Held**
Web: www.toyotires.com
SIC: 5014 Truck tires and tubes
HQ: Toyo Tire Holdings Of Americas Inc.
3565 Harbor Blvd
Costa Mesa CA 92626
714 229-6100

(P-9863)

YOKOHAMA TIRE CORPORATION (DH)

Also Called: Yokohama Tire USA
1 Macarthur Pl Ste 900, Santa Ana (92707)
P.O. Box 4550 (92834-4550)
PHONE.....................714 870-3800
◆ **EMP:** 150 **EST:** 1969
SALES (est): 497.5MM **Privately Held**
Web: www.yokohamatruck.com
SIC: 5014 3011 Automobile tires and tubes; Automobile tires, pneumatic
HQ: Yokohama Corporation Of North America
1 Macarthur Pl
Santa Ana CA 92707

5021 Furniture

(P-9864)

ABBYSON LIVING CORP

Also Called: Yellow Luxury
26500 Agoura Rd Ste 102, Calabasas
(91302-3571)
PHONE.....................805 465-5500
Yavar Rafieha, *Pr*
EMP: 112 **EST:** 2008
SALES (est): 2.47MM **Privately Held**
Web: www.abbyson.com
SIC: 5021 Household furniture

(P-9865)

BENCHPRO INC

Also Called: Bench Depot
13463 Windy Grove Dr, Rancho Cucamonga (91739-2039)
P.O. Box G (91980-0958)
PHONE.....................619 478-9400
Jay David Lissner, *Pr*
▲ **EMP:** 188 **EST:** 2001
SQ FT: 155,000
SALES (est): 24.92MM **Privately Held**
Web: www.benchpro.com
SIC: 5021 Furniture

(P-9866)

BLUMENTHAL DISTRIBUTING INC (PA)

Also Called: Office Star Products
1901 S Archibald Ave, Ontario
(91761-8548)
P.O. Box 3520 (91761-0952)
PHONE.....................909 930-2000
Richard Blumenthal, *CEO*
Richard Blumenthal, *Pr*
Rose Blumenthal, *Stockholder*
Jennifer Blumenthal, *
◆ **EMP:** 150 **EST:** 1983
SQ FT: 200,000
SALES (est): 49.22MM
SALES (corp-wide): 49.22MM **Privately Held**
Web: www.officestar.net
SIC: 5021 2522 Office furniture, nec; Chairs, office: padded or plain: except wood

(P-9867)

CAMBIUM BUSINESS GROUP INC (PA)

Also Called: Fairmont Designs
6950 Noritsu Ave, Buena Park
(90620-1311)
PHONE...............714 670-1171
George Tsai, *Ch*
Jason Liu, *
Kevin Fitzgerald, *
Mark Klingensmith, *
◆ **EMP:** 120 **EST:** 1984
SQ FT: 200,000
SALES (est): 25.94MM
SALES (corp-wide): 25.94MM **Privately Held**
Web: www.fairmontdesignshospitality.com
SIC: 5021 2511 Household furniture; Wood household furniture

(P-9868)

COPPEL CORPORATION

Also Called: Coppel
503 Scaroni Ave, Calexico (92231-9791)
PHONE.....................760 357-3707
David Coppel, *CEO*
Allan Lewis, *
Joaquin Aguirre Ruiz, *
Eugenio Ruben Coppel, *
Diego Alberto Coppel Sullivan, *
▲ **EMP:** 75 **EST:** 1991
SQ FT: 70,000
SALES (est): 760.41MM **Privately Held**
Web: www.coppel.com
SIC: 5021 5137 5136 Household furniture; Women's and children's clothing; Men's and boy's clothing
HQ: Coppel, S.A. De C.V.
Republica Poniente No. 2855
Culiacan SIN 80105

(P-9869)

CUSTOM COMFORT MATTRESS CO INC (PA)

Also Called: Custom Comfort Mattress Co
581 N Batavia St, Orange (92868-1218)
P.O. Box 1769 (92856-0769)
PHONE.....................714 693-6161
EMP: 72 **EST:** 1997
SALES (est): 18.05MM **Privately Held**
Web: www.customcomfortmattress.com
SIC: 5021 5712 Beds; Bedding and bedsprings

(P-9870)

EC GROUP INC (PA)

Also Called: Dennis & Leen
5960 Bowcroft St, Los Angeles
(90016-4302)
PHONE.....................310 815-2700
Richard Hallberg, *Pr*
Daniel Cuevas, *
Barbara Wiseley, *
▲ **EMP:** 80 **EST:** 1985
SQ FT: 18,000
SALES (est): 23.58MM **Privately Held**
Web: www.dennisandleen.com
SIC: 5021 Furniture

(P-9871)

FURNITURE AMERICA CAL INC (PA)

Also Called: Furniture of America
680 S Lemon Ave, City Of Industry
(91789-2934)
PHONE.....................866 923-8500
George Wells, *CEO*
Rocky Yang, *
Jean Chen, *
Jose Palacios, *
◆ **EMP:** 36 **EST:** 2005
SALES (est): 22.12MM **Privately Held**
Web: www.foagroup.com
SIC: 5021 2512 Furniture; Upholstered household furniture

(P-9872)

GOFORTH & MARTI (PA)

Also Called: G/M Business Interiors
110 W A St Ste 140, San Diego
(92101-3702)
PHONE.....................800 686-6583
Laurinda Easley, *CEO*
Josie Donley, *
Stephen L Easley, *
▲ **EMP:** 90 **EST:** 1944
SQ FT: 38,000
SALES (est): 130MM
SALES (corp-wide): 130MM **Privately Held**
Web: www.gmbi.net
SIC: 5021 Office furniture, nec

(P-9873)

GOFORTH & MARTI

Also Called: G/M Business Interiors
1099 W La Cadena Dr, Riverside
(92501-1413)
PHONE.....................951 684-0870

PRODUCTS & SVCS

EMP: 70
SALES (corp-wide): 130MM **Privately Held**
Web: www.gmbi.net
SIC: 5021 Office furniture, nec
PA: Goforth & Marti
110 W A St Ste 140
800 686-6583

(P-9874)
INTEX RECREATION CORP
Also Called: INTEX RECREATION
4001 Via Oro Ave, Long Beach
(90810-1400)
PHONE.....................310 549-5400
Tien P Zee, *CEO*
Jim Lai, *
Bill Smith, *
Bob Howe, *
◆ EMP: 100 EST: 1966
SQ FT: 330,000
SALES (est): 2.3MM,**Privately Held**
Web: www.intexcorp.com
SIC: 5021 5092 5091 5162 Waterbeds;
Toys, nec; Watersports equipment and
supplies; Plastics materials and basic
shapes
PA: Intex Corp.
4001 Via Oro Ave Ste 210

(P-9875)
JANUS ET CIE (PA)
12310 Greenstone Ave, Santa Fe Springs
(90670-4737)
PHONE.....................800 245-2687
Janice K Feldman, *CEO*
Paul Warren, *
Greg Buscher, *
◆ EMP: 110 EST: 1977
SQ FT: 154,000
SALES (est): 47.44MM
SALES (corp-wide): 47.44MM **Privately Held**
Web: www.janusetcie.com
SIC: 5021 5712 Outdoor and lawn furniture,
nec; Outdoor and garden furniture

(P-9876)
KIMLOR MILLS INC
Also Called: Kimlor Innovative HM Fashions
18142 Blue Ridge Dr, Santa Ana
(92705-2056)
PHONE.....................803 531-2037
Wade Svicarovich, *Pr*
Matthew King, *
◆ EMP: 100 EST: 1980
SALES (est): 1.09MM **Privately Held**
Web: www.kimlor.com
SIC: 5021 2392 Household furniture;
Household furnishings, nec

(P-9877)
NEW TANGRAM LLC
Also Called: BKM Total Office of Texas
9200 Sorensen Ave, Santa Fe Springs
(90670-2645)
PHONE.....................562 365-5000
Joseph P Lozowski, *Brnch Mgr*
EMP: 177
SALES (corp-wide): 85.43MM **Privately Held**
Web: www.tangraminteriors.com
SIC: 5021 Office furniture, nec
PA: New Tangram, Llc
9200 Sorensen Ave
562 365-5000

(P-9878)
OFFICE MASTER INC
Also Called: Om Smart Seating

1110 Mildred St, Ontario (91761-3512)
PHONE.....................909 392-5678
◆ EMP: 60 EST: 1986
SALES (est): 9.51MM **Privately Held**
Web: www.omseating.com
SIC: 5021 2522 Office furniture, nec;
Benches, office: except wood

(P-9879)
OMNIA ITALIAN DESIGN LLC
4900 Edison Ave, Chino (91710-5713)
PHONE.....................909 393-4400
Peter Zolferino, *Managing Member*
Luie Nastri, *
◆ EMP: 200 EST: 1989
SQ FT: 110,000
SALES (est): 23.95MM **Privately Held**
Web: www.omnialeather.com
SIC: 5021 Household furniture

(P-9880)
POUNDEX ASSOCIATES CORPORATION
21490 Baker Pkwy, City Of Industry
(91789-5239)
PHONE.....................909 444-5878
Lionel Chen, *Ch*
◆ EMP: 100 EST: 1988
SQ FT: 55,000
SALES (est): 8.3MM **Privately Held**
Web: www.poundex.com
SIC: 5021 Household furniture

(P-9881)
PREMIERE RACK SOLUTIONS INC
4502 Brickell Privado St, Ontario
(91761-7827)
P.O. Box 2205 (94551-2205)
PHONE.....................909 605-6300
EMP: 76
SIC: 5021 Racks

(P-9882)
PRIVILEGE INTERNATIONAL INC
2323 Firestone Blvd, South Gate
(90280-2684)
PHONE.....................323 585-0777
Eddy Sarraf, *CEO*
Eddy Sarraf, *Pr*
Richard Darwish, *
Mark Darwish, *
◆ EMP: 75 EST: 1999
SQ FT: 350,000
SALES (est): 4.11MM **Privately Held**
Web: www.privilegeinc.com
SIC: 5021 Furniture

(P-9883)
SITONIT SEATING INC
6415 Katella Ave, Cypress (90630-5245)
PHONE.....................714 995-4800
Paul Devries, *CEO*
EMP: 151 EST: 2008
SALES (est): 2.55MM **Privately Held**
Web: www.sitonit.net
SIC: 5021 Office furniture, nec
PA: Exemplis Llc
6415 Katella Ave

(P-9884)
UNISOURCE SOLUTIONS LLC (PA)
8350 Rex Rd, Pico Rivera (90660-3785)
PHONE.....................562 654-3500
James Kastner, *
Ken Kastner, *
Jim Kastner, *Ch*
Clem Nieto, *

▲ EMP: 105 EST: 1987
SQ FT: 186,000
SALES (est): 48.15MM
SALES (corp-wide): 48.15MM **Privately Held**
Web: www.unisourceit.com
SIC: 5021 Office furniture, nec

(P-9885)
VIRCO INC (HQ)
2027 Harpers Way, Torrance (90501-1524)
PHONE.....................310 533-0474
Robert Virtue, *CEO*
Robert Dose, *
▼ EMP: 45 EST: 1998
SQ FT: 560,000
SALES (est): 20.3MM
SALES (corp-wide): 269.12MM **Publicly Held**
Web: www.virco.com
SIC: 5021 2599 Furniture; Factory furniture
and fixtures
PA: Virco Mfg. Corporation
2027 Harpers Way
310 533-0474

(P-9886)
WINNERS ONLY INC
1365 Park Center Dr, Vista (92081-8338)
PHONE.....................760 599-0300
Alex Shu, *Ch*
Sheue-wen Lee, *CEO*
Fred Dizon, *
◆ EMP: 200 EST: 1989
SALES (est): 9.49MM **Privately Held**
Web: www.winnersonly.com
SIC: 5021 Office furniture, nec

(P-9887)
WMK OFFICE SAN DIEGO LLC (PA)
4780 Eastgate Mall Ste 100, San Diego
(92121-2063)
PHONE.....................858 569-4700
James Skidmore, *CEO*
William Kuhnert, *
Jim Skidmore, *
EMP: 70 EST: 2003
SQ FT: 100,000
SALES (est): 68.51MM
SALES (corp-wide): 68.51MM **Privately Held**
Web: www.bkmofficeworks.com
SIC: 5021 Office furniture, nec

5023 Homefurnishings

(P-9888)
AMERICAN FAUCET COATINGS CORP
1333 Keystone Way, Vista (92081-8311)
PHONE.....................760 598-5895
Susan E Butler, *Pr*
◆ EMP: 50 EST: 1993
SALES (est): 16MM **Privately Held**
Web: www.afccorp.net
SIC: 5023 3432 Homefurnishings; Plumbing
fixture fittings and trim

(P-9889)
BRADSHAW INTERNATIONAL INC (PA)
Also Called: Bradshaw Home
9409 Buffalo Ave, Rancho Cucamonga
(91730-6012)
PHONE.....................909 476-3884
James Hair, *CEO*
Steve Molineaux, *
Robert Michelson, *

Jeff Megorden, *
Gary Appel, *
◆ EMP: 295 EST: 2010
SQ FT: 313,048
SALES (est): 642.04MM
SALES (corp-wide): 642.04MM **Privately Held**
Web: www.bradshawhome.com
SIC: 5023 Kitchenware

(P-9890)
CONTRACTORS FLRG SVC CAL INC
3403 W Macarthur Blvd, Santa Ana
(92704-6805)
P.O. Box 15106 (92735-0106)
PHONE.....................714 556-6100
Joseph J Ott, *Pr*
EMP: 110 EST: 1996
● SALES (est): 9.74MM **Privately Held**
Web: www.cfsofca.com
SIC: 5023 Floor coverings

(P-9891)
ELIJAH TEXTILES INC
Also Called: Sharp Fabric
1251 E Olympic Blvd Ste 108, Los Angeles
(90021-1860)
PHONE.....................310 666-3443
Kourosh Amirianfar, *Pr*
EMP: 82 EST: 2001
SQ FT: 100,000
SALES (est): 653.57K **Privately Held**
SIC: 5023 5949 Sheets, textile; Fabric stores
piece goods

(P-9892)
EV RAY INC
6400 Variel Ave, Woodland Hills
(91367-2577)
PHONE.....................818 346-5381
Lee Brown, *Pr*
EMP: 50 EST: 1962
SQ FT: 22,000
SALES (est): 6.97MM **Privately Held**
Web: www.rayev.com
SIC: 5023 2211 2591 2391 Draperies;
Draperies and drapery fabrics, cotton;
Drapery hardware and window blinds and
shades; Curtains and draperies

(P-9893)
EVRIHOLDER PRODUCTS LLC (PA)
Also Called: Evriholder
975 W Imperial Hwy Ste 100, Brea
(92821-3846)
PHONE.....................714 490-7878
◆ EMP: 73 EST: 1995
SQ FT: 45,000
SALES (est): 85.83MM **Privately Held**
Web: www.evriholder.com
SIC: 5023 5085 5087 Kitchenware; Bins and
containers, storage; Cleaning and
maintenance equipment and supplies

(P-9894)
GA GERTMENIAN AND SONS LLC (PA)
300 W Avenue 33, Los Angeles
(90031-3503)
PHONE.....................213 250-7777
▲ EMP: 149 EST: 1896
SALES (est): 24.13MM
SALES (corp-wide): 24.13MM **Privately Held**
Web: www.gertmenian.com
SIC: 5023 Rugs

(P-9895)
GALLEHER LLC (PA)
Also Called: Galleher
9303 Greenleaf Ave, Santa Fe Springs
(90670-3029)
PHONE..............................562 944-8885
Sunil Palakodati, *CEO*
Rick Coates, *
David Burke, *
▲ **EMP:** 110 **EST:** 1937
SQ FT: 100,000
SALES (est): 356.59MM
SALES (corp-wide): 356.59MM **Privately Held**
Web: www.galleher.com
SIC: 5023 2426 Wood flooring; Hardwood dimension and flooring mills

(P-9896)
GIBSON OVERSEAS INC (PA)
Also Called: Gibson Homeware
2410 Yates Ave, Commerce (90040-1918)
PHONE..............................323 832-8900
Sol Gabbay, *CEO*
Darioush Gabbay, *
Soloman Gabbay, *
◆ **EMP:** 475 **EST:** 1979
SQ FT: 850,000
SALES (est): 31.46MM
SALES (corp-wide): 31.46MM **Privately Held**
Web: www.gibsonusa.com
SIC: 5023 3269 2511 Glassware; Kitchen and table articles, coarse earthenware; Kitchen and dining room furniture

(P-9897)
GTT INTERNATIONAL INC
1615 Eastridge Ave, Riverside
(92507-7111)
PHONE..............................951 788-8729
Mohammed Arshad, *Pr*
Hafiz Ur Rahaman, *
▲ **EMP:** 35 **EST:** 1991
SALES (est): 1.89MM **Privately Held**
SIC: 5023 2258 Bedspreads; Lace and warp knit fabric mills

(P-9898)
LEDRA BRANDS INC
Also Called: Bruck Lighting Systems
88 Maxwell, Irvine (92618-4641)
PHONE..............................714 259-9959
Alex Ladjevardi, *Pr*
Jade Turney, *
Farah Emami, *
David Derk, *
Jorg Westerheide, *
▲ **EMP:** 112 **EST:** 1993
SALES (est): 21.56MM **Privately Held**
Web: www.ledrabrands.com
SIC: 5023 Lamps: floor, boudoir, desk

(P-9899)
MSRS INC
Also Called: Vm International
945 E Church St, Riverside (92507-1103)
PHONE..............................310 952-9000
Moe Vazin, *CEO*
Roya Vazin, *
◆ **EMP:** 120 **EST:** 1996
SQ FT: 250,000
SALES (est): 30.95MM **Privately Held**
SIC: 5023 5719 Kitchenware; Housewares, nec

(P-9900)
NEXGRILL INDUSTRIES INC (PA)
Also Called: Nexgrill Industries
14050 Laurelwood Pl, Chino (91710-5454)
PHONE..............................909 598-8799
Sherman Lin, *CEO*
◆ **EMP:** 98 **EST:** 1993
SQ FT: 50,000
SALES (est): 22.45MM
SALES (corp-wide): 22.45MM **Privately Held**
Web: www.nexgrill.com
SIC: 5023 3631 Grills, barbecue; Barbecues, grills, and braziers (outdoor cooking)

(P-9901)
NORCAL POTTERY PRODUCTS INC
5700 E Airport Dr, Ontario (91761-8620)
PHONE..............................909 390-3745
Carrie Roberts, *Mgr*
EMP: 135
SALES (corp-wide): 3.2B **Publicly Held**
SIC: 5023 Pottery
HQ: Norcal Pottery Products, Inc.
1000 Washington St
Foxboro MA 02035
510 895-5966

(P-9902)
NORMAN INTERNATIONAL INC
Also Called: Norman Charter
28 Centerpointe Dr Ste 120, La Palma
(90623-2500)
PHONE..............................562 946-0420
Ranjan Mada, *CEO*
◆ **EMP:** 70 **EST:** 2001
SALES (est): 27.64MM
SALES (corp-wide): 42.43MM **Privately Held**
Web: www.normanusa.com
SIC: 5023 Homefurnishings
PA: Norman International Dallas, Llc
28 Centerpointe Dr # 120
562 946-0420

(P-9903)
OMEGA MOULDING WEST LLC
Also Called: Omega
5500 Lindbergh Ln, Bell (90201-6410)
PHONE..............................323 261-3510
Bernard Portnoy, *Managing Member*
◆ **EMP:** 130 **EST:** 1998
SQ FT: 130,000
SALES (est): 2.56MM **Privately Held**
Web: www.omegamoulding.com
SIC: 5023 Frames and framing, picture and mirror

(P-9904)
PACIFIC HERITG HM FASHION INC
Also Called: Home Decor Wholesaler
901 Lawson St, City Of Industry
(91748-1121)
PHONE..............................909 598-5200
Meng Lan Liu, *Pr*
Frank Hsu, *
▲ **EMP:** 25 **EST:** 2002
SALES (est): 4.95MM **Privately Held**
SIC: 5023 2392 Window shades; Blankets, comforters and beddings

(P-9905)
REU DISTRIBUTION LLC
Also Called: Republic Floor
7227 Telegraph Rd, Montebello
(90640-6512)
PHONE..............................323 201-4200
Eliyahu Shuat, *
EMP: 700 **EST:** 2015
SALES (est): 3.42MM **Privately Held**
SIC: 5023 5211 2426 Wood flooring; Flooring, wood; Flooring, hardwood

(P-9906)
SIDS CARPET BARN (PA)
Also Called: Abbey Carpet
132 W 8th St, National City (91950-1197)
PHONE..............................619 477-7000
Allan W Ziman, *Pr*
Allan W Ziman, *Pr*
Don Pasquill, *
Stacy B Ziman, *
Robert Wood, *
EMP: 24 **EST:** 1950
SQ FT: 7,800
SALES (est): 30.14MM
SALES (corp-wide): 30.14MM **Privately Held**
Web: www.sidscarpet.com
SIC: 5023 1771 5713 1389 Carpets; Flooring contractor; Carpets; Construction, repair, and dismantling services

(P-9907)
SOTO PROVISION INC
Also Called: Soto Food Service
488 Parriott Pl W, City Of Industry
(91745-1015)
PHONE..............................626 458-4600
John R Renna Senior, *Pr*
John R Renna Junior, *VP*
Russ Fischer, *CFO*
EMP: 70 **EST:** 1974
SQ FT: 35,000
SALES (est): 47.45MM **Privately Held**
Web: www.sotofoodservice.com
SIC: 5023 5046 Kitchen tools and utensils, nec; Commercial cooking and food service equipment

(P-9908)
TABLETOPS UNLIMITED INC (PA)
Also Called: Tabletops Unlimited
23000 Avalon Blvd, Carson (90745-5017)
PHONE..............................310 549-6000
Mohsen Asgari, *Dir*
Hamid Ebrahimi, *
Daryoush Molayem, *
Ali Alan Asgari, *
Masoud Tehrani, *
◆ **EMP:** 77 **EST:** 1983
SQ FT: 350,000
SALES (est): 17.62MM
SALES (corp-wide): 17.62MM **Privately Held**
Web: www.ttustore.com
SIC: 5023 Kitchenware

(P-9909)
TAE SOOK CHUNG
Also Called: Elim Bedding Town
21080 Golden Springs Dr, Walnut
(01780 3804)
PHONE..............................909 598-6255
Tae Sook Chung, *Owner*
EMP: 76 **EST:** 2002
SALES (est): 873.16K **Privately Held**
SIC: 5023 Blankets

(P-9910)
TEST-RITE PRODUCTS CORP (DH)
1900 Burgundy Pl, Ontario (91761-2308)
PHONE..............................909 605-9899
Kelly Ho, *Pr*
Jack Ho, *
◆ **EMP:** 80 **EST:** 1975
SQ FT: 400,000
SALES (est): 28.42MM **Privately Held**
SIC: 5023 Homefurnishings
HQ: Test-Rite International (U.S.) Co., Ltd.
1900 South Burgundy Pl

Ontario CA 91761

(P-9911)
TIFFANY DALE INC (PA)
14765 Firestone Blvd, La Mirada
(90638-5918)
PHONE..............................714 739-2700
Ye H Chung, *CEO*
Connie Chung, *
▲ **EMP:** 83 **EST:** 1979
SALES (est): 6.96MM
SALES (corp-wide): 6.96MM **Privately Held**
Web: www.daletiffany.com
SIC: 5023 Lamps: floor, boudoir, desk

(P-9912)
TRI-WEST LTD (PA)
12005 Pike St, Santa Fe Springs
(90670-6100)
PHONE..............................562 692-9166
Allen Gage, *Pr*
Randy Sims, *Pt*
John Lubinxki, *Pt*
▲ **EMP:** 200 **EST:** 1976
SQ FT: 300,000
SALES (est): 90.31MM
SALES (corp-wide): 90.31MM **Privately Held**
Web: www.triwestltd.com
SIC: 5023 Floor coverings

(P-9913)
UNIQUE CARPETS LTD
7360 Jurupa Ave, Riverside (92504-1025)
PHONE..............................951 352-8125
Bill D Graves, *Pr*
Robert L Binford, *
Martin Lopez, *
▲ **EMP:** 55 **EST:** 1985
SALES (est): 4.99MM **Privately Held**
Web: www.uniquecarpetsltd.com
SIC: 5023 2273 Carpets; Carpets and rugs

(P-9914)
UNIVERSAL WOOD MOULDING INC (PA)
Also Called: Universal Framing Products
21139 Centre Pointe Pkwy, Santa Clarita
(91350-2994)
PHONE..............................661 362-6262
Jon M Bromberg, *CEO*
Avi Feibenlatt, *Ch Bd*
Mark Gottlieb, *
▲ **EMP:** 50 **EST:** 1995
SALES (est): 24.32MM
SALES (corp-wide): 24.32MM **Privately Held**
Web: www.universalarquati.com
SIC: 5023 3999 Frames and framing, picture and mirror; Atomizers, toiletry

(P-9915)
VENUS GROUP INC (PA)
Also Called: Venus Textiles
25861 Wright, Foothill Ranch (92610-3504)
PHONE..............................949 609-1299
Rajni D Patel, *CEO*
Aman Ullah, *
◆ **EMP:** 78 **EST:** 1971
SALES (est): 24.88MM
SALES (corp-wide): 24.88MM **Privately Held**
Web: www.venusgroup.com
SIC: 5023 2392 5719 Towels; Towels, fabric and nonwoven: made from purchased materials; Towels

PRODUCTS & SVCS

(P-9916)
ZWILLING JA HENCKELS LLC
Also Called: Z Willing J A Henckels
100 Citadel Dr Ste 575, Commerce
(90040-1571)
PHONE..................................323 597-1421
EMP: 244
SALES (corp-wide): 4.45B Privately Held
Web: www.zwilling.com
SIC: 5023 Kitchenware
HQ: Zwilling J.A. Henckels, Llc
270 Marble Ave
Pleasantville NY 10570
914 749-3400

5031 Lumber, Plywood, And Millwork

(P-9917)
48FORTY SOLUTIONS LLC
14966 Whittram Ave, Fontana
(92335-3158)
PHONE..................................909 371-0101
EMP: 299
SALES (corp-wide): 502.24MM Privately Held
Web: www.48forty.com
SIC: 5031 Pallets, wood
PA: 48forty Solutions, Llc
11740 Katy Fwy
678 722-3984

(P-9918)
BUILDERS FENCE COMPANY INC (PA)
8937 San Fernando Rd, Sun Valley
(91352-1410)
P.O. Box 125 (91353-0125)
PHONE..................................818 768-5500
Marshall K Frankel, Pr
▲ EMP: 35 EST: 1959
SQ FT: 6,400
SALES (est): 48.82MM
SALES (corp-wide): 48.82MM Privately Held
Web: www.buildersfence.com
SIC: 5031 1799 3446 Fencing, wood;
Ornamental metal work; Architectural metalwork

(P-9919)
EXPO INDUSTRIES INC
Also Called: Expo Builders Supply
7455 Carroll Rd, San Diego (92121-2379)
P.O. Box 711 (92121)
PHONE..................................858 566-3110
EMP: 95
Web: www.expostucco.com
SIC: 5031 3299 Building materials, exterior;
Stucco

(P-9920)
FOUNDATION BUILDING MTLS INC (HQ)
Also Called: Foundation Building Materials
2520 Redhill Ave, Santa Ana (92705-5542)
PHONE..................................714 380-3127
Ruben Mendoza, Pr
Onur Demirkaya, *
David Opre, *
Richard J Tilley, *
EMP: 255 EST: 2016
SALES (est): 2.23B Privately Held
Web: www.fbmsales.com
SIC: 5031 5033 5039 Building materials,
interior; Roofing, siding, and insulation;
Ceiling systems and products
PA: American Securities Llc
590 Madison Ave Fl 38

(P-9921)
GROVE LUMBER & BLDG SUPS INC (PA)
27126 Watson Rd, Menifee (92585-9792)
PHONE..................................909 947-0277
Raymond G Croll Junior, CEO
EMP: 190 EST: 1979
SQ FT: 3,000
SALES (est): 24.51MM
SALES (corp-wide): 24.51MM Privately Held
Web: www.grovelumber.com
SIC: 5031 5211 Lumber: rough, dressed,
and finished; Lumber products

(P-9922)
HARDY WINDOW COMPANY (PA)
1639 E Miraloma Ave, Placentia
(92870-6623)
PHONE..................................714 996-1807
Chance P Hardy, Pr
EMP: 141 EST: 1998
SQ FT: 14,000
SALES (est): 23.22MM
SALES (corp-wide): 23.22MM Privately Held
Web:
www.orangecountywindowanddoor.com
SIC: 5031 Windows

(P-9923)
JAMES HARDIE BUILDING PDTS INC
10901 Elm Ave, Fontana (92337-7348)
PHONE..................................909 355-6500
Bob Mussleman, Brnch Mgr
EMP: 53
Web: www.jameshardie.com
SIC: 5031 3272 Building materials, exterior;
Areaways, basement window: concrete
HQ: James Hardie Building Products Inc.
303 E Wacker Dr
Chicago IL 60601
312 291-5072

(P-9924)
JELD-WEN INC
Also Called: American Building Supply
120 S Cedar Ave, Rialto (92376-9010)
PHONE..................................909 879-8700
Carlos Duran, Brnch Mgr
EMP: 103
Web: www.abs-abs.com
SIC: 5031 Doors, nec
HQ: Jeld-Wen, Inc.
2645 Silver Crescent Dr
Charlotte NC 28273
800 535-3936

(P-9925)
MCDAVIS AND GUMBYS INC ◆
Also Called: Fleetwood Windows and Doors
1 Fleetwood Way, Corona (92879-5101)
P.O. Box P.O. Box 1086 (92878-1086)
PHONE..................................800 736-7363
EMP: 250 EST: 2023
SALES (est): 25.59MM Publicly Held
Web: www.fleetwoodusa.com
SIC: 5031 3442 Doors and windows; Metal
doors, sash, and trim
HQ: Masonite International Corporation
1242 E 5th Ave
Tampa FL 33605
813 877-2726

(P-9926)
NICHOLS LUMBER & HARDWARE CO
Also Called: Ace Hardware

13470 Dalewood St, Baldwin Park
(91706-5883)
PHONE..................................626 960-4802
Judith A Nichols, Pr
Charles Nichols, *
EMP: 75 EST: 1958
SALES (est): 8.48MM Privately Held
Web: www.nicholslumber.com
SIC: 5031 5251 2421 Lumber: rough,
dressed, and finished; Hardware stores;
Sawmills and planing mills, general

(P-9927)
OREGON PCF BLDG PDTS MAPLE INC
Also Called: Orepac Millwork Products
2401 E Philadelphia St, Ontario
(91761-7743)
PHONE..................................909 627-4043
Douglas Hart, Pr
▲ EMP: 125 EST: 1992
SALES (est): 6.36MM
SALES (corp-wide): 555.25MM Privately Held
Web: www.orepac.com
SIC: 5031 5032 Building materials, exterior;
Brick, stone, and related material
PA: Orepac Holding Company
30170 Sw Ore Pac Ave
503 685-5499

(P-9928)
PANORAMIC DOORS LLC
3265 Production Ave Ste A, Oceanside
(92058-1361)
PHONE..................................760 722-1300
Raffy Timonian, VP
EMP: 90
SALES (corp-wide): 24.77MM Privately Held
Web: www.panoramicdoors.com
SIC: 5031 Windows
PA: Panoramic Doors Llc
15050 Frye Rd
817 952-3500

(P-9929)
RELIABLE WHOLESALE LUMBER INC (PA)
7600 Redondo Cir, Huntington Beach
(92648-1397)
P.O. Box 191 (92648-0191)
PHONE..................................714 848-8222
Jerome M Higman, Pr
Jerome M Higman, Pr
David Higman, *
Will Higman, *
Jerry Higman, Prin
EMP: 90 EST: 1970
SQ FT: 4,500
SALES (est): 92.3MM
SALES (corp-wide): 92.3MM Privately Held
Web: www.rwli.net
SIC: 5031 2421 Lumber: rough, dressed,
and finished; Sawmills and planing mills,
general

(P-9930)
ROBERTS LUMBER SALES INC
Also Called: Robert's Lumber
2661 S Lilac Ave, Bloomington
(92316-3211)
PHONE..................................909 350-9164
Robert Cantero Junior, CEO
Lori Cantero, *
EMP: 57 EST: 1997
SALES (est): 9.09MM Privately Held
Web: www.robertslumbersales.com

SIC: 5031 2448 Lumber: rough, dressed,
and finished; Wood pallets and skids

(P-9931)
ROYAL PLYWOOD COMPANY LLC (PA)
14171 Park Pl, Cerritos (90703-2463)
P.O. Box 728 (90637-0728)
PHONE..................................562 404-2989
Stephen Fuller, *
▲ EMP: 78 EST: 1999
SQ FT: 120,000
SALES (est): 62.2MM
SALES (corp-wide): 62.2MM Privately Held
Web: www.royalplywood.com
SIC: 5031 Lumber: rough, dressed, and
finished

(P-9932)
SHAPP INTERNATIONAL TRDG INC
Also Called: Shapp Internatiooonal
6000 Reseda Blvd, Tarzana (91356-1500)
P.O. Box 893 (91365-0893)
PHONE..................................818 348-3000
Allan Shapiro, Pr
Louis Justin, *
EMP: 118 EST: 1991
SQ FT: 8,000
SALES (est): 1.2MM Privately Held
SIC: 5031 5064 5112 5021 Lumber,
plywood, and millwork; Electrical
appliances, major; Stationery and office
supplies; Furniture

(P-9933)
WALNUT INVESTMENT CORP
Also Called: AMS
2940 E White Star Ave, Anaheim
(92806-2627)
PHONE..................................714 238-9240
▲ EMP: 550
SIC: 5031 5039 5072 Building materials,
exterior; Ceiling systems and products;
Hardware

(P-9934)
WESTSIDE BLDG SAN DIEGO LLC
Also Called: Westside Building Materials
11620 Sorrento Valley Rd, San Diego
(92121-1011)
PHONE..................................858 566-4343
Leana Aluria, Prin
Geraldine Peckham, *
Richard N Peckham, *
EMP: 48 EST: 2007
SALES (est): 4.25MM Privately Held
Web: www.westsidebmc.com
SIC: 5031 3299 Building materials, exterior;
Mica products

(P-9935)
WEYERHAEUSER COMPANY
11100 Hope St, Cypress (90630-5236)
PHONE..................................714 523-3330
EMP: 77
SALES (corp-wide): 7.67B Publicly Held
Web: www.weyerhaeuser.com
SIC: 5031 Lumber: rough, dressed, and
finished
PA: Weyerhaeuser Company
220 Occidental Ave S
206 539-3000

5032 Brick, Stone, And Related Material

(P-9936)
ATLAS CONSTRUCTION SUPPLY INC (PA)
4640 Brinnell St, San Diego (92111-2302)
P.O. Box 178240 (92177)
PHONE..............................858 277-2100
Brian Quinn, *Pr*
James E Wright, *
Tom Vargas, *
▲ **EMP:** 75 **EST:** 1980
SQ FT: 30,000
SALES (est): 49.08MM
SALES (corp-wide): 49.08MM **Privately Held**
Web: www.atlasform.com
SIC: 5032 Concrete building products

(P-9937)
ATLAS CONSTRUCTION SUPPLY INC
7550 Stage Rd, Buena Park (90621-1253)
PHONE..............................714 441-9500
Pat Kelley, *Mgr*
EMP: 29
SALES (corp-wide): 49.08MM **Privately Held**
Web: www.atlasform.com
SIC: 5032 5211 5082 3444 Concrete building products; Masonry materials and supplies; Contractor's materials; Concrete forms, sheet metal
PA: Atlas Construction Supply, Inc.
4640 Brinnell St
858 277-2100

(P-9938)
CARRARA MARBLE CO AMER INC (PA)
15939 Phoenix Dr, City Of Industry (91745-1624)
PHONE..............................626 961-6010
William Cordova, *Pr*
James Hogan, *
▲ **EMP:** 70 **EST:** 1953
SQ FT: 30,000
SALES (est): 5.59MM
SALES (corp-wide): 5.59MM **Privately Held**
Web: www.carrara.com
SIC: 5032 1743 1741 Ceramic wall and floor tile, nec; Marble installation, interior; Masonry and other stonework

(P-9939)
CEMEX CEMENT INC
1201 W Gladstone St, Azusa (91702-5142)
P.O. Box 575 (91702-0575)
PHONE..............................626 969-1747
Steve Hayes, *Mgr*
EMP: 168
SIC: 5032 3273 3251 1411 Concrete mixtures; Ready-mixed concrete; Brick and structural clay tile; Dimension stone
HQ: Cemex Cement, Inc.
10100 Katy Fwy Ste 300
Houston TX 77043
713 650-6200

(P-9940)
CEMEX CONSTRUCTION MTLS INC (DH)
3990 Concours Ste 200, Ontario (91764-7971)
PHONE..............................909 974-5500
Deborah Sue Politte, *Pr*

Gilberto Perez, *
Thomas Edgeller, *
◆ **EMP:** 35 **EST:** 1990
SQ FT: 20,419
SALES (est): 9.17MM **Privately Held**
SIC: 5032 1423 Cement; Crushed and broken granite
HQ: Cemex, Inc.
10100 Katy Fwy Ste 300
Houston TX 77043
713 650-6200

(P-9941)
COAST ROCK PRODUCTS INC
1625 E Donovan Rd, Santa Maria (93454-2500)
P.O. Box 1280 (93456-1280)
PHONE..............................805 925-2505
Ron Root, *Pr*
Steve Will, *
John Will, *
George Hamel, *
EMP: 45 **EST:** 1955
SQ FT: 5,000
SALES (est): 437.09K **Privately Held**
SIC: 5032 3273 3241 2951 Cement; Ready-mixed concrete; Cement, hydraulic; Asphalt paving mixtures and blocks

(P-9942)
CONCRETE TIE INDUSTRIES INC (PA)
Also Called: Concrete Tie
130 E Oris St, Compton (90222-2714)
P.O. Box 5406 (90224-5406)
PHONE..............................310 628-2328
Paul J Schoendienst, *Pr*
Steve Sim, *
EMP: 70 **EST:** 1981
SQ FT: 280,000
SALES (est): 2.75MM
SALES (corp-wide): 2.75MM **Privately Held**
SIC: 5032 3452 Concrete and cinder building products; Bolts, nuts, rivets, and washers

(P-9943)
ELDORADO STONE LLC
24100 Orange Ave, Perris (92570-8791)
PHONE..............................951 601-3838
EMP: 701
Web: www.eldoradostone.com
SIC: 5032 Brick, stone, and related material
HQ: Eldorado Stone Llc
3817 Ocean Ranch Blvd
Oceanside CA 92056
800 925-1491

(P-9944)
EMSER INTERNATIONAL LLC (PA)
8431 Santa Monica Blvd, Los Angeles (90069-4209)
PHONE..............................323 650-2000
Sam Ghodsian, *Managing Member*
Ehsan Ghodsian, *
▲ **EMP:** 70 **EST:** 1967
SQ FT: 50,000
SALES (est): 24.06MM
SALES (corp-wide): 24.06MM **Privately Held**
Web: www.emser.com
SIC: 5032 Ceramic wall and floor tile, nec

(P-9945)
EMSER TILE LLC (PA)
Also Called: Design Made Easy
8431 Santa Monica Blvd, Los Angeles (90069-4209)

PHONE..............................323 650-2000
◆ **EMP:** 275 **EST:** 1968
SALES (est): 273.97MM
SALES (corp-wide): 273.97MM **Privately Held**
Web: www.emser.com
SIC: 5032 5211 Ceramic wall and floor tile, nec; Tile, ceramic

(P-9946)
M S INTERNATIONAL INC (PA)
Also Called: MSI Orange Showroom & Dist Ctr
2095 N Batavia St, Orange (92865-3101)
PHONE..............................714 685-7500
Manahar Shah, *CEO*
Rajesh Shah, *
Rutesh Shah, *
Chandrika Shah, *
◆ **EMP:** 266 **EST:** 1983
SQ FT: 500,000
SALES (est): 513.97MM
SALES (corp-wide): 513.97MM **Privately Held**
Web: www.msisurfaces.com
SIC: 5032 5023 Granite building stone; Floor coverings

(P-9947)
MARJAN STONE INC
2758 Via Orange Way, Spring Valley (91978-1744)
PHONE..............................619 825-6000
Hikmet Pauls, *CEO*
EMP: 25 **EST:** 2006
SQ FT: 1,600
SALES (est): 5.2MM **Privately Held**
Web: www.marjanstone.com
SIC: 5032 3281 Granite building stone; Cut stone and stone products

(P-9948)
NEW GENERATION ENGRG CNSTR INC
22815 Frampton Ave, Torrance (90501-5034)
PHONE..............................424 329-3950
Raul Ocegueda, *Pr*
EMP: 25 **EST:** 2016
SALES (est): 9.76MM **Privately Held**
Web: www.tngec.com
SIC: 5032 1459 3317 3531 Brick, stone, and related material; Clays (common) quarrying ; Steel pipe and tubes; Construction machinery

(P-9949)
PACIFIC CLAY PRODUCTS INC
14741 Lake St, Lake Elsinore (92530-1610)
PHONE..............................661 857-1401
Darry Coley, *Pr*
Kai Chin, *
Dale Kline, *
▲ **EMP:** 160 **EST:** 1930
SQ FT: 200,000
SALES (est): 20.81MM **Privately Held**
Web: www.pacificclay.com
SIC: 5032 3251 Tile and clay products; Paving brick, clay

(P-9950)
PATRICK INDUSTRIES INC
Also Called: Custom Vinyls
13414 Slover Ave, Fontana (92337-6977)
PHONE..............................909 350-4440
Vince Fergan, *Brnch Mgr*
EMP: 41
SALES (corp-wide): 3.47B **Publicly Held**
Web: www.patrickind.com

SIC: 5032 1799 2435 3083 Brick, stone, and related material; Building site preparation; Hardwood veneer and plywood; Laminated plastics plate and sheet
PA: Patrick Industries, Inc.
107 W Franklin St
574 294-7511

(P-9951)
UGM CITATAH INC (PA)
Also Called: Ugmc
13220 Cambridge St, Santa Fe Springs (90670-4902)
PHONE..............................562 921-9549
Viken Dave Yaghjian, *Pr*
Bruce Feaster, *
Irmen Yaghjian, *
▲ **EMP:** 125 **EST:** 1987
SQ FT: 46,000
SALES (est): 5.01MM
SALES (corp-wide): 5.01MM **Privately Held**
Web: www.ugmcstone.com
SIC: 5032 1741 1743 Marble building stone; Stone masonry; Terrazzo, tile, marble and mosaic work

(P-9952)
VALORI SAND & GRAVEL COMPANY
Also Called: Thompson Building Materials
11027 Cherry Ave, Fontana (92337-7118)
P.O. Box 950 (92334-0950)
PHONE..............................909 350-3000
Tom Rievley, *Brnch Mgr*
EMP: 250
SALES (corp-wide): 2.61MM **Privately Held**
Web: www.thompsonbldg.com
SIC: 5032 5211 Brick, stone, and related material; Cement
PA: Valori Sand & Gravel Company Inc
141 W Taft Ave
714 637-0104

(P-9953)
WEST COAST SAND AND GRAVEL INC (PA)
Also Called: West Coast Materials
7282 Orangethorpe Ave, Buena Park (90621-3331)
P.O. Box 5067 (90622-5067)
PHONE..............................714 522-0282
TOLL FREE: 800
Daniel C Reyneveld, *CEO*
Marvin J Struiksma, *
John Struiksma, *
Robert Struiksma, *
Mike Struiksma, *Co-Secretary*
EMP: 71 **EST:** 1968
SQ FT: 4,200
SALES (est): 102.63MM
SALES (corp-wide): 102.63MM **Privately Held**
Web: www.wcsg.com
SIC: 5032 Sand, construction

(P-9954)
WESTERN PACIFIC DISTRG LLC
Also Called: Westpac Materials
341 W Meats Ave, Orange (92865-2623)
PHONE..............................714 974-6837
Mark Hamilton, *Managing Member*
EMP: 157 **EST:** 2001
SALES (est): 19.56MM **Privately Held**
Web: www.westpac.bz
SIC: 5032 Drywall materials

PRODUCTS & SVCS

(P-9955)
WHITEWATER ROCK & SUP CO INC
58645 Old Highway 60, Whitewater (92282-7600)
PHONE..................................760 325-2747
Allan E Bankus Junior, *Pr*
Irene Bankus, *
▲ EMP: 31 EST: 1962
SQ FT: 4,500
SALES (est): 8.93MM **Privately Held**
Web: www.whitewater-rock.com
SIC: 5032 3281 Building stone; Stone, quarrying and processing of own stone products

5033 Roofing, Siding, And Insulation

(P-9956)
BEACON PACIFIC INC
Also Called: Pacific Supply
675 N Batavia St, Orange (92868-1220)
PHONE..................................714 288-1974
EMP: 110
SIC: 5033 5211 Roofing, asphalt and sheet metal; Roofing material

(P-9957)
CARLISLE CONSTRUCTION MTLS LLC
Also Called: Western Insulfoam
5635 Schaefer Ave, Chino (91710-9048)
PHONE..................................909 591-7425
Tom Tartaglione, *Mgr*
EMP: 96
SQ FT: 45,464
SALES (corp-wide): 4.59B **Publicly Held**
Web:
www.carlisleconstructionmaterials.com
SIC: 5033 3086 Insulation materials; Cups and plates, foamed plastics
HQ: Carlisle Construction Materials, Llc
    1285 Ritner Hwy
    Carlisle PA 17013

(P-9958)
INSUL-THERM INTERNATIONAL INC (PA)
Also Called: Insul-Therm
6651 E 26th St, Commerce (90040-3215)
PHONE..................................323 728-0558
▲ EMP: 24 EST: 1982
SALES (est): 23.24MM
SALES (corp-wide): 23.24MM **Privately Held**
Web: www.insultherm.com
SIC: 5033 2899 3296 Insulation, thermal; Insulating compounds; Mineral wool

(P-9959)
PACIFIC AWARD METALS INC
Also Called: Gibraltar
10302 Birtcher Dr, Jurupa Valley (91752-1829)
PHONE..................................909 390-9880
Brian Lipke, *Brnch Mgr*
EMP: 55
SALES (corp-wide): 1.38B **Publicly Held**
Web:
www.gibraltarbuildingproducts.com
SIC: 5033 2952 3444 Roofing and siding materials; Roofing materials; Sheet metalwork
HQ: Pacific Award Metals, Inc.
    1450 Virginia Ave
    Baldwin Park CA 91706
    626 814-4410

5039 Construction Materials, Nec

(P-9960)
BAKERSFIELD SHINGLES WHOLESALE INC
Also Called: Bsw Roofing Contractors
4 P St, Bakersfield (93304-3192)
P.O. Box 70272 (93387-0272)
PHONE..................................661 327-3727
EMP: 85 EST: 1971
SALES (est): 9.6MM **Privately Held**
Web: www.bswroofing.com
SIC: 5039 1761 Eavestroughing, parts and supplies; Roofing contractor

(P-9961)
LSF9 CYPRESS PARENT 2 LLC
2741 Walnut Ave Ste 200, Tustin (92780-7063)
PHONE..................................714 380-3127
EMP: 3500 EST: 2016
SALES (est): 3.08MM
SALES (corp-wide): 3.08MM **Privately Held**
SIC: 5039 5031 5033 Ceiling systems and products; Wallboard; Insulation materials
PA: Lsf9 Cypress L.P.
    2741 Walnut Ave Ste 200
    714 380-3127

(P-9962)
ULTRAGLAS INC
3392 Hampton Ct, Thousand Oaks (91362-1130)
PHONE..................................818 772-7744
Jane Skeeter, *Pr*
▼ EMP: 23 EST: 1972
SALES (est): 4.63MM **Privately Held**
Web: www.ultraglas.com
SIC: 5039 3231 3211 5231 Glass construction materials; Products of purchased glass; Flat glass; Glass, leaded or stained

(P-9963)
WHITE CAP SUPPLY GROUP INC
Also Called: White Cap 301
28255 Kelly Johnson Pkwy, Santa Clarita (91355-5080)
PHONE..................................661 294-7737
Julia Laguardia, *Brnch Mgr*
EMP: 3639
SALES (corp-wide): 7.35B **Privately Held**
Web: www.whitecap.com
SIC: 5039 5072 Air ducts, sheet metal; Hardware
HQ: White Cap Supply Group, Inc.
    6250 Brook Hllow Pkwy Ste
    Norcross GA 30071

5043 Photographic Equipment And Supplies

(P-9964)
AAA IMAGING & SUPPLIES INC
Also Called: AAA Imaging Solutions
2313 S Susan St, Santa Ana (92704-4420)
PHONE..................................714 431-0570
Robert G Noterman, *CEO*
Lou Burgess, *VP*
◆ EMP: 25 EST: 1998
SALES (est): 3.45MM **Privately Held**
Web: www.aaaimaging.com

SIC: 5043 3861 7699 Photographic processing equipment; Processing equipment, photographic; Photographic equipment repair

(P-9965)
CANON USA INC
15955 Alton Pkwy, Irvine (92618-3731)
PHONE..................................949 753-4000
Glen Takahashi, *Mgr*
EMP: 350
Web: usa.canon.com
SIC: 5043 5044 5045 8741 Photographic cameras, projectors, equipment and supplies; Office equipment; Computers, nec ; Management services
HQ: Canon U.S.A., Inc.
    1 Canon Park
    Melville NY 11747
    800 385-2155

(P-9966)
DIAKONT ADVANCED TECH INC
Also Called: Diakont
1662 Ord Way, Oceanside (92056-1500)
PHONE..................................858 551-5551
Edward Petit De Mange, *CEO*
Mikhail Fedosovskiy, *
◆ EMP: 30 EST: 2011
SALES (est): 9.7MM **Privately Held**
Web: www.diakont.com
SIC: 5043 7389 3625 Photographic equipment and supplies; Patrol of electric transmission or gas lines; Actuators, industrial

(P-9967)
JK IMAGING LTD
14067 Stage Rd, Santa Fe Springs (90670-5225)
PHONE..................................310 755-6848
Joe Atick, *CEO*
Mike Feng, *
Shu-ping Wu, *CFO*
▲ EMP: 100 EST: 2012
SALES (est): 9.39MM **Privately Held**
SIC: 5043 Cameras and photographic equipment

(P-9968)
NORITSU-AMERICA CORPORATION (HQ)
6900 Noritsu Ave, Buena Park (90620-1311)
P.O. Box 5039 (90622-5039)
PHONE..................................714 521-9040
Michiro Niikura, *CEO*
Kanichi Nishimoto, *
Akihiko Kuwabara, *
◆ EMP: 115 EST: 1978
SQ FT: 27,500
SALES (est): 35.5MM **Privately Held**
Web: www.noritsu.com
SIC: 5043 Photographic processing equipment
PA: Noritsu Koki Co., Ltd.
    1-10-10, Azabujuban

(P-9969)
PILGRIM OPERATIONS LLC
Also Called: Tailbroom Media Grop
12020 Chandler Blvd Ste 200, North Hollywood (91607-4617)
PHONE..................................818 478-4500
Douglas Liechty, *Managing Member*
EMP: 400 EST: 2012
SALES (est): 6.79MM **Privately Held**
Web: www.pilgrimmediagroup.com
SIC: 5043 Motion picture studio and theater equipment

5044 Office Equipment

(P-9970)
ALLSTATE IMAGING INC (PA)
21621 Nordhoff St, Chatsworth (91311-5828)
PHONE..................................818 678-4550
Alan Jurick, *Pr*
Richard Shapiro, *
Russel Leventhal, *
EMP: 80 EST: 1990
SALES (est): 4.44MM **Privately Held**
SIC: 5044 Office equipment

(P-9971)
CANON BUSINESS SOLUTIONS-WEST INC
110 W Walnut St, Gardena (90248-3100)
P.O. Box 51075 (90074-1075)
PHONE..................................310 217-3000
EMP: 450
SIC: 5044 Office equipment

(P-9972)
CANON SOLUTIONS AMERICA INC
Also Called: Canon
6435 Ventura Blvd Ste C007, Ventura (93003-7228)
PHONE..................................844 443-4636
Suzanne Alpizar, *Mgr*
EMP: 39
Web: csa.canon.com
SIC: 5044 7699 3861 Copying equipment; Photocopy machine repair; Photographic equipment and supplies
HQ: Canon Solutions America, Inc.
    One Canon Park
    Melville NY 11747
    631 330-5000

(P-9973)
IMAGE IV SYSTEMS INC (PA)
512 S Varney St, Burbank (91502-2196)
PHONE..................................818 841-0756
Terry Shayne, *CEO*
Ronald Warren, *
Sue Warren, *
Rickie Miyake Ctrl, *Prin*
EMP: 79 EST: 1984
SQ FT: 4,000
SALES (est): 7.11MM
SALES (corp-wide): 7.11MM **Privately Held**
Web: www.imageiv.com
SIC: 5044 Photocopy machines

(P-9974)
INTEGRUS LLC
Also Called: Advanced Office
14370 Myford Rd Ste 100, Irvine (92606-1015)
PHONE..................................949 538-9211
Mike Dixon, *CEO*
Richard Van Dyke, *Pr*
Tim Wickers, *VP*
EMP: 100 EST: 2011
SALES (est): 23.07MM **Privately Held**
SIC: 5044 Office equipment

(P-9975)
KYOCERA DCMENT SOLUTIONS W LLC
14101 Alton Pkwy, Irvine (92618-1815)
PHONE..................................800 996-9591
Norihiko Ina, *Managing Member*
Mike Graves, *
EMP: 150 EST: 2008

SALES (est): 19.6MM **Privately Held**
Web: www.kyocerawest.com
SIC: **5044** Office equipment
HQ: Kyocera Document Solutions America, Inc.
225 Sand Rd
Fairfield NJ 07004
973 808-8444

(P-9976)
MICROTEK LAB INC (HQ)
13337 South St, Cerritos (90703-7308)
PHONE...............................310 687-5823
Clark Hsu, *Pr*
Stewart Chow, *
▲ EMP: 110 EST: 1980
SQ FT: 126,000
SALES (est): 3.05MM **Privately Held**
Web: www.microtekusa.com
SIC: **5044** Copying equipment
PA: Microtek International Inc.
No.6 Industry E. Road 3 Science-Based Industrial Park

(P-9977)
MR COPY INC (DH)
Also Called: Mrc, Smart Tech Solutions
5657 Copley Dr, San Diego (92111-7903)
PHONE...............................858 573-6300
Bob Leone, *Pr*
EMP: 75 EST: 2009
SQ FT: 18,000
SALES (est): 85.49MM
SALES (corp-wide): 6.89B **Publicly Held**
Web: www.mrc360.com
SIC: **5044** Copying equipment
HQ: Xerox Corporation
201 Merritt 7
Norwalk CT 06851
203 849-5216

(P-9978)
NEW AGE ELECTRONICS INC
21950 Arnold Center Rd, Carson
(90810-1646)
PHONE...............................310 549-0000
▲ EMP: 130
SIC: **5044** 5045 Office equipment; Computers, peripherals, and software

(P-9979)
TOSHIBA AMER BUS SOLUTIONS INC (DH)
Also Called: Toshiba
25530 Commercentre Dr, Lake Forest
(92630-8855)
PHONE...............................949 462-6000
Scott Maccabe, *CEO*
Desmond Allen, *
Mark Mathews, *
Bill Lombard, *
Larry White, *
◆ EMP: 350 EST: 1999
SQ FT: 90,000
SALES (est): 1.38B **Privately Held**
Web: www.toshiba.com
SIC: **5044** Copying equipment
HQ: Toshiba Tec Corporation
1-11-1, Osaki
Shinagawa-Ku TKY 141-0

(P-9980)
UNITED MERCHANT SVCS CAL INC
Also Called: Ums Banking
750 Fairmont Ave Ste 201, Glendale
(91203-1074)
PHONE...............................818 246-6767
Joyce Gaines, *Pr*
Lynda Neuman, *

Bruce Ferguson, *
EMP: 72 EST: 1987
SQ FT: 8,580
SALES (est): 9.95MM **Privately Held**
Web: www.umsbanking.net
SIC: **5044** 5065 7629 Office equipment; Electronic parts and equipment, nec; Electronic equipment repair

(P-9981)
UNITED RIBBON COMPANY INC
Also Called: United Imaging
21201 Oxnard St, Woodland Hills
(91367-5015)
PHONE...............................818 716-1515
TOLL FREE: 800
Michael Cohen, *Pr*
Yigal Avrahamy, *
EMP: 85 EST: 1973
SQ FT: 22,000
SALES (est): 15.64MM **Privately Held**
Web: www.unitedimaging.com
SIC: **5044** 5943 5021 7699 Office equipment ; Office forms and supplies; Office and public building furniture; Office equipment and accessory customizing

(P-9982)
XEROX EDUCATION SERVICES LLC (DH)
2277 E 220th St, Long Beach (90810-1639)
PHONE...............................310 830-9847
J Michael Peffer, *Managing Member*
Mike R Festa, *Managing Member*
EMP: 90 EST: 1970
SALES (est): 16.26MM
SALES (corp-wide): 3.72B **Publicly Held**
Web: www.acs-education.com
SIC: **5044** Office equipment
HQ: Conduent Business Services, Llc
100 Campus Dr Ste 200
Florham Park NJ 07932
973 261-7100

5045 Computers, Peripherals, And Software

(P-9983)
ACCTON MANUFACTURING & SVC INC (HQ)
Also Called: SMC Networks, Inc.
20 Mason, Irvine (92618-2706)
PHONE...............................949 679-8029
Alex Kim, *CEO*
Frank Kuo, *
Inho Kim, *
Lane Ruoff, *
◆ EMP: 80 EST: 1971
SQ FT: 22,650
SALES (est): 6.8MM **Privately Held**
Web: www.smc.com
SIC: **5045** Computer peripheral equipment
PA: Accton Technology Corporation
1 Creation 3rd Rd., Hsinchu Science Park,

(P-9984)
ADESSO INC
Also Called: ADS Techonlogy
20659 Valley Blvd, Walnut (91789-2731)
PHONE...............................909 839-2929
Allen Ku, *Pr*
▲ EMP: 200 EST: 1994
SALES (est): 1.96MM **Privately Held**
Web: www.adesso.com
SIC: **5045** Computer peripheral equipment

(P-9985)
ALTAMETRICS LLC
Also Called: Altametrics
3191 Red Hill Ave Ste 100, Costa Mesa
(92626-3451)
PHONE...............................800 676-1281
Mitesh Gala, *Pr*
Anand Gala, *
Ajay Shiv, *CIO*
EMP: 140 EST: 2001
SQ FT: 6,000
SALES (est): 9.66MM **Privately Held**
Web: www.altametrics.com
SIC: **5045** Computer software

(P-9986)
AMERICAN FUTURE TECH CORP
Also Called: Ibuypower
529 Baldwin Park Blvd, City Of Industry
(91746-1419)
PHONE...............................888 462-3899
Alex Hou, *CEO*
Darren Su, *
▲ EMP: 120 EST: 1997
SQ FT: 25,000
SALES (est): 90.49MM **Privately Held**
Web: www.ibuypower.com
SIC: **5045** Computer peripheral equipment

(P-9987)
AMERICAN SCALE CO INC
Also Called: Scales
21326 E Arrow Hwy, Covina (91724-1442)
P.O. Box 158 (91773-0158)
PHONE...............................800 773-7225
David William Eccles Iii, *CEO*
EMP: 24 EST: 1946
SQ FT: 4,150
SALES (est): 4.8MM **Privately Held**
Web: www.americanscale.com
SIC: **5045** 3596 7699 Computers, peripherals, and software; Scales and balances, except laboratory; Scale repair service

(P-9988)
ATEN TECHNOLOGY INC
Also Called: Iogear
15365 Barranca Pkwy, Irvine (92618-2216)
PHONE...............................949 453-8782
Sun-chung Chen, *CEO*
Holly Garcia, *
Grace Chen, *
Ching-uei Tyan, *CFO*
▲ EMP: 80 EST: 1996
SALES (est): 21.97MM **Privately Held**
Web: www.iogear.com
SIC: **5045** Computer peripheral equipment
PA: Aten International Co., Ltd.
3f, No. 125, Sec. 2, Datong Rd.

(P-9989)
AVATAR TECHNOLOGY INC
339 Cheryl Ln, City Of Industry
(91789-3003)
PHONE...............................909 598-7696
Juanito Pangalilingan, *CEO*
Toresa Lou, *
▲ EMP: 30 EST: 1999
SQ FT: 48,000
SALES (est): 1.48MM **Privately Held**
Web: www.v4me.com
SIC: **5045** 3571 Computers, nec; Electronic computers

(P-9990)
AXIOM MEMORY SOLUTIONS INC
16 Goodyear Ste 120, Irvine (92618-3757)
PHONE...............................949 581-1450

Keith Carpenter, *Pr*
EMP: 75 EST: 1995
SALES (est): 5.32MM **Privately Held**
Web: www.axiomupgrades.com
SIC: **5045** Computer peripheral equipment

(P-9991)
BAKER & TAYLOR HOLDINGS LLC
Also Called: Baker & Taylor Marketing Svc
10350 Barnes Canyon Rd, San Diego
(92121-2708)
PHONE...............................858 457-2500
EMP: 2243
SALES (corp-wide): 371.99MM **Privately Held**
SIC: **5045** 5065 5192 7822 Computer software; Tapes, audio and video recording; Books; Television tape distribution
HQ: Baker & Taylor Holdings, Llc
2810 Coliseum Centre Dr # 300
Charlotte NC 28217
704 998-3100

(P-9992)
BRAINSTORM CORPORATION
Also Called: Skytech Gaming
1600 Proforma Ave, Ontario (91761-7605)
PHONE...............................888 370-8882
Kevin Hsu, *CEO*
◆ EMP: 200 EST: 2005
SALES (est): 4.9MM **Privately Held**
Web: www.brainstormco.com
SIC: **5045** 5065 Computer peripheral equipment; Electronic parts and equipment, nec
PA: Dfi Inc.
10f, No. 97, Xintai 5th Rd., Sec. 1

(P-9993)
BROADWAY TYPEWRITER CO INC
Also Called: Arey Jones Eductl Solutions
1055 6th Ave Ste 101, San Diego
(92101-5229)
PHONE...............................800 998-9199
Michael Scarpella, *Pr*
Peter Scarpella, *
David Scarpella, *
Margaret Scarpella, *
EMP: 80 EST: 1968
SQ FT: 40,000
SALES (est): 139.47MM **Privately Held**
Web: www.areyjones.com
SIC: **5045** 7378 Computers, peripherals, and software; Computer maintenance and repair

(P-9994)
CURVATURE LLC (DH)
7418 Hollister Ave Ste 110, Santa Barbara
(93117-2676)
PHONE...............................800 230-6638
Christopher Adams, *Pr*
Betsy Dellinger, *
Andrew Gehrlein, *
◆ EMP: 300 EST: 2001
SALES (est): 52.45MM **Privately Held**
Web: www.curvature.com
SIC: **5045** 7379 Computer peripheral equipment; Computer related maintenance services
HQ: Nhr Newco Holdings Llc
6500 Hllister Ave Ste 210
Santa Barbara CA 93117
805 964-9975

(P-9995)
D-LINK SYSTEMS INCORPORATED

Also Called: D - Link
14420 Myford Rd Ste 100, Irvine
(92606-1019)
PHONE..................714 885-6000
William Brown, *Pr*
▲ **EMP:** 164 **EST:** 1986
SQ FT: 120,000
SALES (est): 36.19MM **Privately Held**
Web: www.dlink.com
SIC: 5045 3577 Computers, nec; Computer
peripheral equipment, nec
PA: D-Link Corporation
No. 289, Xinhu 3rd Rd.

(P-9996)

DANE ELEC CORP USA (HQ)

Also Called: Gigastone America
17520 Von Karman Ave, Irvine
(92614-6208)
PHONE..................949 450-2900
Michael Wang, *CEO*
◆ **EMP:** 32 **EST:** 1985
SQ FT: 25,000
SALES (est): 1MM **Privately Held**
Web: www.gigastone.com
SIC: 5045 3577 8731 Computer software;
Computer peripheral equipment, nec;
Computer (hardware) development
PA: Gigastone Corporation
4f, No. 166, Xinhu 2nd Rd.

(P-9997)

DATA EXCHANGE CORPORATION (PA)

Also Called: D E X
3600 Via Pescador, Camarillo
(93012-5035)
PHONE..................805 388-1711
Sheldon Malchicoff, *CEO*
Alan Kheel, *
Burcak Sungur, *
▲ **EMP:** 300 **EST:** 1980
SQ FT: 100,000
SALES (est): 70.96MM
SALES (corp-wide): 70.96MM **Privately
Held**
Web: www.dex.com
SIC: 5045 7378 Computers, peripherals, and
software; Computer and data processing
equipment repair/maintenance

(P-9998)

DATALLEGRO INC

85 Enterprise Ste 200, Aliso Viejo
(92656-2614)
PHONE..................949 680-3000
Stuart Frost, *Ch Bd*
Mark Theissen, *
EMP: 100 **EST:** 2003
SQ FT: 16,000
SALES (est): 1.34MM
SALES (corp-wide): 245.12B **Publicly
Held**
Web: www.getlikes.com
SIC: 5045 Computer software
PA: Microsoft Corporation
1 Microsoft Way
425 882-8080

(P-9999)

EN POINTE TECHNOLOGIES SLS LLC

200 N Pacific Coast Hwy Ste 1050, El
Segundo (90245-5605)
PHONE..................310 337-6151
Frank Khulusi, *CEO*
Robert Miley, *
Brandon Laverne, *
EMP: 200 **EST:** 2015
SALES (est): 48.88MM **Publicly Held**

SIC: 5045 Computer peripheral equipment
HQ: Pcm, Inc.
200 N Pacific Coast Hwy # 1050
El Segundo CA 90245
310 354-5600

(P-10000)

ENVIRONMENTAL SYSTEMS RESEARCH INSTITUTE INC (PA)

Also Called: Esri
380 New York St, Redlands (92373-8100)
P.O. Box 7661 (92375-0661)
PHONE..................909 793-2853
EMP: 1900 **EST:** 1973
SALES (est): 872.47MM
SALES (corp-wide): 872.47MM **Privately
Held**
Web: www.esri.com
SIC: 5045 7371 Computer software;
Computer software development and
applications

(P-10001)

EPHESOFT INC

8707 Research Dr, Irvine (92618-4217)
PHONE..................949 335-5335
Ike Kavas, *CEO*
Naren Goel, *
▼ **EMP:** 71 **EST:** 2010
SALES (est): 9.44MM
SALES (corp-wide): 75.49MM **Privately
Held**
Web: www.tungstenautomation.com
SIC: 5045 Computer software
PA: Kofax Limited
15211 Laguna Canyon Rd
949 783-1000

(P-10002)

ESET LLC (HQ)

Also Called: Eset North America
655 W Broadway Ste 700, San Diego
(92101-8480)
PHONE..................619 876-5400
Anton Zajac, *Pr*
Andrew Lee, *
Brett Stapleton, *
Brent Mccarty, *VP*
EMP: 129 **EST:** 1999
SALES (est): 40.2MM **Privately Held**
Web: www.eset.com
SIC: 5045 Computer software
PA: Eset, Spol. S R.O.
Einsteinova 3541/24

(P-10003)

EWORKPLACE MANUFACTURING INC

Also Called: Batchmaster Software
9861 Irvine Center Dr, Irvine (92618-4307)
PHONE..................949 583-1646
Steve Tait, *CEO*
Sahib Dudani, *
EMP: 200 **EST:** 1999
SQ FT: 5,000
SALES (est): 17.82MM **Privately Held**
Web: www.batchmaster.com
SIC: 5045 Computer software

(P-10004)

GAR ENTERPRISES (PA)

Also Called: Kgs Electronics
418 E Live Oak Ave, Arcadia (91006-5619)
PHONE..................626 574-1175
Nathan Sugimoto, *CEO*
Pastor Kazuo G Sugimoto, *Prin*
EMP: 70 **EST:** 1960
SALES (est): 23.35MM
SALES (corp-wide): 23.35MM **Privately
Held**

Web: www.kgselectronics.com
SIC: 5045 3728 Anti-static equipment and
devices; Aircraft assemblies,
subassemblies, and parts, nec

(P-10005)

GBT INC

Also Called: Gigabyte Technology
17358 Railroad St, City Of Industry
(91748-1023)
PHONE..................626 854-9338
Eric C Lu, *Pr*
Eric C Lu, *Pr*
James Liao, *
▲ **EMP:** 130 **EST:** 1990
SQ FT: 35,000
SALES (est): 634.41MM **Privately Held**
Web: www.gigabyte.com
SIC: 5045 Computers and accessories,
personal and home entertainment
PA: Giga-Byte Technology Co., Ltd.
No. 6, Baoqiang Rd.,

(P-10006)

GENERAL MICRO SYSTEMS INC (PA)

Also Called: G M S
8358 Maple Pl, Rancho Cucamonga
(91730-3839)
P.O. Box 3689 (91729-3689)
PHONE..................909 980-4863
Benjamin K Sharfi, *Pr*
EMP: 77 **EST:** 1979
SQ FT: 20,000
SALES (est): 49.09MM
SALES (corp-wide): 49.09MM **Privately
Held**
Web: www.gms4sbc.com
SIC: 5045 Computers, peripherals, and
software

(P-10007)

GENERAL PROCUREMENT INC (PA)

Also Called: Connect Computers
1964 W Corporate Way, Anaheim
(92801-5373)
PHONE..................949 679-7960
Imad Boukai, *CEO*
Sam Boukai, *
Janet Carmona, *
▲ **EMP:** 84 **EST:** 1991
SALES (est): 23MM **Privately Held**
Web: www.generalprocurement.com
SIC: 5045 5065 Computers, peripherals, and
software; Electronic parts

(P-10008)

GENICA CORPORATION

43195 Business Park Dr, Temecula
(92590-3629)
PHONE..................855 433-5747
▲ **EMP:** 334
Web: www.genica.com
SIC: 5045 5734 Computer peripheral
equipment; Modems, monitors, terminals,
and disk drives: computers

(P-10009)

GETAC INC

Also Called: Getac North America
15495 Sand Canyon Ave Ste 350, Irvine
(92618-3153)
PHONE..................949 681-2900
Ming-hang Hwang, *CEO*
Jim Rimay, *
▲ **EMP:** 90 **EST:** 1994
SQ FT: 12,000
SALES (est): 12.99MM **Privately Held**
Web: www.getac.com

SIC: 5045 Mainframe computers
PA: Getac Holdings Corporation
Building A, 5f, No. 209. Sec. 1.
Nangang Rd.

(P-10010)

HITACHI SOLUTIONS AMERICA LTD (DH)

100 Spectrum Center Dr Ste 350, Irvine
(92618-4967)
PHONE..................949 242-1300
Keiho Akiyama, *CEO*
▲ **EMP:** 30 **EST:** 1990
SQ FT: 12,000
SALES (est): 266.41MM **Privately Held**
Web: global.hitachi-solutions.com
SIC: 5045 7372 Computer software;
Prepackaged software
HQ: Hitachi Solutions, Ltd.
4-12-7, Higashishinagawa
Shinagawa-Ku TKY 140-0

(P-10011)

INGRAM MICRO INC (HQ)

Also Called: Im-Logstics An Ingram McRo Div
3351 Michelson Dr Ste 100, Irvine
(92612-0697)
PHONE..................714 566-1000
Paul Bay, *CEO*
Mike Zilis, *
◆ **EMP:** 4000 **EST:** 1979
SALES (est): 32.76B **Privately Held**
Web: www.ingrammicro.com
SIC: 5045 Computer software
PA: Platinum Equity, Llc
360 N Crescent Dr Bldg S

(P-10012)

JAL AVIONET USA (HQ)

300 Continental Blvd # 190, El Segundo
(90245-5045)
PHONE..................310 606-1000
◆ **EMP:** 30 **EST:** 1985
SQ FT: 13,375
SALES (est): 10.17MM **Privately Held**
Web: www.jalavionet.com
SIC: 5045 7372 5065 7377 Computer
software; Prepackaged software;
Communication equipment; Computer
rental and leasing
PA: Japan Airlines Co.,Ltd.
2-4-11, Higashishinagawa

(P-10013)

K-MICRO INC

Also Called: Corpinfo Services
1618 Stanford St, Santa Monica
(90404-4114)
PHONE..................310 442-3200
Michael Sabourian, *Pr*
Ahmad Gramian, *
EMP: 96 **EST:** 1984
SQ FT: 25,000
SALES (est): 16.68MM **Privately Held**
Web: www.kmicro.com
SIC: 5045 7378 7373 7371 Computers and
accessories, personal and home
entertainment; Computer maintenance and
repair; Computer integrated systems design
; Custom computer programming services

(P-10014)

KINGSTON TECHNOLOGY COMPANY INC (HQ)

17600 Newhope St, Fountain Valley
(92708-4298)
PHONE..................714 435-2600
◆ **EMP:** 780 **EST:** 1989
SALES (est): 418.24MM **Privately Held**

Web: www.kingston.com
SIC: **5045** 3674 Computer peripheral
   equipment; Random access memory (RAM)
PA: Kingston Technology Corporation
   17600 Newhope St

(P-10015)
MAGNELL ASSOCIATE INC (DH)
Also Called: A B S
21688 Gateway Center Dr Ste 300,
Diamond Bar (91765-2452)
PHONE..............................800 685-3471
Robert Chang, *CEO*
◆ **EMP:** 130 **EST:** 1990
SALES (est): 89.51MM
SALES (corp-wide): 2.38B **Publicly Held**
Web: www.absgamingpc.com
SIC: **5045** Computers and accessories,
   personal and home entertainment
HQ: Newegg Inc.
   21688 Gtwy Ctr Dr Ste 300
   Diamond Bar CA 91765
   626 271-9700

(P-10016)
MAGNELL ASSOCIATE INC
Also Called: ABS Computer Technologies
18045 Rowland St, City Of Industry
(91748-1205)
PHONE..............................626 271-1580
Fred Chang, *Pr*
EMP: 256
SALES (corp-wide): 2.38B **Publicly Held**
Web: www.absgamingpc.com
SIC: **5045** Computers and accessories,
   personal and home entertainment
HQ: Magnell Associate, Inc.
   21688 Gtwy Ctr Dr Ste 300
   Diamond Bar CA 91765

(P-10017)
MEDIATEK USA INC
10188 Telesis Ct Ste 500, San Diego
(92121-4761)
PHONE..............................858 731-9200
EMP: 147
Web: www.mediatek.com
SIC: **5045** Computer software
HQ: Mediatek Usa Inc.
   2840 Junction Ave
   San Jose CA 95134
   408 526-1899

(P-10018)
**MICRO-TECHNOLOGY
CONCEPTS INC**
Also Called: M T C
17037 Rowland St, City Of Industry
(91748-1122)
PHONE..............................626 839-6800
Roy Han, *Pr*
▲ **EMP:** 85 **EST:** 1989
SQ FT: 42,500
SALES (est): 2.32MM
SALES (corp-wide): 8.55MM **Privately
Held**
Web: www.mtcusa.com
SIC: **5045** Computer peripheral equipment
PA: Mtc Direct, Inc.
   17837 Rowland St
   626 839-6800

(P-10019)
MSI COMPUTER CORP (HQ)
901 Canada Ct, City Of Industry
(91748-1136)
PHONE..............................626 913-0828
Andy Tung, *CEO*
Connie Chang, *
Juting Chang, *

◆ **EMP:** 90 **EST:** 1998
SQ FT: 77,500
SALES (est): 60.97MM **Privately Held**
Web: us.msi.com
SIC: **5045** Computer peripheral equipment
PA: Micro-Star International Co., Ltd.
   No.69, Lide St.,

(P-10020)
MTC WORLDWIDE CORP
17837 Rowland St, City Of Industry
(91748-1122)
PHONE..............................626 839-6800
Roy Han, *CEO*
▲ **EMP:** 79 **EST:** 1989
SQ FT: 42,500
SALES (est): 2.76MM
SALES (corp-wide): 8.55MM **Privately
Held**
Web: www.mtcusa.com
SIC: **5045** 3577 Computer peripheral
   equipment; Computer peripheral
   equipment, nec
PA: Mtc Direct, Inc.
   17837 Rowland St
   626 839-6800

(P-10021)
NZXT INC (PA)
605 E Huntington Dr Ste 213, Monrovia
(91016-6353)
PHONE..............................626 385-8272
Johnny Chun Ju Hou, *CEO*
▲ **EMP:** 330 **EST:** 2015
SALES (est): 73.95MM
SALES (corp-wide): 73.95MM **Privately
Held**
Web: www.nzxt.com
SIC: **5045** 3571 7379 Computers,
   peripherals, and software; Computers,
   digital, analog or hybrid; Computer
   hardware requirements analysis

(P-10022)
PAYDARFAR INDUSTRIES INC
Also Called: Saratech
26054 Acero, Mission Viejo (92691-2768)
PHONE..............................949 481-3267
Saeed Paydarfar Ph.d., *CEO*
EMP: 60 **EST:** 2002
SQ FT: 5,930
SALES (est): 22.86MM **Privately Held**
Web: www.saratech.com
SIC: **5045** 8711 7372 7373 Computer
   software; Engineering services;
   Prepackaged software; Value-added
   resellers, computer systems

(P-10023)
PC SPECIALISTS INC (HQ)
Also Called: Technology Integration Group
11860 Community Rd Ste 160, Poway
(92064-8888)
PHONE..............................858 566-1900
EMP: 117 **EST:** 1983
SALES (est): 467.24MM
SALES (corp-wide): 1.97B **Privately Held**
Web: www.tig.com
SIC: **5045** 3571 7371 Computers,
   peripherals, and software; Electronic
   computers; Custom computer programming
   services
PA: Converge Technology Solutions Corp
   161 Bay St Suite 2325
   416 360-3995

(P-10024)
PRINTSAFE INC
11895 Community Rd Ste B, Poway
(92064-7125)

PHONE..............................858 748-8600
Thomas Hittle, *CEO*
Linda Hittle, *
EMP: 25 **EST:** 1988
SQ FT: 15,000
SALES (est): 1.9MM **Privately Held**
Web: www.printsafe.com
SIC: **5045** 3953 5084 Printers, computer;
   Marking devices; Printing trades machinery,
   equipment, and supplies

(P-10025)
QUARTIC SOLUTIONS LLC
1427 Chalcedony St, San Diego
(92109-2127)
PHONE..............................858 377-8470
Timo Luostarinen, *Pr*
Jodi Luostarinen, *
EMP: 35 **EST:** 2004
SALES (est): 2.28MM **Privately Held**
Web: www.quarticsolutions.com
SIC: **5045** 7372 7389 7371 Computer
   software; Application computer software;
   Mapmaking services; Custom computer
   programming services

(P-10026)
**REGAL TECHNOLOGY
PARTNERS INC**
2921 Daimler St, Santa Ana (92705-5810)
PHONE..............................714 835-1162
Allen Ronk, *Pr*
Paul Sorrentino, *
Jim Allen, *
◆ **EMP:** 110 **EST:** 1988
SQ FT: 26,000
SALES (est): 44.89MM **Privately Held**
Web: www.regaltechnology.com
SIC: **5045** 7379 Computers, nec; Computer
   related consulting services

(P-10027)
**SAMSUNG RESEARCH
AMERICA INC**
18500 Von Karman Ave Ste 700, Irvine
(92612-0543)
PHONE..............................949 468-1143
David Swanson, *Brnch Mgr*
EMP: 378
Web: sra.samsung.com
SIC: **5045** Computers, peripherals, and
   software
HQ: Samsung Research America, Inc.
   665 Clyde Ave
   Mountain View CA 94043

(P-10028)
**SOLID OAK SOFTWARE INC
(PA)**
319 W Mission St, Santa Barbara
(93101-2822)
P.O. Box 6826 (93160-6826)
PHONE..............................805 568-5415
Brian P Milburn Senior, *Pr*
Brian Milburn, *
Mark Kanter, *
EMP: 25 **EST:** 1990
SALES (est): 9.27MM **Privately Held**
Web: www.27labs.com
SIC: **5045** 7372 Computer software;
   Prepackaged software

(P-10029)
SOUTHLAND TECHNOLOGY INC
8053 Vickers St, San Diego (92111-1917)
PHONE..............................858 694-0932
Grace Pedigo, *CEO*
Robert Pedigo, *
EMP: 65 **EST:** 2001

SQ FT: 16,000
SALES (est): 44.12MM **Privately Held**
Web: www.southlandtechnology.com
SIC: **5045** 8748 7373 7379 Computer
   peripheral equipment; Systems engineering
   consultant, ex. computer or professional;
   Computer integrated systems design;
   Computer related maintenance services

(P-10030)
SPEEDATA INC
6520 Platt Ave Ste 804, West Hills
(91307-3218)
PHONE..............................612 743-7960
Dan Eaton, *Prin*
EMP: 70
SALES (est): 1.55MM **Privately Held**
SIC: **5045** Computers, peripherals, and
   software

(P-10031)
**SPIRENT COMMUNICATIONS
INC (HQ)**
Also Called: Spirent Calabasas
27349 Agoura Rd, Calabasas (91301-2413)
PHONE..............................818 676-2300
Eric G Hutchinson, *CEO*
Bill Burns, *
▲ **EMP:** 350 **EST:** 1988
SALES (est): 474.73MM
SALES (corp-wide): 474.3MM **Privately
Held**
Web: www.spirent.com
SIC: **5045** 3663 3829 3825 Computers,
   peripherals, and software; Radio and t.v.
   communications equipment; Measuring and
   controlling devices, nec; Instruments to
   measure electricity
PA: Spirent Communications Plc
   Origin One
   129 376-7676

(P-10032)
SQUARE ENIX INC
999 N Pacific Coast Hwy Fl 3, El Segundo
(90245-2731)
PHONE..............................310 846-0400
Mike Fischer, *Pr*
Clinton Foy, *
Koichiro Hyashi, *
▲ **EMP:** 110 **EST:** 1998
SALES (est): 24.13MM **Privately Held**
Web: www.square-enix.com
SIC: **5045** 7372 Computer software;
   Publisher's computer software
HQ: Square Enix Of America Holdings, Inc.
   999 N Pacific Coast Hwy # 3
   El Segundo CA 90245

(P-10033)
**SYSPRO IMPACT SOFTWARE
INC**
Also Called: Syspro
1735 Flight Way, Tustin (92782-1852)
PHONE..............................714 437-1000
Brian Stein, *CEO*
Joey Benadretti, *
Kristin Valentyn, *CRO*
EMP: 200 **EST:** 1991
SALES (est): 23.5MM **Privately Held**
Web: us.syspro.com
SIC: **5045** 7372 7371 Computer software;
   Prepackaged software; Custom computer
   programming services

(P-10034)
TP-LINK SYSTEMS INC
3760 Kilroy Airport Way Ste 600, Long
Beach (90806-6827)
PHONE..............................562 528-7700

Dana Knight, *Mktg Dir*
EMP: 159
Web: www.tp-link.com
SIC: 5045 Computer peripheral equipment
HQ: Tp-Link Systems Inc.
    10 Mauchly
    Irvine CA 92618
    626 333-0234

(P-10035)
TW SECURITY CORP (HQ)
5 Park Plz Ste 400, Irvine (92614-8524)
PHONE..............................949 932-1000
John Vigouroux, *CEO*
Bruce Green, *
Rodney S Miller, *
William Kilmer, *CMO*
EMP: 120 **EST:** 2008
SQ FT: 28,000
SALES (est): 21.69MM
SALES (corp-wide): 90.96MM **Privately Held**
SIC: 5045 Computer software
PA: Trustwave Holdings, Inc.
    70 W Madison St Ste 600
    312 750-0950

(P-10036)
U2 SCIENCE LABS INC
Also Called: Ubix Labs
400 Spectrum Center Dr, Irvine
(92618-4934)
PHONE..............................949 482-8540
Miles Mahoney, *Pr*
John Burke, *
EMP: 95 **EST:** 2017
SALES (est): 4.32MM **Privately Held**
SIC: 5045 Computer software

(P-10037)
UBIQ SECURITY INC
Also Called: Ubiq
4660 La Jolla Village Dr Ste 100, San Diego
(92122-4604)
PHONE..............................888 434-6674
Wias Issa, *CEO*
Eric Tobias, *
Linda Eigner, *
EMP: 27 **EST:** 2012
SALES (est): 2.9MM **Privately Held**
Web: www.ubiqsecurity.com
SIC: 5045 7372 Computer software;
    Prepackaged software

(P-10038)
VIRTIUM LLC
30052 Tomas, Rcho Sta Marg
(92688-2127)
PHONE..............................949 888-2444
Robert P Healy, *Managing Member*
Sean P Barrette, *
EMP: 100 **EST:** 2015
SALES (est): 25.35MM **Privately Held**
Web: www.virtium.com
SIC: 5045 Computers, peripherals, and
    software

(P-10039)
WHI SOLUTIONS INC
Also Called: D S T Macdonald
28470 Avenue Stanford Ste 200, Valencia
(91355-1465)
PHONE..............................661 257-2120
Bruce Adamson, *Brnch Mgr*
EMP: 140
Web: www.whisolutions.com
SIC: 5045 7371 Computers, nec; Computer
    software development
HQ: Whi Solutions, Inc.
    2145 Hamilton Ave

San Jose CA 95125
914 697-9301

5046 Commercial Equipment, Nec

(P-10040)
AAMP OF FLORIDA INC
Also Called: Aamp of America
7166 Bickmore Ave # 2, Chino
(91708-9157)
PHONE..............................805 338-6800
◆ **EMP:** 48
SALES (corp-wide): 36.71MM **Privately Held**
Web: www.stingersolutions.com
SIC: 5046 3714 3629 Coin-operated
    equipment; Automotive wiring harness sets;
    Battery chargers, rectifying or nonrotating
PA: Aamp Of Florida, Inc.
    15500 Lghtwave Dr Ste 202
    727 572-9255

(P-10041)
BUYEFFICIENT LLC
903 Calle Amanecer Ste 200, San Clemente
(92673-6252)
PHONE..............................949 382-3129
Dennis Baker, *Pr*
EMP: 124 **EST:** 2000
SALES (est): 1.62MM **Publicly Held**
Web: www.avendra.com
SIC: 5046 Hotel equipment and supplies
HQ: Avendra, Llc
    540 Gaither Rd Ste 200
    Rockville MD 20850
    301 825-0500

(P-10042)
DEPENDBLE BREAK RM SLTIONS INC
1431 W 9th St Ste B, Upland (91786-5698)
PHONE..............................909 982-5933
Zachary Oliver, *Pr*
Mark Oliver, *
EMP: 80 **EST:** 1987
SALES (est): 9.06MM **Privately Held**
Web: www.dependablevend.com
SIC: 5046 7389 5963 5078 Vending
    machines, coin-operated; Coffee service;
    Bottled water delivery; Drinking water
    coolers, mechanical

(P-10043)
HANNAM CHAIN USA INC (PA)
Also Called: Hannam Chain Super 1 Market
2740 W Olympic Blvd, Los Angeles
(90006-2633)
PHONE..............................213 382-2922
Kee W Ha, *CEO*
Kee W Ha, *CEO*
Jeong Wan Koo, *Pr*
▲ **EMP:** 105 **EST:** 1987
SQ FT: 22,000
SALES (est): 14.28MM
SALES (corp-wide): 14.28MM **Privately Held**
SIC: 5046 5411 Restaurant equipment and
    supplies, nec; Supermarkets, independent

(P-10044)
HEC ASSET MANAGEMENT INC
29341 Kimberlina Rd, Wasco (93280-7617)
P.O. Box 1200 (93280-8100)
PHONE..............................661 587-2250
Keith B Gardiner, *CEO*
EMP: 100 **EST:** 2011
SALES (est): 17.72MM **Privately Held**

SIC: 5046 Commercial equipment, nec

(P-10045)
INTERSTATE ELECTRIC CO INC
Also Called: IEC
2240 Yates Ave, Commerce (90040-1914)
PHONE..............................800 225-5432
Edward Urlik, *CEO*
▲ **EMP:** 85 **EST:** 1946
SQ FT: 72,000
SALES (est): 23.04MM **Privately Held**
Web: www.iecdelivers.com
SIC: 5046 Signs, electrical

(P-10046)
JETRO HOLDINGS LLC
1611 E Washington Blvd, Los Angeles
(90021-3133)
PHONE..............................213 516-0301
Javier Gomez, *Brnch Mgr*
EMP: 191
Web: www.restaurantdepot.com
SIC: 5046 Restaurant equipment and
    supplies, nec
HQ: Jetro Holdings, Llc
    1710 Whitestone Expy
    Whitestone NY 11357

(P-10047)
JETRO HOLDINGS LLC
7466 Carroll Rd Ste 100, San Diego
(92121-2356)
PHONE..............................858 564-0466
Dan Camacho, *Brnch Mgr*
EMP: 273
Web: www.restaurantdepot.com
SIC: 5046 Restaurant equipment and
    supplies, nec
HQ: Jetro Holdings, Llc
    1710 Whitestone Expy
    Whitestone NY 11357

(P-10048)
JONES SIGNS CO INC
Also Called: Ultrasigns Electrical Advg
9025 Balboa Ave Ste 150, San Diego
(92123-1522)
PHONE..............................858 569-1400
EMP: 120
Web: www.jonessign.com
SIC: 5046 .Signs, electrical

(P-10049)
JUSTMAN PACKAGING & DISPLAY (PA)
5819 Telegraph Rd, Commerce
(90040-1515)
PHONE..............................323 728-8888
Morley Justman, *Pr*
Russell Justman, *VP*
Barbara Cabaret, *CFO*
▲ **EMP:** 65 **EST:** 1989
SALES (est): 25.37MM
SALES (corp-wide): 25.37MM **Privately Held**
Web: www.justmanpackaging.com
SIC: 5046 5113 2752 Display equipment,
    except refrigerated; Corrugated and solid
    fiber boxes; Commercial printing,
    lithographic

(P-10050)
KUBOTA INDUSTRIAL EQUIPMENT
3401 Del Amo Blvd, Torrance (90503-1636)
PHONE..............................817 756-1171
EMP: 148 **EST:** 2017
SALES (est): 12.68MM **Privately Held**
Web: www.kubota.com

SIC: 5046 Commercial equipment, nec

(P-10051)
R W SMITH & CO
Also Called: Trimark R. W. Smith & Co.
10101 Old Grove Rd, San Diego
(92131-1650)
PHONE..............................858 530-1800
EMP: 74
Web: www.rwsmithco.com
SIC: 5046 Restaurant equipment and
    supplies, nec
HQ: R. W. Smith & Co.
    10101 Old Grove Rd
    San Diego CA 92131
    858 530-1800

(P-10052)
SHOPPER INC
2655 Park Center Dr Ste B, Simi Valley
(93065-6333)
PHONE..............................800 344-8830
Bill Bieda, *CEO*
Elliot Bieda, *
Eta Bieda, *
◆ **EMP:** 300 **EST:** 1992
SALES (est): 5.19MM **Privately Held**
Web: www.communityshopper.com
SIC: 5046 Store fixtures

(P-10053)
TOM DREHER SALES INC
Beach Cities Wholesalers
2021 W 17th St, Long Beach (90813-1011)
P.O. Box 41386 (90853-1386)
PHONE..............................562 355-4074
Tom Dreher, *Pr*
EMP: 77
SIC: 5046 5145 Restaurant equipment and
    supplies, nec; Popcorn and supplies
PA: Tom Dreher Sales, Inc.
    2553 W La Palma Ave

(P-10054)
TRIMARK RAYGAL LLC
Also Called: Trimark Orange County
210 Commerce, Irvine (92602-1318)
PHONE..............................949 474-1000
Michael Anthony Costanzo, *Pr*
Eric Smith, *
Dirk Hallett, *Corporate Secretary*
EMP: 220 **EST:** 1971
SQ FT: 62,850
SALES (est): 22.9MM **Privately Held**
Web: www.trimarkusa.com
SIC: 5046 Restaurant equipment and
    supplies, nec
PA: Trimark Usa, Llc
    9 Hampshire St

(P-10055)
TRINITY EQUIPMENT INC
2650 S La Cadena Dr, Colton (92324-3708)
PHONE..............................951 790-1652
Eric Lewis, *CEO*
Robert Sandoval, *
EMP: 75 **EST:** 2016
SALES (est): 2.33MM **Privately Held**
Web: www.trinityequipmentinc.com
SIC: 5046 7353 Commercial equipment, nec
    ; Heavy construction equipment rental

(P-10056)
TRUST 1 SALES INC
Also Called: Sam Sung Fixtures
1737 S Vermont Ave, Los Angeles
(90006-4523)
PHONE..............................323 732-3300
Richard Kim, *CEO*
Young S Kim, *

▲ **EMP:** 100 **EST:** 1984
SQ FT: 12,000
SALES (est): 1.4MM **Privately Held**
Web: www.trust1sales.com
SIC: 5046 7699 Restaurant equipment and
supplies, nec; Restaurant equipment repair

5047 Medical And Hospital Equipment

(P-10057)
A PLUS INTERNATIONAL INC (PA)
5138 Eucalyptus Ave, Chino (91710-9254)
PHONE..................................909 591-5168
Wayne Lin, *Pr*
David Lee, *VP*
◆ **EMP:** 73 **EST:** 1988
SQ FT: 150,000
SALES (est): 7.77MM
SALES (corp-wide): 7.77MM **Privately Held**
Web: www.aplusgroup.net
SIC: 5047 3842 Medical equipment and
supplies; Surgical appliances and supplies

(P-10058)
ALPHAEON CORPORATION
17901 Von Karman Ave Ste 150, Irvine
(92614-5245)
PHONE..................................949 284-4555
Murthy Simhambhatla, *CEO*
Murthy Simhambhatla, *Pr*
Robert E Grant, *Vice Chairman**
Bob Rhatigan, *
William Link, *
EMP: 105 **EST:** 2012
SALES (est): 20.35MM
SALES (corp-wide): 22.62MM **Privately Held**
Web: www.alphaeon.com
SIC: 5047 Hospital equipment and furniture
PA: Strathspey Crown Holdings Llc
4040 Mcrthur Blvd Ste 210
949 260-1700

(P-10059)
AMERICAN MED & HOSP SUP CO INC
Also Called: Am-Touch Dental
28703 Industry Dr, Valencia (91355-5414)
PHONE..................................661 294-1213
Harish Khetarpal, *CEO*
Roma Khetarpal, *
▲ **EMP:** 32 **EST:** 1987
SQ FT: 25,000
SALES (est): 9.27MM **Privately Held**
Web: www.amtouch.com
SIC: 5047 3843 3842 Medical equipment
and supplies; Dental equipment and
supplies; Surgical appliances and supplies

(P-10060)
AMERICAN MEDICAL TECH INC
750 The City Dr S, Orange (92868-4940)
PHONE..................................949 553-0359
Jean Signore, *Pr*
Jerry Signore, *
EMP: 100 **EST:** 1989
SALES (est): 8.34MM **Privately Held**
Web: www.restorixhealth.com
SIC: 5047 Medical equipment and supplies

(P-10061)
AMERICAN TOOTH INDUSTRIES
1200 Stellar Dr, Oxnard (93033-2404)
PHONE..................................805 487-9868
Emilio Pozzi, *CEO*

Bruno Pozzi, *
Victoria Pozzi, *
Roberto Trada, *
Minda Darimbang, *
▲ **EMP:** 98 **EST:** 1985
SQ FT: 28,000
SALES (est): 4.07MM **Privately Held**
Web: www.americantooth.com
SIC: 5047 Dental equipment and supplies

(P-10062)
ARGONAUT MFG SVCS INC
2841 Loker Ave E, Carlsbad (92010-6626)
PHONE..................................888 834-8892
Wayne Woodard, *CEO*
Patrick Yount, *
EMP: 75 **EST:** 2016
SQ FT: 31,000
SALES (est): 12.62MM **Privately Held**
Web: www.argonautms.com
SIC: 5047 Diagnostic equipment, medical

(P-10063)
ARJO INC
17502 Fabrica Way, Cerritos (90703-7014)
PHONE..................................714 412-1170
Harald Stock, *Brnch Mgr*
EMP: 236
Web: www.arjo.com
SIC: 5047 Medical equipment and supplies
HQ: Arjo, Inc.
2349 W Lake St Ste 250
Addison IL 60101
630 785-4490

(P-10064)
ATG - DESIGNING MOBILITY INC (DH)
Also Called: Numotion
11075 Knott Ave Ste B, Cypress
(90630-5150)
PHONE..................................562 921-0258
TOLL FREE: 800
Mike Swinford, *CEO*
EMP: 26 **EST:** 1996
SQ FT: 10,500
SALES (est): 9.69MM
SALES (corp-wide): 770.72MM **Privately Held**
Web: www.numotion.com
SIC: 5047 5999 3842 Medical equipment
and supplies; Medical apparatus and
supplies; Wheelchairs
HQ: Atg Holdings, Inc.
805 Brook St Ste 2
Rocky Hill CT 06067

(P-10065)
AVENUE MEDICAL EQUIPMENT INC
38062 Encanto Rd, Murrieta (92563-3208)
PHONE..................................949 680-7444
Myo Tun, *Pr*
EMP: 35 **EST:** 2015
SALES (est): 487.85K **Privately Held**
Web: www.avenueme.com
SIC: 5047 5021 3842 5048 Medical
equipment and supplies; Furniture;
Orthopedic appliances; Ophthalmic goods

(P-10066)
AVITA MEDICAL AMERICAS LLC
Also Called: AVITA MEDICAL
28159 Avenue Stanford Ste 220, Valencia
(91355-2203)
PHONE..................................661 367-9170
Michael Perry, *Managing Member*
▲ **EMP:** 114 **EST:** 2005
SQ FT: 23,000
SALES (est): 50.14MM **Privately Held**

Web: www.avitamedical.com
SIC: 5047 Medical and hospital equipment
HQ: Avita Medical Pty Limited
L 7 330 Collins St
Melbourne VIC 3000

(P-10067)
BALT USA LLC
Also Called: Blockade Medical
29 Parker Ste 100, Irvine (92618-1667)
PHONE..................................949 788-1443
David A Ferrera, *Pr*
EMP: 90 **EST:** 2011
SQ FT: 47,000
SALES (est): 37.79MM
SALES (corp-wide): 2.4MM **Privately Held**
Web: www.baltgroup.com
SIC: 5047 3841 Medical equipment and
supplies; Surgical and medical instruments
HQ: Balt International
10 Rue De La Croix Vigneron
Montmorency IDF 95160
139894641

(P-10068)
BINDING SITE INC (HQ)
6730 Mesa Ridge Rd, San Diego
(92121-2951)
PHONE..................................858 453-9177
Doug Kurth, *Pr*
Doug Anderson, *
▲ **EMP:** 77 **EST:** 1987
SQ FT: 23,000
SALES (est): 8.6MM
SALES (corp-wide): 42.86B **Publicly Held**
Web: www.thermofisher.com
SIC: 5047 Diagnostic equipment, medical
PA: Thermo Fisher Scientific Inc.
168 3rd Ave
781 622-1000

(P-10069)
BIONIME USA CORPORATION
1450 E Spruce St Ste B, Ontario
(91761-8313)
PHONE..................................909 781-6969
Chun-mu Huang, *Prin*
Alex Wang, *
▲ **EMP:** 25 **EST:** 2008
SALES (est): 2.64MM **Privately Held**
Web: www.bionimeusa.com
SIC: 5047 2835 Diagnostic equipment,
medical; In vitro diagnostics

(P-10070)
BIOSITE INC
9975 Summers Ridge Rd, San Diego
(92121-2997)
PHONE..................................510 683-9063
Yonkin John, *Pr*
EMP: 76 **EST:** 2011
SALES (est): 7.89MM **Privately Held**
Web:
www.pharmaceutical-technology.com
SIC: 5047 Medical equipment and supplies

(P-10071)
CAMERON HEALTH INC
905 Calle Amanecer Ste 300, San Clemente
(92673-6277)
PHONE..................................949 940-4000
EMP: 100
SIC: 5047 Medical equipment and supplies

(P-10072)
CANON MEDICAL SYSTEMS USA INC (DH)
Also Called: Video Sensing Division
2441 Michelle Dr, Tustin (92780-7047)
P.O. Box 2068 (92781-2068)

PHONE..................................714 730-5000
Shuzo Yamamoto, *Pr*
Nader Rad, *VP*
Calum G Cunningham, *VP*
Scott Goodwin, *VP*
John Patterson, *CFO*
◆ **EMP:** 300 **EST:** 1989
SQ FT: 135,000
SALES (est): 496.54MM **Privately Held**
Web: medical.toshiba.com
SIC: 5047 X-ray machines and tubes
HQ: Canon Medical Systems Corporation
1385, Shimoishigami
Otawara TCG 324-0

(P-10073)
CONVAID PRODUCTS LLC
2830 California St, Torrance (90503-3908)
P.O. Box 4209 (90274-9571)
PHONE..................................310 618-0111
Chris Braun, *CEO*
Mervyn M Watkins, *
◆ **EMP:** 89 **EST:** 1976
SALES (est): 22.94MM **Privately Held**
Web: www.etac.com
SIC: 5047 Medical equipment and supplies

(P-10074)
CRAMER-DECKER INDUSTRIES (PA)
Also Called: Prorack Gas Products
1300 E Wakeham Ave Ste A, Santa Ana
(92705-4145)
PHONE..................................714 566-3800
Ryan W Decker, *CEO*
Paul Cramer, *
Lorraine Cramer, *
Christine Decker, *
◆ **EMP:** 23 **EST:** 1980
SQ FT: 42,000
SALES (est): 9.24MM
SALES (corp-wide): 9.24MM **Privately Held**
Web: www.prorackgasproducts.com
SIC: 5047 2813 Medical equipment and
supplies; Oxygen, compressed or liquefied

(P-10075)
DIRECT MEDICAL SUPPLY INC
5 Knowles, Irvine (92603-3446)
PHONE..................................949 823-9565
Michael Shieh, *Pr*
▲ **EMP:** 200 **EST:** 2010
SQ FT: 50,000
SALES (est): 1.27MM **Privately Held**
SIC: 5047 Medical equipment and supplies

(P-10076)
DISCUS DENTAL LLC
1700 S Baker Ave, Ontario (91761-7707)
PHONE..................................310 845-8600
◆ **EMP:** 207 **EST:** 2007
SALES (est): 40.78MM
SALES (corp-wide): 18.51B **Privately Held**
Web: www.discusdental.com
SIC: 5047 Dental equipment and supplies
PA: Koninklijke Philips N.V.
High Tech Campus 52
402791111

(P-10077)
ELECTROMED INC
4590 Ish Dr, Simi Valley (93063-7678)
PHONE..................................805 523-7500
Terry Belford, *Brnch Mgr*
EMP: 75
SALES (corp-wide): 54.72MM **Publicly Held**
Web: www.smartvest.com

PRODUCTS & SVCS

SIC: 5047 Medical equipment and supplies
PA: Electromed, Inc.
500 6th Ave Nw
952 758-9299

(P-10078)
FISHER & PAYKEL HEALTHCARE INC
17400 Laguna Canyon Rd Ste 300, Irvine
(92618-5425)
PHONE.................................949 453-4000
Justin Callahan, Pr
Tony Barclay, *
Bryan Goudzwaard, *
Paul Shearer, *
▲ EMP: 150 EST: 1995
SQ FT: 5,000
SALES (est): 90.27MM Privately Held
Web: www.fphcare.com
SIC: 5047 Medical equipment and supplies
HQ: Fisher & Paykel Healthcare
Corporation Limited
15 Maurice Paykel Pl
Auckland AUK 2013

(P-10079)
GOLDEN STATE MEDICAL SUP INC
5187 Camino Ruiz, Camarillo (93012-8601)
PHONE.................................805 477-9866
Benjamin Hall, *
Thomas S Weaver, *
Shiela Curran, *
Anita Wrublevski, *
Jim Mcmanimie, Sr VP
EMP: 150 EST: 1989
SQ FT: 95,500
SALES (est): 47.53MM
SALES (corp-wide): 47.53MM Privately Held
Web: www.gsms.us
SIC: 5047 Medical equipment and supplies
PA: Gsms, Inc.
5187 Camino Ruiz
805 477-9866

(P-10080)
GORDIAN MEDICAL INC
Also Called: Restorixhealth
750 The City Dr S, Orange (92868-4940)
PHONE.................................714 556-0200
Gerald Del Signore, CEO
Joseph Del Signore, *
David Simon, *
EMP: 290 EST: 2007
SALES (est): 46.64MM Privately Held
Web: www.restorixhealth.com
SIC: 5047 Medical equipment and supplies

(P-10081)
GRIFOLS USA LLC
13111 Temple Ave, City Of Industry
(91746-1500)
PHONE.................................626 435-2600
EMP: 565
Web: www.grifols.com
SIC: 5047 Diagnostic equipment, medical
HQ: Grifols Usa, Llc
2410 Grifols Way
Los Angeles CA 90032
323 225-2221

(P-10082)
H AND H DRUG STORES INC
Also Called: Western Drug Medical Supply
114 E Airport Dr, San Bernardino
(92408-3473)
PHONE.................................909 890-9700
EMP: 80
SALES (corp-wide): 50.91MM Privately Held

Web: www.westerndrug.com
SIC: 5047 Medical equipment and supplies
HQ: H And H Drug Stores, Inc.
3604 San Fernando Rd
Glendale CA 91204
818 956-6691

(P-10083)
H AND H DRUG STORES INC (HQ)
Also Called: Western Drug
3604 San Fernando Rd, Glendale
(91204-2917)
PHONE.................................818 956-6691
Hagop Youredjian, Ch Bd
Haig Youredjian, *
Zarig Youredjian, *
EMP: 70 EST: 1980
SQ FT: 19,000
SALES (est): 50.91MM
SALES (corp-wide): 50.91MM Privately Held
Web: www.westerndrug.com
SIC: 5047 Medical equipment and supplies
PA: Sg Homecare, Inc.
15602 Mosher Ave
949 474-2050

(P-10084)
HARDY DIAGNOSTICS (PA)
1430 W Mccoy Ln, Santa Maria
(93455-1005)
P.O. Box 645264 (45264-5264)
PHONE.................................805 346-2766
Jay R Hardy, Pr
Jeff Schroder, *
◆ EMP: 300 EST: 1980
SQ FT: 75,000
SALES (est): 95.87MM
SALES (corp-wide): 95.87MM Privately Held
Web: www.hardydiagnostics.com
SIC: 5047 2836 Medical equipment and
supplies; Agar culture media

(P-10085)
HORIBAABX INC
Also Called: Horiba Medical
34 Bunsen, Irvine (92618-4210)
PHONE.................................949 453-0500
▲ EMP: 108
Web: www.horiba.com
SIC: 5047 Medical and hospital equipment

(P-10086)
IHEALTH MANUFACTURING INC
15715 Arrow Hwy, Irwindale (91706-2006)
PHONE.................................216 785-0107
EMP: 80 EST: 2022
SALES (est): 8.71MM Privately Held
Web: www.ihealthlabs.com
SIC: 5047 Medical and hospital equipment

(P-10087)
JB DENTAL SUPPLY CO INC (PA)
17000 Kingsview Ave, Carson
(90746-1230)
PHONE.................................310 202-8855
TOLL FREE: 800
Joseph Berman, Pr
Manny Chada, *
EMP: 120 EST: 1973
SQ FT: 26,000
SALES (est): 23.9MM
SALES (corp-wide): 23.9MM Privately Held
SIC: 5047 Dental equipment and supplies

(P-10088)
KLM LABORATORIES INC
Also Called: Klm Orthotic
28280 Alta Vista Ave, Valencia
(91355-0958)
PHONE.................................661 295-2600
Kirk Marshall, Pr
Scott Marshall, *
Kent Marshall, *
EMP: 100 EST: 1974
SQ FT: 35,000
SALES (est): 4.57MM Privately Held
Web: www.klmlabstore.com
SIC: 5047 3842 Medical laboratory
equipment; Foot appliances, orthopedic

(P-10089)
LEVLAD LLC
9200 Mason Ave, Chatsworth (91311-6005)
PHONE.................................818 882-2951
◆ EMP: 215 EST: 1973
SALES (est): 43.75MM Privately Held
Web: www.levlad.com
SIC: 5047 5122 Incontinent care products
and supplies; Cosmetics
PA: Natural Products Group, Llc
9400 Jeronimo Rd

(P-10090)
MCKESSON MDCL-SRGCAL TOP HLDNG
Also Called: Physician Sales & Service
1938 W Malvern Ave, Fullerton
(92833-2105)
PHONE.................................800 300-4350
Mike Baker, Brnch Mgr
EMP: 265
SALES (corp-wide): 308.95B Publicly Held
Web: mms.mckesson.com
SIC: 5047 Medical equipment and supplies
HQ: Mckesson Medical-Surgical Top
Holdings, Inc.
2054 Vista Pkwy Ste 400
West Palm Beach FL 33411
904 332-3000

(P-10091)
MENTOR WORLDWIDE LLC
5425 Hollister Ave, Santa Barbara
(93111-3341)
PHONE.................................805 681-6000
Diane Becker, Mgr
EMP: 500
SALES (corp-wide): 85.16B Publicly Held
Web: www.mentordirect.com
SIC: 5047 Medical and hospital equipment
HQ: Mentor Worldwide Llc
31 Technology Dr Ste 200
Irvine CA 92618
800 636-8678

(P-10092)
MOBILITY SOLUTIONS INC (PA)
7895 Convoy Ct Ste 11, San Diego
(92111-1215)
PHONE.................................858 278-0591
Martin Helsing, Pr
Richard Tuthill, *
▲ EMP: 25 EST: 1994
SALES (est): 17.43MM Privately Held
Web: www.mobility-solutions.com
SIC: 5047 3842 Medical equipment and
supplies; Wheelchairs

(P-10093)
MOOREFORD INC
Also Called: Expressmed
2544 Campbell Pl Ste 200, Carlsbad
(92009-1769)

PHONE.................................877 822-2719
Mark Howard, Ofcr
Tim Cady, Ofcr
EMP: 72 EST: 2016
SALES (est): 9.73MM Privately Held
SIC: 5047 Medical equipment and supplies

(P-10094)
NANTBIOSCIENCE INC
9920 Jefferson Blvd, Culver City
(90232-3506)
PHONE.................................310 883-1300
Patrick Soon-shiong, CEO
EMP: 128 EST: 2013
SALES (est): 7.11MM
SALES (corp-wide): 158.26K Publicly Held
SIC: 5047 8099 Medical laboratory
equipment; Blood related health services
PA: Nantworks, Llc
9920 Jefferson Blvd
310 883-1300

(P-10095)
NIHON KOHDEN AMERICA LLC (HQ)
15353 Barranca Pkwy, Irvine (92618-2216)
PHONE.................................949 580-1555
Eiichi Tanaka, CEO
Shinya Hama, CCO*
Ken Kanzler, *
▲ EMP: 130 EST: 1979
SQ FT: 35,000
SALES (est): 69.27MM Privately Held
Web: us.nihonkohden.com
SIC: 5047 Electro-medical equipment
PA: Nihon Kohden Corporation
1-31-4, Nishiochiai

(P-10096)
NOVA ORTHO-MED INC (PA)
Also Called: Nova Medical Products
1470 Beachey Pl, Carson (90746-4002)
PHONE.................................310 352-3600
Sue Chen, CEO
Ronald Gaudiano, *
▲ EMP: 30 EST: 1993
SQ FT: 5,500
SALES (est): 22.67MM Privately Held
Web: www.novajoy.com
SIC: 5047 3842 Medical equipment and
supplies; Wheelchairs

(P-10097)
OWENS & MINOR DISTRIBUTION INC
452 Sespe Ave, Fillmore (93015-2042)
PHONE.................................805 524-0243
Michael Guelzow, Brnch Mgr
EMP: 473
Web: www.owens-minor.com
SIC: 5047 Medical equipment and supplies
HQ: Owens & Minor Distribution, Inc.
9120 Lockwood Blvd
Mechanicsville VA 23116
804 723-7000

(P-10098)
P M D HOLDING CORP
Also Called: Peerigon Medical Distribution
26672 Towne Centre Dr Ste 310, El Toro
(92610-2828)
PHONE.................................949 595-4777
Frank Schyving, Pr
Charles Kruger, *
Rick Hayes, *
Mike Shaunessy Technical Services, Prin
EMP: 259 EST: 1996
SALES (est): 840.03K Privately Held

SIC: 5047 Medical equipment and supplies

(P-10099)
PACIFIC MEDICAL GROUP INC
Also Called: Avante Health Solutions
212 Avenida Fabricante, San Clemente
(92672-7538)
PHONE..............................866 282-6834
Michael Roux, *CEO*
Matthew Tschanz, *CFO*
Janet Koller, *Sec*
EMP: 100 **EST:** 2005
SALES (est): 23.83MM **Privately Held**
Web: www.pacificmedicalsupply.com
SIC: 5047 Medical equipment and supplies

(P-10100)
PARTER MEDICAL PRODUCTS INC
17015 Kingsview Ave, Carson
(90746-1220)
PHONE..............................310 327-4417
Hormonz Foroughi, *Pr*
Parviz Hassanzadeh, *Stockholder**
▲ **EMP:** 160 **EST:** 1984
SQ FT: 40,000
SALES (est): 24.44MM **Privately Held**
Web: www.partermedical.com
SIC: 5047 Medical equipment and supplies

(P-10101)
PEARSON DENTAL SUPPLIES INC (PA)
Also Called: Pearson Surgical Supply Co
13161 Telfair Ave, Sylmar (91342-3574)
PHONE..............................818 362-2600
Keyhan Kashfian, *Pr*
Parviz Kashfian, *
Nader Kashfian, *
▲ **EMP:** 105 **EST:** 1983
SQ FT: 88,000
SALES (est): 37.03MM
SALES (corp-wide): 37.03MM **Privately Held**
Web: www.pearsondental.com
SIC: 5047 Dental equipment and supplies

(P-10102)
PETER BRASSELER HOLDINGS LLC
Also Called: Comet Medical
4837 Mcgrath St Ste J, Ventura
(93003-8077)
PHONE..............................805 650-5209
Orlando Deleon, *Mgr*
EMP: 73
SALES (corp-wide): 22.1MM **Privately Held**
Web: www.brasselerusa.com
SIC: 5047 3841 3843 Dental equipment and supplies; Surgical and medical instruments; Dental equipment
PA: Peter Brasseler Holdings, Llc
1 Brasseler Blvd
912 925-8525

(P-10103)
POM MEDICAL LLC
5456 Endeavour Ct, Moorpark
(93021-1705)
PHONE..............................805 306-2105
EMP: 99 **EST:** 2012
SALES (est): 4.9MM **Privately Held**
Web: www.proceduraloxygenmask.com
SIC: 5047 Oxygen therapy equipment

(P-10104)
PRI MEDICAL TECHNOLOGIES INC

Also Called: UHS Surgical Services
10939 Pendleton St, Sun Valley
(91352-1522)
PHONE..............................818 394-2800
EMP: 78
Web: www.agilitihealth.com
SIC: 5047 7352 8741 Instruments, surgical and medical; Medical equipment rental; Administrative management

(P-10105)
QUAD-C JH HOLDINGS INC
4593 Ish Dr Ste 320, Simi Valley
(93063-7696)
PHONE..............................800 966-6662
EMP: 172
SALES (corp-wide): 259.82MM **Privately Held**
SIC: 5047 Medical equipment and supplies
HQ: Quad-C Jh Holdings Inc.
2430 Whthall Pk Dr Ste 10
Charlotte NC 28273
800 826-0270

(P-10106)
QUAD-C JH HOLDINGS INC
1055 E Discovery Ln, Anaheim
(92801-1147)
PHONE..............................502 741-0421
EMP: 184
SALES (corp-wide): 259.82MM **Privately Held**
SIC: 5047 Medical and hospital equipment
HQ: Quad-C Jh Holdings Inc.
2430 Whthall Pk Dr Ste 10
Charlotte NC 28273
800 826-0270

(P-10107)
SAKURA FINETEK USA INC (HQ)
1750 W 214th St, Torrance (90501-2857)
PHONE..............................310 972-7800
Takashi Tsuzuki, *CEO*
Anthony C Marotti, *
Kam Patel, *
▲ **EMP:** 109 **EST:** 1986
SQ FT: 68,000
SALES (est): 85.85MM **Privately Held**
Web: www.sakuraus.com
SIC: 5047 Medical laboratory equipment
PA: Sakura Global Holding Co., Ltd.
3-1-9, Nihombashihoncho

(P-10108)
SHIELD-DENVER HEALTH CARE CTR (HQ)
Also Called: Shield Healthcare
27911 Franklin Pkwy, Valencia
(91355-4110)
PHONE..............................661 294-4200
Jim Snell, *Pr*
Jeffery Thompson, *
Cheryl Hornberger, *
EMP: 200 **EST:** 1983
SQ FT: 95,000
SALES (est): 7.06MM **Privately Held**
Web: www.shieldhealthcare.com
SIC: 5047 Medical equipment and supplies
PA: Dharma Ventures Group, Inc
24700 Ave Rockefeller

(P-10109)
SHIMADZU PRECISION INSTRS INC
Shimadzu Medical Systems
20101 S Vermont Ave, Torrance
(90502-1328)
PHONE..............................310 217-8855
Akinori Yamaguchi, *Pr*
EMP: 80

Web: www.shimadzu.com
SIC: 5047 Medical equipment and supplies
HQ: Shimadzu Precision Instruments, Inc.
3645 N Lakewood Blvd
Long Beach CA 90808
562 420-6226

(P-10110)
SUNRISE RESPIRATORY CARE INC
Also Called: Sunrise Respiratory Care
1881 Langley Ave, Irvine (92614-5623)
PHONE..............................949 398-6555
Oscar Munoz, *CEO*
Oscar L Munoz, *
EMP: 110 **EST:** 2010
SALES (est): 17.26MM **Privately Held**
Web: www.sunriseresp.com
SIC: 5047 Medical equipment and supplies

(P-10111)
TEAM POST-OP INC
Also Called: Team Post-Op
17256 Red Hill Ave, Irvine (92614-5628)
PHONE..............................949 253-5500
Jeffrey Salamon, *Pr*
Lisa Salamon, *
EMP: 105 **EST:** 1988
SQ FT: 1,400
SALES (est): 7.02MM
SALES (corp-wide): 1.12B **Privately Held**
Web: www.teampostop.net
SIC: 5047 Orthopedic equipment and supplies
HQ: Hanger Prosthetics & Orthotics, Inc.
10910 Domain Dr Ste 300
Austin TX 78758
512 777-3800

(P-10112)
THERAPAK LLC (DH)
651 Wharton Dr, Claremont (91711-4819)
PHONE..............................909 267-2000
Todd Gates, *Pr*
◆ **EMP:** 70 **EST:** 2000
SQ FT: 24,000
SALES (est): 50.04MM
SALES (corp-wide): 6.97B **Publicly Held**
Web: www.therapak.com
SIC: 5047 Medical equipment and supplies
HQ: Vwr Corporation
100 W Mtsnford Rd Bldg 1
Radnor PA 19087
610 386-1700

(P-10113)
TOTAL HEALTH ENVIRONMENT LLC
743 W Taft Ave, Orange (92865-4229)
PHONE..............................714 637-1010
EMP: 30 **EST:** 2014
SALES (est): 2.53MM **Privately Held**
Web: www.the-gsc.net
SIC: 5047 3843 5021 Medical and hospital equipment; Dental equipment; Office furniture, nec

(P-10114)
TWIN MED INC
5900 Wilshire Blvd Ste 2600, Los Angeles
(90036-5028)
▲ **EMP:** 500
SIC: 5047 Medical equipment and supplies

(P-10115)
VIDENT
Also Called: Vita North America
22705 Savi Ranch Pkwy Ste 100, Yorba
Linda (92887-4604)

PHONE..............................714 221-6700
Emanuel Rauter, *CEO*
James Mcguire, *Dir*
Janet Siwinski, *
▲ **EMP:** 70 **EST:** 1984
SQ FT: 43,000
SALES (est): 15.18MM
SALES (corp-wide): 113.32MM **Privately Held**
Web: www.vitanorthamerica.com
SIC: 5047 Dental equipment and supplies
HQ: Vita Zahnfabrik H. Rauter Gesellschaft
Mit Beschrankter Haftung & Co. Kg
Spitalgasse 3
Bad Sackingen BW 79713
77615620

(P-10116)
ZEST ANCHORS LLC
Also Called: Zest Dental Solutions
2230 Enterprise St, Escondido
(92029-2004)
PHONE..............................760 743-7744
EMP: 182
SALES (corp-wide): 23.64MM **Privately Held**
Web: www.zestdent.com
SIC: 5047 Dental equipment and supplies
PA: Zest Anchors, Llc
2875 Loker Ave E
760 743-7744

5049 Professional Equipment, Nec

(P-10117)
ABC SCHOOL EQUIPMENT INC
Also Called: Platinum Visual Systems
1451 E 6th St, Corona (92879-1715)
PHONE..............................951 817-2200
Gary P Stell Junior, *CEO*
Thomas Mendez, *
EMP: 70 **EST:** 1964
SQ FT: 35,000
SALES (est): 1.7MM **Privately Held**
Web: www.abcse.com
SIC: 5049 3861 2531 School supplies; Photographic equipment and supplies; Public building and related furniture

(P-10118)
INDIO PRODUCTS INC (PA)
Also Called: Seven Sisters of New Orleans
12910 Mulberry Dr Unit A, Whittier
(90602-3455)
PHONE..............................323 720-1188
▲ **EMP:** 130 **EST:** 2010
SALES (est): 26.98MM
SALES (corp-wide): 26.98MM **Privately Held**
Web: www.indioproducts.com
SIC: 5049 3999 Religious supplies; Candles

(P-10119)
LEXICON MARKETING (USA) INC (PA)
Also Called: Lexicon Marketing
640 S San Vicente Blvd, Los Angeles
(90048-4654)
PHONE..............................323 782-8282
Valeria Rico, *Pr*
EMP: 81 **EST:** 1979
SALES (est): 1.76MM **Privately Held**
Web:
beverly-grove-electricians.myfreesites.net
SIC: 5049 5999 School supplies; Education aids, devices and supplies

---

(P-10120)
REM OPTICAL COMPANY INC
Also Called: REM Eye Wear
10941 La Tuna Canyon Rd, Sun Valley
(91352-2012)
PHONE...................................818 504-3950
Alessandro Baronti, *Pr*
Donna Gindy, *COO*
Donna Nakawaki, *CFO*
Claudio Ninotti, *VP*
◆ **EMP:** 149 **EST:** 1977
SQ FT: 42,000
SALES (est): 22.27MM
SALES (corp-wide): 611.9MM **Privately
Held**
Web: www.derigo.us
SIC: 5049 Optical goods
HQ: De Rigo Vision Spa
    Zona Industriale Villanova 12
    Longarone BL 32013

(P-10121)
SAPPHIRE CLEAN ROOMS LLC
2810 E Coronado St, Anaheim
(92806-2503)
PHONE...................................714 316-5036
Hector Garibay, *Pr*
EMP: 136
SALES (corp-wide): 1.08MM **Privately
Held**
Web: www.sapphirecleanrooms.com
SIC: 5049 Laboratory equipment, except
medical or dental
PA: Sapphire Clean Rooms, Llc
    505 Porter Way
    714 316-5036

(P-10122)
TECAN SP INC
14180 Live Oak Ave, Baldwin Park
(91706-1350)
P.O. Box 1608 (91706-7608)
PHONE...................................626 962-0010
Philip A Dimson, *CEO*
Christian Herr, *
▲ **EMP:** 84 **EST:** 1997
SALES (est): 20.88MM **Privately Held**
Web: www.tecan.com
SIC: 5049 Laboratory equipment, except
medical or dental
PA: Tecan Group Ag
    Seestrasse 103

5051 Metals Service Centers And Offices

(P-10123)
**ALUMINUM PRECISION PDTS
INC**
1001 Mcwane Blvd, Oxnard (93033-9016)
PHONE...................................805 488-4401
Richard Hayes, *Brnch Mgr*
EMP: 125
SQ FT: 15,000
SALES (corp-wide): 37.3MM **Privately
Held**
Web: www.aluminumprecision.com
SIC: 5051 Steel
PA: Aluminum Precision Products, Inc.
    3333 W Warner Ave
    714 546-8125

(P-10124)
BERGSEN INC
12241 Florence Ave, Santa Fe Springs
(90670-3805)
PHONE...................................562 236-9787
Thomas Sharpe, *CEO*
◆ **EMP:** 25 **EST:** 1971

SQ FT: 27,000
SALES (est): 14MM **Privately Held**
Web: www.bergsen.com
SIC: 5051 3317 Steel; Boiler tubes (wrought)

(P-10125)
BLUE CHIP STAMPS INC
301 E Colorado Blvd Ste 300, Pasadena
(91101-1921)
PHONE...................................626 585-6700
Robert H Bird, *COO*
Charles T Munger, *CEO*
Jeffrey L Jacobson, *
Kenneth E Wittmeyer, *VP*
EMP: 3074 **EST:** 1956
SQ FT: 123,732
SALES (est): 5.25MM
SALES (corp-wide): 364.48B **Publicly
Held**
SIC: 5051 Steel
PA: Berkshire Hathaway Inc.
    3555 Farnam St Ste 1440
    402 346-1400

(P-10126)
CALIFORNIA STEEL AND TUBE
16049 Stephens St, City Of Industry
(91745-1786)
PHONE...................................626 968-5511
TOLL FREE: 800
Rick Hirsch, *Pr*
Ron Prichard, *VP*
EMP: 108 **EST:** 1952
SQ FT: 108,000
SALES (est): 23.76MM
SALES (corp-wide): 7.56B **Privately Held**
Web: www.californiasteelandtube.com
SIC: 5051 Steel
HQ: Kloeckner Metals Corporation
    500 Clnial Ctr Pkwy Ste 5
    Roswell GA 30076

(P-10127)
**CALIFORNIA STEEL SERVICES
INC**
Also Called: California Steel Services
1212 S Mountain View Ave, San Bernardino
(92408-3001)
PHONE...................................909 796-2222
Parviz Razavian, *CEO*
EMP: 49 **EST:** 1983
SQ FT: 78,000
SALES (est): 22.09MM **Privately Held**
Web: www.calsteel.com
SIC: 5051 3444 3443 Steel; Sheet metalwork
; Fabricated plate work (boiler shop)

(P-10128)
CMC REBAR WEST
5425 Industrial Pkwy, San Bernardino
(92407-1803)
PHONE...................................909 713-1130
Lee Albright, *Mgr*
EMP: 109
SALES (corp-wide): 1.56B **Privately Held**
Web: www.cmc.com
SIC: 5051 Steel
HQ: Cmc Rebar West
    3880 Murphy Canyon Rd # 100
    San Diego CA 92123

(P-10129)
COAST ALUMINUM INC (PA)
Also Called: Coast Aluminum
10628 Fulton Wells Ave, Santa Fe Springs
(90670-3740)
P.O. Box 2144 (90670-0440)
PHONE...................................562 946-6061
TOLL FREE: 800
Thomas C Clark, *CEO*

Bonnie Clark, *
▲ **EMP:** 125 **EST:** 1982
SQ FT: 112,000
SALES (est): 482.99MM **Privately Held**
Web: www.coastaluminum.com
SIC: 5051 Miscellaneous nonferrous
products

(P-10130)
CONQUEST INDUSTRIES INC
12740 Lakeland Rd, Santa Fe Springs
(90670-4633)
PHONE...................................562 906-1111
▲ **EMP:** 25 **EST:** 1979
SALES (est): 2.99MM **Privately Held**
Web: www.conquestind.com
SIC: 5051 3559 Nonferrous metal sheets,
bars, rods, etc., nec; Jewelers' machines

(P-10131)
CREST STEEL CORPORATION
Also Called: Crest Steel
6580 General Rd, Riverside (92509-0103)
PHONE...................................951 727-2600
James Hoffman, *CEO*
Kris Farris, *
Dave Zertuche, *
Paul Worden, *
▲ **EMP:** 90 **EST:** 1964
SQ FT: 12,000
SALES (est): 23.04MM
SALES (corp-wide): 14.81B **Publicly Held**
Web: www.creststeel.com
SIC: 5051 Steel
PA: Reliance, Inc.
    16100 N 71st St Ste 400
    480 564-5700

(P-10132)
**DANIEL GERARD WORLDWIDE
INC**
Also Called: City Wire Cloth
13055 Jurupa Ave, Fontana (92337-6982)
PHONE...................................951 361-1111
TOLL FREE: 800
Todd Snelbaker, *Mgr*
EMP: 71
SQ FT: 50,000
SALES (corp-wide): 49.4MM **Privately
Held**
Web: www.gerarddaniel.com
SIC: 5051 3496 3356 3315 Wire, nec; Mesh,
made from purchased wire; Nonferrous
rolling and drawing, nec; Steel wire and
related products
PA: Gerard Daniel Worldwide, Inc.
    150 Factory St
    800 232-3332

(P-10133)
**DOUGLAS STEEL SUPPLY INC
(PA)**
Also Called: DOUGLAS STEEL SUPPLY CO.
4804 Laurel Canyon Blvd, Valley Village
(91607-3717)
PHONE...................................323 587-7676
Douglas Stein, *CEO*
Donal Hecht, *
EMP: 86 **EST:** 1972
SQ FT: 100,000
SALES (est): 88.5K
SALES (corp-wide): 88.5K **Privately Held**
Web: www.digitaluppercut.com
SIC: 5051 Steel

(P-10134)
**EARLE M JORGENSEN
COMPANY**
350 S Grand Ave Ste 5100, Los Angeles
(90071-3421)

PHONE...................................323 567-1122
Janice Day, *Mgr*
EMP: 93
SALES (corp-wide): 14.81B **Publicly Held**
Web: www.emjmetals.com
SIC: 5051 Steel
HQ: Earle M. Jorgensen Company
    10650 Alameda St
    Lynwood CA 90262
    323 567-1122

(P-10135)
**EARLE M JORGENSEN
COMPANY (HQ)**
Also Called: EMJ Corporate
10650 Alameda St, Lynwood (90262-1754)
PHONE...................................323 567-1122
◆ **EMP:** 120 **EST:** 2006
SALES (est): 442.9MM
SALES (corp-wide): 14.81B **Publicly Held**
Web: www.emjmetals.com
SIC: 5051 Metals service centers and offices
PA: Reliance, Inc.
    16100 N 71st St Ste 400
    480 564-5700

(P-10136)
FRY STEEL COMPANY
13325 Molette St, Santa Fe Springs
(90670-5568)
P.O. Box 4028 (90670-1028)
PHONE...................................562 802-2721
◆ **EMP:** 115 **EST:** 1945
SALES (est): 23.62MM
SALES (corp-wide): 14.81B **Publicly Held**
Web: www.frysteel.com
SIC: 5051 5099 Steel; Brass goods
PA: Reliance, Inc.
    16100 N 71st St Ste 400
    480 564-5700

(P-10137)
GEORG FISCHER LLC (DH)
Also Called: Georg Fischer Piping
9271 Jeronimo Rd, Irvine (92618-1906)
PHONE...................................714 731-8800
◆ **EMP:** 70 **EST:** 1967
SQ FT: 55,000
SALES (est): 167.25MM **Privately Held**
Web: www.gfps.com
SIC: 5051 5085 Pipe and tubing, steel;
Valves and fittings
HQ: George Fischer, Inc.
    5462 Irwindale Ave Ste A
    Baldwin Park CA 91706
    626 571-2770

(P-10138)
GVS ITALY
8616 La Tijera Blvd Ste 512, Los Angeles
(90045-3946)
PHONE...................................424 382-4343
Bruno Montesano, *Mgr*
EMP: 100 **EST:** 2016
SALES (est): 1.73MM **Privately Held**
SIC: 5051 Aluminum bars, rods, ingots,
sheets, pipes, plates, etc.

(P-10139)
HARBOR PIPE AND STEEL INC
Also Called: James Metals
1495 Columbia Ave Bldg 10, Riverside
(92507-2074)
PHONE...................................951 369-3990
Joseph W Beattie, *Pr*
Martha Fournier, *
Teri Stevens, *
P Jay Peterson, *
Tom Liljegren, *
▲ **EMP:** 150 **EST:** 1962

SALES (est): 26.94MM **Privately Held**
Web: www.harborpipe.com
SIC: 5051 Steel

(P-10140)
JACK RUBIN & SONS INC (PA)
13103 S Alameda St, Compton
(90222-2898)
P.O. Box 3005 (90223-3005)
PHONE..............................310 635-5407
Bruce Rubin, *CEO*
Phillip Mandel, *
Michael Rubin, *
▲ **EMP:** 25 **EST:** 1945
SQ FT: 30,000
SALES (est): 24.47MM
SALES (corp-wide): 24.47MM **Privately Held**
Web: www.wirerope.net
SIC: 5051 3496 3999 Rope, wire (not insulated); Woven wire products, nec; Atomizers, toiletry

(P-10141)
JFE SHOJI AMERICA HOLDINGS INC (DH)
301 E Ocean Blvd Ste 1750, Long Beach (90802-4879)
PHONE..............................562 637-3500
Naosuke Oda, *Pr*
Hidehiko Ogawa, *
Toshihiro Kabasawa, *
◆ **EMP:** 85 **EST:** 1965
SQ FT: 7,500
SALES (est): 291.13MM **Privately Held**
Web: www.jfe-shoji-steel-america.com
SIC: 5051 Steel
HQ: Jfe Shoji Corporation
1-9-5, Otemachi
Chiyoda-Ku TKY 100-0

(P-10142)
JIMS SUPPLY CO INC (PA)
3500 Buck Owens Blvd, Bakersfield (93308-4920)
P.O. Box 668 (93302-0668)
PHONE..............................661 616-6977
TOLL FREE: 800
Clay Watson, *CEO*
Jennifer Drake, *
Jennice Boylan, *
Dan Drake, *
Bryan Boylan, *
▲ **EMP:** 82 **EST:** 1959
SQ FT: 25,300
SALES (est): 24.49MM
SALES (corp-wide): 24.49MM **Privately Held**
Web: www.jimssupply.com
SIC: 5051 Steel

(P-10143)
KLOECKNER METALS CORPORATION
Also Called: Gary Steel Division
9804 Norwalk Blvd # A, Santa Fe Springs (90670-2901)
PHONE..............................562 906-2020
John Ganem, *CEO*
EMP: 75
SALES (corp-wide): 7.56B **Privately Held**
Web: www.kloecknermetals.com
SIC: 5051 Steel
HQ: Kloeckner Metals Corporation
500 Clnial Ctr Pkwy Ste 5
Roswell GA 30076

(P-10144)
M-H IRONWORKS INC
1000 S Seaward Ave, Ventura (93001-3735)
P.O. Box 58364 (90058-0364)
▲ **EMP:** 52 **EST:** 1947
SALES (est): 1.31MM **Privately Held**
SIC: 5051 3312 Steel; Blast furnaces and steel mills

(P-10145)
MWS PRECISION WIRE INDS INC
Also Called: Mws Wire Industries
3000 Camino Del Sol, Oxnard (93030-7275)
PHONE..............................818 991-8553
TOLL FREE: 888
Benjamin Konrad, *Pr*
Darrell H Friedman, *
Alan Friedman, *
Lois J Friedman, *
EMP: 52 **EST:** 1968
SQ FT: 32,000
SALES (est): 20.86MM **Privately Held**
Web: www.mwswire.com
SIC: 5051 3351 3357 Copper sheets, plates, bars, rods, pipes, etc., nec; Wire, copper and copper alloy; Nonferrous wiredrawing and insulating

(P-10146)
NEIGHBORHOOD STEEL LLC (HQ)
Also Called: Maas-Hansen Steel
5555 Garden Grove Blvd Ste 250, Westminster (92683-8240)
P.O. Box 58307 (90058)
PHONE..............................714 236-8700
Gary Stein, *Managing Member*
EMP: 30 **EST:** 2015
SALES (est): 8.11MM
SALES (corp-wide): 482.42MM **Privately Held**
Web: www.sss-steel.com
SIC: 5051 3312 Steel; Blast furnaces and steel mills
PA: Triple-S Steel Holdings, Inc.
6000 Jensen Dr
713 697-7105

(P-10147)
NORMAN INDUSTRIAL MTLS INC
Also Called: Industrial Metal Supply Co
2481 Alton Pkwy, Irvine (92606-5030)
PHONE..............................949 250-3343
Jerry Entin, *VP*
EMP: 43
SQ FT: 40,000
SALES (corp-wide): 82.56MM **Privately Held**
Web: www.industrialmetalsupply.com
SIC: 5051 5099 3366 Steel; Brass goods; Bronze foundry, nec
PA: Norman Industrial Materials, Inc.
8300 San Fernando Rd
818 729-3333

(P-10148)
NORMAN INDUSTRIAL MTLS INC (PA)
Also Called: Industrial Metal Supply Co
8300 San Fernando Rd, Sun Valley (91352-3222)
PHONE..............................818 729-3333
TOLL FREE: 800
Eric Steinhauer, *CEO*
David Pace, *
David Berkey, *
Dave Cohen, *
▲ **EMP:** 125 **EST:** 1945

SQ FT: 70,000
SALES (est): 82.56MM
SALES (corp-wide): 82.56MM **Privately Held**
Web: www.industrialmetalsupply.com
SIC: 5051 3441 3449 Metals service centers and offices; Fabricated structural metal; Miscellaneous metalwork

(P-10149)
PACIFIC STEEL GROUP
Also Called: PACIFIC STEEL GROUP
2755 S Willow Ave, Bloomington (92316-3260)
PHONE..............................858 449-7219
EMP: 417
SALES (corp-wide): 123.74MM **Privately Held**
Web: www.pacificsteelgroup.com
SIC: 5051 Iron and steel (ferrous) products
PA: Pacific Steel Group, Llc
4805 Murphy Canyon Rd
858 251-1100

(P-10150)
PUSAN PIPE AMERICA INC
Also Called: Seah Steel America
2100 Main St Ste 100, Irvine (92614-6238)
PHONE..............................949 655-8000
Byung Joon Lee, *CEO*
Jun Lee, *
Howard Lee, *
▲ **EMP:** 357 **EST:** 1978
SALES (est): 7.15MM **Privately Held**
Web: www.seahusa.com
SIC: 5051 Steel

(P-10151)
RAMCAST ORNAMENTAL SUP CO INC
Also Called: Ramcast Steel
1450 E Mission Blvd, Pomona (91766-2229)
PHONE..............................909 469-4767
Ismael Ramirez, *Brnch Mgr*
EMP: 30
SQ FT: 5,478
SALES (corp-wide): 27.6MM **Privately Held**
Web: www.ramcaststeel.net
SIC: 5051 3312 Steel; Stainless steel
PA: Ramcast Ornamental Supply Company, Inc.
2201 Firestone Blvd
323 585-1625

(P-10152)
RELIANCE INC
Also Called: Reliance Steel Company
2537 E 27th St, Los Angeles (90058-1284)
PHONE..............................323 583-0111
John Becknell, *Brnch Mgr*
EMP: 200
SALES (corp-wide): 14.81B **Publicly Held**
Web: www.rsac.com
SIC: 5051 Steel
PA: Reliance, Inc.
16100 N 71st St Ste 400
480 564-5700

(P-10153)
RELIANCE INC
Metal Center
15090 Northam St, La Mirada (90638-5757)
P.O. Box 2101 (90670-0013)
PHONE..............................562 944-3322
Jay Rose, *Brnch Mgr*
EMP: 80
SALES (corp-wide): 14.81B **Publicly Held**
Web: www.rsac.com

SIC: 5051 Steel
PA: Reliance, Inc.
16100 N 71st St Ste 400
480 564-5700

(P-10154)
RELIANCE STEEL & ALUMINUM CO
Bralco Metals
15090 Northam St, La Mirada (90638-5757)
PHONE..............................714 736-4800
TOLL FREE: 800
Michael Hubbart, *Brnch Mgr*
EMP: 118
SALES (corp-wide): 14.81B **Publicly Held**
Web: www.bralco.com
SIC: 5051 Steel
PA: Reliance, Inc.
16100 N 71st St Ste 400
480.564-5700

(P-10155)
ROSSIN STEEL INC
9102 Birch St, Spring Valley (91977-4109)
PHONE..............................619 656-9200
Ted F Rossin, *CEO*
Jeffrey Clinkscleas, *
EMP: 110 **EST:** 2005
SALES (est): 23.94MM **Privately Held**
Web: www.rossinsteelinc.com
SIC: 5051 Steel

(P-10156)
SAC INTERNATIONAL STEEL INC (PA)
6130 Avalon Blvd, Los Angeles (90003-1633)
PHONE..............................323 232-2467
◆ **EMP:** 74 **EST:** 1979
SALES (est): 1.33MM **Privately Held**
Web: www.sacsteel.com
SIC: 5051 Sheets, metal

(P-10157)
STAUB METALS LLC
7747 Rosecrans Ave, Paramount (90723-2509)
P.O. Box 1425 (90723)
PHONE..............................562 602-2200
EMP: 85 **EST:** 1980
SALES (est): 10.75MM **Privately Held**
Web: www.staubmetals.com
SIC: 5051 Steel

(P-10158)
STEEL UNLIMITED INC
Also Called: Sui Companies
4210 Riverwalk Pkwy, Riverside (92505-3305)
PHONE..............................909 873-1222
TOLL FREE: 800
Mike Frabotta, *Pr*
David Sunde, *
▲ **EMP:** 75 **EST:** 1996
SALES (est): 19.96MM **Privately Held**
Web: www.steelunlimited.com
SIC: 5051 Steel

(P-10159)
TA CHEN INTERNATIONAL INC (HQ)
Also Called: Sunland Shutters
5860 N Paramount Blvd, Long Beach (90805-3708)
PHONE..............................562 808-8000
Johnny Hsieh, *CEO*
James Chang, *
John Hellighausen, *
Andrew Chang, *

◆ **EMP:** 172 **EST:** 1989
SALES (est): 917.07MM **Privately Held**
Web: www.tachen.com
SIC: 5051 Steel
PA: Ta Chen Stainless Pipe Co., Ltd.
No. 125, Xintian 2nd St.

(P-10160)
TMX AEROSPACE
12821 Carmenita Rd Unit F, Santa Fe
Springs (90670-4805)
PHONE................................562 215-4410
EMP: 120 **EST:** 2006
SALES (est): 4.43MM **Privately Held**
Web: www.thyssenkrupp-aerospace.com
SIC: 5051 Steel

(P-10161)
TOOL COMPONENTS INC (PA)
Also Called: E-Z Lok Division
240 E Rosecrans Ave, Gardena
(90248-1942)
P.O. Box 2069 (90247-0069)
PHONE................................310 323-5613
TOLL FREE: 800
▲ **EMP:** 38 **EST:** 1956
SALES (est): 21.33MM
SALES (corp-wide): 21.33MM **Privately
Held**
Web: www.tciprecision.com
SIC: 5051 3429 Aluminum bars, rods, ingots,
sheets, pipes, plates, etc.; Metal fasteners

(P-10162)
TOTTEN TUBES INC (PA)
500 W Danlee St, Azusa (91702-2341)
PHONE................................626 812-0220
Tracy N Totten, *CEO*
David Totten, *
Linda Furse, *
Jeffrey Totten, *
EMP: 60 **EST:** 1955
SQ FT: 73,000
SALES (est): 48.57MM
SALES (corp-wide): 48.57MM **Privately
Held**
Web: www.tottentubes.com
SIC: 5051 3498 Pipe and tubing, steel; Coils,
pipe: fabricated from purchased pipe

(P-10163)
TRANSTAR METALS CORP
Also Called: Castle Metals Aerospace
14001 Orange Ave, Paramount
(90723-2017)
PHONE................................562 630-1400
▲ **EMP:** 450
SIC: 5051 Aluminum bars, rods, ingots,
sheets, pipes, plates, etc.

(P-10164)
VER SALES INC (PA)
2509 N Naomi St, Burbank (91504-3236)
PHONE................................818 567-3000
TOLL FREE: 800
Gloria Ryan, *CEO*
James J Ryan, *CEO*
Craig Ryan, *VP*
Paul Ryan, *VP*
Patrick Ryan, *VP*
▲ **EMP:** 45 **EST:** 1972
SQ FT: 30,000
SALES (est): 24.36MM
SALES (corp-wide): 24.36MM **Privately
Held**
Web: www.versales.com
SIC: 5051 5099 3357 Metal wires, ties,
cables, and screening; Safety equipment
and supplies; Nonferrous wiredrawing and
insulating

**5063 Electrical Apparatus
And Equipment**

(P-10165)
ACUITY BRANDS LIGHTING INC
Also Called: Lithonia Lighting Hydrel
12881 Bradley Ave, Sylmar (91342-3828)
PHONE................................818 362-9465
Dwight Hochstein, *VP*
EMP: 137
SALES (corp-wide): 3.84B **Publicly Held**
Web: lithonia.acuitybrands.com
SIC: 5063 Lighting fixtures
HQ: Acuity Brands Lighting, Inc.
1170 Pchtree St Ne Ste 23
Atlanta GA 30309

(P-10166)
ADJ PRODUCTS LLC (PA)
6122 S Eastern Ave, Los Angeles
(90040-3402)
PHONE................................323 582-2650
Toby Velasquez, *Managing Member*
EMP: 120 **EST:** 2012
SALES (est): 15.41MM
SALES (corp-wide): 15.41MM **Privately
Held**
Web: www.adj.com
SIC: 5063 Lighting fixtures

(P-10167)
**ADVANTAGE MANUFACTURING
INC**
Also Called: Electric Motors
616 S Santa Fe St, Santa Ana
(92705-4109)
PHONE................................714 505-1166
Lyann Courant, *CEO*
Michael Collins, *
◆ **EMP:** 30 **EST:** 1992
SQ FT: 25,000
SALES (est): 6.06MM **Privately Held**
Web: www.advantageman.com
SIC: 5063 5091 3621 5999 Motors, electric;
Swimming pools, equipment and supplies;
Motors, electric; Swimming pools, hot tubs,
and sauna equipment and supplies

(P-10168)
ANIXTER INC
Anixter
7140 Opportunity Rd, San Diego
(92111-2202)
PHONE................................800 854-2088
Marshall Merrifield, *Brnch Mgr*
EMP: 76
Web: www.anixter.com
SIC: 5063 Electrical apparatus and
equipment
HQ: Anixter Inc.
2301 Patriot Blvd
Glenview IL 60026
866 746-3519

(P-10169)
**AQ LIGHTING GROUP TEXAS
INC**
Also Called: Aq Lighting Group
28486 Westinghouse Pl Ste 120, Santa
Clarita (91355-0954)
PHONE................................818 534-5300
Cynthia Piana, *Pr*
Tom Piana, *
EMP: 25 **EST:** 2017
SQ FT: 16,000
SALES (est): 21MM **Privately Held**
Web: www.aqlightinggroup.com

SIC: 5063 3645 3612 2599 Light bulbs and
related supplies; Light shades, metal;
Distribution transformers, electric; Factory
furniture and fixtures

(P-10170)
ARCHIPELAGO LIGHTING INC
4615 State St, Montclair (91763-6130)
PHONE................................909 627-5333
Jia H Deng, *CEO*
Jian H Ma, *CFO*
EMP: 70 **EST:** 2005
SQ FT: 40,000
SALES (est): 11.64MM **Privately Held**
Web: www.archipelagolighting.com
SIC: 5063 Lighting fixtures

(P-10171)
BARTCO LIGHTING INC
5761 Research Dr, Huntington Beach
(92649-1616)
PHONE................................714 230-3200
Robert Barton, *CEO*
Dana B Mcke, *Ex VP*
Brian Labbe, *
▲ **EMP:** 70 **EST:** 1998
SALES (est): 23.98MM **Privately Held**
Web: www.bartcolighting.com
SIC: 5063 3648 Lighting fixtures, commercial
and industrial; Airport lighting fixtures:
runway approach, taxi, or ramp

(P-10172)
BAY CITY EQUIPMENT INDS INC
Also Called: John Deere Authorized Dealer
13625 Danielson St, Poway (92064-6829)
PHONE................................619 938-8200
Mark Loftin, *CEO*
Rodney Lee, *
Charles Loftin, *
EMP: 100 **EST:** 1932
SQ FT: 20,000
SALES (est): 28.42MM **Privately Held**
Web: www.bcew.com
SIC: 5063 5082 Generators; Construction
and mining machinery

(P-10173)
BEACON ELECTRIC SUPPLY
9630 Chesapeake Dr, San Diego
(92123-1389)
PHONE................................858 279-9770
EMP: 74
SIC: 5063 Electrical construction materials

(P-10174)
BRITHINEE ELECTRIC
620 S Rancho Ave, Colton (92324-3296)
PHONE................................909 825-7971
Wallace P Brithinee, *Pr*
Donald P Brithinee, *VP*
EMP: 57 **EST:** 1963
SALES (est): 8.77MM **Privately Held**
Web: www.brithinee.com
SIC: 5063 7694 Motors, electric; Electric
motor repair

(P-10175)
CABLECONN INDUSTRIES INC
Also Called: Cableconn
7198 Convoy Ct, San Diego (92111-1019)
PHONE................................858 571-7111
Lisa Coffman, *Pr*
Roger Newman, *
Rod Coffman, *
EMP: 65 **EST:** 1991
SQ FT: 20,000
SALES (est): 22.72MM **Privately Held**
Web: www.cableconn.com

SIC: 5063 3678 3643 Building wire and cable
; Electronic connectors; Current-carrying
wiring services

(P-10176)
**COMMERCIAL LIGHTING INDS
INC**
Also Called: Cli
81161 Indio Blvd, Indio (92201-1931)
PHONE................................800 755-0155
Frank Halcovich, *CEO*
▼ **EMP:** 74 **EST:** 1991
SQ FT: 81,000
SALES (est): 20.98MM **Privately Held**
Web: www.commercial-lighting.net
SIC: 5063 Light bulbs and related supplies

(P-10177)
CORDELIA LIGHTING INC
20101 S Santa Fe Ave, Compton
(90221-5917)
PHONE................................310 886-3490
James Keng, *Pr*
Li-wei Wang, *VP*
▲ **EMP:** 106 **EST:** 1985
SQ FT: 200,000
SALES (est): 8.64MM **Privately Held**
Web: www.cordelia.com
SIC: 5063 Lighting fixtures

(P-10178)
**COUNTY WHL ELC CO LOS
ANGELES**
Also Called: C E D
560 N Main St, Orange (92868-1183)
PHONE................................714 633-3801
Joe Mihelich, *Prin*
EMP: 76 **EST:** 1986
SALES (est): 8.82MM
SALES (corp-wide): 1.5B **Privately Held**
Web: www.countywholesale.com
SIC: 5063 Electrical supplies, nec
PA: Consolidated Electrical Distributors,
Inc.
1920 Westridge Dr
972 582-5300

(P-10179)
CUSTOM POWER LLC
10910 Talbert Ave, Fountain Valley
(92708-6038)
PHONE................................714 962-7600
▲ **EMP:** 70 **EST:** 1965
SALES (est): 24.69MM
SALES (corp-wide): 207.25MM **Privately
Held**
Web: www.custompower.com
SIC: 5063 Batteries, dry cell
PA: Solid State Plc
Ravensbank Business Park
152 783-0800

(P-10180)
EATON AEROSPACE LLC
Eaton Aerospace
4690 Colorado Blvd, Los Angeles
(90039-1106)
PHONE................................818 409-0200
Stephanie Stewart, *Brnch Mgr*
EMP: 256
SQ FT: 41,117
SIC: 5063 3492 Electrical apparatus and
equipment; Fluid power valves and hose
fittings
HQ: Eaton Aerospace Llc
1000 Eaton Blvd
Cleveland OH 44114
818 409-0200

(P-10181)

ECOSENSE LIGHTING INC (PA)
837 N Spring St Ste 103, Los Angeles
(90012-2594)
PHONE..................................855 632-6736
Mark Reynoso, *CEO*
George Mueller, *
Neil Gamble, *
Steven Gelsomini, *
Robert T Mcculley, *VP*
▲ EMP: 95 EST: 2008
SALES (est): 26.32MM
SALES (corp-wide): 26.32MM **Privately Held**
Web: www.ecosenselighting.com
SIC: 5063 Lighting fixtures

(P-10182)

ECOSENSE LIGHTING INC
14811 Myford Rd, Tustin (92780-7227)
PHONE..................................714 823-1014
EMP: 129
SALES (corp-wide): 26.32MM **Privately Held**
Web: www.ecosenselighting.com
SIC: 5063 Lighting fixtures
PA: Ecosense Lighting Inc.
837 N Spring St Ste 103
855 632-6736

(P-10183)

EXPO POWER SYSTEMS INC
Also Called: Enviroguard
5534 Olive St, Montclair (91763-1649)
PHONE..................................800 506-9884
Doug Frazier, *Pr*
EMP: 34 EST: 1993
SQ FT: 15,000
SALES (est): 18.79MM **Privately Held**
Web: www.enviroguard.com
SIC: 5063 3444 Batteries; Sheet metalwork

(P-10184)

GRAYBAR ELECTRIC COMPANY INC
Also Called: Graybar
1370 Valley Vista Dr Ste 100, Diamond Bar
(91765-3921)
PHONE..................................909 451-4300
Bruce Spencer, *Brnch Mgr*
EMP: 153
SALES (corp-wide): 11.04B **Privately Held**
Web: www.graybar.com
SIC: 5063 5065 Electrical supplies, nec;
Telephone equipment
PA: Graybar Electric Company, Inc.
34 N Meramec Ave
314 573-9200

(P-10185)

GRAYBAR ELECTRIC COMPANY INC
8606 Miralani Dr, San Diego (92126-4353)
PHONE..................................858 578-8606
Chris Ruperto, *Mgr*
EMP: 91
SQ FT: 42,973
SALES (corp-wide): 11.04B **Privately Held**
Web: www.graybar.com
SIC: 5063 Electrical supplies, nec
PA: Graybar Electric Company, Inc.
34 N Meramec Ave
314 573-9200

(P-10186)

HOCHIKI AMERICA CORPORATION (HQ)
Also Called: Hochiki
7051 Village Dr Ste 100, Buena Park
(90621-2268)

P.O. Box 514689 (90051-4689)
PHONE..................................714 522-2246
Hisham Harake, *CEO*
Hiroshi Kamei, *VP*
Sunichi Shoji V Pes, *Prin*
Michel Nader, *Dir*
◆ EMP: 95 EST: 1972
SQ FT: 30,000
SALES (est): 48.18MM **Privately Held**
Web: www.hochikiamerica.com
SIC: 5063 3669 Fire alarm systems; Fire
detection systems, electric
PA: Hochiki Corporation
2-10-43, Kamiosaki

(P-10187)

JME INC (PA)
Also Called: T M B
527 Park Ave, San Fernando (91340-2557)
PHONE..................................201 896-8600
Colin R Waters, *CEO*
Thomas M Bissett, *
◆ EMP: 80 EST: 1982
SQ FT: 34,000
SALES (est): 21.39MM
SALES (corp-wide): 21.39MM **Privately Held**
Web: www.tmb.com
SIC: 5063 3499 Lighting fittings and
accessories; Aerosol valves, metal

(P-10188)

KOBERT & COMPANY INC
Also Called: L.H. Dottie Co
6131 Garfield Ave, Commerce
(90040-3610)
PHONE..................................323 725-1000
▲ EMP: 90 EST: 1965
SALES (est): 22.2MM **Privately Held**
Web: www.lhdottie.com
SIC: 5063 5074 Electrical supplies, nec;
Plumbing fittings and supplies

(P-10189)

LIGHTING TECHNOLOGIES INTL LLC
13700 Live Oak Ave, Baldwin Park
(91706-1319)
PHONE..................................626 480-0755
▲ EMP: 190 EST: 2016
SALES (est): 24.06MM **Privately Held**
Web: www.ltilighting.com
SIC: 5063 3648 Lighting fixtures; Lighting
equipment, nec

(P-10190)

LOS ANGELES LTG MFG CO INC
Also Called: L A Lighting
10141 Olney St, El Monte (91731-2311)
PHONE..................................626 454-8300
William D Shapiro, *Pr*
Mieko Shapiro, *VP*
◆ EMP: 70 EST: 1988
SQ FT: 50,000
SALES (est): 22.27MM **Privately Held**
Web: www.lalighting.com
SIC: 5063 3646 Lighting fixtures; Ceiling
systems, luminous

(P-10191)

MAGNETIKA INC (PA)
2041 W 139th St, Gardena (90249-2409)
PHONE..................................310 527-8100
Francis Ishida, *Pr*
Basil P Caloyeras, *
EMP: 80 EST: 1960
SQ FT: 40,000
SALES (est): 23.39MM
SALES (corp-wide): 23.39MM **Privately Held**

Web: www.magnetika.com
SIC: 5063 3612 Transformers, electric;
Ballasts for lighting fixtures

(P-10192)

MAIN ELECTRIC SUPPLY CO LLC
4674 Cardin St, San Diego (92111-1419)
PHONE..................................858 737-7000
Darryl Dalrymple, *Brnch Mgr*
EMP: 44
SALES (corp-wide): 464.19MM **Privately Held**
Web: www.mainelectricsupply.com
SIC: 5063 3699 Electrical supplies, nec;
Electrical equipment and supplies, nec
PA: Main Electric Supply Company Llc
3600 W Segerstrom Ave
949 833-3052

(P-10193)

MAXIM LIGHTING INTL INC (PA)
Also Called: Maxim Lighting
253 Vineland Ave, City Of Industry
(91746-2319)
PHONE..................................626 956-4200
Jacob Sperling, *CEO*
Zvi Sperling, *
Michael S Andrews, *
▲ EMP: 81 EST: 1999
SQ FT: 26,000
SALES (est): 47.04MM
SALES (corp-wide): 47.04MM **Privately Held**
Web: www.maximlighting.com
SIC: 5063 Lighting fixtures

(P-10194)

MINKA LIGHTING LLC (DH)
Also Called: Minka Group
1151 Bradford Cir, Corona (92882-7166)
PHONE..................................951 735-9220
William S Brundage, *Managing Member*
Ian T Graham, *
Marian Tang, *
Kurt Schulzman, *
◆ EMP: 70 EST: 1982
SQ FT: 350,000
SALES (est): 22.9MM
SALES (corp-wide): 29.73B **Privately Held**
Web: www.minkagroup.net
SIC: 5063 Lighting fixtures
HQ: Ferguson Enterprises, Llc
751 Lakefront Cmns
Newport News VA 23606
757 874-7795

(P-10195)

MOTIVE ENERGY LLC (PA)
125 E Commercial St Ste B, Anaheim
(02801 1217)
PHONE..................................714 888-2525
Robert J Istwan, *Pr*
▼ EMP: 80 EST: 1979
SALES (est): 55.28MM
SALES (corp-wide): 55.28MM **Privately Held**
Web: www.motiveenergy.com
SIC: 5063 Storage batteries, industrial

(P-10196)

MULTIQUIP INC (DH)
Also Called: Mq Power
6141 Katella Ave Ste 200, Cypress
(90630-5202)
PHONE..................................310 537-3700
Robert J Graydon, *CEO*
James Henehan, *
◆ EMP: 300 EST: 1973
SALES (est): 214.36MM **Privately Held**

Web: www.multiquip.com
SIC: 5063 5082 3645 Generators; General
construction machinery and equipment;
Garden, patio, walkway and yard lighting
fixtures: electric
HQ: Itochu International Inc.
1251 Ave Of The Amrcas Fl
New York NY 10020
212 818-8000

(P-10197)

MURCAL INC
Also Called: Murcal
41343 12th St W, Palmdale (93551-1442)
PHONE..................................661 272-4700
Robert J Murphy, *Pr*
John H Murphy, *
Essie Murphy, *Stockholder*
EMP: 26 EST: 1958
SQ FT: 20,000
SALES (est): 10.08MM **Privately Held**
Web: www.murcal.com
SIC: 5063 3621 3694 Motor controls,
starters and relays: electric; Storage battery
chargers, motor and engine generator type;
Ignition apparatus, internal combustion
engines

(P-10198)

NORA LIGHTING INC
6505 Gayhart St, Commerce (90040-2507)
PHONE..................................323 767-2600
Fred Farzan, *CEO*
Jill Farzan, *
Neda Farzan, *
◆ EMP: 144 EST: 1989
SQ FT: 150,000
SALES (est): 90MM **Privately Held**
Web: www.noralighting.com
SIC: 5063 3648 5719 Lighting fixtures;
Lighting fixtures, except electric: residential;
Lighting fixtures

(P-10199)

ORBIT INDUSTRIES INC
7533 Garfield Ave, Bell Gardens
(90201-4817)
PHONE..................................213 745-8884
Saeed Nikayin, *CEO*
John Alexandrovic, *
▲ EMP: 98 EST: 1965
SALES (est): 3.92MM **Privately Held**
Web: www.orbitelectric.com
SIC: 5063 Electrical apparatus and
equipment
HQ: Element Materials Technology Group
Limited
Davidson Building, 5 Southampton
Street
London WC2E
800 470-3598

(P-10200)

PACIFIC POWER SYSTEMS INTEGRATION INC
14729 Spring Ave, Santa Fe Springs
(90670-5107)
PHONE..................................562 281-0500
EMP: 23
SIC: 5063 3826 Transformers, electric;
Petroleum product analyzing apparatus

(P-10201)

PLC IMPORTS INC
Also Called: P L C Lighting
9667 Owensmouth Ave Ste 201,
Chatsworth (91311-4818)
PHONE..................................818 349-1600
Daniel Gilardi, *Pr*
Robert Gilardi, *

PRODUCTS & SVCS

▲ **EMP:** 25 **EST:** 1992
SALES (est): 2.23MM **Privately Held**
Web: www.plclighting.com
SIC: 5063 3646 Light bulbs and related
    supplies; Commercial lighting fixtures

(P-10202)
POWER SYSTEMS WEST LLC ✪
13625 Danielson St, Poway (92064-6829)
PHONE...............................208 869-0483
Rodney Lee, *Managing Member*
EMP: 150 **EST:** 2024
SALES (est): 2.63MM **Privately Held**
SIC: 5063 Electrical apparatus and
    equipment

(P-10203)
**PRECISION FLUORESCENT
WEST INC**
Also Called: Precision Energy Efficient Ltg
23281 La Palma Ave, Yorba Linda
(92887-4768)
PHONE...............................352 692-5900
Raymond Pustinger, *Pr*
Dan Rodriguez, *
▲ **EMP:** 95 **EST:** 1995
SQ FT: 31,000
SALES (est): 3.09MM
SALES (corp-wide): 1.6B **Privately Held**
SIC: 5063 Electrical supplies, nec
HQ: Hli Solutions, Inc.
    701 Millennium Blvd
    Greenville SC 29607

(P-10204)
QUANTUM AUTOMATION (PA)
4400 E La Palma Ave, Anaheim
(92807-1807)
P.O. Box 18687 (92817-8687)
PHONE...............................714 854-0800
Brian Gallogly, *Pr*
EMP: 35 **EST:** 1991
SQ FT: 11,000
SALES (est): 13.12MM **Privately Held**
Web: www.quantumautomation.com
SIC: 5063 3825 3613 Electrical apparatus
    and equipment; Electrical power measuring
    equipment; Control panels, electric

(P-10205)
**REGENCY ENTERPRISES INC
(PA)**
Also Called: Regency Supply
9261 Jordan Ave, Chatsworth (91311-5739)
PHONE...............................818 901-0255
Ron Regenstreif, *CEO*
Scott Anderson, *
Isaac Regensreif, *
Judah Regenstreif, *
Mike Goldstone, *
◆ **EMP:** 272 **EST:** 1981
SALES (est): 83.97MM
SALES (corp-wide): 83.97MM **Privately
Held**
Web: www.regencysupply.com
SIC: 5063 Light bulbs and related supplies

(P-10206)
SIEMENS INDUSTRY INC
6141 Katella Ave, Cypress (90630-5202)
PHONE...............................714 761-2200
Eric Ackerman, *Genl Mgr*
EMP: 80
SALES (corp-wide): 84.78B **Privately Held**
Web: www.siemens.com
SIC: 5063 Electrical apparatus and
    equipment
HQ: Siemens Industry, Inc.
    1000 Deerfield Pkwy
    Buffalo Grove IL 60089
    847 215-1000

(P-10207)
**SLOAN ELECTRIC
CORPORATION**
3520 Main St, San Diego (92113-3804)
PHONE...............................619 239-5174
EMP: 28 **EST:** 1985
SALES (est): 9.39MM **Privately Held**
Web: www.sloanelectric.com
SIC: 5063 7694 7629 Motor controls,
    starters and relays; electric; Electric motor
    repair; Generator repair

(P-10208)
SOLARWORLD AMERICAS LLC
4650 Adohr Ln, Camarillo (93012-8508)
PHONE...............................503 844-3400
◆ **EMP:** 75
SIC: 5063 Electrical apparatus and
    equipment

(P-10209)
SUNCO LIGHTING INC
27811 Hancock Pkwy Ste A, Valencia
(91355-4187)
PHONE...............................844 334-9938
Sorush Tahour, *CEO*
EMP: 44 **EST:** 2014
SALES (est): 11.71MM **Privately Held**
Web: www.sunco.com
SIC: 5063 3699 Electrical supplies, nec;
    Electrical equipment and supplies, nec

(P-10210)
UNS ELECTRIC INC
6565 Valley View St, La Palma
(90623-1060)
PHONE...............................714 690-3660
Irene Mitchell, *Prin*
EMP: 26
SALES (corp-wide): 8.38B **Privately Held**
Web: www.uesaz.com
SIC: 5063 3691 Storage batteries, industrial;
    Storage batteries
HQ: Uns Electric, Inc.
    88 E Bradway Blvd Hqe 901
    Tucson AZ 85701
    928 681-8966

(P-10211)
US ELECTRICAL SERVICES INC
Also Called: Wiedenbach-Brown
1501 E Orangethorpe Ave Ste 140,
Fullerton (92831-5252)
PHONE...............................714 982-1534
Scott King, *Mgr*
EMP: 26
SALES (corp-wide): 734.19MM **Privately
Held**
Web: www.usesi.com
SIC: 5063 3645 Lighting fixtures; Residential
    lighting fixtures
HQ: U.S. Electrical Services, Inc.
    701 Middle St
    Middletown CT 06457

(P-10212)
USHIO AMERICA INC (HQ)
5440 Cerritos Ave, Cypress (90630-4567)
PHONE...............................714 236-8600
Tetsuya Nishio, *Pr*
Shinji Kameda, *CFO*
Ako Shimada, *Sec*
Yuichi Asaka, *Prin*
◆ **EMP:** 90 **EST:** 1967
SQ FT: 70,000
SALES (est): 57.83MM **Privately Held**
Web: www.ushio.com
SIC: 5063 Lighting fixtures, commercial and
    industrial
PA: Ushio Inc.
    1-6-5, Marunouchi

(P-10213)
**WALTERS WHOLESALE
ELECTRIC CO (HQ)**
200 N Berry St, Brea (92821-3903)
PHONE...............................714 784-1900
John L Walter, *CEO*
Bill Durkee, *
Roland Wood, *
Nancy Nielsen, *
▼ **EMP:** 50 **EST:** 1953
SALES (est): 374.7MM
SALES (corp-wide): 1.5B **Privately Held**
Web: www.walterswholesale.com
SIC: 5063 3699 1731 Wire and cable;
    Electronic training devices; Lighting
    contractor
PA: Consolidated Electrical Distributors,
    Inc.
    1920 Westridge Dr
    972 582-5300

5064 Electrical Appliances, Television And Radio

(P-10214)
AVA ENTERPRISES INC (PA)
Also Called: Boss Audio Systems
3451 Lunar Ct, Oxnard (93030-8976)
PHONE...............................805 988-0192
Soheil Rabbani, *Pr*
Sheila Rabbani, *VP*
Kam Mobini, *Stockholder*
◆ **EMP:** 85 **EST:** 1988
SQ FT: 70,000
SALES (est): 23.72MM **Privately Held**
Web: www.bossaudio.com
SIC: 5064 Radios, motor vehicle

(P-10215)
DRAGON TRADE INTL CORP
1205 Highland Ave, National City
(91950-3536)
PHONE...............................619 816-6062
Jorge Petit, *CEO*
Carlos Hermida, *
Manuel Hermida Rodriguez, *
EMP: 200 **EST:** 2014
SALES (est): 55MM **Privately Held**
SIC: 5064 Electrical appliances, major

(P-10216)
**E & S INTERNATIONAL ENTPS
INC (PA)**
Also Called: Import Direct
7801 Hayvenhurst Ave, Van Nuys
(91406-1712)
PHONE...............................818 887-0700
Philip Asherian, *CEO*
Farshad Asherian, *
Mike Rad, *COO*
Mark Barron, *
◆ **EMP:** 168 **EST:** 1983
SQ FT: 60,000
SALES (est): 88.54MM
SALES (corp-wide): 88.54MM **Privately
Held**
Web: www.esintl.com
SIC: 5064 Electrical appliances, major

(P-10217)
**EPSILON ELECTRONICS INC
(PA)**
Also Called: Power Acoustik Electronics
1550 S Maple Ave, Montebello
(90640-6508)
PHONE...............................323 722-3333
Jack Rochel, *Pr*
Mossa Rochel, *

◆ **EMP:** 77 **EST:** 1983
SQ FT: 69,000
SALES (est): 7.73MM
SALES (corp-wide): 7.73MM **Privately
Held**
Web: www.epsilonelectronicsinc.com
SIC: 5064 Electrical entertainment equipment

(P-10218)
ETEKCITY CORPORATION
Also Called: Etekcity
1202 N Miller St Unit A, Anaheim
(92806-1956)
PHONE...............................855 686-3835
Grace Yang, *CEO*
Phillip Chen, *
Sean Yang, *CIO*
EMP: 125 **EST:** 2011
SALES (est): 48.53MM **Privately Held**
Web: www.vesync.com
SIC: 5064 Electrical appliances, television
    and radio

(P-10219)
**HARMAN-KARDON
INCORPORATED**
Also Called: Harman-Kardon
8500 Balboa Blvd, Northridge (91325-5802)
P.O. Box 2200 (91328-2200)
PHONE...............................818 841-4600
Tom Mcloughlin, *Pr*
Chet Simon, *VP Fin*
▲ **EMP:** 275 **EST:** 1949
SALES (est): 5.83MM **Privately Held**
Web: www.harman.com
SIC: 5064 3651 High fidelity equipment;
    Household audio and video equipment
HQ: Harman International Industries
    Incorporated
    400 Atlantic St Fl 15
    Stamford CT 06901
    203 328-3500

(P-10220)
HOMELAND HOUSEWARES LLC
Also Called: Magic Bullet
10900 Wilshire Blvd Ste 900, Los Angeles
(90024-6501)
PHONE...............................310 996-7200
Rich Krause, *CEO*
▲ **EMP:** 80 **EST:** 2003
SALES (est): 5.02MM
SALES (corp-wide): 47.46MM **Privately
Held**
Web: www.nutribullet.com
SIC: 5064 5963 Electrical appliances, major;
    Appliance sales, house-to-house
HQ: Capital Brands, Llc
    10900 Wilshire Blvd # 900
    Los Angeles CA 90024

(P-10221)
MEMOREX PRODUCTS INC
17777 Center Court Dr N Ste 800, Cerritos
(90703-8575)
PHONE...............................562 653-2800
Michael Golacinski, *Pr*
Allan Yap, *
Mae Higa, *
Kevin Mcdonnell, *Sr VP*
▲ **EMP:** 159 **EST:** 1993
SQ FT: 212,000
SALES (est): 7.95MM **Publicly Held**
SIC: 5064 5065 5045 3652 Electrical
    entertainment equipment; Radio and
    television equipment and parts; Computer
    peripheral equipment; Prerecorded records
    and tapes
PA: Glassbridge Enterprises, Inc.
    18 E 50th St Ste 700

▲ = Import ▼ = Export
◆ = Import/Export

(P-10222)

PHILIPS NORTH AMERICA LLC

Also Called: Innercool Therapies
3721 Valley Centre Dr, San Diego
(92130-3329)
PHONE..................................858 677-6390
John Dobak, *CEO*
EMP: 85
SALES (corp-wide): 18.51B **Privately Held**
Web: usa.philips.com
SIC: **5064** Television sets
HQ: Philips North America Llc
222 Jacobs St Fl 3
Cambridge MA 02141
617 245-5900

(P-10223)

PIONEER NORTH AMERICA INC

2050 W 190th St Ste 100, Torrance
(90504-6229)
PHONE..................................310 952-2000
EMP: 216
Web: www.pioneerelectronics.com
SIC: **5064** 3651 High fidelity equipment;
Household audio and video equipment
HQ: Pioneer North America, Inc.
970 W 190th St Ste 360
Torrance CA 90502
310 952-2000

(P-10224)

R & B WHOLESALE DISTRS INC (PA)

2350 S Milliken Ave, Ontario (91761-2332)
PHONE..................................909 230-5400
Robert O Burggraf, *Pr*
Masako Burggraf, *
Shamsul Hyder, *
◆ EMP: 75 EST: 1968
SQ FT: 72,000
SALES (est): 95.66MM
SALES (corp-wide): 95.66MM **Privately Held**
Web: www.rbdist.com
SIC: **5064** Electrical appliances, major

(P-10225)

SAMSUNG ELECTRONICS AMER INC

5601 E Slauson Ave Ste 200, Commerce
(90040-2997)
PHONE..................................323 374-6300
EMP: 176
Web: www.samsung.com
SIC: **5064** Electrical appliances, television
and radio
HQ: Samsung Electronics America, Inc.
85 Challenger Rd
Ridgefield Park NJ 07660
201 229-4000

(P-10226)

TTE TECHNOLOGY INC

Also Called: Tcl Electronics
189 Technology Dr, Irvine (92618-2402)
PHONE..................................877 300-8837
Wenhai Zhang, *CEO*
Xiao Chen, *
Chunli Tang, *
Mark Zhang, *
Nicole Feng, *
▲ EMP: 150 EST: 2004
SQ FT: 50,000
SALES (est): 6.01MM
SALES (corp-wide): 293.57K **Privately Held**
Web: www.tcl.com
SIC: **5064** Television sets
HQ: Tcl Electronics Holdings Limited

C/O Maples Corporate Services
Limited
George Town GR CAYMAN KY1-1

5065 Electronic Parts And Equipment, Nec

(P-10227)

ACE WIRELESS & TRADING INC

3031 Orange Ave Ste B, Santa Ana
(92707-4246)
PHONE..................................949 748-5700
◆ EMP: 375
SIC: **5065** Electronic parts

(P-10228)

ADVANCED MP TECHNOLOGY LLC (DH)

27271 Las Ramblas Ste 300, Mission Viejo
(92691-8042)
PHONE..................................800 492-3113
Homayoun Shorooghi, *Pr*
◆ EMP: 126 EST: 1994
SALES (est): 48.74MM
SALES (corp-wide): 410.29MM **Privately Held**
Web: www.a2globalelectronics.com
SIC: **5065** Electronic parts
HQ: America Ii Electronics, Llc
2500 118th Ave N
Saint Petersburg FL 33716
727 573-0900

(P-10229)

AIR ELECTRO INC (PA)

9452 De Soto Ave, Chatsworth
(91311-4950)
P.O. Box 2231 (91313-2231)
PHONE..................................818 407-5400
EMP: 104 EST: 1951
SALES (est): 24.47MM
SALES (corp-wide): 24.47MM **Privately Held**
Web: www.airelectro.com
SIC: **5065** 3674 Electronic parts; Computer
logic modules

(P-10230)

BEAR COMMUNICATIONS INC

Also Called: Bearcom Wireless Worldwide
8290 Vickers St Ste D, San Diego
(92111-2116)
PHONE..................................619 263-2159
Rick Andrews, *Brnch Mgr*
EMP: 90
SALES (corp-wide): 944.26MM **Privately Held**
Web: www.bearcom.com
SIC: **5065** Communication equipment
HQ: Bear Communications, Inc.
4009 Dist Dr Ste 200
Garland TX 75041

(P-10231)

BEAR COMMUNICATIONS INC

Also Called: Bearcom Wireless Worldwide
8584 Venice Blvd, Los Angeles
(90034-2549)
PHONE..................................310 854-2327
TOLL FREE: 800
Stan Cameron, *Brnch Mgr*
EMP: 90
SALES (corp-wide): 944.26MM **Privately Held**
Web: www.bearcom.com
SIC: **5065** Communication equipment
HQ: Bear Communications, Inc.
4009 Dist Dr Ste 200
Garland TX 75041

(P-10232)

BISCO INDUSTRIES INC (HQ)

Also Called: Fastcor
5065 E Hunter Ave, Anaheim (92807-6001)
PHONE..................................800 323-1232
▲ EMP: 85 EST: 1973
SALES (est): 160.95MM
SALES (corp-wide): 356.23MM **Publicly Held**
Web: www.biscoind.com
SIC: **5065** Electronic parts
PA: Eaco Corporation
5065 E Hunter Ave
714 876-2490

(P-10233)

BITCENTRAL INC

Also Called: Bitcentral
4340 Von Karman Ave Ste 410, Newport
Beach (92660-2085)
PHONE..................................949 253-9000
EMP: 85
SIC: **5065** Communication equipment

(P-10234)

BROWNSTONE COMPANIES INC

Also Called: Brownstone Security
2629 Manhattan Beach Blvd 100, Redondo
Beach (90278-1604)
PHONE..................................310 297-3600
EMP: 700
SIC: **5065** Security control equipment and
systems

(P-10235)

BUYERS CONSULTATION SVC INC (PA)

Also Called: B C S
8735 Remmet Ave, Canoga Park
(91304-1519)
P.O. Box 8427 (91372-8427)
PHONE..................................818 341-4820
Jo Manhan, *Pr*
▲ EMP: 75 EST: 1988
SQ FT: 40,000
SALES (est): 28.78MM **Privately Held**
Web: www.scrapdr.com
SIC: **5065** 7389 5093 4953 Electronic parts
and equipment, nec; Auctioneers, fee basis
; Metal scrap and waste materials;
Recycling, waste materials

(P-10236)

CAL SOUTHERN SOUND IMAGE INC (PA)

Also Called: Sound Image
2425 Auto Park Way, Escondido
(92029-1222)
PHONE..................................760 737-3900
David R Shadoan, *CEO*
Ralph Wagner, *
EMP: 65 EST: 1984
SQ FT: 28,000
SALES (est): 49.52MM
SALES (corp-wide): 49.52MM **Privately Held**
Web: www.sound-image.com
SIC: **5065** 3651 5064 Sound equipment,
electronic; Speaker systems; Electrical
appliances, television and radio

(P-10237)

CBOL CORPORATION

19850 Plummer St, Chatsworth
(91311-5652)
PHONE..................................818 704-8200
Howard Nam, *COO*
Kenneth Cheung, *
Lynn Turk, *

Spencer H Kim, *
◆ EMP: 131 EST: 1987
SQ FT: 69,820
SALES (est): 33.25MM **Privately Held**
Web: www.cbol.com
SIC: **5065** 5072 5013 5088 Electronic parts
and equipment, nec; Hardware; Motor
vehicle supplies and new parts;
Transportation equipment and supplies

(P-10238)

CICOIL LLC

28606 Livingston Ave, Valencia
(91355-4186)
PHONE..................................661 295-1295
Mark Twaalfhoven, *CEO*
John Palahnuk, *
Patrick H Albert, *
Preet Ranu, *
EMP: 118 EST: 1956
SQ FT: 16,000
SALES (est): 22.76MM **Privately Held**
Web: www.cicoil.com
SIC: **5065** Electronic parts and equipment,
nec

(P-10239)

CP DOCUMENT TECHNOLOGIES LLC (PA)

Also Called: Copypage
800 W 6th St Ste 1400, Los Angeles
(90017-2718)
PHONE..................................213 617-4040
EMP: 70 EST: 1992
SQ FT: 8,350
SALES (est): 2.58MM **Privately Held**
SIC: **5065** 7334 7374 Electronic parts;
Photocopying and duplicating services;
Optical scanning data service

(P-10240)

CYNERGY PROF SYSTEMS LLC

23187 La Cadena Dr Ste 102, Laguna Hills
(92653-1481)
PHONE..................................800 776-7978
Cynthia Mason, *Pr*
EMP: 30 EST: 2009
SALES (est): 34.81MM **Privately Held**
Web: www.cynergy.pro
SIC: **5065** 7379 3663 3661 Communication
equipment; Computer related maintenance
services; Radio and t.v. communications
equipment; Communication headgear,
telephone

(P-10241)

ELECTRONIC HARDWARE LIMITED (PA)

13257 Saticoy St, North Hollywood
(91605-3486)
PHONE..................................818 982-6100
R E Vudrogivic, *CEO*
Richard Degn, *Pr*
EMP: 33 EST: 1973
SQ FT: 10,000
SALES (est): 1.67MM
SALES (corp-wide): 1.67MM **Privately Held**
Web: www.electronichardware.com
SIC: **5065** 5072 3541 Electronic parts;
Hardware; Machine tools, metal cutting type

(P-10242)

ENERPRO INC

99 Aero Camino, Goleta (93117-3822)
PHONE..................................805 683-2114
Thomas Bourbeau, *Pr*
Frank J Bourbeau, *
Ilse Bourbeau, *
Thomas Bourbeau, *VP*

◆ **EMP:** 25 **EST:** 1983
SQ FT: 27,000
SALES (est): 7.92MM **Privately Held**
Web: www.enerpro-inc.com
SIC: 5065 3699 Electronic parts and equipment, nec; Accelerating waveguide structures

(P-10243)
EQUITY INTERNATIONAL INC
Also Called: B & W
5541 Fermi Ct, Carlsbad (92008-7348)
PHONE..............................978 664-2712
Joseph Atkins, *Pr*
Stephen Curran, *
Cindy Hughes, *
EMP: 574 **EST:** 1993
SALES (est): 2.67MM **Privately Held**
Web: www.equityinternational.com
SIC: 5065 Radio and television equipment and parts
HQ: B & W Group Ltd
Dale Road
Worthing W SUSSEX BN11
190 322-1500

(P-10244)
FOREIGN TRADE CORPORATION
Also Called: Technocel
685 Cochran St Ste 200, Simi Valley (93065-1921)
PHONE..............................805 823-8400
▲ **EMP:** 115
SIC: 5065 Mobile telephone equipment

(P-10245)
GENERAL TRANSISTOR CORPORATION (PA)
Also Called: G T C
12449 Putnam St, Whittier (90602-1023)
PHONE..............................310 578-7344
Albert A Barrios, *Pr*
Ilan Israely, *
EMP: 30 **EST:** 1976
SALES (est): 9.06MM
SALES (corp-wide): 9.06MM **Privately Held**
Web: www.gtcelectronics.com
SIC: 5065 3674 Semiconductor devices; Semiconductor circuit networks

(P-10246)
HARMAN INTERNATIONAL INDS INC
Also Called: Los Angeles Sales Office
8500 Balboa Blvd, Northridge (91325-5802)
PHONE..............................818 893-8411
Jan Quaglia, *Brnch Mgr*
EMP: 434
Web: www.harman.com
SIC: 5065 Radio parts and accessories, nec
HQ: Harman International Industries
Incorporated
400 Atlantic St Fl 15
Stamford CT 06901
203 328-3500

(P-10247)
HEC INC
Also Called: Total Garments
30961 Agoura Rd Ste 311, Westlake Village (91361-5607)
PHONE..............................818 879-7414
Shaukat H Zaidi, *CEO*
Shamim Zaidi, *VP*
EMP: 338 **EST:** 1996
SQ FT: 4,500
SALES (est): 2.34MM **Privately Held**
Web: www.hoorayusa.com
SIC: 5065 Electronic parts

(P-10248)
HIGH TECH PET PRODUCTS
2111 Portola Rd # A, Ventura (93003-7723)
PHONE..............................805 644-1797
Nicholas Donge, *Pr*
▲ **EMP:** 60 **EST:** 1980
SALES (est): 4.4MM **Privately Held**
Web: www.hitecpet.com
SIC: 5065 2399 Electronic parts and equipment, nec; Pet collars, leashes, etc.: non-leather

(P-10249)
HIRSCH ELECTRONICS LLC
1900 Carnegie Ave Ste B, Santa Ana (92705-5557)
PHONE..............................949 250-8888
John Picc, *Managing Member*
John Piccininni, *Managing Member*
Stephen D Healy, *Managing Member*
EMP: 85 **EST:** 1981
SQ FT: 34,600
SALES (est): 4.95MM **Publicly Held**
Web: www.identiv.com
SIC: 5065 Security control equipment and systems
PA: Identiv, Inc.
2201 Walnut Ave Ste 100

(P-10250)
HM ELECTRONICS INC (PA)
Also Called: H M E
2848 Whiptail Loop, Carlsbad (92010-6708)
PHONE..............................858 535-6000
Harrison Y Miyahira, *Ch Bd*
Charles Miyahira, *
◆ **EMP:** 315 **EST:** 1971
SQ FT: 73,000
SALES (est): 452.77MM
SALES (corp-wide): 452.77MM **Privately Held**
Web: www.hme.com
SIC: 5065 Electronic parts and equipment, nec

(P-10251)
I C CLASS COMPONENTS CORP (PA)
Also Called: Classic Components
23605 Telo Ave, Torrance (90505-4028)
PHONE..............................310 539-5500
Jeffrey Klein, *Pr*
Kris Klein, *Ex VP*
Daniel Lee, *VP*
Mike Thomas, *VP*
▲ **EMP:** 100 **EST:** 1985
SQ FT: 53,000
SALES (est): 35.11MM
SALES (corp-wide): 35.11MM **Privately Held**
Web: www.class-ic.com
SIC: 5065 Electronic parts

(P-10252)
IMPACT COMPONENTS A CALIFORNIA LIMITED PARTNERSHIP
Also Called: Impact Components
6010 Cornerstone Ct W Ste 200, San Diego (92121-3762)
PHONE..............................858 634-4800
▲ **EMP:** 30 **EST:** 1897
SALES (est): 10.43MM **Privately Held**
SIC: 5065 3674 Electronic parts; Integrated circuits, semiconductor networks, etc.

(P-10253)
INSULECTRO (PA)
20362 Windrow Dr, Lake Forest (92630-8140)
PHONE..............................949 587-3200
Patrick Redfern, *CEO*
Sean M Redfern, *
Robert Mallord, *
Kenneth Parent, *
Kevin M Miller, *
▲ **EMP:** 70 **EST:** 1991
SQ FT: 40,000
SALES (est): 120.05MM
SALES (corp-wide): 120.05MM **Privately Held**
Web: www.insulectro.com
SIC: 5065 Electronic parts

(P-10254)
INTELLIPOWER INC
Also Called: Ametek Intellipower
1746 N Saint Thomas Cir, Orange (92865-4247)
PHONE..............................714 921-1580
G W Bill Shipman, *CEO*
Dan Rieth, *
Oscar Tang, *
Dan Johnson, *
EMP: 100 **EST:** 1988
SQ FT: 22,000
SALES (est): 21.25MM
SALES (corp-wide): 6.6B **Publicly Held**
Web: www.intellipower.com
SIC: 5065 Electronic parts and equipment, nec
PA: Ametek, Inc.
1100 Cassatt Rd
610 647-2121

(P-10255)
INTERNTIONAL TECH SYSTEMS CORP
Also Called: Itsco
10721 Walker St, Cypress (90630-4720)
PHONE..............................714 761-8886
Stanley Ning, *Pr*
▲ **EMP:** 48 **EST:** 1985
SQ FT: 40,000
SALES (est): 23.41MM **Privately Held**
Web: www.itsco.net
SIC: 5065 3578 Electronic parts and equipment, nec; Point-of-sale devices

(P-10256)
JAE ELECTRONICS INC (HQ)
142 Technology Dr Ste 100, Irvine (92618-2430)
PHONE..............................949 753-2600
Noriyuki Konishi, *Pr*
Shinjiro Ando, *
◆ **EMP:** 36 **EST:** 1977
SQ FT: 20,000
SALES (est): 154.52MM **Privately Held**
Web: www.jaeusa.com
SIC: 5065 3679 3829 3678 Connectors, electronic; Electronic circuits; Measuring and controlling devices, nec; Electronic connectors
PA: Japan Aviation Electronics Industry, Limited
1-21-1, Dogenzaka

(P-10257)
JEB HOLDINGS CORP (PA)
54125 Maranatha Dr, Idyllwild (92549-0075)
P.O. Box 67 (92549-0067)
PHONE..............................951 659-2183
Gordon Brown Senior, *CEO*
EMP: 75 **EST:** 1957
SQ FT: 80,000
SALES (est): 8.59MM
SALES (corp-wide): 8.59MM **Privately Held**

Web: www.southbaycable.com
SIC: 5065 Electronic parts

(P-10258)
JRI INC
Also Called: J R Industries
31280 La Baya Dr, Westlake Village (91362-4005)
PHONE..............................818 706-2424
Craig Pfefferman, *CEO*
▲ **EMP:** 50 **EST:** 1987
SQ FT: 20,000
SALES (est): 9.03MM **Privately Held**
Web: www.jri.com
SIC: 5065 3679 Electronic parts; Harness assemblies, for electronic use: wire or cable

(P-10259)
JVCKENWOOD USA CORPORATION (HQ)
4001 Worsham Ave, Long Beach (90808-1976)
P.O. Box 22745 (90801-5745)
PHONE..............................310 639-9000
Shinya Niina, *Pr*
Joseph Glassett, *
Mark Jasin, *
Craig Geiger, *
Harvey D Mitnick, *
▲ **EMP:** 160 **EST:** 1961
SQ FT: 238,000
SALES (est): 80.58MM **Privately Held**
Web: www.jvckenwood.com
SIC: 5065 Electronic parts and equipment, nec
PA: Jvckenwood Corporation
3-12, Moriyacho, Kanagawa-Ku

(P-10260)
KLEIN ELECTRONICS INC
Also Called: Klein Electronics
349 N Vinewood St, Escondido (92029-1338)
PHONE..............................760 781-3220
Richard Klein, *Pr*
▲ **EMP:** 26 **EST:** 1992
SQ FT: 13,700
SALES (est): 4.68MM **Privately Held**
Web: www.kleinelectronics.com
SIC: 5065 3663 Electronic parts and equipment, nec; Radio broadcasting and communications equipment

(P-10261)
L3HARRIS INTERSTATE ELEC CORP
707 E Vermont Ave A, Anaheim (92805-5600)
PHONE..............................714 758-0500
Richard Paul, *Brnch Mgr*
EMP: 163
SALES (corp-wide): 19.42B **Publicly Held**
Web: www.l3harris.com
SIC: 5065 Electronic parts
HQ: L3harris Interstate Electronics Corporation
602 E Vermont Ave
Anaheim CA 92805
714 758-0500

(P-10262)
LIGHTPOINTE COMMUNICATIONS INC
Also Called: Lightpointe Wireless
8515 Arjons Dr Ste G, San Diego (92126-4358)
PHONE..............................858 834-4083
Heinz A Willerbrand, *Ch Bd*
Lorian Sanders, *

▲ **EMP:** 25 **EST:** 2000
SALES (est): 2.97MM **Privately Held**
Web: www.lightpointe.com
SIC: 5065 3661 Communication equipment;
Fiber optics communications equipment

(P-10263)
LINKSYS LLC
120 Theory, Irvine (92617-3210)
PHONE.............................408 526-4000
EMP: 156
Web: www.linksys.com
SIC: 5065 Electronic parts and equipment,
nec
HQ: Linksys Llc
121 Theory Ste 150
Irvine CA 92617
310 751-5100

(P-10264)
LINKSYS LLC
121 Theory Ste 150, Irvine (92617-3204)
PHONE.............................310 751-5100
EMP: 194
Web: www.linksys.com
SIC: 5065 Electronic parts and equipment,
nec
HQ: Linksys Llc
121 Theory Ste 150
Irvine CA 92617
310 751-5100

(P-10265)
LINKSYS USA INC
121 Theory, Irvine (92617-3209)
PHONE.............................949 270-8500
Jonathan Bettino, *CEO*
EMP: 100 **EST:** 2018
SALES (est): 24.82MM
SALES (corp-wide): 5.3B **Publicly Held**
Web: www.linksys.com
SIC: 5065 3577 Communication equipment;
Data conversion equipment, media-to-
media: computer
PA: Fortinet, Inc.
909 Kifer Rd
408 235-7700

(P-10266)
MAURY MICROWAVE INC (PA)
2900 Inland Empire Blvd, Ontario
(91764-4804)
PHONE.............................909 987-4715
Michael Howo, *CEO*
▲ **EMP:** 200 **EST:** 1957
SQ FT: 6,000
SALES (est): 49.6MM
SALES (corp-wide): 49.6MM **Privately
Held**
Web: www.maurymw.com
SIC: 5065 Electronic parts and equipment,
nec

(P-10267)
MITSUBISHI ELECTRIC US INC
(DH)
Also Called: Meus
5900 Katella Ave Ste A, Cypress
(90630-5019)
P.O. Box 6007 (90630)
PHONE.............................714 220-2500
Mike Corbo, *Pr*
Masahiro Oya, *
Mike Corbo, *Pr*
Jared Baker, *
Perry Pappous, *
◆ **EMP:** 200 **EST:** 2000
SQ FT: 10,400
SALES (est): 931.5MM **Privately Held**
Web: us.mitsubishielectric.com

SIC: 5065 3534 1796 3669 Electronic parts;
Escalators, passenger and freight; Elevator
installation and conversion; Visual
communication systems
HQ: Mitsubishi Electric Us Holdings, Inc.
5900 Katella Ave Ste A
Cypress CA 90630
714 220-2500

(P-10268)
MOBILE LINE
COMMUNICATIONS
CORPORATION
1402 Morgan Cir, Tustin (92780-6423)
▲ **EMP:** 75
SIC: 5065 Telephone equipment

(P-10269)
MOTOROLA MOBILITY LLC
Also Called: Motorola
6450 Sequence Dr, San Diego
(92121-4376)
PHONE.............................858 455-1500
Rick Neal, *Brnch Mgr*
EMP: 73
SQ FT: 30,000
Web: www.motorola.com
SIC: 5065 3663 Communication equipment;
Radio and t.v. communications equipment
HQ: Motorola Mobility Llc
222 W Mdse Mart Plz Ste 1
Chicago IL 60654

(P-10270)
MOTORS & CONTROLS WHSE
INC
Also Called: Sabina Motors & Controls
1440 N Burton Pl, Anaheim (92806-1204)
PHONE.............................714 956-0480
Vincent Tjelmeland, *Pr*
◆ **EMP:** 29 **EST:** 1969
SQ FT: 35,000
SALES (est): 6.93MM **Privately Held**
Web: www.sabinadrives.com
SIC: 5065 3621 Electronic parts; Motors,
electric

(P-10271)
MTROIZ INTERNATIONAL
150 S Kenmore Ave, Los Angeles
(90004-5603)
PHONE.............................661 998-8013
Eun H Chae, *CEO*
Hong Chae, *
Stephen Banks, *
EMP: 32 **EST:** 2011
SALES (est): 1.24MM **Privately Held**
Web: www.mtroiz.com
SIC: 5065 2844 5023 5047 Communication
equipment; Perfumes, cosmetics and other
toilet preparations; Homefurnishings;
Medical and hospital equipment

(P-10272)
NISCAYAH INC
Hamilton Pacific
751 N Todd Ave, Azusa (91702-2244)
PHONE.............................626 683-8167
Diane Frank, *Brnch Mgr*
EMP: 95
SALES (corp-wide): 15.78B **Publicly Held**
SIC: 5065 Security control equipment and
systems
HQ: Niscayah, Inc.
2400 Commerce Ave Ste 500
Duluth GA 30096
678 474-1720

(P-10273)
NORTH AMERICAN VIDEO
CORP (PA)
Also Called: Navco Security Systems
1335 S Acacia Ave, Fullerton (92831-5315)
PHONE.............................714 779-7499
Jason Oakley, *CEO*
William Augustus Groves, *
Margaret Groves, *
William Groves, *
Sharon Bryant, *
◆ **EMP:** 45 **EST:** 1975
SALES (est): 81.67MM
SALES (corp-wide): 81.67MM **Privately
Held**
Web: www.navco.com
SIC: 5065 3812 Video equipment, electronic;
Acceleration indicators and systems
components, aerospace

(P-10274)
NOVACAP LLC (HQ)
25111 Anza Dr, Valencia (91355-3478)
PHONE.............................661 295-5920
Mark Skoog, *CEO*
Shelley Mears, *
▲ **EMP:** 120 **EST:** 1987
SQ FT: 38,000
SALES (est): 38.41MM
SALES (corp-wide): 707.6MM **Publicly
Held**
Web: www.novacap.ca
SIC: 5065 Electronic parts and equipment,
nec
PA: Knowles Corporation
1151 Maplewood Dr
630 250-5100

(P-10275)
OMNITRON SYSTEMS TECH INC
38 Tesla, Irvine (92618-4603)
PHONE.............................949 250-6510
Arie Goldberg, *CEO*
Heidi Cairns, *VP*
EMP: 75 **EST:** 1985
SQ FT: 15,000
SALES (est): 22.66MM **Privately Held**
Web: www.omnitron-systems.com
SIC: 5065 Electronic parts and equipment,
nec

(P-10276)
OTTER PRODUCTS LLC
Also Called: Lifeproof
15110 Avenue Of Science, San Diego
(92128-3405)
PHONE.............................888 533-0735
Jc Richardson, *Brnch Mgr*
EMP: 178
SALES (corp-wide): 368.51MM **Privately
Held**
Web: www.otterbox.com
SIC: 5065 Mobile telephone equipment
PA: Otter Products, Llc
209 S Meldrum St
855 688-7269

(P-10277)
P C A ELECTRONICS INC
16799 Schoenborn St, North Hills
(91343-6194)
PHONE.............................818 892-0761
Morris Weinberg, *Pr*
Benjamin Weinberg, *
EMP: 44 **EST:** 1949
SQ FT: 30,000
SALES (est): 5.82MM **Privately Held**
Web: www.pca.com
SIC: 5065 3674 Electronic parts;
Semiconductors and related devices

(P-10278)
PERILLO INDUSTRIES INC
Also Called: Century Electronics
2150 Anchor Ct Ste A, Newbury Park
(91320-1609)
PHONE.............................805 498-9838
Mary Perillo, *Pr*
EMP: 50 **EST:** 1973
SQ FT: 20,000
SALES (est): 9.73MM **Privately Held**
Web: www.centuryelectronics.us
SIC: 5065 3679 Electronic parts and
equipment, nec; Electronic loads and power
supplies

(P-10279)
PRESIDIO COMPONENTS INC
7169 Construction Ct, San Diego
(92121-2615)
PHONE.............................858 578-9390
Violet Devoe, *Pr*
Daniel Devoe, *
Alan Devoe, *
Lambert Devoe, *
▲ **EMP:** 120 **EST:** 1980
SQ FT: 35,000
SALES (est): 43.47MM **Privately Held**
Web: www.presidiocomponents.com
SIC: 5065 Electronic parts and equipment,
nec

(P-10280)
Q TECH CORPORATION (PA)
6161 Chip Ave, Cypress (90630-5213)
PHONE.............................310 836-7900
Sally Phillips, *Pr*
Richard Taylor, *
EMP: 159 **EST:** 1972
SALES (est): 24.75MM
SALES (corp-wide): 24.75MM **Privately
Held**
Web: www.q-tech.com
SIC: 5065 Electronic parts and equipment,
nec

(P-10281)
QUINSTAR TECHNOLOGY INC
24085 Garnier St, Torrance (90505-5319)
PHONE.............................310 320-1111
Leo Fong, *Pr*
John Kuno, *
▲ **EMP:** 72 **EST:** 1993
SALES (est): 23.14MM **Privately Held**
Web: www.quinstar.com
SIC: 5065 3671 Electronic parts and
equipment, nec; Cathode ray tubes,
including rebuilt

(P-10282)
RAYTHEON CMMAND CTRL
SLTONS LL (DH)
1801 Hughes Dr, Fullerton (92833-2200)
P.O. Box 34055 (92834-9455)
PHONE.............................714 446-3118
Alex Cresswell, *
Don Johnson, *
▲ **EMP:** 700 **EST:** 2001
SALES (est): 312.6K
SALES (corp-wide): 68.92B **Publicly Held**
SIC: 5065 Security control equipment and
systems
HQ: Raytheon Company
870 Winter St
Waltham MA 02451
781 522-3000

(P-10283)
SAMSUNG INTERNATIONAL
INC (DH)

333 H St Ste 6000, Chula Vista
(91910-5565)
PHONE....................619 671-6001
Byaong Gueon Jeon, *CEO*
Wonchul Song, *
Hak Seob Shim, *
◆ EMP: 50 EST: 1983
SALES (est): 14.95MM **Privately Held**
Web: www.samsung.com
SIC: 5065 3663 Mobile telephone equipment
; Mobile communication equipment
HQ: Samsung Electronics America, Inc.
85 Challenger Rd
Ridgefield Park NJ 07660
201 229-4000

(P-10284)
STEREN ELECTRONICS INTL LLC (PA)
Also Called: Steren Electronic Solutions
8445 Camino Santa Fe Ste 203, San Diego
(92121-2650)
PHONE....................800 266-3333
David Shteremberg, *
Vick Soffer, *
Jose Zyman, *
◆ EMP: 100 EST: 1956
SALES (est): 28.31MM
SALES (corp-wide): 28.31MM **Privately Held**
Web: www.sterensolutions.com
SIC: 5065 Connectors, electronic

(P-10285)
SUPERIOR COMMUNICATIONS INC (PA)
Also Called: Puregear
5027 Irwindale Ave Ste 900, Irwindale
(91706-2187)
PHONE....................877 522-4727
Jeffrey Banks, *CEO*
Solomon Chen, *
Robert Chen, *
Keith Kam, *
Jennifer Ju, *Legal Counsel*
▲ EMP: 248 EST: 1991
SQ FT: 11,000
SALES (est): 77.12MM **Privately Held**
Web: www.superiorcommunications.com
SIC: 5065 Communication equipment

(P-10286)
SWANN COMMUNICATIONS USA INC
Also Called: Swann
12636 Clark St, Santa Fe Springs
(90670-3950)
PHONE....................562 777-2551
Michael Lucas, *CEO*
Kimberly Banducci, *
▲ EMP: 70 EST: 2000
SQ FT: 45,000
SALES (est): 22.67MM **Privately Held**
Web: us.swann.com
SIC: 5065 Video equipment, electronic

(P-10287)
TALLEY LLC (DH)
Also Called: Talley & Associates
12976 Sandoval St, Santa Fe Springs
(90670-4061)
P.O. Box 3123 (90670-0123)
PHONE....................562 906-8000
Mark D Talley, *CEO*
John C Gschwind, *
Karen Frankenberg, *
Jeffrey R Talley, *
Richard M Talley, *
◆ EMP: 110 EST: 1968
SQ FT: 80,000

SALES (est): 100.18MM
SALES (corp-wide): 2.67MM **Privately Held**
Web: www.talleycom.com
SIC: 5065 Communication equipment
HQ: Rexel, Inc.
5429 Lyndon B Jhnson Fwy
Dallas TX 75240

(P-10288)
TAMURA CORPORATION OF AMERICA (HQ)
277 Rancheros Dr Ste 190, San Marcos
(92069-2982)
PHONE....................800 472-6624
Norihiko Nanjo, *CEO*
Junko Walker, *Sec*
Tony Shinonuma, *CFO*
Takatoshi Nakakaryia, *Chief Operating Officer Sales*
▲ EMP: 26 EST: 1976
SQ FT: 10,801
SALES (est): 33.09MM **Privately Held**
Web: www.tamuracorp.com
SIC: 5065 5063 3677 Electronic parts;
Electrical apparatus and equipment;
Electronic coils and transformers
PA: Tamura Corporation
1-19-43, Higashioizumi

(P-10289)
TAPE SPECIALTY INC
Also Called: T S I
26017 Huntington Ln Ste C, Valencia
(91355-1116)
PHONE....................661 702-9030
Steve Feldman, *Pr*
Stu Feldman, *
Peggy James, *
▲ EMP: 28 EST: 1976
SALES (est): 4.76MM **Privately Held**
Web: www.tsidm.com
SIC: 5065 3652 7389 Magnetic recording
tape; Magnetic tape (audio): prerecorded;
Music and broadcasting services

(P-10290)
TDK-LAMBDA AMERICAS INC
401 Mile Of Cars Way Ste 325, National City (91950-6614)
PHONE....................619 575-4400
Pascal Shauson, *CEO*
EMP: 200
Web: us.tdk-lambda.com
SIC: 5065 Electronic parts and equipment, nec
HQ: Tdk-Lambda Americas Inc.
405 Essex Rd
Tinton Falls NJ 07753
732 795-4100

(P-10291)
TECH SYSTEMS INC
7372 Walnut Ave Ste J, Buena Park
(90620-1718)
PHONE....................714 523-5404
Raymond Downs, *Mgr*
EMP: 210
SALES (corp-wide): 47.35MM **Privately Held**
Web: www.techsystemsinc.com
SIC: 5065 Closed circuit TV
PA: Tech Systems, Inc.
4942 Summer Oak Dr
770 495-8700

(P-10292)
TECOM INDUSTRIES INCORPORATED
375 Conejo Ridge Ave, Thousand Oaks
(91361-4928)

PHONE....................805 267-0100
◆ EMP: 160
Web: www.smithsinterconnect.com
SIC: 5065 Electronic parts

(P-10293)
TELIT WIRELESS SOLUTIONS INC
7700 Irvine Center Dr, Irvine (92618-2923)
PHONE....................949 461-7150
EMP: 131
Web: www.telit.com
SIC: 5065 Electronic parts
PA: Telit Wireless Solutions, Inc.
5425 Page Rd Ste 120

(P-10294)
TV EARS INC
2701 Via Orange Way Ste 1, Spring Valley
(91978-1702)
PHONE....................619 797-1600
George Dennis, *CEO*
Nancy Nelson, *
Steffens Meeks, *CPO*
▲ EMP: 30 EST: 1998
SALES (est): 9.56MM **Privately Held**
Web: www.tvears.com
SIC: 5065 3651 Sound equipment, electronic
; Television receiving sets

(P-10295)
UNION TECHNOLOGY CORP
718 Monterey Pass Rd, Monterey Park
(91754-3607)
PHONE....................323 266-6871
David I Chu, *CEO*
Robert Boughrum, *
Raj Amin, *
Gary Koniow, *
Benha Choonhauri, *
◆ EMP: 50 EST: 1991
SQ FT: 21,800
SALES (est): 8.61MM **Privately Held**
Web: www.quanticutc.com
SIC: 5065 3675 Electronic parts; Electronic capacitors

(P-10296)
VISHAY SPRAGUE INC
4051 Greystone Dr, Ontario (91761-3100)
PHONE....................909 923-3313
Joseph Tobia, *Brnch Mgr*
EMP: 100
SALES (corp-wide): 3.4B **Publicly Held**
Web: www.vishay.com
SIC: 5065 Electronic parts and equipment, nec
HQ: Sprague Vishay Inc
2813 West Rd
Bennington VT 05201
802 442-5473

(P-10297)
WEXLER CORPORATION
Also Called: Wexler Video
1111 S Victory Blvd, Burbank (91502-2550)
PHONE....................818 846-9381
EMP: 3115 EST: 1980
SALES (est): 4.16MM **Privately Held**
Web: www.reesewexler.com
SIC: 5065 7359 Video equipment, electronic;
Equipment rental and leasing, nec
HQ: H.I.G. Capital, Inc.
1450 Brickell Ave Fl 31
Miami FL 33131
305 379-2322

(P-10298)
WINCHESTER INTERCONNECT EC LLC
Also Called: Elrob LLC
12691 Monarch St, Garden Grove
(92841-3918)
PHONE....................714 230-6122
Arik Vrobel, *Pr*
Roberto Ortega, *Finance CTRL*
▲ EMP: 54 EST: 1960
SQ FT: 38,500
SALES (est): 98.57MM **Privately Held**
Web: www.el-comsystems.com
SIC: 5065 3679 3613 3643 Electronic parts;
Harness assemblies, for electronic use:
wire or cable; Switchgear and switchboard
apparatus; Current-carrying wiring services
HQ: Winchester Interconnect Corporation
185 Plains Rd
Milford CT 06461

(P-10299)
YUNEEC USA INC
Also Called: Yuneec USA
9227 Haven Ave Ste 210, Rancho
Cucamonga (91730-5473)
P.O. Box 970 (94566-0970)
PHONE....................855 284-8888
Mike Kahn, *CEO*
Larry Liu, *
Ryan Borders, *
▲ EMP: 70 EST: 2013
SALES (est): 8.63MM **Privately Held**
Web: www.yuneec.online
SIC: 5065 7629 Video equipment, electronic;
Electrical equipment repair services
HQ: Yuneec International Co., Limited
Rm D 10/F Billion Ctr Twr A
Kowloon Bay KLN

5072 Hardware

(P-10300)
ALLIED INTERNATIONAL LLC
Also Called: Allied International
28955 Avenue Sherman, Valencia
(91355-5446)
PHONE....................818 364-2333
Timothy Florian, *CEO*
Melissa Berninger, *
▲ EMP: 50 EST: 1962
SQ FT: 106,000
SALES (est): 14.87MM **Privately Held**
Web: www.alliedtools.com
SIC: 5072 3499 Hand tools; Stabilizing bars
(cargo), metal

(P-10301)
AMERICAN KAL ENTERPRISES INC (PA)
Also Called: Pro America Premium Tools
4265 Puente Ave, Baldwin Park
(91706-3420)
PHONE....................626 338-7308
John Toshima, *Pr*
Mila Bierotte, *
▲ EMP: 90 EST: 1966
SQ FT: 32,000
SALES (est): 8.76MM
SALES (corp-wide): 8.76MM **Privately Held**
SIC: 5072 3546 3463 3462 Hand tools;
Power-driven handtools; Nonferrous
forgings; Iron and steel forgings

(P-10302)
B & B SPECIALTIES INC
G S Aerospace Division
4321 E La Palma Ave, Anaheim
(92807-1887)

▲ = Import ▼ = Export
◆ = Import/Export

PHONE.....................714 985-3075
Tom Rutan, *Mgr*
EMP: 100
SALES (corp-wide): 22.69MM **Privately Held**
Web: www.bbspecialties.com
SIC: 5072 3429 Miscellaneous fasteners; Hardware, nec
PA: B & B Specialties, Inc.
4321 E La Palma Ave
714 985-3000

(P-10303)
CLARENDON SPECIALTY FAS INC
2180 Temple Ave, Long Beach (90804-1020)
PHONE.....................714 842-2603
Arnaud Zemmour, *Admn*
Michael Lang, *
Jeff Heywood, *
▲ **EMP:** 90 **EST:** 1985
SQ FT: 4,000
SALES (est): 23.06MM **Privately Held**
Web: www.clarendonsf.com
SIC: 5072 3444 Miscellaneous fasteners; Sheet metalwork

(P-10304)
CORONA CLIPPER INC
Also Called: Corona Tools
22440 Temescal Canyon Rd Ste 102, Corona (92883-4200)
PHONE.....................800 847-7863
Thomas A Welke, *CEO*
Al Schulten, *
John Reisveck, *
John J Gordan, *
Eric Prendeville, *
◆ **EMP:** 86 **EST:** 1927
SQ FT: 85,000
SALES (est): 45.24MM
SALES (corp-wide): 26.64MM **Privately Held**
Web: www.coronatools.com
SIC: 5072 3524 Hand tools; Lawn and garden equipment
PA: Natt Tools Group Inc
460 Sherman Ave N
905 549-7433

(P-10305)
E B BRADLEY CO (PA)
5602 Bickett St, Vernon (90058-2826)
P.O. Box 58548 (90058-0548)
PHONE.....................323 585-9917
Don Lorey, *Pr*
Scott Simons, *
Ramn Miramontes, *
David Jackson, *
▲ **EMP:** 48 **EST:** 1946
SQ FT: 45,000
SALES (est): 154.3MM
SALES (corp-wide): 154.3MM **Privately Held**
Web: www.ebbradley.com
SIC: 5072 2452 Hardware; Panels and sections, prefabricated, wood

(P-10306)
EMTEK PRODUCTS GROUP LLC (HQ)
Also Called: Emtek Products
12801 Schabarum Ave, Irwindale (91706-6808)
PHONE.....................626 961-0413
Jason Chau, *CEO*
Ashley E George, *CFO*
◆ **EMP:** 200 **EST:** 1979
SALES (est): 35.71MM

SALES (corp-wide): 4.63B **Publicly Held**
Web: www.emtek.com
SIC: 5072 Hardware
PA: Fortune Brands Innovations, Inc.
520 Lake Cook Rd
847 484-4400

(P-10307)
EMTEK PRODUCTS GROUP LLC
600 Baldwin Park Blvd, City Of Industry (91746-1501)
PHONE.....................626 369-4718
Birk Sorennsen, *Mgr*
EMP: 597
SALES (corp-wide): 4.63B **Publicly Held**
Web: www.emtek.com
SIC: 5072 Hardware
HQ: Emtek Products Group, Llc
12801 Schabarum Ave
Irwindale CA 91706
626 961-0413

(P-10308)
HD SUPPLY DISTRIBUTION SERVICES LLC
Also Called: Crown Bolt
26940 Aliso Viejo Pkwy, Aliso Viejo (92656-2622)
PHONE.....................949 643-4700
◆ **EMP:** 1078
Web: www.hdsupplyhardwaresolutions.com
SIC: 5072 Screws

(P-10309)
INDUSTRIAL THREADED PDTS INC (PA)
Also Called: I T P
515 N Puente St, Brea (92821-2805)
PHONE.....................562 802-4626
Garrett Charles Futrell, *CEO*
Clay Weaver, *
▲ **EMP:** 28 **EST:** 1979
SALES (est): 37.59MM
SALES (corp-wide): 37.59MM **Privately Held**
Web: www.itpbolt.com
SIC: 5072 3599 Nuts (hardware); Machine and other job shop work

(P-10310)
MAKITA USA INC (HQ)
Also Called: Makita
14930 Northam St, La Mirada (90638-5753)
PHONE.....................714 522-8088
Sean Okada, *Pr*
Yuhei Iwanaga, *CFO*
◆ **EMP:** 250 **EST:** 1970
SQ FT: 130,000
SALES (est): 436.01MM **Privately Held**
Web: www.makitatools.com
SIC: 5072 Power handtools
PA: Makita Corporation
3-11-8, Sumiyoshicho

(P-10311)
PENN ELCOM INC (HQ)
Also Called: Penn Elcom Hardware
7465 Lampson Ave, Garden Grove (92841-2903)
PHONE.....................714 230-6200
Philip John Stratford, *CEO*
Roger Willems, *
◆ **EMP:** 35 **EST:** 1993
SQ FT: 28,000
SALES (est): 27MM **Privately Held**
Web: www.penn-elcom.com
SIC: 5072 3429 Hardware; Hardware, nec
PA: Penn Elcom Corporation

C/O Maples Corporate Services (Bvi) Limited

(P-10312)
PORTEOUS ENTERPRISES INC (DH)
1040 E Watson Center Rd, Carson (90745-4202)
PHONE.....................310 549-9180
◆ **EMP:** 175 **EST:** 1969
SALES (est): 11.88MM **Privately Held**
SIC: 5072 Nuts (hardware)
HQ: Brighton-Best International, Inc.
5855 Obispo Ave
Long Beach CA 90805
562 808-8000

(P-10313)
SHAMROCK SUPPLY COMPANY INC (PA)
Also Called: Shamrock Companies, The
3366 E La Palma Ave, Anaheim (92806-2814)
PHONE.....................714 575-1800
John J O'connor, *Co-Secretary*
Michael O'connor, *Pr*
▲ **EMP:** 52 **EST:** 1975
SQ FT: 45,000
SALES (est): 51.94MM
SALES (corp-wide): 51.94MM **Privately Held**
Web: www.shamrocksupply.com
SIC: 5072 5084 3842 Hand tools; Industrial machinery and equipment; Personal safety equipment

(P-10314)
WURTH LOUIS AND COMPANY (DH)
895 Columbia St, Brea (92821-2933)
P.O. Box 2253 (92822-2253)
PHONE.....................714 529-1771
Thomas M Stolmeier, *CEO*
Evangeline De Guzman, *
◆ **EMP:** 90 **EST:** 1975
SQ FT: 116,000
SALES (est): 114.19MM
SALES (corp-wide): 22.17B **Privately Held**
Web: www.wurthlac.com
SIC: 5072 5198 Furniture hardware, nec; Stain
HQ: Wurth Group Of North America Inc.
93 Grant St
Ramsey NJ 07446

5074 Plumbing And Hydronic Heating Supplies

(P-10315)
BURKE ENGINEERING CO
9700 Factorial Way, El Monte (91733-1799)
P.O. Box 928 (92075-0928)
PHONE.....................626 579-6763
EMP: 100
Web: www.burkehvacr.com
SIC: 5074 5084 5075 Heating equipment (hydronic); Controlling instruments and accessories; Warm air heating and air conditioning

(P-10316)
ELMCO SALES INC (PA)
Also Called: Elmco Group
15070 Proctor Ave, City Of Industry (91746-3305)
P.O. Box 3787 (91744-0787)
PHONE.....................626 855-4831
Donald E Morris, *Ch Bd*

Kristin E Kahle, *
EMP: 90 **EST:** 1944
SQ FT: 49,650
SALES (est): 3.7MM
SALES (corp-wide): 3.7MM **Privately Held**
Web: www.elmcoaz.com
SIC: 5074 Plumbing fittings and supplies

(P-10317)
FERGUSON FIRE FABRICATION INC (DH)
Also Called: Pacific Fire Safety
2750 S Towne Ave, Pomona (91766-6205)
PHONE.....................909 517-3085
Leo J Klien, *Pr*
Leo J Klein, *
Dave Keltner, *
▲ **EMP:** 100 **EST:** 1987
SQ FT: 120,000
SALES (est): 232.98MM
SALES (corp-wide): 29.73B **Privately Held**
Web: www.ferguson.com
SIC: 5074 5099 Plumbing fittings and supplies; Safety equipment and supplies
HQ: Ferguson Enterprises, Llc
751 Lakefront Cmns
Newport News VA 23606
757 874-7795

(P-10318)
GLOBAL PLUMBING & FIRE SUPPLY
723 Sonora Ave, Glendale (91201-2431)
PHONE.....................818 550-8444
Armond Sarkissian, *CEO*
EMP: 112 **EST:** 2016
SALES (est): 9.8MM **Privately Held**
Web: www.firesprinklerstore.com
SIC: 5074 Plumbing fittings and supplies

(P-10319)
GREAT WESTERN SALES INC
Also Called: Mega Western Sales
8737 Dice Rd, Santa Fe Springs (90670-2513)
P.O. Box 3427 (90703-3427)
PHONE.....................310 323-7900
▲ **EMP:** 76 **EST:** 1971
SALES (est): 22.24MM **Privately Held**
Web: www.megawestern.com
SIC: 5074 Plumbing fittings and supplies

(P-10320)
GREEN CONVERGENCE (PA)
Also Called: Sunpower By Green Convergence
28476 Westinghouse Pl, Valencia (91355-0929)
PHONE.....................661 294-9495
Mark Clinton Figearo, *CEO*
Donald Schramm, *
Stacy Hitt, *
EMP: 52 **EST:** 2008
SQ FT: 6,000
SALES (est): 24.79MM
SALES (corp-wide): 24.79MM **Privately Held**
Web: www.greenconvergence.com
SIC: 5074 1711 2493 2621 Heating equipment and panels, solar; Solar energy contractor; Roofing board, unsaturated; Roofing felt stock

(P-10321)
H2O INNOVATION USA HOLDING INC
Also Called: H2o Innovation Operation Maint
1048 La Mirada Ct, Vista (92081-7874)
PHONE.....................760 639-4400

Coley Ali, *Brnch Mgr*
EMP: 895
SALES (corp-wide): 220.98MM **Privately Held**
SIC: 5074 7389 Water softeners; Water softener service
HQ: H2o Innovation Usa Holding, Inc.
　　8900 109th Ave N Ste 1000
　　Champlin MN 55316
　　763 566-8961

(P-10322)
HARRINGTON INDUSTRIAL PLAS LLC (PA)
14480 Yorba Ave, Chino (91710-5766)
P.O. Box 5128 (91710)
PHONE.............................909 597-8641
Bob Graham, *CEO*
Dave Abercrombie, *Vice Chairman*
Mike Tourtelot, *CFO*
▼ **EMP:** 85 **EST:** 1959
SQ FT: 50,000
SALES (est): 450.67MM
SALES (corp-wide): 450.67MM **Privately Held**
Web: www.hipco.com
SIC: 5074 Pipes and fittings, plastic

(P-10323)
KEYLINE SALES INC
9768 Firestone Blvd, Downey (90241-5510)
PHONE.............................562 904-3910
Richard Banner, *Pr*
John Shaw, *
Mike Powers, *
EMP: 42 **EST:** 1974
SQ FT: 3,500
SALES (est): 9.77MM **Privately Held**
Web: www.keylinesales.com
SIC: 5074 3822 Plumbing fittings and supplies; Environmental controls

(P-10324)
LARSEN SUPPLY CO (PA)
Also Called: Lasco
12055 Slauson Ave, Santa Fe Springs (90670-2601)
PHONE.............................562 698-0731
John Palumbo, *CEO*
Rella Bodinus, *
Ruth Larsen, *Stockholder*
◆ **EMP:** 100 **EST:** 1930
SQ FT: 60,000
SALES (est): 22.97MM
SALES (corp-wide): 22.97MM **Privately Held**
Web: www.lasco.net
SIC: 5074 5075 Plumbing fittings and supplies; Warm air heating and air conditioning

(P-10325)
MITTAL RAM
100 E Hillcrest Blvd, Inglewood (90301-2415)
PHONE.............................310 769-6669
Ram Mittal, *Owner*
Lillian Mittal, *Prin*
EMP: 95 **EST:** 1989
SALES (est): 1.04MM **Privately Held**
SIC: 5074 Heating equipment and panels, solar

(P-10326)
TA INDUSTRIES INC (HQ)
Also Called: Truaire
11130 Bloomfield Ave, Santa Fe Springs (90670-4603)
P.O. Box 4448 (90670-1460)
PHONE.............................562 466-1000

Yongki Yi, *Prin*
Elizabeth Yi, *VP*
▲ **EMP:** 39 **EST:** 1996
SQ FT: 86,000
SALES (est): 20.63MM
SALES (corp-wide): 792.84MM **Publicly Held**
Web: www.rectorseal.com
SIC: 5074 5075 3567 Heating equipment (hydronic); Air conditioning and ventilation equipment and supplies; Heating units and devices, industrial: electric
PA: Csw Industrials, Inc.
　　5420 Lyndon B Jhnson Fwy
　　214 884-3777

(P-10327)
WATERSTONE FAUCETS LLC
Also Called: Waterstone Faucets
41180 Raintree Ct, Murrieta (92562-7020)
P.O. Box 1240 (92593-1240)
PHONE.............................951 304-0520
Christopher G Kuran, *Managing Member*
Steve Kliewer, *
Bob Santella, *
▲ **EMP:** 131 **EST:** 1999
SQ FT: 42,000
SALES (est): 23.78MM **Privately Held**
Web: www.waterstoneco.com
SIC: 5074 3432 Plumbing fittings and supplies; Faucets and spigots, metal and plastic

---

5075 Warm Air Heating And Air Conditioning

(P-10328)
AC PRO INC (PA)
Also Called: MSI Hvac
11700 Industry Ave, Fontana (92337-6934)
PHONE.............................951 360-7849
Dion Quinn, *CEO*
EMP: 250 **EST:** 1986
SQ FT: 80,000
SALES (est): 107.01MM
SALES (corp-wide): 107.01MM **Privately Held**
Web: www.acpro.com
SIC: 5075 3444 Air conditioning and ventilation equipment and supplies; Sheet metalwork

(P-10329)
BIODEFENSOR CORPORATION
13448 Manhasset Rd Ste 3, Apple Valley (92308-5799)
PHONE.............................888 899-2956
Jose Villalobos, *Pr*
EMP: 25 **EST:** 2018
SALES (est): 1.43MM **Privately Held**
Web: www.biodefensor.com
SIC: 5075 3564 3569 5013 Air filters; Filters, air: furnaces, air conditioning equipment, etc.; Filters; Filters, air and oil

(P-10330)
DAIKIN COMFORT TECH DIST INC
525 Park Ave, San Fernando (91340-2557)
PHONE.............................713 861-2500
Larry Girton, *Brnch Mgr*
EMP: 270
Web: www.goodmanmfg.com
SIC: 5075 Warm air heating and air conditioning
HQ: Daikin Comfort Technologies Distribution, Inc.
　　19001 Kermier Rd
　　Waller TX 77484
　　713 861-2500

(P-10331)
ESPECIAL T HVAC SHTMTL FTTNGS
1239 E Franklin Ave, Pomona (91766-5450)
PHONE.............................909 869-9150
Gerardo Tavarez, *Pr*
Maria Tavarez, *
▲ **EMP:** 30 **EST:** 2001
SQ FT: 12,000
SALES (est): 8.53MM **Privately Held**
Web: www.especialt.com
SIC: 5075 3444 Air conditioning and ventilation equipment and supplies; Sheet metalwork

(P-10332)
FLORENCE FILTER CORPORATION
530 W Manville St, Compton (90220-5587)
PHONE.............................310 637-1137
Adrian M Anhood, *CEO*
Floriana A Anhood, *
Erika A Anhood, *
▲ **EMP:** 60 **EST:** 1971
SQ FT: 55,000
SALES (est): 11.25MM **Privately Held**
Web: www.florencefilter.com
SIC: 5075 3564 5211 Air filters; Filters, air: furnaces, air conditioning equipment, etc.; Lumber and other building materials

(P-10333)
GEORGE T HALL CO INC (PA)
Also Called: California Control Solutions
1605 E Gene Autry Way, Anaheim (92805-6730)
P.O. Box 25269 (92825-5269)
PHONE.............................909 825-9751
Charles Niemann, *Pr*
James Martin, *
Marlyn Niemann, *
▲ **EMP:** 30 **EST:** 1932
SQ FT: 15,000
SALES (est): 25.5MM
SALES (corp-wide): 25.5MM **Privately Held**
Web: www.georgethall.com
SIC: 5075 5085 3613 Warm air heating and air conditioning; Industrial supplies; Control panels, electric

(P-10334)
HEAT TRANSFER PDTS GROUP LLC
Also Called: Htpghnl
1933 S Vineyard Ave, Ontario (91761-7747)
PHONE.............................909 786-3669
EMP: 145
Web: www.htpgusa.com
SIC: 5075 Warm air heating and air conditioning
HQ: Heat Transfer Products Group, Llc
　　3885 Crestwood Pkwy Nw # 50
　　Duluth GA 30096

(P-10335)
HKF INC (PA)
Also Called: Therm Pacific
5983 Smithway St, Commerce (90040-1607)
PHONE.............................323 225-1318
James P Hartfield, *Pr*
▲ **EMP:** 57 **EST:** 1990
SALES (est): 9.67MM
SALES (corp-wide): 9.67MM **Privately Held**

SIC: 5075 3873 5064 3567 Warm air heating and air conditioning; Watches, clocks, watchcases, and parts; Electrical appliances, television and radio; Industrial furnaces and ovens

(P-10336)
INJEN TECHNOLOGY COMPANY LTD
244 Pioneer Pl, Pomona (91768-3275)
PHONE.............................909 839-0706
Ron Delgado, *CEO*
▲ **EMP:** 30 **EST:** 1998
SALES (est): 17.42MM **Privately Held**
Web: www.injen.com
SIC: 5075 3714 Air filters; Filters: oil, fuel, and air, motor vehicle

(P-10337)
US AIRCONDITIONING DISTRIBUTORS INC (PA)
Also Called: U.S. Airconditioning Distrs
16900 Chestnut St, City Of Industry (91748-1012)
P.O. Box 1111 (91749-1111)
PHONE.............................626 854-4500
◆ **EMP:** 150 **EST:** 1964
SALES (est): 108.43MM **Privately Held**
Web: www.us-ac.com
SIC: 5075 1711 Air conditioning equipment, except room units, nec; Plumbing, heating, air-conditioning

---

5078 Refrigeration Equipment And Supplies

(P-10338)
BEVERAGES & MORE INC
6820 Katella Ave, Cypress (90630-5108)
PHONE.............................714 891-1242
Jeff Ruffelo, *Brnch Mgr*
EMP: 114
SALES (corp-wide): 1.61B **Privately Held**
Web: www.bevmo.com
SIC: 5078 Refrigerated beverage dispensers
HQ: Beverages & More, Inc.
　　1401 Wllow Pass Rd Ste 90
　　Concord CA 94520

(P-10339)
BRIO WATER TECHNOLOGY INC
Also Called: Dtwusa
768 Turnbull Canyon Rd, Hacienda Heights (91745-1401)
PHONE.............................800 781-1680
Frank Melkonian, *CEO*
Gerard A Thompson, *Sec*
Arman Melkonian, *Dir*
▲ **EMP:** 30 **EST:** 2013
SALES (est): 15.45MM **Privately Held**
Web: www.dtwusa.com
SIC: 5078 3589 Drinking water coolers, mechanical; Water filters and softeners, household type

(P-10340)
HILL PHOENIX INC
Walk-Ins Western Operations
14680 Monte Vista Ave, Chino (91710-5744)
PHONE.............................909 592-8830
Sangyup Steve Lee, *Mgr*
EMP: 83
SALES (corp-wide): 8.44B **Publicly Held**
Web: www.hillphoenix.com
SIC: 5078 Refrigeration equipment and supplies
HQ: Hill Phoenix, Inc.
　　2016 Gees Mill Rd

Conyers GA 30013

(P-10341)
OMNITEAM INC
4380 Ayers Ave, Vernon (90058-4306)
PHONE.................................562 923-9660
Kans Haasis Junior, *CEO*
Robert Davis, *
Don Hyatt Senior, *VP*
EMP: 125 **EST:** 1999
SALES (est): 7.91MM **Privately Held**
Web: www.omniteaminc.com
SIC: 5078 Commercial refrigeration
equipment

(P-10342)
PEPSI-COLA METRO BTLG CO INC
Also Called: Pepsi-Cola
6659 Sycamore Canyon Blvd, Riverside
(92507-0733)
PHONE.................................951 697-3200
Jerry Sime, *Mgr*
EMP: 26
SALES (corp-wide): 86.39B **Publicly Held**
Web: www.pepsico.com
SIC: 5078 2086 5149 Refrigerated beverage
dispensers; Bottled and canned soft drinks;
Soft drinks
HQ: Pepsi-Cola Metropolitan Bottling
Company, Inc.
700 Anderson Hill Rd
Purchase NY 10577
914 767-6000

(P-10343)
REFRIGERATION HDWR SUP CORP
9255 Deering Ave, Chatsworth
(91311-5804)
PHONE.................................800 537-8300
TOLL FREE: 800
Pamela Sylvester, *Brnch Mgr*
EMP: 52
SALES (corp-wide): 22.94MM **Privately Held**
Web: www.rhsparts.com
SIC: 5078 5722 3585 7699 Refrigeration
equipment and supplies; Household
appliance stores; Refrigeration and heating
equipment; Restaurant equipment repair
PA: Refrigeration Hardware Supply
Corporation
632 Foresight Cir
970 241-2800

(P-10344)
REFRIGERATION SUPPLIES DISTRIBUTOR (PA)
Also Called: R S D
28021 Atlantic Ocean Dr, Lake Forest
(92630-8831)
PHONE.................................949 380-7878
▲ **EMP:** 70 **EST:** 1907
SALES (est): 193.04MM
SALES (corp-wide): 193.04MM **Privately Held**
Web: www.rsd.net
SIC: 5078 5075 Refrigeration equipment and
supplies; Air conditioning and ventilation
equipment and supplies

5082 Construction And Mining Machinery

(P-10345)
CAMERON WEST COAST INC
Also Called: Cameron Surface Systems

4315 Yeager Way, Bakersfield
(93313-2018)
▲ **EMP:** 90 **EST:** 1992
SQ FT: 48,000
SALES (est): 9.33MM **Publicly Held**
SIC: 5082 1389 7353 Oil field equipment; Oil
field services, nec; Oil field equipment,
rental or leasing
HQ: Cameron International Corporation
1333 West Loop S Ste 1700
Houston TX 77027

(P-10346)
DENARDI MACHINERY INC
Also Called: D3 Equipment
1475 Pioneer Way, El Cajon (92020-1627)
PHONE.................................619 749-0039
EMP: 102
SIC: 5082 7699 General construction
machinery and equipment; Construction
equipment repair

(P-10347)
GAMA CONTRACTING SERVICES INC
1835 Floradale Ave, South El Monte
(91733-3605)
PHONE.................................626 442-7200
Jose Sergio Duenas, *Pr*
EMP: 140 **EST:** 2008
SALES (est): 7.75MM **Privately Held**
Web: www.gamacsi.com
SIC: 5082 1795 8744 General construction
machinery and equipment; Wrecking and
demolition work; Environmental remediation

(P-10348)
GOODFELLOW CORPORATION
590 Crane St, Lake Elsinore (92530-2727)
PHONE.................................909 874-2700
Lynn Goodfellow, *Brnch Mgr*
EMP: 72
SALES (corp-wide): 121.33MM **Privately Held**
Web: www.goodfellowcorp.com
SIC: 5082 General construction machinery
and equipment
PA: Goodfellow Corporation
12451 Us 95
702 293-7504

(P-10349)
GOTTSTEIN CORPORATION
3500 Chester Ave, Bakersfield
(93301-1630)
PHONE.................................661 322-8934
Scott Gottstein, *Brnch Mgr*
EMP: 210
SALES (corp-wide): 57MM **Privately Held**
Web: www.gottsteincorporation.com
SIC: 5082 General construction machinery
and equipment
PA: Gottstein Corporation
39 Elm Rd Hmbolt Indus Pk
570 454-7162

(P-10350)
HERCA TELECOMM SERVICES INC
Also Called: Herca Construction Services
18610 Beck St, Perris (92570-9185)
PHONE.................................951 940-5941
Hector R Castellon, *Pr*
Tracy Hertel, *
Raul Castellon, *
Alfredo Castellon, *
Alfonso Catellon, *
EMP: 56 **EST:** 2005
SQ FT: 67,900
SALES (est): 2.12MM **Privately Held**

Web: www.hercatelecomm.com
SIC: 5082 1623 1731 3663 General
construction machinery and equipment;
Communication line and transmission tower
construction; General electrical contractor;
Antennas, transmitting and communications

(P-10351)
JPL GLOBAL LLC
Also Called: Iq Power Tools
4635 Wade Ave, Perris (92571-7494)
P.O. Box 7449 (92552-7449)
PHONE.................................888 274-7744
Paul Guth, *Managing Member*
Scott Craft, *Genl Mgr*
▲ **EMP:** 23 **EST:** 2009
SALES (est): 5.16MM **Privately Held**
Web: www.iqpowertools.com
SIC: 5082 1741 3541 Masonry equipment
and supplies; Masonry and other stonework
; Machine tools, metal cutting type

(P-10352)
MALOOF NAMAN BUILDERS
Also Called: Heavy Civil - Gen Engrg Cnstr
9614 Cozycroft Ave, Chatsworth
(91311-5116)
PHONE.................................818 775-0040
Omar G Maloof, *Pr*
EMP: 52 **EST:** 2009
SALES (est): 2.2MM **Privately Held**
SIC: 5082 3531 1629 8711 Road
construction equipment; Road construction
and maintenance machinery; Dams,
waterways, docks, and other marine
construction; Building construction
consultant

(P-10353)
NAUMANN/HOBBS MTL HDLG CORP II
Also Called: Hawthorne Lift Systems
86998 Avenue 52, Coachella (92236-2710)
PHONE.................................866 266-2244
EMP: 105
SALES (corp-wide): 90MM **Privately Held**
SIC: 5082 5084 General construction
machinery and equipment; Industrial
machinery and equipment
PA: Naumann/Hobbs Material Handling
Corporation Ii, Inc.
4336 S 43rd Pl
602 437-1331

(P-10354)
OAKCROFT ASSOCIATES INC (PA)
Also Called: American Assod Roofg Distrs
750 Monterey Pass Rd, Monterey Park
(91754-3607)
P.O. Box 63309 (90063-0309)
PHONE.................................323 261-5122
James D Yundt, *Pr*
James S Yundt, *VP*
Joellen Yundt, *Sec*
John Carmack, *Dir*
Jonathan Yundt, *VP*
▲ **EMP:** 31 **EST:** 1950
SQ FT: 14,500
SALES (est): 13.82MM
SALES (corp-wide): 13.82MM **Privately Held**
Web: www.roofmaster.com
SIC: 5082 3531 5199 General construction
machinery and equipment; Roofing
equipment; Broom, mop, and paint handles

(P-10355)
QUINN COMPANY
Also Called: Caterpillar Authorized Dealer
1655 Carlotti Dr, Santa Maria (93454-1503)
PHONE.................................805 925-8611
Dan Hunt, *Mgr*
EMP: 75
SALES (corp-wide): 359MM **Privately Held**
Web: www.quinncompany.com
SIC: 5082 5083 5084 7353 General
construction machinery and equipment;
Farm and garden machinery; Industrial
machinery and equipment; Heavy
construction equipment rental
HQ: Quinn Company
10006 Rose Hills Rd
City Of Industry CA 90601
562 463-4000

(P-10356)
QUINN COMPANY
Also Called: Caterpillar Authorized Dealer
801 Del Norte Blvd, Oxnard (93030-8966)
PHONE.................................805 485-2171
Jay Ervine, *Brnch Mgr*
EMP: 81
SALES (corp-wide): 359MM **Privately Held**
Web: www.quinncompany.com
SIC: 5082 5083 5084 7353 General
construction machinery and equipment;
Farm and garden machinery; Industrial
machinery and equipment; Heavy
construction equipment rental
HQ: Quinn Company
10006 Rose Hills Rd
City Of Industry CA 90601
562 463-4000

(P-10357)
QUINN COMPANY
Also Called: Caterpillar Authorized Dealer
2200 Pegasus Dr, Bakersfield
(93308-6801)
PHONE.................................661 393-5800
Steve Eucce, *Brnch Mgr*
EMP: 87
SALES (corp-wide): 359MM **Privately Held**
Web: www.quinncompany.com
SIC: 5082 5083 5084 7353 General
construction machinery and equipment;
Farm and garden machinery; Industrial
machinery and equipment; Heavy
construction equipment rental
HQ: Quinn Company
10006 Rose Hills Rd
City Of Industry CA 90601
562 463-4000

(P-10358)
QUINN SHEPHERD MACHINERY
Also Called: Caterpillar Authorized Dealer
10006 Rose Hills Rd, City Of Industry
(90601-1794)
P.O. Box 226789 (90022-6789)
PHONE.................................562 463-6000
Blake Quinn, *Pr*
▲ **EMP:** 287 **EST:** 1924
SQ FT: 163,000
SALES (est): 24.87MM
SALES (corp-wide): 359MM **Privately Held**
Web: www.quinncompany.com
SIC: 5082 5084 General construction
machinery and equipment; Industrial
machinery and equipment
PA: Quinn Group, Inc.
10006 Rose Hills Rd
562 463-4000

(P-10359)
SABA HOLDING COMPANY LLC
Also Called: Volvo Construction Eqp & Svc
22099 Knabe Rd, Corona (92883-7111)
PHONE..............................951 277-7620
Jason Rhoda, *Brnch Mgr*
EMP: 140
SALES (corp-wide): 52.58B **Privately Held**
Web: www.vcesvolvo.com
SIC: 5082 General construction machinery
and equipment
HQ: Saba Holding Company, Llc
312 Volvo Way
Shippensburg PA 17257
717 532-9181

(P-10360)
THOMPCO INC
899 Mission Rock Rd, Santa Paula
(93060-9800)
PHONE..............................805 933-8048
Dori Thompson, *Pr*
EMP: 27 **EST:** 2008
SALES (est): 2.59MM **Privately Held**
SIC: 5082 1389 Oil field equipment; Oil and
gas field services, nec

5083 Farm And Garden Machinery

(P-10361)
CASCADE TURF LLC
Also Called: Aa Equipment
4811 Brooks St, Montclair (91763-4733)
PHONE..............................909 626-8586
EMP: 79
SIC: 5083 Agricultural machinery and
equipment

(P-10362)
EURODRIP USA INC
7545 Carroll Rd, San Diego (92121-2401)
PHONE..............................559 674-2670
Rowland Wilkinson, *CEO*
◆ **EMP:** 80 **EST:** 1996
SALES (est): 6.43MM **Privately Held**
Web: www.eurodripusa.com
SIC: 5083 3084 Irrigation equipment;
Plastics pipe
HQ: Rivulis A.V.E.G.E.
Athinon - Lamias National Rd (55th
Km), P.O. Box 34
Oinofyta 32011

(P-10363)
I BRANDS LLC
2617 N Sepulveda Blvd, Manhattan Beach
(90266-2737)
PHONE..............................424 336-5216
EMP: 140 **EST:** 2010
SALES (est): 831.75K **Privately Held**
Web: www.skywatchtime.com
SIC: 5083 Agricultural machinery and
equipment

(P-10364)
SPEARS MANUFACTURING CO (PA)
15853 Olden St, Rancho Cascades
(91342-1293)
P.O. Box 9203 (91392-9203)
PHONE..............................818 364-1611
Robert Wayne Spears, *CEO*
Wayne Spears, *
Michael Valasquez, *General Vice President**
Ken Ruggles, *
◆ **EMP:** 134 **EST:** 1970
SQ FT: 119,088

SALES (est): 1.37B
SALES (corp-wide): 1.37B **Privately Held**
Web: www.spearsmanufacturing.com
SIC: 5083 3494 Irrigation equipment; Valves
and pipe fittings, nec

5084 Industrial Machinery And Equipment

(P-10365)
AIRGAS USA LLC
3737 Worsham Ave, Long Beach
(90808-1774)
P.O. Box 7423 (91109-7423)
PHONE..............................562 497-1991
Douglas L Jones, *Reg Pr*
EMP: 1726
SALES (corp-wide): 114.13MM **Privately
Held**
Web: www.airgas.com
SIC: 5084 Welding machinery and equipment
HQ: Airgas Usa, Llc
259 N Rdnor Chster Rd Ste
Radnor PA 19087
216 642-6600

(P-10366)
ALS GROUP INC
Also Called: Capri Tools
1788 W 2nd St, Pomona (91766-1206)
PHONE..............................909 622-7555
Anderson Cheung, *CEO*
▲ **EMP:** 25 **EST:** 2005
SALES (est): 3.48MM **Privately Held**
SIC: 5084 3545 3546 3423 Pneumatic tools
and equipment; Precision measuring tools;
Power-driven handtools; Wrenches, hand
tools

(P-10367)
AMADA AMERICA INC (HQ)
7025 Firestone Blvd, Buena Park
(90621-1869)
PHONE..............................714 739-2111
TOLL FREE: 800
Mike Guarin, *CEO*
Koa Nakata, *CFO*
▲ **EMP:** 75 **EST:** 1971
SQ FT: 103,000
SALES (est): 185.26MM **Privately Held**
Web: www.amada.com
SIC: 5084 6159 Metalworking machinery;
Machinery and equipment finance leasing
PA: Amada Co., Ltd.
200, Ishida

(P-10368)
CDS MOVING EQUIPMENT INC (PA)
Also Called: Cds Packing Solutions
375 W Manville St, Rancho Dominguez
(90220-5617)
PHONE..............................310 631-1100
TOLL FREE: 800
Kara Sidor, *CEO*
Ryan Sidor, *
Dennis Barwick, *
Aaron Barwick, *
▲ **EMP:** 80 **EST:** 1981
SQ FT: 100,000
SALES (est): 55.9MM
SALES (corp-wide): 55.9MM **Privately
Held**
Web: www.cds-usa.com
SIC: 5084 Materials handling machinery

(P-10369)
CENTERLINE INDUSTRIAL INC
2530 Southport Way Ste D, National City
(91950-6676)
PHONE..............................858 505-0838
Joann Loehr, *Pr*
Richard Botkin, *Prin*
Jack Loehr, *Prin*
EMP: 29 **EST:** 1996
SQ FT: 15,000
SALES (est): 1.5MM **Privately Held**
SIC: 5084 3544 Machine tools and
accessories; Special dies, tools, jigs, and
fixtures

(P-10370)
DSI PROCESS SYSTEMS LLC
Also Called: Statco
7595 Reynolds Cir, Huntington Beach
(92647-6787)
PHONE..............................314 382-1525
EMP: 136 **EST:** 2010
SALES (est): 18.06MM **Privately Held**
Web: www.statco-dsi.com
SIC: 5084 Industrial machinery and
equipment
HQ: Statco Engineering & Fabricators Llc
7595 Reynolds Cir
Huntington Beach CA 92647
714 375-6300

(P-10371)
ELEVATOR EQUIPMENT CORPORATION (PA)
Also Called: Eeco
4035 Goodwin Ave, Los Angeles
(90039-1190)
P.O. Box 39714 (90039-0714)
PHONE..............................323 245-0147
Abe Salehpour, *CEO*
Abdul Mozayeni, *
◆ **EMP:** 75 **EST:** 1944
SQ FT: 20,000
SALES (est): 24.17MM
SALES (corp-wide): 24.17MM **Privately
Held**
Web: www.elevatorequipment.com
SIC: 5084 Elevators

(P-10372)
ELLISON TECHNOLOGIES INC
9912 Pioneer Blvd, Santa Fe Springs
(90670-3250)
PHONE..............................562 949-8311
EMP: 112
Web: www.ellisontechnologies.com
SIC: 5084 Machine tools and accessories
HQ: Ellison Technologies, Inc.
9828 Arlee Ave
Santa Fe Springs CA 90670
562 949-8311

(P-10373)
EQUIPMENT DEPOT INC
Also Called: Southern California Mtl Hdlg
16748 Boyle Ave, Fontana (92337-7503)
PHONE..............................562 949-1000
David Turner, *Pr*
EMP: 150
Web: www.eqdepot.com
SIC: 5084 Conveyor systems
HQ: Equipment Depot, Inc.
16330 Air Center Blvd
Houston TX 77032
713 365-2530

(P-10374)
FUELING AND SERVICE TECH INC

Also Called: Fastech
7050 Village Dr Ste D, Buena Park
(90621-2281)
PHONE..............................714 523-0194
M Dan Mcgill, *CEO*
EMP: 75 **EST:** 1994
SQ FT: 15,000
SALES (est): 25.01MM **Privately Held**
Web: www.fastechus.com
SIC: 5084 Petroleum industry machinery

(P-10375)
HARVEY PERFORMANCE COMPANY LLC
28231 Avenue Crocker Ste 90, Valencia
(91355-1276)
PHONE..............................661 467-0440
EMP: 90
SALES (corp-wide): 42.76MM **Privately
Held**
Web: www.harveyperformance.com
SIC: 5084 Industrial machinery and
equipment
PA: Harvey Performance Company Llc
428 Newburyport Tpke
844 393-8665

(P-10376)
HAWTHORNE MACHINERY CO
Also Called: Caterpillar
16945 Camino San Bernardo, San Diego
(92127-2499)
PHONE..............................858 674-7000
Bob Price, *Mgr*
EMP: 111
SALES (corp-wide): 176.69MM **Privately
Held**
Web: www.hawthornecat.com
SIC: 5084 7359 5085 5088 Engines and
parts, air-cooled; Equipment rental and
leasing, nec; Industrial supplies; Marine
crafts and supplies
PA: Hawthorne Machinery Co.
16945 Camino San Bernardo
858 674-7000

(P-10377)
INDUSTRIAL PARTS DEPOT LLC (HQ)
Also Called: Ipd
1550 Charles Willard St, Carson
(90746-4039)
PHONE..............................310 530-1900
Michael Badar, *Pr*
Russell Kneipp, *Managing Member**
◆ **EMP:** 70 **EST:** 1955
SALES (est): 23.18MM
SALES (corp-wide): 44.12MM **Privately
Held**
Web: www.ipdparts.com
SIC: 5084 3519 Engines and parts, diesel;
Parts and accessories, internal combustion
engines
PA: Storm Industries, Inc.
970 W 190th St
310 534-5232

(P-10378)
JOHN TILLMAN COMPANY (DH)
1300 W Artesia Blvd, Compton
(90220-5307)
PHONE..............................310 764-0110
Phillip Mcgreevy, *Pr*
▲ **EMP:** 100 **EST:** 1928
SQ FT: 25,000
SALES (est): 24.24MM
SALES (corp-wide): 14.7B **Privately Held**
Web: www.jtillman.com

SIC: **5084** 3842 3548 Safety equipment;
Personal safety equipment; Welding
apparatus
HQ: Bunzl Distribution Inc.
1 Cityplace Dr Ste 200
Saint Louis MO 63141

(P-10379)
JWC ENVIRONMENTAL INC (DH)
Also Called: Windjmmer Capitl Investors III
2850 Redhill Ave Ste 125, Santa Ana
(92705-5541)
PHONE..............................949 833-3888
Ken Biele, *CEO*
Joe Ruiz, *CFO*
◆ **EMP:** 30 **EST:** 1989
SALES (est): 35.4MM **Privately Held**
Web: www.jwce.com
SIC: **5084** 3589 Industrial machinery and
equipment; Commercial cleaning equipment
HQ: Sulzer Management Ag
Neuwiesenstrasse 15
Winterthur ZH

(P-10380)
KAFCO SALES COMPANY
2300 E 37th St, Vernon (90058-1405)
P.O. Box 58563 (90058-0563)
PHONE..............................323 588-7141
Akira Urakawa, *CEO*
▲ **EMP:** 26 **EST:** 1978
SQ FT: 15,500
SALES (est): 4.54MM **Privately Held**
Web: www.kafcosales.com
SIC: **5084** 3842 Safety equipment; Surgical
appliances and supplies

(P-10381)
MATERIAL HANDLING SUPPLY
INC (HQ)
12900 Firestone Blvd, Santa Fe Springs
(90670-5405)
PHONE..............................562 921-7715
TOLL FREE: 800
Alexander Stephen Lynn, *CEO*
Donn C Lynn Junior, *Ch Bd*
John Hanson, *
EMP: 80 **EST:** 1962
SQ FT: 85,000
SALES (est): 4.58MM
SALES (corp-wide): 5.86MM **Privately
Held**
Web: www.mhs-ca.com
SIC: **5084** 7629 5046 Food industry
machinery; Electrical repair shops;
Commercial equipment, nec
PA: Envicor
12900 Firestone Blvd
562 921-7715

(P-10382)
MAXON LIFT CORP (PA)
11921 Slauson Ave, Santa Fe Springs
(90670-2221)
PHONE..............................562 464-0099
Casey Lugash, *Pr*
Brenda Leung, *VP Fin*
▲ **EMP:** 55 **EST:** 1957
SQ FT: 30,000
SALES (est): 49.53MM **Privately Held**
Web: www.maxonlift.com
SIC: **5084** 3537 3534 Lift trucks and parts;
Industrial trucks and tractors; Elevators and
moving stairways

(P-10383)
MENKE MARKING DEVICES INC
Also Called: Menke Marketing Devices
10440 Pioneer Blvd Ste 4, Santa Fe Springs
(90670-5574)

P.O. Box 2986 (90670-0986)
PHONE..............................562 921-1380
Stephen Menke, *Pr*
EMP: 29 **EST:** 1943
SALES (est): 4.56MM **Privately Held**
Web: www.menkemarking.com
SIC: **5084** 3953 Industrial machinery and
equipment; Marking devices

(P-10384)
MUTUAL LIQUID GAS & EQP CO
INC (PA)
Also Called: Mutual Propane
17117 S Broadway, Gardena (90248-3191)
PHONE..............................310 515-0553
Melvin Moore, *CEO*
Steve Moore, *
EMP: 30 **EST:** 1934
SQ FT: 3,100
SALES (est): 14.31MM
SALES (corp-wide): 14.31MM **Privately
Held**
Web: www.mutualpropane.com
SIC: **5084** 3549 Propane conversion
equipment; Metalworking machinery, nec

(P-10385)
NUWA ROBOTICS INC
9250 1/2 Hall Rd, Downey (90241-5308)
PHONE..............................562 450-0100
Liou Tzung Guo, *CEO*
Chih Chieh Chang, *COO*
Xin Fu Chen, *CDO*
Wei Li Lin, *CSO*
EMP: 102 **EST:** 2022
SALES (est): 2.84MM **Privately Held**
SIC: **5084** Robots, industrial
HQ: Nuwa Robotics (Hk) Limited Taiwan
Branch
6f, No. 102, Dunhua N. Rd.
Taipei City TAP 10540

(P-10386)
OLIVER HEALTHCARE
PACKAGING CO
Also Called: Clean Cut Technologies
1145 N Ocean Cir, Anaheim (92806-1939)
PHONE..............................714 864-3500
Mike Benevento, *Pr*
EMP: 100
SALES (corp-wide): 2.26B **Privately Held**
Web: www.oliverhcp.com
SIC: **5084** 5199 3053 Processing and
packaging equipment; Packaging materials;
Packing materials
HQ: Oliver Healthcare Packaging Company
445 6th St Nw
Grand Rapids MI 49504
833 465-4837

(P-10387)
ONEIL DATA SYSTEMS LLC
12655 Beatrice St, Los Angeles
(90066-7300)
PHONE..............................310 448-6400
▲ **EMP:** 150
SIC: **5084** Fans, industrial

(P-10388)
OTIS ELEVATOR COMPANY
512 Paula Ave Ste A, Glendale
(91201-2363)
PHONE..............................818 241-2828
Sam Goe, *Brnch Mgr*
EMP: 250
SQ FT: 15,000
SALES (corp-wide): 14.21B **Publicly Held**
Web: www.otis.com
SIC: **5084** 7699 Elevators; Elevators:
inspection, service, and repair

HQ: Otis Elevator Company
1 Carrier Pl
Farmington CT 06032
860 674-3000

(P-10389)
OTIS ELEVATOR COMPANY
3949 Viewridge Ave, San Diego (92123)
PHONE..............................858 560-5881
Brian Petler, *Mgr*
EMP: 57
SQ FT: 1,400
SALES (corp-wide): 14.21B **Publicly Held**
Web: www.otis.com
SIC: **5084** 5082 7699 3534 Elevators;
General construction machinery and
equipment; Door and window repair;
Elevators and moving stairways
HQ: Otis Elevator Company
1 Carrier Pl
Farmington CT 06032
860 674-3000

(P-10390)
PALFINGER LIFTGATES LLC
15939 Piuma Ave, Cerritos (90703-1526)
PHONE..............................888 774-5844
Hakan Pettersson, *
▲ **EMP:** 81 **EST:** 2013
SALES (est): 16.65MM **Privately Held**
Web: www.palfinger.com
SIC: **5084** Lift trucks and parts

(P-10391)
PAPE MATERIAL HANDLING INC
2615 Pellissier Pl, City Of Industry
(90601-1508)
PHONE..............................562 463-8000
Jordan Pape, *Brnch Mgr*
EMP: 200
Web: www.papemh.com
SIC: **5084** 7699 7359 Lift trucks and parts;
Industrial machinery and equipment repair;
Industrial truck rental
HQ: Pape' Material Handling, Inc.
355 Goodpasture Island Rd
Eugene OR 97401

(P-10392)
PARKER-HANNIFIN
CORPORATION
Customer Support Military Div
14300 Alton Pkwy, Irvine (92618-1898)
PHONE..............................949 465-4519
Edwin Feick, *Brnch Mgr*
EMP: 138
SALES (corp-wide): 19.93B **Publicly Held**
Web: www.parker.com
SIC: **5084** Hydraulic systems equipment and
supplies
PA: Parker Hannifin Corporation
6035 Parkland Blvd
216 896-3000

(P-10393)
POWELL WORKS INC
Also Called: Powell Works
17807 Maclaren St Ste B, La Puente
(91744-5700)
PHONE..............................909 861-6699
Jerry Wang, *Pr*
▲ **EMP:** 256 **EST:** 2015
SQ FT: 2,500
SALES (est): 1.5MM **Privately Held**
SIC: **5084** Compressors, except air
conditioning

(P-10394)
POWER GENERATION ENTPS
INC
26764 Oak Ave, Canyon Country
(91351-2409)
PHONE..............................818 484-8550
Vartan Seropian, *CEO*
EMP: 110 **EST:** 2014
SALES (est): 8.43MM **Privately Held**
Web: www.powergenenterprises.com
SIC: **5084** Industrial machinery and
equipment

(P-10395)
PRO SAFETY INC
20503 Belshaw Ave, Carson (90746-3505)
PHONE..............................562 364-7450
Catherina Zember, *Pr*
EMP: 148 **EST:** 2015
SQ FT: 88,000
SALES (est): 9.59MM **Privately Held**
Web: www.airprotarservices.com
SIC: **5084** 8331 Industrial machinery and
equipment; Job training and related services

(P-10396)
QUALLS STUD WELDING PDTS
INC
Also Called: Stud Welding Products
9459 Washburn Rd, Downey (90242-2912)
PHONE..............................562 923-7883
Robert Butcher, *Brnch Mgr*
EMP: 23
SALES (corp-wide): 12.92MM **Privately
Held**
Web: www.studweldprod.com
SIC: **5084** 7692 1799 Welding machinery
and equipment; Welding repair; Welding on
site
PA: Quall's Stud Welding Products, Inc.
7820 S 210th St Ste C103
425 656-9787

(P-10397)
RAYMOND HANDLING
SOLUTIONS INC (DH)
Also Called: Raymond West
9939 Norwalk Blvd, Santa Fe Springs
(90670-3321)
P.O. Box 3683 (90670-1683)
PHONE..............................562 944-8067
James Wilcox, *CEO*
EMP: 188 **EST:** 2002
SQ FT: 5,000
SALES (est): 118.87MM **Privately Held**
Web: www.raymondwest.com
SIC: **5084** 7600 7350 Materials handling
machinery; Industrial machinery and
equipment repair; Industrial truck rental
HQ: The Raymond Corporation
22 S Canal St
Greene NY 13778
607 656-2311

(P-10398)
RDM INDUSTRIES
14310 Gannet St, La Mirada (90638-5221)
PHONE..............................714 690-0380
Jaz Manak, *CEO*
Jaz Manak, *Pr*
Dan Gilmore, *Stockholder*
◆ **EMP:** 28 **EST:** 2011
SALES (est): 5.16MM **Privately Held**
Web: www.rdmindustriesinc.com
SIC: **5084** 3565 5162 2671 Industrial
machinery and equipment; Aerating
machines, for beverages; Plastics
materials, nec; Plastic film, coated or
laminated for packaging

(P-10399)
REBAS INC
Also Called: Toyota Material Hdlg Solutions
12012 Burke St, Santa Fe Springs
(90670-2676)
PHONE....................800 794-5438
Shankar Basu, *Ch Bd*
Simon Walker, *
▲ EMP: 104 EST: 1990
SQ FT: 103,000
SALES (est): 37.91MM **Privately Held**
Web: www.toyotamhs.com
SIC: 5084 Materials handling machinery

(P-10400)
REPLANET LLC
800 N Haven Ave Ste 120, Ontario
(91764-4951)
P.O. Box 2893 (95344-0893)
PHONE....................951 520-1700
EMP: 600
Web: www.replanet.com
SIC: 5084 4953 Recycling machinery and
equipment; Refuse systems

(P-10401)
SCHURMAN FINE PAPERS
3333 Bristol St, Costa Mesa (92626-1873)
PHONE....................714 549-0212
EMP: 27
SALES (corp-wide): 38.97MM **Privately Held**
Web: www.srgretail.com
SIC: 5084 2621 Industrial machinery and
equipment; Paper mills
PA: Schurman Fine Papers
300 Oak Bluff Ln
707 425-8006

(P-10402)
SHARP INDUSTRIES INC (PA)
Also Called: Sharp
3501 Challenger St Fl 2, Torrance
(90503-1697)
PHONE....................310 370-5990
James Chen, *Ch Bd*
Nicholas Chen, *CEO*
George Lee, *Sr VP*
Roger Lee, *VP*
▲ EMP: 23 EST: 1976
SQ FT: 40,000
SALES (est): 10.21MM
SALES (corp-wide): 10.21MM **Privately Held**
Web: www.sharp-industries.com
SIC: 5084 3542 Machine tools and
accessories; Arbor presses

(P-10403)
SHIP & SHORE ENVIRONMENTAL INC
2474 N Palm Dr, Signal Hill (90755-4007)
PHONE....................562 997-0233
Anoosheh Mostafaei, *Pr*
Anu D Vij, *
▲ EMP: 38 EST: 2000
SQ FT: 4,000
SALES (est): 12.29MM **Privately Held**
Web: www.shipandshore.com
SIC: 5084 3444 Pollution control equipment,
air (environmental); Awnings and canopies

(P-10404)
SOUTHERN CAL HYDRLIC ENGRG COR
Also Called: S C Hydraulic Engineering
1130 Columbia St, Brea (92821-2921)
PHONE....................714 257-4800
Donna Perez, *Pr*

David Vedder, *
Manuel Perez, *
EMP: 40 EST: 1953
SQ FT: 65,000
SALES (est): 10.16MM **Privately Held**
Web: www.schydraulic.com
SIC: 5084 3594 Pumps and pumping
equipment, nec; Pumps, hydraulic power
transfer

(P-10405)
SOUTHERN CALIFORNIA MATERIAL HANDLING INC
Also Called: Scmh
12393 Slauson Ave, Whittier (90606-2824)
P.O. Box 80770 (91118-8770)
PHONE....................562 949-1006
▲ EMP: 150
Web: www.eqdepot.com
SIC: 5084 Conveyor systems

(P-10406)
STAINLESS STL FABRICATORS INC
Also Called: Cook King
15120 Desman Rd, La Mirada
(90638-5737)
PHONE....................714 739-9904
Craig Miller, *Pr*
Dave Hart, *
Glenna Miller, *
Jennifer Arcos, *Prin*
EMP: 60 EST: 1985
SQ FT: 11,204
SALES (est): 8.35MM **Privately Held**
Web: www.ssfab.net
SIC: 5084 3444 Industrial machinery and
equipment; Restaurant sheet metalwork

(P-10407)
SURFACE PUMPS INC (PA)
3301 Unicorn Rd, Bakersfield (93308-6852)
P.O. Box 5757 (93388-5757)
PHONE....................661 393-1545
Steven J Durrett, *Pr*
David Cook, *
Marty Rushing, *
EMP: 51 EST: 1970
SQ FT: 14,000
SALES (est): 26.27MM
SALES (corp-wide): 26.27MM **Privately Held**
Web: www.surfacepumps.com
SIC: 5084 7699 8711 3519 Pumps and
pumping equipment, nec; Pumps and
pumping equipment repair; Engineering
services; Parts and accessories, internal
combustion engines

(P-10408)
SVF FLOW CONTROLS INC
5595 Fresca Dr, La Palma (90623-1006)
PHONE....................562 802-2255
Wayne Ulanski, *Pr*
David Steel, *
Russell Stern, *Stockholder*
▲ EMP: 40 EST: 1993
SQ FT: 20,000
SALES (est): 4.98MM **Privately Held**
Web: www.svf.net
SIC: 5084 3491 3494 5085 Instruments and
control equipment; Industrial valves; Valves
and pipe fittings, nec; Valves and fittings

(P-10409)
SWARCO MCCAIN INC (DH)
2365 Oak Ridge Way, Vista (92081-8348)
PHONE....................760 727-8100
Jimi Meshulam, *CEO*
Jo Ann Mills, *

▲ EMP: 250 EST: 1987
SQ FT: 6,700
SALES (est): 127MM
SALES (corp-wide): 2.67MM **Privately Held**
Web: www.mccain-inc.com
SIC: 5084 3444 3669 Industrial machinery
and equipment; Sheet metalwork; Traffic
signals, electric
HQ: Swarco Ag
Blattenwaldweg 8
Wattens 6112
522458770

(P-10410)
TESTEQUITY INC
Also Called: Testequity
6100 Condor Dr, Moorpark (93021-2608)
PHONE....................805 498-9933
EMP: 85
SIC: 5084 Measuring and testing equipment,
electrical

(P-10411)
TK ELEVATOR CORPORATION
1965 Gillespie Way Ste 101, El Cajon
(92020-0500)
PHONE....................619 596-7220
Jeff Hansen, *Mgr*
EMP: 86
SALES (corp-wide): 2.67MM **Privately Held**
Web: www.tkelevator.com
SIC: 5084 Elevators
HQ: Tk Elevator Corporation
788 Crcle 75 Pkwy Se Ste
Atlanta GA 30339
678 319-3240

(P-10412)
VALLEY POWER SYSTEMS INC
Also Called: Valley Detriot Diesel
4000 Rosedale Hwy, Bakersfield
(93308-6131)
PHONE....................661 325-9001
Ken Relyea, *Brnch Mgr*
EMP: 106
SALES (corp-wide): 178.72MM **Privately Held**
Web: www.valleypowersystems.com
SIC: 5084 Engines and parts, diesel
PA: Valley Power Systems, Inc.
425 S Hacienda Blvd
626 333-1243

(P-10413)
VALLEY POWER SYSTEMS INC (PA)
Also Called: John Deere Authorized Dealer
425 S Hacienda Blvd, City Of Industry
(91745-1123)
PHONE....................626 333-1243
TOLL FREE: 800
Hampton Clark Lee, *Ch Bd*
Michael Barnett, *Pr*
Robert K Humphryes, *CFO*
Richard Kickliter, *VP*
Bruce Noble, *Marketing*
◆ EMP: 100 EST: 1949
SQ FT: 49,000
SALES (est): 178.72MM
SALES (corp-wide): 178.72MM **Privately Held**
Web: www.valleypowersystems.com
SIC: 5084 Engines and parts, diesel

(P-10414)
VALTRA INC (PA)
Also Called: Strong Hand Tools
8750 Pioneer Blvd, Santa Fe Springs
(90670-2006)

PHONE....................562 949-8625
Harry Hon Wong, *CEO*
▲ EMP: 24 EST: 1983
SQ FT: 24,000
SALES (est): 14.11MM
SALES (corp-wide): 14.11MM **Privately Held**
Web: lp.constantcontactpages.com
SIC: 5084 5085 3452 3429 Industrial
machine parts; Industrial supplies; Bolts,
nuts, rivets, and washers; Hardware, nec

(P-10415)
VAUGHANS INDUSTRIAL REPAIR INC
16224 Garfield Ave, Paramount
(90723-4804)
P.O. Box 1898 (90723-1898)
PHONE....................562 633-2660
Thomas Vaughan, *Pr*
Patricia Vaughan, *
David Newton, *
John L Smith, *
Keven Vaughan, *
EMP: 35 EST: 1978
SQ FT: 20,000
SALES (est): 7.48MM
SALES (corp-wide): 7.48MM **Privately Held**
Web: www.virc1.com
SIC: 5084 1711 3599 Oil refining machinery,
equipment, and supplies; Mechanical
contractor; Machine and other job shop
work
PA: Vss Sales, Inc.
16220 Garfield Ave
562 630-0606

(P-10416)
WASSCO
Also Called: Wassco Sales
12778 Brookprinter Pl, Poway
(92064-6810)
P.O. Box 856 (60076-0856)
PHONE....................858 679-0444
EMP: 106
SIC: 5084 Machine tools and metalworking
machinery

(P-10417)
WASTECH CONTROLS & ENGRG LLC
20600 Nordhoff St, Chatsworth
(91311-6114)
PHONE....................818 998-3500
Paul Nicolas, *Pr*
▲ EMP: 58 EST: 1987
SQ FT: 30,000
SALES (est): 24.8MM **Privately Held**
Web: www.wastechengineering.com
SIC: 5084 3561 3823 3559 Waste
compactors; Pumps, domestic: water or
sump; Industrial flow and liquid measuring
instruments; Anodizing equipment

(P-10418)
WESTAIR GASES & EQUIPMENT INC
Also Called: Westair Gases & Equipment
3901 Buck Owens Blvd, Bakersfield
(93308-4927)
PHONE....................661 387-6800
Steve Castiglione, *Mgr*
EMP: 160
SALES (corp-wide): 80.86MM **Privately Held**
Web: www.westairgases.com
SIC: 5084 Welding machinery and equipment
PA: Westair Gases & Equipment, Inc.
2505 Congress St

▲ = Import ▼ = Export
◆ = Import/Export

866 937-8247

(P-10419)

WESTERN REFINING INC

1201 Baker St, Costa Mesa (92626-3916)
PHONE...............................714 708-2200
EMP: 57
Web: www.wnr.com
SIC: 5084 2911 Metalworking machinery;
  Petroleum refining
HQ: Western Refining, Inc.
  212 N Clark Dr
  El Paso TX 79905

(P-10420)

WESTERN REFINING INC

22232 Wilmington Ave, Carson
(90745-4308)
PHONE...............................310 834-1297
EMP: 57
Web: www.wnr.com
SIC: 5084 2911 Metalworking machinery;
  Petroleum refining
HQ: Western Refining, Inc.
  212 N Clark Dr
  El Paso TX 79905

(P-10421)

WESTERN REFINING INC

4357 E Cesar E Chavez Ave, Los Angeles
(90022-1401)
PHONE...............................323 264-8500
EMP: 57
Web: www.wnr.com
SIC: 5084 2911 Metalworking machinery;
  Petroleum refining
HQ: Western Refining, Inc.
  212 N Clark Dr
  El Paso TX 79905

(P-10422)

WIGGINS LIFT CO INC

2571 Cortez St, Oxnard (93030)
P.O. Box 5187 (93031-5187)
PHONE...............................805 485-7821
Hattie Wiggins, *Ch Bd*
Michael M Wiggins, *
Paul Hurbace, *
Jack Mc Dowell, *General Vice President*
Michelle Mc Dowell, *
◆ EMP: 70 EST: 1951
SQ FT: 55,000
SALES (est): 20MM Privately Held
Web: www.wigginslift.com
SIC: 5084 Materials handling machinery

(P-10423)

**YALE/CHASE EQUIPMENT AND
SERVICES INC**

2615 Pellissier Pl, City Of Industry
(00601 1608)
P.O. Box 1231 (91749-1231)
PHONE...............................562 463-8000
TOLL FREE: 800
◆ EMP: 200
Web: www.pape.com
SIC: 5084 7699 7359 Lift trucks and parts;
  Industrial machinery and equipment repair;
  Industrial truck rental

5085 Industrial Supplies

(P-10424)

**ALLIED HIGH TECH PRODUCTS
INC**

16207 Carmenita Rd, Cerritos
(90703-2212)
P.O. Box 4608 (90220)
PHONE...............................310 635-2466
Clayton A Smith, *CEO*
Shirley A Smith, *
▲ EMP: 70 EST: 1983
SQ FT: 34,000
SALES (est): 25.93MM Privately Held
Web: www.alliedhightech.com
SIC: 5085 Abrasives

(P-10425)

**AMERICAN INDUSTRIAL
SOURCE INC**

15759 Strathern St Ste 1, Van Nuys
(91406-1345)
P.O. Box 8011 (91409-8011)
PHONE...............................800 661-0622
Boris Kofsman, *Pr*
EMP: 90 EST: 2005
SALES (est): 3MM Privately Held
Web:
www.americanindustrialsource.com
SIC: 5085 Industrial supplies

(P-10426)

BDI INC

9917 Gidley St Unit A, El Monte
(91731-1136)
PHONE...............................626 442-8948
EMP: 95
SALES (corp-wide): 1.51B Privately Held
Web: www.bdiexpress.com
SIC: 5085 Hydraulic and pneumatic pistons
  and valves
HQ: Bdi, Inc.
  8000 Hub Pkwy
  Cleveland OH 44125
  216 642-9100

(P-10427)

**BRIDGESTONE HOSEPOWER
LLC**

Also Called: Hose Power USA
2865 Pellissier Pl, City of Industry
(90601-1512)
PHONE...............................562 699-9500
Alfonso Sanchez, *Genl Mgr*
EMP: 24
Web: www.hosepower.com
SIC: 5085 3492 Hose, belting, and packing;
  Hose and tube fittings and assemblies,
  hydraulic/pneumatic
HQ: Bridgestone Hosepower, Llc
  50 Industrial Loop Dr N
  Orange Park FL 32073

(P-10428)

CARPENTER GROUP

Also Called: American Rigging & Supply
2380 Main St, San Diego (92113-3643)
PHONE...............................619 233-5625
Bruce Yoder, *Brnch Mgr*
EMP: 30
SQ FT: 10,000
SALES (corp-wide): 24.59MM Privately
Held
Web: www.thecarpentergroup.com
SIC: 5085 5084 3537 Industrial supplies;
  Industrial machinery and equipment;
  Industrial trucks and tractors
PA: The Carpenter Group
  28800 Hesperian Blvd
  415 285-1954

(P-10429)

**CENTRAL PURCHASING LLC
(HQ)**

Also Called: Harbor Freight Tools
26677 Agoura Rd, Calabasas (91302-1959)
P.O. Box 6010 (93011)
PHONE...............................800 444-3353

Allan Smidt, *
◆ EMP: 500 EST: 1968
SQ FT: 277,000
SALES (est): 166.59MM
SALES (corp-wide): 1.99B Privately Held
Web: go.harborfreight.com
SIC: 5085 5961 5251 Tools, nec; Tools and
  hardware, mail order; Tools
PA: Harbor Freight Tools Usa, Inc.
  26677 Agoura Rd
  818 836-5000

(P-10430)

**CLOVER ENVMTL SOLUTIONS
LLC**

Also Called: Color Laser R&D
9414 Eton Ave, Chatsworth (91311-5862)
PHONE...............................815 431-8100
EMP: 606
SALES (corp-wide): 173.68MM Privately
Held
Web: www.cloverimaging.com
SIC: 5085 Ink, printer's
PA: Clover Environmental Solutions Llc
  4200 Columbus St
  866 734-6548

(P-10431)

**COLUMBIA SPECIALTY
COMPANY INC**

Also Called: Plumbing World
5875 Obispo Ave, Long Beach
(90805-3715)
PHONE...............................562 634-6425
▲ EMP: 78
Web: www.tristarind.com
SIC: 5085 Valves and fittings

(P-10432)

CURIOSITY INK MEDIA LLC

478 Ellis St, Pasadena (91105-1617)
PHONE...............................561 287-5776
EMP: 89 EST: 2017
SALES (est): 157.49K
SALES (corp-wide): 4.04MM Publicly
Held
SIC: 5085 Ink, printer's
PA: Grom Social Enterprises, Inc.
  2060 Nw Boca Rton Blvd St
  561 287-5776

(P-10433)

**CUSTOM BUILDING PRODUCTS
LLC**

1900 Norris Rd, Bakersfield (93308-2229)
PHONE...............................661 393-0422
Kevin Odell, *Brnch Mgr*
EMP: 52
Web: www.custombuildingproducts.com
SIC: 5085 5211 3531 Adhesives, tape and
  plasters; Masonry materials and supplies;
  Construction machinery
HQ: Custom Building Products Llc
  7711 Center Ave Ste 500
  Huntington Beach CA 92647
  800 272-8786

(P-10434)

D & D SAW WORKS INC

Also Called: D & D Tool & Supply
1445 Engineer St Ste 110, Vista
(92081-8846)
EMP: 126
SIC: 5085 Industrial supplies

(P-10435)

DHV INDUSTRIES INC

3451 Pegasus Dr, Bakersfield
(93308-6827)

PHONE...............................661 392-8948
Tingchun Huang, *Pr*
◆ EMP: 52 EST: 1996
SQ FT: 180,000
SALES (est): 10.72MM Privately Held
Web: www.dhvindustries.com
SIC: 5085 3491 Valves and fittings; Industrial
  valves

(P-10436)

DUHIG AND CO INC

Also Called: Duhig Stainless
5071 Telegraph Rd, Los Angeles
(90022-4997)
P.O. Box 226966 (90022-0666)
◆ EMP: 48
Web: www.fergusonindustrial.com
SIC: 5085 5051 3441 Valves and fittings;
  Pipe and tubing, steel; Fabricated structural
  metal

(P-10437)

**FASTENER DIST HOLDINGS LLC
(HQ)**

Also Called: Stealth Aerospace
5200 Sheila St, Commerce (90040-3906)
PHONE...............................213 620-9950
Scott Tucker, *Pr*
EMP: 86 EST: 2014
SALES (est): 399.16MM
SALES (corp-wide): 512.41MM Privately
Held
Web: fdhaerostg.wpenginepowered.com
SIC: 5085 3721 Fasteners, industrial: nuts,
  bolts, screws, etc.; Aircraft
PA: Fdh Aero, Llc
  5200 Sheila St
  213 620-9950

(P-10438)

FASTENER TECHNOLOGY CORP

7415 Fulton Ave, North Hollywood
(91605-4116)
PHONE...............................818 764-6467
Dennis Suedkamp, *CEO*
Thomas Boat, *
EMP: 125 EST: 1979
SQ FT: 24,000
SALES (est): 5MM
SALES (corp-wide): 145.58MM Privately
Held
Web: www.ftc-usa.com
SIC: 5085 3812 5251 Fasteners, industrial:
  nuts, bolts, screws, etc.; Aircraft/aerospace
  flight instruments and guidance systems;
  Tools
HQ: Avantus Aerospace, Inc.
  29101 The Old Rd
  Valencia CA 91355
  661 295-8620

(P-10439)

GENERAL TOOL INC

Also Called: Gt Diamond
2025 Alton Pkwy, Irvine (92606-4904)
PHONE...............................949 261-2322
Jae Woo Kim, *CEO*
▲ EMP: 90 EST: 1984
SQ FT: 40,000
SALES (est): 24.47MM Privately Held
Web: www.gtdiamond.com
SIC: 5085 Diamonds, industrial: natural,
  crude

(P-10440)

**HOWMET GLOBL FSTNING
SYSTEMS I (HQ)**

Also Called: Howmet Fastening Systems
3990a Heritage Oak Ct, Simi Valley
(93063-6711)

PHONE..................805 426-2270
Vagner Finelli, *Pr*
▲ EMP: 120 EST: 1977
SQ FT: 37,000
SALES (corp-wide): 6.64B **Publicly Held**
SIC: 5085 5072 5065 Fasteners and
fastening equipment; Hardware; Electronic
parts and equipment, nec
PA: Howmet Aerospace Inc.
201 Isabella St Ste 200
412 553-1950

(P-10441)
INDUSTRIAL VALCO INC (PA)
3135 E Ana St, Compton (90221-5606)
PHONE..................310 635-0711
Rob C Raban, *Pr*
▲ EMP: 50 EST: 1983
SQ FT: 62,000
SALES (est): 18.07MM
SALES (corp-wide): 18.07MM **Privately
Held**
Web: www.ivalco.com
SIC: 5085 3498 Valves and fittings; Pipe
fittings, fabricated from purchased pipe

(P-10442)
LIBERTY SYNERGISTICS INC
Also Called: Liberty Photo Products
1041 Calle Trepadora, San Clemente
(92673-6204)
PHONE..................949 361-1100
▲ EMP: 55
Web: www.ivokenow.com
SIC: 5085 3861 Industrial supplies;
Photographic equipment and supplies

(P-10443)
LINEAR INDUSTRIES LTD (PA)
1850 Enterprise Way, Monrovia
(91016-4271)
PHONE..................626 303-1130
Anthony Dell Angelica, *Pr*
Savonia Angelica, *
Jean Cade, *
▲ EMP: 36 EST: 1960
SQ FT: 45,000
SALES (est): 20.8MM
SALES (corp-wide): 20.8MM **Privately
Held**
Web: www.linearindustries.com
SIC: 5085 3625 5065 5072 Bearings;
Positioning controls, electric; Electronic
parts; Hardware

(P-10444)
LONESTAR SIERRA LLC
1820 W Orangewood Ave, Orange
(92868-2043)
PHONE..................866 575-5680
EMP: 225
SALES (est): 19.81MM **Privately Held**
Web: www.lonestarsierra.com
SIC: 5085 Refractory material

(P-10445)
LORD & SONS INC
10504 Pioneer Blvd, Santa Fe Springs
(90670-3704)
PHONE..................562 529-2500
Lawrence James, *Mgr*
EMP: 107
SALES (corp-wide): 47.02MM **Privately
Held**
Web: www.lordandsons.com
SIC: 5085 Fasteners, industrial: nuts, bolts,
screws, etc.
PA: Lord & Sons, Inc.
430 E Trimble Rd

408 293-4841

(P-10446)
MCMASTER-CARR SUPPLY COMPANY
9630 Norwalk Blvd, Santa Fe Springs
(90670-2954)
P.O. Box 54960 (90054-0960)
PHONE..................562 692-5911
EMP: 460
SALES (corp-wide): 621.02MM **Privately
Held**
Web: www.mcmaster.com
SIC: 5085 Industrial supplies
PA: Mcmaster-Carr Supply Company
600 N County Line Rd
630 834-9600

(P-10447)
MIDLAND INDUSTRIES
659 E Ball Rd, Anaheim (92805-5910)
PHONE..................800 821-5725
Vince Hodes, *Owner*
EMP: 100 EST: 2020
SALES (est): 1.54MM **Privately Held**
SIC: 5085 Valves, pistons, and fittings

(P-10448)
MILLENNIA STAINLESS INC
10016 Romandel Ave, Santa Fe Springs
(90670-3424)
PHONE..................562 946-3545
Ching-po Li, *CEO*
▲ EMP: 75 EST: 1996
SQ FT: 10,500
SALES (est): 5.82MM **Privately Held**
Web: www.millenniastainless.com
SIC: 5085 5065 5051 Industrial supplies;
Coils, electronic; Steel
PA: Chain Chon Industrial Co., Ltd.
No.178, Daguan Rd.,

(P-10449)
MILLS IRON WORKS
14834 S Maple Ave, Gardena
(90248-1936)
PHONE..................323 321-6520
Jeffrey Griffith, *CEO*
Kenneth E Berger, *
EMP: 75 EST: 1905
SQ FT: 48,000
SALES (est): 9.7MM **Privately Held**
Web: www.millsiron.com
SIC: 5085 Valves and fittings

(P-10450)
MOTION AND FLOW CTRL PDTS INC
Also Called: Mfcp Parker Store
911 N Poinsettia St, Santa Ana
(92701-3827)
PHONE..................714 541-2244
Darrell Sabin, *Brnch Mgr*
EMP: 100
SALES (corp-wide): 539.04MM **Privately
Held**
Web: www.mfcp.com
SIC: 5085 Seals, industrial
PA: Motion And Flow Control Products, Inc.
1772 Prairie Way
720 262-7337

(P-10451)
MOTION INDUSTRIES INC
Also Called: F & L Industrial Solutions
12550 Stowe Dr, Poway (92064-6804)
PHONE..................858 602-1500
Lori Lefeuvre, *Brnch Mgr*
EMP: 23

SALES (corp-wide): 23.09B **Publicly Held**
Web: www.fandl8020.com
SIC: 5085 3355 Bearings; Extrusion ingot,
aluminum: made in rolling mills
HQ: Motion Industries, Inc.
1605 Alton Rd
Birmingham AL 35210
205 956-1122

(P-10452)
NELSON STUD WELDING INC
Also Called: Automatic Screw Mch Pdts Co
630 E Lambert Rd, Brea (92821-4119)
P.O. Box 1608 (35602-1608)
PHONE..................256 353-1931
Mike Selby, *Genl Mgr*
EMP: 113
SALES (corp-wide): 15.78B **Publicly Held**
Web:
www.stanleyengineeredfastening.com
SIC: 5085 Fasteners, industrial: nuts, bolts,
screws, etc.
HQ: Nelson Stud Welding, Inc.
7900 W Ridge Rd
Elyria OH 44035
440 329-0400

(P-10453)
NMC GROUP INC
Also Called: Nylon Molding
300 E Cypress St, Brea (92821-4007)
PHONE..................714 223-3525
Michael Johnson, *Pr*
Wolfgang Hombrecher, *
▲ EMP: 24 EST: 1972
SALES (est): 21.3MM
SALES (corp-wide): 7.94B **Publicly Held**
Web: www.kirkhill.com
SIC: 5085 3089 Fasteners and fastening
equipment; Injection molding of plastics
HQ: Ta Aerospace Co.
28065 Franklin Pkwy
Valencia CA 91355
661 775-1100

(P-10454)
NSK PRECISION AMERICA INC
Also Called: NSK Prcsion Amer Snta Fe
Sprng
13921 Bettencourt St, Cerritos
(90703-1011)
PHONE..................562 968-1000
Philip Jennings, *District Center Manager*
EMP: 84
Web: www.nsk.com
SIC: 5085 Bearings
HQ: Nsk Precision America, Inc.
3450 Bearing Dr
Franklin IN 46131
317 738-5000

(P-10455)
PACIFIC ECHO INC
23540 Telo Ave, Torrance (90505-4098)
PHONE..................310 539-1822
Takeo Ogami, *CEO*
▲ EMP: 90 EST: 1967
SQ FT: 110,000
SALES (est): 16.28MM **Privately Held**
Web: www.pacificecho.com
SIC: 5085 Hose, belting, and packing
HQ: Kakuichi Co., Ltd.
1415, Midoricho, Tsuruga
Nagano NAG 380-0

(P-10456)
PCBC HOLDCO INC
12748 Florence Ave, Santa Fe Springs
(90670-3906)
PHONE..................562 944-9549

Robert Gardner, *Pr*
▲ EMP: 38 EST: 1989
SQ FT: 47,000
SALES (est): 7.99MM **Privately Held**
Web: www.pacificcoastbolt.com
SIC: 5085 3965 3452 5072 Fasteners,
industrial: nuts, bolts, screws, etc.;
Fasteners; Bolts, nuts, rivets, and washers;
Bolts, nuts, and screws

(P-10457)
PENTACON INC
21123 Nordhoff St, Chatsworth
(91311-5816)
PHONE..................818 727-8000
EMP: 300
SIC: 5085 5063 Fasteners and fastening
equipment; Electrical fittings and
construction materials

(P-10458)
RBC TRANSPORT DYNAMICS CORP
3131 W Segerstrom Ave, Santa Ana
(92704-5862)
PHONE..................203 267-7001
Michael Harnett, *Pr*
▲ EMP: 185 EST: 1992
SQ FT: 75,000
SALES (est): 24.27MM
SALES (corp-wide): 1.56B **Publicly Held**
Web: www.rbcbearings.com
SIC: 5085 3728 Bearings; Aircraft
assemblies, subassemblies, and parts, nec
HQ: Roller Bearing Company Of America,
Inc.
102 Willenbrock Rd
Oxford CT 06478
203 267-7001

(P-10459)
REVCO INDUSTRIES INC (PA)
Also Called: Black Stallion Industries
10747 Norwalk Blvd, Santa Fe Springs
(90670-3823)
PHONE..................562 777-1588
C Edward Chu, *Ch Bd*
Steve Hwang, *
Hong Brian Choi, *
Thomas Han, *
Jimmy Wu, *
◆ EMP: 28 EST: 1974
SQ FT: 24,000
SALES (est): 10.57MM
SALES (corp-wide): 10.57MM **Privately
Held**
Web: www.revcoindustries.com
SIC: 5085 5136 3842 Valves and fittings;
Work clothing, men's and boys'; Personal
safety equipment

(P-10460)
RUTLAND TOOL & SUPPLY CO (HQ)
Also Called: MSC Metalworking
2225 Workman Mill Rd, City Of Industry
(90601-1437)
PHONE..................562 566-5000
TOLL FREE: 800
Thomas J Neri, *CEO*
Andrew Verey, *
◆ EMP: 140 EST: 2005
SALES (est): 5.07MM **Publicly Held**
SIC: 5085 5251 Industrial supplies; Tools
PA: Msc Industrial Direct Co., Inc.
515 Brdhollow Rd Ste 1000

(P-10461)

SAN DIEGO SIGN COMPANY INC
Also Called: Wholesale Displays
5960 Pascal Ct, Carlsbad (92008-8808)
PHONE..............................888 748-7446
Eric Steven Van Velzer, *CEO*
Vance Rodney Van Velzer, *
Eric Christopher Van Velzer, *
▲ **EMP:** 28 **EST:** 1963
SQ FT: 15,000
SALES (est): 9.69MM **Privately Held**
Web: www.sdsign.com
SIC: 5085 3993 Signmaker equipment and
   supplies; Signs and advertising specialties

(P-10462)

SAW DAILY SERVICE INC
4481 Firestone Blvd, South Gate
(90280-3320)
P.O. Box 3458 (92834-3458)
PHONE..............................323 564-1791
▲ **EMP:** 50
SIC: 5085 7699 3546 Knives, industrial;
   Industrial machinery and equipment repair;
   Saws and sawing equipment

(P-10463)

SO CAL SANDBAGS INC
12620 Bosley Ln, Corona (92883-6358)
PHONE..............................951 277-3404
Peter Rasinski, *Pr*
EMP: 100 **EST:** 1986
SALES (est): 24.88MM **Privately Held**
Web: www.socalsandbags.com
SIC: 5085 5999 Industrial supplies; Safety
   supplies and equipment

(P-10464)

SOUTHERN CALIFORNIA VALVE INC
Also Called: Scv
13903 Maryton Ave, Santa Fe Springs
(90670-4924)
PHONE..............................562 404-2246
◆ **EMP:** 70 **EST:** 1972
SALES (est): 6.51MM **Privately Held**
Web: www.scvvalve.com
SIC: 5085 Valves and fittings

(P-10465)

SPS TECHNOLOGIES LLC
Also Called: Pb Fasteners
1700 W 132nd St, Gardena (90249-2008)
PHONE..............................310 323-6222
EMP: 260
SALES (corp-wide): 364.48B **Publicly Held**
Web: www.pccfasteners.com
SIC: 5085 Fasteners, industrial: nuts, bolts,
   screws, etc.
HQ: Sps Technologies, Llc
   301 Highland Ave
   Jenkintown PA 19046
   215 572-3000

(P-10466)

SPS TECHNOLOGIES LLC
Shur-Lok Company
2541 White Rd, Irvine (92614-6235)
PHONE..............................949 474-6000
Damian Moreau, *Mgr*
EMP: 428
SALES (corp-wide): 364.48B **Publicly Held**
Web: www.shur-lok.com
SIC: 5085 Fasteners, industrial: nuts, bolts,
   screws, etc.
HQ: Sps Technologies, Llc
   301 Highland Ave
   Jenkintown PA 19046
   215 572-3000

(P-10467)

TEN DAYS MANUFACTURING
Also Called: Daily Manufacturing
458 Commercial Rd, San Bernardino
(92408-3706)
PHONE..............................909 871-5340
EMP: 70
SALES (corp-wide): 2.57MM **Privately Held**
Web: www.dlymfg.com
SIC: 5085 Plastic bottles
PA: Ten Days Manufacturing
   7801 Cherry Ave
   888 222-1575

(P-10468)

THALASINOS ENTERPRISES INC
Also Called: T & T Enterprises
1220 Railroad St, Corona (92882-1837)
PHONE..............................951 340-0911
Brent Thalasinos, *CEO*
John Thalasinos, *Ch Bd*
Alison Siedler, *VP*
▲ **EMP:** 23 **EST:** 1993
SQ FT: 54,000
SALES (est): 8.83MM **Privately Held**
Web: www.ttenterprises.com
SIC: 5085 3452 Fasteners, industrial: nuts,
   bolts, screws, etc.; Nuts, metal

(P-10469)

TRISTAR INDUSTRIAL LLC
Also Called: Columbia Spclty A Trstar Indus
5875 Obispo Ave, Long Beach
(90805-3715)
PHONE..............................562 634-6425
Michael Taylor, *Brnch Mgr*
EMP: 78
Web: www.tristarind.com
SIC: 5085 Valves and fittings
PA: Tristar Industrial, Llc
   501 N 44th St

(P-10470)

TSC AUTO ID TECHNOLOGY AMERICA (HQ)
3040 Saturn St Ste 200, Brea (92821-6231)
PHONE..............................909 468-0100
Hank Wang, *Pr*
▲ **EMP:** 120 **EST:** 2008
SALES (est): 13.29MM **Privately Held**
Web: usca.tscprinters.com
SIC: 5085 Ink, printer's
PA: Tsc Auto Id Technology Co., Ltd.
   9f, No. 95, Minquan Rd.

5087 Service Establishment Equipment

(P-10471)

AMERICAN SANITARY SUPPLY INC
3800 E Miraloma Ave, Anaheim
(92806-2108)
P.O. Box 6436 (92816-0436)
PHONE..............................714 632-3010
Luis Salazar, *CEO*
Silvia Salazar, *
▲ **EMP:** 75 **EST:** 1983
SQ FT: 20,000
SALES (est): 8.31MM **Privately Held**
Web: www.amersan.com
SIC: 5087 Janitors' supplies

(P-10472)

CHIRO INC (PA)
Also Called: Mr Clean Maintenance Systems
1834 Business Center Dr, San Bernardino
(92408-3461)
P.O. Box 31 (92324-0031)
PHONE..............................909 879-1160
Arthur Rose, *CEO*
Denise Peters, *
EMP: 107 **EST:** 1980
SQ FT: 10,000
SALES (est): 16.5MM
SALES (corp-wide): 16.5MM **Privately Held**
Web: www.mrcleansystems.com
SIC: 5087 7349 5169 Cleaning and
   maintenance equipment and supplies;
   Cleaning service, industrial or commercial;
   Chemicals and allied products, nec

(P-10473)

EXTENSIONS PLUS INC
Also Called: Extensions Plus
5428 Reseda Blvd, Tarzana (91356-2606)
PHONE..............................818 881-5611
Helene Stahl, *Pr*
EMP: 30 **EST:** 1994
SALES (est): 6.16MM **Privately Held**
Web: www.extensions-plus.com
SIC: 5087 3999 Beauty parlor equipment
   and supplies; Hair and hair-based products

(P-10474)

GLAMOUR INDUSTRIES CO
100 Wilshire Blvd Ste 700, Santa Monica
(90401-3602)
PHONE..............................213 687-8600
EMP: 100
SALES (corp-wide): 47.77MM **Privately Held**
Web: www.aiibeauty.com
SIC: 5087 Beauty parlor equipment and
   supplies
PA: Glamour Industries, Co.
   2220 Gaspar Ave
   323 728-2999

(P-10475)

KAPLAN INDUS CAR WASH SUPS INC
Also Called: Kaplan Industries Mfg
13875 Mica St, Santa Fe Springs
(90670-5729)
PHONE..............................562 921-5544
Everardo Llamas, *CEO*
Mert Ozkaya, *
EMP: 37 **EST:** 2006
SALES (est): 2.31MM **Privately Held**
SIC: 5087 2841 Carwash equipment and
   supplies; Soap and other detergents

(P-10476)

MALYS OF CALIFORNIA INC
28145 Harrison Pkwy, Valencia
(91355-4165)
PHONE..............................661 295-8317
EMP: 500
SIC: 5087 Barber shop equipment and
   supplies

(P-10477)

NIKKEN GLOBAL INC (HQ)
18301 Von Karman Ave Ste 120, Irvine
(92612-0104)
PHONE..............................949 789-2000
Tom Toshizo Watanabe, *Ch Bd*
Kendall Cho, *
▲ **EMP:** 155 **EST:** 1996
SALES (est): 3.19MM **Privately Held**
Web: na.nikken.com

SIC: 5087 5023 5013 5122 Stress reducing
   equipment, electric; Bedspreads; Seat
   covers; Vitamins and minerals
PA: Nikken International, Inc.
   18301 Von Karman Ave

(P-10478)

SPILO WORLDWIDE INC
Also Called: Spilo Worldwide
100 Wilshire Blvd Ste 700, Santa Monica
(90401-3602)
PHONE..............................213 687-8600
Marc Spilo, *CEO*
◆ **EMP:** 100 **EST:** 1977
SALES (est): 3.24MM
SALES (corp-wide): 1.71B **Publicly Held**
SIC: 5087 Beauty parlor equipment and
   supplies
PA: Enovis Corporation
   2711 Cntrville Rd Ste 400
   301 252-9160

(P-10479)

SWEIS INC (PA)
20000 Mariner Ave, Torrance (90503-1670)
PHONE..............................310 375-0558
Karl Sweis, *Pr*
Theresa Sweis, *
EMP: 70 **EST:** 2000
SALES (est): 23.12MM **Privately Held**
Web: www.sweisinc.com
SIC: 5087 2844 Beauty parlor equipment
   and supplies; Hair preparations, including
   shampoos

(P-10480)

UNITED FABRICARE SUPPLY INC (PA)
1237 W Walnut St, Compton (90220-5009)
P.O. Box 1796 (90001-0796)
PHONE..............................310 537-2096
Steve S Hong, *CEO*
W David Weimer, *
Hae S Hong, *
Mike Fahar, *
Kirby Schnebly, *
▲ **EMP:** 75 **EST:** 1946
SQ FT: 50,000
SALES (est): 24.58MM
SALES (corp-wide): 24.58MM **Privately Held**
Web: www.unitedfabricaresupply.com
SIC: 5087 Laundry equipment and supplies

(P-10481)

WAXIES ENTERPRISES LLC
Also Called: Waxie
905 Wineville Ave, Ontario (91764-8508)
P.O. Box 5926 (92412)
PHONE..............................909 942-3100
Jeff Roberts, *Brnch Mgr*
EMP: 88
SALES (corp-wide): 2.83B **Privately Held**
Web: info.waxie.com
SIC: 5087 Janitors' supplies
HQ: Waxie's Enterprises, Llc
   9353 Waxie Way
   San Diego CA 92123
   800 995-4466

(P-10482)

WAXIES ENTERPRISES LLC (DH)
Also Called: Waxie Sanitary Supply
9353 Waxie Way, San Diego (92123-1036)
P.O. Box 60227 (90060)
PHONE..............................800 995-4466
TOLL FREE: 800
EMP: 140 **EST:** 1945
SALES (est): 522.9MM
SALES (corp-wide): 2.83B **Privately Held**

Web: info.waxie.com
SIC: 5087 Janitors' supplies
HQ: Envoy Solutions, Llc
　　2101 Claire Ct
　　Glenview IL 60025
　　847 832-4000

5088 Transportation Equipment And Supplies

(P-10483)
AIR FRAME MFG & SUPPLY CO INC
Also Called: Air Frame Mfg. & Supply Co.
26135 Technology Dr, Valencia
(91355-1138)
PHONE...................661 257-7728
Yoshinobu Kawamura, *CEO*
Ray Wong, *
Howard Miyoshi, *
Yoshimi Sussan, *
▼ **EMP: 35 EST:** 1964
SQ FT: 30,000
SALES (est): 11.69MM **Privately Held**
Web: www.afmsupply.com
SIC: 5088 3999 3728 Aircraft and parts, nec; Atomizers, toiletry; Accumulators, aircraft propeller

(P-10484)
AIRCRAFT HARDWARE WEST
Also Called: Ahw
2180 Temple Ave, Long Beach
(90804-1020)
PHONE...................562 961-9324
Frank Ioffrida, *CEO*
Krista Wildermuth, *
▲ **EMP: 30 EST:** 2002
SQ FT: 15,000
SALES (est): 14.34MM **Privately Held**
Web: www.ahw-global.com
SIC: 5088 3993 5072 Aircraft and parts, nec; Name plates: except engraved, etched, etc.: metal; Hardware

(P-10485)
AIREY ENTERPRISES LLC
Also Called: A Transportation
5530 Corbin Ave Ste 325, Tarzana
(91356-6037)
P.O. Box 17328 (91416-7328)
PHONE...................818 530-3362
EMP: 160 EST: 2015
SALES (est): 2.82MM **Privately Held**
SIC: 5088 Transportation equipment and supplies

(P-10486)
APICAL INDUSTRIES INC
Also Called: Dart Aerospace
3030 Enterprise Ct Ste A, Vista
(92081-8358)
PHONE...................760 724-5300
Alain Madore, *CEO*
EMP: 100 EST: 1995
SQ FT: 30,000
SALES (est): 21.75MM
SALES (corp-wide): 7.94B **Publicly Held**
Web: www.dartaerospace.com
SIC: 5088 3728 Helicopter parts; Aircraft landing assemblies and brakes
HQ: Dart Aerospace Company
　　310-9900 Boul Cavendish
　　Saint-Laurent QC H4M 2
　　514 907-5959

(P-10487)
BOEING STLLITE SYSTEMS INTL IN (HQ)
Also Called: Boeing Company, The
2260 E Imperial Hwy, El Segundo
(90245-3501)
P.O. Box 92919 (90009-2919)
PHONE...................310 364-4000
Randy Brinkley, *Pr*
Craig R Cooning, *
David Lillington, *
Danny Howard, *
▲ **EMP: 40 EST:** 1967
SALES (est): 106.54MM
SALES (corp-wide): 77.79B **Publicly Held**
Web: www.rvsatellite.com
SIC: 5088 4899 3663 Aircraft and space vehicle supplies and parts; Satellite earth stations; Radio and t.v. communications equipment
PA: The Boeing Company
　　929 Long Bridge Dr
　　703 465-3500

(P-10488)
COM DEV USA LLC
2333 Utah Ave, El Segundo (90245-4818)
PHONE...................424 456-8000
EMP: 100
Web: www.comdev-usa.com
SIC: 5088 3679 Aircraft equipment and supplies, nec; Microwave components

(P-10489)
COMAV LLC (PA)
18499 Phantom St Ste 17, Victorville
(92394-7967)
PHONE...................760 523-5100
Craig Garrick, *Pr*
Jon Day, *CFO*
EMP: 47 EST: 2012
SQ FT: 58,732
SALES (est): 43.18MM
SALES (corp-wide): 43.18MM **Privately Held**
Web: www.comav.com
SIC: 5088 4581 3599 Aircraft and parts, nec; Aircraft maintenance and repair services; Machine and other job shop work

(P-10490)
DESSER TIRE & RUBBER CO LLC
Also Called: Cee Baileys Aircraft Plastics
6900 W Acco St, Montebello (90640-5435)
PHONE...................323 837-1497
Brian Elliott, *Contrlr*
EMP: 30
SALES (corp-wide): 860.49MM **Publicly Held**
Web: www.vansaircrafttires.com
SIC: 5088 3728 Aircraft and space vehicle supplies and parts; Aircraft parts and equipment, nec
HQ: Desser Tire & Rubber Co., Llc
　　6900 W Acco St
　　Montebello CA 90640
　　323 721-4900

(P-10491)
FALCON AEROSPACE HOLDINGS LLC
Also Called: Wesco Aircraft
27727 Avenue Scott, Valencia
(91355-1219)
PHONE...................661 775-7200
Randy J Snyder, *Ch Bd*
Gregory A Hann, *
Tommy Lee, *

EMP: 1250 EST: 2006
SALES (est): 41.12MM **Privately Held**
Web: www.incora.com
SIC: 5088 Aircraft and parts, nec

(P-10492)
INTEGRATED PROCUREMENT TECH (PA)
Also Called: Ipt
7230 Hollister Ave, Goleta (93117-2807)
PHONE...................805 682-0842
Etty Yenni, *CEO*
Ken Krutenat, *
Debbie Martinez, *
◆ **EMP: 85 EST:** 1996
SQ FT: 26,000
SALES (est): 50.75MM **Privately Held**
Web: www.iptsb.com
SIC: 5088 5065 Aircraft and parts, nec; Communication equipment

(P-10493)
ITOCHU AVIATION INC (DH)
222 N Pacific Coast Hwy Ste 2200, El Segundo (90245-5629)
P.O. Box 997 (90245-0997)
PHONE...................310 640-2770
Naoya Osaki, *CEO*
Takehiko Yamada, *
▲ **EMP: 25 EST:** 1973
SALES (est): 43.62MM **Privately Held**
SIC: 5088 3728 Aircraft and parts, nec; Aircraft parts and equipment, nec
HQ: Itochu International Inc.
　　1251 Ave Of The Amrcas Fl
　　New York NY 10020
　　212 818-8000

(P-10494)
JCM ENGINEERING CORP
2690 E Cedar St, Ontario (91761-8533)
PHONE...................909 923-3730
Carlo Moyano, *CEO*
Marcelo Calichio, *
Neil Bishkin, *
EMP: 77 EST: 1979
SQ FT: 140,000
SALES (est): 9.01MM **Privately Held**
Web: www.jcmcorp.com
SIC: 5088 Aeronautical equipment and supplies

(P-10495)
KETTENBURG MARINE CORPORATION
2810 Carleton St, San Diego (92106-2792)
P.O. Box 6448 (92166-0448)
PHONE...................619 224-8211
Tom Fetter, *Pr*
Jane T Fetter, *
▼ **EMP: 140 EST:** 1919
SQ FT: 30,000
SALES (est): 1.07MM **Privately Held**
SIC: 5088 7699 Marine supplies; Boat repair

(P-10496)
LOGISTICAL SUPPORT LLC
20409 Prairie St, Chatsworth (91311-6029)
PHONE...................818 341-3344
Joseph Lucan, *
Jerry Hill, *
EMP: 120 EST: 1997
SQ FT: 14,600
SALES (est): 6.52MM
SALES (corp-wide): 31.13MM **Privately Held**
Web: www.rtcaerospace.com
SIC: 5088 Aircraft and parts, nec
PA: Rtc Aerospace Llc
　　7215 45th St Ct E

918 407-0291

(P-10497)
ONTIC ENGINEERING AND MFG INC (PA)
20400 Plummer St, Chatsworth
(91311-5372)
P.O. Box 2424 (91313)
PHONE...................818 678-6555
Gareth Hall, *CEO*
Peg Billson, *
Toby Richard Woolrych, *
Susan Coates Kroll, *
EMP: 95 EST: 1986
SQ FT: 54,000
SALES (est): 480.55MM
SALES (corp-wide): 480.55MM **Privately Held**
Web: www.ontic.com
SIC: 5088 3728 3812 3563 Aircraft equipment and supplies, nec; Aircraft parts and equipment, nec; Search and navigation equipment; Air and gas compressors

(P-10498)
PROPONENT INC (PA)
Also Called: Proponent
3120 Enterprise St, Brea (92821-6236)
PHONE...................714 223-5400
Andrew Todhunter, *Pr*
Steven Frields, *
Corey Yarnell, *
▲ **EMP: 175 EST:** 1972
SALES (est): 127.06MM
SALES (corp-wide): 127.06MM **Privately Held**
Web: www.proponent.com
SIC: 5088 3728 Aircraft and parts, nec; Aircraft parts and equipment, nec

(P-10499)
REGENT AEROSPACE CORPORATION (PA)
Also Called: Regent
28110 Harrison Pkwy, Valencia
(91355-4109)
PHONE...................661 257-3000
Reza Soltanianzadeh, *CEO*
Reza Soltanian, *
Tim Garvin, *
▲ **EMP: 200 EST:** 1993
SQ FT: 90,000
SALES (est): 95.2MM **Privately Held**
Web: www.regentaerospace.com
SIC: 5088 3728 Aircraft and parts, nec; Aircraft parts and equipment, nec

(P-10500)
SHIMADZU PRECISION INSTRS INC (DH)
Also Called: Shimadzu Medical Systems USA
3645 N Lakewood Blvd, Long Beach
(90808-1797)
PHONE...................562 420-6226
Takashi Ishii, *CEO*
Tina Kang, *CFO*
Tsuyosh Hirai, *Sec*
▲ **EMP: 70 EST:** 1979
SQ FT: 60,000
SALES (est): 98.03MM **Privately Held**
Web: www.spi-inc.com
SIC: 5088 5047 5084 Aircraft equipment and supplies, nec; Medical equipment and supplies; Industrial machinery and equipment
HQ: Shimadzu America, Inc.
　　7102 Riverwood Dr
　　Columbia MD 21046

▲ = Import ▼ = Export
◆ = Import/Export

(P-10501)

STRECH PLASTICS INCORPORATED

900 John St Ste J, Banning (92220-6204)
PHONE..................................951 922-2224
James M Strech, *CEO*
▲ **EMP:** 50 **EST:** 1974
SQ FT: 52,000
SALES (est): 10.21MM **Privately Held**
Web: www.strechplastics.com
SIC: 5088 3949 Golf carts; Sporting and athletic goods, nec

(P-10502)

TELEDYNE RESON INC

5212 Verdugo Way, Camarillo
(93012-8662)
PHONE..................................805 964-6260
Robert Mehrabian, *CEO*
EMP: 33 **EST:** 1985
SALES: 5.4MM
SALES (corp-wide): 5.64B **Publicly Held**
Web: www.teledynemarine.com
SIC: 5088 3812 Navigation equipment and supplies; Sonar systems and equipment
PA: Teledyne Technologies Inc
1049 Camino Dos Rios
805 373-4545

(P-10503)

THORNTON TECHNOLOGY CORP

Also Called: Thornton Technologies
2608 Temple Heights Dr, Oceanside
(92056-3512)
PHONE..................................760 471-9969
William S Thornton, *Prin*
EMP: 23
SALES (corp-wide): 4.59MM **Privately Held**
Web: www.thorntontech.com
SIC: 5088 4581 3812 Aircraft equipment and supplies, nec; Aircraft cleaning and janitorial service; Search and navigation equipment
PA: Thornton Technology Corp
5410 Us Highway 2 W
406 257-7223

(P-10504)

UNITED AERONAUTICAL CORP

7360 Laurel Canyon Blvd, North Hollywood
(91605-3710)
P.O. Box 7102 (91615-0102)
PHONE..................................818 764-2102
Lawrence P Holt, *CEO*
Bradford T Beck, *
◆ **EMP:** 32 **EST:** 1988
SQ FT: 200,000
SALES (est): 14MM **Privately Held**
Web: www.unitedaero.com
SIC: 5088 3812 Aeronautical equipment and supplies; Search and navigation equipment

(P-10505)

UNITED STATES MARINE CORPS

Also Called: Marine Aviation Logistics
Marine Corps Air Stn Bldg 23122 (Camp Pendleton), Oceanside (92049)
PHONE..................................760 725-3564
EMP: 100
Web: www.marines.mil
SIC: 5088 9711 Marine supplies; Marine Corps
HQ: United States Marine Corps
Branch Hlth Clnic Bldg #5
Beaufort SC 29904

(P-10506)

WESCO AIRCRAFT HARDWARE CORP

Also Called: Incora
27727 Avenue Scott, Valencia
(91355-3909)
PHONE..................................661 775-7200
Steve Halford, *Brnch Mgr*
EMP: 400
SALES (corp-wide): 1.33B **Privately Held**
Web: www.incora.com
SIC: 5088 Aircraft and parts, nec
HQ: Wesco Aircraft Hardware Corp.
2601 Meacham Blvd Ste 400
Fort Worth TX 76137
817 284-4449

(P-10507)

WILLIAMS AEROSPACE & MFG INC (DH)

999 Avenida Acaso, Camarillo
(93012-8700)
PHONE..................................805 586-8699
Greg Beason, *CEO*
Richard Drinkward, *
▲ **EMP:** 23 **EST:** 1982
SQ FT: 9,910
SALES (est): 9.03MM
SALES (corp-wide): 156.2MM **Privately Held**
Web: www.goallclear.com
SIC: 5088 3728 3724 Aircraft equipment and supplies, nec; Aircraft parts and equipment, nec; Aircraft engines and engine parts
HQ: Allclear Aerospace & Defense, Inc.
15501 Sw 29th St Ste 101
Miramar FL 33027
954 239-7844

5091 Sporting And Recreation Goods

(P-10508)

AFTCO MFG CO INC

Also Called: Bluewater Wear
2400 S Garnsey St, Santa Ana
(92707-3335)
PHONE..................................949 660-8757
William D Shedd, *CEO*
Casey Shedd, *
Cody Shedd, *
◆ **EMP:** 75 **EST:** 1957
SQ FT: 24,000
SALES (est): 21.52MM **Privately Held**
Web: www.aftco.com
SIC: 5091 Fishing tackle

(P-10509)

AQUA PERFORMANCE INC

Also Called: A.J. Metal Manufacturing
425 N Smith Ave, Corona (92880)
P.O. Box 370 (92878-0370)
PHONE..................................951 340-2056
Sue Curi, *VP*
EMP: 34 **EST:** 1990
SQ FT: 20,000
SALES (est): 5.29MM **Privately Held**
Web: www.aquaperformance.com
SIC: 5091 3339 3444 Watersports equipment and supplies; Primary nonferrous metals, nec; Sheet metalwork

(P-10510)

BIKES ONLINE INC

Also Called: Siskiu
2711 Loker Ave W, Carlsbad (92010-6601)
PHONE..................................650 272-3378
Jonathon Allara, *CEO*

EMP: 95 **EST:** 2019
SALES (est): 2.07MM **Privately Held**
Web: www.bikesonline.com
SIC: 5091 5941 Bicycles; Bicycle and bicycle parts

(P-10511)

BODYKORE INC

7466 Orangewood Ave, Garden Grove
(92841-1413)
PHONE..................................949 325-3088
Leo Chang, *CEO*
EMP: 30 **EST:** 2020
SALES (est): 1MM **Privately Held**
Web: www.bodykore.com
SIC: 5091 5961 3949 5941 Fitness equipment and supplies; Fitness and sporting goods, mail order; Sporting and athletic goods, nec; Sporting goods and bicycle shops

(P-10512)

EASTON DIAMOND SPORTS LLC

112 S Lakeview Canyon Rd, Westlake Village (91362-3925)
PHONE..................................800 632-7866
Ed Kinnaly, *CEO*
EMP: 100 **EST:** 2017
SALES (est): 2.37MM **Privately Held**
Web: easton.rawlings.com
SIC: 5091 Sporting and recreation goods

(P-10513)

FULL-SWING GOLF INC

1905 Aston Ave Ste 100, Carlsbad
(92008-7393)
PHONE..................................858 675-1100
▲ **EMP:** 30 **EST:** 1986
SALES (est): 51.31MM **Privately Held**
Web: www.fullswinggolf.com
SIC: 5091 3949 Golf equipment; Golf equipment

(P-10514)

INTEX PROPERTIES S BAY CORP (PA)

4001 Via Oro Ave Ste 210, Long Beach
(90810-1400)
PHONE..................................310 549-5400
Tien P Zee, *Pr*
◆ **EMP:** 96 **EST:** 1970
SQ FT: 80,000
SALES (est): 91.03MM
SALES (corp-wide): 91.03MM **Privately Held**
Web: www.intexcorp.com
SIC: 5091 5092 5021 3081 Watersports equipment and supplies; Toys, nec; Waterbeds; Vinyl film and sheet

(P-10515)

SHIMANO NORTH AMER HOLDG INC (HQ)

Also Called: Shimano North America Bicycle
1 Holland, Irvine (92618-2597)
PHONE..................................949 951-5003
Hiroshi Matsui, *CEO*
Jim Lafrance, *
Gerriet O'neill, *Contrlr*
▲ **EMP:** 150 **EST:** 1986
SQ FT: 122,000
SALES (est): 91.38MM **Privately Held**
Web: fish.shimano.com
SIC: 5091 Bicycle parts and accessories
PA: Shimano Inc.
77, 3cho, Oimatsucho, Sakai-Ku

(P-10516)

TROY LEE DESIGNS LLC (DH)

155 E Rincon St, Corona (92879-1328)
PHONE..................................951 371-5219
Jason William Steris, *CEO*
▲ **EMP:** 79 **EST:** 1981
SQ FT: 6,000
SALES (est): 27.22MM **Privately Held**
Web: www.troyleedesigns.com
SIC: 5091 7336 Sporting and recreation goods; Graphic arts and related design
HQ: 2 Ride Holding
11 Traverse De La Buzine
Marseille PAC 13011

5092 Toys And Hobby Goods And Supplies

(P-10517)

ANATEX ENTERPRISES INC

Also Called: Anatex
15911 Arminta St, Van Nuys (91406-1807)
PHONE..................................818 908-1888
Fleur Chesler, *Pr*
Mark Chesler, *
▲ **EMP:** 25 **EST:** 1982
SALES (est): 1.52MM **Privately Held**
Web: www.anatex.com
SIC: 5092 3944 Toys, nec; Games, toys, and children's vehicles

(P-10518)

AURORA WORLD INC

Also Called: Aurora
8820 Mercury Ln, Pico Rivera
(90660-6706)
PHONE..................................562 205-1222
TOLL FREE: 800
Heui-yul Noh, *CEO*
Kee Sun Hong, *
◆ **EMP:** 110 **EST:** 1991
SQ FT: 100,000
SALES (est): 22.41MM **Privately Held**
Web: www.auroragift.com
SIC: 5092 Toys, nec
PA: Aurora World Corporation
624 Teheran-Ro, Gangnam-Gu

(P-10519)

BANDAI NAMCO ENTRMT AMER INC

Also Called: Bandai Namco
23 Odyssey, Irvine (92618-3144)
PHONE..................................408 235-2000
Naoki Katashima, *CEO*
Masaaki Tsuji, *
Graeme Bayless, *
Shuji Nakata, *
Hide Irie, *
▲ **EMP:** 200 **EST:** 1990
SQ FT: 51,118
SALES (est): 25.74MM **Privately Held**
Web: shop.bandai.com
SIC: 5092 Video games
HQ: Bandai Namco Holdings Usa Inc.
2120 Park Pl Ste 120
El Segundo CA 90245

(P-10520)

DESIGN INTERNATIONAL GROUP INC

755 Epperson Dr, City Of Industry
(91748-1335)
PHONE..................................626 369-2289
William Yeh, *Pr*
Julie Hwang, *
◆ **EMP:** 25 **EST:** 2003
SALES (est): 8.67MM **Privately Held**

Web: www.luckydig.com
SIC: 5092 5947 2678 Toys and hobby goods
and supplies; Gifts and novelties;
Stationery products

(P-10521)
HORIZON HOBBY LLC
4710 E Guasti Rd Ste A, Ontario
(91761-8121)
PHONE..............................909 390-9595
Yolanda Perry, *Brnch Mgr*
EMP: 77
SALES (corp-wide): 23.08MM **Privately
Held**
Web: www.horizonhobby.com
SIC: 5092 5945 Hobby goods; Hobby and
craft supplies
PA: Horizon Hobby, Llc
2904 Research Rd
217 352-1913

(P-10522)
INTERACTIVE FILMS LLC
12049 Jefferson Blvd, Culver City
(90230-6219)
PHONE..............................310 988-0643
Jim Tsai, *Managing Member*
EMP: 74 EST: 2021
SALES (est): 674.9K **Privately Held**
Web: www.participant.com
SIC: 5092 Video games

(P-10523)
ME & MY BIG IDEAS LLC
Also Called: Happy Planner, The
6261 Katella Ave Ste 150, Cypress
(90630-5249)
PHONE..............................240 348-5240
Tom Shaw, *CEO*
Stephanie Rahmatulla, *
▲ EMP: 101 EST: 1998
SALES (est): 10.66MM **Privately Held**
Web: www.thehappyplanner.com
SIC: 5092 2678 Arts and crafts equipment
and supplies; Notebooks: made from
purchased paper

(P-10524)
MERCHSOURCE LLC (DH)
Also Called: Threesixty Group
7755 Irvine Center Dr Ste 100, Irvine
(92618-2904)
PHONE..............................800 374-2744
Johann Clapp, *Managing Member*
Mike Roberts, *
◆ EMP: 115 EST: 2011
SALES (est): 97.9MM
SALES (corp-wide): 21.53MM **Privately
Held**
Web: www.thethreesixtygroup.com
SIC: 5092 Toys and hobby goods and
supplies
HQ: Threesixty Group Limited
28/F Harbourside Hq
Kowloon Bay KLN

(P-10525)
MGA ENTERTAINMENT INC
9220 Winnetka Ave, Chatsworth
(91311-8172)
PHONE..............................800 222-4685
Isaac Larian, *CEO*
Steve Schultz, *
Elizabeth Risha, *
◆ EMP: 2100 EST: 1980
SALES (est): 310.11MM **Privately Held**
Web: www.mgae.com
SIC: 5092 Toys, nec

(P-10526)
PC WOO INC (PA)
Also Called: Mega Toys
6443 E Slauson Ave, Commerce
(90040-3107)
PHONE..............................323 887-8138
Tak Kwan Woo, *Prin*
Peter Tak Kwan Woo, *
Liwen Kao, *OF SEASONAL DIV*
Charlie Woo, *Head Secretary*
◆ EMP: 83 EST: 1989
SQ FT: 120,000
SALES (est): 22.99MM **Privately Held**
SIC: 5092 Toys, nec

(P-10527)
SEGA OF AMERICA INC (DH)
140 Progress Ste 100, Irvine (92618-0338)
PHONE..............................949 788-0455
Shuji Utsumi, *CEO*
Mitsuhiro Tanaka, *
Jeffrey Shieh, *
▲ EMP: 45 EST: 1985
SALES (est): 44.58MM **Privately Held**
Web: www.sega.com
SIC: 5092 3999 Video games; Coin-
operated amusement machines
HQ: Sega Corporation
1-1-1, Nishishinagawa
Shinagawa-Ku TKY 141-0

(P-10528)
SEGA OF AMERICA INC
2900 W Alameda Ave, Burbank
(91505-4220)
PHONE..............................747 477-3708
EMP: 270
Web: www.sega.com
SIC: 5092 Video games
HQ: Sega Of America, Inc.
140 Progress Ste 100
Irvine CA 92618
949 788-0455

(P-10529)
SMC PRODUCTS INC
Also Called: Hpi Racing
22651 Lambert St Ste 105, Lake Forest
(92630-1611)
PHONE..............................949 753-1099
▲ EMP: 68
SIC: 5092 3944 Toys and hobby goods and
supplies; Electronic toys

(P-10530)
**ULTRA PRO INTERNATIONAL
LLC**
Also Called: Jolly Roger Games
6049 E Slauson Ave, Commerce
(90040-3007)
PHONE..............................323 890-2100
Jay Kuo, *Managing Member*
Marc Lieberman, *
Herman Lee, *
▲ EMP: 122 EST: 2011
SALES (est): 44.78MM **Privately Held**
Web: www.ultrapro.com
SIC: 5092 3944 Toys and hobby goods and
supplies; Games, toys, and children's
vehicles

(P-10531)
VICTORY INTL GROUP LLC
Also Called: M Z J
14748 Pipeline Ave Ste B, Chino Hills
(91709-6024)
PHONE..............................949 407-5888
Dawson Fan, *Pr*
▲ EMP: 230 EST: 2001
SQ FT: 4,960

SALES (est): 896MM **Privately Held**
Web: www.victoryintlgroup.com
SIC: 5092 3843 2389 3842 Toys and hobby
goods and supplies; Dental equipment and
supplies; Hospital gowns; Respiratory
protection equipment, personal

(P-10532)
WHAM-O INC
6301 Owensmouth Ave Ste 700, Woodland
Hills (91367-2265)
PHONE..............................818 963-4200
Raylin Hsieh, *CEO*
Jeff Hsieh, *
Blake Wong, *
◆ EMP: 59 EST: 1997
SALES (est): 1.45MM **Privately Held**
Web: www.wham-o.com
SIC: 5092 5091 3944 3949 Toys and games;
Surfing equipment and supplies; Toy trains,
airplanes, and automobiles; Sporting and
athletic goods, nec

5093 Scrap And Waste
Materials

(P-10533)
75S CORP
Also Called: FMC Metals
800 E 62nd St, Los Angeles (90001-1506)
PHONE..............................323 234-7708
Kevin Armstrong, *CEO*
Octavio Cabrerra, *OK Vice President*
◆ EMP: 42 EST: 1959
SALES (est): 9.79MM **Privately Held**
Web: www.fmcmet.com
SIC: 5093 3341 Nonferrous metals scrap;
Recovery and refining of nonferrous metals

(P-10534)
**AADLEN BROS AUTO
WRECKING INC (PA)**
11590 Tuxford St, Sun Valley (91352-3186)
PHONE..............................323 875-1400
Sam Adlen, *Pr*
Samuel Lewinstein, *
EMP: 79 EST: 1951
SALES (est): 4.05MM
SALES (corp-wide): 4.05MM **Privately
Held**
Web: www.aadlenbros.com
SIC: 5093 Metal scrap and waste materials

(P-10535)
**ATLAS PACIFIC CORPORATION
(PA)**
2803 Industrial Dr, Bloomington
(92316-3249)
P.O. Box 726 (92324-0726)
PHONE..............................909 421-1200
Gregory Woolfson, *Pr*
▼ EMP: 25 EST: 1980
SQ FT: 10,000
SALES (est): 4.4MM
SALES (corp-wide): 4.4MM **Privately Held**
Web: www.atlaspacific.net
SIC: 5093 3341 3339 Nonferrous metals
scrap; Brass smelting and refining
(secondary); Zinc refining (primary),
including slabs & dust

(P-10536)
**B & B PLASTICS RECYCLERS
INC (PA)**
3040 N Locust Ave, Rialto (92377-3706)
PHONE..............................909 829-3606
Baltasar Mejia, *Pr*
Bacilio Mejia, *

EMP: 46 EST: 1998
SQ FT: 100,000
SALES (est): 7.67MM
SALES (corp-wide): 7.67MM **Privately
Held**
Web: www.bbplasticsinc.com
SIC: 5093 2673 Plastics scrap; Bags: plastic,
laminated, and coated

(P-10537)
**CEDARWOOD-YOUNG
COMPANY**
Also Called: Allan Company
14618 Arrow Hwy, Baldwin Park
(91706-1733)
PHONE..............................626 962-4047
Brett Weigand, *Brnch Mgr*
EMP: 55
SQ FT: 10,664
SALES (corp-wide): 252.16MM **Privately
Held**
Web: www.allancompany.com
SIC: 5093 2611 Waste paper; Pulp mills
PA: Cedarwood-Young Company
14620 Joanbridge St
626 962-4047

(P-10538)
GLOBAL PLASTICS INC
145 Malbert St, Perris (92570-8624)
PHONE..............................951 657-5466
Nadim Salim Bahou, *Pr*
Patti Gilmour, *
▲ EMP: 120 EST: 1996
SQ FT: 55,000
SALES (est): 24.21MM **Privately Held**
Web: www.globalpetinc.com
SIC: 5093 4953 3053 Plastics scrap;
Recycling, waste materials; Packing
materials

(P-10539)
**GREENPATH RECOVERY WEST
INC**
Also Called: Greenpath Recovery Recycl
Svcs
330 W Citrus St Ste 250, Colton
(92324-1422)
PHONE..............................909 954-0686
Joe Castro, *Pr*
EMP: 60 EST: 2012
SQ FT: 90,000
SALES (est): 4.38MM **Privately Held**
Web: www.greenpathrecovery.com
SIC: 5093 3089 2821 Scrap and waste
materials; Plastics processing; Plastics
materials and resins

(P-10540)
**PAVEMENT RECYCLING
SYSTEMS INC (PA)**
Also Called: Prsi
10240 San Sevaine Way, Jurupa Valley
(91752-1100)
PHONE..............................951 682-1091
Richard W Gove, *Pr*
Stephen Concannon, *
Nathan Beyler, *Prin*
▲ EMP: 125 EST: 1989
SQ FT: 40,000
SALES (est): 107.14MM **Privately Held**
Web: www.pavementrecycling.com
SIC: 5093 1611 Scrap and waste materials;
Surfacing and paving

(P-10541)
**SELF SERVE AUTO
DISMANTLERS (PA)**
Also Called: Adams Steel

3200 E Frontera St, Anaheim (92806-2822)
P.O. Box 6258 (92816-0258)
PHONE...............................714 630-8901
George Adams Junior, *Pr*
Mike Adams, *
Terry Adams, *
Wendy Adams, *
◆ **EMP:** 120 **EST:** 1987
SQ FT: 41,000
SALES (est): 10.52MM **Privately Held**
SIC: 5093 Ferrous metal scrap and waste

(P-10542)
STRATEGIC MATERIALS INC
Container Recycl Aliance Div
3211 E 26th St, Vernon (90058-8007)
PHONE...............................323 415-0166
Dennis Hinson, *Brnch Mgr*
EMP: 23
SALES (corp-wide): 118.92MM **Privately Held**
Web: www.smi.com
SIC: 5093 3231 Metal scrap and waste
materials; Products of purchased glass
HQ: Strategic Materials, Inc.
17220 Katy Fwy Ste 150
Houston TX 77094

(P-10543)
TST INC
Standards Metals
2132 E Dominguez St, Long Beach
(90810-1022)
PHONE...............................310 835-0115
Andrew G Stein, *CEO*
EMP: 28
SALES (corp-wide): 36.95MM **Privately Held**
Web: www.tst-inc.com
SIC: 5093 3354 Metal scrap and waste
materials; Aluminum extruded products
PA: Tst, Inc.
13428 Benson Ave
951 685-2155

5094 Jewelry And Precious Stones

(P-10544)
A-MARK PRECIOUS METALS INC (PA)
Also Called: A-Mark
2121 Rosecrans Ave Ste 6300, El Segundo
(90245-7528)
PHONE...............................310 587-1477
Gregory N Roberts, *CEO*
Jeffrey D Benjamin, *Ch Bd*
Thor G Gjerdrum, *Pr*
Brian Aquilino, *COO*
Kathleen Simpson Taylor, *Ex VP*
▲ **EMP:** 108 **EST:** 1965
SQ FT: 9,000
SALES (est): 9.7B
SALES (corp-wide): 9.7B **Publicly Held**
Web: www.amark.com
SIC: 5094 Jewelry

(P-10545)
C&C JEWELRY MFG INC
323 W 8th St Fl 4, Los Angeles
(90014-3109)
PHONE...............................213 623-6800
Mikhail Chekhman, *Pr*
Robert Connolly, *
Dmitriy Moskalenko Ctrl, *Prin*
▲ **EMP:** 75 **EST:** 2001
SQ FT: 3,000
SALES (est): 28.36MM **Privately Held**

SIC: 5094 3915 Jewelry; Jewel preparing:
instruments, tools, watches, and jewelry

(P-10546)
CITIZEN WATCH COMPANY OF AMERICA INC (HQ)
Also Called: Citizen Watch America
1000 W 190th St, Torrance (90502-1040)
PHONE...............................800 321-1023
▲ **EMP:** 150 **EST:** 1975
SALES (est): 124.65MM **Privately Held**
Web: www.citizenwatch.com
SIC: 5094 Watches and parts
PA: Citizen Watch Co., Ltd.
6-1-12, Tanashicho

(P-10547)
GOLDCO DIRECT LLC
Also Called: Goldco
24025 Park Sorrento Ste 210, Calabasas
(91302-4025)
PHONE...............................818 343-0186
EMP: 80 **EST:** 2006
SALES (est): 40MM **Privately Held**
Web: www.goldco.com
SIC: 5094 Precious metals

(P-10548)
INDUSTRIAL STRENGTH CORP
6115 Corte Del Cedro, Carlsbad
(92011-1516)
PHONE...............................760 795-1068
Jeffry D Lorenz, *Pr*
EMP: 27 **EST:** 1995
SALES (est): 3.75MM **Privately Held**
Web: www.isbodyjewelry.com
SIC: 5094 3961 3911 Jewelry; Costume
jewelry; Jewelry, precious metal

(P-10549)
MAURICE KRAIEM & COMPANY
Also Called: Mk Luxury Group
228 S Beverly Dr, Beverly Hills
(90212-3805)
PHONE...............................213 629-0038
Moshe Kraiem, *CEO*
▲ **EMP:** 24 **EST:** 1978
SALES (est): 4.78MM **Privately Held**
Web: www.mkdiamonds.com
SIC: 5094 3911 Jewelry; Jewelry, precious
metal

(P-10550)
MEL BERNIE AND COMPANY INC (PA)
Also Called: 1928 Jewelry Company
3000 W Empire Ave, Burbank
(91504-3109)
PHONE...............................818 841-1928
Melvyn Bernie, *CEO*
▲ **EMP:** 250 **EST:** 1968
SQ FT: 65,000
SALES (est): 13.25MM
SALES (corp-wide): 13.25MM **Privately Held**
Web: www.1928.com
SIC: 5094 Jewelry

(P-10551)
NIXON INC (PA)
Also Called: Nixon Watches
2810 Whiptail Loop Ste 1, Carlsbad
(92010-6754)
Rural Route 2810 Whiptail (92010)
PHONE...............................888 455-9200
Andrew Laats, *
▲ **EMP:** 120 **EST:** 1997
SALES (est): 22.23MM
SALES (corp-wide): 22.23MM **Privately Held**

Web: www.nixon.com
SIC: 5094 5611 5136 Watches and parts;
Clothing accessories: men's and boys';
Leather and sheep lined clothing, men's
and boys'

(P-10552)
SIMON G JEWELRY INC
Also Called: Zeghani
528 State St, Glendale (91203-1524)
PHONE...............................818 500-8595
Zaven Ghanimian, *CEO*
Simon Ghanimian, *
Hratch Shahbazian, *
▲ **EMP:** 48 **EST:** 1994
SQ FT: 10,000
SALES (est): 9.85MM **Privately Held**
Web: www.simongjewelry.com
SIC: 5094 3911 Jewelry; Jewelry, precious
metal

(P-10553)
SIMON GOLUB & SONS INC (DH)
Also Called: Lorenzo USA
514 Via De La Valle Ste 210, Solana Beach
(92075-2717)
▲ **EMP:** 90 **EST:** 1923
SQ FT: 40,000
SALES (est): 4.37MM **Privately Held**
Web: www.portlandjewelrysupplies.com
SIC: 5094 3911 Jewelry; Jewelry, precious
metal
HQ: Astral Holdings Inc
5506 6th Ave S
Seattle WA 98108

(P-10554)
SWEDA COMPANY LLC
Also Called: Sweda
17411 E Valley Blvd, City Of Industry
(91744-5159)
PHONE...............................626 357-9999
Brandon Mackay, *CEO*
Seidler Sweda, *
Paul Beck, *
Scott Pearson, *
Kellie Claudio, *
◆ **EMP:** 273 **EST:** 1976
SQ FT: 350,000
SALES (est): 12.93MM **Privately Held**
SIC: 5094 5044 Watches and parts;
Calculators, electronic

5099 Durable Goods, Nec

(P-10555)
C D LISTENING BAR INC
Also Called: Super D Phantom Distribution
17822 Gillette Ave Ste A, Irvine
(92614-0527)
PHONE...............................949 225-1170
EMP: 730
Web: www.ccvideo.com
SIC: 5099 Compact discs

(P-10556)
CENTERLINE WOOD PRODUCTS
15447 Anacapa Rd Ste 102, Victorville
(92392-2481)
PHONE...............................760 246-4530
Michael Rodriguez, *Pr*
EMP: 99 **EST:** 2017
SALES (est): 2.02MM **Privately Held**
Web: www.cwp.cab
SIC: 5099 Wood and wood by-products

(P-10557)
D J AMERICAN SUPPLY INC
Also Called: American Dj Group of
Companies

6122 S Eastern Ave, Commerce
(90040-3402)
PHONE...............................323 582-2650
Charles J Davies, *CEO*
Charles Davies, *CEO*
Toby B Velazquez, *Sec*
◆ **EMP:** 126 **EST:** 1985
SQ FT: 100,000
SALES (est): 6.5MM **Privately Held**
Web: www.americandjsupply.com
SIC: 5099 5719 5999 Firearms and
ammunition, except sporting; Lighting
fixtures; Theatrical equipment and supplies

(P-10558)
DENNIS FOLAND INC (PA)
Also Called: Logo Expressions
1500 S Hellman Ave, Ontario (91761-7634)
P.O. Box 4591 (91761-0822)
PHONE...............................909 930-9900
Dennis Foland, *CEO*
Beverly Foland, *
▲ **EMP:** 50 **EST:** 1979
SQ FT: 140,000
SALES (est): 7.16MM
SALES (corp-wide): 7.16MM **Privately Held**
Web: www.folandgroup.com
SIC: 5099 3944 Souvenirs; Games, toys,
and children's vehicles

(P-10559)
EASTMAN MUSIC COMPANY (PA)
Also Called: Eastmans Guitars
2158 Pomona Blvd, Pomona (91768-3332)
PHONE...............................909 868-1777
Saul Friedgood, *CEO*
Saul Friedgood, *Pr*
Qian Ni, *
▲ **EMP:** 40 **EST:** 2001
SALES (est): 24.14MM
SALES (corp-wide): 24.14MM **Privately Held**
Web: www.eastmanstrings.com
SIC: 5099 3931 Musical instruments;
Accordions and parts

(P-10560)
FAM PPE LLC
5553 Bandini Blvd B, Bell (90201-6421)
PHONE...............................323 888-7755
Frank M Zarabi, *Managing Member*
EMP: 223 **EST:** 2020
SALES (est): 327.37K **Privately Held**
SIC: 5099 Safety equipment and supplies
PA: Fam, Llc
5553 B Bandini Blvd

(P-10561)
FT 2 INC
1211 N Miller St, Anaheim (92806-1933)
PHONE...............................714 765-5555
◆ **EMP:** 170
SIC: 5099 2393 3161 Carrying cases; Textile
bags; Luggage

(P-10562)
GENIUS PRODUCTS INC
3301 Exposition Blvd Ste 100, Santa
Monica (90404-5045)
PHONE...............................310 453-1222
Trevor Drinkwater, *Pr*
Stephen K Bannon, *
Edward J Byrnes, *
▲ **EMP:** 222 **EST:** 2005
SQ FT: 40,520
SALES (est): 5.61MM **Privately Held**
Web: www.geniusproducts.com

P
R
O
D
U
C
T
S
&
S
V
C
S

SIC: **5099** 3652 7819 Video and audio equipment; Prerecorded records and tapes; Video tape or disk reproduction

(P-10563)
GUTHY-RENKER LLC
Also Called: Guthy-Renker Direct
3340 Ocean Park Blvd Fl 2, Santa Monica (90405-3204)
PHONE..................................310 581-6250
Bill Guthy, *Pr*
EMP: 80
Web: www.guthy-renker.com
SIC: **5099** 7812 5999 Tapes and cassettes, prerecorded; Commercials, television: tape or film; Cosmetics
PA: Guthy-Renker Llc
    100 N Pcf Cast Hwy Ste 16

(P-10564)
MONOPRICE INC
11701 6th St, Rancho Cucamonga (91730-6030)
PHONE..................................877 271-2592
EMP: 89
Web: www.monoprice.com
SIC: **5099** Video and audio equipment
HQ: Monoprice, Inc.
    1 Pointe Dr Ste 400
    Brea CA 92821
    909 989-6887

(P-10565)
OLIVET INTERNATIONAL INC (PA)
11015 Hopkins St, Mira Loma (91752-3248)
PHONE..................................951 681-8888
Sean Lin, *Managing Member*
Lydia Hsu, *
David Yu, *
Pei Te Lin, *
▲ **EMP:** 89 **EST:** 1984
SQ FT: 456,000
SALES (est): 172.9MM
SALES (corp-wide): 172.9MM **Privately Held**
Web: www.olivetintl.com
SIC: **5099** 3161 Luggage; Luggage

(P-10566)
PLATINUM DISC LLC
Also Called: Echo Bridge Home Entertainment
10203 Santa Monica Blvd Fl 5, Los Angeles (90067-6405)
PHONE..................................608 784-6620
Nate Hart, *Pr*
Nathan Hart, *
▼ **EMP:** 91 **EST:** 1995
SALES (est): 2.73MM
SALES (corp-wide): 2.73MM **Privately Held**
SIC: **5099** Compact discs
PA: Echo Bridge Entertainment, Llc
    75 2nd Ave Ste 500
    781 444-6767

(P-10567)
RGGD INC (PA)
Also Called: Crystal Art Gallery
4950 S Santa Fe Ave, Vernon (90058-2106)
PHONE..................................323 581-6617
Randy Greenberg, *CEO*
Douglas Song, *
◆ **EMP:** 45 **EST:** 1994
SQ FT: 120,000
SALES (est): 23.59MM
SALES (corp-wide): 23.59MM **Privately Held**
Web: www.crystalartgallery.com

SIC: **5099** 3441 Wood and wood by-products ; Fabricated structural metal

(P-10568)
ROLAND CORPORATION US (HQ)
5100 S Eastern Ave, Los Angeles (90040-2950)
P.O. Box 910921 (90091-0921)
PHONE..................................323 890-3700
Christopher Bristol, *CEO*
Dennis M Houlihan, *
Mark S Malbon, *
Charles L Wright, *
Junpei Yamato, *
◆ **EMP:** 165 **EST:** 1953
SQ FT: 50,000
SALES (est): 49.25MM **Privately Held**
Web: www.roland.com
SIC: **5099** 5045 3931 Musical instruments; Computer peripheral equipment; Organs, all types: pipe, reed, hand, electronic, etc.
PA: Roland Corporation
    2036-1, Hosoechonakagawa, Hamana-Ku

(P-10569)
ROSEN ELECTRONICS LLC
Also Called: Rosen Electronics
2500 E Francis St, Ontario (91761-7730)
PHONE..................................951 898-9808
W Thomas Clements, *Pr*
▲ **EMP:** 75 **EST:** 2003
SALES (est): 1.95MM **Privately Held**
Web: www.voxxelectronics.com
SIC: **5099** 3679 Video and audio equipment; Liquid crystal displays (LCD)

(P-10570)
SUN COAST MERCHANDISE CORP
6405 Randolph St, Commerce (90040-3511)
PHONE..................................323 720-9700
Kumar C Bhavnani, *Pr*
Dilip Bhavnani, *
Vidya Bhavnani, *
◆ **EMP:** 250 **EST:** 1943
SQ FT: 120,000
SALES (est): 8MM **Privately Held**
Web: www.sunscopeusa.com
SIC: **5099** Brass goods

(P-10571)
SUNSCAPE EYEWEAR INC
17526 Von Karman Ave Ste A, Irvine (92614-4258)
PHONE..................................949 553-0590
Ali Adam Rizza, *Pr*
Adam Rizza, *CFO*
Wally Rizza, *VP*
▲ **EMP:** 78 **EST:** 1999
SQ FT: 10,500
SALES (est): 1.74MM **Privately Held**
Web: www.eyeride.com
SIC: **5099** Sunglasses

(P-10572)
TAYLOR-LISTUG INC (PA)
Also Called: Taylor Guitars
1980 Gillespie Way, El Cajon (92020-1096)
PHONE..................................619 258-1207
Kurt Listug, *CEO*
Robert Taylor, *
▲ **EMP:** 245 **EST:** 1968
SQ FT: 86,000
SALES (est): 39.74MM
SALES (corp-wide): 39.74MM **Privately Held**
Web: www.taylorguitars.com

SIC: **5099** 5736 3931 Musical instruments; Musical instrument stores; Guitars and parts, electric and nonelectric

(P-10573)
UNITED STATES LUGGAGE CO LLC
13300 Carmenita Rd, Santa Fe Springs (90670-4815)
PHONE..................................562 293-4400
Anthony Fortunato, *Mgr*
EMP: 71
SALES (corp-wide): 24.35MM **Privately Held**
Web: www.usluggage.com
SIC: **5099** Luggage
PA: United States Luggage Company, Llc
    400 Wireless Blvd
    631 434-7070

(P-10574)
WARNER MUSIC GROUP CORP
777 S Santa Fe Ave, Los Angeles (90021-1750)
PHONE..................................818 953-2600
James Theodoulou, *Mgr*
EMP: 95
Web: www.wmg.com
SIC: **5099** Phonograph records
HQ: Warner Music Group Corp.
    1633 Broadway
    New York NY 10019
    212 275-2000

(P-10575)
YAMAHA CORPORATION OF AMERICA (HQ)
Also Called: Yamaha Music Corporation U S A
6600 Orangethorpe Ave, Buena Park (90620-1396)
PHONE..................................714 522-9011
Hitoshi Fukutome, *CEO*
Terry Lewis, *
Brian Jemelian, *
◆ **EMP:** 300 **EST:** 1958
SALES (est): 427.4MM **Privately Held**
Web: usa.yamaha.com
SIC: **5099** 5065 5091 3931 Musical instruments; Sound equipment, electronic; Sporting and recreation goods; Musical instruments
PA: Yamaha Corporation
    10-1, Nakazawacho, Chuo-Ku

5111 Printing And Writing Paper

(P-10576)
KELLY SPICERS INC (HQ)
Also Called: Kelly Spicers Packaging North
12310 Slauson Ave, Santa Fe Springs (90670-2629)
PHONE..................................562 698-1199
Janice L Gottesman, *CEO*
Rick J Anderson, *
▲ **EMP:** 180 **EST:** 1965
SQ FT: 365,000
SALES (est): 282.36MM
SALES (corp-wide): 2.35B **Privately Held**
Web: www.kellyspicers.com
SIC: **5111** 5199 5087 Fine paper; Packaging materials; Janitors' supplies
PA: Central National Gottesman Inc.
    3 Manhattanville Rd
    914 696-9000

5112 Stationery And Office Supplies

(P-10577)
BANGKIT (USA) INC
Also Called: Bazic Product
10511 Valley Blvd, El Monte (91731-2403)
PHONE..................................626 672-0888
Handy Hioe, *CEO*
Anita Handojo, *
◆ **EMP:** 76 **EST:** 1998
SQ FT: 195,000
SALES (est): 23.88MM **Privately Held**
Web: www.bazicproducts.com
SIC: **5112** Office supplies, nec

(P-10578)
BLUE SKY THE CLOR IMGNTION LLC
Also Called: Day Designer
410 Exchange Ste 250, Irvine (92602-1392)
PHONE..................................714 389-7700
James E Freeman Iii, *CEO*
Warren Vidovich, *Managing Member*
Jeannie M Alich, *
Dennis Marquardt, *
▲ **EMP:** 85 **EST:** 2002
SALES (est): 19.91MM **Privately Held**
Web: www.bluesky.com
SIC: **5112** 5943 Stationery and office supplies; Stationery stores

(P-10579)
CENVEO WORLDWIDE LIMITED
705 Baldwin Park Blvd, City Of Industry (91746-1504)
PHONE..................................626 369-4921
Timothy Hollywood, *Brnch Mgr*
EMP: 419
SALES (corp-wide): 1.04B **Privately Held**
Web: www.cenveo.com
SIC: **5112** Stationery and office supplies
HQ: Cenveo Worldwide Limited
    200 Frst Stamford Pl Fl 2
    Stamford CT 06902
    203 595-3000

(P-10580)
GRAPHIC BUSINESS SOLUTIONS INC
Also Called: House of Magnets
1912 John Towers Ave, El Cajon (92020-1158)
PHONE..................................619 258-4081
Gerald Rivaldi, *CEO*
Kenneth Hamilton, *
▲ **EMP:** 39 **EST:** 1994
SQ FT: 10,000
SALES (est): 16.89MM **Privately Held**
Web: www.gogbs.com
SIC: **5112** 2752 Business forms; Commercial printing, lithographic

(P-10581)
IMAGE SOURCE INC (PA)
Also Called: Bluebird Office Supplies
2110 Pontius Ave, Los Angeles (90025-5726)
P.O. Box 642380 (90064-8094)
PHONE..................................310 477-0700
Faramarz Sadeghi, *CEO*
Ramin Sadeghi, *Treas*
▲ **EMP:** 181 **EST:** 1982
SQ FT: 5,000
SALES (est): 19.23MM
SALES (corp-wide): 19.23MM **Privately Held**
Web: www.bluebirdonline.com

SIC: 5112 5943 Office supplies, nec; Office forms and supplies

(P-10582)
PENTEL OF AMERICA LTD (DH)
2715 Columbia St, Torrance (90503-3861)
PHONE..............................310 320-3831
Chotaro Koumi, *Pr*
Norikazu Hasegama, *
Nobuo Aihara, *CMO*
Toshiro Hemmi, *
◆ EMP: 132 EST: 1966
SQ FT: 46,000
SALES (est): 16.84MM Privately Held
Web: www.pentel.com
SIC: 5112 3951 5199 3952 Pens and/or pencils; Pens and mechanical pencils; Artists' materials; Artists' materials, except pencils and leads
HQ: Pentel Co., Ltd.
7-2, Nihombashikoamicho
Chuo-Ku TKY 103-0

(P-10583)
PRESTIGE GRAPHICS INC
9630 Ridgehaven Ct Ste B, San Diego (92123-5605)
PHONE..............................858 560-8213
Mark Grantham, *Pr*
▲ EMP: 30 EST: 1988
SALES (est): 9.38MM Privately Held
SIC: 5112 2752 Business forms; Offset printing
PA: Pgac Corp.
9630 Ridgehaven Crt Ste B

(P-10584)
PUNCH STUDIO LLC (PA)
6025 W Slauson Ave, Culver City (90230-6507)
P.O. Box 3663 (90231-3663)
PHONE..............................310 390-9900
Todd Brian Kirshner, *CEO*
Nathalie Carrer, *
◆ EMP: 230 EST: 2001
SQ FT: 106,000
SALES (est): 36.25MM Privately Held
Web: www.punchstudio.com
SIC: 5112 Greeting cards

(P-10585)
R R DONNELLEY & SONS COMPANY
Also Called: Moore Business Forms
40610 County Center Dr Ste 100, Temecula (92591-6021)
PHONE..............................951 296-2890
Rick Budge, *Mgr*
EMP: 51
SALES (corp-wide): 15B Privately Held
Web: www.rrd.com
SIC: 5112 2761 2752 Business forms; Manifold business forms; Color lithography
HQ: R. R. Donnelley & Sons Company
35 W Wacker Dr
Chicago IL 60601
312 326-8000

(P-10586)
VIKING OFFICE PRODUCTS INC (DH)
3366 E Willow St, Signal Hill (90755-2311)
PHONE..............................562 490-1000
M Bruce Nelson, *Pr*
Mark R Brown, *Vice-President Information Systems*
Ronald W Weissman, *Senior Vice President Logistics*
▲ EMP: 292 EST: 1960
SQ FT: 187,000

SALES (est): 3.85MM
SALES (corp-wide): 7.83B Publicly Held
Web: www.officedepot.com
SIC: 5112 5021 5045 5087 Office supplies, nec; Office furniture, nec; Computers, peripherals, and software; Janitors' supplies
HQ: Office Depot, Llc
6600 N Military Trl
Boca Raton FL 33496
561 438-4800

(P-10587)
XSE GROUP INC
92 Argonaut Ste 235, Aliso Viejo (92656-4112)
PHONE..............................888 272-8340
EMP: 199
SALES (corp-wide): 31.4MM Privately Held
Web: www.xsegroup.com
SIC: 5112 Office supplies, nec
PA: Xse Group, Inc.
35 Phil Mack Dr
888 272-8340

5113 Industrial And Personal Service Paper

(P-10588)
ANDWIN CORPORATION (PA)
Also Called: Andwin Scientific
167 W Cochran St, Simi Valley (93065-6217)
P.O. Box 689 (91365-0689)
PHONE..............................818 999-2828
Natalie Sarraf, *CEO*
Jesse Palaganas, *
▲ EMP: 62 EST: 1950
SALES (est): 59.75MM
SALES (corp-wide): 59.75MM Privately Held
Web: www.andwincorp.com
SIC: 5113 5199 5087 5047 Shipping supplies ; Art goods and supplies; Janitors' supplies; Hospital equipment and furniture

(P-10589)
BUNZL DISTRIBUTION CAL LLC (DH)
Also Called: Bunzl
3310 E Miraloma Ave, Anaheim (92806-1911)
PHONE..............................714 688-1900
Derek R Goodin, *
Scot Gregory, *
◆ EMP: 98 EST: 1989
SQ FT: 150,000
SALES (est): 4.3MM
SALES (corp-wide): 14.7B Privately Held
Web: www.bunzldistribution.com
SIC: 5113 Paper, wrapping or coarse, and products
HQ: Bunzl Distribution Usa, Llc
1 Cityplace Dr Ste 200
Saint Louis MO 63141

(P-10590)
CALIFORNIA BOX II
8949 Toronto Ave, Rancho Cucamonga (91730-5412)
PHONE..............................909 944-9202
John Widera, *CEO*
Mackey Davis, *
EMP: 80 EST: 1990
SQ FT: 100,000
SALES (est): 5.68MM
SALES (corp-wide): 78.02MM Privately Held
Web: www.calbox.com

SIC: 5113 2653 Corrugated and solid fiber boxes; Boxes, corrugated: made from purchased materials
PA: California Box Company
13901 Carmenita Rd
562 921-1223

(P-10591)
E & S PAPER CO
Also Called: Delta Packaging Products
14110 S Broadway, Los Angeles (90061-1019)
PHONE..............................310 538-8700
TOLL FREE: 800
Spencer Pritkin, *Pr*
Richard Hemmer, *
Rosalind Pritikin, *
EMP: 28 EST: 1964
SQ FT: 21,000
SALES (est): 2.04MM Privately Held
Web: www.deltapackaging.com
SIC: 5113 5085 2679 3086 Paperboard and products; Packing, industrial; Paperboard products, converted, nec; Packaging and shipping materials, foamed plastics

(P-10592)
FRICK PAPER COMPANY LLC
Also Called: Paper Mart Indus & Ret Packg
2164 N Batavia St, Orange (92865-3104)
PHONE..............................714 787-4900
Tom Frick, *Managing Member*
John Frick, *
◆ EMP: 106 EST: 1921
SQ FT: 210,000
SALES (est): 47.01MM Privately Held
Web: www.papermart.com
SIC: 5113 Paper, wrapping or coarse, and products

(P-10593)
GEORGIA-PACIFIC LLC
Also Called: Georgia-Pacific
9206 Santa Fe Springs Rd, Santa Fe Springs (90670-2618)
PHONE..............................562 861-6226
EMP: 275
SALES (corp-wide): 64.37B Privately Held
Web: www.gp.com
SIC: 5113 2653 Corrugated and solid fiber boxes; Boxes, corrugated: made from purchased materials
HQ: Georgia-Pacific Llc
133 Peachtree St Nw
Atlanta GA 30303
404 652-4000

(P-10594)
IMPERIAL BAG & PAPER CO LLC
Also Called: Paper Company, The
550 S 7th Ave, City Of Industry (91746-3120)
PHONE..............................800 834-6248
Julie Scheibe, *VP Opers*
EMP: 98
SALES (corp-wide): 1.65B Privately Held
Web: www.imperialdade.com
SIC: 5113 5199 Containers, paper and disposable plastic; Packaging materials
PA: Imperial Bag & Paper Co. Llc
255 Route 1 & 9
201 437-7440

(P-10595)
OAK PAPER PRODUCTS CO LLC (PA)
Also Called: Acorn Paper Products Co.
3686 E Olympic Blvd, Los Angeles (90023-3146)
P.O. Box 23965 (90023-0965)

PHONE..............................323 268-0507
TOLL FREE: 800
David Weissberg, *CEO*
Max Weissberg, *
▲ EMP: 174 EST: 1959
SQ FT: 250,000
SALES (est): 49.97MM
SALES (corp-wide): 49.97MM Privately Held
Web: www.acorn-paper.com
SIC: 5113 5199 5087 2653 Shipping supplies ; Packaging materials; Janitors' supplies; Corrugated and solid fiber boxes

(P-10596)
OASIS BRANDS INC
100 S Anaheim Blvd Ste 280, Anaheim (92805-3807)
PHONE..............................540 658-2830
Lee Shuchun, *Dir*
▲ EMP: 75 EST: 2009
SALES (est): 1.01MM Privately Held
SIC: 5113 Napkins, paper

(P-10597)
ORORA PACKAGING SOLUTIONS
Also Called: Corru Kraft Buena Pk Div 5058
6200 Caballero Blvd, Buena Park (90620-1124)
PHONE..............................714 562-6002
Jim Wilczek, *Brnch Mgr*
EMP: 149
Web: www.ororacorrugated.com
SIC: 5113 2653 Paper, wrapping or coarse, and products; Boxes, corrugated: made from purchased materials
HQ: Orora Packaging Solutions
6600 Valley View St
Buena Park CA 90620
714 562-6000

(P-10598)
ORORA PACKAGING SOLUTIONS
Also Called: Landsberg Los Angeles Div 1001
1640 S Greenwood Ave, Montebello (90640-6538)
P.O. Box 800 (90640-0800)
PHONE..............................323 832-2000
Jed Wockenfuss, *Mgr*
EMP: 168
Web: www.ororapackagingsolutions.com
SIC: 5113 2653 Paper, wrapping or coarse, and products; Boxes, corrugated: made from purchased materials
HQ: Orora Packaging Solutions
6600 Valley View St
Buena Park CA 90620
714 562-6000

(P-10599)
ORORA PACKAGING SOLUTIONS
Also Called: Mpp San Diego Div 6064
664 N Twin Oaks Valley Rd, San Marcos (92069-1712)
PHONE..............................760 510-7170
Scott Romagnoli, *Mgr*
EMP: 28
Web: www.ororapackagingsolutions.com
SIC: 5113 2653 Paper, wrapping or coarse, and products; Boxes, corrugated: made from purchased materials
HQ: Orora Packaging Solutions
6600 Valley View St
Buena Park CA 90620
714 562-6000

PRODUCTS & SVCS

(P-10600)
ORORA PACKAGING
SOLUTIONS
Also Called: Landsberg Snta Brbara Div 1046
2146 Eastman Ave, Oxnard (93030-5168)
PHONE................................805 278-5040
Terry Mayfield, *Mgr*
EMP: 30
Web: www.ororapackagingsolutions.com
SIC: 5113 2653 Paper, wrapping or coarse,
and products; Boxes, corrugated: made
from purchased materials
HQ: Orora Packaging Solutions
6600 Valley View St
Buena Park CA 90620
714 562-6000

(P-10601)
ORORA PACKAGING
SOLUTIONS
Also Called: Landsberg Flfilment Sltons Div
13397 Marlay Ave, Fontana (92337-6946)
PHONE................................909 770-5400
Jerry Mejia, *Brnch Mgr*
EMP: 46
Web: www.ororapackagingsolutions.com
SIC: 5113 2653 Paper, wrapping or coarse,
and products; Boxes, corrugated: made
from purchased materials
HQ: Orora Packaging Solutions
6600 Valley View St
Buena Park CA 90620
714 562-6000

(P-10602)
ORORA PACKAGING
SOLUTIONS
Mpp Los Angeles Div 6060
3201 W Mission Rd, Alhambra
(91803-1113)
PHONE................................626 284-9524
Marc Fenster, *Mgr*
EMP: 34
Web: www.ororapackagingsolutions.com
SIC: 5113 2653 Paper, wrapping or coarse,
and products; Boxes, corrugated: made
from purchased materials
HQ: Orora Packaging Solutions
6600 Valley View St
Buena Park CA 90620
714 562-6000

(P-10603)
ORORA PACKAGING
SOLUTIONS (HQ)
Also Called: Orora North America
6600 Valley View St, Buena Park
(90620-1145)
PHONE................................714 562-6000
Kelly Barlow, *Pr*
David Conley, *
Lara Coons, *
◆ **EMP:** 100 **EST:** 1951
SQ FT: 300,000
SALES (est): 1.88B **Privately Held**
Web: www.ororapackagingsolutions.com
SIC: 5113 2653 Paper, wrapping or coarse,
and products; Boxes, corrugated: made
from purchased materials
PA: Orora Limited
109 Burwood Rd

(P-10604)
ORORA PACKAGING
SOLUTIONS
Also Called: Landsberg Orange Cnty Div 1025
7001 Village Dr Ste 155, Buena Park
(90621-2276)
PHONE................................714 525-4900

Jerry Mejia, *Mgr*
EMP: 34
Web: www.ororapackagingsolutions.com
SIC: 5113 2653 Paper, wrapping or coarse,
and products; Boxes, corrugated: made
from purchased materials
HQ: Orora Packaging Solutions
6600 Valley View St
Buena Park CA 90620
714 562-6000

(P-10605)
ORORA PACKAGING
SOLUTIONS
Also Called: Mpp Fullerton Div 6061
1901 E Rosslynn Ave, Fullerton
(92831-5141)
PHONE................................714 278-6000
Carol Hortick, *Brnch Mgr*
EMP: 53
Web: www.ororagroup.com
SIC: 5113 2653 Paper, wrapping or coarse,
and products; Boxes, corrugated: made
from purchased materials
HQ: Orora Packaging Solutions
6600 Valley View St
Buena Park CA 90620
714 562-6000

(P-10606)
P & R PAPER SUPPLY CO INC
(HQ)
1898 E Colton Ave, Redlands (92374-9798)
P.O. Box 590 (92373-0201)
PHONE................................909 389-1807
Robert Tillis, *CEO*
Joe Maiberger, *
Luke Maiberger, *
Chris Dirx, *
Paul Cervino, *
▼ **EMP:** 90 **EST:** 1965
SQ FT: 75,000
SALES (est): 81.69MM
SALES (corp-wide): 1.65B **Privately Held**
Web: www.prpaper.com
SIC: 5113 5169 5149 5072 Paper, wrapping
or coarse, and products; Chemicals and
allied products, nec; Groceries and related
products, nec; Hardware
PA: Imperial Bag & Paper Co. Llc
255 Route 1 & 9
201 437-7440

(P-10607)
PERRIN BERNARD SUPOWITZ
LLC (HQ)
Also Called: Fergadis Enterprises
5496 Lindbergh Ln, Bell (90201-6409)
PHONE................................323 981-2800
Ken Sweder, *Ch*
Nigel Kershaw, *
Carl Duhnoski, *CIO**
EMP: 92 **EST:** 1996
SQ FT: 175,000
SALES (est): 517.81MM
SALES (corp-wide): 3.05B **Privately Held**
Web: supplies.individualfoodservice.com
SIC: 5113 Industrial and personal service
paper
PA: Kelso & Company, L.P.
299 Park Ave
212 350-7700

(P-10608)
PIONEER PACKING INC (PA)
2430 S Grand Ave, Santa Ana
(92705-5211)
PHONE................................714 540-9751
Michael S Blower, *Pr*
Ronald Scagliotti, *

▲ **EMP:** 26 **EST:** 1976
SQ FT: 170,000
SALES (est): 52.87MM
SALES (corp-wide): 52.87MM **Privately
Held**
Web: www.pioneerpackinginc.com
SIC: 5113 2653 Shipping supplies; Boxes,
corrugated: made from purchased materials

(P-10609)
SAN DIEGO DIE CUTTING INC
3112 Moore St, San Diego (92110-4480)
PHONE................................619 297-4453
George Thomas Christian, *Pr*
James Roche, *
◆ **EMP:** 34 **EST:** 1956
SQ FT: 12,000
SALES (est): 9.96MM **Privately Held**
Web: www.sddiecutting.com
SIC: 5113 3544 7319 2759 Corrugated and
solid fiber boxes; Special dies and tools;
Display advertising service; Embossing on
paper

(P-10610)
USED CARDBOARD BOXES INC
4032 Wilshire Blvd Ste 402, Los Angeles
(90010-3413)
P.O. Box 10819 (90295)
PHONE................................323 724-2500
Marty Metro, *CEO*
▲ **EMP:** 125 **EST:** 2006
SALES (est): 4.97MM **Privately Held**
Web: www.usedcardboardboxes.com
SIC: 5113 Corrugated and solid fiber boxes

(P-10611)
VALLEY BOX CO INC
10611 Prospect Ave, Santee (92071-4532)
PHONE................................619 449-2882
Robert Eschwege, *Pr*
EMP: 40 **EST:** 1966
SQ FT: 7,000
SALES (est): 1.83MM **Privately Held**
Web: www.valleybox.com
SIC: 5113 2448 2653 2449 Corrugated and
solid fiber boxes; Cargo containers, wood;
Corrugated and solid fiber boxes; Wood
containers, nec

5122 Drugs, Proprietaries,
And Sundries

(P-10612)
AMERISOURCEBERGEN DRUG
CORP
Also Called: ABC Valencia
1851 California Ave, Corona (92881-6477)
PHONE................................951 371-2000
Ron Green, *Mgr*
EMP: 150
SALES (corp-wide): 293.96B **Publicly
Held**
Web: www.amerisourcebergen.com
SIC: 5122 4225 Pharmaceuticals; General
warehousing and storage
HQ: Amerisourcebergen Drug Corporation
1 W 1st Ave
Conshohocken PA 19428
610 727-7000

(P-10613)
AMERISOURCEBERGEN DRUG
CORP
Also Called: Good Neighbor Pharmacy
500 N State College Blvd Ste 900, Orange
(92868-6606)
PHONE................................484 222-9726

Wanisha Eggleston, *Mgr*
EMP: 115
SALES (corp-wide): 293.96B **Publicly
Held**
Web: www.amerisourcebergendrug.com
SIC: 5122 Drugs, proprietaries, and sundries
HQ: Amerisourcebergen Drug Corporation
1 W 1st Ave
Conshohocken PA 19428
610 727-7000

(P-10614)
BAXTER HEALTHCARE
CORPORATION
1 Baxter Way Ste 100, Westlake Village
(91362-3890)
PHONE................................805 372-3000
John Bacich, *Pr*
EMP: 51
SALES (corp-wide): 14.81B **Publicly Held**
Web: www.baxter.com
SIC: 5122 2834 2836 5047 Drugs,
proprietaries, and sundries; Solutions,
pharmaceutical; Biological products, except
diagnostic; Medical equipment and supplies
HQ: Baxter Healthcare Corporation
1 Baxter Pkwy
Deerfield IL 60015
224 948-2000

(P-10615)
BEAUTY 21 COSMETICS INC
Also Called: L A Girl
2021 S Archibald Ave, Ontario
(91761-8535)
PHONE................................909 945-2220
Lan Jack Yu, *CEO*
Chafe Yu Trinh, *
Mahon So Yu, *
◆ **EMP:** 175 **EST:** 1985
SQ FT: 250,000
SALES (est): 49.52MM **Privately Held**
Web: www.lagirlusa.com
SIC: 5122 2844 Cosmetics; Perfumes,
cosmetics and other toilet preparations

(P-10616)
CENCORA INC
1368 Metropolitan Dr, Orange (92868)
P.O. Box 247 (08086-0247)
PHONE................................610 727-7000
Daniel Ramirez, *Mgr*
EMP: 82
SALES (corp-wide): 293.96B **Publicly
Held**
Web: www.cencora.com
SIC: 5122 Pharmaceuticals
PA: Cencora, Inc.
1 W 1st Ave
610 727-7000

(P-10617)
CHEMI-SOURCE INC
Also Called: Metabolic Response Modifiers
2665 Vista Pacific Dr, Oceanside
(92056-3500)
PHONE................................760 477-8177
Mark Olson, *CEO*
Rocky Palamara, *
Kristina Archuleta, *
▲ **EMP:** 38 **EST:** 1996
SQ FT: 24,000
SALES (est): 19.32MM **Privately Held**
Web: www.mrmnutrition.com
SIC: 5122 2833 5499 Vitamins and minerals;
Medicinals and botanicals; Health and
dietetic food stores

▲ = Import ▼ = Export
◆ = Import/Export

(P-10618)
COLORESCIENCE INC
2141 Palomar Airport Rd Ste 200, Carlsbad
(92011-1425)
PHONE..................866 426-5673
Mary Fisher, *CEO*
Josie Juncal, *CCO**
Ted Ebel, *Chief Business Officer**
Steve P Loomis, *
▲ **EMP:** 111 **EST:** 2013
SQ FT: 15,000
SALES (est): 23.8MM **Privately Held**
Web: www.colorescience.com
SIC: 5122 2844 Cosmetics; Cosmetic
   preparations

(P-10619)
CONQUISTADOR INTERNATIONAL LLC
Also Called: Posh'n Bae
21200 Oxnard St Ste 492, Woodland Hills
(91367-5014)
PHONE..................424 249-9304
Andrew Andrew, *Managing Member*
EMP: 100 **EST:** 2018
SALES (est): 1.74MM **Privately Held**
SIC: 5122 Cosmetics

(P-10620)
DAKO NORTH AMERICA INC
6392 Via Real, Carpinteria (93013-2921)
P.O. Box 58059 (93013)
PHONE..................805 566-6655
◆ **EMP:** 325
SIC: 5122 3841 Biologicals and allied
   products; Diagnostic apparatus, medical

(P-10621)
DISTRIBUTION ALTERNATIVES INC
1979 Renaissance Pkwy, Rialto
(92376-2403)
PHONE..................909 770-8900
EMP: 78
SALES (corp-wide): 38.56MM **Privately Held**
Web: www.daserv.com
SIC: 5122 Cosmetics
PA: Distribution Alternatives, Inc.
   6870 21st Ave S
   651 636-9167

(P-10622)
E MANAGEMENT SERVICES LLC
20010 Ventura Blvd, Woodland Hills
(91364-2632)
PHONE..................818 835-9525
Kevin Krivitsky, *Prin*
Kevin Krivitsky, *Prin*
EMP: 75 **EST:** 2019
SALES (est): 2.15MM **Privately Held**
SIC: 5122 Drugs, proprietaries, and sundries

(P-10623)
FFF ENTERPRISES INC (PA)
44000 Winchester Rd, Temecula
(92590-2578)
PHONE..................951 296-2500
Patrick M Schmidt, *CEO*
Wayne Talleur, *
Chris Ground, *
Jonathan Hahn, *CIO**
Michael J Alkire, *
EMP: 300 **EST:** 1988
SQ FT: 162,000
SALES (est): 379.23MM
SALES (corp-wide): 379.23MM **Privately Held**
Web: www.fffenterprises.com

SIC: **5122** Pharmaceuticals

(P-10624)
GLAMOUR INDUSTRIES CO (PA)
Also Called: American International Inds
2220 Gaspar Ave, Los Angeles
(90040-1516)
PHONE..................323 728-2999
Zvi Ryzman, *Pr*
Theresa Cooper, *Ex VP*
Charlie Loveless, *VP*
Betty Ryzman, *Sec*
EMP: 250 **EST:** 1971
SQ FT: 224,000
SALES (est): 47.77MM
SALES (corp-wide): 47.77MM **Privately Held**
Web: www.aiibeauty.com
SIC: 5122 2844 Cosmetics; Cosmetic
   preparations

(P-10625)
H D SMITH LLC
1370 E Victoria St, Carson (90746-7501)
P.O. Box 6231 (90749-6231)
PHONE..................310 641-1885
Bob Schwartz, *Mgr*
EMP: 100
SALES (corp-wide): 293.96B **Publicly Held**
SIC: 5122 5047 Pharmaceuticals; Medical
   and hospital equipment
HQ: H. D. Smith, Llc
   1 W 1st Ave Ste 100
   Conshohocken PA 19428
   866 232-1222

(P-10626)
HATCHBEAUTY PRODUCTS LLC (PA)
Also Called: Hatchbeauty
355 S Grand Ave, Los Angeles
(90071-3152)
P.O. Box 641415 (90064-6415)
PHONE..................310 396-7070
Tracy Holland, *Managing Member*
Benjamin Bennett, *
◆ **EMP:** 83 **EST:** 2009
SALES (est): 38.75MM
SALES (corp-wide): 38.75MM **Privately Held**
Web: www.hatchbeauty.com
SIC: 5122 Cosmetics, perfumes, and hair
   products

(P-10627)
IRISYS INC
6828 Nancy Ridge Dr Ste 100, San Diego
(92121-2224)
PHONE..................858 623-1520
Gina Stack, *Pr*
Robert Ginnini, *
Gerald Yakatan, *Stockholder**
Doug Taylor, *
EMP: 86 **EST:** 2001
SQ FT: 10,000
SALES (est): 9.29MM **Privately Held**
Web: www.societalcdmo.com
SIC: 5122 8748 Pharmaceuticals; Business
   consulting, nec

(P-10628)
JARROW FORMULAS INC (PA)
15233 Ventura Blvd Fl 900, Sherman Oaks
(91403-2250)
PHONE..................310 204-6936
Ojesh Bhalla, *CEO*
Jarrow L Rogovin, *
Michael Jacobs, *
Peilin Guo, *

Clayton Dubose, *
◆ **EMP:** 80 **EST:** 1977
SQ FT: 37,000
SALES (est): 45.08MM
SALES (corp-wide): 45.08MM **Privately Held**
Web: www.jarrow.com
SIC: 5122 Vitamins and minerals

(P-10629)
LIFETECH RESOURCES LLC
Also Called: International Research Labs
700 Science Dr, Moorpark (93021-2012)
PHONE..................805 944-1199
Richard Carieri, *Ch Bd*
Susan Mccarthy, *Pr*
Anna Carieri, *
▲ **EMP:** 85 **EST:** 1990
SQ FT: 152,000
SALES (est): 46MM **Privately Held**
Web: www.lifetechresources.com
SIC: 5122 5149 Cosmetics; Health foods

(P-10630)
MARKWINS BEAUTY BRANDS INC (PA)
22067 Ferrero, City Of Industry
(91789-5214)
PHONE..................909 595-8898
Lina Chen, *CEO*
John Chen, *
◆ **EMP:** 150 **EST:** 1984
SQ FT: 320,000
SALES (est): 270.93MM
SALES (corp-wide): 270.93MM **Privately Held**
Web: www.markwinsbeauty.com
SIC: 5122 Cosmetics

(P-10631)
MCKESSON CORPORATION
Also Called: McKesson Drug Company
9501 Norwalk Blvd, Santa Fe Springs
(90670-2929)
P.O. Box 2116 (90670-0116)
PHONE..................562 463-2100
Todd Kleinow, *Mgr*
EMP: 108
SALES (corp-wide): 308.95B **Publicly Held**
Web: www.mckesson.com
SIC: 5122 Pharmaceuticals
PA: Mckesson Corporation
   6555 State Highway 161
   972 446-4800

(P-10632)
MEDICAL RESEARCH INSTITUTE
Also Called: M R I
21411 Prairie St, Chatsworth (91311-5829)
PHONE..................818 739-6000
Chirag Patel, *CEO*
Patrick S Mccullough, *Pr*
Jenia G Khudagulyan, *
Alfred Baumeler, *CMO**
Kevin J Dwyer, *
EMP: 215 **EST:** 1997
SALES (est): 1.85MM
SALES (corp-wide): 85.54MM **Privately Held**
Web: www.mri-performance.com
SIC: 5122 Vitamins and minerals
PA: Natrol Llc
   15233 Vntura Blvd Ste 900
   800 262-8765

(P-10633)
METAGENICS LLC (PA)
25 Enterprise Ste 200, Aliso Viejo
(92656-2713)

PHONE..................949 366-0818
Pat Smallcombe, *Pr*
Jean M Bellin, *
Dave Tuit, *
John Troup, *CSO**
Sara Gottfried, *CMO**
◆ **EMP:** 150 **EST:** 1983
SQ FT: 88,000
SALES (est): 188.55MM
SALES (corp-wide): 188.55MM **Privately Held**
Web: www.metagenics.com
SIC: 5122 Vitamins and minerals

(P-10634)
MOROCCANOIL INC (PA)
16311 Ventura Blvd Ste 1200, Encino
(91436-2152)
PHONE..................888 700-1817
Jay Elarar, *CEO*
Ofer Tal, *
◆ **EMP:** 188 **EST:** 2010
SQ FT: 25,000
SALES (est): 23.8MM
SALES (corp-wide): 23.8MM **Privately Held**
Web: www.moroccanoil.com
SIC: 5122 Cosmetics

(P-10635)
MURAD LLC
1340 Storm Pkwy, Torrance (90501-5041)
PHONE..................310 726-3300
Howard Murad, *Brnch Mgr*
EMP: 120
SALES (corp-wide): 64.79B **Privately Held**
Web: www.murad.com
SIC: 5122 Cosmetics
HQ: Murad, Llc
   2121 Park Pl Ste 1
   El Segundo CA 90245

(P-10636)
N QIAGEN AMERCN HOLDINGS INC (HQ)
27220 Turnberry Ln Ste 200, Valencia
(91355-1019)
PHONE..................800 426-8157
Peer Schatz, *Pr*
EMP: 250 **EST:** 2000
SALES (est): 106.71MM **Privately Held**
SIC: 5122 Biologicals and allied products
PA: Qiagen N.V.
   Hulsterweg 82

(P-10637)
NATROL LLC
9454 Jordan Ave, Chatsworth (91311-5813)
PHONE..................818 739-6000
EMP: 36
SALES (corp widc): 85.54MM **Privately Held**
Web: www.natrol.com
SIC: 5122 2099 Drugs, proprietaries, and
   sundries; Food preparations, nec
PA: Natrol Llc
   15233 Vntura Blvd Ste 900
   800 262-8765

(P-10638)
NATUREWARE INC
6590 Darin Way, Cypress (90630-5121)
PHONE..................714 251-4510
Eun Ah Shin, *CEO*
Han C Shin, *
EMP: 96 **EST:** 2006
SALES (est): 9.89MM **Privately Held**
SIC: 5122 Vitamins and minerals

(P-10639)
NEW MILANI GROUP LLC (PA)
Also Called: Milani Cosmetics
2035 E 49th St, Vernon (90058-2801)
P.O. Box 58585 (90058-0585)
PHONE....................323 582-9404
Mary Van Praag, *CEO*
Lindsay Shumlas, *CFO*
Evelyn Wang, *CMO*
▲ **EMP: 82 EST:** 2001
SQ FT: 11,893
SALES (est): 21.03MM
SALES (corp-wide): 21.03MM **Privately Held**
Web: www.milanicosmetics.com
SIC: 5122 Cosmetics

(P-10640)
OBAGI COSMECEUTICALS LLC (HQ)
Also Called: Obagi
3760 Kilroy Airport Way Ste 500, Long Beach (90806-2485)
PHONE....................800 636-7546
Steve Dai, *CEO*
Jaime Castle, *
Sue Collins, *
Trish Mentas, *
Lisa Errecart, *
EMP: 82 EST: 2017
SQ FT: 28,352
SALES (est): 5.59MM **Publicly Held**
Web: www.obagi.com
SIC: 5122 Cosmetics
PA: Waldencast Plc
10 Bank St Ste 560
917 546-6828

(P-10641)
ONCOR CORP
Also Called: ONCOR CORP
13115 Barton Rd Ste G-H, Whittier (90605-2762)
PHONE....................562 944-0230
Danne King, *Brnch Mgr*
EMP: 34
Web: www.dannemking.com
SIC: 5122 2844 Toilet preparations; Perfumes, cosmetics and other toilet preparations
PA: Danne Montague King Co
10420 Pioneer Blvd

(P-10642)
OUTDATE RX LLC
1125 Research Dr, Redlands (92374-4562)
PHONE....................855 688-3283
Jacob Record, *Pr*
Keriann Record, *
Lori Granados, *
EMP: 84 EST: 2015
SALES (est): 10.92MM **Privately Held**
Web: www.outdaterx.com
SIC: 5122 4953 Pharmaceuticals; Medical waste disposal

(P-10643)
PAUL MITCHELL JOHN SYSTEMS (PA)
Also Called: Paul Mitchell
20705 Centre Pointe Pkwy, Santa Clarita (91350-2664)
P.O. Box 10597 (90213-3597)
PHONE....................800 793-8790
Michaeline Heydari, *CEO*
John Paul Dejoria, *Dir*
◆ **EMP: 80 EST:** 1980
SQ FT: 90,000
SALES (est): 100.53MM
SALES (corp-wide): 100.53MM **Privately Held**

Web: www.paulmitchell.com
SIC: 5122 5999 Hair preparations; Hair care products

(P-10644)
PHARMERICA CORPORATION
833 Marlborough Ave, Riverside (92507-2133)
PHONE....................951 683-4165
Dale Timmothy, *Prin*
EMP: 517
SALES (corp-wide): 8.83B **Publicly Held**
Web: www.pharmerica.com
SIC: 5122 Pharmaceuticals
HQ: Pharmerica Corporation
805 N Whittington Pkwy
Louisville KY 40222

(P-10645)
PLATINUM PERFORMANCE INC (HQ)
90 Thomas Rd, Buellton (93427-9657)
P.O. Box 990 (93427-0990)
PHONE....................800 553-2400
Mark J Herthel, *Pr*
EMP: 27 EST: 1996
SQ FT: 7,000
SALES (est): 23.45MM
SALES (corp-wide): 8.54B **Publicly Held**
Web: www.platinumperformance.com
SIC: 5122 2023 Vitamins and minerals; Dietary supplements, dairy and non-dairy based
PA: Zoetis Inc.
10 Sylvan Way
973 822-7000

(P-10646)
PPHM INC
Also Called: Avid Bioservices
14282 Franklin Ave, Tustin (92780-7009)
PHONE....................714 508-6100
Nicholas Green, *CEO*
Daniel Hart, *CFO*
Jeffrey Masten, *VP*
EMP: 100 EST: 2002
SALES (est): 44.7MM
SALES (corp-wide): 139.91MM **Publicly Held**
SIC: 5122 Pharmaceuticals
PA: Avid Bioservices, Inc.
14191 Myford Rd
714 508-6100

(P-10647)
PRIMAL ELEMENTS INC
Also Called: Primal Elements
18062 Redondo Cir, Huntington Beach (92648-1326)
PHONE....................714 899-0757
Faith Freeman, *CEO*
Scott Freeman, *
▲ **EMP: 99 EST:** 1993
SQ FT: 56,500
SALES (est): 22.03MM **Privately Held**
Web: www.primalelements.com
SIC: 5122 2841 Cosmetics; Detergents, synthetic organic or inorganic alkaline

(P-10648)
QYK BRANDS LLC
12101 Western Ave, Garden Grove (92841-2914)
PHONE....................833 795-7664
Rakesh Tammabattula, *CEO*
EMP: 189 EST: 2017
SALES (est): 20.76MM **Privately Held**
Web: www.qyk.us

SIC: 5122 2842 3842 2023 Pharmaceuticals; Disinfectants, household or industrial plant; Respiratory protection equipment, personal; Dietary supplements, dairy and non-dairy based

(P-10649)
RUGBY LABORATORIES INC (DH)
311 Bonnie Cir, Corona (92878-5182)
PHONE....................951 270-1400
David C Hsia Ph.d., *Pr*
Michael E Boser, *
Chato Abad, *
Frederick Wilkinson, *
Michel J Feldman, *
EMP: 90 EST: 1961
SALES (est): 3.38MM
SALES (corp-wide): 226.83B **Publicly Held**
SIC: 5122 2834 Pharmaceuticals; Pharmaceutical preparations
HQ: The Harvard Drug Group L L C
341 Mason Rd
La Vergne TN 37086
800 616-2471

(P-10650)
SCIENCE OF SKINCARE LLC
Also Called: Innovative Skin Care
3333 N San Fernando Blvd, Burbank (91504-2531)
PHONE....................818 254-7961
C Bryan Johns, *Managing Member*
Alec Call, *
◆ **EMP: 139 EST:** 2003
SQ FT: 36,000
SALES (est): 33.62MM **Privately Held**
Web: www.isclinical.com
SIC: 5122 Cosmetics

(P-10651)
SOS BEAUTY INC
9100 Wilshire Blvd Ste 500w, Beverly Hills (90212-3426)
PHONE....................424 285-1405
Dustin Cash, *CEO*
Charlene Valledor, *
EMP: 38 EST: 2017
SALES (est): 13.1MM **Privately Held**
Web: www.sosbty.com
SIC: 5122 3221 7389 3172 Cosmetics, perfumes, and hair products; Cosmetic jars, glass; Cosmetic kits, assembling and packaging; Cosmetic bags

(P-10652)
SPA DE SOLEIL INC
10443 Arminta St, Sun Valley (91352-4109)
PHONE....................818 504-3200
Rena Revivo, *CEO*
▲ **EMP: 50 EST:** 1994
SALES (est): 19.82MM **Privately Held**
Web: www.spadesoleil.com
SIC: 5122 2844 Cosmetics; Cosmetic preparations

(P-10653)
STAR NAIL PRODUCTS INC
Also Called: Star Nail International
29120 Avenue Paine, Valencia (91355-5402)
PHONE....................661 257-3376
Tony Cuccio, *CEO*
Elaine Watson, *
Christina Jahn, *
Anthony Cuccio, *
Roberta Cuccio, *
◆ **EMP: 55 EST:** 1982
SQ FT: 14,000

SALES (est): 11.65MM **Privately Held**
Web: www.starnail.com
SIC: 5122 2844 7231 Cosmetics; Perfumes, cosmetics and other toilet preparations; Beauty shops

(P-10654)
UNITE EUROTHERAPY INC
2870 Whiptail Loop Ste 100, Carlsbad (92010-6710)
PHONE....................760 585-1800
Andrew Dale, *Pr*
Andrew Dale, *CEO*
Jerry Trombetta, *
▲ **EMP: 80 EST:** 2002
SALES (est): 9.88MM **Privately Held**
Web: www.unitehairpro.com
SIC: 5122 Hair preparations

(P-10655)
URBAN DECAY COSMETICS LLC
Also Called: Urban Decay
833 W 16th St, Newport Beach (92663-2801)
PHONE....................949 631-4504
▲ **EMP: 70 EST:** 2000
SALES (est): 7.96MM
SALES (corp-wide): 6.5B **Privately Held**
SIC: 5122 Cosmetics
PA: L'oreal
14 Rue Royale
140206000

(P-10656)
VALLEY OF SUN COSMETICS LLC
Also Called: Valley of The Sun Labs
535 Patrice Pl, Gardena (90248-4232)
P.O. Box 3022 (90212)
PHONE....................310 327-9062
Ajmal Shehzad, *
◆ **EMP: 156 EST:** 1994
SQ FT: 10,000
SALES (est): 22.79MM **Privately Held**
Web: www.hollywoodstyleusa.com
SIC: 5122 Cosmetics

(P-10657)
VIVA LIFE SCIENCE INC
350 Paularino Ave, Costa Mesa (92626-4616)
PHONE....................949 645-6100
David Fan, *Pr*
EMP: 220 EST: 1987
SQ FT: 60,000
SALES (est): 2.43MM
SALES (corp-wide): 8.44MM **Privately Held**
Web: www.vivalife.com
SIC: 5122 2833 Vitamins and minerals; Medicinals and botanicals
PA: Westar Nutrition Corp.
350 Paularino Ave
949 645-6100

(P-10658)
WECKERLE COSMETICS USA INC
Also Called: Weckerle Cosmetic
525 Maple Ave, Torrance (90503-3905)
PHONE....................310 328-7000
Thomas Weckerle, *Pr*
Petra Webersberger, *
▲ **EMP: 35 EST:** 1979
SQ FT: 20,000
SALES (est): 22.74MM
SALES (corp-wide): 68.37MM **Privately Held**
Web: www.weckerle.com

SIC: 5122 5084 2844 Cosmetics; Packaging machinery and equipment; Lipsticks
PA: Weckerle Holding Gmbh
Holzhofstr. 26
88192930

(P-10659)
WELLA OPERATIONS US LLC
4500 Park Granada Ste 100, Calabasas (91302-1665)
PHONE....................818 999-5112
Yannis Rodocanachi, *Managing Member*
Sennen Pamich, *
EMP: 500 EST: 2020
SALES (est): 32.37MM
SALES (corp-wide): 261.21MM Privately Held
Web: www.wella.com
SIC: 5122 Cosmetics, perfumes, and hair products
PA: Wella Germany Gmbh
Berliner Allee 65-65a
61513020

5131 Piece Goods And Notions

(P-10660)
A W CHANG CORPORATION (PA)
Also Called: Excalibur International
6945 Atlantic Ave, Long Beach (90805-1415)
PHONE....................310 764-2000
William Chang, *CEO*
Abraham K Chang, *
William Chang, *VP*
▲ EMP: 27 EST: 1989
SQ FT: 12,000
SALES (est): 27.29MM Privately Held
SIC: 5131 5632 2211 Silk piece goods, woven; Apparel accessories; Apparel and outerwear fabrics, cotton

(P-10661)
ALEXANDER HENRY FABRICS INC
1951 N Ontario St, Burbank (91505-1231)
PHONE....................818 562-8200
Marcus De Leon, *Pr*
Kim Dunn, *
EMP: 40 EST: 1992
SALES (est): 5.25MM Privately Held
Web: www.ahfabrics.com
SIC: 5131 2211 Cotton goods; Broadwoven fabric mills, cotton

(P-10662)
BLUE RIDGE HOME FASHIONS INC
15761 Tapia St, Irwindale (91706-2177)
PHONE....................626 960-6069
Ning He, *CEO*
Fred Buonocore, *
Jim England, *
◆ EMP: 39 EST: 1994
SALES (est): 9.44MM Privately Held
Web: www.blueridgehome.com
SIC: 5131 3999 2392 Textiles, woven, nec; Feathers and feather products; Blankets, comforters and beddings

(P-10663)
CHARMING TRIM & PACKAGING
5889 Rickenbacker Rd, Commerce (90040-3027)
PHONE....................415 302-7021
Richard Ringeisen, *Pr*
Barry Chan, *

EMP: 1000 EST: 2011
SALES (est): 14.45MM Privately Held
Web: www.charmingtrim.com
SIC: 5131 3111 Trimmings, apparel; Garment leather

(P-10664)
J ROBERT SCOTT INC (PA)
722 N La Cienega Blvd, West Hollywood (90069-5086)
PHONE....................310 680-4300
Andrew Frumovitz, *CEO*
Sally Lewis, *
Nancy Preller, *
▲ EMP: 120 EST: 1972
SALES (est): 7.04MM
SALES (corp-wide): 7.04MM Privately Held
Web: www.jrobertscott.com
SIC: 5131 2512 2511 Textiles, woven, nec; Upholstered household furniture; Wood household furniture

(P-10665)
L & R DISTRIBUTORS INC
9292 9th St, Rancho Cucamonga (91730-4407)
PHONE....................909 980-3807
EMP: 271
SALES (corp-wide): 465.97MM Privately Held
Web: www.lrdist.com
SIC: 5131 Notions, nec
PA: L. & R. Distributors, Inc.
88 35th St Bldg 4 Fl 5 St
718 272-2100

(P-10666)
M M FAB INC
Also Called: South Seas Imports
2300 E Gladwick St, Compton (90220-6208)
PHONE....................310 763-3800
Richard Friedman, *Prin*
▲ EMP: 85 EST: 1988
SQ FT: 110,000
SALES (est): 4.36MM Privately Held
Web: www.southimports.com
SIC: 5131 Textiles, woven, nec

(P-10667)
MATRIX INTERNATIONAL TEX INC
Also Called: Matrix
1363 S Bonnie Beach Pl, Commerce (90023-4001)
P.O. Box 23484 (90023)
PHONE....................323 502-9100
Kourosh Neman, *Prin*
Kourosh Neman, *CEO*
Chris Neman, *
Kevin Neman, *
Simin Neman, *
◆ EMP: 28 EST: 1997
SQ FT: 60,000
SALES (est): 8.62MM Privately Held
Web: www.matrixtextiles.com
SIC: 5131 2299 Broadwoven fabrics; Apparel filling: cotton waste, kapok, and related material

(P-10668)
MOMENTUM TEXTILES LLC (PA)
Also Called: Momentum Textiles Wallcovering
17811 Fitch, Irvine (92614-6001)
PHONE....................949 833-8886
David Krakoff, *CEO*
Joanne Corrao, *
◆ EMP: 40 EST: 1987
SQ FT: 20,000

SALES (est): 39.66MM
SALES (corp-wide): 39.66MM Privately Held
Web: www.momentumtextilesandwalls.com
SIC: 5131 2221 Upholstery fabrics, woven; Broadwoven fabric mills, manmade

(P-10669)
MORGAN FABRICS CORPORATION (PA)
Also Called: Morgan Fabrics
4265 Exchange Ave, Los Angeles (90058-2604)
P.O. Box 58523 (90058-0523)
PHONE....................323 583-9981
Arnold Gittelson, *Ch*
Michael Gittelson, *Pr*
Robert Gittelson, *VP*
Ken Yang, *CFO*
◆ EMP: 60 EST: 1956
SQ FT: 50,000
SALES (est): 15.58MM
SALES (corp-wide): 15.58MM Privately Held
Web: www.morgan-fabrics.com
SIC: 5131 2759 Textiles, woven, nec; Commercial printing, nec

(P-10670)
PINDLER & PINDLER INC (PA)
Also Called: Pindler
11910 Poindexter Ave, Moorpark (93021-1748)
P.O. Box 8007 (93020-8007)
PHONE....................805 531-9090
Curt R Pindler, *Pr*
S L Crawford Junior, *Ex VP*
Barbara Bick, *
▲ EMP: 95 EST: 1939
SQ FT: 75,000
SALES (est): 27.14MM
SALES (corp-wide): 27.14MM Privately Held
Web: www.pindler.com
SIC: 5131 Drapery material, woven

(P-10671)
RADIX TEXTILE INC
Also Called: Radix
600 E Washington Blvd Ste C2, Los Angeles (90015-3739)
PHONE....................323 234-1667
Arad Shemirani, *Pr*
▲ EMP: 99 EST: 2007
SALES (est): 4.71MM Privately Held
SIC: 5131 2211 Piece goods and other fabrics; Broadwoven fabric mills, cotton

(P-10672)
RDMM LEGACY INC
Also Called: Fabri Cote
724 E 60th St, Los Angeles (90001-1013)
P.O. Box 1856 (90001-0856)
PHONE....................323 232-2147
▲ EMP: 30 EST: 1957
SALES (est): 3.11MM Privately Held
Web: www.fabricote.com
SIC: 5131 2295 Coated fabrics; Coated fabrics, not rubberized

(P-10673)
ROMEX TEXTILES INC (PA)
2454 E 27th St, Vernon (90058-1220)
PHONE....................213 749-9090
Shawn Binafard, *CEO*
▲ EMP: 39 EST: 1993
SALES (est): 10.54MM Privately Held
Web: www.romextex.com

SIC: 5131 2211 Textiles, woven, nec; Apparel and outerwear fabrics, cotton

(P-10674)
SO TECH/SPCL OP TECH INC (PA)
Also Called: Special Operations Tech
206 Star Of India Ln, Carson (90746-1418)
PHONE....................310 202-9007
James W Cragg V, *Pr*
▲ EMP: 32 EST: 1997
SQ FT: 12,000
SALES (est): 2.34MM
SALES (corp-wide): 2.34MM Privately Held
Web: www.sotechtactical.com
SIC: 5131 2396 Nylon piece goods, woven; Apparel findings and trimmings

(P-10675)
SPECIALTY TEXTILE SERVICES LLC
1333 30th St Ste A, San Diego (92154-3484)
PHONE....................619 476-8750
Mark Wilstine, *Mgr*
EMP: 155
Web: www.specialtytextileservices.com
SIC: 5131 Textiles, woven, nec
PA: Specialty Textile Services Llc
737 W Buchanan St

(P-10676)
STEVEN LABEL CORPORATION (PA)
11926 Burke St, Santa Fe Springs (90670-2546)
P.O. Box 3688 (90670-1688)
PHONE....................562 698-9971
EMP: 119 EST: 1954
SALES (est): 24.5MM
SALES (corp-wide): 24.5MM Privately Held
Web: www.stevenlabel.com
SIC: 5131 3643 Labels; Electric switches

(P-10677)
ZI INDUSTRIES INC (PA)
3957 S Hill St Ste A, Los Angeles (90037-1313)
P.O. Box 15218 (90015-0218)
PHONE....................213 749-1215
Alan Faiola, *Pr*
Virginia Acosta, *
▲ EMP: 70 EST: 1940
SQ FT: 43,000
SALES (est): 8.93MM
SALES (corp-wide): 8.93MM Privately Held
Web: www.zabin.com
SIC: 5131 Zippers

5136 Men's And Boy's Clothing

(P-10678)
BLACK BOX INC
371 2nd St Ste 1, Encinitas (92024-3524)
PHONE....................760 804-3300
▲ EMP: 100
SIC: 5136 5137 Men's and boy's clothing; Women's and children's clothing

(P-10679)
BRIXTON LLC
3821 Ocean Ranch Blvd, Oceanside (92056-2601)
PHONE....................866 264-4245

PRODUCTS & SVCS

Seth Ellison, *CEO*
Raphael Peck, *Managing Member**
Jason Young, *
David Stoddard, *
▲ **EMP:** 79 **EST:** 2004
SQ FT: 10,000
SALES (est): 28.4MM
SALES (corp-wide): 465.65MM **Privately Held**
Web: www.brixton.com
SIC: 5136 5611 5137 5621 Work clothing, men's and boys'; Clothing accessories: men's and boys'; Fur clothing, women's and children's; Women's specialty clothing stores
PA: Altamont Capital Partners Llc
    400 Hamilton Ave Ste 230
    650 264-7750

(P-10680)
CHEF WORKS INC
12325 Kerran St # A, Poway (92064-6801)
PHONE.....................858 643-5600
Neil R Gross, *CEO*
Joshua C Gross, *
David Roth, *
David Forster, *
▲ **EMP:** 350 **EST:** 1994
SQ FT: 50,000
SALES (est): 98.84MM **Privately Held**
Web: www.chefworks.com
SIC: 5136 5137 Uniforms, men's and boys'; Uniforms, women's and children's

(P-10681)
COLOSSEUM ATHLETICS CORP
Also Called: Colosseum Athletics
2400 S Wilmington Ave, Compton (90220-5403)
PHONE.....................310 538-8991
Stuart Whang, *CEO*
◆ **EMP:** 85 **EST:** 1992
SQ FT: 64,227
SALES (est): 18.19MM **Privately Held**
Web: www.colosseumathletics.com
SIC: 5136 5137 Sportswear, men's and boys'; Sportswear, women's and children's

(P-10682)
ELIEL & CO
Also Called: Eliel Cycling
2215 La Mirada Dr, Vista (92081-8828)
PHONE.....................760 877-8469
Ryan Eliel Cady, *CEO*
EMP: 24 **EST:** 2014
SALES (est): 1.52MM **Privately Held**
Web: www.elielcycling.com
SIC: 5136 2389 Sportswear, men's and boys'; Men's miscellaneous accessories

(P-10683)
FASHION WORLD INCORPORATED
Also Called: Bijan
420 N Rodeo Dr, Beverly Hills (90210-4502)
PHONE.....................310 273-6544
Manigeh Messa, *Mgr*
EMP: 128
SALES (corp-wide): 2.4MM **Privately Held**
Web: www.bijan.com
SIC: 5136 Men's and boy's clothing
PA: Fashion World, Incorporated
    421 N Rodeo Dr Ph
    310 273-6544

(P-10684)
FORIA INTERNATIONAL INC
18689 Arenth Ave, City Of Industry (91748-1302)

PHONE.....................626 912-8836
◆ **EMP:** 111
Web: www.foria.com
SIC: 5136 Men's and boy's clothing

(P-10685)
HELMET HOUSE LLC (PA)
Also Called: Tour Master
26855 Malibu Hills Rd, Calabasas Hills (91301-5100)
PHONE.....................800 421-7247
Robert M Miller, *CEO*
Philip Bellomy, *
Randy Hutchings, *
◆ **EMP:** 84 **EST:** 1969
SQ FT: 80,000
SALES (est): 20.94MM
SALES (corp-wide): 20.94MM **Privately Held**
Web: www.helmethouse.com
SIC: 5136 3949 3751 Men's and boy's clothing; Helmets, athletic; Motorcycle accessories

(P-10686)
HYBRID PROMOTIONS LLC (PA)
Also Called: Hybrid Promotions
10700 Valley View St, Cypress (90630-4835)
PHONE.....................714 952-3866
William Scott Hutchison, *CEO*
Faith Garcia-ross, *COO*
Ed Massura Csco, *Prin*
◆ **EMP:** 175 **EST:** 1999
SALES (est): 252.15MM
SALES (corp-wide): 252.15MM **Privately Held**
Web: www.hybridapparel.com
SIC: 5136 5137 5611 Sportswear, men's and boys'; Women's and children's clothing; Men's and boys' clothing stores

(P-10687)
M & S TRADING INC
Also Called: 7 Diamonds Clothing
15778 Gateway Cir, Tustin (92780-6469)
PHONE.....................714 241-7190
Sami Khalil, *CEO*
▲ **EMP:** 71 **EST:** 1991
SQ FT: 36,000
SALES (est): 3.67MM **Privately Held**
Web: www.7diamonds.com
SIC: 5136 5137 Sportswear, men's and boys'; Women's and children's clothing

(P-10688)
MEUNDIES INC
9534 Jefferson Blvd, Culver City (90232-2918)
PHONE.....................888 552-6775
Jonathan Shokrian, *CEO*
Sabah Mikha, *
Ariel Stoddard, *CRO**
EMP: 251 **EST:** 2011
SQ FT: 2,500
SALES (est): 19.14MM **Privately Held**
Web: www.meundies.com
SIC: 5136 5137 Underwear, men's and boys'; Women's and children's lingerie and undergarments

(P-10689)
MICHAEL GERALD LTD
Also Called: Mgl
7051 E Avenida De Santiago, Anaheim (92807-5130)
PHONE.....................562 921-9611
Gerald Barnes, *CEO*
▲ **EMP:** 23 **EST:** 1983
SALES (est): 4.91MM **Privately Held**

SIC: 5136 2329 3999 Sweaters, men's and boys'; Men's and boys' sportswear and athletic clothing; Atomizers, toiletry

(P-10690)
MOTENG INC
Also Called: Rax Alar Products
12220 Parkway Centre Dr, Poway (92064-6867)
PHONE.....................858 715-2500
▲ **EMP:** 70
SIC: 5136 5137 5072 5139 Men's and boy's clothing; Women's and children's clothing; Hardware; Footwear

(P-10691)
MOUNTAIN GEAR CORPORATION
Also Called: Tri-Mountain
4889 4th St, Irwindale (91706-2194)
PHONE.....................626 851-2488
Daniel Tsai, *CEO*
Rosie Tsai, *
▲ **EMP:** 125 **EST:** 1994
SQ FT: 300,000
SALES (est): 7.14MM **Privately Held**
Web: www.trimountain.com
SIC: 5136 Sportswear, men's and boys'

(P-10692)
PRANA LIVING LLC (HQ)
Also Called: Prana
3209 Lionshead Ave, Carlsbad (92010-4710)
PHONE.....................866 915-6457
Monica Mirro, *Pr*
▲ **EMP:** 89 **EST:** 1992
SALES (est): 20.14MM
SALES (corp-wide): 3.49B **Publicly Held**
Web: www.prana.com
SIC: 5136 5137 Men's and boy's clothing; Women's and children's clothing
PA: Columbia Sportswear Company
    14375 Nw Science Park Dr
    503 985-4000

(P-10693)
QUAKE CITY CASUALS INC
Also Called: Quake City Caps
1800 S Flower St, Los Angeles (90015-3424)
PHONE.....................213 746-0540
John Glucksman, *CEO*
▲ **EMP:** 125 **EST:** 1977
SQ FT: 11,500
SALES (est): 5.02MM **Privately Held**
Web: www.capstoneheadwear.com
SIC: 5136 Men's and boy's clothing

(P-10694)
ROOCHI TRADERS INCORPORATED
Also Called: Cotton Heritage
6393 E Washington Blvd, Commerce (90040-1817)
PHONE.....................323 722-5592
▲ **EMP:** 75 **EST:** 1982
SALES (est): 22.37MM **Privately Held**
Web: www.cottonheritage.com
SIC: 5136 Sportswear, men's and boys'

(P-10695)
SAYARI SHAHRZAD
Also Called: Blue Bay Industries
4822 Aqueduct Ave, Encino (91436-1621)
PHONE.....................310 903-6368
Shahrzad Sayari, *Owner*
EMP: 25 **EST:** 2017
SALES (est): 647.33K **Privately Held**

SIC: 5136 2339 2329 5651 Men's and boys' sportswear and work clothing; Women's and misses' athletic clothing and sportswear; Ski and snow clothing: men's and boys'; Unisex clothing stores

(P-10696)
SOEX WEST USA LLC
Also Called: Soex Group
3294 E 26th St, Vernon (90058-8008)
PHONE.....................323 264-8300
Nursis Ohanian, *
◆ **EMP:** 300 **EST:** 1981
SQ FT: 120,000
SALES (est): 6.71MM **Privately Held**
SIC: 5136 Men's and boy's clothing

(P-10697)
TRLGGC SERVICES LLC
1888 Rosecrans Ave, Manhattan Beach (90266-3712)
PHONE.....................323 266-3072
EMP: 225 **EST:** 2015
SALES (est): 1.49MM
SALES (corp-wide): 350MM **Privately Held**
SIC: 5136 5137 Work clothing, men's and boys'; Women's and children's dresses, suits, skirts, and blouses
HQ: True Religion Sales, Llc
    500 W 190th St Ste 300
    Gardena CA 90248

(P-10698)
UNI HOSIERY CO INC (PA)
1911 E Olympic Blvd, Los Angeles (90021-2421)
PHONE.....................213 228-0100
Harry Hayog Chung, *CEO*
◆ **EMP:** 120 **EST:** 1988
SQ FT: 500,000
SALES (est): 24.55MM
SALES (corp-wide): 24.55MM **Privately Held**
Web: www.unihosiery.com
SIC: 5136 5137 Hosiery, men's and boys'; Hosiery: women's, children's, and infants'

(P-10699)
VANTAGE CUSTOM CLASSICS INC
Also Called: Vantage Apparel
1815 Ritchey St, Santa Ana (92705-5124)
PHONE.....................714 755-1133
Patty Venny, *Mgr*
EMP: 117
SALES (corp-wide): 16.32MM **Privately Held**
Web: www.vantageapparel.com
SIC: 5136 2397 2395 Sportswear, men's and boys'; Schiffli machine embroideries; Pleating and stitching
PA: Vantage Custom Classics, Inc.
    100 Vantage Dr
    732 340-3000

5137 Women's And Children's Clothing

(P-10700)
2253 APPAREL LLC (PA)
Also Called: Celebrity Pink
1708 Aeros Way, Montebello (90640-6504)
PHONE.....................323 837-9800
Doron Kadosh, *CEO*
Benny Goldstein, *
David Kadosh, *
▲ **EMP:** 55 **EST:** 2004
SQ FT: 50,000

SALES (est): 20.12MM **Privately Held**
Web: www.celebpink.com
SIC: **5137** 2211 2339 Women's and
children's dresses, suits, skirts, and blouses
; Denims; Jeans: women's, misses', and
juniors'

(P-10701)
ALSTYLE AP & ACTIVEWEAR MGT CO (HQ)
1501 E Cerritos Ave, Anaheim
(92805-6400)
PHONE.........................714 765-0400
Rauf Gajiani, *CEO*
Amin Amdani, *
◆ EMP: 1800 EST: 2001
SQ FT: 715,000
SALES (est): 5.89MM
SALES (corp-wide): 3.2B **Privately Held**
SIC: **5137** Women's and children's clothing
PA: Les Vetements De Sport Gildan Inc
600 Boul De Maisonneuve O 33eme
Etage
514 735-2023

(P-10702)
BP CLOTHING LLC
Also Called: Baby Phat
3424 Garfield Ave, Commerce
(90040-3104)
▲ EMP: 150
SIC: **5137** Women's and children's clothing

(P-10703)
CALIFORNIA RAIN COMPANY INC
Also Called: California Rain
1213 E 14th St, Los Angeles (90021-2215)
PHONE.........................213 623-6061
Jack Jhy C Jang, *Pr*
◆ EMP: 90 EST: 1986
SQ FT: 8,600
SALES (est): 4.95MM **Privately Held**
Web: www.californiarainla.com
SIC: **5137** 5136 5699 Sportswear, women's
and children's; Sportswear, men's and boys'
; Customized clothing and apparel

(P-10704)
DAMO TEXTILE INC
Also Called: Damo Clothing Company
12121 Wilshire Blvd Ste 1120, Los Angeles
(90025-1164)
PHONE.........................213 741-1323
James Min, *CEO*
Paul Eeahn, *
Edwin Min, *
▲ EMP: 40 EST: 1999
SALES (est): 5.76MM **Privately Held**
Web: www.damoclothing.com
SIC: **5137** 3000 Women's and children's
clothing; Atomizers, toiletry

(P-10705)
DELTA GALIL USA INC
Also Called: Loomworks Apparel
16912 Von Karman Ave, Irvine
(92606-4972)
PHONE.........................949 296-0380
EMP: 277
Web: www.deltagalil.com
SIC: **5137** Women's and children's lingerie
and undergarments
HQ: Delta Galil Usa Inc.
1 Harmon Plz Fl 5
Secaucus NJ 07094
201 902-0055

(P-10706)
DG BRANDS INC
Also Called: Dreamgirl International
5548 Lindbergh Ln, Bell (90201-6410)
PHONE.........................323 268-0220
▲ EMP: 55 EST: 1978
SALES (est): 8.84MM **Privately Held**
Web: www.dreamgirldirect.com
SIC: **5137** 2389 2329 Lingerie; Costumes;
Athletic clothing, except uniforms: men's,
youths' and boys'

(P-10707)
EDGEMINE INC
Also Called: Mine
1801 E 50th St, Los Angeles (90058-1940)
PHONE.........................323 267-8222
Kevin Chang Kang, *CEO*
Kristen Han, *
Sarah King, *
Daniel Kang, *
▲ EMP: 130 EST: 1994
SQ FT: 200,000
SALES (est): 95MM **Privately Held**
Web: www.edgemine.com
SIC: **5137** 5621 5961 Women's and
children's clothing; Women's specialty
clothing stores; Electronic shopping

(P-10708)
FINAL TOUCH APPAREL INC
Also Called: Final Touch Apparel
116 E 32nd St, Los Angeles (90011-1916)
PHONE.........................323 484-9621
Mark Min Hyuk Kim, *CEO*
June Lim, *
EMP: 25 EST: 2017
SQ FT: 16,000
SALES (est): 1.73MM **Privately Held**
Web: www.finaltouchapparel.com
SIC: **5137** 2331 5632 Women's and
children's clothing; Women's and misses'
blouses and shirts; Apparel accessories

(P-10709)
FOX HEAD INC (HQ)
Also Called: Fox Racing
16752 Armstrong Ave, Irvine (92606-4912)
PHONE.........................949 757-9500
Jeff Mcguane, *CEO*
Andrew Keegan, *
◆ EMP: 492 EST: 1974
SALES (est): 59.42MM
SALES (corp-wide): 2.75B **Publicly Held**
Web: www.foxracing.com
SIC: **5137** 5699 5136 5961 Sportswear,
women's and children's; Sports apparel;
Sportswear, men's and boys'; Mail order
house, nec
PA: Vista Outdoor Inc.
1 Vista Way
763 433-1000

(P-10710)
JOHNNY WAS LLC
395 Santa Monica Pl Ste 124, Santa Monica
(90401-3477)
PHONE.........................310 656-0600
Eli Levite, *Brnch Mgr*
EMP: 98
SALES (corp-wide): 1.57B **Publicly Held**
Web: www.johnnywas.com
SIC: **5137** 2339 Women's and children's
clothing; Women's and misses' accessories
HQ: Johnny Was, Llc
712 S Olive St
Los Angeles CA 90014
866 942-8806

(P-10711)
KAREN KANE INC (PA)
2275 E 37th St, Vernon (90058-1435)
PHONE.........................323 588-0000
Michael Kane, *CEO*
Lonnie Kane, *CFO*
Karen Kane, *Sec*
Cecelia Jenkins, *Treas*
▲ EMP: 130 EST: 1979
SQ FT: 96,000
SALES (est): 19.78MM
SALES (corp-wide): 19.78MM **Privately Held**
Web: www.karenkane.com
SIC: **5137** Women's and children's clothing

(P-10712)
LA DYE & PRINT INC
13416 Estrella Ave, Gardena (90248-1513)
PHONE.........................310 327-3200
George Chaghouri, *CEO*
EMP: 35 EST: 2011
SQ FT: 1,800
SALES (est): 5.4MM **Privately Held**
Web: www.ladyeandprint.com
SIC: **5137** 2269 Women's and children's
dresses, suits, skirts, and blouses; Linen
fabrics: dyeing, finishing, and printing

(P-10713)
LYMI INC (PA)
Also Called: Reformation
2263 E Vernon Ave, Vernon (90058-1631)
PHONE.........................844 701-0139
Hali Borenstein, *CEO*
Jennifer Maclellan, *
Yael Alfalo, *
▲ EMP: 100 EST: 2013
SQ FT: 120,000
SALES (est): 114.03MM
SALES (corp-wide): 114.03MM **Privately Held**
Web: www.thereformation.com
SIC: **5137** 2335 Women's and children's
clothing; Women's, junior's, and misses'
dresses

(P-10714)
MAD ENGINE GLOBAL LLC
6740 Cobra Way Ste 100, San Diego
(92121-4102)
PHONE.........................858 558-5270
EMP: 306 EST: 2020
SALES (est): 33.73MM **Privately Held**
SIC: **5137** Women's and children's clothing

(P-10715)
MATESTA CORPORATION
5620 Knott Ave, Buena Park (90621-1808)
P.O. Box 5395 (90622-5395)
PHONE.........................040 074-0052
Salim Saeed, *CEO*
Robert Abraham, *CFO*
EMP: 106 EST: 2017
SALES (est): 62MM **Privately Held**
Web: www.matesta.com
SIC: **5137** 5136 Women's and children's
clothing; Men's and boy's clothing

(P-10716)
MIAS FASHION MFG CO INC
Also Called: California Basic
1734 Aeros Way, Montebello (90640-6504)
PHONE.........................562 906-1060
Peter D Anh, *Pr*
Brian Song, *
◆ EMP: 252 EST: 1999
SALES (est): 83MM **Privately Held**
Web: www.miasfashion.com

SIC: **5137** Women's and children's clothing

(P-10717)
NEW PRIDE CORPORATION
Also Called: Belinda
5101 Pacific Blvd, Vernon (90058-2217)
PHONE.........................323 584-6608
Miran Byun, *CEO*
Ho Lee, *Pr*
EMP: 55 EST: 2007
SQ FT: 5,000
SALES (est): 4.76MM **Privately Held**
SIC: **5137** 2331 Women's and children's
clothing; Women's and misses' blouses and
shirts

(P-10718)
NYDJ APPAREL LLC (PA)
Also Called: Not Your Daughters Jeans
801 S Figueroa St Ste 2500, Los Angeles
(90017-5504)
PHONE.........................323 581-9040
Lisa Collier, *Pr*
Steve Brink, *
▲ EMP: 73 EST: 2003
SQ FT: 6,000
SALES (est): 25.22MM
SALES (corp-wide): 25.22MM **Privately Held**
Web: www.nydj.com
SIC: **5137** Women's and children's clothing

(P-10719)
NYDJ APPAREL LLC
5401 S Soto St, Vernon (90058-3618)
PHONE.........................877 995-3267
EMP: 127
SALES (corp-wide): 25.22MM **Privately Held**
Web: www.nydj.com
SIC: **5137** Women's and children's clothing
PA: Nydj Apparel, Llc
801 S Fgueroa St Ste 2500
323 581-9040

(P-10720)
O & K INC (PA)
Also Called: One Clothing
2121 E 37th St, Vernon (90058-1416)
PHONE.........................323 846-5700
Chang Ho Ok, *CEO*
Seongeun Kim, *
Chang Ho, *
▲ EMP: 134 EST: 1989
SQ FT: 55,000
SALES (est): 7.22MM **Privately Held**
Web: www.oneclothing.com
SIC: **5137** Women's and children's clothing

(P-10721)
PHOENIX TEXTILE INC (PA)
Also Called: Level 99
14600 S Broadway, Gardena (90248-1812)
PHONE.........................310 715-7090
Cindy Change, *CEO*
Dominic Poon, *CFO*
◆ EMP: 87 EST: 1984
SQ FT: 39,000
SALES (est): 8.96MM
SALES (corp-wide): 8.96MM **Privately Held**
Web: www.level99jeans.com
SIC: **5137** 2337 3144 Women's and
children's accessories; Women's and
misses' capes and jackets; Boots, canvas
or leather: women's

(P-10722)
PIEGE CO (PA)
Also Called: Buffalo

20120 Plummer St, Chatsworth
(91311-5448)
PHONE.............................818 727-9100
Kambiz Zarabi, *CEO*
Morad Zarabi, *
Michael Zarabi, *
Nara Estpanian, *
▲ **EMP: 95 EST:** 1981
SQ FT: 48,000
SALES (est): 36.07MM
SALES (corp-wide): 36.07MM **Privately Held**
Web: www.felina.com
SIC: 5137 5136 5632 Lingerie; Men's and boys' suits and trousers; Lingerie and corsets (underwear)

(P-10723)
RUBY RIBBON INC
4607 Lakeview Canyon Rd Pmb 405,
Westlake Village (91361-4028)
PHONE.............................650 449-4470
Melyn Campbell, *CEO*
▲ **EMP: 25 EST:** 2012
SALES (est): 2.37MM **Privately Held**
Web: www.rubyribbon.com
SIC: 5137 5632 5699 2254 Underwear: women's, children's, and infants'; Lingerie and corsets (underwear); Sports apparel; Shorts, shirts, slips, and panties (underwear): knit

(P-10724)
RUNWAY LIQUIDATION LLC (HQ)
2761 Fruitland Ave, Vernon (90058-3607)
PHONE.............................323 589-2224
Martine Melloul, *
Brian Fleming, *
Bernd Kroeber, *
◆ **EMP: 75 EST:** 1989
SQ FT: 500,000
SALES (est): 56.41MM
SALES (corp-wide): 122.83MM **Privately Held**
Web: www.bcbg.com
SIC: 5137 5621 2335 Women's and children's clothing; Women's clothing stores; Women's, junior's, and misses' dresses
PA: Marquee Brands Llc
330 W 34th St Fl 15
212 203-8135

(P-10725)
SAME SWIM LLC
2333 E 49th St, Vernon (90058-2820)
PHONE.............................323 582-2588
EMP: 90 EST: 2015
SALES (est): 942.52K **Privately Held**
SIC: 5137 Women's and children's sportswear and swimsuits

(P-10726)
SEVEN LICENSING COMPANY LLC
Also Called: Seven7 Brands
801 S Figueroa St Ste 2500, Los Angeles
(90017-5504)
PHONE.............................323 780-8250
▲ **EMP: 102 EST:** 2002
SALES (est): 7.08MM **Privately Held**
Web: www.sunrisebrands.com
SIC: 5137 Women's and children's accessories
PA: Sunrise Brands, Llc
801 S Figueroa St Fl 8

(P-10727)
SIGNAL PRODUCTS INC (PA)
Also Called: Signal Products/Guess Handbags

5600 W Adams Blvd Ste 200, Los Angeles
(90016-2563)
PHONE.............................213 748-0990
▲ **EMP: 86 EST:** 1992
SALES (est): 9.81MM **Privately Held**
Web: www.signalbrands.com
SIC: 5137 Handbags

(P-10728)
SNOWMASS APPAREL INC (PA)
Also Called: County Clothing Company
15225 Alton Pkwy, Irvine (92618-2354)
PHONE.............................949 788-0617
George Wong, *CEO*
Edmond Wong, *
Harry Yip, *
▲ **EMP: 45 EST:** 1984
SALES (est): 1.52MM
SALES (corp-wide): 1.52MM **Privately Held**
SIC: 5137 5136 2339 Women's and children's outerwear; Men's and boys' outerwear; Women's and misses' outerwear, nec

(P-10729)
STANCE INC (PA)
Also Called: Stance
197 Avenida La Pata, San Clemente
(92673-6307)
PHONE.............................949 391-9030
John Wilson, *CEO*
Brian Shea, *
▲ **EMP: 215 EST:** 2009
SALES (est): 32.95MM
SALES (corp-wide): 32.95MM **Privately Held**
Web: www.stance.com
SIC: 5137 Women's and children's clothing

(P-10730)
SWATFAME INC (PA)
Also Called: Kut From The Kloth
16425 Gale Ave, City Of Industry
(91745-1722)
PHONE.............................626 961-7928
Mitchell Quaranta, *CEO*
Jonathan Greenberg, *
Brian Min, *
Bruce Stern, *
▲ **EMP: 290 EST:** 1978
SQ FT: 233,000
SALES (est): 49.71MM
SALES (corp-wide): 49.71MM **Privately Held**
Web: www.swatfame.com
SIC: 5137 2211 2339 Dresses; Denims; Women's and misses' outerwear, nec

(P-10731)
THE TIMING INC
Also Called: Timing Fashion
2807 S Santa Fe Ave, Vernon
(90058-1408)
PHONE.............................323 589-5577
Kevin Kim, *CEO*
Bowhan Kim, *
Alice Kang, *
◆ **EMP: 40 EST:** 1989
SALES (est): 5.11MM **Privately Held**
Web: www.timingfashion.com
SIC: 5137 2331 2335 2339 Women's and children's clothing; Women's and misses' blouses and shirts; Women's, junior's, and misses' dresses; Women's and misses' outerwear, nec

---

5139 Footwear

(P-10732)
ACI INTERNATIONAL (PA)
844 Moraga Dr, Los Angeles (90049-1632)
PHONE.............................310 889-3400
Steven Jackson, *CEO*
David Mankowitz, *
Anna Liau, *
▲ **EMP: 99 EST:** 1952
SQ FT: 40,000
SALES (est): 23.7MM
SALES (corp-wide): 23.7MM **Privately Held**
Web: www.acifootwear.com
SIC: 5139 3021 Shoes; Rubber and plastics footwear

(P-10733)
ASICS AMERICA CORPORATION (HQ)
Also Called: Asics Tiger
7755 Irvine Center Dr Ste 400, Irvine
(92618-2904)
PHONE.............................949 453-8888
Gene Mccarthy, *Pr*
Seiho Gohashi, *
Kenji Sakai, *
◆ **EMP: 109 EST:** 1973
SALES (est): 453.96MM **Privately Held**
Web: www.asics.com
SIC: 5139 5136 5137 2369 Footwear, athletic; Sportswear, men's and boys'; Sportswear, women's and children's; Girl's and children's outerwear, nec
PA: Asics Corporation
7-1-1, Minatojimanakamachi, Chuo-Ku

(P-10734)
CAPE ROBBIN INC
1943 W Mission Blvd, Pomona
(91766-1037)
PHONE.............................626 810-8080
Michael Chen, *CEO*
▲ **EMP: 50 EST:** 2011
SQ FT: 20,000
SALES (est): 4.33MM **Privately Held**
Web: www.caperobbin.com
SIC: 5139 3171 Shoes; Handbags, women's

(P-10735)
CONVERSE INC
1437 3rd Street Promenade 39, Santa
Monica (90401-2321)
PHONE.............................310 451-0314
EMP: 89
SALES (corp-wide): 51.36B **Publicly Held**
Web: www.converse.com
SIC: 5139 5661 Footwear, athletic; Footwear, athletic
HQ: Converse Inc.
1 Love Joy Wharf
Boston MA 02114
617 248-9530

(P-10736)
FORTUNE DYNAMIC INC
21923 Ferrero, City Of Industry
(91789-5210)
PHONE.............................909 979-8318
Carol Lee, *Pr*
James Lee, *
◆ **EMP: 90 EST:** 1986
SQ FT: 150,000
SALES (est): 8.85MM **Privately Held**
Web: www.fortunedynamic.com
SIC: 5139 Shoes

(P-10737)
OSATA ENTERPRISES INC
Also Called: Globe Shoes
18105 Bishop Ave, Carson (90746-4020)
PHONE.............................888 445-6237
Matthew Hill, *Pr*
Gary Valentine, *
▲ **EMP: 100 EST:** 1997
SQ FT: 30,000
SALES (est): 19.88MM **Privately Held**
Web: www.us.globebrand.com
SIC: 5139 Shoes
PA: Globe International Limited
1 Fennell St

(P-10738)
SKECHERS USA INC
Also Called: Skechers Factory Outlet 335
29800 Eucalyptus Ave, Moreno Valley
(92555-6738)
PHONE.............................951 242-4307
Carlette Moore, *Mgr*
EMP: 49
Web: local.skechers.com
SIC: 5139 3021 Footwear; Shoes, rubber or plastic molded to fabric
PA: Skechers U.S.A., Inc.
228 Manhattan Beach Blvd

(P-10739)
SOUTH CONE INC
Also Called: Reef
5935 Darwin Ct, Carlsbad (92008-7302)
PHONE.............................760 431-2300
Mike Jensen, *CEO*
Daniella Turenshine, *CFO*
◆ **EMP: 120 EST:** 1984
SQ FT: 37,583
SALES (est): 7.09MM
SALES (corp-wide): 10.45B **Publicly Held**
Web: www.reef.com
SIC: 5139 3144 3143 Shoes; Women's footwear, except athletic; Men's footwear, except athletic
PA: V.F. Corporation
1551 Wewatta St
720 778-4000

5141 Groceries, General Line

(P-10740)
ACOSTA REMAINCO INC
Also Called: Acosta Sales & Marketing
480 Apollo St Ste C, Brea (92821-3121)
PHONE.............................714 988-1500
Rick Nist, *Brnch Mgr*
EMP: 150
SALES (corp-wide): 1.88B **Privately Held**
Web: www.acosta.com
SIC: 5141 Food brokers
HQ: Acosta Remainco, Inc.
6600 Corporate Ctr Pkwy
Jacksonville FL 32216
904 281-9800

(P-10741)
AFC DISTRIBUTION CORP
19205 S Laurel Park Rd, Rancho
Dominguez (90220-6032)
PHONE.............................310 604-3630
Sadamu Taniguch, *CEO*
EMP: 250 EST: 2016
SALES (est): 29.95MM **Privately Held**
Web: www.afcsushi.com
SIC: 5141 Groceries, general line
PA: Zensho Holdings Co., Ltd.
2-18-1, Konan

▲ = Import ▼ = Export
◆ = Import/Export

(P-10742)
AMK FOODSERVICES INC
Also Called: Kaney Foods
830 Capitolio Way, San Luis Obispo
(93401-7122)
P.O. Box 1188 (93406-1188)
PHONE..........................805 544-7600
John P Kaney, *CEO*
EMP: 130 **EST:** 1988
SQ FT: 35,000
SALES (est): 1.77MM **Privately Held**
SIC: 5141 Food brokers

(P-10743)
ANSAR GALLERY INC
2505 El Camino Rd, Tustin (92782)
PHONE..........................949 220-0000
Ali Akbar Feroozesh, *Prin*
Hussein Saadat, *
▲ **EMP:** 200 **EST:** 2013
SQ FT: 120,000
SALES (est): 2.2MM **Privately Held**
Web: www.ansargallery.us
SIC: 5141 Food brokers
PA: Ansar Mall Llc
Office No M, Al-Ittihad Street-Ansar
Mall, Al-Nahda

(P-10744)
BROOKS RESTAURANT GROUP INC (PA)
Also Called: Dynaco Equipment Co
220 Five Cities Dr, Pismo Beach
(93449-3004)
PHONE..........................559 485-8520
EMP: 35 **EST:** 1973
SALES (est): 23.06MM
SALES (corp-wide): 23.06MM **Privately Held**
SIC: 5141 5087 2011 5812 Groceries, general line; Restaurant supplies; Meat packing plants; Steak restaurant

(P-10745)
BUFFALO MARKET INC
Also Called: Buffalo Market
1439 N Highland Ave, Los Angeles
(90028-7622)
PHONE..........................650 337-0078
Adam Olejniczak, *CEO*
Charmaine Button, *
Sean Howell, *
EMP: 140 **EST:** 2019
SALES (est): 22MM **Privately Held**
Web: www.buffalomarket.com
SIC: 5141 Groceries, general line

(P-10746)
CANTON FOOD CO INC
750 S Alameda St, Los Angeles
(90021 1624)
PHONE..........................213 688-7707
Shiu Lit Kwan, *CEO*
Shui Lit Kwan, *
Cho W Kwan, *
Wai Kam Kwan, *
▲ **EMP:** 106 **EST:** 1979
SQ FT: 96,000
SALES (est): 12.28MM **Privately Held**
Web: www.cantonfoodco.com
SIC: 5141 5146 5411 5421 Food brokers; Seafoods; Grocery stores; Seafood markets

(P-10747)
CHOICE FOODSERVICES INC
8134 Lankershim Blvd, North Hollywood
(91605-1611)
PHONE..........................818 504-8213
EMP: 109
Web: www.choicelunch.com

SIC: 5141 Groceries, general line
PA: Choice Foodservices, Inc.
9000 Crow Canyon Rd Ste S

(P-10748)
CONCORD FOODS INC (HQ)
Also Called: Greco Los Angeles
300 Baldwin Park Blvd, City Of Industry
(91746-1405)
PHONE..........................909 975-2000
Nick J Sciortino Junior, *Pr*
John Sciortino, *VP*
Roy Sciortino, *CFO*
EMP: 89 **EST:** 1985
SQ FT: 67,000
SALES (est): 4.58MM
SALES (corp-wide): 78.84B **Publicly Held**
Web: www.grecoandsons.com
SIC: 5141 Food brokers
PA: Sysco Corporation
1390 Enclave Pkwy
281 584-1390

(P-10749)
DELIVERR INC
307 S Wilson Ave Apt 6, Pasadena
(91106-3238)
PHONE..........................213 534-8686
EMP: 415
SALES (corp-wide): 504.44MM **Privately Held**
Web: www.deliveer.com
SIC: 5141 Groceries, general line
HQ: Deliverr, Inc.
110 Sutter St Fl 9
San Francisco CA 94104
415 475-9175

(P-10750)
DPI SPECIALTY FOODS WEST INC
Also Called: Dpi West
930 S Rockefeller Ave, Ontario
(91761-8149)
PHONE..........................909 975-1019
EMP: 366
SALES (corp-wide): 2.4B **Privately Held**
Web: www.dpispecialtyfoods.com
SIC: 5141 Food brokers
HQ: Dpi Specialty Foods West, Inc.
601 S Rockefeller Ave
Ontario CA 91761
909 975-1019

(P-10751)
FOOD SALES WEST INC
235 Baker St, Costa Mesa (92626-4521)
P.O. Box 10738 (02623 0738)
PHONE..........................714 966-2900
David Lyons, *CEO*
Carl Scharffenberger, *
Mary Ellen Scharffenberger, *
Robert Watkins, *
Michael Berkson, *
EMP: 85 **EST:** 1973
SQ FT: 12,000
SALES (est): 2.51MM **Privately Held**
SIC: 5141 Food brokers

(P-10752)
FOOTHILL PACKING INC
2255 S Broadway, Santa Maria
(93454-7871)
PHONE..........................805 925-7900
Jorge Rivera, *Pr*
EMP: 489
SALES (corp-wide): 9.75MM **Privately Held**
Web: www.foothillpacking.com
SIC: 5141 Food brokers

PA: Foothill Packing, Inc.
1582 Moffett St
831 784-1453

(P-10753)
GOURMET FOODS INC (PA)
2910 E Harcourt St, Compton (90221-5502)
PHONE..........................310 632-3300
Marcel Lagnaz, *Managing Member*
Mitch Rosen, *Managing Member*
◆ **EMP:** 80 **EST:** 1986
SQ FT: 35,000
SALES (est): 21.76MM
SALES (corp-wide): 21.76MM **Privately Held**
Web: www.gourmetfoodsinc.com
SIC: 5141 5812 2099 Food brokers; Eating places; Food preparations, nec

(P-10754)
ICPK CORPORATION
Also Called: Hpp Food Services
1130 W C St, Wilmington (90744-5102)
PHONE..........................310 830-8020
EMP: 70
SALES (corp-wide): 17.78MM **Privately Held**
Web: www.hppfs.com
SIC: 5141 2035 Groceries, general line; Dressings, salad: raw and cooked (except dry mixes)
PA: Icpk Corporation
16700 Valley View Ave # 170
714 321-7025

(P-10755)
MARQUEZ BROTHERS ENTPS INC (PA)
15480 Valley Blvd, City Of Industry
(91746-3325)
PHONE..........................626 330-3310
Gustavo Marquez, *Pr*
Juan Marquez, *VP*
Jaime Marquez, *VP*
◆ **EMP:** 127 **EST:** 1993
SQ FT: 200,000
SALES (est): 22.87MM **Privately Held**
SIC: 5141 Food brokers

(P-10756)
MARTIN-BROWER COMPANY LLC
21489 Baker Pkwy, Walnut (91789-5236)
PHONE..........................909 595-8764
EMP: 90
Web: www.martinbrower.com
SIC: 5141 Food brokers
HQ: The Martin-Brower Company L L C
6250 N River Rd Ste 9000
Rosemont IL 60018
847 227 6500

(P-10757)
MCLANE FOODSERVICE INC
Also Called: McLane Riverside
14813 Meridian Pkwy, Riverside
(92518-3004)
PHONE..........................951 867-3727
Eric Polk, *Brnch Mgr*
EMP: 174
SALES (corp-wide): 364.48B **Publicly Held**
Web: www.mclaneco.com
SIC: 5141 Food brokers
HQ: Mclane Foodservice, Inc.
4747 Mclane Pkwy
Temple TX 76504
254 771-7500

(P-10758)
MCLANE FOODSERVICE DIST INC
Also Called: McLane Inland
1051 Wineville Ave, Ontario (91764-5388)
PHONE..........................909 912-3700
Daniel Lara, *Brnch Mgr*
EMP: 115
SALES (corp-wide): 364.48B **Publicly Held**
Web: www.mclaneco.com
SIC: 5141 Food brokers
HQ: Mclane Foodservice Distribution, Inc.
4747 Mclane Pkwy
Temple TX 76504
254 771-7500

(P-10759)
MCLANE FOODSERVICE DIST INC
Also Called: McLane Rancho Cucamonga
9408 Richmond Pl Ste A, Rancho
Cucamonga (91730-6052)
PHONE..........................909 484-6100
Ron Mcintosh, *Mgr*
EMP: 75
SALES (corp-wide): 364.48B **Publicly Held**
Web: www.mclaneco.com
SIC: 5141 Food brokers
HQ: Mclane Foodservice Distribution, Inc.
4747 Mclane Pkwy
Temple TX 76504
254 771-7500

(P-10760)
MERCADO LATINO INC (PA)
Also Called: International Gourmet
245 Baldwin Park Blvd, City Of Industry
(91746-1404)
P.O. Box 6168 (91734-6168)
PHONE..........................626 333-6862
Richard Rodriguez, *CEO*
Roberto Rodriguez, *
Jorge Rodriguez, *
Angelita Rodriguez, *
◆ **EMP:** 100 **EST:** 1963
SQ FT: 105,000
SALES (est): 32.57MM
SALES (corp-wide): 32.57MM **Privately Held**
Web: www.mercadolatinoinc.com
SIC: 5141 5148 Food brokers; Fresh fruits and vegetables

(P-10761)
NAFTA DISTRIBUTORS
5120 Santa Ana St, Ontario (91761-8632)
PHONE..........................800 956-2382
Samuel Madikians, *CEO*
▲ **EMP:** 75 **EST:** 1994
SQ FT: 12,000
SALES (est): 2.22MM **Privately Held**
Web: www.naftadist.com
SIC: 5141 Food brokers

(P-10762)
NONGSHIM AMERICA INC (HQ)
Also Called: Nongshim
12155 6th St, Rancho Cucamonga
(91730-6115)
PHONE..........................909 481-3698
Dong Y Shin, *CEO*
Joon Park, *
Jongmin Chung, *
Chris Gepford, *
◆ **EMP:** 250 **EST:** 1994
SALES (est): 83.03MM **Privately Held**
Web: www.nongshimusa.com

PRODUCTS & SVCS

SIC: **5141** 2098 Food brokers; Noodles (e.g. egg, plain, and water), dry
PA: Nongshim Co., Ltd.
    112 Yeouidaebang-Ro, Dongjak-Gu

(P-10763)
OTASTY FOODS INC
160 S Hacienda Blvd, City Of Industry (91745-1101)
PHONE..............................626 330-1229
Ming Chao Huang, *Pr*
Ken Chen, *
◆ **EMP: 91 EST:** 1994
SQ FT: 58,000
SALES (est): 16.09MM **Privately Held**
Web: www.otastyfoods.com
SIC: **5141** Food brokers

(P-10764)
PALISADES RANCH INC
Also Called: Goldberg and Solovy Foods Inc
5925 Alcoa Ave, Vernon (90058-3920)
PHONE..............................323 581-6161
Paul Paget, *CEO*
Earl Goldberg, *Pr*
EMP: 285 **EST:** 1974
SQ FT: 70,000
SALES (est): 19.64MM
SALES (corp-wide): 78.84B **Publicly Held**
Web: www.gsfoods.com
SIC: **5141** 5149 5046 5169 Food brokers; Groceries and related products, nec; Restaurant equipment and supplies, nec; Chemicals and allied products, nec
PA: Sysco Corporation
    1390 Enclave Pkwy
    281 584-1390

(P-10765)
PIVEG INC
3525 Del Mar Heights Rd Ste 1069, San Diego (92130-2199)
PHONE..............................858 436-3070
Roberto L Espinoza, *CEO*
▲ **EMP:** 220 **EST:** 2004
SALES (est): 57.3MM **Privately Held**
Web: www.piveg.com
SIC: **5141** Food brokers

(P-10766)
PREMIER FOOD SERVICES INC
14359 Amargosa Rd Ste F, Victorville (92392-2334)
PHONE..............................760 843-8000
David Lopez, *Brnch Mgr*
EMP: 541
SALES (corp-wide): 1.13B **Privately Held**
Web: www.premierfoodservices.com
SIC: **5141** Groceries, general line
HQ: Premier Food Services, Inc.
    9500 Gilman Dr
    La Jolla CA

(P-10767)
REAL MEX FOODS INC
Also Called: El Torito Franchising Company
5660 Katella Ave Ste 200, Cypress (90630-5059)
PHONE..............................714 523-0031
EMP: 100
SIC: **5141** 5182 5087 2099 Food brokers; Wine and distilled beverages; Restaurant supplies; Food preparations, nec

(P-10768)
ROBERT KINSELLA INC
15375 Barranca Pkwy Ste G107, Irvine (92618-2208)
PHONE..............................949 453-9533
Robert Kinsella, *Owner*

EMP: 77
SALES (corp-wide): 2.44MM **Privately Held**
SIC: **5141** Food brokers
PA: Robert Kinsella, Inc.
    535 S Nolen Dr Ste 100
    214 260-8670

(P-10769)
SMART & FINAL STORES LLC (DH)
Also Called: Smart & Final
600 Citadel Dr, Los Angeles (90040-1562)
PHONE..............................323 869-7500
David G Hirz, *Managing Member*
EMP: 97 **EST:** 1991
SALES (est): 1.53B **Privately Held**
Web: www.smartandfinal.com
SIC: **5141** Groceries, general line
HQ: Chedraui Usa, Inc.
    600 Citadel Dr
    Commerce CA 90040
    323 869-7500

(P-10770)
SMART & FINAL STORES LLC
Also Called: Smart & Final
10113 Venice Blvd, Los Angeles (90034-5898)
PHONE..............................310 559-1722
Eddie Preciado, *Mgr*
EMP: 99
SQ FT: 19,886
Web: www.smartandfinal.com
SIC: **5141** Groceries, general line
HQ: Smart & Final Stores Llc
    600 Citadel Dr
    Los Angeles CA 90040

(P-10771)
SMART & FINAL STORES LLC
Also Called: Smart & Final
12210 Santa Monica Blvd, Los Angeles (90025-2518)
PHONE..............................310 207-8688
Jerry Miyamoto, *Mgr*
EMP: 165
SQ FT: 18,263
Web: www.smartandfinal.com
SIC: **5141** Groceries, general line
HQ: Smart & Final Stores Llc
    600 Citadel Dr
    Los Angeles CA 90040

(P-10772)
SMART & FINAL STORES LLC
Also Called: Smart & Final
2308 E 4th St, Los Angeles (90033-4306)
PHONE..............................323 268-9179
Juan Garcia, *Mgr*
EMP: 110
SQ FT: 11,648
Web: www.smartandfinal.com
SIC: **5141** Groceries, general line
HQ: Smart & Final Stores Llc
    600 Citadel Dr
    Los Angeles CA 90040

(P-10773)
SMART & FINAL STORES LLC
1216 Compton Ave, Los Angeles (90021-2331)
PHONE..............................213 747-6697
Lisa Mesias, *Mgr*
EMP: 88
SQ FT: 14,160
Web: www.smartandfinal.com
SIC: **5141** Groceries, general line
HQ: Smart & Final Stores Llc
    600 Citadel Dr

Los Angeles CA 90040

(P-10774)
SMART STORES OPERATIONS LLC
855 N Wilcox Ave, Montebello (90640-1801)
PHONE..............................323 725-2985
EMP: 351
SALES (corp-wide): 4.74B **Privately Held**
Web: www.smartandfinal.com
SIC: **5141** Groceries, general line
HQ: Smart Stores Operations Llc
    600 Citadel Dr
    Los Angeles CA 90040
    323 869-7500

(P-10775)
SMART STORES OPERATIONS LLC
15427 Amar Rd, La Puente (91744-2803)
PHONE..............................626 330-2495
Robert Terry, *Brnch Mgr*
EMP: 351
SALES (corp-wide): 4.74B **Privately Held**
Web: www.smartandfinal.com
SIC: **5141** Groceries, general line
HQ: Smart Stores Operations Llc
    600 Citadel Dr
    Los Angeles CA 90040
    323 869-7500

(P-10776)
SMART STORES OPERATIONS LLC
18555 Devonshire St, Northridge (91324-1308)
PHONE..............................818 368-6409
Marie Teolis, *Brnch Mgr*
EMP: 351
SALES (corp-wide): 4.74B **Privately Held**
Web: www.smartandfinal.com
SIC: **5141** Groceries, general line
HQ: Smart Stores Operations Llc
    600 Citadel Dr
    Los Angeles CA 90040
    323 869-7500

(P-10777)
SMART STORES OPERATIONS LLC
644 Redondo Ave, Long Beach (90814-1453)
PHONE..............................562 438-0450
EMP: 234
SALES (corp-wide): 4.74B **Privately Held**
Web: www.smartandfinal.com
SIC: **5141** Groceries, general line
HQ: Smart Stores Operations Llc
    600 Citadel Dr
    Los Angeles CA 90040
    323 869-7500

(P-10778)
SMART STORES OPERATIONS LLC
615 N Pacific Coast Hwy, Redondo Beach (90277-2107)
PHONE..............................323 497-8528
EMP: 234
SALES (corp-wide): 4.74B **Privately Held**
Web: www.smartandfinal.com
SIC: **5141** Groceries, general line
HQ: Smart Stores Operations Llc
    600 Citadel Dr
    Los Angeles CA 90040
    323 869-7500

(P-10779)
SMART STORES OPERATIONS LLC
240 S Diamond Bar Blvd, Diamond Bar (91765-1605)
PHONE..............................323 855-8434
EMP: 234
SALES (corp-wide): 4.74B **Privately Held**
Web: www.smartandfinal.com
SIC: **5141** Groceries, general line
HQ: Smart Stores Operations Llc
    600 Citadel Dr
    Los Angeles CA 90040
    323 869-7500

(P-10780)
SMART STORES OPERATIONS LLC
3830 W Verdugo Ave, Burbank (91505-3441)
PHONE..............................818 954-8631
EMP: 234
SALES (corp-wide): 4.74B **Privately Held**
Web: www.smartandfinal.com
SIC: **5141** Groceries, general line
HQ: Smart Stores Operations Llc
    600 Citadel Dr
    Los Angeles CA 90040
    323 869-7500

(P-10781)
SMART STORES OPERATIONS LLC
5038 W Avenue N, Palmdale (93551-5729)
PHONE..............................661 722-6210
Danny Omada, *Brnch Mgr*
EMP: 351
SALES (corp-wide): 4.74B **Privately Held**
Web: www.smartandfinal.com
SIC: **5141** Groceries, general line
HQ: Smart Stores Operations Llc
    600 Citadel Dr
    Los Angeles CA 90040
    323 869-7500

(P-10782)
SMART STORES OPERATIONS LLC
13003 Whittier Blvd, Whittier (90602-3046)
PHONE..............................562 907-7037
David Hirs, *Brnch Mgr*
EMP: 351
SALES (corp-wide): 4.74B **Privately Held**
Web: www.smartandfinal.com
SIC: **5141** Groceries, general line
HQ: Smart Stores Operations Llc
    600 Citadel Dr
    Los Angeles CA 90040
    323 869-7500

(P-10783)
SMART STORES OPERATIONS LLC
303 E Foothill Blvd, Azusa (91702-2516)
PHONE..............................626 334-5189
EMP: 351
SALES (corp-wide): 4.74B **Privately Held**
Web: www.smartandfinal.com
SIC: **5141** Groceries, general line
HQ: Smart Stores Operations Llc
    600 Citadel Dr
    Los Angeles CA 90040
    323 869-7500

(P-10784)
SMART STORES OPERATIONS LLC
4550 W Pico Blvd, Los Angeles (90019-4257)

PHONE..............323 549-9586
EMP: 351
SALES (corp-wide): 4.74B **Privately Held**
Web: www.smartandfinal.com
SIC: 5141 Groceries, general line
HQ: Smart Stores Operations Llc
600 Citadel Dr
Los Angeles CA 90040
323 869-7500

(P-10785)
SMART STORES OPERATIONS LLC
1005 W Arrow Hwy, San Dimas (91773-2422)
PHONE..............909 592-2190
EMP: 351
SALES (corp-wide): 4.74B **Privately Held**
Web: www.smartandfinal.com
SIC: 5141 Groceries, general line
HQ: Smart Stores Operations Llc
600 Citadel Dr
Los Angeles CA 90040
323 869-7500

(P-10786)
SMART STORES OPERATIONS LLC (DH)
Also Called: Smart & Final
600 Citadel Dr, Los Angeles (90040-1562)
PHONE..............323 869-7500
David B Kaplan, *Ch Bd*
David G Hirz, *
Richard N Phegley, *
Leland P Smith, *
Edward Wong, *Senior Vice President Supply Chain*
EMP: 447 **EST:** 1900
SQ FT: 81,000
SALES (est): 2.25B
SALES (corp-wide): 4.74B **Privately Held**
Web: www.smartandfinal.com
SIC: 5141 Groceries, general line
HQ: Smart & Final Holdings, Inc.
600 Citadel Dr
Commerce CA 90040
800 894-0511

(P-10787)
SMART STORES OPERATIONS LLC
1308 W Edinger Ave, Santa Ana (92704-4306)
PHONE..............714 549-2362
EMP: 234
SALES (corp-wide): 4.74B **Privately Held**
Web: www.smartandfinal.com
SIC: 5141 Groceries, general line
HQ: Smart Stores Operations Llc
600 Citadel Dr
Los Angeles CA 90040
323 869-7500

(P-10788)
SMART STORES OPERATIONS LLC
26911 Trabuco Rd, Mission Viejo (92691-3506)
PHONE..............949 581-1212
EMP: 351
SALES (corp-wide): 4.74B **Privately Held**
Web: www.smartandfinal.com
SIC: 5141 Groceries, general line
HQ: Smart Stores Operations Llc
600 Citadel Dr
Los Angeles CA 90040
323 869-7500

(P-10789)
SMART STORES OPERATIONS LLC
12339 Poway Rd, Poway (92064-4218)
PHONE..............858 748-0101
EMP: 234
SALES (corp-wide): 4.74B **Privately Held**
Web: www.smartandfinal.com
SIC: 5141 Groceries, general line
HQ: Smart Stores Operations Llc
600 Citadel Dr
Los Angeles CA 90040
323 869-7500

(P-10790)
SMART STORES OPERATIONS LLC
9870 N Magnolia Ave, Santee (92071-1901)
PHONE..............619 449-2396
EMP: 234
SALES (corp-wide): 4.74B **Privately Held**
Web: www.smartandfinal.com
SIC: 5141 Groceries, general line
HQ: Smart Stores Operations Llc
600 Citadel Dr
Los Angeles CA 90040
323 869-7500

(P-10791)
SMART STORES OPERATIONS LLC
150 B Ave, Coronado (92118-1511)
PHONE..............619 522-2014
EMP: 234
SALES (corp-wide): 4.74B **Privately Held**
Web: www.smartandfinal.com
SIC: 5141 Groceries, general line
HQ: Smart Stores Operations Llc
600 Citadel Dr
Los Angeles CA 90040
323 869-7500

(P-10792)
SMART STORES OPERATIONS LLC
13439 Camino Canada, El Cajon (92021-8811)
PHONE..............619 390-1738
EMP: 351
SALES (corp-wide): 4.74B **Privately Held**
Web: www.smartandfinal.com
SIC: 5141 Groceries, general line
HQ: Smart Stores Operations Llc
600 Citadel Dr
Los Angeles CA 90040
323 869-7500

(P-10793)
SMART STORES OPERATIONS LLC
1845 W Vista Way, Vista (92083-6119)
PHONE..............760 732-1480
EMP: 234
SALES (corp-wide): 4.74B **Privately Held**
Web: www.smartandfinal.com
SIC: 5141 Groceries, general line
HQ: Smart Stores Operations Llc
600 Citadel Dr
Los Angeles CA 90040
323 869-7500

(P-10794)
SMART STORES OPERATIONS LLC
955 Carlsbad Village Dr, Carlsbad (92008-1802)
PHONE..............760 434-2449

EMP: 234
SALES (corp-wide): 4.74B **Privately Held**
Web: www.smartandfinal.com
SIC: 5141 Groceries, general line
HQ: Smart Stores Operations Llc
600 Citadel Dr
Los Angeles CA 90040
323 869-7500

(P-10795)
SMART STORES OPERATIONS LLC
933 Sweetwater Rd, Spring Valley (91977-4837)
PHONE..............619 668-9039
EMP: 234
SALES (corp-wide): 4.74B **Privately Held**
Web: www.smartandfinal.com
SIC: 5141 Groceries, general line
HQ: Smart Stores Operations Llc
600 Citadel Dr
Los Angeles CA 90040
323 869-7500

(P-10796)
SMART STORES OPERATIONS LLC
2235 University Ave, San Diego (92104-2717)
PHONE..............619 291-1842
EMP: 351
SALES (corp-wide): 4.74B **Privately Held**
Web: www.smartandfinal.com
SIC: 5141 Groceries, general line
HQ: Smart Stores Operations Llc
600 Citadel Dr
Los Angeles CA 90040
323 869-7500

(P-10797)
SMART STORES OPERATIONS LLC
2800 Fletcher Pkwy, El Cajon (92020-2111)
PHONE..............619 589-7000
EMP: 234
SALES (corp-wide): 4.74B **Privately Held**
Web: www.smartandfinal.com
SIC: 5141 Groceries, general line
HQ: Smart Stores Operations Llc
600 Citadel Dr
Los Angeles CA 90040
323 869-7500

(P-10798)
SMART STORES OPERATIONS LLC
10740 Westview Pkwy, San Diego (92126-2962)
PHONE..............858 578-7343
EMP: 351
SALES (corp-wide): 4.74B **Privately Held**
Web: www.smartandfinal.com
SIC: 5141 Groceries, general line
HQ: Smart Stores Operations Llc
600 Citadel Dr
Los Angeles CA 90040
323 869-7500

(P-10799)
SMART STORES OPERATIONS LLC
13346 Limonite Ave, Eastvale (92880-3360)
PHONE..............909 773-1813
EMP: 234
SALES (corp-wide): 4.74B **Privately Held**
Web: www.smartandfinal.com
SIC: 5141 Groceries, general line
HQ: Smart Stores Operations Llc
600 Citadel Dr

Los Angeles CA 90040
323 869-7500

(P-10800)
SMART STORES OPERATIONS LLC
928 E Ontario Ave, Corona (92881-3616)
PHONE..............323 869-7543
EMP: 234
SALES (corp-wide): 4.74B **Privately Held**
Web: www.smartandfinal.com
SIC: 5141 Groceries, general line
HQ: Smart Stores Operations Llc
600 Citadel Dr
Los Angeles CA 90040
323 869-7500

(P-10801)
SMART STORES OPERATIONS LLC
2121 Spring St, Paso Robles (93446-1455)
PHONE..............805 237-0323
EMP: 351
SALES (corp-wide): 4.74B **Privately Held**
Web: www.smartandfinal.com
SIC: 5141 Groceries, general line
HQ: Smart Stores Operations Llc
600 Citadel Dr
Los Angeles CA 90040
323 869-7500

(P-10802)
SMART STORES OPERATIONS LLC
850 Linden Ave, Carpinteria (93013-2043)
PHONE..............805 566-2174
EMP: 234
SALES (corp-wide): 4.74B **Privately Held**
Web: www.smartandfinal.com
SIC: 5141 Groceries, general line
HQ: Smart Stores Operations Llc
600 Citadel Dr
Los Angeles CA 90040
323 869-7500

(P-10803)
SMART STORES OPERATIONS LLC
5770 Lindero Canyon Rd, Westlake Village (91362-4088)
PHONE..............818 889-8253
EMP: 234
SALES (corp-wide): 4.74B **Privately Held**
Web: www.smartandfinal.com
SIC: 5141 Groceries, general line
HQ: Smart Stores Operations Llc
600 Citadel Dr
Los Angeles CA 90040
323 869-7500

(P-10804)
SMART STORES OPERATIONS LLC
7800 Telegraph Rd, Ventura (93004-1503)
PHONE..............805 647-4276
Brian Gillman, *Brnch Mgr*
EMP: 351
SALES (corp-wide): 4.74B **Privately Held**
Web: www.smartandfinal.com
SIC: 5141 Groceries, general line
HQ: Smart Stores Operations Llc
600 Citadel Dr
Los Angeles CA 90040
323 869-7500

(P-10805)
SMART STORES OPERATIONS LLC

PRODUCTS & SVCS

5135 E Los Angeles Ave, Simi Valley
(93063-3431)
PHONE.................................805 520-6035
EMP: 234
SALES (corp-wide): 4.74B Privately Held
Web: www.smartandfinal.com
SIC: 5141 Groceries, general line
HQ: Smart Stores Operations Llc
　　600 Citadel Dr
　　Los Angeles CA 90040
　　323 869-7500

(P-10806)
**SOUTHWEST TRADERS
INCORPORATED (PA)**
Also Called: Swt Stockton
27565 Diaz Rd, Temecula (92590-3411)
PHONE.................................951 699-7800
Ken Smith, CEO
Lynne Bredemeier, *
▲ EMP: 180 EST: 1977
SQ FT: 130,000
SALES (est): 398.79MM
SALES (corp-wide): 398.79MM Privately
Held
Web: www.southwesttraders.com
SIC: 5141 Food brokers

(P-10807)
SYGMA NETWORK INC
Also Called: Sygma
46905 47th St W, Lancaster (93536-8527)
PHONE.................................661 723-0405
Mike Wren, Brnch Mgr
EMP: 162
SALES (corp-wide): 78.84B Publicly Held
Web: www.sygmanetwork.com
SIC: 5141 Food brokers
HQ: The Sygma Network Inc
　　5550 Blazer Pkwy Ste 300
　　Dublin OH 43017

(P-10808)
SYSCO LOS ANGELES INC
Also Called: Sysco
20701 Currier Rd, Walnut (91789-2904)
PHONE.................................909 595-9595
TOLL FREE: 800
Daniel S Haag, CEO
John Kao, Sr VP
Sal Adelberg, *
◆ EMP: 1000 EST: 1988
SALES (est): 87.78MM
SALES (corp-wide): 78.84B Publicly Held
Web: www.sysco.com
SIC: 5141 5084 Groceries, general line;
　Food industry machinery
PA: Sysco Corporation
　　1390 Enclave Pkwy
　　281 584-1390

(P-10809)
SYSCO RIVERSIDE INC
15750 Meridian Pkwy, Riverside
(92518-3001)
PHONE.................................951 601-5300
Saul Adelsberg, CEO
EMP: 375 EST: 2009
SALES (est): 29.3MM
SALES (corp-wide): 78.84B Publicly Held
Web: www.sysco-riverside.com
SIC: 5141 5142 5143 5144 Food brokers;
　Packaged frozen goods; Dairy products,
　except dried or canned; Poultry and poultry
　products
PA: Sysco Corporation
　　1390 Enclave Pkwy
　　281 584-1390

(P-10810)
SYSCO SAN DIEGO INC
Also Called: Sysco
12180 Kirkham Rd, Poway (92064-6879)
PHONE.................................858 513-7300
Kevin Mangan, CEO
Debra Morey, *
◆ EMP: 370 EST: 1996
SQ FT: 250,000
SALES (est): 23.23MM
SALES (corp-wide): 78.84B Publicly Held
Web: www.sysco.com
SIC: 5141 5142 5147 5148 Food brokers;
　Packaged frozen goods; Meats and meat
　products; Fresh fruits and vegetables
PA: Sysco Corporation
　　1390 Enclave Pkwy
　　281 584-1390

(P-10811)
SYSCO VENTURA INC
Also Called: Sysco
3100 Sturgis Rd, Oxnard (93030-7276)
PHONE.................................805 205-7000
Jerry L Barash, Pr
Manny Fernandez, *
Bill Delaney, *
Brian Beach, *
Twila Day, *
EMP: 300 EST: 2003
SQ FT: 370,000
SALES (est): 39.26MM
SALES (corp-wide): 78.84B Publicly Held
Web: www.sysco.com
SIC: 5141 Food brokers
PA: Sysco Corporation
　　1390 Enclave Pkwy
　　281 584-1390

(P-10812)
TAPIA ENTERPRISES INC (PA)
Also Called: Tapia Brothers Co
6067 District Blvd, Maywood (90270-3560)
PHONE.................................323 560-7415
Raul Tapia, CEO
Francisco Tapia, *
Ramon Tapia, *
▲ EMP: 95 EST: 1985
SQ FT: 40,000
SALES (est): 87.04MM
SALES (corp-wide): 87.04MM Privately
Held
Web: www.tapiabrothers.com
SIC: 5141 Groceries, general line

(P-10813)
**UNION SUP COMSY SOLUTIONS
INC**
2301 E Pacifica Pl, Rancho Dominguez
(90220-6210)
PHONE.................................785 357-5005
Guy Steele, CFO
Kyle Deere, *
EMP: 322 EST: 2012
SALES (est): 18.19MM Publicly Held
Web: www.unionsupply.com
SIC: 5141 5661 2252 Food brokers;
　Footwear, athletic; Men's, boys', and girls'
　hosiery
HQ: Union Supply Group, Inc.
　　2500 Regent Blvd Ste 100
　　Dallas TX 75261

(P-10814)
US FOODS INC
15155 Northam St, La Mirada (90638-5754)
P.O. Box 29283 (85038-9283)
PHONE.................................714 670-3500
David Patterson, Brnch Mgr
EMP: 172

Web: www.usfoods.com
SIC: 5141 5046 3556 2099 Food brokers;
　Commercial equipment, nec; Food products
　machinery; Food preparations, nec
HQ: Us Foods, Inc.
　　9399 W Higgins Rd Ste 500
　　Rosemont IL 60018

(P-10815)
USFI INC
Also Called: Social Talkie
108 W Walnut St Ste 221, Gardena
(90248-3102)
PHONE.................................424 260-9210
Gary Place, Pr
Byung Hak Erick Yoo, *
Steven Choi, *
William Baek, *
▲ EMP: 75 EST: 1998
SQ FT: 4,000
SALES (est): 8.39MM Privately Held
Web: www.usfifoods.com
SIC: 5141 5149 Food brokers; Groceries
　and related products, nec

(P-10816)
VITCO DISTRIBUTORS INC
Also Called: Vitco Food Service
715 E California St, Ontario (91761-1814)
PHONE.................................909 355-1300
Kostas Vitakis, Pr
Emmanuel Vitakis, *
EMP: 199 EST: 2001
SQ FT: 20,000
SALES (est): 88.46MM Privately Held
Web: www.vitcofoods.com
SIC: 5141 Food brokers

(P-10817)
**WISMETTAC ASIAN FOODS INC
(HQ)**
Also Called: Wismettac Fresh Fish
13409 Orden Dr, Santa Fe Springs
(90670-6336)
PHONE.................................562 802-1900
Yuji Sasa, CEO
Hiroyuki Shinkai, *
Toshiyuki Nishikawa, *
Hyoe Yamashita, *
Shingo Shimamura, *
◆ EMP: 200 EST: 1960
SQ FT: 225,000
SALES (est): 496.09MM Privately Held
Web: www.wismettacusa.com
SIC: 5141 Groceries, general line
PA: Nishimoto Co., Ltd.
　　3-2-1, Nihombashimuromachi

5142 Packaged Frozen Goods

(P-10818)
**CONTESSA LIQUIDATING CO
INC**
222 W 6th St Fl 8, San Pedro (90731-3358)
P.O. Box 1950 (90733-1950)
◆ EMP: 113
SIC: 5142 5146 Packaged frozen goods;
　Seafoods

(P-10819)
**CONTESSA PREMIUM FOODS
INC**
5980 Alcoa Ave, Vernon (90058-3925)
PHONE.................................310 832-8000
EMP: 250
SIC: 5142 5146 Packaged frozen goods;
　Fish and seafoods

(P-10820)
EL PRIMO FOODS INC
608 Monterey Pass Rd, Monterey Park
(91754-2419)
PHONE.................................626 289-5054
EMP: 225
SIC: 5142 Packaged frozen goods

(P-10821)
JECKYS BEST INC
Also Called: Jab Foods
26450 Summit Cir, Santa Clarita
(91350-2991)
PHONE.................................661 259-1313
Jecky Bicer, Pr
Eitay Bicer, *
▲ EMP: 30 EST: 1997
SQ FT: 25,000
SALES (est): 5.28MM Privately Held
Web: www.jabfoods.com
SIC: 5142 2038 Bakery products, frozen;
　Frozen specialties, nec

(P-10822)
JON-LIN FROZEN FOODS (PA)
Also Called: Jon-Lin Foods
1620 N 8th St, Colton (92324-1302)
PHONE.................................909 825-8542
Russell H Burch, Pr
Mary Kate Burch, Sec
Joseph Burch, VP
Jan Burch, Treas
EMP: 85 EST: 1962
SALES (est): 1.19MM
SALES (corp-wide): 1.19MM Privately
Held
SIC: 5142 Packaged frozen goods

(P-10823)
**MARIE CLLENDER
WHOLESALERS INC**
170 E Rincon St, Corona (92879-1327)
PHONE.................................951 737-6760
Phillip Ratner, Pr
Gerald Tanaka, *
Kurt Schweickhart, *
EMP: 3423 EST: 1968
SQ FT: 28,000
SALES (est): 1.9MM
SALES (corp-wide): 33.41MM Privately
Held
SIC: 5142 Bakery products, frozen
HQ: Castle Harlan Partners Iii Lp
　　150 E 58th St Fl 38
　　New York NY 10155
　　212 644-8600

(P-10824)
WEI-CHUAN USA INC (PA)
6655 Garfield Ave, Bell Gardens
(90201-1807)
PHONE.................................626 225-7168
Steve Lin, Pr
William Huang, Treas
Benny Chang, Sec
◆ EMP: 120 EST: 1972
SQ FT: 38,000
SALES (est): 59.96MM
SALES (corp-wide): 59.96MM Privately
Held
Web: www.weichuanusa.com
SIC: 5142 2038 Packaged frozen goods;
　Dinners, frozen and packaged

(P-10825)
WEST PICO FOODS INC
5201 S Downey Rd, Vernon (90058-3703)
P.O. Box 58107 (90058-0107)
PHONE.................................323 586-9050
Elias Naghi, Pr

▲ = Import ▼ = Export
◆ = Import/Export

Don Lubitz, *
▲ **EMP:** 125 **EST:** 1969
SQ FT: 42,000
SALES (est): 24.35MM **Privately Held**
Web: www.westpicofoods.com
SIC: 5142 5144 Packaged frozen goods;
Poultry: live, dressed or frozen
(unpackaged)

5143 Dairy Products, Except Dried Or Canned

(P-10826)
CACIQUE DISTRIBUTORS US
Also Called: Cacique
14923 Proctor Ave, La Puente
(91746-3206)
P.O. Box 1047 (91017-1047)
PHONE...............................626 961-3399
EMP: 240
SIC: 5143 Cheese

(P-10827)
CACIQUE FOODS LLC
Also Called: Cacique
14923 Proctor Ave, La Puente
(91746-3206)
P.O. Box 1047 (91017-1047)
PHONE...............................626 961-3399
EMP: 240
SALES (corp-wide): 129.03MM **Privately Held**
Web: www.caciquefoods.com
SIC: 5143 Cheese
PA: Cacique Foods Llc
1410 Westridge Cir N
626 961-3399

(P-10828)
CLEMSON DISTRIBUTION INC (PA)
20722 Currier Rd, City Of Industry
(91789-2903)
PHONE...............................909 595-2770
Rolando T Santos, *Pr*
Emeline Santos, *
▲ **EMP:** 23 **EST:** 1994
SQ FT: 32,000
SALES (est): 60.52MM
SALES (corp-wide): 60.52MM **Privately Held**
Web: www.clemsondistribution.com
SIC: 5143 2013 Ice cream and ices;
Prepared beef products, from purchased beef

(P-10829)
CRYSTAL CREAMERY INC
1629 Carlotti Dr, Santa Maria (93454-1503)
PHONE...............................209 576-3479
Julie Welch, *Mgr*
EMP: 79
SALES (corp-wide): 21.59MM **Privately Held**
Web: www.crystalcreamery.com
SIC: 5143 Dairy products, except dried or canned
PA: Crystal Creamery, Inc.
529 Kansas Ave
209 576-3400

(P-10830)
HOKEY POKEY LLC
Also Called: Hokey Pokey La
1235 24th St Unit 4, Santa Monica
(90404-1329)
PHONE...............................213 361-2503
Bharat Chalmers, *Managing Member*
EMP: 25 **EST:** 2022

SALES (est): 900K **Privately Held**
SIC: 5143 5149 2024 7389 Frozen dairy desserts; Coffee and tea; Dairy based frozen desserts; Business services, nec

(P-10831)
LOS ALTOS FOOD PRODUCTS LLC
Also Called: Los Altos
450 Baldwin Park Blvd, City Of Industry
(91746-1407)
PHONE...............................626 330-6555
Raul Andrade, *Pr*
Raul Andrade, *Pr*
Gloria Andrade, *
EMP: 105 **EST:** 1988
SQ FT: 38,000
SALES (est): 21.68MM **Privately Held**
Web: www.losaltosfoods.com
SIC: 5143 Cheese

(P-10832)
MCCONNELLS FINE ICE CREAMS LLC
800 Del Norte Blvd, Oxnard (93030-8971)
PHONE...............................805 963-8813
Briana Gray, *Managing Member*
Charlie Price, *Managing Member**
Michael Palmer, *Managing Member**
Eva Ein, *Managing Member**
EMP: 38 **EST:** 2011
SQ FT: 184,000
SALES (est): 20.28MM **Privately Held**
Web: www.mcconnells.com
SIC: 5143 2024 Ice cream and ices; Ice cream, bulk

(P-10833)
NESTLE ICE CREAM COMPANY
7301 District Blvd, Bakersfield
(93313-2042)
PHONE...............................661 398-3500
James L Dintaman, *CEO*
▲ **EMP:** 1920 **EST:** 1993
SALES (est): 9.03MM **Privately Held**
SIC: 5143 5451 Ice cream and ices; Ice cream (packaged)
HQ: Nestle Usa, Inc.
1812 N Moore St
Arlington VA 22209
800 225-2270

5144 Poultry And Poultry Products

(P-10834)
EGGS UNLIMITED LLC
Also Called: Eggs Unlimited
17875 Von Karman Ave Ste 450, Irvine
(92614-6212)
PHONE...............................888 554-3977
Timothy Cohen, *Pr*
Timothy John Cohen, *
EMP: 70 **EST:** 2019
SALES (est): 5.09MM **Privately Held**
Web: www.eggsunlimited.com
SIC: 5144 Eggs

(P-10835)
HIDDEN VILLA RANCH PRODUCE INC (HQ)
Also Called: Hidden Villa Ranch
310 N Harbor Blvd Ste 205, Fullerton
(92832-1954)
P.O. Box 34001 (92834-9411)
PHONE...............................714 680-3447
Tim E Luberski, *Pr*
Don Lawson, *

Greg Schneider, *
Michael Sencer, *
Robert J Kelly Bob, *Ex VP*
◆ **EMP:** 270 **EST:** 1995
SQ FT: 21,619
SALES (est): 410MM
SALES (corp-wide): 350MM **Privately Held**
Web: www.hiddenvilla.com
SIC: 5144 Eggs
PA: Luberski, Inc.
310 N Harbor Blvd Ste 205
714 680-3447

(P-10836)
INTERSTATE FOODS INC
310 S Long Beach Blvd, Compton
(90221-3400)
PHONE...............................310 635-2442
Carlos Velasco, *CEO*
EMP: 145 **EST:** 1999
SQ FT: 13,000
SALES (est): 6.47MM **Privately Held**
SIC: 5144 Poultry products, nec

(P-10837)
MOARK LLC
12005 Cabernet Dr, Fontana (92337-7703)
PHONE...............................850 378-2005
Craig Willardson, *Brnch Mgr*
EMP: 93
SALES (corp-wide): 2.89B **Privately Held**
SIC: 5144 Poultry and poultry products
HQ: Moark, Llc
28 Under The Mountain Rd
North Franklin CT 06254
951 332-3300

(P-10838)
ROGERS POULTRY CO
2020 E 67th St, Los Angeles (90001-2169)
PHONE...............................800 585-0802
John C Butler, *COO*
EMP: 80
SALES (corp-wide): 14.29MM **Privately Held**
Web: www.rogerspoultry.com
SIC: 5144 Poultry products, nec
PA: Roger's Poultry Co.
5050 S Santa Fe Ave
323 585-0802

(P-10839)
ROGERS POULTRY CO (PA)
5050 S Santa Fe Ave, Vernon
(90058-2124)
P.O. Box 58641 (90058-0641)
PHONE...............................323 585-0802
TOLL FREE: 800
George V Saffarrans, *CEO*
John C Butler, *
EMP: 100 **EST:** 1979
SQ FT: 15,000
SALES (est): 14.29MM
SALES (corp-wide): 14.29MM **Privately Held**
Web: www.rogerspoultry.com
SIC: 5144 Poultry products, nec

5145 Confectionery

(P-10840)
B B G MANAGEMENT GROUP (PA)
Also Called: Granlund Candies
12164 California St, Yucaipa (92399-4333)
PHONE...............................909 797-9581
R Scott Burkle, *Pr*
Margie Rogan, *

EMP: 50 **EST:** 1961
SQ FT: 10,000
SALES (est): 1.83MM
SALES (corp-wide): 1.83MM **Privately Held**
SIC: 5145 2064 Candy; Candy and other confectionery products

(P-10841)
BALANCE FOODS INC
5743 Smithway St Ste 103, Commerce
(90040-1548)
PHONE...............................323 838-5555
Florencia Cuetara, *CEO*
Theia D Ainlle Esq, *Sr VP*
EMP: 38 **EST:** 2014
SALES (est): 4.46MM **Privately Held**
Web: www.balancefoods.net
SIC: 5145 2096 Snack foods; Potato chips and similar snacks

(P-10842)
CALBEE AMERICA INCORPORATED
3625 Del Amo Blvd Ste 235, Torrance
(90503-1696)
PHONE...............................310 370-2500
EMP: 88
Web: www.calbeena.com
SIC: 5145 Confectionery
HQ: Calbee America Incorporated
2600 Maxwell Way
Fairfield CA 94534
707 427-2500

(P-10843)
CENTURY SNACKS LLC
5560 E Slauson Ave, Commerce
(90040-2921)
PHONE...............................323 278-9578
Valerie Oswalt, *CEO*
David Lowe, *
Tiffany Obenchain, *
Mel Deane, *Vice Chairman**
Stephen Famolaro, *
EMP: 330 **EST:** 1999
SQ FT: 280,000
SALES (est): 18.17MM
SALES (corp-wide): 118.93MM **Privately Held**
Web: www.centurysnacks.com
SIC: 5145 2064 Nuts, salted or roasted; Nuts, candy covered
HQ: Scncs, Llc
5560 E Slauson Ave
Commerce CA 90040
323 278-9578

(P-10844)
CONSOLIDATED SVC DISTRS INC
Also Called: Jacks Candy
777 S Central Ave, Los Angeles
(90021-1507)
PHONE...............................908 687-5800
Steven Simon, *Pr*
Herbert Lefkowitz, *
Mark Leskowitz, *
Bill German, *
▲ **EMP:** 85 **EST:** 1937
SALES (est): 9.51MM **Privately Held**
Web: www.jackscandy.com
SIC: 5145 5194 Candy; Tobacco and tobacco products

(P-10845)
ENERGY CLUB INC
Also Called: Energy Club
12950 Pierce St, Pacoima (91331-2526)
▲ **EMP:** 80 **EST:** 1984

PRODUCTS & SVCS

SALES (est): 3.86MM
SALES (corp-wide): 5.29MM **Privately Held**
SIC: 5145 2099 Confectionery; Food preparations, nec
PA: Shackleton Equity Partners Llc
　　4119 Guardian St
　　310 733-5658

(P-10846)
FRITO-LAY NORTH AMERICA INC
Also Called: Frito-Lay
28801 Highway 58, Bakersfield (93314-9000)
PHONE..............................661 328-6034
Jason Audler, *Mgr*
EMP: 116
SALES (corp-wide): 86.39B **Publicly Held**
Web: www.fritolay.com
SIC: 5145 Snack foods
HQ: Frito-Lay North America, Inc.
　　7701 Legacy Dr
　　Plano TX 75024

(P-10847)
FRITO-LAY NORTH AMERICA INC
Also Called: Frito-Lay
9846 4th St, Rancho Cucamonga (91730-5720)
PHONE..............................909 941-6218
George Smith, *Mgr*
EMP: 31
SALES (corp-wide): 86.39B **Publicly Held**
Web: www.fritolay.com
SIC: 5145 2099 2096 Snack foods; Food preparations, nec; Potato chips and similar snacks
HQ: Frito-Lay North America, Inc.
　　7701 Legacy Dr
　　Plano TX 75024

(P-10848)
FRITO-LAY NORTH AMERICA INC
Also Called: Frito-Lay
9535 Archibald Ave, Rancho Cucamonga (91730-5737)
PHONE..............................909 941-6214
Brian Birrell, *Mgr*
EMP: 500
SALES (corp-wide): 86.39B **Publicly Held**
Web: www.fritolay.com
SIC: 5145 Snack foods
HQ: Frito-Lay North America, Inc.
　　7701 Legacy Dr
　　Plano TX 75024

(P-10849)
LAYMON CANDY CO INC
276 Commercial Rd, San Bernardino (92408-4149)
PHONE..............................909 825-4408
Kenneth Laymon, *Pr*
Paul T Applen, *
▲ **EMP:** 27 **EST:** 1927
SQ FT: 43,000
SALES (est): 8.21MM **Privately Held**
Web: www.laymoncandy.com
SIC: 5145 2064 Candy; Candy and other confectionery products

(P-10850)
S&E GOURMET CUTS INC
Also Called: Country Archer Jerky
1055 E Cooley Ave, San Bernardino (92408-2819)
PHONE..............................909 370-0155

Eugene Kang, *CEO*
Adam Razik, *
Susan Kang, *
EMP: 150 **EST:** 2011
SALES (est): 45.02MM **Privately Held**
Web: www.countryarcher.com
SIC: 5145 2013 Confectionery; Sausages and other prepared meats

(P-10851)
YOUBAR INC (PA)
445 Wilson Way, City Of Industry (91744-3935)
PHONE..............................626 537-1851
Anthony Flynn, *CEO*
Anthony M Flynn, *
EMP: 49 **EST:** 2007
SALES (est): 21.62MM **Privately Held**
Web: www.youbars.com
SIC: 5145 5812 2064 Snack foods; Food bars; Granola and muesli, bars and clusters

---

5146 Fish And Seafoods

(P-10852)
DEL MAR SEAFOODS INC
1449 Spinnaker Dr, Ventura (93001-4355)
PHONE..............................805 850-0421
EMP: 185
Web: www.delmarseafoods.com
SIC: 5146 Seafoods
PA: Del Mar Seafoods, Inc.
　　331 Ford St

(P-10853)
DULCICH INC
Also Called: Pacific Seafood of Los Angeles
605 Flint Ave, Wilmington (90744-6110)
PHONE..............................310 835-4343
Frank M Dulcich, *Brnch Mgr*
EMP: 319
SALES (corp-wide): 647.74MM **Privately Held**
Web: www.pacificseafood.com
SIC: 5146 Fish, cured
PA: Dulcich, Inc.
　　16797 Se 130th Ave
　　503 226-2200

(P-10854)
H & N FOODS INTERNATIONAL INC (HQ)
Also Called: H & N Fish Co.
5580 S Alameda St, Vernon (90058-3426)
PHONE..............................323 586-9300
Hua Thanh Ngo, *Pr*
Christine Ngo, *
Bobby Ngo, *
Dat Trieu, *
◆ **EMP:** 125 **EST:** 1981
SQ FT: 45,000
SALES (est): 13.83MM
SALES (corp-wide): 28.84MM **Privately Held**
Web: www.hngroup.com
SIC: 5146 Seafoods
PA: H & N Group, Inc.
　　5580 S Alameda St
　　323 586-9388

(P-10855)
H & T SEAFOOD INC
Also Called: Global Nature Foods
5598 Lindbergh Ln, Bell (90201-6410)
PHONE..............................323 526-0888
Ivy N Tran, *CEO*
Thong Lu, *
◆ **EMP:** 41 **EST:** 1994
SQ FT: 120,000

SALES (est): 1.86MM **Privately Held**
Web: www.htseafood.com
SIC: 5146 2092 Fish and seafoods; Fresh or frozen fish or seafood chowders, soups, and stews

(P-10856)
KINGS SEAFOOD COMPANY LLC
7691 Edinger Ave, Huntington Beach (92647-3604)
PHONE..............................714 793-1177
Malia Cappuccio, *Brnch Mgr*
EMP: 770
Web: www.kingsseafood.com
SIC: 5146 Seafoods
PA: King's Seafood Company, Llc
　　3185 Airway Ave Ste J

(P-10857)
PLD ENTERPRISES INC
Also Called: Superior Seafood Co
440 Stanford Ave, Los Angeles (90013-2121)
PHONE..............................213 626-4444
Chip Mezin, *Genl Mgr*
EMP: 70
SIC: 5146 Fish and seafoods
PA: P.L.D. Enterprises, Inc.
　　1621 W 25th St Ste 228

(P-10858)
PROSPECT ENTERPRISES INC (PA)
Also Called: American Fish and Seafood
625 Kohler St, Los Angeles (90021-1023)
PHONE..............................213 599-5700
Ernest Y Doizaki, *Ch Bd*
Jack King, *
Paula Eberhardt, *
◆ **EMP:** 160 **EST:** 1947
SQ FT: 20,000
SALES (est): 47.37MM
SALES (corp-wide): 47.37MM **Privately Held**
Web: www.kansasmarine.com
SIC: 5146 2092 Fish, fresh; Fresh or frozen packaged fish

(P-10859)
QUALY PAK SPECIALTY FOODS INC
2208 Signal Pl, San Pedro (90731-7227)
PHONE..............................310 541-3023
◆ **EMP:** 85
Web: www.qualypak.com
SIC: 5146 5142 Fish, fresh; Fish, frozen: packaged

(P-10860)
RED CHAMBER CO (PA)
1912 E Vernon Ave, Vernon (90058-1611)
PHONE..............................323 234-9000
Shan Chun Kou, *Ch Bd*
Shu Chin Kou, *Ch Bd*
Ming Bin Kou, *CEO*
◆ **EMP:** 341 **EST:** 1974
SQ FT: 15,000
SALES (est): 94.16MM
SALES (corp-wide): 94.16MM **Privately Held**
Web: www.redchamber.com
SIC: 5146 4222 Seafoods; Warehousing, cold storage or refrigerated

(P-10861)
SBS ACQUISITION COMPANY LLC ✪
Also Called: Santa Barbara Smokehouse

312 N Nopal St, Santa Barbara (93103-3225)
PHONE..............................805 966-9796
Darcy Zbinovec, *Mgr*
Michael A Foisy, *Mgr*
EMP: 100 **EST:** 2024
SALES (est): 9.13MM
SALES (corp-wide): 32.01MM **Privately Held**
SIC: 5146 Fish, cured
PA: Panos Intermediate Holdings, Llc
　　8888 Kystne Crssing Ste 6

(P-10862)
SHINING OCEAN INC
10888 7th St, Rancho Cucamonga (91730-5421)
PHONE..............................253 826-3700
Daryl Gormley, *CEO*
Michael Beauregard, *
Matthew Lacki, *
◆ **EMP:** 140 **EST:** 1985
SALES (est): 4.73MM
SALES (corp-wide): 6.15MM **Privately Held**
Web: www.kanimi.com
SIC: 5146 Seafoods
PA: Aquamar Holdings, Inc.
　　10888 7th St
　　909 481-4700

(P-10863)
TRI-MARINE FISH COMPANY LLC
220 Cannery St, San Pedro (90731-7308)
PHONE..............................310 547-1144
Vince Torre, *Managing Member*
◆ **EMP:** 75 **EST:** 2001
SQ FT: 30,000
SALES (est): 2.54MM **Privately Held**
SIC: 5146 Seafoods

(P-10864)
TRI-UNION SEAFOODS LLC (DH)
Also Called: Chicken of Sea International
2150 E Grand Ave, El Segundo (90245-5024)
P.O. Box 85568 (92186-5568)
PHONE..............................424 397-8556
Valentin Ramirez, *CEO*
Christie Fleming, *
Jim Cox, *
Ignatius Dharma, *
David E Roszmann, *
◆ **EMP:** 69 **EST:** 1996
SQ FT: 24,000
SALES (est): 139.17MM **Privately Held**
SIC: 5146 2091 Seafoods; Tuna fish: packaged in cans, jars, etc.
HQ: Thai Union North America, Inc.
　　2150 E Grand Ave
　　El Segundo CA 90245
　　424 397-8556

5147 Meats And Meat Products

(P-10865)
BICARA LTD
318 Avenue I Ste 65, Redondo Beach (90277-5601)
PHONE..............................310 316-6222
William Jeffrey Hughes, *CEO*
William D Hughes, *
Raymond Rosenthal, *
◆ **EMP:** 300 **EST:** 1948
SQ FT: 105,000
SALES (est): 4.56MM **Privately Held**

SIC: **5147** 5146 5141 Meats and meat products; Seafoods; Groceries, general line

(P-10866)
BRIDGFORD MARKETING COMPANY (DH)
1308 N Patt St, Anaheim (92801-2551)
P.O. Box 3773 (92803-3773)
PHONE..............................714 526-5533
Allan L Bridgford, *Ch*
Allan L Bridgford Senior, *Ch*
William L Bridgford, *
John Simmons, *
Ray Lancey, *
EMP: 89 **EST:** 1957
SQ FT: 100,000
SALES (est): 10.4MM
SALES (corp-wide): 503.53MM **Publicly Held**
Web: www.bridgford.com
SIC: 5147 5149 Meats and meat products; Bakery products
HQ: Bridgford Foods Corporation
1707 S Good Latimer Expy
Dallas TX 75226
214 428-1535

(P-10867)
DEL MAR HOLDING LLC
1022 Bay Marina Dr # 10, National City (91950-6398)
PHONE..............................313 659-7300
Leon Bergmann, *CEO*
Joel Jorgensen, *
EMP: 1600 **EST:** 2016
SALES (est): 2MM **Privately Held**
SIC: 5147 Meats and meat products

(P-10868)
EASTLAND CORPORATION
Also Called: C & H Meat Company
3017 Bandini Blvd, Vernon (90058-4109)
PHONE..............................323 261-5388
Young Yoo, *Pr*
Young Won, *
EMP: 23 **EST:** 1973
SQ FT: 10,000
SALES (est): 5.8MM **Privately Held**
Web: www.candhmeatco.com
SIC: 5147 2013 Meats, fresh; Cooked meats, from purchased meat

(P-10869)
HARVEST MEAT COMPANY INC
Also Called: HARVEST MEAT COMPANY, INC.
1022 Bay Marina Dr Ste 106, National City (91950-6327)
PHONE..............................619 477-0185
Jonathan Leavy, *Brnch Mgr*
EMP: 100
SALES (corp-wide): 529.51MM **Privately Held**
Web: www.harvestfooddistributors.com
SIC: 5147 Meats, fresh
HQ: Harvest Meat Company Inc
1000 Bay Marina Dr
National City CA 91950

(P-10870)
HARVEST MEAT COMPANY INC (HQ)
Also Called: Harvest Food Distributors
1000 Bay Marina Dr, National City (91950-6302)
PHONE..............................619 477-0185
Leon Bergmann, *CEO*
◆ **EMP:** 80 **EST:** 1994
SQ FT: 60,000
SALES (est): 226.66MM

SALES (corp-wide): 529.51MM **Privately Held**
Web: www.harvestfooddistributors.com
SIC: 5147 Meats, fresh
PA: Del Mar Holdings, L.L.C.
12499 Evergreen Rd
313 659-7300

(P-10871)
HEARTLAND MEAT COMPANY INC
Also Called: H M C
3461 Main St, Chula Vista (91911-5828)
PHONE..............................619 407-3668
TOLL FREE: 800
Joseph E Stidman, *CEO*
James Methey, *
Stephanie Stidman, *
EMP: 70 **EST:** 1971
SQ FT: 49,000
SALES (est): 23.07MM **Privately Held**
Web: www.heartlandmeat.com
SIC: 5147 2013 Meats, fresh; Sausages and other prepared meats

(P-10872)
HV RANDALL FOODS LLC (PA)
2900 Ayers Ave, Vernon (90058-4304)
P.O. Box 2669 (90255)
PHONE..............................323 261-6565
Mike Buccheri, *CEO*
Matt Ellis, *
John Whatley, *
Mario Valdovino, *CIO*
David Minx, *CPO*
EMP: 140 **EST:** 2020
SALES (est): 63.43MM
SALES (corp-wide): 63.43MM **Privately Held**
Web: www.randallfoods.com
SIC: 5147 Meats and meat products

(P-10873)
JENSEN MEAT COMPANY INC
2550 Britannia Blvd Ste 101, San Diego (92154-7408)
PHONE..............................619 754-6400
Abel Olivera, *CEO*
Sam Acuna, *
Jeff Hamann, *
EMP: 95 **EST:** 1958
SQ FT: 25,000
SALES (est): 95.16MM **Privately Held**
Web: www.jensenmeat.com
SIC: 5147 Meats, fresh

(P-10874)
JETRO CASH AND CARRY ENTPS LLC
Also Called: Restaurant Depot
1700 Main St, San Diego (92113-1025)
PHONE..............................619 233-0200
Frank Shapiro, *Brnch Mgr*
EMP: 100
Web: www.restaurantdepot.com
SIC: 5147 5141 5142 5181 Meats, fresh; Groceries, general line; Packaged frozen goods; Beer and other fermented malt liquors
HQ: Jetro Cash And Carry Enterprises, Llc
1710 Whitestone Expy
Whitestone NY 11357
718 762-8700

(P-10875)
L & T MEAT CO
3050 E 11th St, Los Angeles (90023-3606)
PHONE..............................323 262-2815
Chak Por Tea, *Pr*
Bobby Lu, *

EMP: 80 **EST:** 1995
SQ FT: 20,000
SALES (est): 3.65MM **Privately Held**
Web: www.ltmeat.com
SIC: 5147 Meats, fresh

(P-10876)
MPCI HOLDINGS INC
Also Called: Monterrey The Natural Choice
7850 Waterville Rd, San Diego (92154-8205)
P.O. Box 81046 (92138-1046)
PHONE..............................619 294-2222
TOLL FREE: 800
▲ **EMP:** 130
SIC: 5147 5143 5148 5113 Meats, fresh; Cheese; Fresh fruits and vegetables; Disposable plates, cups, napkins, and eating utensils

(P-10877)
NEWPORT MEAT SOUTHERN CAL INC
Also Called: Newport Meat Company
16691 Hale Ave, Irvine (92606-5025)
PHONE..............................949 399-4200
Timothy K Hussman, *CEO*
Denise Van Voorhis, *
EMP: 227 **EST:** 1976
SQ FT: 92,000
SALES (est): 26.75MM
SALES (corp-wide): 78.84B **Publicly Held**
Web: www.newportmeat.com
SIC: 5147 5142 Meats, fresh; Packaged frozen goods
PA: Sysco Corporation
1390 Enclave Pkwy
281 584-1390

(P-10878)
PRODUCERS MEAT AND PROV INC
Also Called: Tarantino Wholesale Fd Distrs
7651 Saint Andrews Ave, San Diego (92154-8209)
PHONE..............................619 232-7593
Rose M Tarantino, *CEO*
▲ **EMP:** 35 **EST:** 1961
SQ FT: 10,000
SALES (est): 3.03MM **Privately Held**
SIC: 5147 2013 Meats, fresh; Sausages and other prepared meats

(P-10879)
RANCHO FOODS INC
2528 E 37th St, Vernon (90058-1725)
P.O. Box 58504 (90058-0504)
PHONE..............................323 585-0503
Annette Mac Donald, *Pr*
John Mac Donald, *VP*
EMP: 100 **EST:** 1972
SQ FT: 26,000
SALES (est): 38.13MM **Privately Held**
Web: www.ranchofoods.com
SIC: 5147 2013 Meats, fresh; Sausages and other prepared meats

(P-10880)
RW ZANT LLC (DH)
1470 E 4th St, Los Angeles (90033-4288)
PHONE..............................323 980-5457
Robert W Zant, *Pr*
William Zant, *
▲ **EMP:** 90 **EST:** 1950
SQ FT: 42,000
SALES (est): 18.62MM
SALES (corp-wide): 1.24B **Privately Held**
Web: www.rwzant.com

SIC: **5147** 5146 5144 4222 Meats, fresh; Fish and seafoods; Poultry and poultry products; Cheese warehouse
HQ: Honor Holdings Inc.
5505 Tacony St
Philadelphia PA 19137
215 236-1700

(P-10881)
STROUK GROUP LLC
Also Called: Monsieur Marcel
6333 W 3rd St Ste 150, Los Angeles (90036-3191)
PHONE..............................323 939-7792
Stephane Strouk, *Pr*
Katrin Strouk, *
EMP: 105 **EST:** 1998
SALES (est): 13.9MM **Privately Held**
Web: www.mrmarcel.com
SIC: 5147 5143 5812 Meats and meat products; Cheese; French restaurant

(P-10882)
SYDNEY & ANNE BLOOM FARMS INC
Also Called: Randall Farms
2900 Ayers Ave, Vernon (90058-4304)
P.O. Box 2669 (90255-8069)
PHONE..............................323 261-6565
EMP: 545 **EST:** 1952
SALES (est): 87.28MM **Privately Held**
Web: www.randallfoods.com
SIC: 5147 7299 Meats and meat products; Butcher service, processing only - does not sell meat

(P-10883)
THREE SONS INC
Also Called: Merit Day Food Service
5201 Industry Ave, Pico Rivera (90660-2505)
P.O. Box 6 (90660-0006)
PHONE..............................562 801-4100
Michael Shannon Day, *CEO*
John Brenan, *
David Day, *Stockholder*
Mariellen Day, *Stockholder*
Michael Day, *Stockholder*
▲ **EMP:** 87 **EST:** 1975
SQ FT: 40,000
SALES (est): 17.03MM **Privately Held**
Web: www.americanmeatcompanies.com
SIC: 5147 2013 2011 Meats, cured or smoked; Sausages and other prepared meats; Meat packing plants

5148 Fresh Fruits And Vegetables

(P-10884)
4 EARTH FARMS LLC (PA)
Also Called: McL Fresh
5555 E Olympic Blvd, Los Angeles (90022-5129)
PHONE..............................323 201-5800
David Lake, *CEO*
Robert Lake, *
◆ **EMP:** 329 **EST:** 1993
SQ FT: 165,000
SALES (est): 31.06MM **Privately Held**
Web: www.4earthfarms.com
SIC: 5148 4783 Fresh fruits and vegetables; Containerization of goods for shipping

(P-10885)
AGRI-EMPIRE
630 W 7th St, San Jacinto (92583-4015)
P.O. Box 490 (92581-0490)
PHONE..............................951 654-7311

Larry J Minor, *Pr*
EMP: 120 **EST:** 1943
SQ FT: 5,000
SALES (est): 10.27MM **Privately Held**
Web: www.agri-empire.com
SIC: 5148 Potatoes, fresh

(P-10886)
ALL ABOUT PRODUCE COMPANY
712 Fiero Ln Ste 30, San Luis Obispo
(93401-8705)
PHONE...............805 543-9000
Guy Demangeon, *Pr*
EMP: 120 **EST:** 1993
SALES (est): 2.09MM **Privately Held**
SIC: 5148 Fruits, fresh
PA: The Berry Man Inc
205 W Montecito St

(P-10887)
BORG PRODUCE SALES LLC
1601 E Olympic Blvd Ste 100, Los Angeles
(90021-1940)
P.O. Box 21008 (90021-0008)
PHONE...............213 624-2674
▲ **EMP:** 170
SIC: 5148 Fresh fruits and vegetables

(P-10888)
BOSKOVICH FRESH CUT LLC
711 Diaz Ave, Oxnard (93030-7247)
P.O. Box 1272 (93032-1272)
PHONE...............805 487-2299
George Boskovich, *CEO*
George Boskovich, *Managing Member*
Lina Perez, *
EMP: 250 **EST:** 2018
SALES (est): 18.23MM **Privately Held**
Web: www.boskovichfarms.com
SIC: 5148 Vegetables, fresh

(P-10889)
BUY FRESH PRODUCE INC
6636 E 26th St, Commerce (90040-3216)
PHONE...............323 796-0127
Ted Kasnetsis, *Pr*
Traci Kasnetsis, *
EMP: 80 **EST:** 2005
SQ FT: 23,500
SALES (est): 9.93MM **Privately Held**
Web: www.buyfreshproduceinc.com
SIC: 5148 Fruits, fresh

(P-10890)
COAST CITRUS DISTRIBUTORS (PA)
Also Called: Coast Tropical
7597 Bristow Ct, San Diego (92154-7419)
P.O. Box 530369 (92153-0369)
PHONE...............619 661-7950
James M Alvarez, *Ch Bd*
Margarita Alvarez, *
◆ **EMP:** 100 **EST:** 1950
SQ FT: 80,000
SALES (est): 87.99MM
SALES (corp-wide): 87.99MM **Privately Held**
Web: www.coasttropical.com
SIC: 5148 Fruits, fresh

(P-10891)
COAST PRODUCE COMPANY (PA)
1791 Bay St, Los Angeles (90021-1655)
P.O. Box 86468 (90086-0468)
PHONE...............213 955-4900
Mike Ito, *CEO*
John K Dunn, *

Rick Uyeno, *
▲ **EMP:** 165 **EST:** 1955
SQ FT: 80,000
SALES (est): 24.82MM
SALES (corp-wide): 24.82MM **Privately Held**
Web: www.coastproduce.com
SIC: 5148 Fruits, fresh

(P-10892)
D&D WHOLESALE DISTRIBUTORS LLC
777 Baldwin Park Blvd, City Of Industry
(91746-1504)
PHONE...............626 333-2111
Joe Dupree, *Pr*
Pamela Dupree, *
EMP: 90 **EST:** 1979
SQ FT: 20,000
SALES (est): 9.77MM **Privately Held**
Web: www.ddwholesale.com
SIC: 5148 5143 Fruits, fresh; Dairy products, except dried or canned

(P-10893)
DAVALAN SALES INC
Also Called: Davalan Fresh
1601 E Olympic Blvd Ste 325, Los Angeles
(90021-1957)
PHONE...............213 623-2500
Alan Frick, *Pr*
Dave Bouton, *
▲ **EMP:** 200 **EST:** 1983
SQ FT: 15,000
SALES (est): 23.92MM **Privately Held**
Web: www.davalanfresh.com
SIC: 5148 Fruits, fresh

(P-10894)
DEL MONTE FRESH PRODUCE CO
10730 Patterson Pl, Santa Fe Springs
(90670-4025)
PHONE...............562 777-1127
Oscar Chawdhry, *Mgr*
EMP: 77
Web: www.freshdelmonte.com
SIC: 5148 Fruits, fresh
HQ: Del Monte Fresh Produce Company
241 Sevilla Ave
Coral Gables FL 33134
305 520-8400

(P-10895)
EVOLUTION FRESH INC
Also Called: Evolution Juice
11655 Jersey Blvd Ste A, Rancho
Cucamonga (91730-4903)
PHONE...............800 794-9986
Chris Bruzzo, *CEO*
Ricki Reves, *CFO*
▲ **EMP:** 180 **EST:** 2010
SQ FT: 70,000
SALES (est): 105.1MM
SALES (corp-wide): 562.6MM **Privately Held**
Web: www.evolutionfresh.com
SIC: 5148 2037 Fruits, fresh; Frozen fruits and vegetables
HQ: Wm. Bolthouse Farms, Inc.
7200 E Brundage Ln
Bakersfield CA 93307
800 467-4683

(P-10896)
FAMILY TREE PRODUCE INC
5510 E La Palma Ave, Anaheim
(92807-2108)
PHONE...............714 693-5688
Fidel Guzman, *Pr*

Christy Guzman, *
EMP: 115 **EST:** 1975
SQ FT: 33,000
SALES (est): 19.87MM **Privately Held**
Web: www.familytreeproduce.com
SIC: 5148 Fruits, fresh

(P-10897)
FIELD FRESH FOODS INCORPORATED
14805 S San Pedro St, Gardena
(90248-2030)
P.O. Box 3877 (90247-7577)
PHONE...............310 719-8422
EMP: 600 **EST:** 1994
SALES (est): 27.39MM **Privately Held**
Web: www.fieldfresh.com
SIC: 5148 Vegetables, fresh
PA: Del Monte Foods Private Limited
First Floor, Tower C-2, Survey No.
155/1 To 157/2,

(P-10898)
FRESHPOINT INC
Also Called: Freshpoint Las Vegas
155 N Orange Ave, City Of Industry
(91744-3432)
PHONE...............626 855-1400
Terry Owen, *Pr*
EMP: 191
SALES (corp-wide): 78.84B **Publicly Held**
Web: www.freshpoint.com
SIC: 5148 Fresh fruits and vegetables
HQ: Freshpoint, Inc.
1390 Enclave Parkway
Houston TX 77077

(P-10899)
FRESHPOINT SOUTHERN CAL INC
Also Called: Freshpoint Southern California
155 N Orange Ave, City Of Industry
(91744-3432)
PHONE...............626 855-1400
Verne L Lusby Junior, *CEO*
Robert Gordon, *
Jim Procuniar, *
Rich Dachman, *
Jeff Ronk, *
EMP: 208 **EST:** 1921
SQ FT: 97,000
SALES (est): 21.81MM
SALES (corp-wide): 78.84B **Publicly Held**
Web: www.freshpoint.com
SIC: 5148 5142 Fruits, fresh; Packaged frozen goods
PA: Sysco Corporation
1390 Enclave Pkwy
281 584-1390

(P-10900)
FRIEDAS INC
Also Called: Friedas Specialty Produce
1765 W Penhall Way, Anaheim
(92801-6728)
PHONE...............714 826-6100
Karen Caplan, *Pr*
Jackie Caplan-wiggins, *VP*
▲ **EMP:** 75 **EST:** 1962
SALES (est): 22.03MM **Privately Held**
Web: www.friedas.com
SIC: 5148 5499 7389 Vegetables, fresh;
Dried fruit; Labeling bottles, cans, cartons, etc.

(P-10901)
FRUIT GROWERS SUPPLY COMPANY
225 S Wineville Ave, Ontario (91761-7891)

PHONE...............909 390-0190
Steve Moore, *Mgr*
EMP: 75
SALES (corp-wide): 122.9MM **Privately Held**
Web: www.fruitgrowers.com
SIC: 5148 Fruits, fresh
PA: Fruit Growers Supply Company Inc
27770 N Entrmt Dr Fl 3 Flr 3
888 997-4855

(P-10902)
GIUMARRA AGRICOM INTL LLC
15651 Old Milky Way, Escondido
(92027-7104)
PHONE...............760 480-8502
Don Corsaro, *Brnch Mgr*
EMP: 1873
SALES (corp-wide): 72.36MM **Privately Held**
Web: www.giumarra.com
SIC: 5148 Fruits
HQ: Giumarra Agricom International Llc
1601 E Olympic Blvd
Los Angeles CA 90021

(P-10903)
GIUMARRA BROS FRUIT CO INC (PA)
Also Called: Giumarra International Berry
1601 E Olympic Blvd Ste 400, Los Angeles
(90021-1943)
P.O. Box 861449 (90086-1449)
PHONE...............213 627-2900
Donald Corsaro, *Ch*
John Giumarra Junior, *Treas*
John Corsaro, *
◆ **EMP:** 74 **EST:** 1950
SQ FT: 8,000
SALES (est): 23.77MM
SALES (corp-wide): 23.77MM **Privately Held**
Web: www.giumarra.com
SIC: 5148 Fresh fruits and vegetables

(P-10904)
GOURMET SPECIALTIES INC
2120 E 25th St, Vernon (90058-1126)
PHONE...............323 587-1734
Abundio Ruiz, *CEO*
EMP: 75 **EST:** 2010
SALES (est): 9.99MM **Privately Held**
SIC: 5148 Fresh fruits and vegetables

(P-10905)
GREEN FARMS INC
Also Called: Worldwide Produce
2652 Long Beach Ave, Los Angeles
(90058-1323)
PHONE...............858 831-7701
Abbas Ghulam, *Brnch Mgr*
EMP: 89
SALES (corp-wide): 116.63MM **Privately Held**
Web: www.wwproduce.com
SIC: 5148 Fresh fruits and vegetables
HQ: Green Farms California, Llc
2652 Long Beach Ave Ste 2
Los Angeles CA 90058

(P-10906)
GRIMMWAY ENTERPRISES INC
Also Called: Cal-Organic Farms
12000 Main St, Lamont (93241-2836)
P.O. Box 81498 (93380-1498)
PHONE...............661 845-3758
Roodzant Steve, *Genl Mgr*
EMP: 404
SALES (corp-wide): 577.4MM **Privately Held**

▲ = Import ▼ = Export
◆ = Import/Export

Web: www.grimmway.com
SIC: 5148 Vegetables, fresh
PA: Grimmway Enterprises, Inc.
12064 Buena Vista Blvd
800 301-3101

(P-10907)
HOLLANDIA OXNARD
Also Called: Pete's
6135 N Rose Ave, Oxnard (93036-1033)
PHONE.........................805 886-1272
Brian Cook, CEO
EMP: 150 EST: 2018
SALES (est): 3.37MM
SALES (corp-wide): 27.56MM **Publicly Held**
SIC: 5148 Fresh fruits and vegetables
PA: Local Bounti Corporation
490 Foley Ln
406 361-3711

(P-10908)
INDEX FRESH INC (PA)
1250 Corona Pointe Ct Ste 401, Corona
(92879-1781)
PHONE.........................909 877-0999
TOLL FREE: 800
Dana L Thomas, Pr
Merrill Causey, *
Giovanni Cavaletto, *
◆ EMP: 52 EST: 1914
SQ FT: 40,000
SALES (est): 42.94MM
SALES (corp-wide): 42.94MM **Privately Held**
Web: www.indexfresh.com
SIC: 5148 2099 Fruits, fresh; Vegetables, peeled for the trade

(P-10909)
INGARDIA BROS PRODUCE INC
700 S Hathaway St, Santa Ana
(92705-4126)
PHONE.........................949 645-1365
EMP: 190 EST: 1973
SALES (est): 21.78MM **Privately Held**
Web: www.ingardiabros.com
SIC: 5148 5146 Fresh fruits and vegetables; Seafoods

(P-10910)
LA SPECIALTY PRODUCE CO (PA)
Also Called: Vesta Foodservice
13527 Orden Dr, Santa Fe Springs
(90670-6338)
P.O. Box 2293 (90670-0293)
PHONE.........................562 711 2200
Michael Glick, CEO
Scott Parra-matthews, CFO
EMP: 375 EST: 1985
SQ FT: 188,000
SALES (est): 210.39MM
SALES (corp-wide): 210.39MM **Privately Held**
Web: www.vestafoodservice.com
SIC: 5148 Fruits, fresh

(P-10911)
LEGACY FARMS LLC
1765 W Penhall Way, Anaheim
(92801-6728)
PHONE.........................714 736-1800
Nick Cancellieri, Managing Member
Ron Shimizu, Managing Member
Michael Sanders, Managing Member
▲ EMP: 100 EST: 1991
SQ FT: 95,000
SALES (est): 17.2MM **Privately Held**
Web: www.legacyproduce.com

SIC: 5148 Fruits, fresh

(P-10912)
NATURES PRODUCE
3305 Bandini Blvd, Vernon (90058-4130)
P.O. Box 58366 (90058-0366)
PHONE.........................323 235-4343
Rick Polisky, CEO
▲ EMP: 110 EST: 2000
SALES (est): 24.07MM **Privately Held**
Web: www.naturesproduce.com
SIC: 5148 Fruits, fresh

(P-10913)
PACIFIC TRELLIS FRUIT LLC (PA)
Also Called: Borg Produce Sales
2301 E 7th St Ste C200, Los Angeles
(90023-1041)
PHONE.........................323 859-9600
Josh Leichter, CEO
David Sullivan, *
▲ EMP: 130 EST: 1999
SQ FT: 10,000
SALES (est): 89.46MM
SALES (corp-wide): 89.46MM **Privately Held**
Web: www.dulcinea.com
SIC: 5148 Fruits, fresh

(P-10914)
PRIMETIME INTERNATIONAL INC
47110 Washington St Ste 103, La Quinta
(92253-2186)
PHONE.........................760 399-4166
Mark Nickerson, Managing Member*
Mike Way, Managing Member*
Jeff Taylor, Managing Member*
▲ EMP: 95 EST: 1994
SALES (est): 9.66MM **Privately Held**
Web: www.primetimeproduce.com
SIC: 5148 4783 Vegetables, fresh; Packing goods for shipping
PA: Sun And Sands Enterprises, Llc
47110 Washington St # 103

(P-10915)
PROFESSIONAL PRODUCE
2570 E 25th St, Los Angeles (90058-1211)
P.O. Box 58308 (90058-0308)
PHONE.........................323 277-1550
Ted Kaplan, CEO
Maribel Reyes, *
◆ EMP: 99 EST: 1994
SQ FT: 5,000
SALES (est): 23.42MM **Privately Held**
Web: www.profproduce.com
SIC: 5148 Fruits, fresh

(P-10916)
SEASON PRODUCE CO INC
1601 E Olympic Blvd Ste 315, Los Angeles
(90021-1942)
PHONE.........................213 689-0008
Patrick R Horwath, Pr
Daniel Horwath, *
Timothy R Horwath, *
EMP: 353 EST: 1958
SQ FT: 20,000
SALES (est): 7.47MM
SALES (corp-wide): 17.86MM **Privately Held**
SIC: 5148 Fresh fruits and vegetables
PA: S & H Packing & Sales Co., Inc.
2590 Harriet St
323 581-7172

(P-10917)
SHAPIRO-GILMAN-SHANDLER CO
Also Called: S G S Produce
739 Decatur St, Los Angeles (90021-1649)
PHONE.........................213 593-1200
Minyi Xu, CEO
Carol C Shandler, *
Morris Shander, *
Muriel Shandler, *
▲ EMP: 101 EST: 1907
SQ FT: 50,000
SALES (est): 22.62MM
SALES (corp-wide): 297.68MM **Privately Held**
Web: www.sgsproduce.com
SIC: 5148 Fruits, fresh
PA: Grubmarket, Inc.
1925 Jerrold Ave
415 986-0523

(P-10918)
SUN PACIFIC MARKETING COOP INC
Also Called: Sun Pacific Farming
31452 Old River Rd, Bakersfield
(93311-9621)
PHONE.........................661 847-1015
Bob Dipiazza, Brnch Mgr
EMP: 395
SALES (corp-wide): 97.84MM **Privately Held**
Web: www.sunpacific.com
SIC: 5148 Fresh fruits and vegetables
PA: Sun Pacific Marketing Cooperative, Inc.
1095 E Green St
213 612-9957

(P-10919)
SUNKIST GROWERS INC (PA)
27770 Entertainment Dr, Valencia
(91355-1092)
PHONE.........................661 290-8900
Russell Hanlin Ii, Pr
Richard G French, VP
Michael Wootton, Sr VP
John Mc Guigan, VP
Russell L Hanlin Ii, VP
◆ EMP: 223 EST: 1893
SQ FT: 50,000
SALES (est): 81.32MM
SALES (corp-wide): 81.32MM **Privately Held**
Web: www.sunkist.com
SIC: 5148 2033 2037 2899 Fruits, fresh; Fruit juices: packaged in cans, jars, etc.; Fruit juice concentrates, frozen; Lemon oil (edible)

(P-10920)
SUNRISE GROWERS INC
701 W Kimberly Ave Ste 210, Placentia
(92870-6354)
PHONE.........................714 706-6090
▼ EMP: 140
SIC: 5148 Fruits

(P-10921)
V & L PRODUCE INC
Also Called: General Produce
2550 E 25th St, Vernon (90058-1211)
PHONE.........................323 589-3125
Victor Mendoza, Pr
▲ EMP: 140 EST: 1984
SQ FT: 12,000
SALES (est): 8.48MM **Privately Held**
Web: www.vlproduce.com
SIC: 5148 Fresh fruits and vegetables

(P-10922)
VAL-PRO INC (PA)
Also Called: Valley Fruit and Produce Co
748 S Alameda St, Los Angeles
(90021-1616)
PHONE.........................213 627-8736
◆ EMP: 170 EST: 1920
SALES (est): 19.42MM
SALES (corp-wide): 19.42MM **Privately Held**
Web: www.valleyproduce.com
SIC: 5148 Fruits, fresh

(P-10923)
VEG-FRESH FARMS LLC (PA)
Also Called: Veg Fresh
1400 W Rincon St, Corona (92878-9205)
PHONE.........................800 422-5535
Lawrence Cancellieri Senior, Managing Member
Mark C Widder, *
Mark Resnikoff, *
EMP: 134 EST: 1989
SQ FT: 94,000
SALES (est): 47.7MM **Privately Held**
Web: www.vegfresh.com
SIC: 5148 Vegetables, fresh

(P-10924)
VENTURA COUNTY LEMON COOP
Also Called: Ventura Pacific Co
2620 Sakioka Dr, Oxnard (93030-5647)
P.O. Box 6986 (93031-6986)
PHONE.........................805 385-3345
Donald Dames, Pr
Milton Daily, Ch Bd
James H Gill, Sec
Jim Waters, Treas
EMP: 80 EST: 1943
SALES (est): 14.18MM **Privately Held**
Web: www.venturapacific.com
SIC: 5148 4783 3999 Fruits, fresh; Containerization of goods for shipping; Fruits, artificial and preserved

(P-10925)
WEST CENTRAL PRODUCE INC
Also Called: West Central Food Service
12840 Leyva St, Norwalk (90650-6852)
P.O. Box 4664 (90607-4664)
PHONE.........................213 629-3600
Michael Dodo, CEO
Jamie Purcell, *
Lance Shiring, *
▲ EMP: 400 EST: 1970
SQ FT: 34,000
SALES (est): 25.76MM **Privately Held**
Web: www.westcentralfoodservice.com
SIC: 5148 5147 5149 5146 Fruits, fresh; Meats and meat products; Dairy products, dried or canned; Seafoods

(P-10926)
WORLD VARIETY PRODUCE INC
Also Called: Melissas World Variety Produce
5325 S Soto St, Vernon (90058-3624)
P.O. Box 514599 (90051-2599)
PHONE.........................800 588-0151
Joe V Hernandez, Prin
Joe V Hernandez, Pr
Sharon Hernandez, *
David Shafer, *
◆ EMP: 325 EST: 1983
SQ FT: 244,000
SALES (est): 32.89MM **Privately Held**
Web: www.melissas.com
SIC: 5148 Fruits, fresh

PRODUCTS & SVCS

5149 Groceries And Related Products, Nec

(P-10927)
APP WHOLESALE LLC
3686 E Olympic Blvd, Los Angeles
(90023-3146)
PHONE..............................323 980-8315
EMP: 500 EST: 2013
SQ FT: 220,000
SALES (est): 13.59MM **Privately Held**
Web: www.app-wholesale.com
SIC: 5149 2741 Specialty food items;
  Business service newsletters: publishing
  and printing

(P-10928)
ASPIRE BAKERIES LLC
Also Called: Fresh Start Bakeries
1220 S Baker Ave, Ontario (91761-7739)
P.O. Box 1283 (91802-1283)
PHONE..............................909 472-3500
Rob Crawford, *Genl Mgr*
EMP: 197
SALES (corp-wide): 1.78B **Privately Held**
Web: www.aspirebakeries.com
SIC: 5149 Bakery products
HQ: Aspire Bakeries Llc
  6701 Center Dr W Ste 850
  Los Angeles CA 90045
  844 992-7747

(P-10929)
ASPIRE BAKERIES LLC
6501 District Blvd, Bakersfield
(93313-2000)
PHONE..............................661 832-0409
EMP: 221
SALES (corp-wide): 1.78B **Privately Held**
Web: www.aspirebakeries.com
SIC: 5149 Bakery products
HQ: Aspire Bakeries Llc
  6701 Center Dr W Ste 850
  Los Angeles CA 90045
  844 992-7747

(P-10930)
BAKEMARK USA LLC (PA)
Also Called: Bakemark
7351 Crider Ave, Pico Rivera (90660-3705)
PHONE..............................562 949-1054
Jim Parker, *Managing Member*
◆ EMP: 103 EST: 1928
SQ FT: 275,000
SALES (est): 563.73MM
SALES (corp-wide): 563.73MM **Privately
Held**
Web: www.yourbakemark.com
SIC: 5149 2045 3556 2099 Bakery products;
  Flours and flour mixes, from purchased flour
  ; Food products machinery; Food
  preparations, nec

(P-10931)
**BAKERY EX SOUTHERN CAL
LLC**
1910 W Malvern Ave, Fullerton
(92833-2105)
PHONE..............................714 446-9470
EMP: 100 EST: 2001
SQ FT: 28,000
SALES (est): 8.71MM **Privately Held**
SIC: 5149 Bakery products

(P-10932)
BLUETRITON BRANDS INC
Also Called: Arrowhead Water
619 N Main St, Orange (92868-1103)

PHONE..............................714 532-6220
Dan Miller, *Mgr*
EMP: 105
SQ FT: 16,312
SALES (corp-wide): 1.3B **Privately Held**
Web: www.bluetriton.com
SIC: 5149 5499 5963 5078 Water, distilled;
  Water: distilled mineral or spring; Bottled
  water delivery; Refrigeration equipment and
  supplies
HQ: Bluetriton Brands, Inc.
  900 Long Ridge Rd Bldg 2
  Stamford CT 06902

(P-10933)
**BUENA VISTA FOOD PRODUCTS
INC (DH)**
823 W 8th St, Azusa (91702-2247)
PHONE..............................626 815-8859
Laura Trujillo, *Pr*
Michelle Reitzin-bass, *Prin*
Peter Woods, *Prin*
Mike Likovich, *Prin*
EMP: 115 EST: 1991
SALES (est): 5.07MM **Privately Held**
Web: www.bvfoods.com
SIC: 5149 Bakery products
HQ: Sterling Foods, Llc
  1075 Arion Pkwy
  San Antonio TX 78216
  210 490-1669

(P-10934)
CALIFORNIA BAKING COMPANY
Also Called: California Bread Co.
681 Anita St, Chula Vista (91911-4663)
PHONE..............................619 591-8289
Abraham Levy, *Pr*
EMP: 300 EST: 2002
SALES (est): 24.87MM **Privately Held**
Web: www.californiabaking.com
SIC: 5149 2051 Bakery products; Sponge
  goods, bakery: except frozen

(P-10935)
**CAPITOL DISTRIBUTION CO
LLC (PA)**
Also Called: Capitol Food Company
12836 Alondra Blvd, Cerritos (90703-2107)
PHONE..............................562 404-4321
Douglas L Levi, *Managing Member*
John Levi, *
Douglas Jensen, *
▲ EMP: 36 EST: 1999
SALES (est): 139.39MM
SALES (corp-wide): 139.39MM **Privately
Held**
Web: www.capitolfoodco.com
SIC: 5149 2041 Bakery products; Biscuit
  dough

(P-10936)
CIBARIA INTERNATIONAL INC
705 Columbia Ave, Riverside (92507-2141)
PHONE..............................951 823-8490
Kathy Griset, *Pr*
Karen Moore, *
▲ EMP: 30 EST: 1998
SQ FT: 55,000
SALES (est): 2.57MM **Privately Held**
Web: www.cibaria-intl.com
SIC: 5149 2899 Cooking oils; Essential oils

(P-10937)
CJ AMERICA INC (HQ)
Also Called: C J Foods
300 S Grand Ave Ste 1100, Los Angeles
(90071-3173)
PHONE..............................213 338-2700
Hyunsoo Shin, *CEO*

Jae Kyung Jeon, *
◆ EMP: 54 EST: 1984
SALES (est): 485.8MM **Privately Held**
Web: www.cjamerica.com
SIC: 5149 1541 3556 5169 Groceries and
  related products, nec; Food products
  manufacturing or packing plant construction
  ; Food products machinery; Food additives
  and preservatives
PA: Cj Cheiljedang Corporation
  330 Dongho-Ro, Jung-Gu

(P-10938)
COASTAL COCKTAILS INC (PA)
Also Called: Modern Gourmet Foods
1920 E Deere Ave Ste 100, Santa Ana
(92705-5717)
PHONE..............................949 250-8951
Boaz Shonfeld, *CEO*
William E Mote, *
▲ EMP: 34 EST: 2009
SALES (est): 59.02MM **Privately Held**
Web: www.coastalcocktails.com
SIC: 5149 2086 Food gift baskets; Bottled
  and canned soft drinks

(P-10939)
**COMPLETELY FRESH FOODS
INC**
4401 S Downey Rd, Vernon (90058-2518)
P.O. Box 58667 (90058-0667)
PHONE..............................323 722-9136
Josh Solovy, *Pr*
Levi Litmanovich, *
Eric Litmanovich, *
EMP: 200 EST: 2006
SQ FT: 15,000
SALES (est): 3.82MM
SALES (corp-wide): 966.1MM **Privately
Held**
Web: www.gwfg.com
SIC: 5149 5046 Specialty food items;
  Commercial equipment, nec
PA: Golden West Food Group, Inc.
  4401 S Downey Rd
  888 807-3663

(P-10940)
**CORE-MARK INTERNATIONAL
INC**
2311 E 48th St, Vernon (90058-2007)
PHONE..............................323 583-6531
Julian Puentes, *Brnch Mgr*
EMP: 174
SALES (corp-wide): 58.28B **Publicly Held**
Web: www.core-mark.com
SIC: 5149 5194 5145 Groceries and related
  products, nec; Tobacco and tobacco
  products; Confectionery
HQ: Core-Mark International, Inc.
  1500 Solana Blvd Ste 3400
  Westlake TX 76262
  650 589-9445

(P-10941)
**CORE-MARK INTERNATIONAL
INC**
200 Coremark Ct, Bakersfield (93307-8402)
P.O. Box 70458 (93387-0458)
PHONE..............................661 366-2673
Caral Parker, *Pr*
EMP: 211
SALES (corp-wide): 58.28B **Publicly Held**
Web: www.core-mark.com
SIC: 5149 Groceries and related products,
  nec
HQ: Core-Mark International, Inc.
  1500 Solana Blvd Ste 3400
  Westlake TX 76262
  650 589-9445

(P-10942)
**CULINARY HISPANIC FOODS
INC**
Also Called: Productos Chata
805 Bow St, Chula Vista (91914)
PHONE..............................619 955-6101
▲ EMP: 1458 EST: 2011
SQ FT: 4,000
SALES (est): 70.89MM **Privately Held**
SIC: 5149 Canned goods: fruit, vegetables,
  seafood, meats, etc.

(P-10943)
DESERT VALLEY DATE LLC
86740 Industrial Way, Coachella
(92236-2718)
PHONE..............................760 398-0999
Greg Willsey, *Managing Member*
EMP: 85 EST: 2020
SALES (est): 10.62MM **Privately Held**
Web: www.desertvalleydate.com
SIC: 5149 5148 Organic and diet food; Fruits

(P-10944)
EL GUAPO SPICES INC (PA)
Also Called: El Guapo Spices and Herbs Pkg
6200 E Slauson Ave, Commerce
(90040-3012)
PHONE..............................213 312-1300
Dan Terrazas, *Pr*
EMP: 100 EST: 1982
SALES (est): 2.55MM
SALES (corp-wide): 2.55MM **Privately
Held**
SIC: 5149 Spices and seasonings

(P-10945)
**GOGLANIAN BAKERIES INC
(HQ)**
Also Called: Goglanian
3401 W Segerstrom Ave, Santa Ana
(92704-6404)
PHONE..............................714 338-1145
◆ EMP: 300 EST: 1978
SQ FT: 71,500
SALES (est): 8.76MM
SALES (corp-wide): 4.81B **Privately Held**
Web: www.richsusa.com
SIC: 5149 Bakery products
PA: Rich Products Corporation
  1 Robert Rich Way
  716 878-8000

(P-10946)
**GOURMET INDIA FOOD
COMPANY LLC**
12220 Rivera Rd Ste A, Whittier
(90606-6206)
PHONE..............................562 698-9763
▲ EMP: 75 EST: 2000
SALES (est): 1.77MM **Privately Held**
Web: www.gourmetindiafood.com
SIC: 5149 Bakery products

(P-10947)
**GUAYAKI SSTNBLE RNFREST
PDTS I (PA)**
Also Called: Guayaki Yerba Mate
215 Rose Ave, Venice (90291-2567)
PHONE..............................888 482-9254
Benjamin Mand, *CEO*
Steve Karr, *
Dave Karr, *
Alex Pryor, *
▲ EMP: 149 EST: 1999
SALES (est): 27.61MM
SALES (corp-wide): 27.61MM **Privately
Held**
Web: www.guayaki.com

SIC: 5149 2095 Beverages, except coffee and tea; Coffee extracts

(P-10948)
HARRIS FREEMAN & CO INC (PA)
Also Called: Harris Tea Company
3110 E Miraloma Ave, Anaheim (92806-1906)
PHONE....................714 765-7525
Anil J Shah, *CEO*
Kevin Shah, *
Meena Shah, *
◆ EMP: 500 EST: 1981
SQ FT: 58,000
SALES (est): 150K
SALES (corp-wide): 150K **Privately Held**
Web: www.harrisfreeman.com
SIC: 5149 2099 Tea; Spices, including grinding

(P-10949)
JANS ENTERPRISES CORPORATION
Also Called: Wira Co
4181 Temple City Blvd Ste A, El Monte (91731-1029)
PHONE....................626 575-2000
Anthony Kartawinata, *Pr*
Nila Prawirawidjaja, *
◆ EMP: 25 EST: 1998
SQ FT: 50,000
SALES (est): 13.67MM **Privately Held**
Web: www.jansfood.com
SIC: 5149 2026 2096 Specialty food items; Milk, ultra-high temperature (longlife); Potato chips and similar snacks

(P-10950)
JFC INTERNATIONAL INC
Also Called: Los Angeles Branch
7140 Bandini Blvd, Commerce (90040-3325)
PHONE....................323 721-6900
Tamaki Saijo, *Brnch Mgr*
EMP: 165
Web: www.jfc.com
SIC: 5149 Specialty food items
HQ: Jfc International Inc.
7101 E Slauson Ave
Commerce CA 90040
323 721-6100

(P-10951)
JFC INTERNATIONAL INC (HQ)
7101 E Slauson Ave, Commerce (90040-3622)
P.O. Box 875349 (90087-0449)
PHONE....................323 721-6100
Yoshiyuki Ishigaki, *CEO*
Hiroyuki Enomoto, *
◆ EMP: 203 EST: 1948
SALES (est): 387.79MM **Privately Held**
Web: www.jfc.com
SIC: 5149 7389 Specialty food items; Labeling bottles, cans, cartons, etc.
PA: Kikkoman Corporation
2-1-1, Nishishimbashi

(P-10952)
K T LUCKY CO INC
10925 Schmidt Rd, El Monte (91733-2707)
PHONE....................626 579-7272
Hang Huynh, *Pr*
▲ EMP: 70 EST: 1986
SQ FT: 12,000
SALES (est): 5MM **Privately Held**
SIC: 5149 Macaroni

(P-10953)
KIDS HEALTHY FOODS LLC
2030 Main St Ste 1300, Irvine (92614-7220)
PHONE....................949 260-4950
Jeff Mcclelland, *CEO*
EMP: 25 EST: 2010
SALES (est): 9.64MM **Privately Held**
Web: www.kidshealthyfoods.com
SIC: 5149 2099 Beverages, except coffee and tea; Tea blending

(P-10954)
LA PROVENCE INC
Also Called: La Provence Bakery
1370 W San Marcos Blvd Ste 130, San Marcos (92078-1601)
PHONE....................760 736-3299
Philip Dardaine, *CEO*
Thierry Bouchereau, *
Karen Dardaine, *
EMP: 95 EST: 1990
SQ FT: 6,000
SALES (est): 17.73MM **Privately Held**
Web: www.laprovenceinc.com
SIC: 5149 Bakery products

(P-10955)
LANGER JUICE COMPANY INC
400 S Stimson Ave, City Of Industry (91745)
PHONE....................626 336-3100
Bruce Langer, *Mgr*
EMP: 106
SALES (corp-wide): 85.1MM **Privately Held**
Web: www.langers.com
SIC: 5149 Juices
PA: Langer Juice Company, Inc.
16195 Stephens St
626 336-3100

(P-10956)
LAZY ACRES NATURAL MARKET
422 W Washington St, San Diego (92103-1933)
PHONE....................619 847-8443
EMP: 76 EST: 2017
SALES (est): 613.29K **Privately Held**
Web: www.lazyacres.com
SIC: 5149 Natural and organic foods

(P-10957)
LEE KUM KEE (USA) INC (DH)
Also Called: Lee's Kitchen
14841 Don Julian Rd, City Of Industry (91746-3110)
PHONE....................626 709-1888
Simon Wu, *CEO*
David H W Lee, *
◆ EMP: 44 EST: 1983
SQ FT: 50,000
SALES (est): 177.39MM **Privately Held**
Web: usa.lkk.com
SIC: 5149 2099 2035 Sauces; Food preparations, nec; Pickles, sauces, and salad dressings
HQ: Lee Kum Kee International Holdings Limited
Tai Po Indl Est
Tai Po NT

(P-10958)
LENORE JOHN & CO (PA)
1250 Delevan Dr, San Diego (92102-2437)
PHONE....................619 232-6136
John G Lenore, *CEO*
Jamie Lenore, *
Karl Hurlbert, *
◆ EMP: 120 EST: 1966

SQ FT: 50,000
SALES (est): 12.65MM
SALES (corp-wide): 12.65MM **Privately Held**
Web: www.johnlenore.com
SIC: 5149 5182 5181 Soft drinks; Wine; Beer and other fermented malt liquors

(P-10959)
MHH HOLDINGS INC
415 S Lake Ave Ste 108, Pasadena (91101-5047)
PHONE....................626 744-9370
Xiomara Bellido, *Prin*
EMP: 217
SALES (corp-wide): 7.74MM **Privately Held**
Web: www.coffeebean.com
SIC: 5149 Tea
PA: Mhh Holdings, Inc.
4580 Calle Alto
805 484-7924

(P-10960)
MHH HOLDINGS INC
5653 Alton Pkwy, Irvine (92618-4058)
PHONE....................949 651-9903
Cynthia Espere, *Brnch Mgr*
EMP: 216
SALES (corp-wide): 7.74MM **Privately Held**
Web: www.coffeebean.com
SIC: 5149 Tea
PA: Mhh Holdings, Inc.
4580 Calle Alto
805 484-7924

(P-10961)
MINH PHUNG INCORPORATED
Also Called: Banh Hoi Minh Phung
15216 Weststate St, Westminster (92683-6531)
PHONE....................714 379-0606
Chuyen Huynh, *Pr*
▲ EMP: 23 EST: 1996
SALES (est): 1.01MM **Privately Held**
SIC: 5149 2098 Pasta and rice; Noodles (e.g. egg, plain, and water), dry

(P-10962)
MONDELEZ GLOBAL LLC
Also Called: Nabisco
5815 Clark St, Ontario (91761-3676)
PHONE....................909 605-0140
Botie Magee, *Brnch Mgr*
EMP: 51
Web: www.mondelezinternational.com
SIC: 5149 2099 2052 Crackers, cookies, and bakery products; Food preparations, nec; Cookies and crackers
HQ: Mondelez Global Llc
905 W Fulton Mkt Ste 200
Chicago IL 60607
847 943-4000

(P-10963)
MONSTER ENERGY COMPANY (HQ)
Also Called: Monster Energy
1 Monster Way, Corona (92879-7101)
PHONE....................866 322-4466
Rodney C Sacks, *CEO*
Hilton H Scholsberg, *
Thomas J Kelly, *
◆ EMP: 258 EST: 1992
SQ FT: 300,000
SALES (est): 485.2MM
SALES (corp-wide): 7.14B **Publicly Held**
Web: www.monsterbevcorp.com
SIC: 5149 Juices

PA: Monster Beverage Corporation
1 Monster Way
951 739-6200

(P-10964)
MUTUAL TRADING CO INC (DH)
Also Called: Mtc Kitchen Home La
4200 Shirley Ave, El Monte (91731-1130)
PHONE....................213 626-9458
Masatoshi Ohata, *Dir*
Atsuko Kanai, *
Yoshihiro Sakata, *
Ami Nakanishi, *Dir*
Minori Mori, *
◆ EMP: 105 EST: 1926
SALES (est): 191.56MM **Privately Held**
Web: www.lamtc.com
SIC: 5149 5141 5023 Groceries and related products, nec; Groceries, general line; Homefurnishings
HQ: Takara Shuzo International Co., Ltd.
20, Naginatabokocho, Higashiiru, Karasuma, Shijodoori, Shimogyo-Kyoto KYO 600-8

(P-10965)
NATURES BEST
6 Pointe Dr Ste 300, Brea (92821-6323)
P.O. Box 2248 (92822-2248)
PHONE....................714 255-4600
▲ EMP: 360
Web: www.kehe.com
SIC: 5149 Health foods

(P-10966)
NEUROBRANDS LLC
Also Called: Neuro Drinks
15303 Ventura Blvd Ste 675, Sherman Oaks (91403-6608)
P.O. Box 55245 (91413)
PHONE....................310 393-6444
Diana Jenkins, *CEO*
Scott Laporta, *
Greg Buscher, *
▲ EMP: 125 EST: 2009
SALES (est): 20.07MM **Privately Held**
Web: www.drinkneuro.com
SIC: 5149 Soft drinks

(P-10967)
OAKHURST INDUSTRIES INC (PA)
Also Called: Freund Baking
2050 S Tubeway Ave, Los Angeles (90040-1624)
P.O. Box 911457 (90091-1238)
PHONE....................323 724-3000
James Freund, *Pr*
Ronald Martin, *
Jonathan Freund, *
Linda F Freund, *
EMP: 140 EST: 1981
SQ FT: 81,000
SALES (est): 72.41MM **Privately Held**
SIC: 5149 Bakery products

(P-10968)
OLDE THOMPSON LLC
2300 Celsius Ave, Oxnard (93030-5572)
PHONE....................805 983-0388
EMP: 26
SALES (corp-wide): 178.36MM **Privately Held**
Web: www.oldethompson.com
SIC: 5149 2099 Groceries and related products, nec; Food preparations, nec
HQ: Olde Thompson, Llc
3250 Camino Del Sol
Oxnard CA 93030
805 983-0388

(P-10969)
PASTA PICCININI INC
950 N Fair Oaks Ave, Pasadena
(91103-3009)
PHONE..................626 798-0841
Stefano Piccinini, *CEO*
▲ **EMP:** 37 **EST:** 1971
SQ FT: 30,000
SALES (est): 9.94MM **Privately Held**
Web: www.pastapiccinini.com
SIC: 5149 5812 2045 Pasta and rice; Eating places; Biscuit dough, prepared; from purchased flour

(P-10970)
PERFECT BAR LLC
Also Called: Perfect Snacks
10505 Roselle St Ste 102, San Diego
(92121-1553)
PHONE..................866 628-8548
Bill Keith, *CEO*
EMP: 200 **EST:** 2005
SQ FT: 16,000
SALES (est): 96.39MM **Publicly Held**
Web: www.perfectsnacks.com
SIC: 5149 Health foods
PA: Mondelez International, Inc.
905 W Fulton Mkt Ste 200

(P-10971)
QUALITY NATURALLY FOODS INC
Also Called: QUALITY NATURALLYU FOODS, INC.
17769 Railroad St, City Of Industry
(91748-1111)
PHONE..................626 854-6363
EMP: 26
SALES (corp-wide): 20.26MM **Privately Held**
Web: www.qnfoods.com
SIC: 5149 2099 2045 Bakery products; Food preparations, nec; Prepared flour mixes and doughs
PA: Quality Naturally Foods, Inc.
18830 San Jose Ave
626 854-6363

(P-10972)
QUALITY NATURALLY FOODS INC (PA)
Also Called: Yum Yum Donut Shop
18830 San Jose Ave, City Of Industry
(91748-1325)
PHONE..................626 854-6363
◆ **EMP:** 24 **EST:** 1971
SALES (est): 20.26MM
SALES (corp-wide): 20.26MM **Privately Held**
Web: www.qnfoods.com
SIC: 5149 2099 2045 Bakery products; Food preparations, nec; Prepared flour mixes and doughs

(P-10973)
RED BULL MEDIA HSE N AMER INC (HQ)
1740 Stewart St, Santa Monica
(90404-4022)
PHONE..................310 393-4647
Stefan Kozak, *CEO*
EMP: 72 **EST:** 2011
SALES (est): 51.97MM
SALES (corp-wide): 11.47B **Privately Held**
SIC: 5149 Beverage concentrates
PA: Red Bull Gmbh
Am Brunnen 1
66265820

(P-10974)
REYES COCA-COLA BOTTLING LLC
Also Called: Coca-Cola
12925 Bradley Ave, Sylmar (91342-3830)
PHONE..................818 362-4307
Larry Campbell, *Brnch Mgr*
EMP: 70
SALES (corp-wide): 850.14MM **Privately Held**
Web: www.reyescocacola.com
SIC: 5149 4225 2086 Soft drinks; General warehousing; Bottled and canned soft drinks
PA: Reyes Coca-Cola Bottling, L.L.C.
3 Park Plz Ste 600
213 744-8616

(P-10975)
ROCKVIEW DAIRIES INC (PA)
Also Called: Motive Nation
7011 Stewart And Gray Rd, Downey
(90241-4347)
P.O. Box 668 (90241-0668)
PHONE..................562 927-5511
Egbert Jim Degroot, *CEO*
Ted De Groot, *
Joe Valadez, *
◆ **EMP:** 188 **EST:** 1966
SALES (est): 42.13MM
SALES (corp-wide): 42.13MM **Privately Held**
Web: www.rockviewfarms.com
SIC: 5149 5143 2026 Dried or canned foods; Milk; Fluid milk

(P-10976)
ROYAL CROWN ENTERPRISES INC
780 Epperson Dr, City Of Industry
(91748-1336)
PHONE..................626 854-8080
◆ **EMP:** 150
SIC: 5149 5141 Canned goods: fruit, vegetables, seafood, meats, etc.; Groceries, general line

(P-10977)
SADIE ROSE BAKING CO
Also Called: Colors Pizza
2614 Temple Heights Dr, Oceanside
(92056-3512)
PHONE..................760 806-7793
Jennifer A Curran, *CEO*
Jennifer Ann Curran, *CEO*
Michael Lipman, *
◆ **EMP:** 70 **EST:** 2004
SQ FT: 23,000
SALES (est): 24.81MM **Privately Held**
Web: www.sadierose.com
SIC: 5149 Bakery products

(P-10978)
SHAMROCK FOODS COMPANY
12400 Riverside Dr, Eastvale (91752-1004)
PHONE..................951 685-6314
Kent Mullison, *Brnch Mgr*
EMP: 403
SALES (corp-wide): 5.86B **Privately Held**
Web: www.shamrockfoods.com
SIC: 5149 Groceries and related products, nec
PA: Shamrock Foods Company
3900 E Camelback Rd # 300
602 233-6400

(P-10979)
SIMPSON LABS LLC
24955 Avenue Kearny, Valencia
(91355-1252)
PHONE..................661 347-4348
Eric Simpson, *Pr*
EMP: 150
SALES (corp-wide): 4.38MM **Privately Held**
Web: www.simpsonlabs.net
SIC: 5149 Groceries and related products, nec
PA: Simpson Labs Llc
27540 Avenue Mentry
661 347-4348

(P-10980)
SOOFER CO INC
Also Called: Sadaf Foods
2828 S Alameda St, Los Angeles
(90058-1347)
PHONE..................323 234-6666
Jamshid Soofer, *Pr*
Dariush Soofer, *
Behrooz David Soofer, *
Ramon Sentimental, *
David Soofer, *
◆ **EMP:** 75 **EST:** 1982
SQ FT: 70,000
SALES (est): 38.84MM **Privately Held**
Web: www.sadaffoods.com
SIC: 5149 Spices and seasonings

(P-10981)
SUGAR FOODS LLC
Also Called: Sugar Foods
3059 Townsgate Rd, Westlake Village
(91361-5861)
PHONE..................805 230-2591
EMP: 89
SALES (corp-wide): 677.96MM **Privately Held**
Web: www.sugarfoods.com
SIC: 5149 Groceries and related products, nec
HQ: Sugar Foods Llc
3059 Townsgate Rd Ste 101
Westlake Village CA 91361
805 396-5000

(P-10982)
SUNFOOD CORPORATION
Also Called: Sunfood Superfoods
1825 Gillespie Way, El Cajon (92020-0501)
PHONE..................619 596-7979
Robert Deupree, *CEO*
▲ **EMP:** 79 **EST:** 2009
SALES (est): 17.98MM **Privately Held**
Web: www.sunfood.com
SIC: 5149 Natural and organic foods

(P-10983)
TADIN INC
Also Called: Tadin Herb & Tea Co.
3345 E Slauson Ave, Vernon (90058-3914)
PHONE..................213 406-8880
▲ **EMP:** 95
Web: www.tadin.com
SIC: 5149 Tea

(P-10984)
TL MONTGOMERY & ASSOCIATES INC
2833 Leonis Blvd Ste 205, Vernon
(90058-3028)
PHONE..................323 583-1645
▼ **EMP:** 110
SIC: 5149 Pet foods

(P-10985)
TLD ACQUISITION CO LLC
Also Called: Tld Distribution Co
505 S 7th Ave, City Of Industry
(91746-3121)

▲ **EMP:** 150
SIC: 5149 5023 5145 5046 Beverages, except coffee and tea; Glassware; Snack foods; Restaurant equipment and supplies, nec

(P-10986)
TRINIDAD/BENHAM CORP
12400 Wilshire Blvd Ste 1180, Los Angeles
(90025-1058)
PHONE..................626 723-2300
EMP: 72
SALES (corp-wide): 468.79MM **Privately Held**
Web: www.trinidadbenham.com
SIC: 5149 Pasta and rice
HQ: Trinidad/Benham Corp.
3650 S Yosemite St # 300
Denver CO 80237
303 220-1400

(P-10987)
US FOODS INC
Also Called: General Cold Stg 4145
8457 Eastern Ave, Bell Gardens
(90201-7137)
PHONE..................562 806-2445
EMP: 159
Web: www.usfoods.com
SIC: 5149 Dried or canned foods
HQ: Us Foods, Inc.
9399 W Higgins Rd Ste 500
Rosemont IL 60018

(P-10988)
US FOODS INC
Also Called: Central Prcss 4140
636 Stanford Ave, Los Angeles
(90021-1006)
PHONE..................213 623-4150
EMP: 159
Web: www.usfoods.com
SIC: 5149 Dried or canned foods
HQ: Us Foods, Inc.
9399 W Higgins Rd Ste 500
Rosemont IL 60018

(P-10989)
US FOODS INC
Also Called: P&O Stg-Carson 4150
1610 E Sepulveda Blvd, Carson
(90745-6120)
PHONE..................310 632-6265
EMP: 159
Web: www.usfoods.com
SIC: 5149 Dried or canned foods
HQ: Us Foods, Inc.
9399 W Higgins Rd Ste 500
Rosemont IL 60018

(P-10990)
VINH - SANH TRADING CORP
13500 Nelson Ave, City Of Industry
(91746-2334)
PHONE..................626 968-6888
Timothy Chen, *CEO*
Kan Wang Chen, *
Stacy Tran, *
▲ **EMP:** 77 **EST:** 1998
SQ FT: 178,000
SALES (est): 10.02MM **Privately Held**
Web: www.vinhsanh.com
SIC: 5149 Groceries and related products, nec

▲ = Import ▼ = Export
◆ = Import/Export

5159 Farm-product Raw Materials, Nec

(P-10991)
805 BEACH BREAKS INC
1053 Highland Way, Grover Beach (93433-3102)
PHONE..............................408 896-4854
Samantha Tabak, *Prin*
EMP: 84 EST: 2017
SALES (est): 926.33K
SALES (corp-wide): 1.13B Privately Held
Web: www.harvesthoc.com
SIC: 5159
PA: Trulieve Cannabis Corp.
6749 Ben Bostic Rd
844 878-5438

(P-10992)
FLUIDS MANUFACTURING INC
11941 Vose St, North Hollywood (91605-5750)
P.O. Box 16297 (91615)
PHONE..............................818 264-4657
Nik Patel, *CEO*
EMP: 150 EST: 2015
SALES (est): 8.73MM Privately Held
SIC: 5159

(P-10993)
IMPERIAL WESTERN PRODUCTS INC A CALIFORNIA CORPORATION (HQ)
86600 Avenue 54, Coachella (92236-3812)
P.O. Box 1110 (92236)
PHONE..............................760 398-0815
▼ EMP: 50 EST: 1966
SALES (est): 86.81MM
SALES (corp-wide): 591.61MM Privately Held
Web: www.imperialwesternproducts.com
SIC: 5159 2841 2869 Cotton merchants and products; Glycerin, crude or refined: from fats; Industrial organic chemicals, nec
PA: Denali Water Solutions Llc
3308 Bernice Ave
479 498-0500

(P-10994)
SOUTH VALLEY ALMOND CO LLC
Also Called: South Valley Farms
15443 Beech Ave, Wasco (93280-7604)
PHONE..............................661 391-9000
Paul C Genho, *Managing Member*
Merrill Dibble, *Managing Member*
✪ EMP: 200 EST: 2007
SQ FT: 4,000
SALES (est): 17.61MM Privately Held
Web: www.southvalleyfarms.com
SIC: 5159 Nuts and nut by-products

5162 Plastics Materials And Basic Shapes

(P-10995)
CIRRUS ENTERPRISES LLC
Also Called: E.V. Roberts
18027 Bishop Ave, Carson (90746-4019)
PHONE..............................310 204-6159
Tracey H Cloud, *
▲ EMP: 52 EST: 1938
SQ FT: 26,000
SALES (est): 8.29MM Privately Held
Web: www.gracoroberts.com

SIC: 5162 2821 2891 5198 Plastics products, nec; Epoxy resins; Adhesives and sealants; Paints, varnishes, and supplies

(P-10996)
CONSOLIDATED PLASTICS CORP (PA)
Also Called: Paragon Plastics Co Div
14954 La Palma Dr, Chino (91710-9695)
PHONE..............................909 393-8222
Jean Bouris, *Pr*
Gloria Jean Bouris, *
EMP: 50 EST: 1973
SQ FT: 45,000
SALES (est): 3.19MM
SALES (corp-wide): 3.19MM Privately Held
Web: www.planetplastics.com
SIC: 5162 3599 Plastics sheets and rods; Machine shop, jobbing and repair

(P-10997)
EDGEBANDING SERVICES INC (PA)
Also Called: E S I
828 W Cienega Ave, San Dimas (91773-2459)
PHONE..............................909 599-2336
◆ EMP: 75 EST: 1988
SALES (est): 25.11MM Privately Held
Web: www.edgebanding-services.com
SIC: 5162 5031 Plastics products, nec; Structural assemblies, prefabricated: wood

(P-10998)
ELKAY PLASTICS CO INC (PA)
Also Called: Lk Packaging
6000 Sheila St, Commerce (90040-2405)
PHONE..............................323 722-7073
Louis Chertkow, *Pr*
Geoffrey Pankau, *
▲ EMP: 100 EST: 1966
SQ FT: 175,000
SALES (est): 101.9MM
SALES (corp-wide): 101.9MM Privately Held
Web: www.lkpkg.com
SIC: 5162 Plastics products, nec

(P-10999)
ORANGE COUNTY INDUS PLAS INC (PA)
Also Called: Ocip
4811 E La Palma Ave, Anaheim (92807-1954)
PHONE..............................714 632-9450
Robert Robinson, *Pr*
▲ EMP: 25 EST: 1985
SQ FT: 70,198
SALES (est): 20.87MM
SALES (corp-wide): 20.87MM Privately Held
Web: www.ocip.com
SIC: 5162 2821 Plastics products, nec; Plastics materials and resins

(P-11000)
PLASTIC SALES SOUTHERN INC
Also Called: Plastic Sales
425 Havana Ave, Long Beach (90814-1928)
PHONE..............................714 375-7900
James Quinn, *Pr*
EMP: 23 EST: 1980
SALES (est): 826.93K Privately Held
SIC: 5162 3089 Plastics sheets and rods; Injection molding of plastics

(P-11001)
REGAL-PIEDMONT PLASTICS LLC
Also Called: Piedmont Plastics
17000 Valley View Ave, La Mirada (90638-5827)
P.O. Box 1274 (90308-1274)
PHONE..............................562 404-4014
TOLL FREE: 800
Carlos Bennett, *Brnch Mgr*
EMP: 34
SALES (corp-wide): 201.65MM Privately Held
Web: www.piedmontplastics.com
SIC: 5162 2396 5169 Plastics sheets and rods; Furniture trimmings, fabric; Silicon lubricants
HQ: Regal-Piedmont Plastics, Llc
5010 W W. T. Harris Blvd
Charlotte NC 28269

(P-11002)
S & W PLASTIC STORES INC (PA)
Also Called: S & W Plastics Supply
14270 Albers Way, Chino (91710-6940)
PHONE..............................909 390-0090
William B Goldstein, *CEO*
David Goldstein, *
▲ EMP: 35 EST: 1964
SQ FT: 25,000
SALES (est): 2.61MM
SALES (corp-wide): 2.61MM Privately Held
Web: www.sandwplastics.com
SIC: 5162 5719 3089 Plastics products, nec; Housewares, nec; Plastics kitchenware, tableware, and houseware

(P-11003)
TRANSCENDIA INC
Also Called: Transilwrap Company
9000 9th St Ste 140, Rancho Cucamonga (91730-4499)
PHONE..............................909 944-9981
Jorge Zaldivar, *Brnch Mgr*
EMP: 44
SQ FT: 41,400
SALES (corp-wide): 290.26MM Privately Held
Web: www.transcendia.com
SIC: 5162 3081 3089 Plastics materials and basic shapes; Unsupported plastics film and sheet; Plastics processing
PA: Transcendia, Inc.
9201 W Belmont Ave
847 678-1800

5169 Chemicals And Allied Products, Nec

(P-11004)
ACCESS BUSINESS GROUP LLC
5600 Beach Blvd, Buena Park (90621-2007)
P.O. Box 5940 (90622-5940)
PHONE..............................714 562-6200
Steve Vanandel, *BD*
EMP: 403
Web: www.amwayglobal.com
SIC: 5169 Chemicals and allied products, nec
HQ: Access Business Group Llc
7575 Fulton St E
Ada MI 49355

(P-11005)
ACCESS BUSINESS GROUP LLC
Also Called: Nutrilite
5609 River Way, Buena Park (90621-1709)
PHONE..............................714 562-7914
EMP: 282
Web: www.amwayglobal.com
SIC: 5169 Chemicals and allied products, nec
HQ: Access Business Group Llc
7575 Fulton St E
Ada MI 49355

(P-11006)
ACCESS BUSINESS GROUP LLC
Also Called: Access Logistics
12825 Leffingwell Ave, Santa Fe Springs (90670-6339)
PHONE..............................808 422-9482
Hee Douglas, *Brnch Mgr*
EMP: 262
Web: www.amwayglobal.com
SIC: 5169 Chemicals and allied products, nec
HQ: Access Business Group Llc
7575 Fulton St E
Ada MI 49355

(P-11007)
BRENNTAG PACIFIC INC (DH)
10747 Patterson Pl, Santa Fe Springs (90670-4043)
PHONE..............................562 903-9626
David Eckelbarger, *CEO*
Steven Pozzi, *
H Edward Boyadjian, *
Julia Tu, *
Leslie Lenhardt, *
▲ EMP: 96 EST: 2003
SALES (est): 391.54MM Privately Held
SIC: 5169 Chemicals, industrial and heavy
HQ: Brenntag North America, Inc.
5083 Pottsville Pike
Reading PA 19605
610 926-6100

(P-11008)
CALWAX LLC (DH)
16511 Knott Ave, La Mirada (90638-6011)
PHONE..............................626 969-4334
John Paraszczak, *Managing Member*
▲ EMP: 37 EST: 1955
SQ FT: 40,000
SALES (est): 4.6MM Privately Held
Web: www.calwax.com
SIC: 5169 2842 Waxes, except petroleum; Waxes for wood, leather, and other materials
HQ: Remet Corporation
210 Commons Rd
Utica NY 13502
315 797-8700

(P-11009)
CHEMBRIDGE CORPORATION (PA)
11199 Sorrento Valley Rd Ste 206, San Diego (92121-1334)
PHONE..............................858 451-7400
Sergey Altshteyn, *Pr*
Eugene Vaisberg, *Sec*
EMP: 260 EST: 1993
SQ FT: 26,000
SALES (est): 6.61MM Privately Held
Web: www.chembridge.com
SIC: 5169 Chemicals and allied products, nec

(P-11010)
CHEMSIL SILICONES INC
21900 Marilla St, Chatsworth (91311-4129)
PHONE..............................818 700-0302
Williams S Patrick, *CEO*
Patrick S Williams, *
Bruce Mcdonald, *General Vice President*
Ian Cleminson, *
Tom Martin, *
◆ **EMP: 26 EST:** 2000
SQ FT: 32,789
SALES (est): 24.6MM
SALES (corp-wide): 1.95B **Publicly Held**
Web: www.chemsil.com
SIC: 5169 2869 Chemicals and allied products, nec; Silicones
PA: Innospec Inc.
　8310 S Valley Hwy Ste 350
　303 792-5554

(P-11011)
CHEROKEE CHEMICAL CO INC (PA)
Also Called: CCI
3540 E 26th St, Vernon (90058-4103)
PHONE..............................323 265-1112
Da Criswell, *CEO*
EMP: 47 **EST:** 1964
SQ FT: 30,000
SALES (est): 28.76MM
SALES (corp-wide): 28.76MM **Privately Held**
Web: www.ccichemical.com
SIC: 5169 2842 2819 Specialty cleaning and sanitation preparations; Polishes and sanitation goods; Industrial inorganic chemicals, nec

(P-11012)
ESE INC
Also Called: Ese
1163 E 12th St, Los Angeles (90021-2205)
PHONE..............................213 614-0102
David Kazemi, *CEO*
▲ **EMP:** 25 **EST:** 1993
SALES (est): 5MM **Privately Held**
Web: www.realklean.com
SIC: 5169 2841 5065 Alcohols and antifreeze compounds; Soap and other detergents; Electronic parts and equipment, nec

(P-11013)
GEO DRILLING FLUIDS INC (PA)
Also Called: Industrial Minerals Company
1431 Union Ave, Bakersfield (93305-5732)
P.O. Box 1478 (93302-1478)
PHONE..............................661 325-5919
Jim Clifford, *Pr*
Dan Bauman, *
Bob French, *
Don Boulet, *
Tom Needham, *
▲ **EMP:** 30 **EST:** 1950
SQ FT: 7,500
SALES (est): 20.68MM
SALES (corp-wide): 20.68MM **Privately Held**
Web: www.geodf.com
SIC: 5169 1389 7389 Chemicals and allied products, nec; Servicing oil and gas wells; Grinding, precision: commercial or industrial

(P-11014)
GURUNANDA LLC (PA)
Also Called: Gurunanda
6645 Caballero Blvd, Buena Park (90620-1131)
PHONE..............................714 256-4050
Puneet Nanda, *Managing Member*

Ajay Bansal, *
EMP: 96 **EST:** 2013
SQ FT: 5,500
SALES (est): 39.15MM
SALES (corp-wide): 39.15MM **Privately Held**
Web: www.gurunanda.com
SIC: 5169 Essential oils

(P-11015)
HENKEL US OPERATIONS CORP
5800 Bristol Pkwy, Culver City (90230-6696)
PHONE..............................424 308-0505
Thomas Keller, *Brnch Mgr*
EMP: 72
SALES (corp-wide): 23.39B **Privately Held**
Web: www.henkel.com
SIC: 5169 5099 Adhesives and sealants; Firearms and ammunition, except sporting
HQ: Henkel Us Operations Corporation
　1 Henkel Way
　Rocky Hill CT 06067
　860 571-5100

(P-11016)
HILL BROTHERS CHEMICAL COMPANY (PA)
Also Called: Hill Brothers Chemical
3000 E Birch St Ste 108, Brea (92821-6261)
PHONE..............................714 998-8800
Adam Hill, *Pr*
Matthew Thorne, *
Thomas F James, *
Kathryn J Waters, *
▲ **EMP:** 150 **EST:** 1935
SALES (est): 80.33MM
SALES (corp-wide): 80.33MM **Privately Held**
Web: www.hillbrothers.com
SIC: 5169 2819 Acids; Calcium chloride and hypochlorite

(P-11017)
NORMAN FOX & CO
5511 S Boyle Ave, Vernon (90058-3932)
P.O. Box 58727 (90058-0727)
PHONE..............................323 973-4900
Alex Kirby, *Brnch Mgr*
EMP: 23
SALES (corp-wide): 30.33MM **Privately Held**
Web: www.norfoxchem.com
SIC: 5169 2841 Industrial chemicals; Soap: granulated, liquid, cake, flaked, or chip
PA: Norman, Fox & Co.
　14970 Don Julian Rd
　800 632-1777

(P-11018)
NORMAN FOX & CO (PA)
Also Called: Norfox
14970 Don Julian Rd, City Of Industry (91746-3111)
PHONE..............................800 632-1777
Stephen Halpin, *CEO*
Bob Code, *
◆ **EMP:** 40 **EST:** 1971
SQ FT: 5,000
SALES (est): 30.33MM
SALES (corp-wide): 30.33MM **Privately Held**
Web: www.norfoxchem.com
SIC: 5169 2841 Chemicals and allied products, nec; Soap: granulated, liquid, cake, flaked, or chip

(P-11019)
R D ABBOTT CO INC
11958 Monarch St, Garden Grove (92841-2112)
PHONE..............................562 944-5354
Keith Arthur Thomas, *CEO*
▲ **EMP:** 91 **EST:** 1949
SALES (est): 21.34MM **Privately Held**
Web: www.rdabbott.com
SIC: 5169 Chemicals and allied products, nec

(P-11020)
SPECTRUM LABORATORY PDTS INC
Also Called: Spectrum Lab & Phrm Pdts
14422 S San Pedro St, Gardena (90248-2027)
PHONE..............................520 292-3103
Elizabeth Brown, *CEO*
EMP: 31
SALES (corp-wide): 86.13MM **Privately Held**
Web: www.spectrumchemical.com
SIC: 5169 2869 2819 Organic chemicals, synthetic; Laboratory chemicals, organic; Industrial inorganic chemicals, nec
PA: Spectrum Laboratory Products, Inc.
　769 Jersey Ave
　732 214-1300

(P-11021)
STRATEGIC SANITATION SVCS INC
25801 Obrero Dr Ste 11, Mission Viejo (92691-3141)
PHONE..............................949 444-9009
Steven Reyes, *Prin*
EMP: 103 **EST:** 2011
SALES (est): 11.53MM **Privately Held**
Web: www.wasteoptimize.com
SIC: 5169 Specialty cleaning and sanitation preparations

(P-11022)
UNIVAR SOLUTIONS USA LLC
2600 Garfield Ave, Commerce (90040-2608)
P.O. Box 512062 (90040)
PHONE..............................323 727-7005
Gary Cramer, *Brnch Mgr*
EMP: 175
SALES (corp-wide): 11.48B **Privately Held**
Web: www.univarsolutions.com
SIC: 5169 Industrial chemicals
HQ: Univar Solutions Usa Llc
　3075 Hghland Pkwy Ste 200
　Downers Grove IL 60515
　331 777-6000

(P-11023)
VALEANT BIOMEDICALS INC (DH)
1 Enterprise, Aliso Viejo (92656-2606)
PHONE..............................949 461-6000
Tim Tyson, *Pr*
EMP: 100 **EST:** 1983
SQ FT: 55,000
SALES (est): 7.34MM
SALES (corp-wide): 8.76B **Privately Held**
SIC: 5169 2835 8731 3826 Chemicals and allied products, nec; Diagnostic substances; Biotechnical research, commercial; Analytical instruments
HQ: Bausch Health Americas, Inc.
　400 Somerset Corp Blvd
　Bridgewater NJ 08807
　908 927-1400

(P-11024)
VIJALL INC
Also Called: Chemtec Chemical Company
21900 Marilla St, Chatsworth (91311-4129)
PHONE..............................818 700-0071
Patrick S Williams, *Pr*
Bruce Mcdonald, *Pr*
Ian Cleminson, *
Tom Martin, *
David E Williams, *
▲ **EMP:** 26 **EST:** 1987
SQ FT: 32,789
SALES (est): 2.62MM
SALES (corp-wide): 1.95B **Publicly Held**
Web: www.chemteccc.com
SIC: 5169 2819 Industrial chemicals; Industrial inorganic chemicals, nec
HQ: Innospec Active Chemicals Llc
　510 W Grimes Ave
　High Point NC 27260
　336 882-3308

5171 Petroleum Bulk Stations And Terminals

(P-11025)
SOUTHERN COUNTIES LLC (DH)
Also Called: SC Fuels
1800 W Katella Ave Ste 210, Orange (92867-3444)
P.O. Box 4159 (92863-4159)
PHONE..............................714 744-7140
TOLL FREE: 800
Shameek Konar, *CEO*
Mimi Taylor, *
David Larimer, *
EMP: 95 **EST:** 1969
SALES (est): 246.93MM
SALES (corp-wide): 364.48B **Publicly Held**
Web: www.scfuels.com
SIC: 5171 5541 5172 Petroleum bulk stations ; Gasoline service stations; Petroleum products, nec
HQ: Pilot Travel Centers Llc
　5508 Lonas Rd
　Knoxville TN 37909
　877 866-7378

(P-11026)
ZECO SYSTEMS INC
Also Called: Greenlots
767 S Alameda St Ste 200, Los Angeles (90021-1664)
PHONE..............................888 751-8560
Andreas Lips, *CEO*
Brett Hauser, *
Lin-dhuang Khoo, *Sr VP*
Harmeet Singh, *
Ron Mahabir, *
EMP: 95 **EST:** 2012
SQ FT: 10,000
SALES (est): 19.38MM
SALES (corp-wide): 316.62B **Privately Held**
Web: www.shellrecharge.com
SIC: 5171 Petroleum bulk stations and terminals
HQ: Zeco Holdings, Inc.
　925 N La Brea Ave
　West Hollywood CA 90038
　888 751-8560

5172 Petroleum Products, Nec

(P-11027)
APEX HOLDING CO

23901 Calabasas Rd Ste 2090, Calabasas
(91302-3306)
PHONE................818 876-0161
Louis Silvers, *Ofcr*
EMP: 73
SALES (corp-wide): 443.36MM **Privately
Held**
SIC: 5172 Petroleum products, nec
PA: Apex Holding Co.
8235 Forsyth Blvd Ste 400
314 889-9600

(P-11028)
ASTRA OIL COMPANY INC
301 Main St Ste 201, Huntington Beach
(92648-5171)
PHONE................714 969-6569
◆ **EMP:** 160
Web: www.astraoil.com
SIC: 5172 Petroleum products, nec

(P-11029)
CASEY COMPANY (PA)
180 E Ocean Blvd Ste 1010, Long Beach
(90802-4711)
PHONE................562 436-9685
Larry Delpit Senior, *Ch*
Betty Jane Blanchette, *
Barbara Odom, *
EMP: 129 **EST:** 1982
SQ FT: 4,000
SALES (est): 86.86MM
SALES (corp-wide): 86.86MM **Privately
Held**
Web: www.caseys.com
SIC: 5172 Petroleum products, nec

(P-11030)
EFUEL LLC
Also Called: Easy Fuel
65 Enterprise 3rd Fl, Aliso Viejo
(92656-2705)
PHONE................949 330-7145
Donald Harper, *CEO*
EMP: 90 **EST:** 2016
SALES (est): 27.28MM
SALES (corp-wide): 149.89B **Publicly
Held**
Web: www.efuelco.com
SIC: 5172 Petroleum products, nec
PA: Phillips 66
2331 Citywest Blvd
281 293-6600

(P-11031)
EMPIRE OIL CO
2756 S Riverside Ave, Bloomington
(92316-3500)
PHONE................909 877-0226
Richard Alden Senior, *CEO*
Richard Scott Alden Junior, *Pr*
Donald Welker, *
EMP: 141 **EST:** 1961
SQ FT: 2,300
SALES (est): 2.46MM **Publicly Held**
SIC: 5172 Diesel fuel
HQ: Northern Tier Energy Lp
1250 W Washington St # 300
Tempe AZ 85288
602 302-5450

(P-11032)
**GENERAL PETROLEUM LLC
(HQ)**
Also Called: G P Resources
19501 S Santa Fe Ave, Compton
(90221-5913)
P.O. Box 2136 (76099-2136)
PHONE................562 983-7300
James A Halsam Iii, *CEO*

Michael Ruehring, *
Sean Kha, *
▲ **EMP:** 150 **EST:** 1946
SQ FT: 5,000
SALES (est): 18.66MM
SALES (corp-wide): 39.9MM **Privately
Held**
SIC: 5172 Crude oil
PA: Pecos, Inc.
19501 S Santa Fe Ave
310 356-2300

(P-11033)
POMA HOLDING COMPANY INC
571 W Slover Ave, Bloomington
(92316-2454)
PHONE................909 877-2441
EMP: 118
Web: www.pomacos.com
SIC: 5172 Petroleum products, nec

(P-11034)
**PREMIER FUEL DISTRIBUTORS
INC**
Also Called: Premier Fuel Delivery Service
156 E La Cadena Dr, Riverside
(92507-8699)
PHONE................760 423-3610
Hugo Rodriguez, *CEO*
EMP: 150 **EST:** 2013
SALES (est): 19.06MM **Privately Held**
SIC: 5172 2869 Petroleum products, nec;
Fuels

(P-11035)
**TESORO REFINING & MKTG CO
LLC**
2101 E Pacific Coast Hwy, Wilmington
(90744-2914)
PHONE................877 837-6762
James Nichols, *Brnch Mgr*
EMP: 215
SIC: 5172 Service station supplies,
petroleum
HQ: Tesoro Refining & Marketing Company
Llc
19100 Ridgewood Pkwy
San Antonio TX 78259
210 626-6000

(P-11036)
TIODIZE CO INC
15701 Industry Ln, Huntington Beach
(92649-1569)
PHONE................714 898-4377
Thomas Adams, *Pr*
EMP: 48
SALES (corp-wide): 9.73MM **Privately
Held**
Web: www.tiodize.com
SIC: 5172 3471 Lubricating oils and greases
; Anodizing (plating) of metals or formed
products
PA: Tiodize Co., Inc.
5858 Engineer Dr
714 898-4377

(P-11037)
**VALLEY PACIFIC PETRO SVCS
INC**
9521 Enos Ln, Bakersfield (93314-8007)
PHONE................661 746-7737
Kat Bowen, *Brnch Mgr*
EMP: 88
SALES (corp-wide): 47.15MM **Privately
Held**
Web: www.valleypacific.com
SIC: 5172 Gasoline
PA: Valley Pacific Petroleum Services, Inc.
152 Frank West Cir # 100

209 948-9412

5181 Beer And Ale

(P-11038)
ADVANCE BEVERAGE CO INC
5200 District Blvd, Bakersfield
(93313-2330)
P.O. Box 9517 (93389-9517)
PHONE................661 833-3783
William K Lazzerini Senior, *Ch Bd*
William K Lazzerini Junior, *Pr*
Anthony Lazzerini, *
◆ **EMP:** 90 **EST:** 1952
SQ FT: 93,000
SALES (est): 11.17MM **Privately Held**
Web: www.advancebeverage.com
SIC: 5181 5182 Beer and other fermented
malt liquors; Wine

(P-11039)
**ALLIED COMPANY HOLDINGS
INC**
28311 Constellation Rd, Santa Clarita
(91355-5048)
P.O. Box 129 (92398-0129)
PHONE................661 510-6533
Kevin R Williams, *Brnch Mgr*
EMP: 187
SALES (corp-wide): 10.69MM **Privately
Held**
Web: www.alliedbeverages.com
SIC: 5181 Beer and other fermented malt
liquors
PA: Allied Company Holdings, Inc.
13235 Golden State Rd
818 493-6400

(P-11040)
**ALLIED COMPANY HOLDINGS
INC (PA)**
Also Called: Best-Way Distributing Co
13235 Golden State Rd, Sylmar
(91342-1129)
PHONE................818 493-6400
Kevin Williams, *CEO*
William L Larson, *
Erin S Gabler, *
Earl J Whitehead, *
◆ **EMP:** 97 **EST:** 1953
SQ FT: 240,000
SALES (est): 10.69MM
SALES (corp-wide): 10.69MM **Privately
Held**
Web: www.alliedbeverages.com
SIC: 5181 Beer and other fermented malt
liquors

(P-11041)
**BEAUCHAMP DISTRIBUTING
COMPANY**
1911 S Santa Fe Ave, Compton
(90221-5306)
PHONE................310 639-5320
Patrick L Beauchamp, *Pr*
Mary S Beauchamp, *
Stacee L Beauchamp, *
Peter J Gumpert, *
▲ **EMP:** 100 **EST:** 1971
SQ FT: 100,000
SALES (est): 19.04MM **Privately Held**
Web: www.beauchampdistributing.com
SIC: 5181 5149 Beer and other fermented
malt liquors; Groceries and related
products, nec

(P-11042)
BENNY ENTERPRISES INC
Also Called: Quality Distributor
1100 N Johnson Ave Ste 110, El Cajon
(92020-1917)
PHONE................619 592-4455
Raad Benny, *CEO*
EMP: 40 **EST:** 1994
SQ FT: 8,000
SALES (est): 9.79MM **Privately Held**
SIC: 5181 5141 5087 5015 Beer and ale;
Groceries, general line; Cleaning and
maintenance equipment and supplies;
Automotive parts and supplies, used

(P-11043)
**CENTRAL COAST
DISTRIBUTING LLC**
815 S Blosser Rd, Santa Maria
(93458-4915)
PHONE................805 922-2108
▲ **EMP:** 90 **EST:** 2001
SQ FT: 51,651
SALES (est): 2.38MM **Privately Held**
Web: www.greatbeer.us
SIC: 5181 Beer and other fermented malt
liquors

(P-11044)
**CLASSIC BEV SOUTHERN CAL
LLC**
120 Puente Ave, City Of Industry
(91746-2301)
PHONE................626 934-3700
Carlos Joseph Sanchez, *CEO*
John Thomas, *
▲ **EMP:** 261 **EST:** 1978
SQ FT: 102,000
SALES (est): 14.17MM **Privately Held**
Web: www.classicdist.com
SIC: 5181 Beer and other fermented malt
liquors

(P-11045)
CREST BEVERAGE LLC
1348 47th St, San Diego (92102-2510)
PHONE................858 452-2300
Steven S Sourapas, *Managing Member*
▲ **EMP:** 400 **EST:** 2009
SALES (est): 11.69MM **Privately Held**
Web: www.crestbeverage.com
SIC: 5181 Beer and other fermented malt
liquors

(P-11046)
**CREST BEVERAGE COMPANY
INC**
3840 Via De La Valle Ste 300, Del Mar
(92014-4268)
P.O. Box 9160 (92067-4160)
PHONE................858 452-2300
Steven S Sourapas Senior, *Pr*
▲ **EMP:** 170 **EST:** 1956
SQ FT: 160,000
SALES (est): 4.9MM **Privately Held**
Web: www.crestbeverage.com
SIC: 5181 5182 5149 Beer and other
fermented malt liquors; Wine; Groceries
and related products, nec

(P-11047)
**GATE CITY BEVERAGE DISTRS
(PA)**
2505 Steele Rd, San Bernardino
(92408-3913)
PHONE................909 799-0281
Leona Aronoff, *Pr*
Barry Aronoff, *
▲ **EMP:** 294 **EST:** 1940

SQ FT: 280,000
SALES (est): 7.39MM
SALES (corp-wide): 7.39MM **Privately Held**
Web: www.gatecitybeverage.com
SIC: 5181 5149 5145 Beer and other fermented malt liquors; Soft drinks; Confectionery

(P-11048)
HARALAMBOS BEVERAGE CO
26717 Palmetto Ave, Redlands (92374-1513)
PHONE...........................562 347-4300
H T Haralambos, *CEO*
Anthony Haralambos, *
Thomas Haralambos, *
Sally Haralambos, * *
▲ **EMP:** 300 **EST:** 1933
SALES (est): 11.61MM **Privately Held**
SIC: 5181 5149 Beer and other fermented malt liquors; Beverages, except coffee and tea

(P-11049)
HARBOR DISTRIBUTING LLC (HQ)
Also Called: Golden Brands
5901 Bolsa Ave, Huntington Beach (92647-2053)
PHONE...........................714 933-2400
Jude Reyes, *
Chris Reyes, *
▲ **EMP:** 200 **EST:** 1989
SQ FT: 150,000
SALES (est): 310.62MM **Privately Held**
Web: www.harbordistributingllc.com
SIC: 5181 Beer and other fermented malt liquors
PA: Reyes Holdings, L.L.C.
6250 N River Rd Ste 9000

(P-11050)
JORDANOS INC (PA)
Also Called: Jordano's Food Service
550 S Patterson Ave, Santa Barbara (93111-2498)
P.O. Box 6803 (93160-6803)
PHONE...........................805 964-0611
Peter Jordano, *CEO*
Michael F Sieckowski, *VP*
Jeffrey S Jordano, *Ex VP*
▲ **EMP:** 250 **EST:** 1915
SQ FT: 80,000
SALES (est): 95.73MM
SALES (corp-wide): 95.73MM **Privately Held**
Web: www.jordanos.com
SIC: 5181 5182 5149 5141 Beer and other fermented malt liquors; Wine; Soft drinks; Groceries, general line

(P-11051)
LIQUID INVESTMENTS INC (PA)
3840 Via De La Valle Ste 300, Del Mar (92014-4268)
PHONE...........................858 509-8510
Ron L Fowler, *CEO*
Terry L Harris, *
Mark Herculson, *
▲ **EMP:** 170 **EST:** 1981
SQ FT: 190,000
SALES (est): 9.6MM
SALES (corp-wide): 9.6MM **Privately Held**
Web: www.nextsolutions.us
SIC: 5181 5145 5182 Beer and other fermented malt liquors; Fountain supplies; Wine

(P-11052)
STRAUB DISTRIBUTING CO LTD (PA)
4633 E La Palma Ave, Anaheim (92807-1909)
PHONE...........................714 779-4000
Michael L Cooper, *Genl Pt*
Don Beightol, *Pt*
Robert K Adams, *Pt*
▲ **EMP:** 150 **EST:** 1948
SQ FT: 32,000
SALES (est): 13.4MM
SALES (corp-wide): 13.4MM **Privately Held**
Web: www.straubdistributing.com
SIC: 5181 Beer and other fermented malt liquors

(P-11053)
TRIANGLE DISTRIBUTING CO
Also Called: Heimark Distributing
12065 Pike St, Santa Fe Springs (90670-6102)
PHONE...........................562 699-3424
▲ **EMP:** 270
SIC: 5181 Beer and other fermented malt liquors

5182 Wine And Distilled Beverages

(P-11054)
BREAKTHRU BEVERAGE CAL LLC (HQ)
6550 E Washington Blvd, Commerce (90040-1822)
P.O. Box 910900 (90091-0900)
PHONE...........................800 331-2829
James P Myerson, *Pr*
◆ **EMP:** 350 **EST:** 1966
SQ FT: 135,000
SALES (est): 18.32MM
SALES (corp-wide): 2.8B **Privately Held**
Web: www.breakthrubevca.com
SIC: 5182 Wine
PA: Breakthru Beverage Group, Llc
60 E 42nd St Ste 1915
212 699-7000

(P-11055)
CUSHMAN WINERY CORPORATION
Also Called: Zaca Mesa Winery
6905 Foxen Canyon Rd, Los Olivos (93441-4530)
P.O. Box 899 (93441-0899)
PHONE...........................805 688-9339
Brook Williams, *Pr*
Susan English, *
▲ **EMP:** 31 **EST:** 1972
SALES (est): 10.58MM **Privately Held**
Web: www.zacamesa.com
SIC: 5182 2084 0172 Wine; Wines; Grapes

(P-11056)
GUARACHI WINE PARTNERS INC
Also Called: Parker Station
27001 Agoura Rd Ste 285, Calabasas (91301-5141)
PHONE...........................818 225-5100
Alejandro Guarachi, *CEO*
▲ **EMP:** 80 **EST:** 1988
SQ FT: 5,000
SALES (est): 13.49MM **Privately Held**
Web: www.guarachiwinepartners.com
SIC: 5182 Wine

(P-11057)
LUCAS & LEWELLEN VINEYARDS INC (PA)
Also Called: Lucas Lwllen Vnyrds Tasting Rm
1645 Copenhagen Dr, Solvang (93463-3742)
P.O. Box 648 (93440-0648)
PHONE...........................805 686-9336
Royce R Lewellen, *Pr*
Louis A Lucas, *
▲ **EMP:** 25 **EST:** 1996
SALES (est): 9.3MM
SALES (corp-wide): 9.3MM **Privately Held**
Web: www.llwine.com
SIC: 5182 2084 Wine; Wines

(P-11058)
MONTESQUIEU CORP
Also Called: Montesquieu Vins & Domaines
888 W E St, San Diego (92101-5912)
PHONE...........................877 705-5669
Fonda Hopkins, *Pr*
Frank Kryger, *
▲ **EMP:** 100 **EST:** 1991
SALES (est): 6.52MM **Privately Held**
Web: www.montesquieu.com
SIC: 5182 8743 Wine; Promotion service

(P-11059)
PERNOD RICARD USA LLC
3333 Michelson Dr Ste 925, Irvine (92612-7652)
PHONE...........................949 242-6800
Ricard Pernod, *Brnch Mgr*
▲ **EMP:** 97
SALES (corp-wide): 494.94MM **Privately Held**
Web: www.pernod-ricard-usa.com
SIC: 5182 Wine
HQ: Pernod Ricard Usa, Llc
250 Park Ave 17th Fl
New York NY 10177
212 372-5400

(P-11060)
REPUBLIC NAT DISTRG CO LLC (PA)
Also Called: Rndc
14402 Franklin Ave, Tustin (92780-7013)
P.O. Box 37100 (40233)
PHONE...........................714 368-4615
Jay Johnson, *Managing Member*
Nicholas Mehall, *
Robert Hendrickson, *
Robert Cornella, *
Sean Halligan, *Co-Executive Vice President*
▲ **EMP:** 144 **EST:** 1998
SALES (est): 1.4B
SALES (corp-wide): 1.4B **Privately Held**
Web: www.rndc-usa.com
SIC: 5182 Wine

(P-11061)
SOUTHERN GLZERS WINE SPRITS LL
Also Called: Southern Glzers Wine Sprits Ca
17101 Valley View Ave, Cerritos (90703-2442)
PHONE...........................562 926-2000
EMP: 500
SALES (corp-wide): 7.27B **Privately Held**
Web: www.southernglazers.com
SIC: 5182 5181 Wine; Beer and ale
HQ: Southern Glazer's Wine And Spirits, Llc
2400 Sw 145th Ave Ste 200
Miramar FL 33027
954 680-4600

(P-11062)
THORNHILL COMPANIES INC
132 E Carrillo St, Santa Barbara (93101-2111)
PHONE...........................805 969-5803
EMP: 90 **EST:** 2016
SALES (est): 2.77MM **Privately Held**
Web: www.thornhillcompanies.com
SIC: 5182 Wine and distilled beverages

(P-11063)
YOUNGS HOLDINGS INC (PA)
15 Enterprise Ste 100, Aliso Viejo (92656-2654)
PHONE...........................714 368-4615
Chris Underwood, *CEO*
Vernon Underwood Junior, *Ch Bd*
EMP: 100 **EST:** 1973
SALES (est): 77.88MM
SALES (corp-wide): 77.88MM **Privately Held**
Web: www.youngsholdings.com
SIC: 5182 Wine

(P-11064)
YOUNGS INTERCO INC
14402 Franklin Ave, Tustin (92780-7013)
PHONE...........................714 368-4615
Chris Underwood, *CEO*
Vernon Underwood, *Ch Bd*
▲ **EMP:** 1606 **EST:** 1989
SQ FT: 250,000
SALES (est): 4.76MM
SALES (corp-wide): 77.88MM **Privately Held**
SIC: 5182 Wine
PA: Young's Holdings, Inc.
15 Enterprise Ste 100
714 368-4615

(P-11065)
YOUNGS MARKET COMPANY LLC
Also Called: Wine Dept
500 S Central Ave, Los Angeles (90013-1715)
PHONE...........................213 629-3929
Mark Sneed, *Brnch Mgr*
EMP: 264
SALES (corp-wide): 1.4B **Privately Held**
Web: www.rndc-usa.com
SIC: 5182 Wine
HQ: Young's Market Company, Llc
14402 Franklin Ave
Tustin CA 92780
800 317-6150

(P-11066)
YOUNGS MARKET COMPANY LLC (HQ)
14402 Franklin Ave, Tustin (92780-7013)
PHONE...........................800 317-6150
Chris Underwood, *CEO*
Dennis Hamann, *
◆ **EMP:** 350 **EST:** 1888
SQ FT: 250,000
SALES (est): 344.83MM
SALES (corp-wide): 1.4B **Privately Held**
Web: www.rndc-usa.com
SIC: 5182 Wine
PA: Republic National Distributing Company, Llc
14402 Franklin Ave
714 368-4615

(P-11067)
YOUNGS MARKET COMPANY LLC
Also Called: Young's Market

6711 Bickmore Ave, Chino (91708-9103)
PHONE..............................909 393-4540
Terrie Young, *Brnch Mgr*
EMP: 72
SALES (corp-wide): 1.4B **Privately Held**
Web: www.rndc-usa.com
SIC: 5182 Wine
HQ: Young's Market Company, Llc
    14402 Franklin Ave
    Tustin CA 92780
    800 317-6150

5191 Farm Supplies

(P-11068)
AG RX (PA)
Also Called: Mountain View Transportation
751 S Rose Ave, Oxnard (93030-5146)
P.O. Box 2008 (93034-2008)
PHONE..............................805 487-0696
Ken Burdullis, *Pr*
EMP: 92 EST: 1993
SQ FT: 45,000
SALES (est): 46.92MM **Privately Held**
Web: www.agrx.com
SIC: 5191 Fertilizer and fertilizer materials

(P-11069)
BFG SUPPLY CO LLC
2552 Shenandoah Way, San Bernardino
(92407-1845)
PHONE..............................909 591-0461
David C Daily, *Pr*
EMP: 190
SALES (corp-wide): 183.31MM **Privately Held**
Web: www.bfgsupply.com
SIC: 5191 2875 2449 5193 Insecticides;
    Potting soil, mixed; Wood containers, nec;
    Flowers and florists supplies
PA: Bfg Supply Co., Llc
    14500 Kinsman Rd
    800 883-0234

(P-11070)
LEACH GRAIN & MILLING CO INC
8131 Pivot St, Downey (90241-4853)
PHONE..............................562 869-4451
Willis R Leach Senior, *Pr*
Roy Leach, *
Willis R Leach Junior, *Sec*
Bruce Leach, *Stockholder*
EMP: 26 EST: 1934
SQ FT: 20,000
SALES (est): 4.73MM **Privately Held**
Web: www.leachgrain.com
SIC: 5191 2047 2048 Farm supplies; Dog
    and cat food; Bird food, prepared

(P-11071)
SEEDS OF CHANGE INC
Also Called: Sustainable Agriculture
31 Mountain Laurel, Trabuco Canyon
(92679-4216)
P.O. Box 4908 (90220)
PHONE..............................310 764-7700
Will Righeimer, *CEO*
◆ EMP: 120 EST: 1997
SALES (est): 2.01MM
SALES (corp-wide): 42.84B **Privately Held**
Web: www.seedsofchange.com
SIC: 5191 0723 Seeds: field, garden, and
    flower; Crop preparation services for market
HQ: Mars Food Us, Llc
    2001 E Cashdan St Ste 201
    Rancho Dominguez CA 90220
    310 933-0670

(P-11072)
SEMINIS VEGETABLE SEEDS INC (DH)
Also Called: Seminis
2700 Camino Del Sol, Oxnard
(93030-7967)
PHONE..............................855 733-3834
Michael J Frank, *CEO*
Kerry Preete, *
◆ EMP: 600 EST: 1962
SQ FT: 370,000
SALES (est): 27.62MM
SALES (corp-wide): 51.78B **Privately Held**
Web: www.seminis-us.com
SIC: 5191 0723 Seeds: field, garden, and
    flower; Crop preparation services for market
HQ: Monsanto Technology Llc.
    800 North Lindbergh Blvd
    Saint Louis MO 63167
    314 694-1000

(P-11073)
TARGET SPECIALTY PRODUCTS INC
15415 Marquardt Ave, Santa Fe Springs
(90670-5711)
P.O. Box 3408 (90670-1408)
PHONE..............................562 865-9541
EMP: 100
Web: www.target-specialty.com
SIC: 5191 Chemicals, agricultural

5192 Books, Periodicals, And Newspapers

(P-11074)
BAKER & TAYLOR LLC
10350 Barnes Canyon Rd Ste 100, San
Diego (92121-2709)
PHONE..............................858 457-2500
James Leidich, *Dir*
EMP: 214
Web: www.baker-taylor.com
SIC: 5192 5099 5199 5045 Books; Tapes
    and cassettes, prerecorded; Calendars;
    Computer software
PA: Baker & Taylor, Llc
    2810 Clseum Cntre Dr Ste

(P-11075)
EL AVISO MAGAZINE
4850 Gage Ave, Bell (90201-1409)
P.O. Box 3360 (90202-3360)
PHONE..............................323 586-9199
Jose Zepeda, *CEO*
EMP: 40 EST: 1988
SALES (est): 616.68K **Privately Held**
Web: www.elaviso.com
SIC: 5192 2721 Magazines; Magazines:
    publishing and printing

(P-11076)
GREAT ATLANTIC NEWS LLC
Also Called: News Group, The
1575 N Main St, Orange (92867-3439)
PHONE..............................770 863-9000
John Seebach, *Brnch Mgr*
EMP: 109
SALES (corp-wide): 28.29B **Privately Held**
SIC: 5192 5994 Periodicals; Magazine stand
HQ: Great Atlantic News L.L.C.
    1962 Highway 160 W # 102
    Fort Mill SC 29708

(P-11077)
MADER NEWS INC
913 Ruberta Ave, Glendale (91201-2346)
PHONE..............................818 551-5000

Avan Mader, *Pr*
EMP: 100 EST: 1980
SALES (est): 3.92MM **Privately Held**
Web: www.madernews.com
SIC: 5192 Newspapers

(P-11078)
WHITE DIGITAL MEDIA INC
Also Called: Wdm Group
3394 Carmel Mountain Rd Ste 250, San
Diego (92121-1072)
PHONE..............................760 827-7800
Brian Smith, *CEO*
Glen White, *
Matthew P Melucci, *Chief Content Officer**
EMP: 150 EST: 2007
SALES (est): 2.22MM **Privately Held**
SIC: 5192 Magazines

5193 Flowers And Florists Supplies

(P-11079)
ALTMAN SPECIALTY PLANTS LLC
Also Called: Altman Flowers
2575 Olive Hill Rd, Fallbrook (92028-9557)
PHONE..............................800 348-4881
EMP: 385
SALES (corp-wide): 225.14MM **Privately Held**
Web: www.altmanplants.com
SIC: 5193 Nursery stock
PA: Altman Specialty Plants, Llc
    3742 Bluebird Canyon Rd
    800 348-4881

(P-11080)
ALTMAN SPECIALTY PLANTS LLC (PA)
Also Called: Altman Plants
3742 Blue Bird Canyon Rd, Vista
(92084-7432)
PHONE..............................800 348-4881
Ken Altman, *CEO*
Deena Altman, *
▲ EMP: 800 EST: 1973
SQ FT: 4,000
SALES (est): 225.14MM
SALES (corp-wide): 225.14MM **Privately Held**
Web: www.altmanplants.com
SIC: 5193 3999 Nursery stock; Atomizers;
    toiletry

(P-11081)
B & B NURSERIES INC
Also Called: Landscape Center
9505 Cleveland Ave, Riverside
(92503-6241)
P.O. Box 7308 (92513)
PHONE..............................951 352-8383
Mark Barrett, *CEO*
EMP: 109 EST: 1985
SALES (est): 9.98MM **Privately Held**
Web: www.tlcnurseries.com
SIC: 5193 0781 Flowers and nursery stock;
    Landscape counseling services

(P-11082)
BANDY RANCH FLORAL CORP
2755 Dos Aarons Way Ste B, Vista
(92081-8359)
PHONE..............................805 757-9905
Steve Dodge, *CEO*
EMP: 115 EST: 2015
SALES (est): 32.25MM **Privately Held**
Web: www.bandyranchfloral.com

SIC: 5193 Flowers, fresh

(P-11083)
BELLA TERRA NURSERY INC
Also Called: Terra Bella Nursery
302 Hollister St, San Diego (92154-4700)
P.O. Box 551 (91912-0551)
PHONE..............................619 585-1118
Jose L Ramos, *Pr*
EMP: 100 EST: 2007
SALES (est): 5.07MM **Privately Held**
Web: www.terrabellanursery.com
SIC: 5193 Flowers and florists supplies

(P-11084)
BOUQS COMPANY
Also Called: Thebouqs.com
4094 Glencoe Ave, Marina Del Rey
(90292-5608)
PHONE..............................888 320-2687
Kimberly Tobman, *CEO*
John Tabis, *Ch Bd*
Jp Montfar, *COO*
EMP: 98 EST: 2012
SALES (est): 14.66MM **Privately Held**
Web: www.bouqs.com
SIC: 5193 Flowers, fresh

(P-11085)
COUNTRY FLORAL SUPPLY INC (PA)
Also Called: Country Furnishings
3802 Weatherly Cir, Westlake Village
(91361-3821)
PHONE..............................805 520-8026
Mark Reese, *Pr*
Debbie Reese, *
▲ EMP: 80 EST: 1982
SQ FT: 60,000
SALES (est): 2.62MM
SALES (corp-wide): 2.62MM **Privately Held**
SIC: 5193 5999 Artificial flowers; Artificial
    flowers

(P-11086)
DELTA FLORAL DISTRIBUTORS INC
6810 West Blvd, Los Angeles (90043-4668)
PHONE..............................323 751-8116
Foti Defterios, *Pr*
▲ EMP: 200 EST: 1984
SQ FT: 30,000
SALES (est): 4.22MM **Privately Held**
SIC: 5193 Flowers, fresh

(P-11087)
GREEN THUMB INTERNATIONAL INC
21812 Sherman Way, Canoga Park
(91303-1940)
PHONE..............................818 340-6400
Del Berquist, *Prin*
EMP: 87
SALES (corp-wide): 24.03MM **Privately Held**
Web: www.greenthumb.com
SIC: 5193 5261 0782 0181 Nursery stock;
    Retail nurseries and garden stores; Lawn
    and garden services; Ornamental nursery
    products
PA: Green Thumb International Inc
    7105 Jordan Ave
    818 340-6400

(P-11088)
GRINGO VENTURES LLC
Also Called: Dos Gringos
3260 Corporate Vw, Vista (92081-8528)

PHONE.................760 477-7999
EMP: 354 EST: 1995
SALES (est): 14.64MM Privately Held
Web: www.dosgringos.com
SIC: 5193 0181 Flowers and florists supplies
; Ornamental nursery products

(P-11089)
GROLINK PLANT COMPANY INC (PA)
Also Called: Grolink
4107 W Gonzales Rd, Oxnard
(93036-7783)
P.O. Box 5506 (93031-5506)
PHONE.................805 984-7958
Anthony Vollering, CEO
Art Gordijin, *
Jerry Van Wingerden, *
Harry Van Wingerden, Stockholder*
Ton Vallering, *
▲ EMP: 149 EST: 1985
SQ FT: 400,000
SALES (est): 1.27MM
SALES (corp-wide): 1.27MM Privately
Held
Web: www.grolink.com
SIC: 5193 0181 Nursery stock; Ornamental
nursery products

(P-11090)
KENDAL FLORAL SUPPLY LLC (PA)
Also Called: Kendal North Bouquet Co
1960 Kellogg Ave, Carlsbad (92008-6581)
PHONE.................888 828-9875
Kenneth X Baca, Pr
▲ EMP: 80 EST: 1973
SALES (est): 23.61MM
SALES (corp-wide): 23.61MM Privately
Held
Web: www.kmsfloral.com
SIC: 5193 Flowers, fresh

(P-11091)
MELLANO & CO
Also Called: Melano Enterprises
734 Wilshire Rd, Oceanside (92057-2111)
P.O. Box 100 (92068-0100)
PHONE.................760 433-9550
Harry M Mellano, Owner
EMP: 108
SALES (corp-wide): 29.69MM Privately
Held
Web: www.mellano.com
SIC: 5193 Flowers, fresh
PA: Mellano & Company
766 Wall St
213 622-0796

(P-11092)
MELLANO & COMPANY (PA)
Also Called: Mellano Enterprises
766 Wall St, Los Angeles (90014-2316)
P.O. Box 100 (92068-0100)
PHONE.................213 622-0796
Michael Anthony Mellano, CEO
H Mike Mellano Senior, VP
Michelle Castellano, *
Bob Mellano, *
EMP: 75 EST: 1975
SALES (est): 29.69MM
SALES (corp-wide): 29.69MM Privately
Held
Web: www.mellano.com
SIC: 5193 Flowers, fresh

(P-11093)
NAKASE BROTHERS WHL NURS LP (PA)

9441 Krepp Dr, Huntington Beach
(92646-2708)
PHONE.................949 855-4388
Shigeo Gary Nakase, Managing Member
▲ EMP: 100 EST: 1965
SALES (est): 3.55MM
SALES (corp-wide): 3.55MM Privately
Held
Web: www.nakasebros.com
SIC: 5193 Nursery stock

(P-11094)
NAKASE BROTHERS WHOLESALE NURS
Also Called: NAKASE BROTHERS
WHOLESALE NURSERY
20621 Lake Forest Dr, Lake Forest
(92630-7743)
PHONE.................949 855-4388
Joann Shurlock, Mgr
EMP: 180
SALES (corp-wide): 22.88MM Privately
Held
Web: www.nakasebros.com
SIC: 5193 Nursery stock
PA: Nakase Brothers Wholesale Nursery Lp
9441 Krepp Dr
949 855-4388

(P-11095)
NORMANS NURSERY INC
5800 Via Real, Carpinteria (93013-2610)
PHONE.................805 684-5442
EMP: 142
SALES (corp-wide): 41.58MM Privately
Held
Web: www.normansnursery.com
SIC: 5193 Nursery stock
PA: Norman's Nursery, Inc.
8665 Duarte Rd
626 285-9795

(P-11096)
NORMANS NURSERY INC
Also Called: Norman's Nursery
20500 Ramona Blvd, Baldwin Park (91706)
PHONE.................626 285-9795
Ricardo Goodman, Mgr
EMP: 143
SALES (corp-wide): 41.58MM Privately
Held
Web: www.nngrower.com
SIC: 5193 Nursery stock
PA: Norman's Nursery, Inc.
8665 Duarte Rd
626 285-9795

(P-11097)
PARDEE TREE NURSERY
30970 Via Puerta Del Sol, Oceanside
(92057)
P.O. Box 240 (92003-0240)
PHONE.................760 630-5400
Lauren Davis, Pr
EMP: 75 EST: 1999
SALES (est): 9.37MM Privately Held
Web: www.pardeetree.com
SIC: 5193 Nursery stock

(P-11098)
PONTO NURSERY
2545 Ramona Dr, Vista (92084-1632)
P.O. Box 536 (92085-0536)
PHONE.................760 724-6003
William Ponto, Pr
Judy Ponto, *
EMP: 70 EST: 1956
SQ FT: 2,000
SALES (est): 768.5K Privately Held
Web: www.pontonursery.com

SIC: 5193 Nursery stock

(P-11099)
PYRAMID FLOWERS INC
3813 Doris Ave, Oxnard (93030-4706)
PHONE.................805 382-8070
Fred Van Wingerden, Pr
Edith Van Wingerden, *
▲ EMP: 120 EST: 1991
SQ FT: 900,000
SALES (est): 16.07MM Privately Held
Web: www.pyramidflowers.com
SIC: 5193 Flowers, fresh

(P-11100)
SPECTRUM EQUIPMENT LLC
Also Called: Spectrum Floral Service
2505 Commerce Way, Vista (92081-8420)
PHONE.................760 599-8849
Gene Aschbrenner, Managing Member
Sarah Aschbrenner, *
William Simon, *
EMP: 80 EST: 2017
SQ FT: 16,000
SALES (est): 3.04MM Privately Held
SIC: 5193 Flowers, fresh

(P-11101)
SUNSHINE FLORAL INC
4595 Foothill Rd, Carpinteria (93013-3096)
PHONE.................805 684-1177
Henry Vanwingerden, Pr
Anthony Vollering, *
▲ EMP: 70 EST: 1972
SALES (est): 1.03MM Privately Held
Web: www.sunshinefloral.com
SIC: 5193 Flowers, fresh

(P-11102)
T - Y NURSERY INC
15335 Highway 76, Pauma Valley
(92061-9583)
P.O. Box 424 (92061-0424)
PHONE.................760 742-2151
Alfonso Ramos, Mgr
EMP: 200
SALES (corp-wide): 23.67MM Privately
Held
Web: www.tynursery.com
SIC: 5193 5261 Plants, potted; Retail
nurseries
PA: T - Y Nursery, Inc.
5221 Arvada St
310 370-2561

(P-11103)
VILLAGE NURSERIES WHL LLC
20099 Santa Rosa Mine Rd, Perris
(92570-7774)
PHONE.................951 657-3940
Joseph Jensen, Brnch Mgr
EMP: 299
SALES (corp-wide): 14.4MM Privately
Held
Web: www.everde.com
SIC: 5193 Nursery stock
PA: Village Nurseries Wholesale, Llc
1045 W Katella Ave
714 279-3100

5194 Tobacco And Tobacco Products

(P-11104)
KRETEK INTERNATIONAL INC (DH)
5449 Endeavour Ct, Moorpark
(93021-1712)

PHONE.................805 531-8888
Hugh R Cassar, CEO
Lynn K Cassar, *
Sean Cassar, *
Donald Gormley, *
Eliot Suied, *
◆ EMP: 90 EST: 1983
SQ FT: 80,000
SALES (est): 45.92MM Privately Held
Web: www.kretek.com
SIC: 5194 Cigarettes
HQ: Pt. Djarum
Jalan Jend. A. Yani No. 28
Kabupaten Kudus JT 59317

(P-11105)
NATIONAL TOBACCO COMPANY LP (DH)
Also Called: National Tobacco Company
1315 Lincoln Blvd, Santa Monica
(90401-1750)
PHONE.................800 579-0975
Thomas Helms Junior, Ch Bd
Robert A Milliken Junior, Pr
▲ EMP: 245 EST: 1988
SQ FT: 550,000
SALES (est): 30.65MM
SALES (corp-wide): 405.39MM Publicly
Held
Web: www.zigzag.com
SIC: 5194 Tobacco and tobacco products
HQ: North Atlantic Trading Company, Inc.
5201 Interchange Way
Louisville KY 40229
502 778-4421

5198 Paints, Varnishes, And Supplies

(P-11106)
BERG LACQUER CO (PA)
Also Called: Pacific Coast Lacquer
3150 E Pico Blvd, Los Angeles
(90023-3632)
PHONE.................323 261-8114
Sandra Berg, Pr
Robert O Berg, *
▲ EMP: 65 EST: 1934
SQ FT: 85,000
SALES (est): 4.22MM
SALES (corp-wide): 4.22MM Privately
Held
SIC: 5198 2851 Paints; Paints and paint
additives

5199 Nondurable Goods, Nec

(P-11107)
99 CENTS ONLY STORES LLC (HQ)
Also Called: 99 Cents Only Stores
1730 Flight Way, Tustin (92782-1850)
PHONE.................323 980-8145
Barry J Feld, *
Felicia Thornton, *
Michael Kvitko, CMO*
Ashok Walia, *
◆ EMP: 500 EST: 1965
SALES (est): 3.36B
SALES (corp-wide): 3.36B Privately Held
Web: www.99only.com
SIC: 5199 5331 4225 General merchandise,
non-durable; Variety stores; General
warehousing and storage
PA: Number Holdings, Inc.
4000 Union Pacific Ave
323 980-8145

(P-11108)
AHI INVESTMENT INC (DH)
Also Called: Linzer Products
675 Glenoaks Blvd, San Fernando
(91340-1471)
P.O. Box 310 (91341-0310)
PHONE....................................818 979-0030
Hisatoshi Ohtsuka, *Prin*
Mark Saji, *Ex VP*
Yuko Waki, *Prin*
◆ **EMP:** 25 **EST:** 1989
SQ FT: 75,000
SALES (est): 52.67MM **Privately Held**
Web: www.linzerproducts.com
SIC: 5199 3991 Broom, mop, and paint
handles; Paintbrushes
HQ: Ohtsuka Brush Mfg.Co., Ltd.
4-1, Yotsuya
Shinjuku-Ku TKY 160-0

(P-11109)
**AMERICAN PAPER & PLASTICS
LLC**
Also Called: American Paper & Provisions
550 S 7th Ave, City Of Industry
(91746-3120)
PHONE....................................626 444-0000
Daniel Emrani, *CEO*
EMP: 119 **EST:** 1982
SQ FT: 300,000
SALES (est): 42.25MM
SALES (corp-wide): 1.65B **Privately Held**
Web: www.appinc.com
SIC: 5199 Packaging materials
PA: Imperial Bag & Paper Co. Llc
255 Route 1 & 9
201 437-7440

(P-11110)
ANNS TRADING COMPANY INC
Also Called: Urban Concepts
5333 S Downey Rd, Vernon (90058-3725)
PHONE....................................323 585-4702
Hyung Don Kim, *CEO*
Daniel Im, *
Mi H Kim, *Sec*
◆ **EMP:** 30 **EST:** 1981
SALES (est): 8.35MM **Privately Held**
Web: www.annstrading.com
SIC: 5199 2335 Gifts and novelties;
Women's, junior's, and misses' dresses

(P-11111)
ARMANI TRADE LLC
21255 Burbank Blvd Ste 120, Woodland
Hills (91367-6669)
PHONE....................................310 849-0067
Nader Abdollahi, *CEO*
EMP: 50 **EST:** 2018
SALES (est): 2.02MM **Privately Held**
SIC: 5199 3699 General merchandise, non-
durable; Electrical equipment and supplies,
nec

(P-11112)
BIO HAZARD INC
6019 Randolph St, Commerce
(90040-3417)
PHONE....................................213 625-2116
EMP: 36 **EST:** 2007
SALES (est): 4.15MM **Privately Held**
Web: www.biohazardinc.com
SIC: 5199 3221 Smokers' supplies; Glass
containers

(P-11113)
BLUEMARK INC
27909 Hancock Pkwy, Valencia
(91355-4116)
PHONE....................................323 230-0770

Joseph Shusterman, *CEO*
Yosef Shusterman, *
EMP: 112 **EST:** 2009
SALES (est): 9.53MM **Privately Held**
Web: www.bluemark.com
SIC: 5199 Advertising specialties

(P-11114)
CLOUDRADIANT CORP (PA)
Also Called: Enbiz International
12 Fuchsia, Lake Forest (92630-1431)
PHONE....................................408 256-1527
Anil Rao, *Pr*
◆ **EMP:** 128 **EST:** 2010
SALES (est): 8.14MM
SALES (corp-wide): 8.14MM **Privately
Held**
SIC: 5199 8748 7371 8711 General
merchandise, non-durable; Business
consulting, nec; Computer software
systems analysis and design, custom;
Consulting engineer

(P-11115)
DOLPHIN HKG LTD (PA)
Also Called: Dolphin International
1125 W Hillcrest Blvd, Inglewood
(90301-2021)
P.O. Box 91081 (90009-1081)
PHONE....................................310 215-3356
Steven Lundblad, *Pr*
Helen Lundblad, *
◆ **EMP:** 70 **EST:** 1970
SQ FT: 12,000
SALES (est): 9.56MM
SALES (corp-wide): 9.56MM **Privately
Held**
Web: www.dolphin-int.com
SIC: 5199 Tropical fish

(P-11116)
EPSILON PLASTICS INC
3100 E Harcourt St, Compton (90221-5506)
PHONE....................................310 609-1320
Jim Gifford, *Mgr*
EMP: 75
SQ FT: 39,963
Web: www.alpha-industries.com
SIC: 5199 Packaging materials
HQ: Epsilon Plastics Inc.
Page & Schuyler Ave # 8
Lyndhurst NJ 07071
201 933-6000

(P-11117)
ERNEST PACKAGING (PA)
Also Called: Ernest Paper
5777 Smithway St, Commerce
(90040-1507)
PHONE....................................800 233-7788
Charles Wilson, *Ch Bd*
Timothy Wilson, *
▲ **EMP:** 130 **EST:** 1947
SQ FT: 300,000
SALES (est): 189.32MM
SALES (corp-wide): 189.32MM **Privately
Held**
Web: www.ernestpackaging.com
SIC: 5199 7389 5113 Packaging materials;
Cosmetic kits, assembling and packaging;
Shipping supplies

(P-11118)
EUROW AND OREILLY CORP
Also Called: Equine Comfort Products
51 Moreland Rd, Simi Valley (93065-1662)
PHONE....................................800 747-7452
Donna O'reilly, *CEO*
Patrice Bonnefoi, *
◆ **EMP:** 32 **EST:** 2000

SQ FT: 60,000
SALES (est): 10.43MM **Privately Held**
Web: www.eurow.com
SIC: 5199 2392 General merchandise, non-
durable; Towels, dishcloths and dust cloths

(P-11119)
EVE HAIR INC (PA)
Also Called: Eve
3935 Paramount Blvd, Lakewood
(90712-4100)
PHONE....................................562 377-1020
Young Soo Cho, *Pr*
Young Soo Cho, *Pr*
Ed Pak, *
◆ **EMP:** 37 **EST:** 1990
SQ FT: 44,000
SALES (est): 1.63MM **Privately Held**
Web: www.evehairinc.com
SIC: 5199 3999 Wigs; Hair and hair-based
products

(P-11120)
EZCARETECH USA INC
21081 S Western Ave Ste 130, Torrance
(90501-1707)
PHONE....................................424 558-3191
Justin Chung, *CEO*
Kyungho Min, *
Justin Park, *
EMP: 350 **EST:** 2019
SALES (est): 964.23K **Privately Held**
Web: www.ezcaretech.com
SIC: 5199 Nondurable goods, nec

(P-11121)
GAJU MARKET CORPORATION
Also Called: Gaju Market
450 S Western Ave, Los Angeles
(90020-4120)
PHONE....................................213 382-9444
David Rhee, *CEO*
EMP: 135 **EST:** 2015
SQ FT: 2,000
SALES (est): 2MM **Privately Held**
Web: www.gajumarketplace.com
SIC: 5199 General merchandise, non-durable

(P-11122)
GIFTING GROUP LLC
42210 Zevo Dr, Temecula (92590-3732)
PHONE....................................951 296-0310
Andrea Stringer, *Managing Member*
Andrea Stringer, *Pr*
▲ **EMP:** 75 **EST:** 2011
SQ FT: 24,575
SALES (est): 11.07MM **Privately Held**
Web: www.aldercrookgiftbackotc.com
SIC: 5199 5149 5145 5947 Gifts and
novelties; Food gift baskets; Candy; Gift
baskets

(P-11123)
GRAPHIC PACKAGING INTL LLC
1600 Barranca Pkwy, Irvine (92606-4823)
PHONE....................................949 250-0900
Wendy Shute, *Brnch Mgr*
EMP: 96
Web: www.graphicpkg.com
SIC: 5199 Packaging materials
HQ: Graphic Packaging International, Llc
1500 Rvredge Pkwy Ste 100
Atlanta GA 30328

(P-11124)
KATZKIN LEATHER INC (PA)
6868 W Acco St, Montebello (90640-5441)
PHONE....................................323 725-1243
Brook Mayberry, *Pr*
Scott Briskie, *

▲ **EMP:** 200 **EST:** 1998
SQ FT: 50,000
SALES (est): 21.59MM
SALES (corp-wide): 21.59MM **Privately
Held**
Web: www.katzkin.com
SIC: 5199 2531 Leather and cut stock;
Seats, automobile

(P-11125)
KHW ENTERPRISES INC
8550 Chetle Ave Ste A, Whittier
(90606-2697)
PHONE....................................562 236-8440
◆ **EMP:** 75
SIC: 5199 Pets and pet supplies

(P-11126)
KOLE IMPORTS
Also Called: Basket Basics
24600 Main St, Carson (90745-6332)
PHONE....................................310 834-0004
Robert Kole, *CEO*
Dan Kole, *
◆ **EMP:** 78 **EST:** 1985
SQ FT: 150,000
SALES (est): 21.56MM **Privately Held**
Web: www.koleimports.com
SIC: 5199 General merchandise, non-durable

(P-11127)
**LEE-MAR AQUARIUM & PET
SUPS**
Also Called: Lee Mar Aquarium & Pet Sups
2459 Dogwood Way, Vista (92081-8421)
PHONE....................................760 727-1300
Terran R Boyd, *Pr*
▲ **EMP:** 100 **EST:** 1971
SQ FT: 67,000
SALES (est): 9.94MM **Privately Held**
Web: www.petwholesaleusa.com
SIC: 5199 3999 Pet supplies; Pet supplies

(P-11128)
LOGOMARK INC
Also Called: Valumark
1201 Bell Ave, Tustin (92780-6420)
PHONE....................................714 675-6100
Trevor Gnesin, *Pr*
▲ **EMP:** 250 **EST:** 1992
SQ FT: 200,000
SALES (est): 21.93MM **Privately Held**
Web: www.logomark.com
SIC: 5199 Advertising specialties

(P-11129)
MIDWAY INTERNATIONAL INC
Also Called: Bobbi Boss
13131 166th St, Cerritos (90703-2202)
PHONE....................................800 826-2383
Ha Chung, *CEO*
◆ **EMP:** 97 **EST:** 1985
SQ FT: 32,700
SALES (est): 21.94MM **Privately Held**
Web: www.bobbiboss.com
SIC: 5199 5047 Wigs; Medical equipment
and supplies

(P-11130)
MISA IMPORTS INC
2343 Saybrook Ave, Commerce
(90040-1721)
PHONE....................................562 281-6773
EMP: 99
SALES (corp-wide): 345.56MM **Privately
Held**
Web: www.misaimports.com
SIC: 5199 Art goods and supplies
PA: Misa Imports Inc.
1502 Viceroy Dr

PRODUCTS & SVCS

972 235-3834

(P-11131)
MODERN CANDLE CO INC
Also Called: Modern Candles
12884 Bradley Ave, Sylmar (91342-3827)
PHONE..................................323 441-0104
Armik Pirijanian, *CEO*
Nora Pirijanian, *
▲ **EMP: 45 EST: 1995**
SALES (est): 6.58MM Privately Held
Web: www.moderncandle.com
SIC: 5199 3999 Candles; Candles

(P-11132)
NW PACKAGING LLC (PA)
Also Called: NW Packaging
1201 E Lexington Ave, Pomona
(91766-5520)
P.O. Box 357 (92871-0357)
PHONE..................................909 706-3627
Robert E Sliter, *Admn*
EMP: 100 EST: 2012
SALES (est): 2.36MM
SALES (corp-wide): 2.36MM Privately Held
Web: www.nwpackagingonline.com
SIC: 5199 Packaging materials

(P-11133)
P2F HOLDINGS
Also Called: Mulen
1760 Apollo Ct, Seal Beach (90740-5617)
PHONE..................................562 296-1055
▲ **EMP: 75**
SIC: 5199 General merchandise, non-durable

(P-11134)
POLYCELL PACKAGING CORPORATION
12851 Midway Pl, Cerritos (90703-2141)
PHONE..................................562 483-6000
Chin Ching Hsu, *Pr*
▲ **EMP: 35 EST: 1995**
SALES (est): 11.82MM Privately Held
Web: www.polycellpkg.com
SIC: 5199 3089 Packaging materials; Blister
or bubble formed packaging, plastics

(P-11135)
PREMIERE PACKAGING INDS INC
Also Called: P P I
12202 Slauson Ave, Santa Fe Springs
(90670-2628)
PHONE..................................562 799-9200
John Luyben, *CEO*
Christi Luyben, *
EMP: 77 EST: 1999
SALES (est): 6.45MM
SALES (corp-wide): 2.35B Privately Held
SIC: 5199 Packaging materials
HQ: Kelly Spicers Inc.
12310 E Slauson Ave
Santa Fe Springs CA 90670

(P-11136)
PRO SPECIALTIES GROUP INC
14055 Kirkham Way, Poway (92064-7162)
PHONE..................................858 541-1100
Cheng Shun Li, *Pr*
I Chin Li, *Sec*
▲ **EMP: 70 EST: 1997**
SALES (est): 24.75MM Privately Held
Web: www.psginc.com
SIC: 5199 Advertising specialties

(P-11137)
PROACTIVE PACKG & DISPLAY LLC
602 S Rockefeller Ave Ste A, Ontario
(91761-8191)
PHONE..................................909 390-5624
Richard Hartman, *CEO*
▲ **EMP: 72 EST: 1994**
SQ FT: 164,000
SALES (est): 23.58MM
SALES (corp-wide): 587.57MM Privately Held
Web: www.newindypackaging.com
SIC: 5199 Packaging materials
HQ: New-Indy Containerboard Llc
3500 Porsche Wy Ste 150
Ontario CA 91764
909 296-3400

(P-11138)
REDBARN PET PRODUCTS INC (PA)
Also Called: Redbarn Premium Pet Products
3229 E Spring St Ste 310, Long Beach
(90806-2478)
PHONE..................................562 495-7315
Jeff Baikie, *CEO*
Howard Bloxam, *
◆ **EMP: 236 EST: 1994**
SQ FT: 50,000
SALES (est): 39.4MM Privately Held
Web: www.redbarn.com
SIC: 5199 2047 Pet supplies; Dog and cat
food

(P-11139)
REVOLTION CNSMR SLTIONS CA LLC (DH)
Also Called: Command Packaging
3840 E 26th St, Los Angeles (90058-4107)
PHONE..................................323 980-0918
◆ **EMP: 114 EST: 1989**
SQ FT: 170,000
SALES (est): 51.14MM
SALES (corp-wide): 303.43MM Privately Held
Web: www.commandpackaging.com
SIC: 5199 Packaging materials
HQ: Delta Plastics Of The South, Llc
8801 Frazier Pike
Little Rock AR 72206

(P-11140)
ROYAL PAPER BOX CO CALIFORNIA (PA)
1105 S Maple Ave, Montebello
(90640-6007)
P.O. Box 458 (90640-0458)
PHONE..................................323 728-7041
Jim Hodges, *CEO*
Darryl Carlson, *VP*
Scott Larson, *VP*
Andy Polanco, *VP*
Steve Perez, *VP*
▲ **EMP: 197 EST: 1940**
SQ FT: 172,500
SALES (est): 900.5K
SALES (corp-wide): 900.5K Privately Held
Web: www.royalpaperbox.com
SIC: 5199 Packaging materials

(P-11141)
RYL INC
2738 Supply Ave, Commerce (90040-2704)
PHONE..................................213 503-7968
James Lee, *CEO*
Ronald Lee, *
Sandra Lee, *
▲ **EMP: 35 EST: 1996**

SQ FT: 31,000
SALES (est): 4.94MM Privately Held
Web: www.colorglasstube.com
SIC: 5199 3221 General merchandise, non-
durable; Glass containers

(P-11142)
SCHROFF INC
7328 Trade St, San Diego (92121-3435)
PHONE..................................858 740-2400
Robert Bradley, *Brnch Mgr*
EMP: 136
Web: schroff.nvent.com
SIC: 5199 Packaging materials
HQ: Schroff, Inc.
170 Commerce Dr
Warwick RI 02886
763 204-7700

(P-11143)
SHIMS BARGAIN INC (PA)
Also Called: J C Sales
2600 S Soto St, Los Angeles (90058-8015)
PHONE..................................323 881-0099
Sesilia Song, *CEO*
Kenneth Suh, *
James Shim, *
Bj Chang, *CFO*
◆ **EMP: 100 EST: 1993**
SQ FT: 420,000
SALES (est): 38.75MM Privately Held
Web: www.jcsalesweb.com
SIC: 5199 General merchandise, non-durable

(P-11144)
SMITH PACKING INC
680 S Simas Rd, Santa Maria
(93455-9700)
P.O. Box 1338 (93456-1338)
PHONE..................................805 348-1817
Alvaro Quesada, *Prin*
EMP: 118
SALES (corp-wide): 4.39MM Privately Held
Web: www.smithpacking.com
SIC: 5199 Packaging materials
PA: Smith Packing, Inc.
111 W Chapel St
805 348-1818

(P-11145)
TARGUS INTERNATIONAL LLC (HQ)
Also Called: Targus
1211 N Miller St, Anaheim (92806-1933)
PHONE..................................714 765-5555
Mikel H Williams, *CEO*
Bill Oppenlander, *
Victor C Streufert, *
◆ **EMP: 175 EST: 1995**
SQ FT: 200,656
SALES (est): 24.83MM Publicly Held
Web: us.targus.com
SIC: 5199 5065 Bags, baskets, and cases;
Electronic parts and equipment, nec
PA: B. Riley Financial, Inc.
11100 Snta Mnica Blvd Ste

(P-11146)
UNIX PACKAGING LLC
5361 Alexander St, Commerce
(90040-3062)
PHONE..................................213 627-5050
EMP: 144
SALES (corp-wide): 90.43MM Privately Held
Web: www.unixpackaging.com
SIC: 5199 Packaging materials
PA: Unix Packaging, Llc
9 Minson Way

213 627-5050

(P-11147)
VICTORY FOAM INC (PA)
3 Holland, Irvine (92618-2506)
PHONE..................................949 474-0690
Frank M Comerford, *CEO*
Myles Comerford, *
Helen Comerford, *
▲ **EMP: 94 EST: 1982**
SQ FT: 53,000
SALES (est): 24.15MM
SALES (corp-wide): 24.15MM Privately Held
Web: www.victoryfoam.com
SIC: 5199 3086 Packaging materials; Cups
and plates, foamed plastics

(P-11148)
WEST BAY IMPORTS INC
Also Called: Euronext Hair Collection
7245 Oxford Way, Commerce (90040-3644)
PHONE..................................323 720-5777
Yong Kyu Yi, *CEO*
◆ **EMP: 30 EST: 1981**
SALES (est): 6.33MM Privately Held
Web: www.westbayinc.com
SIC: 5199 2389 Wigs; Masquerade costumes

5211 Lumber And Other Building Materials

(P-11149)
BOISE CASCADE COMPANY
Also Called: Boise Cascade
7145 Arlington Ave, Riverside
(92503-1508)
PHONE..................................951 343-3000
Mike Bland, *Mgr*
EMP: 82
SALES (corp-wide): 6.84B Publicly Held
Web: www.bc.com
SIC: 5211 5031 Lumber products; Lumber:
rough, dressed, and finished
PA: Boise Cascade Company
1111 W Jffrson St Ste 300
208 384-6161

(P-11150)
DIXIELINE LUMBER COMPANY LLC
2625 Durahart St, Riverside (92507-2654)
PHONE..................................951 224-8491
EMP: 419
SALES (corp-wide): 17.1B Publicly Held
Web: www.dixieline.com
SIC: 5211 5251 2439 5072 Lumber and
other building materials; Builders' hardware
; Trusses, wooden roof; Hardware
HQ: Dixieline Lumber Company Llc
3250 Sports Arena Blvd
San Diego CA 92110
619 224-4120

(P-11151)
DIXIELINE LUMBER COMPANY LLC (DH)
Also Called: Dixieline Probuild
3250 Sports Arena Blvd, San Diego
(92110-4588)
P.O. Box 85307 (92186-5307)
PHONE..................................619 224-4120
William S Cowling Ii, *Ch Bd*
Joe Laurence, *
Don Polich, *
▲ **EMP: 55 EST: 1913**
SQ FT: 12,000
SALES (est): 14.7MM

SALES (corp-wide): 17.1B Publicly Held
Web: www.dixieline.com
SIC: 5211 5251 2439 5072 Lumber and
other building materials; Builders' hardware
; Trusses, wooden roof; Hardware
HQ: Lanoga Corporation
17946 Ne 65th St
Redmond WA 98052
425 883-4125

(P-11152)
EMSER TILE LLC
4546 Stine Rd, Bakersfield (93313-2300)
PHONE...................................661 837-4400
Ghodsian Sah, *Mgr*
EMP: 40
SALES (corp-wide): 273.97MM Privately
Held
Web: www.emser.com
SIC: 5211 5032 3253 Tile, ceramic; Ceramic
wall and floor tile, nec; Ceramic wall and
floor tile
PA: Emser Tile, Llc
8431 Santa Monica Blvd
323 650-2000

(P-11153)
EMSER TILE LLC
42092 Winchester Rd, Temecula
(92590-4805)
PHONE...................................951 296-3671
Ed Combs, *Mgr*
EMP: 31
SALES (corp-wide): 273.97MM Privately
Held
Web: www.emser.com
SIC: 5211 5032 5023 3272 Tile, ceramic;
Tile and clay products; Floor coverings;
Floor tile, precast terrazzo
PA: Emser Tile, Llc
8431 Santa Monica Blvd
323 650-2000

(P-11154)
G & G DOOR PRODUCTS INC
7600 Stage Rd, Buena Park (90621-1226)
PHONE...................................714 228-2008
Bernie Gabel, *Pr*
Lynette Bleeker, *
Chad Gabel, *
Kathy Martens, *
EMP: 35 EST: 1995
SQ FT: 13,500
SALES (est): 6.52MM Privately Held
Web: www.ggdoor.net
SIC: 5211 3442 Doors, storm: wood or metal
; Metal doors, sash, and trim

(P-11155)
GANAHL LUMBER COMPANY
Also Called: Benjamin Moore Authorized Ret
150 W Blaine St, Corona (92878-4047)
P.O. Box 1326 (92878-1326)
PHONE...................................951 278-4000
Mark Ganahl, *Prin*
EMP: 67
SALES (corp-wide): 756.05MM Privately
Held
Web: www.ganahllumber.com
SIC: 5211 2431 5031 1751 Millwork and
lumber; Millwork; Lumber: rough, dressed,
and finished; Window and door
(prefabricated) installation
PA: Ganahl Lumber Company
1220 E Ball Rd
714 772-5444

(P-11156)
HOME DEPOT USA INC
Also Called: Home Depot, The

401 W Ventura Blvd, Camarillo
(93010-9122)
PHONE...................................805 389-9918
Michael Curbelo, *Mgr*
EMP: 286
SALES (corp-wide): 152.67B Publicly
Held
Web: www.homedepot.com
SIC: 5211 7359 Home centers; Tool rental
HQ: Home Depot U.S.A., Inc.
2455 Paces Ferry Rd
Atlanta GA 30339

(P-11157)
HOME DEPOT USA INC
Also Called: Home Depot, The
401 W Esplanade Dr, Oxnard (93036-1298)
PHONE...................................805 983-0653
Chris Barajas, *Mgr*
EMP: 263
SALES (corp-wide): 152.67B Publicly
Held
Web: www.homedepot.com
SIC: 5211 7359 Home centers; Tool rental
HQ: Home Depot U.S.A., Inc.
2455 Paces Ferry Rd
Atlanta GA 30339

(P-11158)
HOME DEPOT USA INC
Also Called: Home Depot, The
1830 W Slauson Ave, Los Angeles
(90047-1126)
PHONE...................................323 292-1397
John Cruz, *Mgr*
EMP: 266
SQ FT: 110,000
SALES (corp-wide): 152.67B Publicly
Held
Web: www.homedepot.com
SIC: 5211 7359 Home centers; Tool rental
HQ: Home Depot U.S.A., Inc.
2455 Paces Ferry Rd
Atlanta GA 30339

(P-11159)
HOME DEPOT USA INC
Also Called: Home Depot, The
2055 N Figueroa St, Los Angeles
(90065-1021)
PHONE...................................323 342-9495
Laud Ashbar, *Mgr*
EMP: 100
SQ FT: 107,880
SALES (corp-wide): 152.67B Publicly
Held
Web: www.homedepot.com
SIC: 5211 7359 Home centers; Tool rental
HQ: Home Depot U.S.A., Inc.
2455 Paces Ferry Rd
Atlanta GA 30339

(P-11160)
HOME DEPOT USA INC
Also Called: Home Depot, The
6400 Alondra Blvd, Paramount
(90723-3726)
PHONE...................................562 272-8055
Raul M Rodriguez, *Brnch Mgr*
EMP: 111
SALES (corp-wide): 152.67B Publicly
Held
Web: www.homedepot.com
SIC: 5211 7359 Home centers; Tool rental
HQ: Home Depot U.S.A., Inc.
2455 Paces Ferry Rd
Atlanta GA 30339

(P-11161)
HOME DEPOT USA INC
Also Called: Home Depot, The
3200 Puente Ave, Baldwin Park
(91706-5526)
PHONE...................................626 813-7131
Chip Dazies, *Mgr*
EMP: 82
SQ FT: 105,920
SALES (corp-wide): 152.67B Publicly
Held
Web: www.homedepot.com
SIC: 5211 7359 Home centers; Tool rental
HQ: Home Depot U.S.A., Inc.
2455 Paces Ferry Rd
Atlanta GA 30339

(P-11162)
HOME DEPOT USA INC
Also Called: Home Depot, The
1625 S Mountain Ave, Monrovia
(91016-4205)
PHONE...................................626 256-0580
Mako Kapaska, *Mgr*
EMP: 275
SALES (corp-wide): 152.67B Publicly
Held
Web: www.homedepot.com
SIC: 5211 7359 Home centers; Tool rental
HQ: Home Depot U.S.A., Inc.
2455 Paces Ferry Rd
Atlanta GA 30339

(P-11163)
HOME DEPOT USA INC
Also Called: Home Depot, The
575 N China Lake Blvd, Ridgecrest
(93555-3581)
PHONE...................................760 375-4614
Garbriel Garcia, *Mgr*
EMP: 72
SALES (corp-wide): 152.67B Publicly
Held
Web: www.homedepot.com
SIC: 5211 7359 Home centers; Tool rental
HQ: Home Depot U.S.A., Inc.
2455 Paces Ferry Rd
Atlanta GA 30339

(P-11164)
HOME DEPOT USA INC
Also Called: Home Depot, The
7121 Firestone Blvd, Downey (90241-4104)
PHONE...................................562 776-2200
Max Hernandez, *Mgr*
EMP: 156
SALES (corp-wide): 152.67B Publicly
Held
Web: www.homedepot.com
SIC: 5211 7359 Home centers; Tool rental
HQ: Home Depot U.S.A., Inc.
2455 Paces Ferry Rd
Atlanta GA 30339

(P-11165)
HOME DEPOT USA INC
Also Called: Home Depot, The
16800 Roscoe Blvd, Van Nuys
(91406-1105)
PHONE...................................818 780-5448
John Cruz, *Mgr*
EMP: 277
SALES (corp-wide): 152.67B Publicly
Held
Web: www.homedepot.com
SIC: 5211 7359 Home centers; Tool rental
HQ: Home Depot U.S.A., Inc.
2455 Paces Ferry Rd
Atlanta GA 30339

(P-11166)
HOME DEPOT USA INC
Also Called: Home Depot, The
3040 E Slauson Ave, Huntington Park
(90255-3138)
PHONE...................................323 587-5520
Ross Manzo, *Mgr*
EMP: 108
SALES (corp-wide): 152.67B Publicly
Held
Web: www.homedepot.com
SIC: 5211 7359 Home centers; Tool rental
HQ: Home Depot U.S.A., Inc.
2455 Paces Ferry Rd
Atlanta GA 30339

(P-11167)
HOME DEPOT USA INC
Also Called: Home Depot, The
3363 W Century Blvd, Inglewood
(90303-1366)
PHONE...................................310 677-1944
Kim Dixon, *Mgr*
EMP: 99
SQ FT: 107,421
SALES (corp-wide): 152.67B Publicly
Held
Web: www.homedepot.com
SIC: 5211 7359 Home centers; Tool rental
HQ: Home Depot U.S.A., Inc.
2455 Paces Ferry Rd
Atlanta GA 30339

(P-11168)
HOME DEPOT USA INC
Also Called: Home Depot, The
110 E Sepulveda Blvd, Carson
(90745-6301)
PHONE...................................310 835-7547
Emily R Simpson, *Mgr*
EMP: 263
SALES (corp-wide): 152.67B Publicly
Held
Web: www.homedepot.com
SIC: 5211 7359 Home centers; Tool rental
HQ: Home Depot U.S.A., Inc.
2455 Paces Ferry Rd
Atlanta GA 30339

(P-11169)
HOME DEPOT USA INC
Also Called: Home Depot, The
12322 Washington Blvd, Whittier
(90606-2503)
PHONE...................................562 789-4121
Ben Deardudin, *Mgr*
EMP: 124
SALES (corp-wide): 152.67B Publicly
Held
Web: www.homedepot.com
SIC: 5211 7359 Home centers; Tool rental
HQ: Home Depot U.S.A., Inc.
2455 Paces Ferry Rd
Atlanta GA 30339

(P-11170)
HOME DEPOT USA INC
Also Called: Home Depot, The
14603 Ocean Gate Ave, Hawthorne
(90250-6744)
PHONE...................................310 644-9600
Jason Oaks, *Mgr*
EMP: 121
SALES (corp-wide): 152.67B Publicly
Held
Web: www.homedepot.com
SIC: 5211 7359 Home centers; Tool rental
HQ: Home Depot U.S.A., Inc.
2455 Paces Ferry Rd
Atlanta GA 30339

(P-11171)
HOME DEPOT USA INC
Also Called: Home Depot, The
7015 Telegraph Rd, Los Angeles
(90040-3225)
PHONE.....................323 727-9600
Sal Prieto, *Mgr*
EMP: 286
SALES (corp-wide): 152.67B **Publicly Held**
Web: www.homedepot.com
SIC: 5211 7359 Home centers; Tool rental
HQ: Home Depot U.S.A., Inc.
2455 Paces Ferry Rd
Atlanta GA 30339

(P-11172)
HOME DEPOT USA INC
Also Called: Home Depot, The
12975 W Jefferson Blvd, Los Angeles
(90066-7023)
PHONE.....................310 822-3330
Bj Powers, *Mgr*
EMP: 263
SALES (corp-wide): 152.67B **Publicly Held**
Web: www.homedepot.com
SIC: 5211 7359 Home centers; Tool rental
HQ: Home Depot U.S.A., Inc.
2455 Paces Ferry Rd
Atlanta GA 30339

(P-11173)
HOME DEPOT USA INC
Also Called: Home Depot, The
12960 Foothill Blvd, San Fernando (91340)
PHONE.....................818 365-7662
Gil Camarena, *Mgr*
EMP: 109
SALES (corp-wide): 152.67B **Publicly Held**
Web: www.homedepot.com
SIC: 5211 7359 Home centers; Tool rental
HQ: Home Depot U.S.A., Inc.
2455 Paces Ferry Rd
Atlanta GA 30339

(P-11174)
HOME DEPOT USA INC
Also Called: Home Depot, The
20642 Golden Triangle Rd, Santa Clarita
(91351-2419)
PHONE.....................661 252-7800
Jeff Rogers, *Mgr*
EMP: 275
SALES (corp-wide): 152.67B **Publicly Held**
Web: www.homedepot.com
SIC: 5211 7359 Home centers; Tool rental
HQ: Home Depot U.S.A., Inc.
2455 Paces Ferry Rd
Atlanta GA 30339

(P-11175)
HOME DEPOT USA INC
Also Called: Home Depot, The
2450 Cherry Ave, Long Beach
(90755-3706)
PHONE.....................562 595-9200
Nick Crooks, *Mgr*
EMP: 105
SALES (corp-wide): 152.67B **Publicly Held**
Web: www.homedepot.com
SIC: 5211 7359 Home centers; Tool rental
HQ: Home Depot U.S.A., Inc.
2455 Paces Ferry Rd
Atlanta GA 30339

(P-11176)
HOME DEPOT USA INC
Also Called: Home Depot, The
3323 Madison St, Riverside (92504-4132)
PHONE.....................951 358-1370
Brian Lay, *Mgr*
EMP: 286
SALES (corp-wide): 152.67B **Publicly Held**
Web: www.homedepot.com
SIC: 5211 7359 Home centers; Tool rental
HQ: Home Depot U.S.A., Inc.
2455 Paces Ferry Rd
Atlanta GA 30339

(P-11177)
HOME DEPOT USA INC
Also Called: Home Depot, The
6140 Hamner Ave, Mira Loma
(91752-3121)
PHONE.....................951 727-0324
Otto Torres, *Mgr*
EMP: 114
SALES (corp-wide): 152.67B **Publicly Held**
Web: www.homedepot.com
SIC: 5211 7359 Home centers; Tool rental
HQ: Home Depot U.S.A., Inc.
2455 Paces Ferry Rd
Atlanta GA 30339

(P-11178)
HOME DEPOT USA INC
Also Called: Home Depot, The
15975 Perris Blvd, Moreno Valley
(92551-4692)
PHONE.....................951 485-5400
Maribel Reyes, *Mgr*
EMP: 97
SALES (corp-wide): 152.67B **Publicly Held**
Web: www.homedepot.com
SIC: 5211 7359 Home centers; Tool rental
HQ: Home Depot U.S.A., Inc.
2455 Paces Ferry Rd
Atlanta GA 30339

(P-11179)
HOME DEPOT USA INC
Also Called: Home Depot, The
25100 Madison Ave, Murrieta (92562-8907)
PHONE.....................951 698-1555
Maria Tub, *Mgr*
EMP: 129
SALES (corp-wide): 152.67B **Publicly Held**
Web: www.homedepot.com
SIC: 5211 7359 Home centers; Tool rental
HQ: Home Depot U.S.A., Inc.
2455 Paces Ferry Rd
Atlanta GA 30339

(P-11180)
HOME DEPOT USA INC
Also Called: Home Depot, The
1355 E Ontario Ave, Corona (92881-6604)
PHONE.....................951 808-0327
Vanessa Muenoz, *Brnch Mgr*
EMP: 127
SALES (corp-wide): 152.67B **Publicly Held**
Web: www.homedepot.com
SIC: 5211 7359 Home centers; Tool rental
HQ: Home Depot U.S.A., Inc.
2455 Paces Ferry Rd
Atlanta GA 30339

(P-11181)
HOME DEPOT USA INC
Also Called: Home Depot, The

7530 Broadway, Lemon Grove
(91945-1604)
PHONE.....................619 589-2999
Terry Ouellette, *Mgr*
EMP: 237
SALES (corp-wide): 152.67B **Publicly Held**
Web: www.homedepot.com
SIC: 5211 7359 Home centers; Tool rental
HQ: Home Depot U.S.A., Inc.
2455 Paces Ferry Rd
Atlanta GA 30339

(P-11182)
HOME DEPOT USA INC
Also Called: Home Depot, The
15150 Bear Valley Rd, Victorville
(92395-8709)
PHONE.....................760 955-2999
Jyll Cowdell, *Mgr*
EMP: 259
SALES (corp-wide): 152.67B **Publicly Held**
Web: www.homedepot.com
SIC: 5211 7359 Home centers; Tool rental
HQ: Home Depot U.S.A., Inc.
2455 Paces Ferry Rd
Atlanta GA 30339

(P-11183)
HOME DEPOT USA INC
Also Called: Home Depot, The
14549 Ramona Ave, Chino (91710-5647)
PHONE.....................909 393-5205
Rich Ramirez, *Prin*
EMP: 275
SALES (corp-wide): 152.67B **Publicly Held**
Web: www.homedepot.com
SIC: 5211 7359 Home centers; Tool rental
HQ: Home Depot U.S.A., Inc.
2455 Paces Ferry Rd
Atlanta GA 30339

(P-11184)
HOME DEPOT USA INC
Also Called: Home Depot, The
11884 Foothill Blvd, Rancho Cucamonga
(91730-3900)
PHONE.....................909 948-9200
Penny Allen, *Mgr*
EMP: 88
SALES (corp-wide): 152.67B **Publicly Held**
Web: www.homedepot.com
SIC: 5211 7359 Home centers; Tool rental
HQ: Home Depot U.S.A., Inc.
2455 Paces Ferry Rd
Atlanta GA 30339

(P-11185)
HOME DEPOT USA INC
Also Called: Home Depot, The
355 Marketplace Ave, San Diego
(92113-1960)
PHONE.....................619 263-1533
Brian Farwell, *Mgr*
EMP: 109
SALES (corp-wide): 152.67B **Publicly Held**
Web: www.homedepot.com
SIC: 5211 7359 Home centers; Tool rental
HQ: Home Depot U.S.A., Inc.
2455 Paces Ferry Rd
Atlanta GA 30339

(P-11186)
HOME DEPOT USA INC
Also Called: Home Depot, The
1475 E Valley Pkwy, Escondido
(92027-2313)

PHONE.....................760 233-1285
Marco Bernardino, *Mgr*
EMP: 105
SALES (corp-wide): 152.67B **Publicly Held**
Web: www.homedepot.com
SIC: 5211 7359 Home centers; Tool rental
HQ: Home Depot U.S.A., Inc.
2455 Paces Ferry Rd
Atlanta GA 30339

(P-11187)
HOME DEPOT USA INC
Also Called: Home Depot, The
1320 Eastlake Pkwy, Chula Vista
(91915-4116)
PHONE.....................619 421-0639
Emil Isvanca, *Mgr*
EMP: 113
SALES (corp-wide): 152.67B **Publicly Held**
Web: www.homedepot.com
SIC: 5211 7359 Home centers; Tool rental
HQ: Home Depot U.S.A., Inc.
2455 Paces Ferry Rd
Atlanta GA 30339

(P-11188)
HOME DEPOT USA INC
Also Called: Home Depot, The
298 Fletcher Pkwy, El Cajon (92020-2506)
PHONE.....................619 401-6610
Bill Walker, *Brnch Mgr*
EMP: 120
SALES (corp-wide): 152.67B **Publicly Held**
Web: www.homedepot.com
SIC: 5211 7359 Home centers; Tool rental
HQ: Home Depot U.S.A., Inc.
2455 Paces Ferry Rd
Atlanta GA 30339

(P-11189)
HOME DEPOT USA INC
Also Called: Home Depot, The
1151 W Lugonia Ave, Redlands
(92374-2000)
PHONE.....................909 748-0505
Kade Kasner, *Brnch Mgr*
EMP: 109
SALES (corp-wide): 152.67B **Publicly Held**
Web: www.homedepot.com
SIC: 5211 7359 Home centers; Tool rental
HQ: Home Depot U.S.A., Inc.
2455 Paces Ferry Rd
Atlanta GA 30339

(P-11190)
HOME DEPOT USA INC
Also Called: Home Depot, The
2300 Harbor Blvd Ste F, Costa Mesa
(92626-6200)
PHONE.....................949 646-4220
Marcella Kinsey, *Mgr*
EMP: 120
SALES (corp-wide): 152.67B **Publicly Held**
Web: www.homedepot.com
SIC: 5211 7359 Home centers; Tool rental
HQ: Home Depot U.S.A., Inc.
2455 Paces Ferry Rd
Atlanta GA 30339

(P-11191)
HOME DEPOT USA INC
Also Called: Home Depot, The
20021 Lake Forest Dr, Lake Forest
(92630-8703)
PHONE.....................949 609-0221

Elizabeth Capippi, *Mgr*
EMP: 108
SALES (corp-wide): 152.67B **Publicly Held**
Web: www.homedepot.com
SIC: 5211 7359 Home centers; Tool rental
HQ: Home Depot U.S.A., Inc.
2455 Paces Ferry Rd
Atlanta GA 30339

(P-11192)
HOME DEPOT USA INC
Also Called: Home Depot, The
27952 Hillcrest, Mission Viejo (92692-3637)
PHONE..................949 364-1900
Dionne Kiloh, *Mgr*
EMP: 125
SALES (corp-wide): 152.67B **Publicly Held**
Web: www.homedepot.com
SIC: 5211 7359 Home centers; Tool rental
HQ: Home Depot U.S.A., Inc.
2455 Paces Ferry Rd
Atlanta GA 30339

(P-11193)
HOME DEPOT USA INC
Also Called: Home Depot, The
27401 La Paz Rd, Laguna Niguel (92677-3739)
PHONE..................949 831-3698
Dan Schneid, *Brnch Mgr*
EMP: 92
SALES (corp-wide): 152.67B **Publicly Held**
Web: www.homedepot.com
SIC: 5211 7359 Home centers; Tool rental
HQ: Home Depot U.S.A., Inc.
2455 Paces Ferry Rd
Atlanta GA 30339

(P-11194)
HOME DEPOT USA INC
Also Called: Home Depot, The
625 S Placentia Ave, Fullerton (92831-5199)
PHONE..................714 459-4909
Pete Canscale, *Mgr*
EMP: 84
SALES (corp-wide): 152.67B **Publicly Held**
Web: www.homedepot.com
SIC: 5211 7359 Home centers; Tool rental
HQ: Home Depot U.S.A., Inc.
2455 Paces Ferry Rd
Atlanta GA 30339

(P-11195)
HOME DEPOT USA INC
Also Called: Home Depot, The
1095 N Pullman St, Anaheim (92807-2516)
PHONE..................714 921-1215
Rob Sholte, *Mgr*
EMP: 89
SALES (corp-wide): 152.67B **Publicly Held**
Web: www.homedepot.com
SIC: 5211 7359 Home centers; Tool rental
HQ: Home Depot U.S.A., Inc.
2455 Paces Ferry Rd
Atlanta GA 30339

(P-11196)
HOME DEPOT USA INC
Also Called: Home Depot, The
600 S Harbor Blvd, La Habra (90631-6166)
PHONE..................562 690-6006
Merna Rosas, *Mgr*
EMP: 97
SALES (corp-wide): 152.67B **Publicly Held**

Web: www.homedepot.com
SIC: 5211 7359 Home centers; Tool rental
HQ: Home Depot U.S.A., Inc.
2455 Paces Ferry Rd
Atlanta GA 30339

(P-11197)
HOME DEPOT USA INC
Also Called: Home Depot, The
3500 W Macarthur Blvd, Santa Ana (92704-6808)
PHONE..................714 966-8551
Beatrice Celazeo, *Genl Mgr*
EMP: 114
SALES (corp-wide): 152.67B **Publicly Held**
Web: www.homedepot.com
SIC: 5211 7359 Home centers; Tool rental
HQ: Home Depot U.S.A., Inc.
2455 Paces Ferry Rd
Atlanta GA 30339

(P-11198)
HOME DEPOT USA INC
Also Called: Home Depot, The
435 W Katella Ave, Orange (92867-4603)
PHONE..................714 538-9600
Michelle Fromholz, *Mgr*
EMP: 119
SALES (corp-wide): 152.67B **Publicly Held**
Web: www.homedepot.com
SIC: 5211 1752 1751 Home centers; Carpet laying; Window and door installation and erection
HQ: Home Depot U.S.A., Inc.
2455 Paces Ferry Rd
Atlanta GA 30339

(P-11199)
HOME DEPOT USA INC
Also Called: Home Depot, The
10801 Garden Grove Blvd, Garden Grove (92843-1201)
PHONE..................714 539-0319
Chris Murray, *Mgr*
EMP: 111
SALES (corp-wide): 152.67B **Publicly Held**
Web: www.homedepot.com
SIC: 5211 7359 Home centers; Tool rental
HQ: Home Depot U.S.A., Inc.
2455 Paces Ferry Rd
Atlanta GA 30339

(P-11200)
HOME DEPOT USA INC
Also Called: Home Depot, The
1750 E Edinger Ave, Santa Ana (92705-5031)
PHONE..................714 259-1030
Rudy Teralta, *Mgr*
EMP: 97
SALES (corp-wide): 152.67B **Publicly Held**
Web: www.homedepot.com
SIC: 5211 7359 Home centers; Tool rental
HQ: Home Depot U.S.A., Inc.
2455 Paces Ferry Rd
Atlanta GA 30339

(P-11201)
J B WHL ROOFG BLDG SUPS INC (DH)
Also Called: J B
21524 Nordhoff St, Chatsworth (91311-5822)
P.O. Box 5289 (91313-5289)
PHONE..................818 998-0440
W Keith Jones, *Pr*

Brian Jones, *Sec*
EMP: 70 **EST:** 1981
SQ FT: 2,000
SALES (est): 20.16MM
SALES (corp-wide): 152.67B **Publicly Held**
Web: www.jbwholesale.com
SIC: 5211 5033 Roofing material; Shingles, except wood
HQ: Srs Distribution Inc.
7440 S Hwy 121
Mckinney TX 75070

(P-11202)
LOWES HOME CENTERS LLC
Also Called: Lowe's
30481 Avenida De Las Flores, Rancho Santa Margari (92688-3923)
PHONE..................949 589-5005
Pete Bradley, *Brnch Mgr*
EMP: 76
SALES (corp-wide): 86.38B **Publicly Held**
Web: www.lowes.com
SIC: 5211 5031 5722 5064 Home centers; Building materials, exterior; Household appliance stores; Electrical appliances, television and radio
HQ: Lowe's Home Centers, Llc
1000 Lowes Blvd
Mooresville NC 28117
336 658-4000

(P-11203)
LOWES HOME CENTERS LLC
Also Called: Lowe's
907 Avenida Pico, San Clemente (92673-3908)
PHONE..................949 369-4644
Sonya Olmedo, *Mgr*
EMP: 103
SALES (corp-wide): 86.38B **Publicly Held**
Web: www.lowes.com
SIC: 5211 5031 5722 5064 Home centers; Building materials, exterior; Household appliance stores; Electrical appliances, television and radio
HQ: Lowe's Home Centers, Llc
1000 Lowes Blvd
Mooresville NC 28117
336 658-4000

(P-11204)
LOWES HOME CENTERS LLC
Also Called: Lowe's
1500 N Lemon St, Anaheim (92801-1204)
PHONE..................714 447-6140
Brian Hefel, *Brnch Mgr*
EMP: 99
SALES (corp-wide): 86.38B **Publicly Held**
Web: www.lowes.com
SIC: 5211 5031 5722 5064 Home centers; Building materials, exterior; Household appliance stores; Electrical appliances, television and radio
HQ: Lowe's Home Centers, Llc
1000 Lowes Blvd
Mooresville NC 28117
336 658-4000

(P-11205)
LOWES HOME CENTERS LLC
Also Called: Lowe's
1380 S Beach Blvd, La Habra (90631-6374)
PHONE..................562 690-5122
Ken Konkel, *Mgr*
EMP: 120
SALES (corp-wide): 86.38B **Publicly Held**
Web: www.lowes.com

SIC: 5211 5031 5722 5064 Home centers; Building materials, exterior; Household appliance stores; Electrical appliances, television and radio
HQ: Lowe's Home Centers, Llc
1000 Lowes Blvd
Mooresville NC 28117
336 658-4000

(P-11206)
LOWES HOME CENTERS LLC
Also Called: Lowe's
8175 Warner Ave, Huntington Beach (92647-8251)
PHONE..................714 907-9006
Jose Rodriquez, *Mgr*
EMP: 70
SALES (corp-wide): 86.38B **Publicly Held**
Web: www.lowes.com
SIC: 5211 5031 5722 5064 Home centers; Building materials, exterior; Household appliance stores; Electrical appliances, television and radio
HQ: Lowe's Home Centers, Llc
1000 Lowes Blvd
Mooresville NC 28117
336 658-4000

(P-11207)
LOWES HOME CENTERS LLC
Also Called: Lowe's
2500 Park Ave, Tustin (92782-2712)
PHONE..................714 913-2663
Nico Zavala, *Mgr*
EMP: 120
SALES (corp-wide): 86.38B **Publicly Held**
Web: www.lowes.com
SIC: 5211 5031 5722 5064 Home centers; Building materials, exterior; Household appliance stores; Electrical appliances, television and radio
HQ: Lowe's Home Centers, Llc
1000 Lowes Blvd
Mooresville NC 28117
336 658-4000

(P-11208)
LOWES HOME CENTERS LLC
Also Called: Lowe's
500 S Mills Rd, Ventura (93003-3459)
PHONE..................805 675-8800
Glen Sueishi, *Mgr*
EMP: 138
SALES (corp-wide): 86.38B **Publicly Held**
Web: www.lowes.com
SIC: 5211 5031 5722 5064 Home centers; Building materials, exterior; Household appliance stores; Electrical appliances, television and radio
HQ: Lowe's Home Centers, Llc
1000 Lowes Blvd
Mooresville NC 28117
336 658-4000

(P-11209)
LOWES HOME CENTERS LLC
Also Called: Lowe's
1275 Simi Town Center Way, Simi Valley (93065-0513)
PHONE..................805 426-2780
Bob Derr, *Mgr*
EMP: 112
SALES (corp-wide): 86.38B **Publicly Held**
Web: www.lowes.com
SIC: 5211 5031 5722 5064 Home centers; Building materials, exterior; Household appliance stores; Electrical appliances, television and radio
HQ: Lowe's Home Centers, Llc
1000 Lowes Blvd
Mooresville NC 28117
336 658-4000

PRODUCTS & SVCS

(P-11210)
LOWES HOME CENTERS LLC
Also Called: Lowe's
2445 Golden Hill Rd, Paso Robles
(93446-6385)
PHONE..................805 602-9051
EMP: 115
SALES (corp-wide): 86.38B Publicly Held
Web: www.lowes.com
SIC: 5211 5031 5722 5064 Home centers;
Building materials, exterior; Household
appliance stores; Electrical appliances,
television and radio
HQ: Lowe's Home Centers, Llc
1000 Lowes Blvd
Mooresville NC 28117
336 658-4000

(P-11211)
LOWES HOME CENTERS LLC
Also Called: Lowe's
11399 Foothill Blvd, Rancho Cucamonga
(91730-7626)
PHONE..................909 476-9697
Jeniffer Lang, Mgr
EMP: 109
SALES (corp-wide): 86.38B Publicly Held
Web: www.lowes.com
SIC: 5211 5031 5722 5064 Home centers;
Building materials, exterior; Household
appliance stores; Electrical appliances,
television and radio
HQ: Lowe's Home Centers, Llc
1000 Lowes Blvd
Mooresville NC 28117
336 658-4000

(P-11212)
LOWES HOME CENTERS LLC
Also Called: Lowe's
14333 Bear Valley Rd, Victorville
(92392-5403)
PHONE..................760 949-9565
Shawn Pierson, Mgr
EMP: 103
SALES (corp-wide): 86.38B Publicly Held
Web: www.lowes.com
SIC: 5211 5031 5722 5064 Home centers;
Building materials, exterior; Household
appliance stores; Electrical appliances,
television and radio
HQ: Lowe's Home Centers, Llc
1000 Lowes Blvd
Mooresville NC 28117
336 658-4000

(P-11213)
LOWES HOME CENTERS LLC
Also Called: Lowe's
1659 W Foothill Blvd, Upland (91786-3533)
PHONE..................909 982-4795
Dan Caganap, Mgr
EMP: 111
SALES (corp-wide): 86.38B Publicly Held
Web: www.lowes.com
SIC: 5211 5031 5722 5064 Home centers;
Building materials, exterior; Household
appliance stores; Electrical appliances,
television and radio
HQ: Lowe's Home Centers, Llc
1000 Lowes Blvd
Mooresville NC 28117
336 658-4000

(P-11214)
LOWES HOME CENTERS LLC
Also Called: Lowe's
16851 Sierra Lakes Pkwy, Fontana
(92336-1226)
PHONE..................909 350-7900

Jan Hardy, Mgr
EMP: 114
SALES (corp-wide): 86.38B Publicly Held
Web: www.lowes.com
SIC: 5211 5031 5722 5064 Home centers;
Building materials, exterior; Household
appliance stores; Electrical appliances,
television and radio
HQ: Lowe's Home Centers, Llc
1000 Lowes Blvd
Mooresville NC 28117
336 658-4000

(P-11215)
LOWES HOME CENTERS LLC
Also Called: Lowe's
1725 W Redlands Blvd, Redlands
(92373-8012)
PHONE..................909 307-8883
Jim Riley, Mgr
EMP: 109
SALES (corp-wide): 86.38B Publicly Held
Web: www.lowes.com
SIC: 5211 5031 5722 5064 Home centers;
Building materials, exterior; Household
appliance stores; Electrical appliances,
television and radio
HQ: Lowe's Home Centers, Llc
1000 Lowes Blvd
Mooresville NC 28117
336 658-4000

(P-11216)
LOWES HOME CENTERS LLC
Also Called: Lowe's
12189 Apple Valley Rd, Apple Valley
(92308-6702)
PHONE..................760 961-3000
Chris Horan, Mgr
EMP: 123
SALES (corp-wide): 86.38B Publicly Held
Web: www.lowes.com
SIC: 5211 5031 5722 5064 Home centers;
Building materials, exterior; Household
appliance stores; Electrical appliances,
television and radio
HQ: Lowe's Home Centers, Llc
1000 Lowes Blvd
Mooresville NC 28117
336 658-4000

(P-11217)
LOWES HOME CENTERS LLC
Also Called: Lowe's
2390 S Grove Ave, Ontario (91761-4808)
PHONE..................909 969-9053
Myama Zega, Mgr
EMP: 112
SALES (corp-wide): 86.38B Publicly Held
Web: www.lowes.com
SIC: 5211 5031 5722 5064 Home centers;
Building materials, exterior; Household
appliance stores; Electrical appliances,
television and radio
HQ: Lowe's Home Centers, Llc
1000 Lowes Blvd
Mooresville NC 28117
336 658-4000

(P-11218)
LOWES HOME CENTERS LLC
Also Called: Lowe's
30472 Haun Rd, Menifee (92584-6810)
PHONE..................951 723-1930
Dave Jenkins, Brnch Mgr
EMP: 118
SALES (corp-wide): 86.38B Publicly Held
Web: www.lowes.com

SIC: 5211 5031 5722 5064 Home centers;
Building materials, exterior; Household
appliance stores; Electrical appliances,
television and radio
HQ: Lowe's Home Centers, Llc
1000 Lowes Blvd
Mooresville NC 28117
336 658-4000

(P-11219)
LOWES HOME CENTERS LLC
Also Called: Lowe's
9851 Magnolia Ave, Riverside
(92503-3528)
PHONE..................951 509-5500
Daniel Mergio, Brnch Mgr
EMP: 140
SALES (corp-wide): 86.38B Publicly Held
Web: www.lowes.com
SIC: 5211 5031 5722 5064 Home centers;
Building materials, exterior; Household
appliance stores; Electrical appliances,
television and radio
HQ: Lowe's Home Centers, Llc
1000 Lowes Blvd
Mooresville NC 28117
336 658-4000

(P-11220)
LOWES HOME CENTERS LLC
Also Called: Lowe's
78865 Highway 111, La Quinta
(92253-2003)
PHONE..................760 771-5566
Ron Stewart, Mgr
EMP: 146
SALES (corp-wide): 86.38B Publicly Held
Web: www.lowes.com
SIC: 5211 5031 5722 5064 Home centers;
Building materials, exterior; Household
appliance stores; Electrical appliances,
television and radio
HQ: Lowe's Home Centers, Llc
1000 Lowes Blvd
Mooresville NC 28117
336 658-4000

(P-11221)
LOWES HOME CENTERS LLC
Also Called: Lowe's
5201 E Ramon Rd, Palm Springs
(92264-3600)
PHONE..................760 866-1901
Robert Richmond, Brnch Mgr
EMP: 106
SALES (corp-wide): 86.38B Publicly Held
Web: www.lowes.com
SIC: 5211 5031 5722 5064 Home centers;
Building materials, exterior; Household
appliance stores; Electrical appliances,
television and radio
HQ: Lowe's Home Centers, Llc
1000 Lowes Blvd
Mooresville NC 28117
336 658-4000

(P-11222)
LOWES HOME CENTERS LLC
Also Called: Lowe's
24701 Madison Ave, Murrieta (92562-9763)
PHONE..................951 461-8916
Scott Holland, Mgr
EMP: 96
SALES (corp-wide): 86.38B Publicly Held
Web: www.lowes.com
SIC: 5211 5031 5722 5064 Home centers;
Building materials, exterior; Household
appliance stores; Electrical appliances,
television and radio
HQ: Lowe's Home Centers, Llc
1000 Lowes Blvd

Mooresville NC 28117
336 658-4000

(P-11223)
LOWES HOME CENTERS LLC
Also Called: Lowe's
12400 Day St, Moreno Valley (92553-7501)
PHONE..................951 656-1859
David Jenkins, Mgr
EMP: 82
SALES (corp-wide): 86.38B Publicly Held
Web: www.lowes.com
SIC: 5211 5031 5722 5064 Home centers;
Building materials, exterior; Household
appliance stores; Electrical appliances,
television and radio
HQ: Lowe's Home Centers, Llc
1000 Lowes Blvd
Mooresville NC 28117
336 658-4000

(P-11224)
LOWES HOME CENTERS LLC
Also Called: Lowe's
40390 Winchester Rd, Temecula
(92591-5519)
PHONE..................951 296-1618
Rose Burns, Mgr
EMP: 85
SALES (corp-wide): 86.38B Publicly Held
Web: www.lowes.com
SIC: 5211 5031 5722 5064 Home centers;
Building materials, exterior; Household
appliance stores; Electrical appliances,
television and radio
HQ: Lowe's Home Centers, Llc
1000 Lowes Blvd
Mooresville NC 28117
336 658-4000

(P-11225)
LOWES HOME CENTERS LLC
Also Called: Lowe's
1285 Magnolia Ave, Corona (92879-2092)
PHONE..................951 256-9004
Jeff Fowler, Brnch Mgr
EMP: 88
SALES (corp-wide): 86.38B Publicly Held
Web: www.lowes.com
SIC: 5211 5031 5722 5064 Home centers;
Building materials, exterior; Household
appliance stores; Electrical appliances,
television and radio
HQ: Lowe's Home Centers, Llc
1000 Lowes Blvd
Mooresville NC 28117
336 658-4000

(P-11226)
LOWES HOME CENTERS LLC
Also Called: Lowe's
350 S Sanderson Ave, Hemet
(92545-9014)
PHONE..................951 492-7000
Randy Scott, Mgr
EMP: 102
SALES (corp-wide): 86.38B Publicly Held
Web: www.lowes.com
SIC: 5211 5031 5722 5064 Home centers;
Building materials, exterior; Household
appliance stores; Electrical appliances,
television and radio
HQ: Lowe's Home Centers, Llc
1000 Lowes Blvd
Mooresville NC 28117
336 658-4000

(P-11227)
LOWES HOME CENTERS LLC
Also Called: Lowe's

▲ = Import ▼ = Export
◆ = Import/Export

29335 Central Ave, Lake Elsinore
(92532-2212)
PHONE.................951 253-6000
A Nuseibtel, *Prin*
EMP: 126
SALES (corp-wide): 86.38B Publicly Held
Web: www.lowes.com
SIC: 5211 5031 5722 5064 Home centers;
Building materials, exterior; Household
appliance stores; Electrical appliances,
television and radio
HQ: Lowe's Home Centers, Llc
1000 Lowes Blvd
Mooresville NC 28117
336 658-4000

(P-11228)
LOWES HOME CENTERS LLC
Also Called: Lowe's
155 Old Grove Rd, Oceanside
(92057-1216)
PHONE.................760 966-7140
Mike Shratz, *Mgr*
EMP: 150
SALES (corp-wide): 86.38B Publicly Held
Web: www.lowes.com
SIC: 5211 5031 5722 5064 Home centers;
Building materials, exterior; Household
appliance stores; Electrical appliances,
television and radio
HQ: Lowe's Home Centers, Llc
1000 Lowes Blvd
Mooresville NC 28117
336 658-4000

(P-11229)
LOWES HOME CENTERS LLC
Also Called: Lowe's
151 Vista Village Dr, Vista (92083-4974)
PHONE.................760 631-6255
Bill Mobley, *Brnch Mgr*
EMP: 114
SALES (corp-wide): 86.38B Publicly Held
Web: www.lowes.com
SIC: 5211 5031 5722 5064 Home centers;
Building materials, exterior; Household
appliance stores; Electrical appliances,
television and radio
HQ: Lowe's Home Centers, Llc
1000 Lowes Blvd
Mooresville NC 28117
336 658-4000

(P-11230)
LOWES HOME CENTERS LLC
Also Called: Lowe's
2225 Otay Lakes Rd, Chula Vista
(91915-1001)
PHONE.................619 739-9060
EMP: 106
SALES (corp-wide): 86.38B Publicly Held
Web: www.lowes.com
SIC: 5211 5031 5722 5064 Home centers;
Building materials, exterior; Household
appliance stores; Electrical appliances,
television and radio
HQ: Lowe's Home Centers, Llc
1000 Lowes Blvd
Mooresville NC 28117
336 658-4000

(P-11231)
LOWES HOME CENTERS LLC
Also Called: Lowe's
9416 Mission Gorge Rd, Santee
(92071-3847)
P.O. Box 710909 (92072-0909)
PHONE.................619 212-4100
Jim Andrews, *Mgr*
EMP: 111
SALES (corp-wide): 86.38B Publicly Held

Web: www.lowes.com
SIC: 5211 5031 5722 5064 Home centers;
Building materials, exterior; Household
appliance stores; Electrical appliances,
television and radio
HQ: Lowe's Home Centers, Llc
1000 Lowes Blvd
Mooresville NC 28117
336 658-4000

(P-11232)
LOWES HOME CENTERS LLC
Also Called: Lowe's
620 W Mission Ave, Escondido
(92025-1611)
PHONE.................760 484-5113
Bill Mobley, *Mgr*
EMP: 123
SALES (corp-wide): 86.38B Publicly Held
Web: www.lowes.com
SIC: 5211 5031 5722 5064 Home centers;
Building materials, exterior; Household
appliance stores; Electrical appliances,
television and radio
HQ: Lowe's Home Centers, Llc
1000 Lowes Blvd
Mooresville NC 28117
336 658-4000

(P-11233)
LOWES HOME CENTERS LLC
Also Called: Lowe's
4777 Chino Hills Pkwy, Chino Hills
(91709-5849)
PHONE.................909 438-9000
EMP: 137
SALES (corp-wide): 86.38B Publicly Held
Web: www.lowes.com
SIC: 5211 5031 5722 5064 Home centers;
Building materials, exterior; Household
appliance stores; Electrical appliances,
television and radio
HQ: Lowe's Home Centers, Llc
1000 Lowes Blvd
Mooresville NC 28117
336 658-4000

(P-11234)
LOWES HOME CENTERS LLC
Also Called: Lowe's
27847 Greenspot Rd, Highland
(92346-4381)
PHONE.................909 557-9010
EMP: 123
SALES (corp-wide): 86.38B Publicly Held
Web: www.lowes.com
SIC: 5211 5031 5722 5064 Home centers;
Building materials, exterior; Household
appliance stores; Electrical appliances,
television and radio
HQ: Lowe's Home Centers, Llc
1000 Lowes Blvd
Mooresville NC 28117
336 658-4000

(P-11235)
LOWES HOME CENTERS LLC
Also Called: Lowe's
2318 Northside Dr, San Diego
(92108-2704)
PHONE.................619 584-5500
Rebecca Young, *Mgr*
EMP: 120
SALES (corp-wide): 86.38B Publicly Held
Web: www.lowes.com
SIC: 5211 5031 5722 5064 Home centers;
Building materials, exterior; Household
appliance stores; Electrical appliances,
television and radio
HQ: Lowe's Home Centers, Llc
1000 Lowes Blvd

Mooresville NC 28117
336 658-4000

(P-11236)
LOWES HOME CENTERS LLC
Also Called: Lowe's
730 W Avenue K, Lancaster (93534-6001)
PHONE.................661 341-9000
Pete Reed, *Genl Mgr*
EMP: 93
SALES (corp-wide): 86.38B Publicly Held
Web: www.lowes.com
SIC: 5211 5031 5722 5064 Home centers;
Building materials, exterior; Household
appliance stores; Electrical appliances,
television and radio
HQ: Lowe's Home Centers, Llc
1000 Lowes Blvd
Mooresville NC 28117
336 658-4000

(P-11237)
LOWES HOME CENTERS LLC
Also Called: Lowe's
19601 Nordhoff St, Northridge
(91324-2422)
PHONE.................818 477-9022
Mark Harrison, *Store Mgr*
EMP: 143
SALES (corp-wide): 86.38B Publicly Held
Web: www.lowes.com
SIC: 5211 5031 5722 5064 Home centers;
Building materials, exterior; Household
appliance stores; Electrical appliances,
television and radio
HQ: Lowe's Home Centers, Llc
1000 Lowes Blvd
Mooresville NC 28117
336 658-4000

(P-11238)
LOWES HOME CENTERS LLC
Also Called: Lowe's
19001 Golden Valley Rd, Santa Clarita
(91387-1471)
PHONE.................661 678-4430
Veronica January, *Brnch Mgr*
EMP: 109
SALES (corp-wide): 86.38B Publicly Held
Web: www.lowes.com
SIC: 5211 5031 5722 5064 Home centers;
Building materials, exterior; Household
appliance stores; Electrical appliances,
television and radio
HQ: Lowe's Home Centers, Llc
1000 Lowes Blvd
Mooresville NC 28117
336 658-4000

(P-11239)
LOWES HOME CENTERS LLC
Also Called: Lowe's
2053 N Imperial Ave, El Centro
(92243-1324)
PHONE.................760 337-6700
Chad Manley, *Mgr*
EMP: 137
SALES (corp-wide): 86.38B Publicly Held
Web: www.lowes.com
SIC: 5211 5031 5722 5064 Home centers;
Building materials, exterior; Household
appliance stores; Electrical appliances,
television and radio
HQ: Lowe's Home Centers, Llc
1000 Lowes Blvd
Mooresville NC 28117
336 658-4000

(P-11240)
LOWES HOME CENTERS LLC
Also Called: Lowe's
1601 Columbus St, Bakersfield
(93305-2133)
PHONE.................661 889-9000
Francisco Dubon, *Brnch Mgr*
EMP: 232
SALES (corp-wide): 86.38B Publicly Held
Web: www.lowes.com
SIC: 5211 5031 5722 5064 Home centers;
Building materials, exterior; Household
appliance stores; Electrical appliances,
television and radio
HQ: Lowe's Home Centers, Llc
1000 Lowes Blvd
Mooresville NC 28117
336 658-4000

(P-11241)
LOWES HOME CENTERS LLC
Also Called: Lowe's
13500 Paxton St, Pacoima (91331-2352)
PHONE.................818 686-4300
Mario Garza, *Brnch Mgr*
EMP: 100
SALES (corp-wide): 86.38B Publicly Held
Web: www.lowes.com
SIC: 5211 5031 5722 5064 Home centers;
Building materials, exterior; Household
appliance stores; Electrical appliances,
television and radio
HQ: Lowe's Home Centers, Llc
1000 Lowes Blvd
Mooresville NC 28117
336 658-4000

(P-11242)
LOWES HOME CENTERS LLC
Also Called: Lowe's
8383 Topanga Canyon Blvd, West Hills
(91304-2343)
PHONE.................818 610-1960
Pete Reed, *Brnch Mgr*
EMP: 125
SALES (corp-wide): 86.38B Publicly Held
Web: www.lowes.com
SIC: 5211 5031 5722 5064 Home centers;
Building materials, exterior; Household
appliance stores; Electrical appliances,
television and radio
HQ: Lowe's Home Centers, Llc
1000 Lowes Blvd
Mooresville NC 28117
336 658-4000

(P-11243)
LOWES HOME CENTERS LLC
Also Called: Lowe's
2000 W Empire Ave, Burbank
(91504-3434)
PHONE.................818 557-2300
Chris Mcgilroy, *Mgr*
EMP: 112
SALES (corp-wide): 86.38B Publicly Held
Web: www.lowes.com
SIC: 5211 5031 5722 5064 Home centers;
Building materials, exterior; Household
appliance stores; Electrical appliances,
television and radio
HQ: Lowe's Home Centers, Llc
1000 Lowes Blvd
Mooresville NC 28117
336 658-4000

(P-11244)
LOWES HOME CENTERS LLC
Also Called: Hawthorne Lowe's
2800 W 120th St, Hawthorne (90250-3338)
PHONE.................323 327-4000

Mike Bryant, *Mgr*
EMP: 128
SALES (corp-wide): 86.38B **Publicly Held**
Web: www.lowes.com
SIC: 5211 5031 5722 5064 Home centers;
Building materials, exterior; Household
appliance stores; Electrical appliances,
television and radio
HQ: Lowe's Home Centers, Llc
1000 Lowes Blvd
Mooresville NC 28117
336 658-4000

(P-11245)
LOWES HOME CENTERS LLC
Also Called: Lowe's
8600 Washington Blvd, Pico Rivera
(90660-3790)
PHONE..............................562 942-9909
Jose Rodriquez, *Brnch Mgr*
EMP: 374
SALES (corp-wide): 86.38B **Publicly Held**
Web: www.lowes.com
SIC: 5211 5031 5722 5064 Home centers;
Building materials, exterior; Household
appliance stores; Electrical appliances,
television and radio
HQ: Lowe's Home Centers, Llc
1000 Lowes Blvd
Mooresville NC 28117
336 658-4000

(P-11246)
LOWES HOME CENTERS LLC
Also Called: Lowe's
39500 Lowes Dr, Palmdale (93551-3754)
PHONE..............................661 267-9888
Veronica Pinkui, *Mgr*
EMP: 129
SQ FT: 133,410
SALES (corp-wide): 86.38B **Publicly Held**
Web: www.lowes.com
SIC: 5211 5031 5722 5064 Home centers;
Building materials, exterior; Household
appliance stores; Electrical appliances,
television and radio
HQ: Lowe's Home Centers, Llc
1000 Lowes Blvd
Mooresville NC 28117
336 658-4000

(P-11247)
LOWES HOME CENTERS LLC
Also Called: Lowe's
22255 S Western Ave, Torrance
(90501-4106)
PHONE..............................310 787-1469
Ricky Garcia, *Mgr*
EMP: 115
SALES (corp-wide): 86.38B **Publicly Held**
Web: www.lowes.com
SIC: 5211 5031 5722 5064 Home centers;
Building materials, exterior; Household
appliance stores; Electrical appliances,
television and radio
HQ: Lowe's Home Centers, Llc
1000 Lowes Blvd
Mooresville NC 28117
336 658-4000

(P-11248)
LOWES HOME CENTERS LLC
Also Called: Lowe's
14873 Carmenita Rd, Norwalk
(90650-5232)
PHONE..............................562 926-0826
Patrick Cosley, *Mgr*
EMP: 122
SALES (corp-wide): 86.38B **Publicly Held**
Web: www.lowes.com

SIC: 5211 5031 5722 5064 Home centers;
Building materials, exterior; Household
appliance stores; Electrical appliances,
television and radio
HQ: Lowe's Home Centers, Llc
1000 Lowes Blvd
Mooresville NC 28117
336 658-4000

(P-11249)
PARAGON INDUSTRIES INC
Also Called: Anaheim Warehouse 125
1515 E Winston Rd, Anaheim (92805-6445)
PHONE..............................714 778-1800
Diana Kelly, *Brnch Mgr*
EMP: 100
SALES (corp-wide): 251.57MM **Privately
Held**
Web: www.bedrosians.com
SIC: 5211 5032 Tile, ceramic; Brick, stone,
and related material
PA: Paragon Industries, Inc.
4285 N Golden State Blvd
559 275-5000

(P-11250)
PAREX USA INC
Also Called: La Habra Stucco
2150 Eastridge Ave, Riverside
(92507-0720)
PHONE..............................951 653-3549
Brian Carrier, *Mgr*
EMP: 31
Web: www.parexusa.com
SIC: 5211 3299 Lumber and other building
materials; Stucco
HQ: Parex Usa, Inc.
2150 Eastridge Ave
Riverside CA 92507
714 778-2266

(P-11251)
SMI ARCHITECTURAL MILLWORK INC
Also Called: SMI Millwork
2116 W Chestnut Ave, Santa Ana
(92703-4306)
PHONE..............................714 567-0112
Robert Stolo, *Pr*
Karen Kawasaki, *
Timothy J Stolo, *
EMP: 35 **EST:** 1997
SQ FT: 1,500
SALES (est): 2MM **Privately Held**
Web: www.smimillwork.com
SIC: 5211 2431 Millwork and lumber;
Millwork

(P-11252)
SUPERIOR READY MIX CONCRETE LP
Also Called: San Diego Ready Mix
9245 Camino Santa Fe, San Diego
(92121-2201)
PHONE..............................858 695-0666
J Frederickson, *Brnch Mgr*
EMP: 71
SALES (corp-wide): 205.26MM **Privately
Held**
Web: www.superiorrm.com
SIC: 5211 3273 Concrete and cinder block;
Ready-mixed concrete
PA: Superior Ready Mix Concrete L.P.
1564 Mission Rd
760 745-0556

(P-11253)
SWAN FENCE INCORPORATED
600 W Manville St, Compton (90220-5508)
PHONE..............................310 669-8000

Shigehiro Hatake, *Pr*
Jun Ando, *
EMP: 25 **EST:** 1988
SQ FT: 50,000
SALES (est): 2.41MM **Privately Held**
Web: www.swanfence.com
SIC: 5211 3315 Fencing; Fence gates,
posts, and fittings: steel
PA: Koiwa Kanaami Co., Ltd.
3-20-14, Nishisakusa

5231 Paint, Glass, And Wallpaper Stores

(P-11254)
DUNN-EDWARDS CORPORATION (DH)
Also Called: Dunn-Dwrds Pints Wallcoverings
6119 E Washington Blvd, Commerce
(90040-2436)
P.O. Box 30389 (90040)
PHONE..............................888 337-2468
Karl Altergott, *Pr*
◆ **EMP:** 150 **EST:** 1925
SALES (est): 325.93MM **Privately Held**
Web: www.dunnedwards.com
SIC: 5231 2851 Paint; Lacquer: bases,
dopes, thinner
HQ: Nippon Paint Holdings Co., Ltd.
2-1-2, Oyodokita, Kita-Ku
Osaka OSK 531-0

(P-11255)
MICROBLEND TECHNOLOGIES INC
4333 Park Terrace Dr, Westlake Village
(91361-4642)
PHONE..............................480 831-0757
John E Tyson, *Ch*
Jeff Pirtle, *CFO*
John Bond, *COO*
Randall Hughes, *Pr*
Thom Davis, *Prin*
▼ **EMP:** 60 **EST:** 2013
SALES (est): 486.17K **Privately Held**
Web: www.microblendtechnologies.com
SIC: 5231 3991 Paint and painting supplies;
Paint rollers

(P-11256)
VISTA PAINT CORPORATION (PA)
2020 E Orangethorpe Ave, Fullerton
(92831-5327)
PHONE..............................714 680-3800
Eddie R Fischer, *Pr*
Eddie R Fischer, *Pr*
Jerome Fischer, *
Joe Wittenberg, *Marketing*
▲ **EMP:** 150 **EST:** 1956
SQ FT: 140,000
SALES (est): 96.51MM
SALES (corp-wide): 96.51MM **Privately
Held**
Web: www.vistapaint.com
SIC: 5231 2851 Paint; Paints and paint
additives

5251 Hardware Stores

(P-11257)
CONSOLIDATED DEVICES INC (HQ)
Also Called: CDI Torque Products
19220 San Jose Ave, City Of Industry
(91748-1417)
PHONE..............................626 965-0668

Michael King, *Pr*
Gary Keefe, *
▲ **EMP:** 25 **EST:** 1968
SQ FT: 90,000
SALES (est): 11.58MM
SALES (corp-wide): 4.73B **Publicly Held**
Web: www.cditorque.com
SIC: 5251 3679 3625 5072 Tools;
Transducers, electrical; Control equipment,
electric; Hardware
PA: Snap-On Incorporated
2801 80th St
262 656-5200

(P-11258)
GEORGE L THROOP CO
Also Called: Do It Best
444 N Fair Oaks Ave, Pasadena
(91103-3619)
P.O. Box 92405 (91109-2405)
PHONE..............................626 796-0285
TOLL FREE: 800
Jeffrey Throop, *Pr*
George L Throop Iii, *VP*
Ann T Comey, *
▲ **EMP:** 32 **EST:** 1921
SQ FT: 10,500
SALES (est): 4.85MM **Privately Held**
Web: www.throop.com
SIC: 5251 3272 3273 Hardware stores;
Concrete products, nec; Ready-mixed
concrete

5261 Retail Nurseries And Garden Stores

(P-11259)
GREEN THUMB INTERNATIONAL INC
Also Called: Green Thumb Nurseries
23734 Newhall Ave, Newhall (91321-3125)
PHONE..............................661 259-1071
Bryan Payne, *Mgr*
EMP: 86
SALES (corp-wide): 24.03MM **Privately
Held**
Web: www.greenthumb.com
SIC: 5261 5712 5193 0782 Nursery stock,
seeds and bulbs; Outdoor and garden
furniture; Nursery stock; Sodding contractor
PA: Green Thumb International Inc
7105 Jordan Ave
818 340-6400

(P-11260)
TREASURE GARDEN INC (PA)
13401 Brooks Dr, Baldwin Park
(91706-2294)
PHONE..............................626 814-0168
Oliver Ma, *Pr*
Margaret Chang, *
◆ **EMP:** 50 **EST:** 1984
SQ FT: 45,000
SALES (est): 23.25MM
SALES (corp-wide): 23.25MM **Privately
Held**
Web: www.treasuregarden.com
SIC: 5261 2514 Retail nurseries and garden
stores; Lawn furniture: metal

5311 Department Stores

(P-11261)
LADESSERTS INC
1433 E Gage Ave, Los Angeles
(90001-1783)
PHONE..............................323 588-2522
EMP: 40

SALES (corp-wide): 10.98MM **Privately Held**
Web: www.theivyrestaurants.com
SIC: 5311 5137 2389 Department stores; Women's and children's clothing; Apparel for handicapped
PA: L.A.Desserts Inc.
113 N Robertson Blvd
310 274-8303

(P-11262)
PENNEY OPCO LLC
Also Called: JC Penney
280 W Hillcrest Dr, Thousand Oaks (91360-4210)
PHONE..............................805 497-6811
M Kline, *Brnch Mgr*
EMP: 86
SALES (corp-wide): 1.93B **Privately Held**
SIC: 5311 7231 5995 Department stores, non-discount; Beauty shops; Optical goods stores
HQ: Penney Opco Llc
6501 Legacy Dr
Plano TX 75024
972 431-4746

(P-11263)
PENNEY OPCO LLC
Also Called: JC Penney
400 S Baldwin Ave Lowr, Arcadia (91007-1909)
PHONE..............................626 445-6454
Jeff Paige, *Mgr*
EMP: 107
SALES (corp-wide): 1.93B **Privately Held**
SIC: 5311 7231 Department stores, non-discount; Beauty shops
HQ: Penney Opco Llc
6501 Legacy Dr
Plano TX 75024
972 431-4746

(P-11264)
PENNEY OPCO LLC
Also Called: JC Penney 1505
1203 Plaza Dr, West Covina (91790-2885)
PHONE..............................626 960-3711
Bob Watanabe, *Brnch Mgr*
EMP: 179
SALES (corp-wide): 1.93B **Privately Held**
SIC: 5311 7231 5995 Department stores, non-discount; Beauty shops; Optical goods stores
HQ: Penney Opco Llc
6501 Legacy Dr
Plano TX 75024
972 431-4746

(P-11265)
WALMART INC
Also Called: Walmart
1366 S Riverside Ave, Rialto (92376-7608)
PHONE..............................909 820-9912
James Wright, *Mgr*
EMP: 93
SQ FT: 180,839
SALES (corp-wide): 648.13B **Publicly Held**
Web: corporate.walmart.com
SIC: 5311 7384 Department stores, discount ; Film developing services
PA: Walmart Inc.
702 Sw 8th St
479 273-4000

5331 Variety Stores

(P-11266)
CPL HOLDINGS LLC
12181 Bluff Creek Dr Ste 250, Playa Vista (90094-3236)
PHONE..............................310 348-6800
Patrick Gregory, *CFO*
Stephen Krenzer, *
EMP: 200 EST: 2012
SQ FT: 40,000
SALES (est): 3.49MM **Privately Held**
Web: www.coredigitalmedia.com
SIC: 5331 6719 5961 Variety stores; Investment holding companies, except banks; Electronic shopping

(P-11267)
GOODWILL INDS SOUTHERN CAL (PA)
342 N San Fernando Rd, Los Angeles (90031-1730)
PHONE..............................323 223-1211
Patrick Mcclenahan, *CEO*
Patrick Mcclenahan, *Pr*
Michelle Tan, *
▲ EMP: 880 EST: 1919
SQ FT: 200,000
SALES (est): 287.98MM
SALES (corp-wide): 287.98MM **Privately Held**
Web: www.goodwillsocal.org
SIC: 5331 8331 Variety stores; Vocational rehabilitation agency

(P-11268)
NUMBER HOLDINGS INC (PA)
4000 Union Pacific Ave, Los Angeles (90023-3202)
PHONE..............................323 980-8145
Christopher J Wells, *CRO*
Frank J Schools, *
▲ EMP: 224 EST: 2011
SALES (est): 3.36B
SALES (corp-wide): 3.36B **Privately Held**
Web: www.99only.com
SIC: 5331 5199 Variety stores; General merchandise, non-durable

(P-11269)
PG USA LLC
Also Called: Pricegrabber.com
5150 W Goldleaf Cir, Los Angeles (90056-1662)
PHONE..............................310 954-1040
◆ EMP: 85 EST: 1999
SALES (est): 2.34MM
SALES (corp-wide): 85.63MM **Privately Held**
SIC: 5331 4813 Variety stores; Online service providers
HQ: Connexity, Inc.
2120 Colorado Ave Ste 400
Santa Monica CA 90404

5399 Miscellaneous General Merchandise

(P-11270)
COSTCO WHOLESALE CORPORATION
Also Called: Costco
1345 N Montebello Blvd, Montebello (90640-2585)
PHONE..............................323 890-1904
EMP: 205

SIC: 5399 5014 Warehouse club stores; Automobile tires and tubes

5411 Grocery Stores

(P-11271)
ALBERTSONS LLC
Also Called: Albertsons 6514
8938 Trautwein Rd Ste A, Riverside (92508-9191)
PHONE..............................951 656-6603
Bill Brown, *Mgr*
EMP: 68
SALES (corp-wide): 79.24B **Publicly Held**
Web: local.albertsons.com
SIC: 5411 2051 Supermarkets, chain; Bread, cake, and related products
HQ: Albertson's Llc
250 E Parkcenter Blvd
Boise ID 83706
208 395-6200

(P-11272)
ALBERTSONS LLC
Also Called: Albertsons 6798
30901 Riverside Dr, Lake Elsinore (92530-4934)
PHONE..............................951 245-4461
Brad Sharp, *Mgr*
EMP: 24
SALES (corp-wide): 79.24B **Publicly Held**
Web: www.starbucks.com
SIC: 5411 5992 2052 2051 Supermarkets, chain; Florists; Cookies and crackers; Bread, cake, and related products
HQ: Albertson's Llc
250 E Parkcenter Blvd
Boise ID 83706
208 395-6200

(P-11273)
ARRIETTA INCORPORATED
Also Called: La Tolteca Mexican Foods
429 N Azusa Ave, Azusa (91702-3442)
PHONE..............................626 334-0302
Benjamin E Arrietta, *Pr*
Jean Arrietta, *
Tim Arrietta, *
Ben D Arrietta, *
EMP: 33 EST: 1948
SQ FT: 19,000
SALES (est): 1.62MM **Privately Held**
Web: www.latoltecaazusa.com
SIC: 5411 2099 5812 Delicatessen stores; Tortillas, fresh or refrigerated; Mexican restaurant

(P-11274)
DIANAS MEXICAN FOOD PDTS INC
Also Called: Labonita Diana's Mexican Food
300 E Sepulveda Blvd, Carson (90745-5923)
PHONE..............................310 834-4886
Carlos Andres, *Mgr*
EMP: 44
SQ FT: 1,660
SALES (corp-wide): 23.78MM **Privately Held**
Web: www.dianas.net
SIC: 5411 2099 5812 Delicatessen stores; Food preparations, nec; Mexican restaurant
PA: Diana's Mexican Food Products, Inc.
16330 Pioneer Blvd
562 926-5802

(P-11275)
DILLON COMPANIES INC
Also Called: Food 4 Less

4250 Van Buren Blvd, Riverside (92503-2602)
PHONE..............................951 352-8353
Rocky Scmit, *Mgr*
EMP: 143
SALES (corp-wide): 150.04B **Publicly Held**
Web: www.dillons.com
SIC: 5411 2051 Supermarkets, chain; Bread, cake, and related products
HQ: Dillon Companies, Llc
2700 E 4th Ave
Hutchinson KS 67504
620 665-5511

(P-11276)
EL TIGRE INC
Also Called: El Tigre Warehouse 2
2909 Coronado Ave, San Diego (92154-2150)
PHONE..............................619 429-8212
M Rodriguez, *Genl Mgr*
EMP: 108
SALES (corp-wide): 2.62MM **Privately Held**
SIC: 5411 2051 Grocery stores, independent ; Bread, cake, and related products
PA: El Tigre, Inc.
1002 Mission Creek Rd
760 728-8800

(P-11277)
GELSONS MARKETS
13455 Maxella Ave, Marina Del Rey (90292-5682)
PHONE..............................310 306-3192
Romel Montero, *Genl Mgr*
EMP: 83
Web: www.gelsons.com
SIC: 5411 2051 5461 Supermarkets, chain; Bread, cake, and related products; Retail bakeries
HQ: Gelson's Markets
13833 Freeway Dr
Santa Fe Springs CA 90670
310 638-2842

(P-11278)
HOLZHEUS EL RANCHO MARKET INC
2886 Mission Dr, Solvang (93463-9444)
PHONE..............................805 688-4300
EMP: 100 EST: 1966
SALES (est): 2.95MM **Privately Held**
Web: www.californiafreshmarket.com
SIC: 5411 5147 Grocery stores, independent ; Meats, fresh

(P-11279)
MAJOR MARKET INC
Also Called: Major Market Ftd Florist
845 S Main Ave, Fallbrook (92028-3347)
PHONE..............................760 723-0857
John Elkon, *Mgr*
EMP: 122
SALES (corp-wide): 4.16MM **Privately Held**
Web: www.majormarketgrocery.com
SIC: 5411 7336 Supermarkets, chain; Commercial art and graphic design
PA: Major Market, Inc.
845 S Main Ave
760 723-0857

(P-11280)
PRESTIGE STATIONS INC (DH)
Also Called: Am/PM Mini Market
4 Centerpointe Dr, La Palma (90623-1015)
PHONE..............................714 670-5145
John Lannan, *VP*

PRODUCTS & SVCS

EMP: 200 **EST:** 1974
SQ FT: 7,000
SALES (est): 270.65MM
SALES (corp-wide): 171.22B **Privately Held**
Web: www.ampm.com
SIC: 5411 7549 5541 Convenience stores, chain; Automotive maintenance services; Filling stations, gasoline
HQ: Atlantic Richfield Company Inc
4 Centerpointe Dr Ste 200
La Palma CA 90623
800 333-3991

(P-11281)
STATER BROS MARKETS
10114 Adams Ave, Huntington Beach
(92646-4907)
PHONE..............................714 963-0949
Kevin Wagner, *Mgr*
EMP: 35
SALES (corp-wide): 1.5B **Privately Held**
Web: www.staterbros.com
SIC: 5411 5912 5992 2052 Supermarkets, chain; Drug stores; Florists; Cookies and crackers
HQ: Stater Bros. Markets
301 S Tippecanoe Ave
San Bernardino CA 92408
909 733-5000

(P-11282)
STATER BROS MARKETS
1131 N State College Blvd, Anaheim
(92806-2704)
PHONE..............................714 991-5310
Scott Jefferson, *Mgr*
EMP: 35
SALES (corp-wide): 1.5B **Privately Held**
Web: www.staterbros.com
SIC: 5411 5912 5992 2051 Supermarkets, chain; Drug stores; Florists; Bread, cake, and related products
HQ: Stater Bros. Markets
301 S Tippecanoe Ave
San Bernardino CA 92408
909 733-5000

(P-11283)
SUPER CENTER CONCEPTS INC
Also Called: Superior Super Warehouse
7300 Atlantic Ave, Cudahy (90201-4305)
PHONE..............................323 562-8980
Peter Buyn, *Brnch Mgr*
EMP: 113
Web: www.superiorgrocers.com
SIC: 5411 5421 2052 2051 Grocery stores, independent; Meat and fish markets; Cookies and crackers; Bread, cake, and related products
PA: Super Center Concepts, Inc.
15510 Carmenita Rd

(P-11284)
SUPER CENTER CONCEPTS INC
Also Called: Superior Warehouse
10211 Avalon Blvd, Los Angeles
(90003-4819)
PHONE..............................323 241-6789
Mat Kovacs, *Brnch Mgr*
EMP: 113
Web: www.superiorgrocers.com
SIC: 5411 2051 5812 5461 Supermarkets, independent; Bread, cake, and related products; Carry-out only (except pizza) restaurant; Retail bakeries
PA: Super Center Concepts, Inc.
15510 Carmenita Rd

(P-11285)
VONS COMPANIES INC
Also Called: Vons 2124
7789 Foothill Blvd, Tujunga (91042-2195)
PHONE..............................818 353-4917
Kevin Micalles, *Mgr*
EMP: 120
SQ FT: 39,200
SALES (corp-wide): 79.24B **Publicly Held**
Web: local.vons.com
SIC: 5411 5912 5992 2051 Supermarkets, chain; Drug stores; Florists; Bread, cake, and related products
HQ: The Vons Companies Inc
5918 Stoneridge Mall Rd
Pleasanton CA 94588
925 467-3000

(P-11286)
VONS COMPANIES INC
Also Called: Vons 2111
24160 Lyons Ave, Newhall (91321-2442)
PHONE..............................661 259-9214
Phil Nakamura, *Mgr*
EMP: 159
SALES (corp-wide): 79.24B **Publicly Held**
Web: www.vons.com
SIC: 5411 5912 2051 Supermarkets, chain; Drug stores; Bread, cake, and related products
HQ: The Vons Companies Inc
5918 Stoneridge Mall Rd
Pleasanton CA 94588
925 467-3000

(P-11287)
VONS COMPANIES INC
Also Called: Vons 2030
25850 The Old Rd, Stevenson Ranch
(91381-1710)
PHONE..............................661 254-3570
Brian Flaherty, *Mgr*
EMP: 139
SALES (corp-wide): 79.24B **Publicly Held**
Web: local.vons.com
SIC: 5411 5912 2051 5461 Supermarkets, chain; Drug stores; Bread, cake, and related products; Retail bakeries
HQ: The Vons Companies Inc
5918 Stoneridge Mall Rd
Pleasanton CA 94588
925 467-3000

(P-11288)
VONS COMPANIES INC
Also Called: Vons 2381
535 N Mckinley St, Corona (92879-1297)
PHONE..............................951 278-8284
Rick Williams, *Mgr*
EMP: 120
SALES (corp-wide): 79.24B **Publicly Held**
Web: local.vons.com
SIC: 5411 5912 2051 5461 Supermarkets, chain; Drug stores; Bread, cake, and related products; Retail bakeries
HQ: The Vons Companies Inc
5918 Stoneridge Mall Rd
Pleasanton CA 94588
925 467-3000

(P-11289)
VONS COMPANIES INC
Also Called: Vons 2560
1758 W Grand Ave, Grover Beach
(93433-2293)
PHONE..............................805 481-2492
Jim Clark, *Mgr*
EMP: 159
SALES (corp-wide): 79.24B **Publicly Held**
Web: local.vons.com

SIC: 5411 5912 3556 Supermarkets, chain; Drug stores; Food products machinery
HQ: The Vons Companies Inc
5918 Stoneridge Mall Rd
Pleasanton CA 94588
925 467-3000

(P-11290)
VONS COMPANIES INC
Also Called: Vons 2407
475 W Main St, Brawley (92227-2244)
PHONE..............................760 351-3002
Frank Huerta, *Mgr*
EMP: 120
SALES (corp-wide): 79.24B **Publicly Held**
Web: www.vons.com
SIC: 5411 5912 2051 7384 Supermarkets, chain; Drug stores; Bread, cake, and related products; Photofinish laboratories
HQ: The Vons Companies Inc
5918 Stoneridge Mall Rd
Pleasanton CA 94588
925 467-3000

5431 Fruit And Vegetable Markets

(P-11291)
LINNS FRUIT BIN INC (PA)
Also Called: Linn's Main Bin
2535 Village Ln Ste A, Cambria
(93428-3428)
PHONE..............................805 927-1499
Maureen Linn, *Pr*
Renee Linn, *
John Linn, *
Aaron Linn, *
EMP: 35 **EST:** 1995
SQ FT: 16,000
SALES (est): 4.58MM
SALES (corp-wide): 4.58MM **Privately Held**
Web: www.linnsfruitbin.com
SIC: 5431 2053 5812 Fruit and vegetable markets; Frozen bakery products, except bread; Eating places

(P-11292)
PIONEER THEATRES INC
Also Called: Roadium Open Air Market
2500 Redondo Beach Blvd, Torrance
(90504-1529)
PHONE..............................310 532-8183
William Fleischman, *Pr*
William Warnick, *
EMP: 110 **EST:** 1949
SQ FT: 3,000
SALES (est): 4.58MM **Privately Held**
Web: www.roadium.com
SIC: 5431 7832 Fruit and vegetable markets; Motion picture theaters, except drive-in

5441 Candy, Nut, And Confectionery Stores

(P-11293)
LEGENDARY FOODS LLC
2601 Colorado Ave, Santa Monica
(90404-3518)
PHONE..............................888 698-1708
Michael Veni, *
Nathan Tudhope, *
EMP: 48 **EST:** 2015
SALES (est): 63.33MM **Privately Held**
Web: www.eatlegendary.com
SIC: 5441 1541 2099 Candy; Food products manufacturing or packing plant construction; Food preparations, nec

5461 Retail Bakeries

(P-11294)
DUDLEYS BAKERY INC
30218 Highway 78, Santa Ysabel
(92070-9733)
P.O. Box 67 (92070-0067)
PHONE..............................760 765-0488
Barry Burnye, *Mgr*
EMP: 38 **EST:** 1946
SQ FT: 6,000
SALES (est): 2.47MM **Privately Held**
Web: www.dudleysbakery.com
SIC: 5461 5149 2051 Bread; Bakery products ; Bread, cake, and related products

(P-11295)
EVKII INC
624 Garrison St Ste1-2, Oceanside
(92054-4844)
PHONE..............................760 721-5200
Heath Squier, *CEO*
EMP: 40 **EST:** 1990
SQ FT: 35,000
SALES (est): 3.78MM **Privately Held**
Web: www.julianbakery.com
SIC: 5461 2053 2023 5149 Bread; Frozen bakery products, except bread; Dietary supplements, dairy and non-dairy based; Organic and diet food

(P-11296)
JESSIE LORD BAKERY LLC
Also Called: Jessie Lord
21100 S Western Ave, Torrance
(90501-1705)
PHONE..............................310 533-6010
Tracy Lee, *
▲ **EMP:** 50 **EST:** 2003
SQ FT: 130,000
SALES (est): 23.66MM **Privately Held**
Web: www.jessielordbakery.com
SIC: 5461 2051 Retail bakeries; Cakes, bakery: except frozen

(P-11297)
KAYLAS CAKE CORPORATION
1311 S Gilbert St, Fullerton (92833-4302)
PHONE..............................714 869-1522
Kayla Lee, *CEO*
EMP: 30 **EST:** 2014
SALES (est): 476.26K **Privately Held**
Web: www.thekaylascake.com
SIC: 5461 5149 2024 Cakes; Bakery products; Ice cream and frozen deserts

(P-11298)
MADONNA INN INC
100 Madonna Rd, San Luis Obispo
(93405-5489)
PHONE..............................805 543-3000
Phyllis Madonna, *CEO*
EMP: 200 **EST:** 1951
SQ FT: 9,200
SALES (est): 10.73MM **Privately Held**
Web: www.madonnainn.com
SIC: 5461 5812 5813 7991 Retail bakeries; Cafe; Bar (drinking places); Spas

(P-11299)
MAMOLOS CNTNTL BAILEY BAKERIES
Also Called: Viktor Benes Bakeries
2734 Townsgate Rd, Westlake Village
(91361-2906)
PHONE..............................805 496-0045
Manigeh Tabataba, *Mgr*
EMP: 141
SALES (corp-wide): 2.84MM **Privately Held**

Web: www.viktorbenesbakery.com
SIC: 5461 5149 Cakes; Bakery products
PA: Mamolo's Continental & Bailey
    Bakeries Inc
    703 S Main St
    818 841-9347

(P-11300)
PORTOS BAKERY BURBANK INC
Also Called: Portos Bakery & Cafe
3614 W Magnolia Blvd, Burbank
(91505-2913)
PHONE..............................818 846-9100
Raul R Porto, CEO
EMP: 50 **EST:** 2006
SALES (est): 10.63MM **Privately Held**
Web: www.portosbakery.com
SIC: 5461 2051 Cakes; Bread, cake, and
related products

(P-11301)
PURITAN BAKERY INC
1624 E Carson St, Carson (90745-2599)
PHONE..............................310 830-5451
Matthew R Grimes, Pr
John G Markulis, *
John John Markulis, *
EMP: 200 **EST:** 1940
SQ FT: 60,000
SALES (est): 24.2MM **Privately Held**
Web: www.puritanbakery.com
SIC: 5461 2051 Retail bakeries; Breads,
rolls, and buns

(P-11302)
SONORA BAKERY INC
4484 Whittier Blvd, Los Angeles
(90022-1534)
PHONE..............................323 269-2253
Hector Oratowski, Pr
Theresa Oratowski, *
Dennis Oratowski, *
EMP: 30 **EST:** 1986
SQ FT: 6,000
SALES (est): 1MM **Privately Held**
Web: www.sonorabakery.com
SIC: 5461 2051 5812 Retail bakeries; Bread,
cake, and related products; Caterers

(P-11303)
WETZELS PRETZELS LLC
Also Called: Store 3
525 Parkway Plz Unit 525, El Cajon
(92020-2531)
PHONE..............................619 588-1074
Linda Holm, Genl Mgr
EMP: 41
SALES (corp-wide): 848.13MM **Privately
Held**
Web: www.wetzels.com
SIC: 5461 2099 Pretzels; Food preparations,
nec
HQ: Wetzel's Pretzels, Llc
    35 Hugus Alley Ste 300
    Pasadena CA 91103

5499 Miscellaneous Food Stores

(P-11304)
COROMEGA COMPANY INC
2525 Commerce Way, Vista (92081-8420)
P.O. Box 131135 (92013-1135)
PHONE..............................760 599-6088
Frank Morley, Pr
Alice Chen, *
▲ **EMP:** 30 **EST:** 1999
SALES (est): 4.81MM **Privately Held**

Web: www.coromega.com
SIC: 5499 2099 Health foods; Food
preparations, nec

(P-11305)
IHERB LLC (PA)
Also Called: Iherb House Brands
17400 Laguna Canyon Rd Ste 400, Irvine
(92618-5425)
PHONE..............................951 616-3600
Emun Zabihi, *
◆ **EMP:** 1942 **EST:** 2001
SQ FT: 336,000
SALES (est): 1.64B
SALES (corp-wide): 1.64B **Privately Held**
Web: www.iherb.com
SIC: 5499 5122 Vitamin food stores; Drugs,
proprietaries, and sundries

(P-11306)
LA COSTA COFFEE ROASTING CO (PA)
Also Called: COSTA COFFEE
6965 El Camino Real Ste 208, Carlsbad
(92009-4102)
PHONE..............................760 438-8160
Douglas Novak, Prin
Douglas Novak, Mng Pt
Paul Novak, Pt
Linda Novak, Pt
EMP: 25 **EST:** 1991
SALES (est): 823.01K **Privately Held**
Web: www.lacostacoffee.com
SIC: 5499 5149 2095 Coffee; Coffee, green
or roasted; Coffee roasting (except by
wholesale grocers)

(P-11307)
LANGER JUICE COMPANY INC (PA)
Also Called: Langers Juice
16195 Stephens St, City Of Industry
(91745-1718)
PHONE..............................626 336-3100
Bruce Langer, CEO
David Langer, CFO
◆ **EMP:** 154 **EST:** 1960
SQ FT: 140,000
SALES (est): 85.1MM
SALES (corp-wide): 85.1MM **Privately
Held**
Web: www.langers.com
SIC: 5499 2033 Juices, fruit or vegetable;
Vegetable juices: fresh

(P-11308)
SOL-TI INC
Also Called: Solti
8380 Miralani Dr, San Diego (92126-4304)
PHONE..............................888 765-8411
Pawan Kalra, Pr
Ryne O'donnell, Ch
EMP: 76 **EST:** 2014
SQ FT: 15,000
SALES (est): 10.01MM **Privately Held**
Web: www.solti.com
SIC: 5499 2033 2037 Juices, fruit or
vegetable; Fruit juices: fresh; Citrus pulp,
dried

(P-11309)
SUJA LIFE LLC (PA)
Also Called: Suja Juice
3841 Ocean Ranch Blvd, Oceanside
(92056-2694)
PHONE..............................855 879-7852
Maria Stipp, CEO
James Brennan, Pr
▲ **EMP:** 48 **EST:** 2012
SALES (est): 59.64MM

SALES (corp-wide): 59.64MM **Privately
Held**
Web: www.sujaorganic.com
SIC: 5499 2033 Juices, fruit or vegetable;
Fruit juices: packaged in cans, jars, etc.

(P-11310)
TONE IT UP LLC
1110 Manhattan Ave, Manhattan Beach
(90266-5313)
P.O. Box 323 (90245-0323)
PHONE..............................310 376-7645
Russell Sternlicht, CEO
Christine Sana, *
▲ **EMP:** 31 **EST:** 2009
SQ FT: 3,000
SALES (est): 6.03MM **Privately Held**
Web: my.toneitup.com
SIC: 5499 2099 5149 Health and dietetic
food stores; Food preparations, nec;
Groceries and related products, nec

(P-11311)
VITA-HERB NUTRICEUTICALS INC
172 E La Jolla St, Placentia (92870-7111)
PHONE..............................714 632-3726
M Bing Baksh, CEO
▲ **EMP:** 35 **EST:** 1999
SQ FT: 11,000
SALES (est): 4.45MM **Privately Held**
Web: www.vhni.com
SIC: 5499 2834 Vitamin food stores;
Pharmaceutical preparations

5511 New And Used Car Dealers

(P-11312)
ADVANTAGE FORD LINCOLN MERCURY
Also Called: Advantage Ford
260 California Ter, Pasadena (91105-1515)
PHONE..............................626 305-9188
Gary W Hoecker, Pr
EMP: 97 **EST:** 1997
SALES (est): 1.31MM **Privately Held**
Web: www.lincolnofduarte.com
SIC: 5511 7532 Automobiles, new and used;
Top and body repair and paint shops

(P-11313)
AL ASHER & SONS INC
5301 Valley Blvd, Los Angeles
(90032-3930)
PHONE..............................800 896-2480
James A Asher, CEO
James A Asher, Pr
Robert L Asher, *
◆ **EMP:** 25 **EST:** 1914
SQ FT: 80,000
SALES (est): 3.55MM **Privately Held**
Web: www.alasher.com
SIC: 5511 7353 3531 Trucks, tractors, and
trailers: new and used; Heavy construction
equipment rental; Construction machinery

(P-11314)
ALHAMBRA MOTORS INC
Also Called: Goudy Honda
1400 W Main St, Alhambra (91801-1952)
PHONE..............................626 576-1114
TOLL FREE: 800
EMP: 156 **EST:** 1958
SALES (est): 45.89MM **Privately Held**
Web: www.goudyhonda.com
SIC: 5511 7521 Automobiles, new and used;
Automobile parking

(P-11315)
ALLEN GWYNN CHEVROLET INC
Also Called: Allen Gwynn Chevrolet
1400 S Brand Blvd, Glendale (91204-2895)
PHONE..............................818 240-0000
Gwynn G Bacon, Pr
James Bacon, Prin
Virginia Bacon, Prin
EMP: 76 **EST:** 1930
SALES (est): 3.96MM **Privately Held**
Web: www.lovemychevy.com
SIC: 5511 7515 Automobiles, new and used;
Passenger car leasing

(P-11316)
AMERICAN SUZUKI MOTOR CORPORATION
3251 E Imperial Hwy, Brea (92821-6722)
P.O. Box 1100 (92822-1100)
PHONE..............................714 996-7040
◆ **EMP:** 382
SIC: 5511 5571 5091 5013 Automobiles,
new and used; Motorcycle dealers;
Outboard motors; Motor vehicle supplies
and new parts

(P-11317)
BARGAIN RENT-A-CAR
Also Called: Lexus of Cerritos
18800 Studebaker Rd, Cerritos
(90703-5339)
PHONE..............................562 865-7447
Afshin Kahensohayegh, Mgr
Lewis M Webb, *
Jerry Heuer, Acting Secretary*
EMP: 130 **EST:** 1960
SALES (est): 3.44MM
SALES (corp-wide): 26.95B **Publicly Held**
Web: www.cerritoslexus.com
SIC: 5511 5521 5012 Automobiles, new and
used; Used car dealers; Automobiles and
other motor vehicles
HQ: Webb Automotive Group, Inc.
    200 Sw 1st Ave
    Fort Lauderdale FL 33301
    954 769-7000

(P-11318)
BOB BAKER VOLKSWAGEN
Also Called: Bob Baker Chrysler-Plymouth
5500 Paseo Del Norte, Carlsbad
(92008-4428)
P.O. Box 2129 (92067-2129)
PHONE..............................760 438-2200
Michael Baker, Pr
Micheal Baker, *
Tom Solomon, *
William Kornik, General Vice President*
Michelle Wagstaff, *
EMP: 90 **EST:** 1975
SALES (est): 2.49MM
SALES (corp-wide): 21.19MM **Privately
Held**
Web:
www.autonationvolkswagencarlsbad.com
SIC: 5511 7538 5531 Automobiles, new and
used; General automotive repair shops;
Automotive parts
PA: Bob Baker Enterprises, Inc.
    591 Camino De La Reina
    619 683-5591

(P-11319)
BOB STALL CHEVROLET
7601 Alvarado Rd, La Mesa (91942-8211)
P.O. Box 339 (91944-0339)
PHONE..............................619 460-1311
John Stall, CEO
Thomas Stall, *

EMP: 110 **EST:** 1958
SALES (est): 8.08MM **Privately Held**
Web: www.bobstall.com
SIC: 5511 7538 Automobiles, new and used;
General automotive repair shops

(P-11320)
BOULEVARD AUTOMOTIVE GROUP (PA)
Also Called: Boulevard Collision Center
2850 Cherry Ave, Signal Hill (90755-1909)
PHONE.................................562 492-1000
EMP: 83 **EST:** 1961
SALES (est): 4.2MM
SALES (corp-wide): 4.2MM **Privately Held**
Web: www.boulevard4u.com
SIC: 5511 Automobiles, new and used;
General automotive repair shops

(P-11321)
BRECHT ENTERPRISES INC
Also Called: Brecht BMW
1555 Auto Park Way, Escondido
(92029-2003)
P.O. Box 461089 (92046-1089)
PHONE.................................760 745-3000
TOLL FREE: 888
EMP: 100 **EST:** 1985
SQ FT: 56,000
SALES (est): 33.49MM **Privately Held**
Web: www.bmwofescondido.com
SIC: 5511 5571 6159 5013 Automobiles,
new and used; Motorcycle dealers;
Equipment and vehicle finance leasing
companies; Automotive supplies and parts

(P-11322)
CABE BROTHERS
Also Called: Cabe Toyota
2895 Long Beach Blvd, Long Beach
(90806-1595)
PHONE.................................562 595-7411
John Cabe, *Pr*
Marilyn Gidden, *
Glenda Favilla, *
Myra Cabe, *
EMP: 81 **EST:** 1956
SQ FT: 11,080
SALES (est): 3.37MM **Privately Held**
Web: www.cabetoyota.com
SIC: 5511 7538 Automobiles, new and used;
General automotive repair shops

(P-11323)
CADILLAC MOTOR DIV AREA
30930 Russell Ranch Rd, Westlake Village
(91362-7378)
PHONE.................................805 373-9575
Mike Jackson, *Mgr*
EMP: 175 **EST:** 1955
SALES (est): 4.31MM **Publicly Held**
Web: www.cadillac.com
SIC: 5511 3711 Automobiles, new and used;
Motor vehicles and car bodies
HQ: General Motors Llc
300 Rnaissance Ctr Ste L1
Detroit MI 48243

(P-11324)
CENTER AUTOMOTIVE INC
Also Called: Center B M W
5201 Van Nuys Blvd, Sherman Oaks
(91401-5618)
P.O. Box 3870 (91031-6870)
PHONE.................................818 907-9995
EMP: 85 **EST:** 1968
SQ FT: 50,000
SALES (est): 27.92MM **Privately Held**
Web: www.bmwshermanoaks.com

SIC: 5511 5012 Automobiles, new and used;
Automobiles and other motor vehicles

(P-11325)
CENTURY WEST LLC
4245 Lankershim Blvd, North Hollywood
(91602-2802)
PHONE.................................818 432-5800
Dennis Lin, *Pr*
EMP: 92 **EST:** 1995
SALES (est): 7.27MM **Privately Held**
Web: www.centurywestbmw.com
SIC: 5511 7538 Automobiles, new and used;
General automotive repair shops

(P-11326)
CITRUS MOTORS ONTARIO INC (PA)
Also Called: Citrus Ford
1375 S Woodruff Way, Ontario
(91761-2233)
P.O. Box 4270 (91761-8970)
PHONE.................................909 390-0930
Dennis Shannon, *Pr*
Alice Van Dentoorn, *
EMP: 211 **EST:** 1950
SALES (est): 10.17MM
SALES (corp-wide): 10.17MM **Privately Held**
Web: www.citrusmotors.com
SIC: 5511 7538 Automobiles, new and used;
General automotive repair shops

(P-11327)
CJM AUTOMOTIVE GROUP INC
Also Called: Bakersfield Mazda
3101 Cattle Dr, Bakersfield (93313-2604)
P.O. Box 41117 (93384-1117)
PHONE.................................661 832-3000
Masoud Bashirtash, *Pr*
James Haddad, *
Farhad Bashirtash, *
Ali Reza Bashirtash, *
EMP: 70 **EST:** 1960
SALES (est): 4.03MM **Privately Held**
Web: www.drivecj.com
SIC: 5511 7538 Automobiles, new and used;
General automotive repair shops

(P-11328)
COUNTY FORD NORTH INC (PA)
Also Called: North County GMC
450 W Vista Way, Vista (92083-5829)
PHONE.................................760 945-9900
James E Crowley, *Pr*
Sean Crowley, *
Jeffrey Friestedt, *
Joseph Weir, *
Scott Crowley, *
▼ **EMP:** 213 **EST:** 1992
SALES (est): 14.41MM **Privately Held**
Web: www.northcountyford.net
SIC: 5511 5521 7538 7515 Automobiles,
new and used; Used car dealers; General
automotive repair shops; Passenger car
leasing

(P-11329)
COURTESY CHEVROLET CENTER
Also Called: Geo Sales-Courtesy Chevrolet
750 Camino Del Rio N, San Diego
(92108-3296)
PHONE.................................619 297-4321
TOLL FREE: 877
William R Gruwell, *Pr*
EMP: 86 **EST:** 1961
SQ FT: 60,000
SALES (est): 4.21MM **Privately Held**
Web: www.courtesysandiego.com

SIC: 5511 7538 5531 7515 Automobiles,
new and used; General automotive repair
shops; Auto and home supply stores;
Passenger car leasing

(P-11330)
CREVIER CLASSICS LLC
1500 Auto Mall Dr, Santa Ana
(92705-4743)
PHONE.................................714 835-3171
EMP: 320 **EST:** 1971
SALES (est): 4.15MM **Privately Held**
Web: www.crevierbmw.com
SIC: 5511 5521 5531 7538 Automobiles,
new and used; Automobiles, used cars only
; Auto and home supply stores; General
automotive repair shops

(P-11331)
D LONGO INC
Also Called: Longo Scion
3534 Peck Rd, El Monte (91731-3526)
PHONE.................................626 580-6000
Greg Penske, *Pr*
EMP: 380 **EST:** 1967
SALES (est): 7.3MM
SALES (corp-wide): 32.13B **Publicly Held**
Web: www.longotoyota.com
SIC: 5511 7538 Automobiles, new and used;
General automotive repair shops
PA: Penske Corporation
2555 Telegraph Rd
248 648-2000

(P-11332)
DAVID A CAMPBELL CORPORATION
Also Called: B M W of Riverside
3060 Adams St, Riverside (92504-4014)
P.O. Box 4007 (92514-4007)
PHONE.................................951 785-4444
Allen David Franklin, *CEO*
Steven Campbell, *
Patrick Campbell, *
EMP: 150 **EST:** 1975
SQ FT: 45,000
SALES (est): 4.13MM **Privately Held**
Web: www.bmwofriverside.com
SIC: 5511 7538 Automobiles, new and used;
General automotive repair shops

(P-11333)
DCH ACURA OF TEMECULA
Also Called: Lithia
26705 Ynez Rd, Temecula (92591-4693)
P.O. Box 9043 (92589-9043)
PHONE.................................877 847-9532
Kenneth Colson, *VP*
EMP: 100 **EST:** 2014
SALES (est): 1.85MM **Privately Held**
Web: www.ohacuraoftemecula.com
SIC: 5511 7539 5531 Automobiles, new and
used; Automotive repair shops, nec;
Automotive parts

(P-11334)
DCH CALIFORNIA MOTORS INC
Also Called: Toyota of Oxnard
1631 Auto Center Dr, Oxnard (93036-8972)
PHONE.................................805 988-7900
Shau-wai Lam, *Pr*
Scott Borg, *
EMP: 95 **EST:** 1991
SALES (est): 3.16MM
SALES (corp-wide): 31.04B **Publicly Held**
Web: www.toyotaofoxnard.com
SIC: 5511 7538 7532 Automobiles, new and
used; General automotive repair shops; Top
and body repair and paint shops
HQ: Dch North America Inc.
955 Rte 9 North

South Amboy NJ
732 727-9168

(P-11335)
DCH GARDENA HONDA
Also Called: Gardena Honda
15541 S Western Ave, Gardena
(90249-4320)
P.O. Box 3758 (90247-7458)
PHONE.................................310 515-5700
TOLL FREE: 800
Shauwai Lam, *Prin*
EMP: 140 **EST:** 1979
SQ FT: 290,000
SALES (est): 2.38MM
SALES (corp-wide): 31.04B **Publicly Held**
Web: www.gardenahonda.com
SIC: 5511 7538 Automobiles, new and used;
General automotive repair shops
HQ: Dch North America Inc.
955 Rte 9 North
South Amboy NJ
732 727-9168

(P-11336)
DIAMOND BAR IMPORTS INC
Also Called: Diamond Honda
17525 Gale Ave, City Of Industry
(91748-1517)
PHONE.................................626 935-1700
Linda Tachdjian, *CEO*
EMP: 89 **EST:** 1994
SALES (est): 12.46MM **Privately Held**
Web: www.diamondhonda.com
SIC: 5511 5012 Automobiles, new and used;
Automobiles

(P-11337)
DICK DEWESE CHEVROLET INC
Also Called: Tom Bell Chevrolet
800 Alabama St, Redlands (92374-2806)
PHONE.................................909 793-2681
Tom O Bell, *Pr*
Derek Hanson, *
Lynn Drysdale, *
EMP: 102 **EST:** 1951
SQ FT: 10,000
SALES (est): 4.36MM **Privately Held**
Web: www.tombellchevrolet.com
SIC: 5511 7538 5531 5521 Automobiles,
new and used; General automotive repair
shops; Auto and home supply stores; Used
car dealers

(P-11338)
DREW FORD
Also Called: Drew Hyundai
8970 La Mesa Blvd, La Mesa (91942-0849)
P.O. Box 188 (91944-0188)
PHONE.................................619 464-7777
William J Drew, *Pr*
EMP: 250 **EST:** 1927
SQ FT: 90,000
SALES (est): 3.69MM **Privately Held**
Web: www.drewauto.com
SIC: 5511 7538 Automobiles, new and used;
General automotive repair shops

(P-11339)
EL CENTRO MOTORS
Also Called: Ford Lincoln Mercury
1520 Ford Dr, El Centro (92243-1603)
P.O. Box 3250 (92244-3250)
PHONE.................................760 336-2100
EMP: 95 **EST:** 1901
SALES (est): 39.31MM **Privately Held**
Web: www.elcentromotors.net
SIC: 5511 7538 5531 Automobiles, new and
used; General automotive repair shops;
Automotive parts

(P-11340)
EL MONTE AUTOMOTIVE GROUP INC
Also Called: Longo Lexus
3530 Peck Rd, El Monte (91731-3526)
PHONE.....................626 580-6200
Greg Penske, *Pr*
EMP: 104 **EST:** 1989
SALES (est): 33.75MM **Privately Held**
Web: www.longolexus.com
SIC: 5511 7532 7515 5521 Automobiles, new and used; Top and body repair and paint shops; Passenger car leasing; Used car dealers

(P-11341)
EL MONTE AUTOMOTIVE GROUP LLC
Also Called: Nelson Honda
3464 Peck Rd, El Monte (91731-3253)
PHONE.....................626 444-0321
TOLL FREE: 800
EMP: 80 **EST:** 1960
SALES (est): 1.86MM **Privately Held**
Web: www.autoserviceelmonte.com
SIC: 5511 7538 7515 5531 Automobiles, new and used; General automotive repair shops; Passenger car leasing; Auto and home supply stores

(P-11342)
EMERGENCY VEHICLE GROUP INC
Also Called: E V G
2883 E Coronado St Ste A, Anaheim (92806-2552)
PHONE.....................714 238-0110
Travis Grinstead, *Pr*
EMP: 25 **EST:** 2005
SQ FT: 15,000
SALES (est): 2.41MM **Privately Held**
Web: www.evginc.net
SIC: 5511 5012 3569 5013 Trucks, tractors, and trailers new and used; Ambulances; Firefighting apparatus; Motor vehicle supplies and new parts

(P-11343)
ESCONDIDO MOTORS LLC
Also Called: Mercedes Benz of Escondido
1101 W 9th Ave, Escondido (92025-3843)
PHONE.....................760 745-5000
Simon Sarriedine, *CEO*
Jack Manukyan, *
EMP: 80 **EST:** 1988
SALES (est): 4.32MM **Privately Held**
Web: www.mbescondido.com
SIC: 5511 5521 7515 5531 Automobiles, new and used; Automobiles, used cars only ; Passenger car leasing; Auto and home supply stores

(P-11344)
EUROPA AUTO IMPORTS INC
Also Called: Mercedes Benz of San Diego
4750 Kearny Mesa Rd, San Diego (92111-2405)
PHONE.....................858 569-6900
Ora Smith, *Pr*
Judy Antrim, *
Duayne Hancock, *
▼ **EMP:** 116 **EST:** 1957
SQ FT: 10,000
SALES (est): 4.95MM **Privately Held**
Web: www.mbsd.com
SIC: 5511 5521 7538 Automobiles, new and used; Used car dealers; General automotive repair shops

(P-11345)
FAA BEVERLY HILLS INC
Also Called: Beverly Hills BMW
5070 Wilshire Blvd, Los Angeles (90036-4381)
PHONE.....................323 801-1430
Step Jones, *Genl Mgr*
EMP: 85 **EST:** 1991
SQ FT: 4,000
SALES (est): 4.29MM
SALES (corp-wide): 14.37MM **Publicly Held**
Web: www.bmwofbeverlyhills.com
SIC: 5511 7538 Automobiles, new and used; General automotive repair shops
PA: Sonic Automotive, Inc.
4401 Colwick Rd
704 566-2400

(P-11346)
FELIX CHEVROLET LP (PA)
Also Called: Felix Chevrolet
714 W Olympic Blvd Ste 1124, Los Angeles (90015-4129)
PHONE.....................213 748-6141
Nicholas N Shammas, *Pt*
George Damaa, *Pt*
EMP: 113 **EST:** 1921
SALES (est): 8.41MM
SALES (corp-wide): 8.41MM **Privately Held**
Web: www.felixchevrolet.com
SIC: 5511 7538 7532 5531 Automobiles, new and used; General automotive repair shops; Top and body repair and paint shops ; Auto and home supply stores

(P-11347)
FIESTA FORD INC
Also Called: Fiesta Ford Lincoln-Mercury
79015 Avenue 40, Indio (92203-9499)
PHONE.....................760 775-7777
Paul J Thiel, *CEO*
EMP: 126 **EST:** 1966
SQ FT: 304,920
SALES (est): 3.43MM **Privately Held**
Web: www.ford.com
SIC: 5511 7538 Automobiles, new and used; General automotive repair shops

(P-11348)
FORD MOTOR COMPANY
Also Called: Ford
3 Glen Bell Way Ste 200, Irvine (92618-3392)
PHONE.....................949 341-5800
Michael O'driscoll, *Pr*
EMP: 76
SALES (corp-wide): 176.19B **Publicly Held**
Web: www.ford.com
SIC: 5511 7549 Automobiles, new and used; Automotive customizing services, nonfactory basis
PA: Ford Motor Company
1 American Rd
313 322-3000

(P-11349)
FORD OF SANTA MONICA INC
Also Called: Ford
1402 Santa Monica Blvd, Santa Monica (90404-1710)
PHONE.....................310 451-1588
Ron Davis, *CEO*
EMP: 92 **EST:** 1948
SALES (est): 2.7MM **Privately Held**
Web: www.smford.com
SIC: 5511 5012 Automobiles, new and used; Ambulances

(P-11350)
FORD OF SIMI VALLEY INC
Also Called: Ford
2440 1st St, Simi Valley (93065-0916)
PHONE.....................805 583-0333
Larry Hibbler, *Pr*
Kathleen Lindsey, *
EMP: 70 **EST:** 2001
SQ FT: 28,000
SALES (est): 6.03MM **Privately Held**
Web: www.ford.com
SIC: 5511 7538 Automobiles, new and used; General automotive repair shops

(P-11351)
FOX HILLS AUTO INC (PA)
Also Called: Airport Marina Ford
5880 W Centinela Ave, Los Angeles (90045-1504)
PHONE.....................310 649-3673
Norris J Bishton Junior, *CEO*
▲ **EMP:** 140 **EST:** 1989
SQ FT: 35,000
SALES (est): 18.74MM **Privately Held**
Web: www.ford.com
SIC: 5511 7538 5531 5521 Automobiles, new and used; General automotive repair shops; Auto and home supply stores; Used car dealers

(P-11352)
GALPIN MOTORS INC (PA)
Also Called: Galpin Ford
15505 Roscoe Blvd, North Hills (91343-6598)
PHONE.....................818 787-3800
Herbert F Boeckman Ii, *Pr*
Karl L Boeckmann, *
Bradley M Boeckmann, *
Alan J Skobin, *
Jane Boeckmann, *
▼ **EMP:** 500 **EST:** 1946
SQ FT: 175,000
SALES (est): 59.63MM
SALES (corp-wide): 59.63MM **Privately Held**
Web: www.galpin.com
SIC: 5511 5521 7538 7515 Automobiles, new and used; Used car dealers; General automotive repair shops; Passenger car leasing

(P-11353)
GENERAL MOTORS LLC
Also Called: General Motors
3050 Lomita Blvd Ste 237, Torrance (90505-5103)
PHONE.....................313 556-5000
Nicholas Herron, *Brnch Mgr*
EMP: 25
Web: www.gm.com
SIC: 5511 3711 Automobiles, new and used; Automobile assembly, including specialty automobiles
HQ: General Motors Llc
300 Rnaissance Ctr Ste L1
Detroit MI 48243

(P-11354)
GEORGE CHEVROLET
Also Called: George Chevrolet
17000 Lakewood Blvd, Bellflower (90706-5594)
PHONE.....................562 925-2500
Jeffery Estabrooks, *Pr*
Patricia Estabrooks, *
EMP: 100 **EST:** 1961
SQ FT: 56,000
SALES (est): 7.28MM **Privately Held**
Web: www.chevrolet.com

SIC: 5511 7515 7538 Automobiles, new and used; Passenger car leasing; General automotive repair shops

(P-11355)
GPI CA-NIII INC
Also Called: Performance Nissan
1434 Buena Vista St, Duarte (91010-2402)
PHONE.....................626 305-3000
John C Rickel, *CEO*
Frank Grese Junior, *Prin*
EMP: 74 **EST:** 1991
SALES (est): 1.06MM **Publicly Held**
Web: www.perfnissan.com
SIC: 5511 7538 7515 5531 Automobiles, new and used; General automotive repair shops; Passenger car leasing; Auto and home supply stores
PA: Group 1 Automotive, Inc.
800 Gessner Rd Ste 500

(P-11356)
GREGORY CONSULTING INC (PA)
6350 Leland St, Ventura (93003-8585)
PHONE.....................805 642-0111
TOLL FREE: 888
Robert Gregory, *Pr*
Nancy Gregory, *
EMP: 135 **EST:** 1986
SQ FT: 54,000
SALES (est): 794.99K
SALES (corp-wide): 794.99K **Privately Held**
Web: www.paradisechevrolet.com
SIC: 5511 7538 5521 Automobiles, new and used; General automotive repair shops; Used car dealers

(P-11357)
H W HUNTER INC (PA)
Also Called: Hunter Dodge Chrysler Jeep Ram
1130 Auto Mall Dr, Lancaster (93534-6302)
P.O. Box 4324 (93539-4324)
PHONE.....................661 948-8411
Timothy H Fuller, *CEO*
EMP: 80 **EST:** 1956
SQ FT: 5,000
SALES (est): 8.72MM
SALES (corp-wide): 8.72MM **Privately Held**
Web: www.hunterdodgechryslerjeep.net
SIC: 5511 7538 Automobiles, new and used; General automotive repair shops

(P-11358)
HABERFELDE FORD (PA)
Also Called: Jim Burke Ford
2001 Oak St, Bakersfield (93301-3010)
P.O. Box 2088 (93303-2088)
PHONE.....................661 328-3600
Daniel George Hay, *Pr*
Michelle Hay, *
Beverly Burke, *
Joe Hay, *
EMP: 236 **EST:** 1913
SQ FT: 102,000
SALES (est): 17.16MM
SALES (corp-wide): 17.16MM **Privately Held**
Web: www.jimburkeford.com
SIC: 5511 7538 Automobiles, new and used; General automotive repair shops

(P-11359)
HARBILL INC
Also Called: Crest Chevrolet
909 W 21st St, San Bernardino (92405-3201)

P.O. Box 501 (92402-0501)
PHONE.............................909 883-8833
D William Bader, *CEO*
Robert Bader, *
Douglas Bader, *
Patty Bader, *
EMP: 93 **EST:** 1958
SQ FT: 20,000
SALES (est): 1.5MM **Privately Held**
Web: www.driveadiamond.com
SIC: 5511 5012 5531 5521 Automobiles, new and used; Automobiles and other motor vehicles; Auto and home supply stores; Used car dealers

(P-11360)
HOEHN COMPANY INC
Also Called: Hoehn Honda
5454 Paseo Del Norte, Carlsbad (92008-4426)
P.O. Box 789 (92018-0789)
PHONE.............................760 438-1818
TOLL FREE: 888
Robert A Hoehn, *Pr*
T William Hoehn Iii, *VP*
Gloria Rediker, *
EMP: 80 **EST:** 1993
SQ FT: 3,000
SALES (est): 3.51MM **Privately Held**
Web: www.hoehnhonda.com
SIC: 5511 7538 Automobiles, new and used; General automotive repair shops

(P-11361)
HONDA WORLD WESTMINSTER
13600 Beach Blvd, Westminster (92683-3202)
PHONE.............................714 890-8900
Jim Kitzmiller, *Pr*
Tom Chadwell, *
EMP: 175 **EST:** 1989
SQ FT: 6,000
SALES (est): 5.86MM
SALES (corp-wide): 23.93MM **Privately Held**
Web: www.honda.com
SIC: 5511 7539 5015 5012 Automobiles, new and used; Automotive repair shops, nec; Motor vehicle parts, used; Automobiles and other motor vehicles
PA: Gee Investments, Inc
21502 E George Gee Ave
509 343-2391

(P-11362)
IDEALAB (HQ)
130 W Union St, Pasadena (91103-3628)
PHONE.............................626 356-3654
Bill Gross, *Ch Bd*
Marcia Goodstein, *
Craig Chrisney, *
Teresa Bridwell, *
Kristen Ding, *
▲ **EMP:** 82 **EST:** 1996
SQ FT: 30,000
SALES (est): 17.03MM
SALES (corp-wide): 35.77MM **Privately Held**
Web: www.idealab.com
SIC: 5511 6726 New and used car dealers; Investment offices, nec
PA: Idealab Holdings, L.L.C.
130 West Union St
626 585-6900

(P-11363)
ISUZU NORTH AMERICA CORP (HQ)
1400 S Douglass Rd Ste 100, Anaheim (92806-6906)

PHONE.............................714 935-9300
Masanori Katayama, *Pr*
Shinichi Takahashi, *
Masatoshi Ito, *
◆ **EMP:** 150 **EST:** 1975
SQ FT: 64,000
SALES (est): 283.94MM **Privately Held**
Web: www.isuzu.com
SIC: 5511 5084 5013 5015 Automobiles, new and used; Engines and parts, diesel; Automotive supplies and parts; Motor vehicle parts, used
PA: Isuzu Motors Limited
1-2-5, Takashima, Nishi-Ku

(P-11364)
JACK GOSCH FORD INC
Also Called: Gosch Ford Lincoln Mercury
150 Carriage Cir, Hemet (92545-9615)
PHONE.............................951 658-3181
TOLL FREE: 800
Jack E Gosch, *Pr*
Mark E Gosch, *
Eric Gosch, *
Marc Gosch, *
Richard Rodgers, *
EMP: 100 **EST:** 1964
SQ FT: 35,000
SALES (est): 2.8MM **Privately Held**
Web: www.goschauto.com
SIC: 5511 7538 Automobiles, new and used; General automotive repair shops

(P-11365)
JACK PWELL CHRYSLER - DDGE INC
Also Called: Jack Pwell Chrysler Ddge Jeep
1625 Auto Park Way, Escondido (92029-2008)
PHONE.............................760 745-2880
Jack Powell Junior, *Pr*
Jack Powell Junior, *Pr*
Judith Powell, *
EMP: 85 **EST:** 1958
SQ FT: 28,000
SALES (est): 3.37MM **Privately Held**
Web: www.dodge.com
SIC: 5511 7538 5531 Automobiles, new and used; General automotive repair shops; Auto and home supply stores

(P-11366)
JEEP CHRYSLER OF ONTARIO
Also Called: Jeep Chrysler Ddge Ram Ontario
1202 Auto Center Dr, Ontario (91761-2208)
PHONE.............................909 390-9898
Richard D Romero, *Ch Bd*
R J Romero, *
Kathy Brown, *
Valerie Romero, *
J B Butterwick, *
EMP: 95 **EST:** 1993
SQ FT: 30,000
SALES (est): 4.54MM **Privately Held**
Web: www.jcofontario.com
SIC: 5511 7538 5531 Automobiles, new and used; General automotive repair shops; Auto and home supply stores

(P-11367)
JOHNSON FORD (PA)
Also Called: Antelope Valley Lincoln
1155 Auto Mall Dr, Lancaster (93534-5867)
PHONE.............................661 206-2597
Michael H Johnson, *Pr*
Doug Killebrew, *
Brooke Powell, *
Bob Heninger, *
EMP: 120 **EST:** 1957
SQ FT: 70,000

SALES (est): 10.3MM
SALES (corp-wide): 10.3MM **Privately Held**
Web: www.diamondfordav.com
SIC: 5511 7538 5561 Automobiles, new and used; General automotive repair shops; Camper and travel trailer dealers

(P-11368)
KEN GRODY REDLANDS LLC
Also Called: Ken Grody Ford - Redlands
1121 W Colton Ave, Redlands (92374-2935)
PHONE.............................909 793-3211
William Raymond, *
Brandi Desherlia, *
EMP: 85 **EST:** 2019
SALES (est): 3.53MM **Privately Held**
Web: www.kengrodyfordredlands.com
SIC: 5511 7538 New and used car dealers; General automotive repair shops

(P-11369)
KEYES MOTORS INC (PA)
Also Called: Keyes Toyota
5855 Van Nuys Blvd, Van Nuys (91401-4219)
PHONE.............................818 782-0122
Howard Keyes, *Pr*
Lawrence Abramson, *
EMP: 80 **EST:** 1968
SQ FT: 20,000
SALES (est): 16.53MM
SALES (corp-wide): 16.53MM **Privately Held**
Web: www.keyestoyota.com
SIC: 5511 7538 7515 5012 Automobiles, new and used; General automotive repair shops; Passenger car leasing; Automobiles and other motor vehicles

(P-11370)
KEYLEX INC (PA)
Also Called: Keyes Lexus
5905 Van Nuys Blvd, Van Nuys (91401-3624)
PHONE.............................818 379-4000
Howard Keyes, *Pr*
EMP: 87 **EST:** 1989
SQ FT: 32,376
SALES (est): 15.19MM **Privately Held**
Web: www.keyeslexus.com
SIC: 5511 7538 7515 5531 Automobiles, new and used; General automotive repair shops; Passenger car leasing; Auto and home supply stores

(P-11371)
KEYSTONE FORD INC (PA)
12000 Firestone Blvd, Norwalk (90650-2907)
PHONE.............................562 868-0825
TOLL FREE: 800
Norman P Stutzke, *Pr*
Lamberto Colon, *
Paul Stutzke, *
EMP: 130 **EST:** 1968
SQ FT: 14,000
SALES (est): 1.6MM
SALES (corp-wide): 1.6MM **Privately Held**
Web: www.ford.com
SIC: 5511 5531 7514 Automobiles, new and used; Automotive parts; Rent-a-car service

(P-11372)
LAKE CHEVROLET
31201 Auto Center Dr, Lake Elsinore (92530-4424)
P.O. Box 4000 (92531-4000)
PHONE.............................951 674-3116

EMP: 133
Web: www.andersonchevroletca.com
SIC: 5511 7515 5521 Automobiles, new and used; Passenger car leasing; Used car dealers

(P-11373)
LEO HOFFMAN CHEVROLET INC (PA)
Also Called: Puente Hills Chevrolet
17300 E Gale Ave, City Of Industry (91748-1512)
P.O. Box 90428 (91715-0428)
PHONE.............................626 968-8411
Thomas L Hoffman, *Pr*
Gary A Campbell, *
Kurt Hoffman, *
EMP: 71 **EST:** 1944
SQ FT: 75,000
SALES (est): 4.99MM
SALES (corp-wide): 4.99MM **Privately Held**
Web: www.chevroletofpuentehills.com
SIC: 5511 7515 Automobiles, new and used; Passenger car leasing

(P-11374)
LOS FELIZ FORD INC (PA)
Also Called: Star Ford Lincoln Mercury
1101 S Brand Blvd, Glendale (91204-2313)
PHONE.............................818 502-1901
Steve Bussjaeger, *Pr*
Tad Okumoto, *
Agnes Gurida, *
EMP: 80 **EST:** 1970
SQ FT: 75,000
SALES (est): 11MM
SALES (corp-wide): 11MM **Privately Held**
Web: www.starford.com
SIC: 5511 7515 Automobiles, new and used; Passenger car leasing

(P-11375)
M K SMITH CHEVROLET
12845 Central Ave, Chino (91710-4120)
P.O. Box 455 (91708-0455)
PHONE.............................909 628-8961
Marc Smith, *CEO*
Carolyn Coble, *
Cheryl Smith, *
Marc Smith, *Ex VP*
EMP: 120 **EST:** 1941
SALES (est): 6.88MM **Privately Held**
Web: www.mksmithchevrolet.com
SIC: 5511 7549 5531 Automobiles, new and used; Automotive maintenance services; Automotive parts

(P-11376)
MAGIC ACQUISITION CORP
Also Called: Autonation Ford Valencia
23920 Creekside Rd, Valencia (91355-1701)
PHONE.............................661 382-4700
Chance Corbitt, *Mgr*
Mark Leccompte, *
EMP: 350 **EST:** 1996
SALES (est): 2.91MM
SALES (corp-wide): 26.95B **Publicly Held**
Web: www.autonationfordvalencia.com
SIC: 5511 7538 5531 New and used car dealers; General automotive repair shops; Auto and home supply stores
HQ: Magic Acquisition Holding, Llc
200 Sw 1st Ave
Fort Lauderdale FL 33301
954 769-7000

(P-11377)
MARK CHRISTOPHER CHEVROLET INC (PA)
Also Called: Mark Christopher Hummer
2131 E Convention Center Way, Ontario
(91764-4495)
PHONE..................909 321-5860
Chris Leggio, *CEO*
Shirley Leggid, *
Loretta Holtz, *
EMP: 132 EST: 1986
SQ FT: 15,000
SALES (est): 44.87MM
SALES (corp-wide): 44.87MM **Privately Held**
Web: www.markchristopher.com
SIC: 5511 5521 3714 Automobiles, new and used; Used car dealers; Motor vehicle parts and accessories

(P-11378)
MARTIN CHEVROLET
23505 Hawthorne Blvd, Torrance
(90505-4739)
P.O. Box 2895 (90509-2895)
PHONE..................323 772-6494
TOLL FREE: 888
Joe Giacomin, *Pr*
Fran Williams, *
EMP: 100 EST: 1947
SQ FT: 10,000
SALES (est): 4.42MM **Privately Held**
Web: www.martinchevrolet.com
SIC: 5511 7538 Automobiles, new and used; General automotive repair shops

(P-11379)
MILLER AUTOMOTIVE GROUP INC (HQ)
Also Called: Miller Nissan
5425 Van Nuys Blvd, Sherman Oaks
(91401-5628)
PHONE..................818 787-8400
Fred Miller, *Ch Bd*
Michael Miller, *
Mark Miller, *
Doug Stewart, *
▲ **EMP: 350 EST:** 1989
SQ FT: 40,000
SALES (est): 8.53MM **Publicly Held**
Web: www.nissanofvannuys.com
SIC: 5511 7538 5521 Automobiles, new and used; General automotive repair shops; Automobiles, used cars only
PA: Group 1 Automotive, Inc.
800 Gessner Rd Ste 500

(P-11380)
MISSION VOLKSWAGEN INC
Also Called: Capistrano Volkswagen
32922 Valle Rd, San Juan Capistrano
(92675-4802)
PHONE..................949 493-4511
Miles Braden, *Pr*
Miles Brandon, *
EMP: 80 EST: 1993
SQ FT: 3,997
SALES (est): 4.11MM **Privately Held**
Web: www.capovw.com
SIC: 5511 7538 Automobiles, new and used; General automotive repair shops

(P-11381)
MOSSY AUTOMOTIVE GROUP INC (PA)
Also Called: Mossy Toyota
4555 Mission Bay Dr, San Diego
(92109-4920)
PHONE..................858 581-4000
Philip Mossy, *Pr*
Peter Mossy, *
EMP: 100 EST: 2002
SALES (est): 32.39MM **Privately Held**
Web: www.mossytoyota.com
SIC: 5511 7538 Automobiles, new and used; General automotive repair shops

(P-11382)
MOSSY FORD INC
Also Called: Quick Lane
4570 Mission Bay Dr, San Diego
(92109-4985)
PHONE..................858 273-7500
Phillip Mossy, *Pr*
John Epps, *
▼ **EMP: 200 EST:** 1988
SQ FT: 10,000
SALES (est): 3.04MM **Privately Held**
Web: www.mossyford.com
SIC: 5511 7538 7532 7515 Automobiles, new and used; General automotive repair shops; Top and body repair and paint shops ; Passenger car leasing

(P-11383)
MOSSY NISSAN INC
Also Called: Mossy Nissan Kearny Mesa
8118 Clairemont Mesa Blvd, San Diego
(92111-1998)
PHONE..................858 565-6608
Mike Obeso, *Mgr*
EMP: 100
Web: www.infinitiofkearnymesa.com
SIC: 5511 5521 7515 Automobiles, new and used; Used car dealers; Passenger car leasing
HQ: Nissan Mossy Inc
2700 National City Blvd
National City CA 91950
619 474-7011

(P-11384)
MOTOR CITY SALES & SERVICE (PA)
Also Called: Motor City GMC Buick Pontiac
3101 Pacheco Rd, Bakersfield
(93313-3214)
P.O. Box 40340 (93384-0340)
PHONE..................661 836-9000
EMP: 111 EST: 1945
SALES (est): 22MM
SALES (corp-wide): 22MM **Privately Held**
Web: www.motorcitywest.com
SIC: 5511 7538 Pickups, new and used; General automotive repair shops

(P-11385)
NGP MOTORS INC
Also Called: Sunrise Ford
5500 Lankershim Blvd, North Hollywood
(91601-2724)
P.O. Box 908 (92334-0908)
PHONE..................818 980-9800
Robert Burncati, *Pr*
Maureen Burncati, *
EMP: 131 EST: 1979
SQ FT: 75,000
SALES (est): 13.82MM **Privately Held**
Web: www.ford.com
SIC: 5511 7539 7538 Automobiles, new and used; Automotive repair shops, nec; General automotive repair shops

(P-11386)
NICK ALEXANDER IMPORTS
6333 S Alameda St, Los Angeles
(90001-2168)
PHONE..................800 800-6425
TOLL FREE: 800

Elizabeth Alexander, *CEO*
Mary Alexander, *
EMP: 110 EST: 1978
SQ FT: 32,500
SALES (est): 6.96MM **Privately Held**
Web: www.bmwdtla.com
SIC: 5511 7549 Automobiles, new and used; Automotive maintenance services

(P-11387)
NISSAN OF TUSTIN
Also Called: Tustin Saab
30 Auto Center Dr, Tustin (92782-8401)
PHONE..................714 669-8282
James H Parkinson, *Pr*
Mark Parkinson, *
EMP: 149 EST: 1972
SQ FT: 30,000
SALES (est): 45.07MM **Privately Held**
Web: www.nissanoftustin.com
SIC: 5511 6159 Automobiles, new and used; Automobile finance leasing

(P-11388)
NOARUS INVESTMENTS INC
Also Called: Airport Honda
5850 W Centinela Ave, Los Angeles
(90045-1504)
PHONE..................310 649-2440
Norris J Bishton, *Pr*
EMP: 100 EST: 1998
SALES (est): 4.96MM **Privately Held**
Web: www.honda.com
SIC: 5511 5521 5531 7538 Automobiles, new and used; Automobiles, used cars only ; Automotive parts; General automotive repair shops

(P-11389)
NOARUS TGG
Also Called: Toyota Scion Place
9444 Trask Ave, Garden Grove
(92844-2824)
PHONE..................714 895-5595
Norris J Bishton, *Pr*
Gary Alwood, *
William Hurst, *General Vice President*
EMP: 97 EST: 1979
SQ FT: 30,000
SALES (est): 6.33MM **Privately Held**
Web: www.toyota.com
SIC: 5511 5531 7538 Automobiles, new and used; Automotive parts; General automotive repair shops

(P-11390)
OCEANSIDE AUTO COUNTRY INC (PA)
Also Called: Toyota Carlsbad
6030 Avenida Encinas Ste 200, Carlsbad
(92011-1062)
PHONE..................760 438-2000
Judith Jones-cone, *CEO*
Olen Woods, *
Michael W Wear, *
EMP: 116 EST: 1972
SQ FT: 3,500
SALES (est): 16.63MM
SALES (corp-wide): 16.63MM **Privately Held**
Web: www.toyotacarlsbad.com
SIC: 5511 7538 7532 Automobiles, new and used; General automotive repair shops; Top and body repair and paint shops

(P-11391)
ONTARIO AUTOMOTIVE LLC
Also Called: Penske Honda Ontario
1401 Auto Center Dr, Ontario (91761-2221)
PHONE..................909 974-3800

Roger Penske, *Ch Bd*
Greg Penske, *
Brian Kobus, *
EMP: 125 EST: 1990
SALES (est): 1.4MM
SALES (corp-wide): 32.13B **Publicly Held**
Web: www.penskehondaontario.com
SIC: 5511 5521 5012 Automobiles, new and used; Used car dealers; Automobiles and other motor vehicles
PA: Penske Corporation
2555 Telegraph Rd
248 648-2000

(P-11392)
PALM SPRINGS MOTORS INC
Also Called: Palm Sprng Ford Lncoln Mercury
69-200a Highway 111, Cathedral City
(92234)
PHONE..................760 699-6695
Paul J Thiel, *CEO*
William S Torrance, *
Joseph A Gibbs, *
EMP: 200 EST: 1950
SALES (est): 746.79K **Privately Held**
Web: www.palmspringslincoln.net
SIC: 5511 7538 Automobiles, new and used; General automotive repair shops

(P-11393)
PARK PLACE FORD LLC
Also Called: Ford
555 W Foothill Blvd, Upland (91786-3853)
PHONE..................909 946-5555
EMP: 83 EST: 2012
SQ FT: 15,000
SALES (est): 3.73MM **Privately Held**
Web: www.ford.com
SIC: 5511 7532 7549 5561 Automobiles, new and used; Collision shops, automotive; Emissions testing without repairs, automotive; Travel trailers: automobile, new and used

(P-11394)
PEARSON FORD CO (PA)
5900 Sycamore Canyon Blvd, Riverside
(92507-0719)
PHONE..................877 743-0421
John Mccallan, *Pr*
EMP: 180 EST: 1940
SQ FT: 275,000
SALES (est): 1.9MM
SALES (corp-wide): 1.9MM **Privately Held**
Web: www.racewayford.com
SIC: 5511 7539 7538 5521 Automobiles, new and used; Automotive repair shops, nec; General automotive repair shops; Used car dealers

(P-11395)
PERRY FORD OF POWAY LLC
Also Called: Perry Ford
12740 Poway Rd, Poway (92064-4404)
PHONE..................858 748-1400
Perry Falk, *Managing Member*
EMP: 100 EST: 1995
SQ FT: 50,000
SALES (est): 24.31MM **Privately Held**
Web: www.ford.com
SIC: 5511 7538 5531 5521 Automobiles, new and used; General automotive repair shops; Auto and home supply stores; Used car dealers

(P-11396)
POMONA MC KENNA MOTORS
Also Called: McKenna Pomona Dodge
25 Rio Rancho Rd, Pomona (91766-4775)
PHONE..................909 620-7370

Daniel J Mckenna, *Pt*
Daniel Berliner, *
Charlott Olivares, *
EMP: 117 **EST:** 1992
SALES (est): 178.84K **Privately Held**
Web: www.dodge.com
SIC: 5511 7539 7538 New and used car
dealers; Automotive repair shops, nec;
General automotive repair shops

(P-11397)
POWAY TOYOTA SCION INC
Also Called: Poway Toyota
13631 Poway Rd, Poway (92064-4703)
PHONE..............................858 486-2900
TOLL FREE: 800
Tim Moran, *Genl Mgr*
EMP: 129 **EST:** 1996
SQ FT: 10,000
SALES (est): 5.48MM **Privately Held**
Web: www.toyotaofpoway.com
SIC: 5511 7538 7515 Automobiles, new and
used; General automotive repair shops;
Passenger car leasing

(P-11398)
R E BARBER-FORD
Also Called: Barber Volkeswagen
3440 E Main St, Ventura (93003-5012)
P.O. Box 1628 (93002-1628)
PHONE..............................805 656-4259
EMP: 135
SIC: 5511 7538 7532 5521 New and used
car dealers; General automotive repair
shops; Top and body repair and paint shops
; Used car dealers

(P-11399)
RACEWAY FORD INC
Also Called: Quick Lane
5900 Sycamore Canyon Blvd, Riverside
(92507-0719)
PHONE..............................951 571-9300
John Barry Mccallan Junior, *Pr*
EMP: 145 **EST:** 1956
SALES (est): 7.05MM **Privately Held**
Web: www.racewayford.com
SIC: 5511 7538 Automobiles, new and used;
General automotive repair shops

(P-11400)
RANCHO FORD INC
Also Called: Rancho
26895 Ynez Rd, Temecula (92591-4695)
PHONE..............................951 699-1302
Eric Gosch, *Pr*
Marc L Gosch, *
Issac Lizarrago, *
EMP: 124 **EST:** 1984
SQ FT: 40,000
SALES (est): 4.31MM **Privately Held**
Web: www.ranchoford.com
SIC: 5511 7532 7515 5521 Automobiles,
new and used; Top and body repair and
paint shops; Passenger car leasing; Used
car dealers

(P-11401)
RHI INC (PA)
Also Called: Robertson Honda
5841 Lankershim Blvd, North Hollywood
(91601-1035)
PHONE..............................818 508-3800
TOLL FREE: 800
Robert Robertson, *Pr*
▼ **EMP:** 99 **EST:** 1970
SQ FT: 130,000
SALES (est): 1.64MM
SALES (corp-wide): 1.64MM **Privately
Held**

Web: www.robertsonhonda.com
SIC: 5511 7538 7532 5531 Automobiles,
new and used; General automotive repair
shops; Body shop, automotive; Automotive
parts

(P-11402)
ROTOLO CHEVROLET INC
16666 S Highland Ave, Fontana
(92336-1213)
P.O. Box 457 (92334-0457)
PHONE..............................866 756-9776
Marie Waddingham, *Pr*
Nina Rotolo, *
Darinda Madeiros, *
EMP: 137 **EST:** 1971
SQ FT: 51,000
SALES (est): 49.17MM **Privately Held**
Web: www.rotolochevy.com
SIC: 5511 5521 7538 Automobiles, new and
used; Used car dealers; General
automotive repair shops

(P-11403)
SAN DIEGO V INC (PA)
Also Called: San Diego Volvo
5350 Kearny Mesa Rd, San Diego
(92111-1802)
PHONE..............................888 308-2260
TOLL FREE: 800
Stephen Hinkle, *CEO*
Wesley G Hinkle, *
Robin Seal, *
EMP: 85 **EST:** 1956
SQ FT: 9,200
SALES (est): 7.63MM
SALES (corp-wide): 7.63MM **Privately
Held**
Web: www.volvocarssandiego.com
SIC: 5511 7532 Automobiles, new and used;
Top and body repair and paint shops

(P-11404)
SAN FERNANDO VALLEY AUTO LLC
Also Called: Rydell Chevrolet-Northridge
18600 Devonshire St, Northridge
(91324-1309)
PHONE..............................818 832-1600
Kelly Cashman, *Dir*
EMP: 195
SALES (corp-wide): 12.74MM **Privately
Held**
Web: www.chevynorthridge.com
SIC: 5511 7538 7532 Automobiles, new and
used; General automotive repair shops;
Body shop, automotive
PA: San Fernando Valley Automotive, Llc
6001 Van Nuys Blvd
818 817-4600

(P-11405)
SEIDNER-MILLER INC
Also Called: Toyota of Glendora
1949 Auto Centre Dr, Glendora
(91740-6714)
PHONE..............................909 305-2000
Murrey Seidner, *Pr*
Peter Miller, *
EMP: 180 **EST:** 1993
SQ FT: 65,000
SALES (est): 8.01MM **Privately Held**
Web: www.toyotaofglendora.com
SIC: 5511 7532 7515 5521 Automobiles,
new and used; Top and body repair and
paint shops; Passenger car leasing; Used
car dealers

(P-11406)
SELMAN CHEVROLET COMPANY
1800 E Chapman Ave, Orange
(92867-7797)
P.O. Box 31 (92856-9031)
PHONE..............................714 633-3521
TOLL FREE: 800
William H Selman Junior, *CEO*
William H Selman Iii, *VP*
Daisy Kan, *
EMP: 107 **EST:** 1951
SQ FT: 4,000
SALES (est): 9.89MM **Privately Held**
Web: www.selmanchevy.com
SIC: 5511 7515 Automobiles, new and used;
Passenger car leasing

(P-11407)
SIMPSON AUTOMOTIVE INC
Also Called: Simpson Buick Pontiac GMC
6600 Auto Center Dr, Buena Park
(90621-2927)
PHONE..............................714 690-6200
David A Simpson, *Pr*
Dianna Ramsey, *
EMP: 91 **EST:** 1951
SQ FT: 46,000
SALES (est): 8.6MM **Privately Held**
Web:
www.simpsonbuickgmcbuenapark.com
SIC: 5511 5531 7539 Automobiles, new and
used; Auto and truck equipment and parts;
Automotive repair shops, nec

(P-11408)
SOUTH BAY FORD INC (PA)
Also Called: Quick Lane
5100 W Rosecrans Ave, Hawthorne
(90250-6620)
P.O. Box 1550 (90251-1550)
PHONE..............................310 644-0211
TOLL FREE: 800
Gary Premeaux, *CEO*
Steve Wood, *
▼ **EMP:** 150 **EST:** 1993
SALES (est): 11.3MM
SALES (corp-wide): 11.3MM **Privately
Held**
Web: www.southbayford.com
SIC: 5511 5531 7538 5521 Automobiles,
new and used; Automotive parts; General
automotive repair shops; Used car dealers

(P-11409)
SOUTH BAY TOYOTA
18416 S Western Ave, Gardena
(90248-3823)
PHONE..............................310 323-7800
David Wilson, *Pr*
David Ortiz, *General Vice President*
EMP: 141 **EST:** 1989
SQ FT: 33,000
SALES (est): 5.47MM **Privately Held**
Web: www.southbaytoyota.com
SIC: 5511 7538 7515 Automobiles, new and
used; General automotive repair shops;
Passenger car leasing

(P-11410)
SOUTH CNTY LXUS AT MSSION VEJO
28242 Marguerite Pkwy, Mission Viejo
(92692-3704)
PHONE..............................949 347-3400
Patrick Lustin, *Genl Mgr*
EMP: 200 **EST:** 2013
SALES (est): 1.63MM **Privately Held**
Web: www.southcountylexus.com

SIC: 5511 7549 Automobiles, new and used;
Automotive maintenance services

(P-11411)
SOUTHBAY EUROPEAN INC
Also Called: Southbay BMW
18800 Hawthorne Blvd, Torrance
(90504-5507)
PHONE..............................310 939-7300
Fritz Hitchcock, *Pr*
Peter Boesen, *
EMP: 100 **EST:** 1968
SQ FT: 150,000
SALES (est): 3.34MM **Privately Held**
Web: www.southbaybmw.com
SIC: 5511 5531 7539 Automobiles, new and
used; Automotive parts; Automotive repair
shops, nec

(P-11412)
SOUTHWEST MATERIAL HDLG INC (PA)
Also Called: Southwest Toyota Lift
3725 Nobel Ct, Jurupa Valley (91752-3267)
P.O. Box 1070 (91752-8070)
PHONE..............................951 727-0477
Kirt Little, *CEO*
Joseph G Little, *
▲ **EMP:** 115 **EST:** 1962
SQ FT: 10,000
SALES (est): 60.98MM
SALES (corp-wide): 60.98MM **Privately
Held**
Web: www.swwarehousesolutions.com
SIC: 5511 7389 7699 7359 Automobiles,
new and used; Design, commercial and
industrial; Industrial machinery and
equipment repair; Equipment rental and
leasing, nec

(P-11413)
STERLING MOTORS LTD
Also Called: Sterling BMW
3000 W Coast Hwy, Newport Beach
(92663-4085)
PHONE..............................949 645-5900
Wayne Minor, *CEO*
John Belanger, *
Steve Army, *
Jim Hutton, *
Doug Janco, *
EMP: 80 **EST:** 1955
SQ FT: 27,000
SALES (est): 6.05MM **Privately Held**
Web: www.sterlingbmw.com
SIC: 5511 7515 Automobiles, new and used;
Passenger car leasing

(P-11414)
SUNLAND FORD INC
Also Called: Sunland Ford-Lincoln-Mercury
15330 Palmdale Rd, Victorville
(92392-2498)
PHONE..............................760 241-7751
Ken Chambers, *Pr*
EMP: 90 **EST:** 1969
SQ FT: 10,000
SALES (est): 3.17MM **Privately Held**
Web: www.sunlandfordinc.com
SIC: 5511 7538 5531 5521 Automobiles,
new and used; General automotive repair
shops; Auto and home supply stores; Used
car dealers

(P-11415)
SUNRISE FORD
Also Called: Quick Lane
16005 Valley Blvd, Fontana (92335-6419)
P.O. Box 310125 (92331-0125)
PHONE..............................909 822-4401

▲ = Import ▼ = Export
◆ = Import/Export

Robert Bruncati, *CEO*
Maureen Bruncati, *
EMP: 200 **EST:** 1944
SQ FT: 100,000
SALES (est): 8.64MM **Privately Held**
Web: www.sunrisefordparts.com
SIC: 5511 5012 7538 Automobiles, new and used; Automobiles and other motor vehicles; General automotive repair shops

(P-11416)
SUZUKI MOTOR OF AMERICA INC (HQ)
Also Called: Suzuki USA
3251 E Imperial Hwy, Brea (92821-6795)
P.O. Box 1100 (92822-1100)
PHONE..............................714 996-7040
Takeshi Hayasaki, *Pr*
Takuya Sato, *
◆ **EMP:** 250 **EST:** 2012
SALES (est): 96.42MM **Privately Held**
Web: www.suzuki.com
SIC: 5511 3519 3799 Automobiles, new and used; Outboard motors; Recreational vehicles
PA: Suzuki Motor Corporation
300, Takatsukacho, Chuo-Ku

(P-11417)
TED FORD JONES INC
Also Called: Ken Grody Ford
5555 Paseo Del Norte, Carlsbad (92008-4429)
P.O. Box 1576 (92018-1576)
PHONE..............................760 438-9171
Kurt Maletych, *Brnch Mgr*
EMP: 150
SALES (corp-wide): 45.03MM **Privately Held**
Web: www.ford.com
SIC: 5511 7538 5521 5012 Automobiles, new and used; General automotive repair shops; Used car dealers; Automobiles and other motor vehicles
PA: Ted Jones Ford, Inc.
6211 Beach Blvd
714 521-3110

(P-11418)
THEODORE ROBINS INC
Also Called: Theodore Robins Ford
2060 Harbor Blvd, Costa Mesa (92627-5556)
P.O. Box 5055 (92628-5055)
PHONE..............................949 642-0010
James M Robins, *Pr*
David Robins, *
Dave Robins Ucod, *Vice Manager*
EMP: 78 **EST:** 1921
SQ FT: 65,000
SALES (est): 21.74MM **Privately Held**
Web: www.robinsford.com
SIC: 5511 5012 Automobiles, new and used; Automobiles and other motor vehicles

(P-11419)
THREE-WAY CHEVROLET CO (PA)
4501 Wible Rd, Bakersfield (93313-2639)
P.O. Box 9609 (93389-9609)
PHONE..............................661 847-6400
EMP: 180 **EST:** 1947
SALES (est): 12.53MM
SALES (corp-wide): 12.53MM **Privately Held**
Web: www.3waychevrolet.com
SIC: 5511 5531 7538 7515 Automobiles, new and used; Automotive parts; General automotive repair shops; Passenger car leasing

(P-11420)
TOMS TRUCK CENTER INC
Also Called: Isuzu Truck Services
1008 E 4th St, Santa Ana (92701-4751)
P.O. Box 88 (92702-0088)
PHONE..............................714 835-1978
TOLL FREE: 800
K C Heidler, *Brnch Mgr*
EMP: 177
SALES (corp-wide): 18.26MM **Privately Held**
Web: www.ttruck.com
SIC: 5511 5012 Automobiles, new and used; Automobiles and other motor vehicles
PA: Tom's Truck Center, Inc.
909 N Grand Ave
800 238-9308

(P-11421)
TOYOTA LOGISTICS SERVICES INC (DH)
19001 S Western Ave, Torrance (90501-1106)
PHONE..............................310 468-4000
Randy Pflughaupt, *CEO*
Allen Decarr, *
Donald Esmond, *
◆ **EMP:** 176 **EST:** 1981
SQ FT: 600
SALES (est): 63.58MM **Privately Held**
Web: www.toyota.com
SIC: 5511 3711 Automobiles, new and used; Motor vehicles and car bodies
HQ: Toyota Motor Sales Usa Inc
6565 Hdqtr Dr Apt W1-3c
Plano TX 75024

(P-11422)
TOYOTA OF ORANGE INC
1400 N Tustin St, Orange (92867-3995)
PHONE..............................714 639-6750
David Wilson, *Pr*
EMP: 135 **EST:** 1972
SQ FT: 38,000
SALES (est): 7.47MM
SALES (corp-wide): 25.87MM **Privately Held**
Web: www.toyotaoforange.com
SIC: 5511 5521 5012 Automobiles, new and used; Used car dealers; Automobiles and other motor vehicles
PA: D W W Co., Inc.
1400 N Tustin St
714 516-3111

(P-11423)
TOYOTA OF RIVERSIDE INC
7870 Indiana Ave, Riverside (92504-4109)
PHONE..............................951 687-1622
David Wilson, *Pr*
EMP: 100 **EST:** 1960
SQ FT: 100,000
SALES (est): 9.7MM **Privately Held**
Web: www.toyotaofriverside.com
SIC: 5511 5531 7538 5521 Automobiles, new and used; Automotive parts; General automotive repair shops; Used car dealers

(P-11424)
TRANSWEST TRUCK CENTER LLC
10150 Cherry Ave, Fontana (92335-5282)
PHONE..............................909 770-5170
EMP: 75 **EST:** 1975
SQ FT: 4,000
SALES (est): 3.06MM
SALES (corp-wide): 233.56MM **Privately Held**
Web: www.trans-west.com

SIC: 5511 5531 5013 Automobiles, new and used; Automotive parts; Motor vehicle supplies and new parts
PA: Los Angeles Truck Centers, Llc
2429 Peck Rd
562 447-1200

(P-11425)
TUTTLE-CLICK FORD INC
Also Called: Tuttle Click Ford
43 Auto Center Dr, Irvine (92618-2898)
PHONE..............................949 855-1704
Bob Tuttle, *Pr*
James H Click, *
Chris Cotter, *
Elvia Morales, *
EMP: 225 **EST:** 1980
SQ FT: 50,000
SALES (est): 9.15MM **Privately Held**
Web: www.tuttleclicklincolnirvine.com
SIC: 5511 5521 7538 Automobiles, new and used; Used car dealers; General automotive repair shops

(P-11426)
VAHI TOYOTA INC (PA)
Also Called: Valley-HI Toyota Honda
14612 Valley Center Dr, Victorville (92395-4205)
P.O. Box 1508 (92393-1508)
PHONE..............................760 241-6484
Kent Browning, *Pr*
EMP: 120 **EST:** 1971
SQ FT: 17,000
SALES (est): 1.46MM
SALES (corp-wide): 1.46MM **Privately Held**
Web: www.valleyhitoyota.com
SIC: 5511 7538 5561 5531 Automobiles, new and used; General automotive repair shops; Recreational vehicle dealers; Auto and home supply stores

(P-11427)
VILLA FORD INC
Also Called: David Wilson's Villa Ford
2550 N Tustin St, Orange (92865-3099)
PHONE..............................714 637-8222
TOLL FREE: 888
Peggy Baldwin-butler, *Pr*
Brian Butler, *
Peggy Butler, *
Karen Baldwin, *
EMP: 132 **EST:** 1970
SQ FT: 38,745
SALES (est): 3.47MM **Privately Held**
Web: www.villaford.com
SIC: 5511 7532 7549 Automobiles, new and used; Body shop, automotive; Automotive maintenance services

(P-11428)
VISTA FORD INC
Also Called: Vista Ford of Oxnard
1501 Auto Center Dr, Oxnard (93036-7916)
PHONE..............................805 983-6511
Randy Haddock, *Mgr*
EMP: 80
SALES (corp-wide): 19.5MM **Privately Held**
Web: www.ford.com
SIC: 5511 5521 7538 Automobiles, new and used; Used car dealers; General automotive repair shops
PA: Vista Ford Inc.
21501 Ventura Blvd
818 884-7600

(P-11429)
VOLKSWAGEN OF VAN NUYS INC
300 Hitchcock Way, Santa Barbara (93105-4002)
PHONE..............................323 873-3311
Ludwig Pflock, *Pr*
EMP: 100 **EST:** 1991
SALES (est): 3.04MM **Privately Held**
Web: www.vw.com
SIC: 5511 7538 Automobiles, new and used; General automotive repair shops

(P-11430)
VOLKSWAGEN SANTA MONICA INC (PA)
Also Called: Lexus Santa Monica
2440 Santa Monica Blvd, Santa Monica (90404-2039)
PHONE..............................310 829-1888
TOLL FREE: 888
Michael Sullivan, *Pr*
Kerry Sullivan, *
Hazel R Sullivan, *
EMP: 170 **EST:** 1964
SQ FT: 10,000
SALES (est): 18.22MM
SALES (corp-wide): 18.22MM **Privately Held**
Web: www.volkswagensantamonica.com
SIC: 5511 7532 7538 Automobiles, new and used; Body shop, automotive; General automotive repair shops

(P-11431)
WALTERS AUTO SALES AND SVC INC
Also Called: Mercedes Benz of Riverside
3213 Adams St, Riverside (92504-4002)
PHONE..............................888 316-4097
Steve Kienle, *Genl Mgr*
Helga Kienle, *
Lothar Wacker, *
EMP: 248 **EST:** 1964
SQ FT: 14,000
SALES (est): 10.22MM **Privately Held**
Web: www.waltersaudi.com
SIC: 5511 5012 Automobiles, new and used; Automobiles and other motor vehicles

(P-11432)
WAYNE GOSSETT FORD INC
Also Called: Encinitas Ford
1424 Encinitas Blvd, Encinitas (92024-2930)
P.O. Box 230945 (92023-0945)
PHONE..............................760 753-6286
TOLL FREE: 800
Mark S Wheeler, *Pr*
EMP: 95 **EST:** 1960
SALES (est): 4.1MM **Privately Held**
Web: www.encinitasford.com
SIC: 5511 7549 Automobiles, new and used; Do-it-yourself garages

(P-11433)
WESTRUX INTERNATIONAL INC (PA)
15555 Valley View Ave, Santa Fe Springs (90670-5718)
PHONE..............................562 404-1020
David M Kenney, *Pr*
John M Reynolds, *
▲ **EMP:** 70 **EST:** 1982
SALES (est): 39.38MM
SALES (corp-wide): 39.38MM **Privately Held**
Web: www.westrux.com

P R O D U C T S & S V C S

SIC: **5511** 5531 7513 7538 Trucks, tractors, and trailers: new and used; Truck equipment and parts; Truck rental, without drivers; Truck engine repair, except industrial

(P-11434)
YORK ENTERPRISES SOUTH INC
Also Called: Huntington Beach Ford
18255 Beach Blvd, Huntington Beach (92648-1351)
PHONE..................................714 842-6611
Oscar Bakhtiari, *CEO*
Donna Graham, *
EMP: 100 **EST:** 1989
SALES (est): 5.08MM **Privately Held**
Web: www.huntingtonbeachford.com
SIC: **5511** 7538 Automobiles, new and used; General automotive repair shops

5521 Used Car Dealers

(P-11435)
CARMAX INC
25560 Madison Ave, Murrieta (92562-9095)
PHONE..................................951 387-3887
EMP: 159
SALES (corp-wide): 26.54B **Publicly Held**
Web: www.carmax.com
SIC: **5521** 7539 Automobiles, used cars only; Automotive repair shops, nec
PA: Carmax, Inc.
        12800 Tuckahoe Creek Pkwy
        804 747-0422

(P-11436)
K MOTORS INC
Also Called: Toyota of El Cajon
965 Arnele Ave, El Cajon (92020-3001)
PHONE..................................619 270-3000
Robert Kaminsky, *Pr*
Gary Kaminsky, *
Greg Kaminsky, *
Kim Kaminsky, *
Gregory Kaminsky, *
EMP: 186 **EST:** 1956
SQ FT: 29,497
SALES (est): 11.2MM **Privately Held**
Web: www.toyotaofelcajon.com
SIC: **5521** 5013 5511 Automobiles, used cars only; Automotive supplies and parts; Automobiles, new and used

5531 Auto And Home Supply Stores

(P-11437)
AKH COMPANY INC
Also Called: Discount Tire Center 038
1647 W Redlands Blvd Ste C, Redlands (92373-8001)
PHONE..................................909 748-5016
Marc Fortin, *Mgr*
EMP: 100
SALES (corp-wide): 22.1MM **Privately Held**
Web: www.discounttirecenters.com
SIC: **5531** 7539 5014 Automotive tires; Wheel alignment, automotive; Automobile tires and tubes
PA: Akh Company, Inc.
        1160 N Anaheim Blvd
        800 999-2878

(P-11438)
AKH COMPANY INC
Also Called: Discount Tire Center 077
23316 Sunnymead Blvd, Moreno Valley (92553-5227)
PHONE..................................951 924-5356
Juan Valdes, *Mgr*
EMP: 100
SALES (corp-wide): 22.1MM **Privately Held**
Web: www.discounttirecenters.com
SIC: **5531** 5014 7539 Automotive tires; Automobile tires and tubes; Wheel alignment, automotive
PA: Akh Company, Inc.
        1160 N Anaheim Blvd
        800 999-2878

(P-11439)
AM-PAC TIRE DIST INC (DH)
Also Called: Tire Pros
51 Moreland Rd, Simi Valley (93065-1662)
P.O. Box 1949 (28070-1949)
PHONE..................................805 581-1311
John Abernethy, *Pr*
Dave Crawford, *
▲ **EMP:** 75 **EST:** 1998
SALES (est): 26.15MM
SALES (corp-wide): 1.82B **Privately Held**
Web: www.amr1.com
SIC: **5531** 5014 Automotive tires; Tires and tubes
HQ: American Tire Distributors, Inc.
        12200 Hrbert Wyne Ct Ste
        Huntersville NC 28078
        704 992-2000

(P-11440)
ATV CANTER LLC (PA)
Also Called: American Tire Depot
2875 Pomona Blvd, Pomona (91768-3281)
PHONE..................................562 977-8565
Ara Tchaghlassian, *Pr*
Craig Anderson, *
◆ **EMP:** 70 **EST:** 1994
SALES (est): 98.81MM **Privately Held**
Web: www.americantiredepot.com
SIC: **5531** 7538 Automotive tires; General automotive repair shops

(P-11441)
CERTIFIED TIRE & SVC CTRS INC
Also Called: Goodyear
23920 Alessandro Blvd Ste A, Moreno Valley (92553-8804)
PHONE..................................951 656-6466
Victor Cervantes, *Mgr*
EMP: 36
SALES (corp-wide): 24.35MM **Privately Held**
Web: www.thetirechoice.com
SIC: **5531** 7534 Automotive tires; Tire retreading and repair shops
PA: Certified Tire & Service Centers, Inc.
        1875 Iowa Ave
        951 369-0025

(P-11442)
CLASSIC CAMARO INC
Also Called: Classic Firebird
18460 Gothard St, Huntington Beach (92648-1229)
PHONE..................................714 847-6887
Jeffrey M Leonard, *CEO*
▲ **EMP:** 115 **EST:** 1977
SQ FT: 30,000
SALES (est): 23.17MM **Privately Held**
Web: www.classicindustries.com

SIC: **5531** 5013 Automotive accessories; Automotive supplies and parts

(P-11443)
DNA MOTOR INC
Also Called: Dna Motoring
801 Sentous Ave, City Of Industry (91744-2543)
PHONE..................................626 965-8898
Jia Jie Chen, *CEO*
◆ **EMP:** 40 **EST:** 2009
SALES (est): 7.14MM **Privately Held**
Web: www.dnamotoring.com
SIC: **5531** 3714 Automotive parts; Motor vehicle parts and accessories

(P-11444)
FORNACA INC (PA)
Also Called: Frank Toyota & Scion
2400 National City Blvd, National City (91950-6628)
P.O. Box 540 (91951-0540)
PHONE..................................866 308-9461
James Fornaca, *CEO*
Gary Fenelli, *
Ronald Fornaca, *
EMP: 140 **EST:** 1978
SQ FT: 150,000
SALES (est): 23.36MM **Privately Held**
Web: www.frankmotors.com
SIC: **5531** 5511 7532 Auto and home supply stores; Automobiles, new and used; Top and body repair and paint shops

(P-11445)
FRED M BOERNER MOTOR CO (PA)
Also Called: Boerner Truck Center
3620 E Florence Ave, Huntington Park (90255-5999)
PHONE..................................323 560-3882
▼ **EMP:** 86 **EST:** 1926
SALES (est): 8.52MM
SALES (corp-wide): 8.52MM **Privately Held**
SIC: **5531** 7538 5012 Truck equipment and parts; General truck repair; Truck bodies

(P-11446)
FREEDOM PRFMCE EXHAUST INC
1255 Railroad St, Corona (92882-1838)
PHONE..................................951 898-4733
Flora Arteaga, *CEO*
Martin Arteaga, *
EMP: 47 **EST:** 2006
SALES (est): 4.94MM **Privately Held**
Web: www.freedomperformexhaust.com
SIC: **5531** 3714 Speed shops, including race car supplies; Mufflers (exhaust), motor vehicle

(P-11447)
GLOBAL TRADE ALLIANCE INC
Also Called: Action Crash Parts
13642 Orden Dr, Santa Fe Springs (90670-6353)
PHONE..................................562 944-6422
Todd Hanson, *Mgr*
EMP: 114
SALES (corp-wide): 13.87B **Publicly Held**
SIC: **5531** 5013 Automotive parts; Automotive supplies and parts
HQ: Global Trade Alliance, Inc.
        2040 S Hamilton Rd
        Columbus OH
        614 751-3100

(P-11448)
KRACO ENTERPRISES LLC
505 E Euclid Ave, Compton (90222-2890)
PHONE..................................310 639-0666
◆ **EMP:** 164
Web: www.kraco.com
SIC: **5531** 3069 5013 Automotive accessories; Hard rubber and molded rubber products; Motor vehicle supplies and new parts

(P-11449)
MOSS MOTORS LTD (PA)
400 Rutherford St, Goleta (93117-3702)
PHONE..................................805 967-4546
◆ **EMP:** 130 **EST:** 1948
SALES (est): 24.14MM
SALES (corp-wide): 24.14MM **Privately Held**
Web: www.mossmotors.com
SIC: **5531** 5013 Automotive parts; Automotive supplies and parts

(P-11450)
ORIGINAL PARTS GROUP INC (PA)
Also Called: Chevelle Classics Parts & ACC
1770 Saturn Way, Seal Beach (90740-5618)
PHONE..................................562 594-1000
David Harry Leonard, *Pr*
Anthony M Genty, *
▲ **EMP:** 84 **EST:** 1984
SQ FT: 100,000
SALES (est): 22.31MM
SALES (corp-wide): 22.31MM **Privately Held**
Web: www.opgi.com
SIC: **5531** 3465 Automotive parts; Body parts, automobile: stamped metal

(P-11451)
PARKHOUSE TIRE SERVICE INC
Also Called: Parkhouse Tire
4660 Ruffner St, San Diego (92111-2220)
PHONE..................................858 565-8473
Janette Fox, *Mgr*
EMP: 39
SALES (corp-wide): 83.75MM **Privately Held**
Web: www.parkhousetire.com
SIC: **5531** 5014 7534 Automotive tires; Tires and tubes; Tire retreading and repair shops
PA: Parkhouse Tire Service, Inc.
        6006 Shull St
        562 928-0421

(P-11452)
PARKHOUSE TIRE SERVICE INC (PA)
Also Called: Parkhouse Tire
6006 Shull St, Bell Gardens (90201-6237)
P.O. Box 2430 (90202)
PHONE..................................562 928-0421
◆ **EMP:** 75 **EST:** 1971
SALES (est): 83.75MM
SALES (corp-wide): 83.75MM **Privately Held**
Web: www.parkhousetire.com
SIC: **5531** 5014 7534 Automotive tires; Automobile tires and tubes; Rebuilding and retreading tires

(P-11453)
PLASTICOLOR MOLDED PDTS INC (PA)
Also Called: Plasticolor
801 S Acacia Ave, Fullerton (92831-5398)
P.O. Box 6985 (92831)

PHONE..............714 525-3880
Matthew Bagne, *CEO*
Shawn Diamond, *
Gayle Deflin, *
◆ **EMP:** 250 **EST:** 1971
SALES (est): 48.61MM
SALES (corp-wide): 48.61MM **Privately Held**
Web: www.plasticolorinc.com
SIC: **5531** 3083 Automotive accessories; Plastics finished products, laminated

(P-11454)
RAMONA AUTO SERVICES INC
Also Called: Firestone
2451 S Euclid Ave, Ontario (91762-6617)
P.O. Box 960 (92546-0960)
PHONE...............909 986-1785
Chris Wyborny, *Brnch Mgr*
EMP: 74
Web: www.ramonatire.com
SIC: **5531** 7538 Automotive tires; General automotive repair shops
PA: Ramona Auto Services, Inc.
2350 W Menlo Ave

(P-11455)
SANTA MARIA TIRE INC (PA)
Also Called: SM Tire
2170 Hutton Rd Bldg A, Nipomo (93444-9717)
P.O. Box 6007 (93456-6007)
PHONE...............805 347-4793
Craig Stephens, *Pr*
Brenee Stephens, *
C Kent Stephens, *
Cameron Stephens, *
Conrad Stephens Attorney, *Prin*
EMP: 75 **EST:** 1946
SALES (est): 20.64MM
SALES (corp-wide): 20.64MM **Privately Held**
Web: www.smtire.com
SIC: **5531** 7534 Automotive tires; Rebuilding and retreading tires

(P-11456)
SOUTHERN CAL DISC TIRE CO INC
Also Called: Discount Tire
4640 Telephone Rd, Ventura (93003-5630)
PHONE...............805 639-0166
Thomas Gensen, *Mgr*
EMP: 109
SQ FT: 4,500
SALES (corp-wide): 3.69B **Privately Held**
Web: www.discounttire.com
SIC: **5531** 7538 Automotive tires; General automotive repair shops
HQ: Southern California Discount Tire Co., Inc.
16100 N Grnway Hyden Loop
Scottsdale AZ 85260
602 996-0201

(P-11457)
SOUTHERN CAL DISC TIRE CO INC
Also Called: Discount Tire
550 N Broadway, Escondido (92025-2720)
PHONE...............760 741-9805
David Benibedez, *Mgr*
EMP: 123
SALES (corp-wide): 3.69B **Privately Held**
Web: www.discounttire.com
SIC: **5531** 5014 5013 Automotive tires; Automobile tires and tubes; Wheels, motor vehicle

HQ: Southern California Discount Tire Co., Inc.
16100 N Grnway Hyden Loop
Scottsdale AZ 85260
602 996-0201

(P-11458)
SOUTHERN CAL DISC TIRE CO INC
Also Called: Discount Tire
780 Grand Ave, San Marcos (92078-1249)
PHONE...............760 744-3526
Brett Harris, *Mgr*
EMP: 95
SALES (corp-wide): 3.69B **Privately Held**
Web: www.discounttire.com
SIC: **5531** 5014 Automotive tires; Automobile tires and tubes
HQ: Southern California Discount Tire Co., Inc.
16100 N Grnway Hyden Loop
Scottsdale AZ 85260
602 996-0201

(P-11459)
SOUTHERN CAL DISC TIRE CO INC
Also Called: Discount Tire
209 S Escondido Blvd, Escondido (92025-4116)
PHONE...............760 741-3801
Pat Fuller, *Mgr*
EMP: 109
SALES (corp-wide): 3.69B **Privately Held**
Web: www.discounttire.com
SIC: **5531** 5014 5013 Automotive tires; Automobile tires and tubes; Wheels, motor vehicle
HQ: Southern California Discount Tire Co., Inc.
16100 N Grnway Hyden Loop
Scottsdale AZ 85260
602 996-0201

(P-11460)
SOUTHERN CAL DISC TIRE CO INC
Also Called: Discount Tire
685 San Rodolfo Dr, Solana Beach (92075-2001)
PHONE...............858 481-6387
Bruce Hopple, *Brnch Mgr*
EMP: 123
SALES (corp-wide): 3.69B **Privately Held**
Web: www.discounttire.com
SIC: **5531** 5014 Automotive tires; Automobile tires and tubes
HQ: Southern California Discount Tire Co., Inc.
16100 N Grnway Hyden Loop
Scottsdale AZ 85260
602 996-0201

(P-11461)
SOUTHERN CAL DISC TIRE CO INC
Also Called: Discount Tire
12651 Poway Rd, Poway (92064-4415)
PHONE...............858 486-3600
Alan Birse, *Brnch Mgr*
EMP: 109
SALES (corp-wide): 3.69B **Privately Held**
Web: www.discounttire.com
SIC: **5531** 5014 5013 Automotive tires; Automobile tires and tubes; Wheels, motor vehicle
HQ: Southern California Discount Tire Co., Inc.
16100 N Grnway Hyden Loop
Scottsdale AZ 85260
602 996-0201

(P-11462)
SOUTHERN CAL DISC TIRE CO INC
Also Called: Discount Tire
1037 S Coast Hwy, Oceanside (92054-5004)
PHONE...............760 439-8539
John Toonds, *Mgr*
EMP: 95
SALES (corp-wide): 3.69B **Privately Held**
Web: www.discounttire.com
SIC: **5531** 5014 Automotive tires; Automobile tires and tubes
HQ: Southern California Discount Tire Co., Inc.
16100 N Grnway Hyden Loop
Scottsdale AZ 85260
602 996-0201

(P-11463)
SOUTHERN CAL DISC TIRE CO INC
Also Called: Discount Tire
600 W Florida Ave, Hemet (92543-4009)
PHONE...............951 929-2130
Josh Mccartner, *Mgr*
EMP: 123
SALES (corp-wide): 3.69B **Privately Held**
Web: www.discounttire.com
SIC: **5531** 5013 Automotive tires; Wheels, motor vehicle
HQ: Southern California Discount Tire Co., Inc.
16100 N Grnway Hyden Loop
Scottsdale AZ 85260
602 996-0201

(P-11464)
SOUTHERN CAL DISC TIRE CO INC
Also Called: Discount Tire
107 N El Camino Real, Encinitas (92024-2802)
PHONE...............760 634-2202
Alan Brise, *Brnch Mgr*
EMP: 123
SALES (corp-wide): 3.69B **Privately Held**
Web: www.discounttire.com
SIC: **5531** 7534 Automotive tires; Tire repair shop
HQ: Southern California Discount Tire Co., Inc.
16100 N Grnway Hyden Loop
Scottsdale AZ 85260
602 996-0201

(P-11465)
SOUTHERN CAL DISC TIRE CO INC
Also Called: Discount Tire
3935 Convoy St, San Diego (92111-3723)
PHONE...............858 278-0661
Mark Leisenring, *Off Mgr*
EMP: 96
SALES (corp-wide): 3.69B **Privately Held**
Web: www.discounttire.com
SIC: **5531** 5014 Automotive tires; Automobile tires and tubes
HQ: Southern California Discount Tire Co., Inc.
16100 N Grnway Hyden Loop
Scottsdale AZ 85260
602 996-0201

(P-11466)
SOUTHERN CAL DISC TIRE CO INC
Also Called: Discount Tire
15672 Springdale St, Huntington Beach (92649-1315)

PHONE...............714 901-8226
Joe Ortiz, *Mgr*
EMP: 109
SALES (corp-wide): 3.69B **Privately Held**
Web: www.discounttire.com
SIC: **5531** 5013 Automotive tires; Wheels, motor vehicle
HQ: Southern California Discount Tire Co., Inc.
16100 N Grnway Hyden Loop
Scottsdale AZ 85260
602 996-0201

(P-11467)
SOUTHERN CAL DISC TIRE CO INC
Also Called: Discount Tire
20741 Avalon Blvd, Carson (90746-3313)
PHONE...............310 324-2569
Arnel Ramos, *Mgr*
EMP: 123
SALES (corp-wide): 3.69B **Privately Held**
Web: www.discounttire.com
SIC: **5531** 5014 5013 Automotive tires; Automobile tires and tubes; Wheels, motor vehicle
HQ: Southern California Discount Tire Co., Inc.
16100 N Grnway Hyden Loop
Scottsdale AZ 85260
602 996-0201

(P-11468)
SOUTHERN CAL DISC TIRE CO INC
Also Called: Discount Tire
705 S Grand Ave, Glendora (91740-4141)
PHONE...............626 335-2883
Abel Ariola, *Mgr*
EMP: 95
SALES (corp-wide): 3.69B **Privately Held**
Web: www.discounttire.com
SIC: **5531** 5013 Automotive tires; Wheels, motor vehicle
HQ: Southern California Discount Tire Co., Inc.
16100 N Grnway Hyden Loop
Scottsdale AZ 85260
602 996-0201

(P-11469)
TIRES WAREHOUSE LLC
18203 Mount Baldy Cir, Fountain Valley (92708-6117)
PHONE...............714 432-8851
Terry Ahlstrom, *Brnch Mgr*
EMP: 313
SALES (corp-wide): 1.56B **Privately Held**
Web: www.usautoforce.com
SIC: **5531** 5014 Automotive tires; Tires and tubes
HQ: Tire's Warehouse, Llc
391 N Main St
Corona CA 92878
951 808-0111

(P-11470)
TOYOTA DOWNTOWN LA
Also Called: Toyota of Downtown L.A.
714 W Olympic Blvd Ste 1131, Los Angeles (90015-2137)
PHONE...............213 342-3646
EMP: 154 **EST:** 1970
SALES (est): 3.03MM **Privately Held**
Web: www.toyotaofdowntownla.com
SIC: **5531** 7538 5511 5521 Batteries, automotive and truck; General automotive repair shops; Automobiles, new and used; Used car dealers

PRODUCTS & SVCS

(P-11471)
TRANSAMERICAN DISSOLUTION LLC (HQ)
Also Called: Four Wheel Parts Wholesalers
400 W Artesia Blvd, Compton (90220-5501)
PHONE..................................310 900-5500
Greg Adler, *Managing Member*
Craig Scanlon, *
◆ EMP: 200 EST: 1959
SQ FT: 120,000
SALES (est): 479.89MM
SALES (corp-wide): 8.93B Publicly Held
Web: www.4wheelparts.com
SIC: 5531 5013 Automotive parts;
   Automotive supplies and parts
PA: Polaris Inc.
   2100 Highway 55
   763 542-0500

(P-11472)
UNITED SYATT AMERICA CORP (PA)
Also Called: Broadway Auto Parts
920 E 1st St, Santa Ana (92701-5365)
PHONE.................................714 568-1938
Ron Hanson, *Pr*
Donna Hanson, *Sec*
EMP: 105 EST: 1955
SQ FT: 27,000
SALES (est): 863.25K
SALES (corp-wide): 863.25K Privately Held
SIC: 5531 5013 Automotive parts;
   Automotive supplies and parts

5541 Gasoline Service Stations

(P-11473)
ATLANTIC RICHFIELD COMPANY (DH)
Also Called: A R C O
4 Centerpointe Dr, La Palma (90623-1015)
PHONE.................................800 333-3991
Robert A Malone, *Pr*
Ian Springett, *
▲ EMP: 2200 EST: 1870
SALES (est): 142.72MM
SALES (corp-wide): 171.22B Privately Held
Web: www.arco.com
SIC: 5541 1321 2911 Filling stations,
   gasoline; Natural gas liquids; Petroleum
   refining
HQ: Bp America Inc
   4101 Winfield Rd Ste 200
   Warrenville IL 60555
   214 210-4835

(P-11474)
CHEVRON CORPORATION
Also Called: Chevron
324 W El Segundo Blvd, El Segundo (90245-3680)
PHONE.................................310 615-5000
William Simok, *Ex Dir*
EMP: 812
SALES (corp-wide): 200.95B Publicly Held
Web: www.chevron.com
SIC: 5541 1311 1382 1321 Filling stations,
   gasoline; Crude petroleum production; Oil
   and gas exploration services; Natural gas
   liquids
PA: Chevron Corporation
   5001 Exec Pkwy Ste 200
   925 842-1000

(P-11475)
EVGO SERVICES LLC
Also Called: Evgo Montgomery Co
11835 W Olympic Blvd Ste 900e, Los Angeles (90064-5088)
P.O. Box 642830 (90064-8287)
PHONE.................................310 954-2900
Cathy Zoi, *CEO*
Olga Shevorenkova, *
Ivo Steklac, *
EMP: 298 EST: 2010
SQ FT: 10,000
SALES (est): 37.36MM Publicly Held
Web: www.evgo.com
SIC: 5541 3694 Gasoline service stations;
   Automotive electrical equipment, nec
HQ: Evgo Inc.
   11835 W Olympic Blvd Ste
   Los Angeles CA 90064
   877 494-3833

(P-11476)
EXXON MOBIL CORPORATION
Also Called: Exxon
12000 Calle Real, Goleta (93117-9708)
PHONE.................................805 961-4093
Bob Barnes, *Brnch Mgr*
EMP: 24
SALES (corp-wide): 344.58B Publicly Held
Web: corporate.exxonmobil.com
SIC: 5541 3533 Filling stations, gasoline; Oil
   and gas field machinery
PA: Exxon Mobil Corporation
   22777 Sprngwoods Vlg Pkwy
   972 940-6000

(P-11477)
PAQ INC
Also Called: Food 4 Less
1465 Creston Rd, Paso Robles (93446-3218)
PHONE.................................805 227-1660
EMP: 112
SALES (corp-wide): 150.04B Publicly Held
Web: www.myfood4less.com
SIC: 5541 5411 5141 Gasoline service
   stations; Grocery stores, chain; Groceries,
   general line
HQ: Paq, Inc
   3021 Reynolds Ranch Pkwy # 230
   Lodi CA 95240

5551 Boat Dealers

(P-11478)
TOLLER ENTERPRISES INC (PA)
Also Called: Electra Craft
2251 Townsgate Rd, Westlake Village (91361-2404)
PHONE.................................805 374-9455
Alex Toller, *Pr*
Cheryl Toller, *Sec*
EMP: 26 EST: 1979
SALES (est): 1.76MM
SALES (corp-wide): 1.76MM Privately Held
Web: www.electracraft.com
SIC: 5551 3732 Motor boat dealers;
   Boatbuilding and repairing

5561 Recreational Vehicle Dealers

(P-11479)
GIANT INLAND EMPIRE RV CTR INC (PA)
Also Called: Giant Rv
9150 Benson Ave, Montclair (91763-1688)
PHONE.................................909 981-0444
TOLL FREE: 800
Behzad Barouti, *CEO*
Nasser Etebar, *
EMP: 125 EST: 1986
SQ FT: 50,000
SALES (est): 12.67MM
SALES (corp-wide): 12.67MM Privately Held
Web: www.giantrv.com
SIC: 5561 7538 Recreational vehicle parts
   and accessories; Recreational vehicle
   repairs

(P-11480)
LA MESA R V CENTER INC (PA)
Also Called: Rec Van
7430 Copley Park Pl, San Diego (92111-1122)
PHONE.................................858 874-8000
James R Kimbrell, *CEO*
James Walters, *
EMP: 130 EST: 1972
SALES (est): 98.28MM
SALES (corp-wide): 98.28MM Privately Held
Web: www.lamesarv.com
SIC: 5561 7538 Motor homes; Recreational
   vehicle repairs

5571 Motorcycle Dealers

(P-11481)
ARCH MOTORCYCLE COMPANY INC
3216 W El Segundo Blvd, Hawthorne (90250-4823)
PHONE.................................970 443-1380
Gard Hollinger, *Prin*
EMP: 39 EST: 2012
SALES (est): 933.37K Privately Held
Web: www.archmotorcycle.com
SIC: 5571 3751 Motorcycles; Bicycles and
   related parts

(P-11482)
JIM ONEAL DISTRIBUTING INC
Also Called: O'Neal U S A
799 Camarillo Springs Rd, Camarillo (93012-9468)
PHONE.................................805 426-3300
Frank Kashare, *Pr*
▲ EMP: 40 EST: 1970
SALES (est): 5.36MM Privately Held
Web: www.oneal.com
SIC: 5571 3751 Motorcycle dealers;
   Motorcycles, bicycles and parts

(P-11483)
KAWASAKI MOTORS CORP USA (HQ)
26972 Burbank, Foothill Ranch (92610-2506)
P.O. Box 25252 (92799-5252)
PHONE.................................949 837-4683
Eigo Konya, *Pr*
Terunori Kitajima, *
Richard N Beattie, *Chief Marketing*
◆ EMP: 400 EST: 1967

SQ FT: 40,000
SALES (est): 267.77MM Privately Held
Web: www.kawasaki.com
SIC: 5571 5013 5084 5091 Motorcycle
   dealers; Motorcycle parts; Engines, gasoline
   ; Boats, canoes, watercrafts, and equipment
PA: Kawasaki Heavy Industries, Ltd.
   1-1-3, Higashikawasakicho, Chuo-Ku

(P-11484)
OCELOT ENGINEERING INC
Also Called: Chaparral Motorsports
555 S H St, San Bernardino (92410-3415)
PHONE.................................800 841-2960
David S Damron, *Pr*
James E Damron, *
Linda J Damron, *
◆ EMP: 160 EST: 1973
SALES (est): 15.79MM Privately Held
Web: www.chapmoto.com
SIC: 5571 5551 5013 3751 Motorcycles; Jet
   skis; Motorcycle parts; Motorcycle
   accessories

(P-11485)
YAMAHA MOTOR CORPORATION USA (HQ)
6555 Katella Ave, Cypress (90630-5101)
PHONE.................................714 761-7300
Mike Chrzanowski, *Pr*
Takuwy Watanabe, *
Jeff Young, *
◆ EMP: 400 EST: 1955
SQ FT: 200,000
SALES (est): 1.47B Privately Held
Web: www.yamaha-motor.com
SIC: 5571 5013 5091 5012 Motorcycle
   dealers; Motor vehicle supplies and new
   parts; Boats, canoes, watercrafts, and
   equipment; Motorcycles
PA: Yamaha Motor Co., Ltd.
   2500, Shingai

5599 Automotive Dealers, Nec

(P-11486)
CARSON TRAILER INC (PA)
Also Called: Carson Trailer Sales
14831 S Maple Ave, Gardena (90248-1935)
PHONE.................................310 835-0876
William Modisette, *Pr*
EMP: 100 EST: 1991
SALES (est): 11.59MM Privately Held
Web: www.carsontrailer.com
SIC: 5599 3792 Utility trailers; Travel trailers
   and campers

(P-11487)
IRWIN INTERNATIONAL INC (PA)
Also Called: Aircraft Spruce & Specialty
225 Airport Cir, Corona (92880)
P.O. Box 4000 (92878-4000)
PHONE.................................951 372-9555
James J Irwin, *Pr*
Elizabeth Irwin, *
▼ EMP: 95 EST: 1965
SQ FT: 5,000
SALES (est): 28.57MM
SALES (corp-wide): 28.57MM Privately Held
Web: www.aircraftspruce.com
SIC: 5599 5088 Aircraft instruments,
   equipment or parts; Aircraft and parts, nec

5611 Men's And Boys' Clothing Stores

(P-11488)
GURU DENIM LLC (DH)
Also Called: True Religion Apparel
500 W 190th St Ste 300, Gardena
(90248-4269)
PHONE.................................323 266-3072
Sandip Grewal, *
Lori Nembirkow, *
▲ EMP: 150 EST: 2002
SALES (est): 50.39MM
SALES (corp-wide): 350MM **Privately Held**
Web: www.truereligion.com
SIC: 5611 5137 Clothing accessories: men's and boys'; Women's and children's clothing
HQ: True Religion Apparel, Inc.
500 W 190th St Ste 300
Gardena CA 90248
855 928-6124

(P-11489)
HUB DISTRIBUTING INC (HQ)
Also Called: Anchor Blue
1260 Corona Pointe Ct, Corona
(92879-5013)
PHONE.................................951 340-3149
Thomas Sands, *CEO*
Elaine Gregg, *
Thomas Shaw, *
▲ EMP: 300 EST: 1947
SQ FT: 500,000
SALES (est): 2.7MM
SALES (corp-wide): 3.46B **Privately Held**
SIC: 5611 5621 5632 5137 Men's and boys' clothing stores; Women's clothing stores; Apparel accessories; Women's and children's clothing
PA: Sun Capital Partners, Inc.
5200 Town Ctr Cr Fl 4
561 394-0550

5621 Women's Clothing Stores

(P-11490)
AMERICAN RAG COMPAGNIE
150 S La Brea Ave, Los Angeles
(90036-2910)
PHONE.................................323 935-3154
Mark Werts Senior, *CEO*
Mark Werts Junior, *CFO*
▲ EMP: 100 EST: 1984
SQ FT: 15,000
SALES (est): 1.43MM **Privately Held**
Web: www.americanrag.com
SIC: 5621 5932 5137 5611 Ready-to-wear apparel, women's; Clothing, secondhand; Women's and children's clothing; Clothing, male: everyday, except suits and sportswear

(P-11491)
COUNTRY CLUB FASHIONS INC
Also Called: Theodore
6083 W Pico Blvd, Los Angeles
(90035-2648)
PHONE.................................323 965-2707
EMP: 45
Web: www.theodorebh.com
SIC: 5621 5611 2337 2331 Ready-to-wear apparel, women's; Clothing, sportswear, men's and boys'; Skirts, separate: women's, misses', and juniors'; Blouses, women's and juniors': made from purchased material

(P-11492)
NASTY GAL INC (HQ)
2049 Century Park E Ste 3400, Los Angeles
(90067-3208)
PHONE.................................213 542-3436
Sheree Waterson, *CEO*
Bob Ross, *
◆ EMP: 23 EST: 2008
SALES (est): 9.47MM
SALES (corp-wide): 1.85B **Privately Held**
Web: www.nastygal.com
SIC: 5621 5139 2389 Ready-to-wear apparel, women's; Shoes; Academic vestments (caps and gowns)
PA: Boohoo Group Plc
The Boohoo Group

(P-11493)
SANCTUARY CLOTHING LLC (PA)
Also Called: Sanctuary Clothing
3611 N San Fernando Blvd, Burbank
(91505-1043)
PHONE.................................818 505-0018
Kenneth Polanco, *Managing Member*
Debra Polanco, *Chief Creative Officer*
Elizabeth Fernando, *Contrlr*
EMP: 41 EST: 2008
SALES (est): 9.93MM
SALES (corp-wide): 9.93MM **Privately Held**
Web: www.sanctuaryclothing.com
SIC: 5621 5137 2211 Ready-to-wear apparel, women's; Women's and children's dresses, suits, skirts, and blouses; Apparel and outerwear fabrics, cotton

(P-11494)
TOPSON DOWNS CALIFORNIA LLC (PA)
Also Called: Topson Downs
3840 Watseka Ave, Culver City
(90232-2633)
PHONE.................................310 558-0300
Joe Wirht, *
Daniel Abramovitch, *
▲ EMP: 250 EST: 1971
SQ FT: 42,000
SALES (est): 45.02MM
SALES (corp-wide): 45.02MM **Privately Held**
Web: www.topsondowns.com
SIC: 5621 5136 2211 2221 Women's clothing stores; Shirts, men's and boys'; Apparel and outerwear fabrics, cotton; Apparel and outerwear fabric, manmade fiber or silk

5632 Women's Accessory And Specialty Stores

(P-11495)
VERA BRADLEY INC
4525 La Jolla Village Dr, San Diego
(92122-1215)
PHONE.................................858 320-9020
EMP: 28
SALES (corp-wide): 470.79MM **Publicly Held**
Web: www.verabradley.com
SIC: 5632 5137 3171 Handbags; Purses; Handbags, women's
PA: Vera Bradley, Inc.
12420 Stonebridge Rd
877 708-8372

(P-11496)
WEN U LUV LIQUIDATION LLC
8383 Wilshire Blvd Ste 800, Beverly Hills
(90211-2440)
PHONE.................................323 456-8821
Alexander Compton, *Managing Member*
EMP: 25 EST: 2010
SALES (est): 165.82K **Privately Held**
SIC: 5632 2339 3911 5199 Handbags; Athletic clothing: women's, misses', and juniors'; Jewelry apparel; General merchandise, non-durable

5651 Family Clothing Stores

(P-11497)
J & M SALES INC
Also Called: Fallas Discount Stores
15001 S Figueroa St, Gardena
(90248-1721)
PHONE.................................310 324-9962
▲ EMP: 2500
SIC: 5651 6531 Unisex clothing stores; Real estate listing services

(P-11498)
WALKING COMPANY HOLDINGS INC (PA)
Also Called: Big Dog Sportswear
1800 Avenue Of The Stars Ste 300, Los Angeles (90067-4204)
PHONE.................................805 963-8727
Andrew D Feshbach, *CEO*
Fred Kayne, *
Roberta J Morris, *
Anthony J Wall, *Executive Business Affairs Vice President*
Lee M Cox Senior, *Retail Operations Vice President*
▲ EMP: 160 EST: 1993
SQ FT: 24,000
SALES (est): 68.88MM **Privately Held**
Web: www.thewalkingcompany.com
SIC: 5651 5961 5136 5137 Family clothing stores; Clothing, mail order (except women's); Sportswear, men's and boys'; Sportswear, women's and children's

5661 Shoe Stores

(P-11499)
SKECHERS USA INC II
228 Manhattan Beach Blvd Ste 200, Manhattan Beach (90266-5356)
PHONE.................................800 746-3411
Robort Croonborg, *CEO*
David Weinberg, *
Philip Paccione, *
◆ EMP: 4000 EST: 1994
SALES (est): 4.98MM **Publicly Held**
Web: www.skechers.com
SIC: 5661 3021 Shoe stores; Shoes, rubber or plastic molded to fabric
PA: Skechers U.S.A., Inc.
228 Manhattan Beach Blvd

(P-11500)
T AND B BOOTS INC
Also Called: Takken's Comfort Shoes
72 S Main St B, Templeton (93465-9787)
PHONE.................................805 434-9904
EMP: 80
SIC: 5661 7251 Men's boots; Shoe repair shop

(P-11501)
VENTURA FEED AND PET SUPS INC
Also Called: Wharf, The
980 E Front St, Ventura (93001-3017)
P.O. Box 1806 (93002-1806)
PHONE.................................805 648-5035
Todd Butterbaugh, *CEO*
Darren Borgstedte, *
EMP: 42 EST: 1953
SQ FT: 13,000
SALES (est): 2.21MM **Privately Held**
Web: store.thewharfonline.com
SIC: 5661 3999 2048 5632 Shoe stores; Pet supplies; Prepared feeds, nec; Apparel accessories

5699 Miscellaneous Apparel And Accessories

(P-11502)
511 INC (DH)
Also Called: 5.11 Tactical Series
3150 Bristol St Ste 300, Costa Mesa
(92626-3088)
PHONE.................................866 451-1726
Francisco Morales, *CEO*
Dan Costa, *
John Wicks, *
James Mcginty, *CFO*
◆ EMP: 26 EST: 2003
SQ FT: 93,000
SALES (est): 97.95MM **Publicly Held**
Web: www.511tactical.com
SIC: 5699 2231 5139 2393 Uniforms; Apparel and outerwear broadwoven fabrics; Boots; Canvas bags
HQ: 5.11 Ta, Inc.
4300 Spyres Way
Modesto CA 95356
209 527-4511

(P-11503)
ADRENALINE LACROSSE INC
24 21st St, San Diego (92102-3802)
PHONE.................................888 768-8479
Alex Cade, *CEO*
Steve Sepeta, *
Parker Anger, *
Rory Doucette, *
Xander Ritz, *
EMP: 29 EST: 2012
SALES (est): 1.73MM **Privately Held**
Web: www.adrln.com
SIC: 5699 2389 Sports apparel; Men's miscellaneous accessories

(P-11504)
AMERICAN SOCCER COMPANY INC (PA)
Also Called: Score Sports
726 E Anaheim St, Wilmington
(90744-3635)
P.O. Box 3579 (90510-3579)
PHONE.................................310 830-6161
Kevin Mahoney, *Pr*
◆ EMP: 127 EST: 1975
SQ FT: 30,000
SALES (est): 24.63MM
SALES (corp-wide): 24.63MM **Privately Held**
Web: www.scoresports.com
SIC: 5699 2329 2339 3949 Uniforms; Men's and boys' athletic uniforms; Uniforms, athletic: women's, misses', and juniors'; Sporting and athletic goods, nec

(P-11505)
ATHLEISURE INC
Also Called: Sun Diego
3126 Micaion Blvd Ste B, San Diego
(92109)
PHONE..................................858 866-0108
Graham Smith, *Brnch Mgr*
EMP: 24
SALES (corp-wide): 24.45MM Privately
Held
Web: www.sundiego.com
SIC: 5699 5941 3021 Sports apparel; Water
sport equipment; Shoes, rubber or plastic
molded to fabric
PA: Athleisure, Inc.
1330 Specialty Dr Ste A1
760 734-3818

(P-11506)
AURELIO FELIX BARRETO III
Also Called: C-28
169 Radio Rd, Corona (92879-1724)
PHONE..................................951 354-9528
▲ EMP: 125
Web: www.c28.com
SIC: 5699 5136 5137 Customized clothing
and apparel; Men's and boy's clothing;
Women's and children's clothing

(P-11507)
CINTAS CORPORATION
Also Called: Cintas Fire
4320 E Miraloma Ave, Anaheim
(92807-1886)
P.O. Box 636525 (45263-6525)
PHONE..................................714 646-2550
Winter Barry, *Genl Mgr*
EMP: 80
SALES (corp-wide): 9.6B Publicly Held
Web: www.cintas.com
SIC: 5699 7389 8711 Uniforms; Fire
protection service other than forestry or
public; Fire protection engineering
PA: Cintas Corporation
6800 Cintas Blvd
513 459-1200

(P-11508)
HOT TOPIC INC (DH)
Also Called: Shockhound
18305 San Jose Ave, City Of Industry
(91748-1237)
PHONE..................................800 892-8674
Steve Vranes, *CEO*
Ash Walia, *
Tiffany Smith, *
◆ EMP: 800 EST: 1988
SQ FT: 250,000
SALES (est): 770.2MM Publicly Held
Web: www.hottopic.com
SIC: 5699 5632 6411 Designers, apparel;
Apparel accessories; Insurance agents,
brokers, and service
HQ: 212f Holdings Llc
120 Orange St
Wilmington DE

(P-11509)
PATAGONIA WORKS (PA)
259 W Santa Clara St, Ventura
(93001-2545)
P.O. Box 150 (93002-0150)
PHONE..................................805 643-8616
◆ EMP: 340 EST: 1966
SALES (est): 415.44MM
SALES (corp-wide): 415.44MM Privately
Held
Web: www.patagonia.com

SIC: 5699 2339 2329 5961 Uniforms and
work clothing; Sportswear, women's; Men's
and boys' sportswear and athletic clothing;
Catalog and mail-order houses

5712 Furniture Stores

(P-11510)
**ABC HOME FURNISHINGS INC
(PA)**
Also Called: A.B.C. Carpet & Home
11111 Santa Monica Blvd, Los Angeles
(90025-3333)
PHONE..................................212 473-3000
Aaron Rose, *CEO*
Paulette Cole, *
▲ EMP: 525 EST: 1985
SALES (est): 5.99MM
SALES (corp-wide): 5.99MM Privately
Held
Web: www.abchome.com
SIC: 5712 5719 5023 Furniture stores;
Beddings and linens; Homefurnishings

(P-11511)
AMES CONSTRUCTION INC
391 N Main St Ste 302, Corona
(92878-4006)
PHONE..................................951 356-1275
EMP: 288
SALES (corp-wide): 313.92MM Privately
Held
Web: www.amesconstruction.com
SIC: 5712 1751 1522 1521 Customized
furniture and cabinets; Cabinet building and
installation; Residential construction, nec;
Single-family housing construction
PA: Ames Construction, Inc.
2500 County Road 42 W
952 435-7106

(P-11512)
BOYD FLOTATION INC
Also Called: Boyd Specialty Sleep
7551 Cherry Ave, Fontana (92336-4276)
PHONE..................................314 997-5222
Alfred Mayen, *Mgr*
EMP: 33
Web: www.boydsleep.com
SIC: 5712 2515 Mattresses; Mattresses and
bedsprings
PA: Boyd Flotation, Inc.
2440 Adie Rd

(P-11513)
**DIAMOND MATTRESS
COMPANY INC (PA)**
Also Called: Diamond Mattress Nf
3112 E Las Hermanas St, Compton
(90221-5578)
PHONE..................................310 638-0363
Shaun Pennington, *Pr*
Breana Pennington, *
Brian Arnold, *
▲ EMP: 38 EST: 1955
SQ FT: 31,000
SALES (est): 33.46MM
SALES (corp-wide): 33.46MM Privately
Held
Web: www.diamondmattress.com
SIC: 5712 2515 Mattresses; Bedsprings,
assembled

(P-11514)
**KAISER FOUNDATION
HOSPITALS**
Also Called: Kaiser Prmnnte Nat Fclties Svc
3355 E 26th St, Vernon (90058-4169)
PHONE..................................323 264-4310

Jose Montero, *Prin*
EMP: 137
SALES (corp-wide): 70.8B Privately Held
Web: www.kaisercenter.com
SIC: 5712 2434 Cabinet work, custom;
Vanities, bathroom: wood
HQ: Kaiser Foundation Hospitals Inc
1 Kaiser Plz
Oakland CA 94612
510 271-6611

(P-11515)
**LIVING SPACES FURNITURE
LLC**
1900 University Dr, Vista (92083-7773)
PHONE..................................760 945-6805
EMP: 114
SALES (corp-wide): 439.91MM Privately
Held
Web: www.livingspaces.com
SIC: 5712 5021 Mattresses; Furniture
PA: Living Spaces Furniture, Llc
14501 Artesia Blvd
877 266-7300

(P-11516)
**LIVING SPACES FURNITURE
LLC (PA)**
14501 Artesia Blvd, La Mirada
(90638-5805)
P.O. Box 2309 (90621-0809)
PHONE..................................877 266-7300
Grover Geiselman, *CEO*
Sharm Schuerman, *
▲ EMP: 230 EST: 2003
SQ FT: 136,000
SALES (est): 439.91MM
SALES (corp-wide): 439.91MM Privately
Held
Web: www.livingspaces.com
SIC: 5712 5021 Mattresses; Furniture

(P-11517)
MODERNICA INC (PA)
Also Called: Modernica
2901 Saco St, Vernon (90058-1433)
PHONE..................................323 826-1600
▲ EMP: 50 EST: 1990
SALES (est): 8.59MM Privately Held
Web: www.modernica.net
SIC: 5712 5021 2511 2512 Furniture stores;
Furniture; Wood household furniture;
Upholstered household furniture

(P-11518)
SEVILLE CLASSICS INC (PA)
19401 Harborgate Way, Torrance
(90501-1322)
PHONE..................................310 533-3800
Jackson Yang, *CEO*
Julie Yang, *CFO*
◆ EMP: 157 EST: 1979
SQ FT: 10,000
SALES (est): 3.66MM
SALES (corp-wide): 3.66MM Privately
Held
Web: www.sevilleclassics.com
SIC: 5712 5021 5085 Office furniture;
Household furniture; Bins and containers,
storage

5713 Floor Covering Stores

(P-11519)
ABC CARPET CO INC (PA)
Also Called: A B C Design Rugs
11111 Santa Monica Blvd, Los Angeles
(90025-3333)
PHONE..................................212 473-3000

Aaron Rose, *CEO*
Paul Chapman, *
◆ EMP: 75 EST: 1897
SALES (est): 7.74MM
SALES (corp-wide): 7.74MM Privately
Held
Web: www.abchome.com
SIC: 5713 5023 Floor covering stores; Floor
coverings

(P-11520)
B & W TILE CO INC (PA)
Also Called: B & W Tile Manufacturing
14600 S Western Ave, Gardena
(90249-3399)
PHONE..................................310 538-9579
Joe Logan, *VP*
Joseph Logan, *
Ralph Logan, *
▲ EMP: 35 EST: 1948
SQ FT: 32,000
SALES (est): 2.37MM
SALES (corp-wide): 2.37MM Privately
Held
Web: www.bwtile.com
SIC: 5713 3253 Floor tile; Floor tile, ceramic

(P-11521)
BLUE RIBBON DRAPERIES INC
Also Called: Drapery Affair
7341 Adams St Ste A, Paramount
(90723-4007)
PHONE..................................562 425-4637
Roy Donald, *CEO*
Gene Donald, *Pr*
Delrose Donald, *Sec*
EMP: 24 EST: 1982
SQ FT: 9,000
SALES (est): 1.86MM Privately Held
Web:
www.draperyaffairandfloorstore.com
SIC: 5713 2391 Floor covering stores;
Cottage sets (curtains), made from
purchased materials

(P-11522)
**CHRISTIAN BROS FLRG
INTRORS IN**
Also Called: Christian Bros Flrg Interiors
12086 Woodside Ave, Lakeside
(92040-2916)
PHONE..................................619 443-9500
Yvonne Castelli, *CEO*
Michael Castelli, *
Mike Sally, *
EMP: 80 EST: 1987
SQ FT: 2,800
SALES (est): 4.55MM Privately Held
Web: www.cbfloorsinc.com
SIC: 5713 1752 Carpets; Carpet laying

(P-11523)
FAIRPRICE ENTERPRISES INC
Also Called: Fair Price Carpets
1070 Center St, Riverside (92507-1016)
PHONE..................................951 684-8578
Kurt Ritz, *CEO*
Donovan Ritz, *
Marlene Ritz, *
EMP: 60 EST: 1957
SQ FT: 28,000
SALES (est): 1.75MM Privately Held
Web: www.fairpricecarpets.com
SIC: 5713 3281 2426 5032 Carpets; Granite,
cut and shaped; Flooring, hardwood;
Ceramic wall and floor tile, nec

(P-11524)
PROVENZA FLOORS INC (PA)
15541 Mosher Ave, Tustin (92780-6424)

PHONE..................949 788-0900
Mohammad Reza Jozi, *CEO*
▲ **EMP:** 70 **EST:** 2006
SALES (est): 2.15MM **Privately Held**
Web: www.provenzafloors.com
SIC: 5713 1771 Floor covering stores;
Flooring contractor

(P-11525)
RM PARTNERS INC
Also Called: Sterling Carpets & Flooring
1439 S State College Blvd, Anaheim
(92806-5718)
PHONE..................714 765-5725
Richard Mandel, *Pr*
John Ernst, *
EMP: 40 **EST:** 1962
SQ FT: 16,000
SALES (est): 4.09MM **Privately Held**
Web: www.sterlingflooring.com
SIC: 5713 1752 2273 Carpets; Carpet laying
; Dyeing and finishing of tufted rugs and
carpets

5719 Miscellaneous Homefurnishings

(P-11526)
AERO SHADE CO INC (PA)
Also Called: A-Z Industries Div
8404 W 3rd St, Los Angeles (90048-4112)
PHONE..................323 938-2314
Jack Pitson, *Pr*
Mario Soulema, *
Shelly Soulema, *
EMP: 25 **EST:** 1942
SQ FT: 2,400
SALES (est): 2.34MM
SALES (corp-wide): 2.34MM **Privately
Held**
Web: www.aeroshadeco.com
SIC: 5719 2591 5023 Window furnishings;
Window shades; Window shades

(P-11527)
ANNAS LINENS INC
Also Called: Annas Linens
3550 Hyland Ave, Costa Mesa
(92626-1438)
PHONE..................714 850-0504
◆ **EMP:** 2500
Web: www.annaslinens.com
SIC: 5719 5714 5023 Linens; Drapery and
upholstery stores; Window covering parts
and accessories

(P-11528)
BEBE STUDIO INC
Also Called: B E B E
10260 Santa Monica Blvd Ste 6, Los
Angeles (90067-6410)
PHONE..................213 362-2323
Manny Mashouf, *Pr*
Gary Bosch, *
Marc So, *
▲ **EMP:** 150 **EST:** 2002
SQ FT: 46,685
SALES (est): 996.92K **Publicly Held**
SIC: 5719 5621 5661 2339 Linens; Women's
clothing stores; Women's shoes; Women's
and misses' accessories
HQ: Bebe Stores, Inc.
400 Valley Dr
Brisbane CA 94005
415 715-3900

(P-11529)
COOKINGCOM INC
1960 E Grand Ave Ste 60, El Segundo
(90245-5000)

PHONE..................310 664-1283
Tracy Randall, *Pr*
Bryan Handlen, *
Larry Sales, *
Laura Shaff, *
Sarah Cohen, *Content Vice President*
EMP: 150 **EST:** 1998
SQ FT: 8,000
SALES (est): 2.47MM **Privately Held**
Web: www.cooking.com
SIC: 5719 5046 Cookware, except aluminum
; Commercial cooking and food service
equipment

(P-11530)
DACOR (DH)
14425 Clark Ave, City Of Industry
(91745-1235)
P.O. Box 90070 (91715-0070)
PHONE..................626 799-1000
Stanley Michael Joseph, *Ch Bd*
Charles J Huebner, *
Steve Joseph, *
Anthony B Joseph Iii, *Prin*
◆ **EMP:** 100 **EST:** 1965
SQ FT: 40,000
SALES (est): 24.6MM **Privately Held**
Web: www.dacor.com
SIC: 5719 3631 Kitchenware; Convection
ovens, including portable: household
HQ: Samsung Electronics America, Inc.
85 Challenger Rd
Ridgefield Park NJ 07660
201 229-4000

(P-11531)
GOOD FELLAS INDUSTRIES INC
Also Called: G F I
4400 Bandini Blvd, Vernon (90058-4310)
P.O. Box 861657 (90086)
PHONE..................323 924-9495
Judd A Shipper, *CEO*
◆ **EMP:** 85 **EST:** 1997
SQ FT: 40,000
SALES (est): 3.99MM **Privately Held**
Web: www.gfi-inc.net
SIC: 5719 1799 2591 Bedding (sheets,
blankets, spreads, and pillows); Drapery
track installation; Shade, curtain, and
drapery hardware

(P-11532)
IMPRESSIONS VANITY COMPANY (PA)
17353 Derian Ave, Irvine (92614-5801)
PHONE..................844 881-0790
Dong Kevin Choi, *CEO*
EMP: 29 **EST:** 2015
SALES (est): 3.29MM
SALES (corp-wide): 3.29MM **Privately
Held**
Web: www.impressionsvanity.com
SIC: 5719 5063 2531 Mirrors; Lighting
fixtures; Chairs, table and arm

(P-11533)
LA LINEN INC
1760 E 15th St, Los Angeles (90021-2716)
PHONE..................213 745-4004
Danny Levy, *CEO*
EMP: 30 **EST:** 2010
SQ FT: 16,500
SALES (est): 2.4MM **Privately Held**
Web: www.lalinen.com
SIC: 5719 2392 2391 Linens; Tablecloths
and table settings; Curtains and draperies

(P-11534)
LINEN SALVAGE ET CIE LLC
1073 Stearns Dr, Los Angeles
(90035-2638)

PHONE..................323 904-3100
Andrea Bernstein, *Prin*
EMP: 36 **EST:** 2018
SALES (est): 790.72K **Privately Held**
Web: www.linensalvage.com
SIC: 5719 2269 Linens; Linen fabrics:
dyeing, finishing, and printing

(P-11535)
NORTH RANCH MANAGEMENT CORP
9754 Deering Ave, Chatsworth
(91311-4301)
PHONE..................800 410-2153
Richard Goldman, *CEO*
▲ **EMP:** 70 **EST:** 2000
SALES (est): 1.86MM **Privately Held**
Web: www.dreamproducts.com
SIC: 5719 3171 3172 4813 Housewares, nec
; Women's handbags and purses; Wallets;
Online service providers

(P-11536)
SKYCO SHADING SYSTEMS INC
3411 W Fordham Ave, Santa Ana
(92704-4422)
PHONE..................714 708-3038
Davide Pesca, *CEO*
Davide Pesca, *CEO*
▲ **EMP:** 28 **EST:** 1994
SQ FT: 16,000
SALES (est): 4.57MM
SALES (corp-wide): 12.53MM **Privately
Held**
Web: www.skycoshade.com
SIC: 5719 2431 Window furnishings; Millwork
PA: Pesca Holding Llc
2517 Manana Dr
469 423-9837

5722 Household Appliance Stores

(P-11537)
JOHNSTONE SUPPLY INC
Also Called: Johnson Contrls Authorized Dlr
8040 Slauson Ave, Montebello
(90640-6620)
PHONE..................323 722-2859
William J Salpaka, *Pr*
EMP: 71
SALES (corp-wide): 1.18B **Privately Held**
Web: www.johnstonesupply.com
SIC: 5722 3585 5075 Gas household
appliances; Parts for heating, cooling, and
refrigerating equipment; Warm air heating
and air conditioning
HQ: Johnstone Supply, Llc
11632 Ne Ainsworth Cir
Portland OR 97220
503 256-3663

5734 Computer And Software Stores

(P-11538)
AXELLIANT LLC
2640 Main St, Irvine (92614-6229)
PHONE..................424 535-1100
Shahzad Munawwar, *COO*
EMP: 93
SALES (corp-wide): 38.03MM **Privately
Held**
Web: www.axelliant.com
SIC: 5734 5045 Computer and software
stores; Computers, peripherals, and
software
PA: Axelliant, Llc
21250 Hwthrne Blvd Ste 50

424 535-1100

(P-11539)
COAST TO COAST CMPT PDTS INC (PA)
4277 Valley Fair St, Simi Valley
(93063-2940)
PHONE..................805 244-9500
Rick Roussin, *Pr*
Wendy Roussin, *Treas*
Stacy Schulman, *VP Sls*
▼ **EMP:** 110 **EST:** 1985
SQ FT: 8,800
SALES (est): 22.71MM
SALES (corp-wide): 22.71MM **Privately
Held**
Web: www.coastcoast.com
SIC: 5734 7373 7371 5112 Magnetic disks;
Computer systems analysis and design;
Computer software systems analysis and
design, custom; Stationery and office
supplies

(P-11540)
GOLDEN STAR TECHNOLOGY INC (PA)
Also Called: G S T
12881 166th St, Cerritos (90703-2103)
PHONE..................562 345-8700
Jia Peir Wang, *CEO*
Alice Wang, *
Dennise Wang, *
▲ **EMP:** 70 **EST:** 1985
SQ FT: 55,000
SALES (est): 197.26MM
SALES (corp-wide): 197.26MM **Privately
Held**
Web: www.gstes.com
SIC: 5734 7378 5045 Computer peripheral
equipment; Computer maintenance and
repair; Computers, peripherals, and
software

(P-11541)
GOSECURE INC (PA)
13220 Evening Creek Dr S Ste 107, San
Diego (92128-4103)
PHONE..................301 442-3432
Neal Creighton, *CEO*
Neal Creighton, *Pr*
Robert J Mccullen, *Ofcr*
Richard Miller, *COO*
Thalia Gietzen, *CFO*
EMP: 178 **EST:** 2004
SALES (est): 22.51MM **Privately Held**
Web: www.gosecure.ai
SIC: 5734 7382 7372 7373 Computer
software and accessories; Protective
devices, security; Publisher's computer
software; Computer systems analysis and
design

(P-11542)
GURUCUL SOLUTIONS LLC
222 N Pacific Coast Hwy Ste 1322, El
Segundo (90245-5629)
PHONE..................213 291-6888
Saryu Nayyar, *
Jasen Meece, *
Nilesh Dherange, *
EMP: 60 **EST:** 2010
SQ FT: 4,360
SALES (est): 5.43MM **Privately Held**
Web: www.gurucul.com
SIC: 5734 7372 Software, business and non-
game; Publisher's computer software

(P-11543)
VELARO INCORPORATED
1234 N La Brea Ave, West Hollywood
(90038-1179)
PHONE...................................800 983-5276
Alex Bloom, *CEO*
Jasen Fici, *
Alex Bloom, *VP*
EMP: 95 **EST:** 2000
SALES (est): 1.56MM **Privately Held**
Web: www.velaro.com
SIC: 5734 7371 Software, business and non-game; Computer software development and applications

---

5736 Musical Instrument Stores

(P-11544)
CARVIN CORP
Also Called: Carvin Guitars & Pro Sound
16262 W Bernardo Dr, San Diego
(92127-1879)
PHONE...................................858 487-1600
Carson Kiesel, *CEO*
Carson L Kiesel, *
Jon Kiesel, *
Paul Kiesel, *
Mark Kiesel, *
◆ **EMP:** 179 **EST:** 1946
SQ FT: 82,000
SALES (est): 2.16MM **Privately Held**
Web: www.carvinaudio.com
SIC: 5736 3931 Musical instrument stores; Guitars and parts, electric and nonelectric

(P-11545)
DEERING BANJO COMPANY INC
3733 Kenora Dr, Spring Valley
(91977-1206)
PHONE...................................619 464-8252
Charles Greg Deering, *Pr*
Janet Deering, *Sec*
▲ **EMP:** 40 **EST:** 1975
SQ FT: 18,000
SALES (est): 2.32MM **Privately Held**
Web: www.deeringbanjos.com
SIC: 5736 3548 Musical instrument stores; Welding and cutting apparatus and accessories, nec

---

5812 Eating Places

(P-11546)
ACAPULCO RESTAURANTS INC
Also Called: Acapulco Mxican Rest Escondido
1541 E Valley Pkwy, Escondido
(92027-2315)
PHONE...................................562 346-1200
Mark Shultden, *Genl Mgr*
EMP: 71
SALES (corp-wide): 113.16MM **Privately Held**
Web: www.acapulcorestaurants.com
SIC: 5812 7299 Mexican restaurant; Banquet hall facilities
HQ: Acapulco Restaurants, Inc.
      4001 Via Oro Ave Ste 200
      Long Beach CA 90810
      310 513-7538

(P-11547)
ACAPULCO RESTAURANTS INC
Also Called: Acapulco Mxican Rest Y Cantina
12625 Frederick St Ste T, Moreno Valley
(92553-5236)
PHONE...................................951 653-8809
Fernando Correa, *Mgr*

EMP: 71
SALES (corp-wide): 113.16MM **Privately Held**
Web: www.acapulcorestaurants.com
SIC: 5812 7299 Mexican restaurant; Banquet hall facilities
HQ: Acapulco Restaurants, Inc.
      4001 Via Oro Ave Ste 200
      Long Beach CA 90810
      310 513-7538

(P-11548)
ACCOR CORP
Also Called: Sofitel Los Angeles
8555 Beverly Blvd, Los Angeles
(90048-3303)
PHONE...................................310 278-5444
Gunter Zweimuller, *Pr*
EMP: 200 **EST:** 1986
SQ FT: 380,000
SALES (est): 8.06MM
SALES (corp-wide): 1.66B **Privately Held**
Web: www.sofitel-los-angeles.com
SIC: 5812 7011 Eating places; Hotels
PA: Accor
      82 Rue H Farman
      146429193

(P-11549)
AIR FAYRE USA INC
1720 W 135th St, Gardena (90249-2508)
PHONE...................................310 808-1061
Stephen Yapp, *CEO*
Joe Golio, *
EMP: 200 **EST:** 2008
SALES (est): 24.56MM
SALES (corp-wide): 715.07K **Privately Held**
Web: www.airfayre.com
SIC: 5812 2099 Caterers; Box lunches, for sale off premises
HQ: Journey Group Limited
      One Bartholomew Close
      London EC1A

(P-11550)
APPLE FARM COLLECTIONS-SLO INC (PA)
2015 Monterey St, San Luis Obispo
(93401-2617)
PHONE...................................805 544-2040
John E King, *Pr*
Carole D King, *
▼ **EMP:** 290 **EST:** 1977
SQ FT: 51,000
SALES (est): 2.78MM
SALES (corp-wide): 2.78MM **Privately Held**
Web: www.applefarm.com
SIC: 5812 7011 5947 Restaurant, family: independent; Motor inn; Gift shop

(P-11551)
BENIHANA INC
Also Called: Benihana 24
16226 Ventura Blvd, Encino (91436-2271)
PHONE...................................818 788-7121
Shugo Kanai, *Genl Mgr*
EMP: 87
Web: www.benihana.com
SIC: 5812 7299 5813 Japanese restaurant; Banquet hall facilities; Cocktail lounge
HQ: Benihana Inc.
      21500 Bscyne Blvd Ste 100
      Miami FL 33180
      305 593-0770

(P-11552)
BOILING CRAB OPERATIONS LLC

Also Called: Boiling Crab, The
5811 Mcfadden Ave, Huntington Beach
(92649-1323)
PHONE...................................714 636-4885
Dada Ngo, *Managing Member*
Sinh Nguyen, *
Angela Nguyen, *
Hai Nguyen, *
EMP: 270 **EST:** 2013
SALES (est): 4.8MM **Privately Held**
Web: www.theboilingcrab.com
SIC: 5812 6794 Cajun restaurant; Franchises, selling or licensing

(P-11553)
BW HOTEL LLC
Also Called: Buffalo Wild Wings
9500 Wilshire Blvd, Beverly Hills
(90212-2405)
PHONE...................................310 275-5200
Kathleen Taylor, *CEO*
▲ **EMP:** 820 **EST:** 1928
SALES (est): 43.14MM **Privately Held**
Web: www.theblvdrestaurant.com
SIC: 5812 7011 Grills (eating places); Hotels and motels

(P-11554)
CARPENTERS SOUTHWEST ADM CORP
Also Called: Pea Soup Andersen's Restaurant
376 Avenue Of The Flags, Buellton
(93427-9704)
P.O. Box 195 (93427-0195)
PHONE...................................805 688-5581
Ed Sarbinie, *Mgr*
EMP: 239
SALES (corp-wide): 24.63MM **Privately Held**
Web: www.carpenterssw.org
SIC: 5812 7299 Eating places; Banquet hall facilities
PA: Carpenters Southwest Administrative Corporation
      533 S Fremont Ave
      213 386-8590

(P-11555)
CASTLE HARLAN PARTNERS III LP
Also Called: Marie Callender's Pie Shops 73
3801 California Ave, Bakersfield
(93309-1007)
PHONE...................................661 863-0305
Michael Lee, *Mgr*
EMP: 5016
SALES (corp-wide): 33.41MM **Privately Held**
Web: www.mariecallenders.com
SIC: 5812 5149 Restaurant, family: chain; Bakery products
HQ: Castle Harlan Partners Iii Lp
      150 E 58th St Fl 38
      New York NY 10155
      212 644-8600

(P-11556)
CASTLE IMPORTING INC
14550 Miller Ave, Fontana (92336-1696)
PHONE...................................909 428-9200
Rosangela Borruso, *CEO*
Marc Zadra, *
Richard White, *
▲ **EMP:** 45 **EST:** 1989
SALES (est): 7.28MM **Privately Held**
Web: www.castleimporting.com
SIC: 5812 2022 Eating places; Processed cheese

(P-11557)
CHEESECAKE FACTORY BAKERY INC
26950 Agoura Rd, Calabasas Hills
(91301-5335)
PHONE...................................818 871-3000
Keith T Carango, *CEO*
David Overton, *
Max Byfuglin, *
▲ **EMP:** 500 **EST:** 1972
SQ FT: 60,000
SALES (est): 27.64MM **Publicly Held**
Web: www.thecheesecakefactorybakery.com
SIC: 5812 2051 Eating places; Cakes, bakery: except frozen
PA: The Cheesecake Factory Incorporated
      26901 Malibu Hills Rd

(P-11558)
CHEESECAKE FACTORY INC (PA)
Also Called: CHEESECAKE FACTORY, THE
26901 Malibu Hills Rd, Calabasas Hills
(91301-5354)
PHONE...................................818 871-3000
David Overton, *Ch Bd*
David M Gordon, *Pr*
Matthew E Clark, *Ex VP*
Scarlett May, *Ex VP*
▲ **EMP:** 350 **EST:** 1972
SQ FT: 88,000
SALES (est): 3.44B **Publicly Held**
Web: www.thecheesecakefactory.com
SIC: 5812 2051 American restaurant; Cakes, bakery: except frozen

(P-11559)
CHOP STOP INC
601 N Glendale Ave, Glendale
(91206-2408)
PHONE...................................818 369-7350
Mark Kulkis, *CEO*
EMP: 97 **EST:** 2010
SALES (est): 5.36MM **Privately Held**
Web: www.chopstop.com
SIC: 5812 6794 Fast food restaurants and stands; Franchises, selling or licensing

(P-11560)
CHOURA VENUE SERVICES
Also Called: Choura Vnue Svcs At Carson Ctr
4101 E Willow St, Long Beach
(90815-1740)
PHONE...................................562 426-0555
James Choura, *CEO*
EMP: 99 **EST:** 2012
SALES (est): 2.47MM **Privately Held**
Web: www.thegrandlb.com
SIC: 5812 7299 Caterers; Facility rental and party planning services

(P-11561)
CHRONIC TACOS ENTERPRISES
Also Called: Chronic Tacos
95 Enterprise Ste 320, Aliso Viejo
(92656-2612)
PHONE...................................949 680-4602
Dan Biello, *Prin*
EMP: 139 **EST:** 2009
SALES (est): 1.63MM **Privately Held**
Web: www.chronictacos.com
SIC: 5812 6794 Mexican restaurant; Franchises, selling or licensing

(P-11562)
CITADEL PANDA EXPRESS INC
Also Called: Panda Express
899 El Centro St Ste 201, South Pasadena
(91030-3101)

PHONE..................626 799-9898
Peggy T Cherng, *CEO*
Andrew Jin Chan Cherng, *Ch Bd*
EMP: 176 **EST:** 1990
SQ FT: 10,000
SALES (est): 1.61MM
SALES (corp-wide): 1.64B **Privately Held**
Web: www.pandaexpress.com
SIC: 5812 6794 Chinese restaurant;
Franchises, selling or licensing
HQ: Panda Express, Inc.
1683 Walnut Grove Ave
Rosemead CA 91770

(P-11563)
CITRUS RESTAURANT LLC
8110 Aero Dr, San Diego (92123-1715)
PHONE..................858 277-8888
Kate Mendez, *Genl Mgr*
EMP: 145 **EST:** 2010
SALES (est): 155.4K **Privately Held**
SIC: 5812 7011 American restaurant; Hotels

(P-11564)
DEL TACO RESTAURANTS INC (PA)
Also Called: Del Taco
25521 Commercentre Dr Ste 200, Lake Forest (92630-8872)
PHONE..................949 462-9300
Lawrence F Levy, *Ch Bd*
Chad Gretzema, *Pr*
Steven L Brake, *Ex VP*
David A Pear, *VP Opers*
M Barry Westrum, *CMO*
EMP: 169 **EST:** 1964
SQ FT: 37,500
SALES (est): 527.36MM
SALES (corp-wide): 527.36MM **Privately Held**
Web: www.deltaco.com
SIC: 5812 6794 Fast-food restaurant, chain;
Franchises, selling or licensing

(P-11565)
DICKEYS BARBECUE REST INC
Also Called: Dickeys Barbecue Pit
17245 17th St, Tustin (92780-1974)
PHONE..................714 602-3874
Roland Dickey, *Brnch Mgr*
EMP: 28
SALES (corp-wide): 94.85MM **Privately Held**
Web: www.dickeys.com
SIC: 5812 2033 Barbecue restaurant;
Tomato products, packaged in cans, jars, etc.
HQ: Dickey's Barbecue Restaurants, Inc.
850 Cntral Pkwy E Ste 140
Plano TX 75074
972 248-9899

(P-11566)
DIFFERENT RULES LLC
Also Called: Jack In The Box
9357 Spectrum Center Blvd, San Diego (92123-1444)
PHONE..................858 571-2121
EMP: 93 **EST:** 2018
SALES (est): 3.59MM **Privately Held**
Web: www.jackinthebox.com
SIC: 5812 6794 Fast-food restaurant, chain;
Franchises, selling or licensing

(P-11567)
DINE BRANDS GLOBAL INC (PA)
Also Called: DINE BRANDS GLOBAL
10 W Walnut St Fl 5, Pasadena (91103-3633)
PHONE..................818 240-6055

Stephen P Joyce, *CEO*
Richard J Dahl, *

Thomas H Song, *CFO*
Bryan R Adel, *Senior Vice President Legal*
Justin Skelton, *CIO*
EMP: 500 **EST:** 1958
SALES (est): 831.07MM
SALES (corp-wide): 831.07MM **Publicly Held**
Web: www.dinebrands.com
SIC: 5812 6794 Restaurant, family: chain;
Franchises, selling or licensing

(P-11568)
EL POLLO LOCO HOLDINGS INC (PA)
Also Called: El Pollo Loco
3535 Harbor Blvd Ste 100, Costa Mesa (92626-1494)
PHONE..................714 599-5000
Elizabeth Williams, *CEO*
William R Floyd, *
Maria Hollandsworth, *COO*
Ira Fils, *CFO*
Bjorn Erland, *CPO*
EMP: 149 **EST:** 1980
SQ FT: 29,880
SALES (est): 468.66MM **Publicly Held**
Web: www.elpolloloco.com
SIC: 5812 6794 Eating places; Franchises, selling or licensing

(P-11569)
FAHETAS LLC (PA)
Also Called: Green Tomato Grill
1419 N Tustin St Ste A, Orange (92867-3922)
PHONE..................949 280-1983
Kyle Markt, *Managing Member*
Chris Stern, *
Michael Moore, *
Bruce Whistnant, *
Nicole Piscetelli, *
EMP: 100 **EST:** 2012
SALES (est): 4MM
SALES (corp-wide): 4MM **Privately Held**
Web: www.greentomatogrill.com
SIC: 5812 7371 Fast-food restaurant, chain;
Computer software development and applications

(P-11570)
FGR 1 LLC
Also Called: Fresh Griller
3191 Red Hill Ave Ste 100, Costa Mesa (92626-3451)
PHONE..................800 653-3517
Anand Gala, *Managing Member*
EMP: 40 **EST:** 2011
SALES (est): 219.34K **Privately Held**
SIC: 5812 7372 American restaurant;
Application computer software

(P-11571)
FISH HOUSE PARTNERS ONE LLC
Also Called: Restaurants Bars & Food Svcs
5955 Melrose Ave, Los Angeles (90038-3623)
PHONE..................323 460-4170
Michael Cimarusti, *Managing Member*
Cristina Echiverri, *
EMP: 96 **EST:** 2015
SALES (est): 1.53MM **Privately Held**
SIC: 5812 6799 Seafood restaurants;
Investors, nec

(P-11572)
FLORENCE MEAT PACKING CO INC
Also Called: F M P
9840 Everest St, Downey (90242-3114)
PHONE..................562 401-0760
EMP: 35
SIC: 5812 2011 Eating places; Meat packing plants

(P-11573)
GAMEWORKS ENTERTAINMENT LLC (PA)
9737 Lurline Ave, Chatsworth (91311-4404)
PHONE..................206 521-0952
EMP: 620
SALES (est): 16.39MM
SALES (corp-wide): 16.39MM **Privately Held**
SIC: 5812 7993 Eating places; Video game arcade

(P-11574)
HIDEAWAY
80440 Hideaway Club Ct, La Quinta (92253-7867)
PHONE..................760 777-7400
Shawn Ygnatowiz, *Genl Mgr*
Mike Finnell, *Prin*
EMP: 150 **EST:** 2006
SALES (est): 1.42MM **Privately Held**
Web: www.hideawaygolfclub.com
SIC: 5812 7041 Grills (eating places);
Residence club, organization

(P-11575)
HUXTABLES KITCHEN INC
Also Called: Huxtable's
2100 E 49th St, Vernon (90058-2825)
P.O. Box 2847 (90058)
PHONE..................323 923-2900
▲ **EMP:** 100
Web: www.huxtables.com
SIC: 5812 2099 2015 2013 Eating places;
Ready-to-eat meals, salads, and sandwiches; Poultry slaughtering and processing; Sausages and other prepared meats

(P-11576)
IL FORNAIO (AMERICA) LLC
16932 Valley View Ave Ste A, La Mirada (90638-5826)
PHONE..................714 752-7052
Luis Espinoza, *Brnch Mgr*
EMP: 160
SALES (corp-wide): 8.04B **Privately Held**
Web: www.ilfornaio.com
SIC: 5812 5813 5149 2051 Italian restaurant
; Drinking places; Bakery products; Bread, cake, and related products
HQ: Il Fornaio (America) Llc
770 Tamalpais Dr Ste 208
Corte Madera CA 94925
415 945-0500

(P-11577)
INTERNATIONAL COFFEE & TEA LLC (HQ)
Also Called: Coffee Bean & Tea Leaf, The
550 S Hope St Ste 2100, Los Angeles (90071-2625)
PHONE..................310 237-2326
John In De Braekt, *CEO*
Jeff Harris, *
Sunny Sassoon, *
Jacques Wizman, *
Mel Elias, *
▲ **EMP:** 75 **EST:** 1963

SQ FT: 20,000
SALES (est): 48.34MM **Privately Held**
Web: www.coffeebean.com
SIC: 5812 5499 6794 Coffee shop; Coffee;
Franchises, selling or licensing
PA: Jollibee Foods Corporation
5th-10th Floor Jollibee Plaza Building

(P-11578)
JACK IN BOX INC (PA)
Also Called: Jack In The Box
9357 Spectrum Center Blvd, San Diego (92123-1524)
P.O. Box 23447 (92193)
PHONE..................858 571-2121
Darin S Harris, *CEO*
David L Goebel, *Non-Executive Chairman of the Board*
Ryan Ostrom, *CMO*
Richard D Cook, *Sr VP*
Sarah Super, *Legal RISK*
▲ **EMP:** 542 **EST:** 1951
SQ FT: 70,000
SALES (est): 1.57B
SALES (corp-wide): 1.57B **Publicly Held**
Web: www.jackinthebox.com
SIC: 5812 6794 Fast-food restaurant, chain;
Franchises, selling or licensing

(P-11579)
JACMAR COMPANIES LLC
Jacmar Foodservice Dist
12761 Schabarum Ave, Baldwin Park (91706-6807)
PHONE..................626 430-9082
Frank Visvikis, *Prin*
EMP: 132
SALES (corp-wide): 259.98MM **Privately Held**
Web: www.jacmar.com
SIC: 5812 5722 5719 5046 Contract food services; Kitchens, complete (sinks, cabinets, etc.); Kitchenware; Restaurant equipment and supplies, nec
PA: The Jacmar Companies Llc
4601 E Guasti Rd
800 834-8806

(P-11580)
JIPCOB INC
Also Called: John's Incredible Pizza Co
3709 Rosedale Hwy, Bakersfield (93308-6251)
PHONE..................661 859-1111
John Parlet, *Pr*
Betty D Parlet, *
EMP: 180 **EST:** 1998
SQ FT: 26,000
SALES (est): 2.73MM **Privately Held**
SIC: 5812 2099 7993 5813 Italian restaurant
; Salads, fresh or refrigerated; Video game arcade; Drinking places

(P-11581)
JMJ ENTERPRISES INC
Also Called: Someone's In The Kitchen
5973 Reseda Blvd, Tarzana (91356-1505)
PHONE..................818 343-5151
Joann Roth Oseary, *Pr*
Jason Perel, *
EMP: 120 **EST:** 1981
SQ FT: 6,000
SALES (est): 4.34MM **Privately Held**
Web: www.jmjenterprises.com
SIC: 5812 7299 7359 Caterers; Party planning service; Sound and lighting equipment rental

(P-11582)

KING TACO RESTAURANT INC (PA)

3421 E 14th St, Los Angeles (90023-3837)
PHONE...............................323 266-3585
Raul D Martinez, *CEO*
Raul O Martinez Senior, *Pr*
EMP: 65 **EST:** 1974
SALES (est): 25.69MM
SALES (corp-wide): 25.69MM **Privately Held**
Web: www.kingtaco.com
SIC: 5812 2099 Mexican restaurant; Food preparations, nec

(P-11583)

KINGS HAWAIIAN BAKERY W INC (HQ)

Also Called: Kings Hawaiian Bakery
1411 W 190th St, Gardena (90248-4324)
PHONE...............................310 533-3250
Mark Taira, *Pr*
Curtis Taira, *
Leatrice Taira, *
Vaughn Taira, *
Stella Taira, *
▲ **EMP:** 25 **EST:** 1950
SALES (est): 62.63MM
SALES (corp-wide): 153.92MM **Privately Held**
Web: www.kingshawaiian.com
SIC: 5812 5142 2051 Restaurant, family: independent; Bakery products, frozen; Bread, cake, and related products
PA: King's Hawaiian Holding Company, Inc.
19161 Harborgate Way
310 533-3250

(P-11584)

LAWRYS RESTAURANTS II INC

Also Called: Tam O'Shanter Inn
2980 Los Feliz Blvd, Los Angeles (90039-1524)
PHONE...............................323 664-0228
Bryan Lytle, *Mgr*
EMP: 174
SALES (corp-wide): 23.63MM **Privately Held**
Web: www.lawrysonline.com
SIC: 5812 7299 Steak restaurant; Banquet hall facilities
PA: Lawry's Restaurants Ii, Inc.
100 N La Cienega Blvd
626 440-5234

(P-11585)

LAWRYS RESTAURANTS II INC

100 N La Cienega Blvd, Beverly Hills (90211-2207)
PHONE...............................310 652-2827
EMP: 87
SALES (corp-wide): 23.63MM **Privately Held**
Web: www.lawrysonline.com
SIC: 5812 7299 7389 Steak restaurant; Banquet hall facilities; Convention and show services
PA: Lawry's Restaurants Ii, Inc.
100 N La Cienega Blvd
626 440-5234

(P-11586)

LOFTY COFFEE INC

97 N Coast Highway 101 Ste 101, Encinitas (92024-3282)
PHONE...............................760 230-6747
Eric Myers, *CEO*
EMP: 100 **EST:** 2011
SALES (est): 1.18MM **Privately Held**
Web: www.loftycoffee.com

SIC: 5812 2095 Coffee shop; Coffee roasting (except by wholesale grocers)

(P-11587)

LOS ALAMITOS RACE COURSE

Also Called: Vessels Club Restaurant
4961 Katella Ave, Cypress (90720-2799)
PHONE...............................714 820-2800
Edward Allred, *Pt*
EMP: 200 **EST:** 1943
SQ FT: 2,000
SALES (est): 4.99MM **Privately Held**
Web: www.losalamitos.com
SIC: 5812 7948 5813 5963 Eating places; Horses, racing; Bar (drinking places); Direct selling establishments

(P-11588)

LOVE AT FIRST BITE CATERING

Also Called: Premere Event Services
18281 Gothard St Ste 108, Huntington Beach (92648-1205)
PHONE...............................714 369-0561
John Labrake, *Pr*
EMP: 70 **EST:** 1982
SQ FT: 2,600
SALES (est): 904.92K **Privately Held**
Web: www.lafbcatering.com
SIC: 5812 7299 Caterers; Party planning service

(P-11589)

MAGIC CASTLES INC

7001 Franklin Ave, Los Angeles (90028-8600)
PHONE...............................323 851-3313
Milton P Larsen, *CEO*
Ron Wilson, *
Bruce Cervon, *
EMP: 100 **EST:** 1962
SQ FT: 20,000
SALES (est): 7.93MM **Privately Held**
Web: www.magiccastle.com
SIC: 5812 7997 7991 Eating places; Membership sports and recreation clubs; Physical fitness facilities

(P-11590)

MEXICALI INC

Also Called: Mexicali Restaurant
631 18th St, Bakersfield (93301-4934)
PHONE...............................661 327-3861
Sunny Crews, *Mgr*
EMP: 115
SALES (corp-wide): 2.14MM **Privately Held**
Web: www.mexicalifood.com
SIC: 5812 5813 7299 Mexican restaurant; Bar (drinking places); Banquet hall facilities
PA: Mexicali, Inc.
419 Baker St
661 327-4218

(P-11591)

MSR DESERT RESORT LP

Also Called: Hotel Associates Palm Springs
49499 Eisenhower Dr, La Quinta (92253-2722)
P.O. Box 659 (92247-0659)
PHONE...............................760 564-5730
Michael Shannon, *Pt*
John Saer, *VP*
Nola Dyal, *VP*
Stephen Elliott, *VP*
Larry Scheerer, *VP*
▲ **EMP:** 1500 **EST:** 1926
SALES (est): 1.92MM **Privately Held**
Web: www.laquintavilla.com

SIC: 5812 7011 7997 5813 Eating places; Motel, franchised; Tennis club, membership; Drinking places

(P-11592)

OSF INTERNATIONAL INC

Also Called: Old Spagetti Factory
111 N Twin Oaks Valley Rd, San Marcos (92069-2950)
PHONE...............................760 471-0155
Sheryl Zumaeta, *Mgr*
EMP: 102
SALES (corp-wide): 145.43MM **Privately Held**
Web: www.osf.com
SIC: 5812 7299 Italian restaurant; Banquet hall facilities
PA: Osf International, Inc.
0715 S W Bancroft St
503 222-5375

(P-11593)

OSF INTERNATIONAL INC

Also Called: Newport Beach Spaghetti
2110 Newport Blvd, Newport Beach (92663-4322)
PHONE...............................949 675-8654
Dean Rakr, *Mgr*
EMP: 72
SALES (corp-wide): 145.43MM **Privately Held**
Web: www.osf.com
SIC: 5812 7011 Italian restaurant; Hotels and motels
PA: Osf International, Inc.
0715 S W Bancroft St
503 222-5375

(P-11594)

PANDA SYSTEMS INC

Also Called: Panda Express
1683 Walnut Grove Ave, Rosemead (91770-3711)
P.O. Box 1159 (91770-1011)
PHONE...............................626 799-9898
Andrew J Cherng, *Ch Bd*
Peggy T Cherng, *
EMP: 130 **EST:** 1988
SQ FT: 10,000
SALES (est): 552.63K
SALES (corp-wide): 1.64B **Privately Held**
Web: www.pandarg.com
SIC: 5812 6794 Chinese restaurant; Franchises, selling or licensing
PA: Panda Restaurant Group, Inc.
1683 Walnut Grove Ave
626 799-9898

(P-11595)

PBF & E LLC

Also Called: Guelaguetza
3014 W Olympic Blvd, Los Angeles (90006-2516)
PHONE...............................213 427-0340
Bricia Lopez, *Managing Member*
EMP: 50 **EST:** 2000
SALES (est): 2.19MM **Privately Held**
Web: www.ilovemole.com
SIC: 5812 2087 Mexican restaurant; Cocktail mixes, nonalcoholic

(P-11596)

PIE RISE LTD

Also Called: Marie Callender's Pie Shops
29051 S Western Ave, Rancho Palos Verdes (90275-0806)
PHONE...............................310 832-4559
Jim Louder, *Pt*
John Turner, *Pt*
EMP: 50 **EST:** 1971

SQ FT: 5,000
SALES (est): 248.41K **Privately Held**
Web: www.mariecallenders.com
SIC: 5812 2051 5461 Restaurant, family: chain; Pies, bakery: except frozen; Retail bakeries

(P-11597)

QDOBA RESTAURANT CORPORATION (HQ)

Also Called: Qdoba Mexican Grill
350 Camino De La Reina Fl 4, San Diego (92108-3007)
PHONE...............................858 766-4900
Susan Daggett, *CFO*
Kevin Carroll, *
Jeremy Vitaro, *Chief Development Officer*
EMP: 125 **EST:** 1995
SALES (est): 128.18MM
SALES (corp-wide): 411.36MM **Privately Held**
Web: www.qdoba.com
SIC: 5812 6794 Mexican restaurant; Franchises, selling or licensing
PA: Modern Restaurant Concepts Holdings, Llc
3001 Brighton Blvd
917 667-7972

(P-11598)

SACCO RESTAURANTS INC

Also Called: Epic Wings
12075 Carmel Mountain Rd Ste 201, San Diego (92128-4613)
PHONE...............................858 451-9464
Sam Sacco, *Prin*
EMP: 70 **EST:** 2016
SALES (est): 253.19K **Privately Held**
Web: www.epicwingsnthings.com
SIC: 5812 6794 Eating places; Franchises, selling or licensing

(P-11599)

SEVERSON GROUP LLC

Also Called: Severson Group, The
950 Boardwalk Ste 202, San Marcos (92078-2600)
PHONE...............................760 550-9976
Robert Severson, *Managing Member*
EMP: 200 **EST:** 2006
SQ FT: 10,000
SALES (est): 738.14K **Privately Held**
Web: www.theseversongroup.com
SIC: 5812 8741 8742 8748 Contract food services; Management services; Management consulting services; Systems engineering consultant, ex. computer or professional

(P-11600)

SLATERS 50/50 INC

Also Called: Slater's 50/50
5801 E Camino Pinzon, Anaheim (92807-3910)
PHONE...............................714 602-8115
Scott D Slater, *CEO*
Scott Slater, *
EMP: 125 **EST:** 2009
SALES (est): 728.91K **Privately Held**
Web: www.slaters5050.com
SIC: 5812 5813 6794 American restaurant; Drinking places; Patent owners and lessors

(P-11601)

SPECIALTY RESTAURANTS CORP

Also Called: Castaway Restaurant, The
1250 E Harvard Rd, Burbank (91501-1002)
PHONE...............................818 843-5013
Saeed Fazeli, *Genl Mgr*

EMP: 253
SALES (corp-wide): 88.08MM **Privately Held**
Web: www.castawayburbank.com
SIC: 5812 7299 American restaurant; Banquet hall facilities
PA: Specialty Restaurants Corporation
150 Paularino Ave Bldg C
714 279-6100

(P-11602)
SYCUAN TRIBAL DEVELOPMENT
Also Called: Sycuan Resort
1530 Hilton Head Rd Ste 210, El Cajon (92019-4655)
PHONE..................619 442-3425
Daniel Tucker, *Ch Bd*
Glen Quiroga, *
Codey Martinez, *
EMP: 250 **EST:** 2001
SALES (est): 1.7MM **Privately Held**
SIC: 5812 7992 7011 Eating places; Public golf courses; Hotels and motels
PA: Sycuan Band Of Kumeyaay Nation
3007 Dehesa Rd
619 445-6002

(P-11603)
TA OPERATING LLC
Also Called: Burger King
4325 E Guasti Rd, Ontario (91761-7807)
PHONE..................909 390-7800
Tom Obrien, *Brnch Mgr*
EMP: 110
SALES (corp-wide): 171.22B **Privately Held**
Web: www.bk.com
SIC: 5812 6794 Fast-food restaurant, chain; Franchises, selling or licensing
HQ: Ta Operating Llc
24601 Center Ridge Rd # 200
Westlake OH 44145

(P-11604)
TACO BELL CORP (HQ)
Also Called: Taco Bell
1 Glen Bell Way, Irvine (92618-3344)
PHONE..................949 863-4500
Sean Tresvant, *CEO*
Sean Tresvan, *
Scott Mezvinsky, *
Julie Davis, *
Melissa Friebe, *
▲ **EMP:** 1025 **EST:** 1962
SQ FT: 278,000
SALES (est): 509.82MM
SALES (corp-wide): 7.08B **Publicly Held**
Web: www.tacobell.com
SIC: 5812 6794 Fast-food restaurant, chain; Franchises, selling or licensing
PA: Yum Brands, Inc.
1441 Gardiner Ln
502 874-8300

(P-11605)
TRE VENEZIE INC
Also Called: Ca'del Sole
4100 Cahuenga Blvd, Toluca Lake (91602-2831)
PHONE..................818 985-4669
Rodolfo Costela, *Pr*
Jean Louis De Mori, *
Rodolfo Costello, *General Vice President*
EMP: 73 **EST:** 1994
SQ FT: 7,000
SALES (est): 2.18MM **Privately Held**
Web: www.cadelsole.com
SIC: 5812 7299 Italian restaurant; Wedding consultant

(P-11606)
TS ENTERPRISES INC
Also Called: La Quinta Cliff House
78250 Highway 111, La Quinta (92253-2074)
PHONE..................760 360-5991
David Potesta, *Brnch Mgr*
EMP: 23
SALES (corp-wide): 23.29MM **Privately Held**
Web: www.laquintacliffhouse.com
SIC: 5812 5699 5261 2791 American restaurant; Custom tailor; Lawn and garden supplies; Typesetting
PA: T.S. Enterprises, Inc
225 W Plaza St Ste 300
858 720-2380

(P-11607)
UNIFIED NUTRIMEALS
5469 Ferguson Dr, Commerce (90022-5118)
PHONE..................323 923-9335
Shabir Kashyap, *Pr*
Hugo Meza, *
Phil Chavez, *
EMP: 85 **EST:** 2005
SALES (est): 2.46MM **Privately Held**
Web: www.unifiednm.com
SIC: 5812 2099 Contract food services; Ready-to-eat meals, salads, and sandwiches

(P-11608)
VIE DE FRANCE YAMAZAKI INC
Also Called: Vie De France 108
3046 E 50th St, Vernon (90058-2918)
PHONE..................323 582-1241
Driss Goulhiane, *Brnch Mgr*
EMP: 911
Web: www.viedefrance.com
SIC: 5812 2051 Restaurant, family: chain; Breads, rolls, and buns
HQ: Vie De France Yamazaki, Inc.
150 Linden Oaks
Rochester NY 14625

(P-11609)
WARNER FOOD MANAGEMENT CO INC
4917 Genesta Ave, Encino (91316-3438)
PHONE..................818 285-2160
Sudesh Sood, *Pr*
Terry O'herrick, *Sec*
EMP: 125 **EST:** 1989
SQ FT: 2,000
SALES (est): 1.63MM **Privately Held**
SIC: 5812 0742 Fast-food restaurant, chain; Restaurant and food services consultants

(P-11610)
WKS RESTAURANT CORPORATION (PA)
Also Called: El Pollo Loco
5856 Corporate Ave Ste 200, Cypress (90630-4754)
P.O. Box 39 (90714)
PHONE..................562 425-1402
Roland Spongberg, *Pr*
Paul Tanner, *CFO*
EMP: 243 **EST:** 1987
SQ FT: 1,200
SALES (est): 432.65MM
SALES (corp-wide): 432.65MM **Privately Held**
Web: www.wksusa.com
SIC: 5812 6794 Mexican restaurant; Franchises, selling or licensing

5813 Drinking Places

(P-11611)
BELCHING BEAVER BREWERY
Also Called: Rocky Point RTD
1334 Rocky Point Dr, Oceanside (92056-5864)
PHONE..................760 599-5832
Tom Vogel, *CEO*
▲ **EMP:** 145 **EST:** 2012
SALES (est): 3.65MM **Privately Held**
Web: www.belchingbeaver.com
SIC: 5813 2082 Bars and lounges; Malt beverages

(P-11612)
BORDER X BREWING LLC
2181 Logan Ave, San Diego (92113-2203)
PHONE..................619 501-0503
David Favela, *Prin*
Martin Favela, *
Marcelino Favela, *
Marcel Favela, *
Mike Fuller, *
EMP: 33 **EST:** 2012
SALES (est): 2.38MM **Privately Held**
Web: www.borderxbrewing.com
SIC: 5813 2082 Bars and lounges; Ale (alcoholic beverage)

(P-11613)
CORONADO BREWING COMPANY INC (PA)
170 Orange Ave, Coronado (92118-1409)
PHONE..................619 437-4452
Ron Chapman, *Pr*
Rick Chapman, *
EMP: 50 **EST:** 1996
SQ FT: 6,000
SALES (est): 10.5MM **Privately Held**
Web: www.coronadobrewing.com
SIC: 5813 2082 Bars and lounges; Malt beverages

(P-11614)
HARLAND BREWING CO LLC
10115 Carroll Canyon Rd, San Diego (92131-1109)
PHONE..................858 800-4566
Jeffrey Hansson, *Managing Member*
EMP: 34 **EST:** 2018
SALES (est): 3.05MM **Privately Held**
Web: www.harlandbeer.com
SIC: 5813 2082 Bars and lounges; Beer (alcoholic beverage)

(P-11615)
LEVITY OF BREA LLC
180 S Brea Blvd, Brea (92821-4902)
PHONE..................714 482-0700
Alireza Ghaemian, *Prin*
EMP: 92 **EST:** 2015
SALES (est): 607.41K **Privately Held**
Web: www.improv.com
SIC: 5813 7997 5812 Bars and lounges; Membership sports and recreation clubs; Buffet (eating places)

(P-11616)
MISSION BREWERY INC
8830 Rehco Rd, San Diego (92121-3263)
PHONE..................619 818-7147
Daniel R Selis, *Pr*
▲ **EMP:** 24 **EST:** 2010
SALES (est): 3.88MM **Privately Held**
Web: www.missionbrewery.com
SIC: 5813 5812 2082 Bars and lounges; Grills (eating places); Malt beverages

(P-11617)
PALOS VERDES GOLF CLUB
Also Called: Palos Verdes Golf & Cntry CLB
3301 Via Campesina, Palos Verdes Peninsu (90274-1468)
PHONE..................310 375-2759
Gerald Kouzmanoff, *CEO*
EMP: 100 **EST:** 1967
SQ FT: 55,000
SALES (est): 11.4MM **Privately Held**
Web: www.pvgc.com
SIC: 5813 5941 7997 5812 Bar (drinking places); Golf goods and equipment; Golf club, membership; Eating places

(P-11618)
SBE ENTERTAINMENT GROUP LLC (HQ)
2535 Las Vegas Blvd S, Los Angeles (90036)
PHONE..................323 655-8000
Sam Nazarian, *Managing Member*
Nikki Mark, *
Sam Bakhshandehpour, *
EMP: 75 **EST:** 2002
SQ FT: 11,000
SALES (est): 39.49MM
SALES (corp-wide): 1.66B **Privately Held**
Web: www.sbe.com
SIC: 5813 7011 5812 Night clubs; Hotels; American restaurant
PA: Accor
82 Rue H Farman
146429193

(P-11619)
STONE BREWING CO LLC (DH)
Also Called: Stone Brewing Co.
1999 Citracado Pkwy, Escondido (92029-4158)
PHONE..................760 294-7866
▲ **EMP:** 24 **EST:** 1996
SALES (est): 175.4MM **Privately Held**
Web: www.stonebrewing.com
SIC: 5813 2082 Bars and lounges; Ale (alcoholic beverage)
HQ: Sapporo Breweries Ltd.
4-20-1, Ebisu
Shibuya-Ku TKY 150-0

(P-11620)
TAVISTOCK RESTAURANTS LLC
Also Called: Alcatraz Brewing Company
20 City Blvd W Ste R1, Orange (92868-3116)
PHONE..................714 939-8686
Jarred Creagan, *Mgr*
EMP: 150
Web: www.tavistockrestaurantcollection.com
SIC: 5813 5812 2082 Bars and lounges; American restaurant; Malt beverages
HQ: Tavistock Restaurants Llc
6900 Tvstock Lkes Blvd St
Orlando FL 32827
407 909-7101

5912 Drug Stores And Proprietary Stores

(P-11621)
KERN VALLEY HOSP FOUNDATION (PA)
Also Called: KERN VALLEY HOSPITAL
6412 Laurel Ave, Lake Isabella (93240-9529)
P.O. Box 1628 (93240-1628)
PHONE..................760 379-2681

PRODUCTS & SVCS

Clarence Semonious, *Pr*
Anne Litz, *
Sally Partin, *
Kay Knight, *
Mary Completo, *
EMP: 300 **EST:** 1964
SQ FT: 65,000
SALES (est): 59.8K
SALES (corp-wide): 59.8K **Privately Held**
Web: www.kvhd.org
SIC: 5912 8051 Drug stores; Extended care
facility

(P-11622)
SANSUM CLINIC
Also Called: Santa Brbara Med Fndtion Clnic
215 Pesetas Ln, Santa Barbara
(93110-1416)
P.O. Box 1200 (93102-1200)
PHONE..............................805 681-7500
Kut Ransolhoff, *CEO*
EMP: 78
SALES (corp-wide): 357.93MM **Privately
Held**
Web: www.sansumclinic.org
SIC: 5912 8011 Drug stores and proprietary
stores; Offices and clinics of medical
doctors
PA: Sansum Clinic
470 S Patterson Ave
805 681-7700

(P-11623)
SHARP HEALTHCARE (PA)
8695 Spectrum Center Blvd, San Diego
(92123-1489)
PHONE..............................858 499-4000
Christopher Howard, *Managing Member*
Michael Murphy, *Managing Member**
Ann Pumpian, *Managing Member**
Daniel L Gross, *Managing Member**
Alison J Fleury, *Managing Member**
EMP: 760 **EST:** 1946
SQ FT: 15,700
SALES (est): 1.9B
SALES (corp-wide): 1.9B **Privately Held**
Web: www.sharp.com
SIC: 5912 8741 6324 8011 Drug stores;
Hospital management; Hospital and
medical service plans; Offices and clinics of
medical doctors

(P-11624)
SHARP HEALTHCARE ACO LLC
Also Called: Sharp Rees-Stealy Pharmacy
2929 Health Center Dr, San Diego
(92123-2762)
PHONE..............................619 688-3543
Christopher Howard, *Brnch Mgr*
EMP: 117
SQ FT: 27,810
SALES (corp-wide): 1.9B **Privately Held**
Web: www.sharp.com
SIC: 5912 8011 Drug stores; Orthopedic
physician
PA: Sharp Healthcare
8695 Spectrum Ctr Blvd
858 499-4000

5921 Liquor Stores

(P-11625)
BEVERAGES & MORE INC
875 E Birch St Ste A, Brea (92821-5769)
PHONE..............................714 990-2060
Kerry Christopher, *Mgr*
EMP: 114
SALES (corp-wide): 1.61B **Privately Held**
Web: www.bevmo.com
SIC: 5921 5149 Wine; Soft drinks

HQ: Beverages & More, Inc.
1401 Wllow Pass Rd Ste 90
Concord CA 94520

(P-11626)
BEVERAGES & MORE INC
2000 N Tustin St, Orange (92865-3902)
PHONE..............................714 279-8131
Lisa Young, *Mgr*
EMP: 114
SALES (corp-wide): 1.61B **Privately Held**
Web: www.bevmo.com
SIC: 5921 5149 Hard liquor; Soft drinks
HQ: Beverages & More, Inc.
1401 Wllow Pass Rd Ste 90
Concord CA 94520

5932 Used Merchandise
Stores

(P-11627)
DESERT AREA RESOURCES
TRAINING (PA)
Also Called: DART
201 E Ridgecrest Blvd, Ridgecrest
(93555-3919)
PHONE..............................760 375-9787
Jinny Deangelis, *CEO*
Robert Beecroft, *
Jeannie Luke, *
Chris Bridges Cof Clieants, *Prin*
EMP: 100 **EST:** 1961
SQ FT: 10,800
SALES (est): 3.07MM
SALES (corp-wide): 3.07MM **Privately
Held**
Web: www.dartontarget.org
SIC: 5932 7349 8322 Clothing and shoes,
secondhand; Janitorial service, contract
basis; Association for the handicapped

(P-11628)
GOODWILL CENTRAL COAST
Also Called: Goodwill Inds San Luis Obispo
880 Industrial Way, San Luis Obispo
(93401-7666)
PHONE..............................805 544-0542
James Burke, *Brnch Mgr*
EMP: 235
SALES (corp-wide): 46.14MM **Privately
Held**
Web: www.ccgoodwill.org
SIC: 5932 8322 Used merchandise stores;
Rehabilitation services
PA: Goodwill Central Coast
1566 Moffett St
831 423-8611

(P-11629)
LABELS-R-US INC
Also Called: Label Shoppe, The
1121 Fullerton Rd, City Of Industry
(91748-1232)
PHONE..............................626 333-4001
Rudolph Gaytan, *CEO*
EMP: 25 **EST:** 1991
SQ FT: 65,000
SALES (est): 2.58MM **Privately Held**
Web: www.labelsrus.com
SIC: 5932 2759 Used merchandise stores;
Commercial printing, nec

5941 Sporting Goods And
Bicycle Shops

(P-11630)
ECI WATER SKI PRODUCTS INC

Also Called: Skylon
224 Malbert St, Perris (92570-6279)
PHONE..............................951 940-9999
Tom Hellwig, *Pr*
Ronna Hellwig, *
EMP: 35 **EST:** 1984
SALES (est): 2.42MM **Privately Held**
Web: www.paradisesocal.com
SIC: 5941 3949 Water sport equipment;
Water skiing equipment and supplies,
except skis

5942 Book Stores

(P-11631)
BNI PUBLICATIONS INC
Also Called: Building News
990 Park Center Dr Ste E, Vista
(92081-8352)
PHONE..............................760 734-1113
William Mahoney, *Pr*
William Dennis Mahoney, *
Norman Peterson, *
Vincent Wilhelm, *
EMP: 38 **EST:** 1946
SQ FT: 2,000
SALES (est): 2.32MM **Privately Held**
Web: www.bnibooks.com
SIC: 5942 2731 8999 Book stores; Book
publishing; Lecturing services

(P-11632)
FORTY-NINER SHOPS INC
Also Called: University Bookstore
6049 E 7th St, Long Beach (90840-0007)
PHONE..............................562 985-5093
Don Penrod, *CEO*
Doctor Mary Ann Takemoto, *Ch*
Ms. Mary Stephens, *Treas*
EMP: 550 **EST:** 1949
SQ FT: 36,000
SALES (est): 19.38MM **Privately Held**
Web: www.fortyninershops.com
SIC: 5942 5943 5812 7021 College book
stores; School supplies; Cafeteria;
Dormitory, commercially operated

(P-11633)
NORTH ORNGE CNTY CMNTY
CLLEGE
Also Called: Fullerton College Bookstore
330 E Chapman Ave, Fullerton
(92832-2087)
PHONE..............................714 992-7008
Nick Karvia, *Brnch Mgr*
EMP: 295
SALES (corp-wide): 92.98MM **Privately
Held**
Web: www.nocccd.edu
SIC: 5942 5045 College book stores;
Computers, peripherals, and software
PA: North Orange County Community
College District
1830 W Romneya Dr
714 808-4500

(P-11634)
PSYCHIC EYE BOOK SHOPS
INC (PA)
13435 Ventura Blvd, Sherman Oaks
(91423-3812)
PHONE..............................818 906-8263
Robert Leysen, *CEO*
Mary Karahalios, *
EMP: 80 **EST:** 1984
SQ FT: 5,000
SALES (est): 1.01MM
SALES (corp-wide): 1.01MM **Privately
Held**

Web: www.pebooks.com
SIC: 5942 5947 7999 Book stores; Gift shop;
Fortune tellers

5943 Stationery Stores

(P-11635)
EC DESIGN LLC
Also Called: Erin Condren
4860 W 147th St, Hawthorne (90250-6706)
PHONE..............................310 220-2362
Eric Howard, *Pr*
EMP: 26
SALES (corp-wide): 76.59MM **Privately
Held**
Web: www.erincondren.com
SIC: 5943 5049 5632 5331 Stationery stores
; School supplies; Apparel accessories;
Variety stores
PA: Ec Design Llc
201 W Howard Ln
512 676-4200

(P-11636)
W B MASON CO INC
5911 E Washington Blvd, Commerce
(90040-2412)
PHONE..............................888 926-2766
EMP: 27
SALES (corp-wide): 1.01B **Privately Held**
Web: www.wbmason.com
SIC: 5943 5712 2752 Office forms and
supplies; Office furniture; Commercial
printing, lithographic
PA: W. B. Mason Co., Inc.
59 Centre St
508 586-3434

(P-11637)
YEBO GROUP LLC
Also Called: Yebo Printing
2652 Dow Ave, Tustin (92780-7208)
PHONE..............................949 502-3317
Andrew Tosh, *Managing Member*
▲ **EMP:** 125 **EST:** 2008
SALES (est): 3.59MM **Privately Held**
Web:
www.customboxesandpackaging.com
SIC: 5943 2652 3086 2752 Stationery stores
; Boxes, newsboard, metal edged: made
from purchased materials; Packaging and
shipping materials, foamed plastics;
Commercial printing, lithographic

5944 Jewelry Stores

(P-11638)
DIAMOND GOLDENWEST
CORPORATION (PA)
Also Called: Jewelry Exchange, The
15732 Tustin Village Way, Tustin
(92780-4924)
PHONE..............................714 542-9000
William S Doddridge, *Pr*
Sylvia Trujillo, *
EMP: 150 **EST:** 1977
SQ FT: 25,000
SALES (est): 32.72MM
SALES (corp-wide): 32.72MM **Privately
Held**
Web: www.jewelryexchange.com
SIC: 5944 5094 Jewelry, precious stones
and precious metals; Jewelry

(P-11639)
ENO BRANDS INC
Also Called: Alamo Rings
6481 Global Dr, Cypress (90630-5227)

▲ = Import ▼ = Export
◆ = Import/Export

PHONE.............................714 220-1318
Guey Miaw Tsao, *CEO*
Chun Tsao, *CFO*
Kevin Tsao, *Sec*
EMP: 24 **EST:** 2005
SQ FT: 5,000
SALES (est): 2.33MM **Privately Held**
Web: www.enobrands.com
SIC: 5944 5094 7389 5632 Jewelry stores;
Jewelry; Design services; Costume jewelry

(P-11640)
LUGANO DIAMONDS & JEWELRY INC (HQ)
545 Newport Center Dr, Newport Beach
(92660-6937)
PHONE.............................949 625-7722
Mordechai Ferder, *CEO*
Joshua Gaynor, *
Idit Ferder, *
Stuart Winston, *CMO**
Scott Sussman, *
EMP: 76 **EST:** 2004
SALES (est): 5.15MM **Publicly Held**
Web: www.luganodiamonds.com
SIC: 5944 3911 Jewelry, precious stones
and precious metals; Jewelry apparel
PA: Compass Diversified Holdings
301 Riverside Ave Fl 2

(P-11641)
M & G JEWELERS INC
10823 Edison Ct, Rancho Cucamonga
(91730-3868)
PHONE.............................909 989-2929
Juan Guevara, *Pr*
Michael Insalago, *
EMP: 68 **EST:** 1991
SQ FT: 8,432
SALES (est): 11.92MM **Privately Held**
Web: www.mandgjewelers.com
SIC: 5944 3911 7631 Jewelry, precious
stones and precious metals; Jewelry,
precious metal; Watch repair

(P-11642)
MONEX DEPOSIT A CAL LTD PARTNR
Also Called: Monex
4910 Birch St, Newport Beach
(92660-8100)
PHONE.............................800 444-8317
Mike Carabini, *Ltd Pt*
Louis E Carabini, *Pt*
EMP: 100 **EST:** 1987
SALES (est): 2.44MM **Privately Held**
SIC: 5944 6722 3324 Jewelry, precious
stones and precious metals; Management
investment, open-end; Steel investment
foundries

(P-11643)
S A TOP-U CORPORATION
1794 Illinois Ave, Perris (92571-9371)
PHONE.............................951 916-4025
Hans Werner Wendel, *Ch*
Pia Wendel, *
◆ **EMP:** 27 **EST:** 1984
SQ FT: 20,000
SALES (est): 833.53K **Privately Held**
Web: www.rdit.com
SIC: 5944 3993 Clock and watch stores;
Signs and advertising specialties

5945 Hobby, Toy, And Game Shops

(P-11644)
POP MART AMERICAS INC
Also Called: Pop Mart
500 N Brand Blvd Ste 2000, Glendale
(91203-3304)
PHONE.............................415 640-8197
Si De, *Pr*
Yang Jingbing, *
Moon Duk II, *Dir*
Lu Yonghui, *
EMP: 89 **EST:** 2022
SALES (est): 4.75MM **Privately Held**
SIC: 5945 7389 Hobby, toy, and game shops
; Business Activities at Non-Commercial
Site
HQ: Beijing Pop Mart Cultural Creative
Corp., Ltd.
Room 3606, Floor 36, Bldg. A, 101,
4-33/F, Building 13, District
Beijing BJ 10001

(P-11645)
SAILING INNOVATION (US) INC
17870 Castleton St Ste 220, City Of Industry
(91748-6795)
PHONE.............................626 965-6665
Steven Goldsmith, *CEO*
Valen Tong, *CFO*
Kiran Smith, *CMO*
EMP: 3187 **EST:** 2014
SALES (est): 380.18K **Privately Held**
SIC: 5945 3651 Toys and games; Audio
electronic systems

5946 Camera And Photographic Supply Stores

(P-11646)
FILMTOOLS INC (PA)
Also Called: Moviola Digital
1015 N Hollywood Way, Burbank
(91505-2546)
PHONE.............................323 467-1116
Joseph Paskal, *Pr*
Randy Paskal, *
Carl Nelson, *
Dana Newman, *
EMP: 50 **EST:** 1923
SQ FT: 30,000
SALES (est): 23.05MM
SALES (corp-wide): 23.05MM **Privately Held**
Web: www.filmtools.com
SIC: 5946 5043 7819 3861 Photographic
supplies; Motion picture equipment; Editing
services, motion picture production;
Photographic equipment and supplies

(P-11647)
FREESTYLE SALES CO LTD PARTNR
Also Called: Freestyle
12231 Florence Ave, Santa Fe Springs
(90670-3805)
P.O. Box 27924 (90027)
PHONE.............................323 660-3460
Ronald M Resch, *Pt*
Leonore King, *Pt*
▲ **EMP:** 90 **EST:** 1946
SALES (est): 3.51MM **Privately Held**
Web: www.freestylephoto.com
SIC: 5946 5043 Photographic supplies;
Photographic equipment and supplies

(P-11648)
SAMYS CAMERA INC (PA)
Also Called: Samy's Digital Imaging
12636 Beatrice St, Los Angeles
(90066-7312)
P.O. Box 48126 (90048-0126)
PHONE.............................310 591-2100
▲ **EMP:** 108 **EST:** 1976
SALES (est): 63.6MM
SALES (corp-wide): 63.6MM **Privately Held**
Web: www.samys.com
SIC: 5946 5731 7699 Cameras; Video
recorders, players, disc players, and
accessories; Camera repair shop

5947 Gift, Novelty, And Souvenir Shop

(P-11649)
ALIN PARTY SUPPLY CO
6493 Magnolia Ave, Riverside
(92506-2409)
PHONE.............................951 682-7441
Sherry Bauer, *Mgr*
EMP: 30
Web: www.alinpartysupply.com
SIC: 5947 7389 2759 Party favors; Balloons,
novelty and toy; Invitation and stationery
printing and engraving
PA: Alin Party Supply Co.
4139 Woodruff Ave

5949 Sewing, Needlework, And Piece Goods

(P-11650)
MICHAEL LEVINE INC
920 Maple Ave, Los Angeles (90015-1812)
PHONE.............................213 622-6259
Laurence A Freidin, *Prin*
Laurence A Freidin, *Prin*
Laurence Freidin, *
▲ **EMP:** 75 **EST:** 2011
SQ FT: 60,000
SALES (est): 967.08K **Privately Held**
Web: www.lowpricefabric.com
SIC: 5949 5131 Fabric, remnants;
Upholstery fabrics, woven

(P-11651)
ROBERT KAUFMAN CO INC (PA)
Also Called: Robert Kaufman Fabrics
129 W 132nd St, Los Angeles
(90061-1619)
P.O. Box 59266 (90059-0266)
PHONE.............................310 538-3482
Kenneth Kaufman, *CEO*
Harvey Kaufman, *
Alvin Kaufman, *
Joseph Kaufman, **
◆ **EMP:** 114 **EST:** 1942
SQ FT: 24,000
SALES (est): 59.89MM
SALES (corp-wide): 59.89MM **Privately Held**
Web: www.robertkaufman.com
SIC: 5949 2299 Fabric stores piece goods;
Linen fabrics

(P-11652)
VICTORY SPORTSWEAR INC
Also Called: Victory Sportswear
2381 Buena Vista St, Irwindale
(91010-3301)
PHONE.............................866 308-0798
Victor Ju, *CEO*
Xiao Can Zhang, *

▲ **EMP:** 25 **EST:** 1999
SQ FT: 22,000
SALES (est): 2.38MM **Privately Held**
Web: www.victorysportswearinc.com
SIC: 5949 2321 2311 2331 Knitting goods
and supplies; Men's and boys' sports and
polo shirts; Men's and boy's suits and coats
; Women's and misses' blouses and shirts

5961 Catalog And Mail-order Houses

(P-11653)
AL GLOBAL CORPORATION (HQ)
Also Called: Youngvity Essntial Lf Sciences
2400 Boswell Rd, Chula Vista
(91914-3553)
PHONE.............................619 934-3980
Stephan Wallach, *CEO*
William Andreoli, *Pr*
Michelle Wallach, *COO*
David Briskie, *CFO*
◆ **EMP:** 36 **EST:** 1996
SQ FT: 70,000
SALES (est): 18.66MM
SALES (corp-wide): 147.44MM **Publicly Held**
Web: www.youngevity.com
SIC: 5961 2043 Catalog and mail-order
houses; Cereal breakfast foods
PA: Youngevity International, Inc.
2400 Boswell Rd
619 934-3980

(P-11654)
HADLEY FRUIT ORCHARDS INC (PA)
48980 Seminole Dr, Cabazon (92230-2112)
P.O. Box 495 (92230-0495)
PHONE.............................951 849-5255
Gerald Bench, *Pr*
John Taylor, *
Dennis Flint, *
James Taylor, *
Fred Bond, *
EMP: 35 **EST:** 1931
SALES (est): 1.01MM
SALES (corp-wide): 1.01MM **Privately Held**
Web: www.hadleyfruitorchards.com
SIC: 5961 2034 5499 5441 Food, mail order;
Fruits, dried or dehydrated, except freeze-
dried; Dried fruit; Nuts

(P-11655)
MELTON INTL TACKLE INC
1376 S State College Blvd, Anaheim
(92806-5728)
PHONE.............................714 978-9192
Tracy M Melton, *Pr*
◆ **EMP:** 28 **EST:** 1993
SALES (est): 2.47MM **Privately Held**
Web: www.meltontackle.com
SIC: 5961 5199 3949 5091 Fishing, hunting
and camping equipment and supplies: by
mail; Advertising specialties; Lures, fishing:
artificial; Boat accessories and parts

(P-11656)
MERQBIZ LLC
300 Continental Blvd Ste 640, El Segundo
(90245-5042)
PHONE.............................855 637-7249
John Fox, *
EMP: 35 **EST:** 2016
SALES (est): 973.04K **Privately Held**
Web: www.voith.com
SIC: 5961 3554 Electronic shopping; Paper
industries machinery

(P-11657)
PASSWORD ENTERPRISE INC
3200 E 29th St, Long Beach (90806-2321)
P.O. Box 90729 (90809-0729)
PHONE.................................562 988-8889
Sophead Naing, *CEO*
Adam Chu, *
EMP: 25 **EST:** 2013
SQ FT: 32,000
SALES (est): 2.45MM **Privately Held**
Web: www.passwordmm.com
SIC: 5961 3369 Automotive supplies and
equipment, mail order; Aerospace castings,
nonferrous: except aluminum

(P-11658)
PCM INC (HQ)
200 N Pacific Coast Hwy Ste 1050, El
Segundo (90245-5605)
PHONE.................................310 354-5600
Glynis A Bryan, *CFO*
EMP: 812 **EST:** 1987
SALES (est): 859.88MM **Publicly Held**
Web: www.insight.com
SIC: 5961 5731 5045 5734 Computer
equipment and electronics, mail order;
Radio, television, and electronic stores;
Computers, peripherals, and software;
Personal computers
PA: Insight Enterprises, Inc.
2701 E Insight Way

(P-11659)
**PERFORMANCE AUTOMOTIVE
WHL INC (PA)**
Also Called: Paw
20235 Nordhoff St, Chatsworth
(91311-6213)
P.O. Box 829 (91319-0829)
PHONE.................................805 499-8973
Keith E Harvie, *CEO*
Brian Mcelroy, *Pr*
EMP: 100 **EST:** 1978
SALES (est): 1.79MM
SALES (corp-wide): 1.79MM **Privately
Held**
Web: www.pawinc.com
SIC: 5961 5013 Automotive supplies and
equipment, mail order; Automotive supplies
and parts

(P-11660)
QUANTUM NETWORKS LLC
3412 Garfield Ave, Commerce
(90040-3104)
PHONE.................................212 993-5899
Jonathan Goldman, *Pr*
Eytan Wiener, *
EMP: 30 **EST:** 2008
SALES (est): 2.57MM **Privately Held**
Web: www.quantumnetworks.com
SIC: 5961 5731 5065 3651 Computer
equipment and electronics, mail order;
Consumer electronic equipment, nec; Video
equipment, electronic; Household audio
and video equipment

(P-11661)
QUILT IN A DAY INC
1955 Diamond St, San Marcos
(92078-5122)
PHONE.................................760 591-0929
TOLL FREE: 800
Eleanor A Burns, *CEO*
▲ **EMP:** 37 **EST:** 1979
SQ FT: 9,000
SALES (est): 4.45MM **Privately Held**
Web: www.quiltinaday.com

SIC: 5961 5949 5192 2731 Books, mail
order (except book clubs); Quilting
materials and supplies; Books; Book
publishing

(P-11662)
**ROAD RUNNER SPORTS INC
(PA)**
Also Called: Road Runner Sports
5549 Copley Dr, San Diego (92111-7904)
PHONE.................................858 974-4200
Michael Gotfredson, *CEO*
Scott Campbell, *
▲ **EMP:** 80 **EST:** 1987
SQ FT: 88,000
SALES (est): 136.68MM
SALES (corp-wide): 136.68MM **Privately
Held**
Web: www.roadrunnersports.com
SIC: 5961 3949 5661 Mail order house, nec;
Sporting and athletic goods, nec; Footwear,
athletic

(P-11663)
RUGGABLE LLC
17809 S Broadway, Gardena (90248-3541)
PHONE.................................310 295-0098
Nathan Baldwin, *CEO*
EMP: 378 **EST:** 2017
SALES (est): 51.95MM **Privately Held**
Web: www.ruggable.com
SIC: 5961 2273 Electronic shopping; Rugs,
hand and machine made

(P-11664)
SPENCER FORREST INC
Also Called: Toppik
11777 San Vicente Blvd Ste 650, Los
Angeles (90049-5051)
▲ **EMP:** 25 **EST:** 1981
SQ FT: 3,000
SALES (est): 1.76MM **Privately Held**
Web: www.toppik.com
SIC: 5961 3999 Cosmetics and perfumes,
mail order; Hair and hair-based products

5963 Direct Selling Establishments

(P-11665)
AVERY GROUP INC
8941 Dalton Ave, Los Angeles
(90047-3631)
PHONE.................................310 217-1070
Leatora Jefferson, *Pr*
EMP: 300 **EST:** 2006
SALES (est): 7.28MM **Privately Held**
Web: www.averygroup-inc.com
SIC: 5963 7349 Food services, direct sales;
Janitorial service, contract basis

(P-11666)
BTG TEXTILES INC
Also Called: Btg Textiles
710 Union St, Montebello (90640-6521)
PHONE.................................323 586-9488
Mohammed Alam, *CEO*
Yed Karim Raza, *
Nawarin Hasib, *
▲ **EMP:** 24 **EST:** 2011
SALES (est): 1.39MM **Privately Held**
Web: www.btgtextiles.com
SIC: 5963 2299 Direct selling establishments
; Towels and towelings, linen and linen-and-
cotton mixtures

(P-11667)
ENAGIC USA INC (PA)
4115 Spencer St, Torrance (90503-2419)
PHONE.................................310 542-7700
Hironari Oshiro, *Pr*
◆ **EMP:** 66 **EST:** 2003
SALES (est): 24.29MM
SALES (corp-wide): 24.29MM **Privately
Held**
Web: www.enagic.com
SIC: 5963 2086 Bottled water delivery;
Mineral water, carbonated: packaged in
cans, bottles, etc.

(P-11668)
STRATA USA LLC
333 City Blvd W Fl 17, Orange
(92868-5905)
PHONE.................................888 878-7282
EMP: 25 **EST:** 2014
SALES (est): 425.62K **Privately Held**
Web: www.strata-usa.com
SIC: 5963 0175 5122 5047 Direct sales,
telemarketing; Deciduous tree fruits;
Medical rubber goods; Hospital equipment
and furniture

5992 Florists

(P-11669)
**FOREST LAWN MEMORIAL-
PARK ASSN (PA)**
Also Called: Forest Lawn Mem Parks
Mortuary
1712 S Glendale Ave, Glendale
(91205-3320)
PHONE.................................323 254-3131
TOLL FREE: 800
Darin B Drabing, *CEO*
Darin B Drabing, *Pr*
Thomas Mckernan, *Ch Bd*
John Llewellyn, *
R Scott Jenkins, *
▲ **EMP:** 300 **EST:** 1906
SQ FT: 450,000
SALES (est): 185.21MM
SALES (corp-wide): 185.21MM **Privately
Held**
Web: www.forestlawn.com
SIC: 5992 6553 7261 Flowers, fresh;
Cemetery association; Funeral service and
crematories

(P-11670)
SAFEWAY INC
200 N Puente St, Brea (92821-3824)
PHONE.................................714 990-8357
EMP: 679
SALES (corp-wide): 79.24B **Publicly Held**
Web: www.safeway.com
SIC: 5992 4225 Florists; General
warehousing and storage
HQ: Safeway Inc.
5918 Stoneridge Mall Rd
Pleasanton CA 94588
925 226-5000

5994 News Dealers And Newsstands

(P-11671)
**HI-DESERT PUBLISHING
COMPANY**
Also Called: Big Bear Grizzly & Big Bear Lf
42007 Fox Farm Rd Ste 3b, Big Bear Lake
(92315-2192)
PHONE.................................909 866-3456

Gerald Wright, *Mgr*
EMP: 41
SALES (corp-wide): 21.91MM **Privately
Held**
Web: www.hidesertstar.com
SIC: 5994 2711 News dealers and
newsstands; Newspapers
HQ: Hi-Desert Publishing Company
56445 29 Palms Hwy
Yucca Valley CA 92284

5995 Optical Goods Stores

(P-11672)
**CONNECTICUT CTR PLASTIC
SURG**
73260 El Paseo Ste 2b, Palm Desert
(92260-4270)
PHONE.................................760 779-9595
Gary Price Md, *Brnch Mgr*
EMP: 76
Web: www.esanamedspa.com
SIC: 5995 8011 8042 Optical goods stores;
Physicians' office, including specialists;
Specialized optometrists
PA: Connecticut Center For Plastic Surgery
330 Orchard St Ste 211

5999 Miscellaneous Retail Stores, Nec

(P-11673)
**AAA FLAG & BANNER MFG CO
INC (PA)**
Also Called: AAA Flag & Banner
8937 National Blvd, Los Angeles
(90034-3307)
PHONE.................................310 836-3200
Howard S Furst, *Pr*
Susan Furst, *
▲ **EMP:** 150 **EST:** 1971
SQ FT: 4,000
SALES (est): 52.47MM
SALES (corp-wide): 52.47MM **Privately
Held**
Web: www.a3visual.com
SIC: 5999 2399 Flags; Banners, pennants,
and flags

(P-11674)
**ARBONNE INTERNATIONAL
LLC (DH)**
21 Technology Dr, Irvine (92618-2335)
PHONE.................................949 770-2610
Tyler Whitehead, *CEO*
Bernadette Chala, *
Amy Humfleet, *
Astrid Van-ruymbeke, *CFO*
Jen Orlando, *GROWTH Innovation*
▲ **EMP:** 25 **EST:** 1984
SQ FT: 37,000
SALES (est): 89.85MM **Privately Held**
Web: www.arbonne.com
SIC: 5999 5961 5499 2834 Cosmetics;
Cosmetics and perfumes, mail order;
Vitamin food stores; Vitamin preparations
HQ: Groupe Rocher Operations
La Croix Des Archers
La Gacilly BRE 56200
299297474

(P-11675)
**ARBONNE INTERNATIONAL
DIST INC**
9400 Jeronimo Rd, Irvine (92618-1907)
PHONE.................................800 272-6663
Tyler Whitehead, *CEO*

EMP: 40 EST: 2006
SALES (est): 6.54MM Privately Held
SIC: 5999 5961 5499 2834 Cosmetics;
Cosmetics and perfumes, mail order;
Vitamin food stores; Vitamin preparations
HQ: Arbonne International, Llc
21 Technology Dr
Irvine CA 92618
949 770-2610

(P-11676)
CALDESSO LLC
Also Called: Therm Core Products
439 S Stoddard Ave, San Bernardino
(92401-2025)
PHONE..............................909 888-2882
Andrew Cameron, CEO
P Anthony Panico, *
▲ EMP: 65 EST: 2010
SQ FT: 23,500
SALES (est): 442.28K Privately Held
SIC: 5999 3567 Hot tub and spa chemicals,
equipment, and supplies; Heating units and
devices, industrial: electric

(P-11677)
CINEMA SECRETS INC
6639 Odessa Ave, Van Nuys (91406-5746)
PHONE..............................818 846-0579
Barbara Stein, Pr
Maurice Stein, *
Michael Stein, *
Daniel Stein, *
▲ EMP: 60 EST: 1985
SALES (est): 4.59MM Privately Held
Web: www.cinemasecrets.com
SIC: 5999 5699 2389 5122 Cosmetics;
Costumes, masquerade or theatrical;
Costumes; Cosmetics

(P-11678)
CMC RESCUE INC
Also Called: CMC
6740 Cortona Dr, Goleta (93117-5574)
PHONE..............................805 562-9120
James A Frank, Ch
Richard M Phillips, *
Elizabeth Henry, *
▲ EMP: 65 EST: 1978
SQ FT: 23,000
SALES (est): 16.6MM Privately Held
Web: www.cmcpro.com
SIC: 5999 5099 3842 8299 Safety supplies
and equipment; Safety equipment and
supplies; Personal safety equipment;
Educational services

(P-11679)
**COSMETIC LABORATORIES OF
AMERICA LLC**
Also Called: Cosmetic Laboratories America
20245 Sunburst St, Chatsworth
(91311-6219)
PHONE..............................818 717-6140
▲ EMP: 400
SIC: 5999 5122 2844 2833 Cosmetics;
Cosmetics; Perfumes, cosmetics and other
toilet preparations; Medicinals and
botanicals

(P-11680)
COWAY USA INC
Also Called: Woongjin Coway USA Inc.
4221 Wilshire Blvd Ste 210, Los Angeles
(90010-3557)
PHONE..............................213 486-1600
Hong Rae Gim, Pr
Hosuk Yoon, *
▲ EMP: 39 EST: 2006
SQ FT: 4,200

SALES (est): 10.99MM Privately Held
Web: www.coway-usa.com
SIC: 5999 3564 Water purification equipment
; Air purification equipment
PA: Coway Co., Ltd.
136-23 Yugumagoksa-Ro, Yugu-Eup

(P-11681)
**DHARMA VENTURES GROUP
INC (PA)**
24700 Avenue Rockefeller, Valencia
(91355-3465)
PHONE..............................661 294-4200
Jim Snell, Pr
Cheryl Horn Berger, *
EMP: 280 EST: 2006
SQ FT: 75,000
SALES (est): 7.06MM Privately Held
Web: www.shieldhealthcare.com
SIC: 5999 6719 Medical apparatus and
supplies; Personal holding companies,
except banks

(P-11682)
DOCUSOURCE INC
Also Called: Equipment Brokers Unlimited
13100 Alondra Blvd Ste 108, Cerritos
(90703-2262)
PHONE..............................562 447-2600
▼ EMP: 80
SIC: 5999 7699 5943 Photocopy machines;
Photocopy machine repair; Office forms
and supplies

(P-11683)
**EVOQUA WATER
TECHNOLOGIES LLC**
1441 E Washington Blvd, Los Angeles
(90021-3039)
PHONE..............................213 748-8511
Gary Cappeline, Interim Chief Executive
Officer
EMP: 27
Web: www.evoqua.com
SIC: 5999 2899 Water purification equipment
; Chemical preparations, nec
HQ: Evoqua Water Technologies Llc
210 6th Ave Ste 3300
Pittsburgh PA 15222
724 772-0044

(P-11684)
GEORGIA-PACIFIC LLC
Also Called: Georgia-Pacific
15500 Valley View Ave, La Mirada
(90638-5230)
P.O. Box 981953 (79998-1953)
PHONE..............................562 926-8888
Sam Shah, Prin
EMP: 28
SALES (corp-wide): 64.37B Privately Held
Web: www.gp.com
SIC: 5999 5113 2653 3275 Alcoholic
beverage making equipment and supplies;
Corrugated and solid fiber boxes;
Corrugated and solid fiber boxes; Gypsum
products
HQ: Georgia-Pacific Llc
133 Peachtree St Nw
Atlanta GA 30303
404 652-4000

(P-11685)
GREATCALL INC
Also Called: Jitterbug
10945 Vista Sorrento Pkwy Ste 120, San
Diego (92130-8649)
P.O. Box 4428 (92018-4428)
PHONE..............................800 733-6632
David Inns, CEO

Bill Yates, CMO*
Lynn Herrick, CLO*
Bryan Adams, CCO*
Anne Murphy, CIO*
EMP: 501 EST: 2005
SQ FT: 29,000
SALES (est): 25.49MM
SALES (corp-wide): 43.45B Publicly Held
Web: www.lively.com
SIC: 5999 4812 Mobile telephones and
equipment; Cellular telephone services
PA: Best Buy Co., Inc.
7601 Penn Ave S
612 291-1000

(P-11686)
**INNOVATIVE DIALYSIS
PARTNERS INC**
1 World Trade Ctr Ste 2500, Long Beach
(90831-2500)
PHONE..............................562 495-8075
EMP: 350
SIC: 5999 8092 Medical apparatus and
supplies; Kidney dialysis centers

(P-11687)
INTELLIGENT BEAUTY LLC
Also Called: Iq Cosmetics
2301 Rosecrans Ave Ste 4110, El Segundo
(90245-4966)
PHONE..............................310 683-0940
▲ EMP: 550
Web: www.ibinc.com
SIC: 5999 2844 Cosmetics; Cosmetic
preparations

(P-11688)
**JAFRA COSMETICS INTL INC
(DH)**
Also Called: Jafra Cosmetics
1 Baxter Way Ste 150, Westlake Village
(91362-3819)
PHONE..............................805 449-3000
Karalee Mora, CEO
Mauro Schnaidman, *
Stacy Wolf, *
Mark Funaki, *
James Christl, *
◆ EMP: 52 EST: 1956
SALES (est): 51.94MM Privately Held
Web: www.jafra.com
SIC: 5999 2844 Cosmetics; Perfumes,
cosmetics and other toilet preparations
HQ: Betterware De Mexico, S.A.P.I. De C.V.
Cruce Carretera Gdl-Ameca-Huaxtla
Km. 5
El Arenal JAL 45350

(P-11689)
JON DAVLER INC
9440 Gidley St, Temple City (91780-4211)
PHONE..............................626 941-6558
David J Sheen, Pr
Christina Yang, *
◆ EMP: 24 EST: 2001
SQ FT: 12,000
SALES (est): 3.04MM Privately Held
Web: www.jondavler.com
SIC: 5999 2844 Cosmetics; Perfumes,
cosmetics and other toilet preparations

(P-11690)
**NAPOLEON PERDIS
COSMETICS INC**
16825 Saticoy St, Van Nuys (91406-2728)
PHONE..............................323 817-3611
Napoleon Perdis, Pr
Soula-marie Perdis, Sec
◆ EMP: 93 EST: 2005

SALES (est): 2.25MM Privately Held
Web: www.napoleonperdis.com
SIC: 5999 5122 Cosmetics; Cosmetics

(P-11691)
**NATIONAL ADVANCED
ENDOSCOPY DE**
22134 Sherman Way, Canoga Park
(91303-1136)
PHONE..............................818 227-2720
Fawzia Dabiri, CEO
John Dawoodjee, *
EMP: 25 EST: 1994
SQ FT: 16,000
SALES (est): 2.64MM Privately Held
Web: www.aed.md
SIC: 5999 3841 5047 7629 Medical
apparatus and supplies; Surgical and
medical instruments; Medical and hospital
equipment; Electrical repair shops

(P-11692)
NICE NORTH AMERICA LLC (DH)
5919 Sea Otter Pl Ste 100, Carlsbad
(92010-6750)
P.O. Box 9003 (92008)
PHONE..............................760 438-7000
Emanuel Bertolini, CEO
Darren Learmonth, *
Senthoor Navaratnam, Chief Product
Officer*
◆ EMP: 200 EST: 1961
SQ FT: 32,000
SALES (est): 63.38MM Privately Held
Web: na.niceforyou.com
SIC: 5999 3699 Alarm and safety equipment
stores; Security control equipment and
systems
HQ: Nice Spa
Via Callalta 1
Oderzo TV 31046

(P-11693)
OFFICIA IMAGING INC (PA)
5636 Ruffin Rd, San Diego (92123-1317)
PHONE..............................858 348-0831
Todd Rogers, Pr
Cary Carlton, *
EMP: 24 EST: 1963
SALES (est): 9.97MM
SALES (corp-wide): 9.97MM Privately
Held
Web: www.office1.com
SIC: 5999 5044 3861 Photocopy machines;
Photocopy machines; Printing equipment,
photographic

(P-11694)
**PLAYBOY ENTERPRISES INC
(HQ)**
Also Called: Playboy
10960 Wilshire Blvd Fl 22, Los Angeles
(90024-3808)
PHONE..............................310 424-1800
Ben Kohn, Pr
Suhail Rizvi, Ch Bd
David Israel, CFO
▲ EMP: 77 EST: 1953
SQ FT: 45,000
SALES (est): 147MM
SALES (corp-wide): 142.95MM Publicly
Held
Web: www.powersergefitness.com
SIC: 5999 5169 Toiletries, cosmetics, and
perfumes; Silicon lubricants
PA: Plby Group, Inc.
10960 Wlshire Blvd Ste 22
310 424-1800

(P-11695)
RELIEF-MART INC
Also Called: Selectabed
28505 Canwood St Ste C, Agoura Hills
(91301-3207)
PHONE.....................805 379-4300
Rick T Swartzburg, *CEO*
Jim Swartzburg, *
▲ **EMP: 42 EST:** 2001
SQ FT: 36,000
SALES (est): 500K **Privately Held**
Web: www.reliefmart.com
SIC: 5999 2515 2392 Medical apparatus and
supplies; Mattresses and foundations;
Cushions and pillows

(P-11696)
SCOPE ORTHTICS PROSTHETICS INC (DH)
Also Called: Scope
7720 Cardinal Ct, San Diego (92123-3333)
PHONE.....................858 292-7448
Loren Saxton, *Pr*
Tony Di Santo, *
Kel Bergmann, *
EMP: 30 **EST:** 1982
SQ FT: 7,400
SALES (est): 9.35MM
SALES (corp-wide): 1.12B **Privately Held**
Web: www.scop.net
SIC: 5999 3842 Orthopedic and prosthesis
applications; Prosthetic appliances
HQ: Hanger Prosthetics & Orthotics, Inc.
10910 Domain Dr Ste 300
Austin TX 78758
512 777-3800

(P-11697)
SEA DWELLING CREATURES INC
5515 W 104th St, Los Angeles
(90045-6013)
PHONE.....................310 676-9697
Bradford Remmer, *Pr*
Eric Cohen, *
Scott Cohen, *
◆ **EMP:** 70 **EST:** 1993
SQ FT: 24,000
SALES (est): 4.13MM **Privately Held**
Web: www.seadwelling.com
SIC: 5999 5199 Tropical fish; Pets and pet
supplies

(P-11698)
SMARTLABS INC
Also Called: Smarthomepro
1621 Alton Pkwy Ste 100, Irvine
(92606-4846)
PHONE.....................800 762-7846
Brian Taylor, *Interim Chief Executive Officer*
Rob Lilleness, *
◆ **EMP:** 85 **EST:** 1993
SQ FT: 59,230
SALES (est): 9.88MM **Privately Held**
Web: www.smartlabsinc.com
SIC: 5999 3822 Electronic parts and
equipment; Environmental controls

(P-11699)
SOUTHWEST BOULDER & STONE INC (PA)
5002 2nd St, Fallbrook (92028-9790)
PHONE.....................760 451-3333
TOLL FREE: 800
Michelle S Mcleod, *Pr*
Michael O Mcleod, *Sec*
▲ **EMP:** 45 **EST:** 1996
SQ FT: 4,500
SALES (est): 26.38MM **Privately Held**

Web: www.southwestboulder.com
SIC: 5999 1422 Rock and stone specimens;
Crushed and broken limestone

(P-11700)
UNITED ACCESS LLC
4797 Ruffner St, San Diego (92111-1519)
PHONE.....................623 879-0800
Richard May, *Pr*
EMP: 70
SALES (corp-wide): 11.55MM **Privately Held**
Web: www.braunability.com
SIC: 5999 5521 7538 Medical apparatus and
supplies; Used car dealers; General
automotive repair shops
HQ: United Access, L.L.C.
500 Nrthwest Plz Dr Ste 9
Saint Ann MO 63074
877 501-8267

(P-11701)
VCA INC (DH)
Also Called: VCA
12401 W Olympic Blvd, Los Angeles
(90064-1022)
PHONE.....................310 571-6500
Doug Drew, *CEO*
Arthur J Antin, *
EMP: 102 **EST:** 1987
SQ FT: 81,000
SALES (est): 2.21B
SALES (corp-wide): 42.84B **Privately Held**
Web: www.vca.com
SIC: 5999 5047 0742 Pets and pet supplies;
Veterinarians' equipment and supplies;
Animal hospital services, pets and other
animal specialties
HQ: Mmi Holdings, Inc.
18101 Se 6th Way
Vancouver WA 98683
360 784-5422

(P-11702)
WAXIES ENTERPRISES LLC
Also Called: Waxie Sanitary Supply
3220 S Fairview St, Santa Ana
(92704-6509)
PHONE.....................714 545-8441
TOLL FREE: 800
Laura Maloney, *Brnch Mgr*
EMP: 80
SQ FT: 78,582
SALES (corp-wide): 2.83B **Privately Held**
Web: info.waxie.com
SIC: 5999 5191 5169 5087 Cleaning
equipment and supplies; Farm supplies;
Chemicals and allied products, nec; Service
establishment equipment
HQ: Waxie's Enterprises, Llc
9353 Waxie Way
San Diego CA 92123
800 995-4466

6011 Federal Reserve Banks

(P-11703)
FEDERAL RSRVE BNK SAN FRNCISCO
Also Called: Los Angeles Branch
950 S Grand Ave Fl 1, Los Angeles
(90015-1467)
P.O. Box 512077 (90051-0077)
PHONE.....................213 683-2300
Mark Mullinix, *Mgr*
EMP: 640
Web: www.frbsf.org
SIC: 6011 Federal Reserve branches

HQ: Federal Reserve Bank Of San
Francisco
101 Market St
San Francisco CA 94105
415 974-2000

6021 National Commercial Banks

(P-11704)
BANA HOME LOAN SERVICING
31303 Agoura Rd, Westlake Village
(91361-4635)
PHONE.....................213 345-7975
Rachel Fiorillo, *Sr VP*
EMP: 900 **EST:** 2016
SALES (est): 4.57MM **Privately Held**
SIC: 6021 National commercial banks

(P-11705)
BANC OF CALIFORNIA INC
9701 Wilshire Blvd Ste 700, Beverly Hills
(90212-2007)
PHONE.....................310 887-8500
Jared M Wolff, *Pr*
EMP: 1700
SALES (corp-wide): 1.52B **Publicly Held**
Web: www.bancofcal.com
SIC: 6021 National commercial banks
PA: Banc Of California, Inc.
11611 San Vcnte Blvd Ste
855 361-2262

(P-11706)
BANC OF CALIFORNIA INC (PA)
11611 San Vicente Blvd Ste 500, Los
Angeles (90049-6505)
P.O. Box 61452 (92602)
PHONE.....................855 361-2262
Jared M Wolff, *V Ch Bd*
John M Eggemeyer Iii, *Ch Bd*
Joseph Kauder, *Ex VP*
Robert G Dyck, *CCO*
Jeffrey Krumpoch, *Interim CAO*
EMP: 120 **EST:** 2002
SALES (est): 1.52B
SALES (corp-wide): 1.52B **Publicly Held**
Web: www.bancofcal.com
SIC: 6021 National commercial banks

(P-11707)
BANK OF HOPE (HQ)
3200 Wilshire Blvd Ste 1400, Los Angeles
(90010-1325)
PHONE.....................213 639-1700
Kevin S Kim, *CEO*
Min J Kim, *Pr*
Scott Yoon-suk Whang, *Ch Bd*
Julianna Balicka, *Ex VP*
▲ **EMP:** 108 **EST:** 1985
SALES (est): 1.09B
SALES (corp-wide): 1.09B **Publicly Held**
Web: www.bankofhope.com
SIC: 6021 National commercial banks
PA: Hope Bancorp, Inc.
3200 Wilshire Blvd S 1400
213 639-1700

(P-11708)
BBCN BANK
Also Called: California Center Bank
3731 Wilshire Blvd, Los Angeles
(90010-2830)
PHONE.....................213 251-2222
▲ **EMP:** 704
SIC: 6021 National commercial banks

(P-11709)
CIT BANK NA (HQ)
75 N Fair Oaks Ave Ste C, Pasadena
(91103-3647)
P.O. Box 7056 (91109-7056)
PHONE.....................626 859-5400
Ellen R Alemany, *Ch Bd*
Joseph Otting, *
Kenneth A Brause, *
Stacey Goodman, *
Carol Hayles, *
EMP: 112 **EST:** 2009
SALES (est): 498.62MM
SALES (corp-wide): 22.47B **Publicly Held**
Web: www.first.bank
SIC: 6021 National commercial banks
PA: First Citizens Bancshares Inc
4300 Six Forks Rd
919 716-7000

(P-11710)
CITIBANK FSB
Also Called: Citibank
1 World Trade Ctr Ste 100, Long Beach
(90831-0100)
PHONE.....................562 999-3453
Jim Drake, *Brnch Mgr*
EMP: 547
SALES (corp-wide): 156.82B **Publicly Held**
Web: www.citigroup.com
SIC: 6021 National commercial banks
HQ: Citibank, F.S.B.
1 Sansome St
San Francisco CA 94104
415 627-6000

(P-11711)
CITY NATIONAL BANK
4605 Lankershim Blvd Ste 150, North
Hollywood (91602-1863)
PHONE.....................818 487-1040
Lisa Kaplan, *Prin*
EMP: 120
SQ FT: 1,815
SALES (corp-wide): 41.52B **Privately Held**
Web: www.cnb.com
SIC: 6021 National commercial banks
HQ: City National Bank
555 S Flower St 21st Flr
Los Angeles CA 90071
310 888-6000

(P-11712)
CITY NATIONAL BANK
12515 Ventura Blvd, Studio City
(91604-2485)
P.O. Box 1765 (91614-0765)
PHONE.....................818 487-7530
Kathi Atkinson, *Brnch Mgr*
EMP: 77
SALES (corp-wide): 41.52B **Privately Held**
Web: www.cnb.com
SIC: 6021 National commercial banks
HQ: City National Bank
555 S Flower St 21st Flr
Los Angeles CA 90071
310 888-6000

(P-11713)
CITY NATIONAL BANK
1315 Lincoln Blvd Ste 110, Santa Monica
(90401-1762)
PHONE.....................424 280-8000
EMP: 77
SALES (corp-wide): 41.52B **Privately Held**
Web: www.cnb.com
SIC: 6021 National commercial banks
HQ: City National Bank
555 S Flower St 21st Flr

Los Angeles CA 90071
310 888-6000

(P-11714)
CITY NATIONAL BANK
100 Oceangate Ste 1000, Long Beach
(90802-4347)
PHONE................................562 624-8600
Phil Bond, *Mgr*
EMP: 77
SALES (corp-wide): 41.52B **Privately Held**
Web: www.cnb.com
SIC: 6021 National commercial banks
HQ: City National Bank
555 S Flower St 21st Flr
Los Angeles CA 90071
310 888-6000

(P-11715)
CITY NATIONAL BANK
Also Called: Pasadena Branch
89 S Lake Ave, Pasadena (91101-2686)
PHONE................................626 432-7100
John Lavier, *Brnch Mgr*
EMP: 103
SALES (corp-wide): 41.52B **Privately Held**
Web: www.cnb.com
SIC: 6021 National commercial banks
HQ: City National Bank
555 S Flower St 21st Flr
Los Angeles CA 90071
310 888-6000

(P-11716)
CITY NATIONAL BANK
Also Called: Fairfax Office 11
8641 Wilshire Blvd Ste 101, Beverly Hills
(90211-2919)
PHONE................................323 634-7200
Fernando Linares, *Mgr*
EMP: 214
SALES (corp-wide): 41.52B **Privately Held**
Web: www.cnb.com
SIC: 6021 National commercial banks
HQ: City National Bank
555 S Flower St 21st Flr
Los Angeles CA 90071
310 888-6000

(P-11717)
CITY NATIONAL BANK
11677 San Vicente Blvd Ste 103, Los
Angeles (90049-5126)
PHONE................................310 855-7960
EMP: 94
SALES (corp-wide): 41.52B **Privately Held**
Web: www.cnb.com
SIC: 6021 National commercial banks
HQ: City National Bank
555 S Flower St 21st Flr
Los Angeles CA 90071
310 888-6000

(P-11718)
CITY NATIONAL BANK
Also Called: Sunset Doheny Office 6
9229 W Sunset Blvd Ste 100, Los Angeles
(90069-3408)
PHONE................................310 888-6800
Jeri O'shea, *Prin*
EMP: 77
SALES (corp-wide): 41.52B **Privately Held**
Web: www.cnb.com
SIC: 6021 National commercial banks
HQ: City National Bank
555 S Flower St 21st Flr
Los Angeles CA 90071
310 888-6000

(P-11719)
CITY NATIONAL BANK
Also Called: Head Office Banking 1
400 N Roxbury Dr, Beverly Hills
(90210-5000)
PHONE................................310 888-6150
Thomas Caballerd, *Brnch Mgr*
EMP: 154
SALES (corp-wide): 41.52B **Privately Held**
Web: www.cnb.com
SIC: 6021 National commercial banks
HQ: City National Bank
555 S Flower St 21st Flr
Los Angeles CA 90071
310 888-6000

(P-11720)
CITY NATIONAL BANK
Also Called: Encino Office 24
16133 Ventura Blvd Ste 100, Encino
(91436-2400)
PHONE................................818 905-4100
Arey Cakarian, *Mgr*
EMP: 103
SALES (corp-wide): 41.52B **Privately Held**
Web: www.cnb.com
SIC: 6021 National commercial banks
HQ: City National Bank
555 S Flower St 21st Flr
Los Angeles CA 90071
310 888-6000

(P-11721)
CITY NATIONAL BANK
Also Called: Residential Mortgage Ctr 39
2100 Park Pl Ste 150, El Segundo
(90245-4912)
P.O. Box 60938 (90060-0938)
PHONE................................310 297-6606
J W Lewis, *Sr VP*
EMP: 77
SALES (corp-wide): 41.52B **Privately Held**
Web: www.cnb.com
SIC: 6021 National commercial banks
HQ: City National Bank
555 S Flower St 21st Flr
Los Angeles CA 90071
310 888-6000

(P-11722)
CITY NATIONAL BANK
Also Called: C N B Real Estate Group
555 S Flower St Ste 2500, Los Angeles
(90071-2326)
P.O. Box 5581 (90209-5581)
PHONE................................310 888-6500
Sam Kaska, *Mgr*
EMP: 488
SALES (corp-wide): 41.52B **Privately Held**
Web: www.cnb.com
SIC: 6021 National commercial banks
HQ: City National Bank
555 S Flower St 21st Flr
Los Angeles CA 90071
310 888-6000

(P-11723)
CITY NATIONAL BANK
24200 Magic Mountain Pkwy Ste 140,
Valencia (91355-4888)
PHONE................................661 291-3160
Elizabeth Hopp, *Brnch Mgr*
EMP: 86
SALES (corp-wide): 41.52B **Privately Held**
Web: www.cnb.com
SIC: 6021 National commercial banks
HQ: City National Bank
555 S Flower St 21st Flr
Los Angeles CA 90071
310 888-6000

(P-11724)
CITY NATIONAL BANK
500 E Esplanade Dr Fl 2, Oxnard
(93036-0581)
PHONE................................805 981-2700
Alice Madrid, *Brnch Mgr*
EMP: 77
SALES (corp-wide): 41.52B **Privately Held**
Web: www.cnb.com
SIC: 6021 National commercial banks
HQ: City National Bank
555 S Flower St 21st Flr
Los Angeles CA 90071
310 888-6000

(P-11725)
CITY NATIONAL BANK
Also Called: C N B Commercial Banking Ctr
4275 Executive Sq Ste 101, La Jolla
(92037-1476)
PHONE................................858 642-4950
Steven Cusato, *Mgr*
EMP: 94
SALES (corp-wide): 41.52B **Privately Held**
Web: www.cnb.com
SIC: 6021 National commercial banks
HQ: City National Bank
555 S Flower St 21st Flr
Los Angeles CA 90071
310 888-6000

(P-11726)
CITY NATIONAL BANK
501 W Broadway Ste 100, San Diego
(92101-8594)
PHONE................................858 875-2030
Glenn Marshall, *Brnch Mgr*
EMP: 120
SALES (corp-wide): 41.52B **Privately Held**
Web: www.cnb.com
SIC: 6021 National commercial banks
HQ: City National Bank
555 S Flower St 21st Flr
Los Angeles CA 90071
310 888-6000

(P-11727)
CITY NATIONAL BANK
Also Called: C N B Commercial Banking Ctr
3484 Central Ave, Riverside (92506-2156)
PHONE................................951 276-8800
Bruce Wachtel, *Mgr*
EMP: 111
SALES (corp-wide): 41.52B **Privately Held**
Web: www.cnb.com
SIC: 6021 National commercial banks
HQ: City National Bank
555 S Flower St 21st Flr
Los Angeles CA 90071
310 888-6000

(P-11728)
CITY NATIONAL BANK
Also Called: C N B Commercial Banking Ctr
3633 Inland Empire Blvd Ste 100, Ontario
(91764-4921)
PHONE................................909 476-7999
Ernie Hwang, *Mgr*
EMP: 77
SALES (corp-wide): 41.52B **Privately Held**
Web: www.cnb.com
SIC: 6021 National commercial banks
HQ: City National Bank
555 S Flower St 21st Flr
Los Angeles CA 90071
310 888-6000

(P-11729)
CITY NATIONAL BANK (DH)
555 S Flower St Ste 2500, Los Angeles
(90071-2326)

PHONE................................310 888-6000
Howard Hammond, *Pr*
Kelly Coffey, *
Greg Carmichael, *
Richard Shier, *
Michael Pagano, *PRIVATE BANK SVCS*
▲ **EMP:** 300 **EST:** 1968
SQ FT: 80,000
SALES (est): 5.02B
SALES (corp-wide): 41.52B **Privately Held**
Web: www.cnb.com
SIC: 6021 6022 National commercial banks;
State commercial banks
HQ: Rbc Usa Holdco Corporation
3 World Financial Center
New York NY 10281
212 858-7200

(P-11730)
CITY NATIONAL BANK
18111 Von Karman Ave Ste 100, Irvine
(92612-7117)
PHONE................................949 223-4000
James Mccloskey, *Prin*
EMP: 214
SALES (corp-wide): 41.52B **Privately Held**
Web: www.cnb.com
SIC: 6021 National commercial banks
HQ: City National Bank
555 S Flower St 21st Flr
Los Angeles CA 90071
310 888-6000

(P-11731)
CITY NATIONAL CORPORATION
555 S Flower St, Los Angeles
(90071-2300)
▲ **EMP:** 3566
Web: www.abmparking.com
SIC: 6021 National commercial banks

(P-11732)
**CITY NATIONAL SECURITIES
INC**
400 N Roxbury Dr Ste 400, Beverly Hills
(90210-5021)
PHONE................................310 888-6393
Michael Nunnelee, *Pr*
EMP: 351 **EST:** 2005
SALES (est): 6.67MM
SALES (corp-wide): 41.52B **Privately Held**
Web: locations.cnb.com
SIC: 6021 National commercial banks
HQ: City National Bank
555 S Flower St 21st Flr
Los Angeles CA 90071
310 888-6000

(P-11733)
FIRST BANK AND TRUST
4040 Atlantic Ave, Long Beach
(90807-2908)
PHONE................................562 595-8775
Kennith P Maness, *Ch Bd*
David Goren, *
Ronald F Clark, *
Clement W Morin, *
EMP: 76 **EST:** 1982
SQ FT: 2,880
SALES (est): 1.8MM **Privately Held**
SIC: 6021 National trust companies with
deposits, commercial

(P-11734)
FIRST COMMUNITY BANCORP
5900 La Place Ct Ste 200, Carlsbad
(92008-8832)
PHONE................................858 756-3023
Andrew Colker, *Prin*
EMP: 99 **EST:** 2018

SALES (est): 1.25MM
SALES (corp-wide): 1.52B **Publicly Held**
SIC: 6021 National commercial banks
PA: Banc Of California, Inc.
11611 San Vcnte Blvd Ste
855 361-2262

(P-11735)
MANHATTAN BANCORP
2141 Rosecrans Ave Ste 1100, El Segundo
(90245-4761)
PHONE....................................310 606-8000
EMP: 187
SIC: 6021 National commercial banks

(P-11736)
MISSION COMMUNITY BANCORP
3380 S Higuera St, San Luis Obispo
(93401-6926)
PHONE....................................805 782-5000
EMP: 111
SIC: 6021 National commercial banks

(P-11737)
MUFG UNION BANK FOUNDATION
445 S Figueroa St, Los Angeles
(90071-1602)
PHONE....................................213 236-5000
Masashi Oka, Pr
John F Harrigan, *
W H Wofford, *
David Anderson, *
Charles D Kenny, *
EMP: 4200 EST: 1967
SALES (est): 8.3MM **Privately Held**
Web: www.mufgamericas.com
SIC: 6021 National commercial banks

(P-11738)
NORTHERN TRUST OF CALIFORNIA (INC)
Also Called: Northern Trust
201 S Lake Ave Ste 600, Pasadena
(91101-3016)
EMP: 285
SIC: 6021 National commercial banks

(P-11739)
PACIFIC WESTERN BANK
Also Called: Rancho Santa Fe
6110 El Tordo, Rancho Santa Fe (92067)
PHONE....................................858 756-3023
EMP: 262
SALES (corp-wide): 1.52B **Publicly Held**
Web: www.pacwest.com
SIC: 6021 6153 National commercial banks;
Purchasers of accounts receivable and
commercial paper
HQ: Pacific Western Bank
9320 Wilshire Blvd
Beverly Hills CA 90212
310 887-8500

(P-11740)
PACWEST BANCORP
9701 Wilshire Blvd Ste 700, Beverly Hills
(90212-2007)
PHONE....................................310 887-8500
EMP: 263
Web: investors.bancofcal.com
SIC: 6021 National commercial banks

(P-11741)
WELLS FARGO SECURITIES LLC
Also Called: Barrington Associates
1800 Century Park E Ste 1100, Los Angeles
(90067-1519)

PHONE....................................310 479-3500
Jim Freedman, Brnch Mgr
EMP: 1251
SALES (corp-wide): 115.34B **Publicly Held**
Web: www.wellsfargo.com
SIC: 6021 National commercial banks
HQ: Wells Fargo Securities, Llc
550 S Tryon St
Charlotte NC 28202

6022 State Commercial Banks

(P-11742)
1ST CENTURY BANCSHARES INC
1875 Century Park E Ste 1400, Los Angeles
(90067-2572)
PHONE....................................310 270-9500
EMP: 71
Web: www.1stcenturybank.com
SIC: 6022 State commercial banks

(P-11743)
AMERICAN BUSINESS BANK
970 W 190th St Ste 850, Torrance
(90502-1059)
PHONE....................................310 808-1200
Debbie Dm, Mgr
EMP: 110
SALES (corp-wide): 169.05MM **Publicly Held**
Web: www.cbbank.com
SIC: 6022 State trust companies accepting
deposits, commercial
PA: American Business Bank
400 S Hope Ste 300
213 430-4000

(P-11744)
AMERICAN BUSINESS BANK
3633 Inland Empire Blvd Ste 720, Ontario
(91764-7979)
PHONE....................................909 919-2040
Elaine Lopez, Brnch Mgr
EMP: 109
SALES (corp-wide): 169.05MM **Publicly Held**
Web: www.americanbb.bank
SIC: 6022 State commercial banks
PA: American Business Bank
400 S Hope Ste 300
213 430-4000

(P-11745)
AMERICAN SECURITY BANK
1401 Dove St Ste 100, Newport Beach
(92660-2425)
PHONE....................................949 440-5200
EMP: 90
SIC: 6022 State commercial banks

(P-11746)
BENEFICIAL STATE BANK
3626 E 1st St, Los Angeles (90063-2326)
PHONE....................................323 264-3310
Bob Hughes, Pr
EMP: 73
Web: www.beneficialstatebank.com
SIC: 6022 State commercial banks
HQ: Beneficial State Bank
1438 Webster St Ste 100
Oakland CA 94612

(P-11747)
BUSA SERVICING INC (PA)
787 W 5th St, Los Angeles (90071-2003)
PHONE....................................310 203-3400
Manuel Sanchez Lugo, Ch Bd

Rebecca Macieira-kaufmann, CEO
Thomas Levine, Senior Vice President
Legal*
Roger Johnston, *
Francisco Moreno, *
▲ EMP: 200 EST: 1963
SALES (est): 5.31MM
SALES (corp-wide): 5.31MM **Privately Held**
Web: www.citigroup.com
SIC: 6022 State commercial banks

(P-11748)
CALIFORNIA BANK & TRUST
11622 El Camino Real, San Diego
(92130-2049)
PHONE....................................858 793-7400
David Blackford, CEO
Gene Louie, *
Steven Borg, *
Frank Lee, *
◆ EMP: 1910 EST: 1952
SALES (est): 558.62MM
SALES (corp-wide): 4.62B **Publicly Held**
SIC: 6022 State trust companies accepting
deposits, commercial
HQ: Zions Bancorporation
1 S Main St Fl 15
Salt Lake City UT 84133
801 844-7637

(P-11749)
CALIFORNIA REPUBLIC BANK
18400 Von Karman Ave Ste 1100, Irvine
(92612-0517)
P.O. Box 25085 (92799-5085)
PHONE....................................949 270-9700
EMP: 270
SIC: 6022 State commercial banks

(P-11750)
CAPITALSOURCE BANK
130 S State College Blvd, Brea
(92821-5807)
P.O. Box 2485 (92822-2485)
PHONE....................................714 989-4600
EMP: 250
SIC: 6022 State commercial banks

(P-11751)
CATHAY BANK (HQ)
777 N Broadway, Los Angeles
(90012-2819)
PHONE....................................626 279-3698
Dunson K Cheng, Ch Bd
Perry P Oei, *
James R Brewer, *
Heng W Chen, *
Irwin Wong, *
▲ EMP: 125 EST: 1962
SALES (est): 1.3B **Publicly Held**
Web: www.cathaybank.com
SIC: 6022 State trust companies accepting
deposits, commercial
PA: Cathay General Bancorp
777 N Broadway

(P-11752)
CATHAY GENERAL BANCORP (PA)
Also Called: Bancorp
777 N Broadway, Los Angeles
(90012-2819)
PHONE....................................213 625-4700
Chang M Liu, Pr
Dunson K Cheng, Ex Ch Bd
Anthony M Tang, V Ch Bd
Peter Wu, V Ch Bd
Heng W Chen, Ex VP
EMP: 129 EST: 1990

SALES (est): 1.31B **Publicly Held**
Web: www.cathaybank.com
SIC: 6022 State commercial banks

(P-11753)
CIT BANK NA
12401 Wilshire Blvd, Los Angeles
(90025-1085)
PHONE....................................310 820-9650
Leonard Rampulla, Brnch Mgr
EMP: 79
SALES (corp-wide): 22.47B **Publicly Held**
Web: www.firstcitizens.com
SIC: 6022 State commercial banks
HQ: Cit Bank, N.A.
75 N Fair Oaks Ave Ste C
Pasadena CA 91103

(P-11754)
CIT BANK NA
7320 Firestone Blvd Ste 101, Downey
(90241-4159)
PHONE....................................323 838-6881
Jonathan Silva, Brnch Mgr
EMP: 79
SALES (corp-wide): 22.47B **Publicly Held**
Web: www.firstcitizens.com
SIC: 6022 State commercial banks
HQ: Cit Bank, N.A.
75 N Fair Oaks Ave Ste C
Pasadena CA 91103

(P-11755)
CIT BANK NA
401 Wilshire Blvd, Santa Monica
(90401-1416)
PHONE....................................310 394-1640
EMP: 79
SALES (corp-wide): 22.47B **Publicly Held**
Web: www.firstcitizens.com
SIC: 6022 State commercial banks
HQ: Cit Bank, N.A.
75 N Fair Oaks Ave Ste C
Pasadena CA 91103

(P-11756)
CIT BANK NA
Also Called: Onewest Bank
10784 Jefferson Blvd, Culver City
(90230-4933)
PHONE....................................310 559-7222
Peter Smith, Brnch Mgr
EMP: 79
SALES (corp-wide): 22.47B **Publicly Held**
Web: www.first.bank
SIC: 6022 State commercial banks
HQ: Cit Bank, N.A.
75 N Fair Oaks Ave Ste C
Pasadena CA 91103

(P-11757)
CIT BANK NA
888 Prospect St Ste 140, La Jolla
(92037-4268)
PHONE....................................858 454-8800
Patrick Dunn, Brnch Mgr
EMP: 79
SALES (corp-wide): 22.47B **Publicly Held**
Web: www.firstcitizens.com
SIC: 6022 State commercial banks
HQ: Cit Bank, N.A.
75 N Fair Oaks Ave Ste C
Pasadena CA 91103

(P-11758)
CITIZENS BUSINESS BANK (HQ)
701 N Haven Ave Ste 280, Ontario
(91764-4920)
P.O. Box 51000 (91761)
PHONE....................................909 980-4030

TOLL FREE: 877
Christopher D Myers, *Pr*
Hal W Oswalt, *
E Allen Nicholson, *
David C Harvey, *
David F Farnsworth, *CCO*
▲ **EMP:** 150 **EST:** 1973
SQ FT: 23,000
SALES (est): 664.92MM **Publicly Held**
Web: www.cbbank.com
SIC: 6022 State trust companies accepting
deposits, commercial
PA: Cvb Financial Corp.
701 N Haven Ave Ste 350

(P-11759)
COMMUNITY BANK
460 Sierra Madre Villa Ave, Pasadena
(91107-2967)
PHONE..............................626 577-1700
▲ **EMP:** 300
Web: www.cbbank.com
SIC: 6022 6029 State trust companies
accepting deposits, commercial;
Commercial banks, nec

(P-11760)
COMMUNITY WEST BANCSHARES
Also Called: Cwbc
445 Pine Ave, Goleta (93117-3709)
PHONE..............................805 692-5821
EMP: 124
SALES (est): 61.27MM **Privately Held**
Web: ir.cvcb.com
SIC: 6022 State commercial banks

(P-11761)
EAST WEST BANCORP INC (PA)
Also Called: East West
135 N Los Robles Ave Fl 7, Pasadena
(91101-4525)
PHONE..............................626 768-6000
Dominic Ng, *Ch Bd*
Douglas P Krause, *Vice Chairman*
Parker Shi, *Ex VP*
Christopher Del Moral-niles, *Ex VP*
Irene H Oh, *CRO*
◆ **EMP:** 268 **EST:** 1998
SALES (est): 3.99B
SALES (corp-wide): 3.99B **Publicly Held**
Web: www.eastwestbank.com
SIC: 6022 State commercial banks

(P-11762)
EAST WEST BANK (HQ)
135 N Los Robles Ave Ste 100, Pasadena
(01101-4626)
PHONE..............................626 768-6000
Dominic Ng, *CEO*
Donald S Chow, *Ex VP*
Douglas P Krause, *Ex VP*
Thomas J Tolda, *CFO*
Irene Oh, *Sr VP*
◆ **EMP:** 300 **EST:** 1973
SQ FT: 18,000
SALES (est): 3.99B
SALES (corp-wide): 3.99B **Publicly Held**
Web: www.eastwestbank.com
SIC: 6022 State commercial banks
PA: East West Bancorp, Inc.
135 N Los Robles Ave Fl 7
626 768-6000

(P-11763)
ENTERPRISE BANK & TRUST
11939 Rancho Bernardo Rd Ste 200, San
Diego (92128-2075)
PHONE..............................858 432-7000
Stephen Marsh, *Brnch Mgr*

EMP: 118
Web: www.enterprisebank.com
SIC: 6022 State trust companies accepting
deposits, commercial
HQ: Enterprise Bank & Trust
150 N Meramec Ave Ste 300
Saint Louis MO 63105
314 725-5500

(P-11764)
ENTERPRISE BANK & TRUST
17785 Center Court Dr N # 750, Cerritos
(90703-9310)
PHONE..............................562 345-9092
EMP: 184
SIC: 6022 State trust companies accepting
deposits, commercial
HQ: Enterprise Bank & Trust
150 N Meramec Ave Ste 300
Saint Louis MO 63105
314 725-5500

(P-11765)
FARMERS MERCHANTS BNK LONG BCH (HQ)
Also Called: F&M Bank
302 Pine Ave, Long Beach (90802-2326)
P.O. Box 1370 (90801-1370)
PHONE..............................562 437-0011
W Henry Walker, *CEO*
Kenneth G Walker, *
John Hinrichs, *
Danile K Walker, *
Michael Hess, *
▲ **EMP:** 130 **EST:** 1907
SQ FT: 150,000
SALES (est): 428.4MM **Privately Held**
Web: www.fmb.com
SIC: 6022 6029 State trust companies
accepting deposits, commercial;
Commercial banks, nec
PA: Palomar Enterprises, Llc
302 Pine Ave

(P-11766)
FB CORPORATION
1211 E Valley Blvd, Alhambra (91801-5235)
PHONE..............................626 300-0880
Tim Wang, *Mgr*
EMP: 261
SALES (corp-wide): 427.66MM **Privately
Held**
Web: www.first.bank
SIC: 6022 State commercial banks
PA: Fb Corporation
135 N Meramec Ave
314 854-4600

(P-11767)
FIRST FOUNDATION INC (PA)
Also Called: Ffi
18101 Von Karman Ave Ste 700, Irvine
(92612-0145)
PHONE..............................949 202-4160
Scott F Kavanaugh, *CEO*
Ulrich E Keller Junior, *Ex Ch Bd*
Amy Djou, *Interim Chief Financial Officer*
Kelly Rentzel, *Ex VP*
EMP: 160 **EST:** 2006
SALES (est): 623.04MM **Publicly Held**
Web: www.firstfoundationinc.com
SIC: 6022 State commercial banks

(P-11768)
HERITAGE OAKS BANCORP
1222 Vine St, Paso Robles (93446-2268)
PHONE..............................805 369-5200
EMP: 283
Web: www.heritageoaksbancorp.com

SIC: 6022 State commercial banks

(P-11769)
HERITAGE OAKS BANK
1222 Vine St, Paso Robles (93446-2268)
PHONE..............................805 239-5200
EMP: 220
SIC: 6022 State commercial banks

(P-11770)
IMPERIAL CAPITAL BANCORP INC (PA)
10618 Edenoaks St, San Diego
(92131-3222)
PHONE..............................858 551-0511
Joseph W Kiley Iii, *Pr*
Anthony A Rusnak, *COO*
EMP: 191 **EST:** 1996
SQ FT: 21,903
SALES (est): 4.34MM **Privately Held**
SIC: 6022 State commercial banks

(P-11771)
MERCHANTS BANK CALIFORNIA N A
1 Civic Plaza Dr Ste 100, Carson
(90745-7958)
P.O. Box 6008 (90806-0008)
PHONE..............................310 549-4350
Joyce Yamasaki, *CEO*
Daniel K Roberts, *
EMP: 75 **EST:** 1989
SQ FT: 5,551
SALES (est): 10.86MM **Privately Held**
Web: www.merchantsbankca.com
SIC: 6022 State commercial banks

(P-11772)
MORGAN STNLEY SMITH BARNEY LLC
74199 El Paseo Ste 201, Palm Desert
(92260-4151)
PHONE..............................760 568-3500
Anthony Maddlina, *Mgr*
EMP: 117
SALES (corp-wide): 96.19B **Publicly Held**
Web: www.morganstanley.com
SIC: 6022 State commercial banks
HQ: Morgan Stanley Smith Barney, Llc
1585 Broadway Ave
New York NY 10036

(P-11773)
PACIFIC PREMIER BANCORP INC
3403 10th St Ste 100, Riverside
(92501-3661)
PHONE..............................951 274-2400
Joe Servi, *Brnch Mgr*
EMP: 350
Web: www.ppbi.com
SIC: 6022 State commercial banks
PA: Pacific Premier Bancorp, Inc.
17901 Von Krman Ave Ste 1

(P-11774)
PACIFIC PREMIER BANCORP INC
102 E 6th St Ste 100, Corona (92879-1450)
PHONE..............................951 272-3590
Kerry Pendergast, *Brnch Mgr*
EMP: 158
Web: www.ppbi.com
SIC: 6022 State commercial banks
PA: Pacific Premier Bancorp, Inc.
17901 Von Krman Ave Ste 1

(P-11775)
PACIFIC PREMIER BANCORP INC (PA)
17901 Von Karman Ave Ste 1200, Irvine
(92614-5248)
PHONE..............................949 864-8000
Steven R Gardner, *Ch Bd*
EMP: 123 **EST:** 1983
SALES (est): 714.07MM **Publicly Held**
Web: www.ppbi.com
SIC: 6022 State commercial banks

(P-11776)
PCB BANK (HQ)
3701 Wilshire Blvd Ste 900, Los Angeles
(90010-2871)
PHONE..............................213 210-2000
Hae Young Cho, *CEO*
Henry Kim, *
Heo Young Cho, *
Andrew Chung, *
Mike Kim, *Chief Lending Officer*
▲ **EMP:** 152 **EST:** 2003
SALES (est): 161.85MM
SALES (corp-wide): 161.86MM **Publicly
Held**
Web: www.mypcbbank.com
SIC: 6022 State commercial banks
PA: Pcb Bancorp
3701 Wlshire Blvd Ste 100
213 210-2000

(P-11777)
SEACOAST CMMERCE BANC HOLDINGS
11939 Rancho Bernardo Rd, San Diego
(92128-2073)
PHONE..............................858 432-7000
Richard Sanborn, *CEO*
Scott R Andrews, *CAO*
S Alan Rosen, *Admn*
EMP: 200 **EST:** 2014
SALES (est): 1.44MM **Publicly Held**
Web: www.scbholdings.com
SIC: 6022 State commercial banks
PA: Enterprise Financial Services Corp
150 N Meramec Ave

(P-11778)
SMBC MANUBANK (DH)
515 S Figueroa St 4th Fl, Los Angeles
(90071-3301)
PHONE..............................213 489-6200
Mitsugu Serizawa, *CEO*
Naresh Sheth, *
Adrian Danescu, *
Ted Mergenthaler, *
Leslie A Lyons, *
▲ **EMP:** 164 **EST:** 1962
SQ FT: 69,206
SALES (est): 297.09MM **Privately Held**
Web: www.smbcmanubank.com
SIC: 6022 State commercial banks
HQ: Smbc Americas Holdings, Inc.
277 Park Ave
New York NY 10172

(P-11779)
STANDARD CHARTERED BANK
601 S Figueroa St Ste 2775, Los Angeles
(90017-5877)
PHONE..............................626 639-8000
Jim Mc Cabe, *CEO*
EMP: 84
SALES (corp-wide): 38.29B **Privately Held**
Web: www.sc.com
SIC: 6022 6282 6029 State trust companies
accepting deposits, commercial; Investment
advisory service; Commercial banks, nec
HQ: Standard Chartered Bank
1 Basinghall Avenue

PRODUCTS & SVCS

London EC2V
207 885-8888

(P-11780)
WILSHIRE BANCORP INC
3200 Wilshire Blvd, Los Angeles
(90010-1333)
PHONE..............................213 387-3200
EMP: 547
SIC: 6022 State commercial banks

(P-11781)
WILSHIRE BANK
Also Called: Wilshire State Bank
3200 Wilshire Blvd Ste 1400, Los Angeles
(90010-1325)
PHONE..............................213 427-1000
▲ EMP: 349
SIC: 6022 State commercial banks

6029 Commercial Banks, Nec

(P-11782)
BANK OF MANHATTAN
2141 Rosecrans Ave Ste 1100, El Segundo
(90245-4761)
PHONE..............................310 606-8000
EMP: 187
SIC: 6029 Commercial banks, nec

(P-11783)
OPUS BANK
19900 Macarthur Blvd Ste 1200, Irvine
(92612-8427)
PHONE..............................949 250-9800
TOLL FREE: 800
▲ EMP: 607
Web: www.ppbi.com
SIC: 6029 Commercial banks, nec

(P-11784)
PLAZA BANK
18200 Von Karman Ave Ste 500, Irvine
(92612-7145)
PHONE..............................949 502-4300
EMP: 78
Web: www.plazabank.com
SIC: 6029 Commercial banks, nec

6035 Federal Savings Institutions

(P-11785)
GREENBOX LOANS INC
Also Called: Greenbox
3250 Wilshire Blvd Ste 1900, Los Angeles
(90010-1616)
PHONE..............................800 919-1086
Raymond Eshaghian, *CEO*
EMP: 87 EST: 2000
SALES (est): 16.87MM **Privately Held**
Web: www.greenboxloans.com
SIC: 6035 6162 Federal savings and loan
associations; Loan correspondents

(P-11786)
ONEWEST BANK GROUP LLC
888 E Walnut St, Pasadena (91101-1895)
P.O. Box 7056 (91109-7056)
PHONE..............................626 535-4870
EMP: 850
SIC: 6035 Federal savings banks

(P-11787)
PACIFIC TRUST BANK
18500 Von Karman Ave Ste 1100, Irvine
(92612-0546)

P.O. Box 61452 (92602-6048)
PHONE..............................949 236-5211
Robert M Franko, *CEO*
Al Majors, *
Hans Ganz, *
James P Sheehy, *
Marangal Domingo, *
EMP: 107 EST: 1941
SQ FT: 12,100
SALES (est): 83.94MM
SALES (corp-wide): 1.52B **Publicly Held**
Web: www.bancofcal.com
SIC: 6035 Federal savings banks
PA: Banc Of California, Inc.
11611 San Vcnte Blvd Ste
855 361-2262

(P-11788)
PAN AMERICAN BANK FSB
18191 Von Karman Ave Ste 300, Irvine
(92612-7106)
PHONE..............................949 224-1917
Jim Vagim, *Pr*
EMP: 350 EST: 1994
SQ FT: 20,000
SALES (est): 96.49MM
SALES (corp-wide): 893.2MM **Publicly
Held**
SIC: 6035 Federal savings and loan
associations
HQ: Vroom Automotive Finance Corporation
1071 Camelback St Ste 100
Newport Beach CA 92660
949 224-1226

(P-11789)
PFF BANCORP INC (PA)
2058 N Mills Ave Pmb 139, Claremont
(91711-2812)
PHONE..............................213 683-6393
Kevin Mccarthy, *Pr*
Robert W Burwell, *Ch Bd*
EMP: 852 EST: 1995
SALES (est): 6.58MM **Privately Held**
SIC: 6035 Federal savings and loan
associations

6061 Federal Credit Unions

(P-11790)
**ALTAONE FEDERAL CREDIT
UNION (PA)**
Also Called: Alta One Fcu
701 S China Lake Blvd, Ridgecrest
(93555-5027)
P.O. Box 1209 (93556-1209)
PHONE..............................760 371-7000
Stephanie Sievers, *Pr*
Denise Mattice, *
EMP: 114 EST: 1947
SQ FT: 33,000
SALES (est): 19.98MM
SALES (corp-wide): 19.98MM **Privately
Held**
Web: www.altaone.org
SIC: 6061 Federal credit unions

(P-11791)
**AMERICAN FIRST CREDIT
UNION (PA)**
6 Pointe Dr Ste 400, Brea (92821-6322)
PHONE..............................562 691-1112
TOLL FREE: 800
Jon Shigematsu, *Prin*
Jon Shigematsu, *CEO*
Julie Glance, *
Brian Thompson, *CAO**
EMP: 96 EST: 1956
SALES (est): 49.43MM

SALES (corp-wide): 49.43MM **Privately
Held**
Web: www.amerfirst.org
SIC: 6061 Federal credit unions

(P-11792)
**ARROWHEAD CENTRAL
CREDIT UNION (PA)**
Also Called: ARROWHEAD CREDIT UNION
8686 Haven Ave, Rancho Cucamonga
(91730-9109)
P.O. Box 4100 (91729-4100)
PHONE..............................866 212-4333
Darin Woinarowicz, *CEO*
Marie A Alonzo, *Ch*
Susan Conjurski, *Ex VP*
Doug Hallen, *Treas*
Raymond Mesler, *CFO*
EMP: 301 EST: 1949
SQ FT: 40,000
SALES (est): 120.31MM
SALES (corp-wide): 120.31MM **Privately
Held**
Web: www.arrowheadcu.org
SIC: 6061 Federal credit unions

(P-11793)
CALIFORNIA CREDIT UNION
503 Telegraph Canyon Rd, Chula Vista
(91910-6436)
P.O. Box 85833 (92186-5833)
PHONE..............................858 769-7369
Lisa Barker, *Prin*
EMP: 72
SALES (corp-wide): 204.85MM **Privately
Held**
Web: www.ccu.com
SIC: 6061 Federal credit unions
PA: The California Credit Union
701 N Brand Blvd Fl 7
818 291-6700

(P-11794)
**CREDIT UNION SOUTHERN CAL
(PA)**
8101 E Kaiser Blvd Ste 300, Anaheim
(92808-2261)
P.O. Box 200 (90608-0200)
PHONE..............................562 698-8326
Dave Gunderson, *Pr*
Peter Putnam, *CFO*
Ed Fost, *COO*
Debbie Childs, *Ex VP*
▲ EMP: 77 EST: 1954
SQ FT: 12,000
SALES (est): 179.48MM
SALES (corp-wide): 179.48MM **Privately
Held**
Web: www.cusocal.org
SIC: 6061 Federal credit unions

(P-11795)
F & A FEDERAL CREDIT UNION
2625 Corporate Pl, Monterey Park
(91754-7645)
P.O. Box 30831 (90030-0831)
PHONE..............................213 268-1226
Richard Andrews, *Pr*
EMP: 70 EST: 1936
SQ FT: 43,000
SALES (est): 73.44MM **Privately Held**
Web: www.fafcu.org
SIC: 6061 Federal credit unions

(P-11796)
**FARMERS INSUR GROUP
FDRAL CR U (PA)**
Also Called: Farmers Insurance
2255 N Ontario St Ste 320, Burbank
(91504-3191)

P.O. Box 2723 (90509)
PHONE..............................323 209-6000
Mark Herter, *CEO*
Laszlo Haredy, *
Jan Larson, *
Laura Campbell, *
EMP: 70 EST: 1936
SQ FT: 12,000
SALES (est): 102.3MM
SALES (corp-wide): 102.3MM **Privately
Held**
Web: www.figfcu.org
SIC: 6061 Federal credit unions

(P-11797)
**FINANCIAL PARTNERS CREDIT
UN (PA)**
Also Called: Financial Partners Credit Un
7800 Imperial Hwy, Downey (90242-3457)
P.O. Box 7005 (90241-7005)
PHONE..............................562 904-3000
John Crites, *Ch Bd*
Nader Moghaddam, *
Michael Patterson, *
Mary Torsney, *
Wanda Williams, *
EMP: 73 EST: 1937
SQ FT: 32,000
SALES (est): 112.97MM
SALES (corp-wide): 112.97MM **Privately
Held**
Web: www.fpcu.org
SIC: 6061 Federal credit unions

(P-11798)
**FIREFIGHTERS FIRST CREDIT
UN (PA)**
1520 W Colorado Blvd, Pasadena
(91105-1413)
PHONE..............................323 254-1700
Dixie Abramian, *CEO*
EMP: 138 EST: 1935
SALES (est): 98.95MM
SALES (corp-wide): 98.95MM **Privately
Held**
Web: www.firefightersfirstcu.org
SIC: 6061 Federal credit unions

(P-11799)
**FIRST ENTERTAINMENT CREDIT
UN (PA)**
6735 Forest Lawn Dr Ste 100, Los Angeles
(90068-1055)
P.O. Box 100 (90078-0100)
PHONE..............................323 851-3673
Charles A Bruen, *Pr*
Lucy Wander-pema, *Ch*
Dennis Tange, *
Michael Edwards, *Vice Chairman**
Irwin Jacobson, *
EMP: 80 EST: 1998
SQ FT: 57,000
SALES (est): 100.25MM
SALES (corp-wide): 100.25MM **Privately
Held**
Web: www.firstent.org
SIC: 6061 Federal credit unions

(P-11800)
**FIRST FINANCIAL FEDERAL CR
UN**
650 Sierra Madre Villa Ave Ste 300,
Pasadena (91107-2073)
PHONE..............................800 537-8491
Dietmar Huesch, *CFO*
EMP: 140 EST: 1974
SALES (est): 5.31MM **Privately Held**
SIC: 6061 Federal credit unions

▲ = Import ▼ = Export
◆ = Import/Export

(P-11801)

FRONTWAVE CREDIT UNION (PA)

1278 Rocky Point Dr, Oceanside
(92056-5867)
PHONE..................760 430-7511
Bill Birnie, *Pr*
Shilpa Edlabadkar, *
Paul Leonhardt, *CLO**
Jennifer Williams, *
EMP: 107 **EST:** 1953
SQ FT: 22,000
SALES (est): 31.72MM
SALES (corp-wide): 31.72MM **Privately Held**
Web: www.frontwavecu.com
SIC: 6061 Federal credit unions

(P-11802)

KINECTA FEDERAL CREDIT UNION (PA)

Also Called: Kinecta
1440 Rosecrans Ave, Manhattan Beach
(90266-3702)
P.O. Box 10003 (90266)
PHONE..................310 643-5400
Keith Sultemeier, *CEO*
Teresa Freeborn, *
Joseph E Whitaker, *
Steven J Glouberman, *
Sharon Moseley, *
EMP: 250 **EST:** 1940
SQ FT: 80,000
SALES (est): 324.27MM
SALES (corp-wide): 324.27MM **Privately Held**
Web: www.kinecta.org
SIC: 6061 Federal credit unions

(P-11803)

LOGIX FEDERAL CREDIT UNION (PA)

2340 N Hollywood Way, Burbank
(91505-1124)
P.O. Box 4130 (91310-4130)
PHONE..................888 718-5328
Ana Fonseca, *CEO*
Jan Franklin, *
Tim Boland, *
Dave Styler, *
Ana Fonseca, *CFO*
EMP: 210 **EST:** 1937
SQ FT: 75,000
SALES (est): 230.72MM
SALES (corp-wide): 230.72MM **Privately Held**
Web: www.logixbanking.com
SIC: 6061 Federal credit unions

(P-11804)

LOS ANGELES FEDERAL CREDIT UN (PA)

Also Called: LOS ANGELES FEDERAL CREDIT UNI
300 S Glendale Ave Ste 100, Glendale
(91205-1752)
PHONE..................818 242-8640
John T Dea, *CEO*
Richard Lie, *
Leta Cook, *
Anthony Cuevas, *
EMP: 100 **EST:** 1936
SQ FT: 40,000
SALES (est): 54.64MM
SALES (corp-wide): 54.64MM **Privately Held**
Web: www.lafcu.org
SIC: 6061 Federal credit unions

(P-11805)

MISSION FEDERAL CREDIT UNION

4250 Clairemont Mesa Blvd Ste B, San Diego (92117-2747)
P.O. Box 910557 (92191-0557)
PHONE..................858 531-5106
EMP: 218
SALES (corp-wide): 119.62MM **Privately Held**
Web: www.missionfed.com
SIC: 6061 Federal credit unions
PA: Mission Federal Credit Union
5785 Oberlin Dr Ste 312
858 546-2184

(P-11806)

MISSION FEDERAL CREDIT UNION

5500 Grossmont Center Dr Ste 113, La Mesa (91942-3070)
PHONE..................858 524-2850
EMP: 125
SALES (corp-wide): 119.62MM **Privately Held**
Web: www.missionfed.com
SIC: 6061 Federal credit unions
PA: Mission Federal Credit Union
5785 Oberlin Dr Ste 312
858 546-2184

(P-11807)

MISSION FEDERAL CREDIT UNION (PA)

5785 Oberlin Dr Ste 312, San Diego
(92121-3752)
PHONE..................858 546-2184
Debra Schwartz, *CEO*
Ron Araujo, *CFO*
Sheila Carpizo, *Acctg Mgr*
EMP: 75 **EST:** 2015
SQ FT: 59,956
SALES (est): 119.62MM
SALES (corp-wide): 119.62MM **Privately Held**
Web: www.missionfed.com
SIC: 6061 Federal credit unions

(P-11808)

MISSION FEDERAL SERVICES LLC (PA)

10325 Meanley Dr, San Diego
(92131-3011)
P.O. Box 919023 (92191-9023)
PHONE..................858 524-2850
Debra Schwartz, *CEO*
Rooc Hartley, *
Richard Hartley, *
Gary M Devan Senior, *Vice-President Information Systems*
Elaine Ziegler, *Senior Vice President Human Resources**
EMP: 150 **EST:** 1961
SQ FT: 55,000
SALES (est): 278.02MM
SALES (corp-wide): 278.02MM **Privately Held**
Web: www.missionfed.com
SIC: 6061 Federal credit unions

(P-11809)

NUVISION FINCL FEDERAL CR UN (PA)

7812 Edinger Ave Ste 100, Huntington Beach (92647-3727)
P.O. Box 1220 (92647-1220)
PHONE..................714 375-8000
Roger Ballard, *CEO*
John Afdem, *CFO*

Robert Geraci, *Treas*
EMP: 137 **EST:** 1935
SALES (est): 98.79MM
SALES (corp-wide): 98.79MM **Privately Held**
Web: www.nuvisionfederal.com
SIC: 6061 Federal credit unions

(P-11810)

ORANGE COUNTYS CREDIT UNION (PA)

1721 E Saint Andrew Pl, Santa Ana
(92705-4934)
P.O. Box 11777 (92711-1777)
PHONE..................714 755-5900
Lucy Ito, *Interim Chief Executive Officer*
Dan Dillon, *
EMP: 157 **EST:** 1938
SALES (est): 118.83MM
SALES (corp-wide): 118.83MM **Privately Held**
Web: www.orangecountyscu.org
SIC: 6061 Federal credit unions

(P-11811)

PARTNERS FEDERAL CREDIT UNION (PA)

100 N First St Ste 400, Burbank
(91502-1818)
PHONE..................800 948-6677
Ricky Otey, *Pr*
Rick Wise, *
EMP: 73 **EST:** 1968
SQ FT: 26,000
SALES (est): 147.4MM
SALES (corp-wide): 147.4MM **Privately Held**
Web: www.partnersfcu.org
SIC: 6061 6163 Federal credit unions; Loan brokers

(P-11812)

RIZE FEDERAL CREDIT UNION (PA)

Also Called: SCE Fcu
12701 Schabarum Ave, Baldwin Park
(91706-6807)
P.O. Box 8017 (91734-2317)
PHONE..................626 960-6888
Dennis Huber, *CEO*
George Poitou, *
Daniel Rader, *
Tony Salse, *
EMP: 90 **EST:** 1952
SQ FT: 30,000
SALES (est): 61.12MM
SALES (corp-wide): 61.12MM **Privately Held**
Web: www.scefcu.org
SIC: 6061 Federal credit unions

(P-11813)

SAN DIEGO COUNTY CREDIT UNION (PA)

Also Called: Sdccu
6545 Sequence Dr, San Diego
(92121-4363)
PHONE..................877 732-2848
Irene Oberbauer, *Pr*
Robert Marchand, *
Heather Moshier, *
Theresa Halleck, *
Tracey Curran, *
▲ **EMP:** 239 **EST:** 1938
SQ FT: 50,000
SALES (est): 447.68MM
SALES (corp-wide): 447.68MM **Privately Held**
Web: www.sdccu.com

SIC: 6061 Federal credit unions

(P-11814)

SCHOOLSFIRST FEDERAL CREDIT UN

Also Called: Consumer Loan Dept
15442 Del Amo Ave, Tustin (92780-6445)
P.O. Box 11547 (92711-1547)
PHONE..................480 777-5995
Rudy Tafoya, *Dir*
EMP: 79
SQ FT: 61,058
SALES (corp-wide): 1.24B **Privately Held**
Web: www.schoolsfirstfcu.org
SIC: 6061 Federal credit unions
PA: Schoolsfirst Federal Credit Union
2115 N Broadway
714 258-4000

(P-11815)

SCHOOLSFIRST FEDERAL CREDIT UN (PA)

2115 N Broadway, Santa Ana (92706-2613)
P.O. Box 11547 (92711-1547)
PHONE..................714 258-4000
Bill Cheney, *CEO*
Jose Lara, *
Jim Phillips, *
Jill Meznarich, *Chief Auditor**
EMP: 270 **EST:** 1934
SALES (est): 1.24B
SALES (corp-wide): 1.24B **Privately Held**
Web: www.schoolsfirstfcu.org
SIC: 6061 Federal credit unions

(P-11816)

STRATA FEDERAL CREDIT UNION

1717 Truxtun Ave, Bakersfield
(93301-5102)
P.O. Box 1667 (93302-1667)
PHONE..................661 327-9461
Brandon Ivie, *CEO*
EMP: 71 **EST:** 1949
SQ FT: 17,000
SALES (est): 18.56MM **Privately Held**
Web: www.kernfcu.org
SIC: 6061 6163 Federal credit unions; Loan brokers

(P-11817)

TELESIS COMMUNITY CREDIT UNION (PA)

9301 Winnetka Ave, Chatsworth
(91311-6069)
PHONE..................818 885-1226
Grace Mayo, *Pr*
Jean Faenza, *
EMP: 90 **EST:** 1993
SQ FT: 17,000
SALES (est): 1.27MM **Privately Held**
Web: www.telesiscu.com
SIC: 6061 6163 Federal credit unions; Loan brokers

(P-11818)

UNITED SVCS AMER FEDERAL CR UN (PA)

Also Called: USA Federal Credit Union
9999 Willow Creek Rd, San Diego
(92131-1117)
PHONE..................858 831-8100
TOLL FREE: 800
Martin Cassell, *Pr*
Ron Davis, *
Jim Bedinger, *
EMP: 90 **EST:** 1953
SQ FT: 42,000
SALES (est): 5.15MM

SALES (corp-wide): 5.15MM **Privately Held**
Web: www.navyfederal.org
SIC: 6061 Federal credit unions

(P-11819)
UNIVERSITY CREDIT UNION
1500 S Sepulveda Blvd, Los Angeles (90025-3312)
PHONE...............................310 477-6628
Charles Bumbarger, *Pr*
Tristan Dion Chen, *CMO**
EMP: 104 **EST:** 1945
SALES (est): 60.52MM **Privately Held**
Web: www.ucu.org
SIC: 6061 Federal credit unions

(P-11820)
VALLEY STRONG CREDIT UNION
6101 Coffee Rd, Bakersfield (93308-9415)
P.O. Box 9506 (93389-9506)
PHONE...............................661 833-7900
Ruth Rubbo, *Mgr*
EMP: 87
SALES (corp-wide): 256.59MM **Privately Held**
Web: www.valleystrong.com
SIC: 6061 Federal credit unions
PA: Valley Strong Credit Union
11500 Bolthouse Dr
661 833-7900

(P-11821)
VENTURA COUNTY CREDIT UNION (PA)
2575 Vista Del Mar Dr Ste 100, Ventura (93001-3956)
PHONE...............................805 477-4000
Joseph Schroeder, *Pr*
Linda Rossi, *
Gavin Bradley, *
Linda Sim, *
EMP: 84 **EST:** 1950
SQ FT: 22,500
SALES (est): 66.66MM
SALES (corp-wide): 66.66MM **Privately Held**
Web: www.vccuonline.net
SIC: 6061 Federal credit unions

6062 State Credit Unions

(P-11822)
ADELFI CREDIT UNION
Also Called: Eccu
135 S State College Blvd Ste 500, Brea (92821-5819)
P.O. Box 2400 (92822-2400)
PHONE...............................714 671-5700
Abel Pomar, *CEO*
Gregory Talbott, *
Susan Rushing, *
Patty Staples, *
Tom Honan, *
EMP: 147 **EST:** 1964
SQ FT: 125,000
SALES (est): 33.02MM **Privately Held**
Web: www.adelfibanking.com
SIC: 6062 State credit unions, not federally chartered

(P-11823)
CALIFORNIA COAST CREDIT UNION (PA)
9201 Spectrum Center Blvd Ste 300, San Diego (92123-1407)
P.O. Box 502080 (92150-2080)
PHONE...............................858 495-1600
Marla Shepard, *CEO*

Ruth Peshkoff, *
Carol Walker, *
Charles Wallace, *
Frederick Schwartz, *
EMP: 74 **EST:** 1929
SALES (est): 152.46MM
SALES (corp-wide): 152.46MM **Privately Held**
Web: www.calcoastcu.org
SIC: 6062 6163 State credit unions, not federally chartered; Loan brokers

(P-11824)
CALIFORNIA CREDIT UNION (PA)
701 N Brand Blvd Fl 7, Glendale (91203-1218)
P.O. Box 29100 (91209)
PHONE...............................818 291-6700
Steve O'connell, *CEO*
Rebecca Collier, *
Hudson Lee, *
EMP: 120 **EST:** 1933
SALES (est): 204.85MM
SALES (corp-wide): 204.85MM **Privately Held**
Web: www.ccu.com
SIC: 6062 6061 State credit unions, not federally chartered; Federal credit unions

(P-11825)
CHRISTIAN COMMUNITY CREDIT UN (PA)
255 N Lone Hill Ave, San Dimas (91773-2308)
P.O. Box 3012 (91722-9012)
PHONE...............................626 915-7551
Marji Hughes, *Interim Chief Executive Officer*
John T Walling, *
David Estridge, *
Linda Tashiro, *
Marji Hughes, *Ex VP*
EMP: 70 **EST:** 1957
SQ FT: 24,000
SALES (est): 38.27MM
SALES (corp-wide): 38.27MM **Privately Held**
Web: www.mycccu.com
SIC: 6062 State credit unions, not federally chartered

(P-11826)
COASTHILLS CREDIT UNION (PA)
Also Called: CSCU
1075 E Betteravia Rd, Santa Maria (93454-7023)
P.O. Box 8000 (93456)
PHONE.............................,.805 733-7600
Jeff York, *Pr*
Dave Upham, *
Scott Coe, *
Marty Chatham, *
Dal Widick, *
EMP: 80 **EST:** 1958
SQ FT: 30,000
SALES (est): 95.87MM
SALES (corp-wide): 95.87MM **Privately Held**
Web: www.coasthills.coop
SIC: 6062 State credit unions, not federally chartered

(P-11827)
CU COOPERATIVE SYSTEMS LLC (PA)
Also Called: Co-Op Solutions
9692 Haven Ave Ste 300, Rancho Cucamonga (91730-0101)
PHONE...............................909 948-2500

Dean Michaels, *Pr*
Grace Mayo, *Vice Chairman*
Tom Sargent, *Ch Bd*
John Bommarito, *Treas*
James Hanisch, *Ex VP*
▲ **EMP:** 285 **EST:** 1981
SALES (est): 185.31MM
SALES (corp-wide): 185.31MM **Privately Held**
Web: www.coop.org
SIC: 6062 State credit unions, not federally chartered

(P-11828)
LBS FINANCIAL CREDIT UNION (PA)
5505 Garden Grove Blvd Ste 500, Westminster (92683-1894)
PHONE...............................562 598-9007
Sean Hardeman, *CEO*
Sean M Hardeman, *
Gene Allen, *
Dug Woog, *
EMP: 120 **EST:** 1935
SQ FT: 63,000
SALES (est): 79.24MM
SALES (corp-wide): 79.24MM **Privately Held**
Web: www.lbsfcu.org
SIC: 6062 State credit unions, not federally chartered

(P-11829)
LOS ANGELES POLICE CREDIT UN (PA)
Also Called: L A P F C U
16150 Sherman Way, Van Nuys (91406-3956)
P.O. Box 10188 (91499)
PHONE...............................818 787-6520
Tyler E Izen, *Ch Bd*
G Michael Padgett, *
Warren D Spayth, *
Angelino Cayanan, *
EMP: 100 **EST:** 1936
SQ FT: 30,000
SALES (est): 72.81MM
SALES (corp-wide): 72.81MM **Privately Held**
Web: www.lapfcu.org
SIC: 6062 6061 State credit unions, not federally chartered; Federal credit unions

(P-11830)
NORTH ISLAND FINANCIAL CREDIT UNION
Also Called: North Island Credit Union
5898 Copley Dr Ste 100, San Diego (92111-7917)
P.O. Box 85833 (92186-5833)
PHONE...............................619 656-6525
EMP: 353
SIC: 6062 State credit unions

(P-11831)
PREMIER AMERICA CREDIT UNION (PA)
Also Called: PREMIER AMERICA WEALTH MANAGEM
19867 Prairie St Lbby, Chatsworth (91311-6532)
P.O. Box 2178 (91313-2178)
PHONE...............................818 772-4000
John M Merlo, *Pr*
James Anderson, *
Nancy Wheeler-chandler, *Vice Chairman*
Liz Condercuri, *
Marge Mcnaught, *Sr VP*
EMP: 135 **EST:** 1957
SQ FT: 80,000

SALES (est): 127.07MM
SALES (corp-wide): 127.07MM **Privately Held**
Web: www.premieramerica.com
SIC: 6062 6163 State credit unions, not federally chartered; Loan brokers

(P-11832)
SESLOC CREDIT UNION (PA)
3855 Broad St, San Luis Obispo (93401-7109)
P.O. Box 5360 (93403-5360)
PHONE...............................805 543-1816
Michael Quamma, *CEO*
Bertha Foxford, *
Andy Bechinsky, *
Micki Myall, *
Kenneth Long, *CRO**
EMP: 77 **EST:** 1942
SQ FT: 19,700
SALES (est): 44.47MM
SALES (corp-wide): 44.47MM **Privately Held**
Web: www.sesloc.org
SIC: 6062 State credit unions

(P-11833)
VISTERRA CREDIT UNION
23520 Cactus Ave, Moreno Valley (92553-8906)
P.O. Box 9500 (92552-9500)
PHONE...............................951 656-4411
EMP: 107
Web: www.visterracu.org
SIC: 6062 State credit unions

(P-11834)
WESCOM CENTRAL CREDIT UNION (PA)
123 S Marengo Ave, Pasadena (91101-2428)
P.O. Box 7058 (91109-7058)
PHONE...............................888 493-7266
TOLL FREE: 888
Darren Williams, *Prin*
Jane P Wood, *Prin*
Keith Pipes, *Prin*
Jonathon Bauman, *Prin*
Jeanne Brown, *Prin*
EMP: 425 **EST:** 1934
SQ FT: 90,000
SALES (est): 329.03MM
SALES (corp-wide): 329.03MM **Privately Held**
Web: www.wescom.org
SIC: 6062 State credit unions, not federally chartered

6091 Nondeposit Trust Facilities

(P-11835)
DEUTSCHE BANK NATIONAL TR CO
1761 E Saint Andrew Pl, Santa Ana (92705-4934)
PHONE...............................714 247-6054
F Jim Della Sala, *Prin*
David West, *
EMP: 75 **EST:** 2007
SALES (est): 8.5MM
SALES (corp-wide): 59.62B **Privately Held**
SIC: 6091 6021 Nondeposit trust facilities; National commercial banks
HQ: Deutsche Bank Trust Company Americas
1 Columbus Cir
New York NY 10019
212 250-2500

(P-11836)
SUNAMERICA INC (HQ)
Also Called: SunAmerica
1 Sun America Ctr Fl 38, Los Angeles
(90067-6101)
PHONE...........................310 772-6000
Eli Broad, *Ch*
Jay S Wintrob, *CEO*
James R Belardi, *Ex VP*
Michael J Akers, *Sr VP*
Mary L Cavanaugh, *Sr VP*
▲ **EMP:** 1000 **EST:** 1957
SQ FT: 95,845
SALES (est): 55.53MM
SALES (corp-wide): 46.8B **Publicly Held**
Web: www.sunamerica.com
SIC: 6091 6311 6211 6282 Nondeposit trust
facilities; Life insurance carriers; Mutual
funds, selling by independent salesperson;
Manager of mutual funds, contract or fee
basis
PA: American International Group, Inc.
1271 Ave Of The Americas
212 770-7000

6099 Functions Related To Depository Banking

(P-11837)
ASSOCTED FGN EXCH
HOLDINGS INC (HQ)
21045 Califa St, Woodland Hills
(91367-5104)
PHONE...........................818 386-2702
Irving Barr, *Ch*
Jan Vliestra, *
Fred Kunik, *
EMP: 89 **EST:** 2006
SALES (est): 112.61MM **Publicly Held**
SIC: 6099 Foreign currency exchange
PA: Corpay, Inc.
3280 Pchtree Rd Ne Ste 24

(P-11838)
CONTINENTAL CURRENCY
SVCS INC (PA)
Also Called: Cash It Here
1108 E 17th St, Santa Ana (92701-2600)
P.O. Box 10970 (92711-0970)
PHONE...........................714 667-6699
Fred Kunik, *Pr*
Irving Barr, *
David Wilder, *
EMP: 80 **EST:** 1977
SQ FT: 12,500
SALES (est): 98.45MM
SALES (corp wide): 08.46MM **Privately**
Held
Web:
www.continentalcurrencyservices.com
SIC: 6099 Check cashing agencies

(P-11839)
DEBISYS INC (PA)
Also Called: Emida Technologies
27442 Portola Pkwy Ste 150, Foothill Ranch
(92610-2860)
PHONE...........................949 699-1401
Dennis Andrews, *CEO*
Jim Wodach, *
EMP: 80 **EST:** 1977
SQ FT: 10,000
SALES (est): 21.09MM
SALES (corp-wide): 21.09MM **Privately**
Held
Web: www.emida.com
SIC: 6099 Automated teller machine (ATM)
network

(P-11840)
HAPPY MONEY INC
Also Called: Payoff
21515 Hawthorne Blvd Ste 200, Torrance
(90503-6512)
PHONE...........................949 430-0630
EMP: 366 **EST:** 2009
SALES (est): 16.62MM **Privately Held**
Web: www.happymoney.com
SIC: 6099 Functions related to deposit
banking

(P-11841)
LENLYN LTD WHICH WILL DO
BUS I (HQ)
Also Called: Ice Currency Services USA
5777 W Century Blvd, Los Angeles
(90045-5600)
P.O. Box 92192 (90009-2192)
PHONE...........................310 417-3432
Bharat Shah, *CEO*
EMP: 75 **EST:** 1984
SQ FT: 1,000
SALES (est): 4.95MM **Privately Held**
SIC: 6099 Foreign currency exchange
PA: Lenlyn Holdings Limited
1st Floor

(P-11842)
POPULUS FINANCIAL GROUP
INC
Also Called: Ace Cash Express
6302 Van Buren Blvd, Riverside
(92503-2051)
PHONE...........................951 509-3506
Michael Mc Knight, *Brnch Mgr*
EMP: 105
Web: www.acecashexpress.com
SIC: 6099 Check cashing agencies
HQ: Populus Financial Group, Inc.
300 E John Carpenter Fwy # 900
Irving TX 75062
972 550-5000

(P-11843)
SAN MNUEL BAND MISSION
INDIANS
Also Called: Yaamava Rsort Csino At San
Mnu
101 Pure Water Ln, Highland (92346-6711)
PHONE...........................909 425-4682
EMP: 118
Web: www.sanmanuel-nsn.gov
SIC: 6099 Check clearing services
PA: San Manuel Band Of Mission Indians
26569 Community Center Dr
909 864-8933

(P-11844)
SERFIN FUNDS TRANSFER (PA)
1000 S Fremont Ave Bldg A-O, Alhambra
(91803-8800)
PHONE...........................626 457-3070
Richard Stevenson, *Pr*
EMP: 100 **EST:** 1994
SALES (est): 9.74MM **Privately Held**
SIC: 6099 Electronic funds transfer network,
including switching

6111 Federal And Federally Sponsored Credit

(P-11845)
DEUTSCHE BANK NATIONAL TR
CO
1999 Avenue Of The Stars Ste 3750, Los
Angeles (90067-4605)

PHONE...........................310 788-6200
EMP: 100 **EST:** 1983
SALES (est): 161.96MM
SALES (corp-wide): 59.62B **Privately Held**
Web: www.deutschewealth.com
SIC: 6111 National Consumer Cooperative
Bank
HQ: Deutsche Bank Trust Company
Americas
1 Columbus Cir
New York NY 10019
212 250-2500

(P-11846)
LAW SCHOOL FINANCIAL INC
Also Called: Law School Loans
175 S Lake Ave Unit 200, Pasadena
(91101-2629)
PHONE...........................626 243-1800
EMP: 190
SQ FT: 25,000
SALES (est): 15.5MM **Privately Held**
Web: www.lawschoolloans.com
SIC: 6111 Student Loan Marketing
Association

6141 Personal Credit Institutions

(P-11847)
AMERICAN HONDA FINANCE
CORP (DH)
Also Called: AMERICAN HONDA
1919 Torrance Blvd, Torrance (90501-2746)
P.O. Box 2200 (90509)
PHONE...........................310 972-2239
Hideo Tamaka, *CEO*
John Weisickle, *
Stephan Smith, *
EMP: 200 **EST:** 1980
SALES (est): 8.4B **Privately Held**
Web: honda.americanhondafinance.com
SIC: 6141 Financing: automobiles, furniture,
etc., not a deposit bank
HQ: American Honda Motor Co., Inc.
1919 Torrance Blvd
Torrance CA 90501
310 783-2000

(P-11848)
AMERICAN HONDA
PROTECTION PROD
20800 Madrona Ave, Torrance
(90503-4915)
P.O. Box 2225 (90509-2225)
PHONE...........................310 972-2200
Michael Ryan, *Treas*
EMP: 75 **EST:** 2013
SALES (est): 4.52MM **Privately Held**
Web: www.honda.com
SIC: 6141 Personal credit institutions

(P-11849)
ASSOCIATES FIRST CAPITAL
CORP
Also Called: Avco Financial
3634 5th Ave, Glendale (91214-2444)
PHONE...........................818 248-7055
EMP: 187
SALES (corp-wide): 156.82B **Publicly**
Held
SIC: 6141 Consumer finance companies
HQ: Associates First Capital Corporation
4000 Regent Blvd
Irving TX 75063
800 922-6235

(P-11850)
CASHCALL INC
Also Called: Chapter Seven Lending
1 City Blvd W Ste 102, Orange
(92868-3621)
P.O. Box 66007 (92816-6007)
PHONE...........................949 752-4600
John Paul Reddam, *CEO*
Ethan Taub, *CMO*
EMP: 1400 **EST:** 2000
SALES (est): 323.43MM **Privately Held**
Web: www.cashcall.com
SIC: 6141 Personal finance licensed loan
companies, small

(P-11851)
CELTIC BANK CORPORATION
32605 Temecula Pkwy Ste 204, Temecula
(92592-6839)
PHONE...........................951 303-3330
EMP: 147
SIC: 6141 6021 Personal credit institutions;
National commercial banks
HQ: Celtic Bank Corporation
268 S State St Ste 300
Salt Lake City UT 84111
801 363-6500

(P-11852)
CIG FINANCIAL LLC
Also Called: Autonation Finance
6 Executive Cir Ste 100, Irvine
(92614-6732)
P.O. Box 19795 (92623-9795)
PHONE...........................877 244-4442
Greg Skjonsby, *Pr*
EMP: 76 **EST:** 2011
SALES (est): 25.73MM
SALES (corp-wide): 26.95B **Publicly Held**
Web: www.cigfinancial.com
SIC: 6141 7389 Consumer finance
companies; Financial services
PA: Autonation, Inc.
200 Sw 1st Ave
954 769-6000

(P-11853)
CITIFINANCIAL CREDIT
COMPANY
Also Called: Citifinancial
2655 Del Vista Dr, City Of Industry
(91745-5244)
PHONE...........................626 712-8780
EMP: 123
SALES (corp-wide): 156.82B **Publicly**
Held
SIC: 6141 Consumer finance companies
HQ: Citifinancial Credit Company
300 Saint Paul Pl Fl 3
Baltimore MD 21202
410 332-3000

(P-11854)
HYUNDAI PROTECTION PLAN
INC
3161 Michelson Dr Ste 1900, Irvine
(92612-4418)
PHONE...........................949 468-4000
Jwa Jin Cho, *Prin*
EMP: 273 **EST:** 2015
SALES (est): 1.57MM **Privately Held**
Web: www.hyundaicapitalamerica.com
SIC: 6141 Automobile loans, including
insurance
HQ: Hyundai Capital America
3161 Michelson Dr # 1900
Irvine CA 92612

PRODUCTS & SVCS

(P-11855)

MITSUBISHI MOTORS CR AMER INC (DH)

Also Called: Mmca
6400 Katella Ave, Cypress (90630-5208)
P.O. Box 689040 (37068-9040)
PHONE.................714 799-4730
Dan Booth, *Pr*
Charles Tredway, *
Ellen Gleberman, *
Hideyuki Kitamura, *
EMP: 394 EST: 1990
SQ FT: 32,256
SALES (est): 9.56MM **Privately Held**
Web: www.mitsubishicars.com
SIC: 6141 6159 Automobile loans, including insurance; Truck finance leasing
HQ: Mitsubishi Motors North America, Inc.
4031 Aspen Grove Drv Ste
Franklin TN 37067
714 799-4730

(P-11856)

MONTEREY FINANCIAL SVCS INC (PA)

Also Called: Monterey Collection Services
4095 Avenida De La Plata, Oceanside (92056-5802)
P.O. Box 5199 (92052-5199)
PHONE.................760 639-3500
Robert Steinke, *Pr*
Mike Gray, *
Kathi Steinke, *
EMP: 110 EST: 1989
SQ FT: 27,000
SALES (est): 21.84MM **Privately Held**
Web: www.montereyfinancial.com
SIC: 6141 8721 7322 8742 Consumer finance companies; Billing and bookkeeping service; Collection agency, except real estate; Financial consultant

(P-11857)

NATIONAL PLANNING CORPORATION

100 N Pacific Coast Hwy Ste 1800, El Segundo (90245-5612)
PHONE.................800 881-7174
John C Johnson, *Pr*
Sarah Corce, *
Jim Dafalco, *
Patricia Mccallop, *CCO*
EMP: 150 EST: 1998
SALES (est): 3.97MM **Privately Held**
Web:
www.nationalplanningholdings.com
SIC: 6141 Automobile and consumer finance companies

(P-11858)

NEW AMERICAN FUNDING LLC (PA)

Also Called: Naf
14511 Myford Rd Ste 100, Tustin (92780-7057)
PHONE.................949 430-7029
Rick Arvielo, *CEO*
Patricia Arvielo, *
Christy Bunce, *
Scott Frommert, *
EMP: 650 EST: 2002
SALES (est): 164.89MM **Privately Held**
Web: www.newamericanfunding.com
SIC: 6141 7371 Licensed loan companies, small; Computer software development and applications

(P-11859)

NORTH AMERICAN ACCEPTANCE CORP

Also Called: An Open Check
3191 Red Hill Ave Ste 100, Costa Mesa (92626-3451)
PHONE.................714 868-3195
Marco J Rasic, *CEO*
Mary Clancey Rasic, *
EMP: 123 EST: 2002
SQ FT: 24,000
SALES (est): 2.14MM **Privately Held**
SIC: 6141 6719 Automobile and consumer finance companies; Personal holding companies, except banks

(P-11860)

PATHWARD NATIONAL ASSOCIATION

1301 Dove St Ste 1000, Newport Beach (92660-2475)
PHONE.................949 756-2600
Jerry Fred, *Brnch Mgr*
EMP: 210
Web: www.pathward.com
SIC: 6141 6282 Personal credit institutions; Investment advice
HQ: Pathward, National Association
5501 S Broadband Ln
Sioux Falls SD 57108
712 732-4117

(P-11861)

PAYOFF INC

Also Called: Happy Money
3200 Park Center Dr Ste 800, Costa Mesa (92626-1979)
PHONE.................949 430-0630
Matt Potere, *CEO*
Christopher Hilliard, *CCO*
Adam Zarlengo, *CPO*
EMP: 89 EST: 2012
SQ FT: 19,500
SALES (est): 24.89MM **Privately Held**
Web: www.happymoney.com
SIC: 6141 Personal credit institutions

(P-11862)

PROFESSIONAL CR REPORTING INC

3560 Hyland Ave, Costa Mesa (92626-1438)
PHONE.................714 556-1570
Tim Nguyen, *Admn*
EMP: 132 EST: 2016
SALES (est): 805.71K
SALES (corp-wide): 303.62MM **Publicly Held**
Web: www.profcredit.com
SIC: 6141 Personal credit institutions
PA: Meridianlink, Inc.
3560 Hyland Ave Ste 200
714 708-6950

(P-11863)

WHEELS FINANCIAL GROUP LLC

Also Called: Loanmart
15400 Sherman Way Ste 300, Van Nuys (91406-4272)
P.O. Box 8075 (91409-8075)
PHONE.................855 422-7412
EMP: 123 EST: 2015
SALES (est): 11.32MM **Privately Held**
Web: www.800loanmart.com
SIC: 6141 Consumer finance companies

6153 Short-term Business Credit

(P-11864)

AMWEST FUNDING CORP

6 Pointe Dr Ste 300, Brea (92821-6323)
PHONE.................714 831-3333
Ryan Kim, *Pr*
EMP: 135 EST: 2017
SALES (est): 16.43MM **Privately Held**
Web: www.amwestfunding.com
SIC: 6153 Working capital financing

(P-11865)

BALBOA CAPITAL CORPORATION (DH)

575 Anton Blvd Ste 1200, Costa Mesa (92626-7685)
PHONE.................949 756-0800
H Palmer Proctor Junior, *CEO*
EMP: 200 EST: 1988
SALES (est): 41.39MM
SALES (corp-wide): 1.52B **Publicly Held**
Web: www.balboacapital.com
SIC: 6153 Working capital financing
HQ: Ameris Bank
300 S Main St
Moultrie GA 31768
800 845-5219

(P-11866)

ENCORE CAPITAL GROUP INC (PA)

Also Called: Encore
350 Camino De La Reina Ste 100, San Diego (92108-3007)
PHONE.................877 445-4581
Ashish Masih, *Pr*
Michael P Monaco, *Non-Executive Chairman of the Board*
Jonathan C Clark, *Ex VP*
Andrew E Asch, *Corporate Secretary*
Monique Dumais-chrisope, *CIO*
EMP: 517 EST: 1990
SQ FT: 118,000
SALES (est): 1.22B
SALES (corp-wide): 1.22B **Publicly Held**
Web: www.encorecapital.com
SIC: 6153 Purchasers of accounts receivable and commercial paper

(P-11867)

HANA COMMERCIAL FINANCE LLC

1000 Wilshire Blvd Ste 570, Los Angeles (90017-2462)
PHONE.................213 240-1234
Sunnie Kim, *Managing Member*
EMP: 85 EST: 2016
SALES (est): 1.73MM **Privately Held**
Web: www.hanafinancial.com
SIC: 6153 Factoring services

(P-11868)

INPUT 1 LLC

Also Called: Digital Payment Services
1 Baxter Way Ste 270, Westlake Village (91362-3895)
PHONE.................888 882-2554
Todd Greenbaum, *Managing Member*
Jeffrey S Greenbaum, *
EMP: 110 EST: 1984
SQ FT: 24,000
SALES (est): 9.69MM **Privately Held**
Web: www.input1.com

SIC: 6153 7371 Short-term business credit institutions, except agricultural; Computer software development and applications

(P-11869)

MIDLAND CREDIT MANAGEMENT INC

Also Called: Midland Credit Management
350 Camino De La Reina Ste 100, San Diego (92108-3007)
P.O. Box 939069 (92193)
PHONE.................877 240-2377
Kenneth A Vecchione, *CEO*
Carl Gregory, *
Robin Pruitt, *
Monique Dumais, *CIO*
EMP: 1800 EST: 1953
SALES (est): 35.06MM
SALES (corp-wide): 1.22B **Publicly Held**
Web: www.midlandcredit.com
SIC: 6153 Short-term business credit institutions, except agricultural
PA: Encore Capital Group, Inc.
350 Cmino De La Rina Ste
877 445-4581

(P-11870)

PACIFIC LIFE GLOBAL FUNDING

700 Newport Center Dr, Newport Beach (92660-6307)
PHONE.................949 219-3011
William Gross, *Prin*
EMP: 82 EST: 2007
SALES (est): 950.26K
SALES (corp-wide): 12.84B **Privately Held**
Web: www.pacificlife.com
SIC: 6153 Short-term business credit institutions, except agricultural
HQ: Pacific Life Insurance Company
700 Newport Center Dr
Newport Beach CA 92660
949 219-3011

(P-11871)

RELIANT SERVICES GROUP LLC

Also Called: Reliant Funding Group
9540 Towne Centre Dr Ste 100, San Diego (92121-1989)
PHONE.................877 850-0998
Steve Kietz, *CEO*
Adam Stettner, *
Paul Norman, *
EMP: 180 EST: 2000
SALES (est): 16.7MM **Privately Held**
Web: www.reliantfunding.com
SIC: 6153 Working capital financing

(P-11872)

RIVIERA FINANCE OF TEXAS INC

10430 Pioneer Blvd Ste 1, Santa Fe Springs (90670-8245)
PHONE.................562 777-1300
Sandy Newman, *Brnch Mgr*
EMP: 87
Web: www.rivierafinance.com
SIC: 6153 Factors of commercial paper
PA: Riviera Finance Of Texas, Inc
220 Avenue I

(P-11873)

SKYVIEW CAPITAL LLC

2000 Avenue Of The Stars Ste 810, Los Angeles (90067-4709)
PHONE.................310 273-6000
Alex Soltani, *CEO*
EMP: 99 EST: 2002
SALES (est): 9.54MM **Privately Held**

Web: www.skyviewcapital.com
SIC: 6153 Direct working capital financing

PHONE.................................310 453-7300
Sean Spring, *
EMP: 99 EST: 2002
SALES (est): 25.82MM
SALES (corp-wide): 115.34B **Publicly Held**
Web: www.wellsfargocapitalfinance.com
SIC: 6159 General and industrial loan institutions
HQ: Wells Fargo Bank, National Association
420 Mntgmery St Frnt San
San Francisco CA 94104
605 575-6900

(P-11874)
STARTENGINE CROWDFUNDING INC
4100 W Alameda Ave Fl 3, Burbank
(91505-4191)
PHONE.................................800 317-2200
Howard Marks, CEO
Ron Miller, Ofcr
Josh Amster, VP
EMP: 72 EST: 2014
SALES (est): 23.39MM **Privately Held**
Web: www.startengine.com
SIC: 6153 Working capital financing

6159 Miscellaneous Business Credit

(P-11875)
CAPITALSOURCE INC
633 W 5th St 33rd Fl, Los Angeles
(90071-2005)
PHONE.................................213 443-7700
EMP: 515
SIC: 6159 General and industrial loan institutions

(P-11876)
CAPNET FINANCIAL SERVICES INC (PA)
Also Called: Capital Network Funding Svcs
11901 Santa Monica Blvd Ste 338, Los Angeles (90025-2767)
PHONE.................................877 980-0558
John Armstron, CEO
Blake Johnson, *
Michael Kromnick, *
Armita Dalal, Head*
EMP: 90 EST: 2001
SQ FT: 23,000
SALES (est): 3.16MM
SALES (corp-wide): 3.16MM **Privately Held**
SIC: 6159 Equipment and vehicle finance leasing companies

(P-11877)
ELECTRONIC COMMERCE LLC
Also Called: Electronic Commerce
4100 Newport Place Dr Ste 500, Newport Beach (92660-1409)
PHONE.................................800 770-5520
Darnell Ponder, Mng Pt
Khaazra Maaranu, *
EMP: 85 EST: 2013
SALES (est): 2.2MM **Privately Held**
SIC: 6159 Intermediate investment banks

(P-11878)
SECURE CHOICE LENDING
Also Called: Coast Home Loans
1650 Spruce St Ste 100, Riverside
(92507-7403)
PHONE.................................951 733-8925
Mark Hossler, Pr
EMP: 75 EST: 2017
SALES (est): 5.48MM **Privately Held**
Web: www.securechoicelending.com
SIC: 6159 General and industrial loan institutions

(P-11879)
WELLS FARGO CAPITAL FIN LLC (DH)
2450 Colorado Ave Ste 3000w, Santa Monica (90404-3597)

6162 Mortgage Bankers And Correspondents

(P-11880)
A-A MORTGAGE OPPORTUNITIES LP
1 Baxter Way, Westlake Village
(91362-3889)
PHONE.................................888 469-0810
James S Furash, CEO
EMP: 738 EST: 2013
SALES (est): 4.4B
SALES (corp-wide): 32.64B **Publicly Held**
Web: www.amerihome.com
SIC: 6162 Mortgage bankers and loan correspondents
PA: Apollo Global Management, Inc.
9 W 57th St Fl 42
212 515-3200

(P-11881)
AMERICAN FINANCIAL NETWORK INC (PA)
Also Called: Gateway Home Realty
10 Pointe Dr Ste 330, Brea (92821-7620)
PHONE.................................714 831-4000
John B Sherman, Pr
John R Sherman, *
▲ EMP: 200 EST: 2001
SQ FT: 8,000
SALES (est): 60.75MM
SALES (corp-wide): 60.75MM **Privately Held**
Web: www.afncorp.com
SIC: 6162 Mortgage bankers

(P-11882)
AMERICAN INTERNET MORTGAGE INC
Also Called: Aimloan.com, A Direct Lender
4121 Camino Del Rio S Ste 200, San Diego
(92108-4103)
PHONE.................................888 411-4246
Vincent J Kasperick, Pr
EMP: 106 EST: 1998
SQ FT: 4,500
SALES (est): 22.56MM **Privately Held**
Web: www.aimloan.com
SIC: 6162 Mortgage bankers

(P-11883)
AMNET ESOP CORPORATION
Also Called: American Mortgage Network
347 Third Ave Fl 2, Chula Vista
(91910-3929)
PHONE.................................877 354-1110
Joseph Sal Restivo, CEO
Shawn Stougard, *
EMP: 144 EST: 2019
SALES (est): 4.57MM **Privately Held**
Web: www.amnetmtg.com
SIC: 6162 Mortgage bankers

(P-11884)
AMNET MORTGAGE LLC
10421 Wateridge Cir Ste 250, San Diego
(92121-5788)
PHONE.................................858 909-1200
John M Robbins, CEO
Jay M Fuller, Parts Vice President*
Lisa Falk, *
EMP: 759 EST: 1997
SQ FT: 40,400
SALES (est): 4.16MM
SALES (corp-wide): 115.34B **Publicly Held**
SIC: 6162 Mortgage bankers and loan correspondents
HQ: Wells Fargo Bank, National Association
420 Mntgmery St Frnt San
San Francisco CA 94104
605 575-6900

(P-11885)
ANCHOR LOANS LP
Also Called: Anchor Nationwide Loans
1 Baxter Way # 220, Westlake Village
(91362-3889)
PHONE.................................310 395-0010
Stephen Pollack, CEO
Bryan Thompson, CFO
EMP: 200 EST: 2015
SALES (est): 19.26MM **Privately Held**
Web: www.anchorloans.com
SIC: 6162 Mortgage bankers and loan correspondents

(P-11886)
ARCS COMMERCIAL MORTGAGE CO LP (DH)
Also Called: Arcs Commercial Mortgage
26901 Agoura Rd Ste 200, Calabasas
(91301-5109)
PHONE.................................818 676-3274
Timothy White, CEO
▲ EMP: 110 EST: 1995
SQ FT: 15,000
SALES (est): 3.71MM
SALES (corp-wide): 31.88B **Publicly Held**
SIC: 6162 Mortgage bankers
HQ: Pnc Bank, National Association
300 5th Ave
Pittsburgh PA 15222
877 762-2000

(P-11887)
BERKSHIRE HTHWAY HM SVCS CAL P
2365 Northside Dr Ste 200, San Diego
(92108-2720)
PHONE.................................619 302-8082
EMP: 114
SALES (corp-wide): 364.48B **Publicly Held**
Web: www.bhhscalifornia.com
SIC: 6162 Mortgage bankers and loan correspondents
HQ: Berkshire Hathaway Home Services California Properties
12770 El Cmino Real Ste 1
San Diego CA 92130
858 792-6085

(P-11888)
BLUFI LENDING CORPORATION
9909 Mira Mesa Blvd Ste 160, San Diego
(92131-3002)
EMP: 120
SIC: 6162 Loan correspondents

(P-11889)
CAKE MORTGAGE CORP
Also Called: Millennial Home Lending
9200 Oakdale Ave Ste 501, Chatsworth
(91311-6562)
PHONE.................................818 812-5150
David Arshak Abelyan, CEO
EMP: 70 EST: 2018
SALES (est): 2.26MM **Privately Held**
Web: www.mhlending.us
SIC: 6162 Mortgage bankers and loan correspondents

(P-11890)
CAL MUTUAL INC
34077 Temecula Creek Rd, Temecula
(92592-5646)
PHONE.................................888 700-4650
Dennis Shane Dailey, Pr
EMP: 87 EST: 2013
SALES (est): 1.97MM **Privately Held**
Web: www.calmutualmortgage.com
SIC: 6162 6531 Mortgage bankers and loan correspondents; Real estate agent, residential

(P-11891)
CALIBER HOME LOANS INC
1500 Ventura Blvd, Oxnard (93036-1880)
PHONE.................................805 983-0904
EMP: 84
SALES (corp-wide): 3.8B **Publicly Held**
Web: www.caliberhomeloans.com
SIC: 6162 Mortgage bankers and loan correspondents
HQ: Caliber Home Loans, Inc.
1525 S Belt Line Rd
Coppell TX 75019

(P-11892)
CARRINGTON MRTG HOLDINGS LLC
1600 S Douglass Rd Ste 110, Anaheim
(92806-5951)
PHONE.................................888 267-0584
Phil Grassbaugh, Prin
Rob Petruska, *
Rick Sharga, *
EMP: 123 EST: 2001
SQ FT: 192,000
SALES (est): 20.53MM
SALES (corp-wide): 43.95MM **Privately Held**
SIC: 6162 Mortgage bankers and loan correspondents
PA: Carrington Capital Management Llc
1700 E Putnam Ave 5th Fl
203 661-6188

(P-11893)
CHANGE LENDING LLC
32 Discovery Ste 160, Irvine (92618-3156)
PHONE.................................949 769-3526
EMP: 92
Web: www.changemtg.com
SIC: 6162 Mortgage bankers and loan correspondents
PA: Change Lending, Llc
175 N Riverview Dr

(P-11894)
COUNTRYWIDE HOME LOANS INC
Also Called: Countrywide
801 N Brand Blvd Ste 750, Glendale
(91203-3218)
PHONE.................................818 550-8700
Lynda Martinlawley, Mgr
EMP: 1755

SALES (corp-wide): 171.91B **Publicly Held**
Web: mortgage-brokers.cmac.ws
SIC: 6162 Mortgage bankers
HQ: Countrywide Home Loans, Inc.
　　31303 Agoura Rd
　　Westlake Village CA 91361

(P-11895)
COUNTRYWIDE HOME LOANS INC (HQ)
Also Called: Countrywide
31303 Agoura Rd, Westlake Village
(91361-4635)
EMP: 700 EST: 1969
SQ FT: 220,000
SALES (est): 50.2MM
SALES (corp-wide): 171.91B **Publicly Held**
Web: www.bankofamerica.com
SIC: 6162 Mortgage bankers
PA: Bank Of America Corporation
　　100 N Tryon St
　　704 386-5681

(P-11896)
CROSSCOUNTRY MORTGAGE LLC
4655 Executive Dr Ste 300, San Diego
(92121-3123)
PHONE.............................858 735-0255
EMP: 103
SALES (corp-wide): 490.47MM **Privately Held**
Web: www.crosscountrymortgage.com
SIC: 6162 Mortgage bankers and loan correspondents
PA: Crosscountry Mortgage, Llc
　　6850 Miller Rd
　　440 845-3700

(P-11897)
DECISION READY SOLUTIONS INC
Also Called: Decision Ready
400 Spectrum Center Dr Ste 2050, Irvine
(92618-5024)
PHONE.............................949 400-1126
Ravi Ramanathan, Pr
Dan Mahler, CSO*
Claudia Sanchez, *
Tom Schmidt, *
EMP: 50 EST: 2011
SALES (est): 6MM **Privately Held**
Web: www.decisionreadysolutions.com
SIC: 6162 7371 7372 Mortgage bankers;
　　Computer software systems analysis and
　　design, custom; Business oriented
　　computer software

(P-11898)
E&S FINANCIAL GROUP INC
Also Called: Capital Mortgage Services
700 E Main St, Ventura (93001-2906)
PHONE.............................805 644-1621
Jordan Eller, Pr
EMP: 70 EST: 2008
SALES (est): 2.42MM **Privately Held**
SIC: 6162 Mortgage bankers and loan correspondents

(P-11899)
EC CLOSING CORP
Also Called: Cal Western Foreclosure Svcs
525 E Main St, El Cajon (92020-4007)
P.O. Box 22004 (92022-9004)
PHONE.............................800 546-1531
EMP: 80
Web: www.rickpatterson.com

SIC: 6162 Loan correspondents

(P-11900)
EMET LENDING GROUP INC
Also Called: Dream Mortgage Group
2601 Saturn St Ste 200, Brea (92821-6702)
PHONE.............................714 933-9800
Julie Ahn, CEO
EMP: 80 EST: 2015
SALES (est): 4.32MM **Privately Held**
Web: www.cartamortgage.com
SIC: 6162 Mortgage bankers

(P-11901)
EQUITY SMART HOME LOANS INC
Also Called: Lending Enterprise
1499 Huntington Dr Ste 500, South Pasadena (91030-5473)
PHONE.............................626 864-8774
Pablo Martinez, CEO
EMP: 84 EST: 2016
SALES (est): 3.25MM **Privately Held**
Web: www.equitysmartloans.com
SIC: 6162 Mortgage bankers

(P-11902)
EXPRESS CAPITAL LENDING
3134 Airway Ave, Costa Mesa
(92626-4610)
PHONE.............................714 429-1025
David Golden, Prin
EMP: 85 EST: 2008
SALES (est): 906.73K **Privately Held**
Web: www.goldencapitalgrp.com
SIC: 6162 6141 Loan correspondents;
　　Personal credit institutions

(P-11903)
FEDERAL HOME LOAN MRTG CORP
Also Called: Freddie Mac
444 S Flower St Fl 44, Los Angeles
(90071-2944)
PHONE.............................213 337-4200
Steve Griffin, Mgr
EMP: 545
SALES (corp-wide): 108.05B **Publicly Held**
Web: www.freddiemac.com
SIC: 6162 Mortgage bankers
PA: Federal Home Loan Mortgage
　　Corporation
　　8200 Jones Branch Dr
　　703 903-2000

(P-11904)
FIRST MORTGAGE CORPORATION
1131 W 6th St Ste 300, Ontario
(91762-1118)
PHONE.............................909 595-1996
EMP: 430
SIC: 6162 Mortgage bankers

(P-11905)
GFS CAPITAL HOLDINGS
6499 Havenwood Cir Ste 720, Huntington Beach (92648-6621)
PHONE.............................714 720-3918
EMP: 280
SIC: 6162 Mortgage brokers, using own money

(P-11906)
GOAL FINANCIAL LLC
Also Called: Education Ln Ctr Alexandria Ci
401 W A St Ste 1300, San Diego
(92101-7906)

PHONE.............................619 684-7600
EMP: 250 EST: 2004
SALES (est): 11.03MM **Privately Held**
Web: www.goalfinancial.net
SIC: 6162 Loan correspondents

(P-11907)
GOLDEN EMPIRE MORTGAGE INC (PA)
2130 Chester Ave, Bakersfield
(93301-4471)
PHONE.............................661 328-1600
Howard Kootstra, CEO
EMP: 100 EST: 1987
SQ FT: 25,000
SALES (est): 19.62MM **Privately Held**
Web: www.gemcorp.com
SIC: 6162 Mortgage bankers

(P-11908)
GOLDEN EMPIRE MORTGAGE INC (PA)
Also Called: Gem Mortgage
1200 Discovery Dr Ste 300, Bakersfield
(93309-7036)
PHONE.............................661 328-1600
John Copeland, Prin
EMP: 80 EST: 2006
SALES (est): 26.64MM **Privately Held**
Web: www.gemcorp.com
SIC: 6162 7371 Mortgage bankers;
　　Computer software development

(P-11909)
GOLDEN EMPIRE MORTGAGE INC
Also Called: Gem
41331 12th St W Ste 102, Palmdale
(93551-1423)
PHONE.............................661 949-3388
Jane Lawrence, Brnch Mgr
EMP: 254
Web: www.gemcorp.com
SIC: 6162 Mortgage bankers
PA: Golden Empire Mortgage, Inc.
　　2130 Chester Ave

(P-11910)
GUARANTEED RATE INC
1455 Frazee Rd Ste 500, San Diego
(92108-4350)
PHONE.............................760 310-6008
Trent Annicharico, Brnch Mgr
EMP: 120
Web: www.rate.com
SIC: 6162 Mortgage bankers
PA: Guaranteed Rate, Inc.
　　3940 N Ravenswood Ave

(P-11911)
GUARANTEED RATE INC
1065 Higuera St Ste 100, San Luis Obispo
(93401-3786)
PHONE.............................805 550-6933
EMP: 120
Web: www.rate.com
SIC: 6162 Mortgage bankers and loan correspondents
PA: Guaranteed Rate, Inc.
　　3940 N Ravenswood Ave

(P-11912)
GUARANTEED RATE INC
230 Commerce, Irvine (92602-1324)
PHONE.............................424 354-5344
EMP: 120
Web: www.rate.com
SIC: 6162 Mortgage bankers and loan correspondents

PA: Guaranteed Rate, Inc.
　　3940 N Ravenswood Ave

(P-11913)
HOMEXPRESS MORTGAGE CORP
1936 E Deere Ave Ste 200, Santa Ana
(92705-5733)
PHONE.............................714 944-3022
Kyle R Walker, CEO
EMP: 245 EST: 2018
SALES (est): 13.22MM **Privately Held**
Web: www.homexmortgage.com
SIC: 6162 Mortgage bankers and loan correspondents

(P-11914)
IMPAC MORTGAGE CORP
Also Called: Impac Mortgage
19500 Jamboree Rd Ste 100, Irvine
(92612-2426)
PHONE.............................949 475-3600
Joseph R Tomkinson, Pr
EMP: 298 EST: 2008
SALES (est): 7.86MM **Privately Held**
Web: www.cashcallmortgage.com
SIC: 6162 Mortgage bankers
PA: Impac Mortgage Holdings, Inc.
　　19500 Jamboree Rd Ste 100

(P-11915)
ISERVE RESIDENTIAL LENDING LLC
Also Called: Idirect Home Loans
10815 Rancho Bernardo Rd, San Diego
(92127-2186)
PHONE.............................858 486-4169
Doug Wilson, Dir
EMP: 100 EST: 2011
SALES (est): 24.68MM **Privately Held**
Web: www.iservelending.com
SIC: 6162 Bond and mortgage companies

(P-11916)
LENDERS INVESTMENT CORP
18101 Von Karman Ave Ste 400, Irvine
(92612-0149)
PHONE.............................714 540-4747
Kerry M Smith, Pr
Bill Ammerman, *
EMP: 86 EST: 2003
SQ FT: 14,000
SALES (est): 646.32K **Privately Held**
SIC: 6162 Mortgage bankers

(P-11917)
LENDSURE MORTGAGE CORP
Also Called: Talis Lending
12230 World Trade Dr Ste 250, San Diego
(92128-3799)
PHONE.............................888 707-7811
Joseph John Lydon, Prin
EMP: 263 EST: 2016
SALES (est): 7.14MM **Privately Held**
Web: www.talislending.com
SIC: 6162 Mortgage bankers and loan correspondents

(P-11918)
LOANDEPOT INC (PA)
Also Called: Loandepot
6561 Irvine Center Dr, Irvine (92618-2118)
PHONE.............................888 337-6888
Frank Martell, Pr
Anthony Hsieh, Ofcr
David Hayes, CFO
Joseph Grassi, CRO
Gregory Smallwood, CLO
EMP: 242 EST: 2010

SQ FT: 144,398
SALES (est): 974.02MM
SALES (corp-wide): 974.02MM **Publicly Held**
Web: www.loandepot.com
SIC: 6162 Mortgage bankers and loan correspondents

(P-11919)
LOANDEPOTCOM LLC (DH)
Also Called: Customer Loan Depot
6561 Irvine Center Dr, Irvine (92618-2118)
PHONE....................888 337-6888
Andrew Dodson, *Pr*
David Norris, *Pr*
Bryan Sullivan, *Ex VP*
Peter Macdonald, *Ex VP*
Harold Gonzalez, *Sr VP*
EMP: 963 **EST:** 2009
SALES (corp-wide): 974.02MM **Publicly Held**
Web: www.ldpersonalloans.com
SIC: 6162 Mortgage bankers
HQ: Ld Holdings Group Llc
    26642 Towne Centre Dr
    Foothill Ranch CA 92610
    888 337-6888

(P-11920)
LOANDEPOTCOM LLC
901 N Palm Canyon Dr Ste 107, Palm Springs (92262-4450)
PHONE....................760 797-6000
EMP: 582
SALES (corp-wide): 974.02MM **Publicly Held**
Web: www.movement.com
SIC: 6162 Mortgage bankers
HQ: Loandepot.Com, Llc
    6561 Irvine Center Dr
    Irvine CA 92618

(P-11921)
LOANDEPOTCOM LLC
42455 10th St W Ste 109, Lancaster (93534-7060)
PHONE....................661 202-1700
EMP: 971
SALES (corp-wide): 974.02MM **Publicly Held**
Web: www.imortgage.com
SIC: 6162 Loan correspondents
HQ: Loandepot.Com, Llc
    6561 Irvine Center Dr
    Irvine CA 92618

(P-11922)
LOWER LLC
Also Called: Georgetown Mortgage
9587 Foothill Blvd, Rancho Cucamonga (91730-3506)
PHONE....................909 527-3736
EMP: 145
SALES (corp-wide): 42.08MM **Privately Held**
Web: www.thrivemortgage.com
SIC: 6162 Mortgage bankers and loan correspondents
PA: Lower, Llc
    5950 Symphony Woods Rd
    240 538-6184

(P-11923)
METROPOLITAN HOME MORTGAGE INC
Also Called: Intelliloan
3090 Bristol St Ste 600, Costa Mesa (92626-7318)
PHONE....................949 428-0161

Daryl Preedge, *Pr*
EMP: 100 **EST:** 1993
SQ FT: 5,000
SALES (est): 2.05MM **Privately Held**
Web: www.metrohmc.com
SIC: 6162 Mortgage bankers and loan correspondents

(P-11924)
MISSION HILLS MORTGAGE CORP (HQ)
Also Called: Mission Hills Mortgage Bankers
18500 Von Karman Ave Ste 1100, Irvine (92612-0546)
PHONE....................714 972-3832
Jay Ledbetter, *Pr*
EMP: 140 **EST:** 1969
SQ FT: 27,000
SALES (est): 6.3MM
SALES (corp-wide): 74.6MM **Privately Held**
Web: www.mhmb.com
SIC: 6162 Mortgage bankers and loan correspondents
PA: Tarbell Financial Corporation
    1403 N Tustin Ave Ste 380
    714 972-0988

(P-11925)
MORTGAGE BANK OF CALIFORNIA
Also Called: Mboc
3555 Voyager St Ste 201, Torrance (90503-1675)
PHONE....................310 498-2700
Michael Dallal, *Prin*
EMP: 82 **EST:** 2015
SALES (est): 4.46MM **Privately Held**
Web: www.mbanc.com
SIC: 6162 Mortgage bankers and loan correspondents

(P-11926)
MOUNTAIN WEST FINANCIAL INC (PA)
Also Called: Mortgage Works Financial
1255 W Colton Ave, Redlands (92374-2861)
PHONE....................909 793-1500
Gary H Martell Junior, *Pr*
Michael W Douglas, *
EMP: 391 **EST:** 1990
SALES (est): 32.51MM **Privately Held**
Web: www.mwfinc.com
SIC: 6162 Mortgage bankers

(P-11927)
NETWORK CAPITAL FUNDING CORP (PA)
Also Called: Network Capital
7700 Irvine Center Dr Fl 3, Irvine (92618-2923)
PHONE....................949 442-0060
Tri Nguyen, *Pr*
✿ **EMP:** 345 **EST:** 2002
SALES (est): 29.83MM
SALES (corp-wide): 29.83MM **Privately Held**
Web: www.networkcapital.com
SIC: 6162 Mortgage bankers

(P-11928)
NEW CENTURY MORTGAGE CORP
Also Called: New Century Mortgage
18400 Von Karman Ave Ste 1000, Irvine (92612-0516)
PHONE....................949 440-7030
Brad A Morrice, *Pr*

Brad A Morrice, *CEO*
Patrick Flanagan, *
Patti M Dodge, *
Daniel P Sussman, *
EMP: 3261 **EST:** 1995
SALES (est): 2.88MM **Privately Held**
SIC: 6162 Mortgage bankers and loan correspondents

(P-11929)
OCMBC INC (PA)
Also Called: Ocmban
19000 Macarthur Blvd Ste 200, Irvine (92612-1420)
PHONE....................949 679-7400
Rabi H Aziz, *CEO*
Madelina L Colon, *Pr*
EMP: 102 **EST:** 2001
SQ FT: 12,500
SALES (est): 272.89MM
SALES (corp-wide): 272.89MM **Privately Held**
Web: www.lsmortgage.com
SIC: 6162 Mortgage bankers

(P-11930)
PLATINUM CAPITAL GROUP (PA)
3500 N Sepulveda Blvd Ste E, Manhattan Beach (90266-3639)
PHONE....................310 406-3505
Mark Moses, *CEO*
Brett Dillenberg, *
Jack Daly E, *Development*
John Bastis, *
EMP: 78 **EST:** 1993
SQ FT: 24,000
SALES (est): 12.27MM **Privately Held**
Web: www.platinumcapitalpartners.com
SIC: 6162 Mortgage bankers and loan correspondents

(P-11931)
PRIVATE NAT MRTG ACCPTANCE LLC (DH)
Also Called: Pennymac
6101 Condor Dr, Agoura Hills (91301)
PHONE....................866 549-3583
EMP: 800 **EST:** 2008
SALES (est): 467.92MM
SALES (corp-wide): 1.4B **Publicly Held**
Web: www.pennymac.com
SIC: 6162 Mortgage bankers
HQ: Pnmac Holdings, Inc.
    3043 Townsgate Rd
    Westlake Village CA 91361
    818 224-7442

(P-11932)
RIGHT START MORTGAGE INC (PA)
Also Called: CFS Home Loans
80 S Lake Ave Ste 520, Pasadena (91101-2481)
PHONE....................855 313-9405
Buster Williams, *Pr*
Michael Goldman, *CEO*
EMP: 78 **EST:** 1989
SALES (est): 6.79MM **Privately Held**
Web: www.rightstartmortgage.com
SIC: 6162 Mortgage bankers and loan correspondents

(P-11933)
RUSHMORE LOAN MGT SVCS LLC (PA)
Also Called: Rushmore Crrspndent Lnding Svc
15480 Laguna Canyon Rd Ste 100, Irvine (92618-2132)

P.O. Box 619079 (75261-9079)
PHONE....................949 727-4798
Terry Smith, *Managing Member*
EMP: 842 **EST:** 2008
SQ FT: 3,000
SALES (est): 165.78MM **Privately Held**
Web: www.rushmorelm.com
SIC: 6162 Mortgage bankers and loan correspondents

(P-11934)
SEA BREEZE FINANCIAL SVCS INC
Also Called: Sea Breeze Mortgage Services
18191 Von Karman Ave Ste 150, Irvine (92612-7104)
P.O. Box 19079 (92817-9079)
PHONE....................949 223-9700
Leonard Hamilton, *Pr*
Curtis Green, *
EMP: 150 **EST:** 1985
SQ FT: 50,000
SALES (est): 2.52MM **Privately Held**
SIC: 6162 Mortgage bankers

(P-11935)
STEARNS LENDING LLC
Also Called: Stearns Home Loans
555 Anton Blvd Ste 300, Costa Mesa (92626-7667)
PHONE....................714 513-7777
Glenn Stearns, *Brnch Mgr*
EMP: 114
SIC: 6162 Mortgage bankers and loan correspondents
PA: Stearns Lending, Llc
    401 E Corp Dr Ste 150

(P-11936)
SUN WEST MORTGAGE COMPANY INC (PA)
Also Called: Lowratscom 1st Lbrty Cal State
18303 Gridley Rd, Cerritos (90703-5400)
PHONE....................833 478-6937
Pavan Agarwal, *CEO*
Hari S Agarwal, *
Sharda Agarwal, *
Jim Trapinski, *
Anita Agarwal, *
EMP: 147 **EST:** 1980
SQ FT: 9,800
SALES (est): 96.09MM
SALES (corp-wide): 96.09MM **Privately Held**
Web: www.swmc.com
SIC: 6162 6163 Mortgage bankers; Loan brokers

(P-11937)
SYNERGY ONE LENDING INC
Also Called: Morelends.com
3131 Camino Del Rio N Ste 150, San Diego (92108-5758)
PHONE....................385 273-5250
EMP: 104 **EST:** 2018
SALES (est): 11.28MM **Privately Held**
Web: www.s1l.com
SIC: 6162 Mortgage bankers and loan correspondents

6163 Loan Brokers

(P-11938)
5 ARCHES LLC
19800 Macarthur Blvd, Irvine (92612-2421)
PHONE....................949 387-8092
Shawn Miller, *CEO*
Gene Clark, *
Steven Davis, *

EMP: 95 EST: 2012
SALES (est): 4.27MM **Publicly Held**
Web: www.corevestfinance.com
SIC: **6163** Mortgage brokers arranging for loans, using money of others
PA: Redwood Trust, Inc.
1 Belvedere Pl Ste 300

(P-11939)
ATHAS CAPITAL GROUP INC
27001 Agoura Rd Ste 100, Agoura Hills (91301-5110)
PHONE..................................877 877-1477
Brian O'shaughnessy, *CEO*
EMP: 196 **EST:** 2007
SALES (est): 15.35MM **Privately Held**
Web: www.athascapital.com
SIC: **6163** Mortgage brokers arranging for loans, using money of others

(P-11940)
BAY-VALLEY MORTGAGE GROUP
Also Called: Bay Valley Mortgage
15020 La Mirada Blvd, La Mirada (90638-4743)
PHONE...................................714 367-5125
John Nelson, *CEO*
Christine Kim, *
EMP: 100 **EST:** 2011
SALES (est): 4MM **Privately Held**
Web: www.pacbaylending.com
SIC: **6163** Mortgage brokers arranging for loans, using money of others

(P-11941)
CARNEGIE MORTGAGE LLC
Also Called: Ovation Home Loans
15480 Laguna Canyon Rd Ste 100, Irvine (92618-2132)
PHONE...................................949 379-7000
Graham Fleming, *Managing Member*
EMP: 300
Web: www.carnegiemtg.com
SIC: **6163** Mortgage brokers arranging for loans, using money of others
PA: Carnegie Mortgage Llc
2297 Highway 33

(P-11942)
CENTER STREET LENDING CORP
18201 Von Karman Ave, Irvine (92612-1000)
PHONE...................................949 244-1090
EMP: 83 **EST:** 2010
SALES (est): 3.52MM **Privately Held**
SIC: **6163** 7371 Loan brokers; Computer software development

(P-11943)
CHANGE LENDING LLC
6265 Greenwich Dr Ste 215, San Diego (92122-5917)
PHONE...................................858 500-3060
EMP: 91
Web: www.changemtg.com
SIC: **6163** Mortgage brokers arranging for loans, using money of others
PA: Change Lending, Llc
175 N Riverview Dr

(P-11944)
CLEARPATH LENDING
Also Called: Clearpath Lending
15635 Alton Pkwy Ste 300, Irvine (92618-7332)
PHONE...................................949 502-3577
Amir Ali Omid, *CEO*

EMP: 130 EST: 2012
SALES (est): 9.45MM **Privately Held**
Web: www.clearpathlending.com
SIC: **6163** Mortgage brokers arranging for loans, using money of others

(P-11945)
DIGNIFIED HOME LOANS LLC
1 Baxter Way Ste 120, Westlake Village (91362-3809)
PHONE...................................818 421-7753
Preston James, *Prin*
EMP: 80 **EST:** 2013
SALES (est): 4.29MM **Privately Held**
Web: www.dignifiedhomeloans.com
SIC: **6163** Mortgage brokers arranging for loans, using money of others

(P-11946)
HOMEBRIDGE FINANCIAL SVCS INC
15301 Ventura Blvd Ste D300, Sherman Oaks (91403-6631)
PHONE...................................818 981-0606
Douglas Rotella, *Pr*
EMP: 1700
Web: www.homebridge.com
SIC: **6163** Mortgage brokers arranging for loans, using money of others
PA: Homebridge Financial Services, Inc.
194 Wood Ave S 9th Fl

(P-11947)
LMB OPCO LLC
Also Called: Lowermybills.com
12181 Bluff Creek Dr Ste 250, Playa Vista (90094-3236)
PHONE...................................310 348-6800
Jeff Hughes, *CEO*
EMP: 320 **EST:** 2016
SALES (est): 15.09MM **Privately Held**
Web: www.quickencompare.com
SIC: **6163** 7389 Mortgage brokers arranging for loans, using money of others; Financial services

(P-11948)
ML MORTGAGE CORP
Also Called: ML Mortgage
8270 Aspen St, Rancho Cucamonga (91730-3271)
PHONE...................................909 652-0780
Kamran Akbar, *Pr*
Jamal Akber, *
EMP: 80 **EST:** 2007
SQ FT: 1,200
SALES (est): 6.23MM **Privately Held**
Web: www.mlmortgage.net
SIC: **6163** Mortgage brokers arranging for loans, using money of others

(P-11949)
PENNYMAC CORP
3043 Townsgate Rd, Westlake Village (91361-3027)
PHONE...................................818 878-8416
Stanford L Kurland, *Pr*
EMP: 501 **EST:** 2010
SALES (est): 2.23MM **Publicly Held**
Web: www.pennymac.com
SIC: **6163** Loan brokers
PA: Pennymac Mortgage Investment Trust
3043 Townsgate Rd

(P-11950)
POPE MORTGAGE & ASSOCIATES INC
2980 Inland Empire Blvd Unit 100, Ontario (91764-6532)

PHONE...................................909 466-5380
Paul Pope, *Pr*
EMP: 72 **EST:** 2003
SQ FT: 14,000
SALES (est): 2.74MM **Privately Held**
SIC: **6163** Mortgage brokers arranging for loans, using money of others

(P-11951)
RMR FINANCIAL LLC (DH)
Also Called: Online Capital
610 Newport Center Dr, Newport Beach (92660-6419)
PHONE...................................408 355-2000
EMP: 84 **EST:** 2000
SQ FT: 11,300
SALES (est): 4.46MM
SALES (corp-wide): 1.07B **Publicly Held**
SIC: **6163** 6162 Mortgage brokers arranging for loans, using money of others; Mortgage bankers
HQ: Phh Corporation
3000 Leadenhall Rd
Mount Laurel NJ 08054
856 917-1744

(P-11952)
SAND CANYON CORPORATION (HQ)
7595 Irvine Center Dr Ste 120, Irvine (92618-2999)
P.O. Box 57080 (92619)
PHONE...................................949 727-9425
Robert Dubrish, *Pr*
William O'neill, *CFO*
Steve Nadon, *
Dale M Sugimoto, *
EMP: 100 **EST:** 1992
SALES (est): 13.7MM
SALES (corp-wide): 3.61B **Publicly Held**
Web: www.sandcanyondentistry.com
SIC: **6163** 6162 Loan brokers; Mortgage bankers and loan correspondents
PA: H & R Block, Inc.
1 H And R Block Way
816 854-3000

(P-11953)
STRATUS REAL ESTATE INC
Also Called: Stratus Realestate
435 Garfield Ave, South Pasadena (91030-2249)
PHONE...................................626 441-5549
Steve Heighimler, *Pr*
EMP: 165
SALES (corp-wide): 758.38MM **Privately Held**
Web: www.stratusrealestate.com
SIC: **6163** Loan brokers
HQ: Stratus Real Estate, Inc.
5311 Topanga Canyon Blvd # 3
Woodland Hills CA 91364

(P-11954)
STRATUS REAL ESTATE INC
Banning Villa Apartments
1100 N Banning Blvd Apt 111, Wilmington (90744-3527)
PHONE...................................310 549-7028
Bernadette Saunder, *Mgr*
EMP: 137
SALES (corp-wide): 758.38MM **Privately Held**
Web: www.stratusrealestate.com
SIC: **6163** 6513 Loan brokers; Apartment building operators
HQ: Stratus Real Estate, Inc.
5311 Topanga Canyon Blvd # 3
Woodland Hills CA 91364

(P-11955)
TARBELL FINANCIAL CORPORATION (PA)
1403 N Tustin Ave Ste 380, Santa Ana (92705-8691)
PHONE...................................714 972-0988
Donald Tarbell, *CEO*
Tina Jimov, *
Elizabeth Tarbell, *
Ronald Tarbell, *
Jin Lee, *
EMP: 100 **EST:** 1982
SQ FT: 60,000
SALES (est): 74.6MM
SALES (corp-wide): 74.6MM **Privately Held**
Web: www.tarbellcareers.com
SIC: **6163** 6531 6099 Mortgage brokers arranging for loans, using money of others; Real estate brokers and agents; Escrow institutions other than real estate

(P-11956)
UNITED VISION FINANCIAL INC
16027 Ventura Blvd Ste 200, Encino (91436-2733)
PHONE...................................818 285-0211
Dan Michaels, *Pr*
EMP: 180 **EST:** 2003
SQ FT: 3,000
SALES (est): 478.52K **Privately Held**
SIC: **6163** Mortgage brokers arranging for loans, using money of others

(P-11957)
VILLA VENETIA
2775 Mesa Verde Dr E, Costa Mesa (92626-4957)
PHONE...................................714 540-1800
United Dominion, *Pr*
EMP: 137 **EST:** 2001
SALES (est): 1.2MM
SALES (corp-wide): 758.38MM **Privately Held**
SIC: **6163** Loan brokers
HQ: Stratus Real Estate, Inc.
5311 Topanga Canyon Blvd # 3
Woodland Hills CA 91364

6211 Security Brokers And Dealers

(P-11958)
AMERIHOME MORTGAGE COMPANY LLC
Also Called: Amerihome Mortgage
1 Baxter Way Ste 300, Westlake Village (91362-3888)
PHONE...................................888 469-0810
James Furash, *CEO*
Thomas Smith, *
Todd Taylor, *
EMP: 704 **EST:** 2014
SALES (est): 43.18MM
SALES (corp-wide): 4.32B **Publicly Held**
Web: www.amerihome.com
SIC: **6211** Mortgages, buying and selling
PA: Western Alliance Bancorporation
1 E Washington St
602 389-3500

(P-11959)
CARRINGTON MORTGAGE SVCS LLC
10370 Commerce Center Dr Ste 140, Rancho Cucamonga (91730-5806)
PHONE...................................909 226-7963
Jaleh Jenkins, *Brnch Mgr*

EMP: 76
Web: www.carringtonwholesale.com
SIC: 6211 6163 Mortgages, buying and selling; Loan brokers
PA: Carrington Mortgage Services, Llc
1600 Douglass Rd Ste 200a

(P-11960)
CENTURION GROUP INC (PA)
Also Called: Coast Group Financial
365 S Rancho Santa Fe Rd # 3rd, San Marcos (92078-2338)
PHONE..............................760 471-8536
Jack Heilbron, *Pr*
Mary Lamoges, *
EMP: 125 **EST:** 1982
SQ FT: 9,000
SALES (est): 1.38MM
SALES (corp-wide): 1.38MM **Privately Held**
SIC: 6211 8111 Brokers, security; Legal services

(P-11961)
CHARLES SCHWAB CORPORATION
Also Called: Charles Schwab
7510 Hazard Center Dr Ste 407, San Diego (92108-4525)
PHONE..............................800 435-4000
Jim Croutch, *Prin*
EMP: 79
SALES (corp-wide): 18.84B **Publicly Held**
Web: www.schwab.com
SIC: 6211 Brokers, security
PA: The Charles Schwab Corporation
3000 Schwab Way
817 859-5000

(P-11962)
CHARLES SCHWAB CORPORATION
Also Called: Charles Schwab
27580 Ynez Rd Ste A, Temecula (92591-4667)
PHONE..............................800 435-4000
Mark Morgan, *Mgr*
EMP: 131
SALES (corp-wide): 18.84B **Publicly Held**
Web: www.schwab.com
SIC: 6211 6282 Brokers, security; Investment advice
PA: The Charles Schwab Corporation
3000 Schwab Way
817 859-5000

(P-11963)
CHARLES SCHWAB CORPORATION
Also Called: Charles Schwab
9757 Wilshire Blvd, Beverly Hills (90212-1821)
PHONE..............................800 435-4000
Jane E Fry, *Brnch Mgr*
EMP: 79
SALES (corp-wide): 18.84B **Publicly Held**
Web: www.schwab.com
SIC: 6211 Brokers, security
PA: The Charles Schwab Corporation
3000 Schwab Way
817 859-5000

(P-11964)
FIRST ALLIED SECURITIES INC (HQ)
Also Called: First Allied
655 W Broadway Fl 11, San Diego (92101-8487)
P.O. Box 85549 (92186-5549)

PHONE..............................619 702-9600
Adam Antoniades, *CEO*
Frank Campanale, *Vice Chairman**
Joel Marks, *Ch*
Kevin Keefe, *
Gregg S Glaser, *
EMP: 75 **EST:** 1994
SALES (est): 70.49MM **Privately Held**
Web: www.cetera.com
SIC: 6211 Brokers, security
PA: Cetera Financial Group, Inc.
655 W Broadway

(P-11965)
GOLD PARENT LP
11111 Santa Monica Blvd Ste 2000, Los Angeles (90025-3354)
PHONE..............................310 954-0444
Jonathan D Sokoloff, *Prin*
EMP: 3400 **EST:** 2016
SALES (est): 5.46MM **Privately Held**
SIC: 6211 Investment bankers

(P-11966)
GOLDMAN SACHS & CO LLC
Also Called: Goldman Sachs
2121 Avenue Of The Stars Ste 2600, Los Angeles (90067-5050)
PHONE..............................310 407-5700
John Mallory, *Brnch Mgr*
EMP: 120
SALES (corp-wide): 108.42B **Publicly Held**
Web: www.goldmansachs.com
SIC: 6211 Investment bankers
HQ: Goldman Sachs & Co. Llc
200 W St
New York NY 10282
212 902-1000

(P-11967)
GORES GROUP LLC (PA)
9800 Wilshire Blvd, Beverly Hills (90212-1804)
PHONE..............................310 209-3010
Alec Gores, *Managing Member*
Joseph Page, *
Vance Diggens, *
Frank Stefanik, *
EMP: 60 **EST:** 2003
SALES (est): 1.81B
SALES (corp-wide): 1.81B **Privately Held**
Web: www.gores.com
SIC: 6211 7372 5734 Investment firm, general brokerage; Prepackaged software; Computer software and accessories

(P-11968)
HYUNDAI ABS FUNDING LLC
3161 Michelson Dr, Irvine (92612-4400)
PHONE..............................949 732-2697
EMP: 11 **EST:** 2016
SALES (est): 4.75MM **Privately Held**
SIC: 6211 Security brokers and dealers
HQ: Hyundai Capital America
3161 Michelson Dr # 1900
Irvine CA 92612

(P-11969)
IMPERIAL CAPITAL LLC (PA)
10100 Santa Monica Blvd Ste 2400, Los Angeles (90067-4136)
PHONE..............................310 246-3700
Randall Wooster, *CEO*
Jason W Reese, *Ch*
Randall E Wooster, *CEO*
Timothy Sullivan, *Pr*
Mark Martis, *COO*
EMP: 85 **EST:** 1997
SALES (est): 43.09MM

SALES (corp-wide): 43.09MM **Privately Held**
Web: www.imperialcapital.com
SIC: 6211 Investment bankers

(P-11970)
INTERLINK SECURITIES CORP
20750 Ventura Blvd Ste 300, Woodland Hills (91364-6236)
P.O. Box 4323 (91365-4323)
PHONE..............................818 992-6700
Barry Wolfe, *Pr*
EMP: 100 **EST:** 1992
SALES (est): 735.03K **Privately Held**
SIC: 6211 6722 Security brokers and dealers ; Management investment, open-end

(P-11971)
LEAR CAPITAL INC
1990 S Bundy Dr Ste 600, Los Angeles (90025-5256)
PHONE..............................310 571-0190
John Ohanesian, *Pr*
Kevin Demeritt, *
EMP: 72 **EST:** 1997
SQ FT: 4,500
SALES (est): 23.93MM **Privately Held**
Web: www.learcapital.com
SIC: 6211 Mineral, oil, and gas leasing and royalty dealers

(P-11972)
LEONARD GREEN & PARTNERS LP (PA)
11111 Santa Monica Blvd Ste 2000, Los Angeles (90025-3354)
PHONE..............................310 954-0444
Jonathan Sokoloff, *Pt*
John Danhakl, *
Peter Nolan, *
Jonathan Seiffer, *
John Baumer, *
▲ **EMP:** 93 **EST:** 1989
SQ FT: 15,000
SALES (est): 3.41B **Privately Held**
Web: www.leonardgreen.com
SIC: 6211 Investment firm, general brokerage

(P-11973)
LERETA LLC (PA)
901 Corporate Center Dr, Pomona (91768-2642)
PHONE..............................626 543-1765
John Walsh, *CEO*
Tyler Page, *
James V Micali, *
Cody Tillack, *
Chris Masten, *
EMP: 350 **EST:** 2009
SALES (est): 12.43MM **Privately Held**
Web: www.lereta.com
SIC: 6211 6541 6361 Tax certificate dealers; Title search companies; Real estate title insurance

(P-11974)
LPL FINANCIAL HOLDINGS INC (PA)
Also Called: Access Overlay
4707 Executive Dr, San Diego (92121-3091)
PHONE..............................800 877-7210
Rich Steinmeier, *Interim Chief Executive Officer*
James S Putnam, *Non-Executive Chairman of the Board*
Matthew J Audette, *CFO*
Sara Dadyar, *Chief Human Capital Officer*
Greg Gates, *Chief Technician*
EMP: 454 **EST:** 1989

SQ FT: 420,000
SALES (est): 10.05B **Publicly Held**
Web: www.lpl.com
SIC: 6211 6282 6091 Brokers, security; Investment advisory service; Nondeposit trust facilities

(P-11975)
M L STERN & CO LLC (DH)
8350 Wilshire Blvd Ste 300, Beverly Hills (90211-2350)
PHONE..............................323 658-4400
Stephen F Kempa, *
EMP: 117 **EST:** 1980
SQ FT: 8,100
SALES (est): 12.92MM
SALES (corp-wide): 1.57B **Publicly Held**
Web: www.mlstern.com
SIC: 6211 Brokers, security
HQ: Hilltop Securities Holdings Llc
200 Crescent Ct Ste 1330
Dallas TX 75201
214 855-2177

(P-11976)
MERRILL LYNCH INV MGT INC
Also Called: Merrill Lynch
10877 Wilshire Blvd Ste 1900, Los Angeles (90024-4374)
PHONE..............................310 209-4000
Robin Mayorkas, *Mgr*
EMP: 187
SALES (corp-wide): 171.91B **Publicly Held**
Web: www.ml.com
SIC: 6211 Security brokers and dealers
HQ: Merrill Lynch Investment Management, Inc.
225 Liberty St Fl 41
New York NY 10281
800 937-0605

(P-11977)
MERRILL LYNCH PRCE FNNER SMITH
Also Called: Merrill Lynch
5080 California Ave Ste 102, Bakersfield (93309-1697)
P.O. Box 9788 (93389-9788)
PHONE..............................661 326-7700
Gary Sampson, *Mgr*
EMP: 141
SALES (corp-wide): 171.91B **Publicly Held**
Web: www.ml.com
SIC: 6211 Security brokers and dealers
HQ: Merrill Lynch, Pierce, Fenner & Smith Incorporated
111 Eighth Ave
New York NY 10281
800 637-7455

(P-11978)
MERRILL LYNCH PRCE FNNER SMITH
Also Called: Merrill Lynch
24200 Magic Mountain Pkwy Ste 115, Valencia (91355-4887)
PHONE..............................661 802-0764
Ann Johnson, *Brnch Mgr*
EMP: 70
SALES (corp-wide): 171.91B **Publicly Held**
Web: www.ml.com
SIC: 6211 Security brokers and dealers
HQ: Merrill Lynch, Pierce, Fenner & Smith Incorporated
111 Eighth Ave
New York NY 10281
800 637-7455

(P-11979)

MERRILL LYNCH PRCE FNNER SMITH

Also Called: Merrill Lynch
2301 Rosecrans Ave Ste 3150, El Segundo (90245-4966)
PHONE.....................310 536-1600
Shawn Soroush, *Mgr*
EMP: 88
SALES (corp-wide): 171.91B **Publicly Held**
Web: www.ml.com
SIC: 6211 Security brokers and dealers
HQ: Merrill Lynch, Pierce, Fenner & Smith Incorporated
111 Eighth Ave
New York NY 10281
800 637-7455

(P-11980)

MERRILL LYNCH PRCE FNNER SMITH

Also Called: Merrill Lynch
800 E Colorado Blvd Ste 400, Pasadena (91101-2136)
PHONE.....................800 637-7455
Mark Mixon, *Mgr*
EMP: 246
SALES (corp-wide): 171.91B **Publicly Held**
Web: www.ml.com
SIC: 6211 Security brokers and dealers
HQ: Merrill Lynch, Pierce, Fenner & Smith Incorporated
111 Eighth Ave
New York NY 10281
800 637-7455

(P-11981)

MERRILL LYNCH PRCE FNNER SMITH

Also Called: Merrill Lynch
650 Town Center Dr # 500, Costa Mesa (92626-1989)
PHONE.....................714 429-2800
EMP: 88
SALES (corp-wide): 93.85B **Publicly Held**
Web: www.ml.com
SIC: 6211 8742 Security brokers and dealers ; Financial consultant
HQ: Merrill Lynch, Pierce, Fenner & Smith Incorporated
111 8th Ave
New York NY 10281
800 637-7455

(P-11982)

MERRILL LYNCH PRCE FNNER SMITH

Also Called: Merrill Lynch
520 Newport Center Dr Ste 1900, Newport Beach (92660-7084)
PHONE.....................949 467-3760
David Gunta, *Brnch Mgr*
EMP: 193
SALES (corp-wide): 171.91B **Publicly Held**
Web: www.ml.com
SIC: 6211 Security brokers and dealers
HQ: Merrill Lynch, Pierce, Fenner & Smith Incorporated
111 Eighth Ave
New York NY 10281
800 637-7455

(P-11983)

MERRILL LYNCH PRCE FNNER SMITH

Also Called: Merrill Lynch

145 S State College Blvd Ste 300, Brea (92821-5844)
PHONE.....................714 257-4400
TOLL FREE: 800
Robert Max, *Mgr*
EMP: 193
SALES (corp-wide): 171.91B **Publicly Held**
Web: www.ml.com
SIC: 6211 Security brokers and dealers
HQ: Merrill Lynch, Pierce, Fenner & Smith Incorporated
111 Eighth Ave
New York NY 10281
800 637-7455

(P-11984)

MERRILL LYNCH PRCE FNNER SMITH

Also Called: Merrill Lynch
3010 Old Ranch Pkwy Ste 150, Seal Beach (90740-2760)
PHONE.....................562 493-1300
Julie Danaho, *Mgr*
EMP: 88
SALES (corp-wide): 171.91B **Publicly Held**
Web: www.ml.com
SIC: 6211 Security brokers and dealers
HQ: Merrill Lynch, Pierce, Fenner & Smith Incorporated
111 Eighth Ave
New York NY 10281
800 637-7455

(P-11985)

MERRILL LYNCH PRCE FNNER SMITH

Also Called: Merrill Lynch
1020 Marsh St, San Luis Obispo (93401-3630)
PHONE.....................805 596-2222
M Barry Epperson, *Dir*
EMP: 70
SALES (corp-wide): 171.91B **Publicly Held**
Web: www.ml.com
SIC: 6211 Security brokers and dealers
HQ: Merrill Lynch, Pierce, Fenner & Smith Incorporated
111 Eighth Ave
New York NY 10281
800 637-7455

(P-11986)

MERRILL LYNCH PRCE FNNER SMITH

Also Called: Merrill Lynch
1096 Coast Village Rd, Santa Barbara (93108-0723)
PHONE.....................805 695-7028
EMP: 106
SALES (corp-wide): 171.91B **Publicly Held**
Web: www.ml.com
SIC: 6211 6021 Security brokers and dealers ; National commercial banks
HQ: Merrill Lynch, Pierce, Fenner & Smith Incorporated
111 Eighth Ave
New York NY 10281
800 637-7455

(P-11987)

MERRILL LYNCH PRCE FNNER SMITH

Also Called: Merrill Lynch
1424 State St, Santa Barbara (93101-2512)
PHONE.....................805 963-0333
Frederick Burrows, *Brnch Mgr*

EMP: 211
SALES (corp-wide): 171.91B **Publicly Held**
Web: www.ml.com
SIC: 6211 Security brokers and dealers
HQ: Merrill Lynch, Pierce, Fenner & Smith Incorporated
111 Eighth Ave
New York NY 10281
800 637-7455

(P-11988)

MERRILL LYNCH PRCE FNNER SMITH

Also Called: Merrill Lynch
2815 Townsgate Rd Ste 300, Westlake Village (91361-3094)
PHONE.....................805 381-2600
TOLL FREE: 800
Brian Riley, *Mgr*
EMP: 88
SALES (corp-wide): 171.91B **Publicly Held**
Web: www.ml.com
SIC: 6211 Security brokers and dealers
HQ: Merrill Lynch, Pierce, Fenner & Smith Incorporated
111 Eighth Ave
New York NY 10281
800 637-7455

(P-11989)

MERRILL LYNCH PRCE FNNER SMITH

Also Called: Merrill Lynch
74800 Us Highway 111, Indian Wells (92210-7116)
PHONE.....................760 862-1400
Robert O Braun, *Brnch Mgr*
EMP: 123
SALES (corp-wide): 171.91B **Publicly Held**
Web: www.ml.com
SIC: 6211 Security brokers and dealers
HQ: Merrill Lynch, Pierce, Fenner & Smith Incorporated
111 Eighth Ave
New York NY 10281
800 637-7455

(P-11990)

MERRILL LYNCH PRCE FNNER SMITH

Also Called: Merrill Lynch
11811 Bernardo Plaza Ct, San Diego (92128-2401)
PHONE.....................858 673-6700
John Lohrenc, *Mgr*
EMP: 106
SALES (corp-wide): 171.91B **Publicly Held**
Web: www.ml.com
SIC: 6211 Security brokers and dealers
HQ: Merrill Lynch, Pierce, Fenner & Smith Incorporated
111 Eighth Ave
New York NY 10281
800 637-7455

(P-11991)

MERRILL LYNCH PRCE FNNER SMITH

Also Called: Merrill Lynch
7825 Fay Ave Ste 300, La Jolla (92037-4255)
PHONE.....................858 456-3600
Paul Sullivan, *Mgr*
EMP: 106
SALES (corp-wide): 171.91B **Publicly Held**

Web: www.ml.com
SIC: 6211 Security brokers and dealers
HQ: Merrill Lynch, Pierce, Fenner & Smith Incorporated
111 Eighth Ave
New York NY 10281
800 637-7455

(P-11992)

MERRILL LYNCH PRCE FNNER SMITH

Also Called: Merrill Lynch
12830 El Camino Real Ste 300, San Diego (92130-2976)
PHONE.....................858 677-1300
Scott Wilson, *Dir*
EMP: 88
SALES (corp-wide): 171.91B **Publicly Held**
Web: www.ml.com
SIC: 6211 Security brokers and dealers
HQ: Merrill Lynch, Pierce, Fenner & Smith Incorporated
111 Eighth Ave
New York NY 10281
800 637-7455

(P-11993)

MERRILL LYNCH PRCE FNNER SMITH

Also Called: Merrill Lynch
701 B St Ste 2350, San Diego (92101-8125)
PHONE.....................619 699-3700
Quinton Ellis, *Brnch Mgr*
EMP: 193
SALES (corp-wide): 171.91B **Publicly Held**
Web: www.ml.com
SIC: 6211 8742 Security brokers and dealers ; Financial consultant
HQ: Merrill Lynch, Pierce, Fenner & Smith Incorporated
111 Eighth Ave
New York NY 10281
800 637-7455

(P-11994)

MERRILL LYNCH PRCE FNNER SMITH

Also Called: Merrill Lynch Carlsbad Office
1000 Aviara Dr Ste 200, Carlsbad (92011-4218)
PHONE.....................760 930-3100
Nick Givogri, *Mgr*
EMP: 88
SALES (corp-wide): 171.91B **Publicly Held**
Web: www.ml.com
SIC: 6211 Security brokers and dealers
HQ: Merrill Lynch, Pierce, Fenner & Smith Incorporated
111 Eighth Ave
New York NY 10281
800 637-7455

(P-11995)

MORGAN STNLEY SMITH BARNEY LLC

5796 Armada Dr Ste 200, Carlsbad (92008-4694)
PHONE.....................760 438-5100
John Condos, *Prin*
EMP: 117
SALES (corp-wide): 96.19B **Publicly Held**
Web: www.morganstanley.com
SIC: 6211 Stock brokers and dealers
HQ: Morgan Stanley Smith Barney, Llc
1585 Broadway Ave
New York NY 10036

▲ = Import ▼ = Export
◆ = Import/Export

(P-11996)
MORGAN STNLEY SMITH BARNEY LLC
1225 Prospect St Ste 202, La Jolla (92037-3687)
PHONE..................212 761-4000
Emily Temporal, *Brnch Mgr*
EMP: 102
SALES (corp-wide): 96.19B **Publicly Held**
Web: www.morganstanley.com
SIC: 6211 Security brokers and dealers
HQ: Morgan Stanley Smith Barney, Llc
1585 Broadway Ave
New York NY 10036

(P-11997)
MORGAN STNLEY SMITH BARNEY LLC
Also Called: Morgan Stanley Smith Barney
101 W Broadway Ste 1800, San Diego (92101-8298)
PHONE..................619 238-1226
Nozomi Ward, *Sr VP*
EMP: 122
SALES (corp-wide): 96.19B **Publicly Held**
Web: www.morganstanley.com
SIC: 6211 Stock brokers and dealers
HQ: Morgan Stanley Smith Barney, Llc
1585 Broadway Ave
New York NY 10036

(P-11998)
MORGAN STNLEY SMITH BARNEY LLC
3750 University Ave Ste 600, Riverside (92501-3323)
PHONE..................951 682-1181
James Gibson, *Mgr*
EMP: 107
SALES (corp-wide): 96.19B **Publicly Held**
Web: www.morganstanley.com
SIC: 6211 Security brokers and dealers
HQ: Morgan Stanley Smith Barney, Llc
1585 Broadway Ave
New York NY 10036

(P-11999)
MORGAN STNLEY SMITH BARNEY LLC
10 Pointe Dr Ste 400, Brea (92821-7620)
PHONE..................714 674-4100
Vincent Daigneault, *Prin*
EMP: 102
SALES (corp-wide): 96.19B **Publicly Held**
Web: www.morganstanley.com
SIC: 6211 Stock brokers and dealers
HQ: Morgan Stanley Smith Barney, Llc
1585 Broadway Ave
New York NY 10036

(P-12000)
MORGAN STNLEY SMITH BARNEY LLC
444 S Flower St Ste 2700, Los Angeles (90071-2971)
PHONE..................213 891-3200
Bruce Brereton, *Brnch Mgr*
EMP: 117
SALES (corp-wide): 96.19B **Publicly Held**
Web: www.morganstanley.com
SIC: 6211 Security brokers and dealers
HQ: Morgan Stanley Smith Barney, Llc
1585 Broadway Ave
New York NY 10036

(P-12001)
MORGAN STNLEY SMITH BARNEY LLC

21650 Oxnard St Ste 1800, Woodland Hills (91367-4944)
PHONE..................818 715-1800
Fred Rucker Esq, *Brnch Mgr*
EMP: 127
SALES (corp-wide): 96.19B **Publicly Held**
Web: www.morganstanley.com
SIC: 6211 Stock brokers and dealers
HQ: Morgan Stanley Smith Barney, Llc
1585 Broadway Ave
New York NY 10036

(P-12002)
MURIEL SIEBERT & CO INC
9378 Wilshire Blvd Ste 300, Beverly Hills (90212-3168)
PHONE..................800 993-2015
Joseph M Ramos, *Ex VP*
EMP: 100
SALES (corp-wide): 124.63MM **Publicly Held**
Web: www.siebert.com
SIC: 6211 Brokers, security
HQ: Muriel Siebert & Co., Inc.
15 Exchange Pl Ste 615
Jersey City NJ 07302
212 644-2400

(P-12003)
NATIONAL FINANCIAL SVCS LLC
19200 Von Karman Ave Ste 400, Irvine (92612-8512)
PHONE..................949 476-0157
Lawrence Goodkind, *Brnch Mgr*
EMP: 880
SALES (corp-wide): 4.35B **Privately Held**
Web: www.fidelity.com
SIC: 6211 Investment firm, general brokerage
HQ: National Financial Services Llc
200 Seaport Blvd Ste 630
Boston MA 02210
800 471-0382

(P-12004)
PACIFIC SELECT DISTRS INC
700 Newport Center Dr Fl 4, Newport Beach (92660-6307)
PHONE..................949 219-3011
Gerald W Robinson, *Pr*
Audrey L Milfs, *
Edward R Byrd, *
Kathy R Gough, *Assistant Vice President Compliance*
Thomas C Sutton, *
EMP: 96 EST: 1969
SQ FT: 300,000
SALES (est): 2.05MM
SALES (corp-wide): 12.84B **Privately Held**
Web: www.pacificlife.com
SIC: 6211 Brokers, security
HQ: Pacific Life Insurance Company
700 Newport Center Dr
Newport Beach CA 92660
949 219-3011

(P-12005)
PLAZA HOME MORTGAGE INC
9808 Scranton Rd, San Diego (92121-3704)
PHONE..................858 346-1208
Kevin Parra, *Pr*
EMP: 93
SALES (corp-wide): 50.27MM **Privately Held**
Web: www.plazahomemortgage.com
SIC: 6211 6162 Mortgages, buying and selling; Loan correspondents
PA: Plaza Home Mortgage, Inc.
4820 Eastgate Mall # 100
858 346-1200

(P-12006)
ROTH CAPITAL PARTNERS LLC (PA)
Also Called: Roth Mkm
888 San Clemente Dr, Newport Beach (92660-6366)
PHONE..................800 678-9147
Byron Roth, *Ch*
Byron Roth, *CEO*
Gordon Roth, *COO*
Warren Dunnavant Ii, *VP*
EMP: 100 EST: 1984
SQ FT: 52,000
SALES (est): 23.61MM
SALES (corp-wide): 23.61MM **Privately Held**
Web: www.roth.com
SIC: 6211 Investment bankers

(P-12007)
TRUST COMPANY OF WEST
865 S Figueroa St Ste 1800, Los Angeles (90017-2593)
PHONE..................213 244-0000
EMP: 515
SIC: 6211 Bond dealers and brokers

(P-12008)
UBS AMERICAS INC
600 W Broadway Ste 2800, San Diego (92101-0906)
PHONE..................619 557-2400
EMP: 142
Web: www.ubs.com
SIC: 6211 Security brokers and dealers
HQ: Ubs Americas Inc.
600 Washington Blvd
Stamford CT 06901
203 719-3000

(P-12009)
WEDBUSH SECURITIES INC (HQ)
1000 Wilshire Blvd Ste 900, Los Angeles (90017-2466)
P.O. Box P.O. Box 30014 (90030-0014)
PHONE..................213 688-8000
Edward W Wedbush, *Pr*
Thomas Ringer, *
Peter Allman-ward, *CFO*
Earl I Feldhorn, *
V Thomas Hale, *
EMP: 300 EST: 1955
SQ FT: 100,000
SALES (est): 224.6MM
SALES (corp-wide): 254.49MM **Privately Held**
Web: www.wedbush.com
SIC: 6211 Brokers, security
PA: Wedbush Capital
1000 Wilshire Blvd
213 688-8080

(P-12010)
WILLIAM ONEIL & CO INC (PA)
12655 Beatrice St, Los Angeles (90066-7302)
PHONE..................310 448-6800
Willaim J Oneil, *CEO*
Don Drake, *CFO*
Randy Watts, *CIS*
EMP: 77 EST: 2010
SQ FT: 5,000
SALES (est): 21.88MM
SALES (corp-wide): 21.88MM **Privately Held**
Web: www.williamoneil.com
SIC: 6211 6282 Brokers, security; Investment advisory service

6221 Commodity Contracts Brokers, Dealers

(P-12011)
CABALLERO & SONS INC
Also Called: Beyond Meat and Company
5753 E Santa Ana Canyon Rd Ste G-380, Anaheim (92807-3230)
PHONE..................562 368-1644
Perpetua Duque-hata, *Pr*
Nathaniel Caballero, *
Marivet Caballero, *
EMP: 25 EST: 2017
SQ FT: 500
SALES (est): 7MM **Privately Held**
SIC: 6221 2392 5141 5149 Commodity traders, contracts; Cushions and pillows; Food brokers; Beverages, except coffee and tea

(P-12012)
INVAPHARM INC (PA)
1320 W Mission Blvd, Ontario (91762-4786)
PHONE..................909 757-1818
Manu Patolia, *CEO*
Kalpesh Bodar, *Dir*
Nirmala Patolia, *Dir*
Mita Bodar, *Sec*
EMP: 26 EST: 2015
SQ FT: 60,000
SALES (est): 11.1MM
SALES (corp-wide): 11.1MM **Privately Held**
Web: www.invapharm.com
SIC: 6221 2023 Commodity brokers, contracts; Dietary supplements, dairy and non-dairy based

6282 Investment Advice

(P-12013)
ADVICEPERIOD
2121 Avenue Of The Stars Ste 2400, Los Angeles (90067-5048)
PHONE..................424 281-3600
Allison Schaengold, *Prin*
EMP: 76 EST: 2014
SALES (est): 6.19MM **Privately Held**
Web: www.adviceperiod.com
SIC: 6282 Investment advisory service

(P-12014)
ALLIANZ GLOBAL INVESTORS OF AMERICA LP
680 Newport Center Dr Ste 250, Newport Beach (92660-4046)
PHONE..................949 219-2200
EMP: 1800
SIC: 6282 Investment advisory service

(P-12015)
ALLIANZ GLOBL INVESTORS US LLC
680 Newport Center Dr Ste 250, Newport Beach (92660-4046)
PHONE..................949 219-2638
EMP: 244
SALES (corp-wide): 28.21B **Privately Held**
Web: www.allianzgi.com
SIC: 6282 Investment advice
HQ: Allianz Global Investors U.S. Llc
1633 Broadway
New York NY 10019
212 739-3000

(P-12016)

ANDERSON KAYNE CAPITAL

1800 Avenue Of The Stars Ste 200 # 3rd,
Los Angeles (90067-4204)
PHONE.............................800 231-7414
Richard Kayne, *Ch*
Robert Sinnott, *CEO*
Edward Cerny, *Mng Pt*
EMP: 300 **EST:** 1994
SALES (est): 2.34MM **Privately Held**
Web: www.kaynecapitalfoundation.org
SIC: 6282 Investment advisory service

(P-12017)

ANGELO GORDON & CO LP

2000 Avenue Of The Stars Ste 1020, Los
Angeles (90067-4710)
PHONE.............................310 777-5440
Angelo Gordon, *Brnch Mgr*
EMP: 1021
SALES (corp-wide): 90.89MM **Privately
Held**
Web: www.angelogordon.com
SIC: 6282 Futures advisory service
PA: Angelo, Gordon & Co., L.P.
245 Park Ave Fl 26
212 692-2000

(P-12018)

BEATING WALL STREET INC
(PA)

20121 Ventura Blvd Ste 305, Woodland Hills
(91364-2559)
PHONE.............................818 332-9696
Hamed Khorsand, *Pr*
EMP: 230 **EST:** 2000
SALES (est): 1.31MM
SALES (corp-wide): 1.31MM **Privately
Held**
Web: www.bwsfinancial.com
SIC: 6282 Investment advisory service

(P-12019)

BLYTHE GLOBAL ADVISORS
LLC

19800 Macarthur Blvd Ste 1180, Irvine
(92612-2460)
PHONE.............................949 757-4180
Marc Blythe, *Prin*
EMP: 78 **EST:** 2009
SALES (est): 993.31K **Privately Held**
Web: www.blytheglobal.com
SIC: 6282 Investment advisory service

(P-12020)

BRANDES INV PARTNERS INC
(PA)

11988 El Camino Real Ste 300, San Diego
(92130-2594)
P.O. Box 919048 (92191-9048)
PHONE.............................858 755-0239
Charles H Brandes, *Ch Bd*
Brent V Woods, *
Glenn R Carlson, *
Jeffrey A Busby, *
Gary Iwamura, *
EMP: 212 **EST:** 1974
SQ FT: 27,000
SALES (est): 22.71MM
SALES (corp-wide): 22.71MM **Privately
Held**
Web: www.brandes.com
SIC: 6282 Investment advisory service

(P-12021)

BRANDES INVESTMENT
PARTNERS LP

4275 Executive Sq Ste 500, La Jolla
(92037-1477)

P.O. Box 919048 (92191)
PHONE.............................858 755-0239
Oliver Murray, *Mng Pt*
EMP: 240 **EST:** 1974
SALES (est): 4.97MM **Privately Held**
Web: www.brandes.com
SIC: 6282 Investment advice

(P-12022)

C2 FINANCIAL CORPORATION

703 Sunset Ct, San Diego (92109-7024)
PHONE.............................858 220-2112
EMP: 162
SALES (corp-wide): 18.16MM **Privately
Held**
Web: www.c2financial.com
SIC: 6282 Investment advice
PA: C2 Financial Corporation
12230 El Camino Real
858 312-4900

(P-12023)

CAPITAL RESEARCH AND MGT
CO (HQ)

333 S Hope St Fl 55, Los Angeles
(90071-3061)
PHONE.............................213 486-9200
R Michael Shanahan, *Ch Bd*
James F Rothenberg, *Ch Bd*
Timothy Armour, *CEO*
Gordon Crawford, *Sr VP*
Gina Despres, *Sr VP*
EMP: 500 **EST:** 1944
SALES (est): 1.61B
SALES (corp-wide): 7.25B **Privately Held**
Web: www.thecapitalgroup.com
SIC: 6282 Investment research
PA: The Capital Group Companies Inc
333 S Hope St Fl 53
213 486-9200

(P-12024)

CITY NATIONAL ROCHDALE
LLC

400 N Roxbury Dr Ste 400, Beverly Hills
(90210-5021)
PHONE.............................310 888-6000
Gregory Kaplan, *Brnch Mgr*
EMP: 128
SALES (corp-wide): 41.52B **Privately Held**
Web: www.rochdale.com
SIC: 6282 Investment advisory service
HQ: City National Rochdale, Llc
400 Park Ave Fl 10
New York NY 10022
212 702-3500

(P-12025)

CYPRESS EQUITY
INVESTMENTS LLC

233 Wilshire Blvd Ste 325, Santa Monica
(90401-1221)
PHONE.............................310 207-1699
Michael Sorochinsky, *Managing Member*
EMP: 100 **EST:** 2003
SALES (est): 5.02MM **Privately Held**
Web: www.cypressequity.com
SIC: 6282 Investment advice

(P-12026)

HOULIHAN LOKEY INC (PA)

10250 Constellation Blvd Fl 5, Los Angeles
(90067-6205)
PHONE.............................310 788-5200
Scott L Beiser, *CEO*
Irwin N Gold, *
Scott J Adelson, *
David A Preiser, *
J Lindsey Alley, *CFO*

EMP: 300 **EST:** 1972
SALES (est): 1.81B
SALES (corp-wide): 1.81B **Publicly Held**
Web: www.hl.com
SIC: 6282 6211 Investment advice; Security
brokers and dealers

(P-12027)

MARLIN EQUITY PARTNERS
LLC (PA)

1301 Manhattan Ave, Hermosa Beach
(90254-3654)
PHONE.............................310 364-0100
David Mcgovern, *Managing Member*
Nick Kaiser, *
Peter Spasov, *
George Kase, *
Steve Johnson, *
EMP: 80 **EST:** 2005
SALES (est): 690.66MM **Privately Held**
Web: www.marlinequity.com
SIC: 6282 3661 Investment advisory service;
Telephones and telephone apparatus

(P-12028)

OAKTREE CAPITAL
MANAGEMENT LP (DH)

333 S Grand Ave Fl 28, Los Angeles
(90071-1530)
PHONE.............................213 830-6300
Todd Molz, *COO*
EMP: 120 **EST:** 2007
SALES (est): 4.86B
SALES (corp-wide): 69.83B **Privately Held**
Web: www.oaktreecapital.com
SIC: 6282 6722 6211 Investment advisory
service; Management investment, open-end
; Security brokers and dealers
HQ: Brookfield Asset Management Llc
250 Vesey St Fl 15
New York NY 10281

(P-12029)

PACIFIC ALTRNTIVE ASSET
MGT LL (HQ)

Also Called: Paamco
660 Newport Center Dr Ste 930, Newport
Beach (92660-6410)
PHONE.............................949 261-4900
Jane Buchan, *CEO*
EMP: 94 **EST:** 2000
SALES (est): 24.49MM
SALES (corp-wide): 37.73MM **Privately
Held**
Web: www.paamcoprisma.com
SIC: 6282 Investment advisory service
PA: Paamco Prisma Holdings, Llc
660 Nwport Ctr Dr Ste 930
949 261-4900

(P-12030)

PAYDEN & RYGEL (PA)

333 S Grand Ave Ste 4000, Los Angeles
(90071-1518)
PHONE.............................213 625-1900
Joan Payden, *CEO*
Scott J Weiner, *Managing Principal
GLOBAL*
Brian Matthews, *Managing Principal
GLOBAL*
Brad Hersh, *
EMP: 140 **EST:** 1983
SALES (est): 24.2MM
SALES (corp-wide): 24.2MM **Privately
Held**
Web: www.payden.com
SIC: 6282 6211 Investment counselors;
Security brokers and dealers

(P-12031)

PLAN MEMBER FINANCIAL
CORP

Also Called: Planmember Services
6187 Carpinteria Ave, Carpinteria
(93013-2805)
PHONE.............................800 874-6910
Jon Ziehl, *CEO*
Terry Janeway, *
Bill Kemble, *
Trish Stone-damon, *Sec*
EMP: 100 **EST:** 1990
SQ FT: 6,000
SALES (est): 23.82MM **Privately Held**
Web: www.planmemberfinancial.com
SIC: 6282 Investment counselors

(P-12032)

RESEARCH AFFILIATES
CAPITAL LP

Also Called: Research Affiliates
660 Newport Center Dr, Newport Beach
(92660-6401)
PHONE.............................949 325-8700
Rob Arnott, *CEO*
Jason Hsu, *CIO*
Katrina F Sherrerd, *COO*
EMP: 82 **EST:** 2002
SALES (est): 6.95MM **Privately Held**
Web: www.researchaffiliates.com
SIC: 6282 Investment advisory service

(P-12033)

RESEARCH AFFILIATES MGT
LLC

Also Called: Research Affiliates
660 Newport Center Dr, Newport Beach
(92660-6401)
PHONE.............................949 325-8700
Rob Arnott, *CEO*
Jason Hsu, *CIO*
Katrina Sherrerd, *COO*
EMP: 80 **EST:** 2002
SALES (est): 8.02MM **Privately Held**
Web: www.researchaffiliates.com
SIC: 6282 Investment counselors

(P-12034)

TCW GROUP INC (PA)

515 S Flower St, Los Angeles
(90071-2201)
PHONE.............................213 244-0000
David Lippman, *Pr*
Richard M Villa, *
Meredith S Jackson, *
David S Devito, *
Jeffrey Engelsman Global, *Chief
Compliance Officer*
EMP: 450 **EST:** 1971
SALES (est): 54.33MM **Privately Held**
SIC: 6282 6211 Investment advisory service;
Security brokers and dealers

(P-12035)

THOMAS JAMES CAPITAL INC

26940 Aliso Viejo Pkwy Ste 100, Aliso Viejo
(92656-2650)
PHONE.............................949 481-7026
Thomas L Beadel, *Pr*
James Quandt, *
EMP: 150 **EST:** 2006
SQ FT: 1,400
SALES (est): 21.25MM **Privately Held**
Web: www.tjh.com
SIC: 6282 6798 Investment advisory service;
Real estate investment trusts

(P-12036)

TRILLER GROUP INC

7119 W Sunset Blvd Pmb 782, Los Angeles
(90046-4411)
PHONE..................310 893-5090
Kevin Mcgurn, *CEO*
Ng Wing Fai Grp, *CEO*
Robert E Diamond Junior, *Ch Bd*
Richard Kong, *GRP*
Shu Pei Huang Act Grp, *CFO*
EMP: 176 **EST:** 2015
SALES (est): 54.19MM **Privately Held**
SIC: 6282 Investment advice

(P-12037)

U S TRUST COMPANY NA

Also Called: US Trust
515 S Flower St Ste 2700, Los Angeles
(90071-2216)
PHONE..................213 861-5000
Tim Leach, *CEO*
EMP: 350 **EST:** 1982
SQ FT: 65,000
SALES (est): 5.06MM
SALES (corp-wide): 171.91B **Publicly Held**
SIC: 6282 6022 Investment advice; State commercial banks
HQ: Bank Of America Pvt Wealth Management
114 W 47th St Ste C-1
New York NY 10036
800 878-7878

6289 Security And Commodity Service

(P-12038)

AMERICAN FUNDS SERVICE COMPANY (DH)

Also Called: Capital Group
6455 Irvine Center Dr, Irvine (92618-4518)
PHONE..................949 975-5000
EMP: 300 **EST:** 1968
SALES (est): 57.07MM
SALES (corp-wide): 7.25B **Privately Held**
Web: www.capitalgroup.com
SIC: 6289 6211 Security transfer agents; Security brokers and dealers
HQ: Capital Research And Management Company
333 S Hope St Fl 55
Los Angeles CA 90071
213 486-9200

(P-12039)

COMPUTERSHARE INC

2335 Alaska Ave, El Segundo
(90245-4808)
PHONE..................800 522 6646
EMP: 185
Web: www.computershare.com
SIC: 6289 Stock transfer agents
HQ: Computershare Inc.
150 Royall St
Canton MA 02021

6311 Life Insurance

(P-12040)

FATCO HOLDINGS LLC

1 First American Way, Santa Ana
(92707-5913)
PHONE..................714 250-3000
EMP: 77 **EST:** 2007
SALES (est): 252.7MM **Publicly Held**
Web: www.firstam.com
SIC: 6311 Life insurance

PA: First American Financial Corporation
1 First American Way

(P-12041)

GOLDEN STATE MUTL LF INSUR CO (PA)

1999 W Adams Blvd, Los Angeles
(90018-3595)
P.O. Box 26894 (94126-6894)
PHONE..................713 526-4361
Larkin Teasley, *Pr*
EMP: 100 **EST:** 1925
SQ FT: 57,000
SALES (est): 3.1MM
SALES (corp-wide): 3.1MM **Privately Held**
SIC: 6311 Mutual association life insurance

(P-12042)

GUARDIAN LIFE INSUR CO AMER

975 San Pasqual St, Pasadena
(91106-3368)
PHONE..................626 792-1935
Bob Daignault, *Brnch Mgr*
EMP: 83
SALES (corp-wide): 3.42B **Privately Held**
Web: www.guardianlife.com
SIC: 6311 Life insurance
PA: Guardian Life Insurance Company Of America
10 Hudson Yards Fl 22
212 598-8000

(P-12043)

GUARDIAN LIFE INSUR CO AMER

510 W 6th St Ste 815, Los Angeles
(90014-1309)
PHONE..................213 624-2002
Charles Bogue, *Brnch Mgr*
EMP: 85
SALES (corp-wide): 3.42B **Privately Held**
Web: www.guardianlife.com
SIC: 6311 Life insurance
PA: Guardian Life Insurance Company Of America
10 Hudson Yards Fl 22
212 598-8000

(P-12044)

JOHN ALDEN LIFE INSURANCE CO

20950 Warner Center Ln Ste A, Woodland Hills (91367-6537)
PHONE..................818 595-7600
Thomas Christenson, *Brnch Mgr*
FMP: 140
SALES (corp-wide): 11.13B **Publicly Held**
SIC: 6311 Life insurance
HQ: Alden John Life Insurance Company
501 W Michigan St
Milwaukee WI 53203
414 271-3011

(P-12045)

JOHN HANCOCK LIFE INSUR CO USA

5000 Birch St Ste 120, Newport Beach
(92660-8117)
PHONE..................949 254-1440
EMP: 347
SALES (corp-wide): 17.45B **Privately Held**
Web: www.johnhancock.com
SIC: 6311 Life insurance
HQ: John Hancock Life Insurance Company (U.S.A.)
865 S Fgueroa St Ste 3320
Los Angeles CA 90017
213 689-0813

(P-12046)

NEW FIRST FINCL RESOURCES LLC

100 Spectrum Center Dr Ste 400, Irvine
(92618-4966)
PHONE..................949 223-2160
EMP: 212 **EST:** 1987
SALES (est): 1.57MM **Privately Held**
Web: www.ffrmembers.com
SIC: 6311 Life insurance

(P-12047)

NORTHWESTERN MUTL FINCL NETWRK (PA)

4225 Executive Sq Ste 1250, La Jolla
(92037-9176)
PHONE..................619 234-3111
Garrett J Bleakley, *Owner*
EMP: 100 **EST:** 1952
SALES (est): 12.26MM **Privately Held**
Web: www.northwesternmutual.com
SIC: 6311 Life insurance

(P-12048)

PACIFIC ASSET HOLDING LLC

700 Newport Center Dr, Newport Beach
(92660-6307)
PHONE..................949 219-3011
EMP: 109 **EST:** 1997
SALES (est): 960.74K
SALES (corp-wide): 12.84B **Privately Held**
SIC: 6311 6371 6321 Life insurance carriers; Pension funds; Accident insurance carriers
HQ: Pacific Life Insurance Company
700 Newport Center Dr
Newport Beach CA 92660
949 219-3011

(P-12049)

PACIFIC LIFE & ANNUITY COMPANY

700 Newport Center Dr, Newport Beach
(92660-6307)
P.O. Box 9000 (92658-9030)
PHONE..................949 219-3011
James Morris, *Pr*
Khanh T Tran, *
Audrey L Milfs, *
Brian Klemens, *
EMP: 650 **EST:** 1982
SQ FT: 125,000
SALES (est): 8.34MM
SALES (corp-wide): 12.84B **Privately Held**
Web: www.pacificlife.com
SIC: 6311 6411 Life insurance carriers; Insurance agents, brokers, and service
HQ: Pacific Life Insurance Company
700 Newport Center Dr
Newport Beach CA 92660
949 219-3011

(P-12050)

PACIFIC LIFE INSURANCE COMPANY

45 Enterprise # 4, Aliso Viejo (92656-2601)
PHONE..................949 219-5200
Evelyn Grant, *Brnch Mgr*
EMP: 82
SALES (corp-wide): 12.84B **Privately Held**
Web: www.pacificlife.com
SIC: 6311 Life insurance carriers
HQ: Pacific Life Insurance Company
700 Newport Center Dr
Newport Beach CA 92660
949 219-3011

(P-12051)

STANDARD INSURANCE COMPANY

500 N State College Blvd Ste 1000, Orange
(92868-1626)
PHONE..................714 634-8200
Joy Giblin, *Mgr*
EMP: 95
Web: www.standard.com
SIC: 6311 Life insurance carriers
HQ: Standard Insurance Company
900 Sw 5th Ave
Portland OR 97204
971 321-7000

(P-12052)

SUNAMERICA LIFE INSURANCE COMPANY

Also Called: SunAmerica
1 Sun America Ctr Fl 36, Los Angeles
(90067-6104)
PHONE..................310 772-6000
EMP: 225
SIC: 6311 Life insurance

(P-12053)

TRANSAMERICA OCCIDENTAL LIFE INSURANCE COMPANY

1150 S Olive St Fl 23, Los Angeles
(90015-2477)
P.O. Box 2101 (90078-2101)
PHONE..................213 742-2111
EMP: 3700
SIC: 6311 6371 6321 6324 Life insurance carriers; Pension funds; Health insurance carriers; Group hospitalization plans

(P-12054)

TRUCK UNDERWRITERS ASSOCIATION

Farmers Insurance
6303 Owensmouth Ave Fl 1, Woodland Hills
(91367-2200)
PHONE..................323 932-3200
Jane Franklin, *VP*
EMP: 1078
SQ FT: 275,000
Web: www.farmers.com
SIC: 6311 6331 6321 Life insurance; Fire, marine, and casualty insurance; Accident and health insurance
HQ: Truck Underwriters Association
4680 Wilshire Blvd
Los Angeles CA 90010
323 932-3200

6321 Accident And Health Insurance

(P-12055)

21ST CENTURY LF & HLTH CO INC (PA)

Also Called: Lifecare Assurance Company
21600 Oxnard St Ste 1500, Woodland Hills
(91367-4972)
P.O. Box 4243 (91365-4243)
PHONE..................818 887-4436
James M Glickman, *Pr*
Alan S Hughes, *
Daniel J Di Sipio, *
Jay R Peters Fsa, *Ex VP*
Pete Diffley, *
▲ **EMP:** 241 **EST:** 1980
SQ FT: 50,000
SALES (est): 22.73MM **Privately Held**
Web: www.lifecareassurance.com

SIC: 6321　Health insurance carriers

(P-12056)
AGENT FRANCHISE LLC
9518 9th St Ste C2, Rancho Cucamonga
(91730-4568)
PHONE.............................949 930-5025
EMP: 101 EST: 2014
SQ FT: 14,980
SALES (est): 2.72MM Privately Held
Web: www.agentfranchise.com
SIC: 6321　Accident and health insurance

(P-12057)
AUTO CLUB ENTERPRISES (PA)
3333 Fairview Rd, Costa Mesa
(92626-1610)
P.O. Box 25001　(92799)
PHONE.............................714 850-5111
John F Boyle, CEO
Raju T Varma, *
Gail C Louis, *
EMP: 1200 EST: 1912
SQ FT: 700,000
SALES (est): 222.44MM
SALES (corp-wide): 222.44MM Privately
Held
Web: www.aaa.com
SIC: 6321　Accident and health insurance

(P-12058)
AUTO CLUB ENTERPRISES
8761 Santa Monica Blvd, West Hollywood
(90069-4538)
PHONE.............................310 914-8500
Bob Szhwab, Mgr
EMP: 500
SALES (corp-wide): 222.44MM Privately
Held
Web: www.aaa.com
SIC: 6321　Accident and health insurance
PA: Auto Club Enterprises
　　3333 Fairview Rd
　　714 850-5111

(P-12059)
CARE 1ST HEALTH PLAN (PA)
601 Potrero Grande Dr Fl 2, Monterey Park
(91755-7430)
PHONE.............................323 889-6638
Maureen Tyson, Pr
Anna Tran, *
Janet Jan, *
Michael Rowan, *
Jamie Ueoka, *
EMP: 165 EST: 1994
SALES (est): 102.5MM Privately Held
Web: www.blueshieldca.com
SIC: 6321　Health insurance carriers

(P-12060)
CARELON HEALTH CALIFORNIA
INC (HQ)
Also Called: Caremore Health Plan
12900 Park Plaza Dr Ste 150, Cerritos
(90703-9329)
PHONE.............................562 622-2950
TOLL FREE: 888
Leeba R Lessin, Sup Chief Executive
　Officer
Allan Hoops, CEO
Sergio Zaldivar, Senior Vice President
　Corporate Development
John Kao, OF MANAGEMENT SERVICES
　ORGANIZATION
Doctor Ken Kin Md, Chief Medical Officer
EMP: 148 EST: 1996
SALES (est): 80.71MM
SALES (corp-wide): 171.34B Publicly
Held

Web: www.carelonhealth.com
SIC: 6321　Health insurance carriers
PA: Elevance Health, Inc.
　　220 Virginia Ave
　　800 331-1476

(P-12061)
CARELON MED BENEFITS MGT
INC
505 N Brand Blvd, Glendale　(91203-1906)
PHONE.............................847 310-0366
EMP: 586
SALES (corp-wide): 171.34B Publicly
Held
Web: www.caroninsights.com
SIC: 6321　Health insurance carriers
HQ: Carelon Medical Benefits
　　Management, Inc.
　　8600 W Bryn Mawr Ave Tw
　　Chicago IL 60631

(P-12062)
INLAND EMPIRE HEALTH PLAN
(PA)
Also Called: Iehp
10801 6th St Ste 120, Rancho Cucamonga
(91730-5987)
P.O. Box 1400　(91729-1400)
PHONE.............................909 890-2000
Jarrod Mcnaughton, CEO
Bob Buster, *
Chet Uma, *
Supriya Sood, *
Randee Roberts, *
EMP: 850 EST: 1994
SQ FT: 72,000
SALES (est): 200.07MM Privately Held
Web: www.iehp.org
SIC: 6321 6324　Health insurance carriers;
　Health Maintenance Organization (HMO),
　insurance only

(P-12063)
LIFECARE ASSURANCE
COMPANY
21600 Oxnard St Fl 16, Woodland Hills
(91367-4976)
PHONE.............................818 887-4436
James Glickman, Pr
Alan S Hughes, *
Daniel J Disipio, *
Peter Diffley, *
Dick Sato, *
EMP: 246 EST: 1988
SQ FT: 35,000
SALES (est): 3.71MM Privately Held
Web: www.lifecareassurance.com
SIC: 6321 6411 6311　Accident and health
　insurance; Insurance agents, brokers, and
　service; Life insurance
PA: 21st Century Life And Health
　　Company, Inc.
　　21600 Oxnard St Ste 1500

(P-12064)
MD CARE INC
Also Called: MD Care Healthplan
1640 E Hill St, Signal Hill　(90755-3612)
P.O. Box 14165　(40512-4165)
PHONE.............................562 344-3400
EMP: 75 EST: 2004
SALES (est): 18.29MM
SALES (corp-wide): 54.38B Publicly Held
SIC: 6321　Health insurance carriers
PA: Humana Inc.
　　500 W Main St Ste 300
　　502 580-1000

(P-12065)
MOLINA HLTHCARE CAL
PRTNER PLA
200 Oceangate Ste 100, Long Beach
(90802-4317)
PHONE.............................562 435-3666
Richard Chambers, CEO
J Mario Molina, *
John Kotal, *
Doctor James Howatt, Chief Medical Officer
Terry Bayer, *
EMP: 131 EST: 1980
SALES (est): 1.07MM
SALES (corp-wide): 34.07B Publicly Held
Web: www.molinahealthcare.com
SIC: 6321 8011　Health insurance carriers;
　Clinic, operated by physicians
PA: Molina Healthcare, Inc.
　　200 Oceangate Ste 100
　　562 435-3666

(P-12066)
SANTA BRBARA SAN LUIS
OBSPO RG
Also Called: Cencal Health
4050 Calle Real, Santa Barbara
(93110-3413)
PHONE.............................800 421-2560
Robert Freeman, CEO
Kashina Bishop, *
EMP: 140 EST: 2009
SALES (est): 24.91MM Privately Held
Web: www.cencalhealth.org
SIC: 6321　Accident and health insurance

(P-12067)
STATE COMPENSATION INSUR
FUND
2901 N Ventura Rd Ste 100, Oxnard
(93036-1126)
PHONE.............................888 782-8338
Martin Goldman, Mgr
EMP: 91
SALES (corp-wide): 2.76B Privately Held
Web: www.statefundca.com
SIC: 6321 9651　Disability health insurance;
　Insurance commission, government
PA: State Compensation Insurance Fund
　　333 Bush St Ste 800
　　888 782-8338

6324 Hospital And Medical
Service Plans

(P-12068)
ADMAR CORPORATION
1551 N Tustin Ave Ste 300, Santa Ana
(92705-8638)
P.O. Box 1049　(92702-1049)
PHONE.............................714 953-9600
Kraig Boysen, Pr
Virginia Pascual, *
Ed Evans, *
EMP: 160 EST: 1973
SQ FT: 37,000
SALES (est): 62.76MM
SALES (corp-wide): 961.52MM Publicly
Held
SIC: 6324　Hospital and medical service plans
PA: Multiplan Corporation
　　640 5th Ave Fl 12
　　212 380-7500

(P-12069)
ALIGNMENT HEALTH PLAN
Also Called: Citizens Choice Health Plan
1100 W Town And Country Rd Ste 1600,
Orange　(92868-4698)

PHONE.............................323 728-7232
Chuck Weber, Pr
Elizabeth Tejada, *
Charlotte Leblanc, CAO*
EMP: 90 EST: 2003
SALES (est): 27.65MM
SALES (corp-wide): 1.82B Publicly Held
Web: www.alignmenthealthplan.com
SIC: 6324　Health Maintenance Organization
　(HMO), insurance only
PA: Alignment Healthcare, Inc.
　　1100 W Town Cntry Rd Ste
　　844 310-2247

(P-12070)
ALIGNMENT HEALTHCARE INC
(PA)
Also Called: Alignment Health
1100 W Town And Country Rd Ste 1600,
Orange　(92868-4698)
PHONE.............................844 310-2247
John Kao, CEO
Joseph Konowiecki, Ch Bd
Thomas Freeman, CFO
Dinesh Kumar, CMO
Richard Cross, Sr VP
EMP: 102 EST: 2013
SQ FT: 89,000
SALES (est): 1.82B
SALES (corp-wide): 1.82B Publicly Held
Web: www.alignmenthealth.com
SIC: 6324 7372　Hospital and medical
　service plans; Prepackaged software

(P-12071)
AMERICAN SPCLTY HLTH
GROUP INC
10221 Wateridge Cir Ste 201, San Diego
(92121-2702)
PHONE.............................858 754-2000
George T Devries, CEO
Robert White, COO
Kevin E Kujawa, CIO
Marcel Danko, CFO
▲ EMP: 500 EST: 1987
SQ FT: 148,000
SALES (est): 46.93MM Privately Held
Web: www.ashcompanies.com
SIC: 6324　Hospital and medical service plans
PA: American Specialty Health
　　Incorporated
　　12800 N Meridian St

(P-12072)
BLUE SHIELD CAL LF HLTH
INSUR
2275 Rio Bonito Way Ste 250, San Diego
(92108-1697)
PHONE.............................619 686-4200
Matthew Leming, Prin
EMP: 1324
SALES (corp-wide): 21.94MM Privately
Held
Web: www.blueshieldca.com
SIC: 6324　Hospital and medical service plans
HQ: Blue Shield Of California Life & Health
　　Insurance Co
　　601 12th St
　　Oakland CA 94607
　　510 607-2000

(P-12073)
CALIFORNIA PHYSICIANS
SERVICE
Also Called: Blue Shield of California
3401 Centre Lake Dr Ste 400, Ontario
(91761-1205)
PHONE.............................909 974-5201
Sue Britton, Mgr
EMP: 75

SALES (corp-wide): 21.94MM **Privately Held**

Web: www.blueshieldca.com

SIC: 6324 Hospital and medical service plans

PA: California Physicians' Service
601 12th St
510 607-2000

(P-12074)
CALIFORNIA PHYSICIANS SERVICE
Also Called: Blue Shield of California
3840 Kilroy Airport Way, Long Beach (90806-2452)
PHONE.................................310 744-2668
Aubrey Chernick, *Brnch Mgr*
EMP: 75
SALES (corp-wide): 21.94MM **Privately Held**
Web: www.blueshieldca.com
SIC: 6324 Hospital and medical service plans
PA: California Physicians' Service
601 12th St
510 607-2000

(P-12075)
CALIFORNIA PHYSICIANS SERVICE
Also Called: Blue Shield of California
6300 Canoga Ave Ste A, Woodland Hills (91367-8000)
PHONE.................................818 598-8000
John Headberg, *Brnch Mgr*
EMP: 225
SALES (corp-wide): 21.94MM **Privately Held**
Web: www.blueshieldca.com
SIC: 6324 Hospital and medical service plans
PA: California Physicians' Service
601 12th St
510 607-2000

(P-12076)
CIGNA BEHAVIORAL HEALTH OF CAL
Also Called: Cigna
450 N Brand Blvd Ste 500, Glendale (91203-4414)
PHONE.................................800 753-0540
EMP: 205 **EST:** 2014
SALES (est): 836.53K
SALES (corp-wide): 195.26B **Publicly Held**
SIC: 6324 Health Maintenance Organization (HMO), insurance only
HQ: Evernorth Behavioral Health, Inc
11095 Viking Dr Ste 350
Eden Prairie MN 55344

(P-12077)
CIGNA HEALTHCARE CAL INC (DH)
Also Called: Cigna
400 N Brand Blvd Ste 400, Glendale (91203-2399)
P.O. Box 188045 (37422-8045)
PHONE.................................818 500-6262
TOLL FREE: 800
Peter Welch, *CEO*
Leroy Volberding, *Pr*
David Yeager, *Contrlr*
Davit Aghazaryan, *CFO*
William Jameson, *Sec*
EMP: 400 **EST:** 1968
SQ FT: 110,000
SALES (est): 17.47MM
SALES (corp-wide): 195.26B **Publicly Held**
Web: www.cigna.com

SIC: 6324 Health Maintenance Organization (HMO), insurance only
HQ: Healthsource, Inc.
1750 Elm St Ste 800
Manchester NH 03104
603 268-7000

(P-12078)
COUNTY OF LOS ANGELES
Also Called: Community Hlth Plan Off MGT Ca
1000 S Fremont Ave Unit 4, Alhambra (91803-8859)
PHONE.................................626 299-5300
Dave Beck, *Dir*
EMP: 90
Web: www.lacounty.gov
SIC: 6324 9431 Hospital and medical service plans; Mental health agency administration, government
PA: County Of Los Angeles
500 W Temple St Ste 437
213 974-1101

(P-12079)
DELTA DENTAL OF CALIFORNIA
Also Called: Delta Dental
1450 Frazee Rd Ste 200, San Diego (92108-4341)
P.O. Box 261391 (92196-1391)
PHONE.................................619 683-2549
Delta California, *Brnch Mgr*
EMP: 122
SALES (corp-wide): 5.84B **Privately Held**
Web: www.deltadental.com
SIC: 6324 Dental insurance
PA: Delta Dental Of California
560 Mission St Ste 1300
415 972-8300

(P-12080)
HEALTH NET LLC (HQ)
21650 Oxnard St, Woodland Hills (91367-7829)
PHONE.................................818 676-6000
Jay M Gellert, *Pr*
James E Woys, *Interim Treasurer**
Juanell Hefner, *
Angelee F Bouchard, *
Rich Hall, *ACTURIAL**
EMP: 250 **EST:** 2015
SQ FT: 115,488
SALES (est): 1.52B **Publicly Held**
Web: www.healthnet.com
SIC: 6324 6311 Hospital and medical service plans; Life insurance carriers
PA: Centene Corporation
7700 Forsyth Blvd

(P-12081)
HEALTH NET LLC
6013 Niles St, Bakersfield (93306-4696)
PHONE.................................661 321-3904
EMP: 174
Web: www.healthnet.com
SIC: 6324 Hospital and medical service plans
HQ: Health Net, Llc
21650 Oxnard St
Woodland Hills CA 91367
818 676-6000

(P-12082)
HEALTH NET INC
21650 Oxnard St, Woodland Hills (91367-7829)
PHONE.................................818 676-6000
EMP: 8014
SIC: 6324 6311 Hospital and medical service plans; Life insurance carriers

(P-12083)
INLAND EMPIRE HEALTH PLAN
805 W 2nd St Ste C, San Bernardino (92410-3255)
P.O. Box 1800 (91729-1800)
PHONE.................................866 228-4347
EMP: 1945
Web: www.iehp.org
SIC: 6324 8742 Health Maintenance Organization (HMO), insurance only; Hospital and health services consultant
PA: Inland Empire Health Plan
10801 Sixth St Ste 120

(P-12084)
KAISER FNDTION HLTH PLAN GA IN
Also Called: Kaiser Foundation Health Plan
1850 California Ave, Corona (92881-3378)
PHONE.................................951 270-1200
Anita Ward, *Mgr*
EMP: 379
SALES (corp-wide): 70.8B **Privately Held**
Web: www.kaiserpermanente.org
SIC: 6324 Health Maintenance Organization (HMO), insurance only
HQ: Kaiser Foundation Health Plan Of Georgia, Inc.
3495 Piedmont Rd Ne # 9
Atlanta GA 30305
404 364-7000

(P-12085)
KAISER FOUNDATION HOSPITALS
Also Called: Kaiser Foundation Health Plan
27309 Madison Ave, Temecula (92590-5685)
PHONE.................................866 984-7483
David Kvancz, *VP*
EMP: 90
SALES (corp-wide): 70.8B **Privately Held**
Web: www.kaiserpermanente.org
SIC: 6324 Hospital and medical service plans
HQ: Kaiser Foundation Hospitals Inc
1 Kaiser Plz
Oakland CA 94612
510 271-6611

(P-12086)
KAISER FOUNDATION HOSPITALS
Also Called: Kaiser Permanente
3750 Grand Ave, Chino (91710-5478)
PHONE.................................888 750-0036
Jonathan Rothchild, *Mgr*
EMP: 97
SALES (corp-wide): 70.8B **Privately Held**
Web: www.kaisercenter.com
SIC: 6324 Hospital and medical service plans
HQ: Kaiser Foundation Hospitals Inc
1 Kaiser Plz
Oakland CA 94612
510 271-6611

(P-12087)
KAISER FOUNDATION HOSPITALS
Also Called: Kaiser Foundation Health Plan
9961 Sierra Ave, Fontana (92335-6720)
P.O. Box None (92335)
PHONE.................................909 427-3910
Gerald Mc Call, *Brnch Mgr*
EMP: 461
SALES (corp-wide): 70.8B **Privately Held**
Web: www.kaisercenter.com
SIC: 6324 Hospital and medical service plans
HQ: Kaiser Foundation Hospitals Inc
1 Kaiser Plz

Oakland CA 94612
510 271-6611

(P-12088)
KAISER FOUNDATION HOSPITALS
Also Called: Kaiser Permanente
12470 Whittier Blvd, Whittier (90602-1017)
PHONE.................................866 340-5974
Beth Lopez, *Prin*
EMP: 126
SALES (corp-wide): 70.8B **Privately Held**
Web: healthy.kaiserpermanente.org
SIC: 6324 Hospital and medical service plans
HQ: Kaiser Foundation Hospitals Inc
1 Kaiser Plz
Oakland CA 94612
510 271-6611

(P-12089)
KAISER FOUNDATION HOSPITALS
Also Called: Kaiser Foundation Health Plan
12200 Bellflower Blvd, Downey (90242-2804)
PHONE.................................562 622-4190
Jim Harrington, *Brnch Mgr*
EMP: 177
SALES (corp-wide): 70.8B **Privately Held**
Web: www.kaiserpermanente.org
SIC: 6324 Hospital and medical service plans
HQ: Kaiser Foundation Hospitals Inc
1 Kaiser Plz
Oakland CA 94612
510 271-6611

(P-12090)
KAISER FOUNDATION HOSPITALS
Also Called: Kaiser Foundation Health Plan
11666 Sherman Way, North Hollywood (91605-5831)
PHONE.................................818 503-7082
Charles Ford, *Mgr*
EMP: 213
SALES (corp-wide): 70.8B **Privately Held**
Web: www.kaiserpermanente.org
SIC: 6324 Hospital and medical service plans
HQ: Kaiser Foundation Hospitals Inc
1 Kaiser Plz
Oakland CA 94612
510 271-6611

(P-12091)
KAISER FOUNDATION HOSPITALS
Also Called: Kaiser Permanente
1249 S Sunset Ave, West Covina (91790-3997)
PHONE.................................866 319-4269
Jane Lau, *Mgr*
EMP: 87
SALES (corp-wide): 70.8B **Privately Held**
Web: healthy.kaiserpermanente.org
SIC: 6324 Hospital and medical service plans
HQ: Kaiser Foundation Hospitals Inc
1 Kaiser Plz
Oakland CA 94612
510 271-6611

(P-12092)
KAISER FOUNDATION HOSPITALS
Also Called: Kaiser Permanente
1011 Baldwin Park Blvd, Baldwin Park (91706-5806)
PHONE.................................626 851-1011
Linda Margarita Gutierrez, *Prin*
EMP: 793

PRODUCTS & SVCS

SALES (corp-wide): 70.8B Privately Held
Web: healthy.kaiserpermanente.org
SIC: 6324 Hospital and medical service plans
HQ: Kaiser Foundation Hospitals Inc
    1 Kaiser Plz
    Oakland CA 94612
    510 271-6611

(P-12093)
LIBERTY DENTAL PLAN CAL INC
340 Commerce Ste 100, Irvine
(92602-1358)
PHONE..................................949 223-0007
Amir Hossein Neshat, *Prin*
Maja Kapic, *
EMP: 300 EST: 2001
SALES (est): 22.56MM Privately Held
Web: www.libertydentalplan.com
SIC: 6324 Dental insurance

(P-12094)
LIBERTY DENTAL PLAN CORP (PA)
340 Commerce Ste 100, Irvine
(92602-1358)
PHONE..................................888 703-6999
Tom Choate, *Pr*
Rohan C Reid, *
Amir Neshat, *
Rosa Roldan, *Chief Dental Officer*
EMP: 100 EST: 2007
SALES (est): 24.12MM
SALES (corp-wide): 24.12MM Privately Held
Web: www.libertydentalplan.com
SIC: 6324 Dental insurance

(P-12095)
LOCAL INTTIVE HLTH AUTH FOR LO
696 W Holt Ave, Pomona (91768-3515)
PHONE..................................909 620-1661
EMP: 437
Web: www.communityresourcecenterla.org
SIC: 6324 Health Maintenance Organization
    (HMO), insurance only
PA: Local Initiative Health Authority For
    Los Angeles County
    1200 W 7th St

(P-12096)
LOCAL INTTIVE HLTH AUTH FOR LO (PA)
Also Called: L.A. Care Health Plan
1200 W 7th St, Los Angeles (90017-2349)
PHONE..................................213 694-1250
John Baackes, *CEO*
Richard Seidman, *CMO*
Dino Kasdagly, *
Marie Montgomery, *
EMP: 463 EST: 1995
SALES (est): 332.56MM Privately Held
Web: www.lacare.org
SIC: 6324 Health Maintenance Organization
    (HMO), insurance only

(P-12097)
MANAGED HEALTH NETWORK
Also Called: Managed Health
7755 Center Ave Ste 700, Huntington
Beach (92647-9126)
PHONE..................................714 934-5519
Carol Mclean, *Brnch Mgr*
EMP: 268
Web: www.mhn.com
SIC: 6324 Hospital and medical service plans
HQ: Managed Health Network
    2370 Kerner Blvd
    San Rafael CA 94901

(P-12098)
MOLINA HEALTHCARE INC
1500 Hughes Way, Long Beach
(90810-1870)
PHONE..................................310 221-3031
EMP: 132
SALES (corp-wide): 34.07B Publicly Held
Web: www.molinahealthcare.com
SIC: 6324 6321 Hospital and medical
    service plans; Accident and health
    insurance
PA: Molina Healthcare, Inc.
    200 Oceangate Ste 100
    562 435-3666

(P-12099)
OPTUMRX INC
Also Called: Prescription Solutions
2858 Loker Ave E Ste 100, Carlsbad
(92010-6673)
P.O. Box 2975 (66201-1375)
PHONE..................................760 804-2399
Sean O'rourke, *Mgr*
EMP: 400
SALES (corp-wide): 371.62B Publicly
Held
Web: www.optumrx.com
SIC: 6324 Hospital and medical service plans
HQ: Optumrx, Inc.
    11000 Optum Cir
    Eden Prairie MN 55344

(P-12100)
PACIFCARE HLTH PLAN ADMNSTRTOR (DH)
Also Called: Pacificare
3120 W Lake Center Dr, Santa Ana
(92704-6917)
P.O. Box 25186 (92799-5186)
PHONE..................................714 825-5200
David Reed, *Ch Bd*
Coy F Baugh, *Treas*
EMP: 400 EST: 1975
SQ FT: 220,000
SALES (est): 46.57MM
SALES (corp-wide): 371.62B Publicly
Held
SIC: 6324 Group hospitalization plans
HQ: Pacificare Health Systems, Llc
    5995 Plaza Dr
    Cypress CA 90630

(P-12101)
PRIVATE MEDICAL-CARE INC
12898 Towne Center Dr, Cerritos
(90703-8546)
PHONE..................................562 924-8311
Robert Elliott, *Pr*
EMP: 575 EST: 1970
SALES (est): 4.93MM
SALES (corp-wide): 5.84B Privately Held
SIC: 6324 Dental insurance
PA: Delta Dental Of California
    560 Mission St Ste 1300
    415 972-8300

(P-12102)
SAFEGUARD HEALTH ENTPS INC (HQ)
95 Enterprise Ste 100, Aliso Viejo
(92656-2605)
PHONE..................................800 880-1800
Steven J Baileys D.d.s., *Ch Bd*
James E Buncher, *Pr*
Stephen J Baker, *Ex VP*
Ronald I Brendzel, *Sr VP*
Dennis L Gates, *Sr VP*
EMP: 355 EST: 1974
SQ FT: 68,000
SALES (est): 18.46MM

SALES (corp-wide): 66.91B Publicly Held
Web: www.metlife.com
SIC: 6324 Dental insurance
PA: Metlife, Inc.
    200 Park Ave
    212 578-9500

(P-12103)
SAG-AFTRA HEALTH PLAN
Also Called: SAG PRODUCERS PENSION
PLAN
3601 W Olive Ave Ste 200, Burbank
(91505-4602)
PHONE..................................800 777-4013
EMP: 138
SALES (est): 490.65MM Privately Held
Web: www.sagaftraplans.org
SIC: 6324 Hospital and medical service plans

(P-12104)
SCAN GROUP (PA)
3800 Kilroy Airport Way Ste 100, Long
Beach (90806-6818)
PHONE..................................562 308-2733
Sachin H Jain, *Pr*
Linda Rosenstock, *
Janet Kornblatt, *
Michael Plumb, *
Deepa Sheth, *Chief Corporate
Development Officer*
EMP: 306 EST: 1983
SALES (est): 6.11MM
SALES (corp-wide): 6.11MM Privately
Held
Web: www.scanhealthplan.com
SIC: 6324 Health Maintenance Organization
    (HMO), insurance only

(P-12105)
SENIOR CARE ACTION NTWRK FNDTI (PA)
Also Called: SCAN HEALTH PLAN
3800 Kilroy Airport Way, Long Beach
(90806-2494)
P.O. Box 22616 (90801-5616)
PHONE..................................562 989-5100
David Schmidt, *CEO*
Dennis Eder, *
▲ EMP: 650 EST: 1978
SQ FT: 119,219
SALES (est): 4.31B
SALES (corp-wide): 4.31B Privately Held
Web: www.scanhealthplan.com
SIC: 6324 Health Maintenance Organization
    (HMO), insurance only

(P-12106)
SHARP HEALTH PLAN
8520 Tech Way Ste 200, San Diego
(92123-1450)
PHONE..................................858 499-8300
Melissa Hayden-cook, *Pr*
Rita Datko, *
Leslie Pels-beck, *VP*
Michael Byrd, *Chief Business Development
Officer*
Doctor Cary Shames, *Chief Medical Officer*
EMP: 98 EST: 1992
SALES (est): 968.14MM
SALES (corp-wide): 1.9B Privately Held
Web: www.sharphealthplan.com
SIC: 6324 Health Maintenance Organization
    (HMO), insurance only
PA: Sharp Healthcare
    8695 Spectrum Ctr Blvd
    858 499-4000

(P-12107)
SOUTHERN CAL PRMNNTE MED GROUP

Also Called: Tustin Executive Center
17542 17th St Ste 300, Tustin
(92780-1960)
PHONE..................................714 734-4500
Adamma Agufoh, *Dir*
EMP: 240
SALES (corp-wide): 70.8B Privately Held
Web: www.permanente.org
SIC: 6324 Hospital and medical service plans
HQ: Southern California Permanente
    Medical Group
    393 Walnut Dr
    Pasadena CA 91107
    626 405-5704

(P-12108)
SOUTHERN CAL PRMNNTE MED GROUP
Also Called: Southern California Permanente
Medical Group
10800 Magnolia Ave, Riverside
(92505-3043)
PHONE..................................866 984-7483
Jeffrey A Weisz, *Prin*
EMP: 133
SALES (corp-wide): 70.8B Privately Held
Web: www.permanente.org
SIC: 6324 Hospital and medical service plans
HQ: Southern California Permanente
    Medical Group
    393 Walnut Dr
    Pasadena CA 91107
    626 405-5704

(P-12109)
SOUTHERN CAL PRMNNTE MED GROUP
Also Called: SOUTHERN CALIFORNIA
PERMANENTE MEDICAL GROUP
6860 Avenida Encinas, Carlsbad
(92011-3201)
PHONE..................................619 528-5000
Walter Borschel, *Admn*
EMP: 174
SALES (corp-wide): 70.8B Privately Held
Web: www.permanente.org
SIC: 6324 Hospital and medical service plans
HQ: Southern California Permanente
    Medical Group
    393 Walnut Dr
    Pasadena CA 91107
    626 405-5704

(P-12110)
SOUTHERN CAL PRMNNTE MED GROUP
Also Called: Kaiser Foundation Health Plan
5855 Copley Dr Ste 250, San Diego
(92111-7908)
PHONE..................................858 974-1000
Tom Cooper, *Mgr*
EMP: 380
SQ FT: 89,984
SALES (corp-wide): 70.8B Privately Held
Web: www.kaiserpermanente.org
SIC: 6324 Health Maintenance Organization
    (HMO), insurance only
HQ: Southern California Permanente
    Medical Group
    393 Walnut Dr
    Pasadena CA 91107
    626 405-5704

(P-12111)
SOUTHERN CAL PRMNNTE MED GROUP
13652 Cantara St, Panorama City
(91402-5423)
PHONE..................................800 272-3500
Arthur Phelps, *Brnch Mgr*

EMP: 627
SALES (corp-wide): 70.8B **Privately Held**
Web: healthy.kaiserpermanente.org
SIC: 6324 Hospital and medical service plans
HQ: Southern California Permanente
Medical Group
393 Walnut Dr
Pasadena CA 91107
626 405-5704

(P-12112)
SOUTHERN CAL PRMNNTE MED GROUP
1511 W Garvey Ave N, West Covina
(91790-2138)
PHONE..............................626 960-4844
EMP: 287
SALES (corp-wide): 70.8B **Privately Held**
Web: healthy.kaiserpermanente.org
SIC: 6324 Hospital and medical service plans
HQ: Southern California Permanente
Medical Group
393 Walnut Dr
Pasadena CA 91107
626 405-5704

(P-12113)
SOUTHERN CAL PRMNNTE MED GROUP
Also Called: S C P M G
1255 W Arrow Hwy, San Dimas
(91773-2340)
PHONE..............................909 394-2505
EMP: 174
SALES (corp-wide): 70.8B **Privately Held**
Web: www.permanente.org
SIC: 6324 Hospital and medical service plans
HQ: Southern California Permanente
Medical Group
393 Walnut Dr
Pasadena CA 91107
626 405-5704

(P-12114)
UHC OF CALIFORNIA (DH)
Also Called: Pacificare Health Systems
5995 Plaza Dr, Cypress (90630-5028)
PHONE..............................952 936-6615
Brad A Bowlus, *Principal Health Plan*
Joseph S Konowiecki, *
Michael Montevideo, *
EMP: 800 **EST:** 1975
SALES (est): 17.97MM
SALES (corp-wide): 371.62B **Publicly Held**
SIC: 6324 8732 Health Maintenance
Organization (HMO), insurance only;
Commercial nonphysical research
HQ: Pacificare Health Systems, Llc
5995 Plaza Dr
Cypress CA 90630

6331 Fire, Marine, And Casualty Insurance

(P-12115)
ALLIANZ GLOBL RISKS US INSUR (DH)
Also Called: Allianz Insurance Company
2350 W Empire Ave Ste 200, Burbank
(91504-3439)
P.O. Box 970 (63366)
PHONE..............................818 260-7500
Hugh Burgess, *CEO*
Randy Renn, *
EMP: 175 **EST:** 1938
SQ FT: 20,000
SALES (est): 70.15MM
SALES (corp-wide): 28.21B **Privately Held**

Web: commercial.allianz.com
SIC: 6331 Property damage insurance
HQ: Fireman's Fund Insurance Company
1 Progress Pt Pkwy Ste 20
O Fallon MO 63368
415 899-2000

(P-12116)
AMERICAN RELIABLE INSURANCE CO
333 S Anita Dr Ste 980, Orange
(92868-3320)
PHONE..............................714 937-2300
Jeff Dailey, *Brnch Mgr*
EMP: 800
SALES (corp-wide): 528.13MM **Privately Held**
Web: www.americanreliable.com
SIC: 6331 Fire, marine, and casualty
insurance
HQ: American Reliable Insurance Company
3 Bala Plz
Bala Cynwyd PA 19004
480 483-8666

(P-12117)
ARROWHEAD GEN INSUR AGCY INC (HQ)
701 B St Ste 2100, San Diego
(92101-8197)
PHONE..............................619 881-8600
Chris L Walker, *CEO*
Steve Boydm, *Prin*
Steve Boyd, *
Scott Marshall, *
Stephen M Lesieur, *
EMP: 240 **EST:** 1983
SQ FT: 74,000
SALES (est): 28.19MM
SALES (corp-wide): 3.57B **Publicly Held**
Web: www.arrowheadgrp.com
SIC: 6331 6411 Automobile insurance;
Insurance agents, brokers, and service
PA: Brown & Brown, Inc.
300 N Beach St
386 252-9601

(P-12118)
GOLDEN EAGLE INSURANCE CORP (DH)
Also Called: Golden Eagle
525 B St Ste 1300, San Diego
(92101-4421)
P.O. Box 85826 (92186-5826)
PHONE..............................619 744-6000
J Paul Condrin Iii, *CEO*
Frank J Kotarba, *
EMP: 250 **EST:** 1997
SALES (est): 26.56MM
SALES (corp-wide): 49.41B **Privately Held**
SIC: 6331 Property damage insurance
HQ: Liberty Mutual Insurance Company
175 Berkeley St
Boston MA 02116
617 357-9500

(P-12119)
GREAT AMERICAN CSTM INSUR SVCS
Also Called: Great American Custom
725 S Figueroa St Ste 3400, Los Angeles
(90017-5434)
PHONE..............................213 430-4300
Neil A Bethel, *Pr*
Phil Levy, *
EMP: 254 **EST:** 1983
SQ FT: 50,000
SALES (est): 8.47MM **Publicly Held**
Web: www.gamcustom.com

SIC: 6331 Fire, marine, and casualty
insurance
HQ: Great American Insurance Company
301 E 4th St
Cincinnati OH 45202
513 369-5000

(P-12120)
HMC ASSETS LLC
2015 Manhattan Beach Blvd Ste 200,
Redondo Beach (90278-1226)
PHONE..............................310 535-9293
EMP: 112 **EST:** 2010
SALES (est): 4.76MM
SALES (corp-wide): 42.58MM **Privately Held**
Web: www.hmcassets.com
SIC: 6331 Property damage insurance
PA: Wedgewood Inc.
2015 Manhattan Beach Blvd # 102
310 640-3070

(P-12121)
ICW GROUP HOLDINGS INC (PA)
15025 Innovation Dr, San Diego
(92128-3455)
P.O. Box 509039 (92150)
PHONE..............................858 350-2400
Kevin M Prior, *CEO*
Ernest Rady, *
Sariborz Rostamian, *
EMP: 89 **EST:** 1974
SQ FT: 160,000
SALES (est): 610.35MM
SALES (corp-wide): 610.35MM **Privately Held**
Web: www.icwgroup.com
SIC: 6331 6411 Fire, marine and casualty
insurance and carriers; Insurance brokers,
nec

(P-12122)
KRAMER-WILSON COMPANY INC (PA)
Also Called: Century National
340 N Westlake Blvd Ste 210, Westlake
Village (91362-7034)
P.O. Box 3999 (91609-0599)
PHONE..............................818 760-0880
Weldon Wilson, *CEO*
Kevin Wilson, *
Daniel Sherrin, *
Mary Ann Wagner, *
◆ **EMP:** 240 **EST:** 1969
SALES (est): 14.07MM
SALES (corp-wide): 14.07MM **Privately Held**
SIC: 6331 Fire, marine and casualty
insurance and carriers

(P-12123)
MERCURY CASUALTY COMPANY (HQ)
Also Called: M C C
555 W Imperial Hwy, Brea (92821-4802)
P.O. Box 54600 (90054-0600)
PHONE..............................323 937-1060
Gabriel Tirador, *CEO*
George Joseph, *
EMP: 600 **EST:** 1962
SALES (est): 492.34MM
SALES (corp-wide): 4.63B **Publicly Held**
Web: www.mercuryinsurance.com
SIC: 6331 6351 Automobile insurance;
Warranty insurance, home
PA: Mercury General Corporation
4484 Wilshire Blvd
323 937-1060

(P-12124)
MERCURY GENERAL CORPORATION (PA)
Also Called: MERCURY GENERAL
4484 Wilshire Blvd, Los Angeles
(90010-3700)
P.O. Box 36662 (90036-0662)
PHONE..............................323 937-1060
Gabriel Tirador, *Pr*
George Joseph, *Ch Bd*
Theodore R Stalick, *Sr VP*
Christopher Graves, *VP*
Abby Hosseini, *VP*
EMP: 634 **EST:** 1961
SQ FT: 41,000
SALES (est): 4.63B
SALES (corp-wide): 4.63B **Publicly Held**
Web: www.mercuryinsurance.com
SIC: 6331 6411 Automobile insurance;
Insurance agents, brokers, and service

(P-12125)
MERCURY INSURANCE COMPANY
1700 Greenbriar Ln, Brea (92821-5971)
PHONE..............................714 255-5000
Ken Kitzmiller, *Brnch Mgr*
EMP: 829
SALES (corp-wide): 4.63B **Publicly Held**
Web: www.mercuryinsurance.com
SIC: 6331 Fire, marine, and casualty
insurance
HQ: Mercury Insurance Company
555 W Imperial Hwy
Brea CA 92821
323 937-1060

(P-12126)
MERCURY INSURANCE COMPANY (HQ)
555 W Imperial Hwy, Brea (92821-4839)
P.O. Box 54600 (90054-0600)
PHONE..............................323 937-1060
Gabe Tirador, *CEO*
Ted Stalick, *
Judith Walters, *
EMP: 160 **EST:** 1972
SQ FT: 40,809
SALES (est): 1.21B
SALES (corp-wide): 4.63B **Publicly Held**
Web: www.mercuryinsurance.com
SIC: 6331 Fire, marine, and casualty
insurance
PA: Mercury General Corporation
4484 Wilshire Blvd
323 937-1060

(P-12127)
MERCURY INSURANCE COMPANY
9635 Granite Ridge Dr Ste 200, San Diego
(92123-2682)
P.O. Box 10730 (92711-0730)
PHONE..............................858 694-4100
Randy Petro, *Mgr*
EMP: 746
SALES (corp-wide): 4.63B **Publicly Held**
Web: www.mercuryinsurance.com
SIC: 6331 6399 Fire, marine, and casualty
insurance; Warranty insurance, automobile
HQ: Mercury Insurance Company
555 W Imperial Hwy
Brea CA 92821
323 937-1060

(P-12128)
MERCURY INSURANCE COMPANY
27200 Tourney Rd Ste 400, Valencia
(91355-4997)

P.O. Box 10730 (92711-0730)
PHONE..............................661 291-6470
David Levy, *Mgr*
EMP: 523
SALES (corp-wide): 4.63B **Publicly Held**
Web: www.mercuryinsurance.com
SIC: 6331 Fire, marine, and casualty
　insurance
HQ: Mercury Insurance Company
　　555 W Imperial Hwy
　　Brea CA 92821
　　323 937-1060

(P-12129)
**MERCURY INSURANCE
COMPANY**
Also Called: Mercury Insurance Broker
1433 Santa Monica Blvd, Santa Monica
(90404-1709)
PHONE..............................310 451-4943
Ken Donaldson, *Owner*
EMP: 195
SALES (corp-wide): 4.63B **Publicly Held**
Web: www.mercuryinsurance.com
SIC: 6331 6411 Fire, marine, and casualty
　insurance; Insurance agents, brokers, and
　service
HQ: Mercury Insurance Company
　　555 W Imperial Hwy
　　Brea CA 92821
　　323 937-1060

(P-12130)
**MID-CENTURY INSURANCE
COMPANY**
6303 Owensmouth Ave Fl 1, Woodland Hills
(91367-2200)
PHONE..............................323 932-7116
Ron Coble, *Sr VP*
Bob Woudstra, *
EMP: 250 **EST:** 1953
SALES (est): 4.5MM **Privately Held**
Web: www.farmers.com
SIC: 6331 6351 Automobile insurance;
　Fidelity insurance
HQ: Farmers Insurance Exchange
　　6301 Owensmouth Ave
　　Woodland Hills CA 91367
　　888 327-6335

(P-12131)
ORION INDEMNITY COMPANY
714 W Olympic Blvd Ste 800, Los Angeles
(90015-1440)
PHONE..............................213 742-8700
Jeanette Shammas, *Ch Bd*
Nicholas J Lannotti, *
Denise M Tyson, *
EMP: 100 **EST:** 1949
SALES (est): 13MM
SALES (corp-wide): 4.63B **Publicly Held**
Web: www.orionindemnity.com
SIC: 6331 Fire, marine, and casualty
　insurance
PA: Mercury General Corporation
　　4484 Wilshire Blvd
　　323 937-1060

(P-12132)
**REPUBLIC INDEMNITY CO
AMER (DH)**
Also Called: Rica
4500 Park Granada Ste 300, Calabasas
(91302-1667)
P.O. Box 20036 (91416-0036)
PHONE..............................818 990-9860
Dwayne Marioni, *CEO*
Marion Chappel, *
Gene J Simpson, *
EMP: 129 **EST:** 1973

SQ FT: 70,000
SALES (est): 703.47MM **Publicly Held**
Web: www.republicindemnity.com
SIC: 6331 Workers' compensation insurance
HQ: Pennsylvania Company Inc
　　1 E 4th St
　　Cincinnati OH 45202
　　513 579-2121

(P-12133)
**REPUBLIC INDEMNITY
COMPANY CAL**
15821 Ventura Blvd Ste 370, Encino
(91436-2909)
P.O. Box 4275 (91365-4275)
PHONE..............................818 990-9860
Dwayne T Marioni, *Pr*
Shila Euper, *
EMP: 127 **EST:** 1982
SALES (est): 2.3MM **Publicly Held**
Web: www.republicindemnity.com
SIC: 6331 Fire, marine, and casualty
　insurance
HQ: Republic Indemnity Company Of
　　America
　　4500 Park Granada Ste 300
　　Calabasas CA 91302
　　818 990-9860

(P-12134)
ROYAL SPECIALTY UNDWRT INC
Also Called: Rsui Group
15303 Ventura Blvd Ste 500, Sherman Oaks
(91403-6619)
PHONE..............................818 922-6700
Christine Chinen, *Admn*
EMP: 103
SALES (corp-wide): 364.48B **Publicly
Held**
Web: www.rsui.com
SIC: 6331 6411 Fire, marine, and casualty
　insurance; Insurance agents, brokers, and
　service
HQ: Royal Specialty Underwriting, Inc.
　　945 E Paces Ferry Rd Ne
　　Atlanta GA 30326

(P-12135)
**STATE COMPENSATION INSUR
FUND**
21300 Victory Blvd Ste 600, Woodland Hills
(91367-8031)
P.O. Box 1950 (91365)
PHONE..............................818 888-4750
Mary Powers, *Brnch Mgr*
EMP: 510
SALES (corp-wide): 2.76B **Privately Held**
Web: www.statefundca.com
SIC: 6331 9651 Workers' compensation
　insurance; Insurance commission,
　government
PA: State Compensation Insurance Fund
　　333 Bush St Ste 800
　　888 782-8338

(P-12136)
**STATE COMPENSATION INSUR
FUND**
Also Called: Los Angles Dst Off Policy Svcs
900 Corporate Center Dr, Monterey Park
(91754-7620)
P.O. Box 65005 (93650-5005)
PHONE..............................323 266-5000
Joe Codron, *Brnch Mgr*
EMP: 224
SALES (corp-wide): 2.76B **Privately Held**
Web: www.statefundca.com
SIC: 6331 9651 Workers' compensation
　insurance; Insurance commission,
　government

PA: State Compensation Insurance Fund
　　333 Bush St Ste 800
　　888 782-8338

(P-12137)
**STATE COMPENSATION INSUR
FUND**
Also Called: Bakersfield District Office
9801 Camino Media Ste 101, Bakersfield
(93311-1312)
P.O. Box 21810 (93390-1810)
PHONE..............................661 664-4000
Robert Kean, *Mgr*
EMP: 92
SALES (corp-wide): 2.76B **Privately Held**
Web: www.statefundca.com
SIC: 6331 9651 Workers' compensation
　insurance; Insurance commission,
　government
PA: State Compensation Insurance Fund
　　333 Bush St Ste 800
　　888 782-8338

(P-12138)
**STATE COMPENSATION INSUR
FUND**
Also Called: Santa Ana District Office
1750 E 4th St Fl 3, Santa Ana
(92705-3929)
PHONE..............................714 565-5000
Liz Glidden, *Mgr*
EMP: 241
SALES (corp-wide): 2.76B **Privately Held**
Web: www.statefundca.com
SIC: 6331 9651 Workers' compensation
　insurance; Insurance commission,
　government
PA: State Compensation Insurance Fund
　　333 Bush St Ste 800
　　888 782-8338

(P-12139)
**STATE COMPENSATION INSUR
FUND**
Also Called: San Diego District Office
10105 Pacific Heights Blvd Ste 120, San
Diego (92121-4246)
PHONE..............................888 782-8338
Lisa Middleton, *Mgr*
EMP: 234
SALES (corp-wide): 2.76B **Privately Held**
Web: www.statefundca.com
SIC: 6331 9651 Workers' compensation
　insurance; Insurance commission,
　government
PA: State Compensation Insurance Fund
　　333 Bush St Ste 800
　　888 782-8338

(P-12140)
**STATE COMPENSATION INSUR
FUND**
Also Called: Riverside District Office
6301 Day St, Riverside (92507-0902)
PHONE..............................888 782-8338
Barbara Katzka, *Mgr*
EMP: 207
SALES (corp-wide): 2.76B **Privately Held**
Web: www.statefundca.com
SIC: 6331 9651 Workers' compensation
　insurance; Insurance commission,
　government
PA: State Compensation Insurance Fund
　　333 Bush St Ste 800
　　888 782-8338

(P-12141)
**TRISTAR INSURANCE GROUP
INC (PA)**

Also Called: Tristar Risk Management
100 Oceangate Ste 700, Long Beach
(90802-4368)
PHONE..............................562 495-6600
Thomas J Veale, *Pr*
Russ O'donnell, *Sec*
Joseph Mclaughlin, *Sr VP*
Denise J Cotter, *CFO*
EMP: 700 **EST:** 1982
SQ FT: 9,000
SALES (est): 258.52MM
SALES (corp-wide): 258.52MM **Privately
Held**
Web: www.tristargroup.net
SIC: 6331 8741 Workers' compensation
　insurance; Management services

(P-12142)
**WESTERN MUTUAL INSURANCE
CO**
27489 Agoura Rd, Agoura Hills
(91301-2419)
PHONE..............................818 879-2142
Joe Crail, *Pr*
EMP: 70 **EST:** 1942
SALES (est): 17.91MM **Privately Held**
SIC: 6331 Fire, marine, and casualty
　insurance: mutual

(P-12143)
**ZENITH INSURANCE COMPANY
(DH)**
Also Called: Zenith A Fairfax Company, The
21255 Califa St, Woodland Hills
(91367-5021)
P.O. Box 9055 (91409-9055)
PHONE..............................818 713-1000
Stanley R Zax, *Ch Bd*
Jack D Miller, *Pr*
Paul Ramont, *Chief Underwriting Officer*
EMP: 400 **EST:** 1950
SQ FT: 120,000
SALES (est): 289.43MM
SALES (corp-wide): 20.88B **Privately Held**
Web: www.thezenith.com
SIC: 6331 Workers' compensation insurance
HQ: Zenith National Insurance Corp.
　　21255 Califa St
　　Woodland Hills CA 91367
　　818 713-1000

6351 Surety Insurance

(P-12144)
**AMERICAN CONTRS INDEMNITY
CO (DH)**
Also Called: HCC Surety Group
801 S Figueroa St Ste 700, Los Angeles
(90017-2523)
PHONE..............................213 330-1309
Adam S Pessin, *Pr*
Michael Budnitsky, *
EMP: 150 **EST:** 1990
SALES (est): 28.46MM **Privately Held**
Web: www.trmhcc.com
SIC: 6351 Surety insurance bonding
HQ: Hcc Insurance Holdings, Inc.
　　13403 Northwest Fwy
　　Houston TX 77040

(P-12145)
CAP-MPT (PA)
333 S Hope St Fl 8, Los Angeles
(90071-3001)
PHONE..............................213 473-8600
Jim Weidner, *CEO*
Michael Wormley Md, *Ch Bd*
Thomas Andre, *
Cindy Belcher, *

Nancy Brusegaard Johnson, *
EMP: 140 **EST:** 1977
SALES (est): 6.2MM
SALES (corp-wide): 6.2MM **Privately Held**
Web: www.capphysicians.com
SIC: 6351 Liability insurance

(P-12146)
DEVELOPERS SURETY INDEMNITY CO (DH)
Also Called: Insco Dico Group , The
17771 Cowan Ste 100, Irvine (92614-6044)
P.O. Box 19725 (92623-9725)
PHONE..............................949 263-3300
Walter Crowell, *Pr*
Harry C Crowell, *
David Rhodes, *
EMP: 70 **EST:** 1936
SQ FT: 25,000
SALES (est): 7.51MM
SALES (corp-wide): 3.82B **Privately Held**
Web: www.amtrustfinancial.com
SIC: 6351 Fidelity or surety bonding
HQ: Insco Insurance Services, Inc.
17771 Cowan St Ste 100
Irvine CA 92614
949 263-3415

(P-12147)
FAR WEST BOND SERVICES CAL INC (PA)
5230 Las Virgenes Rd, Calabasas
(91302-3448)
P.O. Box 4500 (91365-4500)
PHONE..............................818 704-1111
John Savage, *Pr*
Neal Pomp, *
Steve Kay, *
▼ **EMP:** 300 **EST:** 1974
SALES (est): 4.61MM
SALES (corp-wide): 4.61MM **Privately Held**
SIC: 6351 6331 Surety insurance; Fire, marine, and casualty insurance

(P-12148)
SELECT HOME WARRANTY CA INC
222 W 6th St Ste 400, San Pedro
(90731-3345)
PHONE..............................732 835-0110
Joseph Shrem, *CEO*
EMP: 325 **EST:** 2019
SALES (est): 25MM **Privately Held**
SIC: 6351 Warranty insurance, home

6361 Title Insurance

(P-12149)
CHICAGO TITLE INSURANCE CO (HQ)
Also Called: Chicago Title
4050 Calle Real, Santa Barbara
(93110-3413)
PHONE..............................805 565-6900
William Halvorsen Junior, *Pr*
A Larry Sisk, *
Peter G Leemputte, *
EMP: 150 **EST:** 1984
SQ FT: 44,637
SALES (est): 224.43MM **Publicly Held**
SIC: 6361 Real estate title insurance
PA: Fidelity National Financial, Inc.
601 Riverside Ave

(P-12150)
FIRST AMERICAN FINANCIAL CORP (PA)

Also Called: First American
1 First American Way, Santa Ana
(92707-5913)
PHONE..............................714 250-3000
Kenneth D Degiorgio, *CEO*
Dennis J Gilmore, *Ch Bd*
Mark E Seaton, *Ex VP*
Lisa W Cornehl, *CLO*
Matthew F Wajner, *VP*
EMP: 695 **EST:** 1889
SQ FT: 490,000
SALES (est): 6B **Publicly Held**
Web: www.firstam.com
SIC: 6361 6351 Title insurance; Surety insurance

(P-12151)
FIRST AMERICAN MORTGAGE SVCS
3 First American Way, Santa Ana
(92707-5913)
PHONE..............................714 250-4210
EMP: 350 **EST:** 2009
SALES (est): 28.1MM **Privately Held**
Web: www.firstam.com
SIC: 6361 Title insurance

(P-12152)
FIRST AMERICAN TITLE INSUR CO (HQ)
Also Called: First American Mortgage Svcs
1 First American Way, Santa Ana
(92707-5913)
P.O. Box 267 (92702-0267)
PHONE..............................800 854-3643
Curt G Johnson, *V Ch Bd*
Curt Caspersen, *
Mark R Amesen, *
Max Weldex, *
Kurt Pfotenhauer, *Vice Chairman*
EMP: 485 **EST:** 1889
SALES (est): 3.64B **Publicly Held**
Web: www.firstam.com
SIC: 6361 7371 Real estate title insurance; Computer software development
PA: First American Financial Corporation
1 First American Way

(P-12153)
LAWYERS TITLE INSURANCE CORP
2751 Park View Ct, Oxnard (93036-5452)
PHONE..............................805 484-2701
John Arnold, *Mgr*
EMP: 2684
Web: www.ltic.com
SIC: 6361 Guarantee of titles
HQ: Lawyers Title Insurance Corporation
601 Riverside Ave
Jacksonville FL 32204
888 866-3684

(P-12154)
LAWYERS TITLE INSURANCE CORP
Also Called: Lawyers Title Escrow
5000 Birch St, Newport Beach
(92660-2127)
PHONE..............................949 223-5575
Dan Williams, *Owner*
EMP: 424
Web: www.ltic.com
SIC: 6361 Real estate title insurance
HQ: Lawyers Title Insurance Corporation
601 Riverside Ave
Jacksonville FL 32204
888 866-3684

(P-12155)
LAWYERS TITLE INSURANCE CORP
18551 Von Karman Ave Ste 100, Irvine
(92612-1553)
PHONE..............................949 223-5575
Dan Williams, *Brnch Mgr*
EMP: 565
Web: www.ltic.com
SIC: 6361 6541 Real estate title insurance; Title and trust companies
HQ: Lawyers Title Insurance Corporation
601 Riverside Ave
Jacksonville FL 32204
888 866-3684

(P-12156)
STEWART TITLE CALIFORNIA INC (DH)
7676 Hazard Center Dr Ste 1400, San Diego (92108-4516)
PHONE..............................619 692-1600
Shari Schneider, *Pr*
Brian Glaze, *VP*
Gregg Unrath, *VP*
Linda Mundy, *Sec*
EMP: 140 **EST:** 1996
SQ FT: 44,000
SALES (est): 45.92MM
SALES (corp-wide): 2.26B **Publicly Held**
Web: www.stewart.com
SIC: 6361 Guarantee of titles
HQ: Stewart Title Company
1360 Post Oak Blvd Ste 10
Houston TX 77056
713 625-8100

(P-12157)
TITLE365 HOLDING CO (HQ)
5000 Birch St Ste 300, Newport Beach
(92660-2147)
PHONE..............................949 475-3752
Michael Tafoya, *CEO*
EMP: 350 **EST:** 2009
SALES (est): 18.17MM
SALES (corp-wide): 156.85MM **Publicly Held**
Web: www.title365.com
SIC: 6361 6531 Title insurance; Real estate agents and managers
PA: Blend Labs, Inc.
7250 Redwood Blvd Ste 300
650 550-4810

6371 Pension, Health, And Welfare Funds

(P-12158)
ASSOCIATED THIRD PARTY ADMINISTRATORS INC
Also Called: Atpa
222 N Pacific Coast Hwy Ste 2000, El Segundo (90245-5614)
EMP: 390
SIC: 6371 6411 Union welfare, benefit, and health funds; Insurance agents, brokers, and service

(P-12159)
CAL SOUTHERN UNITED FOOD
Also Called: U F C Pension Trust Fund
6425 Katella Ave Ste 100, Cypress
(90630-5248)
P.O. Box 6010 (90630-0010)
PHONE..............................714 220-2297
P Thompson, *Admn*
EMP: 240 **EST:** 1957
SQ FT: 36,000

SALES (est): 7.9MM **Privately Held**
Web: www.scufcwfunds.com
SIC: 6371 Pension funds

(P-12160)
LOS ANGLES CNTY EMPLYEES RTRME (PA)
Also Called: Lacera
300 N Lake Ave Ste 720, Pasadena
(91101-5674)
P.O. Box 7060 (91109-7060)
PHONE..............................626 564-6000
Gregg Rademather, *CEO*
EMP: 200 **EST:** 1938
SQ FT: 85,000
SALES (est): 2.06B
SALES (corp-wide): 2.06B **Privately Held**
Web: www.lacera.com
SIC: 6371 Pension funds

(P-12161)
MOTION PCTURE INDUST PNSION HL
11365 Ventura Blvd Ste 300, Studio City
(91604-3148)
PHONE..............................818 769-0007
David Wescoe, *CEO*
Chuck Killian, *
EMP: 150 **EST:** 1954
SQ FT: 12,500
SALES (est): 12.22MM **Privately Held**
SIC: 6371 Pension, health, and welfare funds

(P-12162)
PRODUCR-WRTERS GILD AMER PNSIO (PA)
2900 W Alameda Ave Unit 1100, Burbank
(91505-4267)
PHONE..............................818 846-1015
Jim Hedges, *Admn*
Wendy Pagnone, *Admn*
EMP: 80 **EST:** 1960
SQ FT: 30,000
SALES (est): 48.31MM
SALES (corp-wide): 48.31MM **Privately Held**
Web: www.wgaplans.org
SIC: 6371 Pension funds

(P-12163)
SCREEN ACTORS GUILD - AMERICAN
Also Called: Screen Actors Guild-Producers
3601 W Olive Ave Fl 2, Burbank
(91505-4662)
P.O. Box 7830 (91510-7830)
PHONE..............................818 954-9400
EMP: 135
SALES (corp-wide): 46.97MM **Privately Held**
Web: www.sagaftra.org
SIC: 6371 6411 Pensions; Pension and retirement plan consultants
PA: Screen Actors Guild - American Federation Of Television And Radio Artists
5757 Wilshire Blvd Fl 7
415 391-7510

(P-12164)
SOUTHWEST ADMINISTRATORS INC
466 Foothill Blvd, La Canada Flintridge
(91011-3518)
EMP: 300
SIC: 6371 Pension funds

6411 Insurance Agents, Brokers, And Service

(P-12165)
21ST CENTURY LIFE INSURANCE CO (DH)
Also Called: 21st Century Insurance
6301 Owensmouth Ave Ste 700, Woodland Hills (91367-2265)
PHONE..............................877 310-5687
Glenn A Pfeil, *CEO*
Michael J Cassanego, *
Dean E Stark, *
Richard R Andre, *
Kathy Doyle, *
EMP: 1800 **EST:** 1955
SQ FT: 412,000
SALES (est): 12.41MM **Privately Held**
Web: www.21st.com
SIC: 6411 Insurance agents, brokers, and service
HQ: 21st Century North America Insurance Company
3 Beaver Valley Rd
Wilmington DE 19803
877 310-5687

(P-12166)
ADMINSURE INC
3380 Shelby St, Ontario (91764-5566)
PHONE..............................909 718-1200
Alithia Vargas-flores, *Pr*
EMP: 130 **EST:** 1982
SQ FT: 30,000
SALES (est): 4.42MM **Privately Held**
Web: www.adminsure.com
SIC: 6411 Insurance agents, nec

(P-12167)
AGIA INC (PA)
Also Called: Agia Affinity
300 E Esplanade Dr Ste 2010, Oxnard (93036-1229)
PHONE..............................805 566-9191
J Christopher Burke, *Pr*
Julie L Capritto, *
Andrew Dowen, *
Susan Roe, *
Carl A Adamek, *Senior Vice President Accounting*
EMP: 231 **EST:** 1965
SALES (est): 19.67MM **Privately Held**
Web: www.agia.com
SIC: 6411 Medical insurance claim processing, contract or fee basis

(P-12168)
AIG DIRECT INSURANCE SVCS INC
Also Called: Matrix Direct Insurance Svcs
9640 Granite Ridge Dr Ste 200, San Diego (92123-2691)
PHONE..............................858 309-3000
Ron Harris, *CEO*
Laura Huffman, *
Kevin Wilshusen, *
Patty Karstein, *
EMP: 275 **EST:** 1995
SQ FT: 24,000
SALES (est): 9.51MM
SALES (corp-wide): 46.8B **Publicly Held**
Web: www.aigdirect.com
SIC: 6411 Insurance agents, nec
HQ: American General Life Insurance Company
2727-A Allen Parkway
Houston TX 77019
713 522-1111

(P-12169)
ALLSTATE FINANCIAL SVCS LLC
Also Called: Allstate
5161 Pomona Blvd Ste 212, Los Angeles (90022-1749)
PHONE..............................323 981-8520
Carlos Godinez, *Prin*
EMP: 96
Web: www.allstate.com
SIC: 6411 Insurance agents, brokers, and service
HQ: Allstate Financial Services, Llc
151 N 8th St
Lincoln NE 68508
402 328-6700

(P-12170)
ALLSTATE FLORAL INC
15928 Commerce Way, Cerritos (90703-2319)
PHONE..............................562 926-2989
EMP: 223
SALES (corp-wide): 18.6MM **Privately Held**
Web: www.allstatefloral.com
SIC: 6411 Insurance agents and brokers
PA: Allstate Floral, Inc.
14101 Park Pl
562 926-2302

(P-12171)
AMERICAN HERITAGE LF INSUR CO
Also Called: American Heritage
400 Exchange Ste 210, Irvine (92602-1340)
PHONE..............................800 753-9227
EMP: 81
Web: www.allstate.com
SIC: 6411 Insurance agents, brokers, and service
HQ: American Heritage Life Insurance Co Inc
1776 Amercn Heritg Lf Dr
Jacksonville FL 32224
904 992-1776

(P-12172)
AMERICAN SPCLTY HLTH PLANS CAL
10221 Wateridge Cir, San Diego (92121-2702)
PHONE..............................619 297-8100
George Devries, *Pr*
Robert White, *
Marcel Danko, *CFO*
EMP: 500 **EST:** 1999
SALES (est): 5.16MM **Privately Held**
Web: www.ashcompanies.com
SIC: 6411 Insurance information and consulting services
PA: American Specialty Health Incorporated
12800 N Meridian St

(P-12173)
ANCHOR GENERAL INSUR AGCY INC
10256 Meanley Dr, San Diego (92131-3009)
P.O. Box 509020 (92150-9020)
PHONE..............................858 527-3600
Abdulla Badani, *Pr*
EMP: 203 **EST:** 1995
SALES (est): 9.3MM **Privately Held**
Web: secure3.anchorgeneral.com
SIC: 6411 Insurance agents, nec

(P-12174)
ATLAS GENERAL INSUR SVCS LLC
Also Called: Nationwide
6165 Greenwich Dr Ste 200, San Diego (92122-5911)
PHONE..............................858 529-6700
EMP: 153 **EST:** 2008
SALES (est): 39.89MM
SALES (corp-wide): 10.07B **Publicly Held**
Web: atlas.us.com
SIC: 6411 Insurance agents, nec
PA: Arthur J. Gallagher & Co.
2850 Golf Rd
630 773-3800

(P-12175)
AUTO INSURANCE SPECIALISTS LLC (DH)
Also Called: Nationwide
17785 Center Court Dr N Ste 110, Cerritos (90703-9326)
PHONE..............................562 345-6247
EMP: 210 **EST:** 1968
SQ FT: 45,000
SALES (est): 9.59MM
SALES (corp-wide): 4.63B **Publicly Held**
Web: www.aisinsurance.com
SIC: 6411 Insurance brokers, nec
HQ: Ais Management, Llc
17785 Center Court Dr N # 250
Cerritos CA 90703

(P-12176)
AUTOMOBILE CLUB SOUTHERN CAL (PA)
Also Called: A A A Automobile Club So Cal
2601 S Figueroa St, Los Angeles (90007-3294)
P.O. Box 25001 (92799-5001)
PHONE..............................213 741-3686
John F Boyle, *CEO*
Zoo Babies, *
Peter R Mcdonald, *Sr VP*
Robert T Bouttier, *
EMP: 150 **EST:** 1900
SQ FT: 425,000
SALES (est): 1.08B
SALES (corp-wide): 1.08B **Privately Held**
Web: ace.aaa.com
SIC: 6411 8699 Insurance agents, nec; Automobile owners' association

(P-12177)
AUTOMOBILE CLUB SOUTHERN CAL
Also Called: A A A Automobile Club So Cal
13331 Jamboree Rd, Irvine (92602)
P.O. Box 11763 (92711-1763)
PHONE..............................714 973-1211
Sid Munger, *Mgr*
EMP: 183
SALES (corp-wide): 1.08B **Privately Held**
Web: ace.aaa.com
SIC: 6411 Insurance agents, brokers, and service
PA: Automobile Club Of Southern California
2601 S Figueroa St
213 741-3686

(P-12178)
AUTOMOBILE CLUB SOUTHERN CAL
Also Called: AAA Auto Club
3333 Fairview Rd, Costa Mesa (92626-1698)
PHONE..............................714 885-1343
Becky Martinez, *Brnch Mgr*
EMP: 200

SALES (corp-wide): 1.08B **Privately Held**
Web: ace.aaa.com
SIC: 6411 Insurance agents, brokers, and service
PA: Automobile Club Of Southern California
2601 S Figueroa St
213 741-3686

(P-12179)
AUTOMOBILE CLUB SOUTHERN CAL
Also Called: AAA
2033b S Broadway, Santa Maria (93454-7809)
P.O. Box 1308 (93454)
PHONE..............................805 922-5731
Keith Pierce, *Mgr*
EMP: 101
SALES (corp-wide): 1.08B **Privately Held**
Web: ace.aaa.com
SIC: 6411 Insurance agents, brokers, and service
PA: Automobile Club Of Southern California
2601 S Figueroa St
213 741-3686

(P-12180)
AUTOMOBILE CLUB SOUTHERN CAL
Also Called: AAA
8765 Fletcher Pkwy, La Mesa (91942-3200)
PHONE..............................619 464-7001
Marria Porter, *Mgr*
EMP: 101
SQ FT: 42,441
SALES (corp-wide): 1.08B **Privately Held**
Web: ace.aaa.com
SIC: 6411 Insurance agents, brokers, and service
PA: Automobile Club Of Southern California
2601 S Figueroa St
213 741-3686

(P-12181)
B&C LIQUIDATING CORP (HQ)
Also Called: Nationwide
3475 E Foothill Blvd Ste 100, Pasadena (91107-6024)
P.O. Box 6030 (91102)
PHONE..............................626 799-7000
EMP: 123 **EST:** 1931
SALES (est): 23.58MM
SALES (corp-wide): 445.49MM **Privately Held**
Web: www.boltonco.com
SIC: 6411 Insurance agents, nec
PA: The Ima Financial Group Inc
1705 17th St Ste 100
316 267-9221

(P-12182)
BARNEY & BARNEY INC
Also Called: Loss and Risk Advisors
9171 Towne Centre Dr Ste 500, San Diego (92122-1238)
P.O. Box 85638 (92186-5638)
PHONE..............................800 321-4696
EMP: 200
SIC: 6411 Property and casualty insurance agent

(P-12183)
BEECHER CARLSON HOLDINGS INC
21650 Oxnard St Ste 1600, Woodland Hills (91367-4940)
PHONE..............................818 598-4200
Rob Glicksteen, *Dir*
EMP: 70

SALES (corp-wide): 3.57B **Publicly Held**
Web: www.bbrown.com
SIC: 6411 Insurance brokers, nec
HQ: Beecher Carlson Holdings, Inc.
6 Concourse Pkwy Ste 2300
Atlanta GA 30328
404 460-1400

(P-12184)
BURNHAM BNEFITS INSUR SVCS LLC
Also Called: Burnham Risk Insurance
15901 Red Hill Ave, Tustin (92780-7318)
PHONE..............................310 370-5000
Kristen Allison, *Brnch Mgr*
EMP: 74
SALES (corp-wide): 11.39MM **Privately Held**
Web: www.burnhambenefits.com
SIC: 6411 Insurance agents, nec
PA: Burnham Benefits Insurance Services, Llc
2211 Michelson Dr # 1200
805 772-7965

(P-12185)
BURNHAM BNEFITS INSUR SVCS LLC (PA)
Also Called: Life Plans
2211 Michelson Dr Ste 1200, Irvine (92612-0304)
PHONE..............................805 772-7965
Kristen Mauger Allison, *Pr*
Scott Aston, *
Janet Vreeland, *
Nooshin George, *
Chris Krusiewicz, *
EMP: 72 EST: 1995
SALES (est): 11.39MM
SALES (corp-wide): 11.39MM **Privately Held**
Web: www.burnhambenefits.com
SIC: 6411 Insurance agents, nec

(P-12186)
CALIFORNIA FAIR PLAN ASSN
725 S Figueroa St Ste 3900, Los Angeles (90017-5439)
PHONE..............................213 487-0111
Stuart M Wilkinson, *Pr*
EMP: 80 EST: 1968
SALES (est): 8.12MM **Privately Held**
Web: www.cfpnet.com
SIC: 6411 Insurance agents, nec

(P-12187)
CALIFRNIA INSUR GUARANTEE ASSN
Also Called: C I G A
330 N Brand Blvd Ste 500, Glendale (01203 2322)
P.O. Box 29066 (91209)
PHONE..............................818 844-4300
Lawrence E Mulryan, *Dir*
Wayne Wilson, *
EMP: 110 EST: 1969
SALES (est): 8.74MM **Privately Held**
Web: www.ciga.org
SIC: 6411 Insurance agents, brokers, and service

(P-12188)
CARELON BHAVIORAL HLTH CAL INC
Also Called: Valueoptions of California Inc
12898 Towne Center Dr, Cerritos (90703-8546)
PHONE..............................800 228-1286
Juan Molina, *VP Opers*

Jolene Myrter, *
Steve Rockowitz, *
EMP: 537 EST: 1989
SALES (est): 2.18MM
SALES (corp-wide): 171.34B **Publicly Held**
Web: www.carelonbehavioralhealthca.com
SIC: 6411 6321 Insurance agents, nec; Accident and health insurance
HQ: Fhc Health Systems, Inc
240 Crporate Blvd Ste 100
Norfolk VA 23502
757 459-5100

(P-12189)
CARL WARREN & COMPANY LLC (HQ)
175 N Riverview Dr Pmb A, Anaheim (92808-1225)
P.O. Box 25180 (92799)
PHONE..............................657 622-4200
Jason Turner, *CEO*
Gordon Pennington, *Pr*
Richard Mcabee, *CMO*
EMP: 118 EST: 1974
SQ FT: 16,000
SALES (est): 27.63MM **Privately Held**
Web: www.carlwarren.com
SIC: 6411 Insurance claim adjusters, not employed by insurance company
PA: Venbrook Group, Llc
6320 Canoga Ave Fl 12

(P-12190)
CARNEGIE AGENCY INC
Also Called: Carnegie General Insur Agcy
2535 W Hillcrest Dr, Newbury Park (91320-2457)
P.O. Box 2595 (91319)
PHONE..............................805 445-1470
John Smith, *Pr*
Chuck Smith, *
EMP: 75 EST: 1988
SALES (est): 3.2MM **Privately Held**
Web: www.cgia.com
SIC: 6411 Insurance agents, nec

(P-12191)
CARTEL MARKETING INC
Also Called: Insure Express Insurance Svc
6345 Balboa Blvd, Encino (91316-1519)
PHONE..............................818 483-1130
Robert M Humphreys, *Ch Bd*
Jack Edelstein, *
William Russell, *
EMP: 101 EST: 1984
SALES (est): 2.23MM
SALES (corp-wide): 16.38MM **Privately Held**
Web: www.cartel.net
SIC: 6411 Insurance agents, nec
HQ: Expresslink, Inc.
16501 Ventura Blvd # 300
Encino CA 91436
818 788-5555

(P-12192)
CBIZ LIFE INSUR SOLUTIONS INC
13500 Evening Creek Dr N Ste 450, San Diego (92128-8125)
PHONE..............................858 444-3100
Timothy Moynihan, *Pr*
EMP: 267 EST: 1974
SALES (est): 3.45MM **Publicly Held**
Web: lifeinsurance.cbiz.com
SIC: 6411 Insurance brokers, nec
PA: Cbiz, Inc.
5959 Rckside Wods Blvd N

(P-12193)
CENTERSTONE INSUR & FINCL SVCS
Also Called: Benefitmall
21550 Oxnard St, Woodland Hills (91367-7100)
PHONE..............................818 348-1200
Cathy Dibble, *Mgr*
EMP: 168
SALES (corp-wide): 24.65MM **Privately Held**
Web: www.benefitmall.com
SIC: 6411 Insurance brokers, nec
PA: Centerstone Insurance And Financial Services
12404 Park Central Dr # 400
469 791-3300

(P-12194)
CENTURY-NATIONAL INSURANCE CO (DH)
16650 Sherman Way Ste 200, Van Nuys (91406-3782)
PHONE..............................818 760-0880
Weldon Wilson, *CEO*
Marie Balicki, *
Judy Osborn, *
EMP: 260 EST: 1955
SQ FT: 41,000
SALES (est): 8.05MM **Publicly Held**
Web: century-company.edan.io
SIC: 6411 Insurance agents, nec
HQ: National General Holdings Corp.
59 Maiden Ln Fl 38
New York NY 10038

(P-12195)
CHOIC ADMINI INSUR SERVI
Also Called: California Choice
721 S Parker St Ste 200, Orange (92868-4772)
PHONE..............................714 542-4200
Michael Close, *Pr*
John M Word, *
Raymond D Godeke, *
Brenda Scott, *
EMP: 500 EST: 1984
SALES (est): 7.3MM **Privately Held**
Web: www.mycalchoice.com
SIC: 6411 Insurance agents, nec

(P-12196)
CONEXIS BNFITS ADMNSTRATORS LP (HQ)
721 S Parker St Ste 300, Orange (92868-4732)
PHONE..............................714 835-5006
EMP: 120 EST: 1988
SQ FT: 57,000
SALES (est): 12.28MM
SALES (corp-wide): 175.25MM **Privately Held**
Web: www.wordandbrown.com
SIC: 6411 Insurance information and consulting services
PA: Word & Brown, Insurance Administrators, Inc.
721 S Parker St Ste 300
714 835-5006

(P-12197)
CONFIE HOLDING II CO (PA)
Also Called: Confie
7711 Center Ave Ste 200, Huntington Beach (92647-9124)
PHONE..............................714 252-2500
Cesar Soriano, *CEO*
Michael Kaplan, *
Darrin Silveria, *CSO*

Tim Clark, *Chief Human Resource Officer*
Joshua Marder, *CMO*
EMP: 160 EST: 2007
SALES (est): 70.61MM
SALES (corp-wide): 70.61MM **Privately Held**
Web: www.confie.com
SIC: 6411 Insurance agents, nec

(P-12198)
CUSTOMZED SVCS ADMNSTRTORS INC
Also Called: Global Care Travel
9797 Aero Dr Ste 300, San Diego (92123-1898)
P.O. Box 939057 (92193-9057)
PHONE..............................858 810-2004
Christopher Carnicelli, *CEO*
John Martini, *
EMP: 140 EST: 1991
SALES (est): 33.53MM
SALES (corp-wide): 6.33B **Privately Held**
Web: shop.generalitravelinsurance.com
SIC: 6411 4724 Insurance agents, nec; Travel agencies
HQ: Generali Global Assistance, Inc.
4330 East West Hwy # 1000
Bethesda MD 20814
240 330-1000

(P-12199)
CYBERPOLICY INC
19584 Pine Valley Ave, Porter Ranch (91326-1408)
PHONE..............................877 626-9991
Keith Moore, *CEO*
EMP: 103 EST: 2016
SALES (est): 917.04K **Privately Held**
Web: www.cyberpolicy.com
SIC: 6411 Insurance agents, brokers, and service

(P-12200)
CYPRESS PNT-RROWHEAD GEN INSUR
2365 Northside Dr Ste 450, San Diego (92108-2719)
PHONE..............................619 681-0560
Bill Trzos, *Pr*
EMP: 75 EST: 2001
SQ FT: 6,000
SALES (est): 362.65K **Privately Held**
SIC: 6411 Insurance agents, nec

(P-12201)
DEDICTED DFNED BENEFT SVCS LLC
550 N Brand Blvd Ste 1610, Glendale (91203-1964)
P.O. Box 219800 (64121-9800)
PHONE..............................415 931-1990
Karen Shapiro, *CEO*
EMP: 127 EST: 2006
SALES (est): 807.08K
SALES (corp-wide): 947.08MM **Privately Held**
Web: www.dedicated-db.com
SIC: 6411 Pension and retirement plan consultants
PA: Ascensus, Llc
200 Dryden Rd E Ste 1000
215 648-8000

(P-12202)
DEWITT STERN GROUP INC
5990 Sepulveda Blvd Ste 550, Van Nuys (91411-2536)
PHONE..............................818 933-2700
Jolyon F Stern, *Brnch Mgr*

EMP: 137
SALES (corp-wide): 1.03B **Privately Held**
Web: www.dewittstern.com
SIC: 6411 Insurance brokers, nec
HQ: Dewitt Stern Group, Inc.
420 Lexington Ave Rm 2700
New York NY 10170
212 867-3550

(P-12203)
DMA CLAIMS INC
Also Called: David Morse & Associates
330 N Brand Blvd Ste 230, Glendale
(91203-2380)
P.O. Box 26004 (91222)
PHONE..............................877 880-3616
Jason Turner, CEO
EMP: 250 **EST:** 1993
SALES (est): 23.37MM **Privately Held**
Web: www.dmaclaims.com
SIC: 6411 Insurance claim adjusters, not
employed by insurance company
PA: Venbrook Group, Llc
6320 Canoga Ave Fl 12

(P-12204)
DMA CLAIMS MANAGEMENT INC
Also Called: David Morse & Assoc.
330 N Brand Blvd Ste 230, Glendale
(91203-2380)
P.O. Box 26004 (91222-6004)
PHONE..............................323 342-6800
Dan Mara, Brnch Mgr
EMP: 77
SALES (corp-wide): 11.32MM **Privately Held**
Web: www.davidmorse.com
SIC: 6411 Insurance claim adjusters, not
employed by insurance company
PA: Dma Claims Management, Inc.
330 N Brand Blvd Ste 230
323 342-6800

(P-12205)
EDGEWOOD PARTNERS INSUR CTR
Also Called: Nationwide
4675 Macarthur Ct, Newport Beach
(92660-1875)
PHONE..............................949 263-0606
Dan Ryan, Brnch Mgr
EMP: 289
SALES (corp-wide): 501.41MM **Privately Held**
Web: www.epicbrokers.com
SIC: 6411 Insurance brokers, nec
HQ: Edgewood Partners Insurance Center
1 California St Ste 400
San Francisco CA 94111

(P-12206)
EPISOURCE LLC
500 W 190th St Ste 400, Gardena
(90248-4269)
PHONE..............................714 452-1961
Sishir Reddy, Prin
Erik Simonsen, *
EMP: 6600 **EST:** 2006
SALES (est): 58.99MM **Privately Held**
Web: www.episource.com
SIC: 6411 Medical insurance claim
processing, contract or fee basis

(P-12207)
FARMERS GROUP INC (HQ)
Also Called: Farmers Insurance
6301 Owensmouth Ave, Woodland Hills
(91367-2216)
P.O. Box 2450 (49501-2450)

PHONE..............................323 932-3200
Raul Vargas, Pr
Giles Harrison, *
Melissa Joye, CMO*
John Griek, *
▲ **EMP:** 2100 **EST:** 1998
SALES (est): 4.96B **Privately Held**
Web: www.farmers.com
SIC: 6411 Insurance agents, brokers, and
service
PA: Zurich Insurance Group Ag
C/O Zurich Versicherungs-Gesellschaft
Ag

(P-12208)
FARMERS GROUP INC 401 K SAV PL
Also Called: Farmers Insurance
4680 Wilshire Blvd, Los Angeles
(90010-3807)
PHONE..............................323 932-3200
EMP: 73 **EST:** 2017
SALES (est): 5.35MM **Privately Held**
Web: www.farmers.com
SIC: 6411 Insurance agents, brokers, and
service

(P-12209)
FARMERS INSURANCE
113 Avondale Ave, Monterey Park
(91754-1797)
PHONE..............................626 288-0870
Yvone Ti, Brnch Mgr
EMP: 179
Web: www.farmers.com
SIC: 6411 Insurance agents and brokers
HQ: Farmers Insurance
6600 Sw Hampton St
Portland OR 97223
503 372-2000

(P-12210)
FARMERS INSURANCE
27433 Tourney Rd Ste 170, Valencia
(91355-5399)
PHONE..............................661 257-0844
Corrine Mirone, Prin
EMP: 179
Web: www.farmers.com
SIC: 6411 Insurance agents, brokers, and
service
HQ: Farmers Insurance
6600 Sw Hampton St
Portland OR 97223
503 372-2000

(P-12211)
FARMERS INSURANCE
3600 Lime St Ste 122, Riverside
(92501-0911)
PHONE..............................951 681-1068
Lucinda Metcalfe, Brnch Mgr
EMP: 179
Web: www.farmers.com
SIC: 6411 Insurance agents, brokers, and
service
HQ: Farmers Insurance
6600 Sw Hampton St
Portland OR 97223
503 372-2000

(P-12212)
FARMERS INSURANCE EXCHANGE (DH)
Also Called: Farmers Insurance
6301 Owensmouth Ave, Woodland Hills
(91367-2216)
PHONE..............................888 327-6335
Jeff Pailey, CEO
Thomas Noh, *

Eric Kappler, CPO*
EMP: 3000 **EST:** 1928
SQ FT: 210,000
SALES (est): 306.01MM **Privately Held**
Web: www.farmers.com
SIC: 6411 Insurance agents, brokers, and
service
HQ: Farmers Group, Inc.
6301 Owensmouth Ave
Woodland Hills CA 91367
323 932-3200

(P-12213)
FIRE INSURANCE EXCHANGE (PA)
6301 Owensmouth Ave, Woodland Hills
(91367-2216)
PHONE..............................323 932-3200
Martin Feinstein, Pr
John Harrington, *
Doren Hohl, *
Ron Myhan, *
EMP: 2300 **EST:** 1942
SALES (est): 2.95MM
SALES (corp-wide): 2.95MM **Privately Held**
Web: www.farmers.com
SIC: 6411 Insurance agents, brokers, and
service

(P-12214)
FMC FINANCIAL GROUP (PA)
4675 Macarthur Ct Ste 1250, Newport
Beach (92660-8803)
PHONE..............................949 225-9369
James Chapel, Owner
▲ **EMP:** 75 **EST:** 1981
SALES (est): 1.98MM **Privately Held**
Web: www.fmcfg.com
SIC: 6411 Insurance agents and brokers

(P-12215)
FREEWAY INSURANCE (PA)
Also Called: South Coast Auto Insurance
7711 Center Ave Ste 200, Huntington Beach
(92647-9124)
P.O. Box 669 (90630-0669)
PHONE..............................714 252-2500
Elias Assaf, Pr
John Klaeb, *
Norm Hudson, *
EMP: 120 **EST:** 1988
SQ FT: 20,000
SALES (est): 10.43MM
SALES (corp-wide): 10.43MM **Privately Held**
Web: www.freeway.com
SIC: 6411 Insurance agents, nec

(P-12216)
GROSVENOR INV MGT US INC
2308 Chelsea Rd, Palos Verdes Estates
(90274-2606)
PHONE..............................310 265-0297
Stephen Waddell, Brnch Mgr
EMP: 80
SALES (corp-wide): 8.48B **Publicly Held**
SIC: 6411 Pension and retirement plan
consultants
HQ: Grosvenor Investment Management
Us Inc.
10 New King St Ste 214
White Plains NY 10604
914 683-3710

(P-12217)
H & H AGENCY INC (PA)
1403 N Tustin Ave Ste 280, Santa Ana
(92705-8691)
PHONE..............................949 260-8840

Michael Weinstein, CEO
EMP: 88 **EST:** 1969
SQ FT: 25,000
SALES (est): 2.43MM
SALES (corp-wide): 2.43MM **Privately Held**
Web: www.hhagency.com
SIC: 6411 Insurance agents, nec

(P-12218)
HEALTHSMART MGT SVCS ORGNZTION
Also Called: Healthsmart Mso
10855 Business Center Dr Ste C, Cypress
(90630-5252)
P.O. Box 6300 (90630-0063)
PHONE..............................714 947-8600
Carol Houchins, Pr
EMP: 90 **EST:** 1996
SALES (est): 4.99MM **Privately Held**
Web: www.healthsmartmso.com
SIC: 6411 8741 8721 Medical insurance
claim processing, contract or fee basis;
Hospital management; Billing and
bookkeeping service

(P-12219)
HOWARDS MBS INC
23909 Sylvan St, Woodland Hills
(91367-1246)
PHONE..............................202 570-4074
Ketsha Thompson, CEO
EMP: 75 **EST:** 2006
SALES (est): 717.87K **Privately Held**
SIC: 6411 7929 Education services,
insurance; Entertainers and entertainment
groups

(P-12220)
INDEMNITY COMPANY CALIFORNIA (DH)
17771 Cowan Ste 100, Irvine (92614-6044)
P.O. Box 19725 (92623-9725)
PHONE..............................949 263-3300
Harry C Crowell, Ch
Walter A Crowell, Sec
Sam Zaza, Treas
Fern Haberman, CFO
EMP: 71 **EST:** 1967
SQ FT: 50,000
SALES (est): 2.56MM
SALES (corp-wide): 3.82B **Privately Held**
SIC: 6411 Insurance agents, nec
HQ: Insco Insurance Services, Inc.
17771 Cowan St Ste 100
Irvine CA 92614
949 263-3415

(P-12221)
INSCO INSURANCE SERVICES INC (DH)
Also Called: Developers Surety Indemnity Co
17771 Cowan Ste 100, Irvine (92614-6044)
P.O. Box 19725 (92614)
PHONE..............................949 263-3415
Harry Crowell, Ch Bd
EMP: 70 **EST:** 1970
SQ FT: 50,000
SALES (est): 14.6MM
SALES (corp-wide): 3.82B **Privately Held**
Web: comingsoon.markmonitor.com
SIC: 6411 6351 Property and casualty
insurance agent; Surety insurance bonding
HQ: Amtrust Financial Services, Inc.
59 Maiden Ln Fl 43
New York NY 10038

(P-12222)
INSURANCE COMPANY OF WEST (HQ)
Also Called: I C W
15025 Innovation Dr, San Diego (92128-3455)
P.O. Box 509039 (92150)
PHONE.................................858 350-2400
Kevin Prior, Pr
Ernest Rady, *
H Michael Freet, *
EMP: 96 **EST:** 1972
SQ FT: 150,000
SALES (est): 78.59MM
SALES (corp-wide): 610.35MM **Privately Held**
Web: www.icwgroup.com
SIC: 6411 Insurance agents, nec
PA: Icw Group Holdings, Inc.
15025 Innovation Dr
858 350-2400

(P-12223)
JOHN HANCOCK LIFE INSUR CO USA (DH)
Also Called: John Hancock
865 S Figueroa St Ste 3320, Los Angeles (90017-5444)
PHONE.................................213 689-0813
Emeritus D'alessandro, CEO
David F D'alessandro, Pr
Robert R Reitano, *
Gregory P Winn, *
▲ **EMP:** 2000 **EST:** 1862
SQ FT: 3,600,000
SALES (est): 471.15MM
SALES (corp-wide): 17.45B **Privately Held**
Web: www.johnhancock.com
SIC: 6411 6351 6371 6321 Insurance agents and brokers; Mortgage guarantee insurance ; Pensions; Accident insurance carriers
HQ: John Hancock Financial Services, Inc.
200 Clarendon St
Boston MA 02117
617 572-6000

(P-12224)
JOHN HANCOCK LIFE INSUR CO USA
Also Called: John Hancock
10180 Telesis Ct, San Diego (92121-2705)
PHONE.................................858 292-1667
EMP: 462
SALES (corp-wide): 17.45B **Privately Held**
Web: www.johnhancock.com
SIC: 6411 Insurance agents and brokers
HQ: John Hancock Life Insurance Company (U.S.A.).
865 S Fgueroa St Ste 3320
Los Angeles CA 90017
213 689-0813

(P-12225)
KEENAN & ASSOCIATES (HQ)
2355 Crenshaw Blvd Ste 200, Torrance (90501-3395)
P.O. Box 4328 (90510-4328)
PHONE.................................310 212-3344
John Keenan, Ch Bd
Sean Smith, *
Henry Loubet, Senior Vice President Strategic Planning*
Keith Pippard, *
Davis Seres, *
EMP: 339 **EST:** 1972
SQ FT: 80,000
SALES (est): 39.79MM **Privately Held**
Web: www.keenan.com
SIC: 6411 Insurance brokers, nec
PA: Assuredpartners, Inc.
450 S Orange Ave Fl 4

(P-12226)
LEXISNEXIS RISK ASSETS INC
Also Called: Choicepoint
2112 Business Center Dr Ste 150, Irvine (92614)
PHONE.................................949 222-0028
Tim Coon, Owner
EMP: 95
SALES (corp-wide): 11.42B **Privately Held**
Web: risk.lexisnexis.com
SIC: 6411 Information bureaus, insurance
HQ: Lexisnexis Risk Assets Inc.
1105 N Market St Ste 501
Wilmington DE 19801
800 458-9410

(P-12227)
LOCKTON CMPNIES LLC - PCF SRIE (HQ)
Also Called: Lockton Insurance Brokers
777 S Figueroa St Ste 5200, Los Angeles (90017-5850)
PHONE.................................213 689-0500
Timothy J Noonan, Pr
Nate Mundy, *
Leonard G Fodemski, *
EMP: 294 **EST:** 2016
SQ FT: 72,300
SALES (est): 38.1MM
SALES (corp-wide): 1.61B **Privately Held**
Web: global.lockton.com
SIC: 6411 Insurance brokers, nec
PA: Lockton, Inc.
444 W 47th St Ste 900
816 960-9000

(P-12228)
MARKEL CORP
Also Called: Associated Intl Insur Co
21600 Oxnard St Ste 900, Woodland Hills (91367-7834)
PHONE.................................818 595-0600
Anthony Markel, Pr
Alan Kirshner, *
Steven Markel, *
EMP: 297 **EST:** 1972
SQ FT: 32,000
SALES (est): 2.15MM
SALES (corp-wide): 15.8B **Publicly Held**
Web: www.markel.com
SIC: 6411 Insurance agents, brokers, and service
HQ: Markel North America, Inc.
4521 Highwoods Pwy
Glen Allen VA 23060
804 747-0136

(P-12229)
MARSH & MCLENNAN AGENCY LLC
Also Called: Marsh
9171 Towne Centre Dr Ste 500, San Diego (92122-1238)
PHONE.................................858 457-3414
Paul Hering, Brnch Mgr
EMP: 200
SALES (corp-wide): 22.74B **Publicly Held**
Web: www.marshma.com
SIC: 6411 Insurance brokers, nec
HQ: Marsh & Mclennan Agency Llc
9850 Nw 41st St Ste 100
Doral FL 33178

(P-12230)
MARSH RISK & INSURANCE SVCS
Also Called: MMC
633 W 5th St Ste 1200, Los Angeles (90017)
PHONE.................................213 624-5555
Melody Schwartz, *
EMP: 687 **EST:** 1883
SALES (est): 2.98MM
SALES (corp-wide): 22.74B **Publicly Held**
SIC: 6411 Insurance brokers, nec
PA: Marsh & Mclennan Companies, Inc.
1166 Ave Of The Americas
212 345-5000

(P-12231)
MEDICAL EYE SERVICES INC
Also Called: Mesvision
345 Baker St, Costa Mesa (92626-4518)
P.O. Box 25209 (92799-5209)
PHONE.................................714 619-4660
Aspasia Shappet, Pr
EMP: 88 **EST:** 1976
SQ FT: 12,000
SALES (est): 7.4MM
SALES (corp-wide): 23.26MM **Privately Held**
Web: www.mesvision.com
SIC: 6411 Insurance claim processing, except medical
PA: The Eye Care Network Of California Inc
345 Baker St
714 619-4660

(P-12232)
MESA INSURANCE SOLUTIONS INC
50 Castilian Dr, Goleta (93117-3080)
PHONE.................................805 308-6308
EMP: 244 **EST:** 2017
SALES (est): 456.47K
SALES (corp-wide): 471.88MM **Publicly Held**
SIC: 6411 Insurance agents, nec
PA: Appfolio, Inc.
70 Castilian Dr
805 364-6093

(P-12233)
MOMENTOUS INSURANCE BRKG INC
5990 Sepulveda Blvd Ste 550, Van Nuys (91411-2536)
PHONE.................................818 933-2700
Diane Brinson Schiele, Pr
Michelle Boyer, Prin
Carla Cave, Prin
Erin Gaston, Sr VP
David Oliver, Sr VP
EMP: 104 **EST:** 2008
SALES (est): 20.27MM
SALES (corp-wide): 22.74B **Publicly Held**
Web: www.momentousino.com
SIC: 6411 Insurance agents, nec
PA: Marsh & Mclennan Companies, Inc.
1166 Ave Of The Americas
212 345-5000

(P-12234)
MONARCH E & S INSURANCE SVCS
2540 Foothill Blvd # 101, La Crescenta (91214-4573)
PHONE.................................559 226-0200
EMP: 70
SALES (est): 12.77MM **Privately Held**
SIC: 6411 Insurance information and consulting services

(P-12235)
MONY LIFE INSURANCE COMPANY
Also Called: Mony Life
333 S Anita Dr Ste 750, Orange (92868-3322)
PHONE.................................714 939-6669
Joseph Moore, Mgr
EMP: 75
Web: www.protective.com
SIC: 6411 Insurance agents, brokers, and service
HQ: Mony Life Insurance Company
1740 Broadway
New York NY 10019
800 487-6669

(P-12236)
MORRIS GRRITANO INSUR AGCY INC
Also Called: Nationwide
1122 Laurel Ln, San Luis Obispo (93401-5895)
P.O. Box 1189 (93406-1189)
PHONE.................................805 543-6887
Brendan Morris, CEO
Gene Garritano, *
Gabe Garcia, *
David Morgan, Stockholder*
Kelly Morgan, Stockholder*
EMP: 85 **EST:** 1916
SQ FT: 14,000
SALES (est): 22.71MM **Privately Held**
Web: www.morrisgarritano.com
SIC: 6411 Insurance agents, nec

(P-12237)
MULLIN TBG INSUR AGCY SVCS LLC (DH)
Also Called: Mullintbg
3333 Michelson Dr Ste 820, Irvine (92612-0655)
EMP: 185 **EST:** 1987
SALES (est): 9.25MM
SALES (corp-wide): 53.98B **Publicly Held**
SIC: 6411 Insurance information and consulting services
HQ: The Prudential Insurance Company Of America
751 Broad St Fl 21
Newark NJ 07102
973 802-6000

(P-12238)
NATIONAL INSURANCE CRIME BUR
15545 Devonshire St Ste 309, Mission Hills (91345-2672)
PHONE.................................818 895-2867
Bob Jones, Dir
EMP: 82
SALES (corp-wide): 19.58MM **Privately Held**
Web: www.nicb.org
SIC: 6411 Insurance agents, brokers, and service
PA: National Insurance Crime Bureau, Inc
1111 E Touhy Ave Ste 400
847 544-7000

(P-12239)
NNA INSURANCE SERVICES LLC
9350 De Soto Ave, Chatsworth (91311-4926)
P.O. Box 2402 (91313-2402)
PHONE.................................818 739-4071
Milton G Valera, Ch Bd
Deborah M Thaw, *
Thomas A Heymann, *
Robert A Clarke, *
▲ **EMP:** 204 **EST:** 1957
SQ FT: 55,000
SALES (est): 1.88MM **Privately Held**
Web: www.nationalnotary.org

PRODUCTS & SVCS

SIC: 6411 Insurance agents, brokers, and service

(P-12240)
NORTHWESTERN MUTL INV MGT LLC
Also Called: Northwestern Mutual Investment
610 Newport Center Dr Ste 850, Newport Beach (92660-6472)
PHONE.....................949 759-5555
Gary Farmer, *Ex Dir*
EMP: 178
SALES (corp-wide): 16.13B Privately Held
Web: www.northwesternmutual.com
SIC: 6411 6282 Insurance agents, brokers, and service; Investment advice
HQ: Northwestern Mutual Investment
　　Management Company, Llc
　　720 E Wisconsin Ave
　　Milwaukee WI 53202
　　414 271-1444

(P-12241)
PACIFIC COMPENSATION INSUR CO
3011 Townsgate Rd Ste 120, Westlake Village (91361-5876)
P.O. Box 5034 (91359-5034)
PHONE.....................818 575-8500
Marc E Schmittlein, *Pr*
EMP: 150 EST: 2002
SALES (est): 7.05MM
SALES (corp-wide): 473.43MM Privately Held
Web: www.copperpoint.com
SIC: 6411 Insurance agents, nec
HQ: Pacific Compensation Corporation
　　3011 Townsgate Rd Ste 120
　　Westlake Village CA 91361

(P-12242)
PACIFIC INDEMNITY COMPANY
Also Called: Chubb
555 S Flower St Ste 300, Los Angeles (90071-2427)
PHONE.....................213 622-2334
John Fennigan, *Pr*
EMP: 300 EST: 1926
SALES (est): 3.17MM Privately Held
Web: www.chubb.com
SIC: 6411 6331 6351 Property and casualty insurance agent; Fire, marine, and casualty insurance; mutual; Surety insurance
HQ: Ina Chubb Holdings Inc
　　436 Walnut St
　　Philadelphia PA 19106
　　215 640-1000

(P-12243)
PACIFIC PIONEER INSUR GROUP (PA)
Also Called: Nationwide
6363 Katella Ave, Cypress (90630-5205)
PHONE.....................714 228-7888
EMP: 80 EST: 1989
SQ FT: 32,000
SALES (est): 9.01MM Privately Held
Web: www.ucageneral.com
SIC: 6411 Insurance agents, nec

(P-12244)
POLISEEK AIS INSUR SLTIONS INC
Also Called: Nationwide
17785 Center Court Dr N Ste 250, Cerritos (90703-8596)
PHONE.....................866 480-7335
Mark Ribisi, *Pr*
Chris Bremer, *CAO*

Romayne Levee, *
Lani Elkin, *
Mark Casas, *
EMP: 85 EST: 2008
SALES (est): 894.98K
SALES (corp-wide): 4.63B Publicly Held
Web: www.nationwide.com
SIC: 6411 Insurance agents, nec
HQ: Ais Management, Llc
　　17785 Center Court Dr N # 250
　　Cerritos CA 90703

(P-12245)
PRECEPT ADVISORY GROUP LLC (DH)
Also Called: Precept Group The
130 Theory Ste 200, Irvine (92617-3065)
PHONE.....................949 955-1430
Wade R Olson, *Pr*
Alex Wasilewski, *Ex VP*
Steve Zarate, *COO*
Christopher H Coulter, *CMO*
Mercedes Meseck, *VP*
EMP: 90 EST: 1987
SQ FT: 32,000
SALES (est): 10.59MM
SALES (corp-wide): 246.86MM Privately Held
Web: www.truist.com
SIC: 6411 Insurance brokers, nec
HQ: Mcgriff Insurance Services, Llc
　　7701 Airport Center Dr
　　Greensboro NC 27409
　　919 716-9907

(P-12246)
PREFERRED EMPLOYERS INSUR CO
9797 Aero Dr Ste 200, San Diego (92123-1898)
P.O. Box 85478 (92186-5478)
PHONE.....................619 688-3900
Linda R Smith, *CEO*
Steven A Gallacher, *
S Akbar Khan, *
EMP: 87 EST: 1997
SALES (est): 5.04MM
SALES (corp-wide): 12.14B Publicly Held
Web: www.peiwc.com
SIC: 6411 Insurance information and consulting services
PA: W. R. Berkley Corporation
　　475 Steamboat Rd
　　203 629-3000

(P-12247)
PREMIER DEALER SERVICES INC
9449 Balboa Ave Ste 300, San Diego (92123-4395)
PHONE.....................858 810-1700
John R Topits, *Pr*
Kurt Wolery, *
A Kurt Wolery, *
EMP: 100 EST: 1998
SALES (est): 2.34MM Privately Held
Web: www.pdsadm.com
SIC: 6411 Insurance agents, brokers, and service

(P-12248)
QUALITAS INSURANCE COMPANY
Also Called: Qualitas Premier Insur Svcs
4545 Murphy Canyon Rd Fl 3, San Diego (92123-4363)
PHONE.....................619 876-4355
Eduardo Pedrero, *CEO*
Robert Blanchard, *
EMP: 70 EST: 2014

SALES (est): 2.89MM Privately Held
Web: www.qualitasinsurance.com
SIC: 6411 Insurance agents, brokers, and service

(P-12249)
R MC CLOSKEY INSURANCE AGENCY
Also Called: Tax and Financial Group
4001 Macarthur Blvd Ste 300, Newport Beach (92660-2508)
PHONE.....................949 223-8100
Richard Mc Closkey, *Pr*
EMP: 120 EST: 1969
SQ FT: 15,000
SALES (est): 5.1MM Privately Held
Web: www.tfgroup.com
SIC: 6411 Insurance agents, nec

(P-12250)
ROBERT MORENO INSURANCE SVCS
3110 E Guasti Rd Ste 500, Ontario (91761-1228)
PHONE.....................714 578-3318
Robert B Moreno, *Owner*
EMP: 140 EST: 1978
SALES (est): 2.18MM Privately Held
Web: www.rmismga.com
SIC: 6411 Insurance agents, nec

(P-12251)
SAFECO INSURANCE COMPANY AMER
Safeco
330 N Brand Blvd Ste 680, Glendale (91203-2385)
PHONE.....................818 956-4250
Don Chambers, *Mgr*
EMP: 234
SALES (corp-wide): 49.41B Privately Held
Web: www.safeco.com
SIC: 6411 Insurance agents, nec
HQ: Safeco Insurance Company Of America
　　1001 Fourth Ave
　　Seattle WA 98185
　　206 545-5000

(P-12252)
SEDGWICK CMS HOLDINGS INC
Also Called: Sedgwick
3633 Inland Empire Blvd, Ontario (91764-4922)
PHONE.....................909 477-5500
Kim Pech, *Brnch Mgr*
EMP: 518
SALES (corp-wide): 2.96B Publicly Held
Web: www.sedgwick.com
SIC: 6411 Insurance claim adjusters, not employed by insurance company
HQ: Sedgwick Cms Holdings, Inc.
　　1100 Rdgway Loop Rd Ste 2
　　Memphis TN 38120

(P-12253)
SENECA FAMILY OF AGENCIES
Also Called: Cys Knship Sneca Tstin Wrprund
1801 Park Court Pl Bldg H, Santa Ana (92701-5028)
PHONE.....................714 881-8600
EMP: 153
SALES (corp-wide): 176.92MM Privately Held
Web: www.senecafoa.org
SIC: 6411 Insurance agents, brokers, and service
PA: Seneca Family Of Agencies
　　8945 Golf Links Rd

510 317-1444

(P-12254)
SENTRY LIFE INSURANCE COMPANY
4720 Aliso Way, Oceanside (92057-6821)
PHONE.....................661 274-4018
Jay Ottersen, *Mgr*
EMP: 191
SALES (corp-wide): 3.07B Privately Held
Web: www.sentry.com
SIC: 6411 Insurance agents, brokers, and service
HQ: Sentry Life Insurance Company
　　1800 N Point Dr
　　Stevens Point WI 54481
　　715 346-6000

(P-12255)
STATE FARM MUTL AUTO INSUR CO
Also Called: State Farm Insurance
900 Old River Rd 400, Bakersfield (93311-9501)
PHONE.....................309 766-2311
EMP: 72
SALES (corp-wide): 39.59B Privately Held
SIC: 6411 Insurance agents and brokers
PA: State Farm Mutual Automobile
　　Insurance Company
　　1 State Farm Plz
　　309 766-2311

(P-12256)
SURECO HLTH LF INSUR AGCY INC
201 Sandpointe Ave Ste 600, Santa Ana (92707-8700)
PHONE.....................949 333-0263
Marc Steven Bablot, *CEO*
EMP: 75 EST: 2016
SALES (est): 4.68MM Privately Held
Web: www.sureco.com
SIC: 6411 7379 7311 Insurance agents, brokers, and service; Online services technology consultants; Advertising agencies

(P-12257)
TEAGUE INSURANCE AGENCY INC
Also Called: Nationwide
7777 Alvarado Rd, La Mesa (91942-8216)
PHONE.....................619 464-6851
Walter Johnston, *Pr*
Elizabeth Bonilla, *
EMP: 74 EST: 1968
SALES (est): 2.48MM Privately Held
Web: www.teagueins.com
SIC: 6411 Insurance agents, nec

(P-12258)
THI HOLDINGS (DELAWARE) INC
2140 E Palmdale Blvd Ste O, Palmdale (93550-1207)
PHONE.....................661 266-7423
Lewis Pelser, *Mgr*
EMP: 401
SALES (corp-wide): 11.75B Privately Held
Web: www.allergycleveland.com
SIC: 6411 Insurance agents, nec
HQ: Thi Holdings (Delaware), Inc.
　　5915 Landerbrook Dr
　　Cleveland OH 44124

(P-12259)

TM CLAIMS SERVICE INC

Also Called: Tokio Marine Michido
800 E Colorado Blvd, Pasadena
(91101-2103)
P.O. Box 7216 (91109-7316)
PHONE..............................626 568-7800
Tommy Hasegawa, *Mgr*
EMP: 96
Web: ebilling.tmclaims.com
SIC: 6411 Insurance brokers, nec
HQ: Tm Claims Service, Inc.
499 Wshngton Blvd Ste 150
Jersey City NJ 07310

(P-12260)

TOKIO MARINE HIGHLAND INSURANCE SERVICES INC (DH)

Also Called: Tm Highland Insurance Services
899 El Centro St, South Pasadena
(91030-3101)
PHONE..............................626 463-6486
EMP: 100 **EST:** 1962
SALES (est): 20.57MM **Privately Held**
Web: www.tokiomarinehighland.com
SIC: 6411 Insurance agents, nec
HQ: Tokio Marine Kiln Insurance Limited
20 Fenchurch Street
London EC3M
207 886-9000

(P-12261)

TOPA INSURANCE COMPANY (HQ)

1800 Avenue Of The Stars Ste 1200, Los
Angeles (90067-4200)
PHONE..............................310 201-0451
John E Anderson, *Ch Bd*
Harry W Degner, *
Noshirwan Marfatia, *
William S Anderson, *
Dan Sherrin, *
EMP: 79 **EST:** 1979
SALES (est): 24.39MM
SALES (corp-wide): 251.02MM **Privately Held**
Web: www.topains.com
SIC: 6411 Insurance agents, nec
PA: Topa Equities, Ltd.
1800 Avenue Of The Stars
310 203-9199

(P-12262)

TRG INSURANCE SERVICES

Also Called: The Rule Group
4675 Macarthur Ct, Newport Beach
(92660-1875)
PHONE..............................949 474-1550
Kent Crawford, *Pr*
EMP: 248 **EST:** 1983
SALES (est): 3.71MM **Privately Held**
SIC: 6411 Insurance brokers, nec
HQ: Integro Usa Inc.
1 State St Fl 9
New York NY 10004
212 295-8000

(P-12263)

TRISTAR SERVICE COMPANY INC (HQ)

100 Oceangate Ste 700, Long Beach
(90802-4368)
PHONE..............................562 495-6600
Thomas J Veale, *Pr*
Denise Cotter, *
Joseph Mclaughlin, *SLS*
Craig Evans, *CIO**
Shana Barrowclough, *Claims Operations
Vice President**

EMP: 375 **EST:** 2002
SQ FT: 9,000
SALES (est): 77.87MM
SALES (corp-wide): 258.52MM **Privately Held**
Web: www.tristarrisk.com
SIC: 6411 8742 Inspection and investigation
services, insurance; Management
consulting services
PA: Tristar Insurance Group, Inc.
100 Oceangate Ste 700
562 495-6600

(P-12264)

VALLEY INSURANCE SERVICE INC

Also Called: Brower Hale
23181 Verdugo Dr Ste 100b, Laguna Hills
(92653-1313)
PHONE..............................949 707-4080
Debbie Hale, *Mgr*
EMP: 241
SALES (corp-wide): 324.14MM **Privately Held**
Web: www.worldsystembuilder.com
SIC: 6411 Insurance agents, nec
HQ: Valley Insurance Service, Inc.
4695 Macarthur Ct Ste 600
Newport Beach CA 92660
626 966-3664

(P-12265)

VENBROOK INSURANCE SERVICES GP

6320 Canoga Ave Fl 12, Woodland Hills
(91367-2584)
PHONE..............................818 598-8900
Jason Turner, *CEO*
EMP: 100 **EST:** 2002
SALES (est): 7.61MM **Privately Held**
SIC: 6411 Insurance agents, brokers, and
service
PA: Venbrook Group, Llc
6320 Canoga Ave Fl 12

(P-12266)

VETERINARY PET INSURANCE SERVICES INC

Also Called: Dvm Insurance Agency
1800 E Imperial Hwy Ste 145, Brea
(92821-6002)
P.O. Box 2344 (92822-2344)
PHONE..............................714 989-0555
EMP: 420
Web: www.petinsurance.com
SIC: 6411 Insurance agents, brokers, and
service

(P-12267)

W BROWN ASSOC INSUR SVCS LLC

19000 Macarthur Blvd Ste 600, Irvine
(92612-1470)
PHONE..............................949 851-2060
John Krebs, *Pr*
William Brown, *
Scott Brown, *
Brian English, *
Tom Bussard, *
EMP: 88 **EST:** 1987
SQ FT: 11,000
SALES (est): 5.32MM **Privately Held**
SIC: 6411 Insurance agents, nec
HQ: Sompo International Holdings Ltd.
C/O Endurance Specialty Insurance Ltd
Hamilton HM08

(P-12268)

WELLS FRGO INSUR SVCS MINN INC

4141 Inland Empire Blvd, Ontario
(91764-5004)
PHONE..............................909 481-3802
EMP: 103
SALES (corp-wide): 94.18B **Publicly Held**
SIC: 6411 Insurance agents, brokers, and
service
HQ: Wells Fargo Insurance Services Of
Minnesota, Inc.
400 Highway 169 S Ste 800
Minneapolis MN 55426
952 563-0600

(P-12269)

WEST COVINA FOSTER FAMILY AGCY

Also Called: A SUNRISE HORIZON
527 E Rowland St Ste 100, Covina
(91723-3230)
PHONE..............................626 814-9085
Sukhwinder Singh, *Ex Dir*
Emmanuel Azariah, *
EMP: 70 **EST:** 1994
SALES (est): 5.23MM **Privately Held**
Web: www.westcovina.org
SIC: 6411 Insurance agents, brokers, and
service

(P-12270)

WESTERN GENERAL INSURANCE CO

5230 Las Virgenes Rd Ste 100, Calabasas
(91302-3447)
P.O. Box 26894 (94126)
PHONE..............................818 880-9070
Robert M Ehrlich, *Pr*
Daniel Mallut, *
John Albanese, *
Denise M Tyson, *
Marleen Kushner, *
EMP: 165 **EST:** 1971
SQ FT: 51,000
SALES (est): 7.55MM **Privately Held**
Web: www.caclo.org
SIC: 6411 Insurance agents, nec

(P-12271)

WESTWOOD INSURANCE AGENCY LLC (HQ)

Also Called: Centex Insurance Agency
6320 Canoga Ave Ste 500, Woodland Hills
(91367-7799)
PHONE..............................818 990-9715
John Flynn, *Pr*
Mark Nettleton, *
EMP: 89 **EST:** 1952
SALES (est): 2.18MM
SALES (corp-wide): 1.22B **Publicly Held**
Web: www.westwoodinsurance.com
SIC: 6411 Insurance agents, nec
PA: The Baldwin Insurance Group Inc
4211 W Boy Scout Blvd Ste
866 279-0698

(P-12272)

WINTERTHUR U S HOLDINGS INC

Also Called: Winterthur
888 S Figueroa St Ste 570, Los Angeles
(90017-5449)
PHONE..............................213 228-0281
Ken Mcclelland, *Brnch Mgr*
EMP: 216
SIC: 6411 6311 6331 Property and casualty
insurance agent; Life insurance; Fire,
marine, and casualty insurance

HQ: Winterthur U. S. Holdings Inc
1 General Dr
Sun Prairie WI 53596
608 837-4440

(P-12273)

WOOD GUTMANN BOGART INSUR BRKG

Also Called: Nationwide
15901 Red Hill Ave Ste 100, Tustin
(92780-7318)
PHONE..............................714 505-7000
Kevin S Bogart, *CEO*
EMP: 93 **EST:** 1984
SALES (est): 6.24MM **Privately Held**
Web: www.burnhamwgb.com
SIC: 6411 Insurance agents, nec

(P-12274)

WOOD GUTMANN BOGART INSUR BRKS

Also Called: Burnham Wgb Insur Solutions
15901 Red Hill Ave Ste 100, Tustin
(92780-7318)
PHONE..............................714 505-7000
EMP: 130 **EST:** 1985
SQ FT: 5,500
SALES (est): 4MM
SALES (corp-wide): 11.39MM **Privately Held**
Web: www.burnhamwgb.com
SIC: 6411 Insurance brokers, nec
PA: Burnham Benefits Insurance Services,
Llc
2211 Michelson Dr # 1200
805 772-7965

(P-12275)

WORD & BROWN INSURANCE ADMINISTRATORS INC (PA)

Also Called: Cobrapro
721 S Parker St Ste 300, Orange
(92868-4732)
PHONE..............................714 835-5006
EMP: 430 **EST:** 1977
SALES (est): 175.25MM
SALES (corp-wide): 175.25MM **Privately Held**
Web: www.wordandbrown.com
SIC: 6411 Insurance brokers, nec

(P-12276)

WORLDWIDE HOLDINGS INC (PA)

725 S Figueroa St Ste 1900, Los Angeles
(90017-5496)
PHONE..............................213 236-4500
Donald R Davis, *Ch*
Davis D Moore, *
Daniel Colacurcio, *
EMP: 85 **EST:** 1970
SQ FT: 23,000
SALES (est): 19.14MM
SALES (corp-wide): 19.14MM **Privately Held**
SIC: 6411 Insurance brokers, nec

6512 Nonresidential Building Operators

(P-12277)

6500 HLLISTER AVE PARTNERS LLC

6500 Hollister Ave, Goleta (93117-3011)
PHONE..............................805 722-1362
EMP: 100 **EST:** 2014
SALES (est): 1.15MM **Privately Held**

PRODUCTS & SVCS

SIC: 6512 Commercial and industrial building operation

(P-12278)
ABBEY-PROPERTIES LLC (PA)
12447 Lewis St Ste 203, Garden Grove (92840-6601)
PHONE..................562 435-2100
▲ EMP: 75 EST: 1989
SQ FT: 276,000
SALES (est): 14.52MM Privately Held
SIC: 6512 Commercial and industrial building operation

(P-12279)
ALPINE VILLAGE
Also Called: Alpine Inn Restaurant
23670 Hawthorne Blvd Ste 208, Torrance (90505-8207)
PHONE..................310 327-4384
Ursula Wilson, CEO
EMP: 250 EST: 1968
SALES (est): 4.15MM Privately Held
SIC: 6512 Commercial and industrial building operation

(P-12280)
AMERICAN ASSETS INC
Also Called: Loma Palisades
2799 Adrian St, San Diego (92110-5713)
PHONE..................619 255-9944
Kim Reisign, Brnch Mgr
EMP: 107
SALES (corp-wide): 34.37MM Privately Held
Web: www.lomapalisades.com
SIC: 6512 6513 Commercial and industrial building operation; Apartment building operators
PA: American Assets, Inc.
11455 El Cmno Rl Ste 140
858 350-2600

(P-12281)
AMERICARE HLTH RETIREMENT INC
Also Called: Silvergate San Marcos
1550 Security Pl Ofc, San Marcos (92078-4063)
PHONE..................760 744-4484
Melba Dunn, Admn
EMP: 150
SQ FT: 51,071
SALES (corp-wide): 9.68MM Privately Held
Web: www.silvergaterr.com
SIC: 6512 8051 Nonresidential building operators; Skilled nursing care facilities
PA: Americare Health & Retirement, Inc.
140 Lomas Santa Fe Dr # 1
858 792-0696

(P-12282)
ARDEN REALTY INC
11601 Wilshire Blvd Fl 5, Los Angeles (90025-0509)
PHONE..................310 966-2600
EMP: 300
Web: www.ardenrealty.com
SIC: 6512 Commercial and industrial building operation

(P-12283)
C & D WAX INC
9353 Waxie Way, San Diego (92123-1036)
P.O. Box 23506 (92193-3506)
PHONE..................858 292-5954
David Wax, Ex VP
Charles Wax, *
EMP: 160 EST: 1987

SALES (est): 1.19MM Privately Held
SIC: 6512 Nonresidential building operators

(P-12284)
CB RICHARD ELLIS STRGC PRTNERS
515 S Flower St Ste 3100, Los Angeles (90071-2233)
PHONE..................213 683-4200
EMP: 100 EST: 2000
SALES (est): 1.81MM Publicly Held
SIC: 6512 Nonresidential building operators
PA: Cbre Group, Inc.
2100 Mcknney Ave Ste 1250

(P-12285)
CDCF III PCF LNDMARK SCRMNTO L
Also Called: Colony Dstrssed Cr Spcial Stto
515 S Flower St 44th Fl, Los Angeles (90071-2201)
PHONE..................310 552-7211
EMP: 241 EST: 2016
SALES (est): 5.06MM Privately Held
SIC: 6512 Commercial and industrial building operation

(P-12286)
COLLINS & COLLINS
Also Called: Leal, Jennifer A
790 E Colorado Blvd Ste 600, Pasadena (91101-2186)
PHONE..................626 243-1100
John J Collins, Pt
Sameul Muir, Pt
Robert Traver, Pt
EMP: 97 EST: 1980
SALES (est): 2.28MM Privately Held
Web: www.ccllp.law
SIC: 6512 Commercial and industrial building operation

(P-12287)
CRMLS LLC
15325 Fairfield Ranch Rd Ste 200, Chino Hills (91709-8834)
PHONE..................909 859-2040
Art Carter, CEO
Edward Zorn, VP
Adrese Roundree, COO
Ray Ewing, Chief
EMP: 106 EST: 2019
SALES (est): 4.73MM Privately Held
Web: go.crmls.org
SIC: 6512 Nonresidential building operators

(P-12288)
DAIKIN COMFORT TECH DIST INC
20035 E Walnut Dr N, Walnut (91789-2922)
PHONE..................626 210-4595
EMP: 315
Web: www.goodmanmfg.com
SIC: 6512 Commercial and industrial building operation
HQ: Daikin Comfort Technologies Distribution, Inc.
19001 Kermier Rd
Waller TX 77484
713 861-2500

(P-12289)
DESERT HOT SPRNG REAL PRPTS IN
Also Called: Desert Hot Springs Spa Hotel
10805 Palm Dr, Desert Hot Springs (92240-2511)
PHONE..................760 329-6000
Lynn Bymes, CEO

EMP: 85 EST: 1988
SQ FT: 44,070
SALES (est): 1.7MM Privately Held
Web: www.dhsspa.com
SIC: 6512 Nonresidential building operators

(P-12290)
DONAHUE SCHRIBER RLTY GROUP LP (PA)
Also Called: Ds Lakeshore
200 Baker St Ste 100, Costa Mesa (92626-4551)
PHONE..................714 545-1400
Patrick S Donahue, CEO
Lisa L Hirose, Ex VP
Lawrence P Casey, Pr
Mark L Whitfield, Ex VP
EMP: 100 EST: 1969
SQ FT: 44,805
SALES (est): 22.01MM
SALES (corp-wide): 22.01MM Privately Held
SIC: 6512 Shopping center, property operation only

(P-12291)
ENTREPRENEURIAL CAPITAL CORP
4100 Newport Place Dr Ste 400, Newport Beach (92660-2450)
PHONE..................949 809-3900
John K Abel, Prin
EMP: 240
SALES (corp-wide): 33.22MM Privately Held
SIC: 6512 Commercial and industrial building operation
PA: Entrepreneurial Capital Corporation
4100 Newport Place Dr # 400
949 809-3900

(P-12292)
FORD MOTOR LAND DEV CORP
Also Called: Ford
3 Glen Bell Way Ste 100, Irvine (92618-3390)
PHONE..................949 242-6606
Dan Werbin, Ex Dir
EMP: 167
SALES (corp-wide): 176.19B Publicly Held
Web: www.fordland.com
SIC: 6512 Commercial and industrial building operation
HQ: Ford Motor Land Development Corporation
17000 Rotunda Dr Fl 1
Dearborn MI 48120
248 200-8804

(P-12293)
FREEDOM PROPERTIES-HEMET LLC
Also Called: Village The
27122b Paseo Espada Ste 1024, San Juan Capistrano (92675-5706)
PHONE..................949 489-0430
Cheryl L Roskamp, Managing Member
Ms. Cheryl L Roskamp, Managing Member
EMP: 250 EST: 1999
SALES (est): 456.08K Privately Held
SIC: 6512 Nonresidential building operators

(P-12294)
GLENDALE ASSOCIATES LTD
Also Called: Apple Store Glendale Galleria
100 W Broadway Ste 100, Glendale (91210-1230)
PHONE..................818 246-6737

EMP: 100 EST: 1976
SALES (est): 2.17MM Privately Held
Web: www.glendalegalleria.com
SIC: 6512 Shopping center, property operation only

(P-12295)
GREYSTAR RS GROUP LLC
Also Called: Royal Equestrian Apartments
1200 W Riverside Dr, Burbank (91506-3158)
PHONE..................818 841-2441
David Page, Brnch Mgr
EMP: 109
SALES (corp-wide): 758.38MM Privately Held
Web: www.allresco.com
SIC: 6512 Commercial and industrial building operation
HQ: Greystar Rs Group, Llc
1201 Elm St Ste 1600
Dallas TX 75270

(P-12296)
GUMBINER SAVETT INC
Also Called: Gumbiner Svett Fnkel Fnglson R
1723 Cloverfield Blvd, Santa Monica (90404-4017)
PHONE..................310 828-9798
Louis Savett, Ch Bd
Charles Gumbiner, *
Gary Finkel, *
David Rose, *
Rodney Fingleson, *
EMP: 90 EST: 1950
SQ FT: 25,000
SALES (est): 6.5MM Privately Held
Web: www.gscpa.com
SIC: 6512 Nonresidential building operators

(P-12297)
INSIGNIA/ESG HT PARTNERS INC (DH)
11150 Santa Monica Blvd Ste 220, Los Angeles (90025-3380)
PHONE..................310 765-2600
Mary Ann Tighe, CEO
John Powers, Pr
EMP: 325 EST: 1993
SALES (est): 49.09MM Publicly Held
SIC: 6512 Property operation, retail establishment
HQ: Cb Richard Ellis Real Estate Services, Llc
200 Park Ave Fl 19
New York NY 10166
212 984-8000

(P-12298)
INTEX RECREATION CORP
Also Called: INTEX RECREATION CORP
1665 Hughes Way, Long Beach (90810-1835)
PHONE..................310 549-5400
Kwai Kenny, Ex Dir
EMP: 158
SALES (corp-wide): 91.03MM Privately Held
Web: www.intexcorp.com
SIC: 6512 Nonresidential building operators
PA: Intex Properties South Bay Corp.
4001 Via Oro Ave Ste 210
310 549-5400

(P-12299)
JORDACHE ENTERPRISES INC
Also Called: US Polo Assn - Otlets At Ornge
20 City Blvd W, Orange (92868-3100)
PHONE..................714 978-1901
Joe Nakash, CEO

EMP: 209
SALES (corp-wide): 249.58MM **Privately Held**
Web: www.simon.com
SIC: 6512 Shopping center, property operation only
PA: Jordache Enterprises Inc.
1385 Broadway Frnt 6
212 643-8400

(P-12300)
KATELLA PROPERTIES
10140 Grayling Ave, Whittier (90603-2607)
PHONE............................562 704-8695
Paige Harrison, *Brnch Mgr*
EMP: 85
SALES (corp-wide): 9.87MM **Privately Held**
Web: www.katellaseniorliving.com
SIC: 6512 Nonresidential building operators
PA: Katella Properties
3952 Katella Ave
562 596-2773

(P-12301)
LERETA LLC
10760 4th St, Rancho Cucamonga (91730-0975)
PHONE............................626 332-1942
EMP: 179
Web: www.lereta.com
SIC: 6512 Commercial and industrial building operation
PA: Lereta, Llc
901 Corporate Center Dr

(P-12302)
LOS ANGLES CNVNTION EXHBTION C
Also Called: Los Angles Dept Cnvtion Trism
1201 S Figueroa St, Los Angeles (90015-1308)
PHONE............................213 741-1151
Brad Gessner, *Genl Mgr*
EMP: 288 **EST:** 1968
SQ FT: 867,000
SALES (est): 3.46MM **Privately Held**
Web: www.lacclink.com
SIC: 6512 Commercial and industrial building operation

(P-12303)
MALIBU CONFERENCE CENTER INC
Also Called: Calamigos Guest Rnch & Bch CLB
327 Latigo Canyon Rd, Malibu (90205-2708)
PHONE............................818 889-6440
Glen Gerson, *Pr*
EMP: 500 **EST:** 1985
SALES (est): 4.44MM **Privately Held**
Web: www.calamigos.com
SIC: 6512 Commercial and industrial building operation

(P-12304)
MILLS CORPORATION
Also Called: Ontario Mills Shopping Center
1 Mills Cir Ste 1, Ontario (91764-5215)
PHONE............................909 484-8300
Laurence Siegel, *Brnch Mgr*
EMP: 145
Web: www.themill.com
SIC: 6512 Shopping center, property operation only
HQ: The Mills Corporation
5425 Wsconsin Ave Ste 300
Chevy Chase MD 20815
301 968-6000

(P-12305)
MILWOOD HEALTHCARE INC
Also Called: MAYWOOD ACRES HEALTHCARE
2641 S C St, Oxnard (93033-4585)
PHONE............................626 274-4345
Alger Brion, *CEO*
EMP: 97 **EST:** 2007
SQ FT: 10,000
SALES (est): 2.46MM **Privately Held**
Web: www.maywoodacres.com
SIC: 6512 Nonresidential building operators

(P-12306)
NEVINS/ADAMS PROPERTIES INC (PA)
Also Called: Nevins Adams Properties
920 Garden St Ste A, Santa Barbara (93101-7465)
PHONE............................805 963-2884
Henry Nevins, *Pr*
David Adams, *
EMP: 250 **EST:** 1992
SALES (est): 2.11MM
SALES (corp-wide): 2.11MM **Privately Held**
SIC: 6512 Commercial and industrial building operation

(P-12307)
OLEN COMMERCIAL REALTY CORP
Also Called: Olen Residential Realty
7 Corporate Plaza Dr, Newport Beach (92660-7904)
PHONE............................949 644-6536
Igor M Olenicoff, *Pr*
Andrei Olenicoff, *
EMP: 400 **EST:** 1974
SQ FT: 44,000
SALES (est): 24.04MM **Privately Held**
Web: www.olen.com
SIC: 6512 Commercial and industrial building operation

(P-12308)
ORANGE BAKERY INC
75 Parker, Irvine (92618-1605)
PHONE............................949 454-1247
EMP: 139
Web: www.orangebakery.com
SIC: 6512 Commercial and industrial building operation
HQ: Orange Bakery, Inc.
17751 Cowan
Irvine CA 92614
949 863-1377

(P-12309)
ORMOND BEACH LP
1259 E Thousand Oaks Blvd, Thousand Oaks (91362-2818)
PHONE............................805 496-4948
Derrick Wada, *Pt*
Rick Schroeder, *Pt*
EMP: 80 **EST:** 2016
SALES (est): 2.49MM **Privately Held**
SIC: 6512 Nonresidential building operators

(P-12310)
PM REALTY GROUP LP
3 Park Plz Ste 450, Irvine (92614-2572)
PHONE............................949 390-5500
Jim Proehl, *VP*
EMP: 90
Web: www.madisonmarquette.com
SIC: 6512 7349 Nonresidential building operators; Building maintenance services, nec

HQ: Pm Realty Group, L.P.
1000 Main St Ste 2400
Houston TX 77002
713 209-5800

(P-12311)
PREMIUM OUTLET PARTNERS LP
Camarillo Premium Outlets
740 Ventura Blvd, Camarillo (93010-5842)
PHONE............................805 445-8520
Brian Hassett, *Genl Mgr*
EMP: 94
Web: www.premiumoutlets.com
SIC: 6512 Shopping center, property operation only
HQ: Premium Outlet Partners, L.P.
225 W Washington St
Indianapolis IN 46204

(P-12312)
PREMIUM OUTLET PARTNERS LP
Desert Hills Premium Outlets
48400 Seminole Dr, Cabazon (92230-2125)
PHONE............................951 849-6641
Kathy Frederiksen, *Brnch Mgr*
EMP: 94
SQ FT: 430,000
Web: www.premiumoutlets.com
SIC: 6512 Shopping center, property operation only
HQ: Premium Outlet Partners, L.P.
225 W Washington St
Indianapolis IN 46204

(P-12313)
PREMIUM OUTLET PARTNERS LP
Also Called: Carlsbad Premium Outlets
5620 Paseo Del Norte Ste 100, Carlsbad (92008-4444)
PHONE............................760 804-9045
Caren Buksbaum, *Mgr*
EMP: 94
Web: www.simon.com
SIC: 6512 Shopping center, property operation only
HQ: Premium Outlet Partners, L.P.
225 W Washington St
Indianapolis IN 46204

(P-12314)
REALTY INCOME CORPORATION (PA)
11995 El Camino Real, San Diego (02130-2530)
PHONE............................858 284-5000
Sumit Roy, *Pr*
Michael D Mckee, *Non-Executive Chairman of the Board*
Jonathan Pong, *Ex VP*
Gregory J Whyte, *Ex VP*
Mark E Hagan, *CIO*
EMP: 105 **EST:** 1969
SALES (est): 4.08B **Publicly Held**
Web: www.realtyincome.com
SIC: 6512 6798 Nonresidential building operators; Real estate investment trusts

(P-12315)
SAN DIEGO THEATRES INC
Also Called: CIVIC THEATRE
233 A St Ste 900, San Diego (92101-4099)
P.O. Box 124920 (92112-4920)
PHONE............................619 615-4007
Carol Wallace, *CEO*
Donald M Telford, *
EMP: 200 **EST:** 2003

SALES (est): 3.53MM **Privately Held**
Web: www.sandiegotheatres.org
SIC: 6512 Theater building, ownership and operation

(P-12316)
SCP HORTON OWNER 1 LLC
10850 Wilshire Blvd Ste 1050, Los Angeles (90024-4326)
PHONE............................310 693-4400
Jennifer Gattey, *Prin*
Steven Yari, *
EMP: 70 **EST:** 2018
SALES (est): 8.24MM **Privately Held**
SIC: 6512 Nonresidential building operators

(P-12317)
SDMV LLC
520 Newport Center Dr Fl 2, Newport Beach (92660-7020)
PHONE............................949 516-0088
Marshall Young, *Pt*
Li Hui Lo, *Pt*
Peiing Lee, *Pt*
EMP: 71 **EST:** 2019
SALES (est): 2.47MM **Privately Held**
SIC: 6512 Nonresidential building operators

(P-12318)
SHEA PROPERTIES MGT CO INC
Also Called: Shea Properties
130 Vantis Dr Ste 200, Aliso Viejo (92656-2691)
P.O. Box 62814 (92602-6093)
PHONE............................949 389-7000
Colm Macken, *CEO*
EMP: 347 **EST:** 2003
SQ FT: 48,000
SALES (est): 9.72MM
SALES (corp-wide): 2.1B **Privately Held**
Web: www.sheaproperties.com
SIC: 6512 Nonresidential building operators
PA: J. F. Shea Co., Inc.
655 Brea Canyon Rd
909 594-9500

(P-12319)
SOLARI ENTERPRISES INC
1507 W Yale Ave, Orange (92867-3447)
PHONE............................714 282-2520
Johrita Solari, *Pr*
Bruce Solari, *
EMP: 140 **EST:** 1986
SQ FT: 8,400
SALES (est): 23.89MM **Privately Held**
Web: www.solari-ent.com
SIC: 6512 Property operation, retail establishment

(P-12320)
SOUTH COAST PLAZA LLC
Also Called: South Coast Plaza Mall
3333 Bristol St Ofc, Costa Mesa (92626-1811)
PHONE............................714 435-2000
David Grant, *Mgr*
EMP: 91
SALES (corp-wide): 48.85MM **Privately Held**
Web: www.southcoastplaza.com
SIC: 6512 Shopping center, property operation only
PA: South Coast Plaza, Llc
3333 Bristol St Ofc
714 546-0110

(P-12321)
TOPA PROPERTY GROUP INC (HQ)
Also Called: Anderson Real Estate

P R O D U C T S & S V C S

1800 Avenue Of The Stars Ste 1400, Los
Angeles (90067-4216)
PHONE...................................310 203-9199
James Brooks, *CEO*
Jim Brooks, *
Paul Gienger, *
Carol Shane, *
Darren Bell, *
EMP: 158 **EST:** 1981
SALES (est): 18.26MM
SALES (corp-wide): 251.02MM **Privately
Held**
Web: www.andersonrealestate.com
SIC: 6512 Commercial and industrial
building operation
PA: Topa Equities, Ltd.
1800 Avenue Of The Stars
310 203-9199

(P-12322)
**UNIBAL-RODAMCO-WESTFIELD
GROUP**
2049 Century Park E 41st Fl, Los Angeles
(90067-3101)
PHONE...................................310 478-4456
EMP: 155 **EST:** 2019
SALES (est): 10.67MM **Privately Held**
Web: www.urw.com
SIC: 6512 Shopping center, property
operation only

(P-12323)
**UNIVERSAL SHOPPING PLAZA
A CA**
6281 Regio Ave, Buena Park (90620-1023)
PHONE...................................714 521-8899
Ho Yuan Chen, *Genl Pt*
EMP: 200 **EST:** 1987
SALES (est): 9.62MM **Privately Held**
SIC: 6512 Shopping center, property
operation only

(P-12324)
**UNIVERSITY BUSINESS CTR
ASSOC**
5383 Hollister Ave Ste 120, Santa Barbara
(93111-2304)
PHONE...................................601 354-3555
David H Hoster Ii, *CEO*
EMP: 80 **EST:** 1996
SALES (est): 650.08K
SALES (corp-wide): 570.59MM **Publicly
Held**
SIC: 6512 Commercial and industrial
building operation
PA: Eastgroup Properties, Inc.
400 W Parkway Pl Ste 100
601 354-3555

(P-12325)
WATT PROPERTIES INC (PA)
Also Called: Watt Commercial Properties
2716 Ocean Park Blvd Ste 2025, Santa
Monica (90405-5209)
PHONE...................................310 314-2430
Janet Watt Van Huisen, *Ch Bd*
James Maginn, *
Susan Rorison, *
J Scott Watt, *
EMP: 78 **EST:** 1973
SQ FT: 8,700
SALES (est): 7.44MM
SALES (corp-wide): 7.44MM **Privately
Held**
Web: www.wattcompanies.com
SIC: 6512 6531 6552 Shopping center,
property operation only; Real estate
managers; Land subdividers and
developers, commercial

(P-12326)
WELLTOWER OM GROUP LLC
301 W Huntington Dr Ste 5, Arcadia
(91007-3462)
PHONE...................................626 254-0552
Heidy Giron, *Brnch Mgr*
EMP: 139
SALES (corp-wide): 5.86B **Publicly Held**
Web: www.welltower.com
SIC: 6512 Commercial and industrial
building operation
HQ: Welltower Om Group Llc
4500 Dorr St
Toledo OH 43615
419 247-2800

(P-12327)
**WEST SIDE REHAB
CORPORATION**
1755 E Martin Luther King Jr Blvd, Los
Angeles (90069-1512)
PHONE...................................323 231-4174
Dean Foley, *Pr*
EMP: 200 **EST:** 1973
SQ FT: 1,500
SALES (est): 461.9K **Privately Held**
SIC: 6512 Commercial and industrial
building operation

(P-12328)
WESTFIELD LLC (DH)
2049 Century Park E 41st Fl, Los Angeles
(90067-3101)
PHONE...................................310 478-4456
Peter Lowy, *CEO*
Gregory Miles, *
Mark Stefanel, *
Rory A Packer, *
EMP: 400 **EST:** 1978
SQ FT: 120,000
SALES (est): 454.77MM
SALES (corp-wide): 206.9MM **Privately
Held**
Web: www.westfield.com
SIC: 6512 Shopping center, property
operation only
HQ: Westfield America, Inc.
2049 Century Park E Fl 41
Los Angeles CA 90067
310 478-4456

(P-12329)
WESTFIELD AMERICA INC (HQ)
2049 Century Park E 41st Fl, Los Angeles
(90067-3101)
PHONE...................................310 478-4456
Peter S Lowy, *CEO*
Jean Marie Tritant, *
Peter R Schwartz, *
Elizabeth Westman, *
Mark A Stefanek, *
EMP: 200 **EST:** 1924
SALES (est): 469.14MM
SALES (corp-wide): 206.9MM **Privately
Held**
Web: www.westfield.com
SIC: 6512 Shopping center, property
operation only
PA: Unibail-Rodamco-Westfield Se
7 Place Du Chancelier Adenauer
145051082

(P-12330)
**WESTFIELD AMERICA LTD
PARTNR**
2049 Century Park E Ste 4100, Los Angeles
(90067-3215)
PHONE...................................310 277-3898
John Widdup, *CEO*
Peter Lowy, *Pt*

EMP: 500 **EST:** 1998
SALES (est): 28.88MM
SALES (corp-wide): 206.9MM **Privately
Held**
Web: www.westfield.com
SIC: 6512 Shopping center, property
operation only
HQ: Westfield, Llc
2049 Century Park E Fl 41
Los Angeles CA 90067

(P-12331)
WILSHIRE KINGSLEY INC
Also Called: Bcd Tofu House
3575 Wilshire Blvd, Los Angeles
(90010-2303)
PHONE...................................213 382-6677
Edward S Lee, *Pr*
Hee Sook Lee, *
EMP: 100 **EST:** 2001
SALES (est): 1.07MM **Privately Held**
Web: www.bcdtofuhouselawsuit.com
SIC: 6512 Commercial and industrial
building operation

6513 Apartment Building
Operators

(P-12332)
**APERTO PROPERTY
MANAGEMENT INC**
17351 Main St, La Puente (91744-5155)
PHONE...................................626 965-1961
EMP: 353
SALES (corp-wide): 15.89MM **Privately
Held**
Web: www.apertoliving.com
SIC: 6513 Apartment building operators
PA: Aperto Property Management, Inc.
2 Venture Ste 525
949 873-4200

(P-12333)
**BARKER MANAGEMENT
INCORPORATED**
Also Called: Senior Garden APT
438 3rd Ave Apt 312, San Diego
(92101-6876)
PHONE...................................619 236-8130
Peter Barker, *Pr*
EMP: 75
SALES (corp-wide): 11.33MM **Privately
Held**
Web: www.barkermgt.com
SIC: 6513 Retirement hotel operation
PA: Barker Management, Incorporated
1101 E Orangewood Ave # 200
714 533-3450

(P-12334)
BV GENERAL INC
Also Called: Leisure Vale Retirement Hotel
413 E Cypress St, Glendale (91205-3334)
PHONE...................................818 244-2323
Polita Barnes, *Dir*
EMP: 73
SQ FT: 10,000
Web: www.leisurevale.com
SIC: 6513 Retirement hotel operation
PA: B.V. General, Inc.
1332 S Glendale Ave

(P-12335)
**CHARLES & CYNTHIA EBERLY
INC**
Also Called: The Eberly Company
8383 Wilshire Blvd Ste 906, Beverly Hills
(90211-2443)

PHONE...................................323 937-6468
Charles Eberly, *Pr*
Cynthia Eberly, *
EMP: 90 **EST:** 1986
SALES (est): 3.22MM **Privately Held**
Web: www.eberlyco.com
SIC: 6513 Apartment building operators

(P-12336)
**CHATEAU LK SAN MRCOS
HMWNERS A**
1502 Circa Del Lago, San Marcos
(92078-7201)
PHONE...................................760 471-0083
Chris Arvanitis, *Pr*
EMP: 75 **EST:** 1985
SQ FT: 240,000
SALES (est): 2.27MM **Privately Held**
Web: www.chateaulakesanmarcos.com
SIC: 6513 Retirement hotel operation

(P-12337)
**COMMUNITY CORP SANTA
MONICA**
1410 2nd St Ste 200, Santa Monica
(90401-3349)
PHONE...................................310 394-8487
Tara Barauskas, *Ex Dir*
Patricia Hoffman, *
Joan C Ling, *
Robert Connell, *
EMP: 120 **EST:** 1982
SQ FT: 3,800
SALES (est): 21.61MM **Privately Held**
Web: www.communitycorp.org
SIC: 6513 Apartment building operators

(P-12338)
EMERITUS CORPORATION
Also Called: Villa Del Rey Retirement Inn
1351 E Washington Ave, Escondido
(92027-1934)
PHONE...................................760 741-3055
Pam Judkins, *Brnch Mgr*
EMP: 104
SQ FT: 60,000
SALES (corp-wide): 2.83B **Publicly Held**
Web: www.emeritus.org
SIC: 6513 Retirement hotel operation
HQ: Emeritus Corporation
6737 W Wash St Ste 2300
Milwaukee WI 53214

(P-12339)
EMERITUS CORPORATION
Also Called: Creston Village
1919 Creston Rd Ofc, Paso Robles
(93446-4475)
PHONE...................................805 239-1313
Tonya Hogue, *Dir*
EMP: 244
SALES (corp-wide): 2.83B **Publicly Held**
Web: www.emeritus.org
SIC: 6513 Retirement hotel operation
HQ: Emeritus Corporation
6737 W Wash St Ste 2300
Milwaukee WI 53214

(P-12340)
**EUGENE BURGER
MANAGEMENT CORP**
Also Called: Village Gardens Apartments
1020 E Avenue R Ofc, Palmdale
(93550-5309)
PHONE...................................661 273-4447
EMP: 90
SALES (corp-wide): 24.49MM **Privately
Held**
Web: www.ebmc.com

SIC: **6513** Apartment building operators
PA: Eugene Burger Management Corp
775 Baywood Dr
707 584-5123

(P-12341)
FFRT RESIDENTIAL LLC
Also Called: Fairfield Properties
5510 Morehouse Dr Ste 200, San Diego
(92121-3700)
PHONE.................................858 457-2123
EMP: 135
SIC: **6513** 6552 6531 1522 Apartment
building operators; Subdividers and
developers, nec; Real estate agents and
managers; Residential construction, nec

(P-12342)
FRONT PORCH COMMUNITIES & SVCS
Also Called: Casa De Manana
849 Coast Blvd, La Jolla (92037-4223)
PHONE.................................858 454-2151
Justin Weber, *Brnch Mgr*
EMP: 187
Web: www.frontporch.net
SIC: **6513** 8052 8361 Retirement hotel
operation; Intermediate care facilities;
Residential care
PA: Front Porch Communities And Services
800 N Brand Blvd Fl 19

(P-12343)
HARVEST MANAGEMENT SUB LLC
Also Called: Las Brisas
1299 Briarwood Dr, San Luis Obispo
(93401-5965)
PHONE.................................805 543-0187
David Dolan, *Brnch Mgr*
EMP: 3223
SALES (corp-wide): 389.7MM **Privately Held**
Web: www.holidayseniorliving.com
SIC: **6513** Retirement hotel operation
PA: Harvest Management Sub Llc
300 E Market St Ste 100
503 370-7070

(P-12344)
HG FENTON COMPANY
7577 Mission Valley Rd Ste 200, San Diego
(92108-4432)
PHONE.................................619 400-0120
Mike Neal, *
Robert Gottlieb, *
Henry Hunte, *
EMP: 215 **EST:** 2008
SALES (est): 23.98MM **Privately Held**
Web: www.hgfenton.com
SIC: **6513** 6519 Apartment building operators
; Real property lessors, nec

(P-12345)
HUMANGOOD SOCAL
Also Called: Royal Oaks
1763 Royal Oaks Dr Ofc, Duarte
(91010-1989)
PHONE.................................626 357-1632
Tina Heaney, *Mgr*
EMP: 111
SALES (corp-wide): 31.22MM **Privately Held**
Web: www.humangood.org
SIC: **6513** Retirement hotel operation
HQ: Humangood Socal
1900 Huntington Dr
Duarte CA 91010
925 924-7138

(P-12346)
HUMANGOOD SOCAL
Also Called: Windsor Manor
1230 E Windsor Rd Ofc, Glendale
(91205-2674)
PHONE.................................818 244-7219
Marc Herrera, *Brnch Mgr*
EMP: 133
SQ FT: 139,840
SALES (corp-wide): 31.22MM **Privately Held**
Web: www.humangood.org
SIC: **6513** Retirement hotel operation
HQ: Humangood Socal
1900 Huntington Dr
Duarte CA 91010
925 924-7138

(P-12347)
HUMANGOOD SOCAL
Also Called: Regents Point
19191 Harvard Ave Ofc, Irvine
(92612-8624)
PHONE.................................949 854-9500
Melinda Forney, *Mgr*
EMP: 133
SALES (corp-wide): 31.22MM **Privately Held**
Web: www.humangood.org
SIC: **6513** 8052 8051 Retirement hotel
operation; Intermediate care facilities;
Skilled nursing care facilities
HQ: Humangood Socal
1900 Huntington Dr
Duarte CA 91010
925 924-7138

(P-12348)
HUNTINGTON BCH SENIOR HSING LP
Also Called: Huntington Gardens
18765 Florida St, Huntington Beach
(92648-1999)
PHONE.................................714 842-4006
Don Jones, *Pt*
EMP: 132 **EST:** 2008
SALES (est): 387.04K
SALES (corp-wide): 6.17MM **Privately Held**
Web: www.huntingtonbeachca.gov
SIC: **6513** Apartment building operators
PA: Living Opportunities Management
Company, Llc
3787 Worsham Ave
562 595-7567

(P-12349)
INTEGRAL SENIOR LIVING LLC (PA)
2333 State St Ste 300, Carlsbad
(02008 1601)
PHONE.................................760 547-2863
Tracee Degrande, *
Collette Valentine, *
Suzanne Foley, *
Vince Limburg, *
EMP: 148 **EST:** 2000
SALES (est): 38.73MM
SALES (corp-wide): 38.73MM **Privately Held**
Web: www.islllc.com
SIC: **6513** Retirement hotel operation

(P-12350)
IRVINE APT COMMUNITIES LP (HQ)
Also Called: I A C
110 Innovation Dr, Irvine (92617-3040)
PHONE.................................949 720-5600

Raymond Watson, *Vice Chairman*
Mike Ellis, *Ex VP*
EMP: 200 **EST:** 1993
SQ FT: 8,316
SALES (est): 45.94MM
SALES (corp-wide): 579.21MM **Privately Held**
Web:
www.irvinecompanyapartments.com
SIC: **6513** 6552 6798 Apartment building
operators; Subdividers and developers, nec
; Real estate investment trusts
PA: The Irvine Company Llc
550 Newport Center Dr
949 720-2000

(P-12351)
IRVINE APT COMMUNITIES LP
Also Called: Rancho Monterey Apartments
100 Robinson Dr, Tustin (92782-1095)
PHONE.................................714 505-7181
Brooks Foy, *Mgr*
EMP: 267
SALES (corp-wide): 579.21MM **Privately Held**
Web:
www.irvinecompanyapartments.com
SIC: **6513** Apartment building operators
HQ: Irvine Apartment Communities, Lp
110 Innovation Dr
Irvine CA 92617

(P-12352)
IRVINE APT COMMUNITIES LP
13212 Magnolia St Ofc, Garden Grove
(92844-1368)
PHONE.................................714 537-8500
Mike Conway, *Brnch Mgr*
EMP: 200
SALES (corp-wide): 579.21MM **Privately Held**
Web: www.ranchomonterey.com
SIC: **6513** Apartment building operators
HQ: Irvine Apartment Communities, Lp
110 Innovation Dr
Irvine CA 92617

(P-12353)
IRVINE APT COMMUNITIES LP
299 N State College Blvd, Orange
(92868-1703)
PHONE.................................714 937-8900
EMP: 201
SALES (corp-wide): 579.21MM **Privately Held**
Web:
www.irvinecompanyapartments.com
SIC: **6513** Apartment building operators
HQ: Irvine Apartment Communities, Lp
110 Innovation Dr
Irvine CA 92617

(P-12354)
IRVINE APT COMMUNITIES LP
Also Called: 1221 Ocean Ave Apartments
1221 Ocean Ave, Santa Monica
(90401-1034)
PHONE.................................310 255-1221
Stephanie Van Dermotter, *Mgr*
EMP: 200
SALES (corp-wide): 579.21MM **Privately Held**
Web:
www.irvinecompanyapartments.com
SIC: **6513** 6531 Apartment building operators
; Rental agent, real estate
HQ: Irvine Apartment Communities, Lp
110 Innovation Dr
Irvine CA 92617

(P-12355)
JOHN COLLINS CO INC
5155 Cedarwood Rd, Bonita (91902-1942)
PHONE.................................818 227-2190
EMP: 97
SALES (corp-wide): 2.67MM **Privately Held**
Web: www.collinscoastalhomes.com
SIC: **6513** Apartment building operators
PA: The John Collins Co Inc
5135 N Harbor Dr

(P-12356)
KISCO SENIOR LIVING LLC
Also Called: KRC Orange
620 S Glassell St, Orange (92866-3000)
PHONE.................................714 997-5355
Bruce Hoggan, *Ex Dir*
EMP: 133
SALES (corp-wide): 138.27MM **Privately Held**
Web: www.kiscoseniorliving.com
SIC: **6513** Retirement hotel operation
PA: Senior Kisco Living Llc
5790 Fleet St Ste 300
760 804-5900

(P-12357)
LIVING OPPORTUNITIES MGT CO
Also Called: LIVING OPPORTUNITIES
MANAGEMENT COMPANY
6900 Seville Ave, Huntington Park
(90255-4970)
PHONE.................................323 589-5956
EMP: 88
SALES (corp-wide): 6.17MM **Privately Held**
Web: www.huntingtonparklocksmith.club
SIC: **6513** Apartment building operators
PA: Living Opportunities Management
Company, Llc
3787 Worsham Ave
562 595-7567

(P-12358)
MARINA CITY CLUB LP A CALI
4333 Admiralty Way, Marina Del Rey
(90292-5469)
PHONE.................................310 822-0611
J H Snyder, *Pt*
Lewis Geyser, *Pt*
Milton Swimmer, *Pt*
Lon Snyder, *Pt*
EMP: 125 **EST:** 1969
SQ FT: 10,000
SALES (est): 4.12MM **Privately Held**
Web: www.marinacityclub.net
SIC: **6513** 7997 4493 Apartment building
operators; Membership sports and
recreation clubs; Marinas

(P-12359)
MONARK LP
2804 W El Segundo Blvd, Gardena
(90249-1551)
PHONE.................................310 769-6669
EMP: 99
SALES (est): 1.91MM **Privately Held**
SIC: **6513** Apartment building operators

(P-12360)
NATIONAL COMMUNITY RENAISSANCE
Also Called: Heritage Pointe
8590 Malven Ave, Rancho Cucamonga
(91730-4669)
PHONE.................................909 948-7579
EMP: 121

SALES (corp-wide): 330 **Privately Held**
Web: www.nationalcore.org
SIC: 6513 Apartment building operators
PA: National Community Renaissance
　　9692 Haven Ave Ste 100
　　909 483-2444

(P-12361)
PARK NEWPORT LTD (PA)
Also Called: Park Newport Apartments
1 Park Newport, Newport Beach
(92660-5004)
PHONE.....................949 644-1900
Gerson Bakar, *Owner*
EMP: 75 EST: 1970
SQ FT: 10,000
SALES (est): 1.4MM
SALES (corp-wide): 1.4MM **Privately Held**
Web: www.parknewportapts.com
SIC: 6513 Apartment hotel operation

(P-12362)
PRC MULTI-FAMILY LLC
Also Called: Park Regency Club Apts
10000 Imperial Hwy, Downey (90242-3243)
PHONE.....................562 803-5000
David Lifschitz, *CEO*
Alfred Somekh, *
EMP: 102 EST: 1984
SALES (est): 3.4MM
SALES (corp-wide): 127.37MM **Privately Held**
SIC: 6513 Apartment building operators
HQ: Gehr Development Corporation
　　5701 S Eastern Ave
　　Commerce CA 90040

(P-12363)
RANCE KING PROPERTIES INC (PA)
Also Called: R K Properties
3737 E Broadway, Long Beach
(90803-6104)
PHONE.....................562 240-1000
William Rance King Junior, *Pr*
Steven King, *
EMP: 104 EST: 1978
SQ FT: 5,000
SALES (est): 17.97MM
SALES (corp-wide): 17.97MM **Privately Held**
Web: www.rkprop.com
SIC: 6513 Apartment building operators

(P-12364)
SAN DIMAS RETIREMENT CENTER (PA)
Also Called: Longwood Management
834 W Arrow Hwy, San Dimas
(91773-2499)
PHONE.....................909 599-8441
Frankie Ramirez, *Admn*
Frankie Ramirez, *Admn*
EMP: 70 EST: 1965
SALES (est): 640.21K
SALES (corp-wide): 640.21K **Privately Held**
Web: www.mytirepros.com
SIC: 6513 8059 Retirement hotel operation; Personal care home, with health care

(P-12365)
SARES RGIS GROUP RSDENTIAL INC
Also Called: Aliso Creek Apts
24152 Hollyoak, Aliso Viejo (92656-6900)
PHONE.....................949 643-8922
Zack Austin, *Brnch Mgr*
EMP: 121

SALES (corp-wide): 95.9MM **Privately Held**
Web: www.sares-regis.com
SIC: 6513 Apartment hotel operation
PA: Sares Regis Group Residential, Inc.
　　3501 Jamboree Rd Ste 300
　　949 756-5959

(P-12366)
SENIOR RESOURCE GROUP LLC
Also Called: La Vida Del Mar Associates
850 Del Mar Downs Rd Apt 338, Solana
Beach (92075-2722)
PHONE.....................858 519-0890
Terry Oquest, *Mgr*
EMP: 202
SALES (corp-wide): 110.02MM **Privately Held**
Web: www.srgseniorliving.com
SIC: 6513 Retirement hotel operation
PA: Senior Resource Group, Llc
　　500 Stevens Ave Ste 100
　　858 792-9300

(P-12367)
STEADFAST MANAGEMENT CO INC
Also Called: Flanders Pointe Apts
15520 Tustin Village Way, Tustin
(92780-4211)
PHONE.....................714 542-2229
EMP: 70
SALES (corp-wide): 36.12MM **Privately Held**
Web: www.steadfastcompanies.com
SIC: 6513 6531 Apartment building operators ; Real estate managers
PA: Steadfast Management Company, Inc.
　　18100 Von Krman Ave Ste 5
　　949 748-3000

(P-12368)
THE PINES LTD
1423 E Washington Ave, El Cajon
(92019-2559)
PHONE.....................619 447-1880
EMP: 111
SALES (est): 4.1MM **Privately Held**
SIC: 6513 Apartment building operators

(P-12369)
TRAMMELL CROW RESIDENTIAL CO
Also Called: Tcr SC Construc 1 Ltd Ptr
949 S Coast Dr Ste 400, Costa Mesa
(92626-7836)
PHONE.....................714 966-9355
Tina Meyer, *Mgr*
EMP: 72
Web: www.crowholdings.com
SIC: 6513 Apartment building operators
PA: Trammell Crow Residential Company
　　3819 Maple Ave

(P-12370)
WAMC COMPANY INC
Also Called: Cal West Enterprises
7420 Clairemont Mesa Blvd, San Diego
(92111-1546)
PHONE.....................858 454-2753
EMP: 94 EST: 1995
SALES (est): 2.33MM **Privately Held**
SIC: 6513 Apartment building operators

(P-12371)
WATERMARK RTRMENT CMMNTIES INC
Also Called: Fountains At The Sea Bluffs

25411 Sea Bluffs Dr, Dana Point
(92629-2190)
PHONE.....................949 443-9543
Connie Smith, *Mgr*
EMP: 88
Web: www.watermarkcommunities.com
SIC: 6513 Retirement hotel operation
HQ: Watermark Retirement Communities, Inc.
　　2020 W Rudasill Rd
　　Tucson AZ 85704

(P-12372)
WILLMARK CMMNTIES UNIV VLG INC (PA)
9948 Hibert St Ste 210, San Diego
(92131-1034)
PHONE.....................858 271-0582
Mark Schmidt, *Pr*
EMP: 78 EST: 1984
SQ FT: 2,000
SALES (est): 4.13MM
SALES (corp-wide): 4.13MM **Privately Held**
SIC: 6513 1522 Apartment building operators ; Multi-family dwellings, new construction

6514 Dwelling Operators, Except Apartments

(P-12373)
ACTION PROPERTY MANAGEMENT INC (PA)
Also Called: Action Property Management
2603 Main St Ste 500, Irvine (92614-4261)
PHONE.....................949 450-0202
Matthew Holbrook, *CEO*
Marianne Simek, *
EMP: 90 EST: 1980
SQ FT: 18,000
SALES (est): 30MM
SALES (corp-wide): 30MM **Privately Held**
Web: www.actionlife.com
SIC: 6514 8641 Residential building, four or fewer units: operation; Homeowners' association

(P-12374)
DAYTON DMH INC
121 Spinnaker Ct, Del Mar (92014-3218)
PHONE.....................858 350-4400
Donald Ambrose, *Pr*
EMP: 172 EST: 1995
SALES (est): 938.9K **Privately Held**
SIC: 6514 Dwelling operators, except apartments

6515 Mobile Home Site Operators

(P-12375)
CAREFREE COMMUNITIES INC
Also Called: Carefree Communities
1251 Old Conejo Rd, Newbury Park
(91320-1031)
PHONE.....................805 498-2612
EMP: 125
SALES (corp-wide): 3.22B **Publicly Held**
Web: www.iamcarefree.com
SIC: 6515 Mobile home site operators
HQ: Carefree Communities Inc.
　　6991 E Camelback Rd B310
　　Scottsdale AZ 85251
　　480 423-5700

6519 Real Property Lessors, Nec

(P-12376)
HG FENTON PROPERTY COMPANY (PA)
Also Called: Silverton Business Center
7577 Mission Valley Rd Ste 200, San Diego
(92108-4432)
PHONE.....................619 400-0120
Mike Neal, *Pr*
Jennifer Tokatyan, *
Geoffrey Swortwood, *
Allen Jones, *
Kevin Hill, *
EMP: 200 EST: 1920
SALES (est): 20.61MM
SALES (corp-wide): 20.61MM **Privately Held**
Web: www.hgfenton.com
SIC: 6519 Real property lessors, nec

(P-12377)
LAACO LTD (HQ)
Also Called: Storage West
4469 Admiralty Way, Marina Del Rey
(90292-5415)
PHONE.....................213 622-1254
Karen L Hathaway, *Pr*
John K Hathaway, *
Steven K Hathaway, *
Bryan J Cusworth, *
EMP: 125 EST: 1986
SALES (est): 195.9K **Publicly Held**
Web: www.laac.com
SIC: 6519 7997 7011 5812 Real property lessors, nec; Yacht club, membership; Hotels; Eating places
PA: Cubesmart
　　5 Old Lancaster Rd

6531 Real Estate Agents And Managers

(P-12378)
ABODE COMMUNITIES LLC
1149 S Hill St Fl 7, Los Angeles
(90015-2219)
PHONE.....................213 629-2702
Robin Hughes, *Pr*
Rick Saperstein, *
Kenneth Krug, *
Sandra Kulli, *Vice Chairman*
Holly Benson, *
▲ EMP: 150 EST: 1968
SQ FT: 10,094
SALES (est): 32.74MM **Privately Held**
Web: www.abodecommunities.org
SIC: 6531 8712 8711 Housing authority operator; Architectural services; Engineering services

(P-12379)
ABSOLUTELY ZERO CORPORATION
1 City Blvd W Ste 1000, Orange
(92868-3611)
PHONE.....................949 269-3300
Ronald Radziminsky, *Pr*
EMP: 275 EST: 2018
SALES (est): 8.53MM **Privately Held**
Web: www.owning.com
SIC: 6531 Real estate brokers and agents
PA: Guaranteed Rate, Inc.
　　3940 N Ravenswood Ave

(P-12380)

ALLIANT ASSET MGT CO LLC (HQ)

26050 Mureau Rd Fl 2, Calabasas (91302-3174)
PHONE..............................818 668-2805
Shawn Horwitz, *Managing Member*
Scott Koticks, *
Brian Goldberg, *Managing Member**
EMP: 81 **EST:** 1997
SALES (est): 21.05MM **Publicly Held**
Web: www.alliantcapital.com
SIC: 6531 Real estate managers
PA: Walker & Dunlop, Inc.
7272 Wscnsin Ave Ste 1300

(P-12381)

AMERICAN DEVELOPMENT CORP (PA)

3605 Long Beach Blvd Ste 410, Long Beach (90807-4026)
PHONE..............................562 989-3730
Marco Gomez, *Pr*
EMP: 87 **EST:** 1994
SQ FT: 8,000
SALES (est): 1.31MM **Privately Held**
SIC: 6531 Real estate agents and managers

(P-12382)

ATLAS HOSPITALITY GROUP

1901 Main St Ste 175, Irvine (92614-0517)
PHONE..............................949 622-3400
Alan Reay, *Pr*
S Shah, *VP*
EMP: 90 **EST:** 1991
SALES (est): 5.53MM **Privately Held**
Web: www.atlashospitality.com
SIC: 6531 Real estate agent, commercial

(P-12383)

AUCTIONCOM INC

Also Called: Auction.com
1 Mauchly Ste 27, Irvine (92618-2305)
PHONE..............................800 499-6199
Jeffrey Frieden, *CEO*
James Corum, *
Virginia Pierce, *
Annamarie Giagunto, *
Joseph Joffrion, *
EMP: 200 **EST:** 1990
SQ FT: 18,000
SALES (est): 1.86MM **Privately Held**
SIC: 6531 Auction, real estate

(P-12384)

AUCTIONCOM LLC (PA)

Also Called: Auction.com
1 Mauchly, Irvine (92618-2305)
PHONE..............................949 859-2777
Jeffrey Frieden, *
Keith Mclane, *Pr*
Eva Tapia, *
Eric Andrew, *
EMP: 142 **EST:** 2008
SALES (est): 53.71MM **Privately Held**
Web: www.auction.com
SIC: 6531 Real estate agents and managers

(P-12385)

AWARD-SUPERSTARS

Also Called: Century 21
1530 Hilton Head Rd Ste 201, El Cajon (92019-4655)
PHONE..............................619 593-4300
Nikki Coppa, *Bmch Mgr*
EMP: 80
SALES (corp-wide): 4.26MM **Privately Held**
Web: www.century21award.com

SIC: 6531 6519 Real estate agent, residential
; Real property lessors, nec
PA: Award-Superstars
7676 Hazard Center Dr # 300
619 471-2000

(P-12386)

BAKERSFIELD WESTWIND CORP

Also Called: Coldwell Banker
1810 Westwind Dr, Bakersfield (93301-3027)
PHONE..............................661 327-2121
John Garone, *Pr*
EMP: 145 **EST:** 1972
SALES (est): 1.51MM **Privately Held**
Web: www.coldwellbanker.com
SIC: 6531 Real estate agent, residential

(P-12387)

BENNION DEVILLE FINE HOMES INC

Also Called: Windermere RE Coachella Vly
74850 Us Highway 111, Indian Wells (92210-7116)
PHONE..............................760 674-3452
Rick Fisk, *Bmch Mgr*
EMP: 378
SALES (corp-wide): 21.06MM **Privately Held**
Web: www.bdhomes.com
SIC: 6531 Real estate brokers and agents
PA: Bennion & Deville Fine Homes, Inc.
71691 Hwy 111
760 770-6801

(P-12388)

BETTA ASSETS INC

Also Called: Carick Lending
17141 Ventura Blvd Ste 205, Encino (91316-4027)
PHONE..............................818 990-7733
Richard Dennis, *Pr*
Carl Marer, *
EMP: 80 **EST:** 1994
SALES (est): 719.95K **Privately Held**
SIC: 6531 6514 Real estate agents and managers; Dwelling operators, except apartments

(P-12389)

BGK EQUITIES INC (HQ)

2000 Avenue Of The Stars Ste 550, Los Angeles (90067-4713)
PHONE..............................505 982-2184
Michael Mahony, *COO*
Ian Brownlow, *
EMP: 70 **EST:** 1995
SALES (est): 1.53MM **Privately Held**
Web: www.geminirosemont.com
SIC: 6531 Real estate agent, commercial
PA: Rosemont Realty, Llc
2000 Avenue Of The Stars # 550

(P-12390)

BIXBY LAND COMPANY

1501 Quail St Ste 230, Newport Beach (92660-2740)
PHONE..............................949 336-7000
William R Halford, *Pr*
Mike Severson, *CIO*
EMP: 115 **EST:** 1896
SALES (est): 12.03MM **Privately Held**
Web: www.bixbyland.com
SIC: 6531 Real estate agents and managers

(P-12391)

BKM DIABLO 227 LLC

1701 Quail St Ste 100, Newport Beach (92660-2796)

PHONE..............................602 688-6409
Brian K Malliet, *Prin*
Rene Velasquez, *
EMP: 85 **EST:** 2018
SALES (est): 1.53MM **Privately Held**
Web: www.bkmmanagementco.com
SIC: 6531 Real estate managers

(P-12392)

BUCHANAN STREET PARTNERS LP

3501 Jamboree Rd Ste 4200, Newport Beach (92660-2958)
PHONE..............................949 721-1414
Robert Brunswick, *CEO*
Timothy Ballard, *
James Gill, *
EMP: 85 **EST:** 2000
SALES (est): 35.55MM **Privately Held**
Web: www.buchananstreet.com
SIC: 6531 Real estate agents and managers

(P-12393)

BURLEIGH POINT LLC

Also Called: Burleigh Point, Ltd.
5600 Argosy Ave Ste 100, Huntington Beach (92649-1063)
PHONE..............................949 428-3200
◆ **EMP:** 200
SIC: 6531 6513 Real estate agent, residential; Residential hotel operation

(P-12394)

C B COAST NEWPORT PROPERTIES

Also Called: Coldwell Bnkr Rsdntial Rfrral
840 Newport Center Dr Ste 100, Newport Beach (92660-6377)
PHONE..............................949 644-1600
Daniel F Bibb, *Pr*
Tom Queen, *
Gary Legrand, *
EMP: 1191 **EST:** 1990
SQ FT: 7,300
SALES (est): 764.34K **Publicly Held**
Web: www.coldwellbanker.com
SIC: 6531 Real estate agent, residential
HQ: Coldwell Banker Residential Referral Network
27271 Las Ramblas
Mission Viejo CA 92691
949 367-1800

(P-12395)

CAMDEN DEVELOPMENT INC

27261 Las Ramblas, Mission Viejo (92691-6441)
PHONE..............................949 427-4674
EMP: 134
Web: www.camdenliving.com
SIC: 6531 Real estate agent, commercial
HQ: Camden Development, Inc.
11 Greenway Plz Ste 2400
Houston TX 77046

(P-12396)

CBABR INC (PA)

Also Called: Coldwell Banker
31620 Railroad Canyon Rd Ste A, Canyon Lake (92587-9476)
PHONE..............................951 640-7056
Budge Huskey, *CEO*
Dennis M Mccoy, *Pr*
Margaret Mccoy, *Sec*
Jody Regus, *
EMP: 73 **EST:** 1983
SQ FT: 4,000
SALES (est): 4.41MM **Privately Held**
Web: www.cbabrlife.com

SIC: 6531 Real estate agent, residential

(P-12397)

CBRE INC

4301 La Jolla Village Dr # 3000, San Diego (92122-1484)
PHONE..............................858 546-4600
EMP: 160
Web: www.cbre.us
SIC: 6531 Real estate agent, commercial
HQ: Cbre, Inc.
400 S Hope St Ste 25
Los Angeles CA 75201
213 613-3333

(P-12398)

CBRE FOUNDATION INC

Also Called: Cbre
2221 Rosecrans Ave Ste 100, El Segundo (90245-4950)
PHONE..............................949 809-3744
Cindy Kee, *Pr*
EMP: 86 **EST:** 2017
SALES (est): 1.63MM **Privately Held**
SIC: 6531 Real estate agent, commercial

(P-12399)

CBRE GLOBL VALUE INVESTORS LLC (DH)

Also Called: Global Innovation Partner
601 S Figueroa St Ste 49, Los Angeles (90017-5253)
PHONE..............................213 683-4200
Ritson Ferguson, *CEO*
Gil Borok, *
Maurice Voskuilen, *
EMP: 150 **EST:** 1972
SALES (est): 6.15MM **Publicly Held**
Web: www.cbreim.com
SIC: 6531 Real estate agent, commercial
HQ: Cbre, Inc.
2100 Mcknney Ave Ste 1250
Dallas TX 75201
866 225-3099

(P-12400)

CBRE GLOBL VALUE INVESTORS LLC

Also Called: Cbre
3501 Jamboree Rd Ste 100, Newport Beach (92660-2940)
PHONE..............................949 725-8500
Steven Swerdlow, *Prin*
EMP: 184
Web: www.cbreim.com
SIC: 6531 Real estate agent, commercial
HQ: Cbre Global Value Investors. Llc
601 S Figueroa St Ste 49
Los Angeles CA 90017
213 683-4200

(P-12401)

CBRE PARTNER INC

400 S Hope St Fl 25, Los Angeles (90071-2801)
PHONE..............................213 613-3333
EMP: 89 **EST:** 2018
SALES (est): 6.78MM **Publicly Held**
Web: www.cbre.com
SIC: 6531 Real estate agent, commercial
PA: Cbre Group, Inc.
2100 Mcknney Ave Ste 1250

(P-12402)

CENTURY 21 A BETTER SVC RLTY

Also Called: Century 21
5831 Firestone Blvd Ste J, South Gate (90280-3718)

PHONE..................562 806-1000
EMP: 97
SQ FT: 4,000
SALES (est): 3.76MM **Privately Held**
Web: www.c21abetterservice.com
SIC: 6531 Real estate agents and managers

(P-12403)
CHARLES DUNN RE SVCS INC (PA)
800 W 6th St Ste 600, Los Angeles
(90017-2709)
PHONE..................213 270-6200
Walter Conn, *CEO*
Patrick Conn, *
EMP: 86 **EST:** 1995
SQ FT: 30,000
SALES (est): 3.49MM
SALES (corp-wide): 3.49MM **Privately Held**
Web: www.charlesdunn.com
SIC: 6531 Real estate brokers and agents

(P-12404)
CHILD DEVELOPMENT INCORPORATED
17341 Jacquelyn Ln, Huntington Beach
(92647-5713)
PHONE..................714 842-4064
EMP: 362
SALES (corp-wide): 4.47MM **Privately Held**
Web: www.catalystkids.org
SIC: 6531 Real estate agents and managers
PA: Child Development Incorporated
350 Woodview Ave
408 556-7300

(P-12405)
CIRRUS ASSET MANAGEMENT INC (PA)
Also Called: Cirrus Property MGT Svcs
20720 Ventura Blvd Ste 300, Woodland Hills
(91364-6266)
PHONE..................818 222-4840
Steve Heimler, *CEO*
Carrie E Roth, *CFO*
EMP: 77 **EST:** 2007
SALES (est): 23.31MM
SALES (corp-wide): 23.31MM **Privately Held**
SIC: 6531 Real estate managers

(P-12406)
CITIVEST INC
Also Called: Hydrotech Construction Group
4350 Von Karman Ave Ste 200, Newport
Beach (92660-2041)
PHONE..................949 705-0420
Dana Haynes, *Pr*
EMP: 90 **EST:** 1987
SALES (est): 4.89MM **Privately Held**
Web: www.citivestinc.com
SIC: 6531 Real estate managers

(P-12407)
COASTAL ALLIANCE HOLDINGS INC
Also Called: Coldwell Banker Coastl Aliance
1650 Ximeno Ave Ste 120, Long Beach
(90804-2179)
PHONE..................562 370-1000
Jack Irvin, *Pr*
EMP: 140 **EST:** 2003
SALES (est): 2.1MM **Privately Held**
Web: www.tristardw.com
SIC: 6531 Real estate agent, residential

(P-12408)
COLDWELL BANKER RESIDENTIAL (DH)
Also Called: Coldwell Banker
27742 Vista Del Lago Ste 1, Mission Viejo
(92692-1119)
PHONE..................949 837-5700
Robert M Becker, *Pr*
Gregory S Campbell, *
Robert J Arrigoni, *
Bruce Zipf, *
Gregory Blackburn, *
EMP: 75 **EST:** 1987
SALES (est): 13.31MM **Publicly Held**
Web: www.coldwellbanker.com
SIC: 6531 Real estate agent, residential
HQ: Nrt Commercial Utah Llc
175 Park Ave
Madison NJ 07940

(P-12409)
COLDWELL BNKR RSDNTIAL RFRRAL
Also Called: Coldwell Banker
201 Marine Ave, Newport Beach
(92662-1203)
P.O. Box 68 (92662-0068)
PHONE..................949 673-8700
Steve Sutherland, *Mgr*
EMP: 1489
Web: www.coldwellbanker.com
SIC: 6531 Real estate agent, residential
HQ: Coldwell Banker Residential Referral
Network
27271 Las Ramblas
Mission Viejo CA 92691
949 367-1800

(P-12410)
COLDWELL BNKR RSDNTIAL RFRRAL (DH)
Also Called: Coldwell Banker
27271 Las Ramblas, Mission Viejo
(92691-8041)
PHONE..................949 367-1800
Robert Becker, *Pr*
Dan Happer, *CFO*
EMP: 410 **EST:** 1984
SQ FT: 6,000
SALES (est): 31.17MM **Publicly Held**
Web: www.coldwellbanker.com
SIC: 6531 Real estate agent, residential
HQ: Nrt Commercial Utah Llc
175 Park Ave
Madison NJ 07940

(P-12411)
COLLEGE PARK REALTY INC (PA)
Also Called: Re/Max
10791 Los Alamitos Blvd, Los Alamitos
(90720-2394)
PHONE..................562 594-6753
Barry Binder, *Pr*
Carol Treadway, *
Betty Binder, *
EMP: 80 **EST:** 1974
SQ FT: 5,000
SALES (est): 2.55MM
SALES (corp-wide): 2.55MM **Privately Held**
Web: www.remax-collegepark-ca.com
SIC: 6531 Real estate agent, residential

(P-12412)
COMMERCIAL RE EXCH INC
Also Called: Crexi
5510 Lincoln Blvd Ste 400, Playa Vista
(90094-1900)

PHONE..................888 273-0423
Michael Degiorgio, *CEO*
Erek Benz, *
Ben Widhelm, *
Hans Ku, *CPO*
Courtney Ettus, *CMO*
EMP: 250 **EST:** 2015
SQ FT: 2,000
SALES (est): 26.49MM **Privately Held**
Web: www.crexi.com
SIC: 6531 Real estate agent, commercial

(P-12413)
COMMON GROUNDS HOLDINGS LLC
6790 Embarcadero Ln Ste 100, Carlsbad
(92011-3278)
PHONE..................760 206-7861
Jacob Bates, *Prin*
EMP: 90 **EST:** 2017
SALES (est): 2.17MM **Privately Held**
Web: www.cgworkplace.com
SIC: 6531 8742 Real estate leasing and rentals; Real estate consultant

(P-12414)
CONAM MANAGEMENT CORPORATION (PA)
3990 Ruffin Rd Ste 100, San Diego
(92123-4805)
PHONE..................858 614-7200
J Bradley Forrester, *CEO*
Daniel Epstein, *
Frazier Crawford, *
Rob Singh, *
E Scott Dupree, *
EMP: 142 **EST:** 1975
SQ FT: 45,634
SALES (est): 159.21MM **Privately Held**
Web: www.conam.com
SIC: 6531 Real estate managers

(P-12415)
CORE REALTY HOLDINGS MGT INC
Also Called: Crh Management
1600 Dove St Ste 450, Newport Beach
(92660-2447)
PHONE..................949 863-1031
Dougless Morehead, *CEO*
EMP: 99 **EST:** 2010
SALES (est): 4.16MM **Privately Held**
Web: www.crhmi.com
SIC: 6531 Real estate managers

(P-12416)
CSL BERKSHIRE OPERATING CO LLC
Also Called: Clearwater Living
5000 Birch St Ste 400, Newport Beach
(92660-8125)
PHONE..................949 333-8580
Anthony Ferrero, *Pr*
EMP: 82 **EST:** 2017
SALES (est): 5.38MM **Privately Held**
SIC: 6531 Real estate agents and managers

(P-12417)
CUBEWORKCOM INC (PA)
Also Called: Cubework
900 Turnbull Canyon Rd, City Of Industry
(91745-1404)
PHONE..................909 991-6669
James Chang, *CEO*
Christine Wei, *CCO*
EMP: 199 **EST:** 2018
SALES (est): 4.78MM
SALES (corp-wide): 4.78MM **Privately Held**

Web: www.cubework.com
SIC: 6531 Real estate leasing and rentals

(P-12418)
CUSHMAN & WAKEFIELD CAL INC
10250 Constellation Blvd Ste 2200, Los
Angeles (90067-6255)
PHONE..................310 556-1805
Eric Olosson, *Mgr*
EMP: 432
SALES (corp-wide): 9.49B **Privately Held**
Web: www.cushmanwakefield.com
SIC: 6531 Real estate agent, commercial
HQ: Cushman & Wakefield Of California, Inc.
1 Maritime Plz Ste 900
San Francisco CA 94111
408 275-6730

(P-12419)
CUSHMAN & WAKEFIELD CAL INC
3760 Kilroy Airport Way, Long Beach
(90806-2443)
PHONE..................562 276-1400
Joe Vargus, *Mgr*
EMP: 432
SALES (corp-wide): 9.49B **Privately Held**
Web: www.cushmanwakefield.com
SIC: 6531 Real estate agent, commercial
HQ: Cushman & Wakefield Of California, Inc.
1 Maritime Plz Ste 900
San Francisco CA 94111
408 275-6730

(P-12420)
CUSHMAN & WAKEFIELD CAL INC
Also Called: Cushman & Wakefield California
7281 Garden Grove Blvd Ste G, Garden
Grove (92841-4212)
PHONE..................714 591-0451
EMP: 336
SALES (corp-wide): 9.49B **Privately Held**
Web: www.cushmanwakefield.com
SIC: 6531 Real estate agent, commercial
HQ: Cushman & Wakefield Of California, Inc.
1 Maritime Plz Ste 900
San Francisco CA 94111
408 275-6730

(P-12421)
CUSHMAN & WAKEFIELD CAL INC
18111 Von Karman Ave Ste 1000, Irvine
(92612-7101)
PHONE..................949 474-4004
Dee Shipley, *Mgr*
EMP: 624
SALES (corp-wide): 9.49B **Privately Held**
Web: www.cushmanwakefield.com
SIC: 6531 Real estate agent, commercial
HQ: Cushman & Wakefield Of California, Inc.
1 Maritime Plz Ste 900
San Francisco CA 94111
408 275-6730

(P-12422)
CUSHMAN & WAKEFIELD CAL INC
3011 Townsgate Rd, Westlake Village
(91361-5820)
PHONE..................805 418-5811
EMP: 384
SALES (corp-wide): 9.49B **Privately Held**

Web: www.cushmanwakefield.com
SIC: 6531 Real estate agent, commercial
HQ: Cushman & Wakefield Of California,
Inc.
1 Maritime Plz Ste 900
San Francisco CA 94111
408 275-6730

(P-12423)
CUSHMAN & WAKEFIELD CAL INC
770 Paseo Camarillo 315, Camarillo
(93010-6095)
PHONE..............................805 322-7244
EMP: 384
SALES (corp-wide): 9.49B Privately Held
Web: www.cushmanwakefield.com
SIC: 6531 Real estate agent, commercial
HQ: Cushman & Wakefield Of California,
Inc.
1 Maritime Plz Ste 900
San Francisco CA 94111
408 275-6730

(P-12424)
CUSHMAN & WAKEFIELD CAL INC
Also Called: Corporate Real Estate Advisors
12830 El Camino Real Ste 100, San Diego
(92130-2976)
PHONE..............................858 452-6500
Steve Rosetta, Mgr
EMP: 864
SALES (corp-wide): 9.49B Privately Held
Web: www.cushmanwakefield.com
SIC: 6531 8742 8732 Real estate agent,
commercial; Real estate consultant; Market
analysis, business, and economic research
HQ: Cushman & Wakefield Of California,
Inc.
1 Maritime Plz Ste 900
San Francisco CA 94111
408 275-6730

(P-12425)
CUSHMAN & WAKEFIELD CAL INC
Also Called: Cushman & Wakefield
3800 Concours Ste 300, Ontario
(91764-5907)
PHONE..............................909 483-0077
EMP: 384
SALES (corp-wide): 9.49B Privately Held
Web: www.cushmanwakefield.com
SIC: 6531 Real estate agent, commercial
HQ: Cushman & Wakefield Of California,
Inc.
1 Maritime Plz Sto 000
San Francisco CA 94111
408 275-6730

(P-12426)
CUSHMAN & WAKEFIELD CAL INC
901 Via Piemonte Ste 200, Ontario
(91764-6597)
PHONE..............................909 980-3781
Luanne Alleman, Mgr
EMP: 480
SALES (corp-wide): 9.49B Privately Held
Web: www.cushmanwakefield.com
SIC: 6531 Real estate agent, commercial
HQ: Cushman & Wakefield Of California,
Inc.
1 Maritime Plz Ste 900
San Francisco CA 94111
408 275-6730

(P-12427)
CUSHMAN REALTY CORPORATION
601 S Figueroa St Ste 4700, Los Angeles
(90017-5752)
PHONE..............................213 627-4700
EMP: 200
SIC: 6531 Real estate brokers and agents

(P-12428)
DAYMARK REALTY ADVISORS INC
Also Called: Daymark Properties Realty
750 B St Ste 2620, San Diego
(92101-8172)
PHONE..............................714 975-2999
Todd A Mikles, CEO
EMP: 400 EST: 2010
SALES (est): 2.33MM Privately Held
SIC: 6531 Real estate brokers and agents

(P-12429)
DEASY PENNER PODLEY
Also Called: Dpp Real Estate
30 N Baldwin Ave, Sierra Madre
(91024-1956)
PHONE..............................626 408-1280
Mike Deasy, Ch Bd
George Penner, *
EMP: 223 EST: 2019
SALES (est): 873.94K Privately Held
Web: www.dppre.com
SIC: 6531 Real estate agent, commercial

(P-12430)
DIAMOND RIDGE CORPORATION
Also Called: Re/Max
121 S Mountain Ave, Upland (91786-6257)
PHONE..............................909 949-0605
Jennifer Lynn Puglisi, CEO
EMP: 165 EST: 2001
SALES (est): 2.25MM Privately Held
Web: www.remax.com
SIC: 6531 Real estate agent, residential

(P-12431)
DILBECK INC (PA)
Also Called: Dilbeck Realtors
1030 Foothill Blvd, La Canada
(91011-3285)
PHONE..............................818 790-6774
Mark Dilbeck, Ch Bd
Mark Dilbeck, Ch Bd
Bruce Dilbeck, *
EMP: 70 EST: 1963
SQ FT: 9,000
SALES (est): 24 46MM
SALES (corp-wide): 24.46MM Privately Held
Web: www.evrealestate.com
SIC: 6531 Real estate agent, commercial

(P-12432)
DONAHUE SCHRBER RLTY GROUP INC (PA)
200 Baker St Ste 100, Costa Mesa
(92626-4551)
PHONE..............................714 545-1400
Thomas Schriber, Ch Bd
Patrick S Donahue, *
Larry Casey, *
EMP: 80 EST: 1954
SQ FT: 20,000
SALES (est): 3.81MM
SALES (corp-wide): 3.81MM Privately Held
Web: www.orangejulius.com
SIC: 6531 Real estate agent, commercial

(P-12433)
E & S RING MANAGEMENT CORP
Also Called: Meadows, The
6300 Green Valley Cir, Culver City
(90230-7009)
PHONE..............................310 670-5983
Kelly Donavan, Mgr
EMP: 73
SALES (corp-wide): 28.19MM Privately Held
Web: www.esring.com
SIC: 6531 6513 Real estate managers;
Apartment hotel operation
PA: E & S Ring Management Corp.
6601 Center Dr W Ste 600
310 337-5400

(P-12434)
EAM ENTERPRISES INC
Also Called: Century 21 Crest
8307 Foothill Blvd, Sunland (91040-2809)
PHONE..............................818 951-6464
Razmik Mira, Owner
EMP: 82
Web: www.century21.com
SIC: 6531 Real estate agent, residential
PA: E.A.M. Enterprises Inc.
4005 Foothill Blvd

(P-12435)
EAM ENTERPRISES INC (PA)
Also Called: Crest R E O & Relocation
4005 Foothill Blvd, La Crescenta
(91214-1623)
PHONE..............................818 248-9100
Razmik Mirzakhanian, CEO
EMP: 100 EST: 1991
SQ FT: 5,000
SALES (est): 2.26MM Privately Held
Web: www.century21.com
SIC: 6531 Real estate agent, residential

(P-12436)
EAPPRAISEIT LLC
12395 First American Way, Poway
(92064-6897)
PHONE..............................800 281-6200
Devid Feildman, Prin
EMP: 185 EST: 2002
SALES (est): 831.79K Privately Held
Web: www.eappraiseit.com
SIC: 6531 Appraiser, real estate

(P-12437)
ENGEL VOLKERS BEVERLY HILLS
340 N Camden Dr, Beverly Hills
(90210-5130)
PHONE..............................310 777-7510
Raphael Earragan, Pr
EMP: 84 EST: 2015
SALES (est): 404.92K Privately Held
Web: federicosalvatori.evusa.com
SIC: 6531 Real estate agent, residential

(P-12438)
EQUITY CONCEPT INC
16902 Bolsa Chica St Ste 203, Huntington
Beach (92649-3590)
PHONE..............................714 374-8859
James Jones, Pr
Boyce Jones, *
EMP: 75 EST: 1997
SALES (est): 924.35K Privately Held
Web: www.equity-concepts.com
SIC: 6531 Rental agent, real estate

(P-12439)
ESSEX PROPERTIES LLC
18012 Sky Park Cir Ste 100, Irvine
(92614-6671)
PHONE..............................949 798-8100
Jim Niger, Pr
Burrel D Magnusson, *
Linda Webber, *
EMP: 75 EST: 1987
SALES (est): 2.26MM Privately Held
SIC: 6531 Real estate agent, commercial

(P-12440)
EVOQ PROPERTIES INC
1318 E 7th St Ste 200, Los Angeles
(90021-1128)
PHONE..............................213 988-8890
Martin Caveroy, CEO
John Charles Maddux, *
Lynn Beckemeyer, Executive Development
Vice President*
Todd Nielsen, Corporate Secretary*
Andrew Murray, *
EMP: 82 EST: 2006
SALES (est): 2.75MM Privately Held
Web: www.evoqproperties.com
SIC: 6531 Real estate agent, commercial

(P-12441)
F M TARBELL CO (HQ)
Also Called: Tarbell Realtors
1403 N Tustin Ave Ste 380, Santa Ana
(92705-8691)
PHONE..............................714 972-0988
TOLL FREE: 800
Tina Jimov, Pr
Donald M Tarbell, *
EMP: 110 EST: 1956
SQ FT: 60,000
SALES (est): 19.33MM
SALES (corp-wide): 74.6MM Privately Held
Web: www.jenniferpoltl.com
SIC: 6531 Real estate agent, residential
PA: Tarbell Financial Corporation
1403 N Tustin Ave Ste 380
714 972-0988

(P-12442)
FIRST AMERCN PROF RE SVCS INC (HQ)
Also Called: Commercial Due Diligence Svcs
200 Commerce, Irvine (92602-5000)
PHONE..............................714 250-1400
Larry Davidson, Pr
EMP: 240 EST: 1997
SQ FT: 28,000
SALES (est): 2.47MM Publicly Held
Web: www.firstam.com
SIC: 6531 Real estate agents and managers
PA: First American Financial Corporation
1 First American Way

(P-12443)
FIRST AMERICAN TEAM REALTY INC (PA)
Also Called: Best Financial, The
2501 Cherry Ave Ste 100, Signal Hill
(90755-2039)
PHONE..............................562 427-7765
Steve S Vong, Pr
EMP: 150 EST: 1995
SQ FT: 3,300
SALES (est): 2.17MM Privately Held
Web: www.firstamericanteam.com
SIC: 6531 Real estate agent, residential

(P-12444)

FIRST TEAM RE - ORANGE CNTY
42 64th Pl, Long Beach (90803-5676)
PHONE....................562 346-5088
EMP: 85
SALES (corp-wide): 486 Privately Held
Web: www.firstteam.com
SIC: 6531 Real estate agent, residential
PA: First Team Real Estate - Orange
County
108 Pacifica Ste 300
949 988-3000

(P-12445)

FIRST TEAM RE - ORANGE CNTY
3626 Long Beach Blvd, Long Beach
(90807-4006)
PHONE....................562 424-2004
EMP: 85
SALES (corp-wide): 486 Privately Held
Web: www.firstteam.com
SIC: 6531 Real estate agent, residential
PA: First Team Real Estate - Orange
County
108 Pacifica Ste 300
949 988-3000

(P-12446)

FIRST TEAM RE - ORANGE CNTY
Also Called: First Team Real Estate
8028 E Santa Ana Canyon Rd, Anaheim
(92808-1108)
PHONE....................714 974-9191
Anna Bennet, *Mgr*
EMP: 85
SALES (corp-wide): 486 Privately Held
Web: www.firstteam.com
SIC: 6531 Real estate agent, residential
PA: First Team Real Estate - Orange
County
108 Pacifica Ste 300
949 988-3000

(P-12447)

FIRST TEAM RE - ORANGE CNTY
Also Called: First Team Real Estate
26711 Aliso Creek Rd Ste 200a, Aliso Viejo
(92656-4822)
PHONE....................949 389-0004
Michele Williams, *Brnch Mgr*
EMP: 150
SALES (corp-wide): 486 Privately Held
Web: www.firstteam.com
SIC: 6531 Real estate agent, residential
PA: First Team Real Estate - Orange
County
108 Pacifica Ste 300
949 988-3000

(P-12448)

**FIRST TEAM RE - ORANGE
CNTY (PA)**
Also Called: First Team Walk-In Realty
108 Pacifica Ste 300, Irvine (92618-7435)
PHONE.:...................949 988-3000
Cameron Merage, *CEO*
Michele Harrington, *
Francisco Galleno, *
EMP: 160 EST: 1976
SQ FT: 8,000
SALES (est): 486
SALES (corp-wide): 486 Privately Held
Web: www.firstteam.com
SIC: 6531 Real estate agent, residential

(P-12449)

FIRST TEAM RE - ORANGE CNTY
12501 Seal Beach Blvd Ste 100, Seal
Beach (90740-2755)
PHONE....................562 596-9911

Judy Sharp, *Mgr*
EMP: 85
SALES (corp-wide): 486 Privately Held
Web: www.firstteam.com
SIC: 6531 Real estate agent, residential
PA: First Team Real Estate - Orange
County
108 Pacifica Ste 300
949 988-3000

(P-12450)

FIRST TEAM RE - ORANGE CNTY
Also Called: First Team Real Estate
4040 Barranca Pkwy Ste 100, Irvine
(92604-4772)
PHONE....................714 485-7984
Dan Sarnecky, *Mgr*
EMP: 127
SALES (corp-wide): 486 Privately Held
Web: www.firstteam.com
SIC: 6531 Real estate agent, residential
PA: First Team Real Estate - Orange
County
108 Pacifica Ste 300
949 988-3000

(P-12451)

FIRST TEAM RE - ORANGE CNTY
32451 Golden Lantern Ste 210, Laguna
Niguel (92677-5344)
PHONE....................949 240-7979
Mark Kojac, *Genl Mgr*
EMP: 212
SALES (corp-wide): 486 Privately Held
Web: www.firstteam.com
SIC: 6531 Real estate agent, residential
PA: First Team Real Estate - Orange
County
108 Pacifica Ste 300
949 988-3000

(P-12452)

FIRST TEAM RE - ORANGE CNTY
Also Called: 1st Team Real Estate
17240 17th St, Tustin (92780-1945)
PHONE....................714 544-5456
Michael Hampton, *Mgr*
EMP: 297
SALES (corp-wide): 486 Privately Held
Web: www.firstteam.com
SIC: 6531 Real estate agent, residential
PA: First Team Real Estate - Orange
County
108 Pacifica Ste 300
949 988-3000

(P-12453)

FIRST TEAM RE - ORANGE CNTY
200 S Main St Ste 100, Corona (92879)
PHONE....................951 270-2800
Linda Rocha, *Prin*
EMP: 85
SALES (corp-wide): 486 Privately Held
Web: www.firstteam.com
SIC: 6531 Real estate agent, residential
PA: First Team Real Estate - Orange
County
108 Pacifica Ste 300
949 988-3000

(P-12454)

**FIRSTSRVICE RSIDENTIAL CAL
LLC (HQ)**
Also Called: Merit Companies The
15241 Laguna Canyon Rd, Irvine
(92618-3146)
PHONE....................949 448-6000
Bob Cardoza, *Pr*
Katie Ward, *Prin*
EMP: 200 EST: 1980

SQ FT: 21,000
SALES (est): 2.89MM
SALES (corp-wide): 4.33B Privately Held
Web: www.fsresidential.com
SIC: 6531 Real estate managers
PA: Firstservice Corporation
600-1255 Bay St
416 960-9566

(P-12455)

**GEMINI-ROSEMONT REALTY
LLC**
2000 Avenue Of The Stars Ste 550, Los
Angeles (90067-4713)
PHONE....................505 992-5100
Julia Golden, *Pr*
EMP: 84 EST: 2017
SALES (est): 10.32MM Privately Held
Web: www.geminirosemont.com
SIC: 6531 Real estate agent, commercial

(P-12456)

GEMMM CORPORATION (PA)
Also Called: Prudential
2860 E Thousand Oaks Blvd, Thousand
Oaks (91362-3201)
PHONE....................805 496-0555
TOLL FREE: 800
Robert L Majorino, *Pr*
Robert Hamilton, *
Anthony Principe, *
Lynn Gilbert, *
EMP: 100 EST: 1990
SQ FT: 12,500
SALES (est): 9.85MM
SALES (corp-wide): 9.85MM Privately
Held
Web: www.bhhscalhomes.com
SIC: 6531 Real estate agent, residential

(P-12457)

GK MANAGEMENT CO INC (PA)
5150 Overland Ave, Culver City
(90230-4914)
PHONE....................310 204-2050
Carole Glodney, *CEO*
Jona Goldrich, *
EMP: 150 EST: 1972
SALES (est): 64.47MM
SALES (corp-wide): 64.47MM Privately
Held
Web: www.goldrichkest.com
SIC: 6531 Real estate managers

(P-12458)

**GRAND PACIFIC RESORTS INC
(PA)**
Also Called: Cove Bar and Grill, The
5900 Pasteur Ct Ste 200, Carlsbad
(92008-7336)
P.O. Box 4068 (92018-4068)
PHONE....................760 431-8500
Timothy J Stripe, *CEO*
David Brown, *
EMP: 250 EST: 1993
SQ FT: 22,000
SALES (est): 45.79MM Privately Held
Web: www.grandpacificresorts.com
SIC: 6531 7011 Time-sharing real estate
sales, leasing and rentals; Hotels and
motels

(P-12459)

**GREYSTAR MANAGEMENT
SVCS LP**
6320 Canoga Ave Ste 1512, Woodland Hills
(91367-2526)
PHONE....................818 596-2180
Grace White, *Owner*

EMP: 116
Web: www.greystar.com
SIC: 6531 Real estate brokers and agents
PA: Greystar Management Services, L.P.
750 Bering Dr Ste 300

(P-12460)

**GREYSTAR MANAGEMENT
SVCS LP**
Also Called: Greystar
620 Newport Center Dr 15th Fl, Newport
Beach (92660-6420)
PHONE....................949 705-0010
Kevin Kaverna, *Dir*
EMP: 812
Web: www.greystar.com
SIC: 6531 Real estate managers
PA: Greystar Management Services, L.P.
750 Bering Dr Ste 300

(P-12461)

GRUBB & ELLIS COMPANY
1551 N Tustin Ave Ste 300, Santa Ana
(92705-8638)
PHONE....................714 667-8252
◆ EMP: 4500
SIC: 6531 8742 6162 Real estate agent,
commercial; Real estate consultant;
Mortgage brokers, using own money

(P-12462)

**GRUBB & ELLIS MANAGEMENT
SERVICES INC**
1551 N Tustin Ave Ste 300, Santa Ana
(92705-8638)
PHONE....................412 201-8200
EMP: 1800
SIC: 6531 Real estate agents and managers

(P-12463)

**HANKEN CONO ASSAD & CO
INC**
Also Called: Wintergreen Apts
1504 Oro Vista Rd Apt 145, San Diego
(92154-4069)
PHONE....................619 575-3100
Martha Alonso, *Mgr*
EMP: 113
SALES (corp-wide): 16.83MM Privately
Held
Web: www.liveatwintergreen.com
SIC: 6531 6513 Condominium manager;
Apartment building operators
PA: Hanken Cono Assad & Co., Inc.
5550 Baltimore Dr Ste 200
619 698-4770

(P-12464)

HELM MANAGEMENT CO (PA)
Also Called: Helm, The
4668 Nebo Dr Ste A, La Mesa
(91941-5200)
PHONE....................619 589-6222
Tom Hensley, *Pr*
EMP: 70 EST: 1979
SQ FT: 1,176
SALES (est): 5.94MM
SALES (corp-wide): 5.94MM Privately
Held
Web: www.helmmanagement.com
SIC: 6531 Real estate managers

(P-12465)

HOUSE SEVEN GABLES RE INC
Also Called: Cole, Norman Anne
5753 E Santa Ana Canyon Rd Ste P,
Anaheim (92807-3230)
PHONE....................714 282-0306
Kelli Ludden, *CFO*

EMP: 91
SALES (corp-wide): 22.27MM **Privately Held**
Web: www.sevengables.com
SIC: 6531 Real estate agent, residential
PA: House Of Seven Gables Real Estate, Inc.
12651 Newport Ave
714 731-3777

(P-12466)
HOUSE SEVEN GABLES RE INC
Also Called: Seven Gables Real Estate
5481 E Santa Ana Canyon Rd, Anaheim (92807-3100)
PHONE...............................714 974-7000
Mike Hickman, *Brnch Mgr*
EMP: 91
SALES (corp-wide): 22.27MM **Privately Held**
Web: www.chinohillsteam.com
SIC: 6531 Real estate agent, residential
PA: House Of Seven Gables Real Estate, Inc.
12651 Newport Ave
714 731-3777

(P-12467)
I D PROPERTY CORPORATION
Also Called: Property I D
1001 Wilshire Blvd Ste 100, Los Angeles (90017-2821)
PHONE...............................213 625-0100
Carlos Siderman, *Pr*
▲ **EMP:** 120 **EST:** 1983
SALES (est): 4.54MM **Privately Held**
Web: www.propertyid.com
SIC: 6531 8742 Real estate listing services; Real estate consultant

(P-12468)
INVESERVE CORPORATION
812 W Las Tunas Dr, San Gabriel (91776-1021)
PHONE...............................626 458-3435
Norman Chang, *Pr*
Amy Chang, *
Michael Fang, *
EMP: 80 **EST:** 1987
SALES (est): 1.91MM **Privately Held**
Web: www.inveserve.com
SIC: 6531 Real estate agent, commercial

(P-12469)
INVITATION HOMES INC
680 E Colorado Blvd, Pasadena (91101-6143)
PHONE...............................805 372-2900
Luke Kochniuk, *Brnch Mgr*
EMP: 80
SALES (corp-wide): 2.43B **Publicly Held**
Web: www.invitationhomes.com
SIC: 6531 Real estate agents and managers
PA: Invitation Homes Inc.
5420 Lyndon B Jhnson Fwy
972 421-3600

(P-12470)
IRVINE APT COMMUNITIES LP
146 Berkeley, Irvine (92612-4618)
PHONE...............................949 854-4942
Kevin Baldridge, *Brnch Mgr*
EMP: 200
SALES (corp-wide): 579.21MM **Privately Held**
Web: www.irvinecompanyapartments.com
SIC: 6531 Real estate managers
HQ: Irvine Apartment Communities, Lp
110 Innovation Dr

Irvine CA 92617

(P-12471)
J & M REALTY COMPANY (PA)
41 Corporate Park Ste 240, Irvine (92606-3125)
PHONE...............................949 261-2727
John Woolley, *Pr*
Michael Aimola, *Genl Mgr*
EMP: 120 **EST:** 1988
SQ FT: 4,000
SALES (est): 1.3MM **Privately Held**
Web: www.cabrokerx.com
SIC: 6531 8641 6798 6519 Real estate managers; Homeowners' association; Real estate investment trusts; Real property lessors, nec

(P-12472)
JAMBOREE REALTY CORP (PA)
Also Called: Jamboree Management
22982 Mill Creek Dr, Laguna Hills (92653-1214)
PHONE...............................949 380-0300
Fred G Sparks, *Pr*
Richard M Tucker, *
Kathleen Tucker, *
EMP: 120 **EST:** 1982
SALES (est): 9.52MM
SALES (corp-wide): 9.52MM **Privately Held**
Web: www.jamboreemanagement.com
SIC: 6531 Real estate managers

(P-12473)
KELLER WLLAMS RLTY BVRLY HILLS
Also Called: Keller Williams Realtors
439 N Canon Dr Ste 300, Beverly Hills (90210-3909)
PHONE...............................310 432-6400
Paul Morris, *Prin*
EMP: 90 **EST:** 2005
SALES (est): 2.69MM **Privately Held**
Web: www.kwbeverlyhills.com
SIC: 6531 Real estate agent, residential

(P-12474)
KENNEDY-WILSON INC (PA)
151 El Camino Dr, Beverly Hills (90212-2704)
PHONE...............................310 887-6400
William Mcmorrow, *Ch Bd*
Justin Enbody, *CFO*
Matt Windisch, *Pr*
John Pradhu, *VP*
EMP: 103 **EST:** 1977
SALES (est): 52.58MM **Privately Held**
Web: www.kennedywilson.com
SIC: 6531 6799 Auction, real estate; Real estate investors, except property operators

(P-12475)
KOR REALTY GROUP LLC (PA)
1212 S Flower St Fl 5, Los Angeles (90015-2123)
PHONE...............................323 930-3700
EMP: 86 **EST:** 2001
SQ FT: 6,500
SALES (est): 2.49MM
SALES (corp-wide): 2.49MM **Privately Held**
Web: www.thekorgroup.com
SIC: 6531 Real estate managers

(P-12476)
LA CIENEGA ASSOCIATES
Also Called: Beverly Center
8500 Beverly Blvd Ste 501, Los Angeles (90048-6277)

PHONE...............................310 854-0071
Laurel Crary-globus, *Genl Mgr*
A Alfred Taubman, *Pt*
Sheldon Gordon, *Pt*
EMP: 75 **EST:** 1982
SQ FT: 2,500
SALES (est): 4.63MM **Privately Held**
Web: www.beverlycenter.com
SIC: 6512 Real estate brokers and agents; Auditorium and hall operation

(P-12477)
LAGUNA WOODS VILLAGE
24351 El Toro Rd, Laguna Woods (92637-4901)
P.O. Box 2220 (92654-2220)
PHONE...............................949 597-4267
Milton John, *Dir*
Russ Disbro, *Dir*
EMP: 1000 **EST:** 1964
SALES (est): 4.44MM **Privately Held**
Web: www.lagunawoodsvillage.com
SIC: 6531 Real estate agents and managers

(P-12478)
LANDMARK DIVIDEND LLC (PA)
Also Called: Landmark Dividend
400 Continental Blvd Ste 500, El Segundo (90245-5078)
PHONE...............................323 306-2683
Arthur P Brazy Junior, *CEO*
EMP: 77 **EST:** 2010
SQ FT: 7,500
SALES (est): 14.75MM
SALES (corp-wide): 14.75MM **Privately Held**
Web: www.landmarkdividend.com
SIC: 6531 Real estate agent, commercial

(P-12479)
LOIS LAUER REALTY (PA)
Also Called: Century 21
1998 Orange Tree Ln, Redlands (92374-2841)
P.O. Box 524 (92373-0161)
PHONE...............................909 748-7000
TOLL FREE: 800
David Coy, *Pr*
Shirley Harrington, *VP*
Ann Bryan, *Sec*
James H Lauer, *Dir*
EMP: 109 **EST:** 1976
SQ FT: 17,000
SALES (est): 9.95MM
SALES (corp-wide): 9.95MM **Privately Held**
Web: www.century21.com
SIC: 6531 Real estate agent, residential

(P-12480)
LOWE ENTERPRISES INC
Also Called: Lowe Enterprises Real Estate
300 Spectrum Center Dr Ste 1460, Irvine (92618-4985)
PHONE...............................949 724-1515
Rachel Pozzi, *Brnch Mgr*
EMP: 90
SALES (corp-wide): 367.25MM **Privately Held**
Web: www.lowe-re.com
SIC: 6531 Real estate brokers and agents
PA: Lowe Enterprises, Inc.
11777 San Vcnte Blvd Ste
310 820-6661

(P-12481)
LOWE ENTERPRISES RLTY SVCS INC
Also Called: Encino Financial Center
16133 Ventura Blvd Ste 535, Encino (91436-2402)

PHONE...............................818 990-9555
Karla Akins, *Brnch Mgr*
EMP: 1895
SALES (corp-wide): 367.25MM **Privately Held**
Web: www.lowe-re.com
SIC: 6531 Real estate managers
HQ: Lowe Enterprises Realty Services, Inc.
11777 San Vicente Blvd
Los Angeles CA 90049
310 820-6661

(P-12482)
LRES CORPORATION (PA)
Also Called: Guardian Solutions
765 The City Dr S, Orange (92868-4942)
PHONE...............................714 520-5737
Roger Beane, *Pr*
Don Mask, *CAO*
Alice Sorenson, *Ex VP*
Paul Abbamonto, *COO*
Richard Cimino, *Sr VP*
EMP: 91 **EST:** 2001
SALES (est): 19.15MM
SALES (corp-wide): 19.15MM **Privately Held**
Web: www.lres.com
SIC: 6531 Real estate managers

(P-12483)
LUXRE REALTY INC
222 Avenida Del Mar, San Clemente (92672-4005)
PHONE...............................949 498-3702
Deborah Gietter, *CEO*
EMP: 71 **EST:** 2011
SALES (est): 1.4MM **Privately Held**
Web: www.luxrerealty.com
SIC: 6531 Real estate agent, residential

(P-12484)
M & S ACQUISITION CORPORATION (PA)
707 Wilshire Blvd Ste 5200, Los Angeles (90017-3614)
PHONE...............................213 385-1515
Mark Santarsiero, *CFO*
Mark Santarsiero, *CEO*
Robert Kerslake, *
Merle Atkins, *
Fred Thomas, *
EMP: 115 **EST:** 1993
SALES (est): 12.92MM
SALES (corp-wide): 12.92MM **Privately Held**
SIC: 6531 8742 Appraiser, real estate; Management consulting services

(P-12485)
MAJESTIC REALTY CO (PA)
Also Called: Majestic Management Co.
13191 Crossroads Pkwy N Ste 600, City Of Industry (91746-3493)
PHONE...............................562 692-9581
EMP: 150 **EST:** 1948
SALES (est): 1.13MM
SALES (corp-wide): 1.13MM **Privately Held**
Web: www.majesticrealty.com
SIC: 6531 6552 Real estate agent, commercial; Subdividers and developers, nec

(P-12486)
MARCUS & MILLICHAP INC (PA)
Also Called: Marcus & Millichap
23975 Park Sorrento Ste 400, Calabasas (91302-4014)
PHONE...............................818 212-2250
Hessam Nadji, *Pr*

Mitchell R Labar, *Ex VP*
Steve Degennaro, *CFO*
Christopher J Zorbas, *Mng Dir*
Andrew Strockis, *CMO*
EMP: 98 **EST:** 1971
SQ FT: 24,028
SALES (est): 645.93MM
SALES (corp-wide): 645.93MM **Publicly Held**
Web: www.marcusmillichap.com
SIC: 6531 Real estate agent, commercial

(P-12487)
MEMCO HOLDINGS INC
10390 Santa Monica Blvd Ste 210, Los Angeles (90025-6964)
PHONE..............................310 277-0057
Mitchell Stein, *Pr*
EMP: 130 **EST:** 1987
SALES (est): 408.94K **Privately Held**
SIC: 6531 Real estate managers

(P-12488)
MESA MANAGEMENT INC
1451 Quail St Ste 201, Newport Beach (92660-2741)
P.O. Box 2990 (92658-9018)
PHONE..............................949 851-0995
Steve Mensinger, *Pr*
Robert Lucas, *
EMP: 70 **EST:** 1977
SQ FT: 5,000
SALES (est): 4.15MM **Privately Held**
Web: www.mesamanagement.net
SIC: 6531 Real estate managers

(P-12489)
MOONSTONE MANAGEMENT CORP (PA)
Also Called: Moonstone Hotel Properties
2905 Burton Dr, Cambria (93428-4001)
PHONE..............................805 927-4200
Dirk Winter, *Pr*
EMP: 175 **EST:** 1995
SQ FT: 5,000
SALES (est): 3.67MM **Privately Held**
Web: www.moonstonehotels.com
SIC: 6531 Real estate managers

(P-12490)
MOSS & COMPANY INC (PA)
15300 Ventura Blvd Ste 405, Sherman Oaks (91403-5856)
PHONE..............................818 305-3600
Cindy Gray, *Pr*
Ronald Tamkin, *Executive Partner**
Chris Gray, *
EMP: 70 **EST:** 1963
SQ FT: 10,000
SALES (est): 9.54MM
SALES (corp-wide): 9.54MM **Privately Held**
SIC: 6531 Real estate managers

(P-12491)
MOSS MANAGEMENT SERVICES INC
15300 Ventura Blvd Ste 405, Sherman Oaks (91403-5856)
PHONE..............................818 990-5999
Cindy Gray, *Pr*
Chris Gray, *Ex VP*
Henriette Saffron, *CFO*
EMP: 82 **EST:** 2006
SALES (est): 2.7MM **Privately Held**
SIC: 6531 Real estate managers

(P-12492)
MOVE SALES INC (DH)
Also Called: Homestore Apartments & Rentals
30700 Russell Ranch Rd Ste 290, Westlake Village (91362-9500)
PHONE..............................805 557-2300
Steve Berkowitz, *CEO*
Maria Pietrosorte, *Pr*
Kristin Pudwill, *VP*
EMP: 75 **EST:** 1996
SALES (est): 13.7MM
SALES (corp-wide): 10.09B **Publicly Held**
Web: www.realtor.com
SIC: 6531 Real estate brokers and agents
HQ: Move, Inc.
3315 Scott Blvd
Santa Clara CA 95054
408 558-7100

(P-12493)
MSE ENTERPRISES INC (PA)
Also Called: Marshall S Ezralow & Assoc
23622 Calabasas Rd Ste 200, Calabasas (91302-1509)
PHONE..............................818 223-3500
Marshall S Ezralow, *Pr*
EMP: 90 **EST:** 1974
SALES (est): 3.48MM
SALES (corp-wide): 3.48MM **Privately Held**
SIC: 6531 Real estate managers

(P-12494)
MURCOR INC
Also Called: Pcv Murcor Real Estate Svcs
740 Corporate Center Dr Ste 100, Pomona (91768-2654)
PHONE..............................909 623-4001
Keith D Murray, *Pr*
Jon D Van Deuren, *
Richard J Barkley, *
Tim Scherf, *
Cindy Nasser, *
EMP: 225 **EST:** 1981
SALES (est): 19.57MM **Privately Held**
Web: www.pcvmurcor.com
SIC: 6531 Appraiser, real estate

(P-12495)
NELSON SHELTON & ASSOCIATES
Also Called: ERA Real Estate
355 N Canon Dr, Beverly Hills (90210-4704)
PHONE..............................310 271-2229
Mark Shelton, *VP*
Elsa Nelson, *Pr*
EMP: 200 **EST:** 1988
SALES (est): 1.78MM **Privately Held**
Web: www.nelsonshelton.com
SIC: 6531 Real estate agent, residential

(P-12496)
NIJJAR REALTY INC (PA)
4900 Santa Anita Ave Ste 2c, El Monte (91731-1490)
P.O. Box 6085 (91734-2085)
PHONE..............................626 575-0062
Daljit Kler, *Prin*
Mike Nijjar, *
Peter Nijjar, *
Swaranjit S Nijjar, *
EMP: 70 **EST:** 1949
SQ FT: 2,000
SALES (est): 2MM
SALES (corp-wide): 2MM **Privately Held**
SIC: 6531 Real estate brokers and agents

(P-12497)
NMS PROPERTIES INC
10599 Wilshire Blvd, Los Angeles (90024-7620)
PHONE..............................310 656-2700
Naum Shekhter, *CEO*
Margot Shekhter, *
Kurt Lietz, *
Scott Walter, *
Dino Ciarmoli, *
EMP: 95 **EST:** 1997
SALES (est): 3.78MM **Privately Held**
Web: www.nmsproperties.com
SIC: 6531 Real estate managers

(P-12498)
ON CENTRAL REALTY INC
1648 Colorado Blvd, Los Angeles (90041-1403)
PHONE..............................323 543-8500
Vazrik Bonyadi, *Brnch Mgr*
EMP: 314
Web: www.cbhallmark.com
SIC: 6531 6519 Real estate brokers and agents; Real property lessors, nec
PA: On Central Realty, Inc.
1625 W Glenoaks Blvd

(P-12499)
PACIFIC MONARCH RESORTS INC (PA)
Also Called: Vacation Interval Realty
4000 Macarthur Blvd Ste 600, Newport Beach (92660-2517)
PHONE..............................949 609-2400
Mark D Post, *CEO*
Carlton Post, *
Nick Baldwin, *
EMP: 100 **EST:** 1987
SQ FT: 20,000
SALES (est): 49.26MM
SALES (corp-wide): 49.26MM **Privately Held**
Web: www.pacificmonarchresorts.com
SIC: 6531 7011 Time-sharing real estate sales, leasing and rentals; Vacation lodges

(P-12500)
PANGO GROUP INC
6100 San Fernando Rd, Glendale (91201-2247)
PHONE..............................818 502-0400
Scott Akerley, *CEO*
Brett Yates, *CFO*
EMP: 74 **EST:** 2009
SQ FT: 6,500
SALES (est): 8.66MM **Privately Held**
Web: www.pangogroup.com
SIC: 6531 Real estate brokers and agents

(P-12501)
PARK REGENCY INC
10146 Balboa Blvd, Granada Hills (91344-7408)
PHONE..............................818 363-6116
Joseph Alexander, *Pr*
Ken Engeron, *
Patrick Pace, *
EMP: 70 **EST:** 1980
SQ FT: 4,500
SALES (est): 2.23MM **Privately Held**
Web: www.parkregency.com
SIC: 6531 Real estate agent, residential

(P-12502)
PATHSTONE FAMILY OFFICE LLC
Also Called: Pathstone Federal Street
1900 Avenue Of The Stars Ste 970, Los Angeles (90067-4661)
PHONE..............................888 750-7284
Steve Braverman, *Prin*
EMP: 91
SALES (corp-wide): 9.23MM **Privately Held**
Web: www.pathstone.com
SIC: 6531 Appraiser, real estate
HQ: Pathstone Family Office, Llc
50 Park Row W Ste 113
Providence RI 02903
888 750-7284

(P-12503)
PCS PROPERTY MANAGMENT LLC
11859 Wilshire Blvd Ste 600, Los Angeles (90025-6621)
PHONE..............................310 231-1000
Michael Ross, *Brnch Mgr*
EMP: 141
Web: www.pcsnorthvalley.com
SIC: 6531 Real estate managers
PA: Pcs Property Managment Llc
4500 Woodman Ave Ofc

(P-12504)
PINNACLE ESTATE PROPERTIES INC (PA)
Also Called: Pinnacle Escrow Company
20065 Rinaldi St Ste 210, Porter Ranch (91326-4917)
PHONE..............................818 993-4707
Dana Potter, *Pr*
Jeff Black, *
EMP: 120 **EST:** 1985
SQ FT: 13,000
SALES (est): 7.21MM
SALES (corp-wide): 7.21MM **Privately Held**
Web: www.pinnacleestate.com
SIC: 6531 Real estate agent, residential

(P-12505)
PITTS & BACHMANN REALTORS INC
1482 E Valley Rd Ste 44, Santa Barbara (93108-1200)
P.O. Box 50816 (93150-0816)
PHONE..............................805 969-5005
Dennis Walsh, *Owner*
EMP: 77
SALES (corp-wide): 1.14MM **Privately Held**
SIC: 6531 Real estate brokers and agents
PA: Pitts & Bachmann Realtors Inc
1165 Coast Village Rd K
805 682-6415

(P-12506)
PITTS & BACHMANN REALTORS INC
1436 State St, Santa Barbara (93101-2512)
PHONE..............................805 963-1391
Patty Tunnicliffe, *Mgr*
EMP: 78
SALES (corp-wide): 1.14MM **Privately Held**
SIC: 6531 Real estate agent, residential
PA: Pitts & Bachmann Realtors Inc
1165 Coast Village Rd K
805 682-6415

(P-12507)
PREFERRED BROKERS INC (PA)
Also Called: Coldwell Banker
9100 Ming Ave Ste 100, Bakersfield (93311-1329)
PHONE..............................661 836-2345
John Mackessey, *Pr*

Gary Belter, *
EMP: 70 **EST:** 1990
SQ FT: 8,000
SALES (est): 2.48MM **Privately Held**
Web: www.coldwellbanker.com
SIC: 6531 Real estate agent, residential

(P-12508)
PRO GROUP INC
Also Called: Keller Williams Realtors
4160 Temescal Canyon Rd Ste 500, Corona
  (92883-4642)
PHONE.........................951 271-3000
James Brown, *Pr*
Jim Brown, *
David Clark, *
Joseph Regan, *
EMP: 195 **EST:** 2003
SQ FT: 18,000
SALES (est): 4.5MM **Privately Held**
Web: www.pgescrow.com
SIC: 6531 Real estate agent, residential

(P-12509)
PROFESSIONAL CMNTY MGT CAL INC
Also Called: P C M
850 Country Club Dr, Banning
  (92220-5306)
PHONE.........................951 845-2191
Mike Bennett, *Mgr*
EMP: 567
SALES (corp-wide): 17.24MM **Privately Held**
Web: www.pcminternet.com
SIC: 6531 Real estate managers
PA: Professional Community Management
Of California, Inc.
27051 Twne Cntre Dr Ste 2
800 369-7260

(P-12510)
PROFESSIONAL CMNTY MGT CAL INC
Also Called: Leisure World Resales
23522 Paseo De Valencia, Laguna Hills
(92653)
P.O. Box 2220 (92654-2220)
PHONE.........................949 597-4200
Gabrielle Velten, *Mgr*
EMP: 98
SALES (corp-wide): 17.24MM **Privately Held**
Web: www.pcminternet.com
SIC: 6531 Real estate managers
PA: Professional Community Management
Of California, Inc.
27051 Twne Cntre Dr Ste 2
800 369-7260

(P-12511)
PROFESSIONAL CMNTY MGT CAL INC
Also Called: Pcm
24351 El Toro Rd, Laguna Woods
(92637-4901)
PHONE.........................949 206-0580
Milt Johns, *Mgr*
EMP: 98
SALES (corp-wide): 17.24MM **Privately Held**
Web: www.pcminternet.com
SIC: 6531 Real estate managers
PA: Professional Community Management
Of California, Inc.
27051 Twne Cntre Dr Ste 2
800 369-7260

(P-12512)
PROLAND PROPERTY MANAGMENT LLC (PA)
Also Called: Hollingshead Management
2510 W 7th St 2nd Fl, Los Angeles
(90057-3802)
PHONE.........................213 738-8175
EMP: 80 **EST:** 1998
SQ FT: 5,000
SALES (est): 3.01MM
SALES (corp-wide): 3.01MM **Privately Held**
SIC: 6531 Real estate managers

(P-12513)
PROPERTY MANAGEMENT ASSOC INC (PA)
Also Called: Capital Commercial Property
6011 Bristol Pkwy, Culver City
(90230-6601)
PHONE.........................323 295-2000
Thomas Spear, *Pr*
Joshua Fein, *
Patrick Lacey, *
EMP: 130 **EST:** 1991
SQ FT: 6,500
SALES (est): 12.12MM **Privately Held**
Web: www.wemanageproperties.com
SIC: 6531 Real estate managers

(P-12514)
RA SNYDER PROPERTIES INC (PA)
2399 Camino Del Rio S Ste 200, San Diego
  (92108-3695)
PHONE.........................619 297-0274
Richard Snyder, *Pr*
Marietta Robinson, *
EMP: 210 **EST:** 1987
SQ FT: 2,400
SALES (est): 16.76MM
SALES (corp-wide): 16.76MM **Privately Held**
Web: www.rasnyder.com
SIC: 6531 Real estate managers

(P-12515)
RAD DIVERSIFIED REIT INC
3110 E Guasti Rd Ste 300, Ontario
(91761-1262)
PHONE.........................813 723-7348
Dutch Mendenhall, *CEO*
Taylor Green, *Prin*
EMP: 80 **EST:** 2017
SALES (est): 2.44MM **Privately Held**
SIC: 6531 Real estate agents and managers

(P-12516)
RE/MAX OF VALENCIA INC (PA)
Also Called: Re/Max
25101 The Old Rd, Santa Clarita
(91381-2206)
PHONE.........................661 255-2650
John O'hare, *Pr*
John Ohare, *Pr*
Alice O'hare, *VP*
EMP: 123 **EST:** 1985
SQ FT: 10,000
SALES (est): 1.48MM
SALES (corp-wide): 1.48MM **Privately Held**
Web: www.remax-valencia-ca.com
SIC: 6531 8742 Real estate agent, residential
  ; Real estate consultant

(P-12517)
REALSELECT INC
3063 W Chapman Ave Apt 6207, Orange
(92868-1758)

PHONE.........................661 803-5188
Ashley Ivey, *Brnch Mgr*
EMP: 151
SALES (corp-wide): 10.09B **Publicly Held**
Web: www.realtor.com
SIC: 6531 Real estate brokers and agents
HQ: Realselect, Inc.
3315 Scott Blvd Ste 250
Santa Clara CA 95054

(P-12518)
RED TAIL RESIDENTIAL LLC (PA)
2082 Michelson Dr Fl 4, Irvine
(92612-1212)
PHONE.........................949 399-2510
EMP: 70 **EST:** 2022
SALES (est): 23.62MM
SALES (corp-wide): 23.62MM **Privately Held**
Web: www.rtacq.com
SIC: 6531 Real estate agents and managers

(P-12519)
REMAX OLSON & ASSOCIATES INC
Also Called: Re/Max
11141 Tampa Ave, Northridge (91326-2254)
PHONE.........................818 366-3300
Todd C Olson, *CEO*
Keith Myers, *Ex VP*
EMP: 175 **EST:** 1987
SQ FT: 30,000
SALES (est): 5.55MM **Privately Held**
Web: www.maxoneproperties.com
SIC: 6531 Real estate agent, residential

(P-12520)
REMN INC
3400 Central Ave Ste 330, Riverside
(92506-2164)
PHONE.........................951 697-8135
EMP: 82
Web: www.homebridge.com
SIC: 6531 6211 Real estate agents and
  managers; Mortgages, buying and selling
PA: Remn , Inc
  194 Wood Ave S Fl 9

(P-12521)
REXFORD INDUS RLTY & MGT INC
11620 Wilshire Blvd Ste 300, Los Angeles
(90025-1769)
PHONE.........................310 966-1690
Howard Schwimmer, *CEO*
Michael S Frankel. *
Richard Ziman, *
EMP: 102 **EST:** 2010
SALES (est): 10.53K
SALES (corp-wide): 797.83MM **Privately Held**
Web: www.rexfordindustrial.com
SIC: 6531 8742 Real estate listing services;
  Real estate consultant
PA: Rexford Industrial Realty, Inc.
11620 Wlshire Blvd Ste 10
310 966-1680

(P-12522)
RGC SERVICES INC
Also Called: Re/Max
601 E Daily Dr Ste 102, Camarillo
(93010-5838)
PHONE.........................805 484-1600
Teresa Toomey, *Mgr*
EMP: 117
Web: www.remax.com

SIC: 6531 Real estate agent, residential
PA: Rgc Services, Inc.
5720 Ralston St Ste 100

(P-12523)
RGC SERVICES INC (PA)
Also Called: Re/Max
5720 Ralston St Ste 100, Ventura
(93003-7845)
PHONE.........................805 644-1242
Glenn Sipes, *Pr*
Michael Sipes, *
Jerry Beebe, *
EMP: 110 **EST:** 1994
SQ FT: 35,000
SALES (est): 24.56MM **Privately Held**
Web: www.remax.com
SIC: 6531 Real estate agent, residential

(P-12524)
RODEO REALTY INC (PA)
Also Called: Paramount Properties
9171 Wilshire Blvd Ste 321, Beverly Hills
(90210-5562)
PHONE.........................818 349-9997
Sydney Leibovitch, *CEO*
Linda Leibovitch, *
EMP: 76 **EST:** 1986
SQ FT: 5,000
SALES (est): 52.07MM **Privately Held**
Web: www.rodeore.com
SIC: 6531 Real estate agent, residential

(P-12525)
ROMAN CTHLIC BSHP OF SAN DIEGO
Also Called: Holy Cross Cemetary
4470 Hilltop Dr, San Diego (92102-3651)
PHONE.........................619 264-3127
Mario Deblasio, *Brnch Mgr*
EMP: 90
SALES (corp-wide): 48.57MM **Privately Held**
Web: www.holycrosssd.com
SIC: 6531 Cemetery management service
PA: The Roman Catholic Bishop Of San
  Diego
3888 Paducah Dr

(P-12526)
ROW MANAGEMENT LTD INC
499 N Canon Dr, Beverly Hills
(90210-4887)
PHONE.........................310 887-3671
Kevin Shahin, *Brnch Mgr*
EMP: 305
SALES (corp-wide): 38.02MM **Privately Held**
Web: www.aboardtheworld.com
SIC: 6531 Real estate agents and managers
PA: Row Management Ltd. Inc.
1551 Sawgrs Corp Pkwy
954 538-8400

(P-12527)
SATELLITE MANAGEMENT CO (PA)
Also Called: Ccts
1010 E Chestnut Ave, Santa Ana
(92701-6497)
PHONE.........................714 558-2411
Ronald Jensen, *CEO*
Mary E Conzelman, *
Helen M Jensen, *
EMP: 121 **EST:** 1963
SQ FT: 800
SALES (est): 21.42MM
SALES (corp-wide): 21.42MM **Privately Held**
Web: www.satellitemanagement.com

PRODUCTS & SVCS

SIC: 6531 Real estate managers

(P-12528)
SFT REALTY GALWAY DOWNS LLC
Also Called: Kentina
38801 Los Corralitos Rd, Temecula (92592-9055)
P.O. Box 4404 Jeremie Dr (92592)
PHONE..................................951 232-1880
Kenneth C Smith, *Managing Member*
EMP: 70 EST: 2013
SQ FT: 2,000
SALES (est): 2.82MM **Privately Held**
Web: www.galwaydowns.com
SIC: 6531 Real estate agents and managers

(P-12529)
SOUTHERN CAL PIPE TRADES ADM
Also Called: Marina Village
1936 Quivira Way Bldg G, San Diego (92109-8315)
PHONE..................................619 224-3125
Gerald Pharest, *Genl Mgr*
EMP: 92
SALES (corp-wide): 158.82MM **Privately Held**
Web: www.scptac.org
SIC: 6531 Real estate agents and managers
PA: Southern California Pipe Trades Administrative Corp
501 Shatto Pl Ste 500
213 385-6161

(P-12530)
SPUS7 125 CAMBRIDGEPARK LP
515 S Flower St Ste 3100, Los Angeles (90071-2233)
PHONE..................................213 683-4200
EMP: 74 EST: 2014
SALES (est): 868.96K **Publicly Held**
SIC: 6531 Real estate agent, commercial
HQ: Cbre Global Value Investors, Llc
601 S Figueroa St Ste 49
Los Angeles CA 90017
213 683-4200

(P-12531)
SPUS7 150 CAMBRIDGEPARK LP
515 S Flower St Ste 3100, Los Angeles (90071-2233)
PHONE..................................213 683-4200
EMP: 110 EST: 2014
SALES (est): 1.19MM **Publicly Held**
SIC: 6531 Real estate agent, commercial
HQ: Cbre Global Value Investors, Llc
601 S Figueroa St Ste 49
Los Angeles CA 90017
213 683-4200

(P-12532)
SRHT PROPERTY HOLDING LLC
Also Called: Skid Row Housing Trust
1317 E 7th St, Los Angeles (90021-1101)
PHONE..................................213 683-0522
Jerrick Holloway, *Dir*
EMP: 150 EST: 2005
SALES (est): 1.67MM **Privately Held**
Web: www.skidrow.org
SIC: 6531 Real estate managers

(P-12533)
STARPINT 1031 PROPERTY MGT LLC
Also Called: Vision Realty Managements

450 N Roxbury Dr Ste 1050, Beverly Hills (90210-4235)
PHONE..................................310 247-0550
EMP: 110 EST: 1997
SALES (est): 3.28MM **Privately Held**
Web: www.starpointproperties.com
SIC: 6531 Real estate agent, commercial

(P-12534)
STEADFAST MANAGEMENT CO INC (PA)
Also Called: Steadfast Companies
18100 Von Karman Ave Ste 500, Irvine (92612-0196)
PHONE..................................949 748-3000
Rodney F Emery, *CEO*
Dinesh K Davar, *
Michael Brown, *
EMP: 82 EST: 2000
SALES (est): 36.12MM
SALES (corp-wide): 36.12MM **Privately Held**
Web: www.steadfastliving.com
SIC: 6531 Real estate managers

(P-12535)
STRATEGIC PROPERTY MANAGEMENT
2055 3rd Ave Ste 200, San Diego (92101-2058)
PHONE..................................619 295-2211
Don Clausson, *Prin*
EMP: 75 EST: 2000
SALES (est): 2.43MM **Privately Held**
Web: www.stratprop.com
SIC: 6531 Real estate managers

(P-12536)
TEN-X FINANCE INC
Also Called: Ten-X
15295 Alton Pkwy, Irvine (92618-2315)
PHONE..................................949 465-8523
Steve Jacobs, *CEO*
EMP: 111 EST: 2013
SALES (est): 430.86K
SALES (corp-wide): 2.46B **Publicly Held**
SIC: 6531 Real estate agents and managers
HQ: Ten-X, Inc.
15295 Alton Pkwy
Irvine CA 92618
949 465-8523

(P-12537)
TERRA VISTA MANAGEMENT INC
Also Called: Terra Vista Management
2211 Pacific Beach Dr, San Diego (92109-5626)
PHONE..................................858 581-4200
Micheal Gelfand, *Brnch Mgr*
EMP: 459
SALES (corp-wide): 12.22MM **Privately Held**
Web: www.campland.com
SIC: 6531 7033 4225 4226 Real estate managers; Trailer parks and campsites; General warehousing and storage; Special warehousing and storage, nec
PA: Vista Terra Management Inc
445 Marine View Ave # 110
323 954-5900

(P-12538)
THOMAS JAMES HOMES LLC
26880 Aliso Viejo Pkwy Ste 200, Aliso Viejo (92656-2623)
PHONE..................................949 424-2356
EMP: 187 EST: 2019
SALES (est): 15.47MM **Privately Held**

Web: www.tjh.com
SIC: 6531 Real estate brokers and agents

(P-12539)
THOMAS PROPERTIES GROUP INC
515 S Flower St Ste 600, Los Angeles (90071-2241)
PHONE..................................213 613-1900
▲ EMP: 141
SIC: 6531 Real estate brokers and agents

(P-12540)
TRG INC
Also Called: Rosenthal Group, The
1350 Abbot Kinney Blvd # 101, Venice (90291-3893)
P.O. Box 837 (90294-0837)
PHONE..................................310 396-6750
EMP: 100
SALES (est): 3.32MM **Privately Held**
Web: www.trgnational.com
SIC: 6531 Real estate agents and managers

(P-12541)
TRIYAR SV LLC (PA)
10850 Wilshire Blvd Ste 1050, Los Angeles (90024-4326)
PHONE..................................310 234-2888
EMP: 300 EST: 2012
SALES (est): 20.05MM **Privately Held**
Web: www.triyar.com
SIC: 6531 Buying agent, real estate

(P-12542)
TROOP REAL ESTATE INC
4165 E Thousand Oaks Blvd Ste 100, Westlake Village (91362-3882)
PHONE..................................805 402-3028
Jeff Rosenblum, *Brnch Mgr*
EMP: 140
SALES (corp-wide): 7.58MM **Privately Held**
Web: www.karentroop.com
SIC: 6531 Real estate agent, residential
PA: Troop Real Estate, Inc.
1308 Madera Rd Ste 8
805 581-3200

(P-12543)
TROOP REAL ESTATE INC
586 W Main St, Santa Paula (93060-3209)
PHONE..................................805 921-0030
Brian Troop, *Owner*
EMP: 125
SALES (corp-wide): 7.58MM **Privately Held**
Web: www.karentroop.com
SIC: 6531 Real estate agent, residential
PA: Troop Real Estate, Inc.
1308 Madera Rd Ste 8
805 581-3200

(P-12544)
TROOP REAL ESTATE INC (PA)
1308 Madera Rd Ste 8, Simi Valley (93065-4044)
PHONE..................................805 581-3200
Brian C Troop, *CEO*
Laura Lee Anthony, *
Deborah Mccarthy, *COO*
EMP: 95 EST: 1987
SALES (est): 7.58MM
SALES (corp-wide): 7.58MM **Privately Held**
Web: www.karentroop.com
SIC: 6531 Real estate agent, residential

(P-12545)
US REAL ESTATE SERVICES INC
Also Called: Res.net
27442 Portola Pkwy Ste 300, Foothill Ranch (92610-2822)
PHONE..................................949 598-9920
Keith Guenther, *CEO*
Michael Bull, *
EMP: 90 EST: 1994
SQ FT: 37,000
SALES (est): 22.15MM **Privately Held**
Web: www.usres.com
SIC: 6531 Real estate brokers and agents

(P-12546)
V TROTH INC
Also Called: Berkshire Hthway Hmsrvces Trot
1801 W Avenue K Ste 101, Lancaster (93534-5999)
P.O. Box 2024 (93539-2024)
PHONE..................................661 948-4646
Debra K Anderson, *Pr*
Donald L Anderson, *
Mark A Troth, *
EMP: 75 EST: 1965
SALES (est): 1.77MM **Privately Held**
Web: www.bhhstroth.com
SIC: 6531 8742 Real estate agent, residential ; Real estate consultant

(P-12547)
WATT COMPANIES INC
1875 Century Park E, Los Angeles (90067-2253)
PHONE..................................310 789-2180
Jamie Bergantz, *Prin*
EMP: 73
SALES (corp-wide): 12.4MM **Privately Held**
Web: www.wattcompanies.com
SIC: 6531 8742 Real estate agent, commercial; General management consultant
PA: Watt Companies, Inc.
2716 Ocean Park Blvd # 20
310 314-2430

(P-12548)
WEST EDGE INC
Also Called: West Edge
1061 Tierra Del Rey, Chula Vista (91910-7880)
PHONE..................................619 475-4095
EMP: 88
Web: www.coldwellbankerwesthomes.com
SIC: 6531 Real estate agent, residential
PA: West Edge, Inc.
4538 Bonita Rd

(P-12549)
WESTERN NATIONAL SECURITIES (PA)
Also Called: Ramada By Wyndham
8 Executive Cir, Irvine (92614-6746)
P.O. Box 19528 (92623-9528)
PHONE..................................949 862-6200
Michael K Hayde, *CEO*
David Stone, *Ch*
Jeff Scott, *CFO*
James Gilly, *
Jerry Lapointe, *
EMP: 120 EST: 1981
SQ FT: 35,000
SALES (est): 223.07MM
SALES (corp-wide): 223.07MM **Privately Held**
Web: www.wng.com
SIC: 6531 7011 Real estate managers; Hotels and motels

(P-12550)
WHV RESORT GROUP INC (HQ)
Also Called: Welk Resort Center
300 Rancheros Dr Ste 310, San Marcos
(92069-2969)
PHONE.................................760 652-4913
Larry Welk, *CEO*
EMP: 89 EST: 1999
SALES (est): 93.71MM Publicly Held
Web: www.sonisrestaurant.com
SIC: 6531 6552 7992 7011 Time-sharing
real estate sales, leasing and rentals;
Subdividers and developers, nec; Public
golf courses; Hotels and motels
PA: Marriott Vacations Worldwide
Corporation
7812 Palm Pkwy

(P-12551)
WOODMAN REALTY INC
Also Called: Sierra Springs Apartments
26030 Base Line St Apt 97, San Bernardino
(92410-7066)
PHONE.................................909 425-5324
Kelly Fox, *Mgr*
EMP: 223
SIC: 6531 Real estate agent, commercial
HQ: Woodman Realty Inc.
2016 Riverside Dr
Los Angeles CA 90039

(P-12552)
YLOPO LLC
4712 Admiralty Way 548, Marina Del Rey
(90292-6905)
PHONE.................................818 915-9150
Howard Tager, *CEO*
EMP: 147 EST: 2014
SALES (est): 14.31MM Privately Held
Web: www.ylopo.com
SIC: 6531 Real estate agents and managers

6541 Title Abstract Offices

(P-12553)
ANYWHERE INTEGRATED SVCS LLC
801 N Brand Blvd, Glendale (91203-1237)
PHONE.................................818 291-4400
EMP: 398
Web: www.anywhereis.re
SIC: 6541 Title and trust companies
HQ: Anywhere Integrated Services Llc
1000 Bishops Gate Ste 100
Mount Laurel NJ 08054

(P-12554)
COMMONWEALTH LAND TITLE INSUR
Also Called: Commonwealth Land Title
6 Executive Cir Ste 100, Irvine
(92614-6732)
PHONE.................................949 460-4500
Carl Brown, *CEO*
EMP: 103
Web: www.cwtitle.com
SIC: 6541 Title and trust companies
HQ: Commonwealth Land Title Corporation
201 Cncourse Blvd Ste 200
Glen Allen VA 23059
904 854-8100

(P-12555)
COMMONWEALTH LAND TITLE INSUR
Also Called: Commonwealth Land Title
41637 Margarita Rd Ste 101, Temecula
(92591-2990)

PHONE.................................951 296-6289
Linda Delaney, *Mgr*
EMP: 103
Web: www.cwtitle.com
SIC: 6541 Title and trust companies
HQ: Commonwealth Land Title Corporation
201 Cncourse Blvd Ste 200
Glen Allen VA 23059
904 854-8100

(P-12556)
EQUITY TITLE COMPANY (DH)
801 N Brand Blvd Ste 400, Glendale
(91203-3261)
PHONE.................................818 291-4400
TOLL FREE: 800
Jim Cossell, *Pr*
EMP: 80 EST: 1979
SALES (est): 2.44MM Publicly Held
Web: www.equitytitle.com
SIC: 6541 Title and trust companies
HQ: Anywhere Integrated Services Llc
1000 Bishops Gate Ste 100
Mount Laurel NJ 08054

(P-12557)
FIDELITY NAT TITLE INSUR CO NY
Also Called: Fidelity National
950 Hampshire Rd, Westlake Village
(91361-2805)
PHONE.................................805 370-1400
EMP: 1382
Web: www.fidelitytitleny.com
SIC: 6541 Title and trust companies
HQ: Fidelity National Title Insurance Co Of
New York
1 Pak Ave Ste 1402
New York NY 10016
904 854-8100

(P-12558)
FIRST AMERICAN TITLE COMPANY
1 First American Way, Santa Ana
(92707-5913)
PHONE.................................714 250-3109
James Boxdell, *VP*
EMP: 6000 EST: 1964
SALES (est): 5.69MM Privately Held
Web: www.firstam.com
SIC: 6541 Title and trust companies

(P-12559)
GREENHEDGE ESCROW
2015 Manhattan Beach Blvd, Redondo
Beach (90278-1226)
PHONE.................................310 640-3040
David Wehrly, *Prin*
EMP: 206 EST: 2016
SALES (est): 565.61K
SALES (corp-wide): 42.58MM Privately
Held
Web: www.greenhedgeescrow.com
SIC: 6541 Title and trust companies
PA: Wedgewood Inc.
2015 Manhattan Beach Blvd # 102
310 640-3070

(P-12560)
GUARDIAN TITLE COMPANY
300 Commerce, Irvine (92602-1308)
PHONE.................................949 495-9306
E Neil Gulley, *CEO*
James Kozel, *
Gregory Blackburn, *
EMP: 100 EST: 1975
SALES (est): 1.14MM Publicly Held
Web: www.equitytitle.com

SIC: 6541 Title and trust companies
HQ: Nrt Commercial Utah Llc
175 Park Ave
Madison NJ 07940

(P-12561)
PROPERTY INSIGHT LLC
2510 Redhill Ave, Santa Ana (92705-5542)
PHONE.................................877 747-2537
John Walsh, *Managing Member*
Ron Sree, *
EMP: 4186 EST: 2004
SALES (est): 444.02K
SALES (corp-wide): 7.99B Publicly Held
Web: www.propertyinsight.biz
SIC: 6541 Title search companies
HQ: Black Knight Real Estate Data
Solutions, Llc
121 Theory Ste 100
Irvine CA 92617
626 808-9000

(P-12562)
STEWART TITLE CALIFORNIA INC
525 N Brand Blvd Ste 200, Glendale
(91203-3993)
PHONE.................................818 502-2700
Steve Lessack, *Group President*
EMP: 125
SALES (corp-wide): 2.26B Publicly Held
Web: www.stewart.com
SIC: 6541 Title and trust companies
HQ: Stewart Title Of California, Inc.
7676 Hazard Center Dr # 1400
San Diego CA 92108
619 692-1600

(P-12563)
WFG NATIONAL TITLE INSUR CO (PA)
Also Called: Alliance Title
700 N Brand Blvd Ste 1100, Glendale
(91203-1208)
PHONE.................................818 476-4000
Jeffrey Fox, *CEO*
Roberto Olivera, *
Art Cheyne, *
Rhio H Weir, *
James Lokay, *
EMP: 75 EST: 1980
SQ FT: 15,000
SALES (est): 17.31MM
SALES (corp-wide): 17.31MM Privately
Held
Web: www.wfgtitle.com
SIC: 6541 Title and trust companies

6552 Subdividers And Developers, Nec

(P-12564)
ARCHIPELAGO DEVELOPMENT INC
P.O. Box 7050 (92067-7050)
PHONE.................................858 699-6272
Mark Edward Benjamin, *CEO*
EMP: 100 EST: 2008
SALES (est): 357.35K Privately Held
SIC: 6552 Subdividers and developers, nec

(P-12565)
CENTURY PACIFIC REALTY CORP
10345 W Olympic Blvd, Los Angeles
(90064-2524)
PHONE.................................310 729-9922
Irwin J Deutch, *Pr*

Charles L Schwennessen, *
Eric Maman, *
EMP: 250 EST: 1987
SQ FT: 3,500
SALES (est): 890.98K Privately Held
SIC: 6552 Subdividers and developers, nec

(P-12566)
GOLDRICH & KEST INDUSTRIES LLC (PA)
5150 Overland Ave, Culver City
(90230-4914)
P.O. Box 3623 (90231-3623)
PHONE.................................310 204-2050
EMP: 750 EST: 1957
SQ FT: 5,000
SALES (est): 9.51MM
SALES (corp-wide): 9.51MM Privately
Held
Web: www.goldrichkest.com
SIC: 6552 Subdividers and developers, nec

(P-12567)
GOLDRICH KEST HIRSCH STERN LLC (PA)
5150 Overland Ave, Culver City
(90230-4914)
P.O. Box 3623 (90231-3623)
PHONE.................................310 204-2050
Jona Goldrich, *Pr*
Sol Kest, *
EMP: 250 EST: 1963
SQ FT: 5,000
SALES (est): 15.82MM
SALES (corp-wide): 15.82MM Privately
Held
Web: www.goldrichkest.com
SIC: 6552 Land subdividers and developers,
commercial

(P-12568)
KING VENTURES
285 Bridge St, San Luis Obispo
(93401-5510)
PHONE.................................805 544-4444
John E King, *Owner*
EMP: 126 EST: 1977
SQ FT: 10,000
SALES (est): 1.56MM Privately Held
Web: www.kingventures.net
SIC: 6552 6512 Land subdividers and
developers, commercial; Commercial and
industrial building operation

(P-12569)
LEWIS GROUP OF COMPANIES
1156 N Mountain Ave, Upland (91785)
P.O. Box 670 (91785-0670)
PHONE.................................909 985-0971
EMP: 445 EST: 2015
SALES (est): 9.47MM Privately Held
Web: www.lewisgroupofcompanies.com
SIC: 6552 Subdividers and developers, nec

(P-12570)
LOWE ENTERPRISES RE GROUP
Also Called: Lowe Enterprises
11777 San Vicente Blvd Ste 900, Los
Angeles (90049-5084)
PHONE.................................310 820-6661
Bob Lowe, *Pr*
EMP: 403 EST: 1994
SQ FT: 10,000
SALES (est): 706.39K
SALES (corp-wide): 367.25MM Privately
Held
Web: www.lowe-re.com
SIC: 6552 6531 Land subdividers and
developers, commercial; Real estate
managers

PA: Lowe Enterprises, Inc.
11777 San Vcnte Blvd Ste
310 820-6661

(P-12571)
LPC COMMERCIAL SERVICES INC
Also Called: LPC COMMERCIAL SERVICES, INC.
915 Wilshire Blvd Ste 250, Los Angeles (90017-3409)
PHONE..............................213 362-9080
David Binswangar, *Brnch Mgr*
EMP: 159
SALES (corp-wide): 1.32B **Privately Held**
Web: www.lpc.com
SIC: 6552 6531 Land subdividers and developers, commercial; Real estate brokers and agents
HQ: Lpc Commercial Services Llc
2000 Mckinney Ave # 1000
Dallas TX 75201

(P-12572)
MAKAR PROPERTIES LLC (PA)
Also Called: Makallon La Jolla Properties
4100 Macarthur Blvd Ste 150, Newport Beach (92660-2063)
P.O. Box 7080 (92658-7080)
PHONE..............................949 255-1100
Paul P Makarechian, *CEO*
Peter Ciaccia, *Pr*
EMP: 75 EST: 2001
SALES (est): 11.52MM
SALES (corp-wide): 11.52MM **Privately Held**
Web: www.makarproperties.com
SIC: 6552 1542 Land subdividers and developers, commercial; Commercial and office building, new construction

(P-12573)
NATIONAL CMNTY RENAISSANCE CAL (PA)
9692 Haven Ave Ste 100, Rancho Cucamonga (91730-0101)
PHONE..............................909 483-2444
Steven J Pontell, *CEO*
Sebastiano Sterpa, *
Orlando Cabrera, *
Tracy Thomas, *
Doretta Bryan, *
EMP: 100 EST: 1992
SALES (est): 17.55MM **Privately Held**
Web: www.nationalcore.org
SIC: 6552 Subdividers and developers, nec

(P-12574)
NATIONAL CMNTY RENAISSANCE CAL
8265 Aspen St Ste 100, Rancho Cucamonga (91730-3291)
PHONE..............................619 223-9222
Rebecca Clark, *Mgr*
EMP: 231
Web: www.nationalcore.org
SIC: 6552 Subdividers and developers, nec
PA: National Community Renaissance Of California
9692 Haven Ave

(P-12575)
OLSON COMPANY LLC (PA)
Also Called: Olson Homes
3010 Old Ranch Pkwy Ste 100, Seal Beach (90740-2750)
PHONE..............................562 596-4770
EMP: 99 EST: 2014
SALES (est): 24.12MM

SALES (corp-wide): 24.12MM **Privately Held**
Web: www.olsonhomes.com
SIC: 6552 Subdividers and developers, nec

(P-12576)
PANATTONI DEVELOPMENT CO INC (PA)
2442 Dupont Dr, Irvine (92612-1523)
PHONE..............................916 381-1561
Carl Panattoni, *Ch*
Dudley Mitchell, *
Jacklyn Shelby, *
Greg Thurman, *
Adon Panattoni, *
EMP: 90 EST: 1986
SALES (est): 25.53MM
SALES (corp-wide): 25.53MM **Privately Held**
Web: www.panattoni.com
SIC: 6552 Subdividers and developers, nec

(P-12577)
PORTSMOUTH SQUARE INC
Also Called: INTERGROUP
1516 S Bundy Dr Ste 200, Los Angeles (90025-6650)
PHONE..............................310 889-2500
John V Winfield, *Ch Bd*
David C Gonzalez, *Pr*
Jolie Kahn, *Sec*
Ann Marie Blair, *Treas*
EMP: 187 EST: 1967
SALES (est): 41.89MM
SALES (corp-wide): 58.14MM **Publicly Held**
Web: www.intergroupcorporation.com
SIC: 6552 7011 Subdividers and developers, nec; Hotels
PA: The Intergroup Corporation
1516 S Bundy Dr Ste 200
310 889-2500

(P-12578)
SHAPELL INDUSTRIES LLC (HQ)
Also Called: S & S Construction Co
8383 Wilshire Blvd Ste 700, Beverly Hills (90211-2407)
PHONE..............................323 655-7330
EMP: 100 EST: 1955
SQ FT: 25,000
SALES (est): 7.95MM
SALES (corp-wide): 9.99B **Publicly Held**
SIC: 6552 6514 1522 Land subdividers and developers, residential; Residential building, four or fewer units: operation; Residential construction, nec
PA: Toll Brothers, Inc.
1140 Virginia Dr
215 938-8000

(P-12579)
SILVER SADDLE RANCH & CLUB INC
Also Called: McQ
7635 N San Fernando Rd, Burbank (91505-1073)
PHONE..............................818 768-8808
Thomas Maney, *Pr*
Justin Child, *
Terry Hansen, *Stockholder*
EMP: 100 EST: 1986
SQ FT: 5,500
SALES (est): 937.79K **Privately Held**
SIC: 6552 7041 Land subdividers and developers, residential; Residence club, organization

(P-12580)
STEELWAVE LLC
4553 Glencoe Ave Ste 300, Marina Del Rey (90292-7914)
PHONE..............................310 821-1111
EMP: 578
SALES (corp-wide): 6.71MM **Privately Held**
Web: www.steelwavellc.com
SIC: 6552 Land subdividers and developers, commercial
PA: Steelwave, Llc
999 Baker Way Ste 200
650 571-2200

(P-12581)
TAYLOR MORRISON CALIFORNIA LLC
100 Spectrum Center Dr Ste 1450, Irvine (92618-4984)
PHONE..............................949 341-1200
Stephen J Wethor, *Mgr*
EMP: 108 EST: 2008
SALES (est): 5.1MM
SALES (corp-wide): 7.42B **Publicly Held**
SIC: 6552 Land subdividers and developers, residential
HQ: Taylor Morrison Home Ii Corporation
4900 N Scottsdale Rd # 2
Scottsdale AZ 85251
480 840-8100

(P-12582)
WEBB DEL CALIFORNIA CORP (DH)
39755 Berkey Dr, Palm Desert (92211-1106)
PHONE..............................760 772-5300
Nancy E Abbott, *Prin*
EMP: 300 EST: 1965
SQ FT: 14,000
SALES (est): 601.22K
SALES (corp-wide): 16.06B **Publicly Held**
SIC: 6552 Subdividers and developers, nec
HQ: Pulte Home Company, Llc
3350 Peachtree Rd Ne # 15
Atlanta GA 30326
248 647-2750

6553 Cemetery Subdividers And Developers

(P-12583)
FOREST LAWN CO
1712 S Glendale Ave, Glendale (91205-3320)
PHONE..............................818 241-4151
John Llewellyn, *Pr*
EMP: 150 EST: 1906
SQ FT: 50,000
SALES (est): 6.2MM **Privately Held**
Web: www.forestlawn.com
SIC: 6553 Real property subdividers and developers, cemetery lots only

(P-12584)
INGLEWOOD PARK CEMETERY (PA)
720 E Florence Ave, Inglewood (90301-1482)
P.O. Box 6042 (90312-6042)
PHONE..............................310 412-6500
Daniel Villa, *Pr*
Cheryl Lewis, *
David Wharmby, *
Kevin Brown, *
Chris Winners, *
EMP: 152 EST: 1905

SQ FT: 14,000
SALES (est): 19.11MM
SALES (corp-wide): 19.11MM **Privately Held**
Web: www.inglewoodparkcemetery.com
SIC: 6553 Cemeteries, real estate operation

(P-12585)
OAKDALE MEMORIAL PARK (PA)
1401 S Grand Ave, Glendora (91740-5406)
PHONE..............................626 335-0281
Genny Delgado, *Mgr*
Genny Delgado, *Genl Mgr*
EMP: 75 EST: 1890
SQ FT: 10,000
SALES (est): 897.33K
SALES (corp-wide): 897.33K **Privately Held**
Web: www.oakdalemortuaryglendora.com
SIC: 6553 Cemeteries, real estate operation

(P-12586)
ROMAN CTHLIC DIOCESE OF ORANGE
Also Called: Good Shepherd Cemetery
8301 Talbert Ave, Huntington Beach (92646-1546)
PHONE..............................714 847-8546
Lupe Ramirez, *Mgr*
EMP: 84
SALES (corp-wide): 41.41MM **Privately Held**
Web: www.occem.org
SIC: 6553 Cemeteries, real estate operation
PA: The Roman Catholic Diocese Of Orange
13280 Chapman Ave
714 282-3000

(P-12587)
ROMAN CTHLIC DIOCESE OF ORANGE
Also Called: Holy Sepulcher Cemetery
7845 E Santiago Canyon Rd, Orange (92869-1830)
PHONE..............................714 532-6551
Mike Wessner, *Dir*
EMP: 126
SALES (corp-wide): 41.41MM **Privately Held**
Web: www.occem.org
SIC: 6553 Cemeteries, real estate operation
PA: The Roman Catholic Diocese Of Orange
13280 Chapman Ave
714 282-3000

(P-12588)
ROSE HILLS COMPANY (DH)
Also Called: Rose Hills Mem Pk & Mortuary
3888 Workman Mill Rd, Whittier (90601-1626)
PHONE..............................562 699-0921
TOLL FREE: 800
Dennis Poulsen, *Ch Bd*
Kenton Woods, *
Mary Guzman, *
EMP: 595 EST: 1996
SQ FT: 143,950
SALES (est): 33.3MM
SALES (corp-wide): 4.1B **Publicly Held**
Web: www.rosehills.com
SIC: 6553 Real property subdividers and developers, cemetery lots only
HQ: Rose Hills Holdings Corp.
3888 Workman Mill Rd
Whittier CA 90601
562 699-0921

(P-12589)
ROSE HILLS HOLDINGS CORP (HQ)
Also Called: Rose Hills Mem Pk & Mortuary
3888 Workman Mill Rd, Whittier
(90601-1626)
PHONE..............................562 699-0921
Pat Monroe, *CEO*
EMP: 500 **EST:** 1996
SQ FT: 143,950
SALES (est): 33.3MM
SALES (corp-wide): 4.1B **Publicly Held**
Web: www.rosehills.com
SIC: 6553 Cemeteries, real estate operation
PA: Service Corporation International
1929 Allen Pkwy
713 522-5141

6712 Bank Holding Companies

(P-12590)
BANAMEX USA BANCORP (DH)
787 W 5th St, Los Angeles (90071-2003)
PHONE..............................310 203-3440
Salvador Villar Junior, *Pr*
Francisco Moreno Senior, *VP*
▲ **EMP:** 210 **EST:** 1977
SALES (est): 2.75MM
SALES (corp-wide): 156.82B **Publicly Held**
Web: www.citigroup.com
SIC: 6712 6029 6022 Bank holding companies; Commercial banks, nec; State commercial banks
HQ: Banco Nacional De Mexico, S.A., Integrante Del Grupo Financiero Banamex
Isabel La Catolica No. 44
Mexico CMX 06000

6719 Holding Companies, Nec

(P-12591)
ALDON INC
1333 E 223rd St, Carson (90745-4314)
▲ **EMP:** 75 **EST:** 1974
SQ FT: 10,000
Web: www.toyota.com
SIC: 6719 Investment holding companies, except banks

(P-12592)
AME-GYU CO LTD
20000 Mariner Ave Ste 500, Torrance
(90503-1670)
PHONE..............................310 214-9572
Ryo Tozu, *CEO*
Hidokazu Soo, *
Hiratsugu Aiba, *
EMP: 1100 **EST:** 2016
SIC: 6719 5812 Investment holding companies, except banks; Japanese restaurant

(P-12593)
AMERICAN ACADEMIC HLTH SYS LLC
222 N Pacific Coast Hwy Ste 900, El Segundo (90245-5670)
PHONE..............................310 414-7200
EMP: 2850 **EST:** 2017
Web: www.paladinhealthcare.com
SIC: 6719 8062 Investment holding companies, except banks; General medical and surgical hospitals

(P-12594)
ASP HENRY HOLDINGS INC
999 N Pacific Coast Hwy Ste 800, El Segundo (90245-2716)
PHONE..............................310 955-9200
Frank Ready, *CEO*
EMP: 600 **EST:** 2016
SALES (corp-wide): 4.59B **Publicly Held**
SIC: 6719 2952 Investment holding companies, except banks; Roof cement: asphalt, fibrous, or plastic
PA: Carlisle Companies Incorporated
16430 N Scttsdale Rd Ste
480 781-5000

(P-12595)
BETHAR CORPORATION
17625 Railroad St, City Of Industry
(91748-1110)
P.O. Box 8445 (91748-0445)
▲ **EMP:** 180 **EST:** 1945
SQ FT: 80,000
SIC: 6719 Investment holding companies, except banks

(P-12596)
CCC PROPERTY HOLDINGS LLC
Also Called: Contractors Cargo Company
7223 Alondra Blvd, Paramount
(90723-3901)
P.O. Box 5290 (90224-5290)
PHONE..............................310 609-1957
Gerald Wheeler, *Ch Bd*
Kim Dorio, *
Carla Ann Wheeler, *
Jerry Wheeler, *
EMP: 121 **EST:** 2009
SIC: 6719 Investment holding companies, except banks

(P-12597)
DESSER HOLDING COMPANY LLC (HQ)
Also Called: Desser Tire & Rubber Co.
6900 W Acco St, Montebello (90640-5435)
P.O. Box 1028 (90640-1028)
PHONE..............................323 721-4900
Christopher Lawler, *Ch*
Steven D Chlavin, *
Joseph Heinmiller, *
EMP: 30 **EST:** 2014
SALES (est): 40.92MM
SALES (corp-wide): 860.49MM **Publicly Held**
Web: www.desser.com
SIC: 6719 3011 3691 Investment holding companies, except banks; Airplane tires, pneumatic; Batteries, rechargeable
PA: Vse Corporation
3361 Enterprise Way
950 430-6600

(P-12598)
FORTRESS HOLDING GROUP LLC
5500 E Santa Ana Canyon Rd Ste 220, Anaheim (92807-3139)
PHONE..............................714 202-8710
Luis Perez, *Ch*
Adam Forbs, *Pr*
EMP: 90 **EST:** 2009
SIC: 6719 Investment holding companies, except banks

(P-12599)
GATEWAY FRESH LLC
Also Called: Baja Fresh
3660 Grand Ave Ste A, Chino Hills
(91709-1477)

P.O. Box 1456 (91709-0049)
PHONE..............................951 378-5439
FAX: 909 548-6602
EMP: 190
SQ FT: 5,000
SIC: 6719 Investment holding companies, except banks

(P-12600)
GH GROUP INC
Also Called: Glass House Group
3645 Long Beach Blvd, Long Beach
(90807-4018)
PHONE..............................562 264-5078
Kyle Kazan, *CEO*
Graham Farrar, *
Daryl Kato, *
Derrek Higgins, *
EMP: 250 **EST:** 2006
Web: www.glasshousebrands.com
SIC: 6719 Investment holding companies, except banks

(P-12601)
HCO HOLDING I CORPORATION (HQ)
999 N Pacific Coast Hwy Ste 800, El Segundo (90245-2716)
PHONE..............................323 583-5000
Mike Kenny, *
Brian C Strauss, *Parent Chief Executive Officer*
Dori M Reap, *
James F Barry, *
Robert D Armstrong, *Senior Vice President Human Resources*
◆ **EMP:** 100 **EST:** 2005
SALES (est): 249.72MM
SALES (corp-wide): 249.72MM **Privately Held**
SIC: 6719 Investment holding companies, except banks
PA: Hnc Parent, Inc.
999 N Splveda Blvd Ste 80
310 955-9200

(P-12602)
HIRSCH3667 CORP
5700 Hannum Ave Ste 250, Culver City
(90230-6548)
PHONE..............................310 641-6690
EMP: 140
SIC: 6719 Investment holding companies, except banks

(P-12603)
MLIM HOLDINGS LLC
350 Camino De La Reina, San Diego
(92108-3007)
PHONE..............................619 299-3131
Douglas Manchester, *Ch*
John Lynch, *Vice Chairman*
EMP: 768 **EST:** 2011
SIC: 6719 Investment holding companies, except banks

(P-12604)
MPI LIMITED INC
1901 E Cooley Dr, Colton (92324-6322)
▲ **EMP:** 100 **EST:** 1977
SQ FT: 33,000
Web: www.microdyneplastics.com
SIC: 6719 Investment holding companies, except banks

(P-12605)
N2 ACQUISITION COMPANY INC
Also Called: N2 Imaging Systems
14440 Myford Rd, Irvine (92606-1001)
PHONE..............................714 942-3563

Tony Bacarella, *CEO*
Timothy Boyle, *CEO*
EMP: 92 **EST:** 2019
SIC: 6719 Investment holding companies, except banks

(P-12606)
NRP HOLDING CO INC (PA)
1 Mauchly, Irvine (92618-2305)
PHONE..............................949 583-1000
Jeffrey P Frieden, *Pr*
Robert Friedman, *
EMP: 200 **EST:** 2003
SQ FT: 40,000
SALES (est): 44.87MM **Privately Held**
Web: www.auction.com
SIC: 6719 Investment holding companies, except banks

(P-12607)
PLATINUM GROUP COMPANIES INC (PA)
Also Called: Top Finance Company
22560 La Quilla Dr, Chatsworth
(91311-1221)
P.O. Box 280518 (91328-0518)
PHONE..............................818 721-3800
David Mandel, *CEO*
Sandy To, *
EMP: 125 **EST:** 2005
SQ FT: 20,000
SALES (est): 8.15MM **Privately Held**
SIC: 6719 Personal holding companies, except banks

(P-12608)
PROJECT SKYLINE INTRMDATE HLDG
360 N Crescent Dr Bldg S, Beverly Hills
(90210-2529)
PHONE..............................310 712-1850
Tom Gores, *Pr*
EMP: 2020 **EST:** 2009
SALES (est): 555K **Privately Held**
SIC: 6719 Investment holding companies, except banks

(P-12609)
PROSPECT MORTGAGE LLC
EMP: 1700 **EST:** 1999
SIC: 6719 Investment holding companies, except banks

(P-12610)
RON RICK HOLDINGS MONTANA LLC
80795 Vista Bonita Trl, La Quinta
(92253-7525)
PHONE..............................406 493-5606
Rick Kerscher, *Pr*
Rick Kerscherm, *Pr*
EMP: 100 **EST:** 2007
SQ FT: 7,000
SIC: 6719 Personal holding companies, except banks

(P-12611)
RSG GROUP USA INC
Also Called: Gold's Gym
7007 Romaine St Ste 101, West Hollywood
(90038-2439)
PHONE..............................214 574-4653
Sebastian Schoepe, *CEO*
EMP: 2000 **EST:** 2020
SALES (corp-wide): 242.12K **Privately Held**
Web: www.goldsgym.com

PRODUCTS & SVCS

SIC: **6719** 7991 Investment holding companies, except banks; Physical fitness facilities
HQ: Rsg Group Gmbh
  Tannenberg 4
  Schlusselfeld BY 96132
  308 379-5500

(P-12612)
SABAN CAPITAL GROUP LLC
11301 W Olympic Blvd Ste 121601, Los Angeles (90064-1653)
PHONE............................310 557-5100
Adam Chesnoss, *COO*
Adam Chesnonss, *COO*
Haim Saban, *Ch*
EMP: 70 EST: 2003
Web: www.saban.com
SIC: **6719** Holding companies, nec

(P-12613)
SHRYNE GROUP INC
728 E Commercial St, Los Angeles (90012-3412)
PHONE............................323 614-4558
Jon Avidor, *CEO*
Tak Sato, *
Elisabeth Baron, *CMO**
John Malone, *
Cary Berger, *CLO**
EMP: 2500 EST: 2019
Web: www.shrynegroup.com
SIC: **6719** Holding companies, nec

(P-12614)
SKEFFINGTON ENTERPRISES INC
2200 S Yale St, Santa Ana (92704-4404)
PHONE............................714 540-1700
William J Skeffington, *Pr*
John Skeffington, *
EMP: 100 EST: 1951
SQ FT: 180,000
Web: www.bensasphalt.com
SIC: **6719** Personal holding companies, except banks

(P-12615)
STANTEC HOLDINGS DEL III INC
Also Called: Stantec Oil and Gas
5500 Ming Ave Ste 300, Bakersfield (93309-4627)
PHONE............................661 396-3770
Robert Gomes, *Pr*
EMP: 460 EST: 2005
SALES (corp-wide): 4.72B **Privately Held**
SIC: **6719** Investment holding companies, except banks
PA: Stantec Inc
  300-10220 103 Ave Nw
  780 917-7000

(P-12616)
SWDS HOLDINGS INC
Also Called: Swds
8659 Research Dr, Irvine (92618-4204)
PHONE............................800 395-5277
Vernon Leake, *CEO*
Michael Okada, *
Aaron Lodge, *
Jill Zack, *
EMP: 317 EST: 1987
Web: www.acrisurepg.com
SIC: **6719** Holding companies, nec

(P-12617)
TRANSOM POST MIDCO LLC
100 N Pacific Coast Hwy # 17, El Segundo (90245-5612)
PHONE............................312 254-3300

Russell Roenick, *Managing Member*
EMP: 200 EST: 2022
SIC: **6719** Personal holding companies, except banks

(P-12618)
TYDG ENTERPRISES INC
10232 Palm Dr, Santa Fe Springs (90670-3368)
PHONE............................562 903-9030
Michael Rashtchi, *CEO*
George Abi-aad, *Pr*
Marianne Abi-aad, *Ex VP*
Johnathan Soon, *
▲ EMP: 95 EST: 1985
SQ FT: 65,000
Web: www.royalcorporation.com
SIC: **6719** Investment holding companies, except banks

(P-12619)
W-GL 1241 OCBC HLDINGS VIII LP
18301 Von Karman Ave Ste 250, Irvine (92612-0106)
PHONE............................949 331-1323
Kari Blevins, *Pt*
Wilbur H Smith Iii, *Pt*
EMP: 80 EST: 2018
SIC: **6719** Holding companies, nec

(P-12620)
WILBUR CURTIS CO INC
6913 W Acco St, Montebello (90640-5403)
PHONE............................800 421-6150
Ray Peden, *CEO*
Michael A Curtis, *Ex VP*
Norman Fujitaki, *CFO*
Joe Laws, *COO*
Shubham Kumar, *Finance*
◆ EMP: 280 EST: 1941
SQ FT: 175,000
SALES (corp-wide): 2.67MM **Privately Held**
Web: www.wilburcurtis.com
SIC: **6719** 3589 Investment holding companies, except banks; Coffee brewing equipment
HQ: Groupe Seb Retailing
  112 Che Du Moulin Carron
  Ecully ARA 69130

(P-12621)
YF ART HOLDINGS GP LLC
9130 W Sunset Blvd, Los Angeles (90069-3110)
PHONE............................678 441-1400
Fred Boehler, *Pr*
EMP: 10600 EST: 2014
SIC: **6719** Investment holding companies, except banks

(P-12622)
YUCAIPA COMPANIES LLC (PA)
9130 W Sunset Blvd, Los Angeles (90069-3110)
PHONE............................310 789-7200
Ronald W Burkle, *Managing Member*
Scott Stedman, *
EMP: 150 EST: 1986
SALES (est): 247.94MM
SALES (corp-wide): 247.94MM **Privately Held**
Web: www.yucaipaco.com
SIC: **6719** 6726 5411 Investment holding companies, except banks; Investment offices, nec; Grocery stores, chain

---

6722 Management Investment, Open-ended

(P-12623)
ABSOLUTE RETURN PORTFOLIO
700 Newport Center Dr, Newport Beach (92660-6307)
P.O. Box 9000 (92658-9030)
PHONE............................800 800-7646
EMP: 1306 EST: 2015
SALES (est): 818.51K
SALES (corp-wide): 12.84B **Privately Held**
SIC: **6722** Money market mutual funds
HQ: Pacific Life Fund Advisors Llc
  700 Newport Center Drive
  Newport Beach CA 92660

(P-12624)
ALLIANCEBERNSTEIN LP
Also Called: Bernstein
1999 Avenue Of The Stars Ste 2150, Los Angeles (90067-6059)
PHONE............................310 286-6000
Alan D Croll, *Brnch Mgr*
EMP: 123
SALES (corp-wide): 10.53B **Publicly Held**
Web: www.alliancebernstein.com
SIC: **6722** Money market mutual funds
HQ: Alliancebernstein L.P.
  501 Commerce St
  Nashville TN 37203
  212 969-1000

(P-12625)
ALTURA HOLDINGS LLC
1335 S Acacia Ave, Fullerton (92831-5315)
PHONE............................714 948-8400
Robert Blazek, *CEO*
Karen Frankenberg, *CFO*
EMP: 300 EST: 2011
SALES (est): 3.28MM **Privately Held**
Web: www.alturacs.com
SIC: **6722** Management investment, open-end
PA: Silver Oak Services Partners, Llc
  1560 Sherman Ave Ste 1200

(P-12626)
AMERICAN FUNDS DISTRS INC (DH)
333 S Hope St Ste Levb, Los Angeles (90071-3003)
PHONE............................213 486-9200
Michael Johnston, *Ch Bd*
Larry Clemmensen, *
J Kelly Webb, *
Dorine Darnell, *
▲ EMP: 116 EST: 1972
SQ FT: 6,000
SALES (est): 1.01B
SALES (corp-wide): 7.25B **Privately Held**
Web: www.capitalgroup.com
SIC: **6722** Mutual fund sales, on own account
HQ: Capital Research And Management Company
  333 S Hope St Fl 55
  Los Angeles CA 90071
  213 486-9200

(P-12627)
AMERICAN MUTUAL FUND
333 S Hope St Fl 51, Los Angeles (90071-1420)
PHONE............................213 486-9200
Jonathan B Lovelace Junior, *Ch Bd*
James K Dunton, *
James W Ratzlaff, *

Robert G O'donnell, *Pr*
Joyce Gordon, *
EMP: 200 EST: 1949
SQ FT: 5,000
SALES (est): 2.02B **Privately Held**
Web: www.capitalgroup.com
SIC: **6722** Money market mutual funds

(P-12628)
ARES MANAGEMENT CORPORATION (PA)
Also Called: Ares
1800 Avenue Of The Stars Ste 1400, Los Angeles (90067-4216)
PHONE............................310 201-4100
Michael J Arougheti, *Pr*
Antony P Ressler, *Ex Ch Bd*
Jarrod Phillips, *CFO*
Ryan Berry, *Chief Marketing*
Naseem Sagati Aghili, *Corporate Secretary*
EMP: 102 EST: 1997
SALES (est): 3.63B
SALES (corp-wide): 3.63B **Publicly Held**
Web: www.aresmgmt.com
SIC: **6722** 6282 Management investment, open-end; Investment advice

(P-12629)
BELLOTA US CORP
22440 Temescal Canyon Rd, Corona (92883-4200)
PHONE............................951 737-6515
▲ EMP: 150
SIC: **6722** Money market mutual funds

(P-12630)
CARMEL PARTNERS LLC
530 Wilshire Blvd Ste 203, Santa Monica (90401-1427)
PHONE............................916 479-5286
EMP: 115
SALES (corp-wide): 66.25MM **Privately Held**
Web: www.carmelpartners.com
SIC: **6722** Management investment, open-end
HQ: Carmel Partners, Llc
  1000 Sansome St Fl 1
  San Francisco CA 94111
  415 273-2900

(P-12631)
CAUSEWAY CAPITAL MGT LLC (PA)
11111 Santa Monica Blvd Fl 15, Los Angeles (90025-5565)
PHONE............................310 231-6100
Gracie Fermelia, *Managing Member*
Sarah Ketterer, *
Harry Hartford, *
EMP: 98 EST: 2001
SALES (est): 16.5MM
SALES (corp-wide): 16.5MM **Privately Held**
Web: www.causewaycap.com
SIC: **6722** Money market mutual funds

(P-12632)
CLEARLAKE CAPITAL GROUP LP (PA)
233 Wilshire Blvd Ste 800, Santa Monica (90401-1207)
PHONE............................310 400-8800
Behdad Eghbali, *Mng Pt*
Jose Feliciano, *Pt*
Paul Huber, *Pt*
Prashant Mehrotra, *Pt*
EMP: 258 EST: 2006
SALES (est): 3.89B **Privately Held**

Web: www.clearlake.com
SIC: 6722 3694 3714 5013 Management investment, open-end; Engine electrical equipment; Motor vehicle parts and accessories; Automotive engines and engine parts

(P-12633)
CLEARLAKE CPITL PARTNERS IV LP
233 Wilshire Blvd Ste 800, Santa Monica (90401-1207)
PHONE.....................310 400-8800
EMP: 180 EST: 2016
SALES (est): 3.86MM Privately Held
Web: www.clearlake.com
SIC: 6722 Management investment, open-end

(P-12634)
GUGGENHEIM PRTNERS INV MGT LLC
100 Wilshire Blvd 5th Fl, Santa Monica (90401-1143)
PHONE.....................310 576-1270
Robert Daviduk, Dir
EMP: 1097
SALES (est): 6.54MM
SALES (corp-wide): 380.53MM Privately Held
Web: www.guggenheiminvestments.com
SIC: 6722 Money market mutual funds
PA: Guggenheim Partners, Llc
330 Madison Ave
212 739-0700

(P-12635)
LOS ANGELES CAPITAL MGT LLC (PA)
Also Called: La Capital
11150 Santa Monica Blvd Ste 200, Los Angeles (90025-0418)
PHONE.....................310 479-9998
Thomas Stevens, Ch Bd
Thomas D Stevens, *
Hal Reynolds, *
David Borger, *
Stuart Matsuda, *
EMP: 80 EST: 2002
SQ FT: 10,192
SALES (est): 105.64K
SALES (corp-wide): 105.64K Privately Held
Web: www.lacapm.com
SIC: 6722 8741 8211 6282 Management investment, open-end; Management services; Elementary and secondary schools; Investment advice

(P-12636)
METWEST TOTAL RETURN BOND FUND
865 S Figueroa St, Los Angeles (90017-2543)
PHONE.....................800 241-4671
EMP: 75 EST: 2016
SALES (est): 974.46K Privately Held
SIC: 6722 Money market mutual funds
HQ: Metropolitan West Asset Management, Llc
865 S Figueroa St
Los Angeles CA 90017
213 244-0000

(P-12637)
OAKTREE HOLDINGS INC
333 S Grand Ave Fl 28, Los Angeles (90071-1530)
PHONE.....................213 830-6300

EMP: 768 EST: 2014
SALES (est): 599.22K Privately Held
Web: www.oaktreecapital.com
SIC: 6722 Money market mutual funds
PA: Oaktree Capital Group Holdings, L.P. 333 S Grand Ave Fl 28

(P-12638)
OAKTREE REAL ESTATE OPPRTNTIES
333 S Grand Ave Fl 28, Los Angeles (90071-1530)
PHONE.....................213 830-6300
EMP: 768 EST: 2014
SALES (est): 1.73MM Privately Held
Web: www.oaktreecapital.com
SIC: 6722 Money market mutual funds
PA: Oaktree Capital Group Holdings, L.P. 333 S Grand Ave Fl 28

(P-12639)
OAKTREE STRATEGIC INCOME LLC
333 S Grand Ave Fl 28, Los Angeles (90071-1530)
PHONE.....................213 830-6300
EMP: 1229 EST: 2015
SALES (est): 1.22MM Privately Held
Web: www.oaktreespecialtylending.com
SIC: 6722 Money market mutual funds
PA: Oaktree Capital Group Holdings, L.P. 333 S Grand Ave Fl 28

(P-12640)
OCM REAL ESTATE OPPRTNTIES FUN
333 S Grand Ave Fl 28, Los Angeles (90071-1530)
PHONE.....................213 830-6300
EMP: 461 EST: 2014
SALES (est): 506.37K Privately Held
SIC: 6722 Money market mutual funds
PA: Oaktree Capital Group Holdings, L.P. 333 S Grand Ave Fl 28

(P-12641)
PACIFIC INVESTMENT MGT CO LLC (DH)
Also Called: Pimco
650 Newport Center Dr, Newport Beach (92660-6392)
P.O. Box 6430 (92658-6430)
PHONE.....................949 720-6000
Emmanuel Roman, CEO
Jeremie Banet, *
Sai S Devabhaktuni, Head OF CORP DISTRESSED PORTFOLIO MGMNT
Mohamed A El-erian, Managing Member
Jay Jacobs, *
EMP: 240 EST: 1969
SQ FT: 25,000
SALES (est): 361.63MM
SALES (corp-wide): 28.21B Privately Held
Web: www.pimco.com
SIC: 6722 Money market mutual funds
HQ: Allianz Asset Management Of America Llc
650 Newport Center Dr
Newport Beach CA 92660
949 219-2200

(P-12642)
SHAMROCK CAPITAL ADVISORS LLC
1100 Glendon Ave Ste 1600, Los Angeles (90024-3567)
PHONE.....................310 974-6600
Stephen Royer, CEO
Peter Rivera, *

Bhuvan Jain, *
Blair Brenton, *
EMP: 400 EST: 2010
SALES (est): 25.68MM Privately Held
Web: www.shamrockcap.com
SIC: 6722 Management investment, open-end

(P-12643)
WESTERN ASSET CORE PLUS BOND P
385 E Colorado Blvd, Pasadena (91101-1923)
PHONE.....................626 844-9400
Larry Clark, Prin
EMP: 118 EST: 2012
SALES (est): 1.24MM
SALES (corp-wide): 8.48B Publicly Held
Web: www.westernasset.com
SIC: 6722 Money market mutual funds
HQ: Western Asset Management Company
385 East Colorado Blvd
Pasadena CA 91101
626 844-9265

6726 Investment Offices, Nec

(P-12644)
ACORNS GROW INCORPORATED (PA)
Also Called: Acorns
5300 California Ave, Irvine (92617-3051)
PHONE.....................949 251-0095
Noah Kerner, CEO
David Hijirida, Pr
Seth Wunder, CIO
Kennedy Reynolds, EDUCATION CONTENT
EMP: 96 EST: 2012
SQ FT: 2,500
SALES (est): 47.49MM
SALES (corp-wide): 47.49MM Privately Held
Web: www.acorns.com
SIC: 6726 Investment offices, nec

(P-12645)
BRIDGEWEST VENTURES LLC (PA)
Also Called: Bridgewest Group, The
7310 Miramar Rd Ste 500, San Diego (92126-4222)
P.O. Box 928769 (92126)
PHONE.....................858 529-6600
Masood Tayebi, CEO
Massih Tayebi, Ch
Kevin M Russell, Chief Legal Counsel
Saum Vahdat, CFO
EMP: 624 EST: 2014
SALES (est): 3.88MM
SALES (corp-wide): 3.88MM Privately Held
Web: www.bridgewestgroup.com
SIC: 6726 Management investment funds, closed-end

(P-12646)
CENTURY PK CAPITL PARTNERS LLC (PA)
880 Apollo St Ste 300, El Segundo (90245-4726)
PHONE.....................310 867-2210
Martin A Sarafa, Managing Member
EMP: 160 EST: 2004
SALES (est): 37.52MM Privately Held
Web: www.centuryparkcapital.com

SIC: 6726 3569 3086 3448 Management investment funds, closed-end; Firefighting and related equipment; Carpet and rug cushions, foamed plastics; Ramps, prefabricated metal

(P-12647)
CHARLES SCHWAB CORPORATION
Also Called: Charles Schwab
10920 Via Frontera Ste 100, San Diego (92127-1730)
PHONE.....................800 435-4000
EMP: 79
SALES (corp-wide): 18.84B Publicly Held
Web: client.schwab.com
SIC: 6726 6211 Investment offices, nec; Brokers, security
PA: The Charles Schwab Corporation
3000 Schwab Way
817 859-5000

(P-12648)
KINGSWOOD CAPITAL MGT LLC (PA)
11111 Santa Monica Blvd Ste 1700, Los Angeles (90025-0449)
PHONE.....................424 744-8238
EMP: 205 EST: 2013
SALES (est): 174.68MM
SALES (corp-wide): 174.68MM Privately Held
Web: www.kingswood-capital.com
SIC: 6726 Investment offices, nec

(P-12649)
OASIS WEST REALTY LLC
Also Called: Espelette Beverly Hills
1800 Century Park E Ste 500, Los Angeles (90067-1508)
PHONE.....................310 274-8066
Samuel Surloff, *
EMP: 502 EST: 2003
SALES (est): 4.76MM Privately Held
Web: www.alagemcapital.com
SIC: 6726 5947 5813 5812 Investment offices, nec; Gift shop; Drinking places; Eating places

(P-12650)
SCHAUMBOND GROUP INC (PA)
225 S Lake Ave Ste 300, Pasadena (91101-3009)
PHONE.....................626 215-4998
Baohua Zheng, Pr
EMP: 450 EST: 1996
SQ FT: 8,000
SALES (est): 3.32MM Privately Held
SIC: 6726 Investment offices, nec

6732 Trusts: Educational, Religious, Etc.

(P-12651)
COUNTY OF LOS ANGELES
Also Called: Extension Services
6300 E State University Dr Ste 104, Long Beach (90815-4678)
PHONE.....................562 985-4687
Marilyn Crego, Dean
EMP: 80
Web: www.lacounty.gov
SIC: 6732 9111 Educational trust management; Executive offices
PA: County Of Los Angeles
500 W Temple St Ste 437
213 974-1101

(P-12652)
EMPOWER OUR YOUTH
Also Called: Eoy
6767 W Sunset Blvd Ste 8-188, Los
Angeles (90028-7177)
PHONE.....................323 203-5436
Ihkisha Levell, *Prin*
EMP: 99 **EST:** 2008
SALES (est): 1.27MM **Privately Held**
SIC: 6732 Trusts: educational, religious, etc.

(P-12653)
**GREATER LOS ANGLES
VTRANS RES**
11301 Wilshire Blvd Bldg 114, Los Angeles
(90073-1003)
PHONE.....................310 312-1554
Jane Cheung, *Ex Dir*
Thoyd Ellis, *
Bonita Krall, *CPO**
Ron Waldorf, *
Leila Ghayouri, *
EMP: 90 **EST:** 2018
SALES (est): 7.08MM **Privately Held**
Web: www.glavref.org
SIC: 6732 Trusts: educational, religious, etc.

(P-12654)
UCLA FOUNDATION
10889 Wilshire Blvd Ste 1100, Los Angeles
(90024-4201)
PHONE.....................310 794-3193
Craig Ehrlich, *Ch*
Peter Hayashida, *
Neal Axelrod, *
Jocelyn Smith, *
EMP: 317 **EST:** 1945
SALES (est): 636.37MM **Privately Held**
Web: www.uclafoundation.org
SIC: 6732 Educational trust management

6733 Trusts, Nec

(P-12655)
**BENEFITS PRGRAM
ADMINSITRATION**
Also Called: Gciu Employer Retirement Fund
13191 Concords Pkwy N Ste 205, City Of
Industry (91746)
PHONE.....................562 463-5000
Mathew Wenner, *Admn*
EMP: 95 **EST:** 1955
SALES (est): 815.22K
SALES (corp-wide): 9.95MM **Privately
Held**
SIC: 6733 Trusts, except educational,
religious, charity: management
PA: Management Applied Programming,
Inc.
13191 Crssrads Pkwy N Ste
562 463-5000

(P-12656)
**CAPITAL GUARDIAN TRUST
COMPANY (HQ)**
333 S Hope St Fl 52, Los Angeles
(90071-3061)
PHONE.....................213 486-9200
Richard C Barker, *Ch Bd*
Robert Ronus, *
EMP: 100 **EST:** 1968
SQ FT: 6,000
SALES (est): 7.15MM
SALES (corp-wide): 7.25B **Privately Held**
SIC: 6733 Trusts, except educational,
religious, charity: management
PA: The Capital Group Companies Inc
333 S Hope St Fl 53
213 486-9200

(P-12657)
EPIDAURUS
Also Called: Amity Foundation
3745 S Grand Ave, Los Angeles
(90007-4332)
PHONE.....................213 743-9075
Mark Schettenger, *Pr*
EMP: 272
Web: www.amityfdn.org
SIC: 6733 Trusts, nec
PA: Epidaurus
721 N 4th Ave

(P-12658)
**GUILD MORTGAGE COMPANY
LLC (HQ)**
Also Called: Guild Mortgage
5887 Copley Dr, San Diego (92111-7906)
P.O. Box 85304 (92186)
PHONE.....................800 365-4441
EMP: 200 **EST:** 1960
SALES (est): 332.86MM
SALES (corp-wide): 655.19MM **Publicly
Held**
Web: www.guildmortgage.com
SIC: 6733 6162 Trusts, except educational,
religious, charity: management; Mortgage
bankers
PA: Guild Holdings Company
5887 Copley Dr
858 560-6330

(P-12659)
IMPAC SECURED ASSETS CORP
19500 Jamboree Rd, Irvine (92612-2411)
PHONE.....................949 475-3600
Ronald Martin Morrison, *Admn*
EMP: 99 **EST:** 2008
SALES (est): 885.81K **Privately Held**
SIC: 6733 Trusts, nec
HQ: Impac Funding Corporation
19500 Jamboree Rd
Irvine CA 92612

(P-12660)
**KAISER FOUNDATION
HOSPITALS**
Also Called: Orange County-Irvine Med Ctr
6640 Alton Pkwy, Irvine (92618-3734)
PHONE.....................949 932-5000
George Disalvo, *Brnch Mgr*
EMP: 191
SALES (corp-wide): 70.8B **Privately Held**
Web: www.kaiserpermanente.org
SIC: 6733 Trusts, nec
HQ: Kaiser Foundation Hospitals Inc
1 Kaiser Plz
Oakland CA 94612
510 271-6611

(P-12661)
**KAISER FOUNDATION
HOSPITALS**
Also Called: Kaiser Permanente
4647 Zion Ave, San Diego (92120-2507)
PHONE.....................619 528-5888
Kathy Roper, *Mgr*
EMP: 679
SALES (corp-wide): 70.8B **Privately Held**
Web: www.kaisercenter.com
SIC: 6733 8062 Trusts, nec; General
medical and surgical hospitals
HQ: Kaiser Foundation Hospitals Inc
1 Kaiser Plz
Oakland CA 94612
510 271-6611

(P-12662)
MANAGEMENT TRUST ASSN INC
9815 Carroll Canyon Rd Ste 103, San Diego
(92131-1123)
PHONE.....................858 547-4373
Diane Houston, *Brnch Mgr*
EMP: 80
Web: www.managementtrust.com
SIC: 6733 Trusts, nec
PA: The Management Trust Association Inc
15661 Red Hl Ave Ste 201

(P-12663)
MANAGEMENT TRUST ASSN INC
4160 Temescal Canyon Rd Ste 202, Corona
(92883-4629)
PHONE.....................951 694-1758
EMP: 80
Web: www.managementtrust.com
SIC: 6733 Trusts, nec
PA: The Management Trust Association Inc
15661 Red Hl Ave Ste 201

(P-12664)
MOELIS & COMPANY LLC
10100 Santa Monica Blvd Ste 1600, Los
Angeles (90067-4119)
PHONE.....................310 443-2300
Stella Hoe, *Brnch Mgr*
EMP: 114
SALES (corp-wide): 854.75MM **Publicly
Held**
Web: www.moelis.com
SIC: 6733 6282 Private estate, personal
investment and vacation fund trusts;
Investment advisory service
HQ: Moelis & Company Llc
399 Park Ave Fl 5
New York NY 10022

(P-12665)
**OPERATING ENGINEERS
FUNDS INC (PA)**
100 Corson St, Pasadena (91103-3892)
P.O. Box 7063 (91109-7063)
PHONE.....................866 400-5200
Mike Roddy, *CEO*
Matt Erieg, *
Chuck Killian, *
EMP: 135 **EST:** 1971
SQ FT: 84,600
SALES (est): 314.23K
SALES (corp-wide): 314.23K **Privately
Held**
Web: www.oefi.org
SIC: 6733 Trusts, except educational,
religious, charity: management

(P-12666)
**PMT CRDIT RISK TRNSF TR
2015-1**
3043 Townsgate Rd, Westlake Village
(91361-3027)
PHONE.....................818 224-7028
EMP: 215 **EST:** 2017
SALES (est): 462.97K **Publicly Held**
Web: pfsi.pennymac.com
SIC: 6733 Trusts, nec
PA: Pennymac Mortgage Investment Trust
3043 Townsgate Rd

(P-12667)
**PMT CRDIT RISK TRNSF TR
2015-2**
3043 Townsgate Rd, Westlake Village
(91361-3027)
PHONE.....................818 224-7442
EMP: 215 **EST:** 2017
SALES (est): 336.72K **Publicly Held**

Web: pfsi.pennymac.com
SIC: 6733 Trusts, nec
PA: Pennymac Mortgage Investment Trust
3043 Townsgate Rd

(P-12668)
**PMT CRDIT RISK TRNSF TR
2019-2**
3043 Townsgate Rd, Westlake Village
(91361-3027)
PHONE.....................818 224-7028
EMP: 143 **EST:** 2019
SALES (est): 416.95K **Publicly Held**
Web: pmt.pennymac.com
SIC: 6733 Trusts, nec
PA: Pennymac Mortgage Investment Trust
3043 Townsgate Rd

(P-12669)
**PMT CRDIT RISK TRNSF TR
2019-3**
3043 Townsgate Rd, Westlake Village
(91361-3027)
PHONE.....................818 224-7028
EMP: 143
SALES (est): 437.1K **Publicly Held**
SIC: 6733 Trusts, nec
PA: Pennymac Mortgage Investment Trust
3043 Townsgate Rd

(P-12670)
**PMT CRDIT RISK TRNSF TR
2020-1**
3043 Townsgate Rd, Westlake Village
(91361-3027)
PHONE.....................818 224-7028
EMP: 143 **EST:** 2020
SALES (est): 405.22K **Publicly Held**
SIC: 6733 Trusts, nec
PA: Pennymac Mortgage Investment Trust
3043 Townsgate Rd

(P-12671)
**PMT CRDIT RISK TRNSF TR
2020-2**
3043 Townsgate Rd, Westlake Village
(91361-3027)
PHONE.....................818 224-7028
EMP: 143
SALES (est): 352.2K **Publicly Held**
SIC: 6733 Trusts, nec
PA: Pennymac Mortgage Investment Trust
3043 Townsgate Rd

(P-12672)
PNMAC GMSR ISSUER TRUST
3043 Townsgate Rd, Westlake Village
(91361-3027)
PHONE.....................818 746-2271
EMP: 759 **EST:** 2017
SALES (est): 645.26K
SALES (corp-wide): 1.4B **Publicly Held**
Web: pfsi.pennymac.com
SIC: 6733 Trusts, nec
HQ: Pnmac Holdings, Inc.
3043 Townsgate Rd
Westlake Village CA 91361
818 224-7442

(P-12673)
QUALITY LOAN SERVICE CORP
2763 Camino Del Rio S, San Diego
(92108-3708)
PHONE.....................619 645-7711
Kevin R Mccarthy, *CEO*
Thomas J Holthus, *
John R Valkus, *
Dave Owen, *
Victoria Logan, *

EMP: 384 **EST:** 1988
SALES (est): 6.63MM **Privately Held**
Web: www.qualityloan.com
SIC: 6733 Trusts, except educational, religious, charity: management

(P-12674)
SOUTHERN CAL PIPE TRADES ADM (PA)
Also Called: Southern Cal Pipe Trades ADM
501 Shatto Pl Ste 500, Los Angeles
(90020-1730)
PHONE......................213 385-6161
Milton D Johnson, *Pr*
EMP: 70 **EST:** 1956
SQ FT: 70,000
SALES (est): 158.82MM
SALES (corp-wide): 158.82MM **Privately Held**
Web: www.scptac.org
SIC: 6733 6513 Trusts, except educational, religious, charity: management; Retirement hotel operation

(P-12675)
VARNER FAMILY LTD PARTNERSHIP (PA)
5900 E Lerdo Hwy, Shafter (93263-4023)
PHONE......................661 399-1163
James Varner, *Genl Pt*
EMP: 80 **EST:** 2000
SALES (est): 22.55MM
SALES (corp-wide): 22.55MM **Privately Held**
SIC: 6733 Private estate, personal investment and vacation fund trusts

---

6794 Patent Owners And Lessors

(P-12676)
ADVANCED FRESH CONCEPTS CORP (PA)
Also Called: A F C
19205 S Laurel Park Rd, Rancho Dominguez (90220-6032)
PHONE......................310 604-3630
Jeffery Seiler, *CEO*
◆ **EMP:** 25 **EST:** 1986
SQ FT: 60,000
SALES (est): 48.2MM
SALES (corp-wide): 48.2MM **Privately Held**
Web: www.afcsushi.com
SIC: 6794 2032 2092 5141 Patent owners and lessors; Chinese foods, nec: packaged in cans, jars, etc.; Fresh or frozen packaged fish; Food brokers

(P-12677)
BRER AFFILIATES LLC (DH)
Also Called: Prudential
18500 Von Karman Ave Ste 400, Irvine (92612-0511)
PHONE......................949 794-7900
John Vanderwall, *Pr*
Patti Ray, *
EMP: 208 **EST:** 2004
SQ FT: 55,500
SALES (est): 17.42MM
SALES (corp-wide): 53.98B **Publicly Held**
SIC: 6794 6531 Franchises, selling or licensing; Real estate agents and managers
HQ: The Prudential Insurance Company Of America
751 Broad St Fl 21
Newark NJ 07102
973 802-6000

(P-12678)
QUALCOMM INTERNATIONAL INC (HQ)
Also Called: Qualcomm
5775 Morehouse Dr, San Diego (92121-1714)
PHONE......................858 587-1121
Steve Altman, *Pr*
Derek Aberle, *
EMP: 4000 **EST:** 1993
SALES (est): 12.92MM
SALES (corp-wide): 38.96B **Publicly Held**
Web: investor.qualcomm.com
SIC: 6794 Patent buying, licensing, leasing
PA: Qualcomm Incorporated
5775 Morehouse Dr
858 587-1121

(P-12679)
UMG RECORDINGS INC
Also Called: Universal Music Enterprises
2220 Colorado Ave, Santa Monica (90404-3506)
PHONE......................310 865-4000
Lucian Grainge, *Ch*
Boyd Murr, *
EMP: 1000 **EST:** 1968
SALES (est): 7.73MM **Privately Held**
SIC: 6794 Music licensing and royalties
HQ: Universal Music Group, Inc.
2220 Colorado Ave
Santa Monica CA 90404
310 865-0770

(P-12680)
UNIVERSAL STDIOS LICENSING LLC
Also Called: Universal Prtnrships Licensing
100 Universal City Plz, Universal City (91608-1085)
PHONE......................818 695-1273
Sheetal Madadi, *Mgr*
Gabriela Kornzweig, *
EMP: 150 **EST:** 2010
SALES (est): 4.36MM
SALES (corp-wide): 121.57B **Publicly Held**
SIC: 6794 Copyright buying and licensing
HQ: Nbcuniversal Media, Llc
30 Rockefeller Plz
New York NY 10112

(P-12681)
WSM INVESTMENTS LLC
Also Called: Topco Sales
3990b Heritage Oak Ct, Simi Valley (93063-6716)
PHONE......................818 332-4600
Scott Tucker, *CEO*
Martin Tucker, *
Michael Siogol, *
▲ **EMP:** 145 **EST:** 2009
SQ FT: 150,000
SALES (est): 4.84MM **Privately Held**
SIC: 6794 5122 5099 4731 Performance rights, publishing and licensing; Cosmetics; Novelties, durable; Freight forwarding
PA: Lover Health Science And Technology Incorporated Co., Ltd
No.1208, Taihu Ave., Changxing Economic Development Zone, Changx

---

6798 Real Estate Investment Trusts

(P-12682)
AMERICAN HEALTHCARE REIT INC (PA)

18191 Von Karman Ave Ste 300, Irvine (92612-7106)
PHONE......................949 270-9200
Danny Prosky, *Pr*
Jeffrey T Hanson, *Non-Executive Chairman of the Board*
Gabriel M Willhite, *COO*
Brian S Peay, *CFO*
Stefan K L Oh, *CIO*
EMP: 97 **EST:** 2015
SALES (est): 1.87B
SALES (corp-wide): 1.87B **Publicly Held**
Web: www.americanhealthcarereit.com
SIC: 6798 Real estate investment trusts

(P-12683)
BIOMED REALTY TRUST INC (PA)
Also Called: Biomed Realty
4570 Executive Dr Ste 400, San Diego (92121-3074)
PHONE......................858 207-2513
Alan D Gold, *Ch Bd*
R Kent Griffin Junior, *Pr*
Greg N Lubushkin, *CFO*
Gary A Kreitzer, *
Charlie Piscitello, *CPO*
EMP: 375 **EST:** 2004
SQ FT: 61,286
SALES (est): 264.45MM
SALES (corp-wide): 264.45MM **Privately Held**
Web: www.biomedrealty.com
SIC: 6798 Real estate investment trusts

(P-12684)
CORESITE LLC
624 S Grand Ave Ste 1800, Los Angeles (90023-1629)
PHONE......................213 327-1231
Thomas Ray, *Brnch Mgr*
EMP: 162
Web: www.coresite.com
SIC: 6798 Real estate investment trusts
HQ: Coresite, L.L.C.
1001 17th St Ste 500
Denver CO 80202
866 777-2673

(P-12685)
EQUITY FUND ADVISORS INC
11995 El Camino Real, San Diego (92130-2539)
PHONE......................602 716-8803
Chris Cole, *Pr*
EMP: 130 **EST:** 2004
SALES (est): 2.94MM **Privately Held**
SIC: 6798 Real estate investment trusts
PA: Vereit, Inc.
11995 El Camino Real

(P-12686)
HUDSON PACIFIC PROPERTIES INC (PA)
11601 Wilshire Blvd Ste 1600, Los Angeles (90025-0317)
PHONE......................310 445-5700
Victor J Coleman, *Ch Bd*
Mark T Lammas, *Pr*
Harout Diramerian, *CFO*
Kay L Tidwell, *CRO*
Dale Shimoda, *VP Fin*
EMP: 71 **EST:** 2009
SALES (est): 952.3MM **Publicly Held**
Web: www.hudsonpacificproperties.com
SIC: 6798 Real estate investment trusts

(P-12687)
IRVINE EASTGATE OFFICE II LLC
Also Called: Irvine Company Office Property
550 Newport Center Dr, Newport Beach (92660-7010)
P.O. Box 2460 (92658-8960)
PHONE......................949 720-2000
Pam Van Nort, *VP*
EMP: 3000 **EST:** 2013
SQ FT: 3,000
SALES (est): 47.6MM **Privately Held**
Web: www.irvinecompany.com
SIC: 6798 Real estate investment trusts

(P-12688)
MACERICH COMPANY (PA)
401 Wilshire Blvd Ste 700, Santa Monica (90401-1452)
PHONE......................310 394-6000
Jackson Hsieh, *Pr*
Steven R Hash, *
Ann C Menard, *CLO*
Douglas J Healey, *Head OF Leasing*
EMP: 233 **EST:** 1965
SALES (est): 884.07MM
SALES (corp-wide): 884.07MM **Publicly Held**
Web: www.macerich.com
SIC: 6798 Real estate investment trusts

(P-12689)
MPG OFFICE TRUST INC
355 S Grand Ave Ste 3300, Los Angeles (90071-1592)
PHONE......................213 626-3300
EMP: 70
SIC: 6798 Real estate investment trusts

(P-12690)
PACIFICA COMPANIES LLC (PA)
Also Called: Pacifica Companies
1775 Hancock St Ste 200, San Diego (92110-2036)
PHONE......................619 296-9000
Deepak Israni, *Pr*
Ashok Israni, *
EMP: 1909 **EST:** 2004
SALES (est): 41.98MM **Privately Held**
Web: www.pacificacompanies.com
SIC: 6798 6512 Real estate investment trusts ; Nonresidential building operators

(P-12691)
PMT ISSUER TRUST - FMSR
3043 Townsgate Rd, Westlake Village (91361-3027)
PHONE......................818 224-7028
EMP: 143 **EST:** 2018
SALES (est): 561.29K **Publicly Held**
Web: pmt.pennymac.com
SIC: 6798 Real estate investment trusts
PA: Pennymac Mortgage Investment Trust
3043 Townsgate Rd

(P-12692)
PRIME ADMINISTRATION LLC
Also Called: Prime Group
357 S Curson Ave, Los Angeles (90036-5201)
P.O. Box 360859 (90036-1359)
PHONE......................323 549-7155
Daniel H James, *Ch*
John C Atwater, *CEO*
EMP: 522 **EST:** 2004
SALES (est): 96.75MM **Privately Held**
Web: www.primegrp.com
SIC: 6798 Real estate investment trusts

PRODUCTS & SVCS

(P-12693)
PUBLIC STORAGE (PA)
701 Western Ave, Glendale (91201-2349)
PHONE..................................818 244-8080
Joseph D Russell Junior, *Pr*
Ronald L Havner Junior, *Ch Bd*
H Thomas Boyle, *CIO*
Natalia N Johnson, *Chief*
Nathaniel A Vitan, *CLO*
EMP: 430 EST: 1980
SALES (est): 4.52B
SALES (corp-wide): 4.52B Publicly Held
Web: www.publicstorage.com
SIC: 6798 Real estate investment trusts

(P-12694)
PUBLIC STORAGE OPERATING CO (DH)
701 Western Ave, Glendale (91201-2349)
PHONE..................................818 244-8080
Joseph D Russell Junior, *Pr*
Ronald L Havner Junior, *Ch Bd*
H Thomas Boyle, *CIO*
Natalia N Johnson, *Chief*
Nathaniel A Vitan, *CLO*
EMP: 430 EST: 1980
SALES (est): 817.16MM
SALES (corp-wide): 4.52B Publicly Held
Web: www.publicstorage.com
SIC: 6798 Real estate investment trusts
HQ: Public Storage Op, L.P.
  701 Western Ave
  Glendale CA 91201
  818 244-8080

(P-12695)
SPIRIT REALTY LP
11995 El Camino Real, San Diego (92130-2539)
PHONE..................................972 476-1900
Jackson Hsieh, *Pr*
Michael Hughes, *Ex VP*
EMP: 82 EST: 2003
SALES (est): 3.4MM Publicly Held
Web: www.realtyincome.com
SIC: 6798 Real estate investment trusts
PA: Realty Income Corporation
  11995 El Camino Real

(P-12696)
VEREIT REAL ESTATE LP
11995 El Camino Real, San Diego (92130-2539)
PHONE..................................602 778-6000
Michele Garrett, *Pt*
Margaret Foster, *
EMP: 99 EST: 2017
SALES (est): 5.03MM Publicly Held
SIC: 6798 Real estate investment trusts
PA: Realty Income Corporation
  11995 El Camino Real

6799 Investors, Nec

(P-12697)
7TH & C INVESTMENTS LLC
404 14th St, San Diego (92101-7508)
PHONE..................................619 233-7327
James W Brennan, *Prin*
EMP: 249 EST: 2010
SALES (corp-wide): 1.03B Publicly Held
Web: www.taogroup.com
SIC: 6799 Investors, nec
PA: Sphere Entertainment Co.
  2 Penn Plz
  725 258-0001

(P-12698)
ARE/CAL-SD REGION NO 62 LLC
26 N Euclid Ave, Pasadena (91101-1961)
PHONE..................................626 578-0777
Mark Butcher, *
EMP: 99 EST: 2019
SALES (est): 595.71K Privately Held
SIC: 6799 Investors, nec

(P-12699)
BACKBONE CAPITAL ADVISORS LLC
4084 Camellia Ave, Studio City (91604-3006)
PHONE..................................818 769-8016
Britt Terrell, *Prin*
EMP: 88 EST: 2011
SALES (est): 364.57K
SALES (corp-wide): 10.39MM Privately Held
Web: www.backbonecap.com
SIC: 6799 Investors, nec
PA: Palm Tree Llc
  11755 Wilshire Blvd
  424 220-6800

(P-12700)
BROADREACH CAPITL PARTNERS LLC
6430 W Sunset Blvd Ste 504, Los Angeles (90028-7908)
PHONE..................................310 691-5760
Andre Ramillon, *Brnch Mgr*
EMP: 998
SALES (corp-wide): 9.94MM Privately Held
Web: www.broadreachcp.com
SIC: 6799 Investors, nec
PA: Broadreach Capital Partners Llc
  885 Oak Grove Ave Ste 206
  650 331-2500

(P-12701)
CALL TO ACTION PARTNERS LLC
11601 Wilshire Blvd Fl 23, Los Angeles (90025-0509)
PHONE..................................310 996-7200
Colin Sapire, *Managing Member*
Lenny Sands, *
Richard Kam, *
▲ EMP: 190 EST: 2009
SQ FT: 9,500
SALES (est): 1.34MM Privately Held
SIC: 6799 Investors, nec

(P-12702)
CLEARVIEW CAPITAL LLC
12100 Wilshire Blvd Ste 800, Los Angeles (90025-7140)
PHONE..................................310 806-9555
Larry Simon, *Brnch Mgr*
EMP: 916
SALES (corp-wide): 26.03MM Privately Held
Web: www.clearviewcap.com
SIC: 6799 Venture capital companies
PA: Clearview Capital, Llc
  1010 Washington Blvd 2-9
  203 698-2777

(P-12703)
CORRIDOR CAPITAL LLC (PA)
12400 Wilshire Blvd Ste 645, Los Angeles (90025-1260)
PHONE..................................310 442-7000
Craig L Enenstein, *CEO*
Edward A Monnier, *

Cameron Reilly, *
Jessamyn Davis, *
EMP: 126 EST: 2005
SALES (est): 21.29MM Privately Held
Web: www.corridor-capital.com
SIC: 6799 Venture capital companies

(P-12704)
CRESTMONT CAPITAL LLC
1422 Edinger Ave Ste 210, Tustin (92780-6298)
PHONE..................................949 537-3882
EMP: 250 EST: 2015
SALES (est): 2.6MM Privately Held
Web: www.crestmontcapital.com
SIC: 6799 Investors, nec

(P-12705)
EMP III INC
Also Called: Duarte Manor
1755 Mrtn Lthr Kng Jr Blv, Los Angeles (90058-1522)
PHONE..................................323 231-4174
Ernie Piltil, *Pr*
Scott Mason, *
Tim English, *
EMP: 80 EST: 2010
SALES (est): 2.47MM Privately Held
SIC: 6799 Real estate investors, except property operators

(P-12706)
FULL STACK FINANCE
2701 Ocean Park Blvd Ste 210, Santa Monica (90405-5241)
PHONE..................................800 941-0356
EMP: 77 EST: 2018
SALES (est): 1.3MM Privately Held
Web: www.fullstackfinance.com
SIC: 6799 Investors, nec

(P-12707)
GOLDEN INTERNATIONAL
424 S Los Angeles St Ste 2, Los Angeles (90013-1470)
PHONE..................................213 628-1388
Gi Hanbae, *Brnch Mgr*
EMP: 2968
SALES (corp-wide): 965.94K Privately Held
SIC: 6799 Investors, nec
PA: Golden International
  36720 Palmdale Rd
  760 568-1912

(P-12708)
GSA DES PLAINES LLC
10100 Santa Monica Blvd Ste 2600, Los Angeles (90067-4000)
PHONE..................................310 557-5100
Daniel Goldstone, *Managing Member*
EMP: 70 EST: 2012
SQ FT: 100
SALES (est): 856.45K Privately Held
SIC: 6799 Real estate investors, except property operators

(P-12709)
HEALTHPOINT CAPITAL LLC (PA)
9920 Pacific Heights Blvd Ste 150, San Diego (92121-4361)
PHONE..................................212 935-7780
John H Foster, *CEO*
Mike Mogul, *
William Johnson, *
EMP: 160 EST: 2002
SALES (est): 1.32MM
SALES (corp-wide): 1.32MM Privately Held

Web: www.healthpointcapital.com
SIC: 6799 Venture capital companies

(P-12710)
IDEALAB HOLDINGS LLC (PA)
130 W Union St, Pasadena (91103-3628)
PHONE..................................626 585-6900
Brent Novak, *
Marcia Goodstein, *
Craig Chrisney, *
Kristen Ding, *
EMP: 626 EST: 1996
SALES (est): 35.77MM
SALES (corp-wide): 35.77MM Privately Held
Web: www.idealab.com
SIC: 6799 5045 5734 Venture capital companies; Computer software; Computer software and accessories

(P-12711)
IMPERIAL CAPITAL GROUP LLC (PA)
2000 Avenue Of The Stars Ste 900s, Los Angeles (90067-4716)
PHONE..................................310 246-3700
Lenny Bianco, *Sr VP*
EMP: 70 EST: 1989
SQ FT: 14,909
SALES (est): 9.68MM Privately Held
Web: www.imperialcapital.com
SIC: 6799 Investors, nec

(P-12712)
INTREPID INV BANKERS LLC
11755 Wilshire Blvd Ste 2200, Los Angeles (90025-1567)
PHONE..................................310 478-9000
Ed Bagdasarian, *CEO*
EMP: 5096 EST: 2010
SALES (est): 8.55MM Privately Held
Web: www.intrepidib.com
SIC: 6799 Investors, nec
HQ: Mufg Americas Holdings Corporation
  1251 Ave Of The Americas
  New York NY 10020
  212 782-6800

(P-12713)
INVENTURE CAPITAL CORPORATION (PA)
Also Called: Tala
429 Santa Monica Blvd Ste 450, Santa Monica (90401-3467)
PHONE..................................213 262-6903
Shivani B Siroya, *CEO*
Jennifer Law, *
EMP: 542 EST: 2014
SQ FT: 4,500
SALES (est): 42.66MM
SALES (corp-wide): 42.66MM Privately Held
Web: www.tala.co
SIC: 6799 Venture capital companies

(P-12714)
LD ACQUISITION COMPANY 16 LLC
400 Continental Blvd Ste 500, El Segundo (90245-5078)
PHONE..................................310 294-8160
Tim Brazy, *CEO*
George Doyle, *
Dan Parsons, *
Josef Bobek, *
EMP: 99 EST: 2017
SALES (est): 1.58MM Privately Held
SIC: 6799 Investors, nec

(P-12715)
MARLIN EQUITY PARTNERS III LP (PA)

1301 Manhattan Ave, Hermosa Beach (90254-3654)
PHONE.....................310 364-0100
David Mcgovern, *Pt*
Nick Kaiser, *Managing Member*
EMP: 181 EST: 2009
SALES (est): 24.21MM **Privately Held**
Web: www.marlinequity.com
SIC: 6799 Venture capital companies

(P-12716)
MATSUSHITA INTERNATIONAL CORP (PA)

1141 Via Callejon, San Clemente (92673-6230)
PHONE.....................949 498-1000
Hiroyuki Matsushita, *Pr*
EMP: 80 EST: 1990
SALES (est): 21.11MM **Privately Held**
SIC: 6799 3711 3714 Real estate investors, except property operators; Automobile assembly, including specialty automobiles; Motor vehicle parts and accessories

(P-12717)
MCMILLIN COMPANIES LLC (PA)

Also Called: McMillin Homes
2750 Womble Rd Ste 102, San Diego (92106-6114)
P.O. Box 21010 (92021-0980)
PHONE.....................619 477-4117
EMP: 80 EST: 1998
SALES (est): 6.22MM
SALES (corp-wide): 6.22MM **Privately Held**
Web: www.mcmillin.com
SIC: 6799 Real estate investors, except property operators

(P-12718)
MEDIMPACT HOLDINGS INC (PA)

10181 Scripps Gateway Ct, San Diego (92131-5152)
PHONE.....................858 566-2727
Frederick Howe, *CEO*
Jim Gollaher, *Accounting Controller*
EMP: 817 EST: 2010
SALES (est): 473.33MM **Privately Held**
Web: www.medimpact.com
SIC: 6799 Investors, nec

(P-12719)
MIRAMAR ACQUISITION CO LLC

Also Called: Rosewood Miramar Bch Montecito
1759 S Jameson Ln, Santa Barbara (93108-2925)
PHONE.....................805 900-8338
Rick J Caruso, *Prin*
EMP: 179 EST: 2015
SALES (est): 2.98MM **Privately Held**
Web: www.rosewoodhotels.com
SIC: 6799 Investors, nec

(P-12720)
MSD CAPITAL LP

Also Called: MSD CAPITAL L.P.
100 Wilshire Blvd Ste 1450, Santa Monica (90401-1197)
PHONE.....................310 458-3600
John Sauter, *Mgr*
EMP: 105
SALES (corp-wide): 2.25B **Privately Held**
Web: www.dellfamilyoffice.com

SIC: 6799 Venture capital companies
HQ: Msd Capital, L.P
51 E 42nd St Fl 26
New York NY 10017
212 303-1650

(P-12721)
MSR HOTELS & RESORTS INC

Also Called: Sheraton Inn Bakersfield
5101 California Ave Ste 204, Bakersfield (93309-1623)
PHONE.....................661 325-9700
Kole Siefken, *Mgr*
EMP: 240
SALES (corp-wide): 96.19B **Publicly Held**
Web: www.cnl.com
SIC: 6799 Investors, nec
HQ: Msr Hotels & Resorts, Inc.
450 S Orange Ave
Orlando FL 32801
407 650-1000

(P-12722)
NAVITAS SEMICONDUCTOR CORP

3520 Challenger St, Torrance (90503-1640)
PHONE.....................844 654-2642
Gene Sheridan, *Ch Bd*
Dan Kinzer, *
Ron Shelton, *Sr VP*
Ranbir Singh, *
EMP: 314 EST: 2020
SALES (est): 79.46MM **Privately Held**
Web: www.navitassemi.com
SIC: 6799 Investors, nec

(P-12723)
NEXUS CAPITAL MANAGEMENT LP

11100 Santa Monica Blvd, Los Angeles (90025-3384)
PHONE.....................424 330-8820
EMP: 925 EST: 2016
SALES (est): 7.82MM **Privately Held**
Web: www.nexuslp.com
SIC: 6799 Investors, nec

(P-12724)
NNN REALTY INVESTORS LLC

19700 Fairchild Ste 300, Irvine (92612-2515)
PHONE.....................714 667-8252
Jeffrey T Hanson, *CIO*
Todd A Mikles, *
EMP: 458 EST: 1998
SQ FT: 18,800
SALES (est): 2.84MM **Privately Held**
SIC: 6799 6531 Investors, nec; Real estate managers

(P-12725)
NOGALES INVESTORS LLC

9229 W Sunset Blvd Ste 900, Los Angeles (90069-3410)
PHONE.....................310 276-7439
Luis Nogales, *Managing Member*
EMP: 275 EST: 2001
SQ FT: 2,500
SALES (est): 368.87K **Privately Held**
SIC: 6799 Investors, nec
PA: Nogales Investors Management, Llc
9229 W Sunset Blvd # 900

(P-12726)
NRLL LLC

Also Called: Land Disposition Company
1 Mauchly, Irvine (92618-2305)
P.O. Box 15534 (92623-5534)
PHONE.....................949 768-7777

SIC: 6799 Venture capital companies
HQ: Msd Capital, L.P
51 E 42nd St Fl 26
New York NY 10017
212 303-1650

EMP: 360 EST: 1995
SQ FT: 18,000
SALES (est): 435.53K **Privately Held**
Web: www.landauction.com
SIC: 6799 Real estate investors, except property operators
PA: Nrp Holding Co., Inc.
1 Mauchly

(P-12727)
OTTS ASIA MOORER DEVON

Also Called: Newshire Investment
10015 Baring Cross St, Los Angeles (90044-4511)
PHONE.....................323 603-6959
Asia Otts, *Owner*
Devon Moorer, *Owner*
EMP: 105 EST: 2016
SALES (est): 606.58K **Privately Held**
SIC: 6799 Investors, nec

(P-12728)
PMC CAPITAL PARTNERS LLC

12243 Branford St, Sun Valley (91352-1010)
PHONE.....................818 896-1101
Michel Tamer, *Mng Pt*
EMP: 1000 EST: 2019
SALES (est): 2.42MM **Privately Held**
Web: www.pmcsg.com
SIC: 6799 Venture capital companies

(P-12729)
PROVIDENCE REST PARTNERS LLC

Also Called: Restaurant Investment
5955 Melrose Ave, Los Angeles (90038-3623)
PHONE.....................323 460-4170
EMP: 88 EST: 2004
SALES (est): 1.12MM **Privately Held**
Web: www.providencela.com
SIC: 6799 5963 Investors, nec; Food services, direct sales

(P-12730)
PYRAMID PEAK CORPORATION

1401 Avocado Ave Ste 709, Newport Beach (92660-8714)
PHONE.....................949 769-8600
Cindy Ragsdale, *Pr*
EMP: 70 EST: 2002
SALES (est): 5.93MM **Privately Held**
SIC: 6799 Investors, nec

(P-12731)
REGENT LP (PA)

9720 Wilshire Blvd Fl 6, Beverly Hills (90212-2025)
PHONE.....................310 299-4100
Michael A Reinstein, *CIO*
Roxanna Sassanian, *CFO*
EMP: 85 EST: 2017
SALES (est): 921.67MM
SALES (corp-wide): 921.67MM **Privately Held**
Web: www.regentlp.com
SIC: 6799 Investors, nec

(P-12732)
RETAIL OPPRTNITY INVSTMNTS PRT

Also Called: ROIC California
11250 El Camino Real Ste 200, San Diego (92130-2677)
PHONE.....................858 677-0900
Stuart A Tanz, *Prin*
Michael B Haines, *Prin*
Richard K Schoebel, *Prin*

EMP: 71 EST: 2020
SALES (est): 327.73MM **Publicly Held**
SIC: 6799 Investors, nec
PA: Retail Opportunity Investments Corp.
11250 El Cmino Real Ste 2

(P-12733)
ROLL PROPERTIES INTL INC

Also Called: Paramout Farms
13646 Highway 33, Lost Hills (93249-9719)
PHONE.....................661 797-6500
Bill Bowers, *Mgr*
EMP: 121
SALES (corp-wide): 15.17MM **Privately Held**
Web: www.thetradelawfirm.com
SIC: 6799 Real estate investors, except property operators
PA: Roll Properties International, Inc.
11444 W Olympic Blvd # 10
310 966-5700

(P-12734)
RUSTIC CANYON GROUP LLC

Also Called: Rustic Canyon Partners
1025 Westwood Blvd, Los Angeles (90024-2902)
PHONE.....................310 998-8000
Nate Redmond, *Managing Member*
David Travers, *
Renee Labran, *
John Staenberg, *
Michael Kim, *
EMP: 75 EST: 2000
SALES (est): 2.96MM **Privately Held**
Web: www.rusticcanyonrestaurant.com
SIC: 6799 Venture capital companies

(P-12735)
SABAL CAPITAL PARTNERS LLC

680 E Colorado Blvd Ste 350, Pasadena (91101-6148)
PHONE.....................949 255-1007
Pat Jackson, *CEO*
EMP: 130 EST: 2015
SALES (est): 6.43MM
SALES (corp-wide): 9.15B **Publicly Held**
Web: www.regions.com
SIC: 6799 Investors, nec
HQ: Regions Bank
1900 5th Ave N
Birmingham AL 35203
205 264-5523

(P-12736)
SOLIS CAPITAL PARTNERS LLC

3371 Calle Tres Vistas Ste 100, Encinitas (92024-0079)
PHONE.....................760 309-9436
Daniel J Lubeck, *Brnch Mgr*
EMP: 86
SALES (corp-wide): 2.73MM **Privately Held**
Web: www.soliscapital.com
SIC: 6799 Venture capital companies
PA: Solis Capital Partners, Llc
23 Corporate Plaza Dr # 215
949 296-2440

(P-12737)
STOCKDALE CAPITAL PARTNERS LLC

11601 Wilshire Blvd Ste 1750, Los Angeles (90025-1754)
PHONE.....................310 693-4400
Barry Bartle, *Pr*
Steven Yari, *Managing Member*
Paula Pfleuger, *VP*
Shawn Yari, *Managing Member*
Sean Blitz, *VP*

EMP: 100 EST: 2013
SALES (est): 21.3MM **Privately Held**
Web: www.stockdalecapital.com
SIC: 6799 Venture capital companies

(P-12738)
STONECALIBRE LLC (PA)
2049 Century Park E Ste 2550, Los Angeles
(90067-3110)
PHONE..............................310 774-0014
Brian Wall, *Pr*
EMP: 100 EST: 2012
SALES (est): 60.5MM **Privately Held**
Web: www.stonecalibre.com
SIC: 6799 Investors, nec

(P-12739)
TAPETECH TOOL COMPANY
Also Called: Tapetech Tool Company
7360 Convoy Ct, San Diego (92111-1110)
PHONE..............................858 268-0656
EMP: 633
SALES (corp-wide): 5.5B **Publicly Held**
Web: www.amestools.com
SIC: 6799 Investors, nec
HQ: Ames Tools Corporation
1327 Nrthbrook Pkwy Ste 4
Suwanee GA 30024

(P-12740)
TCG CAPITAL MANAGEMENT LP
12180 Millennium Ste 500, Playa Vista
(90094-2948)
PHONE..............................310 633-2900
Peter Chernin, *CEO*
EMP: 135 EST: 2018
SALES (est): 2.23MM **Privately Held**
SIC: 6799 Investors, nec

(P-12741)
TENNENBAUM CAPITL PARTNERS LLC (DH)
Also Called: T C P
2951 28th St Ste 1000, Santa Monica
(90405-2993)
PHONE..............................310 566-1000
Lee Landrum, *Mng Pt*
Michael Leitner, *
Rajneesh Vig, *
Howard Levkowitz, *
Philip Tseng, *
EMP: 70 EST: 1999
SQ FT: 15,850
SALES (est): 5.25MM
SALES (corp-wide): 17.86B **Publicly Held**
SIC: 6799 Venture capital companies
HQ: Blackrock Finance, Inc.
50 Hudson Yards
New York NY 10001

(P-12742)
TRANSOM CAPITAL GROUP LLC (PA)
10990 Wilshire Blvd Ste 440, Los Angeles
(90024-3950)
PHONE..............................424 293-2818
Ken Firtel, *Managing Member*
EMP: 47 EST: 2007
SALES (est): 1.32B
SALES (corp-wide): 1.32B **Privately Held**
Web: www.transomcap.com
SIC: 6799 5112 5943 3951 Investors, nec;
Pens and/or pencils; Writing supplies;
Fountain pens and fountain pen desk sets

(P-12743)
TRUAMERICA MULTIFAMILY LLC
Also Called: Solis FL Owner

10100 Santa Monica Blvd Ste 400, Los
Angeles (90067-4108)
PHONE..............................424 325-2750
EMP: 70 EST: 2013
SALES (est): 27.58MM **Privately Held**
Web: www.truamerica.com
SIC: 6799 Investors, nec

(P-12744)
TRUE INVESTMENTS LLC
6535 Caballero Blvd Unit B, Buena Park
(90620-8106)
PHONE..............................949 258-9720
EMP: 26
SALES (corp-wide): 1.54MM **Privately Held**
Web: www.truefamilyenterprises.com
SIC: 6799 7372 Investors, nec; Application
computer software
PA: True Investments, Llc
2260 University Dr
949 258-9720

(P-12745)
TRUE INVESTMENTS LLC (PA)
2260 University Dr, Newport Beach
(92660-3319)
PHONE..............................949 258-9720
Alan True, *CEO*
EMP: 24 EST: 2012
SALES (est): 4.94MM
SALES (corp-wide): 4.94MM **Privately Held**
Web: www.twilatrue.com
SIC: 6799 7372 Investors, nec; Application
computer software

(P-12746)
USA ENTERPRISE INC
9777 Wilshire Blvd Ste 400, Beverly Hills
(90212-1904)
PHONE..............................310 750-4246
Ahmed Sharif, *CEO*
EMP: 350 EST: 1999
SALES (est): 580.43K **Privately Held**
Web: www.usaenterpriseinc.com
SIC: 6799 Real estate investors, except
property operators

(P-12747)
WEDGEWOOD INC (PA)
2015 Manhattan Beach Blvd Ste 100,
Redondo Beach (90278-1230)
PHONE..............................310 640-3070
Gregory L Geiser, *CEO*
David Wehrly, *
Michele Tasker, *
EMP: 81 EST: 1985
SQ FT: 3,200
SALES (est): 42.58MM
SALES (corp-wide): 42.58MM **Privately Held**
Web: www.wedgewood-inc.com
SIC: 6799 Real estate investors, except
property operators

(P-12748)
WINDJMMER CPITL INVSTORS III L
Also Called: Westwind Equity Investors
610 Newport Center Dr Ste 1100, Newport
Beach (92660-6460)
PHONE..............................949 706-9989
J Derek Watson, *
Mike Wattles, *
Jeff Miehe, *
Matt Anderson, *
EMP: 724 EST: 1990
SALES (est): 1.32MM **Privately Held**
Web: www.windjammercapital.com

SIC: 6799 Investors, nec

(P-12749)
WINDJMMER CPITL INVSTORS IV LP
610 Newport Center Dr Ste 1100, Newport
Beach (92660-6460)
PHONE..............................919 706-9989
Bill Herkamp, *Pt*
EMP: 450 EST: 2011
SALES (est): 1.41MM **Privately Held**
Web: www.windjammercapital.com
SIC: 6799 Investors, nec

7011 Hotels And Motels

(P-12750)
1260 BB PROPERTY LLC
Also Called: Four Ssons Rsort Santa Barbara
1260 Channel Dr, Santa Barbara
(93108-2805)
PHONE..............................805 969-2261
H Ty Warner, *CEO*
▲ EMP: 500 EST: 1986
SALES (est): 50.3MM
SALES (corp-wide): 54.92MM **Privately Held**
SIC: 7011 Resort hotel
HQ: Fsb Cal Corp.
280 Chestnut Ave
Westmont IL 60559
630 920-1515

(P-12751)
1835 COLUMBIA STREET LP
Also Called: Porto Vista Hotel
1835 Columbia St, San Diego
(92101-2505)
PHONE..............................619 564-3993
Moe Siry, *Pt*
EMP: 80 EST: 1992
SALES (est): 2.68MM **Privately Held**
Web: www.portovistasd.com
SIC: 7011 Hotels

(P-12752)
1855 S HBR BLVD DRV HLDNGS LLC
Also Called: Sheraton Pk Ht At Anheim Rsort
1855 S Harbor Blvd, Anaheim
(92802-3509)
PHONE..............................714 750-1811
Kunthea Hang, *Prin*
Tony Bruno, *
Ian Gee, *
EMP: 250 EST: 2012
SALES (est): 1.2MM **Privately Held**
Web: four-points.marriott.com
SIC: 7011 Hotels

(P-12753)
51ST ST & 8TH AVE CORP
Also Called: Loews Coronado Bay Resort
4000 Coronado Bay Rd, Coronado
(92118-3290)
PHONE..............................619 424-4000
Johnathan M Tish, *CEO*
▲ EMP: 206 EST: 1994
SALES (est): 22.77MM **Privately Held**
Web: www.loewshotels.com
SIC: 7011 Hotels

(P-12754)
6417 SELMA HOTEL LLC
Also Called: Dream Hollywood
6417 Selma Ave, Los Angeles
(90028-7310)
PHONE..............................323 844-6417

SIC: 6799 Investors, nec

Richard Heyman, *Managing Member*
EMP: 250 EST: 2017
SALES (est): 11.04MM **Privately Held**
Web: www.dreamhotels.com
SIC: 7011 Hotels

(P-12755)
8110 AERO HOLDING LLC
Also Called: Sheraton
8110 Aero Dr, San Diego (92123-1715)
PHONE..............................858 277-8888
Lucy Burni, *Managing Member*
Nabih Geha, *
EMP: 210 EST: 2019
SALES (est): 4.99MM **Privately Held**
Web: www.marriott.com
SIC: 7011 5813 5812 Hotels and motels;
Drinking places; Eating places

(P-12756)
901 WEST OLYMPIC BLVD LTD PRTN
Also Called: Residence Inn By Marriott
901 W Olympic Blvd, Los Angeles
(90015-1327)
PHONE..............................213 443-9200
Greg Steinhauer, *Pt*
Homer Williams, *Pt*
EMP: 110 EST: 2011
SQ FT: 286,000
SALES (est): 3.33MM **Privately Held**
Web: www.marriott.com
SIC: 7011 Hotels and motels

(P-12757)
AGUA CLNTE BAND CHILLA INDIANS
Also Called: Agua Caliente Casino & Resort
32250 Bob Hope Dr, Rancho Mirage
(92270-2704)
PHONE..............................760 321-2000
Ken Kettler, *Brnch Mgr*
EMP: 1000
SALES (corp-wide): 83.82MM **Privately Held**
Web: www.aguacalientecasinos.com
SIC: 7011 Casino hotel
PA: Agua Caliente Band Of Cahuilla
Indians
5401 Dinah Shore Dr
760 699-6800

(P-12758)
AGUA CLNTE BAND CHILLA INDIANS
Also Called: Spa Resort Casino
401 E Amado Rd, Palm Springs
(92262-6403)
PHONE..............................800 854-1279
Ramona Grinager, *Prin*
EMP: 698
SALES (corp-wide): 83.82MM **Privately Held**
Web: www.aguacalientecasinos.com
SIC: 7011 7991 Casino hotel; Spas
PA: Agua Caliente Band Of Cahuilla
Indians
5401 Dinah Shore Dr
760 699-6800

(P-12759)
AMERICAN KOYU CORPORATION
1733 S Anaheim Blvd, Anaheim
(92805-6518)
P.O. Box 1145 (92878-1145)
PHONE..............................626 793-0669
Yoichi Erikawa, *Pr*
EMP: 150 EST: 2002

SALES (est): 19.24MM **Privately Held**
Web: koyucorp.jimdofree.com
SIC: 7011 Hotels

(P-12760)
AMERICAN PRPRTY-MNAGEMENT CORP
Also Called: U. S. Grant Hotel
326 Broadway, San Diego (92101-4812)
PHONE..................................619 232-3121
John Gallegon, *Mgr*
EMP: 1414
SALES (corp-wide): 24.4MM **Privately Held**
Web: www.marriott.com
SIC: 7011 Hotels
PA: American Property-Management Corporation
8910 Univ Ctr Ln Ste 100
858 964-5500

(P-12761)
ANAHEIM - 1855 S HBR BLVD OWNE
Also Called: Sheraton
1855 S Harbor Blvd, Anaheim (92802-3509)
PHONE..................................714 750-1811
Ian Gee, *Prin*
EMP: 99 EST: 2019
SALES (est): 2.62MM **Privately Held**
Web: four-points.marriott.com
SIC: 7011 Hotels

(P-12762)
ASCOT HOTEL LP
Also Called: Hotel Angeleno
170 N Church Ln, Los Angeles (90049-2044)
PHONE..................................310 476-6411
Mark Beccaria, *Pt*
EMP: 125 EST: 2008
SALES (est): 4.28MM **Privately Held**
Web: www.hotelangeleno.com
SIC: 7011 Hotels

(P-12763)
ATLAS HOTELS INC
Also Called: Town and Country
500 Hotel Cir N, San Diego (92108-3005)
PHONE..................................619 291-2232
EMP: 1023
Web: www.towncountry.com
SIC: 7011 5812 5813 Hotels; Eating places; Cocktail lounge

(P-12764)
AVIARA FSRC ASSOCIATES LIMITED
7100 Aviara Resort Dr, Carlsbad (92011-4908)
PHONE..................................760 603-6800
Robert Cima, *Genl Mgr*
Aviara Resort Club, *
EMP: 1200 EST: 1995
SALES (est): 1.6MM **Publicly Held**
Web: www.parkhyattaviara.com
SIC: 7011 Resort hotel
HQ: Aviara Resort Associates Limited Partnership, A California Limited Partnership
7100 Aviara Resort Dr
Carlsbad CA 92011

(P-12765)
AYRES - PASO ROBLES LP
Also Called: Allegretto Vineyard Resort
2700 Buena Vista Dr, Paso Robles (93446-9530)

PHONE..................................714 850-0409
EMP: 120 EST: 2015
SALES (est): 2.11MM **Privately Held**
Web: www.allegrettovineyardresort.com
SIC: 7011 Hotels

(P-12766)
BALDWIN HOSPITALITY LLC
Also Called: Courtyard By Marriott
14635 Baldwin Park Towne Ctr, Baldwin Park (91706-5548)
PHONE..................................626 446-2988
Lina Mita, *Managing Member*
EMP: 80 EST: 1997
SALES (est): 2.53MM **Privately Held**
Web: courtyard.marriott.com
SIC: 7011 Hotels and motels

(P-12767)
BARONA RESORT & CASINO
1932 Wildcat Canyon Rd, Lakeside (92040-1553)
PHONE..................................619 443-2300
Dean Allen, *Sr VP*
Linda Jordan, *Sr VP*
Nick Dillon, *Ex VP*
Troy Simpson, *Ex VP*
Rick Salinas, *Genl Mgr*
EMP: 3500 EST: 2005
SALES (est): 46.51MM **Privately Held**
Web: www.barona.com
SIC: 7011 Resort hotel

(P-12768)
BARTELL HOTELS
Also Called: Hilton San Diego Airport/Hrbr
1960 Harbor Island Dr, San Diego (92101-1013)
PHONE..................................619 291-6700
Luis Barrios, *Genl Mgr*
EMP: 100
SALES (corp-wide): 31.86MM **Privately Held**
Web: www.bartellhotels.com
SIC: 7011 Hotels
PA: Bartell Hotels, A California Limited Partnership
4875 N Harbor Dr
619 224-1556

(P-12769)
BCRA RESORT SERVICES INC
Also Called: Bacara Resorts and Spa
8301 Hollister Ave, Santa Barbara (93117-2474)
PHONE..................................805 571-3176
EMP: 150
Web: www.ritzcarlton.com
SIC: 7011 Hotels

(P-12770)
BEHRINGER HARVARD WILSHIRE BLV
Also Called: Hotel Palomar
10740 Wilshire Blvd, Los Angeles (90024-4493)
PHONE..................................310 475-8711
Ravi Sikand, *Pt*
EMP: 99 EST: 2006
SALES (est): 4.55MM **Privately Held**
Web: www.hotelpalomar-beverlyhills.com
SIC: 7011 6531 Hotels; Real estate agents and managers

(P-12771)
BELVEDERE HOTEL PARTNERSHIP
Also Called: Peninsula Beverly Hill's

9882 Santa Monica Blvd, Beverly Hills (90212-1605)
PHONE..................................310 551-2888
Ali Kasikci, *Mgr*
EMP: 442
Web: www.privatebeverlyhills.com
SIC: 7011 6512 5813 5812 Hotels; Nonresidential building operators; Drinking places; Eating places
PA: The Belvedere Hotel Partnership
421 N Beverly Dr Ste 350

(P-12772)
BELVEDERE PARTNERSHIP
Also Called: Peninsula Beverly Hills, The
9882 Santa Monica Blvd, Beverly Hills (90212-1605)
PHONE..................................310 551-2888
Robert Zarnegan, *Pr*
▲ EMP: 400 EST: 2005
SALES (est): 24.87MM **Privately Held**
Web: www.peninsula.com
SIC: 7011 Bed and breakfast inn

(P-12773)
BEST WESTERN STOVALLS INN (PA)
Also Called: Anaheim Inn
1110 W Katella Ave, Anaheim (92802-2805)
PHONE..................................714 956-4430
James Stovall, *Pt*
Robert Stovall, *Pt*
Minta Pettis-stovall, *Pt*
Bill O'connell, *Pt*
EMP: 90 EST: 1966
SQ FT: 4,800
SALES (est): 9.97MM
SALES (corp-wide): 9.97MM **Privately Held**
Web: www.anaheiminn.com
SIC: 7011 Hotels and motels

(P-12774)
BEVERLY HILLS LUXURY HOTEL LLC
1801 Century Park E Ste 1200, Los Angeles (90067-2334)
PHONE..................................310 274-9999
Kenneth Bordewick, *Managing Member*
EMP: 450 EST: 2002
SALES (est): 4.44MM **Privately Held**
SIC: 7011 Resort hotel

(P-12775)
BH PARTNERSHIP LP (PA)
Also Called: Bahia Resort Hotels
998 W Mission Bay Dr, San Diego (92109-7803)
PHONE..................................858 539-7635
Anne L Evans, *Genl Pt*
William L Evans, *Pt*
Anthony Belefm, *Chief Human Resources Officer*
EMP: 300 EST: 1945
SALES (est): 9.52MM
SALES (corp-wide): 9.52MM **Privately Held**
Web: www.bahiahotel.com
SIC: 7011 6531 5812 Resort hotel; Real estate managers; Eating places

(P-12776)
BRAEMAR PARTNERSHIP
Also Called: Catamaran Resort Hotel
3999 Mission Blvd, San Diego (92109-6959)
PHONE..................................858 488-1081
Robert Gleason, *CFO*
Anne L Evans, *Mgr*
EMP: 350 EST: 1959

SALES (est): 8.92MM **Privately Held**
Web: www.catamaranresort.com
SIC: 7011 5812 5813 Resort hotel; American restaurant; Cocktail lounge

(P-12777)
BRISAM LAX (DE) LLC
Also Called: Holiday Inn
9901 S La Cienega Blvd, Los Angeles (90045-5915)
PHONE..................................310 649-5151
Steve Hostetter, *Genl Mgr*
EMP: 95 EST: 2007
SALES (est): 3.84MM **Privately Held**
Web: www.holidayinn.com
SIC: 7011 Hotels and motels

(P-12778)
BURTON WAY HOTELS LLC
Also Called: Four Seasons Hotels Limited
300 S Doheny Dr, Los Angeles (90048-3704)
PHONE..................................310 273-2222
Isadore Sharp, *Ch*
EMP: 77 EST: 2015
SALES (est): 12.46MM **Privately Held**
SIC: 7011 Hotels

(P-12779)
BURTON WAY HTELS LTD A CAL LTD
Also Called: Four Seasons Ht Westlake Vlg
2 Dole Dr, Westlake Village (91362-7300)
PHONE..................................818 575-3000
Robert Cima, *Brnch Mgr*
EMP: 215
SALES (corp-wide): 3.69MM **Privately Held**
SIC: 7011 Hotels
PA: Burton Way Hotels, Ltd., A California Limited Partnership
2029 Century Park E # 2200
310 552-6623

(P-12780)
BURTON-WAY HOUSE LTD A CA
Also Called: Four Seasons Hotel
300 S Doheny Dr, Los Angeles (90048-3704)
PHONE..................................310 273-2222
Mehdi Efpekari, *Genl Mgr*
EMP: 215
SALES (corp-wide): 3.69MM **Privately Held**
SIC: 7011 5812 Hotels; Eating places
PA: Burton Way Hotels, Ltd., A California Limited Partnership
2029 Century Park E # 2200
310 552-6623

(P-12781)
BY THE BLUE SEA LLC
Also Called: Shutters On The Beach
1 Pico Blvd, Santa Monica (90405-1063)
PHONE..................................310 458-0030
Tim Dubois, *Pr*
Klaus Mennekes, *
EMP: 350 EST: 2001
SALES (est): 23.88MM **Privately Held**
Web: www.shuttersonthebeach.com
SIC: 7011 Hotels

(P-12782)
C W HOTELS LTD
Also Called: JW Marriott Le Merigot
1740 Ocean Ave, Santa Monica (90401-3214)
PHONE..................................310 395-9700
Damien Hirsch, *Genl Mgr*
EMP: 150

P R O D U C T S & S V C S

SALES (corp-wide): 9.39MM **Privately Held**
Web: www.marriott.com
SIC: 7011 Hotels
PA: C W Hotels Ltd
740 Centre View Blvd
859 578-1100

(P-12783)
CABAZON BAND MISSION INDIANS
Fantasy Spring Resort Casino
84245 Indio Springs Dr, Indio (92203-3499)
PHONE..................................760 342-5000
Jim Mccannon, *Mgr*
EMP: 520
Web: www.fantasyspringsresort.com
SIC: 7011 Casino hotel
PA: Cabazon Band Of Cahuilla Indians
84245 Indio Springs Dr

(P-12784)
CALIFORNIA COMMERCE CLUB INC
Also Called: Commerce Casino
6131 Telegraph Rd, Commerce (90040-2501)
PHONE..................................323 721-2100
Haig Papaian, *CEO*
Ralph Wong, *CAO**
Dante Oliveto, *
Harvey Ross, *
Deborah Payne, *
▲ EMP: 2600 EST: 1982
SQ FT: 350,000
SALES (est): 41.95MM **Privately Held**
Web: www.commercecasino.com
SIC: 7011 5812 Casino hotel; Eating places

(P-12785)
CARPENTERS SOUTHWEST ADM CORP (PA)
533 S Fremont Ave, Los Angeles (90071-1712)
P.O. Box 17969 (90017-0969)
PHONE..................................213 386-8590
Douglas Mccarron, *CEO*
EMP: 70 EST: 1982
SQ FT: 25,000
SALES (est): 24.63MM
SALES (corp-wide): 24.63MM **Privately Held**
Web: www.carpenterssw.org
SIC: 7011 Hotels and motels

(P-12786)
CARSON OPERATING COMPANY LLC
Also Called: Doubletree By Hilton Carson
2 Civic Plaza Dr, Carson (90745-2231)
PHONE..................................310 830-9200
Greg Guthrie, *Genl Mgr*
Leroy Russell, *
EMP: 90 EST: 2015
SALES (est): 2.32MM **Privately Held**
Web: www.hilton.com
SIC: 7011 Hotels

(P-12787)
CAVALIER INN INC
Also Called: Cavalier Oceanfront Resort
9415 Hearst Dr, San Simeon (93452-9724)
PHONE..................................805 927-4688
Mona Rigdon, *Prin*
Michael Hanchett, *
EMP: 80 EST: 2016
SALES (est): 1.83MM **Privately Held**
Web: www.cavalierresort.com
SIC: 7011 Motels

(P-12788)
CELEBRITY CASINOS INC
Also Called: Crystal Casino & Hotel
123 E Artesia Blvd, Compton (90220-4921)
PHONE..................................310 631-3838
Mark A Kelegian, *Pr*
Haig Kelegian Junior, *CFO*
Haig Kelegian Senior, *CEO*
EMP: 400 EST: 2005
SQ FT: 190,000
SALES (est): 3.28MM **Privately Held**
Web: www.thecrystalcasino.com
SIC: 7011 Casino hotel

(P-12789)
CENTURY GAMING MANAGEMENT INC
Also Called: Hollywood Park Casino
3883 W Century Blvd, Inglewood (90303-1003)
PHONE..................................310 330-2800
▲ EMP: 710
Web: www.playhpc.com
SIC: 7011 5813 5812 Casino hotel; Drinking places; Eating places

(P-12790)
CHA LA MIRADA LLC
Also Called: Holiday Inn La Mirada
14299 Firestone Blvd, La Mirada (90638-5523)
PHONE..................................714 739-8500
Regina Stryker, *Prin*
Jay Macaluso, *Prin*
EMP: 120 EST: 1984
SALES (est): 4.54MM **Privately Held**
Web: www.holidayinn.com
SIC: 7011 Hotels and motels

(P-12791)
CHAMPION INVESTMENT CORP
12809 Oakfield Way, Poway (92064-1520)
PHONE..................................917 712-7807
Chia-sheng Hou, *Pr*
Pi-lien Hou, *VP*
EMP: 100 EST: 1993
SALES (est): 836.99K **Privately Held**
Web: www.hilton.com
SIC: 7011 Resort hotel

(P-12792)
CIM GROUP LP (PA)
Also Called: Commercial Inv MGT Group
4700 Wilshire Blvd Ste 1, Los Angeles (90010-3854)
PHONE..................................323 860-4900
Avraham Shemesch, *Pt*
Eric P Rubenfeld, *Pt*
EMP: 85 EST: 2000
SALES (est): 46.57MM
SALES (corp-wide): 46.57MM **Privately Held**
Web: www.cimgroup.com
SIC: 7011 6798 6552 Hotels and motels; Real estate investment trusts; Land subdividers and developers, commercial

(P-12793)
CIM/H & H HOTEL LP
Also Called: Renaissance Hollywood Ht & Spa
1755 N Highland Ave, Los Angeles (90028-4403)
PHONE..................................323 856-1200
EMP: 350
Web: www.renaissancehollywood.com
SIC: 7011 Hotels

(P-12794)
CINDERELLA MOTEL
Also Called: Candy Cane Inn
1747 S Harbor Blvd, Anaheim (92802-2315)
PHONE..................................559 432-0118
Ralph Kazarian, *Pr*
EMP: 81
SQ FT: 65,542
SALES (corp-wide): 2.29MM **Privately Held**
Web: www.candycaneinn.net
SIC: 7011 Motels
PA: Cinderella Motel
2416 W Shaw Ave Ste 109
559 432-0118

(P-12795)
CITRUS NORTH VENTURE LLC
6591 Collins Dr Ste E11, Moorpark (93021-1493)
PHONE..................................256 428-2000
Marc Pierguidi, *Sec*
EMP: 99 EST: 2017
SALES (est): 661.59K **Privately Held**
SIC: 7011 Hotel, franchised

(P-12796)
CNI THL PROPCO FE LLC
Also Called: Four Points Bakersfield
5101 California Ave, Bakersfield (93309-1623)
PHONE..................................661 325-9700
EMP: 80 EST: 2017
SALES (est): 932.32K **Privately Held**
Web: www.fourpointsbakersfield.com
SIC: 7011 Hotels and motels

(P-12797)
COLONY PALMS HOTEL LLC
572 N Indian Canyon Dr, Palm Springs (92262-6030)
PHONE..................................760 969-1800
Al Wertheimer, *Prin*
EMP: 70 EST: 2011
SALES (est): 3.9MM **Privately Held**
Web: www.colonypalmshotel.com
SIC: 7011 Resort hotel

(P-12798)
COMFORT CALIFORNIA INC
Also Called: Clarion Hotel
616 W Convention Way, Anaheim (92802-3401)
PHONE..................................714 750-3131
Mike Thomas, *Brnch Mgr*
EMP: 149
SALES (corp-wide): 49.02MM **Privately Held**
Web: www.choicehotels.com
SIC: 7011 Hotels and motels
HQ: Comfort California, Inc.
8171 Maple Lawn Blvd # 380
Fulton MD 20759

(P-12799)
CORE/RELATED GALA RETAIL LLC
Also Called: Conrad Los Angeles
100 S Grand Ave, Los Angeles (90012-4794)
PHONE..................................213 349-8585
EMP: 75 EST: 2018
SQ FT: 1,800
SALES (est): 3.61MM **Privately Held**
SIC: 7011 Hotels and motels

(P-12800)
COURTYARD MANAGEMENT CORP
Also Called: Courtyard By Marriott Irvine
7955 Irvine Center Dr, Irvine (92618-3207)
PHONE..................................949 453-1033
Audun Poulsen, *Genl Mgr*
EMP: 70
SALES (corp-wide): 23.71B **Publicly Held**
Web: www.marriott.com
SIC: 7011 Hotels and motels
HQ: Courtyard Management Llc
7750 Wisconsin Ave
Bethesda MD 20814

(P-12801)
COURTYARD OXNARD
600 E Esplanade Dr, Oxnard (93036-2480)
PHONE..................................805 988-3600
Patricia Tewes, *Genl Mgr*
EMP: 80 EST: 2009
SALES (est): 980.93K **Privately Held**
SIC: 7011 Hotels and motels

(P-12802)
CPH MONARCH HOTEL LLC
Also Called: Waldorf Astria Mnrc Bch Rsort
1 Monarch Beach Resort, Dana Point (92629-4085)
PHONE..................................949 234-3200
Paul Makarechian, *Pr*
▲ EMP: 1100 EST: 2001
SQ FT: 300,000
SALES (est): 17.06MM
SALES (corp-wide): 97.93MM **Privately Held**
Web: www.waldorfastoriamonarchbeach.com
SIC: 7011 Resort hotel
PA: Waldorf Astoria Management Llc
7930 Jones Branch Dr # 1100
703 883-1000

(P-12803)
CRESTLINE HOTELS & RESORTS INC (HQ)
Also Called: Kyoto Grand Hotel and Gardens
120 S Los Angeles St 11, Los Angeles (90012-3724)
PHONE..................................213 629-1200
Richard Gaines, *Genl Mgr*
EMP: 130 EST: 1974
SALES (est): 743.65K
SALES (corp-wide): 370.56MM **Privately Held**
Web: www.kyotograndhotel.com
SIC: 7011 5812 5813 Hotels; Restaurant, family: independent; Drinking places
PA: Crestline Hotels & Resorts, Llc
3950 University Dr # 301
571 529-6100

(P-12804)
CTC GROUP INC (DH)
Also Called: Doubletree Hotel
21333 Hawthorne Blvd, Torrance (90503-5602)
PHONE..................................310 540-0500
John Huang, *CEO*
EMP: 145 EST: 1989
SALES (est): 9.88MM
SALES (corp-wide): 2.7B **Publicly Held**
Web: www.hilton.com
SIC: 7011 Hotels and motels
HQ: Gringteam Inc
21725 Gateway Center Drv
Diamond Bar CA 91765

▲ = Import ▼ = Export
◆ = Import/Export

(P-12805)
CUSTOM HOTEL LLC
Also Called: Hotel June, The
8639 Lincoln Blvd, Los Angeles
(90045-3503)
PHONE...................310 645-0400
Alisa Matthews, *
EMP: 236 **EST:** 2005
SALES (est): 2.58MM **Publicly Held**
Web: www.thehoteljune.com
SIC: 7011 Hotels
HQ: Joie De Vivre Hospitality, Llc
1750 Geary Blvd
San Francisco CA 94115
415 922-6000

(P-12806)
DAVIDSON HOTEL PARTNERS LP
Also Called: Agoura Hills Renaissance Hotel
30100 Agoura Rd, Agoura Hills
(91301-2004)
PHONE...................818 707-1220
Larry Mills, Pt
EMP: 2215
Web: www.davidsonhospitality.com
SIC: 7011 Hotels and motels
PA: Davidson Hotel Partners, L.P
1 Ravinia Dr Ste 1600

(P-12807)
DESTINATION RESIDENCES LLC
Also Called: Shadow Mtn Rsort Rcquet CLB Tn
45750 San Luis Rey Ave, Palm Desert
(92260-4728)
PHONE...................760 346-4647
Sindy Calhoun, Mgr
EMP: 666
SALES (corp-wide): 367.25MM **Privately Held**
Web: www.destinationhotels.com
SIC: 7011 5699 6531 Resort hotel; Sports apparel; Condominium manager
HQ: Destination Residences Llc
10333 E Dry Creek Rd
Englewood CO 80112
303 799-3830

(P-12808)
DIAMOND RESORTS INTL INC
Also Called: Palm Canyon Resort
2800 S Palm Canyon Dr, Palm Springs
(92264-9337)
PHONE...................702 823-7000
David F Palmer, Brnch Mgr
EMP: 80
SALES (corp-wide): 3.90B **Publicly Held**
Web: www.tophotelreservations.com
SIC: 7011 Resort hotel
HQ: Diamond Resorts International, Inc
1450 Center Crossing Rd
Las Vegas NV 89144
877 787-0906

(P-12809)
DIAMOND RESORTS LLC
Also Called: Palm Canyon Resort & Spa
2800 S Palm Canyon Dr, Palm Springs
(92264-9337)
PHONE...................760 866-1800
Allison Wickerham, Managing Member
Carl Ellis, *
EMP: 100 **EST:** 2004
SALES (est): 2.41MM **Privately Held**
Web: www.tophotelreservations.com
SIC: 7011 5812 7991 Resort hotel; American restaurant; Spas

(P-12810)
DIAMONDROCK SAN DEGO TNANT LLC
Also Called: Westin San Diego
400 W Broadway, San Diego (92101-3504)
PHONE...................619 239-4500
EMP: 300 **EST:** 2012
SQ FT: 337,717
SALES (est): 7.56MM
SALES (corp-wide): 1.07B **Publicly Held**
Web: www.westinsandiego.com
SIC: 7011 Hotels
HQ: Diamondrock Hospitality Limited Partnership
3 Bethesda Metro Center,
Bethesda MD 20814

(P-12811)
DISNEY ENTERPRISES INC
Also Called: Disney
1150 W Magic Way, Anaheim (92802-2247)
PHONE...................714 778-6600
Michael D Eisner, Pr
EMP: 3500
SALES (corp-wide): 91.36B **Publicly Held**
Web: en.disneyme.com
SIC: 7011 Resort hotel
HQ: Disney Enterprises, Inc.
500 S Buena Vista St
Burbank CA 91521
818 560-1000

(P-12812)
DISNEYLAND INTERNATIONAL
Also Called: Disneyland
1580 S Disneyland Dr, Anaheim
(92802-2294)
PHONE...................714 956-6746
EMP: 4000
SALES (corp-wide): 91.36B **Publicly Held**
Web: disneyland.disney.go.com
SIC: 7011 Resort hotel
HQ: Disneyland International
1313 S Harbor Blvd
Anaheim CA 92802
714 781-4565

(P-12813)
DKN HOTEL LLC (PA)
42 Corporate Park Ste 200, Irvine
(92606-3104)
PHONE...................714 427-4320
Nilesh Patel, *
John Jorgensen, *
Dahya Lal, *
EMP: 290 **EST:** 2002
SQ FT: 4,000
SALES (est): 23.19MM
SALES (corp-wide): 23.19MM **Privately Held**
Web: www.dknhotels.com
SIC: 7011 Hotels and motels

(P-12814)
DOLPHIN BAY HT & RESIDENCE INC
Also Called: Dolphin Bay Hotel & Residences
2727 Shell Beach Rd, Shell Beach
(93449-1602)
PHONE...................805 773-4300
Richard J Loughead Junior, CEO
EMP: 90 **EST:** 2005
SALES (est): 4.79MM **Privately Held**
Web: www.thedolphinbay.com
SIC: 7011 Resort hotel

(P-12815)
DONALD T STERLING CORPORATION
Also Called: Beverly Hills Plaza Hotel
10300 Wilshire Blvd, Los Angeles
(90024-4772)
PHONE...................310 275-5575
Zair Caceres, Brnch Mgr
EMP: 80
SALES (corp-wide): 2.1MM **Privately Held**
Web: www.beverlyhillsplazahotel.com
SIC: 7011 Hotels
PA: Donald T. Sterling Corporation
9441 Wlshire Blvd Pnthuse
310 278-8000

(P-12816)
DTRS SANTA MONICA LLC
Also Called: Loews Santa Monica Beach Hotel
1700 Ocean Ave, Santa Monica
(90401-3214)
PHONE...................310 458-6700
Younes Atallah, Owner
Younes Atolah, Genl Mgr
Andrei Zotoff, Managing Member
Patrick Mayor, Managing Member
EMP: 300 **EST:** 1989
SQ FT: 300,000
SALES (est): 22.79MM **Privately Held**
Web: santamonica.regenthotels.com
SIC: 7011 Resort hotel

(P-12817)
EDWARD THOMAS COMPANIES
Also Called: Jolly Roger Inn
640 W Katella Ave, Anaheim (92802-3411)
PHONE...................714 782-7500
Fred Kokash, Brnch Mgr
EMP: 110
SALES (corp-wide): 1.22MM **Privately Held**
Web: www.edwardthomasco.com
SIC: 7011 5812 Motels; Eating places
PA: The Edward Thomas Companies
9950 Santa Monica Blvd
310 859-9366

(P-12818)
EDWARD THOMAS HOSPITALITY CORP
Also Called: Shutters On The Beach
1 Pico Blvd, Santa Monica (90405-1063)
PHONE...................310 458-0030
Klaus Mennekes, Brnch Mgr
EMP: 349
SALES (corp-wide): 2.99MM **Privately Held**
Web: www.shuttersonthebeach.com
SIC: 7011 5812 7991 5813 Hotels; Eating places; Physical fitness facilities; Drinking places
PA: The Edward Thomas Hospitality Corp
9950 Santa Monica Blvd
310 859-9366

(P-12819)
EL DORADO ENTERPRISES INC
Also Called: Hustler Casino
1000 W Redondo Beach Blvd, Gardena
(90247-4192)
PHONE...................310 719-9800
Larry C Flynt, CEO
EMP: 760 **EST:** 2000
SALES (est): 24.86MM **Privately Held**
Web: www.hustlercasino.com
SIC: 7011 Casino hotel

(P-12820)
EL ENCANTO INC
Also Called: Belmond El Encanto
800 Alvarado Pl, Santa Barbara
(93103-2176)
PHONE...................805 845-5800
Richard M Levine, CEO
Martin O'grady, CFO
Pedro Dias, *
EMP: 122 **EST:** 2013
SALES (est): 9.33MM **Privately Held**
Web: www.belmond.com
SIC: 7011 Resort hotel

(P-12821)
ENCINA PEPPER TREE JOINT VENTR (PA)
Also Called: Best Western
3850 State St, Santa Barbara (93105-3112)
PHONE...................805 687-5511
Jeanette Webber, Mng Pt
Pamela Webber, Pt
Camille Shaar, Pt
David Potter, Pt
EMP: 70 **EST:** 1951
SQ FT: 100,000
SALES (est): 5.96MM
SALES (corp-wide): 5.96MM **Privately Held**
Web: www.bestwestern.com
SIC: 7011 Hotels and motels

(P-12822)
ENCINA PEPPER TREE JOINT VENTR
Also Called: Best Western
2220 Bath St, Santa Barbara (93105-4322)
PHONE...................805 682-7277
Pam Webber, Owner
EMP: 80
SALES (corp-wide): 5.96MM **Privately Held**
Web: www.bestwestern.com
SIC: 7011 Motels
PA: Pepper Encina Tree Joint Venture
3850 State St
805 687-5511

(P-12823)
ET WHITEHALL SEASCAPE LLC
Also Called: Hotel Casa Del Mar
1910 Ocean Way, Santa Monica
(90405-1083)
PHONE...................310 581-5533
◆ **EMP:** 202 **EST:** 1998
SQ FT: 200,000
SALES (est): 4.35MM **Privately Held**
Web: www.hotelcasadelmar.com
SIC: 7011 5812 Hotels; Eating places

(P-12824)
EVOLUTION HOSPITALITY LLC
Also Called: Queen Mary, The
1126 Queens Hwy, Long Beach
(90802-6331)
PHONE...................562 435-3511
EMP: 315
SALES (corp-wide): 819.71MM **Privately Held**
Web: www.evolutionhospitality.com
SIC: 7011 Hotels and motels
HQ: Evolution Hospitality, Llc
1211 Puerta Del Sol # 170
San Clemente CA 92673
949 325-1350

(P-12825)
FJS INC
Also Called: Anabella Hotel The
888 S Disneyland Dr Ste 400, Anaheim
(92802-1846)
PHONE...................714 905-1050
Francis J Sparolini, CEO
C Y Chan, *
Rachel Moorhead, *

PRODUCTS & SVCS

EMP: 118 EST: 1989
SALES (est): 17.32MM **Privately Held**
SIC: 7011 Resort hotel

(P-12826)
FORTUNA ENTERPRISES LP
Also Called: Hilton
5711 W Century Blvd, Los Angeles
(90045-5672)
PHONE..............................310 410-4000
Henry H Hsu, *Pt*
David Hsu, *Pt*
Christine Hsu, *Pt*
EMP: 450 EST: 1992
SQ FT: 2,700
SALES (est): 40.28MM **Privately Held**
Web: www.hilton.com
SIC: 7011 5812 5813 Hotels and motels;
   Eating places; Bar (drinking places)
HQ: Universal Fortuna Investment, Inc.
   5711 W Century Blvd # 16
   Los Angeles CA 90045

(P-12827)
**GOLDEN DOOR PROPERTIES
LLC**
Also Called: Golden Door
777 Deer Springs Rd, San Marcos
(92069-9757)
PHONE..............................760 744-5777
Joanne Conway, *Managing Member*
Kathy Van Ness, *COO*
▲ EMP: 173 EST: 1958
SQ FT: 50,000
SALES (est): 8.46MM **Privately Held**
Web: www.goldendoor.com
SIC: 7011 Hotels and motels

(P-12828)
**GOLDEN HOTELS LTD
PARTNERSHIP**
Also Called: Atrium Hotel
18700 Macarthur Blvd, Irvine (92612-1409)
PHONE..............................949 833-2770
Mike Wang, *Pt*
John Wang, *
EMP: 140 EST: 1960
SQ FT: 120,000
SALES (est): 2.15MM **Privately Held**
Web: www.atriumhotel.com
SIC: 7011 Resort hotel

(P-12829)
GOLDEN WEST PARTNERS INC
Also Called: Golden West Casino
1001 S Union Ave, Bakersfield
(93307-3641)
PHONE..............................661 324-6936
Jaussauds Maison, *Brnch Mgr*
EMP: 104
Web: www.goldenwestcasino.com
SIC: 7011 Casino hotel
PA: Golden West Partners, Inc.
   200 Spctrum Ctr Dr Ste 12

(P-12830)
GRAND DEL MAR RESORT LP
Also Called: Grand Del Mar
5300 Grand Del Mar Ct, San Diego
(92130-4901)
PHONE..............................858 314-2000
Tom Voss, *Pt*
EMP: 570 EST: 2005
SALES (est): 24.5MM **Privately Held**
Web: www.thegranddelmar.com
SIC: 7011 Resort hotel

(P-12831)
**GRAND PACIFIC CARLSBAD HT
LP**
Also Called: Sheraton Carlsbad Resort & Spa
5480 Grand Pacific Dr, Carlsbad
(92008-4723)
PHONE..............................760 827-2400
Tim Shinkle, *CFO*
Janina Kershaw, *Contrlr*
EMP: 272 EST: 2008
SALES (est): 23.86MM **Privately Held**
Web: www.sheratoncarlsbad.com
SIC: 7011 Resort hotel

(P-12832)
GRAND PACIFIC RESORTS INC
Also Called: Resortime.com
5900 Pasteur Ct Ste 200, Carlsbad
(92008-7336)
PHONE..............................760 431-8500
Sherri Weks, *Mgr*
EMP: 513
Web: www.grandpacificresorts.com
SIC: 7011 Resort hotel
PA: Grand Pacific Resorts, Inc.
   5900 Pasteur Ct Ste 200

(P-12833)
**GRAND PACIFIC RESORTS
SVCS LP**
5900 Pasteur Ct Ste 200, Carlsbad
(92008-7336)
PHONE..............................760 431-8500
Timothy Stripe, *Pt*
David Brown, *Pt*
EMP: 120 EST: 1992
SQ FT: 22,000
SALES (est): 2.16MM **Privately Held**
Web: www.grandpacificresorts.com
SIC: 7011 Resort hotel

(P-12834)
**GREAT WOLF RSORTS
HOLDINGS INC**
12681 Harbor Blvd, Garden Grove
(92840-5857)
PHONE..............................888 960-9653
EMP: 239
SALES (corp-wide): 8.02B **Publicly Held**
Web: www.greatwolf.com
SIC: 7011 Resort hotel
HQ: Great Wolf Resorts Holdings, Inc.
   1255 Fourier Dr Ste 201
   Madison WI 53717
   608 662-4700

(P-12835)
GREENS GROUP INC
16530 Bake Pkwy Ste 200, Irvine
(92618-4685)
PHONE..............................949 829-4902
Ashutosh Kadakia, *CFO*
EMP: 145 EST: 2004
SALES (est): 4.97MM **Privately Held**
SIC: 7011 Resort hotel, franchised

(P-12836)
GRINGTEAM INC
Also Called: Doubletree By Hilton
7450 Hazard Center Dr, San Diego
(92108-4539)
PHONE..............................619 297-5466
Karima Zaki, *Mgr*
EMP: 300
SALES (corp-wide): 2.7B **Publicly Held**
Web: www.hilton.com
SIC: 7011 5812 Hotels and motels; Eating
   places
HQ: Gringteam Inc
   21725 Gateway Center Drv

Diamond Bar CA 91765

(P-12837)
GRINGTEAM INC
Also Called: Doubletree Golf Resort
800 W Ivy St Ste D, San Diego
(92101-1771)
PHONE..............................858 485-4145
Russ Tanakaya, *Genl Mgr*
EMP: 104
SALES (corp-wide): 2.7B **Publicly Held**
Web: www.hilton.com
SIC: 7011 Hotels and motels
HQ: Gringteam Inc
   21725 Gateway Center Drv
   Diamond Bar CA 91765

(P-12838)
GUESTY INC (PA)
440 N Barranca Ave Pmb 9720, Covina
(91723-1722)
PHONE..............................415 244-0277
Amiad Soto, *CEO*
Philip David Aber, *CFO*
EMP: 73 EST: 2013
SALES (est): 3.57MM
SALES (corp-wide): 3.57MM **Privately
Held**
Web: www.guesty.com
SIC: 7011 7371 Vacation lodges; Computer
   software development and applications

(P-12839)
H & H LLC (PA)
1131 S Russell Ave, Santa Maria
(93458-6821)
PHONE..............................805 925-2036
Blanche Hollingsead, *Managing Member*
EMP: 89 EST: 2011
SALES (est): 2.34MM
SALES (corp-wide): 2.34MM **Privately
Held**
Web: www.radissonhotels.com
SIC: 7011 Hotels and motels

(P-12840)
HANDLERY HOTELS INC
Also Called: Handlery Hotels
950 Hotel Cir N, San Diego (92108-2995)
PHONE..............................415 781-4550
John Martin, *Mgr*
EMP: 150
SALES (corp-wide): 18.71MM **Privately
Held**
Web: sd.handlery.com
SIC: 7011 5941 5812 5947 Resort hotel;
   Golf goods and equipment; Eating places;
   Gift, novelty, and souvenir shop
PA: Handlery Hotels, Inc.
   180 Geary St Ste 700
   415 781-4550

(P-12841)
HANFORD HOTELS INC
Also Called: Hotel Hanford, The
3131 Bristol St, Costa Mesa (92626-3037)
PHONE..............................714 557-3000
Tony Eccher, *Ex Dir*
EMP: 239
SQ FT: 65,311
Web: www.hanfordhotels.com
SIC: 7011 Hotels
PA: Hanford Hotels, Inc.
   17542 17th St Ste 450

(P-12842)
**HARBOR VIEW HOTEL
VENTURES LLC**
Also Called: Doubletree Ht San Diego
Dwntwn

1646 Front St, San Diego (92101-2920)
PHONE..............................619 239-6800
Michael Gallegos, *Managing Member*
EMP: 100 EST: 1997
SALES (est): 2.76MM **Privately Held**
Web: www.hilton.com
SIC: 7011 Hotels

(P-12843)
HAVASU LANDING CASINO (PA)
1 Main St, Needles (92363-9216)
PHONE..............................760 858-5380
EMP: 71 EST: 2010
SALES (est): 9.63MM **Privately Held**
Web: www.havasulanding.com
SIC: 7011 Casino hotel

(P-12844)
HAWAIIAN GARDENS CASINO
11871 Carson St, Hawaiian Gardens
(90716-1127)
PHONE..............................562 860-5887
David Moskowitz, *CEO*
Irving Moskowitz, *
▲ EMP: 1000 EST: 1998
SALES (est): 47.26MM **Privately Held**
Web: www.thegardenscasino.com
SIC: 7011 Casino hotel

(P-12845)
**HAWAIIAN HOTELS & RESORTS
INC**
2830 Borchard Rd, Newbury Park
(91320-3810)
PHONE..............................805 480-0052
Edward J Hogan, *Pr*
Glenn Hogan, *
EMP: 145 EST: 2001
SALES (est): 2.26MM
SALES (corp-wide): 1.08B **Privately Held**
Web: www.hawaiihotels.com
SIC: 7011 Resort hotel
HQ: Pleasant Holidays, Llc
   2404 Townsgate Rd
   Westlake Village CA 91361

(P-12846)
HAZENS INVESTMENT LLC
Also Called: Sheraton
6101 W Century Blvd, Los Angeles
(90045-5310)
PHONE..............................310 642-1111
Henry Pekun, *Contrlr*
EMP: 395 EST: 2002
SALES (est): 8.98MM **Privately Held**
Web: four-points.marriott.com
SIC: 7011 Hotels

(P-12847)
HCAL LLC
Also Called: Harrahs Resort Southern Cal
777 S Resort Dr, Valley Center (92082)
PHONE..............................760 751-3100
EMP: 95 EST: 2005
SALES (est): 4.58MM
SALES (corp-wide): 11.53B **Publicly Held**
Web: www.harrahssocal.com
SIC: 7011 Casino hotel
HQ: Caesars Holdings, Inc.
   1 Caesars Palace Dr
   Las Vegas NV 89109

(P-12848)
HEI HOSPITALITY LLC
Also Called: Marriott
21850 Oxnard St, Woodland Hills
(91367-3631)
PHONE..............................818 887-4800
Clay Andrews, *Mgr*
EMP: 167

SALES (corp-wide): 447.39MM **Privately Held**
Web: www.heihotels.com
SIC: 7011 Hotels and motels
PA: Hei Hospitality, Llc
101 Merritt 7
203 849-8844

(P-12849)
HEI LONG BEACH LLC
Also Called: Hilton Hotels
701 W Ocean Blvd, Long Beach
(90831-3100)
PHONE..............................562 983-3400
Clark Christopher, *Prin*
EMP: 125 EST: 2004
SALES (est): 8.61MM
SALES (corp-wide): 447.39MM **Privately Held**
Web: www.hilton.com
SIC: 7011 Hotels
PA: Hei Hospitality, Llc
101 Merritt 7
203 849-8844

(P-12850)
HISTORIC MISSION INN CORP
Also Called: Mission Inn Hotel and Spa, The
3649 Mission Inn Ave, Riverside
(92501-3364)
P.O. Box 1433 (92502-1433)
PHONE..............................951 784-0300
Duane R Roberts, *Pr*
Diana Rosure, *General Vice President**
Richard Shippee, *
Cliff Day, *
EMP: 460 EST: 1992
SALES (est): 33.22MM
SALES (corp-wide): 33.22MM **Privately Held**
Web: www.missioninn.com
SIC: 7011 7991 Resort hotel; Spas
PA: Entrepreneurial Capital Corporation
4100 Newport Place Dr # 400
949 809-3900

(P-12851)
HISTORICAL PROPERTIES INC (PA)
Also Called: Horton Grand Hotel
311 Island Ave, San Diego (92101-6923)
PHONE..............................619 230-8417
Doris J Rose, *Pr*
Santiago Ojeda, *
EMP: 96 EST: 1995
SQ FT: 60,000
SALES (est): 4.92MM **Privately Held**
Web: www.hortongrand.com
SIC: 7011 Hotels

(P-12852)
HOLLYWOOD PARK CASINO CO INC
3883 W Century Blvd, Inglewood
(90303-1003)
PHONE..............................310 330-2800
Terrence E Fancher, *Pr*
EMP: 239 EST: 2007
SALES (est): 25.31MM **Privately Held**
Web: www.playhpc.com
SIC: 7011 Casino hotel

(P-12853)
HONEYMOON REAL ESTATE LP
Also Called: Avalon Hotel
9400 W Olympic Blvd, Beverly Hills
(90212-4552)
PHONE..............................310 277-5221
Brad Korzen, *Pt*
EMP: 90 EST: 1997

SQ FT: 400,000
SALES (est): 4.6MM **Privately Held**
Web: www.avalon-hotel.com
SIC: 7011 Resort hotel

(P-12854)
HOTEL BEL-AIR
701 Stone Canyon Rd, Los Angeles
(90077-2909)
PHONE..............................310 472-1211
EMP: 265 EST: 1994
SQ FT: 30,000
SALES (est): 1.2MM **Privately Held**
Web: www.dorchestercollection.com
SIC: 7011 Hotels
HQ: Kava Holdings, Inc.
701 Stone Canyon Rd
Los Angeles CA 90077
310 472-1211

(P-12855)
HOTEL CIRCLE PROPERTY LLC
Also Called: Town and Country Hotel
500 Hotel Cir N, San Diego (92108-3005)
PHONE..............................619 291-7131
April Shute, *Managing Member*
EMP: 500 EST: 2014
SQ FT: 1,132,560
SALES (est): 38.03MM **Privately Held**
Web: www.towncountry.com
SIC: 7011 Resort hotel

(P-12856)
HOTEL SHANGRI-LA
11400 W Olympic Blvd, Los Angeles
(90064-1544)
PHONE..............................310 394-2791
EMP: 74 EST: 2011
SALES (est): 3.84MM **Privately Held**
SIC: 7011 Resort hotel

(P-12857)
HP LQ INVESTMENT LP
Also Called: La Quinta Resort & Club
49499 Eisenhower Dr, La Quinta
(92253-2722)
PHONE..............................760 564-4111
EMP: 392 EST: 2021
SALES (est): 26.94MM
SALES (corp-wide): 10.23B **Publicly Held**
Web: www.laquintaresort.com
SIC: 7011 Resort hotel
PA: Hilton Worldwide Holdings Inc.
7930 Jones Br Dr Ste 1100
703 883-1000

(P-12858)
HUMNIT HOTEL AT LAX LLC
Also Called: Concorse Ht At Los Angles Arpr
6225 W Century Blvd, Los Angeles
(00046 5311)
PHONE..............................424 702-1234
Jina Luman, *Prin*
Jina Luman, *Asst Tr*
EMP: 99 EST: 2013
SQ FT: 49,500
SALES (est): 994.73K
SALES (corp-wide): 387.41MM **Publicly Held**
SIC: 7011 Hotels
PA: Amalgamated Financial Corp.
275 Seventh Ave
212 255-6200

(P-12859)
HUNTINGTON HOTEL COMPANY
5951 Linea Del Cielo, Rancho Santa Fe
(92067)
PHONE..............................858 756-1131
Scott Jenkins, *CEO*

EMP: 88 EST: 1921
SQ FT: 5,000
SALES (est): 2.34MM **Privately Held**
Web: www.theinnatrsf.com
SIC: 7011 5812 Resort hotel; Eating places

(P-12860)
HUOYEN INTERNATIONAL INC
Also Called: Hotel Fullerton Anaheim, The
1500 S Raymond Ave, Fullerton
(92831-5236)
P.O. Box 1071 (92822-1071)
PHONE..............................714 635-9000
Hsi Jung Yang, *Pr*
EMP: 90 EST: 1995
SQ FT: 144,698
SALES (est): 2.23MM **Privately Held**
SIC: 7011 Hotel, franchised

(P-12861)
HYATT CORP AS AGT BRCP HEF HT
Also Called: Hyatt Hotel
7100 Aviara Resort Dr, Carlsbad
(92011-4908)
PHONE..............................760 603-6851
EMP: 76 EST: 2010
SALES (est): 8.29MM **Privately Held**
Web: www.parkhyattviara.com
SIC: 7011 Resort hotel

(P-12862)
HYATT CORPORATION
Also Called: Hyatt Regency Lajolla
3777 La Jolla Village Dr, San Diego
(92122-1070)
PHONE..............................858 453-0018
Benjie Barin, *Owner*
EMP: 75 EST: 2000
SALES (est): 8.99MM **Privately Held**
Web: www.lajollamom.com
SIC: 7011 Hotels

(P-12863)
HYATT CORPORATION
Also Called: Manchster Grnd Hyatt San Diego
1 Market Pl, San Diego (92101-7714)
PHONE..............................619 232-1234
Ted Kanatas, *Mgr*
EMP: 117
Web: www.hosthotels.com
SIC: 7011 Hotels
HQ: Hyatt Corporation
250 Vesey St
New York NY 10281
312 750-1234

(P-12864)
HYATT CORPORATION
Also Called: Andaz Sandiego
600 F St, San Diego (92101-6310)
PHONE..............................619 849-1234
Rusty Middleton, *Brnch Mgr*
EMP: 98
Web: www.hyatt.com
SIC: 7011 Resort hotel
HQ: Hyatt Corporation
250 Vesey St
New York NY 10281
312 750-1234

(P-12865)
HYATT CORPORATION
Also Called: Hyatt Grand Champion Resort
44600 Indian Wells Ln, Indian Wells
(92210-8707)
PHONE..............................760 341-1000
Allan Farwell, *Mgr*
EMP: 413
Web: www.hyatt.com

SIC: 7011 5813 5812 Hotels; Drinking places
; Eating places
HQ: Hyatt Corporation
250 Vesey St
New York NY 10281
312 750-1234

(P-12866)
HYATT CORPORATION
Also Called: Hyatt Hotel
17900 Jamboree Rd, Irvine (92614-6211)
PHONE..............................949 975-1234
Rod T Schinnerer, *Genl Mgr*
EMP: 83
Web: www.hyatt.com
SIC: 7011 7992 7991 5813 Hotels and motels
; Public golf courses; Physical fitness
facilities; Drinking places
HQ: Hyatt Corporation
250 Vesey St
New York NY 10281
312 750-1234

(P-12867)
HYATT CORPORATION
Also Called: Hyatt Hotel
1107 Jamboree Rd, Newport Beach
(92660-6219)
PHONE..............................949 729-1234
Ruth Benjamin, *Genl Mgr*
EMP: 300
Web: www.hyatt.com
SIC: 7011 5813 5812 Hotels and motels;
Drinking places; Eating places
HQ: Hyatt Corporation
250 Vesey St Fl 15
New York NY 10281
312 750-1234

(P-12868)
HYATT CORPORATION
Also Called: Hyatt Hotel
200 S Pine Ave, Long Beach (90802-4553)
PHONE..............................562 432-0161
Steve Smith, *Mgr*
EMP: 463
Web: www.hyatt.com
SIC: 7011 7299 Hotels and motels; Banquet
hall facilities
HQ: Hyatt Corporation
250 Vesey St
New York NY 10281
312 750-1234

(P-12869)
HYATT CORPORATION
Also Called: Hyatt Hotel
0401 W Sunset Blvd, Los Angeles
(90069-1909)
PHONE..............................323 656-1234
Tim Flodin, *Mgr*
EMP: 105
Web: www.hyattdevelopment.com
SIC: 7011 5812 5813 Hotels and motels;
Restaurant, family: independent; Bar
(drinking places)
HQ: Hyatt Corporation
250 Vesey St
New York NY 10281
312 750-1234

(P-12870)
HYATT CORPORATION
Also Called: Hyatt Los Angeles Airport
6225 W Century Blvd, Los Angeles
(90045-5311)
PHONE..............................312 750-1234
Donald J Henderson, *Mgr*
EMP: 500
Web: www.hyattdevelopment.com

PRODUCTS & SVCS

SIC: 7011 5812 5813 Hotels; Restaurant, family: chain; Bar (drinking places)
HQ: Hyatt Corporation
250 Vesey St
New York NY 10281
312 750-1234

(P-12871)
HYATT EQUITIES LLC
Also Called: Hyatt Hotel
285 Bay St, Long Beach (90802-8178)
PHONE..............................562 436-1047
Tracey Pool, *Brnch Mgr*
EMP: 77
Web: www.hyatt.com
SIC: 7011 Hotels and motels
HQ: Hyatt Equities, L.L.C.
71 S Wacker Dr 14th Fl
Chicago IL 60606
312 750-1234

(P-12872)
HYATT HOTELS MANAGEMENT CORP
Also Called: Hyatt Hotel
285 N Palm Canyon Dr, Palm Springs (92262-5525)
PHONE..............................760 322-9000
Dania Duke, *Mgr*
EMP: 135
Web: www.hyatt.com
SIC: 7011 7299 5812 Hotels; Banquet hall facilities; Caterers
HQ: Hyatt Hotels Management Corporation
71 S Wacker Dr 12f
Chicago IL 60606
312 750-1234

(P-12873)
HYATT REGENCY CENTURY PLAZA
2025 Avenue Of The Stars, Los Angeles (90067-4741)
PHONE..............................310 228-1234
Rakesh Sama, *CEO*
Ken Cruse, *
EMP: 650 **EST:** 2005
SALES (est): 5.63MM **Privately Held**
Web: centuryplaza.hyatt.com
SIC: 7011 Hotels

(P-12874)
IHG MANAGEMENT (MARYLAND) LLC
Also Called: Intercntnntal Los Angles Dwntw
900 Wilshire Blvd, Los Angeles (90017-4701)
PHONE..............................213 688-7777
EMP: 96 **EST:** 2017
SALES (est): 3.18MM **Privately Held**
Web: dtla.intercontinental.com
SIC: 7011 Hotels

(P-12875)
INN OF CHICAGO ASSOCIATES LTD
Also Called: Bestwestren Inn of Chicago
1 Del Mar, Newport Coast (92657-2156)
PHONE..............................312 787-3100
Sam Segal, *Mgr*
EMP: 199
SALES (corp-wide): 699.58K **Privately Held**
Web: www.theinnofchicago.com
SIC: 7011 6512 5813 5812 Hotels and motels ; Nonresidential building operators; Drinking places; Eating places
PA: Inn Of Chicago Associates Ltd
40 Skokie Blvd Ste 350

847 564-4600

(P-12876)
INTERSTATE HOTELS RESORTS INC
Also Called: Santa Barbara Inn
901 E Cabrillo Blvd, Santa Barbara (93103-3642)
P.O. Box 5634 (93150-5634)
PHONE..............................805 966-2285
Clark Sarchet, *Brnch Mgr*
EMP: 75
Web: www.santabarbarainn.com
SIC: 7011 Hotels
HQ: Interstate Hotels & Resorts, Inc.
5301 Headquarters Dr
Plano TX 75024
703 387-3100

(P-12877)
IRP LAX HOTEL LLC
Also Called: Four Pnts By Shrton La Intl Ar
9750 Airport Blvd, Los Angeles (90045-5404)
PHONE..............................310 645-4600
EMP: 240 **EST:** 1994
SQ FT: 337,720
SALES (est): 1.84MM
SALES (corp-wide): 16.11B **Publicly Held**
Web: www.marriott.com
SIC: 7011 Resort hotel
HQ: Tishman Hotel Corporation
100 Park Ave Fl 18
New York NY 10017

(P-12878)
JHC INVESTMENT INC
Also Called: Dt Club Hotel Santa Ana
7 Hutton Centre Dr, Santa Ana (92707-5753)
PHONE..............................714 751-2400
Jung-hsiung Chiu, *Pr*
EMP: 70 **EST:** 1993
SQ FT: 85,000
SALES (est): 2.06MM **Privately Held**
SIC: 7011 Hotels

(P-12879)
JP ALLEN EXTENDED STAY (PA)
Also Called: Days Inn
450 Pioneer Dr, Glendale (91203-1713)
PHONE..............................818 956-0202
Joe Perry, *Owner*
EMP: 76 **EST:** 1945
SQ FT: 4,000
SALES (est): 3.08MM
SALES (corp-wide): 3.08MM **Privately Held**
Web: www.wyndhamhotels.com
SIC: 7011 Hotels and motels

(P-12880)
KAM SANG COMPANY INC
Also Called: New Age Lamirada Inn
14419 Firestone Blvd, La Mirada (90638-5912)
PHONE..............................714 523-2800
Grace Tanji, *Genl Mgr*
EMP: 70
SALES (corp-wide): 4.34MM **Privately Held**
Web: www.kamsangcompany.com
SIC: 7011 Hotel, franchised
PA: Kam Sang Company, Inc.
411 E Huntington Dr # 305
626 446-2988

(P-12881)
KANG FAMILY PARTNERS LLC
Also Called: Santa Ynez Valley Marriott
555 Mcmurray Rd, Buellton (93427-9559)
PHONE..............................805 688-1000
Daphne Kang, *Managing Member*
EMP: 110 **EST:** 1995
SALES (est): 3.83MM **Privately Held**
Web: www.syvmarriott.com
SIC: 7011 Hotel, franchised

(P-12882)
KAVA HOLDINGS INC (DH)
Also Called: Hotel Bel-Air
701 Stone Canyon Rd, Los Angeles (90077-2909)
PHONE..............................310 472-1211
Hj Suharafadzil, *Pr*
Christopher Cowdary, *
Helen Smith, *
Eugenio Pirri, *
Franois Delahaye, *
EMP: 200 **EST:** 1994
SQ FT: 30,000
SALES (est): 42.1MM **Privately Held**
Web: www.dorchestercollection.com
SIC: 7011 Resort hotel
HQ: Dorchester Group Limited
The Dorchester
London W1K 1
207 629-8888

(P-12883)
KEN REAL ESTATE LEASE LTD
Also Called: Anaheim Majestic Garden Hotel
900 S Disneyland Dr, Anaheim (92802-1844)
PHONE..............................714 778-1700
Shigeru Sato, *Pr*
EMP: 99 **EST:** 2005
SALES (est): 9.58MM **Privately Held**
Web: www.ken-pm.com
SIC: 7011 Resort hotel

(P-12884)
KIMPTON HOTEL & REST GROUP LLC
6317 Wilshire Blvd, Los Angeles (90048-5600)
PHONE..............................323 852-6000
Ashley Gochnauer, *Mgr*
EMP: 152
Web: www.hotelwilshire.com
SIC: 7011 Hotels
HQ: Kimpton Hotel & Restaurant Group Llc
3 Ravinia Dr
Atlanta GA 30346
415 397-5572

(P-12885)
KINTETSU ENTERPRISES CO AMER (HQ)
Also Called: Kintetsu Enterprises Co Amer
21241 S Western Ave Ste 100, Torrance (90501-2973)
PHONE..............................310 782-9300
Hisao Hiro, *Pr*
EMP: 200 **EST:** 1961
SALES (est): 16.45MM **Privately Held**
Web: www.kintetsu-enterprises.com
SIC: 7011 6512 Hotel, franchised; Nonresidential building operators
PA: Kintetsu Group Holdings Co.,Ltd.
6-1-55, Uehonmachi, Tennoji-Ku

(P-12886)
KIRKWOOD COLLECTION INC
Also Called: Kirkwood Collection
301 N Canon Dr Ste 302, Beverly Hills (90210-4724)

PHONE..............................424 532-1160
Alex Kirkwood, *CEO*
EMP: 76 **EST:** 2016
SALES (est): 961.04K **Privately Held**
Web: www.kirkwoodcollection.com
SIC: 7011 7389 Hotels; Business Activities at Non-Commercial Site

(P-12887)
KNOTTS BERRY FARM LLC
Also Called: Knott's Berry Farm Hotel
7675 Crescent Ave, Buena Park (90620-3947)
PHONE..............................714 995-1111
Stan Dlander, *Mgr*
EMP: 99
SALES (corp-wide): 1.08B **Publicly Held**
Web: www.knotts.com
SIC: 7011 Resort hotel
HQ: Berry Knott's Farm Llc
8039 Beach Blvd
Buena Park CA 90620
714 827-1776

(P-12888)
KSL RANCHO MIRAGE OPERATING CO INC
Also Called: Rancho Las Palmas Resort & Spa
41000 Bob Hope Dr, Rancho Mirage (92270-4416)
PHONE..............................760 568-2727
EMP: 500
Web: www.rancholaspalmasresort.com
SIC: 7011 Hotels and motels

(P-12889)
KSL RESORTS HOTEL DEL CORONADO
Also Called: Hotel Del Coronado
1500 Orange Ave, Coronado (92118-2986)
PHONE..............................619 435-6611
Bob Antes, *Prin*
EMP: 205 **EST:** 1888
SALES (est): 1.24MM
SALES (corp-wide): 10.23B **Publicly Held**
Web: www.hoteldel.com
SIC: 7011 Resort hotel
HQ: Hilton Supply Management Llc
7926 Jones Br Dr Ste 400
Mclean VA 22102
703 883-1000

(P-12890)
L & O ALISO VIEJO LLC
Also Called: Renaissance Hotel Clubsport
50 Enterprise, Aliso Viejo (92656-6026)
PHONE..............................949 643-6700
Ed Tomlin, *Genl Mgr*
EMP: 128 **EST:** 2008
SALES (est): 8.33MM **Privately Held**
Web: www.evolutionswim.com
SIC: 7011 Hotels and motels

(P-12891)
L-O BEDFORD OPERATING LLC
Also Called: Doubletree Hotel Boston
11755 Wilshire Blvd Ste 1350, Los Angeles (90025-1540)
PHONE..............................781 275-5500
EMP: 200 **EST:** 2011
SALES (est): 894.35K **Privately Held**
Web: www.hilton.com
SIC: 7011 Hotels and motels

(P-12892)
L-O CORONADO HOTEL INC
1500 Orange Ave, Coronado (92118-2918)
PHONE..............................619 435-6611

Tod Shallon, *Pr*
EMP: 73 **EST:** 1886
SALES (est): 309.43K **Privately Held**
Web: www.hoteldel.com
SIC: 7011 5812 5813 5941 Resort hotel;
Eating places; Cocktail lounge; Tennis
goods and equipment

(P-12893)
LA JOLLA BCH & TENNIS CLB INC
Also Called: Shores Restaurant
8110 Camino Del Oro, La Jolla
(92037-3108)
PHONE.............................858 459-8271
John Cambel, *Mgr*
EMP: 285
SALES (corp-wide): 47.87MM **Privately Held**
Web: www.theshoresrestaurant.com
SIC: 7011 5812 5813 7299 Resort hotel;
Restaurant, family: independent; Cocktail
lounge; Banquet hall facilities
PA: La Jolla Beach & Tennis Club, Inc.
2000 Spindrift Dr
858 454-7126

(P-12894)
LA JOLLA COVE HT MTL APRTMNTS
Also Called: La Jolla Cove Motel
1155 Coast Blvd, La Jolla (92037-3627)
P.O. Box 1067 (92038-1067)
PHONE.............................858 459-2621
Helen Jackman, *VP*
EMP: 78 **EST:** 1959
SQ FT: 78,000
SALES (est): 5.05MM **Privately Held**
Web: www.lajollacove.com
SIC: 7011 Hotels

(P-12895)
LAKE ARRWHEAD RSORT OPRTOR INC (HQ)
Also Called: Marriott
27984 Hwy 189, Lake Arrowhead (92352)
PHONE.............................909 336-1511
TOLL FREE: 800
Carmen Rodriguez, *CEO*
Veronique Williams, *
EMP: 115 **EST:** 1982
SALES (est): 4.57MM
SALES (corp-wide): 23.71B **Publicly Held**
Web: www.lakearrowheadresort.com
SIC: 7011 5813 5812 Resort hotel; Drinking
places; Eating places
PA: Marriott International, Inc.
7750 Wisconsin Ave
301 380-3000

(P-12896)
LAV HOTEL CORP
Also Called: Whaling Bar & Grill
1132 Prospect St, La Jolla (92037-4533)
PHONE.............................858 454-0771
Harry Collins, *Pr*
W M Allen Senior, *Bd of Dir*
W M Allen Junior, *VP*
EMP: 250 **EST:** 1928
SQ FT: 1,000
SALES (est): 5.02MM **Privately Held**
Web: www.lavalencia.com
SIC: 7011 Hotels

(P-12897)
LC TRS INC
Also Called: La Costa Resort & Spa
2100 Costa Del Mar Rd, Carlsbad
(92009-6823)

PHONE.............................760 438-9111
EMP: 872
Web: www.theclubatlacosta.com
SIC: 7011 5812 Resort hotel; Eating places

(P-12898)
LFS DEVELOPMENT LLC
Also Called: Intercontinental San Diego
901 Bayfront Ct Ste 1, San Diego
(92101-3050)
PHONE.............................619 501-5400
EMP: 200 **EST:** 1946
SALES (est): 4.76MM **Privately Held**
Web: www.intercontinentalsandiego.com
SIC: 7011 Hotels

(P-12899)
LH INDIAN WELLS OPERATING LLC
4500 Indian Wells Ln, Indian Wells (92210)
PHONE.............................760 341-2200
Bob Low, *Prin*
EMP: 220 **EST:** 2004
SALES (est): 296.37K **Privately Held**
SIC: 7011 7991 Resort hotel; Spas
PA: Lh Indian Wells Holding, Llc
11777 San Vicente Blvd

(P-12900)
LH UNIVERSAL OPERATING LLC
Also Called: Sheraton
333 Universal Hollywood Dr, Universal City
(91608-1001)
PHONE.............................818 980-1212
EMP: 280 **EST:** 1969
SALES (est): 24.75MM **Privately Held**
Web: www.sheratonuniversal.com
SIC: 7011 Hotels

(P-12901)
LHO MSSION BAY RSIE LESSEE INC
Also Called: San Diego Mission Bay Resort
1775 E Mission Bay Dr, San Diego
(92109-6801)
PHONE.............................619 276-4010
Raymond D Martz, *CEO*
Thomas C Fisher, *
Summer Shoemaker, *
EMP: 300 **EST:** 2005
SALES (est): 23.79MM **Publicly Held**
Web: www.giavaratennis.com
SIC: 7011 5812 5947 Resort hotel; Eating
places; Gift, novelty, and souvenir shop
PA: Pebblebrook Hotel Trust
4747 Bthesda Ave Ste 1100

(P-12902)
LHOBERGE LESSEE INC
Also Called: L'Auberge Del Mar
1540 Camino Del Mar, Del Mar
(92014-2411)
PHONE.............................858 259-1515
Jamie Sabatier, *CEO*
Charles Peck, *
Dennis Fischer, *
EMP: 250 **EST:** 1989
SQ FT: 84,312
SALES (est): 10.06MM **Privately Held**
Web: www.laubergedelmar.com
SIC: 7011 Resort hotel
PA: Noble House Hotels & Resorts, Ltd.
600 6th St S

(P-12903)
LIGHTSTONE DT LA LLC
Also Called: Moxy AC Ht Dwntwn Los
Angeles

1260 S Figueroa St, Los Angeles
(90015-2887)
PHONE.............................310 669-9252
EMP: 300 **EST:** 2022
SALES (est): 4.12MM **Privately Held**
SIC: 7011 7389 Hotels; Business services,
nec

(P-12904)
LOEWS HOLLYWOOD HOTEL LLC
1755 N Highland Ave, Hollywood
(90028-4403)
PHONE.............................323 450-2235
Jonathan Tisch, *Ch Bd*
Reggie Dominique, *
EMP: 375 **EST:** 2012
SALES (est): 65.63MM
SALES (corp-wide): 15.9B **Publicly Held**
Web: www.loewshotels.com
SIC: 7011 Hotels
PA: Loews Corporation
667 Madison Ave
212 521-2000

(P-12905)
LONG BEACH GOLDEN SAILS INC
Also Called: Best Western Golden Sails Ht
23545 Crenshaw Blvd Ste 100, Torrance
(90505-5240)
PHONE.............................562 596-1631
TOLL FREE: 800
Luis Vasquez, *Pr*
Ruben Garza, *
Vicki Arreguin, *
▲ **EMP:** 100 **EST:** 1964
SQ FT: 150,000
SALES (est): 2.27MM
SALES (corp-wide): 2.27MM **Privately Held**
Web: www.goldensailshotel.com
SIC: 7011 5812 5813 Hotels and motels;
Restaurant, family: independent; Bar
(drinking places)
PA: Abp Hotel, Llc
2200 W Valley Blvd
562 596-1631

(P-12906)
LONG POINT DEVELOPMENT LLC
Also Called: Terranea Resort
100 Terranea Way, Rancho Palos Verdes
(90275-1013)
PHONE.............................310 265-2800
Terri Haack, *Managing Member*
Jennifer Yang, *
EMP: 1000 **EST:** 2004
SALES (est): 89.79MM **Privately Held**
Web: www.terranea.com
SIC: 7011 Resort hotel

(P-12907)
LOWE ENTERPRISES INC (PA)
Also Called: Lei AG Seattle
11777 San Vicente Blvd Ste 900, Los
Angeles (90049-5084)
PHONE.............................310 820-6661
Robert J Lowe Senior, *Ch*
Robert M Weekley, *Sr VP*
Peter O'keeffe, *Ex VP*
Linda Leonard, *Corporate Secretary*
EMP: 125 **EST:** 1972
SQ FT: 20,000
SALES (est): 367.25MM
SALES (corp-wide): 367.25MM **Privately Held**
Web: www.lowe-re.com

SIC: 7011 6552 Hotels and motels;
Subdividers and developers, nec

(P-12908)
LOWE ENTERPRISES INC
843 2nd St Ste C, Encinitas (92024-4476)
PHONE.............................310 820-6661
EMP: 179
SALES (corp-wide): 367.25MM **Privately Held**
Web: www.lowe-re.com
SIC: 7011 Hotels and motels
PA: Lowe Enterprises, Inc.
11777 San Vcnte Blvd Ste
310 820-6661

(P-12909)
M&C HOTEL INTERESTS INC
530 Pico Blvd, Santa Monica (90405-1223)
PHONE.............................310 399-9344
Lisa Nagahori, *Brnch Mgr*
EMP: 332
Web: www.richfield.com
SIC: 7011 Hotels
HQ: M&C Hotel Interests, Inc.
6560 Grnwood Plz Blvd Ste
Englewood CO 80111

(P-12910)
M4DEV LLC
Also Called: Hilton Grdn Inn San Dego Dwntw
2137 Pacific Hwy Ste A, San Diego
(92101-8472)
PHONE.............................619 696-6300
EMP: 100 **EST:** 2016
SALES (est): 2.64MM **Privately Held**
Web: www.hilton.com
SIC: 7011 Resort hotel

(P-12911)
MAJESTIC INDUSTRY HILLS LLC
Also Called: Pacific Plms Conference Resort
1 Industry Hills Pkwy, City Of Industry
(91744-5160)
PHONE.............................626 810-4455
Scott Huntsman, *Brnch Mgr*
EMP: 547
SALES (corp-wide): 19.22MM **Privately Held**
Web: www.pacificpalmsresort.com
SIC: 7011 7999 7389 7299 Resort hotel;
Tennis courts, outdoor/indoor: non-
membership; Convention and show services
; Banquet hall facilities
PA: Majestic Industry Hills, Llc
1 Industry Hills Pkwy
562 692-9581

(P-12912)
MAKAR ANAHEIM LLC
Also Called: Hilton
777 W Convention Way, Anaheim
(92802-3425)
PHONE.............................714 750-4321
EMP: 1200 **EST:** 1984
SQ FT: 1,000,000
SALES (est): 18.51MM **Privately Held**
Web: www.hilton.com
SIC: 7011 Resort hotel

(P-12913)
MANCHESTER GRAND RESORTS LP
Also Called: Manchster Grnd Hyatt San Diego
1 Market Pl Fl 33, San Diego (92101-7714)
PHONE.............................619 232-1234
Mark S Hoplamazian, *CEO*
Douglas F Manchester, *Pt*

Richard V Gibbons, *Pt*
H Charles Floyd, *Ex VP*
Peter Fulton, *Ex VP*
EMP: 74 **EST:** 1984
SALES (est): 7.62MM
SALES (corp-wide): 5.31B **Publicly Held**
Web:
www.manchestergrandhyattsandiego.com
SIC: 7011 Hotel, franchised
PA: Host Hotels & Resorts, Inc.
4747 Bthesda Ave Ste 1300
240 744-1000

(P-12914)
MARCUS HOTELS INC
Also Called: Holiday Inn
4222 Vineland Ave, North Hollywood
(91602-3318)
PHONE..................818 980-8000
Kroy Walter, *Dir*
EMP: 166
SALES (corp-wide): 729.58MM **Publicly Held**
Web: www.marcushotels.com
SIC: 7011 Hotels and motels
HQ: Marcus Hotels Inc
111 E Kilbourn Ave
Milwaukee WI 53202

(P-12915)
MARRIOTT INTERNATIONAL INC
Also Called: Marriott
5855 W Century Blvd, Los Angeles
(90045-5614)
PHONE..................310 641-5700
Jim Burns, *Genl Mgr*
EMP: 900
SALES (corp-wide): 23.71B **Publicly Held**
Web: www.marriott.com
SIC: 7011 7389 6513 Hotels and motels; Office facilities and secretarial service rental ; Residential hotel operation
PA: Marriott International, Inc.
7750 Wisconsin Ave
301 380-3000

(P-12916)
MARRIOTT INTERNATIONAL INC
Also Called: Marriott
4240 La Jolla Village Dr, La Jolla
(92037-1407)
PHONE..................858 587-1414
Paul Corsinita, *Mgr*
EMP: 337
SALES (corp-wide): 23.71B **Publicly Held**
Web: www.marriott.com
SIC: 7011 Hotels and motels
PA: Marriott International, Inc.
7750 Wisconsin Ave
301 380-3000

(P-12917)
MARRIOTT INTERNATIONAL INC
Also Called: Inn At Mssion San Juan Cpstran
31692 El Camino Real, San Juan Capistrano (92675-2657)
PHONE..................949 503-5700
Arne Sorenson, *CEO*
Kristi Kaib, *
EMP: 90 **EST:** 1997
SALES (est): 2.53MM **Privately Held**
Web: www.marriott.com
SIC: 7011 Hotels and motels

(P-12918)
MARRIOTT INTERNATIONAL INC
Also Called: Marriott
18000 Von Karman Ave, Irvine
(92612-1004)
PHONE..................949 724-3606

Satinder Palpa, *Brnch Mgr*
EMP: 258
SALES (corp-wide): 23.71B **Publicly Held**
Web: www.marriott.com
SIC: 7011 7389 Hotels and motels; Office facilities and secretarial service rental
PA: Marriott International, Inc.
7750 Wisconsin Ave
301 380-3000

(P-12919)
MAVERICK HOSPITALITY INC
17662 Irvine Blvd Ste 4, Tustin
(92780-3132)
PHONE..................714 730-7717
Brad Perrin, *Prin*
EMP: 77 **EST:** 2004
SALES (est): 4.9MM **Privately Held**
SIC: 7011 Hotels and motels

(P-12920)
MBP LAND LLC
Also Called: Courtyard Marriott Mission Vly
595 Hotel Cir S, San Diego (92108-3403)
PHONE..................619 291-5720
John Blem, *Managing Member*
EMP: 2208 **EST:** 2000
SALES (est): 538.2K
SALES (corp-wide): 819.71MM **Privately Held**
Web: courtyard.marriott.com
SIC: 7011 Hotels
HQ: Evolution Hospitality, Llc
1211 Puerta Del Sol # 170
San Clemente CA 92673
949 325-1350

(P-12921)
MERRITT HOSPITALITY LLC
Also Called: Marriott
2701 Nutwood Ave, Fullerton (92831-5400)
PHONE..................714 738-7800
Tom Beebon, *Mgr*
EMP: 241
SALES (corp-wide): 447.39MM **Privately Held**
Web: www.marriott.com
SIC: 7011 7991 5813 5812 Resort hotel; Physical fitness facilities; Drinking places; Eating places
HQ: Merritt Hospitality, Llc
101 Merritt 7 Ste 14
Norwalk CT 06851
203 849-8844

(P-12922)
MERRITT HOSPITALITY LLC
Also Called: Hilton
701 W Ocean Blvd, Long Beach
(90831-3100)
PHONE..................562 983-3400
Grace Sun, *Sls Mgr*
EMP: 174
SALES (corp-wide): 447.39MM **Privately Held**
Web: www.hilton.com
SIC: 7011 7991 5813 5812 Resort hotel; Physical fitness facilities; Drinking places; Eating places
HQ: Merritt Hospitality, Llc
101 Merritt 7 Ste 14
Norwalk CT 06851
203 849-8844

(P-12923)
METROPOLIS HOTEL MGT LLC
Also Called: Hotel Indigo Los Angles Dwntwn
899 Francisco St, Los Angeles
(90017-2534)
PHONE..................213 683-4855

Raymond Vermolen, *Genl Mgr*
EMP: 120 **EST:** 2016
SALES (est): 8.61MM **Privately Held**
Web: www.hotelindigo.com
SIC: 7011 Hotels
HQ: Inter-Continental Hotels Corporation
35016 Avenue D
Yucaipa CA 92399
770 604-5000

(P-12924)
MHF MV OPERATING VI LLC
Also Called: Courtyard San Dego Mssion Vlly
595 Hotel Cir S, San Diego (92108-3403)
PHONE..................619 481-5881
Robert A Indeglia Junior, *Pr*
EMP: 100 **EST:** 2019
SALES (est): 3.6MM **Privately Held**
Web: www.marriott.com
SIC: 7011 Hotels

(P-12925)
MHRP RESORT INC
Also Called: Mountain High Ski Resort
24510 Highway 2, Wrightwood (92397)
P.O. Box 3010 (92397-3010)
PHONE..................760 249-5808
Russel S Bernard, *Pr*
Kenneth Lang, *
Marc Porosoff, *
W Gregory Geiger, *
EMP: 100 **EST:** 1997
SALES (est): 2.92MM **Privately Held**
Web: www.mthigh.com
SIC: 7011 Resort hotel

(P-12926)
MONDRIAN HOLDINGS LLC
8440 W Sunset Blvd, West Hollywood
(90069-1912)
PHONE..................323 848-6004
Steve Del Rosario, *
EMP: 400 **EST:** 1999
SQ FT: 500,000
SALES (est): 5.05MM **Privately Held**
Web: book.ennismore.com
SIC: 7011 Hotels

(P-12927)
MONTAGE HOTELS & RESORTS LLC (PA)
Also Called: Montage Laguna Beach
3 Ada Ste 100, Irvine (92618-2322)
P.O. Box 52031 (85072-2031)
PHONE..................949 715-5002
Alan Fuerstman, *Managing Member*
Jason Herthel, *
Iqbal Bashir, *
James D Bermingham, *
Bill Claypool, *
EMP: 640 **EST:** 2002
SQ FT: 586,000
SALES (est): 153.78MM
SALES (corp-wide): 153.78MM **Privately Held**
Web: www.montage.com
SIC: 7011 Resort hotel

(P-12928)
MONTAGE INTL N AMER LLC
3 Ada Ste 100, Irvine (92618-2322)
PHONE..................800 700-7744
EMP: 78 **EST:** 2018
SALES (est): 2.69MM **Privately Held**
Web: www.montageinternational.com
SIC: 7011 Resort hotel

(P-12929)
MOONSTONE BCH INNVSTORS A CAL
Also Called: Best Wstn Fireside Inn By Sea
6700 Moonstone Beach Dr, Cambria
(93428-1814)
PHONE..................805 927-8661
EMP: 199
Web: www.firesideinncambria.com
SIC: 7011 Hotels
PA: Moonstone Beach Innvstors, A California Limited Partnership
170 Nwport Ctr Dr Ste 245

(P-12930)
MORGANS HOTEL GROUP MGT LLC
Also Called: Miramar Hotel
1555 S Jameson Ln, Santa Barbara
(93108-2918)
PHONE..................805 969-2203
Philip Dailey, *Genl Mgr*
EMP: 190
SALES (corp-wide): 1.66B **Privately Held**
Web: www.sbe.com
SIC: 7011 Hotels
HQ: Morgans Hotel Group Management Llc
475 10th Ave Fl 11
New York NY 10018

(P-12931)
MORGANS HOTEL GROUP MGT LLC
Also Called: Mondrian Hotel
8440 W Sunset Blvd, Los Angeles
(90069-1912)
PHONE..................323 650-8999
David Weidlich, *Genl Mgr*
EMP: 200
SALES (corp-wide): 1.66B **Privately Held**
Web: www.morganshotelgroup.com
SIC: 7011 5813 5812 Hotels; Drinking places ; Eating places
HQ: Morgans Hotel Group Management Llc
475 10th Ave Fl 11
New York NY 10018

(P-12932)
MSR HOTELS & RESORTS INC
Also Called: Residence Inn By Marriott
3701 Torrance Blvd, Torrance (90503-4805)
PHONE..................310 543-4566
David Zimmerman, *Mgr*
EMP: 240
SALES (corp-wide): 96.19B **Publicly Held**
Web: residence-inn.marriott.com
SIC: 7011 Hotels and motels
HQ: Msr Hotels & Resorts, Inc.
450 S Orange Ave
Orlando FL 32801
407 650-1000

(P-12933)
MSR RESORT LODGING TENANT LLC
Also Called: Pga West By Wldorf Astoria MGT
49499 Eisenhower Dr, La Quinta
(92253-2722)
P.O. Box 659 (92247-0659)
PHONE..................760 564-4111
▲ **EMP:** 900
SIC: 7011 Hotels and motels

(P-12934)
NANDI-LAKSH INC
Also Called: Super 8 Motel
901 Real Rd, Bakersfield (93309-1003)
PHONE..................661 322-1012
Mark Grotewohl, *Brnch Mgr*

▲ = Import ▼ = Export
◆ = Import/Export

▲ **EMP:** 150
SALES (corp-wide): 655.54K **Privately Held**
Web: www.wyndhamhotels.com
SIC: 7011 Hotels and motels
PA: Nandi-Laksh. Inc
22561 Wdford Tehachapi Rd

(P-12935)
NARVEN ENTERPRISES INC
Also Called: Rodeway Inn
1430 7th Ave Ste B, San Diego
(92101-2815)
PHONE..............................619 239-2261
Behram Baxter, *Pr*
EMP: 75 **EST:** 1982
SQ FT: 6,000
SALES (est): 2.36MM **Privately Held**
Web: www.narveninc.com
SIC: 7011 Hotels and motels

(P-12936)
NEW FIGUEROA HOTEL INC
Also Called: Figueroa Hotel
1000 S Hope St Apt 201, Los Angeles
(90015-1492)
PHONE..............................213 627-8971
Uno Thimansson, *Pr*
Elyse Omori, *
EMP: 70 **EST:** 1977
SQ FT: 200,000
SALES (est): 2.58MM **Privately Held**
Web: www.hotelfigueroa.com
SIC: 7011 5812 5813 Resort hotel; Eating
places; Bars and lounges

(P-12937)
NEWPORT HOSPITALITY GROUP INC
Also Called: Holiday Inn
801 Truxtun Ave, Bakersfield (93301-4726)
PHONE..............................661 323-1900
Eric Iokal, *Mgr*
EMP: 100
SALES (corp-wide): 1.35MM **Privately Held**
Web: www.holidayinn.com
SIC: 7011 Hotels and motels
PA: Newport Hospitality Group Inc
1048 Irvine Ave Ste 365
949 706-7002

(P-12938)
NHCA INC
Also Called: Crowne Plz Los Angeles Hbr Ht
2330 Grand Ave, Long Beach
(90815-1761)
PHONE..............................310 519-8200
EMP: 151 **EST:** 1997
SALES (est): 4.84MM **Privately Held**
SIC: 7011 Hotels

(P-12939)
NOBLE/UTAH LONG BEACH LLC
Also Called: Westin Long Beach Hotel, The
333 E Ocean Blvd, Long Beach
(90802-4827)
PHONE..............................562 436-3000
Mitesh B Shah, *Managing Member*
EMP: 250 **EST:** 2005
SQ FT: 51,000
SALES (est): 1.2MM **Privately Held**
Web: www.westin.marriott.com
SIC: 7011 Hotels and motels
PA: Noble Investment Group, Llc
3424 Peachtree Rd Ne

(P-12940)
NORTHWEST HOTEL CORPORATION (PA)
Also Called: Howard Johnson
1380 S Harbor Blvd, Anaheim
(92802-2310)
PHONE..............................714 776-6120
James P Edmondson, *Pr*
EMP: 108 **EST:** 1965
SQ FT: 50,000
SALES (est): 4.6MM
SALES (corp-wide): 4.6MM **Privately Held**
Web: www.hojoanaheim.com
SIC: 7011 Hotels and motels

(P-12941)
NREA-TRC 711 LLC
Also Called: Sheraton
711 S Hope St, Los Angeles (90017-3803)
PHONE..............................213 488-3500
EMP: 200 **EST:** 2013
SQ FT: 470,000
SALES (est): 8.57MM **Privately Held**
Web: four-points.marriott.com
SIC: 7011 Hotels

(P-12942)
OAK VALLEY HOTEL LLC
2270 Hotel Cir N, San Diego (92108-2810)
PHONE..............................619 297-1101
EMP: 99 **EST:** 2016
SALES (est): 914.78K **Privately Held**
SIC: 7011 Hotels

(P-12943)
OASIS WEST REALTY LLC
Also Called: Waldorf Astoria Beverly Hills
9850 Wilshire Blvd, Beverly Hills
(90210-3115)
PHONE..............................310 860-6666
Damian Cabotaje, *Managing Member*
EMP: 158 **EST:** 2017
SALES (est): 10.25MM **Privately Held**
Web: waldorfastoria3.hilton.com
SIC: 7011 Hotels

(P-12944)
OCEAN AVENUE LLC
Also Called: Fairmont Miramar Hotel
101 Wilshire Blvd, Santa Monica
(90401-1106)
PHONE..............................310 576-7777
Ellis O'connor, *Managing Member*
Simon A Fricker, *
EMP: 275 **EST:** 1973
SQ FT: 209,000
SALES (est): 26.99MM
SALES (corp-wide): 1.66B **Privately Held**
Web: www.fairmont-miramar.com
SIC: 7011 Hotels
HQ: Accor Services Us Llc
950 Mason St
San Francisco CA 94108
415 772-5000

(P-12945)
OCEAN SANDS HOTEL
Also Called: Comfort Inn
2620 Hotel Ter, Santa Ana (92705-5447)
PHONE..............................714 966-5200
Ravi Khanna, *Mgr*
EMP: 74
Web: www.choicehotels.com
SIC: 7011 Hotels and motels
PA: Ocean Sands Hotel
1024 N Atlantic Ave

(P-12946)
OCEANS ELEVEN CASINO
Also Called: Ocean's Eleven
121 Brooks St, Oceanside (92054-3424)
PHONE..............................760 439-6988
Mark Kelegian, *Mng Pt*
EMP: 367 **EST:** 1996
SQ FT: 30,000
SALES (est): 22.62MM **Privately Held**
Web: www.oceans11.com
SIC: 7011 Casino hotel

(P-12947)
OH SO ORIGINAL INC
Also Called: Express Hotels
150 E Angeleno Ave, Burbank
(91502-1911)
PHONE..............................818 841-4770
Mark Crigler, *Pr*
Rich Reid, *
EMP: 300 **EST:** 2015
SQ FT: 100,000
SALES (est): 11.31MM **Privately Held**
Web: www.jpallenapartments.com
SIC: 7011 6513 8741 Hotel, franchised;
Apartment building operators; Hotel or
motel management

(P-12948)
OHI RESORT HOTELS LLC
Also Called: Wyndham Anaheim Garden
Grove
12021 Harbor Blvd, Garden Grove
(92840-4001)
PHONE..............................714 867-5555
Jeremy Yujuico, *Prin*
EMP: 98 **EST:** 1998
SALES (est): 4.12MM **Privately Held**
Web: anaheim.crowneplaza.com
SIC: 7011 Hotels

(P-12949)
OKA & OKA HAWAII LLC
Also Called: Kona Bay Hotel
1756 Ruhland Ave, Manhattan Beach
(90266-7132)
PHONE..............................808 329-1393
Tracey Kimi, *Mgr*
EMP: 196
SALES (corp-wide): 1.36MM **Privately Held**
SIC: 7011 Hotels
PA: Oka & Oka Hawaii, Llc
75 5744 Alii Dr
808 329-1393

(P-12950)
OLD TOWN FMLY HOSPITALITY CORP
Also Called: Fiesta De Reyes
2754 Calhoun St, San Diego (92110-2706)
PHONE..............................619 246-8010
Chuck Ross, *Pr*
EMP: 240 **EST:** 2009
SQ FT: 1,600
SALES (est): 13.62MM **Privately Held**
Web: www.fiestadereyes.com
SIC: 7011 5812 Hotels; Eating places

(P-12951)
OLS HOTELS & RESORTS LLC
Also Called: Le Parc Suite Hotel
733 N West Knoll Dr, West Hollywood
(90069-5207)
PHONE..............................310 855-1115
Sam Ebeid, *CEO*
EMP: 678
SALES (corp-wide): 34.76MM **Privately Held**
Web: www.leparcsuites.com

SIC: 7011 8741 Hotels; Hotel or motel
management
PA: Ols Hotels & Resorts Llc
16000 Vntura Blvd Ste 101
818 905-8280

(P-12952)
OMNI HOTELS CORPORATION
Also Called: Omni Hotels
41000 Bob Hope Dr, Rancho Mirage
(92270-4416)
PHONE..............................760 568-2727
EMP: 410
Web: www.omnihotels.com
SIC: 7011 Hotels and motels
HQ: Omni Hotels Corporation
4001 Maple Ave Ste 500
Dallas TX 75219
972 871-5600

(P-12953)
OMNI LA COSTA RESORT & SPA LLC (DH)
2100 Costa Del Mar Rd, Carlsbad
(92009-6823)
PHONE..............................760 438-9111
Randy Zupanski, *Managing Member*
EMP: 79 **EST:** 2013
SALES (est): 24.47MM **Privately Held**
Web: www.omnihotels.com
SIC: 7011 Resort hotel
HQ: Omni Hotels Corporation
4001 Maple Ave Ste 500
Dallas TX 75219
972 871-5600

(P-12954)
ORANGEWOOD LLC
Also Called: Doubltree Stes By Hlton Anheim
2085 S Harbor Blvd, Anaheim
(92802-3513)
PHONE..............................714 750-3000
Shirish H Patel, *
EMP: 175 **EST:** 2000
SALES (est): 8.88MM **Privately Held**
Web: www.doubletreeanaheim.com
SIC: 7011 5812 Hotels and motels;
American restaurant

(P-12955)
OVIS LLC
Also Called: Ojai Valley Inn & Spa
905 Country Club Rd, Ojai (93023-3734)
PHONE..............................805 646-5511
TOLL FREE: 888
Stephen Crown, *Managing Member*
EMP: 600 **EST:** 1923
SALES (est): 22.83MM **Privately Held**
Web: www.ojaivalleyinn.com
SIC: 7011 5813 5812 Resort hotel; Drinking
places; Eating places

(P-12956)
OXFORD PALACE HOTEL LLC
745 S Oxford Ave, Los Angeles
(90005-2909)
PHONE..............................213 382-7756
Bowhan Kim, *Prin*
Don W Chang, *
EMP: 96 **EST:** 1992
SALES (est): 3.85MM **Privately Held**
Web: www.oxfordhotel.com
SIC: 7011 5812 Resort hotel; Korean
restaurant

(P-12957)
PACIFIC CAMBRIA INC
Also Called: Cambria Pines Lodge
2905 Burton Dr, Cambria (93428-4001)
PHONE..............................805 927-6114

Dirk Winter, *Pr*
EMP: 90 **EST:** 1975
SQ FT: 70,000
SALES (est): 4.84MM **Privately Held**
Web: www.cambriapineslodge.com
SIC: 7011 5812 5813 Hotels; Restaurant, family: independent; Bar (drinking places)

(P-12958)
PACIFIC CITY HOTEL LLC
Also Called: Pasea Hotel & Spa
21080 Pacific Coast Hwy, Huntington Beach (92648-5305)
PHONE.................714 698-6100
EMP: 300 **EST:** 2015
SALES (est): 2.8MM **Privately Held**
Web: www.paseahotel.com
SIC: 7011 Resort hotel

(P-12959)
PACIFIC HOTEL MANAGEMENT INC
Also Called: Radison Hotel Newport Beach
4545 Macarthur Blvd, Newport Beach (92660-2022)
PHONE.................949 608-1091
Ron Mavaddat, *Pr*
EMP: 140 **EST:** 2003
SALES (est): 3.2MM **Privately Held**
Web: www.radissonhotels.com
SIC: 7011 Hotels

(P-12960)
PACIFIC HUNTINGTON HOTEL CORP
Also Called: Langham Huntington Hotel & Spa
1401 S Oak Knoll Ave, Pasadena (91106-4508)
PHONE.................626 568-3900
Ying Shek Lo, *Pr*
EMP: 600 **EST:** 2000
SQ FT: 21,193
SALES (est): 46.39MM **Privately Held**
Web: www.langhamhotels.com
SIC: 7011 Resort hotel
HQ: Langham Hotels International Limited
33/F Great Eagle Ctr
Wan Chai HK

(P-12961)
PACIFIC MONARCH RESORTS INC
Also Called: Riviera Shores
34630 Pacific Coast Hwy, Capistrano Beach (92624-1301)
PHONE.................949 248-2944
EMP: 90
SALES (corp-wide): 49.26MM **Privately Held**
Web: www.pacificmonarchresorts.com
SIC: 7011 6531 Resort hotel; Time-sharing real estate sales, leasing and rentals
PA: Pacific Monarch Resorts, Inc.
4000 Mcrthur Blvd Ste 600
949 609-2400

(P-12962)
PACIFICA HOSTS INC
Also Called: Radisson Inn
6225 W Century Blvd, Los Angeles (90045-5311)
PHONE.................310 670-9000
Ashok Israni, *Pr*
EMP: 192
SALES (corp-wide): 43.21MM **Privately Held**
Web: www.pacificacompanies.com

SIC: 7011 6552 5813 5812 Hotels; Subdividers and developers, nec; Drinking places; Eating places
PA: Pacifica Hosts, Inc.
1775 Hancock St Ste 200
619 296-9000

(P-12963)
PACIFICA HOSTS INC
717 S Highway 101, Solana Beach (92075-2606)
PHONE.................858 792-8200
Julio Ongpin, *Genl Mgr*
EMP: 179
SALES (corp-wide): 43.21MM **Privately Held**
Web: www.pacificacompanies.com
SIC: 7011 Hotels
PA: Pacifica Hosts, Inc.
1775 Hancock St Ste 200
619 296-9000

(P-12964)
PACKARD REALTY INC
Also Called: Holiday Inn
9901 S La Cienega Blvd, Los Angeles (90045-5915)
PHONE.................310 649-5151
Tommy Spencer, *Genl Mgr*
EMP: 250
Web: www.packard-1.com
SIC: 7011 Hotels and motels
PA: Packard Realty Inc.
8775 Aero Dr Ste 335

(P-12965)
PALA CASINO SPA & RESORT
Also Called: Pala Casino
11154 Highway 76, Pala (92059-2904)
PHONE.................760 510-5100
TOLL FREE: 877
Robert Smith, *Ch Bd*
Bill Bembenek, *
Shauna Anton, *
Stacy Hoover, *
EMP: 1800 **EST:** 2000
SQ FT: 140,000
SALES (est): 77.25MM **Privately Held**
Web: www.palacasino.com
SIC: 7011 Casino hotel

(P-12966)
PAN PCFIC HTELS RSRTS AMER INC
Also Called: Pan Pacific San Diego
400 W Broadway, San Diego (92101-3504)
PHONE.................619 239-4500
Jim Hollister, *Genl Mgr*
EMP: 238
SALES (corp-wide): 9.46MM **Privately Held**
Web: www.wyndhamhotels.com
SIC: 7011 5812 Hotels; Eating places
PA: Pan Pacific Hotels And Resorts America Inc.
500 Post St Ste 800
415 732-7747

(P-12967)
PARADISE LESSEE INC
Also Called: Paradise Point Resort & Spa
1404 Vacation Rd, San Diego (92109-7905)
PHONE.................858 274-4630
Alfred L Young, *CEO*
EMP: 328 **EST:** 1962
SALES (est): 7.62MM **Publicly Held**
Web: www.paradisepoint.com
SIC: 7011 Resort hotel
PA: Pebblebrook Hotel Trust
4747 Bthesda Ave Ste 1100

(P-12968)
PARK MANAGEMENT GROUP LLC
Also Called: Jameson Inn
1825 Gillespie Wy Ste 101, North Hollywood (91601)
PHONE.................404 350-9990
▲ **EMP:** 3500
SIC: 7011 Hotels and motels

(P-12969)
PASADENA HOTEL DEV VENTR LP
Also Called: Sheraton Pasadena
303 Cordova St, Pasadena (91101-2426)
PHONE.................626 449-4000
Ray Serafin, *Prin*
EMP: 99 **EST:** 2008
SALES (est): 1.73MM **Privately Held**
Web: www.sheratonpasadena.com
SIC: 7011 Resort hotel

(P-12970)
PAUMA BAND OF MISSION INDIANS
Casino Pauma
777 Pauma Reservation Rd, Pauma Valley (92061)
P.O. Box 1067 (92061-1067)
PHONE.................760 742-2177
Richard Darder, *CEO*
EMP: 500
Web: www.casinopauma.com
SIC: 7011 Casino hotel
PA: Pauma Band Of Mission Indians
1010 Pauma Reservation Rd

(P-12971)
PECHANGA DEVELOPMENT CORP
Also Called: Pechanga Resort & Casino
45000 Pechanga Pkwy, Temecula (92592-5810)
P.O. Box 9041 (92589-9041)
PHONE.................951 695-4655
Patrick Murphy, *CEO*
Jerry Konchar, *
Randall Bardwell, *
Edith Atwood, *
Jared Munoa, *
◆ **EMP:** 4000 **EST:** 1995
SALES (est): 55.74MM **Privately Held**
Web: www.pechanga.com
SIC: 7011 7929 7999 Casino hotel; Entertainment service; Gambling establishment

(P-12972)
PECHANGA RESORTS INCORPORATED
45000 Pechanga Pkwy, Temecula (92592-5810)
P.O. Box 1477 (92593-1477)
PHONE.................888 732-4264
Edith Atwood, *CEO*
EMP: 77 **EST:** 2018
SALES (est): 5.51MM **Privately Held**
Web: www.pechanga.com
SIC: 7011 Casino hotel

(P-12973)
PHF II BURBANK LLC
Also Called: Burbank Airport Mariott Hotel
2500 N Hollywood Way, Burbank (91505-1019)
PHONE.................818 843-6000
Linda Davey, *Managing Member*
EMP: 220 **EST:** 2006

SALES (est): 4.61MM **Privately Held**
Web: www.ctn-events.com
SIC: 7011 Hotels and motels

(P-12974)
PINNACLE RVRSIDE HSPITALITY LP
Also Called: Riverside Marriott
3400 Market St, Riverside (92501-2826)
PHONE.................951 784-8000
Doctor Bharat Lall, *Genl Pt*
EMP: 190 **EST:** 2007
SALES (est): 9.67MM **Privately Held**
Web: www.marriott.com
SIC: 7011 Hotels

(P-12975)
PLAYA PROPER JV LLC
Also Called: Custom Hotel
8639 Lincoln Blvd, Los Angeles (90045-3503)
PHONE.................310 645-0400
Brad Korzen, *CEO*
Bryan De Lowe, *
Jeffrey Cruz, *
EMP: 80 **EST:** 2017
SALES (est): 2.5MM **Privately Held**
Web: www.thehoteljune.com
SIC: 7011 Hotels

(P-12976)
PORTOFINO INN & SUITES ANAHEIM
1831 S Harbor Blvd, Anaheim (92802-3509)
PHONE.................714 782-7600
Jennifer Reihl, *Dir*
EMP: 1244 **EST:** 2008
SALES (est): 1.43MM
SALES (corp-wide): 87.9MM **Privately Held**
Web: www.portofinoinnanaheim.com
SIC: 7011 Inns
HQ: Tarsadia Hotels
620 Nwport Ctr Dr Ste 140
Newport Beach CA 92660

(P-12977)
PRIME HOSPITALITY LLC
Also Called: Radisson Inn
2200 E Holt Blvd, Ontario (91761-7671)
PHONE.................909 975-5000
Tom Vanwinkle, *Brnch Mgr*
EMP: 84
Web: www.radissonhotels.com
SIC: 7011 Hotels and motels
PA: Prime Hospitality, Llc
2155 E Convention Ctr Way

(P-12978)
PRUTEL JOINT VENTURE
Also Called: Ritz-Carlton Laguna Niguel
1 Ritz Carlton Dr, Dana Point (92629-4205)
PHONE.................949 240-5064
W B Johnson, *Pt*
Prudential Realty San Francisco Ca, *Pt*
Paul Patterson, *CFO*
Kelly Steward, *Genl Mgr*
EMP: 700 **EST:** 1984
SALES (est): 3.3MM **Privately Held**
Web: www.ritzcarlton.com
SIC: 7011 Hotels

(P-12979)
PT GAMING LLC
235 Oregon St, El Segundo (90245-4215)
PHONE.................323 260-5060
Patrick Tierney, *Managing Member*
EMP: 700 **EST:** 2012

▲ = Import ▼ = Export
◆ = Import/Export

SQ FT: 7,000
SALES (est): 4.41MM **Privately Held**
Web: www.ptgaming.com
SIC: 7011 Casino hotel

(P-12980)
QUEENSBAY HOTEL LLC
Also Called: Hotel Maya
700 Queensway Dr, Long Beach
(90802-6343)
PHONE..............................562 481-3910
Cherie Davis, *Mgr*
EMP: 100
SALES (corp-wide): 9.87MM **Privately Held**
Web: www.hotelmayalongbeach.com
SIC: 7011 Hotels
PA: Queensbay Hotel, Llc
444 W Ocean Blvd
562 628-0625

(P-12981)
R P S RESORT CORP
1600 N Indian Canyon Dr, Palm Springs
(92262-4602)
PHONE..............................760 327-8311
Douglas Mccarron, *Pr*
EMP: 684 **EST:** 1990
SALES (est): 392.55K
SALES (corp-wide): 24.63MM **Privately Held**
Web: www.margaritavilleresorts.com
SIC: 7011 Resort hotel
HQ: The San Bernardino Hilton
285 E Hospitality Ln
San Bernardino CA 92408

(P-12982)
RADLAX GATEWAY HOTEL LLC
Also Called: Radisson Inn
6225 W Century Blvd, Los Angeles
(90045-5311)
PHONE..............................310 670-9000
Peter Dumon, *Managing Member*
EMP: 1432 **EST:** 2007
SALES (est): 2.49MM **Privately Held**
Web: www.radissonhotels.com
SIC: 7011 Hotels
PA: Portfolio Hotels & Resorts, Llc
1211 W 22nd St Ste 1002

(P-12983)
RAFFLES LRMITAGE BEVERLY HILLS
Also Called: L'Ermitage Hotel
9291 Burton Way, Beverly Hills
(90210-3709)
PHONE..............................310 278 3344
Jack Naderkhani, *Genl Mgr*
▲ **EMP:** 249 **EST:** 1993
SALES (est): 5.8MM
SALES (corp-wide): 1.66B **Privately Held**
Web: www.lermitagebeverlyhills.com
SIC: 7011 5813 5812 Hotels; Drinking places
; Eating places
HQ: Raffles International Limited
1 Wallich Street
Singapore 07888

(P-12984)
RALEIGH ENTERPRISES INC (PA)
Also Called: Raleigh Holdings
5300 Melrose Ave, Los Angeles
(90038-5111)
PHONE..............................310 899-8900
Kristen J Raleigh, *CEO*
George I Rosenthal, *Ch Bd*
Mark Rosenthal, *Pr*
EMP: 130 **EST:** 1955

SQ FT: 20,000
SALES (est): 25.12MM
SALES (corp-wide): 25.12MM **Privately Held**
Web: www.raleighenterprises.com
SIC: 7011 Hotels

(P-12985)
RANCHO VLNCIA RSORT PRTNERS LL
5921 Valencia Cir, Rancho Santa Fe
(92067-9520)
P.O. Box 9126 (92067-4126)
PHONE..............................858 756-1123
Jeffrey Essakow, *Managing Member*
Hal Jacobs, *
EMP: 300 **EST:** 1989
SALES (est): 21.98MM **Privately Held**
Web: www.ranchovalencia.com
SIC: 7011 Resort hotel

(P-12986)
RBD HOTEL PALM SPRINGS LLC
Also Called: Hyatt Rgency Suites Palm Sprng
285 N Palm Canyon Dr, Palm Springs
(92262-5525)
PHONE..............................760 322-9000
Larry Mills, *Sr VP*
EMP: 75 **EST:** 2009
SALES (est): 950K **Privately Held**
Web: www.hyatt.com
SIC: 7011 Resort hotel

(P-12987)
RED EARTH CASINO
3089 Norm Niver Rd, Thermal
(92274-6550)
PHONE..............................760 395-1200
Larry Drouse, *Genl Mgr*
EMP: 150 **EST:** 2007
SQ FT: 15,000
SALES (est): 8.11MM **Privately Held**
Web: www.redearthcasino.com
SIC: 7011 7993 Casino hotel; Gambling
establishments operating coin-operated
machines

(P-12988)
REMINGTON HOTEL CORPORATION
Also Called: Palm Springs Renaissance
888 E Tahquitz Canyon Way, Palm Springs
(92262-6708)
PHONE..............................760 322-6000
EMP: 214
Web: www.remingtonhospitality.com
SIC: 7011 Hotels
PA: Remington Hotel Corporation
14185 Dllas Pkwy Ste 1150

(P-12989)
REMINGTON HOTEL CORPORATION
Also Called: Holiday Inn
1150 S Beverly Dr, Los Angeles
(90035-1120)
PHONE..............................310 553-6561
Jack Jones, *Brnch Mgr*
EMP: 212
Web: www.remingtonhospitality.com
SIC: 7011 Hotels and motels
PA: Remington Hotel Corporation
14185 Dllas Pkwy Ste 1150

(P-12990)
RENAISSANCE HOTEL OPERATING CO
Also Called: Marriott
9620 Airport Blvd, Los Angeles
(90045-5402)

PHONE..............................310 337-2800
Gregory Lehman, *Mgr*
EMP: 300
SALES (corp-wide): 23.71B **Publicly Held**
Web: www.marriott.com
SIC: 7011 5813 5812 7389 Hotels and motels
; Drinking places; Eating places; Office
facilities and secretarial service rental
HQ: Renaissance Hotel Operating
Company
10400 Fernwood Rd
Bethesda MD 20817

(P-12991)
RENAISSANCE HOTEL OPERATING CO
Also Called: Renaissance Indian Wells
44400 Indian Wells Ln, Indian Wells
(92210-8708)
PHONE..............................760 773-4444
Tom Tabler, *Prin*
EMP: 600
SALES (corp-wide): 23.71B **Publicly Held**
Web: renaissance-hotels.marriott.com
SIC: 7011 Hotels
HQ: Renaissance Hotel Operating
Company
10400 Fernwood Rd
Bethesda MD 20817

(P-12992)
RESIDENCE INN BY MARRIOTT LLC
Also Called: Marriott
38305 Cook St, Palm Desert (92211-1794)
PHONE..............................760 776-0050
Michael Gerano, *Brnch Mgr*
EMP: 83
SALES (corp-wide): 23.71B **Publicly Held**
Web: www.marriott.com
SIC: 7011 Hotels and motels
HQ: Residence Inn By Marriott, Llc
10400 Fernwood Rd
Bethesda MD 20817

(P-12993)
RGC GASLAMP LLC
Also Called: Pendry San Diego
550 J St, San Diego (92101-7020)
PHONE..............................619 738-7000
Michael Odonohue, *Prin*
EMP: 93 **EST:** 2016
SALES (est): 13.53MM **Privately Held**
Web: www.pendry.com
SIC: 7011 Resort hotel

(P-12994)
RIO VISTA DEVELOPMENT CO INC (PA)
Also Called: Holiday Inn
4222 Vineland Ave, North Hollywood
(91602-3318)
PHONE..............................818 980-8000
Scott A Mills, *Prin*
Scott Mills, *
EMP: 133 **EST:** 1971
SQ FT: 100,000
SALES (est): 13.23MM
SALES (corp-wide): 13.23MM **Privately Held**
Web: www.thegarland.com
SIC: 7011 Hotels and motels

(P-12995)
RITZ-CARLTON HOTEL COMPANY LLC
Also Called: Ritz-Carlton
1 Ritz Carlton Dr, Dana Point (92629-4206)
PHONE..............................949 240-5020

Jannie Vanderoy, *Brnch Mgr*
EMP: 348
SALES (corp-wide): 23.71B **Publicly Held**
Web: www.ritzcarlton.com
SIC: 7011 Hotels
HQ: The Ritz-Carlton Hotel Company Llc
7750 Wisconsin Ave
Bethesda MD 20814
301 380-3000

(P-12996)
RITZ-CARLTON HOTEL COMPANY LLC
Also Called: Ritz Carlton Rancho Mirage
68900 Frank Sinatra Dr, Rancho Mirage
(92270-5300)
PHONE..............................760 321-8282
James H Palllin Junior, *Mgr*
EMP: 313
SALES (corp-wide): 23.71B **Publicly Held**
Web: www.ritzcarlton.com
SIC: 7011 Hotels
HQ: The Ritz-Carlton Hotel Company Llc
7750 Wisconsin Ave
Bethesda MD 20814
301 380-3000

(P-12997)
RITZ-CARLTON HOTEL COMPANY LLC
Also Called: Ritz-Carlton
8301 Hollister Ave, Santa Barbara
(93117-2474)
PHONE..............................805 968-0100
EMP: 650
SALES (corp-wide): 23.71B **Publicly Held**
Web: www.ritzcarlton.com
SIC: 7011 Hotels
HQ: The Ritz-Carlton Hotel Company Llc
7750 Wisconsin Ave
Bethesda MD 20814
301 380-3000

(P-12998)
RITZ-CARLTON MARINA DEL REY
Also Called: Ritz-Carlton
4375 Admiralty Way, Marina Del Rey
(90292-5434)
PHONE..............................310 823-1700
Robert Thomas, *Prin*
EMP: 71 **EST:** 2004
SALES (est): 4.85MM **Privately Held**
Web: www.ritzcarlton.com
SIC: 7011 Hotels

(P-12999)
RMS FOUNDATION INC
Also Called: Queen Mary Hotel
1126 Queens Hwy, Long Beach
(90802-6331)
PHONE..............................562 435-3511
Joseph F Prevratil, *Pr*
EMP: 650 **EST:** 1993
SQ FT: 750,000
SALES (est): 45.3MM **Privately Held**
Web: www.queenmary.com
SIC: 7011 Hotels and motels
PA: City Of Long Beach
1800 E Wardlow Rd
562 570-6450

(P-13000)
ROOSEVELT HOTEL LLC
Also Called: Hollywood Roosevelt Hotel
7000 Hollywood Blvd, Los Angeles
(90028-6003)
PHONE..............................323 466-7000
Goodwin Gaw, *Managing Member*

P
R
O
D
U
C
T
S

&

S
V
C
S

David Chan, *
Andrew Jay, *
EMP: 200 **EST:** 1995
SALES (est): 25.87MM **Privately Held**
Web: www.thehollywoodroosevelt.com
SIC: 7011 5813 5812 Hotels; Drinking places
; Eating places

(P-13001)
ROSANNA INC
Also Called: Avenue of Arts Wyndham Hotel
3350 Avenue Of The Arts, Costa Mesa
(92626-1913)
PHONE..............................714 751-5100
Nick Price, *Genl Mgr*
Paul Sanford, *
Rachael Moorhead, *
Rosanna Chan, *
Robin Reid, *OF AUDIT*
EMP: 151 **EST:** 2009
SALES (est): 4.59MM **Privately Held**
Web: www.avenueoftheartshotel.com
SIC: 7011 5812 Hotels; Food bars

(P-13002)
RPD HOTELS 18 LLC
Also Called: Vagabond Inns
1801 S La Cienega Blvd Ste 301, Los
Angeles (90035-4658)
PHONE..............................213 746-1531
Juan Sanchez Llaca, *Pr*
Don Johnson, *
Stewart Rubin, *
EMP: 1310 **EST:** 1998
SALES (est): 4.52MM **Privately Held**
Web: www.vagabondinn.com
SIC: 7011 Motels

(P-13003)
RUFFIN HOTEL CORP OF CAL
Also Called: Long Beach Marriott
4700 Airport Plaza Dr, Long Beach
(90815-1252)
PHONE..............................562 425-5210
Phillip G Ruffin, *Pr*
EMP: 260 **EST:** 1993
SALES (est): 3.94MM **Privately Held**
Web: www.marriott.com
SIC: 7011 5812 5813 Hotels; Eating places;
Drinking places

(P-13004)
S B H HOTEL CORPORATION
285 E Hospitality Ln, San Bernardino
(92408-3411)
PHONE..............................909 889-0133
Douglas Mccarron, *Brnch Mgr*
EMP: 311
SALES (corp-wide): 24.63MM **Privately
Held**
SIC: 7011 Hotels
HQ: S B H Hotel Corporation
520 S Virgil Ave Fl 4
Los Angeles CA

(P-13005)
S W K PROPERTIES LLC
Also Called: Holiday Inn
2726 S Grand Ave Lbby, Santa Ana
(92705-5404)
PHONE..............................714 481-6300
Rod Hurt, *Mgr*
EMP: 129
SALES (corp-wide): 2.7MM **Privately Held**
Web: www.holidayinn.com
SIC: 7011 Hotels and motels
PA: S W K Properties Llc
3807 Wilshire Blvd # 122
213 383-9204

(P-13006)
S W K PROPERTIES LLC (PA)
Also Called: Sheraton
3807 Wilshire Blvd Ste 1226, Los Angeles
(90010-3104)
PHONE..............................213 383-9204
EMP: 70 **EST:** 1998
SQ FT: 3,000
SALES (est): 2.7MM
SALES (corp-wide): 2.7MM **Privately Held**
Web: four-points.marriott.com
SIC: 7011 Hotels

(P-13007)
**SAGE HOSPITALITY
RESOURCES LLC**
Also Called: Courtyard By Mrrott Los Angles
700 W Huntington Dr, Monrovia
(91016-3104)
PHONE..............................626 357-5211
Dennis Hollingdrake, *Mgr*
EMP: 360
SALES (corp-wide): 286.23MM **Privately
Held**
Web: www.marriott.com
SIC: 7011 Hotels and motels
PA: Sage Hospitality Resources L.L.C.
1809 Blake St
303 595-7200

(P-13008)
SAI MANAGEMENT CO INC
Also Called: Desert Inn & Suites
1600 S Harbor Blvd, Anaheim
(92802-2314)
PHONE..............................714 772-5050
Priti Hansji, *Mgr*
EMP: 80
SALES (corp-wide): 4.91MM **Privately
Held**
Web: www.anaheimdesertinn.com
SIC: 7011 Resort hotel
PA: Sai Management Co., Inc.
631 W Katella Ave
714 776-8604

(P-13009)
SAJAHTERA INC
Also Called: Beverly Hills Hotel
9641 Sunset Blvd, Beverly Hills
(90210-2938)
PHONE..............................310 276-2251
Junaidi Masri, *Pr*
Edward Mady, *OF WEST COAST USA*
EMP: 600 **EST:** 1912
SQ FT: 10,758
SALES (est): 57.4MM **Privately Held**
Web: www.dorchestercollection.com
SIC: 7011 Resort hotel
HQ: Dorchester Group Limited
The Dorchester
London W1K 1
207 629-8888

(P-13010)
SAN BERNARDINO HILTON (HQ)
Also Called: Hilton
285 E Hospitality Ln, San Bernardino
(92408-3411)
PHONE..............................909 889-0133
Douglas Mccarron, *Pr*
Morgan Mcpherson, *Ex Dir*
Ronald Schoen, *
EMP: 152 **EST:** 1984
SALES (est): 3.78MM
SALES (corp-wide): 24.63MM **Privately
Held**
Web: www.hilton.com

SIC: 7011 6512 5812 Hotels and motels;
Commercial and industrial building
operation; Eating places
PA: Carpenters Southwest Administrative
Corporation
533 S Fremont Ave
213 386-8590

(P-13011)
**SAN DIEGO HOTEL COMPANY
LLC**
Also Called: Marriott San Dego Gslamp Qrter
660 K St, San Diego (92101-7036)
PHONE..............................619 696-0234
James Evans, *CFO*
▲ **EMP:** 135 **EST:** 1999
SALES (est): 6.85MM **Privately Held**
Web: www.sandiegogaslamphotel.com
SIC: 7011 Hotels

(P-13012)
**SAN PSQUAL BAND MSSION
INDIANS**
Also Called: Valley View Casino
16300 Nyemii Pass Rd, Valley Center
(92082-6769)
P.O. Box 2379 (92082-2379)
PHONE..............................760 291-5500
TOLL FREE: 866
Bruce Howards, *Genl Mgr*
EMP: 242
Web:
www.sanpasqualbandofmissionindians.org
SIC: 7011 Casino hotel
PA: San Pasqual Band Of Mission Indians
16400 Kumeyaay Way

(P-13013)
**SAN YSIDRO BB PROPERTY
LLC**
Also Called: Stonehouse Restaurant
900 San Ysidro Ln, Santa Barbara
(93108-1325)
PHONE..............................805 368-6788
Seamus Mcmanus, *Managing Member*
EMP: 140 **EST:** 2000
SQ FT: 4,415
SALES (est): 4.27MM **Privately Held**
Web: www.sanysidroranch.com
SIC: 7011 5812 Hotels; Eating places

(P-13014)
SAND AND SEA
Also Called: Shore Hotel
1515 Ocean Ave, Santa Monica
(90401-2118)
PHONE..............................310 458-1515
Julie Ward, *Prin*
EMP: 72 **EST:** 2011
SALES (est): 13.49MM **Privately Held**
Web: www.shorehotel.com
SIC: 7011 Resort hotel

(P-13015)
**SANDM SAN DEGO MRRIOTT
DEL MAR**
11966 El Camino Real, San Diego
(92130-2592)
PHONE..............................858 523-1700
Jenessa Schaniel, *Prin*
EMP: 1000 **EST:** 2009
SALES (est): 2.88MM **Privately Held**
Web: www.marriott.com
SIC: 7011 Hotels

(P-13016)
**SANTA MONICA HOTEL OWNER
LLC**
Also Called: Doubltree Stes By Hlton Snta M

1707 4th St, Santa Monica (90401-3301)
PHONE..............................310 395-3332
EMP: 135 **EST:** 2005
SALES (est): 3.27MM **Privately Held**
Web: www.monicaslosangeles.com
SIC: 7011 Hotels

(P-13017)
**SANTA MONICA PROPER JV
LLC**
Also Called: Santa Monica Proper Hotel
700 Wilshire Blvd, Santa Monica
(90401-1708)
PHONE..............................310 620-9990
Brad Korzen, *CEO*
EMP: 250 **EST:** 2016
SALES (est): 17.63MM **Privately Held**
Web: www.properhotel.com
SIC: 7011 Hotels

(P-13018)
SD HOTEL CIRCLE LLC
Also Called: Homewood Suites
2201 Hotel Cir S, San Diego (92108-3315)
PHONE..............................619 881-6800
Mayur Patel, *
Louisa Yeung, *
EMP: 75 **EST:** 2017
SALES (est): 3.16MM **Privately Held**
Web: www.hilton.com
SIC: 7011 Hotels and motels

(P-13019)
**SEATTLE ARPRT HOSPITALITY
LLC**
Also Called: Holiday Inn
170 N Church Ln, Los Angeles
(90049-2044)
PHONE..............................310 476-6411
Robert Buescher, *Genl Mgr*
EMP: 99
Web: www.islandhospitality.com
SIC: 7011 5813 5812 Hotels and motels;
Drinking places; Eating places
PA: Seattle Airport Hospitality, Llc
5847 San Felipe St # 4650

(P-13020)
**SECOND STREET
CORPORATION**
Also Called: Huntley Hotel Santa Monica Bch
1111 2nd St, Santa Monica (90403-5003)
PHONE..............................310 394-5454
Sohrab Sassounian, *Pr*
Dora Levy, *Stockholder*
Helal M El-sherif, *CFO*
Shiva Aghaipour, *
EMP: 250 **EST:** 1964
SQ FT: 185,000
SALES (est): 21.66MM **Privately Held**
Web: www.thehuntleyhotel.com
SIC: 7011 5812 Hotels; Eating places

(P-13021)
SHEN ZHEN NEW WORLD II LLC
Also Called: Sheraton
333 Universal Hollywood Dr, Universal City
(91608)
PHONE..............................818 980-1212
EMP: 99 **EST:** 2011
SALES (est): 1.96MM **Privately Held**
Web: four-points.marriott.com
SIC: 7011 Hotels

(P-13022)
**SHERATON HT SAN DEGO
MSSION VL**
Also Called: Sheraton San Diego Mission Vly
1433 Camino Del Rio S, San Diego
(92108-3521)

▲ = Import ▼ = Export
◆ = Import/Export

PHONE..................619 260-0111
Admiral Cynthia Adams Carlin, *Prin*
Cynthia Adams Carlin, *Admn*
Brooke Vandenbrink, *Contrlr*
EMP: 100 **EST:** 2007
SALES (est): 1.4MM **Privately Held**
Web: www.sheratonmissionvalley.com
SIC: 7011 Hotels

(P-13023)
SILENT VALLEY CLUB INC
46305 Poppet Flats Rd, Banning
(92220-9636)
PHONE..................951 849-4501
Patrick Buhrer, *Park Director*
EMP: 70 **EST:** 1973
SQ FT: 2,200
SALES (est): 3.87MM **Privately Held**
Web: www.silentvalleyclub.com
SIC: 7011 Resort hotel

(P-13024)
SIMI WEST INC
Also Called: Grand Vista Hotel
999 Enchanted Way, Simi Valley
(93065-1998)
PHONE..................760 346-5502
Leo Cook, *Ch Bd*
EMP: 120 **EST:** 1993
SALES (est): 5.19MM **Privately Held**
Web: www.grandvistasimi.com
SIC: 7011 Hotels and motels

(P-13025)
SIX CONTINENTS HOTELS INC
Also Called: Holiday Inn
612 Wainwright Ct, Lebec (93243)
PHONE..................661 343-3316
EMP: 122
Web: www.holidayinn.com
SIC: 7011 Hotels and motels
HQ: Six Continents Hotels, Inc
35016 Avenue D
Yucaipa CA 92399
770 604-5000

(P-13026)
SLS HOTEL AT BEVERLY HILLS
465 S La Cienega Blvd, Los Angeles
(90048-4001)
PHONE..................310 247-0400
Robert Leck, *Genl Mgr*
EMP: 112 **EST:** 2015
SALES (est): 3.12MM
SALES (corp-wide): 58.67MM **Privately Held**
Web: book.ennismore.com
SIC: 7011 Hotels
PA: The Sunrider Corporation
1625 Abalone Ave
310 781-3808

(P-13027)
SMOKE TREE INC
Also Called: Smoke Tree Ranch
1850 Smoke Tree Ln, Palm Springs
(92264-9270)
PHONE..................760 327-1221
Lisa Bell, *Mgr*
Brad Poncher, *
EMP: 85 **EST:** 1945
SALES (est): 3.01MM **Privately Held**
Web: www.smoketreeranch.com
SIC: 7011 Resort hotel

(P-13028)
SNOW SUMMIT LLC (PA)
Also Called: Bear Mountain
880 Summit Blvd, Big Bear Lake (92315)
P.O. Box 77 (92315-0077)

PHONE..................909 866-5766
Wade Reeser, *CEO*
Robert Law, *VP*
Alan Macquoid, *Treas*
Paula Lowery, *Sec*
Robert Tarras, *CFO*
EMP: 150 **EST:** 1960
SQ FT: 10,000
SALES (est): 13.63MM
SALES (corp-wide): 13.63MM **Privately Held**
Web: www.bigbearmountainresort.com
SIC: 7011 5812 Ski lodge; American restaurant

(P-13029)
SOUTH COAST WESTIN HOTEL CO
Also Called: Starwood Hotels & Resorts
686 Anton Blvd, Costa Mesa (92626-1920)
PHONE..................714 540-2500
Steve Heyer, *CEO*
Mike Hall, *
Bob Jenness, *
EMP: 99 **EST:** 1970
SALES (est): 3.29MM
SALES (corp-wide): 23.71B **Publicly Held**
Web: www.marriott.com
SIC: 7011 5812 Hotels; Eating places
HQ: Starwood Hotels & Resorts Worldwide, Llc
7750 Wisconsin Ave
Bethesda MD 20814
203 964-6000

(P-13030)
SPA RESORT CASINO
100 N Indian Canyon Dr, Palm Springs
(92262-6414)
PHONE..................760 883-1034
Max Ross, *CFO*
EMP: 926
SALES (corp-wide): 5.02MM **Privately Held**
Web: www.aguacalientecasinos.com
SIC: 7011 Casino hotel
PA: Spa Resort Casino
401 E Amado Rd
888 999-1995

(P-13031)
SPA RESORT CASINO (PA)
401 E Amado Rd, Palm Springs
(92262-6403)
PHONE..................888 999-1995
Kato Moy, *Genl Mgr*
Agvahgue Eahilla Indian, *Owner*
EMP: 74 **EST:** 2004
SALES (est): 5.02MM
SALES (corp-wide): 5.02MM **Privately Held**
Web: www.aguacalientecasinos.com
SIC: 7011 Resort hotel

(P-13032)
SPECTRUM HOTEL GROUP LLC
Also Called: Doubletree Hotel
90 Pacifica, Irvine (92618-3312)
PHONE..................949 471-8888
Timothy R Busch, *General Member*
EMP: 119 **EST:** 1997
SALES (est): 5.13MM **Privately Held**
Web: www.hilton.com
SIC: 7011 7991 5812 Hotels and motels; Physical fitness facilities; Eating places

(P-13033)
SPF CAPITAL REAL ESTATE LLC
Also Called: Crown Plaza La Harbor Hotel
601 S Palos Verdes St, San Pedro
(90731-3329)

PHONE..................310 519-8200
Tiegang Yin, *Prin*
Tim Yin, *Prin*
EMP: 99 **EST:** 2017
SALES (est): 5.81MM **Privately Held**
Web: www.lawaterfront.org
SIC: 7011 Hotels

(P-13034)
SS HERITAGE INN ONTARIO LLC
3595 E Guasti Rd, Ontario (91761-3705)
PHONE..................909 937-5000
Aimee Fyke, *Managing Member*
EMP: 99 **EST:** 2018
SALES (est): 2.23MM **Privately Held**
SIC: 7011 Inns

(P-13035)
STARWOOD HTELS RSRTS WRLDWIDE
Also Called: Starwood Hotels & Resorts
910 Broadway Cir, San Diego (92101-6114)
PHONE..................619 239-2200
Doug Korn, *Genl Mgr*
EMP: 250
SALES (corp-wide): 23.71B **Publicly Held**
Web: www.starwoodhotels.com
SIC: 7011 7991 6512 5812 Hotels and motels ; Physical fitness facilities; Nonresidential building operators; Eating places
HQ: Starwood Hotels & Resorts Worldwide, Llc
7750 Wisconsin Ave
Bethesda MD 20814
203 964-6000

(P-13036)
STARWOOD HTELS RSRTS WRLDWIDE
Also Called: Sheraton
601 W Mckinley Ave, Pomona
(91768-1635)
PHONE..................909 622-2220
John Gilbert, *Genl Mgr*
EMP: 195
SALES (corp-wide): 23.71B **Publicly Held**
Web: www.starwoodhotels.com
SIC: 7011 Hotels and motels
HQ: Starwood Hotels & Resorts Worldwide, Llc
7750 Wisconsin Ave
Bethesda MD 20814
203 964-6000

(P-13037)
STOCKBRIDGE/SBE HOLDINGS LLC
Also Called: SBE
5900 Wilshire Blvd Ste 3100, Los Angeles
(90036-5030)
PHONE..................323 655-8000
EMP: 3000 **EST:** 2007
SALES (est): 10.08MM **Privately Held**
SIC: 7011 Hotels

(P-13038)
STONEBRIDGE RLTY ADVISORS INC
Also Called: Hampton Inn
27102 Towne Centre Dr, Foothill Ranch
(92610-2801)
PHONE..................949 597-8700
John Matthews, *Mgr*
EMP: 361
Web: www.hilton.com
SIC: 7011 Hotels and motels
PA: Stonebridge Realty Advisors, Inc.
9100 E Pnorama Dr Ste 300

(P-13039)
SUMMERWOOD WINERY & INN INC
2175 Arbor Rd, Paso Robles (93446-8620)
PHONE..................805 227-1365
Mark Uhalley, *Pr*
▲ **EMP:** 33 **EST:** 2002
SALES (est): 2.11MM **Privately Held**
Web: www.summerwoodwine.com
SIC: 7011 2084 Bed and breakfast inn; Wines

(P-13040)
SUN HILL PROPERTIES INC
Also Called: Hilton Los Angls/Nversal Cy Ht
555 Universal Hollywood Dr, Universal City
(91608-1001)
PHONE..................818 506-2500
Denn Hu, *Ch Bd*
▲ **EMP:** 350 **EST:** 1989
SALES (est): 20.84MM **Privately Held**
Web: www.sunhillprop.com
SIC: 7011 Hotels and motels
PA: Universal Paragon Corporation
150 Exctive Pk Blvd Ste 4

(P-13041)
SUNSTONE DURANTE LLC
Also Called: Hilton San Diego/Del Mar
15575 Jimmy Durante Blvd, Del Mar
(92014-1901)
PHONE..................858 792-5200
Scott Sloan, *Managing Member*
Damien Proctor, *Prin*
EMP: 250 **EST:** 2005
SALES (est): 3.17MM **Privately Held**
SIC: 7011 Hotels and motels

(P-13042)
SUNSTONE HOTEL PROPERTIES INC
3805 Murphy Canyon Rd, San Diego
(92123-4404)
PHONE..................858 277-1199
Linda Dimeglio, *Mgr*
EMP: 108
Web: www.sunstonehotels.com
SIC: 7011 Hotels
HQ: Sunstone Hotel Properties Inc
120 Vantis Dr Ste 350
Aliso Viejo CA 92656

(P-13043)
SUNSTONE HOTEL PROPERTIES INC
Also Called: Residence Inn By Marriott
1177 S Beverly Dr, Los Angeles
(90035-1119)
PHONE..................310 228-4100
Tom Deedon, *Genl Mgr*
EMP: 214
Web: www.sunstonehotels.com
SIC: 7011 Hotels and motels
HQ: Sunstone Hotel Properties Inc
120 Vantis Dr Ste 350
Aliso Viejo CA 92656

(P-13044)
SUNSTONE HOTEL PROPERTIES INC (DH)
Also Called: Residence Inn By Marriott
120 Vantis Dr Ste 350, Aliso Viejo
(92656-2686)
PHONE..................949 330-4000
Arthur Buser, *Pr*
EMP: 120 **EST:** 1994
SALES (est): 2.89MM **Privately Held**
Web: www.sunstonehotels.com

PRODUCTS & SVCS

SIC: 7011 Hotels and motels
HQ: Interstate Hotels & Resorts, Inc.
5301 Headquarters Dr
Plano TX 75024
703 387-3100

(P-13045)
SUNSTONE TOP GUN LESSEE INC
Also Called: Embassy Suites
4550 La Jolla Village Dr, San Diego
(92122-1248)
PHONE..................................949 330-4000
Kenneth E Cruse, *CEO*
John V Arabia, *
Lindsay Monge, *
EMP: 150 EST: 2006
SALES (est): 9.27MM **Publicly Held**
Web: www.hilton.com
SIC: 7011 Hotels and motels
HQ: Sunstone Hotel Trs Lessee, Inc.
15 Enterprise
Aliso Viejo CA 92656

(P-13046)
SWVP WESTLAKE LLC
Also Called: Hyatt Westlake
880 S Westlake Blvd, Westlake Village
(91361-2905)
PHONE..................................805 557-1234
David Coonan, *Genl Mgr*
EMP: 250
SALES (corp-wide): 9MM **Privately Held**
Web: www.swvp.com
SIC: 7011 Motels
PA: Swvp Westlake Llc
12790 El Camino Real
858 480-2900

(P-13047)
SYCUAN CASINO
5469 Casino Way, El Cajon (92019-1823)
PHONE..................................619 445-6002
EMP: 1844
SALES (corp-wide): 28.09MM **Privately Held**
Web: www.sycuan.com
SIC: 7011 Casino hotel
PA: Sycuan Casino
5459 Casino Way
619 445-6002

(P-13048)
SYDELL HOTELS LLC
Also Called: Line Hotel, The
3515 Wilshire Blvd, Los Angeles
(90010-2301)
PHONE..................................213 381-7411
Gary J Thomas, *
EMP: 130 EST: 2011
SALES (est): 20.18MM
SALES (corp-wide): 10.23B **Publicly Held**
Web: www.thelinehotel.com
SIC: 7011 Resort hotel
HQ: Sydell Group Llc
276 5th Ave Rm 704
New York NY 10001

(P-13049)
T M MIAN & ASSOCIATES INC
Also Called: Hilton Garden Inn Calabasas
24150 Park Sorrento, Calabasas
(91302-4101)
PHONE..................................818 591-2300
Shawn Nicoles, *Genl Mgr*
EMP: 80
SALES (corp-wide): 10.53MM **Privately Held**
Web: www.hilton.com
SIC: 7011 Resort hotel

PA: T. M. Mian & Associates, Inc.
1055 Regal Row
972 960-2024

(P-13050)
T-12 THREE LLC
Also Called: Hard Rock Hotel
207 5th Ave, San Diego (92101-6908)
PHONE..................................619 702-3000
Nilesh Madhav, *Managing Member*
Matt Greene, *
EMP: 356 EST: 2007
SALES (est): 18.32MM **Privately Held**
Web: hotel.hardrock.com
SIC: 7011 Hotels

(P-13051)
THE LODGE AT TORREY PINES PARTNERSHIP L P
998 W Mission Bay Dr, San Diego
(92109-7803)
EMP: 275 EST: 1961
SALES (est): 905K **Privately Held**
Web: www.lodgetorreypines.com
SIC: 7011 5812 Resort hotel; Coffee shop

(P-13052)
TIC HOTELS INC
Also Called: Best Western Bayside Inn
555 W Ash St, San Diego (92101-3414)
PHONE..................................619 238-7577
Tracey Wicken, *Genl Mgr*
EMP: 77
Web: www.bestwestern.com
SIC: 7011 Hotels
HQ: Tic Hotels, Inc.
1811 State St Ste C
Santa Barbara CA 93101
805 898-0855

(P-13053)
TIC HOTELS INC
Also Called: Shorecliff Properties
2555 Price St, Pismo Beach (93449-2111)
PHONE..................................805 773-4671
Edward Brown, *Mgr*
EMP: 78
Web: www.shorecliff.com
SIC: 7011 5812 5813 Motels; Eating places;
Bar (drinking places)
HQ: Tic Hotels, Inc.
1811 State St Ste C
Santa Barbara CA 93101
805 898-0855

(P-13054)
TODAYS IV
Also Called: Westin Bonaventure Ht & Suites
404 S Figueroa St Ste 516, Los Angeles
(90071-1798)
PHONE..................................213 835-4016
Tee Fong Zen, *CEO*
Peter Zen, *
Ming Nin Zen, *
EMP: 701 EST: 1989
SQ FT: 1,200,000
SALES (est): 18.09MM **Privately Held**
Web: westin.marriott.com
SIC: 7011 5813 5812 Hotels; Drinking places
; Eating places
PA: Today's Hotel Corporation
1500 Van Ness Ave

(P-13055)
TRIGILD INTERNATIONAL INC
Also Called: Ramada Inn
2151 Hotel Cir S, San Diego (92108-3314)
PHONE..................................619 295-6886
Charlie Holiday, *Mgr*
EMP: 111

SALES (corp-wide): 7.73MM **Privately Held**
Web: www.trigild.com
SIC: 7011 Hotels and motels
PA: Trigild International, Inc.
3323 Carmel Mountain Rd # 2
858 720-6700

(P-13056)
TRIGILD INTERNATIONAL INC
Also Called: Days Inn
133 Encinitas Blvd, Encinitas (92024-3641)
PHONE..................................760 944-0260
Maria Rebollar, *Brnch Mgr*
EMP: 118
SALES (corp-wide): 7.73MM **Privately Held**
Web: www.trigild.com
SIC: 7011 Hotels and motels
PA: Trigild International, Inc.
3323 Carmel Mountain Rd # 2
858 720-6700

(P-13057)
UHG LAX PROP LLC
Also Called: Hotel Company
1985 E Grand Ave, El Segundo
(90245-5015)
PHONE..................................310 322-0999
Charu Goyal, *Managing Member*
Jordan Austin, *
Mark Lewis, *
EMP: 125 EST: 2017
SALES (est): 4.27MM **Privately Held**
Web: www.hilton.com
SIC: 7011 5812 Hotels; Restaurant, family:
independent

(P-13058)
UKA LLC
Also Called: Tarsadia Hotels
620 Newport Center Dr Ste 1400, Newport
Beach (92660-8025)
PHONE..................................949 610-8000
B U Patel, *Mgr*
EMP: 495 EST: 1997
SQ FT: 12,000
SALES (est): 235.37K
SALES (corp-wide): 87.9MM **Privately Held**
SIC: 7011 Hotels
HQ: Tarsadia Investments, Llc
520 Newport Center Dr # 2100
Newport Beach CA 92660
949 610-8000

(P-13059)
UNIWELL CORPORATION
Also Called: Holiday Inn
7000 Beach Blvd, Buena Park
(90620-1832)
PHONE..................................714 522-7000
Tracy Myer, *Brnch Mgr*
EMP: 150
SALES (corp-wide): 17.64MM **Privately Held**
Web: www.hibuenapark.com
SIC: 7011 5813 5812 Hotels and motels;
Drinking places; Eating places
PA: Uniwell Corporation
21172 Figueroa St
310 782-8888

(P-13060)
URBAN COMMONS QUEENSWAY LLC
Also Called: Queen Mary, The
1126 Queens Hwy, Long Beach
(90802-6331)
PHONE..................................562 499-1611

EMP: 900 EST: 2016
SALES (est): 2.02MM **Privately Held**
Web: www.queenmary.com
SIC: 7011 Hotels

(P-13061)
US GRANT HOTEL VENTURES LLC
326 Broadway, San Diego (92101-4812)
PHONE..................................619 744-2007
EMP: 80 EST: 2003
SQ FT: 99,999
SALES (est): 2.78MM **Privately Held**
Web: www.grantgrill.com
SIC: 7011 Resort hotel

(P-13062)
US HOTEL AND RESORT MGT INC
Also Called: Regency Inn
2544 Newport Blvd, Costa Mesa
(92627-1331)
PHONE..................................949 650-2988
Peggy Chen, *Mgr*
EMP: 216
SALES (corp-wide): 17.94MM **Privately Held**
Web: www.ramkotacompanies.com
SIC: 7011 Resort hotel
HQ: U.S. Hotel And Resort Management,
Inc.
3211 W Sencore Dr
Sioux Falls SD 57107
605 334-2371

(P-13063)
V TODAYS INC
Also Called: Holiday Inn
19800 S Vermont Ave, Torrance
(90502-1126)
PHONE..................................310 781-9100
Belinda Zen, *CEO*
David Britton, *
EMP: 110 EST: 1986
SQ FT: 95,000
SALES (est): 3.54MM **Privately Held**
Web: www.holidayinn.com
SIC: 7011 Hotels and motels

(P-13064)
VALADON HOTEL LLC
Also Called: Petit Ermitage
8822 Cynthia St, West Hollywood
(90069-4502)
PHONE..................................310 854-1114
Adrian Ashkenazy, *
EMP: 80 EST: 1997
SQ FT: 40,000
SALES (est): 15.16MM **Privately Held**
Web: www.petitermitage.com
SIC: 7011 Hotels

(P-13065)
VENTURA HSPTALITY PARTNERS LLC
Also Called: Crowne Plaza Ventura Beach
450 Harbor Blvd, Ventura (93001-2708)
PHONE..................................805 648-2100
EMP: 140 EST: 2006
SQ FT: 143,000
SALES (est): 9.07MM **Privately Held**
Web: www.ihg.com
SIC: 7011 Hotels

(P-13066)
VICTORVLLE TRSURE HOLDINGS LLC
Also Called: Holiday Inn
15494 Palmdale Rd, Victorville
(92392-2408)

PHONE..............760 245-6565
Benjamin Gonzales, *Genl Mgr*
EMP: 75 **EST:** 2011
SALES (est): 2.25MM **Privately Held**
Web: www.hivictorville.com
SIC: 7011 5812 Hotels and motels;
American restaurant

(P-13067)
VPB OPERATING CO LLC
Also Called: Autograph Collection Hotels
147 Stimson Ave, Pismo Beach
(93449-2643)
PHONE..............805 773-1011
EMP: 84 **EST:** 2021
SALES (est): 812.83K **Privately Held**
Web: autograph-hotels.marriott.com
SIC: 7011 Resort hotel, franchised

(P-13068)
W LODGING INC
Also Called: Ramada Inn
1825 Gillespie Way Ste 10, El Cajon
(92020-0501)
PHONE..............619 258-6565
EMP: 800
SIC: 7011 5812 8741 Hotels and motels;
Eating places; Hotel or motel management

(P-13069)
W LOS ANGELES
Also Called: Westwood Marquis Hotel &
Grdns
930 Hilgard Ave, Los Angeles
(90024-3009)
P.O. Box 14029 (85267-4029)
PHONE..............310 208-8765
George I Rosenthal, *Pr*
Anil Sharma, *
Mark Rosenthal, *
Damien Hirsch, *
EMP: 330 **EST:** 1977
SALES (est): 4.16MM
SALES (corp-wide): 25.12MM **Privately Held**
Web: www.wlosangeles.com
SIC: 7011 Resort hotel
PA: Raleigh Enterprises, Inc.
5300 Melrose Ave Fl 4
310 899-8900

(P-13070)
WALTERS FAMILY PARTNERSHIP
Also Called: Hilton Resort In Palm Spring
400 E Tahquitz Canyon Way, Palm Springs
(92262-6605)
PHONE..............760 320-0000
Lance Walters, *Pt*
EMP: 150 **EST:** 1981
SQ FT: 200,000
SALES (est): 3.49MM **Privately Held**
SIC: 7011 5813 5812 Hotels and motels;
Drinking places; Eating places

(P-13071)
WATERFRONT HOTEL LLC
Also Called: Hilton
21100 Pacific Coast Hwy, Huntington Beach
(92648-5307)
PHONE..............714 845-8000
John Gilbert, *Mgr*
EMP: 298
Web: www.hilton.com
SIC: 7011 5813 5812 7299 Hotels and motels
; Drinking places; Eating places; Banquet
hall facilities
PA: The Waterfront Hotel Llc
660 Nwport Ctr Ste 105

(P-13072)
WCO HOTELS INC
Also Called: Disneys Grnd Clifornian Ht Spa
1600 S Disneyland Dr, Anaheim
(92802-2317)
PHONE..............714 635-2300
Dorothy Stratton, *Brnch Mgr*
EMP: 824
SALES (corp-wide): 91.36B **Publicly Held**
SIC: 7011 Resort hotel
HQ: Wco Hotels, Inc.
1150 W Magic Way
Anaheim CA 92802
323 636-3251

(P-13073)
WELK GROUP INC (PA)
Also Called: Welk Music Group
11400 W Olympic Blvd Ste 760, Los
Angeles (90064-1585)
PHONE..............760 749-3000
Jon Fredricks, *Pr*
Marc L Luzzatto, *
EMP: 345 **EST:** 1955
SQ FT: 6,200
SALES (est): 22.87MM
SALES (corp-wide): 22.87MM **Privately
Held**
Web: www.sonisrestaurant.com
SIC: 7011 5099 Resort hotel; Compact discs

(P-13074)
WELK GROUP INC
Also Called: Welk Resort Center
8860 Lawrence Welk Dr, Escondido
(92026-6403)
PHONE..............760 749-3000
Mario Trejo, *Mgr*
EMP: 400
SALES (corp-wide): 22.87MM **Privately
Held**
Web: www.beachcarswpb.com
SIC: 7011 5812 Motels; Eating places
PA: The Welk Group Inc
11400 W Olympic Blvd # 1450
760 749-3000

(P-13075)
WEST HOLLYWOOD EDITION
9040 W Sunset Blvd, West Hollywood
(90069-1851)
PHONE..............310 795-7103
EMP: 96 **EST:** 2018
SALES (est): 4.4MM **Privately Held**
Web: www.editionhotels.com
SIC: 7011 Hotels

(P-13076)
WESTGROUP SAN DIEGO ASSOCIATES
Also Called: Paradise Point Resort
1404 Vacation Rd, San Diego (92109-7905)
PHONE..............858 274-4630
David Feeney, *Pt*
EMP: 92 **EST:** 1998
SALES (est): 1.92MM **Privately Held**
Web: www.paradisepoint.com
SIC: 7011 Resort hotel

(P-13077)
WESTIN ANAHEIM RESORT
Also Called: Westin
1030 W Katella Ave, Anaheim
(92802-3419)
PHONE..............657 279-9786
EMP: 78 **EST:** 2018
SALES (est): 4.57MM **Privately Held**
Web: www.westinanaheim.com
SIC: 7011 Hotels

(P-13078)
WESTLAKE PROPERTIES INC
Also Called: Westlake Village Inn
31943 Agoura Rd, Westlake Village
(91361-4427)
PHONE..............818 889-0230
John Notter, *Prin*
EMP: 150 **EST:** 1974
SALES (est): 16.76MM **Privately Held**
Web: www.westlakevillageinn.com
SIC: 7011 Resort hotel

(P-13079)
WHB CORPORATION
Also Called: Millennium Biltmore Hotel
506 S Grand Ave, Los Angeles
(90071-2602)
PHONE..............213 624-1011
John Demola, *Brnch Mgr*
EMP: 630
Web: www.millenniumhotels.com
SIC: 7011 5812 5813 Hotels; Eating places;
Drinking places
HQ: Whb Corporation
7600 E Orchard Rd 230s
Greenwood Village CO 80111
303 779-2000

(P-13080)
WHV RESORT GROUP INC
Also Called: Lawrence Welk Desert Oasis
34567 Cathedral Canyon Dr, Cathedral City
(92234-6637)
PHONE..............760 770-9755
Bill Palmer, *Mgr*
EMP: 1004
Web: www.beachcarswpb.com
SIC: 7011 Resort hotel
HQ: Whv Resort Group, Inc.
300 Rancheros Dr Ste 310
San Marcos CA 92069
760 652-4913

(P-13081)
WIN TIME LTD (PA)
Also Called: Holiday Inn Express
9335 Kearny Mesa Rd, San Diego
(92126-4502)
PHONE..............858 695-2300
Herman Lin, *Genl Pt*
Chue-huang Chiu, *Pt*
Yi-ho Huang, *Pt*
EMP: 166 **EST:** 1982
SQ FT: 100,000
SALES (est): 3.93MM
SALES (corp-wide): 3.93MM **Privately
Held**
Web: www.holidayinn.com
SIC: 7011 Hotels and motels

(P-13082)
WINDSOR CAPITAL GROUP INC
Also Called: Embassy Suites
29345 Rancho California Rd, Temecula
(92591-5201)
PHONE..............951 676-5656
Tom Demott, *Genl Mgr*
EMP: 143
SALES (corp-wide): 59.4MM **Privately
Held**
Web: www.hilton.com
SIC: 7011 Hotels and motels
PA: Windsor Capital Group, Inc.
2800 28th St Ste 385
310 566-1100

(P-13083)
WINDSOR CAPITAL GROUP INC
Also Called: Marriott
1510 University Ave, Riverside
(92507-4468)

PHONE..............951 276-1200
Jim Larson, *Genl Mgr*
EMP: 143
SALES (corp-wide): 59.4MM **Privately
Held**
Web: www.marriott.com
SIC: 7011 Hotels and motels
PA: Windsor Capital Group, Inc.
2800 28th St Ste 385
310 566-1100

(P-13084)
WINDSOR CAPITAL GROUP INC
Also Called: Recp/Wndsor Port Hueneme
Ventr
350 E Port Hueneme Rd, Port Hueneme
(93041-3209)
PHONE..............805 986-5353
Silvia Bernard, *Brnch Mgr*
EMP: 96
SALES (corp-wide): 59.4MM **Privately
Held**
Web: www.windsorhospitality.com
SIC: 7011 Hotel, franchised
PA: Windsor Capital Group, Inc.
2800 28th St Ste 385
310 566-1100

(P-13085)
WINDSOR CAPITAL GROUP INC
Also Called: Embassy Suites
900 E Birch St, Brea (92821-5812)
PHONE..............714 990-6000
Regina Samy, *Mgr*
EMP: 143
SQ FT: 48,164
SALES (corp-wide): 59.4MM **Privately
Held**
Web: www.hilton.com
SIC: 7011 Hotels and motels
PA: Windsor Capital Group, Inc.
2800 28th St Ste 385
310 566-1100

(P-13086)
WINDSOR CAPITAL GROUP INC
Also Called: Embassy Suites Arcadia
2800 28th St Ste 385, Santa Monica
(90405-6211)
PHONE..............310 566-1100
EMP: 96
SALES (corp-wide): 59.4MM **Privately
Held**
Web: www.hilton.com
SIC: 7011 Hotels and motels
PA: Windsor Capital Group, Inc.
2800 28th St Ste 385
310 566-1100

(P-13087)
WINDSOR CAPITAL GROUP INC
Also Called: Embassy Suites Lompoc
2800 28th St Ste 385, Santa Monica
(90405-6211)
PHONE..............310 566-1100
EMP: 96
SALES (corp-wide): 59.4MM **Privately
Held**
Web: www.hilton.com
SIC: 7011 Hotels and motels
PA: Windsor Capital Group, Inc.
2800 28th St Ste 385
310 566-1100

(P-13088)
WINDSOR CAPITAL GROUP INC
Also Called: Marriott
2800 28th St Ste 385, Santa Monica
(90405-6211)
PHONE..............209 577-3825

Shawn Williams, *Mgr*
EMP: 96
SALES (corp-wide): 59.4MM **Privately Held**
Web: www.marriott.com
SIC: 7011 Hotels and motels
PA: Windsor Capital Group, Inc.
2800 28th St Ste 385
310 566-1100

(P-13089)
WINDSOR CAPITAL GROUP INC
2800 28th St Ste 385, Santa Monica (90405-6211)
PHONE...............................310 566-1100
EMP: 96
SALES (corp-wide): 59.4MM **Privately Held**
Web: www.windsorhospitality.com
SIC: 7011 Hotels
PA: Windsor Capital Group, Inc.
2800 28th St Ste 385
310 566-1100

(P-13090)
WINDSOR CAPITAL GROUP INC
Also Called: Embassy Suites El Paso
2800 28th St Ste 385, Santa Monica (90405-6211)
PHONE...............................310 566-1100
EMP: 96
SALES (corp-wide): 59.4MM **Privately Held**
Web: www.hilton.com
SIC: 7011 Hotels and motels
PA: Windsor Capital Group, Inc.
2800 28th St Ste 385
310 566-1100

(P-13091)
WJ NEWPORT LLC
Also Called: Marriott
4500 Macarthur Blvd, Newport Beach (92660-2010)
PHONE...............................949 476-2001
EMP: 190 **EST:** 2016
SALES (est): 13.88MM **Privately Held**
Web: www.marriott.com
SIC: 7011 5812 Resort hotel; Family restaurants

(P-13092)
WOODBINE LGACY/PLAYA OWNER LLC
Also Called: Hilton Los Angeles Culver City
6161 W Centinela Ave, Culver City (90230-6306)
PHONE...............................678 292-4962
Lakeisha Walker, *
EMP: 75 **EST:** 2018
SALES (est): 4.59MM **Privately Held**
Web: www.hilton.com
SIC: 7011 Hotels and motels

(P-13093)
WS MMV HOTEL LLC
Also Called: San Diego Marriott Mission Vly
8757 Rio San Diego Dr, San Diego (92108-1620)
PHONE...............................619 692-3800
EMP: 99 **EST:** 2016
SALES (est): 1.68MM **Privately Held**
Web: www.marriott.com
SIC: 7011 Hotels

(P-13094)
WW SAN DIEGO HARBOR ISLAND LLC
Also Called: Hilton

1960 Harbor Island Dr, San Diego (92101-1097)
PHONE...............................619 291-6700
Shahid Kayani, *Genl Mgr*
EMP: 120 **EST:** 1980
SALES (est): 3.08MM
SALES (corp-wide): 45.8MM **Privately Held**
Web: www.hilton.com
SIC: 7011 Resort hotel
PA: Ww Lbv Inc.
2000 Hotel Plaza Blvd
407 828-2424

(P-13095)
YHB LONG BEACH LLC
Also Called: Holiday Inn
2640 N Lakewood Blvd, Long Beach (90815-1715)
PHONE...............................562 597-4401
Traycee Mayer, *Prin*
EMP: 90 **EST:** 2003
SALES (est): 6.65MM **Privately Held**
Web: www.holidayinn.com
SIC: 7011 Hotels and motels

7021 Rooming And Boarding Houses

(P-13096)
AMERICAN CMPUS COMMUNITIES INC
Also Called: Vista Del Campo
62600 Arroyo Dr, Irvine (92617-4387)
PHONE...............................949 854-0900
EMP: 100
SALES (corp-wide): 942.41MM **Privately Held**
Web: www.americancampus.com
SIC: 7021 Rooming and boarding houses
PA: American Campus Communities Llc
12700 Hill Country Blvd T-200
512 732-1000

(P-13097)
M-AURORA WORLDWIDE (US) LP (PA)
2222 Corinth Ave, Los Angeles (90064-1602)
PHONE...............................800 888-0808
▲ **EMP:** 200 **EST:** 1960
SALES (est): 14.13MM
SALES (corp-wide): 14.13MM **Privately Held**
SIC: 7021 6531 Furnished room rental; Real estate brokers and agents

(P-13098)
WORLDWIDE CORPORATE HOUSING LP
Also Called: Oakwood Temporary Housing
1 World Trade Ctr Ste 2400, Long Beach (90831-2400)
PHONE...............................972 392-4747
Howard Ruby, *Pt*
EMP: 493
SALES (corp-wide): 14.13MM **Privately Held**
Web: www.discoverasr.com
SIC: 7021 Furnished room rental
HQ: Worldwide Corporate Housing, Lp
1 World Trade Ctr # 2400
Long Beach CA 90831
562 473-7371

7032 Sporting And Recreational Camps

(P-13099)
ALISAL PROPERTIES (PA)
Also Called: Alisal Guest Ranch
1054 Alisal Rd, Solvang (93463-3033)
PHONE...............................805 688-6411
Palmer Jackson, *Pr*
Joan Y Jackson, *VP*
Susanne Powell, *Sec*
EMP: 243 **EST:** 1946
SQ FT: 10,000
SALES (est): 24.12MM
SALES (corp-wide): 24,12MM **Privately Held**
Web: www.alisalranch.com
SIC: 7032 7997 Sporting camps; Golf club, membership

(P-13100)
BIG LGUE DREAMS CONSULTING LLC
33700 Date Palm Dr, Cathedral City (92234-4731)
PHONE...............................760 324-5600
Steve Navarro, *VP*
EMP: 107
SALES (corp-wide): 15.39MM **Privately Held**
Web: www.bigleaguedreams.com
SIC: 7032 Recreational camps
PA: Big League Dreams Consulting, Llc
16333 Fairfield Ranch Rd
909 287-1700

(P-13101)
COUNTY OF LOS ANGELES
Also Called: Parks & Recreation Dept
7326 Jordan Ave, Canoga Park (91303-1237)
PHONE...............................818 340-2633
Sharon Haseltine, *Mgr*
EMP: 71
Web: www.lacounty.gov
SIC: 7032 Recreational camps
PA: County Of Los Angeles
500 W Temple St Ste 437
213 974-1101

(P-13102)
FOREST HOME INC
Also Called: Forest Home Ministries
40000 Valley Of The Falls Dr, Forest Falls (92339-9674)
PHONE...............................909 389-2300
EMP: 250 **EST:** 1938
SALES (est): 7.54MM **Privately Held**
Web: www.foresthome.org
SIC: 7032 Cabin camp

(P-13103)
INTERVRSITY CHRSTN FLLWSHP/USA
Also Called: Campus By The Sea
Gallager&Apos;S Cove, Avalon (90704)
P.O. Box 466 (90704-0466)
PHONE...............................310 510-0015
Susan Veon, *Dir*
EMP: 496
SALES (corp-wide): 24.9MM **Privately Held**
Web: www.intervarsity.org
SIC: 7032 5942 Bible camp; Book stores
PA: Intervarsity Christian Fellowship/Usa
635 Science Dr
608 274-9001

(P-13104)
LLC WOODWARD WEST
28400 Stallion Springs Dr, Tehachapi (93561-5266)
PHONE...............................661 822-7900
EMP: 143 **EST:** 2002
SALES (est): 3.29MM **Privately Held**
Web: www.woodwardwest.com
SIC: 7032 Sporting and recreational camps

(P-13105)
PALI CAMP
Also Called: Pali Adventures
30778 Hwy 18, Running Springs (92382)
PHONE...............................909 867-5743
Andrew Wexler, *CEO*
EMP: 150 **EST:** 1990
SALES (est): 596.26K **Privately Held**
Web: www.paliadventures.com
SIC: 7032 Summer camp, except day and sports instructional

(P-13106)
WILSHIRE BOULEVARD TEMPLE
11495 Pacific Coast Hwy, Malibu (90265-2006)
PHONE...............................310 457-7861
EMP: 75
SALES (corp-wide): 22.36MM **Privately Held**
Web: www.wbtla.org
SIC: 7032 Sporting and recreational camps
PA: Wilshire Boulevard Temple
3663 Wilshire Blvd
213 388-2401

7033 Trailer Parks And Campsites

(P-13107)
BURLINGAME INDUSTRIES INC (PA)
Also Called: Eagle Roofing Products
3546 N Riverside Ave, Rialto (92377-3878)
PHONE...............................909 355-7000
Robert C Burlingame, *Ch Bd*
Roger D Thompson, *Vice Chairman**
Kevin C Burlingame, *
Seamus P Burlingame, *
William L Robinson, *
▲ **EMP:** 100 **EST:** 1969
SQ FT: 100,000
SALES (est): 54.45MM
SALES (corp-wide): 54.45MM **Privately Held**
Web: www.eagleroofing.com
SIC: 7033 0971 3559 3259 Campgrounds; Hunting preserve; Tile making machines; Roofing tile, clay

(P-13108)
COLORADO RIVER ADVENTURES INC (PA)
Also Called: Yuma Lakes Resort
2715 Parker Dam Rd, Earp (92242-9712)
P.O. Box 1088 (85344-1088)
PHONE...............................760 663-3737
Phil Younis, *Pr*
EMP: 112 **EST:** 1982
SQ FT: 6,500
SALES (est): 4.99MM
SALES (corp-wide): 4.99MM **Privately Held**
Web: www.coloradoriveradventures.com
SIC: 7033 8641 7032 Campgrounds; Social club, membership; Recreational camps

7041 Membership-basis Organization Hotels

(P-13109)

MEDIEVAL TIMES ENTRMT INC (HQ)

7662 Beach Blvd, Buena Park (90620-1838)
PHONE....................714 523-1100
Kenneth H Kim, *Pr*
EMP: 1716 **EST:** 2001
SALES (est): 5.48MM **Privately Held**
Web: www.medievaltimes.com
SIC: 7041 7996 Membership-basis organization hotels; Theme park, amusement
PA: Medieval Times Entertainment, Inc.
5020 Riverside Dr Bldg 3

7211 Power Laundries, Family And Commercial

(P-13110)

ANITSA INC

Also Called: Valet Services
6032 Shull St, Bell Gardens (90201-6237)
PHONE....................213 237-0533
Margo Minisiam, *Pr*
Gary Von, *Corporate Accountant**
EMP: 135 **EST:** 1988
SQ FT: 65,000
SALES (est): 1.35MM **Privately Held**
SIC: 7211 8742 Power laundries, family and commercial; Industry specialist consultants

(P-13111)

RADIANT SERVICES CORP (PA)

651 W Knox St, Gardena (90248-4409)
PHONE....................310 327-6300
Mina Keywanfar, *CEO*
Shahrokh Keywanfar, *
Jamshid Beroukhim, *
EMP: 235 **EST:** 1994
SALES (est): 10.56MM **Privately Held**
Web: www.radiantservices.com
SIC: 7211 7216 Power laundries, family and commercial; Drycleaning plants, except rugs

7213 Linen Supply

(P-13112)

AMERICAN TEXTILE MAINT CO

Also Called: Medico Professional Linen Svc
1705 Hooper Ave, Los Angeles (90021-3111)
P.O. Box 516564 (90051-0596)
PHONE....................213 749-4433
Kenny Immazumi, *Mgr*
EMP: 84
SALES (corp-wide): 62.65MM **Privately Held**
Web: www.medicolinen.com
SIC: 7213 Uniform supply
PA: American Textile Maintenance Company
1667 W Washington Blvd
323 731-3132

(P-13113)

AMERICAN TEXTILE MAINT CO

Also Called: Master-Chef's Linen Rental
1664 W Washington Blvd, Los Angeles (90007-1115)
PHONE....................323 735-1661
Bob Brill, *Brnch Mgr*
EMP: 149

SALES (corp-wide): 62.65MM **Privately Held**
Web: www.republicmasterchefs.com
SIC: 7213 Towel supply
PA: American Textile Maintenance Company
1667 W Washington Blvd
323 731-3132

(P-13114)

AMERIPRIDE SERVICES LLC

5950 Alcoa Ave, Los Angeles (90058-3925)
PHONE....................323 587-3941
TOLL FREE: 800
Ampett Easemero, *Brnch Mgr*
EMP: 110
SALES (corp-wide): 2.81B **Publicly Held**
Web: www.ameripride.com
SIC: 7213 Uniform supply
HQ: Ameripride Services, Llc
115 N First St
Burbank CA 91502
800 750-4628

(P-13115)

BRAUN LINEN SERVICE (PA)

Also Called: A-1 Pomona Linen
16514 Garfield Ave, Paramount (90723-5304)
P.O. Box 348 (90723-0348)
PHONE....................909 623-2678
Richard A Cornwell, *CEO*
William S Cornwell, *
▲ **EMP:** 125 **EST:** 1985
SQ FT: 28,000
SALES (est): 7.71MM
SALES (corp-wide): 7.71MM **Privately Held**
Web: www.braunlinen.com
SIC: 7213 Towel supply

(P-13116)

CINTAS SALES CORPORATION

Also Called: Cintas
2618 Oak St, Santa Ana (92707-3720)
PHONE....................714 957-2852
EMP: 100
SALES (corp-wide): 9.6B **Publicly Held**
Web: www.cintas.com
SIC: 7213 5999 5912 5699 Uniform supply; Alarm and safety equipment stores; Drug stores and proprietary stores; Uniforms and work clothing
HQ: Cintas Sales Corporation
6800 Cintas Blvd
Cincinnati OH 45262

(P-13117)

GBS LINENS INC (PA)

Also Called: GBS Party Linens
305 N Muller St, Anaheim (92801-5445)
PHONE....................714 778-6448
Pravin Mody, *Pr*
Sujata Mody, *
Ameer P Mody, *
Sudha Mody, *
▲ **EMP:** 100 **EST:** 1962
SQ FT: 57,000
SALES (est): 9.13MM
SALES (corp-wide): 9.13MM **Privately Held**
Web: www.gbslinens.com
SIC: 7213 2392 7211 5023 Linen supply; Household furnishings, nec; Power laundries, family and commercial; Homefurnishings

(P-13118)

MISSION LINEN SUPPLY

Also Called: Mission Linen & Uniform Svc

619 W Avenue I, Lancaster (93534-2585)
PHONE....................661 948-5052
Dick Grever, *Mgr*
EMP: 78
SALES (corp-wide): 54.98MM **Privately Held**
Web: www.missionlinen.com
SIC: 7213 Uniform supply
PA: Mission Linen Supply
717 E Yanonali St
805 730-3620

(P-13119)

MISSION LINEN SUPPLY

Also Called: Mission Linen & Uniform Svc
505 Maulhardt Ave, Oxnard (93030-7925)
PHONE....................805 485-6794
Matthew Aguelli, *Mgr*
EMP: 78
SALES (corp-wide): 54.98MM **Privately Held**
Web: www.missionlinen.com
SIC: 7213 Uniform supply
PA: Mission Linen Supply
717 E Yanonali St
805 730-3620

(P-13120)

MISSION LINEN SUPPLY

Also Called: Mission Linen & Uniform Svc
712 E Montecito St, Santa Barbara (93103-3295)
PHONE....................805 962-7687
Curtos Lopez, *Mgr*
EMP: 171
SALES (corp-wide): 54.98MM **Privately Held**
Web: www.missionlinen.com
SIC: 7213 Uniform supply
PA: Mission Linen Supply
717 E Yanonali St
805 730-3620

(P-13121)

MISSION LINEN SUPPLY

Also Called: Mission Linen & Uniform Svc
602 S Western Ave, Santa Maria (93458-5496)
PHONE....................805 922-3579
Bill Bently, *Genl Mgr*
EMP: 93
SALES (corp-wide): 54.98MM **Privately Held**
Web: www.missionlinen.com
SIC: 7213 Uniform supply
PA: Mission Linen Supply
717 E Yanonali St
805 730-3620

(P-13122)

MISSION LINEN SUPPLY

Also Called: Mission Linen & Uniform Svc
2727 Industry St, Oceanside (92054-4810)
PHONE....................760 757-9099
Graig Rogers, *Prin*
EMP: 148
SALES (corp-wide): 54.98MM **Privately Held**
Web: www.missionlinen.com
SIC: 7213 7218 Uniform supply; Industrial launderers
PA: Mission Linen Supply
717 E Yanonali St
805 730-3620

(P-13123)

MISSION LINEN SUPPLY

Also Called: Mission Linen & Uniform Svc
5400 Alton Way, Chino (91710-7601)
PHONE....................909 393-6857

Louis Filveria, *Mgr*
EMP: 140
SALES (corp-wide): 54.98MM **Privately Held**
Web: www.missionlinen.com
SIC: 7213 Uniform supply
PA: Mission Linen Supply
717 E Yanonali St
805 730-3620

(P-13124)

MORGAN SERVICES INC

Also Called: Morgan Linen Service
905 Yale St, Los Angeles (90012-1791)
PHONE....................213 485-9666
Mark Smith, *Brnch Mgr*
EMP: 99
SQ FT: 51,339
SALES (corp-wide): 30.2MM **Privately Held**
Web: www.morganservices.com
SIC: 7213 7218 Linen supply; Industrial launderers
PA: Morgan Services, Inc.
323 N Michigan Ave
312 346-3181

(P-13125)

PARK CLEANERS INC (PA)

Also Called: Park Uniform Rentals
419 Mcgroarty St, San Gabriel (91776-2302)
PHONE....................626 281-5942
James L Brittain, *Pr*
Ted Doll, *
EMP: 75 **EST:** 1946
SQ FT: 7,000
SALES (est): 286.5K
SALES (corp-wide): 286.5K **Privately Held**
SIC: 7213 7216 Uniform supply; Cleaning and dyeing, except rugs

(P-13126)

SOCAL AUTO SUPPLY INC

21418 Osborne St, Canoga Park (91304-1520)
PHONE....................302 360-8373
EMP: 46
SIC: 7213 2676 Towel supply; Towels, napkins, and tissue paper products
PA: Socal Auto Supply Inc
16192 Postal Hwy

(P-13127)

YEE YUEN LAUNDRY AND CLRS INC

Also Called: Yee Yuen Linen Service
2575 S Normandie Ave, Los Angeles (90007-1598)
PHONE....................323 734-7205
Deborah Morikawa, *Pr*
Cynthia Louie, *
Luis Lee, *
EMP: 80 **EST:** 1928
SQ FT: 20,000
SALES (est): 2.02MM **Privately Held**
Web: www.yeeyuenlinen.com
SIC: 7213 Linen supply

7215 Coin-operated Laundries And Cleaning

(P-13128)

ALL VALLEY WASHER SERVICE INC

15008 Delano St, Van Nuys (91411-2016)
PHONE....................818 787-1100
TOLL FREE: 800

Ron Feinstein, *Pr*
Robert Feinstein, *
Billy Feinstein, *
EMP: 70 **EST:** 1961
SQ FT: 11,000
SALES (est): 9.8MM **Privately Held**
Web: www.allvalleywasher.com
SIC: 7215 6531 7359 5087 Laundry, coin-operated; Real estate agents and managers ; Appliance rental; Laundry equipment and supplies

(P-13129)
CSC SERVICEWORKS INC
14426 Bonelli St, City Of Industry
(91746-3020)
PHONE................................626 389-0169
Hal Sazzmann, *Pr*
EMP: 74
SALES (corp-wide): 1.97B **Privately Held**
Web: www.cscsw.com
SIC: 7215 Laundry, coin-operated
HQ: Csc Serviceworks, Inc.
    35 Pinelawn Rd Ste 120w
    Melville NY 11747
    516 349-8555

(P-13130)
PRO-WASH INC
9117 S Main St, Los Angeles (90003-3722)
PHONE................................323 756-6000
Steve Koo, *Pr*
EMP: 70 **EST:** 1991
SQ FT: 20,000
SALES (est): 559.89K **Privately Held**
Web: www.pro-wash.org
SIC: 7215 Laundry, coin-operated

(P-13131)
WASH MLTFMILY LDRY SYSTEMS LLC (PA)
2200 195th St, Torrance (90501-1120)
PHONE................................800 421-6897
TOLL FREE: 800
Jim Gimeson, *CEO*
Arthur J Long, *
Andres De Armas, *CRO*
EMP: 150 **EST:** 2007
SQ FT: 130,000
SALES (est): 84.49MM
SALES (corp-wide): 84.49MM **Privately Held**
Web: www.wash.com
SIC: 7215 Laundry, coin-operated

7216 Drycleaning Plants, Except Rugs

(P-13132)
PICO CLEANERS INC (PA)
9150 W Pico Blvd, Los Angeles
(90035-1320)
PHONE................................310 274-2431
Sharam Jahanbani, *CEO*
Simon Djahanbani, *
EMP: 80 **EST:** 1963
SQ FT: 10,000
SALES (est): 2.28MM
SALES (corp-wide): 2.28MM **Privately Held**
Web: www.picocleaners.com
SIC: 7216 Cleaning and dyeing, except rugs

(P-13133)
STAR LAUNDRY SERVICES INC
Also Called: Star Services
    3410 Main St, San Diego (92113-3803)
PHONE................................619 572-1009
Abraham Yang, *Pr*

EMP: 80 **EST:** 2006
SALES (est): 515.34K **Privately Held**
Web: www.starls.com
SIC: 7216 Cleaning and dyeing, except rugs

7217 Carpet And Upholstery Cleaning

(P-13134)
BONDED INC (PA)
Also Called: Bonded Carpet
    7590 Carroll Rd, San Diego (92121-2415)
    P.O. Box 23910 (92193-3910)
PHONE................................858 576-8400
Mitch Adler, *Pr*
Sherri Adler, *
EMP: 80 **EST:** 1975
SALES (est): 3.22MM
SALES (corp-wide): 3.22MM **Privately Held**
Web: www.bondedinc.com
SIC: 7217 5023 Carpet and furniture cleaning on location; Homefurnishings

(P-13135)
COLT SERVICES INC
Also Called: Stanley Steemer Carpet Cleaner
    9655 Via Excelencia, San Diego
    (92126-4555)
PHONE................................858 271-9910
TOLL FREE: 888
Steven R Thompson, *Pr*
EMP: 100 **EST:** 1979
SQ FT: 33,000
SALES (est): 2.34MM **Privately Held**
Web: www.stanleysteemer.com
SIC: 7217 Carpet and furniture cleaning on location

(P-13136)
EXPRESS CONTRACTORS INC
3810 Wacker Dr, Jurupa Valley
(91752-1142)
    P.O. Box 310279 (92331-0279)
PHONE................................951 360-6500
Amaer Alhamwi, *CEO*
EMP: 100 **EST:** 1992
SQ FT: 10,000
SALES (est): 11.07MM **Privately Held**
Web: www.expresscontractorsinc.com
SIC: 7217 1752 1721 1743 Carpet and rug cleaning and repairing plant; Carpet laying; Painting and paper hanging; Terrazzo, tile, marble and mosaic work

(P-13137)
JOURDUCCI INC
Also Called: Stanley Steemer of Los Angeles
    841 W Foothill Blvd, Azusa (91702-2815)
PHONE................................626 791-9400
TOLL FREE: 800
Kevin Pucci, *Pr*
Jeff Pucci, *
EMP: 104 **EST:** 1947
SALES (est): 793.46K **Privately Held**
Web: www.stanleysteemer.com
SIC: 7217 1799 Carpet and furniture cleaning on location; Post disaster renovations

---

7218 Industrial Launderers

(P-13138)
AMERICAN TEXTILE MAINT CO
2201 E Carson St, Long Beach
(90807-3043)
PHONE................................562 424-1607
Steve Jones, *Mgr*

EMP: 85
SALES (corp-wide): 62.65MM **Privately Held**
Web: www.republicmasterchefs.com
SIC: 7218 7213 Industrial launderers; Uniform supply
PA: American Textile Maintenance Company
    1667 W Washington Blvd
    323 731-3132

(P-13139)
PRUDENTIAL OVERALL SUPPLY
Also Called: Prudential Dust Control
    6997 Jurupa Ave, Riverside (92504-1009)
PHONE................................951 687-0440
Jay Boyer, *Mgr*
EMP: 73
SALES (corp-wide): 83.22MM **Privately Held**
Web: www.prudentialuniforms.com
SIC: 7218 Industrial launderers
PA: Prudential Overall Supply
    1661 Alton Pkwy
    949 250-4855

(P-13140)
PRUDENTIAL OVERALL SUPPLY (PA)
Also Called: Prudential Cleanroom Services
    1661 Alton Pkwy, Irvine (92606-4877)
    P.O. Box 11210 (92711-1210)
PHONE................................949 250-4855
Dan Clark, *CEO*
Thomas C Watts, *
Donald C Lahn, *
▲ **EMP:** 95 **EST:** 1947
SQ FT: 20,000
SALES (est): 83.22MM
SALES (corp-wide): 83.22MM **Privately Held**
Web: www.prudentialuniforms.com
SIC: 7218 Wiping towel supply

(P-13141)
UNIFIRST CORPORATION
Also Called: Unifirst
    700 Etiwanda Ave Ste C, Ontario
    (91761-8608)
PHONE................................909 390-8670
Jeff Martin, *Mgr*
EMP: 130
SALES (corp-wide): 2.43B **Publicly Held**
Web: www.unifirst.com
SIC: 7218 7213 Industrial uniform supply; Uniform supply
PA: Unifirst Corporation
    68 Jonspin Rd
    978 658-8888

(P-13142)
WORKRITE UNIFORM COMPANY INC (DH)
1701 Lombard St Ste 200, Oxnard
(93030-8235)
PHONE................................805 483-0175
Philip C Williamson, *CEO*
Keith Suddaby, *
Mark Adler, *
EMP: 385 **EST:** 1968
SALES (est): 583.29K
SALES (corp-wide): 10.45B **Publicly Held**
Web: www.workrite.com
SIC: 7218 Flame and heat resistant clothing supply
HQ: Vf Outdoor, Llc
    1551 Wewatta St
    Denver CO 80202
    855 500-8639

7219 Laundry And Garment Services, Nec

(P-13143)
CM LAUNDRY LLC
14919 S Figueroa St, Gardena
(90248-1720)
PHONE................................310 436-6170
Ernesto Munoz, *Managing Member*
EMP: 100 **EST:** 2007
SQ FT: 26,500
SALES (est): 2.27MM **Privately Held**
Web: www.cmlaundry.com
SIC: 7219 Laundry, except power and coin-operated

(P-13144)
JOB OPTIONS INCORPORATED
1110 S Washington Ave, San Bernardino
(92408-2244)
PHONE................................909 890-4612
EMP: 820
SQ FT: 35,800
Web: www.joboptionsinc.org
SIC: 7219 Fur garment cleaning, repairing, and storage
PA: Job Options, Incorporated
    3465 Cmino Del Rio S Ste

7221 Photographic Studios, Portrait

(P-13145)
PIXSTER PHOTOBOOTH LLC
4901 Morena Blvd Ste 810, San Diego
(92117-7324)
PHONE................................888 668-5524
Mclain Harvey, *Managing Member*
Ian Cote, *
EMP: 200 **EST:** 2013
SALES (est): 960.69K **Privately Held**
Web: www.pixsterphotobooth.com
SIC: 7221 Photographer, still or video

7231 Beauty Shops

(P-13146)
BEAUTY BARRAGE LLC
4340 Von Karman Ave Ste 240, Newport Beach (92660-1201)
PHONE................................949 771-3399
Sonia Summers, *CEO*
Brady Heyborne, *
Alissa Spencer, *
EMP: 220 **EST:** 2015
SALES (est): 1.94MM **Privately Held**
Web: www.beautybarrage.com
SIC: 7231 8742 Beauty shops; Marketing consulting services

(P-13147)
BELLAMI HAIR LLC
Also Called: Bellami Hair
    21123 Nordhoff St, Chatsworth
    (91311-5816)
PHONE................................844 235-5264
Julius Salerno, *Managing Member*
EMP: 100 **EST:** 2013
SALES (est): 24.76MM
SALES (corp-wide): 25.75MM **Privately Held**
Web: www.bellamihair.com
SIC: 7231 Hairdressers
PA: Beauty Industry Group Opco Llc
    1250 N Flyer Way
    801 206-4781

(P-13148)
ESALONCOM LLC
1910 E Maple Ave, El Segundo
(90245-3411)
PHONE.....................866 550-2424
EMP: 113 **EST:** 2008
SALES (est): 10.09MM **Privately Held**
Web: www.esalon.com
SIC: 7231 Hairdressers

(P-13149)
JLM & MAG ASSOCIATES INC
Also Called: Supercuts
9204 Lakewood Blvd, Downey
(90240-2909)
PHONE.....................562 869-3343
James Miller, *Pr*
EMP: 71
SALES (corp-wide): 1.59MM **Privately
Held**
Web: www.supercuts.com
SIC: 7231 Unisex hair salons
PA: Jlm & Mag Associates, Inc.
22311 Ventura Blvd # 111
818 346-2667

(P-13150)
KLEINTOB INC
Also Called: Supercuts
2691 Tapo Canyon Rd Ste B, Simi Valley
(93063-6845)
PHONE.....................805 527-3389
Daryl Kleintob, *Pr*
Larry Kleintob, *
Carol Johnson, *
EMP: 70 **EST:** 1980
SALES (est): 408.6K **Privately Held**
Web: www.supercuts.com
SIC: 7231 Unisex hair salons

(P-13151)
MINILUXE INC
Also Called: Miniluxe
11965 San Vicente Blvd, Los Angeles
(90049-5003)
PHONE.....................424 442-1630
EMP: 93
SALES (corp-wide): 15MM **Privately Held**
Web: www.miniluxe.com
SIC: 7231 Manicurist, pedicurist
PA: Miniluxe, Inc.
1 Faneuil Hall Sq Fl 7
617 684-2731

(P-13152)
MURAD LLC
Also Called: Murad Spa
2141 Rosecrans Ave Ste 1151, El Segundo
(90245-4759)
PHONE.....................310 726-0470
Howard Murad, *Brnch Mgr*
▲ **EMP:** 108
SALES (corp-wide): 64.79B **Privately Held**
Web: www.murad.com
SIC: 7231 Facial salons
HQ: Murad, Llc
2121 Park Pl Ste 1
El Segundo CA 90245

(P-13153)
**PETROSIAN ESTHETIC ENTPS
LLC**
Also Called: Sev Lasers
2919 W Burbank Blvd, Burbank
(91505-2358)
PHONE.....................818 391-8231
Anineh Petrosian, *COO*
EMP: 180 **EST:** 2013
SALES (est): 10.83MM **Privately Held**

SIC: 7231 7371 Beauty shops; Computer
software development and applications

(P-13154)
SPORT CLIPS INC
Also Called: Sport Clips
4839 Clairemont Dr Ste E, San Diego
(92117-2727)
PHONE.....................858 273-9993
Milan Lidia, *Mgr*
EMP: 1170
Web: www.sportclips.com
SIC: 7231 Beauty shops
PA: Sport Clips, Inc.
110 Sport Clips Way

7261 Funeral Service And Crematories

(P-13155)
FOREST LAWN MORTUARY
66272 Pierson Blvd, Desert Hot Springs
(92240-3658)
PHONE.....................760 329-8737
David Wenzil, *Genl Mgr*
EMP: 482
SALES (corp-wide): 185.21MM **Privately
Held**
Web: www.forestlawn.com
SIC: 7261 Funeral home
HQ: Forest Lawn Mortuary
1712 S Glendale Ave
Glendale CA 91205

(P-13156)
**NORTHSTAR MEMORIAL
GROUP LLC**
2562 State St, Carlsbad (92008-1663)
P.O. Box 616 (90660-0616)
PHONE.....................800 323-1342
EMP: 116
Web: www.nsmg.com
SIC: 7261 Funeral home
PA: Northstar Memorial Group, Llc
1900 St James Pl Ste 300

(P-13157)
PIERCE BROTHERS (DH)
Also Called: SCI
10621 Victory Blvd, North Hollywood
(91606-3918)
PHONE.....................818 763-9121
Oliver Yeo, *Mgr*
R L Waltrip, *
David Anderson, *
Ray Gipson, *
Curtis Briggs, *
EMP: 80 **EST:** 1902
SQ FT: 10,000
SALES (est): 1.6MM
SALES (corp-wide): 4.1B **Publicly Held**
Web: www.portalofthefoldedwings.net
SIC: 7261 6553 Crematory; Cemeteries, real
estate operation
HQ: Sci Funeral Services Of New York, Inc.
1929 Allen Pkwy
Houston TX 77019

(P-13158)
SINAI TEMPLE
Also Called: Mt Sinai Mem Pk & Mortuary
5950 Forest Lawn Dr, Los Angeles
(90068-1010)
PHONE.....................323 469-6000
TOLL FREE: 800
Len Lawrence, *Mgr*
EMP: 125
SQ FT: 22,633
SALES (corp-wide): 44.43MM **Privately
Held**

Web: www.mountsinaiparks.org
SIC: 7261 6553 Funeral home; Cemeteries,
real estate operation
PA: Temple Sinai
10400 Wilshire Blvd
310 474-1518

(P-13159)
**TEMPLE ISRAEL OF
HOLLYWOOD (PA)**
Also Called: Jewish Synagogue
7300 Hollywood Blvd, Los Angeles
(90046-2999)
PHONE.....................323 876-8330
Steve Sloan, *Pr*
Jane Zuckerman, *
Renee Mochkatel, *
David Cremin, *
Nancy Ortenberg, *
EMP: 83 **EST:** 1926
SQ FT: 15,000
SALES (est): 21.83MM
SALES (corp-wide): 21.83MM **Privately
Held**
Web: www.tioh.org
SIC: 7261 8299 8661 Funeral service and
crematories; Religious school; Synagogue

7291 Tax Return Preparation Services

(P-13160)
AHG INC
340 S Lemon Ave 6633, Walnut
(91789-2706)
PHONE.....................703 596-0111
Sanzar Kakar, *Ofcr*
EMP: 300 **EST:** 2018
SALES (est): 148.97K **Privately Held**
SIC: 7291 8721 Tax return preparation
services; Accounting, auditing, and
bookkeeping

(P-13161)
ANDERSEN TAX LLC
400 S Hope St Ste 2000, Los Angeles
(90071-2832)
PHONE.....................213 593-2300
EMP: 129
SALES (corp-wide): 38.88MM **Privately
Held**
Web: www.andersen.com
SIC: 7291 Tax return preparation services
PA: Andersen Tax Llc
333 Bush St Ste 1700
415 764-2700

(P-13162)
CERIDIAN TAX SERVICE INC
Also Called: Ceridian
17390 Brookhurst St, Fountain Valley
(92708-3720)
P.O. Box 20805 (92728-0805)
PHONE.....................714 963-1311
Webster Hill, *Genl Mgr*
EMP: 300 **EST:** 1998
SQ FT: 130,000
SALES (est): 988.05K
SALES (corp-wide): 1.51B **Publicly Held**
Web: www.dayforce.com
SIC: 7291 Tax return preparation services
PA: Dayforce, Inc.
3311 E Old Shakopee Rd
952 853-8100

(P-13163)
EXACTAX INC (PA)
1100 E Orangethorpe Ave Ste 100,
Anaheim (92801-5168)

PHONE.....................714 284-4802
Kevin Love, *Pr*
Michael Leonetti, *
Bob Lynch, *
Richard Johnson, *
Franklin Pang, *Stockholder*
EMP: 74 **EST:** 1989
SALES (est): 441.33K **Privately Held**
Web: www.perfectdomain.com
SIC: 7291 7371 Tax return preparation
services; Computer software development

(P-13164)
H G GROUP INC
4225 Saviers Rd, Oxnard (93033-7158)
PHONE.....................805 486-6463
EMP: 382
SALES (corp-wide): 58.29MM **Privately
Held**
Web: www.hyatt.com
SIC: 7291 Tax return preparation services
HQ: H G Group Inc
71 S Wacker Dr Ste 1000
Chicago IL

(P-13165)
INTERNAL REVENUE SERVICE
2400 E Katella Ave Ste 800, Anaheim
(92806-5955)
PHONE.....................714 512-2818
EMP: 77
Web: www.irs.gov
SIC: 7291 Tax return preparation services
HQ: Internal Revenue Service
1111 Constitution Ave, Nw
Washington DC 20220
202 803-9000

(P-13166)
OPTIMA TAX RELIEF LLC
Also Called: Optima Protection Plan
6 Hutton Centre Dr, Santa Ana
(92707-5745)
PHONE.....................714 361-4636
Harry Langenberg, *
EMP: 180 **EST:** 2010
SALES (est): 22.11MM **Privately Held**
Web: www.optimataxrelief.com
SIC: 7291 Tax return preparation services

7299 Miscellaneous Personal Services

(P-13167)
**AMERICAN FRUITS & FLAVORS
LLC ✪**
510 Park Ave, San Fernando (91340-2527)
PHONE.....................818 899-9574
William Haddad, *Pr*
EMP: 300 **EST:** 2023
SALES (est): 3.07MM
SALES (corp-wide): 7.14B **Publicly Held**
SIC: 7299 House sitting
PA: Monster Beverage Corporation
1 Monster Way
951 739-6200

(P-13168)
BEYOND FINANCE LLC
Also Called: Accredited Debt Relief
9525 Towne Centre Dr Ste 100, San Diego
(92121-1995)
PHONE.....................800 282-7186
Tim Ho, *CEO*
EMP: 558
SALES (corp-wide): 66.51MM **Privately
Held**
Web: www.accrediteddebtrelief.com

SIC: 7299 Debt counseling or adjustment
service, individuals
PA: Beyond Finance, Llc
7322 Southwest Fwy # 1200
800 282-7186

(P-13169)
CIRI - STROUP INC
Also Called: Mile High Valet
25135 Park Lantern, Dana Point
(92629-2878)
PHONE.................949 488-3104
Rob Stroup, *Owner*
EMP: 103
SIC: 7299 7521 Valet parking; Automobile
parking
PA: Ciri - Stroup, Inc.
1 Park Pl Ste 200

(P-13170)
CLOUDSTAFF LLC
26895 Aliso Creek Rd # B-209, Aliso Viejo
(92656-5301)
PHONE.................888 551-5339
EMP: 471
SALES (corp-wide): 2.53MM **Privately
Held**
Web: www.cloudstaffllc.com
SIC: 7299 Personal appearance services
PA: Cloudstaff Llc
1165 E San Antonio Dr
888 551-5339

(P-13171)
DEL MAR FAIRGROUNDS
2260 Jimmy Durante Blvd, Del Mar
(92014-2216)
PHONE.................858 792-4288
EMP: 128 **EST:** 2007
SALES (est): 4.22MM **Privately Held**
Web: www.delmarfairgrounds.com
SIC: 7299 Banquet hall facilities

(P-13172)
DESTINATION RESIDENCES LLC
Also Called: Tesancia La Jlla Ht Spa Resort
9700 N Torrey Pines Rd, La Jolla
(92037-1102)
PHONE.................858 550-1000
Charlie Peck, *Pr*
EMP: 1037
SALES (corp-wide): 367.25MM **Privately
Held**
Web: www.estancialajolla.com
SIC: 7299 7389 7991 7011 Banquet hall
facilities; Convention and show services;
Spas; Hotels
HQ: Destination Residences Llc
10333 E Dry Creek Rd
Englewood CO 80112
303 799-3830

(P-13173)
EHARMONY INC (HQ)
Also Called: Eharmony.com
3583 Hayden Ave, Culver City
(90232-2412)
PHONE.................424 258-1199
Grant Langston, *CEO*
EMP: 119 **EST:** 2000
SALES (est): 5.75MM
SALES (corp-wide): 4.19B **Privately Held**
Web: www.eharmony.com
SIC: 7299 Dating service
PA: Prosiebensat.1 Media Se
Medienallee 7
89950710

(P-13174)
EUROPRO INC
6023 Coffee Rd, Bakersfield (93308-9446)
PHONE.................661 588-5666
EMP: 81
SALES (corp-wide): 4.42MM **Privately
Held**
Web: www.europhoria.com
SIC: 7299 Tanning salon
PA: Europro, Inc.
9539 Langley Rd
661 615-6610

(P-13175)
GLEN IVY HOT SPRINGS
1001 Brea Mall, Brea (92821-5721)
PHONE.................714 990-2090
Jen Breakey, *Mgr*
EMP: 190
SALES (corp-wide): 12.11MM **Privately
Held**
Web: www.glenivy.com
SIC: 7299 7991 5812 5699 Massage parlor;
Spas; Cafe; Bathing suits
PA: Glen Ivy Hot Springs
25000 Glen Ivy Rd
951 277-3529

(P-13176)
**INFORMTION RFRRAL FDRTION
OF L**
Also Called: 211 LA COUNTY
526 W Las Tunas Dr, San Gabriel
(91776-1111)
P.O. Box 726 (91778)
PHONE.................626 350-1841
Maribel Marin, *Ex Dir*
Amy Latzer, *
EMP: 100 **EST:** 1980
SQ FT: 23,000
SALES (est): 21.58MM **Privately Held**
Web: www.211la.org
SIC: 7299 Information services, consumer

(P-13177)
**JC WEIGHT LOSS CENTRES
INC (PA)**
Also Called: Jenny Craig
5770 Fleet St, Carlsbad (92008-4700)
PHONE.................760 696-4000
Kent Kreh, *Ch Bd*
Jenny Craig, *
Dana Fiser, *
Patti Larchet, *
Jenice Lara, *
EMP: 130 **EST:** 1985
SQ FT: 50,000
SALES (est): 49.28MM **Privately Held**
Web: www.jennycraig.com
SIC: 7299 7991 6794 Diet center, without
medical staff; Weight reducing clubs;
Franchises, selling or licensing

(P-13178)
**JET FLEET INTERNATIONAL
CORP**
Also Called: J F I
2370 Westwood Blvd Ste K, Los Angeles
(90064-2150)
PHONE.................310 440-3820
Finn Moller, *Pr*
Arcy Lariz, *
EMP: 28 **EST:** 2003
SALES (est): 1.06MM **Privately Held**
Web: www.jetfleetinternational.com
SIC: 7299 7363 2911 6361 Buyers' club;
Pilot service, aviation; Jet fuels; Title
insurance

(P-13179)
**MASTROIANNI FAMILY ENTPS
LTD**
Also Called: Jay's Catering
10581 Garden Grove Blvd, Garden Grove
(92843-1128)
PHONE.................310 952-1700
Jay Mastroiannis, *Pr*
EMP: 360
SALES (corp-wide): 8.79MM **Privately
Held**
Web: www.jayscatering.com
SIC: 7299 Banquet hall facilities
PA: Mastroianni Family Enterprises Ltd.
10581 Garden Grove Blvd
714 636-6045

(P-13180)
ONE CALL PLUMBER GOLETA
140 Nectarine Ave Apt 4, Goleta
(93117-3359)
PHONE.................805 284-0441
One Call Plumber Goleta, *Owner*
EMP: 99 **EST:** 2001
SALES (est): 236.06K **Privately Held**
Web: www.plumbersgoleta.com
SIC: 7299 Handyman service

(P-13181)
ONE EVENTS INC
8581 Santa Monica Blvd, West Hollywood
(90069-4120)
PHONE.................310 498-5471
Nickolas William Potocic, *CEO*
EMP: 90 **EST:** 2012
SALES (est): 734.94K **Privately Held**
Web: www.oneevents.biz
SIC: 7299 Banquet hall facilities

(P-13182)
OSF INTERNATIONAL INC
Also Called: Old Spaghetti Factory-Duarte
1431 Buena Vista St, Duarte (91010-2458)
PHONE.................626 358-2115
Jennifer Smith, *Mgr*
EMP: 92
SALES (corp-wide): 145.43MM **Privately
Held**
Web: www.osf.com
SIC: 7299 5813 5812 Banquet hall facilities;
Drinking places; Italian restaurant
PA: Osf International, Inc.
0715 S W Bancroft St
503 222-5375

(P-13183)
**PACIFIC COAST
ENTERTAINMENT**
Also Called: Pacific Coast Entertainment
7601 Woodwind Dr, Huntington Beach
(92647-7142)
PHONE.................714 841-6455
Ryan Steidinger, *CEO*
Brandon Domercq, *
EMP: 335 **EST:** 2007
SQ FT: 8,000
SALES (est): 5.59MM **Privately Held**
Web: www.gopce.com
SIC: 7299 Facility rental and party planning
services

(P-13184)
**PACIFIC EVENT PRODUCTIONS
INC (PA)**
Also Called: Pep Creations
6989 Corte Santa Fe, San Diego
(92121-3260)
PHONE.................858 458-9908
Lawrence J Toll, *CEO*

George Duff, *
Joanne Mera, *
EMP: 81 **EST:** 1990
SQ FT: 30,000
SALES (est): 4.48MM **Privately Held**
Web: www.pacificevents.com
SIC: 7299 Party planning service

(P-13185)
PPS PARKING INC
1800 E Garry Ave Ste 107, Santa Ana
(92705-5803)
P.O. Box 16635 (92623-6635)
PHONE.................949 223-8707
Steve Paliska, *Pr*
EMP: 506 **EST:** 1982
SQ FT: 5,000
SALES (est): 912.12K **Privately Held**
Web: www.ppsparkinginc.com
SIC: 7299 8748 Valet parking; Business
consulting, nec

(P-13186)
ROUSE SERVICES LLC
8383 Wilshire Blvd Ste 900, Beverly Hills
(90211-2444)
PHONE.................310 360-9200
Darren Watt, *Mgr*
EMP: 91 **EST:** 2013
SALES (est): 3.94MM
SALES (corp-wide): 3.68B **Publicly Held**
Web: www.rouseservices.com
SIC: 7299 Miscellaneous personal service
PA: Rb Global, Inc.
2 Westbrook Corp Ctr Ste
708 492-7000

(P-13187)
SERVIZ INC
15303 Ventura Blvd Ste 1600, Sherman
Oaks (91403-3133)
PHONE.................818 381-4826
Zorik Gordon, *CEO*
Michael Klien, *
EMP: 70 **EST:** 2014
SQ FT: 8,000
SALES (est): 18.64MM
SALES (corp-wide): 2.66B **Publicly Held**
Web: pro.frontdoor.com
SIC: 7299 Home improvement and
renovation contractor agency
PA: Gannett Co., Inc.
1675 Broadway Fl 23
703 854-6000

(P-13188)
SIGNATURE PARKING LLC
924 Chapala St Ste B, Santa Barbara
(93101-8220)
PHONE.................805 969-7275
EMP: 100 **EST:** 2000
SQ FT: 900
SALES (est): 803K **Privately Held**
Web: www.signatureparking.com
SIC: 7299 Valet parking

(P-13189)
VIBIANA EVENTS LLC
Also Called: Vibiana
214 S Main St, Los Angeles (90012-3708)
PHONE.................213 626-1507
Amy Knoll Fraser, *Managing Member*
EMP: 88 **EST:** 2011
SALES (est): 968.97K **Privately Held**
Web: www.vibiana.com
SIC: 7299 Facility rental and party planning
services

(P-13190)
VISAGE IMAGING INC
12625 High Bluff Dr Ste 205, San Diego
(92130-2053)
PHONE.....................858 345-4410
Sam Hupert, *CEO*
EMP: 75 **EST:** 2007
SQ FT: 1,200
SALES (est): 3.46MM **Privately Held**
Web: www.visageimaging.com
SIC: 7299 7379 Personal document and
   information services; Computer related
   consulting services
PA: Pro Medicus Limited
   450 Swan St

(P-13191)
WESTERN COSTUME CO (HQ)
11041 Vanowen St, North Hollywood
(91605-6314)
PHONE.....................818 760-0900
Eddie Marks, *Pr*
EMP: 48 **EST:** 1912
SQ FT: 150,000
SALES (est): 4.76MM **Privately Held**
Web: www.westerncostume.com
SIC: 7299 2389 Costume rental; Costumes
PA: Ahs Trinity Group, Inc.
   11041 Vanowen St

7311 Advertising Agencies

(P-13192)
180LA LLC
12777 W Jefferson Blvd, Los Angeles
(90066-7048)
PHONE.....................310 382-1400
Alan Moseley, *Managing Member*
Troy Ruhanen, *Managing Member*
EMP: 110 **EST:** 2006
SQ FT: 13,000
SALES (est): 9.4MM
SALES (corp-wide): 14.69B **Publicly Held**
Web: www.180la.com
SIC: 7311 Advertising consultant
HQ: Tbwa Worldwide Inc.
   220 East 42nd St Fl 14
   New York NY 10017

(P-13193)
AD POPULUM LLC (PA)
1234 6th St Apt 410, Santa Monica
(90401-1654)
P.O. Box 212 (90406)
PHONE.....................619 818-7644
EMP: 90 **EST:** 2022
SALES (est): 480.53MM
SALES (corp-wide): 480.53MM **Privately
Held**
SIC: 7311 Advertising agencies

(P-13194)
ADCONION MEDIA INC (PA)
Also Called: Adconion Media Group
3301 Exposition Blvd Fl 1, Santa Monica
(90404-5082)
PHONE.....................310 382-5521
Kristian Wilson, *Pr*
Scott Sullivan, *Global Chief Technology
Officer*
EMP: 119 **EST:** 2007
SALES (est): 8.33MM
SALES (corp-wide): 8.33MM **Privately
Held**
SIC: 7311 Advertising consultant

(P-13195)
**ALCONE MARKETING GROUP
INC (HQ)**

Also Called: Jeep Gear
4 Studebaker, Irvine (92618-2012)
PHONE.....................949 595-5322
William Hahn, *CEO*
Bill Hahn, *
Sean Conciatore, *CCO*
▲ **EMP:** 100 **EST:** 1983
SQ FT: 90,000
SALES (est): 11.39MM
SALES (corp-wide): 14.69B **Publicly Held**
Web: www.alcone.com
SIC: 7311 Advertising consultant
PA: Omnicom Group Inc.
   280 Park Ave
   212 415-3600

(P-13196)
APOLLO INTERACTIVE LLC (PA)
139 Illinois St, El Segundo (90245-4312)
PHONE.....................310 836-9777
David Bohline, *CEO*
Justin Woo, *CEO*
Andrew Shevin, *VP*
Todd Anderson, *Dir*
Matthew Beshear, *Pr*
EMP: 75 **EST:** 1995
SALES (est): 12.49MM **Privately Held**
Web: www.apollointeractive.com
SIC: 7311 Advertising consultant

(P-13197)
AZIRA LLC ✪
80 S Lake Ave Ste 719, Pasadena
(91101-2638)
PHONE.....................606 889-7680
Gladys Kong, *CEO*
EMP: 185 **EST:** 2023
SALES (est): 50MM **Privately Held**
SIC: 7311 Advertising agencies

(P-13198)
CAMPBELL-EWALD COMPANY
Also Called: Campbell-Ewald-West
1840 Century Park E Ste 1600, Los Angeles
(90067-2116)
PHONE.....................310 358-4800
Jeffrey Fisher, *Mgr*
EMP: 82
SALES (corp-wide): 10.89B **Publicly Held**
Web: www.c-e.com
SIC: 7311 Advertising consultant
HQ: Campbell-Ewald Company
   2000 Brush St Ste 601
   Detroit MI 48226
   586 574-3400

(P-13199)
CAUSAL IQ ✪
2945 Townsgate Rd Ste 350, Westlake
Village (91361-5869)
PHONE.....................805 367-6348
Farshad Fardad, *CEO*
Farnam Fardad, *
Lee Lipman, *
EMP: 113 **EST:** 2024
SALES (est): 1.51MM **Privately Held**
SIC: 7311 Advertising consultant

(P-13200)
**CIMARRON PARTNER
ASSOCIATES LLC**
Also Called: Cimarron Group, The
6855 Santa Monica Blvd, Los Angeles
(90038-1119)
PHONE.....................323 337-0300
EMP: 150
Web: www.cimarrongroup.com
SIC: 7311 Advertising agencies

(P-13201)
DAILEY & ASSOCIATES
8687 Melrose Ave Ste G300, West
Hollywood (90069-5701)
P.O. Box 931629 (90093-1629)
PHONE.....................323 490-3847
Jean Grabow, *CEO*
Michelle Wong, *
Bridget Johnson, *
Bradley Johnson, *
Steven Mitchell, *
EMP: 82 **EST:** 1964
SALES (est): 9.65MM **Privately Held**
Web: www.daileyla.com
SIC: 7311 Advertising consultant

(P-13202)
DAVID & GOLIATH LLC
909 N Pacific Coast Hwy Ste 700, El
Segundo (90245-2735)
PHONE.....................310 445-5200
Yumi Prentice, *Pr*
Wells Davis, *Chief Strategy Officer*
Bobby Pearce, *Chief Creative Officer*
Brendan Robertson, *Chief Strategy Officer*
EMP: 200 **EST:** 1999
SQ FT: 1,000
SALES (est): 24.26MM **Privately Held**
Web: www.dng.com
SIC: 7311 Advertising consultant
PA: Innocean Worldwide Inc.
   308 Gangnam-Daero, Gangnam-Gu

(P-13203)
**DAVISELEN ADVERTISING INC
(PA)**
Also Called: Downtown Edit
865 S Figueroa St Ste 1200, Los Angeles
(90017-2596)
PHONE.....................213 688-7000
Mark Davis, *CEO*
Robert Elen, *
Thomas Saltarelli, *
Terry Sullivan, *
EMP: 172 **EST:** 1915
SQ FT: 32,000
SALES (est): 42.44MM
SALES (corp-wide): 42.44MM **Privately
Held**
Web: www.daviselen.com
SIC: 7311 Advertising consultant

(P-13204)
**DDB WRLDWIDE CMMNCTONS
GROUP L**
340 Main St, Venice (90291-2524)
PHONE.....................310 907-1500
Nick Bishop, *Mgr*
EMP: 128
SALES (corp-wide): 14.69B **Publicly Held**
Web: www.ddb.com
SIC: 7311 Advertising consultant
HQ: Ddb Worldwide Communications
   Group Llc
   195 Broadway Fl 7
   New York NY 10007
   212 415-2000

(P-13205)
DEUTSCH LA INC
Also Called: Steelhead
12901 W Jefferson Blvd, Los Angeles
(90066-7023)
PHONE.....................310 862-3000
Mike Sheldon, *CEO*
EMP: 100 **EST:** 1995
SALES (est): 23.89MM
SALES (corp-wide): 10.89B **Publicly Held**
Web: www.steelhead.tv

SIC: 7311 Advertising agencies
PA: The Interpublic Group Of Companies
   Inc
   909 3rd Ave
   212 704-1200

(P-13206)
DGWB INC
Also Called: Dgwb Advg & Communications
217 N Main St Ste 200, Santa Ana
(92701-4843)
PHONE.....................714 881-2300
Mike Wiseman, *CEO*
John Gothold, *
Cindy Melton, *
EMP: 70 **EST:** 1987
SALES (est): 6.84MM **Privately Held**
SIC: 7311 Advertising consultant

(P-13207)
DIGITAS INC
Also Called: Digitaslbi
13031 W Jefferson Blvd Ste 800, Los
Angeles (90094-7002)
PHONE.....................617 867-1000
EMP: 109
SALES (corp-wide): 31.79MM **Privately
Held**
Web: www.digitas.com
SIC: 7311 Advertising agencies
HQ: Digitas, Inc.
   40 Water St
   Boston MA 02109
   617 369-8000

(P-13208)
FORMERLY KNOWN AS LLC
40 E Verdugo Ave, Burbank (91502-1931)
PHONE.....................310 551-3500
Justin Archer, *Prin*
EMP: 80
SALES (corp-wide): 31.79MM **Privately
Held**
Web: www.moxieusa.com
SIC: 7311 Advertising agencies
HQ: Formerly Known As, Llc
   1230 Peachtree St Ne
   Atlanta GA 30309

(P-13209)
GL NEMIROW INC
Also Called: Terry Hines & Assoc
2550 N Hollywood Way Ste 502, Burbank
(91505-5023)
PHONE.....................818 562-9433
Grant W Nemirow, *Pr*
Ralph Terraciano, *
EMP: 07 **EST:** 1900
SALES (est): 4.51MM **Privately Held**
Web: www.terryhines.com
SIC: 7311 Advertising agencies

(P-13210)
GRUPO GALLEGOS
Also Called: Gallegos United
300 Pacific Coast Hwy Ste 200, Huntington
Beach (92648-5150)
PHONE.....................562 256-3600
John Gallegos, *CEO*
Jennifer Mull, *
Pedro Fragata, *
EMP: 90 **EST:** 2004
SALES (est): 9.99MM **Privately Held**
Web: www.gallegosunited.com
SIC: 7311 Advertising consultant

(P-13211)
HAVAS EDGE LLC (DH)
1525 Faraday Ave Ste 250, Carlsbad
(92008-7373)

PHONE.................760 929-0041
Steve Netzley, *CEO*
Jennifer Peabody, *
Greg Johnson, *
Eric Bush, *
EMP: 98 EST: 1988
SALES (est): 44.87MM Privately Held
Web: www.havasedge.com
SIC: 7311 Advertising agencies
HQ: Havas
29-30
Puteaux IDF 92800
158478000

(P-13212)
HORIZON MEDIA INC
Also Called: HORIZON MEDIA, INC.
1888 Century Park E Ste 700, Los Angeles
(90067-1711)
PHONE.................310 282-0909
Zach Rosenberg, *Brnch Mgr*
EMP: 300
Web: www.horizonmedia.com
SIC: 7311 Advertising agencies
PA: Horizon Media Llc
75 Varick St

(P-13213)
ICON MEDIA DIRECT INC (PA)
5910 Lemona Ave, Van Nuys (91411-3006)
P.O. Box 55818 (91413-0818)
PHONE.................818 995-6400
Nancy Lazkani, *CEO*
Seth Klein, *
EMP: 81 EST: 1999
SQ FT: 16,445
SALES (est): 22.03MM
SALES (corp-wide): 22.03MM Privately
Held
Web: www.iconmediadirect.com
SIC: 7311 Advertising consultant

(P-13214)
IGNITE HEALTH LLC (PA)
7535 Irvine Center Dr Ste 200, Irvine
(92618-4951)
PHONE.................949 861-3200
Matt Brown, *Pr*
Richard E Fair, *
Timothy J Riley, *
Fabio Gratton, *
Brian Lefkowitz, *Chief Creative Officer*
EMP: 99 EST: 2000
SQ FT: 15,000
SALES (est): 3.12MM
SALES (corp-wide): 3.12MM Privately
Held
Web: www.ignitehealth.com
SIC: 7311 Advertising consultant

(P-13215)
IGNITED LLC (PA)
111 Penn St, El Segundo (90245-3908)
PHONE.................310 773-3100
William Rosenthal, *
Eric Springer, *Chief Creative Officer*
EMP: 115 EST: 1999
SQ FT: 55,000
SALES (est): 180MM
SALES (corp-wide): 180MM Privately
Held
Web: www.ignitedusa.com
SIC: 7311 Advertising consultant

(P-13216)
INTERACTIVE MEDIA HOLDINGS INC
Also Called: Viant
2722 Michelson Dr Ste 100, Irvine
(92612-8905)

PHONE.................949 861-8888
Timothy C Vanderhook, *Pr*
Roy E Luna, *
Chris Vanderhook, *
Larry Madden, *
EMP: 110 EST: 2004
SALES (est): 20.53MM
SALES (corp-wide): 222.93MM Publicly
Held
SIC: 7311 7313 Advertising consultant;
Newspaper advertising representative
HQ: Viant Technology Llc
2722 Michelson Dr Ste 100
Irvine CA 92612
949 861-8888

(P-13217)
INTERTREND COMMUNICATIONS INC
228 E Broadway, Long Beach
(90802-4840)
PHONE.................562 733-1888
Julia Huang, *CEO*
▲ EMP: 70 EST: 1991
SQ FT: 10,000
SALES (est): 18.34MM Privately Held
Web: www.intertrend.com
SIC: 7311 Advertising consultant

(P-13218)
KATCH LLC
2381 Rosecrans Ave Ste 400, El Segundo
(90245-4920)
PHONE.................310 219-6200
EMP: 70
Web: www.katch.com
SIC: 7311 Advertising agencies

(P-13219)
KERN ORGANIZATION INC
Also Called: Kern Direct Marketing
20955 Warner Center Ln, Woodland Hills
(91367-6511)
PHONE.................818 703-8775
Russell Kern, *Pr*
David Azulay, *
Tom Mackendrick, *
Zeke Ibarbia, *
Steven Orenstein, *
EMP: 80 EST: 2008
SQ FT: 11,350
SALES (est): 19.49MM
SALES (corp-wide): 14.69B Publicly Held
Web: www.thekernorg.com
SIC: 7311 Advertising consultant
PA: Omnicom Group Inc.
280 Park Ave
212 415-3600

(P-13220)
KLIENTBOOST LLC
2787 Bristol St Ste 100, Costa Mesa
(92626-5956)
PHONE.................657 203-7866
J Dane Schuesler, *Managing Member*
Johnathan Dane Schuesler, *Managing Member*
EMP: 127 EST: 2015
SALES (est): 6.29MM Privately Held
Web: www.klientboost.com
SIC: 7311 Advertising consultant

(P-13221)
LIQUID ADVERTISING INC
Also Called: Liquidarcade
138 Eucalyptus Dr, El Segundo
(90245-3819)
PHONE.................310 450-2653
William Akerlof, *CEO*
Marlo Huang, *

Alison Hamon, *
Alison Binetti, *
Shuly Millstein, *
EMP: 91 EST: 2000
SQ FT: 2,000
SALES (est): 8.96MM Privately Held
Web: www.liquidadvertising.com
SIC: 7311 Advertising consultant

(P-13222)
LOCAL CORPORATION (PA)
Also Called: Local.com
7555 Irvine Center Dr, Irvine (92618-2912)
P.O. Box 50700 (92619-0700)
PHONE.................949 784-0800
Frederick G Thiel, *CEO*
Kenneth S Cragun, *CFO*
Erick Herring, *Senior Vice President Technology*
EMP: 80 EST: 1999
SQ FT: 34,612
SALES (est): 12.93MM
SALES (corp-wide): 12.93MM Publicly
Held
Web: www.localcorporation.com
SIC: 7311 Advertising agencies

(P-13223)
MANY LLC
17575 Pacific Coast Hwy, Pacific Palisades
(90272-4148)
PHONE.................310 399-1515
Jens Stoelken, *Pt*
EMP: 71 EST: 2009
SALES (est): 3.49MM Privately Held
Web: www.themany.com
SIC: 7311 Advertising agencies

(P-13224)
MARSHALL ADVERTISING AND DESIGN INC
2729 Bristol St Ste 100, Costa Mesa
(92626-7930)
PHONE.................714 545-5757
EMP: 25
Web: www.marshallad.com
SIC: 7311 7336 2752 Advertising agencies;
Commercial art and graphic design;
Catalogs, lithographed

(P-13225)
MEDIABRANDS WORLDWIDE INC
Also Called: Initiative Media North America
1840 Century Park E, Los Angeles
(90067-2101)
PHONE.................323 370-8000
EMP: 300
SALES (corp-wide): 10.89B Publicly Held
Web: www.ipgmediabrands.com
SIC: 7311 Advertising consultant
HQ: Mediabrands Worldwide, Inc.
100 W 33rd St 3rd Fl
New York NY 10001

(P-13226)
MH SUB I LLC (PA)
Also Called: Internet Brands
909 N Pacific Coast Hwy Fl 11, El Segundo
(90245-2727)
PHONE.................310 280-4000
EMP: 255 EST: 2013
SALES (est): 694.53MM
SALES (corp-wide): 694.53MM Privately
Held
Web: www.internetbrands.com
SIC: 7311 Advertising agencies

(P-13227)
MINDGRUVE HOLDINGS INC
627 8th Ave Ste 300, San Diego
(92101-6453)
PHONE.................619 757-1325
Chad Robley, *CEO*
Dan Helleusch, *
EMP: 102 EST: 2017
SALES (est): 55.36MM Privately Held
Web: www.mindgruve.com
SIC: 7311 Advertising agencies

(P-13228)
MOB SCENE LLC
Also Called: Mob Scene Creative Productions
8447 Wilshire Blvd Ste 100, Beverly Hills
(90211-3228)
PHONE.................323 648-7200
EMP: 135 EST: 2005
SALES (est): 8.47MM Privately Held
Web: www.mobscene.com
SIC: 7311 7929 3993 7812 Advertising
consultant; Entertainment service;
Advertising artwork; Television film
production

(P-13229)
MOVERS AND SHAKERS LLC
1217 Wilshire Blvd, Santa Monica
(90403-5466)
P.O. Box 3327 (90408-3327)
PHONE.................310 893-7051
EMP: 100 EST: 2016
SALES (est): 10.55MM
SALES (corp-wide): 2.53B Publicly Held
Web: www.moversshakers.co
SIC: 7311 Advertising agencies
PA: Stagwell Inc.
1 World Trade Ctr Fl 65
646 429-1800

(P-13230)
MULLENLOWE US INC
12130 Millennium, Los Angeles
(90094-2945)
PHONE.................424 738-6600
EMP: 94
SALES (corp-wide): 10.89B Publicly Held
Web: www.mullenloweglobal.com
SIC: 7311 Advertising consultant
HQ: Mullenlowe U.S., Inc.
2 Drydock Ave Fl 8
Boston MA 02210
617 226-9000

(P-13231)
MULLENLOWE US INC
2121 Park Pl Ste 150, El Segundo
(90245-4843)
PHONE.................424 738-6500
Jennifer Diodonet, *Prin*
EMP: 94
SALES (corp-wide): 10.89B Publicly Held
Web: us.mullenlowe.com
SIC: 7311 8743 8742 8732 Advertising
agencies; Public relations and publicity;
Marketing consulting services; Commercial
nonphysical research
HQ: Mullenlowe U.S., Inc.
2 Drydock Ave Fl 8
Boston MA 02210
617 226-9000

(P-13232)
MUTESIX GROUP INC
Also Called: Mutesix, An Iprospect Company
5800 Bristol Pkwy Ste 500, Culver City
(90230-6899)
PHONE.................800 935-6856
Steve Weiss, *CEO*

Daniel Rutberg, *
EMP: 120 **EST:** 2018
SALES (est): 2.51MM **Privately Held**
SIC: 7311 Advertising agencies
HQ: Dentsu Uk Limited
Regent S Place
London NW1 3
207 070-7700

(P-13233)
NEXSTAR DIGITAL LLC
12777 W Jefferson Blvd Ste B100, Los
Angeles (90066-7048)
PHONE.................................310 971-9300
Morgan Harris, *Brnch Mgr*
EMP: 100
SALES (corp-wide): 4.93B **Publicly Held**
Web: www.nexstardigital.com
SIC: 7311 Advertising agencies
HQ: Nexstar Digital, Llc
545 E John Crptr Fwy Ste
Irving TX 75062
972 373-8800

(P-13234)
ONE & ALL INC (HQ)
Also Called: Regency Group
2 N Lake Ave Ste 600, Pasadena
(91101-1868)
PHONE.................................626 449-6100
EMP: 215 **EST:** 1966
SALES (est): 24.79MM
SALES (corp-wide): 14.69B **Publicly Held**
Web: www.truesense.com
SIC: 7311 Advertising agencies
PA: Omnicom Group Inc.
280 Park Ave
212 415-3600

(P-13235)
PETROL ADVERTISING INC
443 N Varney St, Burbank (91502-1733)
PHONE.................................323 644-3720
EMP: 70
Web: www.petrolad.com
SIC: 7311 Advertising consultant

(P-13236)
POSTAER RUBIN AND ASSOCIATES
2525 Colorado Ave Ste 100, Santa Monica
(90404-5576)
PHONE.................................312 644-3636
Bill Marks, *Owner*
EMP: 216
SALES (corp-wide): 82.31MM **Privately Held**
Web: www.rpa.com
SIC: 7311 Advertising consultant
PA: Rubin Postaer And Associates
2525 Colorado Ave Ste 100
310 394-4000

(P-13237)
PROMOVEO HEALTH LLC
701 Palomar Airport Rd, Carlsbad
(92011-1027)
PHONE.................................760 931-4794
Rolando Collado, *
EMP: 700 **EST:** 2014
SALES (est): 6MM **Privately Held**
Web: www.promoveohealth.com
SIC: 7311 Advertising agencies

(P-13238)
PSB
26012 Atlantic Ocean Dr, Lake Forest
(92630-8843)
PHONE.................................949 465-0772
EMP: 70

Web: www.psblitho.com
SIC: 7311 Advertising agencies

(P-13239)
QUIGLY-SIMPSON HEPPELWHITE INC
Also Called: Quigley-Simpson & Hepplewhite
11601 Wilshire Blvd Ste 710, Los Angeles
(90025-0315)
PHONE.................................310 996-5800
Kathryn Browne, *CFO*
Gerald Bagg, *
Renee Hill Young, *
Alissa Stakgold, *
Duryea Ruffins, *
EMP: 150 **EST:** 2002
SQ FT: 10,500
SALES (est): 22.94MM **Privately Held**
Web: www.quigleysimpson.com
SIC: 7311 7319 Advertising agencies; Media
buying service

(P-13240)
RAPP WORLDWIDE INC
Also Called: Rapp
12777 W Jefferson Blvd Bldg C, Los
Angeles (90066-7048)
PHONE.................................310 563-7200
Collins Rapp, *Brnch Mgr*
EMP: 110
SALES (corp-wide): 14.69B **Publicly Held**
Web: www.rapp.com
SIC: 7311 Advertising consultant
HQ: Rapp Worldwide Inc.
220 E 42nd St Fl 12
New York NY 10017

(P-13241)
REACHLOCAL INC (DH)
Also Called: Reachlocal
21700 Oxnard St Ste 1600, Woodland Hills
(91367-7586)
PHONE.................................818 274-0260
Sharon T Rowlands, *CEO*
Ross G Landsbaum, *
Kris Barton, *CPO* *
Paras Maniar, *CSO* *
EMP: 142 **EST:** 2004
SQ FT: 38,592
SALES (est): 398.01MM
SALES (corp-wide): 2.66B **Publicly Held**
Web: www.localiq.com
SIC: 7311 7375 Advertising consultant;
Online data base information retrieval
HQ: Gannett Media Corp.
7950 Jones Branch Dr
Mclean VA 22102
703 854-6000

(P-13242)
RESCUE AGENCY PUB BENEFT LLC (PA)
2437 Morena Blvd, San Diego
(92110-4152)
PHONE.................................619 231-7555
Kristin Carroll, *CEO*
Jeffrey Jordan, *Pr*
Connor Lynch, *VP*
Steven Andrews, *Dir Fin*
Dennis Triplett, *COO*
EMP: 70 **EST:** 2017
SALES (est): 10.16MM
SALES (corp-wide): 10.16MM **Privately Held**
Web: www.rescueagency.com
SIC: 7311 8732 Advertising agencies;
Sociological research

(P-13243)
RUBIN POSTAER AND ASSOCIATES (PA)
Also Called: R P Direct
2525 Colorado Ave Ste 100, Santa Monica
(90404-5576)
PHONE.................................310 394-4000
Willam C Hagelstein, *CEO*
Gerrold R Rubin, *
Vincent Mancuso, *
Larry Postaer, *
Tom Kirk, *
EMP: 201 **EST:** 1986
SQ FT: 130,000
SALES (est): 82.31MM
SALES (corp-wide): 82.31MM **Privately Held**
Web: www.rpa.com
SIC: 7311 Advertising consultant

(P-13244)
SAATCHI & SAATCHI N AMER LLC
Team One
3501 Sepulveda Blvd, Torrance
(90505-2540)
PHONE.................................310 437-2500
EMP: 250
SALES (corp-wide): 31.79MM **Privately Held**
Web: www.teamone-usa.com
SIC: 7311 Advertising consultant
HQ: Saatchi & Saatchi North America, Llc.
375 Hudson St
New York NY 10014
212 463-2000

(P-13245)
SEISMIC PRODUCTIONS
7010 Santa Monica Blvd, West Hollywood
(90038-1012)
PHONE.................................310 407-0411
David Schneiderman, *Pt*
Kevin Sewelson, *Pt*
EMP: 90 **EST:** 1990
SALES (est): 1.73MM **Privately Held**
Web: www.seismicproductions.com
SIC: 7311 Advertising agencies

(P-13246)
SPECIFICMEDIA INC
2722 Michelson Dr Ste 100, Irvine
(92612-8905)
PHONE.................................949 861-8888
EMP: 90 **EST:** 2016
SALES (est): 5.44MM **Privately Held**
SIC: 7311 Advertising agencies

(P-13247)
STN DIGITAL LLC
Also Called: Digital Marketing
3033 Bunker Hill St, San Diego
(92109-5705)
PHONE.................................619 292-8683
David Brickley, *Managing Member*
EMP: 81 **EST:** 2013
SALES (est): 15MM **Privately Held**
Web: www.stndigital.com
SIC: 7311 Advertising agencies

(P-13248)
SUISSA MILLER ADVERTISING LLC
8687 Melrose Ave, West Hollywood
(90069-5701)
PHONE.................................310 392-9666
EMP: 100 **EST:** 1985
SQ FT: 40,000
SALES (est): 1.93MM **Privately Held**

SIC: 7311 Advertising agencies

(P-13249)
TEAM GARAGE LLC
Also Called: Garage Team Mazda
3200 Bristol St Ste 300, Costa Mesa
(92626-1838)
PHONE.................................714 913-9900
Michael Buttlar, *CEO*
Brian Rogers, *
Tom Nickerson, *
EMP: 70 **EST:** 2012
SALES (est): 4.24MM **Privately Held**
Web: www.vml.com
SIC: 7311 Advertising agencies

(P-13250)
TRAILER PARK INC (PA)
Also Called: Mutiny
6922 Hollywood Blvd Fl 12, Los Angeles
(90028-6132)
P.O. Box 2950 (90078-2950)
PHONE.................................310 845-3000
Rick Eiserman, *Pr*
Tim Nett, *Executive Creative Director* *
Benedict Coulter, *
James Hale, *Stockholder* *
EMP: 100 **EST:** 2005
SQ FT: 8,000
SALES (est): 46.39MM **Privately Held**
Web: www.trailerparkgroup.com
SIC: 7311 Advertising agencies

(P-13251)
VITROROBERTSON LLC
Also Called: Vitro
225 Broadway, San Diego (92101-5005)
PHONE.................................619 234-0408
Tom Sullivan, *
Alan Bonine, *
EMP: 89 **EST:** 2004
SALES (est): 9.03MM
SALES (corp-wide): 2.53B **Publicly Held**
Web: www.vitroagency.com
SIC: 7311 Advertising consultant
PA: Stagwell Inc.
1 World Trade Ctr Fl 65
646 429-1800

(P-13252)
WHEREWECHAT ONLINE SVCS LLC ✪
15442 Ventura Blvd Ste 201-275, Sherman
Oaks (91403-3004)
PHONE.................................302 566-1649
Chibuike Paul, *Managing Member*
EMP: 100 **EST:** 2024
SALES (est): 2.19MM **Privately Held**
SIC: 7311 Advertising agencies

(P-13253)
WONDERFUL AGENCY
11444 W Olympic Blvd Ste 210, Los
Angeles (90064-1559)
PHONE.................................310 966-8600
Stewart A Resnick, *CEO*
Margaret Keene, *Chief Creative Officer*
EMP: 1773 **EST:** 2016
SALES (est): 1.66MM
SALES (corp-wide): 2.04B **Privately Held**
Web: www.wonderful.com
SIC: 7311 Advertising consultant
PA: The Wonderful Company Llc
11444 W Olympic Blvd Fl 1
310 966-5700

(P-13254)
YOUNG & RUBICAM LLC
Also Called: Y&R-Wcj Spectrum
7535 Irvine Center Dr, Irvine (92618-2962)

P
R
O
D
U
C
T
S
&
S
V
C
S

PHONE..................949 754-2000
David Murphy, *Pr*
EMP: 300
SALES (corp-wide): 18.5B **Privately Held**
Web: www.vml.com
SIC: 7311 Advertising consultant
HQ: Young & Rubicam Llc
　　175 Greenwich St Fl 28
　　New York NY 10007
　　212 210-3017

(P-13255)
YOUNG & RUBICAM LLC
Also Called: Landor Associates
7535 Irvine Center Dr, Irvine (92618-2962)
PHONE..................949 754-2100
Rick Eisermas, *Mgr*
EMP: 250
SALES (corp-wide): 18.5B **Privately Held**
Web: www.vml.com
SIC: 7311 Advertising agencies
HQ: Young & Rubicam Llc
　　175 Greenwich St Fl 28
　　New York NY 10007
　　212 210-3017

7312 Outdoor Advertising Services

(P-13256)
BAMKO INC
Also Called: Bamko
11620 Wilshire Blvd Ste 610, Los Angeles
(90025-1267)
PHONE..................310 470-5859
EMP: 150
Web: www.bamko.net
SIC: 7312 7311 Outdoor advertising services
; Advertising agencies

(P-13257)
OUTFRONT MEDIA LLC
1731 Workman St, Los Angeles
(90031-3334)
PHONE..................323 222-7171
Dennis Kuhl, *Mgr*
EMP: 27
SALES (corp-wide): 1.82B **Publicly Held**
Web: www.outfront.com
SIC: 7312 3993 Outdoor advertising services
; Signs and advertising specialties
HQ: Outfront Media Llc
　　405 Lxington Ave 14th Flr
　　New York NY 10174
　　212 297-6400

7313 Radio, Television, Publisher Representatives

(P-13258)
ADACTIVE MEDIA CA INC
Also Called: Thoughtful Asia Limited
14724 Ventura Blvd Ste 1110, Sherman
Oaks (91403-3511)
PHONE..................818 465-7500
Bien Kiat Tan, *CEO*
EMP: 70 **EST:** 2010
SALES (est): 1.98MM
SALES (corp-wide): 8.17MM **Publicly
Held**
Web: www.thoughtmedia.com
SIC: 7313 Electronic media advertising
representatives
HQ: Thoughtful Media Group Incorporated
　　701 S Carson St Ste 200
　　Carson City NV

(P-13259)
ATTN INC
5700 Wilshire Blvd Ste 375, Los Angeles
(90036-7212)
PHONE..................323 413-2878
Jarrett Moreno, *CEO*
Matthew Segel, *
EMP: 200 **EST:** 2014
SQ FT: 100,000
SALES (est): 11.86MM **Privately Held**
Web: www.attn.com
SIC: 7313 Electronic media advertising
representatives

(P-13260)
BEACHBODY LLC (HQ)
Also Called: Beachbody
400 Continental Blvd Ste 400, El Segundo
(90245-5089)
P.O. Box 1227 (90660-1227)
PHONE..................310 883-9000
Carl Daikeler, *Ch*
Jon Congdon, *CMO**
Brad Ramberg, *
Sue Collyns, *
Bryan Muehlberger, *CIO**
▲ **EMP:** 500 **EST:** 1998
SALES (est): 489.45MM
SALES (corp-wide): 527.11MM **Publicly
Held**
Web: www.bodi.com
SIC: 7313 7999 Electronic media advertising
representatives; Physical fitness instruction
PA: The Beachbody Company Inc
　　400 Cntnntal Blvd Ste 400
　　310 883-9000

(P-13261)
**BEACHBODY COMPANY INC
(PA)**
Also Called: Beachbody Company, The
400 Continental Blvd Ste 400, El Segundo
(90245-5089)
PHONE..................310 883-9000
Carl Daikeler, *CEO*
Mark Goldston, *Ex Ch Bd*
Brad Ramberg, *Interim Chief Financial
Officer*
Kathy Vrabeck, *CFO*
EMP: 88 **EST:** 2020
SQ FT: 42,000
SALES (est): 527.11MM
SALES (corp-wide): 527.11MM **Publicly
Held**
Web: www.thebeachbodycompany.com
SIC: 7313 7999 Electronic media advertising
representatives; Physical fitness instruction

(P-13262)
**BLT CMMNCTIONS LLC A LTD
LBLTY**
6430 W Sunset Blvd Ste 800, Los Angeles
(90028-7911)
PHONE..................323 860-4000
EMP: 207 **EST:** 2007
SALES (est): 3.18MM **Privately Held**
Web: www.bltomato.com
SIC: 7313 Electronic media advertising
representatives

(P-13263)
BRITE MEDIA LLC
Also Called: Brite Promotions
16027 Ventura Blvd Ste 210, Encino
(91436-2876)
PHONE..................818 826-5790
Greg Martin, *Brnch Mgr*
EMP: 270
SALES (corp-wide): 11.1MM **Privately
Held**

Web: www.britevision.com
SIC: 7313 Electronic media advertising
representatives
PA: Brite Media Llc
　　350 Frank Ogawa Plz Ste 3
　　877 479-7777

(P-13264)
CANVAS WORLDWIDE LLC
12015 Bluff Creek Dr, Playa Vista
(90094-2930)
PHONE..................424 303-4300
Paul Woolmington, *CEO*
Madhavi Tadikonda, *CIO**
EMP: 250 **EST:** 2015
SALES (est): 54.23MM **Privately Held**
Web: www.canvasworldwide.com
SIC: 7313 Electronic media advertising
representatives
PA: Innocean Worldwide Inc.
　　308 Gangnam-Daero, Gangnam-Gu

(P-13265)
EDMUNDSCOM INC (HQ)
2401 Colorado Ave Ste P1, Santa Monica
(90404-3175)
PHONE..................310 309-6300
Seth Berkowitz, *Pr*
Scott Fanelli, *VP*
Katti Fields, *VP*
Xiao Sun, *VP*
▲ **EMP:** 550 **EST:** 1966
SALES (est): 15.49MM **Privately Held**
Web: www.edmunds.com
SIC: 7313 Electronic media advertising
representatives
PA: Edmunds Holding Company
　　2401 Colorado Ave

(P-13266)
**GHOST MANAGEMENT GROUP
LLC**
41 Discovery, Irvine (92618-3150)
PHONE..................949 870-1400
Doug Francis, *
Albert Lopez, *
Chris Beals, *
Hendrik Davel, *Senior Controller**
EMP: 175 **EST:** 2012
SQ FT: 44,820
SALES (est): 20.79MM
SALES (corp-wide): 215.53MM **Publicly
Held**
SIC: 7313 7371 Electronic media advertising
representatives; Computer software
development and applications
PA: Wm Technology, Inc.
　　41 Discovery
　　646 699-3750

(P-13267)
GRABIT INTERACTIVE INC
Also Called: Kerv Interactive
14724 Ventura Blvd, Sherman Oaks
(91403-3501)
PHONE..................844 472-2488
Gary Mittman, *CEO*
EMP: 34 **EST:** 2016
SALES (est): 681.8K **Privately Held**
Web: www.grabit.media
SIC: 7313 7372 Printed media advertising
representatives; Application computer
software

(P-13268)
KARGO GLOBAL INC
1437 4th St Ste 200, Santa Monica
(90401-2377)
PHONE..................212 979-9000
Natalie Nelson, *Brnch Mgr*

EMP: 139
Web: www.kargo.com
SIC: 7313 7372 7374 Electronic media
advertising representatives; Application
computer software; Computer graphics
service
PA: Kargo Global, Inc.
　　826 Broadway Fl 4

(P-13269)
MEDIAALPHA INC (PA)
Also Called: Mediaalpha
700 S Flower St Ste 640, Los Angeles
(90017-4122)
PHONE..................213 316-6256
Steven Yi, *Pr*
Patrick Thompson, *CFO*
EMP: 129 **EST:** 2020
SALES (est): 388.15MM
SALES (corp-wide): 388.15MM **Publicly
Held**
Web: www.mediaalpha.com
SIC: 7313 Electronic media advertising
representatives

(P-13270)
SHED MEDIA US INC
3000 W Alameda Ave, Burbank
(91505-4400)
PHONE..................323 904-4680
Nick Emmerson, *Pr*
Josh Mills, *
EMP: 98 **EST:** 2009
SALES (est): 2.01MM **Privately Held**
Web: www.shedmedia.com
SIC: 7313 Electronic media advertising
representatives

(P-13271)
STUDIO 71 LP
8383 Wilshire Blvd Ste 1050, Beverly Hills
(90211-2415)
PHONE..................323 370-1500
Michael Green, *
Dan Weinstein, *
Scott Weller, *
Jordan Toplitzky, *
EMP: 150 **EST:** 2011
SQ FT: 15,000
SALES (est): 60MM
SALES (corp-wide): 4.19B **Privately Held**
Web: www.studio71.com
SIC: 7313 Electronic media advertising
representatives
PA: Prosiebensat.1 Media Se
　　Medienallee 7
　　89950710

(P-13272)
WALDBERG INC
Also Called: Refinery, The
3200 W Valhalla Dr, Burbank (91505-1236)
PHONE..................818 843-0004
Adam Waldman, *CEO*
Brad Hochberg, *
EMP: 100 **EST:** 2006
SALES (est): 11.02MM **Privately Held**
Web: www.therefinerycreative.com
SIC: 7313 Electronic media advertising
representatives

7319 Advertising, Nec

(P-13273)
FASTCLICK INC
Also Called: Fastclick.com
530 E Montecito St, Santa Barbara
(93103-3245)
PHONE..................805 689-9839

EMP: 522 **EST:** 2000
SQ FT: 14,900
SALES (est): 7.48MM
SALES (corp-wide): 29.15MM **Privately
Held**
Web: www.epsilon.com
SIC: 7319 Circular and handbill distribution
HQ: Conversant, Llc
101 N Wacker Dr
Chicago IL 60601

(P-13274)
GILS DISTRIBUTING SERVICE
Also Called: Great Western Distributing Svc
718 E 8th St, Los Angeles (90021-1802)
PHONE.....................213 627-0539
Feleciano Gil, *Pr*
Fidel Gil, *
Gloria Gil, *
EMP: 112 **EST:** 1967
SQ FT: 5,000
SALES (est): 1.98MM **Privately Held**
SIC: 7319 4215 Circular and handbill
distribution; Courier services, except by air

(P-13275)
IMAGE OPTIONS (PA)
Also Called: Image Options Painting & Dctg
80 Icon, Foothill Ranch (92610-3000)
PHONE.....................949 586-7665
Barry Polan, *CEO*
Tim Bennett, *Ch Bd*
Brian Hite, *Pr*
Dave Brewer, *VP*
Barry Polan, *CRO*
EMP: 63 **EST:** 1999
SQ FT: 22,000
SALES (est): 24.71MM
SALES (corp-wide): 24.71MM **Privately
Held**
Web: www.imageoptions.net
SIC: 7319 7336 2759 Display advertising
service; Commercial art and graphic design
; Commercial printing, nec

7322 Adjustment And
Collection Services

(P-13276)
AMERICAN RECOVERY
SERVICE INC (DH)
Also Called: Arsi of California
555 Saint Charles Dr Ste 100, Thousand
Oaks (91360-3983)
P.O. Box 1025 (91358-0025)
PHONE.....................805 379-8500
EMP: 200 **EST:** 1986
SALES (est): 24.24MM **Privately Held**
Web: www.arsigroup.com
SIC: 7322 Collection agency, except real
estate
HQ: Firstsource Solutions Limited
5th Floor, Paradigm, B Wing,
Mindspace,
Mumbai MH 40006

(P-13277)
ARS NATIONAL SERVICES INC
(PA)
201 W Grand Ave, Escondido
(92025-2603)
P.O. Box 463023 (92046-3023)
PHONE.....................800 456-5053
Jason Howerton, *Pr*
John Howerton, *
Kathy Howerton, *
John Watson, *
Jim Beck, *
EMP: 150 **EST:** 1987

SQ FT: 33,000
SALES (est): 27.8MM **Privately Held**
Web: www.arsnational.com
SIC: 7322 Collection agency, except real
estate

(P-13278)
ATTORNEY RECOVERY
SYSTEMS INC (PA)
18757 Burbank Blvd Ste 300, Tarzana
(91356-6329)
PHONE.....................818 774-1420
Gene Bloom, *Pr*
EMP: 70 **EST:** 1989
SALES (est): 1.45MM **Privately Held**
Web: www.perfectdomain.com
SIC: 7322 8111 Collection agency, except
real estate; Legal services

(P-13279)
CAINE & WEINER COMPANY
INC (PA)
Also Called: Caine & Weiner
5805 Sepulveda Blvd Fl 4, Sherman Oaks
(91411-2532)
P.O. Box 55848 (91413)
PHONE.....................818 226-6000
Greg A Cohen, *Pr*
Rick Luther, *
Brad Schaffer, *Senior Vice President Client
Services*
Tony Albanesi, *CA*
Steve Simon, *SERVICES*
EMP: 90 **EST:** 1930
SQ FT: 14,400
SALES (est): 22.44MM
SALES (corp-wide): 22.44MM **Privately
Held**
Web: www.caine-weiner.com
SIC: 7322 Collection agency, except real
estate

(P-13280)
CMRE FINANCIAL SERVICES
INC
3075 E Imperial Hwy Ste 200, Brea
(92821-6753)
PHONE.....................714 528-3200
Jeffrey Nieman, *Pr*
EMP: 450 **EST:** 2000
SQ FT: 35,000
SALES (est): 23.01MM **Privately Held**
Web: www.cmrefsi.com
SIC: 7322 Collection agency, except real
estate

(P-13281)
COLLECTION TECHNOLOGY INC
Also Called: C T I
10801 6th St Ste 200, Rancho Cucamonga
(91730-5904)
P.O. Box 2200 (91729-2200)
PHONE.....................800 743-4284
Chris Van Dellen, *CEO*
Paul Van Dellen, *
EMP: 100 **EST:** 1953
SALES (est): 9.77MM **Privately Held**
Web: www.collectiontechnology.com
SIC: 7322 Collection agency, except real
estate

(P-13282)
EGS FINANCIAL CARE INC (DH)
Also Called: Total Debt Management
5 Park Plz Ste 1100, Irvine (92614-8502)
PHONE.....................877 217-4423
Jay King, *Pr*
Steven Winokur, *
Joshua Gindin, *

John R Schwab Treeas, *Prin*
▲ **EMP:** 300 **EST:** 1966
SALES (est): 84.72MM
SALES (corp-wide): 845.12MM **Privately
Held**
SIC: 7322 Collection agency, except real
estate
HQ: Alorica Global Solutions, Inc.
6652 Pinecrest Dr Ste 300
Plano TX 75024

(P-13283)
FCI LENDER SERVICES INC
Also Called: F C I
8180 E Kaiser Blvd, Anaheim (92808-2277)
PHONE.....................800 931-2424
Michael W Griffith, *Pr*
EMP: 190 **EST:** 1982
SQ FT: 19,000
SALES (est): 33.31MM **Privately Held**
Web: www.trustfci.com
SIC: 7322 Adjustment and collection services

(P-13284)
GRANT & WEBER (PA)
Also Called: Grant & Weber Travel
26610 Agoura Rd Ste 209, Calabasas
(91302-2975)
P.O. Box 8669 (91372-8669)
PHONE.....................818 878-7700
Jimi Bingham, *CEO*
Ron Grossblatt, *CDO*
Spencer Weinerman, *
David Weinerman, *
Mary Kempski, *CIO*
▲ **EMP:** 85 **EST:** 1976
SQ FT: 30,000
SALES (est): 24.38MM
SALES (corp-wide): 24.38MM **Privately
Held**
Web: www.grantweber.com
SIC: 7322 Collection agency, except real
estate

(P-13285)
HEALTH ADVOCATES LLC
Also Called: Health Advocates
21540 Plummer St Ste B, Chatsworth
(91311-0888)
PHONE.....................818 995-9500
Al Leibovic, *Managing Member*
Aaron Leibovic, *Managing Member*
EMP: 371 **EST:** 1997
SQ FT: 40,900
SALES (est): 14.59MM **Privately Held**
Web: www.healthadvocates.com
SIC: 7322 Adjustment and collection services

(P-13286)
JJ MAC INTYRE CO INC (PA)
4160 Temescal Canyon Rd Ste 601, Corona
(92883-4626)
P.O. Box 78150 (92877-0138)
PHONE.....................951 898-4300
Scott M Hall, *CEO*
Kenneth A Lee, *
EMP: 115 **EST:** 1959
SQ FT: 28,254
SALES (est): 2.15MM
SALES (corp-wide): 2.15MM **Privately
Held**
SIC: 7322 Collection agency, except real
estate

(P-13287)
RM GALICIA INC
Also Called: Progressive Management
Systems
1521 W Cameron Ave Ste 100, West
Covina (91790-2738)

P.O. Box 2220 (91793-2220)
PHONE.....................626 813-6200
Timothy Chase Banta, *CEO*
William Gutierrez, *Sr VP*
EMP: 125 **EST:** 1978
SQ FT: 20,000
SALES (est): 12.83MM **Privately Held**
Web: www.pmscollects.com
SIC: 7322 Collection agency, except real
estate

(P-13288)
SEQUOIA CONCEPTS INC
Also Called: Sequoia Financial Services
28632 Roadside Dr Ste 110, Agoura Hills
(91301-6074)
PHONE.....................818 409-6000
Roy Duplessis, *Pr*
Denise Duplessis, *
Roy Deplessis Ii, *Sec*
EMP: 75 **EST:** 1992
SQ FT: 9,100
SALES (est): 9.19MM **Privately Held**
Web: www.sequoiafinancial.com
SIC: 7322 Collection agency, except real
estate

(P-13289)
USCB INC (PA)
Also Called: Uscb America
355 S Grand Ave Ste 3200, Los Angeles
(90071-1591)
PHONE.....................213 985-2111
Albert Cadena, *CEO*
Melvin F Shaw, *
Thomas Isgrigg, *
Albert Cadena, *Prin*
Pat Esquivel, *
EMP: 213 **EST:** 1915
SQ FT: 34,000
SALES (est): 31.26MM
SALES (corp-wide): 31.26MM **Privately
Held**
Web: www.uscbamerica.com
SIC: 7322 8741 Collection agency, except
real estate; Management services

(P-13290)
VENGROFF WILLIAMS & ASSOC
INC
2099 S State College Blvd Ste 600,
Anaheim (92806-6137)
PHONE.....................714 889-6200
Robert Sherman, *Brnch Mgr*
EMP: 102
SALES (corp-wide): 11.89MM **Privately
Held**
Web: www.vengroffwilliams.com
SIC: 7322 Collection agency, except real
estate
PA: Vengroff, Williams & Associates, Inc.
2211 Fruitville Rd
941 363-5200

7323 Credit Reporting
Services

(P-13291)
BASEPOINT ANALYTICS LLC
703 Palomar Airport Rd Ste 350, Carlsbad
(92011-1051)
PHONE.....................760 602-4971
EMP: 392 **EST:** 2004
SALES (est): 1.32MM
SALES (corp-wide): 1.64B **Privately Held**
SIC: 7323 Credit reporting services
HQ: Corelogic Systems, Inc.
40 Pacifica Ste 900
Irvine CA 92618
714 250-6400

(P-13292)

CELESTIAL-SATURN PARENT INC (PA)
40 Pacifica, Irvine (92618-7471)
PHONE.................................949 214-1000
EMP: 139 EST: 2021
SALES (est): 1.64B
SALES (corp-wide): 1.64B Privately Held
Web: www.mercuryvmp.com
SIC: 7323 Credit reporting services

(P-13293)

CORELOGIC CREDCO LLC (DH)
Also Called: Corelogic Credco
40 Pacifica Ste 900, Irvine (92618-7487)
PHONE.................................800 255-0792
Jim Balas, CFO
EMP: 220 EST: 2005
SALES (est): 28.36MM
SALES (corp-wide): 1.64B Privately Held
Web: www.credco.com
SIC: 7323 8748 Consumer credit reporting
  bureau; Business consulting, nec
HQ: Corelogic, Inc.
  40 Pacifica Ste 900
  Irvine CA 92618
  866 873-3651

(P-13294)

CORELOGIC CREDCO LLC
2385 Northside Dr, San Diego
(92108-2727)
PHONE.................................619 938-7028
Kathleen Manzione, Brnch Mgr
EMP: 280
SALES (corp-wide): 1.64B Privately Held
Web: www.credco.com
SIC: 7323 Consumer credit reporting bureau
HQ: Corelogic Credco, Llc
  40 Pacifica Ste 900
  Irvine CA 92618
  800 255-0792

(P-13295)

EXPERIAN INFO SOLUTIONS INC (DH)
Also Called: Experian
475 Anton Blvd, Costa Mesa (92626-7037)
P.O. Box 5001 (92628-5001)
PHONE.................................714 830-7000
Chris Callero, CEO
Stephen Burnside, Sr VP
EMP: 3700 EST: 1996
SQ FT: 323,000
SALES (est): 973.87MM
SALES (corp-wide): 7.1B Privately Held
Web: www.experian.com
SIC: 7323 Consumer credit reporting bureau
HQ: Experian Holdings, Inc.
  475 Anton Blvd
  Costa Mesa CA 92626
  714 830-7000

(P-13296)

EXPERIAN MKTG SOLUTIONS LLC
Also Called: Experian Marketing
475 Anton Blvd, Costa Mesa (92626-7037)
PHONE.................................714 830-7000
Kevin Dean, Pr
EMP: 501 EST: 2016
SQ FT: 4,000
SALES (est): 8.52MM
SALES (corp-wide): 380MM Privately
Held
Web: www.experian.com
SIC: 7323 Consumer credit reporting bureau
PA: Vector Capital Management, L.P.
  650 California St

415 293-5000

(P-13297)

THE TAX CREDIT COMPANY
Also Called: Tax Credit Co, The
6464 W Sunset Blvd Ste 1150, Los Angeles
(90028-8021)
PHONE.................................323 927-0750
EMP: 100
SIC: 7323 8721 7291 Credit reporting
  services; Auditing services; Tax return
  preparation services

7331 Direct Mail Advertising Services

(P-13298)

ADVANCED IMAGE DIRECT LLC
Also Called: Fht Printing
1415 S Acacia Ave, Fullerton (92831-5317)
PHONE.................................714 502-3900
Hugo Solorio, *
▲ EMP: 50 EST: 2008
SALES (est): 4.21MM
SALES (corp-wide): 29MM Privately Held
Web: www.advancedimagedirect.com
SIC: 7331 2752 Mailing service; Commercial
  printing, lithographic
PA: Real Estate Image, Inc.
  1415 S Acacia Ave
  714 502-3900

(P-13299)

ADVANTAGE MAILING LLC (PA)
Also Called: Advantage Mailing Service
1600 N Kraemer Blvd, Anaheim
(92806-1410)
P.O. Box 66013 (92816)
PHONE.................................714 538-3881
Tom Ling, Pr
Brett Noss, CFO
EMP: 125 EST: 1994
SQ FT: 60,000
SALES (est): 49.49MM
SALES (corp-wide): 49.49MM Privately
Held
Web: www.advantageinc.com
SIC: 7331 Mailing service

(P-13300)

AST SPORTSWEAR INC
P.O. Box 17219 (92817-7219)
PHONE.................................714 223-2030
EMP: 395
Web: www.astsportswear.com
SIC: 7331 Mailing service
PA: Ast Sportswear, Inc.
  2701 E Imperial Hwy

(P-13301)

DIVERSIFIED MAILING INCORPORATED
Also Called: Diversified Direct
14407 Alondra Blvd, La Mirada
(90638-5504)
P.O. Box 2270777 (75222)
PHONE.................................714 994-6245
TOLL FREE: 800
EMP: 157
SIC: 7331 Direct mail advertising services

(P-13302)

FINANCIAL STATEMENT SVCS INC (PA)
Also Called: Fssi
3300 S Fairview St, Santa Ana
(92704-7004)
PHONE.................................714 436-3326

Jennifer Dietz, CEO
Jon Dietz, *
Karen Elsbury, *
Henry Perez, *
Dan Palmquist, *
EMP: 144 EST: 1984
SQ FT: 167,000
SALES (est): 31.62MM
SALES (corp-wide): 31.62MM Privately
Held
Web: www.fssi-ca.com
SIC: 7331 7374 2759 Mailing service; Data
  processing and preparation; Laser printing

(P-13303)

LOMITA LOGISTICS LLC
Also Called: Xpo
3541 Lomita Blvd, Torrance (90505-5016)
PHONE.................................310 784-8485
EMP: 100
Web: internationalservices.rrd.com
SIC: 7331 Mailing service

(P-13304)

ORANGE COUNTY DIRECT MAIL INC
Also Called: Ocdm
2672 Dow Ave, Tustin (92780-7208)
PHONE.................................714 444-4412
Mark Cretz, CEO
EMP: 45 EST: 1990
SQ FT: 35,000
SALES (est): 8.91MM Privately Held
Web: www.ocdm.com
SIC: 7331 7313 7389 2752 Mailing service;
  Printed media advertising representatives;
  Printers' services: folding, collating, etc.;
  Commercial printing, lithographic

(P-13305)

REAL ESTATE IMAGE INC (PA)
Also Called: Advanced Image Direct
1415 S Acacia Ave, Fullerton (92831-5317)
PHONE.................................714 502-3900
Ty Mcmillin, Pr
Perry Wilson, *
Hugo Solorio, Product Vice President*
EMP: 150 EST: 1981
SQ FT: 136,000
SALES (est): 29MM
SALES (corp-wide): 29MM Privately Held
Web: www.advancedimagedirect.com
SIC: 7331 2752 Mailing service; Commercial
  printing, lithographic

(P-13306)

SPECTRUM INFORMATION SVCS LLC (PA)
3323 Spectrum, Irvine (92618-3374)
PHONE.................................949 752-7070
Curtis Pilon, Pr
Jim Bradford, *
EMP: 70 EST: 1991
SALES (est): 9.32MM Privately Held
Web: www.spectruminformation.com
SIC: 7331 7375 4731 Mailing service;
  Information retrieval services; Shipping
  documents preparation

(P-13307)

TRANSAMERICAN DIRECT INC
Also Called: Transamerican
355 State Pl, Escondido (92029-1359)
PHONE.................................760 745-5343
Paul Barron, CEO
Eleanor Monica, *
▲ EMP: 100 EST: 1987
SALES (est): 9.68MM Privately Held
Web: www.transamericanmailing.com
SIC: 7331 Mailing service

(P-13308)

UNIVERSAL MAIL DELIVERY SVC (PA)
Also Called: Universal Custom Courier
501 S Brand Blvd # 104, San Fernando
(91340-4000)
PHONE.................................818 365-3144
Robert M Reznick, CEO
Bernard Reznick, *
Barbara Reznick, Stockholder*
Saddie Reznick, Stockholder*
EMP: 95 EST: 1953
SQ FT: 1,000
SALES (est): 2.24MM
SALES (corp-wide): 2.24MM Privately
Held
SIC: 7331 Mailing service

7334 Photocopying And Duplicating Services

(P-13309)

AMERICAN LEGAL COPY - OC LLC
655 W Broadway Ste 200, San Diego
(92101-8476)
PHONE.................................415 777-4449
Joe Motz, Prin
EMP: 87 EST: 2003
SALES (est): 311.64K Privately Held
SIC: 7334 Photocopying and duplicating
  services
PA: American Legal Copy-Or, Llc
  1001 4th Ave Ste 300

(P-13310)

ARC DOCUMENT SOLUTIONS LLC
41521 Date St Apt 101, Murrieta
(92562-7088)
PHONE.................................951 445-4480
EMP: 459
SALES (corp-wide): 26.43MM Privately
Held
Web: www.e-arc.com
SIC: 7334 Blueprinting service
PA: Arc Document Solutions, Llc
  12657 Alcsta Blvd Ste 200
  925 949-5100

(P-13311)

CONCORD DOCUMENT SERVICES INC (PA)
1407 W 11th St, Los Angeles (90015-1227)
PHONE.................................213 745-3175
Fernando B Flores, CEO
Hector Flores, *
EMP: 28 EST: 1996
SALES (est): 2.72MM
SALES (corp-wide): 2.72MM Privately
Held
Web: www.concorddt.com
SIC: 7334 3577 Photocopying and
  duplicating services; Optical scanning
  devices

(P-13312)

CP DOCUMENT TECHNOLOGIES LLC
11835 W Olympic Blvd Ste 145, Los
Angeles (90064-5001)
PHONE.................................310 575-6640
Emily Go, Mgr
EMP: 50
SIC: 7334 2754 2759 Photocopying and
  duplicating services; Commercial printing,
  gravure; Commercial printing, nec
PA: Cp Document Technologies, Llc
  800 W 6th St Ste 1400

(P-13313)

DVS MEDIA SERVICES (PA)

Also Called: D V S Mdia Srvces/Intelestream
2625 W Olive Ave, Burbank (91505-4526)
PHONE..................................818 841-6750
Rick Appell, *Managing Member*
EMP: 46 **EST:** 2020
SALES (est): 5.91MM
SALES (corp-wide): 5.91MM **Privately Held**
SIC: 7334 2759 Photocopying and duplicating services; Commercial printing, nec

(P-13314)

LASR INC

Also Called: First Reprographic
1517 Beverly Blvd, Los Angeles (90026-5704)
P.O. Box 749469 (90074-9469)
PHONE..................................877 591-9979
Martin Kayondo, *Pr*
Rick Matsumoto, *
EMP: 120 **EST:** 2002
SALES (est): 2.45MM **Privately Held**
SIC: 7334 Photocopying and duplicating services

(P-13315)

OFFICEMAX NORTH AMERICA INC

Also Called: OfficeMax
7075 Firestone Blvd, Downey (90241-4102)
PHONE..................................562 927-6444
Earl Dadis, *Brnch Mgr*
EMP: 141
SALES (corp-wide): 7.83B **Publicly Held**
SIC: 7334 Photocopying and duplicating services
HQ: Officemax North America, Inc.
    263 Shuman Blvd Ste 145
    Naperville IL 60563
    630 717-0791

(P-13316)

SECOND IMAGE NATIONAL LLC (PA)

170 E Arrow Hwy, San Dimas (91773-3336)
P.O. Box 52969 (77052-2969)
PHONE..................................800 229-7477
Norman Fogwell, *CEO*
EMP: 145 **EST:** 1982
SQ FT: 25,500
SALES (est): 10.05MM
SALES (corp-wide): 10.05MM **Privately Held**
Web: www.ontellus.com
SIC: 7334 Photocopying and duplicating services

(P-13317)

THE ALTERNATIVE COPY SHOP INC

3887 State St Ste 12, Santa Barbara (93105-3125)
PHONE..................................805 569-2116
EMP: 52
SIC: 7334 2759 Photocopying and duplicating services; Commercial printing, nec

---

7335 Commercial Photography

(P-13318)

BRANDED ENTRMT NETWRK INC (PA)

14724 Ventura Blvd Ste 1200, Sherman Oaks (91403-3512)
PHONE..................................310 342-1500
Richard R Butler, *Pr*
Gary Shenk, *CEO*
Joe Schick, *CFO*
Jim Mitchell, *Senior Vice President Corporate Development*
EMP: 233 **EST:** 1989
SALES (est): 16.35MM **Privately Held**
Web: www.bengroup.com
SIC: 7335 Photographic studio, commercial

(P-13319)

GETTY IMAGES INC

Also Called: Gettyone Image Bank
6300 Wilshire Blvd Ste 1600, Los Angeles (90048-5227)
PHONE..................................323 202-4200
Anne Marion, *Brnch Mgr*
EMP: 74
SALES (corp-wide): 916.55MM **Publicly Held**
Web: www.gettyimages.com
SIC: 7335 Photographic studio, commercial
HQ: Getty Images, Inc.
    605 5th Ave S Ste 400
    Seattle WA 98104
    206 925-5000

(P-13320)

ULTRAGRAPHICS INC

2800 N Naomi St, Burbank (91504-2023)
PHONE..................................818 295-3994
E Alexander Kilgo, *CEO*
Jon E Crossley, *
Nancy E Pasch Erlandsen, *
John T Crossley, *
EMP: 44 **EST:** 1980
SQ FT: 19,000
SALES (est): 1.66MM **Privately Held**
Web: www.ultragraphicsla.com
SIC: 7335 2752 Photographic studio, commercial; Offset printing

---

7336 Commercial Art And Graphic Design

(P-13321)

BLT & ASSOCIATES INC

Also Called: BLT
6430 W Sunset Blvd Ste 800, Los Angeles (90028-7911)
PHONE..................................323 860-4000
Clive Baillie, *Pr*
Rick Lynch, *
Dawn Baillie, *
EMP: 170 **EST:** 1992
SQ FT: 15,000
SALES (est): 8.34MM **Privately Held**
SIC: 7336 Graphic arts and related design

(P-13322)

CINNABAR

4571 Electronics Pl, Los Angeles (90039-1007)
PHONE..................................818 842-8190
Jonathan Katz, *Pr*
EMP: 200 **EST:** 1982
SQ FT: 60,000
SALES (est): 6.96MM **Privately Held**
Web: www.cinnabar.com
SIC: 7336 3999 7819 Graphic arts and related design; Theatrical scenery; Sound effects and music production, motion picture

(P-13323)

CONSOLIDATED DESIGN WEST INC

Also Called: Cdw
1345 S Lewis St, Anaheim (92805-6431)
PHONE..................................714 999-1476
Victor John Perrillo, *CEO*
▲ **EMP:** 50 **EST:** 1990
SQ FT: 7,500
SALES (est): 8.4MM **Privately Held**
Web: www.consolidateddesignwest.com
SIC: 7336 2754 Package design; Commercial printing, gravure

(P-13324)

CONTINENTAL GRAPHICS CORP (HQ)

Also Called: Continental Data Graphics
4060 N Lakewood Blvd Bldg 801, Long Beach (90808-1700)
PHONE..................................714 503-4200
David Malmo, *CEO*
Michael Parven, *
James Mills, *
EMP: 200 **EST:** 1986
SQ FT: 45,000
SALES (est): 14.9MM
SALES (corp-wide): 77.79B **Publicly Held**
Web: www.cdgnow.com
SIC: 7336 8741 8711 8999 Commercial art and graphic design; Management services; Engineering services; Technical writing
PA: The Boeing Company
    929 Long Bridge Dr
    703 465-3500

(P-13325)

COUNTY OF LOS ANGELES

Also Called: Gateway
1 Gateway Plz, Los Angeles (90012-3745)
P.O. Box 90012 (90009-0012)
PHONE..................................213 922-6210
Roger Snoball, *Owner*
EMP: 345
Web: www.lacounty.gov
SIC: 7336 9621 Commercial art and graphic design; Transportation department: government, nonoperating
PA: County Of Los Angeles
    500 W Temple St Ste 437
    213 974-1101

(P-13326)

DANDREA VSUAL CMMNCATIONS LLC

Also Called: D'Andrea Graphics
6100 Gateway Dr, Cypress (90630-4840)
PHONE..................................714 947-8444
David D'andrea, *Managing Member*
▲ **EMP:** 80 **EST:** 2005
SQ FT: 25,000
SALES (est): 2.46MM **Privately Held**
Web: www.dandreavisual.com
SIC: 7336 2782 Graphic arts and related design; Account books

(P-13327)

DESIGNORY INC (HQ)

Also Called: Designory
211 E Ocean Blvd Ste 100, Long Beach (90802-4850)
PHONE..................................562 624-0200
Paul Hosea, *CEO*
Janet M Thompson, *
Joel Fuller, *
Christine Ferguson, *
Matt Radigan, *
EMP: 115 **EST:** 1970
SALES (est): 23.06MM
SALES (corp-wide): 14.69B **Publicly Held**
Web: www.designory.com
SIC: 7336 Graphic arts and related design
PA: Omnicom Group Inc.
    280 Park Ave
    212 415-3600

(P-13328)

DIGITAL DOMAIN MEDIA GROUP INC

Also Called: Wyndcrest Dd Florida
12641 Beatrice St, Los Angeles (90066-7003)
EMP: 813
SIC: 7336 7812 7371 7372 Commercial art and graphic design; Non-theatrical motion picture production; Custom computer programming services; Business oriented computer software

(P-13329)

GRAPHIC INK CORP

Also Called: Graphic Ink and Graphic Ink
5382 Industrial Dr, Huntington Beach (92649-1517)
PHONE..................................714 901-2805
Vincent De La Torre, *Pr*
Jenny Lynn Quilico, *
EMP: 45 **EST:** 2005
SQ FT: 6,000
SALES (est): 5.97MM **Privately Held**
Web: www.graphicink.org
SIC: 7336 2262 Commercial art and graphic design; Finishing plants, manmade

(P-13330)

IDENTIGRAPHIX INC

19866 Quiroz Ct, Walnut (91789-2828)
PHONE..................................909 468-4741
A Fred Mendoza, *Pr*
EMP: 25 **EST:** 1982
SQ FT: 17,000
SALES (est): 2.96MM **Privately Held**
Web: www.identigraphix.com
SIC: 7336 2396 Silk screen design; Automotive and apparel trimmings

(P-13331)

MIRUM INC

Also Called: Digitaria
350 10th Ave Ste 1200, San Diego (92101-8702)
PHONE..................................619 237-5552
Daniel Khabie, *CEO*
Doug Hecht, *
Gary Correia, *
EMP: 200 **EST:** 1997
SQ FT: 4,000
SALES (est): 11.82MM
SALES (corp-wide): 18.5B **Privately Held**
SIC: 7336 Graphic arts and related design
HQ: Wunderman Thompson Llc
    175 Greenwich St Fl 16
    New York NY 10007
    212 210-7000

(P-13332)

MOTION THEORY INC

Also Called: Mirada
444 W Ocean Blvd Ste 1400, Long Beach (90802-4522)
PHONE..................................310 396-9433
Andrew Merkin, *Dir*
Matthew Cullen, *
Janell Perez, *
EMP: 110 **EST:** 2000
SQ FT: 25,000
SALES (est): 3.62MM **Privately Held**
Web: www.motiontheory.com
SIC: 7336 7371 7812 Graphic arts and related design; Computer software development and applications; Motion picture production

(P-13333)
MOTIVATIONAL SYSTEMS INC (PA)
2200 Cleveland Ave, National City (91950-6412)
PHONE.....................619 474-8246
Robert D Yound, *CEO*
David Cowan, *
Joe Jordan, *
Anthony Young, *
EMP: 100 EST: 1975
SQ FT: 50,000
SALES (est): 31.24MM
SALES (corp-wide): 31.24MM **Privately Held**
Web: www.motivational.com
SIC: 7336 3993 Graphic arts and related design; Signs and advertising specialties

(P-13334)
PULP STUDIO INCORPORATED
Also Called: CGB
2100 W 139th St, Gardena (90249-2412)
P.O. Box 16231 (90209-2231)
PHONE.....................310 815-4999
Bernard Lax, *CEO*
Lynda N Lax, *
▲ EMP: 60 EST: 1940
SQ FT: 36,000
SALES (est): 15.61MM **Privately Held**
Web: www.pulpstudio.com
SIC: 7336 3229 Commercial art and graphic design; Glass furnishings and accessories

(P-13335)
SESA INC (PA)
Also Called: Signco
20391 Via Guadalupe, Yorba Linda (92887-3133)
PHONE.....................714 779-9700
Elaine M Roach, *CEO*
EMP: 23 EST: 1986
SQ FT: 18,000
SALES (est): 2.15MM
SALES (corp-wide): 2.15MM **Privately Held**
SIC: 7336 2759 3993 2396 Silk screen design; Screen printing; Signs and advertising specialties; Automotive and apparel trimmings

(P-13336)
THINKBASIC INC
Also Called: Basic Agency
350 10th Ave, San Diego (92101-7496)
PHONE.....................858 755-6922
Matthew Faulk, *CEO*
Ashley Reichel, *
Alisa Kuno, *
EMP: 120 EST: 2011
SALES (est): 5.31MM **Privately Held**
Web: www.basicagency.com
SIC: 7336 Graphic arts and related design

(P-13337)
TWENTIETH CNTURY FOX JAPAN INC
Also Called: News Corp - Fox
10201 W Pico Blvd, Los Angeles (90064-2651)
PHONE.....................310 369-4636
Robert B Cohen, *CEO*
EMP: 4000 EST: 1981
SALES (est): 1.42MM
SALES (corp-wide): 91.36B **Publicly Held**
SIC: 7336 Film strip and slide producer
HQ: Tfcf Corporation
1211 Ave Of The Americas
New York NY 10036
212 852-7000

(P-13338)
XX ARTISTS LLC
1214 Abbot Kinney Blvd, Venice (90291-3366)
PHONE.....................503 871-5298
EMP: 70 EST: 2017
SALES (est): 2.69MM **Privately Held**
Web: www.xxartists.com
SIC: 7336 Graphic arts and related design

7338 Secretarial And Court Reporting

(P-13339)
ASAB INC (DH)
500 N Brand Blvd Fl 3, Glendale (91203-4725)
P.O. Box 29054 (91209-9054)
PHONE.....................818 551-7300
Alan Atkinson Baker, *CEO*
Sheila Atkinson-baker, *Pr*
EMP: 150 EST: 1987
SQ FT: 23,000
SALES (est): 2.48MM
SALES (corp-wide): 268.32MM **Privately Held**
Web: www.depo.com
SIC: 7338 Court reporting service
HQ: Veritext, Llc
290 W Mt Plsant Ave Ste 3
Livingston NJ 07039
973 410-4040

(P-13340)
INFOSEND INC (PA)
4240 E La Palma Ave, Anaheim (92807-1816)
PHONE.....................714 993-2690
Mahmood Rezai, *CEO*
Mahmood Rezai, *Pr*
Rusteen Rezai, *COO*
EMP: 49 EST: 1997
SALES (est): 132.63MM
SALES (corp-wide): 132.63MM **Privately Held**
Web: www.infosend.com
SIC: 7338 2732 2741 7389 Stenographic services; Pamphlets: printing only, not published on site; Business service newsletters: publishing and printing; Presorted mail service

(P-13341)
SOFTSCRIPT INC
2215 Campus Dr, El Segundo (90245-0001)
PHONE.....................310 451-2110
Howard Wisnicki, *CEO*
Yuriy Kotlyar, *
EMP: 1200 EST: 1996
SALES (est): 16.05MM **Privately Held**
Web: www.softscript.com
SIC: 7338 Court reporting service

7342 Disinfecting And Pest Control Services

(P-13342)
BANKS PEST CONTROL
7440 District Blvd Ste A, Bakersfield (93313-4821)
P.O. Box 113 (93302-0113)
PHONE.....................661 323-7858
Don Banks, *Pr*
Orland Banks, *
Janet Banks, *
EMP: 167 EST: 1969
SALES (est): 1.22MM

SALES (corp-wide): 3.07B **Publicly Held**
Web: www.bankspest.com
SIC: 7342 Pest control in structures
PA: Rollins, Inc.
2170 Piedmont Rd Ne
404 888-2000

(P-13343)
CARTWRIGHT TRMT PEST CTRL INC
1376 Broadway, El Cajon (92021-5812)
P.O. Box 2398 (92021-0398)
PHONE.....................619 442-9613
Michael Cartwright Ii, *CEO*
Michael Cartwright Senior, *VP*
Ben Cartwright, *
Willard Cartwright, *
EMP: 33 EST: 1962
SQ FT: 2,000
SALES (est): 3.23MM **Privately Held**
Web: www.cartwrightpest.com
SIC: 7342 2879 Exterminating and fumigating ; Insecticides and pesticides

(P-13344)
CATS USA INC
Also Called: Cats U S A Pest Control
5683 Whitnall Hwy, North Hollywood (91601-2213)
P.O. Box 151 (91603-0151)
PHONE.....................818 506-1000
Hirotaka Otomo, *Ch Bd*
EMP: 100 EST: 1971
SQ FT: 3,900
SALES (est): 6.75MM **Privately Held**
Web: www.catspestcontrol.com
SIC: 7342 Pest control in structures
HQ: Cats, Inc.
15-13, Nampeidaicho
Shibuya-Ku TKY 150-0

(P-13345)
CORKYS PEST CONTROL INC
Also Called: Pro Pacific Pest Control
150 Vallecitos De Oro, San Marcos (92069-1435)
PHONE.....................760 432-8801
Corky Mizer, *Pr*
▲ EMP: 60 EST: 1967
SALES (est): 9.35MM **Privately Held**
Web: www.corkyspest.com
SIC: 7342 0782 2879 5211 Pest control in structures; Lawn and garden services; Insecticides and pesticides; Insulation material, building
HQ: Anticimex Inc.
106 Allen Rd Ste 310
Basking Ridge NJ 07920
800 618-2847

(P-13346)
ECOSHELD PEST SLTONS PHNIX LLC
9037 Owensmouth Ave, Canoga Park (91304-1417)
PHONE.....................310 295-9511
EMP: 211
SALES (corp-wide): 9.84MM **Privately Held**
Web: www.ecoshieldpest.com
SIC: 7342 Pest control in structures
PA: Ecoshield Pest Solutions Phoenix, Llc
275 E Rvulon Blvd Ste 106
480 418-4634

(P-13347)
RENTOKIL NORTH AMERICA INC
1160 Sandhill Ave, Carson (90746-1315)

PHONE.....................714 517-9000
EMP: 100
SALES (corp-wide): 6.7B **Privately Held**
Web: www.westernexterminator.com
SIC: 7342 Pest control in structures
HQ: Rentokil North America, Inc.
1125 Berkshire Blvd # 15
Wyomissing PA 19610
470 643-3300

(P-13348)
RENTOKIL NORTH AMERICA INC
Also Called: Target Specialty Products
15415 Marquardt Ave, Santa Fe Springs (90670-5711)
P.O. Box 3408 (90670)
PHONE.....................562 802-2238
Rich Records, *Mgr*
EMP: 100
SALES (corp-wide): 6.7B **Privately Held**
Web: www.westernexterminator.com
SIC: 7342 Pest control in structures
HQ: Rentokil North America, Inc.
1125 Berkshire Blvd # 15
Wyomissing PA 19610
470 643-3300

(P-13349)
RENTOKIL NORTH AMERICA INC
311 N Crescent Way, Anaheim (92801-6709)
PHONE.....................714 563-2450
Julius C Ehrlich, *Brnch Mgr*
EMP: 77
SALES (corp-wide): 6.7B **Privately Held**
Web: www.bugoutservice.com
SIC: 7342 Pest control in structures
HQ: Rentokil North America, Inc.
1125 Berkshire Blvd # 15
Wyomissing PA 19610
470 643-3300

(P-13350)
YOUR WAY FUMIGATION INC
3921 E La Palma Ave Ste N, Anaheim (92807-1718)
PHONE.....................951 699-9116
Jose Manuel Aguilar, *Pr*
EMP: 90 EST: 2006
SALES (est): 4.23MM **Privately Held**
Web: www.ywfumigation.com
SIC: 7342 Pest control in structures

7349 Building Maintenance Services, Nec

(P-13351)
911 RESTORATION ENTPS INC
6932 Gross Ave, West Hills (91307-2432)
PHONE.....................832 887-2582
Ofer Kedem, *Brnch Mgr*
EMP: 202
SALES (corp-wide): 7.96MM **Privately Held**
Web: www.911restorationlosangeles.com
SIC: 7349 Building maintenance services, nec
PA: 911 Restoration Enterprises, Inc.
7721 Densmore Ave
818 373-4880

(P-13352)
ADVANCED CLNROOM MCRCLEAN CORP
Also Called: A C M
3250 S Susan St Ste A, Santa Ana (92704-6807)

▲ = Import ▼ = Export
◆ = Import/Export

PHONE..................714 751-1152
Janet Ford, *CEO*
▲ **EMP:** 200 **EST:** 1982
SQ FT: 3,500
SALES (est): 9.71MM **Privately Held**
Web: www.advancedcleanroom.com
SIC: 7349 8734 Cleaning service, industrial or commercial; Testing laboratories

(P-13353)
ALL-RITE LEASING COMPANY INC
950 S Coast Dr Ste 110, Costa Mesa (92626-1778)
PHONE..................714 957-1822
Chris Schran, *Pr*
Pauline Rosenberg, *
EMP: 269 **EST:** 1991
SALES (est): 2.44MM **Privately Held**
SIC: 7349 Building maintenance services, nec

(P-13354)
AMERI-KLEEN
Also Called: Ameri-Kleen Building Services
1023 E Grand Ave, Arroyo Grande (93420-2504)
PHONE..................805 546-0706
Dan Erpenbach, *Brnch Mgr*
EMP: 220
Web: www.ameri-kleen.com
SIC: 7349 Janitorial service, contract basis
PA: Ameri-Kleen
35 Winham St

(P-13355)
ARAMARK FACILITY SERVICES LLC
Also Called: Aramark
941 W 35th St, Los Angeles (90007-4002)
PHONE..................213 740-8968
Ron Cote, *Mgr*
EMP: 113
Web: www.aramark.es
SIC: 7349 Janitorial service, contract basis
HQ: Aramark Facility Services, Llc
2400 Market St Ste 209
Philadelphia PA 19103
215 238-3000

(P-13356)
ARAYA CONSTRUCTION INC
Also Called: SERVPRO
2870 S Santa Fe Ave, San Marcos (92069-6046)
P.O. Box 730 (92085-0730)
PHONE..................760 758-3454
Juan Araya, *Pr*
Jose Araya, *
EMP: 82 **EST:** 2003
SALES (est): 14.74MM **Privately Held**
Web:
www.servpronesandiegocounty.com
SIC: 7349 7699 Building maintenance services, nec; Miscellaneous building item repair services

(P-13357)
AVALON BUILDING MAINT INC
1832 Commercenter Cir, San Bernardino (92408-3430)
PHONE..................714 693-2407
Steve J Healis, *CEO*
Tom Devlin, *
Tom Poston, *
EMP: 400 **EST:** 1988
SQ FT: 5,000
SALES (est): 2.76MM **Privately Held**
Web:
www.avalonbuildingmaintenance-ie.com

SIC: 7349 Janitorial service, contract basis

(P-13358)
BERGENSONS PROPERTY SVCS INC
Also Called: Solve All Facility Services
3605 Ocean Ranch Blvd Ste 200, Oceanside (92056-2696)
PHONE..................760 631-5111
Mark M Minasian, *CEO*
Aram Minasian, *
EMP: 2000 **EST:** 1984
SQ FT: 2,000
SALES (est): 24.05MM **Privately Held**
Web: www.kbs-services.com
SIC: 7349 Building maintenance, except repairs

(P-13359)
BRITEWORKS INC
Also Called: Briteworks
620 N Commercial Ave, Covina (91723-1309)
PHONE..................626 337-0099
Anita Ron, *Pr*
EMP: 75 **EST:** 2001
SQ FT: 4,800
SALES (est): 4.9MM **Privately Held**
Web: www.briteworks.com
SIC: 7349 Janitorial service, contract basis

(P-13360)
BZYA CORPORATION
3790 Keri Way, Fallbrook (92028-8139)
PHONE..................949 656-3220
Susan Luo, *CEO*
EMP: 325 **EST:** 2017
SALES (est): 443.7K **Privately Held**
SIC: 7349 Janitorial service, contract basis

(P-13361)
C&W FACILITY SERVICES INC
Also Called: Dtz
3011 Townsgate Rd Ste 410, Westlake Village (91361-5882)
PHONE..................805 267-7123
EMP: 1970
SALES (corp-wide): 9.49B **Privately Held**
Web: www.cwservices.com
SIC: 7349 Janitorial service, contract basis
HQ: C&W Facility Services Inc.
140 Kendrick St Ste C120
Needham MA 02494
888 751-9100

(P-13362)
CALICO BUILDING SERVICES INC
Also Called: Calico
15550 Rockfield Blvd Ste C, Irvine (92618-2791)
PHONE..................949 380-8707
Ron Strand, *Pr*
Christopher Guidry, *
Thomas Miquelon, *
Orlando Fernandez, *
EMP: 185 **EST:** 1986
SQ FT: 1,700
SALES (est): 18.18MM **Privately Held**
Web: www.calicoweb.com
SIC: 7349 Janitorial service, contract basis

(P-13363)
CERTIFIED WTR DMAGE RSTRTION E
Also Called: Cwdre
5319 University Dr, Irvine (92612-2965)
PHONE..................800 417-1776
Cyrus Fatoure, *Pr*

EMP: 48 **EST:** 2016
SALES (est): 1.25MM **Privately Held**
SIC: 7349 1389 6331 1521 Building maintenance services, nec; Construction, repair, and dismantling services; Property damage insurance; Repairing fire damage, single-family houses

(P-13364)
COASTAL BUILDING SERVICES INC
1433 W Central Park Ave N, Anaheim (92802-1417)
PHONE..................714 775-2855
Hipolito G Arias, *CEO*
Brett Dunstan, *
EMP: 300 **EST:** 1998
SALES (est): 3.7MM **Privately Held**
Web: www.cbsinc.us
SIC: 7349 Janitorial service, contract basis

(P-13365)
COME LAND MAINT SVC CO INC
1419 N San Fernando Blvd Ste 250, Burbank (91504-4185)
PHONE..................818 567-2455
Grace H Lee, *Pr*
William Lee, *
EMP: 513 **EST:** 1992
SQ FT: 12,750
SALES (est): 1.71MM **Privately Held**
SIC: 7349 Janitorial service, contract basis
PA: Come Land, Inc.
1419 N San Fernando Blvd # 250

(P-13366)
CONTRACT SERVICES GROUP INC
Also Called: Celex Solutions
480 Capricorn St, Brea (92821-3203)
P.O. Box 8815 (92822-5815)
PHONE..................714 582-1800
John Pearce, *CEO*
Casey Pearce, *
EMP: 250 **EST:** 2003
SALES (est): 24.57MM **Privately Held**
Web: www.csgcares.com
SIC: 7349 Janitorial service, contract basis

(P-13367)
CREATIVE MAINTENANCE SYSTEMS
1340 Reynolds Ave Ste 111, Irvine (92614-5503)
PHONE..................949 852-2871
Bill Koop, *Pr*
Christina Alexander, *
EMP: 100 **EST:** 2000
SQ FT: 2,000
SALES (est): 815.71K **Privately Held**
SIC: 7349 Janitorial service, contract basis

(P-13368)
CROWN BUILDING MAINTENANCE CO
Also Called: Able Building Maintenance
14201 Franklin Ave, Tustin (92780-7008)
PHONE..................714 434-9494
Robert Hughes, *CEO*
EMP: 448
SALES (corp-wide): 8.1B **Publicly Held**
SIC: 7349 Janitorial service, contract basis
HQ: Crown Building Maintenance Co.
600 Harrison St Ste 600 # 600
San Francisco CA 94107
415 981-8070

(P-13369)
CROWN BUILDING MAINTENANCE CO
5482 Complex St Ste 108, San Diego (92123-1125)
PHONE..................858 560-5785
EMP: 269
SALES (corp-wide): 8.1B **Publicly Held**
SIC: 7349 8711 Janitorial service, contract basis; Engineering services
HQ: Crown Building Maintenance Co.
600 Harrison St Ste 600 # 600
San Francisco CA 94107
415 981-8070

(P-13370)
CROWN ENERGY SERVICES INC
Also Called: Able Engineering Services
2601 S Figueroa St Bldg 1, Los Angeles (90007)
PHONE..................213 765-7800
EMP: 997
SALES (corp-wide): 8.1B **Publicly Held**
SIC: 7349 Janitorial service, contract basis
HQ: Crown Energy Services, Inc.
600 Harrison St Ste 600 # 600
San Francisco CA 94107

(P-13371)
DIAMOND CONTRACT SERVICES INC
11432 Vanowen St, North Hollywood (91605-6220)
PHONE..................818 565-3554
EMP: 350
Web: www.diamondcontract.com
SIC: 7349 8748 Building maintenance, except repairs; Business consulting, nec

(P-13372)
DMS FACILITY SERVICES INC
Also Called: DMS
2861 E Coronado St, Anaheim (92806-2504)
PHONE..................949 975-1366
Douglas Gregory, *Prin*
EMP: 984
SALES (corp-wide): 24.46MM **Privately Held**
Web: www.dmsfacilityservices.com
SIC: 7349 Janitorial service, contract basis
PA: Dms Facility Services, Inc.
1040 Arroyo Dr
626 305-8500

(P-13373)
ELITE CRAFTSMAN (PA)
Also Called: Stockmar Industrial
2763 Saint Louis Ave, Long Beach (90755-2025)
P.O. Box 90458 (90809-0458)
PHONE..................562 989-3511
William C Stockmar, *Pr*
Linda Pierson, *Sec*
George N Negrete, *VP*
EMP: 130 **EST:** 1972
SQ FT: 10,000
SALES (est): 6.3MM
SALES (corp-wide): 6.3MM **Privately Held**
SIC: 7349 Janitorial service, contract basis

(P-13374)
FLAGSHIP AIRPORT SERVICES INC
1830 W 208th St, Torrance (90501-1807)
PHONE..................310 328-8221
EMP: 71
Web: www.flagshipinc.com

SIC: 7349 Janitorial service, contract basis

P R O D U C T S & S V C S

SIC: 7349 Janitorial service, contract basis
HQ: Flagship Airport Services, Inc.
   1050 N 5th St Ste E
   San Jose CA 95112
   408 977-0155

(P-13375)
GMI BUILDING SERVICES INC
8001 Vickers St, San Diego (92111-1917)
PHONE.............................858 279-6262
Larry Abrams, *Pr*
EMP: 225 EST: 1966
SQ FT: 15,000
SALES (est): 4.05MM **Privately Held**
SIC: 7349 5087 Janitorial service, contract basis; Janitors' supplies

(P-13376)
HAYNES BUILDING SERVICE LLC
16027 Arrow Hwy Ste I, Baldwin Park (91706-2064)
PHONE.............................626 359-6100
TOLL FREE: 800
John P Scharler, *Pr*
Michael Franco, *
EMP: 175 EST: 1982
SQ FT: 20,000
SALES (est): 2.39MM **Privately Held**
Web: www.haynesservices.com
SIC: 7349 Janitorial service, contract basis

(P-13377)
HUNTER EASTERDAY CORPORATION
Also Called: Easterday Building Maintenance
1475 N Hundley St, Anaheim (92806-1323)
PHONE.............................714 238-3400
Sam Easterday, *CEO*
Manny Jones, *
Gilbert Anzaldua, *
Joanne Easterday, *
EMP: 135 EST: 1976
SQ FT: 4,400
SALES (est): 5.3MM **Privately Held**
Web: www.ebmcorp.com
SIC: 7349 5087 Janitorial service, contract basis; Janitors' supplies

(P-13378)
INDUSTRIAL JANITOR SERVICE
Also Called: I J S
221 N San Dimas Ave Ste 217, San Dimas (91773-2664)
PHONE.............................818 782-5658
Darla Drendel, *CEO*
Darla Artura, *
EMP: 100 EST: 1965
SQ FT: 7,500
SALES (est): 1.15MM **Privately Held**
Web: www.ijsclean.com
SIC: 7349 Janitorial service, contract basis

(P-13379)
INNOVATIONS BUILDING SVCS LLC
402 S Orange Ave Apt D, Monterey Park (91755-7554)
PHONE.............................323 787-6068
Helbert Daniel Torres, *Prin*
EMP: 100 EST: 2016
SALES (est): 872.51K **Privately Held**
Web: www.innovationsbuildingservices.com
SIC: 7349 Janitorial service, contract basis

(P-13380)
INNOVATIVE CLEANING SVCS INC

44 Waterworks Way, Irvine (92618-3107)
PHONE.............................949 251-9188
Jennifer Corbett-shramo, *CEO*
John Gambino, *
Jaime Aburto, *
EMP: 500 EST: 2000
SALES (est): 3.66MM **Privately Held**
Web: www.ics-oc.com
SIC: 7349 Cleaning service, industrial or commercial

(P-13381)
K & P JANITORIAL SERVICES
412 S Pacific Coast Hwy Ste 200, Redondo Beach (90277-3712)
PHONE.............................310 540-8878
Kelly Lynch, *Pr*
EMP: 100 EST: 1991
SALES (est): 3.33MM **Privately Held**
Web: www.kandpjanitorial.com
SIC: 7349 Janitorial service, contract basis

(P-13382)
KBM FCLITY SLTONS HOLDINGS LLC
Also Called: Kbm Building Services
7976 Engineer Rd Ste 200, San Diego (92111-1935)
PHONE.............................858 467-0202
Brian Snow, *CEO*
Rene Tuthscher, *
Susan Cologna, *
Shaun Gordon, *
Robert Kennedy Iii, *Dir*
EMP: 500 EST: 1981
SQ FT: 10,000
SALES (est): 20.93MM
SALES (corp-wide): 22.58MM **Privately Held**
Web: www.kbmfs.com
SIC: 7349 Janitorial service, contract basis
PA: Pristine Environments Inc
   3605 Ocean Ranch Blvd # 200
   703 245-4751

(P-13383)
KIMCO FACILITY SERVICES LLC
Also Called: Kimco Services
3605 Ocean Ranch Blvd, Oceanside (92056-2695)
PHONE.............................404 487-1165
Sandeep Gupta, *CEO*
EMP: 3517 EST: 2014
SALES (est): 36.9MM
SALES (corp-wide): 620.83MM **Privately Held**
Web: www.kimcoserv.com
SIC: 7349 Janitorial service, contract basis
PA: Kellermeyer Bergensons Services, Llc
   3605 Ocean Rnch Blvd Ste
   760 631-5111

(P-13384)
LCS JANITORIAL SERVICES LLC
311 F St Ste 207, Chula Vista (91910-2640)
PHONE.............................619 488-7434
Joel Leal, *Pr*
Joel Leal, *Managing Member*
EMP: 159 EST: 2010
SALES (est): 2.82MM **Privately Held**
Web: www.lcsjanitorialservices.com
SIC: 7349 7699 7363 8744 Janitorial service, contract basis; Cleaning services; Temporary help service; Facilities support services

(P-13385)
LEES MAINTENANCE SERVICE INC
14740 Keswick St, Van Nuys (91405-1205)

PHONE.............................818 988-6644
Tyrone P Ingram, *Pr*
EMP: 275 EST: 1961
SQ FT: 3,000
SALES (est): 2.79MM **Privately Held**
Web: www.leesmaint.com
SIC: 7349 5087 Janitorial service, contract basis; Laundry and dry cleaning equipment and supplies

(P-13386)
LIFE CYCLE ENGINEERING INC
7510 Airway Rd Ste 2, San Diego (92154-8303)
PHONE.............................619 785-5990
John Spencer, *Mgr*
EMP: 186
SALES (corp-wide): 48.21MM **Privately Held**
Web: www.lce.com
SIC: 7349 Building maintenance, except repairs
PA: Life Cycle Engineering, Inc.
   4360 Corporate Rd Ste 100
   843 744-7110

(P-13387)
LOS ANGELES UNIFIED SCHOOL DST
Also Called: Central Shop
1240 Naomi Ave, Los Angeles (90021-2393)
PHONE.............................213 763-2900
Herman Perez, *Dir*
EMP: 98
SALES (corp-wide): 1.07MM **Privately Held**
Web: www.laallcityband.com
SIC: 7349 8211 Building maintenance services, nec; Public elementary and secondary schools
PA: Los Angeles Unified School District
   333 S Beaudry Ave
   213 241-1000

(P-13388)
M-N-Z JANITORIAL SERVICES INC
2109 W Burbank Blvd, Burbank (91506-1231)
PHONE.............................323 851-4115
Marc De Mauregne, *Ex VP*
Zorina Russell Kroop, *
Dennis Krebs, *Stockholder**
EMP: 110 EST: 1979
SQ FT: 1,000
SALES (est): 1.2MM **Privately Held**
Web: www.mnz.com
SIC: 7349 1799 Building maintenance, except repairs; Construction site cleanup

(P-13389)
MC-40 (PA)
Also Called: Mintie Technologies
777 N Georgia Ave, Azusa (91702-2207)
PHONE.............................323 225-4111
Kevin J Mintie, *CEO*
James M Mintie, *
EMP: 73 EST: 1940
SALES (est): 9.86MM
SALES (corp-wide): 9.86MM **Privately Held**
Web: www.alliance-enviro.com
SIC: 7349 Building cleaning service

(P-13390)
MERCHANTS BUILDING MAINT CO
Also Called: Merchants Building Maintenance

1639 E Edinger Ave Ste C, Santa Ana (92705-5013)
PHONE.............................714 973-9272
George Rodriguez, *Brnch Mgr*
EMP: 413
SALES (corp-wide): 54.62MM **Privately Held**
Web: www.mbmonline.com
SIC: 7349 Janitorial service, contract basis
PA: Merchants Building Maintenance Company
   1190 Monterey Pass Rd
   323 881-6701

(P-13391)
MERCHANTS BUILDING MAINT CO
Also Called: Merchants Building Maintenance
1995 W Holt Ave, Pomona (91768-3352)
PHONE.............................909 622-8260
Angel Meza, *Brnch Mgr*
EMP: 743
SALES (corp-wide): 54.62MM **Privately Held**
Web: www.mbmonline.com
SIC: 7349 7381 Janitorial service, contract basis; Security guard service
PA: Merchants Building Maintenance Company
   1190 Monterey Pass Rd
   323 881-6701

(P-13392)
MERCHANTS BUILDING MAINT CO
606 Monterey Pass Rd Ste 202, Monterey Park (91754-2419)
PHONE.............................323 881-8902
Michael Anthony Palma, *Bd of Dir*
EMP: 130
SALES (corp-wide): 54.62MM **Privately Held**
Web: www.mbmonline.com
SIC: 7349 7381 Janitorial service, contract basis; Detective and armored car services
PA: Merchants Building Maintenance Company
   1190 Monterey Pass Rd
   323 881-6701

(P-13393)
MERCHANTS BUILDING MAINT CO
9555 Distribution Ave Ste 102, San Diego (92121-2373)
PHONE.............................858 455-0163
Eric Ruiz, *Mgr*
EMP: 371
SALES (corp-wide): 54.62MM **Privately Held**
Web: www.mbmonline.com
SIC: 7349 Janitorial service, contract basis
PA: Merchants Building Maintenance Company
   1190 Monterey Pass Rd
   323 881-6701

(P-13394)
MIDA INDUSTRIES INC
6101 Obispo Ave, Long Beach (90805-3799)
PHONE.............................562 616-1020
Michael T Drake, *Pr*
John Valencia, *
Dawit Kidane, *
EMP: 250 EST: 1989
SQ FT: 10,000
SALES (est): 4.3MM **Privately Held**
Web: www.midaindustries.com

SIC: 7349 1799 Janitorial service, contract basis; Asbestos removal and encapsulation

(P-13395)
MONTEBELLO UNIFIED SCHOOL DST
Also Called: Maintenance & Operation Dept
500 Hendricks St 2nd Fl, Montebello (90640-1566)
PHONE..............................323 887-2140
Virgil Downs, *Prin*
EMP: 90
SALES (corp-wide): 549.74MM Privately Held
Web: www.montebello.k12.ca.us
SIC: 7349 Building maintenance services, nec
PA: Montebello Unified School District
123 S Montebello Blvd
323 887-7900

(P-13396)
NMS MANAGEMENT INC
155 W 35th St Ste A, National City (91950-7922)
PHONE..............................619 425-0440
David Guaderrama, *Pr*
Sophia Guaderrama, *
EMP: 75 EST: 1985
SQ FT: 8,300
SALES (est): 4.48MM Privately Held
Web: www.nms-management.com
SIC: 7349 0781 Building maintenance, except repairs; Landscape services

(P-13397)
ONE SILVER SERVE LLC
Also Called: SERVPRO Encino/Sherman Oaks
16601 Ventura Blvd Fl 4, Encino (91436-1921)
PHONE..............................818 995-6444
Alan Reed, *CEO*
EMP: 80 EST: 2005
SALES (est): 3.46MM Privately Held
Web: www.servproencinoshermanoaks.com
SIC: 7349 Building maintenance services, nec

(P-13398)
OPEN AMERICA INC
Also Called: Openworks
4300 Long Beach Blvd Ste 450, Long Beach (90807-2016)
PHONE..............................562 428-9210
John Palmer, *Brnch Mgr*
EMP: 166
SALES (corp-wide): 18.59MM Privately Held
Web: www.openworksweb.com
SIC: 7349 Janitorial service, contract basis
PA: O.P.E.N. America, Inc.
2355 E Cmlback Rd Ste 600
602 224-0440

(P-13399)
PACIFIC BUILDING CARE INC (HQ)
3001 Red Hill Ave Bldg 6, Costa Mesa (92626-4529)
PHONE..............................949 261-1234
Ian Bress, *CEO*
Ted Geissler, *Pr*
Jennifer Corbett, *VP*
Robin Geissler, *Sec*
Holly Papa, *Treas*
EMP: 117 EST: 1970
SQ FT: 5,200
SALES (est): 3.49MM

SALES (corp-wide): 241MM Privately Held
Web: www.ocde.us
SIC: 7349 Building cleaning service
PA: Commercial Cleaning Systems, Inc.
990 S Broadway Ste 200
303 733-8997

(P-13400)
PARAGON SVCS JNTR ORNGE CNTY L
1111 6th Ave Ste 316, San Diego (92101-5209)
PHONE..............................858 654-0150
Carmen Acosta, *Mgr*
EMP: 100 EST: 2016
SALES (est): 378.92K Privately Held
Web: paragonservices.us.com
SIC: 7349 Janitorial service, contract basis

(P-13401)
PE FACILITY SOLUTIONS LLC (PA)
4217 Ponderosa Ave Ste A, San Diego (92123-1536)
PHONE..............................858 467-0202
Shaun Gordon, *CEO*
EMP: 95 EST: 2017
SQ FT: 18,000
SALES (est): 2.09MM
SALES (corp-wide): 2.09MM Privately Held
SIC: 7349 Janitorial service, contract basis

(P-13402)
PEERLESS MAINTENANCE SVC INC
1100 S Euclid St, La Habra (90631-6807)
P.O. Box 3900 (90632-3900)
PHONE..............................714 871-3380
Linda Gabriel, *Pr*
David Gabriel, *
EMP: 300 EST: 1979
SQ FT: 2,000
SALES (est): 10.13MM Privately Held
Web: www.peerlesssvc.com
SIC: 7349 Janitorial service, contract basis

(P-13403)
PEGASUS BUILDING SVCS CO INC
7966 Arjons Dr Ste A, San Diego (92126-6361)
PHONE..............................858 444-2290
Judith Becker, *Pr*
Mark Tarin, *VP Opers*
Barry Becker, *Dir*
EMP: 350 EST: 1983
SQ FT: 12,800
SALES (est): 24.33MM Privately Held
Web: www.pegasusclean.com
SIC: 7349 Janitorial service, contract basis

(P-13404)
PERFORMANCE BUILDING SERVICES
Also Called: Performance Cleanroom Services
22642 Lambert St Ste 409, Lake Forest (92630-1645)
PHONE..............................949 364-4364
James Chriss, *Pr*
Ron Matthews, *
Robert Lynch, *
EMP: 104 EST: 2001
SALES (est): 4.76MM Privately Held
Web: www.performance-now.com
SIC: 7349 7699 Janitorial service, contract basis; Cleaning services

(P-13405)
PLATINUM CLG INDIANAPOLIS LLC
1522 2nd St, Santa Monica (90401-2303)
PHONE..............................310 584-8000
EMP: 460 EST: 2008
SALES (est): 1.74MM Privately Held
SIC: 7349 Building and office cleaning services

(P-13406)
PRIORITY BUILDING SERVICES LLC (PA)
Also Called: Priority Landscape Services
1524 W Mable St, Anaheim (92802-1022)
PHONE..............................714 255-2963
Simon Rocha, *Pr*
EMP: 71 EST: 2004
SQ FT: 6,000
SALES (est): 9.43MM Privately Held
Web: www.priorityservices.net
SIC: 7349 Janitorial service, contract basis

(P-13407)
PRIORITY BUILDING SERVICES LLC
7313 Carroll Rd Ste G, San Diego (92121-2319)
PHONE..............................858 695-1326
Simon Rocha, *Brnch Mgr*
EMP: 304
Web: www.priorityservices.net
SIC: 7349 Janitorial service, contract basis
PA: Priority Building Services Llc
1524 W Mable St

(P-13408)
PRO BUILDING MAINTENANCE INC (PA)
149 N Maple St Ste H, Corona (92878-3273)
PHONE..............................951 279-3386
Carl Hoff, *CEO*
Christina L Hoff, *Prin*
EMP: 120 EST: 2006
SQ FT: 1,600
SALES (est): 1.73MM Privately Held
Web: www.probuildingmaintenance.com
SIC: 7349 Janitorial service, contract basis

(P-13409)
PROFESSIONAL MAINT SYSTEMS INC
Also Called: Professional Maint Systems
4912 Naples St, San Diego (92110-3820)
P.O. Box 80038 (92138-0038)
PHONE..............................619 276-1150
Karen Berry, *CEO*
EMP: 925 EST: 1983
SQ FT: 9,000
SALES (est): 21.97MM Privately Held
Web: www.pmsjanitorial.com
SIC: 7349 Janitorial service, contract basis

(P-13410)
PRONTO JANITORIAL SVCS INC
12561 Persing Dr, Whittier (90606-2713)
PHONE..............................562 273-5997
Edgar Rodas, *Pr*
EMP: 80 EST: 2019
SALES (est): 610.23K Privately Held
Web: www.prontojsi.com
SIC: 7349 Janitorial service, contract basis

(P-13411)
PROPERTY CARE BUILDING SVC LLC
126 La Porte St Ste F, Arcadia (91006-7190)

P.O. Box 661690 (91066-1690)
PHONE..............................626 623-6420
Everardo Amezcua, *
Victoria Amezcua, *VP*
EMP: 26 EST: 2013
SALES (est): 4.84MM Privately Held
Web: www.propertycarebuildingservice.com
SIC: 7349 2842 7342 Janitorial service, contract basis; Sanitation preparations, disinfectants and deodorants; Disinfecting services

(P-13412)
PROTEC ASSOCIATION SERVICES (PA)
Also Called: Protec Building Services
10180 Willow Creek Rd, San Diego (92131-1636)
PHONE..............................858 569-1080
J David Rauch, *Pr*
Russ Piccoli, *Stockholder**
Scot Clark, *Stockholder**
Libbey Rauch, *Stockholder**
George Vanoofbree, *Stockholder**
EMP: 140 EST: 1996
SQ FT: 12,500
SALES (est): 39.14MM Privately Held
Web: www.protec.com
SIC: 7349 Building maintenance services, nec

(P-13413)
RESOURCE COLLECTION INC
Also Called: Command Guard Services
3771 W 242nd St Ste 205, Torrance (90505-6566)
PHONE..............................310 219-3272
Martin Benom, *Ch Bd*
Paula Benom, *
Marilyn Jacobson, *
Steven Jacobson, *
EMP: 29 EST: 1962
SQ FT: 15,000
SALES (est): 703.29K Privately Held
Web: www.resourcecollection.com
SIC: 7349 7381 0782 3564 Air duct cleaning; Guard services; Lawn and garden services; Air cleaning systems

(P-13414)
RHINO BUILDING SERVICES INC
6650 Flanders Dr Ste K, San Diego (92121-3908)
PHONE..............................858 455-1440
Cody Sears, *Pr*
EMP: 120 EST: 1985
SQ FT: 110
SALES (est): 2.37MM Privately Held
Web: www.rhinoinc.com
SIC: 7349 Janitorial service, contract basis

(P-13415)
SBRM INC (PA)
Also Called: Servicmster Cmplete Rstoration
2342 Meyers Ave, Escondido (92029-1008)
PHONE..............................760 480-0208
TOLL FREE: 800
Barbara Robert, *Pr*
Mike Gamez, *
EMP: 70 EST: 1986
SQ FT: 20,000
SALES (est): 3.85MM Privately Held
Web: www.servicemaster.com
SIC: 7349 1521 Building maintenance services, nec; Repairing fire damage, single-family houses

P R O D U C T S & S V C S

(P-13416)
SCV FACILITIES SERVICES INC
1907 W 75th St, Los Angeles (90047-2325)
PHONE................................310 803-4588
Samuel Valdez, *Owner*
EMP: 72 **EST:** 2013
SALES (est): 3.64MM **Privately Held**
Web: www.scvfs.com
SIC: 7349 7389 Janitorial service, contract
basis; Business Activities at Non-
Commercial Site

(P-13417)
SERVI-TEK INC
Also Called: Servi-Tek Janitorial Services
8765 Sparren Way, San Diego
(92129-4437)
PHONE................................858 638-7735
Kurt G Lester, *
Eric S Friz, *
EMP: 300 **EST:** 2006
SALES (est): 14.26MM **Privately Held**
Web: www.servi-tek.net
SIC: 7349 Janitorial service, contract basis

(P-13418)
SERVICEMASTER BY BEST PROS INC
6474 Western Ave, Riverside (92505-2130)
PHONE................................951 515-9051
Filip Busuioc, *CEO*
EMP: 99 **EST:** 2018
SALES (est): 745.86K **Privately Held**
Web: www.servicemaster.com
SIC: 7349 1799 Building maintenance
services, nec; Construction site cleanup

(P-13419)
SERVICON SYSTEMS INC
3329 Jack Northrop Ave, Hawthorne
(90250-4426)
PHONE................................310 970-0700
Julio E Ramirez, *Brnch Mgr*
EMP: 1472
SALES (corp-wide): 58.77MM **Privately Held**
Web: www.servicon.com
SIC: 7349 Janitorial service, contract basis
PA: Servicon Systems, Inc.
3965 Landmark St
310 204-5040

(P-13420)
SITE CREW INC
3185 Airway Ave Ste G, Costa Mesa
(92626-4601)
PHONE................................714 668-0100
Tina Manavi, *CEO*
EMP: 300 **EST:** 2005
SQ FT: 2,160
SALES (est): 8.3MM **Privately Held**
Web: www.sitecrewinc.com
SIC: 7349 Janitorial service, contract basis

(P-13421)
SO CAL LAND MAINTENANCE INC
3121 E La Palma Ave Ste K, Anaheim
(92806-2804)
PHONE................................714 231-1454
Stephen Guise, *Prin*
EMP: 72 **EST:** 2011
SALES (est): 4.18MM **Privately Held**
SIC: 7349 Building maintenance services,
nec

(P-13422)
SOUTHERN MANAGEMENT CORP

---

808 S Olive St, Los Angeles (90014-3006)
PHONE................................213 312-2268
EMP: 105
SALES (corp-wide): 8.1B **Publicly Held**
SIC: 7349 Building maintenance services,
nec
HQ: Southern Management Corp.
6478e Highway 90
Milton FL 32570

(P-13423)
TRIANGLE SERVICES INC
11065 Penrose St, Sun Valley
(91352-2722)
PHONE................................818 350-7802
EMP: 127
Web: www.triangleservices.com
SIC: 7349 Janitorial service, contract basis
PA: Triangle Services, Inc.
10 5th St Fl 2

(P-13424)
TUTTLE FAMILY ENTERPRISES INC
Also Called: Peerless Building Maint Co
9510 Topanga Canyon Blvd, Chatsworth
(91311-4011)
PHONE................................818 534-2566
Tim Tuttle, *CEO*
EMP: 350 **EST:** 1948
SALES (est): 5.68MM **Privately Held**
SIC: 7349 Building maintenance, except
repairs

(P-13425)
UNISERVE FACILITIES SVCS CORP
1200 Getty Center Dr, Los Angeles
(90049-1678)
PHONE................................310 440-6747
F Jackson, *Operations Staff*
EMP: 325
SALES (corp-wide): 16.38MM **Privately Held**
Web: www.uniservecorp.com
SIC: 7349 Janitorial service, contract basis
PA: Uniserve Facilities Services
Corporation
2363 S Atlantic Blvd
213 533-1000

(P-13426)
UNISERVE FACILITIES SVCS CORP (PA)
Also Called: Union Building Maintenance
2363 S Atlantic Blvd, Commerce
(90040-1256)
PHONE................................213 533-1000
Sam M Hwang, *Ch Bd*
EMP: 500 **EST:** 1966
SQ FT: 5,000
SALES (est): 16.38MM
SALES (corp-wide): 16.38MM **Privately Held**
Web: www.uniservecorp.com
SIC: 7349 Janitorial service, contract basis

(P-13427)
UNIVERSAL SERVICES AMERICA LP
1815 E Wilshire Ave Ste 912, Santa Ana
(92705-4646)
PHONE................................714 923-3700
Mark Olivas, *Brnch Mgr*
EMP: 4347
SALES (corp-wide): 12.86B **Privately Held**
Web: www.aus.com
SIC: 7349 Janitorial service, contract basis
HQ: Universal Services Of America, Lp
450 Exchange

Irvine CA 92602
866 877-1965

(P-13428)
VARSITY CONTRACTORS INC
24155 Laguna Hills Mall, Laguna Hills
(92653-3667)
PHONE................................949 586-8283
EMP: 123
SALES (corp-wide): 620.83MM **Privately Held**
Web: www.kbs-services.com
SIC: 7349 Janitorial service, contract basis
HQ: Varsity Contractors, Inc.
1055 S 3600 W Ste 101
Salt Lake City UT 84104
208 232-8598

(P-13429)
WURMS JANITORIAL SERVICE INC
601 S Milliken Ave, Ontario (91761-7898)
PHONE................................951 582-0003
Larry Stewart, *Pr*
Pam Costa, *
EMP: 80 **EST:** 1986
SALES (est): 2.49MM **Privately Held**
Web: www.ultrashine.com
SIC: 7349 Janitorial service, contract basis

7352 Medical Equipment Rental

(P-13430)
DIGIRAD IMAGING SOLUTIONS INC
13100 Gregg St Ste A, Poway
(92064-7150)
PHONE................................800 947-6134
EMP: 92
SALES (corp-wide): 45.78MM **Publicly Held**
Web: www.digirad.com
SIC: 7352 Medical equipment rental
HQ: Digirad Imaging Solutions Inc
1048 Industrial Ct Ste E
Poway CA 92064
800 947-6134

7353 Heavy Construction Equipment Rental

(P-13431)
BIGGE GROUP
14511 Industry Cir, La Mirada (90638-5814)
PHONE................................714 523-4092
EMP: 106
Web: www.bigge.com
SIC: 7353 Cranes and aerial lift equipment,
rental or leasing
PA: Bigge Group
10700 Bigge Ave

(P-13432)
BRAGG INVESTMENT COMPANY INC
Also Called: Bragg Crane
13188 Dahlia St, Fontana (92337-6903)
PHONE................................909 350-3738
Dyke Leonard, *Mgr*
EMP: 147
SALES (corp-wide): 489.53MM **Privately Held**
Web: www.braggcompanies.com
SIC: 7353 Cranes and aerial lift equipment,
rental or leasing
PA: Bragg Investment Company, Inc.
6251 N Paramount Blvd

---

562 984-2400

(P-13433)
BRAGG INVESTMENT COMPANY INC (PA)
Also Called: Bragg Crane & Rigging
6251 N Paramount Blvd, Long Beach
(90805-3713)
P.O. Box 727 (90801)
PHONE................................562 984-2400
TOLL FREE: 800
M Scott Bragg, *Pr*
Mike Roy, *
Marilynn Bragg, *VP*
Dennis Ferguson, *
Kathleen Pool-ferrin, *Sec*
◆ **EMP:** 300 **EST:** 1946
SQ FT: 50,000
SALES (est): 489.53MM
SALES (corp-wide): 489.53MM **Privately Held**
Web: www.braggcompanies.com
SIC: 7353 4213 7389 1791 Cranes and
aerial lift equipment, rental or leasing;
Heavy hauling, nec; Crane and aerial lift
service; Structural steel erection

(P-13434)
COUNTY OF ORANGE
Also Called: All Access Rental
1631 E Wilshire Ave, Santa Ana
(92705-4504)
PHONE................................714 647-1552
Kevin Aylesworth, *CEO*
EMP: 74
SALES (corp-wide): 5.63B **Privately Held**
Web: www.ocgov.com
SIC: 7353 5599 Cranes and aerial lift
equipment, rental or leasing; Aircraft
instruments, equipment or parts
PA: County Of Orange
400 W. Civic Center Dr
714 834-6200

(P-13435)
GLOBAL RENTAL CO INC
1253 Price Ave, Pomona (91767-5839)
PHONE................................909 469-5160
James Dixon, *Brnch Mgr*
EMP: 120
SALES (corp-wide): 1.21B **Privately Held**
Web: www.altec.com
SIC: 7353 5082 Heavy construction
equipment rental; Contractor's materials
HQ: Global Rental Co., Inc.
33 Inverness Center Pkwy # 250
Hoover AL 35242

(P-13436)
HARBOR INDUSTRIAL SVCS CORP
Also Called: Harbor Industrial
211 N Marine Ave, Wilmington
(90744-5724)
P.O. Box 1487 (90733-1487)
PHONE................................310 522-1193
W Michael Hawk, *Pr*
Maria Gray, *
▲ **EMP:** 80 **EST:** 1993
SALES (est): 10.99MM **Privately Held**
Web: www.harborindustrial.com
SIC: 7353 Cranes and aerial lift equipment,
rental or leasing

(P-13437)
HAWTHORNE MACHINERY CO (PA)
Also Called: Hawthorne Cat
16945 Camino San Bernardo, San Diego
(92127-2499)

PHONE..................858 674-7000
TOLL FREE: 800
Tee K Ness, *Pr*
David Ness, *
◆ **EMP:** 200 **EST:** 1941
SQ FT: 130,000
SALES (est): 176.69MM
SALES (corp-wide): 176.69MM **Privately Held**
Web: www.hawthornecat.com
SIC: 7353 7699 5082 7359 Heavy construction equipment rental; Construction equipment repair; Construction and mining machinery; Equipment rental and leasing, nec

(P-13438)
HAWTHORNE RENT-IT SERVICE (HQ)
Also Called: Caterpillar Authorized Dealer
16945 Camino San Bernardo, San Diego (92127-2405)
PHONE..................858 674-7000
Tee K Ness, *CEO*
Bob Price, *
Paul Hawthorne, *
Mike Johnson, *Product Vice President*
Steve Sager, *
EMP: 100 **EST:** 1974
SQ FT: 130,000
SALES (est): 22.86MM
SALES (corp-wide): 176.69MM **Privately Held**
Web: www.hawthornecat.com
SIC: 7353 5084 Heavy construction equipment rental; Industrial machinery and equipment
PA: Hawthorne Machinery Co.
16945 Camino San Bernardo
858 674-7000

(P-13439)
KING EQUIPMENT LLC
1690 Ashley Way, Colton (92324-4000)
PHONE..................909 986-5300
Diane Quijada, *
EMP: 73 **EST:** 2007
SALES (est): 2.54MM **Privately Held**
Web: www.sunbeltrentals.com
SIC: 7353 Heavy construction equipment rental

(P-13440)
KINGS OIL TOOLS INC (PA)
2235 Spring St, Paso Robles (93446-1404)
PHONE..................805 238-9311
EMP: 30 **EST:** 1982
SALES (est): 11.13MM
SALES (corp-wide): 11.13MM **Privately Held**
Web: www.kingsoiltools.com
SIC: 7353 1389 Oil field equipment, rental or leasing; Oil and gas wells: building, repairing and dismantling

(P-13441)
LLC BREWER CRANE
Also Called: Brewer Crane & Rigging
12570 Highway 67, Lakeside (92040-1159)
PHONE..................619 390-8252
Brent S Brewer, *Pr*
Brent K Garcia, *
EMP: 72 **EST:** 1997
SQ FT: 2,500
SALES (est): 24MM **Privately Held**
Web: www.brewercrane.com
SIC: 7353 Cranes and aerial lift equipment, rental or leasing

(P-13442)
NATIONAL BUSINESS GROUP INC (PA)
Also Called: National Tube & Steel
15319 Chatsworth St, Mission Hills (91345-2040)
PHONE..................818 221-6000
James Mooneyham, *Pr*
◆ **EMP:** 85 **EST:** 1985
SQ FT: 24,000
SALES (est): 16.88MM
SALES (corp-wide): 16.88MM **Privately Held**
Web: www.rentnational.com
SIC: 7353 5039 7359 3496 Earth moving equipment, rental or leasing; Wire fence, gates, and accessories; Garage facility and tool rental; Fencing, made from purchased wire

(P-13443)
NORTHWEST EXCAVATING INC
18201 Napa St, Northridge (91325-3374)
PHONE..................818 349-5861
Susan Groff, *CEO*
Robbie Groff, *
EMP: 72 **EST:** 1959
SQ FT: 2,500
SALES (est): 5.01MM **Privately Held**
Web: www.nwexc.com
SIC: 7353 1794 Heavy construction equipment rental; Excavation and grading, building construction

(P-13444)
WESTERN ENERGY SERVICES CORP
3430 Getty St, Bakersfield (93308-5248)
PHONE..................403 984-5916
Alex R N Macausland, *CEO*
Jeffrey K Bowers, *VP*
EMP: 200 **EST:** 2005
SALES (est): 2.59MM **Privately Held**
Web: www.wesc.ca
SIC: 7353 Oil well drilling equipment, rental or leasing

(P-13445)
WHITES CRANE SERVICE INC
Also Called: White Crane
45524 Towne St, Indio (92201-4446)
PHONE..................760 347-3401
Edwin Neumeyer, *Pr*
EMP: 70 **EST:** 1999
SALES (est): 822.54K
SALES (corp-wide): 10.92MM **Privately Held**
Web: www.whitescraneservice.com
SIC: 7353 Cranes and aerial lift equipment, rental or leasing
PA: White's Steel, Inc.
45524 Towne St
760 347-3401

7359 Equipment Rental And Leasing, Nec

(P-13446)
AFTER-PARTY2 INC (DH)
Also Called: Classic Party Rentals
901 W Hillcrest Blvd, Inglewood (90301-2100)
PHONE..................310 202-0011
Jeff Black, *Pr*
▲ **EMP:** 200 **EST:** 1996
SALES (est): 21.45MM
SALES (corp-wide): 32.64B **Publicly Held**
Web: www.bright.com

SIC: 7359 Party supplies rental services
HQ: Apollo Asset Management, Inc.
9 W 57th St Fl 42
New York NY 10019

(P-13447)
AFTER-PARTY6 INC
Also Called: Classic Party Rentals
901 W Hillcrest Blvd, Inglewood (90301-2100)
PHONE..................310 966-4900
EMP: 130
SIC: 7359 Party supplies rental services

(P-13448)
BRIGHT EVENT RENTALS LLC (PA)
Also Called: Bright Event Rentals
1640 W 190th St Ste A, Torrance (90501-1113)
PHONE..................310 202-0011
Michael Bjornstad, *Managing Member*
▲ **EMP:** 240 **EST:** 2013
SALES (est): 117.71MM
SALES (corp-wide): 117.71MM **Privately Held**
Web: www.bright.com
SIC: 7359 Party supplies rental services

(P-13449)
CELTIC LEASING CORP
Also Called: Celtic Commercial Finance
4 Park Plz Ste 300, Irvine (92614-8511)
PHONE..................949 263-3880
EMP: 80
SIC: 7359 Equipment rental and leasing, nec

(P-13450)
CHOURA EVENTS
540 Hawaii Ave, Torrance (90503-5148)
PHONE..................310 320-6200
James Ryan Choura, *CEO*
EMP: 80 **EST:** 2014
SALES (est): 10.57MM **Privately Held**
Web: www.choura.co
SIC: 7359 Party supplies rental services

(P-13451)
CLASSIC PARTY RENTALS INC
Also Called: Classic Party Rentals
901 W Hillcrest Blvd, Inglewood (90301-2100)
PHONE..................310 966-4900
▲ **EMP:** 2500
SIC: 7359 Party supplies rental services

(P-13452)
CLASSIC/PRIME INC
Also Called: Classic Tents
540 Hawaii Ave, Torrance (90503-5148)
PHONE..................310 328-5060
EMP: 100
SIC: 7359 Tent and tarpaulin rental

(P-13453)
COMPASS GROUP USA INC
Also Called: Canteen Vending
12640 Knott St, Garden Grove (92841-3902)
PHONE..................714 899-2520
Ron Wanamaker, *VP*
EMP: 125
SALES (corp-wide): 39.16B **Privately Held**
Web: www.canteen.com
SIC: 7359 7699 5962 Vending machine rental ; Vending machine repair; Merchandising machine operators
HQ: Compass Group Usa, Inc.
2400 Yorkmont Rd

Charlotte NC 28217

(P-13454)
DIAMOND ENVIRONMENTAL SVCS LP
Also Called: Diamond Environmental Services
807 E Mission Rd, San Marcos (92069-3002)
PHONE..................760 744-7191
EMP: 100 **EST:** 1997
SQ FT: 2,000
SALES (est): 19.63MM **Privately Held**
Web: www.diamondprovides.com
SIC: 7359 Portable toilet rental

(P-13455)
DIRECT CHASSISLINK INC
Also Called: Dcli
7777 Center Ave Ste 325, Huntington Beach (92647-9132)
PHONE..................657 216-5846
Don Peltier, *Mgr*
EMP: 368
SALES (corp-wide): 116.43MM **Privately Held**
Web: www.dcli.com
SIC: 7359 Equipment rental and leasing, nec
PA: Direct Chassislink, Inc.
3525 Whthall Pk Dr Ste 40
704 594-3800

(P-13456)
GUZMAN GRADING AND PAVING CORP
14030 Rose Ave, Fontana (92337-7047)
PHONE..................909 428-5960
Jesus Guzman, *CEO*
EMP: 95 **EST:** 2003
SQ FT: 76,000
SALES (est): 7.14MM **Privately Held**
SIC: 7359 1771 1611 Equipment rental and leasing, nec; Blacktop (asphalt) work; Highway and street construction

(P-13457)
HANA FINANCIAL INC (PA)
1000 Wilshire Blvd Ste 2000, Los Angeles (90017-5645)
PHONE..................213 240-1234
Sunnie S Kim, *CEO*
Young Shim, *
▲ **EMP:** 85 **EST:** 1994
SQ FT: 24,000
SALES (est): 8.23MM **Privately Held**
Web: www.hanafinancial.com
SIC: 7359 6153 6159 Equipment rental and leasing, nec; Factoring services; Small business investment companies

(P-13458)
J L FISHER INC
1000 W Isabel St, Burbank (91506-1404)
PHONE..................818 846-8366
James L Fisher, *Pr*
Cary Clayton, *
▲ **EMP:** 60 **EST:** 1951
SALES (est): 5.28MM **Privately Held**
Web: www.jlfisher.com
SIC: 7359 3861 3663 Equipment rental and leasing, nec; Motion picture apparatus and equipment; Radio and t.v. communications equipment

(P-13459)
L A PARTY RENTS INC
13520 Saticoy St, Van Nuys (91402-6428)
PHONE..................818 989-4300
Gerome Nehus, *Pr*
EMP: 100 **EST:** 1987

SALES (est): 11.67MM **Privately Held**
Web: www.lapartyrents.com
SIC: **7359** Party supplies rental services

(P-13460)
MICROFINANCIAL INCORPORATED
2801 Townsgate Rd, Westlake Village
(91361-3003)
PHONE.....................805 367-8900
Richard Latour, *CEO*
EMP: 106
SALES (corp-wide): 99.27MM **Privately Held**
Web: www.timepayment.com
SIC: **7359** Business machine and electronic equipment rental services
HQ: Microfinancial Incorporated
200 Summit Dr Ste 100
Burlington MA 01803
781 994-4800

(P-13461)
MICROLEASE INC (DH)
6060 Sepulveda Blvd, Van Nuys
(91411-2512)
PHONE.....................866 520-0200
Gordon Curwen, *VP*
EMP: 85 EST: 2001
SQ FT: 20,000
SALES (est): 15.72MM
SALES (corp-wide): 254.4MM **Privately Held**
SIC: **7359** Rental store, general
HQ: Electro Rent Uk Limited
Unit 1, Waverley Industrial Park
Harrow MIDDX HA1 4
208 420-0200

(P-13462)
MUFG AMERICAS LEASING CORP (DH)
445 S Figueroa St Ste 2700, Los Angeles
(90071-1620)
PHONE.....................213 488-3700
Hideya Takaishi, *CEO*
Mark Helman, *General**
Paul Nolan, *
Rory Laughna, *
David A Meehan, *
EMP: 100 EST: 1973
SALES (est): 14.58MM **Privately Held**
Web: www.mufgamericas.com
SIC: **7359** Equipment rental and leasing, nec
HQ: Mufg Americas Holdings Corporation
1251 Ave Of The Americas
New York NY 10020
212 782-6800

(P-13463)
NATIONAL CNSTR RENTALS INC (PA)
Also Called: National Rent A Fence Co.
15319 Chatsworth St, Mission Hills
(91345-2040)
PHONE.....................818 221-6000
James R Mooneyham, *Pr*
W Robert Mooneyham, *Executive President**
◆ EMP: 85 EST: 1961
SQ FT: 23,000
SALES (est): 323.59MM
SALES (corp-wide): 323.59MM **Privately Held**
Web: www.rentnational.com
SIC: **7359** Equipment rental and leasing, nec

(P-13464)
NATIONAL TRENCH SAFETY LLC
Also Called: Trench Plate Rental
13217 Laureldale Ave, Downey
(90242-5140)
PHONE.....................562 602-1642
Dexter Poston, *Brnch Mgr*
EMP: 185
SALES (corp-wide): 104.07MM **Privately Held**
Web: www.ntsafety.com
SIC: **7359** Equipment rental and leasing, nec
PA: National Trench Safety, Llc
260 N Sam Hston Pkwy E St
832 200-0988

(P-13465)
P J J ENTERPRISES INC
1250 Delevan Dr, San Diego (92102-2437)
PHONE.....................619 232-6136
John Lenore, *Pr*
Roger Carey, *
Dorothy Lenore, *
EMP: 150 EST: 1966
SQ FT: 20,000
SALES (est): 908.85K
SALES (corp-wide): 12.65MM **Privately Held**
SIC: **7359** Rental store, general
PA: Lenore John & Co
1250 Delevan Dr
619 232-6136

(P-13466)
PANAVISION INC (PA)
Also Called: Panavision Group
6101 Variel Ave, Woodland Hills
(91367-3722)
PHONE.....................818 316-1000
Ronald O Perelman, *Ch Bd*
Howard Gittis, *V Ch Bd*
Kimberly Snyder, *CEO*
William C Bevins, *Pr*
▲ EMP: 550 EST: 1990
SQ FT: 150,000
SALES (est): 90.43MM **Privately Held**
Web: www.panavision.com
SIC: **7359 3861 3648 5063** Equipment rental and leasing, nec; Cameras and related equipment; Stage lighting equipment; Lighting fixtures

(P-13467)
PORTER HIRE LTD
Also Called: Heavy Equipment Rentals
13013 Temescal Canyon Rd, Corona
(92883-8454)
PHONE.....................951 674-9999
◆ EMP: 46 EST: 1999
SALES (est): 11.55MM **Privately Held**
Web: www.porterrents.com
SIC: **7359 5082 3523** Equipment rental and leasing, nec; Construction and mining machinery; Farm machinery and equipment
HQ: Porter Hire Limited
1 Mark Porter Way, Burbush
Hamilton WKO 3200

(P-13468)
PSAV HOLDINGS LLC (PA)
111 W Ocean Blvd Ste 1110, Long Beach
(90802-4688)
PHONE.....................562 366-0138
J Michael Mcilwain, *CEO*
Ben Erwin, *
Michael Leone, *CCO**
Cathie Kozik, *CIO**
Charlie Young, *Chief Human Resource Officer**

EMP: 122 EST: 2013
SALES (est): 460.08MM
SALES (corp-wide): 460.08MM **Privately Held**
Web: www.encoreglobal.com
SIC: **7359** Audio-visual equipment and supply rental

(P-13469)
RAPHAELS PARTY RENTALS INC (PA)
8606 Miramar Rd, San Diego (92126-4326)
PHONE.....................858 444-1692
Raphael Silverman, *Pr*
Phillip Silverman, *
Kitty Silverman, *
▲ EMP: 175 EST: 1981
SQ FT: 60,000
SALES (est): 9.64MM
SALES (corp-wide): 9.64MM **Privately Held**
Web: www.raphaels.com
SIC: **7359** Party supplies rental services

(P-13470)
SHOWROOM INTERIORS LLC
Also Called: Vesta Luxury Home Staging
8905 Rex Rd, Pico Rivera (90660-3799)
PHONE.....................323 348-1551
Julianne Buckner, *Managing Member*
EMP: 105 EST: 2016
SALES (est): 2.98MM
SALES (corp-wide): 39.09MM **Privately Held**
Web: www.vestahome.com
SIC: **7359** Furniture rental
PA: Showroom, Inc
8905 Rex Rd
323 348-1551

(P-13471)
SIGNATURE PARTY RENTALS LLC
Also Called: Signature Party Rentals
82309 Market St, Indio (92201-2251)
PHONE.....................760 863-0671
EMP: 199
SALES (corp-wide): 53.19MM **Privately Held**
Web: www.signatureparty.com
SIC: **7359** Party supplies rental services
HQ: Signature Party Rentals, Llc
3100 S Susan St
Santa Ana CA 92704
714 545-6777

(P-13472)
SRG HOLDINGS LLC (HQ)
500 Stevens Ave Ste 100, Solana Beach
(92075-2055)
PHONE.....................858 792-9300
J Wickliffe Peterson, *CFO*
Michael Grust, *Pr*
EMP: 261 EST: 1998
SQ FT: 12,300
SALES (est): 13.97MM
SALES (corp-wide): 110.02MM **Privately Held**
SIC: **7359** Business machine and electronic equipment rental services
PA: Senior Resource Group, Llc
500 Stevens Ave Ste 100
858 792-9300

(P-13473)
SUNN AMERICA INC
Also Called: Classe Party Rentals
10280 Indiana Ct, Rancho Cucamonga
(91730-5332)
PHONE.....................909 944-5756

Vishnu Reddy, *Pr*
Saritha Reddy, *
Vishnu Reddy, *CEO*
Ronald Francis, *
EMP: 30 EST: 1999
SALES (est): 3.55MM **Privately Held**
Web: www.classeparty.com
SIC: **7359 7299 3999** Party supplies rental services; Party planning service; Stage hardware and equipment, except lighting

(P-13474)
TOWN & CNTRY EVENT RENTALS INC
Also Called: TOWN & COUNTRY EVENT RENTALS, INC.
3905 State St, Santa Barbara (93105-3138)
PHONE.....................805 770-5729
EMP: 198
SALES (corp-wide): 53.19MM **Privately Held**
Web: www.townandcountry.com
SIC: **7359** Party supplies rental services
PA: Town & Country Event Rentals Llc
7725 Airport Bus Pkwy
818 908-4211

(P-13475)
TOWN & CNTRY EVENT RENTALS LLC (PA) ✪
7725 Airport Business Pkwy, Van Nuys
(91406-1723)
PHONE.....................818 908-4211
Richard Loguercio, *CEO*
Chris Mackey, *
Christopher Keesler, *
Wayne Tay, *
▲ EMP: 400 EST: 2023
SQ FT: 1,100
SALES (est): 53.19MM
SALES (corp-wide): 53.19MM **Privately Held**
Web: www.townandcountry.com
SIC: **7359** Party supplies rental services

(P-13476)
TRAFFIC CONTROL SERVICE INC
Also Called: Allied Trench Shoring Service
4695 Macarthur Ct Ste 1100, Newport Beach (92660-1866)
TOLL FREE: 800
EMP: 207
SIC: **7359 5099 1799** Sign rental; Signs, except electric; Flag pole erection

(P-13477)
VCI EVENT TECHNOLOGY INC
Also Called: Videocam
25172 Arctic Ocean Dr Ste 102, Lake Forest
(92630-8851)
PHONE.....................714 772-2002
TOLL FREE: 888
Kirk Rhinehart, *CEO*
Evan H Goldschlag, *
Kirk Rhinehart, *VP*
▲ EMP: 166 EST: 1993
SALES (est): 18.39MM **Privately Held**
Web: www.vcievents.com
SIC: **7359** Audio-visual equipment and supply rental

(P-13478)
WESTERN OILFIELDS SUPPLY CO
Also Called: Rain For Rent
5101 Office Park Dr Ste 100, Bakersfield
(93309-0615)
P.O. Box File 52541 (90074-0001)

▲ = Import ▼ = Export
◆ = Import/Export

PHONE..............................480 895-9225
EMP: 97
SALES (corp-wide): 250.88MM **Privately Held**
Web: www.rainforrent.com
SIC: 7359 Equipment rental and leasing, nec
PA: Western Oilfields Supply Co Inc
3404 State Rd
661 399-9124

(P-13479)
WESTERN OILFIELDS SUPPLY CO (PA)
Also Called: Rain For Rent
3404 State Rd, Bakersfield (93308-4538)
P.O. Box 2248 (93303-2248)
PHONE..............................661 399-9124
Robert Lake, *CEO*
Maston Cunningham, *CFO*
▲ **EMP:** 150 **EST:** 1934
SQ FT: 57,000
SALES (est): 250.88MM
SALES (corp-wide): 250.88MM **Privately Held**
Web: www.rainforrent.com
SIC: 7359 3523 5083 Equipment rental and leasing, nec; Farm machinery and equipment; Irrigation equipment

7361 Employment Agencies

(P-13480)
24-HOUR MED STAFFING SVCS LLC
1370 Valley Vista Dr Ste 280, Diamond Bar (91765-3923)
PHONE..............................909 895-8960
EMP: 110 **EST:** 2000
SALES (est): 8.71MM **Privately Held**
Web: www.24-hrmed.com
SIC: 7361 Employment agencies

(P-13481)
5 STAR JOBS
12025 Garfield Ave, South Gate (90280-7822)
PHONE..............................562 788-7391
Fernando Carrillo Morales, *CEO*
EMP: 70 **EST:** 2018
SALES (est): 2.15MM **Privately Held**
SIC: 7361 Employment agencies

(P-13482)
ACCESS NURSES INC
5935 Cornerstone Ct W Ste 300, San Diego (92121-3737)
PHONE..............................858 458-4400
Alan Braynin, *CEO*
EMP: 80 **EST:** 2001
SQ FT: 20,000
SALES (est): 7.99MM **Privately Held**
Web: www.accessnurses.com
SIC: 7361 Nurses' registry

(P-13483)
ACT 1 GROUP INC (PA)
Also Called: Agileone
1999 W 190th St, Torrance (90504-6202)
P.O. Box 2886 (90509-2886)
PHONE..............................310 750-3400
Janice B Howroyd, *CEO*
Bernard Howroyd, *
Michael Hoyal, *
Carlton Bryant, *
Tina B Robinson, *
EMP: 90 **EST:** 1978
SQ FT: 18,026
SALES (est): 612MM **Privately Held**
Web: www.actonegroup.com

SIC: 7361 8741 Employment agencies; Administrative management

(P-13484)
ADVANCED MED PRSONNEL SVCS INC
12400 High Bluff Dr Ste 100, San Diego (92130-3077)
PHONE..............................386 756-4395
Jennfier Fuicelli, *CEO*
EMP: 100 **EST:** 1989
SALES (est): 2.98MM
SALES (corp-wide): 3.79B **Publicly Held**
Web: www.amnhealthcare.com
SIC: 7361 7363 Nurses' registry; Medical help service
HQ: Amn Healthcare, Inc.
12400 High Bluff Dr # 100
San Diego CA 92130

(P-13485)
ADVANTAGE RESOURCING AMER INC
11005 Firestone Blvd Ste 105, Norwalk (90650-2224)
PHONE..............................562 465-0099
EMP: 127
Web: www.advantageresourcing.com
SIC: 7361 Employment agencies
HQ: Advantage Resourcing America, Inc.
201 E 4th St Ste 800
Cincinnati OH 45202

(P-13486)
APPLEONE INC
Also Called: Appleone Employment Services
325 W Broadway, Glendale (91204-1301)
PHONE..............................818 240-8688
Marie Rounsavell, *Mgr*
EMP: 120
Web: www.appleone.com
SIC: 7361 Labor contractors (employment agency)
HQ: Appleone, Inc.
327 W Broadway
Glendale CA 91204
818 240-8688

(P-13487)
APPLEONE INC (HQ)
Also Called: Appleone Employment Services
327 W Broadway, Glendale (91204-1301)
PHONE..............................818 240-8688
Janice Bryant Howroyd, *CEO*
Bernard Howroyd, *
Michael Hoyal, *
Brett Howroyd, *
◆ **EMP:** 175 **EST:** 1964
SQ FT: 27,000
SALES (est): 145.38MM **Privately Held**
Web: www.appleone.com
SIC: 7361 Labor contractors (employment agency)
PA: The Act 1 Group Inc
1999 W 190th St

(P-13488)
ASSISTED HOME RECOVERY INC (PA)
Also Called: Assisted Home Care
8550 Balboa Blvd Lbby, Northridge (91325-5808)
PHONE..............................818 894-8117
Elaine S Donley, *Adm/Dir*
Bill Donley, *
EMP: 110 **EST:** 1979
SQ FT: 4,000
SALES (est): 4.25MM
SALES (corp-wide): 4.25MM **Privately Held**

SIC: 7361 Nurses' registry

(P-13489)
ATTORNEY NETWORK SERVICES INC
Also Called: Attorney Network Services
725 S Figueroa St Ste 3065, Los Angeles (90017-5430)
PHONE..............................213 430-0440
Nick Karapetian, *Pr*
Gavin Rubin, *VP*
EMP: 97 **EST:** 1997
SQ FT: 4,000
SALES (est): 1.12MM **Privately Held**
Web: www.karapetianrubin.com
SIC: 7361 Executive placement

(P-13490)
B2 SERVICES LLC
Also Called: At Work
17291 Irvine Blvd Ste 258, Tustin (92780-2949)
PHONE..............................714 363-3481
Lori Brower, *Pr*
EMP: 100 **EST:** 2017
SALES (est): 2.25MM **Privately Held**
Web: www.atwork.com
SIC: 7361 Employment agencies

(P-13491)
BARRETT BUSINESS SERVICES INC
Also Called: B B S I
8880 Rio San Diego Dr Ste 800, San Diego (92108-1642)
PHONE..............................858 314-1100
Milan Todorovic, *Brnch Mgr*
EMP: 4191
SALES (corp-wide): 1.07B **Publicly Held**
Web: www.bbsi.com
SIC: 7361 Employment agencies
PA: Barrett Business Services Inc
8100 Ne Pkwy Dr Ste 200
360 828-0700

(P-13492)
BARRETT BUSINESS SERVICES INC
862 E Hospitality Ln, San Bernardino (92408-3530)
PHONE..............................909 890-3633
EMP: 5003
SALES (corp-wide): 1.07B **Publicly Held**
Web: www.bbsi.com
SIC: 7361 Employment agencies
PA: Barrett Business Services Inc
8100 Ne Pkwy Dr Ste 200
360 828-0700

(P-13493)
BARRETT BUSINESS SERVICES INC
Also Called: Bbsi Camarillo
815 Camarillo Springs Rd Ste C, Camarillo (93012-9457)
PHONE..............................805 987-0331
Dee Levy, *Brnch Mgr*
EMP: 4124
SALES (corp-wide): 1.07B **Publicly Held**
Web: www.bbsi.com
SIC: 7361 8742 Employment agencies; Human resource consulting services
PA: Barrett Business Services Inc
8100 Ne Pkwy Dr Ste 200
360 828-0700

SIC: **7361** Nurses' registry

(P-13494)
BOILING POINT REST S CA INC
Also Called: Boiling Point Rest W Grove
13668 Valley Blvd Unit C2, City Of Industry (91746-2572)
PHONE..............................626 551-5181
Chi How Chou, *Ch*
Michael Lin, *
EMP: 300 **EST:** 2012
SALES (est): 7.54MM **Privately Held**
SIC: 7361 5812 Employment agencies; Chinese restaurant

(P-13495)
BUTLER AMERICA HOLDINGS INC
1125 S Oxnard Blvd, Oxnard (93030-7417)
PHONE..............................805 243-0061
EMP: 195
SALES (corp-wide): 79.52MM **Privately Held**
Web: www.partnerspersonnel.com
SIC: 7361 Employment agencies
PA: Butler America Holdings, Inc.
3820 State St Ste B
805 880-1978

(P-13496)
BUTLER AMERICA HOLDINGS INC
8647 Haven Ave Ste 100, Rancho Cucamonga (91730-4887)
PHONE..............................909 417-3660
Cecilia La Tour, *Brnch Mgr*
EMP: 195
SALES (corp-wide): 42.41MM **Privately Held**
SIC: 7361 Employment agencies
PA: Butler America Holdings, Inc.
3820 State St Ste B
805 880-1978

(P-13497)
BUTLER AMERICA HOLDINGS INC
12625 Frederick St Ste E2, Moreno Valley (92553-5253)
PHONE..............................951 563-0020
EMP: 195
SALES (corp-wide): 42.41MM **Privately Held**
SIC: 7361 Employment agencies
PA: Butler America Holdings, Inc.
3820 State St Ste B
805 880-1978

(P-13498)
BUTLER INTERNATIONAL INC (PA)
3820 State St Ste A, Santa Barbara (93105-3182)
PHONE..............................805 882-2200
Edward M Kopko, *Ch Bd*
Edward M Kopko, *Ch Bd*
James J Beckley, *
Mark Koscinski, *
EMP: 200 **EST:** 1985
SALES (est): 14.08MM
SALES (corp-wide): 14.08MM **Privately Held**
Web: www.butleritresources.com
SIC: 7361 8742 Employment agencies; Management consulting services

(P-13499)
CANON RECRUITING GROUP LLC
27651 Lincoln Pl Ste 250, Santa Clarita (91387-8818)

PHONE..................661 252-7400
Laurie Grayem, *CEO*
Laurie Grayem, *Managing Member*
Tim Grayem, *
EMP: 500 EST: 1980
SQ FT: 7,500
SALES (est): 3.36MM **Privately Held**
Web: www.canonrecruiting.com
SIC: 7361 Executive placement

(P-13500)
CAREER GROUP INC (PA)
Also Called: Fourthfloor Fashion Talent
10100 Santa Monica Blvd Ste 900, Los
Angeles (90067-4138)
PHONE..................310 277-8188
Michael B Levine, *CEO*
Susan Levine, *
Scott H Pick, *
▲ **EMP:** 2100 **EST:** 1980
SQ FT: 11,986
SALES (est): 45.37MM
SALES (corp-wide): 45.37MM **Privately
Held**
Web: www.careergroupcompanies.com
SIC: 7361 Executive placement

(P-13501)
CAREER STRATEGIES TMPRY
INC
575 Anton Blvd Ste 630, Costa Mesa
(92626-1948)
PHONE..................714 824-6840
Mat Mcgowen, *Mgr*
EMP: 104
Web: www.csi4jobs.com
SIC: 7361 Executive placement
PA: Career Strategies Temporary, Inc.
  1 Chisholm Trail Rd # 210

(P-13502)
CAREER STRATEGIES TMPRY
INC
21031 Ventura Blvd Ste 1005, Woodland
Hills (91364-2255)
PHONE..................818 883-0440
Julie Maddox, *VP*
EMP: 104
Web: www.csi4jobs.com
SIC: 7361 Executive placement
PA: Career Strategies Temporary, Inc.
  1 Chisholm Trail Rd # 210

(P-13503)
CAREER STRATEGIES TMPRY
INC
78060 Calle Estado, La Quinta
(92253-2960)
PHONE..................760 564-5959
EMP: 104
Web: www.csi4jobs.com
SIC: 7361 Executive placement
PA: Career Strategies Temporary, Inc.
  1 Chisholm Trail Rd # 210

(P-13504)
CAREER STRATEGIES TMPRY
INC
9267 Haven Ave Ste 225, Rancho
Cucamonga (91730-5458)
PHONE..................909 230-4504
Darin Rado, *Prin*
EMP: 104
Web: www.csipropertymanagement.com
SIC: 7361 Executive placement
PA: Career Strategies Temporary, Inc.
  1 Chisholm Trail Rd # 210

(P-13505)
CENTURY HLTH STAFFING
SVCS INC
1701 Westwind Dr Ste 101, Bakersfield
(93301-3045)
PHONE..................661 322-0606
Richard Ochieng, *Pr*
Lissa Harris-soto, *VP*
EMP: 213 **EST:** 2006
SQ FT: 2,000
SALES (est): 3.42MM **Privately Held**
Web: www.centurynurse.com
SIC: 7361 Nurses' registry

(P-13506)
CREATIVE SOLUTIONS SVCS
LLC
Also Called: Higher Talent
1745 N Vista St, Los Angeles (90046-2234)
PHONE..................646 495-1558
Ashish Kaushal, *Managing Member*
EMP: 212 **EST:** 2016
SALES (est): 7.67MM **Privately Held**
Web: www.css-llc.net
SIC: 7361 Executive placement

(P-13507)
CULVER PERSONNEL
AGENCIES INC
Also Called: Culver Personnel Services
445 Marine View Ave Ste 101, Del Mar
(92014-3951)
P.O. Box 910569 (92191-0569)
PHONE..................888 600-5733
Timothy J Culver, *Pr*
John Weaver, *
EMP: 120 **EST:** 1979
SQ FT: 7,500
SALES (est): 2.3MM **Privately Held**
SIC: 7361 Executive placement

(P-13508)
CYBERCODERS INC
Also Called: Cyberscientific
101 Progress, Irvine (92618-0321)
PHONE..................949 885-5151
Heidi Golledge, *CEO*
Matt Miller, *
EMP: 140 **EST:** 1999
SALES (est): 21.04MM
SALES (corp-wide): 4.45B **Publicly Held**
Web: www.cybercoders.com
SIC: 7361 Executive placement
PA: Asgn Incorporated
  4400 Cox Rd Ste 110
  888 482-8068

(P-13509)
DELTA-T GROUP INC
4420 Hotel Circle Ct Ste 205, San Diego
(92108-3423)
PHONE..................619 543-0556
EMP: 171
Web: www.delta-tgroup.com
SIC: 7361 Employment agencies
PA: Delta-T Group, Inc.
  950 E Hverford Rd Ste 200

(P-13510)
DIVERSITY BUS SOLUTIONS INC
3532 Old Archibald Ranch Rd, Ontario
(91761-9160)
PHONE..................909 395-0243
Sandy Tribby, *CEO*
EMP: 200 **EST:** 2011
SALES (est): 2.24MM **Privately Held**
Web: www.dbsinc.org
SIC: 7361 Employment agencies

(P-13511)
E Z STAFFING INC (PA)
200 N Maryland Ave Ste 303, Glendale
(91206-4276)
PHONE..................818 845-2500
Abraham F Abirafeh, *Pr*
EMP: 298 **EST:** 1994
SALES (est): 3.69MM **Privately Held**
Web: www.ezstaffing.com
SIC: 7361 Nurses' registry

(P-13512)
EASTERN STAFFING LLC
Also Called: Select Staffing
301 Mentor Dr # 210, Santa Barbara
(93111-3339)
PHONE..................805 882-2200
Stephen Sorensen, *Managing Member*
EMP: 417 **EST:** 2004
SALES (est): 521.62K
SALES (corp-wide): 14.08MM **Privately
Held**
Web: www.select.com
SIC: 7361 Employment agencies
PA: Butler International, Inc.
  3820 State St Ste A
  805 882-2200

(P-13513)
EMPLOYNET INC
123 E 9th St Ste 103, Upland (91786-6033)
PHONE..................909 458-0961
EMP: 1327
SALES (corp-wide): 21.33MM **Privately
Held**
Web: www.employnet.com
SIC: 7361 Employment agencies
PA: Employnet, Inc.
  2555 Garden Rd Ste H
  866 527-4473

(P-13514)
EPLICA INC
17785 Center Court Dr N, Cerritos
(90703-8573)
PHONE..................562 977-4300
Jade Jenkins, *Brnch Mgr*
EMP: 120
SALES (corp-wide): 139MM **Privately
Held**
Web: www.eplicaservices.com
SIC: 7361 Employment agencies
PA: Eplica, Inc.
  2385 Northside Dr Ste 250
  619 260-2000

(P-13515)
EPLICA CORPORATE SERVICES
INC
Also Called: Eastridge Workforce Solutions
2385 Northside Dr Ste 250, San Diego
(92108-2716)
PHONE..................619 282-1400
Seth Stein, *CEO*
EMP: 1433 **EST:** 2010
SALES (est): 3.9MM
SALES (corp-wide): 139MM **Privately
Held**
SIC: 7361 Employment agencies
PA: Eplica, Inc.
  2385 Northside Dr Ste 250
  619 260-2000

(P-13516)
ESPARZA ENTERPRISES INC
51335 Cesar Chavez St Ste 112, Coachella
 (92236-1528)
PHONE..................760 398-0349
Manuel Padilla, *Mgr*
EMP: 792

SALES (corp-wide): 135MM **Privately
Held**
Web: www.esparzainc.com
SIC: 7361 Labor contractors (employment
agency)
PA: Esparza Enterprises, Inc.
  3851 Fruitvale Ave
  661 831-0002

(P-13517)
ESPARZA ENTERPRISES INC
222 S Union Ave, Bakersfield (93307-3325)
PHONE..................661 631-0347
EMP: 792
SALES (corp-wide): 135MM **Privately
Held**
Web: www.esparzainc.com
SIC: 7361 Labor contractors (employment
agency)
PA: Esparza Enterprises, Inc.
  3851 Fruitvale Ave
  661 831-0002

(P-13518)
EXECUTIVE PERSONNEL
SERVICES
1526 Brookhollow Dr Ste 83, Santa Ana
(92705-5421)
PHONE..................714 310-9506
Mario Mendoza, *Pr*
Alinne Espinoza, *
EMP: 300 **EST:** 2013
SALES (est): 1.34MM **Privately Held**
SIC: 7361 Executive placement

(P-13519)
EXPERIAN EMPLOYER
SERVICES INC
475 Anton Blvd, Costa Mesa (92626-7037)
P.O. Box 1180 (03053-1180)
PHONE..................866 997-0422
Jay Rooney, *CEO*
Timothy Rooney, *
EMP: 165 **EST:** 2008
SQ FT: 6,000
SALES (est): 6.74MM **Privately Held**
Web: www.aaautokirkland.com
SIC: 7361 Employment agencies

(P-13520)
GARICH INC (PA)
Also Called: The Tristaff Group
841 Quails Trail Rd, Vista (92081-7500)
PHONE..................858 453-1331
Gary O Van Eik, *Pr*
Richard N Papike, *
EMP: 295 **EST:** 1971
SALES (est): 23.07MM
SALES (corp-wide): 23.07MM **Privately
Held**
Web: www.tristaff.com
SIC: 7361 8742 Executive placement;
  Management consulting services

(P-13521)
GARICH INC
Also Called: Tristaff Group
504 E Alvarado St Ste 201, Fallbrook
(92028-2364)
PHONE..................951 302-4750
Trevor Nevis, *Mgr*
EMP: 365
SALES (corp-wide): 10.58MM **Privately
Held**
Web: www.tristaff.com
SIC: 7361 Employment agencies
PA: Garich, Inc.
  841 Quails Trail Rd
  858 453-1331

(P-13522)
GO-STAFF INC
9878 Complex Dr, Oceanside (92054)
PHONE..............................760 730-8520
EMP: 1234
SALES (corp-wide): 15.74MM **Privately Held**
Web: www.go-staff.com
SIC: 7361 Executive placement
PA: Go-Staff, Inc.
8798 Complex Dr
858 292-8562

(P-13523)
GO-STAFF INC
240 W Lincoln Ave, Anaheim (92805-2903)
PHONE..............................657 242-9350
EMP: 1234
SALES (corp-wide): 15.74MM **Privately Held**
Web: www.go-staff.com
SIC: 7361 Executive placement
PA: Go-Staff, Inc.
8798 Complex Dr
858 292-8562

(P-13524)
GRANITE SOLUTIONS GROUPE INC (PA)
26565 Agoura Rd Ste 200, Calabasas (91302-1990)
P.O. Box 3399 (95619-3399)
PHONE..............................415 963-3999
Daniel Hector L'abbe, *CEO*
Ann Bauer, *
John Henning, *
EMP: 207 EST: 1998
SQ FT: 3,582
SALES (est): 19.14MM
SALES (corp-wide): 19.14MM **Privately Held**
Web: www.granitesolutionsgroupe.com
SIC: 7361 8742 Executive placement; Management consulting services

(P-13525)
HRN SERVICES INC
520 N Brand Blvd Ste 200, Glendale (91203-4734)
PHONE..............................323 951-1450
EMP: 95
Web: www.hrnservices.com
SIC: 7361 Nurses' registry

(P-13526)
HUNTINGTON BEACH UNION HIGH
7180 Yorktown Ave, Huntington Beach (92648-2680)
P.O. Box 787 (92648-0787)
PHONE..............................714 478-7684
EMP: 103
SALES (corp-wide): 359.57MM **Privately Held**
Web: www.hbuhsd.edu
SIC: 7361 Placement agencies
PA: Huntington Beach Union High School District
5832 Bolsa Ave
714 903-7000

(P-13527)
IBFTECH INC
Also Called: Image Business Forms
343 Main St, El Segundo (90245-3814)
PHONE..............................424 217-8010
John Koch, *Pr*
EMP: 100 EST: 1979
SQ FT: 4,000

SALES (est): 1.13MM **Privately Held**
Web: www.chiptonross.com
SIC: 7361 Executive placement

(P-13528)
IDEAL PROGRAM SERVICES INC
Also Called: Ideal Day Program H73485
3970 W Martin Luther King Jr Blvd, Los Angeles (90008-1732)
PHONE..............................323 296-2255
Omolara Okunubi, *CEO*
EMP: 71 EST: 1989
SQ FT: 8,880
SALES (est): 4.83MM **Privately Held**
Web: www.idealprogramsservices.org
SIC: 7361 5999 8322 Employment agencies; Technical aids for the handicapped; Social services for the handicapped

(P-13529)
INNOVATIVE PLACEMENTS INC
Also Called: Ipi Travel
12400 High Bluff Dr Ste 100, San Diego (92130-3077)
PHONE..............................800 322-9796
Letha Engelman, *Pr*
Retha Clark, *
John Engelman, *
EMP: 150 EST: 1999
SALES (est): 1.85MM **Privately Held**
SIC: 7361 Placement agencies

(P-13530)
JOBOT LLC
3101 W Coast Hwy Ste 200, Newport Beach (92663-4160)
PHONE..............................949 688-2000
Heidi Golledge, *Prin*
EMP: 600 EST: 2018
SALES (est): 23.9MM **Privately Held**
Web: www.jobot.com
SIC: 7361 Employment agencies

(P-13531)
JT RESOURCES INC
26372 Ruether Ave, Santa Clarita (91350-2990)
PHONE..............................661 367-6827
Darren Jackson, *Prin*
EMP: 110 EST: 2015
SALES (est): 9MM **Privately Held**
Web: www.jtresources.com
SIC: 7361 Labor contractors (employment agency)

(P-13532)
KIMCO STAFFING SERVICES INC
Also Called: Kimco Services
4295 Jurupa St Ste 107, Ontario (91761-1429)
PHONE..............................909 390-9881
Pammy Burton, *Mgr*
EMP: 974
SALES (corp-wide): 45.91MM **Privately Held**
Web: www.kimco.com
SIC: 7361 Labor contractors (employment agency)
PA: Kimco Staffing Services, Inc.
17872 Cowan
949 331-1199

(P-13533)
KIMCO STAFFING SERVICES INC
Also Called: Kimco Staffing Solutions
1770 Iowa Ave Ste 160, Riverside (92507-7400)

P.O. Box 25190 (92799-5190)
PHONE..............................951 686-3800
Silvia Roberts, *Mgr*
EMP: 1218
SALES (corp-wide): 45.91MM **Privately Held**
Web: www.kimco.com
SIC: 7361 Employment agencies
PA: Kimco Staffing Services, Inc.
17872 Cowan
949 331-1199

(P-13534)
KIMCO STAFFING SERVICES INC
3415 S Sepulveda Blvd Ste 1100, Los Angeles (90034-7090)
PHONE..............................310 622-1616
EMP: 487
SALES (corp-wide): 45.91MM **Privately Held**
Web: www.kimco.com
SIC: 7361 Placement agencies
PA: Kimco Staffing Services, Inc.
17872 Cowan
949 331-1199

(P-13535)
KINETICOM INC (PA)
333 H St, Chula Vista (91910-5555)
PHONE..............................619 330-3100
Michael Wager, *CEO*
William Coyman, *
Casey Marquand, *
Blair Bode, *
Michael Steadman, *
EMP: 80 EST: 1999
SALES (est): 13.01MM
SALES (corp-wide): 13.01MM **Privately Held**
Web: www.kineticom.com
SIC: 7361 Executive placement

(P-13536)
KORE1 LLC
36 Discovery, Irvine (92618-3751)
PHONE..............................949 706-6990
Steven Quarles, *Managing Member*
EMP: 153 EST: 2017
SALES (est): 35.75MM **Privately Held**
Web: www.kore1.com
SIC: 7361 Executive placement

(P-13537)
KORN FERRY (PA)
Also Called: Korn Ferry
1900 Avenue Of The Stars Ste 1500, Los Angeles (90067-4400)
PHONE..............................310 552-1834
Gary D Burnison, *Pr*
Robert P Rozok, *CCO*
EMP: 200 EST: 1060
SALES (est): 2.8B
SALES (corp-wide): 2.8B **Publicly Held**
Web: www.kornferry.com
SIC: 7361 8742 Employment agencies; Management consulting services

(P-13538)
L&T STAFFING INC
Also Called: Staffing Solutions
2122 W Whittier Blvd, Montebello (90640-4013)
PHONE..............................323 727-9056
Fortino Rivera, *Brnch Mgr*
EMP: 313
SALES (corp-wide): 3.11MM **Privately Held**
Web: www.staffingsolutions.us

SIC: 7361 Employment agencies
PA: L&T Staffing, Inc.
950 W 17th St Ste E
714 558-1821

(P-13539)
LA COSTA GLEN CRLSBAD CCRC LLC (PA)
Also Called: La Costa Glen
1940 Levante St, Carlsbad (92009-5174)
PHONE..............................760 704-6400
Richard D Aschenbrenner, *Managing Member*
E Justin Wilson Iii, *Managing Member*
Warren E Spieker Junior, *Managing Member*
EMP: 97 EST: 1991
SALES (est): 53.17MM
SALES (corp-wide): 53.17MM **Privately Held**
Web: www.continuinglife.com
SIC: 7361 Employment agencies

(P-13540)
LATERAL LINK GROUP INC
940 E 2nd St Apt 2, Los Angeles (90012-4348)
PHONE..............................310 405-0092
EMP: 100 EST: 2018
SALES (est): 3.6MM **Privately Held**
Web: www.laterallink.com
SIC: 7361 Executive placement

(P-13541)
LOAN ADMINISTRATION NETWRK INC
Also Called: Lani
2082 Business Center Dr Ste 250, Irvine (92612-1190)
PHONE..............................949 752-5246
Charlene Nichols, *Pr*
EMP: 100 EST: 1992
SALES (est): 2.16MM **Privately Held**
Web: www.lani.com
SIC: 7361 8742 Employment agencies; Financial consultant

(P-13542)
MCM HARVESTERS INC
1585 Lirio Ave, Ventura (93004-3227)
P.O. Box 4731 (93007-0731)
PHONE..............................805 659-6833
EMP: 300
SQ FT: 4,000
SALES (est): 11.48MM **Privately Held**
SIC: 7361 Labor contractors (employment agency)

(P-13543)
MEDISCAN DIAGNOSTIC SVCS LLC
Also Called: Mediscan Staffing Services
21050 Califa St Ste 100, Woodland Hills (91367-5103)
PHONE..............................818 758-4224
Val Serebryany, *Pr*
EMP: 100 EST: 1995
SALES (est): 998.49K
SALES (corp-wide): 2.02B **Publicly Held**
Web: www.mediscan.net
SIC: 7361 Employment agencies
HQ: Mediscan Nursing Staffing, Llc
21050 Califa St Ste 100
Woodland Hills CA 91367
818 758-8680

(P-13544)
MERRITT HAWKINS & ASSOC LLC (HQ)

12400 High Bluff Dr Ste 100, San Diego
(92130-3077)
PHONE.................................858 792-0711
Susan Salka Fka Nowakowski, CEO
Brian Scott, *
Denise Jackson, *
John Dillon, *
Maria Creps, *
EMP: 120 EST: 1987
SQ FT: 96,000
SALES (est): 25.96MM
SALES (corp-wide): 3.79B Publicly Held
Web: www.merritthawkins.com
SIC: 7361 Executive placement
PA: Amn Healthcare Services, Inc.
　　2999 Olympus Blvd Ste 500
　　866 871-8519

(P-13545)

MHS CUSTOMER SERVICES INC

7586 Trade St Ste C, San Diego
(92121-2427)
PHONE.................................858 695-2151
Don T Fryer, Pr
Theresa Phebes, *
EMP: 75 EST: 1985
SQ FT: 8,600
SALES (est): 4.72MM Privately Held
Web: www.callmhs.com
SIC: 7361 1542 1531 7299 Labor
　　contractors (employment agency);
　　Nonresidential construction, nec; Operative
　　builders; Handyman service

(P-13546)

**NORTH AMRCN STAFFING
GROUP INC**

3 Pointe Dr Ste 100, Brea (92821-7623)
PHONE.................................714 599-8399
Fred Flores, Pr
Cesar Hindu, VP
EMP: 70 EST: 2014
SALES (est): 1.04MM Privately Held
Web: www.nasg.com
SIC: 7361 8742 Employment agencies;
　　Management consulting services

(P-13547)

NURSECHOICE

12400 High Bluff Dr, San Diego
(92130-3077)
PHONE.................................866 557-6050
EMP: 89 EST: 2019
SALES (est): 470.61K Privately Held
Web: www.amnhealthcare.com
SIC: 7361 Employment agencies

(P-13548)

NURSEFINDERS LLC

Also Called: Nursefinders
1832 Commercenter Cir B, San Bernardino
(92408-3430)
PHONE.................................909 890-2286
TOLL FREE: 877
FAX: 909 890-2346
EMP: 150
SALES (corp-wide): 1.9B Publicly Held
SIC: 7361 7363 Employment agencies;
　　Temporary help service
HQ: Nursefinders, Llc
　　12400 High Bluff Dr
　　San Diego CA 92130
　　858 314-7427

(P-13549)

NURSEFINDERS LLC (HQ)

Also Called: Nursefinders
12400 High Bluff Dr, San Diego
(92130-3077)
P.O. Box 919024 (92191-9024)

PHONE.................................858 314-7427
Susan Salka, CEO
Ralph S Henderson, Pr
Denise L Jackson, Sr VP
Chad W, Reg Dir
Meredith M, Brnch Mgr
EMP: 110 EST: 1975
SQ FT: 22,000
SALES (est): 89.79MM
SALES (corp-wide): 3.79B Publicly Held
Web: www.nursefinders.com
SIC: 7361 8082 7363 8049 Placement
　　agencies; Home health care services; Help
　　supply services; Nurses, registered and
　　practical
PA: Amn Healthcare Services, Inc.
　　2999 Olympus Blvd Ste 500
　　866 871-8519

(P-13550)

OFFICEWORKS INC

11801 Pierce St Fl 2, Riverside
(92505-4400)
PHONE.................................951 784-2534
EMP: 85
SALES (corp-wide): 26.27MM Privately
Held
Web: www.officeworksrx.com
SIC: 7361 Employment agencies
PA: Officeworks, Inc.
　　3200 E Guasti Rd Ste 100
　　909 606-4100

(P-13551)

OSI STAFFING INC

10913 La Reina Ave Ste B, Downey
(90241-3654)
PHONE.................................562 261-5753
Jose Vazquez, CEO
Sid Dakoria, *
EMP: 100 EST: 2018
SALES (est): 9.39MM Privately Held
Web: www.osistaff.net
SIC: 7361 Placement agencies

(P-13552)

**PARTNERS PRSNNEL - MGT
SVCS LL**

Also Called: Nexem Staffing
3820 State St Ste B, Santa Barbara
(93105-3182)
PHONE.................................805 689-8191
EMP: 16932 EST: 2017
SALES (est): 10.12MM
SALES (corp-wide): 15.63MM Privately
Held
Web: www.partnerspersonnel.com
SIC: 7361 Employment agencies
PA: Staffing Partners Holdings Inc.
　　3820 State St Ste B
　　805 880-1900

(P-13553)

**PARTNERSHIP STAFFING SVCS
INC**

Also Called: Partnership Staffing Solutions
19431 Soledad Canyon Rd A3, Santa
Clarita (91351-2632)
PHONE.................................661 542-7074
Judith Robledo, CEO
Richard Schonfeld, CFO
EMP: 710 EST: 2020
SALES (est): 38MM Privately Held
Web: www.partnershipstaffing.net
SIC: 7361 Employment agencies

(P-13554)

PDS DEFENSE INC

3100 S Harbor Blvd Ste 135, Santa Ana
(92704-6813)

PHONE.................................214 647-9600
Dj Englert, Mgr
EMP: 274
Web: www.pdstech.com
SIC: 7361 Employment agencies
HQ: Pds Defense, Inc.
　　545 E John Carpenter Fwy
　　Irving TX 75062
　　214 647-9600

(P-13555)

**PIONEER HEALTHCARE SVCS
LLC**

Also Called: Pioneer H.S. LLC
6255 Ferris Sq # F, San Diego
(92121-3232)
PHONE.................................800 683-1209
Daniel Rietti, CEO
Daniel Rietti, Managing Member
EMP: 300 EST: 2012
SALES (est): 9.35MM Privately Held
Web: www.pioneer-healthcare.com
SIC: 7361 8049 8099 Employment agencies;
　　Physical therapist; Blood related health
　　services

(P-13556)

**PREFERRED HLTHCARE
RGISTRY INC**

4909 Murphy Canyon Rd Ste 210, San
Diego (92123-9600)
P.O. Box 17860 (92177-7860)
PHONE.................................800 787-6787
Melanie Reiten, Pr
Jennifer Hawk, *
Robyn Burlingame, *
EMP: 170 EST: 1994
SQ FT: 2,100
SALES (est): 26.36MM Privately Held
Web: www.mypreferred.com
SIC: 7361 7363 Employment agencies;
　　Temporary help service

(P-13557)

PRIME ONE INC

22410 Hawthorne Blvd Ste 4, Torrance
(90505-2596)
PHONE.................................310 378-1944
Elvira Musell, Pr
EMP: 156 EST: 2001
SQ FT: 1,000
SALES (est): 1.31MM Privately Held
SIC: 7361 Employment agencies

(P-13558)

**PROFESSNAL RGISTRY
NETWRK CORP**

Also Called: Gem Medical Management
17592 17th St Ste 225, Tustin
(92780-7913)
PHONE.................................714 832-5776
George Makridis, Pr
EMP: 75 EST: 2004
SALES (est): 2.03MM Privately Held
SIC: 7361 Employment agencies

(P-13559)

**PSG GLOBAL SOLUTIONS LLC
(HQ)**

4551 Glencoe Ave Ste 150, Marina Del Rey
(90292-7921)
PHONE.................................310 405-0340
Brian Cotter, Pr
Maureen Maranca, VP Fin
EMP: 1331 EST: 2008
SALES (est): 30.33MM
SALES (corp-wide): 236.27MM Privately
Held
Web: www.psgglobalsolutions.com

SIC: 7361 Executive placement
PA: Teleperformance Se
　　Du NAo 21 Au 25
　　153680566

(P-13560)

PTS ADVANCE

Also Called: Pts
1775 Flight Way Ste 100, Tustin
(92782-1845)
PHONE.................................949 268-4000
June Stein, Pr
Ronald Stein, *
Russell Stein, *
David Stein, *
EMP: 220 EST: 1995
SALES (est): 10.54MM Privately Held
Web: www.ptsadvance.com
SIC: 7361 Employment agencies

(P-13561)

**QUANTUM WORLD
TECHNOLOGIES INC**

4281 Katella Ave Ste 102, Los Alamitos
(90720-3592)
PHONE.................................805 834-0532
Rakesh Srivastava, CFO
EMP: 450 EST: 2016
SALES (est): 41.92MM Privately Held
Web: www.quantumworldit.com
SIC: 7361 Placement agencies

(P-13562)

R&D CONSULTING GROUP LLC

Also Called: R & D Partners
8910 University Center Ln Ste 400, San
Diego (92122-1025)
PHONE.................................570 277-7066
Mike Barnard, Ex Dir
Nancy Baltzer, *
EMP: 125 EST: 2012
SALES (est): 9.39MM Privately Held
Web: www.r-dpartners.com
SIC: 7361 Labor contractors (employment
　　agency)

(P-13563)

RAMCO ENTERPRISES LP

325 Plaza Dr Ste 1, Santa Maria
(93454-6929)
PHONE.................................805 922-9888
EMP: 446
SALES (corp-wide): 32.34MM Privately
Held
Web: www.ramcoenterpriseslp.com
SIC: 7361 Executive placement
PA: Ramco Enterprises, L.P.
　　710 La Guardia St
　　831 758-5272

(P-13564)

READYLINK INC

72030 Metroplex Dr, Thousand Palms
(92276-3384)
PHONE.................................760 343-7000
Daniel Caliendo, Prin
EMP: 99 EST: 2017
SALES (est): 9.85MM Privately Held
Web: www.readylinkstaffing.com
SIC: 7361 Employment agencies

(P-13565)

READYLINK HEALTHCARE

72030 Metroplex Dr, Thousand Palms
(92276-3384)
P.O. Box 1047 (92276-1047)
PHONE.................................760 343-7000
Barry L Treash, Pr
EMP: 85 EST: 2002
SALES (est): 8.98MM Privately Held

Web: www.readylinkstaffing.com
SIC: 7361 Nurses' registry

(P-13566)
RECRUIT 360
457 Ogle St, Costa Mesa (92627-3243)
PHONE..........................949 250-4420
Greg Kennedy, *Pr*
EMP: 115 **EST:** 2007
SALES (est): 1.51MM **Privately Held**
Web: www.recruit360.net
SIC: 7361 Executive placement

(P-13567)
REDLANDS EMPLOYMENT SERVICES
Also Called: Redlands Staffing Services
4295 Jurupa St Ste 110, Ontario
(91761-1429)
PHONE..........................951 688-0083
Matt Tahlmeyer, *Pr*
EMP: 344
Web: www.arrowstaffing.com
SIC: 7361 Placement agencies
PA: Redlands Employment Services Inc
499 W State St

(P-13568)
REHABABILITIES INC
Also Called: Social Service Professionals
11835 W Olympic Blvd Ste 1090e, Los
Angeles (90064-5006)
PHONE..........................310 473-4448
Ms. Meryl Stern, *Brnch Mgr*
EMP: 235
SALES (corp-wide): 1.82MM **Privately Held**
Web: www.rehababilities.com
SIC: 7361 Registries
PA: Rehababilities, Inc.
22936 Mirabel Dr
909 989-5699

(P-13569)
SE SCHER CORPORATION
Also Called: Acrobat Staffing
2525 Camino Del Rio S Ste 200, San Diego
(92108-3719)
PHONE..........................858 546-8300
Marc Caplan, *Brnch Mgr*
EMP: 663
SALES (corp-wide): 2.49MM **Privately Held**
SIC: 7361 Executive placement
PA: S.E. Scher Corporation
303 Hegenberger Rd # 300
415 431-8826

(P-13570)
SELECT TEMPORARIES LLC (DH)
Also Called: Select Personnel Services
3820 State St, Santa Barbara (93105-3182)
PHONE..........................805 882-2200
Thomas A Bickes, *Pr*
Paul Galleberg, *
Shawn W Poole, *
▲ **EMP:** 90 **EST:** 1985
SQ FT: 30,000
SALES (est): 37.59MM
SALES (corp-wide): 32.64B **Publicly Held**
Web: www.select.com
SIC: 7361 6794 Employment agencies;
Franchises, selling or licensing
HQ: Employment Solutions Management,
Inc.
1845 Satellite Blvd
Duluth GA 30097
770 671-1900

(P-13571)
SIGNATURE SELECT PERSONNEL LLC
138 W Bonita Ave Ste 207, San Dimas
(91773-3083)
P.O. Box 4309 (91723-4309)
PHONE..........................626 940-3351
Kenji Morinaga, *Managing Member*
Robert Morinaga, *
EMP: 500 **EST:** 2019
SALES (est): 14.18MM **Privately Held**
SIC: 7361 Employment agencies

(P-13572)
SIRACUSA ENTERPRISES INC
Also Called: Quality Temp Staffing
17737 Chatsworth St Ste 200, Granada Hills
(91344-5628)
PHONE..........................818 831-1130
Joe Alas, *Pr*
Marie Alas, *
EMP: 70 **EST:** 1988
SALES (est): 2.62MM **Privately Held**
Web: www.qualitytempstaffing.com
SIC: 7361 Employment agencies

(P-13573)
SOURCE ONE STAFFING LLC
5312 Irwindale Ave Ste 1h, Baldwin Park
(91706-2076)
PHONE..........................626 337-0560
EMP: 9500
Web: www.s1staffing.com
SIC: 7361 Employment agencies

(P-13574)
STAFF ASSISTANCE INC
Also Called: Assisted Home Care
72 Moody Ct Ste 100, Thousand Oaks
(91360-7426)
PHONE..........................805 371-9980
Elaine Thinney, *Brnch Mgr*
EMP: 300
Web: www.assistedcares.com
SIC: 7361 8082 Nurses' registry; Home
health care services
PA: Staff Assistance, Inc.
72 Moody Ct Ste 100

(P-13575)
TEAM-ONE STAFFING SERVICES INC
Also Called: Teamone Employment
16030 Ventura Blvd Ste 430, Encino
(91436-4457)
PHONE..........................951 616-3515
EMP: 2829
Web: www.teamone.com
SIC: 7361 Placement agencies
PA: Team-One Staffing Services, Inc.
24318 Hemlock Ave Ste C1

(P-13576)
TEG STAFFING INC
Also Called: Eastridge Workforce Solutions
2385 Northside Dr Ste 250, San Diego
(92108-2716)
PHONE..........................800 918-1678
Seth Stein, *CEO*
Brandon Stanford, *
Erin Medina, *CLO*
Kasey Hadjis, *CAO*
Jairo Carrion, *
EMP: 1600 **EST:** 1971
SALES (est): 4.18MM
SALES (corp-wide): 139MM **Privately Held**
Web: www.eastridge.com

SIC: 7361 Employment agencies
PA: Eplica, Inc.
2385 Northside Dr Ste 250
619 260-2000

(P-13577)
TEMPUS LLC
Also Called: Emerald Health Services
2041 Rosecrans Ave Ste 245, El Segundo
(90245-7509)
PHONE..........................800 917-5055
Mark Siegel, *CEO*
Mark Stagen, *
EMP: 70 **EST:** 2002
SALES (est): 20.97MM **Privately Held**
Web: www.epictravelstaffing.com
SIC: 7361 Nurses' registry

(P-13578)
TETRA TECH EXECUTIVE SVCS INC
3475 E Foothill Blvd, Pasadena
(91107-6024)
PHONE..........................626 470-2400
Sam Box, *Prin*
EMP: 162 **EST:** 2013
SALES (est): 2.36MM
SALES (corp-wide): 4.52B **Publicly Held**
Web: www.tetratech.com
SIC: 7361 Employment agencies
PA: Tetra Tech, Inc.
3475 E Foothill Blvd
626 351-4664

(P-13579)
TWOMAGNETS LLC
Also Called: Clipboard Health
440 N Barranca Ave Pmb 5028, Covina
(91723-1722)
PHONE..........................408 837-0116
Wei Deng, *CEO*
EMP: 650 **EST:** 2016
SALES (est): 48.53MM **Privately Held**
Web: www.clipboardhealth.com
SIC: 7361 Employment agencies

(P-13580)
VISH CONSULTING SERVICES INC
9655 Granite Ridge Dr Ste 200, San Diego
(92123-2676)
PHONE..........................916 800-3762
Dhruv Bindra, *Pr*
EMP: 80 **EST:** 2011
SALES (est): 40.57MM **Privately Held**
Web: www.vishusa.com
SIC: 7361 7363 Employment agencies;
Temporary help service

(P-13581)
WILLIAM MRRIS ENDVOR ENTRMT LL (DH)
Also Called: Wme
9601 Wilshire Blvd, Beverly Hills
(90210-5213)
PHONE..........................212 586-5100
Walter Zifkin, *CEO*
Norman Brokaw, *
Jerry Katzman, *
Leonard Hirshan, *
Owen Laster, *
EMP: 200 **EST:** 1898
SQ FT: 46,000
SALES (est): 728.47MM
SALES (corp-wide): 5.96B **Publicly Held**
Web: www.wmeagency.com
SIC: 7361 Employment agencies
HQ: Endeavor Operating Company, Llc
11 Madison Ave

New York NY 10010
212 586-5100

(P-13582)
WMBE PAYROLLING INC
Also Called: Tcwglobal
3545 Aero Ct, San Diego (92123-5700)
PHONE..........................858 810-3000
Samer Khouli, *CEO*
EMP: 130 **EST:** 2009
SALES (est): 349.34MM **Privately Held**
Web: www.tcwglobal.com
SIC: 7361 Placement agencies

(P-13583)
WORKWAY INC
19742 Macarthur Blvd Ste 235, Irvine
(92612-2446)
PHONE..........................949 553-8700
Jill Burdock, *Brnch Mgr*
EMP: 227
Web: www.workway.com
SIC: 7361 Labor contractors (employment
agency)
PA: Workway, Inc.
5151 Belt Line Rd

(P-13584)
WORKWAY INC
3111 Camino Del Rio N Ste 400, San Diego
(92108-5724)
PHONE..........................619 278-0012
Bea Ogle, *Mgr*
EMP: 226
Web: www.workway.com
SIC: 7361 Executive placement
PA: Workway, Inc.
5151 Belt Line Rd

(P-13585)
XL STAFFING INC
Also Called: Excell Staffing & SEC Svcs
826 Jackman St, El Cajon (92020-3053)
PHONE..........................619 579-0442
William Mackey, *Pr*
EMP: 200 **EST:** 1996
SALES (est): 5.29MM **Privately Held**
Web: www.xlstaffing.com
SIC: 7361 7381 Executive placement;
Security guard service

7363 Help Supply Services

(P-13586)
A P R INC
Also Called: Alpha Professional Resources
100 E Thousand Oaks Blvd Ste 240,
Thousand Oaks (91360-8107)
PHONE..........................805 379-3400
Salvador Ramirez, *Pr*
Cliff Goodwin, *
EMP: 125 **EST:** 1993
SQ FT: 1,100
SALES (est): 2.45MM **Privately Held**
Web: www.alphaprotemps.com
SIC: 7363 7361 Temporary help service;
Employment agencies

(P-13587)
ADECCO EMPLOYMENT SERVICES
25301 Cabot Rd Ste 214, Aliso Viejo
(92653-5512)
PHONE..........................949 586-2342
Tina Robinson, *Brnch Mgr*
EMP: 150
Web: www.adeccousa.com

PRODUCTS & SVCS

SIC: 7363 Temporary help service
HQ: Adecco Employment Services, Inc
4800 Deerwood Campus Pkwy # 800
Jacksonville FL 32246
631 844-7100

(P-13588)
ADO STAFFING INC
Also Called: Adecco Staffing
850 Lagoon Dr Bldg 99a, Chula Vista
(91910-2001)
PHONE..................619 691-3659
Susannah Wright, Mgr
EMP: 200
Web: www.olsten.com
SIC: 7363 Temporary help service
HQ: Ado Staffing, Inc.
4800 Deerwood Campus Pkwy # 800
Jacksonville FL 32246
631 844-7800

(P-13589)
ALTECH SERVICES INC
400 Continental Blvd Fl 6, El Segundo
(90245-5074)
PHONE..................888 725-8324
EMP: 296
Web: www.altechts.com
SIC: 7363 7361 Help supply services; Labor
contractors (employment agency)
PA: Altech Services, Inc.
695 Us Highway 46

(P-13590)
ANDERSON ASSOC STAFFING CORP (PA)
8200 Wilshire Blvd Ste 200, Beverly Hills
(90211-2331)
PHONE..................323 930-3170
Tom Anderson, Pr
EMP: 200 EST: 1997
SALES (est): 1.19MM
SALES (corp-wide): 1.19MM Privately Held
SIC: 7363 Temporary help service

(P-13591)
AYA HEALTHCARE INC (PA)
5930 Cornerstone Ct W Ste 300, San Diego
(92121-3772)
PHONE..................858 458-4410
Alan Braynin, Pr
EMP: 242 EST: 2009
SQ FT: 20,000
SALES (est): 6B Privately Held
Web: www.ayahealthcare.com
SIC: 7363 8049 Temporary help service;
Nurses, registered and practical

(P-13592)
B2B STAFFING SERVICES INC
Also Called: B2b Payroll Services
4501 Cerritos Ave Ste 201, Cypress
(90630-4215)
PHONE..................714 243-4104
Brian Wigdor, Pr
Bruce Underwood, *
EMP: 350 EST: 2006
SALES (est): 4.9MM Privately Held
Web: www.b2bstaffingservices.com
SIC: 7363 Temporary help service

(P-13593)
BUTLER SERVICE GROUP INC (HQ)
3820 State St Ste A, Santa Barbara
(93105-3182)
PHONE..................201 891-5312
EMP: 100 EST: 1965

SQ FT: 82,000
SALES (est): 146.12MM
SALES (corp-wide): 242.14MM Privately Held
SIC: 7363 8711 8748 3661 Engineering help
service; Engineering services;
Communications consulting; Telephone and
telegraph apparatus
PA: Butler International, Inc.
3820 State St Ste A
805 882-2200

(P-13594)
CARDINAL POINT CAPTAINS INC
Also Called: Cardinal Point Captains
5005 Texas St Ste 104, San Diego
(92108-3722)
PHONE..................760 438-7361
Jordan E Cousino, CEO
Bill Green, CDO*
Heather Jenkins, ACCT AND CONTRACTS*
EMP: 56 EST: 2008
SQ FT: 2,633
SALES (est): 5.39MM Privately Held
Web: www.cpcperforms.com
SIC: 7363 3812 Boat crew service; Search
and navigation equipment

(P-13595)
CARE STFFING PROFESSIONALS INC
2151 E Convention Center Way Ste 204,
Ontario (91764-5429)
PHONE..................909 906-2060
D'andre Lampkin, CEO
EMP: 80 EST: 2016
SALES (est): 4.65MM Privately Held
Web:
www.carestaffingprofessionals.com
SIC: 7363 7361 8049 8082 Medical help
service; Nurses' registry; Nurses and other
medical assistants; Visiting nurse service

(P-13596)
EPLICA INC (PA)
Also Called: Eastridge Workforce Solutions
2385 Northside Dr Ste 250, San Diego
(92108-2716)
PHONE..................619 260-2000
Robert Svet, Pr
EMP: 175 EST: 1971
SQ FT: 15,000
SALES (est): 139MM
SALES (corp-wide): 139MM Privately Held
Web: www.eplicaservices.com
SIC: 7363 7361 Temporary help service;
Employment agencies

(P-13597)
GARICH INC
Also Called: Tristaff Group, The
27540 Ynez Rd, Temecula (92591-5601)
PHONE..................951 699-2899
Claudia Delreal, Mgr
EMP: 364
SALES (corp-wide): 10.58MM Privately Held
Web: www.tristaff.com
SIC: 7363 Help supply services
PA: Garich, Inc.
841 Quails Trail Rd
858 453-1331

(P-13598)
HEALTHCARE RESOURCE GROUP
6571 Altura Blvd Ste 200, Buena Park
(90620-1020)

PHONE..................562 945-7224
Mahabir Atwall Ph.d., Brnch Mgr
EMP: 192
SALES (corp-wide): 339.44MM Publicly Held
Web: www.trubridge.com
SIC: 7363 Medical help service
HQ: Healthcare Resource Group, Inc
12610 E Mirabeau Pkwy # 900
Spokane Valley WA 99216

(P-13599)
HOST HEALTHCARE INC
4225 Executive Sq Ste 1500, La Jolla
(92037-1487)
P.O. Box 927190 (92192-7190)
PHONE..................858 999-3579
Adam Francis, CEO
William Bulger, *
EMP: 525 EST: 2012
SQ FT: 1,400
SALES (est): 37.4MM Privately Held
Web: www.hosthealthcare.com
SIC: 7363 Help supply services

(P-13600)
I N C BUILDERS INC
Also Called: Acme Staffing
1560 Ocotillo Dr Ste L, El Centro
(92243-4237)
PHONE..................760 352-4200
Rebecca Deal, Mgr
EMP: 350
SALES (corp-wide): 11.06MM Privately Held
Web: www.acmestaffing.com
SIC: 7363 Temporary help service
PA: I N C Builders, Inc.
550 E 32nd St Ste 5a
928 344-8367

(P-13601)
JOSHUA A SIEMBIEDA MD PC
Also Called: Emsoc
1310 W Stewart Dr Ste 212, Orange
(92868-3837)
PHONE..................714 543-8911
Matthey Mallarky, Managing Member
Mark Falcone Parnter, Prin
Jonathen Blair, *
Courtney Aldama, *
EMP: 88 EST: 1976
SALES (est): 5.77MM Privately Held
Web: www.emsoc.net
SIC: 7363 Medical help service

(P-13602)
JUNE GROUP LLC
Also Called: Qualstaff Resources
10089 Willow Creek Rd, San Diego
(92131-1697)
PHONE..................858 450-4290
R Scott Silver-hill, Managing Member
EMP: 100 EST: 2003
SALES (est): 1.91MM Privately Held
Web: www.qualstaffresources.com
SIC: 7363 Temporary help service

(P-13603)
LLOYD STAFFING INC
18000 Studebaker Rd Ste 700, Cerritos
(90703-2684)
PHONE..................631 777-7600
Luly Santana, Pr
EMP: 257
SALES (corp-wide): 14.14MM Privately Held
Web: www.lloydstaffing.com
SIC: 7363 Temporary help service
PA: Lloyd Staffing, Inc.
445 Broadhollow Rd # 119

631 777-7600

(P-13604)
MAGNIT RS INC
Also Called: Rightsourcing of Rhode Island
9 Executive Cir Ste 290, Irvine
(92614-4704)
PHONE..................800 660-9544
Kevin Akeroyd, CEO
Maria Luoni, *
EMP: 77 EST: 2003
SALES (est): 44.27MM Privately Held
Web: www.rightsourcingusa.com
SIC: 7363 Help supply services
PA: Magnit, Llc
2635 Iron Pt Rd Ste 270

(P-13605)
MAXIM HEALTHCARE SERVICES INC
Also Called: Temecula Homecare
27555 Ynez Rd, Temecula (92591-4687)
PHONE..................951 694-0100
Jeff Abbott, Mgr
EMP: 140
Web: www.maximhealthcare.com
SIC: 7363 Medical help service
PA: Maxim Healthcare Services, Inc.
7227 Lee Deforest Dr

(P-13606)
MAXIM HEALTHCARE SERVICES INC
Also Called: Riverside Companion Services
1845 Business Center Dr Ste 112, San
Bernardino (92408-3447)
PHONE..................951 684-4148
Elijah Hall, Mgr
EMP: 84
Web: www.maximhealthcare.com
SIC: 7363 Medical help service
PA: Maxim Healthcare Services, Inc.
7227 Lee Deforest Dr

(P-13607)
MAXIM HEALTHCARE SERVICES INC
879 W 190th St, Gardena (90248-4220)
PHONE..................310 329-9115
EMP: 138
Web: www.maximhealthcare.com
SIC: 7363 Medical help service
PA: Maxim Healthcare Services, Inc.
7227 Lee Deforest Dr

(P-13608)
MAXIM HEALTHCARE SERVICES INC
Also Called: Bakersfield Respite Homecare
4540 California Ave, Bakersfield
(93309-7022)
PHONE..................661 322-3039
Reyes Robles, Brnch Mgr
EMP: 84
Web: www.maximhealthcare.com
SIC: 7363 Medical help service
PA: Maxim Healthcare Services, Inc.
7227 Lee Deforest Dr

(P-13609)
MAXIM HEALTHCARE SERVICES INC
28470 Avenue Stanford Ste 250, Valencia
(91355-0916)
PHONE..................661 964-6350
Kowalczyk David, Mgr
EMP: 84
Web: www.maximhealthcare.com

▲ = Import ▼ = Export
◆ = Import/Export

SIC: **7363** 8099 8748 Medical help service;
Blood related health services; Testing
services
PA: Maxim Healthcare Services, Inc.
7227 Lee Deforest Dr

(P-13610)
MAXIM HEALTHCARE SERVICES INC
801 Corporate Center Dr Ste 210, Pomona
(91768-2627)
PHONE.............................626 962-6453
Kirk Grant, *Mgr*
EMP: 84
Web: www.maximhealthcare.com
SIC: **7363** 7361 Medical help service;
Nurses' registry
PA: Maxim Healthcare Services, Inc.
7227 Lee Deforest Dr

(P-13611)
MAXIM HEALTHCARE SERVICES INC
104 Traffic Way Ste A, Arroyo Grande
(93420-3451)
PHONE.............................805 489-2685
Jeremiah Lee, *Brnch Mgr*
EMP: 84
Web: www.maximhealthcare.com
SIC: **7363** 8099 8748 Medical help service;
Blood related health services; Testing
services
PA: Maxim Healthcare Services, Inc.
7227 Lee Deforest Dr

(P-13612)
MAXIM HEALTHCARE SERVICES INC
300 E Esplanade Dr Ste 1500, Oxnard
(93036-0244)
PHONE.............................805 278-4593
EMP: 81
Web: www.maximhealthcare.com
SIC: **7363** Medical help service
PA: Maxim Healthcare Services, Inc.
7227 Lee Deforest Dr

(P-13613)
MED SOURCE VENTURES INC
Also Called: Med Source Prof Personnel
3750 Convoy St Ste 155, San Diego
(92111-3739)
PHONE.............................858 560-9941
Mark M Perry, *Pr*
Mark Perry, *
Eric Meyers, *
EMP: 300 **EST:** 1988
SQ FT: 5,000
SALES (est): 10.22MM
SALES (corp-wide): 10.7MM **Privately
Held**
SIC: **7363** Medical help service
PA: First Call Team / Nurses Prn
4321 W College Ave # 200
920 830-8811

(P-13614)
MEK INDUSTRIES INC
11491 Woodside Ave, Santee (92071-4724)
PHONE.............................858 610-9601
Marc Kranz, *CEO*
EMP: 200 **EST:** 2019
SALES (est): 4.24MM **Privately Held**
SIC: **7363** Manpower pools

(P-13615)
PERSONNEL PLUS INC
12052 Imperial Hwy Ste 200, Norwalk
(90650-3093)

P.O. Box 817 (90651-0817)
PHONE.............................562 712-5490
EMP: 155
Web: www.ppitemps.com
SIC: **7363** 7361 Temporary help service;
Employment agencies

(P-13616)
PHOENIX ENGINEERING CO INC
Also Called: Phoenix Personnel
2480 Armacost Ave, Los Angeles
(90064-2714)
P.O. Box 66395 (90066-0395)
PHONE.............................310 532-1134
Silvia Maron, *Pr*
Silvia Lugo, *
EMP: 100 **EST:** 1974
SQ FT: 1,700
SALES (est): 1.29MM **Privately Held**
Web: www.phoenix-engineering.com
SIC: **7363** 7361 Office help supply service;
Employment agencies

(P-13617)
PLATINUM EMPIRE GROUP INC
Also Called: Platinum Healthcare Staffing
2430 Amsler St Ste B, Torrance
(90505-5302)
P.O. Box 10338 (90505)
PHONE.............................310 821-5888
Arun Mahtani, *Pr*
Maluh Silvano, *
Aaron Quiboloy, *
EMP: 120 **EST:** 2005
SALES (est): 9.19MM **Privately Held**
Web:
www.platinumhealthcarestaffing.com
SIC: **7363** Temporary help service

(P-13618)
REMEDYTEMP INC (DH)
Also Called: Remedy Intelligent Staffing
101 Enterprise Ste 100, Aliso Viejo
(92656-2604)
PHONE.............................949 425-7630
David Stephen Sorensen, *CEO*
Richard Hulme, *Ex VP*
Jeff R Mitchell, *CFO*
EMP: 143 **EST:** 1974
SQ FT: 51,000
SALES (est): 38.24MM
SALES (corp-wide): 32.64B **Publicly Held**
Web: www.remedystaff.com
SIC: **7363** 7361 Temporary help service;
Employment agencies
HQ: Employbridge, Llc
301 Mentor Dr Ste 210
Santa Barbara CA 93111

(P-13619)
ROTH STAFFING COMPANIES LP (PA)
Also Called: Ultimate Staffing Services
450 N State College Blvd, Orange
(92868-1708)
PHONE.............................714 939-8600
Adam Roth, *CEO*
Ben Roth, *
Pam Sexauer, *
◆ **EMP:** 80 **EST:** 1994
SALES (est): 97.49MM **Privately Held**
Web: www.rothstaffing.com
SIC: **7363** Help supply services

(P-13620)
RX PRO HEALTH LLC
12400 High Bluff Dr Ste 100, San Diego
(92130-3077)
PHONE.............................858 369-4050
Susan R Salka, *CEO*

EMP: 1800 **EST:** 2003
SQ FT: 175,000
SALES (est): 2.22MM
SALES (corp-wide): 3.79B **Publicly Held**
SIC: **7363** Medical help service
PA: Amn Healthcare Services, Inc.
2999 Olympus Blvd Ste 500
866 871-8519

(P-13621)
SFN GROUP INC
Also Called: Spherion Prof Recruiting Group
4660 La Jolla Village Dr Ste 910, San Diego
(92122-4608)
PHONE.............................858 458-9200
Bobby Nerini, *Mgr*
EMP: 859
SALES (corp-wide): 27.64B **Privately Held**
Web: www.spherion.com
SIC: **7363** Temporary help service
HQ: Sfn Group, Inc.
2050 Spectrum Blvd
Fort Lauderdale FL 33309
954 308-7600

(P-13622)
SFN GROUP INC
114 Pacifica Ste 210, Irvine (92618-3320)
PHONE.............................949 727-8500
Tammy Hawkins, *Mgr*
EMP: 736
SALES (corp-wide): 27.64B **Privately Held**
Web: www.spherion.com
SIC: **7363** Temporary help service
HQ: Sfn Group, Inc.
2050 Spectrum Blvd
Fort Lauderdale FL 33309
954 308-7600

(P-13623)
SOUTHERN HOME CARE SVCS INC
Also Called: Kelly Services
2900 Bristol St Ste D107, Costa Mesa
(92626-5940)
PHONE.............................714 979-7413
Vicki Demirozu, *Dir*
EMP: 85
SALES (corp-wide): 8.83B **Publicly Held**
Web: www.kellyservices.com
SIC: **7363** 8082 Temporary help service;
Home health care services
HQ: Southern Home Care Services, Inc.
805 N Whttngton Pkwy Ste
Louisville KY 40222
502 394-2100

(P-13624)
STABILITY HEALTHCARE INC
Also Called: Stability Healthcare
87 E Groen St Ste 302, Pasadena
(91105-2072)
PHONE.............................626 568-1540
Jason Casani, *CEO*
EMP: 384 **EST:** 2009
SALES (est): 12.54MM **Privately Held**
Web: www.stabilityhealthcare.com
SIC: **7363** 7361 Temporary help service;
Employment agencies

(P-13625)
TAD PGS INC
12062 Valley View St Ste 108, Garden
Grove (92845-1737)
PHONE.............................800 261-3779
Latonya Walker, *Dir*
EMP: 797
Web: www.tadpgs.com
SIC: **7363** Temporary help service
HQ: Tad Pgs, Inc.
1001 3rd Ave W Ste 460

Bradenton FL 34205
941 746-4434

(P-13626)
TAD PGS INC
10805 Holder St Ste 250, Cypress
(90630-5142)
PHONE.............................571 451-2428
Wendy Harkins, *CFO*
EMP: 797
Web: www.tadpgs.com
SIC: **7363** Temporary help service
HQ: Tad Pgs, Inc.
1001 3rd Ave W Ste 460
Bradenton FL 34205
941 746-4434

(P-13627)
TRIPOD INC
Also Called: Brightstar Care Oxnard Cmrllo
1545 W 5th St Ste 200, Oxnard
(93030-6510)
PHONE.............................805 585-2273
EMP: 75
SALES (corp-wide): 1.76MM **Privately
Held**
SIC: **7363** Medical help service
PA: Tripod Inc.
148 N Brent St Ste 201

(P-13628)
USA STAFFING INC
505 Higuera St, San Luis Obispo
(93401-6107)
PHONE.............................805 269-2677
Susan Elson, *Mgr*
EMP: 75 **EST:** 2010
SALES (est): 2.11MM **Privately Held**
Web: www.unitedwestaff.com
SIC: **7363** Temporary help service

(P-13629)
VASINDA INVESTMENTS INC
Also Called: Around The Clock Care
5353 Truckston Ave, Bakersfield (93309)
PHONE.............................661 324-4277
Mary Vasinda, *Pr*
John Vasinda, *VP*
EMP: 75 **EST:** 1994
SALES (est): 2.45MM **Privately Held**
Web: www.bakersfieldcare.com
SIC: **7363** Domestic help service

(P-13630)
VAYA WORKFORCE SOLUTIONS LLC
5930 Cornerstone Ct W Ste 300, San Diego
(92121-3772)
PHONE.............................866 687-7390
Alan Braynin, *Pr*
EMP: 150 **EST:** 2021
SALES (est): 22.66MM **Privately Held**
Web: www.vayaworkforce.com
SIC: **7363** Temporary help service
PA: Aya Healthcare, Inc.
5930 Crnrstone Ct W Ste 3

(P-13631)
VOLT MANAGEMENT CORP
Also Called: Volt Workforce Solutions
7676 Hazard Center Dr Ste 1000, San
Diego (92108-4517)
PHONE.............................858 576-3140
Rhona Driggs, *Brnch Mgr*
EMP: 92
SALES (corp-wide): 885.39MM **Privately
Held**
Web: www.volt.com

SIC: 7363 Temporary help service
HQ: Volt Management Corp.
　　1455 Lincoln Pkwy E
　　Atlanta GA 30346

(P-13632)
VOLT MANAGEMENT CORP
Also Called: Volt Temporary Services
2411 N Glassell St, Orange (92865-2717)
PHONE.................................800 654-2624
Rhona Driggs, *Brnch Mgr*
EMP: 300
SALES (corp-wide): 885.39MM **Privately Held**
Web: www.volt.com
SIC: 7363 7373 Temporary help service; Computer integrated systems design
HQ: Volt Management Corp.
　　1455 Lincoln Pkwy E
　　Atlanta GA 30346

(P-13633)
VOLT MANAGEMENT CORP
Also Called: Volt Workforce Solutions
1400 N Harbor Blvd Ste 103, Fullerton (92835-4107)
PHONE.................................714 879-9330
Scott Giroux, *Brnch Mgr*
EMP: 81
SQ FT: 11,000
SALES (corp-wide): 885.39MM **Privately Held**
Web: www.volt.com
SIC: 7363 Temporary help service
HQ: Volt Management Corp.
　　1455 Lincoln Pkwy E
　　Atlanta GA 30346

(P-13634)
VOLT MANAGEMENT CORP
Also Called: Volt Workforce Solutions
1701 Solar Dr, Oxnard (93030-0134)
PHONE.................................805 560-8658
Scott Giroux, *Brnch Mgr*
EMP: 81
SALES (corp-wide): 885.39MM **Privately Held**
Web: www.volt.com
SIC: 7363 Temporary help service
HQ: Volt Management Corp.
　　1455 Lincoln Pkwy E
　　Atlanta GA 30346

(P-13635)
WORK FORCE SERVICES INC
Also Called: Work Force Staffing
3612 Coffee Rd Ste B, Bakersfield (93308-5084)
PHONE.................................661 327-5019
Brooks Whitehead, *Pr*
EMP: 250 **EST:** 1981
SALES (est): 2.51MM **Privately Held**
Web: www.workforcestaffing1.com
SIC: 7363 Temporary help service

(P-13636)
WORKFORCE MANAGEMENT GROUP INC
800 N Haven Ave Ste 330, Ontario (91764-4976)
PHONE.................................909 718-8915
Andrew D Hernandez Senior, *CEO*
EMP: 539 **EST:** 2018
SALES (est): 42MM **Privately Held**
SIC: 7363 Manpower pools

7371 Custom Computer Programming Services

(P-13637)
1NTEGER LLC
Also Called: Kharon
10351 Santa Monica Blvd Ste 405, Los Angeles (90025-6908)
PHONE.................................424 320-2977
EMP: 130 **EST:** 2016
SALES (est): 16.92MM **Privately Held**
Web: www.kharon.com
SIC: 7371 Computer software systems analysis and design, custom

(P-13638)
3DNA CORP (PA)
Also Called: Nationbuilder
750 W 7th St Ste 201, Los Angeles (90017-3710)
P.O. Box 811428 (90081-0008)
PHONE.................................213 992-4809
Lea Endres, *CEO*
EMP: 127 **EST:** 2007
SALES (est): 8.4MM
SALES (corp-wide): 8.4MM **Privately Held**
Web: www.nationbuilder.com
SIC: 7371 Computer software development

(P-13639)
3I INFOTECH INC
Also Called: 3I INFOTECH INC
555 Chorro St Ste B, San Luis Obispo (93405-2398)
PHONE.................................805 544-8327
Mathew Philip, *CFO*
EMP: 45
Web: www.3i-infotech.com
SIC: 7371 7372 7373 7379 Computer software development; Prepackaged software; Computer integrated systems design; Computer related consulting services
HQ: 3i Infotech Inc.
　　110 Fieldcrest Ave Ste 25
　　Edison NJ 08837

(P-13640)
A BETTER LIFE RECOVERY LLC
30310 Rancho Viejo Rd, San Juan Capistrano (92675-1576)
PHONE.................................866 278-8804
EMP: 342 **EST:** 2019
SALES (est): 14.73MM **Privately Held**
Web: www.abetterliferecovery.com
SIC: 7371 8093 8361 Computer software development; Substance abuse clinics (outpatient); Residential care

(P-13641)
A R SANTEX LLC (PA)
Also Called: Santex Group
6790 Embarcadero Ln Ste 100, Carlsbad (92011-3278)
PHONE.................................888 622-7098
Juan Santiago, *CEO*
Gabriela Fernandez, *CFO*
EMP: 39 **EST:** 1999
SALES (est): 4.31MM
SALES (corp-wide): 4.31MM **Privately Held**
Web: www.santexgroup.com
SIC: 7371 7372 7373 Computer software systems analysis and design, custom; Business oriented computer software; Systems software development services

(P-13642)
ABACUS DATA SYSTEMS INC (PA)
Also Called: Abacusnext
2010 Jimmy Durante Blvd Ste 130, Del Mar (92014-2260)
PHONE.................................858 452-4280
Keri Gohman, *CEO*
Jerome Fodor, *
Eric Cutler, *Chief Sales & Marketing Officer**
Tomas Suros, *SOLN'S**
Chris Cardinal, *OF Software ENG'G**
EMP: 158 **EST:** 1983
SQ FT: 10,000
SALES (est): 44.26MM
SALES (corp-wide): 44.26MM **Privately Held**
Web: www.getcaret.com
SIC: 7371 7374 Computer software systems analysis and design, custom; Data processing and preparation

(P-13643)
ADAPTAMED LLC
6699 Alvarado Rd Ste 2301, San Diego (92120-5241)
PHONE.................................877 478-7773
EMP: 120 **EST:** 2011
SALES (est): 1.11MM **Privately Held**
Web: www.ehryourway.com
SIC: 7371 Computer software development

(P-13644)
ADCOLONY INC
11400 W Olympic Blvd # 1200, Los Angeles (90064-1583)
PHONE.................................650 625-1262
EMP: 100 **EST:** 2008
SALES (est): 20.51MM **Publicly Held**
Web: www.digitalturbine.com
SIC: 7371 Computer software development
HQ: Adcolony Holdings Us, Inc.
　　901 Mariners Blvd Ste 250
　　San Mateo CA 94404
　　650 625-1262

(P-13645)
ADVENT RESOURCES INC
235 W 7th St, San Pedro (90731-3321)
P.O. Box 1740 (90733-1740)
PHONE.................................310 241-1500
Ysidro Salinas, *Ch Bd*
Timothy Gill, *
EMP: 80 **EST:** 1984
SQ FT: 22,000
SALES (est): 9.64MM **Privately Held**
Web: www.adventresources.com
SIC: 7371 Computer software development

(P-13646)
AKKODIS INC
Also Called: Modis
801 N Brand Blvd Ste 250, Glendale (91203-3251)
PHONE.................................818 546-2848
Lisa Bertram, *Brnch Mgr*
EMP: 108
Web: www.modis.com
SIC: 7371 Computer software systems analysis and design, custom
HQ: Akkodis, Inc.
　　4800 Drwood Cmpus Pkwy Bl
　　Jacksonville FL 32256
　　904 360-2300

(P-13647)
ALGORITHMIC OBJECTIVE CORP
Also Called: Algotive

8910 University Center Ln Ste 400, San Diego (92122-1025)
PHONE.................................858 249-9580
Pablo Castillon, *CEO*
Pablo Antonio Castillon, *
EMP: 32 **EST:** 2019
SALES (est): 1.03MM **Privately Held**
Web: www.algotive.ai
SIC: 7371 7372 Computer software development; Prepackaged software

(P-13648)
ALOGENT HOLDINGS INC
Also Called: Alogent
5868 Owens Ave Ste 200, Carlsbad (92008-5517)
PHONE.................................760 410-9000
EMP: 80
SALES (corp-wide): 25.38MM **Privately Held**
Web: www.alogent.com
SIC: 7371 Computer software development
PA: Alogent Holdings, Inc.
　　35 Technology Pkwy S # 200
　　770 752-6400

(P-13649)
ALTIUM INC (DH)
4225 Executive Sq Ste 800, La Jolla (92037-9150)
PHONE.................................858 864-1500
Aram Mirkazemi, *CEO*
Ted Pawela, *
Joe Bedewi, *
EMP: 83 **EST:** 1988
SQ FT: 11,000
SALES (est): 19.3MM **Privately Held**
Web: www.altium-na.com
SIC: 7371 Computer software development
HQ: Altium Pty Ltd
　　Tower B The Zenith L 6 821 Pacific Hwy
　　Chatswood NSW 2067

(P-13650)
ALVARIA INC
101 Academy Ste 130, Irvine (92617-3081)
PHONE.................................408 595-5002
James Foy, *Owner*
EMP: 110
SALES (corp-wide): 110.02MM **Privately Held**
Web: www.alvaria.com
SIC: 7371 Computer software development
PA: Alvaria, Inc.
　　211 Perimeter Ctr Pkwy Ne
　　978 250-7900

(P-13651)
AMAZON STUDIOS LLC
9336 Washington Blvd, Culver City (90232-2628)
PHONE.................................818 804-0884
Jen Salke, *CEO*
EMP: 149
Web: press.amazonstudios.com
SIC: 7371 Computer software development and applications
HQ: Amazon Studios Llc
　　410 Terry Avenue N
　　Seattle WA 98109
　　310 573-2305

(P-13652)
AMERICAN SUNRISE INC
12646 Carmel Country Rd Unit 153, San Diego (92130-2169)
PHONE.................................858 610-4766
John Zhang, *Pr*
EMP: 100 **EST:** 2002

SQ FT: 4,000
SALES (est): 2.4MM **Privately Held**
SIC: 7371 7361 7379 Computer software development; Employment agencies; Computer related consulting services

(P-13653)
ANAMEX CORPORATION (PA)
250 S Peralta Way, Anaheim (92807-3618)
PHONE.................714 779-7055
Cung Phan, *Pr*
EMP: 47 **EST:** 1986
SQ FT: 10,000
SALES (est): 2.29MM **Privately Held**
SIC: 7371 7372 8711 Computer software development; Prepackaged software; Electrical or electronic engineering

(P-13654)
ANJANA SOFTWARE SOLUTIONS INC
1445 E Los Angeles Ave Ste 305, Simi Valley (93065-7818)
PHONE.................805 583-0121
Saravana Kumarasamy, *Pr*
Muthu Palanisamy, *Sr VP*
Venkatesh Ramachandran, *
Kritik A Govindan, *
▲ **EMP:** 75 **EST:** 2000
SQ FT: 3,000
SALES (est): 1.68MM **Privately Held**
Web: www.anjanasoft.com
SIC: 7371 Computer software development
PA: Anjana Software Solutions Private Limited
Module No. 306, Nsic Software Technology Park

(P-13655)
ANRE TECHNOLOGIES INC
Also Called: Anre Tech
741 W Woodbury Rd, Altadena (91001-5310)
PHONE.................818 627-5433
Roubina Keshish-moses, *Ch Bd*
Roubina Keshish-moses, *Pr*
Eugean Hacopians, *
EMP: 150 **EST:** 2010
SQ FT: 600
SALES (est): 2.98MM **Privately Held**
Web: www.anretech.com
SIC: 7371 7376 7379 Computer software development and applications; Computer facilities management; Computer related maintenance services

(P-13656)
APPLIED COMPUTER SOLUTIONS (DH)
110 Progress, Irvine (92618-0333)
PHONE.................714 801-2200
Elaine Bellock, *Pr*
Michael Davis, *
Warren Barnes, *
EMP: 70 **EST:** 1989
SALES (est): 25.85MM **Privately Held**
Web: www.prosysis.com
SIC: 7371 Custom computer programming services
HQ: Pivot Technology Solutions, Inc
200-55 Renfrew Dr
Markham ON L3R 8
416 360-4777

(P-13657)
APPLIED ENTERPRISE MGT CORP
Also Called: Aem
760 Paseo Camarillo Ste 101, Camarillo (93010-6002)

P.O. Box 1263 (93011)
PHONE.................805 484-1909
Anne Morgan, *Brnch Mgr*
EMP: 250
SALES (corp-wide): 45.39MM **Privately Held**
Web: www.aemcorp.com
SIC: 7371 Computer software development
PA: Applied Enterprise Management Corporation
11951 Freedom Dr
703 464-7030

(P-13658)
ARTIC SENTINEL INC
1700 E Walnut Ave Ste 200, El Segundo (90245-2648)
PHONE.................310 227-8230
EMP: 85
SIC: 7371 7379 Computer software development and applications; Online services technology consultants

(P-13659)
ASHUNYA INC
642 N Eckhoff St, Orange (92868-1004)
PHONE.................714 385-1900
Melanie Merchant, *Prin*
EMP: 88 **EST:** 2001
SALES (est): 6.05MM **Privately Held**
Web: www.ashunya.com
SIC: 7371 7372 7373 Computer software development and applications; Application computer software; Office computer automation systems integration

(P-13660)
ASPIREZ INC
Also Called: Pegasus One
1440 N Harbor Blvd Ste 900, Fullerton (92835-4122)
PHONE.................714 485-8104
Tushar Puri, *CEO*
EMP: 87 **EST:** 2010
SALES (est): 1.96MM **Privately Held**
SIC: 7371 7373 7379 7372 Custom computer programming services; Computer integrated systems design; Computer related maintenance services; Prepackaged software

(P-13661)
AUDITBOARD INC (PA)
12900 Park Plaza Dr Ste 200, Cerritos (90703-9329)
PHONE.................877 769-5444
Scott Arnold, *Pr*
Josh Harding, *CFO*
John Reese, *CMO*
EMP: 100 **EST:** 2014
SQ FT: 10,000
SALES (est): 25.65MM
SALES (corp-wide): 25.65MM **Privately Held**
Web: www.auditboard.com
SIC: 7371 Computer software development

(P-13662)
AUGUSTINE GAMING MGT CORP
Also Called: Augustine Casino
84001 Avenue 54, Coachella (92236-9780)
PHONE.................760 391-9500
Jeff Bauer, *Genl Mgr*
John Corrigan, *Finance*
EMP: 99
SALES (est): 7.4MM **Privately Held**
Web: www.augustinecasino.com
SIC: 7371 Computer software development and applications

(P-13663)
AVAMAR TECHNOLOGIES INC
135 Technology Dr, Irvine (92618-2402)
PHONE.................949 743-5100
EMP: 100
SIC: 7371 Computer software development

(P-13664)
AVANQUEST NORTH AMERICA LLC (HQ)
Also Called: Nova Development
23801 Calabasas Rd Ste 2005, Calabasas (91302-3320)
PHONE.................818 591-9600
Roger Bloxberg, *CEO*
Todd Helfstein, *
Sharon Chiu, *
▲ **EMP:** 80 **EST:** 1984
SQ FT: 12,000
SALES (est): 85.97MM
SALES (corp-wide): 4.02MM **Privately Held**
Web: www.avanquest.com
SIC: 7371 Computer software development
PA: Claranova S.E.
Immeuble Adamas
962557603

(P-13665)
AVEVA SOFTWARE LLC
5850 El Camino Real, Carlsbad (92008-8816)
PHONE.................760 268-7700
Chris Porter, *Brnch Mgr*
EMP: 154
SALES (corp-wide): 1.09K **Privately Held**
Web: www.wonderware.com
SIC: 7371 5045 Computer software development; Computer software
HQ: Aveva Software, Llc
26561 Rancho Pkwy S
Lake Forest CA 92630

(P-13666)
AXON NETWORKS INC (PA)
15420 Laguna Canyon Rd Ste 150, Irvine (92618-2128)
PHONE.................949 310-4429
Martin Manniche, *CEO*
EMP: 97 **EST:** 2020
SALES (est): 2.47MM
SALES (corp-wide): 2.47MM **Privately Held**
Web: www.axon-networks.com
SIC: 7371 8742 Custom computer programming services; General management consultant

(P-13667)
B JACQUELINE AND ASSOC INC
Also Called: J B A
1192 N Lake Ave, Pasadena (91104-3739)
PHONE.................626 844-1400
Jacqueline Buickians, *Pr*
Gary Buickians, *
EMP: 70 **EST:** 1979
SQ FT: 4,000
SALES (est): 1.8MM **Privately Held**
Web: www.jba.com
SIC: 7371 7379 Computer software development and applications; Computer related consulting services

(P-13668)
BABYFIRST AMERICAS LLC
10390 Santa Monica Blvd Ste 310, Los Angeles (90025-5091)
PHONE.................310 442-9853
Guy Oranim, *CEO*
Sharon Rechter, *Pr*

Karl Knipliy, *CFO*
EMP: 75 **EST:** 2010
SALES (est): 2.4MM
SALES (corp-wide): 2.4MM **Privately Held**
Web: www.babyfirsttv.com
SIC: 7371 Computer software development and applications
PA: Bftv, Llc
10390 Santa Monica Blvd # 310
310 442-9853

(P-13669)
BAHARE
11769 W Sunset Blvd, Los Angeles (90049-6903)
PHONE.................516 472-1457
Bahareh Saleh Nia, *CEO*
EMP: 105 **EST:** 2021
SALES (est): 835.45K **Privately Held**
SIC: 7371 7389 Computer software development and applications; Business Activities at Non-Commercial Site

(P-13670)
BAKBONE SOFTWARE INC (HQ)
9540 Towne Centre Dr Ste 100, San Diego (92121-1989)
PHONE.................858 450-9009
Michael S Dell, *CEO*
Stephen J Felice, *
Brian Tgladden, *
Kenneth Horner, *Senior Vice President Corporate Development & Strategy*
Roy Hogsed, *Senior Vice President Worldwide Sales*
EMP: 72 **EST:** 1999
SQ FT: 22,600
SALES (est): 4.82MM
SALES (corp-wide): 647.68MM **Privately Held**
Web: www.quest.com
SIC: 7371 7375 Computer software systems analysis and design, custom; Information retrieval services
PA: Quest Software Inc.
20 Enterprise Ste 100
949 754-8000

(P-13671)
BATIA INFOTECH
Also Called: Proprofs
3101 Ocean Park Blvd Ste 100 Pmb 187, Santa Monica (90405-3029)
PHONE.................855 776-7763
Sameer Bhatia, *CEO*
Malini Bhatia, *
EMP: 180 **EST:** 2003
SALES (est): 10.04MM **Privately Held**
Web: www.proprofs.com
SIC: 7371 Computer software development

(P-13672)
BELLROCK MEDIA INC (PA)
11500 W Olympic Blvd Ste 400, Los Angeles (90064-1525)
PHONE.................310 315-2727
Peter Levin, *Pr*
EMP: 26 **EST:** 2005
SALES (est): 3.88MM **Privately Held**
SIC: 7371 3661 Software programming applications; Headsets, telephone

(P-13673)
BEN GROUP INC
14724 Ventura Blvd Ste 1200, Sherman Oaks (91403-3512)
PHONE.................310 342-1500
Richard Ray Butler, *CEO*
Keith Moffatt, *
Ted Sheffield, *

P R O D U C T S & S V C S

EMP: 420 **EST:** 2017
SALES (est): 100MM **Privately Held**
SIC: 7371 7311 Custom computer
programming services; Advertising agencies

(P-13674)
BIOSERO (PA)
4770 Ruffner St, San Diego (92111-1520)
PHONE....................858 880-7376
Thomas Gilman, *Pr*
Andrea Salazar, *
Tony Morand, *
Daniel Schumann, *
Ryan Bernhardt, *CCO*
▲ **EMP:** 33 **EST:** 2003
SQ FT: 6,000
SALES (est): 9.52MM
SALES (corp-wide): 9.52MM **Privately
Held**
Web: www.biosero.com
SIC: 7371 3569 Computer software
development and applications; Assembly
machines, non-metalworking

(P-13675)
BIS COMPUTER SOLUTIONS INC (PA)
Also Called: Business Information Systems
5500 Alta Canyada Rd, La Canada
Flintridge (91011-1610)
PHONE....................818 248-4282
Miro J Macho, *Pr*
EMP: 25 **EST:** 1971
SALES (est): 5.18MM
SALES (corp-wide): 5.18MM **Privately
Held**
Web: www.biscomputer.com
SIC: 7371 7379 5045 7372 Computer
software development; Computer related
consulting services; Computers,
peripherals, and software; Prepackaged
software

(P-13676)
BLAZE SOLUTIONS INC
155 N Riverview Dr, Anaheim (92808-1225)
PHONE....................415 964-5689
Chris Violas, *CEO*
Justin Kirk, *CPO*
EMP: 75 **EST:** 2018
SALES (est): 700K **Privately Held**
Web: www.blaze.me
SIC: 7371 Computer software development

(P-13677)
BLUEBEAM INC (PA)
443 S Raymond Ave, Pasadena
(91105-2630)
PHONE....................626 788-4100
Usman Shuja, *CEO*
Richard Lee, *
Jim Atkinson, *
Miekie Liebenberg, *
EMP: 200 **EST:** 2002
SALES (est): 47.98MM
SALES (corp-wide): 47.98MM **Privately
Held**
Web: www.bluebeam.com
SIC: 7371 Computer software development

(P-13678)
BOULEVARD LABS INC
626 Wilshire Blvd Ste 410, Los Angeles
(90005-3983)
PHONE....................323 310-2093
Matthew Danna, *CEO*
EMP: 115 **EST:** 2016
SALES (est): 9.85MM **Privately Held**
Web: www.joinblvd.com

SIC: 7371 7389 7372 Computer software
development and applications; Business
Activities at Non-Commercial Site;
Prepackaged software

(P-13679)
BPO MANAGEMENT SERVICES INC (PA)
8175 E Kaiser Blvd # 100, Anaheim
(92808-2214)
PHONE....................714 972-2670
Patrick A Dolan, *Ch Bd*
James Cortens, *Pr*
Donald W Rutherford, *CFO*
EMP: 73 **EST:** 1982
SQ FT: 5,871
SALES (est): 16.91MM
SALES (corp-wide): 16.91MM **Privately
Held**
SIC: 7371 Computer software development

(P-13680)
BRAIN CORPORATION
10182 Telesis Ct Ste 100, San Diego
(92121-4777)
PHONE....................858 689-7600
Eugene Izhikevich, *CEO*
David Pinn, *CFO*
Leah Davis, *VP*
EMP: 220 **EST:** 2009
SALES (est): 40MM **Privately Held**
Web: www.braincorp.com
SIC: 7371 Computer software development

(P-13681)
BUDDY GROUP INC
7 Studebaker, Irvine (92618-2013)
P.O. Box 1021 (92609-1021)
PHONE....................949 468-0042
Peter R Deutschman, *Pr*
EMP: 142 **EST:** 2007
SALES (est): 3.99MM **Privately Held**
Web: www.thebuddygroup.com
SIC: 7371 Computer software development
and applications

(P-13682)
CAREER ENGAGEMENT GROUP LLC
Also Called: Fuel50
30025 Alicia Pkwy, Laguna Niguel
(92677-2090)
PHONE....................212 235-1470
Anne Fulton, *CEO*
EMP: 70 **EST:** 2013
SALES (est): 2.53MM **Privately Held**
SIC: 7371 Computer software development
and applications

(P-13683)
CHEQUE GUARD INC
512 S Verdugo Dr, Burbank (91502-2344)
PHONE....................818 563-9335
Emil Ramzy, *Pr*
Alfred Ramzi, *
Louris Khalaf, *
EMP: 54 **EST:** 2002
SQ FT: 6,000
SALES (est): 2.52MM **Privately Held**
Web: www.cheque-guard.com
SIC: 7371 2893 Computer software
development; Printing ink

(P-13684)
CHROMACODE INC
2330 Faraday Ave Ste 100, Carlsbad
(92008-7244)
PHONE....................442 244-4369
Mark Mcdonough, *CEO*

Mark Mcdonough, *CEO*
Alex Dickinson, *
Lynne Rollins, *
EMP: 27 **EST:** 2014
SALES (est): 8.45MM **Privately Held**
Web: www.chromacode.com
SIC: 7371 3841 8731 Computer software
development; Diagnostic apparatus, medical
; Biological research

(P-13685)
CHROME RIVER TECHNOLOGIES INC
5757 Wilshire Blvd Ste 270, Los Angeles
(90036-5814)
PHONE....................888 781-0088
Eric Friedrichsen, *CEO*
Nord Samuelson, *Pr*
Adriana Carpenter, *CFO*
Courtney Ryan, *CPO*
EMP: 109 **EST:** 2007
SALES (est): 11.67MM **Privately Held**
Web: www.chromeriver.com
SIC: 7371 Computer software development

(P-13686)
CINCOM SYSTEMS INC (PA)
Also Called: Cincom
871 Marlborough Ave, Riverside
(92507-2131)
PHONE....................513 612-2300
Thomas M Nies, *Ch Bd*
Donald Vick, *
Kenneth L Byrne, *
▲ **EMP:** 300 **EST:** 1968
SALES (est): 27.31MM
SALES (corp-wide): 27.31MM **Privately
Held**
Web: www.cincom.com
SIC: 7371 Computer software development

(P-13687)
CITRIX ONLINE LLC
Also Called: Citrix Online Group
7414 Hollister Ave, Goleta (93117-2583)
PHONE....................805 690-6400
EMP: 500
SIC: 7371 Computer software development

(P-13688)
CITRUSBYTE LLC
Also Called: Theorem LLC
21550 Oxnard St Ste 300 # 11, Woodland
Hills (91367-7109)
PHONE....................888 969-2983
William Jessup, *Managing Member*
EMP: 30 **EST:** 2015
SALES (est): 5.11MM **Privately Held**
Web: www.theoremone.co
SIC: 7371 7372 7373 Computer software
development and applications; Business
oriented computer software; Computer
integrated systems design

(P-13689)
CODAZEN INC
Also Called: Codazen
60 Bunsen, Irvine (92618-4210)
PHONE....................949 916-6266
Michael Merchant, *Pr*
Michael H Merchant, *
Angela Merchant, *
EMP: 85 **EST:** 2007
SALES (est): 4.89MM **Privately Held**
Web: www.codazen.com
SIC: 7371 Computer software development

(P-13690)
COLSA CORPORATION
Digital Wizards Division
2727 Camino Del Rio S Ste 340, San Diego
(92108-3741)
PHONE....................619 553-0031
Patricia Hodges, *Prin*
EMP: 70
SALES (corp-wide): 362.72MM **Privately
Held**
Web: www.colsa.com
SIC: 7371 8711 Computer software
development; Engineering services
PA: Colsa Corporation
6728 Odyssey Dr
256 964-5361

(P-13691)
COMPULINK MANAGEMENT CTR INC (PA)
Also Called: Laserfiche Document Imaging
3443 Long Beach Blvd, Long Beach
(90807-4432)
PHONE....................562 988-1688
Nien-ling Wacker, *Pr*
Christopher Wacker, *
Jim Haney, *
▲ **EMP:** 197 **EST:** 1976
SALES (est): 24.35MM
SALES (corp-wide): 24.35MM **Privately
Held**
Web: www.laserfiche.com
SIC: 7371 Computer software development

(P-13692)
COMPUTRITION INC (HQ)
Also Called: Dfm Dietary Food Management
8521 Fallbrook Ave Ste 100, Canoga Park
(91304-3236)
PHONE....................818 961-3999
Scott Saklad, *Pr*
Kim C Goldberg, *Marketing*
EMP: 60 **EST:** 1981
SQ FT: 16,763
SALES (est): 13.33MM
SALES (corp-wide): 8.41B **Privately Held**
Web: www.computrition.com
SIC: 7371 7372 Computer software
development; Prepackaged software
PA: Constellation Software Inc
20 Adelaide St E Suite 1200
416 861-9677

(P-13693)
CORDIAL
402 W Broadway Ste 700, San Diego
(92101-8572)
PHONE....................619 501-5548
EMP: 72 **EST:** 2017
SALES (est): 3.14MM **Privately Held**
Web: www.cordial.com
SIC: 7371 Computer software development

(P-13694)
CORDIAL EXPERIENCE INC
402 W Broadway Ste 700, San Diego
(92101-8572)
P.O. Box 307 (92040-0307)
PHONE....................619 793-9787
Jeremy Swift, *CEO*
Stephanie Robotham, *CMO*
EMP: 70 **EST:** 2014
SALES (est): 7.48MM **Privately Held**
Web: www.cordial.com
SIC: 7371 Computer software systems
analysis and design, custom

(P-13695)

CORELATION INC

2305 Historic Decatur Rd Ste 300, San
Diego (92106-6073)
PHONE.................619 876-5074
John F Landis, *CEO*
Theresa Benavidez, *
Harold Barnabas, *
Lori Paige, *
Dwayne Jacobs, *
EMP: 200 EST: 2007
SALES (est): 28.4MM Privately Held
Web: www.corelationinc.com
SIC: 7371 Computer software development

(P-13696)

CORPTAX LLC

21550 Oxnard St Ste 700, Woodland Hills
(91367-7170)
PHONE.................818 316-2400
EMP: 120
Web: www.corptax.com
SIC: 7371 Computer software development
PA: Corptax, Llc
2100 E Lake Cook Rd # 800

(P-13697)

COUNTY OF LOS ANGELES

Also Called: Internal Services
1100 N Eastern Ave, Los Angeles
(90063-3200)
PHONE.................562 940-4324
David Wesolik, *Genl Mgr*
EMP: 2000
Web: www.lacounty.gov
SIC: 7371 Computer software development
and applications
PA: County Of Los Angeles
500 W Temple St Ste 437
213 974-1101

(P-13698)

CRESCENTONE INC (HQ)

200 Continental Blvd Fl 3, El Segundo
(90245-4510)
PHONE.................310 563-7000
Chikara Ono, *CEO*
Jim Errington, *Ex VP*
Masahiro Cho, *CFO*
EMP: 150 EST: 1970
SQ FT: 53,000
SALES (est): 21.25MM
SALES (corp-wide): 8.41B Privately Held
Web: www.glovia.com
SIC: 7371 7372 Computer software
development; Prepackaged software
PA: Constellation Software Inc
20 Adelaide St E Suite 1200
416 861-9677

(P-13699)

CU DIRECT CORPORATION (PA)

Also Called: Cudc
2855 E Guasti Rd Ste 500, Ontario
(91761-1253)
P.O. Box 51482 (91761-0082)
PHONE.................833 908-0121
Antony Boutelle, *Pr*
Keith Sultemeier, *
Jim Laffoon, *Vice Chairman*
Jerry Neemann, *
Craig S Montesanti, *
EMP: 175 EST: 1994
SQ FT: 30,000
SALES (est): 45.13MM
**SALES (corp-wide): 45.13MM Privately
Held**
Web: www.cudirect.com
SIC: 7371 Computer software development

(P-13700)

CUBIC TRNSP SYSTEMS INC (DH)

Also Called: Cubic
9233 Balboa Ave, San Diego (92123-1513)
P.O. Box 85587 (92186-5587)
PHONE.................858 268-3100
Stephen O Shewmaker, *CEO*
Walter C Zable, *
Raymond De Kozan, *
Steve Purcell, *
◆ **EMP: 550 EST:** 1950
SALES (est): 244.67MM
SALES (corp-wide): 1.48B **Privately Held**
Web: www.cubic.com
SIC: 7371 1731 3829 Custom computer
programming services; Telephone and
telephone equipment installation; Fare
registers, for street cars, buses, etc.
HQ: Cubic Corporation
9233 Balboa Ave
San Diego CA 92123
858 277-6780

(P-13701)

DATA PROCESSING DESIGN INC

Also Called: Goldfax
1409 Glenneyre St Ste B, Laguna Beach
(92651-3171)
PHONE.................714 695-1000
Brendan Nolan, *CEO*
Tom Politowski, *
EMP: 31 EST: 1976
SALES (est): 3.13MM Privately Held
Web: www.egoldfax.com
SIC: 7371 7372 Computer software
development; Prepackaged software

(P-13702)

DATADIRECT NETWORKS INC (PA)

Also Called: D D N
9351 Deering Ave, Chatsworth
(91311-5858)
PHONE.................818 700-7600
Alex Bouzari, *CEO*
Paul Bloch, *
Ian Angelo, *
Robert Triendl, *
Bret Weber, *
▲ **EMP: 120 EST:** 1988
SQ FT: 50,000
SALES (est): 175.84MM
SALES (corp-wide): 175.84MM **Privately
Held**
Web: www.ddn.com
SIC: 7371 7374 Custom computer
programming services; Data processing
service

(P-13703)

DAYBREAK GAME COMPANY LLC

Also Called: Daybreak
13500 Evening Creek Dr N Ste 300, San
Diego (92128-8125)
PHONE.................858 239-0500
▲ **EMP: 450 EST:** 2006
SALES (est): 49.21MM
**SALES (corp-wide): 194.51MM Privately
Held**
Web: www.daybreakgames.com
SIC: 7371 Computer software development
PA: Enad Global 7 Ab (Publ)
Sveavagen 17, Plan 5
738204439

(P-13704)

DAZ SYSTEMS LLC

Also Called: Daz
1003 E 4th Pl Ste 800, Los Angeles
(90013-2775)
PHONE.................310 640-1300
Walt Zipperman, *CEO*
Deborah Arnold, *
David Binkley, *
EMP: 375 EST: 1995
SALES (est): 14.39MM Privately Held
SIC: 7371 7372 Computer software
development; Prepackaged software
HQ: Accenture Llp
500 W Madison St
Chicago IL 60661
312 693-5009

(P-13705)

DENA CORP

360 N Pacific Coast Hwy, El Segundo
(90245-4460)
PHONE.................415 375-3170
Shintaro Asako, *Prin*
EMP: 99 EST: 2014
SALES (est): 2.15MM Privately Held
SIC: 7371 Computer software development
and applications

(P-13706)

DESIGN SCIENCE INC

444 W Ocean Blvd Ste 800, Long Beach
(90802-4529)
PHONE.................562 442-4779
Paul Topping, *Pr*
EMP: 30 EST: 1986
SALES (est): 2.6MM Privately Held
Web: www.wiris.com
SIC: 7371 7379 3572 5045 Computer
software development; Computer related
consulting services; Prepackaged software;
Computers, peripherals, and software

(P-13707)

DISCOVERY OPCO LLC

41 Discovery, Irvine (92618-3150)
PHONE.................844 933-3627
EMP: 115 EST: 2017
SALES (est): 258.31K
**SALES (corp-wide): 215.53MM Publicly
Held**
Web: www.weedmaps.com
SIC: 7371 Computer software development
and applications
PA: Wm Technology, Inc.
41 Discovery
646 699-3750

(P-13708)

DISNEY INTERACTIVE STUDIOS INC

Also Called: Disney Interactive Studios
681 W Buena Vista St, Burbank
(91521-0001)
PHONE.................818 553-5000
Gram Hoper, *Brnch Mgr*
EMP: 270
SALES (corp-wide): 91.36B Publicly Held
Web: www.thewaltdisneycompany.com
SIC: 7371 Computer software development
HQ: Disney Interactive Studios, Inc.
500 S Buena Vista St
Burbank CA 91521
818 560-1000

(P-13709)

DISNEY INTERACTIVE STUDIOS INC

601 Circle Seven Dr, Glendale
(91201-2332)

PHONE.................818 560-1000
Peter Casciani, *Mgr*
EMP: 270
SALES (corp-wide): 91.36B Publicly Held
Web: www.thewaltdisneycompany.com
SIC: 7371 Computer software development
HQ: Disney Interactive Studios, Inc.
500 S Buena Vista St
Burbank CA 91521
818 560-1000

(P-13710)

DISTILLERY TECH INC

Also Called: Distillery
1500 Rosecrans Ave Ste 500, Manhattan
Beach (90266-3771)
PHONE.................310 776-6234
Andrey Kudievskiy, *Pr*
EMP: 220 EST: 2012
SALES (est): 13.7MM Privately Held
Web: www.distillery.com
SIC: 7371 7372 7373 Computer software
development; Application computer software
; Computer systems analysis and design

(P-13711)

DOCUPACE TECHNOLOGIES LLC (PA)

400 Corporate Pointe Ste 300, Culver City
(90230-7620)
P.O. Box 92117 (89193)
PHONE.................310 445-7722
Michael Pinsker, *Managing Member*
John Cunningham, *CIO*
James Caulkins, *CRO*
EMP: 200 EST: 2002
SQ FT: 1,500
SALES (est): 18.78MM
SALES (corp-wide): 18.78MM **Privately
Held**
Web: www.docupace.com
SIC: 7371 Computer software development

(P-13712)

DRAY ALLIANCE INC

111 W Ocean Blvd Ste 1000, Long Beach
(90802-4686)
PHONE.................844 767-6776
Haobo Wen, *CEO*
Sammi Liu, *COO*
EMP: 70 EST: 2018
SALES (est): 4.1MM Privately Held
Web: www.drayalliance.com
SIC: 7371 Computer software development
and applications

(P-13713)

DYNASTY MARKETPLACE INC

716 Hampton Dr, Venice (90291-3019)
PHONE.................804 837-0119
Elliot Burns, *CEO*
EMP: 244 EST: 2016
SALES (est): 479.18K
**SALES (corp-wide): 471.88MM Publicly
Held**
SIC: 7371 Computer software development
and applications
PA: Appfolio, Inc.
70 Castilian Dr
805 364-6093

(P-13714)

DZKICORP INC

Also Called: Dozuki
762 Higuera St Ste 216, San Luis Obispo
(93401-3573)
P.O. Box 642 (92334-0642)
PHONE.................805 464-0573
Richard Crawford, *CEO*
EMP: 75 EST: 2019

SALES (est): 12.88MM **Privately Held**
SIC: **7371** Computer software development

(P-13715)
ECOTRAK LLC
Also Called: Ecotrak
18004 Sky Park Cir Ste 100, Irvine
(92614-6494)
PHONE.................888 219-0000
Matt Singer, *CEO*
David Bennett, *
EMP: 70 EST: 2018
SALES (est): 2.65MM **Privately Held**
Web: www.ecotrak.com
SIC: **7371** Computer software development

(P-13716)
EIGHTEENTH MERIDIAN INC
Also Called: Secure-Dmz
200 Spectrum Center Dr Ste 300, Irvine
(92618-5004)
PHONE.................714 706-3643
Erol Karabeg, *Pr*
Dino Beslic, *
EMP: 500 EST: 1998
SALES (est): 9.01MM **Privately Held**
SIC: **7371** Custom computer programming
services

(P-13717)
EINSTEIN INDUSTRIES INC
Also Called: Einstein Dental
6825 Flanders Dr, San Diego (92121-2905)
P.O. Box 27149 (92198-1149)
PHONE.................858 459-1182
Robert C Silkey, *Pr*
Ted Ricasa, *General Vice President*
EMP: 180 EST: 1995
SALES (est): 24.7MM **Privately Held**
Web: www.einsteinmedical.com
SIC: **7371** 8742 8322 Computer software
development; Marketing consulting services
; Referral service for personal and social
problems

(P-13718)
ELLIE MAE INC
Also Called: ELLIE MAE, INC.
24025 Park Sorrento Ste 210, Calabasas
(91302-4025)
PHONE.................818 223-2000
EMP: 389
SALES (corp-wide): 7.99B **Publicly Held**
Web: www.icemortgagetechnology.com
SIC: **7371** Computer software systems
analysis and design, custom
HQ: Ice Mortgage Technology, Inc.
4420 Rosewood Dr Ste 500
Pleasanton CA 94588
855 224-8572

(P-13719)
EMIDS TECH PRIVATE LTD CORP
6320 Canoga Ave, Woodland Hills
(91367-2526)
PHONE.................805 304-5986
EMP: 3257
Web: www.emids.com
SIC: **7371** Computer software development
PA: Emids Technologies Private Limited
Corp.
318 Seaboard Ln Ste 110

(P-13720)
ENOAH ISOLUTIONS INC
2955 E Hillcrest Dr Ste 124, Westlake
Village (91362-3178)
PHONE.................805 285-3418
Muthukumar Balasubramanian, *CEO*
EMP: 90 EST: 2006

SALES (est): 6.82MM **Privately Held**
Web: www.enoahisolution.com
SIC: **7371** Computer software development

(P-13721)
EPITEC INC
515 Olive Ave, Vista (92083-3439)
PHONE.................760 650-2515
William Grivas, *Pr*
EMP: 900
SALES (corp-wide): 19.12MM **Privately
Held**
Web: www.epitec.com
SIC: **7371** Computer software systems
analysis and design, custom
PA: Epitec, Inc.
26555 Evergreen Rd # 1700
248 353-6800

(P-13722)
EQUATOR LLC (HQ)
Also Called: Equator Business Solutions
6060 Center Dr Ste 500, Los Angeles
(90045-8857)
PHONE.................310 469-9500
Chris Saitta, *CEO*
EMP: 200 EST: 2003
SALES (est): 3.7MM
SALES (corp-wide): 2.67MM **Privately
Held**
Web: www.equator.com
SIC: **7371** Computer software development
and applications
PA: Altisource Portfolio Solutions S.A.
Boulevard Prince Henri 33

(P-13723)
ERGOMOTION INC (PA)
6790 Navigator Way, Goleta (93117-3656)
P.O. Box 8330 (93118)
PHONE.................888 550-3746
Guohai Tang, *CEO*
Zhifan Yang, *
Guilherme Peres, *
▲ EMP: 70 EST: 2006
SALES (est): 22.44MM
SALES (corp-wide): 22.44MM **Privately
Held**
Web: www.ergomotion.com
SIC: **7371** Computer software development
and applications

(P-13724)
ERP INTEGRATED SOLUTIONS LLC
Also Called: SHIPERP
5000 Airport Plaza Dr Ste 230, Long Beach
(90815-1290)
PHONE.................562 425-7800
Joseph Cabrera, *Pr*
Doug Cole, *
Anthony Raimo, *
EMP: 100 EST: 2008
SALES (est): 623.4K **Privately Held**
Web: www.shiperp.com
SIC: **7371** Computer software development

(P-13725)
EVERNOTE CORPORATION (PA)
4231 Balboa Ave # 1008, San Diego
(92117-5504)
PHONE.................650 216-7700
Chris O'neill, *CEO*
Phil Libin, *Ofcr*
Stepan Pachikov Fundr, *Prin*
Jeff Shotts, *CFO*
▲ EMP: 358 EST: 2004
SALES (est): 20.96MM
SALES (corp-wide): 20.96MM **Privately
Held**

Web: www.evernote.com
SIC: **7371** Computer software development

(P-13726)
FAIR FINANCIAL CORP (PA)
1540 2nd St Ste 200, Santa Monica
(90401-3513)
P.O. Box 409 (10523-0409)
PHONE.................800 584-5000
Bradley Stewart, *CEO*
Georg Bauer, *
Craig Nehamen, *
EMP: 82 EST: 2015
SALES (est): 23.16MM
SALES (corp-wide): 23.16MM **Privately
Held**
SIC: **7371** Computer software development
and applications

(P-13727)
FAMILY ZONE INC
Also Called: Linewize
10803 Thornmint Rd Ste 100, San Diego
(92127-2406)
PHONE.................844 723-3932
Tim Levy, *Pr*
EMP: 78 EST: 2014
SALES (est): 4.57MM **Privately Held**
Web: www.linewize.com
SIC: **7371** Computer software development
PA: Qoria Limited
L 3 45 St Georges Tce

(P-13728)
FATTAIL INC (HQ)
23586 Calabasas Rd Ste 102, Calabasas
(91302-1322)
PHONE.................818 615-0380
Douglas Huntington, *CEO*
Barry Witkow, *
EMP: 30 EST: 2001
SQ FT: 3,500
SALES (est): 5.77MM
SALES (corp-wide): 5.77MM **Privately
Held**
Web: www.fattail.com
SIC: **7371** 7372 Computer software
development; Business oriented computer
software
PA: Eventures International, Llc
23586 Clabasas Rd Ste 102

(P-13729)
FENDER DIGITAL LLC
1575 N Gower St Ste 170, Los Angeles
(90028-7179)
PHONE.................323 462-2198
EMP: 75 EST: 2015
SQ FT: 25,000
SALES (est): 3.73MM
SALES (corp-wide): 1.87B **Privately Held**
Web: www.fenderdigital.com
SIC: **7371** Computer software development
and applications
HQ: Fender Musical Instruments
Corporation
17600 N Perimeter Dr # 100
Scottsdale AZ 85255
480 596-9690

(P-13730)
FIDELIS SECURITY LLC
871 Marlborough Ave Ste 100, Riverside
(92507-2131)
PHONE.................240 650-2041
Marty Deconcilis, *Prin*
Ivan Dolensky, *VP*
Jennifer Welesko, *CFO*
EMP: 77 EST: 2002
SALES (est): 1.37MM **Privately Held**

SIC: **7371** Computer software development
and applications

(P-13731)
FINANCIAL INFO NETWRK INC
Also Called: F I N
11164 Bertrand Ave, Granada Hills
(91344-4005)
P.O. Box 7954 (91409-7954)
PHONE.................818 782-0331
Jerry Sears, *Pr*
EMP: 25 EST: 1969
SQ FT: 6,000
SALES (est): 1.7MM **Privately Held**
Web: www.fingps.com
SIC: **7371** 7372 Custom computer
programming services; Prepackaged
software

(P-13732)
FOREMAY INC (PA)
225 S Lake Ave Ste 300, Pasadena
(91101-3009)
PHONE.................408 228-3468
Haining Fan, *CEO*
Tiffany Fan, *Pr*
EMP: 46 EST: 2002
SALES (est): 4.66MM **Privately Held**
Web: www.foremay.net
SIC: **7371** 7373 3572 Computer software
systems analysis and design, custom;
Computer systems analysis and design;
Computer storage devices

(P-13733)
FRONTECH N FUJITSU AMER INC (DH)
Also Called: Ffna
36 Technology Dr Ste 150, Irvine
(92618-5308)
PHONE.................877 766-7545
Shuhei Oyake, *Pr*
▲ EMP: 219 EST: 1990
SALES (est): 57.67MM **Privately Held**
Web: www.fujitsufrontechna.com
SIC: **7371** Computer software development
and applications
HQ: Fujitsu Frontech Limited
1776, Yanokuchi
Inagi TKY 206-0

(P-13734)
G2 SOFTWARE SYSTEMS INC
4025 Hancock St Ste 105, San Diego
(92110-5167)
PHONE.................619 222-8025
Georgia D Griffiths, *CEO*
William Long, *
EMP: 140 EST: 1898
SQ FT: 4,000
SALES (est): 12.56MM **Privately Held**
Web: www.g2ss.com
SIC: **7371** Computer software development

(P-13735)
GAN LIMITED (PA)
Also Called: Gan
400 Spectrum Center Dr Ste 1900, Irvine
(92618-5025)
PHONE.................833 565-0550
Seamus Mcgill, *CEO*
David Goldberg, *
Giuseppe Gardali, *B2B*
Endre Nesset, *B2C*
Brian Chang, *CFO*
EMP: 563 EST: 2002
SALES (est): 129.42MM
SALES (corp-wide): 129.42MM **Publicly
Held**
Web: www.gan.com

SIC: 7371 7374 Custom computer programming services; Data processing and preparation

(P-13736)
GEHRY TECHNOLOGIES INC
12181 Bluff Creek Dr, Los Angeles (90094-2992)
PHONE..............................310 862-1200
Meaghan Lloyd, *CEO*
Michael Lin, *CFO*
Dhruba Kalita, *CIO*
EMP: 95 EST: 2002
SQ FT: 2,000
SALES (est): 7.43MM
SALES (corp-wide): 3.8B **Publicly Held**
Web: www.trimbleconsulting.com
SIC: 7371 Computer software development and applications
PA: Trimble Inc.
    10368 Westmoor Dr
    720 887-6100

(P-13737)
GENEX (DH)
800 Corporate Pointe Ste 100, Culver City (90230-7671)
PHONE..............................424 672-9500
Walter Schild, *CEO*
Gretchen Humbert, *
EMP: 130 EST: 1995
SQ FT: 12,000
SALES (est): 3.44MM
SALES (corp-wide): 3.28B **Publicly Held**
Web: www.genex.com
SIC: 7371 7379 4813 Computer software development and applications; Computer related consulting services; Online service providers
HQ: Hawkeye Acquisition, Inc.
    1716 Locust St
    Des Moines IA 50309
    515 284-3000

(P-13738)
GLOBAL SERVICE RESOURCES INC
Also Called: Computerworks Technologies
711 S Victory Blvd, Burbank (91502-2426)
P.O. Box 4057 (91503-4057)
PHONE..............................800 679-7658
Nick Sefayan, *Pr*
▲ EMP: 80 EST: 1991
SQ FT: 7,000
SALES (est): 1.39MM **Privately Held**
Web: www.globalserviceresources.com
SIC: 7371 7363 Computer software development; Labor resource services

(P-13739)
GOOD SPORTS PLUS LTD
Also Called: ARC
370 Amapola Ave Ste 208, Torrance (90501-7241)
PHONE..............................310 671-4400
Gary Lipsky, *
Kitty Cohen, *
EMP: 300 EST: 2002
SQ FT: 3,500
SALES (est): 15.92MM **Privately Held**
Web: www.arc-experience.com
SIC: 7371 7997 Computer software development and applications; Outdoor field clubs

(P-13740)
GRINDR LLC
750 N San Vicente Blvd, West Hollywood (90069-5788)
P.O. Box 69176 (90069)

PHONE..............................310 776-6680
George Arison, *CEO*
EMP: 206 EST: 2010
SALES (est): 16.73MM
SALES (corp-wide): 259.69MM **Publicly Held**
Web: www.grindr.com
SIC: 7371 Computer software development
PA: Grindr Inc.
    750 N San Vcnte Blvd Ste
    310 776-6680

(P-13741)
H & R ACCOUNTS INC
Also Called: Avadyne Health
3131 Camino Del Rio N Ste 1500, San Diego (92108-5716)
PHONE..............................619 819-8844
Linda Hevern, *Brnch Mgr*
EMP: 125
SALES (corp-wide): 24.67MM **Privately Held**
Web: www.avadynehealth.com
SIC: 7371 Computer software development
HQ: H & R Accounts, Inc.
    5320 22nd Ave
    Moline IL 61265
    309 736-2255

(P-13742)
HOME JUNCTION INC
1 Venture Ste 300, Irvine (92618-7416)
PHONE..............................858 777-9533
John Perkins, *CEO*
EMP: 88 EST: 2013
SALES (est): 3.16MM
SALES (corp-wide): 17.24MM **Privately Held**
Web: www.helpudevelop.com
SIC: 7371 Computer software development
PA: Attom Data Solutions, Llc
    530 Technology Dr Ste 100
    949 502-8300

(P-13743)
HONEY SCIENCE LLC
Also Called: Honey
963 E 4th St Ste 100, Los Angeles (90013-2645)
PHONE..............................949 795-1695
George Ruan, *Managing Member*
Ryan Hudson, *
EMP: 112 EST: 2012
SALES (est): 9.7MM
SALES (corp-wide): 29.77B **Publicly Held**
Web: www.joinhoney.com
SIC: 7371 Software programming applications
PA: Paypal Holdings, Inc.
    2211 N 1st St
    408 967-1000

(P-13744)
HVANTAGE TECHNOLOGIES INC (PA)
22048 Sherman Way Ste 306, Canoga Park (91303-3011)
PHONE..............................818 661-6301
Krishna Baderia, *CEO*
EMP: 79 EST: 2011
SALES (est): 4.62MM
SALES (corp-wide): 4.62MM **Privately Held**
Web: www.hvantagetechnologies.com
SIC: 7371 8748 7372 7373 Computer software development; Systems engineering consultant, ex. computer or professional; Application computer software ; Systems engineering, computer related

(P-13745)
IBASET FEDERAL SERVICES LLC (PA)
27442 Portola Pkwy Ste 300, Foothill Ranch (92610-2822)
PHONE..............................949 598-5200
Ladeira Poonian, *Ch*
Vic Sial, *
Naveen Poonian, *
EMP: 75 EST: 1986
SQ FT: 30,000
SALES (est): 7.01MM **Privately Held**
Web: www.ibaset.com
SIC: 7371 Computer software development

(P-13746)
ID ANALYTICS LLC
10089 Willow Creek Rd Ste 120, San Diego (92131-1698)
PHONE..............................858 312-6200
Rick Trainor, *CEO*
EMP: 140 EST: 2002
SALES (est): 23.72MM
SALES (corp-wide): 11.42B **Privately Held**
Web: risk.lexisnexis.com
SIC: 7371 Computer software development
HQ: Lexisnexis Risk Solutions Inc.
    1000 Alderman Dr
    Alpharetta GA 30005
    678 694-6000

(P-13747)
IMAGE-X ENTERPRISES INC
Also Called: Image X
6464 Hollister Ave Ste 7g, Goleta (93117-3110)
PHONE..............................805 964-3535
Mohammed Shaikh, *Ch Bd*
EMP: 30 EST: 1989
SQ FT: 4,000
SALES (est): 1.12MM **Privately Held**
Web: www.imagexusa.com
SIC: 7371 3577 Computer software development; Computer peripheral equipment, nec

(P-13748)
INFOMAGNUS LLC
5882 Bolsa Ave Ste 210, Huntington Beach (92649-5700)
PHONE..............................714 810-3430
Sal Manzo, *Managing Member*
Kaveh Mahjoob, *
EMP: 90 EST: 2013
SALES (est): 2.28MM **Privately Held**
Web: www.infomagnus.com
SIC: 7371 7379 Software programming applications; Computer related consulting services

(P-13749)
INNOVASYSTEMS INTL LLC
850 Beech St Unit 1006, San Diego (92101-2895)
PHONE..............................619 955-5890
EMP: 198
SALES (corp-wide): 46.49MM **Privately Held**
Web: www.innovasi.com
SIC: 7371 Computer software development
HQ: Innovasystems International Llc
    2385 Northside Dr Ste 300
    San Diego CA 92108
    619 955-5800

(P-13750)
INSEEGO CORP (PA)
Also Called: Inseego
9710 Scranton Rd Ste 200, San Diego (92121-1744)

PHONE..............................858 812-3400
Philip G Brace, *
Steven Gatoff, *CFO*
Doug Kahn, *Ofcr*
James Paul Mcclaskey, *Principal Accounting Officer*
EMP: 72 EST: 1996
SQ FT: 25,000
SALES (est): 195.69MM
SALES (corp-wide): 195.69MM **Publicly Held**
Web: www.inseego.com
SIC: 7371 Software programming applications

(P-13751)
INTELEX SYSTEMS INC
21900 Burbank Blvd Ste 3087, Woodland Hills (91367-6469)
PHONE..............................818 992-2969
Saritha Myadam, *CEO*
Sarith Myadam, *CFO*
EMP: 84 EST: 2009
SALES (est): 3.41MM **Privately Held**
Web: www.intelexsystemsinc.com
SIC: 7371 Computer software development

(P-13752)
INTELLECTYX INC
Also Called: Intellectyx
680 E Colorado Blvd Ste 180, Pasadena (91101-6144)
PHONE..............................720 256-7540
Raj Joseph, *CEO*
EMP: 70 EST: 2010
SALES (est): 1.87MM **Privately Held**
Web: www.intellectyx.com
SIC: 7371 Computer software development

(P-13753)
INTERNATIONAL LOTTERY & TOTALIZATOR SYSTEMS INC
Also Called: Ilts California
2310 Cousteau Ct, Vista (92081-8346)
PHONE..............................760 598-1655
EMP: 33
Web: www.ilts.com
SIC: 7371 7372 3572 Custom computer programming services; Prepackaged software; Computer storage devices

(P-13754)
INTERNTNAL LTTERY TTLZTOR SYST
Also Called: Ilts Delaware
2310 Cousteau Ct, Vista (92081-8346)
PHONE..............................760 598-1655
Theodore A Johnson, *
▲ EMP: 33 EST: 1999
SALES (est): 10.03MM **Privately Held**
Web: www.ilts.com
SIC: 7371 7372 3572 Custom computer programming services; Prepackaged software; Computer storage devices
PA: Berjaya Lottery Management (Hk) Limited
    5/F Manulife Place

(P-13755)
IRISE (PA)
2381 Rosecrans Ave Ste 100, El Segundo (90245-7903)
PHONE..............................800 556-0399
Emmet B Keeffe Iii, *CEO*
Maurice Martin, *
Jacques Marine, *
Stephen Brickley, *
Dean Terry, *
▲ EMP: 94 EST: 1997
SALES (est): 9.54MM

SALES (corp-wide): 9.54MM **Privately Held**
Web: www.irise.com
SIC: 7371 Computer software development

(P-13756)
ISAAC FAIR CORPORATION
Also Called: Mindwave Software
3661 Valley Centre Dr, San Diego
(92130-3321)
PHONE..............................858 369-8000
Steve Gutschow, *Prin*
EMP: 88
SALES (corp-wide): 1.72B **Publicly Held**
Web: www.fico.com
SIC: 7371 Computer software development
PA: Fair Isaac Corporation
5 W Mendenhall Ste 105
406 982-7276

(P-13757)
ITREX GROUP USA CORPORATION
120 Vantis Dr Ste 545, Aliso Viejo
(92656-2679)
PHONE..............................213 436-7785
EMP: 274
SALES (corp-wide): 2.95MM **Privately Held**
Web: www.itrexgroup.com
SIC: 7371 Computer software development
PA: Itrex Group Usa Corporation
1120 Vantis Dr Ste 545
213 436-7785

(P-13758)
JUNGO INC
3033 5th Ave, San Diego (92103-5856)
PHONE..............................619 727-4600
Michael Gulitz, *CEO*
EMP: 88 EST: 2018
SALES (est): 1.65MM **Privately Held**
Web: www.ijungo.com
SIC: 7371 Computer software development

(P-13759)
KINSTA INC
8605 Santa Monica Blvd # 92581, West Hollywood (90069-4109)
PHONE..............................310 736-9306
Mark Gavalda, *CEO*
EMP: 74
SALES (est): 8.82MM **Privately Held**
Web: www.kinsta.com
SIC: 7371 Computer software development

(P-13760)
KRG TECHNOLOGIES INC (PA)
25000 Avenue Stanford Ste 243, Valencia
(91355-4598)
PHONE..............................661 257-9967
Balamurugan Subbiah, *Pr*
Hemalatha Rajagopala, *CEO*
EMP: 490 EST: 2003
SQ FT: 780
SALES (est): 25.93MM
SALES (corp-wide): 25.93MM **Privately Held**
Web: www.krgtech.com
SIC: 7371 Computer software development and applications

(P-13761)
KTB SOFTWARE LLC ✪
11101 W Olympic Blvd, Los Angeles
(90064-1805)
PHONE..............................505 306-0390
Diop Mckenzie, *Managing Member*
EMP: 84 EST: 2023
SALES (est): 2.24MM **Privately Held**

Web: www.ktbsoftwareweb.com
SIC: 7371 Computer software development and applications

(P-13762)
LOCAI INC
Also Called: Petvisor
2044 1st Ave Ste 200, San Diego
(92101-2089)
PHONE..............................469 834-5364
Kenneth Tsui, *Prin*
EMP: 113 EST: 2015
SALES (est): 2.65MM **Privately Held**
Web: www.petvisor.com
SIC: 7371 Computer software development and applications

(P-13763)
LOGILITY INC
4885 Greencraig Ln 200, San Diego
(92123-1664)
PHONE..............................858 565-4238
EMP: 55
SALES (corp-wide): 102.52MM **Publicly Held**
Web: www.logility.com
SIC: 7371 7372 Computer software development; Prepackaged software
HQ: Logility, Inc.
470 E Paces Ferry Rd
Atlanta GA 30305
800 762-5207

(P-13764)
LUMIRADX INC
444 S Cedros Ave Ste 101, Solana Beach
(92075-1966)
PHONE..............................951 201-9384
Jarrod Provins, *Prin*
EMP: 137
Web: www.lumiradx.com
SIC: 7371 Custom computer programming services
HQ: Lumiradx, Inc.
221 Crescent St Ste 502
Waltham MA 02453
617 621-9775

(P-13765)
MAINTECH INCORPORATED
2401 N Glassell St, Orange (92865-2705)
P.O. Box 13500 (92857-8500)
PHONE..............................714 921-8000
Tony Donato, *VP*
EMP: 200
SQ FT: 1,200
SALES (corp-wide): 27.04MM **Privately Held**
Web: www.maintech.com
SIC: 7371 3577 Computer software systems analysis and design, custom; Computer peripheral equipment, nec
PA: Maintech, Incorporated
14 Commerce Dr Ste 200
973 330-3200

(P-13766)
MANGO TECHNOLOGIES INC (PA)
Also Called: Clickup
350 10th Ave Ste 500, San Diego
(92101-7497)
PHONE..............................888 625-4258
Brian Evans, *CEO*
Dan Zhang, *
Derek Dahlin, *
EMP: 694 EST: 2016
SALES (est): 99.03MM
SALES (corp-wide): 99.03MM **Privately Held**

Web: www.clickup.com
SIC: 7371 Computer software development and applications

(P-13767)
MARKET SCAN INFO SYSTEMS INC
Also Called: Market Scan
815 Camarillo Springs Rd, Camarillo
(93012-9457)
PHONE..............................800 658-7226
Russell West, *Pr*
Carsten Preisz, *Chief Business Officer**
Mathew Hermann, *
EMP: 85 EST: 1987
SQ FT: 10,500
SALES (est): 10.84MM
SALES (corp-wide): 12.5B **Publicly Held**
Web: www.marketscan.com
SIC: 7371 Computer software development
PA: S&P Global Inc.
55 Water St
212 438-1000

(P-13768)
MELISSA DATA CORPORATION (PA)
Also Called: Mailers Software
22382 Avenida Empresa, Rcho Sta Marg
(92688-2112)
PHONE..............................949 858-3000
EMP: 90 EST: 1985
SALES (est): 10.71MM
SALES (corp-wide): 10.71MM **Privately Held**
Web: www.melissa.com
SIC: 7371 Computer software development

(P-13769)
MELLMO INC
Also Called: Roambi
131 Aberdeen Dr, Cardiff By The Sea
(92007-1821)
PHONE..............................858 847-3272
EMP: 140
SIC: 7371 Custom computer programming services

(P-13770)
MERIDIANLINK INC (PA)
Also Called: Meridianlink
3560 Hyland Ave Ste 200, Costa Mesa
(92626-1438)
PHONE..............................714 708-6950
Nicolaas Vlok, *CEO*
Edward H Mcdermott, *Non-Executive Chairman of the Board*
Laurence E Katz, *Pr*
Timothy Nguyen, *CSO*
Elias Olmeta, *CFO*
EMP: 58 EST: 1998
SQ FT: 19,838
SALES (est): 303.62MM
SALES (corp-wide): 303.62MM **Publicly Held**
Web: www.meridianlink.com
SIC: 7371 7372 Computer software development; Prepackaged software

(P-13771)
MIR3 INC
3398 Carmel Mountain Rd Ste 100, San Diego (92121-1044)
PHONE..............................858 724-1200
EMP: 90
SIC: 7371 Computer software development and applications

(P-13772)
MODERN CAMPUS USA INC (PA)
1320 Flynn Rd Ste 100, Camarillo
(93012-8745)
PHONE..............................805 484-9400
Brian Kibby, *CEO*
Tom Nalevanko, *
EMP: 60 EST: 1982
SQ FT: 6,600
SALES (est): 12.37MM
SALES (corp-wide): 12.37MM **Privately Held**
Web: www.moderncampus.com
SIC: 7371 7372 Computer software development; Prepackaged software

(P-13773)
MYEVALUATIONSCOM INC
11111 W Olympic Blvd Ste 401, Los Angeles
(90064-1824)
PHONE..............................646 422-0554
David Melamed, *Ex Dir*
EMP: 25 EST: 2005
SALES (est): 595.93K **Privately Held**
Web: www.myevaluations.com
SIC: 7371 7372 Computer software systems analysis and design, custom; Educational computer software

(P-13774)
MYTHICAL ENTERTAINMENT LLC
2121 Avenue Of The Stars Ste 1300, Los Angeles (90067-5081)
PHONE..............................818 859-7398
Charles L Neal, *CEO*
Rhett J Mclaughlin, *Sec*
EMP: 98 EST: 2017
SALES (est): 10.17MM **Privately Held**
Web: www.mythical.com
SIC: 7371 7829 Computer software development and applications; Motion picture distribution services

(P-13775)
NC AMERICA LLC ✪
400 Spectrum Center Dr Fl 18, Irvine
(92618-4934)
PHONE..............................949 447-6287
Taekhun Kim, *CEO*
Taekhun Kim, *Managing Member*
Eunjung Kim, *
EMP: 26 EST: 2023
SALES (est): 1.12MM **Privately Held**
SIC: 7371 7372 Computer software development and applications; Prepackaged software

(P-13776)
NEONROOTS LLC
8560 W Sunset Blvd Ste 500, West Hollywood (90069-2342)
PHONE..............................310 907-9210
Benjamin C Lee, *CEO*
EMP: 125 EST: 2012
SALES (est): 1.15MM **Privately Held**
Web: www.neonroots.com
SIC: 7371 Computer software development and applications

(P-13777)
NEUBLOC LLC (PA)
125 S Highway 101, Solana Beach
(92075-1872)
PHONE..............................858 674-8701
Alexander Nawrocki, *Pt*
EMP: 70 EST: 2005
SALES (est): 2.22MM **Privately Held**
Web: www.neubloc.com

SIC: 7371 Computer software development

(P-13778)
NEUDESIC LLC (HQ)
Also Called: Neuron Esb
200 Spectrum Center Dr Ste 2000, Irvine
(92618-5013)
PHONE.....................949 754-4500
Parsa Rohani, *CEO*
Tim Marshall, *
EMP: 125 EST: 2001
SQ FT: 15,150
SALES (est): 25.72K
SALES (corp-wide): 61.86B **Publicly Held**
Web: www.neudesic.com
SIC: 7371 Computer software development
PA: International Business Machines
Corporation
1 New Orchard Rd
914 499-1900

(P-13779)
NEUINTEL LLC (PA)
Also Called: Pricespider
20 Pacifica Ste 1000, Irvine (92618-7462)
PHONE.....................949 625-6117
Anthony Ferry, *CEO*
Jon Pfortmiller, *Pr*
Lucas Baerg, *CFO*
EMP: 80 EST: 2004
SQ FT: 17,000
SALES (est): 24.77MM
SALES (corp-wide): 24.77MM **Privately
Held**
Web: www.pricespider.com
SIC: 7371 Computer software development

(P-13780)
NEW CAM COMMERCE
SOLUTIONS LLC
222 S Harbor Blvd Ste 1015, Anaheim
(92805-3760)
PHONE.....................714 338-0200
Doug Roberson, *Managing Member*
Ann Gao, *
EMP: 77 EST: 2010
SALES (est): 6.72MM
SALES (corp-wide): 19.7MM **Privately
Held**
SIC: 7371 Computer software development
PA: Celerant Technology, Corp.
485 Route 1 S Bldg B Fl 2
715 804-2369

(P-13781)
NEXXEN INC
10100 Santa Monica Blvd, Los Angeles
(90067-4003)
PHONE.....................310 382-8909
EMP: 81
Web: www.amoboo.com
SIC: 7371 Computer software development
HQ: Nexxen Inc
100 Redwood Shores Pkwy
Redwood City CA 94065

(P-13782)
NGA 911 LLC
Also Called: Telecommunication
8383 Wilshire Blvd Ste 800, Beverly Hills
(90211-2440)
PHONE.....................877 899-8337
Don Ferguson, *CEO*
Jackie Barnes, *
EMP: 120 EST: 2016
SALES (est): 27.11MM **Privately Held**
Web: www.nga911.com
SIC: 7371 Computer software development
and applications

(P-13783)
NLYTE SOFTWARE AMERICAS
LTD
1380 El Cajon Blvd Ste 220, El Cajon
(92020-5760)
PHONE.....................866 386-5983
Bernard Liautaud, *Ch*
EMP: 85
SALES (corp-wide): 22.1B **Publicly Held**
Web: www.nlyte.com
SIC: 7371 Computer software development
HQ: Nlyte Software Americas Limited
275 Raritan Center Pkwy
Edison NJ 08837

(P-13784)
NOREDINK CORP
442 N Barranca Ave Ste 153, Covina
(91723-1722)
PHONE.....................844 667-3346
Jeff Scheur, *CEO*
EMP: 76 EST: 2013
SALES (est): 10.12MM **Privately Held**
Web: www.noredink.com
SIC: 7371 Computer software development

(P-13785)
NORTRIDGE SOFTWARE LLC
Also Called: Nortridge Software
27422 Portola Pkwy Ste 360, Foothill Ranch
(92610-2837)
PHONE.....................714 263-7251
Greg Hindson, *CEO*
Chris Ewoldt, *
EMP: 90 EST: 2010
SALES (est): 1.52MM **Privately Held**
Web: www.nortridge.com
SIC: 7371 Computer software development

(P-13786)
NOVALOGIC INC
27489 Agoura Rd Ste 300, Agoura Hills
(91301-2419)
PHONE.....................818 880-1997
John Garcia, *CEO*
David Seeholzer, *
John Butrovich, *
Kyle Freeman, *
EMP: 100 EST: 1985
SALES (est): 2.1MM **Privately Held**
Web: www.novalogic.com
SIC: 7371 5734 7372 Computer software
development; Software, business and non-
game; Prepackaged software

(P-13787)
NUCLEUSHEALTH LLC
Also Called: Statrad - Radconnect
13280 Evening Creek Dr S Ste 110, San
Diego (92128-4109)
PHONE.....................858 251-3400
Neil De Crescenzo, *Pr*
EMP: 98 EST: 2008
SQ FT: 8,413
SALES (est): 20.19MM
SALES (corp-wide): 371.62B **Publicly
Held**
Web: www.statrad.com
SIC: 7371 8748 Computer software
development; Business consulting, nec
HQ: Change Healthcare Inc.
424 Church St Ste 1400
Nashville TN 37219
615 932-3000

(P-13788)
NUMERADE LABS INC ✪
1155 Rexford Ave, Pasadena (91107-1712)
PHONE.....................213 536-1489
EMP: 75 EST: 2023

SALES (est): 2.14MM **Privately Held**
SIC: 7371 Computer software development
and applications

(P-13789)
OPERATION TECHNOLOGY INC
Also Called: Etap
17 Goodyear Ste 100, Irvine (92618-1822)
PHONE.....................949 462-0100
Farrokh Shokooh, *Pr*
Nikta Nikzad Shokooh, *Corporate
Secretary*
EMP: 90 EST: 1986
SQ FT: 32,000
SALES (est): 20.14MM **Privately Held**
Web: www.etap.com
SIC: 7371 8732 8249 Computer software
development; Research services, except
laboratory; Business training services

(P-13790)
ORANGE LOGIC LLC
4199 Campus Dr Ste 550, Irvine
(92612-4694)
PHONE.....................949 396-2233
Patty Le, *
EMP: 70 EST: 2012
SALES (est): 9.26MM **Privately Held**
Web: www.orangelogic.com
SIC: 7371 Computer software development

(P-13791)
OSHYN INC
10601 Walker St, Cypress (90630-4733)
PHONE.....................213 483-1770
Diego Rebosio, *CEO*
EMP: 75 EST: 2001
SALES (est): 3.46MM **Privately Held**
Web: www.oshyn.com
SIC: 7371 Computer software development

(P-13792)
PACIFIC TECH SOLUTIONS LLC
15530 Rockfield Blvd Ste B4, Irvine
(92618-2723)
PHONE.....................949 830-1623
Frederick Minturn, *Managing Member*
EMP: 76 EST: 1987
SQ FT: 3,000
SALES (est): 1.17MM **Privately Held**
Web: www.pts1.com
SIC: 7371 Computer software development
HQ: Msx International Rns Llc
26555 Evergreen Rd # 1300
Southfield MI 48076
248 829-6300

(P-13793)
PARALLEL 6 INC (PA)
1455 Frazee Rd Ste 900, San Diego
(92108-4310)
PHONE.....................619 452-1750
Allan Camaisa, *CEO*
Adam Halbridge, *
EMP: 30 EST: 2009
SQ FT: 28,000
SALES (est): 3.19MM
SALES (corp-wide): 3.19MM **Privately
Held**
Web: www.parallel6.com
SIC: 7371 7372 Computer software
development; Business oriented computer
software

(P-13794)
PATIENTFI LLC
530 Technology Dr Ste 350, Irvine
(92618-3504)
PHONE.....................949 441-5484
EMP: 71 EST: 2017

SALES (est): 6.8MM **Privately Held**
Web: www.patientfi.com
SIC: 7371 Computer software development
and applications

(P-13795)
PHONE CHECK SOLUTIONS
LLC
Also Called: Software
16027 Ventura Blvd Ste 605, Encino
(91436-4404)
PHONE.....................310 365-1855
Chris Sabeti, *CEO*
EMP: 358 EST: 2016
SALES (est): 2.59MM **Privately Held**
Web: www.phonecheck.com
SIC: 7371 Software programming
applications

(P-13796)
PLATFORM SCIENCE INC (PA)
9560 Towne Centre Dr # 200, San Diego
(92121-1972)
PHONE.....................844 475-8724
John C Kennedy Iii, *CEO*
Chris Sultemeier, *
Greg Ivancich, *
Gerald Choung, *CRO*
EMP: 140 EST: 2015
SALES (est): 27.19MM
SALES (corp-wide): 27.19MM **Privately
Held**
Web: www.platformscience.com
SIC: 7371 7372 Custom computer
programming services; Business oriented
computer software

(P-13797)
PLAYHAVEN LLC
1447 2nd St Ste 200, Santa Monica
(90401-3404)
PHONE.....................310 308-9668
Mike Jones, *Pr*
Greg Gilman, *
Tom Dare, *
EMP: 99 EST: 2014
SQ FT: 15,000
SALES (est): 522.79K **Privately Held**
SIC: 7371 7311 Computer software
development and applications; Advertising
agencies
PA: Rockyou, Inc.
3305 Jerusalem Ave # 201

(P-13798)
PROCORE TECHNOLOGIES INC
(PA)
6309 Carpinteria Ave, Carpinteria
(93013-2924)
PHONE.....................866 477-6267
Craig F Courtemanche Junior, *CEO*
Howard Fu, *CFO*
Benjamin C Singer, *CLO*
Lawrence J Stack, *CRO*
Joy D Durling, *CDO*
EMP: 3386 EST: 2002
SQ FT: 176,000
SALES (est): 950.01MM
SALES (corp-wide): 950.01MM **Publicly
Held**
Web: www.procore.com
SIC: 7371 7372 Computer software
development; Prepackaged software

(P-13799)
PRODEGE LLC (PA)
Also Called: Swagbucks
2030 E Maple Ave Ste 200, El Segundo
(90245-5171)
PHONE.....................310 294-9599

PRODUCTS & SVCS

EMP: 77 **EST:** 2005
SALES (est): 50.71MM
SALES (corp-wide): 50.71MM **Privately Held**
Web: www.prodege.com
SIC: 7371 8742 Computer software development and applications; Marketing consulting services

(P-13800)
PROLIFICS TESTING INC
24025 Park Sorrento Ste 405, Calabasas (91302-4037)
PHONE..............................925 485-9535
Danis Yadegar, *Pr*
Dale Lampson, *VP*
Rutesh Shah, *VP*
Armen Tekerian, *VP*
Claude Fenner, *VP*
EMP: 26 **EST:** 1988
SQ FT: 6,500
SALES (est): 1.9MM **Privately Held**
Web: www.prolifics.com
SIC: 7371 7372 Computer software development; Prepackaged software
HQ: Prolifics Application Services, Inc.
24025 Park Sorrento # 405
Calabasas CA 91302
646 201-4967

(P-13801)
PSYONIX LLC
Also Called: Rocket League
401 W A St Ste 2400, San Diego (92101-7909)
PHONE..............................619 622-8772
David F Hagewood, *CEO*
Jessica Hagewood, *Sec*
EMP: 83 **EST:** 2012
SQ FT: 40,000
SALES (est): 11.26MM **Privately Held**
Web: www.psyonix.com
SIC: 7371 Computer software development
PA: Epic Games, Inc.
620 Crossroads Blvd

(P-13802)
QXV PROGRAMMING LLC ✪
6565 W Sunset Blvd, Los Angeles (90028-7206)
PHONE..............................213 344-2031
Diop Mckenzie, *Managing Member*
EMP: 71 **EST:** 2023
SALES (est): 609.51K **Privately Held**
SIC: 7371 Custom computer programming services

(P-13803)
QXV SOFTWARE LLC ✪
215 N Marengo Ave, Pasadena (91101-1503)
PHONE..............................626 219-0522
Diop Mckenzie, *Managing Member*
EMP: 74 **EST:** 2023
SALES (est): 410K **Privately Held**
SIC: 7371 Computer software development

(P-13804)
REAPPLICATIONS INC
8910 University Center Ln Ste 300, San Diego (92122-1024)
PHONE..............................619 230-0209
Richard Boyle, *CEO*
EMP: 90 **EST:** 1996
SALES (est): 1.45MM
SALES (corp-wide): 2.46B **Publicly Held**
Web: www.reapplications.com
SIC: 7371 Computer software development
HQ: Loopnet, Inc.
101 California St # 4300

San Francisco CA 94111

(P-13805)
RECIPROCAL LABS CORP
Also Called: Propeller Health
9001 Spectrum Center Blvd, San Diego (92123-1438)
PHONE..............................608 251-0470
David Van Sickle, *CEO*
Chris Hogg, *Chief Commercial Officer**
Greg Tracy, *
EMP: 72 **EST:** 2013
SALES (est): 1.77MM **Publicly Held**
Web: www.propellerhealth.com
SIC: 7371 Software programming applications
PA: Resmed Inc.
9001 Spectrum Center Blvd

(P-13806)
ROOTSTRAP INC
8306 Wilshire Blvd Ste 249, Beverly Hills (90211-2304)
PHONE..............................310 907-9210
David Jarrett, *CEO*
Fernando Colman, *
Anthony Figueroa, *
EMP: 134 **EST:** 2015
SALES (est): 2.28MM **Privately Held**
Web: www.rootstrap.com
SIC: 7371 Computer software development

(P-13807)
SAALEX CORP
27525 Enterprise Cir W Ste 101a, Temecula (92590-4885)
PHONE..............................951 543-9259
EMP: 359
SALES (corp-wide): 119.25MM **Privately Held**
Web: www.saalex.com
SIC: 7371 Custom computer programming services
PA: Saalex Corp.
811 Camarillo Springs Rd A
805 482-1070

(P-13808)
SAFRAN PASS INNOVATIONS LLC (HQ)
Also Called: Zodiac Inflight Innovations US
3151 E Imperial Hwy, Brea (92821-6720)
PHONE..............................714 854-8600
Matt Smith, *CEO*
Ed Barrera, *
Steve Hawkins, *
EMP: 73 **EST:** 1996
SALES (est): 61.68MM
SALES (corp-wide): 940.23MM **Privately Held**
Web: www.safran-group.com
SIC: 7371 Computer software systems analysis and design, custom
PA: Safran
2 Boulevard Du General Martial Valin

(P-13809)
SAGO MINI INC
5880 W Jefferson Blvd Ste A, Los Angeles (90016-3160)
PHONE..............................416 731-8586
Anne-sophie Brieger, *Admn*
EMP: 76 **EST:** 2021
SALES (est): 1.29MM **Privately Held**
SIC: 7371 Custom computer programming services

(P-13810)
SAMEDAY TECHNOLOGIES INC
Also Called: Sameday Health
523 Victoria Ave, Venice (90291-4832)
PHONE..............................310 697-8126
Felix Huettenbach, *Pr*
EMP: 230 **EST:** 2021
SALES (est): 5.41MM **Privately Held**
Web: app.samedayhealth.com
SIC: 7371 Computer software development and applications

(P-13811)
SANTA MONICA STUDIOS
Also Called: Santa Monica Productions
3025 Olympic Blvd, Santa Monica (90404-5011)
PHONE..............................310 453-5046
David Rose, *CEO*
Todd Hess, *
EMP: 99 **EST:** 1993
SQ FT: 60,000
SALES (est): 2.11MM **Privately Held**
Web: www.onsetcoaching.com
SIC: 7371 7812 7822 Computer software development and applications; Motion picture production; Motion picture distribution

(P-13812)
SCHOOL-LINK TECHNOLOGIES INC
1437 6th St, Santa Monica (90401-2509)
P.O. Box 2410 (90407-2410)
PHONE..............................310 434-2700
EMP: 90
Web: www.sl-tech.net
SIC: 7371 Computer software development

(P-13813)
SCIFORMA CORPORATION
600 B St Ste 300, San Diego (92101-4505)
P.O. Box 9502 (95157-0502)
PHONE..............................408 899-0398
Yann Lebihan, *CEO*
Roger Meade, *
Charles Meade, *
Dan Karleskint, *
EMP: 28 **EST:** 2002
SALES (est): 5.48MM
SALES (corp-wide): 4.63MM **Privately Held**
Web: www.sciforma.com
SIC: 7371 7372 Computer software development; Prepackaged software
PA: Sciforma Holdco
9 Rue Ybry
178945570

(P-13814)
SCRATCHPADSAAS
440 N Barranca Ave # 9418, Covina (91723-1722)
PHONE..............................415 707-3325
EMP: 200 **EST:** 2019
SALES (est): 1.74MM **Privately Held**
SIC: 7371 Custom computer programming services

(P-13815)
SECUREAUTH CORPORATION (PA)
49 Discovery Ste 220, Irvine (92618-6713)
PHONE..............................949 777-6959
Joseph Dhanapal, *CEO*
Jeff Lo, *
Darin Pendergraft, *
Nick Mansour, *Executive Worldwide Sales Vice-President**

Keith Graham, *
EMP: 186 **EST:** 2005
SALES (est): 29.13MM **Privately Held**
Web: www.secureauth.com
SIC: 7371 Computer software development

(P-13816)
SELECT DATA INC
Also Called: Select Data
4175 E La Palma Ave Ste 205, Anaheim (92807-1842)
PHONE..............................714 577-1000
Edward A Buckley, *CEO*
Pam Hernandez, *
Tawny Nichols, *
Ted A Schulte, *
Pete Poulis, *
EMP: 151 **EST:** 1991
SALES (est): 17.52MM **Privately Held**
Web: www.selectdata.com
SIC: 7371 7372 Computer code authors; Prepackaged software

(P-13817)
SERCO SERVICES INC
Also Called: Lompoc-Vandenberg Afb
701 E North Ave Ste A, Lompoc (93437-6210)
PHONE..............................805 736-3584
Nedra Engleson, *Brnch Mgr*
EMP: 94
SALES (corp-wide): 6.07B **Privately Held**
SIC: 7371 8711 7375 Computer software development; Petroleum engineering; Data base information retrieval
HQ: Serco Services, Inc.
12930 Worldgate Dr # 600
Herndon VA 20170
703 939-6000

(P-13818)
SERVICETITAN INC (PA)
Also Called: Servicetitan
800 N Brand Blvd Ste 100, Glendale (91203-1245)
PHONE..............................855 899-0970
Ara Mahdessian, *Ch Bd*
Vahe Kuzoyan, *
Dave Sherry, *CFO*
EMP: 2725 **EST:** 2015
SALES (est): 363.32MM
SALES (corp-wide): 363.32MM **Publicly Held**
Web: www.servicetitan.com
SIC: 7371 Computer software development

(P-13819)
SETSCHEDULE LLC
100 Spectrum Center Dr Fl 9, Irvine (92618-4962)
PHONE..............................888 222-0011
Udi Dorner, *Managing Member*
EMP: 123 **EST:** 2014
SALES (est): 5.02MM **Privately Held**
Web: www.setschedule.com
SIC: 7371 Computer software development

(P-13820)
SHIPPING TREE LLC
14339 Whittram Ave, Fontana (92335-3071)
PHONE..............................310 404-9502
EMP: 81
SALES (corp-wide): 236.89MM **Privately Held**
Web: www.shippingtree.co
SIC: 7371 Custom computer programming services
HQ: Shipping Tree, Llc
10731 Walker St

Cypress CA 90630
800 728-9984

(P-13821)
SMART ENERGY SYSTEMS INC
Michelson Dr Ste 3370, Irvine (92612)
PHONE...............................909 703-9609
EMP: 119
SALES (corp-wide): 10.19MM **Privately Held**
Web: www.sew.ai
SIC: 7371 Computer software development
PA: Smart Energy Systems, Inc.
　　15495 Sand Cyn Ave Ste 10
　　909 703-9609

(P-13822)
SMART UTILITY SYSTEMS INC
Also Called: Smart Energy Water
19900 Macarthur Blvd Ste 370, Irvine
(92612-8404)
PHONE...............................909 217-3344
Kurt Sweetser, *Prin*
EMP: 100 **EST:** 2014
SALES (est): 10.17MM **Privately Held**
SIC: 7371 7373 8741 Computer software development; Systems software development services; Management services

(P-13823)
SMARTDRIVE SYSTEMS INC (PA)
9515 Towne Centre Dr, San Diego
(92121-1973)
PHONE...............................858 225-5550
Steve Mitgang, *CEO*
Jason Palmer, *
Michael J Baker, *
Dan Lehman, *CORP Development**
▲ **EMP:** 97 **EST:** 2005
SALES (est): 19.07MM **Privately Held**
Web: www.smartdrive.net
SIC: 7371 Computer software development and applications

(P-13824)
SNAIL INC (PA)
Also Called: Snail Games
12049 Jefferson Blvd, Culver City
(90230-6219)
PHONE...............................310 988-0643
Hai Shi, *CSO*
Heidy K Chow, *CFO*
Peter Kang, *OF Business Development Operations*
▲ **EMP:** 49 **EST:** 2009
SQ FT: 7,163
SALES (est): 60.9MM **Publicly Held**
Web: www.snail.com
SIC: 7371 5092 7372 Computer software development; Video games; Prepackaged software

(P-13825)
SNAP INC (PA)
Also Called: SNAPCHAT
3000 31st St Ste C, Santa Monica
(90405-3046)
PHONE...............................310 399-3339
Evan Spiegel, *CEO*
Michael Lynton, *
Derek Andersen, *CFO*
Robert Murphy, *
Rebecca Morrow, *CAO*
EMP: 520 **EST:** 2010
SQ FT: 718,000
SALES (est): 4.61B
SALES (corp-wide): 4.61B **Publicly Held**
Web: www.snap.com

SIC: 7371 7372 Computer software development and applications; Application computer software

(P-13826)
SNAPCOMMS INC
155 N Lake Ave Fl 9, Pasadena
(91101-1849)
PHONE...............................805 715-0300
Chris Leonard, *CEO*
EMP: 80 **EST:** 2012
SALES (est): 1.75MM
SALES (corp-wide): 448.79MM **Privately Held**
Web: www.snapcomms.com
SIC: 7371 Computer software development
PA: Everbridge, Inc.
　　155 N Lake Ave Ste 900
　　818 230-9700

(P-13827)
SOCIALEDGE INC (PA)
Also Called: Creatoriq
177 E Colorado Blvd Fl 2, Pasadena
(91105-1986)
PHONE...............................213 212-7079
Chris Harrington, *CEO*
Dan Murray, *Pr*
Max Powers, *Pr*
Conor Begley, *Chief Strategy Officer*
Bhavin Desai, *Chief Product Officer*
EMP: 336 **EST:** 2013
SALES (est): 53MM
SALES (corp-wide): 53MM **Privately Held**
Web: www.creatoriq.com
SIC: 7371 Custom computer programming services

(P-13828)
SOFTWARE MANAGEMENT CONS LLC
Also Called: Smci
959 S Coast Dr Ste 415, Costa Mesa
(92626-7839)
PHONE...............................714 662-1841
Cesar Sanchez, *Prin*
EMP: 142
SALES (corp-wide): 253.48MM **Privately Held**
Web: www.milestone.tech
SIC: 7371 Computer software development
HQ: Software Management Consultants, Llc
　　500 N Brand Blvd
　　Glendale CA 91203
　　818 240-3177

(P-13829)
SPERASOFT INC
1115 S Flower St, Burbank (91502-2022)
PHONE...............................408 715-6615
Igor Efremov, *CEO*
Alexei Kudriashov, *
EMP: 375 **EST:** 2005
SQ FT: 15,000
SALES (est): 9.97MM
SALES (corp-wide): 848.32MM **Privately Held**
Web: www.sperasoft.com
SIC: 7371 Software programming applications
HQ: Keywords International Limited
　　Whelan House
　　Dublin D18 T

(P-13830)
STARTEL CORPORATION (PA)
16 Goodyear B-125, Irvine (92618-3758)
PHONE...............................949 863-8700
William Lane, *Pr*
EMP: 60 **EST:** 1980

SQ FT: 27,000
SALES (est): 9.63MM
SALES (corp-wide): 9.63MM **Privately Held**
Web: www.startel.com
SIC: 7371 3661 Computer software development; Communication headgear, telephone .

(P-13831)
STEADY PLATFORM INC
5636 Fallsgrove St, Los Angeles
(90016-5027)
PHONE...............................678 792-8364
Adam Roseman, *CEO*
Nancy Bush, *
Adam Roseman, *Sec*
EMP: 70 **EST:** 2017
SALES (est): 2.4MM **Privately Held**
Web: www.steadyapp.com
SIC: 7371 Custom computer programming services

(P-13832)
STRATACARE LLC
Also Called: Stratacare
17838 Gillette Ave Ste D, Irvine
(92614-6502)
P.O. Box 19600 (92623-9600)
PHONE...............................949 743-1200
Scott R Green, *CEO*
John Zavoli, *Chief Compliance Officer**
Dave Perbix, *
Michael Josephs, *
Robert Mccaffrey, *SALES*
▲ **EMP:** 250 **EST:** 1998
SALES (est): 12.26MM
SALES (corp-wide): 3.72B **Publicly Held**
Web: www.conduent.com
SIC: 7371 Computer software development
HQ: Conduent Workers Compensation Holdings, Inc.
　　17838 Gillette Ave
　　Irvine CA 92614

(P-13833)
STRATCOM SYSTEMS INC
Also Called: Sims Software
2701 Loker Ave W Ste 130, Carlsbad
(92010-6637)
P.O. Box 607 (92075-0607)
PHONE...............................858 481-9292
Michael Struttmann, *Pr*
EMP: 24 **EST:** 1983
SQ FT: 2,500
SALES (est): 3.15MM **Privately Held**
Web: www.simssoftware.com
SIC: 7371 7372 Computer software development; Prepackaged software

(P-13834)
STRATGIC HLTHCARE PROGRAMS LLC
6500 Hollister Ave Ste 210, Goleta
(93117-5554)
PHONE...............................805 963-9446
Barbara Rosenblum, *CEO*
EMP: 112 **EST:** 2012
SALES (est): 5.69B
SALES (corp-wide): 6.18B **Publicly Held**
Web: www.shpdata.com
SIC: 7371 Computer software development
PA: Roper Technologies, Inc.
　　6496 University Pkwy
　　941 556-2601

(P-13835)
SYMITAR SYSTEMS INC
8985 Balboa Ave, San Diego (92123-1507)
PHONE...............................619 542-6700

Kathy Burress, *Prin*
EMP: 220 **EST:** 1984
SALES (est): 10.32MM
SALES (corp-wide): 2.22B **Publicly Held**
Web: www.jackhenry.com
SIC: 7371 Computer software development
PA: Jack Henry & Associates, Inc.
　　663 Highway 60
　　417 235-6652

(P-13836)
SYSTECH SOLUTIONS INC (PA)
500 N Brand Blvd Ste 1900, Glendale
(91203-3308)
PHONE...............................818 550-9690
Arun Gollapudi, *Pr*
Srinivasan Ramaswamy, *
Ashish Parikh, *
EMP: 81 **EST:** 1993
SQ FT: 1,500
SALES (est): 7.59MM
SALES (corp-wide): 7.59MM **Privately Held**
Web: www.systechusa.com
SIC: 7371 Computer software systems analysis and design, custom

(P-13837)
TALENT & ACQUISITION LLC
Also Called: Stand 8 Technology Services
3020 Old Ranch Pkwy Ste 300, Seal Beach
(90740-2751)
PHONE...............................888 970-9575
Quinn Fillmon, *Managing Member*
EMP: 150 **EST:** 2009
SALES (est): 10.43MM **Privately Held**
Web: www.stand8.io
SIC: 7371 7379 7363 7361 Computer software development and applications; Computer related consulting services; Help supply services; Employment agencies

(P-13838)
TAPESTRY SOLUTIONS INC (HQ)
6910 Carroll Rd, San Diego (92121-2211)
PHONE...............................858 503-1990
Geoff Evans, *Pr*
Vince Monteparpe, *
Mark Young, *
Mary Ann Wagner, *
EMP: 125 **EST:** 1993
SQ FT: 36,073
SALES (est): 45.25MM
SALES (corp-wide): 77.79B **Publicly Held**
Web: www.tapestrysolutions.com
SIC: 7371 5045 Custom computer programming services; Computer software
PA: The Boeing Company
　　929 Long Bridge Dr
　　703 465-3500

(P-13839)
TCG SOFTWARE SERVICES INC
320 Commerce Ste 200, Irvine
(92602-1363)
PHONE...............................714 665-6200
Greg Blevins, *Brnch Mgr*
EMP: 278
Web: www.tcgdigital.com
SIC: 7371 Custom computer programming services
PA: Tcg Software Services, Inc.
　　265 Davidson Ave Ste 220

(P-13840)
TEBRA TECHNOLOGIES INC (PA)
Also Called: Kareo PM
1111 Bayside Dr, Corona Del Mar
(92625-1714)

P.O. Box 1922 (92616)
PHONE..............................888 775-2736
Daniel Rodrigues, *CEO*
Tom Giannulli, *CMO**
Tom Patterson, *
James Armijo, *
Jason Leu, *
EMP: 239 **EST:** 2004
SALES (est): 44.55MM **Privately Held**
Web: www.kareo.com
SIC: 7371 Computer software development

(P-13841)
TECHNOSSUS LLC
5000 Birch St, Newport Beach
(92660-2127)
PHONE..............................949 769-3500
Giri Kalluri, *Prin*
EMP: 80 **EST:** 2014
SALES (est): 7.1MM **Privately Held**
Web: www.technossus.com
SIC: 7371 Computer software development

(P-13842)
TENANT INC
Also Called: Storage Front
4920 Campus Dr Ste B, Newport Beach
(92660-2110)
PHONE..............................949 894-4500
Lance Watkins, *CEO*
EMP: 79 **EST:** 2019
SALES (est): 1.97MM **Privately Held**
Web: www.storagefront.com
SIC: 7371 Computer software development

(P-13843)
THOMAS GALLAWAY CORPORATION (PA)
Also Called: Technologent
100 Spectrum Center Dr Ste 700, Irvine
(92618-4970)
PHONE..............................949 517-9500
Lezlie Gallaway, *CEO*
Thomas Gallaway, *
Marco Mohajer, *
Mike Mclaughlin, *VP*
Jim Bevis, *
EMP: 70 **EST:** 2002
SQ FT: 4,500
SALES (est): 471.27MM
SALES (corp-wide): 471.27MM **Privately Held**
Web: www.technologent.com
SIC: 7371 Computer software development

(P-13844)
THOMAS HEMMINGS
1620 5th Ave Ste 400, San Diego
(92101-2738)
PHONE..............................303 489-3259
Thomas Hemmings, *Admn*
Admiral Reed Mccalmon, *Prin*
EMP: 90 **EST:** 2018
SALES (est): 3.2MM **Privately Held**
Web: www.deckard.com
SIC: 7371 Computer software writing
services

(P-13845)
TP-LINK SYSTEMS INC
Also Called: Tp-Link USA
10 Mauchly, Irvine (92618-2306)
PHONE..............................866 225-8139
Jianjun Zhao, *CEO*
Li Pingji, *CEO*
Deyi Shu, *
EMP: 200 **EST:** 2008
SALES (est): 4.76MM **Privately Held**
SIC: 7371 Computer software development
and applications

(P-13846)
TRACKR INC
7410 Hollister Ave, Santa Barbara
(93117-2583)
PHONE..............................855 981-1690
Christopher G Herbert, *CEO*
Christian J Smith, *
Nathan Kelly, *
Matthew Pigeon, *
EMP: 100 **EST:** 2009
SQ FT: 40,000
SALES (est): 8.78MM **Privately Held**
Web: www.thetrackr.com
SIC: 7371 Computer software development

(P-13847)
TRADE DESK INC (PA)
Also Called: THETRADEDESK
42 N Chestnut St, Ventura (93001-2662)
PHONE..............................805 585-3434
Jeff T Green, *Ch Bd*
Samantha Jacobson, *CSO*
Laura Schenkein, *CFO*
Jay R Grant, *CLO*
EMP: 271 **EST:** 2009
SALES (est): 1.95B
SALES (corp-wide): 1.95B **Publicly Held**
Web: www.thetradedesk.com
SIC: 7371 7372 Software programming
applications; Prepackaged software

(P-13848)
TRI-TECH SYSTEMS INC (PA)
Also Called: Triad Systems International
23801 Calabasas Rd Ste 2022, Calabasas
(91302-1568)
PHONE..............................818 222-6811
Cyril Cianflone, *Pr*
John Gerber, *VP*
Thomas Pickett, *Sec*
EMP: 395 **EST:** 1992
SQ FT: 3,500
SALES (est): 2.57MM
SALES (corp-wide): 2.57MM **Privately Held**
Web: www.triadsystems.com
SIC: 7371 7373 Custom computer
programming services; Computer
integrated systems design

(P-13849)
TRIBRIDGE HOLDINGS LLC
523 W 6th St Ste 830, Los Angeles
(90014-1243)
PHONE..............................813 287-8887
Criatritinia Valentin, *Brnch Mgr*
EMP: 295
SALES (corp-wide): 13.67B **Publicly Held**
Web: www.dxc.com
SIC: 7371 Computer software development
HQ: Tribridge Holdings, Llc
20408 Bashan Dr Ste 231
Ashburn VA 20147

(P-13850)
TRINUS CORPORATION
35 N Lake Ave Ste 710, Pasadena
(91101-4185)
PHONE..............................818 246-1143
Sanjay Kucheria, *CEO*
Harshada Kucheria, *
EMP: 150 **EST:** 1995
SALES (est): 9.35MM **Privately Held**
Web: www.trinus.com
SIC: 7371 Custom computer programming
services

(P-13851)
TROVATA INC (PA)
Also Called: Trovata

312 S Cedros Ave Ste 312, Solana Beach
(92075-1943)
P.O. Box 1b (92662)
PHONE..............................312 914-8106
Brett Turner, *CEO*
Scott Harrington, *
Joseph Drambarean, *
EMP: 87 **EST:** 2016
SALES (est): 9.57MM
SALES (corp-wide): 9.57MM **Privately
Held**
Web: www.trovata.io
SIC: 7371 Computer software development

(P-13852)
TRUECAR INC (PA)
Also Called: TRUECAR
225 Santa Monica Blvd Fl 12, Santa Monica
(90401-2219)
PHONE..............................800 200-2000
Jantoon E Reigersman, *Pr*
Barbara A Carbone, *
Jeffrey J Swart, *Ex VP*
Jill Angel, *COO*
Oliver M Foley, *CFO*
EMP: 172 **EST:** 2005
SALES (est): 158.71MM **Publicly Held**
Web: www.truecar.com
SIC: 7371 7299 Custom computer
programming services; Information
services, consumer

(P-13853)
TUNGSTEN AUTOMATION CORP (PA)
15211 Laguna Canyon Rd, Irvine
(92618-3146)
PHONE..............................949 783-1000
Reynolds Bish, *CEO*
Cort Townsend, *
Howard Dratler, *
Anthony Macciola, *
Grant Johnson, *
▼ **EMP:** 500 **EST:** 1985
SQ FT: 100,000
SALES (est): 289.38MM
SALES (corp-wide): 289.38MM **Privately
Held**
Web: www.tungstenautomation.com
SIC: 7371 3577 Computer software
development; Input/output equipment,
computer

(P-13854)
UNISYS CORPORATION
9701 Jeronimo Rd Ste 100, Irvine
(92618-2076)
PHONE..............................949 380-5000
Carmen Lynch, *Mgr*
EMP: 196
SALES (corp-wide): 1.98B **Publicly Held**
Web: www.unisys.com
SIC: 7371 Computer software development
PA: Unisys Corporation
801 Lakeview Dr Ste 100
215 986-4011

(P-13855)
UNITED SUPPORT SERVICES INC
3252 Holiday Ct Ste 110, La Jolla
(92037-1807)
PHONE..............................858 373-9500
Michael Fernandez, *Pr*
EMP: 190 **EST:** 2003
SQ FT: 2,600
SALES (est): 15MM **Privately Held**
Web: www.usscompany.com

SIC: 7371 8711 Custom computer
programming services; Consulting engineer

(P-13856)
UPKEEP TECHNOLOGIES INC
10880 Wilshire Blvd Ste 850, Los Angeles
(90024-4109)
PHONE..............................323 880-0280
EMP: 103 **EST:** 2018
SALES (est): 7.7MM **Privately Held**
Web: www.upkeep.com
SIC: 7371 Computer software development

(P-13857)
UST GLOBAL INC (HQ)
Also Called: UST
5 Polaris Way, Aliso Viejo (92656-5374)
PHONE..............................949 716-8757
Krishna Sudheendra, *CEO*
Paras Chandaria, *
Arun Narayanan, *
Sunil Kanchi, *CIO**
Murali Gopalan, *CCO**
EMP: 100 **EST:** 2007
SQ FT: 20,000
SALES (est): 511.51MM **Privately Held**
SIC: 7371 Computer software development
PA: Ust Holdings Ltd
C/O R&H Services Limited

(P-13858)
VEGATEK CORPORATION
Also Called: Intellective
7545 Irvine Center Dr Ste 200, Irvine
(92618-2933)
P.O. Box 436057 (40253-6057)
PHONE..............................949 502-0090
Matthew Barnickle, *CEO*
Boris Zhilin, *
EMP: 70 **EST:** 2005
SALES (est): 8.38MM **Privately Held**
Web: www.intellective.com
SIC: 7371 7379 6411 Computer software
development; Computer related consulting
services; Insurance information and
consulting services

(P-13859)
VENDOR DIRECT SOLUTIONS LLC (PA)
515 S Figueroa St Ste 1900, Los Angeles
(90071-3336)
PHONE..............................213 362-5622
Jules Buenabenta, *Managing Member*
Jim Young, *
Ron Mcelhaney, *Dir Opers*
Angel E Nevarez, *
Stephanie Simmons, *
EMP: 247 **EST:** 2006
SQ FT: 1,200
SALES (est): 19.58MM **Privately Held**
Web: www.teamvds.com
SIC: 7371 Computer software development

(P-13860)
VERITAS TECHNOLOGIES LLC
16501 Ventura Blvd Ste 400, Encino
(91436-2067)
PHONE..............................310 202-0757
EMP: 200
SALES (corp-wide): 2.96B **Publicly Held**
Web: www.veritas.com
SIC: 7371 7375 Computer software
development and applications; Data base
information retrieval
HQ: Veritas Technologies Llc
2625 Augustine Dr
Santa Clara CA 95054
866 837-4827

(P-13861)
VERSEIO INC
Also Called: Short Sale Agent Finder
550 W B St Fl 4, San Diego (92101-3537)
PHONE.................888 373-9942
Tal David, *CEO*
EMP: 90 EST: 2012
SALES (est): 9.75MM **Privately Held**
Web: www.verse.ai
SIC: 7371 Software programming
   applications

(P-13862)
VIDA HEALTH INC
20500 Belshaw Ave, Carson (90746-3506)
PHONE.................415 989-1017
Stephanie Tilenius, *CEO*
Cynthia Mark, *CCO**
EMP: 100 EST: 2013
SALES (est): 23.4MM **Privately Held**
Web: www.vida.com
SIC: 7371 Computer software development
   and applications

(P-13863)
VISION SOLUTIONS INC (HQ)
15300 Barranca Pkwy, Irvine (92618-2200)
PHONE.................949 253-6500
Nicolaas Vlok, *Pr*
Alan Arnold, *
Don Scott, *
Robert Johnson, *
Wm Edward Vesely, *CMO**
▲ EMP: 90 EST: 1989
SQ FT: 25,000
SALES (est): 24.21MM
SALES (corp-wide): 446.91MM **Privately Held**
SIC: 7371 7373 Computer software
   development; Systems integration services
PA: Precisely Software Incorporated
   1700 District Ave Ste 300
   978 436-8900

(P-13864)
WATT INC
Also Called: Northstar
8605 Santa Monica Blvd Pmb 65044, West
Hollywood (90069-4109)
PHONE.................310 896-8197
William Peng, *CEO*
Matthew Mattison, *Pr*
EMP: 70 EST: 2016
SALES (est): 10.36MM **Privately Held**
Web: www.northstarmoney.com
SIC: 7371 Computer software development
   and applications

(P-13865)
X1 DISCOVERY INC
251 S Lake Ave Ste 800, Pasadena
(91101-3052)
PHONE.................877 999-1347
John Patzakis, *CEO*
EMP: 36 EST: 2011
SQ FT: 2,000
SALES (est): 6.75MM **Privately Held**
Web: www.x1.com
SIC: 7371 7372 Computer software
   development; Prepackaged software

(P-13866)
YARDI SYSTEMS INC (PA)
430 S Fairview Ave, Santa Barbara
(93117-3637)
PHONE.................805 699-2040
Anant Yardi, *CEO*
Gordon Morrell, *
Fritz Schindelbeck, *
John Pendergast, *

Robert Teel, *
EMP: 380 EST: 1982
SQ FT: 160,000
SALES (est): 856.64MM
SALES (corp-wide): 856.64MM **Privately
Held**
Web: www.yardi.com
SIC: 7371 Computer software development

(P-13867)
ZESTFINANCE INC
Also Called: Zest.ai
3900 W Alameda Ave Ste 1600, Burbank
(91505-4387)
PHONE.................323 450-3000
Mike De Vere, *CEO*
Douglas Merrill, *
EMP: 85 EST: 2012
SALES (est): 10.37MM **Privately Held**
Web: www.zest.ai
SIC: 7371 Computer software development

7372 Prepackaged Software

(P-13868)
1ON1 LLC
8730 Wilshire Blvd Ste 350, Beverly Hills
(90211-2723)
PHONE.................310 998-7473
Susan Josephson, *Managing Member*
EMP: 50 EST: 2016
SALES (est): 3.36MM **Privately Held**
SIC: 7372 Application computer software

(P-13869)
ACTIVISION BLIZZARD INC (HQ)
Also Called: Activision Blizzard
2701 Olympic Blvd Bldg B, Santa Monica
(90404-4183)
PHONE.................310 255-2000
Brian G Kelly, *Ch Bd*
Armin Zerza, *CFO*
Brian Bulatao, *Chief*
Julie Hodges, *CPO*
Lulu Meservey, *Chief Communications
Officer*
EMP: 333 EST: 1979
SALES (est): 7.53B
SALES (corp-wide): 245.12B **Publicly
Held**
Web: www.activisionblizzard.com
SIC: 7372 Prepackaged software
PA: Microsoft Corporation
   1 Microsoft Way
   425 882-8080

(P-13870)
ACTIVISION BLIZZARD INC
Blizzard Entertainment
3 Blizzard, Irvine (92606)
P.O. Box 18979 (92623-8979)
PHONE.................949 955-1380
Frank Pearce, *Prin*
EMP: 85
SALES (corp-wide): 245.12B **Publicly
Held**
Web: www.activisionblizzard.com
SIC: 7372 Prepackaged software
HQ: Activision Blizzard, Inc.
   2701 Olympic Blvd Bldg B
   Santa Monica CA 90404
   310 255-2000

(P-13871)
ADEXA INC (PA)
5777 W Century Blvd Ste 1100, Los
Angeles (90045-5643)
PHONE.................310 642-2100
Khosrow Cyrus Hadavi, *Ch*

Kameron Hadavi, *
Mario Disandro, *
Tim Field, *
John Hosford, *OF SVCS**
EMP: 50 EST: 1994
SQ FT: 31,000
SALES (est): 9.19MM **Privately Held**
Web: www.adexa.com
SIC: 7372 Business oriented computer
   software

(P-13872)
ADVISYS INC
3 Corporate Park Ste 240, Irvine
(92606-5163)
PHONE.................949 250-0794
Kenneth Kerr, *CEO*
Richard M Kettley, *
Dane Parker, *
Gregg Janes, *
Sherelyn Kettley, *
EMP: 28 EST: 1979
SALES (est): 4.51MM **Privately Held**
Web: www.advisys.com
SIC: 7372 Application computer software

(P-13873)
AGENCYCOM LLC
5353 Grosvenor Blvd, Los Angeles
(90066-6913)
PHONE.................415 817-3800
Chan Suh, *CEO*
Rob Elliott, *CFO*
EMP: 400 EST: 1995
SQ FT: 130,000
SALES (est): 2.47MM
SALES (corp-wide): 14.69B **Publicly Held**
SIC: 7372 Application computer software
PA: Omnicom Group Inc.
   280 Park Ave
   212 415-3600

(P-13874)
AIRA TECH CORP
Also Called: Aira Tech
3451 Via Montebello Ste 192 Pmb 214,
Carlsbad (92009-8492)
PHONE.................800 835-1934
Troy Otillio, *CEO*
EMP: 200 EST: 2015
SALES (est): 17.34MM **Privately Held**
Web: www.aira.io
SIC: 7372 Application computer software

(P-13875)
ALTUMIND INC
10620 Treena St Ste 230, San Diego
(92131-1140)
PHONE.................858 382-3956
Ali Naderi, *Managing Member*
EMP: 50 EST: 2021
SALES (est): 2.54MM **Privately Held**
Web: www.altumindtech.com
SIC: 7372 Application computer software

(P-13876)
AMBER HOLDING INC
1601 Cloverfield Blvd Ste 600s, Santa
Monica (90404-4087)
PHONE.................603 324-3000
Charles E Moran, *Pr*
Tom Mcdonald, *CFO*
Jerry Nine, *
EMP: 49 EST: 2009
SALES (est): 4.87MM
SALES (corp-wide): 553.24MM **Publicly
Held**
SIC: 7372 Prepackaged software
HQ: Skillsoft (Us) Llc
   300 Innvative Way Ste 201

Nashua NH 03062
603 324-3000

(P-13877)
ANCORA SOFTWARE INC (PA)
402 W Broadway Ste 400, San Diego
(92101-3554)
PHONE.................888 476-4839
Noel Flynn, *CEO*
Jane Christie, *COO*
David Pintsov, *COO*
Nick Bova, *VP*
EMP: 27 EST: 2015
SALES (est): 2.25MM
SALES (corp-wide): 2.25MM **Privately
Held**
Web: www.ancorasoftware.com
SIC: 7372 Prepackaged software

(P-13878)
APOTHEKA SYSTEMS INC
14040 Panay Way, Marina Del Rey
(90292-6697)
P.O. Box 1251 (90213-1251)
PHONE.................844 777-4455
Dennis Maliani, *CEO*
EMP: 30 EST: 2018
SALES (est): 1.81MM **Privately Held**
Web: www.apotheka.co
SIC: 7372 Application computer software

(P-13879)
APPFOLIO INC (PA)
Also Called: Appfolio
70 Castilian Dr, Santa Barbara
(93117-3027)
PHONE.................805 364-6093
Jason Randall, *Pr*
Andreas Von Blottnitz, *
Jonathan Walker, *
Matt Mazza, *CLO**
Marcy Campbell, *CRO**
EMP: 340 EST: 2006
SALES (est): 471.88MM
SALES (corp-wide): 471.88MM **Publicly
Held**
Web: www.appfolio.com
SIC: 7372 Business oriented computer
   software

(P-13880)
APPFOLIO INC
Also Called: Mycase
2305 Historic Decatur Rd, San Diego
(92106-6050)
PHONE.................866 648-1536
Troy Alford, *Eng/Dir*
EMP: 102
SALES (corp-wide): 471.88MM **Publicly
Held**
Web: www.appfolio.com
SIC: 7372 Prepackaged software
PA: Appfolio, Inc.
   70 Castilian Dr
   805 364-6093

(P-13881)
**APPLIED BIOSYSTEMS LLC
(DH)**
Also Called: Applied Biosystems
5791 Van Allen Way, Carlsbad
(92008-7321)
▲ EMP: 120 EST: 1937
SQ FT: 51,000
SALES (est): 136.9MM
SALES (corp-wide): 42.86B **Publicly Held**
Web: www.thermofisher.com
SIC: 7372 3826 Prepackaged software; Gas
   chromatographic instruments
HQ: Life Technologies Corporation
   5781 Van Allen Way

Carlsbad CA 92008
760 603-7200

(P-13882)
APPLIED BUSINESS SOFTWARE INC
Also Called: A B S
7755 Center Ave, Huntington Beach
(92647-3007)
PHONE.....................562 426-2188
Jerry Delgado, *Pr*
Edimia Delgado, *Sec*
Gerardo Delgado, *VP*
Eddy Delgado, *VP*
Nelson Noahk, *Contrlr*
EMP: 60 **EST:** 1979
SALES (est): 3.88MM **Privately Held**
Web: www.themortgageoffice.com
SIC: 7372 5045 5734 Prepackaged software
; Computers, peripherals, and software;
Computer and software stores

(P-13883)
APPLIED STATISTICS & MGT INC
Also Called: Md-Staff
32848 Wolf Store Rd Ste A, Temecula
(92592-8277)
P.O. Box 2738 (92593)
PHONE.....................951 699-4600
Nick Phan, *Pr*
Nickolaus Phan, *
EMP: 95 **EST:** 1982
SQ FT: 4,000
SALES (est): 9.29MM **Privately Held**
Web: www.mdstaff.com
SIC: 7372 7371 Prepackaged software;
Computer software systems analysis and
design, custom

(P-13884)
ARTKIVE
16225 Huston St, Encino (91436-1323)
PHONE.....................310 975-9809
EMP: 41 **EST:** 2012
SALES (est): 1.32MM **Privately Held**
Web: www.artkiveapp.com
SIC: 7372 Prepackaged software

(P-13885)
ASCENDER SOFTWARE INC
8885 Rio San Diego Dr Ste 270, San Diego
(92108-1627)
PHONE.....................877 561-7501
Theodore Kye, *Prin*
EMP: 210 **EST:** 2006
SALES (est): 1.12MM
SALES (corp-wide): 94.72MM **Privately Held**
Web: www.matrixmedicalnetwork.com
SIC: 7372 Prepackaged software
PA: Community Care Health Network, Llc
9201 E Mtn View Rd Ste 22
877 564-3627

(P-13886)
ASTEA INTERNATIONAL INC
8 Hughes, Irvine (92618-2072)
PHONE.....................949 784-5000
Carl Smith, *Brnch Mgr*
EMP: 45
SALES (corp-wide): 485.81K **Privately Held**
Web: www.astea.com
SIC: 7372 Business oriented computer
software
HQ: Astea International Inc.
300 Park Blvd Ste 350
Itasca IL 60143
888 437-4968

(P-13887)
ATELIERE CREATIVE TECH INC
315 S Beverly Dr Ste 315, Beverly Hills
(90212-4309)
PHONE.....................800 921-4252
EMP: 25 **EST:** 2020
SALES (est): 2.63MM **Privately Held**
Web: www.ateliere.com
SIC: 7372 Application computer software

(P-13888)
ATLANTIS COMPUTING INC
900 Glenneyre St, Laguna Beach
(92651-2707)
PHONE.....................650 917-9471
Jason Donahue, *Pr*
EMP: 35 **EST:** 2006
SQ FT: 5,000
SALES (est): 8.86MM **Privately Held**
Web: www.hiveio.com
SIC: 7372 Business oriented computer
software

(P-13889)
BITMAX
6600 W Sunset Blvd, Los Angeles
(90028-7160)
PHONE.....................323 978-7878
EMP: 47 **EST:** 2019
SALES (est): 6.45MM **Privately Held**
Web: www.bitmax.net
SIC: 7372 Prepackaged software

(P-13890)
BLACKLINE INC (PA)
Also Called: Blackline
21300 Victory Blvd Fl 12, Woodland Hills
(91367-7734)
PHONE.....................818 223-9008
Owen Ryan, *Ch Bd*
Mark Partin, *CFO*
Karole Morgan-prager, *Legal*
Mark Woodhams, *CRO*
EMP: 1557 **EST:** 2001
SQ FT: 89,000
SALES (est): 590MM
SALES (corp-wide): 590MM **Publicly Held**
Web: www.blackline.com
SIC: 7372 Business oriented computer
software

(P-13891)
BLIND SQUIRREL GAMES INC
7545 Irvine Center Dr Ste 150, Irvine
(92618-2935)
PHONE.....................714 460-0860
Bradford Hendricks, *CEO*
EMP: 23 **EST:** 2010
SALES (est): 11.07MM **Privately Held**
Web:
www.blindsquirrelentertainment.com
SIC: 7372 Home entertainment computer
software

(P-13892)
BLITZ ROCKS INC
750 B St Ste 3300, San Diego
(92101-8188)
PHONE.....................310 883-5183
Mauricio Duran, *CEO*
EMP: 25 **EST:** 2016
SALES (est): 880.69K
SALES (corp-wide): 4.2MM **Privately Held**
Web: www.blitzrocks.com
SIC: 7372 Business oriented computer
software
PA: Sieena, Inc.
600 B St Ste 300
310 455-6188

(P-13893)
BLIZZARD ENTERTAINMENT INC (DH)
1 Blizzard, Irvine (92618-3628)
P.O. Box 18979 (92623-8979)
PHONE.....................949 955-1380
Mike Morhaime, *CEO*
Johanna Faries, *
Chris Metzen, *
Todd Pawlowski, *
Eric Roeder, *
▲ **EMP:** 85 **EST:** 2004
SALES (est): 155.37MM
SALES (corp-wide): 245.12B **Publicly Held**
Web: careers.blizzard.com
SIC: 7372 5734 7819 Prepackaged software
; Software, computer games; Reproduction
services, motion picture production
HQ: Activision Blizzard, Inc.
2701 Olympic Blvd Bldg B
Santa Monica CA 90404
310 255-2000

(P-13894)
BMC
300 Continental Blvd Ste 570, El Segundo
(90245-5072)
PHONE.....................310 321-5555
Sean Allen, *CEO*
EMP: 37 **EST:** 2009
SALES (est): 190.6K **Privately Held**
Web: www.bmc.com
SIC: 7372 Prepackaged software

(P-13895)
BPOMS/HRO INC (HQ)
8175 E Kaiser Blvd # 100, Anaheim
(92808-2214)
PHONE.....................714 974-2670
Patrick Dolan, *Ch Bd*
James Cortens, *COO*
Don Rutherford, *CFO*
EMP: 55 **EST:** 2008
SQ FT: 3,500
SALES (est): 3.33MM
SALES (corp-wide): 16.91MM **Privately Held**
SIC: 7372 7371 Prepackaged software;
Custom computer programming services
PA: Bpo Management Services, Inc.
8175 E Kaiser Blvd 100
714 972-2670

(P-13896)
BQE SOFTWARE INC
3825 Del Amo Blvd, Torrance (90503-2118)
PHONE.....................310 602-4020
Shafat Qazi, *CEO*
Austin Miller, *CMO**
EMP: 95 **EST:** 1995
SQ FT: 20,000
SALES (est): 12.55MM **Privately Held**
Web: www.bqe.com
SIC: 7372 5734 Application computer
software; Software, business and non-game

(P-13897)
CALAMP CORP (PA)
Also Called: Calamp
15635 Alton Pkwy Ste 250, Irvine
(92618-7328)
PHONE.....................949 600-5600
Christopher R Adams, *Pr*
Henry J Maier, *Ch Bd*
Jikun Kim, *Sr VP*
Jeffrey Clark, *CPO*
◆ **EMP:** 101 **EST:** 1981
SQ FT: 23,000
SALES (est): 294.95MM

SALES (corp-wide): 294.95MM **Privately Held**
Web: www.calamp.com
SIC: 7372 Application computer software

(P-13898)
CATAPULT COMMUNICATIONS CORP (DH)
26601 Agoura Rd, Calabasas (91302-1959)
PHONE.....................818 871-1800
Richard A Karp, *Ch Bd*
David Mayfield, *Pr*
Chris Stephenson, *VP*
Barbara J Fairhurst, *VP Opers*
Terry Eastham, *SUPPORT*
▲ **EMP:** 37 **EST:** 1985
SQ FT: 39,000
SALES (est): 5.94MM
SALES (corp-wide): 5.46B **Publicly Held**
SIC: 7372 3661 Application computer
software; Telephone and telegraph
apparatus
HQ: Ixia
26601 Agoura Rd
Calabasas CA 91302
818 871-1800

(P-13899)
CHATMETER INC
225 Broadway Ste 2200, San Diego
(92101-5011)
PHONE.....................619 300-1050
Collin Holmes, *CEO*
John Fitzgerald, *
EMP: 80 **EST:** 2009
SALES (est): 11MM **Privately Held**
Web: www.chatmeter.com
SIC: 7372 Prepackaged software

(P-13900)
CHOWNOW INC (PA)
3585 Hayden Ave, Culver City
(90232-2412)
PHONE.....................888 707-2469
Kanika Soni, *CEO*
Eric Jaffe, *
Stuart Hathaway, *
Andre Mancl, *
EMP: 70 **EST:** 2010
SQ FT: 25,000
SALES (est): 24.96MM
SALES (corp-wide): 24.96MM **Privately Held**
Web: www.chownow.com
SIC: 7372 Business oriented computer
software

(P-13901)
CLASSY INC
Also Called: Classy
350 10th Ave Ste 1300, San Diego
(92101-8703)
PHONE.....................619 961-1892
Chris Himes, *CEO*
EMP: 142 **EST:** 2006
SALES (est): 10.38MM
SALES (corp-wide): 23MM **Privately Held**
Web: www.classy.org
SIC: 7372 Prepackaged software
PA: Gofundme Inc.
1010 Doyle St Ste 250
650 260-3436

(P-13902)
CLEARLAKE CAPITAL PARTNERS
233 Wilshire Blvd Ste 800, Santa Monica
(90401-1207)
PHONE.....................310 400-8800
John A Mckenna Junior, *Pr*

EMP: 1832 **EST:** 2012
SALES (est): 3.88MM **Privately Held**
SIC: 7372 Prepackaged software

(P-13903)

CLOUDCOVER IOT INC (PA)

Also Called: Cloudcover
14 Goodyear Ste 125b, Irvine (92618-3759)
PHONE.....................888 511-2022
Jeffrey Huggins, *CEO*
EMP: 35 **EST:** 2015
SALES (est): 14.71MM
SALES (corp-wide): 14.71MM **Privately Held**
Web: www.cloudcover.it
SIC: 7372 7379 7373 Prepackaged software
; Computer related maintenance services;
Systems engineering, computer related

(P-13904)

CLOUDVIRGA INC

5291 California Ave Ste 300, Irvine
(92617-3221)
PHONE.....................949 799-2643
Daniel Akiva, *CEO*
Maria Moskver, *Legal**
EMP: 59 **EST:** 2015
SALES (est): 19.59MM
SALES (corp-wide): 2.26B **Publicly Held**
Web: www.cloudvirga.com
SIC: 7372 Prepackaged software
PA: Stewart Information Services
Corporation
1360 Post Oak Blvd Ste 10
713 625-8100

(P-13905)

CLUB SPEED LLC (PA)

300 Spectrum Center Dr, Irvine
(92618-4925)
PHONE.....................951 817-7073
Romir Bosu, *CEO*
Caleb Everett, *Pr*
Eric Novakovich, *Chief Strategy Officer*
EMP: 38 **EST:** 2007
SALES (est): 5.54MM
SALES (corp-wide): 5.54MM **Privately Held**
Web: www.clubspeed.com
SIC: 7372 Prepackaged software

(P-13906)

COMPUGROUP MEDICAL INC

25b Technology Dr Ste 200, Irvine
(92618-2302)
PHONE.....................949 789-0500
John Tangredi, *COO*
EMP: 35
SALES (corp-wide): 1.29B **Privately Held**
Web: www.cgm.com
SIC: 7372 Prepackaged software
HQ: Compugroup Medical, Inc.
10901 Stonelake Blvd
Austin TX 78759
855 270-6700

(P-13907)

COMPULINK BUSINESS SYSTEMS INC (PA)

Also Called: Compulink Healthcare Solutions
1100 Business Center Cir, Newbury Park
(91320-1124)
PHONE.....................805 446-2050
Link Wilson, *Pr*
EMP: 117 **EST:** 1985
SQ FT: 15,000
SALES (est): 8.1MM
SALES (corp-wide): 8.1MM **Privately Held**
Web: www.compulinkadvantage.com

SIC: 7372 Business oriented computer
software

(P-13908)

CONSENSUS CLOUD SOLUTIONS INC (PA)

700 S Flower St Fl 15, Los Angeles
(90017-4101)
PHONE.....................323 860-9200
Scott Turicchi, *CEO*
John Nebergall, *COO*
Steve Emberland, *Contrlr*
James Malone, *CFO*
EMP: 92 **EST:** 2021
SALES (est): 362.56MM
SALES (corp-wide): 362.56MM **Publicly
Held**
Web: www.consensus.com
SIC: 7372 Prepackaged software

(P-13909)

CONVERSIONPOINT HOLDINGS INC

840 Newport Center Dr Ste 450, Newport
Beach (92660-6384)
PHONE.....................888 706-6764
Robert Tallack, *Pr*
Don Walker Barrett Iii, *COO*
Raghu Kilambi, *CFO*
EMP: 85 **EST:** 2018
SALES (est): 812.26K **Privately Held**
SIC: 7372 Prepackaged software .

(P-13910)

CORNERSTONE ONDEMAND INC (HQ)

Also Called: Cornerstone
1601 Cloverfield Blvd Ste 620s, Santa
Monica (90404-4178)
PHONE.....................310 752-0200
Himanshu Palsule, *CEO*
Scott Mcdermott, *Chief Accounting Officer*
Toya Del Valle, *Chief Customer Officer*
EMP: 247 **EST:** 1999
SQ FT: 94,000
SALES (est): 740.92MM
SALES (corp-wide): 740.92MM **Privately
Held**
Web: www.cornerstoneondemand.com
SIC: 7372 Business oriented computer
software
PA: Sunshine Software Holdings, Inc.
1601 Cloverf Blvd Ste 62

(P-13911)

D3PUBLISHER OF AMERICA INC

Also Called: D3 Go
15910 Ventura Blvd Ste 800, Encino
(91436-2810)
PHONE.....................310 268-0820
Yoji Takenaka, *Pr*
Yuji Itoh, *Non-Executive Chairman of the
Board*
Hidetaka Tachibana, *CFO*
EMP: 63 **EST:** 2004
SQ FT: 6,129
SALES (est): 4.98MM **Privately Held**
Web: www.d3go.com
SIC: 7372 Home entertainment computer
software
HQ: D3 Publisher Inc.
3-5-2, Kandakajicho
Chiyoda-Ku TKY 101-0

(P-13912)

DASSAULT SYSTEMES BIOVIA CORP (DH)

Also Called: Biovia
5005 Wateridge Vista Dr, San Diego
(92121-5780)

PHONE.....................858 799-5000
Max Carnecchia, *CEO*
Michael Piraino, *Ex VP*
Jason Gray, *Corporate Secretary*
Mathew Hahn, *Sr VP*
Judith Ohrn Hicks, *Senior Vice President
Human Resources*
EMP: 43 **EST:** 1993
SQ FT: 68,436
SALES (est): 93.77MM
SALES (corp-wide): 2.08B **Privately Held**
Web: www.3ds.com
SIC: 7372 Application computer software
HQ: 3ds Acquisition Corp.
175 Wyman St
Waltham MA 02451
781 810-5011

(P-13913)

DAVE INC (PA)

1265 S Cochran Ave, Los Angeles
(90019-2846)
PHONE.....................844 857-3283
Jason Wilk, *Pr*
Kyle Beilman, *CFO*
Kevin Frisch, *CMO*
EMP: 279 **EST:** 2015
SQ FT: 36,000
SALES (est): 259.09MM
SALES (corp-wide): 259.09MM **Publicly
Held**
Web: www.dave.com
SIC: 7372 7389 Prepackaged software;
Financial services

(P-13914)

DECISIONLOGIC LLC

13500 Evening Creek Dr N Ste 600, San
Diego (92128-8125)
PHONE.....................858 586-0202
David Evans, *Pr*
EMP: 23 **EST:** 2011
SALES (est): 2.34MM **Privately Held**
Web: www.decisionlogic.com
SIC: 7372 Business oriented computer
software

(P-13915)

DIGITAL ARBITRAGE DIST INC (PA)

Also Called: Cloudbeds
3033 5th Ave Ste 100, San Diego
(92103-5828)
PHONE.....................888 392-9478
Adam Harris, *CEO*
EMP: 30 **EST:** 2017
SALES (est): 7.7MM
SALES (corp-wide): 7.7MM **Privately Held**
Web: www.cloudbeds.com
SIC: 7372 Prepackaged software

(P-13916)

DINCLOUD INC

27520 Hawthorne Blvd Ste 185, Rllng Hls
Est (90274-3543)
PHONE.....................310 929-1101
Mark Briggs, *CEO*
Ali M Dincmo, ***
Mike L Chase, ***
EMP: 53 **EST:** 2011
SQ FT: 1,500
SALES (est): 6.33MM
SALES (corp-wide): 15.51MM **Privately
Held**
Web: www.dincloud.com
SIC: 7372 Business oriented computer
software
PA: Premier Bpo, Inc.
128 N 2nd St Ste 210
931 551-8888

(P-13917)

DORADO NETWORK SYSTEMS CORP

Also Called: Corelogic Dorado
40 Pacifica, Irvine (92618-7471)
PHONE.....................650 227-7300
Dain Ehring, *CEO*
Karen Camp, ***
EMP: 140 **EST:** 1998
SALES (est): 5.2MM
SALES (corp-wide): 1.64B **Privately Held**
Web: www.corelogic.com
SIC: 7372 Application computer software
HQ: Corelogic, Inc.
40 Pacifica Ste 900
Irvine CA 92618
866 873-3651

(P-13918)

DREAMSTART LABS INC

2907 Shelter Island Dr Ste 105, San Diego
(92106-2797)
PHONE.....................408 914-1234
Wes Wasson, *CEO*
EMP: 30 **EST:** 2016
SALES (est): 400K **Privately Held**
Web: www.dreamstartlabs.com
SIC: 7372 Application computer software

(P-13919)

EAGLE TOPCO LP

18200 Von Karman Ave, Irvine
(92612-1023)
PHONE.....................949 585-4329
EMP: 4000
SIC: 7372 Business oriented computer
software

(P-13920)

EDGATE HOLDINGS INC

4655 Cass St, San Diego (92109-2809)
PHONE.....................858 712-9341
Peter Sibley, *CEO*
EMP: 32 **EST:** 2021
SALES (est): 1.45MM **Privately Held**
Web: www.edgate.com
SIC: 7372 Educational computer software

(P-13921)

EDGEWAVE INC

4225 Executive Sq Ste 1600, La Jolla
(92037-1487)
PHONE.....................800 782-3762
EMP: 100
Web: www.gosecure.ai
SIC: 7372 Operating systems computer
software

(P-13922)

EGL HOLDCO INC

18200 Von Karman Ave Ste 1000, Irvine
(92612-1061)
PHONE.....................800 678-7423
EMP: 4000
SIC: 7372 Prepackaged software

(P-13923)

EKNOWLEDGE GROUP INC

160 W Foothill Pkwy Ste 105, Corona
(92882-8545)
PHONE.....................951 256-4076
Scott Hildebrandt, *Pr*
EMP: 35 **EST:** 1999
SALES (est): 350.42K **Privately Held**
SIC: 7372 Educational computer software

(P-13924)

ELECTRONIC CLEARING HOUSE INC (HQ)

730 Paseo Camarillo, Camarillo
(93010-6064)
PHONE.....................805 419-8700
Charles J Harris, *Pr*
Alice L Cheung, *
Rick Slater, *
William Wied, *CIO*
Karl Asplund, *
EMP: 100 **EST:** 1981
SQ FT: 32,669
SALES (est): 2.42MM
SALES (corp-wide): 16.29B **Publicly Held**
Web: www.echo-inc.com
SIC: 7372 Business oriented computer
software
PA: Intuit Inc.
2700 Coast Ave
650 944-6000

(P-13925)

EPIRUS INC

19145 Gramercy Pl, Torrance (90501-1128)
P.O. Box 3927 (90277)
PHONE.....................310 620-8678
Andy Lowery, *CEO*
Harry Marr, *
Joseph Lonsdale, *
John Tenet, *
Daniel Thompson, *
EMP: 26 **EST:** 2018
SALES (est): 1MM **Privately Held**
Web: www.epirusinc.com
SIC: 7372 7373 0781 1771 Prepackaged
software; Computer integrated systems
design; Landscape counseling and planning
; Stucco, gunite, and grouting contractors

(P-13926)

EQUIMINE

Also Called: Propstream
26457 Rancho Pkwy S, Lake Forest
(92630-8326)
PHONE.....................877 204-9040
Brian Tepfer, *CEO*
EMP: 41 **EST:** 2006
SALES (est): 13.61MM
SALES (corp-wide): 2.26B **Publicly Held**
Web: www.propstream.com
SIC: 7372 3429 Business oriented computer
software; Keys, locks, and related hardware
PA: Stewart Information Services
Corporation
1360 Post Oak Blvd Ste 10
713 625-8100

(P-13927)

ESTIFY INC

5023 Parkway Calabasas, Calabasas
(91302-1421)
PHONE.....................801 341-1911
EMP: 41 **EST:** 2017
SALES (est): 2.02MM **Privately Held**
Web: new.estify.com
SIC: 7372 Prepackaged software

(P-13928)

ETURNS INC

19700 Fairchild Ste 290, Irvine
(92612-2521)
PHONE.....................949 265-2626
Richard Rockwell, *CEO*
EMP: 32 **EST:** 2010
SALES (est): 2.02MM **Privately Held**
Web: www.eturns.com
SIC: 7372 7371 Application computer
software; Computer software development
and applications

(P-13929)

EVENTSCOM INC

Also Called: Bump.me
811 Prospect St, La Jolla (92037-4207)
P.O. Box 1209 (92038)
PHONE.....................858 257-2300
Mitchell Thrower, *CEO*
Paul Brown, *CFO*
Stephen Partridge, *Sec*
EMP: 45 **EST:** 2009
SALES (est): 5.01MM **Privately Held**
Web: www.events.com
SIC: 7372 Publisher's computer software

(P-13930)

EVERBRIDGE INC (PA)

155 N Lake Ave Ste 900, Pasadena
(91101-1849)
PHONE.....................818 230-9700
David Wagner, *Pr*
Noah Webster, *Dir*
David Rockvam, *Dir*
Dominic Jones Senior, *Development*
John Di Leo, *COO*
EMP: 111 **EST:** 2002
SQ FT: 45,000
SALES (est): 448.79MM
SALES (corp-wide): 448.79MM **Privately Held**
Web: www.everbridge.com
SIC: 7372 4899 Prepackaged software; Data
communication services

(P-13931)

EVOCATIVE INC

26 Centerpointe Dr, La Palma
(90623-1072)
PHONE.....................888 365-2656
Patrick Rigney, *CEO*
Erin Mac Arthur, *
EMP: 75 **EST:** 1996
SALES (est): 15.96MM
SALES (corp-wide): 67.28MM **Privately Held**
Web: www.evocative.com
SIC: 7372 Application computer software
PA: Evodc, Llc
26 Centerpointe Dr
888 365-2656

(P-13932)

FACEFIRST LLC ✪

31416 Agoura Rd Ste 250, Westlake Village
(91361-5654)
PHONE.....................805 482-8428
EMP: 30 **EST:** 2023
SALES (est): 3.56MM **Privately Held**
SIC: 7372 Prepackaged software

(P-13933)

FOUNDATION 9 ENTERTAINMENT INC (PA)

30211 Avenida De Las Bandera Ste 200,
Rancho Santa Margari. (92688-2159)
PHONE.....................949 698-1500
James N Hearn, *CEO*
John Goldman, *
David Mann, *
EMP: 200 **EST:** 2005
SALES (est): 14.55MM **Privately Held**
SIC: 7372 Home entertainment computer
software

(P-13934)

FOUNDATION INC

Also Called: Foundation Ai
19800 Macarthur Blvd Ste 300, Irvine
(92612-2479)
P.O. Box 344 (92655-0344)
PHONE.....................310 294-8955

Vivek Rao, *CEO*
Victor Gebhardt, *
Vamsi Kasivajjala, *
EMP: 38 **EST:** 2017
SALES (est): 6.96MM **Privately Held**
Web: www.foundationai.com
SIC: 7372 7371 Prepackaged software;
Custom computer programming services

(P-13935)

FREIGHTGATE INC

Also Called: Edi Ideas
10055 Slater Ave Ste 231, Fountain Valley
(92708-4722)
PHONE.....................714 799-2833
Martin Hubert, *Pr*
EMP: 32 **EST:** 2000
SALES (est): 4.64MM
SALES (corp-wide): 4.64MM **Privately Held**
Web: www.freightgate.com
SIC: 7372 7371 Application computer
software; Computer software development
and applications
PA: Edi Ideas Inc
16051 Springdale St # 111
714 841-2833

(P-13936)

GAIKAI INC

65 Enterprise, Aliso Viejo (92656-2705)
EMP: 51
Web: www.gaikai.com
SIC: 7372 Home entertainment computer
software

(P-13937)

GAMEMINE LLC

439 Carroll Canal, Venice (90291-4683)
PHONE.....................310 310-3105
Flaviu Rus, *Managing Member*
Daneil Starr, *
EMP: 35 **EST:** 2017
SALES (est): 3.5MM **Privately Held**
Web: www.gamemine.com
SIC: 7372 7389 Publisher's computer
software; Business services, nec

(P-13938)

GENASYS INC (PA)

Also Called: GENASYS
16262 W Bernardo Dr, San Diego
(92127-1879)
PHONE.....................858 676-1112
Richard S Danforth, *CEO*
Richard H Osgood Iii, *Ch Bd*
Dennis D Klahn, *CFO*
◆ **EMP:** 90 **EST:** 1980
SQ FT: 55,766
SALES (est): 24.01MM
SALES (corp-wide): 24.01MM **Publicly Held**
Web: www.genasys.com
SIC: 7372 3651 Prepackaged software;
Amplifiers: radio, public address, or musical
instrument

(P-13939)

GLOBAL CASH CARD INC

3972 Barranca Pkwy Ste J610, Irvine
(92606-1204)
PHONE.....................949 751-0360
EMP: 165
SIC: 7372 Business oriented computer
software

(P-13940)

GOVERNMENTJOBSCOM INC (PA)

Also Called: Neogov

2120 Park Pl Ste 100, El Segundo
(90245-4741)
PHONE.....................877 204-4442
Shane Evangelist, *CEO*
Alex Chun, *CFO*
David Eisler, *Sec*
EMP: 55 **EST:** 2000
SQ FT: 5,000
SALES (est): 23.8MM
SALES (corp-wide): 23.8MM **Privately Held**
Web: www.neogov.com
SIC: 7372 Prepackaged software

(P-13941)

GREEN HILLS SOFTWARE LLC (HQ)

Also Called: Green Hills Software
30 W Sola St, Santa Barbara (93101-2599)
PHONE.....................805 965-6044
Daniel O Dowd, *CEO*
Daniel O'dowd, *CEO*
Jeffrey Hazarian, *
EMP: 105 **EST:** 1986
SALES (est): 41MM
SALES (corp-wide): 51.22MM **Privately Held**
Web: www.ghs.com
SIC: 7372 Prepackaged software
PA: Ghs Holding Company
30 W Sola St
805 965-6044

(P-13942)

GREMLIN INC

Also Called: Gremlin Software, Inc.
440 N Barranca Ave Ste 3101, Walnut
(91789)
PHONE.....................408 214-9885
Josh Leslie, *CEO*
Kolton Andrus, *
EMP: 80 **EST:** 2016
SALES (est): 9.57MM **Privately Held**
Web: www.gremlin.com
SIC: 7372 8742 Prepackaged software;
Management consulting services

(P-13943)

GUIDANCE SOFTWARE INC (HQ)

1055 E Colorado Blvd Ste 400, Pasadena
(91106-2375)
PHONE.....................626 229-9191
Patrick Dennis, *Pr*
Barry Plaga, *
Michael Harris, *CMO*
Alfredo Gomez, *Corporate Secretary*
EMP: 215 **EST:** 2006
SQ FT: 90,000
SALES (est): 51.33MM
SALES (corp-wide): 5.77B **Privately Held**
Web: www.opentext.com
SIC: 7372 3572 Business oriented computer
software; Computer storage devices
PA: Open Text Corporation
275 Frank Tompa Dr
519 888-7111

(P-13944)

GUMGUM SPORTS INC

1314 7th St Fl 4, Santa Monica
(90401-1608)
PHONE.....................310 400-0396
Brian Kim, *CEO*
EMP: 45 **EST:** 2021
SALES (est): 1.11MM **Privately Held**
Web: www.gumgum.com
SIC: 7372 Business oriented computer
software

(P-13945)

IAMPLUS ELECTRONICS INC (PA)

809 N Cahuenga Blvd, Los Angeles (90038-3703)
PHONE................323 210-3852
Will Adams, *CEO*
Phil Molyneux, *
Chandrasekar Rathakrishnan, *
Rosemary Peschken, *
EMP: 38 **EST:** 2013
SQ FT: 6,000
SALES (est): 9.1MM
SALES (corp-wide): 9.1MM **Privately Held**
Web: www.iamplus.com
SIC: 7372 Prepackaged software

(P-13946)

ILLUMNATE EDUCATN HOLDINGS INC (PA)

6531 Irvine Center Dr Ste 100, Irvine (92618-2145)
PHONE................949 656-3133
Christine Willig, *CEO*
Shawn Mahoney, *Chief Product Officer*
Jane Snyder, *CMO*
Dick Davidson, *
EMP: 28 **EST:** 2009
SALES (est): 9.91MM
SALES (corp-wide): 9.91MM **Privately Held**
Web: www.illuminateed.com
SIC: 7372 Educational computer software

(P-13947)

INFOR (US) LLC

Also Called: MAI Systems
26250 Enterprise Way Ste 220, Lake Forest (92630-8400)
PHONE................678 319-8000
Barbara Nolan, *Pr*
EMP: 23
SALES (corp-wide): 64.37B **Privately Held**
Web: www.infor.com
SIC: 7372 Business oriented computer software
HQ: Infor (Us), Llc
641 Ave Of The Americas
New York NY 10011
866 244-5479

(P-13948)

INSTRUMENTL INC

440 N Barranca Ave, Covina (91723-1722)
PHONE................909 258-9291
Gauri Manglik, *CEO*
EMP: 48 **EST:** 2015
SALES (est): 2.5MM **Privately Held**
Web: www.instrumentl.com
SIC: 7372 Prepackaged software

(P-13949)

INTUIT INC

21650 Oxnard St Ste 2200, Woodland Hills (91367-7824)
PHONE................818 436-7800
Michael Ermi, *Brnch Mgr*
EMP: 39
SALES (corp-wide): 16.29B **Publicly Held**
Web: www.intuit.com
SIC: 7372 Business oriented computer software
PA: Intuit Inc.
2700 Coast Ave
650 944-6000

(P-13950)

INTUIT INC

7535 Torrey Santa Fe Rd, San Diego (92129-5704)

PHONE................858 780-2846
Brian Bequette, *Prin*
EMP: 311
SALES (corp-wide): 16.29B **Publicly Held**
Web: www.intuit.com
SIC: 7372 Business oriented computer software
PA: Intuit Inc.
2700 Coast Ave
650 944-6000

(P-13951)

INTUIT INC

Also Called: Turbotax
7545 Torrey Santa Fe Rd, San Diego (92129-5704)
PHONE................858 215-8000
Jason Jackson, *Brnch Mgr*
EMP: 300
SALES (corp-wide): 16.29B **Publicly Held**
Web: www.intuit.com
SIC: 7372 Business oriented computer software
PA: Intuit Inc.
2700 Coast Ave
650 944-6000

(P-13952)

IPR SOFTWARE INC

Also Called: Ipr Software
16501 Ventura Blvd Ste 424, Encino (91436-2077)
PHONE................310 499-0544
J D Bowles, *Pr*
James Madden Senior, *Treas*
EMP: 24 **EST:** 2000
SQ FT: 10,000
SALES (est): 1.69MM **Privately Held**
Web: www.iprsoftware.com
SIC: 7372 Application computer software

(P-13953)

IQMS LLC (HQ)

2231 Wisteria Ln, Paso Robles (93446-9820)
PHONE................805 227-1122
Gary Nemmers, *Pr*
Matt Ouska, *
Steve Bieszczat, *CMO*
Dan Vertachnik, *CRO*
Dan Radunz, *
EMP: 130 **EST:** 1989
SQ FT: 60,000
SALES (est): 15.94MM
SALES (corp-wide): 2.08B **Privately Held**
Web: www.iqms-erp-software.com
SIC: 7372 Prepackaged software
PA: Dassault Systemes
10 Rue Marcel Dassault
161626162

(P-13954)

ISOLUTECOM INC (PA)

9 Northam Ave, Newbury Park (91320-3323)
PHONE................805 498-6259
Byron Nutley, *Interim Chief Executive Officer*
Don Hyun, *
Thomas Mangle, *
Michael Brown, *
EMP: 50 **EST:** 1999
SALES (est): 1.75MM
SALES (corp-wide): 1.75MM **Privately Held**
SIC: 7372 Business oriented computer software

(P-13955)

ITC SFTWARE SLUTIONS GROUP LLC (PA)

Also Called: Itc Solutions & Services Group
201 Sandpointe Ave Ste 305, Santa Ana (92707-5766)
PHONE................877 248-2774
Del Husain, *CEO*
Ray Jandga, *Pr*
Guru Gurumoorthy, *VP*
EMP: 326 **EST:** 2008
SQ FT: 3,000
SALES (est): 22.21MM
SALES (corp-wide): 22.21MM **Privately Held**
Web: www.itcssg.com
SIC: 7372 7371 7373 Prepackaged software ; Computer software systems analysis and design, custom; Systems software development services

(P-13956)

JAM CITY INC

2255 N Ontario St, Burbank (91504-3187)
PHONE................804 920-8760
Tiffany Van Decker, *Prin*
EMP: 69
SALES (corp-wide): 59.07MM **Privately Held**
Web: www.jamcity.com
SIC: 7372 Prepackaged software
PA: Jam City, Inc.
3562 Eastham Dr
310 205-4800

(P-13957)

JURNY INC

6600 W Sunset Blvd, Los Angeles (90028-7160)
PHONE................888 875-8769
Luca Zambello, *CEO*
EMP: 24 **EST:** 2018
SALES (est): 5.02MM **Privately Held**
Web: www.jurny.com
SIC: 7372 Prepackaged software

(P-13958)

JUSTENOUGH SOFTWARE CORP INC (HQ)

15440 Laguna Canyon Rd Ste 100, Irvine (92618-2139)
PHONE................949 706-5400
Malcolm Buxton, *Pr*
Robert Rackleff, *CFO*
EMP: 30 **EST:** 2001
SALES (est): 3.31MM
SALES (corp-wide): 48.98MM **Privately Held**
Web: www.justenoughsoftware.com
SIC: 7372 Prepackaged software
PA: MI9 Retail Inc.
1 Financial Plz Ste 601
888 326-8579

(P-13959)

KINGCOM(US) LLC (DH)

3100 Ocean Park Blvd, Santa Monica (90405-3032)
PHONE................424 744-5697
EMP: 44 **EST:** 2016
SALES (est): 8.41MM
SALES (corp-wide): 245.12B **Publicly Held**
SIC: 7372 Home entertainment computer software
HQ: Activision Blizzard, Inc.
2701 Olympic Blvd Bldg B
Santa Monica CA 90404
310 255-2000

(P-13960)

KINTERA INC (HQ)

Also Called: Blackbaud Internet Solutions
9605 Scranton Rd Ste 200, San Diego (92121-1768)
PHONE................858 795-3000
Marc E Chardon, *CEO*
Richard Labarbera, *
Alfred R Berkeley Iii, *Ch Bd*
Richard Davidson, *CFO*
EMP: 217 **EST:** 2000
SQ FT: 38,000
SALES (est): 14.11MM
SALES (corp-wide): 1.11B **Publicly Held**
SIC: 7372 Business oriented computer software
PA: Blackbaud, Inc.
65 Fairchild St
843 216-6200

(P-13961)

KIVE COMPANY

Also Called: Artkive
15800 Arminta St, Van Nuys (91406-1918)
PHONE................747 212-0337
Jedd Gold, *CEO*
EMP: 40 **EST:** 2018
SALES (est): 5.09MM **Privately Held**
Web: www.artkiveapp.com
SIC: 7372 Prepackaged software

(P-13962)

KLENTYSOFT INC

440 N Barranca Ave # 2331, Covina (91723-1722)
PHONE................707 518-9640
Vengat Krishnaraj, *CEO*
Praveen Kumar, *
Bhuvanesh Ram, *
EMP: 109 **EST:** 2015
SALES (est): 1.55MM **Privately Held**
SIC: 7372 Business oriented computer software

(P-13963)

KOFAX LIMITED (PA)

15211 Laguna Canyon Rd, Irvine (92618-3146)
PHONE................949 783-1000
Reynolds C Bish, *CEO*
Cort Townsend, *CFO*
EMP: 1309 **EST:** 1985
SQ FT: 91,000
SALES (est): 75.49MM
SALES (corp-wide): 75.49MM **Privately Held**
Web: www.tungstenautomation.com
SIC: 7372 Business oriented computer software

(P-13964)

KONAMI DIGITAL ENTRMT INC (DH)

Also Called: Konami
1 Konami Way, Hawthorne (90250-1144)
PHONE................310 220-8100
Tomohiro Uesugi, *CEO*
Kazumi Kitaue, *
Takahiro Azuma, *
Chris Bartee, *
▲ **EMP:** 23 **EST:** 1996
SALES (est): 22.81MM **Privately Held**
SIC: 7372 Home entertainment computer software
HQ: Konami Digital Entertainment Co., Ltd.
1-11-1, Ginza
Chuo-Ku TKY 104-0

PRODUCTS & SVCS

(P-13965)
KYRIBA CORP (PA)
4435 Eastgate Mall Ste 200, San Diego
(92121-1980)
PHONE...................858 210-3560
Melissa Di Donato, *Ch*
Edi Poloniato, *
Catherine Moore, *
Remy Dubois, *
Fabrice Lvy, *
EMP: 50 **EST:** 2000
SALES (est): 64.65MM
SALES (corp-wide): 64.65MM **Privately Held**
Web: www.kyriba.com
SIC: 7372 Prepackaged software

(P-13966)
LEADCRUNCH INC (PA)
Also Called: Leadcrunch
750 B St Ste 1630, San Diego
(92101-8131)
P.O. Box 712979 (92171-2979)
PHONE...................888 708-6649
Olin Hyde, *CEO*
David Toth, *Ch Bd*
Sanjit Singh, *COO*
EMP: 27 **EST:** 2018
SALES (est): 7.5MM
SALES (corp-wide): 7.5MM **Privately Held**
Web: www.getrev.ai
SIC: 7372 Business oriented computer software

(P-13967)
LEADS360 LLC
207 Hindry Ave, Inglewood (90301-1519)
PHONE...................888 843-1777
Nick Hedges, *CEO*
Charles Chase, *
Jeff Solomon, *
Christopher Adams, *
Alan Lang, *
EMP: 30 **EST:** 2005
SALES (est): 1.5MM **Privately Held**
SIC: 7372 7371 Prepackaged software; Computer software development

(P-13968)
LIVEOFFICE LLC
Also Called: Advisorsquare
900 Corporate Pointe, Culver City
(90230-7609)
PHONE...................877 253-2793
Matt Smith, *
Nikhil Menta, *
Jeffrey W Hausman, *
Matt Hardy, *
EMP: 29 **EST:** 2007
SQ FT: 15,000
SALES (est): 22.45MM
SALES (corp-wide): 3.81B **Publicly Held**
Web: www.liveoffice.com
SIC: 7372 Prepackaged software
PA: Gen Digital Inc.
60 E Rio Slado Pkwy Ste 1
650 527-8000

(P-13969)
LUMENOVA AI INC
1419 Beaudry Blvd, 1419 Beaudry Blvd,
Glendale (91208)
PHONE...................310 694-2461
Cosmin Andriescu, *Pr*
EMP: 25 **EST:** 2022
SALES (est): 1.03MM **Privately Held**
SIC: 7372 Prepackaged software

(P-13970)
M NEXON INC
Also Called: Nexon America
222 N Pacific Coast Hwy Ste 300, El
Segundo (90245-5614)
PHONE...................213 858-5930
John Robinson, *CEO*
EMP: 30 **EST:** 2011
SALES (est): 5.8MM **Privately Held**
Web: www.nexon.com
SIC: 7372 5092 Application computer software; Video games
PA: Nexon Co., Ltd.
1-4-5, Roppongi

(P-13971)
MAGIC TOUCH SOFTWARE INTL
950 Boardwalk Ste 200, San Marcos
(92078-2600)
P.O. Box 142 (92079-0142)
PHONE...................800 714-6490
Gary Bagheri, *CEO*
Gary Bagheri, *Pr*
George Peiov, *
EMP: 25 **EST:** 2007
SQ FT: 1,500
SALES (est): 1.22MM **Privately Held**
Web: www.magictouchsoftware.com
SIC: 7372 Business oriented computer software

(P-13972)
MEDATA LLC (HQ)
5 Peters Canyon Rd Ste 250, Irvine
(92606-1793)
PHONE...................714 918-1310
Cy King, *CEO*
Tom Herndon, *
T Don Theis, *CSO*
Elizabeth King, *
Tori Henson, *
EMP: 51 **EST:** 1975
SQ FT: 17,192
SALES (est): 39.08MM **Privately Held**
Web: www.medata.com
SIC: 7372 6411 Business oriented computer software; Medical insurance claim processing, contract or fee basis
PA: Medrisk, Llc
2701 Renaissance Blvd

(P-13973)
MICROSOFT CORPORATION
Also Called: Microsoft
3 Park Plz Ste 1800, Irvine (92614-8541)
PHONE...................949 263-3000
Sandy Thomas, *Genl Mgr*
EMP: 25
SALES (corp-wide): 245.12B **Publicly Held**
Web: www.microsoft.com
SIC: 7372 Application computer software
PA: Microsoft Corporation
1 Microsoft Way
425 882-8080

(P-13974)
MINDSHOW INC
811 W 7th St Ste 500, Los Angeles
(90017-3416)
PHONE...................213 531-0277
EMP: 46 **EST:** 2014
SALES (est): 4.49MM **Privately Held**
Web: www.mindshow.com
SIC: 7372 Prepackaged software

(P-13975)
MITEK SYSTEMS INC (PA)
Also Called: Mitek
770 1st Ave Ste 425, San Diego
(92101-6169)
PHONE...................619 269-6800
Edward West, *CEO*
Scott Carter, *Ch Bd*
David Lyle, *CAO*
Jason L Gray, *CLO*
Michael E Diamond, *Sr VP*
EMP: 98 **EST:** 1986
SQ FT: 29,000
SALES (est): 172.08MM
SALES (corp-wide): 172.08MM **Publicly Held**
Web: www.miteksystems.com
SIC: 7372 3577 Prepackaged software; Computer peripheral equipment, nec

(P-13976)
MITRATECH HOLDINGS INC
5900 Wilshire Blvd Ste 1500, Los Angeles
(90036-5031)
PHONE...................323 964-0000
Jason Parkman, *CEO*
EMP: 125
SALES (corp-wide): 103.85MM **Privately Held**
Web: www.mitratech.com
SIC: 7372 Business oriented computer software
PA: Mitratech Holdings, Inc.
13301 Gllria Cir Ste 200
512 382-7322

(P-13977)
MIXMODE INC
111 W Micheltorena St Ste 300-A, Santa
Barbara (93101-3095)
P.O. Box 92041 (93190-2041)
PHONE...................858 225-2352
John Keister, *CEO*
John Keister, *Pr*
Fred Wilmot, *
Mark Rotolo, *CRO*
Karen Buffo, *CMO*
EMP: 40 **EST:** 2012
SALES (est): 7.29MM **Privately Held**
Web: www.mixmode.ai
SIC: 7372 Business oriented computer software

(P-13978)
MSCSOFTWARE CORPORATION
5161 California Ave Ste 200, Irvine
(92617-8002)
PHONE...................714 540-8900
EMP: 855
SALES (est): 125.34MM **Privately Held**
Web: www.hexagon.com
SIC: 7372 Business oriented computer software

(P-13979)
MUSICMATCH INC
16935 W Bernardo Dr Ste 270, San Diego
(92127-1635)
PHONE...................858 485-4300
Dennis Mudd, *CEO*
Peter Csathy, *
Gary Acord, *
Don Leigh, *
Chris Allen Senior Vp Mkting Stragic
Planning, *Prin*
EMP: 140 **EST:** 1997
SQ FT: 20,000
SALES (est): 3.82MM **Privately Held**
SIC: 7372 5734 Prepackaged software; Software, business and non-game
PA: Altaba Inc.
140 E 45th St Fl 15

(P-13980)
MY EYE MEDIA LLC
2211 N Hollywood Way, Burbank
(91505-1113)
PHONE...................818 559-7200
Michael Kadenacy, *Pr*
Rodd Feingold, *CFO*
EMP: 80 **EST:** 2004
SQ FT: 20,000
SALES (est): 6.07MM
SALES (corp-wide): 20.42MM **Privately Held**
Web: www.myeyemedia.com
SIC: 7372 Business oriented computer software
HQ: Eurofins Product Testing Us Holdings, Inc.
11720 N Creek Pkwy N Ste
Bothell WA 98011
800 383-0085

(P-13981)
NATIONWIDE TECHNOLOGIES INC
3684 W Uva Ln, San Bernardino
(92407-1968)
PHONE...................909 340-2770
Ajaydev Singh, *CEO*
Rares Sfetcu, *
EMP: 25 **EST:** 2019
SALES (est): 802.19K **Privately Held**
SIC: 7372 7389 Business oriented computer software; Business Activities at Non-Commercial Site

(P-13982)
NC4 SOLTRA LLC
21515 Hawthorne Blvd Ste 520, Torrance
(90503-6566)
PHONE...................408 489-5579
Tommy Mcdowell, *Managing Member*
EMP: 67 **EST:** 2016
SALES (est): 1.04MM
SALES (corp-wide): 9.82MM **Privately Held**
SIC: 7372 Prepackaged software
PA: Celerium Inc.
21515 Hawthorne Blvd # 520
408 489-5579

(P-13983)
NETSOL TECHNOLOGIES INC (PA)
Also Called: NETSOL
16000 Ventura Blvd Ste 770, Encino
(91436-2758)
PHONE...................818 222-9195
Najeeb Ghauri, *Ch Bd*
Naeem Ghauri, *Pr*
Roger Almond, *CFO*
Erik Wagner, *CMO*
Patti L W Mcglasson, *Sr VP*
EMP: 120 **EST:** 1997
SQ FT: 2,400
SALES (est): 61.39MM
SALES (corp-wide): 61.39MM **Publicly Held**
Web: www.netsoltech.com
SIC: 7372 7373 7299 Business oriented computer software; Computer integrated systems design; Personal document and information services

(P-13984)
NETWORK AUTOMATION INC
3530 Wilshire Blvd Ste 1800, Los Angeles
(90010-2335)
PHONE...................213 738-1700
Dustin Snell, *CEO*
Graham Taylor, *

EMP: 50 **EST:** 2004
SQ FT: 9,000
SALES (est): 1.81MM
SALES (corp-wide): 1.88MM **Privately Held**
Web: www.fortra.com
SIC: 7372 Business oriented computer software
HQ: Fortra, Llc
11095 Viking Dr Ste 100
Eden Prairie MN 55344
952 933-0609

(P-13985)
NETWRIX CORPORATION
300 Spectrum Center Dr Ste 200, Irvine (92618-4987)
PHONE..................888 638-9749
Steve Dickson, *Brnch Mgr*
EMP: 65
SALES (corp-wide): 942.12MM **Privately Held**
Web: www.netwrix.com
SIC: 7372 Prepackaged software
HQ: Netwrix Corporation
6160 Warren Pkwy Ste 100
Frisco TX 75034

(P-13986)
NEW BI US GAMING LLC
10920 Via Frontera Ste 420, San Diego (92127-1732)
PHONE..................858 592-2472
Ian Bonner, *CEO*
Russell Schechter, *
Kimberly Armstrong, *
EMP: 92 **EST:** 2012
SALES (est): 2.05MM **Privately Held**
Web: www.vizexplorer.com
SIC: 7372 Prepackaged software

(P-13987)
NEXOGY INC
10967 Via Frontera, San Diego (92127-1703)
PHONE..................305 358-8952
Felipe Lahrssen, *VP*
EMP: 65 **EST:** 2005
SALES (est): 2.8MM
SALES (corp-wide): 31.62MM **Publicly Held**
Web: www.vervecloud.com
SIC: 7372 8741 Business oriented computer software; Management services
HQ: T3 Communications, Inc.
1610 Royal Palm Ave
Fort Myers FL 33901
239 333-0000

(P-13988)
NEXTGEN HEALTHCARE INC (HQ)
18111 Von Karman Ave Ste 600, Irvine (92612-7100)
PHONE..................949 255-2600
David Sides, *Pr*
Jeffrey H Margolis, *Ch Bd*
James R Arnold Junior, *Ex VP*
Srinivas S Velamoor, *Chief Growth Vice President*
Mitchell L Waters, *Executive Commercial Vice President*
EMP: 475 **EST:** 1974
SALES (est): 653.17MM **Privately Held**
Web: www.nextgen.com
SIC: 7372 7373 Prepackaged software; Computer integrated systems design
PA: Thoma Bravo, L.P.
110 N Wacker Dr Fl 32

(P-13989)
NILE AI INC
15260 Ventura Blvd Ste 1410, Sherman Oaks (91403-5348)
PHONE..................818 689-9107
Artin Davidian, *Admn*
EMP: 25 **EST:** 2020
SALES (est): 1.46MM
SALES (corp-wide): 1.04B **Privately Held**
SIC: 7372 Application computer software
HQ: Ucb Holdings, Inc.
1950 Lake Park Dr
Smyrna GA 30080
770 970-7500

(P-13990)
NIS AMERICA INC
4 Hutton Centre Dr Ste 650, Santa Ana (92707-8726)
PHONE..................714 540-1122
Souhei Niikawa, *CEO*
Harusato Akenaga, *
Mitsuharu Hiraoka, *
Johanna Hirota, *
▲ **EMP:** 40 **EST:** 2003
SQ FT: 1,000
SALES (est): 8.83MM **Privately Held**
Web: www.nisamerica.com
SIC: 7372 Publisher's computer software

(P-13991)
NORTH BEAM INC
222 N Pacific Coast Hwy Ste 2000, El Segundo (90245-5614)
PHONE..................860 940-4569
Austin Harrison, *CEO*
EMP: 48 **EST:** 2019
SALES (est): 4.89MM **Privately Held**
SIC: 7372 7389 Prepackaged software; Business Activities at Non-Commercial Site

(P-13992)
NOVASTOR CORPORATION (PA)
29209 Canwood St Ste 200, Agoura Hills (91301-1908)
PHONE..................805 579-6700
Peter Means, *Pr*
Martin Albert, *
EMP: 30 **EST:** 1987
SQ FT: 7,800
SALES (est): 4.17MM
SALES (corp-wide): 4.17MM **Privately Held**
Web: www.novastor.com
SIC: 7372 7371 5734 Business oriented computer software; Custom computer programming services; Software, business and non-game

(P-13993)
NTRUST INFOTECH INC
230 Commerce Ste 180, Irvine (92602-1336)
PHONE..................562 207-1600
Srikanth Ramachandran, *CEO*
EMP: 65 **EST:** 2003
SALES (est): 5.59MM **Privately Held**
Web: www.ntrustinfotech.com
SIC: 7372 7371 Business oriented computer software; Computer software development and applications

(P-13994)
NUMECENT INC
18565 Jamboree Rd, Irvine (92612-2532)
PHONE..................949 833-2800
Tom Lagatta, *CEO*
Osman Kent, *
Ed Corrente, *
Hildy Shandell, *

EMP: 30 **EST:** 2012
SALES (est): 4.43MM **Privately Held**
Web: www.numecent.com
SIC: 7372 Application computer software

(P-13995)
NWP SERVICES CORPORATION (DH)
535 Anton Blvd Ste 1100, Costa Mesa (92626-7699)
P.O. Box 19661 (92623-9661)
PHONE..................949 253-2500
Ron Reed, *Pr*
Lana Reeve, *CLO**
Mike Haviken, *
EMP: 141 **EST:** 1995
SQ FT: 21,171
SALES (est): 13.88MM **Privately Held**
Web: www.mynwpsc.com
SIC: 7372 8721 Utility computer software; Billing and bookkeeping service
HQ: Realpage, Inc.
2201 Lakeside Blvd
Richardson TX 75082
972 820-3000

(P-13996)
NXGN MANAGEMENT LLC
18111 Von Karman Ave Ste 600, Irvine (92612-7100)
PHONE..................949 255-2600
EMP: 41 **EST:** 2021
SALES (est): 11.23MM **Privately Held**
Web: www.nextgen.com
SIC: 7372 Prepackaged software
HQ: Nextgen Healthcare, Inc.
18111 Von Krman Ave Ste 6
Irvine CA 92612
949 255-2600

(P-13997)
OMNITRACS MIDCO LLC
9276 Scranton Rd Ste 200, San Diego (92121-7703)
PHONE..................858 651-5812
EMP: 30 **EST:** 2013
SALES (est): 2.64MM **Privately Held**
Web: www.omnitracs.com
SIC: 7372 Business oriented computer software

(P-13998)
ONTRAPORT INC
2030 Alameda Padre Serra Ste 200, Santa Barbara (93103-1704)
PHONE..................855 668-7276
Landon Ray, *CEO*
Lena Requist, *
EMP: 98 **EST:** 2006
SQ FT: 35,000
SALES (est): 20.78MM **Privately Held**
Web: www.ontraport.com
SIC: 7372 Business oriented computer software

(P-13999)
OPEN SYSTEMS INC
5250 Lankershim Blvd Ste 620, North Hollywood (91601-3188)
PHONE..................317 566-6662
EMP: 46
SALES (corp-wide): 957.93MM **Privately Held**
Web: www.aptean.com
SIC: 7372 Business oriented computer software
HQ: Open Systems, Inc.
4325 Alexander Dr Ste 100
Alpharetta GA 30022
952 403-5700

(P-14000)
ORACLE CORPORATION
Also Called: Oracle
1 Bolero, Mission Viejo (92692-5164)
PHONE..................626 315-7513
Hemesh Surana, *Brnch Mgr*
EMP: 302
SALES (corp-wide): 52.96B **Publicly Held**
Web: www.oracle.com
SIC: 7372 Prepackaged software
PA: Oracle Corporation
2300 Oracle Way
737 867-1000

(P-14001)
OSR ENTERPRISES INC
1910 E Stowell Rd, Santa Maria (93454-8002)
P.O. Box 7200 (93456)
PHONE..................805 925-1831
James O Rice, *CEO*
Owen S Rice, *
Betty E Rice, *
EMP: 45 **EST:** 1937
SQ FT: 1,500
SALES (est): 11.09MM **Privately Held**
Web: www.osrenterprises.com
SIC: 7372 Publisher's computer software

(P-14002)
PAPAYA
14140 Ventura Blvd Ste 209, Sherman Oaks (91423-2774)
PHONE..................310 740-6774
Dan Mintz, *Prin*
EMP: 33 **EST:** 2019
SALES (est): 5.11MM **Privately Held**
Web: www.papayaclothing.com
SIC: 7372 Prepackaged software

(P-14003)
PARENTSQUARE INC
6144 Calle Real Ste 200a, Goleta (93117-2012)
PHONE..................888 496-3168
Sohit Wadhwa, *CEO*
Anupama Vaid, *Prin*
EMP: 65 **EST:** 2011
SALES (est): 5.71MM **Privately Held**
Web: www.parentsquare.com
SIC: 7372 Educational computer software

(P-14004)
PATIENTPOP INC
214 Wilshire Blvd, Santa Monica (90401-1202)
PHONE..................844 487-8399
Travis Schneider, *CEO*
Luke Kervin, *
David Mcneil, *Pr*
Jason Gardner, *
Taylor Timmer, *
EMP: 51 **EST:** 2015
SALES (est): 5.59MM **Privately Held**
Web: www.tebra.com
SIC: 7372 Business oriented computer software

(P-14005)
PATRON SOLUTIONS LLC
5171 California Ave Ste 200, Irvine (92617-3068)
PHONE..................949 823-1700
Steve Shaw, *Owner*
EMP: 245 **EST:** 2015
SALES (est): 8.66MM **Privately Held**
SIC: 7372 Application computer software

(P-14006)
PLANET DDS INC (PA)
Also Called: Planet DDS
17872 Gillette Ave Ste 250, Irvine
(92614-6573)
PHONE.....................800 861-5098
Eric Giesecke, *CEO*
Stephen Fong, *CFO*
Matt Zelen, *COO*
EMP: 33 **EST:** 2004
SALES (est): 14.22MM
SALES (corp-wide): 14.22MM **Privately Held**
Web: www.planetdds.com
SIC: 7372 Application computer software

(P-14007)
PLUGG ME LNC
18100 Von Karman Ave Ste 850, Irvine
(92612-8110)
PHONE.....................949 705-4472
Clarissa Watkins, *CEO*
EMP: 25 **EST:** 2019
SALES (est): 1.06MM **Privately Held**
SIC: 7372 Application computer software

(P-14008)
POWERDMS INC
Also Called: Innovative Data Solutions
2120 Park Pl, El Segundo (90245-4740)
P.O. Box 2468 (32802-2468)
PHONE.....................407 992-6000
David Digiacomo, *CEO*
Joshua J Brown, *
EMP: 75 **EST:** 2000
SQ FT: 15,506
SALES (est): 11.57MM
SALES (corp-wide): 23.8MM **Privately Held**
Web: www.powerdms.com
SIC: 7372 Prepackaged software
PA: Governmentjobs.Com, Inc.
2120 Park Pl Ste 100
877 204-4442

(P-14009)
PRISM SOFTWARE CORPORATION
184 Technology Dr Ste 201, Irvine
(92618-2434)
PHONE.....................949 855-3100
Carl S Von Bibra, *Ch*
David Ayres, *
Conrad Von Bibra, *
Michael Cheever, *
EMP: 25 **EST:** 1970
SALES (est): 5.04MM **Privately Held**
Web: www.prismsoftware.com
SIC: 7372 Publisher's computer software

(P-14010)
QAD INC (HQ)
Also Called: Qad
101 Innovation Pl, Santa Barbara
(93108-2268)
PHONE.....................805 566-6000
Anton Chilton, *CEO*
Peter R Van Cuylenburg, *
Pamela M Lopker, *
Daniel Lender, *Ex VP*
Kara Bellamy, *CAO*
EMP: 219 **EST:** 1979
SALES (est): 307.87MM
SALES (corp-wide): 307.87MM **Privately Held**
Web: www.qad.com
SIC: 7372 Prepackaged software
PA: Qad Parent, Llc
101 Innovation Pl
805 566-6000

(P-14011)
QDOS INC
Also Called: Desksite
200 Spectrum Center Dr Ste 300, Irvine
(92618-5004)
PHONE.....................949 362-8888
Richard Gillam, *CEO*
Patricia Bender, *
EMP: 26 **EST:** 2003
SQ FT: 6,000
SALES (est): 2.33MM **Privately Held**
Web: www.directsportsnetwork.com
SIC: 7372 7812 7313 7922 Home
entertainment computer software; Motion
picture and video production; Radio,
television, publisher representatives;
Television program, including commercial
producers

(P-14012)
QED SOFTWARE LLC
Also Called: Trinium Technologies
211 E Ocean Blvd, Long Beach
(90802-4809)
PHONE.....................310 214-3118
Michael Thomas, *CEO*
Barry Assadi, *
▲ **EMP:** 27 **EST:** 2001
SALES (est): 13.34MM **Privately Held**
Web: www.triniumtech.com
SIC: 7372 Business oriented computer
software
PA: Wisetech Global Limited
U 3 72 O'riordan St

(P-14013)
QUADROTECH SOLUTIONS INC (PA)
Also Called: Quest
20 Enterprise, Aliso Viejo (92656-7104)
PHONE.....................949 754-8000
Thomas Madsen, *CEO*
EMP: 25 **EST:** 2013
SALES (est): 9.39MM
SALES (corp-wide): 9.39MM **Privately Held**
Web: www.quest.com
SIC: 7372 Application computer software

(P-14014)
QUALER INC
9477 Waples St, San Diego (92121-2934)
PHONE.....................858 224-9516
Alex Spector, *CEO*
Darren Crochet, *
Ruslan Auvad, *
Michael Morozov Ce, *Prin*
EMP: 30 **EST:** 2018
SALES (est): 2.42MM **Privately Held**
Web: www.qualer.com
SIC: 7372 Prepackaged software

(P-14015)
QUEST SOFTWARE INC
Also Called: Cloud Automation Division
20 Enterprise, Aliso Viejo (92656-7104)
PHONE.....................949 754-8000
EMP: 80
SALES (corp-wide): 647.68MM **Privately Held**
Web: www.quest.com
SIC: 7372 Prepackaged software
PA: Quest Software Inc.
20 Enterprise Ste 100
949 754-8000

(P-14016)
RAILSTECH INC
730 Arizona Ave, Santa Monica
(90401-1702)

PHONE.....................267 315-2998
Dov Marmor Coe, *Prin*
Dov Marmor, *CEO*
EMP: 23 **EST:** 2020
SALES (est): 2.43MM
SALES (corp-wide): 6.76MM **Privately Held**
SIC: 7372 Business oriented computer
software
PA: Railsbank Technology Limited
Suite 3 Regency House

(P-14017)
REAL SOFTWARE SYSTEMS LLC (PA)
21255 Burbank Blvd Ste 220, Woodland
Hills (91367-6681)
P.O. Box 7046 (91365-7046)
PHONE.....................818 313-8000
Kent Sahin, *Managing Member*
EMP: 50 **EST:** 1993
SALES (est): 9.03MM **Privately Held**
Web: www.rightsline.com
SIC: 7372 Business oriented computer
software

(P-14018)
RED GATE SOFTWARE INC
144 W Colorado Blvd Ste 200, Pasadena
(91105-1953)
PHONE.....................626 993-3949
Tom Curtis, *Pr*
EMP: 23 **EST:** 2011
SQ FT: 5,500
SALES (est): 5.54MM
SALES (corp-wide): 89.76MM **Privately Held**
Web: www.red-gate.com
SIC: 7372 Business oriented computer
software
HQ: Red Gate Software Limited
C Cavendish House
Cambridge CAMBS CB4 0
122 343-8500

(P-14019)
RELATIONAL CENTER
2717 S Robertson Blvd Apt 1, Los Angeles
(90034-2451)
PHONE.....................323 935-1807
Traci Bivens Davis, *Prin*
EMP: 47 **EST:** 2008
SALES (est): 1.14MM **Privately Held**
Web: www.relationalcenter.org
SIC: 7372 Prepackaged software

(P-14020)
REVCO PRODUCTS
7221 Acacia Ave, Garden Grove
(92841-3908)
PHONE.....................714 891-6688
▲ **EMP:** 51 **EST:** 1977
SALES (est): 9.21MM **Privately Held**
Web: www.revcoproducts.com
SIC: 7372 Operating systems computer
software

(P-14021)
RIOT GAMES INC (DH)
Also Called: Riot Games
12333 W Olympic Blvd, Los Angeles
(90064-1021)
PHONE.....................310 207-1444
Nicolas Laurent, *CEO*
Marc Merrill, *
Dylan Jadeja, *
Mark Sottosanti, *
Daniel Chang, *
▲ **EMP:** 36 **EST:** 2006
SALES (est): 798.36MM **Privately Held**

Web: www.riotgames.com
SIC: 7372 5734 Prepackaged software;
Software, computer games
HQ: Tencent Holdings Limited
29/F Three Pacific Place
Wan Chai HK

(P-14022)
SAGE SOFTWARE HOLDINGS INC (HQ)
6561 Irvine Center Dr, Irvine (92618-2118)
PHONE.....................866 530-7243
Stev Swenson, *CEO*
Doug Meyer, *
Mack Lout, *
Stephen Kelly, *Prin*
Steve Hare, *Prin*
EMP: 400 **EST:** 2000
SALES (est): 870.22MM
SALES (corp-wide): 3.09B **Privately Held**
SIC: 7372 7371 Business oriented computer
software; Custom computer programming
services
PA: The Sage Group Plc.
C23 - 5 & 6 Cobalt Park Way
800 923-0344

(P-14023)
SALESCATCHER LLC
Also Called: Salescatcher
1570 N Batavia St, Orange (92867-3507)
PHONE.....................714 376-6700
Augustin Gohil, *Managing Member*
EMP: 50 **EST:** 2009
SALES (est): 3.23MM **Privately Held**
Web: www.salescatcher.io
SIC: 7372 Application computer software

(P-14024)
SALESFORCECOM INC
Also Called: SALESFORCE.COM, INC.
1442 2nd St, Santa Monica (90401-2302)
PHONE.....................310 752-7000
Andy Demari, *Mgr*
EMP: 40
SALES (corp-wide): 34.86B **Publicly Held**
Web: www.salesforce.com
SIC: 7372 Business oriented computer
software
PA: Salesforce, Inc.
415 Mission St Fl 3
415 901-7000

(P-14025)
SAVIYNT INC (PA)
1301 E El Segundo Blvd Ste D, El Segundo
(90245-4303)
PHONE.....................310 641-1664
Sachin Nayyar, *CEO*
Paul Zolfaghari, *
Shankar Ganapathy, *
James Jackson, *
EMP: 491 **EST:** 2011
SQ FT: 10,786
SALES (est): 79.73MM
SALES (corp-wide): 79.73MM **Privately Held**
Web: www.saviynt.com
SIC: 7372 Prepackaged software

(P-14026)
SCOPELY INC (DH)
3505 Hayden Ave, Culver City
(90232-2412)
PHONE.....................323 400-6618
Tim Obrien, *CRO*
Roxane Lukas, *CPO*
EMP: 200 **EST:** 2011
SALES (est): 97.61MM **Privately Held**
Web: www.scopely.com

SIC: 7372 Home entertainment computer
software
HQ: Savvy Games Group
Office 2.14 B, 6th Floor, Kafd, King
Fahad Road
Riyadh

(P-14027)
SCORELATE INC
91301 Fairview Pl Ste 2, Agoura Hills
(91301)
PHONE................818 602-9176
Sean Bar, *CEO*
EMP: 25
SALES (est): 441.68K **Privately Held**
SIC: 7372 Business oriented computer
software

(P-14028)
SEISMIC SOFTWARE INC (HQ)
12390 El Camino Real Ste 300, San Diego
(92130-3162)
PHONE................714 404-7069
John Douglas Winter, *CEO*
EMP: 54 EST: 2010
SALES (est): 52.61MM
SALES (corp-wide): 151.4MM **Privately
Held**
Web: www.seismic.com
SIC: 7372 Prepackaged software
PA: Seismic Software Holdings, Inc.
11455 El Cmino Real Ste 3

(P-14029)
SEQUELAE INC
101 W Bdwy Fl 9, San Diego (92101)
P.O. Box 431002 (92101)
PHONE................801 628-0256
Ken Ehlert, *CEO*
Lyle Parry, *
EMP: 80 EST: 2022
SALES (est): 1.95MM **Privately Held**
SIC: 7372 Prepackaged software

(P-14030)
SHORTCUTS SOFTWARE INC
7711 Center Ave Ste 550, Huntington Beach
(92647-3075)
PHONE................714 622-6600
Rebecca Randall, *CEO*
Paul Tate, *
Malcom Raward, *
EMP: 30 EST: 2005
SALES (est): 5.47MM
SALES (corp-wide): 8.41B **Privately Held**
Web: www.shortcuts.net
SIC: 7372 Business oriented computer
software
HQ: Shortcuts Software Pty Ltd
L 2 South Tower 10 Browning St
South Brisbane QLD 4101

(P-14031)
SHRED LABS LLC
8033 W Sunset Blvd # 1112, Los Angeles
(90046-2401)
PHONE................781 285-8622
EMP: 23 EST: 2018
SALES (est): 4.45MM **Privately Held**
Web: www.shred.app
SIC: 7372 7389 Application computer
software; Business services, nec

(P-14032)
SNAP INC
579 Toyopa Dr, Pacific Palisades
(90272-4470)
PHONE................310 745-0632
EMP: 77
SALES (corp-wide): 4.61B **Publicly Held**

Web: www.snap.com
SIC: 7372 Application computer software
PA: Snap Inc.
3000 31st St
310 399-3339

(P-14033)
SOLV ENERGY LLC
Also Called: Swinerton Builders
16798 W Bernardo Dr, San Diego
(92128-2850)
PHONE................858 622-4040
Danielle Hammersmith, *Mgr*
EMP: 243
Web: www.swinertonrenewable.com
SIC: 7372 Prepackaged software
HQ: Solv Energy, Llc
16680 W Bernardo Dr
San Diego CA 92127
858 251-4888

(P-14034)
SONENDO ACQUISITION CORP
Also Called: Tdo Software, Inc.
6235 Lusk Blvd, San Diego (92121-2731)
PHONE................858 558-3696
Luiz Motta, *Genl Mgr*
EMP: 25 EST: 2004
SQ FT: 3,600
SALES (est): 6.89MM
SALES (corp-wide): 300K **Privately Held**
Web: www.tdo4endo.com
SIC: 7372 Prepackaged software
HQ: Valsoft Corporation Inc.
7405 Rte Transcanadienne Bureau 100
Saint-Laurent QC H4T 1
514 316-7647

(P-14035)
SPARKTECH SOFTWARE LLC
1419 Beaudry Blvd, Glendale (91208-1707)
PHONE................818 330-9098
Cosmin Andriescu, *Prin*
EMP: 39 EST: 2010
SALES (est): 1.26MM **Privately Held**
Web: www.sparktechsoft.com
SIC: 7372 Prepackaged software

(P-14036)
SPATIAL LABS INC
12555 W Jefferson Blvd Ste 220, Los
Angeles (90066-7032)
PHONE................424 289-0275
Iddris Sandu, *CEO*
EMP: 32
SALES (est): 1.71MM **Privately Held**
SIC: 7372 Prepackaged software

(P-14037)
SPECIALISTS IN CSTM SFTWR INC
2574 Wellesley Ave, Los Angeles
(90064-2738)
PHONE................310 315-9660
Helen Russell, *Pr*
Melissa Vance, *
EMP: 27 EST: 1979
SQ FT: 2,400
SALES (est): 3.47MM **Privately Held**
Web: www.scs-mbs.com
SIC: 7372 Prepackaged software

(P-14038)
SPRING TECHNOLOGIES CORP
10170 Culver Blvd, Culver City
(90232-3152)
PHONE................310 230-4000
Jonathan Finestone, *CEO*
EMP: 30 EST: 2022
SALES (est): 980.3K **Privately Held**

SIC: 7372 Business oriented computer
software

(P-14039)
SRAX INC (PA)
1014 S Westlake Blvd # 14-299, Westlake
Village (91361-3108)
PHONE................323 205-6109
Christopher Miglino, *Ch Bd*
EMP: 43 EST: 2009
SALES (est): 27.86MM
SALES (corp-wide): 27.86MM **Publicly
Held**
SIC: 7372 Prepackaged software

(P-14040)
STRATEGY COMPANION CORP
100 Pacifica Ste 220, Irvine (92618-7441)
PHONE................714 460-8398
Robert Sterling, *Pr*
EMP: 70 EST: 2006
SALES (est): 3.15MM **Privately Held**
Web: www.strategycompanion.com
SIC: 7372 Prepackaged software
PA: Strategy Companion Corp.
Scotia Centre 4th Floor

(P-14041)
STREET SMART LLC
Also Called: Street Smart 247
100 N Pacific Coast Hwy, El Segundo
(90245-4359)
PHONE................866 924-4644
Cicero Lucas, *CEO*
EMP: 27 EST: 2019
SALES (est): 1.44MM
SALES (corp-wide): 14.18MM **Privately
Held**
Web: www.versaterm.com
SIC: 7372 Prepackaged software
HQ: Fivepoint Payments Llc
204 Caughman Farm Ln # 201
Lexington SC 29072
803 951-2094

(P-14042)
STROMASYS INC
871 Marlborough Ave Ste 100, Riverside
(92507-2131)
PHONE................919 239-8450
George Koukis, *Ch Bd*
John Prot, *
Chris Pavlou, *
Serge Pavoncello, *
EMP: 78 EST: 2008
SALES (est): 3.94MM
SALES (corp-wide): 600K **Privately Held**
Web: www.stromasys.com
SIC: 7372 5734 Operating systems
computer software; Software, business and
non-game
HQ: Stromasys Sa
Avenue Louis-Casal 18
GenCve GE 1209

(P-14043)
SUBJECT TECHNOLOGIES INC
Also Called: Subject
345 N Maple Dr, Beverly Hills (90210-3869)
PHONE................310 243-6484
Felix Ruano, *Prin*
EMP: 50 EST: 2020
SALES (est): 6.1MM **Privately Held**
Web: www.subject.com
SIC: 7372 Educational computer software

(P-14044)
SUGARSYNC INC
Also Called: Sharpcast
6922 Hollywood Blvd Ste 500, Los Angeles
(90028-6125)

PHONE................650 571-5105
Laura Yecies, *Pr*
Peter Chantel, *
EMP: 30 EST: 2004
SQ FT: 11,000
SALES (est): 4.9MM **Privately Held**
Web: www.sugarsync.com
SIC: 7372 Business oriented computer
software

(P-14045)
SUNGARD TREASURY SYSTEMS INC
Also Called: Sungard
23975 Park Sorrento Ste 100, Calabasas
(91302-4013)
PHONE................818 223-2300
EMP: 250
SIC: 7372 Prepackaged software

(P-14046)
SYSTEM1 INC (PA)
4235 Redwood Ave, Los Angeles
(90066-5605)
PHONE................310 924-6037
Michael Blend, *Ch Bd*
Paul Filsinger, *Pr*
Tridivesh Kidambi, *CFO*
Brian Coppola, *Chief Product Officer*
EMP: 400 EST: 2020
SALES (est): 401.97MM
SALES (corp-wide): 401.97MM **Publicly
Held**
Web: www.system1.com
SIC: 7372 Business oriented computer
software

(P-14047)
TELESIGN HOLDINGS INC (DH)
13274 Fiji Way Ste 600, Marina Del Rey
(90292-7293)
PHONE................310 740-9700
Ryan Disraeli, *CEO*
Philipp Gast, *
Tom Powledge, *Chief Product Officer*
Justin Hart, *
EMP: 30 EST: 2016
SALES (est): 49.06MM **Privately Held**
Web: www.telesign.com
SIC: 7372 Prepackaged software
HQ: Belgacom International Carrier
Services
Boulevard Du Roi Albert Ii 27
Bruxelles 1030

(P-14048)
TERADATA CORPORATION (PA)
Also Called: Teradata
17095 Via Del Campo, San Diego
(92127-1711)
PHONE................866 548-8348
Stephen Mcmillan, *Pr*
Claire Bramley, *CFO*
Richard Petley, *CRO*
Kathleen Cullen-cote, *CPO*
Margaret Treese, *CLO*
EMP: 951 EST: 1979
SALES (est): 1.83B **Publicly Held**
Web: www.teradata.com
SIC: 7372 3572 7371 3571 Prepackaged
software; Computer storage devices;
Software programming applications;
Mainframe computers

(P-14049)
TESSITURA NETWORK INC
2295 Fletcher Pkwy Ste 101, El Cajon
(92020-2140)
PHONE................888 643-5778
Andrew Recinos, *Pr*

Laura Bowden Vp People, *Prin*
Dahlia Kang, *
EMP: 287 **EST:** 2002
SALES (est): 52.16MM **Privately Held**
Web: www.tessitura.com
SIC: 7372 Prepackaged software

(P-14050)
TEXICAN INC
21031 Ventura Blvd Ste 1000, Woodland Hills (91364-2227)
PHONE..................310 384-7000
Tony Reyna, *CEO*
EMP: 50 **EST:** 2013
SALES (est): 698.26K **Privately Held**
Web: www.texicaninc.com
SIC: 7372 Prepackaged software

(P-14051)
THQ INC
Also Called: Thq San Diego
21900 Burbank Blvd, Woodland Hills (91367-6469)
PHONE..................818 591-1310
EMP: 1088
Web: www.thqnordic.com
SIC: 7372 Prepackaged software

(P-14052)
THRIO INC
5230 Las Virgenes Rd Ste 210, Calabasas (91302-3465)
PHONE..................858 299-7191
Edwin K Margulies, *CEO*
Rose M Sinicrope, *
Ran Ezerzer, *
EMP: 25 **EST:** 2017
SALES (est): 4.07MM **Privately Held**
Web: www.thrio.com
SIC: 7372 Prepackaged software
PA: Nextiva, Inc.
9451 E Via De Ventura

(P-14053)
THURSBY SOFTWARE SYSTEMS LLC
1900 Carnegie Ave, Santa Ana (92705-5557)
PHONE..................817 478-5070
William Thursby, *CEO*
EMP: 28 **EST:** 1986
SALES (est): 3.15MM **Publicly Held**
Web: shop.thursby.com
SIC: 7372 Prepackaged software
PA: Identiv, Inc.
2201 Walnut Ave Ste 100

(P-14054)
TI LIMITED LLC (PA)
20335 Ventura Blvd Ste 231-239, Woodland Hills (91364-2444)
PHONE..................323 877-5991
Alberto Gamez, *
EMP: 52 **EST:** 2016
SQ FT: 9,000
SALES (est): 2.63MM
SALES (corp-wide): 2.63MM **Privately Held**
SIC: 7372 8748 Business oriented computer software; Business consulting, nec

(P-14055)
TIMEVALUE SOFTWARE
22 Mauchly, Irvine (92618-2306)
P.O. Box 50250 (92619-0250)
PHONE..................949 727-1800
Michael Applegate, *Pr*
Charles Miller, *
EMP: 25 **EST:** 1983
SQ FT: 18,000

SALES (est): 4.65MM **Privately Held**
Web: www.timevalue.com
SIC: 7372 7371 Prepackaged software; Computer software development

(P-14056)
TRAFFIC MANAGEMENT PDTS INC
Also Called: Fivesixtwo Inc
4900 Airport Plaza Dr Ste 300, Long Beach (90815-1375)
PHONE..................800 763-3999
Jonathan E Spano, *CEO*
Ed Barrera, *
Christopher H Spano, *
EMP: 887 **EST:** 2015
SALES (est): 3.78MM **Privately Held**
SIC: 7372 Prepackaged software
PA: Traffic Management, Llc
4900 Arprt Plz Dr Ste 300

(P-14057)
TRAXERO NORTH AMERICA LLC
1730 E Holly Ave Ste 740, El Segundo (90245-4404)
PHONE..................423 497-1164
Mark Sedgley, *Managing Member*
EMP: 90 **EST:** 2020
SALES (est): 5.82MM **Privately Held**
SIC: 7372 Business oriented computer software

(P-14058)
UNBROKEN STUDIOS LLC
2120 Park Pl Ste 110, El Segundo (90245-4741)
PHONE..................310 741-2670
Paul Ohanian, *CEO*
Anthony Scott, *
EMP: 80 **EST:** 2018
SALES (est): 8.64MM
SALES (corp-wide): 13.85MM **Privately Held**
Web: www.unbrokenstudios.com
SIC: 7372 Prepackaged software
PA: Pound Sand, Llc
2120 Park Pl Ste 110
310 741-2670

(P-14059)
UNEEKOR INC
15770 Laguna Canyon Rd Ste 100, Irvine (92618-3187)
PHONE..................888 262-6498
Jey Ho Suk, *CEO*
Uinam Choi, *Sec*
EMP: 58 **EST:** 2018
SALES (est): 1.55MM **Privately Held**
Web: www.uneekor.com
SIC: 7372 Prepackaged software

(P-14060)
UNLIMITED INNOVATIONS INC
Also Called: Cerecons
180 N Rverview Dr Ste 320, Anaheim (92808)
PHONE..................714 998-0866
FAX: 714 998-5641
EMP: 30
SQ FT: 5,000
SALES (est): 2.35MM
SALES (corp-wide): 12.81B **Privately Held**
Web: www.cerecons.com
SIC: 7372 Prepackaged software
HQ: Medecision, Inc.
550 E Swedesford Rd # 220
Wayne PA 19087
484 588-0102

(P-14061)
UPSTANDING LLC
Also Called: Mobilityware
440 Exchange Ste 100, Irvine (92602-1390)
PHONE..................949 788-9900
John Libby, *
EMP: 180 **EST:** 1990
SQ FT: 48,000
SALES (est): 5.02MM **Privately Held**
Web: www.mobilityware.com
SIC: 7372 Business oriented computer software

(P-14062)
VIDEOAMP INC (PA)
12121 Bluff Creek Dr, Playa Vista (90094-2994)
PHONE..................424 272-7774
Peter Liguori, *
Peter Bradbury Ccgo, *Prin*
Josh Hudgins, *CPO*
Sharon Lee, *Ex VP*
EMP: 86 **EST:** 2014
SALES (est): 36.08MM
SALES (corp-wide): 36.08MM **Privately Held**
Web: www.videoamp.com
SIC: 7372 Prepackaged software

(P-14063)
VISIONARY VR INC
409 N Plymouth Blvd, Los Angeles (90004-3001)
PHONE..................323 868-7443
Gil Baron, *Prin*
EMP: 24 **EST:** 2014
SALES (est): 131.37K **Privately Held**
Web: www.visionaryvr.com
SIC: 7372 Prepackaged software

(P-14064)
WEBMETRO
Also Called: Multivest
160 Via Verde Ste 1, San Dimas (91773-3901)
PHONE..................909 599-8885
EMP: 85
Web: www.perfectdomain.com
SIC: 7372 7311 Prepackaged software; Advertising agencies

(P-14065)
WM TECHNOLOGY INC (PA)
Also Called: WM TECHNOLOGY
41 Discovery, Irvine (92618-3150)
PHONE..................646 699-3750
Douglas Francis, *Ex Ch Bd*
Mary Hoitt, *Interim Chief Financial Officer*
EMP: 26 **EST:** 2008
SALES (est): 215.53MM
SALES (corp-wide): 215.53MM **Publicly Held**
Web: www.weedmaps.com
SIC: 7372 Prepackaged software

(P-14066)
WME BI LLC
17075 Camino, San Diego (92127)
PHONE..................877 592-2472
EMP: 60 **EST:** 2012
SALES (est): 2.45MM **Privately Held**
SIC: 7372 Operating systems computer software

(P-14067)
WONDERWARE CORPORATION (DH)
26561 Rancho Pkwy S, Lake Forest (92630-8301)

PHONE..................949 727-3200
Rick Bullotta, *VP*
Brian Dibenedetto, *
Karen Hamilton, *
Peter Kent, *
Dave Pickett, *
EMP: 300 **EST:** 1993
SQ FT: 32,000
SALES (est): 13.82MM
SALES (corp-wide): 1.09K **Privately Held**
Web: www.wonderware.com
SIC: 7372 Prepackaged software
HQ: Aveva Software, Llc
26561 Rancho Pkwy S
Lake Forest CA 92630

(P-14068)
YARDI KUBE INC
Also Called: Wun
430 S Fairview Ave, Goleta (93117-3637)
PHONE..................805 699-2040
EMP: 52 **EST:** 2018
SALES (est): 5.52MM **Privately Held**
Web: www.yardikube.com
SIC: 7372 Prepackaged software

(P-14069)
ZWIFT INC (PA)
111 W Ocean Blvd Ste 1800, Long Beach (90802-7936)
PHONE..................855 469-9438
Eric Min, *CEO*
EMP: 282 **EST:** 2014
SALES (est): 26.51MM
SALES (corp-wide): 26.51MM **Privately Held**
Web: www.zwift.com
SIC: 7372 5961 Publisher's computer software; Fitness and sporting goods, mail order

---

7373 Computer Integrated Systems Design

(P-14070)
ALTERYX INC (PA)
Also Called: Alteryx
3347 Michelson Dr Ste 400, Irvine (92612-0691)
PHONE..................888 836-4274
Andy Macmillan, *CEO*
Dean A Stoecker, *
Robert S Jones, *Pr*
Scott Davidson, *COO*
EMP: 25 **EST:** 1997
SQ FT: 180,000
SALES (est): 970MM
SALES (corp-wide): 970MM **Privately Held**
Web: www.alteryx.com
SIC: 7373 7372 Systems software development services; Prepackaged software

(P-14071)
AUTOMATION HOLDCO INC
10815 Rancho Bernardo Rd Ste 102, San Diego (92127-2187)
PHONE..................858 967-8650
Leo Castaneda, *Pr*
EMP: 80 **EST:** 2013
SALES (est): 3.36MM **Privately Held**
SIC: 7373 Systems integration services

(P-14072)
AVEVA SOFTWARE LLC (DH)
Also Called: Wonderware
26561 Rancho Pkwy S, Lake Forest (92630-8301)

PHONE..................949 727-3200
Ravi Gopinath, *Pr*
James Danley, *
Mary B Kibble, *
EMP: 350 **EST:** 2014
SALES (est): 220.34MM
SALES (corp-wide): 1.09K **Privately Held**
Web: www.wonderware.com
SIC: 7373 Computer integrated systems
   design
HQ: Aveva Inc.
   920 Mmrial Cy Way Ste 120
   Houston TX 77024
   713 977-1225

(P-14073)
CACI ENTERPRISE SOLUTIONS LLC
1455 Frazee Rd Ste 700, San Diego
(92108-4308)
PHONE..................619 881-6000
J P London, *CEO*
EMP: 254
SALES (corp-wide): 7.66B **Publicly Held**
Web: www.caci.com
SIC: 7373 Computer integrated systems
   design
HQ: Caci Enterprise Solutions, Llc
   1100 N Glebe Rd Ste 200
   Arlington VA 22201
   703 841-7800

(P-14074)
CAPTIVA SOFTWARE CORPORATION (DH)
10145 Pacific Heights Blvd, San Diego
(92121-4234)
PHONE..................858 320-1000
Reynolds C Bish, *Pr*
Patrick L Edsell, *
Rick E Russo, *CFO*
Jim Nicol, *Executive Product Development Vice President*
Howard Dratler, *OK Vice President*
EMP: 80 **EST:** 1986
SQ FT: 25,000
SALES (est): 9.02MM **Publicly Held**
SIC: 7373 7372 Office computer automation
   systems integration; Prepackaged software
HQ: Emc Corporation
   176 S St
   Hopkinton MA 01748
   508 435-1000

(P-14075)
CLINICOMP INTERNATIONAL INC (PA)
9655 Towne Centre Dr, San Diego
(92121-1964)
PHONE..................858 546-8202
Chris Haudenschild, *CEO*
Eloisa Haudenschild, *CFO*
William Mcdonald, *Contrlr*
Jiao Fan Ph.d., *VP*
Kelley Malott, *VP*
EMP: 99 **EST:** 1983
SQ FT: 42,000
SALES (est): 21.96MM
SALES (corp-wide): 21.96MM **Privately Held**
Web: www.clinicomp.com
SIC: 7373 7371 3571 Systems software
   development services; Custom computer
   programming services; Electronic
   computers

(P-14076)
COGNIZANT TRZTTO SFTWR GROUP I
3631 S Harbor Blvd Ste 200, Santa Ana
(92704-7936)

PHONE..................714 481-0396
Kathy Kantocello, *Contrlr*
EMP: 190
SIC: 7373 4813 Systems software
   development services; Internet connectivity
   services
HQ: Cognizant Trizetto Software Group, Inc.
   9655 Maroon Cir
   Englewood CO 80112

(P-14077)
COMPUTER TECH RESOURCES INC
16 Technology Dr Ste 202, Irvine
(92618-2329)
PHONE..................714 665-6507
Alok Mundra, *Brnch Mgr*
EMP: 192
SALES (corp-wide): 48.1MM **Privately Held**
Web: www.astcorporation.com
SIC: 7373 Computer integrated systems
   design
HQ: Computer Technology Resources, Inc.
   8333 Clairemont Mesa Blvd
   San Diego CA
   858 492-1400

(P-14078)
CORE BTS INC
5250 Lankershim Blvd Ste 620, North
Hollywood (91601-3188)
PHONE..................818 766-2400
EMP: 106
Web: www.corebts.com
SIC: 7373 Systems integration services
HQ: Core Bts, Inc.
   5875 Castle Creek Parkway
   Indianapolis IN 46250
   317 566-6200

(P-14079)
CUBIC CORPORATION
Also Called: Cubic Defense Systems
9233 Balboa Ave, San Diego (92123-1513)
PHONE..................858 277-6780
Brigitte Jen, *Brnch Mgr*
EMP: 2000
SALES (corp-wide): 1.48B **Privately Held**
Web: www.cubic.com
SIC: 7373 Computer integrated systems
   design
HQ: Cubic Corporation
   9233 Balboa Ave
   San Diego CA 92123
   858 277-6780

(P-14080)
ELECTRONIC ONLINE SYSTEMS INTERNATIONAL
Also Called: E O S International
2292 Faraday Ave Frnt, Carlsbad
(92008-7237)
PHONE..................760 431-8400
EMP: 64 **EST:** 1981
SALES (est): 3.52MM **Privately Held**
SIC: 7373 7371 7372 Turnkey vendors,
   computer systems; Computer software
   development; Prepackaged software

(P-14081)
FILENET CORPORATION
3565 Harbor Blvd, Costa Mesa
(92626-1405)
PHONE..................800 345-3638
EMP: 1695
SIC: 7373 7372 Computer integrated
   systems design; Business oriented
   computer software

(P-14082)
GBL SYSTEMS CORPORATION
760 Paseo Camarillo Ste 401, Camarillo
(93010-6002)
PHONE..................805 987-4345
James Buscemi, *Pr*
EMP: 35 **EST:** 1990
SQ FT: 8,228
SALES (est): 7.46MM **Privately Held**
Web: www.gblsys.com
SIC: 7373 Computer integrated
   systems design; Electronic component
   making machinery

(P-14083)
GEMALTO COGENT INC (HQ)
2964 Bradley St, Pasadena (91107-1560)
PHONE..................626 325-9600
Alan Pelligrini, *Pr*
Antonio Lo Brutto, *
Daniel Asraf, *
Ramsey Billups, *
Alex Woods, *
▲ **EMP:** 95 **EST:** 2004
SQ FT: 151,000
SALES (est): 21.43MM
SALES (corp-wide): 269.57MM **Privately Held**
SIC: 7373 Computer-aided system services
PA: Thales
   4 Rue De La Verrerie
   157778000

(P-14084)
GENEA ENERGY PARTNERS INC
19100 Von Karman Ave Ste 550, Irvine
(92612-6571)
PHONE..................714 694-0536
Michal Pasula, *Admn*
Jon Haahr, *
Keith Voysey, *
David Balkin, *
EMP: 120 **EST:** 2006
SQ FT: 10,000
SALES (est): 10.4MM **Privately Held**
Web: www.getgenea.com
SIC: 7373 Systems software development
   services

(P-14085)
HUBB SYSTEMS LLC
Also Called: Data 911
12305 Crosthwaite Cir, Poway
(92064-6817)
PHONE..................510 865-9100
Abigail Baker, *CEO*
Donald R Hubbard, *
Brian Mccown, *CFO*
EMP: 75 **EST:** 1982
SALES (est): 3.74MM
SALES (corp-wide): 23.63MM **Privately Held**
SIC: 7373 7379 Turnkey vendors, computer
   systems; Computer related consulting
   services
PA: Broadcast Microwave Services, Llc
   13475 Dnielson St Ste 130
   858 391-3050

(P-14086)
I3DNET LLC
7 N Fair Oaks Ave, Pasadena
(91103-3608)
PHONE..................800 482-6910
Yves Guillemot, *Managing Member*
EMP: 676 **EST:** 2011
SALES (est): 1.4MM
SALES (corp-wide): 2.22B **Privately Held**
Web: www.i3d.net

(P-14087)
ICL SYSTEMS INC
19782 Macarthur Blvd Ste 260, Irvine
(92612-2486)
PHONE..................877 425-8725
Thomas Swennes, *Prin*
Thomas Swennes, *VP*
Brian Hook, *
Pat Donahoe, *
EMP: 98 **EST:** 2000
SALES (est): 3.35MM **Privately Held**
Web: www.iclsystems.com
SIC: 7373 Systems integration services

(P-14088)
INFORMATION MGT RESOURCES INC (PA)
Also Called: Imri
85 Argonaut Ste 215, Aliso Viejo
(92656-4105)
PHONE..................949 215-8889
Martha Daniel, *CEO*
EMP: 132 **EST:** 1986
SQ FT: 5,000
SALES (est): 16.61MM **Privately Held**
Web: www.imri.com
SIC: 7373 8742 7371 Computer integrated
   systems design; Management consulting
   services; Computer software systems
   analysis and design, custom

(P-14089)
INTERNET CORP FOR ASSGNED NMES (PA)
Also Called: Icann
12025 Waterfront Dr Ste 300, Los Angeles
(90094-3224)
PHONE..................310 823-9358
Cherine Chalaby, *Ch*
Chris Disspain, *Vice Chairman*
EMP: 146 **EST:** 1998
SALES (est): 46.76MM
SALES (corp-wide): 46.76MM **Privately Held**
Web: www.iana.org
SIC: 7373 Systems software development
   services

(P-14090)
KOAM ENGINEERING SYSTEMS INC
Also Called: K E S
7807 Convoy Ct Ste 200, San Diego
(92111-1213)
PHONE..................858 292-0922
John S Yi, *Pr*
Richard Comber, *
Erica Tofson, *
John Schiltz, *
Jim Meadows, *
EMP: 105 **EST:** 1994
SQ FT: 5,700
SALES (est): 9.73MM **Privately Held**
Web: www.kes.com
SIC: 7373 Computer integrated systems
   design

(P-14091)
LIFERAY INC (PA)
Also Called: Liferay
1400 Montefino Ave Ste 100, Diamond Bar
(91765-5501)

PHONE..........................877 543-3729
Brian Chan, *CEO*
Bryan Cheung, *CMO**
Jc Choi, *CFO*
Caris Chan, *CAO*
Michael Han, *Dir*
EMP: 1207 **EST:** 2006
SALES (est): 120K
SALES (corp-wide): 120K **Privately Held**
Web: www.liferay.com
SIC: 7373 Systems software development services

(P-14092)
MESFIN ENTERPRISES
Also Called: Transnational Computer Tech
222 N Pacific Coast Hwy Ste 1570, El Segundo (90245-5648)
PHONE..........................310 615-0881
Wond Wossen Mesfin, *Pr*
EMP: 376 **EST:** 1978
SQ FT: 11,250
SALES (est): 35.33MM **Privately Held**
SIC: 7373 7376 5734 Systems integration services; Computer facilities management; Software, business and non-game

(P-14093)
MIRO TECHNOLOGIES INC
5643 Copley Dr, San Diego (92111-7903)
P.O. Box 3707 (98124-2207)
PHONE..........................858 677-2100
EMP: 150
SIC: 7373 Turnkey vendors, computer systems

(P-14094)
MITCHELL INTERNATIONAL INC (PA)
Also Called: Enlyte
9771 Clairemont Mesa Blvd Ste A, San Diego (92124-1332)
P.O. Box 229001 (92192)
PHONE..........................866 389-2069
Alex Sun, *CEO*
Nina Smith, *
Debbie Day, *
Dave Torrence, *
Erez Nir, *
EMP: 229 **EST:** 1977
SQ FT: 141,000
Web: www.mitchell.com
SIC: 7373 Systems software development services

(P-14095)
MIVA INC
Also Called: Miva Merchant
16870 W Bernardo Dr Ste 100, San Diego (92127-1671)
PHONE..........................858 490-2570
Rick Wilson, *CEO*
Nathan Osborne, *
David Hubbard, *
EMP: 120 **EST:** 2007
SALES (est): 17.84MM **Privately Held**
Web: www.miva.com
SIC: 7373 5961 Systems software development services; Catalog and mail-order houses

(P-14096)
MOBISYSTEMS INC
4501 Mission Bay Dr Ste 3a, San Diego (92109-4926)
PHONE..........................858 350-0315
Stanislav Minchev, *CEO*
Stoyan Gogov, *
EMP: 150 **EST:** 2001
SQ FT: 1,200
SALES (est): 3.53MM **Privately Held**
Web: www.mobisystems.com
SIC: 7373 Systems software development services

(P-14097)
MORPHOTRAK LLC (DH)
Also Called: Safran
5515 E La Palma Ave Ste 100, Anaheim (92807-2127)
PHONE..........................714 238-2000
Celeste Thomasson, *Managing Member*
Clark Nelson, *VP*
Katie Murphy, *Sec*
Florian Hebras, *CFO*
EMP: 175 **EST:** 1985
SQ FT: 32,000
SALES (est): 7.69MM
SALES (corp-wide): 4.59B **Privately Held**
Web: www.morphotrak.com
SIC: 7373 Computer integrated systems design
HQ: Idemia Identity & Security France
2 Place Samuel De Champlain
Courbevoie IDF 92400

(P-14098)
NANTWORKS LLC (PA)
9920 Jefferson Blvd, Culver City (90232-3506)
PHONE..........................310 883-1300
Charles N Kenworthy, *Managing Member*
EMP: 78 **EST:** 2011
SALES (est): 158.26K
SALES (corp-wide): 158.26K **Publicly Held**
Web: www.nantworks.com
SIC: 7373 Computer-aided system services

(P-14099)
NETAPP INC
6320 Canoga Ave Ste 1500, Woodland Hills (91367-2517)
PHONE..........................818 227-5025
James Mccormick Iii, *Mgr*
EMP: 209
Web: www.netapp.com
SIC: 7373 Computer integrated systems design
PA: Netapp, Inc.
3060 Olsen Dr

(P-14100)
NETWORK INTGRTION PARTNERS INC
Also Called: Nic Partners
11981 Jack Benny Dr Ste 103, Rancho Cucamonga (91739-9232)
PHONE..........................909 919-2800
Franklin P Spaeth, *Pr*
EMP: 80 **EST:** 2007
SQ FT: 6,000
SALES (est): 10.07MM **Privately Held**
Web: www.nicpartnersinc.com
SIC: 7373 Local area network (LAN) systems integrator

(P-14101)
OBERMAN TIVOLI & PICKERT INC
Also Called: Media Services
500 S Sepulveda Blvd Ste 500, Los Angeles (90049-3500)
PHONE..........................310 440-9600
Robert Oberman, *Pr*
Barry Oberman, *
Alan Tivoli, *VP*
Sanaa Wadsworth, *
EMP: 230 **EST:** 1989
SALES (est): 6.24MM **Privately Held**

Web: www.mediaservices.com
SIC: 7373 8721 8741 Systems software development services; Payroll accounting service; Business management

(P-14102)
PAT V MACK INC
Also Called: Pvm
2305 Historic Decatur Rd Ste 100, San Diego (92106-6071)
PHONE..........................619 930-5473
Patrick Mack, *Pr*
Sydney Metzmaker, *Prin*
Marivic Watson, *Prin*
EMP: 92 **EST:** 2010
SALES (est): 1.81MM **Privately Held**
Web: www.pvmit.com
SIC: 7373 Computer integrated systems design

(P-14103)
QUEST SOFTWARE INC (PA)
20 Enterprise Ste 100, Aliso Viejo (92656-7104)
PHONE..........................949 754-8000
Patrick Nichols, *CEO*
Carolyn Mccarthy, *CFO*
EMP: 600 **EST:** 1987
SQ FT: 170,000
SALES (est): 647.68MM
SALES (corp-wide): 647.68MM **Privately Held**
Web: www.quest.com
SIC: 7373 7379 7372 Computer integrated systems design; Computer related consulting services; Business oriented computer software

(P-14104)
RESULT GROUP INC
2603 Main St Ste 710, Irvine (92614-4263)
PHONE..........................480 777-7130
William Derick Robson, *Pr*
David Griffiths, *
EMP: 83 **EST:** 2003
SALES (est): 912.32K
SALES (corp-wide): 8.41B **Privately Held**
Web: www.rentalresult.com
SIC: 7373 7372 Systems software development services; Business oriented computer software
HQ: Wynne Systems, Inc.
2601 Main St Ste 270
Irvine CA 92614

(P-14105)
SCIENCE APPLICATIONS INTL CORP
Also Called: Saic
4015 Hancock St, San Diego (92110-5121)
PHONE..........................858 826-3061
Gordon Saakamodo, *Mgr*
EMP: 600
SALES (corp-wide): 7.44B **Publicly Held**
Web: www.saic.com
SIC: 7373 Systems engineering, computer related
PA: Science Applications International Corporation
12010 Sunset Hills Rd
703 676-4300

(P-14106)
SECOM INTERNATIONAL (PA)
Also Called: Secom
15905 S Broadway, Gardena (90248-2405)
PHONE..........................310 641-1290
Ted Burton, *Pr*
Terry Bixler, *
Linda Vose, *

EMP: 52 **EST:** 1978
SALES (est): 8.27MM
SALES (corp-wide): 8.27MM **Privately Held**
Web: www.spdprk.com
SIC: 7373 3446 3559 7371 Turnkey vendors, computer systems; Architectural metalwork; Parking facility equipment and supplies; Computer software systems analysis and design, custom

(P-14107)
SOFTWARE DYNAMICS INCORPORATED
8501 Fallbrook Ave Ste 200, Canoga Park (91304-3235)
PHONE..........................818 992-3299
Matthew Hale, *Pr*
Christopher J Stein, *
Richard Dobb, *
Geoffrey Gill, *
EMP: 71 **EST:** 1982
SQ FT: 40,000
SALES (est): 1.53MM **Publicly Held**
SIC: 7373 7371 Computer systems analysis and design; Computer software development
HQ: S1 Corporation
705 Westech Dr
Norcross GA 30092
678 966-9499

(P-14108)
SOLUGENIX CORPORATION (PA)
Also Called: Solugenix
601 Valencia Ave Ste 260, Brea (92823-6358)
PHONE..........................866 749-7658
Shashi Jasthi, *CEO*
Damola Akinola, *
EMP: 138 **EST:** 2004
SQ FT: 1,600
SALES (est): 54.83MM
SALES (corp-wide): 54.83MM **Privately Held**
Web: www.solugenix.com
SIC: 7373 Computer integrated systems design

(P-14109)
SURVIOS INC
4501 Glencoe Ave, Marina Del Rey (90292-6372)
PHONE..........................310 736-1503
Seth Gerson, *CEO*
Joshua Green, *
Tq Jefferson, *Chief Product Officer**
Alex Silkin, *Prin*
EMP: 24 **EST:** 2013
SALES (est): 6.9MM **Privately Held**
Web: www.survios.com
SIC: 7373 7372 5092 Systems software development services; Prepackaged software; Video games

(P-14110)
TECHNET PARTNERS INC
Also Called: Technet Partners
6116 Innovation Way, Carlsbad (92009-1728)
PHONE..........................760 683-8393
Brian Schumann, *CEO*
Floyd Auten, *
Ryan Hardesty, *
EMP: 184 **EST:** 2011
SALES (est): 31.81MM **Privately Held**
Web: www.technetpartners.com

SIC: **7373** 1731 8748 Local area network (LAN) systems integrator; Fiber optic cable installation; Systems engineering consultant, ex. computer or professional

(P-14111)
TRACE3 LLC (HQ)
Also Called: Trace3
7505 Irvine Center Dr Ste 100, Irvine (92618-3078)
PHONE.............................949 333-2300
Rich Fennessy, *CEO*
Tyler Beecher, *
Kevin Manzo, *
EMP: 100 **EST**: 2001
SALES (est): 467.46MM
SALES (corp-wide): 583.64MM **Privately Held**
Web: www.trace3.com
SIC: **7373** Computer systems analysis and design
PA: Escape Velocity Holdings, Inc.
7505 Irvine Ctr Dr Ste 10
949 333-2381

(P-14112)
TRANSCENTRA INC
20500 Belshaw Ave, Carson (90746-3506)
PHONE.............................310 603-0105
Dwayne Moore, *Brnch Mgr*
EMP: 530
SALES (corp-wide): 1.06B **Publicly Held**
Web: www.exelatech.com
SIC: **7373** Systems software development services
HQ: Transcentra, Inc.
4145 Shackleford Rd # 330
Norcross GA 30093
678 728-2500

(P-14113)
TUSIMPLE INC
9191 Towne Centre Dr, San Diego (92122-1225)
PHONE.............................520 989-7911
EMP: 410
SALES (corp-wide): 9.37MM **Publicly Held**
Web: www.tusimple.com
SIC: **7373** 4213 Computer integrated systems design; Trucking, except local
HQ: Tusimple, Inc.
9191 Twne Cntre Dr Ste 60
San Diego CA 92122
619 916-3144

(P-14114)
TUSIMPLE HOLDINGS INC (PA)
Also Called: TUSIMPLE
9191 Towne Centre Dr Ste 600, San Diego (92122-6207)
PHONE.............................619 916-3144
Cheng Lu, *CEO*
Eric Tapia, *CAO*
Susan Marsch, *Interim General Counsel*
EMP: 486 **EST**: 2015
SQ FT: 80,000
SALES (est): 9.37MM
SALES (corp-wide): 9.37MM **Publicly Held**
Web: www.tusimple.com
SIC: **7373** Computer integrated systems design

(P-14115)
ULTISAT INC
Also Called: A Speedcast Co
11839 Sorrento Valley Rd, San Diego (92121-1040)
PHONE.............................240 243-5107

EMP: 1238
SALES (corp-wide): 60.64MM **Privately Held**
Web: www.ultisat.com
SIC: **7373** Systems integration services
PA: Ultisat, Inc.
14399 Penrose Pl Ste 410
240 243-5100

(P-14116)
URBAN INSIGHT INC
3530 Wilshire Blvd Ste 1285, Los Angeles (90010-2341)
PHONE.............................213 792-2000
Chris Steins, *CEO*
Abhijeet Chavan, *COO*
EMP: 37 **EST**: 1997
SQ FT: 4,000
SALES (est): 2.31MM **Privately Held**
Web: www.urbaninsight.com
SIC: **7373** 7372 7371 8748 Computer integrated systems design; Business oriented computer software; Custom computer programming services; Systems engineering consultant, ex. computer or professional

(P-14117)
WEST PUBLISHING CORPORATION
Also Called: Elite
800 Corporate Pointe Ste 150, Culver City (90230-7676)
P.O. Box 51606 (90051-5906)
PHONE.............................424 243-2100
Salim Sunderji, *VP*
EMP: 1205
SALES (corp-wide): 10.66B **Publicly Held**
Web: store.legal.thomsonreuters.com
SIC: **7373** 7371 Computer integrated systems design; Custom computer programming services
HQ: West Publishing Corporation
2900 Ames Crssing Rd Ste
Eagan MN 55121
651 687-7000

(P-14118)
WHOVA INC
10182 Telesis Ct Ste 500, San Diego (92121-4738)
PHONE.............................858 227-0877
Soyeon Park, *Admn*
Yuanyuan Zhou, *
EMP: 160 **EST**: 2013
SALES (est): 13.01MM **Privately Held**
Web: www.whova.com
SIC: **7373** Systems software development services

(P-14119)
YANG-MING INTERNATIONAL CORP
Also Called: Rackmountpro.com
595 Yorbita Rd, La Puente (91744-5956)
PHONE.............................626 956-0100
Betty B Shou, *Pr*
Stephen Shou, *
◆ **EMP**: 25 **EST**: 1994
SQ FT: 10,000
SALES (est): 8.23MM **Privately Held**
Web: www.rackmountpro.com
SIC: **7373** 3571 Systems integration services ; Electronic computers

(P-14120)
ZMICRO INC (PA)
Also Called: Z Microsystems
9820 Summers Ridge Rd, San Diego (92121-3083)

PHONE.............................858 831-7000
Jack Wade, *CEO*
John Howell, *COO*
Jason Wade, *Pr*
Rick Elliott, *VP*
Angi Smart, *Contrlr*
EMP: 57 **EST**: 1986
SQ FT: 36,800
SALES (est): 25.14MM
SALES (corp-wide): 25.14MM **Privately Held**
Web: www.zmicro.com
SIC: **7373** 3577 3572 Computer integrated systems design; Computer peripheral equipment, nec; Computer storage devices

7374 Data Processing And Preparation

(P-14121)
AMAZON PROCESSING LLC
Also Called: Appstar Financial
4619 Viewridge Ave Ste C, San Diego (92123-5611)
PHONE.............................858 565-1135
EMP: 210 **EST**: 2002
SALES (est): 12.08MM **Privately Held**
Web: www.appstar.net
SIC: **7374** Data processing service

(P-14122)
AUTOMATIC DATA PROCESSING INC
Also Called: ADP
3972 Barranca Pkwy Ste J610, Irvine (92606-1204)
PHONE.............................949 751-0360
EMP: 165
SALES (corp-wide): 18.01B **Publicly Held**
Web: www.adp.com
SIC: **7374** Data processing service
PA: Automatic Data Processing, Inc.
1 Adp Blvd
973 974-5000

(P-14123)
AUTOMATIC DATA PROCESSING INC
Also Called: ADP
400 W Covina Blvd, San Dimas (91773-2976)
PHONE.............................800 225-5237
Rodney Hroblak, *Prin*
EMP: 117
SALES (corp-wide): 18.01B **Publicly Held**
Web: www.adp.com
SIC: **7374** 8721 Data processing service; Accounting, auditing, and bookkeeping
PA: Automatic Data Processing, Inc.
1 Adp Blvd
973 974-5000

(P-14124)
BLACK KNIGHT INFOSERV LLC
2500 Redhill Ave Ste 100, Santa Ana (92705-5518)
PHONE.............................904 854-5100
Miriam Moore, *Brnch Mgr*
EMP: 472
SALES (corp-wide): 7.99B **Publicly Held**
Web: www.icemortgagetechnology.com
SIC: **7374** Data processing and preparation
HQ: Black Knight Infoserv, Llc
601 Riverside Ave
Jacksonville FL 32204

(P-14125)
CCH INCORPORATED
2050 W 190th St, Torrance (90504-6228)
PHONE.............................310 800-9800
EMP: 1943
SQ FT: 280,000
SALES (corp-wide): 6.07B **Privately Held**
Web: www.wolterskluwer.com
SIC: **7374** 7372 7371 Data processing and preparation; Prepackaged software; Custom computer programming services
HQ: Cch Incorporated
2700 Lake Cook Rd
Riverwoods IL 60015
847 267-7000

(P-14126)
COMPUSHARE INC
3 Hutton Centre Dr Ste 700, Santa Ana (92707-8752)
PHONE.............................714 427-1000
EMP: 141
Web: www.compushare.com
SIC: **7374** Data processing and preparation

(P-14127)
COUNTY OF LOS ANGELES
Also Called: Voter Prcnct Vter Rgstrtion Of
12400 Imperial Hwy, Norwalk (90650-3134)
PHONE.............................562 462-2094
Connie Mccormack, *Brnch Mgr*
EMP: 71
Web: www.lacounty.gov
SIC: **7374** 9111 Data entry service; Executive offices
PA: County Of Los Angeles
500 W Temple St Ste 437
213 974-1101

(P-14128)
CYBER-PRO SYSTEMS INC
Also Called: Medical Data Exchange
2121 S Towne Centre Pl Ste 200, Anaheim (92806-6123)
PHONE.............................562 256-3800
Gerry Ibanez, *CEO*
Scott H Kramer, *
EMP: 162 **EST**: 1985
SALES (est): 3.69MM
SALES (corp-wide): 4.32B **Publicly Held**
Web: www.mdxnet.com
SIC: **7374** Data processing service
PA: Agilon Health, Inc.
6210 E Hwy 290 Ste 450
562 256-3800

(P-14129)
DESIGN PEOPLE INC
Also Called: Redux Labs
1700 E Walnut Ave Ste 400, El Segundo (90245-2609)
PHONE.............................800 969-5799
Jon Krabbe, *Pr*
Tiger Bitanga, *
Jon Krabbe, *CFO*
Luigi Amante, *
EMP: 160 **EST**: 1998
SQ FT: 9,200
SALES (est): 11.66MM **Privately Held**
Web: www.thedesignpeople.com
SIC: **7374** Computer graphics service

(P-14130)
EDATA SOLUTIONS INC
17100 Pioneer Blvd, Artesia (90701-2776)
PHONE.............................510 574-5380
Manan Kothari, *CEO*
EMP: 1000 **EST**: 2014
SALES (est): 3.46MM **Privately Held**
Web: www.edataweb.com

P R O D U C T S & S V C S

SIC: 7374 7371 Data processing service; Computer software development and applications

(P-14131)
ELEVATED RESOURCES INC (PA)
3990 Westerly Pl Ste 270, Newport Beach (92660-2348)
PHONE...............................949 419-6632
Robert Morris, *CEO*
Mike Willner, *
Bruce Ferguson, *
EMP: 220 EST: 2007
SQ FT: 1,900
SALES (est): 3.47MM **Privately Held**
Web: www.elevatedresources.com
SIC: 7374 Data processing and preparation

(P-14132)
EMERALD CONNECT LLC (HQ)
15050 Avenue Of Science Ste 200, San Diego (92128-3419)
PHONE...............................800 233-2834
Adam D Amsterdam, *Managing Member*
Sharon Greener, *
Heather Hinkle, *
Heidi Saucier, *OF DIGITAL STRAT*
EMP: 100 EST: 1986
SQ FT: 35,000
SALES (est): 3.7MM **Publicly Held**
Web: www.broadridge.com
SIC: 7374 7331 Data processing service; Mailing service
PA: Broadridge Financial Solutions, Inc.
   5 Dakota Dr Ste 300

(P-14133)
ENCLARITY INC
16815 Von Karman Ave Ste 125, Irvine (92606-2412)
PHONE...............................949 797-7160
Sean Downs, *CEO*
Thomas Suk, *
Warren Gouk Andrea, *
Paul Perleberg, *
Scott Marber, *
EMP: 301 EST: 2005
SQ FT: 3,500
SALES (est): 6.24MM
SALES (corp-wide): 11.42B **Privately Held**
Web: risk.lexisnexis.com
SIC: 7374 Data processing service
HQ: Lexisnexis Risk Solutions Inc.
   1000 Alderman Dr
   Alpharetta GA 30005
   678 694-6000

(P-14134)
EPOCHCOM LLC
Also Called: Epoch.com
3110 Main St Ste 220, Santa Monica (90405-5353)
PHONE...............................310 664-5700
Joel Hall, *Managing Member*
Esther Martinez, *
EMP: 150 EST: 2004
SQ FT: 22,000
SALES (est): 8.78MM **Privately Held**
Web: www.epoch.com
SIC: 7374 Data processing service

(P-14135)
GOODRX HOLDINGS INC (PA)
Also Called: GOODRX
2701 Olympic Blvd, Santa Monica (90404-4183)
PHONE...............................855 268-2822
Scott Wagner, *Interim Chief Executive Officer*

Trevor Bezdek, *
Douglas Hirsch, *CMO*
Karsten Voermann, *CFO*
Romin Nabiey, *CAO*
EMP: 215 EST: 2011
SQ FT: 132,000
SALES (est): 750.26MM
SALES (corp-wide): 750.26MM **Publicly Held**
Web: www.goodrx.com
SIC: 7374 Computer processing services

(P-14136)
GREENSOFT TECHNOLOGY INC
155 S El Molino Ave Ste 100, Pasadena (91101-2563)
PHONE...............................323 254-5961
Larry Yen, *Pr*
Jon Wu, *
EMP: 121 EST: 2002
SALES (est): 4.56MM **Privately Held**
Web: www.greensofttech.com
SIC: 7374 Data processing service

(P-14137)
HONK TECHNOLOGIES INC
2251 Barry Ave, Los Angeles (90064-1401)
P.O. Box 910 (90078-0910)
PHONE...............................800 979-3162
Corey Brundage, *CEO*
Dan Rosenthal, *
EMP: 151 EST: 2014
SQ FT: 8,000
SALES (est): 75MM **Privately Held**
Web: www.honkforhelp.com
SIC: 7374 7372 7331 Data processing and preparation; Business oriented computer software; Custom computer programming services

(P-14138)
IKANO COMMUNICATIONS INC (PA)
Also Called: A & S Technologies
9221 Corbin Ave Ste 260, Northridge (91324-1625)
PHONE...............................801 924-0900
Jim Murphy, *CEO*
Sam Ghahremanpour, *
George Mitsopoulos, *
Dean Russ, *
EMP: 91 EST: 1991
SQ FT: 50,000
SALES (est): 17.46MM **Privately Held**
Web: www.ikano.com
SIC: 7374 Data processing and preparation

(P-14139)
INFOCROSSING LLC
6320 Canoga Ave Ste 600, Woodland Hills (91367-2511)
PHONE...............................714 986-8722
EMP: 70
Web: www.infocrossing.com
SIC: 7374 Data processing service
HQ: Infocrossing, Llc
   20 Mercer St
   Hackensack NJ 07601

(P-14140)
LEAF GROUP LTD (HQ)
Also Called: Leaf Group
1655 26th St, Santa Monica (90404-4016)
PHONE...............................310 394-6400
EMP: 133 EST: 2006
SALES (est): 64.57MM
SALES (corp-wide): 4.41B **Publicly Held**
Web: www.demandmedia.com
SIC: 7374 Data processing and preparation
PA: Graham Holdings Company
   1300 17th St N Ste 1700 F

703 345-6300

(P-14141)
LEGALZOOMCOM INC (PA)
Also Called: LEGALZOOM
101 N Brand Blvd Fl 11, Glendale (91203-2638)
PHONE...............................323 962-8600
Jeffrey Stibel, *Ch Bd*
Noel Watson, *CFO*
Nicole Miller, *CLO*
EMP: 300 EST: 2000
SQ FT: 56,000
SALES (est): 660.73MM **Publicly Held**
Web: www.legalzoom.com
SIC: 7374 8111 Data processing and preparation; Legal services

(P-14142)
MANAGEMENT APPLIED PRGRM INC (PA)
Also Called: Benefit Programs ADM
13191 Crossroads Pkwy N Ste 205, City Of Industry (91746-3434)
PHONE...............................562 463-5000
Phiroze Dalal, *CEO*
Hormazd Dalal, *
EMP: 95 EST: 1964
SALES (est): 9.95MM
SALES (corp-wide): 9.95MM **Privately Held**
Web: www.mapinc.com
SIC: 7374 Data processing service

(P-14143)
MERCURY DEFENSE SYSTEMS INC
Also Called: Mercury Systems
10855 Business Center Dr Ste A, Cypress (90630-5252)
PHONE...............................714 898-8200
EMP: 85
Web: www.mrcy.com
SIC: 7374 Data processing service

(P-14144)
MERCURY SYSTEMS INC
10855 Business Center Dr Ste A, Cypress (90630-5252)
PHONE...............................714 898-8200
EMP: 85
SALES (corp-wide): 835.27MM **Publicly Held**
Web: www.mrcy.com
SIC: 7374 Data processing service
PA: Mercury Systems, Inc.
   50 Minuteman Rd
   978 256-1300

(P-14145)
MERCURY TECHNOLOGY GROUP INC
6430 Oak Cyn Ste 100, Irvine (92618-5227)
PHONE...............................949 417-0260
EMP: 70
Web: www.mercurytechnology.com
SIC: 7374 Data processing and preparation

(P-14146)
MINDBODY INC (PA)
Also Called: Mindbody
651 Tank Farm Rd, San Luis Obispo (93401-7062)
PHONE...............................877 755-4279
Richard Stollmeyer, *Ch Bd*
Josh Mccarter, *Pr*
Michael Mansbach, *
Brett White, *
Kimberly Lytikainen, *CLO*

EMP: 109 EST: 2001
SALES (est): 456.62MM **Privately Held**
Web: www.mindbodyonline.com
SIC: 7374 7372 8741 Data processing and preparation; Business oriented computer software; Business management

(P-14147)
MOCEAN LLC
Also Called: Mocean
2440 S Sepulveda Blvd Ste 150, Los Angeles (90064-1786)
PHONE...............................310 481-0808
Craig R Murray, *Managing Member*
Michael Mcintyre, *Pr*
EMP: 200 EST: 2000
SALES (est): 24.18MM **Privately Held**
Web: www.moceanla.com
SIC: 7374 7822 Computer graphics service; Motion picture distribution

(P-14148)
MULLEN AUTOMOTIVE INC (PA)
Also Called: Net Element
1405 Pioneer St, Brea (92821-3721)
PHONE...............................714 613-1900
David Michery, *Ch Bd*
Jonathan New, *CFO*
Mary Winter, *Sec*
Chester Bragado, *CAO*
EMP: 150 EST: 2010
SQ FT: 24,730
SALES (est): 92.12K
SALES (corp-wide): 92.12K **Publicly Held**
Web: investors.mullenusa.com
SIC: 7374 Data processing and preparation

(P-14149)
ORDERMARK INC
12045 Waterfront Dr Ste 400 # 3, Playa Vista (90094-3226)
P.O. Box 260206 (91426-0206)
PHONE...............................833 673-3762
Alex Canter, *CEO*
Mike Jacobs, *COO*
Paul Allen, *Ofcr*
EMP: 236 EST: 2017
SALES (est): 5.64MM **Privately Held**
Web: www.ordermark.com
SIC: 7374 Data processing and preparation

(P-14150)
PAYMENT CLOUD LLC
Also Called: Paymentcloud
16501 Ventura Blvd Ste 300, Encino (91436-2067)
PHONE...............................800 988-2215
Shawnn Silver, *CEO*
Shawn Silver, *CEO*
EMP: 81 EST: 2017
SALES (est): 3.38MM
SALES (corp-wide): 27.19MM **Privately Held**
Web: www.paymentcloudinc.com
SIC: 7374 Data processing and preparation
PA: Electronic Merchant Systems, Llc
   250 W Huron Rd Ste 300
   216 524-0900

(P-14151)
ROCKSTAR SAN DIEGO INC
2200 Faraday Ave Ste 200, Carlsbad (92008-7233)
PHONE...............................760 929-0700
Allan Wasserman, *Pr*
EMP: 54 EST: 1984
SQ FT: 24,000
SALES (est): 6.89MM **Publicly Held**
SIC: 7374 7372 Computer graphics service; Prepackaged software

PA: Take-Two Interactive Software, Inc.
110 W 44th St

(P-14152)
RUITENG INTERNET TECHNOLOGY CO
1344 W Foothill Blvd Ste D, Azusa
(91702-2846)
PHONE..............................302 597-7438
Canzhi Zhen, *Prin*
Chris Zhang, *
Wendy Huang, *
◆ **EMP:** 220 **EST:** 2018
SQ FT: 500
SALES (est): 894.46K **Privately Held**
SIC: 7374 Computer graphics service

(P-14153)
S E O P INC
1621 Alton Pkwy Ste 150, Irvine
(92606-4875)
PHONE..............................949 682-7906
Gary Hagins, *CEO*
Rhonda Spears, *
EMP: 150 **EST:** 2001
SALES (est): 9.63MM **Privately Held**
Web: www.seop.com
SIC: 7374 Computer graphics service

(P-14154)
SAN DIEGO DATA PROCESSING CORPORATION INC
202 C St 3rd Fl, San Diego (92101-4806)
PHONE..............................858 581-9600
EMP: 11130
Web: www.sddpc.org
SIC: 7374 Data processing service

(P-14155)
SECURE ONE DATA SOLUTIONS LLC
11090 Artesia Blvd Ste D, Cerritos
(90703-2545)
PHONE..............................562 924-7056
David Sandobal, *Pr*
EMP: 90
Web: www.secure1data.com
SIC: 7374 Keypunch service
PA: Secure One Data Solutions, Llc
2801 N 33rd Ave Ste 1

(P-14156)
SONY PICTURES IMAGEWORKS INC
Also Called: Imageworks
9050 Washington Blvd, Culver City
(90232-2518)
PHONE..............................310 840-8000
Michelle Grady, *Pr*
Ken Ralston, *
EMP: 1000 **EST:** 1992
SALES (est): 45.12MM **Privately Held**
Web: www.imageworks.com
SIC: 7374 Computer graphics service
HQ: Sony Pictures Entertainment, Inc.
10202 W Washington Blvd
Culver City CA 90232
310 244-4000

(P-14157)
STARK SERVICES
12444 Victory Blvd Ste 300, North
Hollywood (91606-3173)
PHONE..............................818 985-2003
Maricel Zabel, *Pr*
Steve Pugh, *
EMP: 75 **EST:** 1975
SALES (est): 3.08MM **Privately Held**
Web: www.starkservices.com

SIC: 7374 Data processing service

(P-14158)
TEALIUM INC (PA)
9605 Scranton Rd Ste 600, San Diego
(92121-1770)
PHONE..............................858 779-1344
Jeffrey W Lunsford, *CEO*
Ali Behnam, *
Doug Lindroth, *
Peter Ching, *
Ted Purcell, *CRO* *
EMP: 101 **EST:** 2008
SQ FT: 40,864
SALES (est): 33.77MM **Privately Held**
Web: www.tealium.com
SIC: 7374 7371 Computer graphics service;
Computer software development

(P-14159)
TECHNOSOCIALWORKCOM LLC
Also Called: Stria
4300 Resnik Ct Unit 103, Bakersfield
(93313-4836)
P.O. Box 21660 (93390-1660)
PHONE..............................661 617-6601
Jim Damian, *Managing Member*
EMP: 75 **EST:** 2002
SQ FT: 10,000
SALES (est): 9.42MM **Privately Held**
Web: www.stria.com
SIC: 7374 Computer graphics service

(P-14160)
TEGRA118 WEALTH SOLUTIONS INC (HQ)
700 N San Vicente Blvd Ste G605, West
Hollywood (90069-5078)
PHONE..............................888 800-0188
Cheryl Nash, *Pr*
Andrew Schwartz, *
EMP: 100 **EST:** 2011
SALES (est): 24.06MM
SALES (corp-wide): 256.18MM **Privately Held**
SIC: 7374 7371 Data processing service;
Computer software development and
applications
PA: Investcloud, Inc.
700 N San Vcnte Blvd Ste
310 385-7394

(P-14161)
TOTAL CMMNICATOR SOLUTIONS INC
Also Called: Spark Compass
11160 Sta Monica Sta 600, Los Angeles
(90025)
PHONE..............................619 277-1488
Brent Erik Biojegard, *CEO*
EMP: 95 **EST:** 2012
SALES (est): 5MM **Privately Held**
Web: www.sparkcompass.com
SIC: 7374 Data processing service

(P-14162)
UNIVERSITY CAL SAN DIEGO
Also Called: San Diego Supercomputer
Center
10100 Hopkins Dr, La Jolla (92093-0001)
P.O. Box 85608 (92186-5608)
PHONE..............................858 534-5000
Michael Norman, *Dir*
EMP: 769
SALES (corp-wide): 534.4MM **Privately Held**
Web: www.sdsc.edu

SIC: 7374 8731 8221 9411 Data processing
and preparation; Commercial physical
research; University; Administration of
educational programs
HQ: University Of California, San Diego
9500 Gilman Dr
La Jolla CA 92093
858 534-2230

(P-14163)
VERIZON CONNECT TELO INC (DH)
15505 Sand Canyon Ave, Irvine
(92618-3114)
PHONE..............................844 617-1100
Ralph Mason, *CEO*
A Newth Morris Iv, *TELOGIS ROUTE & TELOGIS NAV*
Jason Koch, *TELOGIS FLEET* *
Susan Heystee, *
Ted Serentelos, *
▼ **EMP:** 150 **EST:** 2001
SALES (est): 20.66MM
SALES (corp-wide): 133.97B **Publicly Held**
Web: www.verizonconnect.com
SIC: 7374 Data processing and preparation
HQ: Verizon Connect Inc.
5055 N Point Pkwy
Alpharetta GA 30022
404 573-5800

(P-14164)
YP HOLDINGS LLC
Also Called: Yp
611 N Brand Blvd Ste 500, Glendale
(91203-1379)
P.O. Box 619810 (75261-9810)
PHONE..............................818 649-8772
EMP: 810
SALES (corp-wide): 916.96MM **Publicly Held**
Web: www.thryv.com
SIC: 7374 7389 7313 Computer graphics
service; Telephone directory distribution,
contract or fee basis; Electronic media
advertising representatives
HQ: Yp Holdings Llc
2247 Northlake Pkwy Fl 10
Tucker GA 30084
866 570-8863

(P-14165)
Z57 INC
Also Called: Z57, INC.
2443 Impala Dr Ste B, Carlsbad
(92010-7227)
PHONE..............................850 623-5577
EMP: 105
SALES (corp-wide): 8.41B **Privately Held**
Web: www.z57.com
SIC: 7374 Computer graphics service
HQ: Z57, Llc
11350 Mccrmick Ep 3 Rd St
Hunt Valley MD 21031
858 623-5577

7375 Information Retrieval Services

(P-14166)
ACCURATE BACKGROUND LLC (PA)
200 Spectrum Center Dr Ste 1100, Irvine
(92618-5006)
PHONE..............................800 784-3911
Tim Dowd, *CEO*
David C Dickerson, *
Brian Fujioka, *

Rashid Ismail, *
Aaron Hayes, *
EMP: 315 **EST:** 1998
SQ FT: 98,024
SALES (est): 90.95MM
SALES (corp-wide): 90.95MM **Privately Held**
Web: www.accurate.com
SIC: 7375 Information retrieval services

(P-14167)
COUNTY OF LOS ANGELES
Also Called: Department of Mental Health
320 W Temple St Fl 9, Los Angeles
(90012-3217)
PHONE..............................213 974-0515
Jacqueline Criddell, *Mgr*
EMP: 150
Web: www.lacounty.gov
SIC: 7375 9131 Information retrieval services
; Executive and legislative combined, level
of government
PA: County of Los Angeles
500 W Temple St Ste 437
213 974-1101

(P-14168)
DIGITAL INSIGHT CORPORATION
5601 Lindero Canyon Rd Ste 100,
Westlake Village (91362-6494)
PHONE..............................818 879-1010
Paul Nieman, *Prin*
EMP: 71
SALES (corp-wide): 3.83B **Publicly Held**
Web: www.ncr.com
SIC: 7375 Information retrieval services
HQ: Digital Insight Corporation
1300 Seaport Blvd Ste 300
Redwood City CA 94063

(P-14169)
E-TIMES CORPORATION (PA)
601 S Figueroa St Ste 5000, Los Angeles
(90017-3883)
PHONE..............................213 452-6720
Chiharu Nakahara, *Pr*
EMP: 280 **EST:** 2003
SALES (est): 737.64K
SALES (corp-wide): 737.64K **Privately Held**
Web: www.etimesltd.com
SIC: 7375 7374 8742 Information retrieval
services; Computer graphics service;
Administrative services consultant

(P-14170)
EDMUNDS HOLDING COMPANY (PA)
Also Called: Edmunds.com
2401 Colorado Ave, Santa Monica
(90404-3585)
PHONE..............................310 309-6300
Avi Steinlauf, *CEO*
Seth Berkowitz, *Pr*
Charles Farrell, *CFO*
EMP: 650 **EST:** 1962
SALES (est): 24.78MM **Privately Held**
Web: www.edmunds.com
SIC: 7375 Information retrieval services

(P-14171)
ELAVON INC
700 S Western Ave, Los Angeles
(90005-5112)
PHONE..............................865 403-7000
John Macht, *Brnch Mgr*
EMP: 400
SALES (corp-wide): 40.62B **Publicly Held**
Web: www.elavon.com

PRODUCTS & SVCS

SIC: 7375 Information retrieval services
HQ: Elavon, Inc.
    2 Concourse Pkwy Ste 800
    Atlanta GA 30328

(P-14172)
GROUNDWORK OPEN SOURCE INC
23332 Mill Creek Dr Ste 155, Laguna Hills
(92653-7911)
PHONE.................................415 992-4500
Dave Lilly, *CEO*
EMP: 100 EST: 2004
SALES (est): 2.23MM
SALES (corp-wide): 1.88MM **Privately Held**
Web: www.gwos.com
SIC: 7375 7371 On-line data base
    information retrieval; Custom computer
    programming services
HQ: Fox Technologies, Inc.
    6455 City West Pkwy
    Eden Prairie MN 55344
    800 328-1000

(P-14173)
LIFESCRIPT INC
Also Called: Lifescript
4000 Macarthur Blvd Ste 800, Newport
Beach (92660-2544)
PHONE.................................949 454-0422
EMP: 110
Web: www.everydayhealth.com
SIC: 7375 Information retrieval services

(P-14174)
LOGICMONITOR INC (PA)
820 State St Fl 5, Santa Barbara
(93101-3271)
PHONE.................................805 394-8632
Christina Kosmowski, *CEO*
Kevin Mcgibben, *Ofcr*
Steven Francis, *CPO*
Carol Lee, *CFO*
EMP: 152 EST: 2007
SALES (est): 21.97MM **Privately Held**
Web: www.logicmonitor.com
SIC: 7375 Information retrieval services

(P-14175)
LOWERMYBILLS INC
Also Called: Lowermybills.com
12181 Bluff Creek Dr Ste 250, Playa Vista
(90094-3236)
PHONE.................................310 348-6800
EMP: 200
SIC: 7375 Information retrieval services

(P-14176)
RELATIONEDGE LLC
10120 Pacific Heights Blvd Ste 110, San
Diego (92121-4210)
PHONE.................................858 451-4665
Matthew Stoyka, *CEO*
EMP: 125 EST: 2013
SALES (est): 3.24MM
SALES (corp-wide): 2.96B **Publicly Held**
SIC: 7375 On-line data base information
    retrieval
HQ: Rackspace Us, Inc.
    1718 Dry Creek Way Ste 11
    San Antonio TX 78259
    800 961-4454

(P-14177)
REPRINTS DESK INC
15821 Ventura Blvd Ste 165, Encino
(91436-5208)
PHONE.................................310 477-0354
Alan Urban, *CFO*

EMP: 92 EST: 2006
SQ FT: 2,500
SALES (est): 2.44MM **Publicly Held**
Web: www.researchsolutions.com
SIC: 7375 Information retrieval services
PA: Research Solutions, Inc.
    16350 Vntura Blvd Ste D #

(P-14178)
SAGE SOFTWARE INC
Sage
7595 Irvine Center Dr Ste 200, Irvine
(92618-2963)
PHONE.................................949 753-1222
John Kang, *Brnch Mgr*
EMP: 47
SALES (corp-wide): 3.09B **Privately Held**
Web: na.sage.com
SIC: 7375 7374 7372 3089 Information
    retrieval services; Data processing and
    preparation; Prepackaged software;
    Plastics processing
HQ: Sage Software, Inc.
    271 17th St Nw Ste 1100
    Atlanta GA 30363
    866 996-7243

(P-14179)
TROJAN PROFESSIONAL SVCS INC
11075 Knott Ave Ste A, Cypress
(90630-5150)
P.O. Box 1270 (90720-1270)
PHONE.................................714 816-7169
Mark Dunn, *CEO*
Ingrid M Kidd, *
Chris Iseri, *
EMP: 99 EST: 1976
SALES (est): 10.12MM **Privately Held**
Web: www.trojanonline.com
SIC: 7375 Data base information retrieval

(P-14180)
WEBX360 INC
6871 Laurelton Ave, Garden Grove
(92845-1418)
PHONE.................................714 896-8004
Shawn M Youngquist, *Pr*
EMP: 78 EST: 2005
SALES (est): 2.22MM **Privately Held**
Web: www.webfx.com
SIC: 7375 On-line data base information
    retrieval

(P-14181)
WESTERN FELD INVSTIGATIONS INC (PA)
Also Called: Releasepoint
405 W Foothill Blvd Ste 204, Claremont
(91711-2728)
P.O. Box 246 (91740-0246)
PHONE.................................800 999-9589
Gerard F Halvey, *Pr*
Clair Halvey, *VP*
Derrick Halvey, *VP*
EMP: 94 EST: 1972
SALES (est): 8.1MM
SALES (corp-wide): 8.1MM **Privately Held**
Web: www.wfi-inc.com
SIC: 7375 Information retrieval services

(P-14182)
ZOOMINFO TECHNOLOGIES LLC
Dept La 24789, Pasadena (91185-0001)
PHONE.................................360 783-6924
Henry Schuck, *Managing Member*
EMP: 554
SALES (corp-wide): 1.24B **Publicly Held**
Web: www.zoominfo.com

SIC: 7375 Information retrieval services
HQ: Zoominfo Technologies Llc
    805 Broadway St Ste 900
    Vancouver WA 98660
    360 783-6800

7376 Computer Facilities Management

(P-14183)
TPUSA - FHCS INC (DH)
Also Called: Teleperformance
215 N Marengo Ave Ste 160, Pasadena
(91101-1524)
PHONE.................................213 873-5100
Jeff Balagna, *Pr*
Dean Duncan, *
Peter Phan, *
EMP: 187 EST: 1998
SQ FT: 1,029,146
SALES (est): 102.09K
SALES (corp-wide): 236.27MM **Privately Held**
Web: www.teleperformance.com
SIC: 7376 7373 Computer facilities
    management; Systems integration services
HQ: Tpusa, Inc.
    1991 S 4650 W
    Salt Lake City UT 84104
    801 257-5800

7378 Computer Maintenance And Repair

(P-14184)
ALQUEST TECHNOLOGIES INC
1687 Curtiss Ct, La Verne (91750-5848)
PHONE.................................909 392-9209
Henry Wojcik, *Pr*
EMP: 70 EST: 2000
SALES (est): 5.74MM **Privately Held**
Web: www.alquestonline.com
SIC: 7378 Computer maintenance and repair

(P-14185)
BCP SYSTEMS INC
1560 S Sinclair St, Anaheim (92806-5933)
PHONE.................................714 202-3900
Carlos P Torres, *CEO*
William W Price, *
EMP: 60 EST: 1994
SALES (est): 9.03MM **Privately Held**
Web: www.bcpsystems.com
SIC: 7378 3571 5063 Computer and data
    processing equipment repair/maintenance;
    Electronic computers; Electrical apparatus
    and equipment

(P-14186)
FAKOURI ELECTRICAL ENGRG INC
Also Called: F E E
30001 Comercio, Rcho Sta Marg
(92688-2106)
PHONE.................................949 888-2400
Maryam Ewalt, *Pr*
Charles Ewalt, *
John Oveisi, *
▲ EMP: 79 EST: 1979
SQ FT: 15,000
SALES (est): 11.59MM **Privately Held**
Web: www.fee-ups.com
SIC: 7378 8742 Computer maintenance and
    repair; Maintenance management
    consultant

(P-14187)
HYUNDAI AUTOEVER AMERICA LLC
Also Called: Haea
10550 Talbert Ave 3rd Fl, Fountain Valley
(92708-6031)
PHONE.................................714 965-3000
EMP: 519 EST: 2004
SQ FT: 20,000
SALES (est): 82.79MM **Privately Held**
Web: www.haeaus.com
SIC: 7378 Computer and data processing
    equipment repair/maintenance
HQ: Hyundai Motor America
    10550 Talbert Ave
    Fountain Valley CA 92708
    714 965-3000

(P-14188)
INHOUSEIT INC
400 Exchange Ste 100, Irvine (92602-1340)
PHONE.................................949 660-5655
Glen Ackerman, *CEO*
Steve Bender, *
EMP: 70 EST: 1998
SALES (est): 9.65MM **Privately Held**
Web: www.inhouse-it.com
SIC: 7378 Computer and data processing
    equipment repair/maintenance

(P-14189)
QUEST INTL MONITOR SVC INC (PA)
Also Called: Quest International
60 Parker 65, Irvine (92618-1604)
PHONE.................................949 581-9900
Shahnam Arshadi, *Pr*
Kamyar Katouzian, *
▲ EMP: 60 EST: 1985
SALES (est): 20.86MM
SALES (corp-wide): 20.86MM **Privately Held**
Web: www.questinc.com
SIC: 7378 7379 7371 7373 Computer
    maintenance and repair; Computer related
    maintenance services; Custom computer
    programming services; Systems integration
    services

(P-14190)
RAKWORX INC
1 Mason, Irvine (92618-2514)
PHONE.................................949 215-1362
Yue Cong, *VP*
Zhiyong Ding, *
EMP: 150 EST: 2016
SALES (est): 1.56MM **Privately Held**
Web: www.rakworx.com
SIC: 7378 3577 Computer and data
    processing equipment repair/maintenance;
    Data conversion equipment, media-to-
    media: computer

(P-14191)
VALTRON TECHNOLOGIES INC
28309 Avenue Crocker, Santa Clarita
(91355-1251)
PHONE.................................805 257-0333
Andrew Hart, *Pr*
Steve Nober, *
EMP: 95 EST: 1988
SQ FT: 48,000
SALES (est): 393.3K **Privately Held**
SIC: 7378 5734 Computer and data
    processing equipment repair/maintenance;
    Modems, monitors, terminals, and disk
    drives: computers

7379 Computer Related Services, Nec

(P-14192)
A P R CONSULTING INC
17852 17th St Ste 206, Tustin
(92780-2143)
PHONE..........................714 544-3696
Darryl Stone, *Brnch Mgr*
EMP: 787
Web: www.aprconsulting.com
SIC: 7379 7371 Computer related
maintenance services; Custom computer
programming services
PA: A P R Consulting, Inc.
1370 Valley Vista Dr # 280

(P-14193)
ADAMS COMM & ENGRG TECH INC
1875 Century Park E Ste 1130, Los Angeles
(90067-2543)
PHONE..........................301 861-5000
Charles Adams, *Pr*
EMP: 107
SALES (corp-wide): 44.6MM **Privately Held**
Web: www.adamscomm.com
SIC: 7379 Online services technology
consultants
PA: Adams Communication & Engineering
Technology, Inc.
10740 Parkridge Blvd # 700
443 345-5285

(P-14194)
ADCOM INTERACTIVE MEDIA INC
Also Called: Admedia
6320 Canoga Ave Ste 200, Woodland Hills
(91367-7745)
PHONE..........................800 296-7104
Danny E Bibi, *CEO*
EMP: 100 EST: 2009
SALES (est): 10.03MM **Privately Held**
Web: www.admedia.com
SIC: 7379 Online services technology
consultants

(P-14195)
AJILON LLC
4590 Macarthur Blvd, Newport Beach
(92660-2030)
PHONE..........................949 955-0100
EMP: 237
Web: www.lhh.com
SIC: 7379 Diskette duplicating service
HQ: Ajilon Llc
4800 Deerwood Campus Pkwy
Jacksonville FL 32246
631 844-7800

(P-14196)
ALPHABOLD INC
2011 Palomar Airport Rd Ste 305, Carlsbad
(92011-1432)
PHONE..........................909 979-1425
Muhammad Tayyab Ali, *Prin*
EMP: 84 EST: 2017
SALES (est): 2.66MM **Privately Held**
Web: www.alphabold.com
SIC: 7379 Computer related consulting
services

(P-14197)
ASSIGN CORPORATION
Also Called: Blockaire
200 N Maryland Ave Ste 204, Glendale
(91206-4274)

PHONE..........................818 247-7100
Umesh Lalwani, *CEO*
EMP: 120 EST: 1997
SQ FT: 1,300
SALES (est): 2.36MM **Privately Held**
SIC: 7379 Online services technology
consultants

(P-14198)
AUTOVITALS INC
4141 Jutland Dr Ste 300, San Diego
(92117-3658)
PHONE..........................866 949-2848
Jon Belmonte, *CEO*
EMP: 70 EST: 2009
SALES (est): 6.97MM **Privately Held**
Web: www.autovitals.com
SIC: 7379 Computer related services, nec

(P-14199)
AVIDEX INDUSTRIES LLC
20382 Hermana Cir, Lake Forest
(92630-8701)
PHONE..........................949 428-6333
Mike Stammire, *Brnch Mgr*
EMP: 100
Web: www.avidex.com
SIC: 7379 1731 Computer related consulting
services; Electrical work
HQ: Avidex Industries, L.L.C.
1100 Crescent Green # 200
Cary NC 27518
919 772-8604

(P-14200)
BE STRUCTURED TECH GROUP INC
Also Called: Bstg
500 S Grand Ave Ste 2200, Los Angeles
(90071-2656)
PHONE..........................323 331-9452
Chad Alan Lauterbach, *CEO*
EMP: 71 EST: 2011
SALES (est): 5.17MM **Privately Held**
Web: www.bestructured.com
SIC: 7379 Computer related consulting
services

(P-14201)
BLYTHECO INC (PA)
530 Technology Dr Ste 100, Irvine
(92618-1350)
PHONE..........................949 583-9500
Stephen P Blythe, *CEO*
Lori Seal, *
EMP: 45 EST: 1980
SALES (est): 9.61MM
SALES (corp-wide): 9.01MM **Privately
Held**
Web: www.blytheco.com
SIC: 7379 7372 7371 Computer related
consulting services; Prepackaged software;
Computer software systems analysis and
design, custom

(P-14202)
BOUGHTS INC
5927 Balfour Ct, Carlsbad (92008-7375)
PHONE..........................619 895-7246
Amir Tafreshi, *Pr*
EMP: 30 EST: 2011
SALES (est): 777.69K **Privately Held**
SIC: 7379 3842 Online services technology
consultants; Respirators

(P-14203)
CALIFRNIA CRTIVE SOLUTIONS INC (PA)
Also Called: CCS Global Tech

13475 Danielson St Ste 230, Poway
(92064-8859)
PHONE..........................458 208-4131
Raminder Singh, *CEO*
EMP: 72 EST: 1997
SALES (est): 24.83MM
SALES (corp-wide): 24.83MM **Privately
Held**
Web: www.ccsglobaltech.com
SIC: 7379 Computer related consulting
services

(P-14204)
CAYLENT INC (PA)
4521 Campus Dr Ste 344, Irvine
(92612-2621)
PHONE..........................800 215-9124
Lori Williams, *CEO*
Valerie Henderson, *Pr*
Jacob Hill, *CFO*
Ginger Siedschlag, *COO*
EMP: 164 EST: 2015
SQ FT: 450
SALES (est): 9.45MM
SALES (corp-wide): 9.45MM **Privately
Held**
Web: www.caylent.com
SIC: 7379 Computer related consulting
services

(P-14205)
CITRIX ONLINE SVC PRVDER GROUP
7414 Hollister Ave, Goleta (93117-2583)
PHONE..........................805 690-6400
EMP: 126 EST: 2015
SALES (est): 782.72K
SALES (corp-wide): 4.38B **Privately Held**
SIC: 7379 Online services technology
consultants
HQ: Cloud Software Group Holdings, Inc.
851 W Cypress Creek Rd
Fort Lauderdale FL 33309
954 267-3000

(P-14206)
CLOUD CREATIONS INC
301 N Lake Ave Ste 600, Pasadena
(91101-5129)
PHONE..........................800 951-7651
Justin Davis, *CEO*
Justin Paul Davis, *
EMP: 74 EST: 2015
SQ FT: 5,000
SALES (est): 2.6MM **Privately Held**
Web: www.cloudcreations.com
SIC: 7379 Computer related consulting
services

(P-14207)
COGNIZANT TRIZETTO
567 San Nicolas Dr Ste 360, Newport
Beach (92660-6500)
PHONE..........................949 719-2200
Jeffrey Margolis, *Mgr*
EMP: 97
SIC: 7379 Computer related consulting
services
HQ: Cognizant Trizetto Software Group, Inc.
9655 Maroon Cir
Englewood CO 80112

(P-14208)
CPUTER INC
Also Called: Ground Force One
2110 Artesia Blvd, Redondo Beach
(90278-3073)
PHONE..........................844 394-1538
Nikolai Nedovodin, *CEO*
EMP: 84 EST: 2013

SALES (est): 1.74MM **Privately Held**
Web: www.cputer.com
SIC: 7379 4119 Computer related consulting
services; Limousine rental, with driver

(P-14209)
CROWDSTRIKE INC
400 Continental Blvd Ste 275, El Segundo
(90245-5073)
PHONE..........................888 512-8906
EMP: 104
SALES (corp-wide): 3.06B **Publicly Held**
Web: www.crowdstrike.com
SIC: 7379 Computer related maintenance
services
HQ: Crowdstrike, Inc.
150 Mathilda Pl Ste 300
Sunnyvale CA 94086

(P-14210)
CROWDSTRIKE INC
15440 Laguna Canyon Rd Ste 250, Irvine
(92618-2142)
PHONE..........................888 512-8906
EMP: 104
SALES (corp-wide): 3.06B **Publicly Held**
Web: www.crowdstrike.com
SIC: 7379 Computer related maintenance
services
HQ: Crowdstrike, Inc.
150 Mathilda Pl Ste 300
Sunnyvale CA 94086

(P-14211)
CROWDSTRIKE INC
15441 Laguna Canyon Rd, Ste 260, Irvine
(92618)
PHONE..........................888 512-8906
EMP: 104
SALES (corp-wide): 3.06B **Publicly Held**
Web: www.crowdstrike.com
SIC: 7379 Computer related maintenance
services
HQ: Crowdstrike, Inc.
150 Mathilda Pl Ste 300
Sunnyvale CA 94086

(P-14212)
DEFENSEWEB TECHNOLOGIES INC
Also Called: Nliven
10188 Telesis Ct Ste 300, San Diego
(92121-4779)
P.O. Box 14601 (40214-0601)
PHONE..........................858 272-8505
EMP: 90
Web: www.transcendinsights.com
SIC: 7379 7371 Computer related consulting
services; Computer software development

(P-14213)
DELTA COMPUTER CONSULTING
25550 Hawthorne Blvd Ste 106, Torrance
(90505-6831)
PHONE..........................310 541-9440
Marzieh Daneshvar, *Pr*
Masih Hakimpour, *
EMP: 180 EST: 1987
SQ FT: 2,000
SALES (est): 8.67MM **Privately Held**
Web: www.deltacci.com
SIC: 7379 Computer related consulting
services

(P-14214)
DRATA INC
4660 La Jolla Village Dr Ste 100, San Diego
(92122-4604)
PHONE..........................858 754-8811
Adam Markowitz, *CEO*

PRODUCTS & SVCS

EMP: 120 **EST:** 2020
SALES (est): 17.65MM **Privately Held**
Web: www.drata.com
SIC: 7379 Online services technology
consultants

(P-14215)
DYNTEK INC (DH)
Also Called: Arctiq
5241 California Ave Ste 150, Irvine
(92617-3215)
PHONE.............................949 271-6700
Paul Kerr, *CEO*
Michael Gullard, *Ch*
Karen S Rosenberger, *CFO*
Kevin O'hare, *Sec*
EMP: 105 **EST:** 1989
SQ FT: 10,250
SALES (est): 58.9MM
SALES (corp-wide): 113.8MM **Privately
Held**
Web: www.arctiq.com
SIC: 7379 Online services technology
consultants
HQ: Arctiq, Inc.
5241 Cal Ave Ste 150
Irvine CA 92617
949 271-6700

(P-14216)
EDGECAST INC
13031 W Jefferson Blvd Ste 900, Los
Angeles (90094-7002)
PHONE.............................310 396-7400
EMP: 501
SALES (est): 57.18MM **Privately Held**
Web: www.yahooinc.com
SIC: 7379 Online services technology
consultants

(P-14217)
ETHERWAN SYSTEMS INC
2301 E Winston Rd, Anaheim (92806-5542)
P.O. Box 1048 (92781-1048)
PHONE.............................714 779-3800
Mitch Yang, *Pr*
▲ **EMP:** 100 **EST:** 1996
SQ FT: 5,000
SALES (est): 9.65MM
SALES (corp-wide): 3.74B **Privately Held**
Web: www.etherwan.com
SIC: 7379 3577 Computer related
maintenance services; Computer peripheral
equipment, nec
HQ: Etherwan Systems, Inc.
8f, No. 2, Alley 6, Lane 235, Baoqiao
Rd.
New Taipei City TAP 23102

(P-14218)
EXOIS INC
Also Called: Datadivider
2567 Ingleton Ave, Carlsbad (92009-3060)
PHONE.............................408 777-6630
Jonathan Clark, *CEO*
John D Clark, *
EMP: 249 **EST:** 2004
SQ FT: 2,000
SALES (est): 1.11MM
SALES (corp-wide): 44.89MM **Privately
Held**
Web: www.exois.com
SIC: 7379 Computer related consulting
services
PA: Sharedlabs, Inc.
6 E Bay St Fl 4
800 960-0149

(P-14219)
FUSIONZONE AUTOMOTIVE INC
1011 Swarthmore Ave Ste T-10, Pacific
Palisades (90272-2552)
PHONE.............................888 576-1136
Brett Sutherlin, *CEO*
Karen Sutherlin, *
Kevin Maloy, *
Steve Greenfield, *
Dick Bradley, *
EMP: 215 **EST:** 2009
SQ FT: 3,000
SALES (est): 411.41K **Privately Held**
Web: www.dealeron.com
SIC: 7379 Computer related consulting
services
PA: Dealeron, Inc.
7361 Calhoun Pl Ste 250

(P-14220)
GDR GROUP INC
3 Park Plz Ste 1700, Irvine (92614-8540)
PHONE.............................949 453-8818
Ellen Dorse, *Prin*
Bruce Greenburg, *
Robert Redwitz, *
Tony S, *
Karen S, *
EMP: 76 **EST:** 1997
SALES (est): 18.19MM **Privately Held**
Web: www.gdrgroup.com
SIC: 7379 Online services technology
consultants

(P-14221)
GEEK SQUAD INC
Also Called: Geek Squad
12989 Park Plaza Dr, Cerritos
(90703-8565)
PHONE.............................562 402-1555
EMP: 88
SALES (corp-wide): 43.45B **Publicly Held**
Web: www.bestbuy.com
SIC: 7379 Computer related consulting
services
HQ: Geek Squad, Inc.
1213 Washington Ave N
Minneapolis MN 55401

(P-14222)
**GENERAL NETWORKS
CORPORATION**
Also Called: Compass365
3524 Ocean View Blvd, Glendale
(91208-1212)
PHONE.............................818 249-1962
Robert Todd Withers, *Pr*
Todd Withers, *
David Horwatt, *
Randall C Wise, *
Cort Baker, *
EMP: 60 **EST:** 1986
SQ FT: 3,600
SALES (est): 11.74MM **Privately Held**
Web: www.gennet.com
SIC: 7379 5045 7372 Computer related
consulting services; Terminals, computer;
Prepackaged software

(P-14223)
IDRIVE INC
Also Called: Ibackup.com
26115 Mureau Rd Ste A, Calabasas
(91302-3179)
PHONE.............................818 594-5972
Raghu Kulkarni, *Prin*
EMP: 70 **EST:** 1995
SALES (est): 12.78MM **Privately Held**
Web: www.idrive.com

SIC: 7379 Computer related maintenance
services

(P-14224)
INFOGEN LABS INC
25350 Magic Mountain Pkwy Ste 300,
Valencia (91355-1356)
PHONE.............................323 816-4813
Sanjeev Kuwadeker, *Pr*
Sid Patti, *
EMP: 70 **EST:** 2017
SALES (est): 4.99MM **Privately Held**
Web: corp.infogen-labs.com
SIC: 7379 Computer related consulting
services
HQ: Ciklum Holding Uk Limited
Lincoln's Inn
London WC2A
203 912-2825

(P-14225)
**INTEGRATED INTERMODAL
SVCS INC**
8600 Banana Ave, Fontana (92335-3033)
PHONE.............................909 355-4100
Greg Philip Stefflre, *Pr*
EMP: 100 **EST:** 1991
SALES (est): 2.23MM **Privately Held**
SIC: 7379 Computer related maintenance
services

(P-14226)
INVISION NETWORKING LLC
333 City Blvd W Ste 1700, Orange
(92868-5905)
PHONE.............................949 309-3441
Justin Johnson, *CEO*
EMP: 135 **EST:** 2006
SALES (est): 1.67MM **Privately Held**
Web: www.invisionnetworking.com
SIC: 7379 Computer related consulting
services

(P-14227)
ITEK SERVICES INC
25501 Arctic Ocean Dr, Lake Forest
(92630-8827)
PHONE.............................949 770-4835
Donald W Rowley, *CEO*
John Curl, *
EMP: 100 **EST:** 2004
SQ FT: 12,000
SALES (est): 11.54MM **Privately Held**
Web: www.itekservices.com
SIC: 7379 Computer related maintenance
services

(P-14228)
KAIZEN SYNDICATE LLC
10413 Magical Waters Ct, Spring Valley
(91978-2037)
PHONE.............................858 309-2028
EMP: 103 **EST:** 2019
SALES (est): 833.95K **Privately Held**
Web: www.kaizensecurity.life
SIC: 7379 5047 Online services technology
consultants; Medical equipment and
supplies

(P-14229)
KINDERSYSTEMS INC
101 State Pl Ste Q, Escondido
(92029-1365)
PHONE.............................760 975-9750
Norbert Haupt, *Pr*
EMP: 70 **EST:** 1996
SALES (est): 11.07MM **Privately Held**
Web: www.kindersystems.com

SIC: 7379 7371 Computer related consulting
services; Computer software systems
analysis and design, custom

(P-14230)
KODELLA LLC
17922 Fitch Ste 200, Irvine (92614-1611)
PHONE.............................844 563-3552
Chris Heath, *CEO*
EMP: 104 **EST:** 2016
SALES (est): 5.96MM **Privately Held**
Web: www.kodella.com
SIC: 7379 8243 Computer related consulting
services; Software training, computer

(P-14231)
KORE1 INC
36 Discovery, Irvine (92618-3751)
PHONE.............................949 706-6990
Brian Hunt, *CEO*
Steven Quarles, *
EMP: 100 **EST:** 2005
SALES (est): 35.75MM **Privately Held**
Web: www.kore1.com
SIC: 7379 Online services technology
consultants

(P-14232)
**LEIDOS GOVERNMENT
SERVICES INC**
500 N Via Val Verde, Montebello
(90640-2358)
PHONE.............................323 721-6979
Nate Sadorian, *Brnch Mgr*
EMP: 145
SIC: 7379 7372 Computer related consulting
services; Prepackaged software
HQ: Leidos Government Services, Inc.
9737 Washingtonian Blvd
Gaithersburg MD 20878
856 486-5156

(P-14233)
**LOGIN CONSULTING SERVICES
INC**
300 Continental Blvd Ste 405, El Segundo
(90245-5042)
PHONE.............................310 607-9091
Elece J Otten, *Pr*
EMP: 75 **EST:** 1996
SQ FT: 3,200
SALES (est): 8.13MM **Privately Held**
Web: www.loginconsult.com
SIC: 7379 Online services technology
consultants

(P-14234)
**MISSION CLOUD SERVICES INC
(PA)**
9350 Wilshire Blvd Ste 203, Beverly Hills
(90212-3204)
PHONE.............................855 647-7466
Simon Anderson, *CEO*
EMP: 104 **EST:** 2017
SALES (est): 28.1MM
SALES (corp-wide): 28.1MM **Privately
Held**
Web: www.missioncloud.com
SIC: 7379 Computer related consulting
services

(P-14235)
NC INTERACTIVE LLC
Also Called: Ncsoft
660 Newport Center Dr Ste 800, Newport
Beach (92660-6409)
PHONE.............................512 623-8700
Songyee Yoon, *Prin*
EMP: 100

SIC: 7379 Computer related consulting services
HQ: Nc Interactive Llc
3180 139th Ave Se Ste 500
Bellevue WA 98005
206 588-7200

(P-14236)
NOWCOM LLC
Also Called: Hankey Group
4751 Wilshire Blvd Ste 115, Los Angeles (90010-3872)
PHONE.........................323 746-6888
Jay Kamdar, Pr
Vimal Kumar Nair, *
EMP: 165 EST: 1996
SQ FT: 4,800
SALES (est): 25.47MM
SALES (corp-wide): 352.68MM Privately Held
Web: www.nowcom.com
SIC: 7379 Online services technology consultants
PA: Hankey Investment Company, Lp
4751 Wlshire Blvd Ste 110
323 692-4008

(P-14237)
ONEHEALTH SOLUTIONS INC
420 Stevens Ave Ste 200, Solana Beach (92075-2078)
PHONE.........................858 947-6333
Bruce Springer, Pr
John Shade, *
Jeff Goe, *
Chuck Mitchell, *
EMP: 133 EST: 2011
SALES (est): 1.61MM Privately Held
SIC: 7379 Online services technology consultants
HQ: Simplywell, Inc.
10670 N Cntl Expy Ste 700
Dallas TX 75231
214 827-4400

(P-14238)
OSI DIGITAL INC (PA)
26745 Malibu Hills Rd, Agoura Hills (91301-5355)
PHONE.........................818 992-2700
Kumar Yamani, CEO
Bob Ree, *
EMP: 40 EST: 1995
SALES (est): 24.49MM Privately Held
Web: www.osidigital.com
SIC: 7379 7372 7371 8741 Online services technology consultants; Application computer software; Computer software development; Management services

(P-14239)
OUTLOOK AMUSEMENTS INC
3746 Foothill Blvd, La Crescenta (91214-1740)
PHONE.........................818 433-3800
Jason Freeland, CEO
Tim Youd, *
Thomas Wszalek, *
Tom Wszalek, *
EMP: 150 EST: 2003
SALES (est): 30.53MM Privately Held
Web: www.outlookamusements.com
SIC: 7379 Online services technology consultants

(P-14240)
OVATION TECH INC
Also Called: L M S
17551 Von Karman Ave, Irvine (92614-6207)

PHONE.........................949 271-0054
Stacey Powell, CEO
Jon Schmidt, *
Jeff Greene, *
Steve Youngblood, *
Minh Vu, *
EMP: 110 EST: 2000
SQ FT: 20,000
SALES (est): 8.74MM Privately Held
Web: www.lmsservice.com
SIC: 7379 Computer related consulting services

(P-14241)
PARTNERS INFORMATION TECH (HQ)
Also Called: Calance
888 S Disneyland Dr Ste 500, Anaheim (92802-1846)
PHONE.........................714 736-4287
Amit Govil, Ch
Bill Darden, *
Asit Govil, *
EMP: 100 EST: 2011
SALES (est): 16.44MM Privately Held
SIC: 7379 Online services technology consultants
PA: Calance Software Private Limited
Sez Unit: Unit No 4, 2nd Floor, Tower 1

(P-14242)
PEGASUS SQUIRE INC
12021 Wilshire Blvd Ste 770, Los Angeles (90025-1206)
PHONE.........................866 208-6837
Scott Cooper, CEO
EMP: 100 EST: 2002
SALES (est): 3.47MM Privately Held
Web: www.pegasussquire.com
SIC: 7379 Computer related consulting services

(P-14243)
POSITIONING UNIVERSAL INC
7071 Convoy Ct Ste 300, San Diego (92111-1023)
PHONE.........................619 639-0235
Mark Wells, CEO
Mark Levey, *
Greg Gower, *
EMP: 76 EST: 2013
SALES (est): 7.77MM Privately Held
Web: www.positioninguniversal.com
SIC: 7379 Computer hardware requirements analysis

(P-14244)
PRAMIRA INC
404 N Berry St, Brea (92821-3104)
PHONE.........................800 678-1169
Omar Houari, CEO
EMP: 125 EST: 2014
SALES (est): 15.53MM Privately Held
Web: www.pramira.com
SIC: 7379 8711 Computer related consulting services; Engineering services

(P-14245)
PRECISEQ INC
11601 Wilshire Blvd Ste 500, Los Angeles (90025-1741)
PHONE.........................310 709-6094
Mark Dorner, Mng Pt
Guy Livneh, *
EMP: 80 EST: 2015
SQ FT: 1,200
SALES (est): 2.46MM Privately Held
SIC: 7379 Computer related consulting services

(P-14246)
PRO-TEK CONSULTING (PA)
21300 Victory Blvd Ste 240, Woodland Hills (91367-7714)
PHONE.........................805 807-5571
Raj Kessireddy, CEO
Divya Reddy Pyreddy, *
EMP: 110 EST: 2010
SQ FT: 2,400
SALES (est): 4.66MM
SALES (corp-wide): 4.66MM Privately Held
Web: www.pro-tekconsulting.com
SIC: 7379 Online services technology consultants

(P-14247)
PROSITES INC
38977 Sky Canyon Dr Ste 200, Murrieta (92563-2682)
PHONE.........................888 932-3644
Jeffry Tobin, Pr
EMP: 152 EST: 2003
SALES (est): 15.59MM Privately Held
Web: www.prosites.com
SIC: 7379 Computer related maintenance services

(P-14248)
SADA SYSTEMS LLC (HQ)
Also Called: Sada
5250 Lankershim Blvd Ste 720, North Hollywood (91601-3188)
PHONE.........................818 766-2400
Tony Safoian, CEO
Annie Safoian, *
Hovig Safoian, *
Matt Lawrence, *
Dana Berg, *
EMP: 105 EST: 2000
SQ FT: 10,503
SALES (est): 26.27MM Publicly Held
Web: www.sada.com
SIC: 7379 Computer related consulting services
PA: Insight Enterprises, Inc.
2701 E Insight Way

(P-14249)
SCIENCE APPLICATIONS INTL CORP
Also Called: Saic Government Solutions
4065 Hancock St, San Diego (92110-5151)
PHONE.........................703 676-4300
EMP: 99
SALES (corp-wide): 7.44B Publicly Held
Web: www.saic.com
SIC: 7379 Computer related consulting services
PA: Science Applications International Corporation
12010 Sunset Hills Rd
703 676-4300

(P-14250)
SENSATA TECHNOLOGIES INC
Also Called: BEI Industrial Encoders
1461 Lawrence Dr, Thousand Oaks (91320-1303)
PHONE.........................805 716-0322
Glenn Avolio, Division Head
EMP: 70
SALES (corp-wide): 4.05B Privately Held
Web: www.sensata.com
SIC: 7379 3827 3663 Computer related maintenance services; Optical instruments and lenses; Radio and t.v. communications equipment
HQ: Sensata Technologies, Inc.
529 Pleasant St

Attleboro MA 02703

(P-14251)
SENTEK CONSULTING INC
Also Called: Sentek Global
2811 Nimitz Blvd Ste G, San Diego (92106-4311)
PHONE.........................619 543-9550
Eric Basu, CEO
Jason Galetti, *
Peter Kuebler, *
EMP: 129 EST: 2001
SALES (est): 15.12MM Privately Held
Web: www.sentekglobal.com
SIC: 7379 Online services technology consultants
HQ: Deloitte Consulting Llp
30 Rockefeller Plz
New York NY 10112
212 492-4000

(P-14252)
SIMULSTAT INCORPORATED
440 Stevens Ave Ste 200, Solana Beach (92075-2059)
PHONE.........................858 546-4337
C Adam Sharp, Pr
EMP: 86 EST: 2001
SALES (est): 3.46MM Privately Held
Web: www.simulstat.com
SIC: 7379 Computer related consulting services

(P-14253)
SOCAL TECHNOLOGIES LLC
1305 Oakdale Ave, El Cajon (92021-8540)
PHONE.........................619 635-1128
Marwa Hasan Farhan, CEO
Saif Farhan, Managing Member
EMP: 23 EST: 2019
SALES (est): 344.62K Privately Held
Web: www.socal-technologies.com
SIC: 7379 1389 1799 1442 Computer related consulting services; Construction, repair, and dismantling services; Construction site cleanup; Construction sand mining

(P-14254)
SOFTWARE MANAGEMENT CONS LLC (HQ)
Also Called: Smci
500 N Brand Blvd, Glendale (91203-1923)
PHONE.........................818 240-3177
Spencer L Karpf, CEO
EMP: 320 EST: 1976
SALES (est): 16.12MM
SALES (corp-wide): 253.48MM Privately Held
Web: www.milestone.tech
SIC: 7379 7361 Computer related consulting services; Placement agencies
PA: Milestone Technologies Inc.
2201 Walnut Ave Ste 290
510 651-2454

(P-14255)
STRATA INFORMATION GROUP INC (PA)
3935 Harney St Ste 203, San Diego (92110-2849)
P.O. Box 16990 (92176)
PHONE.........................619 296-0170
Brent Rhymes, CEO
EMP: 73 EST: 1988
SQ FT: 2,000
SALES (est): 11.81MM
SALES (corp-wide): 11.81MM Privately Held
Web: www.sigcorp.com

SIC: 7379 Online services technology consultants

(P-14256)
STUDIO DESIGNER
1110 N Virgil Ave, Los Angeles (90029-2016)
PHONE.................................310 896-5689
Keith Granet, *CEO*
EMP: 84 EST: 2015
SALES (est): 8.17MM **Privately Held**
Web: www.studiodesigner.com
SIC: 7379 7371 Computer related consulting services; Computer software development and applications

(P-14257)
SYNECTIC SOLUTIONS INC (PA)
Also Called: S S I
771 E Daily Dr Ste 200, Camarillo (93010-0783)
PHONE.................................805 483-4800
Lynn Dines, *Pr*
Toby Doane, *
Joel Dines, *
EMP: 78 EST: 1997
SALES (est): 10.9MM
SALES (corp-wide): 10.9MM **Privately Held**
Web: www.synecticsolutions.com
SIC: 7379 8331 Online services technology consultants; Job training services

(P-14258)
TACTICAL ENGRG & ANALIS INC (PA)
6050 Santo Rd Ste 250, San Diego (92124-6104)
P.O. Box 421425 (92142-1425)
PHONE.................................858 573-9869
Lawrence Massaro, *Pr*
Lawrence Massaro, *VP*
Robert Rosado, *
EMP: 82 EST: 1998
SQ FT: 14,000
SALES (est): 43.44MM
SALES (corp-wide): 43.44MM **Privately Held**
Web: www.tac-eng.com
SIC: 7379 8711 Computer related consulting services; Engineering services

(P-14259)
TAHEEM JOHNSON INC
1237 S Victoria Ave, Oxnard (93035-1292)
PHONE.................................818 835-3785
Taheem M Johnson, *CEO*
EMP: 80 EST: 2021
SALES (est): 1.48MM **Privately Held**
Web: corp.taheemjohnson.com
SIC: 7379 Online services technology consultants

(P-14260)
TENSORIOT INC
625 The City Dr S Ste 485, Orange (92868-4924)
PHONE.................................909 342-2459
Ravikumar Raghunathan, *CEO*
EMP: 100 EST: 2017
SALES (est): 2.23MM **Privately Held**
Web: www.tensoriot.com
SIC: 7379 7371 Computer related consulting services; Computer software development and applications

(P-14261)
TIGERCONNECT INC (PA)
2054 Broadway, Santa Monica (90404-2910)

PHONE.................................310 401-1820
Jeffrey Evans, *CEO*
Sean Whiteley, *COO*
John Friedman, *Dir*
Herbert Madan, *Dir*
EMP: 58 EST: 2010
SALES (est): 20.92MM
SALES (corp-wide): 20.92MM **Privately Held**
Web: www.tigerconnect.com
SIC: 7379 7372 7373 Computer related maintenance services; Publisher's computer software; Computer systems analysis and design

(P-14262)
UNITED STATES TECHNICAL SVCS
Also Called: Usts
16541 Gothard St Ste 214, Huntington Beach (92647-4436)
PHONE.................................714 374-6300
Bob Polk, *Pr*
John Courtney, *
Cynthia Dugger, *
EMP: 122 EST: 1998
SQ FT: 2,500
SALES (est): 8.26MM **Privately Held**
Web: www.usts.com
SIC: 7379 Online services technology consultants

(P-14263)
US DATA MANAGEMENT LLC (PA)
Also Called: Usdm Life Science
535 Chapala St, Santa Barbara (93101-3411)
PHONE.................................888 231-0816
Kevin Brown, *CEO*
Kevin Brown, *Managing Member*
Vega Finucan, *
EMP: 100 EST: 2000
SQ FT: 4,000
SALES (est): 17.75MM
SALES (corp-wide): 17.75MM **Privately Held**
Web: www.akanewmedia.com
SIC: 7379 Computer related consulting services

(P-14264)
VERYS LLC
Also Called: Verys
1251 E Dyer Rd Ste 210, Santa Ana (92705-5660)
PHONE.................................949 423-3295
Christopher B Antonius, *CEO*
Mike Alan Zerkel, *Pr*
EMP: 125 EST: 2012
SQ FT: 15,500
SALES (est): 3.11MM
SALES (corp-wide): 332.34MM **Privately Held**
Web: www.verys.com
SIC: 7379 7371 7372 Online services technology consultants; Computer software development and applications; Application computer software
PA: West Monroe Partners, Llc
311 W Monroe St 14th Fl
312 602-4000

(P-14265)
WE SEE DRAGONS LLC
1100 Glendon Ave Ste 1700, Los Angeles (90024-3588)
PHONE.................................310 361-5700
Zack Zalon, *Mng Pt*
EMP: 105 EST: 2014

SALES (est): 1.47MM **Privately Held**
Web: www.weseedragons.com
SIC: 7379 Computer related maintenance services

7381 Detective And Armored Car Services

(P-14266)
ABM ONSITE SERVICES INC
3337 Michelson Dr Ste Cn7, Irvine (92612-1699)
PHONE.................................949 863-9100
EMP: 939
SALES (corp-wide): 8.1B **Publicly Held**
Web: www.abm.com
SIC: 7381 7521 8711 7349 Security guard service; Automobile parking; Engineering services; Janitorial service, contract basis
HQ: Abm Onsite Services, Inc.
1 Liberty Plz Fl 7
New York NY 10006

(P-14267)
ACCURATE EMPLYMENT SCRNING LLC
Also Called: Cbes
200 Spectrum Center Dr Ste 1100, Irvine (92618-5006)
PHONE.................................847 255-1852
Tim Dowd, *CEO*
EMP: 170 EST: 1991
SALES (est): 8.12MM
SALES (corp-wide): 90.95MM **Privately Held**
SIC: 7381 Private investigator
PA: Accurate Background, Llc
200 Spctrum Ctr Dr Ste 11
800 784-3911

(P-14268)
AEGIS SEC & INVESTIGATIONS INC
10866 Washington Blvd Ste 308, Culver City (90232-3610)
PHONE.................................310 838-2787
Jeffrey Nathaniel Zisner, *CEO*
EMP: 102 EST: 2010
SALES (est): 4.83MM **Privately Held**
Web: www.aegis.com
SIC: 7381 Security guard service

(P-14269)
ALLIED PROTECTION SERVICES INC
Also Called: Armed/Xctive Prtction Armed Un
24303 Berendo Ave, Harbor City (90710-1839)
PHONE.................................310 330-8314
Leon Brooks, *Pr*
EMP: 178 EST: 1999
SALES (est): 7.13MM **Privately Held**
Web: www.alliedprotection.com
SIC: 7381 Security guard service

(P-14270)
AMERICAN EGLE PRTCTIVE SVCS IN
Also Called: American Eagle Protective Svcs
425 W Kelso St, Inglewood (90301-2539)
PHONE.................................310 412-0019
Joelle Fopoussi Epoh, *CEO*
Alma Serrano, *
EMP: 90 EST: 2011
SALES (est): 3.72MM **Privately Held**
Web: www.aeprotectiveservices.com
SIC: 7381 Security guard service

(P-14271)
AMERICAN GUARD SERVICES INC (PA)
1125 W 190th St, Gardena (90248-4303)
PHONE.................................310 645-6200
Sherine Assal, *Pr*
EMP: 400 EST: 1997
SQ FT: 28,000
SALES (est): 97.91MM
SALES (corp-wide): 97.91MM **Privately Held**
Web: www.americanguardservices.com
SIC: 7381 Security guard service

(P-14272)
AMERICAN POWER SEC SVC INC
1451 Rimpau Ave Ste 207, Corona (92879-7522)
PHONE.................................866 974-9994
Mohamed Faty, *Pr*
EMP: 85 EST: 2015
SALES (est): 817.47K **Privately Held**
Web: www.americanpowersecurity.com
SIC: 7381 Security guard service

(P-14273)
AMERICAN PROTECTION GROUP INC (PA)
Also Called: Apg
8741 Van Nuys Blvd Ste 202, Panorama City (91402-2440)
P.O. Box 4518 (91412)
PHONE.................................818 279-2433
Anthony Brown, *Pr*
EMP: 107 EST: 2012
SALES (est): 5.4MM
SALES (corp-wide): 5.4MM **Privately Held**
Web: www.apg-svcs.com
SIC: 7381 5063 7382 Security guard service; Alarm systems, nec; Burglar alarm maintenance and monitoring

(P-14274)
AMERICAN PRTCTIVE SVCS INVSTGT
12471 Balsam Rd, Victorville (92395-9474)
P.O. Box 4640 (91765-0640)
PHONE.................................626 705-8600
Allan Bailey, *Pr*
EMP: 225 EST: 1998
SALES (est): 1.31MM **Privately Held**
SIC: 7381 Security guard service

(P-14275)
ANDREWS INTERNATIONAL INC
Also Called: Vance Executive Protection
11601 Wilshire Blvd Ste 500, Los Angeles (90025-1741)
PHONE.................................310 575-4844
Rocco Barnes, *Dir*
EMP: 454
SALES (corp-wide): 946.48MM **Privately Held**
SIC: 7381 Security guard service
HQ: Andrews International, Inc.
5870 Trinity Pkwy Ste 300
Centreville VA 20120
703 592-1400

(P-14276)
ANDREWS INTERNATIONAL INC (HQ)
455 N Moss St, Burbank (91502-1727)
PHONE.................................818 487-4060
Randy Andrews, *Pr*
Roger Andrews, *
Michael Topf, *

Ty Richmond, *
James Wood, *
EMP: 1700 **EST:** 1986
SQ FT: 5,000
SALES (est): 82.13MM
SALES (corp-wide): 946.48MM **Privately Held**
Web: www.andrewsinternational.com
SIC: 7381 Security guard service
PA: Allied Security Holdings Llc
161 Washington St Ste 600
484 351-1300

(P-14277)
ATI SYSTEMS INTERNATIONAL INC
8807 Complex Dr, San Diego (92123-1403)
PHONE..................858 715-8484
Tony Vasquez, *Brnch Mgr*
EMP: 5023
SALES (corp-wide): 170.74MM **Privately Held**
Web: www.garda.com
SIC: 7381 Detective and armored car services
HQ: Ati Systems International, Inc.
2000 Nw Corp Blvd Ste 101
Boca Raton FL 33431
561 939-7000

(P-14278)
BABYLON SECURITY SERVICES INC
6032 One Half Vineland Ave, North Hollywood (91606)
PHONE..................818 766-8122
Arvin Younan, *Prin*
EMP: 85 **EST:** 1997
SALES (est): 2MM **Privately Held**
Web: www.babylonsecurity.com
SIC: 7381 Security guard service

(P-14279)
BARRYS SECURITY SERVICES INC (PA)
16739 Van Buren Blvd, Riverside (92504-5744)
PHONE..................951 789-7575
Michelle Barry, *CEO*
Martin Morales, *
EMP: 188 **EST:** 1999
SQ FT: 5,000
SALES (est): 5.41MM
SALES (corp-wide): 5.41MM **Privately Held**
Web: www.weguard.biz
SIC: 7381 Security guard service

(P-14280)
BLACK KNIGHT PATROL INC
Also Called: Harbor Area Security Training
505 S Pacific Ave Ste 201, San Pedro (90731-2656)
PHONE..................213 985-6499
Manuel Jimenez, *CEO*
EMP: 70 **EST:** 2015
SALES (est): 9.04MM **Privately Held**
Web: www.blackknightpatrol.com
SIC: 7381 Security guard service

(P-14281)
BOYD AND ASSOCIATES (PA)
2191 E Thompson Blvd, Ventura (93001-3538)
PHONE..................818 752-1888
Raymond G Boyd Senior, *Ch Bd*
Barbara K Boyd, *
Daniel Boyd, *
EMP: 160 **EST:** 1967

SQ FT: 8,000
SALES (est): 14.27MM
SALES (corp-wide): 14.27MM **Privately Held**
Web: www.boydsecurity.com
SIC: 7381 7382 Security guard service; Security systems services

(P-14282)
BRINKS INCORPORATED
Also Called: Brink's
7191 Patterson Dr, Garden Grove (92841-1415)
PHONE..................714 903-9272
Al Kent, *Mgr*
EMP: 120
SALES (corp-wide): 4.87B **Publicly Held**
Web: us.brinks.com
SIC: 7381 Armored car services
HQ: Brink's, Incorporated
1801 Bayberry Ct Ste 400
Richmond VA 23226
804 289-9600

(P-14283)
CALIFRNIA STHLAND PRVATE SEC L
1818 S State College Blvd, Anaheim (92806-6053)
PHONE..................714 367-4005
Alessandro Hickey, *CEO*
Alessandro Hickey, *Managing Member*
Juan Arevalo, *
Joesph Fasano, *
EMP: 200 **EST:** 2019
SALES (est): 3.45MM **Privately Held**
Web: www.californiasouthlandinc.com
SIC: 7381 Security guard service

(P-14284)
CITIGUARD INC
22736 Vanowen St Ste 300, West Hills (91307-2656)
PHONE..................800 613-5903
Sammy Nomir, *Pr*
EMP: 475 **EST:** 2015
SALES (est): 9.67MM **Privately Held**
Web: www.mysecurityguards.com
SIC: 7381 Security guard service

(P-14285)
COMMERCIAL PROTECTIVE SVCS INC
Also Called: CPS Security
17215 Studebaker Rd Ste 205, Cerritos (90703-2523)
PHONE..................310 515-5290
Christopher Coffey, *Pr*
William R Babcock, *
EMP: 1800 **EST:** 1997
SALES (est): 7.82MM **Privately Held**
SIC: 7381 Security guard service

(P-14286)
COMMUNITY PATROL INC
1420 E Edinger Ave Ste 213, Santa Ana (92705-4816)
PHONE..................657 247-4744
Alicia Ledesma, *Owner*
EMP: 90 **EST:** 2019
SALES (est): 2.29MM **Privately Held**
SIC: 7381 Security guard service

(P-14287)
CONSTRUCTION PROTECTIVE SERVICES INC (PA)
Also Called: Commercial Protective Services
436 W Walnut St, Gardena (90248-3137)
PHONE..................800 257-5512

EMP: 700 **EST:** 1992
SALES (est): 24.1MM **Privately Held**
Web: www.garda.com
SIC: 7381 7382 Security guard service; Confinement surveillance systems maintenance and monitoring

(P-14288)
CONTEMPORARY SERVICES CORP (PA)
Also Called: C S C
17101 Superior St, Northridge (91325-1961)
PHONE..................818 885-5150
Damon Zumwalt, *CEO*
Jim Granger, *
▲ **EMP:** 410 **EST:** 1972
SQ FT: 20,000
SALES (est): 98.12MM
SALES (corp-wide): 98.12MM **Privately Held**
Web: www.csc-usa.com
SIC: 7381 Security guard service

(P-14289)
CORNERSTONE PROTECTIVE SVCS
1327 Crenshaw Blvd, Torrance (90501-2432)
PHONE..................888 848-4791
Maxwell Okoh, *Pr*
Maxwell Okoh, *CEO*
EMP: 200 **EST:** 2020
SALES (est): 1.92MM **Privately Held**
Web: www.cornerstoneprotectiveservices.com
SIC: 7381 Security guard service

(P-14290)
COTTRELL PAUL ENTERPRISES LLC (PA)
Also Called: Unique Protective Services
16654 Soledad Canyon Rd Ste 233, Santa Clarita (91387-3217)
PHONE..................661 212-2357
Paul Cottrell, *Managing Member*
EMP: 120 **EST:** 1997
SQ FT: 400
SALES (est): 1.6MM **Privately Held**
SIC: 7381 Security guard service

(P-14291)
CROSSING GUARD COMPANY
10440 Pioneer Blvd Ste 5, Santa Fe Springs (90670-8238)
PHONE..................310 202-8284
EMP: 1762 **EST:** 2011
SALES (est): 441.87K
SALES (corp-wide): 12.42MM **Privately Held**
Web: www.thecrossingguardcompany.com
SIC: 7381 Security guard service
PA: All-City Management Services, Inc.
10440 Pioneer Blvd Ste 5
310 202-8284

(P-14292)
CYPRESS PRIVATE SECURITY LP
9926 Pioneer Blvd Ste 106, Santa Fe Springs (90670-6243)
PHONE..................562 222-4197
Kes Narbutas, *CEO*
EMP: 75
SALES (corp-wide): 12.86B **Privately Held**
Web: www.cypress-security.com
SIC: 7381 Security guard service
HQ: Cypress Private Security, Lp
478 Tehama St

San Francisco CA 94103
866 345-1277

(P-14293)
DAVID SHIELD SECURITY INC
Also Called: Dss
23945 Calabasas Rd Ste 102, Calabasas (91302-1590)
PHONE..................310 849-4950
Athan Bazaz, *Pr*
Snir Warshaziak, *
EMP: 100 **EST:** 2015
SALES (est): 5MM **Privately Held**
Web: www.davidshieldsecurity.com
SIC: 7381 Security guard service

(P-14294)
DIPLOMATIC SECURITY SVCS LLC
7581 Etiwanda Ave, Rancho Cucamonga (91739)
PHONE..................909 463-8409
EMP: 99 **EST:** 2014
SQ FT: 1,500
SALES (est): 784.5K **Privately Held**
SIC: 7381 Security guard service

(P-14295)
DREW CHAIN SECURITY CORP
55 S Raymond Ave Ste 303, Alhambra (91801-7100)
PHONE..................626 457-8626
Kenneth Y Lee, *Pr*
EMP: 71 **EST:** 2004
SQ FT: 800
SALES (est): 2.41MM **Privately Held**
Web: www.drewchain.com
SIC: 7381 Security guard service

(P-14296)
EAGLE EYE SEC SOLUTIONS INC
Also Called: Eess
1045 Bay Blvd Ste B, Chula Vista (91911-1627)
PHONE..................800 372-8142
Juan Francisco Gonzalez, *CEO*
EMP: 100 **EST:** 2013
SQ FT: 7,000
SALES (est): 3.19MM **Privately Held**
Web: www.eagleeyeinternationalprotectiveservices.com
SIC: 7381 Security guard service

(P-14297)
EAGLE SECURITY SERVICES INC
12903 S Normandie Ave, Gardena (90249-2123)
PHONE..................310 642-0050
Mohsen Kamel, *Pr*
EMP: 150 **EST:** 2003
SQ FT: 5,000
SALES (est): 5.11MM **Privately Held**
Web: www.eagless.com
SIC: 7381 Security guard service

(P-14298)
ELITE ENFRCMENT SEC SLTONS INC
29970 Technology Dr Ste 117d, Murrieta (92563-2647)
PHONE..................866 354-8308
Kevin Roncevich, *Brnch Mgr*
EMP: 112
SALES (corp-wide): 1.48MM **Privately Held**

SIC: 7381 Security guard service
PA: Elite Enforcement Security Solutions, Inc.
1290 N Hancock St Ste 101
866 354-8308

(P-14299)
ELITE SHOW SERVICES INC
2878 Camino Del Rio S Ste 260, San Diego (92108-3855)
PHONE.............................619 574-1589
John Kontopuls, *CEO*
John Kontopuls, *Pr*
Gus Kontopuls, *
EMP: 3123 EST: 1995
SALES (est): 31.57MM **Privately Held**
Web: www.elitesecuritystaffing.com
SIC: 7381 Security guard service

(P-14300)
FPK SECURITY INC
Also Called: Fpk Investigaions
28348 Constellation Rd Ste 880, Valencia (91355-5097)
P.O. Box 55597 (91385-0597)
PHONE.............................661 702-9091
Mark David, *CEO*
Robert Esquivel, *
EMP: 365 EST: 2005
SQ FT: 1,200
SALES (est): 13.99MM **Privately Held**
Web: www.fpksecurity.com
SIC: 7381 Security guard service

(P-14301)
GARDA CL WEST INC (HQ)
Also Called: Gcl W
1612 W Pico Blvd, Los Angeles (90015-2410)
PHONE.............................213 383-3611
Stephan Cretier, *Pr*
Chris W Jamroz, *
▲ EMP: 375 EST: 2015
SQ FT: 25,000
SALES (est): 48.1MM
SALES (corp-wide): 437.24MM **Privately Held**
SIC: 7381 Security guard service
PA: Gardaworld Cash Services, Inc.
2000 Nw Corporate Blvd
561 939-7000

(P-14302)
GARDAWORLD
20325 E Walnut Dr N, City Of Industry (91789-2916)
PHONE.............................909 468-2229
EMP: 72
SALES (corp-wide): 28.55MM **Privately Held**
Web: www.garda.com
SIC: 7381 Armored car services
PA: Gardaworld
2000 Nw Corporate Blvd
561 939-7000

(P-14303)
GOLDEN WEST SECURITY
Also Called: Golden West K-9
12502 Van Nuys Blvd Ste 215, Pacoima (91331-1341)
PHONE.............................818 897-5965
Chris Monica, *CEO*
Ralf Santarelli, *Pr*
EMP: 120 EST: 1971
SALES (est): 3.4MM **Privately Held**
Web: www.goldenwestsecurityinc.com
SIC: 7381 Security guard service

(P-14304)
GUARD MANAGEMENT INC
Also Called: G M I
8001 Vickers St, San Diego (92111-1917)
PHONE.............................858 279-8282
Larry Abrams, *Pr*
EMP: 170 EST: 1992
SALES (est): 2.34MM **Privately Held**
Web: www.gmiweb.com
SIC: 7381 Security guard service

(P-14305)
GUARD-SYSTEMS INC
1910 S Archibald Ave Ste M2, Ontario (91761-8502)
PHONE.............................909 947-5400
Patrick Crawford, *Mgr*
EMP: 567
SALES (corp-wide): 4.35MM **Privately Held**
Web: www.guardsystemsinc.com
SIC: 7381 Protective services, guard
PA: Guard-Systems, Inc.
1190 Monterey Pass Rd
626 443-0031

(P-14306)
GUARD-SYSTEMS INC
Also Called: Guard Systems District 1
1190 Monterey Pass Rd, Monterey Park (91754-3690)
PHONE.............................323 881-6715
Theodore Haas, *Owner*
EMP: 568
SALES (corp-wide): 4.35MM **Privately Held**
Web: www.guardsystemsinc.com
SIC: 7381 Security guard service
PA: Guard-Systems, Inc.
1190 Monterey Pass Rd
626 443-0031

(P-14307)
GUARDIAN INTL SOLUTIONS
Also Called: Patrol and Security Services
3415 S Sepulveda Blvd Ste 1100, Los Angeles (90034-7090)
PHONE.............................323 528-6555
Rodney Finnell, *CEO*
EMP: 95 EST: 2017
SALES (est): 5.67MM **Privately Held**
SIC: 7381 Security guard service

(P-14308)
GUARDSMARK LLC (DH)
1551 N Tustin Ave Ste 650, Santa Ana (92705-8664)
PHONE.............................714 619-9700
Steven S Jones, *CEO*
EMP: 99 EST: 2002
SQ FT: 32,107
SALES (est): 195.15MM
SALES (corp-wide): 12.86B **Privately Held**
SIC: 7381 8742 2721 Security guard service; Industry specialist consultants; Periodicals, publishing only
HQ: Universal Protection Service, Lp
450 Exchange
Irvine CA 92602
866 877-1965

(P-14309)
HORSEMEN INC
16911 Algonquin St, Huntington Beach (92649-3812)
PHONE.............................714 847-4243
Patrick Carroll, *Pr*
EMP: 100 EST: 1995
SALES (est): 6.01MM **Privately Held**
Web: www.horsemeninc.com

SIC: 7381 Private investigator

(P-14310)
INTER-CON SECURITY SYSTEMS INC (PA)
210 S De Lacey Ave, Pasadena (91105-2048)
PHONE.............................626 535-2200
Enrique Hernandez Junior, *Ch Bd*
Roland A Hernandez, *
EMP: 20532 EST: 1973
SQ FT: 17,000
SALES (est): 362.19MM
SALES (corp-wide): 362.19MM **Privately Held**
Web: www.icsecurity.com
SIC: 7381 Security guard service

(P-14311)
LANDMARK EVENT STAFFING
4790 Irvine Blvd Ste 105, Irvine (92620-1998)
PHONE.............................714 293-4248
Peter Kranske, *Pr*
EMP: 1259
Web: www.aus.com
SIC: 7381 Security guard service
PA: Landmark Event Staffing Services, Inc.
4131 Harbor Walk Dr

(P-14312)
LANTZ SECURITY SYSTEMS INC
101 N Westlake Blvd Ste 200, Westlake Village (91362-3753)
PHONE.............................805 496-5775
Terry Oestreich, *Mgr*
EMP: 147
Web: www.lantzsecurity.com
SIC: 7381 7382 Security guard service; Security systems services
PA: Lantz Security Systems, Inc.
43440 Sahuayo St

(P-14313)
LAO-HMONG SECURITY AGENCY INC
10682 Trask Ave, Garden Grove (92843-2407)
PHONE.............................714 533-6776
Mouasu Bliaya, *Pr*
George Moua, *
EMP: 100 EST: 1981
SALES (est): 2.41MM **Privately Held**
Web: www.l-hsa.com
SIC: 7381 Security guard service

(P-14314)
LEVEL ONE PROTECTION INC
5861 Pine Ave, Chino Hills (91709-6540)
PHONE.............................949 514-4182
George Aristizabal, *CEO*
EMP: 104 EST: 2016
SALES (est): 5.28MM **Privately Held**
Web: www.leveloneprotection.com
SIC: 7381 Security guard service

(P-14315)
LOCATOR SERVICES INC
Also Called: Able Patrol & Guard
4616 Mission Gorge Pl, San Diego (92120-4133)
PHONE.............................619 229-6100
George Grauer, *Pr*
Diane G Edwards, *
George Grauer Junior, *VP*
Deborah L Kopki, *
EMP: 120 EST: 1964
SQ FT: 4,500
SALES (est): 5.29MM **Privately Held**

Web: www.ablepatrolandguard.com
SIC: 7381 Security guard service

(P-14316)
M & S SECURITY SERVICES INC
Also Called: Westside Security Patrol
2900 L St, Bakersfield (93301-2351)
PHONE.............................661 397-9616
Marvin Fuller Senior, *CEO*
Steve Fuller, *
Darlene Fuller, *
EMP: 100 EST: 1972
SQ FT: 3,000
SALES (est): 5.01MM **Privately Held**
Web: www.mssecurityservices.com
SIC: 7381 7382 1731 Protective services, guard; Security systems services; Fire detection and burglar alarm systems specialization

(P-14317)
MASTER LIGHTNING SEC SOLUTIONS
545 N Mountain Ave Ste 207, Upland (91786-5055)
PHONE.............................626 337-2915
Peter Suaez, *Prin*
EMP: 70 EST: 2011
SALES (est): 3.17MM **Privately Held**
Web: www.mlsscorp.com
SIC: 7381 Security guard service

(P-14318)
MULHOLLAND SEC & PATROL INC
Also Called: Centurion Group, The
11454 San Vicente Blvd, Los Angeles (90049-6208)
PHONE.............................818 755-0202
David Rosenberg, *Pr*
Steven Lemmer, *
Daniel Campbell, *
EMP: 350 EST: 1992
SQ FT: 2,500
SALES (est): 15.72MM **Privately Held**
Web: www.tcgla.com
SIC: 7381 Protective services, guard

(P-14319)
MUTUAL SECURITES INC
807 Camarillo Springs Rd, Camarillo (93012-9463)
P.O. Box 2864 (93011-2864)
PHONE.............................800 750-7862
Mitchell Craig Voss, *Pr*
EMP: 75 EST: 2010
SALES (est): 6.72MM **Privately Held**
Web: www.mutual.group
SIC: 7381 Guard services

(P-14320)
NAFEES MEMON
Also Called: Nafees Mmon Cmmand Intl SEC Sv
6819 Sepulveda Blvd Ste 312, Van Nuys (91405-4464)
PHONE.............................818 997-1666
Nafees Memon, *Owner*
EMP: 90 EST: 2008
SQ FT: 700
SALES (est): 3MM **Privately Held**
Web: www.commandinternational.com
SIC: 7381 Security guard service

(P-14321)
NASTEC INTERNATIONAL INC
23875 Ventura Blvd Ste 204, Calabasas (91302-1420)
PHONE.............................818 222-0355

Shiraya Ben-menahem, *Ex Dir*
Shiraya Honig, *
▼ **EMP:** 100 **EST:** 1994
SQ FT: 3,109
SALES (est): 9.51MM **Privately Held**
Web: www.nastec.com
SIC: 7381 1731 6411 Detective services;
Safety and security specialization;
Inspection and investigation services,
insurance

(P-14322)
NATIONWIDE GUARD SERVICES INC
9327 Fairway View Pl Ste 200, Rancho
Cucamonga (91730-0969)
PHONE.................................909 608-1112
James Woolen, *CEO*
John Woolen, *
EMP: 350 **EST:** 1984
SALES (est): 5.32MM **Privately Held**
Web: www.nwguards.com
SIC: 7381 Security guard service

(P-14323)
NICOLON CORPORATION
165 Castilian Dr, Goleta (93117-3025)
PHONE.................................805 968-1510
EMP: 357
SALES (corp-wide): 600K **Privately Held**
Web: www.tencatego.com
SIC: 7381 Detective and armored car
services
HQ: Nicolon Corporation
365 S Holland Dr
Pendergrass GA 30567
706 693-2226

(P-14324)
NORTH AMRCN SEC INVESTIGATIONS
550 E Carson Plaza Dr Ste 222, Carson
(90746-7371)
PHONE.................................323 634-1911
Kenny Hillman, *Pr*
Arthur Lopez, *
EMP: 100 **EST:** 2004
SQ FT: 6,000
SALES (est): 3.01MM **Privately Held**
Web: www.nasi-pi.com
SIC: 7381 Security guard service

(P-14325)
OFF DUTY OFFICERS INC
2365 La Mirada Dr, Vista (92081-7863)
PHONE.................................888 408-5900
Aram Minasian. *Pr*
Paul Jones, *
Terry Degelder, *
Darren Smith, *
Kevin Hansen, *
EMP: 1300 **EST:** 1993
SQ FT: 4,000
SALES (est): 4.7MM **Privately Held**
Web: www.offdutyofficers.com
SIC: 7381 8742 Security guard service;
Management consulting services

(P-14326)
OLINN SECURITY INCORPORATED
1027 S Palm Canyon Dr, Palm Springs
(92264-8378)
PHONE.................................760 320-5303
Kimberly Olinn, *CEO*
Kimberly S Olinn, *
EMP: 130 **EST:** 1985
SALES (est): 2.48MM **Privately Held**
Web: www.olinnsecurityinc.com

SIC: 7381 Security guard service

(P-14327)
OPSEC SPECIALIZED PROTECTION
Also Called: Opsec Spclized Protecttion Inc
44262 Division St Ste A, Lancaster
(93535-3548)
PHONE.................................661 942-3999
Fred Porras, *Owner*
Jeannie Groff, *
EMP: 99 **EST:** 2001
SALES (est): 4.66MM **Privately Held**
Web: www.opsecpro.com
SIC: 7381 Security guard service

(P-14328)
PACIFIC NATIONAL SECURITY INC
3719 Robertson Blvd, Culver City
(90232-2304)
PHONE.................................310 842-7073
EMP: 225
Web: www.pacificnationalsecurity.com
SIC: 7381 Security guard service

(P-14329)
PICORE BRISTAIN INITIATIVE INC
Also Called: Pbi
23679 Calabasas Rd # 215, Calabasas
(91302-1502)
PHONE.................................818 888-3659
Dana Picore, *CEO*
Gemma Beristain, *
EMP: 100 **EST:** 2010
SQ FT: 3,000
SALES (est): 2.87MM **Privately Held**
SIC: 7381 Security guard service

(P-14330)
PROFESSIONAL SECURITY CONS (PA)
Also Called: Professional Security Cons
11454 San Vicente Blvd 2nd Fl, Los
Angeles (90049-6208)
PHONE.................................310 207-7729
Moshe Alon, *Pr*
Ilene Alon, *
EMP: 100 **EST:** 1985
SALES (est): 25.3MM **Privately Held**
Web: www.pscsite.com
SIC: 7381 7382 Security guard service;
Security systems services

(P-14331)
PROTECT-US
1801 N Bellflower Blvd, Long Beach
(90815-3002)
PHONE.................................714 721-8127
Nadiya Aziz, *Prin*
EMP: 180 **EST:** 2018
SALES (est): 3.94MM **Privately Held**
Web: www.protect.us
SIC: 7381 Security guard service

(P-14332)
REEL SECURITY CALIFORNIA INC
15303 Ventura Blvd Ste 1080, Sherman
Oaks (91403-5800)
PHONE.................................818 928-4737
Mario Inez Ramirez, *CEO*
Bradley Bush, *
EMP: 99 **EST:** 2017
SALES (est): 3.11MM **Privately Held**
Web: www.reelsecurity.com

SIC: 7381 Security guard service

(P-14333)
RICHMAN MANAGEMENT CORPORATION
35400 Bob Hope Dr Ste 107, Rancho
Mirage (92270-1772)
PHONE.................................760 832-8520
EMP: 358
SALES (corp-wide): 168.49K **Privately Held**
Web: www.therichmangroup.com
SIC: 7381 Security guard service
HQ: Richman Management Corporation
7840 Mssion Ctr Ct Ste 10
San Diego CA 92108
619 275-7007

(P-14334)
RICHMAN MANAGEMENT CORPORATION
Also Called: Heritage Security Services
41743 Entp Cir N Ste 209, Temecula
(92590)
PHONE.................................909 296-6189
EMP: 287
SALES (corp-wide): 168.49K **Privately Held**
Web: www.therichmangroup.com
SIC: 7381 Security guard service
HQ: Richman Management Corporation
7840 Mssion Ctr Ct Ste 10
San Diego CA 92108
619 275-7007

(P-14335)
RJN INVESTIGATIONS INC
360 E 1st St Ste 696, Tustin (92780-3211)
P.O. Box 55451 (92517-0451)
PHONE.................................951 686-7638
Robert Nagle, *Pr*
Fred Martino, *
EMP: 80 **EST:** 1992
SALES (est): 2.32MM **Privately Held**
Web: www.rjninv.com
SIC: 7381 Detective agency

(P-14336)
SAFEGUARD ON DEMAND INC
Also Called: Security and Patrol Services
11037 Warner Ave # 297, Fountain Valley
(92708-4007)
PHONE.................................800 640-2327
Ahmad B Nawabi, *CEO*
Ahmad Nawabi, *
EMP: 125 **EST:** 2015
SALES (est): 2.43MM **Privately Held**
Web: www.safeguardondemand.com
SIC: 7381 Security guard service

(P-14337)
SECTRAN SECURITY INCORPORATED (PA)
Also Called: Sectran Armored Truck Service
7633 Industry Ave, Pico Rivera
(90660-4301)
P.O. Box 7267 (90022-0967)
PHONE.................................562 948-1446
Fred Kunik, *Pr*
Irving Barr, *
EMP: 141 **EST:** 1982
SQ FT: 19,736
SALES (est): 17.38MM
SALES (corp-wide): 17.38MM **Privately Held**
Web: www.sectransecurity.com
SIC: 7381 Armored car services

(P-14338)
SECURE NET ALLIANCE
Also Called: Security Company
601 S Glenoaks Blvd Ste 409, Burbank
(91502-2783)
PHONE.................................818 848-4900
Jonathan Kraut, *CEO*
Jonathan Kraut, *Pt*
Levi Quintana, *CEO*
EMP: 85 **EST:** 2007
SALES (est): 3.16MM **Privately Held**
Web: www.securenetprotect.com
SIC: 7381 Security guard service

(P-14339)
SECURITAS SEC SVCS USA INC
Also Called: Western Operations Center
4330 Park Terrace Dr, Westlake Village
(91361-4630)
PHONE.................................818 706-6800
Edie Stafford, *Mgr*
EMP: 350
SALES (corp-wide): 253.67MM **Privately Held**
Web: www.securitasinc.com
SIC: 7381 Security guard service
HQ: Securitas Security Services Usa, Inc.
9 Campus Dr
Parsippany NJ 07054
973 267-5300

(P-14340)
SECURITECH SECURITY SVCS INC
2733 N San Fernando Rd, Los Angeles
(90065-1318)
P.O. Box 65097 (90065-0097)
PHONE.................................213 387-5050
Serge Tachdjian, *Pr*
Adriana Alvarez, *
EMP: 110 **EST:** 1999
SALES (est): 4.19MM **Privately Held**
Web: www.securitechguards.com
SIC: 7381 Security guard service

(P-14341)
SECURITY INDUST SPCIALISTS INC
477 N Oak St, Inglewood (90302-3314)
PHONE.................................323 924-9147
EMP: 984
SALES (corp-wide): 48.26MM **Privately Held**
Web: www.sis.us
SIC: 7381 Detective services
PA: Security Industry Specialists, Inc.
6071 Bristol Pkwy
310 215-5100

(P-14342)
SECURITY INDUST SPCIALISTS INC (PA)
Also Called: SIS
6071 Bristol Pkwy, Culver City
(90230-6601)
PHONE.................................310 215-5100
John Spesak, *CEO*
Tom Seltz, *
Kit Knudsen, *
EMP: 96 **EST:** 1999
SQ FT: 9,000
SALES (est): 48.26MM
SALES (corp-wide): 48.26MM **Privately Held**
Web: www.sis.us
SIC: 7381 5065 Security guard service;
Security control equipment and systems

(P-14343)
SHIELD SECURITY INC (DH)
1551 N Tustin Ave Ste 650, Santa Ana
(92705-8664)
PHONE.....................714 210-1501
Ed Klosterman Junior, *Pr*
Kenneth Klosterman, *
EMP: 300 **EST:** 1964
SQ FT: 5,500
SALES (est): 8.93MM
SALES (corp-wide): 12.86B **Privately Held**
Web: www.clementshieldsecurity.com
SIC: 7381 Security guard service
HQ: Universal Protection Service, Lp
450 Exchange
Irvine CA 92602
866 877-1965

(P-14344)
SHIELD SECURITY INC
265 N Euclid Ave, Upland (91786-6038)
PHONE.....................909 920-1173
Paul Srankowski, *Mgr*
EMP: 322
SALES (corp-wide): 12.86B **Privately Held**
Web: www.clementshieldsecurity.com
SIC: 7381 Security guard service
HQ: Shield Security, Inc.
1551 N Tustin Ave Ste 650
Santa Ana CA 92705
714 210-1501

(P-14345)
SHIELD SECURITY INC
21110 Vanowen St, Canoga Park
(91303-2821)
PHONE.....................818 239-5800
Kenneth Klosterman, *Brnch Mgr*
EMP: 218
SALES (corp-wide): 12.86B **Privately Held**
Web: www.clementshieldsecurity.com
SIC: 7381 Security guard service
HQ: Shield Security, Inc.
1551 N Tustin Ave Ste 650
Santa Ana CA 92705
714 210-1501

(P-14346)
SHIELD SECURITY INC
150 E Wardlow Rd, Long Beach
(90807-4417)
PHONE,.....................562 283-1100
Leo Green, *Mgr*
EMP: 460
SALES (corp-wide): 12.86B **Privately Held**
Web: www.clementshieldsecurity.com
SIC: 7381 Security guard service
HQ: Shield Security, Inc.
1551 N Tustin Ave Ste 650
Santa Ana CA 92705
714 210-1501

(P-14347)
SIGNAL 88 LLC
Also Called: Signal 88
821 S Rockefeller Ave, Ontario
(91761-8119)
PHONE.....................714 713-5306
Mark Anderson, *Brnch Mgr*
EMP: 874
SALES (corp-wide): 25.51MM **Privately Held**
Web: www.teamsignal.com
SIC: 7381 Security guard service
PA: Signal 88, Llc
3880 S 149th St Ste 102
877 498-8494

(P-14348)
SILVINO NIETO
2990 Inland Empire Blvd, Ontario
(91764-4899)
PHONE.....................909 948-0279
Jery Winkfield, *Brnch Mgr*
EMP: 104
Web: www.pacwestsecurity.com
SIC: 7381 Security guard service
PA: Silvino Nieto
3303 Harbor Blvd Ste A103

(P-14349)
SILVINO NIETO
1545 Wilshire Blvd Ste 302, Los Angeles
(90017-4504)
PHONE.....................213 413-3500
Salvador Crespo, *Brnch Mgr*
EMP: 155
Web: www.pacwestsecurity.com
SIC: 7381 Security guard service
PA: Silvino Nieto
3303 Harbor Blvd Ste A103

(P-14350)
SOS SECURITY INCORPORATED
3000 S Robertson Blvd Ste 100, Los
Angeles (90034-3145)
PHONE.....................310 392-9600
Doug Hamilton, *Mgr*
EMP: 133
SALES (corp-wide): 20.58MM **Privately Held**
Web: www.sossecurity.com
SIC: 7381 Security guard service
PA: Sos Security Incorporated
1915 Us Highway 46 Ste 1
973 402-6600

(P-14351)
SOUTHWEST PATROL INC
1800 E Lambert Rd Ste 155, Brea
(92821-4396)
PHONE.....................909 861-1884
TOLL FREE: 800
John Stirn, *Pr*
Richard Stirn, *
EMP: 86 **EST:** 1992
SALES (est): 8.9MM **Privately Held**
Web: www.southwestpatrol.com
SIC: 7381 Security guard service

(P-14352)
SOUTHWEST PROTECTIVE SVCS INC
Also Called: Southwest Security
404 W Heil Ave, El Centro (92243-3328)
P.O. Box 2915 (92244-2915)
PHONE.....................760 996-1285
Jason Jackson, *CEO*
EMP: 250 **EST:** 2015
SALES (est): 4.21MM **Privately Held**
Web: www.southwestsecurity.net
SIC: 7381 Security guard service

(P-14353)
SPECTRUM SECURITY SERVICES INC (PA)
13967 Campo Rd Ste 101, Jamul
(91935-3232)
P.O. Box 744 (91935-0744)
PHONE.....................619 669-6660
Sam Ersan, *Pr*
Porter Erent, *
EMP: 212 **EST:** 1989
SQ FT: 1,200
SALES (est): 2.42MM **Privately Held**
Web:
www.spectrumdetentionservices.com

SIC: 7381 Security guard service

(P-14354)
STAFF PRO INC
675 Convention Way, San Diego
(92101-7805)
PHONE.....................619 544-1774
Mike Hernandez, *Mgr*
EMP: 300
Web: www.staffpro.com
SIC: 7381 Security guard service
PA: Staff Pro Inc.
15272 Newsboy Cir

(P-14355)
STAR PRO SECURITY PATROL INC
3303 Harbor Blvd Ste B3, Costa Mesa
(92626-1517)
PHONE.....................714 617-5056
Sally Covington, *Pr*
EMP: 124 **EST:** 2016
SALES (est): 4.47MM **Privately Held**
Web: www.starprosecurity.com
SIC: 7381 Security guard service

(P-14356)
TRANS-WEST SERVICES INC
8503 Crippen St, Bakersfield (93311-8993)
PHONE.....................661 381-2900
Brooke L Antonioni, *Pr*
Duane Williams, *
Katy Williams, *
EMP: 300 **EST:** 1973
SQ FT: 8,500
SALES (est): 22.58MM **Privately Held**
Web: www.twsecurityservices.com
SIC: 7381 Security guard service

(P-14357)
UNITED FACILITY SOLUTIONS INC
Also Called: Command Gard Srvces Wsa
Srvces
19208 S Vermont Ave Ste 200, Gardena
(90248-4414)
PHONE.....................310 743-3000
Martin Benom, *CEO*
Mark Myers, *Pr*
EMP: 400 **EST:** 2015
SALES (est): 5.43MM **Privately Held**
Web: www.commandguards.com
SIC: 7381 7349 Security guard service;
Janitorial service, contract basis

(P-14358)
UNITED GUARD SECURITY INC
473 E Carnegie Dr Ste 200, San Bernardino
(92408)
PHONE.....................909 402-0754
Ismael Zita, *CEO*
EMP: 128
SALES (corp-wide): 6.36MM **Privately Held**
Web: www.ugssecurity.com
SIC: 7381 Security guard service
PA: United Guard Security Inc.
879 W 190th St Ste 280
800 228-2505

(P-14359)
UNITED GUARD SECURITY INC
1100 W Town And Country Rd Ste 1250,
Orange (92868-4633)
PHONE.....................714 242-4051
Ismael Zita, *CEO*
EMP: 128
SALES (corp-wide): 6.36MM **Privately Held**

Web: www.ugssecurity.com
SIC: 7381 Security guard service
PA: United Guard Security Inc.
879 W 190th St Ste 280
800 228-2505

(P-14360)
UNIVERSAL PROTECTION SVC LP (HQ)
Also Called: Allied Universal Security Svcs
450 Exchange, Irvine (92602-5002)
PHONE.....................866 877-1965
Brian Cescolini, *Pt*
Steve Jones, *Pt*
EMP: 88 **EST:** 2009
SALES (est): 571.19MM
SALES (corp-wide): 12.86B **Privately Held**
Web: www.aus.com
SIC: 7381 Security guard service
PA: Atlas Ontario Lp
4000-199 Bay St
484 351-1586

(P-14361)
UNIVERSAL SERVICES AMERICA LP (HQ)
Also Called: Allied Universal
450 Exchange, Irvine (92602-5002)
PHONE.....................866 877-1965
Steve Jones, *CEO*
EMP: 100 **EST:** 2001
SALES (est): 1.22B
SALES (corp-wide): 12.86B **Privately Held**
Web: www.aus.com
SIC: 7381 7349 Security guard service;
Janitorial service, contract basis
PA: Atlas Ontario Lp
4000-199 Bay St
484 351-1586

(P-14362)
UNIVERSAL SERVICES AMERICA LP
77725 Enfield Ln, Palm Desert
(92211-0468)
PHONE.....................760 200-2865
EMP: 5028
SALES (corp-wide): 12.86B **Privately Held**
Web: www.aus.com
SIC: 7381 Security guard service
HQ: Universal Services Of America, Lp
450 Exchange
Irvine CA 92602
866 877-1965

(P-14363)
US SECURITY ASSOCIATES INC
2275 W 190th St Ste 100, Torrance
(90504-6007)
PHONE.....................714 352-0773
Richard L Wyckoff, *Brnch Mgr*
EMP: 215
SALES (corp-wide): 946.48MM **Privately Held**
Web: www.ussecurityassociates.com
SIC: 7381 Security guard service
HQ: U.S. Security Associates, Inc.
200 Mansell Ct E Fl 5
Roswell GA 30076

(P-14364)
US SECURITY ASSOCIATES INC
Also Called: US Security Associates
455 N Moss St, Burbank (91502-1727)
PHONE.....................818 697-1809
EMP: 215
SALES (corp-wide): 946.48MM **Privately Held**
Web: www.ussecurityassociates.com

▲ = Import ▼ = Export
◆ = Import/Export

SIC: **7381** Security guard service
HQ: U.S. Security Associates, Inc.
200 Mansell Ct E Fl 5
Roswell GA 30076

(P-14365)
VENUE MANAGEMENT SYSTEMS INC
Also Called: V M S
2041 E Gladstone St Ste A, Glendora (91740-5385)
P.O. Box 25 (91773-0025)
PHONE......................626 445-6000
Charles E Mcintyre, *Pr*
EMP: 6000 **EST:** 2001
SQ FT: 35,000
SALES (est): 2.76MM **Privately Held**
Web: www.venueservices.com
SIC: **7381 7363 8742** Detective and armored car services; Employee leasing service; Human resource consulting services

(P-14366)
VESCOM CORPORATION (PA)
1125 W 190th St, Gardena (90248-4303)
PHONE......................207 945-5051
Sherif Assal, *Pr*
Pamela J Treadwell, *
EMP: 622 **EST:** 1986
SALES (est): 9.08MM **Privately Held**
Web: www.vescom.com
SIC: **7381** Security guard service

(P-14367)
VETS SECURING AMERICA INC
1125 W 190th St, Gardena (90248-4303)
PHONE......................310 645-6200
Gerald A Gregory, *Pr*
EMP: 4000 **EST:** 2008
SALES (est): 17.51MM **Privately Held**
Web: www.vetssecuringamerica.com
SIC: **7381** Security guard service

(P-14368)
WHELAN SECURITY CO
400 Continental Blvd, El Segundo (90245-5076)
PHONE......................310 343-8628
Gregory Twardowski, *Brnch Mgr*
EMP: 201
SALES (corp-wide): 170.74MM **Privately Held**
Web: www.garda.com
SIC: **7381** Security guard service
HQ: Whelan Security Co.
1699 S Hanley Rd Ste 350
Saint Louis MO 63144
314 644-3227

(P-14369)
WORLD PRIVATE SECURITY INC
16921 Parthenia St Ste 201, Northridge (91343-4568)
PHONE......................818 894-1800
Fred Youssif, *Pr*
Jeannette Youssif, *
EMP: 200 **EST:** 1997
SALES (est): 3.38MM **Privately Held**
Web: www.worldsecurityinc.com
SIC: **7381** Security guard service

(P-14370)
WORLDWIDE SECURITY ASSOC INC (HQ)
10311 S La Cienega Blvd, Los Angeles (90045-6109)
PHONE......................310 743-3000
EMP: 300 **EST:** 1991
SQ FT: 5,000

SALES (est): 55.12MM **Privately Held**
SIC: **7381** Security guard service
PA: Wsa Group Inc
19208 S Vermont Ave 200

(P-14371)
WSA GROUP INC
19208 S Vermont Ave # 200, Gardena (90248-4414)
PHONE......................310 743-3000
Andres Martinez, *Pr*
James E Bush, *
EMP: 2000 **EST:** 1991
SQ FT: 10,000
SALES (est): 13.23MM **Privately Held**
Web: www.worldseoagency.com
SIC: **7381 7349** Security guard service; Janitorial service, contract basis

---

7382 Security Systems Services

(P-14372)
313 ACQUISITION LLC
1111 Citrus St Ste 1, Riverside (92507-1735)
PHONE......................801 234-6374
Jakob Imig, *Brnch Mgr*
EMP: 4888
SALES (corp-wide): 7.4MM **Privately Held**
SIC: **7382** Security systems services
PA: 313 Acquisition Llc
4931 N 300 W
877 404-4129

(P-14373)
ADT LLC
Also Called: Protection One
1120 Palmyrita Ave Ste 280, Riverside (92507-1709)
PHONE......................951 782-6900
Ray Llewellyn, *Mgr*
EMP: 167
SALES (corp-wide): 4.98B **Publicly Held**
Web: www.adt.com
SIC: **7382 5999 5063 1731** Burglar alarm maintenance and monitoring; Alarm signal systems; Burglar alarm systems; Safety and security specialization
HQ: Adt Llc
1501 Yamato Rd
Boca Raton FL 33431
561 988-3600

(P-14374)
ADT LLC
Also Called: ADT Security Services
1808 Commercenter W Ste E, San Bernardino (92408-3302)
PHONE......................951 824-7205
EMP: 103
SALES (corp-wide): 4.98B **Publicly Held**
Web: www.adt.com
SIC: **7382** Burglar alarm maintenance and monitoring
HQ: Adt Llc
1501 Yamato Rd
Boca Raton FL 33431
561 988-3600

(P-14375)
ADT LLC
731 E Ball Rd, Anaheim (92805-5950)
PHONE......................714 450-6461
EMP: 98
SALES (corp-wide): 4.98B **Publicly Held**
Web: www.adt.com
SIC: **7382** Security systems services
HQ: Adt Llc
1501 Yamato Rd

Boca Raton FL 33431
561 988-3600

(P-14376)
ADT LLC
Also Called: Home Security and HM Ctrl Svcs
475 N Muller St, Anaheim (92801-5452)
PHONE......................626 593-1020
EMP: 150
SALES (corp-wide): 4.98B **Publicly Held**
Web: www.adt.com
SIC: **7382** Burglar alarm maintenance and monitoring
HQ: Adt Llc
1501 Yamato Rd
Boca Raton FL 33431
561 988-3600

(P-14377)
ADT LLC
26074 Avenue Hall Ste 1, Valencia (91355-3444)
PHONE......................818 373-6200
Ron Bogen, *Brnch Mgr*
EMP: 104
SALES (corp-wide): 4.98B **Publicly Held**
Web: www.adt.com
SIC: **7382 5999** Burglar alarm maintenance and monitoring; Alarm and safety equipment stores
HQ: Adt Llc
1501 Yamato Rd
Boca Raton FL 33431
561 988-3600

(P-14378)
ADT LLC
9201 Oakdale Ave Ste 100, Chatsworth (91311-6543)
PHONE......................818 464-5001
EMP: 104
SALES (corp-wide): 4.98B **Publicly Held**
Web: www.adt.com
SIC: **7382** Security systems services
HQ: Adt Llc
1501 Yamato Rd
Boca Raton FL 33431
561 988-3600

(P-14379)
ADVANCED PROTECTION INDS LLC
Also Called: National Monitoring Center
25341 Commercentre Dr, Lake Forest (92630-8856)
PHONE......................800 662-1711
Woodie Andrawos, *Pr*
Todd Shuff, *
Frank Farag, *
EMP: 102 **EST:** 2018
SALES (est): 20.30MM **Privately Held**
Web: www.nmccentral.com
SIC: **7382** Burglar alarm maintenance and monitoring

(P-14380)
AERO PORT SERVICES INC (PA)
216 W Florence Ave, Inglewood (90301-1213)
PHONE......................310 623-8230
Chris Paik, *Pr*
Robert Yim, *
Julie Hong, *
Stephan Park, *
▲ **EMP:** 848 **EST:** 2002
SALES (est): 15.63MM
SALES (corp-wide): 15.63MM **Privately Held**
Web: www.aeroportservices.com

SIC: **7382** Security systems services

(P-14381)
AMERICAN SECURITY FORCE INC
Also Called: Security Services
5430 E Olympic Blvd, Commerce (90022-5113)
PHONE......................323 722-8585
Albert Williams, *CEO*
Albert Williams, *Pr*
EMP: 100 **EST:** 1993
SQ FT: 3,700
SALES (est): 1.52MM **Privately Held**
Web: www.americansecurityforce.com
SIC: **7382 7381** Burglar alarm maintenance and monitoring; Protective services, guard

(P-14382)
ARCULES INC
17875 Von Karman Ave Ste 450, Irvine (92614-6212)
PHONE......................949 439-0053
Andreas Pettersson, *CEO*
Nigel Waterton, *CRO*
EMP: 70 **EST:** 2017
SALES (est): 12.61MM **Privately Held**
Web: www.arcules.com
SIC: **7382** Confinement surveillance systems maintenance and monitoring

(P-14383)
ARECONT VISION COSTAR LLC
1801 Highland Ave, Duarte (91010-2839)
PHONE......................818 937-0700
EMP: 87
Web: www.arecontvision.com
SIC: **7382** Security systems services
HQ: Arecont Vision Costar, Llc
7330 Trade St
San Diego CA 92121
818 937-0700

(P-14384)
AUTONOMOUS DEFENSE TECH CORP
Also Called: Swarm Aero
2889 W 5th St Ste 111, Oxnard (93030-6448)
PHONE......................805 616-2030
Daniel Goodman, *CEO*
Peter Kalogiannis, *
EMP: 32 **EST:** 2022
SALES (est): 5.6MM **Privately Held**
Web: www.swarm.aero
SIC: **7382 7371 3721** Security systems services; Software programming applications; Aircraft

(P-14385)
BOLIDE TECHNOLOGY GROUP INC
Also Called: Bolide International
468 S San Dimas Ave, San Dimas (91773-4045)
PHONE......................909 305-8889
TOLL FREE: 800
David Liu, *Pr*
◆ **EMP:** 70 **EST:** 1994
SQ FT: 16,000
SALES (est): 4.35MM **Privately Held**
Web: www.bolideco.com
SIC: **7382** Security systems services

(P-14386)
BRIGHTCLOUD INC
4370 La Jolla Village Dr Ste 820, San Diego (92122-1277)
PHONE......................858 652-4803

Quinn Curtis, *Pr*
EMP: 219 **EST:** 2005
SALES (est): 1.74MM
SALES (corp-wide): 5.77B **Privately Held**
Web: www.brightcloud.com
SIC: 7382 Security systems services
HQ: Webroot Inc.
385 Interlocken Cres # 800
Broomfield CO 80021
303 442-3813

(P-14387)
CAMSTAR INTERNATIONAL INC
479 Ballena Dr, Diamond Bar (91765-1804)
PHONE.....................909 931-2540
Bingqing Li, *Pr*
◆ **EMP:** 75 **EST:** 2007
SALES (est): 1.41MM **Privately Held**
Web: www.camstarusa.com
SIC: 7382 Security systems services
PA: Yuxin Technology Company
Dayao Village

(P-14388)
CONTEMPORARY SERVICES CORP
369 Van Ness Way Ste 702, Torrance
(90501-6245)
PHONE.....................310 320-8418
Roy Sukimoto, *Brnch Mgr*
EMP: 444
SALES (corp-wide): 98.12MM **Privately Held**
Web: www.csc-usa.com
SIC: 7382 7381 7299 Security systems services; Guard services; Party planning service
PA: Contemporary Services Corporation
17101 Superior St
818 885-5150

(P-14389)
CORPORATE ALNCE STRATEGIES INC
3410 La Sierra Ave Ste F244, Riverside
(92503-5270)
PHONE.....................877 777-7487
Leah L Pinto, *Dir*
Leah Pinto, *
EMP: 115 **EST:** 2015
SALES (est): 3.6MM **Privately Held**
Web:
www.corporatealliancestrategies.com
SIC: 7382 Security systems services

(P-14390)
DARK HORSE SERVICES
12955 Glenoaks Blvd, Sylmar
(91342-4026)
P.O. Box 920801 (91342)
PHONE.....................949 779-0219
Ryan Pugh, *Pr*
Ryan Patrick Pugh, *
James Mckain, *CFO*
EMP: 115 **EST:** 2021
SALES (est): 1.9MM **Privately Held**
SIC: 7382 Security systems services

(P-14391)
DELTA SCIENTIFIC CORPORATION (PA)
40355 Delta Ln, Palmdale (93551-3616)
PHONE.....................661 575-1100
Harry D Dickinson, *CEO*
David Dickinson, *
Richard I Winger, *
Keith Bobrosky, *
◆ **EMP:** 188 **EST:** 1974
SQ FT: 200,000
SALES (est): 24.6MM

SALES (corp-wide): 24.6MM **Privately Held**
Web: www.deltascientific.com
SIC: 7382 Security systems services

(P-14392)
DIAL SECURITY INC (PA)
Also Called: Dial Communications
760 W Ventura Blvd, Camarillo
(93010-8382)
P.O. Box 34781 (20827-0781)
PHONE.....................805 389-6700
William H Dundas, *Pr*
EMP: 250 **EST:** 1974
SQ FT: 12,000
SALES (est): 8.77MM
SALES (corp-wide): 8.77MM **Privately Held**
Web: www.dialcomm.com
SIC: 7382 7381 Protective devices, security; Detective and armored car services

(P-14393)
DTIQ HOLDINGS INC
Also Called: Dtt
1755 N Main St, Los Angeles (90031-2516)
PHONE.....................323 576-1400
Sam Naficy, *CEO*
Jeffrey Moran, *
Thomas M Moran, *
Michael Sutton, *
Adam Watson, *
EMP: 116 **EST:** 2009
SALES (est): 2MM **Privately Held**
Web: www.dtiq.com
SIC: 7382 Confinement surveillance systems maintenance and monitoring

(P-14394)
EASTERNCCTV (USA) LLC
Also Called: Ens Security
525 Parriott Pl W, City Of Industry
(91745-1033)
PHONE.....................626 961-8999
Xianjie Xiong, *Pr*
EMP: 76
SALES (corp-wide): 16.67MM **Privately Held**
Web: www.enssecurity.com
SIC: 7382 Security systems services
PA: Easterncctv (Usa), Llc
50 Commercial St
516 870-3779

(P-14395)
EDGEWORTH INTEGRATION LLC
2360 Shasta Way Ste F, Simi Valley
(93065-1800)
PHONE.....................805 915-0211
EMP: 89
SALES (corp-wide): 8.75MM **Privately Held**
Web: www.edgeworthsecurity.com
SIC: 7382 Security systems services
PA: Edgeworth Integration, Llc
1000 Commerce Dr Fl 2
800 421-9130

(P-14396)
ELITE INTRACTIVE SOLUTIONS INC
1200 W 7th St Ste L1-180, Los Angeles
(90017-6411)
PHONE.....................310 740-5426
Aria Kozak, *Pr*
Jordan Lippel, *Chief Business Development Officer*
John Valdez, *Chief Business Development Officer*

Michael Zatulov, *
EMP: 32 **EST:** 2001
SQ FT: 8,000
SALES (est): 6.74MM **Privately Held**
Web: www.eliteisi.com
SIC: 7382 1731 3629 3669 Burglar alarm maintenance and monitoring; Electrical work ; Electronic generation equipment; Visual communication systems

(P-14397)
EMERGENCY TECHNOLOGIES INC
Also Called: American Two-Way
7345 Varna Ave, North Hollywood
(91605-4009)
PHONE.....................818 765-4421
Christopher Baskin, *CEO*
EMP: 72 **EST:** 1995
SQ FT: 13,000
SALES (est): 5.71MM **Privately Held**
SIC: 7382 Security systems services

(P-14398)
ENTERPRISE SECURITY INC (PA)
Also Called: Enterprise Security Solutions
22860 Savi Ranch Pkwy, Yorba Linda
(92887-4610)
PHONE.....................714 630-9100
Samuel Troy Laughlin, *CEO*
Troy Laughlin, *
Daniel Steiner, *
Joseph Emens, *
EMP: 74 **EST:** 2000
SALES (est): 10.73MM **Privately Held**
Web: www.entersecurity.com
SIC: 7382 3699 3429 6211 Protective devices, security; Security devices; Security cable locking systems; Dealers, security

(P-14399)
EVENT INTELLIGENCE GROUP
4140 Jackson Ave, Culver City
(90232-3234)
PHONE.....................310 237-5375
Allen Cook, *CEO*
EMP: 70 **EST:** 2014
SALES (est): 415.19K **Privately Held**
SIC: 7382 Security systems services
PA: Tourtechsupport, Inc.
1723 Round Rock Dr

(P-14400)
EZVIZ INC
18639 Railroad St, City Of Industry
(91748-1317)
PHONE.....................855 693-9849
Shengyang Jin, *CEO*
Jeffrey He, *
Hsin Lin, *
Yuying Wang, *
EMP: 200 **EST:** 2015
SQ FT: 32,000
SALES (est): 2.53MM **Privately Held**
Web: www.ezviz.com
SIC: 7382 Confinement surveillance systems maintenance and monitoring
HQ: Hikvision Usa Inc.
18639 Railroad St
City Of Industry CA 91748
909 895-0400

(P-14401)
G4S JUSTICE SERVICES LLC
Also Called: G4s Government Services
1290 N Hancock St Ste 103, Anaheim
(92807-1925)
PHONE.....................800 589-6003
EMP: 51 **EST:** 1995

SALES (est): 4.43MM
SALES (corp-wide): 104.73MM **Privately Held**
SIC: 7382 3669 Fire alarm maintenance and monitoring; Emergency alarms
PA: Sentinel Offender Services Llc
1220 N Simon Cir
949 453-1550

(P-14402)
GLARE TECHNOLOGY USA INC
30898 Wealth St, Murrieta (92563-2534)
PHONE.....................909 437-6999
Laith Salih, *CEO*
EMP: 120 **EST:** 2015
SALES (est): 3.96MM **Privately Held**
Web: www.glaretechusa.com
SIC: 7382 Security systems services

(P-14403)
GREATER ALARM COMPANY INC (DH)
3750 Schaufele Ave Ste 200, Long Beach
(90808-1779)
PHONE.....................949 474-0555
TOLL FREE: 800
George De Marco, *Pr*
James De Marco, *
EMP: 71 **EST:** 1981
SQ FT: 11,500
SALES (est): 1.75MM
SALES (corp-wide): 234.6MM **Privately Held**
SIC: 7382 Security systems services
HQ: Interface Security Systems, Llc
1844 Lackland Hill Pkwy
Saint Louis MO 63146
314 595-0100

(P-14404)
GUARDIAN INTEGRATED SEC INC (PA)
Also Called: San Diego Cctv Pros
9701 Topanga Canyon Pl, Chatsworth
(91311-4135)
PHONE.....................800 400-3167
Abraham Ramzan, *CEO*
EMP: 120 **EST:** 2014
SALES (est): 9.47MM
SALES (corp-wide): 9.47MM **Privately Held**
Web:
www.guardianintegratedsecurity.com
SIC: 7382 Security systems services

(P-14405)
HARRISON IYKE
Also Called: Diplomatic Security Services
7611 Etiwanda Ave, Rancho Cucamonga
(91739-9715)
PHONE.....................909 463-8409
EMP: 99
SALES (est): 4.7MM **Privately Held**
SIC: 7382 Security systems services

(P-14406)
HIKVISION USA INC (HQ)
18639 Railroad St, City Of Industry
(91748-1317)
PHONE.....................909 895-0400
Jeffrey He, *CEO*
Ning Tang, *
Tony Yang, *
▲ **EMP:** 120 **EST:** 2007
SALES (est): 44.12MM **Privately Held**
Web: www.hikvision.com
SIC: 7382 Confinement surveillance systems maintenance and monitoring

PA: Hangzhou Hikvision Digital Technology Co., Ltd.
No.518, Wulianwang Street, Binjiang District

(P-14407)

IDENTITY INTLLIGENCE GROUP LLC

Also Called: Idiq
43454 Business Park Dr, Temecula (92590-5530)
PHONE......................626 522-7993
Scott Hermann, *Managing Member*
EMP: 232 **EST:** 2010
SALES (est): 12.55MM **Privately Held**
Web: www.idiq.com
SIC: 7382 Security systems services

(P-14408)

JOHNSON CNTRLS SEC SLTIONS LLC

3870 Murphy Canyon Rd Ste 140, San Diego (92123-4446)
PHONE......................561 988-3600
Greg Pavlicek, *Mgr*
EMP: 100
Web: www.adt.com
SIC: 7382 Burglar alarm maintenance and monitoring
HQ: Johnson Controls Security Solutions Llc
6600 Congress Ave
Boca Raton FL 33487
561 264-2071

(P-14409)

JOHNSON CONTROLS

12728 Shoemaker Ave, Santa Fe Springs (90670-6345)
PHONE......................562 405-3817
Andy Bernot, *Mgr*
EMP: 150
SIC: 7382 1731 1711 Security systems services; Fire detection and burglar alarm systems specialization; Plumbing, heating, air-conditioning
HQ: Johnson Controls Fire Protection Lp
6600 Congress Ave
Boca Raton FL 33487
561 988-7200

(P-14410)

KESA INCORPORATED

Also Called: Constrction Instlltion Mint Gr
960 E Discovery Ln, Anaheim (92801-1149)
PHONE......................714 956-2827
Nancy L Rojo, *Pr*
William B Morrill, *
EMP: 40 **EST:** 2003
SALES (est): 6.42MM **Privately Held**
Web: www.oimgroupinc.com
SIC: 7382 3577 Burglar alarm maintenance and monitoring; Computer peripheral equipment, nec

(P-14411)

KRATOS PUBLIC SAFETY & SECURITY SOLUTIONS INC

4820 Eastgate Mall Ste 200, San Diego (92121-1993)
PHONE......................858 812-7300
EMP: 99
SIC: 7382 Security systems services

(P-14412)

LIFE ALERT EMRGNCY RSPONSE INC (PA)

Also Called: Life Alert
16027 Ventura Blvd Ste 400, Encino (91436-2747)
PHONE......................800 247-0000
Isaac Shepher, *Pr*
Miriam Shepher, *
Felix Leung, *
▲ **EMP:** 175 **EST:** 1987
SQ FT: 29,489
SALES (est): 54.5MM
SALES (corp-wide): 54.5MM **Privately Held**
Web: www.lifealert.com
SIC: 7382 5731 Confinement surveillance systems maintenance and monitoring; Consumer electronic equipment, nec

(P-14413)

LOUROE ELECTRONICS INC

6955 Valjean Ave, Van Nuys (91406-4716)
PHONE......................818 994-6498
Louis Weiss, *Pr*
Richard S Brent, *
Donald Schiffer, *
Pilar Frickey, *
Cameron Javdani, *
▼ **EMP:** 28 **EST:** 1979
SQ FT: 17,000
SALES (est): 6.55MM **Privately Held**
Web: www.louroe.com
SIC: 7382 3651 Burglar alarm maintenance and monitoring; Audio electronic systems

(P-14414)

NAVTRAK LLC

20 Enterprise Ste 100, Aliso Viejo (92656-7104)
PHONE......................410 548-2337
EMP: 97
SIC: 7382 Security systems services

(P-14415)

POST ALARM SYSTEMS (PA)

Also Called: Post Alarm Systems Patrol Svcs
47 E Saint Joseph St, Arcadia (91006-2861)
PHONE......................626 446-7159
William Post, *Pr*
Bill Post, *
Lois Post, *
EMP: 98 **EST:** 1956
SQ FT: 10,500
SALES (est): 12.46MM
SALES (corp-wide): 12.46MM **Privately Held**
Web: www.postalarm.com
SIC: 7382 1731 5063 Burglar alarm maintenance and monitoring; Fire detection and burglar alarm systems specialization; Electrical apparatus and equipment

(P-14416)

REALDEFENSE LLC (PA)

Also Called: PC Cleaner
150 S Los Robles Ave Ste 400, Pasadena (91101-4675)
PHONE......................801 895-7907
Gary Guseinov, *CEO*
Sean Whiteley, *Pr*
EMP: 30 **EST:** 2017
SALES (est): 74.63MM
SALES (corp-wide): 74.63MM **Privately Held**
Web: www.realdefen.se
SIC: 7382 7372 Security systems services; Prepackaged software

(P-14417)

RTI SYSTEMS INC

7635 N San Fernando Rd, Burbank (91505-1073)
PHONE......................213 599-8470
Paul Thompson, *Pr*

EMP: 76 **EST:** 2017
SALES (est): 9.33MM **Privately Held**
Web: www.rtisystems.com
SIC: 7382 Protective devices, security

(P-14418)

SAFESMART ACCESS INC

13238 Florence Ave, Santa Fe Springs (90670-4510)
PHONE......................310 410-1525
EMP: 27 **EST:** 2017
SALES (est): 466.3K **Privately Held**
Web: www.safesmartaccess.com
SIC: 7382 3446 Security systems services; Ornamental metalwork

(P-14419)

SECURITAS TECHNOLOGY CORP

7002 Convoy Ct, San Diego (92111-1017)
PHONE......................858 812-7349
EMP: 99
SALES (corp-wide): 253.67MM **Privately Held**
Web: www.securitastechnology.com
SIC: 7382 Security systems services
HQ: Securitas Technology Corporation
3800 Tabs Dr
Uniontown OH 44685
704 509-0844

(P-14420)

SENTINEL MONITORING CORP (HQ)

220 Technology Dr Ste 200, Irvine (92618-2424)
PHONE......................949 453-1550
Robert Contestabile, *Pr*
EMP: 100 **EST:** 1993
SALES (est): 2.09MM
SALES (corp-wide): 104.73MM **Privately Held**
Web: www.sentinelnet.net
SIC: 7382 Confinement surveillance systems maintenance and monitoring
PA: Sentinel Offender Services Llc
1220 N Simon Cir
949 453-1550

(P-14421)

SENTINEL OFFENDER SERVICES LLC (PA)

1220 N Simon Cir, Anaheim (92806-1854)
PHONE......................949 453-1550
EMP: 85 **EST:** 1993
SALES (est): 104.73MM
SALES (corp-wide): 104.73MM **Privately Held**
Web: www.sentineladvantage.com
SIC: 7382 Confinement surveillance systems maintenance and monitoring

(P-14422)

STAFF PRO INC (PA)

Also Called: Allied Universal Event Svcs
15272 Newsboy Cir, Huntington Beach (92649-1202)
PHONE......................714 230-7200
Cory Meredith, *Pr*
EMP: 700 **EST:** 1987
SALES (est): 32.32MM **Privately Held**
Web: www.staffpro.com
SIC: 7382 8741 Security systems services; Management services

(P-14423)

STAFF PRO INC

Also Called: Allied Universal Services
900 N Broadway, Santa Ana (92701-3452)

PHONE......................323 528-1929
Kerrick Darren Kohn, *Owner*
EMP: 300
SIC: 7382 Security systems services
PA: Staff Pro Inc.
15272 Newsboy Cir

(P-14424)

SYMONS FIRE PROTECTION INC

Also Called: Fire Sprnklr Fire Alarm Dsign
9475 Chesapeake Dr Ste A, San Diego (92123-1337)
PHONE......................619 588-6364
Jamil Shamoon, *Pr*
David Symons, *
EMP: 110 **EST:** 1993
SALES (est): 9.24MM **Privately Held**
Web: www.symonsfp.com
SIC: 7382 1731 8711 7389 Fire alarm maintenance and monitoring; Fire detection and burglar alarm systems specialization; Building construction consultant; Inspection and testing services

(P-14425)

VONNIC INC

16610 Gale Ave, City Of Industry (91745-1801)
PHONE......................626 964-2345
Kim Por Lin, *CEO*
Kitty Lam, *Sec*
▲ **EMP:** 23 **EST:** 2008
SALES (est): 4.57MM **Privately Held**
Web: www.vonnic.com
SIC: 7382 3861 Protective devices, security; Cameras and related equipment

7383 News Syndicates

(P-14426)

BUENA VISTA TELEVISION (DH)

Also Called: Buena Vista TV Advg Sls
500 S Buena Vista St, Burbank (91521-0003)
PHONE......................818 560-1878
Janice Marinelli, *CEO*
Mort Marcus, *
Marsha Reed, *
Jed Cohen, *
Anne L Buettner, *
▲ **EMP:** 129 **EST:** 1985
SALES (est): 20.81MM
SALES (corp-wide): 91.36B **Publicly Held**
Web: www.gargoyles-fans.org
SIC: 7383 News feature syndicate
HQ: Disney Enterprises, Inc.
500 S Buena Vista St
Burbank CA 91521
818 560-1000

(P-14427)

THE COPLEY PRESS INC

Also Called: Copley Newspapers
7776 Ivanhoe Ave, La Jolla (92037-4572)
P.O. Box 1530 (92038-1530)
PHONE......................858 454-0411
EMP: 4170
SIC: 7383 2711 7011 News syndicates; Newspapers, publishing and printing; Resort hotel

7384 Photofinish Laboratories

(P-14428)

COLOREDGE

3520 W Valhalla Dr, Burbank (91505-1126)
PHONE......................818 842-1121

Mike Lannin, *CEO*
EMP: 78 **EST:** 1957
SQ FT: 60,000
SALES (est): 1.11MM **Privately Held**
Web: www.coloredge.com
SIC: 7384 Photofinish laboratories
HQ: Coloredge, Inc.
190 Jony Dr
Carlstadt NJ 07072
212 594-4800

(P-14429)
JAKE HEY INCORPORATED
Also Called: A & I Color Laboratory
257 S Lake St, Burbank (91502-2111)
PHONE.....................323 856-5280
David Alexander, *Pr*
James Ishihara, *
EMP: 144 **EST:** 1978
SQ FT: 16,000
SALES (est): 621.45K **Privately Held**
Web: www.aandibooks.com
SIC: 7384 Photofinishing laboratory

(P-14430)
TECHNICOLOR INC
Also Called: Technicolor Lab
2255 N Ontario St Ste 180, Burbank
(91504-4509)
PHONE.....................818 260-4577
Joe Berchtold, *Pr*
EMP: 400 **EST:** 1966
SALES (est): 9.77MM **Privately Held**
SIC: 7384 Photofinish laboratories

7389 Business Services, Nec

(P-14431)
1111 6TH AVE LLC
1111 6th Ave Ste 102, San Diego
(92101-5214)
PHONE.....................312 283-3683
William Bennett, *Managing Member*
Kayley Dicicco, *Managing Member*
EMP: 75 **EST:** 2019
SALES (est): 1.66MM **Privately Held**
SIC: 7389 Office facilities and secretarial
service rental

(P-14432)
A J PARENT COMPANY INC (PA)
Also Called: Americas Printer.com
6910 Aragon Cir Ste 6, Buena Park
(90620-8103)
PHONE.....................714 521-1100
Arthur Parent, *CEO*
EMP: 88 **EST:** 1997
SALES (est): 3.18MM
SALES (corp-wide): 3.18MM **Privately
Held**
Web: www.americasprinter.com
SIC: 7389 2752 Printers' services: folding,
collating, etc.; Commercial printing,
lithographic

(P-14433)
**AARON THOMAS COMPANY
INC (PA)**
Also Called: Aaron Thomas
7421 Chapman Ave, Garden Grove
(92841-2115)
PHONE.....................714 894-4468
Aerick Bacon, *Pr*
James T Chang, *
Thomas Bacon, *
Jean Chang, *
Linda Bacon, *
▲ **EMP:** 125 **EST:** 1973
SQ FT: 207,000

SALES (est): 48.42MM
SALES (corp-wide): 48.42MM **Privately
Held**
Web: www.packaging.com
SIC: 7389 Packaging and labeling services

(P-14434)
**ABI DOCUMENT SUPPORT
SVCS LLC**
Also Called: ABI Document Support Services
10459 Mountain View Ave Ste E, Loma
Linda (92354-2033)
PHONE.....................909 793-0613
David Benge, *Brnch Mgr*
EMP: 94
Web: www.abidss.com
SIC: 7389 5044 Microfilm recording and
developing service; Office equipment
HQ: Abi Document Support Services, Llc
3534 E Sunshine St Ste L
Springfield MO 65809

(P-14435)
**ADVANSTAR
COMMUNICATIONS INC**
2901 28th St Ste 100, Santa Monica
(90405-2975)
PHONE.....................310 857-7500
Danny Phillips, *Mgr*
EMP: 50
SALES (corp-wide): 3.98B **Privately Held**
Web: epay.advanstar.com
SIC: 7389 2721 7331 Trade show
arrangement; Magazines: publishing only,
not printed on site; Direct mail advertising
services
HQ: Advanstar Communications Inc.
2501 Colorado Ave Ste 280
Santa Monica CA 90404
310 857-7500

(P-14436)
**ADVANSTAR
COMMUNICATIONS INC (DH)**
Also Called: Advanstar Global
2501 Colorado Ave Ste 280, Santa Monica
(90404-3754)
PHONE.....................310 857-7500
◆ **EMP:** 177 **EST:** 1987
SALES (est): 21.62MM
SALES (corp-wide): 3.98B **Privately Held**
Web: epay.advanstar.com
SIC: 7389 2721 7331 Trade show
arrangement; Magazines: publishing only,
not printed on site; Direct mail advertising
services
HQ: Ubm Limited
240 Blackfriars Road
London SE1 8

(P-14437)
**AFFINITY AUTO PROGRAMS
INC**
Also Called: Costco Auto Program
10251 Vista Sorrento Pkwy Ste 300, San
Diego (92121-3769)
PHONE.....................858 643-9324
Jeff Skeen, *Pr*
Gary Drean, *
EMP: 266 **EST:** 1988
SQ FT: 34,000
SALES (est): 3.71MM **Privately Held**
Web: www.costcoauto.com
SIC: 7389 Advertising, promotional, and
trade show services

(P-14438)
**AFM & SG-FTRA INTLLCTUAL
PRPRT**

4705 Laurel Canyon Blvd Ste 400, Valley
Village (91607-5902)
PHONE.....................818 255-7980
Dennis Dreith, *Ex Dir*
Shari Hoffman, *
Jennifer Leblanc, *
EMP: 70 **EST:** 2011
SQ FT: 21,600
SALES (est): 8.07MM **Privately Held**
Web: www.afmsagaftrafund.org
SIC: 7389 Fund raising organizations

(P-14439)
ALL-PRO BAIL BONDS INC
Also Called: All Pro Bail Bonds
530 Hacienda Dr Ste 104d, Vista
(92081-6640)
PHONE.....................760 512-1969
Steffan Gibbs, *Brnch Mgr*
EMP: 100
SALES (corp-wide): 11.67MM **Privately
Held**
Web: www.allprobailbond.com
SIC: 7389 Bail bonding
PA: All-Pro Bail Bonds Inc.
512 Via De La Vlle Ste 30 Valle
858 481-1200

(P-14440)
ALORICA CUSTOMER CARE INC
8885 Rio San Diego Dr Ste 107, San Diego
(92108-1625)
PHONE.....................619 298-7103
EMP: 100
SALES (corp-wide): 845.12MM **Privately
Held**
SIC: 7389 Telemarketing services
HQ: Alorica Customer Care, Inc.
5085 W Park Blvd Ste 300
Plano TX

(P-14441)
ALORICA CUSTOMER CARE INC
5161 California Ave Ste 100, Irvine
(92617-8002)
PHONE.....................941 906-9000
EMP: 175
SALES (corp-wide): 845.12MM **Privately
Held**
Web: www.alorica.com
SIC: 7389 Telemarketing services
HQ: Alorica Customer Care, Inc.
5085 W Park Blvd Ste 300
Plano TX

(P-14442)
ALORICA INC (PA)
5161 California Ave Ste 100, Irvine
(92617-8002)
PHONE.....................866 256-7422
Chris Crowley, *Chief Commercial Officer*
Steve Phillips, *CIO*
Shawn Stacy, *CCO*
▲ **EMP:** 100 **EST:** 1999
SALES (est): 845.12MM
SALES (corp-wide): 845.12MM **Privately
Held**
Web: www.alorica.com
SIC: 7389 Telephone answering service

(P-14443)
ALTEC PRODUCTS INC (PA)
23422 Mill Creek Dr Ste 225, Laguna Hills
(92653-7910)
PHONE.....................949 727-1248
Mark Ford, *CEO*
Brandt Morell, *
Mark Tague, *
Frank Sansone, *
Bill Brown, *

EMP: 79 **EST:** 1985
SQ FT: 12,500
SALES (est): 12.96MM
SALES (corp-wide): 12.96MM **Privately
Held**
Web: doclink.beyond.ai
SIC: 7389 Telemarketing services

(P-14444)
**ALTERNATIVE IRA SERVICES
LLC**
Also Called: Bitcoin Ira
15303 Ventura Blvd Ste 1060, Sherman
Oaks (91403-3100)
PHONE.....................877 936-7175
EMP: 100 **EST:** 2016
SALES (est): 1.67MM **Privately Held**
Web: www.bitcoinira.com
SIC: 7389 Financial services

(P-14445)
**AMERICAN COPAK
CORPORATION**
9175 Eton Ave, Chatsworth (91311-5806)
PHONE.....................818 576-1000
Steven A Brooker, *Pr*
EMP: 150 **EST:** 1987
SQ FT: 150,000
SALES (est): 1.03MM **Privately Held**
Web: www.americancopak.com
SIC: 7389 Packaging and labeling services

(P-14446)
**AMERICAN HEALTH
CONNECTION**
8484 Wilshire Blvd Ste 501, Beverly Hills
(90211-3243)
PHONE.....................424 226-0420
Yuriy Koltyar, *CEO*
Azabeh Williamson, *
EMP: 850 **EST:** 2011
SQ FT: 3,500
SALES (est): 10.16MM **Privately Held**
Web:
www.americanhealthconnection.com
SIC: 7389 Telemarketing services

(P-14447)
AMERICOR FUNDING LLC (PA)
Also Called: Americor Financial
18200 Von Karman Ave Fl 6, Irvine
(92612-1023)
PHONE.....................888 211-2660
Banir Ganatra, *Managing Member*
EMP: 170 **EST:** 2008
SALES (est): 11MM
SALES (corp-wide): 11MM **Privately Held**
Web: www.americor.com
SIC: 7389 Financial services

(P-14448)
AMKOM DESIGN GROUP INC
2598 Fortune Way Ste J, Vista
(92081-8442)
PHONE.....................760 295-1957
Ernest Kasparov, *CEO*
Shlaen Gregory, *
Greg Shlaen, *
Henry Belkin, *
EMP: 25 **EST:** 2016
SALES (est): 1.16MM **Privately Held**
Web: www.amkominc.com
SIC: 7389 3663 Design services; Radio and
t.v. communications equipment

(P-14449)
**ANDREW LAUREN COMPANY
INC**
15225 Alton Pkwy Unit 300, Irvine
(92618-2345)

PHONE.....................949 861-4222
Mark Noonan, *Prin*
EMP: 117
Web: www.andrewlauren.com
SIC: 7389 5713 Interior design services;
Carpets
PA: The Andrew Lauren Company Inc
8909 Kenamar Dr Ste 101

(P-14450)
ANHEUSER-BUSCH LLC
Also Called: Anheuser-Busch
15800 Roscoe Blvd, Van Nuys
(91406-1379)
PHONE.....................805 381-4700
Charles Cindric, *Mgr*
EMP: 232
SALES (corp-wide): 1.7B **Privately Held**
Web: www.budweisertours.com
SIC: 7389 Office facilities and secretarial
service rental
HQ: Anheuser-Busch, Llc
1 Busch Pl
Saint Louis MO 63118
800 342-5283

(P-14451)
ANSWER FINANCIAL INC (HQ)
15910 Ventura Blvd Fl 6, Encino
(91436-2803)
PHONE.....................818 644-4000
Robert J Slingerland, *CEO*
Daniel John Bryce, *
Peter Foley, *
John E Galaviz, *
Craig Lozofsky, *
EMP: 200 **EST:** 2006
SQ FT: 45,000
SALES (est): 15.88MM **Publicly Held**
Web: www.answerfinancial.com
SIC: 7389 6411 Brokers, business: buying
and selling business enterprises; Property
and casualty insurance agent
PA: The Allstate Corporation
3100 Sanders Rd

(P-14452)
ARRIVAL COMMUNICATIONS
INC (DH)
1800 19th St, Bakersfield (93301-4315)
PHONE.....................661 716-2100
Richard Jalkut, *CEO*
Tony Distefano, *
Warren Heffelfinger, *
Geoffrey Whynot, *
David Riordan, *
EMP: 75 **EST:** 1991
SQ FT: 4,000
SALES (est): 965.93K **Privately Held**
Web: www.arrivalcommunications.com
SIC: 7389 Design services
HQ: U.S. Telepacific Corp.
303 Colorado St Ste 2075
Austin TX 78701
877 487-8722

(P-14453)
ARVATO USA LLC
2053 E Jay St, Ontario (91764-1847)
PHONE.....................502 356-8063
Dominik Dittrich, *Brnch Mgr*
EMP: 113
SALES (corp-wide): 54.57MM **Privately
Held**
Web: www.arvato.com
SIC: 7389 Telephone answering service
HQ: Arvato Usa Llc
51 Sawyer Rd Ste 620
Waltham MA 02453
661 702-2700

(P-14454)
ASSOCTED LDSCP DSPLAY
GROUP IN
Also Called: Associated Group
1005 Mateo St, Los Angeles (90021-1715)
PHONE.....................714 558-6100
Laurie Resnick, *Pr*
Greg Salmeri, *
Angelica Arreola Seasonal Display, *Dir*
Angela Hicks, *
EMP: 90 **EST:** 1986
SALES (est): 9MM **Privately Held**
Web: www.ag-ca.com
SIC: 7389 0781 Plant care service;
Landscape services

(P-14455)
AUTOCRIB INC
2882 Dow Ave, Tustin (92780-7258)
PHONE.....................714 274-0400
Stephen Pixley, *CEO*
▲ **EMP:** 150 **EST:** 1999
SQ FT: 58,000
SALES (est): 24.39MM
SALES (corp-wide): 4.73B **Publicly Held**
Web: www.autocrib.com
SIC: 7389 3581 Inventory computing service
; Automatic vending machines
PA: Snap-On Incorporated
2801 80th St
262 656-5200

(P-14456)
AZTECS TELECOM INC
Also Called: Aztecs Telecom
1353 Walker Ln, Corona (92879-1775)
PHONE.....................714 373-1560
Robert Lopez, *CEO*
EMP: 80 **EST:** 2000
SALES (est): 807.33K **Privately Held**
Web: www.aztecs.net
SIC: 7389 1731 Telephone services;
Communications specialization

(P-14457)
B RILEY FINANCIAL INC (PA)
Also Called: B. Riley
11100 Santa Monica Blvd Ste 800, Los
Angeles (90025-3979)
PHONE.....................310 966-1444
Bryant R Riley, *Ch Bd*
Kenneth Young, *Pr*
Phillip J Ahn, *CFO*
Alan N Forman, *Ex VP*
EMP: 89 **EST:** 1973
SALES (est): 1.64B **Publicly Held**
Web: www.brileyfin.com
SIC: 7389 Financial services

(P-14458)
BANKCARD SERVICES (PA)
21281 S Western Ave, Torrance
(90501-2958)
PHONE.....................213 365-1122
EMP: 110 **EST:** 2012
SALES (est): 4.85MM
SALES (corp-wide): 4.85MM **Privately
Held**
Web: www.navyz.com
SIC: 7389 Credit card service

(P-14459)
BANKCARD USA MERCHANT
SRVC
5701 Lindero Canyon Rd, Westlake Village
(91362-4060)
PHONE.....................818 597-7000
Shawn Skelton, *Pr*
Alan Griefer, *

EMP: 85 **EST:** 1993
SQ FT: 20,000
SALES (est): 146.14K **Privately Held**
Web: www.bankcardusa.com
SIC: 7389 Credit card service

(P-14460)
BAXALTA US INC
17511 Armstrong Ave, Irvine (92614-5725)
PHONE.....................949 474-6301
EMP: 202
SIC: 7389 Personal service agents, brokers,
and bureaus
HQ: Baxalta Us Inc.
1200 Lakeside Dr
Bannockburn IL

(P-14461)
BEAUMONT NIELSEN MARINE
INC
2420 Shelter Island Dr, San Diego
(92106-3112)
P.O. Box 6633 (92166-0633)
PHONE.....................619 223-2628
Don Beaumont, *Pr*
Thomas A Nielsen, *
EMP: 29 **EST:** 1979
SALES (est): 3.76MM **Privately Held**
Web: www.nielsenbeaumont.com
SIC: 7389 3732 Repossession service;
Yachts, building and repairing

(P-14462)
BENRICH SERVICE COMPANY
INC (PA)
3190 Airport Loop Dr Ste G, Costa Mesa
(92626-3403)
PHONE.....................714 241-0284
Peter W Bendheim, *Pr*
Redge Henn, *
EMP: 27 **EST:** 1958
SALES (est): 4.33MM
SALES (corp-wide): 4.33MM **Privately
Held**
Web: www.benrichservice.com
SIC: 7389 3433 Water softener service;
Heating equipment, except electric

(P-14463)
BEST SIGNS INC (PA)
1550 S Gene Autry Trl, Palm Springs
(92264-3505)
PHONE.....................760 320-3042
Jesse Cross, *VP*
Jim Cross, *
EMP: 26 **EST:** 1960
SQ FT: 6,000
SALES (est): 5.26MM
SALES (corp-wide): 5.26MM **Privately
Held**
Web: www.bestsignsinc.com
SIC: 7389 3993 1799 Sign painting and
lettering shop; Signs and advertising
specialties; Sign installation and
maintenance

(P-14464)
BOOST MOBILE LLC
6316 Irvine Blvd, Irvine (92620-2102)
PHONE.....................949 451-1563
EMP: 1290
SIC: 7389 Telephone services

(P-14465)
CALIFORNIA TRAFFIC CONTROL
Also Called: California Traffic Ctrl Svcs
3333 Cherry Ave, Long Beach
(90807-4901)
PHONE.....................562 595-7575

Delores Kepl, *CFO*
EMP: 70 **EST:** 2010
SALES (est): 4.49MM **Privately Held**
Web: www.californiatrafficcontrol.com
SIC: 7389 Flagging service (traffic control)

(P-14466)
CALIFRNIA GRNHSE FRM II LTD
PR
17712 Adobe Rd, Bakersfield (93307-9756)
PHONE.....................949 715-3987
Li Hui Lo, *Pr*
EMP: 78 **EST:** 2012
SALES (est): 258.42K **Privately Held**
SIC: 7389 Business Activities at Non-
Commercial Site

(P-14467)
CARDSERVICE INTERNATIONAL
INC (DH)
5898 Condor Dr # 220, Moorpark
(93021-2603)
EMP: 450 **EST:** 2002
SQ FT: 34,000
SALES (est): 9.45MM
SALES (corp-wide): 19.09B **Publicly Held**
SIC: 7389 6153 Credit card service; Short-
term business credit institutions, except
agricultural
HQ: First Data Corporation
600 N Vel R Phillips Ave
Milwaukee WI 53203

(P-14468)
CARECREDIT LLC
555 Anton Blvd Ste 700, Costa Mesa
(92626-7659)
PHONE.....................800 300-3046
EMP: 120 **EST:** 1996
SALES (est): 5.65MM
SALES (corp-wide): 21B **Publicly Held**
Web: www.carecredit.com
SIC: 7389 8742 Financial services; Banking
and finance consultant
PA: Synchrony Financial
777 Long Ridge Rd
203 585-2400

(P-14469)
CAW COWIE INC (PA)
Also Called: Colin Cowie Lifestyle
7 Ginger Root Ln, Rancho Palos Verdes
(90275-5907)
PHONE.....................212 396-9007
Colin Cowie, *CEO*
Stuart Brownstein, *
David Berke, *
EMP: 25 **EST:** 1994
SALES (est): 1.62MM
SALES (corp-wide): 1.62MM **Privately
Held**
Web: www.rsclarkenergy.com
SIC: 7389 7299 5023 2731 Interior design
services; Party planning service; Decorative
home furnishings and supplies; Book
publishing

(P-14470)
CERAMIC DECORATING
COMPANY INC
4651 Sheila St, Commerce (90040-1003)
PHONE.....................323 268-5135
Chad A Johnson, *CEO*
Burnell D Johnson, *
W Allan Johnson, *
Allan Johnson, *
EMP: 50 **EST:** 1934
SQ FT: 30,290
SALES (est): 2.57MM **Privately Held**

Web: www.ceramicdecoratingco.com
SIC: 7389 2396 Labeling bottles, cans, cartons, etc.; Automotive and apparel trimmings

(P-14471)
CETERA FINANCIAL GROUP INC (PA)
655 W Broadway Ste 1680, San Diego (92101-8495)
PHONE..............................866 489-3100
Adam Antoniades, *Pr*
Jeffrey Buchheister, *CFO*
Michael Zuna, *CMO*
Jeannie Finkel, *Chief Human Resource Officer*
EMP: 215 **EST:** 2014
SQ FT: 70,000
SALES (est): 2.44B **Privately Held**
Web: www.cetera.com
SIC: 7389 6282 Financial services; Investment advisory service

(P-14472)
CIRTECH INC
Also Called: Apct Anaheim
250 E Emerson Ave, Orange (92865-3317)
PHONE..............................714 921-0860
Brad Reese, *Pr*
Frank E Reese, *
EMP: 50 **EST:** 1965
SQ FT: 30,000
SALES (est): 6.05MM
SALES (corp-wide): 87.73MM **Privately Held**
Web: www.apct.com
SIC: 7389 3672 Printed circuitry graphic layout; Printed circuit boards
PA: Apct Holdings, Llc
3495 De La Cruz Blvd
408 727-6442

(P-14473)
CLIQ INC
2900 Bristol St Ste F, Costa Mesa (92626-7911)
PHONE..............................714 361-1900
Andrew M Phillips, *Pr*
EMP: 75 **EST:** 2008
SALES (est): 9.83MM **Privately Held**
Web: www.cliq.com
SIC: 7389 Credit card service

(P-14474)
CLOVIS SKILLED CARE LLC
1817 Avenida Del Diablo, Escondido (92029-3112)
PHONE..............................559 299-2591
EMP: 93
SALES (corp-wide): 558.23K **Privately Held**
SIC: 7389 Business Activities at Non-Commercial Site
PA: Clovis Skilled Care Llc
111 Barstow Ave
559 299-2591

(P-14475)
COASTAL INTL HOLDINGS LLC
Also Called: Coastal International
2832 Walnut Ave Ste B, Tustin (92780-7002)
PHONE..............................714 635-1200
Robert Hill, *Brnch Mgr*
EMP: 285
SALES (corp-wide): 3.3MM **Privately Held**
Web: www.coastalintl.com
SIC: 7389 Trade show arrangement
PA: Coastal International Holdings, Llc
3 Harbor Dr

415 339-1700

(P-14476)
CONDUIT LNGAGE SPECIALISTS INC
22720 Ventura Blvd Ste 100, Woodland Hills (91364-1374)
PHONE..............................859 299-3178
Art Mathews, *Brnch Mgr*
EMP: 93
SALES (corp-wide): 776.06K **Privately Held**
Web: www.conduitlanguage.com
SIC: 7389 Translation services
PA: Conduit Language Specialists, Inc.
110 Augusta Way
818 389-4333

(P-14477)
CONSOLDTED FIRE PROTECTION LLC (HQ)
153 Technology Dr Ste 200, Irvine (92618-2461)
PHONE..............................949 727-3277
Keith Fielding, *
Steve Shaffer, *
EMP: 800 **EST:** 1999
SALES (est): 15.05MM **Privately Held**
Web: www.cfpfire.com
SIC: 7389 Fire protection service other than forestry or public
PA: Mx Holdings Us, Inc.
153 Technology Dr Ste 200

(P-14478)
CONTINENTAL EXCH SOLUTIONS INC
Also Called: Ria Financial Services
7001 Village Dr Ste 200, Buena Park (90621-2232)
PHONE..............................562 345-2100
EMP: 70
Web: www.riamoneytransfer.com
SIC: 7389 Financial services
HQ: Dandelion Payments, Inc.
7000 Village Dr Ste 200
Buena Park CA 90621

(P-14479)
CONTRACT LABELING SERVICE INC
13885 Ramona Ave, Chino (91710-5426)
PHONE..............................909 937-0344
Trevor Metcalf, *CEO*
Alexander Riff, *
Carolyn Johnson, *
▲ **EMP:** 48 **EST:** 1992
SALES (est): 4.06MM **Privately Held**
Web: www.contractlabel.com
SIC: 7389 3552 Packaging and labeling services; Silk screens for textile industry

(P-14480)
COUNTRY VILLA SERVICE CORP
39950 Vista Del Sol, Rancho Mirage (92270-3206)
PHONE..............................760 340-0053
Georgeanne Slapper, *Brnch Mgr*
EMP: 102
SALES (corp-wide): 88.5MM **Privately Held**
Web: www.evictionlawyer.com
SIC: 7389 Personal service agents, brokers, and bureaus
PA: Country Villa Service Corp.
2400 E Katella Ave # 800
310 574-3733

(P-14481)
COUNTY OF LOS ANGELES
Also Called: Internal Services Dept
1100 N Eastern Ave, Los Angeles (90063-3200)
PHONE..............................323 267-2771
Linnette Bookman, *Superintnt*
EMP: 81
Web: www.lacounty.gov
SIC: 7389 9631 Telephone services; Communications commission, government
PA: County Of Los Angeles
500 W Temple St Ste 437
213 974-1101

(P-14482)
COUNTY OF SAN DIEGO
Also Called: Public Works
5510 Overland Ave Ste 410, San Diego (92123-1239)
PHONE..............................858 694-2960
Wayne Williams, *Mgr*
EMP: 158
Web: www.sdrp.org
SIC: 7389 Personal service agents, brokers, and bureaus
PA: County Of San Diego
1600 Pacific Hwy Ste 209
619 531-5880

(P-14483)
CREATIVE DESIGN CONSULTANTS (PA)
Also Called: C D C
2915 Red Hill Ave Ste G201, Costa Mesa (92626-5955)
PHONE..............................714 641-4868
Dana Eggerts, *Prin*
Christie Pettus, *Prin*
Julie Ann Stark, *Prin*
Lisa Kells, *Prin*
Cassie Nguyen, *Prin*
EMP: 95 **EST:** 1994
SQ FT: 9,988
SALES (est): 4.77MM
SALES (corp-wide): 4.77MM **Privately Held**
Web: www.cdcdesigns.com
SIC: 7389 Interior designer

(P-14484)
CREDIBILITY CORP
22761 Pacific Coast Hwy, Malibu (90265-5098)
PHONE..............................310 456-8271
EMP: 732
Web: www.credibility.com
SIC: 7389 Financial services

(P-14485)
CREDIT CARD SERVICES INC (PA)
Also Called: Bankcard Services
21281 S Western Ave, Torrance (90501-2958)
PHONE..............................213 365-1122
Patrick S Hong, *CEO*
EMP: 95 **EST:** 1996
SQ FT: 17,000
SALES (est): 8.97MM **Privately Held**
Web: www.navyz.com
SIC: 7389 Credit card service

(P-14486)
DA VINCI SCHOOLS FUND
201 N Douglas St, El Segundo (90245-4637)
PHONE..............................310 725-5800
Matthew Wunder, *Admn*

EMP: 221 **EST:** 2017
SALES (est): 35.36MM **Privately Held**
Web: www.davincischools.org
SIC: 7389 Design services

(P-14487)
DATA COUNCIL LLC
Also Called: Logix3
15310 Barranca Pkwy Ste 100, Irvine (92618-2237)
PHONE..............................904 512-3200
John Kocher, *Pr*
Lloyd Kammerer, *Prin*
EMP: 100 **EST:** 2014
SALES (est): 1.28MM
SALES (corp-wide): 31.31MM **Privately Held**
Web: www.thedatacouncil.com
SIC: 7389 Commodity inspection
PA: Spins, Llc
222 W Hubbard St Ste 300
312 281-5100

(P-14488)
DEKRA-LITE INDUSTRIES INC
Also Called: DI Imaging
3102 W Alton Ave, Santa Ana (92704-6817)
PHONE..............................714 436-0705
Jeffrey Lopez, *CEO*
▲ **EMP:** 80 **EST:** 1987
SQ FT: 30,000
SALES (est): 9.35MM **Privately Held**
Web: www.dekra-lite.com
SIC: 7389 5999 3999 Decoration service for special events; Art, picture frames, and decorations; Advertising curtains

(P-14489)
DF ONE OPERATOR LLC
11 Via Santanella, Rancho Mirage (92270-5817)
PHONE..............................310 961-9739
EMP: 80
SALES (corp-wide): 2.45MM **Privately Held**
SIC: 7389 Personal service agents, brokers, and bureaus
PA: Df One Operator Llc
65441 Two Bunch Palms Trl
605 472-5422

(P-14490)
DIBA FASHIONS INC
472 N Bowling Green Way, Los Angeles (90049-2820)
PHONE..............................323 232-3775
John Gir Daneshrad, *Pr*
Shahin Daneshrad, *
EMP: 70 **EST:** 1980
SQ FT: 22,400
SALES (est): 317.15K **Privately Held**
SIC: 7389 2339 Sewing contractor; Women's and misses' outerwear, nec

(P-14491)
DOCMAGIC INC
Also Called: Document Systems
1800 W 213th St, Torrance (90501-2832)
PHONE..............................800 649-1362
Dominic Iannitti, *Pr*
Alan Brisbane, *Chief of Staff**
Mike Zarrilli, *Operations**
Michael Morford, *OF INTEGRATION SVCS**
Gavin Ales, *Chief Compliance Officer**
EMP: 79 **EST:** 1987
SQ FT: 20,000
SALES (est): 23.12MM **Privately Held**
Web: www.docmagic.com

SIC: 7389 Legal and tax services

(P-14492)
E & C FASHION INC
Also Called: Pacific Concept Laundry
1420 Esperanza St, Los Angeles
(90023-3914)
PHONE..............................323 262-0099
William Moo Han Bae, *CEO*
Maria Bae, *
Elizabeth Bae, *
Claudia Kye, *
▲ EMP: 300 EST: 1989
SALES (est): 3.45MM **Privately Held**
Web: www.atomicdenim.com
SIC: 7389 Sewing contractor

(P-14493)
**EAGLE MED PCKG
STRLIZATION INC**
Also Called: Eagle Med Packg Sterilization
2921 Union Rd Ste A, Paso Robles
(93446-7316)
P.O. Box 1228 (93447-1228)
PHONE..............................805 238-7401
Doyle Timmons, *Pr*
EMP: 35 EST: 1992
SQ FT: 10,000
SALES (est): 2.38MM **Privately Held**
Web: www.eaglemed.com
SIC: 7389 3841 Packaging and labeling
services; Surgical and medical instruments

(P-14494)
FACTER DIRECT LTD
4751 Wilshire Blvd Ste 140, Los Angeles
(90010-3838)
PHONE..............................323 634-1999
Larry Keefer, *Contrlr*
EMP: 252
SALES (corp-wide): 2.19MM **Privately
Held**
SIC: 7389 8742 Telemarketing services;
Marketing consulting services
PA: Facter Direct Ltd
11500 W Olympic Blvd
310 788-9000

(P-14495)
**FLAGSHIP CREDIT
ACCEPTANCE LLC**
7525 Irvine Center Dr, Irvine (92618-3066)
PHONE..............................949 748-7172
EMP: 98
Web: www.flagshipcredit.com
SIC: 7389 Financial services
PA: Flagship Credit Acceptance Llc
3 Christy Dr Ste 203

(P-14496)
FNTECH
3000 W Segerstrom Ave, Santa Ana
(92704-6526)
PHONE..............................714 429-7833
Jeremy Muir, *CEO*
EMP: 91 EST: 2010
SALES (est): 10.16MM **Privately Held**
Web: www.fntech.com
SIC: 7389 Decoration service for special
events

(P-14497)
FREEMAN EXPOSITIONS LLC
Also Called: Freeman
2170 S Towne Centre Pl Ste 100, Anaheim
(92806-6191)
PHONE..............................714 254-3400
Pattie Balding, *Mgr*
EMP: 200

SALES (corp-wide): 1.56B **Privately Held**
Web: www.freeman.com
SIC: 7389 Trade show arrangement
HQ: Freeman Expositions, Llc
1600 Viceroy Dr Ste 100
Dallas TX 75235
214 445-1000

(P-14498)
FREEMAN EXPOSITIONS LLC
Also Called: Freeman Company
2170 S Towne Centre Pl Ste 100, Anaheim
(92806-6191)
PHONE..............................858 320-7800
Tom Robbins, *Genl Mgr*
EMP: 132
SALES (corp-wide): 1.56B **Privately Held**
Web: www.freeman.com
SIC: 7389 Convention and show services
HQ: Freeman Expositions, Llc
1600 Viceroy Dr Ste 100
Dallas TX 75235
214 445-1000

(P-14499)
**FURNITURE FACTORY
HOLDING LLC (HQ)**
11111 Santa Monica Blvd, Los Angeles
(90025-3333)
PHONE..............................918 427-0241
Larry Zigerelli, *Pr*
EMP: 181 EST: 2016
SALES (est): 18.46MM
SALES (corp-wide): 22.12MM **Privately
Held**
SIC: 7389 Personal service agents, brokers,
and bureaus
PA: Furniture Factory Ultimate Holding, Lp
5200 Town Ctr Cir 4th Fl
561 394-0550

(P-14500)
**GELFAND RENNERT &
FELDMAN LLP (DH)**
1880 Century Park E Ste 1600, Los Angeles
(90067-1699)
PHONE..............................310 553-1707
Tyson Beem, *CEO*
EMP: 200 EST: 1967
SALES (est): 9.96MM
SALES (corp-wide): 14.54B **Privately Held**
Web: www.grfllp.com
SIC: 7389 8721 8741 Legal and tax services
; Accounting, auditing, and bookkeeping;
Business management
HQ: Focus Financial Partners Inc.
875 3rd Ave Fl 28
New York NY 10022
646 519-2456

(P-14501)
**GLOBAL CUSTOMER
SERVICES INC**
17373 Lilac St, Hesperia (92345-5162)
PHONE..............................760 995-7949
David Syfrig, *CEO*
Kevin Senart, *
Ernie Bernard, *
Alejandro Joffroy, *
EMP: 100 EST: 2021
SALES (est): 15MM
SALES (corp-wide): 53.94MM **Privately
Held**
Web: www.go-gcs.com
SIC: 7389 Flagging service (traffic control)
PA: Arizona Pipeline Company
17372 Lilac St
760 244-8212

(P-14502)
**GLOBAL EXPRNCE
SPECIALISTS INC**
Also Called: Ges
18504 Beach Blvd Unit 511, Huntington
Beach (92648-0915)
PHONE..............................619 498-6300
Tom Robins, *Mgr*
EMP: 166
Web: www.ges.com
SIC: 7389 Convention and show services
HQ: Global Experience Specialists, Inc.
7000 Lindell Rd
Las Vegas NV 89118
702 515-5500

(P-14503)
**GLOBAL LANGUAGE
SOLUTIONS LLC**
19800 Macarthur Blvd, Irvine (92612-2421)
PHONE..............................949 798-1400
Olga Smirnova, *CEO*
Inna Kassatkina, *
EMP: 100 EST: 1994
SQ FT: 7,500
SALES (est): 825.42K **Privately Held**
SIC: 7389 Translation services
PA: Welocalize, Inc.
136 Madison Ave 6th Fl

(P-14504)
**GOODWILL STHERN LOS
ANGLES CNT (PA)**
Also Called: LINKS SIGN LANGUAGE
INTERPRETI
800 W Pacific Coast Hwy, Long Beach
(90806-5243)
PHONE..............................562 435-3411
Janet Mccarthy, *CEO*
EMP: 100 EST: 1939
SQ FT: 80,000
SALES (est): 33.63MM
SALES (corp-wide): 33.63MM **Privately
Held**
Web: www.linksinterpreting.com
SIC: 7389 8331 5932 Translation services;
Job training and related services; Used
merchandise stores

(P-14505)
GRANDALL DISTRIBUTING LLC
321 El Bonito Ave, Glendale (91204-2707)
PHONE..............................818 242-6640
Jose M Granda, *Pr*
Melisa J Granda, *
Joseph J Granda, *
Jessica J Granda, *
EMP: 30 EST: 1966
SQ FT: 18,000
SALES (est): 2.01MM **Privately Held**
Web: www.grandall.com
SIC: 7389 2844 Cosmetic kits, assembling
and packaging; Cosmetic preparations

(P-14506)
HARINGA INC (PA)
Also Called: Premier Packaging/Assembly
14422 Best Ave, Santa Fe Springs
(90670-5133)
P.O. Box 4707 (90703-4707)
PHONE..............................800 499-9991
Victoria Haringa, *CEO*
Vicki Haringa, *
Randy Haringa, *
▲ EMP: 77 EST: 1991
SQ FT: 200,000
SALES (est): 4.72MM
SALES (corp-wide): 4.72MM **Privately
Held**

Web: www.getwellpsychiatry.com
SIC: 7389 Packaging and labeling services

(P-14507)
HCT PACKAGING INC (PA)
Also Called: Hct Group
2800 28th St Ste 240, Santa Monica
(90405-6214)
PHONE..............................310 260-7680
Tim Thorpe, *Pr*
◆ EMP: 125 EST: 1996
SQ FT: 1,500
SALES (est): 17.17MM
SALES (corp-wide): 17.17MM **Privately
Held**
Web: www.hctgroup.com
SIC: 7389 Packaging and labeling services

(P-14508)
HERITAGE AUCTIONS INC
9478 W Olympic Blvd, Beverly Hills
(90212-4246)
PHONE..............................310 300-8390
Greg Rohan, *Pr*
EMP: 100 EST: 2010
SALES (est): 946.24K **Privately Held**
Web: www.ha.com
SIC: 7389 Auctioneers, fee basis

(P-14509)
HIRSCH/BEDNER INTL INC (PA)
Also Called: Hba International
3216 Nebraska Ave, Santa Monica
(90404-4214)
PHONE..............................310 829-9087
Rene G Kaerskov, *CEO*
Michael J Bedner, *
Howard Pharr, *
Bruce Jones, *
EMP: 70 EST: 1964
SQ FT: 14,000
SALES (est): 21.04MM
SALES (corp-wide): 21.04MM **Privately
Held**
Web: www.hba.com
SIC: 7389 Interior designer

(P-14510)
**HOLLYWOOD SPORTS PARK
LLC**
Also Called: Giant Sportz Paintball Park
9030 Somerset Blvd, Bellflower
(90706-3402)
PHONE..............................562 867-9600
Dennis Bukowski, *Managing Member*
▲ EMP: 100 EST: 1999
SQ FT: 20,000
SALES (est): 2.24MM **Privately Held**
Web: www.hollywoodsports.com
SIC: 7389 Personal service agents, brokers,
and bureaus

(P-14511)
**HUNTER DOUGLAS
FABRICATION CO**
12975 Brookprinter Pl Ste 210, Poway
(92064-8895)
PHONE..............................858 679-7500
TOLL FREE: 800
Bob Madden, *Genl Mgr*
EMP: 70
Web: www.hunterdouglasgroup.com
SIC: 7389 5023 Window trimming service;
Vertical blinds
HQ: Hunter Douglas Fabrication Co
1 Blue Hill Plz Ste 1569
Pearl River NY 10965
845 664-7000

(P-14512)
HYDROPROCESSING ASSOCIATES LLC
Also Called: Hpa-USA
19122 S Santa Fe Ave, Compton (90221-5910)
PHONE...............................310 667-6456
Kees Ooms, *Brnch Mgr*
EMP: 81
SALES (corp-wide): 468.64MM **Privately Held**
Web: www.hpa-usa.com
SIC: 7389 Petroleum refinery inspection service
HQ: Hydroprocessing Associates, Llc
40492 Cannon Rd
Gonzales LA 70737

(P-14513)
INCIRCLE LLC
44000 Winchester Rd, Temecula (92590-2578)
PHONE...............................800 843-7477
EMP: 597 EST: 2018
SALES (est): 198.79K
SALES (corp-wide): 379.23MM **Privately Held**
SIC: 7389 Business Activities at Non-Commercial Site
PA: Fff Enterprises, Inc.
44000 Winchester Rd
951 296-2500

(P-14514)
INDUSTRIAL STITCHTECH INC
520 Library St, San Fernando (91340-2524)
PHONE...............................818 361-6319
Ed Perez, *Pr*
EMP: 150 EST: 1996
SQ FT: 35,000
SALES (est): 2.12MM **Privately Held**
Web: www.industrialstitchtech.com
SIC: 7389 Sewing contractor

(P-14515)
INNOVATION SPECIALTIES
Also Called: Clockparts
11869 Teale St Ste 302, Culver City (90230-7701)
PHONE...............................888 827-2387
EMP: 198
SALES (corp-wide): 28.37MM **Privately Held**
Web: www.clockparts.com
SIC: 7389 Product endorsement service
PA: Innovation Specialties
11869 Teale St
310 398-8116

(P-14516)
INSPECTORATE AMERICA CORP
Also Called: INSPECTORATE AMERICA CORPORATION
3401 Jack Northrop Ave, Hawthorne (90250-4428)
PHONE...............................800 424-0099
EMP: 148
SALES (corp-wide): 339.85MM **Privately Held**
Web: www.bvna.com
SIC: 7389 Petroleum refinery inspection service
HQ: Bureau Veritas Commodities And Trade, Inc.
1300 Hercules Ave Ste 105
Houston TX 77034
713 944-2000

(P-14517)
INTERIOR SPECIALISTS INC
15822 Bernardo Center Dr Ste 1, San Diego (92127-2362)
PHONE...............................909 983-5386
EMP: 300
SALES (corp-wide): 499.75MM **Privately Held**
Web: www.interiorlogicgroup.com
SIC: 7389 Interior designer
HQ: Interior Specialists, Inc.
5830 Granite Pkwy
Plano TX 75024
800 959-8333

(P-14518)
IPAYMENT INC
3325 Wilshire Blvd Ste 535, Los Angeles (90010-1756)
PHONE...............................213 387-1353
Guillermo Ramirez, *Brnch Mgr*
EMP: 190
SALES (corp-wide): 243.26MM **Privately Held**
Web: www.ipaymentinc.com
SIC: 7389 Credit card service
HQ: Ipayment, Inc.
30721 Rssell Rnch Rd Ste
Westlake Village CA 91362
212 802-7200

(P-14519)
ISOVAC ENGINEERING INC
614 Justin Ave, Glendale (91201-2327)
PHONE...............................818 552-6200
George R Neff, *Pr*
EMP: 25 EST: 1957
SALES (est): 2.44MM **Privately Held**
Web: www.isovac.com
SIC: 7389 3825 3829 3826 Inspection and testing services; Semiconductor test equipment; Measuring and controlling devices, nec; Analytical instruments

(P-14520)
JENCO PRODUCTIONS LLC (PA)
401 S J St, San Bernardino (92410-2605)
PHONE...............................909 381-9453
Jennifer Imbriani, *Pr*
◆ EMP: 160 EST: 1995
SQ FT: 50,000
SALES (est): 24.08MM
SALES (corp-wide): 24.08MM **Privately Held**
Web: www.jencoproductions.com
SIC: 7389 2789 2653 7331 Packaging and labeling services; Bookbinding and related work; Boxes, corrugated: made from purchased materials; Mailing service

(P-14521)
JMS INTERIORS INC
10735 Prospect Ave, Santee (92071-4536)
PHONE...............................619 749-5098
James Michael Snyder, *Prin*
EMP: 75 EST: 2016
SALES (est): 3.42MM **Privately Held**
Web: www.jmsinteriorsinc.com
SIC: 7389 Interior design services

(P-14522)
KIRSCHENMAN ENTERPRISES SLS LP
12826 Edison Hwy, Edison (93220)
P.O. Box 27 (93220-0027)
PHONE...............................661 366-5736
Wayde Kirschenman, *Genl Pt*
EMP: 120 EST: 2009
SQ FT: 5,000
SALES (est): 100MM **Privately Held**

Web: www.kirschenman.com
SIC: 7389 Brokers, business: buying and selling business enterprises

(P-14523)
KNOX ATTORNEY SERVICE INC (PA)
Also Called: Knox Services
1550 Hotel Cir N Ste 440, San Diego (92108-2933)
PHONE...............................619 233-9700
Stephen Knox, *Pr*
Steve Knox, *
Robert Porambo, *
James Nemec, *
EMP: 165 EST: 1972
SQ FT: 165,929
SALES (est): 6.91MM
SALES (corp-wide): 6.91MM **Privately Held**
Web: www.knoxservices.com
SIC: 7389 7381 7334 8111 Process serving service; Private investigator; Photocopying and duplicating services; Legal services

(P-14524)
KOOS MANUFACTURING INC
Also Called: Big Star
2741 Seminole Ave, South Gate (90280-5550)
PHONE...............................323 249-1000
U Yul Ku, *CEO*
John Hur, *
Nathan Aroonprapun, *
▲ EMP: 639 EST: 1985
SQ FT: 180,000
SALES (est): 23.78MM **Privately Held**
Web: www.koos.com
SIC: 7389 2325 2339 2369 Sewing contractor; Jeans: men's, youths', and boys'; Jeans: women's, misses', and juniors'; Jeans: girls', children's, and infants'

(P-14525)
KPWR RADIO LLC
9550 Firestone Blvd Ste 105, Downey (90241-5560)
PHONE...............................562 745-2300
Alex Meruelo, *Managing Member*
EMP: 150 EST: 2017
SALES (est): 1.04MM
SALES (corp-wide): 10.73MM **Privately Held**
SIC: 7389 Music and broadcasting services
PA: Meruelo Group Llc
9550 Firestone Blvd # 105
562 745-2300

(P-14526)
LA JOLLA GROUP INC (PA)
Also Called: Ljg
14350 Myford Rd, Irvine (92606-1002)
PHONE...............................949 428-2800
Michael Pratt, *CEO*
▲ EMP: 421 EST: 1993
SALES (est): 38.41MM
SALES (corp-wide): 38.41MM **Privately Held**
Web: www.lajollagroup.com
SIC: 7389 6794 2326 Apparel designers, commercial; Copyright buying and licensing; Men's and boy's work clothing

(P-14527)
LAKEWOOD PARK HEALTH CTR INC (PA)
12023 Lakewood Blvd, Downey (90242-2699)
PHONE...............................562 869-0978
Daniel Zilafro, *Pr*

EMP: 285 EST: 1985
SALES (est): 4.94MM **Privately Held**
Web: www.lwhealthcare.com
SIC: 7389 Personal service agents, brokers, and bureaus

(P-14528)
LENDINGUSA LLC
15303 Ventura Blvd Ste 850, Sherman Oaks (91403-6630)
PHONE...............................800 994-6177
Camilo Concha, *CEO*
Manoj Mathew, *
Johannes Haze, *CMO*
Vale Gardi, *
EMP: 78 EST: 2015
SALES (est): 6.5MM **Privately Held**
Web: www.lendingusa.com
SIC: 7389 Financial services

(P-14529)
LFP ECOMMERCE LLC
210 N Sunset Ave, West Covina (91790-2257)
PHONE...............................314 428-5069
EMP: 74
SALES (corp-wide): 195.15K **Privately Held**
SIC: 7389 Personal service agents, brokers, and bureaus
PA: Lfp Ecommerce, Llc
8484 Wilshire Blvd # 900
323 651-5400

(P-14530)
LINDSEY & SONS
Also Called: Flo-CHI
1226 E 76th St, Los Angeles (90001-2416)
PHONE...............................657 306-5369
Andre Lindsey Senior, *Pr*
EMP: 100 EST: 2021
SALES (est): 366.3K **Privately Held**
SIC: 7389 Business Activities at Non-Commercial Site

(P-14531)
LITIGTION RSRCES OF AMERICA-CA (PA)
Also Called: Legal Enterprise
4232-1 Las Virgenes Rd Ste 100, Calabasas (91302-3589)
PHONE...............................818 878-9227
Tony Maddocks, *Pr*
Rick Matsumoto, *
EMP: 75 EST: 1993
SALES (est): 431.18K **Privately Held**
SIC: 7389 8111 Document storage service; General practice attorney, lawyer

(P-14532)
LIVE NATION ENTERTAINMENT INC (PA)
Also Called: Live Nation
9348 Civic Center Dr Lbby, Beverly Hills (90210-3642)
PHONE...............................310 867-7000
Michael Rapino, *Pr*
Gregory B Maffei, *Non-Executive Chairman of the Board*
Joe Berchtold, *Pr*
Brian Capo, *CAO*
▲ EMP: 200 EST: 2005
SALES (est): 22.75B **Publicly Held**
Web: www.livenation.com
SIC: 7389 7922 7941 Promoters of shows and exhibitions; Entertainment promotion; Sports clubs, managers, and promoters

(P-14533)

LOS ANGELES APPAREL INC

902 E 59th St, Los Angeles (90001-1008)
PHONE....................323 561-8518
EMP: 173
SALES (corp-wide): 33.41MM Privately Held
Web: www.losangelesapparel.net
SIC: 7389 Styling of fashions, apparel, furniture, textiles, etc.
PA: Los Angeles Apparel, Inc.
1020 E 59th St
213 275-3120

(P-14534)

MABIE MARKETING GROUP INC

Also Called: California Marketing
8352 Clairemont Mesa Blvd, San Diego (92111-1302)
P.O. Box 33708 (92163-3708)
PHONE....................858 279-5585
John Mabie, Pr
Ramyar Ravansari, *
EMP: 200 EST: 1984
SALES (est): 7.65MM Privately Held
Web: www.calmarketinggroup.com
SIC: 7389 Telemarketing services

(P-14535)

MACADAMIA HOLDINGS LLC

Also Called: Trellis Chino
5454 Walnut Ave, Chino (91710-2600)
PHONE....................909 465-0246
EMP: 128
SALES (est): 1.59MM
SALES (corp-wide): 3.11B Publicly Held
SIC: 7389 Business services, nec
HQ: California Opco, Llc
100 E San Marcos Blvd
San Marcos CA

(P-14536)

MACRO-PRO INC (PA)

Also Called: Micro-Pro Microfilming Svcs
2400 Grand Ave, Long Beach (90815-1762)
P.O. Box 90459 (90809-0459)
PHONE....................562 595-0900
Patty Waldeck, Pr
EMP: 140 EST: 1988
SQ FT: 24,000
SALES (est): 3.3MM
SALES (corp-wide): 3.3MM Privately Held
Web: www.macropro.com
SIC: 7389 7334 Legal and tax services; Photocopying and duplicating services

(P-14537)

MARINE CORPS UNITED STATES

Also Called: Marine Corps Air Stn Miramar
11 3dmaw, San Diego (92145-0001)
PHONE....................858 307-3434
John D Park, Ofcr
EMP: 257
Web: lejeune.marines.mil
SIC: 7389 Business Activities at Non-Commercial Site
HQ: United States Marine Corps
Branch Hlth Clnic Bldg #5
Beaufort SC 29904

(P-14538)

MARINE TECHNICAL SERVICES INC

Also Called: Dockside Machine & Ship Repair
211 N Marine Ave, Wilmington (90744-5724)
P.O. Box 1301 (90733-1301)
PHONE....................310 549-8030
Dianne Marie Hawke, Pr
▼ EMP: 75 EST: 1989
SQ FT: 20,000
SALES (est): 5.94MM Privately Held
Web: www.marinetechserv.com
SIC: 7389 7699 Crane and aerial lift service; Nautical repair services

(P-14539)

MARINER SYSTEMS INC (PA)

114 C Ave, Coronado (92118-1435)
PHONE....................305 266-7255
Carlos M Collazo, Pr
Carlos M Collazo, Ch Bd
Neil Park, *
EMP: 50 EST: 1982
SALES (est): 2.37MM
SALES (corp-wide): 2.37MM Privately Held
Web: www.carlocksmithcoronado.com
SIC: 7389 7374 7372 7371 Telephone services; Data processing service; Prepackaged software; Custom computer programming services

(P-14540)

MATH HOLDINGS INC (PA)

Also Called: Motivtnal Flfllment Lgstics Sv
15820 Euclid Ave, Chino (91708-9162)
PHONE....................909 517-2200
Hal Altman, CEO
Andrea Stuhley, Ex VP
Anthony Altman, Sr VP
Tony Altman, VP
Jessie Ortiz, VP
▲ EMP: 229 EST: 1977
SQ FT: 300,000
SALES (est): 24.97MM Privately Held
Web: www.mfals.com
SIC: 7389 8748 4225 Telemarketing services ; Business consulting, nec; General warehousing and storage

(P-14541)

MB COATINGS INC

1540 S Lewis St, Anaheim (92805-6423)
PHONE....................714 625-2118
Michael Bartle, Pr
Amanda Bartle, *
EMP: 80 EST: 1996
SALES (est): 4.85MM Privately Held
Web: www.mbcoatings.com
SIC: 7389 Hand painting, textile

(P-14542)

MEDHOLDINGS OF NEWNAN LLC

Also Called: Capitol Records
1750 Vine St, Los Angeles (90028-5209)
PHONE....................213 462-6252
EMP: 1500
Web: www.capitolrecords.com
SIC: 7389 8999 Music and broadcasting services; Music arranging and composing

(P-14543)

MEDUSIND SOLUTIONS INC (PA)

31103 Rancho Viejo Rd Ste 2150, San Juan Capistrano (92675-1759)
PHONE....................949 240-8895
Rajiv Sahney, Ch
Vipul Bansal, *
Robert Beck, *
Dhiren Kapadia, *
Kranti Munje, *
EMP: 80 EST: 2002
SALES (est): 2.87MM
SALES (corp-wide): 2.87MM Privately Held

Web: www.medusind.com
SIC: 7389 Personal service agents, brokers, and bureaus

(P-14544)

MEGA APPRAISERS INC

14724 Ventura Blvd Ste 800, Sherman Oaks (91403-3508)
PHONE....................818 246-7370
Levon Hairapetian, Pr
EMP: 600 EST: 2003
SALES (est): 806.11K Privately Held
Web: www.megaappraisers.com
SIC: 7389 Appraisers, except real estate

(P-14545)

MERCHANT OF TENNIS INC

1625 Proforma Ave, Ontario (91761-7607)
PHONE....................909 923-3388
Larry Khemlani, Prin
EMP: 634
SALES (corp-wide): 342.82MM Privately Held
Web: www.merchantoftennis.com
SIC: 7389 Packaging and labeling services
HQ: The Merchant Of Tennis Inc
8737 Wilshire Blvd
Beverly Hills CA 90211
310 228-4000

(P-14546)

MERIBEAR PRODUCTIONS INC

Also Called: Meredith Baer & Associates
4100 Ardmore Ave, South Gate (90280-3246)
PHONE....................310 204-5353
Meridith Baer, Pr
▲ EMP: 90 EST: 1980
SQ FT: 55,000
SALES (est): 14.97MM Privately Held
Web: www.meridithbaer.com
SIC: 7389 Interior design services

(P-14547)

MERICAL LLC

447 W Freedom Ave, Orange (92865-2644)
PHONE....................714 685-0977
Jeffrey Stallings, Brnch Mgr
EMP: 152
SALES (corp-wide): 207.85MM Privately Held
Web: www.merical.com
SIC: 7389 Packaging and labeling services
HQ: Merical, Llc
2995 E Miraloma Ave
Anaheim CA 92806
714 238-7225

(P-14548)

MERICAL LLC

Also Called: Merical/Vita-Pak
233 E Bristol Ln, Orange (92865-2715)
PHONE....................714 283-9551
EMP: 216
SALES (corp-wide): 207.85MM Privately Held
Web: www.merical.com
SIC: 7389 Packaging and labeling services
HQ: Merical, Llc
2995 E Miraloma Ave
Anaheim CA 92806
714 238-7225

(P-14549)

MERICAL LLC

445 W Freedom Ave, Orange (92865-2644)
PHONE....................714 238-7225
Roshni Patel, Mgr
EMP: 137
SALES (corp-wide): 207.85MM Privately Held

Web: www.merical.com
SIC: 7389 Packaging and labeling services
HQ: Merical, Llc
2995 E Miraloma Ave
Anaheim CA 92806
714 238-7225

(P-14550)

METROPOLITAN IMPORTS LLC

19560 Eagle Ridge Ln, Porter Ranch (91326-3878)
PHONE....................646 980-5343
Starr King Williams Iii, Managing Member
EMP: 144 EST: 2014
SALES (est): 52MM Privately Held
Web: www.metropolitanimports.com
SIC: 7389 7999 Yacht brokers; Pleasure boat rental

(P-14551)

MKTG INC

Also Called: MKTG, INC.
5800 Bristol Pkwy Ste 500, Culver City (90230-6899)
PHONE....................310 972-7900
Patty Hubbard, Brnch Mgr
EMP: 1364
Web: www.mktg.com
SIC: 7389 Advertising, promotional, and trade show services
HQ: 'mktg, Inc.'
150 E 42nd St 14th Fl
New York NY 10017

(P-14552)

MODERN DEV CO A LTD PARTNR

Also Called: Paramount Swap Meet
7900 All America City Way, Paramount (90723-3400)
PHONE....................949 646-6400
Darren Kurkowski, Brnch Mgr
EMP: 79
SALES (corp-wide): 11.22MM Privately Held
Web: www.paramountswap.com
SIC: 7389 Flea market
PA: Modern Development Co, A Limited Partnership
496 N Coast Hwy Ste A
949 646-6400

(P-14553)

MOSS & ASSOCIATES LLC

100 Wonsan Dr, Oceanside (92058-8208)
PHONE....................760 385-4535
EMP: 155
SALES (corp-wide): 565.39MM Privately Held
Web: www.moss.com
SIC: 7309 6531 Appraisers, except real estate; Appraiser, real estate
PA: Moss & Associates, Llc
2101 N Andrews Ave
954 524-5678

(P-14554)

MVENTIX INC (PA)

Also Called: Mventix
21600 Oxnard St Ste 1700, Woodland Hills (91367-4972)
PHONE....................818 337-3747
Kristian Beloff, CEO
Vesselin Kavrakov, Research & Development*
Pavel Monev, *
EMP: 70 EST: 2004
SQ FT: 6,606
SALES (est): 2.71MM
SALES (corp-wide): 2.71MM Privately Held

PRODUCTS & SVCS

Web: www.mventix.com
SIC: 7389 8732 7372 Advertising, promotional, and trade show services; Survey service: marketing, location, etc.; Business oriented computer software

(P-14555)
NETWORK TELEPHONE SERVICES INC (PA)
Also Called: N T S
21135 Erwin St, Woodland Hills (91367-3713)
PHONE....................800 742-5687
Joseph Preston, CEO
Daniel Coleman, *
Connie Binyon, *
EMP: 87 EST: 1988
SQ FT: 70,000
SALES (est): 8.35MM
SALES (corp-wide): 8.35MM Privately Held
Web: www.nts.net
SIC: 7389 4813 7374 Telephone services; Internet connectivity services; Data processing and preparation

(P-14556)
NEW CREW PRODUCTION CORP
1100 W 135th St, Gardena (90247-1919)
PHONE....................323 234-8880
Kris Park, Pr
Joseph Park, *
▲ EMP: 110 EST: 2002
SALES (est): 2.01MM Privately Held
Web: www.newcrewproductioncorp.com
SIC: 7389 Sewing contractor

(P-14557)
NEWPORT DIVERSIFIED INC
Santa Fe Springs Swap Meet
13963 Alondra Blvd, Santa Fe Springs (90670-5814)
PHONE....................562 921-4359
EMP: 101
SQ FT: 10,846
SALES (corp-wide): 30.33MM Privately Held
Web: www.nd-inc.com
SIC: 7389 5932 Flea market; Used merchandise stores
PA: Newport Diversified, Inc.
4695 Macarthur Ct # 1420
949 851-1355

(P-14558)
NEWPORT DIVERSIFIED INC
Also Called: Parkway Bowl
1286 Fletcher Pkwy, El Cajon (92020-1826)
PHONE....................619 448-4111
Tony Casarrubia, Mgr
EMP: 101
SALES (corp-wide): 30.33MM Privately Held
Web: www.boardwalk-parkway.com
SIC: 7389 7933 7996 Flea market; Bowling centers; Amusement parks
PA: Newport Diversified, Inc.
4695 Macarthur Ct # 1420
949 851-1355

(P-14559)
NOR-CAL BEVERAGE CO INC
Also Called: Norcal Beverage Co
1226 N Olive St, Anaheim (92801-2543)
PHONE....................714 526-8600
William Mcfarland, Mgr
EMP: 92
SALES (corp-wide): 46.69MM Privately Held
Web: www.mannabev.com

SIC: 7389 2033 Packaging and labeling services; Canned fruits and specialties
PA: Nor-Cal Beverage Co., Inc.
2150 Stone Blvd
916 372-0600

(P-14560)
OCEANX LLC (PA)
100 N Pacific Coast Hwy Ste 1500, El Segundo (90245-5661)
PHONE....................310 774-4088
Steve Adams, Managing Member
EMP: 98 EST: 2015
SALES (est): 46.63MM
SALES (corp-wide): 46.63MM Privately Held
Web: www.oceanx.com
SIC: 7389 4731 Subscription fulfillment services: magazine, newspaper, etc.; Freight transportation arrangement

(P-14561)
OCS AMERICA INC (DH)
Also Called: Ocs Bookstore
22912 Lockness Ave, Torrance (90501-5117)
PHONE....................310 417-0650
Yutaka Otake, Ch Bd
Susan Onuman, *
Takuya Hiraiwa, *
▲ EMP: 39 EST: 1972
SALES (est): 7.78MM Privately Held
Web: www.ocsworld.com
SIC: 7389 5192 2711 5942 Courier or messenger service; Newspapers; Newspapers: publishing only, not printed on site; Books, foreign
HQ: Overseas Courier Service Co., Ltd.
3-9-27, Tatsumi
Koto-Ku TKY 135-0

(P-14562)
ONTARIO CONVENTION CENTER CORP
Also Called: Smg Management Facility
2000 E Convention Center Way, Ontario (91764-5633)
PHONE....................909 937-3000
EMP: 211 EST: 1995
SQ FT: 225,000
SALES (est): 1.19MM
SALES (corp-wide): 536.58MM Privately Held
Web: www.gocvb.org
SIC: 7389 Convention and show services
PA: City Of Ontario
303 E "b" Street
909 395-2012

(P-14563)
ORANGE COAST TITLE COMPANY (PA)
1551 N Tustin Ave Ste 300, Santa Ana (92705-3798)
P.O. Box 11825 (92711)
PHONE....................714 558-2836
Mike Kaluger, Pr
EMP: 100 EST: 1973
SQ FT: 24,000
SALES (est): 96.89MM Privately Held
Web: www.octitle.com
SIC: 7389 6361 6541 Personal service agents, brokers, and bureaus; Title insurance; Title and trust companies

(P-14564)
ORANGE COURIER INC
Also Called: Asbury
15300 Desman Rd, La Mirada (90638-5762)

P.O. Box 5308 (92704)
PHONE....................714 384-3600
Evell T Stanley, Pr
▲ EMP: 300 EST: 1992
SALES (est): 21.51MM Privately Held
Web: www.orangecourier.com
SIC: 7389 4213 4225 Courier or messenger service; Trucking, except local; General warehousing and storage

(P-14565)
OST TRUCKS AND CRANES INC
Also Called: Ost Crane Service
2951 N Ventura Ave, Ventura (93001-1210)
P.O. Box 237 (93002-0237)
PHONE....................805 643-9963
TOLL FREE: 800
L Dennis Zermeno, Pr
Don D Zermeno, *
Ron J Zermeno, *
EMP: 73 EST: 1962
SQ FT: 3,000
SALES (est): 9.01MM Privately Held
Web: www.ostcranes.com
SIC: 7389 4212 4225 Crane and aerial lift service; Local trucking, without storage; General warehousing and storage

(P-14566)
PACIFIC ASIAN ENTERPRISES INC (PA)
Also Called: Nordhavn Yachts
25001 Dana Dr, Dana Point (92629-3005)
P.O. Box 874 (92629-0874)
PHONE....................949 496-4848
Dan Streech, Pr
Jeffrey Leishman, Sec
James Leishman, CFO
◆ EMP: 30 EST: 1978
SQ FT: 3,500
SALES (est): 4.62MM
SALES (corp-wide): 4.62MM Privately Held
Web: www.nordhavn.com
SIC: 7389 3732 Yacht brokers; Yachts, building and repairing

(P-14567)
PAR WESTERN LINE CONTRS LLC
11276 5th St Ste 100, Rancho Cucamonga (91730-0922)
PHONE....................760 737-0925
Jim Stapp, Pr
Irene Anderson, CTRL*
Travis Walser, *
Kody Kilshaw, *
EMP: 550 EST: 2000
SQ FT: 800
SALES (est): 1.17MM
SALES (corp-wide): 20.88B Publicly Held
Web: www.parwlc.com
SIC: 7389 8711 1731 1623 Mapmaking services; Engineering services; General electrical contractor; Oil and gas line and compressor station construction
PA: Quanta Services, Inc.
2727 North Loop W
713 629-7600

(P-14568)
PARADIGM INDUSTRIES INC
2522 E 37th St, Vernon (90058-1725)
PHONE....................310 965-1900
William Jun, CEO
Chu Kim, *
▲ EMP: 80 EST: 2000
SALES (est): 2.32MM Privately Held
Web: www.paradigmindustries.net

SIC: 7389 Textile and apparel services

(P-14569)
PARTNERS CAPITAL GROUP INC (PA)
Also Called: Partners Capital Group
201 Sandpointe Ave Ste 500, Santa Ana (92707-8716)
PHONE....................949 916-3900
Mark Davin, CEO
EMP: 80 EST: 2005
SQ FT: 25,000
SALES (est): 6.99MM Privately Held
Web: www.partnerscapitalgrp.com
SIC: 7389 Financial services

(P-14570)
PASADENA CENTER OPERATING CO
Also Called: Pasadena Convention Center
300 E Green St, Pasadena (91101-2308)
PHONE....................626 795-9311
Michael Ross, CEO
EMP: 116 EST: 1973
SQ FT: 32,000
SALES (est): 24.24MM Privately Held
Web: www.visitpasadena.com
SIC: 7389 Convention and show services

(P-14571)
PERFECT IMPRESSION INC
Also Called: Perfect Banner, The
27111 Aliso Creek Rd Ste 145, Aliso Viejo (92656-5349)
PHONE....................949 305-0797
Suzie Abrahams, Pr
EMP: 28 EST: 2008
SALES (est): 899.3K Privately Held
Web: www.theperfectimpression.com
SIC: 7389 2395 Embroidery advertising; Embroidery and art needlework

(P-14572)
PHONE WARE INC
8902 Activity Rd Ste A, San Diego (92126-4471)
PHONE....................858 530-8550
William J Nassir, Pr
Hazel Nassir, *
EMP: 366 EST: 1974
SQ FT: 20,000
SALES (est): 23.72MM Privately Held
Web: www.phonewareinc.com
SIC: 7389 8742 Telemarketing services; Marketing consulting services

(P-14573)
PIXAR
500 N Buena Vista St, Burbank (91505-3209)
PHONE....................510 922-4075
Jody B Silverman, Brnch Mgr
EMP: 272
SALES (corp-wide): 91.36B Publicly Held
Web: www.pixar.com
SIC: 7389 Business Activities at Non-Commercial Site
HQ: Pixar
1200 Pk Ave
Emeryville CA 94608
510 922-3000

(P-14574)
PMC INC
3816 E La Palma Ave, Anaheim (92807-1713)
PHONE....................714 967-7230
Walter Buttkus, Brnch Mgr
EMP: 141

SALES (corp-wide): 1.71B **Privately Held**
Web: www.pmcglobalinc.com
SIC: 7389 Financial services
HQ: Pmc, Inc.
12243 Branford St
Sun Valley CA 91352
818 896-1101

(P-14575)
PRODUCTIVE PLAYHOUSE INC (PA)
100 N Brand Blvd, Glendale (91203-2641)
PHONE................................323 250-3445
Harry Ralston, *CEO*
EMP: 248 **EST:** 2009
SALES (est): 1.99MM
SALES (corp-wide): 1.99MM **Privately Held**
Web: www.productiveplayhouse.com
SIC: 7389 Translation services

(P-14576)
PROLOGIC RDMPTION SLUTIONS INC (PA)
2121 Rosecrans Ave, El Segundo (90245-4743)
PHONE................................310 322-7774
William Atkinson, *CEO*
Paul Cooley, *Pr*
John Mccurry, *Ex VP*
Robb Warwick, *CFO*
Kelly Fuller, *CCO*
EMP: 700 **EST:** 2008
SALES (est): 1.3MM
SALES (corp-wide): 1.3MM **Privately Held**
SIC: 7389 Coupon redemption service

(P-14577)
PROMPT DELIVERY INC
Also Called: Southern California Messenger
5757 Wilshire Blvd Ph 3, Los Angeles (90036-3681)
PHONE................................858 549-8000
Mike Dysland, *Mgr*
EMP: 100
Web: www.messengers.com
SIC: 7389 4212 Courier or messenger service; Delivery service, vehicular
PA: Prompt Delivery, Inc.
5757 Wilshire Blvd # 210

(P-14578)
PSC ENVIRONMENTAL SERVICES LLC
1601 Perrino Pl Ste D, Los Angeles (90023-2674)
PHONE................................323 266-6448
EMP: 76
SALES (corp-wide): 20.43B **Publicly Held**
SIC: 7389 Personal service agents, brokers, and bureaus
HQ: Psc Environmental Services, Llc
5151 San Felipe Ste 1100
Houston TX 77056
713 623-8777

(P-14579)
PUFF GLOBAL INC
Also Called: Puff Candy,
402 W Broadway Ste 400, San Diego (92101-3554)
PHONE................................619 520-3499
David Soria, *CEO*
▲ **EMP:** 80 **EST:** 2013
SALES (est): 444.74K **Privately Held**
SIC: 7389 Business Activities at Non-Commercial Site

(P-14580)
QOLOGY DIRECT LLC
Also Called: Centerfield Media
12130 Millennium Ste 600, Los Angeles (90094-2945)
PHONE................................310 341-4420
Brett Cravatt, *Pr*
Jason Cohen, *Pr*
EMP: 170 **EST:** 2012
SQ FT: 90,000
SALES (est): 1.41MM
SALES (corp-wide): 45.02MM **Privately Held**
Web: www.centerfield.com
SIC: 7389 Telephone services
HQ: Qology Direct Holdings, Inc.
12130 Millennium Ste 600
Los Angeles CA 90094

(P-14581)
QUIDEL CARDIOVASCULAR INC
9975 Summers Ridge Rd, San Diego (92121-2997)
PHONE................................858 552-1100
Douglas C Bryant, *CEO*
EMP: 74 **EST:** 2017
SALES (est): 17.85MM
SALES (corp-wide): 3B **Publicly Held**
Web: www.quidelortho.com
SIC: 7389 Inspection and testing services
HQ: Quidel Corporation
9975 Summers Ridge Rd
San Diego CA 92121
858 552-1100

(P-14582)
R G CANNING ENTERPRISES INC
4515 E 59th Pl, Maywood (90270-3201)
PHONE................................323 560-7469
Richard G Canning, *Pr*
Charles R Canning, *
EMP: 215 **EST:** 1955
SQ FT: 50,000
SALES (est): 2.36MM **Privately Held**
Web: www.rgcshows.com
SIC: 7389 Promoters of shows and exhibitions

(P-14583)
REASON FOUNDATION
5737 Mesmer Ave, Los Angeles (90230-6316)
PHONE................................310 391-2245
David Nott, *Pr*
Mike Alissi, *
EMP: 35 **EST:** 1968
SQ FT: 6,300
SALES (est): 15.46MM **Privately Held**
Web: www.reason.org
SIC: 7389 2741 2721 Speakers' bureau; Newsletter publishing; Magazines: publishing and printing

(P-14584)
REGUS BUSINESS CENTRE LLC
Also Called: Plaza Tower 1
600 Anton Blvd Ste 1100, Costa Mesa (92626-7100)
PHONE................................714 371-4000
Karen Barbeau, *Mgr*
EMP: 163
SALES (corp-wide): 3.69B **Privately Held**
Web: www.regus.com
SIC: 7389 Office facilities and secretarial service rental
HQ: Regus Business Centre Llc
15455 Dallas Pkwy Ste 600
Addison TX 75001
972 361-8100

(P-14585)
RGIS LLC
Also Called: Rgis, Llc
1937 W Chapman Ave, Orange (92868-2632)
PHONE................................714 938-0663
EMP: 133
SALES (corp-wide): 156.24MM **Privately Held**
Web: fr.rgis.be
SIC: 7389 Inventory computing service
PA: Wis Ivs, Llc
2000 Taylor Rd
248 221-4000

(P-14586)
ROSE & SHORE INC
5151 Alcoa Ave, Vernon (90058-3715)
P.O. Box 58225 (90058-0225)
PHONE................................323 826-2144
Irwin Miller, *Pr*
Carol Miller, *
EMP: 320 **EST:** 1968
SQ FT: 60,000
SALES (est): 27.41MM **Privately Held**
Web: www.roseandshore.com
SIC: 7389 5147 Packaging and labeling services; Meats, cured or smoked

(P-14587)
RVL PACKAGING INC
31330 Oak Crest Dr, Westlake Village (91361-4632)
PHONE................................818 735-5000
▼ **EMP:** 200
SIC: 7389 2396 2241 Packaging and labeling services; Automotive and apparel trimmings; Narrow fabric mills

(P-14588)
SAN DEGO CNVNTION CTR CORP INC (PA)
Also Called: Convention Center
111 W Harbor Dr, San Diego (92101-7899)
PHONE................................619 782-4388
Clifford R Rippetoe, *CEO*
Mardeen Mattix, *
▲ **EMP:** 281 **EST:** 1984
SALES (est): 44.3MM
SALES (corp-wide): 44.3MM **Privately Held**
Web: www.visitsandiego.com
SIC: 7389 Convention and show services

(P-14589)
SAN MNUEL BAND MISSION INDIANS
Also Called: San Manuel Fire Dept
26540 Indian Service Rd, Highland (92346-1714)
PHONE................................909 864-6928
EMP: 118
Web: www.sanmanuel-nsn.gov
SIC: 7389 Fire protection service other than forestry or public
PA: San Manuel Band Of Mission Indians
26569 Community Center Dr
909 864-8933

(P-14590)
SCOTTXSCOTT INC
3453 Union Pacific Ave, Los Angeles (90023-3834)
PHONE................................310 622-2775
Brandon J Scott, *CEO*
Sarah Scott, *
EMP: 24 **EST:** 2015
SALES (est): 1.12MM **Privately Held**
Web: www.scottxscott.com

SIC: 7389 2329 Apparel designers, commercial; Athletic clothing, except uniforms: men's, youths' and boys'

(P-14591)
SD&A TELESERVICES INC (HQ)
Also Called: Fulldeck
5757 W Century Blvd Ste 300, Los Angeles (90045-6432)
EMP: 300 **EST:** 2004
SALES (est): 3.53MM
SALES (corp-wide): 103.51MM **Privately Held**
Web: www.sdats.com
SIC: 7389 Telemarketing services
PA: Robert W. Woodruff Arts Center, Inc.
1280 Peachtree St Ne
404 733-4200

(P-14592)
SERVICING SOLUTIONS LLC
1 City Blvd W Ste 200, Orange (92868-3689)
PHONE................................844 907-6583
EMP: 80
SALES (corp-wide): 4.19MM **Privately Held**
Web: www.servicingsolutions.com
SIC: 7389 Process serving service
PA: Servicing Solutions, Llc
3660 Regent Blvd Ste 200
844 907-6583

(P-14593)
SEVEN ONE INC (PA)
Also Called: Professional Tele Answering Svc
21540 Prairie St Ste E, Chatsworth (91311-5814)
PHONE................................818 904-3435
James Thompson, *Pr*
EMP: 83 **EST:** 1983
SQ FT: 4,000
SALES (est): 682.51K **Privately Held**
Web: www.answer24live.com
SIC: 7389 Telephone answering service

(P-14594)
SHINWOO P&C USA INC (HQ)
2177 Britannia Blvd Ste 203, San Diego (92154-8307)
PHONE................................619 407-7164
Il Kim, *CEO*
▲ **EMP:** 348 **EST:** 2007
SQ FT: 300
SALES (est): 29.91MM **Privately Held**
SIC: 7389 Packaging and labeling services
PA: Shinan Packaging Co.,Ltd.
19b-5l, Banwol Industrial Complex

(P-14595)
SIGNATURE RESOLUTION
633 W 5th St Ste 1000, Los Angeles (90071-3509)
PHONE................................213 622-1002
EMP: 100 **EST:** 2017
SALES (est): 2.24MM **Privately Held**
Web: www.signatureresolution.com
SIC: 7389 Arbitration and conciliation service

(P-14596)
SIGUE CORPORATION (PA)
Also Called: Sigue
13190 Telfair Ave, Sylmar (91342-3573)
P.O. Box 750 (91341)
PHONE................................818 837-5939
Guillermo Dela Vina, *CEO*
Alfredo Dela Vina, *
Christina M Pappas, *
EMP: 100 **EST:** 1996
SQ FT: 3,000

P
R
O
D
U
C
T
S
&
S
V
C
S

SALES (est): 109.03MM
SALES (corp-wide): 109.03MM **Privately Held**
Web: www.sigue.com
SIC: **7389** 4822 Financial services; Telegraph and other communications

(P-14597)
SIMPLE SCIENCE INC
1626 Ohms Way, Costa Mesa (92627-4329)
PHONE...........................949 335-1099
Christian Henderson, *Pr*
EMP: 40 EST: 2009
SALES (est): 5.67MM **Privately Held**
Web: www.simple.science
SIC: **7389** 7812 7371 7311 Design services; Video production; Software programming applications; Advertising agencies

(P-14598)
SINECERA INC
Also Called: Crown Vly Precision Machining
5397 3rd St, Irwindale (91706-2085)
PHONE...........................626 962-1087
Donald Brown, *CEO*
Dale B Mikus, *CFO*
EMP: 80 EST: 1984
SQ FT: 10,500
SALES (est): 11.45MM
SALES (corp-wide): 93.1MM **Privately Held**
Web: www.crownprecision.com
SIC: **7389** 3492 Grinding, precision: commercial or industrial; Control valves, aircraft: hydraulic and pneumatic
PA: H-D Advanced Manufacturing Company
2418 Greens Rd
346 219-0320

(P-14599)
SOBOBA BAND LUISENO INDIANS
Also Called: Soboba Casino
22777 Soboba Rd, San Jacinto (92583-2935)
PHONE...........................951 665-1000
TOLL FREE: 888
Richard Kline, *Brnch Mgr*
EMP: 900
Web: www.soboba.com
SIC: **7389** 7011 Personal service agents, brokers, and bureaus; Casino hotel
PA: Soboba Band Of Luiseno Indians
23906 Soboba Rd
951 654-2765

(P-14600)
SOCIAL JUNKY INC
7874 Palmetto Ave, Fontana (92336-2744)
PHONE...........................213 999-1275
Shannon Bryant, *CEO*
EMP: 43 EST: 2021
SALES (est): 232.91K **Privately Held**
SIC: **7389** 2836 7929 Business Activities at Non-Commercial Site; Culture media; Entertainers and entertainment groups

(P-14601)
SPECRIGHT INC
1785 Flight Way, Tustin (92782-1838)
PHONE...........................866 290-6952
Matthew Wright, *CEO*
Kathrine Furgal, *VP*
EMP: 101 EST: 2016
SALES (est): 5.68MM **Privately Held**
Web: www.specright.com
SIC: **7389** Inspection and testing services

(P-14602)
STRATEGIC OPERATIONS INC
4705 Ruffin Rd, San Diego (92123-1611)
PHONE...........................858 244-0559
Stuart Segall, *CEO*
EMP: 250 EST: 2002
SQ FT: 12,000
SALES (est): 24.34MM **Privately Held**
Web: www.strategic-operations.com
SIC: **7389** Personal service agents, brokers, and bureaus

(P-14603)
SUGAR FOODS LLC
6190 E Slauson Ave, Commerce (90040-3010)
PHONE...........................818 768-7900
Stephen Odell, *Pt*
EMP: 200
SALES (corp-wide): 677.96MM **Privately Held**
Web: www.sugarfoods.com
SIC: **7389** 2099 2062 Packaging and labeling services; Food preparations, nec; Cane sugar refining
HQ: Sugar Foods Llc
3059 Townsgate Rd Ste 101
Westlake Village CA 91361
805 396-5000

(P-14604)
SUPER CENTER CONCEPTS INC
Also Called: Superior Grocers
133 W Avenue 45, Los Angeles (90065-3022)
PHONE...........................323 223-3878
Chris Gonzalez, *Dist Mgr*
EMP: 151
Web: www.superiorgrocers.com
SIC: **7389** Design services
PA: Super Center Concepts, Inc.
15510 Carmenita Rd

(P-14605)
SUPER CENTER CONCEPTS INC
1130 W 6th St, Corona (92882-3133)
PHONE...........................951 372-9485
EMP: 79
Web: www.superiorgrocers.com
SIC: **7389** Design services
PA: Super Center Concepts, Inc.
15510 Carmenita Rd

(P-14606)
SWIFT MEDIA ENTERTAINMENT INC
5340 Alla Rd Ste 101, Los Angeles (90066-7036)
PHONE...........................310 308-3694
Andy Dinh, *CEO*
EMP: 75 EST: 2017
SALES (est): 4.03MM **Privately Held**
SIC: **7389** Advertising, promotional, and trade show services

(P-14607)
TBWA CHIAT/DAY INC
5353 Grosvenor Blvd, Los Angeles (90066-6913)
PHONE...........................310 305-5000
Lee Clow, *Mgr*
EMP: 374
SALES (corp-wide): 14.69B **Publicly Held**
Web: www.tbwachiatdayla.com
SIC: **7389** Interior design services
HQ: Tbwa Chiat/Day Inc.
220 E 42nd St
New York NY 10017
212 804-1000

(P-14608)
TECHNICON DESIGN CORPORATION
30011 Ivy Glenn Dr Ste 115, Laguna Niguel (92677-5016)
PHONE...........................949 218-1300
Frank Goodchild,, *Pr*
Danton Fitch, *
Helen Carstens, *
EMP: 120 EST: 1989
SALES (est): 20.36MM
SALES (corp-wide): 1.62MM **Privately Held**
Web: www.technicondesign.com
SIC: **7389** Design services
PA: Technicon Design Limited
Technicon House
158 250-6600

(P-14609)
TECMA GROUP LLC
6020 Progressive Ave Ste 200, San Diego (92154-6633)
PHONE...........................619 333-5856
EMP: 974
Web: www.tecma.com
SIC: **7389** Brokers' services
PA: The Tecma Group L L C
2000 Wyoming Ave Ste A

(P-14610)
THOUSAND OAKS PRTG & SPC INC
Also Called: T/O Printing
5334 Sterling Center Dr, Westlake Village (91361-4612)
PHONE...........................818 706-8330
Steve Mahr, *Pr*
▲ EMP: 140 EST: 1981
SQ FT: 60,000
SALES (est): 3.85MM
SALES (corp-wide): 15B **Privately Held**
Web: www.rrd.com
SIC: **7389** 2752 Printing broker; Offset printing
HQ: Consolidated Graphics, Inc.
5858 Westheimer Rd # 200
Houston TX 77057

(P-14611)
THYDE INC (PA)
300 El Sobrante Rd, Corona (92879-5757)
PHONE...........................951 817-2300
Tim Hyde, *Pr*
EMP: 200 EST: 1984
SQ FT: 70,000
SALES (est): 16.93MM
SALES (corp-wide): 16.93MM **Privately Held**
SIC: **7389** Packaging and labeling services

(P-14612)
TRAFFIC MANAGEMENT LLC (PA)
4900 Airport Plaza Dr Ste 300, Long Beach (90815-1375)
PHONE...........................562 595-4278
Christopher H Spano, *CEO*
Jonathan Spano, *
▲ EMP: 144 EST: 1992
SALES (est): 105.24MM **Privately Held**
Web: www.trafficmanagement.com
SIC: **7389** 8741 Flagging service (traffic control); Business management

(P-14613)
TRANSPAK INC
Also Called: Transpak Los Angeles
2601 S Garnsey St, Santa Ana (92707-3338)

PHONE...........................408 254-0500
Charles Frasier, *Prin*
EMP: 108
SALES (corp-wide): 82.99MM **Privately Held**
Web: www.transpak.com
SIC: **7389** Packaging and labeling services
PA: Transpak, Inc.
520 Marburg Way
408 254-0500

(P-14614)
TRANSPRTTION OPRTION MGT SLTON ✪
1917 Palomar Oaks Way Ste 110, Carlsbad (92008-5513)
PHONE...........................858 391-0260
Lee Wilcox, *Pr*
Steve Haddix, *
Brad White, *
Cindy Adamos, *
EMP: 250 EST: 2023
SALES (est): 45MM **Privately Held**
SIC: **7389** Personal service agents, brokers, and bureaus

(P-14615)
TRITON MANAGEMENT SERVICES LLC
Also Called: Aladdin Bail Bonds
1000 Aviara Dr Ste 300, Carlsbad (92011-4218)
PHONE...........................760 431-9911
Bob Lloyd, *Prin*
EMP: 73 EST: 2012
SALES (est): 9.33MM **Privately Held**
Web: www.tritonmanagementservices.com
SIC: **7389** Bail bonding

(P-14616)
TWO JINN INC (PA)
Also Called: Aladdin Bail Bonds
1000 Aviara Dr Ste 300, Carlsbad (92011-4218)
PHONE...........................760 431-9911
Robert H Hayes, *Ch Bd*
Leah Taniguchi, *
EMP: 75 EST: 2004
SALES (est): 21.21MM
SALES (corp-wide): 21.21MM **Privately Held**
Web: www.aladdinbailbonds.com
SIC: **7389** Bail bonding

(P-14617)
UNITED TALENT AGENCY LLC
Also Called: United Talent Agency, LLC
9336 Civic Center Dr, Beverly Hills (90210-3604)
PHONE...........................310 776-8160
EMP: 81
SALES (corp-wide): 34.87MM **Privately Held**
Web: www.unitedtalent.com
SIC: **7389** Personal service agents, brokers, and bureaus
PA: United Talent Agency Holdings, Inc.
888 7th Ave Ste 922
310 273-6700

(P-14618)
UNIVERSAL CARD INC
Also Called: Merchant Services
9012 Research Dr Ste 200, Irvine (92618-4254)
PHONE...........................949 861-4000
Jason Moore, *Pr*
Jason W Moore, *
Robert Parisi, *

EMP: 400 EST: 2000
SQ FT: 40,000
SALES (est): 4.36MM Privately Held
Web: www.merchantsvcs.com
SIC: 7389 Credit card service

(P-14619)
UNIVERSAL MUS GROUP DIST CORP
111 Universal Hollywood Dr Ste 1420, Universal City (91608-1152)
PHONE....................818 508-9550
Clarence Mcdonald, *Brnch Mgr*
EMP: 124
Web: www.universalmusic.com
SIC: 7389 Music recording producer
HQ: Universal Music Group Distribution, Corp.
2220 Colorado Ave
Santa Monica CA 90404
310 235-4700

(P-14620)
UNIVERSAL MUS INVESTMENTS INC (HQ)
2220 Colorado Ave, Santa Monica (90404-3506)
PHONE....................888 583-7176
Lucian C Grainge, *CEO*
Joe Arambula, *
▲ EMP: 80 EST: 1996
SALES (est): 93.57MM Privately Held
Web: www.universalmusic.com
SIC: 7389 7929 Music recording producer; Musical entertainers
PA: Vivendi Se
42 Avenue De Friedland

(P-14621)
UNIVERSAL MUSIC GROUP INC (HQ)
2220 Colorado Ave, Santa Monica (90404-3506)
PHONE....................310 865-0770
Lucian Grainge, *CEO*
Jeffrey Harleston, *
Philippe Flageul, *
Boyd Muir, *
▲ EMP: 100 EST: 1998
SALES (est): 549.4MM Privately Held
Web: www.universalmusic.com
SIC: 7389 2741 Music recording producer; Miscellaneous publishing
PA: Universal Music Group N.V.
S-Gravelandseweg 80

(P-14622)
UNSPOKEN LANGUAGE SERVICES INC
1370 Valley Vista Dr Ste 200, Diamond Bar (91765-3921)
PHONE....................626 532-8096
Amanda Martin, *
EMP: 498 EST: 2019
SALES (est): 816.45K Privately Held
Web: www.unspokenasl.com
SIC: 7389 Translation services

(P-14623)
UPS STORE INC (HQ)
Also Called: Mail Boxes Etc
6060 Cornerstone Ct W, San Diego (92121-3712)
PHONE....................858 455-8800
Walter T Davis, *CEO*
Michelle Van Slyke, *
EMP: 313 EST: 1980
SQ FT: 66,000
SALES (est): 154.51MM

SALES (corp-wide): 90.96B Publicly Held
Web: www.theupsstore.com
SIC: 7389 8742 4783 Mailbox rental and related service; Business management consultant; Packing goods for shipping
PA: United Parcel Service, Inc.
55 Glenlake Pkwy Ne
404 828-6000

(P-14624)
US BANKCARD SERVICES INC
17171 Gale Ave Ste 110, City Of Industry (91745-1822)
PHONE....................888 888-8872
Christopher J Chang, *Pr*
▲ EMP: 75 EST: 1996
SQ FT: 3,000
SALES (est): 5.89MM Privately Held
Web: www.usbsi.com
SIC: 7389 Credit card service

(P-14625)
VASTEK INC
1230 Columbia St Ste 1180, San Diego (92101-8520)
PHONE....................925 948-5701
Vikash Mishra, *CEO*
EMP: 171 EST: 2015
SQ FT: 1,600
SALES (est): 8.03MM Privately Held
Web: www.vastekgroup.com
SIC: 7389 7371 Air pollution measuring service; Custom computer programming services

(P-14626)
VINTAGE DESIGN LLC
8310 Juniper Creek Ln, San Diego (92126-1072)
PHONE....................858 695-9544
Elizabeth Casey, *Brnch Mgr*
EMP: 94
Web: www.vintagedesigninc.com
SIC: 7389 Interior decorating
HQ: Vintage Design, Llc
25200 Commercentre Dr
Lake Forest CA 92630
949 900-5400

(P-14627)
VISUAL PAK SAN DIEGO LLC
2320 Paseo De Las Americas Ste 201, San Diego (92154-7273)
PHONE....................847 689-1000
David Waldron, *Managing Member*
▲ EMP: 250 EST: 2012
SALES (est): 1.75MM Privately Held
Web: www.visualpak.com
SIC: 7389 Packaging and labeling services

(P-14628)
VOLCOM LLC (HQ)
Also Called: Stone Entertainment
1740 Monrovia Ave, Costa Mesa (92627-4407)
PHONE....................949 646-2175
Todd Hymel, *CEO*
Jason Steris, *
John W Fearnley, *
Tom D Ruiz, *
Ryan Immegart, *
EMP: 200 EST: 1991
SQ FT: 104,000
SALES (est): 134.77MM Privately Held
Web: www.volcom.com
SIC: 7389 2253 7822 5136 Design services; Bathing suits and swimwear, knit; Motion picture and tape distribution; Men's and boy's clothing
PA: Authentic Brands Group Llc
1411 Broadway Fl 21

(P-14629)
VXI GLOBAL SOLUTIONS LLC (PA)
Also Called: Vxi Global Solutions
515 S Figueroa St Ste 600, Los Angeles (90071-3339)
PHONE....................213 739-4720
David Zhou, *CEO*
Jared Morrison, *
Frank Yao, *CCO*
EMP: 1200 EST: 1998
SALES (est): 342.05MM
SALES (corp-wide): 342.05MM Privately Held
Web: www.vxi.com
SIC: 7389 Telemarketing services

(P-14630)
WARNER BROS RECORDS INC (DH)
777 S Santa Fe Ave, Los Angeles (90021-1750)
PHONE....................818 846-9090
Livia Tortella, *
Rob Cavallo, *
Lenny Warnoker, *
Murray Gitlin, *
EMP: 460 EST: 1958
SALES (est): 24.85MM Publicly Held
Web: www.warnerrecords.com
SIC: 7389 Music recording producer
HQ: Warner Music Inc.
1633 Broadway
New York NY 10019

(P-14631)
WASHINGTON INVENTORY SERVICE
Also Called: Wis
9265 Sky Park Ct Ste 100, San Diego (92123-4375)
PHONE....................858 565-8111
Jim Rose, *CEO*
Howard L Madden, *
Tom Compogiannis, *
EMP: 1000 EST: 1960
SQ FT: 30,000
SALES (est): 24.52MM Publicly Held
SIC: 7389 Inventory computing service
HQ: Western Inventory Service Ltd.
102-335 Britannia Rd E
Mississauga ON L4Z 1
905 677-1947

(P-14632)
WE PACK IT ALL LLC
2745 Huntington Dr, Duarte (91010-2302)
PHONE....................626 301-9214
George Gellert, *
Robert Gellert, *
Sharon Bershtel, *
Mark Lebovitz, *
EMP: 155 EST: 1972
SQ FT: 50,000
SALES (est): 24.88MM Privately Held
Web: www.wepackitall.com
SIC: 7389 Packaging and labeling services

(P-14633)
WELLS FARGO CAPITAL FINANCE INC
Also Called: Wcf Technology E2040-030
2450 Colo Ave 3000w 3rd Fl, Santa Monica (90404)
PHONE....................310 453-7300
▲ EMP: 195
SIC: 7389 Financial services

(P-14634)
WET (PA)
Also Called: Wet Design
10847 Sherman Way, Sun Valley (91352-4829)
PHONE....................818 769-6200
Mark W Fuller, *CEO*
Shemi Hart, *
Tania Avedissian, *
Helen Park, *
Maria Villamil, *
▲ EMP: 184 EST: 1983
SQ FT: 112,000
SALES (est): 47.23MM
SALES (corp-wide): 47.23MM Privately Held
Web: www.wetdesign.com
SIC: 7389 8711 3443 Design services; Engineering services; Metal parts

(P-14635)
XO BABYPLUTO FADED PARADISE XO
3442 E 8th St, Los Angeles (90023-3025)
PHONE....................650 750-5025
Brandon Aceituno, *CEO*
Brandon Aceituno, *Managing Member*
EMP: 25 EST: 2019
SALES (est): 206.68K Privately Held
SIC: 7389 8641 8299 7372 Business Activities at Non-Commercial Site; Youth organizations; Music school; Educational computer software

(P-14636)
YAPSTONE INC (PA)
Also Called: Rentpayment.com
1902 Wright Pl Ste 231, Carlsbad (92008-6583)
PHONE....................866 289-5977
Tom Villante, *CEO*
Bryan Murphy, *
Kelly Kay, *
Mary Hentges, *
John Malnar, *
EMP: 92 EST: 1999
SALES (est): 47.29MM
SALES (corp-wide): 47.29MM Privately Held
Web: www.yapstone.com
SIC: 7389 Credit card service

(P-14637)
YELLOWPAGESCOM LLC (DH)
Also Called: Dexyp
611 N Brand Blvd Ste 500, Glendale (91203-1379)
PHONE....................818 937-5500
Williams Clenney, *
Brad Mohs, *
EMP: 200 EST: 2004
SALES (est): 9.92MM
SALES (corp-wide): 916.96MM Publicly Held
SIC: 7389 Telephone directory distribution, contract or fee basis
HQ: Thryv, Inc.
2200 W Airfield Dr
Dfw Airport TX 75261
972 453-7000

(P-14638)
ZODIAC POOL SYSTEMS LLC
19319 Harvill Ave, Perris (92570-4901)
PHONE....................760 213-4647
EMP: 123
Web: www.fluidrausa.com
SIC: 7389 Swimming pool and hot tub service and maintenance
HQ: Zodiac Pool Systems Llc
2882 Whptail Loop Ste 100

PRODUCTS & SVCS

Carlsbad CA 92010
760 599-9600

7513 Truck Rental And Leasing, Without Drivers

(P-14639)
PENSKE MOTOR GROUP LLC
Also Called: Penske
2010 E Garvey Ave S, West Covina (91791-1911)
PHONE..............626 859-1200
Glen Hightman, *Brnch Mgr*
EMP: 277
SALES (corp-wide): 32.13B **Publicly Held**
Web: www.penskemotorgroup.com
SIC: 7513 7538 Truck rental and leasing, no drivers; General automotive repair shops
HQ: Penske Motor Group, Llc
3534 N Peck Rd
El Monte CA 91731

(P-14640)
PENSKE TRANSPORTATION MGT LLC
2280 Wardlow Cir, Corona (92878-9078)
PHONE..............844 847-9518
EMP: 116
SALES (corp-wide): 2.11B **Privately Held**
Web: www.penskelogistics.com
SIC: 7513 Truck rental and leasing, no drivers
HQ: Penske Transportation Management Llc
2675 Morgantown Rd
Reading PA 19607
800 529-6531

(P-14641)
ROLLINS LEASING LLC
Also Called: Rollins Truck Rental-Leasing
18305 Arenth Ave, City Of Industry (91748-1226)
PHONE..............626 913-7186
Dave Bettson, *Mgr*
EMP: 86
SQ FT: 10,370
SALES (corp-wide): 2.11B **Privately Held**
Web: www.penisketruckrental.com
SIC: 7513 Truck rental and leasing, no drivers
HQ: Rollins Leasing Llc
2200 Concord Pike
Wilmington DE 19803
302 426-2700

(P-14642)
RP AUTOMOTIVE II INC
Also Called: Penske Ford Chula Vista
560 Auto Park Dr, Chula Vista (91911-6026)
PHONE..............619 656-2500
Roger S Penske Junior, *Brnch Mgr*
EMP: 90
SALES (corp-wide): 10.99MM **Privately Held**
Web: www.kia.com
SIC: 7513 Truck rental and leasing, no drivers
PA: Rp Automotive Ii, Inc.
9136 Firestone Blvd
626 430-9011

(P-14643)
U-HAUL BUSINESS CONSULTANTS
Also Called: U-Haul
314 E 6th St, Corona (92879-1520)

PHONE..............951 736-7811
Erick Weaver, *Mgr*
EMP: 233
SALES (corp-wide): 5.63B **Publicly Held**
Web: offline.uhaul.com
SIC: 7513 Truck rental and leasing, no drivers
HQ: U-Haul Business Consultants, Inc
2727 N Central Ave
Phoenix AZ 85004
602 263-6011

7514 Passenger Car Rental

(P-14644)
ENTERPRISE RNT--CAR LOS ANGLES (DH)
Also Called: Enterprise Rent-A-Car
333 City Blvd W Ste 1000, Orange (92868-5917)
PHONE..............657 221-4400
Andrew C Taylor, *
Pamela Nicholson, *
Greg Stubblefield, *
William W Snyder, *
▲ **EMP:** 90 **EST:** 1957
SQ FT: 30,000
SALES (est): 47.01MM
SALES (corp-wide): 7.04B **Privately Held**
Web: www.enterprise.com
SIC: 7514 7513 5511 Rent-a-car service; Truck rental and leasing, no drivers; Trucks, tractors, and trailers: new and used
HQ: Enterprise Holdings, Inc.
600 Corporate Pk Dr
Saint Louis MO 63105
314 512-5000

(P-14645)
FOX RENT A CAR INC
1776 E Holt Blvd, Ontario (91761-2110)
PHONE..............909 635-6390
Syed Mahdi, *Brnch Mgr*
EMP: 94
SALES (corp-wide): 350.31B **Privately Held**
Web: www.foxrentacar.com
SIC: 7514 Rent-a-car service
HQ: Fox Rent A Car, Inc.
4135 S 100th E Ave
Tulsa OK 74146

(P-14646)
FOX RENT A CAR INC
Also Called: Europcar
5500 W Century Blvd, Los Angeles (90045-5914)
PHONE..............310 342-5155
Allen Rezapour, *Pr*
EMP: 123
SALES (corp-wide): 350.31B **Privately Held**
Web: www.foxrentacar.com
SIC: 7514 Passenger car rental
HQ: Fox Rent A Car, Inc.
4135 S 100th E Ave
Tulsa OK 74146

(P-14647)
FOX RENT A CAR INC
325 Baker St, Costa Mesa (92626-4518)
PHONE..............310 342-5155
Trent Dennis, *Brnch Mgr*
EMP: 71
SALES (corp-wide): 350.31B **Privately Held**
Web: www.foxrentacar.com
SIC: 7514 Passenger car rental
HQ: Fox Rent A Car, Inc.
4135 S 100th E Ave

Tulsa OK 74146

(P-14648)
GALPIN MOTORS INC
Galpin Studio Rentals
1763 Ivar Ave, Los Angeles (90028-5105)
PHONE..............323 957-3333
Bill Wernli, *Mgr*
EMP: 91
SALES (corp-wide): 59.63MM **Privately Held**
Web: www.galpinstudiorentals.com
SIC: 7514 Rent-a-car service
PA: Galpin Motors, Inc.
15505 Roscoe Blvd
818 787-3800

(P-14649)
MIDWAY RENT A CAR INC
2263 Pacific Hwy, San Diego (92101-1744)
PHONE..............619 238-9600
EMP: 71
Web: www.midwaycarrental.com
SIC: 7514 Rent-a-car service
PA: Midway Rent A Car, Inc.
4751 Wilshire Blvd # 120

7515 Passenger Car Leasing

(P-14650)
EL CAJON MOTORS (PA)
Also Called: El Cajon Ford
1595 E Main St, El Cajon (92021-5994)
P.O. Box 1236 (92022-1236)
PHONE..............619 579-8888
Paul F Leader, *Pr*
Andrew Breech, *
John Blake, *
▲ **EMP:** 100 **EST:** 1946
SQ FT: 311,226
SALES (est): 3.12MM
SALES (corp-wide): 3.12MM **Privately Held**
Web: www.elcajonford.com
SIC: 7515 5511 7538 Passenger car leasing; Automobiles, new and used; General automotive repair shops

(P-14651)
EXECUTIVE CAR LEASING COMPANY (PA)
Also Called: Newco Auto Leasing
7807 Santa Monica Blvd, West Hollywood (90046-5398)
P.O. Box 933009 (90093-3009)
PHONE..............800 800-3932
EMP: 100 **EST:** 1953
SALES (est): 9.26MM
SALES (corp-wide): 9.26MM **Privately Held**
Web: www.executivecarleasing.com
SIC: 7515 7513 Passenger car leasing; Truck leasing, without drivers

(P-14652)
MIDWAY RENT A CAR INC
Also Called: Midway Car Rental
4201 Lankershim Blvd, North Hollywood (91602-2856)
PHONE..............818 985-9770
Jeff Riesenberg, *Brnch Mgr*
EMP: 70
Web: www.midwaycarrental.com
SIC: 7515 7514 Passenger car leasing; Passenger car rental
PA: Midway Rent A Car, Inc.
4751 Wilshire Blvd # 120

7519 Utility Trailer Rental

(P-14653)
EL MONTE RENTS INC (HQ)
Also Called: El Monte Rv
12818 Firestone Blvd, Santa Fe Springs (90670-5404)
PHONE..............562 404-9300
Kenneth Schork, *CEO*
EMP: 110 **EST:** 1970
SALES (est): 48.03MM **Privately Held**
Web: www.elmonterv.com
SIC: 7519 5561 Motor home rental; Motor homes
PA: Tourism Holdings Limited
L 1 83 Beach Rd

7521 Automobile Parking

(P-14654)
ABM PARKING SERVICES INC
Also Called: Ampco Airport Parking
1150 S Olive St Fl 19, Los Angeles (90015-2479)
PHONE..............213 284-7600
▲ **EMP:** 9469
SIC: 7521 7349 Parking lots; Janitorial service, contract basis

(P-14655)
AMERIPARK LLC
17165 Von Karman Ave Ste 110, Irvine (92614-0905)
PHONE..............949 279-7525
Josh Hess, *Brnch Mgr*
EMP: 300
SALES (corp-wide): 464.37MM **Privately Held**
Web: www.ameripark.com
SIC: 7521 Parking lots
HQ: Ameripark, Llc
233 Peachtree St Ne # 2600
Atlanta GA 30303

(P-14656)
EVERPARK INC
3470 Wilshire Blvd Ste 940, Los Angeles (90010-3900)
PHONE..............310 987-6922
Alazar Asmamaw, *CEO*
Abiy Wouldgerema, *
Abbi Abebe, *
EMP: 200 **EST:** 2007
SALES (est): 1.21MM **Privately Held**
Web: www.everpark.com
SIC: 7521 Parking lots

(P-14657)
L AND R AUTO PARKS INC
Also Called: Joe's Auto Parks
707 Wilshire Blvd Ste 4300, Los Angeles (90017-3622)
PHONE..............213 784-3018
Charles Bassett, *Pr*
Mark Funk, *
Jeff Matsuno, *
Gabriel Rubin, *
Stuart Rubin Board, *Prin*
EMP: 250 **EST:** 1951
SQ FT: 5,000
SALES (est): 19.79MM **Privately Held**
Web: www.joesautoparks.com
SIC: 7521 7542 7371 Parking lots; Carwashes; Computer software development and applications

(P-14658)
LAZ KARP ASSOCIATES LLC
1400 Ivar Ave, Los Angeles (90028-8122)
PHONE.....................323 464-4190
EMP: 175
Web: www.lazparking.com
SIC: 7521 Parking lots
PA: Laz Karp Associates, Llc
1 Financial Plz

(P-14659)
MODERN PARKING INC
14110 Palawan Way, Marina Del Rey
(90292-6231)
PHONE.....................310 821-1081
Arisur Rahnan, Prin
EMP: 167
Web: www.modernparking.com
SIC: 7521 Parking garage
PA: Modern Parking, Inc.
303 S Union Ave Fl 1

(P-14660)
MODERN PARKING INC
4955 Van Nuys Blvd Frnt, Van Nuys
(91403-1813)
PHONE.....................818 783-3143
EMP: 167
Web: www.modernparking.com
SIC: 7521 Parking garage
PA: Modern Parking, Inc.
303 S Union Ave Fl 1

(P-14661)
MODERN PARKING INC
1025 W Laurel St Ste 105, San Diego
(92101-1254)
PHONE.....................619 233-0412
Richard Viera, Brnch Mgr
EMP: 167
Web: www.modernparking.com
SIC: 7521 Parking garage
PA: Modern Parking, Inc.
303 S Union Ave Fl 1

(P-14662)
**PARKING COMPANY OF
AMERICA**
Also Called: Pcamp
3165 Garfield Ave, Commerce
(90040-3217)
PHONE.....................562 862-2118
Alex Martin Chaves Junior, Pr
Eric Chaves, *
EMP: 100 EST: 1990
SALES (est): 9.34MM Privately Held
Web: www.parkpca.com
SIC: 7521 Parking lots

(P-14663)
PARKING CONCEPTS INC
1020 W Civic Center Dr, Santa Ana
(92703-2303)
PHONE.....................714 543-5725
Gilbert Bernick, Brnch Mgr
EMP: 101
SALES (corp-wide): 44.42MM Privately
Held
Web: www.parkingconcepts.com
SIC: 7521 Parking lots
PA: Parking Concepts, Inc.
12 Mauchly Ste I
949 753-7525

(P-14664)
PARKING CONCEPTS INC
33 E Green St, Pasadena (91105-2022)
PHONE.....................626 577-8963
EMP: 101

SALES (corp-wide): 44.42MM Privately
Held
Web: www.parkingconcepts.com
SIC: 7521 Parking lots
PA: Parking Concepts, Inc.
12 Mauchly Ste I
949 753-7525

(P-14665)
PARKING CONCEPTS INC
1801 Georgia St, Los Angeles
(90015-3477)
PHONE.....................213 746-5764
Bob Hindle, Mgr
EMP: 201
SALES (corp-wide): 44.42MM Privately
Held
Web: www.parkingconcepts.com
SIC: 7521 8748 Parking lots; Traffic
consultant
PA: Parking Concepts, Inc.
12 Mauchly Ste I
949 753-7525

(P-14666)
PARKING CONCEPTS INC
14110 Palawan Way, Venice (90292-6231)
PHONE.....................310 821-1081
Frank Vargas, Genl Mgr
EMP: 100
SALES (corp-wide): 44.42MM Privately
Held
Web: www.parkingconcepts.com
SIC: 7521 8741 Parking lots; Management
services
PA: Parking Concepts, Inc.
12 Mauchly Ste I
949 753-7525

(P-14667)
PARKING CONCEPTS INC
1036 Broxton Ave, Los Angeles
(90024-2824)
PHONE.....................310 208-1611
Jorge Lopez, Mgr
EMP: 100
SALES (corp-wide): 44.42MM Privately
Held
Web: www.parkingconcepts.com
SIC: 7521 Parking lots
PA: Parking Concepts, Inc.
12 Mauchly Ste I
949 753-7525

(P-14668)
PCAM LLC
Also Called: PCA Med
3165 Garfield Ave, Commerce
(90040-3217)
PHONE.....................562 862-2118
Eric Chaves, Prin
EMP: 93 EST: 2011
SALES (est): 3.26MM Privately Held
Web: www.parkpca.com
SIC: 7521 Parking lots

(P-14669)
PROFESSIONAL PARKING
309 Palm St, Newport Beach (92661-1200)
PHONE.....................949 723-4027
Ralph Caldin, Brnch Mgr
EMP: 115
SIC: 7521 Parking garage
HQ: Professional Parking
2799 E 21st St
Signal Hill CA 90755

(P-14670)
**RESORT PARKING SERVICES
INC**

39755 Berkey Dr # B, Palm Desert
(92211-1106)
PHONE.....................760 328-4041
Mario Gardner, Pr
EMP: 120 EST: 1973
SQ FT: 1,100
SALES (est): 2.53MM Privately Held
Web: www.resortparkingservices.com
SIC: 7521 7299 Parking lots; Personal item
care and storage services

(P-14671)
**VALET PARKING SVC A CAL
PARTNR (PA)**
Also Called: Valet Parking Service
6933 Hollywood Blvd, Los Angeles
(90028-6146)
PHONE.....................323 465-5873
Anthony Policella, CEO
EMP: 1268 EST: 1946
SQ FT: 10,000
SALES (est): 1.85MM
SALES (corp-wide): 1.85MM Privately
Held
Web: www.valetparkingservice.com
SIC: 7521 7299 Parking lots; Valet parking

7532 Top And Body Repair
And Paint Shops

(P-14672)
**CALIBER BODYWORKS TEXAS
LLC**
Also Called: Caliber Collision
5 Auto Center Dr, Tustin (92782-8402)
PHONE.....................714 665-3905
David Adams, Brnch Mgr
EMP: 100
Web: www.caliber.com
SIC: 7532 Body shop, automotive
HQ: Caliber Bodyworks Of Texas Llc
2941 Lake Vista Dr
Lewisville TX 75067
469 794-5653

(P-14673)
**GREENWLDS ATBODY
FRMEWORKS INC**
2850 Erie St, San Diego (92117-6143)
PHONE.....................619 477-2600
Daniel Greenwald, Prin
EMP: 70 EST: 1986
SALES (est): 709.72K Privately Held
Web: www.greenwaldsautobody.com
SIC: 7532 Body shop, automotive

(P-14674)
**HOLMES BODY SHOP-
ALHAMBRA INC**
Also Called: Holmes Body Shop Riverside
3860 Buchanan St, Riverside (92503-4821)
PHONE.....................951 734-9920
Rick Bender, Brnch Mgr
EMP: 90
SALES (corp-wide): 1.99MM Privately
Held
Web: www.holmesbodyshop.com
SIC: 7532 Body shop, automotive
PA: Holmes Body Shop-Alhambra, Inc.
466 Foothill Blvd
626 795-6447

(P-14675)
M2 AUTOMOTIVE
1100 Colorado Ave 2nd Fl, Santa Monica
(90401-3010)
PHONE.....................310 399-3887
D Hunt Ramsbottom Junior, CEO

EMP: 750 EST: 1996
SALES (est): 197.84K Privately Held
SIC: 7532 Collision shops, automotive

(P-14676)
**MAIMONE LIQUIDATING CORP
(PA)**
Also Called: Marco's Auto Body
1390 E Palm St, Altadena (91001-2042)
PHONE.....................626 286-5691
Marco G Maimone, Pr
Carl Canzano, *
Lillian Maimone, *
EMP: 100 EST: 1974
SQ FT: 14,000
SALES (est): 927.53K
SALES (corp-wide): 927.53K Privately
Held
Web: www.caliber.com
SIC: 7532 7539 Body shop, automotive;
Frame and front end repair services

(P-14677)
METRO TRUCK BODY INC
240 Citation Cir, Corona (92878-5022)
PHONE.....................310 532-5570
Vincent Xavier Rigali, CEO
▲ EMP: 47 EST: 1968
SQ FT: 20,000
SALES (est): 2.68MM Privately Held
Web: www.metrotruckbody.com
SIC: 7532 3713 5012 5531 Body shop,
automotive; Truck bodies (motor vehicles);
Truck bodies; Truck equipment and parts

(P-14678)
PLATINUM PERFORMANCE INC
760 Mcmurray Rd, Buellton (93427-2510)
PHONE.....................800 553-2400
Kristin Peck, CEO
Kate Russo, *
EMP: 80 EST: 1997
SALES (est): 144.11K Privately Held
Web: www.platinumperformance.com
SIC: 7532 Body shop, automotive

(P-14679)
REDLANDS FORD INC
1121 W Colton Ave, Redlands
(92374-2935)
PHONE.....................909 793-3211
Steve Rojas, CEO
Steve Rojas, Pr
Tracey Hooper, *
EMP: 85 EST: 2002
SALES (est): 1.35MM Privately Held
Web: www.redlandsford.com
SIC: 7532 5511 Body shop, automotive;
Automobiles, new and used

(P-14680)
**SAN DIEGO SATURN
RETAILERS INC**
Miramar Collision Center
9985 Huennekens St, San Diego
(92121-2918)
PHONE.....................858 373-3001
Gary Leger, Mgr
EMP: 94
SQ FT: 24,766
Web: www.teamkiaofelcajon.com
SIC: 7532 Collision shops, automotive
PA: San Diego Saturn Retailers, Inc.
541 N Johnson Ave

PRODUCTS & SVCS

7534 Tire Retreading And Repair Shops

(P-14681)
BRIDGESTONE AMERICAS
Also Called: GCR Tires & Service 185
14521 Hawthorne Ave, Fontana
(92335-2508)
PHONE....................909 770-8523
EMP: 36
Web: www.bridgestoneamericas.com
SIC: 7534 5531 Tire repair shop; Automotive tires
HQ: Bridgestone Americas Tire Operations, Llc
200 4th Ave S Ste 100
Nashville TN 37201
615 937-1000

(P-14682)
NEW PRIDE TIRE LLC
1511 E Orangethorpe Ave Ste D, Fullerton
(92831-5204)
PHONE....................310 631-7000
Edward Eunjong Kim, *Pr*
EMP: 50
Web: www.newpridetire.com
SIC: 7534 1799 Rebuilding and retreading tires; Antenna installation
HQ: New Pride Tire, Llc
2900 Main St Bldg 137
Alameda CA 94501
510 567-8800

(P-14683)
TARULLI TIRE INC (PA)
376 Broadway, Costa Mesa (92627-2344)
PHONE....................714 630-4722
Dan Tarulli, *CEO*
Rick Tarulli, *
EMP: 23 EST: 1979
SQ FT: 25,000
SALES (est): 1.55MM
SALES (corp-wide): 1.55MM Privately Held
SIC: 7534 5014 5531 Rebuilding and retreading tires; Tires and tubes; Automotive tires

7537 Automotive Transmission Repair Shops

(P-14684)
H & A TRANSMISSIONS INC
8727 Rochester Ave, Rancho Cucamonga
(91730-4908)
P.O. Box 4378 (91729-4378)
PHONE....................909 941-9020
Gilbert H Dickason, *CEO*
Corina Dickason, *
▲ EMP: 26 EST: 1992
SQ FT: 3,500
SALES (est): 6.05MM Privately Held
Web: www.handatrans.com
SIC: 7537 3714 Automotive transmission repair shops; Axle housings and shafts, motor vehicle

7538 General Automotive Repair Shops

(P-14685)
ALLIED LUBE INC
Also Called: Jiffy Lube
3087 Edinger Ave, Tustin (92780-7240)
PHONE....................949 651-8814

Lillian Kline, *Acctnt*
EMP: 183
Web: www.jiffylube.com
SIC: 7538 7549 General automotive repair shops; Lubrication service, automotive
PA: Allied Lube, Inc.
27240 La Paz Rd

(P-14686)
BRAKE DEPOT SYSTEMS INC
Also Called: Brake &TIre Depot
1205 E 1st St, Santa Ana (92701-6324)
PHONE....................714 835-4833
EMP: 280
Web: www.tiredepotcompany.com
SIC: 7538 General automotive repair shops
PA: Brake Depot Systems Inc
8901 Sw Canyon Rd

(P-14687)
CENTRAL CALIFORNIA POWER
19487 Broken Ct, Shafter (93263-3146)
P.O. Box 1934 (93303-1934)
PHONE....................661 589-2870
Rhoderick E Headley, *CEO*
Rhoderick E Headley, *Pr*
Blake Headley, *
EMP: 25 EST: 1982
SQ FT: 15,000
SALES (est): 8.8MM Privately Held
Web: www.gensets.com
SIC: 7538 7359 3569 Truck engine repair, except industrial; Equipment rental and leasing, nec; Gas generators

(P-14688)
CITY CHEVROLET OF SAN DIEGO
Also Called: City Chevrolet of Volkswagen
2111 Morena Blvd, San Diego (92110-3440)
P.O. Box 85345 (92186-5345)
PHONE....................619 276-6171
EMP: 148 EST: 2016
SALES (est): 8.51MM Privately Held
Web: www.courtesysandiego.com
SIC: 7538 5511 7515 5015 General automotive repair shops; Automobiles, new and used; Passenger car leasing; Automotive supplies, used: wholesale and retail

(P-14689)
CITY OF BURBANK
Also Called: Public Works Equipment
124 S Lake St, Burbank (91502-2108)
P.O. Box 6459 (91510-6459)
PHONE....................818 238-3838
Ari Omessi, *Mgr*
EMP: 82
SALES (corp-wide): 282.12MM Privately Held
Web: www.burbankca.gov
SIC: 7538 9111 General automotive repair shops; Executive offices
PA: City Of Burbank
275 E Olive Ave
818 238-5800

(P-14690)
GRIMMWAY ENTERPRISES INC
2171 W Bannister Rd, Brawley
(92227-9653)
PHONE....................760 344-0204
Cheryl Chaney, *Prin*
EMP: 70
SALES (corp-wide): 577.4MM Privately Held
Web: www.grimmway.com
SIC: 7538 General automotive repair shops
PA: Grimmway Enterprises, Inc.
12064 Buena Vista Blvd

800 301-3101

(P-14691)
HAMBLINS BDY PNT FRAME SP INC
Also Called: Hamblin's Auto & Body Shop
7590 Cypress Ave, Riverside (92503-1904)
PHONE....................951 689-8440
Rod Perry, *Pr*
EMP: 70 EST: 1965
SALES (est): 2.41MM Privately Held
Web: www.kaizenautocare.com
SIC: 7538 7532 General automotive repair shops; Body shop, automotive

(P-14692)
IRONMAN RENEWAL LLC
2535 Anselmo Dr, Corona (92879-8092)
PHONE....................951 735-3710
EMP: 87
SIC: 7538 Truck engine repair, except industrial

(P-14693)
LANCASTER CMNTY SVCS FNDTION I
Also Called: Development Services
46008 7th St W, Lancaster (93534-7602)
PHONE....................661 723-6230
Randy Williams, *Mgr*
EMP: 200
Web: www.cityoflancasterca.org
SIC: 7538 9111 General automotive repair shops; Mayors' office
PA: The Lancaster Community Services Foundation Inc
44933 Fern Ave
661 723-6000

(P-14694)
LOS ANGELES TRUCK CENTERS LLC (PA)
Also Called: Velocity Vehicle Group
2429 Peck Rd, Whittier (90601-1605)
P.O. Box 101284 (91189)
PHONE....................562 447-1200
EMP: 90 EST: 1998
SALES (est): 233.56MM
SALES (corp-wide): 233.56MM Privately Held
Web: www.velocitytruckcenters.com
SIC: 7538 5012 5013 7532 Truck engine repair, except industrial; Trucks, commercial; Truck parts and accessories; Body shop, trucks

(P-14695)
MISSION SERVICE INC
1800 Avenue Of The Stars Ste 1400, Los Angeles (90067-4216)
PHONE....................323 266-2593
John E Anderson, *Pr*
John E Anderson Junior, *Treas*
EMP: 1160 EST: 1976
SALES (est): 312.01K
SALES (corp-wide): 251.02MM Privately Held
SIC: 7538 Truck engine repair, except industrial
PA: Topa Equities, Ltd.
1800 Avenue Of The Stars
310 203-9199

(P-14696)
NEWPORT BEACH AUTO GROUP LLC
Also Called: Bugatti Newport Beach
44 Auto Center Dr, Irvine (92618-2802)
PHONE....................888 703-7226

EMP: 98 EST: 2018
SALES (est): 1.97MM Privately Held
Web: www.koenigseggnb.com
SIC: 7538 General automotive repair shops

(P-14697)
QUALIS AUTOMOTIVE LLC
21046 Figueroa St, Carson (90745-1906)
PHONE....................859 689-7772
EMP: 100
SALES (corp-wide): 70.48MM Privately Held
Web: www.centricparts.com
SIC: 7538 General automotive repair shops
PA: Qualis Automotive, L.L.C.
14528 Bonelli St
310 218-1082

(P-14698)
R&C MOTOR CORPORATION
Also Called: Claremont Toyota
601 Auto Center Dr, Claremont
(91711-5470)
PHONE....................909 625-1500
EMP: 200 EST: 1992
SALES (est): 9.89MM Privately Held
Web: www.claremonttoyota.com
SIC: 7538 5511 General automotive repair shops; Automobiles, new and used

(P-14699)
SANGERA BUICK INC
Also Called: Mercedes Benz of Bakersfield
5600 Gasoline Alley Dr, Bakersfield
(93313-3737)
PHONE....................661 833-5200
Damon Culbertson, *Pr*
Mehnga Sangera, *
Hardev Sangera, *
EMP: 85 EST: 1969
SQ FT: 20,000
SALES (est): 4.73MM Privately Held
Web: www.sangera.com
SIC: 7538 5531 5511 General automotive repair shops; Automotive parts; Automobiles, new and used

(P-14700)
TED FORD JONES INC (PA)
Also Called: Ken Grody Ford
6211 Beach Blvd, Buena Park
(90621-2307)
P.O. Box 2154 (90621-0654)
PHONE....................714 521-3110
Kenneth B Grody, *Pr*
Ken Grody, *
Curt Maletych, *
▼ EMP: 110 EST: 1995
SQ FT: 4,500
SALES (est): 45.03MM
SALES (corp-wide): 45.03MM Privately Held
Web: www.quicklane.com
SIC: 7538 5511 General automotive repair shops; Automobiles, new and used

7539 Automotive Repair Shops, Nec

(P-14701)
AIRDRAULICS INC
13261 Saticoy St, North Hollywood
(91605-3401)
PHONE....................818 982-1400
Dan Tracey, *CEO*
Devin Tracey, *
EMP: 25 EST: 1986
SQ FT: 5,000
SALES (est): 5.83MM Privately Held

Web: www.airdraulicsinc.com
SIC: **7539** 3599 5013 5084 Automotive repair shops, nec; Machine and other job shop work; Automotive servicing equipment ; Industrial machinery and equipment

(P-14702)
AKH COMPANY INC
Also Called: Discount Tire Center 025
7120 Laurel Canyon Blvd, North Hollywood (91605-5740)
PHONE...................818 691-1978
Leo Gonzalez, *Mgr*
EMP: 74
SALES (corp-wide): 22.1MM **Privately Held**
Web: www.discounttirecenters.com
SIC: **7539** 5014 5531 Wheel alignment, automotive; Automobile tires and tubes; Automotive tires
PA: Akh Company, Inc.
1160 N Anaheim Blvd
800 999-2878

(P-14703)
ST GEORGE AUTO CENTER INC
Also Called: Stg Auto Group
13861 Harbor Blvd, Garden Grove (92843-4043)
P.O. Box 2129 (91763-0629)
PHONE...................657 212-5042
EMP: 99
SALES (corp-wide): 5.16MM **Privately Held**
SIC: **7539** Automotive repair shops, nec
PA: St. George Auto Center, Inc.
10325 Central Ave
909 341-1189

7542 Carwashes

(P-14704)
BLUE BEACON USA LP
Also Called: Blue Beacon of Wheeler Ridge
5831 Santa Elena Dr, Arvin (93203-9705)
PHONE...................661 858-2090
Jose Gonzalez, *Mgr*
EMP: 104
SALES (corp-wide): 38MM **Privately Held**
Web: www.bluebeacon.com
SIC: **7542** Truck wash
PA: Blue Beacon U.S.A., L.P.
500 Graves Blvd
785 825-2221

(P-14705)
CAR WASH PARTNERS INC
Also Called: CAR WASH PARTNERS, INC.
2619 Mount Vernon Ave, Bakersfield (93306-2900)
PHONE...................661 377-1020
EMP: 246
SALES (corp-wide): 927.07MM **Publicly Held**
Web: www.mistercarwash.com
SIC: **7542** Washing and polishing, automotive
HQ: Car Wash Partners, Llc
222 E 5th St
Tucson AZ 85705
520 615-4000

(P-14706)
CAR WASH PARTNERS INC
Also Called: CAR WASH PARTNERS INC.
5375 Olive Dr, Bakersfield (93308-2921)
PHONE...................661 231-3689
EMP: 74
SALES (corp-wide): 1.13B **Privately Held**

Web: www.mistercarwash.com
SIC: **7542** Washing and polishing, automotive
HQ: Car Wash Partners, Llc
1503 S Collins St
Plant City FL 33563

(P-14707)
DYNAMIC AUTO IMAGES INC
Also Called: Dynamic Detail
2860 Michelle Ste 140, Irvine (92606-1007)
PHONE...................714 771-3400
Tom Miller, *Pr*
EMP: 300 EST: 2004
SALES (est): 7.41MM **Privately Held**
Web: www.dentwizard.com
SIC: **7542** 7532 Washing and polishing, automotive; Collision shops, automotive

(P-14708)
EXECUTIVE AUTO RECONDITIONING
Also Called: Dealership Auto Dtail Rstrtons
522 E Duarte Rd, Monrovia (91016-4604)
P.O. Box 33 (90640-0033)
PHONE...................626 416-3322
Miguel Alvarado, *CEO*
EMP: 45 EST: 2017
SALES (est): 468.96K **Privately Held**
SIC: **7542** 7532 3842 Carwashes; Body shop, automotive; Cosmetic restorations

(P-14709)
GREEN-N-CLEAN EX CAR WASH INC
Also Called: H2go Car Wash
28622 Oso Pkwy Pmb C, Rcho Sta Marg (92688-5540)
PHONE...................949 749-4977
Ryan Blanchard, *CEO*
EMP: 75 EST: 2010
SALES (est): 8MM **Privately Held**
Web: www.h2gocarwash.com
SIC: **7542** Carwashes

(P-14710)
SAN RAMON SERVICES INC
Also Called: Sponges Car Wash
12101 Palms Blvd, Los Angeles (90066-1925)
P.O. Box 1736 (94583-6736)
PHONE...................925 901-1400
Jack Levine, *Pr*
EMP: 90 EST: 1993
SALES (est): 450.21K **Privately Held**
Web: www.dsrsd.com
SIC: **7542** Carwashes

7549 Automotive Services, Nec

(P-14711)
ALLIANCE INSPTN MGT HOLDG INC (PA)
330 Golden Shore Ste 400, Long Beach (90802-4271)
PHONE...................562 495-8853
Steve Lambert, *Pr*
EMP: 600 EST: 2005
SALES (est): 36.47MM
SALES (corp-wide): 36.47MM **Privately Held**
SIC: **7549** 6719 Inspection and diagnostic service, automotive; Investment holding companies, except banks

(P-14712)
AMERIT FLEET SOLUTIONS INC
15325 Manila St, Fontana (92337-7261)
PHONE...................909 357-0100
David Kristy, *Mgr*
EMP: 665
Web: www.ameritfleetsolutions.com
SIC: **7549** Inspection and diagnostic service, automotive
HQ: Amerit Fleet Solutions Inc.
1333 N California Blvd
Walnut Creek CA 94596
877 512-6374

(P-14713)
AUTOMOTIVE TSTG & DEV SVCS INC (PA)
400 Etiwanda Ave, Ontario (91761-8637)
PHONE...................909 390-1100
Devon Larry Smith, *CEO*
Kay Smith, *
▲ EMP: 185 EST: 1989
SQ FT: 24,000
SALES (est): 9.38MM **Privately Held**
Web: www.automotivetesting.com
SIC: **7549** 8734 8711 Emissions testing without repairs, automotive; Testing laboratories; Engineering services

(P-14714)
COMPLETE COACH WORKS
42882 Ivy St, Murrieta (92562-7218)
PHONE...................800 300-3751
EMP: 230
SALES (corp-wide): 25.1MM **Privately Held**
Web: www.completecoach.com
SIC: **7549** Trailer maintenance
HQ: Complete Coach Works
1863 Service Ct
Riverside CA 92507

(P-14715)
EZ LUBE LLC
Also Called: Valvoline Instant Oil Change
3599 Harbor Blvd, Costa Mesa (92626-1405)
PHONE...................714 966-1647
Abdul Keium, *Brnch Mgr*
EMP: 126
SALES (corp-wide): 21.83MM **Privately Held**
Web: www.expresscare.com
SIC: **7549** Lubrication service, automotive
PA: Ez Lube, Llc
3540 Howard Way Ste 200

(P-14716)
EZ LUBE LLC
Also Called: EZ Lube- Costco
13421 Washington Blvd, Marina Del Rey (90292-5658)
PHONE...................310 821-2517
Doug Paysse, *Mgr*
EMP: 136
SALES (corp-wide): 9.84MM **Privately Held**
Web: www.ezlube.com
SIC: **7549** Lubrication service, automotive
PA: Ez Lube, Llc
3540 Howard Way Ste 200

(P-14717)
KEYSTONE TOWING INC
Also Called: Keystone
7817 Woodley Ave, Van Nuys (91406-1703)
PHONE...................818 782-1996
Mark Henninger, *Pr*
EMP: 70 EST: 2005

SQ FT: 120,000
SALES (est): 1.95MM **Privately Held**
Web: www.keystonetowing.com
SIC: **7549** Towing service, automotive
PA: Old Towing Company
16325 Crawford Ave

(P-14718)
METROPRO ROAD SERVICES INC
Also Called: A & P Towing-Metropro Rd Svcs
957 W 17th St, Costa Mesa (92627-4402)
PHONE...................714 556-7600
TOLL FREE: 800
Bradley T Humphreys, *CEO*
Jody Campbell, *
EMP: 100 EST: 1998
SALES (est): 2.78MM **Privately Held**
Web: www.metro-pro.com
SIC: **7549** Towing service, automotive

(P-14719)
SINGER VEHICLE DESIGN LLC (PA)
19500 S Vermont Ave, Torrance (90502-1120)
PHONE...................213 592-2728
Mazen Fawaz, *CEO*
Robert Peter Dickinson, *CPO*
Jason Grant, *CFO*
Jason Franklin, *COO*
EMP: 250 EST: 2009
SALES (est): 25.24MM
SALES (corp-wide): 25.24MM **Privately Held**
Web: www.singervehicledesign.com
SIC: **7549** 3714 Automotive customizing services, nonfactory basis; Acceleration equipment, motor vehicle

(P-14720)
SUNBELT TOWING INC (PA)
Also Called: Western Towing
4370 Pacific Hwy, San Diego (92110-3106)
PHONE...................619 297-8697
Steven Hendrickson, *Pr*
EMP: 70 EST: 1978
SALES (est): 5.23MM
SALES (corp-wide): 5.23MM **Privately Held**
Web: www.westerntowing.com
SIC: **7549** 7532 Towing service, automotive; Top and body repair and paint shops

(P-14721)
VALVOLINE INSTANT OIL CHNGE FR
Also Called: Valvoline Instant Oil Change
9520 John St, Santa Fe Springs (90670-2904)
PHONE...................562 906-6200
Brian Nichols, *Brnch Mgr*
EMP: 76
Web: www.valvoline.com
SIC: **7549** Lubrication service, automotive
HQ: Valvoline Instant Oil Change Franchising, Inc.
100 Valvoline Way
Lexington KY 40509

7622 Radio And Television Repair

(P-14722)
DISH FOR ALL INC
148 S Escondido Blvd, Escondido (92025-4115)
PHONE...................760 690-3869

Ahed Ihmud, *Pr*
Rania Abedel Whab, *
Mike Arfat, *
EMP: 30 **EST:** 2007
SQ FT: 4,000
SALES (est): 187.89K **Privately Held**
Web: www.dishforall.com
SIC: 7622 5731 3679 Radio and television receiver installation; Radio, television, and electronic stores; Antennas, satellite: household use

7623 Refrigeration Service And Repair

(P-14723)
ARCTICOM GROUP RFRGN LLC
Also Called: PMC Southwest LLC
3675 De Forest Cir, Jurupa Valley (91752-1139)
PHONE...............................916 484-3190
Sean Patrick, *Pr*
EMP: 406 **EST:** 2017
SALES (est): 34.44MM
SALES (corp-wide): 209.88MM **Privately Held**
Web: www.pmc-southwest.com
SIC: 7623 Refrigeration service and repair
PA: The Arcticom Group Llc
1676 N California Blvd
925 334-7222

(P-14724)
CLIMA-TECH INC
1820 Town And Country Dr, Norco (92860-3616)
PHONE...............................909 613-5513
William C Valenzuela, *CEO*
Husein Aziz, *
Ada Roberts, *
EMP: 89 **EST:** 2004
SALES (est): 6.97MM **Privately Held**
Web: www.climatechref.com
SIC: 7623 1711 Refrigeration service and repair; Refrigeration contractor

(P-14725)
CONTROL AIR ENTERPRISES LLC
1390 Armorlite Dr, San Marcos (92069-1342)
PHONE...............................760 744-2727
Mike Eepn, *Brnch Mgr*
EMP: 477
SALES (corp-wide): 277.7MM **Privately Held**
Web: www.controlac.com
SIC: 7623 1711 Refrigeration service and repair; Heating systems repair and maintenance
PA: Control Air Enterprises Llc
5200 E La Palma Ave
714 777-8600

7629 Electrical Repair Shops

(P-14726)
5 STAR SERVICE INC
Also Called: E Appliance Repair and Hvac
18723 Via Princessa, Santa Clarita (91387-4954)
PHONE...............................323 647-7777
Sardor Umrdinov, *CEO*
EMP: 50 **EST:** 2018
SALES (est): 211.98K **Privately Held**
SIC: 7629 1389 Electrical household appliance repair; Construction, repair, and dismantling services

(P-14727)
ABLE CABLE INC (PA)
Also Called: A C I Communications
5115 Douglas Fir Rd Ste A, Calabasas (91302-2588)
PHONE...............................818 223-3600
Russell Ramas, *Pr*
Russell Ramas, *CEO*
Michael Collette, *
David Gardner, *
EMP: 175 **EST:** 1983
SQ FT: 3,500
SALES (est): 4.57MM
SALES (corp-wide): 4.57MM **Privately Held**
Web: www.acicommunications.com
SIC: 7629 1731 4813 Telephone set repair; Telephone and telephone equipment installation; Telephone communication, except radio

(P-14728)
AUTHORIZED CELLULAR SERVICE
Also Called: ACS
8808 S Sepulveda Blvd, Los Angeles (90045-4810)
PHONE...............................310 466-4144
EMP: 100 **EST:** 1993
SQ FT: 10,000
SALES (est): 492.95K **Privately Held**
SIC: 7629 5999 Telephone set repair; Telephone equipment and systems

(P-14729)
BSH HOME APPLIANCES CORP (DH)
1901 Main St Ste 600, Irvine (92614-0521)
PHONE...............................949 440-7100
TOLL FREE: 800
Christofer Von Nagel, *Pr*
Stefan Koss, *
◆ **EMP:** 220 **EST:** 1996
SQ FT: 52,000
SALES (est): 119.28MM
SALES (corp-wide): 391.51MM **Privately Held**
Web: www.bosch-home.com
SIC: 7629 Electrical household appliance repair
HQ: Bsh Hausgerate Gmbh
Carl-Wery-Str. 34
Munchen BY 81739
89459001

(P-14730)
SCHROFF INC
Also Called: Pentair Equipment Protection
7328 Trade St, San Diego (92121-3435)
PHONE...............................858 740-2400
Robert Bradley, *Brnch Mgr*
EMP: 120
Web: schroff.nvent.com
SIC: 7629 3469 Telecommunication equipment repair (except telephones); Electronic enclosures, stamped or pressed metal
HQ: Schroff, Inc.
170 Commerce Dr
Warwick RI 02886
763 204-7700

(P-14731)
SCOTTEL VOICE & DATA INC
Also Called: Black Box Network Services
6100 Center Dr Ste 720, Los Angeles (90045-9228)
PHONE...............................310 737-7300
George Robertson, *Genl Mgr*
EMP: 130 **EST:** 1984

SQ FT: 5,200
SALES (est): 4.92MM **Privately Held**
Web: www.blackbox.com
SIC: 7629 1731 Telecommunication equipment repair (except telephones); Telephone and telephone equipment installation
HQ: Black Box Corporation
2701 N Dllas Pkwy Ste 510
Plano TX 75093
724 746-5500

(P-14732)
STANDARD CALIBRATIONS INC
681 Anita St Ste 103, Chula Vista (91911-4663)
PHONE...............................619 477-1668
Victor Lewis, *Brnch Mgr*
EMP: 72
Web: www.standardcal.com
SIC: 7629 Electrical measuring instrument repair and calibration
PA: Standard Calibrations, Inc.
501 Resource Row

(P-14733)
TELENET VOIP INC
Also Called: Telenet
850 N Park View Dr, El Segundo (90245-4914)
PHONE...............................310 253-9000
TOLL FREE: 800
Asghar Ghassemy, *Pr*
Nicol Payab, *
EMP: 65 **EST:** 1977
SQ FT: 11,000
SALES (est): 9.69MM **Privately Held**
Web: www.telenetvoip.com
SIC: 7629 7379 7382 3612 Telephone set repair; Computer related consulting services; Security systems services; Transmission and distribution voltage regulators

(P-14734)
TESTEQUITY LLC (HQ)
Also Called: Techni-Tools
6100 Condor Dr, Moorpark (93021-2608)
PHONE...............................805 498-9933
Ruzz Frazee, *Pr*
Nick Hawtrey, *
Aftan Lorick, *
▲ **EMP:** 99 **EST:** 1971
SQ FT: 75,000
SALES (est): 163.89MM
SALES (corp-wide): 1.57B **Publicly Held**
Web: www.testequity.com
SIC: 7629 3825 Electrical equipment repair services; Test equipment for electronic and electrical circuits
PA: Distribution Solutions Group, Inc.
301 Commerce St Ste 1700
888 611-9888

7641 Reupholstery And Furniture Repair

(P-14735)
GUYS PATIO INC
Also Called: Patio Guys
845 N Elm St, Orange (92867-7909)
PHONE...............................844 968-7485
Jan Vanderlinden, *Pr*
EMP: 25 **EST:** 1978
SALES (est): 1.42MM **Privately Held**
Web: www.patioguys.com
SIC: 7641 5712 5021 2514 Furniture repair and maintenance; Furniture stores; Outdoor and lawn furniture, nec; Metal household furniture

(P-14736)
MOYES CUSTOM FURNITURE INC
1884 Pomona Rd, Corona (92878-3278)
PHONE...............................714 729-0234
Brian Moyes, *Pr*
Jane Moyes, *
David Moyes Secratry, *Prin*
EMP: 50 **EST:** 1961
SQ FT: 59,000
SALES (est): 1.72MM **Privately Held**
Web: www.moyesfurniture.com
SIC: 7641 2512 Reupholstery; Upholstered household furniture

7692 Welding Repair

(P-14737)
CAMERON WELDING SUPPLY (PA)
Also Called: Cameron Welding
11061 Dale Ave, Stanton (90680-3247)
P.O. Box 266 (90680-0266)
PHONE...............................714 530-9353
Elizabeth Perry, *CEO*
Joseph Churilla, *
▲ **EMP:** 36 **EST:** 1963
SQ FT: 4,500
SALES (est): 6.19MM
SALES (corp-wide): 6.19MM **Privately Held**
Web: www.cameronwelding.com
SIC: 7692 5999 Welding repair; Welding supplies

(P-14738)
CLP INC (PA)
Also Called: Rick's Hitches & Welding
1546 E Main St, El Cajon (92021-5901)
PHONE...............................619 444-3105
Richard Preston, *Pr*
Betty Preston, *
EMP: 30 **EST:** 1974
SQ FT: 23,500
SALES (est): 294.2K
SALES (corp-wide): 294.2K **Privately Held**
Web: www.cwclp.org
SIC: 7692 7533 7699 Welding repair; Muffler shop, sale or repair and installation; Recreational vehicle repair services

(P-14739)
CW INDUSTRIES INC (PA)
1735 Santa Fe Ave, Long Beach (90813-1242)
PHONE...............................562 432-5421
Craig Wildvank, *Pr*
EMP: 49 **EST:** 1979
SQ FT: 22,000
SALES (est): 7.8MM **Privately Held**
Web: www.cwindustries.us
SIC: 7692 Welding repair

(P-14740)
HANSENS WELDING INC
358 W 168th St, Gardena (90248-2733)
PHONE...............................310 329-6888
Gary D Hansen, *CEO*
Robert Hansen, *
Shauna Hansen, *
EMP: 25 **EST:** 1949
SQ FT: 26,000
SALES (est): 2.52MM **Privately Held**
Web: www.hansenswelding.com
SIC: 7692 Welding repair

(P-14741)
HAYES WELDING INC (PA)
Also Called: Valew Welding & Fabrication
12522 Violet Rd, Adelanto (92301-2704)
P.O. Box 310 (92301-0310)
PHONE..................760 246-4878
Roger L Hayes, *CEO*
Velma D Hayes, *
Vernon L Hayes, *
▲ **EMP:** 91 **EST:** 1954
SQ FT: 45,000
SALES (est): 10.73MM
SALES (corp-wide): 10.73MM **Privately Held**
Web: www.valew.com
SIC: 7692 3465 3714 3713 Welding repair; Automotive stampings; Fuel systems and parts, motor vehicle; Truck and bus bodies

(P-14742)
IRONMAN INC
20555 Superior St, Chatsworth (91311-4418)
PHONE..................818 341-0980
Joe Salem, *CEO*
Ziva Salem, *
Ben Salem, *
Tish Byrne, *
EMP: 25 **EST:** 1987
SALES (est): 4.49MM **Privately Held**
Web: www.ironmaninc.net
SIC: 7692 Welding repair

(P-14743)
RETTIG MACHINE INC
301 Kansas St, Redlands (92373-8153)
P.O. Box 7460 (92375-0460)
PHONE..................909 793-7811
Franz A Rettig Senior, *Pr*
Robert A Rettig, *
Franz A Rettig Junior, *VP*
Susan L Rettig, *
EMP: 25 **EST:** 1952
SQ FT: 37,000
SALES (est): 2.19MM **Privately Held**
Web: www.rettigmachine.com
SIC: 7692 3599 Welding repair; Machine shop, jobbing and repair

(P-14744)
SOUTHCOAST WELDING & MFG LLC
2591 Faivre St Ste 1, Chula Vista (91911-7146)
PHONE..................619 429-1337
Patrick Shoup, *Pr*
Jay Parast, *
Leo Mathieu, *
EMP: 270 **EST:** 2004
SQ FT: 82,000
SALES (est): 44.01MM **Privately Held**
Web: www.southcoastwelding.net
SIC: 7692 Welding repair

(P-14745)
T L FABRICATIONS LP
2921 E Coronado St, Anaheim (92806-2502)
PHONE..................562 802-3980
Ryan Kerrigan, *Pr*
Michael Hsu, *
▲ **EMP:** 60 **EST:** 1980
SQ FT: 30,000
SALES (est): 2.43MM **Privately Held**
SIC: 7692 Welding repair

(P-14746)
WELDLOGIC INC
Also Called: Weldlogic Gas & Supply
2651 Lavery Ct, Newbury Park (91320-1502)
PHONE..................805 375-1670
Robert Elizarraz, *Pr*
Jack Froschauer, *
▲ **EMP:** 65 **EST:** 1980
SQ FT: 25,000
SALES (est): 9.89MM **Privately Held**
Web: www.weldlogic.com
SIC: 7692 Welding repair

(P-14747)
WEST COAST WLDG & PIPING INC
Also Called: Pipline
760 W Hueneme Rd, Oxnard (93033-9013)
PHONE..................805 246-5841
Gabriel Nunez, *Managing Member*
Jose Vargas, *
Mike Barbey, *
EMP: 80 **EST:** 2018
SALES (est): 1.21MM **Privately Held**
Web: www.wcwpiping.com
SIC: 7692 Welding repair

(P-14748)
WYMORE INC
697 S Dogwood Rd, El Centro (92243-9747)
P.O. Box 2618 (92244-2618)
PHONE..................760 352-2045
Marla Wymore Stilwell, *Pr*
Michael Mouser, *
Richard C Wymore, *
Thomas A Wymore, *
EMP: 30 **EST:** 1947
SQ FT: 25,200
SALES (est): 2.27MM **Privately Held**
Web: www.wymoreinc.com
SIC: 7692 3599 5251 5085 Welding repair; Machine shop, jobbing and repair; Tools; Tools, nec

7694 Armature Rewinding Shops

(P-14749)
GRECH MOTORS LLC (PA)
6915 Arlington Ave, Riverside (92504-1905)
PHONE..................951 688-8347
Edward P Grech, *Managing Member*
EMP: 25 **EST:** 2012
SALES (est): 24.57MM
SALES (corp-wide): 24.57MM **Privately Held**
Web: www.grechmotors.com
SIC: 7694 Electric motor repair

(P-14750)
R A REED ELECTRIC COMPANY (PA)
Also Called: Reed Electric & Field Service
5503 S Boyle Ave, Vernon (90058-3997)
PHONE..................323 587-2284
John A Richard Junior, *Pr*
Dorothy J Richard, *
Alex Wong, *
EMP: 29 **EST:** 1929
SQ FT: 55,000
SALES (est): 10.95MM
SALES (corp-wide): 10.95MM **Privately Held**
SIC: 7694 5063 Electric motor repair; Motors, electric

(P-14751)
SULZER ELCTR-MCHNCAL SVCS US I
620 S Rancho Ave, Colton (92324-3243)
PHONE..................909 825-7971
Gary Patton, *Brnch Mgr*
EMP: 50
Web: www.sulzer.com
SIC: 7694 5063 Electric motor repair; Motors, electric
HQ: Sulzer Electro-Mechanical Services (Us) Inc.
1910 Jasmine Dr
Pasadena TX 77503
713 473-3231

7699 Repair Services, Nec

(P-14752)
ACTION CLEANING CORPORATION
1668 Newton Ave, San Diego (92113-1013)
PHONE..................619 233-1881
Roberto Victoria, *Pr*
EMP: 40 **EST:** 1982
SALES (est): 7.15MM **Privately Held**
Web: www.action-cleaning.com
SIC: 7699 4212 3732 Tank and boiler cleaning service; Hazardous waste transport ; Boatbuilding and repairing

(P-14753)
AER TECHNOLOGIES INC
Also Called: Aer Logistics
650 Columbia St, Brea (92821-2912)
PHONE..................714 871-7357
Kim Quick, *CEO*
Michael Mcgroarty, *Pr*
Ingrid Osborne, *
EMP: 320 **EST:** 1953
SQ FT: 50,000
SALES (est): 24.98MM **Privately Held**
Web: www.aertech.com
SIC: 7699 Precision instrument repair

(P-14754)
AEROWORX INC
Also Called: Aero Worx
2565 W 237th St, Torrance (90505-5216)
PHONE..................310 891-0300
Gary E Furlong, *Pr*
Carol Furlong, *
▼ **EMP:** 30 **EST:** 1999
SQ FT: 38,800
SALES (est): 5.02MM **Privately Held**
Web: www.aero-worx.com
SIC: 7699 3569 3492 3724 Industrial equipment services; Industrial shock absorbers; Control valves, aircraft: hydraulic and pneumatic; Pumps, aircraft engine

(P-14755)
AI PHATECH GENERAL INC
Also Called: Ametek-Ameron
4750 Littlejohn St, Baldwin Park (91706-2274)
PHONE..................626 337-4640
EMP: 90
SIC: 7699 3812 Aircraft and heavy equipment repair services; Aircraft/ aerospace flight instruments and guidance systems

(P-14756)
AMERICAN VISION WINDOWS INC
Also Called: American Vision Baths
2125 N Madera Rd Ste A, Simi Valley (93065-7709)
PHONE..................805 582-1833
William Herren, *CEO*
Monica Estrada, *
Al Alfieri, *
EMP: 215 **EST:** 1999
SALES (est): 24.92MM **Privately Held**
Web: www.americanvisionwindows.com
SIC: 7699 1799 5031 Door and window repair; Home/office interiors finishing, furnishing and remodeling; Metal doors, sash and trim

(P-14757)
AMKO SERVICE COMPANY
17909 Adelanto Rd, Adelanto (92301-1745)
PHONE..................760 246-3600
Michael Medsker, *Mgr*
EMP: 70
Web: www.amkotech.com
SIC: 7699 Tank repair and cleaning services
HQ: Amko Service Company
3211 Brightwood Rd
Midvale OH 44653
330 364-8857

(P-14758)
BRIDPORT ERIE AVIATION INC
Also Called: Amsafe Bridport
6900 Orangethorpe Ave, Buena Park (90620-1390)
PHONE..................714 634-8801
Sal Valle, *Genl Mgr*
Keith Mcconnell, *Pr*
Dennis Gilbert, *VP*
Harold Handelsman, *Sec*
Habib Enayetullah, *Treas*
EMP: 25 **EST:** 2000
SALES (est): 1.19MM **Privately Held**
Web: www.amsafebridport.com
SIC: 7699 7363 3728 Aircraft and heavy equipment repair services; Pilot service, aviation; Aircraft body and wing assemblies and parts

(P-14759)
CHROMALLOY SAN DIEGO CORP
7007 Consolidated Way, San Diego (92121-2604)
PHONE..................858 877-2800
Armand F Lauzon Junior, *CEO*
Carlo Luzzatto, *
David G Albert, *
Michael Beffel, *
John Mckirdy, *VP*
EMP: 120 **EST:** 1986
SQ FT: 120,000
SALES (est): 16.69MM
SALES (corp-wide): 517.74MM **Privately Held**
Web: www.chromalloy.com
SIC: 7699 3724 Aircraft and heavy equipment repair services; Aircraft engines and engine parts
HQ: Chromalloy American Llc
330 Blaisdell Rd
Orangeburg NY 10962
845 230-7355

(P-14760)
COLLECTORS UNIVERSE INC (PA)
Also Called: Collectors Universe
1600 E Saint Andrew Pl, Santa Ana (92705-4926)
P.O. Box 6280 (92658-6280)
PHONE..................949 567-1234
Nathaniel Turner, *CEO*
Bruce A Stevens, *
Jason Harinstein, *CFO*
Roxana Jamshidi, *Sec*
EMP: 182 **EST:** 1986
SQ FT: 62,755

PRODUCTS & SVCS

SALES (est): 78.89MM
SALES (corp-wide): 78.89MM **Privately Held**
Web: www.collectors.com
SIC: **7699** Hobby and collectors services

(P-14761)
CROTHALL SERVICES GROUP
14710 Northam St, La Mirada (90638-5620)
PHONE....................714 562-9275
Frank Arcos, *Brnch Mgr*
EMP: 1310
SALES (corp-wide): 39.16B **Privately Held**
Web: www.crothall.com
SIC: **7699** Hospital equipment repair services
HQ: Crothall Services Group
　　1500 Lbrty Rdge Dr Ste 21
　　Wayne PA 19087

(P-14762)
CURTISS-WRIGHT CORPORATION
Also Called: Sgt Dresser-Rand
1675 Brandywine Ave Ste E, Chula Vista
(91911-6064)
PHONE....................619 656-4740
Joshua Guedsse, *Service Center Manager*
EMP: 44
SALES (corp-wide): 2.85B **Publicly Held**
Web: www.curtisswright.com
SIC: **7699 3731** Industrial machinery and equipment repair; Shipbuilding and repairing
PA: Curtiss-Wright Corporation
　　130 Harbour Pl Dr Ste 300
　　704 869-4600

(P-14763)
EDN AVIATION INC
6720 Valjean Ave, Van Nuys (91406-5818)
PHONE....................818 988-8826
Motti Kurzweil, *Pr*
EMP: 45 EST: 1987
SQ FT: 15,000
SALES (est): 4.07MM
SALES (corp-wide): 168.68MM **Privately Held**
Web: www.ednaviation.com
SIC: **7699 3728** Aircraft and heavy equipment repair services; R and D by manuf., aircraft parts and auxiliary equipment
HQ: Velocity Aerospace Group, Inc.
　　495 Lake Mirror Rd
　　Atlanta GA 30349
　　214 988-9898

(P-14764)
ENBIO CORP
150 E Olive Ave Ste 114, Burbank
(91502-1849)
PHONE....................818 953-9976
Arthur Zenian, *CEO*
Greg Aghamanoukian, *
◆ EMP: 142 EST: 2008
SQ FT: 1,500
SALES (est): 2.51MM **Privately Held**
Web: www.enbiocorp.com
SIC: **7699** Medical equipment repair, non-electric

(P-14765)
EVANS HYDRO INC
Also Called: Evans Hydro
18128 S Santa Fe Ave, Compton
(90221-5517)
PHONE....................310 608-5801
James R Byrom, *Pr*
EMP: 28 EST: 1929
SQ FT: 16,000
SALES (est): 4.11MM

SALES (corp-wide): 90.74MM **Privately Held**
Web: www.hydroinc.com
SIC: **7699 7694 5084** Pumps and pumping equipment repair; Armature rewinding shops; Pumps and pumping equipment, nec
PA: Hydro, Inc.
　　834 W Madison St
　　312 738-3000

(P-14766)
EXCEL PICTURE FRAMES INC
647 E 59th St, Los Angeles (90001-1001)
PHONE....................323 231-0244
Rafael Delgado, *CEO*
Antonio Delgado Senior, *Pr*
EMP: 50 EST: 1992
SALES (est): 2.37MM **Privately Held**
Web: www.excelimagegroup.com
SIC: **7699 2791** Picture framing, custom; Photocomposition, for the printing trade

(P-14767)
FLEETWOOD MOTOR HOMES-CALIFINC
Also Called: Fleetwood Homes
2350 Fleetwood Dr, Riverside (92509-2409)
PHONE....................951 274-2000
David Lewis, *Brnch Mgr*
EMP: 185
SIC: **7699 5271** Mobile home repair; Mobile home dealers
HQ: Fleetwood Motor Homes-Calif.Inc
　　3125 Myers St
　　Riverside CA 92503
　　951 354-3000

(P-14768)
GENERAL CONVEYOR INC
Also Called: Cleveland Tramrail So Calif
13385 Estelle St, Corona (92879-1881)
PHONE....................951 734-3460
▼ EMP: 35
Web: tf.click.com.cn
SIC: **7699 1796 3531 3536** Industrial machinery and equipment repair; Machinery installation; Backhoes, tractors, cranes, plows, and similar equipment; Hoists, cranes, and monorails

(P-14769)
GENESIS TECH PARTNERS LLC
21540 Plummer St Ste A, Chatsworth
(91311-4143)
PHONE....................800 950-2647
EMP: 240 EST: 1998
SQ FT: 3,000
SALES (est): 382.1K
SALES (corp-wide): 3.7B **Privately Held**
SIC: **7699** Medical equipment repair, non-electric
HQ: Cohr, Inc.
　　10510 Twin Lakes Pkwy
　　Charlotte NC 28269
　　704 948-5700

(P-14770)
GUITAR CENTER HOLDINGS INC
24961 Pico Canyon Rd, Stevenson Ranch
(91381-1708)
PHONE....................661 222-7521
EMP: 75
Web: stores.guitarcenter.com
SIC: **7699 5736** Musical instrument repair services; Musical instrument stores
PA: Guitar Center Holdings, Inc.
　　5795 Lindero Canyon Rd

(P-14771)
HAWKER PACIFIC AEROSPACE
11240 Sherman Way, Sun Valley
(91352-4942)
PHONE....................818 765-6201
Bernd Riggers, *CEO*
Brian Carr, *
Troy Trower, *
◆ EMP: 355 EST: 1980
SQ FT: 193,000
SALES (est): 23.83MM
SALES (corp-wide): 38.52B **Privately Held**
Web: www.lufthansa-technik.com
SIC: **7699 5088 3728** Hydraulic equipment repair; Aircraft and parts, nec; Aircraft parts and equipment, nec
HQ: Lufthansa Technik Ag
　　Weg Beim Jager 193
　　Hamburg HH 22335
　　4050700

(P-14772)
HRD AERO SYSTEMS INC (PA)
25555 Avenue Stanford, Valencia
(91355-1101)
PHONE....................661 295-0670
Tom Salamone, *Pr*
Tim Mcbride, *CFO*
◆ EMP: 101 EST: 1986
SQ FT: 70,000
SALES (est): 12.22MM **Privately Held**
Web: www.hrd-aerosystems.com
SIC: **7699 8711** Aircraft and heavy equipment repair services; Aviation and/or aeronautical engineering

(P-14773)
HYDRALIC SYSTEMS CMPONENTS INC
Also Called: Rupe's Hydraulics Sales & Svc
725 N Twin Oaks Valley Rd, San Marcos
(92069-1713)
PHONE....................760 744-9350
Patrick John Maluso, *CEO*
Stephanie Jennison, *
▲ EMP: 29 EST: 1977
SQ FT: 36,000
SALES (est): 5.12MM **Privately Held**
Web: www.rupeshydraulics.com
SIC: **7699 5084 3559** Hydraulic equipment repair; Hydraulic systems equipment and supplies; Ammunition and explosives, loading machinery

(P-14774)
KONE INC
1540 Scenic Ave # 100, Costa Mesa
(92626-1408)
PHONE....................714 890-7080
Jeff Schultz, *Mgr*
EMP: 41
Web: www.kone.us
SIC: **7699 3534 1796** Elevators: inspection, service, and repair; Elevators and moving stairways; Installing building equipment
HQ: Kone Inc.
　　3333 Warrenville Rd
　　Lisle IL 60532
　　630 577-1650

(P-14775)
MARINE GROUP BOAT WORKS LLC
Also Called: Marine Group Boat Works
997 G St, Chula Vista (91910-3414)
PHONE....................619 427-6767
Herb Engel, *Managing Member*
Arthur E Engel, *
Todd Roberts, *
▲ EMP: 115 EST: 2008

SALES (est): 21.68MM **Privately Held**
Web: www.marinegroupbw.com
SIC: **7699** Boat repair

(P-14776)
MCKENNA BOILER WORKS INC
2601 Industry St, Oceanside (92054-4808)
PHONE....................323 221-1171
Howard Smith, *Pr*
Richard R Smith, *
James F Smith, *
EMP: 35 EST: 1921
SALES (est): 4.53MM **Privately Held**
Web: www.mckennaboiler.com
SIC: **7699 3823** Boiler repair shop; Boiler controls: industrial, power, and marine type

(P-14777)
NORTHFIELD MEDICAL INC
13631 Pawnee Rd, Apple Valley
(92308-5880)
PHONE....................248 268-2500
EMP: 160
SALES (corp-wide): 1.23B **Privately Held**
Web: www.agilitihealth.com
SIC: **7699** Hospital equipment repair services
HQ: Northfield Medical, Inc.
　　30275 Hudson Dr
　　Novi MI 48377

(P-14778)
O & S PROPERTIES INC (PA)
1817 Chico Ave, South El Monte
(91733-2943)
P.O. Box 3246 (91733-0246)
PHONE....................626 579-1084
TOLL FREE: 800
Ozzie Levine, *Pr*
EMP: 80 EST: 1983
SQ FT: 200,000
SALES (est): 9.65MM
SALES (corp-wide): 9.65MM **Privately Held**
Web: www.tldrumco.com
SIC: **7699 4959 3412** Industrial equipment services; Sanitary services, nec; Metal barrels, drums, and pails

(P-14779)
OMNI OPTICAL PRODUCTS INC
22605 La Palma Ave Ste 505, Yorba Linda
(92887-6712)
PHONE....................714 692-1400
Jeffrey Frank, *Brnch Mgr*
EMP: 31
SALES (corp-wide): 1.9MM **Privately Held**
Web: www.omnisurvey.com
SIC: **7699 5048 3827** Photographic and optical goods equipment repair services; Optometric equipment and supplies; Optical instruments and lenses
PA: Omni Optical Products, Inc.
　　17282 Eastman
　　714 634-5700

(P-14780)
OXYHEAL HEALTH GROUP INC
3224 Hoover Ave, National City
(91950-7224)
PHONE....................619 336-2022
EMP: 250
SIC: **7699** Industrial equipment services

(P-14781)
PASSPORT TECHNOLOGY USA INC
Also Called: Asai
400 N Brand Blvd Ste 800, Glendale
(91203-2366)
PHONE....................818 957-5471

Cleve Tzung, *CEO*
Scott Dowty, *
John Steely, *Chief Operations**
Paul Nielsen, *
Jason H King, *CRO**
EMP: 33 **EST:** 1997
SQ FT: 1,200
SALES (est): 1.55MM **Privately Held**
Web: www.passporttechnology.com
SIC: 7699 3578 6099 Automated teller machine (ATM) repair; Automatic teller machines (ATM); Automated teller machine (ATM) network

(P-14782)
PEGGS COMPANY INC (PA)
4851 Felspar St, Riverside (92509-3024)
P.O. Box 907 (91752)
PHONE..............................800 242-8416
Brett Nelson, *Pr*
Chresten Revelle Nelson, *
John L Peggs, *
◆ **EMP:** 137 **EST:** 1964
SQ FT: 80,000
SALES (est): 32.15MM
SALES (corp-wide): 32.15MM **Privately Held**
Web: www.thepeggscompany.com
SIC: 7699 3496 5046 7359 Shopping cart repair; Miscellaneous fabricated wire products; Commercial equipment, nec; Equipment rental and leasing, nec

(P-14783)
PKL SERVICES INC
14265 Danielson St, Poway (92064-8818)
PHONE..............................858 679-1755
Samuel Flores Junior, *Pr*
Linda Young, *
David K Howell, *
Michael Nisley, *
Paul Callan, *
EMP: 160 **EST:** 2003
SQ FT: 6,000
SALES (est): 10.3MM **Privately Held**
Web: www.pklservices.com
SIC: 7699 Aircraft and heavy equipment repair services

(P-14784)
PORTER BOILER SERVICE INC
1166 E 23rd St, Signal Hill (90755-3447)
PHONE..............................562 426-2528
George Hrebien, *Pr*
Nooshin Singhal, *
EMP: 25 **EST:** 1958
SQ FT: 5,000
SALES (est): 2.32MM **Privately Held**
Web: www.porterboiler.com
SIC: 7699 1711 3443 Boiler repair shop; Boiler maintenance contractor; Fabricated plate work (boiler shop)

(P-14785)
PROPULSION CONTROLS ENGRG (PA)
1620 Rigel St, San Diego (92113-3832)
P.O. Box 13606 (92170-3606)
PHONE..............................619 235-0961
David P Clapp, *CEO*
John P Reilly Iii, *Sec*
EMP: 70 **EST:** 1974
SQ FT: 22,000
SALES (est): 23.33MM
SALES (corp-wide): 23.33MM **Privately Held**
Web: www.propulsioncontrols.com
SIC: 7699 Boiler repair shop

(P-14786)
R & S OVRHD DOORS SO-CAL INC
Also Called: Door Doctor
1617 N Orangethorpe Way, Anaheim (92801-1228)
PHONE..............................714 680-0600
TOLL FREE: 800
David Fowler, *Pr*
EMP: 25 **EST:** 1991
SALES (est): 1.23MM **Privately Held**
Web: www.rsdoorsofsocal.com
SIC: 7699 1731 3446 1751 Door and window repair; Access control systems specialization; Gates, ornamental metal; Garage door, installation or erection

(P-14787)
REDMAN EQUIPMENT & MFG CO
19800 Normandie Ave, Torrance (90502-1182)
PHONE..............................310 329-1134
Gerald E Redman, *
Janelle Redman, *
▲ **EMP:** 48 **EST:** 1962
SQ FT: 8,000
SALES (est): 3.19MM
SALES (corp-wide): 12.58B **Publicly Held**
Web: www.redmaneq.com
SIC: 7699 3443 Boiler and heating repair services; Heat exchangers, condensers, and components
HQ: Ohmstede Ltd.
895 N Main St
Beaumont TX 77701
409 833-6375

(P-14788)
RUSSELL-WARNER INC
Also Called: Roto-Rooter
24971 Avenue Stanford, Valencia (91355-1278)
P.O. Box 74 (89411-0074)
PHONE..............................661 257-9200
EMP: 240
SIC: 7699 6794 1711 Sewer cleaning and rodding; Patent owners and lessors; Plumbing, heating, air-conditioning

(P-14789)
SA CAMP PUMP COMPANY
Also Called: SA Camp Pump and Drilling Co
17876 Zerker Rd, Bakersfield (93308-9221)
P.O. Box 82575 (93380-2575)
PHONE..............................661 399-2976
James S Camp, *Pr*
EMP: 60 **EST:** 1952
SQ FT: 10,000
SALES (est): 10.64MM
SALES (corp-wide): 22.14MM **Privately Held**
Web: www.sacampcompanies.com
SIC: 7699 3561 Agricultural equipment repair services; Pumps and pumping equipment
PA: S A Camp Companies
17876 Zerker Rd
661 399-4451

(P-14790)
SAM SCHAFFER INC
Also Called: Weld-It Co
3015 E Echo Hill Way, Orange (92867-1905)
PHONE..............................323 263-7524
Stephen Schaffer, *VP*
EMP: 43 **EST:** 1946
SALES (est): 2.5MM **Privately Held**
Web: www.welditco.com

SIC: 7699 3559 Industrial machinery and equipment repair; Petroleum refinery equipment

(P-14791)
SCHINDLER ELEVATOR CORPORATION
16450 Foothill Blvd Ste 200, Sylmar (91342-1088)
PHONE..............................818 336-3000
Lance Howard, *Mgr*
EMP: 240
Web: www.schindler.com
SIC: 7699 Elevators: inspection, service, and repair
HQ: Schindler Elevator Corporation
20 Whippany Rd
Morristown NJ 07960
973 397-6500

(P-14792)
SOUTH BAY SAND BLSTG TANK CLG
Also Called: Sbsbtc
326 W 30th St, National City (91950-7206)
P.O. Box 13009 (92170-3009)
PHONE..............................619 238-8338
Canuto Lopez, *CEO*
EMP: 100 **EST:** 1991
SQ FT: 60,000
SALES (est): 8.88MM **Privately Held**
Web: www.sbsbtc.com
SIC: 7699 4212 Ship boiler and tank cleaning and repair, contractors; Hazardous waste transport

(P-14793)
STAVROS ENTERPRISES INC
Also Called: Facilitec West
681 Arrow Grand Cir, Covina (91722-2146)
PHONE..............................888 463-2293
Anthony Emanuel Stavros, *CEO*
EMP: 30 **EST:** 2006
SALES (est): 2.07MM **Privately Held**
Web: www.facilitecwest.com
SIC: 7699 3272 Cleaning services; Grease traps, concrete

(P-14794)
SUNVAIR AEROSPACE GROUP INC (PA)
29145 The Old Rd, Valencia (91355-1015)
PHONE..............................661 294-3777
Udo Reider, *CEO*
Glenn Miller, *
EMP: 80 **EST:** 2014
3Q FT: 77,000
SALES (est): 30.17MM
SALES (corp-wide): 30.17MM **Privately Held**
Web: www.aerospaceplating.com
SIC: 7699 Aircraft and heavy equipment repair services

(P-14795)
SURVIVAL SYSTEMS INTL INC (PA)
Also Called: Ssi
34140 Valley Center Rd, Valley Center (92082-6017)
P.O. Box 1855 (92082)
PHONE..............................760 749-6800
George Beatty, *CEO*
Mark Beatty, *
Colin Hooper, *
▲ **EMP:** 95 **EST:** 1968
SQ FT: 100,000
SALES (est): 20.08MM
SALES (corp-wide): 20.08MM **Privately Held**

Web: www.survivalsystemsinternational.com
SIC: 7699 3531 3086 Industrial equipment services; Winches; Plastics foam products

(P-14796)
TARSCO HOLDINGS LLC
11905 Regentview Ave, Downey (90241-5515)
PHONE..............................562 869-0200
Terry S Warren, *Managing Member*
EMP: 121 **EST:** 2007
SALES (est): 1.84MM
SALES (corp-wide): 164.48MM **Privately Held**
Web: www.tfwarren.com
SIC: 7699 Tank repair
PA: T.F. Warren Group Inc
57 Old Onondaga Rd W
519 756-8222

(P-14797)
TECH KNOWLEDGE ASSOCIATES LLC
Also Called: Tka
1 Centerpointe Dr Ste 200, La Palma (90623-2529)
PHONE..............................714 735-3810
Joe Randolph, *CEO*
Ed Wong, *
Steve Gilbert, *
EMP: 80 **EST:** 2011
SALES (est): 7.8MM
SALES (corp-wide): 55.69MM **Privately Held**
Web: www.ii-techknow.com
SIC: 7699 Medical equipment repair, non-electric
HQ: St. Joseph Health System
3345 Michaelson Dr #100
Irvine CA 92612
949 381-4000

(P-14798)
UNITED STATES DEPT OF NAVY
Also Called: Maintenance Dept
311 Navy Base Ventura County, Port Hueneme (93042-0001)
PHONE..............................805 989-1328
Art Baulyut, *Mgr*
EMP: 250
Web: www.navy.mil
SIC: 7699 9711 Aircraft and heavy equipment repair services; Navy
HQ: United States Department Of The Navy
1200 Navy Pentagon
Washington DC 20350

(P-14799)
UPWIND BLADE SOLUTIONS INC
2869 Historic Decatur Rd Ste 100, San Diego (92106-6176)
PHONE..............................866 927-3142
Marty Crotty, *CEO*
Bo Thisted, *
Bryan Coggins, *
EMP: 288 **EST:** 2011
SALES (est): 1.86MM
SALES (corp-wide): 16.73B **Privately Held**
SIC: 7699 Pumps and pumping equipment repair
HQ: Upwind Solutions, Inc.
1417 Nw Everett St
Portland OR 97209

(P-14800)
WARDLOW 2 LP (PA)
333 S Grand Ave Ste 4070, Los Angeles (90071-1544)

PHONE.............................562 432-8066
Steven B Mcleod, *Pt*
Joe Gregorio, *Pt*
EMP: 99 **EST:** 2007
SALES (est): 20.38MM **Privately Held**
SIC: 7699 Construction equipment repair

(P-14801)
WESTERN PUMP INC (PA)
Also Called: Competrol A Western Pump Co
3235 F St, San Diego (92102-3315)
PHONE.............................619 239-9988
Dennis Rethmeier, *CEO*
Ryan Rethmeier, *
Janice C Rethmeier, *
▲ **EMP:** 55 **EST:** 1988
SQ FT: 10,000
SALES (est): 22.99MM
SALES (corp-wide): 22.99MM **Privately Held**
Web: www.westernpump.com
SIC: 7699 5084 1799 3728 Tank repair and
cleaning services; Petroleum industry
machinery; Petroleum storage tanks,
pumping and draining; Aircraft parts and
equipment, nec

(P-14802)
WHITING DOOR MFG CORP
301 S Milliken Ave, Ontario (91761-7800)
PHONE.............................909 877-0120
Abdullah Eren, *Brnch Mgr*
EMP: 92
SQ FT: 5,400
SALES (corp-wide): 37.53MM **Privately Held**
Web: www.whitingdoor.com
SIC: 7699 3713 5531 5211 Door and window
repair; Truck and bus bodies; Truck
equipment and parts; Garage doors, sale
and installation
PA: Whiting Door Mfg Corp
113 Cedar St
716 542-5427

7812 Motion Picture And Video Production

(P-14803)
ABC FAMILY WORLDWIDE INC (HQ)
Also Called: ABC Family
500 S Buena Vista St, Burbank
(91521-0001)
PHONE.............................818 560-1000
EMP: 500 **EST:** 1996
SALES (est): 15.61MM
SALES (corp-wide): 91.36B **Publicly Held**
Web: www.freeform.com
SIC: 7812 4841 Cartoon production,
television; Cable and other pay television
services
PA: The Walt Disney Company
500 S Buena Vista St
818 560-1000

(P-14804)
ADVANCED DIGITAL SERVICES INC (PA)
Also Called: A D S
948 N Cahuenga Blvd, Los Angeles
(90038-2615)
PHONE.............................323 962-8585
Thomas Engdahl, *Pr*
Andrew Mcintyre, *Ch Bd*
Brad Weyl, *
▲ **EMP:** 87 **EST:** 1989
SQ FT: 33,000
SALES (est): 3.88MM **Privately Held**

Web: www.adshollywood.com
SIC: 7812 7819 Video tape production; Film
processing, editing, and titling: motion
picture

(P-14805)
ALLIED ENTERTAINMENT GROUP INC (PA)
Also Called: Allied Artists International
273 W Allen Ave, City Of Industry (91746)
PHONE.............................626 330-0600
Greg Hammond, *Pr*
John Mason, *
Ashley D Posner, *
Kim Richards, *
Robert Fitzpatrick, *
◆ **EMP:** 325 **EST:** 1999
SQ FT: 60,000
SALES (est): 231.21K
SALES (corp-wide): 231.21K **Privately Held**
Web: www.alliedentertainment.com
SIC: 7812 Video production

(P-14806)
AND SYNDICATED PRODUCTIONS INC
3500 W Olive Ave Ste 1000, Burbank
(91505-5515)
PHONE.............................818 308-5200
Hilary Estey Mcloughlin, *Prin*
Hilary Estey Mcloughlin, *Pr*
▲ **EMP:** 100 **EST:** 1998
SALES (est): 94.52K **Privately Held**
SIC: 7812 Television film production

(P-14807)
ARTISAN ENTERTAINMENT INC
2700 Colorado Ave Ste 200, Santa Monica
(90404-5502)
PHONE.............................310 449-9200
Wayne Levin, *Pr*
James W Barge, *
Brian James Gladstone, *
Kristine Klimczak, *
EMP: 1000 **EST:** 1988
SALES (est): 3.28MM
SALES (corp-wide): 3.85B **Privately Held**
SIC: 7812 Motion picture production
HQ: Lions Gate Entertainment Inc.
2700 Colorado Ave Ste 200
Santa Monica CA 90404
310 449-9200

(P-14808)
BENTO BOX ENTERTAINMENT LLC
5161 Lankershim Blvd Ste 120, North
Hollywood (91601-4962)
PHONE.............................818 333-7700
Scott Greenberg, *CEO*
Brett Coker, *COO*
EMP: 300 **EST:** 2009
SALES (est): 12.8MM
SALES (corp-wide): 13.98B **Publicly Held**
Web: www.bentoboxent.com
SIC: 7812 Motion picture production and
distribution
HQ: Fox Television Stations, Inc.
1999 S Bundy Dr
Los Angeles CA 90025
310 584-2000

(P-14809)
BRILLSTEIN ENTRMT PARTNERS LLC (HQ)
Also Called: Brillstein Grey Entertainment
9150 Wilshire Blvd Ste 350, Beverly Hills
(90212-3453)

PHONE.............................310 205-5100
Brad Grey, *Pr*
EMP: 90 **EST:** 1980
SALES (est): 16.29MM
SALES (corp-wide): 116.26MM **Privately Held**
Web: www.bepmedia.com
SIC: 7812 Television film production
PA: Wasserman Media Group, Llc
10900 Wilshire Blvd Ste 12
310 407-0200

(P-14810)
BUNIM-MURRAY PRODUCTIONS
Also Called: Bmp
1015 Grandview Ave, Glendale
(91201-2205)
PHONE.............................818 756-5100
Jon Murray, *
Gil Goldschein, *
Mark Lebowitz, *
Julie Pizzi, *
▲ **EMP:** 150 **EST:** 1989
SQ FT: 20,000
SALES (est): 21.81MM
SALES (corp-wide): 12.61MM **Privately Held**
Web: www.bunim-murray.com
SIC: 7812 Television film production
HQ: Banijay Entertainment
5 Rue Francois 1er
Paris 75008
143189191

(P-14811)
CABIN EDITING COMPANY LLC
1754 14th St, Santa Monica (90404-4341)
PHONE.............................310 752-0520
Greg Lapidus, *Prin*
EMP: 71 **EST:** 2017
SALES (est): 1.62MM **Privately Held**
Web: www.cabinedit.com
SIC: 7812 Video production

(P-14812)
CBS STUDIOS INC
4024 Radford Ave, Studio City
(91604-2190)
PHONE.............................818 655-5160
David Stapf, *CEO*
Eris Gray, *CFO*
Christa A D'alimonte, *Sec*
EMP: 150 **EST:** 2005
SALES (est): 2.71MM **Privately Held**
Web: www.radfordsc.com
SIC: 7812 Motion picture and video
production

(P-14813)
COLUMBIA PICTURES INDS INC
4024 Radford Ave, Studio City
(91604-2101)
PHONE.............................818 655-5820
Cynthia Phillips, *Prin*
EMP: 85
SIC: 7812 Motion picture and video
production
HQ: Columbia Pictures Industries, Inc.
10202 W Washington Blvd
Culver City CA 90232
310 244-4000

(P-14814)
COLUMBIA PICTURES INDS INC (DH)
Also Called: Columbia Pictures
10202 Washington Blvd, Culver City
(90232-3119)
PHONE.............................310 244-4000
Tom Rothman, *CEO*

Ronald Jacobi, *Ex VP*
Doug Belgrad, *Pr*
Philip Rowley, *CFO*
EMP: 200 **EST:** 1987
SALES (est): 23.92MM **Privately Held**
SIC: 7812 Motion picture production and
distribution
HQ: Sony Pictures Entertainment, Inc.
10202 W Washington Blvd
Culver City CA 90232
310 244-4000

(P-14815)
CRAFTY APES LLC (PA)
127 Lomita St, El Segundo (90245-4114)
PHONE.............................310 837-3900
EMP: 542 **EST:** 2011
SALES (est): 6.65MM
SALES (corp-wide): 6.65MM **Privately Held**
Web: www.craftyapes.com
SIC: 7812 Video production

(P-14816)
CREATORUP INC
525 S Hewitt St, Los Angeles (90013-2217)
PHONE.............................323 300-4725
Michael Tringe, *CEO*
EMP: 72 **EST:** 2014
SALES (est): 2.29MM **Privately Held**
Web: www.creatorup.com
SIC: 7812 Video production

(P-14817)
CRUNCHYROLL LLC (DH)
Also Called: Funimation Entertainment
10202 Washington Blvd, Culver City
(90232-3119)
PHONE.............................972 355-7300
General Fukunaga, *Pr*
Greg Stevenson, *CFO*
▲ **EMP:** 82 **EST:** 1994
SALES (est): 9.31MM **Privately Held**
Web: www.crunchyroll.com
SIC: 7812 4813 7822 Cartoon production,
television; Internet host services; Video
tapes, recorded: wholesale
HQ: Sony Pictures Entertainment, Inc.
10202 W Washington Blvd
Culver City CA 90232
310 244-4000

(P-14818)
DIGITAL DOMAIN 30 INC (PA)
12641 Beatrice St, Los Angeles
(90066-7003)
PHONE.............................213 797-3100
Daniel Seah, *CEO*
Od Welch, *
Amit Chopra, *
Rich Flier Md, *Prin*
John Lagerling, *
EMP: 300 **EST:** 2012
SALES (est): 14.89MM
SALES (corp-wide): 14.89MM **Privately Held**
Web: www.digitaldomain.com
SIC: 7812 Video production

(P-14819)
DISNEY ENTERPRISES INC
Also Called: Disney
1313 S Harbor Blvd, Anaheim
(92802-2309)
PHONE.............................407 397-6000
Marlene Madrid, *Mgr*
EMP: 100
SALES (corp-wide): 91.36B **Publicly Held**
Web: en.disneyme.com

SIC: **7812** Motion picture production and distribution, television
HQ: Disney Enterprises, Inc.
500 S Buena Vista St
Burbank CA 91521
818 560-1000

(P-14820)
DISNEY ENTERPRISES INC
Also Called: Disney
700 W Ball Rd, Anaheim (92802-1843)
P.O. Box 3232 (92803-3232)
PHONE..............................714 781-1651
Matt Ouimet, *Brnch Mgr*
EMP: 132
SALES (corp-wide): 91.36B **Publicly Held**
Web: en.disneyme.com
SIC: **7812** Motion picture production and distribution
HQ: Disney Enterprises, Inc.
500 S Buena Vista St
Burbank CA 91521
818 560-1000

(P-14821)
DISNEY ENTERPRISES INC
Also Called: Disney
1101 Flower St, Glendale (91201-2415)
PHONE..............................818 553-4103
EMP: 113
SALES (corp-wide): 91.36B **Publicly Held**
Web: en.disneyme.com
SIC: **7812** Motion picture production and distribution, television
HQ: Disney Enterprises, Inc.
500 S Buena Vista St
Burbank CA 91521
818 560-1000

(P-14822)
DISNEY INCORPORATED (DH)
Also Called: Disney
500 S Buena Vista St, Burbank (91521-0007)
PHONE..............................818 560-1000
Matthew L Mcginnis, *CEO*
Sanford M Litvack, *
▲ **EMP:** 150 **EST:** 1952
SALES (est): 62.46MM
SALES (corp-wide): 91.36B **Publicly Held**
Web: www.disney.com
SIC: **7812** Motion picture production and distribution
HQ: Disney Enterprises, Inc.
500 S Buena Vista St
Burbank CA 91521
818 560-1000

(P-14823)
DREAMWORKS ANIMATION PUBG LLC
1000 Flower St, Glendale (91201-3007)
PHONE..............................818 695-5000
EMP: 1036 **EST:** 2014
SALES (est): 177.72K
SALES (corp-wide): 121.57B **Publicly Held**
Web: www.dreamworks.com
SIC: **7812** Motion picture and video production
HQ: Dwa Holdings, Llc
1000 Flower St
Glendale CA 91201
818 695-5000

(P-14824)
DWA HOLDINGS LLC (DH)
1000 Flower St, Glendale (91201-3007)
PHONE..............................818 695-5000
Mellody Hobson, *Prin*

Jeffrey Katzenberg, *CEO*
Ann Daly, *Pr*
Fazal Merchant, *CFO*
Steven A Adams, *CAO*
EMP: 85 **EST:** 1994
SQ FT: 500,000
SALES (est): 76.11MM
SALES (corp-wide): 121.57B **Publicly Held**
Web: research.dreamworks.com
SIC: **7812** Cartoon motion picture production
HQ: Nbcuniversal Media, Llc
30 Rockefeller Plz
New York NY 10112

(P-14825)
EFILM LLC
Also Called: E Film Digital Labratories
1144 N Las Palmas Ave, Los Angeles (90038-1209)
PHONE..............................323 463-7041
Dominik J Schmidt, *
EMP: 150 **EST:** 2002
SALES (est): 3.6MM **Privately Held**
Web: www.company3.com
SIC: **7812** Video production

(P-14826)
FANCY LIFE ENTERPRISES LLC (PA)
Also Called: Fancy Life Studios
8030 La Mesa Blvd Pmb 3039, La Mesa (91942-0335)
PHONE..............................619 560-9890
Seana Earls, *Managing Member*
EMP: 125 **EST:** 2022
SALES (est): 12MM
SALES (corp-wide): 12MM **Privately Held**
SIC: **7812** Television film production

(P-14827)
FILM ROMAN LLC
6320 Canoga Ave Ste 450, Woodland Hills (91367-2561)
PHONE..............................818 748-4000
Dana Booton, *Mgr*
EMP: 214
SQ FT: 87,000
SALES (corp-wide): 3.85B **Privately Held**
Web: www.filmroman.com
SIC: **7812** Cartoon motion picture production
HQ: Film Roman, Llc.
8900 Liberty Cir
Englewood CO 80112
720 852-6327

(P-14828)
FOCUS FEATURES LLC (DH)
Also Called: Focus-Gramercy Film Music
1540 2nd St Ste 200, Santa Monica (90401-3513)
PHONE..............................310 315-1722
Peter Schlessel, *CEO*
EMP: 89 **EST:** 1999
SQ FT: 30,000
SALES (est): 1.78MM
SALES (corp-wide): 121.57B **Publicly Held**
Web: www.focusfeatures.com
SIC: **7812** Motion picture production and distribution
HQ: Nbcuniversal Media, Llc
30 Rockefeller Plz
New York NY 10112

(P-14829)
FOX NET INC
Also Called: 20th Century Fox Studio
10201 W Pico Blvd, Los Angeles (90064-2606)

PHONE..............................310 369-1000
Chase Carey, *Pr*
EMP: 4804 **EST:** 1992
SALES (est): 15.96MM
SALES (corp-wide): 91.36B **Publicly Held**
Web: www.foxcredit.org
SIC: **7812** Motion picture and video production
HQ: Twentieth Television, Inc.
10201 W Pico Blvd
Los Angeles CA 90064

(P-14830)
HARPO PRODUCTIONS INC
Also Called: Harpo Entertainment Group
7619 N Patriot Way, Van Nuys (91405-5648)
P.O. Box 29610 (90029-0610)
PHONE..............................312 633-1000
Oprah Winfrey, *Ch Bd*
Tim Bennett, *
Doug Pattison, *
Bill Becker, *General Vice President*
EMP: 200 **EST:** 1988
SALES (est): 351.65K **Privately Held**
SIC: **7812** Television film production

(P-14831)
HERZOG & COMPANY
4640 Lankershim Blvd Ste 400, North Hollywood (91602-1844)
PHONE..............................818 762-4640
Jonathan Buss, *Dir*
EMP: 79 **EST:** 2015
SALES (est): 4.88MM **Privately Held**
Web: www.herzogcompany.com
SIC: **7812** Television film production

(P-14832)
HIGH TECHNOLOGY VIDEO INC
Also Called: H T V
10900 Ventura Blvd, Studio City (91604-3340)
PHONE..............................323 969-8822
Jim Hardy, *CEO*
Steve Weiner, *
EMP: 73 **EST:** 1995
SQ FT: 30,000
SALES (est): 10MM **Privately Held**
Web: www.illuminatehollywood.com
SIC: **7812** Video production

(P-14833)
HUNGRY HEART MEDIA INC
Also Called: Wondros
5450 W Washington Blvd, Los Angeles (90016-1135)
PHONE..............................323 951-0010
Jesse Dylan, *Pr*
EMP: 140 **EST:** 2011
SALES (est): 6.7MM **Privately Held**
Web: www.wondros.com
SIC: **7812** 8742 Motion picture and video production; Marketing consulting services

(P-14834)
IGNITION CREATIVE LLC
1201 W 5th St Ste T1100, Los Angeles (90017-5158)
PHONE..............................310 315-6300
EMP: 128 **EST:** 2003
SALES (est): 5.63MM **Privately Held**
Web: www.ignitioncreative.com
SIC: **7812** Video production

(P-14835)
IYUNO USA INC (HQ)
Also Called: S.D.I. Media USA Inc.
2901 W Alameda Ave, Burbank (91505-4407)

PHONE..............................310 388-8800
Mark Howorth, *Pr*
EMP: 95 **EST:** 1974
SALES (est): 18.06MM
SALES (corp-wide): 18.06MM **Privately Held**
Web: www.iyuno.com
SIC: **7812** Video production
PA: Iyuno Media Group
2901 W Alameda Ave
818 812-1213

(P-14836)
LIONS GATE FILMS INC
2700 Colorado Ave, Santa Monica (90404-3553)
PHONE..............................310 449-9200
Jon Feltheimer, *Pr*
James Keegan, *
Steve Beeks, *
EMP: 147 **EST:** 1998
SQ FT: 30,000
SALES (est): 10.65MM
SALES (corp-wide): 3.85B **Privately Held**
Web: www.lionsgate.com
SIC: **7812** Motion picture production
HQ: Lions Gate Entertainment Inc.
2700 Colorado Ave Ste 200
Santa Monica CA 90404
310 449-9200

(P-14837)
LIONSGATE STUDIOS CORP (PA)
2700 Colorado Ave, Santa Monica (90404-3553)
PHONE..............................877 848-3866
Jon Feltheimer, *CEO*
Michael Burns, *V Ch Bd*
James W Barge, *CFO*
Brian Goldsmith, *COO*
Bruce Tobey, *Ex VP*
EMP: 1075 **EST:** 1997
SQ FT: 19,258
SALES (est): 1.13MM
SALES (corp-wide): 1.13MM **Publicly Held**
SIC: **7812** Motion picture and video production

(P-14838)
METRO-GOLDWYN-MAYER INC (DH)
Also Called: MGM
245 N Beverly Dr, Beverly Hills (90210-5319)
PHONE..............................310 449-3000
Gary Barber, *CEO*
Ken Schapiro, *
Katie Martin Kelley, *Chief Communications Officer*
EMP: 300 **EST:** 1996
SQ FT: 131,400
SALES (est): 184.6MM **Publicly Held**
Web: www.mgm.com
SIC: **7812** Motion picture production and distribution
HQ: Mgm Holdings Ii, Inc.
245 N Beverly Dr
Beverly Hills CA 90210
310 449-3000

(P-14839)
MIRAMAX LLC
1901 Avenue Of The Stars Ste 2000, Los Angeles (90067-6021)
PHONE..............................310 409-4321
Jonathan Glickman, *Pr*
EMP: 108 **EST:** 2011
SALES (est): 2.92MM **Privately Held**
Web: www.miramax.com

SIC: 7812 Motion picture production and distribution
PA: Bein Media Group WII
Behind Ahli Hospital, Al Asmakh Tower No. 864, Zone 63

(P-14840)
NBC UNIVERSAL INC
100 Universal City Plz, Universal City (91608-1002)
◆ **EMP:** 532
SIC: 7812 Motion picture production and distribution

(P-14841)
NW ENTERTAINMENT INC (PA)
Also Called: New Wave Entertainment
2660 W Olive Ave, Burbank (91505-4525)
PHONE..............................818 295-5000
Paul Apel, *CEO*
Alan Duke, *
Greg Woertz, *
Brian Volk-weiss, *Pr*
Matt Sample, *
▲ **EMP:** 97 **EST:** 1986
SQ FT: 40,000
SALES (est): 37.24MM
SALES (corp-wide): 37.24MM **Privately Held**
SIC: 7812 Motion picture production

(P-14842)
ORION PICTURES CORPORATION
245 N Beverly Dr, Beverly Hills (90210-5319)
PHONE..............................310 449-3000
Alex Yemenidjian, *Ch Bd*
Daniel J Taylor, *
EMP: 1000 **EST:** 1995
SALES (est): 1.05MM **Publicly Held**
Web: www.mgm.com
SIC: 7812 Motion picture production and distribution
HQ: Metro-Goldwyn-Mayer, Inc.
245 N Beverly Dr
Beverly Hills CA 90210

(P-14843)
PARAMOUNT PICTURES CORPORATION (HQ)
Also Called: Paramount Studios
5555 Melrose Ave, Los Angeles (90038-3197)
PHONE..............................323 956-5000
David Ellison, *CEO*
Jim Gianopulos, *Ch Bd*
Rob Moore, *V Ch Bd*
Brian Robbins, *Pr*
Courtney Armstrong, *COO*
◆ **EMP:** 1700 **EST:** 1912
SALES (est): 528.55MM
SALES (corp-wide): 29.65B **Publicly Held**
Web: www.paramountstudiotour.com
SIC: 7812 4833 7829 5099 Motion picture production and distribution, television; Television broadcasting stations; Motion picture distribution services; Video cassettes, accessories and supplies
PA: Paramount Global
1515 Broadway
212 258-6000

(P-14844)
PASH PORTFOLIO INC
1453 3rd Street Promenade Ste 400, Santa Monica (90401-3428)
PHONE..............................310 888-8738
Payam Shohadai, *Pr*
John Betdul, *

EMP: 171 **EST:** 2002
SALES (est): 8.85MM **Privately Held**
Web: www.lumapictures.com
SIC: 7812 Motion picture and video production

(P-14845)
PILGRIM STUDIOS INC
12020 Chandler Blvd Ste 200, North Hollywood (91607-4617)
PHONE..............................818 728-8800
Craig M Piligian, *CEO*
EMP: 71 **EST:** 2013
SALES (est): 2.44MM **Privately Held**
Web: www.pilgrimmediagroup.com
SIC: 7812 Video production

(P-14846)
PLAYBOY ENTRMT GROUP INC (DH)
2300 W Empire Ave, Burbank (91504-3341)
PHONE..............................323 276-4000
Brinda Viloa, *Dir*
James Griffiths, *
EMP: 139 **EST:** 1984
SALES (est): 3.8MM
SALES (corp-wide): 142.95MM **Publicly Held**
Web: www.criticalcontent.com
SIC: 7812 Video tape production
HQ: Playboy Enterprises, Inc.
10960 Wlshire Blvd Ste 22
Los Angeles CA 90024
310 424-1800

(P-14847)
POINT360
1133 N Hollywood Way, Burbank (91505-2528)
PHONE..............................818 556-5700
Brian Ehrlich, *Mgr*
EMP: 96
Web: www.point360.com
SIC: 7812 Video production
PA: Point.360
2701 Media Center Dr

(P-14848)
POWER STUDIOS INC
Also Called: Digital Domain
300 Rose Ave, Venice (90291-2628)
PHONE..............................310 314-2800
EMP: 200
SIC: 7812 7819 Motion picture production; Services allied to motion pictures

(P-14849)
PRAGER UNIVERSITY FOUNDATION
15021 Ventura Blvd Ste 552, Sherman Oaks (91403-2442)
PHONE..............................833 772-4378
Marissa Streit, *CEO*
EMP: 77 **EST:** 2011
SALES (est): 68.68MM **Privately Held**
Web: www.prageru.com
SIC: 7812 Motion picture and video production

(P-14850)
RESPAWN ENTERTAINMENT LLC
20131 Prairie St, Chatsworth (91311-6106)
PHONE..............................818 960-4400
Jason West, *Managing Member*
▲ **EMP:** 212 **EST:** 2010
SALES (est): 3.93MM
SALES (corp-wide): 7.43B **Publicly Held**

Web: www.respawn.com
SIC: 7812 Video production
PA: Electronic Arts Inc.
209 Redwood Shores Pkwy
650 628-1500

(P-14851)
RHYTHM AND HUES INC (PA)
Also Called: Rhythm & Hues Studios
2100 E Grand Ave Ste A, El Segundo (90245-5055)
PHONE..............................310 448-7500
John Hughes, *Pr*
Pauline Tso, *Sec*
Keith Goldfarb, *Stockholder**
EMP: 83 **EST:** 1987
SALES (est): 4.45MM
SALES (corp-wide): 4.45MM **Privately Held**
SIC: 7812 Cartoon production, television

(P-14852)
RODAX DISTRIBUTORS
7230 Coldwater Canyon Ave, North Hollywood (91605-4203)
P.O. Box 16539 (91615-6539)
PHONE..............................818 765-6400
Daniel Mamane, *Pr*
Tom Yofee, *
EMP: 78 **EST:** 1995
SALES (est): 155.76K **Privately Held**
SIC: 7812 Video tape production

(P-14853)
ROUNDABOUT ENTERTAINMENT INC
Also Called: Secuto Music
217 S Lake St, Burbank (91502-2111)
PHONE..............................818 842-9300
Craig S Clark, *CEO*
EMP: 84 **EST:** 1992
SQ FT: 6,000
SALES (est): 6.59MM **Privately Held**
Web: www.roundabout.com
SIC: 7812 Video production

(P-14854)
SAINT JSEPH COMMUNICATIONS INC (PA)
Also Called: Catholic Resource Center
1243 E Shamwood St, West Covina (91790-2348)
P.O. Box 720 (91793-0720)
PHONE..............................626 331-3549
Terry Barber, *Pr*
EMP: 25 **EST:** 1988
SALES (est): 2.46MM
SALES (corp-wide): 2.46MM **Privately Held**
Web: www.saintjoe.com
SIC: 7812 2741 7822 Motion picture and video production; Miscellaneous publishing; Motion picture and tape distribution

(P-14855)
SCANLINE VFX INC
6087 W Sunset Blvd, Los Angeles (90028-6434)
PHONE..............................310 827-1555
Stephan Trojansky, *Pr*
EMP: 1200 **EST:** 2019
SALES (est): 3.68MM **Privately Held**
Web: www.scanlinevfx.com
SIC: 7812 Video production

(P-14856)
SCANLINEVFX LA LLC
Also Called: Eyeline Studios
6087 W Sunset Blvd, Los Angeles (90028-6434)

PHONE..............................310 827-1555
EMP: 179 **EST:** 2007
SALES (est): 1.86MM **Publicly Held**
Web: www.scanlinevfx.com
SIC: 7812 Video production
PA: Netflix, Inc.
121 Albright Way

(P-14857)
SONY MEDIA CLOUD SERVICES LLC
10202 Washington Blvd, Culver City (90232-3119)
PHONE..............................877 683-9124
EMP: 50 **EST:** 2013
SALES (est): 294.4K **Privately Held**
Web: www.cloud19.com
SIC: 7812 7372 Video production; Business oriented computer software
PA: Sony Group Corporation
1-7-1, Konan

(P-14858)
SONY PICTURES ENTRMT INC (DH)
Also Called: Sony Pictures Studios
10202 Washington Blvd, Culver City (90232-3119)
PHONE..............................310 244-4000
Tony Vinciquerra, *Ch*
Ravi Ahuja, *
Drew Shearer, *
Tahra Grant, *CCO**
Jon Hookstratten, *Operations**
▲ **EMP:** 3000 **EST:** 1982
SALES (est): 1.55B **Privately Held**
Web: www.sonypictures.com
SIC: 7812 7822 7832 Motion picture production and distribution; Distribution, exclusive of production: motion picture; Motion picture theaters, except drive-in
HQ: Sony Corporation Of America
25 Madison Ave Fl 27
New York NY 10010

(P-14859)
SONY PICTURES TELEVISION INC (DH)
Also Called: Columbia TV Advertiser Sls
10202 Washington Blvd, Culver City (90232-3195)
PHONE..............................310 244-7625
Ravi Ahuja, *Ch*
Keith Le Goy, *
Jeff Frost, *
Jason Clodfelter, *
Wayne Garvie, *
▲ **EMP:** 300 **EST:** 1982
SALES (est): 7.16MM **Privately Held**
Web: www.sonypicturestelevision.com
SIC: 7812 Motion picture production and distribution, television
HQ: Sony Pictures Entertainment, Inc.
10202 W Washington Blvd
Culver City CA 90232
310 244-4000

(P-14860)
STARZ ENTERTAINMENT LLC (DH)
Also Called: Starz Encore Group
2700 Colorado Ave Ste 200, Santa Monica (90404-5502)
PHONE..............................720 852-7700
Jeffrey Hirsch, *CEO*
Scott D Macdonald, *
EMP: 587 **EST:** 1991
SQ FT: 300,000
SALES (est): 73.47MM
SALES (corp-wide): 3.85B **Privately Held**

Web: www.starz.com
SIC: 7812 Motion picture production and distribution, television
HQ: Starz, L.L.C.
   8900 Liberty Cir
   Englewood CO 80112

(P-14861)
STUDIO DISTRIBUTION SVCS LLC
4000 Warner Blvd, Burbank (91522-0001)
PHONE...........................818 954-6000
Eddie Cunningham, *Managing Member*
EMP: 140 **EST:** 2020
SALES (est): 2.42MM **Privately Held**
Web: www.sds.media
SIC: 7812 Motion picture production and distribution

(P-14862)
STX FINANCING LLC
Also Called: Stx Entertainment
3900 W Alameda Ave Fl 32, Burbank (91505-4316)
PHONE...........................310 742-2300
Noah Fogelson, *CEO*
Robert Simonds, *Ch*
Andrew Warren, *CFO*
EMP: 103 **EST:** 2014
SALES (est): 22.78MM **Privately Held**
Web: www.stxentertainment.com
SIC: 7812 Motion picture production and distribution, television
PA: Najafi Companies, Llc
   2525 E Camelback Rd Ste 8

(P-14863)
TWENTETH CNTURY FOX HM ENTRMT (PA)
10201 W Pico Blvd, Los Angeles (90064-2606)
PHONE...........................310 369-1000
EMP: 1000 **EST:** 1953
SQ FT: 25,000
SALES (est): 2.86MM **Privately Held**
SIC: 7812 Television film production

(P-14864)
TWENTIETH CNTURY FOX FILM CORP (DH)
Also Called: Fox Films Entertainment
10201 W Pico Blvd, Los Angeles (90064-2651)
P.O. Box 900 (90213-0900)
◆ **EMP:** 75 **EST:** 1915
SQ FT: 25,000
SALES (est): 28.87MM
SALES (corp-wide): 91.36B **Publicly Held**
SIC: 7812 Motion picture production and distribution
HQ: Fox Entertainment Group, Llc
   1211 Ave Of The Americas
   New York NY 10036
   212 852-7000

(P-14865)
UNIVERSAL CITY STUDIOS LLLP
Also Called: Universal Studios
100 Universal City Plz, Universal City (91608-1085)
PHONE...........................818 622-8477
▲ **EMP:** 7400
SIC: 7812 7996 Motion picture production and distribution; Theme park, amusement

(P-14866)
UNIVERSAL CY STDIOS PRDCTONS L (DH)
Also Called: Nbcuniversal Television Dist

100 Universal City Plz, Universal City (91608-1085)
PHONE...........................818 777-1000
Ron Meyer, *Pr*
Maren Christensen, *Ex VP*
Kenneth L Kahrs, *Ex VP*
Lynn A Calpeter, *Ex VP*
Rick Finkelstein, *Ex VP*
▲ **EMP:** 25 **EST:** 2002
SALES (est): 38.1K
SALES (corp-wide): 121.57B **Publicly Held**
SIC: 7812 3652 2741 5947 Motion picture production and distribution; Phonograph records, prerecorded; Music, sheet: publishing and printing; Gift shop
HQ: Vivendi Universal Entertainment Lllp
   30 Rockefeller Plaza
   New York NY 10112
   212 664-4444

(P-14867)
UNIVERSAL PCTRES HM ENTRMT LLC (DH)
100 Universal City Plz Bldg 1440/7, Universal City (91608-1002)
PHONE...........................818 777-1000
Ed Cunningham, *Pr*
Kathleen Gallagher, *Ex VP*
EMP: 76 **EST:** 1965
SALES (est): 4.61MM
SALES (corp-wide): 121.57B **Publicly Held**
Web: www.uphe.com
SIC: 7812 Motion picture and video production
HQ: Nbcuniversal, Llc
   1221 Ave Of The Amrcas St
   New York NY 10020
   212 664-4444

(P-14868)
UNIVERSAL STUDIOS COMPANY LLC (DH)
100 Universal City Plz, North Hollywood (91608-1085)
PHONE...........................818 777-1000
Adam Fogelson, *Ch*
Donna Langley, *
Ron Meyer, *
Sean Gamble, *
▲ **EMP:** 720 **EST:** 1958
SQ FT: 100,000
SALES (est): 452.4MM
SALES (corp-wide): 121.57B **Publicly Held**
Web: www.universalstudioshollywood.com
SIC: 7812 3652 2741 5947 Motion picture production and distribution; Phonograph records, prerecorded; Music, sheet: publishing and printing; Gift shop
HQ: Nbcuniversal Media, Llc
   30 Rockefeller Plz
   New York NY 10112

(P-14869)
VIACOM NETWORKS
Also Called: Mtv Networks
1575 N Gower St Ste 100, Los Angeles (90028-6488)
PHONE...........................310 752-8000
Anthony Disanto, *Pr*
EMP: 110 **EST:** 2010
SALES (est): 1.7MM **Privately Held**
SIC: 7812 7822 Television film production; Motion picture and tape distribution

(P-14870)
WALT DISNEY MUSIC COMPANY (DH)
Also Called: Disney
500 S Buena Vista St, Burbank (91521-0007)
P.O. Box 3232 (92803-3232)
PHONE...........................818 560-1000
Tom Macdougall, *Pr*
Robert Cavallo, *Ch Bd*
Cathleen Tass, *Treas*
Cathleen M Taff, *CEO*
▲ **EMP:** 148 **EST:** 1947
SALES (est): 48.56MM
SALES (corp-wide): 91.36B **Publicly Held**
Web: www.thewaltdisneycompany.com
SIC: 7812 Motion picture and video production
HQ: Disney Enterprises, Inc.
   500 S Buena Vista St
   Burbank CA 91521
   818 560-1000

(P-14871)
WALT DISNEY PICTURES
Also Called: Disney
811 Sonora Ave, Glendale (91201-2433)
PHONE...........................818 409-2200
Meredith Roberts, *Sr VP*
EMP: 300 **EST:** 1983
SQ FT: 461,000
SALES (est): 7.56MM
SALES (corp-wide): 91.36B **Publicly Held**
Web: www.disneyanimation.com
SIC: 7812 Motion picture and video production
PA: The Walt Disney Company
   500 S Buena Vista St
   818 560-1000

(P-14872)
WALT DISNEY RECORDS DIRECT (DH)
Also Called: Disney
500 S Buena Vista St, Burbank (91521-0001)
PHONE...........................818 560-1000
Alan H Bergman, *Sr VP*
Rob Moore, *
Nick Franklin, *
Marsha Reed, *
◆ **EMP:** 2990 **EST:** 1996
SQ FT: 600,000
SALES (est): 55.66MM
SALES (corp-wide): 91.36B **Publicly Held**
Web: www.thewaltdisneycompany.com
SIC: 7812 Motion picture production and distribution
HQ: Disney Enterprises, Inc.
   500 S Buena Vista St
   Burbank CA 91521
   818 560-1000

(P-14873)
WARNER BROS ENTERTAINMENT INC (DH)
Also Called: Victory Studio
4000 Warner Blvd, Burbank (91522-0001)
P.O. Box 29113 (71903-9113)
PHONE...........................818 954-6000
Ann Sarnoff, *CEO*
Alan Horn, *
John Schulman, *
Barry M Meyer, *
Gunnar Wiedenfels, *
◆ **EMP:** 84 **EST:** 2001
SALES (est): 542.49MM **Publicly Held**
Web: www.warnerbros.com
SIC: 7812 Television film production
HQ: Warner Media, Llc
   30 Hudson Yards

New York NY 10001

(P-14874)
WARNER BROS HOME ENTRMT INC (DH)
4000 Warner Blvd Bldg 160, Burbank (91522-0001)
P.O. Box 9153 (02021-9153)
PHONE...........................818 954-6000
James Cardwell, *Pr*
Edward Byrnes, *
Frank Walsh, *
Timmy Treu, *
Ronald J Sanders, *
▲ **EMP:** 80 **EST:** 1978
SQ FT: 12,000
SALES (est): 7.49MM **Publicly Held**
SIC: 7812 Television film production
HQ: Warner Bros. Entertainment Inc.
   4000 Warner Blvd
   Burbank CA 91522
   818 954-6000

(P-14875)
WARNER BROS INTL TV DIST INC
4000 Warner Blvd, Burbank (91522-0001)
PHONE...........................818 954-6000
Robert Blair, *Pr*
Margee Schubert, *
EMP: 99 **EST:** 2003
SALES (est): 655.14K **Publicly Held**
SIC: 7812 Television film production
HQ: Warner Bros. Entertainment Inc.
   4000 Warner Blvd
   Burbank CA 91522
   818 954-6000

(P-14876)
WESTBROOK OPS LLC
24151 Ventura Blvd Ste 200, Calabasas (91302-1277)
PHONE...........................818 832-2300
EMP: 78 **EST:** 2019
SALES (est): 233.66K **Privately Held**
SIC: 7812 Motion picture and video production

(P-14877)
YOBS TECHNOLOGIES INC
Also Called: Yobs
615 Childs Way Tro 370, Los Angeles (90089-0024)
PHONE...........................213 713-3825
Raphael Danilo, *Pr*
Federico Dubini, *
EMP: 50 **EST:** 2016
SALES (est): 383.47K **Privately Held**
Web: www.yobstech.com
SIC: 7812 8742 7389 3652 Educational motion picture production; Programmed instruction service; Business Activities at Non-Commercial Site; Prerecorded records and tapes

(P-14878)
ZOIC INC
Also Called: Zoic Studios
3582 Eastham Dr, Culver City (90232-2409)
PHONE...........................310 838-0770
Loni Peristere, *CEO*
Chris Jones, *
Tim Mcbride, *Treas*
EMP: 125 **EST:** 2002
SQ FT: 15,000
SALES (est): 4.3MM **Privately Held**
Web: www.zoicstudios.com
SIC: 7812 Video production

(P-14879)
ZOO DIGITAL PRODUCTION LLC
Also Called: Zoo
2201 Park Pl Ste 100, El Segundo
(90245-5167)
PHONE.....................310 220-3939
Laura Herbers, *Adm/Asst*
EMP: 215 EST: 2010
SALES (est): 9.24MM **Privately Held**
Web: www.zoodigital.com
SIC: 7812 Video production

7819 Services Allied To Motion Pictures

(P-14880)
A FILML INC
Also Called: Filml.a
4024 Radford Ave, Studio City
(91604-2101)
PHONE.....................213 977-8600
Paul Audley, *Pr*
Denise Gutches, *
EMP: 95 EST: 1995
SALES (est): 13.07MM **Privately Held**
Web: www.filmla.com
SIC: 7819 Services allied to motion pictures

(P-14881)
ALAN GORDON ENTERPRISES INC
5625 Melrose Ave, Los Angeles
(90038-3909)
PHONE.....................323 466-3561
Grant Loucks, *Pr*
Don Sahlein, *
◆ EMP: 24 EST: 1945
SQ FT: 15,000
SALES (est): 2.45MM **Privately Held**
Web: www.alangordon.com
SIC: 7819 3861 Equipment rental, motion picture; Photographic equipment and supplies

(P-14882)
CARA COMMUNICATIONS LLC
Also Called: Vin Di Bona Productions
12233 W Olympic Blvd Ste 170, Los Angeles (90064-1035)
PHONE.....................310 442-5600
Vincent Dibona, *Pr*
EMP: 78 EST: 1989
SALES (est): 3.78MM
SALES (corp-wide): 10.84MM **Privately Held**
Web: www.vindibonaproductions.com
SIC: 7819 7812 7922 Directors, independent: motion picture; Television film production; Television program, including commercial producers
PA: V10 Entertainment Holdings Lp
12233 W Olympic Blvd
310 442-5600

(P-14883)
CHAPMN/LNARD STDIO EQP CNADA I (PA)
12950 Raymer St, North Hollywood
(91605-4211)
PHONE.....................323 877-5309
Leonard Chapman, *Pr*
Michael Chapman, *
▲ EMP: 145 EST: 1945
SQ FT: 300,000
SALES (est): 20.97MM
SALES (corp-wide): 20.97MM **Privately Held**
Web: www.chapman-leonard.com

(P-14884)
CONDOR PRODUCTIONS LLC
245 N Beverly Dr, Beverly Hills
(90210-5319)
PHONE.....................310 449-3000
EMP: 99 EST: 2016
SQ FT: 5,000
SALES (est): 121.9K **Privately Held**
SIC: 7819 TV tape services: editing, transfers, etc.

(P-14885)
DIRECTORS GUILD AMERICA INC (PA)
Also Called: Đ G A
7920 W Sunset Blvd, Los Angeles
(90046-3347)
PHONE.....................310 289-2000
Jay D Roth, *Ex Dir*
Lesli Linka Glatter, *
Ed Sherin, *
Martha Coolidge, *
Max Schindler, *
EMP: 110 EST: 1936
SQ FT: 100,000
SALES (est): 39.52MM
SALES (corp-wide): 39.52MM **Privately Held**
Web: www.dga.org
SIC: 7819 8631 Directors, independent: motion picture; Labor organizations

(P-14886)
DNEG NORTH AMERICA INC (PA)
Also Called: Prime Focus World
5750 Hannum Ave Ste 100, Culver City
(90230-6666)
PHONE.....................323 461-7887
Namit Malhotra, *CEO*
Robert Hummel, *
Sue Murphree, *
Oliver Welch, *
Anshul Doshi, *Prin*
EMP: 85 EST: 1985
SQ FT: 50,000
SALES (est): 4.09MM
SALES (corp-wide): 4.09MM **Privately Held**
SIC: 7819 Sound effects and music production, motion picture

(P-14887)
DTS INC (DH)
5220 Las Virgenes Rd, Calabasas
(91302-1064)
PHONE.....................818 436-1000
Jon E Kirchner, *CEO*
Melvin L Flanigan, *
Blake A Welcher, *
Kevin Doohan, *CMO*
Kris M Graves, *
▲ EMP: 150 EST: 1990
SQ FT: 89,000
SALES (est): 29.43MM
SALES (corp-wide): 388.79MM **Publicly Held**
Web: www.dts.com
SIC: 7819 3651 Services allied to motion pictures; Household audio and video equipment
HQ: Adeia Holdings Inc.
3025 Orchard Pkwy
San Jose CA 95134
408 473-2500

(P-14888)
EXILE LLC
4203 Redwood Ave, Los Angeles
(90066-5621)
PHONE.....................310 450-2255
Carol Lynn Weaver, *Prin*
EMP: 100 EST: 2014
SALES (est): 953.58K **Privately Held**
Web: www.exileedit.com
SIC: 7819 Services allied to motion pictures

(P-14889)
FIFTH SEASON LLC
11355 W Olympic Blvd Ste 1000w, Los Angeles (90064-1632)
PHONE.....................862 432-3068
Graham Taylor, *CEO*
Chris Rice, *Pr*
EMP: 126 EST: 2017
SALES (est): 16.3MM **Privately Held**
Web: www.fifthseason.com
SIC: 7819 Services allied to motion pictures
PA: Cj Cheiljedang Corporation
330 Dongho-Ro, Jung-Gu

(P-14890)
FILM DEPARTMENT LMU
1 Lmu Dr, Los Angeles (90045-2650)
PHONE.....................310 258-5465
Event Scheduling, *Prin*
EMP: 76 EST: 2011
SALES (est): 2.28MM **Privately Held**
Web: www.lmu.edu
SIC: 7819 Services allied to motion pictures

(P-14891)
FOR CALI PRODUCTIONS LLC
5555 Melrose Ave Bldg 213, Los Angeles
(90038-3996)
PHONE.....................323 956-9500
EMP: 287
SIC: 7819 Services allied to motion pictures
HQ: For Cali Productions, Llc
5808 W Sunset Blvd
Los Angeles CA 90028
323 956-9508

(P-14892)
FOTO-KEM INDUSTRIES INC (PA)
Also Called: Foto Kem Film & Video
2801 W Alameda Ave, Burbank
(91505-4405)
P.O. Box 7755 (91510-7755)
PHONE.....................818 846-3102
William F Brodersen, *CEO*
Christine M Burdick, *
Gerald D Brodersen Junior, *VP*
▲ EMP: 249 EST: 1963
SQ FT: 43,000
SALES (est): 52.5MM
SALES (corp-wide): 52.5MM **Privately Held**
Web: www.fotokem.com
SIC: 7819 Laboratory service, motion picture

(P-14893)
FUSEFX LLC
Also Called: Fusefx
5161 Lankershim Blvd, North Hollywood
(91601-4962)
PHONE.....................818 237-5052
David Altenau, *CEO*
Tim Jacobsen, *Chief Development Officer*
Jason Fotter, *
EMP: 300 EST: 2006
SALES (est): 23.37MM **Privately Held**
Web: www.fusefx.com

SIC: 7819 Visual effects production

(P-14894)
HOLLYWOOD RNTALS PROD SVCS LLC (PA)
5300 Melrose Ave, Los Angeles
(90038-5111)
PHONE.....................818 407-7800
Mark A Rosenthal, *Managing Member*
▲ EMP: 100 EST: 2000
SQ FT: 100,000
SALES (est): 4.58MM
SALES (corp-wide): 4.58MM **Privately Held**
Web: www.the-mbsgroup.com
SIC: 7819 Equipment rental, motion picture

(P-14895)
INDUSTRIAL MEDIA INC (PA)
6007 Sepulveda Blvd, Van Nuys
(91411-2502)
PHONE.....................310 777-1940
Peter Hurwitz, *CEO*
Scott Frosch, *
EMP: 205 EST: 2016
SALES (est): 9.64MM
SALES (corp-wide): 9.64MM **Privately Held**
Web: www.ien.com
SIC: 7819 Reproduction services, motion picture production

(P-14896)
LOMA LINDA UNIVERSITY
Also Called: Loma Linda Broadcasting
11125 Campus St Ste 100, Loma Linda
(92354-3227)
P.O. Box A (92354)
PHONE.....................909 558-8611
Ganim Hanna, *Pr*
EMP: 96
SALES (corp-wide): 379.88MM **Privately Held**
Web: www.llu.edu
SIC: 7819 8221 Video tape or disk reproduction; University
PA: Loma Linda University
11060 Andrson St Bldg Mga
909 558-4540

(P-14897)
NEP BEXEL INC (HQ)
Also Called: Bexel
7850 Ruffner Ave Ste B, Van Nuys
(91406-1619)
PHONE.....................818 565-4399
EMP: 80 EST: 1980
SALES (est): 24.93MM
SALES (corp-wide): 421.16MM **Privately Held**
Web: www.bexel.com
SIC: 7819 5731 5065 Equipment rental, motion picture; Video cameras and accessories; Electronic parts and equipment, nec
PA: Nep Group, Inc.
2 Beta Dr
412 826-1414

(P-14898)
OLIVE AVENUE PRODUCTIONS LLC
4000 Warner Blvd, Burbank (91522-0001)
PHONE.....................770 214-7052
EMP: 500 EST: 2018
SALES (est): 563.34K **Privately Held**
SIC: 7819 Developing and laboratory services, motion picture

(P-14899)

OMEGA/CINEMA PROPS INC
1515 E 15th St, Los Angeles (90021-2711)
PHONE..........................323 466-8201
E Jay Krause, *Pr*
Cheryl Jordan, *
▲ **EMP:** 90 **EST:** 1967
SQ FT: 300,000
SALES (est): 5.77MM **Privately Held**
Web: www.omegacinemaprops.com
SIC: 7819 Equipment rental, motion picture

(P-14900)

PHORUS INC
5220 Las Virgenes Rd, Calabasas
(91302-1064)
PHONE..........................310 995-2521
Jon Kirchner, *CEO*
▲ **EMP:** 100 **EST:** 2012
SALES (est): 724.63K
SALES (corp-wide): 388.79MM **Publicly Held**
Web: www.phorus.com
SIC: 7819 3651 Services allied to motion pictures; Household audio and video equipment
HQ: Adeia Holdings Inc.
3025 Orchard Pkwy
San Jose CA 95134
408 473-2500

(P-14901)

PIXOMONDO LLC
10202 Washington Blvd, Culver City
(90232-3119)
PHONE..........................310 394-0555
Jonny Slow, *CEO*
EMP: 662 **EST:** 2008
SALES (est): 18.06MM **Privately Held**
Web: www.pixomondo.com
SIC: 7819 Visual effects production
HQ: Sony Pictures Entertainment, Inc.
10202 W Washington Blvd
Culver City CA 90232
310 244-4000

(P-14902)

POINT360 (PA)
Also Called: Digital Film Labs
2701 Media Center Dr, Los Angeles
(90065-1700)
PHONE..........................818 565-1400
Haig S Bagerdjian, *Ch Bd*
Alan R Steel, *Executive Vice President Finance & Administration*
EMP: 82 **EST:** 1997
SQ FT: 64,600
SALES (est): 20.63MM **Privately Held**
Web: www.point360.com
SIC: 7819 7822 7829 Video tape or disk reproduction; Motion picture and tape distribution; Motion picture distribution services

(P-14903)

POST GROUP INC (PA)
Also Called: Post Group Production Suites
1415 N Cahuenga Blvd, Los Angeles
(90028-8198)
P.O. Box 3870 (91617-3870)
PHONE..........................323 462-2300
Frederic Rheinstein, *Ch*
Vincent Lyons, *
Duke Gallagher, *
EMP: 110 **EST:** 1974
SQ FT: 40,000
SALES (est): 3.12MM
SALES (corp-wide): 3.12MM **Privately Held**
Web: www.postgroup.com

SIC: 7819 7812 Editing services, motion picture production; Motion picture and video production

(P-14904)

STAR WAGGONS LLC
13334 Ralston Ave, Sylmar (91342-7608)
PHONE..........................818 367-5946
EMP: 87 **EST:** 1979
SALES (est): 6.46MM **Publicly Held**
Web: www.quixote.com
SIC: 7819 Studio property rental, motion picture
PA: Hudson Pacific Properties, Inc.
11601 Wlshire Blvd Ste 16

(P-14905)

STREAMLAND MEDIA LLC
Also Called: Ghost Vfx
3900 W Alameda Ave Fl 10, Burbank
(91505-4316)
PHONE..........................818 855-7467
EMP: 83 **EST:** 2018
SALES (est): 2.13MM **Privately Held**
Web: www.pictureshop.com
SIC: 7819 Services allied to motion pictures

(P-14906)

TECHNCLOR CRATIVE SVCS USA INC
Also Called: Technicolor Creative Studios
8921 Lindblade St, Culver City
(90232-2438)
PHONE..........................818 260-1214
Timothy Sarnoff, *CEO*
Richard Andrews, *
Claude Gagnon, *
John Hancock, *
EMP: 450 **EST:** 1980
SQ FT: 25,000
SALES (est): 8.47MM **Privately Held**
Web: www.mikrosanimation.com
SIC: 7819 Video tape or disk reproduction

(P-14907)

TECHNICOLOR THOMSON GROUP INC (HQ)
Also Called: Technicolor Entertainment Svcs
2233 N Ontario St Ste 300, Burbank
(91504-4500)
◆ **EMP:** 291 **EST:** 1922
SALES (est): 101.85MM **Privately Held**
SIC: 7819 7384 Video tape or disk reproduction; Photofinish laboratories
PA: Vantiva
10 Boulevard De Grenelle

(P-14908)

TEN PUBLISHING MEDIA LLC (PA)
831 S Douglas St, El Segundo
(90245-4902)
PHONE..........................310 531-9900
Scott P Dickey, *CEO*
Peter H Englehart, *Ch Bd*
Chris Argentieri, *Pr*
John B Bode, *Ex VP*
Stephanie S Justice, *Ex VP*
EMP: 230 **EST:** 1991
SALES (est): 8.75MM **Privately Held**
SIC: 7819 Visual effects production

(P-14909)

TESTRONIC INC
Also Called: Testronic Labs
111 N First St Ste 204, Burbank
(91502-1851)
PHONE..........................818 845-3223
Dominic Wheatley, *CEO*

▲ **EMP:** 132 **EST:** 1996
SALES (est): 4.85MM **Privately Held**
Web: www.testroniclabs.com
SIC: 7819 Video tape or disk reproduction

(P-14910)

VANTIVA SCS MEMPHIS INC (DH)
Also Called: Technclor Vdocassette Mich Inc
3601 Calle Tecate Ste 120, Camarillo
(93012-5057)
PHONE..........................805 445-1122
Lanni Ormonvo, *Pr*
John H Oliphant, *
▲ **EMP:** 500 **EST:** 1987
SALES (est): 2.38MM **Privately Held**
SIC: 7819 Video tape or disk reproduction
HQ: Technicolor Thomson Group, Inc
2233 N Ontario St
Burbank CA 91504

(P-14911)

VANTIVA SUP CHAIN SLUTIONS INC (HQ)
Also Called: Technicolor Video Services
3601 Calle Tecate Ste 120, Camarillo
(93012-5057)
PHONE..........................805 445-1122
Lanny Raimondo, *CEO*
Orlando F Raimondo, *Pr*
Patricia Dave, *CFO*
◆ **EMP:** 500 **EST:** 1983
SALES (est): 480.55MM **Privately Held**
SIC: 7819 Video tape or disk reproduction
PA: Vantiva
10 Boulevard De Grenelle

(P-14912)

VANTIVA SUP CHAIN SLUTIONS INC
Also Called: Technicolor
461 Rood Rd Ste A, Calexico (92231-9768)
PHONE..........................760 357-3372
EMP: 79
SIC: 7819 Video tape or disk reproduction
HQ: Vantiva Supply Chain Solutions, Inc.
3601 Calle Tecate Ste 120
Camarillo CA 93012

(P-14913)

VANTIVA SUP CHAIN SLUTIONS INC
Also Called: Accounts Payable Department
5491 E Philadelphia St, Ontario
(91761-2807)
P.O. Box 2459 (91729-2459)
PHONE..........................909 974-2016
EMP: 95
SIC: 7819 Video tape or disk reproduction
HQ: Vantiva Supply Chain Solutions, Inc.
3601 Calle Tecate Ste 120
Camarillo CA 93012

(P-14914)

WALT DSNEY IMGNRING RES DEV IN (DH)
Also Called: Disney
1401 Flower St, Glendale (91201-2421)
P.O. Box 25020 (91221-5020)
PHONE..........................818 544-6500
Thomas O Staggs, *CEO*
Craig Russell, *DESIGN DELIVERY*
Bruce Vaughn, *CREATIVE*
Martin A Sklar, *
Jessica Hodgins, *
◆ **EMP:** 1011 **EST:** 1986
SQ FT: 100,000
SALES (est): 54.47MM
SALES (corp-wide): 91.36B **Publicly Held**

Web: www.disneyimaginations.com
SIC: 7819 8712 1542 8741 Visual effects production; Architectural services; Custom builders, non-residential; Management services
HQ: Disney Enterprises, Inc.
500 S Buena Vista St
Burbank CA 91521
818 560-1000

7822 Motion Picture And Tape Distribution

(P-14915)

20TH CENTURY STUDIOS INC
10201 W Pico Blvd, Los Angeles
(90064-2651)
PHONE..........................888 223-4369
Paige W Olson, *CEO*
Carlos A Gomez, *
Chakira H Gavazzi, *
EMP: 104 **EST:** 2020
SALES (est): 1.83MM
SALES (corp-wide): 91.36B **Publicly Held**
Web: www.20thcenturystudios.com
SIC: 7822 Motion picture and tape distribution
HQ: Buena Vista International Inc
500 S Buena Vista St
Burbank CA 91521
818 560-1000

(P-14916)

CREATIVE PARK PRODUCTIONS LLC
Also Called: Universal Studios
100 Universal City Plz, Universal City
(91608-1002)
PHONE..........................818 622-3702
EMP: 105 **EST:** 2002
SALES (est): 19.77MM **Privately Held**
Web: www.universalstudioslot.com
SIC: 7822 Motion picture and tape distribution

(P-14917)

DELUXE NMS INC
4499 Glencoe Ave, Marina Del Rey
(90292-6357)
PHONE..........................310 760-8500
Cyril Drabinsky, *CEO*
EMP: 200 **EST:** 2010
SQ FT: 20,000
SALES (est): 1.15MM
SALES (corp-wide): 2.19B **Publicly Held**
Web: www.dadcdigital.com
SIC: 7822 7374 Motion picture and tape distribution; Data processing and preparation
PA: Deluxe Corporation
801 Marquette Ave
651 483-7111

(P-14918)

JAMES ALLEN PRODUCTIONS LLC
Also Called: J P Allen Co
11801 Pierce St, Riverside (92505-4408)
PHONE..........................951 944-2564
James Allen, *Managing Member*
EMP: 100 **EST:** 2019
SALES (est): 247.92K **Privately Held**
SIC: 7822 Motion picture and tape distribution

(P-14919)

LFP BROADCASTING LLC (PA)
8484 Wilshire Blvd Ste 900, Beverly Hills
(90211-3218)

PHONE..................323 852-5020
EMP: 75 **EST:** 2004
SALES (est): 40MM
SALES (corp-wide): 40MM **Privately Held**
SIC: 7822 Distribution, for television: motion picture

(P-14920)
LIONSGATE PRODUCTIONS INC
2700 Colorado Ave Ste 200, Santa Monica (90404-5502)
PHONE..................310 255-3937
Jon Feltheimer, *CEO*
Steve Beeks, *
Wayne Levin, *
Michael Burns, *Vice Chairman*
Wayne Levin, *Chief Strategic Officer*
EMP: 118 **EST:** 2010
SALES (est): 13.3MM
SALES (corp-wide): 3.85B **Privately Held**
SIC: 7822 Motion picture and tape distribution
HQ: Lions Gate Entertainment Inc.
2700 Colorado Ave Ste 200
Santa Monica CA 90404
310 449-9200

(P-14921)
SONAR ENTERTAINMENT INC (PA)
2834 Colorado Ave Ste 300, Santa Monica (90404-3644)
PHONE..................424 230-7140
Thomas F Lesinski, *CEO*
Henry S Hoberman, *
William J Aliber, *
Joel E Denton, *Distributor*
EMP: 80 **EST:** 2007
SALES (est): 6.21MM
SALES (corp-wide): 6.21MM **Privately Held**
Web: www.sonarent.com
SIC: 7822 Motion picture and tape distribution

(P-14922)
TWENTETH CNTURY FOX HM ENTRMT
Also Called: Fox
1440 S Sepulveda Blvd 3rd Fl, Los Angeles (90025-3458)
PHONE..................310 369-1000
Jeff Shell, *Brnch Mgr*
EMP: 250
Web: www.fox.com
SIC: 7822 Motion picture distribution
PA: Twentieth Century Fox Home Entertainment Llc
10201 W Pico Blvd

(P-14923)
TWENTIETH CENTURY FOX HOME E
2121 Avenue Of The Stars Ste 2500, Los Angeles (90067-5049)
PHONE..................310 369-3900
Paul Provenzano, *Ex Dir*
EMP: 250
SIC: 7822 7922 Motion picture distribution; Television program, including commercial producers
PA: Twentieth Century Fox Home Entertainment Llc
10201 W Pico Blvd

(P-14924)
TWENTIETH CNTURY FOX INTL CORP (HQ)
Also Called: Fox

10201 W Pico Blvd Bldg 1, Los Angeles (90064-2606)
Rural Route 900 (90213)
PHONE..................310 369-1000
Robert A Iger, *CEO*
◆ **EMP:** 98 **EST:** 1972
SQ FT: 115,000
SALES (est): 1.31MM
SALES (corp-wide): 91.36B **Publicly Held**
Web: www.thefoxgroupre.com
SIC: 7822 7922 Motion picture distribution; Television program, including commercial producers
PA: The Walt Disney Company
500 S Buena Vista St
818 560-1000

(P-14925)
UNITED ARTISTS PRODUCTIONS INC
10250 Constellation Blvd Fl 19, Los Angeles (90067-6219)
PHONE..................310 449-3000
Christopher Mcgurk, *Pr*
EMP: 212 **EST:** 1995
SALES (est): 1.45MM **Publicly Held**
SIC: 7822 Distribution, exclusive of production: motion picture
HQ: United Artists Pictures Inc.
10250 Constellation Blvd
Los Angeles CA 90067

(P-14926)
UNITED ARTISTS TELEVISION CORP
10250 Constellation Blvd Fl 27, Los Angeles (90067-6227)
PHONE..................310 449-3000
EMP: 255 **EST:** 1931
SALES (est): 802.07K **Publicly Held**
SIC: 7822 Distribution, exclusive of production: motion picture
HQ: United Artists Pictures Inc.
10250 Constellation Blvd
Los Angeles CA 90067

(P-14927)
WARNER BROS TRANSATLANTIC INC
Also Called: Warner Bros
3300 W Olive Ave Ste 200, Burbank (91505-4658)
PHONE..................818 977-6384
Scott Levy, *Brnch Mgr*
EMP: 110
Web: www.warnerbroscanada.com
SIC: 7822 Distribution, exclusive of production: motion picture
HQ: Warner Bros. (Transatlantic), Inc.
4000 Warner Blvd
Burbank CA 91522

7829 Motion Picture Distribution Services

(P-14928)
OUR ALCHEMY LLC
Also Called: Alchemy
5900 Wilshire Blvd Fl 18, Los Angeles (90036-5013)
PHONE..................310 893-6289
Kelly Summers, *
Scott Guthrie, *
EMP: 80 **EST:** 2010
SQ FT: 30,000
SALES (est): 981.32K **Privately Held**
Web: www.ouralchemy.com

SIC: 7829 Motion picture distribution services

7832 Motion Picture Theaters, Except Drive-in

(P-14929)
CARMIKE CINEMAS LLC
Also Called: Carmike Cinemas
166 W Hillcrest Dr, Thousand Oaks (91360-4209)
PHONE..................805 494-4702
EMP: 118
Web: www.amctheatres.com
SIC: 7832 Exhibitors, itinerant: motion picture
HQ: Carmike Cinemas, Llc
11500 Ash St
Leawood KS 66211
913 213-2000

(P-14930)
CENTURY THEATRES INC
7777 Edinger Ave Ste 170, Huntington Beach (92647-8690)
PHONE..................714 373-4573
EMP: 248
Web: www.cinemark.com
SIC: 7832 Motion picture theaters, except drive-in
HQ: Century Theatres, Inc
3900 Dallas Pkwy Ste 500
Plano TX 75093
972 665-1000

(P-14931)
DECURION CORPORATION (PA)
120 N Robertson Blvd Fl 3, Los Angeles (90048-3115)
PHONE..................310 659-9432
Michael R Forman, *Pr*
Jerome Forman, *
James Cotter, *
EMP: 100 **EST:** 1966
SQ FT: 31,000
SALES (est): 15.68MM
SALES (corp-wide): 15.68MM **Privately Held**
Web: www.decurion.com
SIC: 7832 7833 Motion picture theaters, except drive-in; Drive-in motion picture theaters

(P-14932)
EDWARDS THEATRES INC
Also Called: Kaleidioscope Stadium Cinema
27741 Crown Valley Pkwy Ste 301, Mission Viejo (92691-6598)
PHONE..................949 582-4078
EMP: 166
SALES (corp-wide): 1.13B **Privately Held**
SIC: 7832 Motion picture theaters, except drive-in
HQ: Edwards Theatres, Inc.
300 Newport Center Dr
Newport Beach CA 92660
949 640-4600

(P-14933)
EDWARDS THEATRES INC
Also Called: La Verne Cinema 12
1950 Foothill Blvd, La Verne (91750-3557)
PHONE..................844 462-7342
EMP: 180
SALES (corp-wide): 1.13B **Privately Held**
Web: www.regmovies.com
SIC: 7832 Motion picture theaters, except drive-in
HQ: Edwards Theatres, Inc.
300 Newport Center Dr
Newport Beach CA 92660
949 640-4600

(P-14934)
EDWARDS THEATRES INC (DH)
Also Called: Edwards Theatres Circuit, Inc.
300 Newport Center Dr, Newport Beach (92660-7529)
PHONE..................949 640-4600
James Edwards Iii, *Ch Bd*
Steve Coffey, *
Joan Randolph, *
Marcella Sheldon, *
EMP: 118 **EST:** 1930
SQ FT: 30,000
SALES (est): 30.55MM
SALES (corp-wide): 1.13B **Privately Held**
SIC: 7832 Motion picture theaters, except drive-in
HQ: Regal Cinemas, Inc.
101 E Blount Ave
Knoxville TN 37920

(P-14935)
EDWARDS THEATRES CIRCUIT INC
Also Called: Rancho San Diego Cinema 16
2951 Jamacha Rd, El Cajon (92019-4342)
PHONE..................619 660-3460
EMP: 180
SALES (corp-wide): 1.13B **Privately Held**
SIC: 7832 Motion picture theaters, except drive-in
HQ: Edwards Theatres, Inc.
300 Newport Center Dr
Newport Beach CA 92660
949 640-4600

(P-14936)
EDWARDS THEATRES CIRCUIT INC
Also Called: Temecula Stadium Cinemas 15
40750 Winchester Rd, Temecula (92591-5524)
PHONE..................951 296-0144
EMP: 166
SALES (corp-wide): 1.13B **Privately Held**
SIC: 7832 Motion picture theaters, except drive-in
HQ: Edwards Theatres, Inc.
300 Newport Center Dr
Newport Beach CA 92660
949 640-4600

(P-14937)
EDWARDS THEATRES CIRCUIT INC
Also Called: Mesa Pointe Stadium 12
901 S Coast Dr, Costa Mesa (92626-1747)
PHONE..................714 428-0962
Minh Duong, *Brnch Mgr*
EMP: 166
SALES (corp-wide): 1.13B **Privately Held**
SIC: 7832 Motion picture theaters, except drive-in
HQ: Edwards Theatres, Inc.
300 Newport Center Dr
Newport Beach CA 92660
949 640-4600

(P-14938)
EDWARDS THEATRES CIRCUIT INC
Also Called: Edwards Cinemas University
4245 Campus Dr, Irvine (92612-2752)
PHONE..................949 854-8811
Mike Peterson, *Brnch Mgr*
EMP: 151
SALES (corp-wide): 1.13B **Privately Held**
SIC: 7832 Motion picture theaters, except drive-in
HQ: Edwards Theatres, Inc.
300 Newport Center Dr

Newport Beach CA 92660
949 640-4600

(P-14939)
**KRIKORIAN PREMIERE
THEATRE LLC**
8290 La Palma Ave, Buena Park (90620)
PHONE.....................714 826-7469
Ted Goldbeck, *Brnch Mgr*
EMP: 94
SALES (corp-wide): 7.62MM **Privately Held**
SIC: 7832 Motion picture theaters, except drive-in
PA: Krikorian Premiere Theatre Llc
2275 W 190th St
310 856-1270

(P-14940)
**KRIKORIAN PREMIERE
THEATRE LLC**
25 Main St, Vista (92083-5800)
PHONE.....................760 945-7469
EMP: 93
SALES (corp-wide): 7.62MM **Privately Held**
SIC: 7832 Motion picture theaters, except drive-in
PA: Krikorian Premiere Theatre Llc
2275 W 190th St
310 856-1270

(P-14941)
**KRIKORIAN PREMIERE
THEATRE LLC**
8540 Whittier Blvd, Pico Rivera (90660-2520)
PHONE.....................562 205-3456
Todd Cummings, *Brnch Mgr*
EMP: 93
SALES (corp-wide): 7.62MM **Privately Held**
SIC: 7832 Motion picture theaters, except drive-in
PA: Krikorian Premiere Theatre Llc
2275 W 190th St
310 856-1270

(P-14942)
**METROPOLITAN THEATRES
CORP**
Also Called: Camelot Theatres
789 E Tahquitz Canyon Way, Palm Springs (92262-6705)
PHONE.....................760 323-3221
Carl Kilebrew, *Brnch Mgr*
EMP: 92
SALES (corp-wide): 140.61K **Privately Held**
Web: www.metrotheatres.com
SIC: 7832 Motion picture theaters, except drive-in
PA: Metropolitan Theatres Corporation
8727 W 3rd St Ste 301
310 858-2800

(P-14943)
**READING ENTERTAINMENT INC
(HQ)**
500 Citadel Dr Ste 300, Commerce (90040-1575)
PHONE.....................213 235-2226
Robert F Smerling, *Pr*
S Craig Tompkins, *Vice Chairman*
Ellen Cotter, *Business Affairs Vice President*
Andrzej Matyczynski, *CFO*
Charles Grohon, *OF FINS*
▲ **EMP:** 78 **EST:** 1996
SQ FT: 3,300

SALES (est): 381.22K
SALES (corp-wide): 222.74MM **Publicly Held**
SIC: 7832 Motion picture theaters, except drive-in
PA: Reading International, Inc.
189 2nd Ave Apt 2s
213 235-2240

(P-14944)
WESTSTAR CINEMAS INC
Also Called: Plant 16
7876 Van Nuys Blvd, Van Nuys (91402-6069)
PHONE.....................818 779-0323
Randy Dingwall, *Brnch Mgr*
EMP: 74
SALES (corp-wide): 2.07MM **Privately Held**
SIC: 7832 Motion picture theaters, except drive-in
PA: Weststar Cinemas, Inc.
16530 Ventura Blvd # 500
818 784-6266

(P-14945)
WESTSTAR CINEMAS INC
Also Called: Augora Hills 8 Cinema Center
29045 Agoura Rd, Agoura Hills (91301-2572)
PHONE.....................818 707-8987
Raymond Cornelio, *Genl Mgr*
EMP: 76
SALES (corp-wide): 2.07MM **Privately Held**
SIC: 7832 Motion picture theaters, except drive-in
PA: Weststar Cinemas, Inc.
16530 Ventura Blvd # 500
818 784-6266

(P-14946)
WESTSTAR CINEMAS INC
Also Called: Man Theateres
180 Promenade Way Ste R, Westlake Village (91362-3826)
PHONE.....................805 379-8966
Joseph Leptore, *Mgr*
EMP: 114
SALES (corp-wide): 2.07MM **Privately Held**
SIC: 7832 Motion picture theaters, except drive-in
PA: Weststar Cinemas, Inc.
16530 Ventura Blvd # 500
818 784-6266

(P-14947)
WESTSTAR CINEMAS INC
Also Called: Buenaventura 6
1440 Eastman Ave, Ventura (93003-7784)
PHONE.....................805 658-6544
Lyndon Golin, *Brnch Mgr*
EMP: 105
SALES (corp-wide): 2.07MM **Privately Held**
SIC: 7832 Motion picture theaters, except drive-in
PA: Weststar Cinemas, Inc.
16530 Ventura Blvd # 500
818 784-6266

7833 Drive-in Motion Picture Theaters

(P-14948)
CENTURY THEATRES INC
Also Called: Century Downtown 10
555 E Main St, Ventura (93001-2628)

PHONE.....................805 641-6555
EMP: 331
Web: www.cinemark.com
SIC: 7833 7832 Drive-in motion picture theaters; Motion picture theaters, except drive-in
HQ: Century Theatres, Inc
3900 Dallas Pkwy Ste 500
Plano TX 75093
972 665-1000

(P-14949)
CENTURY THEATRES INC
Also Called: Century 8
12827 Victory Blvd, North Hollywood (91606-3012)
PHONE.....................818 508-1943
Terrell Hammack, *Brnch Mgr*
EMP: 347
Web: www.cinemark.com
SIC: 7833 7832 Drive-in motion picture theaters; Motion picture theaters, except drive-in
HQ: Century Theatres, Inc
3900 Dallas Pkwy Ste 500
Plano TX 75093
972 665-1000

(P-14950)
**NATIONWIDE THEATRES CORP
(HQ)**
120 N Robertson Blvd Fl 3, Los Angeles (90048-3115)
PHONE.....................310 657-8420
Christopher Forman, *Pr*
Nora Dashwood, *
EMP: 75 **EST:** 1956
SQ FT: 25,000
SALES (est): 8.31MM
SALES (corp-wide): 15.68MM **Privately Held**
SIC: 7833 7832 Drive-in motion picture theaters; Motion picture theaters, except drive-in
PA: The Decurion Corporation
120 N Robertson Blvd Fl 3
310 659-9432

7841 Video Tape Rental

(P-14951)
**EROS STX GLOBAL
CORPORATION**
3900 W Alameda Ave Fl 32, Burbank (91505-4316)
PHONE.....................818 524-7000
Kishore Lulla, *C Executive*
Rishika Lulla Singh, *
Andrew Warren, *CFO*
EMP: 502 **EST:** 1977
SALES (est): 639.47K **Privately Held**
Web: www.erosstx.com
SIC: 7841 Video disk/tape rental to the general public

7922 Theatrical Producers And Services

(P-14952)
**ADVENTIST MEDIA CENTER
INC (PA)**
Also Called: It Is Written
11291 Pierce St, Riverside (92505-2705)
P.O. Box 101 (93062-0101)
PHONE.....................805 955-7777
Daniel R Jackson, *CEO*
Marshall Chase, *
Warren Judd, *

Daniel Jackson, *
▲ **EMP:** 183 **EST:** 1972
SQ FT: 76,000
SALES (est): 566.81K
SALES (corp-wide): 566.81K **Privately Held**
Web: www.adventistmediaministries.com
SIC: 7922 Television program, including commercial producers

(P-14953)
AEG PRESENTS LLC (DH)
Also Called: AEG Presents
425 W 11th St, Los Angeles (90015-3459)
PHONE.....................323 930-5700
Jay Marciano, *Ch*
Jorge Melendez, *
John Meglen, *
Paul Gongaware, *
Shawn A Trell, *
▲ **EMP:** 140 **EST:** 2002
SQ FT: 16,400
SALES (est): 9.15MM **Privately Held**
Web: www.aegpresents.com
SIC: 7922 Entertainment promotion
HQ: Anschutz Entertainment Group, Inc.
800 W Olympic Blvd Ste 30
Los Angeles CA 90015
213 763-7700

(P-14954)
**AGENCY FOR PERFORMING
ARTS INC (PA)**
405 S Beverly Dr Ste 500, Beverly Hills (90212-4425)
PHONE.....................310 557-9049
James Gosnell, *Pr*
EMP: 100 **EST:** 1962
SALES (est): 15.56MM
SALES (corp-wide): 15.56MM **Privately Held**
Web: www.independentartistgroup.com
SIC: 7922 Theatrical producers and services

(P-14955)
AUTHENTIC ENTERTAINMENT
5200 Lankershim Blvd Ste 200, North Hollywood (91601-3180)
PHONE.....................747 529-8800
Tom Rogan, *Ex Dir*
Lauren Lexton, *VP*
EMP: 83 **EST:** 2000
SALES (est): 744.96K **Privately Held**
Web: www.banijayamericas.com
SIC: 7922 7812 Television program, including commercial producers; Motion picture and video production

(P-14956)
**CENTER THTRE GROUP LOS
ANGELES (PA)**
601 W Temple St, Los Angeles (90012-2621)
PHONE.....................213 972-7344
Meghan Pressman, *CEO*
Stephen Rountree, *
William Ahmanson, *
Kiki Gindler, *
Brindell Gottlieb, *
▲ **EMP:** 130 **EST:** 1966
SQ FT: 20,000
SALES (est): 15.78MM
SALES (corp-wide): 15.78MM **Privately Held**
Web: www.centertheatregroup.org
SIC: 7922 Theatrical companies

(P-14957)
CITY OF DOWNEY
Also Called: Downey Civic Theatre
8435 Firestone Blvd, Downey (90241-3843)
P.O. Box 607 (90241-0607)
PHONE..................................562 861-8211
Gerald Caton, *Mgr*
EMP: 102
SALES (corp-wide): 149.66MM **Privately Held**
Web: www.downeyca.org
SIC: 7922 Legitimate live theater producers
PA: City Of Downey
11111 Brookshire Ave
562 869-7331

(P-14958)
CREATIVE ARTSTS AGCY HLDNGS LL (DH)
Also Called: C A A
2000 Avenue Of The Stars Ste 100, Los Angeles (90067-4705)
PHONE..................................424 288-2000
Bryan Lourd, *CEO*
Jim Burtson, *
EMP: 800 **EST:** 1975
SALES (est): 220.99MM **Privately Held**
Web: www.caa.com
SIC: 7922 Agent or manager for entertainers
HQ: Artemis
6 B Rue Bernard Palissy
Saint-Germain-En-Laye IDF

(P-14959)
FANDANGO INC (HQ)
Also Called: Fandangonow
12200 W Olympic Blvd Ste 400, Los Angeles (90064-1047)
PHONE..................................310 954-0278
Chuck Davis, *CEO*
Paul Yanover, *
Arthur Levitt Iii, *Pr*
Walter Williams, *
Daniel V Murray, *
EMP: 71 **EST:** 1996
SQ FT: 10,000
SALES (corp-wide): 121.57B **Publicly Held**
Web: www.fandango.com
SIC: 7922 Ticket agency, theatrical
PA: Comcast Corporation
1 Comcast Ctr
215 286-1700

(P-14960)
FRIENDS OF CULTURAL CENTER INC
Also Called: MCCALLUM THEATRE
73000 Fred Waring Dr, Palm Desert (92260-2899)
PHONE..................................760 346-6505
Jamie Grant, *Pr*
William Towers, *
Harold Matzner, *Vice Chairman*
Ron Gregroire, *
Robert Mcconnaughey, *CFO*
EMP: 100 **EST:** 1973
SQ FT: 66,000
SALES (est): 19.37MM **Privately Held**
Web: www.mccallumtheatre.org
SIC: 7922 Legitimate live theater producers

(P-14961)
GERSH AGENCY LLC (PA)
9465 Wilshire Blvd Fl 6, Beverly Hills (90212-2605)
PHONE..................................310 274-6611
Robert Gersh, *Pr*
David Gersh, *VP*

Beatrice Gersh, *VP*
EMP: 100 **EST:** 1949
SQ FT: 15,000
SALES (est): 7.63MM
SALES (corp-wide): 7.63MM **Privately Held**
Web: www.gersh.com
SIC: 7922 Talent agent, theatrical

(P-14962)
INDUSTRY ENTRMT PARTNERS
955 Carrillo Dr Ste 300, Los Angeles (90048-5400)
PHONE..................................323 954-9000
Keith Addis, *Pt*
EMP: 81 **EST:** 1982
SALES (est): 459.13K **Privately Held**
Web: www.diannefraser.com
SIC: 7922 Talent agent, theatrical

(P-14963)
INNOVTIVE ARTSTS TLENT LTRARY (PA)
1505 10th St, Santa Monica (90401-2805)
PHONE..................................310 656-0400
Scott Harris, *Pr*
EMP: 75 **EST:** 1982
SALES (est): 4.01MM
SALES (corp-wide): 4.01MM **Privately Held**
Web: www.innovativeartists.com
SIC: 7922 7819 Talent agent, theatrical; Casting bureau, motion picture

(P-14964)
LAGUNA PLAYHOUSE (PA)
606 Laguna Canyon Rd, Laguna Beach (92651-1898)
P.O. Box 1747 (92652-1747)
PHONE..................................949 497-2787
Karen Wood, *CEO*
Richard Stein, *
Bob Crowson, *
EMP: 225 **EST:** 1920
SQ FT: 19,000
SALES (est): 2.83MM
SALES (corp-wide): 2.83MM **Privately Held**
Web: www.lagunaplayhouse.com
SIC: 7922 Legitimate live theater producers

(P-14965)
LOS ANGELES OPERA COMPANY
135 N Grand Ave Ste 327, Los Angeles (90012-3018)
PHONE..................................213 972-7219
▲ **EMP:** 500 **EST:** 1966
SALES (est): 39.71MM **Privately Held**
Web: www.laopera.org
SIC: 7922 Theatrical producers and services

(P-14966)
NBC STUDIOS INC
Also Called: NBC
100 Universal City Plz Fl 3, Universal City (91608-1002)
PHONE..................................818 777-1000
EMP: 1000
SIC: 7922 Television program, including commercial producers

(P-14967)
OLD GLOBE THEATRE
Also Called: Old Globe
1363 Old Globe Way, San Diego (92101-1696)
P.O. Box 122171 (92112-2171)
PHONE..................................619 234-5623

Michael G Murphy, *CEO*
Louis Spisto, *
Mark Somers, *
▲ **EMP:** 500 **EST:** 1937
SALES (est): 34.22MM **Privately Held**
Web: www.theoldglobe.org
SIC: 7922 Performing arts center production

(P-14968)
PARADIGM MUSIC LLC (PA)
Also Called: Paradigm
360 N Crescent Dr, Beverly Hills (90210-4874)
PHONE..................................310 288-8000
Sam Gores, *Ch Bd*
Lucy Stille, *
EMP: 70 **EST:** 1993
SALES (est): 3.8MM **Privately Held**
SIC: 7922 Talent agent, theatrical

(P-14969)
PARADIGM TALENT AGENCY LLC
6725 W Sunset Blvd, Los Angeles (90028-7119)
PHONE..................................310 288-8000
Sam Gores, *Brnch Mgr*
EMP: 72
SALES (corp-wide): 4.37MM **Privately Held**
Web: www.paradigmagency.com
SIC: 7922 Talent agent, theatrical
PA: Paradigm Talent Agency, Llc
700 N Vicnte Blvd
310 288-8000

(P-14970)
PERFORMING ARTS CTR LOS ANGLES
Also Called: Music Center
135 N Grand Ave Ste 314, Los Angeles (90012-3018)
PHONE..................................213 972-7512
John Emerson, *Ch Bd*
Stephen Rountree, *
William Taylor, *
Lisa Whitney, *Prin*
Lisa Specht, *
▲ **EMP:** 250 **EST:** 1961
SQ FT: 24,000
SALES (est): 6.45MM
SALES (corp-wide): 15.38MM **Privately Held**
Web: www.musiccenter.org
SIC: 7922 Theatrical production services
PA: The Music Center Of Los Angeles County Inc
135 N Grand Ave Ste 201
213 972-8007

(P-14971)
PRDCTIONS N FREMANTLE AMER INC (DH)
Also Called: Fremantle Media
2900 W Alameda Ave Unit 800, Burbank (91505-4262)
PHONE..................................818 748-1100
Thom Beers, *CEO*
Dan Goldberg, *
Donna Redier Linsk, *
Ellen Goldstein, *
EMP: 100 **EST:** 1995
SALES (est): 2.59MM
SALES (corp-wide): 54.57MM **Privately Held**
Web: www.fremantle.com
SIC: 7922 Television program, including commercial producers
HQ: Fremantlemedia Group Limited
Fao Gillian Ahluwalia

London W1T 1
207 691-6000

(P-14972)
PREMIERE RADIO NETWORK INC (DH)
Also Called: Prn Radio Networks
15260 Ventura Blvd Ste 400, Sherman Oaks (91403-5300)
PHONE..................................818 377-5300
Stephen C Lehman, *CEO*
Kraig T Kitchin, *
Timothy M Kelly, *
EMP: 200 **EST:** 1987
SQ FT: 15,000
SALES (est): 11.19MM **Publicly Held**
Web: www.premierenetworks.com
SIC: 7922 7389 4832 Radio producers; Advertising, promotional, and trade show services; Radio broadcasting stations
HQ: Jacor Communications Company
200 E Basse Rd
San Antonio TX 78209
210 822-2828

(P-14973)
PROFESSNAL INTRCTIVE ENTRMT IN
Also Called: Global Gaming League
6080 Center Dr Ste 600, Los Angeles (90045-1540)
PHONE..................................310 823-4445
Brett W Hawkins Junior, *CEO*
Ted Owen, *
Greg Johnson, *CMO*
EMP: 75 **EST:** 2002
SALES (est): 477K **Privately Held**
SIC: 7922 Entertainment promotion

(P-14974)
RADFORD STUDIO CENTER LLC
Also Called: CBS Studio Center
4024 Radford Ave, Studio City (91604-2101)
PHONE..................................818 655-5000
Michael Klausman, *Pr*
Nina Tassler, *
EMP: 300 **EST:** 1927
SALES (est): 41.13MM
SALES (corp-wide): 29.65B **Publicly Held**
Web: www.radfordsc.com
SIC: 7922 6512 7999 Television program, including commercial producers; Nonresidential building operators; Martial arts school, nec
HQ: Cbs Broadcasting Inc.
524 W 57th St
New York NY 10019
212 975-4321

(P-14975)
ROSE BRAND WIPERS INC
11440 Sheldon St, Sun Valley (91352-1121)
PHONE..................................818 505-6290
Tina Carlin, *Prin*
EMP: 72
SALES (corp-wide): 43.88MM **Privately Held**
Web: www.rosebrand.com
SIC: 7922 Costume and scenery design services
PA: Rose Brand Wipers, Inc.
4 Emerson Ln
201 809-1730

(P-14976)
SAN DEGO REPERTORY THEATRE INC
79 Horton Plz, San Diego (92101-6188)

PHONE..................................619 231-3586
Samuel Woodhouse, *Dir*
EMP: 127 **EST:** 1976
SQ FT: 40,000
SALES (est): 6.02MM **Privately Held**
Web: www.sdrep.org
SIC: 7922 Legitimate live theater producers

(P-14977)
SAN DIEGO OPERA ASSOCIATION
Also Called: Scenic Studio
3064 Commercial St, San Diego
(92113-1413)
PHONE..................................619 232-5911
Ron Allen, *Mgr*
EMP: 225
SQ FT: 35,000
SALES (corp-wide): 7.24MM **Privately Held**
Web: www.sdopera.com
SIC: 7922 Legitimate live theater producers
PA: San Diego Opera Association Inc
233 A St Ste 500
619 232-7636

(P-14978)
SAN DIEGO OPERA ASSOCIATION
3074 Commercial St, San Diego
(92113-1413)
PHONE..................................619 232-5911
EMP: 225
SALES (corp-wide): 7.24MM **Privately Held**
Web: www.sdopera.org
SIC: 7922 Opera company
PA: San Diego Opera Association Inc
233 A St Ste 500
619 232-7636

(P-14979)
SENCLUB LLC
788 Mountain Shadows Dr, Corona
(92881-3554)
PHONE..................................626 317-8073
EMP: 75
SALES (est): 261.45K **Privately Held**
SIC: 7922 7389 Entertainment promotion; Business services, nec

(P-14980)
TENNIS CHANNEL INC (DH)
3003 Exposition Blvd, Santa Monica
(90404-5026)
PHONE..................................310 392-1920
Ken Solomon, *CEO*
William Simon, *
EMP: 70 **EST:** 2001
SALES (est): 24.8MM
SALES (corp-wide): 3.13B **Publicly Held**
Web: www.tennis.com
SIC: 7922 Television program, including commercial producers
HQ: Sinclair Broadcast Group, Llc
10706 Beaver Dam Rd
Hunt Valley MD 21030
410 568-1500

(P-14981)
TICKETSCOM LLC (DH)
2100 E Grand Ave Ste 600, El Segundo
(90245-5150)
PHONE..................................714 327-5400
Joe Choti, *CEO*
Joe Choti, *Pr*
Cristine Hurley, *CFO*
Curt Clausen, *Sec*
Larry D Witherspoon, *Pr*
EMP: 25 **EST:** 1995

SALES (est): 4.89MM
SALES (corp-wide): 4.71MM **Privately Held**
Web: www.tickets.com
SIC: 7922 7372 Ticket agency, theatrical; Application computer software
HQ: Mlb Advanced Media, L.P.
1271 Ave Of The Americas
New York NY 10020
212 485-3444

(P-14982)
WESTSTAR CINEMAS INC
742 W Lancaster Blvd, Lancaster
(93534-3130)
PHONE..................................661 723-9392
EMP: 114
SALES (corp-wide): 2.07MM **Privately Held**
SIC: 7922 Theatrical companies
PA: Weststar Cinemas, Inc.
16530 Ventura Blvd # 500
818 784-6266

(P-14983)
WILLIAM MRRIS ENDVOR ENTRMT FN (DH)
9601 Wilshire Blvd Fl 3, Beverly Hills
(90210-5219)
PHONE..................................310 285-9000
Tom Strickler, *Pr*
Richard Rosen, *
Adam Venit, *
Phillip Raskind, *
EMP: 180 **EST:** 2000
SALES (est): 6.31MM
SALES (corp-wide): 5.96B **Publicly Held**
Web: www.wmeagency.com
SIC: 7922 7829 Talent agent, theatrical; Motion picture distribution services
HQ: William Morris Endeavor
Entertainment, Llc
9601 Wilshire Blvd
Beverly Hills CA 90210
212 586-5100

(P-14984)
WILLIAM MRRIS ENDVOR ENTRMT LL
Also Called: William Morris Consulting
9601 Wilshire Blvd Fl 3, Beverly Hills
(90210-5219)
PHONE..................................310 285-9000
Chris Newman, *Brnch Mgr*
EMP: 393
SALES (corp-wide): 5.96B **Publicly Held**
Web: www.wmeagency.com
SIC: 7922 Talent agent, theatrical
HQ: William Morris Endeavor
Entertainment, Llc
9601 Wilshire Blvd
Beverly Hills CA 90210
212 586-5100

7929 Entertainers And Entertainment Groups

(P-14985)
ANSCHUTZ ENTRMT GROUP INC (HQ)
Also Called: AEG Worldwide
800 W Olympic Blvd Ste 305, Los Angeles
(90015-1366)
PHONE..................................213 763-7700
Tim Leiweke, *Pr*
Dan Beckerman, *
Tracy Hartman, *
Dennis Dennehy, *CCO**
EMP: 154 **EST:** 1994

SALES (est): 431.33K **Privately Held**
Web: www.cryptoarena.com
SIC: 7929 Entertainment service
PA: The Anschutz Corporation
555 17th St Ste 2400

(P-14986)
EASE ENTERTAINMENT SERVICES LP
8383 Wilshire Blvd Ste 90, Beverly Hills
(90211-2430)
PHONE..................................310 469-7300
EMP: 75
SIC: 7929 Entertainers and entertainment groups

(P-14987)
ESL GAMING AMERICA INC (DH)
Also Called: Esl
3111 Winona Ave Unit 105, Burbank
(91506)
PHONE..................................213 235-7079
Craig Levine, *CEO*
EMP: 99 **EST:** 2014
SALES (est): 4.73MM **Privately Held**
Web: www.esl.com
SIC: 7929 Entertainment service
HQ: Savvy Games Group
Office 2.14 B, 6th Floor, Kafd, King Fahad Road
Riyadh

(P-14988)
FIRESTARTER ENTERTAINMENT LLC
4304 Wildwest Cir, Moorpark (93021-2343)
PHONE..................................805 907-6428
Juanita Pryor Hall, *Brnch Mgr*
EMP: 81
SALES (corp-wide): 383.81K **Privately Held**
Web: www.firestarterentertainment.com
SIC: 7929 Entertainers and entertainment groups
PA: Firestarter Entertainment, Llc
21550 Oxnard St Ste 300

(P-14989)
HOB ENTERTAINMENT LLC (DH)
Also Called: House of Blues
7060 Hollywood Blvd, Los Angeles
(90028-6014)
PHONE..................................323 769-4600
Michael Rapino, *CEO*
Joseph C Kaczorowski, *
Peter Cyffka, *
EMP: 172 **EST:** 1993
SQ FT: 53,000
SALES (est): 87.73MM **Publicly Held**
Web: www.houseofblues.com
SIC: 7929 Entertainment service
HQ: Live Nation Worldwide, Inc.
430 W 15th St
New York NY 10014
917 421-5100

(P-14990)
HOB ENTERTAINMENT LLC
Also Called: House of Blues Anaheim
400 W Disney Way Ste 337, Anaheim
(92802-2912)
PHONE..................................714 520-2310
Darryl Taketa, *Brnch Mgr*
EMP: 216
Web: www.houseofblues.com
SIC: 7929 Entertainment service
HQ: Hob Entertainment, Llc
7060 Hollywood Blvd
Los Angeles CA 90028

(P-14991)
HOB ENTERTAINMENT LLC
1055 5th Ave, San Diego (92101-5101)
PHONE..................................619 299-2583
Jim Biasore, *Mgr*
EMP: 72
Web: www.houseofblues.com
SIC: 7929 Entertainment service
HQ: Hob Entertainment, Llc
7060 Hollywood Blvd
Los Angeles CA 90028

(P-14992)
HOUSE OF BLUES CONCERTS INC (DH)
6255 W Sunset Blvd Fl 16, Los Angeles
(90028-7403)
PHONE..................................323 769-4977
Joe Kazoworski, *Pr*
EMP: 150 **EST:** 1978
SALES (est): 19.21MM **Publicly Held**
Web: www.houseofblues.com
SIC: 7929 Entertainment service
HQ: Hob Entertainment, Llc
7060 Hollywood Blvd
Los Angeles CA 90028

(P-14993)
INMOTION ENTRMT GROUP LLC
3225 N Harbor Dr, San Diego (92101-1072)
PHONE..................................904 332-0459
EMP: 119
Web: www.inmotionstores.com
SIC: 7929 Entertainers
HQ: Inmotion Entertainment Group, Llc
3755 W Sunset Rd Ste A
Las Vegas NV 89118
904 332-0450

(P-14994)
LIVE NATION WORLDWIDE INC
Also Called: Clear Channel Entertainment
325 N Maple Dr Ste 100, Beverly Hills
(90210-3429)
PHONE..................................310 867-7000
Jennifer Scott, *Mgr*
EMP: 300
Web: www.livenation.com
SIC: 7929 Entertainers and entertainment groups
HQ: Live Nation Worldwide, Inc.
430 W 15th St
New York NY 10014
917 421-5100

(P-14995)
LIVE NATION WORLDWIDE INC (HQ)
Also Called: Observatory, The
9348 Civic Center Dr Lbby, Beverly Hills
(90210-3642)
PHONE..................................310 867-7000
Kathy Willard, *CEO*
EMP: 300 **EST:** 1997
SALES (est): 1.59MM **Publicly Held**
Web: www.livenationentertainment.com
SIC: 7929 Entertainers and entertainment groups
PA: Live Nation Entertainment, Inc.
9348 Civic Center Dr

(P-14996)
LOS ANGELES PHILHARMONIC ASSN
Also Called: Hollywood Bowl
2301 N Highland Ave, Los Angeles
(90068-2742)
PHONE..................................323 850-2060
Ed Tom, *Dir*

EMP: 899
SALES (corp-wide): 208.06MM **Privately Held**
Web: www.laphil.com
SIC: 7929 Entertainment group
PA: Los Angeles Philharmonic Association
151 S Grand Ave
213 972-7300

(P-14997)
LOS ANGELES PHILHARMONIC ASSN (PA)
Also Called: L A Philharmonic
151 S Grand Ave, Los Angeles
(90012-3034)
P.O. Box 1951 (90078-1951)
PHONE...................213 972-7300
Chad Smith, *CEO*
Thomas L Beckmen, *
Alan Wayte, *
Ben Cadwallader, *
Gail Samuel, *HOLLYWOOD BOWL*
EMP: 200 **EST:** 1934
SQ FT: 13,467
SALES (est): 208.06MM
SALES (corp-wide): 208.06MM **Privately Held**
Web: www.laphil.com
SIC: 7929 Symphony orchestra

(P-14998)
MAKER STUDIOS LLC (DH)
3515 Eastham Dr, Culver City
(90232-2440)
PHONE...................310 606-2182
Courtney Holt, *CEO*
Lisa Donovan, *
EMP: 250 **EST:** 2009
SQ FT: 20,000
SALES (est): 7.66MM
SALES (corp-wide): 91.36B **Publicly Held**
SIC: 7929 Entertainment service
HQ: Twdc Enterprises 18 Corp.
500 S Buena Vista St
Burbank CA 91521

(P-14999)
MING ENTERTAINMENT GROUP LLC
2082 Business Center Dr Ste 292, Irvine
(92612-1154)
PHONE...................949 679-2089
EMP: 96 **EST:** 2007
SALES (est): 431.9K **Privately Held**
Web: www.mingentertainment.com
SIC: 7929 Entertainers and entertainment groups

(P-15000)
NEDERLNDER CNCRTS SAN DEGO LLC
6233 Hollywood Blvd, Los Angeles
(90028-5310)
PHONE...................323 468-1700
James L Nederlander, *Managing Member*
EMP: 97 **EST:** 2007
SALES (est): 384.47K **Privately Held**
Web: www.nederlanderconcerts.com
SIC: 7929 Entertainment service

(P-15001)
RED BULL NORTH AMERICA INC (HQ)
Also Called: Red Bull TV
1630 Stewart St, Santa Monica
(90404-4020)
PHONE...................310 460-5356
▲ **EMP:** 100 **EST:** 1995
SALES (est): 412.82MM

SALES (corp-wide): 11.47B **Privately Held**
Web: www.redbull.com
SIC: 7929 Entertainment service
PA: Red Bull Gmbh
Am Brunnen 1
66265820

(P-15002)
ROUND ONE ENTERTAINMENT INC (HQ)
Also Called: Round 1 Bowling and Amusement
3070 Saturn St Ste 200, Brea (92821-6296)
PHONE...................714 924-7800
Tamiya Sakamoto, *CEO*
Shintaro Kaji, *
Noriaki Tanabe, *
▲ **EMP:** 785 **EST:** 2009
SALES (est): 37.38MM **Privately Held**
Web: www.round1usa.com
SIC: 7929 7933 Entertainment service; Bowling centers
PA: Round One Corporation
5-1-60, Namba, Chuo-Ku

(P-15003)
SAN DEGO SYMPHONY ORCHSTRA ASS
1245 7th Ave, San Diego (92101-4398)
PHONE...................619 235-0800
Edward B Gill, *Ex Dir*
EMP: 110 **EST:** 1928
SALES (est): 92.96MM **Privately Held**
Web: www.sandiegosymphony.org
SIC: 7929 Symphony orchestra

(P-15004)
SAN DIEGO SYMPHONY FOUNDATION
1245 7th Ave, San Diego (92101-4398)
PHONE...................619 235-0800
Robert Caplan, *Prin*
EMP: 153 **EST:** 2011
SALES (est): 925.95K **Privately Held**
Web: www.sandiegosymphony.org
SIC: 7929 Symphony orchestra

(P-15005)
SPECIAL EVENT AUDIO SVCS INC
35889 Shetland Hls E, Fallbrook
(92028-6519)
PHONE...................800 518-9144
Mitchell J Grant, *CEO*
EMP: 24 **EST:** 2014
SALES (est): 3.88MM **Privately Held**
Web: www.seaspro.com
SIC: 7929 5099 3651 Orchestras or bands, nec; Video and audio equipment; Audio electronic systems

(P-15006)
SPSV ENTERTAINMENT LLC
Also Called: Skypark At Santa's Village
28950 State Highway 18, Skyforest
(92385-0460)
P.O. Box 369 (92385-0369)
PHONE...................909 744-9373
William Johnson, *Managing Member*
EMP: 99 **EST:** 2016
SALES (est): 2.41MM **Privately Held**
Web: www.skyparksantasvillage.com
SIC: 7929 Entertainers and entertainment groups

(P-15007)
TRI STAR SPT ENTRMT GROUP INC

9255 W Sunset Blvd Fl 2, West Hollywood
(90069-3308)
PHONE...................615 309-0969
Louise Taylor, *Prin*
EMP: 79
SALES (corp-wide): 1.11MM **Privately Held**
Web: www.team-tristar.com
SIC: 7929 Entertainers and entertainment groups
PA: Tri Star Sports And Entertainment Group, Inc.
55 Music Sq W Fl 2
615 309-0969

(P-15008)
TWENTY MILE PRODUCTIONS LLC
11833 Mississippi Ave Ste 101, Los Angeles
(90025-6135)
PHONE...................412 251-0767
Margaret Ellison, *
EMP: 150 **EST:** 2013
SALES (est): 288.5K **Privately Held**
SIC: 7929 Entertainment group

(P-15009)
TWO BIT CIRCUS DAL LLC
Also Called: Two Bit Circus
634 Mateo St, Los Angeles (90021-1312)
PHONE...................323 438-9808
Brent Bushnell, *Prin*
Eric Co Gradam, *Prin*
Kimberly Schaefer, *
Christopher Ogilvie, *
EMP: 80 **EST:** 2018
SALES (est): 671.32K **Privately Held**
Web: www.twobitcircus.com
SIC: 7929 Entertainment service

(P-15010)
ZEUS NETWORKS LLC
Also Called: Zeus
11713 Riverside Dr, Valley Village
(91607-4020)
PHONE...................323 910-4420
EMP: 75 **EST:** 2018
SALES (est): 20MM **Privately Held**
SIC: 7929 Entertainment service

7933 Bowling Centers

(P-15011)
GABLE HOUSE INC
Also Called: Gable House Bowl
1611 S Pacific Coast Hwy Ste 306,
Redondo Beach (90277-5614)
PHONE...................310 378-2265
Michael Mickey Cogan, *Pr*
EMP: 100 **EST:** 1959
SALES (est): 2.66MM **Privately Held**
Web: www.gablehousebowl.com
SIC: 7933 5813 5812 Ten pin center; Bar (drinking places); Snack bar

(P-15012)
LUCKY STRIKE ENTERTAINMENT INC
800 W Olympic Blvd Ste 250, Los Angeles
(90015-1366)
PHONE...................213 542-4880
Bobby Braydoy, *Brnch Mgr*
EMP: 355
Web: www.bowlluckystrike.com
SIC: 7933 5813 5812 Ten pin center; Tavern (drinking places); American restaurant
PA: Lucky Strike Entertainment, Inc.
15260 Ventura Blvd # 1110

(P-15013)
LUCKY STRIKE ENTERTAINMENT LLC
6801 Hollywood Blvd Ste 143, Los Angeles
(90028-6138)
PHONE...................818 933-3752
David Bradley, *Genl Mgr*
EMP: 77
SALES (corp-wide): 1.15B **Publicly Held**
Web: www.bowlluckystrike.com
SIC: 7933 Ten pin center
HQ: Lucky Strike Entertainment, Llc
16350 Ventura Blvd Ste D
Encino CA 91436
818 933-3752

(P-15014)
LUCKY STRIKE ENTERTAINMENT LLC
20 City Blvd W Ste G2, Orange
(92868-3131)
PHONE...................248 374-3420
Ismail Saleem, *Brnch Mgr*
EMP: 120
SALES (corp-wide): 1.15B **Publicly Held**
Web: www.bowlluckystrike.com
SIC: 7933 Ten pin center
HQ: Lucky Strike Entertainment, Llc
16350 Ventura Blvd Ste D
Encino CA 91436
818 933-3752

(P-15015)
NATIONWIDE THEATRES CORP
Also Called: Cal Coffee Shop
2500 Carson St, Lakewood (90712-4107)
PHONE...................562 421-8448
Tom Moeller, *Mgr*
EMP: 2720
SALES (corp-wide): 15.68MM **Privately Held**
Web: www.calbowl.com
SIC: 7933 5813 5812 Ten pin center; Cocktail lounge; Coffee shop
HQ: Nationwide Theatres Corp.
120 N Robertson Blvd Fl 3
Los Angeles CA 90048
310 657-8420

7941 Sports Clubs, Managers, And Promoters

(P-15016)
ANAHEIM ARENA MANAGEMENT LLC
Also Called: AAM
2695 E Katella Ave, Anaheim (92806-5904)
PHONE...................714 704-2400
Michael Schulman, *
Angela Wergechik, *
James Pearson, *
EMP: 600 **EST:** 2001
SQ FT: 106,000
SALES (est): 22.91MM **Privately Held**
Web: www.hondacenter.com
SIC: 7941 Sports field or stadium operator, promoting sports events

(P-15017)
ANAHEIM DUCKS HOCKEY CLUB LLC (PA)
2695 E Katella Ave, Anaheim (92806-5904)
PHONE...................714 940-2900
Michel Schulman, *Managing Member*
Doug Heller, *
Bob Murray, *
Tim Ryan, *
David Mcnab, *Sr VP*

EMP: 81 EST: 2005
SALES (est): 7.82MM **Privately Held**
Web: www.anaheimteamstore.com
SIC: 7941 Sports clubs, managers, and promoters

(P-15018)
ANGELS BASEBALL LP (PA)
Also Called: Los Angeles Angels of Anaheim
2000 E Gene Autry Way, Anaheim (92806-6143)
PHONE...............714 940-2000
Dennis Kuhl, *Genl Pt*
Bill Beverage, *Pt*
Molly Jolly, *Pt*
Tim Mead, *Pt*
Richard Mcclemmy, *Pt*
EMP: 790 EST: 1996
SALES (est): 14.36MM
SALES (corp-wide): 14.36MM **Privately Held**
Web: www.mlb.com
SIC: 7941 Baseball club, professional and semi-professional

(P-15019)
BIG LGUE DREAMS CONSULTING LLC
2155 Trumble Rd, Perris (92571-9211)
PHONE...............619 846-8855
EMP: 107
SALES (corp-wide): 15.39MM **Privately Held**
Web: www.bigleaguedreams.com
SIC: 7941 Sports field or stadium operator, promoting sports events
PA: Big League Dreams Consulting, Llc
16333 Fairfield Ranch Rd
909 287-1700

(P-15020)
BIG LGUE DREAMS CONSULTING LLC
2100 S Azusa Ave, West Covina (91792-1507)
PHONE...............626 839-1100
Jeffrey Odekirk, *Prin*
EMP: 107
SALES (corp-wide): 15.39MM **Privately Held**
Web: www.bigleaguedreams.com
SIC: 7941 Sports field or stadium operator, promoting sports events
PA: Big League Dreams Consulting, Llc
16333 Fairfield Ranch Rd
909 287-1700

(P-15021)
CALIFORNIA SPORTSERVICE INC
Also Called: San Diego Padres
100 Park Blvd, San Diego (92101-7405)
PHONE...............619 795-5000
Jeremy M Jacobs, *Pr*
EMP: 581 EST: 1940
SALES (est): 3.75MM
SALES (corp-wide): 2.9B **Privately Held**
Web: www.mlb.com
SIC: 7941 Baseball club, professional and semi-professional
HQ: Delaware North Companies Sportservice, Inc.
250 Delaware Ave
Buffalo NY 14202
716 858-5000

(P-15022)
CHARGERS FOOTBALL COMPANY LLC (PA)

Also Called: Los Angeles Chargers
One Chargers Way, El Segundo (90245)
PHONE...............714 540-7100
Dean A Spanos, *Pr*
Dean A Spanos, *Managing Member*
Jim Steeg, *
Jeanne M Bonk, *
George Pernicano, *
EMP: 70 EST: 1959
SALES (est): 691.7K
SALES (corp-wide): 691.7K **Privately Held**
Web: www.chargers.com
SIC: 7941 Football club

(P-15023)
CITY OF SAN DIEGO
Also Called: Petco Park
100 Park Blvd, San Diego (92101-7405)
PHONE...............619 795-5000
John Morris, *Pr*
EMP: 207
SALES (corp-wide): 2.9B **Privately Held**
Web: www.petcoparkinsider.com
SIC: 7941 Sports field or stadium operator, promoting sports events
PA: City Of San Diego
202 C St
619 236-6330

(P-15024)
ENDEAVOR GROUP HOLDINGS INC (PA)
9601 Wilshire Blvd Fl 3, Beverly Hills (90210-5219)
PHONE...............310 285-9000
Ariel Emanuel, *CEO*
Patrick Whitesell, *Ex Ch Bd*
Egon Durban, *Ch Bd*
Mark Shapiro, *Pr*
Jason Lublin, *CFO*
EMP: 90 EST: 2019
SALES (est): 5.96B
SALES (corp-wide): 5.96B **Publicly Held**
Web: www.imgacademy.com
SIC: 7941 Sports field or stadium operator, promoting sports events

(P-15025)
FOX BASEBALL HOLDINGS INC
1000 Vin Scully Ave, Los Angeles (90012-2112)
PHONE...............323 224-1500
Frank Mccourt, *Pr*
EMP: 740 EST: 2000
SALES (est): 125.12K
SALES (corp-wide): 91.36B **Publicly Held**
SIC: 7941 Baseball club, professional and semi-professional
HQ: Fox Entertainment Group, Llc
1211 Ave Of The Americas
New York NY 10036
212 852-7000

(P-15026)
FOX BSB HOLDCO INC (HQ)
Also Called: Dodger Stadium
1000 Vin Scully Ave, Los Angeles (90012)
PHONE...............323 224-1500
Steve Soboroff, *Vice Chairman*
Ron Wheeler, *
Santiago Fernandez, *
Dannis Mannion, *
Peter Wilhelm, *CFO*
EMP: 204 EST: 1971
SQ FT: 20,000
SALES (est): 5.17MM
SALES (corp-wide): 380.53MM **Privately Held**
Web: www.mlb.com

SIC: 7941 Baseball club, professional and semi-professional
PA: Guggenheim Partners, Llc
330 Madison Ave
212 739-0700

(P-15027)
IMMORTALS LLC
6100 Center Dr Ste 1050, Los Angeles (90045-9200)
P.O. Box 641729 (90064-6729)
PHONE...............310 554-8267
Noah Whinston, *CEO*
Ari Segal, *COO*
Jonathan Stein, *
EMP: 85 EST: 2015
SQ FT: 30,000
SALES (est): 961.56K **Privately Held**
Web: www.cityofimmortals.com
SIC: 7941 Professional and semi-professional sports clubs

(P-15028)
INLAND EMPIRE 66ERS BSBAL CLB
280 Se St, San Bernardino (92401-2009)
PHONE...............909 888-9922
David Elmore, *Ch*
Donna Tuttle, *
Jhon Fonsaker, *
EMP: 110 EST: 1993
SQ FT: 600
SALES (est): 37.76K
SALES (corp-wide): 34.1MM **Privately Held**
Web: inlandempire.66ers.milb.com
SIC: 7941 Baseball club, professional and semi-professional
PA: The Elmore Group Ltd
19 N Grant St Ste 2
630 325-6228

(P-15029)
LA CLIPPERS LLC
3930 W Century Blvd, Inglewood (90303-1012)
PHONE...............213 742-7500
Steven A Ballmer, *Managing Member*
EMP: 251 EST: 2014
SALES (est): 4.74MM **Privately Held**
Web: www.clippers.com
SIC: 7941 Basketball club

(P-15030)
LA SPORTS PROPERTIES INC
Also Called: Los Angeles Clippers
1212 S Flower St Fl 5, Los Angeles (90015-2123)
PHONE...............213 742-7500
Dick Parsons, *Interim Chief Executive Officer*
Andrew Roeser, *Ex VP*
EMP: 195 EST: 1946
SQ FT: 5,000
SALES (est): 10.03MM **Privately Held**
Web: www.sportsproperties.com
SIC: 7941 Basketball club

(P-15031)
LOS ANGELES RAMS LLC (PA)
Also Called: St Louis Rams
29899 Agoura Rd, Agoura Hills (91301-2493)
PHONE...............314 982-7267
E Stanley Kroenke, *Managing Member*
Kevin Demoff, *Managing Member*
Les Snead, *Managing Member*
Tony Pastoors, *Managing Member*
EMP: 100 EST: 1939
SALES (est): 1.23MM

SALES (corp-wide): 1.23MM **Privately Held**
Web: www.therams.com
SIC: 7941 Football club

(P-15032)
NFL PROPERTIES LLC
Also Called: Nfl Network
10950 Washington Blvd Ste 100, Culver City (90232-4032)
PHONE...............310 840-4635
Steve Bernstein, *Prin*
EMP: 100
SALES (corp-wide): 372.43MM **Privately Held**
Web: www.nfl.com
SIC: 7941 Football club
PA: Nfl Properties Llc
345 Park Ave
212 450-2000

(P-15033)
NIKE USA INC
222 E Redondo Beach Blvd Ste C, Gardena (90248-2302)
PHONE...............310 670-6770
EMP: 2490
SALES (corp-wide): 51.36B **Publicly Held**
Web: www.nike.com
SIC: 7941 Sports clubs, managers, and promoters
HQ: Nike Usa, Inc.
1 Bowerman Dr
Beaverton OR 97005

(P-15034)
PADRES LP
Also Called: San Diego Padres
100 Park Blvd Petco Park, San Diego (92101)
P.O. Box 122000 (92112-2000)
PHONE...............619 795-5000
EMP: 1100 EST: 1969
SQ FT: 3,000
SALES (est): 82.8MM **Privately Held**
Web: www.mlb.com
SIC: 7941 Baseball club, professional and semi-professional

(P-15035)
PSE HOLDING LLC (DH)
Also Called: The Palace of Auburn Hills
360 N Crescent Dr, Beverly Hills (90210-4874)
PHONE...............248 377-0165
EMP: 300 EST: 1985
SALES (est): 23.84MM **Privately Held**
Web: www.pse.com
SIC: 7941 7922 Stadium event operator services; Summer theater
HQ: Pistons Palace Holdings, Llc
360 N Crescent Dr
Beverly Hills CA 90210
310 228-9521

(P-15036)
SOCAL SPORTSNET LLC
100 Park Blvd, San Diego (92101-7405)
PHONE...............619 795-5000
EMP: 588 EST: 2012
SALES (est): 181.49K
SALES (corp-wide): 312.41K **Privately Held**
Web: www.mlb.com
SIC: 7941 Baseball club, professional and semi-professional
PA: Padre Time, Llc
100 Park Blvd
619 795-5000

PRODUCTS & SVCS

(P-15037)
WME IMG LLC (DH)
Also Called: International Merchandising
9601 Wilshire Blvd, Beverly Hills
(90210-5213)
PHONE....................212 586-5100
Ari Emanuel, *CEO*
Patrick Whitesell, *
Richard Miao, *
Neil Graff, *
Jason Lublin, *
EMP: 284 **EST:** 1961
SALES (est): 15.39MM
SALES (corp-wide): 5.96B **Publicly Held**
Web: www.endeavorco.com
SIC: **7941** 8742 Sports promotion; Business
planning and organizing services
HQ: William Morris Endeavor
     Entertainment, Llc
     9601 Wilshire Blvd
     Beverly Hills CA 90210
     212 586-5100

7948 Racing, Including Track Operation

(P-15038)
DEL MAR THOROUGHBRED CLUB
Also Called: Surfside Race Place At Del Mar
2260 Jimmy Durante Blvd, Del Mar
(92014-2216)
P.O. Box 700 (92014-0700)
PHONE....................858 755-1141
Joe Harper, *Pr*
Craig Fravel, *
Mike Ernst, *
Tom Robbins, *
Craig Dado, *
▲ **EMP:** 400 **EST:** 1970
SALES (est): 39.09MM **Privately Held**
Web: www.dmtc.com
SIC: **7948** Thoroughbred horse racing

(P-15039)
LOS ANGELES TURF CLUB INC (DH)
Also Called: Santa Anita Park
285 W Huntington Dr, Arcadia
(91007-3439)
P.O. Box 60014 (91066-6014)
PHONE....................626 574-6330
Gregory C Avioli, *CEO*
Frank Stronach, *Ch Bd*
George Haines Ii, *Pr*
Frank Demarco Junior, *VP*
▲ **EMP:** 80 **EST:** 1964
SALES (est): 6.2MM
SALES (corp-wide): 42.8B **Privately Held**
Web: www.santaanita.com
SIC: **7948** Horse race track operation
HQ: Magna Car Top Systems Of America,
     Inc.
     456 Wimpole Dr
     Rochester Hills MI 48309
     248 836-4500

(P-15040)
NATIONAL HOT ROD ASSOCIATION (PA)
Also Called: Nhra
140 Via Verde Ste 100, San Dimas
(91773-5117)
P.O. Box 5555 (91740)
PHONE....................626 914-4761
Wally Parks, *Dir*
Richard Wells, *
EMP: 200 **EST:** 1951
SQ FT: 30,000

SALES (est): 88.81MM
SALES (corp-wide): 88.81MM **Privately Held**
Web: www.nhra.com
SIC: **7948** 2711 2741 Auto race track
operation; Newspapers: publishing only, not
printed on site; Miscellaneous publishing

7991 Physical Fitness Facilities

(P-15041)
24 HOUR FITNESS USA LLC (HQ)
Also Called: 24 Hour Fitness
1265 Laurel Tree Ln Ste 200, Carlsbad
(92011-4221)
PHONE....................925 543-3100
Karl Sanft, *CEO*
Tony Ueber, *
Frank Napolitano, *
Patrick Flanagan, *
▲ **EMP:** 183 **EST:** 1983
SALES (est): 326.31MM
SALES (corp-wide): 326.31MM **Privately Held**
Web: careers.24hourfitness.com
SIC: **7991** Health club
PA: All Day Holdings Llc
     1265 Laurel Tree Ln # 200
     925 543-3100

(P-15042)
24 HOUR FITNESS WORLDWIDE INC
1265 Laurel Tree Ln Ste 200, Carlsbad
(92011-4221)
PHONE....................925 543-3100
EMP: 7184
Web: www.24hourfit.com
SIC: **7991** Health club

(P-15043)
ASPYR HOLDINGS LLC
Also Called: Aspyr
270 Baker St Ste 300, Costa Mesa
(92626-4584)
PHONE....................714 651-1840
Marc Thomas, *CEO*
Peter Felner, *
Ryan Kersten, *
EMP: 450 **EST:** 2019
SALES (est): 2.61MM **Privately Held**
SIC: **7991** 6794 Physical fitness facilities;
Patent owners and lessors

(P-15044)
BALLY TOTAL FITNESS CORPORATION
Also Called: Bally Total Fitness
12440 Imperial Hwy Ste 300, Norwalk
(90650-3178)
P.O. Box 739 (60039)
PHONE....................562 484-2000
▲ **EMP:** 12340
SIC: **7991** Health club

(P-15045)
BLISS WORLD LLC
6250 Hollywood Blvd Fl 4, Los Angeles
(90028-5325)
PHONE....................323 500-0921
EMP: 70
Web: www.blissworld.com
SIC: **7991** Spas
HQ: Bliss World Llc
     111 W 33rd St
     New York NY 10001
     212 931-6383

(P-15046)
CHOPRA GLOBAL LLC
6451 El Camino Real Ste A, Carlsbad
(92009-2800)
P.O. Box 1944 (10156-1944)
PHONE....................760 494-1604
Tonia O'connor, *Managing Member*
Richard Wallach, *
EMP: 72 **EST:** 2004
SALES (est): 17MM **Privately Held**
Web: www.chopra.com
SIC: **7991** Spas

(P-15047)
EQUINOX-76TH STREET INC
5400 W Rosecrans Ave Ste Uppr,
Hawthorne (90250-6682)
PHONE....................310 727-9543
Larry Schneider, *Brnch Mgr*
EMP: 76
SALES (corp-wide): 611.7MM **Privately Held**
SIC: **7991** Health club
HQ: Equinox-76th Street, Inc.
     895 Broadway Fl 3
     New York NY 10003

(P-15048)
EQUINOX-76TH STREET INC
1835 S Sepulveda Blvd, Los Angeles
(90025-6941)
PHONE....................310 479-5200
Tonya Jacobs, *Mgr*
EMP: 104
SALES (corp-wide): 611.7MM **Privately Held**
SIC: **7991** Health club
HQ: Equinox-76th Street, Inc.
     895 Broadway Fl 3
     New York NY 10003

(P-15049)
EQUINOX-76TH STREET INC
Also Called: Equinox Fitness Club
10250 Santa Monica Blvd, Los Angeles
(90067-6410)
PHONE....................310 552-0420
Mathew Herbert, *Brnch Mgr*
EMP: 76
SALES (corp-wide): 611.7MM **Privately Held**
SIC: **7991** Health club
HQ: Equinox-76th Street, Inc.
     895 Broadway Fl 3
     New York NY 10003

(P-15050)
EQUINOX-76TH STREET INC
Also Called: Equinox Fitness Club
19540 Jamboree Rd, Irvine (92612-8448)
PHONE....................949 296-1700
Herb Umphreyville, *Genl Mgr*
EMP: 90
SALES (corp-wide): 611.7MM **Privately Held**
SIC: **7991** Health club
HQ: Equinox-76th Street, Inc.
     895 Broadway Fl 3
     New York NY 10003

(P-15051)
JAZZERCISE INC (PA)
Also Called: Jazzercise
2460 Impala Dr, Carlsbad (92010-7226)
PHONE....................760 476-1750
Judi Sheppard Missett, *CEO*
Sally Baldridge, *
Shanna Missett Nelson, *
EMP: 100 **EST:** 1972
SQ FT: 24,228

SALES (est): 7.16MM
SALES (corp-wide): 7.16MM **Privately Held**
Web: www.jazzercise.com
SIC: **7991** 6794 5961 Aerobic dance and
exercise classes; Franchises, selling or
licensing; Fitness and sporting goods, mail
order

(P-15052)
LA BOXING FRANCHISE CORP
1241 E Dyer Rd Ste 100, Santa Ana
(92705-5611)
PHONE....................714 668-0911
Anthony Geisler, *Pr*
▲ **EMP:** 155 **EST:** 1992
SALES (est): 250.28K
SALES (corp-wide): 18.35MM **Privately Held**
SIC: **7991** Physical fitness facilities
PA: U Gym, Llc
     1501 Quail St Ste 100
     714 668-0911

(P-15053)
LA WORKOUT INC
Also Called: La Workout Camarillo West
500 Paseo Camarillo, Camarillo
(93010-5900)
PHONE....................805 482-8884
Steve Rivera, *Brnch Mgr*
EMP: 115
Web: www.perfectdomain.com
SIC: **7991** Health club
PA: La Workout, Inc.
     2510g Las Posas Rd Ste 44

(P-15054)
LIFE TIME INC
1055 Wall St, La Jolla (92037-4400)
PHONE....................858 459-0281
EMP: 96
SALES (corp-wide): 2.22B **Publicly Held**
Web: www.lifetime.life
SIC: **7991** Health club
HQ: Life Time, Inc.
     2902 Corporate Pl
     Chanhassen MN 55317

(P-15055)
LIFE TIME INC
Also Called: Life Time Fitness
111 Avenida Vista Montana, San Clemente
(92672-6094)
PHONE....................949 492-1515
Steve Johnson, *Pr*
EMP: 120
SALES (corp-wide): 2.22B **Publicly Held**
Web: www.lifetime.life
SIC: **7991** Health club
HQ: Life Time, Inc.
     2902 Corporate Pl
     Chanhassen MN 55317

(P-15056)
LOS ANGELES ATHLETIC CLUB INC
431 W 7th St, Los Angeles (90014-1691)
PHONE....................213 625-2211
Karen Hathaway, *Pr*
Bryan Cusworth, *
EMP: 182 **EST:** 1986
SALES (est): 195.9K **Publicly Held**
Web: www.laac.com
SIC: **7991** Athletic club and gymnasiums,
membership
HQ: Laaco, Ltd.
     4469 Admiralty Way
     Marina Del Rey CA 90292
     213 622-1254

(P-15057)
MUSCLEBOUND INC
Also Called: Golds Gym
19835 Nordhoff St, Northridge
(91324-3331)
PHONE..................818 349-0123
Angel J Banos, *Pr*
William Banos, *
EMP: 350 **EST:** 1990
SQ FT: 8,625
SALES (est): 3.38MM **Privately Held**
Web: www.goldsgym.com
SIC: 7991 Physical fitness facilities

(P-15058)
OLYMPIX FITNESS LLC
4101 E Olympic Plz, Long Beach
(90803-2807)
PHONE..................562 366-4600
EMP: 91 **EST:** 2016
SALES (est): 212K **Privately Held**
Web: www.iconixfit.com
SIC: 7991 Physical fitness facilities

(P-15059)
RACHAS INC
Also Called: Chuze Fitness
135 N Beach Blvd, Anaheim (92801-6135)
PHONE..................714 290-0636
Cory Brightwell, *Brnch Mgr*
EMP: 73
SALES (corp-wide): 84.04MM **Privately Held**
Web: www.chuzefitness.com
SIC: 7991 Health club
PA: Rachas, Inc.
1011 Cmino Del Rio S Ste
619 780-0141

(P-15060)
ROW HOUSE FRANCHISE LLC
Also Called: Row House
17877 Von Karman Ave Ste 100, Irvine
(92614-4227)
PHONE..................949 341-5585
Eric Von Frohlich, *CEO*
EMP: 97 **EST:** 2017
SALES (est): 860.95K **Privately Held**
Web: www.therowhouse.com
SIC: 7991 6794 Physical fitness clubs with training equipment; Franchises, selling or licensing

(P-15061)
RSG GROUP NORTH AMERICA LP
7007 Romaine St Ste 101, West Hollywood
(90038-2439)
PHONE..................714 609-0572
Sebastian Schoepe, *CEO*
EMP: 220 **EST:** 2016
SALES (est): 1.59MM **Privately Held**
SIC: 7991 Physical fitness facilities

(P-15062)
SALVATION ARMY RAY & JOAN
Also Called: Salvation Army
6845 University Ave, San Diego
(92115-5829)
PHONE..................619 287-5762
James Knaggs, *Pr*
David Hudson, *
EMP: 300 **EST:** 1998
SALES (est): 1.48MM
SALES (corp-wide): 424.11MM **Privately Held**
Web: www.kroccenter.org

SIC: 7991 8661 7032 7922 Physical fitness clubs with training equipment; Miscellaneous denomination church; Sporting and recreational camps; Community theater production
PA: The Salvation Army National Corporation
615 Slaters Ln
703 684-5500

(P-15063)
SPA HAVENS LP
Also Called: Cal-A-Vie
29402 Spa Haven Way, Vista (92084-2234)
PHONE..................760 945-2055
John Havens, *Owner*
▲ **EMP:** 105 **EST:** 1984
SALES (est): 4.81MM **Privately Held**
Web: www.cal-a-vie.com
SIC: 7991 Spas

(P-15064)
SPECTRUM CLUBS INC
840 Apollo St Ste 100, El Segundo
(90245-4641)
PHONE..................310 727-9300
EMP: 1600
SIC: 7991 Health club

(P-15065)
THINK TOGETHER
12016 Telegraph Rd, Santa Fe Springs
(90670-3784)
PHONE..................562 236-3835
EMP: 344
SALES (corp-wide): 75.71MM **Privately Held**
Web: www.thinktogether.org
SIC: 7991 Physical fitness facilities
PA: Think Together
2101 E 4th St #b-200
714 543-3807

(P-15066)
TRI-CITY HOSPITAL DISTRICT
Also Called: Tri-City Wellness Center
6250 El Camino Real, Carlsbad
(92009-1603)
PHONE..................760 931-3171
EMP: 374
SALES (corp-wide): 319.28MM **Privately Held**
Web: www.tricitymed.org
SIC: 7991 Health club
PA: Tri-City Medical Center
4002 Vista Way
760 724-8411

(P-15067)
TW HOLDINGS INC
10805 Rancho Bernardo Rd Ste 120, San Diego (92127-5702)
PHONE..................858 217-8750
Gene Lamott, *CEO*
Karen Wischmann, *
Rob Zielinski, *
EMP: 600 **EST:** 2007
SALES (est): 2.9MM **Privately Held**
SIC: 7991 Physical fitness clubs with training equipment

(P-15068)
U GYM LLC (PA)
Also Called: Ufc Gym
1501 Quail St Ste 100, Newport Beach
(92660-2797)
PHONE..................714 668-0911
Adam Sedlack, *CEO*
Brent Leffel, *
Mark Mastrov, *

Michael Pilatos, *
EMP: 70 **EST:** 2008
SALES (est): 18.35MM
SALES (corp-wide): 18.35MM **Privately Held**
Web: www.ufcgym.com
SIC: 7991 5699 6794 Health club; Shirts, custom made; Franchises, selling or licensing

(P-15069)
WORLD GYM INTERNATIONAL LLC
Also Called: World Gym Fitness Centers
1901 Avenue Of The Stars Ste 1100, Los Angeles (90067-6002)
PHONE..................310 557-8804
Lewis Stanton, *CEO*
Guy Cammilleri, *Ex Ch Bd*
Jarrod Saracco, *COO*
EMP: 100 **EST:** 2008
SALES (est): 699.33K **Privately Held**
Web: www.worldgym.com
SIC: 7991 6794 Health club; Franchises, selling or licensing

(P-15070)
XI ENTERPRISE INC
2140 E Palmdale Blvd, Palmdale
(93550-1202)
PHONE..................661 266-3200
Shah Roshan, *CEO*
EMP: 74 **EST:** 2011
SALES (est): 316.59K **Privately Held**
SIC: 7991 Physical fitness facilities

(P-15071)
XPONENTIAL FITNESS INC (PA)
17877 Von Karman Ave Ste 100, Irvine
(92614-4227)
PHONE..................949 346-3000
Mark King, *CEO*
Mark Grabowski, *Non-Executive Chairman of the Board*
Sarah Luna, *Pr*
Ryan Junk, *COO*
John Meloun, *CFO*
EMP: 270 **EST:** 2017
SALES (est): 318.66MM
SALES (corp-wide): 318.66MM **Publicly Held**
Web: www.xponential.com
SIC: 7991 Athletic club and gymnasiums, membership

7992 Public Golf Courses

(P-15072)
CHAPMAN GOLF DEVELOPMENT LLC
Also Called: Tradition Golf Club
78505 Avenue 52, La Quinta (92253-2802)
PHONE..................760 564-8723
David Chapman, *Managing Member*
EMP: 100 **EST:** 1999
SALES (est): 583.56K **Privately Held**
SIC: 7992 Public golf courses

(P-15073)
CITY OF HUNTINGTON BEACH
Also Called: Meadowlark Golf Course
16782 Graham St, Huntington Beach
(92649-3754)
PHONE..................714 846-4450
Nick Beck, *Mgr*
EMP: 70
SALES (corp-wide): 386.07MM **Privately Held**
Web: www.huntingtonbeachca.gov

SIC: 7992 Public golf courses
PA: City Of Huntington Beach
2000 Main St
714 536-5202

(P-15074)
COUNTY OF LOS ANGELES
Also Called: Parks and Recreation Dept
1875 Fairplex Dr, Pomona (91768-1240)
PHONE..................909 231-0549
Chad Hackman, *Genl Mgr*
EMP: 172
Web: www.mountainmeadowsgc.com
SIC: 7992 9512 7299 Public golf courses; Recreational program administration, government; Wedding chapel, privately operated
PA: County Of Los Angeles
500 W Temple St Ste 437
213 974-1101

(P-15075)
CROCKETT & COINC
Also Called: Bonita Golf Club
5540 Sweetwater Rd, Bonita (91902-2137)
PHONE..................619 267-1103
Clayton Crockett, *Prin*
EMP: 80
SALES (corp-wide): 2.09MM **Privately Held**
Web: www.bonitagolfclub.com
SIC: 7992 5812 Public golf courses; Eating places
PA: Crockett & Co.Inc.
5120 Robinwood Rd Ste A22
619 267-6410

(P-15076)
DESERT WILLOW GOLF RESORT INC
Also Called: Desert Willow Golf Course
38995 Desert Willow Dr, Palm Desert
(92260-1674)
PHONE..................760 346-0015
Richard Mogensen, *Genl Mgr*
EMP: 150 **EST:** 1997
SQ FT: 33,000
SALES (est): 358.56K **Privately Held**
Web: www.desertwillow.com
SIC: 7992 Public golf courses

(P-15077)
EAGLE VNES VNYRDS GOLF CLB LLC
1733 S Anaheim Blvd, Anaheim
(92805-6518)
P.O. Box 2398 (94558-0239)
PHONE..................707 257-4470
Nobu Mizuhara, *General Vice President*
EMP: 70 **EST:** 2010
SALES (est): 1.83MM **Privately Held**
Web: www.eaglevinesgolfclub.com
SIC: 7992 Public golf courses

(P-15078)
EL PRADO GOLF COURSE LP
6555 Pine Ave, Chino (91708-9163)
PHONE..................909 597-1751
Bruce Jenke, *Genl Pt*
G Barton Heuler, *Pt*
Anthony Foo, *Pt*
Walter Heuler, *Pt*
EMP: 80 **EST:** 1975
SQ FT: 5,000
SALES (est): 2.27MM **Privately Held**
Web: www.elpradogolfcourses.com
SIC: 7992 Public golf courses

(P-15079)

ESTATES AT TRUMP NAT GOLF CLB

Also Called: Trump Nat Golf CLB Los Angeles
1 Trump National Dr, Rancho Palos Verdes (90275-6173)
PHONE..................................310 265-5000
Jill Martin, *CEO*
Mike Vandergles, *Prin*
EMP: 170 EST: 2002
SALES (est): 1.51MM
SALES (corp-wide): 2.44MM **Privately Held**
Web: www.trumpnationallosangeles.com
SIC: 7992 Public golf courses
HQ: Trump Golf Management Llc
    725 5th Ave Bsmt A
    New York NY 10022
    212 832-2000

(P-15080)

FOUR SEASONS RESORT AVIARA

Also Called: Aviar Golf Club
7447 Batiquitos Dr, Carlsbad (92011-4732)
PHONE..................................760 603-6900
James Bellington, *Mgr*
EMP: 91
SALES (corp-wide): 98.06MM **Privately Held**
Web: www.parkhyattaviara.com
SIC: 7992 7011 Public golf courses; Hotels
PA: Four Seasons Hotels Limited
    1165 Leslie St
    416 449-1750

(P-15081)

GLEN ANNIE GOLF CLUB

Also Called: Annie Golf Club
405 Glen Annie Rd, Goleta (93117-1427)
PHONE..................................805 968-6400
Richard Nahas, *Genl Mgr*
EMP: 80 EST: 1997
SALES (est): 462.1K **Privately Held**
Web: www.glenanniegolf.com
SIC: 7992 Public golf courses

(P-15082)

GOLF MANAGEMENT OPERATING LLC

50200 Avenida Vista Bonita, La Quinta (92253-2600)
PHONE..................................760 777-4839
Jim Hinckley, *Pr*
Doug Howe, *
Greg Adair, *
Jack Marquardt, *
Melissa Mckibben, *Prin*
EMP: 2800 EST: 2022
SALES (est): 164.31K **Privately Held**
SIC: 7992 Public golf courses

(P-15083)

GREEN RIVER GOLF CORPORATION

Also Called: Green River Golf Course
5215 Green River Rd, Corona (92878-9404)
PHONE..................................714 970-8411
Judy Saguchi, *Pr*
EMP: 100 EST: 1977
SQ FT: 30,000
SALES (est): 2.06MM **Privately Held**
Web: www.fairviewevents.com
SIC: 7992 5941 5813 5812 Public golf courses; Sporting goods and bicycle shops; Drinking places; Eating places
PA: Courseco, Inc.
    5341 Old Rdwood Hwy Ste 2

(P-15084)

HERITAGE GOLF GROUP LLC

Also Called: Valencia Country Club
27330 Tourney Rd, Valencia (91355-1806)
PHONE..................................661 254-4401
Jim Fitzsimmons, *Mgr*
EMP: 107
SALES (corp-wide): 29.68MM **Privately Held**
SIC: 7992 Public golf courses
PA: Heritage Golf Group, Llc
    12750 High Bluff Dr Fl 4
    858 720-0694

(P-15085)

HERITAGE GOLF GROUP LLC

Also Called: Talega Golf Club
990 Avenida Talega, San Clemente (92673-6849)
PHONE..................................949 369-6226
David Foster, *Brnch Mgr*
EMP: 87
SALES (corp-wide): 29.68MM **Privately Held**
SIC: 7992 Public golf courses
PA: Heritage Golf Group, Llc
    12750 High Bluff Dr Fl 4
    858 720-0694

(P-15086)

KSL RECREATION MANAGEMENT OPERATIONS LLC

50905 Avenida Bermudas, La Quinta (92253-8910)
PHONE..................................760 564-8000
EMP: 8000
SIC: 7992 7011 Public golf courses; Hotels and motels

(P-15087)

LAKESIDE GOLF CLUB

4500 W Lakeside Dr, Burbank (91505-4088)
P.O. Box Po Box 2386 (91610-0386)
PHONE..................................818 984-0601
Jerry Fard, *Mgr*
Michael E Henry, *CEO*
EMP: 98 EST: 1924
SQ FT: 25,000
SALES (est): 13.49MM **Privately Held**
Web: www.lakesidegolfclub.com
SIC: 7992 Public golf courses

(P-15088)

LOS SERRANOS GOLF CLUB

Also Called: Los Serranos Golf & Cntry CLB
15656 Yorba Ave, Chino Hills (91709-3129)
PHONE..................................909 597-1769
John A Kramer Junior, *CEO*
John A Kramer Senior, *Pr*
Ronald Kramer, *
Gloria Kramer, *Stockholder*
Kevin Sullivan, *
EMP: 135 EST: 1953
SQ FT: 41,896
SALES (est): 2.23MM **Privately Held**
Web: www.losserranoscountryclub.com
SIC: 7992 5812 5813 Public golf courses; American restaurant; Cocktail lounge

(P-15089)

MADERAS GOLF CLUB

17750 Old Coach Rd, Poway (92064-6621)
PHONE..................................858 451-8100
Bill Obrien, *Genl Mgr*
EMP: 78 EST: 2006
SALES (est): 2.28MM **Privately Held**
Web: www.maderasgolf.com

SIC: 7992 Public golf courses

(P-15090)

MADISON CLUB OWNERS ASSN

Also Called: Madison Club, The
53035 Meriwether Way, La Quinta (92253-5535)
P.O. Box 1558 (92247-1558)
PHONE..................................760 777-9320
Douglas Siebold, *CEO*
Brian Ellis, *
EMP: 125 EST: 2006
SQ FT: 70,000
SALES (est): 2.23MM
SALES (corp-wide): 435.04MM **Privately Held**
Web: www.madisonclubca.com
SIC: 7992 Public golf courses
PA: Discovery Land Company, Llc
    14605 N 73rd St
    480 624-5200

(P-15091)

MCMILLIN COMMUNITIES INC

Also Called: Temeku Hills
41687 Temeku Dr, Temecula (92591-3909)
PHONE..................................951 506-3303
Sonia Howard, *Brnch Mgr*
EMP: 946
SALES (corp-wide): 6.83MM **Privately Held**
Web: www.mcmillin.com
SIC: 7992 Public golf courses
PA: Mcmillin Communities, Inc.
    2750 Womble Rd Ste 102
    619 477-4117

(P-15092)

MESA VERDE PARTNERS

Also Called: Costa Mesa Country Club
1701 Golf Course Dr, Costa Mesa (92626-5049)
PHONE..................................714 540-7500
Scott Henderson, *Pt*
EMP: 120 EST: 1992
SQ FT: 12,000
SALES (est): 1.63MM
SALES (corp-wide): 8.81MM **Privately Held**
Web: www.costamesacountryclub.com
SIC: 7992 7997 5813 5812 Public golf courses; Membership sports and recreation clubs; Drinking places; Eating places
PA: Santa Anita Associates
    405 S Santa Anita Ave
    626 447-2764

(P-15093)

MILE SQUARE GOLF COURSE

10401 Warner Ave, Fountain Valley (92708-1604)
PHONE..................................714 962-5541
David A Rainville, *Pt*
EMP: 109 EST: 1969
SQ FT: 12,000
SALES (est): 4.4MM **Privately Held**
Web: www.milesquaregolfcourse.com
SIC: 7992 7999 5812 Public golf courses; Golf driving range; American restaurant

(P-15094)

MONARCH BEACH GOLF LINKS (HQ)

50 Monarch Beach Resort N, Dana Point (92629-4084)
PHONE..................................949 240-8247
Hale Kelly, *Dir*
EMP: 80 EST: 1983
SALES (est): 843.93K **Privately Held**
Web: www.monarchbeachgolf.com

SIC: 7992 Public golf courses
PA: Troon Golf, L.L.C.
    15044 N Scttsdale Rd Ste

(P-15095)

QUARRY AT LA QUINTA INC

1 Quarry Ln, La Quinta (92253-8004)
PHONE..................................760 777-1100
Jay Head, *Mgr*
William Morrow, *
EMP: 86 EST: 1993
SALES (est): 15.92MM **Privately Held**
Web: www.thequarrygc.com
SIC: 7992 Public golf courses

(P-15096)

SILVER ROCK RESORT GOLF CLUB

79179 Ahmanson Ln, La Quinta (92253-5715)
PHONE..................................760 777-8884
EMP: 100 EST: 2005
SALES (est): 170.04K
SALES (corp-wide): 102.13MM **Privately Held**
Web: www.silverrock.org
SIC: 7992 Public golf courses
PA: City Of La Quinta
    78495 Calle Tampico
    760 777-7000

(P-15097)

UNITED STATES MARINE CORPS

Also Called: Marine Memorial Golf Course
Golf Course Rd Bldg 18415, Camp Pendleton (92055)
P.O. Box 555020 (92055-5020)
PHONE..................................760 725-4704
Jody Coor, *Genl Mgr*
EMP: 308
Web: pendleton.usmc-mccs.org
SIC: 7992 9711 Public golf courses; Marine Corps
HQ: United States Marine Corps
    Branch Hlth Clinic Bldg #5
    Beaufort SC 29904

(P-15098)

WELK GROUP INC

Also Called: Foutains Executive Course
8860 Lawrence Welk Dr, Escondido (92026-6403)
PHONE..................................760 749-3225
Larry Welk Junior, *VP*
EMP: 159
SALES (corp-wide): 22.87MM **Privately Held**
Web: www.beachcarswpb.com
SIC: 7992 7011 Public golf courses; Resort hotel
PA: The Welk Group Inc
    11400 W Olympic Blvd # 1450
    760 749-3000

7993 Coin-operated Amusement Devices

(P-15099)

CAMPO BAND MISSIONS INDIANS

Also Called: Golden Acorn Casino & Trvl Ctr
1800 Golden Acorn Way, Campo (91906-2301)
P.O. Box 310 (91906-0310)
PHONE..................................619 938-6000
Don Trimble, *Mgr*
EMP: 330
Web: www.goldenacorncasino.com

SIC: 7993 5812 Gambling establishments operating coin-operated machines; American restaurant
PA: Campo Band Of Missions Indians 36190 Church Rd

(P-15100)
PLAYERS WEST AMUSEMENTS INC (PA)
Also Called: Toy Barn
2360 Sturgis Rd Ste A, Oxnard (93030-8956)
PHONE..............................805 983-1400
Jack G Mann, *Pr*
▲ EMP: 38 EST: 1991
SALES (est): 784.54K Privately Held
Web: www.toybarn.com
SIC: 7993 5092 3942 Amusement machine rental, coin-operated; Toys and hobby goods and supplies; Dolls and stuffed toys

(P-15101)
SEGA ENTERTAINMENT USA INC
600 N Brand Blvd 5th Fl, Glendale (91203-4207)
PHONE..............................310 217-9500
▲ EMP: 1550
SIC: 7993 Coin-operated amusement devices

7996 Amusement Parks

(P-15102)
CITY OF LANCASTER
Also Called: Big Eight
43011 10th St W, Lancaster (93534-6012)
PHONE..............................661 723-6071
Jeff Campbell, *Brnch Mgr*
EMP: 149
Web: www.big8.org
SIC: 7996 Amusement parks
PA: City Of Lancaster 44933 Fern Ave

(P-15103)
DISNEYLAND INTERNATIONAL (DH)
Also Called: Disneyland
1313 S Harbor Blvd, Anaheim (92802-2309)
PHONE..............................714 781-4565
James Thomas, *Pr*
James Cora, *Ch Bd*
Michael Eisner, *Dir*
Richard Nunis, *Dir*
Doris Smith, *Sec*
EMP: 200 EST: 1961
SALES (est): 44.73MM
SALES (corp-wide): 91.36B Publicly Held
Web: disneyland.disney.go.com
SIC: 7996 Theme park, amusement
HQ: Disney Enterprises, Inc.
500 S Buena Vista St
Burbank CA 91521
818 560-1000

(P-15104)
KNOTTS BERRY FARM LLC (HQ)
Also Called: Knott's Berry Farm
8039 Beach Blvd, Buena Park (90620-3225)
P.O. Box 5002 (90620)
PHONE..............................714 827-1776
Jack Falfas, *Pt*
▲ EMP: 500 EST: 1997
SQ FT: 5,000
SALES (est): 44.51MM
SALES (corp-wide): 1.08B Publicly Held
Web: www.knotts.com

SIC: 7996 Theme park, amusement
PA: Six Flags Entertainment Corporation 8701 Red Oak Blvd
419 626-0830

(P-15105)
LEGOLAND CALIFORNIA LLC
Also Called: Legoland California Resort
1 Legoland Dr, Carlsbad (92008-4610)
PHONE..............................760 450-3661
▲ EMP: 400 EST: 1994
SALES (est): 32.4MM
SALES (corp-wide): 2.65B Privately Held
Web: www.legoland.com
SIC: 7996 Theme park, amusement
HQ: Merlin Entertainments Group Limited
16th Floor Arbor House
London SE1 9

(P-15106)
RAGING WATERS GROUP INC
Also Called: Raging Waters
111 Raging Waters Dr, San Dimas (91773-3998)
PHONE..............................909 802-2200
EMP: 1092 EST: 2000
SALES (est): 9.97MM
SALES (corp-wide): 53.97MM Privately Held
Web: www.ragingwaters.com
SIC: 7996 Theme park, amusement
PA: Alfa Smartparks, Inc
1 W Adams St Ste 200
904 358-1027

(P-15107)
RAVINE WATERPARK LLC
Also Called: Ravine Waterpark, The
2301 Airport Rd, Paso Robles (93446-8549)
PHONE..............................805 237-8500
James Walsh, *Prin*
EMP: 205 EST: 2004
SALES (est): 2.19MM Privately Held
Web: www.ravinewaterpark.com
SIC: 7996 Theme park, amusement

(P-15108)
SANTA MONICA AMUSEMENTS LLC
Also Called: Pacific Park
380 Santa Monica Pier, Santa Monica (90401-3128)
PHONE..............................310 451-9641
Mary Ann Powell, *CEO*
Jeff Klocke, *
David Gillam, *
Dana Wyatt, *
EMP: 325 EST: 1992
SQ FT: 70,000
SALES (est): 24.01MM Privately Held
Web: www.pacpark.com
SIC: 7996 Theme park, amusement

(P-15109)
SIX FLAGS MAGIC MOUNTAIN INC
26101 Magic Mountain Pkwy, Valencia (91355-1095)
P.O. Box 5500 (91380-5500)
PHONE..............................661 255-4100
Larry B Cochran, *CEO*
EMP: 85 EST: 1979
SALES (est): 4.24MM Privately Held
Web: www.sixflags.com
SIC: 7996 Theme park, amusement

(P-15110)
WALT DISNEY COMPANY (PA)
Also Called: Disney
500 S Buena Vista St, Burbank (91521-0007)
PHONE..............................818 560-1000
Robert A Iger, *CEO*
Mark G Parker, *Ch Bd*
Kevin A Lansberry, *Interim Chief Financial Officer*
Horacio E Gutierrez, *Chief Compliance Officer*
Sonia L Coleman, *Chief Human Resources Officer*
EMP: 1132 EST: 1923
SALES (est): 91.36B
SALES (corp-wide): 91.36B Publicly Held
Web: www.thewaltdisneycompany.com
SIC: 7996 4841 Amusement parks; Cable television services

7997 Membership Sports And Recreation Clubs

(P-15111)
1334 PARTNERS LP
Also Called: Manhattan Country Club
1330 Park View Ave, Manhattan Beach (90266-3704)
PHONE..............................310 546-5656
Keith Brackpool, *Pt*
EMP: 100 EST: 1982
SQ FT: 80,000
SALES (est): 2.31MM Privately Held
Web: www.bayclubs.com
SIC: 7997 6512 7991 5813 Country club, membership; Commercial and industrial building operation; Physical fitness facilities ; Drinking places

(P-15112)
AGI HOLDING CORP (PA)
Also Called: Affinity Group
2575 Vista Del Mar Dr, Ventura (93001-3900)
P.O. Box 6888 (80155-6888)
PHONE..............................805 667-4100
Stephen Adams, *CEO*
Joe Mcadams, *Pr*
Mark Boggess, *
Michael Schneider, *
Mister Stephen Adams, *Prin*
◆ EMP: 52 EST: 1988
SQ FT: 74,000
SALES (est): 6.59MM
SALES (corp-wide): 6.59MM Privately Hold
Web: www.goodsam.com
SIC: 7997 2741 Membership sports and recreation clubs; Directories, nec; publishing and printing

(P-15113)
ALTADENA TOWN AND COUNTRY CLUB
2290 Country Club Dr, Altadena (91001-3202)
PHONE..............................626 345-9088
David Edens, *Pr*
EMP: 80 EST: 1946
SQ FT: 50,000
SALES (est): 5.98MM Privately Held
Web: www.altaclub.com
SIC: 7997 Country club, membership

(P-15114)
AMERICAN GOLF CORPORATION (HQ)

909 N Pacific Coast Hwy Ste 650, El Segundo (90245-2732)
PHONE..............................310 664-4000
Mike Compton, *Pr*
Meng Lai, *
Kim Wong, *
Keith Brown, *
Jim Allison, *
EMP: 150 EST: 1973
SALES (est): 281.77MM Privately Held
Web: www.americangolf.com
SIC: 7997 7999 5812 5941 Golf club, membership; Golf services and professionals; Eating places; Golf goods and equipment
PA: Drive Shack Inc.
10670 N Cntl Expy Ste 700

(P-15115)
ANNANDALE GOLF CLUB
1 N San Rafael Ave, Pasadena (91105-1299)
PHONE..............................626 796-6125
Christoff Granger, *Genl Mgr*
EMP: 125 EST: 1905
SQ FT: 10,000
SALES (est): 11.75MM Privately Held
Web: www.annandalegolf.com
SIC: 7997 Golf club, membership

(P-15116)
ANTELOPE VLY CNTRY CLB IMPRV
39800 Country Club Dr, Palmdale (93551-2970)
PHONE..............................661 947-3142
Mark Range, *
EMP: 150 EST: 1952
SQ FT: 22,000
SALES (est): 2.27MM Privately Held
Web: www.antelopevalleycountryclub.com
SIC: 7997 Country club, membership

(P-15117)
BAKERSFIELD COUNTRY CLUB
4200 Country Club Dr, Bakersfield (93306-3700)
P.O. Box 6007 (93386-6007)
PHONE..............................661 871-4000
Jon Van Boening, *Pr*
EMP: 75 EST: 1948
SQ FT: 30,000
SALES (est): 5.66MM Privately Held
Web: www.bakersfieldcountryclub.com
SIC: 7997 5812 5813 Country club, membership; Eating places; Bar (drinking places)

(P-15118)
BALBOA BAY CLUB INC (HQ)
1221 W Coast Hwy, Newport Beach (92663-5092)
PHONE..............................949 645-5000
David Wooten, *Pr*
W D Ray, *
EMP: 260 EST: 1948
SALES (est): 2.74MM
SALES (corp-wide): 18.67MM Privately Held
Web: www.balboabayclub.com
SIC: 7997 7011 Country club, membership; Resort hotel
PA: International Bay Clubs, Llc
1221 W Coast Hwy Ste 145
949 645-5000

(P-15119)
BAY CLUBS COMPANY LLC
2250 Park Pl, Thousand Oaks (91362-1717)

PHONE..............................310 643-6878
Alyce Jones, *Brnch Mgr*
EMP: 133
SALES (corp-wide): 47.27MM **Privately Held**
Web: www.bayclubs.com
SIC: 7997 Membership sports and recreation clubs
PA: The Bay Clubs Company Llc
　　1 Lombard St
　　415 781-1874

(P-15120)
BAY CLUBS COMPANY LLC
Also Called: Sanctuary Spa
12000 Carmel Country Rd, San Diego (92130-6101)
PHONE..............................858 509-9933
EMP: 259
SALES (corp-wide): 47.27MM **Privately Held**
Web: www.bayclubs.com
SIC: 7997 Membership sports and recreation clubs
PA: The Bay Clubs Company Llc
　　1 Lombard St
　　415 781-1874

(P-15121)
BEL-AIR BAY CLUB LTD
16801 Pacific Coast Hwy, Pacific Palisades (90272-3399)
PHONE..............................310 230-4700
William Howard, *CEO*
EMP: 200 EST: 1927
SQ FT: 7,500
SALES (est): 9.75MM **Privately Held**
Web: www.belairbayclub.com
SIC: 7997 Membership sports and recreation clubs

(P-15122)
BEL-AIR COUNTRY CLUB
10768 Bellagio Rd, Los Angeles (90077-3799)
PHONE..............................310 472-9563
Joseph Wagner, *Genl Mgr*
Peter Best, *
EMP: 140 EST: 1924
SQ FT: 10,000
SALES (est): 16.94MM **Privately Held**
Web: www.bel-aircc.golf
SIC: 7997 5941 Country club, membership; Golf goods and equipment

(P-15123)
BELLA COLLINA SAN CLEMENTE
200 Avenida La Pata, San Clemente (92673-6301)
PHONE..............................949 498-6604
Mark Freilich, *Managing Member*
EMP: 80 EST: 2009
SALES (est): 2.27MM **Privately Held**
Web: www.bellacollinasanclemente.com
SIC: 7997 Country club, membership

(P-15124)
BIG CANYON COUNTRY CLUB
1 Big Canyon Dr, Newport Beach (92660-5299)
PHONE..............................949 644-5404
Donald Tippett, *CEO*
William Stamply, *
EMP: 180 EST: 1971
SQ FT: 50,000
SALES (est): 24.83MM **Privately Held**
Web: www.bigcanyoncc.org
SIC: 7997 Country club, membership

(P-15125)
BIGHORN GOLF CLUB CHARITIES
255 Palowet Dr, Palm Desert (92260-7311)
PHONE..............................760 773-2468
Carl T Cardinalli, *Pr*
Joe Curtis, *
EMP: 190 EST: 1990
SALES (est): 1.66MM **Privately Held**
Web: www.bighorngolf.com
SIC: 7997 7992 Country club, membership; Public golf courses

(P-15126)
BRAEMAR COUNTRY CLUB INC
Also Called: Braemar Country Club
4001 Reseda Blvd, Tarzana (91356-5330)
P.O. Box 570217 (91357-0217)
PHONE..............................323 873-6880
Steven Held, *Mgr*
EMP: 199 EST: 1959
SQ FT: 20,000
SALES (est): 9.13MM
SALES (corp-wide): 2.44B **Privately Held**
Web: www.invitedclubs.com
SIC: 7997 Country club, membership
HQ: Clubcorp Usa, Inc.
　　5215 N O Connor Blvd # 2
　　Irving TX 75039
　　972 243-6191

(P-15127)
BRENTWOOD COUNTRY CLUB LOS ANGELES
Also Called: BRENTWOOD COUNTRY CLUB
590 S Burlingame Ave, Los Angeles (90049-4896)
PHONE..............................310 451-8011
EMP: 100 EST: 1948
SALES (est): 20.27MM **Privately Held**
Web: www.brentwoodcc.net
SIC: 7997 Country club, membership

(P-15128)
CITY OF DOWNEY
Also Called: Independence Park
12334 Bellflower Blvd, Downey (90242-2805)
PHONE..............................562 803-4982
EMP: 80
SALES (corp-wide): 149.66MM **Privately Held**
Web: www.downeyca.org
SIC: 7997 Tennis club, membership
PA: City Of Downey
　　11111 Brookshire Ave
　　562 869-7331

(P-15129)
CLAREMONT TENNIS CLUB
Also Called: Claremont Club, The
1777 Monte Vista Ave, Claremont (91711-2916)
P.O. Box 157 (91785-0157)
PHONE..............................909 625-9515
Michael G Alpert, *Pr*
Geoffrey Clark, *
EMP: 200 EST: 1973
SQ FT: 40,000
SALES (est): 2.12MM **Privately Held**
Web: www.claremontclub.com
SIC: 7997 7991 5812 Membership sports and recreation clubs; Health club; Eating places

(P-15130)
COMEDY CLUB OXNARD LLC
Also Called: Levity Live
591 Collection Blvd, Oxnard (93036-5454)

PHONE..............................805 535-5400
Alireza Ghaemian, *Prin*
EMP: 88 EST: 2015
SALES (est): 277.61K **Privately Held**
SIC: 7997 Membership sports and recreation clubs

(P-15131)
DEL MAR COUNTRY CLUB INC
6001 Clubhouse Dr, Rancho Santa Fe (92067-9589)
P.O. Box 9866 (92067-4866)
PHONE..............................858 759-5500
Madeleine Pickens, *Pr*
EMP: 90 EST: 1993
SQ FT: 18,000
SALES (est): 8.96MM **Privately Held**
Web: www.delmarcountryclub.com
SIC: 7997 Country club, membership

(P-15132)
DHCCNP
Also Called: DESERT HORIZONS COUNTRY CLUB
44900 Desert Horizons Dr, Indian Wells (92210-7401)
PHONE..............................760 340-4646
Jurgen Gross, *Mgr*
EMP: 86 EST: 1979
SQ FT: 30,000
SALES (est): 5.47MM **Privately Held**
Web: www.deserthorizons.org
SIC: 7997 7992 5812 Country club, membership; Public golf courses; Eating places

(P-15133)
EL CABALLERO COUNTRY CLUB
18300 Tarzana Dr, Tarzana (91356-4216)
PHONE..............................818 654-3000
Bary West, *Pr*
Gary Diamond, *
Peter Jimenez, *
EMP: 125 EST: 1956
SQ FT: 20,000
SALES (est): 12.85MM **Privately Held**
Web: www.elcaballerocc.com
SIC: 7997 7992 5812 Country club, membership; Public golf courses; Eating places

(P-15134)
ELDORADO COUNTRY CLUB
46000 E Eldorado Dr, Indian Wells (92210-8631)
PHONE..............................760 346-8081
Geoff Hasley, *Pr*
EMP: 200 EST: 1959
SQ FT: 50,000
SALES (est): 25.74MM **Privately Held**
Web: www.eldoradocc.org
SIC: 7997 5812 Golf club, membership; Eating places

(P-15135)
FAIRBANKS RANCH CNTRY CLB INC
15150 San Dieguito Rd, Rancho Santa Fe (92067)
P.O. Box 8586 (92067-8586)
PHONE..............................858 259-8811
Mike Kendall, *CEO*
Brad Forrester, *
Stan Kinsey, *
Robert Macier, *
EMP: 180 EST: 1983
SQ FT: 35,000
SALES (est): 2.94MM **Privately Held**
Web: www.bayclubs.com

SIC: 7997 Country club, membership

(P-15136)
FRIENDLY HLLS CNTRY CLB FNDTIO
8500 Villaverde Dr, Whittier (90605-1398)
PHONE..............................562 698-0331
Dave Goodrich, *COO*
Chris Banner, *
EMP: 110 EST: 1969
SQ FT: 42,000
SALES (est): 608.97K **Privately Held**
Web: www.friendlyhillscc.com
SIC: 7997 Country club, membership

(P-15137)
GLENDORA COUNTRY CLUB
2400 Country Club Drive, Glendora (91741)
PHONE..............................626 335-4051
Jack Stoughton, *CEO*
Jim Leahy, *
Mike Kerstetter, *
Bill Mckinley, *Treas*
Susan Taylor, *
EMP: 90 EST: 1954
SQ FT: 10,000
SALES (est): 6.98MM **Privately Held**
Web: www.glendoracountryclub.com
SIC: 7997 5812 5813 Country club, membership; Eating places; Drinking places

(P-15138)
HACIENDA GOLF CLUB
718 East Rd, La Habra Heights (90631-8199)
PHONE..............................562 694-1081
Frank Cordeiro, *Genl Mgr*
EMP: 95 EST: 1919
SQ FT: 30,000
SALES (est): 9.14MM **Privately Held**
Web: www.haciendagolfclub.com
SIC: 7997 5812 5813 Golf club, membership; American restaurant; Bar (drinking places)

(P-15139)
HIDEAWAY CLUB
Also Called: Hideaway
80440 Hideaway Club Ct, La Quinta (92253-7867)
P.O. Box 1540 (92247-1540)
PHONE..............................760 777-7400
Brian J Ellis, *CEO*
EMP: 609 EST: 2015
SALES (est): 2.34MM
SALES (corp-wide): 435.04MM **Privately Held**
Web: www.hideawaygolfclub.com
SIC: 7997 6531 Membership sports and recreation clubs; Real estate agents and managers
PA: Discovery Land Company, Llc
　　14605 N 73rd St
　　480 624-5200

(P-15140)
HILLCREST COUNTRY CLUB
10000 W Pico Blvd, Los Angeles (90064-3400)
PHONE..............................310 553-8911
John Jameson, *Pr*
John Goldsmith, *CEO*
Tom Driefus, *CFO*
Richard Powell, *Prin*
Leonard Fisher, *Prin*
EMP: 180 EST: 1920
SQ FT: 69,081
SALES (est): 29.41MM **Privately Held**
Web: www.hcc-la.com
SIC: 7997 Country club, membership

(P-15141)

JONATHAN CLUB

Also Called: Jonathan Beach Club
850 Palisades Beach Rd, Santa Monica
(90403-1008)
PHONE...................310 393-9245
Ernie Dunn, *Mgr*
EMP: 100
SQ FT: 12,784
SALES (corp-wide): 33.42MM **Privately Held**
Web: www.jc.org
SIC: 7997 5812 8641 Beach club, membership; Grills (eating places); Civic and social associations
PA: Jonathan Club
545 S Figueroa St
213 624-0881

(P-15142)

LA CANADA FLINTRIDGE CNTRY CLB

5500 Godbey Dr, La Canada (91011-1899)
PHONE...................818 790-0611
Gilbert Dreyfus, *Pr*
Evelyn Dreyfus, *
EMP: 80 **EST:** 1977
SQ FT: 24,000
SALES (est): 3.46MM **Privately Held**
Web: www.lcfcountryclub.com
SIC: 7997 Country club, membership

(P-15143)

LA CUMBRE COUNTRY CLUB

4015 Via Laguna, Santa Barbara
(93110-2298)
PHONE...................805 687-2421
Brian Bahman, *Genl Mgr*
EMP: 100 **EST:** 1956
SQ FT: 8,000
SALES (est): 22.92MM **Privately Held**
Web: www.lacumbrecc.org
SIC: 7997 Country club, membership

(P-15144)

LA JOLLA BCH & TENNIS CLB INC (PA)

Also Called: Marine Room Restaurant
2000 Spindrift Dr, La Jolla (92037-3283)
PHONE...................858 454-7126
William J Kellogg, *CEO*
Jeannie Porter, *
▲ **EMP:** 165 **EST:** 1940
SQ FT: 3,500
SALES (est): 19.41MM
SALES (corp-wide): 19.41MM **Privately Held**
Web: www.ljbtc.com
SIC: 7997 8742 Membership sports and recreation clubs; Food and beverage consultant

(P-15145)

LAKES COUNTRY CLUB ASSN INC (PA)

Also Called: Lakes Country Club, The
161 Old Ranch Rd, Palm Desert
(92211-3211)
PHONE...................760 568-4321
Gerald Lee Hagood, *Pr*
Ron Phipps, *
Sandy Seddon, *
Frank Melon, *
EMP: 125 **EST:** 1982
SQ FT: 3,600
SALES (est): 6.01MM
SALES (corp-wide): 6.01MM **Privately Held**
Web: www.thelakescc.com

(P-15146)

LAS POSAS COUNTRY CLUB

Also Called: Lpcc
955 Fairway Dr, Camarillo (93010-8499)
PHONE...................805 482-4518
Todd Keefer, *Genl Mgr*
EMP: 146 **EST:** 1957
SALES (est): 2.29MM
SALES (corp-wide): 14.78MM **Privately Held**
Web: www.lasposascc.com
SIC: 7997 7992 5812 0781 Country club, membership; Public golf courses; Eating places; Landscape counseling and planning
PA: Century Golf Partners Management Lp
5430 Lyndon B Johnson Fwy
972 419-1400

(P-15147)

LOS ANGELES COUNTRY CLUB

10101 Wilshire Blvd, Los Angeles
(90024-4703)
PHONE...................310 276-6104
Kirk O Reese, *Prin*
EMP: 250 **EST:** 1898
SQ FT: 75,000
SALES (est): 37.88MM **Privately Held**
Web: www.thelacc.org
SIC: 7997 Country club, membership

(P-15148)

LOS ANGLES RYAL VSTA GOLF CRSE

Also Called: Los Angles Ryal Vsta Golf Crse
20055 Colima Rd, Walnut (91789-3502)
PHONE...................909 595-7441
TOLL FREE: 800
Don Crooker, *Mgr*
EMP: 74
SALES (corp-wide): 2.34MM **Privately Held**
Web: www.larv.com
SIC: 7997 5941 Golf club, membership; Golf goods and equipment
HQ: Los Angeles Royal Vista Golf Courses, Inc.
770 Kapiolani Blvd # 506
Honolulu HI 96813
808 592-4800

(P-15149)

MESA VERDE COUNTRY CLUB

3000 Club House Rd, Costa Mesa
(92020-3599)
PHONE...................714 549-0377
John Hayhoe, *CEO*
Robert Heflin, *
Diane Burnes, *
EMP: 125 **EST:** 1959
SQ FT: 34,000
SALES (est): 11.86MM **Privately Held**
Web: www.mesaverdecc.com
SIC: 7997 Country club, membership

(P-15150)

MISSION HILLS COUNTRY CLUB INC

34600 Mission Hills Dr, Rancho Mirage
(92270-1300)
PHONE...................760 324-9400
Josh Tanner, *Genl Mgr*
Doug Howe, *
EMP: 130 **EST:** 1983
SQ FT: 75,000
SALES (est): 2.05MM
SALES (corp-wide): 2.44B **Privately Held**

Web: www.invitedclubs.com
SIC: 7997 7992 5812 Country club, membership; Public golf courses; Eating places
HQ: Clubcorp Usa, Inc.
5221 N Ocnnor Blvd Ste 30
Irving TX 75039
972 243-6191

(P-15151)

MISSION VIEJO COUNTRY CLUB

26200 Country Club Dr, Mission Viejo
(92691-5905)
PHONE...................949 582-1550
Michael Lance Kennedy, *Managing Member*
Chad Pettit, *
Enrique Martinez, *
Scot Dey, *
Veronica Alva Roman, *
EMP: 103 **EST:** 1969
SALES (est): 9.05MM **Privately Held**
Web: www.missionviejocc.com
SIC: 7997 7991 5812 7299 Country club, membership; Physical fitness facilities; Eating places; Banquet hall facilities

(P-15152)

MONTECITO COUNTRY CLUB INC

920 Summit Rd, Santa Barbara
(93108-2326)
PHONE...................805 969-0800
Tai Warner, *Pr*
Hiro Suzuki, *
EMP: 100 **EST:** 1921
SQ FT: 10,000
SALES (est): 4.06MM **Privately Held**
Web: www.montecitoclub1918.com
SIC: 7997 5812 5813 Country club, membership; Eating places; Bar (drinking places)
PA: Tsukamoto Corporation Co., Ltd.
1-6-5, Nihombashihoncho

(P-15153)

NEW PVCC INC

15835 Pauma Valley Dr, Pauma Valley
(92061-1612)
PHONE...................760 742-1230
Butt Suze, *Pr*
EMP: 76 **EST:** 1961
SQ FT: 3,000
SALES (est): 2.18MM **Privately Held**
Web: www.paumavalleycc.com
SIC: 7997 Country club, membership

(P-15154)

NEWPORT BEACH COUNTRY CLUB INC

Also Called: Newport Beach Country Club
1 Clubhouse Dr, Newport Beach
(92660-7107)
PHONE...................949 644-9550
David Wooten, *Pr*
Jerry Anderson, *General Vice President*
Gerald Johnson, *
EMP: 90 **EST:** 1985
SALES (est): 2.23MM
SALES (corp-wide): 18.67MM **Privately Held**
Web: www.newportbeachcc.com
SIC: 7997 7991 5941 5813 Country club, membership; Physical fitness facilities; Sporting goods and bicycle shops; Drinking places
PA: International Bay Clubs, Llc
1221 W Coast Hwy Ste 145
949 645-5000

(P-15155)

NORTH RANCH COUNTRY CLUB

4761 Valley Spring Dr, Westlake Village
(91362-4399)
PHONE...................818 889-3531
Mark Bagaaso, *CEO*
Scott London, *
EMP: 160 **EST:** 1976
SQ FT: 53,000
SALES (est): 14.71MM **Privately Held**
Web: www.northranchcc.org
SIC: 7997 5812 5941 Country club, membership; Eating places; Sporting goods and bicycle shops

(P-15156)

OAKMONT COUNTRY CLUB

3100 Country Club Dr, Glendale
(91208-1799)
PHONE...................818 542-4260
Pat Dahlson, *CEO*
John Schiller, *
Michael Hyler, *
EMP: 125 **EST:** 1955
SQ FT: 37,000
SALES (est): 15.16MM **Privately Held**
Web: www.oakmontcc.com
SIC: 7997 Country club, membership

(P-15157)

PACIFIC GOLF & COUNTRY CLUB

200 Avenida La Pata, San Clemente
(92673-6301)
PHONE...................949 498-6604
Tom Frost, *Cnslt*
EMP: 77 **EST:** 1986
SQ FT: 27,000
SALES (est): 65.98K
SALES (corp-wide): 672.64K **Privately Held**
Web: www.bellacollinasanclemente.com
SIC: 7997 7992 Golf club, membership; Public golf courses
PA: Golf Investment Llc
200 Avenida La Pata
949 498-6604

(P-15158)

PORTER VALLEY COUNTRY CLUB INC

Also Called: Porter Valley Catering
19216 Singing Hills Dr, Northridge
(91326-1799)
PHONE...................818 360-1071
Robert H Dedman, *Ch Bd*
John Beckett, *
Doug Howe, *
EMP: 110 **EST:** 1966
SQ FT: 18,000
SALES (est): 916.92K
SALES (corp-wide): 2.44B **Privately Held**
Web: www.invitedclubs.com
SIC: 7997 5812 5941 Golf club, membership; Steak restaurant; Sporting goods and bicycle shops
HQ: Clubcorp Usa, Inc.
5221 N Ocnnor Blvd Ste 30
Irving TX 75039
972 243-6191

(P-15159)

PREMIER AQUATIC SERVICES LLC

Also Called: Premier Aquatics
6 Journey Ste 200, Aliso Viejo
(92656-5321)
PHONE...................949 716-3333
Daniel Berzansky, *Pr*

EMP: 73 EST: 2011
SALES (est): 1.12MM Privately Held
Web: www.swimoc.com
SIC: 7997 Swimming club, membership

(P-15160)
RANCHO SANTA FE
ASSOCIATION
Also Called: Rancho Sante Fe Golf Club
5827 Viadelacumere, Rancho Santa Fe
(92067).
P.O. Box A (92067-0359)
PHONE...........................858 756-1182
Stephen Nordstrom, Mgr
EMP: 100
SALES (corp-wide): 27.67MM Privately
Held
Web: www.rsfgc.com
SIC: 7997 Golf club, membership
PA: Rancho Santa Fe Association
17022 Avenida De Acacias
858 756-1174

(P-15161)
RED HILL COUNTRY CLUB
8358 Red Hill Country Club Dr, Rancho
Cucamonga (91730-1899)
PHONE...........................909 982-1358
Rob Mocksley, Pr
EMP: 92 EST: 1921
SQ FT: 20,000
SALES (est): 7.19MM Privately Held
Web: www.redhillcc.com
SIC: 7997 5812 Country club, membership;
Eating places

(P-15162)
REDLANDS COUNTRY CLUB
1749 Garden St, Redlands (92373-7248)
PHONE...........................909 793-2661
Scott Reding, Pr
Jason Murphy, *
EMP: 80 EST: 1946
SQ FT: 22,000
SALES (est): 7.7MM Privately Held
Web: www.redlandscountryclub.com
SIC: 7997 5812 5813 Country club,
membership; Snack shop; Bar (drinking
places)

(P-15163)
RESERVE CLUB
49400 Desert Butte Trl, Indian Wells
(92210-7075)
PHONE...........................760 674-2222
Michael Kelly, CEO
Hayden Eaves, *
EMP: 80 EST: 1998
SQ FT: 10,000
SALES (est): 576.65K Privately Held
Web: www.thereserveclub.com
SIC: 7997 Country club, membership

(P-15164)
RIVIERA GOLF & TENNIS INC
1250 Capri Dr, Pacific Palisades
(90272-4001)
PHONE...........................310 454-6591
Noboru Watanabe, Pr
Todd Yoshitake, Dir
Satoko Stachowicz, Ex VP
EMP: 79 EST: 1989
SALES (est): 30.28K Privately Held
Web: www.therivieracountryclub.com
SIC: 7997 Country club, membership

(P-15165)
ROLLING HILLS COUNTRY CLUB
Also Called: Rolling Hlls Cntry CLB Golf Sp
1 Chandler Ranch Rd, Rolling Hills Estate
(90274-3301)

PHONE...........................424 903-0000
EMP: 82 EST: 1965
SALES (est): 17.41MM Privately Held
Web: www.rollinghillscc.com
SIC: 7997 5941 Country club, membership;
Golf goods and equipment

(P-15166)
ROSE BOWL AQUATICS CENTER
360 N Arroyo Blvd, Pasadena (91103-3201)
PHONE...........................626 564-0330
Judy Biggs, Ex Dir
Kurt Knop, *
Robert Kamins, *
Alison Laster, *
Lyn Beckett Cacciatore, *
EMP: 80 EST: 1992
SALES (est): 9.48MM Privately Held
Web: www.rosebowlaquatics.org
SIC: 7997 Swimming club, membership

(P-15167)
SAN DIEGO STATE UNIVERSITY
Also Called: San Diego State Aztecs
5302 55th St, San Diego (92182-0001)
PHONE...........................619 594-4263
John Jentz, CEO
EMP: 200
SALES (corp-wide): 534.4MM Privately
Held
Web: www.sdsu.edu
SIC: 7997 7922 4832 Membership sports
and recreation clubs; Theatrical producers
and services; Sports
HQ: San Diego State University
5500 Campanile Dr
San Diego CA 92182

(P-15168)
SAN GABRIEL COUNTRY CLUB
350 E Hermosa Dr, San Gabriel
(91775-2346)
PHONE...........................626 287-9671
Tom Dukes, Pr
EMP: 80 EST: 1904
SQ FT: 48,000
SALES (est): 8.99MM Privately Held
Web: www.sangabrielcc.com
SIC: 7997 Country club, membership

(P-15169)
SAN LUIS OBISPO GOLF CNTRY
CLB
Also Called: Slogcc
255 Country Club Dr, San Luis Obispo
(93401-8939)
PHONE...........................805 543-3400
David Cole, Pr
Carol Kerwin, *
Christopher Simpson, *
EMP: 110 EST: 1958
SQ FT: 10,000
SALES (est): 1.8MM Privately Held
Web: www.slocountryclub.com
SIC: 7997 Country club, membership

(P-15170)
SANTA ANA COUNTRY CLUB
20382 Newport Blvd, Santa Ana
(92707-5396)
PHONE...........................714 556-3000
Joseph Jj Wagner, Prin
Joseph J Wagner, CEO
EMP: 100 EST: 1914
SALES (est): 12.21MM Privately Held
Web: www.santaanacc.org
SIC: 7997 Country club, membership

(P-15171)
SANTALUZ CLUB INC
8170 Caminito Santaluz E, San Diego
(92127-2577)
PHONE...........................858 759-3120
Steve Cowell, CEO
James Hoselton, *
Michael Forsum, *
Timothy A Kaehr, *
Terry D Randall, *
EMP: 120 EST: 2000
SQ FT: 19,000
SALES (est): 496.56K Privately Held
Web: www.thesantaluzclub.com
SIC: 7997 Country club, membership

(P-15172)
SATICOY COUNTRY CLUB
4450 Clubhouse Dr, Somis (93066-9798)
PHONE...........................805 647-1153
Douglas Taxton, Pr
Kathy Sube, *
James R Van Wyck, *
EMP: 80 EST: 1921
SALES (est): 2.33MM Privately Held
Web: www.thesaticoyclub.com
SIC: 7997 Country club, membership

(P-15173)
SEVEN OAKS COUNTRY CLUB
2000 Grand Lakes Ave, Bakersfield
(93311-2931)
P.O. Box 11165 (93389-1165)
PHONE...........................661 664-6404
David H Murdock, CEO
Bruce Freeman, *
Don Ciota, *
EMP: 125 EST: 1991
SQ FT: 39,000
SALES (est): 9.01MM Privately Held
Web: www.sevenoakscountryclub.com
SIC: 7997 Country club, membership

(P-15174)
SHADY CANYON GOLF CLUB
INC
100 Shady Canyon Dr, Irvine (92603-0301)
PHONE...........................949 856-7000
James T Wood, CEO
Thomas Heggi, *
Robert Leenhouts, *
EMP: 108 EST: 2003
SALES (est): 269.42K Privately Held
Web: www.shadycanyongolfclub.com
SIC: 7997 Country club, membership

(P-15175)
SOUTH HILLS COUNTRY CLUB
2655 S Citrus St, West Covina
(91791-3405)
PHONE...........................626 339-1231
James Wendoll, CEO
EMP: 78 EST: 1852
SQ FT: 34,000
SALES (est): 6.52MM Privately Held
Web: www.southhillscountryclub.org
SIC: 7997 5813 5812 Country club,
membership; Bar (drinking places);
American restaurant

(P-15176)
SPANISH HILLS CLUB LLC
999 Crestview Ave, Camarillo (93010-8493)
PHONE...........................805 388-5000
Alain O'connor, Managing Member
EMP: 99 EST: 2019
SALES (est): 458.85K Privately Held
Web: www.thespanishhillsclub.com

SIC: 7997 Country club, membership

(P-15177)
SPANISH HILLS COUNTRY
CLUB (PA)
999 Crestview Ave, Camarillo (93010-8493)
PHONE...........................805 389-1644
Joe Topper, Pr
Steve Thomas, *
EMP: 150 EST: 1989
SQ FT: 42,000
SALES (est): 2.33MM Privately Held
Web: www.thespanishhillsclub.com
SIC: 7997 Country club, membership

(P-15178)
STOCKDALE COUNTRY CLUB
7001 Stockdale Hwy, Bakersfield
(93309-1313)
P.O. Box 9727 (93389-9727)
PHONE...........................661 832-0310
Sam Monroe, Pr
Linda Voiland, *
Michael Davis, *
EMP: 100 EST: 1925
SQ FT: 12,000
SALES (est): 7.44MM Privately Held
Web: www.stockdalecc.com
SIC: 7997 Country club, membership

(P-15179)
TAMARISK COUNTRY CLUB (PA)
70240 Frank Sinatra Dr, Rancho Mirage
(92270-2599)
PHONE...........................760 328-2141
Michael Miller, CEO
David Pelzman, Genl Mgr
EMP: 125 EST: 1951
SQ FT: 32,000
SALES (est): 5.15MM
SALES (corp-wide): 5.15MM Privately
Held
Web: www.tamariskcc.com
SIC: 7997 Country club, membership

(P-15180)
TEAM SO-CAL INC
1811 Knoll Dr Ste A, Ventura (93003-7321)
PHONE...........................805 650-9946
Essam Hishmeh, CEO
EMP: 400 EST: 2009
SALES (est): 1.07MM Privately Held
SIC: 7997 Membership sports and recreation
clubs

(P-15181)
THE SAN DIEGO YACHT CLUB
1011 Anchorage Ln, San Diego
(92106-3005)
PHONE...........................619 221-8400
EMP: 120 EST: 1886
SALES (est): 8.84MM Privately Held
Web: www.sdyc.org
SIC: 7997 Yacht club, membership

(P-15182)
TOSCANA COUNTRY CLUB INC
76009 Via Club Villa, Indian Wells
(92210-7851)
PHONE...........................760 404-1444
Paul K Levy, CEO
EMP: 150 EST: 2004
SALES (est): 8.98MM Privately Held
Web: www.toscanacc.com
SIC: 7997 Country club, membership

(P-15183)
VICTORIA CLUB
2521 Arroyo Dr, Riverside (92506-1598)

▲ = Import ▼ = Export
◆ = Import/Export

PHONE...............................951 683-5323
EMP: 105 **EST:** 1903
SALES (est): 5.07MM **Privately Held**
Web: www.victoriaclub.com
SIC: 7997 Country club, membership

(P-15184)
VINTAGE CLUB
75001 Vintage Dr W, Indian Wells
(92210-7352)
PHONE...............................760 340-0500
John Buttemiller Broker Sales E, *Prin*
Marc D Ray, *
John Buttemiller Broker, *Sls Dir*
Carmen Wolfe, *Marketing TRANSACTION**
Jamie Shelton, *PGA Professional**
EMP: 90 **EST:** 1979
SQ FT: 86,000
SALES (est): 27.08MM **Privately Held**
Web: www.thevintageclub.com
SIC: 7997 5813 5812 5941 Country club,
membership; Bar (drinking places);
American restaurant; Golf goods and
equipment

(P-15185)
**VIRGINIA CNTRY CLB OF LONG
BCH**
4602 N Virginia Rd, Long Beach
(90807-1999)
PHONE...............................562 427-0924
Jamie Mulligan, *CEO*
EMP: 110 **EST:** 1909
SQ FT: 15,000
SALES (est): 10.47MM **Privately Held**
Web: www.vcc1909.org
SIC: 7997 Country club, membership

(P-15186)
WELK GROUP INC
Also Called: Meadow Lake Country Club
10333 Meadow Glen Way E, Escondido
(92026-6918)
PHONE...............................760 749-0983
Brad Van Horn, *Mgr*
EMP: 250
SQ FT: 5,000
SALES (corp-wide): 22.87MM **Privately
Held**
Web: www.beachcarswpb.com
SIC: 7997 Country club, membership
PA: The Welk Group Inc
11400 W Olympic Blvd # 1450
760 749-3000

(P-15187)
WESTGROUP KONA KAI LLC
Also Called: Kona Kai Resort Hotel
1551 Shelter Island Dr, San Diego
(92106-3102)
PHONE...............................610 221 8000
EMP: 99 **EST:** 2011
SALES (est): 4.89MM **Privately Held**
Web: www.resortkonakai.com
SIC: 7997 7011 Membership sports and
recreation clubs; Resort hotel
PA: Noble House Hotels & Resorts, Ltd.
600 6th St S

(P-15188)
WILSHIRE COUNTRY CLUB
301 N Rossmore Ave, Los Angeles
(90004-2499)
PHONE...............................323 934-6050
Jeffrey Ornstein, *CEO*
Norman Branchflower, *
Doctor Mirion Bowers Md, *VP*
EMP: 94 **EST:** 1919
SQ FT: 50,000
SALES (est): 12.18MM **Privately Held**

Web: www.wilshirecountryclub.com
SIC: 7997 5941 5812 Country club,
membership; Sporting goods and bicycle
shops; Eating places

(P-15189)
**YOUNG MNS CHRSTN ASSN
ORNGE CN**
Also Called: South Coast YMCA
29831 Crown Valley Pkwy, Laguna Niguel
(92677-1944)
PHONE...............................949 495-9622
Jennifer Heinen, *Brnch Mgr*
EMP: 75
SALES (corp-wide): 50.06MM **Privately
Held**
Web: www.ymcaoc.org
SIC: 7997 8641 Membership sports and
recreation clubs; Civic and social
associations
PA: Young Men's Christian Association Of
Orange County
13821 Newport Ave Ste 200
714 549-9622

7999 Amusement And
Recreation, Nec

(P-15190)
29 PALMS ENTERPRISES CORP
Also Called: Spotlight 29 Casino
46200 Harrison Pl, Coachella (92236-2031)
PHONE...............................760 775-5566
Darrel Mike, *Pr*
EMP: 600 **EST:** 1995
SQ FT: 70,000
SALES (est): 19.04MM **Privately Held**
Web: www.spotlight29.com
SIC: 7999 5812 Gambling establishment;
Eating places

(P-15191)
ADVENTURE CITY INC
1238 S Beach Blvd, Anaheim (92804-4828)
PHONE...............................714 821-3311
Allan Ansdell Junior, *Pr*
Yvonne Ansdell, *
EMP: 100 **EST:** 1992
SALES (est): 5.59MM **Privately Held**
Web: www.adventurecity.com
SIC: 7999 7996 Tourist attractions,
amusement park concessions and rides;
Amusement parks

(P-15192)
**ANSCHUTZ STHERN CAL SPT
CMPLX**
Also Called: Stop Hop Center
18400 Avalon Blvd Ste 100, Carson
(90746-2180)
PHONE...............................310 630-2000
Katherine Pandolfo, *Genl Mgr*
Anschutz Grp, *
Kedie Pendolfo, *
EMP: 160 **EST:** 2000
SALES (est): 346.8K **Privately Held**
Web: www.dignityhealthsportspark.com
SIC: 7999 7941 Exhibition and carnival
operation services; Sports field or stadium
operator, promoting sports events
HQ: Anschutz Entertainment Group, Inc.
800 W Olympic Blvd Ste 30
Los Angeles CA 90015
213 763-7700

(P-15193)
ARIZONA CHANNEL ISLA
300 W 9th St, Oxnard (93030-7060)

PHONE...............................480 788-0755
EMP: 75
SQ FT: 60,000
SALES (est): 282.99K **Privately Held**
SIC: 7999 Amusement and recreation, nec

(P-15194)
**BELL GARDENS BICYCLE
CLUB INC**
Also Called: Bicycle Club Casino
888 Bicycle Casino Dr, Bell Gardens
(90201-7617)
PHONE...............................562 806-4646
George Hardie, *Pr*
George G Hardie, *
EMP: 1300 **EST:** 1984
SQ FT: 110,000
SALES (est): 2.43MM **Privately Held**
Web: www.thebike.com
SIC: 7999 5812 Card rooms; Coffee shop

(P-15195)
**CAESARS ENTRTNMENT
OPRTING INC**
Also Called: Harrah's
777 Harrahs Rincon Way, Valley Center
(92082-5343)
PHONE...............................760 751-3100
Janet Deronio, *Brnch Mgr*
EMP: 1400
SALES (corp-wide): 11.53B **Publicly Held**
Web: www.harrahssocal.com
SIC: 7999 7011 Gambling establishment;
Casino hotel
HQ: Caesars Entertainment Operating
Company, Inc.
One Caesars Palace Dr
Las Vegas NV 89109
702 407-6000

(P-15196)
**CAHUILLA CREEK REST &
CASINO**
Also Called: Cahuilla Creek Casino
52702 Us Highway 371, Anza
(92539-8707)
PHONE...............................951 763-1200
Leonardo Pasquarelli, *Genl Mgr*
Jon Gregory, *
EMP: 103 **EST:** 1996
SQ FT: 14,000
SALES (est): 18.88MM **Privately Held**
Web: www.cahuillacasinohotel.com
SIC: 7999 5812 5813 Gambling
establishment; American restaurant; Bar
(drinking places)

(P-15197)
CTOUR HOLIDAY LLC
222 E Huntington Dr Ste 105, Monrovia
(91016-8014)
PHONE...............................323 261-8811
Charlie Lu, *Managing Member*
EMP: 300 **EST:** 2016
SALES (est): 1.53MM **Privately Held**
Web: www.seagullholiday.com.cn
SIC: 7999 Tour and guide services

(P-15198)
**DISNEY REGIONAL ENTRMT INC
(DH)**
Also Called: Disney
500 S Buena Vista St, Burbank
(91521-0001)
PHONE...............................818 560-1000
Arthur Levitt, *Pr*
Gary Marcotte, *
EMP: 200 **EST:** 1996
SALES (est): 1.28MM

SALES (corp-wide): 91.36B **Publicly Held**
Web: www.dgepress.com
SIC: 7999 5812 5813 Recreation center;
Eating places; Drinking places
HQ: Twdc Enterprises 18 Corp.
500 S Buena Vista St
Burbank CA 91521

(P-15199)
DROPZONE WATERPARK
2165 Trumble Rd, Perris (92571-9211)
PHONE...............................951 210-1600
Erica Bice, *Dir*
EMP: 150 **EST:** 2014
SALES (est): 204.87K **Privately Held**
Web: www.dropzonewaterpark.com
SIC: 7999 Recreation services

(P-15200)
**EAST VALLEY TOURIST DEV
AUTH**
Also Called: Fantasy Springs Resort Casino
84245 Indio Springs Dr, Indio (92203-3405)
PHONE...............................760 342-5000
John James, *Ch Bd*
Mark Benitez, *
Brenda Soulliere, *
Angela Roosevelt, *
EMP: 1200 **EST:** 1983
SQ FT: 94,000
SALES (est): 22.76MM **Privately Held**
Web: www.fantasyspringsresort.com
SIC: 7999 Gambling establishment

(P-15201)
EASTBIZ CORPORATION
3501 Jack Northrop Ave, Hawthorne
(90250-4444)
PHONE...............................310 212-7134
EMP: 114
SIC: 7999 5091 Sporting goods rental, nec;
Sporting and recreation goods

(P-15202)
FAIRPLEX ENTERPRISES INC
1101 W Mckinley Ave, Pomona
(91768-1650)
PHONE...............................909 623-3111
James Henwood, *Pr*
▲ **EMP:** 151 **EST:** 2011
SALES (est): 2.3MM
SALES (corp-wide): 74.99MM **Privately
Held**
Web: www.fairplex.com
SIC: 7999 Fair, nsk
PA: Los Angeles County Fair Association
1101 W Mckinley Ave
909 623-3111

(P-15203)
FAZE CLAN INC
9950 Jefferson Blvd, Culver City
(90232-3530)
PHONE...............................818 688-6373
Richard Bengtson, *CEO*
EMP: 496 **EST:** 2016
SALES (est): 45.5MM
SALES (corp-wide): 9.01MM **Privately
Held**
Web: www.fazeclan.com
SIC: 7999 5961 Games, instruction;
Electronic shopping
PA: Gamesquare Esports Inc
1008-150 York St
647 670-2500

(P-15204)
FAZE HOLDINGS INC
Also Called: Faze Clan
9950 Jefferson Blvd Ste 3, Culver City
(90232-3531)

PHONE..............................818 688-6373
Christoph Pachler, *COO*
Christoph Pachler, *Interim Chief Executive Officer*
Erik Anderson, *Pr*
EMP: 112 **EST:** 2020
SALES (est): 70.02MM
SALES (corp-wide): 52MM **Publicly Held**
Web: www.themuseumofweed.com
SIC: 7999 5961 Games, instruction; Electronic shopping
PA: Gamesquare Holdings, Inc.
　　6775 Cowboys Way Ste 1335
　　216 464-6400

(P-15205)
FLOATIES SWIM SCHOOL LLC
Also Called: Floaties Swim School
13180 Poway Rd, Poway (92064-4612)
PHONE..............................877 277-7946
Kira La Forgia, *Dir Opers*
EMP: 75 **EST:** 2006
SALES (est): 387.76K **Privately Held**
Web: www.floatiesswimschool.com
SIC: 7999 Swimming instruction

(P-15206)
FORTISS LLC
888 Bicycle Casino Dr, Bell Gardens (90201-7617)
PHONE..............................323 415-4900
John Park, *Managing Member*
Michael Vasey, *
EMP: 103 **EST:** 2004
SALES (est): 4.02MM **Privately Held**
Web: www.fortiss.com
SIC: 7999 Card and game services

(P-15207)
HAWAIIAN GARDENS CASINO
11871 Carson St, Hawaiian Gardens (90716-1127)
PHONE..............................562 860-5887
FAX: 562 860-5823
EMP: 840
SALES (corp-wide): 63.26MM **Privately Held**
SIC: 7999 Card and game services
PA: Hawaiian Gardens Casino
　　21520 Pioneer Blvd # 305
　　562 860-5887

(P-15208)
KIDS EMPIRE USA LLC
Also Called: Kids Empire
8605 Santa Monica Blvd, West Hollywood (90069-4109)
PHONE..............................424 527-1039
Haim Elbaz, *CEO*
EMP: 97 **EST:** 2017
SALES (est): 5.45MM **Privately Held**
Web: www.kidsempire.com
SIC: 7999 6794 Recreation services; Franchises, selling or licensing

(P-15209)
KINEMA FITNESS INC
2450 Colorado Ave Ste 100e, Santa Monica (90404-5535)
PHONE..............................866 608-5704
Joshua Love, *Pr*
EMP: 80 **EST:** 2009
SALES (est): 774.53K **Privately Held**
Web: www.kinemafitness.com
SIC: 7999 7991 7389 Physical fitness instruction; Physical fitness facilities; Business Activities at Non-Commercial Site

(P-15210)
LOS ANGELES COUNTY FAIR ASSN (PA)
Also Called: Fairplex Rv Park
1101 W Mckinley Ave, Pomona (91768-1639)
PHONE..............................909 623-3111
Ronald Bolding, *Dir*
Micheal Seder, *
EMP: 100 **EST:** 1922
SALES (est): 74.99MM
SALES (corp-wide): 74.99MM **Privately Held**
Web: www.fairplex.com
SIC: 7999 8412 Fair, nsk; Museums and art galleries

(P-15211)
MARINE CORPS COMMUNITY SVCS
Also Called: Marine Corps Cmnty Svcs Dept
2273 Elrod Ave, San Diego (92145-0001)
P.O. Box 452008 (92145-2008)
PHONE..............................858 577-1061
Mary Bradford, *Dir*
EMP: 389
Web: www.marines.mil
SIC: 7999 9711 Recreation center; Marine Corps
HQ: Marine Corps Community Services
　　3044 Catlin Ave
　　Quantico VA 22134
　　703 432-0109

(P-15212)
MARINE CORPS COMMUNITY SVCS
Also Called: Moral Welfare and Recreation
Acs Mccs Attn Semper Fi Box 555020
Marine Corp Base, Camp Pendleton (92055)
PHONE..............................760 725-6195
Mike Wilkinson, *Department Director*
EMP: 148
SQ FT: 1,152
Web: www.marines.mil
SIC: 7999 9711 Recreation services; Marine Corps
HQ: Marine Corps Community Services
　　3044 Catlin Ave
　　Quantico VA 22134
　　703 432-0109

(P-15213)
MORONGO BAND MISSION INDIANS
Also Called: Morongo Casino Resort Spa
49500 Seminole Dr, Cabazon (92230-2202)
P.O. Box 366 (92230-0366)
PHONE..............................951 849-3080
Dual Cooper, *Brnch Mgr*
EMP: 91
Web: www.morongocasinoresort.com
SIC: 7999 9131 Gambling establishment; Indian Reservation
PA: Morongo Band Of Mission Indians
　　12700 Pumarra Road
　　951 849-4697

(P-15214)
MOUNT SAN JCNTO WINTER PK CORP
1 Tramway Rd, Palm Springs (92262-1827)
PHONE..............................760 325-1449
Nancy Nichols, *Pr*
Rob Parkins, *
Marjorie Dela Cruz, *
Tara Meinkey, *
▲ **EMP:** 73 **EST:** 1945

SQ FT: 50,000
SALES (est): 1.75MM **Privately Held**
Web: www.pstramway.com
SIC: 7999 Aerial tramway or ski lift, amusement or scenic

(P-15215)
MOUNTAIN VISTA GOLF COURSE AT
38180 Del Webb Blvd, Palm Desert (92211-1256)
PHONE..............................760 200-2200
Andrea Goodwin, *Pr*
John Celli, *
Ron Delgado, *
Bill Wirian, *
Chuck Carpenter, *
EMP: 85 **EST:** 1992
SQ FT: 300
SALES (est): 30MM **Privately Held**
Web: www.mountainvistagolfclub.com
SIC: 7999 Golf services and professionals

(P-15216)
QUECHAN INDIAN TRIBE
Also Called: Quechan Gaming Commission
450 Quechan Rd, Winterhaven (92283-9676)
P.O. Box 2737 (85366-2573)
PHONE..............................760 572-2413
Mike Jackson, *Pr*
EMP: 101
Web: www.quechantribe.com
SIC: 7999 5812 Gambling establishment; Eating places
PA: Quechan Indian Tribe
　　350 Picacho Rd
　　760 572-0213

(P-15217)
RIVIERA COUNTRY CLUB INC
Also Called: Grand Slam Tennis Program
1250 Capri Dr, Pacific Palisades (90272-4099)
PHONE..............................310 454-6591
Noboru Watanabe, *CEO*
EMP: 77 **EST:** 1989
SALES (est): 3.14MM **Privately Held**
Web: www.therivieracountryclub.com
SIC: 7999 7997 Tennis club, non-membership; Membership sports and recreation clubs

(P-15218)
ROCKIN JUMP HOLDINGS LLC
Also Called: Rockin' Jump Trampoline
1301 W Rancho Vista Blvd Ste B, Palmdale (93551-3101)
PHONE..............................661 233-9907
EMP: 293
SALES (corp-wide): 50.09MM **Privately Held**
Web: www.rockinjump.com
SIC: 7999 Trampoline operation
HQ: Rockin' Jump Holdings, Llc
　　18 Crow Canyon Ct Ste 350
　　San Ramon CA 94583
　　925 401-7200

(P-15219)
S J S ENTERPRISE INC
Also Called: S C Village
9030 Somerset Blvd, Bellflower (90706-3402)
PHONE..............................949 489-9000
Dennis Bukowski, *Pr*
Judy Bukowski, *
EMP: 150 **EST:** 1987
SALES (est): 502.77K **Privately Held**
Web: www.scvillage.com

SIC: 7999 Indoor court clubs

(P-15220)
SAN BRNRDINO CNTY RGONAL PARKS
777 E Rialto Ave, San Bernardino (92415-1005)
PHONE..............................909 387-2583
EMP: 99 **EST:** 2020
SALES (est): 479.45K **Privately Held**
Web: parks.sbcounty.gov
SIC: 7999 Recreation center

(P-15221)
SAN MANUEL ENTERTAINMENT AUTH (PA)
Also Called: Yaamava Rsort Csino At San Mnu
777 San Manuel Blvd, Highland (92346-6713)
PHONE..............................909 864-5050
TOLL FREE: 800
James Ramos, *Ch*
Rebecca Spalding, *CFO*
Jimmy Starcher, *Ex Dir*
Steve Lengeo, *Ex Dir*
Rikki Tanenbaum, *COO*
▲ **EMP:** 2950 **EST:** 1987
SALES (est): 93.09MM
SALES (corp-wide): 93.09MM **Privately Held**
Web: www.yaamava.com
SIC: 7999 Bingo hall

(P-15222)
SNOW SUMMIT SKI CORPORATION
Also Called: Snow Summit Mountain Resort
43101 Goldmine Dr, Big Bear City (92314)
P.O. Box 77 (92315-0077)
PHONE..............................909 585-2517
Richard C Kun, *Brnch Mgr*
EMP: 85
SALES (corp-wide): 13.63MM **Privately Held**
Web: www.bigbearmountainresort.com
SIC: 7999 7011 5941 7992 Aerial tramway or ski lift, amusement or scenic; Ski lodge; Skiing equipment; Public golf courses
PA: Snow Summit, Llc
　　880 Summit Blvd
　　909 866-5766

(P-15223)
SYCUAN CASINO (PA)
Also Called: Sycuan Resort and Casino
5459 Casino Way, El Cajon (92019)
PHONE..............................619 445-6002
John Denius, *Genl Mgr*
Angela Scantling, *
EMP: 156 **EST:** 1983
SQ FT: 236,000
SALES (est): 28.09MM
SALES (corp-wide): 28.09MM **Privately Held**
Web: www.sycuan.com
SIC: 7999 7997 Gambling establishment; Membership sports and recreation clubs

(P-15224)
T ALLANCE ONE - PALM SPRNG LLC
Also Called: Doubltree Palm Sprng Golf Rsor
67967 Vista Chino, Cathedral City (92234-7408)
PHONE..............................760 322-7000
EMP: 99 **EST:** 2013
SALES (est): 2.98MM **Privately Held**
Web: www.doubletreepalmsprings.com

SIC: 7999 Golf professionals

(P-15225)
TICKETMANAGER
26635 Agoura Rd Ste 200, Calabasas (91302-3810)
PHONE..............................818 698-3616
EMP: 96 EST: 2016
SALES (est): 2.07MM Privately Held
Web: www.ticketmanager.com
SIC: 7999 Ticket sales office for sporting events, contract

(P-15226)
TICKETMASTER CORPORATION
Also Called: Ticketmaster
7060 Hollywood Blvd Ste 2, Los Angeles (90028-6030)
PHONE..............................323 769-4600
EMP: 4390
SIC: 7999 7922 Ticket sales office for sporting events, contract; Theatrical producers and services

(P-15227)
TICKETMASTER ENTERTAINMENT LLC
8800 W Sunset Blvd, West Hollywood (90069-2105)
PHONE..............................800 653-8000
Ron Bension, Managing Member
EMP: 4390 EST: 2010
SALES (est): 3.5MM Publicly Held
SIC: 7999 Ticket sales office for sporting events, contract
PA: Live Nation Entertainment, Inc.
9348 Civic Center Dr

(P-15228)
TICKETMASTER GROUP INC
Also Called: Ticketmaster
3701 Wilshire Blvd Fl 9, Los Angeles (90010-2804)
PHONE..............................800 745-3000
EMP: 4390
SIC: 7999 Ticket sales office for sporting events, contract

(P-15229)
TICKETMSTER NEW VNTRES HLDNGS (HQ)
Also Called: Ticketmaster
325 N Maple Dr, Beverly Hills (90210-3428)
PHONE..............................800 653-8000
Irving Azoff, CEO
EMP: 102 EST: 1996
SALES (est): 7.68MM Publicly Held
Web: www.ticketmaster.com
SIC: 7999 Ticket sales office for sporting events, contract
PA: Live Nation Entertainment, Inc.
9348 Civic Center Dr

(P-15230)
TIERRA DEL SOL FOUNDATION
Also Called: Tierra Del Soul
250 W 1st St Ste 120, Claremont (91711-4741)
PHONE..............................909 626-8301
Rebecca Hamm, Brnch Mgr
EMP: 85
SALES (corp-wide): 24.72MM Privately Held
Web: www.tierradelsol.org
SIC: 7999 5999 Art gallery, commercial; Art dealers
PA: Tierra Del Sol Foundation
9919 Sunland Blvd
818 352-1419

(P-15231)
VOLUME SERVICES INC
5333 Zoo Dr, Los Angeles (90027-1451)
PHONE..............................323 644-6038
Greg Edgar, Mgr
EMP: 260
SALES (corp-wide): 246.43MM Privately Held
Web: us.sodexo.com
SIC: 7999 Concession operator
HQ: Volume Services, Inc.
2187 Atlantic St Ste 6
Stamford CT 06902

(P-15232)
VOLUME SERVICES INC
111 W Harbor Dr, San Diego (92101-7822)
PHONE..............................619 525-5800
EMP: 260
SALES (corp-wide): 246.43MM Privately Held
Web: us.sodexo.com
SIC: 7999 Concession operator
HQ: Volume Services, Inc.
2187 Atlantic St Ste 6
Stamford CT 06902

(P-15233)
WATERSAFE SWIM SCHOOL INC
Also Called: Watersafe Swim School
345 10th St, Seal Beach (90740-6401)
PHONE..............................562 596-8608
Nathanael Najarian, CEO
EMP: 89 EST: 1978
SALES (est): 327.62K Privately Held
Web: www.watersafe.com
SIC: 7999 Swimming instruction

8011 Offices And Clinics Of Medical Doctors

(P-15234)
ALL CARE MEDICAL GROUP INC
Also Called: Professional Svcs Med Group
31 Crescent Street, Huntington Park (90255)
PHONE..............................408 278-3550
Samuel Rotenberg Md, Dir
EMP: 85 EST: 1946
SQ FT: 33,000
SALES (est): 1.37MM Privately Held
Web: www.allcaremg.com
SIC: 8011 Physicians' office, including specialists

(P-15235)
ALTAMED HEALTH SERVICES CORP
Also Called: Senior Health and Activity Ctr
5425 Pomona Blvd, Los Angeles (90022-1716)
PHONE..............................323 728-0411
Mariela Bauer, Brnch Mgr
EMP: 302
SQ FT: 24,369
SALES (corp-wide): 1.25B Privately Held
Web: www.altamedfoundation.org
SIC: 8011 8099 Gynecologist; Medical services organization
PA: Altamed Health Services Corporation
2040 Camfield Ave
323 725-8751

(P-15236)
ALTAMED HEALTH SERVICES CORP
2219 E 1st St, Los Angeles (90033-3901)
PHONE..............................323 269-0421
Shi Y Wong, Brnch Mgr
EMP: 151
SALES (corp-wide): 1.25B Privately Held
Web: www.altamed.org
SIC: 8011 8099 Gynecologist; Medical services organization
PA: Altamed Health Services Corporation
2040 Camfield Ave
323 725-8751

(P-15237)
ALTAMED HEALTH SERVICES CORP
Also Called: Ultimate
1500 Hughes Way Ste A150, Long Beach (90810-1883)
PHONE..............................562 923-9414
Chikita Emel, Dir
EMP: 90
SALES (corp-wide): 1.25B Privately Held
Web: www.altamed.org
SIC: 8011 Gynecologist
PA: Altamed Health Services Corporation
2040 Camfield Ave
323 725-8751

(P-15238)
ALTAMED HEALTH SERVICES CORP
Also Called: Altamed Adhc Golden Age
3820 Martin Luther King Jr Blvd, Lynwood (90262-3625)
PHONE..............................310 632-0415
Peter M Feldman, Prin
EMP: 110
SALES (corp-wide): 1.25B Privately Held
Web: www.altamed.org
SIC: 8011 8099 Gynecologist; Medical services organization
PA: Altamed Health Services Corporation
2040 Camfield Ave
323 725-8751

(P-15239)
ALTAMED HEALTH SERVICES CORP
5427 Whittier Blvd, Los Angeles (90022-4101)
PHONE..............................323 980-4466
Irene Avilar, Prin
EMP: 160
SALES (corp-wide): 1.25B Privately Held
Web: www.altamed.org
SIC: 8011 Clinic, operated by physicians
PA: Altamed Health Services Corporation
2040 Camfield Ave
323 725-8751

(P-15240)
ALTAMED HEALTH SERVICES CORP
2720 S Bristol St, Santa Ana (92704-6207)
PHONE..............................714 426-5400
EMP: 81
SALES (corp-wide): 1.25B Privately Held
Web: www.altamed.org
SIC: 8011 Gynecologist
PA: Altamed Health Services Corporation
2040 Camfield Ave
323 725-8751

(P-15241)
ALTAMED HEALTH SERVICES CORP (PA)
2040 Camfield Ave, Los Angeles (90040-1574)
PHONE..............................323 725-8751
Castulo De La Rocha, CEO
Zoila D Escobar, *
Marie S Torres, *
Jose U Esparza, *
EMP: 135 EST: 1970
SQ FT: 27,345
SALES (est): 1.25B
SALES (corp-wide): 1.25B Privately Held
Web: www.altamed.org
SIC: 8011 8099 Gynecologist; Medical services organization

(P-15242)
AMEN CLINICS INC A MED CORP (PA)
959 S Coast Dr, Costa Mesa (92626-7736)
PHONE..............................888 564-2700
Daniel Amen, Pr
▲ EMP: 75 EST: 2000
SALES (est): 25.27MM
SALES (corp-wide): 25.27MM Privately Held
Web: www.amenclinics.com
SIC: 8011 Psychiatric clinic

(P-15243)
AMN HEALTHCARE INC (HQ)
12400 High Bluff Dr Ste 100, San Diego (92130-3077)
PHONE..............................858 792-0711
Susan R Nowakowski, CEO
Susan R Salka, Pr
Julie Fletcher, VP
Marcia Faller, VP
Denise L Jackson, VP
EMP: 265 EST: 1985
SALES (est): 486.43MM
SALES (corp-wide): 3.79B Publicly Held
Web: www.amnhealthcare.com
SIC: 8011 Primary care medical clinic
PA: Amn Healthcare Services, Inc.
2999 Olympus Blvd Ste 500
866 871-8519

(P-15244)
ANESTHSIA MED GROUP SNTA BRBAR
Also Called: Anesthsia Med Group Snta Brbar
514 W Pueblo St Fl 2, Santa Barbara (93105-6219)
PHONE..............................805 682-7751
Eric Amador, Dir
Douglas Etsel, *
John King, *
Clinton Lagrange, *
Derrick Willsey, *
EMP: 78 EST: 1970
SALES (est): 3.47MM Privately Held
Web: www.amgsb.com
SIC: 8011 Anesthesiologist

(P-15245)
ANTELOPE VALLEY HOSPITAL INC
Ob Clinic
1600 W Avenue J, Lancaster (93534-2894)
PHONE..............................661 726-6180
Vikki Haley, Prin
EMP: 449
SALES (corp-wide): 522.79MM Privately Held
Web: www.avmc.org

SIC: 8011 Offices and clinics of medical doctors
PA: Antelope Valley Health Care District
1600 W Ave J
661 949-5000

(P-15246)
ARROYO VSTA FMLY HLTH FNDATION
Also Called: Arroyo Vista Family Health Ctr
2411 N Broadway, Los Angeles
(90031-2218)
PHONE.....................323 224-2188
Line Fernandez, *Mgr*
EMP: 100
SQ FT: 13,435
Web: www.arroyovista.org
SIC: 8011 Clinic, operated by physicians
PA: Arroyo Vista Family Health Foundation
6000 N Figueroa St

(P-15247)
ASSOCIATED STUDENTS UCLA
Also Called: Ucla Mdcn SC Phrmclgy
650 Charles Young Dr S Rm 23120, Los Angeles (90095-0001)
PHONE.....................310 825-9451
Michael Phelps, *Prin*
EMP: 90
SALES (corp-wide): 55.96MM **Privately Held**
Web: asucla.ucla.edu
SIC: 8011 General and family practice, physician/surgeon
PA: Associated Students U.C.L.A.
308 Westwood Plz
310 794-8836

(P-15248)
BAKERSFIELD FAMILY MEDICAL GROUP INC (PA)
Also Called: Bakersfield Family Medical Ctr
4580 California Ave, Bakersfield
(93309-7013)
P.O. Box 12022 (93389-2022)
PHONE.....................661 327-4411
EMP: 94 EST: 1984
SALES (est): 21.7MM
SALES (corp-wide): 21.7MM **Privately Held**
Web: www.bfmc.com
SIC: 8011 Medical centers

(P-15249)
BALBOA NPHROLOGY MED GROUP INC
4225 Executive Sq Ste 450, La Jolla
(92037-8411)
PHONE.....................858 810-8000
EMP: 222
SALES (est): 11.24MM **Privately Held**
Web: www.balboacare.com
SIC: 8011 Nephrologist

(P-15250)
BEAVER MEDICAL CLINIC INC (PA)
1615 Orange Tree Ln, Redlands
(92374-2804)
P.O. Box 10069 (92423-0069)
PHONE.....................909 793-3311
Robert Klein, *Pr*
EMP: 190 EST: 1945
SQ FT: 79,212
SALES (est): 23.09MM
SALES (corp-wide): 23.09MM **Privately Held**
Web: bmg.optum.com

SIC: 8011 Clinic, operated by physicians

(P-15251)
BEAVER MEDICAL GROUP LP (HQ)
Also Called: Beaver Medical Clinic
7000 Boulder Ave, Highland (92346-3348)
PHONE.....................909 425-3321
John Goodman, *CEO*
Robert Rentschler, *
James Watson Md, *Ltd Pt*
Robert Bourne Md, *Ltd Pt*
EMP: 155 EST: 1995
SALES (est): 23.26MM **Privately Held**
Web: bmg.optum.com
SIC: 8011 General and family practice, physician/surgeon
PA: Epic Management Services, Llc
1615 Orange Tree Ln

(P-15252)
BECKMAN RES INST OF THE CY HOP
Also Called: BECKMAN RESEARCH INSTITUTE OF
1500 Duarte Rd, Duarte (91010-3012)
PHONE.....................626 359-8111
Michael A Friedman, *CEO*
Harlan Levine, *
Robert Stone, *
Terry Blackwood, *
Ric Magnuson, *
EMP: 250 EST: 1979
SALES (est): 229.09MM
SALES (corp-wide): 330.02MM **Privately Held**
Web: www.cityofhope.org
SIC: 8011 Offices and clinics of medical doctors
PA: City Of Hope
1500 E Duarte Rd
626 256-4673

(P-15253)
BORREGO CMNTY HLTH FOUNDATION (PA)
Also Called: BORREGO MEDICAL CENTER
587 Palm Canyon Dr Ste 208, Borrego Springs (92004-4000)
P.O. Box 2369 (92004)
PHONE.....................855 436-1234
Isaac Lee, *CRO*
Bruce E Smith, *
Dianna Troncoso, *
EMP: 140 EST: 1990
SQ FT: 8,054
SALES (est): 120.17MM
SALES (corp-wide): 120.17MM **Privately Held**
Web: www.borregohealth.org
SIC: 8011 Offices and clinics of medical doctors

(P-15254)
BORREGO CMNTY HLTH FOUNDATION
1121 E Washington Ave, Escondido
(92025-2214)
PHONE.....................760 466-1080
EMP: 139
SALES (corp-wide): 120.17MM **Privately Held**
Web: www.borregohealth.org
SIC: 8011 Clinic, operated by physicians
PA: Borrego Community Health Foundation
587 Palm Canyon Suite 208
855 436-1234

SIC: 8011 Clinic, operated by physicians

(P-15255)
BORREGO CMNTY HLTH FOUNDATION
Also Called: Borrego Health
651 N State St Ste 5, San Jacinto
(92583-6574)
PHONE.....................951 487-8506
Michael D Dew, *Brnch Mgr*
EMP: 140
SALES (corp-wide): 120.17MM **Privately Held**
Web: www.borregohealth.org
SIC: 8011 Clinic, operated by physicians
PA: Borrego Community Health Foundation
587 Palm Canyon Suite 208
855 436-1234

(P-15256)
BORREGO CMNTY HLTH FOUNDATION
11750 Cholla Dr Ste B, Desert Hot Springs
(92240-3066)
PHONE.....................760 251-0044
EMP: 140
SALES (corp-wide): 120.17MM **Privately Held**
Web: www.borregohealth.org
SIC: 8011 Clinic, operated by physicians
PA: Borrego Community Health Foundation
587 Palm Canyon Suite 208
855 436-1234

(P-15257)
BRIGHT HEALTH PHYSICIANS (PA)
15725 Whittier Blvd Ste 500, Whittier
(90603-2350)
PHONE.....................562 947-8478
William H Stimmler Md, *Ch Bd*
Keith Miyamoto Md, *VP*
Berent Gray Md, *Sec*
EMP: 140 EST: 1991
SQ FT: 50,000
SALES (est): 38.79MM **Privately Held**
Web: www.brighthealth.com
SIC: 8011 Physicians' office, including specialists

(P-15258)
CABRILLO CRDOLGY MED GROUP INC
2241 Wankel Way Ste C, Oxnard
(93030-0191)
PHONE.....................805 983-0922
David Schmidt Md, *Pr*
David E Schmidt, *
Richard Rothchild Md, *Treas*
Scott Zager, *
Esam Obed, *
EMP: 71 EST: 1971
SALES (est): 9.92MM **Privately Held**
Web: www.cabrillocardiology.com
SIC: 8011 Cardiologist and cardio-vascular specialist

(P-15259)
CAL SOUTHERN MED CTR INC
14550 Haynes St, Van Nuys (91411-1613)
PHONE.....................818 650-6700
Sheila Busheri, *CEO*
EMP: 97 EST: 2011
SALES (est): 12.35MM **Privately Held**
Web: www.scmedcenter.org
SIC: 8011 Clinic, operated by physicians

(P-15260)
CANCER CENTER OF SANTA BARBARA

Also Called: THE CANCER CENTER OF SANTA BARBARA
2410 Fletcher Ave Ste 104, Santa Barbara
(93105-4875)
PHONE.....................805 898-2182
Karen Wallace, *Brnch Mgr*
EMP: 76
SALES (corp-wide): 7.3MM **Privately Held**
Web: www.ridleytreecc.org
SIC: 8011 Clinic, operated by physicians
PA: Cancer Foundation Of Santa Barbara
300 W Pueblo St
805 682-7300

(P-15261)
CARDIONET INC
Also Called: CARDIONET, INC.
750 B St Ste 1400, San Diego
(92101-8190)
PHONE.....................619 243-7500
Jim Sweeney, *Prin*
EMP: 82
SALES (corp-wide): 18.51B **Privately Held**
Web: www.gobio.com
SIC: 8011 Cardiologist and cardio-vascular specialist
HQ: Cardionet, Llc
1000 Cedar Hollow Rd # 10
Malvern PA 19355
610 729-7000

(P-15262)
CAREMARK RX INC
Also Called: US Family Care
1851 N Riverside Ave, Rialto (92376-8069)
PHONE.....................909 822-1164
Steve Heide, *Admn*
EMP: 70
SALES (corp-wide): 357.78B **Publicly Held**
SIC: 8011 General and family practice, physician/surgeon
HQ: Caremark Rx, Inc.
445 Great Cir Rd
Nashville TN 37228

(P-15263)
CAREMORE MEDICAL GROUP
420 W Central Ave Ste A, Brea
(92821-3001)
PHONE.....................714 529-3971
Janice E Clark Md, *Pt*
EMP: 72
SALES (corp-wide): 22.87MM **Privately Held**
Web: www.caremoremedicalgroup.com
SIC: 8011 General and family practice, physician/surgeon
PA: Caremore Medical Group
12898 Towne Center Dr
562 741-4557

(P-15264)
CB TANG MD INCORPORATED
Also Called: Long Beach Medical Clinic
1250 Pacific Ave, Long Beach
(90813-3026)
PHONE.....................562 437-0831
EMP: 96
Web: www.tangandcompany.com
SIC: 8011 Occupational and industrial specialist, physician/surgeon

(P-15265)
CEDARS-SINAI MEDICAL CENTER
Also Called: Radiation Onclogy - Cdrs-Snai
8720 Beverly Blvd Lowr Level, Los Angeles
(90048-1804)
PHONE.....................310 423-4208

Palmer Burnison Hakami, *Prin*
EMP: 74
SALES (corp-wide): 4.66B **Privately Held**
Web: www.cedars-sinai.edu
SIC: 8011 Physicians' office, including specialists
PA: Cedars-Sinai Medical Center
8700 Beverly Blvd
310 423-3277

(P-15266)
CEDARS-SINAI MEDICAL CENTER
Also Called: Cardiac Noninvasive Laboratory
127 S San Vicente Blvd Rm 3417, Los Angeles (90048-3311)
PHONE...............................310 423-3849
Timothy Henry, *Dir*
EMP: 274
SALES (corp-wide): 4.66B **Privately Held**
Web: www.cedars-sinai.edu
SIC: 8011 Cardiologist and cardio-vascular specialist
PA: Cedars-Sinai Medical Center
8700 Beverly Blvd
310 423-3277

(P-15267)
CEDARS-SINAI MEDICAL CENTER
8631 W 3rd St # 800-E, Los Angeles (90048-5901)
PHONE...............................310 423-7900
Carla Wesley, *Brnch Mgr*
EMP: 76
SALES (corp-wide): 4.66B **Privately Held**
Web: www.cedars-sinai.edu
SIC: 8011 Neurologist
PA: Cedars-Sinai Medical Center
8700 Beverly Blvd
310 423-3277

(P-15268)
CENTRAL CARDIOLOGY MED CLINIC
2901 Sillect Ave Ste 100, Bakersfield (93308-6372)
P.O. Box 1139 (93302-1139)
PHONE...............................661 395-0000
Brijesh Bahmbi, *Pt*
William Nyitray Md, *Pt*
Peter Nalos Md, *Pt*
EMP: 120 **EST:** 1974
SALES (est): 4.51MM **Privately Held**
Web: www.heart24.com
SIC: 8011 Cardiologist and cardio-vascular specialist

(P-15269)
CENTRO DE SLUD DE LA CMNDAD DE
Also Called: San Ysidro Health Center
2400 E 8th St, National City (91950-2956)
PHONE...............................619 662-4118
EMP: 365
SALES (corp-wide): 99.89MM **Privately Held**
Web: www.syhealth.org
SIC: 8011 Clinic, operated by physicians
PA: Centro De Salud De La Comunidad De San Ysidro, Inc.
1601 Precision Park Ln
619 428-4463

(P-15270)
CENTRO DE SLUD DE LA CMNDAD DE
Also Called: San Ysidro Health
316 25th St, San Diego (92102-3016)

PHONE...............................619 662-4100
EMP: 365
SALES (corp-wide): 99.89MM **Privately Held**
Web: www.syhealth.org
SIC: 8011 Clinic, operated by physicians
PA: Centro De Salud De La Comunidad De San Ysidro, Inc.
1601 Precision Park Ln
619 428-4463

(P-15271)
CHA HEALTH SYSTEMS INC (PA)
Also Called: Cha Renetative Medicine
3731 Wilshire Blvd Ste 850, Los Angeles (90010-2851)
PHONE...............................213 487-3211
Doctor K Cha, *CEO*
Jean Yi, *COO*
Thomas J May, *CAO*
EMP: 1250 **EST:** 2004
SALES (est): 27.08MM **Privately Held**
Web: www.hollywoodpresbyterian.com
SIC: 8011 Clinic, operated by physicians

(P-15272)
CHEN DVID MD DGNSTC MED GROUP
Also Called: Diagnostic Medical Group
208 N Garfield Ave, Monterey Park (91754-1705)
PHONE...............................626 288-8029
Anthony Tsun, *CEO*
EMP: 80
Web: www.dmg.net
SIC: 8011 Radiologist
PA: Chen, David Md Diagnostic Medical Group Inc
1129 S San Gabriel Blvd

(P-15273)
CHILDRENS CLNIC SRVING CHLDREN
701 E 28th St Ste 200, Long Beach (90806-2784)
PHONE...............................562 264-4638
Elisa A Nicholas, *Ex Dir*
Maria Y Chandler, *
Jina Lee Lawler, *
Knut P Thune, *
Albert P Ocampo, *
EMP: 320 **EST:** 1939
SQ FT: 24,000
SALES (est): 45.71MM **Privately Held**
Web: www.thechildrensclinic.org
SIC: 8011 Clinic, operated by physicians

(P-15274)
CHILDRENS HEALTHCARE CAL
Also Called: Pediatric Cancer Research
455 3 Main St, Orange (92808-3835)
P.O. Box 5700 (92863-5700)
PHONE...............................714 997-3000
Kimberly Crite, *CEO*
EMP: 300
Web: www.choc.org
SIC: 8011 Pediatrician
PA: Children's Healthcare Of California
1201 W La Veta Ave

(P-15275)
CHILDRENS ONCOLOGY GROUP
1333 S Mayflower Ave Ste 260, Monrovia (91016-5239)
PHONE...............................626 241-1500
Joseph Woelkers, *CEO*
EMP: 131 **EST:** 2013
SALES (est): 4.92MM **Privately Held**
Web: www.childrensoncologygroup.org
SIC: 8011 Oncologist

(P-15276)
CHILDRENS SPCLSTS OF SAN DEGO (PA)
Also Called: Childrens Associated Med Group
3020 Childrens Way, San Diego (92123-4223)
PHONE...............................858 576-1700
Michael Segall Md, *Pr*
Robin Steinhorn, *
EMP: 350 **EST:** 1978
SALES (est): 1.56MM
SALES (corp-wide): 1.56MM **Privately Held**
Web: www.rchsd.org
SIC: 8011 Physicians' office, including specialists

(P-15277)
CHINO MEDICAL GROUP INC
5475 Walnut Ave, Chino (91710-2699)
PHONE...............................909 591-6446
J Alex Lira Md, *Pr*
Fidel F Pinzon Md, *VP*
Jeffrey R Unger Md, *VP*
Steven Pulverman, *
EMP: 100 **EST:** 1977
SQ FT: 36,000
SALES (est): 1.96MM **Privately Held**
Web: www.myfamilymg.com
SIC: 8011 8031 Clinic, operated by physicians; Offices and clinics of osteopathic physicians

(P-15278)
CITY HOPE MEDICAL FOUNDATION
Also Called: BECKMAN RESEARCH INSTITUTE OF
1500 Duarte Rd, Duarte (91010-3000)
PHONE...............................626 256-4673
Robert W Stone, *Pr*
EMP: 521 **EST:** 2011
SALES (est): 766.82MM
SALES (corp-wide): 330.02MM **Privately Held**
Web: www.cityofhope.org
SIC: 8011 Offices and clinics of medical doctors
PA: City Of Hope
1500 E Duarte Rd
626 256-4673

(P-15279)
CITY OF HOPE
320 W 6th St, Corona (92882-3349)
PHONE...............................951 898-2828
EMP: 81 **EST:** 2014
SALES (est): 1.4MM **Privately Held**
Web: www.cityofhope.org
SIC: 8011 Offices and clinics of medical doctors

(P-15280)
CLINIC INC
Also Called: TO HELP EVERYONE HEALTH AND WE
3834 S Western Ave, Los Angeles (90062-1104)
PHONE...............................323 730-1920
Jamesina E Henderson, *Ex Dir*
EMP: 85 **EST:** 1974
SQ FT: 26,000
SALES (est): 22.7MM **Privately Held**
Web: www.tohelpeveryone.org
SIC: 8011 Clinic, operated by physicians

(P-15281)
CLINICA SIERRA VISTA
Also Called: Clinica Srra Vsta Adult Mntal

8787 Hall Rd, Lamont (93241-1953)
P.O. Box 457 (93241-0457)
PHONE...............................661 845-3717
Mercedes Macias, *Brnch Mgr*
EMP: 95
SALES (corp-wide): 182.02MM **Privately Held**
Web: www.clinicasierravista.org
SIC: 8011 Clinic, operated by physicians
PA: Clinica Sierra Vista
1430 Truxtun Ave 400
661 635-3050

(P-15282)
CLINICA SIERRA VISTA (PA)
Also Called: Lamont Community Health Center
1430 Truxtun Ave Ste 400, Bakersfield (93301-5220)
P.O. Box 1559 (93302-1559)
PHONE...............................661 635-3050
Stacy Ferreira, *CEO*
Stacy Ferreira, *Chief Human Resource Officer*
Matthew Clark, *
EMP: 90 **EST:** 1971
SQ FT: 14,599
SALES (est): 182.02MM
SALES (corp-wide): 182.02MM **Privately Held**
Web: www.clinicasierravista.org
SIC: 8011 Clinic, operated by physicians

(P-15283)
COASTAL RDTION ONCLOGY MED GRO
1240 S Westlake Blvd Ste 103, Westlake Village (91361-1975)
PHONE...............................805 494-4483
Kimberly Commins, *Dir*
Lauren Lovett, *Dir*
EMP: 99 **EST:** 2018
SALES (est): 910.24K **Privately Held**
Web: www.coastalradiationoncology.com
SIC: 8011 Oncologist

(P-15284)
COMMUNITY HEALTH GROUP
2420 Fenton St Ste 100, Chula Vista (91914-3516)
PHONE...............................800 224-7766
Norma A Diaz, *CEO*
William Rice, *
EMP: 140 **EST:** 1982
SQ FT: 26,000
SALES (est): 99.92MM **Privately Held**
Web: www.chgsd.com
SIC: 8011 Health maintenance organization

(P-15285)
COMMUNITY HEALTH SYSTEMS INC
Also Called: Moreno Valley Family Hlth Ctr
21801 Alessandro Blvd, Moreno Valley (92553-8202)
PHONE...............................951 571-2300
Lori Holeman, *CEO*
Yolanda Gomez, *
EMP: 130 **EST:** 1984
SALES (est): 32.27MM **Privately Held**
Web: www.chsica.org
SIC: 8011 Primary care medical clinic

(P-15286)
COMMUNITY HLTHCARE PARTNER INC
Also Called: COLORADO RIVER MEDICAL CENTER
1401 Bailey Ave, Needles (92363-3103)

PRODUCTS & SVCS

PHONE..................760 326-4531
Bing Lum, *Ex VP*
Knaya Tabora, *Prin*
EMP: 100 **EST:** 1999
SQ FT: 46,000
SALES (est): 8.86MM **Privately Held**
Web: www.crmccares.com
SIC: 8011 8062 Clinic, operated by
physicians; General medical and surgical
hospitals

(P-15287)
COR MEDICA TECHNOLOGY
Also Called: Cor Medica
188 Technology Dr Ste F, Irvine
(92618-2459)
PHONE..................949 353-4554
Fouad Ghaly, *CEO*
David Sestini, *
Rachel Everett, *
Robert Prestwood, *
Katalina Csoka, *
EMP: 26 **EST:** 2015
SQ FT: 2,200
SALES (est): 302.99K **Privately Held**
SIC: 8011 3841 Cardiologist and cardio-
vascular specialist; Diagnostic apparatus,
medical

(P-15288)
CORE MED STAFF
3946 Wilshire Blvd, Los Angeles
(90010-3303)
PHONE..................213 382-5550
Therece Nery, *Pr*
EMP: 98 **EST:** 2005
SALES (est): 667.04K **Privately Held**
Web: www.core.la
SIC: 8011 General and family practice,
physician/surgeon

(P-15289)
CORONA REGIONAL MED CTR LLC
800 S Main St, Corona (92882-3420)
PHONE..................951 737-4343
Alistair Machoka, *CEO*
EMP: 147 **EST:** 2009
SALES (est): 10.7MM **Privately Held**
SIC: 8011 Medical centers

(P-15290)
COUNTY OF LOS ANGELES
Also Called: Hudson H Clude Cmplete Hlth Ct
2829 S Grand Ave, Los Angeles
(90007-3304)
PHONE..................213 744-3919
Michael Mills, *Admn*
EMP: 81
Web: www.lacounty.gov
SIC: 8011 9431 8093 Medical centers;
Administration of public health programs;
Specialty outpatient clinics, nec
PA: County Of Los Angeles
500 W Temple St Ste 437
213 974-1101

(P-15291)
COUNTY OF LOS ANGELES
Also Called: Health Services, Dept of
15930 Central Ave Ste 100, La Puente
(91744-5410)
PHONE..................626 968-3711
Mary Anne Moreno, *Mgr*
EMP: 72
Web: www.lacounty.info
SIC: 8011 9431 Medical centers;
Administration of public health programs
PA: County Of Los Angeles
500 W Temple St Ste 437

213 974-1101

(P-15292)
COUNTY OF LOS ANGELES
Also Called: Health Services, Dept of
10005 Flower St, Bellflower (90706-5412)
PHONE..................562 804-8111
Earnst Espinoza, *Dir*
EMP: 71
Web: dhs.lacounty.gov
SIC: 8011 9431 Medical centers;
Administration of public health programs
PA: County Of Los Angeles
500 W Temple St Ste 437
213 974-1101

(P-15293)
COUNTY OF LOS ANGELES
Also Called: Health Services, Dept of
1900 Zonal Ave, Los Angeles (90033-1033)
P.O. Box 866001 (90086-6001)
PHONE..................323 226-7131
Linda Guerra, *Mgr*
EMP: 517
Web: www.lacounty.gov
SIC: 8011 9431 Offices and clinics of
medical doctors; Administration of public
health programs
PA: County Of Los Angeles
500 W Temple St Ste 437
213 974-1101

(P-15294)
COUNTY OF RIVERSIDE
Also Called: Rubidoux Family Care Center
5256 Mission Blvd, Riverside (92509-4624)
PHONE..................951 955-0840
Koen Brown, *Ex Dir*
EMP: 154
SALES (corp-wide): 5.07B **Privately Held**
Web: www.ruhealth.org
SIC: 8011 Clinic, operated by physicians
PA: County Of Riverside
4080 Lemon St Fl 11
951 955-1110

(P-15295)
COUNTY OF RIVERSIDE
Also Called: Public Social Services
26520 Cactus Ave, Moreno Valley
(92555-3927)
PHONE..................951 486-4000
Donna Matney, *Admn*
EMP: 540
SALES (corp-wide): 5.07B **Privately Held**
Web: www.rivco.org
SIC: 8011 9431 Medical centers; Mental
health agency administration, government
PA: County Of Riverside
4080 Lemon St Fl 11
951 955-1110

(P-15296)
COUNTY OF RIVERSIDE
Also Called: Community Health Agency
26520 Cactus Ave, Moreno Valley
(92555-3927)
PHONE..................951 486-4000
TOLL FREE: 800
Jim Watkins, *Prin*
EMP: 605
SALES (corp-wide): 5.07B **Privately Held**
Web: www.ruhealth.org
SIC: 8011 9431 Medical centers; Public
health agency administration, government
PA: County Of Riverside
4080 Lemon St Fl 11
951 955-1110

(P-15297)
CUROLOGY INC
5717 Pacific Center Blvd Ste 200, San
Diego (92121-4250)
PHONE..................617 959-2480
EMP: 436
SALES (corp-wide): 99.35MM **Privately
Held**
Web: www.curology.com
SIC: 8011 Dermatologist
PA: Curology, Inc
6195 Lusk Blvd
858 859-1188

(P-15298)
DAVITA MAGAN MANAGEMENT INC (DH)
Also Called: M M C
420 W Rowland St, Covina (91723-2943)
PHONE..................626 331-6411
Bradley J Rosenberg, *Prin*
Howard Ort Md, *Ex VP*
EMP: 250 **EST:** 1975
SQ FT: 66,000
SALES (est): 22.07MM
SALES (corp-wide): 371.62B **Publicly
Held**
Web: www.optum.com
SIC: 8011 Clinic, operated by physicians
HQ: Optumcare Management, Llc
2175 Park Pl
El Segundo CA 90245

(P-15299)
DESERT MEDICAL GROUP INC (PA)
Also Called: Desert Oasis Healthcare
275 N El Cielo Rd Ste D-402, Palm Springs
(92262-6972)
PHONE..................760 320-8814
Richard E Merkin Md, *Pr*
EMP: 240 **EST:** 1981
SQ FT: 13,000
SALES (est): 49.93MM
SALES (corp-wide): 49.93MM **Privately
Held**
SIC: 8011 General and family practice,
physician/surgeon

(P-15300)
DESERT ORTHPD CTR A MED GROUP (PA)
39000 Bob Hope Dr Ste W301, Rancho
Mirage (92270-7036)
PHONE..................760 568-2684
Ronald Lamb Md, *Pr*
Robert Murphy Md, *Ch Bd*
Stephen O'connell Md, *CFO*
Adrian Graff-radford Md, *Sec*
David Friscia, *
EMP: 78 **EST:** 1990
SQ FT: 23,000
SALES (est): 3.5MM **Privately Held**
Web: www.desertortho.com
SIC: 8011 Orthopedic physician

(P-15301)
DESERT VALLEY MED GROUP INC (DH)
Also Called: Desert Valley Medical Group
16850 Bear Valley Rd, Victorville (92392)
PHONE..................760 241-8000
Prem Reddy Md, *CEO*
Lex Reddy, *Pr*
M Mansukhani, *CFO*
EMP: 300 **EST:** 1981
SQ FT: 15,000
SALES (est): 28.93MM
SALES (corp-wide): 878.52MM **Privately
Held**

Web: www.desertvalleymedicalgroup.com
SIC: 8011 Physicians' office, including
specialists
HQ: Prime Healthcare Services Inc
3480 E Guasti Rd
Ontario CA 91761

(P-15302)
DIAGNSTIC INTRVNTNAL SRGCAL CT
13160 Mindanao Way Ste 150, Marina Del
Rey (90292-6393)
PHONE..................310 574-0400
Robert S Bray Junior, *Pr*
Keren Reiter, *
EMP: 100 **EST:** 2006
SALES (est): 2.65MM **Privately Held**
Web: www.discmdgroup.com
SIC: 8011 Orthopedic physician

(P-15303)
EISENHOWER MEDICAL CENTER
Also Called: Eisenhower-Memory-Care-center
34450 Gateway Dr, Palm Desert
(92211-0843)
PHONE..................760 836-0232
EMP: 180
SALES (corp-wide): 1.04B **Privately Held**
Web: www.eisenhowerhealth.org
SIC: 8011 Medical centers
PA: Eisenhower Medical Center
39000 Bob Hope Dr
760 340-3911

(P-15304)
EISENHOWER MEDICAL CENTER
Also Called: Dessert Cancer Care
57475 29 Palms Hwy Ste 104, Yucca Valley
(92284-2906)
PHONE..................760 228-9900
EMP: 90
SALES (corp-wide): 1.04B **Privately Held**
Web: www.eisenhowerhealth.org
SIC: 8011 Medical centers
PA: Eisenhower Medical Center
39000 Bob Hope Dr
760 340-3911

(P-15305)
EMANATE HEALTH
Also Called: Emanate Health
1722 Desire Ave Ste 206, Rowland Heights
(91748-2970)
PHONE..................626 912-5282
EMP: 151
SALES (corp-wide): 548.21MM **Privately
Held**
Web: www.cvhp.org
SIC: 8011 Physicians' office, including
specialists
PA: Emanate Health Medical Center
1115 S Sunset Ave
626 962-4011

(P-15306)
ENKI HEALTH AND RES SYSTEMS
Also Called: Enki Health Care
160 S 7th Ave, La Puente (91746-3211)
PHONE..................626 961-8971
Maria M Carmichael, *Dir*
EMP: 70
SALES (corp-wide): 22.76MM **Privately
Held**
Web: www.enkihealth.org

SIC: 8011 8733 Psychiatric clinic; Medical research
PA: Enki Health And Research Systems
150 E Olive Ave Ste 203
818 973-4899

(P-15307)
FAMILY HLTH CTRS SAN DIEGO INC
1845 Logan Ave, San Diego (92113-2111)
PHONE................619 515-2526
Gracie Duran, Brnch Mgr
EMP: 347
SALES (corp-wide): 147.12MM Privately Held
Web: www.fhcsd.org
SIC: 8011 Clinic, operated by physicians
PA: Family Health Centers Of San Diego, Inc.
823 Gateway Center Way
619 515-2303

(P-15308)
FAMILY HLTH CTRS SAN DIEGO INC
2391 Island Ave, San Diego (92102-2941)
PHONE................619 515-2435
Martha Barba, Mgr
EMP: 348
SALES (corp-wide): 147.12MM Privately Held
Web: www.fhcsd.org
SIC: 8011 Clinic, operated by physicians
PA: Family Health Centers Of San Diego, Inc.
823 Gateway Center Way
619 515-2303

(P-15309)
FAMILY HLTH CTRS SAN DIEGO INC
5379 El Cajon Blvd, San Diego (92115-4730)
PHONE................619 515-2400
Tom Murray, Owner
EMP: 348
SALES (corp-wide): 147.12MM Privately Held
Web: www.fhcsd.org
SIC: 8011 Clinic, operated by physicians
PA: Family Health Centers Of San Diego, Inc.
823 Gateway Center Way
619 515-2303

(P-15310)
FAMILY HLTH CTRS SAN DIEGO INC
Also Called: Family Health Center San Diego
8788 Jamacha Rd, Spring Valley (91977-4035)
PHONE................619 515-2555
EMP: 348
SQ FT: 10,970
SALES (corp-wide): 147.12MM Privately Held
Web: www.fhcsd.org
SIC: 8011 Clinic, operated by physicians
PA: Family Health Centers Of San Diego, Inc.
823 Gateway Center Way
619 515-2303

(P-15311)
FAMILY HLTH CTRS SAN DIEGO INC
Also Called: Beach Area Family Health Ctr
3705 Mission Blvd, San Diego (92109-7104)

PHONE................619 515-2444
Gracie Duram, Dir
EMP: 348
SALES (corp-wide): 147.12MM Privately Held
Web: www.fhcsd.org
SIC: 8011 Clinic, operated by physicians
PA: Family Health Centers Of San Diego, Inc.
823 Gateway Center Way
619 515-2303

(P-15312)
GARDEN GROVE ADVANCED IMAGING
1510 Cotner Ave, Los Angeles (90025-3303)
PHONE................310 445-2800
EMP: 128 EST: 2015
SALES (est): 2.53MM Publicly Held
Web: www.radnet.com
SIC: 8011 Radiologist
HQ: Radnet Management Iii, Inc.
1510 Cotner Ave
Los Angeles CA 90025
310 445-2800

(P-15313)
GARFIELD IMAGING CENTER INC
555 N Garfield Ave, Monterey Park (91754-1202)
PHONE................626 572-0912
Clark Gardner Md, Pr
EMP: 116 EST: 1980
SQ FT: 3,000
SALES (est): 825.69K
SALES (corp-wide): 359.96MM Privately Held
Web: www.garfieldimaging.com
SIC: 8011 Radiologist
HQ: Insight Health Services Corp.
5775 Wayzata Blvd 400
Minneapolis MN 55416

(P-15314)
GERALD J ALEXANDER MD
Also Called: Orthopaedic Specialty Inst
280 S Main St Ste 200, Orange (92868-3852)
PHONE................714 634-4567
Gerald Alexander, Prin
EMP: 71 EST: 2010
SALES (est): 16.34MM Privately Held
Web: www.geraldalexandermd.com
SIC: 8011 Orthopedic physician

(P-15315)
GLENWOOD SURGICAL CENTER LP
Also Called: Healthsuth Glnwood Srgical Ctr
8945 Magnolia Ave Ste 200, Riverside (92503-4436)
PHONE................951 689-2647
EMP: 99 EST: 1984
SQ FT: 7,180
SALES (est): 6.4MM
SALES (corp-wide): 4.8B Publicly Held
Web: www.glenwoodsurgerycenter.com
SIC: 8011 Surgeon
PA: Encompass Health Corporation
9001 Liberty Pkwy
205 967-7116

(P-15316)
GRACELIGHT COMMUNITY HEALTH
Also Called: Queenscare Fmly Clnics - Estsi
4618 Fountain Ave, Los Angeles (90029-1830)

PHONE................323 780-4510
Evelyn Moody, Mgr
EMP: 82
SALES (corp-wide): 12.14MM Privately Held
Web: www.queenscare.org
SIC: 8011 Clinic, operated by physicians
PA: Gracelight Community Health
950 Suth Grnd Ave Fl 2 Flr 2
323 669-4301

(P-15317)
GRACELIGHT COMMUNITY HEALTH
4618 Fountain Ave, Los Angeles (90029-1830)
PHONE................323 644-6180
Guillermo Diaz, Brnch Mgr
EMP: 83
SALES (corp-wide): 12.14MM Privately Held
Web: www.queenscare.org
SIC: 8011 Clinic, operated by physicians
PA: Gracelight Community Health
950 Suth Grnd Ave Fl 2 Flr 2
323 669-4301

(P-15318)
GRAYBILL MEDICAL GROUP INC (PA)
225 E 2nd Ave, Escondido (92025-4212)
PHONE................866 228-2236
Floyd Farley, CEO
David Borecky, *
Marvin V Beddoe, *
George A Pleitez, *
EMP: 180 EST: 1932
SALES (est): 20.56MM
SALES (corp-wide): 20.56MM Privately Held
Web: www.graybill.org
SIC: 8011 General and family practice, physician/surgeon

(P-15319)
GROVE DIAGNSTC IMAGING CTR INC
8805 Haven Ave Ste 120, Rancho Cucamonga (91730-5149)
PHONE................909 982-8638
Broc Larouche, Genl Mgr
EMP: 158
Web: www.radnet.com
SIC: 8011 Radiologist
HQ: Grove Diagnostic Imaging Center, Inc.
8283 Grove Ave Ste 101
Rancho Cucamonga CA 91730

(P-15320)
HEALTHSMART PACIFIC INC
Also Called: Health Smart Clinic
2683 Pacific Ave, Long Beach (90806-2610)
PHONE................562 595-1911
Mike Drobot, CEO
EMP: 294
SALES (corp-wide): 11.99MM Privately Held
Web: www.pacificclinics.org
SIC: 8011 Clinic, operated by physicians
PA: Healthsmart Pacific, Inc.
5150 E Pacific Cst Hwy # 200
562 595-1911

(P-15321)
HEMODIALYSIS INC
Also Called: Hunnington Dialysis Center
806 S Fair Oaks Ave, Pasadena (91105-2601)

PHONE................626 792-0548
Susan Burkhart, Mgr
EMP: 75
SALES (corp-wide): 2.82MM Privately Held
Web: www.hemodialysis-inc.com
SIC: 8011 8092 Hematologist; Kidney dialysis centers
PA: Hemodialysis, Inc.
710 W Wilson Ave
818 500-8736

(P-15322)
HENRY MAYO NEWHALL MEM HOSP
Also Called: Henry Mayo Diagnostic Imaging
23845 Mcbean Pkwy, Valencia (91355-2083)
PHONE................661 253-8400
Emily Phirman, Prin
EMP: 98
SALES (corp-wide): 454.17MM Privately Held
Web: www.henrymayo.com
SIC: 8011 Radiologist
PA: Henry Mayo Newhall Memorial Hospital
23845 Mcbean Pkwy
661 253-8000

(P-15323)
HERALD CHRISTIAN HEALTH CENTER (PA)
3401 Aero Jet Ave, El Monte (91731-2801)
PHONE................626 286-8700
David Lee, CEO
Emily Szeto, *
Carolin Eng, *
EMP: 80 EST: 2005
SALES (est): 15.14MM Privately Held
Web: www.hchcla.org
SIC: 8011 8021 Primary care medical clinic; Dental clinics and offices

(P-15324)
HIGH DSERT MED CORP A MED GROU (PA)
Also Called: Heritage Health Care
43839 15th St W, Lancaster (93534-4756)
P.O. Box 7007 (93539-7007)
PHONE................661 945-5984
Richard N Merkin, CEO
Charles M Lim, Dir
Rafael Gonzalez, Admn
Don V Parazo, Dir
Anthony J Dulgeroff, Dir
EMP: 120 EST: 1984
SQ FT: 25,000
SALES (est): 24.78MM
SALES (corp-wide): 24.78MM Privately Held
Web: www.hdmg.net
SIC: 8011 Clinic, operated by physicians

(P-15325)
HIV NEURAL BEHAVIORAL CENTER
150 W Washington St, La Jolla (92093-0001)
PHONE................619 543-5000
Igor Grant, Dir
EMP: 70
SALES (est): 497.49K Privately Held
SIC: 8011 Medical centers

(P-15326)
HOUSE EAR CLINIC INC (PA)
Also Called: House Ear
1245 Wilshire Blvd Ste 812, Los Angeles (90017-4808)

P.O. Box 52001 (85072-2001)
PHONE........................213 483-9930
Derald E Brackmann Md, *Pr*
John W House Md, *Treas*
Antonio De La Cruz Md, *Sec*
EMP: 88 EST: 1969
SALES (est): 8.96MM
SALES (corp-wide): 8.96MM **Privately Held**
Web: www.hifla.org
SIC: 8011 5999 Ears, nose, and throat specialist: physician/surgeon; Hearing aids

(P-15327)
HUNTINGTON MEDICAL FOUNDATION
10 Congress St Ste 208, Pasadena (91105-3027)
PHONE........................626 795-4210
Donna Ellis, *Mgr*
EMP: 106
Web: www.huntingtonmedical.com
SIC: 8011 Internal medicine, physician/surgeon
PA: The Huntington Medical Foundation 100 W California Blvd

(P-15328)
ILINGO2COM INC
800 Los Vallecitos Blvd Ste N, San Marcos (92069-1433)
P.O. Box 2197 (92085-2197)
PHONE........................800 311-8331
Robert Contreras, *Prin*
EMP: 70 EST: 2014
SALES (est): 3.99MM **Privately Held**
Web: www.ilingo2.com
SIC: 8011 Offices and clinics of medical doctors

(P-15329)
IMAGING HLTHCARE SPCALISTS LLC
6386 Alvarado Ct, San Diego (92120-4905)
PHONE........................619 229-2299
EMP: 130
Web: www.imaginghealthcare.com
SIC: 8011 Radiologist
PA: Imaging Healthcare Specialists, Llc 150 W Washington St

(P-15330)
INDIAN HEALTH COUNCIL INC (PA)
50100 Golsh Rd, Valley Center (92082-5338)
P.O. Box 406 (92061-0406)
PHONE........................760 749-1410
Orvin Hanson, *CEO*
EMP: 96 EST: 1970
SALES (est): 37.93MM **Privately Held**
Web: www.indianhealth.com
SIC: 8011 Clinic, operated by physicians

(P-15331)
INLAND EYE INST MED GROUP INC (PA)
1900 E Washington St, Colton (92324-4698)
P.O. Box 1427 (92324-0836)
PHONE........................909 825-3425
TOLL FREE: 800
Loren Denler Md, *Pr*
Wayne B Isaeff, *
Harold P Wallar, *
EMP: 70 EST: 1976
SQ FT: 12,500
SALES (est): 3MM
SALES (corp-wide): 3MM **Privately Held**

Web: www.inlandeye.com
SIC: 8011 Opthalmologist

(P-15332)
INMODE
17 Hughes, Irvine (92618-1902)
PHONE........................949 387-5711
EMP: 90 EST: 2021
SALES (est): 4.94MM **Privately Held**
Web: www.inmodemd.com
SIC: 8011 Dermatologist

(P-15333)
INSITE DIGESTIVE HEALTH CARE
21250 Hawthorne Blvd, Torrance (90503-5506)
PHONE........................626 817-2900
Alaa Abousaif, *Brnch Mgr*
EMP: 42
SALES (corp-wide): 22.36MM **Privately Held**
Web: www.mygenesishealth.com
SIC: 8011 2834 General and family practice, physician/surgeon; Chlorination tablets and kits (water purification)
PA: Insite Digestive Health Care 5525 Etiwanda Ave Ste 110 818 437-8105

(P-15334)
IPC HEALTHCARE INC (DH)
4605 Lankershim Blvd Ste 617, North Hollywood (91602-1856)
PHONE........................888 447-2362
Adam D Singer, *CEO*
R Jeffrey Taylor, *
Richard H Kline Iii, *CFO*
Kerry E Weiner, *CMO**
Richard G Russell, *CDO**
EMP: 173 EST: 1995
SALES (est): 107.2MM
SALES (corp-wide): 3.6B **Privately Held**
SIC: 8011 Physicians' office, including specialists
HQ: Team Health Holdings, Inc. 265 Brkview Cntre Way Ste Knoxville TN 37919 865 693-1000

(P-15335)
JOHN DIGIOVANNI DDS MS
1401 Avocado Ave, Newport Beach (92660-7720)
PHONE........................949 640-0202
Lloyd Rasner, *Brnch Mgr*
EMP: 84
Web: www.braceyourself.org
SIC: 8011 8021 Offices and clinics of medical doctors; Offices and clinics of dentists
PA: John Digiovanni Dds Ms 1166 Glenneyre St

(P-15336)
KAISER FOUNDATION HOSPITALS
Also Called: Kaiser Permanente
3401 S Harbor Blvd, Santa Ana (92704-7933)
PHONE........................714 830-6500
Kip Taylor, *Brnch Mgr*
EMP: 76
SALES (corp-wide): 70.8B **Privately Held**
Web: healthy.kaiserpermanente.org
SIC: 8011 Medical centers
HQ: Kaiser Foundation Hospitals Inc 1 Kaiser Plz Oakland CA 94612 510 271-6611

(P-15337)
KAISER FOUNDATION HOSPITALS
Also Called: La Palma Medical Offices
5 Centerpointe Dr, La Palma (90623-1050)
PHONE........................714 562-3420
Josefina Guzman-inouye, *Mgr*
EMP: 108
SALES (corp-wide): 70.8B **Privately Held**
Web: healthy.kaiserpermanente.org
SIC: 8011 Medical centers
HQ: Kaiser Foundation Hospitals Inc 1 Kaiser Plz Oakland CA 94612 510 271-6611

(P-15338)
KAISER FOUNDATION HOSPITALS
Also Called: Lakeview Medical Offices
411 N Lakeview Ave, Anaheim (92807-3028)
PHONE........................714 279-4675
Suzie Characky, *Mgr*
EMP: 79
SALES (corp-wide): 70.8B **Privately Held**
Web: healthy.kaiserpermanente.org
SIC: 8011 Medical centers
HQ: Kaiser Foundation Hospitals Inc 1 Kaiser Plz Oakland CA 94612 510 271-6611

(P-15339)
KAISER FOUNDATION HOSPITALS
Also Called: Aliso Viejo Medical Offices
24502 Pacific Park Dr, Aliso Viejo (92656-3033)
PHONE........................949 425-3150
Bruce Sogioka, *Brnch Mgr*
EMP: 72
SALES (corp-wide): 70.8B **Privately Held**
Web: www.kaisercenter.com
SIC: 8011 Medical centers
HQ: Kaiser Foundation Hospitals Inc 1 Kaiser Plz Oakland CA 94612 510 271-6611

(P-15340)
KAISER FOUNDATION HOSPITALS
Also Called: Kaiser Permanente
12100 Euclid St, Garden Grove (92840-3304)
PHONE........................714 741-3448
Betty Bohner, *Admn*
EMP: 126
SALES (corp-wide): 70.8B **Privately Held**
Web: www.kaisercenter.com
SIC: 8011 Medical centers
HQ: Kaiser Foundation Hospitals Inc 1 Kaiser Plz Oakland CA 94612 510 271-6611

(P-15341)
KAISER FOUNDATION HOSPITALS
Also Called: Kaiser Permanente
780 Shadowridge Dr, Vista (92083-7986)
PHONE........................619 528-5000
TOLL FREE: 800
Leslei Oliver, *Mgr*
EMP: 112
SALES (corp-wide): 70.8B **Privately Held**
Web: healthy.kaiserpermanente.org
SIC: 8011 Medical centers

HQ: Kaiser Foundation Hospitals Inc 1 Kaiser Plz Oakland CA 94612 510 271-6611

(P-15342)
KAISER FOUNDATION HOSPITALS
Also Called: El Cajon Medical Offices
250 Travelodge Dr, El Cajon (92020-4126)
PHONE........................619 528-5000
Carolyn Bonner, *Admn*
EMP: 87
SQ FT: 47,486
SALES (corp-wide): 70.8B **Privately Held**
Web: www.kaisercenter.com
SIC: 8011 Medical centers
HQ: Kaiser Foundation Hospitals Inc 1 Kaiser Plz Oakland CA 94612 510 271-6611

(P-15343)
KAISER FOUNDATION HOSPITALS
Also Called: Escondido Medical Offices
732 N Broadway, Escondido (92025-1897)
PHONE........................619 528-5000
Han Kim, *Mgr*
EMP: 119
SALES (corp-wide): 70.8B **Privately Held**
Web: healthy.kaiserpermanente.org
SIC: 8011 Medical centers
HQ: Kaiser Foundation Hospitals Inc 1 Kaiser Plz Oakland CA 94612 510 271-6611

(P-15344)
KAISER FOUNDATION HOSPITALS
Also Called: Kaiser Permanente
1301 California St, Redlands (92374-2910)
PHONE........................888 750-0036
Cindy Wong, *Dir*
EMP: 123
SALES (corp-wide): 70.8B **Privately Held**
Web: www.lluh.org
SIC: 8011 Medical centers
HQ: Kaiser Foundation Hospitals Inc 1 Kaiser Plz Oakland CA 94612 510 271-6611

(P-15345)
KAISER FOUNDATION HOSPITALS
Also Called: Kaiser Foundation Health Plan
14011 Park Ave, Victorville (92392-2413)
PHONE........................888 750-0036
EMP: 76
SALES (corp-wide): 70.8B **Privately Held**
Web: www.kaisercenter.com
SIC: 8011 Medical centers
HQ: Kaiser Foundation Hospitals Inc 1 Kaiser Plz Oakland CA 94612 510 271-6611

(P-15346)
KAISER FOUNDATION HOSPITALS
Also Called: Ontario Vineyard Medical Offs
2295 S Vineyard Ave, Ontario (91761-7925)
PHONE........................909 724-5000
EMP: 138
SALES (corp-wide): 70.8B **Privately Held**
Web: www.kaisercenter.com

SIC: 8011 Medical centers
HQ: Kaiser Foundation Hospitals Inc
1 Kaiser Plz
Oakland CA 94612
510 271-6611

(P-15347)
KAISER FOUNDATION HOSPITALS
Also Called: Kaiser Permanente
9961 Sierra Ave, Fontana (92335-6794)
PHONE...............................909 427-5000
William Meyer, *Prin*
EMP: 1191
SALES (corp-wide): 70.8B **Privately Held**
Web: healthy.kaiserpermanente.org
SIC: 8011 Medical centers
HQ: Kaiser Foundation Hospitals Inc
1 Kaiser Plz
Oakland CA 94612
510 271-6611

(P-15348)
KAISER FOUNDATION HOSPITALS
10800 Magnolia Ave, Riverside
(92505-3000)
PHONE...............................951 353-3790
Laura Estrada, *Brnch Mgr*
EMP: 101
SALES (corp-wide): 70.8B **Privately Held**
Web: healthy.kaiserpermanente.org
SIC: 8011 Offices and clinics of medical
doctors
HQ: Kaiser Foundation Hospitals Inc
1 Kaiser Plz
Oakland CA 94612
510 271-6611

(P-15349)
KAISER FOUNDATION HOSPITALS
Also Called: Riverside Medical Center
10800 Magnolia Ave, Riverside
(92505-3000)
PHONE...............................951 353-2000
Vita Willett, *Dir*
EMP: 1773
SALES (corp-wide): 70.8B **Privately Held**
Web: www.kp.org
SIC: 8011 8062 Medical centers; General
medical and surgical hospitals
HQ: Kaiser Foundation Hospitals Inc
1 Kaiser Plz
Oakland CA 94612
510 271-6611

(P-15350)
KAISER FOUNDATION HOSPITALS
Also Called: Kaiser Prmnnte Mreno Vly Med C
27300 Iris Ave, Moreno Valley
(92555-4802)
PHONE...............................951 243-0811
Tom Mc Ciltock, *Mgr*
EMP: 1830
SALES (corp-wide): 70.8B **Privately Held**
Web: healthy.kaiserpermanente.org
SIC: 8011 Medical centers
HQ: Kaiser Foundation Hospitals Inc
1 Kaiser Plz
Oakland CA 94612
510 271-6611

(P-15351)
KAISER FOUNDATION HOSPITALS
13652 Cantara St, Panorama City
(91402-5497)

PHONE...............................818 375-4023
Andrea D Mason O T R, *Brnch Mgr*
EMP: 195
SALES (corp-wide): 70.8B **Privately Held**
Web: healthy.kaiserpermanente.org
SIC: 8011 Internal medicine practitioners
HQ: Kaiser Foundation Hospitals Inc
1 Kaiser Plz
Oakland CA 94612
510 271-6611

(P-15352)
KAISER FOUNDATION HOSPITALS
6041 Cadillac Ave, Los Angeles
(90034-1700)
PHONE...............................323 857-2000
Kenneth Nudelman, *Brnch Mgr*
EMP: 160
SALES (corp-wide): 70.8B **Privately Held**
Web: www.kaisercenter.com
SIC: 8011 Physicians' office, including
specialists
HQ: Kaiser Foundation Hospitals Inc
1 Kaiser Plz
Oakland CA 94612
510 271-6611

(P-15353)
KAISER FOUNDATION HOSPITALS
Also Called: Kaiser Prmnnte W Los Angles
Me
6041 Cadillac Ave, Los Angeles
(90034-1700)
PHONE...............................323 857-2000
Howard Fullman, *Dir*
EMP: 1412
SALES (corp-wide): 70.8B **Privately Held**
Web: www.kaisercenter.com
SIC: 8011 Medical centers
HQ: Kaiser Foundation Hospitals Inc
1 Kaiser Plz
Oakland CA 94612
510 271-6611

(P-15354)
KAISER FOUNDATION HOSPITALS
Also Called: Kaiser Permanente
13651 Willard St, Panorama City (91402)
PHONE...............................818 375-2000
Dev Mahadevan, *Prin*
EMP: 2740
SALES (corp-wide): 70.8B **Privately Held**
Web: thrive.kaiserpermanente.org
SIC: 8011 Medical centers
HQ: Kaiser Foundation Hospitals Inc
1 Kaiser Plz
Oakland CA 94612
510 271-6611

(P-15355)
KAISER FOUNDATION HOSPITALS
Also Called: Orchard Medical Offices
9449 Imperial Hwy, Downey (90242-2814)
PHONE...............................800 823-4040
Leon Randolph, *Pr*
EMP: 79
SALES (corp-wide): 70.8B **Privately Held**
Web: healthy.kaiserpermanente.org
SIC: 8011 Medical centers
HQ: Kaiser Foundation Hospitals Inc
1 Kaiser Plz
Oakland CA 94612
510 271-6611

(P-15356)
KAISER FOUNDATION HOSPITALS
Also Called: Stockdale Medical Offices
3501 Stockdale Hwy, Bakersfield
(93309-2150)
PHONE...............................661 398-5011
Ky P Ho, *Prin*
EMP: 101
SALES (corp-wide): 70.8B **Privately Held**
Web: healthy.kaiserpermanente.org
SIC: 8011 Medical centers
HQ: Kaiser Foundation Hospitals Inc
1 Kaiser Plz
Oakland CA 94612
510 271-6611

(P-15357)
KAISER FOUNDATION HOSPITALS
Also Called: Kaiser Permanente
5055 California Ave Ste 110, Bakersfield
(93309-0700)
P.O. Box 12099 (93389-2099)
PHONE...............................661 334-2020
EMP: 90
SALES (corp-wide): 70.8B **Privately Held**
Web: www.kaisercenter.com
SIC: 8011 Medical centers
HQ: Kaiser Foundation Hospitals Inc
1 Kaiser Plz
Oakland CA 94612
510 271-6611

(P-15358)
KAISER FOUNDATION HOSPITALS
1011 Baldwin Park Blvd, Baldwin Park
(91706-5806)
PHONE...............................310 922-8916
Abdalla Mallouk, *Brnch Mgr*
EMP: 149
SALES (corp-wide): 70.8B **Privately Held**
Web: healthy.kaiserpermanente.org
SIC: 8011 Physicians' office, including
specialists
HQ: Kaiser Foundation Hospitals Inc
1 Kaiser Plz
Oakland CA 94612
510 271-6611

(P-15359)
KAISER FOUNDATION HOSPITALS
9521 Dalen St, Downey (90242-4894)
PHONE...............................817 372-8201
EMP: 112
SALES (corp-wide): 70.8B **Privately Held**
Web: healthy.kaiserpermanente.org
SIC: 8011 Offices and clinics of medical
doctors
HQ: Kaiser Foundation Hospitals Inc
1 Kaiser Plz
Oakland CA 94612
510 271-6611

(P-15360)
KAISER FOUNDATION HOSPITALS
Also Called: Kaiser Permanente
12001 W Washington Blvd, Los Angeles
(90066-5801)
PHONE...............................310 915-5000
James Corb, *Ex Dir*
EMP: 87
SQ FT: 46,281
SALES (corp-wide): 70.8B **Privately Held**
Web: www.kaisercenter.com
SIC: 8011 Medical centers

HQ: Kaiser Foundation Hospitals Inc
1 Kaiser Plz
Oakland CA 94612
510 271-6611

(P-15361)
KAISER FOUNDATION HOSPITALS
Also Called: Kaiser Permanente
25825 Vermont Ave, Harbor City
(90710-3518)
PHONE...............................310 325-5111
Mary Ann Barnes, *Brnch Mgr*
EMP: 975
SALES (corp-wide): 70.8B **Privately Held**
Web: www.kaisercenter.com
SIC: 8011 Medical centers
HQ: Kaiser Foundation Hospitals Inc
1 Kaiser Plz
Oakland CA 94612
510 271-6611

(P-15362)
KAISER FOUNDATION HOSPITALS
1550 N Edgemont St, Los Angeles
(90027-5210)
PHONE...............................323 783-7955
EMP: 112
SALES (corp-wide): 70.8B **Privately Held**
Web: healthy.kaiserpermanente.org
SIC: 8011 Offices and clinics of medical
doctors
HQ: Kaiser Foundation Hospitals Inc
1 Kaiser Plz
Oakland CA 94612
510 271-6611

(P-15363)
KAISER FOUNDATION HOSPITALS
Also Called: Glendale Medical Offices
444 W Glenoaks Blvd, Glendale
(91202-2917)
PHONE...............................818 552-3000
Avetis Tashyan, *Brnch Mgr*
EMP: 123
SALES (corp-wide): 70.8B **Privately Held**
Web: healthy.kaiserpermanente.org
SIC: 8011 Medical centers
HQ: Kaiser Foundation Hospitals Inc
1 Kaiser Plz
Oakland CA 94612
510 271-6611

(P-15364)
KAISER FOUNDATION HOSPITALS
Also Called: Kaiser Prmnnte Psadena Med Off
3280 E Foothill Blvd, Pasadena
(91107-3103)
P.O. Box 7005 (91109-7005)
PHONE...............................626 440-5639
EMP: 177
SALES (corp-wide): 70.8B **Privately Held**
Web: www.kaisercenter.com
SIC: 8011 Medical centers
HQ: Kaiser Foundation Hospitals Inc
1 Kaiser Plz
Oakland CA 94612
510 271-6611

(P-15365)
KAISER FOUNDATION HOSPITALS
5300 Mcconnell Ave, Los Angeles
(90066-7026)
PHONE...............................833 574-2273
EMP: 72

SALES (corp-wide): 70.8B **Privately Held**
Web: www.kaiserpermanente.org
SIC: **8011** Medical centers
HQ: Kaiser Foundation Hospitals Inc
　　1 Kaiser Plz
　　Oakland CA 94612
　　510 271-6611

(P-15366)
KAISER FOUNDATION HOSPITALS
Also Called: Kaiser Permanente
1515 N Vermont Ave Fl 3, Los Angeles
(90027-5337)
PHONE...............323 783-8306
Cecilia Militante, *Prin*
EMP: 283
SALES (corp-wide): 70.8B **Privately Held**
Web: www.kaisercenter.com
SIC: **8011** Dermatologist
HQ: Kaiser Foundation Hospitals Inc
　　1 Kaiser Plz
　　Oakland CA 94612
　　510 271-6611

(P-15367)
KAISER FOUNDATION HOSPITALS
Also Called: Kaiser Permanente
27107 Tourney Rd, Santa Clarita
(91355-1860)
PHONE...............661 222-2323
Pat Kenney, *Prin*
EMP: 126
SQ FT: 70,835
SALES (corp-wide): 70.8B **Privately Held**
Web: healthy.kaiserpermanente.org
SIC: **8011** Medical centers
HQ: Kaiser Foundation Hospitals Inc
　　1 Kaiser Plz
　　Oakland CA 94612
　　510 271-6611

(P-15368)
KAISER FOUNDATION HOSPITALS
Also Called: Kaiser Permanente
110 N La Brea Ave, Inglewood
(90301-1708)
PHONE...............310 419-3303
Victor Ahaiwe, *Pr*
EMP: 87
SALES (corp-wide): 70.8B **Privately Held**
Web: healthy.kaiserpermanente.org
SIC: **8011** Medical centers
HQ: Kaiser Foundation Hospitals Inc
　　1 Kaiser Plz
　　Oakland CA 94612
　　510 271-6611

(P-15369)
KAISER PRMNNTE SCHL ANESTHESIA
100 S Los Robles Ste 501, Pasadena
(91101-2453)
PHONE...............626 564-3016
Kaiser Permanente, *Owner*
EMP: 96 EST: 2009
SALES (est): 20.09MM **Privately Held**
Web: www.kpsan.org
SIC: **8011** Anesthesiologist

(P-15370)
KERLAN-JOBE ORTHOPEDIC CLINIC (PA)
6801 Park Ter Ste 500, Los Angeles
(90045-9212)
PHONE...............310 665-7200
Ralph A Gambardella, *CEO*

Stephen Lombardo, *
EMP: 78 EST: 1973
SQ FT: 37,000
SALES (est): 13.81MM
SALES (corp-wide): 13.81MM **Privately Held**
Web: www.kerlanjobe.org
SIC: **8011** Orthopedic physician

(P-15371)
KERN HEALTH SYSTEMS INC
Also Called: Kern Family Helathcare
2900 Buck Owens Blvd, Bakersfield
(93308-6316)
P.O. Box 85000 (93380)
PHONE...............661 664-5000
Carol L Sorrell, *CEO*
EMP: 98 EST: 1995
SQ FT: 16,000
SALES (est): 30.54MM **Privately Held**
Web: www.kernfamilyhealthcare.com
SIC: **8011** Clinic, operated by physicians

(P-15372)
KERN RDLGY IMAGING SYSTEMS INC
4100 Truxtun Ave Ste 306, Bakersfield
(93309-0657)
PHONE...............661 322-9958
John M Gundzik, *Prin*
EMP: 70
SALES (corp-wide): 27.2MM **Privately Held**
Web: www.radnet.com
SIC: **8011** Radiologist
PA: Kern Radiology Imaging Systems, Inc.
　　2301 Bahamas Dr
　　661 326-9600

(P-15373)
LA JOLLA CSMTC SRGERY CNTRE IN
9850 Genesee Ave Ste 130, La Jolla
(92037-1206)
PHONE...............858 452-1981
R Merrel Olesen, *Prin*
EMP: 72 EST: 1997
SALES (est): 3.59MM **Privately Held**
Web: www.ljcsc.com
SIC: **8011** Plastic surgeon

(P-15374)
LA MAESTRA FAMILY CLINIC INC (PA)
Also Called: LA MAESTRA COMMUNITY HEALTH CE
4060 Fairmount Ave, San Diego
(92105-1608)
PHONE...............619 584-1612
Zara Marselian, *CEO*
Samuel Mirelles, *
Carlos Hanessian, *
Alex Pantoja, *
Alejandrina Areizaga, *
EMP: 197 EST: 1991
SQ FT: 5,000
SALES (est): 80.71MM **Privately Held**
Web: www.lamaestra.org
SIC: **8011** Clinic, operated by physicians

(P-15375)
LA PEER SURGERY CENTER LLC
Also Called: La Peer Health Systems
8920 Wilshire Blvd Ste 101, Beverly Hills
(90211-2001)
PHONE...............310 360-9119
Doctor Siamak Tabib, *Managing Member*
EMP: 78 EST: 2000

SQ FT: 2,300
SALES (est): 6.61MM
SALES (corp-wide): 2.74B **Publicly Held**
Web: www.lapeerhealth.com
SIC: **8011** Surgeon
PA: Surgery Partners, Inc.
　　340 Sven Sprng Way Ste 60
　　615 234-5900

(P-15376)
LAC & USC MEDICAL CENTER
2051 Marengo St, Los Angeles
(90033-1352)
P.O. Box 861749 (90086-1749)
PHONE...............323 409-2345
Marisa Danbee, *Prin*
EMP: 121 EST: 2009
SALES (est): 22.47MM **Privately Held**
Web: dhs.lacounty.gov
SIC: **8011** Primary care medical clinic

(P-15377)
LANCASTER CRDLGY MED GROUP INC (PA)
Also Called: Physicians Referral Service
43847 Heaton Ave Ste B, Lancaster
(93534-4922)
PHONE...............661 726-3058
Shun K Sunder Md, *Pr*
E Ekong Md, *VP*
Kanagaratham Sivalingam Md, *Sec*
EMP: 80 EST: 1976
SQ FT: 30,000
SALES (est): 4.5MM
SALES (corp-wide): 4.5MM **Privately Held**
Web: www.firstvalleymedicalgroup.com
SIC: **8011** Cardiologist and cardio-vascular specialist

(P-15378)
LIFEMD INC
Also Called: Lifemd
5882 Bolsa Ave Ste 100, Huntington Beach
(92649-5702)
PHONE...............800 852-1575
EMP: 70
SALES (corp-wide): 152.55MM **Publicly Held**
Web: www.lifemd.com
SIC: **8011** Offices and clinics of medical doctors
PA: Lifemd, Inc.
　　236 5th Ave Ste 400
　　866 351-5907

(P-15379)
LOMA LINDA UNIVERSITY
Also Called: Loma Lnda Univ Ansthsology Med
11234 Anderson St Ste 2532, Loma Linda
(92354-2871)
PHONE...............909 558-4475
Richard H Hart, *Pr*
EMP: 224
SALES (corp-wide): 379.88MM **Privately Held**
Web: www.llu.edu
SIC: **8011** Anesthesiologist
PA: Loma Linda University
　　11060 Andrson St Bldg Mga
　　909 558-4540

(P-15380)
LOMA LINDA UNIVERSITY MED CTR
11234 Anderson St, Loma Linda
(92354-2871)
PHONE...............877 558-6248
Trevor G Wright, *CEO*
EMP: 158 EST: 1967

SALES (est): 10.3MM **Privately Held**
Web: www.lluh.org
SIC: **8011** Offices and clinics of medical doctors
PA: Loma Linda University Medical
　　11234 Anderson St

(P-15381)
LOMA LNDA UNIV MED CTR - MRRET
28062 Baxter Rd, Murrieta (92563-1401)
PHONE...............951 672-1010
Peter Baker, *CEO*
EMP: 440 EST: 2018
SALES (est): 316.88MM **Privately Held**
Web: www.llumcmurrieta.org
SIC: **8011** Medical centers

(P-15382)
LOS ANGELES FREE CLINIC
5205 Melrose Ave, Los Angeles
(90038-3144)
PHONE...............323 653-1990
EMP: 110
SALES (corp-wide): 52.77MM **Privately Held**
Web: www.sabancommunityclinic.org
SIC: **8011** Clinic, operated by physicians
PA: The Los Angeles Free Clinic
　　8405 Beverly Blvd
　　323 653-8622

(P-15383)
LOS ANGELES FREE CLINIC (PA)
Also Called: SABAN COMMUNITY CLINIC
8405 Beverly Blvd, Los Angeles
(90048-3476)
PHONE...............323 653-8622
Jeffrey Bujer, *CEO*
EMP: 79 EST: 1967
SQ FT: 26,615
SALES (est): 52.77MM
SALES (corp-wide): 52.77MM **Privately Held**
Web: www.sabancommunityclinic.org
SIC: **8011** Clinic, operated by physicians

(P-15384)
LOS ROBLES REGIONAL MED CTR
150 Via Merida, Westlake Village
(91362-3816)
PHONE...............805 370-4531
Simin Shandiz, *Prin*
EMP: 261
Web: www.losrobleshospital.com
SIC: **8011** Medical centers
HQ: Los Robles Regional Medical Center
　　215 W Janss Rd
　　Thousand Oaks CA 91360

(P-15385)
LOS ROBLES REGIONAL MED CTR
Also Called: Neuroscience Gamma Knife Ctr
2200 Lynn Rd, Thousand Oaks
(91360-2071)
PHONE...............805 494-0880
Cherrie De La La Cruz, *Prin*
EMP: 261
Web: www.californiagammaknife.com
SIC: **8011** Neurologist
HQ: Los Robles Regional Medical Center
　　215 W Janss Rd
　　Thousand Oaks CA 91360

(P-15386)
MAINSTAY MEDICAL LIMITED
2159 India St Ste 200, San Diego
(92101-1766)

PHONE..............619 261-9144
Jason Hannon, *CEO*
EMP: 92 **EST:** 2008
SALES (est): 1.05MM **Privately Held**
Web: www.mainstaymedical.com
SIC: 8011 Primary care medical clinic

(P-15387)
MEMORIAL ORTHPDIC SRGCAL GROUP
Also Called: Southern Cal Ctr For Spt Mdcin
2760 Atlantic Ave, Long Beach
(90806-2755)
PHONE..............562 424-6666
Peter R Kurzweil, *CEO*
Douglas W Jackson Md, *Pr*
Curtis W Spencer Iii Md, *VP*
David Morrison Md, *Mgr*
David S Morrison Md, *Sec*
▲ **EMP:** 70 **EST:** 1977
SQ FT: 12,000
SALES (est): 9.91MM **Privately Held**
Web: www.memorialorthopaedic.com
SIC: 8011 Orthopedic physician

(P-15388)
MEMORLCARE SRGCAL CTR AT ORNGE
Also Called: Orange Coast Ctr For Surgl Cr
18111 Brookhurst St Ste 3200, Fountain
Valley (92708-6728)
PHONE..............714 369-1100
Dana Pratt, *CEO*
EMP: 119 **EST:** 2011
SALES (est): 9.63MM
SALES (corp-wide): 371.62B **Publicly Held**
Web: www.orangecoastcenter.com
SIC: 8011 Surgeon
PA: Unitedhealth Group Incorporated
9900 Bren Rd E
800 328-5979

(P-15389)
MING TSUANG DR
Also Called: Ucsd
9500 Gillman Dr Mc 0603, La Jolla
(92093-5004)
PHONE..............858 822-2464
Doctor Ming Tsuang, *Owner*
▲ **EMP:** 89 **EST:** 2004
SALES (est): 17.55MM **Privately Held**
SIC: 8011 8299 Psychiatrist; Educational
services

(P-15390)
MISSION INTERNAL MED GROUP INC
Also Called: Arthur Loussararian MD
26800 Crown Valley Pkwy Ste 103, Mission
Viejo (92691-6389)
PHONE..............949 364-3570
Arthur Loussararian, *Prin*
EMP: 90
SALES (corp-wide): 19.19MM **Privately Held**
SIC: 8011 Primary care medical clinic
PA: Mission Internal Medical Group, Inc.
26732 Crown Valley Pkwy # 351
949 282-1600

(P-15391)
MISSION INTERNAL MED GROUP INC
Also Called: West Coast Physical Therapy
27882 Forbes Rd Ste 110, Laguna Niguel
(92677-1267)
PHONE..............949 364-3605
Joan Shrum-brown, *Prin*

EMP: 91
SALES (corp-wide): 19.19MM **Privately Held**
SIC: 8011 8049 Cardiologist and cardio-
vascular specialist; Physical therapist
PA: Mission Internal Medical Group, Inc.
26732 Crown Valley Pkwy # 351
949 282-1600

(P-15392)
MOLINA HEALTHCARE INC (PA)
Also Called: Molina Healthcare
200 Oceangate Ste 100, Long Beach
(90802-4317)
P.O. Box 22813 (90801-5813)
PHONE..............562 435-3666
Joseph M Zubretsky, *Pr*
Dale B Wolf, *Non-Executive Chairman of
the Board*
Ronna E Romney, *
Mark L Keim, *CFO*
James E Woys, *COO*
EMP: 2800 **EST:** 1980
SALES (est): 34.07B
SALES (corp-wide): 34.07B **Publicly Held**
Web: www.molinahealthcare.com
SIC: 8011 6324 Health maintenance
organization; Hospital and medical service
plans

(P-15393)
MOLINA HEALTHCARE CALIFORNIA
200 Oceangate Ste 100, Long Beach
(90802-4317)
PHONE..............800 526-8196
EMP: 620 **EST:** 2016
SALES (est): 742.78K
SALES (corp-wide): 34.07B **Publicly Held**
Web: www.molinahealthcare.com
SIC: 8011 Offices and clinics of medical
doctors
PA: Molina Healthcare, Inc.
200 Oceangate Ste 100
562 435-3666

(P-15394)
MOLINA HEALTHCARE NEW YORK INC
200 Oceangate Ste 100, Long Beach
(90802-4317)
PHONE..............888 562-5442
Richard Chambers, *Pr*
EMP: 98 **EST:** 2019
SALES (est): 545.34K
SALES (corp-wide): 34.07B **Publicly Held**
SIC: 8011 Health maintenance organization
PA: Molina Healthcare, Inc.
200 Oceangate Ste 100
562 435-3666

(P-15395)
MOLINA PATHWAYS LLC
200 Oceangate Ste 100, Long Beach
(90802-4317)
PHONE..............562 491-5773
Craig Bass, *CEO*
EMP: 294 **EST:** 2011
SALES (est): 751.89K
SALES (corp-wide): 34.07B **Publicly Held**
SIC: 8011 Health maintenance organization
PA: Molina Healthcare, Inc.
200 Oceangate Ste 100
562 435-3666

(P-15396)
MONARCH HEALTHCARE A MEDICAL (HQ)
11 Technology Dr, Irvine (92618-2302)

PHONE..............949 923-3200
Bartley Asner, *CEO*
Jay J Cohen Md, *VP*
Steven Rudy Md, *VP*
James Selevan Md, *Mgr*
Marvin Gordon Md, *CFO*
EMP: 94 **EST:** 1986
SQ FT: 75,000
SALES (est): 26.57MM
SALES (corp-wide): 371.62B **Publicly Held**
Web: www.optum.com
SIC: 8011 Group health association
PA: Unitedhealth Group Incorporated
9900 Bren Rd E
800 328-5979

(P-15397)
MONARCH HEALTHCARE A MEDICAL
675 Camino De Los Mares Ste 300, San
Clemente (92673-2836)
PHONE..............949 489-1960
Adam Crawford D.o.s., *Brnch Mgr*
EMP: 161
SALES (corp-wide): 371.62B **Publicly Held**
Web: www.optum.com
SIC: 8011 Group health association
HQ: Monarch Healthcare, A Medical Group,
Inc.
11 Technology Dr
Irvine CA 92618

(P-15398)
N S C CHANNEL ISLANDS INC
Also Called: HealthSouth
2300 Wankel Way, Oxnard (93030-2665)
PHONE..............805 485-1908
Susan Clark, *Admn*
EMP: 476 **EST:** 1995
SQ FT: 14,000
SALES (est): 4.6MM
SALES (corp-wide): 4.8B **Publicly Held**
Web:
www.channelislandssurgicenter.com
SIC: 8011 Surgeon
HQ: Healthsouth Rehabilitation Hospital Of
Cypress, Llc
9001 Liberty Pkwy
Birmingham AL 35242

(P-15399)
NEIGHBORHOOD HEALTHCARE (PA)
Also Called: NEIGHBORHOOD
HEALTHCARE- RIVER
215 S Hickory St, Escondido (92025-4359)
PHONE..............833 867-4642
Rakesh Patel, *CEO*
Tracy Roam, *
Johnny Watson, *
Richard Marino, *
Lisa Daigle, *
EMP: 100 **EST:** 1971
SQ FT: 17,000
SALES (est): 218.21MM
SALES (corp-wide): 218.21MM **Privately Held**
Web: www.nhcare.org
SIC: 8011 Clinic, operated by physicians

(P-15400)
NEIGHBORHOOD HEALTHCARE
460 N Elm St, Escondido (92025-3002)
PHONE..............760 737-2000
Gail Thomsky, *Mgr*
EMP: 268
SQ FT: 9,288
SALES (corp-wide): 218.21MM **Privately Held**

Web: www.nhcare.org
SIC: 8011 Clinic, operated by physicians
PA: Neighborhood Healthcare
215 S Hickory St
833 867-4642

(P-15401)
NEIGHBORHOOD HEALTHCARE
26926 Cherry Hills Blvd Ste B, Menifee
(92586-2500)
PHONE..............951 216-2200
EMP: 110
SQ FT: 4,871
SALES (corp-wide): 218.21MM **Privately Held**
Web: www.nhcare.org
SIC: 8011 Clinic, operated by physicians
PA: Neighborhood Healthcare
215 S Hickory St
833 867-4642

(P-15402)
NEIGHBORHOOD HEALTHCARE
855 E Madison Ave, El Cajon (92020-3819)
PHONE..............619 440-2751
Alex Nunez, *Dir Opers*
EMP: 79
SQ FT: 9,198
SALES (corp-wide): 218.21MM **Privately Held**
Web: www.nhcare.org
SIC: 8011 Clinic, operated by physicians
PA: Neighborhood Healthcare
215 S Hickory St
833 867-4642

(P-15403)
NEIGHBORHOOD HEALTHCARE
28477 Lizard Rocks Rd Ste 200, Valley
Center (92082-6220)
PHONE..............760 742-9919
Nicholas Jauregui Md, *Prin*
EMP: 89
SALES (corp-wide): 218.21MM **Privately Held**
Web: www.nhcare.org
SIC: 8011 Clinic, operated by physicians
PA: Neighborhood Healthcare
215 S Hickory St
833 867-4642

(P-15404)
NEWPORT BEACH SURGERY CTR LLC
361 Hospital Rd Ste 124, Newport Beach
(92663-3521)
PHONE..............949 631-0988
Perter Broekelschen, *Managing Member*
Harvey Heinrichs, *Managing Member*
Bruce Albert, *
Robert Anderson, *
EMP: 120 **EST:** 1992
SQ FT: 10,000
SALES (est): 15.69MM **Privately Held**
Web:
www.newportbeachsurgerycenter.com
SIC: 8011 Surgeon

(P-15405)
NORTH CAST SRGERY CTR LTD A CA
3903 Waring Rd, Oceanside (92056-4405)
PHONE..............760 940-0997
Doctor Bruce Hochman, *Pt*
Doctor Bruce Hochman, *Mng Pt*
EMP: 79 **EST:** 1985
SQ FT: 11,000
SALES (est): 4.5MM
SALES (corp-wide): 371.62B **Publicly Held**

Web: www.northcoastsurgerycenter.com
SIC: 8011 Surgeon
PA: Unitedhealth Group Incorporated
9900 Bren Rd E
800 328-5979

(P-15406)
NORTH COUNTY HEALTH PRJ INC
605 Crouch St Bldg C, Oceanside (92054-4415)
PHONE.............................760 757-4566
Alicia Santos, *Mgr*
EMP: 74
SALES (corp-wide): 97.36MM **Privately Held**
Web: www.northcoastpatrol.com
SIC: 8011 8093 Clinic, operated by physicians; Family planning and birth control clinics
PA: North County Health Project Incorporated
150 Valpreda Rd
760 736-6755

(P-15407)
NORTH COUNTY HEALTH PRJ INC
1130 2nd St, Encinitas (92024-5008)
PHONE.............................760 736-6767
Patricia Cheu, *Prin*
EMP: 127
SQ FT: 7,513
SALES (corp-wide): 97.36MM **Privately Held**
Web: www.truecare.org
SIC: 8011 Clinic, operated by physicians
PA: North County Health Project Incorporated
150 Valpreda Rd
760 736-6755

(P-15408)
NORTH COUNTY HEALTH PRJ INC (PA)
Also Called: North County Services
150 Valpreda Rd Frnt, San Marcos (92069-2944)
PHONE.............................760 736-6755
Irma Cota, *CEO*
Kathy Martinez, *
EMP: 221 **EST:** 1973
SQ FT: 69,880
SALES (est): 97.36MM
SALES (corp-wide): 97.36MM **Privately Held**
Web: www.northcoastpatrol.com
SIC: 8011 Clinic, operated by physicians

(P-15409)
OAK GROVE INST FOUNDATION INC (PA)
Also Called: OAK GROVE CENTER
24275 Jefferson Ave, Murrieta (92562-7285)
PHONE.............................951 677-5599
Tamara L Wilson, *CEO*
Barry Soper, *
Fe Santiago, *
EMP: 148 **EST:** 1986
SQ FT: 39,000
SALES (est): 24.45MM **Privately Held**
Web: www.oakgrovecenter.org
SIC: 8011 8211 8361 Psychiatric clinic; Specialty education; Residential care

(P-15410)
OLIVE VIEW-UCLA MEDICAL CENTER (PA)
Also Called: Valley Care Olive View Med Ctr
14445 Olive View Dr, Sylmar (91342-1438)
PHONE.............................818 364-1555
Carolyn Rhee, *CEO*
EMP: 99 **EST:** 2001
SALES (est): 48.91MM
SALES (corp-wide): 48.91MM **Privately Held**
Web: www.uclaoliveview.org
SIC: 8011 Medical centers

(P-15411)
OMNI FAMILY HEALTH (PA)
Also Called: Community Health Center
4900 California Ave Ste 400b, Bakersfield (93309-7081)
P.O. Box 1060 (93263-1060)
PHONE.............................661 459-1900
Francisco L Castillon, *CEO*
Novira Irawan, *
Petrus Tjandra, *
Aurora Cooper, *
EMP: 80 **EST:** 1978
SQ FT: 14,000
SALES (est): 139.05MM
SALES (corp-wide): 139.05MM **Privately Held**
Web: www.omnifamilyhealth.org
SIC: 8011 Clinic, operated by physicians

(P-15412)
ONCOLOGY INST CA A PROF CORP (PA)
Also Called: Women's Cancer Care
18000 Studebaker Rd Ste 800, Cerritos (90703-2671)
PHONE.............................323 278-4400
Hilda Agajanian, *Pr*
EMP: 670 **EST:** 2007
SALES (est): 20.4MM **Privately Held**
Web: www.theoncologyinstitute.com
SIC: 8011 Oncologist

(P-15413)
ONRAD INC
Also Called: Onrad Medical Group
1770 Iowa Ave Ste 280, Riverside (92507-7401)
PHONE.............................800 848-5876
David Engert, *Pr*
Samuel Salen, *
Scott Castle, *CFO*
EMP: 79 **EST:** 2008
SQ FT: 1,500
SALES (est): 5.36MM **Privately Held**
Web: www.onradinc.com
SIC: 8011 Radiologist

(P-15414)
OPERATION SAMAHAN INC
Also Called: Camino Ruiz Suite 235
10737 Camino Ruiz Ste 235138, San Diego (92126-2359)
PHONE.............................619 477-4451
Dirk Virbel, *CEO*
EMP: 128
SALES (corp-wide): 15.49MM **Privately Held**
Web: www.operationsamahan.org
SIC: 8011 8021 Clinic, operated by physicians; Offices and clinics of dentists
PA: Operation Samahan, Inc.
1428 Highland Ave
619 477-4451

(P-15415)
OPTUMCARE MANAGEMENT LLC (HQ)
Also Called: Healthcare Partners Med Group
2175 Park Pl, El Segundo (90245-4705)

PHONE.............................310 354-4200
Robert J Margolis, *CEO*
Matthew Mazdyasni, *
Zan F Calhoun, *
EMP: 600 **EST:** 1994
SQ FT: 38,000
SALES (est): 128.28MM
SALES (corp-wide): 371.62B **Publicly Held**
SIC: 8011 Group health association
PA: Unitedhealth Group Incorporated
9900 Bren Rd E
800 328-5979

(P-15416)
OPTUMCARE MANAGEMENT LLC
502 Torrance Blvd, Redondo Beach (90277-3413)
PHONE.............................310 316-0811
Mark Moser, *Brnch Mgr*
EMP: 79
SQ FT: 23,000
SALES (corp-wide): 371.62B **Publicly Held**
Web: www.optum.com
SIC: 8011 General and family practice, physician/surgeon
HQ: Optumcare Management, Llc
2175 Park Pl
El Segundo CA 90245

(P-15417)
OPTUMCARE MANAGEMENT LLC
Harriman Jones Medical
2600 Redondo Ave Ste 405, Long Beach (90806-2330)
PHONE.............................562 988-7000
Jill R Cortese, *Prin*
EMP: 127
SALES (corp-wide): 371.62B **Publicly Held**
SIC: 8011 Clinic, operated by physicians
HQ: Optumcare Management, Llc
2175 Park Pl
El Segundo CA 90245

(P-15418)
PACIFIC CLINICS
Also Called: Asian Pacific Family Center
9353 Valley Blvd Ste C, Rosemead (91770-1923)
PHONE.............................626 287-2988
Terry Gock, *Dir*
EMP: 92
SALES (corp-wide): 245.37MM **Privately Held**
Web: www.pacificclinics.org
SIC: 8011 8322 8093 Clinic, operated by physicians; Individual and family services; Mental health clinic, outpatient
PA: Pacific Clinics
251 Llewellyn Ave
408 379-3790

(P-15419)
PAVILION SURGERY CENTER LLC
Also Called: Pavilion Surgery Center
1140 W La Veta Ave Ste 300, Orange (92868-4226)
PHONE.............................714 744-8850
David Yomtoob, *Ch Bd*
EMP: 70 **EST:** 2016
SQ FT: 49,000
SALES (est): 14.37MM **Privately Held**
Web: www.pavilionsurgery.com
SIC: 8011 Surgeon

(P-15420)
PEDIATRIC AND FAMILY MED CTR
Also Called: Eisner Pediatric Fmly Med Ctr
1530 S Olive St, Los Angeles (90015-3023)
PHONE.............................213 342-3325
Carl Coan, *CEO*
Kevin Rossi, *
Edward Matthews Iii, *V Ch*
Irma Avila, *
Carl Edward Coan, *
EMP: 160 **EST:** 1920
SQ FT: 21,000
SALES (est): 63.74MM **Privately Held**
Web: www.eisnerhealth.org
SIC: 8011 Clinic, operated by physicians

(P-15421)
PEOPLE CREATING SUCCESS INC
380 Arneill Rd, Camarillo (93010-6406)
PHONE.............................805 644-9480
Marie Mcmanus, *Brnch Mgr*
EMP: 99
SALES (corp-wide): 4.53MM **Privately Held**
Web: www.pcs-services.org
SIC: 8011 Offices and clinics of medical doctors
PA: People Creating Success, Inc.
2585 Teller Rd
805 375-9222

(P-15422)
PERLMAN CLINIC
3900 5th Ave Ste 110, San Diego (92103-3122)
PHONE.............................858 554-1212
EMP: 216 **EST:** 2010
SALES (est): 5.51MM **Privately Held**
Web: www.perlmanclinic.com
SIC: 8011 General and family practice, physician/surgeon

(P-15423)
PERMANENTE MEDICAL GROUP INC
Also Called: S C P M G
25825 Vermont Ave, Harbor City (90710-3518)
PHONE.............................310 325-5111
TOLL FREE: 800
Leroy Foster, *Mgr*
EMP: 626
SALES (corp-wide): 70.8B **Privately Held**
Web: www.permanente.org
SIC: 8011 Medical centers
HQ: The Permanente Medical Group Inc
1950 Franklin St Fl 18
Oakland CA 94612
866 858-2226

(P-15424)
PROGRESSIVE HEALTH CARE SYSTEM
Also Called: P H S
8510 Balboa Blvd Ste 150, Northridge (91325-5810)
PHONE.............................818 707-9603
EMP: 100 **EST:** 1999
SQ FT: 10,000
SALES (est): 4.49MM **Privately Held**
Web: www.msophs.com
SIC: 8011 Offices and clinics of medical doctors

(P-15425)

PROSPECT MEDICAL HOLDINGS INC (PA)

3824 Hughes Ave, Los Angeles (90034-6981)
PHONE.................310 943-4500
Samuel Lee, *Ch Bd*
Mike Heather, *CFO*
Donna Vigil, *VP*
Linda Hodges, *Ex VP*
EMP: 211 **EST:** 1993
SALES (est): 3.91B
SALES (corp-wide): 3.91B **Privately Held**
Web: www.pmh.com
SIC: 8011 Health maintenance organization

(P-15426)

PROVIDNCE FACEY MED FOUNDATION (PA)

15451 San Fernando Mission Blvd, Mission Hills (91345-1368)
PHONE.................818 365-9531
Bill Gill, *CEO*
Jim Corwin, *
EMP: 170 **EST:** 1991
SQ FT: 306,000
SALES (est): 91.37MM
SALES (corp-wide): 91.37MM **Privately Held**
Web: www.facey.com
SIC: 8011 Physicians' office, including specialists

(P-15427)

PROVIDNCE FACEY MED FOUNDATION

27924 Seco Canyon Rd, Santa Clarita (91350-3870)
PHONE.................661 513-2100
Joan Rhee, *Mgr*
EMP: 88
SALES (corp-wide): 91.37MM **Privately Held**
Web: www.facey.com
SIC: 8011 Physicians' office, including specialists
PA: Providence Facey Medical Foundation
15451 San Frnndo Mssion B
818 365-9531

(P-15428)

PROVIDNCE FACEY MED FOUNDATION

11165 Sepulveda Blvd, Mission Hills (91345-1125)
PHONE.................818 365-9531
Judy Broon, *Brnoh Mgr*
EMP: 117
SALES (corp-wide): 91.37MM **Privately Held**
Web: www.facey.com
SIC: 8011 Physicians' office, including specialists
PA: Providence Facey Medical Foundation
15451 San Frnndo Mssion B
818 365-9531

(P-15429)

RADIOLOGY PARTNERS INC (HQ)

Also Called: Cirpa Radiology Management
2101 E El Segundo Blvd Ste 401, El Segundo (90245-4519)
PHONE.................424 290-8004
Richard Whitney, *CEO*
EMP: 500 **EST:** 2012
SALES (est): 93.24MM
SALES (corp-wide): 96.78MM **Privately Held**

Web: www.radpartners.com
SIC: 8011 Radiologist
PA: Radiology Partners Holdings, Llc
2330 Utah Ave Ste 200
424 290-8004

(P-15430)

RADIOLOGY PRTNERS HOLDINGS LLC (PA)

2330 Utah Ave Ste 200, El Segundo (90245-4817)
PHONE.................424 290-8004
Rich Whitney, *CEO*
Jay Bronner, *
Steve Tumbarello, *
Anthony Gabriel, *
Krishna Nallamshetty, *CMO*
EMP: 118 **EST:** 2013
SALES (est): 96.78MM
SALES (corp-wide): 96.78MM **Privately Held**
Web: www.radpartners.com
SIC: 8011 Radiologist

(P-15431)

RADNET MANAGEMENT III INC

72855 Fred Waring Dr, Palm Desert (92260-9368)
PHONE.................760 346-1130
David E Conston, *Brnch Mgr*
EMP: 80
Web: www.radnet.com
SIC: 8011 Radiologist
HQ: Radnet Management Iii, Inc.
1510 Cotner Ave
Los Angeles CA 90025
310 445-2800

(P-15432)

RADNET MANAGEMENT III INC

12677 Hesperia Rd Ste 190, Victorville (92395-7754)
PHONE.................760 243-1234
Rainilda Valencia, *Pr*
EMP: 80
Web: www.radnet.com
SIC: 8011 Radiologist
HQ: Radnet Management Iii, Inc.
1510 Cotner Ave
Los Angeles CA 90025
310 445-2800

(P-15433)

RADNET MANAGEMENT III INC

8750 Wilshire Blvd Ste 100, Beverly Hills (90211-2708)
PHONE.................323 549-3000
Taryn D Dartz, *Brnoh Mgr*
EMP: 80
Web: www.radnet.com
SIC: 8011 Radiologist
HQ: Radnet Management Iii, Inc.
1510 Cotner Ave
Los Angeles CA 90025
310 445-2800

(P-15434)

RAVI PATEL MD INC

Also Called: Comprehensive Blood Cancer Ctr
6501 Truxtun Ave, Bakersfield (93309-0633)
PHONE.................661 862-7113
EMP: 250 **EST:** 1987
SALES (est): 24.34MM **Privately Held**
Web: www.cbccusa.com
SIC: 8011 Medical centers

(P-15435)

REDWOOD FAMILY CARE NETWRK INC

13920 City Center Dr, Chino Hills (91709-5432)
PHONE.................909 942-0218
David Catrell, *Pr*
EMP: 2300 **EST:** 2021
SALES (est): 12.76MM **Privately Held**
Web: www.redwoodfcn.com
SIC: 8011 Medical centers

(P-15436)

RIVERSD-SAN BRNRDINO CNTY INDI (PA)

11980 Mount Vernon Ave, Grand Terrace (92313-5172)
PHONE.................909 864-1097
Jackie Wisespirit, *Pr*
Charles Castello, *
Faith Morreo, *
Brandie Miranda, *
Bill Thomsen, *
EMP: 99 **EST:** 1974
SQ FT: 38,000
SALES (est): 73.51MM
SALES (corp-wide): 73.51MM **Privately Held**
Web: www.rsbcihi.org
SIC: 8011 8093 Clinic, operated by physicians; Specialty outpatient clinics, nec

(P-15437)

RIVERSD-SAN BRNRDINO CNTY INDI

Also Called: Soboba Indian Health Clinic
607 Donna Way, San Jacinto (92583-5517)
PHONE.................951 654-0803
Maria Adams, *Mgr*
EMP: 143
SALES (corp-wide): 73.51MM **Privately Held**
Web: www.rsbcihi.org
SIC: 8011 Clinic, operated by physicians
PA: Riverside-San Bernardino County Indian Health, Inc.
11980 Mount Vernon Ave
909 864-1097

(P-15438)

RIVERSIDE MEDICAL CLINIC INC (PA)

Also Called: Riverside Med Clnic Ptient Ctr
3660 Arlington Ave, Riverside (92505-3987)
PHONE.................951 683-6370
Steven E Larson, *Pr*
Judy Carpenter, *
Steven E Larson, *Pr*
EMP: 80 **EST:** 1993
SQ FT: 65,000
SALES (est): 56.26MM
SALES (corp-wide): 56.26MM **Privately Held**
Web: www.riversidemedicalclinic.com
SIC: 8011 Clinic, operated by physicians

(P-15439)

ROBIN RED BREAST INC

6616 Lexington Ave, Los Angeles (90038-1306)
PHONE.................323 466-7800
Jesse Meoli, *Admn*
EMP: 72 **EST:** 2010
SALES (est): 1.23MM **Privately Held**
Web: www.titmouse.net
SIC: 8011 General and family practice, physician/surgeon

(P-15440)

RUME MEDICAL GROUP INC

Also Called: Covid Clinic
18800 Delaware St Ste 800, Huntington Beach (92648-6019)
PHONE.................714 406-1887
Matthew Abinante, *CEO*
EMP: 83 **EST:** 2021
SALES (est): 10.22MM **Privately Held**
SIC: 8011 Offices and clinics of medical doctors

(P-15441)

SAINT JHNS HLTH CTR FOUNDATION

Wayne, John Cancer Institute
2200 Santa Monica Blvd, Santa Monica (90404-2312)
PHONE.................310 315-6111
Donald Mortan, *Dir*
EMP: 125
SQ FT: 7,100
SALES (corp-wide): 10.75B **Privately Held**
Web: www.providence.org
SIC: 8011 8731 Primary care medical clinic; Commercial physical research
HQ: Saint John's Health Center Foundation.
2121 Santa Monica Blvd
Santa Monica CA 90404
310 829-5511

(P-15442)

SAN DEGO PTHLGSTS MED GROUP IN

7592 Metropolitan Dr Ste 406, San Diego (92108-4428)
PHONE.................619 297-4012
Carla Stayboldt Md, *Pr*
Bruce Robbins Md, *Ex VP*
Ralph Shishido Md, *Sec*
Slavek Niewiadomski Md, *Treas*
David Francis Md, *VP*
EMP: 120 **EST:** 1969
SQ FT: 3,500
SALES (est): 3.82MM **Privately Held**
Web: www.sdpath.com
SIC: 8011 Pathologist

(P-15443)

SAN DEGO SPT MDCINE FMLY HLTH

6699 Alvarado Rd Ste 2100, San Diego (92120-5238)
PHONE.................619 229-3909
Jo Baxter, *Mgr*
EMP: 71 **EST:** 2002
SALES (est): 3.94MM **Privately Held**
Web: www.sdsm.com
SIC: 8011 Clinic, operated by physicians

(P-15444)

SAN DIEGO FAMILY CARE (PA)

Also Called: LINDA VISTA HEALTH CARE CENTER
6973 Linda Vista Rd, San Diego (92111-6342)
PHONE.................858 279-0925
Roberta L Feinberg, *CEO*
Manuel Quintanar, *
EMP: 93 **EST:** 1972
SALES (est): 34.22MM
SALES (corp-wide): 34.22MM **Privately Held**
Web: www.sdfamilycare.org
SIC: 8011 Clinic, operated by physicians

(P-15445)

SAN GBRIEL AMBLTORY SRGERY CTR

PRODUCTS & SVCS

207 S Santa Anita St Ste G16, San Gabriel
(91776-1147)
PHONE..............................626 300-5300
Brenda Durgin, *Mgr*
EMP: 251 **EST:** 2003
SALES (est): 1.84MM
SALES (corp-wide): 19.17B **Publicly Held**
Web: www.acuityeyegroup.com
SIC: 8011 Opthalmologist
HQ: United Surgical Partners International, Inc.
14201 Dallas Pkwy
Dallas TX 75254
972 713-3500

(P-15446)
SANTA MONICA BAY
PHYSICIANS HE (PA)
Also Called: Bay Area Community Med Group
5767 W Century Blvd, Los Angeles
(90045-5631)
PHONE..............................310 417-5900
Eileen Mcgrath, *Pr*
Doctor Steven Seizer, *VP* *
Doctor David Cutler, *Sec*
Doctor Richard Zachrich, *Treas*
EMP: 85 **EST:** 1985
SALES (est): 9.96MM
SALES (corp-wide): 9.96MM **Privately Held**
Web: www.uclahealth.org
SIC: 8011 Clinic, operated by physicians

(P-15447)
SB WATERMAN HOLDINGS INC
(PA)
1700 N Waterman Ave, San Bernardino
(92404-5115)
PHONE..............................909 883-8611
James Malin, *CEO*
James W Malin, *
Paul G Godfrey Md, *VP*
Thomas Hellwig, *
Louis Francisco Md, *Treas*
EMP: 150 **EST:** 1954
SQ FT: 55,000
SALES (est): 10.4MM
SALES (corp-wide): 10.4MM **Privately Held**
Web: www.optum.com
SIC: 8011 Clinic, operated by physicians

(P-15448)
SBC MEDICAL GROUP
HOLDINGS INC
Also Called: SBC
200 Spectrum Center Dr Ste 300, Irvine
(92618-5004)
PHONE..............................949 593-0250
Yoshiyuki Aikawa, *Ch Bd*
Yuya Yoshida, *
Ryoji Murata, *CFO*
Akira Komatsu, *CSO*
EMP: 665 **EST:** 2000
SALES (est): 193.54MM
SALES (corp-wide): 193.54MM **Publicly Held**
SIC: 8011 Offices and clinics of medical doctors
PA: Mehana Capital Llc
4348 Waialae Ave Pmb 632

(P-15449)
SCRIBEMD LLC
1310 W Stewart Dr Ste 212, Orange
(92868-3837)
PHONE..............................714 543-8911
Coutney Aldama, *CEO*
Matthew Mullarky, *
EMP: 90 **EST:** 2009

SALES (est): 498.82K **Privately Held**
Web: www.scribemd.com
SIC: 8011 Offices and clinics of medical doctors

(P-15450)
SERRA COMMUNITY MED
CLINIC INC
Also Called: Serra Community Medical Clinic
9375 San Fernando Rd, Sun Valley
(91352-1418)
PHONE..............................818 768-3000
Sadayappa K Durairaj, *CEO*
Doctor Arnold Jacobs, *Treas*
Doctor Carlos Jimenez, *Sec*
Dan Bumgarner, *
Kumar Soundar, *
EMP: 163 **EST:** 1975
SQ FT: 60,000
SALES (est): 7.03MM **Privately Held**
Web: www.serramedicalgroup.com
SIC: 8011 Clinic, operated by physicians

(P-15451)
SGRY LLC
Also Called: Specialty Surgical of Westlake
696 Hampshire Rd Ste 100, Westlake
Village (91361-4456)
PHONE..............................805 413-7920
Kelly Kapp, *Brnch Mgr*
EMP: 134
Web: www.sscwestlake.com
SIC: 8011 Surgeon
HQ: Sgry, Llc
340 Seven Springs Way
Brentwood,TN 37027
615 234-5900

(P-15452)
SHARP HEALTHCARE
8860 Center Dr Ste 450, La Mesa
(91942-7001)
PHONE..............................619 460-6200
Scott Musicant, *Brnch Mgr*
EMP: 94
SALES (corp-wide): 1.9B **Privately Held**
Web: www.sharp.com
SIC: 8011 Cardiologist and cardio-vascular specialist
PA: Sharp Healthcare
8695 Spectrum Ctr Blvd
858 499-4000

(P-15453)
SHARP REES STALY RNCHO
BRNARDO
16899 W Bernardo Dr, San Diego
(92127-1603)
PHONE..............................858 521-2300
EMP: 76 **EST:** 2012
SALES (est): 2.8MM **Privately Held**
Web: www.sharp.com
SIC: 8011 Physicians' office, including specialists

(P-15454)
SHARP RES-STEALY MED
GROUP INC
3555 Kenyon St Ste 200, San Diego
(92110-5341)
PHONE..............................619 221-9547
Betty Thompson, *Mgr*
EMP: 177
Web: www.sharp.com
SIC: 8011 Physicians' office, including specialists
PA: Sharp Rees-Stealy Medical Group, Inc.
300 Fir St

(P-15455)
SHARP RES-STEALY MED
GROUP INC
7862 El Cajon Blvd Ste C, La Mesa
(91942-6712)
PHONE..............................619 644-6405
Behrooz Akbarnia, *Prin*
EMP: 176
Web: www.sharp.com
SIC: 8011 Internal medicine practitioners
PA: Sharp Rees-Stealy Medical Group, Inc.
300 Fir St

(P-15456)
SLEEP DATA SERVICES LLC
5471 Kearny Villa Rd Ste 200, San Diego
(92123-1143)
PHONE..............................619 299-6299
Gaston Sanchez, *Prin*
EMP: 90 **EST:** 2017
SALES (est): 6.24MM **Privately Held**
Web: www.betternight.com
SIC: 8011 Offices and clinics of medical doctors

(P-15457)
SOUTH CENTRAL FAMILY HLTH
CTR
4425 S Central Ave, Los Angeles
(90011-3629)
PHONE..............................323 908-4200
Richard Veloz, *Pr*
Paul Ramos, *
Ruby Raya Morones, *CMO**
Sandra Tatum Green, *
EMP: 92 **EST:** 1983
SQ FT: 13,000
SALES (est): 39.21MM **Privately Held**
Web: www.scfhc.org
SIC: 8011 Clinic, operated by physicians

(P-15458)
SOUTH CNTY ORTHPD
SPCLSTS A ME
Also Called: Orthowest
24331 El Toro Rd Ste 200, Laguna Hills
(92637-3116)
PHONE..............................949 586-3200
James Mullen, *Pr*
Lance J Wrobel, *
Larry M Gursten, *
Lonnie J Moskow, *
Kyle W Coker, *
EMP: 86 **EST:** 1994
SALES (est): 19.06MM **Privately Held**
Web: www.scosortho.com
SIC: 8011 Orthopedic physician

(P-15459)
SOUTHERN CAL HLTH
RHBLTTION PR
2610 Industry Way Ste A, Lynwood
(90262-4028)
PHONE..............................310 631-8004
Doctor Jack M Barbour, *CFO*
Rita Floyd, *
EMP: 165 **EST:** 1993
SQ FT: 6,000
SALES (est): 4.32MM **Privately Held**
Web: www.scharpca.com
SIC: 8011 Psychiatric clinic

(P-15460)
SOUTHERN CAL ORTHPD INST
LP (PA)
6815 Noble Ave, Van Nuys (91405-3796)
PHONE..............................818 901-6600
Marc J Friedman, *Pt*

EMP: 135 **EST:** 1992
SALES (est): 171.1K **Privately Held**
Web: www.scoi.com
SIC: 8011 8249 Orthopedic physician; Medical training services

(P-15461)
SOUTHERN CAL PRMNNTE MED
GROUP
3501 Stockdale Hwy, Bakersfield
(93309-2150)
PHONE..............................661 398-5085
EMP: 127
SALES (corp-wide): 70.8B **Privately Held**
Web: www.permanente.org
SIC: 8011 Medical centers
HQ: Southern California Permanente
Medical Group
393 Walnut Dr
Pasadena CA 91107
626 405-5704

(P-15462)
SOUTHERN CAL PRMNNTE MED
GROUP
5055 California Ave, Bakersfield
(93309-0701)
PHONE..............................661 334-2020
Doctor Geckeley, *Prin*
EMP: 180
SALES (corp-wide): 70.8B **Privately Held**
Web: www.permanente.org
SIC: 8011 Medical centers
HQ: Southern California Permanente
Medical Group
393 Walnut Dr
Pasadena CA 91107
626 405-5704

(P-15463)
SOUTHERN CAL PRMNNTE MED
GROUP
Also Called: S C P M G
5620 Mesmer Ave, Culver City
(90230-6315)
PHONE..............................310 737-4900
Olive Goldsmith, *Mgr*
EMP: 133
SALES (corp-wide): 70.8B **Privately Held**
Web: www.permanente.org
SIC: 8011 Medical centers
HQ: Southern California Permanente
Medical Group
393 Walnut Dr
Pasadena CA 91107
626 405-5704

(P-15464)
SOUTHERN CAL PRMNNTE MED
GROUP
Also Called: S C P M G
110 N La Brea Ave, Inglewood
(90301-1708)
PHONE..............................310 419-3306
Helen Jones, *Mgr*
EMP: 133
SALES (corp-wide): 70.8B **Privately Held**
Web: www.permanente.org
SIC: 8011 Medical centers
HQ: Southern California Permanente
Medical Group
393 Walnut Dr
Pasadena CA 91107
626 405-5704

(P-15465)
SOUTHERN CAL PRMNNTE MED
GROUP
Also Called: S C P M G

7825 Atlantic Ave, Cudahy (90201-5022)
PHONE..............................323 562-6459
Maria Gonzalez, *Prin*
EMP: 167
SALES (corp-wide): 70.8B Privately Held
Web: www.permanente.org
SIC: 8011 Medical centers
HQ: Southern California Permanente
  Medical Group
  393 Walnut Dr
  Pasadena CA 91107
  626 405-5704

(P-15466)

SOUTHERN CAL PRMNNTE MED GROUP

Also Called: S C P M G
21263 Erwin St, Woodland Hills
(91367-3715)
PHONE..............................818 592-3038
Cary Glass, *Brnch Mgr*
EMP: 214
SALES (corp-wide): 70.8B Privately Held
Web: www.permanente.org
SIC: 8011 Medical centers
HQ: Southern California Permanente
  Medical Group
  393 Walnut Dr
  Pasadena CA 91107
  626 405-5704

(P-15467)

SOUTHERN CAL PRMNNTE MED GROUP

Also Called: S C P M G
27107 Tourney Rd, Santa Clarita
(91355-1860)
PHONE..............................661 222-2150
EMP: 180
SALES (corp-wide): 70.8B Privately Held
Web: www.permanente.org
SIC: 8011 Medical centers
HQ: Southern California Permanente
  Medical Group
  393 Walnut Dr
  Pasadena CA 91107
  626 405-5704

(P-15468)

SOUTHERN CAL PRMNNTE MED GROUP

6041 Cadillac Ave, Los Angeles
(90034-1702)
PHONE..............................323 857-2000
Larry Poston, *Dir*
EMP: 220
SALES (corp-wide): 70.8B Privately Held
Web: www.permanente.org
SIC: 8011 Radiologist
HQ: Southern California Permanente
  Medical Group
  393 Walnut Dr
  Pasadena CA 91107
  626 405-5704

(P-15469)

SOUTHERN CAL PRMNNTE MED GROUP

25825 Vermont Ave, Harbor City
(90710-3518)
PHONE..............................800 780-1230
EMP: 167
SALES (corp-wide): 70.8B Privately Held
Web: www.permanente.org
SIC: 8011 Medical centers
HQ: Southern California Permanente
  Medical Group
  393 Walnut Dr
  Pasadena CA 91107
  626 405-5704

(P-15470)

SOUTHERN CAL PRMNNTE MED GROUP

4841 Hollywood Blvd, Los Angeles
(90027-5301)
PHONE..............................323 783-5455
EMP: 287
SALES (corp-wide): 70.8B Privately Held
Web: www.permanente.org
SIC: 8011 Medical centers
HQ: Southern California Permanente
  Medical Group
  393 Walnut Dr
  Pasadena CA 91107
  626 405-5704

(P-15471)

SOUTHERN CAL PRMNNTE MED GROUP

Also Called: Orthopedics Department
4760 W Sunset Blvd, Los Angeles
(90027-6063)
PHONE..............................323 783-4893
Dolores Cobbarrubias, *Off Mgr*
EMP: 194
SALES (corp-wide): 70.8B Privately Held
Web: www.permanente.org
SIC: 8011 Orthopedic physician
HQ: Southern California Permanente
  Medical Group
  393 Walnut Dr
  Pasadena CA 91107
  626 405-5704

(P-15472)

SOUTHERN CAL PRMNNTE MED GROUP

18081 Beach Blvd, Huntington Beach
(92648-1304)
PHONE..............................714 841-7293
EMP: 133
SALES (corp-wide): 70.8B Privately Held
Web: www.permanente.org
SIC: 8011 Medical centers
HQ: Southern California Permanente
  Medical Group
  393 Walnut Dr
  Pasadena CA 91107
  626 405-5704

(P-15473)

SOUTHERN CAL PRMNNTE MED GROUP

Also Called: S C P M G
411 N Lakeview Ave, Anaheim
(92807-3028)
PHONE..............................714 270-4675
Ryan Williams, *Mgr*
EMP: 147
SALES (corp-wide): 70.8B Privately Held
Web: www.permanente.org
SIC: 8011 Medical centers
HQ: Southern California Permanente
  Medical Group
  393 Walnut Dr
  Pasadena CA 91107
  626 405-5704

(P-15474)

SOUTHERN CAL PRMNNTE MED GROUP

Also Called: S C P M G
30400 Camino Capistrano, San Juan
Capistrano (92675-1300)
PHONE..............................949 234-2139
EMP: 133
SALES (corp-wide): 70.8B Privately Held
Web: www.permanente.org
SIC: 8011 Medical centers

HQ: Southern California Permanente
  Medical Group
  393 Walnut Dr
  Pasadena CA 91107
  626 405-5704

(P-15475)

SOUTHERN CAL PRMNNTE MED GROUP

Also Called: S C P M G
1900 E 4th St, Santa Ana (92705-3910)
PHONE..............................714 967-4760
Julie White-dahlgren, *Brnch Mgr*
EMP: 133
SALES (corp-wide): 70.8B Privately Held
Web: www.permanente.org
SIC: 8011 8049 Obstetrician; Psychiatric
  social worker
HQ: Southern California Permanente
  Medical Group
  393 Walnut Dr
  Pasadena CA 91107
  626 405-5704

(P-15476)

SOUTHERN CAL PRMNNTE MED GROUP

6 Willard, Irvine (92604-4694)
PHONE..............................949 262-5780
Debra Dannemeyer, *Admn*
EMP: 174
SALES (corp-wide): 70.8B Privately Held
Web: www.permanente.org
SIC: 8011 Clinic, operated by physicians
HQ: Southern California Permanente
  Medical Group
  393 Walnut Dr
  Pasadena CA 91107
  626 405-5704

(P-15477)

SOUTHERN CAL PRMNNTE MED GROUP

Also Called: Kaiser Permanente
4647 Zion Ave, San Diego (92120-2507)
PHONE..............................619 528-5000
Terry Belmont, *Prin*
EMP: 414
SALES (corp-wide): 70.8B Privately Held
Web: www.kpsan.org
SIC: 8011 Medical centers
HQ: Southern California Permanente
  Medical Group
  393 Walnut Dr
  Pasadena CA 91107
  626 405-5704

(P-15478)

SOUTHERN CAL PRMNNTE MED GROUP

Also Called: S C P M G
789 E Cooley Dr, Colton (92324-4007)
PHONE..............................909 370-2501
EMP: 154
SALES (corp-wide): 70.8B Privately Held
Web: www.permanente.org
SIC: 8011 Medical centers
HQ: Southern California Permanente
  Medical Group
  393 Walnut Dr
  Pasadena CA 91107
  626 405-5704

(P-15479)

SOUTHERN CAL PRMNNTE MED GROUP

Also Called: S C P M G
1630 E Main St, El Cajon (92021-5204)
PHONE..............................619 528-5000

Brenda Scott-mead, *Mgr*
EMP: 174
SALES (corp-wide): 70.8B Privately Held
Web: www.permanente.org
SIC: 8011 Medical centers
HQ: Southern California Permanente
  Medical Group
  393 Walnut Dr
  Pasadena CA 91107
  626 405-5704

(P-15480)

SOUTHERN CAL PRMNNTE MED GROUP

Also Called: S C P M G
4405 Vandever Ave, San Diego
(92120-3315)
PHONE..............................619 516-6000
Thomas Volle, *Mgr*
EMP: 214
SALES (corp-wide): 70.8B Privately Held
Web: www.permanente.org
SIC: 8011 Medical centers
HQ: Southern California Permanente
  Medical Group
  393 Walnut Dr
  Pasadena CA 91107
  626 405-5704

(P-15481)

SOUTHERN CAL PRMNNTE MED GROUP

Also Called: S C P M G
732 N Broadway, Escondido (92025-1870)
PHONE..............................760 839-7200
Alex Anderson, *Mgr*
EMP: 133
SALES (corp-wide): 70.8B Privately Held
Web: www.permanente.org
SIC: 8011 Medical centers
HQ: Southern California Permanente
  Medical Group
  393 Walnut Dr
  Pasadena CA 91107
  626 405-5704

(P-15482)

ST JSEPH HERITG MED GROUP LLC (PA)

Also Called: Yorba Park Medical Group
2212 E 4th St Ste 201, Santa Ana
(92705-3872)
PHONE..............................714 633-1011
Charles Foster, *Pr*
Benjamin Harper Md, *Prin*
C R Burke, *
Ivan Nichols Md, *Prin*
Dennis Long Md, *Treas*
▲ EMP: 134 EST: 1964
SQ FT: 58,000
SALES (est): 9.86MM
SALES (corp-wide): 9.86MM Privately
Held
Web: www.sjhmg.org
SIC: 8011 General and family practice,
  physician/surgeon

(P-15483)

SUCCESS HEALTHCARE 1 LLC

Also Called: Acute Psychiatric Hospital
7500 Hellman Ave, Rosemead
(91770-2216)
PHONE..............................626 288-1160
EMP: 633
SALES (corp-wide): 87.5MM Privately
Held
Web: www.silverlakemc.com
SIC: 8011 Offices and clinics of medical
  doctors
PA: Success Healthcare 1, Llc
  1711 W Temple St

213 989-6100

(P-15484)
SULPIZIO CARDIOVASCULAR CENTER
9434 Medical Center Dr, La Jolla
(92037-1337)
PHONE..............................858 657-7000
EMP: 75 EST: 2015
SALES (est): 589.58K
SALES (corp-wide): 534.4MM **Privately Held**
Web: health.ucsd.edu
SIC: 8011 Cardiologist and cardio-vascular specialist
HQ: University Of California, San Diego
9500 Gilman Dr
La Jolla CA 92093
858 534-2230

(P-15485)
SUN HEALTHCARE GROUP INC (DH)
27442 Portola Pkwy Ste 200, Foothill Ranch
(92610-2822)
PHONE..............................949 255-7100
George V Hager Junior, *CEO*
Richard Edwards, *
▲ EMP: 300 EST: 1993
SALES (est): 2.28B
SALES (corp-wide): 5.86B **Publicly Held**
Web: www.genesishcc.com
SIC: 8011 8322 Medical insurance plan; Referral service for personal and social problems
HQ: Genesis Hc Llc
101 E State St
Kennett Square PA 19348
610 444-6350

(P-15486)
TEMPLETON SURGERY CENTER LLC
1911 Johnson Ave, San Luis Obispo
(93401-4131)
PHONE..............................805 434-3550
Brenda Gray, *Managing Member*
EMP: 179 EST: 2005
SALES (est): 1.95MM
SALES (corp-wide): 19.17B **Publicly Held**
SIC: 8011 Surgeon
HQ: United Surgical Partners International, Inc.
14201 Dallas Pkwy
Dallas TX 75254
972 713-3500

(P-15487)
TENET HEALTHSYSTEM MEDICAL INC
Also Called: Lakewood Regional Medical Ctr
3700 South St, Lakewood (90712-1419)
PHONE..............................562 531-2550
Carol Mammolite, *Brnch Mgr*
EMP: 1022
SALES (corp-wide): 19.17B **Publicly Held**
Web: www.tenethealth.com
SIC: 8011 8062 Medical centers; General medical and surgical hospitals
HQ: Tenet Healthsystem Medical, Inc.
14201 Dallas Pkwy
Dallas TX 75254
469 893-2000

(P-15488)
TENET HEALTHSYSTEM MEDICAL INC
Los Alamitos Med Ctr
3751 Katella Ave, Los Alamitos
(90720-3113)

PHONE..............................805 546-7698
Michelle Finney, *Prin*
EMP: 446
SALES (corp-wide): 19.17B **Publicly Held**
Web: www.tenethealth.com
SIC: 8011 8062 Offices and clinics of medical doctors; General medical and surgical hospitals
HQ: Tenet Healthsystem Medical, Inc.
14201 Dallas Pkwy
Dallas TX 75254
469 893-2000

(P-15489)
TENET HEALTHSYSTEM MEDICAL INC
Also Called: Leisure World Pharmacy
1661 Golden Rain Rd, Seal Beach
(90740-4907)
P.O. Box 2685 (90740-1685)
PHONE..............................562 493-9581
EMP: 120
SALES (corp-wide): 20.55B **Publicly Held**
Web: www.mygnp.com
SIC: 8011 5912 Offices and clinics of medical doctors; Drug stores
HQ: Tenet Healthsystem Medical, Inc.
14201 Dallas Pkwy
Dallas TX 75254
469 893-2000

(P-15490)
THE ORTHOPEDIC INSTITUTE OF
616 Witmer St, Los Angeles (90017-2395)
PHONE..............................213 977-2010
Andrew B Leeka, *CEO*
EMP: 5009 EST: 1990
SALES (est): 1.17MM
SALES (corp-wide): 20.43MM **Privately Held**
SIC: 8011 Orthopedic physician
HQ: Pih Health Good Samaritan Hospital
1225 Wilshire Blvd
Los Angeles CA 90017
213 977-2121

(P-15491)
TRANSLTNAL PLMNARY IMMNLOGY RE
Also Called: Southern Cal Fd Allergy Inst
701 E 28th St Ste 419, Long Beach
(90806-2775)
PHONE..............................562 490-9900
Doctor Inderpal Randhawa, *Prin*
EMP: 90 EST: 2016
SALES (est): 14.47MM **Privately Held**
Web: www.foodallergyinstitute.com
SIC: 8011 Allergist

(P-15492)
TWIN CITIES COMMUNITY HOSP INC
1100 Las Tablas Rd, Templeton
(93465-9796)
PHONE..............................805 434-3500
Eleze Armstrong, *CEO*
Paul Posmosga, *
EMP: 450 EST: 1977
SQ FT: 120,000
SALES (est): 17.75K
SALES (corp-wide): 19.17B **Publicly Held**
Web: www.adventisthealth.org
SIC: 8011 8062 Medical centers; General medical and surgical hospitals
PA: Tenet Healthcare Corporation
14201 Dallas Pkwy
469 893-2000

(P-15493)
UNITED FMLY CARE INC A MED COR
8110 Mango Ave Ste 104, Fontana
(92335-3603)
PHONE..............................909 874-1679
Keith Schauermann, *Pr*
EMP: 120 EST: 1999
SALES (est): 3.96MM **Privately Held**
Web: pmg.optum.com
SIC: 8011 General and family practice, physician/surgeon

(P-15494)
UNITED MEDICAL DOCTORS
Also Called: United Gastroenterologists
28078 Baxter Rd Ste 530, Murrieta
(92563-1405)
PHONE..............................951 566-5229
Samantha Cottrell, *Prin*
EMP: 123 EST: 2003
SALES (est): 14.46MM **Privately Held**
Web: www.unitedmd.com
SIC: 8011 Gastronomist

(P-15495)
UNITED MEDICAL IMAGING INC (PA)
10436 Santa Monica Blvd, Los Angeles
(90025-6933)
PHONE..............................310 943-8400
Nasser Hiekali, *CEO*
EMP: 78 EST: 2006
SALES (est): 11.59MM **Privately Held**
Web: www.umih.com
SIC: 8011 Radiologist

(P-15496)
UNITED STATES DEPT OF NAVY
Also Called: Branch Medical Center
19871 Mitscher Way, San Diego
(92145-5103)
P.O. Box 452002 (92145-2002)
PHONE..............................858 577-9849
EMP: 300
Web: www.navy.mil
SIC: 8011 9711 Medical centers; Navy
HQ: United States Department Of The Navy
1200 Navy Pentagon
Washington DC 20350

(P-15497)
UNIVERSITY CALIFORNIA IRVINE
Also Called: UIC
101 The City Dr S Ste 313, Orange
(92868-3201)
PHONE..............................714 456-6966
Sharon Mccarthy, *Mgr*
EMP: 72
SALES (corp-wide): 534.4MM **Privately Held**
Web: www.uci.edu
SIC: 8011 8221 9411 Surgeon; University; Administration of educational programs
HQ: University Of California, Irvine
510 Aldrich Hall
Irvine CA 92697
949 824-5011

(P-15498)
UNIVERSITY CALIFORNIA IRVINE
Also Called: Uc Irvine Hlth Rgonal Burn Ctr
101 The City Dr S Bldg 1a, Orange
(92868-3201)
PHONE..............................714 456-6170
EMP: 1757
SALES (corp-wide): 534.4MM **Privately Held**

Web: www.ucihealth.org
SIC: 8011 8221 9411 Medical centers; University; Administration of educational programs
HQ: University Of California, Irvine
510 Aldrich Hall
Irvine CA 92697
949 824-5011

(P-15499)
UNIVERSITY CALIFORNIA IRVINE
Also Called: UCI Family Health Center
800 N Main St, Santa Ana (92701-3576)
PHONE..............................714 480-2443
Nancy Downey Hurtado, *Mgr*
EMP: 287
SQ FT: 49,361
SALES (corp-wide): 534.4MM **Privately Held**
Web: www.uci.edu
SIC: 8011 8221 9411 Medical centers; University; Administration of educational programs
HQ: University Of California, Irvine
510 Aldrich Hall
Irvine CA 92697
949 824-5011

(P-15500)
UNIVERSITY CALIFORNIA IRVINE
43 Cambria Dr, Corona Del Mar
(92625-1004)
PHONE..............................949 644-5245
EMP: 72
SALES (corp-wide): 534.4MM **Privately Held**
Web: www.uci.edu
SIC: 8011 Offices and clinics of medical doctors
HQ: University Of California, Irvine
510 Aldrich Hall
Irvine CA 92697
949 824-5011

(P-15501)
UNIVERSITY CALIFORNIA IRVINE
1640 Newport Blvd Ste 340, Costa Mesa
(92627-7730)
PHONE..............................949 646-2267
Olivia Reil, *Brnch Mgr*
EMP: 72
SALES (corp-wide): 534.4MM **Privately Held**
Web: www.uci.edu
SIC: 8011 8221 9411 Gynecologist; University; Administration of educational programs
HQ: University Of California, Irvine
510 Aldrich Hall
Irvine CA 92697
949 824-5011

(P-15502)
UNIVERSITY CALIFORNIA IRVINE
Also Called: Barr, Ronald J MD /UCI Med Gro
101 The City Dr S, Orange (92868-3201)
PHONE..............................714 456-7890
Ronald J Barr Md Dermatology, *Brnch Mgr*
EMP: 92
SALES (corp-wide): 534.4MM **Privately Held**
Web: www.ucihealth.org
SIC: 8011 8221 9411 Dermatologist; University; Administration of educational programs
HQ: University Of California, Irvine
510 Aldrich Hall

Irvine CA 92697
949 824-5011

(P-15503)
US DERMATOLOGY MEDICAL MANAGEMENT INC
1401 N Batavia St Ste 204, Orange
(92867-3500)
P.O. Box 7587 (78683-7587)
PHONE.................................817 962-2157
EMP: 92
SIC: 8011 Dermatologist

(P-15504)
VALLEY COMMUNITY HEALTHCARE
6801 Coldwater Canyon Ave Ste 1b, North Hollywood (91605-5164)
PHONE.................................818 763-8836
Paula Wilson, CEO
Lee Huey, *
EMP: 300 EST: 1970
SQ FT: 15,000
SALES (est): 30.93MM Privately Held
Web:
www.valleycommunityhealthcare.org
SIC: 8011 Clinic, operated by physicians

(P-15505)
VANGUARD HEALTH SYSTEMS INC
Also Called: North Anaheim Surgery Center
1154 N Euclid St, Anaheim (92801-1955)
PHONE.................................714 635-6272
J Rasmussen, Admn
Jeanette Rasmussen, Admn
EMP: 456 EST: 1991
SQ FT: 12,000
SALES (est): 3.09MM
SALES (corp-wide): 19.17B Publicly Held
SIC: 8011 5999 Ambulatory surgical center; Medical apparatus and supplies
HQ: Vanguard Health Systems, Inc.
20 Burton Hlls Blvd Ste 2
Nashville TN 37215
615 665-6000

(P-15506)
VENICE FAMILY CLINIC (PA)
604 Rose Ave, Venice (90291-2767)
PHONE.................................310 664-7703
Mitesh Popat, CEO
Lee Rosenberg, *
Karl Keener, *
Gordon Lee, *
William Flumenbaum, Ch
EMP: 116 EST: 1974
SALES (est): 91.07MM
SALES (corp-wide): 91.07MM Privately Held
Web: www.venicefamilyclinic.org
SIC: 8011 Clinic, operated by physicians

(P-15507)
VETERANS HEALTH ADMINISTRATION
Also Called: Loma Linda Healthcare Sys 605
11201 Benton St, Loma Linda
(92357-0001)
PHONE.................................909 825-7084
Debbie Romero, Brnch Mgr
EMP: 826
Web: benefits.va.gov
SIC: 8011 9451 Medical centers; Administration of veterans' affairs, Federal government
HQ: Veterans Health Administration
810 Vermont Ave Nw
Washington DC 20420

(P-15508)
VETERANS HEALTH ADMINISTRATION
Also Called: West Los Angeles V A Med Ctr
11301 Wilshire Blvd, Los Angeles
(90073-1003)
PHONE.................................310 478-3711
Donna Beiter, Dir
EMP: 1906
Web: benefits.va.gov
SIC: 8011 9451 Clinic, operated by physicians; Administration of veterans' affairs, Federal government
HQ: Veterans Health Administration
810 Vermont Ave Nw
Washington DC 20420

(P-15509)
WATTS HEALTHCARE CORPORATION (PA)
Also Called: WATTS HEALTH
10300 Compton Ave, Los Angeles
(90002-3628)
PHONE.................................323 564-4331
Roderick Seamster, Pr
Roderick Seamster, Pr
Carroll J Mcneely, CFO
EMP: 180 EST: 2002
SALES (est): 39.6MM
SALES (corp-wide): 39.6MM Privately Held
Web: www.wattshealth.org
SIC: 8011 Clinic, operated by physicians

(P-15510)
WEST COVINA MEDICAL CLINIC INC (PA)
1500 W West Covina Pkwy Ste 100, West Covina (91790-2729)
PHONE.................................626 960-8614
Ziad Dabuni, Pr
Doctor Ziad Dabuni, Pr
Doctor Shivani Shah, Ex VP
Doctor Lucio Sanchez, Sec
Doctor Suntheetha Ali, Treas
EMP: 222 EST: 1950
SQ FT: 50,000
SALES (est): 1.91MM
SALES (corp-wide): 1.91MM Privately Held
Web: www.covinaarthritisclinic.com
SIC: 8011 Clinic, operated by physicians

(P-15511)
WESTERN UNIV HLTH SCIENCES
Also Called: Mission Medical Clinic
360 E Mission Blvd, Pomona (01766 1847)
PHONE.................................909 865-2565
Alan D Cundari, Prin
EMP: 78
SALES (corp-wide): 241.37MM Privately Held
Web: www.westernu.edu
SIC: 8011 8221 Clinic, operated by physicians; University
PA: Western University Of Health Sciences
309 E 2nd St
909 623-6116

(P-15512)
WHITE MEMORIAL MED GROUP INC (PA)
1701 E Cesar E Chavez Ave Ste 510, Los Angeles (90033-2488)
P.O. Box 51741 (90033)
PHONE.................................323 987-1300
Alan Lau, Pr
EMP: 71 EST: 1983
SQ FT: 20,000

SALES (est): 7.55MM
SALES (corp-wide): 7.55MM Privately Held
Web: www.adventisthealth.org
SIC: 8011 8742 Medical centers; Hospital and health services consultant

(P-15513)
WHITE MEMORIAL MEDICAL CENTER
1720 E Cesar E Chavez Ave, Los Angeles
(90033-2481)
PHONE.................................323 260-5739
Beth D Zachary, Brnch Mgr
EMP: 800
SALES (corp-wide): 805.07MM Privately Held
Web: www.adventisthealth.org
SIC: 8011 Medical centers
HQ: White Memorial Medical Center Inc
1720 E Cesar E Chavez Ave
Los Angeles CA 90033
323 268-5000

8021 Offices And Clinics Of Dentists

(P-15514)
ACCESS DENTAL PLAN (PA)
Also Called: Access Dental Centers
530 S Main St, Orange (92868-4525)
PHONE.................................916 922-5000
Reza M Abbaszadeh, Pr
Teri Abbaszadeh, *
▲ EMP: 70 EST: 1989
SALES (est): 9.47MM Privately Held
Web: www.westerndental.com
SIC: 8021 Dental clinic

(P-15515)
BOYD DENTAL CORPORATION
362 E Vanderbilt Way, San Bernardino
(92408-3593)
PHONE.................................909 890-0421
EMP: 101
SALES (corp-wide): 1.2MM Privately Held
Web: www.idcsanbernardino.com
SIC: 8021 Dentists' office
PA: Boyd Dental Corporation
599 Inland Center Dr # 110
909 384-1111

(P-15516)
CHROMIUM DENTAL II LLC
Also Called: Labs.dental
1524 Brookhollow Dr, Santa Ana
(92705-5426)
PHONE.................................949 733-3111
Charbel Louis Karam, Managing Member
EMP: 220 EST: 2018
SALES (est): 10.16MM Privately Held
SIC: 8021 Dentists' office

(P-15517)
FAMILY HLTH CTRS SAN DIEGO INC
1809 National Ave, San Diego
(92113-2113)
PHONE.................................619 515-2300
Brian Woolford Md, Dir
EMP: 348
SALES (corp-wide): 147.12MM Privately Held
Web: www.fhcsd.org
SIC: 8021 Offices and clinics of dentists
PA: Family Health Centers Of San Diego, Inc.
823 Gateway Center Way

619 515-2303

(P-15518)
INTERDENT SERVICE CORPORATION
3630 Central Ave, Riverside (92506-5908)
PHONE.................................951 682-1720
Carlos Espadas, Brnch Mgr
EMP: 99
SALES (corp-wide): 83.93MM Privately Held
Web: www.interdent.com
SIC: 8021 Dental clinic
HQ: Interdent Service Corporation
9800 S La Cnega Blvd Ste
Inglewood CA 90301

(P-15519)
JADE GILBERT DENTAL CORP
1197 E Los Angeles Ave Ste E, Simi Valley
(93065-2868)
PHONE.................................805 583-5700
Katayoun Setarehshenas, Brnch Mgr
EMP: 161
Web: www.firststreetdental.com
SIC: 8021 Dentists' office
PA: Jade Gilbert Dental Corporation
17000 Red Hill Ave

(P-15520)
LEONID M GLSMAN DDS A DNTL COR
Also Called: Dentalville
5021 Florence Ave, Bell (90201-3802)
PHONE.................................323 560-4514
EMP: 130
SALES (corp-wide): 2.41MM Privately Held
Web: www.panoramacitydentistca.com
SIC: 8021 Dentists' office
PA: Leonid M. Glosman, D.D.S., A Dental Corporation
7864 Van Nuys Blvd
323 266-1000

(P-15521)
MARINE CORPS COMMUNITY SVCS
Camp Pendleton Marine Corps Base, Oceanside (92055)
P.O. Box 555221 (92055-5221)
PHONE.................................760 725-5187
EMP: 167
Web: marcorsyscom.marines.mil
SIC: 8021 9711 Offices and clinics of dentists; Marine Corps
HQ: Marine Corps Community Services
3044 Catlin Ave
Quantico VA 22134
703 432 0100

(P-15522)
MY KIDS DENTIST
24635 Madison Ave Ste E, Murrieta
(92562-7556)
PHONE.................................951 600-1062
Theresa Gomez, Brnch Mgr
EMP: 400
SALES (corp-wide): 13.98MM Privately Held
Web: www.mkdmurrieta.com
SIC: 8021 Dentists' office
PA: My Kid's Dentist
17000 Red Hill Ave
909 854-1437

(P-15523)
PACIFIC DENTAL SERVICES LLC (PA)

Also Called: Pds
17000 Red Hill Ave, Irvine (92614-5626)
P.O. Box 19723 (92623-9723)
PHONE..................714 845-8500
Stephen E Thorne Iv, Pr
Brady Aase, *
Scott Beck, Vice Chairman*
Dan Burke, *
Joe Feldsien, *
▲ EMP: 300 EST: 1991
SQ FT: 40,000
SALES (est): 1.77MM Privately Held
Web: www.pacificdentalservices.com
SIC: 8021 6794 Dental clinic; Franchises,
selling or licensing

(P-15524)
PACIFIC DNTL SVCS HOLDG CO INC
17000 Red Hill Ave, Irvine (92614-5626)
PHONE..................714 845-8500
Stephen E Thorne Iv, CEO
EMP: 140 EST: 2013
SALES (est): 4.75MM Privately Held
Web: www.pacificdentalservices.com
SIC: 8021 6794 Dental clinic; Franchises,
selling or licensing

(P-15525)
PETER WYLAN DDS
Also Called: Bellflower Dental Group
10318 Rosecrans Ave, Bellflower
(90706-2702)
PHONE..................562 925-3765
Peter Wylan D.d.s., Owner
EMP: 100 EST: 1955
SQ FT: 2,000
SALES (est): 922.99K Privately Held
Web: www.bellflowerdentalgroup.com
SIC: 8021 8072 Dentists' office; Dental
laboratories

(P-15526)
PREMIER DENTAL HOLDINGS INC (PA)
Also Called: Sonrava
530 S Main St Ste 600, Orange
(92868-4544)
P.O. Box 14227 (92863-1227)
PHONE..................714 480-3000
Daniel Crowley, CEO
EMP: 180 EST: 2010
SALES (est): 452.07MM
SALES (corp-wide): 452.07MM Privately
Held
Web: www.orangepremierdental.com
SIC: 8021 Dental clinic

(P-15527)
ST JOHNS COMMUNITY HEALTH (PA)
Also Called: SAINT JOHN'S WELL CHILD
CENTER
808 W 58th St, Los Angeles (90037-3632)
PHONE..................323 541-1411
James J Mangia, CEO
Elizabeth Meisler, *
Joanne Choi, *
EMP: 170 EST: 1963
SALES (est): 151.28MM Privately Held
Web: www.sjch.org
SIC: 8021 8011 Dental clinic; Offices and
clinics of medical doctors

(P-15528)
TOAN D NGUYEN DDS INC
Also Called: TOAN D NGUYEN DDS INC
213 N San Dimas Ave, San Dimas
(91773-2649)

PHONE..................909 599-3398
EMP: 87
SALES (corp-wide): 280.72K Privately
Held
Web: www.sandimasdentistry.com
SIC: 8021 Dentists' office
PA: Toan D. Nguyen, D.D.S., Inc.
511 E 1st St Ste C
562 926-3354

(P-15529)
WESTERN DENTAL SERVICES INC (HQ)
Also Called: Western Dental & Orthodontics
530 S Main St Ste 600, Orange
(92868-4544)
P.O. Box 14227 (92863-1227)
PHONE..................714 480-3000
TOLL FREE: 800
Daniel D Crowley, CEO
Jeffrey Miller, CLO*
John Luther, Chief Dental Officer*
Preet M Takkar, *
William Dembereckyj, *
EMP: 350 EST: 1984
SALES (est): 451.12MM
SALES (corp-wide): 452.07MM Privately
Held
Web: www.westerndental.com
SIC: 8021 Dentists' office
PA: Premier Dental Holdings, Inc.
530 S Main St Ste 600
714 480-3000

8031 Offices And Clinics Of Osteopathic Physicians

(P-15530)
ARTEMIS INST FOR CLNCAL RES LL
770 Washington St Ste 300, San Diego
(92103-2209)
PHONE..................858 278-3647
EMP: 72 EST: 2008
SALES (est): 7.85MM Privately Held
Web: www.artemis-research.com
SIC: 8031 8011 Offices and clinics of
osteopathic physicians; Psychiatrist

(P-15531)
PROVIDNCE FACEY MED FOUNDATION
Also Called: Exer
2655 1st St, Simi Valley (93065-1547)
PHONE..................805 206-2000
EMP: 88
SALES (corp-wide): 91.37MM Privately
Held
Web: www.facey.com
SIC: 8031 8011 Offices and clinics of
osteopathic physicians; Offices and clinics
of medical doctors
PA: Providence Facey Medical Foundation
15451 San Frnndo Mssion B
818 365-9531

(P-15532)
PROVIDNCE FACEY MED FOUNDATION
191 S Buena Vista St, Burbank
(91505-4554)
PHONE..................818 861-7831
Jennifer Sung Md, Brnch Mgr
EMP: 88
SALES (corp-wide): 91.37MM Privately
Held
Web: www.facey.com

SIC: 8031 8011 Offices and clinics of
osteopathic physicians; Offices and clinics
of medical doctors
PA: Providence Facey Medical Foundation
15451 San Frnndo Mssion B
818 365-9531

(P-15533)
VISTA COMMUNITY CLINIC (PA)
Also Called: Lake Elsnore Dntl Spcalty Care
1000 Vale Terrace Dr, Vista (92084-5297)
PHONE..................760 631-5000
Fernando Sanudo, CEO
Michele Lambert, *
EMP: 280 EST: 1972
SQ FT: 60,000
SALES (est): 98.04MM
SALES (corp-wide): 98.04MM Privately
Held
Web: www.vistacommunityclinic.org
SIC: 8031 8011 Offices and clinics of
osteopathic physicians; Medical centers

8041 Offices And Clinics Of Chiropractors

(P-15534)
CHIROTECH INC
Also Called: Chirotouch
9265 Sky Park Ct Ste 200, San Diego
(92123-4312)
PHONE..................619 528-0040
Ron Nielle, Owner
EMP: 225 EST: 2007
SALES (est): 9.56MM Privately Held
Web: www.chirotouch.com
SIC: 8041 Offices and clinics of chiropractors

8042 Offices And Clinics Of Optometrists

(P-15535)
JAMES G MEYERS & ASSOCIATES
Also Called: Eye Exam of California
4353 La Jolla Village Dr Ste 180, San Diego
(92122-1259)
PHONE..................858 622-2165
Elliott Shapiro, Owner
EMP: 30
SALES (corp-wide): 11.7MM Privately
Held
Web: www.shapirofamilyoptometry.com
SIC: 8042 3851 Offices and clinics of
optometrists; Contact lenses
PA: James G Meyers & Associates
11700 Princeton Pike
513 671-0111

(P-15536)
TOTAL VISION LLC
27271 Las Ramblas Ste 200a, Mission Viejo
(92691-8041)
PHONE..................949 652-7242
Scott Strachan, Pr
Doug Lattime, VP Fin
Broke Jakovich, VP Opers
EMP: 194 EST: 2014
SQ FT: 3,000
SALES (est): 19MM
SALES (corp-wide): 19MM Privately Held
Web: www.yourtotalvision.com
SIC: 8042 Group and corporate practice,
optometrist
PA: Total Vision Holdings, Llc
277 Park Ave Fl 27
212 704-5364

8049 Offices Of Health Practitioner

(P-15537)
CASA CLINA HOSP CTRS FOR HLTHC
910 E Alosta Ave, Azusa (91702-2709)
PHONE..................626 334-8735
EMP: 149
SALES (corp-wide): 136.57MM Privately
Held
Web: www.casacolina.org
SIC: 8049 Physical therapist
HQ: Casa Colina Hospital And Centers For
Healthcare
255 E Bonita Ave
Pomona CA 91767
909 596-7733

(P-15538)
CHE SNIOR PSYCHLOGICAL SVCS PC
4929 Wilshire Blvd Ste 510, Los Angeles
(90010-3820)
PHONE..................888 307-0893
Joe Tritel, Brnch Mgr
EMP: 81
SALES (corp-wide): 22.32MM Privately
Held
Web: www.cheservices.com
SIC: 8049 Clinical psychologist
PA: Che Senior Psychological Services,
P.C.
3512 Quentin Rd
718 854-8370

(P-15539)
CTR FOR AUTISM RLTD DISORDERS
21600 Oxnard St Ste 1800, Woodland Hills
(91367-7807)
PHONE..................209 618-1253
EMP: 72 EST: 2020
SALES (est): 4MM Privately Held
Web: www.centerforautism.com
SIC: 8049 Clinical psychologist

(P-15540)
EMPERORS CLLEGE TRDTNAL ORNTAL
Also Called: Emperors Cllege Clnic Trdtnal
1807 Wilshire Blvd Ste B, Santa Monica
(90403-5678)
PHONE..................310 453-8383
Yun Kim, Pr
Bong Dal Kim, Stockholder*
EMP: 82 EST: 1983
SQ FT: 10,000
SALES (est): 2.35MM Privately Held
Web: www.emperors.edu
SIC: 8049 Acupuncturist

(P-15541)
EQUINOX-76TH STREET INC
Also Called: Health Fitness America
1980 Main St Fl 4, Irvine (92614-7200)
PHONE..................949 975-8400
Ian Mcfodden, Mgr
EMP: 85
SALES (corp-wide): 611.7MM Privately
Held
SIC: 8049 7991 Physical therapist; Health
club
HQ: Equinox-76th Street, Inc.
895 Broadway Fl 3
New York NY 10003

▲ = Import ▼ = Export
◆ = Import/Export

(P-15542)
HYPERION HEALING LLC
20660 Bahama St, Chatsworth
(91311-6101)
PHONE..................................818 626-9078
EMP: 84 **EST:** 2018
SALES (est): 292.83K
SALES (corp-wide): 1.13B **Privately Held**
SIC: 8049 Offices of health practitioner
PA: Trulieve Cannabis Corp.
6749 Ben Bostic Rd
844 878-5438

(P-15543)
IN STEPPS INC
Also Called: SUPPORT, TREATMENT, &
EDUCATIO
10 Skypark Circle, Suite 110, Irvine (92614)
PHONE..................................949 474-1493
Y E M Bruinsma, *Ex Dir*
Yvonne E M Bruinsma, *Ex Dir*
Lindsey Lewis, *Reg Dir*
EMP: 82 **EST:** 2010
SALES (est): 175K **Privately Held**
Web: www.instepps.com
SIC: 8049 Occupational therapist

(P-15544)
**INLAND VALLEY PARTNERS
LLC**
Also Called: Inland Valley Care & Rehab Ctr
250 W Artesia St, Pomona (91768-1807)
PHONE..................................909 623-7100
EMP: 250 **EST:** 1998
SALES (est): 31.86MM **Privately Held**
Web: www.inlandvalleyhopepartners.org
SIC: 8049 Nurses and other medical
assistants

(P-15545)
**INSTITUTE FOR APPLIED
BHVIOR A (PA)**
Also Called: Iaba
5601 W Slauson Ave, Culver City
(90230-6582)
PHONE..................................310 649-0499
Gary W Lavigna Ph.d., *Pr*
▲ **EMP:** 140 **EST:** 1982
SALES (est): 19.66MM
SALES (corp-wide): 19.66MM **Privately
Held**
Web: www.iaba.com
SIC: 8049 8741 8093 Clinical psychologist;
Management services; Specialty outpatient
clinics, nec

(P-15546)
**INSTITUTE FOR APPLIED
BHVIOR A**
Also Called: Iaba
2310 E Ponderosa Dr Ste 1, Camarillo
(93010-4747)
PHONE..................................805 987-5886
Gary Lavigna, *Dir*
EMP: 84
SALES (corp-wide): 25.84MM **Privately
Held**
Web: www.iaba.com
SIC: 8049 8399 Clinical psychologist;
Community development groups
PA: Institute For Applied Behavior
Analysis, A Psychological Corporation
5601 W Slauson Ave # 290
310 649-0499

(P-15547)
**INSTITUTE FOR APPLIED
BHVIOR A**
9221 Corbin Ave, Northridge (91324-2483)

PHONE..................................818 341-1933
EMP: 83
SALES (corp-wide): 19.66MM **Privately
Held**
Web: www.iaba.com
SIC: 8049 Nutrition specialist
PA: Institute For Applied Behavior
Analysis, A Psychological Corporation
5601 W Slauson Ave # 290
310 649-0499

(P-15548)
INTERCARE THERAPY INC
4221 Wilshire Blvd Ste 300a, Los Angeles
(90010-3537)
PHONE..................................323 866-1880
Naomi Heller, *Pr*
Eri Heller, *
EMP: 130 **EST:** 1979
SALES (est): 9.78MM **Privately Held**
Web: www.intercaretherapy.com
SIC: 8049 Psychologist, psychotherapist and
hypnotist

(P-15549)
INTERFACE REHAB INC
774 S Placentia Ave Ste 200, Placentia
(92870-6838)
PHONE..................................714 646-8300
Anant B Desai, *CEO*
Falguni Desai, *
EMP: 1000 **EST:** 1995
SQ FT: 10,000
SALES (est): 28.13MM **Privately Held**
Web: www.interfacerehab.com
SIC: 8049 Physical therapist

(P-15550)
LOCUMS UNLIMITED LLC
4141 Jutland Dr Ste 305, San Diego
(92117-3658)
PHONE..................................619 550-3763
EMP: 802 **EST:** 2015
SALES (est): 452.4K **Privately Held**
Web: www.locumsunlimited.com
SIC: 8049 Nurses and other medical
assistants
PA: Aya Healthcare, Inc.
5930 Crnrstone Ct W Ste 3

(P-15551)
**MICHAEL G FRTNSCE PHYSCL
THRAP**
Also Called: Fortanasce & Associates
24630 Washington Ave Ste 200, Murrieta
(92562-6177)
P.O. Box 661150 (91066-1150)
PHONE..................................626 446-7027
Michael Fortanasce, *Pr*
EMP: 120 **EST:** 1981
SALES (est): 1.35MM **Privately Held**
SIC: 8049 Physiotherapist

(P-15552)
**PHYSICAL RHBLTATION
NETWRK LLC (PA)**
Also Called: Cal Rehab
2035 Corte Del Nogal Ste 200, Carlsbad
(92011-1445)
PHONE..................................760 931-8310
Ajay Gupta, *CEO*
Rob Pace, *
Nick Poan, *
EMP: 75 **EST:** 1992
SALES (est): 37.71MM **Privately Held**
Web: www.prnpt.com
SIC: 8049 8011 8093 Physiotherapist;
Sports medicine specialist, physician;
Rehabilitation center, outpatient treatment

(P-15553)
**QUANTUM BHVIORAL
SOLUTIONS INC (PA)**
445 S Figueroa St Ste 3100, Los Angeles
(90071-1635)
PHONE..................................626 531-6999
Gevork Gevojanyan, *Prin*
EMP: 71 **EST:** 2012
SALES (est): 779.54K
SALES (corp-wide): 779.54K **Privately
Held**
Web:
www.quantumbehavioralsolutions.com
SIC: 8049 Clinical psychologist

(P-15554)
**QUANTUM BHVIORAL
SOLUTIONS INC**
2400 E Katella Ave Ste 800, Anaheim
(92806-5955)
PHONE..................................626 531-6999
EMP: 70
SALES (corp-wide): 779.54K **Privately
Held**
Web:
www.quantumbehavioralsolutions.com
SIC: 8049 Clinical psychologist
PA: Quantum Behavioral Solutions, Inc.
445 S Figueroa St # 3100
626 531-6999

(P-15555)
**RANCHO PHYSICAL THERAPY
INC**
Also Called: Rancho Physical Therapy
277 Rancheros Dr, San Marcos
(92069-2976)
PHONE..................................760 752-1011
James Lin, *Brnch Mgr*
EMP: 166
SALES (corp-wide): 9.79MM **Privately
Held**
Web: www.ranchopt.com
SIC: 8049 8011 Physical therapist; Offices
and clinics of medical doctors
PA: Rancho Physical Therapy, Inc.
24630 Washington Ave # 200
951 696-9353

(P-15556)
**ROBERT BALLARD REHAB
HOSPITAL (HQ)**
Also Called: Ballard Rehabilitation Hospital
1760 W 16th St, San Bernardino
(92411-1150)
PHONE..................................909 473-1200
Edward Palacios, *CEO*
Mary Hunt, *COO*
▲ **EMP:** 90 **EST:** 1993
SALES (est): 24.54MM
SALES (corp-wide): 434.59MM **Privately
Held**
Web: www.ballardrehab.com
SIC: 8049 8051 8069 Physical therapist;
Skilled nursing care facilities; Specialty
hospitals, except psychiatric
PA: Vibra Healthcare, Llc
4600 Lena Dr
717 591-5700

(P-15557)
THERAPYTRAVELERS LLC
355 Redondo Ave, Long Beach
(90814-2656)
PHONE..................................888 223-8002
EMP: 73 **EST:** 2017
SALES (est): 1.99MM **Privately Held**
Web:
www.epicspecialeducationstaffing.com

SIC: 8049 Biofeedback therapist

(P-15558)
**VENTURA COUNTY MEDICAL
CENTER**
300 Hillmont Ave, Ventura (93003-1651)
PHONE..................................805 652-6729
Myung Ryang, *Prin*
EMP: 77
SALES (corp-wide): 21.77MM **Privately
Held**
Web: www.vchca.org
SIC: 8049 Clinical psychologist
PA: Ventura County Medical Center
3291 Loma Vista Rd
805 652-6000

(P-15559)
VISTA JV PARTNERS LLC ✪
2035 Corte Del Nogal Ste 200, Carlsbad
(92011-1445)
PHONE..................................214 738-2771
Ajay Gupta, *CEO*
Herschel Sharp, *Sr VP*
EMP: 300 **EST:** 2023
SALES (est): 2MM **Privately Held**
SIC: 8049 Physical therapist

**8051 Skilled Nursing Care
Facilities**

(P-15560)
**ACCREDITED NURSING
SERVICES**
Also Called: Accredited Nursing Care
80 S Lake Ave Ste 630, Pasadena
(91101-4971)
PHONE..................................626 573-1234
Teresa Salvino, *Mgr*
EMP: 185
SALES (corp-wide): 2.91MM **Privately
Held**
SIC: 8051 Skilled nursing care facilities
PA: Accredited Nursing Services
17141 Ventura Blvd # 201
818 986-6017

(P-15561)
AG SEAL BEACH LLC
Also Called: Seal Bch Hlth Rhbilitation Ctr
3000 N Gate Rd, Seal Beach (90740-2535)
PHONE..................................562 592-2477
EMP: 205 **EST:** 2003
SALES (est): 900.81K **Privately Held**
SIC: 8051 Skilled nursing care facilities

(P-15562)
**AHMC GARFIELD MEDICAL CTR
LP**
Also Called: WHITTIER HOSPITAL MEDICAL
CENT
525 N Garfield Ave, Monterey Park
(91754-1205)
PHONE..................................626 573-2222
Patrick Petre, *CEO*
Steve Maekewa, *Pt*
EMP: 150 **EST:** 1997
SALES (est): 182.95MM
SALES (corp-wide): 325.41MM **Privately
Held**
Web: www.ahmchealth.com
SIC: 8051 8062 Skilled nursing care facilities
; General medical and surgical hospitals
PA: Ahmc Healthcare Inc.
506 W Valley Blvd Ste 300
626 943-7526

(P-15563)
AIR FORCE VILLAGE WEST INC
Also Called: Village West Health Center
17050 Arnold Dr, Riverside (92518-2806)
PHONE.................................951 697-2000
Mary Carruthers, *CEO*
James L Melin, *Prin*
Charles Dalton, *
Ervin Reed, *
EMP: 350 EST: 1985
SQ FT: 494,000
SALES (est): 5.76MM **Privately Held**
Web: www.westmontliving.com
SIC: 8051 8052 Convalescent home with continuous nursing care; Intermediate care facilities

(P-15564)
ALAMITOS-BELMONT REHAB INC
Also Called: ALAMITOS BELMONT REHABILITATIO
3901 E 4th St, Long Beach (90814-1699)
PHONE.................................562 434-8421
Shaun Dahl, *Admn*
Darian Dahl, *
EMP: 150 EST: 1969
SQ FT: 30,000
SALES (est): 8.03MM **Privately Held**
Web: www.alamitosbelmont.com
SIC: 8051 Skilled nursing care facilities

(P-15565)
AMADA ENTERPRISES INC
Also Called: View Heights Convalescent Hosp
12619 Avalon Blvd, Los Angeles (90061-2727)
PHONE.................................323 757-1881
Shedrick D Jones, *CEO*
John Jones, *
EMP: 135 EST: 1968
SQ FT: 36,600
SALES (est): 9.84MM **Privately Held**
Web: www.viewheights.com
SIC: 8051 Convalescent home with continuous nursing care

(P-15566)
AMERICAN RETIREMENT CORP
2107 Ocean Ave, Santa Monica (90405-2299)
PHONE.................................310 399-3227
EMP: 102
SALES (corp-wide): 2.83B **Publicly Held**
Web: www.brookdale.com
SIC: 8051 Skilled nursing care facilities
HQ: American Retirement Corporation
111 Westwood Pl Ste 200
Brentwood TN 37027
615 221-2250

(P-15567)
ANAHEIM HEALTHCARE CENTER LLC
Also Called: Anaheim Healthcare Center
501 S Beach Blvd, Anaheim (92804-1810)
PHONE.................................714 816-0540
EMP: 143 EST: 1995
SALES (est): 31.75MM **Privately Held**
Web: www.anaheimhealthcare.com
SIC: 8051 Convalescent home with continuous nursing care

(P-15568)
ANTELOPE VLY RETIREMENT HM INC
Also Called: Antelope Vly Retirement Manor
44523 15th St W, Lancaster (93534-2847)
PHONE.................................661 949-5584
Mark Aronoss, *Brnch Mgr*
EMP: 179
SALES (corp-wide): 3.97MM **Privately Held**
Web: www.avrv.org
SIC: 8051 8361 Skilled nursing care facilities ; Residential care
PA: Antelope Valley Retirement Home, Inc.
44523 15th St W
661 949-5584

(P-15569)
ARCADIA CONVALESCENT HOSP INC
Also Called: Shadow Hills Convalescent Home
10158 Sunland Blvd, Sunland (91040-1651)
PHONE.................................818 352-4438
Orlando Clarizio, *Admn*
EMP: 74
SALES (corp-wide): 18.4MM **Privately Held**
Web: www.arcadiahcc.com
SIC: 8051 Convalescent home with continuous nursing care
PA: Arcadia Convalescent Hospital, Inc.
1601 S Baldwin Ave
626 445-2170

(P-15570)
ASCENT HEALTH SERVICES LLC
27101 Puerta Real Ste 450, Mission Viejo (92691-8566)
PHONE.................................719 250-0824
EMP: 92 EST: 2019
SALES (est): 2.67MM
SALES (corp-wide): 3.73B **Publicly Held**
SIC: 8051 Skilled nursing care facilities
PA: The Ensign Group Inc
29222 Rncho Vejo Rd Ste 1
949 487-9500

(P-15571)
ASH HOLDINGS LLC
Also Called: Redlands Healthcare Center
1620 W Fern Ave, Redlands (92373-4918)
PHONE.................................909 793-2609
Novie Sitanggang, *Managing Member*
EMP: 85 EST: 1999
SALES (est): 9.03MM
SALES (corp-wide): 3.11B **Publicly Held**
Web: www.redlandshealthcarecenter.com
SIC: 8051 Skilled nursing care facilities
HQ: California Opco, Llc
100 E San Marcos Blvd
San Marcos CA

(P-15572)
ASMB LLC
Also Called: Berkley East Healthcare Center
2021 Arizona Ave, Santa Monica (90404-1335)
PHONE.................................949 347-7100
Ryan Case, *CEO*
Jeffrey Bradshaw, *
EMP: 99 EST: 2019
SALES (est): 7.39MM **Privately Held**
Web: www.berkleyeast.com
SIC: 8051 Convalescent home with continuous nursing care

(P-15573)
ATHERTON BAPTIST HOMES
214 S Atlantic Blvd, Alhambra (91801-3298)
PHONE.................................626 863-1710
Craig Statton, *Pr*
Dennis E Mcfadden, *Pr*
Jackie Pascual, *
Angela Paniagua, *
Dale Torry, *
EMP: 200 EST: 1914
SQ FT: 42,000
SALES (est): 26.09MM **Privately Held**
Web: www.abh.org
SIC: 8051 Convalescent home with continuous nursing care

(P-15574)
ATLANTIC MEM HLTHCARE ASSOC IN (HQ)
Also Called: Atlantic Mem Healthcare Ctr
2750 Atlantic Ave, Long Beach (90806-2713)
PHONE.................................562 424-8101
Jake Rothey, *Pr*
EMP: 75 EST: 2002
SALES (est): 12.36MM
SALES (corp-wide): 3.73B **Publicly Held**
Web: www.atlanticmemorial.com
SIC: 8051 Convalescent home with continuous nursing care
PA: The Ensign Group Inc
29222 Rncho Vejo Rd Ste 1
949 487-9500

(P-15575)
ATLANTIC MEM HLTHCARE ASSOC IN
Also Called: Marlora Convalescent Hospital
3801 E Anaheim St, Long Beach (90804-4004)
PHONE.................................562 494-3311
Marrilyn Hauser, *Admn*
EMP: 100
SQ FT: 23,000
SALES (corp-wide): 3.73B **Publicly Held**
Web: www.atlanticmemorial.com
SIC: 8051 Convalescent home with continuous nursing care
HQ: Atlantic Memorial Healthcare Associates, Inc.
2750 Atlantic Ave
Long Beach CA 90806
562 424-8101

(P-15576)
B-SPRING VALLEY LLC
Also Called: Brighton Place Spring Valley
9009 Campo Rd, Spring Valley (91977-1112)
PHONE.................................619 797-3991
EMP: 91 EST: 2006
SALES (est): 9.5MM **Privately Held**
Web: www.brightonplacesv.com
SIC: 8051 Convalescent home with continuous nursing care

(P-15577)
BAKERSFELD HLTHCARE WLLNESS CN
Also Called: Rehabilitation Ctr Bakersfield
2211 Mount Vernon Ave, Bakersfield (93306-3309)
PHONE.................................661 872-2121
EMP: 99 EST: 2009
SALES (est): 9.82MM **Privately Held**
Web: www.rcbakersfield.org
SIC: 8051 Convalescent home with continuous nursing care

(P-15578)
BAKERSFIELDIDENCE OPCO LLC
Also Called: Kern River Transitional Care
5151 Knudsen Dr, Bakersfield (93308-7199)
PHONE.................................661 399-2472
Jason Murray, *Prin*
Mark Hancock, *
EMP: 85 EST: 2016
SALES (est): 8.38MM
SALES (corp-wide): 3.11B **Publicly Held**
Web: www.kernrivertc.com
SIC: 8051 Convalescent home with continuous nursing care
HQ: Providence Group North, Llc
262 N University Ave
Farmington UT 84025
801 447-9829

(P-15579)
BAYSHORE HEALTHCARE INC
Also Called: Bella Vsta Trnstional Care Ctr
3033 Augusta St, San Luis Obispo (93401-5820)
PHONE.................................805 544-5100
Benjamin Flinders, *CEO*
Johannah Tamba, *
Paul Mclean, *Sec*
EMP: 160 EST: 1975
SQ FT: 43,000
SALES (est): 1.61MM **Privately Held**
Web: www.compass-health.com
SIC: 8051 Convalescent home with continuous nursing care

(P-15580)
BAYSIDE HEALTHCARE INC
Also Called: South Bay Post Acute Care
553 F St, Chula Vista (91910-3515)
PHONE.................................619 426-8611
Glenn Matthews, *Prin*
Perris Bennett, *
EMP: 176 EST: 2014
SALES (est): 4.8MM **Privately Held**
SIC: 8051 Skilled nursing care facilities

(P-15581)
BELL VILLA CARE ASSOCIATES LLC
Also Called: Rose Villa Healthcare Center
9028 Rose St, Bellflower (90706-6418)
PHONE.................................562 925-4252
David Howell, *Ex Dir*
EMP: 95 EST: 2003
SALES (est): 4.96MM **Privately Held**
Web: www.rosevillahealthcare.com
SIC: 8051 Convalescent home with continuous nursing care

(P-15582)
BEVERLY WEST HEALTH CARE INC
1020 S Fairfax Ave, Los Angeles (90019-4409)
PHONE.................................323 938-2451
Louise Koss, *Pr*
Lydia Cruz, *
EMP: 85 EST: 1981
SQ FT: 23,848
SALES (est): 9.28MM **Privately Held**
SIC: 8051 Convalescent home with continuous nursing care

(P-15583)
BRETHREN HILLCREST HOMES
Also Called: Hillcrest
2705 Mountain View Dr Ofc, La Verne (91750-4398)
PHONE.................................909 593-4917
Matthew Neely, *Pr*
Barbara Feliciano, *
EMP: 230 EST: 1947
SQ FT: 34,000
SALES (est): 30.44MM **Privately Held**
Web: www.livingathillcrest.org

SIC: 8051 8059 8361 Extended care facility; Nursing home, except skilled and intermediate care facility; Rest home, with health care incidental

(P-15584)

BURLINGTON CONVALESCENT HOSP (PA)

Also Called: View Park Convalescent Center
845 S Burlington Ave, Los Angeles (90057-4296)
PHONE......................213 381-5585
Jacob Friedman, *Pr*
Ervin Friedman, *
Kathleen Becker, *
EMP: 100 EST: 1967
SQ FT: 5,000
SALES (est): 8.31MM
SALES (corp-wide): 8.31MM **Privately Held**
Web: www.burlingtonconvalescent.com
SIC: 8051 8059 8052 Convalescent home with continuous nursing care; Convalescent home; Intermediate care facilities

(P-15585)

BURLINGTON CONVALESCENT HOSP

Also Called: View Park Convalescent Center
3737 Don Felipe Dr, Los Angeles (90008-4210)
PHONE......................323 295-7737
Joe Voltes, *Mgr*
EMP: 179
SQ FT: 40,000
SALES (corp-wide): 8.31MM **Privately Held**
Web: www.alternativesforseniors.com
SIC: 8051 Convalescent home with continuous nursing care
PA: Burlington Convalescent Hospital
845 S Burlington Ave
213 381-5585

(P-15586)

CALIMESA OPERATIONS LLC

Also Called: CALIMESA POST ACUTE
13542 2nd St, Yucaipa (92399-5396)
PHONE......................909 795-2421
Covey Christensen, *
EMP: 105 EST: 2015
SALES (est): 9.66MM **Privately Held**
SIC: 8051 Skilled nursing care facilities

(P-15587)

CAMBRIDGE SIERRA HOLDINGS LLC

Also Called: RECHE CANYON REGIONAL REHAB CE
1350 Reche Canyon Rd, Colton (92324-9528)
PHONE......................909 370-4411
Rb Bridges, *CEO*
EMP: 350 EST: 1991
SALES (est): 26.56MM **Privately Held**
SIC: 8051 Convalescent home with continuous nursing care

(P-15588)

CEDAR HOLDINGS LLC

Also Called: Highland Palms Healthcare Ctr
7534 Palm Ave, Highland (92346-3736)
PHONE......................909 862-0611
Ryan Mccook, *Managing Member*
EMP: 99 EST: 2001
SALES (est): 4.27MM
SALES (corp-wide): 3.11B **Publicly Held**
Web: www.highlandpalmshc.com

SIC: 8051 Convalescent home with continuous nursing care
HQ: California Opco, Llc
100 E San Marcos Blvd
San Marcos CA

(P-15589)

CEDAR OPERATIONS LLC

Also Called: Cedar Mountain Post Acute
11970 4th St, Yucaipa (92399-2720)
PHONE......................909 790-2273
EMP: 140 EST: 2001
SALES (est): 13.56MM
SALES (corp-wide): 13.56MM **Privately Held**
Web: www.cedarmountainpa.org
SIC: 8051 Skilled nursing care facilities
PA: Madison Creek Partners, Llc
26522 La Alameda Ste 300
949 449-2500

(P-15590)

CENTINELA SKLLED NRSING WLLNES

950 S Flower St, Inglewood (90301-4111)
PHONE......................310 674-3216
Nichole Tons, *VP*
EMP: 99 EST: 2008
SQ FT: 6,000
SALES (est): 4.94MM **Privately Held**
Web: www.centinelanursingwest.com
SIC: 8051 Skilled nursing care facilities

(P-15591)

CHA HOLLYWOOD MEDICAL CTR LP

4636 Fountain Ave, Los Angeles (90029-1830)
PHONE......................213 413-3000
Annette Brunin, *Brnch Mgr*
EMP: 1440
Web: www.hollywoodpresbyterian.com
SIC: 8051 Skilled nursing care facilities
HQ: Cha Hollywood Medical Center Lp
1300 N Vermont Ave
Los Angeles CA 90027
213 413-3000

(P-15592)

COASTAL HEALTH CARE INC

Also Called: BRENTWOOD HEALTH CARE CENTER
1321 Franklin St, Santa Monica (90404-2603)
PHONE......................310 828-5596
John Sorensen, *Pr*
Tim Paulsen, *Ex VP*
EMP: 75 EST: 1987
SALES (est): 10.48MM **Privately Held**
Web: www.brentwoodnursing.com
SIC: 8051 Convalescent home with continuous nursing care

(P-15593)

COASTAL VIEW HALTHCARE CTR LLC

Also Called: Coastal View Healthcare Center
4904 Telegraph Rd, Ventura (93003-4109)
PHONE......................805 642-4101
EMP: 96 EST: 2012
SALES (est): 10.96MM **Privately Held**
Web: www.coastalviewhcc.com
SIC: 8051 Convalescent home with continuous nursing care

(P-15594)

COLDWATER CARE CENTER LLC

Also Called: Sherman Village Hlth Care Ctr

12750 Riverside Dr, North Hollywood (91607-3319)
PHONE......................818 766-6105
Elvira Posada, *Mgr*
Brenan Lowery, *Mgr*
EMP: 170 EST: 2010
SALES (est): 14.62MM **Privately Held**
Web: www.shermanvillagehc.com
SIC: 8051 Convalescent home with continuous nursing care

(P-15595)

COMMUNITY CARE CENTER

8665 La Mesa Blvd, La Mesa (91942-9593)
PHONE......................619 465-0702
EMP: 95 EST: 2019
SALES (est): 19.44MM **Privately Held**
Web: www.communitycarectr.com
SIC: 8051 Convalescent home with continuous nursing care

(P-15596)

COMMUNITY CARE ON PALM RVRSIDE

4768 Palm Ave, Riverside (92501-4012)
PHONE......................951 686-9001
Ezequiel Bercovich, *Prin*
EMP: 85 EST: 2020
SALES (est): 4.93MM **Privately Held**
Web: www.cconpalm.com
SIC: 8051 Convalescent home with continuous nursing care

(P-15597)

COMPASS HEALTH INC

Also Called: Compas Health
290 Heather Ct, Templeton (93465-9738)
PHONE......................805 434-3035
Mark Woolpert, *Pr*
EMP: 155
Web: www.compass-health.com
SIC: 8051 Convalescent home with continuous nursing care
PA: Compass Health, Inc.
200 S 13th St Ste 208

(P-15598)

COMPASS HEALTH INC

Also Called: Mission View Health Center
1425 Woodside Dr, San Luis Obispo (93401-5936)
PHONE......................805 543-0210
Linda Lindsey, *Mgr*
EMP: 155
Web: www.compass-health.com
SIC: 8051 Skilled nursing care facilities
PA: Compass Health, Inc.
200 S 13th St Ste 208

(P-15599)

COMPASS HEALTH INC

Also Called: Bayside Care Center
1405 Teresa Dr, Morro Bay (93442-2457)
PHONE......................805 772-7372
Harold Carder, *Mgr*
EMP: 155
Web: www.compass-health.com
SIC: 8051 Skilled nursing care facilities
PA: Compass Health, Inc.
200 S 13th St Ste 208

(P-15600)

COMPASS HEALTH INC

Also Called: Arroyo Grande Care Center
1212 Farroll Ave, Arroyo Grande (93420-3718)
PHONE......................805 489-8137
Harold Carder, *Admn*
EMP: 155
Web: www.compass-health.com

SIC: 8051 Skilled nursing care facilities
PA: Compass Health, Inc.
200 S 13th St Ste 208

(P-15601)

COMPASS HEALTH INC

Also Called: Danish Care Center
10805 El Camino Real, Atascadero (93422-8868)
PHONE......................805 466-9254
Mark Woolpert, *Pr*
EMP: 155
Web: www.compass-health.com
SIC: 8051 Skilled nursing care facilities
PA: Compass Health, Inc.
200 S 13th St Ste 208

(P-15602)

COMPASS HEALTH INC

Also Called: Alto Lucero Transitional Care
3880 Via Lucero, Santa Barbara (93110-1605)
PHONE......................805 687-6651
Kirk Klotthor, *Admn*
EMP: 155
Web: www.compass-health.com
SIC: 8051 Convalescent home with continuous nursing care
PA: Compass Health, Inc.
200 S 13th St Ste 208

(P-15603)

COUNTRY HILLS HEALTH CARE INC

Also Called: Country Hills Post Acute
1580 Broadway, El Cajon (92021-5124)
PHONE......................619 441-8745
Glen Larson, *Pr*
EMP: 247 EST: 1991
SALES (est): 34.85MM **Privately Held**
Web: www.countryhills.com
SIC: 8051 Convalescent home with continuous nursing care

(P-15604)

COUNTRY OAKS CARE CENTER INC

830 E Chapel St, Santa Maria (93454-4699)
PHONE......................805 922-6657
John Henning, *Adm/Dir*
Sharon Henning, *
EMP: 70 EST: 1968
SQ FT: 14,000
SALES (est): 4.89MM **Privately Held**
Web: www.countryoakscarecenter.com
SIC: 8051 Convalescent home with continuous nursing care

(P-15605)

COUNTRY VILLA NURSING CTR INC

Also Called: Country Vlla Nrsing Rhbltton
340 S Alvarado St, Los Angeles (90001)
PHONE......................213 484-9730
Stephen Reissman, *CEO*
Steven Reissman, *CEO*
Diane Reissman, *Sr VP*
Eddie Rowles, *VP*
EMP: 125 EST: 1990
SQ FT: 18,000
SALES (est): 22.3MM **Privately Held**
Web: www.losangelesrehabwc.com
SIC: 8051 Convalescent home with continuous nursing care

(P-15606)

COUNTRY VILLA SERVICE CORP

400 W Huntington Dr, Arcadia (91007-3470)

PHONE..............................626 445-2421
Shelly Andresen, *Prin*
EMP: 102
SALES (corp-wide): 28.62MM **Privately Held**
Web: www.huntingtondrivehcc.com
SIC: 8051 Convalescent home with continuous nursing care
PA: Country Villa Service Corp.
2400 E Katella Ave # 800
310 574-3733

(P-15607)
COUNTRY VILLA SERVICE CORP
3611 E Imperial Hwy, Lynwood (90262-2608)
PHONE..............................310 537-2500
Jacob Wintner, *Brnch Mgr*
EMP: 102
SALES (corp-wide): 88.5MM **Privately Held**
Web: www.evictionlawyer.com
SIC: 8051 Convalescent home with continuous nursing care
PA: Country Villa Service Corp.
2400 E Katella Ave # 800
310 574-3733

(P-15608)
COUNTRY VILLA SERVICE CORP
1208 S Central Ave, Glendale (91204-2504)
PHONE..............................818 246-5516
Adam Mitchel, *Admn*
EMP: 102
SALES (corp-wide): 28.62MM **Privately Held**
Web: www.evictionlawyer.com
SIC: 8051 Skilled nursing care facilities
PA: Country Villa Service Corp.
2400 E Katella Ave # 800
310 574-3733

(P-15609)
COUNTY OF SAN DIEGO
Also Called: Health & Human Services- Aging
9065 Edgemoor Dr, Santee (92071-3037)
PHONE..............................619 956-2800
Gwen Marie Hilleary, *Mgr*
EMP: 96
Web: www.sandiegocounty.gov
SIC: 8051 9431 Skilled nursing care facilities ; Administration of public health programs, County government
PA: County Of San Diego
1600 Pacific Hwy Ste 209
619 531-5880

(P-15610)
COVENANT CARE CALIFORNIA LLC
Also Called: St. Edna Sb-Cute Rhbltton Ctr
1929 N Fairview St, Santa Ana (92706-2205)
PHONE..............................714 554-9700
Joshua Torres, *Mgr*
EMP: 86
Web: www.stedna.com
SIC: 8051 Convalescent home with continuous nursing care
HQ: Covenant Care California, Llc
120 Vantis Dr Ste 200
Aliso Viejo CA 92656

(P-15611)
COVENANT CARE CALIFORNIA LLC
Also Called: Huntington Park Nursing Center
6425 Miles Ave, Huntington Park (90255-4315)

PHONE..............................323 589-5941
Toni Mazzeo, *Brnch Mgr*
EMP: 92
Web: www.huntingtonparknursingcenter.com
SIC: 8051 Convalescent home with continuous nursing care
HQ: Covenant Care California, Llc
120 Vantis Dr Ste 200
Aliso Viejo CA 92656

(P-15612)
COVENANT CARE CALIFORNIA LLC
Also Called: Royal Care Skilled Nursing Ctr
2725 Pacific Ave, Long Beach (90806-2612)
PHONE..............................562 427-7493
Nasreen Pervaiz, *Brnch Mgr*
EMP: 99
Web: www.royalcare.com
SIC: 8051 Convalescent home with continuous nursing care
HQ: Covenant Care California, Llc
120 Vantis Dr Ste 200
Aliso Viejo CA 92656

(P-15613)
COVENANT CARE CALIFORNIA LLC
Also Called: Shoreline Care Center
5225 S J St, Oxnard (93033-8320)
PHONE..............................805 488-3696
Cindy Poulsen, *Ex Dir*
EMP: 92
Web: www.shorelinecarecenter.com
SIC: 8051 Convalescent home with continuous nursing care
HQ: Covenant Care California, Llc
120 Vantis Dr Ste 200
Aliso Viejo CA 92656

(P-15614)
COVENANT CARE CALIFORNIA LLC
Also Called: Buena Vista Care Center
160 S Patterson Ave, Santa Barbara (93111-2006)
PHONE..............................805 964-4871
David Hibarger, *Brnch Mgr*
EMP: 135
Web: www.buenavistacarecenter.net
SIC: 8051 Convalescent home with continuous nursing care
HQ: Covenant Care California, Llc
120 Vantis Dr Ste 200
Aliso Viejo CA 92656

(P-15615)
COVENANT CARE LA JOLLA LLC
Also Called: La Jolla Nrsing Rhbltation Ctr
2552 Torrey Pines Rd Ste 1, La Jolla (92037-3432)
PHONE..............................858 453-5810
Lisa Parker, *Admn*
Carol Tiaadwai, *Admn*
EMP: 200 EST: 2005
SALES (est): 12.23MM **Privately Held**
Web: www.lajollanursingandrehab.com
SIC: 8051 Convalescent home with continuous nursing care
HQ: Covenant Care California, Llc
120 Vantis Dr Ste 200
Aliso Viejo CA 92656

(P-15616)
COVENANT CARE LLC (PA)
120 Vantis Dr Ste 200, Aliso Viejo (92656-2677)

PHONE..............................949 349-1200
EMP: 413 EST: 1994
SALES (est): 502.11MM **Privately Held**
Web: www.covenantcare.com
SIC: 8051 Skilled nursing care facilities

(P-15617)
COVENANT RTIREMENT COMMUNITIES
Also Called: COVENANT RETIREMENT COMMUNITIES
2550 Treasure Dr, Santa Barbara (93105-4148) ·
PHONE..............................805 687-0701
Rick K Fisk, *Pr*
EMP: 80
Web: www.covliving.org
SIC: 8051 Skilled nursing care facilities
HQ: Covenant Living West
5700 Old Orchrd Rd Ste 10
Skokie IL 60077

(P-15618)
COVENTRY COURT HEALTH CENTER
2040 S Euclid St, Anaheim (92802-3111)
PHONE..............................714 636-2800
Saun Dohl, *CEO*
EMP: 200 EST: 2000
SALES (est): 4.44MM **Privately Held**
Web: www.coventrycourt.org
SIC: 8051 Skilled nursing care facilities

(P-15619)
COVINA REHABILITATION CENTER
Also Called: Regency Health Services
261 W Badillo St, Covina (91723-1907)
PHONE..............................626 967-3874
Teresa Dearmond, *Dir*
Agnes Maron, *
EMP: 110 EST: 1971
SQ FT: 27,800
SALES (est): 11.96MM **Privately Held**
SIC: 8051 Skilled nursing care facilities

(P-15620)
CULVER WEST HEALTH CENTER LLC
4035 Grand View Blvd, Los Angeles (90066-5211)
PHONE..............................310 390-9506
EMP: 90 EST: 1996
SQ FT: 25,000
SALES (est): 9.4MM **Privately Held**
Web: www.culverwest.com
SIC: 8051 Convalescent home with continuous nursing care

(P-15621)
DEL RIO SANITARIUM INC
Also Called: Del Rio Convalescent
7002 Gage Ave, Bell Gardens (90201-2014)
PHONE..............................562 927-6586
Joy Thune, *Pr*
EMP: 150 EST: 1963
SALES (est): 11.37MM **Privately Held**
SIC: 8051 Skilled nursing care facilities

(P-15622)
DOUGLAS FIR HOLDINGS LLC
Also Called: Huntington Vly Healthcare Ctr
8382 Newman Ave, Huntington Beach (92647-7038)
PHONE..............................714 842-5551
Brad Truhar, *Admn*
EMP: 145 EST: 2000
SALES (est): 18.28MM

SALES (corp-wide): 3.11B **Publicly Held**
Web: www.hvhcc.com
SIC: 8051 Convalescent home with continuous nursing care
HQ: California Opco, Llc
100 E San Marcos Blvd
San Marcos CA

(P-15623)
DOWNEY COMMUNITY HEALTH CENTER
8425 Iowa St, Downey (90241-4984)
P.O. Box 340 (90241-0340)
PHONE..............................562 862-6506
Rich Coberly, *Admn*
Stanley Diller, *
EMP: 175 EST: 1980
SQ FT: 60,000
SALES (est): 21.79MM **Privately Held**
Web: www.downeycommunityhealthcenter.com
SIC: 8051 Convalescent home with continuous nursing care

(P-15624)
EAST LOS ANGLES HEALTHCARE LLC (HQ)
Also Called: Costa Del Sol Healthcare
1016 S Record Ave, Los Angeles (90023-2533)
PHONE..............................323 268-0106
EMP: 75 EST: 1971
SQ FT: 15,000
SALES (est): 8.37MM
SALES (corp-wide): 3.11B **Publicly Held**
SIC: 8051 Convalescent home with continuous nursing care
PA: Pacs Group, Inc.
262 N University Ave
801 447-9829

(P-15625)
ELDER CARE ALLIANCE CAMARILLO
Also Called: Almavia of Camarillo
2500 Ponderosa Dr N, Camarillo (93010-2383)
PHONE..............................510 769-2700
Jesse Jantzen, *CEO*
EMP: 75 EST: 1999
SALES (est): 6.31MM **Privately Held**
Web: www.eldercarealliance.org
SIC: 8051 Skilled nursing care facilities

(P-15626)
ELDORADO CARE CENTER LP
Also Called: Stillwater Post Acute
510 E Washington Ave, El Cajon (92020-5324)
PHONE..............................619 440-1211
Jacob Graff, *Pt*
EMP: 298 EST: 2008
SALES (est): 6.45MM **Privately Held**
Web: www.avocadopostacute.com
SIC: 8051 8322 Convalescent home with continuous nursing care; Adult day care center

(P-15627)
EMERITUS CORPORATION
Also Called: Brookdale Clairemont
5219 Clairemont Mesa Blvd, San Diego (92117-2206)
PHONE..............................858 292-8044
S Wheeler, *Ex Dir*
EMP: 192
SALES (corp-wide): 2.83B **Publicly Held**
Web: www.brookdale.com

SIC: 8051 Skilled nursing care facilities
HQ: Emeritus Corporation
6737 W Wash St Ste 2300
Milwaukee WI 53214

(P-15628)
EMERITUS CORPORATION
1001 N Lyon Ave, Hemet (92545-1753)
PHONE......................951 744-9861
EMP: 96
SALES (corp-wide): 2.83B **Publicly Held**
Web: www.emeritus.org
SIC: 8051 Skilled nursing care facilities
HQ: Emeritus Corporation
6737 W Wash St Ste 2300
Milwaukee WI 53214

(P-15629)
EMERITUS CORPORATION
Also Called: Terrace, The
22325 Barton Rd, Grand Terrace
(92313-5006)
PHONE......................909 420-0153
Larry Smith, *Dir*
EMP: 165
SALES (corp-wide): 2.83B **Publicly Held**
Web: www.emeritus.org
SIC: 8051 Skilled nursing care facilities
HQ: Emeritus Corporation
6737 W Wash St Ste 2300
Milwaukee WI 53214

(P-15630)
EMERITUS CORPORATION
Also Called: Emeritus At San Dimas
1740 S San Dimas Ave, San Dimas
(91773-5108)
PHONE......................909 394-0304
George Dualan, *Brnch Mgr*
EMP: 165
SALES (corp-wide): 2.83B **Publicly Held**
Web: www.brookdale.com
SIC: 8051 Skilled nursing care facilities
HQ: Emeritus Corporation
6737 W Wash St Ste 2300
Milwaukee WI 53214

(P-15631)
EMERITUS CORPORATION
Also Called: Emeritus At Casa Glendale
426 Piedmont Ave, Glendale (91206-3448)
PHONE......................818 246-7457
David Wilkens, *Brnch Mgr*
EMP: 165
SALES (corp-wide): 2.83B **Publicly Held**
Web: www.emeritus.org
SIC: 8051 Skilled nursing care facilities
HQ: Emeritus Corporation
6737 W Wash St Ste 2300
Milwaukee WI 53214

(P-15632)
EMERITUS CORPORATION
Also Called: Emeritus At Villa Colima
19850 Colima Rd, Walnut (91789-3411)
PHONE......................909 595-5030
Wanda Reynolds, *Brnch Mgr*
EMP: 131
SALES (corp-wide): 2.83B **Publicly Held**
Web: www.brookdale.com
SIC: 8051 Skilled nursing care facilities
HQ: Emeritus Corporation
6737 W Wash St Ste 2300
Milwaukee WI 53214

(P-15633)
EMERITUS CORPORATION
142 S Prospect St, Orange (92869-3842)
PHONE......................714 639-3590
Bernice Holmes, *Ex Dir*

EMP: 113
SALES (corp-wide): 2.83B **Publicly Held**
Web: www.emeritus.org
SIC: 8051 Skilled nursing care facilities
HQ: Emeritus Corporation
6737 W Wash St Ste 2300
Milwaukee WI 53214

(P-15634)
EMERITUS CORPORATION
Also Called: Rosewood Court
411 E Commonwealth Ave, Fullerton
(92832-2018)
PHONE......................714 441-0644
Jane Kim, *Off Mgr*
EMP: 165
SALES (corp-wide): 2.83B **Publicly Held**
Web: www.emeritus.org
SIC: 8051 Skilled nursing care facilities
HQ: Emeritus Corporation
6737 W Wash St Ste 2300
Milwaukee WI 53214

(P-15635)
ENDURA HEALTHCARE INC
29222 Rancho Viejo Rd Ste 127, San Juan
Capistrano (92675-1049)
PHONE......................949 487-9500
EMP: 219 EST: 2014
SALES (est): 3.06MM
SALES (corp-wide): 3.73B **Publicly Held**
SIC: 8051 Skilled nursing care facilities
PA: The Ensign Group Inc
29222 Rncho Vejo Rd Ste 1
949 487-9500

(P-15636)
ENSIGN GROUP INC
32232 Paseo Adelanto Ste 100, San Juan
Capistrano (92675-3600)
PHONE......................949 487-9500
Stapley Gregory, *Brnch Mgr*
EMP: 92
SALES (corp-wide): 3.73B **Publicly Held**
Web: www.ensigngroup.net
SIC: 8051 Convalescent home with
continuous nursing care
PA: The Ensign Group Inc
29222 Rncho Vejo Rd Ste 1
949 487-9500

(P-15637)
ENSIGN GROUP INC
340 Victoria St, Costa Mesa (92627-1914)
PHONE......................949 642-0387
Cindy Ramirez, *Dir*
EMP: 92
SALES (corp-wide): 3.73B **Publicly Held**
Web: www.ensigngroup.net
SIC: 8051 Convalescent home with
continuous nursing care
PA: The Ensign Group Inc
29222 Rncho Vejo Rd Ste 1
949 487-9500

(P-15638)
ENSIGN GROUP INC
Also Called: Downey Care Center
13007 Paramount Blvd, Downey
(90242-4329)
PHONE......................562 923-9301
Marc Brian, *Prin*
EMP: 598
SALES (corp-wide): 3.73B **Publicly Held**
Web: www.ensigngroup.net
SIC: 8051 Convalescent home with
continuous nursing care
PA: The Ensign Group Inc
29222 Rncho Vejo Rd Ste 1
949 487-9500

(P-15639)
ENSIGN GROUP INC
Also Called: Panaroma Gardens
9541 Van Nuys Blvd, Panorama City
(91402-1315)
PHONE......................818 893-6385
Alicia Gamero, *Admn*
EMP: 656
SALES (corp-wide): 3.73B **Publicly Held**
Web: www.ensigngroup.net
SIC: 8051 Convalescent home with
continuous nursing care
PA: The Ensign Group Inc
29222 Rncho Vejo Rd Ste 1
949 487-9500

(P-15640)
ENSIGN GROUP INC
Also Called: Whittier Hills Health Care Ctr
10426 Bogardus Ave, Whittier
(90603-2642)
PHONE......................562 947-7817
Lisa Matarazzo, *Admn*
EMP: 460
SQ FT: 36,316
SALES (corp-wide): 3.73B **Publicly Held**
Web: www.ensigngroup.net
SIC: 8051 8059 Convalescent home with
continuous nursing care; Rest home, with
health care
PA: The Ensign Group Inc
29222 Rncho Vejo Rd Ste 1
949 487-9500

(P-15641)
ENSIGN GROUP INC
Also Called: Mission Care Center
4800 Delta Ave, Rosemead (91770-1127)
PHONE......................626 607-2400
Tin Nelson, *Dir*
EMP: 253
SALES (corp-wide): 3.73B **Publicly Held**
Web: www.missioncareandrehab.com
SIC: 8051 Convalescent home with
continuous nursing care
PA: The Ensign Group Inc
29222 Rncho Vejo Rd Ste 1
949 487-9500

(P-15642)
ENSIGN GROUP INC
Also Called: Palomar Vista Healthcare Ctr
201 N Fig St, Escondido (92025-3416)
PHONE......................760 746-0303
William Adams, *Mgr*
EMP: 115
SALES (corp-wide): 3.73B **Publicly Held**
Web: www.ensigngroup.net
SIC: 8051 Convalescent home with
continuous nursing care
PA: The Ensign Group Inc
29222 Rncho Vejo Rd Ste 1
949 487-9500

(P-15643)
ENSIGN GROUP INC
4343 N Sierra Way, San Bernardino
(92407-3822)
PHONE......................909 886-4731
Barry R Port, *Brnch Mgr*
EMP: 104
SALES (corp-wide): 3.73B **Publicly Held**
Web: www.ensigngroup.net
SIC: 8051 Convalescent home with
continuous nursing care
PA: The Ensign Group Inc
29222 Rncho Vejo Rd Ste 1
949 487-9500

(P-15644)
ENSIGN PALM I LLC
Also Called: ENSIGN
2990 E Ramon Rd, Palm Springs
(92264-7931)
PHONE......................760 323-2638
Soon Burnam, *Treas*
Leeron Hever, *Admn*
EMP: 242 EST: 2001
SALES (est): 10.26MM
SALES (corp-wide): 3.73B **Publicly Held**
Web: www.premiercarecenter.net
SIC: 8051 Convalescent home with
continuous nursing care
PA: The Ensign Group Inc
29222 Rncho Vejo Rd Ste 1
949 487-9500

(P-15645)
ENSIGN SERVICES INC
29222 Rancho Viejo Rd Ste 127, San Juan
Capistrano (92675-1049)
PHONE......................949 487-9500
Christopher Christensen, *CEO*
Chad Keetch, *
Beverly B Wittekind, *
EMP: 90 EST: 2002
SALES (est): 83.21MM
SALES (corp-wide): 3.73B **Publicly Held**
Web: www.ensigngroup.net
SIC: 8051 Convalescent home with
continuous nursing care
PA: The Ensign Group Inc
29222 Rncho Vejo Rd Ste 1
949 487-9500

(P-15646)
ENSIGN SOUTHLAND LLC
Also Called: Southland Care
29222 Rancho Viejo Rd Ste 127, San Juan
Capistrano (92675-1049)
PHONE......................949 487-9500
EMP: 92 EST: 2000
SALES (est): 9.43MM
SALES (corp-wide): 3.73B **Publicly Held**
Web: www.ensigngroup.net
SIC: 8051 Extended care facility
PA: The Ensign Group Inc
29222 Rncho Vejo Rd Ste 1
949 487-9500

(P-15647)
ENSIGN WHITTIER EAST LLC
Also Called: ENSIGN
10426 Bogardus Ave, Whittier
(90603-2642)
PHONE......................562 947-7817
EMP: 219 EST: 2001
SALES (est): 19.32MM
SALES (corp-wide): 3.73B **Publicly Held**
Web: www.whittierhillshealthcare.com
SIC: 0051 Convalescent home with
continuous nursing care
PA: The Ensign Group Inc
29222 Rncho Vejo Rd Ste 1
949 487-9500

(P-15648)
**EPISCOPAL COMMUNITIES &
SERVIC**
Also Called: Canterbury, The
5801 Crestridge Rd, Pls Vrds Pnsl
(90275-4961)
PHONE......................310 544-2204
Consuelo Haire, *Brnch Mgr*
EMP: 100
SALES (corp-wide): 86.44MM **Privately
Held**
Web: www.ecsforseniors.org

SIC: 8051 8361·8059 Extended care facility;
Aged home; Personal care home, with
health care
PA: Episcopal Communities & Services For
Seniors
605 E Hntngton Dr Ste 207
626 403-5880

(P-15649)
ESTRELLA INC
Also Called: Woodruff Convalescent Center
6712 Alamitos Cir, Huntington Beach
(92648-1537)
PHONE....................562 925-6418
Liberation De Leon Md, *Pr*
EMP: 110 EST: 1969
SALES (est): 1.74MM **Privately Held**
Web: www.estrella.com
SIC: 8051 Convalescent home with
continuous nursing care

(P-15650)
EVERGREEN AT LAKEPORT
LLC
Also Called: Evergreen Healthcare Center
6212 Tudor Way, Bakersfield (93306-7067)
PHONE....................661 871-3133
Gloria Melliti, *Mgr*
EMP: 100
SALES (corp-wide): 9.4MM **Privately Held**
SIC: 8051 Convalescent home with
continuous nursing care
PA: Evergreen At Lakeport, L.L.C.
1291 Craig Ave
707 263-6382

(P-15651)
EVERGREEN HEALTH CARE LLC
323 Campus Dr, Arvin (93203-1047)
PHONE....................661 854-4475
Cody Rasmussen, *Ex Dir*
Rush Melliti, *
EMP: 1013 EST: 1985
SALES (est): 3.25MM
SALES (corp-wide): 256.35MM **Privately**
Held
SIC: 8051 Convalescent home with
continuous nursing care
HQ: Evergreen At Chico, L.L.C.
4601 Ne 77th Ave Ste 300
Vancouver WA 98662
530 342-4885

(P-15652)
FAR WEST INC
Also Called: Medical Center
467 E Gilbert St, San Bernardino
(92404-5318)
PHONE....................909 884-4781
Frank De Leosa, *Mgr*
EMP: 91
Web: www.medcentercare.com
SIC: 8051 8059 Convalescent home with
continuous nursing care; Rest home, with
health care
HQ: Far West, Inc.
4020 Sierra College Blvd
Rocklin CA 95677

(P-15653)
FIVE STAR QULTY CARE-CA II
LLC (DH)
Also Called: THOUSAND OAKS HEALTH
CARE CENTER
93 W Avenida De Los Arboles, Thousand
Oaks (91360-2939)
PHONE....................805 492-2444
Eugene Tito, *Admn*
EMP: 76 EST: 2004
SALES (est): 14.71MM

SALES (corp-wide): 934.59MM **Privately**
Held
Web: www.fivestarseniorliving.com
SIC: 8051 Skilled nursing care facilities
HQ: Alerislife Inc.
255 Washington St Ste 300
Newton MA 02458

(P-15654)
FIVE STAR SENIOR LIVING INC
Also Called: Somerford Place Encinitas
1350 S El Camino Real, Encinitas
(92024-4904)
PHONE....................760 479-1818
Terry Records, *Mgr*
EMP: 104
SALES (corp-wide): 934.59MM **Privately**
Held
Web: www.fivestarseniorliving.com
SIC: 8051 Skilled nursing care facilities
HQ: Alerislife Inc.
255 Washington St Ste 300
Newton MA 02458

(P-15655)
FIVE STAR SENIOR LIVING INC
Also Called: Remington Club I & II
16925 Hierba Dr, San Diego (92128-2688)
PHONE....................858 673-6300
Kristen Crinigan, *Ex Dir*
EMP: 197
SALES (corp-wide): 934.59MM **Privately**
Held
Web: www.theremingtonclub.com
SIC: 8051 Skilled nursing care facilities
HQ: Alerislife Inc.
255 Washington St Ste 300
Newton MA 02458

(P-15656)
FIVE STAR SENIOR LIVING INC
Also Called: Flagship Health Care Center
466 Flagship Rd, Newport Beach
(92663-3635)
PHONE....................949 642-8044
Bonny Christino, *Mgr*
EMP: 75
SALES (corp-wide): 934.59MM **Privately**
Held
Web: www.fivestarseniorliving.com
SIC: 8051 Skilled nursing care facilities
HQ: Alerislife Inc.
255 Washington St Ste 300
Newton MA 02458

(P-15657)
FREEDOM VILLAGE
HEALTHCARE CTR
Also Called: REHABWORKS AT FREEDOM
VILLAGE
23442 El Toro Rd Bldg 2, Lake Forest
(92630-6992)
PHONE....................949 472-4733
Joel Niblett, *Admn*
Teresa Leleux, *Admn*
Chery Roscamp, *CFO*
Christine Hall, *Contrlr*
EMP: 140 EST: 1977
SALES (est): 23.54MM **Privately Held**
Web: www.freedomvillage.org
SIC: 8051 8052 Convalescent home with
continuous nursing care; Intermediate care
facilities

(P-15658)
FRONT PORCH COMMUNITIES
& SVCS
Also Called: Fredericka Manor Care Center
111 Third Ave, Chula Vista (91910-1822)
PHONE....................619 427-2777

Loraine Wiencek, *Brnch Mgr*
EMP: 123
Web: www.frontporch.net
SIC: 8051 Convalescent home with
continuous nursing care
PA: Front Porch Communities And Services
800 N Brand Blvd Fl 19

(P-15659)
FULLERTON HLTHCARE
WLLNESS CNT
Also Called: Evergreen Fullerton Healthcare
2222 N Harbor Blvd, Fullerton
(92835-2605)
PHONE....................714 992-5701
Shlomo Rechnitz, *Pt*
Sarrod Brooks, *Pt*
EMP: 125 EST: 2013
SALES (est): 22.73MM **Privately Held**
Web: www.sunnyhillshc.com
SIC: 8051 Convalescent home with
continuous nursing care

(P-15660)
GARDEN CREST CNVLSCENT
HOSP IN
Also Called: GARDEN CREST
RETIREMENT RESIDE
909 Lucile Ave, Los Angeles (90026-1511)
PHONE....................323 663-8281
Paul Barron, *CEO*
Vera Barron, *
EMP: 90 EST: 1954
SQ FT: 30,000
SALES (est): 6.95MM **Privately Held**
Web: www.gardencrestweb.com
SIC: 8051 8059 8322 Convalescent home
with continuous nursing care; Convalescent
home; Old age assistance

(P-15661)
GARDEN GROVE MEDICAL
INVESTORS (HQ)
Also Called: Garden Grove Rehabilitation
12332 Garden Grove Blvd, Garden Grove
(92843-1804)
PHONE....................714 534-1041
Nelia Yonzen, *Ex Dir*
EMP: 93 EST: 1976
SQ FT: 10,000
SALES (est): 130.3K
SALES (corp-wide): 139.21MM **Privately**
Held
Web: www.gardengrovehospital.com
SIC: 8051 8069 Convalescent home with
continuous nursing care; Specialty
hospitals, except psychiatric
PA: Life Care Centers Of America, Inc.
3570 Keith St Nw
423 472-9585

(P-15662)
GATE THREE HEALTHCARE LLC
Also Called: Palm Ter Hlthcare Rhblttion Ct
24962 Calle Aragon, Laguna Hills
(92637-3883)
PHONE....................949 587-9000
EMP: 172 EST: 2004
SALES (est): 14.43MM
SALES (corp-wide): 3.73B **Publicly Held**
Web: www.palmterracecares.com
SIC: 8051 Convalescent home with
continuous nursing care
PA: The Ensign Group Inc
29222 Rncho Vejo Rd Ste 1
949 487-9500

(P-15663)
GENESIS HEALTHCARE LLC
425 Barcellus Ave, Santa Maria
(93454-6901)
PHONE....................805 922-3558
EMP: 897
Web: www.genesishcc.com
SIC: 8051 Convalescent home with
continuous nursing care
HQ: Genesis Healthcare Llc
101 E State St
Kennett Square PA 19348

(P-15664)
GENESIS HEALTHCARE LLC
Also Called: Spring Senior Assisted Living
20900 Earl St Ste 100, Torrance
(90503-4309)
PHONE....................310 370-3594
EMP: 491
Web: www.genesishcc.com
SIC: 8051 Convalescent home with
continuous nursing care
HQ: Genesis Healthcare Llc
101 E State St
Kennett Square PA 19348

(P-15665)
GERI-CARE INC
Also Called: Harbor Post Accute Care Center
21521 S Vermont Ave, Torrance
(90502-1939)
PHONE....................310 320-0961
Emmanuel David, *Pr*
EMP: 100 EST: 1975
SQ FT: 30,000
SALES (est): 10.81MM **Privately Held**
Web: www.harborpostacute.com
SIC: 8051 Convalescent home with
continuous nursing care

(P-15666)
GLIMMER HEALTHCARE INC
Also Called: Ramona Nrsing Rhbilitation Ctr
11900 Ramona Blvd, El Monte
(91732-2314)
PHONE....................626 442-5721
Kevin Niccum, *Pr*
Craig Fitch, *Sec*
Soon Burnam, *Treas*
EMP: 104 EST: 2022
SALES (est): 5.98MM
SALES (corp-wide): 3.73B **Publicly Held**
SIC: 8051 Skilled nursing care facilities
PA: The Ensign Group, Inc.
29222 Rncho Vejo Rd Ste 1
949 487-9500

(P-15667)
GOLDEN STATE HABILITATION
CONV (PA)
Also Called: Golden State Care Center
1758 Big Dalton Ave, Baldwin Park
(91706-5910)
PHONE....................626 962-3274
Eden Salceda, *Pr*
Emmanual David, *
Claudio Hernandez, *
EMP: 175 EST: 1971
SALES (est): 9.1MM **Privately Held**
Web: www.gsccdd.com
SIC: 8051 8361 8052 Convalescent home
with continuous nursing care; Residential
care; Intermediate care facilities

(P-15668)
GPH MEDICAL & LEGAL
SERVICES (PA)
Also Called: G P H Medical Services

468 N Camden Dr, Beverly Hills
(90210-4507)
PHONE..............................213 207-2700
Summer Reed, *Pr*
Michael Mcbay Md, *VP*
Doctor Samuel Wesley, *Sec*
Olen Maxwell Ph.d., *Stockholder*
William Maxwell Ph.d., *Stockholder*
▲ **EMP:** 187 **EST:** 1986
SQ FT: 4,000
SALES (est): 2.14MM **Privately Held**
Web: www.nulegal.com
SIC: 8051 8059 7361 7812 Skilled nursing
care facilities; Convalescent home; Nurses'
registry; Television film production

(P-15669)
GR8 CARE INC
14518 Los Angeles St, Baldwin Park
(91706-2636)
PHONE..............................626 337-7229
Edwin Raquel, *CEO*
Napoleon Garcia, *
EMP: 73 **EST:** 2007
SQ FT: 9,710
SALES (est): 2.56MM **Privately Held**
SIC: 8051 Skilled nursing care facilities

(P-15670)
GRIFFITH PK RHBLTATION CTR
LLC
Also Called: Griffith Park Healthcare Ctr
201 Allen Ave, Glendale (91201-2803)
PHONE..............................818 845-8507
EMP: 75 **EST:** 2015
SALES (est): 13.19MM **Privately Held**
SIC: 8051 Convalescent home with
continuous nursing care

(P-15671)
HARBOR GLEN CARE CENTER
Also Called: Arbor Glen Care Center
1033 E Arrow Hwy, Glendora (91740-6110)
PHONE..............................626 963-7531
Kevin Thomas, *Owner*
EMP: 196 **EST:** 2000
SALES (est): 4.79MM
SALES (corp-wide): 3.73B **Publicly Held**
Web: www.arborglencare.com
SIC: 8051 Convalescent home with
continuous nursing care
PA: The Ensign Group Inc
29222 Rncho Vejo Rd Ste 1
949 487-9500

(P-15672)
HCR MANORCARE MED SVCS
FLA LLC
Also Called: Manorcare Health Services
24962 Calle Aragon, Aliso Viejo (92653)
PHONE..............................949 587-9000
EMP: 150
SALES (corp-wide): 2.27B **Publicly Held**
SIC: 8051 Skilled nursing care facilities
HQ: Hcr Manorcare Medical Services Of
Florida, Llc
333 N Summit St Ste 100
Toledo OH 43604
419 252-5500

(P-15673)
HEALTHCARE CTR OF DOWNEY
LLC
Also Called: Lakewood Healthcare Center
12023 Lakewood Blvd, Downey
(90242-2635)
PHONE..............................562 869-0978
Vince Hambright, *CEO*
Ken Lehmann, *

EMP: 250 **EST:** 2011
SQ FT: 1,076,391
SALES (est): 11.32MM **Privately Held**
Web: www.lwhealthcare.com
SIC: 8051 Mental retardation hospital

(P-15674)
HEALTHCARE INVESTMENTS
INC
Also Called: Rosecrans Care Center
1140 W Rosecrans Ave, Gardena
(90247-2664)
PHONE..............................310 323-3194
Pompeyo Rosales, *Pr*
Gonzalo Delrosario, *
EMP: 106 **EST:** 1991
SALES (est): 12.64MM **Privately Held**
SIC: 8051 Convalescent home with
continuous nursing care

(P-15675)
HEALTHCARE MANAGEMENT
SYSTEMS INC
Also Called: Bradley Court
900 Lane Ave Ste 190, Chula Vista
(91914-4558)
PHONE..............................619 521-9641
EMP: 120
Web: www.erwincablayan.com
SIC: 8051 Skilled nursing care facilities

(P-15676)
HERITAGE HEALTH CARE INC
Also Called: Heritage Gardens Hlth Care Ctr
25271 Barton Rd, Loma Linda
(92354-3013)
PHONE..............................909 796-0216
Stephen Flood, *CEO*
Stephen Flood, *Dir*
Gregory S Goings, *
Jim Kilian, *
EMP: 150 **EST:** 1963
SALES (est): 10.93MM **Privately Held**
Web: www.progressivecarecenters.com
SIC: 8051 8059 Skilled nursing care facilities
; Rest home, with health care

(P-15677)
HIGHLAND HLTHCARE CMLLIA
GRDNS
Also Called: Camellia Gardens Care Center
1920 N Fair Oaks Ave, Pasadena
(91103-1623)
PHONE..............................626 798-6777
Samuel Chazanow, *CEO*
Bernard Friedman, *
EMP: 130 **EST:** 2019
SALES (est): 9.93MM **Privately Held**
Web: www.camelliagardenscc.com
SIC: 8051 Convalescent home with
continuous nursing care

(P-15678)
HIGHLAND PK SKLLED NRSING
WLLN
5125 Monte Vista St, Los Angeles
(90042-3931)
PHONE..............................323 254-6125
EMP: 72 **EST:** 2008
SALES (est): 6.86MM **Privately Held**
Web: www.highlandparkwc.com
SIC: 8051 Convalescent home with
continuous nursing care

(P-15679)
HYDE PK REHABILITATION CTR
LLC
6520 West Blvd, Los Angeles (90043-4311)

PHONE..............................323 753-1354
EMP: 90
SALES (est): 3.15MM **Privately Held**
SIC: 8051 Skilled nursing care facilities

(P-15680)
IMAGINATIVE HORIZONS INC
Also Called: Hillcrest Manor Sanitarium
1889 National City Blvd, National City
(91950-5517)
PHONE..............................619 477-1176
Gary Byrnes, *Pr*
Rosella Byrnes, *
EMP: 84 **EST:** 1930
SQ FT: 30,000
SALES (est): 4.29MM **Privately Held**
Web: website1.specialized-care.com
SIC: 8051 Skilled nursing care facilities

(P-15681)
INLAND CHRSTN HM
FUNDATION INC
1950 S Mountain Ave Ofc, Ontario
(91762-6709)
PHONE..............................909 395-9322
David Stienstra, *Pr*
Karen Miedema, *
EMP: 114 **EST:** 1973
SQ FT: 100,000
SALES (est): 73.56K **Privately Held**
Web: www.ichome.org
SIC: 8051 8052 6513 8361 Skilled nursing
care facilities; Intermediate care facilities;
Retirement hotel operation; Residential care

(P-15682)
INTERCOMMUNITY CARE CTRS
INC
Also Called: Intercommunity Care Center
2626 Grand Ave, Long Beach
(90815-1707)
PHONE..............................562 427-8915
Russel Boydston, *Brnch Mgr*
EMP: 141
SQ FT: 32,159
SALES (corp-wide): 9.57MM **Privately**
Held
Web: www.iccare.org
SIC: 8051 Convalescent home with
continuous nursing care
PA: Intercommunity Care Centers, Inc.
2660 Grand Ave
562 426-1368

(P-15683)
J P H CONSULTING INC
4616 Huntington Dr S, Los Angeles
(90032-1940)
PHONE..............................323 934-5660
EMP: 177
SALES (corp-wide): 14.22MM **Privately**
Held
SIC: 8051 Skilled nursing care facilities
PA: J P H Consulting, Inc.
1101 Crenshaw Blvd
323 934-5660

(P-15684)
JEWISH HM FOR THE AGING
ORNGE
Also Called: HERITAGE POINTE
27356 Bellogente, Mission Viejo
(92691-6341)
PHONE..............................949 364-9685
David Zarnow, *VP*
Rena Loveless, *
EMP: 120 **EST:** 1969
SQ FT: 88,928
SALES (est): 11.82MM **Privately Held**

Web: www.heritagepointe.org
SIC: 8051 Skilled nursing care facilities

(P-15685)
KATELLA PROPERTIES
Also Called: Alamitos W Convalescent Hosp
3902 Katella Ave, Los Alamitos
(90720-3304)
PHONE..............................562 596-5561
Marilyn Gelgincolin, *Dir*
EMP: 85
SALES (corp-wide): 9.87MM **Privately**
Held
Web: www.katellaseniorliving.com
SIC: 8051 Convalescent home with
continuous nursing care
PA: Katella Properties
3952 Katella Ave
562 596-2773

(P-15686)
KNOLLS CONVALESCENT HOSP
INC (PA)
Also Called: Desert Knlls Convalescent Hosp
16890 Green Tree Blvd, Victorville
(92395-5652)
PHONE..............................760 245-5361
Gary L Bechtold, *Pr*
Larry Bechtold, *
Fred Bechtold, *
EMP: 130 **EST:** 1971
SQ FT: 5,421
SALES (est): 9.48MM
SALES (corp-wide): 9.48MM **Privately**
Held
Web: www.knollswestpostacute.com
SIC: 8051 8052 Convalescent home with
continuous nursing care; Intermediate care
facilities

(P-15687)
KNOLLS WEST ENTERPRISE
Also Called: Knolls West Residential Care
16890 Green Tree Blvd, Victorville
(92395-5618)
PHONE..............................760 245-0107
Larry Bechtold, *Pt*
Gary Bechtold, *Pt*
Fred Bechtold, *Pt*
EMP: 158 **EST:** 1979
SQ FT: 44,000
SALES (est): 3.05MM
SALES (corp-wide): 9.48MM **Privately**
Held
Web: www.knollswestpostacute.com
SIC: 8051 Convalescent home with
continuous nursing care
PA: Knolls Convalescent Hospital, Inc.
16890 Green Tree Blvd
760 245-5361

(P-15688)
KSM HEALTHCARE INC
Also Called: Dreier's Nursing Care Center
1400 W Glenoaks Blvd, Glendale
(91201-1911)
PHONE..............................818 242-1183
John Haedrich, *CEO*
EMP: 76 **EST:** 1947
SQ FT: 40,000
SALES (est): 7.74MM **Privately Held**
Web: www.nursing-care.com
SIC: 8051 Skilled nursing care facilities

(P-15689)
LA JOLLA SKILLED INC
Also Called: ENSIGN
3884 Nobel Dr, San Diego (92122-5700)
PHONE..............................858 625-8700
Glenn Matthews, *CEO*

PRODUCTS & SVCS

Craig Fitch, *
Soon Burnam, *
EMP: 322 **EST:** 2014
SALES (est): 9.59MM
SALES (corp-wide): 3.73B **Publicly Held**
Web: www.sprlj.com
SIC: 8051 Convalescent home with
continuous nursing care
PA: The Ensign Group Inc
29222 Rncho Vejo Rd Ste 1
949 487-9500

(P-15690)
LEMON GROVE HEALTH ASSOC LLC
Also Called: Lemon Grove Care Rhbltition Ctr
8351 Broadway, Lemon Grove
(91945-2009)
PHONE..............................619 463-0294
Preet Kambo, *Ex Dir*
Mason Hunter, *
EMP: 298 **EST:** 2004
SALES (est): 9.85MM
SALES (corp-wide): 3.73B **Publicly Held**
Web: www.lemongrovecare.com
SIC: 8051 Convalescent home with
continuous nursing care
PA: The Ensign Group Inc
29222 Rncho Vejo Rd Ste 1
949 487-9500

(P-15691)
LIFE CARE CENTERS AMERICA INC
27555 Rimrock Rd, Barstow (92311-4230)
PHONE..............................760 252-2515
EMP: 201
SALES (corp-wide): 139.21MM **Privately Held**
Web: www.lcca.com
SIC: 8051 Convalescent home with
continuous nursing care
PA: Life Care Centers Of America, Inc.
3570 Keith St Nw
423 472-9585

(P-15692)
LIFE CARE CENTERS AMERICA INC
Also Called: Life Care Centers of Escondido
1980 Felicita Rd, Escondido (92025-5922)
PHONE..............................760 741-6109
Trent Weaver, *Admn*
EMP: 130
SALES (corp-wide): 139.21MM **Privately Held**
Web: www.lcca.com
SIC: 8051 Convalescent home with
continuous nursing care
PA: Life Care Centers Of America, Inc.
3570 Keith St Nw
423 472-9585

(P-15693)
LIFE CARE CENTERS AMERICA INC
Also Called: Imperial Convalescent
11926 La Mirada Blvd, La Mirada
(90638-1303)
PHONE..............................562 943-7156
Ted Stultz, *Mgr*
EMP: 184
SALES (corp-wide): 139.21MM **Privately Held**
Web: www.lcca.com
SIC: 8051 8741 Convalescent home with
continuous nursing care; Management
services
PA: Life Care Centers Of America, Inc.
3570 Keith St Nw

423 472-9585

(P-15694)
LIFE CARE CENTERS AMERICA INC
Also Called: Bel Tren Vlla Cnvalescent Hosp
16910 Woodruff Ave, Bellflower
(90706-6036)
PHONE..............................562 867-1761
Tooren Bel, *Mgr*
EMP: 121
SALES (corp-wide): 139.21MM **Privately Held**
Web: www.lcca.com
SIC: 8051 Convalescent home with
continuous nursing care
PA: Life Care Centers Of America, Inc.
3570 Keith St Nw
423 472-9585

(P-15695)
LIFE CARE CENTERS AMERICA INC
Also Called: Life Care Center of Norwalk
12350 Rosecrans Ave, Norwalk
(90650-5064)
PHONE..............................562 921-6624
Steve Ramsdel, *VP*
EMP: 79
SALES (corp-wide): 139.21MM **Privately Held**
Web: www.lcca.com
SIC: 8051 Convalescent home with
continuous nursing care
PA: Life Care Centers Of America, Inc.
3570 Keith St Nw
423 472-9585

(P-15696)
LIFE CARE CENTERS AMERICA INC
Also Called: Mirada Hlls Rehb Cnvlscent Hos
12200 La Mirada Blvd, La Mirada
(90638-1306)
PHONE..............................562 947-8691
Selina Stewart, *Ex Dir*
EMP: 134
SALES (corp-wide): 139.21MM **Privately Held**
Web: www.lcca.com
SIC: 8051 Convalescent home with
continuous nursing care
PA: Life Care Centers Of America, Inc.
3570 Keith St Nw
423 472-9585

(P-15697)
LIFE CARE CENTERS AMERICA INC
Also Called: Life Care Center of La Habra
1233 W La Habra Blvd, La Habra
(90631-5226)
PHONE..............................562 690-0852
Daniel Husband, *Admn*
EMP: 251
SALES (corp-wide): 139.21MM **Privately Held**
Web: www.lcca.com
SIC: 8051 Convalescent home with
continuous nursing care
PA: Life Care Centers Of America, Inc.
3570 Keith St Nw
423 472-9585

(P-15698)
LIFE GNERATIONS HEALTHCARE LLC
Also Called: Arbor Hills Nursing Center
7800 Parkway Dr, La Mesa (91942-2001)

PHONE..............................619 460-2330
EMP: 99
SALES (corp-wide): 72.62MM **Privately Held**
Web: www.lifegen.net
SIC: 8051 Convalescent home with
continuous nursing care
PA: Life Generations Healthcare Llc
6 Hutton Cntre Dr Ste 400
714 241-5600

(P-15699)
LIGHTHOUSE HEALTHCARE CTR LLC
2222 Santa Ana S, Los Angeles
(90059-1350)
PHONE..............................323 564-4461
EMP: 99 **EST:** 2007
SALES (est): 16.01MM **Privately Held**
SIC: 8051 Skilled nursing care facilities

(P-15700)
LITTLE SSTERS OF THE POOR LOS
Also Called: Jeanne Jugan, A Residence
2100 S Western Ave, San Pedro
(90732-4389)
PHONE..............................310 548-0625
Margaret Mcarthy, *Pr*
Michael Mugan, *
Clotilde Jardim, *
EMP: 100 **EST:** 1905
SQ FT: 145,530
SALES (est): 2.39MM **Privately Held**
Web:
www.littlesistersofthepoorsanpedro.org
SIC: 8051 8361 8052 Extended care facility;
Residential care; Intermediate care facilities

(P-15701)
LONG BEACH CARE CENTER INC
2615 Grand Ave, Long Beach
(90815-1708)
PHONE..............................562 426-6141
William A Nelson, *Pr*
EMP: 108 **EST:** 2003
SQ FT: 43,962
SALES (est): 18.54MM **Privately Held**
Web: www.iccare.org
SIC: 8051 Convalescent home with
continuous nursing care

(P-15702)
LONGWOOD MANAGEMENT CORP
Also Called: Magnolia Grdns Convalescent HM
17922 San Fernando Mission Blvd,
Granada Hills (91344-4043)
PHONE..............................818 360-1864
Ojijoji Gervacio, *Prin*
EMP: 99
SALES (corp-wide): 41.31MM **Privately Held**
Web: www.magnoliagardenshc.com
SIC: 8051 Convalescent home with
continuous nursing care
PA: Longwood Management Llc
4032 Wilshire Blvd Fl 6
213 389-6900

(P-15703)
LONGWOOD MANAGEMENT CORP
Also Called: Green Acres Lodge
8101 Hill Dr, Rosemead (91770-4169)
PHONE..............................626 280-2293
Karen Fugate, *Admn*

EMP: 128
SALES (corp-wide): 41.31MM **Privately Held**
Web: www.greenacreshealthcare.com
SIC: 8051 Convalescent home with
continuous nursing care
PA: Longwood Management Llc
4032 Wilshire Blvd Fl 6
213 389-6900

(P-15704)
LONGWOOD MANAGEMENT CORP
Also Called: San Gabriel Convalescent Ctr
8035 Hill Dr, Rosemead (91770-4116)
PHONE..............................626 280-4820
Gigi Garcia, *Brnch Mgr*
EMP: 99
SALES (corp-wide): 41.31MM **Privately Held**
Web: www.sangabrielhealth.com
SIC: 8051 Convalescent home with
continuous nursing care
PA: Longwood Management Llc
4032 Wilshire Blvd Fl 6
213 389-6900

(P-15705)
LONGWOOD MANAGEMENT CORP
Also Called: Crenshaw Nursing
1900 S Longwood Ave, Los Angeles
(90016-1408)
PHONE..............................323 933-1560
Gilbert Fimbres, *Mgr*
EMP: 102
SALES (corp-wide): 41.31MM **Privately Held**
Web: www.longwoodmgmt.com
SIC: 8051 8052 Convalescent home with
continuous nursing care; Intermediate care
facilities
PA: Longwood Management Llc
4032 Wilshire Blvd Fl 6
213 389-6900

(P-15706)
LONGWOOD MANAGEMENT CORP
Also Called: Imperial Crest Healthcare Ctr
11834 Inglewood Ave, Hawthorne
(90250-2731)
PHONE..............................310 679-1461
Robert Villalub, *Admn*
EMP: 125
SALES (corp-wide): 41.31MM **Privately Held**
Web: www.longwoodmgmt.com
SIC: 8051 Convalescent home with
continuous nursing care
PA: Longwood Management Llc
4032 Wilshire Blvd Fl 6
213 389-6900

(P-15707)
LOS ANGLES JEWISH HM FOR AGING
Also Called: Eisenberg Village
18855 Victory Blvd, Reseda (91335-6445)
PHONE..............................818 774-3000
Kathleen Glass, *Mgr*
EMP: 500
SALES (corp-wide): 46.31MM **Privately Held**
Web: www.lajhealth.org
SIC: 8051 Convalescent home with
continuous nursing care
PA: Los Angeles Jewish Home For The
Aging
7150 Tampa Ave

818 774-3000

(P-15708)

LOS ANGLES JEWISH HM FOR AGING (PA)

Also Called: GRANCELL VILLAGE
7150 Tampa Ave, Reseda (91335-3798)
PHONE..............................818 774-3000
Andrew Berman, *Ch Bd*
Jeffrey Glassman, *
Molly Forrest, *
Sherri B Cunningham, *
Shelly J Ryan, *
EMP: 400 **EST:** 1912
SQ FT: 35,000
SALES (est): 46.31MM
SALES (corp-wide): 46.31MM **Privately Held**
Web: www.lajhealth.org
SIC: 8051 8361 Skilled nursing care facilities ; Residential care

(P-15709)

MARINER HEALTH CARE INC

Also Called: Monterey Palms Health Care Ctr
44610 Monterey Ave, Palm Desert (92260-3326)
PHONE..............................760 776-7700
J Simanjunt, *Admn*
EMP: 178
SALES (corp-wide): 497.49MM **Privately Held**
Web: www.marinerhealthcare.com
SIC: 8051 Extended care facility
PA: Mariner Health Care, Inc.
3060 Mrcer Univ Dr Ste 20
678 443-7000

(P-15710)

MARINER HEALTH CARE INC

Also Called: Verdugo Vista Healthcare Ctr
3050 Montrose Ave, La Crescenta (91214-3619)
PHONE..............................818 957-0850
Jeri-enn Shelton, *Admn*
EMP: 131
SALES (corp-wide): 497.49MM **Privately Held**
Web: www.marinerhealthcare.com
SIC: 8051 Extended care facility
PA: Mariner Health Care, Inc.
3060 Mrcer Univ Dr Ste 20
678 443-7000

(P-15711)

MARINER HEALTH CARE INC

Also Called: Driftwood Health Care Ctr
4109 Emerald St, Torrance (90503-3105)
PHONE..............................310 371-4628
Jennifer Torgrude, *Mgr*
EMP: 101
SALES (corp-wide): 497.49MM **Privately Held**
Web: www.driftwoodhc.com
SIC: 8051 Convalescent home with continuous nursing care
PA: Mariner Health Care, Inc.
3060 Mrcer Univ Dr Ste 20
678 443-7000

(P-15712)

MARINER HEALTH CARE INC

Also Called: Inglewood Health Care Center
100 S Hillcrest Blvd, Inglewood (90301-1313)
PHONE..............................310 677-9114
Amanda Arevalo, *Admn*
EMP: 102
SALES (corp-wide): 497.49MM **Privately Held**

(P-15713)

MARINER HEALTH CARE INC

Also Called: Skyline Health Care Ctr
3032 Rowena Ave, Los Angeles (90039-2005)
PHONE..............................323 665-1185
Kathleen Glass, *Admn*
EMP: 94
SALES (corp-wide): 497.49MM **Privately Held**
Web: www.marinerhealthcare.com
SIC: 8051 Extended care facility
PA: Mariner Health Care, Inc.
3060 Mrcer Univ Dr Ste 20
678 443-7000

(P-15714)

MARINER HEALTH CARE INC

Also Called: Autumn Hills Convalescent Home
430 N Glendale Ave, Glendale (91206-3309)
PHONE..............................818 246-5677
Jenik Akopian, *Prin*
EMP: 131
SALES (corp-wide): 497.49MM **Privately Held**
Web: www.marinerhealthcare.com
SIC: 8051 Extended care facility
PA: Mariner Health Care, Inc.
3060 Mrcer Univ Dr Ste 20
678 443-7000

(P-15715)

MARINER HEALTH CARE INC

Also Called: El Rancho Vista Hlth Care Ctr
8925 Mines Ave, Pico Rivera (90660-3006)
PHONE..............................562 942-7019
Richard Widerynski, *Mgr*
EMP: 126
SALES (corp-wide): 497.49MM **Privately Held**
Web: www.elranchovista.com
SIC: 8051 Convalescent home with continuous nursing care
PA: Mariner Health Care, Inc.
3060 Mrcer Univ Dr Ste 20
678 443-7000

(P-15716)

MARK & FRED ENTERPRISES

Also Called: West Anaheim Care Center
045 3 Beach Blvd, Anaheim (92804-3102)
PHONE..............................714 821-1993
Mark Landry, *Mng Pt*
Connie Black, *Pt*
EMP: 125 **EST:** 1989
SQ FT: 39,000
SALES (est): 9.5MM **Privately Held**
Web: www.beachcreekpostacute.com
SIC: 8051 Convalescent home with continuous nursing care

(P-15717)

MARLORA INVESTMENTS LLC

Also Called: Marlora Post Accute Rhblttion
3801 E Anaheim St, Long Beach (90804-4084)
PHONE..............................562 494-3311
EMP: 100 **EST:** 1998
SQ FT: 22,118
SALES (est): 8.57MM **Privately Held**
Web: www.marlora.com
SIC: 8051 Convalescent home with continuous nursing care

(P-15718)

MARY HLTH OF SICK CNVLSCENT NR

2929 Theresa Dr, Newbury Park (91320-3136)
PHONE..............................805 498-3644
Jody Rupp, *Admn*
Sister Purificaion Fererro, *
Diane Zimanski, *
EMP: 92 **EST:** 1964
SQ FT: 5,000
SALES (est): 8.04MM **Privately Held**
Web: www.maryhealth.com
SIC: 8051 Convalescent home with continuous nursing care

(P-15719)

MEK ESCONDIDO LLC

Also Called: Escondido Post Acute Rehab
421 E Mission Ave, Escondido (92025-1909)
PHONE..............................760 747-0430
EMP: 180 **EST:** 2000
SALES (est): 8.84MM **Privately Held**
SIC: 8051 Convalescent home with continuous nursing care

(P-15720)

MESA VRDE CNVALESCENT HOSP INC

Also Called: Mesa Verde Prosecute Care
661 Center St, Costa Mesa (92627-2708)
PHONE..............................949 548-5584
Rita Simms, *Admn*
Joseph Munoz, *
Joye Tsuchiyama, *
EMP: 200 **EST:** 1972
SALES (est): 8.58MM **Privately Held**
Web: www.mesaverdehealthcare.com
SIC: 8051 Convalescent home with continuous nursing care

(P-15721)

MIRAMONTE ENTERPRISES LLC

Also Called: San Jacinto Healthcare
275 N San Jacinto St, Hemet (92543-4453)
PHONE..............................951 658-9441
Emmanuel B David, *Pr*
EMP: 134 **EST:** 2005
SQ FT: 22,968
SALES (est): 8.3MM **Privately Held**
Web: www.yolocare2.com
SIC: 8051 Convalescent home with continuous nursing care

(P-15722)

MISSION HILLS HEALTH CARE INC

Also Called: Mission Hills Healthcare Ctr
726 Torrance St, San Diego (92103-3813)
PHONE..............................619 297-4086
Patrick Higgins, *Admn*
Leah Higgins, *
EMP: 92 **EST:** 1990
SALES (est): 10.56MM **Privately Held**
Web: www.missionhillshealthcare.com
SIC: 8051 Convalescent home with continuous nursing care

(P-15723)

MONTECITO RETIREMENT ASSN

Also Called: Casa Dorinda
300 Hot Springs Rd, Santa Barbara (93108-2037)
PHONE..............................805 969-8011
Robin Drew, *CFO*
EMP: 265 **EST:** 1973
SQ FT: 350,000

SALES (est): 27.7MM **Privately Held**
Web: www.casadorinda.org
SIC: 8051 8052 8361 Skilled nursing care facilities; Personal care facility; Rest home, with health care incidental

(P-15724)

MORENO VALLEY SNF LLC

Also Called: Rancho Bellagio Post Acute
26940 E Hospital Rd, Moreno Valley (92555-3923)
PHONE..............................951 363-5434
EMP: 156 **EST:** 2020
SALES (est): 2.47MM
SALES (corp-wide): 3.11B **Publicly Held**
Web: www.ranchobellagiopa.com
SIC: 8051 Skilled nursing care facilities
HQ: Providence Group, Inc.
262 N University Ave
Farmington UT 84025
801 447-9829

(P-15725)

MT RUBIDOUXIDENCE OPCO LLC

Also Called: Jurupa Hills Post Acute
6401 33rd St, Riverside (92509-1404)
PHONE..............................951 681-2200
Jason Murray, *Prin*
Mark Hancock, *
Debra Gogerty, *
EMP: 199 **EST:** 2015
SALES (est): 8.13MM
SALES (corp-wide): 3.11B **Publicly Held**
SIC: 8051 Skilled nursing care facilities
HQ: Providence Group Of Southern California, Llc
262 N University Ave
Farmington UT 84025
801 447-9829

(P-15726)

NAVIGAGE FOUNDATION (PA)

849 Foothill Blvd Ste 8, La Canada (91011-3368)
PHONE..............................818 790-2522
Judy Vallas, *CEO*
EMP: 100 **EST:** 1932
SQ FT: 90,000
SALES (est): 707.1K
SALES (corp-wide): 707.1K **Privately Held**
SIC: 8051 8059 8052 Skilled nursing care facilities; Rest home, with health care; Intermediate care facilities

(P-15727)

OCEANSIDE HARBOR HOLDINGS LLC

Also Called: Beach Creek Post-Acute
645 S Beach Blvd, Anaheim (92804-3102)
PHONE..............................760 331-3177
Curt Rodriguez, *
EMP: 200 **EST:** 2022
SALES (est): 10.21MM **Privately Held**
SIC: 8051 Skilled nursing care facilities

(P-15728)

ORANGE HLTHCARE WLLNESS CNTRE

920 W La Veta Ave, Orange (92868-4302)
PHONE..............................714 633-3568
EMP: 110 **EST:** 2009
SALES (est): 9.39MM **Privately Held**
Web: www.orangerehabilitation.com
SIC: 8051 Convalescent home with continuous nursing care

(P-15729)
ORCHARD - POST ACUTE CARE CTR
12385 Washington Blvd, Whittier (90606-2502)
PHONE....................562 693-7701
Rich Jorgensen, *Prin*
EMP: 173 **EST:** 2011
SALES (est): 6.49MM
SALES (corp-wide): 3.73B **Publicly Held**
Web: www.theorchardpostacute.com
SIC: 8051 Convalescent home with continuous nursing care
PA: The Ensign Group Inc
29222 Rncho Vejo Rd Ste 1
949 487-9500

(P-15730)
PACS GROUP INC
Also Called: Mirage Post Acute
44445 15th St W, Lancaster (93534-2801)
PHONE....................661 948-7501
EMP: 224
SALES (corp-wide): 3.11B **Publicly Held**
SIC: 8051 Skilled nursing care facilities
PA: Pacs Group, Inc.
262 N University Ave
·801 447-9829

(P-15731)
PACS GROUP INC
Also Called: Artesia Palms Care Center
11900 Artesia Blvd, Artesia (90701-4039)
PHONE....................562 865-0271
EMP: 156
SALES (corp-wide): 3.11B **Publicly Held**
SIC: 8051 Convalescent home with continuous nursing care
PA: Pacs Group, Inc.
262 N University Ave
801 447-9829

(P-15732)
PACS GROUP INC
Also Called: Beverly Hlls Rhbltation Centre
580 S San Vicente Blvd, Los Angeles (90048-4621)
PHONE....................323 782-1500
EMP: 156
SALES (corp-wide): 3.11B **Publicly Held**
SIC: 8051 Convalescent home with continuous nursing care
PA: Pacs Group, Inc.
262 N University Ave
801 447-9829

(P-15733)
PACS GROUP INC
Also Called: Antelope Valley Care Center
44567 15th St W, Lancaster (93534-2803)
PHONE....................661 949-5524
EMP: 156
SALES (corp-wide): 3.11B **Publicly Held**
SIC: 8051 Convalescent home with continuous nursing care
PA: Pacs Group, Inc.
262 N University Ave
801 447-9829

(P-15734)
PACS GROUP INC
Also Called: Bakersfield Post Acute
6212 Tudor Way, Bakersfield (93306-7067)
PHONE....................661 873-9267
EMP: 185
SALES (corp-wide): 3.11B **Publicly Held**
Web: www.bakersfieldpostacute.com
SIC: 8051 Convalescent home with continuous nursing care
PA: Pacs Group, Inc.
262 N University Ave

801 447-9829

(P-15735)
PACS GROUP INC
Also Called: Arvin Post Acute
323 Campus Dr, Arvin (93203-1047)
PHONE....................661 854-4475
EMP: 166
SALES (corp-wide): 3.11B **Publicly Held**
SIC: 8051 Convalescent home with continuous nursing care
PA: Pacs Group, Inc.
262 N University Ave
801 447-9829

(P-15736)
PACS GROUP INC
Also Called: Windsor Gardens of Long Beach
3232 E Artesia Blvd, Long Beach (90805-2811)
PHONE....................562 422-9219
Calcin Warren, *Admn*
EMP: 253
SALES (corp-wide): 3.11B **Publicly Held**
Web: www.windsorgardenslongbeach.com
SIC: 8051 Convalescent home with continuous nursing care
PA: Pacs Group, Inc.
262 N University Ave
801 447-9829

(P-15737)
PACS GROUP INC
Also Called: Loma Linda Post Acute
25393 Cole St, Loma Linda (92354-3103)
PHONE....................909 478-7894
EMP: 97
SALES (corp-wide): 3.11B **Publicly Held**
Web: www.lindavalleyal.com
SIC: 8051 Skilled nursing care facilities
PA: Pacs Group, Inc.
262 N University Ave
801 447-9829

(P-15738)
PACS GROUP INC
Also Called: Hemet Hills Post Acute
1717 W Stetson Ave, Hemet (92545-6882)
PHONE....................951 925-9171
EMP: 195
SALES (corp-wide): 3.11B **Publicly Held**
SIC: 8051 Convalescent home with continuous nursing care
PA: Pacs Group, Inc.
262 N University Ave
801 447-9829

(P-15739)
PACS GROUP INC
Also Called: Sunrise Post Acute
3476 W Wilson St, Banning (92220-3420)
PHONE....................951 849-4723
EMP: 156
SALES (corp-wide): 3.11B **Publicly Held**
SIC: 8051 Convalescent home with continuous nursing care
PA: Pacs Group, Inc.
262 N University Ave
801 447-9829

(P-15740)
PACS GROUP INC
Also Called: San Jacinto Valley Post Acute
275 N San Jacinto St, Hemet (92543-4453)
PHONE....................951 658-9441
EMP: 156
SALES (corp-wide): 3.11B **Publicly Held**
SIC: 8051 Convalescent home with continuous nursing care

PA: Pacs Group, Inc.
262 N University Ave
801 447-9829

(P-15741)
PACS GROUP INC
Also Called: Sundance Creek Post Acute
5800 W Wilson St, Banning (92220-3042)
PHONE....................951 845-1606
EMP: 156
SALES (corp-wide): 3.11B **Publicly Held**
SIC: 8051 Convalescent home with continuous nursing care
PA: Pacs Group, Inc.
262 N University Ave
801 447-9829

(P-15742)
PACS GROUP INC
Also Called: Willow Springs Healthcare Ctr
74350 Country Club Dr, Palm Desert (92260-1608)
PHONE....................760 341-0261
EMP: 156
SALES (corp-wide): 3.11B **Publicly Held**
SIC: 8051 Convalescent home with continuous nursing care
PA: Pacs Group, Inc.
262 N University Ave
801 447-9829

(P-15743)
PACS GROUP INC
Also Called: Vista Real Post Acute
1665 E Eighth St, Beaumont (92223-2512)
PHONE....................951 845-3125
EMP: 146
SALES (corp-wide): 3.11B **Publicly Held**
SIC: 8051 Convalescent home with continuous nursing care
PA: Pacs Group, Inc.
262 N University Ave
801 447-9829

(P-15744)
PACS GROUP INC
Also Called: Oak Glen Post Acute
9246 Avenida Miravilla, Beaumont (92223-3835)
PHONE....................951 845-3194
EMP: 156
SALES (corp-wide): 3.11B **Publicly Held**
SIC: 8051 Convalescent home with continuous nursing care
PA: Pacs Group, Inc.
262 N University Ave
801 447-9829

(P-15745)
PACS GROUP INC
Also Called: Fountain Valley Post Acute
11680 Warner Ave, Fountain Valley (92708-2513)
PHONE....................714 241-9800
EMP: 175
SALES (corp-wide): 3.11B **Publicly Held**
SIC: 8051 Convalescent home with continuous nursing care
PA: Pacs Group, Inc.
262 N University Ave
801 447-9829

(P-15746)
PALMCREST GRAND CARE CTR INC
3501 Cedar Ave, Long Beach (90807-3809)
PHONE....................562 595-4551
William Nelson, *Pr*
EMP: 99 **EST:** 2004
SALES (est): 1.74MM **Privately Held**

Web: www.palmcrestgrandretirement.com
SIC: 8051 Skilled nursing care facilities

(P-15747)
PALMCREST MEDALLION CONVALESC
3355 Pacific Pl, Long Beach (90806-1239)
PHONE....................562 595-4336
FAX: 562 424-6499
EMP: 85
SQ FT: 30,000
SALES (est): 1.71MM **Privately Held**
SIC: 8051 Skilled nursing care facilities

(P-15748)
PARKVIEW JLIAN CNVLESCENT HOSP
1801 Julian Ave, Bakersfield (93304-6453)
PHONE....................661 831-9150
Ligia Denham, *VP*
Douglas Rice, *
EMP: 130 **EST:** 1971
SQ FT: 8,000
SALES (est): 12.37MM **Privately Held**
Web: www.parkviewjulian-snf.com
SIC: 8051 Convalescent home with continuous nursing care

(P-15749)
PARKVIEW JULIAN LLC
Also Called: Parkview Julian Healthcare Ctr
1801 Julian Ave, Bakersfield (93304-6419)
PHONE....................661 831-9150
David Levy, *Managing Member*
Moshe Frankel, *Managing Member*
EMP: 150 **EST:** 2017
SALES (est): 8.63MM **Privately Held**
SIC: 8051 Convalescent home with continuous nursing care

(P-15750)
PASADENA HOSPITAL ASSN LTD
Also Called: Huntington Extended Care Ctr
716 S Fair Oaks Ave, Pasadena (91105-2618)
PHONE....................626 397-3322
Ken Hoff, *Mgr*
EMP: 386
SALES (corp-wide): 764.47MM **Privately Held**
Web: www.huntingtonhealth.org
SIC: 8051 Skilled nursing care facilities
PA: Pasadena Hospital Association, Ltd.
100 W California Blvd
626 397-5000

(P-15751)
PASADENA MADOWS NURSING CTR LP
150 Bellefontaine St, Pasadena (91105-3102)
PHONE....................626 796-1103
Pnina Graff, *Pt*
EMP: 99 **EST:** 2012
SALES (est): 5.08MM **Privately Held**
Web: www.pasadenameadows.com
SIC: 8051 Convalescent home with continuous nursing care

(P-15752)
PCI CARE VENTURE I
Also Called: Prestige Asssted Lving At Lncs
43454 30th St W Ofc, Lancaster (93536-5307)
PHONE....................661 949-2177
Pat Elliott, *Mgr*
EMP: 85
SALES (corp-wide): 381.63MM **Privately Held**

Web: www.prestigecare.com
SIC: 8051 Skilled nursing care facilities
HQ: Pci Care Venture I
    7700 Ne Parkway Dr # 300
    Vancouver WA 98662

(P-15753)
PENNANT GROUP INC
Also Called: Mainplace Senior Living
1800 W Culver Ave, Orange (92868-4127)
PHONE.............................714 978-2534
EMP: 157
SALES (corp-wide): 544.89MM **Publicly Held**
Web: www.pennantgroup.com
SIC: 8051 Convalescent home with continuous nursing care
PA: The Pennant Group Inc
    1675 E Rvrside Dr Ste 150
    208 506-6100

(P-15754)
PLUM HEALTHCARE GROUP LLC
100 E San Marcos Blvd Ste 200, San Marcos (92069-2987)
PHONE.............................760 471-0388
EMP: 223 EST: 1999
SALES (est): 26.31MM
SALES (corp-wide): 3.11B **Publicly Held**
Web: www.plumhealthcaregroup.com
SIC: 8051 Skilled nursing care facilities
HQ: Bay Bridge Capital Partners, Llc
    262 N University Ave
    Farmington UT 84025
    801 447-9829

(P-15755)
POINT LOMA RHBLITATION CTR LLC
Also Called: Pavilion At Ocean Point, The
3202 Duke St, San Diego (92110-5401)
PHONE.............................619 308-3200
EMP: 130 EST: 2006
SQ FT: 30,895
SALES (est): 5.82MM **Privately Held**
Web: www.pointlomarehab.com
SIC: 8051 Convalescent home with continuous nursing care

(P-15756)
POMERADO OPERATIONS LLC
Also Called: BOULDER CREEK POST ACUTE
12696 Monte Vista Rd, Poway (92064-2500)
PHONE.............................858 487-6242
Covey Christensen, CEO
Travis Greenwood, *
Leland Bruce, *
James Garnett, *
EMP: 99 EST: 2014
SALES (est): 18.52MM **Privately Held**
Web: www.bouldercreekpa.care
SIC: 8051 Convalescent home with continuous nursing care

(P-15757)
POWERS PARK HEALTHCARE INC
Also Called: Channel Islands Post Acute
3880 Via Lucero, Santa Barbara (93110-1605)
PHONE.............................805 687-6651
Cory Monette, Ex Dir
EMP: 99 EST: 2019
SALES (est): 17.3MM **Privately Held**
Web: www.channelislandspa.com

SIC: 8051 Convalescent home with continuous nursing care

(P-15758)
RAMONA CARE INC
Also Called: RAMONA NURSING & REHABILITATIO
11900 Ramona Blvd, El Monte (91732-2314)
PHONE.............................626 442-5721
Michael Hyer, Pr
Victor Lundquist, *
Jeffrey Daly, *
EMP: 140 EST: 1990
SQ FT: 35,000
SALES (est): 2.46MM **Privately Held**
Web: www.ramonarehab.com
SIC: 8051 Convalescent home with continuous nursing care

(P-15759)
REHABLTION CNTRE OF BVRLY HLLS
580 S San Vicente Blvd, Los Angeles (90048-4621)
PHONE.............................323 782-1500
Eldon Teper, Pr
EMP: 200 EST: 1998
SALES (est): 16.62MM **Privately Held**
Web: www.rehabcentre.com
SIC: 8051 Convalescent home with continuous nursing care

(P-15760)
REHABLTTION CTR OF ORNGE CNTY
Also Called: Healthcare Center Orange Cnty
9021 Knott Ave, Buena Park (90620-4138)
PHONE.............................714 826-2330
Peter Madigan, Pr
Robert Nelson, *
EMP: 125 EST: 1967
SALES (est): 8.97MM **Privately Held**
SIC: 8051 8059 Convalescent home with continuous nursing care; Rest home, with health care

(P-15761)
RIVERA SANATARIUM INC
Also Called: Colonial Gardens Nursing Home
7246 Rosemead Blvd, Pico Rivera (90660-4010)
P.O. Box 2098 (90662-2098)
PHONE.............................562 949-2591
Elizabeth Stephens, Pr
Kent Stephens, *
EMP: 86 EST: 1959
SQ FT: 30,000
SALES (est): 5.62MM **Privately Held**
SIC: 8051 Convalescent home with continuous nursing care

(P-15762)
RIVERSIDE CARE INC
Also Called: Valencia Gardens Health Care Center
4301 Caroline Ct, Riverside (92506-2902)
PHONE.............................951 683-7111
Ted Holt, Pr
Jenny Ortiz, *
Spencer E Olsen, *
EMP: 130 EST: 1971
SALES (est): 10.92MM **Privately Held**
Web: www.valenciagardenshealth.com
SIC: 8051 Convalescent home with continuous nursing care
PA: North American Client Services, Inc.
    25910 Acero Ste 350

(P-15763)
RIVERSIDE EQUITIES LLC
Also Called: SUN MAR HEALTH CARE
8487 Magnolia Ave, Riverside (92504-3222)
PHONE.............................951 688-2222
Frank Johnson, CEO
Irving Bauman, *
EMP: 380 EST: 2008
SALES (est): 8.75MM **Privately Held**
Web: www.missioncarecenter.com
SIC: 8051 Convalescent home with continuous nursing care
PA: Sun Mar Management Services
    3050 Saturn St Ste 201

(P-15764)
RIVIERA NURSING & CONVA
Also Called: Riviera Health Care Center
8203 Telegraph Rd, Pico Rivera (90660-4981)
PHONE.............................562 806-2576
Morris Weiss, Pr
Bessie Weiss, *
EMP: 118 EST: 1966
SQ FT: 60,000
SALES (est): 3.25MM **Privately Held**
Web: www.rivierahealthcare.com
SIC: 8051 8059 Convalescent home with continuous nursing care; Convalescent home

(P-15765)
ROWLAND CONVALESCENT HOSP INC
Also Called: ROWLAND, THE
330 W Rowland St, Covina (91723-2941)
PHONE.............................626 967-2741
Anthony Kalomas, Pr
EMP: 100 EST: 1979
SQ FT: 30,000
SALES (est): 6.92MM **Privately Held**
Web: www.rowlandconvalescent.com
SIC: 8051 Convalescent home with continuous nursing care

(P-15766)
RRT ENTERPRISES LP
Also Called: RRT ENTERPRISES LP
855 N Fairfax Ave, Los Angeles (90046-7207)
PHONE.............................323 653-1521
Stephen Reissman, Brnch Mgr
EMP: 225
SALES (corp-wide): 16.4MM **Privately Held**
SIC: 8051 Skilled nursing care facilities
PA: Rrt Enterprises L.P.
    3966 Marcasel Avenue
    310 397-2372

(P-15767)
RRT ENTERPRISES LP (PA)
Also Called: Country Vlla Mar Vsta Nrsing C
3966 Marcasel Ave, Los Angeles (90001)
PHONE.............................310 397-2372
Stephen Reissman, Genl Pt
Diane Reissman, Genl Pt
EMP: 125 EST: 1972
SQ FT: 18,000
SALES (est): 16.4MM
SALES (corp-wide): 16.4MM **Privately Held**
SIC: 8051 Skilled nursing care facilities

(P-15768)
SAN DIEGO HEBREW HOMES (PA)
Also Called: LEICHTAG ASSISTED LIVING

211 Saxony Rd, Encinitas (92024-2791)
PHONE.............................760 942-2695
Yehudi Gaffen, Ch
Betty Byrnes, Vice Chairman*
Mitchell Berner, Vice Chairman*
Pam Ferris, *
Robin P Israel, *
EMP: 180 EST: 1944
SQ FT: 219,000
SALES: 21.89MM
SALES (corp-wide): 21.89MM **Privately Held**
Web: www.seacrestvillage.org
SIC: 8051 8059 6513 Skilled nursing care facilities; Rest home, with health care; Retirement hotel operation

(P-15769)
SAN PEDRO CONVALESCENT HM INC
Also Called: Los Palos Convalescent Hosp
1430 W 6th St, San Pedro (90732-3503)
PHONE.............................310 832-6431
Celia Valdomar, Pr
EMP: 90 EST: 1963
SQ FT: 10,000
SALES (est): 8.28MM **Privately Held**
Web: www.lpconv.com
SIC: 8051 Convalescent home with continuous nursing care

(P-15770)
SANTA ANITA CNVLSCENT HOSP RTR
5522 Gracewood Ave, Temple City (91780)
PHONE.............................626 579-0310
Martin J Weiss, Pr
Jacob Kasirer, *
Ronni J Mayer, *
EMP: 150 EST: 1968
SQ FT: 88,615
SALES: 8.47MM
SALES (corp-wide): 39.78MM **Privately Held**
Web: www.santaanita-convalescent.com
SIC: 8051 Convalescent home with continuous nursing care
PA: Golden State Health Centers, Inc.
    13347 Ventura Blvd
    818 385-3200

(P-15771)
SEA BREEZE HEALTH CARE INC
7781 Garfield Ave, Huntington Beach (92648-2026)
PHONE.............................714 847-9671
Seth Braithwaite, Pr
Victor Lundquist, *
Jeffrey Daly, *
EMP: 132 EST: 2003
SQ FT: 14,895
SALES (est): 2.68MM **Privately Held**
Web: www.beachsidenursing.com
SIC: 8051 Convalescent home with continuous nursing care

(P-15772)
SEACREST CONVALESCENT HOSP INC
Also Called: Seacrest Convalescent Hospital
1416 W 6th St, San Pedro (90732-3550)
PHONE.............................310 833-3526
Cecelia Valdomar, Pr
Cecelia D Valdomar, *
David B David, *
Joy Nacionales, *
Jose Valdomar, *
EMP: 70 EST: 1962
SALES (est): 5.83MM **Privately Held**

PRODUCTS & SVCS

Web: www.scconv.com
SIC: 8051 Convalescent home with
continuous nursing care

(P-15773)
SELA HEALTHCARE INC
Also Called: Holiday Manor Care Center
20554 Roscoe Blvd, Canoga Park
(91306-1746)
PHONE..................818 341-9800
Victorio Ocbena Sosing, *Prin*
EMP: 310
SALES (corp-wide): 4.59MM **Privately
Held**
SIC: 8051 Convalescent home with
continuous nursing care
PA: Sela Healthcare, Inc.
867 E 11th St
909 985-1981

(P-15774)
SELA HEALTHCARE INC (PA)
Also Called: Holiday Manor Care Center
867 E 11th St, Upland (91786-4867)
PHONE..................909 985-1981
Philip Weinberger, *CEO*
Marylnynn Mahan, *
EMP: 140 EST: 2002
SQ FT: 60,000
SALES (est): 4.59MM
SALES (corp-wide): 4.59MM **Privately
Held**
SIC: 8051 Skilled nursing care facilities

(P-15775)
SILVERADO SENIOR LIVING INC
Also Called: Escondido Memory Care Cmnty
1500 Borden Rd, Escondido (92026-2373)
PHONE..................760 456-5137
Jean Busher, *Admn*
EMP: 70
SQ FT: 33,000
SALES (corp-wide): 130.57K **Privately
Held**
Web: www.silverado.com
SIC: 8051 Skilled nursing care facilities
PA: Senior Silverado Living Inc
6400 Oak Canyon Ste 200
949 240-7200

(P-15776)
SILVERADO SENIOR LIVING INC
Also Called: Huntington Memory Care Cmnty
1118 N Stoneman Ave, Alhambra
(91801-1007)
PHONE..................626 872-3941
Vida Gwin, *Admn*
EMP: 84
SALES (corp-wide): 130.57K **Privately
Held**
Web: www.silverado.com
SIC: 8051 Skilled nursing care facilities
PA: Senior Silverado Living Inc
6400 Oak Canyon Ste 200
949 240-7200

(P-15777)
SILVERADO SENIOR LIVING INC
Also Called: Calabasas Memory Care Cmnty
25100 Calabasas Rd, Calabasas
(91302-1435)
PHONE..................818 746-2583
Rachel Dardeau, *Admn*
EMP: 84
SALES (corp-wide): 130.57K **Privately
Held**
Web: www.silverado.com
SIC: 8051 Skilled nursing care facilities
PA: Senior Silverado Living Inc
6400 Oak Canyon Ste 200

949 240-7200

(P-15778)
SILVERADO SENIOR LIVING INC
Also Called: Newport Mesa Memory Care
Cmnty
350 W Bay St, Costa Mesa (92627-2020)
PHONE..................949 945-0189
Michelle Egrer, *Prin*
EMP: 75
SQ FT: 20,331
SALES (corp-wide): 130.57K **Privately
Held**
Web: www.silverado.com
SIC: 8051 Skilled nursing care facilities
PA: Senior Silverado Living Inc
6400 Oak Canyon Ste 200
949 240-7200

(P-15779)
**SKILLED HEALTHCARE LLC
(DH)**
27442 Portola Pkwy Ste 200, Foothill Ranch
(92610-2822)
PHONE..................949 282-5800
Richard Edwards, *
EMP: 98 EST: 1963
SQ FT: 22,000
SALES (est): 292.09MM **Privately Held**
Web: www.skilledhealthcare.com
SIC: 8051 6513 5122 Convalescent home
with continuous nursing care; Retirement
hotel operation; Drugs, proprietaries, and
sundries
HQ: Genesis Healthcare Llc
101 E State St
Kennett Square PA 19348

(P-15780)
**SKYLINE HLTHCARE WLLNESS
CTR L**
Also Called: SKYLINE HEALTHCARE
CENTER
3032 Rowena Ave, Los Angeles
(90039-2005)
PHONE..................323 665-1185
Bernon Aguilar, *Admn*
Sharrod Brooks, *
EMP: 99 EST: 2010
SALES (est): 7.69MM **Privately Held**
Web: www.skylinehc.com
SIC: 8051 Convalescent home with
continuous nursing care

(P-15781)
SOLVANG LUTHERAN HOME INC
Also Called: Atterdag Village of Solvang
636 Atterdag Rd, Solvang (93463-2687)
PHONE..................805 688-3263
EMP: 120 EST: 1951
SALES (est): 16.41MM **Privately Held**
Web: www.peoplewhocare.com
SIC: 8051 8052 6513 Skilled nursing care
facilities; Intermediate care facilities;
Apartment building operators

(P-15782)
**SPRING VALLEY POST ACUTE
LLC**
14973 Hesperia Rd, Victorville
(92395-3923)
PHONE..................760 245-6477
David Johnson, *Managing Member*
Thomas Chambers, *Managing Member**
Matheson Chambers, *Managing Member**
EMP: 200 EST: 2013
SALES (est): 20.09MM **Privately Held**
Web: www.springvalleypostacute.com

SIC: 8051 Convalescent home with
continuous nursing care

(P-15783)
STERLING CARE INC
Also Called: Paradise Valley Manor
2575 E 8th St, National City (91950-2913)
PHONE..................619 470-6700
Kenneth M Funk, *Prin*
EMP: 187
SALES (est): 4.29MM
SALES (corp-wide): 3.11B **Publicly Held**
SIC: 8051 Convalescent home with
continuous nursing care
HQ: Providence Group, Inc.
262 N University Ave
Farmington UT 84025
801 447-9829

(P-15784)
**STJOHN GOD RTIREMENT
CARE CTR**
2468 S St Andrews Pl, Los Angeles
(90018-2042)
PHONE..................323 731-0641
Admiral Michael Bessimer, *Prin*
Michael Bessimer, *Admn*
EMP: 200 EST: 1942
SQ FT: 99,392
SALES (est): 28.44MM **Privately Held**
Web: www.stjog.org
SIC: 8051 8052 Skilled nursing care facilities
; Intermediate care facilities

(P-15785)
SUNRISE SENIOR LIVING LLC
Also Called: Sunrise of Woodland Hills
5501 Newcastle Ave Apt 130, Encino
(91316-2176)
PHONE..................818 346-9046
Tom Colomaria, *Mgr*
EMP: 71
SALES (corp-wide): 433.05MM **Privately
Held**
Web: www.sunriseseniorliving.com
SIC: 8051 8361 Skilled nursing care facilities
; Residential care
HQ: Sunrise Senior Living, Llc
7902 Westpark Dr
Mclean VA 22102

(P-15786)
**TORRANCE CARE CENTER
WEST INC**
4333 Torrance Blvd, Torrance (90503-4401)
PHONE..................310 370-4561
Vicki P Rollins, *Pr*
EMP: 180 EST: 1999
SALES (est): 21.96MM **Privately Held**
Web: www.torranceca.gov
SIC: 8051 Convalescent home with
continuous nursing care

(P-15787)
**TOWN CNTRY MNOR OF
CHRSTN MSSN**
555 E Memory Ln Side, Santa Ana
(92706-1710)
PHONE..................714 547-7581
Dirk De Wolfe, *Admn*
EMP: 210 EST: 1975
SQ FT: 208,000
SALES (est): 26.78MM **Privately Held**
Web: www.tcmanor.com
SIC: 8051 8059 8052 Skilled nursing care
facilities; Nursing home, except skilled and
intermediate care facility; Intermediate care
facilities

(P-15788)
TRINITY HEALTH SYSTEMS (PA)
Also Called: Villa Maria Care Center
14318 Ohio St, Baldwin Park (91706-2553)
PHONE..................626 960-1971
Randal Kleis, *Pr*
EMP: 80 EST: 1989
SQ FT: 35,000
SALES (est): 11.47MM
SALES (corp-wide): 11.47MM **Privately
Held**
Web: www.sierraviewcarecenter.com
SIC: 8051 Convalescent home with
continuous nursing care

(P-15789)
UPLAND COMMUNITY CARE INC
Also Called: ENSIGN
1221 E Arrow Hwy, Upland (91786-4911)
PHONE..................909 985-1903
Owen Hammond, *CEO*
EMP: 276 EST: 2008
SALES (est): 28.05MM
SALES (corp-wide): 3.73B **Publicly Held**
Web: www.uplandcare.com
SIC: 8051 Convalescent home with
continuous nursing care
PA: The Ensign Group Inc
29222 Rncho Vejo Rd Ste 1
949 487-9500

(P-15790)
US SKILLSERVE INC
Also Called: Community Cnvlscent Hosp
Mntcl
9620 Fremont Ave, Montclair (91763-2320)
PHONE..................909 621-4751
Johannes Simanjuntak, *Brnch Mgr*
EMP: 987
SALES (corp-wide): 23.84MM **Privately
Held**
Web: www.communityech.com
SIC: 8051 Convalescent home with
continuous nursing care
PA: U.S. Skillserve Inc
4115 E Broadway Ste A
562 930-0777

(P-15791)
**VALLEY VSTA NRSING
TRNSTNAL CA**
Also Called: Valley Vsta Nrsing Trnstnal Ca
6120 Vineland Ave, North Hollywood
(91606-4914)
PHONE..................818 763-6275
EMP: 170 EST: 2017
SALES (est): 7.48MM **Privately Held**
SIC: 8051 Convalescent home with
continuous nursing care

(P-15792)
VICTORIA CARE CENTER
5445 Everglades St, Ventura (93003-6523)
PHONE..................805 642-1736
Scott Porter, *Ex Dir*
Jay Brady, *
EMP: 100 EST: 1987
SQ FT: 85,000
SALES (est): 6.22MM **Privately Held**
Web: www.victoriacarecenter.com
SIC: 8051 Convalescent home with
continuous nursing care
PA: Beverly Health Care Corporation
5445 Everglades St

(P-15793)
**VICTORIA VNTURA
HEALTHCARE LLC**
Also Called: Victoria Care Center

5445 Everglades St, Ventura (93003-6523)
PHONE..................805 642-1736
Tim Cooley, Ex Dir
EMP: 262 EST: 2003
SALES (est): 4.51MM Privately Held
Web: www.victoriacarecenter.com
SIC: 8051 Convalescent home with continuous nursing care

(P-15794)
VILLA CONVALESCENT HOSP INC
Also Called: VILLA CONVALESCENT HOSPITAL
8965 Magnolia Ave, Riverside (92503-3943)
PHONE..................951 689-5788
Admiral Jacob Paulson, Prin
EMP: 90 EST: 1971
SQ FT: 25,000
SALES (est): 9.4MM Privately Held
Web: www.villahealthcare.com
SIC: 8051 Convalescent home with continuous nursing care

(P-15795)
VILLA SERENA HEALTHCARE CENTER
723 E 9th St, Long Beach (90813-4611)
PHONE..................562 437-2797
Matt Carp, Pr
EMP: 70 EST: 2014
SALES (est): 6.05MM Privately Held
Web: www.villaserenahealthcare.com
SIC: 8051 Skilled nursing care facilities

(P-15796)
VISTA PACIFICA ENTERPRISES INC (PA)
Also Called: Vista Pacifica Center
3674 Pacific Ave, Jurupa Valley (92509-1948)
PHONE..................951 682-4833
Cheryl Jumonville, CEO
A L Braswell Junior, Pr
Ruth Braswell, Stockholder*
James Braswell, Stockholder*
EMP: 180 EST: 1988
SALES (est): 19.68MM Privately Held
Web: www.vistapacificaent.com
SIC: 8051 8059 Convalescent home with continuous nursing care; Domiciliary care

(P-15797)
VISTA WOODS HEALTH ASSOC LLC
Also Called: Vista Knoll Spclzed Care Fclty
2000 Westwood Rd, Vista (92083-5123)
PHONE..................760 630-2273
Ron Cook, Managing Member
EMP: 173 EST: 2003
SALES (est): 3.55MM
Web: www.vistaknoll.com
SIC: 8051 Convalescent home with continuous nursing care
PA: The Ensign Group Inc
29222 Rncho Vejo Rd Ste 1
949 487-9500

(P-15798)
WATERMAN CONVALESCENT HOSP INC (PA)
Also Called: Mt Rubidoux Convalescent Hosp
1850 N Waterman Ave, San Bernardino (92404-4895)
PHONE..................909 882-1215
Thomas Plott, Pr
Mister Terry Steege, Acct Ex

Elizabeth Plott, *
EMP: 109 EST: 1964
SQ FT: 13,000
SALES (est): 3.67MM
SALES (corp-wide): 3.67MM Privately Held
SIC: 8051 Convalescent home with continuous nursing care

(P-15799)
WATERMARK RTRMENT CMMNTIES INC
Also Called: Fountains At The Carlotta, The
41505 Carlotta Dr, Palm Desert (92211-3279)
PHONE..................760 346-5420
EMP: 96
Web: www.watermarkcommunities.com
SIC: 8051 8052 Skilled nursing care facilities ; Intermediate care facilities
HQ: Watermark Retirement Communities, Inc.
2020 W Rudasill Rd
Tucson AZ 85704

(P-15800)
WEST CNTINELA VLY CARE CTR INC
Also Called: Centinela Skld Nrng Wlns Cntr
950 S Flower St, Inglewood (90301-4186)
PHONE..................310 674-3216
EMP: 99
SALES (est): 5.7MM Privately Held
SIC: 8051 Skilled nursing care facilities

(P-15801)
WESTLAKE HEALTH CARE CENTER
1101 Crenshaw Blvd, Los Angeles (90019-3112)
PHONE..................805 494-1233
Jeoung Lee, Pr
EMP: 279 EST: 2001
SALES (est): 4.97MM
SALES (corp-wide): 14.22MM Privately Held
SIC: 8051 Skilled nursing care facilities
PA: J P H Consulting, Inc.
1101 Crenshaw Blvd
323 934-5660

(P-15802)
WESTVIEW SERVICES INC
Also Called: Westview Cmnty Arts Program
1701 S Euclid St Ste E, Anaheim (92802-2408)
PHONE..................714 956 4100
Britain Semain, Mgr
EMP: 81
SALES (corp-wide): 12.13MM Privately Held
Web: www.westviewservices.org
SIC: 8051 8322 Mental retardation hospital; Adult day care center
PA: Westview Services, Inc
10522 Katella Ave
714 517-6606

(P-15803)
WINDSOR ANAHEIM HEALTHCARE (PA)
Also Called: Windsor Grdns Cnvlescent Ctr A
3415 W Ball Rd, Anaheim (92804-3708)
PHONE..................714 826-8950
Lee Samson, Pr
EMP: 164 EST: 1996
SQ FT: 37,245
SALES (est): 6.64MM Privately Held
Web: www.anaheimhealthcare.com

SIC: 8051 Convalescent home with continuous nursing care

(P-15804)
WINDSOR ANAHEIM HEALTHCARE
Also Called: Southwest Convalesant
13922 Cerise Ave, Hawthorne (90250-8118)
PHONE..................310 675-3304
Michael Gamet, Admn
EMP: 100
Web: www.anaheimhealthcare.com
SIC: 8051 Convalescent home with continuous nursing care
PA: Windsor Anaheim Healthcare, Ltd
3415 W Ball Rd

(P-15805)
WINDSOR TWIN PLMS HLTHCARE CTR
Also Called: Windsor Palms Care Center of Artesia
11900 Artesia Blvd, Artesia (90701-4039)
PHONE..................562 865-0271
EMP: 133 EST: 2005
SALES (est): 28.44MM Privately Held
Web: www.windsorartesia.com
SIC: 8051 Convalescent home with continuous nursing care
PA: Lexington Group International, Inc
9200 W Sunset Blvd # 950

8052 Intermediate Care Facilities

(P-15806)
ARCADIA GARDENS MGT CORP
Also Called: Indepndnt Asstd Lvng & Memory
720 W Camino Real Ave, Arcadia (91007-7839)
PHONE..................626 574-8571
Julie Chirikian, Pr
David Chirikian, *
EMP: 100 EST: 2004
SQ FT: 120,320
SALES (est): 9.11MM Privately Held
Web:
www.arcadiagardensretirement.com
SIC: 8052 Intermediate care facilities

(P-15807)
AVALON AT NEWPORT LLC
23 Corporate Plaza Dr Ste 190, Newport Beach (92660-7943)
PHONE..................949 719-4002
EMP: 100 EST: 2000
SQ FT: 95,000
SALES (est): 2.22MM Privately Held
SIC: 8052 Intermediate care facilities

(P-15808)
BLYTH/WNDSOR CNTRY PK HLTHCARE
3232 E Artesia Blvd, Long Beach (90805-2811)
PHONE..................310 385-1090
Jon Peralez, Prin
EMP: 99 EST: 2013
SALES (est): 1.01MM Privately Held
SIC: 8052 Intermediate care facilities

(P-15809)
COUNTY OF ORANGE
405 W 5th St Ofc, Santa Ana (92701-4519)
PHONE..................714 834-6021
David L Riley, Dir
EMP: 87

SALES (corp-wide): 5.63B Privately Held
Web: www.ocgov.com
SIC: 8052 Intermediate care facilities
PA: County Of Orange
400 W. Civic Center Dr
714 834-6200

(P-15810)
DEL ROSA VILLAIDENCE OPCO LLC
Also Called: Del Rosa Villa
2018 Del Rosa Ave, San Bernardino (92404-5642)
PHONE..................909 885-3261
Jason Murray, Prin
Mark Hancock, *
EMP: 143 EST: 2014
SALES (est): 5.22MM
SALES (corp-wide): 3.11B Publicly Held
Web: www.delrosavillapostacute.com
SIC: 8052 Intermediate care facilities
HQ: Providence Group Of Southern California, Llc
262 N University Ave
Farmington UT 84025
801 447-9829

(P-15811)
GENTIVA HOSPICE
5001 E Commercecenter Dr Ste 140, Bakersfield (93309-1687)
PHONE..................661 324-1232
EMP: 72 EST: 2013
SALES (est): 2.42MM
SALES (corp-wide): 14.03B Privately Held
Web: www.gentivahs.com
SIC: 8052 Personal care facility
HQ: Kindred Healthcare, Llc
680 S 4th St
Louisville KY 40202
502 596-7300

(P-15812)
HILLSIDE HOUSE
1235 Veronica Springs Rd, Santa Barbara (93105-4522)
PHONE..................805 687-0788
Michael Rassler, CEO
Pam Flynt, *
Craig Olson, *
Peter Troesch, *
Chuck Klein, *
EMP: 98 EST: 1945
SQ FT: 24,000
SALES (est): 8.24MM Privately Held
Web: www.hillsidesb.org
SIC: 8052 Home for the mentally retarded, with health care

(P-15813)
LEISURE CARE LLC
Also Called: Fairwinds-West Hills
8138 Woodlake Ave, West Hills (91304-3500)
PHONE..................818 713-0900
Pat Luc, Genl Mgr
EMP: 132
SALES (corp-wide): 305.08K Privately Held
Web: www.leisurecare.com
SIC: 8052 Intermediate care facilities
HQ: Leisure Care, Llc
999 3rd Ave Ste 4550
Seattle WA 98104
206 436-7827

(P-15814)
LOS ANGLES CNTY RNCHO LOS AMGO
7601 Imperial Hwy, Downey (90242-3456)

PHONE..................562 385-7111
Jorge Orozco, *CEO*
EMP: 1400 **EST:** 2009
SALES (est): 10.32MM **Privately Held**
Web: dhs.lacounty.gov
SIC: 8052 Personal care facility
PA: Rancho Los Amigos National
Rehabiliatation Center
7601 Imperial Hwy

(P-15815)
**NEW VISTA BEHAVIORAL HLTH
LLC**
3 Park Plz Ste 550, Irvine (92614-2537)
PHONE..................949 284-0095
Jennifer Hale, *Brnch Mgr*
EMP: 99
SALES (corp-wide): 10.44MM **Privately
Held**
Web:
www.newvistabehavioralhealth.com
SIC: 8052 Home for the mentally retarded,
with health care
PA: New Vista Behavioral Health, Llc
1901 Newport Blvd Ste 204
888 316-3665

(P-15816)
**OJAI HEALTHIDENCE OPCO
LLC**
Also Called: Ojai Health & Rehabilitation
601 N Montgomery St, Ojai (93023-2751)
PHONE..................805 646-8124
EMP: 85 **EST:** 2014
SALES (est): 6.55MM
SIC: 8052 Intermediate care facilities
HQ: Providence Group North, Llc
262 N University Ave
Farmington UT 84025
801 447-9829

(P-15817)
ONTARIOIDENCE OPCO LLC
Also Called: Las Colinas Post Acute
800 E 5th St, Ontario (91764-2432)
PHONE..................909 984-8629
Jason Murray, *Prin*
Mark Hancock, *
EMP: 174 **EST:** 2014
SALES (est): 9.54MM
SALES (corp-wide): 3.11B **Publicly Held**
SIC: 8052 Intermediate care facilities
HQ: Providence Group Of Southern
California, Llc
262 N University Ave
Farmington UT 84025
801 447-9829

(P-15818)
**ORANGE TREEIDENCE OPCO
LLC**
Also Called: Riverwalk Post Acute
4000 Harrison St, Riverside (92503-3514)
PHONE..................951 785-6060
Jason Murray, *Prin*
Mark Hancock, *
EMP: 133 **EST:** 2014
SALES (est): 10.1MM
SALES (corp-wide): 3.11B **Publicly Held**
SIC: 8052 Intermediate care facilities
HQ: Providence Group Of Southern
California, Llc
262 N University Ave
Farmington UT 84025
801 447-9829

(P-15819)
PARKSIDE HEALTHCARE INC
Also Called: Parkside Health & Wellness Ctr
444 W Lexington Ave, El Cajon
(92020-4416)
PHONE..................619 442-7744
Matthew Oldroyd, *Prin*
EMP: 85 **EST:** 2014
SALES (est): 1.26MM **Privately Held**
Web: www.parksidehealth.net
SIC: 8052 Intermediate care facilities

(P-15820)
**RANCHO VISTA HEALTH
CENTER**
Also Called: Rancho Vista
200 Grapevine Rd Apt 15, Vista
(92083-4042)
PHONE..................760 941-1480
Alan Shigley, *Ex Dir*
EMP: 88 **EST:** 1983
SALES (est): 7.29MM
SALES (corp-wide): 29.14MM **Privately
Held**
Web: www.elranchovista.com
SIC: 8052 8051 8361 Intermediate care
facilities; Skilled nursing care facilities;
Residential care
PA: Activcare Living, Inc.
10603 Rancho Bernardo Rd
858 565-4424

(P-15821)
RES-CARE INC
45691 Monroe St Ste 6, Indio (92201-3943)
PHONE..................760 775-2887
EMP: 87
SALES (corp-wide): 8.83B **Publicly Held**
Web: www.rescare.com
SIC: 8052 Home for the mentally retarded,
with health care
HQ: Res-Care, Inc.
805 N Whittington Pkwy
Louisville KY 40222
502 394-2100

(P-15822)
RES-CARE INC
22635 Alessandro Blvd, Moreno Valley
(92553-8550)
PHONE..................951 653-1311
EMP: 116
SALES (corp-wide): 8.83B **Publicly Held**
Web: www.rescare.com
SIC: 8052 Home for the mentally retarded,
with health care
HQ: Res-Care, Inc.
805 N Whittington Pkwy
Louisville KY 40222
502 394-2100

(P-15823)
RES-CARE INC
2120 Foothill Blvd Ste 205, La Verne
(91750-2949)
PHONE..................909 596-5360
Jill Crowell, *Mgr*
EMP: 135
SALES (corp-wide): 8.83B **Publicly Held**
Web: www.rescare.com
SIC: 8052 Home for the mentally retarded,
with health care
HQ: Res-Care, Inc.
805 N Whittington Pkwy
Louisville KY 40222
502 394-2100

(P-15824)
VALLEY VILLAGE
8727 Fenwick St, Sunland (91040-1952)
PHONE..................818 446-0366
EMP: 113
SALES (corp-wide): 24.89MM **Privately
Held**
Web: www.valleyvillage.org
SIC: 8052 Intermediate care facilities
PA: Valley Village
20830 Sherman Way
818 587-9450

(P-15825)
**VITAS HEALTHCARE
CORPORATION**
9106 Pulsar Ct Ste D, Corona
(92883-4632)
PHONE..................858 805-6254
EMP: 107
SALES (corp-wide): 2.26B **Publicly Held**
Web: www.vitas.com
SIC: 8052 Personal care facility
HQ: Vitas Healthcare Corporation
201 S Bscyne Blvd Ste 400
Miami FL 33131
305 374-4143

(P-15826)
**VITAS HEALTHCARE
CORPORATION**
333 N Lantana St Ste 124, Camarillo
(93010-9007)
PHONE..................805 437-2100
Rita Peddycoart, *Mgr*
EMP: 115
SALES (corp-wide): 2.26B **Publicly Held**
Web: www.vitas.com
SIC: 8052 Personal care facility
HQ: Vitas Healthcare Corporation
201 S Bscyne Blvd Ste 400
Miami FL 33131
305 374-4143

(P-15827)
WATERMANIDENCE OPCO LLC
Also Called: Waterman Canyon Post Acute
1850 N Waterman Ave, San Bernardino
(92404-4831)
PHONE..................909 882-1215
Jason Murray, *Prin*
Mark Hancock, *
EMP: 164 **EST:** 2014
SALES (est): 5.14MM
SALES (corp-wide): 3.11B **Publicly Held**
SIC: 8052 Intermediate care facilities
HQ: Providence Group Of Southern
California, Llc
262 N University Ave
Farmington UT 84025
801 447-9829

(P-15828)
**WATTS HEALTH FOUNDATION
INC (PA)**
Also Called: Uhp Healthcare
3405 W Imperial Hwy Ste 304, Inglewood
(90303-2219)
PHONE..................310 424-2220
Doctor Clyde W Oden, *Pr*
Jennifer Stapalding, *CEO*
Ron Bolding V Press, *Business Operations*
EMP: 400 **EST:** 1967
SALES (est): 6.55MM
SALES (corp-wide): 6.55MM **Privately
Held**
Web: www.wattshealth.org

SIC: 8052 8011 8741 Intermediate care
facilities; Health maintenance organization;
Management services

(P-15829)
**WEST VALLEYIDENCE OPCO
LLC**
Also Called: West Valley Post Acute
7057 Shoup Ave, West Hills (91307-2335)
PHONE..................818 348-8422
Jason Murray, *Prin*
Mark Hancock, *
EMP: 85 **EST:** 2015
SALES (est): 8.53MM
SALES (corp-wide): 3.11B **Publicly Held**
SIC: 8052 Intermediate care facilities
HQ: Providence Group North, Llc
262 N University Ave
Farmington UT 84025
801 447-9829

8059 Nursing And Personal
Care, Nec

(P-15830)
**AMBERWOOD CONVALESCENT
HOSP**
6071 York Blvd, Los Angeles (90042-3503)
PHONE..................323 254-3407
Jeanie Barrett, *Admn*
Ben Garrett, *
EMP: 100 **EST:** 1967
SALES (est): 620.41K
SALES (corp-wide): 1.25MM **Privately
Held**
Web:
www.yorkhealthcareandwellness.com
SIC: 8059 Convalescent home
PA: Casner Consolidated, Llc.
1020 Huntington Dr
626 282-8443

(P-15831)
**ANTELOPE VLY RETIREMENT
HM INC**
Also Called: Antelope Vly Convalecent Hosp
44445 15th St W, Lancaster (93534-2801)
PHONE..................661 948-7501
Marsha Weldon, *Dir*
EMP: 178
SALES (corp-wide): 3.97MM **Privately
Held**
Web: www.avrv.org
SIC: 8059 8051 Convalescent home; Skilled
nursing care facilities
PA: Antelope Valley Retirement Home, Inc.
44523 15th St W
661 949-5584

(P-15832)
**ANTELOPE VLY RETIREMENT
HM INC**
Also Called: A V Nursing Care Center
44567 15th St W, Lancaster (93534-2803)
PHONE..................661 949-5524
Alfred Jones, *Mgr*
EMP: 178
SALES (corp-wide): 3.97MM **Privately
Held**
Web: www.avrv.org
SIC: 8059 8051 Convalescent home; Skilled
nursing care facilities
PA: Antelope Valley Retirement Home, Inc.
44523 15th St W
661 949-5584

▲ = Import ▼ = Export
◆ = Import/Export

(P-15833)
ARARAT HOME LOS ANGELES INC
Also Called: Ararat Nursing Facility
15099 Mission Hills Rd, Mission Hills
(91345-1102)
PHONE...............818 837-1800
M Kebhichien, *Admn*
EMP: 120
SALES (corp-wide): 53.22MM **Privately Held**
Web: www.ararathome.org
SIC: 8059 8051 Nursing home, except skilled and intermediate care facility; Skilled nursing care facilities
PA: Ararat Home Of Los Angeles, Inc.
15105 Mission Hills Rd
818 365-3000

(P-15834)
ARARAT HOME LOS ANGELES INC
Also Called: Ararat Convalescent Hospital
2373 Colorado Blvd, Los Angeles
(90041-1157)
PHONE...............323 256-8012
Violette Alahaidoyan, *Brnch Mgr*
EMP: 120
SQ FT: 9,104
SALES (corp-wide): 53.22MM **Privately Held**
Web: www.ararathome.org
SIC: 8059 8051 Convalescent home; Skilled nursing care facilities
PA: Ararat Home Of Los Angeles, Inc.
15105 Mission Hills Rd
818 365-3000

(P-15835)
ARCADIA CONVALESCENT HOSP INC (PA)
Also Called: Arcadia Health Care Center
1601 S Baldwin Ave, Arcadia (91007-7910)
PHONE...............626 445-2170
Orlando Clarizio Junior, *CEO*
EMP: 117 EST: 1962
SQ FT: 21,342
SALES (est): 18.4MM
SALES (corp-wide): 18.4MM **Privately Held**
Web: www.arcadiahcc.com
SIC: 8059 8051 Convalescent home; Skilled nursing care facilities

(P-15836)
ARTESIA CHRISTIAN HOME INC
11614 183rd St, Artesia (00701 6606)
PHONE...............562 865-5218
Elroy Van Derley, *Ex Dir*
EMP: 140 EST: 1947
SQ FT: 43,223
SALES (est): 13.17MM **Privately Held**
Web: www.achome.org
SIC: 8059 8052 8051 Convalescent home; Intermediate care facilities; Skilled nursing care facilities

(P-15837)
BERKELEY E CONVALESCENT HOSP
Also Called: Berkeley E Convalescent Hosp
2021 Arizona Ave, Santa Monica
(90404-1335)
PHONE...............310 829-5377
Paul Bartolucce, *Adm/Dir*
Saul Galper, *
EMP: 150 EST: 1965
SQ FT: 10,000
SALES (est): 9.74MM **Privately Held**

SIC: 8059 Convalescent home

(P-15838)
BERNARDO HTS HEALTHCARE INC
Also Called: Carmel Mtn Rhab Healthcare Ctr
11895 Avenue Of Industry, San Diego
(92128-3423)
PHONE...............858 673-0101
Christopher R Christensen, *CEO*
Covey C Christensen, *
Matt Rutter, *
EMP: 253 EST: 2005
SALES (est): 21.34MM
SALES (corp-wide): 3.73B **Publicly Held**
Web: www.carmelmountain.net
SIC: 8059 8051 8011 Nursing home, except skilled and intermediate care facility; Skilled nursing care facilities; Clinic, operated by physicians
PA: The Ensign Group Inc
29222 Rncho Vejo Rd Ste 1
949 487-9500

(P-15839)
BRIERWOOD TERRACE VENTURA INC
Also Called: Ventura Convalescent Center
4904 Telegraph Rd, Ventura (93003-4109)
PHONE...............805 642-4101
Brett Watson, *Admn*
EMP: 77
SALES (corp-wide): 800.19K **Privately Held**
Web: www.theventuran.com
SIC: 8059 8051 Convalescent home; Skilled nursing care facilities
HQ: Brierwood Terrace Ventura, Inc.
4904 Telegraph Rd
Ventura CA 93003
805 642-4101

(P-15840)
BRIGHTON CONVALESCENT LLC
Also Called: Brighton Convalescent Center
1836 N Fair Oaks Ave, Pasadena
(91103-1619)
PHONE...............626 798-9124
Alex Makabuhay, *Admn*
Rose Wilson Ctrl, *Prin*
EMP: 100 EST: 1992
SALES (est): 10.71MM **Privately Held**
Web: www.brighton1836.com
SIC: 8059 8051 Convalescent home; Skilled nursing care facilities

(P-15841)
BUENA VENTURA CARE CENTER INC
Also Called: Leisure Glen Convalescent Ctr
1505 Colby Dr, Glendale (91205-3307)
PHONE...............818 247-4476
Yolanda Wise, *Admn*
EMP: 80
SALES (corp-wide): 3.11B **Publicly Held**
SIC: 8059 8051 Convalescent home; Skilled nursing care facilities
HQ: East Los Angeles Healthcare, Llc
1016 S Record Ave
Los Angeles CA 90023
323 268-0106

(P-15842)
CARE CHOICE HEALTH SYSTEMS INC
Also Called: Care Choice Home Care
1151 S Santa Fe Ave, Vista (92083-7228)
PHONE...............760 798-4508

Tara Pardo, *CEO*
EMP: 120 EST: 2015
SALES (est): 4.43MM **Privately Held**
Web: www.carechoicehomecare.com
SIC: 8059 8082 Personal care home, with health care; Home health care services

(P-15843)
CLEAR VIEW SANITARIUM INC
Also Called: Clear View Sanitarium
15823 S Western Ave, Gardena
(90247-3703)
PHONE...............310 538-2323
Mark D Towns, *CEO*
Jeffrey B Towns, *
EMP: 200 EST: 1937
SQ FT: 40,000
SALES (est): 15.28MM **Privately Held**
Web: www.clearviewcare.com
SIC: 8059 Home for the mentally retarded, ex. skilled or intermediate

(P-15844)
COUNTRY VILLA SERVICE CORP
112 E Broadway, San Gabriel (91776-1805)
PHONE...............626 285-2165
J Caballero, *Admn*
EMP: 102
SALES (corp-wide): 28.62MM **Privately Held**
Web: www.evictionlawyer.com
SIC: 8059 Nursing home, except skilled and intermediate care facility
PA: Country Villa Service Corp.
2400 E Katella Ave # 800
310 574-3733

(P-15845)
COUNTRY VILLA TERRACE (PA)
Also Called: Country Vlla Convalescent Hosp
6050 W Pico Blvd, Los Angeles
(90035-2647)
PHONE...............323 653-3980
Steven Reissman, *Pr*
Diana Reissman, *
EMP: 75 EST: 1963
SQ FT: 6,000
SALES (est): 7.42MM
SALES (corp-wide): 7.42MM **Privately Held**
SIC: 8059 8361 Convalescent home; Residential care

(P-15846)
CPCC INC
Also Called: Chatsworth Park Hlth Care Ctr
10610 Owensmouth Ave, Chatsworth
(91311-2151)
PHONE...............818 882-3200
John Sorensen, *Pr*
Greg Ethington, *
EMP: 99 EST: 1982
SALES (est): 4.74MM **Privately Held**
Web: www.chatsworthparkcare.com
SIC: 8059 8051 Convalescent home; Skilled nursing care facilities

(P-15847)
CRESTWOOD BEHAVIORAL HLTH INC
Also Called: 1115 Bakersfield Mhrc
6700 Eucalyptus Dr Ste A, Bakersfield
(93306-6076)
PHONE...............661 363-8127
Sukhdeep Kaur, *Prin*
EMP: 82
SALES (corp-wide): 278.96MM **Privately Held**
Web:
www.crestwoodbehavioralhealth.com

SIC: 8059 Home for the mentally retarded, ex. skilled or intermediate
PA: Crestwood Behavioral Health, Inc.
520 Capitol Mall Ste 800
209 955-2326

(P-15848)
CRESTWOOD BEHAVIORAL HLTH INC
Also Called: 1154 San Diego Mhrc
5550 University Ave Ste A, San Diego
(92105-2307)
PHONE...............619 481-6790
Robyn Ramsey, *Admn*
EMP: 155
SALES (corp-wide): 278.96MM **Privately Held**
Web:
www.crestwoodbehavioralhealth.com
SIC: 8059 Home for the mentally retarded, ex. skilled or intermediate
PA: Crestwood Behavioral Health, Inc.
520 Capitol Mall Ste 800
209 955-2326

(P-15849)
CRESTWOOD BEHAVIORAL HLTH INC
Also Called: 1167 Fallbrook Mhrc
624 E Elder St, Fallbrook (92028-3004)
PHONE...............760 451-4165
Corey Hise, *Admn*
EMP: 132
SALES (corp-wide): 278.96MM **Privately Held**
Web:
www.crestwoodbehavioralhealth.com
SIC: 8059 Home for the mentally retarded, ex. skilled or intermediate
PA: Crestwood Behavioral Health, Inc.
520 Capitol Mall Ste 800
209 955-2326

(P-15850)
ENSIGN SAN DIMAS LLC
Also Called: Arbor Glen Care Center
1033 E Arrow Hwy, Glendora (91740-6110)
PHONE...............626 963-7531
Steve Powell, *Operations*
Don R Bybee, *Prin*
EMP: 104 EST: 2010
SALES (est): 10.65MM
SALES (corp-wide): 3.73B **Publicly Held**
Web: www.arborglencare.com
SIC: 8059 Convalescent home
PA: The Ensign Group Inc
29222 Rncho Vejo Rd Ste 1
949 487-9500

(P-15851)
FAMILY TIES HOME CARE LLC
1350 Lahtte Dr, Oak Park (91377-4718)
PHONE...............818 565-9147
EMP: 75 EST: 2020
SALES (est): 3.38MM **Privately Held**
Web: www.familytieshomecare.com
SIC: 8059 8082 Personal care home, with health care; Home health care services

(P-15852)
FRONT PORCH COMMUNITIES & SVCS
3775 Modoc Rd, Santa Barbara
(93105-4474)
PHONE...............805 687-0793
Roberta Jacobsen, *Brnch Mgr*
EMP: 111
SQ FT: 68,000
Web: www.frontporch.net

SIC: 8059 8051 Rest home, with health care; Skilled nursing care facilities
PA: Front Porch Communities And Services
800 N Brand Blvd Fl 19

(P-15853)
FRONT PRCH CMMNTIES OPRTING GR
Also Called: FREDERICKA MANOR CARE CENTER
800 N Brand Blvd Fl 19, Glendale (91203-1231)
PHONE..............................800 233-3709
John Woodward, *CEO*
EMP: 190 EST: 2013
SALES (est): 80.38MM **Privately Held**
Web: www.frontporch.net
SIC: 8059 Nursing and personal care, nec

(P-15854)
GENESIS HEALTHCARE LLC
Also Called: Fountain View Cnvalescent Hosp
5310 Fountain Ave, Los Angeles (90029-1005)
PHONE..............................323 461-9961
EMP: 1047
Web: www.genesishcc.com
SIC: 8059 8051 8069 Convalescent home; Skilled nursing care facilities; Specialty hospitals, except psychiatric
HQ: Genesis Healthcare Llc
101 E State St
Kennett Square PA 19348

(P-15855)
GERI-CARE II INC
Also Called: Vermont Care Center
22035 S Vermont Ave, Torrance (90502-2120)
P.O. Box 6069 (90504-0069)
PHONE..............................310 328-0812
Emmanuel David, *Pr*
Engelica Vivillanueva, *
EMP: 250 EST: 1989
SQ FT: 40,000
SALES (est): 10.76MM **Privately Held**
Web: www.vermonthc.com
SIC: 8059 8051 Convalescent home; Skilled nursing care facilities

(P-15856)
GIBRALTAR CNVALESCENT HOSP INC
Also Called: Sunset Manor Convalescent Hosp
2720 Nevada Ave, El Monte (91733-2318)
PHONE..............................626 443-9425
Marcel Morales, *Mgr*
EMP: 100
SALES (corp-wide): 4.69MM **Privately Held**
Web: www.sunsetmanorcare.com
SIC: 8059 8051 Convalescent home; Skilled nursing care facilities
PA: Gibraltar Convalescent Hospital, Inc.
3050 Saturn St Ste 201
714 577-3880

(P-15857)
GOLDEN CARE INC
Also Called: Valley Manor Convalescent Hosp
6120 Vineland Ave, North Hollywood (91606-4914)
PHONE..............................818 763-6275
Evelyn Del Rosario, *Pr*
Gonzalo Del Rosario, *
EMP: 80 EST: 1963
SQ FT: 32,000
SALES (est): 1.75MM **Privately Held**

SIC: 8059 8361 Convalescent home; Residential care

(P-15858)
GOLDEN STATE HEALTH CTRS INC
Also Called: Ocean View Convelesent Hosp
1340 15th St, Santa Monica (90404-1802)
PHONE..............................310 451-9706
Dina Closas R.n., *Dir*
EMP: 200
SALES (corp-wide): 39.78MM **Privately Held**
Web: www.oceanpointehealth.com
SIC: 8059 8051 Convalescent home; Skilled nursing care facilities
PA: Golden State Health Centers, Inc.
13347 Ventura Blvd
818 385-3200

(P-15859)
HILLSDALE GROUP LP
Also Called: Sherman Village Hlth Care Ctr
12750 Riverside Dr, North Hollywood (91607-3319)
PHONE..............................818 623-2170
Rich Terrell, *Prin*
EMP: 249
SALES (corp-wide): 6.54MM **Privately Held**
SIC: 8059 8051 8093 8011 Convalescent home; Skilled nursing care facilities; Rehabilitation center, outpatient treatment; Clinic, operated by physicians
PA: The Hillsdale Group L P
1199 Howard Ave Ste 200

(P-15860)
HUMANGOOD (PA)
Also Called: Terraces At Squaw Peak
1900 Huntington Dr, Duarte (91010-2694)
PHONE..............................602 906-4024
John Cochran, *CEO*
EMP: 110 EST: 1959
SALES (est): 31.22MM
SALES (corp-wide): 31.22MM **Privately Held**
Web: www.humangood.org
SIC: 8059 8051 8322 Rest home, with health care; Skilled nursing care facilities; Old age assistance

(P-15861)
HUMANGOOD NORCAL
Also Called: Rosewood Retirement Community
1401 New Stine Rd, Bakersfield (93309-3530)
PHONE..............................661 834-0620
Ellen Renner, *Brnch Mgr*
EMP: 253
SALES (corp-wide): 31.22MM **Privately Held**
Web: www.humangood.org
SIC: 8059 8052 8051 Rest home, with health care; Intermediate care facilities; Skilled nursing care facilities
HQ: Humangood Norcal
1900 Huntington Dr
Duarte CA 91010
925 924-7100

(P-15862)
HUMANGOOD NORCAL
Also Called: Plymouth Village
900 Salem Dr, Redlands (92373-6147)
PHONE..............................909 793-1233
Keith Kasin, *Brnch Mgr*
EMP: 225
SQ FT: 8,000

SALES (corp-wide): 31.22MM **Privately Held**
Web: www.humangood.org
SIC: 8059 8051 Rest home, with health care; Skilled nursing care facilities
HQ: Humangood Norcal
1900 Huntington Dr
Duarte CA 91010
925 924-7100

(P-15863)
LIFE CARE CENTERS AMERICA INC
Also Called: Vista Del Mar Health Centers
304 N Melrose Dr, Vista (92083-4814)
PHONE..............................760 724-8222
Michael Ramstead, *Brnch Mgr*
EMP: 243
SALES (corp-wide): 139.21MM **Privately Held**
Web: www.lcca.com
SIC: 8059 8051 Convalescent home; Skilled nursing care facilities
PA: Life Care Centers Of America, Inc.
3570 Keith St Nw
423 472-9585

(P-15864)
LIFE GNERATIONS HEALTHCARE LLC
Also Called: Stanford Crt Nrsing Cntr-Sntee
8778 Cuyamaca St, Santee (92071-4255)
PHONE..............................619 449-5555
Andy Ashton, *Admn*
EMP: 87
SALES (corp-wide): 72.62MM **Privately Held**
Web: www.lifegen.net
SIC: 8059 8051 8049 Convalescent home; Skilled nursing care facilities; Physical therapist
PA: Life Generations Healthcare Llc
6 Hutton Cntre Dr Ste 400
714 241-5600

(P-15865)
LONGWOOD MANAGEMENT CORP
Also Called: Western Convelescence
2190 W Adams Blvd, Los Angeles (90018-2039)
PHONE..............................323 737-7778
Emma Camanag, *Admn*
EMP: 91
SALES (corp-wide): 41.31MM **Privately Held**
Web: www.longwoodmgmt.com
SIC: 8059 6512 Convalescent home; Commercial and industrial building operation
PA: Longwood Management Llc
4032 Wilshire Blvd Fl 6
213 389-6900

(P-15866)
LONGWOOD MANAGEMENT CORP
Also Called: Aldon Ter Convalsent Hosptial
1240 S Hoover St, Los Angeles (90006-3606)
PHONE..............................213 382-8461
John Sicat, *Prin*
EMP: 120
SALES (corp-wide): 41.31MM **Privately Held**
Web: www.longwoodmgmt.com
SIC: 8059 8051 Convalescent home; Skilled nursing care facilities
PA: Longwood Management Llc
4032 Wilshire Blvd Fl 6

213 389-6900

(P-15867)
LONGWOOD MANAGEMENT CORP
Also Called: Imperial Care Center
11429 Ventura Blvd, Studio City (91604-3143)
PHONE..............................818 980-8200
Emma Dellanuoni, *Mgr*
EMP: 174
SQ FT: 29,525
SALES (corp-wide): 41.31MM **Privately Held**
Web: www.studiocityrehab.com
SIC: 8059 8051 Convalescent home; Skilled nursing care facilities
PA: Longwood Management Llc
4032 Wilshire Blvd Fl 6
213 389-6900

(P-15868)
LONGWOOD MANAGEMENT CORP
Also Called: Live Oak Rehab
537 W Live Oak St, San Gabriel (91776-1149)
PHONE..............................626 289-3763
Ranita Phan, *Mgr*
EMP: 117
SALES (corp-wide): 41.31MM **Privately Held**
Web: www.liveoakrehab.com
SIC: 8059 8051 Convalescent home; Skilled nursing care facilities
PA: Longwood Management Llc
4032 Wilshire Blvd Fl 6
213 389-6900

(P-15869)
LONGWOOD MANAGEMENT CORP
Also Called: Colonial Care Center
1913 E 5th St, Long Beach (90802-2024)
PHONE..............................562 432-5751
Laura Mccuphen, *Mgr*
EMP: 102
SALES (corp-wide): 41.31MM **Privately Held**
Web: www.longwoodmgmt.com
SIC: 8059 8051 Convalescent home; Skilled nursing care facilities
PA: Longwood Management Llc
4032 Wilshire Blvd Fl 6
213 389-6900

(P-15870)
LONGWOOD MANAGEMENT CORP
Also Called: Sunny View Care Center
2000 W Washington Blvd, Los Angeles (90018-1637)
PHONE..............................323 735-5146
Amber Gooden, *Admn*
EMP: 106
SALES (corp-wide): 41.31MM **Privately Held**
Web: www.longwoodmgmt.com
SIC: 8059 Convalescent home
PA: Longwood Management Llc
4032 Wilshire Blvd Fl 6
213 389-6900

(P-15871)
LONGWOOD MANAGEMENT CORP
Also Called: Broadway Manor Care Center
605 W Broadway, Glendale (91204-1007)
PHONE..............................818 246-7174

Dolly Piper, *Mgr*
EMP: 138
SQ FT: 7,000
SALES (corp-wide): 41.31MM **Privately Held**
Web: www.broadwaymanorhc.com
SIC: 8059 8051 Convalescent home; Skilled nursing care facilities
PA: Longwood Management Llc
4032 Wilshire Blvd Fl 6
213 389-6900

(P-15872)
MAGNOLIA RHBLTTION NURSING CTR
Also Called: Magnolia Convalescent Hospital
8133 Magnolia Ave, Riverside
(92504-3409)
PHONE...................951 688-4321
Larry Mays, *Pr*
Bennie J Mays, *
Bobbie N Mays, *
Grant Edgeson, *
EMP: 140 **EST:** 1971
SQ FT: 25,000
SALES (est): 4.46MM **Privately Held**
Web:
www.woodcrestpostacuterehab.com
SIC: 8059 8051 Convalescent home; Skilled nursing care facilities

(P-15873)
MARLINDA MANAGEMENT INC (PA)
Also Called: Sherwood Guest Home
3351 E Imperial Hwy, Lynwood
(90262-3305)
PHONE...................310 631-6122
Martha Lang, *Pr*
Linda Gassoumis, *
EMP: 120 **EST:** 1961
SALES (est): 1.66MM
SALES (corp-wide): 1.66MM **Privately Held**
SIC: 8059 Convalescent home

(P-15874)
MARNA HEALTH SERVICES INC
Also Called: Sillcrest Nursing Home
4280 Cypress Dr, San Bernardino
(92407-2960)
PHONE...................909 882-2965
Maria Barrios, *Pr*
Napoleon Garcia, *
EMP: 70 **EST:** 2013
SQ FT: 120
SALES (est): 8.18MM **Privately Held**
SIC: 8059 7389 8049 Personal care home, with health care; Business Activities at Non-Commercial Site; Physical therapist

(P-15875)
NEW VISTA HEALTH SERVICES
Also Called: New Vsta Nrsing Rhbltation Ctr
8647 Fenwick St, Sunland (91040-1957)
PHONE...................818 352-1421
Robert Craig, *Pr*
EMP: 224
SALES (corp-wide): 8.23MM **Privately Held**
Web: www.newvista.us
SIC: 8059 8361 Nursing home, except skilled and intermediate care facility; Rehabilitation center, residential: health care incidental
PA: New Vista Health Services, Inc
1987 Vartikian Ave
559 298-3236

(P-15876)
NEW VISTA HEALTH SERVICES
Also Called: New Vsta Post Acute Care Ctr W
1516 Sawtelle Blvd, Los Angeles
(90025-3207)
PHONE...................310 477-5501
Eugene Tipo, *Admn*
EMP: 224
SALES (corp-wide): 8.23MM **Privately Held**
Web: www.newvista.us
SIC: 8059 8051 Nursing home, except skilled and intermediate care facility; Skilled nursing care facilities
PA: New Vista Health Services, Inc
1987 Vartikian Ave
559 298-3236

(P-15877)
OLYMPIA CONVALESCENT HOSPITAL
1100 S Alvarado St, Los Angeles
(90006-4188)
PHONE...................213 487-3000
Otto Schwartz, *Admn*
Sam Lidell, *
Andre Pollak, *
EMP: 115 **EST:** 1971
SQ FT: 25,000
SALES (est): 12.59MM **Privately Held**
Web: www.olympia-convalescent.com
SIC: 8059 8051 Convalescent home; Skilled nursing care facilities

(P-15878)
ORANGE CNTY RYALE CNVLSCENT HO (PA)
Also Called: Royale Convalescent Hospital
1030 W Warner Ave, Santa Ana
(92707-3198)
PHONE...................714 546-6450
Mitchell Kantor, *Pr*
Donald Connelly Admtr, *Prin*
EMP: 330 **EST:** 1965
SQ FT: 87,000
SALES (est): 17.01MM
SALES (corp-wide): 17.01MM **Privately Held**
Web: www.royalehealth.com
SIC: 8059 8051 Convalescent home; Skilled nursing care facilities

(P-15879)
PACIFIC HAVEN CONVALESCENT HM
12072 Trask Ave, Garden Grove
(92843-3881)
PHONE...................714 534-1942
Mike Uranga, *Admn*
EMP: 100 **EST:** 1978
SALES (est): 3.82MM **Privately Held**
Web: www.pachaven.com
SIC: 8059 8051 Convalescent home; Skilled nursing care facilities

(P-15880)
PARK MARINO CONVALESCENT CTR
2585 E Washington Blvd, Pasadena
(91107-1499)
PHONE...................626 463-4105
Admiral William Kite, *Prin*
EMP: 146 **EST:** 1966
SALES (est): 1.11MM
SALES (corp-wide): 4.36MM **Privately Held**
Web: www.parkmarino.com
SIC: 8059 8051 Convalescent home; Skilled nursing care facilities

PA: Diversified Health Services (Del)
136 Washington Ave
510 231-6200

(P-15881)
PILGRIM PLACE IN CLAREMONT (PA)
625 Mayflower Rd, Claremont
(91711-4240)
PHONE...................909 399-5500
William R Cunitz, *Pr*
Joyce Yarborough, *
Sue Fairley, *
Bernard Valek, *
Mary Ann Macias, *
EMP: 175 **EST:** 1914
SQ FT: 2,000
SALES (est): 25.1MM
SALES (corp-wide): 25.1MM **Privately Held**
Web: www.pilgrimplace.org
SIC: 8059 8051 8052 Rest home, with health care; Skilled nursing care facilities; Intermediate care facilities

(P-15882)
RINALDI CONVALESCENT HOSPITAL
16553 Rinaldi St, Granada Hills
(91344-3798)
PHONE...................818 360-1003
EMP: 175 **EST:** 1967
SQ FT: 25,000
SALES (est): 7.39MM **Privately Held**
Web: www.rinaldicares.com
SIC: 8059 8051 Convalescent home; Skilled nursing care facilities

(P-15883)
SAN BERNARDINO CARE COMPANY
467 E Gilbert St, San Bernardino
(92404-5318)
PHONE...................909 884-4781
Jenq Chen, *Pr*
EMP: 110 **EST:** 2004
SALES (est): 2.14MM **Privately Held**
SIC: 8059 Convalescent home

(P-15884)
SAN DEGO CTR FOR CHLDREN FNDTI (PA)
3002 Armstrong St, San Diego
(92111-5702)
PHONE...................858 277-9550
Moises Baron, *CEO*
EMP: 90 **EST:** 1887
SQ FT: 38,000
SALES (est): 24.56MM
SALES (corp wide): 24.56MM **Privately Held**
Web: www.centerforchildren.org
SIC: 8059 8361 Personal care home, with health care; Residential care

(P-15885)
TEMPLE PK CNVALESCENT HOSP INC
2411 W Temple St, Los Angeles
(90026-4899)
PHONE...................213 380-2035
Barry Kohn, *Pr*
Toby Kohn, *
EMP: 77 **EST:** 1976
SALES (est): 9.92MM **Privately Held**
SIC: 8059 Convalescent home

(P-15886)
TWO PALMS NURSING CENTER INC
Also Called: Marlinda Imperial Hospital
150 Bellefontaine St, Pasadena
(91105-3102)
PHONE...................626 796-1103
EMP: 185
SQ FT: 28,955
SALES (corp-wide): 3.22MM **Privately Held**
Web: www.pasadenameadows.com
SIC: 8059 8051 Convalescent home; Skilled nursing care facilities
PA: Two Palms Nursing Center, Inc.
2637 E Washington Blvd
626 798-8991

(P-15887)
UNITED CONVALESCENT FACILITIES
Also Called: University Park Healthcare Ctr
230 E Adams Blvd, Los Angeles
(90011-1426)
PHONE...................213 748-0491
Doug Easton, *Owner*
EMP: 80 **EST:** 1998
SQ FT: 1,300
SALES (est): 8.1MM **Privately Held**
SIC: 8059 Nursing home, except skilled and intermediate care facility

(P-15888)
UNITED MEDICAL MANAGEMENT INC
Also Called: Valley Healthcare
1680 N Waterman Ave, San Bernardino
(92404-5113)
PHONE...................909 886-5291
Alan Hull, *Admn*
EMP: 125 **EST:** 1982
SQ FT: 30,000
SALES (est): 4.42MM **Privately Held**
Web: www.progressivecarecenters.com
SIC: 8059 8051 8322 Convalescent home; Skilled nursing care facilities; Rehabilitation services

(P-15889)
VALLE VSTA CNVLESCENT HOSP INC
1025 W 2nd Ave, Escondido (92025-3839)
PHONE...................760 745-1288
Kristina Kuivon, *CEO*
EMP: 85 **EST:** 1961
SQ FT: 19,000
SALES (est): 4.45MM **Privately Held**
SIC: 8059 Convalescent home
PA: Covenant Care, Llc
120 Vantis Dr Ste 200

(P-15890)
VILLA DE LA MAR INC
Also Called: Bel Vista Healthcare Center
5001 E Anaheim St, Long Beach
(90804-3214)
PHONE...................562 494-5001
Alan Anderson, *Pr*
Dorothy Erickson, *
EMP: 160 **EST:** 1983
SALES (est): 6.65MM
SALES (corp-wide): 3.11B **Publicly Held**
Web: www.belvista.com
SIC: 8059 Convalescent home
HQ: Providence Group, Inc.
262 N University Ave
Farmington UT 84025
801 447-9829

PRODUCTS & SVCS

(P-15891)
WINDSOR CYPRESS GRDNS HLTHCARE
Also Called: Windsor Cypress Garden
9025 Colorado Ave, Riverside
(92503-2157)
PHONE...............................951 688-3643
Lee Samson, *CEO*
Stanley Angermeir, *
Edward Erzen, *
EMP: 2567 EST: 1972
SALES (est): 11.29MM **Privately Held**
Web: www.windsorcypressgardens.com
SIC: 8059 8051 Convalescent home; Skilled nursing care facilities
PA: S&F Management Company, Llc
   1901 Avenue Of The Stars # 1060

8062 General Medical And Surgical Hospitals

(P-15892)
ADVENTIST HEALTH DELANO
Also Called: Delano Regional Medical Center
1205 Garces Hwy Ste 208, Delano
(93215-3658)
PHONE...............................661 721-5337
Ester Bumabod, *Mgr*
EMP: 131
SALES (corp-wide): 805.07MM **Privately Held**
Web: www.adventisthealth.org
SIC: 8062 5047 General medical and surgical hospitals; Therapy equipment
HQ: Adventist Health Delano
   1401 Garces Hwy
   Delano CA 93215
   661 725-4800

(P-15893)
ADVENTIST HEALTH DELANO (HQ)
Also Called: Delano Regional Medical Center
1401 Garces Hwy, Delano (93215-3660)
P.O. Box 460 (93216-0460)
PHONE...............................661 725-4800
EMP: 523 EST: 1973
SALES (est): 91.67MM
SALES (corp-wide): 805.07MM **Privately Held**
Web: www.adventisthealth.org
SIC: 8062 General medical and surgical hospitals
PA: Adventist Health System/West, Corporation
   One Adventist Health Way
   844 574-5686

(P-15894)
ADVENTIST HEALTH MED TEHACHAPI (PA)
305 S Robinson St, Tehachapi
(93561-1726)
P.O. Box 669 (93581-0669)
PHONE...............................661 750-4848
Eugene Suksi, *CEO*
Allen Burgess, *
EMP: 105 EST: 1949
SQ FT: 18,000
SALES (est): 2.95MM
SALES (corp-wide): 2.95MM **Privately Held**
Web: www.tvhd.org
SIC: 8062 General medical and surgical hospitals

(P-15895)
ADVENTIST HLTH SYSTM/WEST CORP
Also Called: Bakersfield Heart Hospital
3001 Sillect Ave, Bakersfield (93308-6337)
PHONE...............................661 316-6000
Kerry Heinrich, *Brnch Mgr*
EMP: 336
SALES (corp-wide): 805.07MM **Privately Held**
Web: www.adventisthealth.org
SIC: 8062 General medical and surgical hospitals
PA: Adventist Health System/West, Corporation
   One Adventist Health Way
   844 574-5686

(P-15896)
AHM GEMCH INC
Also Called: WHITTIER HOSPITAL MEDICAL CENT
1701 Santa Anita Ave, El Monte
(91733-3411)
PHONE...............................626 579-7777
Jeffrey Flocken, *CEO*
Patrick Steinhauser, *COO*
Gary Louis, *CFO*
EMP: 180 EST: 1973
SQ FT: 71,500
SALES (est): 62.04MM
SALES (corp-wide): 325.41MM **Privately Held**
Web: www.greaterelmonte.com
SIC: 8062 General medical and surgical hospitals
PA: Ahmc Healthcare Inc.
   506 W Valley Blvd Ste 300
   626 943-7526

(P-15897)
AHMC ANHEIM RGIONAL MED CTR LP
Also Called: Cardiac Unit
1111 W La Palma Ave, Anaheim
(92801-2804)
PHONE...............................714 774-1450
EMP: 425
SALES (corp-wide): 325.41MM **Privately Held**
Web: www.ahmchealth.com
SIC: 8062 General medical and surgical hospitals
HQ: Ahmc Anaheim Regional Medical Center Lp
   1111 W La Palma Ave
   Anaheim CA 92801
   714 774-1450

(P-15898)
AHMC ANHEIM RGIONAL MED CTR LP
Also Called: Ahmc
1211 W La Palma Ave, Anaheim
(92801-2815)
PHONE...............................714 999-3847
Patrick Petre, *Brnch Mgr*
EMP: 425
SALES (corp-wide): 325.41MM **Privately Held**
Web: www.ahmchealth.com
SIC: 8062 General medical and surgical hospitals
HQ: Ahmc Anaheim Regional Medical Center Lp
   1111 W La Palma Ave
   Anaheim CA 92801
   714 774-1450

(P-15899)
AHMC ANHEIM RGIONAL MED CTR LP
1111 W La Palma Ave, Anaheim
(92801-2804)
PHONE...............................714 774-1450
Barry Arbuckle, *Prin*
Jane Cutler, *
Donald Lorack, *
Kathy Doi, *
▲ EMP: 2957 EST: 1959
SQ FT: 500
SALES (est): 8.17MM
SALES (corp-wide): 325.41MM **Privately Held**
Web: www.ahmchealth.com
SIC: 8062 General medical and surgical hospitals
PA: Ahmc Healthcare Inc.
   506 W Valley Blvd Ste 300
   626 943-7526

(P-15900)
AHMC HEALTHCARE INC (PA)
Also Called: Whittier Hospital Medical Ctr
506 W Valley Blvd Ste 300, San Gabriel
(91776-5716)
PHONE...............................626 943-7526
Jonathan Wu Md, *CEO*
EMP: 150 EST: 2004
SALES (est): 325.41MM
SALES (corp-wide): 325.41MM **Privately Held**
Web: www.ahmchealth.com
SIC: 8062 8641 General medical and surgical hospitals; Civic and social associations

(P-15901)
AHMC HEALTHCARE INC
1701 Santa Anita Ave, South El Monte
(91733-3411)
PHONE...............................626 579-7777
EMP: 137
SALES (corp-wide): 325.41MM **Privately Held**
Web: www.ahmchealth.com
SIC: 8062 General medical and surgical hospitals
PA: Ahmc Healthcare Inc.
   506 W Valley Blvd Ste 300
   626 943-7526

(P-15902)
AHMC WHITTIER HOSP MED CTR LP
9080 Colima Rd, Whittier (90605-1600)
PHONE...............................562 945-3561
Richard Castro, *CEO*
EMP: 850 EST: 2001
SQ FT: 16,782
SALES (est): 22.32MM
SALES (corp-wide): 325.41MM **Privately Held**
Web: www.ahmchealth.com
SIC: 8062 General medical and surgical hospitals
PA: Ahmc Healthcare Inc.
   506 W Valley Blvd Ste 300
   626 943-7526

(P-15903)
ALAKOR HEALTHCARE LLC
Also Called: Monrovia Memorial Hospital
323 S Heliotrope Ave, Monrovia
(91016-2914)
PHONE...............................626 408-9800
Jon Woods, *
Ron Kupferstein, *
EMP: 126 EST: 2004

SQ FT: 10,000
SALES (est): 15.69MM **Privately Held**
Web: www.monroviamemorial.com
SIC: 8062 General medical and surgical hospitals

(P-15904)
ALHAMBRA HOSPITAL MED CTR LP
Also Called: WHITTIER HOSPITAL MEDICAL CENT
100 S Raymond Ave, Alhambra
(91801-3166)
PHONE...............................626 570-1606
Iris Lai, *Managing Member*
EMP: 160 EST: 1920
SQ FT: 200,000
SALES (est): 86.01MM
SALES (corp-wide): 325.41MM **Privately Held**
Web: www.alhambrahospital.com
SIC: 8062 General medical and surgical hospitals
PA: Ahmc Healthcare Inc.
   506 W Valley Blvd Ste 300
   626 943-7526

(P-15905)
ALTA HEALTHCARE SYSTEM LLC (HQ)
4081 E Olympic Blvd, Los Angeles
(90023-3330)
PHONE...............................323 267-0477
David Topper, *Managing Member*
Sam Lee, *
EMP: 250 EST: 1998
SALES (est): 35.05MM
SALES (corp-wide): 3.91B **Privately Held**
Web: www.sch-culvercity.com
SIC: 8062 General medical and surgical hospitals
PA: Prospect Medical Holdings, Inc.
   3415 S Sepulveda Blvd
   310 943-4500

(P-15906)
ALTA HOSPITALS SYSTEM LLC
Also Called: Foothill Regional Medical Ctr
14662 Newport Ave, Tustin (92780-6064)
PHONE...............................714 619-7700
EMP: 575
SALES (corp-wide): 3.91B **Privately Held**
Web: www.pmh.com
SIC: 8062 General medical and surgical hospitals
HQ: Prospect Medical Holdings Inc
   3824 Hughes Ave
   Culver City CA 90232

(P-15907)
ALVARADO HOSPITAL LLC (DH)
6655 Alvarado Rd, San Diego
(92120-5296)
PHONE...............................619 287-3270
Darlene Wetton, *
Gudrun Moll, *
EMP: 232 EST: 1989
SALES (est): 39.06MM
SALES (corp-wide): 534.4MM **Privately Held**
Web: health.ucsd.edu
SIC: 8062 General medical and surgical hospitals
HQ: University Of California, San Diego
   9500 Gilman Dr
   La Jolla CA 92093
   858 534-2230

(P-15908)

ALVARADO HOSPITAL MED CTR INC

6655 Alvarado Rd, San Diego
(92120-5208)
PHONE................619 287-3270
Sharilee Smith, *Pr*
EMP: 791 **EST:** 2000
SALES (est): 17.33MM
SALES (corp-wide): 534.4MM **Privately Held**
Web: health.ucsd.edu
SIC: 8062 General medical and surgical hospitals
HQ: Uc San Diego Health Accountable Care Network, Inc.
9300 Campus Point Dr
La Jolla CA 92037
858 657-7000

(P-15909)

AMERICAN HLTHCARE SYSTEMS CORP (PA)

505 N Brand Blvd Ste 1110, Glendale
(91203-3932)
PHONE................818 646-9933
Michael Sarian, *Dir*
Aimee Gill, *VP*
Aramais Paronyan, *CMO*
Jonathan Burket, *CCO*
EMP: 293 **EST:** 2021
SALES (est): 143.23MM
SALES (corp-wide): 143.23MM **Privately Held**
Web: www.amhealthsystems.com
SIC: 8062 General medical and surgical hospitals

(P-15910)

AMI-HTI TRZANA ENCINO JINT VNT

Also Called: A M I Encn-Trzana Rgnal Med Ce
18321 Clark St, Tarzana (91356-3501)
PHONE................818 881-0800
Dale Surowitz, *Mng Pt*
EMP: 148 **EST:** 1993
SQ FT: 180,000
SALES (est): 10.39MM **Privately Held**
SIC: 8062 General medical and surgical hospitals

(P-15911)

AMISUB OF CALIFORNIA INC (DH)

Also Called: TENET
18321 Clark St, Tarzana (91356-3501)
PHONE................818 881-0800
Dale Surowitz, *CEO*
Don Kreitz, *
Nick Lymboropolouo, *
EMP: 000 **EST:** 1979
SQ FT: 180,000
SALES (est): 506.51K
SALES (corp-wide): 19.17B **Publicly Held**
SIC: 8062 General medical and surgical hospitals
HQ: Tenet Healthsystem Medical, Inc.
14201 Dallas Pkwy
Dallas TX 75254
469 893-2000

(P-15912)

ANAHEIM GLOBAL MEDICAL CENTER

1025 S Anaheim Blvd, Anaheim
(92805-5806)
PHONE................714 533-6220
Jamie You, *CEO*
Marven E Howard, *

Jason Liu, *
EMP: 975 **EST:** 1981
SALES (est): 97.63MM **Privately Held**
Web: www.anaheimglobalmedicalcenter.com
SIC: 8062 General medical and surgical hospitals
HQ: Kpc Healthcare, Inc.
1301 N Tustin Ave
Santa Ana CA 92705
714 953-3652

(P-15913)

ANTELOPE VALLEY HEALTH CARE DI (PA)

Also Called: Avmc
1600 W Avenue J, Lancaster (93534-2814)
P.O. Box 7001 (93539)
PHONE................661 949-5000
Edward Mirzabegian, *CEO*
Abdallah Farrukh, *
Dennis Empey, *
Slavka Rehacek, *
EMP: 1660 **EST:** 1955
SQ FT: 300,000
SALES (est): 522.79MM
SALES (corp-wide): 522.79MM **Privately Held**
Web: www.avmc.com
SIC: 8062 General medical and surgical hospitals

(P-15914)

ANTELOPE VALLEY HLTH CARE DST

Also Called: Antelope Valley Home Care
44335 Lowtree Ave, Lancaster
(93534-4167)
PHONE................661 949-5936
Patti Sheldon, *Mgr*
EMP: 135
SALES (corp-wide): 522.79MM **Privately Held**
Web: www.avmc.org
SIC: 8062 8082 General medical and surgical hospitals; Home health care services
PA: Antelope Valley Health Care District
1600 W Ave J
661 949-5000

(P-15915)

ANTELOPE VALLEY HOSPITAL INC

Also Called: Antelope Valley Hlth Care Dst
44335 Lowtree Ave, Lancaster
(93534-4167)
PHONE................661 949-5000
Cheryl Akerly, *Brnch Mgr*
EMP: 157
SALES (corp-wide): 522.79MM **Privately Held**
Web: www.avmc.org
SIC: 8062 General medical and surgical hospitals
PA: Antelope Valley Health Care District
1600 W Ave J
661 949-5000

(P-15916)

ANTELOPE VALLEY HOSPITAL INC

Antelope Otpatient Imaging Ctr
44105 15th St W Ste 100, Lancaster
(93534-4090)
PHONE................661 726-6050
Veronica Munoz-rivera, *Brnch Mgr*
EMP: 157
SALES (corp-wide): 522.79MM **Privately Held**

Web: www.avmc.org
SIC: 8062 General medical and surgical hospitals; Medical services organization
PA: Antelope Valley Health Care District
1600 W Ave J
661 949-5000

(P-15917)

ARROWHEAD REGIONAL MEDICAL CTR

Also Called: Armc
400 N Pepper Ave, Colton (92324-1819)
PHONE................909 580-1000
Andrew Goldfrach, *CEO*
Patrick Petre, *
Sam Hessami, *CMO**
EMP: 2500 **EST:** 1952
SQ FT: 950,000
SALES (est): 496.16MM
SALES (corp-wide): 4.01B **Privately Held**
Web: www.arrowheadmedcenter.org
SIC: 8062 General medical and surgical hospitals
PA: San Bernardino County
385 N Arrowhead Ave
909 387-3841

(P-15918)

ARROYO GRANDE COMMUNITY HOSPITAL

Also Called: Emergency Dept Dignity Hlth
345 S Halcyon Rd, Arroyo Grande
(93420-3899)
PHONE................805 473-7626
EMP: 400
Web: www.dignityhealth.org
SIC: 8062 General medical and surgical hospitals

(P-15919)

AUXILARY OF MSSION HOSP MSSION

Also Called: MISSION HOSPITAL
27700 Medical Center Rd, Mission Viejo
(92691-6426)
PHONE................949 364-1400
Eduardo Jordan, *Ch Bd*
Kenn Mcfarland, *Pr*
Vicki J Veal, *
EMP: 1242 **EST:** 2011
SALES (est): 247.33K
SALES (corp-wide): 690.3MM **Privately Held**
Web: www.mission4health.com
SIC: 8062 General medical and surgical hospitals
PA: Mission Hospital Regional Medical Center Inc
27700 Medical Center Rd
949 364-1400

(P-15920)

AVALON MEDICAL DEV CORP

Also Called: CATALINA ISLAND MEDICAL CENTER
100 Falls Canyon Rd, Avalon (90704-2990)
P.O. Box 1563 (90704-1563)
PHONE................310 510-0700
Jason Paret, *CEO*
William M Greene, *
EMP: 100 **EST:** 1987
SQ FT: 11,500
SALES (est): 20.95MM **Privately Held**
Web: www.catalinaislandhealth.org
SIC: 8062 Hospital, AMA approved residency

(P-15921)

BAKERSFELD MEM HOSP FOUNDATION

420 34th St, Bakersfield (93301-2237)
PHONE................661 327-4647
Ken Keller, *Prin*
Ken Keller, *CEO*
Tracy Kiser, *1st*
David Morton Second, *Vice Chairman*
Andrew Paulden, *Treas*
EMP: 98 **EST:** 1980
SALES (est): 4.51MM **Privately Held**
Web: www.supportbakersfield.org
SIC: 8062 General medical and surgical hospitals

(P-15922)

BAKERSFIELD MEMORIAL HOSPITAL

Also Called: Memorial Center
420 34th St, Bakersfield (93301-2298)
P.O. Box 1888 (93303-1888)
PHONE................661 327-1792
Jon Van Boening, *CEO*
Gordon K Foster, *
EMP: 1100 **EST:** 1953
SQ FT: 364,000
SALES (est): 620.57MM **Privately Held**
Web: www.dignityhealth.org
SIC: 8062 Hospital, affiliated with AMA residency
HQ: Dignity Health
185 Berry St Ste 200
San Francisco CA 94107
415 438-5500

(P-15923)

BEAR VLY CMNTY HEALTHCARE DST (PA)

41870 Garstin Dr, Big Bear Lake
(92315-2088)
PHONE................909 866-6501
Raymond Hino, *CEO*
Donna Nicely, *
Barbara Espinoza, *
Christopher Fagan, *
EMP: 150 **EST:** 1985
SQ FT: 25,000
SALES (est): 341.35K
SALES (corp-wide): 341.35K **Privately Held**
Web: www.bvchd.com
SIC: 8062 General medical and surgical hospitals

(P-15924)

BEVERLY COMMUNITY HOSP ASSN

101 E Beverly Blvd Ste 104, Montebello
(90640-4314)
PHONE................323 889-2452
Norma Valdez, *Brnch Mgr*
EMP: 295
SALES (corp-wide): 805.07MM **Privately Held**
Web: www.beverly.org
SIC: 8062 8011 General medical and surgical hospitals; Clinic, operated by physicians
HQ: Beverly Community Hospital Association
309 W Beverly Blvd
Montebello CA 90640
323 726-1222

(P-15925)

BEVERLY COMMUNITY HOSP ASSN

Also Called: Kelpien Health Care

1920 W Whittier Blvd, Montebello
(90640-4009)
PHONE...................323 725-1519
Wendy Torres, *Mgr*
EMP: 295
SALES (corp-wide): 805.07MM **Privately Held**
Web: www.beverly.org
SIC: 8062 General medical and surgical hospitals
HQ: Beverly Community Hospital Association
309 W Beverly Blvd
Montebello CA 90640
323 726-1222

(P-15926)
BEVERLY COMMUNITY HOSP ASSN (HQ)
Also Called: ADVENTIST HEALTH
309 W Beverly Blvd, Montebello
(90640-4308)
P.O. Box 619002 (90640)
PHONE...................323 726-1222
Alice Cheng, *CEO*
Gary Kiff, *
Renee D Martinez, *
David I Chambers, *
Mohammad A, *
EMP: 406 **EST:** 1949
SQ FT: 274,000
SALES (est): 38.72MM
SALES (corp-wide): 805.07MM **Privately Held**
Web: www.beverly.org
SIC: 8062 General medical and surgical hospitals
PA: Adventist Health System/West, Corporation
One Adventist Health Way
844 574-5686

(P-15927)
BIO-MED SERVICES INC
Also Called: Prime Healthcare Services
3300 E Guasti Rd, Ontario (91761-8655)
PHONE...................909 235-4400
Prem Reddy, *CEO*
EMP: 85 **EST:** 2006
SALES (est): 29.17MM
SALES (corp-wide): 878.52MM **Privately Held**
Web: www.biomedservicesinc.com
SIC: 8062 General medical and surgical hospitals
HQ: Prime Healthcare Services Inc
3480 E Guasti Rd
Ontario CA 91761

(P-15928)
BROTMAN MEDICAL CENTER INC
Also Called: Southern Cal Hosp At Culver Cy
3828 Delmas Ter, Culver City (90232-6806)
PHONE...................310 836-7000
TOLL FREE: 800
Michael Klepin, *CEO*
EMP: 300 **EST:** 1961
SQ FT: 183,000
SALES (est): 24.23MM
SALES (corp-wide): 3.91B **Privately Held**
Web: www.sch-culvercity.com
SIC: 8062 General medical and surgical hospitals
PA: Prospect Medical Holdings, Inc.
3415 S Sepulveda Blvd
310 943-4500

(P-15929)
CALIFRNIA HOSP MED CTR FNDTION
1401 S Grand Ave, Los Angeles
(90015-3010)
PHONE...................213 742-5867
Phillip C Hill, *Ch Bd*
Nathan R Nusbaum, *
Clark Underwood, *
David Milovich, *
Linda Bolor, *
▲ **EMP:** 1500 **EST:** 1926
SQ FT: 800,000
SALES (est): 46.68MM **Privately Held**
Web: www.supportcaliforniahospital.org
SIC: 8062 Hospital, med school affiliated with nursing and residency
HQ: Dignity Health
185 Berry St Ste 200
San Francisco CA 94107
415 438-5500

(P-15930)
CALIFRNIA RHBLITATION INST LLC
Also Called: SELECT MEDICAL
2070 Century Park E, Los Angeles
(90067-1907)
P.O. Box 2034 (17055-0793)
PHONE...................424 363-1003
Michael Tarvin, *VP*
EMP: 1242 **EST:** 2014
SALES (est): 143.99MM
SALES (corp-wide): 6.66B **Publicly Held**
Web: www.californiarehabinstitute.com
SIC: 8062 General medical and surgical hospitals
PA: Select Medical Holdings Corporation
4714 Gettysburg Rd
717 972-1100

(P-15931)
CASA CLINA HOSP CTRS FOR HLTHC (HQ)
Also Called: Casa Clina Ctrs For Rhbltation
255 E Bonita Ave, Pomona (91767-1923)
P.O. Box 6001 (91769-6001)
PHONE...................909 596-7733
Kelly Linden, *Pr*
Steve Norin, *
Randy Blackman, *Vice Chairman*
Mary Lou Jensen, *
Stephen Graeber, *
▲ **EMP:** 500 **EST:** 1936
SQ FT: 90,000
SALES (est): 92.94MM
SALES (corp-wide): 136.57MM **Privately Held**
Web: www.casacolina.org
SIC: 8062 General medical and surgical hospitals
PA: Casa Colina, Inc.
255 E Bonita Ave
909 596-7733

(P-15932)
CATHOLIC HLTHCARE W STHERN CAL (HQ)
1050 Linden Ave, Long Beach
(90813-3321)
PHONE...................562 491-9000
EMP: 125
SALES (est): 43.27MM
SALES (corp-wide): 7.06B **Privately Held**
SIC: 8062 General medical and surgical hospitals
PA: Dignity Health
185 Berry St Ste 300
415 438-5500

(P-15933)
CEDARS-SINAI MARINA HOSPITAL
Also Called: Centinela Frman Rgonal Med Ctr
555 E Hardy St, Inglewood (90301-4011)
PHONE...................310 673-4660
Michael Rembis, *Brnch Mgr*
EMP: 653
SALES (corp-wide): 4.66B **Privately Held**
Web: www.marinahospital.com
SIC: 8062 General medical and surgical hospitals
HQ: Marina Cedars-Sinai Hospital
4650 Lincoln Blvd
Marina Del Rey CA 90292

(P-15934)
CEDARS-SINAI MARINA HOSPITAL
Also Called: Centinela Frman Rgonal Med Ctr
4650 Lincoln Blvd, Marina Del Rey
(90292-6306)
PHONE...................310 823-8911
EMP: 979
SQ FT: 150,000
SALES (corp-wide): 4.66B **Privately Held**
Web: www.marinahospital.com
SIC: 8062 General medical and surgical hospitals
HQ: Marina Cedars-Sinai Hospital
4650 Lincoln Blvd
Marina Del Rey CA 90292

(P-15935)
CEDARS-SINAI MARINA HOSPITAL
Also Called: Centinela Frman Rgonal Med Ctr
4640 Admiralty Way Ste 650, Marina Del Rey (90292-6667)
PHONE...................310 448-7800
Bob Bokern, *Prin*
EMP: 1088
SALES (corp-wide): 4.66B **Privately Held**
Web: www.marinahospital.com
SIC: 8062 General medical and surgical hospitals
HQ: Marina Cedars-Sinai Hospital
4650 Lincoln Blvd
Marina Del Rey CA 90292

(P-15936)
CEDARS-SINAI MEDICAL CENTER
8730 Alden Dr 220, Los Angeles
(90048-3690)
PHONE...................310 423-2587
EMP: 151
SALES (corp-wide): 4.66B **Privately Held**
Web: www.cedars-sinai.edu
SIC: 8062 General medical and surgical hospitals
PA: Cedars-Sinai Medical Center
8700 Beverly Blvd
310 423-3277

(P-15937)
CEDARS-SINAI MEDICAL CENTER
Also Called: Clinical Translational RES Ctr
8723 Alden Dr, Los Angeles (90048-3692)
PHONE...................310 423-8965
EMP: 249
SALES (corp-wide): 4.66B **Privately Held**
Web: www.cedars-sinai.org
SIC: 8062 General medical and surgical hospitals
PA: Cedars-Sinai Medical Center
8700 Beverly Blvd
310 423-3277

(P-15938)
CEDARS-SINAI MEDICAL CENTER
Also Called: Di Vizio Lab
110 N George Burns Rd, Los Angeles
(90048-1830)
PHONE...................310 659-3732
EMP: 151
SALES (corp-wide): 4.66B **Privately Held**
Web: www.cedars-sinai.org
SIC: 8062 General medical and surgical hospitals
PA: Cedars-Sinai Medical Center
8700 Beverly Blvd
310 423-3277

(P-15939)
CEDARS-SINAI MEDICAL CENTER
Anesthesiology Department
8700 Beverly Blvd Ste 8211, Los Angeles
(90048-1865)
PHONE...................310 423-5841
EMP: 151
SALES (corp-wide): 4.66B **Privately Held**
Web: www.cedars-sinai.edu
SIC: 8062 3841 General medical and surgical hospitals; Anesthesia apparatus
PA: Cedars-Sinai Medical Center
8700 Beverly Blvd
310 423-3277

(P-15940)
CEDARS-SINAI MEDICAL CENTER
8700 Beverly Blvd Ste 2216, Los Angeles
(90048-1865)
PHONE...................310 423-5147
EMP: 101
SALES (corp-wide): 4.66B **Privately Held**
Web: www.cedars-sinai.edu
SIC: 8062 General medical and surgical hospitals
PA: Cedars-Sinai Medical Center
8700 Beverly Blvd
310 423-3277

(P-15941)
CEDARS-SINAI MEDICAL CENTER
310 N San Vicente Blvd, West Hollywood
(90048-1810)
PHONE...................310 423-9310
Sylvia Salgado Estrada, *Prin*
EMP: 125
SALES (corp-wide): 4.66B **Privately Held**
Web: www.cedars-sinai.edu
SIC: 8062 General medical and surgical hospitals
PA: Cedars-Sinai Medical Center
8700 Beverly Blvd
310 423-3277

(P-15942)
CEDARS-SINAI MEDICAL CENTER
99 N La Cienega Blvd Ste Mezz, Beverly Hills (90211-2283)
PHONE...................310 967-1884
Lloyd Greig, *Brnch Mgr*
EMP: 125
SALES (corp-wide): 4.66B **Privately Held**
Web: www.cedars-sinai.edu
SIC: 8062 General medical and surgical hospitals
PA: Cedars-Sinai Medical Center
8700 Beverly Blvd
310 423-3277

792   2025 Southern California
Business Directory and Buyers Guide   ▲ = Import ▼ = Export
◆ = Import/Export

(P-15943)

CEDARS-SINAI MEDICAL CENTER

Also Called: Cedars-Sinai Home Care
8635 W 3rd St Ste.1165w, Los Angeles (90048-6134)
PHONE.....................310 423-3277
Sheldon King, *Pr*
EMP: 569
SALES (corp-wide): 4.66B **Privately Held**
Web: www.cedars-sinai.edu
SIC: 8062 General medical and surgical hospitals
PA: Cedars-Sinai Medical Center
  8700 Beverly Blvd
  310 423-3277

(P-15944)

CEDARS-SINAI MEDICAL CENTER

Also Called: Medical Genetics
444 S San Vicente Blvd Ste 1001, Los Angeles (90048-4170)
PHONE.....................310 423-9520
David Rimoin, *Mgr*
EMP: 446
SALES (corp-wide): 4.66B **Privately Held**
Web: www.cedars-sinai.edu
SIC: 8062 8099 General medical and surgical hospitals; Health screening service
PA: Cedars-Sinai Medical Center
  8700 Beverly Blvd
  310 423-3277

(P-15945)

CEDARS-SINAI MEDICAL CENTER

4100 W 190th St, Torrance (90504-5513)
PHONE.....................310 967-1900
Clyde Goldman, *Prin*
EMP: 544
SALES (corp-wide): 4.66B **Privately Held**
Web: www.cedars-sinai.edu
SIC: 8062 8011 General medical and surgical hospitals; Medical centers
PA: Cedars-Sinai Medical Center
  8700 Beverly Blvd
  310 423-3277

(P-15946)

CEDARS-SINAI MEDICAL CENTER

Also Called: Health System Medical Network
250 N Robertson Blvd #.101, Beverly Hills (90211-1788)
PHONE.....................310 385-3400
Tom Gordon, *CEO*
EMP: 520
SALES (corp-wide): 4.66B **Privately Held**
Web: www.cedars-sinai.edu
SIC: 8062 8011 General medical and surgical hospitals; Offices and clinics of medical doctors
PA: Cedars-Sinai Medical Center
  8700 Beverly Blvd
  310 423-3277

(P-15947)

CEDARS-SINAI MEDICAL CENTER

8797 Beverly Blvd Ste 220, West Hollywood (90048-1892)
PHONE.....................310 423-5468
EMP: 98
SALES (corp-wide): 4.66B **Privately Held**
Web: www.cedars-sinai.edu
SIC: 8062 General medical and surgical hospitals
PA: Cedars-Sinai Medical Center
  8700 Beverly Blvd

---

310 423-3277

(P-15948)

CEDARS-SINAI MEDICAL CENTER

8727 W 3rd St, Los Angeles (90048-3843)
PHONE.....................310 423-6451
Eric Fee, *Genl Mgr*
EMP: 102
SALES (corp-wide): 4.66B **Privately Held**
Web: www.cedars-sinai.edu
SIC: 8062 General medical and surgical hospitals
PA: Cedars-Sinai Medical Center
  8700 Beverly Blvd
  310 423-3277

(P-15949)

CEDARS-SINAI MEDICAL CENTER

Emergency Services
8700 Beverly Blvd Ste 1103, West Hollywood (90048-1865)
PHONE.....................310 423-8780
Joel Giderman, *Dir*
EMP: 125
SALES (corp-wide): 4.66B **Privately Held**
Web: www.cedars-sinai.edu
SIC: 8062 General medical and surgical hospitals
PA: Cedars-Sinai Medical Center
  8700 Beverly Blvd
  310 423-3277

(P-15950)

CEDARS-SINAI MEDICAL CENTER

Also Called: Nephrology
8635 W 3rd St Ste 1195, Los Angeles (90048-6146)
P.O. Box 48956 (90048-0956)
PHONE.....................310 824-3664
Larry Froch, *Prin*
EMP: 457
SALES (corp-wide): 4.66B **Privately Held**
Web: www.cedars-sinai.edu
SIC: 8062 General medical and surgical hospitals
PA: Cedars-Sinai Medical Center
  8700 Beverly Blvd
  310 423-3277

(P-15951)

CEDARS-SINAI MEDICAL CENTER

Also Called: Cedars Surgical Research Ctr
8700 Beverly Blvd # 4018, West Hollywood (90048-1865)
PHONE.....................310 855-7701
Linda Proctor, *Div Mgr*
EMP: 241
SALES (corp-wide): 4.66B **Privately Held**
Web: www.cedars-sinai.edu
SIC: 8062 8733 General medical and surgical hospitals; Medical research
PA: Cedars-Sinai Medical Center
  8700 Beverly Blvd
  310 423-3277

(P-15952)

CHAPMAN GLOBAL MEDICAL CTR INC

Also Called: Chapman Family Health
2601 E Chapman Ave, Orange (92869-3206)
PHONE.....................714 633-0011
TOLL FREE: 800
Matt Whaley, *CEO*
Robert Heinemeier, *

EMP: 425 EST: 1968
SQ FT: 96,000
SALES (est): 98.36K **Privately Held**
Web: www.chapmanglobalmedicalcenter.com
SIC: 8062 General medical and surgical hospitals
HQ: Kpc Healthcare, Inc.
  1301 N Tustin Ave
  Santa Ana CA 92705
  714 953-3652

(P-15953)

CHILDRENS HOSPITAL LOS ANGELES

Also Called: Saban Research Institute, The
4661 W Sunset Blvd, Los Angeles (90027-6042)
PHONE.....................323 361-2751
Cheryl Saban, *Brnch Mgr*
EMP: 450
SALES (corp-wide): 1.74B **Privately Held**
Web: www.chla.org
SIC: 8062 General medical and surgical hospitals
PA: The Childrens Hospital Los Angeles
  4650 Sunset Blvd
  323 660-2450

(P-15954)

CHILDRENS HOSPITAL ORANGE CNTY

Also Called: Choc Mission
455 S Main St, Orange (92868-3835)
PHONE.....................949 365-2416
Kerri Ruppert Schiller, *Prin*
EMP: 528
SALES (corp-wide): 1.55B **Privately Held**
Web: www.choc.org
SIC: 8062 General medical and surgical hospitals
PA: Children's Hospital Of Orange County
  1201 W La Veta Ave
  714 509-8300

(P-15955)

CHILDRENS HOSPITAL ORANGE CNTY

980 Roosevelt, Irvine (92620-3672)
PHONE.....................949 387-2586
EMP: 203
SALES (corp-wide): 1.55B **Privately Held**
Web: www.choc.org
SIC: 8062 8099 8082 6321 General medical and surgical hospitals; Childbirth preparation clinic; Home health care services; Accident and health insurance
PA: Children's Hospital Of Orange County
  1201 W La Veta Ave
  714 509-8300

(P-15956)

CHILDRENS HOSPITAL ORANGE CNTY

Also Called: Choc Childern's
10602 Chapman Ave Ste 200, Garden Grove (92840-3147)
PHONE.....................714 638-5990
Gina Sue Cadogan, *Brnch Mgr*
EMP: 284
SALES (corp-wide): 1.55B **Privately Held**
Web: www.choc.org
SIC: 8062 General medical and surgical hospitals
PA: Children's Hospital Of Orange County
  1201 W La Veta Ave
  714 509-8300

(P-15957)

CHILDRENS HOSPITAL ORANGE CNTY

15785 Laguna Canyon Rd Ste 120, Irvine (92618-3166)
PHONE.....................949 769-6473
EMP: 203
SALES (corp-wide): 1.55B **Privately Held**
Web: www.choc.org
SIC: 8062 General medical and surgical hospitals
PA: Children's Hospital Of Orange County
  1201 W La Veta Ave
  714 509-8300

(P-15958)

CHILDRENS HOSPITAL ORANGE CNTY (PA)

Also Called: Choc
1201 W La Veta Ave, Orange (92868-4203)
PHONE.....................714 509-8300
Kimberly Cripe, *Pr*
L Kenneth Heuler D.d.s., *Ch Bd*
Jessica L Miley, *CDO**
Kim Milstien, *
EMP: 1527 EST: 1950
SQ FT: 328,200
SALES (est): 1.55B
SALES (corp-wide): 1.55B **Privately Held**
Web: www.choc.org
SIC: 8062 General medical and surgical hospitals

(P-15959)

CITY HOPE NATIONAL MEDICAL CTR (HQ)

Also Called: City of Hope Corona
1500 Duarte Rd, Duarte (91010-3000)
PHONE.....................626 553-8061
Marcel Van Den Brink, *Pr*
Robert Stone, *
Jo Ann Escasa-haigh, *CFO*
Cristin O'callahan, *Sec*
Angelique L Richard, *
EMP: 500 EST: 1948
SALES (est): 2.54B
SALES (corp-wide): 330.02MM **Privately Held**
Web: www.cityofhope.org
SIC: 8062 General medical and surgical hospitals
PA: City of Hope
  1500 E Duarte Rd
  626 256-4673

(P-15960)

COAST PLZ DCTORS HOSP A CAL LT (DH)

13100 Studebaker Rd, Norwalk (90050-2501)
PHONE.....................562 868-3751
John Ferrelli, *Ltd Pt*
Craig B Garner, *
Mihi Lee, *
EMP: 75 EST: 1968
SQ FT: 58,000
SALES (est): 7.64MM
SALES (corp-wide): 554.75MM **Privately Held**
Web: www.pipelinehealth.us
SIC: 8062 Hospital, medical school affiliation
HQ: Avanti Hospitals, Llc
  898 N Pcf Cast Hwy Ste 70
  El Segundo CA 90245

(P-15961)

COLLEGE HOSPITAL COSTA MESA MSO INC (HQ)

Also Called: COLLEGE HOSPITAL CERRITOS

301 Victoria St, Costa Mesa (92627-7131)
PHONE..............................949 642-2734
EMP: 100 EST: 1968
SALES (est): 27.76MM
SALES (corp-wide): 72.33MM **Privately Held**
Web: www.chc.la
SIC: **8062** General medical and surgical hospitals
PA: College Hospital, Inc.
　10802 College Pl
　562 924-9581

(P-15962)
COMMUNITY HOSP SAN BERNARDINO (DH)
1805 Medical Center Dr, San Bernardino (92411-1214)
PHONE..............................909 887-6333
June Collisone, *Pr*
Ed Sorenson, *
Darryl Vanzenbosch, *CFO*
EMP: 350 EST: 1938
SALES (est): 306.07MM **Privately Held**
Web: www.dignityhealth.org
SIC: **8062** Hospital, affiliated with AMA residency
HQ: Dignity Health
　185 Berry St Ste 200
　San Francisco CA 94107
　415 438-5500

(P-15963)
COMMUNITY HOSPITAL LONG BEACH
Also Called: Community Hospital
1760 Termino Ave Ste 105, Long Beach (90804-2157)
P.O. Box 92456 (90809-2456)
PHONE..............................562 494-0600
John Bishop, *CEO*
Krikor Jansian, *
Julie Shepard Resources, *Coordtr*
Kevin Peterson, *
EMP: 570 EST: 2000
SALES (est): 21.94MM **Privately Held**
Web: www.chlbfoundation.org
SIC: **8062** Hospital, affiliated with AMA residency
PA: Memorial Health Services
　17360 Brkhurst St Ste 160

(P-15964)
COMMUNITY MEMORIAL HEALTH SYS
Also Called: Ojai Valley Community Hospital
1306 Maricopa Hwy, Ojai (93023-3131)
PHONE..............................805 646-1401
Gary Wilde, *Pr*
EMP: 120
SALES (corp-wide): 552.08MM **Privately Held**
Web: www.mycmh.org
SIC: **8062** General medical and surgical hospitals
PA: Community Memorial Health System
　147 N Brent St
　805 652-5011

(P-15965)
COMMUNITY MEMORIAL HEALTH SYS (PA)
Also Called: Community Memorial Hospital
147 N Brent St, Ventura (93003-2854)
PHONE..............................805 652-5011
Gary Wilde, *Pr*
Adam Thunell, *
David Glyar, *
▲ EMP: 1881 EST: 1933
SQ FT: 174,000

SALES (est): 552.08MM
SALES (corp-wide): 552.08MM **Privately Held**
Web: www.mycmh.org
SIC: **8062** General medical and surgical hospitals

(P-15966)
COTTAGE HEALTH
2050 Viborg Rd, Solvang (93463-2220)
PHONE..............................805 688-6432
EMP: 109
SALES (corp-wide): 152.81MM **Privately Held**
Web: www.cottagehealth.org
SIC: **8062** General medical and surgical hospitals
PA: Cottage Health
　400 W Pueblo St
　805 682-7111

(P-15967)
COUNTY OF KERN
Public Health Dept
1700 Mount Vernon Ave, Bakersfield (93306-4018)
P.O. Box 3519 (93385-3519)
PHONE..............................661 326-2054
Peter Bryan, *CEO*
EMP: 800
Web: www.kerncounty.com
SIC: **8062** 9431 General medical and surgical hospitals; Administration of public health programs
PA: County Of Kern
　1115 Truxtun Ave Rm 505
　661 868-3690

(P-15968)
COUNTY OF LOS ANGELES
Also Called: Health Services Dept
1100 N Mission Rd Rm 236, Los Angeles (90033-1017)
PHONE..............................323 226-6021
Scott Drewgan, *Dir*
EMP: 122
Web: www.lacounty.gov
SIC: **8062** 9431 General medical and surgical hospitals; Administration of public health programs
PA: County Of Los Angeles
　500 W Temple St Ste 437
　213 974-1101

(P-15969)
COUNTY OF LOS ANGELES
Also Called: Los Angles Cnty Cntl Jail Hosp
450 Bauchet St, Los Angeles (90012-2907)
PHONE..............................213 473-6100
Don Knable, *Ch Bd*
EMP: 91
Web: www.lacounty.gov
SIC: **8062** 9431 General medical and surgical hospitals; Administration of public health programs, County government
PA: County Of Los Angeles
　500 W Temple St Ste 437
　213 974-1101

(P-15970)
COUNTY OF LOS ANGELES
Also Called: Health Services Dept
1000 W Carson St 8th Fl, Palos Verdes Peninsu (90274)
PHONE..............................310 222-2401
Miguel Ortiz Marroquin, *CEO*
EMP: 172
Web: www.lacounty.gov

SIC: **8062** 9431 General medical and surgical hospitals; Administration of public health programs
PA: County Of Los Angeles
　500 W Temple St Ste 437
　213 974-1101

(P-15971)
COUNTY OF LOS ANGELES
Also Called: Health Services, Dept of
12025 Wilmington Ave, Los Angeles (90059-3019)
PHONE..............................310 668-4545
Willie T May, *Ex Dir*
EMP: 233
Web: www.lacounty.gov
SIC: **8062** 9431 General medical and surgical hospitals; Administration of public health programs
PA: County Of Los Angeles
　500 W Temple St Ste 437
　213 974-1101

(P-15972)
COUNTY OF SAN LUIS OBISPO
Also Called: County General Hospital
2180 Johnson Ave, San Luis Obispo (93401-4558)
PHONE..............................805 781-4753
Nancy Rosen, *Mgr*
EMP: 114
SQ FT: 4,500
Web: slocounty.ca.gov
SIC: **8062** 8721 General medical and surgical hospitals; Accounting, auditing, and bookkeeping
PA: County Of San Luis Obispo
　Government Center Rm 300
　805 781-5040

(P-15973)
DEANCO HEALTHCARE LLC
Also Called: MISSION COMMUNITY HOSPITAL
14850 Roscoe Blvd, Panorama City (91402-4618)
PHONE..............................818 787-2222
EMP: 700 EST: 2010
SALES (est): 156.97MM **Privately Held**
Web: www.mchonline.org
SIC: **8062** General medical and surgical hospitals

(P-15974)
DESERT REGIONAL MED CTR INC (HQ)
Also Called: Tenet
1150 N Indian Canyon Dr, Palm Springs (92262-4872)
P.O. Box 2739 (92263-2739)
PHONE..............................760 323-6511
TOLL FREE: 888
Michele Finney, *Pr*
Frank Ercoli, *
Ralph M Steiger, *
EMP: 1200 EST: 1948
SQ FT: 400,000
SALES (est): 212.81MM
SALES (corp-wide): 19.17B **Publicly Held**
Web: www.continentaleb5.com
SIC: **8062** General medical and surgical hospitals
PA: Tenet Healthcare Corporation
　14201 Dallas Pkwy
　469 893-2000

(P-15975)
DESERT VALLEY HOSPITAL INC (DH)
16850 Bear Valley Rd, Victorville (92395-5795)

PHONE..............................760 241-8000
Margaret R Peterson, *CEO*
Roger Krissman, *
▲ EMP: 181 EST: 1985
SQ FT: 63,000
SALES (est): 208.51MM
SALES (corp-wide): 878.52MM **Privately Held**
Web: www.dvmc.com
SIC: **8062** General medical and surgical hospitals
HQ: Prime Healthcare Services Inc
　3480 E Guasti Rd
　Ontario CA 91761

(P-15976)
DIGNITY HEALTH
Also Called: Marian Regional Medical Center
1400 E Church St, Santa Maria (93454-5906)
PHONE..............................805 739-3000
Charles Cova, *Pr*
EMP: 400
Web: www.dignityhealth.org
SIC: **8062** 8011 General medical and surgical hospitals; Offices and clinics of medical doctors
HQ: Dignity Health
　185 Berry St Ste 200
　San Francisco CA 94107
　415 438-5500

(P-15977)
DIGNITY HEALTH
Also Called: St. Johns Pleasant Valley Hosp
2309 Antonio Ave, Camarillo (93010-1414)
PHONE..............................805 389-5800
Daniel Herlinger, *Brnch Mgr*
EMP: 250
Web: www.dignityhealth.org
SIC: **8062** General medical and surgical hospitals
HQ: Dignity Health
　185 Berry St Ste 200
　San Francisco CA 94107
　415 438-5500

(P-15978)
DIGNITY HEALTH
Also Called: St Johns Regional Medical Ctr
1600 N Rose Ave, Oxnard (93030-3722)
PHONE..............................805 988-2500
George West, *Brnch Mgr*
EMP: 1900
Web: www.dignityhealth.org
SIC: **8062** General medical and surgical hospitals
HQ: Dignity Health
　185 Berry St Ste 200
　San Francisco CA 94107
　415 438-5500

(P-15979)
DIGNITY HEALTH
Also Called: Pedi Center
400 Old River Rd, Bakersfield (93311-9781)
P.O. Box 119 (93302-0119)
PHONE..............................661 663-6000
Kirk Douglas, *Brnch Mgr*
EMP: 219
Web: www.dignityhealth.org
SIC: **8062** 8099 8011 General medical and surgical hospitals; Childbirth preparation clinic; Offices and clinics of medical doctors
HQ: Dignity Health
　185 Berry St Ste 200
　San Francisco CA 94107
　415 438-5500

(P-15980)
DIGNITY HEALTH
Also Called: Saint John's Hospital X Ray
200 Oceangate, Long Beach (90802-4302)
PHONE..............................805 988-2868
Steve Higgs Managing, *Brnch Mgr*
EMP: 474
Web: www.dignityhealth.org
SIC: 8062 General medical and surgical
hospitals
HQ: Dignity Health
185 Berry St Ste 200
San Francisco CA 94107
415 438-5500

(P-15981)
DIGNITY HEALTH
Also Called: Northridge Hospital Med Ctr
18300 Roscoe Blvd, Northridge
(91325-4105)
PHONE..............................818 885-8500
Paul Watkins, *Pr*
EMP: 1750
Web: www.dignityhealth.org
SIC: 8062 General medical and surgical
hospitals
HQ: Dignity Health
185 Berry St Ste 200
San Francisco CA 94107
415 438-5500

(P-15982)
DIGNITY HEALTH
Also Called: Saint Mary Medical Center
1050 Linden Ave, Long Beach
(90813-3321)
PHONE..............................562 491-9000
Chris Diccio, *Prin*
EMP: 229
Web: www.dignityhealth.org
SIC: 8062 General medical and surgical
hospitals
HQ: Dignity Health
185 Berry St Ste 200
San Francisco CA 94107
415 438-5500

(P-15983)
DOCTORS HOSPITAL W COVINA INC
Also Called: WEST COVINA PHYSICAL
THERAPY
725 S Orange Ave, West Covina
(91790-2614)
PHONE..............................626 338-8481
Pareed Mohamed, *CEO*
Akbar Omar Md, *VP*
Jong Kim Md, *Treas*
Pareed Aliyar Md, *Sec*
EMP: 155 **EST:** 1958
3Q FT: 50,000
SALES (est): 25MM **Privately Held**
SIC: 8062 8049 General medical and
surgical hospitals; Physical therapist

(P-15984)
EAST LOS ANGLES DCTORS HOSP IN
4060 Whittier Blvd, Los Angeles
(90023-2526)
EMP: 350 **EST:** 1978
SALES (est): 74.22MM
SALES (corp-wide): 216.87MM **Privately
Held**
Web: www.eladoctorshospital.com
SIC: 8062 Hospital, affiliated with AMA
residency
PA: Pipeline Health, Llc
898 N Pcf Cast Hwy Ste 70
310 379-2134

(P-15985)
EAST VALLEY GLENDORA HOSP LLC
Also Called: Glendora Oaks Bhvral Hlth Hosp
150 W Route 66, Glendora (91740-6207)
PHONE..............................626 852-5000
Robert Gordon, *
EMP: 448 **EST:** 1957
SQ FT: 60,592
SALES (est): 17.26MM **Privately Held**
Web: www.glendorahospital.com
SIC: 8062 General medical and surgical
hospitals
PA: College Health Enterprises, Llc
11627 Telg Rd Ste 200

(P-15986)
EISENHOWER MEDICAL CENTER
45280 Seeley Dr, La Quinta (92253-6834)
PHONE..............................760 610-7200
EMP: 226
SALES (corp-wide): 1.04B **Privately Held**
Web: www.eisenhowerhealth.org
SIC: 8062 General medical and surgical
hospitals
PA: Eisenhower Medical Center
39000 Bob Hope Dr
760 340-3911

(P-15987)
EISENHOWER MEDICAL CENTER
555 E Tachevah Dr, Palm Springs
(92262-5750)
PHONE..............................760 325-6621
EMP: 180
SALES (corp-wide): 1.04B **Privately Held**
Web: www.eisenhowerhealth.org
SIC: 8062 General medical and surgical
hospitals
PA: Eisenhower Medical Center
39000 Bob Hope Dr
760 340-3911

(P-15988)
EISENHOWER MEDICAL CENTER (PA)
Also Called: EISENHOWER HEALTH
39000 Bob Hope Dr, Rancho Mirage
(92270-3221)
PHONE..............................760 340-3911
G Aubrey Serfling, *CEO*
Martin Massiello, *
Kimberly Osborne, *
Liz Guignier, *
Joseph Scherger, *
▲ **EMP:** 2000 **EST:** 1971
SQ FT: 240,000
SALES (est): 1.04B
SALES (corp-wide): 1.04B **Privately Held**
Web: www.eisenhowerhealth.org
SIC: 8062 8082 General medical and
surgical hospitals; Home health care
services

(P-15989)
EL CENTRO RGNAL MED CTR FNDTIO (PA)
Also Called: E C R M C
1415 Ross Ave, El Centro (92243-4398)
PHONE..............................760 339-7100
Pablo Velez, *CEO*
Robert R Frantz, *
David Momberg, *
Barbara Blevins, *
Debra Drifkill, *
EMP: 603 **EST:** 2005
SQ FT: 187,044

SALES (est): 145.92MM **Privately Held**
Web: www.ecrmc.org
SIC: 8062 General medical and surgical
hospitals

(P-15990)
EMANATE HEALTH
Also Called: Queen of The Valley Campus
1115 S Sunset Ave, West Covina
(91790-3940)
PHONE..............................626 962-4011
Debbie Segaram, *Brnch Mgr*
EMP: 679
Web: www.cvhp.org
SIC: 8062 General medical and surgical
hospitals
PA: Emanate Health
210 W San Bernardino Rd

(P-15991)
EMANATE HEALTH
Also Called: Citrus Vly Hlth Care Partners
427 W Carroll Ave, Glendora (91741-4214)
PHONE..............................626 857-3477
Sue Benson, *Dir*
EMP: 452
SALES (corp-wide): 548.21MM **Privately
Held**
Web: www.emanatehealth.org
SIC: 8062 General medical and surgical
hospitals
PA: Emanate Health Medical Center
1115 S Sunset Ave
626 962-4011

(P-15992)
EMANATE HEALTH (PA)
Also Called: Emanate Hlth Intr-Cmmnity Hosp
210 W San Bernardino Rd, Covina (91722)
P.O. Box 6108 (91722)
PHONE..............................626 331-7331
Robert Curry, *CEO*
James Yoshioka, *
Alvia Polk, *
Lois Conyers, *
Paveljit Bindra, *CMO*
EMP: 1200 **EST:** 1983
SQ FT: 237,000
SALES (est): 684.84MM **Privately Held**
Web: www.cvhp.org
SIC: 8062 General medical and surgical
hospitals

(P-15993)
EMANATE HEALTH MEDICAL CENTER (PA)
Also Called: Emanate Health
1115 S Sunset Ave, West Covina
(91790-3940)
P.O. Box 6108 (91722-5108)
PHONE..............................626 962-4011
Robert Curry, *Pr*
Elvia Foulke, *
Roger Sharma, *
EMP: 1229 **EST:** 1959
SQ FT: 285,000
SALES (est): 548.21MM
SALES (corp-wide): 548.21MM **Privately
Held**
Web: www.cvhp.org
SIC: 8062 General medical and surgical
hospitals

(P-15994)
EMANATE HEALTH MEDICAL CENTER
Also Called: Human Resources Department
140 W College St, Covina (91723-2007)
PHONE..............................626 858-8515
Robert H Curry, *Admn*

EMP: 527
SALES (corp-wide): 548.21MM **Privately
Held**
Web: www.cvhp.org
SIC: 8062 General medical and surgical
hospitals
PA: Emanate Health Medical Center
1115 S Sunset Ave
626 962-4011

(P-15995)
EMANATE HEALTH MEDICAL CENTER
Also Called: Queen of The Valley Hospital
1115 S Sunset Ave, West Covina
(91790-3940)
PHONE..............................626 963-8411
Robert Curry, *Pr*
EMP: 301
SALES (corp-wide): 548.21MM **Privately
Held**
Web: www.cvhp.org
SIC: 8062 General medical and surgical
hospitals
PA: Emanate Health Medical Center
1115 S Sunset Ave
626 962-4011

(P-15996)
EMANATE HEALTH MEDICAL CENTER
Also Called: Inter Community Hospital
210 W San Bernardino Rd, Covina
(91723-1515)
PHONE..............................626 331-7331
TOLL FREE: 877
Jim Yoshioka, *Pr*
EMP: 829
SALES (corp-wide): 548.21MM **Privately
Held**
Web: www.cvhp.org
SIC: 8062 General medical and surgical
hospitals
PA: Emanate Health Medical Center
1115 S Sunset Ave
626 962-4011

(P-15997)
EMANATE HLTH FTHILL PRSBT HOSP (PA)
Also Called: Foothill Presbyterian Hospital
250 S Grand Ave, Glendora (91741-4218)
PHONE..............................626 857-3145
Robert Curry, *Pr*
Earl Washington Cmh, *Prin*
Admiral Diana Zenner, *Prin*
Ed Tronez, *
Melissa Howard, *Chief Nurse*
EMP: 97 **EST:** 1973
SQ FT: 104,371
SALES (est): 122.66MM
SALES (corp-wide): 122.66MM **Privately
Held**
Web: www.cvhp.org
SIC: 8062 Hospital, affiliated with AMA
residency

(P-15998)
FOOTHILL REGIONAL MEDICAL CTR
Also Called: NEWPORT SPECIALTY
HOSPITAL
14662 Newport Ave, Tustin (92780-6064)
PHONE..............................310 943-4500
EMP: 117 **EST:** 2014
SALES (est): 78.64MM **Privately Held**
Web:
www.foothillregionalmedicalcenter.com
SIC: 8062 General medical and surgical
hospitals

P
R
O
D
U
C
T
S

&
S
V
C
S

(P-15999)
FOUNTAIN VLY RGNAL HOSP MED CT
17100 Euclid St, Fountain Valley (92708-4043)
P.O. Box 8010 (92708)
PHONE.................................714 966-7200
Clay Farell, *CEO*
Andrew Pete, *
Richard Wang, *
C J Lee, *Chief Strategy Officer*
EMP: 1200 **EST:** 1969
SALES (est): 64.48MM
SALES (corp-wide): 19.17B **Publicly Held**
Web: www.ucihealth.org
SIC: 8062 Hospital, affiliated with AMA residency
HQ: Tenet Healthsystem Medical, Inc.
14201 Dallas Pkwy
Dallas TX 75254
469 893-2000

(P-16000)
FRENCH HOSPITAL MEDICAL CENTER (DH)
1911 Johnson Ave, San Luis Obispo (93401-4197)
PHONE.................................805 543-5353
Sue Andersen, *Pr*
Jim Copeland, *
EMP: 480 **EST:** 1946
SQ FT: 80,000
SALES (est): 196.54MM **Privately Held**
Web: www.dignityhealth.org
SIC: 8062 Hospital, affiliated with AMA residency
HQ: Dignity Health
185 Berry St Ste 200
San Francisco CA 94107
415 438-5500

(P-16001)
GARDENA HOSPITAL LP
Also Called: Memorial Hospital of Gardena
1145 W Redondo Beach Blvd, Gardena (90247-3511)
PHONE.................................310 532-4200
Kathy Wojno, *CEO*
John N Loizeaux-witte, *Pt*
David Lee, *CFO*
EMP: 760 **EST:** 1999
SALES (est): 141.92MM
SALES (corp-wide): 216.87MM **Privately Held**
Web: www.memorialhospitalgardena.com
SIC: 8062 General medical and surgical hospitals
PA: Pipeline Health, Llc
898 N Pcf Cast Hwy Ste 70
310 379-2134

(P-16002)
GARDENS REGIONAL HOSPITAL AND MEDICAL CENTER INCORPORATED
Also Called: Gardens Regional Hosp Med Ctr
21530 Pioneer Blvd, Hawaiian Gardens (90716-2608)
PHONE.................................877 877-1104
EMP: 350
Web: www.tcrmc.org
SIC: 8062 General medical and surgical hospitals

(P-16003)
GLENDALE ADVENTIST MEDICAL CTR (HQ)
1509 Wilson Ter, Glendale (91206-4098)

PHONE.................................818 409-8000
Kevin A Roberts, *Pr*
Irene Bourdon, *
Warren Tetz, *
Kelly Turner, *
Judy Blair, *
EMP: 2550 **EST:** 1905
SQ FT: 700,000
SALES (est): 486.07MM
SALES (corp-wide): 805.07MM **Privately Held**
Web: www.adventisthealth.org
SIC: 8062 8093 8011 General medical and surgical hospitals; Mental health clinic, outpatient; Freestanding emergency medical center
PA: Adventist Health System/West, Corporation
One Adventist Health Way
844 574-5686

(P-16004)
GLENDALE MEM HLTH FOUNDATION
1420 S Central Ave, Glendale (91204-2594)
PHONE.................................818 502-2375
Carmen Rezak, *Prin*
EMP: 96 **EST:** 1981
SALES (est): 213.36MM **Privately Held**
Web: www.supportglendale.org
SIC: 8062 General medical and surgical hospitals
HQ: Dignity Health
185 Berry St Ste 200
San Francisco CA 94107
415 438-5500

(P-16005)
GLENDALE MEMORIAL HEALTH CORP
Also Called: Glendale Memorial Breast Ctr
222 W Eulalia St, Glendale (91204-2849)
PHONE.................................818 502-2323
FAX: 818 502-4747
EMP: 1000
SALES (corp-wide): 7.06B **Privately Held**
SIC: 8062 8099 General medical and surgical hospitals; Medical services organization
HQ: Glendale Memorial Health Corporation
1420 S Central Ave
Glendale CA 91204
818 502-1900

(P-16006)
GLENDALE MEMORIAL HEALTH CORPORATION
Also Called: Glendale Memorial Center
1420 S Central Ave, Glendale (91204-2594)
PHONE.................................818 502-1900
EMP: 1245
Web: www.supportglendale.org
SIC: 8062 General medical and surgical hospitals

(P-16007)
GLENOAKS CONVALESCENT HOSPITAL
409 W Glenoaks Blvd, Glendale (91202-2989)
PHONE.................................818 240-4300
Elaine Levine, *Pt*
EMP: 85 **EST:** 1984
SQ FT: 22,306
SALES (est): 6.06MM **Privately Held**
Web: www.gshci.com
SIC: 8062 General medical and surgical hospitals

(P-16008)
GOLETA VALLEY COTTAGE HOSP AUX
Also Called: Cottage Health System
351 S Patterson Ave, Santa Barbara (93111-2496)
P.O. Box 689 (93102-0689)
PHONE.................................805 681-6468
Ronald C Werft, *Pr*
Robert Knight, *
Diane Wisby, *
Joan Bricher, *
Joanne Rapp, *
EMP: 300 **EST:** 1966
SQ FT: 92,273
SALES (est): 117.55MM
SALES (corp-wide): 152.81MM **Privately Held**
SIC: 8062 General medical and surgical hospitals
PA: Cottage Health
400 W Pueblo St
805 682-7111

(P-16009)
GOOD SMRTAN HOSP A CAL LTD PRT
901 Olive Dr, Bakersfield (93308-4144)
P.O. Box 85002 (93380-5002)
PHONE.................................661 903-9555
Amandeep Basra, *Pr*
Andrew B Leeka, *
Anand Manohara, *
Sakrepatna Manohara, *
David Huff, *
EMP: 400 **EST:** 1965
SQ FT: 49,001
SALES (est): 23.75MM **Privately Held**
Web: www.goodsamhospital.com
SIC: 8062 8063 8069 General medical and surgical hospitals; Psychiatric hospitals; Specialty hospitals, except psychiatric

(P-16010)
GROSSMONT HOSPITAL CORPORATION (HQ)
5555 Grossmont Center Dr, La Mesa (91942-3077)
PHONE.................................619 740-6000
Dan Gross, *CEO*
EMP: 1740 **EST:** 1953
SQ FT: 494,000
SALES (est): 1.01B
SALES (corp-wide): 1.9B **Privately Held**
Web: www.sharp.com
SIC: 8062 General medical and surgical hospitals
PA: Sharp Healthcare
8695 Spectrum Ctr Blvd
858 499-4000

(P-16011)
GROSSMONT HOSPITAL CORPORATION
Also Called: Grossmont Home Hlth & Hospice
8881 Fletcher Pkwy Ste 105, La Mesa (91942-3132)
PHONE.................................619 667-1900
Jean Cruise, *Mgr*
EMP: 342
SALES (corp-wide): 1.9B **Privately Held**
Web: www.sharp.com
SIC: 8062 8082 General medical and surgical hospitals; Home health care services
HQ: Grossmont Hospital Corporation
5555 Grossmont Ctr Dr
La Mesa CA 91942
619 740-6000

(P-16012)
HDMC HOLDINGS LLC
Also Called: Hi-Desert Medical Center
6601 White Feather Rd, Joshua Tree (92252-6607)
PHONE.................................760 366-3711
Jeffrey Koury, *CEO*
EMP: 81 **EST:** 2015
SALES (est): 20.22MM
SALES (corp-wide): 19.17B **Publicly Held**
Web: www.desertcarenetwork.com
SIC: 8062 General medical and surgical hospitals
PA: Tenet Healthcare Corporation
14201 Dallas Pkwy
469 893-2000

(P-16013)
HEALTH INVESTMENT CORPORATION
14642 Newport Ave Ste 388, Tustin (92780-6059)
PHONE.................................714 669-2085
EMP: 1700
SIC: 8062 General medical and surgical hospitals

(P-16014)
HEALTH RESOURCES CORP
Also Called: Coastal Community Hospital
2701 S Bristol St, Santa Ana (92704-6201)
PHONE.................................714 754-5454
Trevor Fetter, *Pr*
EMP: 400 **EST:** 1984
SALES (est): 3.29MM **Privately Held**
Web: www.kpchealth.com
SIC: 8062 General medical and surgical hospitals
HQ: Kpc Healthcare, Inc.
1301 N Tustin Ave
Santa Ana CA 92705
714 953-3652

(P-16015)
HEALTHSMART PACIFIC INC (PA)
Also Called: Long Beach Pain Center
5150 E Pacific Coast Hwy Ste 200, Long Beach (90804-3399)
PHONE.................................562 595-1911
TOLL FREE: 800
Michael D Drobot, *
G William Hammer, *Prin*
EMP: 610 **EST:** 1932
SALES (est): 11.99MM
SALES (corp-wide): 11.99MM **Privately Held**
SIC: 8062 General medical and surgical hospitals

(P-16016)
HEMET VALLEY MEDICAL CENTER-EDUCATION
Also Called: Hemet Valley Medical Center
1117 E Devonshire Ave, Hemet (92543-3083)
PHONE.................................951 652-2811
EMP: 1200
Web: www.hemetvalleyurology.com
SIC: 8062 General medical and surgical hospitals

(P-16017)
HENRY MAYO NEWHALL MEM HOSP (PA)
23845 Mcbean Pkwy, Valencia (91355-2083)
PHONE.................................661 253-8000
Roger E Seaver, *Pr*

Elizabeth Hopp, *Ch Bd*
Robert Pretzlaff, *CMO*
EMP: 935 **EST:** 1972
SQ FT: 210,000
SALES (est): 454.17MM
SALES (corp-wide): 454.17MM **Privately Held**
Web: www.henrymayo.com
SIC: 8062 General medical and surgical hospitals

(P-16018)
HENRY MAYO NWHALL MEM HLTH FND
Also Called: HENRYMAYO NEWHALL MEMORIAL HOS
23845 Mcbean Pkwy, Valencia (91355-2001)
P.O. Box P O Box 55279 (91385-0279)
PHONE..............................661 253-8000
Roger Seaver, *Pr*
EMP: 1500 **EST:** 1972
SALES (est): 5.35MM **Privately Held**
SIC: 8062 General medical and surgical hospitals

(P-16019)
HOAG CLINIC
Also Called: HOAG CORPORATE HEALTH
1 Hoag Dr, Newport Beach (92663-4162)
P.O. Box 6100 (92658-6100)
PHONE..............................949 764-1888
EMP: 720 **EST:** 1995
SALES (est): 258.15MM **Privately Held**
Web: www.hoag.org
SIC: 8062 General medical and surgical hospitals

(P-16020)
HOAG FAMILY CANCER INSTITUTE
1190 Baker St, Costa Mesa (92626-4108)
PHONE..............................949 764-7777
Inga Barillas, *Brnch Mgr*
EMP: 154
Web: www.hoag.org
SIC: 8062 General medical and surgical hospitals
PA: Hoag Family Cancer Institute
1 Hoag Dr Bldg 41

(P-16021)
HOAG HOSPITAL IRVINE
16200 Sand Canyon Ave, Irvine (92618-3714)
PHONE..............................949 764-4624
EMP: 85 **EST:** 2009
SALES (est): 14.39MM **Privately Held**
Web: www.hoag.org
SIC: 8062 General medical and surgical hospitals

(P-16022)
HOAG MEMORIAL HOSPITAL PRESBT (PA)
1 Hoag Dr, Newport Beach (92658)
P.O. Box 6100 (92658-6100)
PHONE..............................949 764-4624
Robert Braithwaite, *Pr*
Flynn A Andrizzi, *
Kathy Azeez-narain, *Chief Digital Officer*
EMP: 3600 **EST:** 1944
SALES (est): 1.65B **Privately Held**
Web: www.hoag.org
SIC: 8062 General medical and surgical hospitals

(P-16023)
HOAG ORTHOPEDIC INSTITUTE LLC
Also Called: Hoag Orthpd Inst Srgery Ctr -
22 Corporate Plaza Dr Ste 150, Newport Beach (92660-7999)
PHONE..............................949 515-0708
James Caillouette, *Ch Bd*
EMP: 234
SALES (corp-wide): 143.89MM **Privately Held**
Web: www.hoagorthopedicinstitute.com
SIC: 8062 General medical and surgical hospitals
PA: Hoag Orthopedic Institute, Llc
16250 Sand Canyon Ave
949 764-8690

(P-16024)
HOLLYWOOD CMNTY HOSP MED CTR I
Also Called: Hollywood Cmnty Hosp Hollywood
6245 De Longpre Ave, Los Angeles (90028-8253)
PHONE..............................323 462-2271
Robert Starling, *CEO*
Ron Messenger, *
Manfred Krukemeyer, *
EMP: 220 **EST:** 1982
SQ FT: 100,000
SALES (est): 8.41MM
SALES (corp-wide): 3.91B **Privately Held**
Web: www.sch-hollywood.com
SIC: 8062 Hospital, affiliated with AMA residency
HQ: Southern California Healthcare System, Inc.
3415 S Sepulveda Blvd 9thf
Los Angeles CA 90034

(P-16025)
HOLLYWOOD MEDICAL CENTER LP
Also Called: Hollywood Presbyterian Med Ctr
1300 N Vermont Ave, Los Angeles (90027-6098)
PHONE..............................213 413-3000
Jeff Nelson, *Pt*
EMP: 1250 **EST:** 1928
SALES (est): 15.64MM **Privately Held**
Web: www.hollywoodpresbyterian.com
SIC: 8062 General medical and surgical hospitals
PA: Cha Health Systems, Inc
3731 Wilshire Blvd # 850

(P-16026)
HOSPITAL OF BARSTOW INC (DH)
Also Called: Barstow Community Hospital
820 E Mountain View St, Barstow (92311-3004)
PHONE..............................760 256-1761
Justin Sheridan, *CEO*
Shawn Curtis, *
EMP: 99 **EST:** 1958
SQ FT: 54,000
SALES (est): 66.23MM
SALES (corp-wide): 13.15K **Privately Held**
Web: www.barstowhospital.com
SIC: 8062 Hospital, affiliated with AMA residency
HQ: Qhc California Holdings, Llc
1573 Mallory Ln
Brentwood TN

(P-16027)
HUNTINGTON MEDICAL FOUNDATION
65 N Madison Ave Ste 800, Pasadena (91101-2038)
PHONE..............................626 792-3141
Laura Hernandez, *Mgr*
EMP: 106
Web: www.huntingtonmedical.com
SIC: 8062 General medical and surgical hospitals
PA: The Huntington Medical Foundation
100 W California Blvd

(P-16028)
INLAND VLY RGIONAL MED CTR INC
36485 Inland Valley Dr, Wildomar (92595-9700)
PHONE..............................951 677-1111
Alan B Miller, *CEO*
Barry Thorfinnson, *
EMP: 500 **EST:** 1983
SQ FT: 77,000
SALES (est): 30.02MM
SALES (corp-wide): 14.28B **Publicly Held**
Web: www.inlandvalleymedcenter.com
SIC: 8062 8011 General medical and surgical hospitals; Clinic, operated by physicians
PA: Universal Health Services, Inc.
367 S Gulph Rd
610 768-3300

(P-16029)
JFK MEMORIAL HOSPITAL INC
47111 Monroe St, Indio (92201-6739)
PHONE..............................760 347-6191
Gary Honts, *Pr*
EMP: 106 **EST:** 2001
SALES (est): 20.85MM
SALES (corp-wide): 19.17B **Publicly Held**
SIC: 8062 General medical and surgical hospitals
PA: Tenet Healthcare Corporation
14201 Dallas Pkwy
469 893-2000

(P-16030)
JOHN F KENNEDY MEM HOSP AUX
Also Called: DES PERES HOSPITAL, INC.
47111 Monroe St, Indio (92201-6799)
PHONE..............................760 347-6191
TOLL FREE: 800
Gary Honts, *CEO*
EMP: 650 **EST:** 1906
SALES (est): 1.44MM
SALES (corp-wide): 72.97MM **Privately Held**
SIC: 8062 Hospital, affiliated with AMA residency
HQ: St. Luke's Des Peres Episcopal-Presbyterian Hospital
2345 Dougherty Ferry Rd
Saint Louis MO 63122
314 966-9100

(P-16031)
JUPITER BELLFLOWER DOCTORS HOSPITAL
Also Called: Bellflower Medical Center
3699 Wilshire Blvd Ste 540, Los Angeles (90010-2723)
EMP: 500
SIC: 8062 General medical and surgical hospitals

(P-16032)
KAISER FOUNDATION HOSPITALS
Also Called: Cudahy Medical Offices
7825 Atlantic Ave, Cudahy (90201-5022)
PHONE..............................323 562-6400
Karen Warren, *Mgr*
EMP: 134
SALES (corp-wide): 70.8B **Privately Held**
Web: healthy.kaiserpermanente.org
SIC: 8062 General medical and surgical hospitals
HQ: Kaiser Foundation Hospitals Inc
1 Kaiser Plz
Oakland CA 94612
510 271-6611

(P-16033)
KAISER FOUNDATION HOSPITALS
Also Called: Gardena Medical Offices
15446 S Western Ave, Gardena (90249-4319)
PHONE..............................310 517-2956
Mary Mauch, *Mgr*
EMP: 123
SQ FT: 114,575
SALES (corp-wide): 70.8B **Privately Held**
Web: healthy.kaiserpermanente.org
SIC: 8062 General medical and surgical hospitals
HQ: Kaiser Foundation Hospitals Inc
1 Kaiser Plz
Oakland CA 94612
510 271-6611

(P-16034)
KAISER FOUNDATION HOSPITALS
Also Called: Erwin Street Medical Offices
5601 De Soto Ave, Woodland Hills (91367-6701)
PHONE..............................818 592-3100
Karen Kim, *Ofcr*
EMP: 76
SALES (corp-wide): 70.8B **Privately Held**
Web: healthy.kaiserpermanente.org
SIC: 8062 General medical and surgical hospitals
HQ: Kaiser Foundation Hospitals Inc
1 Kaiser Plz
Oakland CA 94612
510 271-6611

(P-16035)
KAISER FOUNDATION HOSPITALS
20000 Rinaldi St, Porter Ranch (91326-4900)
PHONE..............................833 574-2273
EMP: 72
SALES (corp-wide): 70.8B **Privately Held**
Web: healthy.kaiserpermanente.org
SIC: 8062 General medical and surgical hospitals
HQ: Kaiser Foundation Hospitals Inc
1 Kaiser Plz
Oakland CA 94612
510 271-6611

(P-16036)
KAISER FOUNDATION HOSPITALS
Also Called: Kaiser Permanente
8800 Ming Ave, Bakersfield (93311-1308)
PHONE..............................661 412-6777
EMP: 137
SALES (corp-wide): 70.8B **Privately Held**
Web: healthy.kaiserpermanente.org

SIC: 8062 General medical and surgical hospitals
HQ: Kaiser Foundation Hospitals Inc
1 Kaiser Plz
Oakland CA 94612
510 271-6611

(P-16037)
KAISER FOUNDATION HOSPITALS
Also Called: Kaiser Permanente
1055 E Colorado Blvd Ste 100, Pasadena (91106-2368)
PHONE..............................626 440-5659
Jeanine Boudakian, *Brnch Mgr*
EMP: 500
SALES (corp-wide): 70.8B **Privately Held**
Web: healthy.kaiserpermanente.org
SIC: 8062 General medical and surgical hospitals
HQ: Kaiser Foundation Hospitals Inc
1 Kaiser Plz
Oakland CA 94612
510 271-6611

(P-16038)
KAISER FOUNDATION HOSPITALS
Also Called: Kaiser Permanente
250 W San Jose Ave, Claremont (91711-5295)
PHONE..............................888 750-0036
Bell Pacific, *Mgr*
EMP: 112
SQ FT: 17,908
SALES (corp-wide): 70.8B **Privately Held**
Web: www.kaisercenter.com
SIC: 8062 General medical and surgical hospitals
HQ: Kaiser Foundation Hospitals Inc
1 Kaiser Plz
Oakland CA 94612
510 271-6611

(P-16039)
KAISER FOUNDATION HOSPITALS
Also Called: Kaiser Permanente
5601 De Soto Ave, Woodland Hills (91367-6701)
PHONE..............................818 719-2000
Cathy Casas, *Admn*
EMP: 1200
SALES (corp-wide): 70.8B **Privately Held**
Web: thrive.kaiserpermanente.org
SIC: 8062 General medical and surgical hospitals
HQ: Kaiser Foundation Hospitals Inc
1 Kaiser Plz
Oakland CA 94612
510 271-6611

(P-16040)
KAISER FOUNDATION HOSPITALS
Also Called: Kaiser Permanente
43112 15th St W, Lancaster (93534-6219)
PHONE..............................661 726-2500
Barbara Fordice, *Genl Mgr*
EMP: 484
SALES (corp-wide): 70.8B **Privately Held**
Web: healthy.kaiserpermanente.org
SIC: 8062 Hospital, affiliated with AMA residency
HQ: Kaiser Foundation Hospitals Inc
1 Kaiser Plz
Oakland CA 94612
510 271-6611

(P-16041)
KAISER FOUNDATION HOSPITALS
Also Called: Kaiser Prmnente Downey Med Ctr
9333 Imperial Hwy, Downey (90241)
PHONE..............................562 657-9000
Gemma Abad, *Brnch Mgr*
EMP: 410
SALES (corp-wide): 70.8B **Privately Held**
Web: thrive.kaiserpermanente.org
SIC: 8062 General medical and surgical hospitals
HQ: Kaiser Foundation Hospitals Inc
1 Kaiser Plz
Oakland CA 94612
510 271-6611

(P-16042)
KAISER FOUNDATION HOSPITALS
400 S Sepulveda Blvd, Manhattan Beach (90266-6814)
PHONE..............................310 937-4311
EMP: 159
SALES (corp-wide): 70.8B **Privately Held**
Web: www.beachcitiesortho.com
SIC: 8062 General medical and surgical hospitals
HQ: Kaiser Foundation Hospitals Inc
1 Kaiser Plz
Oakland CA 94612
510 271-6611

(P-16043)
KAISER FOUNDATION HOSPITALS
4733 W Sunset Blvd Fl 2, Los Angeles (90027-6021)
PHONE..............................323 783-4011
EMP: 227
SALES (corp-wide): 70.8B **Privately Held**
Web: healthy.kaiserpermanente.org
SIC: 8062 General medical and surgical hospitals
HQ: Kaiser Foundation Hospitals Inc
1 Kaiser Plz
Oakland CA 94612
510 271-6611

(P-16044)
KAISER FOUNDATION HOSPITALS
Also Called: Kaiser Permanente
1255 W Arrow Hwy, San Dimas (91773-2340)
PHONE..............................909 394-2530
Will Tatum, *Mgr*
EMP: 138
SQ FT: 23,801
SALES (corp-wide): 70.8B **Privately Held**
Web: healthy.kaiserpermanente.org
SIC: 8062 8011 General medical and surgical hospitals; General and family practice, physician/surgeon
HQ: Kaiser Foundation Hospitals Inc
1 Kaiser Plz
Oakland CA 94612
510 271-6611

(P-16045)
KAISER FOUNDATION HOSPITALS
Also Called: Antelope Valley Hospital
1600 W Avenue J, Lancaster (93534-2814)
PHONE..............................661 949-5000
Harriet R Lee, *Admn*
EMP: 94
SALES (corp-wide): 70.8B **Privately Held**

Web: healthy.kaiserpermanente.org
SIC: 8062 General medical and surgical hospitals
HQ: Kaiser Foundation Hospitals Inc
1 Kaiser Plz
Oakland CA 94612
510 271-6611

(P-16046)
KAISER FOUNDATION HOSPITALS
Also Called: Kaiser Permanente
3951 Van Buren Blvd, Riverside (92503-3620)
PHONE..............................951 352-0292
Nancy Kingson, *Brnch Mgr*
EMP: 83
SALES (corp-wide): 70.8B **Privately Held**
Web: thrive.kaiserpermanente.org
SIC: 8062 General medical and surgical hospitals
HQ: Kaiser Foundation Hospitals Inc
1 Kaiser Plz
Oakland CA 94612
510 271-6611

(P-16047)
KAISER FOUNDATION HOSPITALS
Also Called: Wildomar Medical Offices
36450 Inland Valley Dr Ste 204, Wildomar (92595-7721)
PHONE..............................951 353-2000
Geoffrey Gomez, *Prin*
EMP: 144
SALES (corp-wide): 70.8B **Privately Held**
Web: healthy.kaiserpermanente.org
SIC: 8062 General medical and surgical hospitals
HQ: Kaiser Foundation Hospitals Inc
1 Kaiser Plz
Oakland CA 94612
510 271-6611

(P-16048)
KAISER FOUNDATION HOSPITALS
325 W Hospitality Ln Ste 312, San Bernardino (92408-3212)
PHONE..............................909 386-5500
EMP: 166
SALES (corp-wide): 70.8B **Privately Held**
Web: healthy.kaiserpermanente.org
SIC: 8062 General medical and surgical hospitals
HQ: Kaiser Foundation Hospitals Inc
1 Kaiser Plz
Oakland CA 94612
510 271-6611

(P-16049)
KAISER FOUNDATION HOSPITALS
Also Called: Kaiser Permanente
4405 Vandever Ave Fl 5, San Diego (92120-3315)
PHONE..............................619 528-2583
David Mandler, *Mgr*
EMP: 231
SALES (corp-wide): 70.8B **Privately Held**
Web: healthy.kaiserpermanente.org
SIC: 8062 General medical and surgical hospitals
HQ: Kaiser Foundation Hospitals Inc
1 Kaiser Plz
Oakland CA 94612
510 271-6611

(P-16050)
KAISER FOUNDATION HOSPITALS
Also Called: Kaiser Permanente
9455 Clairemont Mesa Blvd, San Diego (92123-1297)
PHONE..............................858 573-1504
EMP: 188
SALES (corp-wide): 70.8B **Privately Held**
Web: healthy.kaiserpermanente.org
SIC: 8062 8011 General medical and surgical hospitals; Medical centers
HQ: Kaiser Foundation Hospitals Inc
1 Kaiser Plz
Oakland CA 94612
510 271-6611

(P-16051)
KAISER FOUNDATION HOSPITALS
Also Called: La Mesa Medical Offices
8080 Parkway Dr, La Mesa (91942-2104)
PHONE..............................619 528-5000
Caroline Wu, *Prin*
EMP: 144
SALES (corp-wide): 70.8B **Privately Held**
Web: healthy.kaiserpermanente.org
SIC: 8062 General medical and surgical hospitals
HQ: Kaiser Foundation Hospitals Inc
1 Kaiser Plz
Oakland CA 94612
510 271-6611

(P-16052)
KAISER FOUNDATION HOSPITALS
Also Called: Bostonia Medical Offices
1630 E Main St, El Cajon (92021-5204)
PHONE..............................619 528-5000
EMP: 160
SALES (corp-wide): 70.8B **Privately Held**
Web: healthy.kaiserpermanente.org
SIC: 8062 General medical and surgical hospitals
HQ: Kaiser Foundation Hospitals Inc
1 Kaiser Plz
Oakland CA 94612
510 271-6611

(P-16053)
KAISER FOUNDATION HOSPITALS
Also Called: Kaiser Prmnnte San Mrcos Med C
360 Rush Dr, San Marcos (92078-7901)
PHONE..............................442 385-7000
EMP: 90
SALES (corp-wide): 70.8B **Privately Held**
SIC: 8062 General medical and surgical hospitals
HQ: Kaiser Foundation Hospitals Inc
1 Kaiser Plz
Oakland CA 94612
510 271-6611

(P-16054)
KAISER FOUNDATION HOSPITALS
Also Called: Bonita Medical Offices
3955 Bonita Rd, Bonita (91902-1230)
PHONE..............................619 409-6405
James Lentz, *Prin*
EMP: 72
SQ FT: 67,760
SALES (corp-wide): 70.8B **Privately Held**
Web: healthy.kaiserpermanente.org
SIC: 8062 General medical and surgical hospitals

HQ: Kaiser Foundation Hospitals Inc
1 Kaiser Plz
Oakland CA 94612
510 271-6611

(P-16055)
KAISER FOUNDATION HOSPITALS
Also Called: Kaiser Prmnnte Ornge Cnty-Nhei
3440 E La Palma Ave, Anaheim
(92806-2020)
PHONE..................714 644-2000
Patrick Steinhauser, *Brnch Mgr*
EMP: 4408
SQ FT: 125,000
SALES (corp-wide): 70.8B **Privately Held**
Web: www.kaisercenter.com
SIC: **8062** 8011 General medical and
surgical hospitals; General and family
practice, physician/surgeon
HQ: Kaiser Foundation Hospitals Inc
1 Kaiser Plz
Oakland CA 94612
510 271-6611

(P-16056)
KAISER FOUNDATION HOSPITALS
Also Called: Kaiser Permanente
1900 E 4th St, Santa Ana (92705-3910)
PHONE..................714 967-4700
Martha Bieser, *Prin*
EMP: 130
SALES (corp-wide): 70.8B **Privately Held**
Web: healthy.kaiserpermanente.org
SIC: **8062** General medical and surgical
hospitals
HQ: Kaiser Foundation Hospitals Inc
1 Kaiser Plz
Oakland CA 94612
510 271-6611

(P-16057)
KAISER FOUNDATION HOSPITALS
Also Called: Barranca Medical Offices
6 Willard, Irvine (92604-4694)
PHONE..................949 262-5780
George Disalvo, *Owner*
EMP: 170
SQ FT: 51,080
SALES (corp-wide): 70.8B **Privately Held**
Web: healthy.kaiserpermanente.org
SIC: **8062** General medical and surgical
hospitals
HQ: Kaiser Foundation Hospitals Inc
1 Kaiser Plz
Oakland CA 94612
510 271-6611

(P-16058)
KAISER FOUNDATION HOSPITALS
Also Called: Kaiser Permanente
12620 Prescott Ave, Tustin (92782-1066)
PHONE..................951 353-4000
Danh V Le, *Dir*
EMP: 105
SALES (corp-wide): 70.8B **Privately Held**
Web: healthy.kaiserpermanente.org
SIC: **8062** General medical and surgical
hospitals
HQ: Kaiser Foundation Hospitals Inc
1 Kaiser Plz
Oakland CA 94612
510 271-6611

(P-16059)
KECK HOSPITAL OF USC
1500 San Pablo St, Los Angeles
(90033-5313)
PHONE..................800 872-2273
Thomas E Jackiewicz, *CEO*
James J Uli Junior, *CFO*
▲ EMP: 623 EST: 2009
SALES (est): 1.13B **Privately Held**
Web: www.keckmedicine.org
SIC: **8062** General medical and surgical
hospitals

(P-16060)
KENNETH CORP
Also Called: Garden Grove Hospital
12601 Garden Grove Blvd, Garden Grove
(92843-1908)
PHONE..................714 537-5160
Edward Mirzabegian, *CEO*
Hassan Alkhouli, *
EMP: 615 EST: 1951
SQ FT: 133,083
SALES (est): 76.84MM **Privately Held**
Web: www.gardengrovehospital.com
SIC: **8062** General medical and surgical
hospitals

(P-16061)
KERN COUNTY HOSPITAL AUTHORITY (PA)
1700 Mount Vernon Ave, Bakersfield
(93306-4018)
PHONE..................661 326-2102
Russell Judd, *CEO*
Tyler Whitezell, *Admn Execs*
Andrew Cantu, *CFO*
EMP: 508 EST: 1865
SQ FT: 29,800
SALES (est): 45.43MM
SALES (corp-wide): 45.43MM **Privately
Held**
Web: www.kernmedical.com
SIC: **8062** General medical and surgical
hospitals

(P-16062)
KINDRED HEALTHCARE LLC
Also Called: Kindred Hospital Paramount
16453 Colorado Ave, Paramount
(90723-5011)
PHONE..................562 531-3110
EMP: 225
SALES (corp-wide): 14.03B **Privately Held**
Web: www.kindredhospitals.com
SIC: **8062** General medical and surgical
hospitals
HQ: Kindred Healthcare, Llc
680 S 4th St
Louisville KY 40202
502 596-7300

(P-16063)
KINDRED HEALTHCARE LLC
2224 Medical Center Dr, Perris
(92571-2638)
PHONE..................951 436-3535
James Linhares, *CEO*
EMP: 379
SALES (corp-wide): 14.03B **Privately Held**
Web: www.kindredhospitals.com
SIC: **8062** General medical and surgical
hospitals
HQ: Kindred Healthcare, Llc
680 S 4th St
Louisville KY 40202
502 596-7300

(P-16064)
KINDRED HEALTHCARE LLC
Also Called: Kindred
1503 30th St, San Diego (92102-1503)
PHONE..................619 546-9653
EMP: 90
SALES (corp-wide): 14.03B **Privately Held**
Web: www.barkindred.com
SIC: **8062** General medical and surgical
hospitals
HQ: Kindred Healthcare, Llc
680 S 4th St
Louisville KY 40202
502 596-7300

(P-16065)
KINDRED HEALTHCARE LLC
Also Called: Kindred Hospital Santa Ana
1901 College Ave, Santa Ana (92706-2334)
PHONE..................714 564-7800
EMP: 72
SALES (corp-wide): 14.03B **Privately Held**
Web: www.kindredhospitals.com
SIC: **8062** 8011 General medical and
surgical hospitals; Offices and clinics of
medical doctors
HQ: Kindred Healthcare, Llc
680 S 4th St
Louisville KY 40202
502 596-7300

(P-16066)
KND DEVELOPMENT 55 LLC
Also Called: KINDRED HOSPITAL - RANCHO
10841 White Oak Ave, Rancho Cucamonga
(91730-3817)
PHONE..................909 581-6400
Miller Debroah, *Dir*
EMP: 92 EST: 2007
SALES (est): 26.22MM **Privately Held**
Web: www.kindredhospitals.com
SIC: **8062** General medical and surgical
hospitals

(P-16067)
KPC GLOBAL MEDICAL CENTERS INC (DH)
Also Called: PHH
1117 E Devonshire Ave, Hemet
(92543-3083)
PHONE..................714 953-3500
Kali Chaudhuri, *Ch*
Sreenivasa Nakka, *
Ashok Agarwal, *
Kali Priyo Chaudhuri, *
Rakesh Gupta, *
EMP: 153 EST: 2009
SALES (est): 169.46MM **Privately Held**
Web: www.hemetglobalmedcenter.com
SIC: **8062** General medical and surgical
hospitals
HQ: Kpc Healthcare, Inc.
1301 N Tustin Ave
Santa Ana CA 92705
714 953-3652

(P-16068)
LA METROPOLITAN MEDICAL CENTER
2231 Southwest Dr, Los Angeles
(90043-4523)
PHONE..................323 730-7300
TOLL FREE: 800
EMP: 600
Web: www.lammc.com
SIC: **8062** General medical and surgical
hospitals

(P-16069)
LA PALMA HOSPITAL MEDICAL CENTER
Also Called: La Palma Intercommunity Hosp
7901 Walker St, La Palma (90623-1764)
PHONE..................714 670-7400
TOLL FREE: 800
EMP: 400
Web:
www.lapalmaintercommunityhospital.com
SIC: **8062** General medical and surgical
hospitals

(P-16070)
LAC USC MEDICAL CENTER
Also Called: Los Angeles County Hospital
1200 N State St Rm 5250, Los Angeles
(90089-1001)
P.O. Box 63 (90078-0063)
EMP: 113 EST: 1992
SALES (est): 26.52MM **Privately Held**
Web: www.usc.edu
SIC: **8062** 6324 General medical and
surgical hospitals; Hospital and medical
service plans

(P-16071)
LAKEWOOD REGIONAL MED CTR INC
Also Called: Lakewood Regional Medical Ctr
3700 South St, Lakewood (90712-1498)
P.O. Box 6070 (90714-6070)
PHONE..................562 531-2550
John Grah, *CEO*
Ronald Galonsky, *
Mark Korth, *
Lani Dickinson, *
Michael Paul Amos, *
EMP: 900 EST: 2001
SALES (est): 37.68MM
SALES (corp-wide): 19.17B **Publicly Held**
Web: www.ucihealth.org
SIC: **8062** Hospital, affiliated with AMA
residency
PA: Tenet Healthcare Corporation
14201 Dallas Pkwy
469 893-2000

(P-16072)
LANCASTER HOSPITAL CORPORATION
Also Called: Palmdale Regional Medical Ctr
38600 Medical Center Dr, Palmdale
(93551-4483)
PHONE..................661 948-4781
Nana Deeb, *CEO*
Steve Fillon, *
EMP: 1350 EST: 1953
SQ FT: 95,000
SALES (est): 218.28MM
SALES (corp-wide): 14.28B **Publicly Held**
Web: www.swhpalmdaleregional.com
SIC: **8062** General medical and surgical
hospitals
PA: Universal Health Services, Inc.
367 S Gulph Rd
610 768-3300

(P-16073)
LINDA LOMA UNIV HLTH CARE (HQ)
11370 Anderson St Ste 3900, Loma Linda
(92354-3450)
P.O. Box 2000 (92354-0200)
PHONE..................909 558-2806
Richard Hart, *Pr*
Rosita Fike, *
EMP: 125 EST: 1967
SALES (est): 208.25MM

P
R
O
D
U
C
T
S

&

S
V
C
S

SALES (corp-wide): 379.88MM **Privately Held**
Web: www.llu.edu
SIC: 8062 8011 8051 5999 Hospital, medical school affiliated with residency; Medical centers; Extended care facility; Convalescent equipment and supplies
PA: Loma Linda University
11060 Andrson St Bldg Mga
909 558-4540

(P-16074)
LITTLE COMPANY MARY HOSPITAL
Also Called: Leader Drug Store
4101 Torrance Blvd, Torrance (90503-4664)
PHONE....................310 540-7676
Joseph Zanetta, *CEO*
Elizabeth Zuanich, *
▲ **EMP:** 1200 **EST:** 1957
SQ FT: 300,000
SALES (est): 18.03MM
SALES (corp-wide): 55.69MM **Privately Held**
SIC: 8062 8051 General medical and surgical hospitals; Skilled nursing care facilities
HQ: Providence Health System-Southern California
1801 Lind Ave Sw
Renton WA 98057
425 525-3355

(P-16075)
LITTLE COMPANY OF MARY HEALTH SERVICES
Also Called: Little Company Mary Svc Area
4101 Torrance Blvd, Torrance (90503-4664)
PHONE....................310 540-7676
EMP: 2946
SIC: 8062 8741 General medical and surgical hospitals; Hospital management

(P-16076)
LOMA LINDA UNIVERSITY MED CTR
11370 Anderson St, Loma Linda (92354-3400)
P.O. Box 728 (92354-0728)
PHONE....................909 558-4385
EMP: 92
SALES (corp-wide): 379.88MM **Privately Held**
Web: www.llu.edu
SIC: 8062 General medical and surgical hospitals
HQ: Loma Linda University Medical Center
11234 Anderson St
Loma Linda CA 92354
909 558-4000

(P-16077)
LOMA LINDA UNIVERSITY MED CTR
Also Called: Loma Linda Community Hospital
25333 Barton Rd, Loma Linda (92350-0210)
PHONE....................909 796-0167
Todd Nelson, *Mgr*
EMP: 84
SQ FT: 79,580
SALES (corp-wide): 379.88MM **Privately Held**
Web: www.llu.edu
SIC: 8062 General medical and surgical hospitals
HQ: Loma Linda University Medical Center
11234 Anderson St
Loma Linda CA 92354
909 558-4000

(P-16078)
LOMA LINDA UNIVERSITY MED CTR (DH)
Also Called: Llumc
11234 Anderson St, Loma Linda (92354-2871)
P.O. Box 2000 (92354-0200)
PHONE....................909 558-4000
TOLL FREE: 800
Richard H Hart, *CEO*
James Jesse, *
Richard Catalano, *
Noni Patchett, *
EMP: 4600 **EST:** 1967
SQ FT: 630,000
SALES (est): 1.72B
SALES (corp-wide): 379.88MM **Privately Held**
Web: www.lluh.org
SIC: 8062 8011 8051 5999 Hospital, medical school affiliated with residency; Medical centers; Extended care facility; Medical apparatus and supplies
HQ: Loma Linda University Health Care
11370 Anderson St # 3900
Loma Linda CA 92354
909 558-2806

(P-16079)
LOMA LINDA UNIVERSITY MED CTR
26780 Barton Rd, Redlands (92373-4308)
PHONE....................909 558-4000
EMP: 80
SALES (corp-wide): 379.88MM **Privately Held**
Web: www.llu.edu
SIC: 8062 General medical and surgical hospitals
HQ: Loma Linda University Medical Center
11234 Anderson St
Loma Linda CA 92354
909 558-4000

(P-16080)
LOMA LINDA UNIVERSITY MED CTR
Also Called: Behavioral Medicine Center
1710 Barton Rd, Redlands, (92373-5304)
PHONE....................909 558-9275
Ruthita Fike, *Mgr*
EMP: 107
SQ FT: 62,476
SALES (corp-wide): 379.88MM **Privately Held**
Web: www.lluh.org
SIC: 8062 8221 Hospital, medical school affiliation; University
HQ: Loma Linda University Medical Center
11234 Anderson St
Loma Linda CA 92354
909 558-4000

(P-16081)
LOMA LNDA - INLAND EMPIRE CNSR
Also Called: Loma Linda University Med Ctr
11234 Anderson St, Loma Linda (92354-2804)
PHONE....................909 558-4000
Daniel Giang, *Pr*
EMP: 141 **EST:** 2013
SALES (est): 6.98MM **Privately Held**
SIC: 8062 Hospital, medical school affiliated with residency

(P-16082)
LOMPOC VALLEY MEDICAL CENTER

Also Called: Mammography Center
1111 E Ocean Ave Ste 2, Lompoc (93436-2500)
PHONE....................805 735-9229
Jim Raggio, *Brnch Mgr*
EMP: 139
SALES (corp-wide): 144.98MM **Privately Held**
Web: www.lompcvmc.com
SIC: 8062 General medical and surgical hospitals
PA: Lompoc Valley Medical Center
1515 E Ocean Ave
805 737-3300

(P-16083)
LOMPOC VALLEY MEDICAL CENTER (PA)
Also Called: Lompoc Skilled Care Center
1515 E Ocean Ave, Lompoc (93436-7092)
P.O. Box Po Box 1058 (93438-1058)
PHONE....................805 737-3300
Jim Raggio, *CEO*
Naishadh Buch, *
Jayne Scalise, *
Brian Smolskis, *
EMP: 325 **EST:** 1947
SQ FT: 150,000
SALES (est): 144.98MM
SALES (corp-wide): 144.98MM **Privately Held**
Web: www.lompcvmc.com
SIC: 8062 8051 Hospital, affiliated with AMA residency; Skilled nursing care facilities

(P-16084)
LONG BEACH MEDICAL CENTER
Also Called: Infusion Care
450 E Spring St Ste 11, Long Beach (90806-1625)
PHONE....................562 933-7701
Gerald Nichrossan, *Brnch Mgr*
EMP: 292
Web: www.memorialcare.org
SIC: 8062 General medical and surgical hospitals
HQ: Long Beach Medical Center
2801 Atlantic Ave Fl 2
Long Beach CA 90806
562 933-2000

(P-16085)
LONG BEACH MEDICAL CENTER
1720 Termino Ave, Long Beach (90804-2104)
PHONE....................562 933-0085
Tom Collins, *Pr*
EMP: 341
Web: www.memorialcare.org
SIC: 8062 General medical and surgical hospitals
HQ: Long Beach Medical Center
2801 Atlantic Ave Fl 2
Long Beach CA 90806
562 933-2000

(P-16086)
LONG BEACH MEDICAL CENTER (HQ)
Also Called: Miller Children's Hospital
2801 Atlantic Ave Fl 2, Long Beach (90806-1701)
PHONE....................562 933-2000
John Bishop, *CEO*
Barry Arbuckle Ph.d., *Pr*
Judy Fix, *
Scott Joslyn, *CIO*
Thomas Poole, *
EMP: 2000 **EST:** 1907
SQ FT: 1,100,000

SALES (est): 633.63MM **Privately Held**
Web: www.memorialcare.org
SIC: 8062 General medical and surgical hospitals
PA: Memorial Health Services
17360 Brkhurst St Ste 160

(P-16087)
LONG BEACH MEMORIAL MED CTR
Also Called: LONG BEACH MEMORIAL MEDICAL CENTER
1057 Pine Ave, Long Beach (90813-3118)
PHONE....................562 933-0432
Renee May, *Brnch Mgr*
EMP: 316
Web: www.thechildrensclinic.org
SIC: 8062 General medical and surgical hospitals
HQ: Long Beach Medical Center
2801 Atlantic Ave Fl 2
Long Beach CA 90806
562 933-2000

(P-16088)
LONGWOOD MANAGEMENT CORP
Also Called: Shea Convalescent Hospital
7716 Pickering Ave, Whittier (90602-2001)
PHONE....................562 693-5240
Richard Esconrias, *Mgr*
EMP: 94
SALES (corp-wide): 41.31MM **Privately Held**
Web: www.longwoodmgmt.com
SIC: 8062 8051 8011 General medical and surgical hospitals; Skilled nursing care facilities; Offices and clinics of medical doctors
PA: Longwood Management Llc
4032 Wilshire Blvd Fl 6
213 389-6900

(P-16089)
LONGWOOD MANAGEMENT CORP
Also Called: Northridge Nursing Center
7836 Reseda Blvd, Reseda (91335-1902)
PHONE....................818 881-7414
Deffie Biczi, *Genl Mgr*
EMP: 76
SALES (corp-wide): 41.31MM **Privately Held**
Web: www.longwoodmgmt.com
SIC: 8062 General medical and surgical hospitals
PA: Longwood Management Llc
4032 Wilshire Blvd Fl 6
213 389-6900

(P-16090)
LOS ALAMITOS MEDICAL CTR INC (HQ)
3751 Katella Ave, Los Alamitos (90720-3164)
P.O. Box 533 (90720-0533)
PHONE....................714 826-6400
TOLL FREE: 800
Kent Clayton, *CEO*
Margaret Watkins, *
Alice Livingood Co, *President Elect*
EMP: 1100 **EST:** 1970
SQ FT: 900
SALES (est): 167.97MM
SALES (corp-wide): 19.17B **Publicly Held**
Web: www.ucihealth.org
SIC: 8062 General medical and surgical hospitals
PA: Tenet Healthcare Corporation
14201 Dallas Pkwy

▲ = Import ▼ = Export
◆ = Import/Export

469 893-2000

(P-16091)

LOS ROBLES REGIONAL MED CTR (DH)
Also Called: Los Robles Hospital & Med Ctr
215 W Janss Rd, Thousand Oaks
(91360-1847)
PHONE............................805 497-2727
Natalie Mussi, *CEO*
◆ **EMP:** 917 **EST:** 1978
SQ FT: 475
SALES (est): 334.05K **Publicly Held**
Web: www.losrobleshospital.com
SIC: 8062 General medical and surgical
    hospitals
HQ: Hca Inc.
    1 Park Plz
    Nashville TN 37203
    615 344-9551

(P-16092)

MARIAN MEDICAL CENTER
Also Called: Marian Regional Medical Center
1400 E Church St, Santa Maria
(93454-5906)
PHONE............................805 739-3000
EMP: 1000
Web: www.supportmarianmedical.org
SIC: 8062 General medical and surgical
    hospitals

(P-16093)

MARINE CORPS UNITED STATES
Air Ground Combat Ctr, #1145, Twentynine
Palms (92278)
P.O. Box 788250 (92278-8250)
PHONE............................760 830-6000
EMP: 257
Web: www.marines.mil
SIC: 8062 9711 General medical and
    surgical hospitals; Marine Corps
HQ: United States Marine Corps
    Branch Hlth Clinic Bldg #5
    Beaufort SC 29904

(P-16094)

MEMORIAL HEALTH SERVICES (PA)
Also Called: Memorial Care Medical Centers
17360 Brookhurst St Ste 160, Fountain
Valley (92708-3720)
P.O. Box 20894 (92728-0894)
PHONE............................714 377-2900
Barry Arbuckle, *Pr*
Diana Laird, *
Rick Graniere, *CIO*
Karen Testman, *
Terri Cammarano, *
EMP: 460 **EST:** 1937
SALES (est): 3.03B **Privately Held**
Web: www.memorialcare.org
SIC: 8062 General medical and surgical
    hospitals

(P-16095)

MEMORIAL HLTH SVCS - UNIV CAL (PA)
2801 Atlantic Ave, Long Beach
(90806-1701)
PHONE............................562 933-2000
Edward Quilligan, *CEO*
Diana Hendel, *
Darrel Brownell, *
EMP: 1522 **EST:** 1907
SQ FT: 1,000,000
SALES (est): 422.1MM
SALES (corp-wide): 422.1MM **Privately Held**

Web: www.memorialcare.org
SIC: 8062 8741 General medical and
    surgical hospitals; Management services

(P-16096)

MEMORIAL HOSPITAL OF GARDENA
4060 Woody Blvd, Los Angeles (90023)
PHONE............................323 268-5514
EMP: 400
SIC: 8062 Hospital, affiliated with AMA
    residency

(P-16097)

METHODIST HOSPITAL OF S CA
300 W Huntington Dr, Arcadia
(91007-3473)
P.O. Box 60016 (91066-6016)
PHONE............................626 574-3755
Dennis Lee, *Prin*
EMP: 72 **EST:** 2009
SALES (est): 20.89MM **Privately Held**
Web: www.uscarcadiahospital.org
SIC: 8062 General medical and surgical
    hospitals

(P-16098)

MISSION HOSP REGIONAL MED CTR (PA)
Also Called: MISSION HOSPITAL
27700 Medical Center Rd, Mission Viejo
(92691-6426)
PHONE............................949 364-1400
Seth Peigen, *CEO*
EMP: 1349 **EST:** 1941
SQ FT: 750,000
SALES (est): 690.3MM
SALES (corp-wide): 690.3MM **Privately Held**
Web: www.mission4health.com
SIC: 8062 General medical and surgical
    hospitals

(P-16099)

MLK COMMUNITY HOSPITAL
1680 E 120th St, Los Angeles
(90059-3026)
PHONE............................424 338-8000
Cynthia Moore Oliver, *CEO*
Rhonda Bean, *COO*
Steven Ciampa, *CFO*
EMP: 161 **EST:** 2013
SALES (est): 2.29MM **Privately Held**
Web: www.mlkch.org
SIC: 8062 Hospital, affiliated with AMA
    residency

(P-16100)

MOHAWK MEDICAL GROUP INC
9500 Stockdale Hwy Ste 200, Bakersfield
(93311-3621)
PHONE............................661 324-4747
Jorge Deltoro, *Pr*
Luis Cousin, *
EMP: 80 **EST:** 1985
SQ FT: 18,500
SALES (est): 4.79MM **Privately Held**
Web: www.dignityhealth.org
SIC: 8062 General medical and surgical
    hospitals

(P-16101)

MONTEREY PARK HOSPITAL
Also Called: WHITTIER HOSPITAL MEDICAL
CENT
900 S Atlantic Blvd, Monterey Park
(91754-4780)
PHONE............................626 570-9000
Philip A Cohen, *CEO*

Robert M Dubbs, *
Robert W Fleming Junior, *Sr VP*
EMP: 150 **EST:** 1972
SQ FT: 90,575
SALES (est): 108.18MM
SALES (corp-wide): 325.41MM **Privately Held**
Web: www.ahmchealth.com
SIC: 8062 General medical and surgical
    hospitals
PA: Ahmc Healthcare Inc.
    506 W Valley Blvd Ste 300
    626 943-7526

(P-16102)

MOTION PICTURE AND TV FUND (PA)
Also Called: Bob Hope Health Center
23388 Mulholland Dr, Woodland Hills
(91364-2733)
P.O. Box 51151 (90051-5451)
PHONE............................818 876-1777
Robert Beitcher, *CEO*
Bob Pisano, *
Joseph Fischer, *
Jay Roth, *
EMP: 500 **EST:** 1921
SQ FT: 50,000
SALES (est): 29.84MM
SALES (corp-wide): 29.84MM **Privately Held**
Web: www.mptf.com
SIC: 8062 8051 8011 8351 General medical
    and surgical hospitals; Convalescent home
    with continuous nursing care; Medical
    centers; Child day care services

(P-16103)

MOUNTAIN VIEW CHILD CARE INC (PA)
Also Called: Totally Kids Rhbilitation Hosp
1720 Mountain View Ave, Loma Linda
(92354-1799)
PHONE............................909 796-6915
Doug Pagett, *CEO*
Cynthia Capetillo, *
Donald Nydam, *
Hal Karlin, *
Loma Linda, *
EMP: 275 **EST:** 1972
SALES (est): 48.34MM **Privately Held**
Web: www.totallykids.com
SIC: 8062 8052 8051 General medical and
    surgical hospitals; Intermediate care
    facilities; Skilled nursing care facilities

(P-16104)

MOUNTNS CMNTY HOSP FNDTION IN
Also Called: MOUNTAINS COMMUNITY
HOSPITAL
29101 Hospital Rd, Lake Arrowhead
(92352-9706)
P.O. Box 70 (92352-0070)
PHONE............................909 336-3651
Don Willerth, *CEO*
EMP: 180 **EST:** 1957
SQ FT: 18,500
SALES (est): 31.36MM **Privately Held**
Web: www.mchcares.com
SIC: 8062 8051 General medical and
    surgical hospitals; Skilled nursing care
    facilities

(P-16105)

NIX HOSPITALS SYSTEM LLC (HQ)
Also Called: Nix Healthcare System
3415 S Sepulveda Blvd Ste 900, Los
Angeles (90034-6981)

PHONE............................210 271-1800
John F Strieby, *Pr*
Rob Elders, *Sec*
EMP: 108 **EST:** 2011
SALES (est): 8.94MM
SALES (corp-wide): 3.91B **Privately Held**
Web: www.nixhealth.com
SIC: 8062 General medical and surgical
    hospitals
PA: Prospect Medical Holdings, Inc.
    3415 S Sepulveda Blvd
    310 943-4500

(P-16106)

NORTH KERN S TULARE HOSP DST
Also Called: Delano Dst Sklled Nrsing Fclty
1430 6th Ave, Delano (93215-3008)
PHONE............................661 720-2101
Silva Soto, *Pr*
Dio Telmo, *Admn*
Elson De Guzman, *Contrlr*
Jaime Mendoza, *Prin*
Femme Adebayo, *Prin*
EMP: 230 **EST:** 1966
SALES (est): 14.4MM **Privately Held**
Web: www.nksthd.org
SIC: 8062 General medical and surgical
    hospitals

(P-16107)

OLYMPIA HEALTH CARE LLC
Also Called: Olympia Medical Center
5900 W Olympic Blvd, Los Angeles
(90036-4671)
P.O. Box 351209 (90035-9609)
PHONE............................323 938-3161
Karen Knueven, *
Babur Ozkan, *
EMP: 875 **EST:** 2004
SQ FT: 500,000
SALES (est): 185.86MM **Privately Held**
Web: www.aplahealth.org
SIC: 8062 Hospital, affiliated with AMA
    residency
PA: Alecto Healthcare Services Llc
    101 N Brand Blvd Ste 1920

(P-16108)

ORANGE CNTY GLOBL MED CTR AUX (DH)
Also Called: Western Medical Center Aux
1301 N Tustin Ave, Santa Ana
(92705-8619)
PHONE............................714 835-3555
Dan Brothman, *CEO*
Patricia Stites, *
EMP: 200 **EST:** 1998
SALES (est): 49.01MM **Privately Held**
Web:
www.orangecountyglobalmedicalcenter.com
SIC: 8062 General medical and surgical
    hospitals
HQ: Kpc Healthcare, Inc.
    1301 N Tustin Ave
    Santa Ana CA 92705
    714 953-3652

(P-16109)

ORANGE COAST MEMORIAL MED CTR (HQ)
Also Called: MEMORIAL CARE MEDICAL
CENTERS
9920 Talbert Ave, Fountain Valley
(92708-5153)
P.O. Box 20894 (92708)
PHONE............................714 378-7000
TOLL FREE: 888
Marcia Manker, *Pr*
Steve Mcnamara, *CFO*

P
R
O
D
U
C
T
S
&
S
V
C
S

Aaron Coley, *
EMP: 508 **EST:** 1995
SQ FT: 40,361
SALES (est): 346.99MM **Privately Held**
Web: www.memorialcare.org
SIC: 8062 General medical and surgical hospitals
PA: Memorial Health Services
17360 Brkhurst St Ste 160

(P-16110)
ORANGTREE CNVALESCENT HOSP INC
Also Called: Plott Family Care Centers
4000 Harrison St, Riverside (92503-3599)
PHONE..............................951 785-6060
Elizabeth Plott, *Pr*
EMP: 120 **EST:** 1983
SALES (est): 3.22MM **Privately Held**
SIC: 8062 8051 General medical and surgical hospitals; Skilled nursing care facilities

(P-16111)
ORTHOPAEDIC HOSPITAL (PA)
Also Called: Orthopaedic Inst For Children
403 W Adams Blvd, Los Angeles (90007-2697)
P.O. Box 60132 (90060-0132)
PHONE..............................213 742-1000
Anthony A Scaduto, *Pr*
Diane Moon, *
EMP: 168 **EST:** 1923
SQ FT: 105,000
SALES (est): 13.5MM
SALES (corp-wide): 13.5MM **Privately Held**
Web: www.luskinoic.org
SIC: 8062 8011 General medical and surgical hospitals; Primary care medical clinic

(P-16112)
PACIFIC HEALTH CORPORATION
Also Called: Tustin Hospital
14642 Newport Ave, Tustin (92780-6057)
PHONE..............................714 838-9600
EMP: 1700
Web: www.hawaiipacifichealth.org
SIC: 8062 General medical and surgical hospitals

(P-16113)
PACIFICA OF VALLEY CORPORATION
Also Called: Pacifica Hospital of Valley
9449 San Fernando Rd, Sun Valley (91352-1421)
PHONE..............................818 767-3310
Paul Tuft, *Ch Bd*
Ayman Mousa, *
EMP: 607 **EST:** 1996
SQ FT: 148,020
SALES (est): 97.12MM **Privately Held**
Web: www.pacificahospital.com
SIC: 8062 Hospital, affiliated with AMA residency

(P-16114)
PALO VERDE HEALTH CARE DST
Also Called: Palo Verde Hospital
250 N 1st St, Blythe (92225-1702)
PHONE..............................760 922-4115
Sandra J Anaya, *CEO*
Dennis Rutherford, *
EMP: 180 **EST:** 1938
SALES (est): 23.8MM **Privately Held**
Web: www.paloverdehospital.org

SIC: 8062 8069 General medical and surgical hospitals; Specialty hospitals, except psychiatric

(P-16115)
PALO VERDE HOSPITAL ASSN
250 N 1st St, Blythe (92225-1702)
PHONE..............................760 922-4115
Sandra J Anaya, *CEO*
Larry Blitz, *
Jim Carney, *
David Conejo, *
Beatrice Pinon, *
EMP: 135 **EST:** 1948
SQ FT: 44,000
SALES (est): 24.24MM **Privately Held**
Web: www.paloverdehospital.org
SIC: 8062 General medical and surgical hospitals

(P-16116)
PALOMAR HEALTH
Also Called: Patient Business Services
152255 Innovation Dr, San Diego (92128)
PHONE..............................858 675-5218
Laurie Rose, *Mgr*
EMP: 300
SALES (corp-wide): 679.43K **Privately Held**
Web: www.palomarhealth.org
SIC: 8062 General medical and surgical hospitals
PA: Palomar Health
2125 Ctrcado Pkwy Ste 300
442 281-5000

(P-16117)
PALOMAR HEALTH (PA)
Also Called: Palomar Medical Center
2125 Citracado Pkwy Ste 300, Escondido (92029-4159)
PHONE..............................442 281-5000
Doug Moir, *Pr*
Tanya Howell, *
EMP: 180 **EST:** 1950
SALES (est): 679.43K
SALES (corp-wide): 679.43K **Privately Held**
Web: www.palomarhealth.org
SIC: 8062 8059 General medical and surgical hospitals; Convalescent home

(P-16118)
PALOMAR HEALTH
Also Called: Palomar Medical Center
15615 Pomerado Rd, Poway (92064-2405)
PHONE..............................760 739-3000
Michael Covert, *CEO*
EMP: 1200
SALES (corp-wide): 679.43K **Privately Held**
Web: www.palomarhealth.org
SIC: 8062 General medical and surgical hospitals
PA: Palomar Health
2125 Ctrcado Pkwy Ste 300
442 281-5000

(P-16119)
PALOMAR HEALTH
Also Called: Pomerado Hospital
15615 Pomerado Rd, Poway (92064-2405)
PHONE..............................858 613-3000
TOLL FREE: 800
Jim Flinn, *Admn*
EMP: 211
SALES (corp-wide): 679.43K **Privately Held**
Web: www.pph.org

SIC: 8062 General medical and surgical hospitals
PA: Palomar Health
2125 Ctrcado Pkwy Ste 300
442 281-5000

(P-16120)
PALOMAR HEALTH MEDICAL GROUP (HQ)
Also Called: Arch Health Partners
15611 Pomerado Rd Ste 575, Poway (92064-2438)
PHONE..............................858 675-3100
Deanna Kyrimis, *CEO*
Hugh King, *
Matt Niedzwiecki, *
EMP: 169 **EST:** 2009
SALES (est): 163.61MM
SALES (corp-wide): 679.43K **Privately Held**
Web: www.palomarhealthmedicalgroup.org
SIC: 8062 General medical and surgical hospitals
PA: Palomar Health
2125 Ctrcado Pkwy Ste 300
442 281-5000

(P-16121)
PALOMAR HEALTH TECHNOLOGY INC
2140 Enterprise St, Escondido (92029-2000)
PHONE..............................442 281-5000
Diane Hansen, *CEO*
EMP: 211 **EST:** 2011
SALES (est): 27.23MM
SALES (corp-wide): 679.43K **Privately Held**
Web: www.palomarhealth.org
SIC: 8062 General medical and surgical hospitals
PA: Palomar Health
2125 Ctrcado Pkwy Ste 300
442 281-5000

(P-16122)
PALOMAR MEDICAL CENTER
Also Called: PALOMAR MEDICAL CENTER
15615 Pomerado Rd, Poway (92064-2405)
PHONE..............................858 613-4000
Dianne Hansen, *CEO*
EMP: 266 **EST:** 2013
SALES (est): 194.84K
SALES (corp-wide): 679.43K **Privately Held**
Web: www.palomarhealth.org
SIC: 8062 General medical and surgical hospitals
PA: Palomar Health
2125 Ctrcado Pkwy Ste 300
442 281-5000

(P-16123)
PAMC LTD (PA)
Also Called: Pamc Health Foundation
531 W College St, Los Angeles (90012-2315)
PHONE..............................213 624-8411
John Edwards, *CEO*
EMP: 530 **EST:** 1989
SQ FT: 75,600
SALES (est): 19.13MM **Privately Held**
Web: www.pamc.net
SIC: 8062 General medical and surgical hospitals

(P-16124)
PARACLSUS LOS ANGLES CMNTY HOS

SIC: 8062 General medical and surgical hospitals
PA: Palomar Health
2125 Ctrcado Pkwy Ste 300
442 281-5000

Also Called: LOS ANGELES COMMUNITY HOSPITAL
4081 E Olympic Blvd, Los Angeles (90023-3330)
PHONE..............................323 267-0477
EMP: 250 **EST:** 1983
SALES (est): 194.63MM **Privately Held**
Web: www.lach-la.com
SIC: 8062 General medical and surgical hospitals

(P-16125)
PARADISE VALLEY HOSPITAL (PA)
2400 E 4th St, National City (91950-2098)
PHONE..............................619 470-4100
Alan Soderblom, *CEO*
Luin Leon, *
Robert Carmen, *
Prem Reddy, *
Neerav Jadeja, *
EMP: 925 **EST:** 1904
SQ FT: 230,000
SALES (est): 140.77MM
SALES (corp-wide): 140.77MM **Privately Held**
Web: www.paradisevalleyhospital.net
SIC: 8062 General medical and surgical hospitals

(P-16126)
PARADISE VALLEY HOSPITAL
Also Called: West Health Care
180 Otay Lakes Rd Ste 100, Bonita (91902-2464)
PHONE..............................619 472-7474
Connie Mayo, *Dir*
EMP: 251
SALES (corp-wide): 140.77MM **Privately Held**
Web: www.paradisevalleyhospital.net
SIC: 8062 General medical and surgical hospitals
PA: Paradise Valley Hospital
2400 E 4th St
619 470-4100

(P-16127)
PARKVIEW CMNTY HOSP MED CTR
3865 Jackson St, Riverside (92503-3919)
PHONE..............................951 354-7404
Norm Martin, *Pr*
Doug Drumwright, *
EMP: 1149 **EST:** 1966
SQ FT: 132,651
SALES (est): 162.74MM
SALES (corp-wide): 162.74MM **Privately Held**
Web: www.ahmchealth.com
SIC: 8062 8011 General medical and surgical hospitals; Offices and clinics of medical doctors
PA: Doctors Hospital Of Riverside Llc
3865 Jackson St
951 354-7404

(P-16128)
PASADENA HOSPITAL ASSN LTD (PA)
Also Called: HUNTINGTON MEMORIAL HOSPITAL
100 W California Blvd, Pasadena (91105-3010)
P.O. Box 440746 (77244)
PHONE..............................626 397-5000
Lori J Morgan, *CEO*
Lois Matthews, *
Stephen A Ralph, *
Jim Noble, *

Jane Haderlein, *
EMP: 2100 **EST:** 1892
SQ FT: 928,000
SALES (est): 764.47MM
SALES (corp-wide): 764.47MM **Privately Held**
Web: www.huntingtonhealth.org
SIC: 8062 General medical and surgical hospitals

(P-16129)
PERRIS VALLEY CMNTY HOSP LLC

Also Called: Vista Hospital Riverside
10841 White Oak Ave, Rancho Cucamonga (91730-3817)
PHONE..............................909 581-6400
Edward L Kuntz, CEO
EMP: 227
Web: www.kindredhospitals.com
SIC: 8062 General medical and surgical hospitals
PA: Perris Valley Community Hospital, Llc
2224 Medical Center Dr

(P-16130)
PIH HEALTH INC (PA)

Also Called: INTEGRATED HEALTHCARE DELIVERY
12401 Washington Blvd, Whittier (90602-1006)
PHONE..............................562 698-0811
Jane Dicus, Ch
Richard Atwood, Vice Chairman*
Efrain Aceves, *
Kenton Woods, *
Ronald Yoshihara, *
EMP: 1100 **EST:** 1981
SQ FT: 500,000
SALES (est): 20.43MM
SALES (corp-wide): 20.43MM **Privately Held**
Web: www.laiic.com
SIC: 8062 8011 General medical and surgical hospitals; Offices and clinics of medical doctors

(P-16131)
PIH HEALTH DOWNEY HOSPITAL (HQ)

Also Called: INTEGRATED HEALTHCARE DELIVERY
11500 Brookshire Ave, Downey (90241-4917)
PHONE..............................562 698-0811
James R West, Pr
Bryan Smolskis, *
Efrain Aceves, *
Kenton Woods, *
Peggy Chulack, CAO*
EMP: 254 **EST:** 1956
SQ FT: 225,000
SALES (est): 197.27MM
SALES (corp-wide): 20.43MM **Privately Held**
SIC: 8062 General medical and surgical hospitals
PA: Pih Health, Inc.
12401 Washington Blvd
562 698-0811

(P-16132)
PIH HEALTH GOOD SAMARITAN HOSP (HQ)

Also Called: General Acute Care Hospital
1225 Wilshire Blvd, Los Angeles (90017-1901)
PHONE..............................213 977-2121
James West, CEO
Charles Munger, *

Alan Ino, *
▲ **EMP:** 1255 **EST:** 1885
SQ FT: 10,000
SALES (est): 379.14MM
SALES (corp-wide): 20.43MM **Privately Held**
SIC: 8062 Hospital, affiliated with AMA residency
PA: Pih Health, Inc.
12401 Washington Blvd
562 698-0811

(P-16133)
PIH HEALTH HOSPITAL - WHITTI

Also Called: Downey Regional Medical Center
11500 Brookshire Ave, Downey (90241-4917)
PHONE..............................562 904-5482
James R West, CEO
EMP: 1150
SALES (corp-wide): 20.43MM **Privately Held**
SIC: 8062 8071 General medical and surgical hospitals; Medical laboratories
HQ: Pih Health Whittier Hospital
12401 Washington Blvd
Whittier CA 90602
562 698-0811

(P-16134)
PIH HEALTH WHITTIER HOSPITAL (HQ)

Also Called: General Acute Care Hospital
12401 Washington Blvd, Whittier (90602-1006)
PHONE..............................562 698-0811
James R West, CEO
Anita Chou, *
Ramona Pratt, *
EMP: 1900 **EST:** 1954
SQ FT: 500,000
SALES (est): 874.07MM
SALES (corp-wide): 20.43MM **Privately Held**
SIC: 8062 General medical and surgical hospitals
PA: Pih Health, Inc.
12401 Washington Blvd
562 698-0811

(P-16135)
PIONEERS MEM HEALTHCARE DST (PA)

Also Called: Pioneers Memorial Hospital
207 W Legion Rd, Brawley (92227-7780)
PHONE..............................760 351-3333
Daniel Heckathorne, *
Justina Aguirre, *
EMP: 571 **EST:** 1947
SQ FT: 171,445
SALES (est): 163.86MM
SALES (corp-wide): 163.86MM **Privately Held**
Web: www.pmhd.org
SIC: 8062 Hospital, affiliated with AMA residency

(P-16136)
PIPELINE HEALTH LLC (PA)

898 N Pacific Coast Hwy Ste 700, El Segundo (90245-2742)
PHONE..............................310 379-2134
EMP: 94 **EST:** 2014
SALES (est): 216.87MM
SALES (corp-wide): 216.87MM **Privately Held**
Web: www.pipelinehealth.us
SIC: 8062 General medical and surgical hospitals

(P-16137)
POMONA VALLEY HOSPITAL MED CTR (PA)

Also Called: Pvhmc
1798 N Garey Ave, Pomona (91767-2918)
PHONE..............................909 865-9500
Richard E Yochum, CEO
Alan Smith, *
Michael Nelson, *
Kurt Weinmeister, *
EMP: 2121 **EST:** 1903
SQ FT: 362,000
SALES (est): 784.65MM
SALES (corp-wide): 784.65MM **Privately Held**
Web: www.pvhmc.org
SIC: 8062 Hospital, medical school affiliated with residency

(P-16138)
PRIME HALTHCARE FOUNDATION INC (PA)

3480 E Guasti Rd, Ontario (91761-7684)
PHONE..............................909 235-4400
Prem Reddy, CEO
EMP: 107 **EST:** 2006
SALES (est): 878.52MM
SALES (corp-wide): 878.52MM **Privately Held**
Web: www.primehealthcare.com
SIC: 8062 General medical and surgical hospitals

(P-16139)
PRIME HEALTHCARE ANAHEIM LLC

Also Called: West Anaheim Medical Center
3033 W Orange Ave, Anaheim (92804-3156)
PHONE..............................714 827-3000
Virg Narbutas, CEO
Kora Guoyavatin, *
EMP: 800 **EST:** 1963
SQ FT: 180,000
SALES (est): 139.44MM
SALES (corp-wide): 878.52MM **Privately Held**
Web: www.westanaheimmedctr.com
SIC: 8062 Hospital, affiliated with AMA residency
HQ: Prime Healthcare Services Inc
3480 E Guasti Rd
Ontario CA 91761

(P-16140)
PRIME HEALTHCARE CENTINELA LLC

Also Called: Centinela Hospital Medical Center
555 E Hardy St, Inglewood (90301-4011)
PHONE..............................310 673-4000
Linda Bradley, CEO
Barbara Kokolowski, SVS
EMP: 1000 **EST:** 1952
SALES (est): 262.74MM
SALES (corp-wide): 878.52MM **Privately Held**
Web: www.centinelamed.com
SIC: 8062 General medical and surgical hospitals
HQ: Prime Healthcare Services Inc
3480 E Guasti Rd
Ontario CA 91761

(P-16141)
PRIME HEALTHCARE SERVICES-MONT

5000 San Bernardino St, Montclair (91763-2326)

PHONE..............................909 625-5411
EMP: 3024
SALES (est): 188.46MM
SALES (corp-wide): 878.52MM **Privately Held**
Web: www.montclair-hospital.org
SIC: 8062 General medical and surgical hospitals
PA: Prime Healthcare Foundation, Inc.
3480 E. Guasti Rd
909 235-4400

(P-16142)
PRIME HLTHCARE HNTNGTON BCH LL

Also Called: Huntington Beach Hospital
17772 Beach Blvd, Huntington Beach (92647-6819)
PHONE..............................714 843-5000
EMP: 480 **EST:** 1957
SQ FT: 100,000
SALES (est): 61.25MM
SALES (corp-wide): 878.52MM **Privately Held**
Web: www.hbhospital.org
SIC: 8062 General medical and surgical hospitals
HQ: Prime Healthcare Services Inc
3480 E Guasti Rd
Ontario CA 91761

(P-16143)
PRIME HLTHCARE SRVCS-MNTCLAIR

Also Called: Urgent Care Center
5000 San Bernardino St, Montclair (91763-2326)
PHONE..............................909 625-5411
David Chu, Mgr
EMP: 216
SALES (corp-wide): 878.52MM **Privately Held**
Web: www.montclair-hospital.org
SIC: 8062 General medical and surgical hospitals
HQ: Prime Healthcare Services-Montclair, Llc
5000 San Bernardino St
Montclair CA 91763
909 625-5411

(P-16144)
PRIME HLTHCARE SRVCS-MNTCLAIR (DH)

Also Called: Montclair Hospital Medical Center
5000 San Bernardino St, Montclair (91763-2326)
PHONE..............................909 625-5411
Jennifer Ramirez, Ex Sec
Prem Reddy, *
EMP: 234 **EST:** 1999
SALES (est): 62.26MM
SALES (corp-wide): 878.52MM **Privately Held**
Web: www.montclair-hospital.org
SIC: 8062 General medical and surgical hospitals
HQ: Prime Healthcare Services Inc
3480 E Guasti Rd
Ontario CA 91761

(P-16145)
PRIME HLTHCARE SVCS - ENCINO H

16237 Ventura Blvd, Encino (91436-2201)
PHONE..............................818 995-5000
Bockhi Park, CEO
Bockhi Park, Prin
Prem Reddy, *

EMP: 400 **EST:** 2008
SALES (est): 91.24MM
SALES (corp-wide): 878.52MM **Privately Held**
Web: www.encinomed.org
SIC: 8062 General medical and surgical hospitals
HQ: Prime Healthcare Services Inc
3480 E Guasti Rd
Ontario CA 91761

(P-16146)
PRIME HLTHCARE SVCS - PMPA LLC (DH)
Also Called: Pampa Regional Medical Center
3300 E Guasti Rd Ste 300, Ontario (91761-8657)
PHONE..................909 235-4400
Brad Morse, *CEO*
Steven Smith, *
Harsha Upadhyay, *
EMP: 149 **EST:** 1960
SQ FT: 150,000
SALES (est): 41.36MM
SALES (corp-wide): 878.52MM **Privately Held**
Web: www.primehealthcare.com
SIC: 8062 General medical and surgical hospitals
HQ: Prime Healthcare Services Inc
3480 E Guasti Rd
Ontario CA 91761

(P-16147)
PRIME HLTHCARE SVCS - SAN DMAS
Also Called: San Dimas Community Hospital
1350 W Covina Blvd, San Dimas (91773-3245)
PHONE..................909 599-6811
TOLL FREE: 800
Gregory Brentano, *CEO*
Harold Way, *
EMP: 350 **EST:** 1982
SQ FT: 90,000
SALES (est): 58.27MM
SALES (corp-wide): 878.52MM **Privately Held**
Web: www.sandimashospital.com
SIC: 8062 General medical and surgical hospitals
HQ: Prime Healthcare Services Inc
3480 E Guasti Rd
Ontario CA 91761

(P-16148)
PRIME HLTHCARE SVCS - SHRMAN O
Also Called: Sherman Oaks Hospital
4929 Van Nuys Blvd, Sherman Oaks (91403-1702)
PHONE..................818 981-7111
Prem Reddy, *CEO*
John Deady, *CFO*
EMP: 500 **EST:** 2004
SQ FT: 36,000
SALES (est): 97.87MM
SALES (corp-wide): 878.52MM **Privately Held**
Web: www.shermanoakshospital.org
SIC: 8062 General medical and surgical hospitals
HQ: Prime Healthcare Services Inc
3480 E Guasti Rd
Ontario CA 91761

(P-16149)
PROVIDENCE HEALTH & SVCS - ORE
Also Called: Providence Holy Cross Med Ctr

15031 Rinaldi St, Mission Hills (91345-1207)
PHONE..................818 365-8051
David Mast, *Brnch Mgr*
EMP: 931
SALES (corp-wide): 55.69MM **Privately Held**
Web: www.providence.org
SIC: 8062 General medical and surgical hospitals
HQ: Providence Health & Services - Oregon
1801 Lind Ave Sw
Renton WA 98057
425 525-3355

(P-16150)
PROVIDENCE HEALTH SYSTEM
Providence St Joseph Med Ctr
501 S Buena Vista St, Burbank (91505-4809)
PHONE..................818 843-5111
Georgianne Johnson, *COO*
EMP: 2000
SALES (corp-wide): 55.69MM **Privately Held**
Web: www.providence.org
SIC: 8062 General medical and surgical hospitals
HQ: Providence Health System-Southern California
1801 Lind Ave Sw
Renton WA 98057
425 525-3355

(P-16151)
PROVIDENCE HOLY CROSS MEDICAL (PA)
Also Called: Providence
15031 Rinaldi St, Mission Hills (91345-1285)
PHONE..................818 365-8051
Lee Kanon Alpert, *Ch*
June E Drake, '
Jodi Hein, *
▲ **EMP:** 439 **EST:** 1960
SALES (est): 557.56MM
SALES (corp-wide): 557.56MM **Privately Held**
SIC: 8062 General medical and surgical hospitals

(P-16152)
PROVIDENCE MEDICAL FOUNDATION (DH)
Also Called: PROVIDENCE HOME HEALTH ORANGE
200 W Center Street Promenade Ste 800, Anaheim (92805-3960)
PHONE..................714 712-3308
EMP: 150 **EST:** 1961
SALES (est): 1.24B
SALES (corp-wide): 55.69MM **Privately Held**
Web: www.psjhmedgroups.org
SIC: 8062 General medical and surgical hospitals
HQ: St. Joseph Health System
3345 Michaelson Dr #100
Irvine CA 92612
949 381-4000

(P-16153)
PROVIDENCE ST JOHNS HLTH CTR
Also Called: St. John's Health Center
2121 Santa Monica Blvd, Santa Monica (90404-2303)
PHONE..................971 268-7643
Marcel Loh, *CEO*
Donald Larsen Junior, *Chief Medical Officer*

Brian Anderson, *Contracts Director*
Guadalupe Martinez, *Finance*
EMP: 350 **EST:** 1940
SQ FT: 60,000
SALES (est): 401MM **Privately Held**
Web: california.providence.org
SIC: 8062 General medical and surgical hospitals

(P-16154)
PROVIDENCE TARZANA MEDICAL CTR
18321 Clark St, Tarzana (91356-3521)
PHONE..................818 881-0800
Dale Surowitz, *CEO*
Nick Lymberopoulos, *
EMP: 1300 **EST:** 1973
SALES (est): 291.91MM **Privately Held**
Web: www.tarzanacme.com
SIC: 8062 General medical and surgical hospitals

(P-16155)
PROVIDNCE HLTH SVCS FNDTN/ SAN
Also Called: Providnce Holy Cross Fundation
501 S Buena Vista St, Burbank (91505-4809)
PHONE..................818 843-5111
Patricia Modrzejewski, *CEO*
Lee Kanon Alpert, *
Thomas Mcdevitt, *Contrlr*
EMP: 2000 **EST:** 1980
SALES (est): 7.58MM **Privately Held**
Web: foundation.providence.org
SIC: 8062 General medical and surgical hospitals

(P-16156)
RADY CHILDRENS HOSP & HLTH CTR (PA)
Also Called: Children's Hospital
3020 Childrens Way, San Diego (92123-4223)
PHONE..................858 576-1700
TOLL FREE: 800
Donald B Kearns, *Pr*
Irvin A Kaufman, *CMO*
Margareta E Norton, *
Roger G Roux, *
Nicholas Holmes, *
EMP: 1700 **EST:** 1980
SALES (est): 1.79B **Privately Held**
Web: www.rchsd.org
SIC: 8062 General medical and surgical hospitals

(P-16157)
RADY CHLD HOSPITAL-SAN DIEGO (HQ)
3020 Childrens Way, San Diego (92123-4223)
PHONE..................858 576-1700
Donald Kearns, *CEO*
Jill Strickland, *CAO*
EMP: 2000 **EST:** 1952
SQ FT: 276,000
SALES (est): 1.69B **Privately Held**
Web: www.rchsd.org
SIC: 8062 General medical and surgical hospitals
PA: Rady Children's Hospital And Health Center
3020 Childrens Way

(P-16158)
RAMONA RHBLTTION POST ACUTE CA
Also Called: Ramona Rhbltton Post Acute Ca

485 W Johnston Ave, Hemet (92543-7012)
PHONE..................951 652-0011
Stan Leland, *Pr*
Heidi Vickers, *
EMP: 120 **EST:** 1995
SQ FT: 30,000
SALES (est): 9.68MM **Privately Held**
Web: www.ramona-rehab.com
SIC: 8062 8051 General medical and surgical hospitals; Convalescent home with continuous nursing care

(P-16159)
REDLANDS COMMUNITY HOSPITAL (PA)
350 Terracina Blvd, Redlands (92373-4897)
PHONE..................909 335-5500
James R Holmes, *CEO*
EMP: 97 **EST:** 1927
SALES (est): 416.82MM **Privately Held**
Web: www.redlandshospital.org
SIC: 8062 General medical and surgical hospitals

(P-16160)
RIDGECREST REGIONAL HOSPITAL (PA)
Also Called: Southern Sierra Medical Clinic
1081 N China Lake Blvd, Ridgecrest (93555-3130)
PHONE..................760 446-3551
James A Suver, *CEO*
Donna Kiser, *
EMP: 470 **EST:** 1962
SQ FT: 80,000
SALES (est): 146.96MM
SALES (corp-wide): 146.96MM **Privately Held**
Web: www.rrh.org
SIC: 8062 General medical and surgical hospitals

(P-16161)
RIVERSIDE CMNTY HLTH SYSTEMS (DH)
Also Called: HCA HEALTHCARE
4445 Magnolia Ave 6th Fl, Riverside (92501-4199)
P.O. Box 550 (37202)
PHONE..................951 788-3000
Peter Hemstead, *CEO*
Tracey Fernandez, *
Partrick Brilliant, *
Mike Hoyt, *
Jesse Roque, *
EMP: 1195 **EST:** 1901
SQ FT: 386,100
SALES (est): 4.04MM **Publicly Held**
Web: www.riversidecommunityhospital.com
SIC: 8062 8011 General medical and surgical hospitals; Offices and clinics of medical doctors
HQ: Hca Inc.
1 Park Plz
Nashville TN 37203
615 344-9551

(P-16162)
RIVERSIDE UNIV HLTH SYS FNDTIO (PA)
Also Called: Riverside Cnty Rgional Med Ctr
4065 County Circle Dr, Riverside (92503-3410)
PHONE..................951 358-5000
Douglas D Bagley, *CEO*
David Runke, *
Ellie Bennett, *
EMP: 473 **EST:** 1989
SALES (est): 5.11MM **Privately Held**

Web: www.ruhealth.org
SIC: **8062** General medical and surgical hospitals

(P-16163)
RIVERSIDE UNIVERSITY HEALTH

Also Called: Ruhs-Emergency Department
26520 Cactus Ave, Moreno Valley
(92555-3927)
PHONE...............................951 486-4000
Bret Powers D.o.s., *Prin*
EMP: 327
Web: www.ruhealth.org
SIC: **8062** General medical and surgical hospitals
PA: Riverside University Health System Foundation
4065 County Circle Dr

(P-16164)
SADDLEBACK MEMORIAL MED CTR (HQ)

Also Called: MEMORIAL CARE MEDICAL CENTERS
24451 Health Center Dr Fl 1, Laguna Hills
(92653-3689)
P.O. Box 20894 (92653)
PHONE...............................949 837-4500
Steve Geidt, *CEO*
Barry Arbuckle, *
Karen Testman, *
Rick Graniere, *
Adolfo Chanez, *
EMP: 1020 **EST:** 1969
SQ FT: 195,000
SALES (est): 369.51MM **Privately Held**
Web: www.memorialcare.org
SIC: **8062** 8011 8093 8099 General medical and surgical hospitals; Medical centers; Rehabilitation center, outpatient treatment; Blood related health services
PA: Memorial Health Services
17360 Brkhurst St Ste 160

(P-16165)
SAINT JOHNS HEALTH CENTER FOUNDATION (DH)

Also Called: Saint John's Health Center
2121 Santa Monica Blvd, Santa Monica
(90404-2303)
PHONE...............................310 829-5511
TOLL FREE: 888
EMP: 1100 **EST:** 1942
SALES (est): 69.62MM
SALES (corp-wide): 10.75B **Privately Held**
Web: www.providence.org
SIC: **8062** General medical and surgical hospitals
HQ: Sisters Of Charity Of Leavenworth Health System, Inc.
500 Eldorado Blvd Ste 6300
Broomfield CO 80021
303 813-5000

(P-16166)
SAN ANTONIO REGIONAL HOSPITAL (PA)

999 San Bernardino Rd, Upland
(91786-4992)
PHONE...............................909 985-2811
John Chapman, *CEO*
Jim Milhiser, *
Wah-chung Hsu, *CFO*
✿ **EMP:** 1900 **EST:** 1920
SQ FT: 349,000
SALES (est): 467.09MM
SALES (corp-wide): 467.09MM **Privately Held**
Web: www.sarh.org

SIC: **8062** 5912 General medical and surgical hospitals; Drug stores and proprietary stores

(P-16167)
SAN GABRIEL VALLEY MEDICAL CTR

438 W Las Tunas Dr, San Gabriel (91778)
PHONE...............................626 289-5454
Thomas Mone, *CEO*
Harold Way, *
Edward Shuey, *
Richard Polver, *
EMP: 850 **EST:** 1964
SQ FT: 42,000
SALES (est): 174.2MM **Privately Held**
Web: www.ahmchealth.com
SIC: **8062** General medical and surgical hospitals
HQ: Dignity Health
185 Berry St Ste 200
San Francisco CA 94107
415 438-5500

(P-16168)
SAN GORGONIO MEMORIAL HOSPITAL

600 N Highland Springs Ave, Banning
(92220-3090)
PHONE...............................951 845-1121
Steve Barron, *CEO*
EMP: 819 **EST:** 1990
SALES (est): 80.2MM **Privately Held**
Web: www.sgmh.org
SIC: **8062** General medical and surgical hospitals

(P-16169)
SAN GRGNIO MEM HOSP FOUNDATION (PA)

600 N Highland Springs Ave, Banning
(92220-3046)
PHONE...............................951 845-1121
Steven Barron, *CEO*
Jerilynn Kaibel, *
Denae Reagins, *
Olivia Hershey, *
Dorothy Ellis, *
EMP: 244 **EST:** 1982
SQ FT: 76,000
SALES (est): 212.63K
SALES (corp-wide): 212.63K **Privately Held**
Web: www.sgmh.org
SIC: **8062** Hospital, affiliated with AMA residency

(P-16170)
SAN JOAQUIN COMMUNITY HOSPITAL (HQ)

Also Called: Adventist Health Bakersfield
2615 Chester Ave, Bakersfield
(93301-2014)
PHONE...............................661 395-3000
Sharlet Briggs, *Pr*
EMP: 850 **EST:** 1910
SQ FT: 137,000
SALES (est): 492.07MM
SALES (corp-wide): 805.07MM **Privately Held**
Web: www.adventisthealth.org
SIC: **8062** 8011 General medical and surgical hospitals; Offices and clinics of medical doctors
PA: Adventist Health System/West, Corporation
One Adventist Health Way
844 574-5686

(P-16171)
SAN PEDRO PENINSULA HOSPITAL

Also Called: Little Co Mary- San Pedro Hosp
1300 W 7th St, San Pedro (90732-3593)
PHONE...............................310 832-3311
EMP: 880
SIC: **8062** 8051 5912 General medical and surgical hospitals; Skilled nursing care facilities; Drug stores

(P-16172)
SANTA BARBARA COTTAGE HOSPITAL

Pathology Department
400 W Pueblo St, Santa Barbara
(93105-4390)
P.O. Box 689 (93102-0689)
PHONE...............................805 569-7367
Ron Werdt, *Pr*
EMP: 169
SALES (corp-wide): 152.81MM **Privately Held**
Web: www.missionpathology.com
SIC: **8062** General medical and surgical hospitals
HQ: Santa Barbara Cottage Hospital Foundation
400 W Pueblo St
Santa Barbara CA 93105
805 682-7111

(P-16173)
SANTA BRBARA CTTAGE HOSP FNDTI

Respiratory Care
400 W Pueblo St, Santa Barbara
(93105-4353)
PHONE...............................805 569-7224
Doctor Phillip Michael, *Dir*
EMP: 149
SALES (corp-wide): 152.81MM **Privately Held**
Web: www.countyofsb.org
SIC: **8062** General medical and surgical hospitals
HQ: Santa Barbara Cottage Hospital Foundation
400 W Pueblo St
Santa Barbara CA 93105
805 682-7111

(P-16174)
SANTA BRBARA CTTAGE HOSP FNDTI

Also Called: Santa Barbara Cnty Social Svcs
2125 Centerpointe Pkwy, Santa Maria
(93455-1337)
PHONE...............................805 346-7135
Charlene Chase, *Dir*
EMP: 157
SALES (corp-wide): 152.81MM **Privately Held**
Web: www.cottagehealth.org
SIC: **8062** General medical and surgical hospitals
HQ: Santa Barbara Cottage Hospital Foundation
400 W Pueblo St
Santa Barbara CA 93105
805 682-7111

(P-16175)
SANTA BRBARA CTTAGE HOSP FNDTI (HQ)

Also Called: Cottage Childrens Medical Ctr
400 W Pueblo St, Santa Barbara
(93105-4353)
P.O. Box 689 (93102-0689)

PHONE...............................805 682-7111
Ronald C Werft, *CEO*
Steven Fellows, *
Brett Tande, *
EMP: 829 **EST:** 1982
SQ FT: 485,874
SALES (est): 772.02MM
SALES (corp-wide): 152.81MM **Privately Held**
Web: www.pacbiztimes.com
SIC: **8062** Hospital, AMA approved residency
PA: Cottage Health
400 W Pueblo St
805 682-7111

(P-16176)
SANTA TERESITA INC (PA)

Also Called: MANOR AT SANTA TERESITA HOSPIT
819 Buena Vista St, Duarte (91010-1703)
PHONE...............................626 359-3243
Sister Mary Clare Mancini, *CEO*
EMP: 276 **EST:** 1955
SQ FT: 232,165
SALES (est): 5.8MM
SALES (corp-wide): 5.8MM **Privately Held**
Web: www.santa-teresita.org
SIC: **8062** 8051 General medical and surgical hospitals; Skilled nursing care facilities

(P-16177)
SANTA YNEZ VLY CTTAGE HOSP INC

2050 Viborg Rd, Solvang (93463-2295)
P.O. Box 689 (93102-0689)
PHONE...............................805 688-6431
Ron Werft, *Pr*
EMP: 75 **EST:** 1962
SQ FT: 30,000
SALES (est): 29.39MM
SALES (corp-wide): 152.81MM **Privately Held**
Web: www.santaynezvalley.com
SIC: **8062** General medical and surgical hospitals
PA: Cottage Health
400 W Pueblo St
805 682-7111

(P-16178)
SCRIPPS CLINIC

12395 El Camino Real Ste 112, San Diego
(92130-3084)
P.O. Box 2469 (92038-2469)
PHONE...............................858 794-1250
Chris Van Gorder, *CEO*
Doctor Hubert Greenway, *CEO*
James Collins, *Pr*
EMP: 104 **EST:** 1999
SALES (est): 18.51MM **Privately Held**
Web: www.scripps.org
SIC: **8062** General medical and surgical hospitals

(P-16179)
SCRIPPS HEALTH

Also Called: Scripps Mercy Hospital
4077 5th Ave, San Diego (92103-2105)
PHONE...............................619 294-8111
Jacqueline Saucier, *Dir*
EMP: 78
SALES (corp-wide): 4.14B **Privately Held**
Web: www.scripps.org
SIC: **8062** General medical and surgical hospitals
PA: Scripps Health
10140 Cmpus Pt Dr Cpa 415
800 727-4777

PRODUCTS & SVCS

(P-16180)
SCRIPPS HEALTH
Also Called: Scripps Rancho Bernardo
15004 Innovation Dr, San Diego
(92128-3491)
PHONE..................................858 271-9770
Melody Stewart, *Admn*
EMP: 98
SALES (corp-wide): 4.14B **Privately Held**
Web: www.scripps.org
SIC: 8062 General medical and surgical
hospitals
PA: Scripps Health
10140 Cmpus Pt Dr Cpa 415
800 727-4777

(P-16181)
SCRIPPS HEALTH
Also Called: Scripps Mem Hosp - Encinatas
354 Santa Fe Dr, Encinitas (92024-5142)
P.O. Box 230817 (92023-0817)
PHONE..................................760 753-6501
Rebecca Ropchan, *Brnch Mgr*
EMP: 250
SALES (corp-wide): 4.14B **Privately Held**
Web: www.scripps.org
SIC: 8062 5912 General medical and
surgical hospitals; Drug stores
PA: Scripps Health
10140 Cmpus Pt Dr Cpa 415
800 727-4777

(P-16182)
SCRIPPS HEALTH
Also Called: Scripps Mercy Hospitals
435 H St, Chula Vista (91910-4383)
PHONE..................................619 691-7000
Pott Hoff, *COO*
EMP: 102
SALES (corp-wide): 4.14B **Privately Held**
Web: www.scripps.org
SIC: 8062 General medical and surgical
hospitals
PA: Scripps Health
10140 Cmpus Pt Dr Cpa 415
800 727-4777

(P-16183)
SCRIPPS HEALTH
Also Called: Scripps Green Hospital
10666 N Torrey Pines Rd, La Jolla
(92037-1027)
PHONE..................................858 455-9100
Robin Brown, *Brnch Mgr*
EMP: 326
SALES (corp-wide): 4.14B **Privately Held**
Web: www.scripps.org
SIC: 8062 General medical and surgical
hospitals
PA: Scripps Health
10140 Cmpus Pt Dr Cpa 415
800 727-4777

(P-16184)
SCRIPPS HEALTH
Also Called: Scripps Mem Hospital-La Jolla
9888 Genesee Ave, La Jolla (92037-1200)
PHONE..................................858 626-6150
James Bruffey, *Brnch Mgr*
EMP: 326
SALES (corp-wide): 4.14B **Privately Held**
Web: www.scripps.org
SIC: 8062 General medical and surgical
hospitals
PA: Scripps Health
10140 Cmpus Pt Dr Cpa 415
800 727-4777

(P-16185)
SCRIPPS HEALTH
Also Called: Scripps Mem Hosp - La Jolla
9888 Genesee Ave, La Jolla (92037-1200)
PHONE..................................858 626-4123
Gary Fybel, *CEO*
EMP: 120
SALES (corp-wide): 4.14B **Privately Held**
Web: www.scripps.org
SIC: 8062 General medical and surgical
hospitals
PA: Scripps Health
10140 Cmpus Pt Dr Cpa 415
800 727-4777

(P-16186)
SCRIPPS HEALTH (PA)
10140 Campus Point Dr, San Diego
(92121-1520)
PHONE..................................800 727-4777
Chris D Van Gorder, *Pr*
Brett Tande, *
Richard Sheridan, *
A Brent Eastman Md, *Chief Medical Officer*
John B Engle, *Chief Development Officer**
EMP: 2514 **EST:** 1924
SQ FT: 95,000
SALES (est): 4.14B
SALES (corp-wide): 4.14B **Privately Held**
Web: www.scripps.org
SIC: 8062 8049 8042 8043 General medical
and surgical hospitals; Physical therapist;
Offices and clinics of optometrists; Offices
and clinics of podiatrists

(P-16187)
SCRIPPS MERCY HOSPITAL
4077 5th Ave # Mer35, San Diego
(92103-2180)
PHONE..................................619 294-8111
Andrew C Ping, *Prin*
EMP: 156 **EST:** 2004
SALES (est): 708.46MM **Privately Held**
Web: www.scripps.org
SIC: 8062 General medical and surgical
hospitals

(P-16188)
SCRIPPS MMRAL-XIMED MED
CTR LP
Also Called: Scripps Health
9850 Genesee Ave Ste 900, La Jolla
(92037-1220)
PHONE..................................858 882-8350
Brian Huizar, *Prin*
EMP: 118 **EST:** 1991
SALES (est): 17.9MM **Privately Held**
SIC: 8062 8049 General medical and
surgical hospitals; Physical therapist

(P-16189)
SGRY LLC
Also Called: Specialty Sugical Ctr Encino
16501 Ventura Blvd Ste 103, Encino
(91436-2064)
PHONE..................................818 501-1080
Michael Roub, *Brnch Mgr*
EMP: 149
Web: www.surgerypartners.com
SIC: 8062 General medical and surgical
hospitals
HQ: Sgry, Llc
340 Seven Springs Way
Brentwood TN 37027
615 234-5900

(P-16190)
SHARP CHULA VISTA MEDICAL
CTR

8695 Spectrum Center Blvd, San Diego
(92123-1489)
PHONE..................................858 499-5150
Chris Boyd, *CEO*
EMP: 99 **EST:** 2007
SALES (est): 2.23MM **Privately Held**
Web: www.sharp.com
SIC: 8062 General medical and surgical
hospitals

(P-16191)
SHARP CHULA VISTA MEDICAL
CTR
Also Called: Sharp Chula Vista Medical Ctr
751 Medical Center Ct, Chula Vista
(91911-6617)
PHONE..................................619 502-5800
Chris Boyd, *CEO*
Michael Murphy, *
Rick King, *
EMP: 1600 **EST:** 1944
SQ FT: 270,205
SALES (est): 503.43MM
SALES (corp-wide): 1.9B **Privately Held**
Web: www.sharp.com
SIC: 8062 General medical and surgical
hospitals
PA: Sharp Healthcare
8695 Spectrum Ctr Blvd
858 499-4000

(P-16192)
SHARP CORONADO HOSPITAL
& HEALTHCARE CENTER
Also Called: Coronado Hospital
250 Prospect Pl, Coronado (92118-1943)
PHONE..................................619 522-3600
EMP: 550 **EST:** 1938
SALES (est): 170.94MM
SALES (corp-wide): 1.9B **Privately Held**
Web: www.sharp.com
SIC: 8062 General medical and surgical
hospitals
PA: Sharp Healthcare
8695 Spectrum Ctr Blvd
858 499-4000

(P-16193)
SHARP HEALTHCARE
Also Called: Birch Ptrick Convalescent Cntr
751 Medical Center Ct, Chula Vista
(91911-6617)
PHONE..................................858 499-2000
Lily Reyes, *Dir*
EMP: 151
SALES (corp-wide): 1.9B **Privately Held**
Web: www.sharp.com
SIC: 8062 General medical and surgical
hospitals
PA: Sharp Healthcare
8695 Spectrum Ctr Blvd
858 499-4000

(P-16194)
SHARP HEALTHCARE
Also Called: Sharp Rees-Stealy
8008 Frost St Ste 106, San Diego
(92123-4229)
PHONE..................................858 939-5434
EMP: 159
SALES (corp-wide): 1.9B **Privately Held**
Web: www.sharp.com
SIC: 8062 General medical and surgical
hospitals
PA: Sharp Healthcare
8695 Spectrum Ctr Blvd
858 499-4000

(P-16195)
SHARP HEALTHCARE ACO LLC
Also Called: Sharp Rees-Stealy Div
300 Fir St, San Diego (92101-2327)
PHONE..................................619 446-1575
Donna Mills, *Admn*
EMP: 291
SQ FT: 61,608
SALES (corp-wide): 1.9B **Privately Held**
Web: www.sharp.com
SIC: 8062 General medical and surgical
hospitals
PA: Sharp Healthcare
8695 Spectrum Ctr Blvd
858 499-4000

(P-16196)
SHARP HEALTHCARE ACO LLC
Also Called: Sharp Health Care
3554 Ruffin Rd Ste Soca, San Diego
(92123-2596)
PHONE..................................858 627-5152
Alison Fleury, *Brnch Mgr*
EMP: 789
SALES (corp-wide): 1.9B **Privately Held**
Web: www.sharp.com
SIC: 8062 General medical and surgical
hospitals
PA: Sharp Healthcare
8695 Spectrum Ctr Blvd
858 499-4000

(P-16197)
SHARP MARY BIRCH H
3003 Health Center Dr, San Diego
(92123-2700)
PHONE..................................858 939-3400
Trisha Khaleghi, *CEO*
EMP: 99 **EST:** 2004
SALES (est): 5.31MM **Privately Held**
Web: www.sharp.com
SIC: 8062 General medical and surgical
hospitals

(P-16198)
SHARP MEMORIAL HOSPITAL
(HQ)
7901 Frost St, San Diego (92123-2786)
PHONE..................................858 939-3636
Tim Smith, *CEO*
▲ **EMP:** 3000 **EST:** 1957
SALES (est): 1.54B
SALES (corp-wide): 1.9B **Privately Held**
Web: www.sharp.com
SIC: 8062 General medical and surgical
hospitals
PA: Sharp Healthcare
8695 Spectrum Ctr Blvd
858 499-4000

(P-16199)
SIERRA VISTA HOSPITAL INC
(HQ)
Also Called: Sierra Vista Regional Med Ctr
1010 Murray Ave, San Luis Obispo
(93405-8801)
P.O. Box 1367 (93406-1367)
PHONE..................................805 546-7600
Joseph Deschryver, *CEO*
Candace Markwith, *
Richard Phillips, *
Rollie Pirkl, *
Michael Keleman, *
EMP: 575 **EST:** 1968
SQ FT: 138,690
SALES (est): 150.01MM
SALES (corp-wide): 19.17B **Publicly Held**
Web: www.adventisthealth.org
SIC: 8062 General medical and surgical
hospitals

PA: Tenet Healthcare Corporation
14201 Dallas Pkwy
469 893-2000

(P-16200)
SIMI VLY HOSP & HLTH CARE SVCS

Also Called: Aspen Surgery Center
2750 Sycamore Dr, Simi Valley
(93065-1502)
PHONE...............805 955-6000
EMP: 548
SALES (corp-wide): 805.07MM Privately Held
Web: www.simivalleyhospital.com
SIC: 8062 General medical and surgical hospitals
HQ: Simi Valley Hospital And Health Care Services
2975 N Sycamore Dr
Simi Valley CA 93065

(P-16201)
SIMI VLY HOSP & HLTH CARE SVCS (HQ)

Also Called: Simi Vly Hosp & Hlth Care Svcs
2975 Sycamore Dr, Simi Valley
(93065-1201)
PHONE...............805 955-6000
Margaret Peterson, Pr
Caroline Esparza, *
Clif Patten, *
EMP: 242 EST: 1960
SALES (est): 199.33MM
SALES (corp-wide): 805.07MM Privately Held
Web: www.simivalleyhospital.com
SIC: 8062 General medical and surgical hospitals
PA: Adventist Health System/West, Corporation
One Adventist Health Way
844 574-5686

(P-16202)
SOUTHERN CAL HALTHCARE SYS INC

Also Called: Southern Cal Hosp At Culver Cy
3828 Delmas Ter, Culver City (90232-2713)
PHONE...............310 836-7000
EMP: 74
SALES (corp-wide): 3.91B Privately Held
Web: www.sch-culvercity.com
SIC: 8062 General medical and surgical hospitals
HQ: Southern California Healthcare System, Inc.
3415 S Sepulveda Blvd 9thf
Los Angeles CA 90034

(P-10203)
SOUTHERN CAL HALTHCARE SYS INC (HQ)

3415 S Sepulveda Blvd 9th Fl, Los Angeles
(90034-6060)
PHONE...............310 943-4500
David R Topper, *
EMP: 189 EST: 1998
SALES (est): 42.18MM
SALES (corp-wide): 3.91B Privately Held
SIC: 8062 General medical and surgical hospitals
PA: Prospect Medical Holdings, Inc.
3415 S Sepulveda Blvd
310 943-4500

(P-16204)
SOUTHERN CAL PRMNNTE MED GROUP

Also Called: Kaiser Permanente
9353 Imperial Hwy Garden Medical Bldg Flr 3, Downey (90242-2812)
PHONE...............562 657-2200
EMP: 581
SALES (corp-wide): 70.8B Privately Held
Web: healthy.kaiserpermanente.org
SIC: 8062 General medical and surgical hospitals
HQ: Southern California Permanente Medical Group
393 Walnut Dr
Pasadena CA 91107
626 405-5704

(P-16205)
SOUTHERN CAL PRMNNTE MED GROUP

3830 Martin Luther King Jr Blvd, Lynwood
(90262-3625)
PHONE...............310 604-5700
EMP: 133
SALES (corp-wide): 70.8B Privately Held
Web: thrive.kaiserpermanente.org
SIC: 8062 General medical and surgical hospitals
HQ: Southern California Permanente Medical Group
393 Walnut Dr
Pasadena CA 91107
626 405-5704

(P-16206)
SOUTHERN CAL PRMNNTE MED GROUP

26415 Carl Boyer Dr, Santa Clarita
(91350-5824)
PHONE...............661 290-3100
EMP: 214
SALES (corp-wide): 70.8B Privately Held
Web: www.permanente.org
SIC: 8062 General medical and surgical hospitals
HQ: Southern California Permanente Medical Group
393 Walnut Dr
Pasadena CA 91107
626 405-5704

(P-16207)
SOUTHERN CAL PRMNNTE MED GROUP

Also Called: S C P M G
9961 Sierra Ave, Fontana (92335-6720)
PHONE...............909 427-5000
Gerald Mccall, Brnch Mgr
EMP: 454
SALES (corp-wide): 70.8B Privately Held
Web: www.permanente.org
SIC: 8062 General medical and surgical hospitals
HQ: Southern California Permanente Medical Group
393 Walnut Dr
Pasadena CA 91107
626 405-5704

(P-16208)
SOUTHERN CAL SPCIALTY CARE INC

Also Called: Kindred Hospital La Mirata
845 N Lark Ellen Ave, West Covina
(91791-1069)
PHONE...............626 339-5451
Nenda Estudillo, Dir
EMP: 250
SQ FT: 34,082
SALES (corp-wide): 14.03B Privately Held
Web: www.kindredhospitals.com

SIC: 8062 General medical and surgical hospitals
HQ: Southern California Specialty Care, Llc
14900 E Imperial Hwy
La Mirada CA 90638

(P-16209)
SOUTHERN CAL SPCIALTY CARE INC

Also Called: Kindred Hospital Santa Ana
1901 College Ave, Santa Ana (92706-2334)
PHONE...............714 564-7800
Rich Mccarthy, Prin
EMP: 250
SALES (corp-wide): 14.03B Privately Held
Web: www.kindredhospitals.com
SIC: 8062 General medical and surgical hospitals
HQ: Southern California Specialty Care, Llc
14900 E Imperial Hwy
La Mirada CA 90638

(P-16210)
SOUTHERN CAL SPCIALTY CARE LLC (DH)

Also Called: Kindred Hospital La Mirada
14900 Imperial Hwy, La Mirada
(90638-2172)
PHONE...............562 944-1900
Ty Richardson, Pr
Robin Rapp, Admn
Judie Sheldon, CCO
George Burkley, COO
EMP: 100 EST: 1994
SQ FT: 74,074
SALES (est): 103.16MM
SALES (corp-wide): 14.03B Privately Held
Web: www.kindredhospitals.com
SIC: 8062 General medical and surgical hospitals
HQ: Specialty Healthcare Services, Inc
680 S 4th St
Louisville KY 40202
502 596-7300

(P-16211)
SOUTHWEST HEALTHCARE SYS AUX

Also Called: Business Department
38977 Sky Canyon Dr Ste 200, Murrieta
(92563-2682)
PHONE...............800 404-6627
Paula Dalbeck, Contrlr
EMP: 712
SALES (corp-wide): 14.28B Publicly Held
Web: www.southwesthealthcare.com
SIC: 8062 General medical and surgical hospitals
HQ: Southwest Healthcare System Auxiliary
25500 Medical Center Dr
Murrieta CA 92562

(P-16212)
SOUTHWEST HEALTHCARE SYS AUX (HQ)

Also Called: Rancho Springs Medical Center
25500 Medical Center Dr, Murrieta
(92562-5965)
PHONE...............951 696-6000
Brad Neet, CEO
Diane Moon, *
Barry Thorfenson, *
▲ EMP: 450 EST: 1989
SALES (est): 72.54K
SALES (corp-wide): 14.28B Publicly Held
Web: www.swranchosprings.com
SIC: 8062 8051 8059 4119 General medical and surgical hospitals; Skilled nursing care facilities; Convalescent home; Ambulance service

PA: Universal Health Services, Inc.
367 S Gulph Rd
610 768-3300

(P-16213)
ST BERNARDINE MED CTR AUX INC

Also Called: Inland Empire Heart Institute
2101 N Waterman Ave, San Bernardino
(92404-4836)
PHONE...............909 881-4320
TOLL FREE: 877
Ed Langden, Dir
EMP: 107
Web: www.dignityhealth.org
SIC: 8062 General medical and surgical hospitals
HQ: St. Bernardine Medical Center Auxiliary, Inc.
2101 N Waterman Ave
San Bernardino CA 92404
909 883-8711

(P-16214)
ST JOSEPH HOSPITAL OF ORANGE (DH)

Also Called: PROVIDENCE HOME HEALTH ORANGE
1100 W Stewart Dr, Orange (92868-3891)
P.O. Box 5600 (92863-5600)
PHONE...............714 633-9111
Larry K Ainsworth, Pr
Jim Cora, *
Warren D Johnson, *
Tina Nycroft, *
Martin J Feldman, Chief of Staff*
EMP: 2100 EST: 1929
SQ FT: 448,000
SALES (est): 669.42MM
SALES (corp-wide): 55.69MM Privately Held
Web: www.sjo.org
SIC: 8062 General medical and surgical hospitals
HQ: St. Joseph Health System
3345 Michaelson Dr #100
Irvine CA 92612
949 381-4000

(P-16215)
ST JOSEPH HOSPITAL OF ORANGE

Also Called: Business Office
3345 Michelson Dr Ste 100, Irvine
(92612-0693)
PHONE...............714 568-5500
Marina Lopez, Mgr
EMP: 208
SALES (corp-wide): 55.69MM Privately Held
Web: www.sjo.org
SIC: 8062 General medical and surgical hospitals
HQ: St. Joseph Hospital Of Orange
1100 W Stewart Dr
Orange CA 92868
714 633-9111

(P-16216)
ST JOSEPH HOSPITAL OF ORANGE

Also Called: Renal Center
1100 W Stewart Dr, Orange (92868-3891)
P.O. Box 5600 (92863-5600)
PHONE...............714 771-8037
Mary Mckenzie, Dir
EMP: 119
SALES (corp-wide): 55.69MM Privately Held
Web: www.sjo.org

PRODUCTS & SVCS

SIC: 8062 General medical and surgical
hospitals
HQ: St. Joseph Hospital Of Orange
1100 W Stewart Dr
Orange CA 92868
714 633-9111

(P-16217)
**ST JOSEPH HOSPITAL OF
ORANGE**
Also Called: St Josephs Physical Rehab Svcs
1310 W Stewart Dr Ste 203, Orange
(92868-3837)
PHONE..................................714 771-8222
Paul Pursell, *Ex Dir*
EMP: 134
SALES (corp-wide): 55.69MM **Privately
Held**
Web: www.sjo.org
SIC: 8062 8322 General medical and
surgical hospitals; Rehabilitation services
HQ: St. Joseph Hospital Of Orange
1100 W Stewart Dr
Orange CA 92868
714 633-9111

(P-16218)
**ST JOSEPH HOSPITAL OF
ORANGE**
Also Called: Information Systems
363 S Main St Ste 211, Orange
(92868-3825)
PHONE..................................714 771-8006
Dennise Masiello, *Dir*
EMP: 134
SQ FT: 15,605
SALES (corp-wide): 55.69MM **Privately
Held**
Web: www.sjo.org
SIC: 8062 General medical and surgical
hospitals
HQ: St. Joseph Hospital Of Orange
1100 W Stewart Dr
Orange CA 92868
714 633-9111

(P-16219)
ST JUDE HOSPITAL (DH)
Also Called: PROVIDENCE HOME HEALTH
ORANGE
101 E Valencia Mesa Dr, Fullerton
(92835-3875)
PHONE..................................714 871-3280
TOLL FREE: 800
Robert Fraschetti, *Pr*
Lee Penrose, *
Doreen Dann, *
▲ EMP: 2582 EST: 1942
SQ FT: 190,000
SALES (est): 620.21MM
SALES (corp-wide): 55.69MM **Privately
Held**
Web: www.stjudemedicalcenter.org
SIC: 8062 General medical and surgical
hospitals
HQ: St. Joseph Health System
3345 Michaelson Dr #100
Irvine CA 92612
949 381-4000

(P-16220)
**ST MARY MEDICAL CENTER
(DH)**
Also Called: St Mary's School Of Nursing
1050 Linden Ave, Long Beach
(90813-3393)
P.O. Box 887 (90801-0887)
PHONE..................................562 491-9000
Trammie Mcmann, *CEO*
Tammie Mcmann, *CEO*

Ed S Engessers, *
Alan Garrett, *
Tiffany Caster, *
EMP: 1929 EST: 1924
SQ FT: 700,000
SALES (est): 387.5MM **Privately Held**
Web: www.stmarymed.com
SIC: 8062 Hospital, med school affiliated
with nursing and residency
HQ: Dignity Health
185 Berry St Ste 200
San Francisco CA 94107
415 438-5500

(P-16221)
**ST MARY MEDICAL CENTER
LLC (HQ)**
18300 Us Highway 18, Apple Valley
(92307-2206)
PHONE..................................760 242-2311
David Klein, *Pr*
Marilyn Drone, *
Tracey Fernandez, *
Kelly Linden, *
Judy Wagner, *
EMP: 217 EST: 1956
SQ FT: 92,000
SALES (est): 403.72MM
SALES (corp-wide): 55.69MM **Privately
Held**
Web: www.stmaryapplevalley.com
SIC: 8062 General medical and surgical
hospitals
PA: Providence St. Joseph Health
1801 Lind Ave Sw
425 525-3355

(P-16222)
**ST MARY MEDICAL CENTER
LLC**
Also Called: Materals MGT At St Mary Med Ct
16000 Kasota Rd, Apple Valley
(92307-2208)
P.O. Box 7025 (92307-0731)
PHONE..................................760 946-8767
Leland Glisson, *Mgr*
EMP: 1133
SALES (corp-wide): 55.69MM **Privately
Held**
Web: www.stmaryapplevalley.com
SIC: 8062 General medical and surgical
hospitals
HQ: St. Mary Medical Center, Llc
18300 Us Highway 18
Apple Valley CA 92307
760 242-2311

(P-16223)
TEAM HEALTH HOLDINGS INC
Also Called: Sharp Grssmont Hosp Emrgncy
Ca
5555 Grossmont Center Dr, La Mesa
(91942-3019)
PHONE..................................619 740-4401
EMP: 1766
SALES (corp-wide): 3.6B **Privately Held**
Web: www.sharp.com
SIC: 8062 General medical and surgical
hospitals
HQ: Team Health Holdings, Inc.
265 Brkview Cntre Way Ste
Knoxville TN 37919
865 693-1000

(P-16224)
**TEMECULA VALLEY HOSPITAL
INC**
Also Called: UHS
31700 Temecula Pkwy, Temecula
(92592-5896)

P.O. Box 61558 (19406-0958)
PHONE..................................951 331-2200
Marvin Pember, *CEO*
Neil Colica, *Chief Nurse*
Barry Thornfinnson, *
Laura Culbertson, *
Marcia Jackson, *
EMP: 440 EST: 2012
SALES (est): 237.98MM
SALES (corp-wide): 14.28B **Publicly Held**
Web: www.temeculavalleyhospital.com
SIC: 8062 General medical and surgical
hospitals
PA: Universal Health Services, Inc.
367 S Gulph Rd
610 768-3300

(P-16225)
**TEMPLE HOSPITAL
CORPORATION**
Also Called: Temple Community Hospital
242 N Hoover St, Los Angeles
(90004-3628)
PHONE..................................213 355-3200
EMP: 350
Web: www.templecommunityhospital.com
SIC: 8062 General medical and surgical
hospitals

(P-16226)
**TENET HEALTH SYSTEMS
NORRIS**
Also Called: KENNETH NORRIS CANCER
HOSPITAL
1441 Eastlake Ave, Los Angeles
(90089-1019)
PHONE..................................323 865-3000
Scott Evans, *CEO*
Strawn Steele, *
EMP: 352 EST: 1982
SQ FT: 175,000
SALES (est): 280.59MM **Privately Held**
Web: www.keckmedicine.org
SIC: 8062 General medical and surgical
hospitals

(P-16227)
**TENET HEALTHSYSTEM
MEDICAL INC**
Also Called: Irvine Regional Hospital
1400 S Douglass Rd Ste 250, Anaheim
(92806-6907)
PHONE..................................714 428-6800
Donald Lorack, *CEO*
EMP: 344
SALES (corp-wide): 19.17B **Publicly Held**
Web: www.tenethealth.com
SIC: 8062 General medical and surgical
hospitals
HQ: Tenet Healthsystem Medical, Inc.
14201 Dallas Pkwy
Dallas TX 75254
469 893-2000

(P-16228)
**THOUSAND OAKS SURGICAL
HOSP LP**
401 Rolling Oaks Dr, Thousand Oaks
(91361-1050)
PHONE..................................805 777-7750
Micheal Bass, *Pt*
EMP: 100 EST: 1999
SQ FT: 50,000
SALES (est): 9.4MM **Privately Held**
Web: www.losrobleshospital.com
SIC: 8062 General medical and surgical
hospitals

(P-16229)
**TORRANCE HEALTH ASSN INC
(PA)**
Also Called: Physician Office Support Svcs
3330 Lomita Blvd, Torrance (90505-5002)
P.O. Box 13717 (90503-0717)
PHONE..................................310 325-9110
John Mcnamara, *Sr VP*
Bill Larson, *
Sally Eberhard, *
Bernadette Reid, *
EMP: 3000 EST: 1985
SQ FT: 180,000
SALES (est): 913.85MM **Privately Held**
Web: www.thipa.org
SIC: 8062 General medical and surgical
hospitals

(P-16230)
**TORRANCE MEMORIAL
MEDICAL CTR (HQ)**
3330 Lomita Blvd, Torrance (90505-5073)
PHONE..................................310 325-9110
Keith Hobbs, *Pr*
EMP: 1500 EST: 1925
SALES (est): 839.79MM **Privately Held**
Web: www.torrancememorial.org
SIC: 8062 Hospital, affiliated with AMA
residency
PA: Torrance Health Association, Inc.
3330 Lomita Blvd

(P-16231)
**TORRANCE MEMORIAL
MEDICAL CTR**
Also Called: Torrance Memorial Breast Diagn
855 Manhattan Beach Blvd Ste 208,
Manhattan Beach (90266-4965)
PHONE..................................310 939-7847
Shireen Alwani, *Brnch Mgr*
EMP: 422
Web: www.torrancememorial.org
SIC: 8062 General medical and surgical
hospitals
HQ: Torrance Memorial Medical Center
3330 Lomita Blvd
Torrance CA 90505
310 325-9110

(P-16232)
**TORRANCE MEMORIAL
MEDICAL CTR**
3333 Skypark Dr Ste 200, Torrance
(90505-5035)
PHONE..................................310 784-6316
EMP: 493
Web: www.torrancememorial.org
SIC: 8062 General medical and surgical
hospitals
HQ: Torrance Memorial Medical Center
3330 Lomita Blvd
Torrance CA 90505
310 325-9110

(P-16233)
**TORRANCE MEMORIAL
MEDICAL CTR**
22411 Hawthorne Blvd, Torrance
(90505-2507)
PHONE..................................310 784-3740
EMP: 352
Web: www.torrancememorial.org
SIC: 8062 Hospital, affiliated with AMA
residency
HQ: Torrance Memorial Medical Center
3330 Lomita Blvd
Torrance CA 90505
310 325-9110

(P-16234)
TUSTIN HOSPITAL AND MEDICAL CENTER
Also Called: Newport Specialty Hospital
3699 Wilshire Blvd Ste 540, Los Angeles
(90010-2723)
PHONE..............................714 619-7700
EMP: 360
SIC: **8062** General medical and surgical hospitals

(P-16235)
UC SAN DEGO HLTH ACCNTBLE CARE (DH)
Also Called: Jacobs Med Ctr At Uc San Dego
9300 Campus Point Dr, La Jolla
(92037-1300)
PHONE..............................858 657-7000
Paul Viviano, *CEO*
Linda Olson, *Pr*
Karandeep Singh, *HEALTH ARTIFICIAL INTELLIGENCE*
EMP: 148 **EST:** 2013
SALES (est): 203.76MM
SALES (corp-wide): 534.4MM **Privately Held**
Web: health.ucsd.edu
SIC: **8062** General medical and surgical hospitals
HQ: University Of California, San Diego
9500 Gilman Dr
La Jolla CA 92093
858 534-2230

(P-16236)
UCLA HEALTH
Also Called: Ronald Reagan Building
757 Westwood Plz, Los Angeles
(90095-8358)
PHONE..............................310 825-9111
Doctor David T Feinberg, *CEO*
EMP: 211 **EST:** 2012
SALES (est): 38.12MM **Privately Held**
Web: www.uclahealth.org
SIC: **8062** General medical and surgical hospitals

(P-16237)
UCLA HEALTHCARE
1821 Wilshire Blvd Fl 6, Santa Monica
(90403-5618)
PHONE..............................310 319-4560
Tami Dennis, *Ex Dir*
EMP: 77 **EST:** 2007
SALES (est): 14.74MM
SALES (corp-wide): 534.4MM **Privately Held**
Web: www.ucla.edu
SIC: **8062** 9411 General medical and surgical hospitals; Administration of educational programs
HQ: University Of California, Los Angeles
405 Hilgard Ave
Los Angeles CA 90095

(P-16238)
UHS-CORONA INC (HQ)
Also Called: Corona Regional Med Ctr Hosp
800 S Main St, Corona (92882-3420)
PHONE..............................951 737-4343
Marvin Pember, *CEO*
Ken Rivers, *
Alan B Miller, *
Kevan Metcalf, *
▲ EMP: 900 **EST:** 1978
SALES (est): 220.6MM
SALES (corp-wide): 14.28B **Publicly Held**
Web: www.coronaregional.com
SIC: **8062** General medical and surgical hospitals

PA: Universal Health Services, Inc.
367 S Gulph Rd
610 768-3300

(P-16239)
UNITED STATES DEPT OF NAVY
Also Called: Naval Medical Center
34800 Bob Wilson Dr, San Diego
(92134-1098)
PHONE..............................619 532-6400
Esther Lynn, *Brnch Mgr*
EMP: 4250
Web: www.navy.mil
SIC: **8062** 9711 General medical and surgical hospitals; Navy
HQ: United States Department Of The Navy
1200 Navy Pentagon
Washington DC 20350

(P-16240)
UNIVERSITY CAL LOS ANGELES
Also Called: Ronald Reagan Ucla Medical Ctr
757 Westwood Plz, Los Angeles
(90095-8358)
PHONE..............................310 825-9111
Tatiana Orloff, *Brnch Mgr*
EMP: 2056
SALES (corp-wide): 534.4MM **Privately Held**
Web: www.uclahealth.org
SIC: **8062** 8221 9411 General medical and surgical hospitals; University; Administration of educational programs
HQ: University Of California, Los Angeles
405 Hilgard Ave
Los Angeles CA 90095

(P-16241)
UNIVERSITY CAL SAN DIEGO
Also Called: Medical Center
200 W Arbor Dr Frnt, San Diego
(92103-9000)
PHONE..............................619 543-6654
Richard Likeweg, *Mgr*
EMP: 4000
SALES (corp-wide): 534.4MM **Privately Held**
Web: www.ucsd.edu
SIC: **8062** 8221 9411 General medical and surgical hospitals; University; Administration of educational programs
HQ: University Of California, San Diego
9500 Gilman Dr
La Jolla CA 92093
858 534-2230

(P-16242)
UNIVERSITY CAL SAN DIEGO
Also Called: Ucsd Thornton Hospital
9300 Campus Point Dr, La Jolla
(92037-1300)
P.O. Box 409 (92075-0409)
PHONE..............................858 657-7000
Paul Hensler, *Dir*
EMP: 1704
SALES (corp-wide): 534.4MM **Privately Held**
Web: www.ucsd.edu
SIC: **8062** 8221 9411 General medical and surgical hospitals; University; Administration of educational programs
HQ: University Of California, San Diego
9500 Gilman Dr
La Jolla CA 92093
858 534-2230

(P-16243)
UNIVERSITY CAL SAN DIEGO
Also Called: U C S D Medical Center
402 Dickinson St Ste 380, San Diego
(92103-6902)

PHONE..............................619 543-6170
Doctor Kenneth Kaushkay, *Ch*
EMP: 211
SALES (corp-wide): 534.4MM **Privately Held**
Web: www.ucsd.edu
SIC: **8062** 8221 9411 General medical and surgical hospitals; University; Administration of educational programs
HQ: University Of California, San Diego
9500 Gilman Dr
La Jolla CA 92093
858 534-2230

(P-16244)
UNIVERSITY CALIFORNIA IRVINE
Also Called: Uc Irvine Medical Center
101 The City Dr S, Orange (92868-3201)
PHONE..............................714 456-6011
Mary Piccione, *Ex Dir*
EMP: 3000
SALES (corp-wide): 534.4MM **Privately Held**
Web: www.ucihealth.org
SIC: **8062** 8221 9411 General medical and surgical hospitals; University; Administration of educational programs, State government
HQ: University Of California, Irvine
510 Aldrich Hall
Irvine CA 92697
949 824-5011

(P-16245)
UNIVERSITY CALIFORNIA IRVINE
Also Called: Irvine Medical Center
200 S Manchester Ave Ste 400, Orange
(92868-3220)
PHONE..............................714 456-5558
Joy Grosse, *Dir*
EMP: 102
SALES (corp-wide): 534.4MM **Privately Held**
Web: law.uci.edu
SIC: **8062** 8221 9411 General medical and surgical hospitals; University; Administration of educational programs
HQ: University Of California, Irvine
510 Aldrich Hall
Irvine CA 92697
949 824-5011

(P-16246)
UNIVERSITY CALIFORNIA IRVINE
Also Called: UCI Cancer Center
101 The City Dr S, Orange (92868-3201)
PHONE..............................714 456-8000
Michael Lekawa, *Pr*
EMP: 663
SALES (corp-wide): 534.4MM **Privately Held**
Web: www.uciurology.com
SIC: **8062** General medical and surgical hospitals
HQ: University Of California, Irvine
510 Aldrich Hall
Irvine CA 92697
949 824-5011

(P-16247)
UNIVERSITY CALIFORNIA IRVINE
Also Called: UCI Westminster Medical Center
15355 Brookhurst St Ste 102, Westminster
(92683-7071)
PHONE..............................714 775-3066
TOLL FREE: 888

Nhu Ngo, *Mgr*
EMP: 195
SALES (corp-wide): 534.4MM **Privately Held**
Web: www.uci.edu
SIC: **8062** 8221 9411 General medical and surgical hospitals; University; Administration of educational programs
HQ: University Of California, Irvine
510 Aldrich Hall
Irvine CA 92697
949 824-5011

(P-16248)
UNIVERSITY SOUTHERN CALIFORNIA
Also Called: Usc University Hospital
1500 San Pablo St, Los Angeles
(90033-5313)
PHONE..............................323 442-8500
Paul Vivano, *Dir*
EMP: 875
SALES (corp-wide): 7.46B **Privately Held**
Web: www.usc.edu
SIC: **8062** 8011 General medical and surgical hospitals; Offices and clinics of medical doctors
PA: University Of Southern California
3551 Trsdale Pkwy Ste 102
213 740-2101

(P-16249)
USC ARCADIA HOSPITAL (PA)
Also Called: METHODIST HOSPITAL
300 W Huntington Dr, Arcadia
(91007-3402)
PHONE..............................626 898-8000
TOLL FREE: 800
Ikenna Mmeje, *Pr*
Steven A Sisto, *
William E Grigg, *
Clifford R Daniels, *
EMP: 933 **EST:** 1903
SQ FT: 100,000
SALES (est): 305.97MM
SALES (corp-wide): 305.97MM **Privately Held**
Web: www.uscarcadiahospital.org
SIC: **8062** General medical and surgical hospitals

(P-16250)
USC VERDUGO HILLS HOSPITAL LLC
1812 Verdugo Blvd, Glendale (91208-1409)
PHONE..............................818 790-7100
Armand Dorian, *CEO*
Debbie Walsh, *
Cynthia Trousdale, *
Thomas Jackiewicz, *
Ilack Lash, *
EMP: 750 **EST:** 2013
SQ FT: 45,000
SALES (est): 43.18MM
SALES (corp-wide): 7.46B **Privately Held**
Web: www.uscvhh.org
SIC: **8062** Hospital, affiliated with AMA residency
PA: University Of Southern California
3551 Trsdale Pkwy Ste 102
213 740-2101

(P-16251)
USC VRDUGO HLLS HOSP FUNDATION (HQ)
Also Called: U S C
1812 Verdugo Blvd, Glendale (91208-1409)
PHONE..............................800 872-2273
TOLL FREE: 800
Paul Craig, *CEO*

Debbie L Walsh, *Pr*
EMP: 446 **EST:** 1947
SQ FT: 225,000
SALES (est): 891.27K
SALES (corp-wide): 7.46B **Privately Held**
Web: www.keckmedicine.org
SIC: 8062 General medical and surgical
hospitals
PA: University Of Southern California
3551 Trsdale Pkwy Ste 102
213 740-2101

(P-16252)
VALLEY HOSPITAL MEDICAL CENTER FOUNDATION
Also Called: Calex
18300 Roscoe Blvd, Northridge
(91325-4105)
PHONE..................818 885-8500
EMP: 1000
Web: www.dignityhealth.org
SIC: 8062 General medical and surgical
hospitals

(P-16253)
VALLEY PRESBYTERIAN HOSPITAL
Also Called: V P H
15107 Vanowen St, Van Nuys
(91405-4597)
PHONE..................818 782-6600
Gustavo Valdespino, *CEO*
Ray Moss, *CIO*
Michelle Quigley, *VP*
Jean Rico, *Sr VP*
Norma Resneder, *Sr VP*
EMP: 1600 **EST:** 1948
SQ FT: 400,000
SALES (est): 481.61MM **Privately Held**
Web: www.valleypres.org
SIC: 8062 General medical and surgical
hospitals

(P-16254)
VERDUGO HILLS HOSPITAL INC
1812 Verdugo Blvd, Glendale (91208-1409)
PHONE..................818 790-7100
Leonard Labella, *Pr*
EMP: 144 **EST:** 1947
SALES (est): 162.4MM **Privately Held**
Web: www.uscvhh.org
SIC: 8062 Hospital, affiliated with AMA
residency

(P-16255)
VERITAS HEALTH SERVICES INC
Also Called: Chino Valley Medical Center
5451 Walnut Ave, Chino (91710-2609)
PHONE..................909 464-8600
Parrish Scarboro, *CEO*
Irv E Edwards, *
EMP: 600 **EST:** 2000
SALES (est): 106.21MM
SALES (corp-wide): 878.52MM **Privately
Held**
Web: www.cvmc.com
SIC: 8062 General medical and surgical
hospitals
HQ: Prime Healthcare Services Inc
3480 E Guasti Rd
Ontario CA 91761

(P-16256)
VIBRA HEALTHCARE LLC
Also Called: Vibra Hospital of San Diego
555 Washington St, San Diego
(92103-2289)
PHONE..................619 260-8300

TOLL FREE: 800
Meeta Jones, *CEO*
EMP: 156
SALES (corp-wide): 434.59MM **Privately
Held**
Web: www.vibrahealthcare.com
SIC: 8062 8069 8322 General medical and
surgical hospitals; Specialty hospitals,
except psychiatric; Rehabilitation services
PA: Vibra Healthcare, Llc
4600 Lena Dr
717 591-5700

(P-16257)
VICTOR VLY HOSP ACQISITION INC
Also Called: Victor Valley Global Med Ctr
15248 Eleventh St, Victorville (92395-3787)
PHONE..................760 245-8691
Suzanne Richards, *CEO*
EMP: 78 **EST:** 2010
SALES (est): 44.28MM **Privately Held**
Web:
www.victorvalleyglobalmedicalcenter.com
SIC: 8062 General medical and surgical
hospitals
HQ: Kpc Healthcare, Inc.
1301 N Tustin Ave
Santa Ana CA 92705
714 953-3652

(P-16258)
VINCENT-HAYLEY ENTERPRISES INC
Also Called: St Vincent Health Care
1810 N Fair Oaks Ave, Pasadena
(91103-1619)
PHONE..................626 398-8182
Rob Barrett, *Pr*
Cipriano Baustista, *
EMP: 75 **EST:** 1990
SALES (est): 11.28MM **Privately Held**
SIC: 8062 General medical and surgical
hospitals

(P-16259)
WHITE MEMORIAL MEDICAL CENTER (HQ)
Also Called: CECILLA GONZALEZ DE AL
HOYA CA
1720 E Cesar E Chavez Ave, Los Angeles
(90033-2481)
PHONE..................323 268-5000
Beth D Zachary, *CEO*
Terri Day, *
John G Raffoul, *
Roland Fargo, *
Mary Anne Chern, *
EMP: 1200 **EST:** 1913
SQ FT: 454,000
SALES (est): 491.61MM
SALES (corp-wide): 805.07MM **Privately
Held**
Web: www.adventisthealth.org
SIC: 8062 General medical and surgical
hospitals
PA: Adventist Health System/West,
Corporation
One Adventist Health Way
844 574-5686

(P-16260)
WHITTIER HOSPITAL MED CTR INC
9080 Colima Rd, Whittier (90605-1600)
PHONE..................562 945-3561
Richard Castro, *CEO*
EMP: 180 **EST:** 1962
SQ FT: 144,000
SALES (est): 24.76MM

SALES (corp-wide): 325.41MM **Privately
Held**
Web: www.ahmchealth.com
SIC: 8062 General medical and surgical
hospitals
PA: Ahmc Healthcare Inc.
506 W Valley Blvd Ste 300
626 943-7526

8063 Psychiatric Hospitals

(P-16261)
ALISO RDGE BEHAVIORAL HLTH LLC
Also Called: Aliso Ridge Behavioral Health
200 Freedom Ln, Aliso Viejo (92656-5876)
PHONE..................949 415-9218
Phillip Franks, *Managing Member*
EMP: 95 **EST:** 2016
SALES (est): 9.57MM **Privately Held**
Web: www.ocspecialtyhealth.com
SIC: 8063 Psychiatric hospitals

(P-16262)
ALTA HLLYWOOD CMNTY HOSP VAN N
14433 Emelita St, Van Nuys (91401-4213)
PHONE..................818 787-1511
Irving Loube, *Pr*
Claude Lowen, *
EMP: 517 **EST:** 1969
SQ FT: 34,192
SALES (est): 2.3MM
SALES (corp-wide): 3.91B **Privately Held**
Web: www.sch-vannuys.com
SIC: 8063 Psychiatric hospitals
HQ: Southern California Healthcare
System, Inc.
3415 S Sepulveda Blvd 9thf
Los Angeles CA 90034

(P-16263)
AURORA - SAN DIEGO LLC (DH)
Also Called: MAGELLAN
11878 Avenue Of Industry, San Diego
(92128-3423)
PHONE..................858 487-3200
Jim Plummer, *CEO*
Jane Jones, *
EMP: 72 **EST:** 1986
SQ FT: 50,000
SALES (est): 36.83MM **Publicly Held**
Web: www.aurorasandiego.com
SIC: 8063 8069 Psychiatric hospitals; Drug
addiction rehabilitation hospital
HQ: Magellan Health, Inc.
6303 Cowboys Way
Frisco TX 75034
800 642-1716

(P-16264)
AURORA BEHAVIORAL HEALTH CARE
Also Called: AURORA BEHAVIORAL
HEALTH CARE
2900 E Del Mar Blvd, Pasadena
(91107-4375)
PHONE..................818 515-4735
EMP: 78
Web: www.lasencinashospital.com
SIC: 8063 Psychiatric hospitals
HQ: Aurora - San Diego, Llc
11878 Avenue Of Industry
San Diego CA 92128
858 487-3200

(P-16265)
AURORA CHRTR OAK - LOS ANGLES
1161 E Covina Blvd, Covina (91724-1523)
PHONE..................626 966-1632
Todd Smith, *Prin*
EMP: 152 **EST:** 2017
SALES (est): 13.05MM **Privately Held**
Web: www.charteroakhospital.com
SIC: 8063 Psychiatric hospitals

(P-16266)
AURORA LAS ENCINAS LLC
Also Called: Aurora Las Encinas Hospital
2900 E Del Mar Blvd, Pasadena
(91107-4375)
PHONE..................626 795-9901
EMP: 236 **EST:** 1903
SQ FT: 132,000
SALES (est): 31.46MM **Publicly Held**
Web: www.lasencinashospital.com
SIC: 8063 8069 Mental hospital, except for
the mentally retarded; Alcoholism
rehabilitation hospital
HQ: Hca Inc.
1 Park Plz
Nashville TN 37203
615 344-9551

(P-16267)
BAKERSFELD BHVRAL HLTHCARE HOS
5201 White Ln, Bakersfield (93309-6200)
PHONE..................661 398-1800
Jeff Chinn, *CEO*
EMP: 235 **EST:** 2015
SALES (est): 18.72MM **Privately Held**
Web: www.bakersfieldbehavioral.com
SIC: 8063 8011 Psychiatric hospitals;
Medical centers

(P-16268)
CALIFRNIA DEPT STATE HOSPITALS
Also Called: Fairview Developmental Center
2501 Harbor Blvd, Costa Mesa
(92626-6143)
PHONE..................714 957-5000
Michael Hatton, *Prin*
EMP: 951
SALES (corp-wide): 534.4MM **Privately
Held**
Web: dds.ca.gov
SIC: 8063 9431 Mental hospital, except for
the mentally retarded; Mental health
agency administration, government
HQ: California Department Of State
Hospitals
1600 9th St Rm 350
Sacramento CA 95814

(P-16269)
CALIFRNIA DEPT STATE HOSPITALS
Also Called: Patton State Hospital
3102 E Highland Ave, Patton (92369-7813)
PHONE..................909 425-7000
Bruce Parks, *Dir*
EMP: 1110
SALES (corp-wide): 534.4MM **Privately
Held**
Web: dsh.ca.gov
SIC: 8063 9431 Mental hospital, except for
the mentally retarded; Mental health
agency administration, government
HQ: California Department Of State
Hospitals
1600 9th St Rm 350
Sacramento CA 95814

(P-16270)
CALIFRNIA DEPT STATE HOSPITALS
Also Called: Atascadero State Hospital
10333 El Camino Real, Atascadero
(93422-5808)
P.O. Box 7001 (93423-7001)
PHONE..............................805 468-2000
John De Morales, *Brnch Mgr*
EMP: 1349
SALES (corp-wide): 534.4MM **Privately Held**
Web: www.ca.gov
SIC: **8063** 9431 8062 Mental hospital, except for the mentally retarded; Mental health agency administration, government; General medical and surgical hospitals
HQ: California Department Of State Hospitals
1600 9th St Rm 350
Sacramento CA 95814

(P-16271)
CANYON RIDGE HOSPITAL INC
Also Called: UHS
5353 G St, Chino (91710-5250)
PHONE..............................909 590-3700
Peggy Minnick, *CEO*
EMP: 372 EST: 1990
SALES (est): 46.67MM
SALES (corp-wide): 14.28B **Publicly Held**
Web: www.canyonridgehospital.com
SIC: **8063** 8093 Mental hospital, except for the mentally retarded; Mental health clinic, outpatient
HQ: Willow Springs, Llc
6640 Crthers Pkwy Ste 400
Franklin TN 37067
615 312-5700

(P-16272)
COLLEGE HOSPITAL INC (PA)
Also Called: College Hospital Cerritos
10802 College Pl, Cerritos (90703-1579)
PHONE..............................562 924-9581
TOLL FREE: 800
Stephen A Witt, *Pr*
Bessie Weiss, *
EMP: 300 EST: 1973
SQ FT: 60,000
SALES (est): 72.33MM
SALES (corp-wide): 72.33MM **Privately Held**
Web: www.chc.la
SIC: **8063** Mental hospital, except for the mentally retarded

(P-16273)
COUNTY OF SAN DIEGO
Also Called: Health & Human Services
3853 Rosecrans St, San Diego
(92110-3115)
PHONE..............................619 692-8200
Karen Hogan, *CEO*
EMP: 342
Web: www.sandiegocounty.gov
SIC: **8063** 9431 Psychiatric hospitals; Administration of public health programs
PA: County Of San Diego
1600 Pacific Hwy Ste 209
619 531-5880

(P-16274)
GATEWAYS HOSP MENTAL HLTH CTR (PA)
1891 Effie St, Los Angeles (90026-1711)
PHONE..............................323 644-2000
Mara Pelsman, *CEO*
Jeff Emery, *
EMP: 150 EST: 1953

SQ FT: 40,000
SALES (est): 41.77MM
SALES (corp-wide): 41.77MM **Privately Held**
Web: www.gatewayshospital.org
SIC: **8063** 8093 Mental hospital, except for the mentally retarded; Mental health clinic, outpatient

(P-16275)
KAISER FOUNDATION HOSPITALS
Also Called: Kaiser Mental Health Center
765 W College St, Los Angeles
(90012-1181)
PHONE..............................213 580-7200
Kurt Hastings, *Mgr*
EMP: 205
SQ FT: 66,697
SALES (corp-wide): 70.8B **Privately Held**
Web: thrive.kaiserpermanente.org
SIC: **8063** Psychiatric hospitals
HQ: Kaiser Foundation Hospitals Inc
1 Kaiser Plz
Oakland CA 94612
510 271-6611

(P-16276)
KEDREN COMMUNITY HLTH CTR INC (PA)
Also Called: Kedren Acute Psychtric Hosp Cm
4211 Avalon Blvd, Los Angeles
(90011-5622)
PHONE..............................323 233-0425
John Griffith, *Pr*
John Griffith Ph.d., *Pr*
Lupe Ross, *
Robert Lawson, *
EMP: 400 EST: 1965
SQ FT: 144,000
SALES (est): 21.22MM
SALES (corp-wide): 21.22MM **Privately Held**
Web: www.kedren.org
SIC: **8063** 8093 Mental hospital, except for the mentally retarded; Specialty outpatient clinics, nec

(P-16277)
LANDMARK MEDICAL SERVICES INC
Also Called: Landmark Medical Center
2030 N Garey Ave, Pomona (91767-2795)
PHONE..............................909 593-2585
Rose Horsman, *Pr*
EMP: 100 EST: 1971
SQ FT: 27,500
SALES (est): 4.57MM **Privately Held**
Web: www.landmarkmedicalcenter.net
SIC: **8063** Mental hospital, except for the mentally retarded

(P-16278)
PINE GROVE HOSPITAL CORP
9449 San Fernando Rd, Sun Valley
(91352-1421)
PHONE..............................818 348-0500
Paul R Tuft, *Pr*
EMP: 180 EST: 1998
SALES (est): 862.16K **Privately Held**
SIC: **8063** Psychiatric hospitals

(P-16279)
SHARP MEMORIAL HOSPITAL
Also Called: Sharp Mesa Vista Hospital
7850 Vista Hill Ave, San Diego
(92123-2717)
PHONE..............................858 278-4110
Carolyn Mason, *Dir*

EMP: 250
SALES (corp-wide): 2.37B **Privately Held**
Web: www.sharp.com
SIC: **8063** 8069 8093 Psychiatric hospitals; Substance abuse hospitals; Specialty outpatient clinics, nec
HQ: Sharp Memorial Hospital
7901 Frost St
San Diego CA 92123
858 939-3636

(P-16280)
VISTA BEHAVIORAL HEALTH INC
Also Called: ACADIA HEALTHCARE
5900 Brockton Ave, Riverside
(92506-1862)
PHONE..............................800 992-0901
Nelson Smith, *CEO*
EMP: 89 EST: 2015
SALES (est): 19.44MM **Publicly Held**
Web: www.pacificgrovehospital.com
SIC: **8063** Psychiatric hospitals
PA: Acadia Healthcare Company, Inc.
6100 Tower Cir Ste 1000

8069 Specialty Hospitals, Except Psychiatric

(P-16281)
AHMC ANHEIM RGIONAL MED CTR LP (HQ)
Also Called: WHITTIER HOSPITAL MEDICAL CENT
1111 W La Palma Ave, Anaheim
(92801-2804)
PHONE..............................714 774-1450
Patrick Petre, *CEO*
Deborah Webber, *
Kathy Doi, *
Marie Trembath, *
EMP: 350 EST: 1958
SALES (est): 158.21MM
SALES (corp-wide): 325.41MM **Privately Held**
Web: www.ahmchealth.com
SIC: **8069** 8062 Childrens' hospital; General medical and surgical hospitals
PA: Ahmc Healthcare Inc.
506 W Valley Blvd Ste 300
626 943-7526

(P-16282)
AKUA BEHAVIORAL HEALTH INC (PA)
Also Called: Akua Mind & Body
20271 Sw Birch St Ste 200, Newport Beach
(92660-1752)
PHONE..............................949 777-2283
Stephen Mercurio, *CEO*
EMP: 107 EST: 2014
SALES (est): 15.66MM
SALES (corp-wide): 15.66MM **Privately Held**
Web: www.akuamindbody.com
SIC: **8069** 8322 Drug addiction rehabilitation hospital; Rehabilitation services

(P-16283)
BARLOW GROUP (PA)
Also Called: BARLOW RESPITORY HOSPITAL
2000 Stadium Way, Los Angeles
(90026-2696)
PHONE..............................213 250-4200
Margaret W Crane, *CEO*
EMP: 250 EST: 1994
SALES (est): 5.95MM
SALES (corp-wide): 5.95MM **Privately Held**

Web: www.barlowhospital.org
SIC: **8069** 7389 8733 Specialty hospitals, except psychiatric; Fund raising organizations; Medical research

(P-16284)
BARLOW RESPIRATORY HOSPITAL
12401 Washington Blvd, Whittier
(90602-1006)
PHONE..............................562 698-0811
Priscilla Jahangiri, *Brnch Mgr*
EMP: 1650
SALES (corp-wide): 65.76MM **Privately Held**
Web: www.barlowhospital.org
SIC: **8069** Specialty hospitals, except psychiatric
PA: Barlow Respiratory Hospital
2000 Stadium Way
213 250-4200

(P-16285)
BARLOW RESPIRATORY HOSPITAL (PA)
2000 Stadium Way, Los Angeles
(90026-2696)
PHONE..............................213 250-4200
Margaret W Crane, *CEO*
Edward Engesser, *
EMP: 250 EST: 1902
SQ FT: 80,000
SALES (est): 65.76MM
SALES (corp-wide): 65.76MM **Privately Held**
Web: www.barlowhospital.org
SIC: **8069** Specialty hospitals, except psychiatric

(P-16286)
BEVERLY HLLS ONCLOGY MED GROUP
Also Called: Beverly Hlls Cncierge Hlth Ctr
8900 Wilshire Blvd, Beverly Hills
(90211-1958)
PHONE..............................310 432-8900
Afshin Gabayan, *CEO*
EMP: 74 EST: 2007
SALES (est): 4.34MM **Privately Held**
Web: www.bhcancercenter.com
SIC: **8069** Cancer hospital

(P-16287)
CHILDRENS HEALTHCARE CAL (PA)
Also Called: CHOC CHILDREN'S
1201 W La Veta Ave, Orange (92868-4203)
PHONE..............................714 997-3000
Kimberly C Cripe, *Pr*
Maria Minon Md, *VP*
Kerri Ruppert, *CFO*
Thomas Brotherton, *COO*
EMP: 1500 EST: 1986
SALES (est): 39.52MM **Privately Held**
Web: www.choc.org
SIC: **8069** Childrens' hospital

(P-16288)
CHILDRENS HOSPITAL LOS ANGELES (PA)
4650 W Sunset Blvd, Los Angeles
(90027-6062)
PHONE..............................323 660-2450
Richard Cordova, *Pr*
Lannie Tonnu, *
Alexandra Carter, *CDO*
Lara Khouri, *
Conrad Band, *CIO*
▲ EMP: 2212 EST: 1901

P R O D U C T S & S V C S

SQ FT: 750,000
SALES (est): 1.74B
SALES (corp-wide): 1.74B **Privately Held**
Web: www.chla.org
SIC: 8069 8062 Childrens' hospital; General medical and surgical hospitals

(P-16289)
CORNERSTONE SOUTHERN CAL
1950 E 17th St Ste 150, Santa Ana (92705-6852)
PHONE.............................714 998-3574
EMP: 95 **EST:** 2015
SALES (est): 2.69MM **Privately Held**
Web: www.cornerstonesocal.com
SIC: 8069 Drug addiction rehabilitation hospital

(P-16290)
COUNTY OF LOS ANGELES
Also Called: Health Services, Dept of
30500 Arrastre Canyon Rd, Acton (93510-2160)
P.O. Box 25 (93510-0025)
PHONE.............................661 223-8700
Suzanna Kassinger, *Admn*
EMP: 111
Web: www.lacounty.info
SIC: 8069 9431 8361 Alcoholism rehabilitation hospital; Administration of public health programs; Residential care
PA: County Of Los Angeles
500 W Temple St Ste 437
213 974-1101

(P-16291)
COUNTY OF LOS ANGELES
Also Called: Department of Health Services
1240 N Mission Rd, Los Angeles (90033-1019)
PHONE.............................323 226-3468
Barbara Oliver, *Ex Dir*
EMP: 101
Web: www.lacounty.gov
SIC: 8069 9431 8062 Specialty hospitals, except psychiatric; Administration of public health programs; General medical and surgical hospitals
PA: County Of Los Angeles
500 W Temple St Ste 437
213 974-1101

(P-16292)
COUNTY OF LOS ANGELES
515 E 6th St, Los Angeles (90021-1009)
PHONE.............................213 974-7284
Maria Lopez, *Mgr*
EMP: 71
Web: www.lacounty.gov
SIC: 8069 9111 Tuberculosis hospital; Executive offices
PA: County Of Los Angeles
500 W Temple St Ste 437
213 974-1101

(P-16293)
COUNTY OF LOS ANGELES
Also Called: Health Services, Dept of
38200 Lake Hughes Rd, Castaic (91384-4100)
PHONE.............................661 223-8700
Lynne Dahl, *Admn*
EMP: 101
Web: www.lacounty.gov
SIC: 8069 9431 Drug addiction rehabilitation hospital; Administration of public health programs
PA: County Of Los Angeles
500 W Temple St Ste 437
213 974-1101

(P-16294)
GOODEN CENTER
191 N El Molino Ave, Pasadena (91101-1804)
PHONE.............................626 356-0078
Thomas Mcnulty, *Prin*
Budd Williams, *
EMP: 85 **EST:** 1962
SALES (est): 9.41MM **Privately Held**
Web: www.goodencenter.org
SIC: 8069 8361 8093 Alcoholism rehabilitation hospital; Rehabilitation center, residential: health care incidental; Mental health clinic, outpatient

(P-16295)
KOREAN COMMUNITY SERVICES INC
Also Called: Kc Services
451 W Lincoln Ave Ste 100, Anaheim (92805-2912)
PHONE.............................714 527-6561
Ellen Ahn, *CEO*
Ellen Ahn, *Ex Dir*
Kay Ahn, *
EMP: 120 **EST:** 1977
SALES (est): 8.12MM **Privately Held**
Web: www.kcsinc.org
SIC: 8069 8322 8011 Drug addiction rehabilitation hospital; Social service center ; Offices and clinics of medical doctors

(P-16296)
MARINE CORPS UNITED STATES
Also Called: Camp Pendleton Hospital
Camp Pendleton, Oceanside (92055)
P.O. Box 555191 (92055-5191)
PHONE.............................760 725-1304
Richard R Jeffries, *Mgr*
EMP: 1000
Web: www.marines.mil
SIC: 8069 9711 Specialty hospitals, except psychiatric; Marine Corps
HQ: United States Marine Corps
Branch Hlth Clnic Bldg #5
Beaufort SC 29904

(P-16297)
PALOMAR HEALTH
800 W Valley Pkwy Ste 201, Escondido (92025-2557)
PHONE.............................760 740-6311
Bob Henker, *CEO*
EMP: 201
SALES (corp-wide): 679.43K **Privately Held**
Web: www.pph.org
SIC: 8069 Specialty hospitals, except psychiatric
PA: Palomar Health
2125 Ctrcado Pkwy Ste 300
442 281-5000

(P-16298)
SHARP MCDONALD CENTER
7989 Linda Vista Rd, San Diego (92111-5106)
PHONE.............................858 637-6920
Daniel L Gross, *Ex VP*
EMP: 800 **EST:** 2001
SALES (est): 5.04MM
SALES (corp-wide): 1.9B **Privately Held**
Web: www.sharp.com
SIC: 8069 Drug addiction rehabilitation hospital
PA: Sharp Healthcare
8695 Spectrum Ctr Blvd
858 499-4000

(P-16299)
SHIELDS FOR FAMILIES (PA)
Also Called: Shields
11601 S Western Ave, Los Angeles (90047-5006)
P.O. Box 59129 (90059-0129)
PHONE.............................323 242-5000
Kathryn S Icenhower, *CEO*
Xylina Bean Md, *Pr*
Norma Mtume, *
Charlene K Smith, *
Gerald Phillips, *
EMP: 82 **EST:** 1991
SALES (est): 27.55MM
SALES (corp-wide): 27.55MM **Privately Held**
Web: www.shieldsforfamilies.org
SIC: 8069 Drug addiction rehabilitation hospital

(P-16300)
SHRINERS HSPITALS FOR CHILDREN
3160 Genieva St, Montrose (91020)
PHONE.............................213 368-3302
Frank Labonte, *Dir*
EMP: 287
SALES (corp-wide): 7.02MM **Privately Held**
Web: www.shrinerschildrens.org
SIC: 8069 8062 Childrens' hospital; General medical and surgical hospitals
HQ: Shriners Hospitals For Children
2900 N Rocky Point Dr
Tampa FL 33607

(P-16301)
SHRINERS HSPITALS FOR CHILDREN
Also Called: Shriner's Hospital
909 S Fair Oaks Ave, Pasadena (91105-2625)
PHONE.............................626 389-9300
Wendy Hill, *Brnch Mgr*
EMP: 255
SALES (corp-wide): 7.02MM **Privately Held**
Web: www.shrinerschildrens.org
SIC: 8069 8062 Childrens' hospital; General medical and surgical hospitals
HQ: Shriners Hospitals For Children
2900 N Rocky Point Dr
Tampa FL 33607

(P-16302)
TENET HEALTHSYSTEM MEDICAL INC
Also Called: Placentia Linda Hospital
1301 N Rose Dr, Placentia (92870-3802)
PHONE.............................714 993-2000
Kent Clayton, *CEO*
EMP: 390
SALES (corp-wide): 19.17B **Publicly Held**
Web: www.tenethealth.com
SIC: 8069 8011 8062 Specialty hospitals, except psychiatric; Offices and clinics of medical doctors; General medical and surgical hospitals
HQ: Tenet Healthsystem Medical, Inc.
14201 Dallas Pkwy
Dallas TX 75254
469 893-2000

8071 Medical Laboratories

(P-16303)
ADVANCED MEDICAL ANALYSIS LLC

1941 Walker Ave, Monrovia (91016-4846)
PHONE.............................626 301-0126
EMP: 75
Web: www.amalab.net
SIC: 8071 Medical laboratories

(P-16304)
ALLIANCE HEALTHCARE SVCS INC (DH)
Also Called: Alliance
18201 Von Karman Ave Ste 600, Irvine (92612-1176)
P.O. Box 19532 (92623)
PHONE.............................800 544-3215
Rhonda Longmore Grund, *CEO*
Percy C Tomlinson, *
Laurie R Miller, *
Richard W Johns, *
EMP: 250 **EST:** 1983
SALES (est): 480.48MM
SALES (corp-wide): 786.27MM **Privately Held**
Web: www.akumin.com
SIC: 8071 Ultrasound laboratory
HQ: Akumin Operating Corp.
8300 W Sunrise Blvd
Plantation FL 33322
855 332-2390

(P-16305)
BIOTHERANOSTICS INC (HQ)
9640 Towne Centre Dr Ste 200, San Diego (92121-1987)
P.O. Box 749249 (90074-9249)
PHONE.............................877 886-6739
Stephen P Macmillan, *Pr*
EMP: 40 **EST:** 1996
SALES (est): 24.64MM
SALES (corp-wide): 4.03B **Publicly Held**
Web: www.biotheranostics.com
SIC: 8071 2835 Medical laboratories; In vitro diagnostics
PA: Hologic, Inc.
250 Campus Dr
508 263-2900

(P-16306)
CAP DIAGNOSTICS LLC
Also Called: Pathnostics
15545 Sand Canyon Ave, Irvine (92618-3114)
PHONE.............................714 966-1221
Matt Tate, *
EMP: 187 **EST:** 2014
SALES (est): 25.57MM **Privately Held**
Web: www.pathnostics.com
SIC: 8071 Medical laboratories

(P-16307)
CEDARS-SINAI MEDICAL CENTER
Also Called: Cedar Snai Bomanufacturing Ctr
8687 Melrose Ave Ste B227, West Hollywood (90069-5701)
PHONE.............................814 758-5466
EMP: 151
SALES (corp-wide): 4.66B **Privately Held**
Web: www.cedars-sinai.org
SIC: 8071 Medical laboratories
PA: Cedars-Sinai Medical Center
8700 Beverly Blvd
310 423-3277

(P-16308)
CLARIENT INC
Also Called: Chromavision Medical Systems
33171 Paseo Cerveza, San Juan Capistrano (92675-4870)
PHONE.............................949 445-7300
FAX: 949 443-3366

EMP: 201
SALES (est): 808.69K
SALES (corp-wide): 244.08MM **Publicly Held**
SIC: 8071 Biological laboratory
HQ: Clarient Diagnostic Services Inc
31 Columbia
Aliso Viejo CA 92656
949 445-7300

(P-16309)
CONSOLDTED MED BO-ANALYSIS INC (PA)
Also Called: Cmb Laboratory
10700 Walker St, Cypress (90630-4703)
P.O. Box 2369 (90630-1869)
PHONE.....................714 657-7369
Chin Kuo Fan, *Pr*
Cam Chinh Fan, *Sr VP*
Michelle Fan, *
Gloria Fan, *Stockholder*
EMP: 100 **EST:** 1979
SQ FT: 11,000
SALES (est): 9.55MM
SALES (corp-wide): 9.55MM **Privately Held**
Web: www.cmblabs.com
SIC: 8071 Testing laboratories

(P-16310)
CURATIVE-KORVA LLC
605 E Huntington Dr, Monrovia
(91016-6352)
PHONE.....................424 645-7575
Jonathan Martin, *Managing Member*
EMP: 85 **EST:** 2020
SALES (est): 3.67MM **Privately Held**
SIC: 8071 Medical laboratories

(P-16311)
DECIPHER CORP
6925 Lusk Blvd Ste 200, San Diego
(92121-2789)
PHONE.....................888 975-4540
Tina Nova, *CEO*
Doug Dolginow, *Prin*
Brent Vetter, *CFO*
Elai Davicioni, *Pr*
EMP: 100 **EST:** 2012
SQ FT: 15,000
SALES (est): 23.62MM
SALES (corp-wide): 5.41MM **Privately Held**
Web: www.genomedx.com
SIC: 8071 Biological laboratory
PA: Genomedx Biosciences Inc
430-1152 Mainland St
888 975-4540

(P-16312)
DR SYSTEMS INC
Also Called: Dominator Radiology Systems
10140 Mesa Rim Rd, San Diego
(92121-2914)
PHONE.....................858 625-3344
EMP: 205
SIC: 8071 Testing laboratories

(P-16313)
EISENHOWER MEDICAL CENTER
Also Called: Clinical Research
39000 Bob Hope Dr Frnt, Rancho Mirage
(92270-3230)
PHONE.....................760 773-1364
Lile Matthews, *Dir*
EMP: 135
SALES (corp-wide): 1.04B **Privately Held**
Web: www.eisenhowerhealth.org

SIC: 8071 Medical laboratories
PA: Eisenhower Medical Center
39000 Bob Hope Dr
760 340-3911

(P-16314)
EPIC SCIENCES INC
9381 Judicial Dr Ste 200, San Diego
(92121-3832)
PHONE.....................858 356-6610
Lloyd Sanders, *Pr*
Michael Rodriguez, *
Mike Coward, *
Michael Giske, *CIO*
Chockalingam Palaniappan, *CIO*
EMP: 80 **EST:** 2008
SALES (est): 14.58MM **Privately Held**
Web: www.epicsciences.com
SIC: 8071 Blood analysis laboratory

(P-16315)
EXAGEN INC
1261 Liberty Way Ste C, Vista
(92081-8356)
PHONE.....................505 272-7966
Robert Mignatti, *Pr*
EMP: 130
SALES (corp-wide): 52.55MM **Publicly Held**
Web: www.exagen.com
SIC: 8071 Medical laboratories
PA: Exagen Inc.
1221 Liberty Way
760 560-1501

(P-16316)
EXAMONE WORLD WIDE INC
Also Called: Examone
7480 Mission Valley Rd Ste 101, San Diego
(92108-4433)
PHONE.....................619 299-3926
EMP: 100
SALES (corp-wide): 9.25B **Publicly Held**
Web: www.myexamone.com
SIC: 8071 Testing laboratories
HQ: Examone World Wide, Inc.
10101 Renner Blvd
Lenexa KS 66219
913 888-1770

(P-16317)
EXQUISITE DENTAL TECHNOLOGY
4816 Temple City Blvd, Temple City
(91780-4235)
PHONE.....................626 237-0107
Ron Tsai, *Pr*
EMP: 70 **EST:** 2001
SQ FT: 920
SALES (est): 1.2MM **Privately Held**
SIC: 8071 Medical laboratories

(P-16318)
FOCUS DIAGNOSTICS INC
Also Called: Focus Diagnostics
11331 Valley View St Ste 150, Cypress
(90630-5300)
PHONE.....................714 220-1900
John Hurrell Ph.d., *Pr*
EMP: 400 **EST:** 1978
SQ FT: 36,000
SALES (est): 10.29MM
SALES (corp-wide): 9.25B **Publicly Held**
Web: int.diasorin.com
SIC: 8071 Testing laboratories
PA: Quest Diagnostics Incorporated
500 Plaza Dr
973 520-2700

(P-16319)
IMMUNALYSIS CORPORATION
829 Towne Center Dr, Pomona
(91767-5901)
PHONE.....................909 482-0840
Kahi Luu, *Prin*
EMP: 80 **EST:** 1975
SALES (est): 11.03MM **Privately Held**
Web: www.immunalysis.com
SIC: 8071 Testing laboratories

(P-16320)
KAISER FOUNDATION HOSPITALS
Also Called: Kaiser Permanente
22750 Wildomar Trl, Wildomar
(92595-9048)
PHONE.....................833 574-2273
Michael Neri Junior Managing, *Brnch Mgr*
EMP: 87
SALES (corp-wide): 70.8B **Privately Held**
SIC: 8071 Medical laboratories
HQ: Kaiser Foundation Hospitals Inc
1 Kaiser Plz
Oakland CA 94612
510 271-6611

(P-16321)
KAN-DI-KI LLC (HQ)
Also Called: Diagnostic Labs & Rdlgy
12612 Raymer St, North Hollywood
(91605-4307)
PHONE.....................818 549-1880
David F Smith Iii, *Managing Member*
EMP: 84 **EST:** 2008
SQ FT: 7,000
SALES (est): 37.71MM **Privately Held**
Web: www.tridentcare.com
SIC: 8071 Testing laboratories
PA: Trident Usa Health Services, Llc
930 Ridgebrook Rd Fl 3

(P-16322)
LATARA ENTERPRISE INC (PA)
Also Called: Foundation Laboratory
1716 W Holt Ave, Pomona (91768-3333)
PHONE.....................909 623-9301
Stepan Vartanian, *CEO*
Linda Vartanian, *Prin*
Taleen Vartanian, *Prin*
Lala Vartanian, *Prin*
Ara Vartanian, *Treas*
EMP: 120 **EST:** 1966
SQ FT: 19,000
SALES (est): 16.22MM
SALES (corp-wide): 16.22MM **Privately Held**
Web: www.foundationlaboratory.com
SIC: 8071 Pathological laboratory

(P-16323)
LOTUS CLINICAL RESEARCH LLC
100 W California Blvd, Pasadena
(91105-3010)
PHONE.....................626 381-9830
Neil Singla, *CSO*
Sonia Kaur D.o.s., *Dir*
Anne Arriaga, *
EMP: 100 **EST:** 2008
SALES (est): 11.47MM **Privately Held**
Web: www.lotuscr.com
SIC: 8071 Medical laboratories

(P-16324)
NICHOLS INST REFERENCE LABS (DH)
33608 Ortega Hwy, San Juan Capistrano
(92675-2042)

PHONE.....................949 728-4000
Douglas Harrington, *Pr*
Charles Olson, *
Murugan R Pandian, *Senior Science Director*
Chuck Miller, *
Michael O'gorman, *Supply Vice President*
EMP: 525 **EST:** 1971
SQ FT: 240,000
SALES (est): 4.63MM
SALES (corp-wide): 9.25B **Publicly Held**
Web: www.questdiagnostics.com
SIC: 8071 Testing laboratories
HQ: Quest Diagnostics Nichols Institute
33608 Ortega Hwy
San Juan Capistrano CA 92675
949 728-4000

(P-16325)
ONCOLOGY INSTITUTE INC (PA)
Also Called: Toi
18000 Studebaker Rd Ste 800, Cerritos
(90703-2671)
PHONE.....................562 735-3226
Daniel Virnich, *CEO*
Richard Barasch, *Ch Bd*
Brad Hively, *V Ch Bd*
Jeremy Castle, *COO*
Rob Carter, *CFO*
EMP: 800 **EST:** 2019
SALES (est): 324.24MM
SALES (corp-wide): 324.24MM **Publicly Held**
Web: www.theoncologyinstitute.com
SIC: 8071 8731 Medical laboratories; Medical research, commercial

(P-16326)
PACIFIC TOXICOLOGY LABS
Also Called: Forensic Toxicology Associates
9348 De Soto Ave, Chatsworth
(91311-4926)
PHONE.....................818 598-3110
Jeff Lanzolatta, *CEO*
Greg Carroll, *
Sue Barbosa, *
Neil Patel Carroll, *
Bert Cohen, *
EMP: 75 **EST:** 1984
SQ FT: 19,000
SALES (est): 9.94MM **Privately Held**
Web: www.pactox.com
SIC: 8071 Testing laboratories

(P-16327)
POLYPEPTIDE LABORATORIES INC (DH)
365 Maple Ave, Torrance (90503-2002)
PHONE.....................310 782-3569
Timothy Culbreth, *Pr*
Jane Salik, *
Michael Verlander, *
Nagana Goud, *
▲ **EMP:** 25 **EST:** 1996
SQ FT: 19,200
SALES (est): 34.69MM **Privately Held**
Web: www.polypeptide.com
SIC: 8071 2836 8731 2834 Medical laboratories; Biological products, except diagnostic; Biotechnical research, commercial; Pharmaceutical preparations
HQ: Polypeptide Group Ag
Neuhofstrasse 24
Baar ZG 6340

(P-16328)
PRIMEX CLINICAL LABS INC (PA)
16742 Stagg St Ste 120, Van Nuys
(91406-1641)

PHONE.................424 213-8019
Oshin Hartoonian, *Pr*
Ara Hartoonian, *VP*
Erik Avaniss-aghajano, *VP*
Bianca Gharimian, *
EMP: 80 **EST:** 1996
SQ FT: 3,000
SALES (est): 24.69MM **Privately Held**
Web: www.primexlab.com
SIC: 8071 Blood analysis laboratory

(P-16329)
PROFORM INC
Also Called: Proform Labs
1140 S Rockefeller Ave, Ontario
(91761-2201)
PHONE.................707 752-9010
Sean Phillip Thomas, *CEO*
EMP: 100 **EST:** 2016
SALES (est): 1.67MM **Privately Held**
SIC: 8071 Biological laboratory

(P-16330)
Q SQUARED SOLUTIONS LLC
Also Called: Biorepository
28454 Livingston Ave, Valencia
(91355-4172)
PHONE.................919 405-2248
EMP: 88
Web: www.q2labsolutions.com
SIC: 8071 Medical laboratories
HQ: Q Squared Solutions Llc
2400 Ellis Rd
Durham NC

(P-16331)
QUEST DIAGNOSTICS NICHOLS INST (HQ)
Also Called: Quest Diagnostics
33608 Ortega Hwy, San Juan Capistrano
(92675-2042)
PHONE.................949 728-4000
Catherine T Doherty, *CEO*
Nicholas Conti, *
Timothy Sharpe, *
Dan Haemmerle, *
Mark Garawitz, *
EMP: 1000 **EST:** 1971
SQ FT: 240,000
SALES (est): 36.19MM
SALES (corp-wide): 9.25B **Publicly Held**
Web: www.questdiagnostics.com
SIC: 8071 Testing laboratories
PA: Quest Diagnostics Incorporated
500 Plaza Dr
973 520-2700

(P-16332)
RADNET INC (PA)
Also Called: Radnet
1510 Cotner Ave, Los Angeles
(90025-3303)
PHONE.................310 478-7808
Howard G Berger, *Ch Bd*
Mark D Stolper, *
Mital Patel, *PLANNING ANALYSIS**
Michael M Murdock, *Ofcr*
David J Katz, *CLO**
EMP: 486 **EST:** 1985
SQ FT: 21,500
SALES (est): 1.62B **Publicly Held**
Web: www.radnet.com
SIC: 8071 Ultrasound laboratory

(P-16333)
SAMARITAN IMAGING CENTER
1245 Wilshire Blvd Ste 205, Los Angeles
(90017-4812)
PHONE.................213 977-2140
Andrew B Leeka, *CEO*

EMP: 5005 **EST:** 2010
SALES (est): 1.93MM
SALES (corp-wide): 20.43MM **Privately Held**
Web: www.samaritanimagingcenter.com
SIC: 8071 Medical laboratories
HQ: Pih Health Good Samaritan Hospital
1225 Wilshire Blvd
Los Angeles CA 90017
213 977-2121

(P-16334)
SEQUENOM CTR FOR MLCLAR MDCINE
Also Called: Sequenom Laboratories
3595 John Hopkins Ct, San Diego
(92121-1121)
PHONE.................858 202-9051
Jeffrey D Linton, *Sec*
Carolyn D Beaver, *
Kelly L Perez, *
Daniel Grosu, *
◆ **EMP:** 344 **EST:** 2008
SALES (est): 5.17MM
SALES (corp-wide): 12.18B **Publicly Held**
Web: womenshealth.labcorp.com
SIC: 8071 Medical laboratories
HQ: Sequenom, Inc.
3595 John Hopkins Ct
San Diego CA 92121

(P-16335)
SPECIALTY LABORATORIES INC (DH)
Also Called: Quest Dgnstics Nchls Inst Vln
27027 Tourney Rd, Valencia (91355-5386)
PHONE.................661 799-6543
R Keith Laughman, *Pr*
Vicki Difrancesco, *
▲ **EMP:** 633 **EST:** 1975
SALES (est): 18.91MM
SALES (corp-wide): 9.25B **Publicly Held**
Web: www.questdiagnostics.com
SIC: 8071 Testing laboratories
HQ: Ameripath, Inc.
7108 Fairway Dr Ste 335
Palm Beach Gardens FL 33418
561 712-6200

(P-16336)
THAIHOT INVESTMENT CO US LTD
18201 Von Karman Ave Ste 600, Irvine
(92612-1176)
PHONE.................949 242-5300
EMP: 2450 **EST:** 2017
SALES (est): 5.52MM **Privately Held**
SIC: 8071 Medical laboratories
PA: Tahoe Investment Group Co., Ltd.
No.333, Wusi North Road

(P-16337)
UNILAB CORPORATION (HQ)
Also Called: Quest Diagnostics
8401 Fallbrook Ave, West Hills
(91304-3226)
PHONE.................818 737-6000
Mark E Delaney, *CEO*
Sandip R Patel, *
EMP: 400 **EST:** 1992
SALES (est): 118.21MM
SALES (corp-wide): 9.25B **Publicly Held**
Web: www.questdiagnostics.com
SIC: 8071 Testing laboratories
PA: Quest Diagnostics Incorporated
500 Plaza Dr
973 520-2700

(P-16338)
UNITED LAB SERVICES INC
2479 S Vicentia Ave, Corona (92882-5934)
PHONE.................951 444-0467
Anabelle Myers, *CEO*
EMP: 80 **EST:** 2015
SALES (est): 2.26MM **Privately Held**
SIC: 8071 Medical laboratories

(P-16339)
UNIVERSITY CALIFORNIA IRVINE
B35 Rowland Hall, Irvine (92697-0001)
PHONE.................949 202-7580
Barbara Chisholm, *Prin*
EMP: 102
SALES (corp-wide): 534.4MM **Privately Held**
Web: www.uci.edu
SIC: 8071 Medical laboratories
HQ: University Of California, Irvine
510 Aldrich Hall
Irvine CA 92697
949 824-5011

(P-16340)
UNIVERSITY CALIFORNIA IRVINE
Also Called: Department of Dermatology
118 Med Surge I, Irvine (92697-4375)
PHONE.................909 358-5774
EMP: 102
SALES (corp-wide): 534.4MM **Privately Held**
Web: www.uci.edu
SIC: 8071 Medical laboratories
HQ: University Of California, Irvine
510 Aldrich Hall
Irvine CA 92697
949 824-5011

8072 Dental Laboratories

(P-16341)
BURBANK DENTAL LABORATORY INC
Also Called: Advanced Technology Center
2101 Floyd St, Burbank (91504-3411)
PHONE.................818 841-2256
Anatony Sedler, *CEO*
Tony Sedler, *
Robert Vartanian, *
David French, *
▲ **EMP:** 175 **EST:** 1980
SALES (est): 22.59MM **Privately Held**
Web: www.burbankdental.com
SIC: 8072 Dental laboratories

(P-16342)
GKY DENTAL ARTS INC (PA)
4212 Artesia Blvd, Torrance (90504-3106)
PHONE.................310 214-8007
Glen Yamamoto, *Pr*
Kiichi Yamamoto, *
▲ **EMP:** 79 **EST:** 1982
SQ FT: 4,500
SALES (est): 5.14MM
SALES (corp-wide): 5.14MM **Privately Held**
Web: www.gkydentalarts.com
SIC: 8072 Crown and bridge production

(P-16343)
JAMES R GLDWELL DNTL CRMICS IN (PA)
Also Called: Glidewell Laboratories
4141 Macarthur Blvd, Newport Beach
(92660-2015)

PHONE.................800 854-7256
James R Glidewell, *CEO*
Jim Shuck, *
Glenn Sasaki, *
Greg Minzenmayer, *
Gary M Pritchard, *
▲ **EMP:** 1100 **EST:** 1969
SQ FT: 72,000
SALES (est): 460.81MM
SALES (corp-wide): 460.81MM **Privately Held**
Web: www.glidewelldental.com
SIC: 8072 Crown and bridge production

(P-16344)
KEATING DENTAL ARTS INC
Also Called: Keating Dental Lab
16881 Hale Ave Ste A, Irvine (92606-5068)
PHONE.................949 955-2100
Shaun Keating, *Pr*
EMP: 105 **EST:** 2002
SQ FT: 26,000
SALES (est): 8.63MM **Privately Held**
Web: www.keatingdentallab.com
SIC: 8072 Crown and bridge production

(P-16345)
NOBEL BIOCARE USA LLC
200 S Kraemer Blvd Unit E, Brea
(92821-6208)
PHONE.................714 282-4800
Thomas Olsen, *Pr*
Frederick Walther, *Treas*
▲ **EMP:** 500 **EST:** 2004
SQ FT: 150,000
SALES (est): 98.65MM
SALES (corp-wide): 2.57B **Publicly Held**
Web: www.nobelbiocare.com
SIC: 8072 Dental laboratories
PA: Envista Holdings Corporation
200 S Kraemer Blvd Bldg E
714 817-7000

(P-16346)
POSCA BROTHERS DENTAL LAB INC
641 W Willow St, Long Beach
(90806-2832)
PHONE.................562 427-1811
Alex Posca, *Pr*
Angel Jorge Posca, *
Yanette Posca, *
▲ **EMP:** 55 **EST:** 1965
SQ FT: 5,000
SALES (est): 2.31MM **Privately Held**
Web: www.poscabrothers.com
SIC: 8072 3843 Dental laboratories; Teeth,
artificial (not made in dental laboratories)

(P-16347)
TRIDENT LABS LLC
Also Called: Trident Dental Labratories
12000 Aviation Blvd, Hawthorne
(90250-3438)
PHONE.................310 915-9121
Laurence K Fishman, *Pr*
Richard B Mc Donald, *
▲ **EMP:** 125 **EST:** 1988
SQ FT: 16,000
SALES (est): 21.52MM
SALES (corp-wide): 21.52MM **Privately Held**
Web: www.tridentlab.com
SIC: 8072 Crown and bridge production
PA: Gdc Holdings, Inc.
1701 Military Trl
763 398-0654

(P-16348)
WEST COAST DENTAL LABS LLC
12002 Aviation Blvd, Hawthorne (90250-3438)
PHONE....................855 220-5600
Chuck Stapleton, *Genl Mgr*
EMP: 855 EST: 2017
SALES (est): 1.27MM
SALES (corp-wide): 339.71MM **Privately Held**
Web: www.wcdlabs.com
SIC: 8072 Crown and bridge production
PA: National Dentex Labs Llc
1701 Military Trl
561 537-8300

8082 Home Health Care Services

(P-16349)
365 HOME CARE
10225 Austin Dr Ste 208, Spring Valley (91978-1522)
PHONE....................310 908-5179
Ebele Enunwa, *CEO*
EMP: 80 EST: 2020
SALES (est): 2.3MM **Privately Held**
Web: www.365homecareca.com
SIC: 8082 Home health care services

(P-16350)
ABC HOME HEALTH CARE LLC
5090 Shoreham Pl Ste 209, San Diego (92122-5935)
PHONE....................858 455-5000
Joseph Monteforte, *Ex Dir*
Hamideh F Panabi, *Managing Member*
Hamid Alebrahim, *Managing Member*
EMP: 125 EST: 1993
SALES (est): 3.17MM **Privately Held**
Web: www.bridgehh.com
SIC: 8082 7371 Home health care services; Computer software development and applications

(P-16351)
ACCENTCARE INC
5050 Murphy Canyon Rd Ste 200, San Diego (92123-4399)
PHONE....................858 576-7410
EMP: 525
SALES (corp-wide): 4.59B **Privately Held**
Web: www.accentcare.com
SIC: 8082 7389 Home health care services; Business services, nec
HQ: Accentcare, Inc.
17855 N Dallas Pkwy
Dallas TX 75287
800 834-3059

(P-16352)
ACCENTCARE HM HLTH EL CNTRO IN
2344 S 2nd St Ste A, El Centro (92243-5606)
PHONE....................760 352-4022
Melanie Ihler, *CEO*
EMP: 270 EST: 1994
SALES (est): 3.07MM
SALES (corp-wide): 4.59B **Privately Held**
Web: www.accentcare.com
SIC: 8082 Home health care services
HQ: Accentcare Home Health, Inc.
135 Technology Dr Ste 150
Irvine CA 92618

(P-16353)
ACCENTCARE HOME HLTH YUMA INC
1455 Auto Center Dr Ste 125, Ontario (91761-2250)
PHONE....................909 605-7000
Connie Morris, *Pr*
Melanie Ihler, *
Anna Trappett, *
EMP: 424 EST: 1992
SALES (est): 2.02MM
SALES (corp-wide): 4.59B **Privately Held**
Web: www.accentcare.com
SIC: 8082 Home health care services
HQ: Accentcare Home Health, Inc.
135 Technology Dr Ste 150
Irvine CA 92618

(P-16354)
ACCREDITED FMS INC
5955 De Soto Ave Ste 136, Woodland Hills (91367-5122)
PHONE....................818 435-4200
EMP: 284 EST: 2012
SALES (est): 815.53K
SALES (corp-wide): 1.9B **Publicly Held**
SIC: 8082 Home health care services
PA: Aveanna Healthcare Holdings Inc.
400 Intrstate N Pkwy Se S
770 441-1580

(P-16355)
ACCREDITED NURSING SERVICES
Also Called: Accredited Nursing Care
950 S Coast Dr Ste 215, Costa Mesa (92626-7850)
PHONE....................714 973-1234
Meryll Jones, *Mgr*
EMP: 244
SALES (corp-wide): 2.91MM **Privately Held**
Web: www.aveanna.com
SIC: 8082 Home health care services
PA: Accredited Nursing Services
17141 Ventura Blvd # 201
818 986-6017

(P-16356)
ACCREDITED NURSING SERVICES
Also Called: Accredited Nursing Care
3570 Camino Del Rio N Ste 108, San Diego (92108-1747)
PHONE....................818 986-1234
Carol Speakman, *Mgr*
EMP: 173
SALES (corp-wide): 2.91MM **Privately Held**
Web: www.aveanna.com
SIC: 8082 Home health care services
PA: Accredited Nursing Services
17141 Ventura Blvd # 201
818 986-6017

(P-16357)
ACTION HLTH CARE PRSNNEL SVCS
3020 Old Ranch Pkwy Ste 300, Seal Beach (90740-2751)
PHONE....................562 799-5523
Renee Steele, *CEO*
EMP: 150 EST: 1977
SALES (est): 666.71K **Privately Held**
SIC: 8082 Home health care services

(P-16358)
AEGIS SENIOR COMMUNITIES LLC
Also Called: Aegis of Granada Hills
10801 Lindley Ave, Granada Hills (91344-4441)
PHONE....................818 363-3373
Bill Phelps, *Brnch Mgr*
EMP: 151
SALES (corp-wide): 137.42MM **Privately Held**
Web: www.aegisliving.com
SIC: 8082 8052 8051 8361 Home health care services; Intermediate care facilities; Skilled nursing care facilities; Residential care
PA: Senior Aegis Communities Llc
415 118th Ave Se
866 688-5829

(P-16359)
AEGIS SENIOR COMMUNITIES LLC
Also Called: Aegis of Ventura
4964 Telegraph Rd, Ventura (93003-8181)
PHONE....................805 650-1114
Hugh Carter, *Mgr*
EMP: 88
SALES (corp-wide): 137.42MM **Privately Held**
Web: www.aegisliving.com
SIC: 8082 8051 Home health care services; Skilled nursing care facilities
PA: Senior Aegis Communities Llc
415 118th Ave Se
866 688-5829

(P-16360)
ALL VALLEY HOME HLTH CARE INC
Also Called: All Valley Home Care
3665 Ruffin Rd Ste 103, San Diego (92123-1871)
PHONE....................619 276-8001
Glen Amador, *Pr*
Michael Drake, *
EMP: 100 EST: 2013
SQ FT: 2,500
SALES (est): 1.19MM **Privately Held**
SIC: 8082 Home health care services

(P-16361)
ALLCARE NURSING SERVICES INC
3675 Huntington Dr Ste 228, Pasadena (91107-5669)
PHONE....................626 432-1999
Paciencia De Guzman, *CEO*
Mary Jane Gumaboa, *
EMP: 100 EST: 2004
SALES (est): 8MM **Privately Held**
Web: www.allcarenursing.com
SIC: 8082 Home health care services

(P-16362)
AMADA SENIOR CARE
901 Calle Amanecer Ste 350, San Clemente (92673-4212)
PHONE....................949 284-8036
Tafa Jefferson, *Prin*
EMP: 80 EST: 2016
SALES (est): 2.92MM **Privately Held**
Web: www.amadaseniorcare.com
SIC: 8082 Home health care services

(P-16363)
AMERICAN PRIVATE DUTY INC
Also Called: American Untd HM Care Crp-Priv
13111 Ventura Blvd Ste 100, Studio City (91604-2218)
PHONE....................818 386-6358
Ann Koshy, *Pr*
EMP: 80 EST: 1999
SALES (est): 761.51K **Privately Held**
SIC: 8082 Visiting nurse service

(P-16364)
AMERICARE HOME HEALTH INC
16501 Sherman Way Ste 225, Van Nuys (91406-3787)
PHONE....................818 881-0005
Karo Yepremian, *CEO*
EMP: 99 EST: 2012
SALES (est): 5.9MM **Privately Held**
Web: www.americarehhinc.com
SIC: 8082 Home health care services

(P-16365)
ANGELS IN MOTION LLC
Also Called: Visiting Angels
13768 Roswell Ave, Chino (91710-1401)
PHONE....................909 590-9102
Dominique Alvarez, *Managing Member*
EMP: 70 EST: 2010
SALES (est): 3.5MM **Privately Held**
Web: www.visitingangels.com
SIC: 8082 Home health care services

(P-16366)
AXELACARE HOLDINGS INC
12604 Hiddencreek Way Ste C, Cerritos (90703-2137)
PHONE....................714 522-8802
EMP: 337
SIC: 8082 Home health care services
PA: Axelacare Holdings, Inc.
15529 College Blvd

(P-16367)
BARRY & TAFFY INC
Also Called: Accredited Home Care
5955 De Soto Ave Ste 160, Woodland Hills (91367-5101)
PHONE....................818 986-1234
Millette Arrendondo, *Pr*
EMP: 1494 EST: 2010
SALES (est): 5.01MM
SALES (corp-wide): 1.9B **Publicly Held**
SIC: 8082 Home health care services
PA: Aveanna Healthcare Holdings Inc.
400 Intrstate N Pkwy Se S
770 441-1580

(P-16368)
BERGER INC
Also Called: Accredited Home Care
5955 De Soto Ave Ste 160, Woodland Hills (91367-5101)
PHONE....................818 986-1234
EMP: 5186 EST: 1980
SALES (est): 2.97MM
SALES (corp-wide): 1.9B **Publicly Held**
Web: www.aveanna.com
SIC: 8082 Home health care services
PA: Aveanna Healthcare Holdings Inc.
400 Intrstate N Pkwy Se S
770 441-1580

(P-16369)
BJZ LLC
Also Called: Always Best Care Desert Cities
45150 Club Dr, Indian Wells (92210-8806)
PHONE....................760 851-0740
Neil Zwack, *Admn*
Neil Zwack, *Managing Member*
Bonnie Zwack, *Managing Member**
EMP: 140 EST: 2013
SALES (est): 3.16MM **Privately Held**
Web: www.alwaysbestcare.com

SIC: 8082 Home health care services

(P-16370)
BRANLYN PROMINENCE INC
Also Called: Home Instead Senior Care
13334 Amargosa Rd, Victorville
(92392-8504)
PHONE..............................760 843-5655
Chris Parmelee, Genl Mgr
EMP: 130
SQ FT: 1,800
Web: www.homeinstead.com
SIC: 8082 Home health care services
PA: Branlyn Prominence, Inc.
9213 Archibald Ave

(P-16371)
BRANLYN PROMINENCE INC (PA)
Also Called: Home Instead Senior Care
9213 Archibald Ave, Rancho Cucamonga
(91730-5207)
P.O. Box 8176 (91701)
PHONE..............................909 476-9030
Brandi Johnson, CEO
Lynda Patriquin, *
EMP: 100 EST: 2000
SALES (est): 3.72MM Privately Held
Web: www.homeinstead.com
SIC: 8082 Home health care services

(P-16372)
BRIDGE HOME HEALTH LLC
5090 Shoreham Pl Ste 109, San Diego
(92122-5934)
PHONE..............................858 277-5200
EMP: 120 EST: 2017
SALES (est): 15.58MM Privately Held
Web: www.bridgehh.com
SIC: 8082 Home health care services

(P-16373)
BUENA VISTA MGT SVCS LLC
Also Called: Windward Life Care
2045 1st Ave, San Diego (92101-2011)
P.O. Box 87371 (92138-7371)
PHONE..............................619 450-4300
Norman Hannay, Owner
Norman J Hannay, Owner
EMP: 130 EST: 2004
SQ FT: 2,000
SALES (est): 4.39MM Privately Held
Web: www.windwardlifecare.com
SIC: 8082 Home health care services

(P-16374)
CAERUS MARKETING GROUP LLC
Also Called: Studykik
409 Santa Monica Blvd Ste 2a, Santa
Monica (90401-2234)
PHONE..............................800 792-1015
Brian Klay, CEO
Kim Odle, *
Greg Christie, CPO*
Tarra Shingler, CCO*
Will Rigsbee, *
EMP: 70 EST: 2013
SALES (est): 25MM
SALES (corp-wide): 5.39B Privately Held
SIC: 8082 Home health care services
PA: Syneos Health, Inc.
1030 Sync St
919 876-9300

(P-16375)
CARE UNLIMITED HEALTH SVCS INC
1025 W Arrow Hwy Ste 103, Glendora
(91740-5407)

PHONE..............................626 332-3767
Carol Wedderburn, CEO
EMP: 90 EST: 1995
SALES (est): 4.36MM Privately Held
Web: www.careunltd.com
SIC: 8082 Home health care services

(P-16376)
CENTERWELL HEALTH SERVICES INC
9444 Balboa Ave Ste 290, San Diego
(92123-4901)
PHONE..............................858 565-2499
EMP: 103
SALES (corp-wide): 106.37B Publicly Held
Web: www.gentivahs.com
SIC: 8082 Home health care services
HQ: Centerwell Health Services, Inc.
3350 Rvrwood Pkwy Ste 140
Atlanta GA 30339
770 951-6450

(P-16377)
CENTRAL HEALTH PLAN CAL INC
200 Oceangate Ste 100, Long Beach
(90802-4317)
PHONE..............................866 314-2427
Abbie Totten, CEO
Amy Park, CFO
EMP: 175 EST: 2001
SQ FT: 16,144
SALES (corp-wide): 1.16B Publicly Held
Web: www.centralhealthplan.com
SIC: 8082 Home health care services
PA: Neuehealth, Inc.
9250 Nw 36th St Ste 420
612 238-1321

(P-16378)
CLINICS ON DEMAND INC
1001 Gayley Ave Unit 24673, Los Angeles
(90024-3490)
PHONE..............................310 709-7355
Shahrouz Ghodsian, CEO
EMP: 81 EST: 2015
SALES (est): 1.95MM Privately Held
SIC: 8082 Home health care services

(P-16379)
COASTAL CMNTY SENIOR CARE LLC
Also Called: Home Instead Senior Care
5500 E Atherton St Ste 216, Long Beach
(90815-4017)
PHONE..............................562 596-4884
Donald Pierce, Managing Member
EMP: 140 EST: 2015
SQ FT: 2,300
SALES (est): 3.79MM Privately Held
Web: www.homeinstead.com
SIC: 8082 Home health care services

(P-16380)
COMPETENT CARE INC
Also Called: Competent Care HM Hlth
Nursing
2900 Bristol St Ste D107, Costa Mesa
(92626-5940)
PHONE..............................714 545-4818
TOLL FREE: 800
Lynett Laroche, Pr
EMP: 70 EST: 1988
SALES (est): 1.33MM Privately Held
Web: www.competentcare.com
SIC: 8082 7299 Visiting nurse service;
Information services, consumer

(P-16381)
CONFIDO LLC
Also Called: 123 Home Care
1055 E Colorado Blvd, Pasadena
(91106-2327)
PHONE..............................310 361-8558
Graeme Freeman, CEO
Ryan Baxter, *
Mark Schellinger, *
EMP: 1900 EST: 2018
SALES (est): 2.23MM Privately Held
Web: www.thekey.com
SIC: 8082 Home health care services

(P-16382)
CORE HOLDINGS INC
Also Called: Maxin
17291 Irvine Blvd Ste 404, Tustin
(92780-2932)
PHONE..............................714 969-2342
Ryan Dammieir, CEO
EMP: 250 EST: 1992
SQ FT: 1,200
SALES (est): 431.61K Privately Held
SIC: 8082 Home health care services

(P-16383)
COX ENTERPRISES LLC
Also Called: Home Helpers of North County
325 W 3rd Ave Ste 101, Escondido
(92025-4140)
PHONE..............................858 822-8587
Christopher Cox, Managing Member
EMP: 80 EST: 2018
SALES (est): 2.25MM Privately Held
Web: www.homehelpershomecare.com
SIC: 8082 Home health care services

(P-16384)
CRESCENT HEALTHCARE INC (HQ)
11980 Telegraph Rd Ste 100, Santa Fe
Springs (90670-6089)
PHONE..............................714 520-6300
Paul Mastrapa, CEO
William P Forster, *
Pamela Bowen, CIO*
EMP: 150 EST: 1992
SQ FT: 26,000
SALES (est): 9.88MM Publicly Held
Web: www.crescenthealthcare.com
SIC: 8082 Home health care services
PA: Option Care Health, Inc.
3000 Lakeside Dr Ste 300n

(P-16385)
DUNN & BERGER INC
Also Called: Accredited Nursing Care
5955 De Soto Ave Ste 160, Woodland Hills
(91367-5101)
PHONE..............................818 986-1234
Barry Berger, Pr
EMP: 500 EST: 1980
SALES (est): 4.85MM
SALES (corp-wide): 1.9B Publicly Held
SIC: 8082 Home health care services
PA: Aveanna Healthcare Holdings Inc.
400 Intrstate N Pkwy Se S
770 441-1580

(P-16386)
DYNAMIC HOME CARE SERVICE INC (PA)
Also Called: DYNAMIC HOME CARE
14260 Ventura Blvd Ste 301, Sherman Oaks
(91423-2734)
PHONE..............................818 981-4446
Nissan Pardo, CEO
Carol Silver, *

EMP: 100 EST: 1987
SALES (est): 8.32MM Privately Held
Web: www.dynamicnursing.com
SIC: 8082 Visiting nurse service

(P-16387)
EISENHOWER MEDICAL CENTER
Also Called: Eisenhower Health Services
39000 Bob Hope Dr Ste 102, Rancho
Mirage (92270-3221)
PHONE..............................760 773-1888
Joel M Hirschberg Md, Mgr
EMP: 180
SALES (corp-wide): 1.04B Privately Held
Web: www.eisenhowerhealth.org
SIC: 8082 8062 Home health care services;
General medical and surgical hospitals
PA: Eisenhower Medical Center
39000 Bob Hope Dr
760 340-3911

(P-16388)
ELIZABETH HOSPICE INC (PA)
800 W Valley Pkwy, Escondido
(92025-2557)
PHONE..............................760 737-2050
Sarah Mcspadden, CEO
Laura Miller, *
Kiprian Skavinski, *
Jan Jones, *
Andrea Goodwin, *
EMP: 200 EST: 1978
SALES (est): 34.27MM
SALES (corp-wide): 34.27MM Privately
Held
Web: www.elizabethhospice.org
SIC: 8082 Home health care services

(P-16389)
FAITH JONES & ASSOCIATES INC (PA)
Also Called: Aall Care In Home Services
7801 Mission Center Ct Ste 106, San Diego
(92108-1314)
PHONE..............................619 297-9601
Faith Jones, Pr
Norman Jones, *
EMP: 90 EST: 1995
SQ FT: 1,200
SALES (est): 1.66MM
SALES (corp-wide): 1.66MM Privately
Held
Web: www.aallcare.com
SIC: 8082 Home health care services

(P-16390)
FIRST MERIDIAN CARE SVCS INC
Also Called: 1st Meridian Medical Transport
4545 Murphy Canyon Rd Ste 204, San
Diego (92123-4363)
PHONE..............................858 529-1886
EMP: 73 EST: 2013
SALES (est): 3.6MM Privately Held
Web: www.1stmeridiancareservices.com
SIC: 8082 Home health care services

(P-16391)
FIRSTAT NURSING SERVICES INC
411 Camino Del Rio S Ste 100, San Diego
(92108-3508)
PHONE..............................619 220-7600
Linnea Goodrich, Owner
Kathleen Tickle, *
EMP: 105 EST: 1997
SQ FT: 1,800
SALES (est): 1.81MM Privately Held

Web: www.firstatofsandiego.com
SIC: 8082 Visiting nurse service

(P-16392)
FORESIDE MANAGEMENT COMPANY
26023 Acero Ste 100, Mission Viejo (92691-7942)
PHONE...............................949 966-1933
Mark Woodsum, *CEO*
Mark Woodsum, *Prin*
EMP: 300 EST: 2014
SALES (est): 9.15MM **Privately Held**
Web: www.brightstarcare.com
SIC: 8082 Home health care services

(P-16393)
GRANDCARE HEALTH SERVICES LLC (PA)
3452 E Foothill Blvd Ste 700, Pasadena (91107-3167)
PHONE...............................866 554-2447
David Bell, *Managing Member*
EMP: 150 EST: 2014
SALES (est): 9.21MM
SALES (corp-wide): 9.21MM **Privately Held**
Web: www.grandcarehealth.com
SIC: 8082 Home health care services

(P-16394)
HELP UNLMTED PERSONNEL SVC INC
Also Called: Help Unlimited
3202 E Ojai Ave, Ojai (93023-9320)
PHONE...............................805 962-4646
Leanna Mcnealy, *Mgr*
EMP: 675
Web: www.arosacare.com
SIC: 8082 7363 Visiting nurse service; Medical help service
PA: Help Unlimited Personnel Service, Inc.
1957 Eastman Ave

(P-16395)
HUNTINGTON CARE LLC
Also Called: Huntington Home Care
3452 E Foothill Blvd Ste 760, Pasadena (91107-6043)
PHONE...............................877 405-6990
Carlo Stepanians, *CEO*
Sergio Varela, *
EMP: 175 EST: 2007
SALES (est): 1.48MM
SALES (corp-wide): 9.21MM **Privately Held**
Web: www.muv.life
SIC: 8082 Home health care services
PA: Grandcare Health Services Llc
3452 E Fthill Blvd Ste 70
866 554-2447

(P-16396)
INTEGRITY HLTHCARE SLTIONS INC
5625 Ruffin Rd, San Diego (92123-1395)
PHONE...............................760 432-9811
Wendy Olayvar, *Pr*
EMP: 75
Web: www.interimhealthcare.com
SIC: 8082 Home health care services
PA: Integrity Healthcare Solutions, Inc.
1551 Sawgrass Corp Pkwy

(P-16397)
INTERHEALTH SERVICES INC (HQ)
Also Called: Presbyterian Inter Cmnty Hosp

12401 Washington Blvd, Whittier (90602-1006)
PHONE...............................562 698-0811
Daniel F Adams, *Pr*
Gary Koger, *
Peggy Chulack, *
Jim West, *
EMP: 143 EST: 1983
SQ FT: 1,000
SALES (est): 22.41MM
SALES (corp-wide): 20.43MM **Privately Held**
SIC: 8082 8062 Home health care services; General medical and surgical hospitals
PA: Pih Health, Inc.
12401 Washington Blvd
562 698-0811

(P-16398)
INTERIM HEALTHCARE INC
Also Called: Interim Services
7000 Indiana Ave Ste 107, Riverside (92506-4153)
PHONE...............................951 684-6111
Marianne Thompson, *Mgr*
EMP: 127
SQ FT: 2,000
Web: www.interimhealthcare.com
SIC: 8082 Home health care services
PA: Interim Healthcare Inc.
1551 Swgrass Corp Pkwy St

(P-16399)
JAMES REBECCA PROUTY ENTPS INC
Also Called: Always Best Care Temecula Vly
43980 Margarita Rd Ste 102, Temecula (92592-2783)
PHONE...............................951 292-9777
Rebecca Prouty, *Pr*
Rebecca Prouty, *Prin*
James Prouty, *
EMP: 80 EST: 2013
SALES (est): 1.38MM **Privately Held**
Web: www.alwaysbestcare.com
SIC: 8082 Home health care services

(P-16400)
LAGUNA HOME HEALTH SVCS LLC
Also Called: Team Select Home Care
25411 Cabot Rd Ste 205, Laguna Hills (92653-5525)
PHONE...............................949 707-5023
Michael Lovell, *Pr*
EMP: 133 EST: 2008
SALES (est): 905.45K **Privately Held**
SIC: 8082 Home health care services

(P-16401)
LIBERTY RESIDENTIAL SVCS INC
12700 Stowe Dr Ste 110, Poway (92064-8875)
PHONE...............................858 500-0852
Herbert T Caskey, *Pr*
EMP: 100 EST: 2007
SALES (est): 1.5MM
SALES (corp-wide): 14.06MM **Privately Held**
Web: www.libertyhealthcare.com
SIC: 8082 Home health care services
PA: Liberty Healthcare Corporation
401 E City Ave Ste 820
610 668-8800

(P-16402)
LIVHOME INC (PA)
Also Called: Arosa

5670 Wilshire Blvd Ste 500, Los Angeles (90036-5682)
PHONE...............................800 807-5854
TOLL FREE: 877
Mike Nicholson, *Ch Bd*
Cody D Legler, *Chief Clinical Officer*
EMP: 1299 EST: 1999
SQ FT: 7,454
SALES (est): 29.93MM
SALES (corp-wide): 29.93MM **Privately Held**
Web: www.livhome.com
SIC: 8082 Home health care services

(P-16403)
MAXIM HEALTHCARE SERVICES INC
3580 Wilshire Blvd Ste 1000, Los Angeles (90010-2544)
PHONE...............................866 465-5678
EMP: 334
Web: www.maximhealthcare.com
SIC: 8082 Home health care services
PA: Maxim Healthcare Services, Inc.
7227 Lee Deforest Dr

(P-16404)
MAXIM HEALTHCARE SERVICES INC
Also Called: Poway Homecare
3111 Camino Del Rio N Ste 1200, San Diego (92108-5747)
PHONE...............................619 299-9350
Jeremy Vanleeuwen, *Mgr*
EMP: 335
Web: www.networthrealtyusa.com
SIC: 8082 Home health care services
PA: Maxim Healthcare Services, Inc.
7227 Lee Deforest Dr

(P-16405)
MAXIM HEALTHCARE SERVICES INC
Also Called: Victorville Homecare
560 E Hospitality Ln Ste 400, San Bernardino (92408-3545)
PHONE...............................760 243-3377
Angie R Wiechert, *Mgr*
EMP: 168
Web: www.maximhealthcare.com
SIC: 8082 Home health care services
PA: Maxim Healthcare Services, Inc.
7227 Lee Deforest Dr

(P-16406)
MISSION HM HLTH SAN DIEGO LLC
Also Called: Mission Healthcare
2365 Northside Dr Ste 200, San Diego (92108-2720)
PHONE...............................619 757-2700
Kerry E Pawl, *CEO*
Brad Parrish, *
Todd Fontenot, *
Mag Vanoosten, *COO*
EMP: 85 EST: 2009
SALES (est): 27.01MM **Privately Held**
Web: www.homewithmission.com
SIC: 8082 Home health care services

(P-16407)
NO ORDINARY MOMENTS INC
16742 Gothard St Ste 115, Huntington Beach (92647-4564)
PHONE...............................714 848-3800
Luis Pena, *Pr*
EMP: 86 EST: 1996
SALES (est): 2.39MM **Privately Held**
Web: www.noordinarymoments.com

SIC: 8082 8322 Home health care services; Emergency social services

(P-16408)
NORTH COAST HOME CARE INC
Also Called: Homewatch Caregivers
5927 Balfour Ct Ste 111, Carlsbad (92008-7376)
PHONE...............................760 260-8700
Tanya Finnerty, *Pr*
Michael Finnerty, *
EMP: 80 EST: 2011
SQ FT: 1,000
SALES (est): 4.31MM **Privately Held**
Web: www.homewatchcaregivers.com
SIC: 8082 Home health care services

(P-16409)
PACIFICARE HEALTH SYSTEMS LLC (HQ)
Also Called: Pacificare Health Systems
5995 Plaza Dr, Cypress (90630-5028)
PHONE...............................714 952-1121
Howard Phanstiel, *CEO*
Joseph S Konowiecki, *
Gregory W Scott, *
Robert W Oberrender, *
EMP: 550 EST: 1996
SQ FT: 104,000
SALES (est): 95.95MM
SALES (corp-wide): 371.62B **Publicly Held**
Web: www.unitedhealthgroup.com
SIC: 8082 6321 Home health care services; Accident and health insurance carriers
PA: Unitedhealth Group Incorporated
9900 Bren Rd E
800 328-5979

(P-16410)
PEGASUS HM HLTH CARE A CAL COR
Also Called: Pegasus Home Health Services
505 N Brand Blvd Ste 1000, Glendale (91203-3924)
PHONE...............................818 551-1932
Pamela Spiszman, *Pr*
▼ EMP: 80 EST: 1994
SALES (est): 11.91MM **Privately Held**
Web: www.pegasushomecare.com
SIC: 8082 Visiting nurse service

(P-16411)
PEOPLES CARE INC
Also Called: PEOPLE'S CARE INC.
13001 Amargosa Rd Ste 101, Victorville (92392-2409)
PHONE...............................760 962-1900
Stacey Minwalla, *Owner*
EMP: 183
SALES (corp-wide): 22.6MM **Privately Held**
Web: www.peoplescare.com
SIC: 8082 Home health care services
PA: Peoples Care Inc.
13920 City Center Dr # 290
855 773-6753

(P-16412)
PREMIER HEALTHCARE SVCS LLC (DH)
Also Called: Phs Staffing
3030 Old Ranch Pkwy Ste 100, Seal Beach (90740-2752)
PHONE...............................626 204-7930
Anthony H Strange, *CEO*
EMP: 200 EST: 2005
SALES (est): 15.23MM

P
R
O
D
U
C
T
S
&
S
V
C
S

SALES (corp-wide): 1.9B **Publicly Held**
Web: www.premier-homehealth.com
SIC: 8082 Home health care services
HQ: Aveanna Healthcare Llc
　　400 Intrstate N Pkwy Se S
　　Atlanta GA 30339
　　770 441-1580

(P-16413)
PREMIER INFSION HLTHCARE SVCS
Also Called: Premier Infusion Care
19500 Normandie Ave, Torrance
(90502-1108)
PHONE..................310 328-3897
Saman Refua, *CEO*
EMP: 99 EST: 2004
SALES (est): 14.91MM **Privately Held**
Web: www.premierinfusion.com
SIC: 8082 Home health care services

(P-16414)
RAMONA COMMUNITY SERVICES CORP (HQ)
Also Called: Ramona Vna & Hospice
890 W Stetson Ave Ste A, Hemet
(92543-7311)
PHONE..................951 658-9288
Patricia Mcbe, *Brnch Mgr*
Carol Wood, *
Patrick Searl, *
Mark Fredrickson, *
John Brudin, *
EMP: 150 EST: 1987
SQ FT: 14,000
SALES (est): 4.36MM **Privately Held**
SIC: 8082 Visiting nurse service
PA: Kpc Group Inc.
　　9 Kpc Pkwy 301

(P-16415)
RES-CARE INC
3187 Red Hill Ave Ste 115, Costa Mesa
(92626-3480)
PHONE..................714 662-3075
Tara Ackley, *Brnch Mgr*
EMP: 97
SALES (corp-wide): 8.83B **Publicly Held**
Web: www.rescare.com
SIC: 8082 Home health care services
HQ: Res-Care, Inc.
　　805 N Whittington Pkwy
　　Louisville KY 40222
　　502 394-2100

(P-16416)
ROCK CANYON HEALTHCARE INC
Also Called: Riverwalk PST-Cute Rhblitation
27101 Puerta Real Ste 450, Mission Viejo
(92691-8566)
PHONE..................719 404-1000
Dave Jorgensen, *Pr*
Beverly Wittekind, *
Soon Burnam, *
Ron Cook, *
EMP: 250 EST: 2014
SALES (est): 19.22MM
SALES (corp-wide): 3.73B **Publicly Held**
Web: www.rockcanyonrehab.com
SIC: 8082 Home health care services
PA: The Ensign Group Inc
　　29222 Rncho Vejo Rd Ste 1
　　949 487-9500

(P-16417)
SAILS WASHINGTON INC
13920 City Center Dr Ste 290, Chino Hills
(91709-5444)

P.O. Box 1026 (98014)
PHONE..................425 333-4114
Michael Kaiser, *CEO*
Anthony Keuter, *
Matthew Cottrell, *
EMP: 500 EST: 2004
SALES (est): 2.34MM **Privately Held**
Web: www.sailswashington.com
SIC: 8082 Home health care services

(P-16418)
SAN DIEGO HOSPICE & PALLIATIVE CARE CORPORATION
Also Called: San Diego Hospice & Palliative
4311 3rd Ave, San Diego (92103-7499)
P.O. Box 3008 (91944-3008)
PHONE..................619 688-1600
TOLL FREE: 866
EMP: 600
Web: www.tibbiaromatik2018.org
SIC: 8082 Home health care services

(P-16419)
SCRIPPS HEALTH
3811 Valley Centre Dr, San Diego
(92130-3318)
PHONE..................858 764-3000
Robert B Sarnoff Md, *Pr*
EMP: 71
SALES (corp-wide): 4.14B **Privately Held**
Web: www.scripps.org
SIC: 8082 Home health care services
PA: Scripps Health
　　10140 Cmpus Pt Dr Cpa 415
　　800 727-4777

(P-16420)
SELECT HOME CARE
128 Erten St, Thousand Oaks
(91360-1809)
PHONE..................805 777-3855
EMP: 100 EST: 2007
SALES (est): 3.13MM **Privately Held**
Web: www.selecthomecare.com
SIC: 8082 Home health care services

(P-16421)
SOUTH BAY SENIOR SERVICES INC
Also Called: Homewatch Caregivers
8929 S Sepulveda Blvd Ste 314, Los
Angeles (90045-3642)
PHONE..................310 338-8558
Richard Williams, *Pr*
Patricia Greaney, *
EMP: 77 EST: 2006
SQ FT: 700
SALES (est): 1.73MM **Privately Held**
Web: www.homewatchcaregivers.com
SIC: 8082 Home health care services

(P-16422)
ST JOSEPH HEALTH PER CARE SVCS
1315 Corona Pointe Ct Ste 201, Corona
(92879-1789)
PHONE..................800 365-1110
Greg Henderson, *Prin*
EMP: 99
SALES (corp-wide): 2.37MM **Privately Held**
Web: www.nursenextdoor.com
SIC: 8082 Home health care services
PA: St Joseph Health Personal Care
　　Services
　　200 W Center St Promenade
　　714 712-7100

(P-16423)
ST JSEPH HLTH SYS HM CARE SVC
200 W Center Street Promenade, Anaheim
(92805-3960)
PHONE..................714 712-9500
Jeffrey Hammond, *Managing Member*
Susan Harvey, *
EMP: 800 EST: 2015
SALES (est): 6.1MM
SALES (corp-wide): 55.69MM **Privately Held**
SIC: 8082 Home health care services
HQ: St. Joseph Health System
　　3345 Michaelson Dr #100
　　Irvine CA 92612
　　949 381-4000

(P-16424)
STAFF ASSISTANCE INC (PA)
Also Called: Staff Assistance
72 Moody Ct Ste 100, Thousand Oaks
(91360-7426)
PHONE..................818 894-7879
Bill Donley, *Ch Bd*
Elaine S Donley, *
EMP: 300 EST: 1992
SQ FT: 800
SALES (est): 24.72MM **Privately Held**
Web: www.assistedcares.com
SIC: 8082 Home health care services

(P-16425)
TIFFANY HOMECARE INC (PA)
Also Called: Always Right Home Care
9700 Reseda Blvd Ste 105, Northridge
(91324-5516)
PHONE..................818 886-1602
Larry S Spaeter, *CEO*
EMP: 497 EST: 2003
SQ FT: 1,200
SALES (est): 4.04MM
SALES (corp-wide): 4.04MM **Privately Held**
SIC: 8082 Home health care services

(P-16426)
UCLA HEALTH AUXILIARY
10920 Wilshire Blvd Ste 400, Los Angeles
(90024-6544)
PHONE..................310 267-4327
David T Feinberg, *Pr*
Patricia Kapur, *
Patty Cuen, *
EMP: 325 EST: 1981
SALES (est): 58.2MM **Privately Held**
Web: www.uclahealth.org
SIC: 8082 Home health care services

(P-16427)
ULTRACARE SERVICES LLC
11539 Hawthorne Blvd Ste 500, Hawthorne
(90250-2353)
PHONE..................818 266-9668
EMP: 94 EST: 2014
SALES (est): 3.72MM **Privately Held**
SIC: 8082 Home health care services

(P-16428)
UNIVERSAL HOME CARE INC
151 N San Vicente Blvd Ste 200, Beverly
Hills (90211-2323)
PHONE..................323 653-9222
Marina Greenberg, *CEO*
Stephen Shapiro Md, *Medical Vice President*
EMP: 200 EST: 1995
SALES (est): 4.23MM **Privately Held**
Web: www.universalhomecare.org

SIC: 8082 Home health care services

(P-16429)
US CARENET SERVICES LLC
42225 10th St W Ste 2b, Lancaster
(93534-7080)
PHONE..................661 945-7350
Michelle Shah, *Dir*
EMP: 106
SALES (corp-wide): 54.48MM **Privately Held**
SIC: 8082 Visiting nurse service
HQ: Us Carenet Services, Llc
　　699 Broad St Ste 1001
　　Augusta GA 30901

(P-16430)
VISITING NRSE ASSN OF INLAND C (PA)
Also Called: Vnaic
600 W Santa Ana Blvd Ste 114, Santa Ana
(92701-4514)
P.O. Box 1649 (92502-1649)
PHONE..................951 413-1200
Mike A Rusnak, *Pr*
EMP: 720 EST: 1960
SALES (est): 11.4MM
SALES (corp-wide): 11.4MM **Privately Held**
Web: www.vnacalifornia.org
SIC: 8082 Visiting nurse service

(P-16431)
VISITING NURSE & HOSPICE CARE (PA)
Also Called: VISITING NURSE & HOSPICE CARE
509 E Montecito St Ste 200, Santa Barbara
(93103-3293)
PHONE..................805 965-5555
Lynda Tanner, *CEO*
Michelle Martinich, *
Rick Keith, *
Neil Levinson, *
Mary Pritchard, *
EMP: 87 EST: 1910
SQ FT: 13,765
SALES (est): 32.91MM
SALES (corp-wide): 32.91MM **Privately Held**
Web: www.vna.health
SIC: 8082 Home health care services

(P-16432)
VNA OF GREATER LOS ANGELES INC
17682 Mitchell N Ste 100, Irvine
(92614-6037)
PHONE..................951 252-5314
Rajnit Walia, *CEO*
EMP: 99 EST: 2005
SALES (est): 1.2MM **Privately Held**
SIC: 8082 Home health care services

(P-16433)
VNACARE (PA)
Also Called: VNA PRIVATE DUTY CARE
412 E Vanderbilt Way Ste 100, San
Bernardino (92408-3552)
P.O. Box 908 (91711)
PHONE..................909 624-3574
Marsha Fox, *Pr*
EMP: 93 EST: 1952
SALES (est): 19.77MM
SALES (corp-wide): 19.77MM **Privately Held**
Web: www.vnacare.com
SIC: 8082 Visiting nurse service

8092 Kidney Dialysis Centers

(P-16434)
DAVITA INC
15271 Laguna Canyon Rd, Irvine
(92618-3146)
PHONE..............................949 930-4400
Viki Anderson, *Brnch Mgr*
EMP: 270
Web: www.davita.com
SIC: 8092 Kidney dialysis centers
PA: Davita Inc.
2000 16th St

(P-16435)
**HARBOR-UCLA MED
FOUNDATION INC**
Also Called: Ucla Hbr Dlysis Ctr Med Fndtio
21602 S Vermont Ave, Torrance
(90502-1940)
PHONE..............................310 533-0413
Patricia Hall, *Mgr*
EMP: 300
Web: www.harbor-ucla.org
SIC: 8092 Kidney dialysis centers
PA: Harbor-Ucla Medical Foundation, Inc.
21840 Normandie Ave Ste 1

(P-16436)
HEMODIALYSIS INC
Also Called: Holy Cross Renal Center
14901 Rinaldi St Ste 100, Mission Hills
(91345-1253)
PHONE..............................818 365-6961
John R Depalma, *Brnch Mgr*
EMP: 75
SALES (corp-wide): 8.93MM **Privately
Held**
Web: www.hemodialysis-inc.com
SIC: 8092 Kidney dialysis centers
PA: Hemodialysis, Inc.
710 W Wilson Ave
818 500-8736

8093 Specialty Outpatient Clinics, Nec

(P-16437)
ABC RECOVERY CENTER INC
44359 Palm St, Indio (92201-3116)
PHONE..............................760 342-6616
Christopher Yingling, *CEO*
J David Likens, *
David Liken, *
Sandra Spence, *
EMP: 86 **EST:** 1963
SQ FT: 30,000
SALES (est): 7.64MM **Privately Held**
Web: www.abcrecoverycenter.org
SIC: 8093 8361 8322 Alcohol clinic,
outpatient; Rehabilitation center, residential;
health care incidental; Substance abuse
counseling

(P-16438)
ACCEL THERAPIES INC
1845 W Orangewood Ave Ste 101, Orange
(92868-2085)
PHONE..............................855 443-3822
Patrick Moynihan, *Admn*
EMP: 91 **EST:** 2005
SALES (est): 5.73MM **Privately Held**
Web: www.acceltherapies.com
SIC: 8093 Rehabilitation center, outpatient
treatment

(P-16439)
**ADDICTION TREATMENT TECH
LLC**
Also Called: Care Solace
120 Birmingham Dr Ste 200, Cardiff
(92007-1753)
PHONE..............................818 437-5609
Chad Castruita, *CEO*
Mike Dodge, *COO*
Ya-yung Cheng, *CMO*
EMP: 70
SALES (est): 5.23MM **Privately Held**
SIC: 8093 Mental health clinic, outpatient

(P-16440)
**ALPINE CONVALESCENT
CENTER INC**
Also Called: Alpine Special Treatment Ctr
2120 Alpine Blvd, Alpine (91901-2113)
PHONE..............................619 659-3120
Michael E Doyle, *CEO*
EMP: 100 **EST:** 1972
SQ FT: 15,000
SALES (est): 22.67MM **Privately Held**
Web: www.astci.com
SIC: 8093 Rehabilitation center, outpatient
treatment

(P-16441)
**AMANECER CMNTY CNSLING
SVC A N**
1200 Wilshire Blvd Ste 200, Los Angeles
(90017-1930)
PHONE..............................213 481-7464
Tim Ryder, *Ex Dir*
Frank Chargualaf, *
EMP: 100 **EST:** 1975
SALES (est): 11.26MM **Privately Held**
Web: www.amanecerla.org
SIC: 8093 Mental health clinic, outpatient

(P-16442)
ARC - IMPERIAL VALLEY
340 E 1st St, Calexico (92231-2732)
PHONE..............................760 768-1944
Alex King, *Prin*
EMP: 42
SALES (corp-wide): 15.5MM **Privately
Held**
Web: www.arciv.org
SIC: 8093 4783 2051 5812 Rehabilitation
center, outpatient treatment; Packing goods
for shipping; Bakery: wholesale or
wholesale/retail combined; Delicatessen
(eating places)
PA: Arc - Imperial Valley
298 E Ross Ave
760 352-0180

(P-16443)
**ART AUTISM RELATED
THERAPY LLC**
10134 6th St Ste I, Rancho Cucamonga
(91730-5857)
PHONE..............................909 304-1039
Sandra Palomo, *Prin*
EMP: 90 **EST:** 2018
SALES (est): 3.5MM **Privately Held**
SIC: 8093 Rehabilitation center, outpatient
treatment

(P-16444)
**BEHAVIORAL HEALTH WORKS
INC**
1301 E Orangewood Ave, Anaheim
(92805-6807)
PHONE..............................800 249-1266
Robert Douk, *CEO*

EMP: 99 **EST:** 2011
SALES (est): 17.11MM **Privately Held**
Web: www.bhwcares.com
SIC: 8093 Mental health clinic, outpatient

(P-16445)
BETTY FORD CENTER (HQ)
39000 Bob Hope Dr, Rancho Mirage
(92270-3221)
P.O. Box 1560 (92270-1056)
PHONE..............................760 773-4100
TOLL FREE: 800
Mark Mishek, *Pr*
James Blaha, *
Jim Steinhagen, *
EMP: 250 **EST:** 1983
SALES (est): 11.12MM
SALES (corp-wide): 222.98MM **Privately
Held**
Web: www.hazeldenbettyford.org
SIC: 8093 Substance abuse clinics
(outpatient)
PA: Hazelden Betty Ford Foundation
15251 Pleasant Valley Rd
651 213-4000

(P-16446)
BH-SD OPCO LLC (PA)
Also Called: Alvarado Parkway Institute
7050 Parkway Dr, La Mesa (91942-1535)
PHONE..............................619 465-4411
Patrick Ziemer, *CEO*
Chad Engbrecht, *
James Adamson, *
EMP: 94 **EST:** 2014
SALES (est): 30.95MM
SALES (corp-wide): 30.95MM **Privately
Held**
Web: www.apibhs.com
SIC: 8093 Mental health clinic, outpatient

(P-16447)
**CARRICO PEDIATRIC THERAPY
INC**
1301 W Arrow Hwy, San Dimas
(91773-2330)
PHONE..............................562 607-1937
Lan Carrico, *Prin*
EMP: 72 **EST:** 2015
SALES (est): 1.71MM **Privately Held**
Web: www.carricopediatrictherapy.com
SIC: 8093 Rehabilitation center, outpatient
treatment

(P-16448)
CASA PALMERA LLC
14750 El Camino Real, Del Mar
(92014-4299)
PHONE..............................888 481-4481
Lee Johnson Mbr, *Mgr*
EMP: 94 **EST:** 2001
SALES (est): 2.52MM **Privately Held**
Web: www.casapalmera.com
SIC: 8093 Substance abuse clinics
(outpatient)

(P-16449)
**CENTER FOR ATISM RES
EVLTION S**
Also Called: Cares
8787 Complex Dr Ste 300, San Diego
(92123-1453)
PHONE..............................858 444-8823
Olanderia Brown, *Mgr*
EMP: 78 **EST:** 2007
SALES (est): 1.93MM
SALES (corp-wide): 33.56MM **Privately
Held**
Web: www.caresnpa.com

SIC: 8093 Mental health clinic, outpatient
PA: Fred Finch Youth Center
3800 Coolidge Ave
510 773-6669

(P-16450)
**CENTRE FOR NEURO SKILLS
(PA)**
5215 Ashe Rd, Bakersfield (93313-2069)
PHONE..............................661 872-3408
David Harrington, *CEO*
Mark J Ashley, *
Ken Chief Strategy Diashyn, *Development
Officer*
EMP: 450 **EST:** 1980
SQ FT: 14,000
SALES (est): 320.23K
SALES (corp-wide): 320.23K **Privately
Held**
Web: www.neuroskills.com
SIC: 8093 Rehabilitation center, outpatient
treatment

(P-16451)
**CENTRO DE SLUD DE LA
CMNDAD DE**
Also Called: San Ysidro Health Center
4004 Beyer Blvd, San Ysidro (92173-2007)
PHONE..............................619 205-6341
Bill Parker, *Dir*
EMP: 365
SALES (corp-wide): 99.89MM **Privately
Held**
Web: www.syhealth.org
SIC: 8093 Specialty outpatient clinics, nec
PA: Centro De Salud De La Comunidad De
San Ysidro, Inc.
1601 Precision Park Ln
619 428-4463

(P-16452)
**CENTRO DE SLUD DE LA
CMNDAD DE**
Also Called: National City Family Clinic
1136 D Ave, National City (91950-3412)
PHONE..............................619 336-2300
Joe Robledo, *Mgr*
EMP: 365
SQ FT: 4,712
SALES (corp-wide): 99.89MM **Privately
Held**
Web: www.syhealth.org
SIC: 8093 Specialty outpatient clinics, nec
PA: Centro De Salud De La Comunidad De
San Ysidro, Inc.
1601 Precision Park Ln
619 428-4463

(P-16453)
**CENTRO DE SLUD DE LA
CMNDAD DE (PA)**
Also Called: San Ysidro Health
1601 Precision Park Ln, San Diego
(92173-1345)
PHONE..............................619 428-4463
Kevin Mattson, *CEO*
Ed Martinez, *
M Gutierrez, *
EMP: 80 **EST:** 1969
SQ FT: 2,000
SALES (est): 99.89MM
SALES (corp-wide): 99.89MM **Privately
Held**
Web: www.syhealth.org
SIC: 8093 8011 Specialty outpatient clinics,
nec; Offices and clinics of medical doctors

(P-16454)
CHILD AND FAMILY GUIDANCE CTR (PA)
Also Called: Northpoint Day Treatment Sch
9650 Zelzah Ave, Northridge (91325-2003)
PHONE.....................818 739-5140
Roy Marshall, *Ex Dir*
Russell Jones, *
Robert Garcia, *
Stephen J Howard Ph.d., *VP*
Bonnie Weissman, *
EMP: 200 EST: 1961
SQ FT: 35,000
SALES (est): 29.83MM
SALES (corp-wide): 29.83MM **Privately Held**
Web: www.childguidance.org
SIC: 8093 Mental health clinic, outpatient

(P-16455)
CHILD GUIDANCE CENTER INC
600 W Santa Ana Blvd, Santa Ana (92701-4558)
PHONE.....................714 953-4455
Lori Pack, *Ex Dir*
Christine Kiehl, *
EMP: 106 EST: 2008
SALES (est): 9.75MM **Privately Held**
Web: www.childguidancecenteroc.org
SIC: 8093 Mental health clinic, outpatient

(P-16456)
CLEAR RECOVERY CENTER
Also Called: Clear Behavioral Health
18119 Prairie Ave Ste 102, Torrance (90504-3740)
PHONE.....................310 318-2122
EMP: 71 EST: 2015
SALES (est): 3.73MM **Privately Held**
Web: www.clearbehavioralhealth.com
SIC: 8093 Substance abuse clinics (outpatient)

(P-16457)
COMMUNITY ACTION PRTNR SAN LUI
Also Called: E O C Health Services
705 Grand Ave, San Luis Obispo (93401-2639)
PHONE.....................805 544-2478
Janice Wolf, *Mgr*
EMP: 127
SALES (corp-wide): 104.15MM **Privately Held**
Web: www.capslo.org
SIC: 8093 Family planning clinic
PA: Community Action Partnership Of San Luis Obispo County, Inc.
1030 Southwood Dr
805 544-4355

(P-16458)
COMPREHENSIVE CANCER CENTERS INC
8201 Beverly Blvd, Los Angeles (90048-4541)
PHONE.....................323 966-3400
EMP: 120
SIC: 8093 Specialty outpatient clinics, nec

(P-16459)
COUNTY OF IMPERIAL
Also Called: Imperial County Mental Health
202 N 8th St, El Centro (92243-2302)
PHONE.....................760 482-4120
Rudy Lopez, *Dir*
EMP: 75
SALES (corp-wide): 445.2MM **Privately Held**

Web: www.imperialcountyced.com
SIC: 8093 9111 Mental health clinic, outpatient; County supervisors' and executives' office
PA: County Of Imperial
940 W Main St Ste 208
760 482-4556

(P-16460)
COUNTY OF LOS ANGELES
Also Called: Mental Health Dept of
17707 Studebaker Rd, Artesia (90703-2640)
PHONE.....................562 402-0688
Latisha Guvman, *Mgr*
EMP: 71
Web: www.lacounty.gov
SIC: 8093 9431 Specialty outpatient clinics, nec; Administration of public health programs
PA: County Of Los Angeles
500 W Temple St Ste 437
213 974-1101

(P-16461)
COUNTY OF LOS ANGELES
Also Called: Health Services, Dept of
5205 Melrose Ave, Los Angeles (90038-3144)
PHONE.....................323 769-7800
Rosa Pinon, *Brnch Mgr*
EMP: 71
Web: www.lacounty.gov
SIC: 8093 9431 Family planning and birth control clinics; Administration of public health programs
PA: County Of Los Angeles
500 W Temple St Ste 437
213 974-1101

(P-16462)
COUNTY OF LOS ANGELES
Also Called: Health Services, Dept of
7601 Imperial Hwy, Downey (90242-3456)
PHONE.....................562 401-7088
Valeria Orange, *Dir*
EMP: 415
Web: www.lacounty.gov
SIC: 8093 9431 Rehabilitation center, outpatient treatment; Administration of public health programs, County government
PA: County Of Los Angeles
500 W Temple St Ste 437
213 974-1101

(P-16463)
COUNTY OF LOS ANGELES
Also Called: Health Dept
5850 S Main St, Los Angeles (90003-1215)
PHONE.....................323 897-6187
Floretta Taylor, *Dir*
EMP: 263
Web: www.lacounty.gov
SIC: 8093 9431 8011 Specialty outpatient clinics, nec; Administration of public health programs; Offices and clinics of medical doctors
PA: County Of Los Angeles
500 W Temple St Ste 437
213 974-1101

(P-16464)
CRC HEALTH CORPORATE
Also Called: Recovery Solutions Santa Ana
2101 E 1st St, Santa Ana (92705-4007)
PHONE.....................714 542-3581
Tfu Bach Tran, *Mgr*
EMP: 1318
Web: www.ctcprograms.com

SIC: 8093 Drug clinic, outpatient
HQ: Crc Health Corporate
20400 Stevns Crk Blvd
Cupertino CA 95014
408 367-0044

(P-16465)
CRC HEALTH GROUP INC
1560 Capalina Clinic, San Marcos (92069)
PHONE.....................760 744-2104
EMP: 80
Web: www.acadiahealthcare.com
SIC: 8093 Mental health clinic, outpatient
HQ: Crc Health Group, Inc.
6100 Tower Cir Ste 1000
Franklin TN 37067

(P-16466)
CRC HEALTH GROUP INC
1021 W La Cadena Dr, Riverside (92501-1413)
PHONE.....................951 784-8010
Tammy Elkins, *Brnch Mgr*
EMP: 159
Web: www.acadiahealthcare.com
SIC: 8093 Mental health clinic, outpatient
HQ: Crc Health Group, Inc.
6100 Tower Cir Ste 1000
Franklin TN 37067

(P-16467)
DEL AMO HOSPITAL INC
Also Called: Del AMO Hospital
23700 Camino Del Sol, Torrance (90505-5000)
PHONE.....................310 530-1151
TOLL FREE: 800
Lisa Moncen, *CEO*
Alan B Miller, *
Kirk E Gorman, *
Sidney Miller, *
EMP: 300 EST: 1991
SQ FT: 88,000
SALES (est): 45.01MM
SALES (corp-wide): 14.28B **Publicly Held**
Web: www.delamobehavioralhealth.com
SIC: 8093 Mental health clinic, outpatient
PA: Universal Health Services, Inc.
367 S Gulph Rd
610 768-3300

(P-16468)
DEVEREUX FOUNDATION
Also Called: Devereux California Center
7055 Seaway Dr, Goleta (93117-4358)
P.O. Box 6784 (93160-6784)
PHONE.....................805 968-2525
Amy Evans, *Prin*
EMP: 269
SALES (corp-wide): 587.41MM **Privately Held**
Web: www.devereux.org
SIC: 8093 Mental health clinic, outpatient
PA: Devereux Foundation
444 Devereux Dr
610 542-3057

(P-16469)
DISCOVERY PRACTICE MGT INC
Also Called: Center For Discovery
18401 Von Karman Ave Ste 500, Irvine (92612-8531)
PHONE.....................714 828-1800
Craig Brown, *CEO*
Mark Hobbins, *Pr*
Robert Weitzman, *CFO*
Jennifer Gorman, *Dir Opers*
EMP: 627 EST: 2007
SALES (est): 32.01MM **Privately Held**
Web: www.centerfordiscovery.com

SIC: 8093 Mental health clinic, outpatient

(P-16470)
DUAL DIAGNOSIS TRTMNT CTR INC (PA)
Also Called: Sovereign Health of California
1211 Puerta Del Sol Ste 200, San Clemente (92673-6342)
PHONE.....................949 276-5553
Tonmoy Sharma, *CEO*
Rishi Barkataki, *
EMP: 178 EST: 1983
SALES (est): 18.94MM
SALES (corp-wide): 18.94MM **Privately Held**
Web: www.sovcal.com
SIC: 8093 Mental health clinic, outpatient

(P-16471)
ENCOMPASS HEALTH CORPORATION
Also Called: HealthSouth
15120 Kensington Park Dr, Tustin (92782-1801)
PHONE.....................714 832-9200
Cathline Smith, *Brnch Mgr*
EMP: 123
SALES (corp-wide): 4.8B **Publicly Held**
Web: www.encompasshealth.com
SIC: 8093 Rehabilitation center, outpatient treatment
PA: Encompass Health Corporation
9001 Liberty Pkwy
205 967-7116

(P-16472)
ENCOMPASS HEALTH CORPORATION
HealthSouth
614 W Duarte Rd, Arcadia (91007-7601)
PHONE.....................626 445-4714
Sara Gamm, *Admn*
EMP: 75
SALES (corp-wide): 4.8B **Publicly Held**
Web: www.encompasshealth.com
SIC: 8093 8011 Rehabilitation center, outpatient treatment; Clinic, operated by physicians
PA: Encompass Health Corporation
9001 Liberty Pkwy
205 967-7116

(P-16473)
ENKI HEALTH AND RES SYSTEMS
3208 Rosemead Blvd Ste 100, El Monte (91731-2830)
PHONE.....................626 227-7001
Daniel Guzman, *Brnch Mgr*
EMP: 70
SALES (corp-wide): 22.76MM **Privately Held**
Web: www.enkihealth.org
SIC: 8093 Mental health clinic, outpatient
PA: Enki Health And Research Systems
150 E Olive Ave Ste 203
818 973-4899

(P-16474)
FELD CARE THERAPY INC
Also Called: Feldcare Connects
100 E Thousand Oaks Blvd, Thousand Oaks (91360-5713)
PHONE.....................818 926-9057
Randi Peled, *CEO*
EMP: 75 EST: 2016
SALES (est): 3.05MM **Privately Held**
Web: www.feldcareconnects.com

SIC: **8093** 7371 Rehabilitation center, outpatient treatment; Computer software development and applications

(P-16475)
GREATER VALLEY MED GROUP INC
Also Called: Healthcare Partners
14600 Sherman Way Ste 300, Van Nuys (91405-2272)
PHONE...............................818 781-7097
Cris Kalal, *Mgr*
EMP: 147
SALES (corp-wide): 5MM **Privately Held**
SIC: **8093** 8011 Specialty outpatient clinics, nec; Offices and clinics of medical doctors
PA: Greater Valley Medical Group Incorporated
11600 Indian Hills Rd # 300
818 838-4500

(P-16476)
GREATER VALLEY MED GROUP INC (PA)
11600 Indian Hills Rd 300, Mission Hills (91345-1225)
PHONE...............................818 838-4500
Don Rebhun Md, *Pr*
Howard Sawyer Md, *Sec*
Mohyi Soleiman Md, *VP*
EMP: 75 **EST:** 1977
SALES (est): 5MM
SALES (corp-wide): 5MM **Privately Held**
SIC: **8093** Specialty outpatient clinics, nec

(P-16477)
HELIX HEALTHCARE INC
Also Called: Alvarado Parkway Institute
7050 Parkway Dr, La Mesa (91942-1535)
PHONE...............................619 465-4411
Roy Rodriguez, *CEO*
Mohammed Bari, *
Saleem Ishaque, *
Robert Sanders, *Stockholder* *
EMP: 310 **EST:** 2003
SQ FT: 37,354
SALES (est): 4.67MM **Privately Held**
Web: www.apibhs.com
SIC: **8093** Mental health clinic, outpatient

(P-16478)
HELP GROUP WEST (PA)
13130 Burbank Blvd, Sherman Oaks (91401-6037)
PHONE...............................818 781-0360
Barbara Firestone, *Pr*
Susan Berman Ph, *Ex VP*
Michael Love, *
EMP: 200 **EST:** 1999
SQ FT: 100,000
SALES (est): 17.88MM
SALES (corp-wide): 17.88MM **Privately Held**
Web: www.thehelpgroup.org
SIC: **8093** Speech defect clinic

(P-16479)
HILLVIEW MENTAL HEALTH CTR INC
12450 Van Nuys Blvd Ste 200, Pacoima (91331-1393)
PHONE...............................818 896-1161
Eva S Mccraven, *Pr*
Beth K Meltzer, *
Julie E Jones, *
Jack L Avila, *
Konstantinos N Tripodis, *
EMP: 80 **EST:** 1984
SQ FT: 17,600

SALES (est): 10.08MM **Privately Held**
Web: www.hillviewmhc.org
SIC: **8093** Mental health clinic, outpatient

(P-16480)
INLAND VLY DRG ALCHOL RCVERY S (PA)
Also Called: ADMINISTRATIVE OFFICES
1260 E Arrow Hwy, Upland (91786-4982)
PHONE...............................909 932-1069
Tina Hughes, *CEO*
Ellen Davis, *
EMP: 75 **EST:** 1962
SALES (est): 12.07MM
SALES (corp-wide): 12.07MM **Privately Held**
Web: www.inlandvalleyrecovery.org
SIC: **8093** Substance abuse clinics (outpatient)

(P-16481)
INSTITUTE FOR BHVORAL HLTH INC
1905 Business Center Dr Ste 100, San Bernardino (92408-3460)
PHONE...............................909 289-1041
Azadeh K Jebelli, *Pr*
EMP: 265 **EST:** 2013
SALES (est): 2.23MM **Privately Held**
Web: www.ibhcare.com
SIC: **8093** Mental health clinic, outpatient

(P-16482)
INTERSTATE RHBLTATION SVCS LLC
333 E Glenoaks Blvd Ste 204, Glendale (91207-2098)
PHONE...............................818 244-5656
Sandy Pietsch, *
EMP: 120 **EST:** 1986
SALES (est): 3.75MM **Privately Held**
Web: www.interstaterehab.com
SIC: **8093** Rehabilitation center, outpatient treatment

(P-16483)
KAISER FOUNDATION HOSPITALS
Also Called: Kaiser Permanente
23621 Main St, Carson (90745-5743)
PHONE...............................310 513-6707
Lora Griffin, *Brnch Mgr*
EMP: 123
SALES (corp-wide): 70.8B **Privately Held**
Web: healthy.kaiserpermanente.org
SIC: **8093** 8062 Specialty outpatient clinics, nec; General medical and surgical hospitals
HQ: Kaiser Foundation Hospitals Inc
1 Kaiser Plz
Oakland CA 94612
510 271-6611

(P-16484)
KERN COUNTY HOSPITAL AUTHORITY
1902 B St, Bakersfield (93301-3526)
P.O. Box 3519 (93385-3519)
PHONE...............................661 843-7980
EMP: 492
SALES (corp-wide): 45.43MM **Privately Held**
Web: www.refinemdspa.com
SIC: **8093** Mental health clinic, outpatient
PA: Kern County Hospital Authority
1700 Mount Vernon Ave
661 326-2102

(P-16485)
MENTAL HEALTH SYSTEMS INC (PA)
Also Called: MHS
9465 Farnham St, San Diego (92123-1308)
PHONE...............................858 573-2600
James Callaghan Junior, *CEO*
EMP: 70 **EST:** 1978
SQ FT: 18,000
SALES (est): 99.1MM
SALES (corp-wide): 99.1MM **Privately Held**
Web: www.mhsinc.org
SIC: **8093** Mental health clinic, outpatient

(P-16486)
MHM SERVICES INC
230 Station Way, Arroyo Grande (93420-3358)
PHONE...............................805 904-6678
EMP: 188
Web: www.teamcenturion.com
SIC: **8093** Mental health clinic, outpatient
HQ: Mhm Services, Inc.
1593 Spring Hl Rd Ste 600
Vienna VA 22182
703 749-4600

(P-16487)
NATIONAL THERAPEUTIC SVCS INC (PA)
Also Called: Northbound Treatment Services
3822 Campus Dr Ste 100, Newport Beach (92660-2674)
PHONE...............................866 311-0003
Michael Neatherton, *Pr*
Paul Alexander, *
Ray Pacini, *
David Allen Gates, *
Devon Wayt, *
EMP: 98 **EST:** 1995
SALES (est): 22.39MM
SALES (corp-wide): 22.39MM **Privately Held**
Web: www.livingsober.com
SIC: **8093** Alcohol clinic, outpatient

(P-16488)
PEDIATRIC THERAPY NETWORK
1815 W 213th St Ste 100, Torrance (90501-2852)
PHONE...............................310 328-0276
Zoe Mailloux, *Ex Dir*
EMP: 136 **EST:** 1996
SQ FT: 20,000
SALES (est): 9.6MM **Privately Held**
Web: www.pediatrictherapynetwork.org
SIC: **8093** Rehabilitation center, outpatient treatment

(P-16489)
PHOENIX HOUSES LOS ANGELES INC
11600 Eldridge Ave, Lake View Terrace (91342-6506)
PHONE...............................818 686-3000
Winifred Wechsler, *Pr*
EMP: 99 **EST:** 2000
SALES (est): 8.79MM
SALES (corp-wide): 16.69MM **Privately Held**
Web: www.phoenixhouseca.org
SIC: **8093** Substance abuse clinics (outpatient)
PA: Phoenix Houses Of California, Inc.
11600 Eldridge Ave
818 896-1121

(P-16490)
PLANNED PARENTHOOD LOS ANGELES (PA)
400 W 30th St, Los Angeles (90007-3320)
PHONE...............................213 284-3200
Sue Dunlap, *Pr*
Mark Kimura, *
Adrianne Black, *
Linda Pahl, *
EMP: 80 **EST:** 1965
SQ FT: 30,000
SALES (est): 117.19MM
SALES (corp-wide): 117.19MM **Privately Held**
Web: www.plannedparenthood.org
SIC: **8093** Family planning clinic

(P-16491)
PLANNED PRNTHOOD OF PCF STHWES
1964 Via Ctr, Vista (92081-6056)
PHONE...............................619 881-4500
Darrah D Johnson, *Mgr*
EMP: 100
SALES (corp-wide): 125.72MM **Privately Held**
Web: www.planned.org
SIC: **8093** Family planning clinic
PA: Planned Parenthood Of The Pacific Southwest
1075 Camino Del Rio
619 881-4500

(P-16492)
PLANNED PRNTHOOD OF PCF STHWES
4501 Mission Bay Dr Ste 1c, San Diego (92109-4924)
PHONE...............................619 881-4652
Darrah D Johnson, *Mgr*
EMP: 100
SALES (corp-wide): 125.72MM **Privately Held**
Web: www.planned.org
SIC: **8093** Family planning clinic
PA: Planned Parenthood Of The Pacific Southwest
1075 Camino Del Rio
619 881-4500

(P-16493)
PLANNED PRNTHOOD OF PCF STHWES (PA)
1075 Camino Del Rio S Ste 100, San Diego (92108-3539)
PHONE...............................619 881-4500
Darrah Johnson, *CEO*
Len Dodson, *CFO*
EMP: 100 **EST:** 1964
SQ FT: 24,000
SALES (est): 125.72MM
SALES (corp-wide): 125.72MM **Privately Held**
Web: www.planned.org
SIC: **8093** Family planning clinic

(P-16494)
POSITIVE BEHAVIOR STEPS CORP
Also Called: Positive Behavior Steps
675 Cliffside Dr, San Dimas (91773-2957)
PHONE...............................626 940-5180
David Sandoval, *CEO*
David Alberto Sandoval, *
EMP: 73 **EST:** 2017
SALES (est): 5.24MM **Privately Held**
Web: www.pbxsteps.org
SIC: **8093** Mental health clinic, outpatient

(P-16495)
PRIME MSO LLC
550 N Brand Blvd Ste 900, Glendale
(91203-4721)
PHONE..................818 937-9969
Raffi Tchamanian, *CEO*
Shadi Yassine, *Acctnt*
Steven Dien Purchaser, *Prin*
EMP: 100 EST: 1998
SALES (est): 20.14MM **Privately Held**
Web: www.primemso.com
SIC: 8093 Specialty outpatient clinics, nec

(P-16496)
REIMAGINE NETWORK (PA)
Also Called: Rehablitation Inst Orange Cnty
1601 E Saint Andrew Pl, Santa Ana
(92705-4940)
PHONE..................714 633-7400
Praim S Singh, *Dir*
EMP: 130 EST: 1950
SALES (est): 12.18MM
SALES (corp-wide): 12.18MM **Privately Held**
Web: www.riorehab.org
SIC: 8093 Rehabilitation center, outpatient treatment

(P-16497)
RESILIENCE TREATMENT CENTER
9663 Santa Monica Blvd, Beverly Hills
(90210-4303)
PHONE..................310 963-2065
EMP: 81 EST: 2015
SALES (est): 1.55MM **Privately Held**
Web: www.lightfully.com
SIC: 8093 Mental health clinic, outpatient

(P-16498)
RIO
Also Called: Rehablttion Inst Sthern Cal Ri
1601 E Saint Andrew Pl Ste A, Santa Ana
(92705-4940)
PHONE..................714 633-7400
Glenn Motola, *Ex Dir*
Parim Singh, *
John Berry, *
EMP: 233 EST: 1964
SALES (est): 1.43MM **Privately Held**
Web: www.reimagineoc.org
SIC: 8093 8351 Rehabilitation center, outpatient treatment; Child day care services

(P-16499)
RIVERSIDE-SAN BERNARDINO
11555 1/2 Potrero Rd, Banning
(92220-6946)
PHONE..................951 849-4761
EMP: 108
SALES (corp-wide): 73.51MM **Privately Held**
Web: www.rsbcihi.org
SIC: 8093 8011 Specialty outpatient clinics, nec; Offices and clinics of medical doctors
PA: Riverside-San Bernardino County Indian Health, Inc.
11980 Mount Vernon Ave
909 864-1097

(P-16500)
SAFE REFUGE
Also Called: Sobriety House
4510 E Pacific Coast Hwy, Long Beach
(90804-3279)
PHONE..................562 987-5722
Kathryn Romo, *Ex Dir*
EMP: 80 EST: 1998
SALES (est): 8.36MM **Privately Held**

Web: www.saferefuge.info
SIC: 8093 Substance abuse clinics (outpatient)

(P-16501)
SAN FERNANDO CITY OF INC
10605 Balboa Blvd Ste 100, Granada Hills
(91344-6367)
PHONE..................818 832-2400
Wendi Tovey, *Brnch Mgr*
EMP: 97
SALES (corp-wide): 49.4MM **Privately Held**
Web: ci.san-fernando.ca.us
SIC: 8093 9111 Mental health clinic, outpatient; County supervisors' and executives' office
PA: San Fernando, City Of Inc
117 Macneil St
818 898-1201

(P-16502)
SANCTARY CTRS SNTA BARBARA INC
222 W Valerio St, Santa Barbara
(93101-2930)
PHONE..................805 569-2785
Susan Pease Brown, *Prin*
EMP: 82 EST: 2004
SALES (est): 5.79MM **Privately Held**
Web: www.sanctuarycenters.org
SIC: 8093 Mental health clinic, outpatient

(P-16503)
SOUTH BAYLO UNIVERSITY
Also Called: South Baylo Acupuncture Clinic
2727 W 6th St, Los Angeles (90057-3111)
PHONE..................213 999-0297
David J Park, *Pr*
EMP: 136
SALES (corp-wide): 4.43MM **Privately Held**
Web: www.southbaylo.edu
SIC: 8093 8221 8049 Specialty outpatient clinics, nec; University; Acupuncturist
PA: South Baylo University
1126 N Brookhurst St
714 533-1495

(P-16504)
SOUTH CNTL HLTH RHBLTTION PRGR
Also Called: Barbour & Floyd Medical Assoc
2620 Industry Way, Lynwood (90262-4024)
PHONE..................310 667-4070
Jack M Barbour, *Prin*
EMP: 97
Web: www.scharpca.org
SIC: 8093 Rehabilitation center, outpatient treatment
PA: South Central Health & Rehabilitation Program
2610 Industry Way Ste A

(P-16505)
SOUTH COAST CHILDRENS SOC INC
24950 Redlands Blvd, Loma Linda
(92354-4032)
PHONE..................909 478-3377
EMP: 186
SALES (corp-wide): 36.84MM **Privately Held**
Web: www.sccskids.org
SIC: 8093 Mental health clinic, outpatient
PA: South Coast Children's Society, Inc.
25910 Acero Ste 160
714 966-8650

(P-16506)
SOUTHERN INDIAN HEALTH COUNCIL (PA)
4058 Willows Rd, Alpine (91901-1668)
P.O. Box 2128 (91903-2128)
PHONE..................619 445-1188
Laura Caswell, *CEO*
Carolina Monsano, *
Donna James, *
EMP: 100 EST: 1980
SQ FT: 11,000
SALES (est): 26.72MM
SALES (corp-wide): 26.72MM **Privately Held**
Web: www.sihc.org
SIC: 8093 Specialty outpatient clinics, nec

(P-16507)
TARZANA TREATMENT CENTERS INC
320 E Palmdale Blvd, Palmdale
(93550-4598)
PHONE..................818 654-3815
Albert Senella, *Pr*
EMP: 79
SALES (corp-wide): 110.26MM **Privately Held**
Web: www.tarzanatc.org
SIC: 8093 Substance abuse clinics (outpatient)
PA: Tarzana Treatment Centers, Inc.
18646 Oxnard St
818 996-1051

(P-16508)
TARZANA TREATMENT CENTERS INC
Also Called: Tarzana Trtmnt Ctrs LNG Bch O
5190 Atlantic Ave, Lakewood (90805-6510)
PHONE..................562 428-4111
EMP: 80
SALES (corp-wide): 110.26MM **Privately Held**
Web: www.tarzanatc.org
SIC: 8093 8299 Substance abuse clinics (outpatient); Airline training
PA: Tarzana Treatment Centers, Inc.
18646 Oxnard St
818 996-1051

(P-16509)
TARZANA TREATMENT CENTERS INC
2101 Magnolia Ave, Long Beach
(90806-4521)
PHONE..................562 218-1868
Angela Knox, *Brnch Mgr*
EMP: 107
SQ FT: 11,482
SALES (corp-wide): 110.26MM **Privately Held**
Web: www.tarzanatc.org
SIC: 8093 Substance abuse clinics (outpatient)
PA: Tarzana Treatment Centers, Inc.
18646 Oxnard St
818 996-1051

(P-16510)
TARZANA TREATMENT CENTERS INC
Also Called: Tarzana Treatment Ctr
44447 10th St W, Lancaster (93534-3324)
PHONE..................661 726-2630
Theresa Scott, *Dir*
EMP: 107
SALES (corp-wide): 110.26MM **Privately Held**
Web: www.tarzanatc.org

SIC: 8093 8069 8011 Drug clinic, outpatient; Drug addiction rehabilitation hospital; Clinic, operated by physicians
PA: Tarzana Treatment Centers, Inc.
18646 Oxnard St
818 996-1051

(P-16511)
TARZANA TREATMENT CENTERS INC (PA)
18646 Oxnard St, Tarzana (91356-1486)
PHONE..................818 996-1051
TOLL FREE: 800
Albert Senella, *Pr*
Sylvia Cadena, *
Bobbi Sloan, *
EMP: 160 EST: 1972
SQ FT: 14,000
SALES (est): 110.26MM
SALES (corp-wide): 110.26MM **Privately Held**
Web: www.tarzanatc.org
SIC: 8093 8322 8063 Mental health clinic, outpatient; Individual and family services; Psychiatric hospitals

(P-16512)
TELECARE CORPORATION
Also Called: La Casa Mhrc
6060 N Paramount Blvd, Long Beach
(90805-3711)
PHONE..................562 630-8672
Anne Bakar, *CEO*
EMP: 85 EST: 1965
SALES (est): 9.77MM
SALES (corp-wide): 440.9MM **Privately Held**
Web: www.telecarecorp.com
SIC: 8093 Mental health clinic, outpatient
PA: Telecare Corporation
1080 Mrina Vlg Pkwy Ste 1
510 337-7950

(P-16513)
TRI-CITY MENTAL HEALTH AUTH (PA)
Also Called: Tri City Mental Health Center
2008 N Garey Ave, Pomona (91767-2722)
PHONE..................909 623-6131
TOLL FREE: 866
Antonette Navarro, *Ex Dir*
Diana Acosta, *
EMP: 85 EST: 1960
SQ FT: 12,000
SALES (est): 10.29MM
SALES (corp-wide): 10.29MM **Privately Held**
Web: www.tricitymhs.org
SIC: 8093 8322 Mental health clinic, outpatient; Individual and family services

(P-16514)
UHS-CORONA INC
Also Called: Corona Rgnal Med Ctr Rhbltion
730 Magnolia Ave, Corona (92879-3117)
PHONE..................951 736-7200
Pat Sanders, *Dir*
EMP: 200
SALES (corp-wide): 14.28B **Publicly Held**
Web: www.coronaregional.com
SIC: 8093 8062 8069 8051 Rehabilitation center, outpatient treatment; General medical and surgical hospitals; Specialty hospitals, except psychiatric; Skilled nursing care facilities
HQ: Uhs-Corona, Inc.
800 S Main St
Corona CA 92882
951 737-4343

(P-16515)
UNITED AMRCN INDIAN INVLVMENT (PA)
1125 W 6th St Ste 103, Los Angeles (90017-1896)
PHONE.................................213 202-3970
Joseph Quintana, *Dir*
Carrie Johnson Ph.d., *Dir*
David L Rambeau, *
EMP: 100 **EST:** 1974
SQ FT: 26,000
SALES (est): 10.38MM
SALES (corp-wide): 10.38MM **Privately Held**
Web: www.uaii.org
SIC: 8093 Rehabilitation center, outpatient treatment

(P-16516)
UNIVERSAL CARE INC (HQ)
Also Called: Brand New Day
200 Oceangate Ste 100, Long Beach (90802-4317)
PHONE.................................866 255-4795
Abbie Totten, *CEO*
Jay Davis, *
Jeffrey Davis, *
Amy Park, *
EMP: 350 **EST:** 1983
SQ FT: 73,000
SALES (est): 23.98MM
SALES (corp-wide): 1.16B **Publicly Held**
Web: www.bndhmo.com
SIC: 8093 Specialty outpatient clinics, nec
PA: Neuehealth, Inc.
9250 Nw 36th St Ste 420
612 238-1321

(P-16517)
VICTOR CMNTY SUPPORT SVCS INC
1105 E Florida Ave, Hemet (92543-4512)
PHONE.................................951 212-1770
EMP: 169
SALES (corp-wide): 82.66MM **Privately Held**
Web: www.victor.org
SIC: 8093 Mental health clinic, outpatient
PA: Victor Community Support Services, Inc.
1360 E Lassen Ave
530 893-0758

(P-16518)
VICTOR CMNTY SUPPORT SVCS INC
15095 Amargosa Rd Ste 201, Victorville (92394-1875)
PHONE.................................760 987-8225
Angie R Wiechert, *Mgr*
EMP: 203
SALES (corp-wide): 82.66MM **Privately Held**
Web: www.victor.org
SIC: 8093 Mental health clinic, outpatient
PA: Victor Community Support Services, Inc.
1360 E Lassen Ave
530 893-0758

(P-16519)
VICTOR CMNTY SUPPORT SVCS INC
Also Called: Desert Mountain Fics
14360 St Andrews Dr Ste 11, Victorville (92395-4341)
PHONE.................................760 245-4695
Alan Mann, *Brnch Mgr*
EMP: 120

SALES (corp-wide): 82.66MM **Privately Held**
Web: www.victor.org
SIC: 8093 Mental health clinic, outpatient
PA: Victor Community Support Services, Inc.
1360 E Lassen Ave
530 893-0758

(P-16520)
VICTOR CMNTY SUPPORT SVCS INC
Also Called: San Bernardino Fics
1908 Business Center Dr Ste 109, San Bernardino (92408-3469)
PHONE.................................909 890-5930
Paula Quijano, *Brnch Mgr*
EMP: 120
SALES (corp-wide): 82.66MM **Privately Held**
Web: www.victor.org
SIC: 8093 Mental health clinic, outpatient
PA: Victor Community Support Services, Inc.
1360 E Lassen Ave
530 893-0758

(P-16521)
WAVELENGTHS RECOVERY INC
703 California St, Huntington Beach (92648-4715)
PHONE.................................714 312-1011
Warren Boyd, *CEO*
EMP: 70 **EST:** 2013
SALES (est): 2.67MM **Privately Held**
Web: www.wavelengths.com
SIC: 8093 Substance abuse clinics (outpatient)

(P-16522)
WORKING WITH AUTISM INC
14724 Ventura Blvd Ste 1110, Sherman Oaks (91403-3511)
PHONE.................................818 501-4240
Jennifer Sabin, *Dir*
EMP: 100 **EST:** 1997
SALES (est): 4.95MM **Privately Held**
Web: www.workingwithautism.com
SIC: 8093 Mental health clinic, outpatient

8099 Health And Allied Services, Nec

(P-16523)
365 HLTHCARE STAFFING SVCS INC
25550 Hawthorne Blvd Ste 211, Torrance (90505-6832)
PHONE.................................310 436-3650
Aaron Mark Kasdorf, *CEO*
EMP: 82 **EST:** 2014
SALES (est): 2.33MM **Privately Held**
Web: www.365healthstaffing.com
SIC: 8099 Health and allied services, nec

(P-16524)
ABLE HEALTH GROUP LLC
41990 Cook St Ste 2004, Palm Desert (92211-6105)
PHONE.................................760 610-2093
Gilbert Mwansa, *Admn*
EMP: 80 **EST:** 2017
SALES (est): 2.8MM **Privately Held**
SIC: 8099 Health and allied services, nec

(P-16525)
ACCOUNTBLE HLTH CARE IPA A PRO

2525 Cherry Ave Ste 225, Signal Hill (90755-2057)
PHONE.................................562 435-3333
EMP: 166 **EST:** 1993
SALES (est): 974.9K **Publicly Held**
SIC: 8099 Physical examination and testing services
HQ: Apc-Lsma Designated Shareholder Medical Corporation
1668 S Garfield Ave Fl 2
Alhambra CA 91801
626 282-0288

(P-16526)
AHMC HEALTHCARE INC
506 W Valley Blvd Ste 300, San Gabriel (91776-5716)
PHONE.................................626 248-3452
EMP: 182
SALES (corp-wide): 325.41MM **Privately Held**
Web: www.ahmchealth.com
SIC: 8099 8062 Blood bank; General medical and surgical hospitals
PA: Ahmc Healthcare Inc.
506 W Valley Blvd Ste 300
626 943-7526

(P-16527)
AHMC HEALTHCARE INC
900 S Atlantic Blvd, Monterey Park (91754-4716)
PHONE.................................626 570-9000
EMP: 137
SALES (corp-wide): 325.41MM **Privately Held**
Web: www.ahmchealth.com
SIC: 8099 Childbirth preparation clinic
PA: Ahmc Healthcare Inc.
506 W Valley Blvd Ste 300
626 943-7526

(P-16528)
ALTAMED HEALTH SERVICES CORP
Also Called: Alta Med Health Services
10418 Valley Blvd Ste B, El Monte (91731-3600)
PHONE.................................626 453-8466
Juan Esquivez, *Brnch Mgr*
EMP: 81
SALES (corp-wide): 1.25B **Privately Held**
Web: www.altamed.org
SIC: 8099 8011 Medical services organization; Gynecologist
PA: Altamed Health Services Corporation
2040 Camfield Ave
323 725-8751

(P-16529)
ALTAMED HEALTH SERVICES CORP
Also Called: Altamed Med & Dntl Group Bell
8627 Atlantic Ave, South Gate (90280-3501)
PHONE.................................323 562-6700
Erika Sockaci, *Brnch Mgr*
EMP: 141
SALES (corp-wide): 1.25B **Privately Held**
Web: www.altamed.org
SIC: 8099 8011 Medical services organization; Gynecologist
PA: Altamed Health Services Corporation
2040 Camfield Ave
323 725-8751

(P-16530)
ALTAMED HEALTH SERVICES CORP

Also Called: Altamed Med Dntl Grp Whttier W
3945 Whittier Blvd, Los Angeles (90023-2440)
PHONE.................................323 307-0400
Angela Arredondo, *Brnch Mgr*
EMP: 141
SALES (corp-wide): 1.25B **Privately Held**
Web: www.altamed.org
SIC: 8099 8011 Medical services organization; Gynecologist
PA: Altamed Health Services Corporation
2040 Camfield Ave
323 725-8751

(P-16531)
ALTAMED HEALTH SERVICES CORP
Also Called: Slauson Plaza Med Group
9436 Slauson Ave, Pico Rivera (90660-4748)
PHONE.................................562 949-8717
Alfredo Nunez, *Brnch Mgr*
EMP: 151
SALES (corp-wide): 1.25B **Privately Held**
Web: www.altamed.org
SIC: 8099 8011 Medical services organization; Clinic, operated by physicians
PA: Altamed Health Services Corporation
2040 Camfield Ave
323 725-8751

(P-16532)
ARBORMED INC (PA)
725 W Town And Country Rd, Orange (92868-4703)
PHONE.................................714 689-1500
Charles Morf, *Pr*
Scott Everson, *
William Shaw, *
EMP: 123 **EST:** 1995
SQ FT: 11,000
SALES (est): 5.32MM **Privately Held**
SIC: 8099 8742 Medical services organization; Management consulting services

(P-16533)
ASTIVA HEALTH INC
765 The City Dr S Ste 200, Orange (92868-4955)
PHONE.................................858 707-5111
Viet Tran, *Ex Dir*
Viet Tran, *Sec*
EMP: 75 **EST:** 2019
SALES (est): 4.79MM **Privately Held**
Web: www.astivahealth.com
SIC: 8099 Health and allied services, nec

(P-16534)
AYA LOCUMS SERVICES INC
5930 Cornerstone Ct W Ste 300, San Diego (92121-3772)
PHONE.................................866 687-7390
Alan Braynin, *Pr*
EMP: 713 **EST:** 2018
SALES (est): 558.41K **Privately Held**
SIC: 8099 Medical services organization
PA: Aya Healthcare, Inc.
5930 Crnrstone Ct W Ste 3

(P-16535)
BAYMARK HEALTH SERVICES LA INC
11682 Atlantic Ave, Lynwood (90262-3832)
PHONE.................................310 761-4762
EMP: 139
SALES (corp-wide): 106.29MM **Privately Held**
Web: www.baymark.com

SIC: **8099** Childbirth preparation clinic
PA: Baymark Health Services Of
Louisiana, Inc.
1720 Lakepointe Dr # 117
214 379-3300

(P-16536)
BHC ALHAMBRA HOSPITAL INC
Also Called: Bhc Alhambra Hospital
4619 Rosemead Blvd, Rosemead
(91770-1478)
PHONE..............................626 286-1191
EMP: 350
SALES (est): 21.89MM **Privately Held**
Web: www.bhcalhambra.com
SIC: **8099** Blood related health services

(P-16537)
BIO-MEDICS INC
371 W Highland Ave, San Bernardino
(92405-4011)
PHONE..............................909 883-9501
Gary Crandall, *Mgr*
EMP: 121
SIC: **8099** Blood bank
PA: Bio-Medics, Inc.
2187 Monitor Dr

(P-16538)
BMS HEALTHCARE INC
8925 Mines Ave, Pico Rivera (90660-3006)
PHONE..............................562 942-7019
Mordechai Stock, *Prin*
EMP: 130 EST: 2010
SALES (est): 1.73MM **Privately Held**
SIC: **8099** Health and allied services, nec

(P-16539)
CALIFORNIA CRYOBANK LLC
(DH)
Also Called: Generate Life Sciences Co
11915 La Grange Ave, Los Angeles
(90025-5213)
PHONE..............................310 496-5691
TOLL FREE: 800
Richards Jennings, *CEO*
Pamela Richardson, *
Brian Rizkallah, *
EMP: 75 EST: 1977
SQ FT: 21,300
SALES (est): 51.19MM
SALES (corp-wide): 3.9B **Publicly Held**
Web: www.cryobank.com
SIC: **8099** Sperm bank
HQ: Coopersurgical, Inc.
75 Corporate Dr
Trumbull CT 06611

(P-16540)
CALIFRNIA DEPT DVLPMENTAL
SVCS
Also Called: CA Department Development
Svc
696 Ramon, Cathedral City (92234)
PHONE..............................760 770-6248
Kathleen Waegner, *Dir*
EMP: 456
SALES (corp-wide): 534.4MM **Privately Held**
Web: dds.ca.gov
SIC: **8099** Physical examination and testing
services
HQ: California Department Of
Developmental Services
1215 O St
Sacramento CA 95814

(P-16541)
CALIFRNIA FRNSIC MED
GROUP INC
2801 Meadow Lark Dr, San Diego
(92123-2709)
PHONE..............................858 694-4690
Penny Looper, *Genl Mgr*
EMP: 70
SALES (corp-wide): 4.17MM **Privately
Held**
SIC: **8099** 9223 Medical services
organization; Jail, government
PA: California Forensic Medical Group,
Incorporated
1283 Murfreesboro Pike # 500
831 649-8994

(P-16542)
CALIFRNIA FRNSIC MED
GROUP INC
800 S Victoria Ave, Ventura (93009-0001)
PHONE..............................805 654-3343
Elaine Hustedt, *VP*
EMP: 91
SALES (corp-wide): 4.17MM **Privately
Held**
SIC: **8099** Medical services organization
PA: California Forensic Medical Group,
Incorporated
1283 Murfreesboro Pike # 500
831 649-8994

(P-16543)
CALMEDCASVS INC
Also Called: California Med Caregiver Svcs
6507 Winnetka Ave, Canoga Park
(91306-4202)
PHONE..............................818 888-0700
Dylan Lichter, *Prin*
EMP: 75 EST: 2014
SALES (est): 2MM **Privately Held**
SIC: **8099** Health and allied services, nec

(P-16544)
CAPRICOR INC
10865 Road To The Cure Ste 150, San
Diego (92121-1156)
PHONE..............................310 358-3200
Linda Marban, *CEO*
Karen Krasney, *Ex VP*
EMP: 83 EST: 2005
SALES (est): 9.33MM
SALES (corp-wide): 25.18MM **Publicly
Held**
Web: www.capricor.com
SIC: **8099** Blood related health services
PA: Capricor Therapeutics, Inc.
10865 Rd To The Cure Ste
858 727-1755

(P-16545)
CENTRO DE SLUD DE LA
CMNDAD DE
Also Called: San Ysidro Health Center
1180 Third Ave Ste C2, Chula Vista
(91911-3139)
PHONE..............................619 662-4161
Ed Estrada, *Brnch Mgr*
EMP: 365
SALES (corp-wide): 99.89MM **Privately
Held**
Web: www.syhealth.org
SIC: **8099** Blood related health services
PA: Centro De Salud De La Comunidad De
San Ysidro, Inc.
1601 Precision Park Ln
619 428-4463

(P-16546)
CERNA HEALTHCARE LLC
2151 Michelson Dr Ste 225, Irvine
(92612-1307)
PHONE..............................949 298-3200
Nick Payzant, *CEO*
EMP: 200 EST: 2008
SALES (est): 5.97MM **Privately Held**
Web: www.cernahomecare.com
SIC: **8099** 8082 Blood related health services
; Home health care services

(P-16547)
CHARLES RVER LABS CELL
SLTONS (HQ)
Also Called: Hemacare Corporation
8500 Balboa Blvd Ste 130, Northridge
(91325-5802)
PHONE..............................877 310-0717
James C Foster, *Pr*
EMP: 93 EST: 1978
SQ FT: 19,600
SALES (est): 26.28MM
SALES (corp-wide): 4.13B **Publicly Held**
Web: www.hemacaredonorcenter.com
SIC: **8099** 5122 Blood related health services
; Blood plasma
PA: Charles River Laboratories
International, Inc.
251 Ballardvale St
781 222-6000

(P-16548)
CITRUS VLY HLTH PARTNERS
INC
Also Called: CITRUS VALLEY HEALTH
PARTNERS, INC.
1325 N Grand Ave Ste 300, Covina
(91724-4046)
PHONE..............................626 732-3100
Carol Eaton, *Prin*
EMP: 509
Web: www.cvhp.org
SIC: **8099** Blood related health services
PA: Emanate Health
210 W San Bernardino Rd

(P-16549)
COAST HEALTH PLAN GOLD
711 E Daily Dr Ste 106, Camarillo
(93010-6082)
PHONE..............................888 301-1228
EMP: 275 EST: 2013
SALES (est): 4.44MM **Privately Held**
Web: www.goldcoasthealthplan.org
SIC: **8099** Health and allied services, nec

(P-16550)
CORTICA HEALTHCARE INC
7090 Miratech Dr, San Diego (92121-3109)
PHONE..............................858 304-6440
EMP: 91 EST: 2017
SALES (est): 11.54MM **Privately Held**
Web: www.corticacare.com
SIC: **8099** Health and allied services, nec

(P-16551)
COUNTY OF IMPERIAL
Also Called: Public Health Department
935 Broadway Ave, El Centro (92243-2349)
PHONE..............................760 482-4441
Evon Smith, *Dir*
EMP: 75
SALES (corp-wide): 445.2MM **Privately
Held**
Web: www.icphd.org
SIC: **8099** 9111 Health screening service;
County supervisors' and executives' office
PA: County Of Imperial
940 W Main St Ste 208

760 482-4556

(P-16552)
COUNTY OF LOS ANGELES
Also Called: Los Angeles County Pub Works
5525 Imperial Hwy, South Gate
(90280-7417)
PHONE..............................562 861-0316
Phil Doudar, *Mgr*
EMP: 81
Web: www.lacounty.gov
SIC: **8099** 9111 Blood related health services
; Executive offices
PA: County Of Los Angeles
500 W Temple St Ste 437
213 974-1101

(P-16553)
DAVID-KLEIS II LLC
Also Called: PALM GROVE HEALTHCARE
1665 E Eighth St, Beaumont (92223-2512)
PHONE..............................951 845-3125
EMP: 86 EST: 2013
SALES (est): 6.72MM **Privately Held**
Web: www.yolocare2.com
SIC: **8099** Health and allied services, nec

(P-16554)
DISCOVERY HEALTH SERVICES
LLC
Also Called: Discovery Medical Staffing
5726 La Jolla Blvd Ste 104, La Jolla
(92037-7342)
PHONE..............................858 459-0785
Jeffrey Sternberg, *CEO*
Preston A Moreno, *
Lisa Hargrove, *
EMP: 286 EST: 2012
SALES (est): 2.02MM **Privately Held**
Web: www.discoveryhealthus.com
SIC: **8099** Blood related health services

(P-16555)
DOCTOR ON DEMAND INC
9454 Wilshire Blvd Ste 803, Beverly Hills
(90212-2925)
PHONE..............................310 988-2882
Kevin Rosenbloom, *Brnch Mgr*
EMP: 78
SALES (corp-wide): 103.94MM **Privately
Held**
Web: www.doctorondemand.com
SIC: **8099** Physical examination and testing
services
HQ: Doctor On Demand, Inc.
3033 Campus Dr Ste 225
Minneapolis MN 55441
415 935-4447

(P-16556)
DUAL DIAGNOSIS TRTMNT CTR
INC
Also Called: Sovereign Health
69640 Highway 111, Rancho Mirage
(92270-2868)
PHONE..............................949 324-4531
Tonmoy Sharma, *Brnch Mgr*
EMP: 194
SALES (corp-wide): 18.94MM **Privately
Held**
Web: www.sovcal.com
SIC: **8099** Childbirth preparation clinic
PA: Dual Diagnosis Treatment Center, Inc.
1211 Prta Del Sol Ste 200
949 276-5553

(P-16557)
EASY CARE MSO LLC
3780 Kilroy Airport Way Ste 530, Long
Beach (90806-2459)

PHONE.................562 676-9600
Michelle Bui, *Pr*
EMP: 262 **EST:** 2014
SALES (est): 3.29MM
SALES (corp-wide): 34.07B **Publicly Held**
Web: www.easycaremso.com
SIC: 8099 Medical services organization
PA: Molina Healthcare, Inc.
200 Oceangate Ste 100
562 435-3666

(P-16558)
ELECTRONIC HEALTH PLANS INC
Also Called: Ehp Administrators
9131 Oakdale Ave Ste 150, Chatsworth
(91311-6502)
P.O. Box 4449 (91313-4449)
PHONE.................818 734-4700
Alina Green, *VP*
EMP: 78
SALES (corp-wide): 4.97MM **Privately Held**
Web: www.electronichealthplans.com
SIC: 8099 Medical services organization
PA: Electronic Health Plans, Inc.
1111 Route 1110 Ste 378
631 845-5680

(P-16559)
ELIZABETH GLASER PEDIA
16130 Ventura Blvd Ste 250, Encino
(91436-2529)
PHONE.................310 231-0400
Charles Lyons, *Brnch Mgr*
EMP: 457
SALES (corp-wide): 172.48MM **Privately Held**
Web: www.pedaids.org
SIC: 8099 Medical services organization
PA: Elizabeth Glaser Pediatric Aids
Foundation
1350 Eye St Nw Ste 400
920 770-0103

(P-16560)
FAMILY HLTH CTRS SAN DIEGO INC
7592 Broadway, Lemon Grove
(91945-1604)
PHONE.................619 515-2550
Elizabeth A Samuels, *Pr*
EMP: 348
SALES (corp-wide): 147.12MM **Privately Held**
Web: www.fhcsd.org
SIC: 8099 Blood related health services
PA: Family Health Centers Of San Diego, Inc.
823 Gateway Center Way
619 515-2303

(P-16561)
GAMEDAY MENS HEALTH LLC
2753 Jefferson St Ste 204, Carlsbad
(92008-1704)
PHONE.................858 252-9202
Evan Miller, *Prin*
EMP: 91 **EST:** 2018
SALES (est): 5.68MM **Privately Held**
Web: www.gamedaymenshealth.com
SIC: 8099 Health and allied services, nec

(P-16562)
GOOD HEALTH INC
Also Called: Premier Pharmacy Service
410 Cloverleaf Dr, Baldwin Park
(91706-6511)
PHONE.................714 961-7930
Stephen Edward Samuel, *CEO*

EMP: 115 **EST:** 1971
SALES (est): 11.02MM **Privately Held**
Web:
www.premierpharmacyservices.com
SIC: 8099 Blood related health services

(P-16563)
GRIFOLS BIO SUPPLIES INC
980 Park Center Dr Ste F, Vista
(92081-8351)
PHONE.................760 651-4042
Mark Viray, *Mgr*
EMP: 195
SALES (corp-wide): 40.07MM **Privately Held**
Web: www.interstatebloodbank.com
SIC: 8099 Blood bank
PA: Grifols Bio Supplies Inc.
2410 Grifols Way
901 384-6200

(P-16564)
GRIFOLS WRLDWIDE OPRTONS USA I
13111 Temple Ave, City Of Industry
(91746-1500)
PHONE.................626 435-2600
Red Fredericksen, *Genl Mgr*
EMP: 70
Web: www.grifols.com
SIC: 8099 Blood bank
HQ: Grifols Worldwide Operations Usa, Inc.
5555 Valley Blvd
Los Angeles CA 90032
323 225-2221

(P-16565)
HARBOR HEALTH SYSTEMS LLC
3501 Jamboree Rd Ste 540, Newport Beach
(92660-2950)
P.O. Box 1145 (60009-1145)
PHONE.................949 273-7020
EMP: 516 **EST:** 2001
SALES (est): 1.27MM **Privately Held**
Web: www.harborhealthsytems.com
SIC: 8099 7372 Blood related health services
; Business oriented computer software
PA: One Call Medical, Inc.
841 Prudential Dr Ste 204

(P-16566)
HEADLIGHT HEALTH INC
5060 Shoreham Pl Ste 330, San Diego
(92122-5976)
PHONE.................503 961-4406
Emily Hawk, *CPO**
EMP: 202 **EST:** 2021
SALES (est): 5.22MM **Privately Held**
Web: www.headlight.health
SIC: 8000 Health and allied services, nec

(P-16567)
HEALTHY MEDICAL SOLUTIONS INC
5943 Rhodes Ave, Valley Village
(91607-1131)
PHONE.................818 974-1980
Mori Bennissan, *CEO*
EMP: 77 **EST:** 2005
SALES (est): 1.14MM **Privately Held**
SIC: 8099 Childbirth preparation clinic

(P-16568)
HENRY MAYO NEWHALL MEM HOSP
Also Called: Santa Clarita Health Care Ctr
23845 Mcbean Pkwy, Santa Clarita
(91355-2083)

PHONE.................661 253-8227
David R Tumilty, *Prin*
EMP: 130
SALES (corp-wide): 454.17MM **Privately Held**
Web: www.henrymayo.com
SIC: 8099 Childbirth preparation clinic
PA: Henry Mayo Newhall Memorial Hospital
23845 Mcbean Pkwy
661 253-8000

(P-16569)
HERITAGE MEDICAL GROUP
Also Called: HERITAGE MEDICAL GROUP
12370 Hesperia Rd Ste 6, Victorville
(92395-4787)
PHONE.................760 956-1286
Stanley Wohl, *Brnch Mgr*
EMP: 261
Web: www.bfmc.com
SIC: 8099 Blood related health services
PA: Heritage Medical Group, Inc.
4580 California Ave

(P-16570)
HUNTINGTON HEALTH PHYSICIANS
100 W California Blvd, Pasadena
(91105-3010)
PHONE.................626 397-8300
EMP: 73 **EST:** 2017
SALES (est): 4.52MM **Privately Held**
Web: www.huntingtonhealth.org
SIC: 8099 Health and allied services, nec

(P-16571)
HWAVE
5702 Bolsa Ave, Huntington Beach
(92649-1128)
PHONE.................714 843-0463
EMP: 95 **EST:** 2018
SALES (est): 1.68MM **Privately Held**
Web: www.h-wave.com
SIC: 8099 Health and allied services, nec

(P-16572)
INDUSTRIAL MEDICAL SUPPORT INC
3320 E Airport Way, Long Beach
(90806-2410)
PHONE.................877 878-9185
Michael Donoghue, *CEO*
Ryan La Bounty, *
EMP: 800 **EST:** 2014
SALES (est): 3.96MM **Privately Held**
SIC: 8099 Medical services organization

(P-16573)
JWCH INSTITUTE INC
14371 Clark Ave, Bellflower (90706-2901)
PHONE.................562 867-7999
Alvaro Ballesteros, *Brnch Mgr*
EMP: 177
SALES (corp-wide): 112.81MM **Privately Held**
Web: www.jwchinstitute.org
SIC: 8099 Blood related health services
PA: Jwch Institute, Inc.
5650 Jillson St
323 477-1171

(P-16574)
JWCH INSTITUTE INC
8530 Firestone Blvd, Downey (90241-4926)
PHONE.................562 862-1000
EMP: 178
SALES (corp-wide): 112.81MM **Privately Held**
Web: www.jwchinstitute.org

SIC: 8099 Childbirth preparation clinic
PA: Jwch Institute, Inc.
5650 Jillson St
323 477-1171

(P-16575)
KAISER FOUNDATION HOSPITALS
Also Called: Kaiser Foundation Health Plan
2055 Kellogg Ave, Corona (92879-3111)
PHONE.................866 984-7483
Ruth Jasse, *Admn*
EMP: 76
SALES (corp-wide): 70.8B **Privately Held**
Web: healthy.kaiserpermanente.org
SIC: 8099 Childbirth preparation clinic
HQ: Kaiser Foundation Hospitals Inc
1 Kaiser Plz
Oakland CA 94612
510 271-6611

(P-16576)
KAISER ONTARIO SURGICAL CENTER
2295 S Vineyard Ave Ste A, Ontario
(91761-7926)
PHONE.................909 724-5000
Vincent Mckinley, *Prin*
EMP: 81 **EST:** 2002
SALES (est): 6.39MM **Privately Held**
SIC: 8099 Health and allied services, nec

(P-16577)
KAISER PRMNNTE BRNARD J TYSON
98 S Los Robles Ave, Pasadena
(91101-2433)
PHONE.................888 576-3348
John L Dalrymple, *CEO*
Vanessa M Benavides, *Sec*
Hong Sze A Yu Asstt, *Sec*
Hong-sze A Yu, *Sec*
EMP: 172 **EST:** 2016
SALES (est): 12.04MM **Privately Held**
Web: medschool.kp.org
SIC: 8099 7371 Health and allied services, nec; Computer software development

(P-16578)
KELLY THOMAS MD UCSD HLTH CARE
Also Called: Ucsd
200 W Arbor Dr, San Diego (92103-1911)
PHONE.................619 543-2885
Lydia Ikeda, *Prin*
Ed Babakaian Md, *Prin*
EMP: 96 **EST:** 2001
SALES (est): 21.13MM **Privately Held**
Web: www.ucsd.edu
SIC: 8099 Childbirth preparation clinic

(P-16579)
LANDMARK HEALTH LLC
3131 Camino Del Rio N, San Diego
(92108-5701)
PHONE.................619 274-8200
EMP: 131
SALES (corp-wide): 371.62B **Publicly Held**
Web: www.landmarkhealth.org
SIC: 8099 Blood related health services
HQ: Landmark Health, Llc
7755 Center Ave Ste 630
Huntington Beach CA 92647
657 237-2450

(P-16580)

LEGACY HEALTHCARE CENTER LLC

1570 N Fair Oaks Ave, Pasadena
(91103-1822)
PHONE..............................626 798-0558
Raphael Oscherowitz, *Prin*
Dov Jacobs, *
EMP: 90 **EST:** 2016
SALES (est): 2.24MM **Privately Held**
SIC: 8099 Health and allied services, nec

(P-16581)

LIFE TIME FITNESS INC

Also Called: LIFE TIME FITNESS, INC.
28221 Crown Valley Pkwy, Laguna Niguel
(92677-1427)
PHONE..............................949 238-2700
EMP: 215
SALES (corp-wide): 2.22B **Publicly Held**
Web: www.lifetime.life
SIC: 8099 7991 7299 Nutrition services;
Physical fitness clubs with training
equipment; Personal appearance services
HQ: Life Time, Inc.
2902 Corporate Pl
Chanhassen MN 55317

(P-16582)

LIFESTREAM BLOOD BANK (HQ)

Also Called: Blood Bnk San Brnrdino Rvrside
384 W Orange Show Rd, San Bernardino
(92412)
P.O. Box 1429 (92402-1429)
PHONE..............................909 885-6503
Frederick B Axelrod, *CEO*
Joseph Dunn, *
Susan Marquez, *
EMP: 240 **EST:** 1951
SQ FT: 50,000
SALES (est): 66.4MM
SALES (corp-wide): 526.62MM **Privately Held**
Web: www.lstream.org
SIC: 8099 2836 Blood bank; Blood
derivatives
PA: Vitalant
9305 E Via De Ventura
800 288-2199

(P-16583)

LOS ANGLES CNTY DVLPMNTAL SVCS

Also Called: FRANK D LANTERMAN
REGIONAL CEN
3303 Wilshire Blvd Ste 700, Los Angeles
(90010-4000)
PHONE..............................213 383-1300
Dianne Anand, *Ex Dir*
EMP: 180 **EST:** 1979
SQ FT: 80,000
SALES (est): 324.23MM **Privately Held**
Web: www.lanterman.org
SIC: 8099 8322 8093 Medical services
organization; Individual and family services;
Mental health clinic, outpatient

(P-16584)

MARTIN LTHER KING JR-LOS ANGLE

Also Called: MARTIN LUTHER KING, JR.
COMMUN
1680 E 120th St, Los Angeles
(90059-3026)
PHONE..............................424 338-8000
Elaine E Batchlor, *CEO*
EMP: 207 **EST:** 2010
SALES (est): 377.77MM **Privately Held**
Web: www.mlkch.org

SIC: 8099 Childbirth preparation clinic

(P-16585)

MAXIMA THRAPY SPECH CLINIC INC

3940 Laurel Canyon Blvd # 456, Studio City
(91604-3709)
PHONE..............................818 287-8875
Anthony Rainin, *CEO*
EMP: 200 **EST:** 2008
SALES (est): 381.97K **Privately Held**
SIC: 8099 Health and allied services, nec

(P-16586)

MEDASEND BIOMEDICAL INC (PA)

1402 Daisy Ave, Long Beach (90813-1521)
PHONE..............................800 200-3581
Steve Grand, *CEO*
Stephanie Harrison, *VP*
EMP: 150 **EST:** 1999
SQ FT: 10,000
SALES (est): 1.15MM
SALES (corp-wide): 1.15MM **Privately Held**
Web: www.medasend.com
SIC: 8099 4953 Health screening service;
Hazardous waste collection and disposal

(P-16587)

MOLINA HEALTHCARE INC

604 Pine Ave, Long Beach (90802-1329)
PHONE..............................888 562-5442
EMP: 99
SALES (corp-wide): 34.07B **Publicly Held**
Web: www.molinahealthcare.com
SIC: 8099 Blood related health services
PA: Molina Healthcare, Inc.
200 Oceangate Ste 100
562 435-3666

(P-16588)

MOLINA HEALTHCARE INC

1 Golden Shore, Long Beach (90802-4202)
PHONE..............................562 435-3666
Sriram Bharadwaj, *Brnch Mgr*
EMP: 522
SALES (corp-wide): 34.07B **Publicly Held**
Web: www.molinahealthcare.com
SIC: 8099 Blood related health services
PA: Molina Healthcare, Inc.
200 Oceangate Ste 100
562 435-3666

(P-16589)

MOLINA HEALTHCARE INC

9275 Sky Park Ct Ste 190, San Diego
(92123-4386)
PHONE..............................858 614-1580
Lisa Ferrari, *Mgr*
EMP: 229
SALES (corp-wide): 34.07B **Publicly Held**
Web: www.molinahealthcare.com
SIC: 8099 Blood related health services
PA: Molina Healthcare, Inc.
200 Oceangate Ste 100
562 435-3666

(P-16590)

MONARCH HLTHCARE A MED GROUP I

2562 State St, Carlsbad (92008-1663)
PHONE..............................760 730-9448
EMP: 120
SALES (corp-wide): 371.62B **Publicly Held**
Web: www.optum.com
SIC: 8099 Blood related health services

HQ: Monarch Healthcare, A Medical Group,
Inc.
11 Technology Dr
Irvine CA 92618

(P-16591)

NALU MEDICAL INC

2320 Faraday Ave Ste 100, Carlsbad
(92008-7241)
PHONE..............................760 603-8466
Earl R Fender, *Pr*
Keegan Harper, *Ch Bd*
EMP: 182 **EST:** 2015
SALES (est): 10.68MM **Privately Held**
Web: www.nalumed.com
SIC: 8099 Childbirth preparation clinic

(P-16592)

NEIGHBORHOOD HEALTHCARE

41840 Enterprise Cir N, Temecula
(92590-5654)
PHONE..............................951 225-6400
EMP: 123
SALES (corp-wide): 218.21MM **Privately Held**
Web: www.nhcare.org
SIC: 8099 Childbirth preparation clinic
PA: Neighborhood Healthcare
215 S Hickory St
833 867-4642

(P-16593)

NEIGHBORHOOD HEALTHCARE

10039 Vine St Ste A, Lakeside
(92040-3122)
PHONE..............................619 390-9975
Tracy Ream, *Brnch Mgr*
EMP: 103
SALES (corp-wide): 218.21MM **Privately Held**
Web: www.nhcare.org
SIC: 8099 8011 Health screening service;
Clinic, operated by physicians
PA: Neighborhood Healthcare
215 S Hickory St
833 867-4642

(P-16594)

NEIGHBORHOOD HEALTHCARE

401 E Valley Pkwy, Escondido
(92025-3317)
PHONE..............................760 737-6903
EMP: 233
SALES (corp-wide): 218.21MM **Privately Held**
Web: www.nhcare.org
SIC: 8099 Childbirth preparation clinic
PA: Neighborhood Healthcare
215 S Hickory St
833 867-4642

(P-16595)

NOVA SKILLED HOME HEALTH INC

3300 N San Fernando Blvd Ste 201,
Burbank (91504-2530)
PHONE..............................323 658-6232
Nelson Aguilar, *CEO*
Julita Fraley, *
Carol Vega, *
EMP: 136 **EST:** 2018
SALES (est): 647.22K **Privately Held**
SIC: 8099 Health and allied services, nec

(P-16596)

ONELEGACY

1303 W Optical Dr, Irwindale (91702-3251)
PHONE..............................213 229-5600
EMP: 98
SALES (corp-wide): 105.54MM **Privately Held**

Web: www.onelegacy.org
SIC: 8099 Organ bank
PA: Onelegacy
1303 W Optical Dr

(P-16597)

OPTUMCARE MANAGEMENT LLC

Also Called: Family Health Program
4910 Airport Plaza Dr, Long Beach
(90815-1376)
PHONE..............................562 429-2473
Rhonda Luster, *Dir*
EMP: 79
SALES (corp-wide): 371.62B **Publicly Held**
SIC: 8099 8011 Medical services
organization; Clinic, operated by physicians
HQ: Optumcare Management, Llc
2175 Park Pl
El Segundo CA 90245

(P-16598)

OPTUMCARE MANAGEMENT LLC

3501 S Harbor Blvd, Santa Ana
(92704-6919)
PHONE..............................714 964-6229
Francis Gale, *Mgr*
EMP: 79
SALES (corp-wide): 371.62B **Publicly Held**
SIC: 8099 Blood related health services
HQ: Optumcare Management, Llc
2175 Park Pl
El Segundo CA 90245

(P-16599)

OPTUMCARE MANAGEMENT LLC

1236 N Magnolia Ave, Anaheim
(92801-2607)
PHONE..............................714 995-1000
Kathy Porter, *Mgr*
EMP: 79
SALES (corp-wide): 371.62B **Publicly Held**
Web: www.optum.com
SIC: 8099 8011 Medical services
organization; Offices and clinics of medical
doctors
HQ: Optumcare Management, Llc
2175 Park Pl
El Segundo CA 90245

(P-16600)

OPTUMCARE MANAGEMENT LLC

19066 Magnolia St, Huntington Beach
(92646-2232)
PHONE..............................714 968-0068
Robert Hunn, *Prin*
EMP: 79
SALES (corp-wide): 371.62B **Publicly Held**
Web: www.optum.com
SIC: 8099 Medical services organization
HQ: Optumcare Management, Llc
2175 Park Pl
El Segundo CA 90245

(P-16601)

OPTUMCARE MANAGEMENT LLC

Also Called: Talbert Medical Center
901 W Civic Center Dr Ste 120, Santa Ana
(92703-2380)
PHONE..............................714 835-8501
Linda Journet, *Mgr*

EMP: 79
SALES (corp-wide): 371.62B **Publicly Held**
SIC: 8099 8011 Medical services organization; General and family practice, physician/surgeon
HQ: Optumcare Management, Llc
2175 Park Pl
El Segundo CA 90245

(P-16602)
PANCRTIC CNCER ACTION NTWRK IN (PA)
Also Called: Pancan
1500 Rosecrans Ave Ste 200, Manhattan Beach (90266-3721)
PHONE..............................310 725-0025
Julie Fleshman, *Pr*
Jeanne Weaver Ruesch, *Ch Bd*
Michael Korengold, *
Megan Gordon Don, *VP*
Jenny Isaacson, *VP*
EMP: 79 **EST:** 1999
SALES (est): 52.93MM
SALES (corp-wide): 52.93MM **Privately Held**
Web: www.pancan.org
SIC: 8099 8399 Medical services organization; Social service information exchange

(P-16603)
PPONEXT WEST INC
1501 Hughes Way Ste 400, Long Beach (90810-1881)
PHONE..............................888 446-6098
Barbara E Rodin Ph.d., *Pr*
EMP: 385 **EST:** 1999
SALES (est): 745.21K
SALES (corp-wide): 961.52MM **Publicly Held**
SIC: 8099 Medical services organization
HQ: Beech Street Corporation
25550 Cmmrcntre Dr Ste 20
Lake Forest CA 92630
949 672-1000

(P-16604)
PROVIDNCE FACEY MED FOUNDATION
11211 Sepulveda Blvd, Mission Hills (91345-1115)
PHONE..............................818 837-5677
Cathy Hawes, *Brnch Mgr*
EMP: 147
SALES (corp-wide): 91.37MM **Privately Held**
Web: www.facey.com
SIC: 8099 8042 8011 Medical services organization; Offices and clinics of optometrists; Offices and clinics of medical doctors
PA: Providence Facey Medical Foundation
15451 San Frnndo Mssion B
818 365-9531

(P-16605)
PROVIDNCE FACEY MED FOUNDATION
Also Called: Marshall, Spector MD
1237 E Main St, San Gabriel (91776)
PHONE..............................626 576-0800
Ana Ventura, *Mgr*
EMP: 88
SALES (corp-wide): 91.37MM **Privately Held**
Web: www.facey.com
SIC: 8099 8011 Medical services organization; Pediatrician
PA: Providence Facey Medical Foundation
15451 San Frnndo Mssion B

818 365-9531

(P-16606)
PROVISIO MEDICAL INC
10815 Rancho Bernardo Rd Ste 110, San Diego (92127-2187)
PHONE..............................508 740-9940
Stephen Eric Ryan, *CEO*
EMP: 44 **EST:** 2014
SALES (est): 6.44MM **Privately Held**
Web: www.provisiomedical.com
SIC: 8099 3841 Medical services organization; Surgical and medical instruments

(P-16607)
PUBLIC HLTH FNDATION ENTPS INC
8666 Whittier Blvd, Pico Rivera (90660-2655)
PHONE..............................562 801-2323
Nicolle Fevere, *Prin*
EMP: 140
SALES (corp-wide): 49.53MM **Privately Held**
Web: www.helunahealth.org
SIC: 8099 Blood related health services
PA: Public Health Foundation Enterprises, Inc.
13300 Crssrads Pkwy N Ste
800 201-7320

(P-16608)
PUBLIC HLTH FNDATION ENTPS INC
1649 W Washington Blvd, Los Angeles (90007-1116)
PHONE..............................323 733-9381
Eloise Jenks, *Pr*
EMP: 140
SALES (corp-wide): 49.53MM **Privately Held**
Web: www.helunahealth.org
SIC: 8099 Blood related health services
PA: Public Health Foundation Enterprises, Inc.
13300 Crssrads Pkwy N Ste
800 201-7320

(P-16609)
PUBLIC HLTH FNDATION ENTPS INC
125 E Anaheim St, Wilmington (90744-4590)
PHONE..............................310 518-2835
EMP: 140
SALES (corp-wide): 49.53MM **Privately Held**
Web: www.helunahealth.org
SIC: 8099 Blood related health services
PA: Public Health Foundation Enterprises, Inc.
13300 Crssrads Pkwy N Ste
800 201-7320

(P-16610)
PUBLIC HLTH FNDATION ENTPS INC
Also Called: Wic
12781 Shama Rd, El Monte (91732)
PHONE..............................626 856-6618
Juan Chong, *Brnch Mgr*
EMP: 140
SALES (corp-wide): 49.53MM **Privately Held**
Web: www.phfewic.org
SIC: 8099 Blood related health services

PA: Public Health Foundation Enterprises, Inc.
13300 Crssrads Pkwy N Ste
800 201-7320

(P-16611)
QTC MANAGEMENT INC (DH)
924 Overland Ct, San Dimas (91773-1742)
PHONE..............................800 682-9701
Elizabeth Porter, *CEO*
▼ **EMP:** 99 **EST:** 1981
SQ FT: 20,000
SALES (est): 99.61MM **Publicly Held**
Web: www.qtcm.com
SIC: 8099 Medical services organization
HQ: Qtc Holdings Inc.
9737 Washingtonian Blvd
Gaithersburg MD 20878
909 859-2100

(P-16612)
QTC MDCAL GROUP INC A MED CORP
Also Called: Qtc Medical Group
924 Overland Ct, San Dimas (91773-1742)
PHONE..............................800 260-1515
Brant Kim, *CEO*
EMP: 1000 **EST:** 1984
SALES (est): 2.78MM **Privately Held**
Web: www.qtcm.com
SIC: 8099 Medical services organization

(P-16613)
REGENTS OF THE UNIVERSITY CAL
Also Called: Santa Monica Ucla Medical Ctr
1250 16th St, Santa Monica (90404-1249)
PHONE..............................310 267-9308
Johnese Spisso, *Prin*
Felicia Rue, *
Paul Staton, *
EMP: 99 **EST:** 1996
SALES (est): 4.38MM **Privately Held**
Web: www.uclahealth.org
SIC: 8099 Health and allied services, nec

(P-16614)
SAN BRNRDINO CY UNFIED SCHL DS
Also Called: Nutrition Services
1257 Northpark Blvd, San Bernardino (92407-2946)
PHONE..............................909 881-8000
Adrian Robles, *Brnch Mgr*
EMP: 79
SALES (corp-wide): 1.2B **Privately Held**
Web: www.cbcucd.org
SIC: 8099 8211 Nutrition services; Elementary school, nec
PA: San Bernardino City Unified School District
777 N F St
909 381-1100

(P-16615)
SAN DIEGO BLOOD BANK (PA)
Also Called: San Diego Blood Bnk Foundation
3636 Gateway Center Ave Ste 100, San Diego (92102-4508)
PHONE..............................619 400-8132
TOLL FREE: 800
Ramona Walker, *CEO*
▲ **EMP:** 155 **EST:** 1950
SQ FT: 132,000
SALES (est): 41.12MM
SALES (corp-wide): 41.12MM **Privately Held**
Web: www.sandiegobloodbank.org

PA: Public Health Foundation Enterprises, Inc.
13300 Crssrads Pkwy N Ste
800 201-7320

SIC: 8099 8071 Blood bank; Medical laboratories

(P-16616)
SCRIBEAMERICA LLC
840 Apollo St Ste 231, El Segundo (90245-4762)
PHONE..............................877 819-5900
Michael Murphy, *Brnch Mgr*
EMP: 700
Web: www.scribeamerica.com
SIC: 8099 Blood related health services
HQ: Scribeamerica, Llc
1200 E Las Olas Blvd # 201
Fort Lauderdale FL 33301

(P-16617)
SOUTHERN CAL PRMNNTE MED GROUP
Also Called: SOUTHERN CALIFORNIA PERMANENTE MEDICAL GROUP
23781 Maquina, Mission Viejo (92691-2716)
PHONE..............................949 376-8619
EMP: 147
SALES (corp-wide): 70.8B **Privately Held**
Web: www.permanente.org
SIC: 8099 Blood related health services
HQ: Southern California Permanente Medical Group
393 Walnut Dr
Pasadena CA 91107
626 405-5704

(P-16618)
STAR OF CA LLC
15260 Ventura Blvd Ste 1140, Sherman Oaks (91403-5346)
PHONE..............................818 986-7827
Alison Stanley, *Brnch Mgr*
EMP: 95
SALES (corp-wide): 165.05MM **Privately Held**
Web: www.starofca.com
SIC: 8099 Medical services organization
HQ: Star Of Ca, Llc
184 High St
Boston MA 02110

(P-16619)
STAR OF CA LLC
8834 Morro Rd, Atascadero (93422-3953)
PHONE..............................805 466-1638
EMP: 95
SALES (corp-wide): 165.05MM **Privately Held**
Web: www.starofca.com
SIC: 8099 Medical services organization
HQ: Star Of Ca, Llc
184 High St
Boston MA 02110

(P-16620)
STAR OF CA LLC
501 Marin St Ste 225, Thousand Oaks (91360-4301)
PHONE..............................805 379-1401
Doug Moes, *Brnch Mgr*
EMP: 94
SALES (corp-wide): 165.05MM **Privately Held**
Web: www.starofca.com
SIC: 8099 Medical services organization
HQ: Star Of Ca, Llc
184 High St
Boston MA 02110

PRODUCTS & SVCS

(P-16621)
SYNERGY ORTHPD
SPECIALISTS INC
4445 Eastgate Mall Ste 103, San Diego
(92121-1979)
PHONE....................858 450-7118
Brent Noon, *CEO*
EMP: 83 **EST:** 2012
SALES (est): 6.13MM **Privately Held**
Web: www.synergysmg.com
SIC: 8099 Blood related health services

(P-16622)
TRI-CITY MEDICAL CENTER (PA)
Also Called: Tri-City Healthcare District
4002 Vista Way, Oceanside (92056-4506)
PHONE....................760 724-8411
Gene Ma, *Pr*
Janice Gurley, *
Jeremy Raimo, *
Roger L Cortez, *CPO**
Mark Albright, *CIO**
EMP: 2100 **EST:** 1957
SQ FT: 50,000
SALES (est): 319.28MM
SALES (corp-wide): 319.28MM **Privately Held**
Web: www.tricitymed.org
SIC: 8099 Medical services organization

(P-16623)
UNITED STATES DEPT OF NAVY
Also Called: Naval Hosp Twntynine Plms Gfeb
1145 Sturgis Rd, Twentynine Palms
(92278)
PHONE....................760 830-2124
Eugene Dearstine, *CFO*
EMP: 99
Web: www.navy.mil
SIC: 8099 Blood related health services
HQ: United States Department Of The Navy
1200 Navy Pentagon
Washington DC 20350

(P-16624)
UNIVERSITY CALIFORNIA
IRVINE
31865 Circle Dr, Laguna Beach
(92651-6860)
PHONE....................949 939-7106
EMP: 71
SALES (corp-wide): 534.4MM **Privately Held**
Web: www.uci.edu
SIC: 8099 Blood related health services
HQ: University Of California, Irvine
510 Aldrich Hall
Irvine CA 92697
949 824-5011

(P-16625)
UNIVERSITY CALIFORNIA
IRVINE
Also Called: UCI Health Blood Donor Center
106 B Student Ctr, Irvine (92697-0001)
PHONE....................949 824-2662
EMP: 72
SALES (corp-wide): 534.4MM **Privately Held**
Web: www.uci.edu
SIC: 8099 Blood donor station
HQ: University Of California, Irvine
510 Aldrich Hall
Irvine CA 92697
949 824-5011

(P-16626)
VENTURA CNTY MD-CAL
MNGED CARE

Also Called: Gold Coast Health Plan
711 E Daily Dr Ste 106, Camarillo
(93010-6082)
PHONE....................888 301-1228
Michael P Engelhard, *CEO*
EMP: 119 **EST:** 2010
SALES (est): 43.37MM **Privately Held**
Web: www.goldcoasthealthplan.org
SIC: 8099 Medical services organization

(P-16627)
WELBE HEALTH LLC
1220 E 4th St, Long Beach (90802-1831)
PHONE....................888 530-4415
EMP: 139
SALES (corp-wide): 20.91MM **Privately Held**
Web: www.welbehealth.com
SIC: 8099 Childbirth preparation clinic
PA: Welbe Health, Llc
405 El Cmino Real Ste 248
650 862-6371

(P-16628)
WEST HEALTH INCUBATOR INC
10350 N Torrey Pines Rd, La Jolla
(92037-1018)
PHONE....................858 535-7000
Shelley Lyford, *CEO*
EMP: 103 **EST:** 2012
SALES (est): 5.06MM **Privately Held**
Web: www.westhealth.org
SIC: 8099 Blood related health services

(P-16629)
WESTLAKE OAKS
HEALTHCARE LLC
Also Called: Sherwood Oaks Post Acute
250 Fairview Rd, Thousand Oaks
(91361-2456)
PHONE....................805 494-1233
EMP: 281 **EST:** 2020
SALES (est): 5.85MM
SALES (corp-wide): 3.11B **Publicly Held**
SIC: 8099 Health and allied services, nec
HQ: Providence Group, Inc.
262 N University Ave
Farmington UT 84025
801 447-9829

8111 Legal Services

(P-16630)
A BUCHALTER PROFESSIONAL
CORP (PA)
1000 Wilshire Blvd Ste 1500, Los Angeles
(90017-1730)
PHONE....................213 891-0700
Adam Bass, *CEO*
EMP: 209 **EST:** 1970
SQ FT: 84,000
SALES (est): 66.32MM
SALES (corp-wide): 66.32MM **Privately Held**
Web: www.buchalter.com
SIC: 8111 General practice law office

(P-16631)
AKERMAN LLP
633 W 5th St, Los Angeles (90071-2005)
PHONE....................213 688-9500
Justin Balser, *Office Managing Partner*
EMP: 80
SALES (corp-wide): 46.48MM **Privately Held**
Web: www.akerman.com
SIC: 8111 General practice attorney, lawyer
PA: Akerman Llp
98 Se 7th St Ste 1100

305 374-5600

(P-16632)
ALBERT & MACKENZIE LLP (PA)
Also Called: Albert & Mackenzie
28216 Dorothy Dr Ste 200, Agoura Hills
(91301-2605)
PHONE....................818 575-9876
Bruce Albert, *Mng Pt*
Bruce Albert, *Pt*
Peter Mackenzie, *Pt*
EMP: 76 **EST:** 2000
SALES (est): 19.12MM
SALES (corp-wide): 19.12MM **Privately Held**
Web: www.albmac.com
SIC: 8111 Real estate law

(P-16633)
ALDRIDGE PITE LLP
4375 Jutland Dr Ste 200, San Diego
(92117-3600)
P.O. Box 17935 (92177-7923)
PHONE....................858 750-7700
EMP: 410
SALES (corp-wide): 22.65MM **Privately Held**
Web: www.aldridgepite.com
SIC: 8111 Real estate law
PA: Aldridge Pite Llp
3575 Piedmont Rd Ne 15-500
404 994-7400

(P-16634)
ALEXANDRA LZANO
IMMGRTION LAW
5800 S Eastern Ave Ste 270, Commerce
(90040-4019)
PHONE....................323 524-9944
Alexandra Lozano, *Governor*
EMP: 212
SALES (corp-wide): 150MM **Privately Held**
Web: www.abogadaalexandra.com
SIC: 8111 Immigration and naturalization law
PA: Alexandra Lozano Immigration Law,
Pllc
6720 Fort Dent Way Ste 23
206 406-3068

(P-16635)
ALLEN MTKINS LECK GMBLE
MLLORY (PA)
Also Called: Allen Matkins
865 S Figueroa St Ste 2800, Los Angeles
(90017-2795)
PHONE....................213 622-5555
David L Osias, *Mng Pt*
Frederick L Allen, *Pt*
Michael L Matkins, *Pt*
John C Gamble, *Pt*
Richard C Mallory, *Pt*
EMP: 130 **EST:** 1986
SQ FT: 40,000
SALES (est): 13.14MM
SALES (corp-wide): 13.14MM **Privately Held**
Web: www.allenmatkins.com
SIC: 8111 General practice law office

(P-16636)
ARNOLD PORTER KAYE
SCHOLER LLP
Also Called: Arnold & Porter
777 S Figueroa St Ste 4400, Los Angeles
(90017-5844)
PHONE....................213 243-4000
Peter Blinkley, *Brnch Mgr*
EMP: 153

Web: www.arnoldporter.com
SIC: 8111 General practice attorney, lawyer
HQ: Arnold & Porter Kaye Scholer Llp
601 Massachusetts Ave Nw
Washington DC 20001
202 942-5000

(P-16637)
ATKINSON ANDLSON LOYA
RUUD ROM (PA)
Also Called: Atkinson Andelson Loya
12800 Center Court Dr S Ste 300, Cerritos
(90703-9364)
PHONE....................562 653-3200
James C Romo, *CEO*
Steven Atkinson, *
Steven Andelson, *
Paul Loya, *
EMP: 150 **EST:** 1979
SALES (est): 38.23MM
SALES (corp-wide): 38.23MM **Privately Held**
Web: www.aalrr.com
SIC: 8111 General practice attorney, lawyer

(P-16638)
AUSTIN SIDLEY CA LLP
350 S Grand Ave, Los Angeles
(90071-3406)
PHONE....................213 896-6000
Dan Clivner, *Pt*
EMP: 125 **EST:** 2001
SALES (est): 8.15MM
SALES (corp-wide): 188.94MM **Privately Held**
SIC: 8111 General practice attorney, lawyer
PA: Sidley Austin Llp
1 S Dearborn
312 853-7000

(P-16639)
BAKER & HOSTETLER LLP
1900 Avenue Of The Stars, Los Angeles
(90067-4301)
PHONE....................310 820-8800
John F Cermak Junior, *Mng Pt*
EMP: 136
SALES (corp-wide): 309.55K **Privately Held**
Web: www.bakerlaw.com
SIC: 8111 General practice attorney, lawyer
PA: Baker & Hostetler Llp
127 Public Sq Ste 2000
216 621-0200

(P-16640)
BAKER & HOSTETLER LLP
600 Anton Blvd Ste 900, Costa Mesa
(92626-7193)
PHONE....................714 754-6600
George T Mooradian, *Pt*
EMP: 90
SQ FT: 6,000
SALES (corp-wide): 309.55K **Privately Held**
Web: www.bakerlaw.com
SIC: 8111 General practice attorney, lawyer
PA: Baker & Hostetler Llp
127 Public Sq Ste 2000
216 621-0200

(P-16641)
BAKER & MCKENZIE LLP
10250 Constellation Blvd Ste 1850, Los
Angeles (90067-6200)
PHONE....................310 201-4728
EMP: 125
SALES (corp-wide): 75.75MM **Privately Held**
Web: www.bakermckenzie.com

SIC: 8111 General practice law office
PA: Baker & Mckenzie Llp
300 E Randolph St # 5000
312 861-8000

(P-16642)
BALLARD SPAHR LLP
2029 Century Park E Ste 1400, Los Angeles
(90002-3076)
PHONE...................424 204-4400
Alan Petlak, *Brnch Mgr*
EMP: 76
SALES (corp-wide): 23.37MM **Privately
Held**
Web: www.ballardspahr.com
SIC: 8111 General practice attorney, lawyer
PA: Ballard Spahr Llp
1735 Market St Fl 51
215 665-8500

(P-16643)
BARNES & THORNBURG LLP
2029 Century Park E Ste 300, Los Angeles
(90067-2904)
PHONE...................310 284-3880
EMP: 113
SALES (corp-wide): 93.48MM **Privately
Held**
Web: www.btlaw.com
SIC: 8111 General practice attorney, lawyer
PA: Barnes & Thornburg Llp
240 E Jckson Blvd Ste 200
574 293-0681

(P-16644)
BD&J PC
9701 Wilshire Blvd Ste 630, Beverly Hills
(90212-2158)
PHONE...................855 906-3699
Kourosh Danesh Moghadam, *CEO*
EMP: 115 EST: 2007
SALES (est): 7.41MM **Privately Held**
Web: www.bdjinjurylawyers.com
SIC: 8111 General practice law office

(P-16645)
**BERGER KAHN A LAW
CORPORATION (PA)**
Also Called: Simon and Gladstone A Prof
1 Park Plz Ste 340, Irvine (92614-2511)
PHONE...................949 474-1880
Craig Simon, *CEO*
Leon J Gladstone, *
▲ EMP: 70 EST: 1928
SQ FT: 22,250
SALES (est): 5.49MM
SALES (corp-wide): 5.49MM **Privately
Held**
Web: www.bergerkahn.com
SIC: 8111 General practice attorney, lawyer

(P-16646)
**BLAKELY SOKOLOFF TAYLOR &
ZAFMAN LLP**
Also Called: Bstz
12400 Wilshire Blvd Ste 700, Los Angeles
(90025-1040)
PHONE...................310 207-3800
EMP: 240
Web: www.womblebonddickinson.com
SIC: 8111 Specialized law offices, attorneys

(P-16647)
BMC GROUP INC
Also Called: Bankruptcy Management Cons
300 Continental Blvd Ste 570, El Segundo
(90245-5072)
PHONE...................310 321-5555
Shawn Allen, *Pr*

EMP: 100
Web: www.bmcgroup.com
SIC: 8111 Bankruptcy referee
PA: The Bmc Group Inc
3732 W 120th St

(P-16648)
**BONNE BRDGES MLLER OKEFE
NCHOL (PA)**
355 S Grand Ave Ste 1750, Los Angeles
(90071-1562)
PHONE...................213 480-1900
David J O'keefe, *Pr*
James D Nichols, *
George Peterson, *
EMP: 100 EST: 1961
SALES (est): 4.94MM
SALES (corp-wide): 4.94MM **Privately
Held**
Web: www.bonnebridges.com
SIC: 8111 General practice attorney, lawyer

(P-16649)
**BOOTH MITCHEL & STRANGE
LLP**
979 Osos St Ste C1, San Luis Obispo
(93401-3253)
PHONE...................805 400-0703
Christpher Levwi, *Brnch Mgr*
EMP: 76
SALES (corp-wide): 3.12MM **Privately
Held**
Web: www.boothmitchel.com
SIC: 8111 General practice law office
PA: Booth Mitchel & Strange, L.L.P.
707 Wilshire Blvd # 3000
213 738-0100

(P-16650)
**BRYAN CAVE LIGHTON
PAISNER LLP**
120 Broadway Ste 300, Santa Monica
(90401-2386)
PHONE...................310 576-2100
Louise Caplan, *Mgr*
EMP: 88
SALES (corp-wide): 84K **Privately Held**
Web: www.bclplaw.com
SIC: 8111 General practice attorney, lawyer
PA: Bryan Cave Leighton Paisner Llp
One Metropolitan Sq 211 N
314 259-2000

(P-16651)
**BURKE WILLIAMS & SORENSEN
LLP (PA)**
Also Called: Burke
444 S Flower St Ste 2400, Los Angeles
(90071-2953)
PHONE...................213 236-0600
John J Welsh, *Mng Pt*
James T Bradshaw Junior, *Pt*
Carl K Newton, *Pt*
Leland C Dolley, *Pt*
Neil F Yeager, *Pt*
EMP: 90 EST: 1927
SQ FT: 51,000
SALES (est): 6.34MM
SALES (corp-wide): 6.34MM **Privately
Held**
Web: www.bwslaw.com
SIC: 8111 General practice attorney, lawyer

(P-16652)
**CALIFORNIA CITY SAN
BERNARDINO (PA)**
290 N D St, San Bernardino (92401-1734)
PHONE...................909 384-7272
R Carey Davis, *Mayor*

Mark Scoth, *
Gigi Hannah, *City Clerk*
David Kennedy, *City Treasurer*
Gary Saiz, *City Attorney*
EMP: 352 EST: 1854
SALES (est): 275.93MM
SALES (corp-wide): 275.93MM **Privately
Held**
Web: www.sbcity.org
SIC: 8111 Administrative and government law

(P-16653)
**CARPENTER ZUCKERMAN &
ROWLEY**
8827 W Olympic Blvd, Beverly Hills
(90211-3613)
PHONE...................310 273-1230
Paul Zuckerman, *Pt*
EMP: 128 EST: 2011
SALES (est): 11.01MM **Privately Held**
Web: www.cz.law
SIC: 8111 Labor and employment law

(P-16654)
**CARSON KURTZMAN
CONSULTANTS (DH)**
Also Called: K C C
2335 Alaska Ave, El Segundo
(90245-4808)
PHONE...................310 823-9000
Johnathan Carson, *
EMP: 180 EST: 2001
SQ FT: 46,000
SALES (est): 54.98MM **Privately Held**
Web: www.kccllc.com
SIC: 8111 Specialized legal services
HQ: Computershare Inc.
150 Royall St
Canton MA 02021

(P-16655)
**CHILDRENS LAW CENTER CAL
(PA)**
101 Centre Plaza Dr, Monterey Park
(91754-2155)
PHONE...................323 980-8700
Leslie Starr Heimov, *CEO*
EMP: 88 EST: 1989
SALES (est): 73.27MM **Privately Held**
Web: www.clccal.org
SIC: 8111 Legal aid service

(P-16656)
**CHRISTIE PARKER & HALE LLP
(PA)**
655 N Central Ave Ste 2300, Glendale
(01203-1445)
P.O. Box 29001 (91209-9001)
PHONE...................626 795-9900
EMP: 130 EST: 1946
SALES (est): 2.4MM
SALES (corp-wide): 2.4MM **Privately Held**
Web: www.lewisroca.com
SIC: 8111 General practice attorney, lawyer

(P-16657)
CLARKSON LAW FIRM PC
22255 Pacific Coast Hwy Ste 102, Malibu
(90265-5807)
PHONE...................213 788-4050
Ryan J Clarkson Esq, *Prin*
EMP: 81 EST: 2015
SALES (est): 2.49MM **Privately Held**
Web: www.clarksonlawfirm.com
SIC: 8111 General practice law office

(P-16658)
**COMPEX LEGAL SERVICES INC
(PA)**
Also Called: Compex Legal Services
325 Maple Ave, Torrance (90503-2602)
PHONE...................310 782-1801
Paul Boroditsch, *CEO*
Nitin Mehta, *
Anthony Bazurto, *
Humildad Pasimio, *
Rajesh Rangaswamy, *
▲ EMP: 120 EST: 1972
SQ FT: 47,740
SALES (est): 36.49MM
SALES (corp-wide): 36.49MM **Privately
Held**
Web: www.cpxlegal.com
SIC: 8111 7338 7334 Specialized legal
services; Secretarial and court reporting;
Photocopying and duplicating services

(P-16659)
**COOKSEY TLEN GAGE DFFY
WOOG A (PA)**
535 Anton Blvd Fl 10, Costa Mesa
(92626-1947)
PHONE...................714 431-1100
David Cooksey, *Pr*
Robert L Toolen, *VP*
EMP: 91 EST: 1970
SALES (est): 9.19MM
SALES (corp-wide): 9.19MM **Privately
Held**
Web: www.cookseylaw.com
SIC: 8111 General practice attorney, lawyer

(P-16660)
COUNTY OF LOS ANGELES
Also Called: Public Defender Administration
210 W Temple St Fl 19, Los Angeles
(90012-3231)
PHONE...................213 974-2811
Ronald Brown, *Brnch Mgr*
EMP: 81
Web: www.lacounty.gov
SIC: 8111 9222 Legal services; Public
defenders' office
PA: County Of Los Angeles
500 W Temple St Ste 437
213 974-1101

(P-16661)
COUNTY OF LOS ANGELES
Also Called: District Attys Off - Cntl Tral
210 W Temple St Rm 18-1144, Los Angeles
(90012-3210)
PHONE...................213 974-3812
Jackie Lazey, *Brnch Mgr*
EMP: 111
Web: www.lasd.org
SIC: 8111 9222 General practice attorney,
lawyer; District attorneys' office
PA: County Of Los Angeles
500 W Temple St Ste 437
213 974-1101

(P-16662)
COUNTY OF RIVERSIDE
Also Called: Public Defender- Main Office
4075 Main St, Riverside (92501-3701)
PHONE...................951 955-6000
Gary Windom, *Admn*
EMP: 200
SALES (corp-wide): 5.07B **Privately Held**
Web: www.rivco.org
SIC: 8111 9222 Legal services; Public
defenders' office
PA: County Of Riverside
4080 Lemon St Fl 11
951 955-1110

PRODUCTS & SVCS

(P-16663)
COUNTY OF SAN DIEGO
District Attorney
330 W Broadway Ste 1020, San Diego
(92101-3827)
PHONE..................619 531-4040
Steven Silva, *Sec*
EMP: 82
Web: www.sandiegocounty.gov
SIC: 8111 9222 Specialized legal services;
District attorneys' office
PA: County Of San Diego
1600 Pacific Hwy Ste 209
619 531-5880

(P-16664)
COVINGTON & BURLING LLP
1999 Avenue Of The Stars Ste 3500, Los
Angeles (90067-4643)
PHONE..................424 332-4800
Michelle Liffman, *Brnch Mgr*
EMP: 102
SALES (corp-wide): 345.07MM **Privately
Held**
Web: www.cov.com
SIC: 8111 General practice law office
PA: Covington & Burling Llp
1 City Ctr 850 10th St Nw
202 662-6000

(P-16665)
COX CASTLE & NICHOLSON LLP (PA)
Also Called: Cox Castle
2029 Century Park E Ste 2100, Los Angeles
(90067-3007)
PHONE..................310 284-2200
Gary A Glick, *Pt*
Edward F Quigley, *Pt*
David W Wensley, *Pt*
Mathew A Wyman, *Pt*
Marlene Goodfried, *Pt*
EMP: 165 EST: 1968
SQ FT: 60,000
SALES (est): 20.16MM
SALES (corp-wide): 20.16MM **Privately
Held**
Web: www.coxcastle.com
SIC: 8111 General practice attorney, lawyer

(P-16666)
CROWELL & MORING LLP
3 Park Plz Ste 2000, Irvine (92614-2591)
PHONE..................949 263-8400
Daniel Sasse, *Mgr*
EMP: 124
SALES (corp-wide): 107.51MM **Privately
Held**
Web: www.crowell.com
SIC: 8111 Specialized law offices, attorneys
PA: Crowell & Moring Llp
1001 Pennsylvania Ave Nw
202 624-2500

(P-16667)
CROWELL & MORING LLP
515 S Flower St Ste 4000, Los Angeles
(90071-2258)
PHONE..................213 622-4750
Mark Neighbor, *Brnch Mgr*
EMP: 113
SALES (corp-wide): 107.51MM **Privately
Held**
Web: www.crowell.com
SIC: 8111 Specialized law offices, attorneys
PA: Crowell & Moring Llp
1001 Pennsylvania Ave Nw
202 624-2500

(P-16668)
DANNING GILL DAMND KOLLITZ LLP
1901 Avenue Of The Stars Ste 450, Los
Angeles (90067-6006)
PHONE..................310 277-0077
David A Gill, *Pt*
Richard K Diamond, *
Howard Kollitz, *
Eric P Israel Pc, *Pt*
David M Poitras, *
EMP: 70 EST: 1952
SALES (est): 6.95MM **Privately Held**
Web: www.danninggill.com
SIC: 8111 General practice law office

(P-16669)
DAVIS WRIGHT TREMAINE LLP
865 S Figueroa St Ste 2400, Los Angeles
(90017-2566)
PHONE..................213 633-6800
Mary Haas, *Pt*
EMP: 121
SALES (corp-wide): 238.76MM **Privately
Held**
Web: www.dwt.com
SIC: 8111 General practice attorney, lawyer
PA: Davis Wright Tremaine Llp
920 5th Ave Ste 3300
206 622-3150

(P-16670)
DEFENSE SPECIALISTS LLC
Also Called: Defense Specialist, The
924 W Washington Blvd, Los Angeles
(90015-3312)
P.O. Box 2266 (90251-2266)
PHONE..................818 270-7162
Emilio Pensado Junior, *CEO*
Elba Aguila, *Prin*
EMP: 55 EST: 2016
SALES (est): 376.61K **Privately Held**
Web: www.thedefensespecialist.com
SIC: 8111 7381 3812 7389 Legal services;
Security guard service; Defense systems
and equipment; Explosives recovery or
extraction services

(P-16671)
DENTONS US LLP
Also Called: A Dentons Innovation Wirthlin
601 S Figueroa St Ste 2500, Los Angeles
(90017-5709)
PHONE..................213 623-9300
Edwin Reeser, *Genl Mgr*
EMP: 150
SALES (corp-wide): 49.92MM **Privately
Held**
Web: www.dentons.com
SIC: 8111 Specialized law offices, attorneys
PA: Dentons Us Llp
233 S Wacker Dr Ste 5900
312 876-8000

(P-16672)
DLA PIPER LLP (US)
2000 Avenue Of The Stars Ste 400n, Los
Angeles (90067-4735)
PHONE..................310 595-3000
Ronnie Decesare, *Brnch Mgr*
EMP: 93
Web: www.dlapiper.com
SIC: 8111 Corporate, partnership and
business law
HQ: Dla Piper Llp (Us)
650 S Exeter St
Baltimore MD 21202
410 580-3000

(P-16673)
DOMINGUEZ LAW GROUP PC
Also Called: Law Offices Juan J. Dominguez
3250 Wilshire Blvd Ste 2200, Los Angeles
(90010-1612)
PHONE..................213 388-7788
Juan J Dominguez, *Pr*
EMP: 100 EST: 1988
SQ FT: 5,000
SALES (est): 12.3MM **Privately Held**
Web: www.dominguezfirm.com
SIC: 8111 General practice attorney, lawyer

(P-16674)
DUCKOR MTZGER WYNNE A PROF LAW
101 W Broadway Ste 1700, San Diego
(92101-8289)
PHONE..................619 209-3000
Michael J Duckor, *Pr*
Gary J Spradling, *
Scott Metzger, *
EMP: 70 EST: 1977
SQ FT: 25,000
SALES (est): 2.15MM **Privately Held**
Web: www.dmwplc.com
SIC: 8111 General practice law office

(P-16675)
ELKINS KALT WNTRAUB RBEN GRTSI
10345 W Olympic Blvd, Los Angeles
(90064-2524)
PHONE..................310 746-4431
EMP: 91 EST: 2019
SALES (est): 7.33MM **Privately Held**
Web: www.elkinskalt.com
SIC: 8111 General practice attorney, lawyer

(P-16676)
ELLIS GRGE CPLLONE OBRIEN ANNG
2121 Avenue Of The Stars Fl 30, Los
Angeles (90067-5010)
PHONE..................310 274-7100
Eric George, *Mng Pt*
Allen Browne, *Pt*
Peter Ross, *Pt*
EMP: 100 EST: 1985
SALES (est): 6.15MM **Privately Held**
Web: www.bgrfirm.com
SIC: 8111 General practice law office

(P-16677)
ENGSTROM LIPSCOMB AND LACK A (PA)
10100 Santa Monica Blvd, Los Angeles
(90067-4003)
PHONE..................310 552-3800
Paul Engstrom, *Pr*
Lee G Lipscomb, *
Walter J Lack, *
EMP: 70 EST: 1974
SQ FT: 22,000
SALES (est): 8.05MM
SALES (corp-wide): 8.05MM **Privately
Held**
Web: www.elllaw.com
SIC: 8111 General practice law office

(P-16678)
EPSTEIN BECKER & GREEN PC
1925 Century Park E Ste 500, Los Angeles
(90067-2706)
PHONE..................415 398-3500
Bill Helvestine, *Mng Pt*
EMP: 85
SALES (corp-wide): 87.71MM **Privately
Held**
Web: www.ebglaw.com
SIC: 8111 General practice attorney, lawyer
PA: Epstein Becker & Green, P.C.
875 Third Ave
212 351-4500

(P-16679)
EPSTEIN BECKER & GREEN PC
1875 Century Park E Ste 500, Los Angeles
(90067-2500)
PHONE..................310 556-8861
Sandy Siciliano, *Mgr*
EMP: 127
SALES (corp-wide): 87.71MM **Privately
Held**
Web: www.ebglaw.com
SIC: 8111 General practice attorney, lawyer
PA: Epstein Becker & Green, P.C.
875 Third Ave
212 351-4500

(P-16680)
FEDERAL DFENDERS SAN DIEGO INC (PA)
225 Broadway Ste 900, San Diego
(92101-5030)
PHONE..................619 234-8467
Jami Ferrara, *CEO*
Shereen J Charlick, *
EMP: 75 EST: 1971
SALES (est): 33.13MM
SALES (corp-wide): 33.13MM **Privately
Held**
Web: www.fdsdi.com
SIC: 8111 General practice law office

(P-16681)
FENNEMORE CRAIG PC
Also Called: Fennemore Craig, P.C.
600 B St Ste 1700, San Diego
(92101-4507)
PHONE..................619 794-0050
EMP: 88
SALES (corp-wide): 11.18MM **Privately
Held**
Web: www.greshamsavage.com
SIC: 8111 General practice attorney, lawyer
PA: Craig Fennemore Foundation
2394 E Cmlback Rd Ste 600
602 916-5000

(P-16682)
FENNEMORE CRAIG PC
Also Called: Fennemore Craig, P.c.
550 E Hospitality Ln Ste 300, San
Bernardino (92408-4205)
PHONE..................619 794-0050
EMP: 80
SALES (corp-wide): 11.18MM **Privately
Held**
Web: www.fennemorelaw.com
SIC: 8111 General practice law office
PA: Craig Fennemore Foundation
2394 E Cmlback Rd Ste 600
602 916-5000

(P-16683)
FISH & RICHARDSON PC
12390 El Camino Real, San Diego
(92130-3162)
PHONE..................858 678-5070
Cindy Winters, *Mgr*
EMP: 189
SALES (corp-wide): 132.63MM **Privately
Held**
Web: www.fr.com
SIC: 8111 General practice law office
PA: Fish & Richardson P.C.
1 Marina Park Dr Ste 1700
617 542-5070

(P-16684)
FISHER & PHILLIPS LLP
2050 Main St Ste 1000, Irvine
(92614-8240)
PHONE..................949 851-2424
James Mcdonald, Pt
EMP: 105
SALES (corp-wide): 87.03MM **Privately Held**
Web: www.fisherphillips.com
SIC: 8111 General practice attorney, lawyer
PA: Fisher & Phillips Llp
1230 Peachtree St Ne # 3300
404 231-1400

(P-16685)
FULWIDER AND PATTON LLP
111 W Ocean Blvd Ste 1510, Long Beach
(90802-7907)
PHONE..................310 824-5555
Richard A Bardin, Mng Pt
Katherine Mcdaniel, *
David Pitman, *
Scott Hansen, *
EMP: 100 EST: 1938
SALES (est): 1.99MM **Privately Held**
Web: www.fulpat.com
SIC: 8111 General practice law office

(P-16686)
GIBBS GIDEN LOCHER
1880 Century Park E Ste 1200, Los Angeles
(90067-1621)
PHONE..................310 552-3400
Richard J Wittbrodt, Prin
Kenneth C Gibbs, Prin
Joseph M Giden, Prin
William D Locher, Prin
EMP: 70 EST: 1978
SQ FT: 27,000
SALES (est): 3.69MM **Privately Held**
Web: www.gibbsgiden.com
SIC: 8111 General practice attorney, lawyer

(P-16687)
GIBSON DUNN & CRUTCHER LLP (PA)
333 S Grand Ave, Los Angeles
(90071-3197)
PHONE..................213 229-7000
Kenneth M Doran, Prin
Dan Mummery, *
M Sean Royall, *
Frederick Brown, *
Theodore B Olson, *
EMP: 500 EST: 1880
SQ FT: 250,000
SALES (est): 1.97MM
SALES (corp-wide): 1.97MM **Privately Held**
Web: www.gibsondunn.com
SIC: 8111 General practice law office

(P-16688)
GIBSON DUNN & CRUTCHER LLP
2029 Century Park E Ste 4000, Los Angeles
(90002-3076)
PHONE..................310 552-8500
Julie Denton, Genl Mgr
EMP: 125
SALES (corp-wide): 1.97MM **Privately Held**
Web: www.gibsondunn.com
SIC: 8111 General practice law office
PA: Gibson, Dunn & Crutcher Llp
333 S Grand Ave
213 229-7000

(P-16689)
GIBSON DUNN & CRUTCHER LLP
3161 Michelson Dr Ste 1200, Irvine
(92612-4412)
PHONE..................949 451-3800
Karen Kubani, Brnch Mgr
EMP: 121
SALES (corp-wide): 1.97MM **Privately Held**
Web: www.gibsondunn.com
SIC: 8111 General practice law office
PA: Gibson, Dunn & Crutcher Llp
333 S Grand Ave
213 229-7000

(P-16690)
GILBERT KLLY CRWLEY JNNETT LLP (PA)
550 S Hope St Ste 2200, Los Angeles
(90071-3200)
PHONE..................213 615-7000
Jon H Tisdale, Mng Pt
Paul Bigley, *
Arthur J Mc Keon Iii, Pt
Timothy Kenna, *
EMP: 75 EST: 1936
SQ FT: 30,000
SALES (est): 3.5MM
SALES (corp-wide): 3.5MM **Privately Held**
SIC: 8111 General practice law office

(P-16691)
GIPSON HFFMAN PNCONE A PROF CO
1901 Avenue Of The Stars Ste 1100, Los Angeles (90067-6002)
PHONE..................310 556-4660
Lawrence R Barnett, Pr
Robert E Gipson, *
Kenneth I Sidle, *
Robert H Steinberg, *
EMP: 70 EST: 1982
SQ FT: 27,000
SALES (est): 4.68MM **Privately Held**
Web: www.ghplaw.com
SIC: 8111 General practice attorney, lawyer

(P-16692)
GIRARDI KEESE (PA)
1126 Wilshire Blvd, Los Angeles
(90017-1904)
PHONE..................213 977-0211
Thomas V Girardi, Pt
Robert M Keese, Pt
EMP: 95 EST: 1976
SQ FT: 5,000
SALES (est): 3.91MM
SALES (corp-wide): 3.91MM **Privately Held**
Web: www.girardikeese.com
SIC: 8111 General practice law office

(P-16693)
GLASER WEIL FINK JACOBS (PA)
10250 Constellation Blvd Fl 19, Los Angeles
(90067-6219)
PHONE..................310 553-3000
Terry Christensen, Mng Pt
Barry E Fink, *
Patricia L Glaser, *
Peter Weil, *
Allen Gilbert, *
EMP: 160 EST: 1988
SQ FT: 76,000
SALES (est): 21.41MM
SALES (corp-wide): 21.41MM **Privately Held**

Web: www.glaserweil.com
SIC: 8111 General practice law office

(P-16694)
GORDON REES SCULLY MANSUKHANI
633 W 5th St 52nd Fl, Los Angeles
(90071-2005)
PHONE..................213 576-5000
Scott Sirlin, Brnch Mgr
EMP: 117
SALES (corp-wide): 75.52MM **Privately Held**
Web: www.grsm.com
SIC: 8111 Specialized law offices, attorneys
PA: Gordon Rees Scully Mansukhani, Llp.
315 Pacific Ave
415 986-5900

(P-16695)
GORDON REES SCULLY MANSUKHANI
101 W Broadway Ste 1600, San Diego
(92101-8217)
PHONE..................619 696-6700
Gary Zacher, Mng Pt
EMP: 112
SQ FT: 7,000
SALES (corp-wide): 75.52MM **Privately Held**
Web: www.grsm.com
SIC: 8111 Specialized law offices, attorneys
PA: Gordon Rees Scully Mansukhani, Llp.
315 Pacific Ave
415 986-5900

(P-16696)
GREENBERG GLSKER FLDS CLMAN MC
2049 Century Park E Ste 2600, Los Angeles
(90067-3200)
PHONE..................310 553-3610
Jonathan R Fitzgarrald, Prin
Arthur N Greenberg, Pt
Stephen Claman, Pt
Bert Fields, Pt
Ricardo P Cestero, Pt
EMP: 200 EST: 1959
SQ FT: 80,000
SALES (est): 19.28MM **Privately Held**
Web: www.greenbergglusker.com
SIC: 8111 General practice attorney, lawyer

(P-16697)
GREENBERG TRAURIG LLP
Also Called: Greenberg Traurig
18565 Jamboree Rd Ste 500, Irvine
(92612-2562)
PHONE..................949 732-6500
Ray Lee, Mng Pt
EMP: 98
SALES (corp-wide): 853.02MM **Privately Held**
Web: www.gtlaw.com
SIC: 8111 General practice attorney, lawyer
HQ: Greenberg Traurig, Llp
One Intrntnal Pl Ste 2000
Boston MA 02110

(P-16698)
GREENBERG TRAURIG LLP
1840 Century Park E Ste 1900, Los Angeles
(90067-2121)
PHONE..................310 586-7708
Richard Rowan, Brnch Mgr
EMP: 76
SALES (corp-wide): 853.02MM **Privately Held**
Web: www.gtlaw.com

SIC: 8111 General practice attorney, lawyer
HQ: Greenberg Traurig, Llp
One Intrntnal Pl Ste 2000
Boston MA 02110

(P-16699)
HAIGHT BROWN & BONESTEEL LLP (PA)
Also Called: Haight
555 S Flower St Ste 4500, Los Angeles
(90071-2441)
PHONE..................213 542-8000
S Christian Stouder, Mng Pt
Carolyn Harper, CFO
EMP: 80 EST: 1980
SQ FT: 36,265
SALES (est): 4.93MM
SALES (corp-wide): 4.93MM **Privately Held**
Web: www.hbblaw.com
SIC: 8111 General practice law office

(P-16700)
HAYNES & BOONE LLP
600 Anton Blvd Ste 700, Costa Mesa
(92626-7651)
PHONE..................949 202-3000
Mike Boone, Pt
EMP: 72 EST: 2009
SALES (est): 2.4MM **Privately Held**
Web: www.haynesboone.com
SIC: 8111 General practice attorney, lawyer

(P-16701)
HIGGS FLETCHER & MACK LLP
Also Called: Goproto
401 W A St Ste 2600, San Diego
(92101-7913)
PHONE..................619 236-1551
John Morrell, Genl Pt
Anna F Roppo, Pt
Phillip C Samouis, Pt
EMP: 150 EST: 1939
SQ FT: 45,000
SALES (est): 21.24MM **Privately Held**
Web: www.higgslaw.com
SIC: 8111 General practice attorney, lawyer

(P-16702)
HILL FARRER & BURRILL
Also Called: One California Plaza
300 S Grand Ave Fl 37, Los Angeles
(90071-3147)
PHONE..................213 620-0460
Scott Gilmore, Pt
Jack R White, Pt
Kyle D Brown, Pt
William M Bitting, Pt
Stanley E Tobin, Pt
EMP: 100 EST: 1923
SQ FT: 32,000
SALES (est): 13.7MM **Privately Held**
Web: www.hillfarrer.com
SIC: 8111 General practice law office

(P-16703)
HOLLAND & KNIGHT LLP
400 S Hope St Ste 800, Los Angeles
(90071-2809)
PHONE..................213 896-2400
Maita Prout, Mgr
EMP: 102
SALES (corp-wide): 146.18MM **Privately Held**
Web: foundation.hklaw.com
SIC: 8111 General practice attorney, lawyer
PA: Holland & Knight Llp
524 Grand Regency Blvd
813 901-4200

PRODUCTS & SVCS

(P-16704)
HUESTON HENNIGAN LLP
523 W 6th St Ste 400, Los Angeles
(90014-1208)
PHONE..................213 788-4340
Marshall A Camp, *Pt*
Douglas J Dixon, *
Alexander C D Giza, *
Brian J Hennigan, *
John C Hueston, *
EMP: 80 **EST:** 2015
SQ FT: 25,000
SALES (est): 10.7MM **Privately Held**
Web: www.hueston.com
SIC: 8111 General practice attorney, lawyer

(P-16705)
IMHOFF & ASSOCIATES PC
Also Called: Miller and Associates
12424 Wilshire Blvd Ste 770, Los Angeles
(90025-1065)
PHONE..................310 691-2200
Jim Stefanucci, *Mgr*
EMP: 100 **EST:** 2001
SALES (est): 2.11MM **Privately Held**
Web: www.criminalattorney.com
SIC: 8111 General practice law office

(P-16706)
IMMIGRANT DEFENDERS LAW CENTER
Also Called: IMMDEF
634 S Spring St Fl 10, Los Angeles
(90014-3912)
PHONE..................213 634-0999
Lindsay Toczylowski, *Ex Dir*
Susan Alva, *
EMP: 85 **EST:** 2015
SALES (est): 12.13MM **Privately Held**
Web: www.immdef.org
SIC: 8111 Legal services

(P-16707)
IRELL & MANELLA LLP
840 Newport Center Dr Ste 400, Newport Beach (92660-6396)
PHONE..................949 760-0991
Nancy Adams, *Mgr*
EMP: 365
SALES (corp-wide): 30.1MM **Privately Held**
Web: www.irell.com
SIC: 8111 General practice attorney, lawyer
PA: Irell & Manella Llp
       1800 Avenue Of The Stars # 900
       310 277-1010

(P-16708)
IRELL & MANELLA LLP (PA)
1800 Avenue Of The Stars Ste 900, Los Angeles (90067-4276)
PHONE..................310 277-1010
Keith Orso, *Pt*
Ben Hattenbach, *Pt*
Lisa Glasser, *Pt*
Matt Ashley, *Ofcr*
Thomas Edwards, *Ex Dir*
EMP: 185 **EST:** 1941
SQ FT: 154,000
SALES (est): 30.1MM
SALES (corp-wide): 30.1MM **Privately Held**
Web: www.irell.com
SIC: 8111 General practice law office

(P-16709)
JACKOWAY TYRMAN WRTHMER ASTEN
1925 Century Park E 2nd Fl, Los Angeles
(90067-2701)

PHONE..................310 553-0305
Barry Hirsch, *Pr*
EMP: 100 **EST:** 1976
SQ FT: 3,000
SALES (est): 3.44MM **Privately Held**
Web: www.jtwamm.com
SIC: 8111 General practice law office

(P-16710)
JEFFER MNGELS BTLR MTCHELL LLP (PA)
Also Called: Jmbm
1900 Avenue Of The Stars Fl 7, Los Angeles (90067-4308)
PHONE..................310 203-8080
Bruce P Jeffer, *Managing Member*
Bruce P Jeffer, *Mng Pt*
Robert E Mangels, *Pt*
James R Butler Junior, *Pt*
Mark Marmaro, *Pt*
▲ **EMP:** 190 **EST:** 1981
SALES (est): 21.07MM
SALES (corp-wide): 21.07MM **Privately Held**
Web: www.jmbm.com
SIC: 8111 General practice attorney, lawyer

(P-16711)
JONES DAY
555 S Flower St Fl 50, Los Angeles
(90071-2452)
PHONE..................213 489-3939
Brian A Sun, *Pt*
EMP: 106
SALES (corp-wide): 84.88MM **Privately Held**
Web: www.jonesday.com
SIC: 8111 7389 General practice attorney, lawyer; Personal service agents, brokers, and bureaus
PA: Jones Day
       N Point 901 Lakeside Ave
       216 586-3939

(P-16712)
K&L GATES LLP
10100 Santa Monica Blvd Ste 700, Los Angeles (90067-4104)
PHONE..................310 552-5000
Karen Doyle, *Mgr*
EMP: 85
SALES (corp-wide): 1.18B **Privately Held**
Web: www.klgates.com
SIC: 8111 General practice law office
PA: K&L Gates Llp
       210 Sixth Ave
       412 355-6500

(P-16713)
KATTEN MUCHIN ROSENMAN LLP
2121 Avenue Of The Stars, Los Angeles
(90067-5010)
PHONE..................310 788-4400
Tanya Russell, *Brnch Mgr*
EMP: 108
SALES (corp-wide): 13.91MM **Privately Held**
Web: www.katten.com
SIC: 8111 General practice law office
PA: Katten Muchin Rosenman Llp
       525 W Monroe Ste 1900
       312 902-5200

(P-16714)
KEESAL YOUNG LOGAN A PROF CORP (PA)
400 Oceangate, Long Beach (90802-4307)
PHONE..................562 436-2000

Samuel A Keesal Junior, *CEO*
J Stephen Young, *
EMP: 90 **EST:** 1970
SQ FT: 65,000
SALES (est): 10.57K
SALES (corp-wide): 10.57K **Privately Held**
Web: www.kyl.com
SIC: 8111 General practice law office

(P-16715)
KIMBALL TIREY & ST JOHN LLP (PA)
7676 Hazard Center Dr Ste 900, San Diego
(92108-4515)
PHONE..................619 234-1690
Theodore C Kimball, *Pt*
Leslie Mason, *Prin*
EMP: 70 **EST:** 1977
SQ FT: 6,000
SALES (est): 5.46MM
SALES (corp-wide): 5.46MM **Privately Held**
Web: www.kts-law.com
SIC: 8111 General practice attorney, lawyer

(P-16716)
KING & SPALDING LLP
633 W 5th St Ste 1600, Los Angeles
(90071-2030)
PHONE..................213 443-4355
EMP: 80
SALES (corp-wide): 248.84MM **Privately Held**
Web: www.kslaw.com
SIC: 8111 General practice law office
PA: King & Spalding Llp
       1180 Peachtree St
       404 572-4600

(P-16717)
KIRKLAND & ELLIS LLP
333 S Hope St Ste 3000, Los Angeles
(90071-3039)
PHONE..................213 680-8400
Cynthia Barnes, *Off Mgr*
EMP: 494
SALES (corp-wide): 487.95MM **Privately Held**
Web: www.kirkland.com
SIC: 8111 General practice law office
PA: Kirkland & Ellis Llp
       333 W Wolf Point Plz
       312 862-2000

(P-16718)
KIRKLAND & ELLIS LLP
2049 Century Park E Ste 3700, Los Angeles
(90067-3211)
PHONE..................310 552-4200
EMP: 103
SALES (corp-wide): 487.95MM **Privately Held**
Web: www.kirkland.com
SIC: 8111 General practice attorney, lawyer
PA: Kirkland & Ellis Llp
       333 W Wolf Point Plz
       312 862-2000

(P-16719)
KIRKLAND & ELLIS LLP
555 S Flower St Ste 3700, Los Angeles
(90071-2432)
PHONE..................213 680-8400
EMP: 160
SALES (corp-wide): 487.95MM **Privately Held**
Web: www.kirkland.com
SIC: 8111 General practice attorney, lawyer
PA: Kirkland & Ellis Llp
       333 W Wolf Point Plz

---

312 862-2000

(P-16720)
KNIGHT LAW GROUP LLP
10250 Constellation Blvd Ste 2500, Los Angeles (90067-6225)
P.O. Box 512906 (90051-0906)
PHONE..................424 355-1155
EMP: 114 **EST:** 2018
SALES (est): 9.09MM **Privately Held**
Web: www.lemonlawhelp.com
SIC: 8111 General practice law office

(P-16721)
KNOBBE MARTENS OLSON BEAR LLP (PA)
2040 Main St Fl 14, Irvine (92614-8214)
PHONE..................949 760-0404
Steven J Nataupsky, *Mng Pt*
Steven Nataupsky, *
James B Bear, *
William B Bunker, *
William H Nieman, *
EMP: 350 **EST:** 1962
SQ FT: 120,000
SALES (est): 49.24MM
SALES (corp-wide): 49.24MM **Privately Held**
Web: www.knobbe.com
SIC: 8111 General practice law office

(P-16722)
KNOBBE MARTENS OLSON BEAR LLP
12790 El Camino Real Ste 100, San Diego
(92130-2217)
PHONE..................858 707-4000
Wesly Pettus, *Brnch Mgr*
EMP: 74
SALES (corp-wide): 49.24MM **Privately Held**
Web: www.knobbe.com
SIC: 8111 Patent, trademark and copyright law
PA: Knobbe Martens Olson & Bear, Llp
       2040 Main St Fl 14
       949 760-0404

(P-16723)
LA FOLLTTE JHNSON DE HAAS FSLE (PA)
701 N Brand Blvd Ste 600, Glendale
(91203-9877)
PHONE..................213 426-3600
Daren T Johnson, *Pr*
Louis De Haas Junior, *VP*
Don Fesler, *
Brian Birnie, *
Alfred Gerisch Junior, *Treas*
EMP: 105 **EST:** 1953
SALES (est): 7.68MM
SALES (corp-wide): 7.68MM **Privately Held**
Web: www.ljdfa.com
SIC: 8111 General practice law office

(P-16724)
LATHAM & WATKINS LLP
12670 High Bluff Dr Ste 100, San Diego
(92130-3086)
PHONE..................858 523-5400
Bruce Shepard, *Pt*
EMP: 101
SALES (corp-wide): 242.07MM **Privately Held**
Web: www.lw.com
SIC: 8111 General practice attorney, lawyer
PA: Latham & Watkins Llp
       555 W 5th Street Ste 300

---

213 485-1234

213 250-1800

312 782-0600

David C Frauman, *Dir*
EMP: 120
SQ FT: 40,000
SALES (corp-wide): 115.89MM **Privately Held**
Web: www.milbank.com
SIC: 8111 Corporate, partnership and business law
PA: Milbank Llp
55 Hudson Yards
212 530-5000

(P-16725)
LATHAM & WATKINS LLP
650 Town Center Dr Ste 2000, Costa Mesa (92626-7135)
PHONE..............................714 540-1235
Shayne Kennedy, *Mng Pt*
EMP: 456
SALES (corp-wide): 242.07MM **Privately Held**
Web: www.lw.com
SIC: 8111 General practice attorney, lawyer
PA: Latham & Watkins Llp
555 W 5th Street Ste 300
213 485-1234

(P-16726)
LATHAM & WATKINS LLP (PA)
555 W 5th St Ste 300, Los Angeles (90013-1020)
PHONE..............................213 485-1234
David Gordon, *Pt*
John Clair, *Pt*
Allen Wang, *Pt*
Philip Rossetti, *Pt*
Jean Paul Poitras, *Pt*
EMP: 570 **EST:** 1934
SALES (est): 242.07MM
SALES (corp-wide): 242.07MM **Privately Held**
Web: www.lw.com
SIC: 8111 General practice attorney, lawyer

(P-16727)
LAW OFFCES LES ZEVE A PROF COR
30 Corporate Park Ste 450, Irvine (92606-3401)
PHONE..............................714 848-7920
Les Zieve, *Prin*
Mark Kayton, *
EMP: 105 **EST:** 1991
SQ FT: 1,000
SALES (est): 1.89MM **Privately Held**
Web: www.zbslaw.com
SIC: 8111 General practice attorney, lawyer

(P-16728)
LEGAL SOLUTIONS HOLDINGS INC
Also Called: Getmedlegal
955 Overland Ct Ste 200, San Dimas (91773-1747)
PHONE..............................800 244-3495
Greg Webber, *CEO*
Kenneth Gleockler, *
Keahi Kakugawa, *
Harren Investors Ii Lp, *Prin*
Harren Investors Ii-b Lp, *Prin*
EMP: 237 **EST:** 1986
SALES (est): 2.32MM **Privately Held**
Web: www.getmedlegal.com
SIC: 8111 Legal services

(P-16729)
LEWIS BRSBOIS BSGARD SMITH LLP
650 Town Center Dr Ste 1400, Costa Mesa (92626-7020)
PHONE..............................714 545-9200
Shawn Derfer, *Mgr*
EMP: 90
SALES (corp-wide): 23.87MM **Privately Held**
Web: www.lewisbrisbois.com
SIC: 8111 General practice law office
PA: Lewis Brisbois Bisgaard & Smith Llp
633 W Fifth St Ste 4000

(P-16730)
LEWIS BRSBOIS BSGARD SMITH LLP (PA)
633 W 5th St Ste 4000, Los Angeles (90071-2074)
PHONE..............................213 250-1800
Robert F Lewis, *Mng Pt*
Roy M Brisbois, *Pt*
Christopher P Bisgaard, *Pt*
EMP: 650 **EST:** 1979
SQ FT: 80,000
SALES (est): 23.87MM
SALES (corp-wide): 23.87MM **Privately Held**
Web: www.lewisbrisbois.com
SIC: 8111 General practice law office

(P-16731)
LEWIS BRSBOIS BSGARD SMITH LLP
701 B St Ste 1900, San Diego (92101-8198)
PHONE..............................619 233-1006
Susan O' Brien, *Mgr*
EMP: 119
SALES (corp-wide): 23.87MM **Privately Held**
Web: www.lewisbrisbois.com
SIC: 8111 General practice law office
PA: Lewis Brisbois Bisgaard & Smith Llp
633 W Fifth St Ste 4000
213 250-1800

(P-16732)
LINER LLP
Also Called: Liner Law
1100 Glendon Ave 14th, Los Angeles (90024-3503)
PHONE..............................310 500-3500
Stuart A Liner, *Mng Pt*
EMP: 104 **EST:** 1996
SQ FT: 21,000
SALES (est): 4.63MM **Privately Held**
Web: www.linerlawgroup.com
SIC: 8111 General practice law office
HQ: Dla Piper Llp (Us)
650 S Exeter St
Baltimore MD 21202
410 580-3000

(P-16733)
LLC BATES WHITE
322 8th St, Del Mar (92014-2807)
PHONE..............................858 523-2150
Dorris Ballentine, *Brnch Mgr*
EMP: 130
SALES (corp-wide): 21.63MM **Privately Held**
Web: www.bateswhite.com
SIC: 8111 General practice attorney, lawyer
PA: Bates White, Llc
2001 K St Nw Bldg Ste 5
202 747-1436

(P-16734)
LLP MAYER BROWN
Also Called: Mayer Brown & Platt
350 S Grand Ave Ste 2500, Los Angeles (90071-3486)
PHONE..............................213 229-9500
Jim Tancula, *Mgr*
EMP: 430
SALES (corp-wide): 96.88MM **Privately Held**
Web: www.mayerbrown.com
SIC: 8111 General practice attorney, lawyer
PA: Mayer Brown Llp
71 S Wacker Dr

(P-16735)
LOEB & LOEB LLP (PA)
Also Called: Loeb & Loeb
10100 Santa Monica Blvd Ste 2200, Los Angeles (90067-4120)
PHONE..............................310 282-2000
Barry I Slotnick, *Ch*
Jerry Post, *Chief*
Kenneth B Anderson, *Pt*
Stan Johnson, *Pt*
Robert A Meyer, *Ch*
EMP: 134 **EST:** 1909
SALES (est): 14.57MM
SALES (corp-wide): 14.57MM **Privately Held**
Web: www.loeb.com
SIC: 8111 General practice attorney, lawyer

(P-16736)
MALCOLM & CISNEROS A LAW CORP
Also Called: Malcolm Cisneros
2112 Business Center Dr Ste 100, Irvine (92612-7136)
PHONE..............................949 252-9400
William Malcolm, *CEO*
Arturo Cisneros, *
EMP: 110 **EST:** 1992
SALES (est): 4.9MM **Privately Held**
Web: www.malcolmcisneros.com
SIC: 8111 General practice law office

(P-16737)
MANATT PHELPS & PHILLIPS LLP (PA)
2049 Century Park E Ste 1700, Los Angeles (90067-3119)
PHONE..............................310 312-4000
EMP: 420 **EST:** 1965
SALES (est): 38.81MM
SALES (corp-wide): 38.81MM **Privately Held**
Web: www.manatt.com
SIC: 8111 General practice law office

(P-16738)
MANNING KASS ELLROD RMREZ TRST (PA)
801 S Figueroa St 15th Fl, Los Angeles (90017-5504)
PHONE..............................213 624-6900
Steven D Manning, *Mng Pt*
EMP: 150 **EST:** 1994
SALES (est): 8.34MM **Privately Held**
Web: www.manningllp.com
SIC: 8111 General practice attorney, lawyer

(P-16739)
MED-LEGAL LLC
955 Overland Ct Ste 200, San Dimas (91773-1747)
PHONE..............................626 653-5160
Moonesh Arora, *CEO*
Michael Salzano, *
Kenneth E Gleockler, *
EMP: 150 **EST:** 2010
SALES (est): 8.22MM **Privately Held**
Web: www.med-legal.com
SIC: 8111 Legal aid service

(P-16740)
MILBANK TWEED HDLEY MCCLOY LLP
Also Called: Milbank Global Securities
2029 Century Park E, Los Angeles (90002-3076)
PHONE..............................424 386-4000

(P-16741)
MINTZ LEVIN COHN FERRIS GL
3580 Carmel Mountain Rd Ste 300, San Diego (92130-6768)
PHONE..............................858 314-1500
EMP: 100
SALES (corp-wide): 199.9MM **Privately Held**
Web: www.mintz.com
SIC: 8111 General practice law office
PA: Mintz, Levin, Cohn, Ferris, Glovsky And Popeo, P.C.
1 Financial Ctr
617 348-4951

(P-16742)
MITCHELL SILBERBERG KNUPP LLP (PA)
Also Called: Mitchell Slbrberg Knupp Fndtio
2049 Century Park E Fl 18, Los Angeles (90067-3120)
PHONE..............................310 312-2000
Jeffrey K Eisen, *Prin*
Thomas P Lambert, *Mng Pt*
Kevin E Gaut, *COO*
Jerry Kaufman, *Ex Dir*
EMP: 198 **EST:** 1908
SALES (est): 23.52MM
SALES (corp-wide): 23.52MM **Privately Held**
Web: www.msk.com
SIC: 8111 General practice law office

(P-16743)
MORRIS POLICH & PURDY LLP (PA)
1055 W 7th St Ste 2400, Los Angeles (90017-2550)
PHONE..............................213 891-9100
Theodore D Levin, *Pt*
Douglas C Purdy, *Pt*
Walter Lipsman, *Pt*
Jeff Barron, *Pt*
James Chantland, *Pt*
EMP: 100 **EST:** 1969
SQ FT: 40,000
SALES (est): 5.01MM
SALES (corp-wide): 5.01MM **Privately Held**
Web: www.mpplaw.com
SIC: 8111 General practice attorney, lawyer

(P-16744)
MORRISON & FOERSTER LLP
Also Called: MORRISON & FOERSTER LLP
12531 High Bluff Dr Ste 100, San Diego (92130-3014)
PHONE..............................858 720-5100
Mark Zebrowski, *Mng Pt*
EMP: 413
SALES (corp-wide): 144.28MM **Privately Held**
Web: www.mofo.com
SIC: 8111 General practice attorney, lawyer
PA: Morrison & Foerster
425 Market St
415 268-7000

(P-16745)
MORRISON & FOESTER
Also Called: Morrison & Foerster
707 Wilshire Blvd, Los Angeles
(90017-3501)
PHONE..............................213 892-5200
Gregory Koltun, *Mng Pt*
EMP: 250
SALES (corp-wide): 144.28MM **Privately Held**
Web: www.mofo.com
SIC: 8111 General practice attorney, lawyer
PA: Morrison & Foerster
425 Market St
415 268-7000

(P-16746)
MUNGER TOLLES & OLSON LLP
350 S Grand Ave Fl 50, Los Angeles
(90071-3426)
PHONE..............................213 683-9100
Sandra Seville-jones Mng Ptrn, *Prin*
EMP: 134 EST: 2001
SALES (est): 24.76MM **Privately Held**
Web: www.mto.com
SIC: 8111 Corporate, partnership and business law

(P-16747)
MUNGER TOLLES OLSON FOUNDATION (PA)
350 S Grand Ave Fl 50, Los Angeles
(90071-3426)
PHONE..............................213 683-9100
O'malley M Miller, *CEO*
Robert Johnson, *
Bart Williams, *
Mark Helm, *
Steven B Weisburd, *
EMP: 420 EST: 1962
SQ FT: 100,000
SALES (est): 1.97MM
SALES (corp-wide): 1.97MM **Privately Held**
Web: www.mto.com
SIC: 8111 General practice attorney, lawyer

(P-16748)
MURCHISON & CUMMING LLP (PA)
Also Called: M & C
801 S Grand Ave Ste 900, Los Angeles
(90017-4624)
PHONE..............................213 623-7400
Friedrich W Seitz, *Pt*
Michael D Mc Evoy, *Sr Pt*
Michael Lawler, *Sr Pt*
Steven L Smilay, *Sr Pt*
Kenneth Moreno, *Sr Pt*
EMP: 100 EST: 1952
SQ FT: 30,000
SALES (est): 6.49MM
SALES (corp-wide): 6.49MM **Privately Held**
Web: www.murchisonlaw.com
SIC: 8111 General practice law office

(P-16749)
MUSICK PEELER & GARRETT LLP (PA)
333 S Hope St Ste 2900, Los Angeles
(90071-3048)
PHONE..............................213 629-7600
R Joseph De Briyn, *Mng Pt*
Wayne Littlefied, *Pt*
Gary Overstreet, *Pt*
Edward Landrey, *Pt*
Peter J Diedrich, *Pt*
EMP: 168 EST: 1937

SQ FT: 100,000
SALES (est): 9.58MM
SALES (corp-wide): 9.58MM **Privately Held**
Web: www.musickpeeler.com
SIC: 8111 General practice law office

(P-16750)
NATIONAL ATTNY COLLECTION SVCS
700 N Brand Blvd Fl 2, Glendale
(91203-1247)
PHONE..............................818 547-9760
A Donovan, *CEO*
John Weinstein, *
EMP: 251 EST: 2005
SALES (est): 9.29MM **Privately Held**
SIC: 8111 Debt collection law

(P-16751)
NEWMEYER & DILLION LLP (PA)
895 Dove St Ste 500, Newport Beach
(92660-2999)
PHONE..............................949 854-7000
Gregory L Dillion, *Pt*
Thomas F Newmeyer, *Pt*
John A O Hara, *Pt*
Michael S Cucchissi, *Pt*
Joseph A Ferrentino, *Pt*
EMP: 115 EST: 1984
SQ FT: 52,000
SALES (est): 6.97MM **Privately Held**
Web: www.newmeyeranddillion.com
SIC: 8111 General practice attorney, lawyer

(P-16752)
NOSSAMAN LLP (PA)
Also Called: Nossaman Consults
777 S Figueroa St Ste 3400, Los Angeles
(90017-5834)
PHONE..............................213 612-7800
E George Joseph, *Mng Pt*
EMP: 74 EST: 1944
SQ FT: 20,000
SALES (est): 10.75MM
SALES (corp-wide): 10.75MM **Privately Held**
Web: www.nossaman.com
SIC: 8111 General practice attorney, lawyer

(P-16753)
OMELVENY & MYERS LLP (PA)
Also Called: O'Melveny
400 S Hope St 18th Fl, Los Angeles
(90071-2801)
PHONE..............................213 430-6000
Arthur Culvahouse Junior, *Mng Pt*
Arthur Culvahouse Junior, *Managing Member*
Bradley Butwin, *Managing Member**
Stephen Brody, *
Chuck Diamond, *
EMP: 850 EST: 1885
SQ FT: 250,000
SALES (est): 125.69MM
SALES (corp-wide): 125.69MM **Privately Held**
Web: www.omm.com
SIC: 8111 General practice law office

(P-16754)
OMELVENY & MYERS LLP
1999 Avenue Of The Stars Fl 8, Los Angeles (90067-6022)
PHONE..............................310 553-6700
Jodi Yamada, *Mgr*
EMP: 143
SALES (corp-wide): 125.69MM **Privately Held**
Web: www.omm.com

SIC: 8111 General practice attorney, lawyer
PA: O'melveny & Myers Llp
400 S Hope St Fl 18th
213 430-6000

(P-16755)
PACHULSKI STANG ZEHL JONES LLP (PA)
Also Called: Pszyjw
10100 Santa Monica Blvd Ste 1100, Los Angeles (90067-4111)
PHONE..............................310 277-6910
Richard M Pachulski, *Pr*
Dean A Ziehl, *
James I Stang, *
EMP: 90 EST: 1983
SQ FT: 21,000
SALES (est): 23.03MM **Privately Held**
Web: www.pszjlaw.com
SIC: 8111 General practice law office

(P-16756)
PALMIERI TYLER WNER WLHELM WLD
1900 Main St Ste 700, Irvine (92614-7328)
P.O. Box 19712 (92623-9712)
PHONE..............................949 851-9400
James E Wilhelm, *Pt*
Dennis Tyler, *
Alan Wiener, *
Mike Greene, *
Robert Ihrke, *
EMP: 100 EST: 1986
SQ FT: 34,000
SALES (est): 8.18MM **Privately Held**
Web: www.ptwww.com
SIC: 8111 General practice attorney, lawyer

(P-16757)
PAUL HASTINGS LLP (PA)
515 S Flower St Fl 25, Los Angeles
(90071-2228)
PHONE..............................213 683-6000
Greg Nitzkowski, *Pt*
Seth M Zachary, *
Elena R Baca, *
EMP: 1890 EST: 2011
SQ FT: 209,000
SALES (est): 429.41MM
SALES (corp-wide): 429.41MM **Privately Held**
Web: www.paulhastings.com
SIC: 8111 General practice law office

(P-16758)
PAUL HASTINGS LLP
4747 Executive Dr Ste 1200, San Diego
(92121-3114)
PHONE..............................858 458-3000
Craig Price, *Admn*
EMP: 104
SALES (corp-wide): 429.41MM **Privately Held**
Web: www.paulhastings.com
SIC: 8111 General practice law office
PA: Paul Hastings Llp
515 S Flower St Fl 25
213 683-6000

(P-16759)
PILLSBURY WNTHROP SHAW PTTMAN
Also Called: Pillsbury
725 S Figueroa St Ste 2800, Los Angeles
(90017-5406)
PHONE..............................213 488-7100
Melissa Burton, *Admn*
EMP: 128
SALES (corp-wide): 61.11MM **Privately Held**

Web: www.pillsburylaw.com
SIC: 8111 General practice law office
PA: Pillsbury Winthrop Shaw Pittman Llp
31 W 52nd St Fl 29
212 858-1000

(P-16760)
PIRCHER NICHOLS & MEEKS (PA)
1925 Century Park E Ste 1700, Los Angeles
(90067-2740)
PHONE..............................310 201-0132
Gary Laughlin, *Sr Pt*
Leo Pircher, *Sr Pt*
Eugene Leone, *Sr Pt*
Stevens Carey, *Sr Pt*
EMP: 95 EST: 1983
SQ FT: 35,000
SALES (est): 2.42MM
SALES (corp-wide): 2.42MM **Privately Held**
Web: www.hklaw.com
SIC: 8111 General practice attorney, lawyer

(P-16761)
POLSINELLI PC
Also Called: Polsinelli LLP
2049 Century Park E Ste 2300, Los Angeles
(90067-3125)
PHONE..............................310 556-1801
Norma Ayala, *Admn*
EMP: 70
SALES (corp-wide): 227.61MM **Privately Held**
Web: www.polsinelli.com
SIC: 8111 General practice attorney, lawyer
PA: Polsinelli Pc
900 W 48th Pl Ste 900 # 900
816 753-1000

(P-16762)
PRICE LAW GROUP A PROF CORP (PA)
Also Called: Plg Law Group
15760 Ventura Blvd Ste 800, Encino
(91436-3018)
PHONE..............................818 995-4540
Stuart M Price, *Pr*
EMP: 115 EST: 1991
SQ FT: 15,000
SALES (est): 6.07MM **Privately Held**
Web: www.resolvelawgroup.com
SIC: 8111 General practice law office

(P-16763)
PRINDLE DECKER & AMARO LLP (PA)
310 Golden Shore Fl 4, Long Beach
(90802-4232)
P.O. Box 22711 (90801-5711)
PHONE..............................562 436-3946
R J Decker, *Pt*
Michael Amaro, *Pt*
Kenneth Prindle, *Pt*
R Joseph Decker, *Pt*
EMP: 85 EST: 1990
SALES (est): 8.45MM **Privately Held**
Web: www.pdalaw.com
SIC: 8111 Specialized law offices, attorneys

(P-16764)
PROBER & RAPHAEL A LAW CORP
Also Called: Prober & Raphael, ALC
20750 Ventura Blvd Ste 100, Woodland Hills
(91364-6207)
P.O. Box 4365 (91365-4365)
PHONE..............................818 227-0100
Dean R Prober, *Pr*

Lee S Raphael, *
EMP: 70 **EST:** 1984
SALES (est): 4.48MM **Privately Held**
Web: www.pralc.com
SIC: 8111 General practice attorney, lawyer

(P-16765)
PROCOPIO CORY HARGREAVES & SAVITCH LLP (PA)
530 B St Ste 2200, San Diego (92101-4435)
PHONE..............................619 238-1900
EMP: 215 **EST:** 1946
SALES (est): 7.89MM
SALES (corp-wide): 7.89MM **Privately Held**
Web: www.procopio.com
SIC: 8111 General practice law office

(P-16766)
PUBLIC COUNSEL
610 S Ardmore Ave, Los Angeles (90005-2322)
PHONE....................213 385-2977
Kathryn Eidmann, *Pr*
Madaline Kleiner, *
EMP: 94 **EST:** 1970
SQ FT: 12,000
SALES (est): 17.3MM **Privately Held**
Web: www.publiccounsel.org
SIC: 8111 Specialized law offices, attorneys

(P-16767)
QUINN EMNUEL URQHART SLLVAN LL (PA)
Also Called: Quinn Emmanuel Trial Lawyers
865 S Figueroa St Fl 10, Los Angeles (90017-5003)
PHONE..............................213 443-3000
John B Quinn, *Pt*
Christopher Tayback, *Pt*
William Burck, *Co-Managing Partner*
Michael Carlinsky, *Co-Managing Partner*
Kevin J Arquit, *Pt*
EMP: 366 **EST:** 1986
SALES (est): 24.99MM
SALES (corp-wide): 24.99MM **Privately Held**
Web: www.quinnemanuel.com
SIC: 8111 Specialized law offices, attorneys

(P-16768)
REED SMITH LLP
355 S Grand Ave Ste 2900, Los Angeles (90071-1514)
PHONE..............................213 457-8000
Peter Kennedy, *Office Managing Partner*
EMP: 158
SALES (corp-wide): 487.57MM **Privately Held**
Web: www.reedsmith.com
SIC: 8111 General practice attorney, lawyer
PA: Reed Smith Llp
  225 5th Ave
  412 288-3131

(P-16769)
RICHARDS WTSON GRSHON A PROF C (PA)
Also Called: RW&g
355 S Grand Ave 40th Fl, Los Angeles (90071-1560)
PHONE..............................213 626-8484
Laurence S Wiener, *CEO*
Kayser O Sume Cmb, *Prin*
James L Markman, *
Craig A Steele, *
William L Strausz, *

▲ **EMP:** 120 **EST:** 1954
SQ FT: 45,000
SALES (est): 17.44MM
SALES (corp-wide): 17.44MM **Privately Held**
Web: www.rwglaw.com
SIC: 8111 General practice law office

(P-16770)
ROBBINS GELLER RUDMAN DOWD LLP (PA)
655 W Broadway Ste 1900, San Diego (92101-8498)
PHONE..............................619 231-1058
Michael J Dowd, *
Darren J Robbins, *
Paul J Geller, *
Samuel H Rudman, *
EMP: 300 **EST:** 2004
SQ FT: 135,000
SALES (est): 42.06MM
SALES (corp-wide): 42.06MM **Privately Held**
Web: www.rgrdlaw.com
SIC: 8111 Corporate, partnership and business law

(P-16771)
ROPERS MAJESKI A PROF CORP
445 S Figueroa St Ste 3000, Los Angeles (90071-1619)
PHONE..............................213 312-2000
Allan Anderson, *Mgr*
EMP: 217
SALES (corp-wide): 5.2MM **Privately Held**
Web: www.ropers.com
SIC: 8111 General practice law office
PA: Ropers Majeski, A Professional Corporation
  535 Middlefield Rd # 245
  650 364-8200

(P-16772)
RUSS AUGUST & KABAT LLP
12424 Wilshire Blvd Ste 1200, Los Angeles (90025-1031)
PHONE..............................310 826-7474
Larry C Russ, *Prin*
Jules L Kabat, *
Laura K Stanton, *
Richard L August, *
Even Kent, *
EMP: 97 **EST:** 1981
SALES (est): 9.8MM **Privately Held**
Web: www.raklaw.com
SIC: 8111 General practice attorney, lawyer

(P-16773)
RUTAN & TUCKER LLP (PA)
18575 Jamboree Rd Ste 900, Irvine (92612-2559)
P.O. Box 1950 (92628-1950)
PHONE..............................714 641-5100
Richard Boden, *Managing Member*
Paul F Marx, *Managing Member**
Jodi Brooks, *Managing Member**
Tony Malkani, *Managing Member**
EMP: 265 **EST:** 1935
SALES (est): 48.58MM
SALES (corp-wide): 48.58MM **Privately Held**
Web: www.rutan.com
SIC: 8111 General practice attorney, lawyer

(P-16774)
SAUL EWING ARNSTEIN & LEHR LLP
Also Called: Saul Ewing Arnstein & Lehr LLP

1888 Century Park E Fl 19, Los Angeles (90067-1702)
PHONE..............................310 398-6100
EMP: 94
SALES (corp-wide): 20.47MM **Privately Held**
Web: www.saul.com
SIC: 8111 General practice law office
PA: Saul Ewing Llp
  1500 Market St Fl 38
  215 972-7777

(P-16775)
SELMAN LCHNGER EDSON HSU NWMAN
11766 Wilshire Blvd, Los Angeles (90025-6538)
PHONE..............................310 445-0800
Sheryl Leichenger, *Pt*
EMP: 70
SALES (est): 1.57MM **Privately Held**
SIC: 8111 Legal services

(P-16776)
SELTZER CPLAN MCMHON VTEK A LA (PA)
750 B St Ste 2100, San Diego (92101-8177)
PHONE..............................619 685-3003
Robert Caplan, *Pr*
Gerald L Mc Mahon, *
John H Alspaugh, *
Neal P Panish, *
EMP: 165 **EST:** 1970
SQ FT: 78,000
SALES (est): 7.77MM
SALES (corp-wide): 7.77MM **Privately Held**
Web: www.scmv.com
SIC: 8111 General practice attorney, lawyer

(P-16777)
SEYFARTH SHAW LLP
2029 Century Park E Ste 3300, Los Angeles (90002-3076)
PHONE..............................310 277-7200
Sandy Abrahamian, *Brnch Mgr*
EMP: 200
SALES (corp-wide): 474.05MM **Privately Held**
Web: www.seyfarth.com
SIC: 8111 General practice law office
PA: Seyfarth Shaw Llp
  233 S Wacker Dr Ste 8000
  312 460-5000

(P-16778)
SHEPPARD MLLIN RCHTER HMPTON L
501 W Broadway Fl 19, San Diego (92101-8541)
PHONE..............................619 338-6500
Robert Sbardellati, *Brnch Mgr*
EMP: 93
SALES (corp-wide): 37.19MM **Privately Held**
Web: www.sheppardmullin.com
SIC: 8111 General practice law office
PA: Sheppard, Mullin, Richter & Hampton, Llp
  333 S Hope St Fl 43
  213 620-1780

(P-16779)
SHEPPARD MLLIN RCHTER HMPTON L
12275 El Camino Real Ste 100, San Diego (92130-4092)
PHONE..............................858 720-8900

Shannon Petersen, *Brnch Mgr*
EMP: 80
SALES (corp-wide): 37.19MM **Privately Held**
Web: www.sheppardmullin.com
SIC: 8111 General practice law office
PA: Sheppard, Mullin, Richter & Hampton, Llp
  333 S Hope St Fl 43
  213 620-1780

(P-16780)
SHEPPARD MLLIN RCHTER HMPTON L (PA)
Also Called: Sheppard Mullin
333 S Hope St Fl 43, Los Angeles (90071-1422)
PHONE..............................213 620-1780
Guy N Halgren, *Ch Bd*
Robert Beall, *Administrative Partner*
Robert Zuber, *Ex Dir*
Lawrence Braun, *Pt*
Charles Barker, *Pt*
EMP: 370 **EST:** 1927
SQ FT: 52,820
SALES (est): 37.19MM
SALES (corp-wide): 37.19MM **Privately Held**
Web: www.sheppardmullin.com
SIC: 8111 General practice law office

(P-16781)
SHOOK HARDY & BACON LLP
5 Park Plz Ste 1600, Irvine (92614-2546)
PHONE..............................949 475-1500
Michelle Fujimoto, *Mgr*
EMP: 239
SALES (corp-wide): 47.6MM **Privately Held**
Web: www.shb.com
SIC: 8111 General practice law office
PA: Shook, Hardy & Bacon L.L.P.
  2555 Grand Blvd
  816 474-6550

(P-16782)
SIDLEY AUSTIN LLP
1999 Avenue Of The Stars Ste 1700, Los Angeles (90067-4622)
PHONE..............................310 284-6618
EMP: 80
SALES (corp-wide): 188.94MM **Privately Held**
Web: www.sidley.com
SIC: 8111 General practice attorney, lawyer
PA: Sidley Austin Llp
  1 S Dearborn
  312 853 7000

(P-16783)
SINGLETON SCHREIBER LLP ✪
Also Called: Singlton Schrber Frless Advcac
591 Camino De La Reina Ste 1025, San Diego (92108-3112)
PHONE..............................619 771-3473
Gerald Singleton, *Mng Pt*
Brett Schreiber, *Pt*
Brian Coln, *Mng Pt*
Andrew Bluth, *Pt*
Mark Fleming, *Pt*
EMP: 152 **EST:** 2023
SALES (est): 16.39MM **Privately Held**
SIC: 8111 General practice law office

(P-16784)
SKADDEN ARPS SLATE MEAGHER & F
300 S Grand Ave Ste 3400, Los Angeles (90071-3137)
PHONE..............................213 687-5000

PRODUCTS & SVCS

Rand S April, *Pt*
EMP: 250
Web: www.skadden.com
SIC: 8111 General practice attorney, lawyer
HQ: Skadden, Arps, Slate, Meagher &
Flom Llp
1 Manhttan W 395 9th Ave
New York NY 10001
212 735-3000

(P-16785)
SNELL & WILMER LLP
Also Called: Snell & Wilmer
600 Anton Blvd Ste 1400, Costa Mesa
(92626-7689)
PHONE..................714 427-7000
Andrea Bryant, *Prin*
EMP: 75
SQ FT: 3,000
SALES (corp-wide): 49.02MM **Privately
Held**
Web: www.swlaw.com
SIC: 8111 General practice attorney, lawyer
PA: Snell & Wilmer L.L.P.
1 E Wshington St Ste 2700
602 382-6000

(P-16786)
STRADLING YCCA CRLSON RUTH A P (PA)
660 Newport Center Dr Ste 1600, Newport
Beach (92660-6458)
PHONE..................949 725-4000
John F Cannon, *Prin*
Nick E Yocca, *
William Rauth, *
Keith C Schaaf, *
Rick C Goodman, *
EMP: 200 **EST:** 1975
SQ FT: 64,000
SALES (est): 40.69MM
SALES (corp-wide): 40.69MM **Privately
Held**
Web: www.stradlinglaw.com
SIC: 8111 General practice law office

(P-16787)
STRETTO INC (PA)
410 Exchange Ste 100, Irvine (92602-1331)
PHONE..................949 222-1212
Steve Moore, *CEO*
Brian Soper, *Development*
Avid S Watkins, *Vice Chairman*
Rod Ennico, *CFO*
Ajay A Parikh, *
EMP: 77 **EST:** 2003
SALES (est): 34.25MM
SALES (corp-wide): 34.25MM **Privately
Held**
Web: www.stretto.com
SIC: 8111 Bankruptcy referee

(P-16788)
STUTMAN TRSTER GLATT PROF CORP
Also Called: Stutman Treister Glatt Prof Co
1901 Avenue Of The Stars Ste 200, Los
Angeles (90067-6015)
PHONE..................310 228-5600
Scott H Yun, *CEO*
Robert A Greenfield, *
Charles D Axelrod, *
Theodore B Stolman, *
Isaac M Pachulski, *
EMP: 75 **EST:** 1969
SQ FT: 40,000
SALES (est): 1.63MM **Privately Held**
SIC: 8111 General practice law office

(P-16789)
THARPE & HOWELL (PA)
15250 Ventura Blvd Fl 9, Sherman Oaks
(91403-3221)
PHONE..................818 205-9955
John Maile, *Mng Pt*
Edgar Allen Tharpe Iii, *Pt*
Todd R Howell, *Pt*
Christopher P Ruiz, *Pt*
Christopher S Maile, *Pt*
EMP: 78 **EST:** 1977
SQ FT: 13,500
SALES (est): 5.13MM
SALES (corp-wide): 5.13MM **Privately
Held**
Web: www.tharpe-howell.com
SIC: 8111 General practice law office

(P-16790)
TOBIN LUCKS A PROF CORP (PA)
Also Called: Tobin Lucks
8511 Fallbrook Ave Ste 400, West Hills
(91304-3267)
P.O. Box 4502 (91365)
PHONE..................818 226-3400
Irvin Lucks, *Mng Pt*
Donald Tobin, *
Irvin Lucks, *Pt*
Edwin Lucks, *
EMP: 97 **EST:** 1982
SALES (est): 9.35MM
SALES (corp-wide): 9.35MM **Privately
Held**
Web: www.tobinlucks.com
SIC: 8111 General practice law office

(P-16791)
TROUTMAN PPPER HMLTON SNDERS L
Also Called: Troutman Sanders
100 Spectrum Center Dr Ste 1500, Irvine
(92618-4984)
PHONE..................949 622-2700
David B Allen, *Pt*
EMP: 86
SALES (corp-wide): 106.22MM **Privately
Held**
Web: www.troutman.com
SIC: 8111 General practice attorney, lawyer
PA: Troutman Pepper Hamilton Sanders Llp
600 Peachtree St Ne # 300
404 885-3000

(P-16792)
TROYGOULD PC
1801 Century Park E Ste 1600, Los Angeles
(90067-2367)
PHONE..................310 553-4441
Sanford J Hillsberg, *Prin*
Diane Gordon, *
EMP: 80 **EST:** 1970
SQ FT: 24,000
SALES (est): 9.96MM **Privately Held**
Web: www.troygould.com
SIC: 8111 General practice attorney, lawyer

(P-16793)
WASSERMAN COMDEN & CASSELMAN (PA)
5567 Reseda Blvd Ste 330, Tarzana
(91356-2699)
P.O. Box 7033 (91357-7033)
PHONE..................323 872-0995
Steve Wasserman, *Pt*
David B Casselman, *
Clifford H Pearson, *
Leonard J Comden, *
EMP: 88 **EST:** 1976

SQ FT: 15,000
SALES (est): 4.55MM
SALES (corp-wide): 4.55MM **Privately
Held**
Web: www.wassermanlawgroup.com
SIC: 8111 General practice law office

(P-16794)
WHITE & CASE LLP
555 S Flower St Ste 2700, Los Angeles
(90071-2433)
PHONE..................213 620-7724
EMP: 98
SALES (corp-wide): 88.63MM **Privately
Held**
Web: www.whitecase.com
SIC: 8111 General practice law office
PA: White & Case Llp
1221 Ave Of The Amrcas St
212 819-8200

(P-16795)
WINGERT GRBING BRBKER JSTKIE L
1230 Columbia St Ste 400, San Diego
(92101-8502)
PHONE..................619 232-8151
Stephen Grebing, *Pt*
Charles Grebing, *Pt*
Michael Anello, *Pt*
Alan Brubaker, *Pt*
James Goodwin, *Pt*
EMP: 100 **EST:** 1974
SALES (est): 8.62MM **Privately Held**
Web: www.wingertlaw.com
SIC: 8111 General practice attorney, lawyer

(P-16796)
WITHERS BERGMAN LLP
Also Called: Withers Bergman
12830 El Camino Real Ste 350, San Diego
(92130-2977)
PHONE..................203 974-0412
EMP: 398
Web: www.withersworldwide.com
SIC: 8111 General practice attorney, lawyer
HQ: Withers Bergman Llp
157 Church St Fl 19
New Haven CT 06510
203 789-1320

(P-16797)
WOMBLE BOND DICKINSON (US) LLP
400 Spectrum Center Dr, Irvine
(92618-4934)
PHONE..................310 207-3800
EMP: 240
SALES (corp-wide): 218.48MM **Privately
Held**
Web: www.womblebonddickinson.com
SIC: 8111 Specialized law offices, attorneys
PA: Womble Bond Dickinson (Us) Llp
One W 4th St
336 721-3600

(P-16798)
ZBS LAW LLP
30 Corporate Park Ste 450, Irvine
(92606-3401)
PHONE..................714 848-7920
Les Zieve, *Pt*
Paul Kim, *Prin*
EMP: 85 **EST:** 2020
SALES (est): 2.4MM **Privately Held**
Web: www.zbslaw.com
SIC: 8111 Real estate law

(P-16799)
ZIFFREN B B F G-L S&C FND
1801 Century Park W Fl 7, Los Angeles
(90067-6406)
PHONE..................310 552-3388
Kenneth Ziffren, *Owner*
Kenneth Ziffren, *Prin*
Harry M Brittenham, *
John G Branca, *
Dennis Luderer, *
EMP: 103 **EST:** 1979
SQ FT: 33,000
SALES (est): 17.17MM **Privately Held**
Web: www.ziffrenlaw.com
SIC: 8111 General practice law office

8211 Elementary And Secondary Schools

(P-16800)
ADAT ARI EL
Also Called: Adat ARI El Day School
12020 Burbank Blvd, Valley Village
(91607-2198)
PHONE..................818 766-4992
Joanne Klein, *Ex Dir*
EMP: 150 **EST:** 1938
SALES (est): 10.03MM **Privately Held**
Web: www.aaedayschool.org
SIC: 8211 8661 8351 8299 Private
elementary school; Temples; Montessori
child development center; Religious school

(P-16801)
BALDWIN PARK UNIFIED SCHL DST
Also Called: Baldwin Pk Unified Schl Dst Chl
13529 Francisquito Ave, Baldwin Park
(91706-4834)
PHONE..................626 337-2711
Russhell Martinez, *Dir*
EMP: 71
SALES (corp-wide): 313.47MM **Privately
Held**
Web: www.bpusd.net
SIC: 8211 8351 Public elementary and
secondary schools; Child day care services
PA: Baldwin Park Unified School District
3699 N Holly Ave
626 939-4000

(P-16802)
BEAUMONT UNFIED SCHL DST PUB F
Also Called: Community Day School
126 W Fifth St, Beaumont (92223-2142)
PHONE..................951 845-6580
Douglas Walter, *Prin*
EMP: 367
SALES (corp-wide): 227.6MM **Privately
Held**
Web: www.beaumontusd.us
SIC: 8211 8351 Public elementary and
secondary schools; Group day care center
PA: Beaumont Unified School District
Public Facilities Corporation
350 W Brookside Ave
951 845-1631

(P-16803)
BRAWLEY UNION HIGH SCHOOL DIST (PA)
480 N Imperial Ave, Brawley (92227-1690)
PHONE..................760 312-6068
Hasnik Danielian, *Superintnt*
Jenifer Layaye, *
EMP: 88 **EST:** 1908

SALES (est): 46.69MM
SALES (corp-wide): 46.69MM **Privately Held**
Web: www.brawleyhigh.org
SIC: 8211 8351 High school, junior or senior, nec; Preschool center

(P-16804)
CHRISTIAN ARCADIA SCHOOL
Also Called: Christian Schl Soc of Arcadia
1900 S Santa Anita Ave, Arcadia (91006-4620)
PHONE.................................626 574-8229
Edward Limon, *Prin*
Steve Blankenship, *
Ryan Tungate, *
Greg Saltzer, *
EMP: 70 EST: 1945
SALES (est): 5.21MM **Privately Held**
Web: www.arcadiachristianschool.org
SIC: 8211 8351 Private elementary school; Preschool center

(P-16805)
COMPTON UNIFIED SCHOOL DST
Also Called: Edward G Chester Adult Center
1104 E 148th St, Compton (90220-1339)
PHONE.................................310 898-6470
Saundra T Bishop, *Dir*
EMP: 73
SALES (corp-wide): 530.25MM **Privately Held**
Web: www.compton.k12.ca.us
SIC: 8211 8322 Public elementary and secondary schools; Adult day care center
PA: Compton Unified School District
501 S Santa Fe Ave
310 639-4321

(P-16806)
DUBNOFF CTR FOR CHILD DEV EDCT (PA)
10526 Dubnoff Way, North Hollywood (91606-3921)
PHONE.................................818 755-4950
Sandra Babcock, *Pr*
Sandra Sternig-babcock, *Pr*
EMP: 94 EST: 1948
SQ FT: 13,968
SALES (est): 1.42MM
SALES (corp-wide): 1.42MM **Privately Held**
SIC: 8211 8093 8361 Specialty education; Specialty outpatient clinics, nec; Residential care

(P 16807)
GARDEN GROVE UNIFIED SCHL DST
Also Called: Alamitos Intermediate School
12381 Dale St, Garden Grove (92841-3219)
PHONE.................................714 663-6101
Christina Pflughoft, *Prin*
EMP: 59
SALES (corp-wide): 994.66MM **Privately Held**
Web: www.ggusd.k12.ca.us
SIC: 8211 2731 Public junior high school; Book publishing
PA: Garden Grove Unified School District
10331 Stanford Ave
714 663-6000

(P-16808)
GOLDEN DAY SCHOOLS INC
Also Called: Golden Day Pre-School
4508 Crenshaw Blvd, Los Angeles (90043-1289)

PHONE.................................323 296-6280
Clark E Parker, *Prin*
Clarke Parker, *
EMP: 100 EST: 1966
SQ FT: 35,000
SALES (est): 2.39MM **Privately Held**
SIC: 8211 8351 Private elementary and secondary schools; Preschool center

(P-16809)
GUADALUPE UNION SCHOOL DST (PA)
4465 9th St, Guadalupe (93434-1436)
P.O. Box 788 (93434-0788)
PHONE.................................805 343-2114
Ed Cora, *Superintnt*
Celia Ramos, *
Jeffrey Alvarez, *
EMP: 114 EST: 1890
SALES (est): 34.5MM
SALES (corp-wide): 34.5MM **Privately Held**
Web: www.guadusd.org
SIC: 8211 8741 Public elementary school; Management services

(P-16810)
HEMET UNIFIED SCHOOL DISTRICT
Also Called: Nutrition Services
2075 W Acacia Ave, Hemet (92545-3746)
PHONE.................................951 765-5100
Kathy Anderson, *Brnch Mgr*
EMP: 80
SALES (corp-wide): 551.01MM **Privately Held**
Web: www.hemetusd.org
SIC: 8211 8734 Public elementary and secondary schools; Testing laboratories
PA: Hemet Unified School District
1791 W Acacia Ave
951 765-5100

(P-16811)
HEMET UNIFIED SCHOOL DISTRICT
Also Called: Santa Fe Middle School
985 N Cawston Ave, Hemet (92545-1551)
P.O. Box 881 (92546-0881)
PHONE.................................951 765-6287
Todd Biggert, *Prin*
EMP: 80
SALES (corp-wide): 551.01MM **Privately Held**
Web: ranchoviejo.hemetusd.org
SIC: 8211 8699 Public elementary and secondary schools; Personal interest organization
PA: Hemet Unified School District
1791 W Acacia Ave
951 765 5100

(P-16812)
INCLUSIVE EDCATN CMNTY PRTNR I
Also Called: Iecp
2323 Roosevelt Blvd Apt 3, Oxnard (93035-4480)
PHONE.................................805 985-4808
Rick B Clemens, *Pr*
Rick Clemens, *
EMP: 300 EST: 2002
SALES (est): 3.51MM **Privately Held**
Web: www.iecp.us
SIC: 8211 8351 Specialty education; Preschool center

(P-16813)
LAGUNA BLANCA SCHOOL (PA)
4125 Paloma Dr, Santa Barbara (93110-2146)
PHONE.................................805 687-2461
Sue Smith, *Mgr*
EMP: 94 EST: 1933
SQ FT: 24,857
SALES (est): 20.82MM
SALES (corp-wide): 20.82MM **Privately Held**
Web: www.lagunablanca.org
SIC: 8211 8748 Private elementary and secondary schools; Business consulting, nec

(P-16814)
LONG BEACH UNIFIED SCHOOL DST
Also Called: Muir Elementary School
3038 Delta Ave, Long Beach (90810-2843)
PHONE.................................562 426-5571
Sophia Griffieth, *Prin*
EMP: 97
SALES (corp-wide): 375.96MM **Privately Held**
Web: www.lbschools.net
SIC: 8211 6531 Public junior high school; Rental agent, real estate
PA: Long Beach Unified School District
1515 Hughes Way
562 997-8000

(P-16815)
LOS ANGELES UNIFIED SCHOOL DST
Also Called: West Valley Occupational Ctr
6200 Winnetka Ave, Woodland Hills (91367-3826)
PHONE.................................818 346-3540
Candace Lee, *Prin*
EMP: 126
SALES (corp-wide): 1.07MM **Privately Held**
Web: www.wvoc.net
SIC: 8211 8299 8331 Public elementary and secondary schools; Educational service, nondegree granting: continuing educ.; Job training and related services
PA: Los Angeles Unified School District
333 S Beaudry Ave
213 241-1000

(P-16816)
LYNWOOD UNIFIED SCHOOL DST
Also Called: Lindbergh Child Care Center
12120 Lindbergh Ave, Lynwood (90262-4701)
PHONE.................................310 631-7308
Maria Noriega, *Dir*
EMP: 88
SQ FT: 3,790
SALES (corp-wide): 236.59MM **Privately Held**
Web: www.mylusd.org
SIC: 8211 8351 Public elementary and secondary schools; Child day care services
PA: Lynwood Unified School District
11321 Bullis Rd
310 886-1600

(P-16817)
NATIONAL SCHOOL DISTRICT
Also Called: Maintenace Operations Svc Ctr
1400 N Ave, National City (91950-4825)
PHONE.................................619 336-7770
Jerry O'hara, *Prin*
EMP: 199

SALES (corp-wide): 118.85MM **Privately Held**
Web: www.nsd.us
SIC: 8211 7349 Public elementary and secondary schools; School custodian, contract basis
PA: National School District
1500 N Ave
619 336-7500

(P-16818)
OJAI VALLEY SCHOOL (PA)
Also Called: OVS
723 El Paseo Rd, Ojai (93023-2498)
PHONE.................................805 646-1423
EMP: 83 EST: 1911
SALES (est): 17.54MM
SALES (corp-wide): 17.54MM **Privately Held**
Web: www.ovs.org
SIC: 8211 8351 Private combined elementary and secondary school; Child day care services

(P-16819)
PAGE PRIVATE SCHOOL
419 S Robertson Blvd, Beverly Hills (90211-3690)
PHONE.................................323 272-3429
Janice Kim, *Prin*
EMP: 81
SQ FT: 7,074
SALES (corp-wide): 4.29MM **Privately Held**
Web: www.pageacademyca.com
SIC: 8211 8351 Private elementary school; Group day care center
PA: Page Private School
657 Victoria St
949 515-1700

(P-16820)
POLYTECHNIC SCHOOL
1030 E California Blvd, Pasadena (91106-4099)
PHONE.................................626 792-2147
John W Bracker, *Head of School*
Wendy Munger, *
EMP: 331 EST: 1907
SALES (est): 53.44MM **Privately Held**
Web: www.polytechnic.org
SIC: 8211 8351 Kindergarten; Preschool center

(P-16821)
ROMAN CTHLIC DIOCESE OF ORANGE
Also Called: St Josephs School
801 N Bradford Ave, Placentia (92870-4515)
PHONE.................................714 528-1794
Joann Telles, *Prin*
EMP: 142
SALES (corp-wide): 41.41MM **Privately Held**
Web: www.rcbo.org
SIC: 8211 8661 7389 Catholic junior high school; Catholic Church; Fund raising organizations
PA: The Roman Catholic Diocese Of Orange
13280 Chapman Ave
714 282-3000

(P-16822)
ROMAN CTHLIC DIOCESE OF ORANGE
Also Called: Saint Cecilia School
1311 Sycamore Ave, Tustin (92780-6276)
PHONE.................................714 544-1533

Mary Alvarado, *Prin*
EMP: 117
SALES (corp-wide): 41.41MM **Privately Held**
Web: www.morethanschool.org
SIC: 8211 8351 Catholic combined elementary and secondary school; Preschool center
PA: The Roman Catholic Diocese Of Orange
　　13280 Chapman Ave
　　714 282-3000

(P-16823)
ROMAN CTHLIC DIOCESE OF ORANGE
Also Called: Santa Mrgrita Cthlic High Schl
22062 Antonio Pkwy, Rcho Sta Marg (92688-1993)
PHONE..............................949 766-6000
Mary B Dougherty, *Prin*
EMP: 200
SQ FT: 142,959
SALES (corp-wide): 92.62MM **Privately Held**
Web: www.smhs.org
SIC: 8211 2721 Catholic senior high school; Periodicals
PA: The Roman Catholic Diocese Of Orange
　　13280 Chapman Ave
　　714 282-3000

(P-16824)
SAN DIEGO CMNTY COLLEGE DST
Also Called: Cesar Chavez Center
1960 National Ave, San Diego (92113-2116)
PHONE..............................619 388-4850
Rudy Kastelic, *Brnch Mgr*
EMP: 102
SQ FT: 4,521
SALES (corp-wide): 139.48MM **Privately Held**
Web: www.sdccd.edu
SIC: 8211 8742 Public adult education school ; Management consulting services
PA: San Diego Community College District
　　3375 Camino Del Rio S
　　619 388-6500

(P-16825)
SIERRA CANYON INC
Also Called: Sierra Canyon Day Camp
11052 Independence Ave, Chatsworth (91311-1562)
PHONE..............................818 882-8121
Jim Skruneis, *Pr*
Howard Wang, *
Stephen Horwitz, *
EMP: 89 **EST:** 1971
SQ FT: 35,000
SALES (est): 981.61K **Privately Held**
Web: www.sierracanyondaycamp.com
SIC: 8211 7999 Private elementary and secondary schools; Day camp

(P-16826)
TEMECULA VLY UNIFIED SCHL DST
Also Called: Pauba Valley Elem. School
33125 Regina Dr, Temecula (92592-1473)
PHONE..............................951 302-5140
Kelli Sutherlands, *Prin*
EMP: 70
SALES (corp-wide): 481.5MM **Privately Held**
Web: www.tvusd.k12.ca.us

SIC: 8211 8641 Public elementary school; Parent-teachers' association
PA: Temecula Valley Unified School District School Facilities Corporation
　　31350 Rancho Vista Rd
　　951 676-2661

(P-16827)
TUSTIN UNIFIED SCHOOL DISTRICT
Also Called: Lestonnac Preschool
16791 E Main St, Tustin (92780-4034)
PHONE..............................714 542-4271
Sharon Lamtrecht, *Prin*
EMP: 117
SALES (corp-wide): 436.42MM **Privately Held**
Web: www.sjdlschool.com
SIC: 8211 8351 Public elementary and secondary schools; Preschool center
PA: Tustin Unified School District
　　300 S C St
　　714 730-7515

(P-16828)
VISTA DEL MAR CHILD FMLY SVCS (PA)
3200 Motor Ave, Los Angeles (90034-3710)
PHONE..............................310 836-1223
Roosevelena Wilson, *CEO*
EMP: 231 **EST:** 1908
SQ FT: 100,000
SALES (est): 40.28MM
SALES (corp-wide): 40.28MM **Privately Held**
Web: www.vistadelmar.org
SIC: 8211 8361 Elementary and secondary schools; Mentally handicapped home

(P-16829)
WEST ANGELES CH GOD IN CHRST
Also Called: West Angeles Christian Academy
3010 Crenshaw Blvd, Los Angeles (90016-4263)
PHONE..............................323 731-2567
Deloris A Dumbar, *Prin*
EMP: 152
SALES (corp-wide): 21.89MM **Privately Held**
Web: www.westa.org
SIC: 8211 6512 Private elementary school; Theater building, ownership and operation
PA: West Angeles Church Of God In Christ
　　3045 Crenshaw Blvd
　　323 733-8300

(P-16830)
WHITTIER UNION HIGH SCHL DIST
Also Called: Capc Adult Services
7200 Greenleaf Ave Ste 170, Whittier (90602-1391)
PHONE..............................562 693-8826
Dan Hulbert, *Dir*
EMP: 106
SALES (corp-wide): 206.51MM **Privately Held**
Web: www.wuhsd.org
SIC: 8211 8322 Public elementary and secondary schools; Social services for the handicapped
PA: Whittier Union High School Dist
　　9401 Painter Ave
　　562 698-8121

8221 Colleges And Universities

(P-16831)
ASSOCIATED STUDENTS UCLA
Also Called: Ucla Dept of Design Media
11000 Kinross Ave Ave Ste 245, Los Angeles (90095-2000)
P.O. Box 951615 (90095-1615)
PHONE..............................310 206-8282
Diane Mills, *Prin*
EMP: 208
SALES (corp-wide): 55.96MM **Privately Held**
Web: asucla.ucla.edu
SIC: 8221 7336 University; Graphic arts and related design
PA: Associated Students U.C.L.A.
　　308 Westwood Plz
　　310 794-8836

(P-16832)
CHAPMAN UNIVERSITY
Also Called: Chapman Academic Center
39115 Trade Center Dr # 203, Palmdale (93551-3649)
PHONE..............................661 267-2001
Jerry Witte, *Mgr*
EMP: 106
SALES (corp-wide): 518.62MM **Privately Held**
Web: www.chapman.edu
SIC: 8221 8742 College, except junior; Training and development consultant
PA: Chapman University
　　One University Dr
　　714 997-6815

(P-16833)
MARSHALL B KETCHUM UNIVERSITY (PA)
Also Called: Eye Care Center, The
2575 Yorba Linda Blvd, Fullerton (92831-1699)
PHONE..............................714 463-7567
EMP: 160 **EST:** 1911
SALES (est): 41.85MM
SALES (corp-wide): 41.85MM **Privately Held**
Web: www.ketchum.edu
SIC: 8221 8042 Professional schools; Offices and clinics of optometrists

(P-16834)
SAN DIEGO STATE UNIVERSITY
Also Called: K P B S
5200 Campanile Dr, San Diego (92182-1901)
PHONE..............................619 594-1515
Tom Karlo, *Mgr*
EMP: 100
SALES (corp-wide): 534.4MM **Privately Held**
Web: www.kpbs.org
SIC: 8221 9411 4832 University; Administration of educational programs, State government; Educational
HQ: San Diego State University
　　5500 Campanile Dr
　　San Diego CA 92182

(P-16835)
UNIVERSITY CAL LOS ANGELES
Tanms Engineering Research Ctr
420 Westwood Plz Rm 7702, Los Angeles (90095-8357)
PHONE..............................310 825-7852
EMP: 200
SALES (corp-wide): 534.4MM **Privately Held**

Web: www.ucla.edu
SIC: 8221 8733 9411 University; Noncommercial research organizations; Administration of educational programs
HQ: University Of California, Los Angeles
　　405 Hilgard Ave
　　Los Angeles CA 90095

(P-16836)
UNIVERSITY CALIFORNIA IRVINE
Also Called: Social Sciences
3151 Social Science Plz, Irvine (92697-5100)
PHONE..............................949 824-7725
Barbara Venook, *Prin*
EMP: 205
SALES (corp-wide): 534.4MM **Privately Held**
Web: www.uci.edu
SIC: 8221 9411 8062 University; Administration of educational programs; General medical and surgical hospitals
HQ: University Of California, Irvine
　　510 Aldrich Hall
　　Irvine CA 92697
　　949 824-5011

(P-16837)
UNIVERSITY CALIFORNIA IRVINE
Also Called: UCI Halth Neuropsychiatric Ctr
3800 W Chapman Ave Ste 7200, Orange (92868-1623)
PHONE..............................714 456-2332
EMP: 92
SALES (corp-wide): 534.4MM **Privately Held**
SIC: 8221 8071 Colleges and universities; Neurological laboratory
HQ: University Of California, Irvine
　　510 Aldrich Hall
　　Irvine CA 92697
　　949 824-5011

(P-16838)
VANGUARD UNIV SOUTHERN CAL
55 Fair Dr, Costa Mesa (92626-6597)
PHONE..............................714 668-6163
Michael Beals, *CEO*
EMP: 200 **EST:** 1921
SQ FT: 420,000
SALES (est): 94.81MM **Privately Held**
Web: www.vanguard.edu
SIC: 8221 8699 College, except junior; Charitable organization

---

8222 Junior Colleges

(P-16839)
SAN DIEGO CMNTY COLLEGE DST
Also Called: San Diego City College
1313 Park Blvd, San Diego (92101-4712)
PHONE..............................619 388-3453
Terrence J Burgess, *Prin*
EMP: 148
SALES (corp-wide): 139.48MM **Privately Held**
Web: www.sdccd.edu
SIC: 8222 8641 Community college; Civic and social associations
PA: San Diego Community College District
　　3375 Camino Del Rio S
　　619 388-6500

(P-16840)

SAN DIEGO CMNTY COLLEGE DST

Also Called: San Diego Mesa College
7250 Mesa College Dr, San Diego
(92111-4999)
PHONE..............................619 388-2600
Pamela Luster, *Pr*
EMP: 1500
SALES (corp-wide): 139.48MM **Privately Held**
Web: www.sdccd.edu
SIC: 8222 8412 Community college; Museums and art galleries
PA: San Diego Community College District
3375 Camino Del Rio S
619 388-6500

(P-16841)

SANTA BRBARA CMNTY COLLEGE DST

Also Called: Academy of Cosmetology
525 Anacapa St, Santa Barbara
(93101-1603)
PHONE..............................805 683-4191
Ben Partee, *Mgr*
EMP: 497
SALES (corp-wide): 82.58MM **Privately Held**
Web: www.sbcc.edu
SIC: 8222 7231 Community college; Cosmetology school
PA: Santa Barbara Community College District
721 Cliff Dr
805 965-0581

8231 Libraries

(P-16842)

HUNTINGTON LIB ART MSUMS BTNCA

Also Called: HUNTINGTON, THE
1151 Oxford Rd, San Marino (91108-1218)
PHONE..............................626 405-2100
Robert F Erburu, *Ch Bd*
Robert Skotheim, *
Steve Koblik, *
Laurie Sowd, *
▲ **EMP:** 380 **EST:** 1919
SALES (est): 167.96MM **Privately Held**
Web: www.huntington.org
SIC: 8231 8412 8422 Public library; Art gallery, noncommercial; Botanical garden

8243 Data Processing Schools

(P-16843)

IT DIVISION INC

Also Called: Apeiro Technologies
9170 Irvine Center Dr Ste 200, Irvine
(92618-4614)
PHONE..............................678 648-2709
Lavanya Nilagiri, *CEO*
Neeta Prasad, *
Shruti Nilagiri, *
Vivek Jaiswal, *
EMP: 103 **EST:** 2006
SALES (est): 1.52MM **Privately Held**
Web: www.apeiro.us
SIC: 8243 7371 7373 Software training, computer; Computer software systems analysis and design, custom; Systems software development services

(P-16844)

NEW HRZNS SRVING INDVDALS WITH (PA)

Also Called: NEW HORIZONS CENTER & WORKSHOP
15725 Parthenia St, North Hills
(91343-4913)
PHONE..............................818 894-9301
Cynthia Kawa, *CEO*
▲ **EMP:** 100 **EST:** 1954
SQ FT: 60,000
SALES (est): 16.73MM
SALES (corp-wide): 16.73MM **Privately Held**
Web: www.newhorizons-sfv.org
SIC: 8243 2052 Software training, computer; Cookies

8249 Vocational Schools, Nec

(P-16845)

GEMOLOGICAL INSTITUTE AMER INC (PA)

Also Called: Gemological Institute America
5345 Armada Dr, Carlsbad (92008-4602)
PHONE..............................760 603-4000
Susan M Jacques, *Pr*
Tom Moses, *LABORATORY Research*
David Tearle, *
EMP: 1000 **EST:** 1931
SQ FT: 300,000
SALES (est): 291.06MM
SALES (corp-wide): 291.06MM **Privately Held**
Web: www.gia.edu
SIC: 8249 8733 Trade school; Noncommercial research organizations

(P-16846)

REAL ESTATE TRAINERS INC

212 Towne Centre Pl Ste 100, Anaheim
(92806)
PHONE..............................800 282-2352
Jerry Mcharg, *Pr*
EMP: 35 **EST:** 1972
SQ FT: 17,000
SALES (est): 245.27K
SALES (corp-wide): 2.16MM **Privately Held**
Web: www.retrainersca.com
SIC: 8249 2721 Real estate and insurance school; Periodicals
PA: Universal Training Corporation
2121 S Twne Cntre Pl Ste
714 972-2211

(P-16847)

THE CODING SOURCE LLC

Also Called: Altegra Health
3415 S Sepulveda Blvd Ste 900, Los
Angeles (90034-6981)
PHONE..............................866 235-7553
EMP: 250
Web: www.thecodingsource.com
SIC: 8249 7374 8331 7361 Medical training services; Data entry service; Job training and related services; Employment agencies

(P-16848)

UNIVERSAL TECHNICAL INST INC

Also Called: Uti
9494 Haven Ave, Rancho Cucamonga
(91730-5843)
PHONE..............................909 484-1929
EMP: 206
SALES (corp-wide): 732.69MM **Publicly Held**
Web: www.uti.edu

SIC: 8249 7389 Trade school; Personal service agents, brokers, and bureaus
PA: Universal Technical Institute, Inc.
4225 E Wndrose Dr Ste 200
623 445-9500

8299 Schools And Educational Services

(P-16849)

AMERICAN ASSN CRTCAL CARE NRSE

Also Called: A A C N
27071 Aliso Creek Rd, Aliso Viejo
(92656-3399)
PHONE..............................949 362-2000
Dana Woods, *CEO*
Teri Lynn Kiss, *President Elect*
Michael Willett, *
Mary Zellinger, *
Linda Bay, *
EMP: 128 **EST:** 1969
SALES (est): 35.75MM **Privately Held**
Web: www.aacn.org
SIC: 8299 8331 8621 Educational services; Job training and related services; Professional organizations

(P-16850)

AMERICAN JUSTICE SOLUTIONS INC

Also Called: Correctivesolutions
25910 Acero Ste 100, Mission Viejo
(92691-2777)
P.O. Box 3026 (92690-1026)
PHONE..............................949 369-6210
Mats Jonsson, *CEO*
Karl Jonsson, *
Karen Boyd, *
Kristy Silguero, *
EMP: 70 **EST:** 2014
SQ FT: 20,000
SALES (est): 2.41MM **Privately Held**
Web: www.correctivesolutions.org
SIC: 8299 8748 Educational service, nondegree granting: continuing educ.; Educational consultant

(P-16851)

BOYS GRLS CLUBS GRDN GROVE INC (PA)

10540 Chapman Ave, Garden Grove
(92840-3101)
PHONE..............................714 530-0430
Mark Surmanian, *CEO*
EMP: 225 **EST:** 1952
SQ FT: 12,000
SALES (est): 11.91MM
SALES (corp-wide): 11.91MM **Privately Held**
Web: www.bgcgg.org
SIC: 8299 8699 Educational services; Charitable organization

(P-16852)

CHRISTAN COMMUNITY THEATRE

Also Called: CHRISTIAN YOUTH THEATER
1545 Pioneer Way, El Cajon (92020-1637)
PHONE..............................619 588-0206
Sheryl Russell, *Pr*
Paul Russell, *
EMP: 78 **EST:** 1980
SQ FT: 11,000
SALES (est): 296.61K **Privately Held**
SIC: 8299 7922 Dramatic school; Legitimate live theater producers

(P-16853)

CROSSRADS CHRSTN SCHOLS CORONA

2380 Fullerton Ave, Corona (92881-3111)
PHONE..............................951 278-3199
Dough Husen, *Superintnt*
EMP: 145 **EST:** 2001
SQ FT: 1,088
SALES (est): 1.21MM **Privately Held**
Web: www.crossroadsschool.org
SIC: 8299 8211 8351 8699 Religious school; High school, junior or senior, nec; Preschool center; Charitable organization

(P-16854)

GREENWOOD HALL INC

6230 Wilshire Blvd Ste 136, Los Angeles
(90048-5126)
PHONE..............................310 905-8300
John Hall, *Ch Bd*
Bill Bradfield, *
EMP: 111 **EST:** 1997
SALES (est): 5.39MM **Privately Held**
Web: www.answernet.com
SIC: 8299 8741 8742 7374 Educational services; Management services; Management consulting services; Data processing service

(P-16855)

LEARNING OVATIONS INC

16 Coltrane Ct, Irvine (92617-4131)
PHONE..............................734 904-1459
Jay Connor, *CEO*
Elliot Amiel, *
Alia Gates, *
Nick Voegeli, *
EMP: 28 **EST:** 2013
SALES (est): 6.68MM
SALES (corp-wide): 1.59B **Publicly Held**
Web: www.learningovations.com
SIC: 8299 7372 Educational services; Educational computer software
PA: Scholastic Corporation
557 Broadway
212 343-6100

(P-16856)

MUSIC ACADEMY OF WEST

1070 Fairway Rd, Santa Barbara
(93108-2899)
PHONE..............................805 969-4726
Nancybell Coe, *Pr*
Benjamin J Cohen, *
John Burgee, *
Barbara Robertson, *
James Davidson, *
EMP: 76 **EST:** 1947
SQ FT: 8,000
SALES (est): 12.86MM **Privately Held**
Web: www.musicacademy.org
SIC: 8299 7929 Music school; Entertainers and entertainment groups

(P-16857)

NAPCA FOUNDATION

2600 W Olive Ave Ste 500, Burbank
(91505-4572)
PHONE..............................800 799-4640
Aaron Smith, *Ex Dir*
EMP: 563 **EST:** 2012
SALES (est): 10.94MM **Privately Held**
Web: www.napcafoundation.org
SIC: 8299 8732 7999 8742 Educational services; Educational research; Instruction schools, camps, and services; School, college, university consultant

PRODUCTS & SVCS

(P-16858)
SOUTHERN CAL PRMNNTE MED GROUP
1465 E 103rd St, Los Angeles (90002-3306)
PHONE....................323 564-7911
Joanne Robinson, *Dir*
EMP: 113
SALES (corp-wide): 70.8B **Privately Held**
Web: www.permanente.org
SIC: 8299 6324 8351 Educational services; Group hospitalization plans; Preschool center
HQ: Southern California Permanente Medical Group
393 Walnut Dr
Pasadena CA 91107
626 405-5704

(P-16859)
VISTA HILL FOUNDATION
Also Called: Stein Sam & Rose Education Ctr
6145 Decena Dr, San Diego (92120-3511)
PHONE....................619 281-5511
Joan Richard, *Prin*
EMP: 90
SALES (corp-wide): 38.47MM **Privately Held**
Web: www.vistahill.org
SIC: 8299 8351 8093 Educational services; Child day care services; Mental health clinic, outpatient
PA: Vista Hill Foundation
8910 Clairemont Mesa Blvd
585 514-5100

8322 Individual And Family Services

(P-16860)
ABRAZAR INC
Also Called: Abrazar Elderly Assistance
7101 Wyoming St, Westminster (92683-3811)
PHONE....................714 893-3581
Mario Ortega, *CEO*
Gloria Reyes, *
Mario Ortega, *COO*
EMP: 180 **EST:** 1975
SALES (est): 9.59MM **Privately Held**
Web: www.abrazarinc.com
SIC: 8322 Social service center

(P-16861)
ADVANCMENT THRUGH OPRTNTY KNWL
Also Called: CHILDREN, YOUTH & FAMILY COLLA
1200 W 37th Pl, Los Angeles (90007-4220)
PHONE....................323 730-9400
Lydia Templeton, *CEO*
EMP: 70 **EST:** 1993
SALES (est): 2.11MM **Privately Held**
Web: www.cyfcla.org
SIC: 8322 Social service center

(P-16862)
AIDS PROJECT LOS ANGELES (PA)
Also Called: Aids Project La
611 S Kingsley Dr, Los Angeles (90005-2319)
PHONE....................213 201-1600
Craig E Thompson, *CEO*
Robyn Goldman, *
EMP: 90 **EST:** 1983
SALES (est): 55.51MM
SALES (corp-wide): 55.51MM **Privately Held**

Web: www.aplahealth.org
SIC: 8322 Social service center

(P-16863)
ALPHA PROJECT FOR HOMELESS
Also Called: Casa Raphael
993 Postal Way, Vista (92083-6945)
PHONE....................760 630-9922
Margaret Larson, *Mgr*
EMP: 156
Web: www.alphaproject.org
SIC: 8322 8361 Community center; Halfway group home, persons with social or personal problems
PA: Alpha Project For The Homeless
3737 5th Ave Ste 203

(P-16864)
AMERICAN NATIONAL RED CROSS
Also Called: American Nat Red Crss-Blood Sv
100 Red Cross Cir, Pomona (91765)
PHONE....................909 859-7006
Joan Manning, *Genl Mgr*
EMP: 129
SALES (corp-wide): 3.18B **Privately Held**
Web: www.redcross.org
SIC: 8322 Social service center
PA: The American National Red Cross
431 18th St
202 737-8300

(P-16865)
AMERICAN NATIONAL RED CROSS
Also Called: Red Cross
1450 S Central Ave, Los Angeles (90021-2627)
PHONE....................310 445-9900
Enrique Rivera, *Off Mgr*
EMP: 86
SALES (corp-wide): 3.18B **Privately Held**
Web: www.redcross.org
SIC: 8322 Social service center
PA: The American National Red Cross
431 18th St
202 737-8300

(P-16866)
AMERICAN NATIONAL RED CROSS
Also Called: American Nat Red Cross - Blood
3150 E 29th St, Long Beach (90806-2319)
PHONE....................562 595-6341
Shonte Jessick, *Mgr*
EMP: 86
SQ FT: 15,336
SALES (corp-wide): 3.18B **Privately Held**
Web: www.redcross.org
SIC: 8322 Social service center
PA: The American National Red Cross
431 18th St
202 737-8300

(P-16867)
AMERICAN RED CROSS LOS ANGLES (PA)
Also Called: American Red Cross
1320 Newton St, Los Angeles (90021-2724)
PHONE....................310 445-9900
TOLL FREE: 800
Roger Dixon, *CEO*
Kirk Richard Hyde, *
William Niese, *
Thomas E Stephenson, *
Michelle Mccarthy, *Chief Financial*
EMP: 150 **EST:** 1916

SALES (est): 2.07MM
SALES (corp-wide): 2.07MM **Privately Held**
Web: www.redcross.org
SIC: 8322 Social service center

(P-16868)
AMERICAN RED CROSS SAN DG-MPRI (PA)
Also Called: American Red Cross
3950 Calle Fortunada, San Diego (92123-1827)
PHONE....................858 309-1200
Joe Craver, *CEO*
EMP: 90 **EST:** 1898
SALES (est): 1.23MM
SALES (corp-wide): 1.23MM **Privately Held**
Web: www.redcross.org
SIC: 8322 Social service center

(P-16869)
AMIGO BABY INC
Also Called: Healthcare
1901 N Rice Ave Ste 325, Oxnard (93030-7912)
P.O. Box 6757 (91359)
PHONE....................805 901-1237
Pablo Velez, *CEO*
EMP: 80 **EST:** 2004
SALES (est): 2.48MM **Privately Held**
Web: www.amigobaby.com
SIC: 8322 8099 Social service center; Health and allied services, nec

(P-16870)
ASSOCIATED STUDENTS INC (PA)
Also Called: ASSICIATED STUDENTS
University Union Bldg 65, San Luis Obispo (93407)
PHONE....................805 756-1281
Richard Johnson, *Ex Dir*
Dwayne Brummett, *
EMP: 70 **EST:** 1964
SQ FT: 110,000
SALES (est): 3.15MM
SALES (corp-wide): 3.15MM **Privately Held**
Web: www.calpoly.edu
SIC: 8322 8221 Multi-service center; Colleges and universities

(P-16871)
AUTISM OTRACH SOUTHERN CAL LLC
3110 Camino Del Rio S Ste 307, San Diego (92108-3832)
PHONE....................619 795-9925
Abigail R Bun, *Mgr*
EMP: 75 **EST:** 2013
SALES (est): 894.66K **Privately Held**
Web: www.mebefamily.com
SIC: 8322 Individual and family services

(P-16872)
AUTISM SPCTRUM INTRVNTIONS LLC
713 W Commonwealth Ave Ste A, Fullerton (92832-1612)
PHONE....................562 972-4846
Timothy M Prior, *Prin*
EMP: 130 **EST:** 2008
SALES (est): 1.92MM **Privately Held**
Web: www.asiautism.org
SIC: 8322 Individual and family services

(P-16873)
AVIVA FAMILY & CHILDRENS SVCS (PA)
1701 Camino Palmero St, Los Angeles (90046-2902)
PHONE....................323 876-0550
Ira J Kruskol, *Dir*
EMP: 99 **EST:** 1976
SALES (est): 4.52MM
SALES (corp-wide): 4.52MM **Privately Held**
Web: www.aviva.org
SIC: 8322 Social service center

(P-16874)
AYA LIVING INC
1450 Frazee Rd, San Diego (92108-4337)
PHONE....................619 446-6469
Matthew Williams, *Ex Dir*
EMP: 120 **EST:** 2010
SALES (est): 4MM **Privately Held**
Web: www.ayaliving.com
SIC: 8322 Individual and family services

(P-16875)
BEHAVIORAL LEARNING CENTER INC
13400 Riverside Dr Ste 209, Sherman Oaks (91423-2545)
PHONE....................818 308-6226
Jody Stiegemeyer, *CEO*
EMP: 220
SALES (corp-wide): 165.05MM **Privately Held**
Web: www.blcca.com
SIC: 8322 Child related social services
HQ: Behavioral Learning Center, Inc.
184 High St
Boston MA 02110
661 254-7086

(P-16876)
BLC RESIDENTIAL CARE INC
1455 W 112th St, Los Angeles (90047-4926)
PHONE....................310 722-7541
Brenda Chandler, *Pr*
EMP: 80 **EST:** 2004
SALES (est): 1.58MM **Privately Held**
SIC: 8322 Adult day care center

(P-16877)
BRAILLE INSTITUTE AMERICA INC (PA)
Also Called: Braille Institute
741 N Vermont Ave, Los Angeles (90029-3594)
PHONE....................323 663-1111
Lester M Sussman, *Ch Bd*
Les Stocker, *
Peter Mindnich, *
Rezaur Rahman, *
EMP: 208 **EST:** 1919
SQ FT: 167,079
SALES (est): 29.58MM
SALES (corp-wide): 29.58MM **Privately Held**
Web: www.brailleinstitute.org
SIC: 8322 8231 2731 2759 Individual and family services; Specialized libraries; Textbooks: publishing and printing; Commercial printing, nec

(P-16878)
CAROLYN E WYLIE CTR FOR CHLDRE
4164 Brockton Ave, Riverside (92501-3400)
PHONE....................951 683-5193

▲ = Import ▼ = Export
◆ = Import/Export

Mickey Rubinson, *CEO*
Melody Amaral, *
EMP: 100 **EST:** 1976
SQ FT: 3,000
SALES (est): 3.04MM **Privately Held**
Web: www.wyliecenter.org
SIC: 8322 8093 8049 Individual and family services; Mental health clinic, outpatient; Psychotherapist, except M.D.

(P-16879)

CASA CLINA HOSP CTRS FOR HLTHC

Also Called: Rancho Pino Verdi
11981 Midway Ave, Lucerne Valley (92356-7517)
P.O. Box 1760 (92356-1760)
PHONE..............................760 248-6245
Michael Stayer, *Mgr*
EMP: 149
SQ FT: 2,934
SALES (corp-wide): 136.57MM **Privately Held**
Web: www.casacolina.org
SIC: 8322 Rehabilitation services
HQ: Casa Colina Hospital And Centers For Healthcare
255 E Bonita Ave
Pomona CA 91767
909 596-7733

(P-16880)

CASA COLINA INC (PA)

Also Called: Casa Clina Hosp Ctrs For Hlthc
255 E Bonita Ave, Pomona (91767-1933)
PHONE..............................909 596-7733
EMP: 800 **EST:** 1981
SALES (est): 136.57MM
SALES (corp-wide): 136.57MM **Privately Held**
Web: www.casacolina.org
SIC: 8322 8011 Rehabilitation services; Ambulatory surgical center

(P-16881)

CASA PCFICA CTRS FOR CHLDREN F (PA)

Also Called: CASA PACIFICA
1722 S Lewis Rd, Camarillo (93012-8520)
PHONE..............................805 482-3260
Shawna Morris, *CEO*
Felice Ginsberg, *
Michael Redard, *
EMP: 175 **EST:** 1988
SQ FT: 63,000
SALES (est): 37.28MM **Privately Held**
Web: www.casapacifica.org
SIC: 8322 8361 8211 Child related social services; Residential care for children; Specialty education

(P-16882)

CATHOLIC CHRTIES SNTA CLARA CN

Also Called: Catholic Charities
303 N Ventura Ave Ste A, Ventura (93001-1961)
PHONE..............................805 643-4694
Robert Batdazian, *Dir*
EMP: 88
SALES (corp-wide): 56.18MM **Privately Held**
Web: www.ccscc.org
SIC: 8322 Social service center
PA: Catholic Charities Of Santa Clara County
2625 Zanker Rd Ste 200
408 468-0100

(P-16883)

CENTRO DE SALUD DE LA COMUNI

1420 E Plaza Blvd Ste E4, National City (91950-3636)
PHONE..............................619 477-0165
Marie Mulhall, *Prin*
EMP: 365
SALES (corp-wide): 99.89MM **Privately Held**
Web: www.syhealth.org
SIC: 8322 Individual and family services
PA: Centro De Salud De La Comunidad De San Ysidro, Inc.
1601 Precision Park Ln
619 428-4463

(P-16884)

CHILD & FAMILY CENTER

21545 Centre Pointe Pkwy, Santa Clarita (91350-2947)
PHONE..............................661 259-9439
Joan Aschoff, *CEO*
Victor Chavira, *
Bert Paras, *
Evelyn Vega-aguilar, *Dir*
EMP: 120 **EST:** 1976
SQ FT: 26,581
SALES (est): 14.17MM **Privately Held**
Web: www.childfamilycenter.org
SIC: 8322 8099 8093 8049 Family counseling services; Childbirth preparation clinic; Mental health clinic, outpatient; Clinical psychologist

(P-16885)

CHILD CARE RESOURCE CENTER INC (PA)

20001 Prairie St, Chatsworth (91311-6508)
PHONE..............................818 717-1000
Michael Olenick, *CEO*
Michael Olenick, *Pr*
Lorraine Schrag, *
Casey Quinn, *
Ellen Cervantes, *
EMP: 130 **EST:** 1976
SALES (est): 404.36MM
SALES (corp-wide): 404.36MM **Privately Held**
Web: www.ccrcca.org
SIC: 8322 Child related social services

(P-16886)

CHILD CARE RESOURCE CENTER INC

250 Grand Cypress Ave Ste 601, Palmdale (93551-3675)
PHONE..............................661 723-3246
Ann Bubont, *Prin*
EMP: 230
SALES (corp-wide): 404.36MM **Privately Held**
Web: www.ccrcca.org
SIC: 8322 Child related social services
PA: Child Care Resource Center, Inc.
20001 Prairie St
818 717-1000

(P-16887)

CHILD DEV RSRCES OF VNTURA CNT (PA)

Also Called: C D R
221 Ventura Blvd, Oxnard (93036-0277)
PHONE..............................805 485-7878
Jack Hinojosa, *CEO*
EMP: 200 **EST:** 1974
SQ FT: 67,007
SALES (est): 62.02MM
SALES (corp-wide): 62.02MM **Privately Held**

Web: www.cdrv.org
SIC: 8322 8699 Child guidance agency; Charitable organization

(P-16888)

CHILD DEVELOPMENT INSTITUTE

Also Called: CDI
18050 Vanowen St, Reseda (91335-5638)
PHONE..............................818 888-4559
Joan Samaltese, *Ex Dir*
Dana Kalek, *
Steve Lenhert, *
Tessa Graham, *
EMP: 93 **EST:** 1995
SALES (est): 5.36MM **Privately Held**
Web: www.cdikids.org
SIC: 8322 Child related social services

(P-16889)

CHILDNET YOUTH & FMLY SVCS INC (PA)

Also Called: CHILDNET
3545 Long Beach Blvd Ste 200, Long Beach (90807-3900)
P.O. Box 4550 (90804)
PHONE..............................562 498-5500
Kathy L Hughes, *CEO*
EMP: 177 **EST:** 1970
SALES (est): 35.76MM
SALES (corp-wide): 35.76MM **Privately Held**
Web: www.childnet.net
SIC: 8322 Child related social services

(P-16890)

CHILDRENS BUREAU SOUTHERN CAL (PA)

1910 Magnolia Ave, Los Angeles (90007-1220)
PHONE..............................213 342-0100
Alex Morales, *Pr*
Sona Chandwani, *
EMP: 107 **EST:** 1904
SQ FT: 43,000
SALES (est): 51.84MM
SALES (corp-wide): 51.84MM **Privately Held**
Web: www.all4kids.org
SIC: 8322 Child related social services

(P-16891)

CHILDRENS INST LOS ANGELES

679 S New Hampshire Ave, Los Angeles (90005-1355)
PHONE..............................213 383-2765
Mary Emmons, *Brnch Mgr*
EMP: 850
SALES (corp-wide): 392.05K **Privately Held**
Web: www.childrensinstitute.org
SIC: 8322 Social service center
PA: Children's Institute Of Los Angeles
2121 W Temple St
213 385-5100

(P-16892)

CHILDRENS INSTITUTE INC (PA)

2121 W Temple St, Los Angeles (90026-4915)
PHONE..............................213 385-5100
Martine Singer, *CEO*
Eugene Straub, *CFOO*
Todd Sosna, *CPO*
James Colon, *
EMP: 190 **EST:** 1906
SQ FT: 18,000
SALES (est): 93.49MM
SALES (corp-wide): 93.49MM **Privately Held**

Web: www.childrensinstitute.org
SIC: 8322 8699 Child related social services; Charitable organization

(P-16893)

CITY OF BAKERSFIELD

Rabobank Arena Thter Cnvntion
1001 Truxtun Ave, Bakersfield (93301-4714)
PHONE..............................661 852-7300
John Dorman, *Genl Mgr*
EMP: 113
SALES (corp-wide): 519.74MM **Privately Held**
Web: www.mechanicsbankarena.com
SIC: 8322 9111 6512 Community center; Mayors' office; Nonresidential building operators
PA: City Of Bakersfield
1600 Truxtun Ave 2nd Fl
661 326-3000

(P-16894)

COACHELLA VLY RESCUE MISSION

Also Called: CVRM
82873 Via Venecia, Indio (92201-6971)
P.O. Box 10660 (92202-2564)
PHONE..............................760 347-3512
Floyd Rhoades, *Ch Bd*
Jim Parrish, *
Darla Burkett, *
Joseph Hayes, *Board Treasurer*
Erik Jensen, *Corporate Secretary*
EMP: 72 **EST:** 1971
SQ FT: 43,000
SALES (est): 13.68MM **Privately Held**
Web: www.cvrm.org
SIC: 8322 8661 Social service center; Nonchurch religious organizations

(P-16895)

COALITION FOR FAMILY HARMONY

1000 Town Center Dr, Oxnard (93036-1100)
PHONE..............................805 983-6014
Cherie Douval, *Pr*
EMP: 72 **EST:** 1978
SALES (est): 2.83MM **Privately Held**
Web: www.thecoalition.org
SIC: 8322 Social service center

(P-16896)

COMMUNITY ACTION PARTNERSHIP

3970 Short St, San Luic Obispo (93401-7567)
PHONE..............................805 541-4122
EMP: 97
SALES (corp-wide): 104.15MM **Privately Held**
Web: www.capslo.org
SIC: 8322 Individual and family services
PA: Community Action Partnership Of San Luis Obispo County, Inc.
1030 Southwood Dr
805 544-4355

(P-16897)

COMMUNITY ACTION PRTNR ORNGE C

Also Called: OC FOOD BANK
11870 Monarch St, Garden Grove (92841-2113)
PHONE..............................714 897-6670
Gregory C Scott, *CEO*
Caroline Coleman, *
EMP: 105 **EST:** 1965

PRODUCTS & SVCS

SQ FT: 86,300
SALES (est): 47.32MM **Privately Held**
Web: www.capoc.org
SIC: 8322 Social service center

(P-16898)
COMMUNITY FOOD CONNECTION
14047 Twin Peaks Rd, Poway
(92064-3039)
PHONE.............................858 751-4613
William Rearick, *Prin*
Kim Rearick, *
EMP: 80 EST: 2014
SALES (est): 198.27K **Privately Held**
Web:
www.thecommunityfoodconnection.com
SIC: 8322 Social service center

(P-16899)
COMMUNITY INTERFACE SERVICES
981 Vale Terrace Dr, Vista (92084-5213)
PHONE.............................760 729-3866
Rose Mueller Hanson, *Pr*
EMP: 100 EST: 1983
SALES (est): 13.68MM **Privately Held**
Web:
www.communityinterfaceservices.org
SIC: 8322 Social service center

(P-16900)
COMMUNITY SUPPORT OPTIONS INC
1401 Poso Dr, Wasco (93280-2584)
P.O. Box 8018 (93280-8108)
PHONE.............................661 758-5331
John Stockton, *CEO*
Anna Poggi, *
Jose Hernandez, *
Ben Goosen, *
Violet Ratzlass, *
EMP: 102 EST: 1974
SQ FT: 9,000
SALES (est): 2.19MM **Privately Held**
Web: www.cso-svd.org
SIC: 8322 Association for the handicapped

(P-16901)
CORE CMNTY ORGNZED RLIEF EFFOR
Also Called: CORE
910 N Hill St, Los Angeles (90012-1715)
PHONE.............................323 934-4400
Sean Penn, *Ch Bd*
Ann Young Lee, *
EMP: 400 EST: 2010
SALES (est): 31.66MM **Privately Held**
Web: www.coreresponse.org
SIC: 8322 Temporary relief service

(P-16902)
COUNCIL ON AGING - STHERN CAL
2 Executive Cir Ste 175, Irvine
(92614-6773)
PHONE.............................714 479-0107
Lisa Wright Jenkins, *CEO*
EMP: 83 EST: 1973
SALES (est): 7.48MM **Privately Held**
Web: www.coasc.org
SIC: 8322 Senior citizens' center or association

(P-16903)
COUNTRY VILLA SERVICE CORP
3000 N Gate Rd, Seal Beach (90740-2535)
PHONE.............................562 598-2477
Jennifer Rose, *Brnch Mgr*

EMP: 103
SALES (corp-wide): 28.62MM **Privately Held**
Web: www.evictionlawyer.com
SIC: 8322 8011 Rehabilitation services; Medical centers
PA: Country Villa Service Corp.
2400 E Katella Ave # 800
310 574-3733

(P-16904)
COUNTRY VLLA RNCHO MRAGE HLTHC
39950 Vista Del Sol, Rancho Mirage
(92270-3210)
PHONE.............................760 340-0053
Scott Gillis, *Admn*
EMP: 200 EST: 2007
SALES (est): 1.55MM **Privately Held**
Web: www.ranchomiragehcc.com
SIC: 8322 Rehabilitation services

(P-16905)
COUNTY OF LOS ANGELES
Also Called: Department of Social Services
530 12th St 1st Fl, Paso Robles
(93446-2201)
PHONE.............................805 237-3110
Michelle Chambers, *Mgr*
EMP: 71
Web: www.lacounty.gov
SIC: 8322 Social service center
PA: County Of Los Angeles
500 W Temple St Ste 437
213 974-1101

(P-16906)
COUNTY OF LOS ANGELES
Also Called: Probation Department
300 E Walnut St Dept 200, Pasadena
(91101-1584)
PHONE.............................626 356-5281
Diana Cunningham, *Prin*
EMP: 81
Web: www.lacounty.gov
SIC: 8322 9199 Probation office; General government administration, County government
PA: County Of Los Angeles
500 W Temple St Ste 437
213 974-1101

(P-16907)
COUNTY OF LOS ANGELES
Also Called: Probation Dept
320 W Temple St Ste 1101, Los Angeles
(90012-3289)
PHONE.............................213 974-9331
Mike Verilla, *Dir*
EMP: 81
Web: www.lacounty.gov
SIC: 8322 9223 8093 Probation office; Correctional institutions; Mental health clinic, outpatient
PA: County Of Los Angeles
500 W Temple St Ste 437
213 974-1101

(P-16908)
COUNTY OF LOS ANGELES
Also Called: La County Probation
8240 Broadway Ave, Whittier (90606-3120)
PHONE.............................562 908-3119
Donna Rose, *Mgr*
EMP: 81
Web: www.lacounty.gov
SIC: 8322 9111 Probation office; County supervisors' and executives' office
PA: County Of Los Angeles
500 W Temple St Ste 437

213 974-1101

(P-16909)
COUNTY OF LOS ANGELES
Also Called: Probation Department
1601 Eastlake Ave, Los Angeles
(90033-1009)
PHONE.............................323 226-8511
Taula Heath, *Dir*
EMP: 91
Web: www.lacounty.gov
SIC: 8322 Probation office
PA: County Of Los Angeles
500 W Temple St Ste 437
213 974-1101

(P-16910)
COUNTY OF LOS ANGELES
Also Called: Children & Family Svcs Dept
510 S Vermont Ave Fl 1, Los Angeles
(90020-1912)
PHONE.............................213 351-5600
Jackie Contreras, *Dir*
EMP: 71
Web: www.lacounty.gov
SIC: 8322 9441 Child related social services; Administration of social and manpower programs
PA: County Of Los Angeles
500 W Temple St Ste 437
213 974-1101

(P-16911)
COUNTY OF LOS ANGELES
Also Called: Probation Department
5300 W Avenue I, Lancaster (93536-8312)
PHONE.............................661 940-4181
Willie Doyle, *Dir*
EMP: 80
Web: www.lacounty.gov
SIC: 8322 9223 Probation office; Correctional institutions
PA: County Of Los Angeles
500 W Temple St Ste 437
213 974-1101

(P-16912)
COUNTY OF LOS ANGELES
Also Called: Child Support Services
5770 S Eastern Ave 4th Fl, Commerce
(90040-2948)
PHONE.............................323 889-3405
Steven Golightly, *Mgr*
EMP: 213
Web: www.lacounty.gov
SIC: 8322 9441 Child related social services; Administration of social and manpower programs
PA: County Of Los Angeles
500 W Temple St Ste 437
213 974-1101

(P-16913)
COUNTY OF LOS ANGELES
Also Called: Children & Family Svcs Dept
10355 Slusher Dr, Santa Fe Springs
(90670-7353)
PHONE.............................562 903-5000
Barbara Betlem, *Dir*
EMP: 71
Web: www.lacounty.gov
SIC: 8322 9441 Child related social services; Administration of social and manpower programs, level of governme
PA: County Of Los Angeles
500 W Temple St Ste 437
213 974-1101

(P-16914)
COUNTY OF LOS ANGELES
Also Called: Dept Children and Family Svcs
4060 Watson Plaza Dr, Lakewood
(90712-4033)
PHONE.............................562 497-3500
Joy Russell, *Admn*
EMP: 91
Web: www.lacounty.info
SIC: 8322 9111 Childrens' aid society; Executive offices
PA: County Of Los Angeles
500 W Temple St Ste 437
213 974-1101

(P-16915)
COUNTY OF LOS ANGELES
Also Called: Community & Senior Svcs
777 W Jackman St, Lancaster
(93534-2419)
PHONE.............................661 948-2320
Nusun Muhamad, *Mgr*
EMP: 71
Web: www.lacounty.gov
SIC: 8322 9441 Senior citizens' center or association; Administration of social and manpower programs
PA: County Of Los Angeles
500 W Temple St Ste 437
213 974-1101

(P-16916)
COUNTY OF LOS ANGELES
Also Called: Probation Information Ctr Pic
9150 Imperial Hwy, Downey (90242-2835)
PHONE.............................562 940-2470
EMP: 81
Web: www.lacounty.gov
SIC: 8322 Probation office
PA: County Of Los Angeles
500 W Temple St Ste 437
213 974-1101

(P-16917)
COUNTY OF LOS ANGELES
Also Called: Probation Department
7285 Quill Dr, Downey (90242-2001)
PHONE.............................562 940-6856
Sheryl Cooke, *Superintnt*
EMP: 81
Web: www.lacounty.gov
SIC: 8322 9223 Probation office; Correctional institutions
PA: County Of Los Angeles
500 W Temple St Ste 437
213 974-1101

(P-16918)
COUNTY OF LOS ANGELES
Also Called: County Los Angles Prbtion Dept
1660 W Mission Blvd, Pomona
(91766-1200)
PHONE.............................909 469-4500
Lorraine Hubbard-johns, *Mgr*
EMP: 81
Web: www.lacounty.gov
SIC: 8322 9223 Probation office; Correctional institutions
PA: County Of Los Angeles
500 W Temple St Ste 437
213 974-1101

(P-16919)
COUNTY OF LOS ANGELES
Also Called: Probation Dept
1725 Main St Rm 125, Santa Monica
(90401-3267)
PHONE.............................310 266-3711
Ernest P Gonzalez, *Brnch Mgr*
EMP: 81

Web: www.lacounty.gov
SIC: **8322** 9223 Probation office;
Correctional institutions
PA: County Of Los Angeles
500 W Temple St Ste 437
213 974-1101

(P-16920)
COUNTY OF LOS ANGELES
Also Called: Probation Dept
14414 Delano St, Van Nuys (91401-2703)
PHONE...................................818 374-2000
Ed Johnson, *Dir*
EMP: 91
Web: probation.lacounty.gov
SIC: **8322** 9223 Probation office;
Correctional institutions
PA: County Of Los Angeles
500 W Temple St Ste 437
213 974-1101

(P-16921)
COUNTY OF LOS ANGELES
Also Called: Probation Dept
4849 Civic Center Way, Los Angeles
(90022-1679)
PHONE...................................323 780-2185
Debbie Nelson, *Dir*
EMP: 132
Web: www.lacounty.gov
SIC: **8322** 9223 Probation office;
Correctional institutions
PA: County Of Los Angeles
500 W Temple St Ste 437
213 974-1101

(P-16922)
COUNTY OF LOS ANGELES
Also Called: Department Children Fmly Svcs
501 Shatto Pl Ste 301, Los Angeles
(90020-1749)
PHONE...................................213 351-7257
Bill Browning, *Dir*
EMP: 81
Web: www.lacounty.gov
SIC: **8322** 9111 Senior citizens' center or
association; Executive offices
PA: County Of Los Angeles
500 W Temple St Ste 437
213 974-1101

(P-16923)
COUNTY OF LOS ANGELES
Also Called: Probation Dept
8526 Grape St, Los Angeles (90001-4134)
PHONE...................................323 586-6469
Mark Garcia, *Dir*
EMP: 01
Web: www.lacounty.gov
SIC: **8322** 9223 Probation office;
Correctional institutions
PA: County Of Los Angeles
500 W Temple St Ste 437
213 974-1101

(P-16924)
COUNTY OF LOS ANGELES
Also Called: Probation Dept
200 W Compton Blvd Ste 300, Compton
(90220-3136)
PHONE...................................310 603-7311
Peggy May, *Dir*
EMP: 81
Web: www.lacounty.gov
SIC: **8322** 9223 Probation office;
Correctional institutions
PA: County Of Los Angeles
500 W Temple St Ste 437
213 974-1101

(P-16925)
COUNTY OF LOS ANGELES
Also Called: Probation Dept
199 N Euclid Ave, Pasadena (91101-1757)
PHONE...................................626 356-5281
Steve Yoder, *Dir*
EMP: 81
Web: www.lacounty.gov
SIC: **8322** 9223 Probation office;
Correctional institutions
PA: County Of Los Angeles
500 W Temple St Ste 437
213 974-1101

(P-16926)
COUNTY OF LOS ANGELES
200 W Woodward Ave, Alhambra
(91801-3459)
PHONE...................................626 308-5542
Roger Fernandez, *Brnch Mgr*
EMP: 81
Web: www.lacounty.gov
SIC: **8322** 9111 Probation office; County
supervisors' and executives' office
PA: County Of Los Angeles
500 W Temple St Ste 437
213 974-1101

(P-16927)
COUNTY OF LOS ANGELES
Also Called: Camp Glenn Rocky
1900 Sycamore Canyon Rd, San Dimas
(91773-1220)
PHONE...................................909 599-2391
Ed Silva, *Dir*
EMP: 101
Web: www.lacounty.gov
SIC: **8322** 9111 Probation office; Executive
offices
PA: County Of Los Angeles
500 W Temple St Ste 437
213 974-1101

(P-16928)
COUNTY OF RIVERSIDE
Also Called: Community Action Prtnr Rvrside
2038 Iowa Ave Ste 102, Riverside
(92507-2471)
PHONE...................................951 955-4900
Maria Y Juarez, *Mgr*
EMP: 71
SALES (corp-wide): 5.07B **Privately Held**
Web: www.capriverside.org
SIC: **8322** 9441 Individual and family
services; Administration of social and
manpower programs
PA: County Of Riverside
4000 Lemon St Fl 11
951 955-1110

(P-16929)
COUNTY OF SAN DIEGO
Also Called: Probation Dept
330 W Broadway Ste 1100, San Diego
(92101-3827)
P.O. Box 23596 (92193-3596)
PHONE...................................619 515-8202
Don Blevins, *Dir*
EMP: 308
Web: www.sdcda.org
SIC: **8322** 9431 Probation office;
Administration of public health programs
PA: County Of San Diego
1600 Pacific Hwy Ste 209
619 531-5880

(P-16930)
COUNTY OF VENTURA
Also Called: County Ventura Human
Resources

800 S Victoria Ave, Ventura (93009-0003)
PHONE...................................805 654-2561
Jodi Lee Prior, *Brnch Mgr*
EMP: 104
SALES (corp-wide): 2.03B **Privately Held**
Web: www.ventura.org
SIC: **8322** 9441 Individual and family
services; Administration of social and
human resources
PA: County Of Ventura
800 S Victoria Ave
805 654-2644

(P-16931)
COUNTY OF VENTURA
Also Called: Medical Center
3291 Loma Vista Rd, Ventura (93003-3099)
PHONE...................................805 652-6000
EMP: 81
SALES (corp-wide): 2.03B **Privately Held**
Web: www.ventura.org
SIC: **8322** 9431 Individual and family
services; Administration of public health
programs
PA: County Of Ventura
800 S Victoria Ave
805 654-2644

(P-16932)
CRYSTAL STAIRS INC (PA)
5110 W Goldleaf Cir Ste 150, Los Angeles
(90056-1287)
PHONE...................................323 299-8998
Jackie B Majors, *CEO*
Dianna Torres, *
Doctor Karen Hill-scott, *Pr*
Carolyn Moultrie, *
Javier La Fianza, *
EMP: 330 **EST:** 1980
SQ FT: 83,000
SALES (est): 297.78MM
SALES (corp-wide): 297.78MM **Privately
Held**
Web: www.crystalstairs.org
SIC: **8322** Social service center

(P-16933)
DESERTARC
Also Called: Desert Valley Industries
73255 Country Club Dr, Palm Desert
(92260-2309)
PHONE...................................760 346-1611
Kurt Parish, *Admn*
Ruth Goodsell, *
Robin Keagen, *
Robert Anzalone, *
Rosemary Fausel, *
EMP: 256 **EST:** 1959
SQ FT: 12,000
SALES (est): 17.72MM **Privately Held**
Web: www.desertarc.org
SIC: **8322** Association for the handicapped

(P-16934)
DIDI HIRSCH PSYCHIATRIC SVC
(PA)
Also Called: Didi Hrsch Cmnty Mntal Hlth Ct
4760 Sepulveda Blvd, Culver City
(90230-4820)
PHONE...................................310 390-6612
Michael Wierwille, *Ch*
Kita S Curry, *
Andrew Rubin, *
John Mcgann, *VP Fin*
Martin Frank, *
EMP: 150 **EST:** 1944
SQ FT: 35,000
SALES (est): 85.73MM
SALES (corp-wide): 85.73MM **Privately
Held**

Web: www.didihirsch.org
SIC: **8322** 8093 Family counseling services;
Mental health clinic, outpatient

(P-16935)
DIVERSE JOURNEYS INC (PA)
525 S Douglas St Ste 210, El Segundo
(90245-4827)
PHONE...................................310 643-7403
Amanda Gerhart, *Pr*
Laura Broderrick, *
EMP: 78 **EST:** 2005
SQ FT: 2,000
SALES (est): 5.6MM
SALES (corp-wide): 5.6MM **Privately Held**
Web: www.diversejourneys.org
SIC: **8322** Social services for the
handicapped

(P-16936)
EAST LOS ANGLES RMRKBLE
CTZENS
Also Called: EL ARCA
3839 Selig Pl, Los Angeles (90031-3143)
PHONE...................................323 223-3079
Carlos Madrid, *Ex Dir*
John Menchaca, *
EMP: 100 **EST:** 1969
SQ FT: 23,360
SALES (est): 4.08MM **Privately Held**
Web: www.elarcainc.org
SIC: **8322** Social services for the
handicapped

(P-16937)
EASTERN LOS ANGLES RGNAL
CTR F (PA)
1000 S Fremont Ave Unit 23, Alhambra
(91803-8646)
P.O. Box 7916 (91802-7916)
PHONE...................................626 299-4700
Gloria Wong, *Ex Dir*
EMP: 242 **EST:** 1969
SQ FT: 31,704
SALES (est): 355.05MM
SALES (corp-wide): 355.05MM **Privately
Held**
Web: www.elarc.org
SIC: **8322** Association for the handicapped

(P-16938)
EGGLESTON YOUTH CENTERS
INC (PA)
256 W Badillo St, Covina (91723-1906)
P.O. Box 638 (91706)
PHONE...................................626 480-8107
Clarence Brown, *Ex Dir*
Don Gutierrez, *
April Mitchell, *Brand President**
EMP: 90 **EST:** 1975
SQ FT: 7,616
SALES (est): 12.8MM
SALES (corp-wide): 12.8MM **Privately
Held**
Web: www.egglestonyouthcenter.org
SIC: **8322** Social service center

(P-16939)
EL NIDO FAMILY CENTERS (PA)
10200 Sepulveda Blvd Ste 350, Mission
Hills (91345-3318)
PHONE...................................818 830-3646
Liz Herrera, *Dir*
EMP: 130 **EST:** 1957
SQ FT: 3,650
SALES (est): 13.44MM
SALES (corp-wide): 13.44MM **Privately
Held**
Web: www.elnidofamilycenters.org

SIC: 8322 Social service center

(P-16940)
ESSENCE OF AMERICA
1855 1st Ave Ste 103, San Diego
(92101-2650)
P.O. Box 23682 (92193-3682)
PHONE..............................312 805-9365
Shannon Davis, *Pr*
EMP: 25 EST: 2011
SALES (est): 200K **Privately Held**
SIC: 8322 5812 2099 2599 Meal delivery
  program; Restaurant, family: independent;
  Syrups; Food wagons, restaurant

(P-16941)
FAMILY ASSISTANCE PROGRAM
Also Called: Our House
15075 Seventh St, Victorville (92395-3810)
PHONE..............................760 843-0701
Darryl Evey, *CEO*
Darryl Evey, *Ex Dir*
Elsa Scott, *
EMP: 148 EST: 1985
SQ FT: 4,960
SALES (est): 10.88MM **Privately Held**
Web: www.familyassist.org
SIC: 8322 Social service center

(P-16942)
FAMILY SVC AGCY SNTA BRBARA CN
123 W Gutierrez St, Santa Barbara
(93101-3424)
PHONE..............................805 965-1001
Denise Cicourel, *Admn*
EMP: 100 EST: 1901
SALES (est): 15.17MM **Privately Held**
Web: www.fsacares.org
SIC: 8322 Social service center

(P-16943)
FIRST 5 LA
750 N Alameda St Ste 300, Los Angeles
(90012-3870)
PHONE..............................213 482-5920
Kim Belsh, *Prin*
EMP: 157 EST: 2008
SALES (est): 9.36MM **Privately Held**
Web: www.first5la.org
SIC: 8322 Child guidance agency

(P-16944)
FOOTHILL FAMILY SERVICE
3629 Santa Anita Ave Ste 201, El Monte
(91731-3635)
PHONE..............................626 246-1240
EMP: 120
SALES (corp-wide): 32.95MM **Privately Held**
Web: www.foothillfamily.org
SIC: 8322 Family counseling services
PA: Foothill Family Service
  2500 E Fthill Blvd Ste 30
  626 993-3000

(P-16945)
FOOTHILL FAMILY SERVICE
2500 E Foothill Blvd Ste 300, Pasadena
(91107-7102)
PHONE..............................626 795-6907
Helen Morran-wolf, *Mgr*
EMP: 120
SALES (corp-wide): 32.95MM **Privately Held**
Web: www.foothillfamily.org
SIC: 8322 Family counseling services
PA: Foothill Family Service
  2500 E Fthill Blvd Ste 30
  626 993-3000

(P-16946)
G&L PENASQUITOS INC
Also Called: Arbors, The
10584 Rancho Carmel Dr, San Diego
(92128-3629)
PHONE..............................858 538-0802
Gary Penovich, *Ex Dir*
EMP: 934 EST: 1998
SQ FT: 48,685
SALES (est): 839.26K
SALES (corp-wide): 14.71MM **Privately Held**
SIC: 8322 Individual and family services
PA: G&L Realty Corp, Llc
  439 N Bedford Dr
  310 273-9930

(P-16947)
GRASSHOPPER HOUSE PARTNERS LLC
Also Called: Passages
6428 Meadows Ct, Malibu (90265-4492)
PHONE..............................310 589-2880
Pax Prentiss, *
EMP: 105 EST: 2000
SQ FT: 16,000
SALES (est): 5.12MM **Privately Held**
Web: www.passagesmalibu.com
SIC: 8322 Rehabilitation services

(P-16948)
HATHAWY-SYCMRES CHILD FMLY SVC
Also Called: Hathaway Children and Family
12502 Van Nuys Blvd Ste 120, Pacoima
(91331-1340)
PHONE..............................626 395-7100
Muriel Gaudin, *Mgr*
EMP: 225
SALES (corp-wide): 62.46MM **Privately Held**
Web: www.sycamores.org
SIC: 8322 Child related social services
PA: Hathaway-Sycamores Child And
  Family Services
  100 W Walnut St Ste 375
  626 395-7100

(P-16949)
HATHAWY-SYCMRES CHILD FMLY SVC
3741 Stocker St Ste 101, View Park
(90008-5150)
PHONE..............................323 733-0322
Debbie Manners, *Brnch Mgr*
EMP: 207
SALES (corp-wide): 62.46MM **Privately Held**
Web: www.sycamores.org
SIC: 8322 Child related social services
PA: Hathaway-Sycamores Child And
  Family Services
  100 W Walnut St Ste 375
  626 395-7100

(P-16950)
HELP CHILDREN WORLD FOUNDATION
Also Called: INTERNATIONAL CHILDREN'S
CHARI
26500 Agoura Rd Ste 657, Calabasas
(91302-1952)
PHONE..............................818 706-9848
Lev M Leznik, *Pr*
Andrew Grey, *
Veronica Duval, *
Michael Teilmann, *
EMP: 300 EST: 1991
SQ FT: 2,200

SALES (est): 224.39K **Privately Held**
SIC: 8322 Childrens' aid society

(P-16951)
HILLSIDES
940 Avenue 64, Pasadena (91105-2711)
PHONE..............................323 254-2274
Joseph M Costa, *CEO*
Ryan Herren, *
Amy Ley-sanchez, *Ex VP*
EMP: 460 EST: 1913
SQ FT: 18,217
SALES (est): 37.73MM **Privately Held**
Web: www.hillsides.org
SIC: 8322 Individual and family services

(P-16952)
HOMEBOY INDUSTRIES (PA)
Also Called: Homeboy Bakery
130 Bruno St, Los Angeles (90012-1815)
PHONE..............................323 526-1254
Greg Boyle, *Ex Dir*
Thomas Vozzo, *Prin*
Jack Faherty, *
John Brady, *
EMP: 270 EST: 2000
SQ FT: 3,690
SALES (est): 25.34MM **Privately Held**
Web: www.homeboyindustries.org
SIC: 8322 Rehabilitation services

(P-16953)
HORRIGAN ENTERPRISES INC
Also Called: Crossrads Adult Day Hlth Care
7945 Cartilla Ave, Rancho Cucamonga
(91730-3076)
PHONE..............................909 481-9663
Judy Lowe, *Mgr*
EMP: 153
SALES (corp-wide): 4.74MM **Privately Held**
Web: www.industry386.com
SIC: 8322 Adult day care center
PA: Horrigan Enterprises, Inc.
  1636 Country Club Dr
  909 484-5561

(P-16954)
HUMAN SERVICES ASSOCIATION (PA)
Also Called: HSA BELL GARDENS LAUP
6800 Florence Ave, Bell (90201-4958)
PHONE..............................562 806-5400
Susanne Sundberg, *Prin*
EMP: 75 EST: 1940
SQ FT: 10,000
SALES (est): 30.76MM
SALES (corp-wide): 30.76MM **Privately Held**
Web: www.hsala.org
SIC: 8322 Social service center

(P-16955)
IN-ROADS CREATIVE PROGRAMS
9057 Arrow Rte Ste 120, Rancho
Cucamonga (91730-4452)
PHONE..............................909 989-9944
Sharon Barton, *Brnch Mgr*
EMP: 419
Web: www.in-roads.net
SIC: 8322 Adult day care center
PA: In-Roads Creative Programs, Inc
  7955 Webster St Ste 7

(P-16956)
IN-ROADS CREATIVE PROGRAMS
1951 E Saint Andrews Dr, Ontario
(91761-6447)

PHONE..............................909 947-9142
Sharon Barton, *Brnch Mgr*
EMP: 315
Web: www.in-roads.net
SIC: 8322 Childrens' aid society
PA: In-Roads Creative Programs, Inc
  7955 Webster St Ste 7

(P-16957)
INCLUSION SERVICES LLC
Also Called: Inclusion Services
7255 Greenleaf Ave Ste 20, Whittier
(90602-1340)
PHONE..............................562 945-2000
Cesar Torres, *Managing Member*
Israel Ibenez, *Managing Member*
EMP: 103 EST: 2009
SALES (est): 3.01MM **Privately Held**
Web: www.inclusionsvs.org
SIC: 8322 8331 Social services for the
  handicapped; Skill training center

(P-16958)
INLAND CNTIES REGIONAL CTR INC (PA)
Also Called: Inland Regional Center
1365 S Waterman Ave, San Bernardino
(92408-2804)
P.O. Box 19037 (92423-9037)
PHONE..............................909 890-3000
Carol A Fitzgibbons, *CEO*
Carol Fitzgibbons, *
EMP: 173 EST: 1971
SQ FT: 82,000
SALES (est): 853.46MM
SALES (corp-wide): 853.46MM **Privately Held**
Web: www.inlandrc.org
SIC: 8322 Social service center

(P-16959)
INTERFACE COMMUNITY (PA)
Also Called: INTERFACE CHILDREN
FAMILY SERV
4001 Mission Oaks Blvd Ste I, Camarillo
(93012-5121)
PHONE..............................805 485-6114
Charles T Watson, *Pr*
Dale Stoeber, *
Terryl Miller, *CPO*
EMP: 88 EST: 1975
SQ FT: 3,000
SALES (est): 15.42MM
SALES (corp-wide): 15.42MM **Privately Held**
Web: www.icfs.org
SIC: 8322 Social service center

(P-16960)
INTERFAITH COMMUNITY SVCS INC
Also Called: INTERFAITH COMMUNITY
SERVICES
250 N Ash St, Escondido (92025)
PHONE..............................760 489-6380
Greg Anglea, *Ex Dir*
Leonard Jacobson, *
Suzanne Pohlman, *
EMP: 100 EST: 1982
SALES (est): 25.19MM **Privately Held**
Web: www.interfaithservices.org
SIC: 8322 Social service center

(P-16961)
INTERNATIONAL MEDICAL CORPS (PA)
Also Called: IMC
12400 Wilshire Blvd Ste 1500, Los Angeles
(90025-1030)

PHONE..............................310 826-7800
Nancy Aossey, *Pr*
Ingrid Renaud, *
Ky Luu, *Ofcr*
EMP: 4500 **EST:** 1984
SALES (est): 223.95MM
SALES (corp-wide): 223.95MM **Privately Held**
Web: www.internationalmedicalcorps.org
SIC: 8322 Disaster service

(P-16962)
JEWISH COMMUNITY CTR LONG BCH
Also Called: Jewish Community Center
3801 E Willow St, Long Beach
(90815-1791)
PHONE..............................562 426-7601
Gordon Lentzner, *Pr*
EMP: 150 **EST:** 1948
SQ FT: 90,000
SALES (est): 5.29MM **Privately Held**
Web: www.alpertjcc.org
SIC: 8322 Community center

(P-16963)
JEWISH FAMILY SVC LOS ANGELES
Also Called: Senior Nutrition Program
330 N Fairfax Ave, Los Angeles
(90036-2109)
PHONE..............................323 937-5900
Eileen Mccouliffe, *Dir*
EMP: 139
SALES (corp-wide): 87.85MM **Privately Held**
Web: www.jfla.org
SIC: 8322 Social service center
PA: Jewish Family Service Of Los Angeles
330 N Fairfax Ave
323 761-8800

(P-16964)
JEWISH FAMILY SVC SAN DIEGO (PA)
Also Called: Jewish Family Service
8804 Balboa Ave, San Diego (92123-1506)
PHONE..............................858 637-3000
Michael Hopkins, *CEO*
Emily Jennewein, *
Felicia Mandelbaum, *
EMP: 204 **EST:** 1936
SQ FT: 25,000
SALES (est): 81.99MM
SALES (corp-wide): 81.99MM **Privately Held**
Web: www.jfssd.org
SIC: 8322 Social service center

(P-16965)
JONI AND FRIENDS FOUNDATION (PA)
30009 Ladyface Ct, Agoura (91301-2583)
PHONE..............................818 707-5664
Joni E Tada, *CEO*
Douglas Mazza, *
Billy Burnett, *
◆ **EMP:** 84 **EST:** 1979
SQ FT: 30,000
SALES (est): 2.51MM
SALES (corp-wide): 2.51MM **Privately Held**
Web: www.joniandfriends.org
SIC: 8322 Association for the handicapped

(P-16966)
JWCH INSTITUTE INC
Also Called: Jwch Medical Center
3591 E Imperial Hwy, Lynwood
(90262-2654)

PHONE..............................310 223-1035
Al Basceros, *Mgr*
EMP: 178
SALES (corp-wide): 112.81MM **Privately Held**
Web: www.jwchinstitute.org
SIC: 8322 8093 Individual and family services; Family planning clinic
PA: Jwch Institute, Inc.
5650 Jillson St
323 477-1171

(P-16967)
KEDREN COMMUNITY HLTH CTR INC
3800 S Figueroa St, Los Angeles
(90037-1206)
PHONE..............................323 524-0634
John Griffith, *Pr*
EMP: 133
SALES (corp-wide): 21.22MM **Privately Held**
Web: www.kedren.org
SIC: 8322 Community center
PA: Kedren Community Health Center, Inc.
4211 Avalon Blvd
323 233-0425

(P-16968)
KINGDOM CAUSES INC
Also Called: City Net
4508 Atlantic Ave Ste 292, Long Beach
(90807-1520)
P.O. Box 90243 (90809-0243)
PHONE..............................714 904-0167
Brad Fieldhouse, *Pr*
David Boder, *
Anthony Flynn, *
Arthur Gray, *
Tranece Harris, *
EMP: 250 **EST:** 2003
SALES (est): 10.8MM **Privately Held**
Web: www.kcbellflower.org
SIC: 8322 Community center

(P-16969)
LA ASCCION NCNAL PRO PRSNAS MY
Also Called: National Assn For Hispanic
1452 W Temple St Ste 100, Los Angeles
(90026-5649)
PHONE..............................213 202-5900
Zecia Soto, *Prin*
EMP: 703
SALES (corp-wide): 10.03MM **Privately Held**
SIC: 8322 7361 8611 Social service center; Employment agencies; Business associations
PA: La Asociacion Nacional Pro Personas Mayores
234 E Colo Blvd Ste 300
626 564-1988

(P-16970)
LAURAS HOUSE
33 Journey Ste 150, Aliso Viejo
(92656-5364)
PHONE..............................949 361-3775
Margaret Bayston, *Ex Dir*
EMP: 92 **EST:** 1994
SALES (est): 2.08MM **Privately Held**
Web: www.laurashouse.org
SIC: 8322 Social service center

(P-16971)
LIFE STEPS FOUNDATION INC
500 E 4th St, Long Beach (90802-2501)
PHONE..............................562 436-0751
Kristine Engels, *Dir*

EMP: 97
Web: www.lifestepsfoundation.org
SIC: 8322 8399 Social service center; Community development groups
PA: Life Steps Foundation, Inc.
5757 W Cntury Blvd Ste 88

(P-16972)
LIFE STEPS FOUNDATION INC
1107 Johnson Ave, San Luis Obispo
(93401-3303)
PHONE..............................805 549-0150
Virginia Franco, *Brnch Mgr*
EMP: 77
Web: www.lifestepsfoundation.org
SIC: 8322 Social service center
PA: Life Steps Foundation, Inc.
5757 W Cntury Blvd Ste 88

(P-16973)
LIFE STEPS FOUNDATION INC
Also Called: Santa Maria Wisdom Center
2255 S Depot St, Santa Maria
(93455-1216)
PHONE..............................805 349-9810
Susan Chang, *Brnch Mgr*
EMP: 77
Web: www.lifestepsfoundation.org
SIC: 8322 Social service center
PA: Life Steps Foundation, Inc.
5757 W Cntury Blvd Ste 88

(P-16974)
LOS ANGELES HOMELESS SVCS AUTH
Also Called: L A H S A
707 Wilshire Blvd Ste 1000, Los Angeles
(90017-3729)
PHONE..............................213 683-3333
Heidi Marston, *Ex Dir*
EMP: 558 **EST:** 1993
SALES (est): 46.39MM **Privately Held**
Web: www.lahsa.org
SIC: 8322 Social service center

(P-16975)
LOS ANGELES REGIONAL FOOD BANK
1734 E 41st St, Los Angeles (90058-1502)
PHONE..............................323 234-3030
Michael Flood, *Pr*
Michael Flood, *Pr*
Czarina Luna, *
EMP: 185 **EST:** 1977
SALES (est): 261.13MM **Privately Held**
Web: www.lafoodbank.org
SIC: 8322 8699 Meal delivery program; Charitable organization

(P-16976)
LUMINA ALLIANCE
Also Called: STAND STRONG
51 Zaca Ln Ste 150, San Luis Obispo
(93401-7319)
P.O. Box 125 (93406)
PHONE..............................805 781-6400
Jennifer Adams, *CEO*
Marianne Kennedy, *
EMP: 75 **EST:** 2001
SALES (est): 5.65MM **Privately Held**
Web: www.luminaalliance.org
SIC: 8322 Social service center

(P-16977)
MARK 1 RESTORATION SERVICE LLC
3360 E La Palma Ave, Anaheim
(92806-2814)
PHONE..............................714 283-9990

Gary Moore, *Managing Member*
EMP: 78 **EST:** 2020
SALES (est): 626.95K **Privately Held**
Web: www.atirestoration.com
SIC: 8322 Disaster service
PA: Ati Restoration, Llc
3360 E La Palma Ave

(P-16978)
MEXICAN AMRCN OPRTNTY FNDATION (PA)
Also Called: MAOF
401 N Garfield Ave, Montebello
(90640-2901)
P.O. Box 4602 (90640-9311)
PHONE..............................323 890-9600
Martin Vasquez Castro, *Pr*
Carlos J Viramontes, *
EMP: 100 **EST:** 1963
SQ FT: 25,000
SALES (est): 141.24MM
SALES (corp-wide): 141.24MM **Privately Held**
Web: www.maof.org
SIC: 8322 Social service center

(P-16979)
MIXTEC/NDGENA CMNTY ORGNZING P
Also Called: MICOP
135 Magnolia Ave, Oxnard (93030-5336)
P.O. Box 20543 (93034)
PHONE..............................805 483-1166
Arcenio Lopez, *Ex Dir*
Donna Foster, *
EMP: 75 **EST:** 2008
SALES (est): 10.79MM **Privately Held**
Web: www.mixteco.org
SIC: 8322 Social service center

(P-16980)
MYHHBS INC
237 N Central Ave Ste A, Glendale
(91203-3526)
PHONE..............................888 969-4427
Khrist Kakosimidi, *Prin*
EMP: 85 **EST:** 2016
SALES (est): 2.55MM **Privately Held**
Web: www.myhhbs.com
SIC: 8322 General counseling services

(P-16981)
NEIGHBORHOOD HOUSE ASSOCIATION (PA)
Also Called: N H A
5660 Copley Dr, San Diego (92111-7902)
PHONE..............................858 715 2642
Rudolph A Johnson Iii, *CEO*
EMP: 500 **EST:** 1914
SQ FT: 60,000
SALES (est): 120.41MM
SALES (corp-wide): 120.41MM **Privately Held**
Web: www.neighborhoodhouse.org
SIC: 8322 Neighborhood center

(P-16982)
NEW ALTERNATIVES INCORPORATED
8755 Aero Dr Ste 230, San Diego
(92123-1750)
PHONE..............................619 863-5855
EMP: 581
SALES (corp-wide): 53.12MM **Privately Held**
Web: www.newalternativesfund.com
SIC: 8322 Social service center
PA: New Alternatives, Incorporated
3589 4th Ave

619 543-0293

(P-16983)
NEW DIRECTIONS INC (PA)
Also Called: NEW DIRECTIONS FOR
VETERANS
11303 Wilshire Blvd Bldg 116, Los Angeles
(90073)
P.O. Box 25536 (90025-0536)
PHONE..................................310 914-4045
Edgar H Howell, *CEO*
Tony Reinis, *
Usha Murthy, *
EMP: 80 EST: 1989
SQ FT: 60,000
SALES (est): 9.62MM Privately Held
Web: www.ndvets.org
SIC: 8322 Substance abuse counseling

(P-16984)
NORTHEAST VALLEY HEALTH
CORP (PA)
1172 N Maclay Ave, San Fernando
(91340-1328)
PHONE..................................818 898-1388
Kimberly Wyard, *CEO*
Nelson Wong, *
Irma Morales, *
Antonio Lugo, *
Patricia Moraga, *
EMP: 75 EST: 1971
SALES (est): 149.24MM
SALES (corp-wide): 149.24MM Privately
Held
Web: www.nevhc.org
SIC: 8322 Community center

(P-16985)
OAK GROVE INST FOUNDATION
INC
1251 N A St, Perris (92570-1911)
PHONE..................................951 238-6022
EMP: 240
Web: www.oakgrovecenter.org
SIC: 8322 Child related social services
PA: Oak Grove Institute Foundation, Inc.
24275 Jefferson Ave

(P-16986)
OPTIMA FAMILY SERVICES INC
253 N San Gabriel Blvd, Pasadena
(91107-3429)
PHONE..................................323 300-6066
Oscar A Carvajal, *Prin*
EMP: 178 EST: 2008
SALES (est): 2.37MM Privately Held
Web: www.optimafamilyservices.com
SIC: 8322 General counseling services

(P-16987)
ORANGE CNTY ADULT
ACHVMENT CTR
Also Called: MY DAY COUNTS
225 W Carl Karcher Way, Anaheim
(92801-2499)
PHONE..................................714 744-5301
Michael Galliano, *CEO*
Patrick Faraday, *
Richard Farmer, *
Laurie Vinkavich, *
Jack Salseda, *
▲ EMP: 135 EST: 1955
SQ FT: 57,000
SALES (est): 9.15MM Privately Held
Web: www.mydaycounts.org
SIC: 8322 Social service center

(P-16988)
ORANGEWOOD FOUNDATION
1575 E 17th St, Santa Ana (92705-8506)
P.O. Box 10341 (92711)
PHONE..................................714 619-0200
Chris Simonsen, *CEO*
John Luker, *
EMP: 85 EST: 1980
SQ FT: 22,340
SALES (est): 24.46MM Privately Held
Web: www.orangewoodfoundation.org
SIC: 8322 Child related social services

(P-16989)
PACIFIC CLINICS
800 S Santa Anita Ave, Arcadia
(91006-3536)
PHONE..................................626 254-5000
Kathryn Mccarthy, *Pr*
EMP: 581
SALES (corp-wide): 245.37MM Privately
Held
Web: www.pacificclinics.org
SIC: 8322 Individual and family services
PA: Pacific Clinics
251 Llewellyn Ave
408 379-3790

(P-16990)
PATH
340 N Madison Ave, Los Angeles
(90004-3504)
PHONE..................................323 644-2216
Joel John Roberts, *Pr*
Jennifer Hark Dietz, *
Sandy Oluwek, *
Sarah Kolish, *
La Keishia Childers, *
EMP: 828 EST: 1984
SALES (est): 159.51MM Privately Held
Web: www.epath.org
SIC: 8322 Social service center

(P-16991)
PEOPLE CONCERN
526 S San Pedro St, Los Angeles
(90013-2102)
P.O. Box 57484 (90057)
PHONE..................................310 874-2806
EMP: 131
SALES (corp-wide): 83.33MM Privately
Held
Web: www.thepeopleconcern.org
SIC: 8322 Social service center
PA: The People Concern
2116 Arlngton Ave Ste 100
323 334-9000

(P-16992)
PEOPLE CONCERN
Daybreak
1751 Cloverfield Blvd, Santa Monica
(90404-4007)
PHONE..................................310 450-0650
Anya Booker, *Dir*
EMP: 131
SALES (corp-wide): 83.33MM Privately
Held
Web: www.thepeopleconcern.org
SIC: 8322 Community center
PA: The People Concern
2116 Arlngton Ave Ste 100
323 334-9000

(P-16993)
PEOPLE CONCERN
Safe Haven
1751 Cloverfield Blvd, Santa Monica
(90404-4007)
PHONE..................................310 883-1222

Andrew Schwich, *Dir*
EMP: 131
SALES (corp-wide): 83.33MM Privately
Held
Web: www.thepeopleconcern.org
SIC: 8322 Emergency shelters
PA: The People Concern
2116 Arlngton Ave Ste 100
323 334-9000

(P-16994)
PEOPLE CREATING SUCCESS
INC
1607 E Palmdale Blvd Ste H, Palmdale
(93550-7801)
PHONE..................................661 225-9700
Robert Donery, *Brnch Mgr*
EMP: 99
SALES (corp-wide): 4.53MM Privately
Held
Web: www.pcs-services.org
SIC: 8322 Individual and family services
PA: People Creating Success, Inc.
2585 Teller Rd
805 375-9222

(P-16995)
PEOPLE CREATING SUCCESS
INC
5350 Hollister Ave Ste I, Santa Barbara
(93111-2326)
PHONE..................................805 692-5290
Brian Fay, *Mgr*
EMP: 99
SALES (corp-wide): 14.09MM Privately
Held
Web: www.pcs-services.org
SIC: 8322 Social service center
PA: People Creating Success, Inc.
2585 Teller Rd
805 375-9222

(P-16996)
PRIORITY CTR ENDING THE
GNRTNA
Also Called: WELCOME BABY
1940 E Deere Ave Ste 100, Santa Ana
(92705-5718)
PHONE..................................714 543-4333
Scott Trotter, *Ex Dir*
Stephanie Enano, *
EMP: 99 EST: 1983
SALES (est): 9.35MM Privately Held
Web: www.theprioritycenter.org
SIC: 8322 Child related social services

(P-16997)
PROJECT CONCERN
INTERNATIONAL (PA)
Also Called: PCI
5151 Murphy Canyon Rd Ste 320, San
Diego (92123-4339)
PHONE..................................858 279-9690
Carrie Hessler-radelet, *Pr*
George Guimaraes, *
Kote Lomidze, *
Janine Schooley, *
Mark O Donnell, *
EMP: 124 EST: 1961
SQ FT: 12,000
SALES (est): 12.21MM
SALES (corp-wide): 12.21MM Privately
Held
Web: www.pciglobal.org
SIC: 8322 Social service center

(P-16998)
PROTOTYPES CENTERS FOR
INNOV

Also Called: Prototypes
1000 N Alameda St Ste 390, Los Angeles
(90012-1804)
PHONE..................................213 542-3838
Cassandra Loch, *Pr*
Maryann Fraser, *
EMP: 250 EST: 1986
SQ FT: 8,400
SALES (est): 20.14MM Privately Held
Web: www.healthright360.org
SIC: 8322 General counseling services

(P-16999)
PUBLIC HLTH FNDATION ENTPS
INC
13181 Crossroads Pkwy N, City Of Industry
(91746-3419)
PHONE..................................626 856-6600
Eliose Jenks, *Brnch Mgr*
EMP: 140
SALES (corp-wide): 49.53MM Privately
Held
Web: www.helunahealth.org
SIC: 8322 Social service center
PA: Public Health Foundation Enterprises,
Inc.
13300 Crssrads Pkwy N Ste
800 201-7320

(P-17000)
ROWI USA LLC
3155 Old Conejo Rd, Thousand Oaks
(91320-2151)
PHONE..................................805 356-3372
Candice Feinberg, *CEO*
EMP: 70 EST: 2019
SALES (est): 835.97K Privately Held
Web: www.rowiteen.com
SIC: 8322 General counseling services

(P-17001)
SALVATION ARMY (HQ)
Also Called: Salvation Army Western Ttry
30840 Hawthorne Blvd, Rancho Palos
Verdes (90275-5300)
PHONE..................................562 264-3600
James M Knaggs, *CEO*
Commissioner Carolyn R Knaggs
Territorial, *MINISTRIES**
Colonel David E Hudson, *Chief Secretary**
Susan Lawrence, *
Kenneth Hodder, *
▼ EMP: 140 EST: 1865
SALES (est): 516.57K
SALES (corp-wide): 424.11MM Privately
Held
Web: www.salvationarmy.org
SIC: 8322 Social service center
PA: The Salvation Army National
Corporation
615 Slaters Ln
703 684-5500

(P-17002)
SAN BRNRDINO CNTY PRBTION
OFFC
4370 Hallmark Pkwy Ste 105, San
Bernardino (92407-1848)
PHONE..................................909 887-2544
Laura Pleasant, *VP*
EMP: 407 EST: 2007
SALES (est): 638.38K Privately Held
Web:
www.sanbernardinocountyprobation.org
SIC: 8322 Probation office

(P-17003)
SAN DEGO SECOND CHANCE
PROGRAM
6145 Imperial Ave, San Diego
(92114-4213)

PHONE.................619 266-2506
Robert Coleman, *Ex Dir*
Scott Silverman, *
EMP: 35 EST: 1992
SALES (est): 3.92MM **Privately Held**
Web: www.secondchanceprogram.org
SIC: 8322 7361 3965 Social service center;
Employment agencies; Fasteners, buttons,
needles, and pins

(P-17004)
SAN DG-MPRIAL CNTIES
DVLPMNTAL (PA)
4355 Ruffin Rd Ste 220, San Diego
(92123-4308)
PHONE.................858 576-2996
Carlos Flores, *Ex Dir*
Judy Wallace Patton, *
Edward Kenney, *
EMP: 286 EST: 1982
SQ FT: 62,000
SALES (est): 709.64MM
SALES (corp-wide): 709.64MM **Privately Held**
Web: www.sdrc.org
SIC: 8322 Social services for the
handicapped

(P-17005)
SAN GBRL/PMONA VLLEYS
DVLPMNTA
Also Called: SAN GABRIEL/POMONA
REGIONAL CE
75 Rancho Camino Dr, Pomona
(91766-4728)
PHONE.................909 620-7722
R Keith Penman, *Ex Dir*
R Keith Penman, *Ex Dir*
Carol Tomblin, *
John Hunt, *
EMP: 323 EST: 1986
SQ FT: 100,000
SALES (est): 320.15MM **Privately Held**
Web: www.sgprc.org
SIC: 8322 Social service center

(P-17006)
SANTEE SENIOR RETIREMENT
COM
Also Called: Pointe At Lantern Crest, The
400 Lantern Crest Way, Santee
(92071-4633)
PHONE.................619 955-0901
Kaan Ciftci, *Ex Dir*
EMP: 104
Web:
www.lanterncrestseniorlivingsantee.com
SIC: 8322 Senior citizens' center or
association
PA: Santee Senior Retirement
Communities, Llc
8510 Railroad Ave

(P-17007)
SBCS CORPORATION
430 F St, Chula Vista (91910-3711)
PHONE.................619 420-3620
Kathryn Lembo, *Ex Dir*
EMP: 200 EST: 1971
SQ FT: 2,900
SALES (est): 51.48MM **Privately Held**
Web: www.case-5-19-cv-07071.info
SIC: 8322 Social service center

(P-17008)
SECOND HRVEST FD BNK
ORNGE CNT
8014 Marine Way, Irvine (92618-2235)
PHONE.................949 653-2900

Claudia Bonilla Keller, *CEO*
Chrislynn Vanskiver, *
Joyce Foley, *
EMP: 80 EST: 2008
SALES (est): 89.95MM **Privately Held**
Web: www.feedoc.org
SIC: 8322 Social service center

(P-17009)
SENECA FAMILY OF AGENCIES
6850 Morro Rd, Atascadero (93422-4123)
PHONE.................805 434-2449
EMP: 152
SALES (corp-wide): 176.92MM **Privately Held**
Web: www.senecafoa.org
SIC: 8322 Social service center
PA: Seneca Family Of Agencies
8945 Golf Links Rd
510 317-1444

(P-17010)
SENECA FAMILY OF AGENCIES
2130 N Ventura Rd, Oxnard (93036-2246)
PHONE.................805 278-0355
EMP: 152
SALES (corp-wide): 176.92MM **Privately Held**
Web: www.senecafoa.org
SIC: 8322 Social service center
PA: Seneca Family Of Agencies
8945 Golf Links Rd
510 317-1444

(P-17011)
SEXUAL RECOVERY INSTITUTE
INC
1964 Westwood Blvd Ste 400, Los Angeles
(90025-4695)
PHONE.................310 360-0130
EMP: 305 EST: 1955
SALES (est): 8.01MM
SALES (corp-wide): 72MM **Privately Held**
Web: www.sexualrecovery.com
SIC: 8322 General counseling services
PA: Elements Behavioral Health, Inc.
5000 Arprt Plz Dr Ste 100
562 741-6470

(P-17012)
SOCIAL ADVCTES FOR YUTH
SAN DE
4275 El Cajon Blvd Ste 101, San Diego
(92105-1293)
PHONE.................619 283-9624
Nancy G Hornberger, *CEO*
EMP: 202
SALES (corp-wide): 21.94MM **Privately Held**
Web: www.saysandiego.org
SIC: 8322 Social service center
PA: Social Advocates For Youth, San
Diego, Inc.
4775 Viewridge Ave
858 565-4148

(P-17013)
SOUTH BAY CTR FOR
COUNSELING
Also Called: SOUTH BAY CENTER FOR
COMMUNITY
540 N Marine Ave, Wilmington
(90744-5528)
PHONE.................310 414-2090
Colleen Mooney, *Ex Dir*
Maria Lomibao, *
EMP: 90 EST: 1974
SALES (est): 6MM **Privately Held**
Web: www.sbccthrivela.org

SIC: 8322 General counseling services

(P-17014)
ST JOSEPH CENTER
Also Called: SAINT JOSEPH CENTER
VOLUNTEER
204 Hampton Dr, Venice (90291-8633)
PHONE.................310 396-6468
Felecia Adams, *VP*
Va Lecia Adams Kellum, *Ex Dir*
Paul Rubenstein, *
Tifara Monroe, *
John Mcgann, *CFO*
EMP: 85 EST: 1976
SQ FT: 32,000
SALES (est): 51.82MM **Privately Held**
Web: www.stjosephctr.org
SIC: 8322 8331 8351 Social service center;
Job training services; Child day care
services

(P-17015)
STRAIGHT TALK INC
Also Called: Straight Talk Counseling Ctr
13710 La Mirada Blvd, La Mirada
(90638-3028)
PHONE.................562 943-0195
Meg Kalugan, *Mgr*
EMP: 90
SALES (corp-wide): 2.68MM **Privately Held**
Web: www.straighttalkcounseling.org
SIC: 8322 General counseling services
PA: Straight Talk Clinic, Incorporated
5712 Camp St
714 828-2000

(P-17016)
TEAM LOGIC IF LA W
HOLLYWOOD
751 N Formosa Ave, Los Angeles
(90046-7609)
PHONE.................310 292-0063
EMP: 71 EST: 2010
SALES (est): 294.12K **Privately Held**
Web: www.teamlogicit.com
SIC: 8322 General counseling services

(P-17017)
TOWARD MAXIMUM
INDEPENDENCE (PA)
Also Called: T M I
4740 Murphy Canyon Rd Ste 300, San
Diego (92123-4385)
PHONE.................858 467-0600
Kerby Wohlander, *Dir*
EMP: 125 EST: 1981
SQ FT: 5,700
SALES (est): 21.42MM **Privately Held**
Web: www.tmi-inc.org
SIC: 8322 Social services for the
handicapped

(P-17018)
TRI-CNTIES ASSN FOR
DVLPMNTLLY
Also Called: Tri-Counties Regional Center
1146 Farmhouse Ln, San Luis Obispo
(93401-8362)
PHONE.................805 543-2833
Frank Bush, *Dir*
EMP: 101
SALES (corp-wide): 452.74MM **Privately Held**
Web: www.tri-counties.org
SIC: 8322 Association for the handicapped
PA: Tri-Counties Association For The
Developmentally Disabled, Inc.
520 E Montecito St

805 962-7881

(P-17019)
TURNING POINT MINISTRIES
Also Called: TURNING POINT COUNSELING
1370 Brea Blvd Ste 245, Fullerton
(92835-4173)
PHONE.................800 998-6329
TOLL FREE: 800
EMP: 73 EST: 1983
SQ FT: 2,500
SALES (est): 1.15MM **Privately Held**
Web: www.turningpointcounseling.org
SIC: 8322 Family counseling services

(P-17020)
UNITED CRBRAL PLSY ASSN
ORNGE
Also Called: Ucp of Orange County
1251 E Dyer Rd Ste 150, Santa Ana
(92705-5662)
PHONE.................949 333-6400
Ramin Baschshi, *CEO*
EMP: 400 EST: 1953
SQ FT: 5,000
SALES (est): 6.38MM **Privately Held**
Web: www.uptheimpact.org
SIC: 8322 Social service center

(P-17021)
UNITED CRBRAL PLSY ASSN
SAN LU
Also Called: Ride On Transportation
3620 Sacramento Dr Ste 201, San Luis
Obispo (93401-7215)
PHONE.................805 543-2039
Mark Shaffer, *Ex Dir*
EMP: 100 EST: 1991
SQ FT: 1,600
SALES (est): 6.02MM **Privately Held**
Web: www.ride-on.org
SIC: 8322 Social service center

(P-17022)
VALLEY VILLAGE (PA)
20830 Sherman Way, Winnetka
(91306-2707)
PHONE.................818 587-9450
Debra Donovan, *Ex Dir*
EMP: 75 EST: 1973
SQ FT: 14,000
SALES (est): 24.89MM
SALES (corp-wide): 24.89MM **Privately Held**
Web: www.valleyvillage.org
SIC: 8322 Individual and family services

(P-17023)
VINTAGE SENIOR
MANAGEMENT INC
2721 W Willow St, Durbank (91505-4544)
PHONE.................818 954-9500
Brian Flornes, *Brnch Mgr*
EMP: 832
Web: www.vintagehousing.com
SIC: 8322 Geriatric social service
PA: Senior Vintage Management Inc
23 Corporate Plaza Dr # 190

(P-17024)
VISTA CARE GROUP LLC (PA)
Also Called: Vista Gardens
1863 Devon Pl, Vista (92084-7624)
PHONE.................760 295-3900
Avelen Delgado, *Admn*
Harry Crowell, *
Joe Balbas, *
EMP: 80 EST: 2010
SALES (est): 5.12MM

PRODUCTS & SVCS

SALES (corp-wide): 5.12MM **Privately Held**
Web:
www.vistagardensmemorycare.com
SIC: 8322 Senior citizens' center or association

(P-17025)
VISTA HILL FOUNDATION
4125 Alpha St, San Diego (92113-4553)
PHONE..............................619 266-0166
EMP: 90
SALES (corp-wide): 38.47MM **Privately Held**
Web: www.vistahill.org
SIC: 8322 8051 Geriatric social service; Skilled nursing care facilities
PA: Vista Hill Foundation
8910 Clairemont Mesa Blvd
585 514-5100

(P-17026)
VITACARE PRESCRIPTION SVCS INC
Also Called: Vps
2701 Olympic Blvd, Santa Monica (90404-4183)
PHONE..............................800 350-3819
John Milligan, *CEO*
EMP: 437 **EST:** 2015
SALES (est): 1.27MM
SALES (corp-wide): 750.26MM **Publicly Held**
Web: www.goodrx.com
SIC: 8322 Individual and family services
PA: Goodrx Holdings, Inc.
2701 Olympic Blvd
855 268-2822

(P-17027)
VOLUNTEERS OF AMER LOS ANGELES
Also Called: Volunteers of America
1032 W 18th St, Los Angeles (90015-3324)
PHONE..............................213 749-0362
Ernest Green, *Dir*
EMP: 105
SALES (corp-wide): 87.55MM **Privately Held**
Web: www.voala.org
SIC: 8322 Social service center
PA: Volunteers Of America Of Los Angeles
3600 Wlshire Blvd Ste 150
213 389-1500

(P-17028)
VOLUNTEERS OF AMER LOS ANGELES
Also Called: Volunteers of America
10896 Lehigh Ave, Pacoima (91331-2584)
PHONE..............................818 834-9097
Paloma Cisneros, *Mgr*
EMP: 79
SALES (corp-wide): 87.55MM **Privately Held**
Web: www.voala.org
SIC: 8322 Social service center
PA: Volunteers Of America Of Los Angeles
3600 Wlshire Blvd Ste 150
213 389-1500

(P-17029)
VOLUNTEERS OF AMER LOS ANGELES
Also Called: Volunteers of America
522 N Dangler Ave, Los Angeles (90022-1218)
PHONE..............................323 780-3770
EMP: 80

SALES (corp-wide): 87.55MM **Privately Held**
Web: www.voala.org
SIC: 8322 Social service center
PA: Volunteers Of America Of Los Angeles
3600 Wlshire Blvd Ste 150
213 389-1500

(P-17030)
VOLUNTEERS OF AMER LOS ANGELES
Also Called: Volunteers of America
1760 W Cameron Ave Ste 104, West Covina (91790-2739)
PHONE..............................626 337-9878
EMP: 106
SALES (corp-wide): 87.55MM **Privately Held**
Web: www.voala.org
SIC: 8322 Social service center
PA: Volunteers Of America Of Los Angeles
3600 Wlshire Blvd Ste 150
213 389-1500

(P-17031)
VOLUNTEERS OF AMER LOS ANGELES
Also Called: Volunteers of America
25141 Avenida Rondel, Valencia (91355-3205)
PHONE..............................661 290-2829
EMP: 80
SALES (corp-wide): 87.55MM **Privately Held**
Web: www.voala.org
SIC: 8322 Social service center
PA: Volunteers Of America Of Los Angeles
3600 Wlshire Blvd Ste 150
213 389-1500

(P-17032)
VOLUNTEERS OF AMER LOS ANGELES
Also Called: Voa Plainview Head Start
10819 Plainview Ave, Tujunga (91042-1633)
PHONE..............................818 352-5974
EMP: 80
SALES (corp-wide): 87.55MM **Privately Held**
Web: www.voala.org
SIC: 8322 Social service center
PA: Volunteers Of America Of Los Angeles
3600 Wlshire Blvd Ste 150
213 389-1500

(P-17033)
VOLUNTEERS OF AMER LOS ANGELES
Also Called: Volunteers of America
6724 Tujunga Ave, North Hollywood (91606-1910)
PHONE..............................818 769-3617
EMP: 106
SALES (corp-wide): 87.55MM **Privately Held**
Web: www.voala.org
SIC: 8322 Social service center
PA: Volunteers Of America Of Los Angeles
3600 Wlshire Blvd Ste 150
213 389-1500

(P-17034)
VOLUNTEERS OF AMER LOS ANGELES
Also Called: Maud Booth Family Center
11243 Kittridge St, North Hollywood (91606-2605)
PHONE..............................818 506-0597

Felix Cruz, *Mgr*
EMP: 133
SALES (corp-wide): 87.55MM **Privately Held**
Web: www.voala.org
SIC: 8322 Social service center
PA: Volunteers Of America Of Los Angeles
3600 Wlshire Blvd Ste 150
213 389-1500

(P-17035)
VOLUNTEERS OF AMER LOS ANGELES
Also Called: Voa
515 E 6th St Fl 9, Los Angeles (90021-1009)
PHONE..............................213 627-8002
Jim Howat, *Dir*
EMP: 106
SQ FT: 15,346
SALES (corp-wide): 87.55MM **Privately Held**
Web: www.voala.org
SIC: 8322 Social service center
PA: Volunteers Of America Of Los Angeles
3600 Wlshire Blvd Ste 150
213 389-1500

(P-17036)
VOLUNTEERS OF AMER LOS ANGELES
Also Called: Volunteers of America
12550 Van Nuys Blvd, Pacoima (91331-1354)
PHONE..............................818 834-8957
Letecia Aguirre, *Prin*
EMP: 80
SALES (corp-wide): 87.55MM **Privately Held**
Web: www.voala.org
SIC: 8322 Social service center
PA: Volunteers Of America Of Los Angeles
3600 Wlshire Blvd Ste 150
213 389-1500

(P-17037)
VOLUNTEERS OF AMER LOS ANGELES
Also Called: Volunteers of America
334 Figueroa St, Wilmington (90744-4804)
PHONE..............................310 830-3404
EMP: 106
SALES (corp-wide): 87.55MM **Privately Held**
Web: www.voala.org
SIC: 8322 Social service center
PA: Volunteers Of America Of Los Angeles
3600 Wlshire Blvd Ste 150
213 389-1500

(P-17038)
VOLUNTEERS OF AMER LOS ANGELES
Also Called: Volunteers of America
2100 N Broadway Ste 300, Santa Ana (92706-2624)
PHONE..............................714 426-9834
EMP: 80
SALES (corp-wide): 87.55MM **Privately Held**
Web: www.voala.org
SIC: 8322 Social service center
PA: Volunteers Of America Of Los Angeles
3600 Wlshire Blvd Ste 150
213 389-1500

(P-17039)
WATTS LABOR COMMUNITY ACTION

Also Called: Wlcac
4142 Palmwood Dr Apt 11, Los Angeles (90008-2355)
PHONE..............................323 563-5639
Timothy Watkins, *CEO*
EMP: 163
SALES (corp-wide): 25.85MM **Privately Held**
Web: www.wlcac.org
SIC: 8322 7299 Social service center; Handyman service
PA: Watts Labor Community Action Committee
10950 S Central Ave
323 563-5639

(P-17040)
WEINGART CENTER ASSOCIATION
Also Called: Weingart Center For Homeless
566 S San Pedro St, Los Angeles (90013-2102)
PHONE..............................213 622-6359
Kevin Murray, *Pr*
Warren Loui, *
Tim Groff, *
EMP: 150 **EST:** 1984
SQ FT: 175,000
SALES (est): 29.86MM **Privately Held**
Web: www.weingart.org
SIC: 8322 Emergency social services

(P-17041)
WELLNEST EMTONAL HLTH WELLNESS (PA)
3031 S Vermont Ave, Los Angeles (90007-3033)
PHONE..............................323 373-2400
Charlene Dimas-peinado, *CEO*
EMP: 110 **EST:** 1924
SALES (est): 32.12MM
SALES (corp-wide): 32.12MM **Privately Held**
Web: www.wellnestla.org
SIC: 8322 Child guidance agency

(P-17042)
WISE & HEALTHY AGING
23388 Mulholland Dr Stop 60, Woodland Hills (91364-2733)
PHONE..............................818 876-1402
Grace Cheng Braun, *Prin*
Charles Hardie, *
Molly Davies, *
Phyllis Amaral, *
EMP: 70 **EST:** 1972
SALES (est): 362.26K **Privately Held**
Web: www.wiseandhealthyaging.org
SIC: 8322 Senior citizens' center or association

8331 Job Training And Related Services

(P-17043)
ABILITY COUNTS INC (PA)
775 Trademark Cir Ste 101, Corona (92879-2084)
PHONE..............................951 734-6595
Joyce Hearn, *CEO*
EMP: 99 **EST:** 1980
SQ FT: 28,000
SALES (est): 7.51MM
SALES (corp-wide): 7.51MM **Privately Held**
Web: www.abilitycounts.org
SIC: 8331 Sheltered workshop

▲ = Import ▼ = Export
◆ = Import/Export

(P-17044)
ADVOCACY FOR RSPECT CHICE - LO (PA)
Also Called: Hillside Entps - AR C Long Bch
4519 E Stearns St, Long Beach
(90815-2540)
PHONE..................................562 597-7716
Marion Lieberman, *CEO*
EMP: 81 **EST:** 1952
SQ FT: 35,000
SALES (est): 5.9MM
SALES (corp-wide): 5.9MM **Privately Held**
Web: www.powwowlongbeach.com
SIC: 8331 Sheltered workshop

(P-17045)
APPRENTICE JRNYMEN TRNING TR F
Also Called: COMPTON TRAINING CENTER
7850 Haskell Ave, Van Nuys (91406-1907)
PHONE..................................310 604-0892
Raymond Levangie Iii, *Ex Dir*
EMP: 222 **EST:** 1956
SALES (est): 30.36MM **Privately Held**
Web: www.ajtraining.edu
SIC: 8331 Job training services

(P-17046)
ARC LOS ANGELES & ORANGE CNTY (PA)
Also Called: Southeast Industries
12049 Woodruff Ave, Downey
(90241-5669)
PHONE..................................562 803-4606
Emilio Sosa, *CEO*
Brittany Javier Managing, *Prin*
EMP: 75 **EST:** 1962
SQ FT: 9,800
SALES (est): 2.08MM
SALES (corp-wide): 2.08MM **Privately Held**
Web: www.thearclaoc.org
SIC: 8331 5932 Skill training center; Used merchandise stores

(P-17047)
ASIAN REHABILITATION SVC INC
Also Called: ARS
312 N Spring St Ste B30, Los Angeles
(90012-3152)
PHONE..................................213 680-3790
George Allen, *Mgr*
EMP: 120
SALES (corp-wide): 2.25MM **Privately Held**
Web: www.asianrehab.org
SIC: 8331 Vocational rehabilitation agency
PA: Asian Rehabilitation Service, Inc.
750 E Green St Ste 301
562 632-1141

(P-17048)
BENEFITVISION INC
5550 Topanga Canyon Blvd, Woodland Hills
(91367-6478)
PHONE..................................818 348-3100
Terry Fuzue, *Brnch Mgr*
EMP: 75
SALES (corp-wide): 4.92MM **Privately Held**
Web: www.benefitvision.com
SIC: 8331 Job training and related services
PA: Benefitvision, Inc.
4522 Rfd
877 737-5526

(P-17049)
BEST OPPORTUNITIES INC
Also Called: BEST OPPORTUNITIES
22450 Headquarters Ave, Apple Valley
(92307-4304)
PHONE..................................760 628-0111
Karin Etheridge, *CEO*
Richard O'brien, *Pr*
EMP: 140 **EST:** 1981
SQ FT: 5,000
SALES (est): 6.4MM **Privately Held**
Web: www.bestopportunities.org
SIC: 8331 Vocational rehabilitation agency

(P-17050)
BUFFINI & COMPANY (PA)
6349 Palomar Oaks Ct, Carlsbad
(92011-1428)
PHONE..................................760 827-2100
Brian Buffini, *Ch Bd*
Beverly Buffini, *
EMP: 182 **EST:** 1995
SALES (est): 24.24MM **Privately Held**
Web: www.buffini.com
SIC: 8331 Job training services

(P-17051)
CALIFRNIA DEPT DVLPMENTAL SVCS
Also Called: Fairview Developmental Center
2501 Harbor Blvd, Costa Mesa
(92626-6179)
PHONE..................................714 957-5151
Bill Wilson, *Ex Dir*
EMP: 765
SALES (corp-wide): 534.4MM **Privately Held**
Web: dds.ca.gov
SIC: 8331 9431 8361 Job training and related services; Administration of public health programs; Residential care
HQ: California Department Of Developmental Services
1215 O St
Sacramento CA 95814

(P-17052)
CHINATOWN SERVICE CENTER (PA)
767 N Hill St Ste 400, Los Angeles
(90012-2381)
PHONE..................................213 808-1701
Peter Ng, *CEO*
Peter Ng, *Pr*
Lawrence Lue, *
Henry Kwong, *
Gloria Tang, *
EMP: 80 **EST:** 1975
SQ FT: 20,000
SALES (est): 14.7MM
SALES (corp-wide): 14.7MM **Privately Held**
Web: www.cscla.org
SIC: 8331 8322 8011 Job counseling; Family (marriage) counseling; Clinic, operated by physicians

(P-17053)
CITY OF SANTA ANA
Also Called: Santa Ana Job Training Program
1000 E Santa Ana Blvd Ste 107, Santa Ana
(92701-3900)
PHONE..................................714 647-6545
Judy Shenlee, *Mgr*
EMP: 80
SALES (corp-wide): 51.21MM **Privately Held**
Web: www.santa-ana.org
SIC: 8331 9111 Job training services; Mayors' office

HQ: City Of Santa Ana
20 Civic Center Plz Fl 8
Santa Ana CA 92701
714 647-5400

(P-17054)
CONSERVATION CORPS LONG BEACH
340 Nieto Ave, Long Beach (90814-1845)
PHONE..................................562 986-1249
Samara Ashley, *Prin*
Mike Bassett, *
Mario R Beas, *
EMP: 165 **EST:** 1987
SQ FT: 10,000
SALES (est): 6.78MM **Privately Held**
Web: www.cclb-corps.org
SIC: 8331 8322 Community service employment training program; Individual and family services

(P-17055)
COUNTY OF RIVERSIDE
Also Called: County Rvrside Wrkfrce Dev Div
1325 Spruce St Ste 400, Riverside
(92507-0506)
P.O. Box 553 (92502-0553)
PHONE..................................951 955-3434
Selicia Slournoy, *Dir*
EMP: 77
SALES (corp-wide): 5.07B **Privately Held**
Web: www.rivcoworkforce.org
SIC: 8331 9441 Skill training center; Administration of social and manpower programs
PA: County Of Riverside
4080 Lemon St Fl 11
951 955-1110

(P-17056)
EXCEPTIONAL CHLD FOUNDATION (PA)
Also Called: PAR SERVICES
5350 Machado Ln, Culver City
(90230-8800)
PHONE..................................310 204-3300
Veronica Arteaga, *Pr*
EMP: 120 **EST:** 1946
SQ FT: 45,000
SALES (est): 28.26MM
SALES (corp-wide): 28.26MM **Privately Held**
Web: www.ecf.net
SIC: 8331 Vocational training agency

(P-17057)
EXCEPTIONAL CHLD FOUNDATION
Also Called: Par Services
1430 Venice Blvd, Los Angeles
(90006-4818)
PHONE..................................213 748-3556
Nanette Cruz, *Prin*
EMP: 219
SALES (corp-wide): 28.26MM **Privately Held**
Web: www.ecf.net
SIC: 8331 Job training and related services
PA: Exceptional Children's Foundation
5350 Machado Ln
310 204-3300

(P-17058)
FOCUS ON INTERVENTION LLC
12612 Rue Sienne Nord, San Diego
(92131-2225)
PHONE..................................858 578-0769
EMP: 256
SALES (corp-wide): 1.75MM **Privately Held**

Web: www.briotix.com
SIC: 8331 Vocational rehabilitation agency
PA: Focus On Intervention, Llc
270f N El Cmino Real Ste
858 578-0769

(P-17059)
FONTANA RESOURCES AT WORK
9460 Sierra Ave, Fontana (92335-2411)
P.O. Box 848 (92334)
PHONE..................................909 428-3833
Joseph Varela, *Ex Dir*
EMP: 44 **EST:** 1965
SQ FT: 22,600
SALES (est): 1.73MM **Privately Held**
Web: www.industrial-support.org
SIC: 8331 3444 Vocational rehabilitation agency; Sheet metalwork

(P-17060)
GOODWILL INDS ORANGE CNTY CAL
Also Called: Goodwill Industries
5880 Edinger Ave, Huntington Beach
(92649-1705)
PHONE..................................714 881-3986
EMP: 95
SALES (corp-wide): 107.8MM **Privately Held**
Web: www.ocgoodwill.org
SIC: 8331 Job training and related services
PA: Goodwill Industries Of Orange County, California
410 N Fairview St
714 547-6308

(P-17061)
LINCOLN TRNING CTR RHBLTTION W
Also Called: Lincoln Training Center
2643 Loma Ave, South El Monte
(91733-1419)
PHONE..................................626 442-0621
Judith Angelo, *CEO*
Eric Brown, *
David Nelson, *Vice Chairman*
Judy Angelo, *
EMP: 85 **EST:** 1964
SQ FT: 30,000
SALES (est): 28.09MM **Privately Held**
Web: www.lincolntc.org
SIC: 8331 Vocational rehabilitation agency

(P-17062)
METROPLTAN AREA ADVSORY CMMTTE (PA)
Also Called: M A A C Project
1355 Third Ave, Chula Vista (91911-4302)
PHONE..................................619 426-3595
Arnulfo Manriquez, *CEO*
Antonio Pizano, *
Austin Foye, *
EMP: 100 **EST:** 1965
SQ FT: 820,000
SALES (est): 55.89MM
SALES (corp-wide): 55.89MM **Privately Held**
Web: www.maacproject.org
SIC: 8331 8351 8748 Job training services; Head Start center, except in conjunction with school; Energy conservation consultant

(P-17063)
OPTIONS FOR ALL INC
4250 Pacific Hwy, San Diego (92110-3216)
PHONE..................................858 565-9870
Richard Gutierrez, *CFO*
EMP: 426

SALES (corp-wide): 22.21MM **Privately Held**
Web: www.optionsforall.org
SIC: 8331 Job training and related services
PA: Options For All, Inc.
4250 Pacific Hwy
858 565-9870

(P-17064)
OWL EDUCATION AND TRAINING INC
2465 Campus Dr, Irvine (92612-1502)
PHONE...............................949 797-2000
Gregory J Burden, *Pr*
Stephen Seastrom, *
EMP: 183 EST: 2005
SQ FT: 22,800
SALES (est): 458.03K
SALES (corp-wide): 27.37MM **Privately Held**
Web: www.owlcompanies.com
SIC: 8331 Job training and related services
PA: Owl Companies
2465 Campus Dr
949 797-2000

(P-17065)
PACIFIC ASIAN CNSRTIUM IN EMPL (PA)
Also Called: P A C E
1055 Wilshire Blvd Ste 1475, Los Angeles (90017-5652)
PHONE...............................213 353-3982
Kerry N Doi, *Ex Dir*
EMP: 130 EST: 1976
SQ FT: 20,000
SALES (est): 34.98MM
SALES (corp-wide): 34.98MM **Privately Held**
Web: www.pacela.org
SIC: 8331 8322 7361 1521 Community service employment training program; Individual and family services; Labor contractors (employment agency); New construction, single-family houses

(P-17066)
SPECIAL SERVICE FOR GROUPS INC (PA)
Also Called: Special Service For Groups Ssg
905 E 8th St, Los Angeles (90021-1848)
PHONE...............................213 368-1888
Herbert K Hatanaka, *CEO*
Donna Wong, *
Donald A Kincey, *
EMP: 100 EST: 1952
SALES (est): 133.16MM
SALES (corp-wide): 133.16MM **Privately Held**
Web: www.ssg.org
SIC: 8331 8093 8399 Vocational rehabilitation agency; Mental health clinic, outpatient; Advocacy group

(P-17067)
ST MADELEINE SOPHIES CENTER
2119 E Madison Ave, El Cajon (92019-1111)
PHONE...............................619 442-5129
Debra Turner, *Ex Dir*
EMP: 70 EST: 1957
SQ FT: 13,092
SALES (est): 8.73MM **Privately Held**
Web: www.stmsc.org
SIC: 8331 Vocational training agency

(P-17068)
SUCCESS STRATEGIES INST INC
Also Called: Tom Ferry Your Coach
6 Hutton Centre Dr Ste 700, Santa Ana (92707-5735)
PHONE...............................949 721-6808
Thomas Ferry, *Pr*
EMP: 70 EST: 2005
SALES (est): 8.83MM **Privately Held**
Web: www.tomferry.com
SIC: 8331 Job training and related services

(P-17069)
VALLEY LGHT CTR FOR SCIAL ADVN
Also Called: Valley Light Industries
109 W 6th St, Azusa (91702-2875)
PHONE...............................626 337-6200
Sheryl Newman, *CEO*
EMP: 80 EST: 1970
SALES (est): 3.17MM **Privately Held**
Web: www.valleylight.org
SIC: 8331 Job training and related services

(P-17070)
VALLEY RESOURCE CENTER INC (PA)
Also Called: Valley Resource Center
1285 N Santa Fe St, Hemet (92543-1823)
PHONE...............................951 766-8659
Lee Trisler, *CEO*
EMP: 50 EST: 1979
SQ FT: 80,000
SALES (est): 8.09MM
SALES (corp-wide): 8.09MM **Privately Held**
Web: www.weexceed.org
SIC: 8331 2389 Vocational training agency; Apparel for handicapped

(P-17071)
VOCATIONAL IMPRV PROGRAM INC (PA)
9210 Rochester Ave, Rancho Cucamonga (91730-5521)
PHONE...............................909 483-5924
Wendy A Rogina, *CEO*
Rick Rogina, *
M Stephen Cho, *
Christopher J Mcardle, *Treas*
EMP: 90 EST: 1986
SQ FT: 23,000
SALES (est): 20.59MM **Privately Held**
Web: www.vipsolutions.com
SIC: 8331 Vocational rehabilitation agency

(P-17072)
VOCATIONAL VISIONS
26041 Pala, Mission Viejo (92691-2705)
PHONE...............................949 837-7280
Joan Mckinney, *CEO*
Kathryn Hebel, *
EMP: 170 EST: 1975
SQ FT: 17,000
SALES (est): 8.92MM **Privately Held**
Web: www.vocationalvisions.org
SIC: 8331 Sheltered workshop

(P-17073)
VTC ENTERPRISES (PA)
2445 A St, Santa Maria (93455-1401)
P.O. Box 1187 (93456-1187)
PHONE...............................805 928-5000
Jason Telander, *CEO*
Doctor Mark Malangko, *Pr*
Henry M Grennan, *
Lisa Walker, *
Cole Kinney, *
EMP: 96 EST: 1962

SQ FT: 21,093
SALES (est): 11.38MM
SALES (corp-wide): 11.38MM **Privately Held**
Web: www.vtc-sm.org
SIC: 8331 Vocational rehabilitation agency

(P-17074)
WESTVIEW SERVICES INC
Also Called: Westview Vocational Services
1655 S Euclid St Ste A, Anaheim (92802-2400)
PHONE...............................714 635-2444
Greg Gann, *CEO*
EMP: 81
SQ FT: 5,952
SALES (corp-wide): 12.13MM **Privately Held**
Web: www.westviewservices.org
SIC: 8331 Vocational rehabilitation agency
PA: Westview Services, Inc
10522 Katella Ave
714 517-6606

(P-17075)
WESTVIEW SERVICES INC
Also Called: Starlight Educational Center
9421 Edinger Ave, Westminster (92683-7426)
PHONE...............................714 418-2090
Lourdis Painter, *Prin*
EMP: 81
SQ FT: 3,775
SALES (corp-wide): 12.13MM **Privately Held**
Web: www.westviewservices.org
SIC: 8331 8244 Community service employment training program; Business and secretarial schools
PA: Westview Services, Inc
10522 Katella Ave
714 517-6606

(P-17076)
WESTVIEW SERVICES INC
1515 W Cameron Ave Ste 310, West Covina (91790-2726)
PHONE...............................626 962-0956
Patricia Stock, *Mgr*
EMP: 81
SALES (corp-wide): 12.13MM **Privately Held**
Web: www.westviewservices.org
SIC: 8331 5999 Job training and related services; Technical aids for the handicapped
PA: Westview Services, Inc
10522 Katella Ave
714 517-6606

(P-17077)
WESTVIEW SERVICES INC
Also Called: Westview Vocational Services
27576 Commerce Center Dr Ste 103, Temecula (92590-2537)
PHONE...............................951 699-0047
Mary Radecki, *Dir*
EMP: 81
SALES (corp-wide): 12.13MM **Privately Held**
Web: www.westviewservices.org
SIC: 8331 8322 Vocational rehabilitation agency; Social services for the handicapped
PA: Westview Services, Inc
10522 Katella Ave
714 517-6606

8351 Child Day Care Services

(P-17078)
CALIFORNIA CHILDRENS ACADEMY
Also Called: Early Learning Center
233 N Breed St, Los Angeles (90033-2902)
PHONE...............................323 263-3846
Monica Barahona, *Dir*
EMP: 144
Web: www.californiachildrensacademy.org
SIC: 8351 Preschool center
PA: California Children's Academy
2701 N Main St

(P-17079)
CALVARY CHURCH SANTA ANA INC
1010 N Tustin Ave, Santa Ana (92705-3598)
PHONE...............................714 973-4800
Pastor Michael Welles, *Prin*
Michael Welles, *Executive Pastor*
EMP: 160 EST: 1932
SQ FT: 133,000
SALES (est): 4.19MM **Privately Held**
Web: www.calvarylife.org
SIC: 8351 8661 Nursery school; Miscellaneous denomination church

(P-17080)
CAROUSEL CHILD CARE CORP
8333 Airport Blvd, Los Angeles (90045-4244)
PHONE...............................310 216-6641
Sandy Montano, *Brnch Mgr*
EMP: 103
SALES (corp-wide): 5.92MM **Privately Held**
Web: www.carouselschool.com
SIC: 8351 Preschool center
PA: Carousel Child Care Corporation
7899 La Tijera Blvd
310 645-9222

(P-17081)
CHILD CARE RESOURCE CENTER INC
Also Called: Volunteers America Head Start
454 S Kalisher St, San Fernando (91340-3535)
PHONE...............................818 837-0097
EMP: 191
SALES (corp-wide): 404.36MM **Privately Held**
Web: www.ccrcca.org
SIC: 8351 Child day care services
PA: Child Care Resource Center, Inc.
20001 Prairie St
818 717-1000

(P-17082)
CHILD DEVELOPMENT ASSOC INC
Also Called: Childrens Co
380 Telegraph Canyon Rd, Chula Vista (91910-6334)
PHONE...............................619 422-7115
Lili Torres, *Dir*
EMP: 213
SALES (corp-wide): 163.05MM **Privately Held**
Web: www.cdasd.org
SIC: 8351 Preschool center
PA: Child Development Associates, Incorporated
180 Otay Lakes Rd Ste 310
619 427-4411

(P-17083)

CHILD DEVELOPMENT INCORPORATED

Also Called: Turtle Rock Cdc
5151 Amalfi Dr, Irvine (92603-3443)
PHONE...............................949 854-5060
Mindy Ho, *Dir*
EMP: 363
SALES (corp-wide): 4.47MM **Privately Held**
Web: www.catalystkids.org
SIC: 8351 Preschool center
PA: Child Development Incorporated
350 Woodview Ave
408 556-7300

(P-17084)

CHILDRENS HOSPITAL ORANGE CNTY

500 Superior Ave, Newport Beach
(92663-3657)
PHONE...............................949 631-2062
EMP: 277
SALES (corp-wide): 1.55B **Privately Held**
Web: www.choc.org
SIC: 8351 Child day care services
PA: Children's Hospital Of Orange County
1201 W La Veta Ave
714 509-8300

(P-17085)

COMMUNITY ACTION PRTNR SAN LUI

Also Called: Day Care Center
805 Fiero Ln Ste A, San Luis Obispo
(93401-8911)
PHONE...............................805 541-2272
Sheri Wilson, *Dir*
EMP: 127
SALES (corp-wide): 104.15MM **Privately Held**
Web: www.capslo.org
SIC: 8351 Head Start center, except in
conjunction with school
PA: Community Action Partnership Of San
Luis Obispo County, Inc.
1030 Southwood Dr
805 544-4355

(P-17086)

COMMUNITY ACTION PRTNR SAN LUI (PA)

1030 Southwood Dr, San Luis Obispo
(93401-5813)
PHONE...............................805 544-4355
Anita Robinson, *Ch Bd*
Fran Coughon, *Vice Chairman*
Frances I Coughlin, *
Elizabeth Biz Steinberg, *
Santos Arrona, *
EMP: 72 **EST:** 1965
SQ FT: 20,000
SALES (est): 104.15MM
SALES (corp-wide): 104.15MM **Privately Held**
Web: www.capslo.org
SIC: 8351 Head Start center, except in
conjunction with school

(P-17087)

COMMUNITY DEV INST HEAD START

12988 Bowron Rd, Poway (92064-5790)
PHONE...............................858 668-2985
EMP: 294
SALES (corp-wide): 73.75MM **Privately Held**
Web: www.cditeam.org

SIC: 8351 Head Start center, except in
conjunction with school
PA: Community Development Institute
Head Start
10065 E Hrvard Ave Ste 70
720 747-5100

(P-17088)

DESERT SNDS UNFIED SCHL DST SC

Also Called: Early Childhood Education
47950 Dune Palms Rd, La Quinta
(92253-4000)
PHONE...............................760 777-4200
Debra Loukatos, *Prin*
EMP: 72
SALES (corp-wide): 646.48MM **Privately Held**
Web: www.dsusd.us
SIC: 8351 Preschool center
PA: Desert Sands Unified School District
School Building Corporation
47950 Dune Palms Dr
760 777-4200

(P-17089)

DREAM BIG CHILDRENS CENTER

612 S Myrtle Ave, Monrovia (91016-3406)
PHONE...............................626 239-0138
EMP: 70 **EST:** 2016
SALES (est): 1.93MM **Privately Held**
Web: www.dreambigchildren.com
SIC: 8351 Child day care services

(P-17090)

FAMILY CARE NETWORK INC (PA)

1255 Kendall Rd, San Luis Obispo
(93401-8750)
PHONE...............................805 503-6240
James Robert, *CEO*
Bobbie Boyer, *
Jonathan Nibbio, *
EMP: 71 **EST:** 1989
SQ FT: 2,600
SALES (est): 17.09MM
SALES (corp-wide): 17.09MM **Privately Held**
Web: www.fcni.org
SIC: 8351 Child day care services

(P-17091)

GARDEN GROVE UNIFIED SCHL DST

Also Called: Bryant Elementary School
8371 Orangewood Ave, Garden Grove
(92841-1517)
PHONE...............................714 663-6437
Sharon Hazelleaf, *Prin*
EMP: 117
SALES (corp-wide): 994.66MM **Privately Held**
Web: bryant.ggusd.us
SIC: 8351 Preschool center
PA: Garden Grove Unified School District
10331 Stanford Ave
714 663-6000

(P-17092)

HARMONIUM INC (PA)

Also Called: EPICENTRE
5440 Morehouse Dr Ste 1000, San Diego
(92121-6701)
PHONE...............................858 684-3080
Rosa Ana Lozada, *CEO*
Melinda Mallie, *
EMP: 150 **EST:** 1975
SALES (est): 11.84MM

SALES (corp-wide): 11.84MM **Privately Held**
Web: www.harmoniumsd.org
SIC: 8351 Preschool center

(P-17093)

LEPORT EDUCATIONAL INST INC

Also Called: Leport Schools
1 Technology Dr Bldg A, Irvine
(92618-2350)
PHONE...............................914 374-8860
Ramandeep S Girn, *CEO*
EMP: 255 **EST:** 2000
SALES (est): 2.66MM **Privately Held**
Web: www.leportschools.com
SIC: 8351 Montessori child development
center

(P-17094)

MARINE CORPS COMMUNITY SVCS

Also Called: Browne Child Development Ctr
202860 San Jacinto Rd, Oceanside
(92054)
PHONE...............................760 725-2817
Maria Langlie, *Dir*
EMP: 111
Web: www.usmc-mccs.org
SIC: 8351 9711 Child day care services;
Marine Corps
HQ: Marine Corps Community Services
3044 Catlin Ave
Quantico VA 22134
703 432-0109

(P-17095)

MARINE CORPS COMMUNITY SVCS

Also Called: San Onofre Child Care Center
Basilone Rd Bldg 51080, Camp Pendleton
(92055)
P.O. Box 555020 (92055-5020)
PHONE...............................760 725-7311
Kanoe Serguson, *Dir*
EMP: 111
Web: www.usmc-mccs.org
SIC: 8351 9711 Child day care services;
Marine Corps
HQ: Marine Corps Community Services
3044 Catlin Ave
Quantico VA 22134
703 432-0109

(P-17096)

MARYVALE DAY CARE CENTER

Also Called: Maryvale Edcatn Fmly Rsrce Ctr
2502 Huntington Dr, Duarte (91010-2221)
PHONE...............................626 357-1514
Steve Gunther, *Dir*
EMP: 122
SALES (corp-wide): 17.27MM **Privately Held**
Web: www.maryvale.org
SIC: 8351 Preschool center
PA: Maryvale Day Care Center
1050 Maryvale Drive
626 280-6511

(P-17097)

MOTION PICTURE AND TV FUND

Also Called: Samuel Goldwyn Child Care Ctr
2114 Pontius Ave, Los Angeles
(90025-5726)
PHONE...............................310 445-8993
Kae Connors, *Dir*
EMP: 95
SQ FT: 9,743
SALES (corp-wide): 29.84MM **Privately Held**

Web: www.mptf.com
SIC: 8351 Child day care services
PA: Motion Picture And Television Fund
23388 Mlhlland Dr Ste 200
818 876-1777

(P-17098)

MOUNTAIN VIEW CHILD CARE INC

Also Called: Totally Kids Spcalty Hlth Care
10716 La Tuna Canyon Rd, Sun Valley
(91352-2130)
PHONE...............................818 252-5863
Michelle Nydam, *Brnch Mgr*
EMP: 150
Web: www.totallykids.com
SIC: 8351 Child day care services
PA: Mountain View Child Care, Inc.
1720 Mountain View Ave

(P-17099)

MULBERRY CHILD CARE CTRS INC

10250 Kidd St, Riverside (92503-3413)
PHONE...............................951 688-4242
Cristy Martinez, *Mgr*
EMP: 70
SALES (corp-wide): 967.64MM **Privately Held**
SIC: 8351 Group day care center
HQ: Mulberry Child Care Centers, Inc.
990 Washington St Ste 104
Dedham MA 02026

(P-17100)

MULBERRY CHILD CARE CTRS INC

Also Called: Leport Montessori Academy
23721 La Palma Ave, Yorba Linda
(92887-5538)
PHONE...............................714 692-1111
Jennifer Mendoza, *Brnch Mgr*
EMP: 70
SALES (corp-wide): 967.64MM **Privately Held**
SIC: 8351 Group day care center
HQ: Mulberry Child Care Centers, Inc.
990 Washington St Ste 104
Dedham MA 02026

(P-17101)

NAVY EXCHANGE SERVICE COMMAND

Also Called: Naval Station Child Dev Ctr
2375 Recreation Way, San Diego
(92136-5518)
PHONE...............................619 556-7466
Phylis Williams, *Dir*
EMP: 98
Web: www.mynavyexchange.com
SIC: 8351 9711 Child day care services;
Navy
HQ: Navy Exchange Service Command
3280 Virginia Beach Blvd
Virginia Beach VA 23452
757 463-6200

(P-17102)

ONEGENERATION (PA)

Also Called: Onegenrtion Adult Dycare Chldc
17400 Victory Blvd, Van Nuys
(91406-5349)
PHONE...............................818 708-6625
Lawrence Gordon, *Ex Dir*
EMP: 73 **EST:** 1978
SALES (est): 9.09MM
SALES (corp-wide): 9.09MM **Privately Held**
Web: www.onegeneration.org

SIC: 8351 8322 Child day care services;
Senior citizens' center or association

(P-17103)
ORANGE COUNTY HEAD START INC (PA)
2501 Pullman St, Santa Ana (92705-5515)
P.O. Box 9269 (92728-9269)
PHONE.........................714 241-8920
Colleen Versteeg, *Ex Dir*
Loyal Sharp, *
EMP: 75 EST: 1965
SQ FT: 20,000
SALES (est): 40.1MM
SALES (corp-wide): 40.1MM **Privately Held**
Web: www.ochsinc.org
SIC: 8351 Head Start center, except in
conjunction with school

(P-17104)
PACIFIC CLINICS HEAD START
171 N Altadena Dr, Pasadena
(91107-7318)
PHONE.........................626 254-5000
Wassy Tesfa, *Ex Dir*
EMP: 130 EST: 2021
SALES (est): 919.62K **Privately Held**
Web: www.headstartprogram.us
SIC: 8351 Head Start center, except in
conjunction with school

(P-17105)
PEOPLES CARE INC
Also Called: PEOPLE'S CARE INC.
12215 Telegraph Rd Ste 208, Santa Fe
Springs (90670-3344)
PHONE.........................562 320-0174
Torres Cesaer, *Prin*
EMP: 138
SALES (corp-wide): 22.6MM **Privately Held**
Web: www.peoplescare.com
SIC: 8351 Child day care services
PA: Peoples Care Inc.
13920 City Center Dr # 290
855 773-6753

(P-17106)
PLAZA DE LA RAZA CHILD DEV SVC (PA)
13300 Crossroads Pkwy N Ste 440, La
Puente (91746-3440)
PHONE.........................562 776-1301
Anthony Rendon, *Ex Dir*
Rosalina Fine, *
EMP: 72 EST: 1965
SALES (est): 18.45MM
SALES (corp-wide): 18.45MM **Privately Held**
Web: www.plazadelaraza.info
SIC: 8351 Head Start center, except in
conjunction with school

(P-17107)
PLAZA DE LA RAZA CHILD DEVELOP
225 N Avenue 25, Los Angeles
(90031-1794)
PHONE.........................323 224-1788
EMP: 72
SALES (corp-wide): 18.45MM **Privately Held**
Web: www.plazadelaraza.info
SIC: 8351 Head Start center, except in
conjunction with school
PA: Plaza De La Raza Child Development
Services, Inc.
13300 Crssrads Pkwy N Ste

562 776-1301

(P-17108)
PLAZA DE LA RAZA CHILD DEVELOP
6411 Norwalk Blvd, Whittier (90606-1502)
PHONE.........................562 695-1070
Adriana Gonzalez, *Pr*
EMP: 71
SALES (corp-wide): 18.45MM **Privately Held**
Web: www.plazadelaraza.info
SIC: 8351 Head Start center, except in
conjunction with school
PA: Plaza De La Raza Child Development
Services, Inc.
13300 Crssrads Pkwy N Ste
562 776-1301

(P-17109)
PREGEL AMERICA INC
116 S Brent Cir, Walnut (91789-3050)
PHONE.........................909 598-8980
EMP: 115
SALES (corp-wide): 184.98MM **Privately Held**
Web: www.pregelamerica.com
SIC: 8351 5149 Child day care services;
Groceries and related products, nec
HQ: Pregel America, Inc.
4450 Fortune Ave Nw
Concord NC 28027
704 707-0300

(P-17110)
PRIME HEALTH CARE
Also Called: San Dimas Community Hospital
1350 W Covina Blvd, San Dimas
(91773-3245)
PHONE.........................909 394-2727
Prim Reddy, *Owner*
EMP: 80 EST: 2010
SALES (est): 4.44MM **Privately Held**
Web: www.primehealthcare.com
SIC: 8351 8062 Child day care services;
General medical and surgical hospitals

(P-17111)
TEMPLE JDEA OF W SAN FRNNDO VL
Also Called: Temple Judea Nursery School
5429 Lindley Ave, Tarzana (91356-3703)
PHONE.........................818 758-3800
Margie Ipp, *Dir*
EMP: 94
SALES (corp-wide): 1.8MM **Privately Held**
Web: www.templejudea.com
SIC: 8351 8661 Child day care services;
Synagogue
PA: Temple Judea Of The West San
Fernando Valley
5429 Lindley Ave
818 758-3800

(P-17112)
TENET HEALTHSYSTEM MEDICAL INC
555 E Hardy St, Inglewood (90301-4011)
P.O. Box 720 (90312-6720)
PHONE.........................310 673-4660
Steve Barker, *Brnch Mgr*
EMP: 93
SALES (corp-wide): 19.17B **Publicly Held**
Web: www.tenethealth.com
SIC: 8351 Child day care services
HQ: Tenet Healthsystem Medical, Inc.
14201 Dallas Pkwy
Dallas TX 75254
469 893-2000

(P-17113)
THINK TOGETHER
800 S Barranca Ave Ste 120, Covina
(91723-3680)
PHONE.........................626 373-2311
Tom Lopez, *Brnch Mgr*
EMP: 345
SALES (corp-wide): 75.71MM **Privately Held**
Web: www.thinktogether.org
SIC: 8351 Child day care services
PA: Think Together
2101 E 4th St #b-200
714 543-3807

(P-17114)
THINK TOGETHER
22620 Goldencrest Dr Ste 104, Moreno
Valley (92553-9032)
PHONE.........................951 571-9944
EMP: 345
SALES (corp-wide): 75.71MM **Privately Held**
Web: www.thinktogether.org
SIC: 8351 Child day care services
PA: Think Together
2101 E 4th St #b-200
714 543-3807

(P-17115)
THINK TOGETHER
202 E Airport Dr Ste 200, San Bernardino
(92408-3429)
PHONE.........................909 723-1400
EMP: 344
SALES (corp-wide): 75.71MM **Privately Held**
Web: www.thinktogether.org
SIC: 8351 Child day care services
PA: Think Together
2101 E 4th St #b-200
714 543-3807

(P-17116)
TUTOR TIME LEARNING CTRS LLC
5855 De Soto Ave, Woodland Hills
(91367-5202)
PHONE.........................818 710-1677
EMP: 163
Web: www.tutortime.com
SIC: 8351 Preschool center
HQ: Tutor Time Learning Centers, Llc
21333 Haggerty Rd Ste 300
Novi MI 48375
248 697-9000

(P-17117)
TUTOR TIME LEARNING CTRS LLC
5805 Corporate Ave, Cypress
(90630-4730)
PHONE.........................714 484-1000
Jennifer Gardea, *Dir*
EMP: 243
Web: www.tutortime.com
SIC: 8351 Preschool center
HQ: Tutor Time Learning Centers, Llc
21333 Haggerty Rd Ste 300
Novi MI 48375
248 697-9000

8361 Residential Care

(P-17118)
AEGIS SENIOR COMMUNITIES LLC
Also Called: Aegis of Laguna Niguel

32170 Niguel Rd, Laguna Niguel
(92677-4264)
PHONE.........................949 496-8080
Pamela Kerr, *Ex Dir*
EMP: 151
SALES (corp-wide): 137.42MM **Privately Held**
Web: www.aegisliving.com
SIC: 8361 Residential care
PA: Senior Aegis Communities Llc
415 118th Ave Se
866 688-5829

(P-17119)
ALLIANCE CHILDRENS SERVICES
Also Called: Mentor California
1001 Tower Way Ste 110, Bakersfield
(93309-1586)
PHONE.........................661 863-0350
Andretta Stokes, *Mgr*
EMP: 114
SALES (corp-wide): 979.67K **Privately Held**
SIC: 8361 Mentally handicapped home
PA: Alliance Children's Services Inc
313 Congress St Fl 5
617 790-4800

(P-17120)
ARDCORE SENIOR LIVING
Also Called: Canyon Hills Club
525 S Anaheim Hills Rd, Anaheim
(92807-4721)
PHONE.........................714 974-2226
J Bert Sprenger, *Mgr*
EMP: 352
Web: www.obayashi.co.jp
SIC: 8361 6513 Aged home; Apartment
building operators
PA: Obayashi Corporation
2-15-2, Konan

(P-17121)
ASCEND HEALTHCARE LLC
Also Called: Ascend Healthcare
11515 W Washington Blvd, Los Angeles
(90066-5913)
PHONE.........................310 598-1840
Joseph Essas, *Managing Member*
EMP: 86 EST: 2016
SALES (est): 16.07MM **Privately Held**
Web: www.ascendhc.com
SIC: 8361 Rehabilitation center, residential:
health care incidental

(P-17122)
AVANTGARDE SENIOR LIVING
5645 Lindley Ave, Tarzana (91356-2557)
PHONE.........................818 881-0055
Jason Adelman, *Prin*
EMP: 102 EST: 2010
SALES (est): 6.2MM **Privately Held**
Web: www.avantgardeseniorliving.com
SIC: 8361 Aged home

(P-17123)
BOYS REPUBLIC (PA)
Also Called: GIRLS REPUBLIC
1907 Boys Republic Dr, Chino Hills
(91709-5447)
PHONE.........................909 902-6690
Dennis Slattery, *CEO*
Timothy J Kay, *
Robert Key, *
Jeff Seymour, *
Nadine Bosen, *
EMP: 150 EST: 1907
SQ FT: 173,000
SALES (est): 21.75MM

SALES (corp-wide): 21.75MM **Privately
Held**
Web: www.boysrepublic.org
SIC: **8361** Group foster home

(P-17124)
BRITTANY HOUSE LLC
5401 E Centralia St, Long Beach
(90808-1494)
PHONE..................562 421-4717
Colleen Rosatti, *Ex Dir*
EMP: 199 EST: 1989
SQ FT: 43,018
SALES (est): 1.47MM
SALES (corp-wide): 29.14MM **Privately
Held**
Web: www.activcareliving.com
SIC: **8361** Aged home
PA: Activcare Living, Inc.
10603 Rancho Bernardo Rd
858 565-4424

(P-17125)
CALIFORNIA FRIENDS HOMES
Also Called: QUAKER GARDENS
12151 Dale Ave, Stanton (90680-3889)
PHONE..................714 530-9100
Randy Brown, *CEO*
Gina Kolb, *
Glenda Hementiza, *
EMP: 315 EST: 1962
SQ FT: 10,000
SALES (est): 18.84MM **Privately Held**
Web: www.rowntreegardens.org
SIC: **8361** 8051 Aged home; Convalescent
home with continuous nursing care

(P-17126)
CASA DE AMPARO (PA)
325 Buena Creek Rd, San Marcos
(92069-9679)
PHONE..................760 754-5500
Sharon Delphenich, *Ex Dir*
Tamara Fleck-myers, *Ex Dir*
Debbie Slattery, *
EMP: 74 EST: 1979
SQ FT: 25,000
SALES (est): 10.83MM
SALES (corp-wide): 10.83MM **Privately
Held**
Web: www.casadeamparo.org
SIC: **8361** 8351 Residential care; Child day
care services

(P-17127)
**CASA DE LAS CAMPANAS INC
(PA)**
18655 W Bernardo Dr, San Diego
(92127-3099)
PHONE..................858 451-9152
Jill Sorenson, *Ex Dir*
Robert L Reeves, *
David Johnson, *
EMP: 97 EST: 1988
SQ FT: 709,627
SALES (est): 43.84MM
SALES (corp-wide): 43.84MM **Privately
Held**
Web: www.casadelascampanas.com
SIC: **8361** 8052 8051 6513 Aged home;
Intermediate care facilities; Skilled nursing
care facilities; Apartment building operators

(P-17128)
CASA-PACIFICA INC
Also Called: Freedom Properties
2200 W Acacia Ave Ofc, Hemet
(92545-3737)
PHONE..................951 658-3369
Mary Ann Casino, *Dir*

EMP: 251
SALES (corp-wide): 17.83MM **Privately
Held**
Web: www.casapacifica.org
SIC: **8361** 8059 Geriatric residential care;
Rest home, with health care
PA: Casa-Pacifica, Inc
23442 El Toro Rd
949 489-0430

(P-17129)
CASA-PACIFICA INC
Also Called: Freedom Properties Village
2400 W Acacia Ave, Hemet (92545-3743)
PHONE..................951 766-5116
Valeria Machain, *Genl Mgr*
EMP: 251
SALES (corp-wide): 17.83MM **Privately
Held**
Web: www.casapacifica.org
SIC: **8361** 8052 8051 6513 Aged home;
Intermediate care facilities; Skilled nursing
care facilities; Apartment building operators
PA: Casa-Pacifica, Inc
23442 El Toro Rd
949 489-0430

(P-17130)
CHILDHELP INC
Also Called: Child Help Head Start Center
14700 Manzanita Rd, Beaumont
(92223-3026)
P.O. Box 247 (92223-0247)
PHONE..................951 845-6737
Klara Pakózdi, *Mgr*
EMP: 126
SALES (corp-wide): 41.46MM **Privately
Held**
Web: www.childhelp.org
SIC: **8361** Children's home
PA: Childhelp, Inc.
6730 N Scttsdale Rd Ste 1
480 922-8212

(P-17131)
CLIFF VIEW TERRACE INC
Also Called: Mission Terrace
623 W Junipero St, Santa Barbara
(93105-4213)
PHONE..................805 682-7443
Eve Murphy, *Mgr*
EMP: 83
SALES (corp-wide): 5.77MM **Privately
Held**
Web: www.missionterracesb.com
SIC: **8361** 8051 Aged home; Convalescent
home with continuous nursing care
PA: Cliff View Terrace, Inc.
1020 Cliff Dr
805 963-7556

(P-17132)
**COLLWOOD TER STELLAR
CARE INC**
4518 54th St, San Diego (92115-3527)
PHONE..................619 287-2920
Chris Cho, *Pr*
EMP: 90 EST: 2008
SALES (est): 1.24MM **Privately Held**
Web: www.stellarcaresd.com
SIC: **8361** Aged home

(P-17133)
**COMMUNITY ACTION PARTNR
KERN**
1611 1st St, Bakersfield (93304-2901)
PHONE..................661 336-5300
Aniko Matis, *Dir*
EMP: 71
SALES (corp-wide): 117.9MM **Privately
Held**

Web: www.capk.org
SIC: **8361** Rehabilitation center, residential;
health care incidental
PA: Community Action Partnership Of Kern
1300 18th St
661 336-5236

(P-17134)
COMPASS HEALTH INC
Also Called: Wyndham Residence
222 S Elm St, Arroyo Grande (93420-6012)
PHONE..................805 474-7260
Mark Woolpert, *Pr*
EMP: 155
Web: www.wyndhamresidence.com
SIC: **8361** Aged home
PA: Compass Health, Inc.
200 S 13th St Ste 208

(P-17135)
CORECARE III
Also Called: Morningside of Fullerton
800 Morningside Dr, Fullerton (92835-3597)
PHONE..................714 256-8000
Carl Wilkins, *Admn*
EMP: 130 EST: 1989
SQ FT: 24,000
SALES (est): 10.49MM **Privately Held**
Web: www.morningsideoffullerton.com
SIC: **8361** 8052 Aged home; Intermediate
care facilities

(P-17136)
**COUNSELING AND RESEARCH
ASSOC (PA)**
Also Called: MASADA HOMES
108 W Victoria St, Gardena (90248-3523)
P.O. Box 47001 (90247-6801)
PHONE..................310 715-2020
George Igi, *Ex Dir*
Bernard Smith, *
EMP: 125 EST: 1966
SQ FT: 2,500
SALES (est): 19.04MM
SALES (corp-wide): 19.04MM **Privately
Held**
Web: www.masadahomes.org
SIC: **8361** Children's home

(P-17137)
COUNTY OF LOS ANGELES
1605 Eastlake Ave, Los Angeles
(90033-1009)
PHONE..................323 226-8611
Richard Shumsky, *Mgr*
EMP: 91
Web: www.lacounty.gov
SIC: **8361** 9111 Juvenile correctional facilities
; Executive offices
PA: County Of Los Angeles
500 W Temple St Ste 437
213 974-1101

(P-17138)
COUNTY OF LOS ANGELES
Also Called: San Fernando Juvenile Hall
16350 Filbert St, Sylmar (91342-1002)
PHONE..................818 364-2011
Dan Torres, *Superintnt*
EMP: 71
Web: www.lacounty.gov
SIC: **8361** 9223 8093 Juvenile correctional
home; Correctional institutions; Mental
health clinic, outpatient
PA: County Of Los Angeles
500 W Temple St Ste 437
213 974-1101

(P-17139)
COUNTY OF SAN DIEGO
Also Called: Health & Human Svcs
1255 Imperial Ave Ste 433, San Diego
(92101-7404)
PHONE..................619 338-2558
Shirley Downs, *Brnch Mgr*
EMP: 103
Web: www.sandiegocounty.gov
SIC: **8361** 9441 Aged home; Administration
of social and manpower programs
PA: County Of San Diego
1600 Pacific Hwy Ste 209
619 531-5880

(P-17140)
COVENANT HOUSE CALIFORNIA
Also Called: CHC
1325 N Western Ave, Hollywood
(90027-5615)
PHONE..................323 461-3131
Luz Juan, *CEO*
George Lozano, *
Patrick S Mccabe, *Ex Dir*
EMP: 150 EST: 1986
SQ FT: 16,000
SALES (est): 22.33MM **Privately Held**
Web: www.covenanthousecalifornia.org
SIC: **8361** Children's home

(P-17141)
COVENANT LIVING WEST
Also Called: Covenant Living At Mt Miguel
325 Kempton St, Spring Valley
(91977-5810)
PHONE..................619 931-1114
Thad Rothrock, *Mgr*
EMP: 80
Web: www.covlivingmountmiguel.org
SIC: **8361** Aged home
HQ: Covenant Living West
5700 Old Orchrd Rd Ste 10
Skokie IL 60077

(P-17142)
COVENANT LIVING WEST
Also Called: Covenant Living At Samarkand
2550 Treasure Dr, Santa Barbara
(93105-4148)
PHONE..................805 687-0701
Kenneth D Noreen, *Admn*
EMP: 80
Web: www.covlivingsamarkand.org
SIC: **8361** 8059 Aged home; Rest home,
with health care
HQ: Covenant Living West
5700 Old Orchrd Rd Ste 10
Skokio IL 60077

(P-17143)
**CRESTWOOD BEHAVIORAL
HLTH INC**
Also Called: 1170 Lompoc Mhrc
303 S C St, Lompoc (93436-7305)
PHONE..................805 308-8720
Charlotte Acosta, *Admn*
EMP: 85
SALES (corp-wide): 278.96MM **Privately
Held**
Web:
www.crestwoodbehavioralhealth.com
SIC: **8361** Residential care
PA: Crestwood Behavioral Health, Inc.
520 Capitol Mall Ste 800
209 955-2326

(P-17144)
CRI-HELP INC (PA)
Also Called: Cri Help Drug Rehabilitation
11027 Burbank Blvd, North Hollywood
(91601-2431)

PRODUCTS & SVCS

P.O. Box 899 (91603-0899)
PHONE.................................818 985-8323
Jack Bernstein, *Pr*
Markus Sola, *
Anthony Edmonson, *
EMP: 71 **EST:** 1971
SQ FT: 40,000
SALES (est): 10.37MM
SALES (corp-wide): 10.37MM **Privately Held**
Web: www.cri-help.org
SIC: 8361 8069 Rehabilitation center, residential: health care incidental; Drug addiction rehabilitation hospital

(P-17145)
DAVID AND MARGARET HOME INC
Also Called: DAVID & MARGARET YOUTH AND FAM
1350 3rd St, La Verne (91750-5299)
PHONE.................................909 596-5921
Arun Tolia, *Pr*
Cindy Walkenbach, *
Charles C Rich, *
Timothy Evans, *
Sabina Sullivan, *
EMP: 240 **EST:** 1910
SQ FT: 40,000
SALES (est): 16.38MM **Privately Held**
Web: www.davidandmargaret.org
SIC: 8361 8322 Emotionally disturbed home; Individual and family services

(P-17146)
DEVELPMNTAL SVCS CONTINUUM INC
7944 Golden Ave, Lemon Grove (91945-1810)
PHONE.................................619 460-7333
Elaine Lewis, *Pr*
EMP: 75 **EST:** 1982
SALES (est): 4.91MM **Privately Held**
SIC: 8361 Group foster home

(P-17147)
E R I T INC (PA)
Also Called: TERI COMMON GROUNDS CAFE & COF
251 Airport Rd, Oceanside (92058-1201)
PHONE.................................760 433-6024
Cheryl Kilmer, *Ex Dir*
William E Mara, *
EMP: 85 **EST:** 1980
SQ FT: 15,000
SALES (est): 28.9MM
SALES (corp-wide): 28.9MM **Privately Held**
Web: www.teriinc.org
SIC: 8361 Retarded home

(P-17148)
ENCOMPASS HEALTH CORPORATION
Also Called: HealthSouth
5001 Commerce Dr, Bakersfield (93309-0648)
PHONE.................................661 323-5500
Rosa Arriola, *Mgr*
EMP: 72
SALES (corp-wide): 4.8B **Publicly Held**
Web: www.encompasshealth.com
SIC: 8361 8069 Rehabilitation center, residential: health care incidental; Specialty hospitals, except psychiatric
PA: Encompass Health Corporation
9001 Liberty Pkwy
205 967-7116

(P-17149)
ENCORE SENIOR LIVING III LLC
Also Called: Sierra Vista
13815 Rodeo Dr Ofc, Victorville (92395-5648)
PHONE.................................760 243-2271
Jana Herrera, *Admn*
EMP: 84
Web: www.sierravistaseniorliving.com
SIC: 8361 Aged home
PA: Encore Senior Living Iii, Llc
400 Locust St Ste 820

(P-17150)
ENSIGN GROUP INC
1405 E Main St, Santa Maria (93454-4801)
PHONE.................................805 925-8713
Shawn Taylor, *Brnch Mgr*
EMP: 380
SALES (corp-wide): 3.73B **Publicly Held**
Web: www.santamariaterrace.net
SIC: 8361 6513 Geriatric residential care; Retirement hotel operation
PA: The Ensign Group Inc
29222 Rncho Vejo Rd Ste 1
949 487-9500

(P-17151)
EVOLVE GROWTH INITIATIVES LLC
Also Called: Evolve Treatment Centers
820 Moraga Dr, Los Angeles (90049-1632)
PHONE.................................424 281-5000
Menachem Baron, *CEO*
EMP: 148 **EST:** 2014
SQ FT: 1,700
SALES (est): 3.02MM **Privately Held**
Web: www.evolvetreatment.com
SIC: 8361 8093 Rehabilitation center, residential: health care incidental; Mental health clinic, outpatient

(P-17152)
FIVE ACRES - THE BYS GRLS AID
Also Called: FIVE ACRES
760 Mountain View St, Altadena (91001-4925)
PHONE.................................626 798-6793
Chanel W Boutakidis, *CEO*
Daniel Braun, *
Cathy Clement, *OF PHILANTHROPHY*
Robert A Ketch, *Executive Director Emeritus*
Kim Hutchigs, *
EMP: 419 **EST:** 1888
SQ FT: 70,000
SALES (est): 40.79MM **Privately Held**
Web: www.5acres.org
SIC: 8361 8322 8211 Children's home; Public welfare center; Public combined elementary and secondary school

(P-17153)
FLORENCE CRTTNTON SVCS ORNGE C
Also Called: CRITTENTON SERVICES FOR CHILDR
801 E Chapman Ave Ste 203, Fullerton (92831-3846)
P.O. Box 9 (92836-0009)
PHONE.................................714 680-9000
Joyce Capelle, *CEO*
EMP: 320 **EST:** 1966
SALES (est): 37.78MM **Privately Held**
Web: www.crittentonsocal.org
SIC: 8361 Residential care for children

(P-17154)
FRONT PORCH COMMUNITIES & SVCS
Also Called: Carlsbad By The Sea
2855 Carlsbad Blvd, Carlsbad (92008-2902)
PHONE.................................760 729-4983
Tim Wetzel, *Brnch Mgr*
EMP: 149
Web: www.frontporch.net
SIC: 8361 Aged home
PA: Front Porch Communities And Services
800 N Brand Blvd Fl 19

(P-17155)
FRONT PORCH COMMUNITIES & SVCS
Also Called: Kingsley Manor
1055 N Kingsley Dr, Los Angeles (90029-1207)
PHONE.................................323 661-1128
Cindy Gonzales, *Prin*
EMP: 136
SQ FT: 106,521
Web: www.frontporch.net
SIC: 8361 Aged home
PA: Front Porch Communities And Services
800 N Brand Blvd Fl 19

(P-17156)
GOOD SHEPHERD LUTHERAN HM OF W
2949 Alamo St, Simi Valley (93063-2185)
PHONE.................................805 526-2482
Brian Dietrich, *Prin*
EMP: 135
SALES (corp-wide): 2.61MM **Privately Held**
Web: www.gsls-simi.com
SIC: 8361 8059 Residential care for the handicapped; Personal care home, with health care
PA: Good Shepherd Lutheran Home Of The West
24800 Chrisanta Dr # 250
559 791-2000

(P-17157)
HAMBURGER HOME (PA)
Also Called: AVIVA FAMILY & CHILDREN'S SERV
7120 Franklin Ave, Los Angeles (90046-3002)
PHONE.................................323 876-0550
Regina Bette, *Pr*
EMP: 90 **EST:** 1915
SQ FT: 25,000
SALES (est): 16.84MM
SALES (corp-wide): 16.84MM **Privately Held**
Web: www.aviva.org
SIC: 8361 Children's home

(P-17158)
HARBOR HEALTH CARE INC
9461 Flower St, Bellflower (90706-5705)
PHONE.................................562 866-7054
Cheryl Hutchins, *Pr*
EMP: 200 **EST:** 1999
SALES (est): 9.36MM **Privately Held**
Web: www.harborhealthcare.org
SIC: 8361 Mentally handicapped home

(P-17159)
HATHAWY-SYCMRES CHILD FMLY SVC
840 N Avenue 66, Los Angeles (90042-1508)
PHONE.................................323 257-9600

Jim Cheney, *Pr*
EMP: 121
SALES (corp-wide): 62.46MM **Privately Held**
Web: www.sycamores.org
SIC: 8361 8093 Emotionally disturbed home; Mental health clinic, outpatient
PA: Hathaway-Sycamores Child And Family Services
100 W Walnut St Ste 375
626 395-7100

(P-17160)
HAYNES FAMILY PROGRAMS INC
Also Called: LEROY HAYNES CENTER
233 Baseline Rd, La Verne (91750-2353)
P.O. Box 400 (91750-0400)
PHONE.................................909 593-2581
Daniel Maydeck, *Pr*
Tony Williams, *
Frank Linebaugh, *
EMP: 125 **EST:** 1946
SQ FT: 72,466
SALES (est): 18.89MM **Privately Held**
Web: www.leroyhaynes.org
SIC: 8361 8211 8099 Boys' towns; Specialty education; Medical services organization

(P-17161)
HEALTHVIEW INC (PA)
Also Called: Harbor View House
921 S Beacon St, San Pedro (90731-3740)
PHONE.................................310 638-4113
Susan Jane Major, *CEO*
EMP: 135 **EST:** 1965
SQ FT: 110,000
SALES (est): 4.73MM
SALES (corp-wide): 4.73MM **Privately Held**
Web: www.hvi.com
SIC: 8361 8052 Mentally handicapped home ; Home for the mentally retarded, with health care

(P-17162)
HOLLENBECK PALMS
Also Called: HOLLENBECK HOME FOR THE AGED
24431 Lyons Ave Apt 336, Newhall (91321-2360)
PHONE.................................323 263-6195
William G Heideman Junior, *Pr*
Johnny Young, *Contrlr*
Morris Shockley, *VP*
EMP: 170 **EST:** 1890
SALES (est): 25.02MM **Privately Held**
Web: www.hollenbeckpalms.com
SIC: 8361 Aged home

(P-17163)
HOME GUIDING HANDS CORPORATION (PA)
1908 Friendship Dr, El Cajon (92020-1129)
PHONE.................................619 938-2850
Mark Klaus, *CEO*
Carol A Fitzgibbons, *
Jan Adams, *
EMP: 266 **EST:** 1961
SALES (est): 31.62MM
SALES (corp-wide): 31.62MM **Privately Held**
Web: www.guidinghands.org
SIC: 8361 8052 Residential care for the handicapped; Intermediate care facilities

(P-17164)
HOPE HSE FOR MLTPLE HNDCPPED I (PA)

▲ = Import ▼ = Export
◆ = Import/Export

Also Called: Schmitt House
4215 Peck Rd, El Monte (91732-2113)
PHONE...................................626 443-1313
D Bernstein, *Ex Dir*
David Bernstein, *
EMP: 100 EST: 1963
SQ FT: 15,000
SALES (est): 4.54MM
SALES (corp-wide): 4.54MM **Privately
Held**
Web: www.hopehouse.org
SIC: 8361 Residential care for the
handicapped

(P-17165)
HUMANGOOD SOCAL
Also Called: Buena Vista Manor
802 Buena Vista St, Duarte (91010-1702)
PHONE...................................626 359-8141
Judy Phornkein, *Mgr*
EMP: 155
SALES (corp-wide): 31.22MM **Privately
Held**
Web: www.humangood.org
SIC: 8361 Aged home
HQ: Humangood Socal
1900 Huntington Dr
Duarte CA 91010
925 924-7138

(P-17166)
HUMANGOOD SOCAL
Also Called: Redwood Senior Homes & Svcs
710 W 13th Ave, Escondido (92025-5511)
PHONE...................................760 747-4306
Gary Boriero, *Mgr*
EMP: 266
SQ FT: 8,552
SALES (corp-wide): 31.22MM **Privately
Held**
Web: www.humangood.org
SIC: 8361 Aged home
HQ: Humangood Socal
1900 Huntington Dr
Duarte CA 91010
925 924-7138

(P-17167)
HUMANGOOD SOCAL
Also Called: White Sands of La Jolla Clinic
7450 Olivetas Ave Ofc, La Jolla
(92037-4900)
PHONE...................................858 454-4201
Wendy Matalon, *Brnch Mgr*
EMP: 266
SALES (corp-wide): 31.22MM **Privately
Held**
Web: www.humangood.org
SIC: 8361 8051 Aged home; Skilled nursing
care facilities
HQ: Humangood Socal
1900 Huntington Dr
Duarte CA 91010
925 924-7138

(P-17168)
INDEPENDENT OPTIONS INC
5095 Murphy Canyon Rd, San Diego
(92123-4346)
PHONE...................................858 598-5260
EMP: 115
SALES (corp-wide): 15.69MM **Privately
Held**
Web: www.independentoptions.org
SIC: 8361 Mentally handicapped home
PA: Independent Options, Inc.
391 Corporate Terrace Cir # 102
951 279-2585

(P-17169)
INDEPENDENT OPTIONS INC
2625 Sherwood Ave, Fullerton
(92831-1418)
PHONE...................................714 738-4991
P Dennis Mattson, *Pr*
EMP: 91
SALES (corp-wide): 15.69MM **Privately
Held**
Web: www.independentoptions.org
SIC: 8361 8059 Mentally handicapped home
; Personal care home, with health care
PA: Independent Options, Inc.
391 Corporate Terrace Cir # 102
951 279-2585

(P-17170)
ISL EMPLOYEES INC
Also Called: Integral Senior Living
2333 State St Ste 300, Carlsbad
(92008-1691)
PHONE...................................760 547-2863
Sue Farrow, *CEO*
Tracee Degrande, *
Collette Valentine, *
EMP: 71 EST: 2011
SALES (est): 8.57MM **Privately Held**
Web: www.islllc.com
SIC: 8361 Residential care

(P-17171)
LAMP INC
Also Called: Lamp Community
2116 Arlington Ave Lbby, Los Angeles
(90018-1365)
PHONE...................................213 488-9559
Donna Gallup, *CEO*
Kim Carson, *
EMP: 110 EST: 1985
SQ FT: 4,500
SALES (est): 3.21MM **Privately Held**
Web: www.shopgreyarea.com
SIC: 8361 Residential care for the
handicapped

(P-17172)
LAS VILLAS DEL NORTE
1325 Las Villas Way, Escondido
(92026-1946)
PHONE...................................760 741-1047
Jolene M Farish, *Ex Dir*
EMP: 180 EST: 1989
SALES (est): 2.78MM **Privately Held**
Web:
www.lasvillasdelnorteseniorliving.com
SIC: 8361 8051 Geriatric residential care;
Skilled nursing care facilities

(P-17173)
LEISURE CARE LLC
Also Called: Wellington Crt Asscted Lving C
601 Sunset Blvd, Arcadia (91007-6310)
PHONE...................................626 447-0106
Tamara Pribble, *Mgr*
EMP: 104
SALES (corp-wide): 305.08K **Privately
Held**
Web: www.leisurecare.com
SIC: 8361 Aged home
HQ: Leisure Care, Llc
999 3rd Ave Ste 4550
Seattle WA 98104
206 436-7827

(P-17174)
LEISURE CARE LLC
Also Called: Nohl Ranch Inn
380 S Anaheim Hills Rd Ofc, Anaheim
(92807-4062)
PHONE...................................714 974-1616

Wanda Reynolds, *Brnch Mgr*
EMP: 131
SQ FT: 82,222
SALES (corp-wide): 305.08K **Privately
Held**
Web: www.leisurecare.com
SIC: 8361 8051 Aged home; Skilled nursing
care facilities
HQ: Leisure Care, Llc
999 3rd Ave Ste 4550
Seattle WA 98104
206 436-7827

(P-17175)
LONGWOOD MANAGEMENT
CORP
Also Called: Rosecrans Villa
14110 Cordary Ave, Hawthorne
(90250-8005)
PHONE...................................310 675-9163
Boris Blumkin, *Mgr*
EMP: 76
SALES (corp-wide): 41.31MM **Privately
Held**
Web: www.longwoodmgmt.com
SIC: 8361 Aged home
PA: Longwood Management Llc
4032 Wilshire Blvd Fl 6
213 389-6900

(P-17176)
LOS ANGELES MISSION INC
(PA)
303 E 5th St, Los Angeles (90013-1505)
P.O. Box 55900 (90055)
PHONE...................................213 629-1227
Troy Vaughn, *CEO*
Herb Smith, *
Steve Kennedy, *
EMP: 77 EST: 1977
SALES (est): 21.51MM
SALES (corp-wide): 21.51MM **Privately
Held**
Web: www.losangelesmission.org
SIC: 8361 Destitute home

(P-17177)
LOS ANGELES RESIDENTIAL
COMM F
29890 Bouquet Canyon Rd, Santa Clarita
(91390-5111)
PHONE...................................661 296-8636
Kathy Sturky, *Ex Dir*
EMP: 85 EST: 1959
SQ FT: 5,000
SALES (est): 1.92MM **Privately Held**
Web: www.larcfoundation.org
SIC: 8361 8322 8051 Mentally handicapped
home; Individual and family services;
Skilled nursing care facilities

(P-17178)
MARYVALE
7600 Graves Ave, Rosemead (91770-3453)
P.O. Box 1039 (91770-1000)
PHONE...................................626 280-6510
Steve Gunter, *CEO*
EMP: 156 EST: 2011
SALES (est): 16.3MM **Privately Held**
Web: www.maryvale.org
SIC: 8361 8322 Residential care for children;
Public welfare center

(P-17179)
MCKINLEY CHILDRENS CENTER
INC (PA)
180 Via Verde Ste 200, San Dimas
(91773-3993)
PHONE...................................909 599-1227

Anil Vadatary, *CEO*
Michael Frazer, *
EMP: 190 EST: 1890
SALES (est): 36.19MM
SALES (corp-wide): 36.19MM **Privately
Held**
Web: www.mckinleycc.org
SIC: 8361 8211 Boys' towns; Private
elementary and secondary schools

(P-17180)
MEADOWBROOK VLG CHRSTN
RTRMENT
100 Holland Gln, Escondido (92026-1354)
PHONE...................................760 746-2500
Jacob Bronwer, *Pr*
Sarah Rogh, *
EMP: 109 EST: 2004
SALES (est): 10.79MM **Privately Held**
Web: www.meadowbrookvillage.org
SIC: 8361 Aged home

(P-17181)
MONTE VISTA GROVE HOMES
2889 San Pasqual St, Pasadena
(91107-5364)
PHONE...................................626 796-6135
M Helen Baatz, *Ex Dir*
EMP: 85 EST: 1924
SQ FT: 12,000
SALES (est): 8.53MM **Privately Held**
Web: www.mvgh.org
SIC: 8361 Aged home

(P-17182)
MORNINGSTAR SENIOR MGT
LLC
Also Called: Morningstar of Mission Viejo
28570 Marguerite Pkwy, Mission Viejo
(92692-3713)
PHONE...................................949 298-3675
Dyan Summerell, *Ex Dir*
EMP: 117
SALES (corp-wide): 95.1MM **Privately
Held**
Web: www.morningstarseniorliving.com
SIC: 8361 Residential care
PA: Morningstar Senior Management, Llc
7887 E Belleview Ave
303 750-5522

(P-17183)
NATIONAL MENTOR HOLDINGS
INC
Also Called: Horrigan Cole Enterprises
30033 Technology Dr, Murrieta
(92563-3520)
PHONE...................................951 677-1453
EMP: 636
SALES (corp-wide): 345.57MM **Privately
Held**
Web: www.sevitahealth.com
SIC: 8361 Residential care
HQ: National Mentor Holdings, Inc.
1 Batterymarch Park
Quincy MA 02169
617 790-4800

(P-17184)
NURSECORE MANAGEMENT
SVCS LLC
1010 S Broadway Ste A, Santa Maria
(93454-6600)
PHONE...................................805 938-7660
Veronica Aburto, *Brnch Mgr*
EMP: 551
Web: www.nursecore.com

SIC: **8361** 8082 8049 7361 Residential care; Home health care services; Nurses and other medical assistants; Nurses' registry
PA: Nursecore Management Services, Llc
2201 Brookhllw Plz Dr # 450

(P-17185)
OLIVE CREST (PA)
Also Called: OLIVE CREST
2130 E 4th St Ste 200, Santa Ana (92705-3818)
PHONE...............................714 543-5437
Donald A Verleur, *CEO*
Lois Verleur, *
EMP: 300 EST: 1973
SQ FT: 40,000
SALES (est): 80.16MM
SALES (corp-wide): 80.16MM **Privately Held**
Web: www.olivecrest.org
SIC: **8361** 8322 Emotionally disturbed home; Individual and family services

(P-17186)
PACIFIC LODGE YOUTH SVCS INC
Also Called: PACIFIC LODGE BOY'S HOME
4900 Serrania Ave, Woodland Hills (91364-3300)
P.O. Box 308 (91364)
PHONE...............................818 347-1577
Leslie King, *Ch*
Lisa Alegria, *
EMP: 110 EST: 1923
SQ FT: 22,634
SALES (est): 3.01K **Privately Held**
Web: www.oyhfs.org
SIC: **8361** Residential care

(P-17187)
PEPPERMINT RIDGE (PA)
Also Called: Ridge
825 Magnolia Ave, Corona (92879-3129)
PHONE...............................951 273-7320
Danette Mccarnes, *Ex Dir*
EMP: 83 EST: 1965
SQ FT: 25,000
SALES (est): 11.13MM
SALES (corp-wide): 11.13MM **Privately Held**
Web: www.peppermintridge.org
SIC: **8361** 8322 Mentally handicapped home; Individual and family services

(P-17188)
RANCHO SAN ANTONIO BOYS HM INC (PA)
21000 Plummer St, Chatsworth (91311-4903)
PHONE...............................818 882-6400
Aubree Sweeney, *Ex Dir*
Brother John Crowe, *
Nicholas Rizzo, *Finance*
EMP: 100 EST: 1933
SALES (est): 20.01MM
SALES (corp-wide): 20.01MM **Privately Held**
Web: www.ranchosanantonio.org
SIC: **8361** Boys' towns

(P-17189)
REDWOOD ELDERLINK SCPH
Also Called: Redwood Elderlink & Homelink
710 W 13th Ave, Escondido (92025-5511)
PHONE...............................760 480-1030
Kurt Norden, *Dir*
Tom Vedvick, *Ch*
Dan Johnson, *Pr*
Fran Hillebrecht, *Treas*
Doug Best, *Sec*

EMP: 222 EST: 1989
SQ FT: 200,000
SALES (est): 912.45K
SALES (corp-wide): 31.22MM **Privately Held**
Web: www.humangood.org
SIC: **8361** 8742 Aged home; Compensation and benefits planning consultant
HQ: Humangood Socal
1900 Huntington Dr
Duarte CA 91010
925 924-7138

(P-17190)
REGENT ASSISTED LIVING INC
Also Called: Regent Senior Living W Covina
150 S Grand Ave Ofc, West Covina (91791-2355)
PHONE...............................626 332-3344
Lorena Arechiga, *Mgr*
EMP: 89
SIC: **8361** Aged home
PA: Regent Assisted Living, Inc.
121 Sw Morrison Ste 950

(P-17191)
RES-CARE INC
611 S Central Ave, Glendale (91204-2008)
PHONE...............................818 637-7727
Michael Sowerby, *Mgr*
EMP: 116
SALES (corp-wide): 8.83B **Publicly Held**
Web: www.rescarecommunityliving.com
SIC: **8361** Residential care
HQ: Res-Care, Inc.
805 N Whittington Pkwy
Louisville KY 40222
502 394-2100

(P-17192)
ROSEMARY CHILDRENS SERVICES (PA)
36 S Kinneloa Ave # 200, Pasadena (91107-3853)
PHONE...............................626 844-3033
Greg Wessels, *Ex Dir*
Sungo Wang, *
Lynn Lu, *
Veronica Fuentes, *
Lesley Evangelista, *
EMP: 101 EST: 1920
SQ FT: 9,000
SALES (est): 4.42MM
SALES (corp-wide): 4.42MM **Privately Held**
Web: www.rosemarychildren.org
SIC: **8361** Emotionally disturbed home

(P-17193)
S L START AND ASSOCIATES LLC
Also Called: Pacific Place Retirement
3500 Lake Blvd, Oceanside (92056-4600)
PHONE...............................760 414-9411
Ree Marina, *Dir*
EMP: 83
SALES (corp-wide): 9.99MM **Privately Held**
Web: www.slstart.com
SIC: **8361** Residential care for the handicapped
PA: S. L. Start And Associates Llc
528 E Spokane Falls Blvd
509 328-2740

(P-17194)
SILVERADO SNIOR LVING HLDNGS
6400 Oak Cyn Ste 200, Irvine (92618-5233)

PHONE...............................949 240-7200
Loren B Shook, *CEO*
Kristina Hulsey, *Chief Compliance Officer*
EMP: 4000 EST: 2010
SALES (est): 15.82MM **Privately Held**
Web: www.silverado.com
SIC: **8361** Aged home

(P-17195)
SISTERS OF NZARETH LOS ANGELES
3333 Manning Ave, Los Angeles (90064-4804)
PHONE...............................310 839-2361
Margarette Brody, *Admn*
EMP: 100 EST: 1935
SQ FT: 62,558
SALES (est): 9.99MM **Privately Held**
Web: www.sistersofnazareth.com
SIC: **8361** Aged home

(P-17196)
SOLHEIM LUTHERAN HOME
2236 Merton Ave, Los Angeles (90041-1915)
PHONE...............................323 257-7518
James Graunke, *Prin*
Norma Heaton, *
Antonio Davila, *
Sherry Wait, *
EMP: 185 EST: 1923
SQ FT: 82,591
SALES (est): 15.16MM **Privately Held**
Web: www.solheimsenior.org
SIC: **8361** Aged home

(P-17197)
ST ANNES FAMILY SERVICES
155 N Occidental Blvd, Los Angeles (90026-4641)
PHONE...............................213 381-2931
Lorna Little, *Pr*
Mike Cazares, *CFO*
Janice Kanellis Cpoo, *Prin*
EMP: 158 EST: 1941
SQ FT: 100,000
SALES (est): 30.77MM **Privately Held**
Web: www.stannes.org
SIC: **8361** Rehabilitation center, residential: health care incidental

(P-17198)
ST PAULS EPISCOPAL HOME INC
2635 2nd Ave Ofc, San Diego (92103-6597)
PHONE...............................619 239-2097
EMP: 72
SALES (corp-wide): 34.55MM **Privately Held**
Web: www.stpaulseniors.org
SIC: **8361** Aged home
PA: St. Paul's Episcopal Home, Inc.
328 Maple St
619 239-6900

(P-17199)
ST PAULS EPISCOPAL HOME INC
Saint Pauls Health Care Center
235 Nutmeg St, San Diego (92103-6201)
PHONE...............................619 239-8687
Ben Geske, *Mgr*
EMP: 72
SQ FT: 1,100
SALES (corp-wide): 34.55MM **Privately Held**
Web: www.stpaulseniors.org

SIC: **8361** 8051 Rest home, with health care incidental; Skilled nursing care facilities
PA: St. Paul's Episcopal Home, Inc.
328 Maple St
619 239-6900

(P-17200)
ST PAULS EPISCOPAL HOME INC
Also Called: St Paul's Villa
2700 E 4th St, National City (91950-3006)
PHONE...............................619 232-2996
Cheryl Wilson, *Dir*
EMP: 72
SALES (corp-wide): 34.55MM **Privately Held**
Web: www.stpaulseniors.org
SIC: **8361** Aged home
PA: St. Paul's Episcopal Home, Inc.
328 Maple St
619 239-6900

(P-17201)
SUSAN J HARRIS INC
Also Called: Therapy Specialist
344 F St Ste 100, Chula Vista (91910-2645)
PHONE...............................619 498-8450
EMP: 211
SALES (corp-wide): 21.68MM **Privately Held**
Web: www.therapyspecialists.net
SIC: **8361** 8049 Rehabilitation center, residential: health care incidental; Occupational therapist
PA: New Life Physical Therapy Services San Diego, Inc.
344 F St Ste 202
858 514-0375

(P-17202)
TIERRA DEL SOL FOUNDATION (PA)
9919 Sunland Blvd, Sunland (91040-1599)
PHONE...............................818 352-1419
Steve Miller, *Ex Dir*
EMP: 95 EST: 1971
SQ FT: 20,000
SALES (est): 24.72MM
SALES (corp-wide): 24.72MM **Privately Held**
Web: www.tierradelsol.org
SIC: **8361** 8211 8322 Mentally handicapped home; Public special education school; Individual and family services

(P-17203)
VICTOR TREATMENT CENTERS INC
Also Called: Victor Treatment Centers
1053 N D St, San Bernardino (92410-3521)
PHONE...............................951 436-5200
Jana Trew, *Brnch Mgr*
EMP: 79
SALES (corp-wide): 18.99MM **Privately Held**
Web: www.victor.org
SIC: **8361** Emotionally disturbed home
PA: Victor Treatment Centers, Inc.
1360 E Lassen Ave
530 893-0758

(P-17204)
VILLAGE AT NORTHRIDGE
9222 Corbin Ave, Northridge (91324-2409)
PHONE...............................818 514-4497
EMP: 112 EST: 2008
SALES (est): 7.93MM
SALES (corp-wide): 110.02MM **Privately Held**

Web: www.srgseniorliving.com
SIC: 8361 Aged home
PA: Senior Resource Group, Llc
500 Stevens Ave Ste 100
858 792-9300

(P-17205)
VILLAS DE CRLSBAD LTD A CAL LT
Also Called: Las Villas De Carlsbad
3500 Lake Blvd, Oceanside (92056-4600)
PHONE..............................760 434-7116
Jack Rowe, *Owner*
EMP: 97
SIC: 8361 Aged home
PA: Villas De Carlsbad, Ltd., A California
Limited Partnership
9619 Chesapeake Dr # 103

(P-17206)
VISTA DEL MAR CHILD FMLY SVCS
1533 Euclid St, Santa Monica (90404-3306)
PHONE..............................310 836-1223
Louis Josephson, *Brnch Mgr*
EMP: 269
SALES (corp-wide): 40.28MM **Privately Held**
Web: www.vistadelmar.org
SIC: 8361 Mentally handicapped home
PA: Vista Del Mar Child And Family
Services
3200 Motor Ave
310 836-1223

(P-17207)
WALDEN HOUSE INC
845 E Arrow Hwy, Pomona (91767-2535)
PHONE..............................626 258-0300
Grace Gerarto, *Mgr*
EMP: 128
SALES (corp-wide): 12.86MM **Privately Held**
Web: www.healthright360.org
SIC: 8361 Group foster home
PA: Walden House, Inc.
520 Townsend St
415 554-1100

(P-17208)
WESTMONT LIVING INC
11141 Washington Blvd, Culver City
(90232-3918)
PHONE..............................310 736-4118
EMP: 139
SALES (corp-wide): 46.22MM **Privately Held**
SIC: 8361 Residential care
PA: Westmont Living, Inc.
3636 Nobel Dr
858 450-1200

(P-17209)
WHITE RABBIT PARTNERS INC
9000 W Sunset Blvd Ste 1500, West
Hollywood (90069-5815)
PHONE..............................310 975-1450
Andrew W Spanswick, *CEO*
Andrew William Spanswick, *CEO*
EMP: 150 **EST:** 2009
SALES (est): 1.63MM **Privately Held**
SIC: 8361 Residential care

8399 Social Services, Nec

(P-17210)
ANTI-RECIDIVISM COALITION
1320 E 7th St, Los Angeles (90021-1132)
PHONE..............................213 955-5885
Scott Budnick, *Admn*
EMP: 87 **EST:** 2013
SALES (est): 8.46MM **Privately Held**
Web: www.antirecidivism.org
SIC: 8399 Advocacy group

(P-17211)
ARC OF SAN DIEGO (PA)
Also Called: ARC ENTERPRISES
3030 Market St, San Diego (92102-3230)
PHONE..............................619 685-1175
David W Schneider, *CEO*
Anthony J Desalis, *
Rich Coppa, *
Chad Lyle, *
Jennifer Bates Navarra, *
▲ **EMP:** 200 **EST:** 1953
SQ FT: 55,093
SALES (est): 43.12MM
SALES (corp-wide): 43.12MM **Privately Held**
Web: www.arc-sd.com
SIC: 8399 8351 8361 8322 Advocacy group;
Child day care services; Retarded home;
Individual and family services

(P-17212)
ARC OF SAN DIEGO
Also Called: ARC - SD E Cnty Training Ctrs
1855 John Towers Ave, El Cajon
(92020-1116)
PHONE..............................619 448-2415
Millie Oveross, *Mgr*
EMP: 238
SALES (corp-wide): 43.12MM **Privately Held**
Web: www.arc-sd.com
SIC: 8399 8361 Advocacy group; Physically
handicapped home
PA: The Arc Of San Diego
3030 Market St
619 685-1175

(P-17213)
ARC OF SAN DIEGO
1336 Rancheros Dr Ste 100, San Marcos
(92069-3089)
PHONE..............................760 740-6800
Laura Orcutt, *Dir*
EMP: 674
SALES (corp-wide): 43.12MM **Privately Held**
Web: www.arc-sd.com
SIC: 8399 8322 Advocacy group;
Association for the handicapped
PA: The Arc Of San Diego
3030 Market St
619 685-1175

(P-17214)
ASSOCIATED STUDENTS UCLA
924 Westwood Blvd, Los Angeles
(90024-2910)
PHONE..............................310 794-0242
Roseanna P Malone, *Brnch Mgr*
EMP: 235
SALES (corp-wide): 55.96MM **Privately Held**
Web: www.uclahealth.org
SIC: 8399 Council for social agency
PA: Associated Students U.C.L.A.
308 Westwood Plz
310 794-8836

(P-17215)
ASSOCIATED STUDENTS UCLA (PA)
Also Called: UCLA STUDENT STORE
308 Westwood Plz, Los Angeles
(90095-8355)
PHONE..............................310 794-8836
Pouria Abbassi, *Ex Dir*
Donna Baker, *Finance*
EMP: 500 **EST:** 1919
SQ FT: 200,000
SALES (est): 55.96MM
SALES (corp-wide): 55.96MM **Privately Held**
Web: asucla.ucla.edu
SIC: 8399 5942 Council for social agency;
Book stores

(P-17216)
BEACH CITIES HEALTH DISTRICT
1200 Del Amo St, Redondo Beach
(90277-3050)
PHONE..............................310 374-3426
Tom Bakaly, *Mgr*
Tom Bakaly, *CEO*
Monica Suua, *
EMP: 147 **EST:** 1955
SALES (est): 7.31MM **Privately Held**
Web: www.bchd.org
SIC: 8399 Health systems agency

(P-17217)
CALIFORNIA ENDOWMENT (PA)
1000 N Alameda St, Los Angeles
(90012-1804)
PHONE..............................213 928-8800
Robert K Ross, *Pr*
Dan C Deleon, *
Martha Jimenez, *
EMP: 80 **EST:** 1995
SQ FT: 110,000
SALES (est): 361.9MM **Privately Held**
Web: www.calendow.org
SIC: 8399 Fund raising organization, non-fee
basis

(P-17218)
CITY OF HOPE
City Hope Development Center
1500 Duarte Rd, Duarte (91010-3012)
PHONE..............................213 202-5735
Kathleen Cane, *Brnch Mgr*
EMP: 145
SALES (corp-wide): 330.02MM **Privately Held**
Web: www.cityofhope.org
SIC: 8399 9532 Fund raising organization,
non-fee basis; Urban and community
development
PA: City Of Hope
1500 E Duarte Rd
626 256-4673

(P-17219)
COMMUNITY ACTION PARTNR KERN
315 Stine Rd, Bakersfield (93309-3268)
PHONE..............................661 835-5405
Luz Adams, *Brnch Mgr*
EMP: 84
SALES (corp-wide): 117.9MM **Privately Held**
Web: www.capk.org
SIC: 8399 Community action agency
PA: Community Action Partnership Of Kern
1300 18th St
661 336-5236

(P-17220)
COMMUNITY ACTION PARTNR KERN
814 N Norma St, Ridgecrest (93555-3509)
PHONE..............................760 371-1469
Maria Harley, *Brnch Mgr*
EMP: 85
SALES (corp-wide): 117.9MM **Privately Held**
Web: www.capk.org
SIC: 8399 8351 Community action agency;
Child day care services
PA: Community Action Partnership Of Kern
1300 18th St
661 336-5236

(P-17221)
COMMUNITY ACTION PRTNR SAN BRN
Also Called: CAPSBC
696 S Tippecanoe Ave, San Bernardino
(92408-2607)
PHONE..............................909 723-1500
Patricia L Nickols, *CEO*
Richard Schmidt, *
Joanne Gilbert, *
Socorro Enriquez, *Vice Chairman*
Ammie Hines, *
EMP: 88 **EST:** 1965
SALES (est): 32.04MM **Privately Held**
Web: www.capsbc.org
SIC: 8399 8699 Community action agency;
Charitable organization

(P-17222)
COMMUNITY PARTNERS (PA)
1000 N Alameda St Ste 240, Los Angeles
(90012-1804)
PHONE..............................213 346-3200
Paul Vandeventer, *Pr*
Gary Erickson, *
Janet Elliott, *
EMP: 198 **EST:** 1990
SALES (est): 114.17MM **Privately Held**
Web: www.communitypartners.org
SIC: 8399 Social service information
exchange

(P-17223)
COUNTY OF LOS ANGELES
9668 Valley Blvd Ste 104, Rosemead
(91770-1598)
PHONE..............................626 291-2200
EMP: 71
Web: www.lacounty.gov
SIC: 8399 Community development groups
PA: County Of Los Angeles
500 W Temple St Ste 437
213 974-1101

(P-17224)
DVEAL CORPORATION
Also Called: D'Veal Family and Youth Svcs
2750 E Washington Blvd Ste 230,
Pasadena (91107-1449)
P.O. Box 40255 (91114-7255)
PHONE..............................626 296-8900
John Mccall, *Ex Dir*
EMP: 107 **EST:** 1996
SQ FT: 7,500
SALES (est): 8.62MM **Privately Held**
Web: www.dveal.org
SIC: 8399 Community action agency

(P-17225)
ESSENTIAL ACCESS HEALTH (PA)
Also Called: Cfhc
3600 Wilshire Blvd Ste 600, Los Angeles
(90010-2610)

P R O D U C T S & S V C S

PHONE..................213 386-5614
Julie Rabinovitz, *Pr*
Nomsa Khalfani, *
Brenda Flores, *
Ron Frezieres, *
Amy Moy, *
EMP: 81 **EST:** 1968
SQ FT: 18,000
SALES (est): 9.57MM
SALES (corp-wide): 9.57MM **Privately Held**
Web: www.essentialaccess.org
SIC: 8399 8011 8099 Fund raising organization, non-fee basis; Primary care medical clinic; Medical services organization

(P-17226)
GOFUNDME GIVING FUND
Also Called: Gofund.me
3223 Greyling Dr, San Diego (92123-2229)
PHONE..................650 260-3436
EMP: 82 **EST:** 2020
SALES (est): 5.13MM **Privately Held**
Web: www.gofundme.com
SIC: 8399 Advocacy group

(P-17227)
GREATER LOS ANGELES ZOO ASSN
Also Called: GLAZA
5333 Zoo Dr, Los Angeles (90027-1451)
PHONE..................323 644-4200
Connie M Morgan, *Pr*
Jeb Bonner, *
Genie Vasels, *
Eugenia Vasels, *
Phyllis Kupferstein, *
EMP: 100 **EST:** 1963
SQ FT: 8,200
SALES (est): 26.83MM **Privately Held**
Web: www.lazoo.org
SIC: 8399 7999 Fund raising organization, non-fee basis; Concession operator

(P-17228)
HARBOR DVLPMNTAL DSBLTIES FNDT
Also Called: Harbor Regional Center
21231 Hawthorne Blvd, Torrance (90503-5501)
P.O. Box 2930 (90509-2930)
PHONE..................310 540-1711
Judy Wada, *CFO*
EMP: 225 **EST:** 1977
SQ FT: 60,000
SALES (est): 349.67MM **Privately Held**
Web: www.harborrc.org
SIC: 8399 Council for social agency

(P-17229)
INTERNTNAL FNDTION FOR KREA UN
3435 Wilshire Blvd Ste 480, Los Angeles (90010-1918)
PHONE..................213 550-2182
Willie Wang-pyo Seung, *CEO*
EMP: 300 **EST:** 2016
SALES (est): 202.98K **Privately Held**
Web: www.ifku.org
SIC: 8399 Advocacy group

(P-17230)
INTOUCH TECHNOLOGIES INC (HQ)
Also Called: Intouch Health
7402 Hollister Ave, Goleta (93117-2583)
PHONE..................805 562-8686
Yulun Wang, *Ch*
Paul Evans, *

Michael Chan, *
Charles S Jordan, *
David Adornetto, *
EMP: 92 **EST:** 2002
SQ FT: 1,600
SALES (est): 16.07MM **Publicly Held**
Web: www.teladochealth.com
SIC: 8399 7379 Health systems agency; Computer related consulting services
PA: Teladoc Health, Inc.
2 Manhttnville Rd Ste 203

(P-17231)
KERN REGIONAL CENTER (PA)
3200 N Sillect Ave, Bakersfield (93308-6333)
P.O. Box 2536 (93303-2536)
PHONE..................661 327-8531
TOLL FREE: 800
Michal Clark, *Ex Dir*
Jerry Bowman, *
Duane Law, *
EMP: 147 **EST:** 1971
SQ FT: 33,000
SALES (est): 231.95MM
SALES (corp-wide): 231.95MM **Privately Held**
Web: www.kernrc.org
SIC: 8399 Social service information exchange

(P-17232)
KEYSTONE NPS LLC
Also Called: Keystone Educatn & Youth Svcs
9994 County Farm Rd, Riverside (92503-3518)
PHONE..................951 785-0504
Holly Fields, *Brnch Mgr*
EMP: 247
SALES (corp-wide): 14.28B **Publicly Held**
SIC: 8399 8211 Advocacy group; Private elementary and secondary schools
HQ: Keystone Nps Llc
11980 Mount Vernon Ave
Grand Terrace CA 92313
909 633-6354

(P-17233)
KEYSTONE NPS LLC (DH)
Also Called: Keystone Schools-Ramona
11980 Mount Vernon Ave, Grand Terrace (92313-5172)
PHONE..................909 633-6354
Alfredo Alvarado, *Prin*
Martha Petrey, *
Don Whitfield, *
EMP: 100 **EST:** 1978
SALES (est): 1.87MM
SALES (corp-wide): 14.28B **Publicly Held**
SIC: 8399 Advocacy group
HQ: Children's Comprehensive Services, Inc.
3401 West End Ave Ste 400
Nashville TN 37203
615 250-0000

(P-17234)
LAWRENCE FMLY JWISH CMNTY CTRS (PA)
4126 Executive Dr, La Jolla (92037-1348)
PHONE..................858 362-1144
Craig Schluss, *Pr*
David Wax, *
Nancy Johnson, *
EMP: 150 **EST:** 1945
SALES (est): 12.04MM
SALES (corp-wide): 12.04MM **Privately Held**
Web: www.lfjcc.org

SIC: 8399 8351 Community development groups; Child day care services

(P-17235)
LOS ANGELES LGBT CENTER (PA)
Also Called: L.A. GAY & LESBIAN CENTER
1625 Schrader Blvd, Los Angeles (90028-6213)
P.O. Box 2988 (90078-2988)
PHONE..................323 993-7618
Lorri L Jean, *CEO*
Michael Holtzman, *
EMP: 148 **EST:** 1972
SQ FT: 45,000
SALES (est): 162.44MM
SALES (corp-wide): 162.44MM **Privately Held**
Web: www.lalgbtcenter.org
SIC: 8399 Advocacy group

(P-17236)
NEW ADVNCES FOR PPLE WITH DSBL
Also Called: Napd
4032 Jewett Ave, Bakersfield (93301-1114)
PHONE..................661 322-9735
Lou Lopez, *Brnch Mgr*
EMP: 106
SALES (corp-wide): 7.52MM **Privately Held**
Web: www.napd-bak.org
SIC: 8399 Community development groups
PA: New Advances For People With Disabilities
3400 N Sillect Ave
661 395-1361

(P-17237)
NEW ADVNCES FOR PPLE WITH DSBL
Also Called: Center For Achievement Center
1120 21st St, Bakersfield (93301-4613)
PHONE..................661 327-0188
Linda Waninger, *Mgr*
EMP: 76
SALES (corp-wide): 7.52MM **Privately Held**
Web: www.napd-bak.org
SIC: 8399 Community development groups
PA: New Advances For People With Disabilities
3400 N Sillect Ave
661 395-1361

(P-17238)
ORTHALLIANCE INC
Also Called: Orthalliances
21535 Hawthorne Blvd Ste 200, Torrance (90503-6612)
PHONE..................310 792-1300
Sam Westover, *Pr*
Paul H Hayase, *
James C Wilson, *
EMP: 1700 **EST:** 1996
SQ FT: 4,200
SALES (est): 573.35K **Privately Held**
Web: www.orthalliance.com
SIC: 8399 8742 8741 Advocacy group; Management consulting services; Business management
PA: Orthosynetics, Inc.
3850 N Cswy Blvd Ste 800

(P-17239)
PENNY LANE CENTERS (PA)
15305 Rayen St, North Hills (91343-5117)
P.O. Box 2548 (91343)
PHONE..................818 892-3423

Arthur Barr, *Pr*
Ivelise Markovits, *
Peter Padin, *Assistant Executive Director*
EMP: 275 **EST:** 1967
SQ FT: 7,000
SALES (est): 54.11MM
SALES (corp-wide): 54.11MM **Privately Held**
Web: www.pennylane.org
SIC: 8399 Social service information exchange

(P-17240)
PREMIER DISABILITY SVCS LLC
909 N Pacific Coast Hwy Fl 11, El Segundo (90245-2727)
PHONE..................310 280-4000
Robert N Brisco, *Mgr*
EMP: 99 **EST:** 2020
SALES (est): 437.64K **Privately Held**
Web: www.premierdisability.com
SIC: 8399 Advocacy group

(P-17241)
SAN DIEGO RESCUE MISSION INC (PA)
Also Called: CITY RESCUE MISSION
299 17th St, San Diego (92101-7665)
P.O. Box 80427 (92138-0427)
PHONE..................619 819-1880
Herb Johnson, *CEO*
John Suderman, *
Shari Finney Houser, *
C Greg Helton, *
Cathy Christianson, *
EMP: 99 **EST:** 1955
SALES (est): 25.34MM
SALES (corp-wide): 25.34MM **Privately Held**
Web: www.sdrescue.org
SIC: 8399 5932 8322 Social change association; Used merchandise stores; Emergency shelters

(P-17242)
SOUTH CNTL LOS ANGLES RGNAL CT
650 W Adams Blvd, Los Angeles (90007-2580)
PHONE..................231 744-8484
Terrence Payne, *Brnch Mgr*
EMP: 128
SALES (corp-wide): 532.53MM **Privately Held**
Web: www.sclarc.org
SIC: 8399 Health and welfare council
PA: South Central Los Angeles Regional Center For Developmentally Disabled Persons, Inc.
2500 S Western Av
213 744-7000

(P-17243)
SOUTH CNTL LOS ANGLES RGNAL CT (PA)
Also Called: Sclarc
2500 S Western Ave, Los Angeles (90018-2609)
PHONE..................213 744-7000
Dexter Henderson, *CEO*
Roy Doronila, *
EMP: 107 **EST:** 1983
SQ FT: 110,470
SALES (est): 532.53MM
SALES (corp-wide): 532.53MM **Privately Held**
Web: www.sclarc.org
SIC: 8399 Health and welfare council

(P-17244)
SPECIAL SERVICE FOR GROUPS INC
Also Called: Occupational Therapy Training
879 W 190th St, Gardena (90248-4220)
PHONE..............................310 323-6887
Sarah Bream, *Brnch Mgr*
EMP: 132
SALES (corp-wide): 133.16MM **Privately Held**
Web: www.ssg.org
SIC: 8399 8322 Community action agency; Individual and family services
PA: Special Service For Groups, Inc.
905 E 8th St
213 368-1888

(P-17245)
SPECIAL SERVICE FOR GROUPS INC
520 S La Fayette Park Pl # 30, Los Angeles (90057-1607)
PHONE..............................213 553-1800
Herbert Hatanaka, *Brnch Mgr*
EMP: 131
SALES (corp-wide): 133.16MM **Privately Held**
Web: www.ssg.org
SIC: 8399 Community development groups
PA: Special Service For Groups, Inc.
905 E 8th St
213 368-1888

(P-17246)
UNITED WAY INC (PA) ✲
Also Called: UNITED WAY OF GREATER LOS ANGE
1150 S Olive St Ste T-500, Los Angeles (90015-2481)
PHONE..............................213 808-6220
Caroline W Nahas, *Ch Bd*
Elise Buik, *
Les Brockhurst, *
Alicia Lara, *
Mae Tuck, *
▲ EMP: 95 EST: 1962
SQ FT: 40,000
SALES (est): 47.41MM
SALES (corp-wide): 47.41MM **Privately Held**
Web: www.unitedwayla.org
SIC: 8399 Fund raising organization, non-fee basis

(P-17247)
WESTSIDE JEWISH CMNTY CTR INC
Also Called: J La, The
5870 W Olympic Blvd, Los Angeles (90036-4698)
PHONE..............................323 938-2531
Brian Greene, *Ex Dir*
EMP: 600 EST: 1932
SQ FT: 150,000
SALES (est): 2.31MM **Privately Held**
Web: www.westsidejcc.org
SIC: 8399 8641 8322 Community development groups; Civic and social associations; Individual and family services

---

8412 Museums And Art Galleries

(P-17248)
ARMAND HMMER MSEUM OF ART CLTR
Also Called: HAMMER MUSEUM
10899 Wilshire Blvd, Los Angeles (90024-4343)

PHONE..............................310 443-7000
Michael Rubel, *Dir*
Steven A Olsen, *
▲ EMP: 101 EST: 1989
SQ FT: 20,000
SALES (est): 28.73MM **Privately Held**
Web: hammer.ucla.edu
SIC: 8412 Museum

(P-17249)
AUTRY MUSEUM OF AMERICAN WEST
Also Called: Autry Museum
4700 Western Heritage Way, Los Angeles (90027-1462)
PHONE..............................323 667-2000
Richard West, *Prin*
Richard West, *Pr*
Robert Caragher, *
Maren Dougherty, *
Susan Harlow, *
EMP: 140 EST: 1984
SQ FT: 144,000
SALES (est): 6.23MM **Privately Held**
Web: www.theautry.org
SIC: 8412 5947 5812 6512 Museum; Gift shop; Cafeteria; Theater building, ownership and operation

(P-17250)
CALIFRNIA CTR FOR ARTS ESCNDID
340 N Escondido Blvd, Escondido (92025-2600)
PHONE..............................760 839-4138
Vicky Basehore, *Pr*
Lee Cavell Board, *Prin*
EMP: 185 EST: 1989
SALES (est): 5.23MM **Privately Held**
Web: www.artcenter.org
SIC: 8412 5999 Arts or science center; Art dealers

(P-17251)
CALIFRNIA SCNCE CTR FOUNDATION
700 Exposition Park Dr, Los Angeles (90037-1210)
PHONE..............................213 744-2545
Jeffrey N Rudolph, *Pr*
Cynthia Pygin, *
EMP: 260 EST: 1949
SALES (est): 28.6MM
SALES (corp-wide): 534.4MM **Privately Held**
Web: asucla.ucla.edu
SIC: 8412 7832 5947 Museum; Motion picture theaters, except drive-in; Gifts and novelties
HQ: California Natural Resources Agency
715 P St
Sacramento CA 95814

(P-17252)
CHARLES W BOWERS MUSEUM CORP
Also Called: BOWERS MUSEUM
2002 N Main St, Santa Ana (92706-2776)
PHONE..............................714 567-3600
Peter C Keller, *Pr*
▲ EMP: 72 EST: 1936
SALES (est): 9.95MM **Privately Held**
Web: www.bowers.org
SIC: 8412 Museum

(P-17253)
DISCOVERY SCNCE CTR ORNGE CNTY
2500 N Main St, Santa Ana (92705-6600)

PHONE..............................866 552-2823
Daniel Bolar, *Ch Bd*
Joseph Adams, *Pr*
▲ EMP: 135 EST: 1998
SALES (est): 12.79MM **Privately Held**
Web: www.discoverycube.org
SIC: 8412 Museum

(P-17254)
KIDSPCE A PRTICIPATORY MUSEUM
Also Called: KIDSPACE
480 N Arroyo Blvd, Pasadena (91103-3269)
PHONE..............................626 449-9144
Jane Popovich, *Pr*
Chris Morphy, *
Mark Mckinley, *Treas*
Nam Jack, *
Stephen H Baumann, *
EMP: 83 EST: 1979
SALES (est): 5.92MM **Privately Held**
Web: www.kidspacemuseum.org
SIC: 8412 Museum

(P-17255)
LUCAS MUSEUM OF NARRATIVE ART
700 S Flower St Ste 2400, Los Angeles (90017-4211)
P.O. Box 29137 (94129-0137)
PHONE..............................831 566-9332
Andrea Wishom, *CEO*
EMP: 94 EST: 2012
SALES (est): 3.75MM **Privately Held**
Web: www.lucasmuseum.org
SIC: 8412 Museum

(P-17256)
MUSEUM ASSOCIATES
Also Called: La County Museum of Art
5905 Wilshire Blvd, Los Angeles (90036-4504)
PHONE..............................323 857-6172
Michael Gavin, *Dir*
EMP: 400 EST: 1938
SALES (est): 198.52MM **Privately Held**
Web: www.lacma.org
SIC: 8412 Museum

(P-17257)
MUSEUM OF CONTEMPORARY ART (PA)
250 S Grand Ave, Los Angeles (90012-3021)
PHONE..............................213 626-6222
Johanna Burton, *CEO*
Heather Podesta, *
Meredith King, *
▲ EMP: 150 EST: 1979
SQ FT: 100,000
SALES (est): 17MM
SALES (corp-wide): 17MM **Privately Held**
Web: www.moca.org
SIC: 8412 Museum

(P-17258)
NEW CHILDRENS MUSEUM
200 W Island Ave, San Diego (92101-6850)
PHONE..............................619 233-8792
Judy Forrester, *Ex Dir*
Kay Wagner, *
Robert Sain, *
Rachel Teagle, *
Julianne Markow, *
EMP: 90 EST: 1981
SQ FT: 50,000
SALES (est): 6.55MM **Privately Held**
Web: www.thinkplaycreate.org
SIC: 8412 Museum

(P-17259)
NORTON SMON MSEUM ART AT PSDEN
411 W Colorado Blvd, Pasadena (91105-1825)
PHONE..............................626 449-6840
Ronald H Dykhuizen, *Prin*
Jennifer J Simon, *
Walter W Timoshuk, *
Robert Walker, *
▲ EMP: 100 EST: 1924
SQ FT: 70,000
SALES (est): 8.12MM **Privately Held**
Web: www.nortonsimon.org
SIC: 8412 Museum

(P-17260)
PALM SPRINGS ART MUSEUM INC
101 N Museum Dr, Palm Springs (92262-5659)
P.O. Box 2310 (92263-2310)
PHONE..............................760 322-4800
Donna Macmillan, *Ch Bd*
Rochelle Steinerm, *Chief Curator*
Adam Lerner, *
▲ EMP: 96 EST: 1938
SQ FT: 75,000
SALES (est): 8.92MM **Privately Held**
Web: www.psmuseum.org
SIC: 8412 Museum

(P-17261)
REUBEN H FLEET SCIENCE CENTER
1875 El Prado, San Diego (92101-1625)
P.O. Box 33303 (92163-3303)
PHONE..............................619 238-1233
Gary Thomas Phillips, *CEO*
Jeffrey Kirsch, *
Craig A Blower, *
EMP: 105 EST: 1957
SQ FT: 93,500
SALES (est): 8.49MM **Privately Held**
Web: www.fleetscience.org
SIC: 8412 Museum

(P-17262)
RONALD RGAN PRSDNTIAL FNDTION
Also Called: RONALD REAGAN PRESIDENTIAL LIB
40 Presidential Dr Ste 200, Simi Valley (93065-0600)
PHONE..............................805 522-2977
TOLL FREE: 800
Glenn Baker, *CFO*
John Heubusch, *
Cary L Garman, *
Joanne Drake, *Chief of Staff*
EMP: 70 EST: 1985
SQ FT: 225,000
SALES (est): 37.04MM **Privately Held**
Web: www.reaganfoundation.org
SIC: 8412 8231 5947 8399 Museum; Public library; Gifts and novelties; Community development groups

(P-17263)
SAN DEGO SOC OF NTURAL HISTORY
Also Called: SAN DIEGO NATURAL HISTORY MUSE
1788 El Prado, San Diego (92101-1624)
P.O. Box 121390 (92112-1390)
PHONE..............................619 232-3821
Michael W Hager, *CEO*
George Gonyer, *
Susan Loveall, *

▲ **EMP:** 70 **EST:** 1874
SQ FT: 60,000
SALES (est): 27.26MM **Privately Held**
Web: www.sdnhm.org
SIC: 8412 5047 Museum; Dental equipment
and supplies

(P-17264)
SAN DIEGO AIR & SPACE MUSEUM

2001 Pan American Plz, San Diego
(92101-1636)
PHONE.................................619 234-8291
James Kidrick, *Pr*
▼ **EMP:** 75 **EST:** 1961
SQ FT: 105,000
SALES (est): 6.26MM **Privately Held**
Web: www.sandiegoairandspace.org
SIC: 8412 5947 Museum; Souvenirs

(P-17265)
SAN DIEGO MUSEUM OF ART

1450 El Prado, San Diego (92112)
P.O. Box 122107 (92112-2107)
PHONE.................................619 696-1909
Philip Tom Gildred, *CEO*
Roxanna Velasquez, *
Reed Viekerman, *Asst Dir*
▲ **EMP:** 82 **EST:** 1925
SQ FT: 96,278
SALES (est): 10.45MM **Privately Held**
Web: www.sdmart.org
SIC: 8412 Museum

(P-17266)
SANTA BRBARA MSEUM NTRAL HSTOR

2559 Puesta Del Sol, Santa Barbara
(93105-2998)
PHONE.................................805 682-4711
Luke Swetland, *CEO*
Karl Hutterer, *
Brian Storr, *
Palmer Jackson Junior, *Pr*
Carolyn Chandler, *
EMP: 95 **EST:** 1916
SALES (est): 8.95MM **Privately Held**
Web: www.sbnature.org
SIC: 8412 Museum

(P-17267)
SKIRBALL CULTURAL CENTER

Also Called: SKIRBALL CULTURAL CENTER
2701 N Sepulveda Blvd, Los Angeles
(90049-6833)
PHONE.................................310 440-4500
Uri D Herscher, *Pr*
Leslie K Johnson, *
▲ **EMP:** 150 **EST:** 1995
SQ FT: 65,000
SALES (est): 22.07MM **Privately Held**
Web: www.skirball.org
SIC: 8412 Museum

(P-17268)
THE J PAUL GETTY TRUST (PA)

Also Called: Getty Publications
1200 Getty Center Dr Ste 500, Los Angeles
(90049-1695)
PHONE.................................310 440-7300
▲ **EMP:** 1431 **EST:** 1953
SALES (est): 370.25MM
SALES (corp-wide): 370.25MM **Privately
Held**
Web: www.getty.edu
SIC: 8412 Museums and art galleries

8422 Botanical And Zoological Gardens

(P-17269)
AQUARIUM OF PACIFIC (PA)

100 Aquarium Way, Long Beach
(90802-8126)
PHONE.................................562 590-3100
Jerry R Schubel, *Pr*
Anthony Brown, *
Cecile Fisher, *
Perry Hampton, *
David Bader, *
▲ **EMP:** 220 **EST:** 1997
SQ FT: 10,000
SALES (est): 51.75MM **Privately Held**
Web: www.aquariumofpacific.org
SIC: 8422 Aquarium

(P-17270)
LIVING DESERT

47900 Portola Ave, Palm Desert
(92260-6156)
PHONE.................................760 346-5694
Allen Monroe, *CEO*
Terrie Correll, *
Dwight Middendorf, *
Sarah Clapp, *
Peter Siminski, *
EMP: 124 **EST:** 1970
SQ FT: 1,700
SALES (est): 34.59MM **Privately Held**
Web: www.livingdesert.org
SIC: 8422 5947 Aquariums and zoological
gardens; Gift shop

(P-17271)
RANCHO SANTA ANA BOTANIC GRDN

Also Called: CALIFORNIA BOTANIC
GARDEN
1500 N College Ave, Claremont
(91711-3157)
PHONE.................................909 625-8767
Lucinda Mcdade, *Ex Dir*
Clement Hamilton, *
Richard Grant, *
Sonja Evensen, *
EMP: 75 **EST:** 1927
SQ FT: 30,000
SALES (est): 6.51MM **Privately Held**
Web: www.calbg.org
SIC: 8422 Botanical garden

(P-17272)
SANTA BRBARA ZLGCAL FOUNDATION

Also Called: Santa Barbara Zoo
500 Ninos Dr, Santa Barbara (93103-3798)
PHONE.................................805 962-1673
Yul Vanek, *CEO*
Nancy Mctoldridge, *COO*
Carol Bedford, *
Fred Clough, *
Diane Pearson, *
▲ **EMP:** 130 **EST:** 1961
SQ FT: 1,200
SALES (est): 16.61MM **Privately Held**
Web: www.sbzoo.org
SIC: 8422 Zoological garden, noncommercial

(P-17273)
ZOOLOGICAL SOCIETY SAN DIEGO (PA)

Also Called: SAN DIEGO ZOO WILDLIFE
ALLIANC
2920 Zoo Dr, San Diego (92101-1646)
P.O. Box 120551 (92112-0551)
PHONE.................................619 231-1515
Paul Baribault, *CEO*
Shawn Dixon, *
David Franco, *
◆ **EMP:** 1500 **EST:** 1916
SALES (est): 411.02MM
SALES (corp-wide): 411.02MM **Privately
Held**
Web:
www.sandiegozoowildlifealliance.org
SIC: 8422 Aquarium

(P-17274)
ZOOLOGICAL SOCIETY SAN DIEGO

Also Called: San Diego Wild Animal Park
15500 San Pasqual Valley Rd, Escondido
(92027-7017)
PHONE.................................760 747-8702
Robert Mcclure, *Mgr*
EMP: 191
SALES (corp-wide): 411.02MM **Privately
Held**
Web:
www.sandiegozoowildlifealliance.org
SIC: 8422 7999 Animal and reptile exhibit;
Tourist attraction, commercial
PA: Zoological Society Of San Diego
2920 Zoo Dr
619 231-1515

(P-17275)
ZOOLOGICAL SOCIETY SAN DIEGO

Also Called: San Diego Zoo
2920 Zoo Dr, San Diego (92101-1646)
P.O. Box 120551 (92112-0551)
PHONE.................................619 744-3325
Richard Farrar, *Dir*
EMP: 179
SALES (corp-wide): 411.02MM **Privately
Held**
Web:
www.sandiegozoowildlifealliance.org
SIC: 8422 Botanical and zoological gardens
PA: Zoological Society Of San Diego
2920 Zoo Dr
619 231-1515

(P-17276)
ZOOLOGICAL SOCIETY SAN DIEGO

Also Called: San Diego Zoo
10946 Willow Ct Ste 200, San Diego
(92127-2417)
PHONE.................................619 231-1515
Janet Matsuura, *Dir*
EMP: 153
SALES (corp-wide): 411.02MM **Privately
Held**
Web:
www.sandiegozoowildlifealliance.org
SIC: 8422 Animal and reptile exhibit
PA: Zoological Society Of San Diego
2920 Zoo Dr
619 231-1515

8611 Business Associations

(P-17277)
ALL STATE ASSOCIATION INC

11487 San Fernando Rd, San Fernando
(91340-3406)
PHONE.................................877 425-2558
Steve Avetyan, *CEO*
Alfred Megrabyan, *
Armen Karibyan, *
EMP: 250 **EST:** 2003
SALES (est): 748.32K **Privately Held**

SIC: 8611 Trade associations

(P-17278)
CALIFORNIA ASSN REALTORS INC (PA)

525 S Virgil Ave, Los Angeles
(90020-1403)
PHONE.................................213 739-8200
Phil Hawkins, *CEO*
Don Flyn, *
Don Faught, *
EMP: 110 **EST:** 1907
SQ FT: 52,000
SALES (est): 51.06MM
SALES (corp-wide): 51.06MM **Privately
Held**
Web: www.car.org
SIC: 8611 8742 Real estate board; Real
estate consultant

(P-17279)
CALIFORNIA RE ASSN INC

Also Called: California Real Estate
525 S Virgil Ave, Los Angeles
(90020-1403)
PHONE.................................213 739-8200
Joel Singer, *Pr*
Don Flymn, *CFO*
EMP: 85 **EST:** 1996
SQ FT: 52,000
SALES (est): 352.37K
SALES (corp-wide): 51.06MM **Privately
Held**
SIC: 8611 Real estate board
PA: California Association Of Realtors, Inc.
525 S Virgil Ave
213 739-8200

(P-17280)
CITY ORANGE POLICE ASSN INC

1107 N Batavia St, Orange (92867-4615)
P.O. Box 906 (92856-6906)
PHONE.................................714 457-5340
John Mancini, *Pr*
EMP: 216 **EST:** 1980
SALES (est): 390.11K **Privately Held**
Web: www.copa33.org
SIC: 8611 Business associations

(P-17281)
ELECTRA OWNERS ASSOC

700 W E St, San Diego (92101-5984)
PHONE.................................619 236-3310
J E Martin, *Prin*
EMP: 117 **EST:** 2008
SALES (est): 338.38K
SALES (corp-wide): 30MM **Privately Held**
Web: www.electrahoa.com
SIC: 8611 Business associations
PA: Action Property Management, Inc.
2603 Main St Ste 500
949 450-0202

(P-17282)
EPSILON SYSTEMS SOLUTIONS INC

2101 Haffley Ave # A, National City
(91950-6416)
PHONE.................................619 474-3252
Robert Duran, *Brnch Mgr*
EMP: 118
SALES (corp-wide): 110MM **Privately
Held**
Web: www.epsilonsystems.com
SIC: 8611 Shipping and steamship company
association
PA: Epsilon Systems Solutions, Inc.
9444 Balboa Ave Ste 100
619 702-1700

▲ = Import ▼ = Export
◆ = Import/Export

(P-17283)

INSTITUTE OF ELEC ELEC ENGNERS

Also Called: Ieee Computer Society
10662 Los Vaqueros Cir, Los Alamitos
(90720-2513)
P.O. Box 3014 (90720-1314)
PHONE...................714 821-8380
Linda Ashworth, *Admn*
EMP: 85
SALES (corp-wide): 566.43MM **Privately Held**
Web: www.ieee.org
SIC: 8611 Trade associations
PA: The Institute Of Electrical And
Electronics Engineers Incorporated
445 Hoes Ln
212 419-7900

(P-17284)

LOS ANGLES AREA CHMBER CMMERCE

350 S Bixel St, Los Angeles (90017-1418)
PHONE...................213 580-7500
Maria S Salinas, *Pr*
Gary Toebben, *Pr*
David Eads, *COO*
Benjamin Stilp, *CFO*
Mark Louchheim, *Ch Bd*
EMP: 85 **EST:** 2009
SALES (est): 5.71MM **Privately Held**
Web: www.lachamber.com
SIC: 8611 Chamber of Commerce

(P-17285)

MERCY HOUSE LIVING CENTERS

Also Called: MERCY HOUSE
TRANSITIONAL LIVIN
807 N Garfield St, Santa Ana (92701-3821)
P.O. Box 1905 (92702-1905)
PHONE...................714 836-7188
Larry Haynes, *Ex Dir*
Jerome Karcher, *
Carrie Delaurie, *
EMP: 170 **EST:** 1988
SQ FT: 19,000
SALES (est): 54.57MM **Privately Held**
Web: www.mercyhouse.net
SIC: 8611 Community affairs and services

(P-17286)

MISSION EDGE SAN DIEGO

2820 Roosevelt Rd Ste 104, San Diego
(92106-6146)
P.O. Box 12319 (92112)
PHONE...................877 232 4541
Ken Davenport, *CEO*
David Lynn, *
EMP: 90 **EST:** 2010
SALES (est): 10.2MM **Privately Held**
Web: www.missionedge.org
SIC: 8611 8742 Business associations;
Management consulting services

(P-17287)

SATICOY LEMON ASSOCIATION

600 E 3rd St, Oxnard (93030-6001)
P.O. Box 46 (93061-0046)
PHONE...................805 654-6543
Kevin Colvard, *Manager*
EMP: 99
SALES (corp-wide): 21.99MM **Privately Held**
Web: www.saticoylemon.com
SIC: 8611 Growers' associations
PA: Saticoy Lemon Association
103 N Peck Rd
805 654-6500

(P-17288)

SOUTHLAND RGNAL ASSN RLTORS IN (PA)

7232 Balboa Blvd, Van Nuys (91406-2701)
PHONE...................818 786-2110
James Link, *Ex VP*
Brian Paul, *
Rob Schwab, *
Chuck Nickerson, *
Steve White, *
EMP: 72 **EST:** 1957
SQ FT: 25,000
SALES (est): 2.1MM
SALES (corp-wide): 2.1MM **Privately Held**
Web: www.srar.com
SIC: 8611 Real estate board

(P-17289)

SPECILTY EQP MKT ASSN PRFMCE R (PA)

Also Called: Sema
1575 Valley Vista Dr, Diamond Bar
(91765-3914)
PHONE...................909 610-2030
Mike Spagnola, *CEO*
George Afremow, *
Ryan Stutzman, *
David Speicher, *
EMP: 70 **EST:** 1963
SQ FT: 23,000
SALES (est): 18.33MM
SALES (corp-wide): 18.33MM **Privately Held**
Web: www.sema.org
SIC: 8611 Trade associations

(P-17290)

WESTERN GROWERS ASSOCIATION (PA)

Also Called: W G A
6501 Irvine Center Dr, Irvine (92618-2133)
P.O. Box 57089 (92619)
PHONE...................949 863-1000
Tom A Nassif, *CEO*
Steve Patricio, *
Matt Mcinerney, *Ex VP*
Ward Kennedy, *
Dave Puglia, *
EMP: 150 **EST:** 1926
SALES (est): 19.72MM
SALES (corp-wide): 19.72MM **Privately Held**
Web: www.wga.com
SIC: 8611 8111 Growers' associations; Legal services

(P-17291)

WONDERFUL CITRUS COOPERATIVE

4060 7th Standard Rd, Shafter
(93263-9800)
PHONE...................661 720-2400
EMP: 520
Web: www.wonderfulcitrus.com
SIC: 8611 Growers' marketing advisory service
PA: Wonderful Citrus Cooperative
1901 S Lexington St

8621 Professional Organizations

(P-17292)

ACADEMY MPIC ARTS & SCIENCES (PA)

8949 Wilshire Blvd, Beverly Hills
(90211-1972)
PHONE...................310 247-3000
Dawn Hudson, *CEO*
Bruce Davis, *
Andy Horn, *
Meredith Shea Chief Membership Impact
Industry, *Ofcr*
Teni Melidonian, *OSCARS**
EMP: 100 **EST:** 1927
SQ FT: 35,000
SALES (est): 266.68MM
SALES (corp-wide): 266.68MM **Privately Held**
Web: www.oscars.org
SIC: 8621 7819 8611 Professional
organizations; Services allied to motion
pictures; Business associations

(P-17293)

ATTAINMENT HOLDCO LLC

Also Called: Instride
840 Apollo St, El Segundo (90245-4723)
PHONE...................310 954-1578
Stephen Chu, *Managing Member*
Jonathan Lau, *COO*
Dan Bock, *CCO*
Jeff Stark, *CFO*
EMP: 175 **EST:** 2019
SALES (est): 9.24MM **Privately Held**
Web: www.instride.com
SIC: 8621 Education and teacher association

(P-17294)

CALIFORNIA CANCER SPECIALISTS MEDICAL GROUP INC

1333 S Mayflower Ave Ste 200, Monrovia
(91016-5266)
PHONE...................626 775-3200
EMP: 320
SIC: 8621 7389 Medical field-related
associations; Financial services

(P-17295)

CALIFRNIA ASSN HLTH EDCATN LNK

17800 Us Highway 18, Apple Valley
(92307-1221)
PHONE...................760 955-3536
Jenae Holt, *CEO*
EMP: 99 **EST:** 2020
SALES (est): 184.87K **Privately Held**
SIC: 8621 Education and teacher association

(P-17296)

CAPITAL INVSTMNTS VNTURES CORP (PA)

Also Called: Civco
30151 Tomas, Rcho Sta Marg
(92688-2125)
PHONE...................949 858-0647
Drew Richardson, *Pr*
Gary Prenovost, *
Marjorie Kelso Int'l, *Prs Dir*
Brian Cronin, *
◆ **EMP:** 195 **EST:** 1975
SQ FT: 95,000
SALES (est): 23.01MM
SALES (corp-wide): 23.01MM **Privately Held**
Web: www.padi.com
SIC: 8621 4724 Professional organizations;
Travel agencies

(P-17297)

COOPERTIVE AMRCN PHYSCIANS INC (PA)

Also Called: Cap-Mpt
333 S Hope St Fl 8, Los Angeles
(90071-1406)
PHONE...................213 473-8600
James Weidner, *CEO*
Thomas Andrem, *VP*
Cindy Belcher, *COO*
Nancy Brusegaard Johnson, *Sr VP*
John Donaldson, *CFO*
EMP: 100 **EST:** 1975
SALES (est): 21.15MM
SALES (corp-wide): 21.15MM **Privately Held**
Web: www.capphysicians.com
SIC: 8621 Medical field-related associations

(P-17298)

COUNTY OF LOS ANGELES

313 N Figueroa St 9th Fl, Los Angeles
(90012-2602)
PHONE...................213 240-8412
Thomas L Garthwaite, *Brnch Mgr*
EMP: 101
Web: www.lacounty.gov
SIC: 8621 9431 Professional organizations;
Prenatal (maternity) health program
administration, govt.
PA: County Of Los Angeles
500 W Temple St Ste 437
213 974-1101

(P-17299)

LEIGHTON GROUP INC

75450 Gerald Ford Dr Ste 301, Palm Desert
(92211-6022)
PHONE...................760 776-4192
EMP: 165
SALES (corp-wide): 470.14MM **Privately Held**
Web: www.leightongroup.com
SIC: 8621 Professional organizations
HQ: Leighton Group, Inc.
2600 Michelson Dr Ste 400
Irvine CA 92612
949 250-1421

(P-17300)

LOS ANGELES COUNTY BAR ASSN (PA)

Also Called: LOS ANGELES LAWYER
MAGAZINE
444 S Flower St, Los Angeles
(90071-2901)
P.O. Box 55020 (90055-2020)
PHONE...................213 627-2727
Paul R Kiesel, *Pr*
Sally Suchil, *
▲ **EMP:** 85 **EST:** 1878
SALES (est): 8.13MM
SALES (corp-wide): 8.13MM **Privately Held**
Web: www.lacba.org
SIC: 8621 Bar association

(P-17301)

MEDIMPACT HLTHCARE SYSTEMS INC (HQ)

10181 Scripps Gateway Ct, San Diego
(92131-5152)
PHONE...................800 788-2949
Frederick Howe, *Ch Bd*
James Gollaher, *CFO*
EMP: 146 **EST:** 1989
SQ FT: 100,000
SALES (est): 46.36MM **Privately Held**
Web: www.medimpact.com
SIC: 8621 Medical field-related associations
PA: Medimpact Holdings, Inc.
10181 Scripps Gateway Ct

(P-17302)

NATIONAL NOTARY ASSOCIATION

Also Called: Nna Insurance Services
9350 De Soto Ave, Chatsworth
(91311-4926)
PHONE..................800 876-6827
EMP: 204 **EST:** 1984
SALES (est): 10.46MM **Privately Held**
SIC: 8621 Professional organizations

(P-17303)
ORANGE CNTY HLTH AUTH A PUB AG
Also Called: Orange County Health Authority
505 City Pkwy W, Orange (92868-2924)
PHONE..................714 246-8500
Richard Chambers, *CEO*
Michael Schrader, *
Richard Helmer, *Chief Medical Officer*
Ladan Khamseh, *
EMP: 432 **EST:** 1994
SQ FT: 200,000
SALES (est): 50.01MM **Privately Held**
Web: www.caloptima.org
SIC: 8621 Professional organizations

(P-17304)
ORANGE COUNTY HEALTH CARE AGCY
405 W 5th St Ste 700, Santa Ana
(92701-4534)
PHONE..................714 568-5683
Jenny Qian, *Prin*
EMP: 99 **EST:** 2014
SALES (est): 2.48MM **Privately Held**
Web: www.ochealthinfo.com
SIC: 8621 Health association

(P-17305)
REGAL MEDICAL GROUP INC (PA)
Also Called: Heritage California Aco
8510 Balboa Blvd Ste 275, Northridge
(91325-5809)
PHONE..................818 654-3400
Richard N Merkin, *CEO*
EMP: 104 **EST:** 1986
SALES (est): 46.35MM **Privately Held**
Web: www.regalmed.com
SIC: 8621 Medical field-related associations

(P-17306)
ROCKBLUE
601 Foothill Rd, Ojai (93023-1765)
PHONE..................703 314-0208
Peter Macy, *Pr*
Satish Menon, *
Richard Noth, *
Chris Fahlin, *
Shannon Roxborough, *
EMP: 75 **EST:** 2021
SALES (est): 792.92K **Privately Held**
SIC: 8621 Professional organizations

(P-17307)
SHARP COMMUNITY MEDICAL GROUP
Also Called: SCMG
8695 Spectrum Center Blvd, San Diego
(92123-1489)
PHONE..................858 499-4525
Kenneth Roth, *Pr*
EMP: 200 **EST:** 1989
SALES (est): 606.67MM
SALES (corp-wide): 1.9B **Privately Held**
Web: www.scmg.org
SIC: 8621 Professional organizations
PA: Sharp Healthcare
8695 Spectrum Ctr Blvd
858 499-4000

(P-17308)
STATE BAR OF CALIFORNIA
755 Santa Rosa St Ste 310, San Luis
Obispo (93401-4805)
PHONE..................805 544-7551
EMP: 92
SALES (corp-wide): 46.74MM **Privately Held**
Web: calbar.ca.gov
SIC: 8621 Bar association
PA: State Bar Of California
180 Howard St
415 538-2000

(P-17309)
STATE BAR OF CALIFORNIA
845 S Figueroa St, Los Angeles
(90017-2515)
PHONE..................213 765-1520
EMP: 93
SALES (corp-wide): 46.74MM **Privately Held**
Web: calbar.ca.gov
SIC: 8621 Bar association
PA: State Bar Of California
180 Howard St
415 538-2000

(P-17310)
TRUCK UNDERWRITERS ASSOCIATION (DH)
4680 Wilshire Blvd, Los Angeles
(90010-3807)
PHONE..................323 932-3200
Leonard H Gelfand, *Pr*
Gerald Faulwell, *
Martin Feinstein, *
John Lynch, *
Jason Katz, *
EMP: 1767 **EST:** 1935
SALES (est): 2.67MM **Privately Held**
SIC: 8621 Professional organizations
HQ: Farmers Group, Inc.
6301 Owensmouth Ave
Woodland Hills CA 91367
323 932-3200

8631 Labor Organizations

(P-17311)
INTERNTIONAL UN OPER ENGINEERS
Also Called: Local 12
3935 Normal St, San Diego (92103-3418)
PHONE..................619 295-3186
Dan Hawn, *Mgr*
EMP: 476
SQ FT: 4,500
SALES (corp-wide): 8.11MM **Privately Held**
Web: www.iuoelocal841.com
SIC: 8631 Labor union
PA: International Union Of Operating
Engineers
1121 L St Ste 401
916 444-6880

(P-17312)
INTERNTIONAL UN OPER ENGINEERS
Also Called: Local 12
1647 W Lugonia Ave, Redlands
(92374-2048)
PHONE..................909 307-8700
Ron Sikroski, *Mgr*
EMP: 713
SALES (corp-wide): 8.11MM **Privately Held**
Web: www.oefi.org

SIC: 8631 Labor union
PA: International Union Of Operating
Engineers
1121 L St Ste 401
916 444-6880

(P-17313)
SEIU LOCAL 721
1545 Wilshire Blvd Ste 100, Los Angeles
(90017-4510)
PHONE..................213 368-8660
Annelle Grajeda, *Owner*
EMP: 184 **EST:** 2007
SALES (est): 142.29K **Privately Held**
Web: www.seiu721.org
SIC: 8631 Labor union

(P-17314)
SOUTHWEST CARPTR TRAINING FUND
533 S Fremont Ave Ste 700, Los Angeles
(90071-1714)
PHONE..................213 386-8590
Matt Dunphy, *Admn*
EMP: 81 **EST:** 2012
SALES (est): 39.18MM **Privately Held**
Web: www.swmsctf.org
SIC: 8631 Labor union

(P-17315)
SOUTHWEST RGNAL CNCIL CRPNTERS
Also Called: Southwest Regional Council of
Carpenters
7111 Firestone Blvd, Buena Park
(90621-2958)
PHONE..................714 571-0449
EMP: 92
SALES (corp-wide): 96.12MM **Privately Held**
Web: www.wscarpenters.org
SIC: 8631 Labor union
PA: Western States Regional Council Of
Carpenters
533 S Fremont Ave Fl 10
213 385-1457

(P-17316)
TEMPORARY STAFFING UNION
19800 Macarthur Blvd Ste 300, Irvine
(92612-2479)
PHONE..................714 728-5186
Veronica Lake, *CEO*
Fe Santos, *
EMP: 4000 **EST:** 2018
SQ FT: 1,500
SALES (est): 299.21K **Privately Held**
SIC: 8631 Labor union

(P-17317)
UNITED FARM WORKERS AMERICA (PA)
29700 Woodford Tehachapi Rd, Keene
(93531-8007)
P.O. Box 62 (93531-0062)
PHONE..................661 822-5571
Arturo Rodriguez, *Pr*
Irv Hershenbaum, *
Tanis Ybarra, *
Liz Villarino, *
EMP: 110 **EST:** 1966
SQ FT: 5,000
SALES (est): 9.96MM
SALES (corp-wide): 9.96MM **Privately Held**
Web: www.ufw.org
SIC: 8631 Labor union

(P-17318)
UNITED TEACHERS-LOS ANGELES
Also Called: U T L A
3303 Wilshire Blvd Fl 10, Los Angeles
(90010-1794)
PHONE..................213 487-5560
Aj Duffy, *Pr*
Ana Valencia, *
Joshua Pechthalt, *
David Goldburg, *
Betty Forrester, *
EMP: 72 **EST:** 1970
SQ FT: 144,000
SALES (est): 56.22MM **Privately Held**
Web: www.utla.net
SIC: 8631 Labor union

(P-17319)
WRITERS GUILD AMERICA WEST INC
7000 W 3rd St, Los Angeles (90048-4321)
PHONE..................323 951-4000
David Young, *CEO*
David Weiss, *Prin*
Elias Davis, *Sec*
David Young, *Ex Dir*
Chris Keyser, *Prin*
EMP: 160 **EST:** 1954
SQ FT: 67,000
SALES (est): 48.31MM
SALES (corp-wide): 48.31MM **Privately Held**
Web: www.wga.org
SIC: 8631 Labor union
PA: Producer-Writers Guild Of America
Pension Plan
2900 W Almeda Ave Ste 110
818 846-1015

8641 Civic And Social Associations

(P-17320)
21515 HAWTHORNE OWNER LLC
21535 Hawthorne Blvd Ste 100, Torrance
(90503-6624)
PHONE..................310 406-3730
Margaret Powell, *
Jenny Blanchart, *
EMP: 100 **EST:** 2014
SALES (est): 812.17K **Privately Held**
SIC: 8641 Dwelling-related associations

(P-17321)
ACTION PROPERTY MANAGEMENT INC
530 S Hewitt St, Los Angeles (90013-2286)
PHONE..................800 400-2284
Mary Moore, *Brnch Mgr*
EMP: 98
SALES (corp-wide): 30MM **Privately Held**
Web: www.actionlife.com
SIC: 8641 Homeowners' association
PA: Action Property Management, Inc.
2603 Main St Ste 500
949 450-0202

(P-17322)
AFRICAN WOMEN RISING
801 Cold Springs Rd, Santa Barbara
(93108-1016)
PHONE..................415 278-1784
Linda Cole, *CEO*
EMP: 200 **EST:** 2007
SALES (est): 2.12MM **Privately Held**
Web: www.africanwomenrising.org

SIC: 8641 Civic and social associations

(P-17323)
ARMED SERVICES YMCA OF USA
3293 Santo Rd, San Diego (92124-3340)
PHONE..................858 751-5755
Kim Ney, *Ex Dir*
EMP: 124
SALES (corp-wide): 25.58MM **Privately Held**
Web: www.asymca.org
SIC: 8641 Youth organizations
PA: Armed Services Ymca Of The U.S.A.
14040 Central Loop # B
703 445-3986

(P-17324)
BEAR VALLEY SPRINGS ASSN
29541 Rollingoak Dr, Tehachapi (93561-7133)
PHONE..................661 821-5537
Todd Lander, *Pr*
Terry Quinn, *
Larry Thompson, *
Tim Hawkins, *
EMP: 200 EST: 1970
SQ FT: 2,000
SALES (est): 8.47MM **Privately Held**
Web: www.bvsa.org
SIC: 8641 Homeowners' association

(P-17325)
BOYS & GIRLS CLUBS SOUTH CNTY
847 Encina Ave, Imperial Beach (91932-2135)
P.O. Box 520 (91932)
PHONE..................619 424-2266
Ken Blinsman, *Pr*
EMP: 100 EST: 1982
SALES (est): 2.87MM **Privately Held**
Web: www.bgcscounty.org
SIC: 8641 5812 Youth organizations; Eating places

(P-17326)
BOYS GIRLS CLUBS OF KERN CNTY
Also Called: BOY'S & GIRL'S CLUB OF BAKERSF
801 Niles St, Bakersfield (93305-4419)
PHONE..................661 325-3730
Zane Smith, *Dir*
Ed Kuhn, *
Bill Campbell, *
Craig Stickler, *
Tricia Ceccarill, *
EMP: 500 EST: 1971
SALES (est): 13.87MM **Privately Held**
Web: www.bgckc.org
SIC: 8641 8322 Boy Scout organization; Individual and family services

(P-17327)
BOYS GRLS CLB BRBANK GRTER E V
300 E Angeleno Ave, Burbank (91502-1311)
PHONE..................818 842-9333
Shanna Warren, *CEO*
Shannon Warren, *
EMP: 99 EST: 1994
SQ FT: 6,000
SALES (est): 3.15MM **Privately Held**
Web: www.bgcburbank.org
SIC: 8641 Youth organizations

(P-17328)
BOYS GRLS CLB SNTA MONICA INC
Also Called: Boys Girls Clubs Santa Monica
1220 Lincoln Blvd, Santa Monica (90401-1704)
PHONE..................310 361-8500
Aaron Young, *Dir*
EMP: 83 EST: 1943
SQ FT: 6,000
SALES (est): 3.03MM **Privately Held**
Web: www.smbgc.org
SIC: 8641 7997 Youth organizations; Membership sports and recreation clubs

(P-17329)
BOYS GRLS CLUBS HUNTINGTON VLY (PA)
Also Called: BOYS & GIRLS CLUBS OF HUNTINGT
16582 Brookhurst St, Fountain Valley (92708-2353)
PHONE..................714 531-2582
Tanya Hoxsie, *Pr*
EMP: 89 EST: 1967
SALES (est): 13.52MM **Privately Held**
Web: www.bgchv.com
SIC: 8641 Youth organizations

(P-17330)
CALIFORNIA CLUB
538 S Flower St, Los Angeles (90071-2548)
PHONE..................213 622-1391
Robert C Baker, *CEO*
EMP: 185 EST: 1888
SALES (est): 8.86MM **Privately Held**
Web: www.californiaclub.org
SIC: 8641 7041 Business persons club; Residence club, organization

(P-17331)
CHANNEL ISLNDS YUNG MNS CHRSTN
301 W Figueroa St, Santa Barbara (93101-3632)
PHONE..................805 963-8775
Teri Bradford Rouse, *Brnch Mgr*
EMP: 87
SALES (corp-wide): 19.27MM **Privately Held**
Web: www.ciymca.org
SIC: 8641 Youth organizations
PA: Channel Islands Young Men's Christian Association
1180 Eugenia Pl
805 560 1103

(P-17332)
CHANNEL ISLNDS YUNG MNS CHRSTN
Also Called: Lompoc Family YMCA
201 W College Ave, Lompoc (93436-4415)
PHONE..................805 736-3483
Dan Powell, *Brnch Mgr*
EMP: 87
SALES (corp-wide): 19.27MM **Privately Held**
Web: www.ciymca.org
SIC: 8641 7991 8351 7032 Youth organizations; Physical fitness facilities; Child day care services; Youth camps
PA: Channel Islands Young Men's Christian Association
1180 Eugenia Pl
805 569-1103

(P-17333)
CHANNEL ISLNDS YUNG MNS CHRSTN
Also Called: Santa Barbara Family YMCA
36 Hitchcock Way, Santa Barbara (93105-3102)
PHONE..................805 687-7727
Tim Hardy, *Brnch Mgr*
EMP: 88
SALES (corp-wide): 19.27MM **Privately Held**
Web: www.ciymca.org
SIC: 8641 7991 8351 7032 Youth organizations; Physical fitness facilities; Child day care services; Youth camps
PA: Channel Islands Young Men's Christian Association
1180 Eugenia Pl
805 569-1103

(P-17334)
CHANNEL ISLNDS YUNG MNS CHRSTN
Also Called: Montecito Family YMCA
591 Santa Rosa Ln, Santa Barbara (93108-2145)
PHONE..................805 969-3288
Yvonne Rubio, *Dir*
EMP: 88
SALES (corp-wide): 19.27MM **Privately Held**
Web: www.ciymca.org
SIC: 8641 7991 8351 7032 Youth organizations; Physical fitness facilities; Child day care services; Youth camps
PA: Channel Islands Young Men's Christian Association
1180 Eugenia Pl
805 569-1103

(P-17335)
CHANNEL ISLNDS YUNG MNS CHRSTN
Also Called: Stuart C. Gildred Family YMCA
900 N Refugio Rd, Santa Ynez (93460-9314)
PHONE..................805 686-2037
Paula Parisotto, *Brnch Mgr*
EMP: 88
SALES (corp-wide): 19.27MM **Privately Held**
Web: www.ciymca.org
SIC: 8641 7991 8351 7032 Youth organizations; Physical fitness facilities; Child day care services; Youth camps
PA: Channel Islands Young Men's Christian Association
1180 Eugenia Pl
805 569-1103

(P-17336)
CHANNEL ISLNDS YUNG MNS CHRSTN
Also Called: Camarillo Family YMCA
3111 Village Park Dr, Camarillo (93012)
PHONE..................805 484-0423
Marge Castellano, *Dir*
EMP: 88
SALES (corp-wide): 19.27MM **Privately Held**
Web: www.ciymca.org
SIC: 8641 7991 8351 7032 Youth organizations; Physical fitness facilities; Child day care services; Youth camps
PA: Channel Islands Young Men's Christian Association
1180 Eugenia Pl
805 569-1103

(P-17337)
CHANNEL ISLNDS YUNG MNS CHRSTN
Also Called: Ventura Family YMCA
3760 Telegraph Rd, Ventura (93003-3421)
PHONE..................805 484-0423
Sarah Abrams, *Dir*
EMP: 88
SALES (corp-wide): 19.27MM **Privately Held**
Web: www.ciymca.org
SIC: 8641 7991 8351 7032 Youth organizations; Physical fitness facilities; Child day care services; Youth camps
PA: Channel Islands Young Men's Christian Association
1180 Eugenia Pl
805 569-1103

(P-17338)
COUNTY OF RIVERSIDE
Also Called: Riverside Crona Rsrce Cnsrvtio
4500 Glenwood Dr Ste A, Riverside (92501-3066)
PHONE..................951 683-7691
Shelli Lamb, *Dist Mgr*
EMP: 148
SALES (corp-wide): 5.07B **Privately Held**
Web: www.rcrcd.org
SIC: 8641 9512 Environmental protection organization; Land, mineral, and wildlife conservation, County government
PA: County Of Riverside
4080 Lemon St Fl 11
951 955-1110

(P-17339)
CRESCENTA-CANADA YMCA
Also Called: Learning Tree Pre-School
6840 Foothill Blvd, Tujunga (91042-2711)
PHONE..................818 352-3255
Kathi Brink, *Brnch Mgr*
EMP: 130
SALES (corp-wide): 10.67MM **Privately Held**
Web: www.ymcafoothills.org
SIC: 8641 7991 8351 7032 Youth organizations; Physical fitness facilities; Child day care services; Youth camps
PA: Crescenta-Canada Ymca
1930 Foothill Blvd
818 790-0123

(P-17340)
CRESCENTA-CANADA YMCA (PA)
Also Called: YMCA CRESCENTA-CANADA
1930 Foothill Blvd, La Canada (91011-1933)
PHONE..................818 790-0123
Larry Hall, *CEO*
Ken Gorvetzian, *
EMP: 150 EST: 1953
SALES (est): 10.67MM
SALES (corp-wide): 10.67MM **Privately Held**
Web: www.ymcafoothills.org
SIC: 8641 7991 8351 7032 Youth organizations; Physical fitness facilities; Child day care services; Youth camps

(P-17341)
DS LAKESHORE LP
200 Baker St Ste 100, Costa Mesa (92626-4551)
PHONE..................916 286-5231
Patrick S Donahue, *Pt*
Trina Perales, *Pt*
EMP: 99 EST: 2019
SALES (est): 177.4K **Privately Held**

SIC: 8641 Civic and social associations

(P-17342)
ELIZABETH GLSER PDTRIC AIDS FN
2950 31st St Ste 125, Santa Monica (90405-3098)
PHONE.................................310 593-0047
Jeff Gaffney, *Brnch Mgr*
EMP: 457
SALES (corp-wide): 172.48MM **Privately Held**
Web: www.pedaids.org
SIC: 8641 Civic and social associations
PA: Elizabeth Glaser Pediatric Aids Foundation
1350 Eye St Nw Ste 400
920 770-0103

(P-17343)
EXCEPTIONAL CHLD FOUNDATION
11124 Fairbanks Way, Culver City (90230-4945)
PHONE.................................310 915-6606
EMP: 110
SALES (corp-wide): 28.26MM **Privately Held**
Web: www.ecf.net
SIC: 8641 Civic and social associations
PA: Exceptional Children's Foundation
5350 Machado Ln
310 204-3300

(P-17344)
GIRL SCUTS CLFRNIAS CNTL COAST
Also Called: GIRL SCOUTS
1500 Palma Dr # 110, Ventura (93003-6451)
PHONE.................................831 633-4877
Sharon B Reece, *Pr*
Brenda Whitsett, *Ex Dir*
Donna Brown, *Sec*
Manuela Kolpin, *Treas*
EMP: 81 **EST:** 1924
SALES (est): 5.47MM **Privately Held**
Web: www.girlscoutsccc.org
SIC: 8641 Girl Scout organization

(P-17345)
GIRL SCUTS GREATER LOS ANGELES (PA)
423 N La Brea Ave, Inglewood (90302-3408)
PHONE.................................626 677-2265
Lise Luttgens, *CEO*
Sylvia Rosenberger, *
Christa Weddle, *
Emily Ausbrook Chief Mission Delivery, *Ofcr*
EMP: 114 **EST:** 1924
SALES (est): 25.69MM
SALES (corp-wide): 25.69MM **Privately Held**
Web: www.girlscoutsla.org
SIC: 8641 Girl Scout organization

(P-17346)
GIRL SCUTS SAN DG-MPRIAL CNCIL (PA)
Also Called: GIRL SCOUTS SAN DIEGO
1231 Upas St, San Diego (92103-5127)
PHONE.................................619 610-0751
Jo Dee C Jacob, *CEO*
▼ **EMP:** 94 **EST:** 1917
SQ FT: 7,926
SALES (est): 13.27MM
SALES (corp-wide): 13.27MM **Privately Held**

Web: www.sdgirlscouts.org
SIC: 8641 Girl Scout organization

(P-17347)
GREATER LOS ANGLES AREA CNCIL (PA)
Also Called: BOY SCOUTS OF AMERICA
2333 Scout Way, Los Angeles (90026-4912)
PHONE.................................213 413-4400
Cash Sutton, *Pr*
EMP: 93 **EST:** 1935
SALES (est): 14.47MM
SALES (corp-wide): 14.47MM **Privately Held**
Web: www.glaacbsa.org
SIC: 8641 Boy Scout organization

(P-17348)
HEAL BAY
1444 9th St, Santa Monica (90401-2707)
PHONE.................................310 451-1500
Alix Hobbs, *Pr*
Kim Francis, *
Sue Sattin, *
Sarah Abramson Sikich, *
EMP: 85 **EST:** 1986
SALES (est): 4.65MM **Privately Held**
Web: www.healthebay.org
SIC: 8641 Environmental protection organization

(P-17349)
JEWISH CMNTY FNDTION LOS ANGLE (PA)
6505 Wilshire Blvd Ste 1150, Los Angeles (90048-4906)
PHONE.................................323 761-8700
Richard V Sandler, *Ch Bd*
Leslie E Bider, *
J Sanderson, *
Arlene Freedman, *
Jack Klein, *
EMP: 150 **EST:** 1937
SQ FT: 100,000
SALES (est): 49.73MM
SALES (corp-wide): 49.73MM **Privately Held**
Web: www.jewishla.org
SIC: 8641 8661 Community membership club ; Religious organizations

(P-17350)
JONATHAN CLUB (PA)
545 S Figueroa St, Los Angeles (90071-1704)
PHONE.................................213 624-0881
Gregory J Dumas, *Pr*
James Abbott, *
Norm Rich, *
Randolph P Sinnott, *
◆ **EMP:** 200 **EST:** 1895
SQ FT: 230,276
SALES (est): 33.42MM
SALES (corp-wide): 33.42MM **Privately Held**
Web: www.jc.org
SIC: 8641 Social club, membership

(P-17351)
KOOJI INTL MINORITY EDUCATN
6896 Magnolia Ave, Riverside (92506-2843)
PHONE.................................951 313-7403
Metropolitan Marcos, *Ch*
EMP: 75 **EST:** 2015
SALES (est): 157.22K **Privately Held**
SIC: 8641 Civic and social associations

(P-17352)
KPMG NEW YORK FOUNDATION INC
Also Called: Kpmg
550 S Hope St Ste 1500, Los Angeles (90071-2629)
PHONE.................................212 758-9700
Bijay Kim, *Pr*
EMP: 176 **EST:** 1971
SALES (est): 2.53MM **Privately Held**
Web: www.kpmg.com
SIC: 8641 8721 Civic and social associations ; Accounting, auditing, and bookkeeping

(P-17353)
LAKE FREST NO II MSTR HMWNERS
Also Called: SUN & SAIL CLUB
24752 Toledo Ln, Lake Forest (92630-2399)
PHONE.................................949 586-0860
Sonny Morper, *Pr*
Ted Brackez, *
Terri Graham, *
Ken Hedge, *
EMP: 80 **EST:** 1971
SQ FT: 9,000
SALES (est): 6.41MM **Privately Held**
Web: www.liveinlakeforest.com
SIC: 8641 Homeowners' association

(P-17354)
LAKE MISSION VIEJO ASSOCIATION
22555 Olympiad Rd, Mission Viejo (92692-1177)
PHONE.................................949 770-1313
Fred Mellenbruch, *Pr*
Jane Chadburn, *
Senator Jeff Miklaus, *VP*
Wayne Dunn, *
Sid Wittenberg, *
EMP: 90 **EST:** 1978
SQ FT: 7,400
SALES (est): 9.68MM **Privately Held**
Web: www.lakemissionviejo.org
SIC: 8641 Homeowner's association

(P-17355)
MARAVILLA FOUNDATION (PA)
5729 Union Pacific Ave, Commerce (90022-5134)
PHONE.................................323 721-4162
Alex M Sotomayor, *CEO*
Paul Lopez, *
Robert Lagunas, *
George Ross, *
EMP: 151 **EST:** 1967
SQ FT: 30,000
SALES (est): 16.57MM
SALES (corp-wide): 16.57MM **Privately Held**
Web: www.maravilla.org
SIC: 8641 Civic and social associations

(P-17356)
MILKEN FAMILY FOUNDATION
1250 4th St Fl 1, Santa Monica (90401-1418)
PHONE.................................310 570-4800
Lowell J Milken, *Pr*
Susan Fox, *
EMP: 200 **EST:** 1986
SALES (est): 5.05MM **Privately Held**
Web: www.mff.org
SIC: 8641 Civic and social associations

(P-17357)
MORNINGSIDE COMMUNITY ASSN
82 Mayfair Dr, Rancho Mirage (92270-2562)
PHONE.................................760 328-3323
M Abdelnour, *Genl Mgr*
Michelle Abdelnour, *
EMP: 73 **EST:** 1983
SQ FT: 3,500
SALES (est): 3.32MM **Privately Held**
Web: www.morningsideca.com
SIC: 8641 Homeowners' association

(P-17358)
OXNARD POLICE DEPARTMENT
251 S C St, Oxnard (93030-5789)
PHONE.................................805 385-8300
EMP: 350 **EST:** 1960
SALES (est): 9.72MM **Privately Held**
Web: www.oxnardpd.org
SIC: 8641 Veterans' organization

(P-17359)
PALM DESERT GREENS ASSOCIATION
73750 Country Club Dr, Palm Desert (92260-8698)
PHONE.................................760 346-8005
Roberta Hollingsworth, *Genl Mgr*
Mal Sinclair, *
Ken Dobson, *
EMP: 75 **EST:** 1971
SQ FT: 12,400
SALES (est): 8.91MM **Privately Held**
Web: www.pdgcc.org
SIC: 8641 Homeowners' association

(P-17360)
PUBLIC HLTH FNDATION ENTPS INC (PA)
Also Called: Heluna Health
13300 Crossroads Pkwy N Ste 450, City Of Industry (91746-3405)
PHONE.................................800 201-7320
Blain Cutler, *Pr*
Eric Ramanathan, *
Devecchio Finley, *Vice Chairman*
Robert Jenks, *
Tamara Joseph, *
EMP: 177 **EST:** 1968
SQ FT: 25,000
SALES (est): 49.53MM
SALES (corp-wide): 49.53MM **Privately Held**
Web: www.helunahealth.org
SIC: 8641 Civic and social associations

(P-17361)
PUBLIC HLTH FNDATION ENTPS INC
277 S Atlantic Blvd, Los Angeles (90022-1734)
PHONE.................................323 263-0262
Laurie Hill, *Prin*
EMP: 140
SALES (corp-wide): 49.53MM **Privately Held**
Web: www.helunahealth.org
SIC: 8641 Civic and social associations
PA: Public Health Foundation Enterprises, Inc.
13300 Crssrads Pkwy N Ste
800 201-7320

(P-17362)
PUBLIC HLTH FNDATION ENTPS INC

Also Called: Wic
1640 W Carson St Ste G, Torrance
(90501-3877)
PHONE.............................310 320-5215
EMP: 140
SALES (corp-wide): 49.53MM **Privately
Held**
Web: www.helunahealth.org
SIC: 8641 Civic and social associations
PA: Public Health Foundation Enterprises,
Inc.
13300 Crssroads Pkwy N Ste
800 201-7320

(P-17363)
SAN DIEGO COUNTRY ESTATES ASSN
Also Called: SAN VICENTE INN & GOLF
CLUB
24157 San Vicente Rd, Ramona
(92065-4199)
PHONE.............................760 789-3788
Jim Piva, *Pr*
EMP: 147 **EST:** 1972
SQ FT: 14,000
SALES (est): 13.53MM **Privately Held**
Web: www.sanvicenteresort.com
SIC: 8641 7997 7992 7011 Homeowners'
association; Membership sports and
recreation clubs; Public golf courses;
Vacation lodges

(P-17364)
SAN LUIS OBISPO COUNTY YMCA
5785 Los Ranchos Rd, San Luis Obispo
(93401-8247)
PHONE.............................805 544-7225
Mike Robertson, *Dir*
EMP: 72
SALES (corp-wide): 2.97MM **Privately
Held**
Web: www.ciymca.org
SIC: 8641 7991 8351 7032 Youth
organizations; Physical fitness facilities;
Child day care services; Youth camps
PA: San Luis Obispo County Ymca Inc
1020 Southwood Dr
805 543-8235

(P-17365)
SAVICE INC
30052 Tomas, Rcho Sta Marg
(92688-2127)
PHONE.............................949 888-2444
Phu Hoang, *Prin*
EMP: 98 **EST:** 2008
SALES (est): 71K **Privately Held**
SIC: 8641 Civic and social associations

(P-17366)
SHRINERS INTERNATIONAL
Also Called: Shriners Hsspitals For Children
909 S Fair Oaks Ave, Pasadena
(91105-2625)
PHONE.............................626 389-9300
EMP: 94
SALES (corp-wide): 7.02MM **Privately
Held**
Web: www.shrinerschildrens.org
SIC: 8641 Fraternal associations
HQ: Shriners Hospitals For Children
2900 N Rocky Point Dr
Tampa FL 33607

(P-17367)
SILVER LAKES ASSOCIATION
Also Called: Homeowners Association
15273 Orchard Hill Ln, Helendale
(92342-7824)

P.O. Box 179 (92342-0179)
PHONE.............................760 245-1606
Michael Bennett, *Genl Mgr*
EMP: 90 **EST:** 1976
SQ FT: 3,000
SALES (est): 5.02MM **Privately Held**
Web: www.silverlakesassociation.com
SIC: 8641 Homeowners' association

(P-17368)
SUN CITY PALM DSERT CMNTY ASSN (PA)
Also Called: Palm Desert Community Assn
38180 Del Webb Blvd, Palm Desert
(92211-1256)
PHONE.............................760 200-2100
Helen Mcenerney, *Pr*
EMP: 80 **EST:** 1992
SQ FT: 4,000
SALES (est): 16.7MM **Privately Held**
Web: www.scpdca.com
SIC: 8641 7992 7997 Dwelling-related
associations; Public golf courses; Country
club, membership

(P-17369)
THEATER ARTS FNDTION SAN DEGO
Also Called: LA JOLLA PLAYHOUSE
2910 La Jolla Village Dr, La Jolla
(92093-5100)
P.O. Box 12039 (92039-2039)
PHONE.............................858 623-3306
Jeffrey Ressler Ch Person, *Prin*
Steven Libman, *
Lynelle Lynch Ch Person, *Prin*
Tim Scott Ch Person, *Prin*
Michael Bartell, *
EMP: 250 **EST:** 1954
SQ FT: 1,440
SALES (est): 6.05MM **Privately Held**
Web: www.lajollaplayhouse.org
SIC: 8641 7922 Civic associations;
Theatrical producers and services

(P-17370)
U C RIVERSIDE FOUNDATION
900 University Ave, Riverside (92521-9800)
PHONE.............................951 827-6389
Peter Hayashida, *Pr*
EMP: 185 **EST:** 2011
SALES (est): 18.34MM **Privately Held**
Web: www.ucr.edu
SIC: 8641 8699 Civic and social associations
; Charitable organization

(P-17371)
UNITED BYS GRLS CLUBS SNTA BRB
Also Called: Boys & Girls Club
5701 Hollister Ave, Goleta (93117-3420)
P.O. Box 1485 (93102-1485)
PHONE.............................805 967-1612
Sal Rodriguez, *Ex Dir*
EMP: 71
SALES (corp-wide): 3.73MM **Privately
Held**
Web: www.unitedbg.org
SIC: 8641 8351 Bars and restaurants,
members only; Child day care services
PA: United Boys And Girls Clubs Of Santa
Barbara County
1124 Castillo St
805 681-1315

(P-17372)
URBAN CORPS SAN DIEGO COUNTY
3127 Jefferson St, San Diego (92110-4422)

P.O. Box 80156 (92138-0156)
PHONE.............................619 235-6884
Sam Duran, *CEO*
Michael Sterns, *
EMP: 132 **EST:** 1989
SQ FT: 25,000
SALES (est): 14.3MM **Privately Held**
Web: www.urbancorpssd.org
SIC: 8641 Youth organizations

(P-17373)
VALLEY HUNT CLUB
520 S Orange Grove Blvd, Pasadena
(91105-1799)
PHONE.............................626 793-7134
David Mole, *CEO*
Donald F Crumrine, *
EMP: 85 **EST:** 1888
SQ FT: 40,000
SALES (est): 8.39MM **Privately Held**
Web: www.valleyhuntclub.com
SIC: 8641 Social club, membership

(P-17374)
VETERANS MED RES FNDTION SAN D
3350 La Jolla Village Dr Ste 151a, San
Diego (92161-0002)
PHONE.............................858 642-3080
Kerstin B Lynam, *CEO*
Barabara Dovenbarger, *
EMP: 250 **EST:** 1986
SALES (est): 15.91MM **Privately Held**
Web: www.vmrf.org
SIC: 8641 Civic and social associations

(P-17375)
VTS INDUSTRIES
1049 Elkelton Blvd, Spring Valley
(91977-4720)
PHONE.............................619 337-9244
William D Mudd, *Pr*
Bernard Bandish, *
Clifford Caldwell, *
Donald Pouliot, *
EMP: 100 **EST:** 1967
SQ FT: 8,000
SALES (est): 14.35MM **Privately Held**
Web: www.davveteransthriftstores.com
SIC: 8641 5932 Veterans' organization;
Clothing, secondhand

(P-17376)
WEST END YUNG MNS CHRISTN ASSN
Also Called: Ontario/Montclair YMCA
1257 E D St, Ontario (91764-4329)
P.O. Box 3220 (91761-0922)
PHONE.............................909 477-2780
Dianna Lee-mitchell, *Dir*
EMP: 115
SALES (corp-wide): 4.94MM **Privately
Held**
Web: www.weymca.org
SIC: 8641 7991 8351 7032 Youth
organizations; Physical fitness facilities;
Child day care services; Youth camps
PA: West End Young Men's Christian
Association Inc
1150 E Foothill Blvd
909 481-0722

(P-17377)
WEST END YUNG MNS CHRISTN ASSN
Also Called: Chino Valley YMCA
5665 Edison Ave, Chino (91710-9051)
PHONE.............................909 597-7445
Deb Anderson, *Dir*

EMP: 115
SALES (corp-wide): 4.94MM **Privately
Held**
Web: www.weymca.org
SIC: 8641 7991 8351 7032 Youth
organizations; Physical fitness facilities;
Child day care services; Youth camps
PA: West End Young Men's Christian
Association Inc
1150 E Foothill Blvd
909 481-0722

(P-17378)
YMCA OF EAST VALLEY (PA)
500 E Citrus Ave, Redlands (92373-5285)
PHONE.............................909 798-9622
Darwin Barnett, *CEO*
Ken Stein, *
Perry Mecate, *
Doug Thorne, *
Carmen Barney, *
EMP: 125 **EST:** 1887
SQ FT: 100,000
SALES (est): 19.76MM
SALES (corp-wide): 19.76MM **Privately
Held**
Web: www.ymcaeastvalley.org
SIC: 8641 Youth organizations

(P-17379)
YMCA OF EAST VALLEY
Also Called: YMCA Camp Edwards
42842 Jenks Lake Rd E, Angelus Oaks
(92305-9769)
P.O. Box 277 (92305-0277)
PHONE.............................909 794-1702
Loren Werner, *Dir*
EMP: 119
SALES (corp-wide): 19.76MM **Privately
Held**
Web: www.ymcaeastvalley.org
SIC: 8641 7991 8351 7032 Youth
organizations; Physical fitness facilities;
Child day care services; Youth camps
PA: Ymca Of The East Valley
500 E Citrus Ave
909 798-9622

(P-17380)
YMCA OF EAST VALLEY
Also Called: San Bernardino Family YMCA
808 E 21st St, San Bernardino
(92404-4874)
PHONE.............................909 881-9622
Bill Blank, *Dir*
EMP: 119
SALES (corp-wide): 19.76MM **Privately
Held**
Web: www.ymcaeastvalley.org
SIC: 8641 7991 8351 7032 Youth
organizations; Physical fitness facilities;
Child day care services; Youth camps
PA: Ymca Of The East Valley
500 E Citrus Ave
909 798-9622

(P-17381)
YMCA OF SAN DIEGO COUNTY
Also Called: Y M C A Childcare Resource Ser
1310 Union Plaza Ct Ste 200, Oceanside
(92054-5655)
PHONE.............................760 754-6042
Job Moraido, *Brnch Mgr*
EMP: 99
SALES (corp-wide): 155.53MM **Privately
Held**
Web: www.ymca.org
SIC: 8641 7991 8351 7032 Youth
organizations; Physical fitness facilities;
Child day care services; Youth camps
HQ: Ymca Of San Diego County
3708 Ruffin Rd

San Diego CA 92123
858 292-9622

(P-17382)
YMCA OF SAN DIEGO COUNTY
Also Called: Toby Wells YMCA
5105 Overland Ave, San Diego
(92123-1238)
PHONE....................858 496-9622
EMP: 91
SALES (corp-wide): 155.53MM **Privately Held**
Web: www.ymcasd.org
SIC: 8641 Youth organizations
HQ: Ymca Of San Diego County
3708 Ruffin Rd
San Diego CA 92123
858 292-9622

(P-17383)
YMCA OF SAN DIEGO COUNTY
Also Called: La Jolla YMCA
8355 Cliffridge Ave, La Jolla (92037-2107)
PHONE....................858 453-3483
Sam Wurtzbacher, Dir
EMP: 228
SALES (corp-wide): 155.53MM **Privately Held**
Web: www.ymca.org
SIC: 8641 8351 7997 Youth organizations; Child day care services; Membership sports and recreation clubs
HQ: Ymca Of San Diego County
3708 Ruffin Rd
San Diego CA 92123
858 292-9622

(P-17384)
YMCA OF SAN DIEGO COUNTY
Also Called: Gymnastics Center
6100 Avenida Encinas Ste B, Carlsbad
(92011-1052)
PHONE....................760 804-8170
Ellen Morelli, Dir
EMP: 95
SALES (corp-wide): 155.53MM **Privately Held**
Web: www.ymca.org
SIC: 8641 8322 Youth organizations; Youth center
HQ: Ymca Of San Diego County
3708 Ruffin Rd
San Diego CA 92123
858 292-9622

(P-17385)
YMCA OF SAN DIEGO COUNTY
Also Called: Borderview Y M C A
3085 Beyer Blvd Ste 105, San Diego
(92154-3479)
PHONE....................619 428-1168
Mauricio Gonzalez, Ex Dir
EMP: 152
SALES (corp-wide): 155.53MM **Privately Held**
Web: www.ymcasd.org
SIC: 8641 7991 8351 7032 Youth organizations; Physical fitness facilities; Child day care services; Youth camps
HQ: Ymca Of San Diego County
3708 Ruffin Rd
San Diego CA 92123
858 292-9622

(P-17386)
YMCA OF SAN DIEGO COUNTY
Also Called: Pelomar Family YMCA
200 Saxony Rd, Encinitas (92024-2720)
PHONE....................760 745-7490
Alfredo Velasco, Mgr

EMP: 218
SALES (corp-wide): 155.53MM **Privately Held**
Web: www.ymcasd.org
SIC: 8641 7991 8351 7032 Youth organizations; Physical fitness facilities; Child day care services; Youth camps
HQ: Ymca Of San Diego County
3708 Ruffin Rd
San Diego CA 92123
858 292-9622

(P-17387)
YMCA OF SAN DIEGO COUNTY
Also Called: Young Mens Christn Assocation
8881 Dallas St, La Mesa (91942-3297)
PHONE....................619 464-1323
Steve Rowe, Ex Dir
EMP: 165
SALES (corp-wide): 155.53MM **Privately Held**
Web: www.ymcasd.org
SIC: 8641 7991 8351 7032 Youth organizations; Physical fitness facilities; Child day care services; Youth camps
HQ: Ymca Of San Diego County
3708 Ruffin Rd
San Diego CA 92123
858 292-9622

(P-17388)
YMCA OF SAN DIEGO COUNTY
Also Called: Copley Family YMCA
5505 Friars Rd, San Diego (92110-2682)
PHONE....................619 280-9622
Kischa Hill, Dir
EMP: 243
SALES (corp-wide): 155.53MM **Privately Held**
Web: www.ymcasd.org
SIC: 8641 7991 8351 7032 Youth organizations; Physical fitness facilities; Child day care services; Youth camps
HQ: Ymca Of San Diego County
3708 Ruffin Rd
San Diego CA 92123
858 292-9622

(P-17389)
YMCA OF SAN DIEGO COUNTY
Also Called: Magdalena Ecke Family YMCA
200 Saxony Rd, Encinitas (92024-2720)
PHONE....................858 292-4034
Susan J Cocke, Brnch Mgr
EMP: 295
SALES (corp-wide): 155.53MM **Privately Held**
Web: www.ymca.org
SIC: 8641 8351 8322 7997 Youth organizations; Child day care services; Youth center; Membership sports and recreation clubs
HQ: Ymca Of San Diego County
3708 Ruffin Rd
San Diego CA 92123
858 292-9622

(P-17390)
YMCA OF SAN DIEGO COUNTY
Also Called: YMCA Youth & Family Services
2927 Meade Ave, San Diego (92116-4251)
PHONE....................619 281-8313
Cesar Marcano, Ex Dir
EMP: 153
SALES (corp-wide): 155.53MM **Privately Held**
Web: www.ymcasd.org
SIC: 8641 7991 8351 7032 Youth organizations; Physical fitness facilities; Child day care services; Youth camps
HQ: Ymca Of San Diego County
3708 Ruffin Rd

San Diego CA 92123
858 292-9622

(P-17391)
YMCA OF SAN DIEGO COUNTY
Also Called: Peninsula Family YMCA Sunshine
2150 Beryl St Ste 18, San Diego
(92109-3617)
PHONE....................619 226-8888
Andrea Sanchez, Dir
EMP: 194
SQ FT: 3,500
SALES (corp-wide): 155.53MM **Privately Held**
Web: www.ymcasd.org
SIC: 8641 8322 Youth organizations; Individual and family services
HQ: Ymca Of San Diego County
3708 Ruffin Rd
San Diego CA 92123
858 292-9622

(P-17392)
YMCA OF SAN DIEGO COUNTY
Also Called: Jackie Robinson Family YMCA
5505 Friars Rd, San Diego (92110-2682)
PHONE....................619 264-0144
Mike Brunker, Ex Dir
EMP: 141
SALES (corp-wide): 155.53MM **Privately Held**
Web: www.ymcasd.org
SIC: 8641 7991 8351 7032 Youth organizations; Physical fitness facilities; Child day care services; Youth camps
HQ: Ymca Of San Diego County
3708 Ruffin Rd
San Diego CA 92123
858 292-9622

(P-17393)
YMCA OF SAN DIEGO COUNTY
Also Called: YMCA Child Care Resource Svcs
3333 Camino Del Rio S Ste 400, San Diego
(92108-3839)
PHONE....................619 521-3055
Debbie Macdonald, Dir
EMP: 180
SALES (corp-wide): 155.53MM **Privately Held**
Web: www.ymcasd.org
SIC: 8641 7991 8351 7032 Youth organizations; Physical fitness facilities; Child day care services; Youth camps
HQ: Ymca Of San Diego County
3708 Ruffin Rd
San Diego CA 92123
858 292-9622

(P-17394)
YMCA OF SAN DIEGO COUNTY
Also Called: YMCA Overnight Camp
4761 Pine Hills Rd, Julian (92036)
P.O. Box 2440 (92036-2440)
PHONE....................760 765-0642
Thomas Madeyski, Ex Dir
EMP: 148
SALES (corp-wide): 155.53MM **Privately Held**
Web: www.ymca.org
SIC: 8641 7991 8351 7032 Youth organizations; Physical fitness facilities; Child day care services; Youth camps
HQ: Ymca Of San Diego County
3708 Ruffin Rd
San Diego CA 92123
858 292-9622

(P-17395)
YMCA OF SAN DIEGO COUNTY
Also Called: Oz San Diego
3304 Idlewild Way, San Diego
(92117-3508)
PHONE....................858 270-8213
Laura Sutter, Mgr
EMP: 95
SALES (corp-wide): 155.53MM **Privately Held**
Web: www.ymcasd.org
SIC: 8641 7991 8351 7032 Youth organizations; Physical fitness facilities; Child day care services; Youth camps
HQ: Ymca Of San Diego County
3708 Ruffin Rd
San Diego CA 92123
858 292-9622

(P-17396)
YMCA OF SAN DIEGO COUNTY
Also Called: Mission Valley YMCA
5505 Friars Rd, San Diego (92110-2682)
PHONE....................619 298-3576
Dick Webster, Mgr
EMP: 299
SALES (corp-wide): 155.53MM **Privately Held**
Web: www.ymcasd.org
SIC: 8641 7997 Youth organizations; Membership sports and recreation clubs
HQ: Ymca Of San Diego County
3708 Ruffin Rd
San Diego CA 92123
858 292-9622

(P-17397)
YMCA OF SAN DIEGO COUNTY
Also Called: Joe & Mary Mottino YMCA
200 Saxony Rd, Encinitas (92024-2720)
PHONE....................760 758-0808
Jeff Guzzardo, Brnch Mgr
EMP: 161
SALES (corp-wide): 155.53MM **Privately Held**
Web: www.ymcasd.org
SIC: 8641 8322 Youth organizations; Individual and family services
HQ: Ymca Of San Diego County
3708 Ruffin Rd
San Diego CA 92123
858 292-9622

(P-17398)
YMCA OF SAN DIEGO COUNTY
Also Called: Santa Margarita YMCA Garrison
333 Garrison St, Oceanside (92054-4700)
PHONE....................760 757-8270
Margie Oliver, Brnch Mgr
EMP: 95
SALES (corp-wide): 155.53MM **Privately Held**
Web: www.ymca.org
SIC: 8641 7991 8351 7032 Youth organizations; Physical fitness facilities; Child day care services; Youth camps
HQ: Ymca Of San Diego County
3708 Ruffin Rd
San Diego CA 92123
858 292-9622

(P-17399)
YMCA OF SAN DIEGO COUNTY
Also Called: Y M C A
River Rock Dr, Santee (92071)
PHONE....................619 449-9622
Debbie Lenz, Dir
EMP: 99
SALES (corp-wide): 155.53MM **Privately Held**

Web: www.ymca.org
SIC: **8641** 7991 8351 7032 Youth organizations; Physical fitness facilities; Child day care services; Youth camps
HQ: Ymca Of San Diego County
3708 Ruffin Rd
San Diego CA 92123
858 292-9622

(P-17400)
YMCA OF SAN DIEGO COUNTY
Also Called: Oz North Coast Y M C A
215 Barnes St, Oceanside (92054-3472)
PHONE...............................760 721-8930
Kim Morgan, *Mgr*
EMP: 148
SQ FT: 3,567
SALES (corp-wide): 155.53MM **Privately Held**
Web: www.ymca.org
SIC: **8641** 7991 8351 7032 Youth organizations; Physical fitness facilities; Child day care services; Youth camps
HQ: Ymca Of San Diego County
3708 Ruffin Rd
San Diego CA 92123
858 292-9622

(P-17401)
YMCA OF SAN DIEGO COUNTY (HQ)
Also Called: Y, The
3708 Ruffin Rd, San Diego (92123-1812)
PHONE...............................858 292-9622
Todd Tibbits, *Pr*
John Merritt, *
Charmaine Carter, *
EMP: 78 EST: 1882
SQ FT: 19,600
SALES (est): 391K
SALES (corp-wide): 155.53MM **Privately Held**
Web: www.ymcasd.org
SIC: **8641** Youth organizations
PA: National Council Of Young Men's Christian Associations Of The United States Of America
101 N Wacker Dr Ste 1600
312 419-8456

(P-17402)
YOUNG MNS CHRSTN ASSN BRBANK C (PA)
321 E Magnolia Blvd, Burbank (91502-1132)
PHONE...............................818 845-8551
Mary Cutone, *CEO*
Bryan Snodgrasss, *
EMP: 100 EST: 1924
SQ FT: 47,000
SALES (est): 7.21MM
SALES (corp-wide): 7.21MM **Privately Held**
Web: www.burbankymca.org
SIC: **8641** 7991 8351 7032 Youth organizations; Physical fitness facilities; Child day care services; Youth camps

(P-17403)
YOUNG MNS CHRSTN ASSN GLNDALE
Also Called: GLENDALE YMCA SWIM SCHOOL
140 N Louise St, Glendale (91206-4226)
PHONE...............................818 484-8256
Tom Tyler, *CEO*
EMP: 86 EST: 1924
SQ FT: 15,000
SALES (est): 5.36MM **Privately Held**
Web: www.glendaleymca.org

SIC: **8641** Youth organizations

(P-17404)
YOUNG MNS CHRSTN ASSN MTRO LOS
Also Called: YMCA of Westchester
8015 S Sepulveda Blvd, Los Angeles (90045-2940)
PHONE...............................310 216-9036
Patricia De Frelice, *Ex Dir*
EMP: 70
SALES (corp-wide): 80.43MM **Privately Held**
Web: www.ymcala.org
SIC: **8641** 8322 Youth organizations; Individual and family services
PA: Young Men's Christian Association Of Metropolitan Los Angeles
625 S New Hampshire Ave
213 380-6448

(P-17405)
YOUNG MNS CHRSTN ASSN MTRO LOS
Also Called: YMCA
2900 Sepulveda Blvd, Torrance (90505-2804)
PHONE...............................310 325-5885
Steve Macaller, *Ex Dir*
EMP: 82
SALES (corp-wide): 80.43MM **Privately Held**
Web: www.ymcala.org
SIC: **8641** 7997 Youth organizations; Membership sports and recreation clubs
PA: Young Men's Christian Association Of Metropolitan Los Angeles
625 S New Hampshire Ave
213 380-6448

(P-17406)
YOUNG MNS CHRSTN ASSN MTRO LOS
Also Called: National Fitness Testing
1553 Schrader Blvd, Los Angeles (90028-7203)
PHONE...............................323 467-4161
Rosa Najera, *Brnch Mgr*
EMP: 105
SALES (corp-wide): 80.43MM **Privately Held**
Web: www.ymcala.org
SIC: **8641** Youth organizations
PA: Young Men's Christian Association Of Metropolitan Los Angeles
625 S New Hampshire Ave
213 380-6448

(P-17407)
YOUNG MNS CHRSTN ASSN MTRO LOS (PA)
Also Called: YMCA
625 S New Hampshire Ave, Los Angeles (90005-1342)
PHONE...............................213 380-6448
Alan Hostrup, *Pr*
Stephen Meier, *
W J Ellison, *
Dan Cooper, *
EMP: 70 EST: 1887
SQ FT: 16,000
SALES (est): 80.43MM
SALES (corp-wide): 80.43MM **Privately Held**
Web: www.ymcala.org
SIC: **8641** Youth organizations

(P-17408)
YOUNG MNS CHRSTN ASSN OF FTHLL
Also Called: YMCA OF THE FOOTHILLS
1930 Foothill Blvd, La Canada (91011-1933)
PHONE...............................818 790-0123
Tyler Wright, *CEO*
Mark Skeehan, *Finance*
Linden Katherine, *Prin*
EMP: 72 EST: 1957
SALES (est): 7.85MM **Privately Held**
Web: www.ymcafoothills.org
SIC: **8641** Youth organizations

(P-17409)
YOUNG MNS CHRSTN ASSN ORNGE CN
Also Called: Saddle Back Valley YMCA
27341 Trabuco Cir, Mission Viejo (92692-1939)
PHONE...............................949 859-9622
Mary J Goodrick, *Ex Dir*
EMP: 105
SALES (corp-wide): 50.06MM **Privately Held**
Web: www.ymcaoc.org
SIC: **8641** 7991 8351 7032 Youth organizations; Physical fitness facilities; Child day care services; Youth camps
PA: Young Men's Christian Association Of Orange County
13821 Newport Ave Ste 200
714 549-9622

(P-17410)
YOUNG MNS CHRSTN ASSN ORNGE CN
Also Called: YMCA
2300 University Dr, Newport Beach (92660-3313)
PHONE...............................949 642-9990
Joy Hyde, *Genl Mgr*
EMP: 90
SQ FT: 17,976
SALES (corp-wide): 50.06MM **Privately Held**
Web: www.ymcaoc.org
SIC: **8641** 7991 Youth organizations; Physical fitness facilities
PA: Young Men's Christian Association Of Orange County
13821 Newport Ave Ste 200
714 549-9622

(P-17411)
YOUNG WNS CHRSTN ASSN GRTER LO
Also Called: Angeles Mesa YWCA Chldren Lrng
2519 W Vernon Ave, Los Angeles (90008-3927)
PHONE...............................323 295-4288
Hertistine Taylor, *Dir*
EMP: 132
SALES (corp-wide): 14.57MM **Privately Held**
Web: www.ywcagla.org
SIC: **8641** 8351 Youth organizations; Child day care services
PA: Young Women's Christian Association Of Greater Los Angeles, California
1020 S Olive St 7th Fl
213 365-2991

(P-17412)
YOUNG WNS CHRSTN ASSN GRTER LO
Also Called: YWCA

2501 W Vernon Ave, Los Angeles (90008-3927)
PHONE...............................323 295-4280
EMP: 116
SALES (corp-wide): 14.57MM **Privately Held**
Web: www.ywcagla.org
SIC: **8641** Youth organizations
PA: Young Women's Christian Association Of Greater Los Angeles, California
1020 S Olive St 7th Fl
213 365-2991

8661 Religious Organizations

(P-17413)
CRENSHAW CHRSTN CTR CH LOS ANG (PA)
Also Called: Ever Increasing Faith Ministry
7901 S Vermont Ave, Los Angeles (90044-3531)
P.O. Box 90000 (90009-9201)
PHONE...............................323 758-3777
Frederick K C Price, *CEO*
Angela Evans, *
Craig Hays, *
Cheryl Price, *
Jeanette Fant, *
▲ EMP: 294 EST: 1973
SALES (est): 9.99MM
SALES (corp-wide): 9.99MM **Privately Held**
Web: www.crenshawchristiancenter.net
SIC: **8661** 7812 Community Church; Motion picture and video production

(P-17414)
CRYSTAL CATHEDRAL MINISTRIES (PA)
12901 Lewis St, Garden Grove (92840-6207)
P.O. Box 100 (92842-0100)
PHONE...............................714 622-2900
Robert V Schuller, *CEO*
Fred Southard, *
▲ EMP: 250 EST: 1955
SQ FT: 135,000
SALES (est): 2.63MM
SALES (corp-wide): 2.63MM **Privately Held**
Web: www.christcathedralcalifornia.org
SIC: **8661** 7812 Apostolic Church; Television film production

(P-17415)
HOSPITLLER ORDER OF ST JOHN GO
2468 S St Andrews Pl, Los Angeles (90018-2042)
PHONE...............................323 731-0041
Arlene De Guzman Hospitaller, *Prin*
EMP: 362 EST: 2009
SALES (est): 138.81K **Privately Held**
SIC: **8661** 8399 Religious organizations; Health and welfare council

(P-17416)
INTERNTNAL CH OF FRSQARE GOSPL (PA)
Also Called: Foursquare International
1910 W Sunset Blvd, Los Angeles (90026-3275)
P.O. Box 26902 (90026-0176)
PHONE...............................714 701-1818
Glenn C Burris Junior, *Pr*
Jared Roth, *
James C Scott Junior, *VP*
Sterling Brackett, *
Tammy Dunahoo, *

P R O D U C T S & S V C S

▲ **EMP:** 100 **EST:** 1921
SQ FT: 110,000
SALES (est): 74.92MM
SALES (corp-wide): 74.92MM **Privately Held**
Web: www.foursquare.org
SIC: 8661 6512 7032 8211 Miscellaneous denomination church; Nonresidential building operators; Sporting and recreational camps; Elementary and secondary schools

(P-17417)
MORRIS CRULLO WORLD EVANGELISM (PA)
875 Hotel Cir S # 2, San Diego (92108-3406)
P.O. Box 85277 (92186-5277)
PHONE...................858 277-2200
Reverend Morris Cerullo, *Pr*
Lynn Hodge, *
Teresa Cerullo, *
EMP: 77 **EST:** 1961
SALES (est): 9.56MM
SALES (corp-wide): 9.56MM **Privately Held**
Web: www.mcwe.com
SIC: 8661 2741 Churches, temples, and shrines; Miscellaneous publishing

(P-17418)
SELF-REALIZATION FELLOWSHIP CH (PA)
Also Called: Self Realization Fellowship
3880 San Rafael Ave, Los Angeles (90065-3298)
PHONE...................323 225-2471
Faye Wright, *Pr*
Mrinalini Mata, *
▲ **EMP:** 35 **EST:** 1935
SALES (est): 20.63MM
SALES (corp-wide): 20.63MM **Privately Held**
Web: www.yogananda.org
SIC: 8661 2741 Miscellaneous denomination church; Miscellaneous publishing

(P-17419)
SINAI TEMPLE (PA)
Also Called: Mt Sinai Mem Pk & Mortuary
10400 Wilshire Blvd, Los Angeles (90024-4600)
PHONE...................310 474-1518
Howard Lesner, *Admn*
Howard Lesner, *Ex Dir*
Joel Weinstein, *
EMP: 300 **EST:** 1908
SQ FT: 100,000
SALES (est): 44.43MM
SALES (corp-wide): 44.43MM **Privately Held**
Web: www.sinaiakiba.org
SIC: 8661 7261 5947 Synagogue; Funeral service and crematories; Gift shop

(P-17420)
SISTERS OF ST JOSEPH ORANGE
240 Ocean Ave, Seal Beach (90740-6029)
PHONE...................562 430-4638
Catherine Gray, *Prin*
EMP: 2572
SALES (corp-wide): 55.69MM **Privately Held**
Web: www.csjorange.org
SIC: 8661 8062 Convent; General medical and surgical hospitals
HQ: Sisters Of St. Joseph Of Orange
480 S Batavia St
Orange CA 92868
714 633-8121

(P-17421)
ST JHNS LTHRAN CH BAKERSFIELD
Also Called: St Johns Lthran Schl Chldren C
4500 Buena Vista Rd, Bakersfield (93311-9702)
PHONE...................661 665-7815
Pastor Dennis Hilken, *Prin*
Eric Van Scharrel, *
Evan Anwyl, *
Mike Kinsey, *
EMP: 105 **EST:** 1904
SQ FT: 40,000
SALES (est): 7MM **Privately Held**
Web: www.sjlchurch.org
SIC: 8661 8211 7371 Lutheran Church; Private elementary school; Computer software development and applications

(P-17422)
WILSHIRE BOULEVARD TEMPLE
4334 Whittier Blvd, Los Angeles (90023-2019)
PHONE...................323 261-6135
Carol J Bova, *Mgr*
EMP: 75
SALES (corp-wide): 22.36MM **Privately Held**
Web: www.wbtla.org
SIC: 8661 6553 7261 Temples; Cemetery subdividers and developers; Funeral service and crematories
PA: Wilshire Boulevard Temple
3663 Wilshire Blvd
213 388-2401

(P-17423)
YOUNG MEN CHRSTN ASSOC W SAN G (PA)
Also Called: YMCA
401 Corto St, Alhambra (91801-4553)
PHONE...................626 576-0226
Valarie Gomez, *CEO*
EMP: 70 **EST:** 1912
SQ FT: 17,000
SALES (est): 893.34K
SALES (corp-wide): 893.34K **Privately Held**
Web: www.wsgvymca.org
SIC: 8661 8322 Religious organizations; Youth center

8699 Membership Organizations, Nec

(P-17424)
AFFINITY DEVELOPMENT GROUP INC
Also Called: A D G
10590 W Ocean Air Dr Ste 300, San Diego (92130-4682)
PHONE...................858 643-9324
Jeff Skeen, *Pr*
Gary Drean, *
Greg Siebenthal, *
Eric Campbell, *CSO*
EMP: 120 **EST:** 1997
SALES (est): 17.41MM **Privately Held**
Web: www.affinitydev.com
SIC: 8699 Automobile owners' association

(P-17425)
AGUA CLNTE BAND CHILLA INDIANS (PA)
5401 Dinah Shore Dr, Palm Springs (92264-5970)
PHONE...................760 699-6800
Jeff L Grubbe, *Ch*

Larry N Olinger, *Vice Chairman**
Vincent Gonzales Iii, *Sec*
EMP: 495 **EST:** 1988
SALES (est): 83.82MM
SALES (corp-wide): 83.82MM **Privately Held**
Web: www.dwa.org
SIC: 8699 6552 7999 Reading rooms and other cultural organizations; Subdividers and developers, nec; Tour and guide services

(P-17426)
AUTOMOBILE CLUB SOUTHERN CAL
Also Called: AAA
5402 Philadelphia St Ste A, Chino (91710-2489)
P.O. Box 1846 (91708-1846)
PHONE...................909 591-9451
Tim Irwin, *Mgr*
EMP: 122
SALES (corp-wide): 1.08B **Privately Held**
Web: ace.aaa.com
SIC: 8699 Automobile owners' association
PA: Automobile Club Of Southern California
2601 S Figueroa St
213 741-3686

(P-17427)
AUTOMOBILE CLUB SOUTHERN CAL
Also Called: AAA
4973 Clairemont Dr Ste C, San Diego (92117-2793)
P.O. Box 17527 (92177-7527)
PHONE...................858 483-4960
Thomas Mckernan, *Brnch Mgr*
EMP: 223
SALES (corp-wide): 1.08B **Privately Held**
Web: ace.aaa.com
SIC: 8699 Automobile owners' association
PA: Automobile Club Of Southern California
2601 S Figueroa St
213 741-3686

(P-17428)
AUTOMOBILE CLUB SOUTHERN CAL
Also Called: AAA
2440 Hotel Cir N Ste 100, San Diego (92108-2823)
PHONE...................619 233-1000
Jill Clark, *Mgr*
EMP: 101
SALES (corp-wide): 1.08B **Privately Held**
Web: ace.aaa.com
SIC: 8699 Automobile owners' association
PA: Automobile Club Of Southern California
2601 S Figueroa St
213 741-3686

(P-17429)
AUTOMOBILE CLUB SOUTHERN CAL
Also Called: A A A Automobile Club So Cal
3330 Vista Way, Oceanside (92056-3799)
P.O. Box 1128 (92051-1128)
PHONE...................760 433-6261
Carolyn Tsuida, *Mgr*
EMP: 81
SQ FT: 10,240
SALES (corp-wide): 1.08B **Privately Held**
Web: ace.aaa.com
SIC: 8699 Automobile owners' association
PA: Automobile Club Of Southern California
2601 S Figueroa St
213 741-3686

(P-17430)
AUTOMOBILE CLUB SOUTHERN CAL
Also Called: AAA
800 La Terraza Blvd, Escondido (92025-3898)
PHONE...................760 745-2124
Theresa Tentschert, *Mgr*
EMP: 122
SQ FT: 49,100
SALES (corp-wide): 1.08B **Privately Held**
Web: ace.aaa.com
SIC: 8699 Automobile owners' association
PA: Automobile Club Of Southern California
2601 S Figueroa St
213 741-3686

(P-17431)
AUTOMOBILE CLUB SOUTHERN CAL
Also Called: AAA
12630 Sabre Springs Pkwy Ste 301, San Diego (92128-4129)
PHONE...................858 486-0786
Jill Clark Gregory, *Mgr*
EMP: 81
SQ FT: 7,000
SALES (corp-wide): 1.08B **Privately Held**
Web: ace.aaa.com
SIC: 8699 Automobile owners' association
PA: Automobile Club Of Southern California
2601 S Figueroa St
213 741-3686

(P-17432)
AUTOMOBILE CLUB SOUTHERN CAL
3700 Central Ave, Riverside (92506-2421)
P.O. Box 2217 (92516-2217)
PHONE...................951 684-4250
Richard Meyer, *Brnch Mgr*
EMP: 101
SALES (corp-wide): 1.08B **Privately Held**
Web: ace.aaa.com
SIC: 8699 Automobile owners' association
PA: Automobile Club Of Southern California
2601 S Figueroa St
213 741-3686

(P-17433)
AUTOMOBILE CLUB SOUTHERN CAL
Also Called: A A A Automobile Club So Cal
450 W Stetson Ave, Hemet (92543-7328)
PHONE...................951 652-6202
EMP: 81
SALES (corp-wide): 1.08B **Privately Held**
Web: ace.aaa.com
SIC: 8699 Automobile owners' association
PA: Automobile Club Of Southern California
2601 S Figueroa St
213 741-3686

(P-17434)
AUTOMOBILE CLUB SOUTHERN CAL
1170 El Camino Ave, Corona (92879-1761)
PHONE...................951 808-9624
EMP: 81
SALES (corp-wide): 1.08B **Privately Held**
Web: ace.aaa.com
SIC: 8699 Automobile owners' association
PA: Automobile Club Of Southern California
2601 S Figueroa St
213 741-3686

(P-17435)

AUTOMOBILE CLUB SOUTHERN CAL

2730 Santa Monica Blvd, Santa Monica (90404-2408)
PHONE.................................310 453-1909
Vasile Dejeu, *Mgr*
EMP: 142
SQ FT: 10,000
SALES (corp-wide): 1.08B **Privately Held**
Web: ace.aaa.com
SIC: 8699 Automobile owners' association
PA: Automobile Club Of Southern California
2601 S Figueroa St
213 741-3686

(P-17436)

AUTOMOBILE CLUB SOUTHERN CAL

Also Called: A A A Automobile Club So Cal
4800 Airport Plaza Dr Ste 100, Long Beach (90815-1274)
PHONE.................................562 425-8350
Susan Dabinett, *Mgr*
EMP: 81
SQ FT: 7,200
SALES (corp-wide): 1.08B **Privately Held**
Web: ace.aaa.com
SIC: 8699 Automobile owners' association
PA: Automobile Club Of Southern California
2601 S Figueroa St
213 741-3686

(P-17437)

AUTOMOBILE CLUB SOUTHERN CAL

Also Called: AAA
18642 Gridley Rd, Artesia (90701-5441)
PHONE.................................562 924-6636
Diane Ruiz, *Brnch Mgr*
EMP: 81
SQ FT: 12,960
SALES (corp-wide): 1.08B **Privately Held**
Web: ace.aaa.com
SIC: 8699 Automobile owners' association
PA: Automobile Club Of Southern California
2601 S Figueroa St
213 741-3686

(P-17438)

AUTOMOBILE CLUB SOUTHERN CAL

Also Called: AAA
8761 Santa Monica Blvd, West Hollywood (90069-4538)
PHONE.................................323 525-0018
Randy Miller, *Mgr*
EMP: 101
SALES (corp-wide): 1.08B **Privately Held**
Web: ace.aaa.com
SIC: 8699 Automobile owners' association
PA: Automobile Club Of Southern California
2601 S Figueroa St
213 741-3686

(P-17439)

AUTOMOBILE CLUB SOUTHERN CAL

Also Called: AAA
1500 Commercial Way, Bakersfield (93309-0625)
PHONE.................................661 327-4661
Jeff Goldsmith, *Brnch Mgr*
EMP: 81
SALES (corp-wide): 1.08B **Privately Held**
Web: ace.aaa.com
SIC: 8699 Automobile owners' association
PA: Automobile Club Of Southern California
2601 S Figueroa St

213 741-3686

(P-17440)

AUTOMOBILE CLUB SOUTHERN CAL

Also Called: AAA
23001 Hawthorne Blvd, Torrance (90505-3702)
P.O. Box 4298 (90510-4298)
PHONE.................................310 325-3111
Bud Hudson, *Brnch Mgr*
EMP: 101
SQ FT: 34,720
SALES (corp-wide): 1.08B **Privately Held**
Web: ace.aaa.com
SIC: 8699 Automobile owners' association
PA: Automobile Club Of Southern California
2601 S Figueroa St
213 741-3686

(P-17441)

AUTOMOBILE CLUB SOUTHERN CAL

Also Called: AAA
1301s S Grand Ave, Glendora (91740-5040)
PHONE.................................626 963-8531
Connie Stelzer, *Mgr*
EMP: 81
SQ FT: 8,261
SALES (corp-wide): 1.08B **Privately Held**
Web: ace.aaa.com
SIC: 8699 Automobile owners' association
PA: Automobile Club Of Southern California
2601 S Figueroa St
213 741-3686

(P-17442)

AUTOMOBILE CLUB SOUTHERN CAL

Also Called: AAA
9440 Reseda Blvd, Northridge (91324-6014)
PHONE.................................818 993-1616
EMP: 81
SQ FT: 15,624
SALES (corp-wide): 1.08B **Privately Held**
Web: ace.aaa.com
SIC: 8699 Automobile owners' association
PA: Automobile Club Of Southern California
2601 S Figueroa St
213 741-3686

(P-17443)

AUTOMOBILE CLUB SOUTHERN CAL

Also Called: AAA
8223 Firestone Blvd, Downey (90241-4809)
PHONE.................................562 904-5970
Mirtha Rodriguez, *Brnch Mgr*
EMP: 81
SALES (corp-wide): 1.08B **Privately Held**
Web: ace.aaa.com
SIC: 8699 Automobile owners' association
PA: Automobile Club Of Southern California
2601 S Figueroa St
213 741-3686

(P-17444)

AUTOMOBILE CLUB SOUTHERN CAL

Also Called: AAA
700 S Aviation Blvd, Manhattan Beach (90266-7106)
PHONE.................................310 376-0521
John Dm, *Mgr*
EMP: 122
SQ FT: 7,815
SALES (corp-wide): 1.08B **Privately Held**

Web: ace.aaa.com
SIC: 8699 Automobile owners' association
PA: Automobile Club Of Southern California
2601 S Figueroa St
213 741-3686

(P-17445)

AUTOMOBILE CLUB SOUTHERN CAL

Also Called: A A A Automobile Club So Cal
801 E Union St, Pasadena (91101-1885)
PHONE.................................626 795-0601
Teresa Martinez, *Mgr*
EMP: 81
SQ FT: 12,326
SALES (corp-wide): 1.08B **Privately Held**
Web: ace.aaa.com
SIC: 8699 Automobile owners' association
PA: Automobile Club Of Southern California
2601 S Figueroa St
213 741-3686

(P-17446)

AUTOMOBILE CLUB SOUTHERN CAL

Also Called: AAA
22708 Victory Blvd, Woodland Hills (91367-1697)
PHONE.................................818 883-2660
Glenn Lumley, *Brnch Mgr*
EMP: 81
SQ FT: 15,624
SALES (corp-wide): 1.08B **Privately Held**
Web: ace.aaa.com
SIC: 8699 4724 6331 Automobile owners' association; Travel agencies; Fire, marine, and casualty insurance
PA: Automobile Club Of Southern California
2601 S Figueroa St
213 741-3686

(P-17447)

AUTOMOBILE CLUB SOUTHERN CAL

Also Called: A A A Automobile Club So Cal
1234 Centinela Ave, Inglewood (90302-1138)
PHONE.................................310 673-5170
Lola Nix, *Brnch Mgr*
EMP: 81
SQ FT: 11,228
SALES (corp-wide): 1.08B **Privately Held**
Web: ace.aaa.com
SIC: 8699 Automobile owners' association
PA: Automobile Club Of Southern California
2601 S Figueroa St
213 741-3686

(P-17448)

AUTOMOBILE CLUB SOUTHERN CAL

Also Called: AAA
16041 Whittier Blvd, Whittier (90603-2526)
P.O. Box 4766 (90607-4766)
PHONE.................................562 698-3721
Velia Garcia, *Mgr*
EMP: 81
SALES (corp-wide): 1.08B **Privately Held**
Web: ace.aaa.com
SIC: 8699 4724 6331 Automobile owners' association; Travel agencies; Fire, marine, and casualty insurance
PA: Automobile Club Of Southern California
2601 S Figueroa St
213 741-3686

(P-17449)

AUTOMOBILE CLUB SOUTHERN CAL

Web: ace.aaa.com
SIC: 8699 Automobile owners' association
PA: Automobile Club Of Southern California
2601 S Figueroa St
213 741-3686

(P-17450)

AUTOMOBILE CLUB SOUTHERN CAL

Also Called: A A A Automobile Club So Cal
23770 Valencia Blvd Ste 100, Valencia (91355-2185)
PHONE.................................661 259-6222
Kelly Clark, *Brnch Mgr*
EMP: 101
SALES (corp-wide): 1.08B **Privately Held**
Web: ace.aaa.com
SIC: 8699 Automobile owners' association
PA: Automobile Club Of Southern California
2601 S Figueroa St
213 741-3686

(P-17450)

AUTOMOBILE CLUB SOUTHERN CAL

Also Called: AAA
1445 Calle Joaquin, San Luis Obispo (93405-7203)
PHONE.................................805 543-6454
Darlene Lair, *Brnch Mgr*
EMP: 81
SALES (corp-wide): 1.08B **Privately Held**
Web: ace.aaa.com
SIC: 8699 Automobile owners' association
PA: Automobile Club Of Southern California
2601 S Figueroa St
213 741-3686

(P-17451)

AUTOMOBILE CLUB SOUTHERN CAL

3712 State St, Santa Barbara (93105-3104)
PHONE.................................805 682-5811
Nancy Alexander, *Brnch Mgr*
EMP: 121
SALES (corp-wide): 1.08B **Privately Held**
Web: ace.aaa.com
SIC: 8699 Automobile owners' association
PA: Automobile Club Of Southern California
2601 S Figueroa St
213 741-3686

(P-17452)

AUTOMOBILE CLUB SOUTHERN CAL

525 W Central Ave, Lompoc (93436-2836)
PHONE.................................805 735-2731
EMP: 81
SALES (corp-wide): 1.08B **Privately Held**
Web: ace.aaa.com
SIC: 8699 Automobile owners' association
PA: Automobile Club Of Southern California
2601 S Figueroa St
213 741-3686

(P-17453)

AUTOMOBILE CLUB SOUTHERN CAL

Also Called: AAA
100 E Wilbur Rd, Thousand Oaks (91360-5564)
P.O. Box 1046 (91358-0046)
PHONE.................................805 497-0911
Chris Davis, *Brnch Mgr*
EMP: 81
SALES (corp-wide): 1.08B **Privately Held**
Web: www.bestappliancela.com
SIC: 8699 Automobile owners' association
PA: Automobile Club Of Southern California
2601 S Figueroa St
213 741-3686

(P-17454)

AUTOMOBILE CLUB SOUTHERN CAL

Also Called: AAA
420 N Euclid St, Anaheim (92801-5505)
PHONE.................................714 774-2392

PRODUCTS & SVCS

Conny Kuhm, *Mgr*
EMP: 101
SALES (corp-wide): 1.08B **Privately Held**
Web: ace.aaa.com
SIC: 8699 Automobile owners' association
PA: Automobile Club Of Southern California
2601 S Figueroa St
213 741-3686

(P-17455)
AUTOMOBILE CLUB SOUTHERN CAL

3880 Birch St, Newport Beach
(92660-2669)
PHONE................................949 476-8880
Cindy Kitchens, *Mgr*
EMP: 81
SQ FT: 14,794
SALES (corp-wide): 1.08B **Privately Held**
Web: ace.aaa.com
SIC: 8699 Automobile owners' association
PA: Automobile Club Of Southern California
2601 S Figueroa St
213 741-3686

(P-17456)
AUTOMOBILE CLUB SOUTHERN CAL

Also Called: AAA
638 Camino De Los Mares Ste E100, San
Clemente (92673-2833)
PHONE................................949 489-5572
Cindy Colter, *Brnch Mgr*
EMP: 81
SALES (corp-wide): 1.08B **Privately Held**
Web: ace.aaa.com
SIC: 8699 Automobile owners' association
PA: Automobile Club Of Southern California
2601 S Figueroa St
213 741-3686

(P-17457)
AUTOMOBILE CLUB SOUTHERN CAL

Also Called: A A A Automobile Club So Cal
25181 Paseo De Alicia, Laguna Hills
(92653-4670)
PHONE................................949 951-1400
Cindy Raymond, *Mgr*
EMP: 81
SQ FT: 13,948
SALES (corp-wide): 1.08B **Privately Held**
Web: ace.aaa.com
SIC: 8699 Automobile owners' association
PA: Automobile Club Of Southern California
2601 S Figueroa St
213 741-3686

(P-17458)
BEST FRIENDS ANIMAL SOCIETY

1845 Pontius Ave, Los Angeles
(90025-4305)
PHONE................................818 643-3989
Marc Peralta, *Mgr*
EMP: 246
Web: www.bestfriends.org
SIC: 8699 Animal humane society
PA: Best Friends Animal Society
5001 Angel Canyon Road

(P-17459)
BRILLIANT CORNERS TERI ENOMOTO

527 W 7th St Rm 1100, Los Angeles
(90014-2503)
PHONE................................213 232-0134
EMP: 71 **EST:** 2015
SALES (est): 2.4MM **Privately Held**

Web: www.brilliantcorners.org
SIC: 8699 Charitable organization

(P-17460)
CARLSBAD FIREFIGHTERS ASSN

2560 Orion Way, Carlsbad (92010-7280)
P.O. Box 945 (92018-0945)
PHONE................................760 729-3730
Josh Clark, *Pr*
EMP: 80 **EST:** 1970
SALES (est): 230.09K **Privately Held**
Web: www.carlsbadfdf.org
SIC: 8699 Charitable organization

(P-17461)
CHARITBLE ADULT RIDES SVCS INC

Also Called: CARS
4669 Murphy Canyon Rd Ste 100, San
Diego (92123-4333)
PHONE................................858 300-2900
Howard Pearo, *CEO*
EMP: 80 **EST:** 2010
SQ FT: 6,500
SALES (est): 11.76MM **Privately Held**
Web: www.careasy.org
SIC: 8699 Charitable organization

(P-17462)
CHG FOUNDATION

740 Bay Blvd, Chula Vista (91910-5254)
PHONE................................619 422-0422
Sheila Martz, *Dir*
EMP: 372 **EST:** 1999
SALES (est): 1.25B **Privately Held**
SIC: 8699 Charitable organization

(P-17463)
GOODWILL INDS SAN DIEGO CNTY

Also Called: Goodwill Industries
3841 Plaza Dr Ste 902, Oceanside
(92056-4649)
PHONE................................760 806-7670
Tim Hurley, *Mgr*
EMP: 97
SALES (corp-wide): 78.91MM **Privately Held**
Web: www.sdgoodwill.org
SIC: 8699 8331 5932 Charitable organization
; Vocational rehabilitation agency; Used
merchandise stores
PA: Goodwill Industries Of San Diego
County
3663 Rosecrans St
619 225-2200

(P-17464)
INLAND EMPIRE CHPTR-SSCTION CR

2210 E Route 66, Glendora (91740-4661)
PHONE................................512 478-9000
Todd Christopher Landry Cfe C.p.a., *Prin*
EMP: 82 **EST:** 2009
SALES (est): 4.13K **Privately Held**
SIC: 8699 Membership organizations, nec

(P-17465)
LOS ANGELES MEM COLISEUM COMM

Also Called: La Sports Arena
3911 S Figueroa St, Los Angeles
(90037-1207)
PHONE................................213 747-7111
Kevin Daly, *Admn*
Don Knabe, *
Gregory Hellmold, *

John Sandbrook, *
EMP: 500 **EST:** 1923
SQ FT: 2,000
SALES (est): 21.59MM **Privately Held**
Web: www.lacoliseum.com
SIC: 8699 Athletic organizations

(P-17466)
MEMORIAL MEDICAL CENTER FOUNDATION

Also Called: MILLER CHILDREN'S
HOSPITAL
2801 Atlantic Ave, Long Beach
(90806-1799)
P.O. Box 1428 (90801-1428)
PHONE................................562 933-2273
EMP: 2313 **EST:** 1964
SALES (est): 9.66MM **Privately Held**
Web: www.memorialcare.org
SIC: 8699 Charitable organization
HQ: Long Beach Medical Center
2801 Atlantic Ave Fl 2
Long Beach CA 90806
562 933-2000

(P-17467)
PASADENA HUMANE SOCIETY

361 S Raymond Ave, Pasadena
(91105-2687)
PHONE................................626 792-7151
Steven R Mc Nall, *Pr*
EMP: 70 **EST:** 1903
SQ FT: 26,000
SALES (est): 16.43MM **Privately Held**
Web: www.pasadenahumane.org
SIC: 8699 0752 Animal humane society;
Animal specialty services

(P-17468)
PLAY VERSUS INC

Also Called: Playvs
2236 S Barrington Ave Ste A, Los Angeles
(90064-1231)
PHONE................................949 636-4193
Jon Chapman, *CEO*
EMP: 107 **EST:** 2018
SALES (est): 3.84MM **Privately Held**
Web: www.playvs.com
SIC: 8699 Amateur sports promotion

(P-17469)
RESCUE MISSION ALLIANCE (PA)

Also Called: MISSION BARGAIN CENTER
315 N A St, Oxnard (93030-4901)
P.O. Box 5545 (93031-5545)
PHONE................................805 487-1234
Gary Gray, *Pr*
Jim Ownes, *
Brian Elster, *Vice Chairman**
Andy Stay, *
David Chittenden, *
EMP: 77 **EST:** 1972
SQ FT: 30,000
SALES (est): 29.11MM **Privately Held**
Web: www.erescuemission.org
SIC: 8699 Charitable organization

(P-17470)
SOCIETY OF ST VNCENT DE PAUL C (PA)

Also Called: ST VINCENT DE PAUL
SOCIETY OF
210 N Avenue 21, Los Angeles
(90031-1713)
PHONE................................323 226-9645
David Garcia, *Ex Dir*
Susana Santana, *Deputy Executive
Director**

EMP: 77 **EST:** 1908
SQ FT: 108,000
SALES (est): 18.24MM
SALES (corp-wide): 18.24MM **Privately
Held**
Web: www.svdpla.org
SIC: 8699 Charitable organization

(P-17471)
THINK TOGETHER

17270 Bear Valley Rd Ste 103, Victorville
(92395-7751)
PHONE................................760 269-1230
EMP: 344
SALES (corp-wide): 75.71MM **Privately
Held**
Web: www.thinktogether.org
SIC: 8699 8351 Charitable organization;
Child day care services
PA: Think Together
2101 E 4th St #b-200
714 543-3807

(P-17472)
U C SAN DIEGO FOUNDATION

Also Called: UC SAN DIEGO
9500 Gilman Dr, La Jolla (92093-5004)
PHONE................................858 534-1032
Steve Gamer, *Pr*
Kathy Drucquer Duff, *
Marlene D Shaver, *
I-ju Tracy, *Contrlr*
EMP: 87 **EST:** 1972
SALES (est): 217.35MM **Privately Held**
Web: www.ucsd.edu
SIC: 8699 Charitable organization

(P-17473)
VICTORIA PLACE COMMUNITY ASSN

195 N Euclid Ave, Upland (91786-6055)
PHONE................................909 981-4131
John Melcher, *Pr*
EMP: 75 **EST:** 2008
SALES (est): 128.66K **Privately Held**
SIC: 8699 Membership organizations, nec

(P-17474)
VITAMIN ANGEL ALLIANCE INC

Also Called: VITAMIN ANGEL
6500 Hollister Ave Ste 130, Goleta
(93117-5556)
P.O. Box 4490 (93140-4490)
PHONE................................805 564-8400
Peter Van Stolk, *CEO*
Howard Schiffer, *
Bonnie Forssel, *
Caterinia Cellis, *
EMP: 92 **EST:** 2010
SALES (est): 132.05MM **Privately Held**
Web: www.vitaminangels.org
SIC: 8699 5122 Charitable organization;
Vitamins and minerals

(P-17475)
WORLD VISION INTERNATIONAL (PA)

800 W Chestnut Ave, Monrovia
(91016-3198)
P.O. Box 9716 (98063-9716)
PHONE................................626 303-8811
Andrew Morley, *CEO*
Kevin Jenkins, *
Valdir Steuernagel, *
Denis St Amour, *
▼ **EMP:** 196 **EST:** 1977
SQ FT: 94,000
SALES (est): 34.65MM
SALES (corp-wide): 34.65MM **Privately
Held**

▲ = Import ▼ = Export
◆ = Import/Export

Web: www.wvi.org
SIC: 8699 Charitable organization

8711 Engineering Services

(P-17476)
ABM FACILITY SERVICES LLC
Also Called: A B M
152 Technology Dr, Irvine (92618-2401)
PHONE...........................949 330-1555
EMP: 1391
SIC: 8711 Engineering services

(P-17477)
ABS CONSULTING INC
Also Called: ABS Group
420 Exchange Ste 200, Irvine (92602-1319)
PHONE...........................714 734-4242
Doug Frazier, CEO
Peter Yanev, Pr
Jim Johnson, COO
George Reitter, CFO
EMP: 100 EST: 1970
SALES (est): 4.85MM
SALES (corp-wide): 487.78MM Privately Held
Web: www.abs-group.com
SIC: 8711 8742 Consulting engineer; Management consulting services
HQ: Abs Group Of Companies, Inc.
1701 City Plaza Dr
Spring TX 77389

(P-17478)
ACCUNEX INC
Also Called: Accurate Electronics
20700 Lassen St, Chatsworth (91311-4507)
PHONE...........................818 882-5858
Farid Jadali, Pr
Roxana Coronado, *
▲ EMP: 50 EST: 1998
SQ FT: 25,000
SALES (est): 12.15MM Privately Held
Web: www.accurate-elec.com
SIC: 8711 3679 Engineering services; Electronic circuits

(P-17479)
AIR LIQUIDE ELECTRONICS US LP
Also Called: Air Lquide Globl E C Solutions
1831 Carnegie Ave, Santa Ana (92705-5528)
PHONE...........................713 624-8000
EMP: 3930
SALES (corp-wide): 114.13MM Privately Held
Web: engineering.airliquide.com
SIC: 8711 Engineering services
HQ: Air Liquide Electronics U.S. Lp
9101 Lyndon B Jhnson Fwy
Dallas TX 75243
972 301-5200

(P-17480)
ALBERT A WEBB ASSOCIATES (PA)
Also Called: Webb
3788 Mccray St, Riverside (92506-2927)
PHONE...........................951 686-1070
A Hubert Webb, Ch
Matt Webb, *
Scott Webb, *
Roger D Prend Pe, *
Todd R Smith, *
EMP: 127 EST: 1949
SQ FT: 20,000
SALES (est): 24.96MM
SALES (corp-wide): 24.96MM Privately Held

Web: www.webbassociates.com
SIC: 8711 Civil engineering

(P-17481)
ALLEN ENGINEERING CONTRACTOR INC
1655 Riverview Dr, San Bernardino (92408-3016)
PHONE...........................909 478-5500
EMP: 165
Web: www.allenec.com
SIC: 8711 Construction and civil engineering

(P-17482)
AME UNMANNED AIR SYSTEMS INC
Also Called: Lockheed Martin Unmndd
125 Venture Dr Ste 110, San Luis Obispo (93401-9103)
PHONE...........................805 541-4448
EMP: 80
Web: www.ameuas.com
SIC: 8711 Aviation and/or aeronautical engineering

(P-17483)
AMERESCO SOLAR LLC
42261 Zevo Dr, Temecula (92590-3733)
PHONE...........................888 967-6527
EMP: 470
Web: www.ameresco.com
SIC: 8711 Energy conservation engineering
HQ: Ameresco Solar Llc
111 Speen St Ste 410
Framingham MA 01701
508 661-2200

(P-17484)
AMERICAN TECHNICAL SVCS INC
20384 Via Mantua, Porter Ranch (91326-4441)
PHONE...........................951 372-9664
Alen Petrossian, Pr
EMP: 70 EST: 2004
SQ FT: 2,040
SALES (est): 2.4MM Privately Held
Web: www.atspage.com
SIC: 8711 Consulting engineer

(P-17485)
APPLIED COMPANIES
28020 Avenue Stanford, Santa Clarita (91355-1105)
P.O. Box 802078 (91380-2078)
PHONE...........................661 257-0090
Mary Elizabeth Klinger, CEO
Joseph Klinger, Development*
EMP: 50 EST: 1962
SQ FT: 50,000
SALES (est): 13.71MM Privately Held
Web: www.appliedcompanies.net
SIC: 8711 3585 3443 3621 Mechanical engineering; Ice making machinery; Cylinders, pressure: metal plate; Motors and generators

(P-17486)
ARIA GROUP INCORPORATED
17395 Daimler St, Irvine (92614-5510)
PHONE...........................949 475-2915
Clive Hawkins, Pr
EMP: 70 EST: 1995
SQ FT: 45,489
SALES (est): 11.73MM Privately Held
Web: www.aria-group.com
SIC: 8711 Consulting engineer

(P-17487)
ARQ LLC
Also Called: Arq
555 Anton Blvd, Costa Mesa (92626-7811)
EMP: 85 EST: 2008
SALES (est): 10.37MM Privately Held
Web: www.arqwireless.com
SIC: 8711 Electrical or electronic engineering

(P-17488)
ARUP NORTH AMERICA LIMITED
12777 W Jefferson Blvd Ste 300, Los Angeles (90066-7034)
PHONE...........................310 578-4182
Tony Panossian, Brnch Mgr
EMP: 299
Web: www.arup.com
SIC: 8711 Consulting engineer
HQ: Arup North America Limited
560 Mission St Fl 7
San Francisco CA 94105

(P-17489)
ASHLEY & VANCE ENGINEERING INC
1229 Carmel St, San Luis Obispo (93401-3814)
PHONE...........................805 545-0010
Truitt Vance, Prin
EMP: 90 EST: 2008
SALES (est): 3.08MM Privately Held
Web: www.ashleyvance.com
SIC: 8711 Civil engineering

(P-17490)
ASTRION
4125 Market St Ste 12, Ventura (93003-5642)
PHONE...........................805 644-2191
Timothy Minniear, Brnch Mgr
EMP: 493
SALES (corp-wide): 25.27MM Privately Held
Web: www.astrion.us
SIC: 8711 Marine engineering
PA: Astrion
800 Maine Ave Sw
781 676-7333

(P-17491)
AUSGAR TECHNOLOGIES INC
10721 Treena St Ste 100, San Diego (92131-1016)
PHONE...........................855 428-7427
Jonathan Dien, Pr
Karen Dien, *
Eric Lofgren, *
Saul Dien, *
EMP: 115 EST: 2003
SQ FT: 16,000
SALES (est): 9.17MM Privately Held
Web: www.ausgar.com
SIC: 8711 7371 7373 7379 Consulting engineer; Custom computer programming services; Computer integrated systems design; Computer related consulting services

(P-17492)
BAE SYSTEMS MARITIME ENGINEERING & SERVICES INC
7330 Engineer Rd Ste A, San Diego (92111-1434)
P.O. Box 13308 (92170-3308)
PHONE...........................619 238-1000
EMP: 370
SIC: 8711 Engineering services

(P-17493)
BERT W SALAS INC
11203 Highway 67, Lakeside (92040-1409)
PHONE...........................619 562-7711
Bob Salaz, Pr
EMP: 115 EST: 1956
SALES (est): 20.75MM Privately Held
SIC: 8711 Construction and civil engineering

(P-17494)
BKF ENGINEERS/AGS
Also Called: BKF ENGINEERS/AGS
4675 Macarthur Ct Ste 400, Newport Beach (92660-8834)
PHONE...........................949 526-8400
Isaac Kontorovsky, Brnch Mgr
EMP: 72
SALES (corp-wide): 28.61MM Privately Held
Web: www.bkf.com
SIC: 8711 Civil engineering
PA: Bkf Engineers
255 Shoreline Dr Ste 200
650 482-6300

(P-17495)
BOYLE ENGINEERING CORPORATION
999 W Town And Country Rd, Orange (92868-4713)
PHONE...........................949 476-3300
EMP: 400
SIC: 8711 8712 Engineering services; Architectural engineering

(P-17496)
BRINDERSON LLC (DH)
18841 S Broadwick St, Compton (90220-6429)
PHONE...........................714 466-7100
William Gary, CEO
EMP: 150 EST: 1993
SALES (est): 54.02MM Privately Held
Web: www.brockgroup.com
SIC: 8711 1629 Engineering services; Dams, waterways, docks, and other marine construction
HQ: Brock Holdings Iii, Llc
10343 Sam Hston Pk Dr Ste
Houston TX 77064
281 807-8200

(P-17497)
BURNS & MCDONNELL INC
145 S State College Blvd Ste 600, Brea (92821-5833)
PHONE...........................714 256-1595
Ken Gerling, Brnch Mgr
EMP: 80
SALES (corp-wide): 1.26B Privately Held
Web: www.burnsmcd.com
SIC: 8711 Consulting engineer
PA: Burns & Mcdonnell, Inc.
9450 Ward Pkwy
816 333-9400

(P-17498)
C D LYON CONSTRUCTION INC (PA)
380 W Stanley Ave, Ventura (93001-1350)
P.O. Box 1456 (93002-1456)
PHONE...........................805 653-0173
Christopher D Lyon, CEO
Debra C Lyon, *
EMP: 80 EST: 1986
SALES (est): 21.22MM
SALES (corp-wide): 21.22MM Privately Held
Web: www.cdlyon.com

PRODUCTS & SVCS

SIC: 8711 Petroleum engineering

(P-17499)
CALIFORNIA MFG TECH CONSULTING
Also Called: CMTC
3760 Kilroy Airport Way Ste 450, Long
Beach (90806-6858)
PHONE..............................310 263-3060
James Watson, *CEO*
James Watson, *Pr*
Patrick Billiter, *
EMP: 74 EST: 1994
SQ FT: 10,000
SALES (est): 31.02MM **Privately Held**
Web: www.cmtc.com
SIC: 8711 8742 Consulting engineer;
Marketing consulting services

(P-17500)
CALIFORNIA SEMICONDUCTOR TECH
Also Called: Calsemi
429 Santa Monica Blvd, Santa Monica
(90401-3401)
PHONE..............................310 579-2939
Antonio Garcia, *CEO*
Jose Luis Lopez, *
EMP: 120 EST: 2013
SALES (est): 6.79MM **Privately Held**
Web: www.calsemi-tech.com
SIC: 8711 Engineering services

(P-17501)
CDM CONSTRUCTORS INC
9220 Cleveland Ave Ste 100, Rancho
Cucamonga (91730-8561)
PHONE..............................909 579-3500
Joyce Jackson, *Brnch Mgr*
EMP: 90
SALES (corp-wide): 1.42B **Privately Held**
Web: www.cdmsmith.com
SIC: 8711 Consulting engineer
HQ: Cdm Constructors Inc.
75 State St, Suite 701
Boston MA 02109

(P-17502)
CITY OF GLENDALE
Also Called: Engineering Public Works
633 E Broadway Ste 205, Glendale
(91206-4310)
PHONE..............................818 548-3945
Lou Le Blanc, *Dir*
EMP: 74
SALES (corp-wide): 390.24MM **Privately
Held**
Web: www.glendaleca.gov
SIC: 8711 9511 Engineering services; Air,
water, and solid waste management
PA: City Of Glendale
141 N Glendale Ave Fl 2
818 548-2085

(P-17503)
CONCEPT TECHNOLOGY INC
2941 W Macarthur Blvd Ste 136, Santa Ana
(92704-6952)
PHONE..............................949 851-6550
EMP: 430
SALES (corp-wide): 4.61MM **Privately
Held**
Web: www.concepttechnologyinc.com
SIC: 8711 Consulting engineer
PA: Concept Technology, Inc.
895 Dove St 3rd Fl
949 854-7047

(P-17504)
CONCEPT TECHNOLOGY INC (PA)
895 Dove St 3rd Fl, Newport Beach
(92660-2941)
PHONE..............................949 854-7047
Mahesh P Badani, *Pr*
▲ EMP: 60 EST: 1981
SALES (est): 4.61MM
SALES (corp-wide): 4.61MM **Privately
Held**
Web: m.conceptechnology.com
SIC: 8711 3599 8742 3825 Consulting
engineer; Machine shop, jobbing and repair
; Management information systems
consultant; Radio frequency measuring
equipment

(P-17505)
COUNTY OF LOS ANGELES
Also Called: Engineering Division
44933 Fern Ave, Lancaster (93534-2461)
PHONE..............................661 723-6088
Bert Perry, *Brnch Mgr*
EMP: 122
Web: www.lacounty.gov
SIC: 8711 9111 Engineering services;
Executive offices
PA: County Of Los Angeles
500 W Temple St Ste 437
213 974-1101

(P-17506)
COUNTY OF LOS ANGELES
Public Works, Dept of
14747 Ramona Blvd, Baldwin Park
(91706-3435)
PHONE..............................626 337-1277
William Wolfer, *Brnch Mgr*
EMP: 81
Web: www.lacounty.gov
SIC: 8711 9199 Engineering services;
General government administration
PA: County Of Los Angeles
500 W Temple St Ste 437
213 974-1101

(P-17507)
CURTISS-WRGHT CNTRLS ELCTRNIC
28965 Avenue Penn, Santa Clarita
(91355-4185)
PHONE..............................661 257-4430
Val Zarov, *Brnch Mgr*
EMP: 194
SALES (corp-wide): 2.85B **Publicly Held**
Web: www.curtisswright.com
SIC: 8711 Engineering services
HQ: Curtiss-Wright Controls Electronic
Systems, Inc.
28965 Avenue Penn
Santa Clarita CA 91355
661 257-4430

(P-17508)
CUSTOM BUILT MACHINERY INC
Also Called: C B M
2614 S Hickory St, Santa Ana
(92707-3714)
PHONE..............................714 424-9250
Milan Chrena, *CEO*
Victor Escobedo, *
Milan Chrena, *Pr*
Pete Marloski, *Stockholder*
EMP: 25 EST: 1995
SQ FT: 11,000
SALES (est): 2.84MM **Privately Held**

SIC: 8711 3559 Engineering services;
Pharmaceutical machinery

(P-17509)
DAIKIN COMFORT TECH DIST INC
5160 Richton St Ste A, Montclair
(91763-1315)
PHONE..............................909 946-0632
Michael Rowe, *Mgr*
EMP: 405
Web: www.goodmanmfg.com
SIC: 8711 5099 Heating and ventilation
engineering; Firearms and ammunition,
except sporting
HQ: Daikin Comfort Technologies
Distribution, Inc.
19001 Kermier Rd
Waller TX 77484
713 861-2500

(P-17510)
DCS CORPORATION
137 W Drummond Ave Ste C, Ridgecrest
(93555-3583)
PHONE..............................760 384-5600
Charles Faris, *Brnch Mgr*
EMP: 119
SALES (corp-wide): 196.63MM **Privately
Held**
Web: www.dcscorp.com
SIC: 8711 Consulting engineer
PA: Dcs Corporation
6909 Metro Pk Dr Ste 500
571 227-6000

(P-17511)
DESIGNWORKS/USA INC
2201 Corporate Center Dr, Newbury Park
(91320-1421)
PHONE..............................805 499-9590
Laurenz Schaffer, *Pr*
EMP: 78 EST: 1971
SQ FT: 78,000
SALES (est): 3.72MM
SALES (corp-wide): 169.02B **Privately
Held**
Web: www.bmwgroupdesignworks.com
SIC: 8711 Designing: ship, boat, machine,
and product
PA: Bayerische Motoren Werke Ag
Petuelring 130
893820

(P-17512)
DEVELOPMENT RESOURCE CONS INC (PA)
160 S Old Springs Rd Ste 210, Anaheim
(92808-1226)
PHONE..............................714 685-6860
Lawrence Gates, *Pr*
EMP: 90 EST: 1997
SQ FT: 12,000
SALES (est): 15.5MM
SALES (corp-wide): 15.5MM **Privately
Held**
SIC: 8711 Civil engineering

(P-17513)
DEX CORPORATION
Also Called: Data Exchange
3600 Via Pescador, Camarillo
(93012-5035)
PHONE..............................805 388-1711
Sheldon Malchiconfqs, *CEO*
EMP: 150 EST: 2015
SQ FT: 100,000
SALES (est): 7.73MM **Privately Held**
Web: www.dex.com

SIC: 8711 5065 Engineering services;
Electronic parts

(P-17514)
DIVERGENT TECHNOLOGIES INC (PA)
Also Called: Divergent 3d
19601 Hamilton Ave, Torrance
(90502-1309)
PHONE..............................424 542-2158
Kevin Czinger, *Pr*
Ursula Ster, *CFO*
EMP: 350 EST: 2021
SALES (est): 62.2MM
SALES (corp-wide): 62.2MM **Privately
Held**
Web: www.divergent3d.com
SIC: 8711 Mechanical engineering

(P-17515)
DIVERSIFIED PRJ SVCS INTL INC (PA)
5351 Olive Dr Ste 100, Bakersfield
(93308-2926)
PHONE..............................661 371-2800
Robert Chambers, *Pr*
EMP: 80 EST: 2007
SALES (est): 11.24MM
SALES (corp-wide): 11.24MM **Privately
Held**
Web: www.dpsiinc.com
SIC: 8711 Consulting engineer

(P-17516)
DMS FACILITY SERVICES LLC
2861 E Coronado St, Anaheim
(92806-2504)
PHONE..............................949 975-1366
Richard E Dotts, *Brnch Mgr*
EMP: 807
Web: www.dmsfacilityservices.com
SIC: 8711 Engineering services
PA: Dms Facility Services, Llc
1040 Arroyo Dr

(P-17517)
DMS FACILITY SERVICES LLC
5735 Kearny Villa Rd Ste 108, San Diego
(92123-1138)
PHONE..............................858 560-4191
John Harris, *Brnch Mgr*
EMP: 538
Web: www.dmsfacilityservices.com
SIC: 8711 7349 0781 Engineering services;
Janitorial service, contract basis;
Landscape services
PA: Dms Facility Services, Llc
1040 Arroyo Dr

(P-17518)
DUDEK INC (PA)
605 3rd St, Encinitas (92024-3513)
PHONE..............................760 942-5147
Joseph Monaco, *CEO*
Eric Wilson, *
Christine Moore, *
Emily Hart, *
Helder Guimaraes, *
EMP: 100 EST: 1980
SQ FT: 50,000
SALES (est): 132.78MM
SALES (corp-wide): 132.78MM **Privately
Held**
Web: www.dudek.com
SIC: 8711 8748 Civil engineering;
Environmental consultant

(P-17519)
EDSI
700 Ammunition Rd Bldg 103, Fallbrook
(92028-3187)
PHONE.............................760 731-3501
Rick Lengerke, *Brnch Mgr*
EMP: 118
SALES (corp-wide): 9.25MM **Privately
Held**
Web: www.edsi.com
SIC: 8711 Engineering services
PA: Edsi
22835 Savi Ranch Pkwy F
951 272-8689

(P-17520)
EICHLEAY INC
500 N State College Blvd, Orange
(92868-1604)
PHONE.............................562 256-8600
Lori M Lofstrom, *Brnch Mgr*
EMP: 149
Web: www.eichleay.com
SIC: 8711 Consulting engineer
PA: Eichleay, Inc.
1390 Wllow Pass Rd Ste 60

(P-17521)
EMBEE PROCESSING LLC
Also Called: Embee Plating
2158 S Hathaway St, Santa Ana
(92705-5249)
PHONE.............................714 546-9842
Michael Coburn, *CEO*
Scott Chrisman, *
Derek Watson, *
▲ EMP: 385 EST: 1947
SQ FT: 100,000
SALES (est): 23.51MM **Privately Held**
Web: www.embee.com
SIC: 8711 3398 3479 8734 Aviation and/or
aeronautical engineering; Shot peening
(treating steel to reduce fatigue); Coating of
metals and formed products; Metallurgical
testing laboratory

(P-17522)
ENCORE SEMI INC
7310 Miramar Rd Ste 410, San Diego
(92126-4226)
PHONE.............................858 225-4993
Behrooz Abdi, *Ch Bd*
Olivier Lauvray, *
Angeline Trang Dof, *Prin*
EMP: 67 EST: 2011
SALES (est): 2.04MM **Privately Held**
Web: www.encoresemi.com
SIC: 8711 3674 Engineering services;
Integrated circuits, semiconductor
networks, etc.

(P-17523)
ENGINEERING PARTNERS INC
Also Called: E P I
10150 Meanley Dr Ste 200, San Diego
(92131-3008)
PHONE.............................858 824-1761
Romeo Flores, *Pr*
EMP: 95 EST: 1985
SQ FT: 2,500
SALES (est): 10.69MM **Privately Held**
Web: www.engineeringpartners.com
SIC: 8711 Consulting engineer

(P-17524)
**ENGINRING SFTWR SYS
SLTONS INC (PA)**
Also Called: E S 3
600 B St, San Diego (92101-4501)
PHONE.............................619 338-0380

Teri Sgammato, *Pr*
Chuck Dahms, *
Doug Wiser, *
Craig Edwards, *
EMP: 80 EST: 2001
SALES (est): 24.72MM
SALES (corp-wide): 24.72MM **Privately
Held**
Web: www.es3inc.com
SIC: 8711 Engineering services

(P-17525)
**EPSILON SYSTEMS SLTONS
MSSION**
9242 Lightwave Ave Ste 100, San Diego
(92123-6402)
PHONE.............................619 702-1700
Alan Stewart, *CFO*
Robin Nordberg, *
EMP: 99 EST: 2011
SALES (est): 1.69MM **Privately Held**
Web: www.epsilonsystems.com
SIC: 8711 Electrical or electronic engineering

(P-17526)
**EPSILON SYSTEMS SOLUTIONS
INC (PA)**
9444 Balboa Ave Ste 100, San Diego
(92123-4351)
PHONE.............................619 702-1700
Bryan Min, *CEO*
Joe Quinn, *
EMP: 100 EST: 1990
SQ FT: 50,000
SALES (est): 110MM
SALES (corp-wide): 110MM **Privately
Held**
Web: www.epsilonsystems.com
SIC: 8711 Engineering services

(P-17527)
**ES ENGINEERING SERVICES
LLC**
4 Park Plz Ste 790, Irvine (92614-5262)
PHONE.............................949 988-3500
Vijay Menthripragada, *CEO*
EMP: 85 EST: 2015
SALES (est): 4.2MM
SALES (corp-wide): 624.21MM **Publicly
Held**
SIC: 8711 8748 Engineering services;
Systems analysis and engineering
consulting services
PA: Montrose Environmental Group, Inc.
5120 Northshore Dr
501 602-7008

(P-17528)
FFS TECH INC
Also Called: First Fire Systems
6000 Venice Blvd, Los Angeles
(90034-2233)
PHONE.............................323 965-9300
Yahooda Roshanzamir, *CEO*
EMP: 94 EST: 2014
SALES (est): 1.81MM **Privately Held**
Web: www.ffstech.com
SIC: 8711 1799 Fire protection engineering;
Fire escape installation

(P-17529)
**FIRE PROTECTION GROUP
AMER INC**
3712 W Jefferson Blvd, Los Angeles
(90016-4208)
P.O. Box 180520 (90018-9682)
PHONE.............................323 732-4200
George Saadian, *Pr*
Louise Tchaman, *

EMP: 40 EST: 1985
SQ FT: 20,000
SALES (est): 2.2MM **Privately Held**
Web: www.firesprinkler.com
SIC: 8711 1711 3569 1731 Fire protection
engineering; Fire sprinkler system
installation; Firefighting and related
equipment; Fire detection and burglar alarm
systems specialization

(P-17530)
FLINT ENERGY SERVICES INC
1999 Avenue Of The Stars Ste 2600, Los
Angeles (90067-6033)
PHONE.............................213 593-8000
EMP: 113
SALES (corp-wide): 16.11B **Publicly Held**
Web: www.aecom.com
SIC: 8711 Engineering services
HQ: Flint Energy Services Inc.
7595 E Technology Way # 200
Denver CO 80237
918 294-3030

(P-17531)
FLUOR CORPORATION
Also Called: Trs Staffing Solutions
3 Polaris Way, Aliso Viejo (92656-5338)
PHONE.............................949 349-2000
Tim Kirk, *Prin*
EMP: 99
SALES (corp-wide): 15.47B **Publicly Held**
Web: www.fluor.com
SIC: 8711 7363 Engineering services; Help
supply services
PA: Fluor Corporation
6700 Las Colinas Blvd
469 398-7000

(P-17532)
**FLUOR PLANT SERVICES INTL
INC**
Also Called: Fluor Daniel
1 Enterprise, Aliso Viejo (92656-2606)
PHONE.............................949 349-2000
D Michael Steuert, *CFO*
EMP: 100 EST: 1900
SALES (est): 7.95MM
SALES (corp-wide): 15.47B **Publicly Held**
Web: www.microsemi.com
SIC: 8711 Engineering services
PA: Fluor Corporation
6700 Las Colinas Blvd
469 398-7000

(P-17533)
**FORWARD SLOPE
INCORPORATED (PA)**
Also Called: Forward Slope.
2020 Camino Del Rio N Ste 400, San Diego
(92108-1543)
PHONE.............................619 299-4400
Carlos Persichetti, *Pr*
Kevin Noonan, *VP*
EMP: 80 EST: 1997
SALES (est): 22.33MM
SALES (corp-wide): 22.33MM **Privately
Held**
Web: www.forwardslope.com
SIC: 8711 7371 7389 Consulting engineer;
Software programming applications;
Financial services

(P-17534)
FTI CONSULTING INC
350 S Grand Ave Ste 3000, Los Angeles
(90071-3424)
PHONE.............................213 689-1200
Stewart Kahn, *Pr*
EMP: 80

SALES (corp-wide): 3.49B **Publicly Held**
Web: www.fticonsulting.com
SIC: 8711 8748 8742 Consulting engineer;
Business consulting, nec; Management
consulting services
PA: Fti Consulting, Inc.
555 12th St Nw Ste 700
202 312-9100

(P-17535)
FUSCOE ENGINEERING INC (PA)
15535 Sand Canyon Ave, Irvine
(92618-3114)
PHONE.............................949 474-1960
Patrick Fuscoe, *Pr*
EMP: 85 EST: 1992
SALES (est): 21.57MM **Privately Held**
Web: www.fuscoe.com
SIC: 8711 Civil engineering

(P-17536)
**GARRETT J GENTRY GEN
ENGRG INC**
1297 W 9th St, Upland (91786-5706)
PHONE.............................909 693-3391
Garrett J Gentry, *Pr*
Bryan Copping, *
EMP: 100 EST: 2013
SALES (est): 26.16MM **Privately Held**
Web: www.gjgentry.com
SIC: 8711 Acoustical engineering

(P-17537)
GEOCON INCORPORATED
6960 Flanders Dr, San Diego (92121-3992)
PHONE.............................858 558-6900
Joesph Vettel, *CEO*
Michael Chapin, *
William Lydon, *
EMP: 100 EST: 1971
SALES (est): 18.42MM **Privately Held**
Web: www.geoconinc.com
SIC: 8711 Consulting engineer

(P-17538)
GEORGE G SHARP INC
1065 Bay Blvd Ste D, Chula Vista
(91911-1626)
PHONE.............................619 425-4211
EMP: 75
SALES (corp-wide): 32.11MM **Privately
Held**
SIC: 8711 Consulting engineer
PA: George G. Sharp, Inc.
160 Broadway Rm 800
212 732-2800

(P-17539)
**GLENN A RICK ENGRG & DEV
CO (PA)**
Also Called: Rick Engineering Company
5620 Friars Rd, San Diego (92110-2513)
PHONE.............................619 291-0708
Roger Ball, *Prin*
Paul J Iezzi, *
Robert A Stockton, *
Dennis C Bowling, *
Deborah B Ragione, *
EMP: 212 EST: 1955
SQ FT: 50,000
SALES (est): 22.59MM
SALES (corp-wide): 22.59MM **Privately
Held**
Web: www.rickengineering.com
SIC: 8711 Civil engineering

(P-17540)
**GLOBAL SOLUTIONS
INTEGRATION**

Also Called: Gsico
26632 Towne Centre Dr Ste 300, Foothill Ranch (92610-2814)
PHONE..............949 307-1849
Cel Esmundi, *Pr*
EMP: 75 EST: 2016
SQ FT: 3,000
SALES (est): 1.51MM **Privately Held**
Web: www.gsico.net
SIC: 8711 Engineering services

(P-17541)
GRADIENT ENGINEERS INC
Also Called: Leighton & Associates
17781 Cowan Ste 140, Irvine (92614-6009)
PHONE..............949 477-0555
EMP: 156 EST: 1996
SALES (est): 325.55K
SALES (corp-wide): 154.82MM **Privately Held**
SIC: 8711 8744 Consulting engineer; Environmental remediation
HQ: Leighton Group, Inc.
2600 Michelson Dr Ste 400
Irvine CA 92612
949 250-1421

(P-17542)
GRYPHON MARINE LLC
Also Called: Gryphon
694 Moss St, Chula Vista (91911-1616)
PHONE..............619 407-4010
Ms. Karlovic, *CEO*
EMP: 90
SALES (corp-wide): 2.52B **Privately Held**
Web: www.mantech.com
SIC: 8711 Engineering services
HQ: Gryphon Marine, Llc
4600 Village Ave Ste 100
Norfolk VA 23502
757 763-6666

(P-17543)
HETHERINGTON ENGINEERING (PA)
4333 Apache St, Oceanside (92056-2913)
PHONE..............760 931-1917
Mark Hetherington, *Pr*
EMP: 227 EST: 1986
SALES (est): 2.54MM
SALES (corp-wide): 2.54MM **Privately Held**
Web: www.hetheringtonengineering.com
SIC: 8711 Consulting engineer

(P-17544)
HIGHBURY DEFENSE GROUP LLC
2725 Congress St Ste 1m, San Diego (92110-2766)
PHONE..............619 316-7979
Andrew Nugent, *CEO*
EMP: 76 EST: 2012
SALES (est): 3.57MM **Privately Held**
Web: www.highbury-defense.com
SIC: 8711 7382 Engineering services; Security systems services

(P-17545)
HII FLEET SUPPORT GROUP LLC
131 W 33rd St Ste 100a, National City (91950-7266)
PHONE..............619 474-8820
Suliman Haidar, *Mgr*
EMP: 178
SIC: 8711 Engineering services
HQ: Hii Fleet Support Group Llc
5701 Cleveland St
Virginia Beach VA 23462
757 463-6666

(P-17546)
HMS CONSTRUCTION INC (PA)
Also Called: HMS
2885 Scott St, Vista (92081-8547)
PHONE..............760 727-9808
Michael C High, *CEO*
Ian High, *
Sharon High, *
Carla Sims, *
Chris Morales, *
EMP: 75 EST: 1996
SQ FT: 5,200
SALES (est): 40.22MM
SALES (corp-wide): 40.22MM **Privately Held**
Web: www.hmsconco.com
SIC: 8711 1781 1731 Engineering services; Geothermal drilling; Electrical work

(P-17547)
HNTB CORPORATION
6 Hutton Centre Dr Ste 500, Santa Ana (92707-6725)
PHONE..............714 460-1600
EMP: 119
SALES (corp-wide): 449.19MM **Privately Held**
Web: www.hntb.com
SIC: 8711 Consulting engineer
HQ: Hntb Corporation
715 Kirk Dr
Kansas City MO 64105
816 472-1201

(P-17548)
HNTB GERWICK WATER SOLUTIONS
200 Sandpointe Ave, Santa Ana (92707-5751)
PHONE..............714 460-1600
EMP: 150
SALES (est): 3.78MM **Privately Held**
SIC: 8711 8712 Consulting engineer; Architectural services

(P-17549)
HOLMES & NARVER INC (HQ)
999 W Town And Country Rd, Orange (92868-4713)
P.O. Box 6240 (92863-6240)
PHONE..............714 567-2400
Danny Seal, *CEO*
Raymond Landy, *
Dennis Deslatte, *
Tina Clugston, *
EMP: 250 EST: 1933
SQ FT: 100,000
SALES (est): 2.42MM
SALES (corp-wide): 16.11B **Publicly Held**
SIC: 8711 8742 8741 1542 Engineering services; Training and development consultant; Construction management; Nonresidential construction, nec
PA: Aecom
13355 Noel Rd Ste 400
972 788-1000

(P-17550)
HSA & ASSOCIATES INC
301 N Lake Ave Ste 500, Pasadena (91101-5134)
PHONE..............626 521-9931
Rafik Gerges, *Prin*
EMP: 81 EST: 2019
SALES (est): 4.08MM **Privately Held**
Web: www.hsaassociates.com
SIC: 8711 Consulting engineer

(P-17551)
HUNSAKER & ASSOC IRVINE INC (PA)
Also Called: Hunsaker & Associates
3 Hughes, Irvine (92618-2082)
PHONE..............949 583-1010
Richard Hunsaker, *CEO*
Douglas Snyder, *
Kamal Karam, *
Doug Staley, *
EMP: 100 EST: 1976
SQ FT: 27,000
SALES (est): 15.41MM
SALES (corp-wide): 15.41MM **Privately Held**
Web: www.hnagi.com
SIC: 8711 8713 Civil engineering; Surveying services

(P-17552)
HUNSAKER & ASSOC IRVINE INC
2900 Adams St Ste A15, Riverside (92504-4337)
PHONE..............951 352-7200
Brad Hay, *Brnch Mgr*
EMP: 300
SALES (corp-wide): 15.41MM **Privately Held**
Web: www.hnagi.com
SIC: 8711 Civil engineering
PA: Hunsaker & Associates Irvine, Inc.
3 Hughes
949 583-1010

(P-17553)
HYUNDAI AMER TECHNICAL CTR INC
Also Called: Kia Design Center America
101 Peters Canyon Rd, Irvine (92606-1790)
PHONE..............734 337-2500
EMP: 113
Web: www.hatci.com
SIC: 8711 8734 Designing: ship, boat, machine, and product; Automobile proving and testing ground
HQ: Hyundai America Technical Center Incorporated
6800 Geddes Rd
Ypsilanti MI 48198
734 337-2500

(P-17554)
IMEG CONSULTANTS CORP
222 S Harbor Blvd Ste 800, Anaheim (92805-3715)
PHONE..............714 490-5555
Albert Chiu, *Brnch Mgr*
EMP: 71
SALES (corp-wide): 141.33MM **Privately Held**
Web: www.imegcorp.com
SIC: 8711 Consulting engineer
PA: Imeg Consultants Corp.
623 26th Ave
309 788-0673

(P-17555)
INDUS TECHNOLOGY INC
2243 San Diego Ave Ste 200, San Diego (92110-2070)
PHONE..............619 299-2555
James B Lasswell, *Pr*
Will Nevilles, *
Eric Macgregor, *
Jan Perez, *
Rebecca Spane, *
EMP: 230 EST: 1991
SQ FT: 12,000

SALES (est): 20.78MM **Privately Held**
Web: www.industechnology.com
SIC: 8711 Engineering services

(P-17556)
INGENIUM TECHNOLOGIES CORP
5665 Oberlin Dr Ste 202, San Diego (92121-1739)
PHONE..............858 227-4422
Duane Wingate, *Prin*
EMP: 80
SALES (corp-wide): 8.75MM **Privately Held**
Web: www.ingeniumtech.com
SIC: 8711 Consulting engineer
PA: Ingenium Technologies Corp.
4216 Maray Dr
815 399-8803

(P-17557)
INNOVATIVE ENGRG SYSTEMS INC (PA)
Also Called: Ies Engineering
8800 Crippen St, Bakersfield (93311-9686)
P.O. Box 20610 (93390-0610)
EMP: 100 EST: 2002
SQ FT: 20,000
SALES (est): 23.85MM **Privately Held**
Web: www.agilitechgroup.com
SIC: 8711 1731 Consulting engineer; Electrical work

(P-17558)
INTERNATIONAL ENERGY SERVICES USA INC
Also Called: International Energy Svcs Co
3445 Kashiwa St, Torrance (90505-4024)
PHONE..............310 257-8222
EMP: 200
SIC: 8711 Engineering services

(P-17559)
IRIS TECHNOLOGY CORPORATION
2811 Mcgaw Ave Ste A, Irvine (92614-0101)
P.O. Box 15115 (92623-5115)
PHONE..............949 975-8410
Edward O'rourke, *CEO*
Marguerite Slater, *
EMP: 70 EST: 1986
SQ FT: 4,000
SALES (est): 14.26MM **Privately Held**
Web: www.iristechnology.com
SIC: 8711 Aviation and/or aeronautical engineering

(P-17560)
JACOBS CIVIL INC
1500 Hughes Way Ste B400, Long Beach (90810-1882)
PHONE..............310 847-2500
EMP: 229
SALES (corp-wide): 11.5B **Publicly Held**
SIC: 8711 Consulting engineer
HQ: Jacobs Civil Inc.
501 N Broadway
Saint Louis MO

(P-17561)
JACOBS ENGINEERING COMPANY
1111 S Arroyo Pkwy, Pasadena (91105-3254)
P.O. Box 7084 (91109-7084)
PHONE..............626 449-2171
EMP: 4000 EST: 1979

SALES (est): 42.54MM
SALES (corp-wide): 14.09B **Publicly Held**
SIC: **8711** 1629 Engineering services; Chemical plant and refinery construction
HQ: Jacobs Engineering Group Inc.
1999 Bryan St Ste 1200
Dallas TX 75201
214 583-8500

(P-17562)
JACOBS ENGINEERING GROUP INC
2600 Michelson Dr Ste 500, Irvine (92612-6506)
PHONE..................................949 224-7500
Dan Grubb, *Brnch Mgr*
EMP: 88
SALES (corp-wide): 11.5B **Publicly Held**
Web: www.jacobs.com
SIC: **8711** Consulting engineer
HQ: Jacobs Engineering Group Inc.
1999 Bryan St Ste 3500
Dallas TX 75201
214 583-8500

(P-17563)
JACOBS ENGINEERING GROUP INC
1111 S Arroyo Pkwy, Pasadena (91105-3254)
P.O. Box 7084 (91109-7084)
PHONE..................................626 578-3500
EMP: 89
SALES (corp-wide): 11.5B **Publicly Held**
Web: www.jacobs.com
SIC: **8711** Consulting engineer
HQ: Jacobs Engineering Group Inc.
1999 Bryan St Ste 3500
Dallas TX 75201
214 583-8500

(P-17564)
JACOBS ENGINEERING INC (DH)
155 N Lake Ave, Pasadena (91101-1849)
P.O. Box 7084 (91109-7084)
PHONE..................................626 578-3500
Craig L Martin, *CEO*
Noel G Watson, *
EMP: 161 EST: 1971
SALES (est): 34.66MM
SALES (corp-wide): 11.5B **Publicly Held**
Web: www.jacobs.com
SIC: **8711** Consulting engineer
HQ: Jacobs Engineering Group Inc.
1999 Bryan St Ste 3500
Dallas TX 75201
214 583-8500

(P-17565)
JACOBS INTERNATIONAL LTD INC
155 N Lake Ave Ste 800, Pasadena (91101-1857)
P.O. Box 7084 (91109-7084)
PHONE..................................626 578-3500
Craig Martin, *Pr*
Jeff Sanders, *
John W Prosser Junior, *Treas*
EMP: 300 EST: 2002
SQ FT: 120,000
SALES (est): 13.11MM
SALES (corp-wide): 11.5B **Publicly Held**
SIC: **8711** Consulting engineer
HQ: Jacobs Engineering Group Inc.
1999 Bryan St Ste 3500
Dallas TX 75201
214 583-8500

(P-17566)
JACOBS PROJECT MANAGEMENT CO
2600 Michelson Dr Ste 500, Irvine (92612-6506)
PHONE..................................949 224-7695
Les Steinberger, *Mgr*
Frank Joyce, *
EMP: 99 EST: 2008
SALES (est): 2.37MM
SALES (corp-wide): 11.5B **Publicly Held**
Web: www.jacobs.com
SIC: **8711** Consulting engineer
HQ: Jacobs Engineering Group Inc.
1999 Bryan St Ste 3500
Dallas TX 75201
214 583-8500

(P-17567)
JSL TECHNOLOGIES INC
1701 Pacific Ave Ste 270, Oxnard (93033-1887)
PHONE..................................805 985-7700
Joseph T Black Iii, *Pr*
Ben Fujikawa, *
Jed Williams, *
EMP: 305 EST: 2008
SQ FT: 22,155
SALES (est): 28MM **Privately Held**
Web: www.jsltechinc.com
SIC: **8711** Consulting engineer

(P-17568)
JT3 LLC
190 S Wolfe Ave Bldg 1260, Edwards (93524-6501)
PHONE..................................661 277-4900
James Tedeschi, *Mgr*
EMP: 1340
SALES (corp-wide): 150MM **Privately Held**
Web: www.jt4llc.com
SIC: **8711** Engineering services
PA: Jt3, L.L.C.
821 Grier Dr
704 492-2181

(P-17569)
K&B ELECTRIC LLC
Also Called: K&B Engineering
290 Corporate Terrace Cir Ste 200, Corona (92879-6033)
PHONE..................................951 808-9501
Sandee Gibbs, *Managing Member*
Trey Gibbs, *
EMP: 158 EST: 2011
SALES (est): 5.87MM **Privately Held**
Web: www.kbeng.net
SIC: **8711** Consulting engineer

(P-17570)
KIEWIT CORPORATION
10704 Shoemaker Ave, Santa Fe Springs (90670-4040)
PHONE..................................907 222-9350
EMP: 94
SALES (corp-wide): 10.41B **Privately Held**
Web: www.kiewit.com
SIC: **8711** Consulting engineer
HQ: Kiewit Corporation
1550 Mike Fahey St
Omaha NE 68102
402 342-2052

(P-17571)
KINEMETRICS INC (DH)
222 Vista Ave, Pasadena (91107-3295)
PHONE..................................626 795-2220
Tadashi Jimbo, *CEO*
Melvin Lund, *

Ogie Kuraica, *
Ian Standley, *
Michelle Harrington, *
EMP: 59 EST: 1969
SQ FT: 50,000
SALES (est): 26.8MM **Privately Held**
Web: www.kinemetrics.com
SIC: **8711** 3829 Engineering services; Seismographs
HQ: Oyo Corporation U.S.A.
245 N Carmelo Ave Ste 101
Pasadena CA 91107

(P-17572)
KLEINFELDER INC (HQ)
Also Called: Kleinfelder
770 1st Ave Ste 400, San Diego (92101-6171)
P.O. Box 51958 (90051-6258)
PHONE..................................619 831-4600
John Murphy, *CFO*
Deborah Butera, *
Carl Lowman, *
Daniel Brockman, *
Lisa Millet, *Central Division*
EMP: 160 EST: 1962
SQ FT: 5,000
SALES (est): 249.41MM
SALES (corp-wide): 458.93MM **Privately Held**
Web: www.kleinfelder.com
SIC: **8711** 8712 Consulting engineer; Architectural engineering
PA: The Kleinfelder Group Inc
770 First Ave Ste 400
619 831-4600

(P-17573)
KLEINFELDER GROUP INC (PA)
770 1st Ave Ste 400, San Diego (92101-6171)
PHONE..................................619 831-4600
Louis Armstrong, *Pr*
Lisa Millet, *Ex VP*
Jeff Hill, *Dist Vice President*
Ann Masey, *Prin*
Erik Soderquist, *Ex VP*
EMP: 175 EST: 1985
SALES (est): 458.93MM
SALES (corp-wide): 458.93MM **Privately Held**
Web: www.kleinfelder.com
SIC: **8711** Consulting engineer

(P-17574)
KPFF INC
K P F F Consulting Engineers
18500 Von Karman Ave Ste 1000, Irvine (92612-0527)
PHONE..................................949 252-1022
Roger Young, *Prin*
EMP: 01
SALES (corp-wide): 108.51MM **Privately Held**
Web: www.kpff.com
SIC: **8711** Consulting engineer
PA: Kpff, Inc.
1601 5th Ave Ste 1300
206 225-2980

(P-17575)
KRATOS TECH TRNING SLTIONS INC (HQ)
10680 Treena St Ste 600, San Diego (92131-2440)
PHONE..................................858 812-7300
Eric M Demarco, *Pr*
Deanna H Lund, *Ex VP*
Laura L Siegal, *Corporate Controller*
Deborah S Butera, *Sec*

Phil Carrai, *VP Opers*
EMP: 94 EST: 1966
SQ FT: 25,000
SALES (est): 72.92MM **Publicly Held**
Web: www.kratosdefense.com
SIC: **8711** Engineering services
PA: Kratos Defense & Security Solutions, Inc.
10680 Treena St Ste 600

(P-17576)
L3 MARIPRO INC
1522 Cook Pl, Goleta (93117-3124)
PHONE..................................805 683-3881
EMP: 90
SIC: **8711** Marine engineering

(P-17577)
LAMER STREET KREATIONS CORP
Also Called: Calwest Mfg and Lsk Suspension
13815 Arrow Blvd, Fontana (92335-0255)
PHONE..................................909 305-4824
Aaron Rifkin, *Pr*
Aaron Riskin, *
Van Syverud, *
EMP: 25 EST: 2012
SALES (est): 5.98MM **Privately Held**
Web: www.lsksuspension.com
SIC: **8711** 3499 3569 Sanitary engineers; Fire- or burglary-resistive products; Robots, assembly line: industrial and commercial

(P-17578)
LASH CONSTRUCTION INC
721 Carpinteria St, Santa Barbara (93103-3623)
P.O. Box 4640 (93140-4640)
PHONE..................................805 963-3553
EMP: 99 EST: 1978
SALES (est): 4.77MM **Privately Held**
Web: www.lashconstruction.com
SIC: **8711** 1623 Engineering services; Underground utilities contractor

(P-17579)
LOCKHEED MARTIN SERVICES LLC
Also Called: Lockheed Martin
645 Marsat Ct Ste D, Chula Vista (91911-7141)
PHONE..................................619 271-9831
EMP: 350
SIC: **8711** Engineering services
HQ: Lockheed Martin Services, Llc
700 N Frederick Ave
Gaithersburg MD 20879

(P-17580)
LOS ANGELES ENGINEERING INC
633 N Barranca Ave, Covina (91723-1229)
PHONE..................................626 869-1400
Henry Angus O'brien, *Pr*
Henry Angus O'brien, *Pr*
Aaron O'brien, *VP*
Beth Ballard, *
Melody Turner, *
EMP: 110 EST: 1987
SQ FT: 33,000
SALES (est): 47.57MM **Privately Held**
Web: www.laeng.net
SIC: **8711** 1622 Construction and civil engineering; Bridge, tunnel, and elevated highway construction

(P-17581)
MANGAN INC (PA)
Also Called: Barry D. Payne and Associates

P
R
O
D
U
C
T
S

&

S
V
C
S

3901 Via Oro Ave, Long Beach
(90810-1800)
PHONE.................310 835-8080
Richard D Mangan, *Pr*
Russell Seward, *
Amin Solehjou, *
Christopher Lopez, *
Christine Said, *
EMP: 90 **EST:** 1991
SQ FT: 15,000
SALES (est): 37.92MM **Privately Held**
Web: www.manganinc.com
SIC: 8711 Consulting engineer

(P-17582)
MARVIN ENGINEERING CO INC (PA)
Also Called: Marvin Group, The
261 W Beach Ave, Inglewood (90302-2904)
PHONE.................310 674-5030
Howard Gussman, *CEO*
Ariel Lechter, *
Craig Snaguski, *
▲ **EMP:** 580 **EST:** 1963
SQ FT: 300,000
SALES (est): 149.54MM
SALES (corp-wide): 149.54MM **Privately Held**
Web: www.marvingroup.com
SIC: 8711 Consulting engineer

(P-17583)
MDS CONSULTING (PA)
17320 Red Hill Ave Ste 350, Irvine
(92614-5671)
PHONE.................949 251-8821
Stanley C Morse, *Ch*
Stanley C Morse, *Owner*
Jerry R Schultz, *
EMP: 71 **EST:** 1976
SQ FT: 8,837
SALES (est): 3.93MM
SALES (corp-wide): 3.93MM **Privately Held**
Web: www.mdsconsulting.net
SIC: 8711 Civil engineering

(P-17584)
MERUELO GROUP LLC (PA)
Also Called: Meruelo Group
9550 Firestone Blvd Ste 105, Downey
(90241-5560)
PHONE.................562 745-2300
EMP: 75 **EST:** 2015
SALES (est): 10.73MM
SALES (corp-wide): 10.73MM **Privately Held**
Web: www.meruelogroup.com
SIC: 8711 Engineering services

(P-17585)
MESA ASSOCIATES INC
3670 W Temple Ave Ste 152, Pomona
(91768-2588)
PHONE.................909 979-6609
Brad Hoy, *Brnch Mgr*
EMP: 79
Web: www.mesainc.com
SIC: 8711 8712 Consulting engineer; Architectural services
PA: Mesa Associates, Inc.
480 Production Ave

(P-17586)
MICHAEL BAKER INTERNATIONAL INC (DH)
5 Hutton Centre Dr Ste 500, Santa Ana
(92707-6736)
Rural Route 57057 (92619)
PHONE.................949 472-3505

EMP: 350 **EST:** 1944
SALES (est): 43.61MM
SALES (corp-wide): 1.04B Privately Held
Web: www.mbakerintl.com
SIC: 8711 8713 Civil engineering; Surveying services
HQ: Michael Baker International Holdco Corporation
100 Airside Dr
Moon Township PA 15108
412 269-6300

(P-17587)
MICROWAVE APPLICATIONS GROUP
Also Called: M A G
3030 Industrial Pkwy, Santa Maria
(93455-1881)
PHONE.................805 928-5711
Steven Van Dyke, *CEO*
Tom Janzen, *
Scott Mckechnie, *VP*
Robin Hopp, *
EMP: 26 **EST:** 1969
SQ FT: 22,000
SALES (est): 4.42MM **Privately Held**
Web: www.magsmx.com
SIC: 8711 3679 Engineering services; Microwave components

(P-17588)
MNS ENGINEERS INC (PA)
201 N Calle Cesar Chavez Ste 300, Santa Barbara (93103-3256)
PHONE.................805 692-6921
James A Salvito, *CEO*
Mark E Reinhardt, *
Gregory A Chelini, *
Jeffrey L Edwards, *
Shawn M Kowalewski, *
EMP: 94 **EST:** 1962
SQ FT: 7,000
SALES (est): 17.99MM
SALES (corp-wide): 17.99MM **Privately Held**
Web: www.mnsengineers.com
SIC: 8711 8713 Civil engineering; Surveying services

(P-17589)
MOBILENET SERVICES INC (PA)
18 Morgan Ste 200, Irvine (92618-2074)
PHONE.................949 951-4444
Richard Grant, *Pr*
Eugene Powell, *
Edward Krol, *
Lorenzo Mills, *
Rodelio Santos, *
EMP: 180 **EST:** 2002
SQ FT: 17,500
SALES (est): 9.12MM
SALES (corp-wide): 9.12MM **Privately Held**
Web: www.mobilenet.net
SIC: 8711 4813 Engineering services; Telephone communication, except radio

(P-17590)
MODELO GROUP INC
16751 Millikan Ave, Irvine (92606-5009)
PHONE.................562 446-5091
Jose Vazquez, *CEO*
EMP: 25 **EST:** 2004
SALES (est): 1MM **Privately Held**
SIC: 8711 7373 3999 Engineering services; Computer-aided design (CAD) systems service; Barber and beauty shop equipment

(P-17591)
MOFFATT & NICHOL
Also Called: Moffatt & Nichol
555 Anton Blvd Ste 400, Costa Mesa
(92626-7667)
PHONE.................657 261-2699
Eric Nichol, *CEO*
EMP: 70
SALES (corp-wide): 126.34MM **Privately Held**
Web: www.moffattnichol.com
SIC: 8711 Structural engineering
PA: Moffat & Nichol
4225 E Conant St Ste 101
562 590-6500

(P-17592)
MSM INDUSTRIES INC
12660 Magnolia Ave, Riverside
(92503-4636)
PHONE.................951 735-0834
Darryl Clare, *Pr*
Peter Taylor, *
Craig Sparling, *
Carl Maas, *
EMP: 31 **EST:** 2002
SALES (est): 6.44MM **Privately Held**
Web: www.msm-ind.com
SIC: 8711 2891 2515 Engineering services; Epoxy adhesives; Mattresses, containing felt, foam rubber, urethane, etc.

(P-17593)
NATIONAL SECURITY TECH LLC
5520 Ekwill St Ste B, Goleta (93111-2335)
PHONE.................805 681-2432
EMP: 553
SALES (corp-wide): 61.46MM **Privately Held**
Web: www.nstec.com
SIC: 8711 1629 Civil engineering; Industrial plant construction
PA: National Security Technologies, Llc
2621 Losee Rd
702 295-1000

(P-17594)
NATIONAL TELECONSULTANTS INC
1830 Avenida Del Mundo, Coronado
(92118-3003)
PHONE.................818 265-4400
Eliot P Graham, *Managing Member*
Charles C Phelan, *
Peter Adamiak, *
EMP: 108 **EST:** 1981
SALES (est): 5.41MM **Privately Held**
Web: www.ntc.com
SIC: 8711 Electrical or electronic engineering

(P-17595)
NAVAL FACILITIES ENGINEER COMM
1220 Pacific Hwy, San Diego (92132-5101)
PHONE.................619 532-1158
Shahraam Plaseied, *Prin*
Nancy Wright, *Acctnt*
Captain Darius Banaji, *COO*
EMP: 99 **EST:** 2014
SQ FT: 4,000
SALES (est): 3.31MM **Privately Held**
SIC: 8711 1623 8744 Pollution control engineering; Underground utilities contractor; Base maintenance (providing personnel on continuing basis)

(P-17596)
NEST PARENT INC
2125 E Katella Ave Ste 250, Anaheim
(92806-6024)

PHONE.................310 551-0101
Gerald L Parsky, *Pr*
John T Mapes, *
EMP: 1207 **EST:** 2012
SALES (est): 2.25MM **Privately Held**
SIC: 8711 Consulting engineer

(P-17597)
NV5 INC
Also Called: Nolte, George S & Associates
15092 Avenue Of Science # 200, San Diego
(92128-3404)
PHONE.................858 385-0500
Carmen Kasmer, *Dir*
EMP: 200
SALES (corp-wide): 861.74MM **Publicly Held**
Web: www.nv5.com
SIC: 8711 8713 Civil engineering; Surveying services
HQ: Nv5, Inc.
2150 River Plaza Dr
Sacramento CA 95833
916 641-9100

(P-17598)
ONCORE MANUFACTURING LLC (HQ)
Also Called: Neo Tech
9340 Owensmouth Ave, Chatsworth
(91311-6915)
PHONE.................818 734-6500
Sudesh Arora, *Pr*
Laura Siegal, *
Kunal Sharma, *
David Brakenwagen Csmo, *Prin*
David Lane, *
▲ **EMP:** 700 **EST:** 2001
SALES (est): 146.23MM
SALES (corp-wide): 1.43B **Privately Held**
Web: www.neotech.com
SIC: 8711 3672 Electrical or electronic engineering; Printed circuit boards
PA: Natel Engineering Company, Llc
9340 Owensmouth Ave
818 495-8617

(P-17599)
ONE SUN POWER INC
3451 Via Montebello Ste 511, Carlsbad
(92009-8492)
PHONE.................844 360-9600
James Joseph Holmes, *CEO*
EMP: 3231 **EST:** 2017
SALES (est): 1.99MM **Privately Held**
SIC: 8711 Energy conservation engineering

(P-17600)
P2S LP
4660 La Jolla Village Dr Ste 600, San Diego
(92122-4605)
PHONE.................562 497-2999
EMP: 195
Web: www.p2sinc.com
SIC: 8711 Consulting engineer
PA: P2s Lp
5000 E Spring St Ste 800

(P-17601)
PACIFIC ADVNCED CVIL ENGRG INC (PA)
17520 Newhope St Ste 200, Fountain Valley
(92708-8206)
PHONE.................714 481-7300
Mark E Krebs, *Pr*
Andy Komor, *
James Matthews, *
Michael Krebs, *
Cory Severson, *
EMP: 73 **EST:** 1987

SQ FT: 18,254
SALES (est): 3.62MM
SALES (corp-wide): 3.62MM **Privately Held**
Web: www.pacewater.com
SIC: 8711 Civil engineering

(P-17602)
PACIFIC HYDROTECH CORPORATION
314 E 3rd St, Perris (92570-2225)
PHONE..............................951 943-8803
J Kirk Harris, *Pr*
Sean Finnegan, *
Bobby Owens, *
Joselito Guintu, *
Dale Mckay, *VP*
EMP: 135 EST: 1987
SQ FT: 1,500
SALES (est): 45.48MM **Privately Held**
Web: www.pachydro.com
SIC: 8711 Construction and civil engineering

(P-17603)
PACIFICA SERVICES INC
106 S Mentor Ave Ste 200, Pasadena (91106-2931)
PHONE..............................626 405-0131
Ernest M Camacho, *Pr*
Stephen Caropino, *
EMP: 84 EST: 1979
SQ FT: 15,000
SALES (est): 4.88MM **Privately Held**
Web: www.pacificaservices.com
SIC: 8711 7629 8741 Civil engineering; Electronic equipment repair; Construction management

(P-17604)
PANASONIC AVIONICS CORPORATION (DH)
3347 Michelson Dr Ste 100, Irvine (92612-0661)
PHONE..............................949 672-2000
Kenneth W Sain, *CEO*
Seigo Tada, *
Jessica L Hodkinson, *
▲ EMP: 400 EST: 1990
SQ FT: 20,000
SALES (est): 461.89MM **Privately Held**
Web: www.panasonic.aero
SIC: 8711 3728 Aviation and/or aeronautical engineering; Aircraft parts and equipment, nec
HQ: Panasonic Corporation Of North America
Two Riverfront Plz Fl 7
Newark NJ 07102
201 348-7000

(P-17605)
PARSONS ENGRG SCIENCE INC (DH)
100 W Walnut St, Pasadena (91124-0002)
P.O. Box 88954 (60695-1954)
PHONE..............................626 440-2000
Charles Harrington, *CEO*
Mary Ann Hopkins, *
Curtis A Bower, *
Nicholas L Presecan, *
Gary L Stone, *
EMP: 500 EST: 1946
SALES (est): 36.61MM
SALES (corp-wide): 5.44B **Publicly Held**
Web: www.parsons.com
SIC: 8711 Consulting engineer
HQ: Parsons Government Services Inc.
5875 Trinity Pkwy Ste 230
Centreville VA 20120
703 988-8500

(P-17606)
PARSONS GOVERNMENT SVCS INC
525 B St Ste 1600, San Diego (92101-4413)
PHONE..............................619 685-0085
Christopher Bush, *VP*
EMP: 301
SALES (corp-wide): 5.44B **Publicly Held**
Web: www.parsons.com
SIC: 8711 Engineering services
HQ: Parsons Government Services Inc.
5875 Trinity Pkwy Ste 230
Centreville VA 20120
703 988-8500

(P-17607)
PARSONS INTL CAYMAN ISLANDS
100 W Walnut St, Pasadena (91124-0001)
PHONE..............................626 440-6000
William E Hall, *Pr*
EMP: 2000 EST: 1994
SALES (est): 31.57MM
SALES (corp-wide): 5.44B **Publicly Held**
Web: www.parsons.com
SIC: 8711 8741 Engineering services; Management services
HQ: Parsons Government Services Inc.
5875 Trinity Pkwy Ste 230
Centreville VA 20120
703 988-8500

(P-17608)
PARSONS SERVICE CORPORATION
100 W Walnut St, Pasadena (91124-0001)
PHONE..............................626 440-2000
Geoge L Ball, *Prin*
EMP: 797 EST: 1977
SALES (est): 7.99MM **Privately Held**
Web: www.parsons.com
SIC: 8711 Construction and civil engineering

(P-17609)
PENFIELD & SMITH ENGINEERS INC
Also Called: Penfield & Smith
111 E Victoria St, Santa Barbara (93101-2072)
P.O. Box 98 (93102-0098)
PHONE..............................805 963-9532
EMP: 80
SIC: 8711 8713 Civil engineering; Surveying services

(P-17610)
PHG ENGINEERING SERVICES LLC
27481 Ganso, Mission Viejo (92691-3646)
PHONE..............................714 283-8288
EMP: 100 EST: 2017
SALES (est): 1.73MM **Privately Held**
SIC: 8711 Engineering services

(P-17611)
PHOTON RESEARCH ASSOCIATES INC
9985 Pacific Heights Blvd Ste 200, San Diego (92121-4310)
PHONE..............................858 455-9741
EMP: 187
SIC: 8711 5045 8733 Aviation and/or aeronautical engineering; Computer software; Scientific research agency

(P-17612)
PLUMP ENGINEERING INC
914 E Katella Ave, Anaheim (92805-6615)
PHONE..............................714 385-1835
Richard Plump, *Pr*
EMP: 70 EST: 1997
SQ FT: 6,623
SALES (est): 16.76MM **Privately Held**
Web: www.peica.com
SIC: 8711 Consulting engineer

(P-17613)
PROCESSES UNLIMITED INTERNATIONAL INC
Also Called: Processes Unlimited
5500 Ming Ave Ste 400, Bakersfield (93309-9119)
PHONE..............................661 396-3770
EMP: 330
SIC: 8711 Engineering services

(P-17614)
PROTOTYPE ENGINEERING AND MANUFACTURING INC
140 E 162nd St, Gardena (90248-2802)
PHONE..............................310 532-6305
EMP: 24
Web: www.prototypeengineering.com
SIC: 8711 3825 Electrical or electronic engineering; Test equipment for electronic and electric measurement

(P-17615)
PTSI MANAGED SERVICES INC
100 W Walnut St, Pasadena (91124-0001)
PHONE..............................626 440-3118
Mary Ann Hopkins, *Pr*
EMP: 99 EST: 1983
SALES (est): 4.67MM
SALES (corp-wide): 5.44B **Publicly Held**
Web: www.parsons.com
SIC: 8711 Engineering services
PA: The Parsons Corporation
14291 Pk Madow Dr Ste 100
703 988-8500

(P-17616)
QUARTUS ENGINEERING INC (PA)
9689 Towne Centre Dr, San Diego (92121-1964)
PHONE..............................858 875-6000
John Williams, *CEO*
Mark Stabb, *
Chris Flanigan, *
Doug Botos, *
Jeff Frantz, *
EMP: 95 EST: 1997
SQ FT: 3,100
SALES (est): 24.39MM
SALES (corp-wide): 24.39MM **Privately Held**
Web: www.quartus.com
SIC: 8711 Consulting engineer

(P-17617)
R AND L LOPEZ ASSOCIATES INC (PA)
Also Called: Lopez & Associates Engineers
3649 Tyler Ave, El Monte (91731-2505)
PHONE..............................626 330-5296
Lourdes P Lopez, *Pr*
Remberto Lopez, *
EMP: 80 EST: 1979
SQ FT: 2,700
SALES (est): 2.37MM **Privately Held**
SIC: 8711 Consulting engineer

(P-17618)
RAYTHEON SECURE INFORMATION SYSTEMS LLC
Also Called: Raytheon
2000 E El Segundo Blvd, El Segundo (90245-4501)
PHONE..............................310 647-9438
EMP: 226
SIC: 8711 Electrical or electronic engineering

(P-17619)
RIALTO BIOENERGY FACILITY LLC
5780 Fleet St Ste 310, Carlsbad (92008-4714)
PHONE..............................760 436-8870
Arun Sharma, *Managing Member*
EMP: 250 EST: 2013
SQ FT: 12,937
SALES (est): 9.37MM
SALES (corp-wide): 9.37MM **Privately Held**
Web: www.anaergia.com
SIC: 8711 Energy conservation engineering
PA: Sevana Bioenergy Llc
9169 W State St Pmb 710
415 463-1333

(P-17620)
ROCK WEST COMPOSITES INC
7625 Panasonic Way, San Diego (92154-8204)
PHONE..............................858 537-6260
James Gormican, *Brnch Mgr*
EMP: 25
Web: www.rockwestcomposites.com
SIC: 8711 3624 Engineering services; Carbon and graphite products
PA: Rock West Composites, Inc.
7625 Panasonic Way

(P-17621)
ROVE ENGINEERING INC
398 E Aurora Dr, El Centro (92243-9603)
PHONE..............................760 425-0001
Steven Eugenio, *CEO*
Yessenia Galindo Eugenio, *VP*
EMP: 95 EST: 2018
SALES (est): 2.21MM **Privately Held**
SIC: 8711 Engineering services

(P-17622)
SAALEX CORP (PA)
Also Called: Saalex Solutions
811 Camarillo Springs Rd Ste A, Camarillo (93012-9466)
PHONE..............................805 482-1070
Travis Mack, *Pr*
Elaine Reese, *
Lisa Cortes, *
EMP: 245 EST: 1999
SQ FT: 7,000
SALES (est): 119.25MM
SALES (corp-wide): 119.25MM **Privately Held**
Web: www.saalex.com
SIC: 8711 7379 Consulting engineer; Computer related consulting services

(P-17623)
SABRE SYSTEMS INC
3111 Camino Del Rio N Ste 400, San Diego (92108-5724)
PHONE..............................619 528-2226
EMP: 87
Web: www.sabresystems.com
SIC: 8711 Engineering services
PA: Sabre Systems, Inc.
125 Cunty Line Rd Ste 180

(P-17624)

SAN DIEGO COMPOSITES INC

9220 Activity Rd Ste 100, San Diego
(92126-4420)
PHONE.....................858 751-0450
Marc Duvall, *CEO*
Jeff Murphy, *
EMP: 70 **EST:** 2003
SQ FT: 70,000
SALES (est): 26.39MM
SALES (corp-wide): 189.21MM **Privately Held**
Web: www.appliedcomposites.com
SIC: 8711 8734 3761 3764 Consulting engineer; Testing laboratories; Guided missiles and space vehicles; Space propulsion units and parts
PA: Applied Composites Holdings, Llc
25692 Atlantic Ocean Dr
949 716-3511

(P-17625)

SAN DIEGO SERVICES LLC

Also Called: Paragon Services Engineering
5415 Oberlin Dr, San Diego (92121-1716)
PHONE.....................858 654-0102
Rosemary Dymek, *Prin*
Wesley S Dymek, *Prin*
EMP: 150 **EST:** 1999
SQ FT: 2,477
SALES (est): 10.07MM **Privately Held**
Web: paragonservices.us.com
SIC: 8711 Engineering services

(P-17626)

SC WRIGHT CONSTRUCTION INC

3838 Camino Del Rio N Ste 370, San Diego
(92108-1764)
P.O. Box 3250 (91944-3250)
PHONE.....................619 698-6909
Steven C Wright, *Pr*
EMP: 400 **EST:** 1997
SALES (est): 6.88MM **Privately Held**
Web: www.scwright.com
SIC: 8711 Building construction consultant

(P-17627)

SCICON TECHNOLOGIES CORP (PA)

27525 Newhall Ranch Rd Ste 2, Valencia
(91355-4003)
PHONE.....................661 295-8630
Thomas J Bulger, *Pr*
Marie Bulger, *
▲ **EMP:** 50 **EST:** 1989
SQ FT: 25,000
SALES (est): 3.4MM **Privately Held**
Web: www.scicontech.com
SIC: 8711 3999 Mechanical engineering; Models, except toy

(P-17628)

SEP GROUP INC

11374 Turtleback Ln, San Diego
(92127-2009)
P.O. Box 270475 (92198-2475)
PHONE.....................858 876-4621
Abtin Sepehri, *CEO*
EMP: 25 **EST:** 1998
SALES (est): 907.87K **Privately Held**
SIC: 8711 1611 1542 1389 Construction and civil engineering; General contractor, highway and street construction; Commercial and office building contractors; Construction, repair, and dismantling services

(P-17629)

SERCO INC

9350 Waxie Way Ste 400, San Diego
(92123-1056)
PHONE.....................858 569-8979
Kent Brown, *Brnch Mgr*
EMP: 132
SALES (corp-wide): 6.07B **Privately Held**
Web: www.serco.com
SIC: 8711 Engineering services
HQ: Serco Inc.
12930 Wrldgate Dr Ste 600
Herndon VA 20170

(P-17630)

SIA ENGINEERING (USA) INC

7001 W Imperial Hwy, Los Angeles
(90045-6313)
PHONE.....................310 957-2928
Chandra Nair, *CEO*
Cheng Hian Tan, *
Chiuyen Tseng, *
EMP: 151 **EST:** 2008
SALES (est): 19.94MM **Privately Held**
SIC: 8711 Consulting engineer
HQ: Sia Engineering Company Limited
31 Airline Road
Singapore 81983

(P-17631)

SITESOL

Also Called: Site Sltions Cnstr Integration
7372 Sycamore Canyon Blvd, Riverside
(92508-2335)
P.O. Box 91747 (90809-1747)
PHONE.....................562 746-5884
Kristine Glaeser, *CEO*
Peter Glaeser, *
EMP: 85 **EST:** 2010
SALES (est): 3.56MM **Privately Held**
Web: www.sitesol.us
SIC: 8711 Construction and civil engineering

(P-17632)

SONATECH LLC

879 Ward Dr, Santa Barbara (93111-2958)
PHONE.....................805 683-1431
John Mather, *
Charles Randall, *
EMP: 104 **EST:** 2016
SQ FT: 10,000
SALES (est): 25MM **Privately Held**
Web: www.sonatech.com
SIC: 8711 Acoustical engineering

(P-17633)

SONIC INDUSTRIES INC

Also Called: Airframer R
20030 Normandie Ave, Torrance
(90502-1210)
PHONE.....................310 532-8382
Jamie King, *CEO*
▲ **EMP:** 150 **EST:** 1966
SQ FT: 65,000
SALES (est): 11.26MM
SALES (corp-wide): 1.56B **Publicly Held**
Web: www.rbcbearings.com
SIC: 8711 7699 Machine tool design; Aviation propeller and blade repair
HQ: Roller Bearing Company Of America, Inc.
102 Willenbrock Rd
Oxford CT 06478
203 267-7001

(P-17634)

SPEARMAN AEROSPACE INC

9215 Greenleaf Ave, Santa Fe Springs
(90670-3028)
PHONE.....................714 523-4751
Urio Zanetti, *Pr*
EMP: 25 **EST:** 2013
SALES (est): 10MM **Privately Held**
Web: www.spearmanaerospace.com
SIC: 8711 3721 Aviation and/or aeronautical engineering; Aircraft

(P-17635)

SPEC SERVICES INC

10540 Talbert Ave Ste 100e, Fountain Valley (92708-6051)
PHONE.....................714 963-8077
Kim R Henry, *Pr*
Dan Letcher, *
Chuck Lake, *
EMP: 290 **EST:** 1981
SQ FT: 16,000
SALES (est): 19.24MM **Privately Held**
Web: www.specservices.com
SIC: 8711 Consulting engineer

(P-17636)

STANTEC CONSULTING SVCS INC

300 N Lake Ave Ste 400, Pasadena
(91101-4169)
PHONE.....................626 796-9141
Paul Boulos, *Brnch Mgr*
EMP: 79
SALES (corp-wide): 4.72B **Privately Held**
Web: www.stantec.com
SIC: 8711 Consulting engineer
HQ: Stantec Consulting Services Inc.
475 5th Ave Fl 12
New York NY 10017
212 366-5600

(P-17637)

STEARNS CONRAD AND SCHMIDT CONSULTING ENGINEERS INC (PA)

Also Called: Scs Engineers
3900 Kilroy Airport Way Ste 100, Long Beach (90806-6816)
PHONE.....................562 426-9544
EMP: 100 **EST:** 1970
SALES (est): 497.42MM
SALES (corp-wide): 497.42MM **Privately Held**
Web: www.scsengineers.com
SIC: 8711 1541 8748 Consulting engineer; Industrial buildings, new construction, nec; Environmental consultant

(P-17638)

SUMARIA SYSTEMS LLC

105 13th St, Vandenberg Afb (93437-5209)
PHONE.....................805 606-4973
EMP: 82
SALES (corp-wide): 74.06MM **Privately Held**
Web: www.sumaria.com
SIC: 8711 Consulting engineer
PA: Sumaria Systems, Llc
8 Essex Center Dr
978 739-4200

(P-17639)

SYSTEMS & TECHNOLOGY RES LLC

Also Called: Str
1808 Aston Ave Ste 180, Carlsbad
(92008-7364)
PHONE.....................844 204-0963
EMP: 74
Web: www.str.us
SIC: 8711 Engineering services
PA: Systems & Technology Research Llc
600 W Cummings Park # 1075

(P-17640)

SYSTEMS APPLICATION & TECH INC

Also Called: Sa-Tech
1000 Town Center Dr Ste 110, Oxnard
(93036-1153)
P.O. Box 25 (93044-0025)
PHONE.....................805 487-7373
Geoff Dezavala, *Sr VP*
EMP: 80
Web: www.sa-techinc.com
SIC: 8711 Consulting engineer
PA: Systems Application & Technologies, Inc.
1101 Merc Ln Ste 200

(P-17641)

SYSTEMS ENGINEERING & MGT CO (PA)

Also Called: Semco
1430 Vantage Ct, Vista (92081-8568)
PHONE.....................760 727-7800
William M Tincup, *Pr*
Doug Ocull, *
Michael Samuels, *
▼ **EMP:** 35 **EST:** 1982
SQ FT: 42,000
SALES (est): 14.14MM
SALES (corp-wide): 14.14MM **Privately Held**
Web: www.semco.com
SIC: 8711 3812 3825 3663 Consulting engineer; Search and navigation equipment ; Instruments to measure electricity; Radio and t.v. communications equipment

(P-17642)

T2 UES INC

Also Called: T2 Utility Engineers
5622 Research Dr Ste A, Huntington Beach
(92649-1633)
PHONE.....................714 487-5786
EMP: 122
SALES (corp-wide): 9.2MM **Privately Held**
Web: www.t2ue.com
SIC: 8711 Consulting engineer
PA: T2 Ues, Inc.
7217 E 87th St
855 222-8283

(P-17643)

TECHNIP USA INC

Also Called: TP USA
555 W Arrow Hwy, Claremont (91711-4805)
PHONE.....................909 447-3600
Gary Keyser, *Brnch Mgr*
EMP: 400
Web: www.technipfmc.com
SIC: 8711 Petroleum engineering
PA: Technip Energies Usa, Inc.
11720 Katy Fwy

(P-17644)

TEN STONE WBSTER PRCESS TECH

555 W Arrow Hwy, Claremont (91711-4805)
PHONE.....................909 447-3600
Gary Keyser, *Brnch Mgr*
EMP: 395
Web: www.ten.com
SIC: 8711 Chemical engineering
HQ: T.En Stone & Webster Process Technology, Inc.
11720 Katy Fwy Ste 100
Houston TX 77079
281 870-1111

▲ = Import ▼ = Export
◆ = Import/Export

(P-17645)
TETRA TECH INC
17885 Von Karman Ave Ste 500, Irvine
(92614-5227)
PHONE....................949 263-0846
Jack Chicca, *Brnch Mgr*
EMP: 85
SALES (corp-wide): 4.52B **Publicly Held**
Web: www.tetratech.com
SIC: 8711 Consulting engineer
PA: Tetra Tech, Inc.
3475 E Foothill Blvd
626 351-4664

(P-17646)
TETRA TECH INC (PA)
Also Called: Tetra Tech
3475 E Foothill Blvd, Pasadena
(91107-6024)
PHONE....................626 351-4664
Dan L Batrack, *Ch*
Dan L Batrack, *Ch*
Jill Hudkins, *Pr*
Steven M Burdick, *Ex VP*
Leslie Shoemaker, *SUSTAINABILITY & LEADERSHIP*
EMP: 540 **EST:** 1966
SALES (est): 4.52B
SALES (corp-wide): 4.52B **Publicly Held**
Web: www.tetratech.com
SIC: 8711 Engineering services

(P-17647)
THERMAL ENGRG INTL USA INC (HQ)
Also Called: Thermal Engineering
18000 Studebaker Rd Ste 400, Cerritos
(90703-2691)
PHONE....................323 726-0641
Kenneth Murakoshi, *CEO*
Thomas Richardson, *
Micahel D Leclair, *
William J Ferguson Junior, *Law Vice President*
Scott Leeman, *
◆ **EMP:** 70 **EST:** 1969
SQ FT: 18,000
SALES (est): 43.84MM
SALES (corp-wide): 509.03MM **Privately Held**
Web: www.thermalengint.com
SIC: 8711 3443 Professional engineer; Air coolers, metal plate
PA: Babcock Power Inc.
222 Rosewood Drive 3rd F
978 646-3300

(P 17648)
THORPE TECHNOLOGIES INC (DH)
449 W Allen Ave Ste 119, San Dimas
(91773-1453)
PHONE....................562 903-8230
John E Allen, *Pr*
Thomas A Carpenter, *
EMP: 25 **EST:** 1988
SALES (est): 3.95MM
SALES (corp-wide): 57.35MM **Privately Held**
Web: www.thorpetech.com
SIC: 8711 3567 Engineering services; Industrial furnaces and ovens
HQ: Thorpe Holding Company
9905 Painter Ave # D
Whittier CA 90605

(P-17649)
TOYON RESEARCH CORPORATION (PA)
6800 Cortona Dr, Goleta (93117-3139)
PHONE....................805 968-6787
Kevin Sullivan, *
Dave Wright, *
Paul Castleberg, *
Chuck Nardo, *
EMP: 200 **EST:** 1980
SQ FT: 16,000
SALES (est): 19.22MM
SALES (corp-wide): 19.22MM **Privately Held**
Web: www.toyon.com
SIC: 8711 7371 Electrical or electronic engineering; Custom computer programming services

(P-17650)
TRANSTECH ENGINEERS INC (PA)
13367 Benson Ave, Chino (91710-5246)
PHONE....................909 595-8599
Allen Cayir, *Pr*
Sybil Cayir, *
EMP: 85 **EST:** 1989
SQ FT: 10,000
SALES (est): 8.26MM **Privately Held**
Web: www.transtech.org
SIC: 8711 Civil engineering

(P-17651)
TRI STAR ENGINEERING INC
6774 Calle De Linea Ste 106, San Diego
(92154-8020)
PHONE....................619 710-8038
Alfred Lybred, *Mgr*
EMP: 86
Web: www.star3.com
SIC: 8711 Engineering services
PA: Tri Star Engineering, Inc.
1801 S Liberty Dr Ste 200

(P-17652)
TRUST AUTOMATION INC
125 Venture Dr Ste 110, San Luis Obispo
(93401-9103)
PHONE....................805 544-0761
Ty Safreno, *CEO*
Trudie Safreno, *
Brett Keegan, *
Chuck Kass, *
Dave Rennie, *
▲ **EMP:** 65 **EST:** 1990
SQ FT: 100,000
SALES (est): 25.94MM **Privately Held**
Web: www.trustautomation.com
SIC: 8711 3812 3731 3621 Machine tool design; Antennas, radar or communications; Submersible marine robots, manned or unmanned; Generators for gas-electric or oil-electric vehicles

(P-17653)
TTG ENGINEERS
Also Called: Mbe
300 N Lake Ave Fl 14, Pasadena
(91101-4164)
PHONE....................626 463-2800
▲ **EMP:** 350
SIC: 8711 Consulting engineer

(P-17654)
UCI CONSTRUCTION INC
3900 Fruitvale Ave, Bakersfield
(93308-5114)
PHONE....................661 587-0192
David Krugh, *Brnch Mgr*
EMP: 98
SALES (corp-wide): 26.79MM **Privately Held**
Web: www.uciconstruction.com

SIC: 8711 Professional engineer
PA: U.C.I. Construction, Inc.
167 Grobric Ct
925 370-9808

(P-17655)
UES PROFESSIONAL SOLUTIONS INC
14538 Meridian Pkwy Ste A, Riverside
(92518-3018)
PHONE....................951 571-4081
Vincent Patula, *Brnch Mgr*
EMP: 156
SALES (corp-wide): 533.93MM **Privately Held**
Web: www.teamues.com
SIC: 8711 Civil engineering
HQ: Ues Professional Solutions, Inc.
1441 Montiel Rd Ste 115
Escondido CA 92026

(P-17656)
UNITED INDUSTRIES GROUP INC
Also Called: U I G
11 Rancho Cir, Lake Forest (92630-8324)
P.O. Box 8009 (92658-8009)
PHONE....................949 759-3200
James P Mansour, *Pr*
John Mensell, *
EMP: 26 **EST:** 1969
SQ FT: 10,000
SALES (est): 4.98MM **Privately Held**
Web: www.unitedind.com
SIC: 8711 3589 Engineering services; Water treatment equipment, industrial

(P-17657)
URS GROUP INC
Also Called: URS
3995 Via Oro Ave, Long Beach
(90810-1869)
PHONE....................562 420-2933
Wilfrido Simbol, *Brnch Mgr*
EMP: 186
SALES (corp-wide): 16.11B **Publicly Held**
Web: www.aecom.com
SIC: 8711 8712 Structural engineering; Architectural engineering
HQ: Urs Group, Inc.
300 S Grand Ave Suite 900
Los Angeles CA 90067
213 593-8000

(P-17658)
UTILITY TRAFFIC SERVICES LLC
2845 E Spring St, Long Beach
(90806-2417)
PHONE....................562 264-2355
Ed Barrera, *Managing Member*
EMP: 273 **EST:** 2020
SALES (est): 981.56K **Privately Held**
Web: www.utilitytraffic.com
SIC: 8711 Consulting engineer
PA: Traffic Management, Llc
4900 Arprt Plz Dr Ste 300

(P-17659)
VT MILCOM INC
1660 Logan Ave Ste 2, San Diego
(92113-1044)
PHONE....................619 424-9024
Brian Upthegrove, *Brnch Mgr*
EMP: 100
SALES (corp-wide): 827.24MM **Privately Held**
Web: www.mlupino.com
SIC: 8711 Engineering services
HQ: Vt Milcom Inc.
448 Viking Dr Ste 350

Virginia Beach VA 23452
757 463-2800

(P-17660)
W M LYLES CO
2810 Unicorn Rd, Bakersfield (93308-6853)
PHONE....................661 387-1600
Mike Burson, *Pr*
EMP: 113
SALES (corp-wide): 17.85MM **Privately Held**
Web: www.wmlylesco.com
SIC: 8711 1623 Engineering services; Pipeline construction, nsk
HQ: W. M. Lyles Co.
525 W Alluvial Ave
Fresno CA 93711
559 441-1900

(P-17661)
WESTWIND ENGINEERING INC
625 Esplanade Unit 70, Redondo Beach
(90277-4150)
PHONE....................310 831-3454
Mary Anne Graves, *CEO*
Carl Graves, *
EMP: 150 **EST:** 1992
SQ FT: 2,400
SALES (est): 5.83MM **Privately Held**
Web: www.westwind111.com
SIC: 8711 7363 Engineering services; Temporary help service

(P-17662)
WILLDAN GROUP INC (PA)
Also Called: Willdan
2401 E Katella Ave Ste 300, Anaheim
(92806-5909)
PHONE....................800 424-9144
Michael A Bieber, *Pr*
Thomas D Brisbin, *Ch Bd*
Creighton K Early, *Ex VP*
Micah H Chen, *Ex VP*
EMP: 116 **EST:** 1964
SQ FT: 18,000
SALES (est): 510.1MM
SALES (corp-wide): 510.1MM **Publicly Held**
Web: www.willdan.com
SIC: 8711 8748 Civil engineering; Urban planning and consulting services

(P-17663)
WSP USA INC
Also Called: Odeh Engineers
15231 Laguna Canyon Rd, Irvine
(92618-7714)
PHONE....................714 973-4000
Charline Talmer, *Genl Mgr*
EMP: 100
SALES (corp-wide): 10.51B **Privately Held**
Web: www.wsp.com
SIC: 8711 Consulting engineer
HQ: Wsp Usa Inc.
250 W 34th St Fl 4
New York NY 10119
212 465-5000

8712 Architectural Services

(P-17664)
5 DESIGN INC (PA)
Also Called: 5design
6161 Santa Monica Blvd Ste 208, Los
Angeles (90038-4406)
PHONE....................323 308-3558
Stanley Russell Hathaway, *Pr*
Arthur Benedetti Junior, *VP*
Michael Ellis, *

Tim Magill, *
EMP: 72 **EST:** 2005
SALES (est): 3.55MM **Privately Held**
Web: www.5plusdesign.com
SIC: 8712 Architectural engineering

(P-17665)
AECOM SERVICES INC (HQ)
300 S Grand Ave Ste 900, Los Angeles
(90071-3135)
PHONE....................213 593-8000
Michael S Burke, *CEO*
Raymond Landy, *Pr*
Kelly Olson, *VP*
Paul Steinke, *Ex VP*
Deborah Klem, *Sr VP*
EMP: 250 **EST:** 1946
SALES (est): 190.66MM
SALES (corp-wide): 16.11B **Publicly Held**
Web: www.aecom.com
SIC: 8712 8741 8711 Architectural services;
Management services; Engineering services
PA: Aecom
13355 Noel Rd Ste 400
972 788-1000

(P-17666)
ARCHITECTS ORANGE INC
Also Called: Ao
144 N Orange St, Orange (92866-1400)
PHONE.................714 639-9860
Jack Selman, *Sr Pt*
Darrel Hebenstreit, *
Hugh Rose, *
Jim Dietze, *
Rc Alley Iii, *Pt*
EMP: 200 **EST:** 1973
SQ FT: 10,000
SALES (est): 24.65MM **Privately Held**
Web: www.aoarchitects.com
SIC: 8712 Architectural engineering

(P-17667)
ARCHITECTURAL MTLS USA INC
4025 Camino Del Rio S Ste 300, San Diego
(92108-4108)
PHONE.................888 219-2126
Greg Romine, *CEO*
Serhan Emre, *
EMP: 70 **EST:** 1997
SALES (est): 2.39MM **Privately Held**
Web: www.architecturalmaterials.com
SIC: 8712 3999 3211 5039 Architectural
engineering; Barber and beauty shop
equipment; Construction glass;
Prefabricated structures

(P-17668)
AUSTIN VEUM RBBINS
PRTNERS INC (PA)
501 W Broadway Ste A, San Diego
(92101-3562)
PHONE.................619 231-1960
Douglas H Austin Faia, *CEO*
Randy Robbins, *
Chris Vium, *
Jeffrey Parshalle, *
Doreen Deen Austin, *CFO*
EMP: 83 **EST:** 1995
SQ FT: 12,500
SALES (est): 2.46MM **Privately Held**
SIC: 8712 Architectural engineering

(P-17669)
DLR GROUP INC (HQ)
700 S Flower St Ste 2200, Los Angeles
(90017-4209)
PHONE.................213 800-9400
Adrian O Cohen, *Pr*
Daniel A Munn, *

Jon P Anderson, *
Darrell L Stelling, *
Pamela Touschner, *
EMP: 140 **EST:** 1997
SALES (est): 24.79MM
SALES (corp-wide): 183.73MM **Privately
Held**
Web: www.dlrgroup.com
SIC: 8712 8711 Architectural engineering;
Engineering services
PA: Dlr Holding Company
6457 Frances St Ste 200
402 393-4100

(P-17670)
GEHRY PARTNERS LLP
12541 Beatrice St, Los Angeles
(90066-7001)
PHONE.................310 482-3000
Frank Gehry, *Pt*
Berta Gehry, *
Brian Aamoth, *
John Bowers, *
Anand Devarajan, *
EMP: 130 **EST:** 2001
SQ FT: 12,100
SALES (est): 21.66MM **Privately Held**
Web: www.foga.com
SIC: 8712 Architectural services

(P-17671)
GKK CORPORATION (PA)
Also Called: Gkkworks
2355 Main St Ste 220, Irvine (92614-4251)
PHONE.................949 250-1500
Praful Kulkarni, *Pr*
David Hunt, *
Mike Helton, *Prin*
Sam Porter, *Prin*
EMP: 85 **EST:** 1991
SQ FT: 11,000
SALES (est): 4.85MM **Privately Held**
SIC: 8712 8711 Architectural engineering;
Building construction consultant

(P-17672)
GRUEN ASSOCIATES INC
Also Called: Gruen Assoc Archtects Planners
6330 San Vicente Blvd Ste 200, Los
Angeles (90048-5441)
PHONE.................323 937-4270
Ki Suh Park, *Pt*
Michael Enomoto, *
EMP: 75 **EST:** 1947
SQ FT: 14,000
SALES (est): 4.56MM **Privately Held**
Web: www.gruenassociates.com
SIC: 8712 Architectural engineering

(P-17673)
HAWKINS BROWN USA INC
3415 S Sepulveda Blvd, Los Angeles
(90034-6060)
PHONE.................310 600-2695
Matthew Ollier, *Prin*
EMP: 276 **EST:** 2017
SALES (est): 2.44MM **Privately Held**
Web: www.hawkinsbrown.com
SIC: 8712 Architectural engineering

(P-17674)
HELLMUTH OBATA &
KASSABAUM INC
757 S Alameda St, Los Angeles
(90021-1670)
PHONE.................310 838-9555
Jeff Mayer, *Mgr*
EMP: 97
SALES (corp-wide): 457.53MM **Privately
Held**

Web: www.hok.com
SIC: 8712 8711 Architectural engineering;
Engineering services
HQ: Hellmuth, Obata & Kassabaum, Inc.
1 Bush St Ste 200
San Francisco CA 94104

(P-17675)
HMC GROUP (HQ)
Also Called: HMC Architects
3546 Concours, Ontario (91764-5584)
PHONE.................909 989-9979
Brian Staton, *CEO*
▲ **EMP:** 165 **EST:** 1941
SQ FT: 58,000
SALES (est): 22.54MM
SALES (corp-wide): 36.51MM **Privately
Held**
Web: www.hmcarchitects.com
SIC: 8712 Architectural engineering
PA: Hmc Holdings, Inc.
3546 Concours
909 989-9979

(P-17676)
HPI ARCHITECTURE
12636 High Bluff Dr Ste 100, San Diego
(92130-2071)
PHONE.................858 203-4999
EMP: 122
SALES (corp-wide): 7.9MM **Privately Held**
Web: www.hpiarchitecture.com
SIC: 8712 Architectural engineering
PA: Hpi Architecture
115 22nd St
949 675-6442

(P-17677)
JOHNSON FAIN INC
Also Called: Johnson Fain
1201 N Broadway, Los Angeles
(90012-1407)
PHONE.................323 224-6000
R Scott Johnson, *
Sherry Miller, *
EMP: 80 **EST:** 1950
SQ FT: 26,000
SALES (est): 8.66MM **Privately Held**
Web: www.johnsonfain.com
SIC: 8712 7389 Architectural engineering;
Interior design services

(P-17678)
KTGY GROUP INC (PA)
Also Called: Ktgy Architecture Planning
17911 Von Karman Ave Ste 200, Irvine
(92614-6240)
PHONE.................949 851-2133
Tricia Esser, *CEO*
Stan Braden, *Pr*
Brittany Choisnet, *Sec*
EMP: 70 **EST:** 1991
SQ FT: 21,000
SALES (est): 23.27MM **Privately Held**
Web: www.ktgy.com
SIC: 8712 Architectural engineering

(P-17679)
LAMAR JHNSON
COLLABORATIVE INC
8590 National Blvd, Culver City
(90232-2443)
PHONE.................424 361-3960
EMP: 114
SALES (corp-wide): 878.7MM **Privately
Held**
Web: www.theljc.com
SIC: 8712 Architectural engineering
HQ: The Lamar Johnson Collaborative Inc
35 E Wacker Dr Ste 1300

Chicago IL 60601
312 429-0400

(P-17680)
LEE BURKHART LIU INC
5510 Lincoln Blvd # 250, Playa Vista
(90094-2034)
PHONE.................310 829-2249
Kenneth Lee, *Pr*
Erich Burkart, *
Ken Liu, *
EMP: 75 **EST:** 1986
SQ FT: 11,000
SALES (est): 2.56MM **Privately Held**
SIC: 8712 Architectural engineering

(P-17681)
LPA INC (PA)
Also Called: Lpa Design Group, Inc.
5301 California Ave Ste 100, Irvine
(92617-3226)
PHONE.................949 261-1001
Wendy Rogers, *CEO*
Dan Heinfeld, *
James Kelly, *
Charles Pruitt, *
◆ **EMP:** 180 **EST:** 1971
SQ FT: 33,700
SALES (est): 36.63MM
SALES (corp-wide): 36.63MM **Privately
Held**
Web: www.lpadesignstudios.com
SIC: 8712 8711 0781 Architectural
engineering; Engineering services;
Landscape counseling and planning

(P-17682)
M ARTHUR GENSLER JR
ASSOC INC
Also Called: Gensler and Associates
500 S Figueroa St, Los Angeles
(90071-1705)
PHONE.................213 927-3600
Rob Jernigan, *Brnch Mgr*
EMP: 249
SALES (corp-wide): 1.88B **Privately Held**
Web: www.gensler.com
SIC: 8712 7389 Architectural engineering;
Design, commercial and industrial
PA: M. Arthur Gensler Jr. & Associates, Inc.
220 Montgomery St Ste 200
415 433-3700

(P-17683)
M ARTHUR GENSLER JR
ASSOC INC
Also Called: Gensler
4675 Macarthur Ct Ste 100, Newport Beach
(92660-8811)
PHONE.................949 863-9434
Kim Graham, *Brnch Mgr*
EMP: 83
SALES (corp-wide): 1.88B **Privately Held**
Web: www.gensler.com
SIC: 8712 Architectural engineering
PA: M. Arthur Gensler Jr. & Associates, Inc.
220 Montgomery St Ste 200
415 433-3700

(P-17684)
MARMOL RDZNER AN
ARCHTCTRAL CO
12210 Nebraska Ave, Los Angeles
(90025-3620)
PHONE.................310 826-6222
Ron Radziner, *CEO*
Leo Marmol, *
EMP: 70 **EST:** 1989
SQ FT: 6,500

SALES (est): 9.87MM **Privately Held**
Web: www.marmol-radziner.com
SIC: **8712** 1521 1542 Architectural
engineering; General remodeling, single-
family houses; Commercial and office
building, new construction

(P-17685)
MARTIN AC PARTNERS INC
444 S Flower St Ste 1200, Los Angeles
(90071-2977)
PHONE..............................213 683-1900
Robert Newsom, *Pr*
Christopher C Martin, *
David C Martin, *
EMP: 116 EST: 1906
SALES (est): 9.49MM **Privately Held**
Web: www.acmartin.com
SIC: **8712** Architectural services

(P-17686)
**NEWMAN GARRISON +
PARTNERS INC**
3100 Bristol St Ste 400, Costa Mesa
(92626-7333)
PHONE..............................949 756-0818
Kevin Newman, *Ch*
Donald J Meeks, *
EMP: 70 EST: 1974
SQ FT: 7,000
SALES (est): 2.14MM **Privately Held**
Web: www.nggpartners.com
SIC: **8712** Architectural engineering

(P-17687)
NTD ARCHITECTS
Also Called: NTD Architecture
9665 Chesapeake Dr Ste 365, San Diego
(92123-1352)
PHONE..............................858 565-4440
EMP: 98
Web: www.ntd.com
SIC: **8712** Architectural services

(P-17688)
RDC-S111 INC (PA)
Also Called: Perkowitz & Ruth Architects
245 E 3rd St, Long Beach (90802-3141)
PHONE..............................562 628-8000
Bradley Williams, *CEO*
Ian Denny, *
Brian Wolfe, *
EMP: 72 EST: 1979
SALES (est): 25.96MM
SALES (corp-wide): 25.96MM **Privately
Held**
Web: www.rdcollaborative.com
SIC: **8712** Architectural engineering

(P-17689)
RRM DESIGN GROUP (PA)
3765 S Higuera St Ste 102, San Luis
Obispo (93401-1577)
PHONE..............................805 439-0442
Victor Montgomery, *Ch Bd*
John Wilbanks, *
Keith Gurnee, *
EMP: 99 EST: 1973
SQ FT: 23,000
SALES (est): 9.31MM
SALES (corp-wide): 9.31MM **Privately
Held**
Web: www.rrmdesign.com
SIC: **8712** Architectural engineering

(P-17690)
STANTEC ARCHITECTURE INC
300 N Lake Ave Ste 400, Pasadena
(91101-4169)
PHONE..............................626 796-9141

Simon Bluestone, *Brnch Mgr*
EMP: 88
SALES (corp-wide): 4.72B **Privately Held**
Web: www.stantec.com
SIC: **8712** Architectural services
HQ: Stantec Architecture Inc.
224 S Michigan Ave # 1400
Chicago IL 60604
336 714-7413

(P-17691)
**STANTEC CONSULTING SVCS
INC**
38 Technology Dr Ste 250, Irvine
(92618-5311)
PHONE..............................949 923-6000
Bob Gomes, *Brnch Mgr*
EMP: 117
SALES (corp-wide): 4.72B **Privately Held**
Web: www.stantec.com
SIC: **8712** 8711 Architectural services;
Engineering services
HQ: Stantec Consulting Services Inc.
475 5th Ave Fl 12
New York NY 10017
212 366-5600

(P-17692)
STEINBERG HART (PA)
Also Called: Steinberg Architects
818 W 7th St Ste 1100, Los Angeles
(90017-3461)
PHONE..............................213 629-0500
David Hart, *Pr*
Robert Steinberg, *
Ernest Yamana, *
EMP: 74 EST: 1953
SQ FT: 14,000
SALES (est): 14.69MM
SALES (corp-wide): 14.69MM **Privately
Held**
Web: www.steinberghart.com
SIC: **8712** Architectural engineering

(P-17693)
STV ARCHITECTS INC
1055 W 7th St Ste 3150, Los Angeles
(90017-2556)
PHONE..............................213 482-9444
Wagih Andraos, *Mgr*
EMP: 156
SALES (corp-wide): 261.09MM **Privately
Held**
Web: www.stvinc.com
SIC: **8712** 8742 8711 Architectural
engineering; Transportation consultant;
Consulting engineer
HQ: Stv Architects Inc
205 W Welsh Dr
Douglassville PA 19518
610 385-8200

(P-17694)
THE JERDE PARTNERSHIP INC
Also Called: Jerde Partnership Intl
601 W 5th St Ste 500, Los Angeles
(90071-2045)
PHONE..............................310 399-1987
EMP: 70 EST: 1977
SALES (est): 5MM **Privately Held**
Web: www.jerde.com
SIC: **8712** Architectural services

(P-17695)
WARE MALCOMB (PA)
10 Edelman, Irvine (92618-4312)
PHONE..............................949 660-9128
Kenneth Wink, *CEO*
Lawrence R Armstrong, *
Jay Todisco, *

Matthew Brady, *
Tobin Sloane, *
▲ EMP: 137 EST: 1972
SQ FT: 22,000
SALES (est): 49.67MM
SALES (corp-wide): 49.67MM **Privately
Held**
Web: www.waremalcomb.com
SIC: **8712** 7336 8711 7389 Architectural
engineering; Commercial art and graphic
design; Civil engineering; Interior design
services

(P-17696)
**WILLIAM HZMLHLCH
ARCHTCTS INC**
Also Called: Wha
200 Commerce, Irvine (92602-5000)
PHONE..............................949 250-0607
William Hezmalhalch, *CEO*
EMP: 75 EST: 1986
SALES (est): 12.69MM **Privately Held**
Web: www.whainc.com
SIC: **8712** Architectural engineering

(P-17697)
**ZIMMER GNSUL FRSCA
ARCHTCTS LL**
Also Called: Zimmer Gnsul Frsca Partnr Amer
515 S Flower St Ste 3700, Los Angeles
(90071-2221)
PHONE..............................213 617-1901
Rachel Morris, *Mgr*
EMP: 118
SALES (corp-wide): 24.62MM **Privately
Held**
SIC: **8712** 7389 Architectural engineering;
Interior designer
PA: Zimmer Gunsul Frasca Architects Llp
1223 Sw Wash St Ste 200
503 224-3860

8713 Surveying Services

(P-17698)
PSOMAS (PA)
Also Called: Pfeiler Psomas
865 S Figueroa St Ste 3200, Los Angeles
(90017-5431)
PHONE..............................213 223-1400
Ryan Mclean, *Pr*
EMP: 125 EST: 1946
SALES (est): 47.17MM
SALES (corp-wide): 47.17MM **Privately
Held**
Web: www.psomas.com
SIC: **8713** 8711 Surveying services;
Engineering services

(P-17699)
PSOMAS
Also Called: Bonterra Psomas
5 Hutton Centre Dr Ste 300, Santa Ana
(92707-8708)
PHONE..............................714 751-7373
Ryan Mclean, *Mgr*
EMP: 132
SALES (corp-wide): 47.17MM **Privately
Held**
Web: www.psomas.com
SIC: **8713** 8711 Surveying services;
Consulting engineer
PA: Psomas
865 S Figueroa St
213 223-1400

8721 Accounting, Auditing, And Bookkeeping

(P-17700)
**ACCLARA HOLDINGS GROUP
INC**
Also Called: Medical Specialty Billing
770 The City Dr S, Orange (92868-4900)
PHONE..............................714 571-5000
Lincoln Popp, *CEO*
Lauren Newman, *
EMP: 115 EST: 1990
SQ FT: 29,000
SALES (est): 8.76MM
SALES (corp-wide): 2.25B **Privately Held**
Web: www.acclara.com
SIC: **8721** Billing and bookkeeping service
PA: R1 Rcm Inc.
434 W Ascension Way Fl 6
312 324-7820

(P-17701)
ARMANINO LLP
11766 Wilshire Blvd Fl 9, Los Angeles
(90025-6538)
PHONE..............................310 478-4148
EMP: 284
SALES (corp-wide): 52.58MM **Privately
Held**
Web: www.armanino.com
SIC: **8721** Certified public accountant
PA: Armanino Llp
2700 Camino Ramon Ste 350
925 790-2600

(P-17702)
ARMANINO LLP
2101 E El Segundo Blvd Ste 400, El
Segundo (90245-4519)
PHONE..............................310 822-8552
EMP: 80
SALES (corp-wide): 52.58MM **Privately
Held**
Web: www.armanino.com
SIC: **8721** Certified public accountant
PA: Armanino Llp
2700 Camino Ramon Ste 350
925 790-2600

(P-17703)
BAKER TILLY US LLP
6320 Canoga Ave, Woodland Hills
(91367-2526)
PHONE..............................818 981-2600
William Wolf, *Brnch Mgr*
FMP: 437
SALES (corp-wide): 178.7MM **Privately
Held**
Web: www.bakertilly.com
SIC: **8721** Certified public accountant
PA: Baker Tilly Us, Llp
205 N Mich Ave Ste 2800
312 729-8000

(P-17704)
BAKER TILLY US LLP
11150 Santa Monica Blvd Ste 600, Los
Angeles (90025-0479)
PHONE..............................310 826-4474
Lew Thomashaw, *Brnch Mgr*
EMP: 980
SALES (corp-wide): 178.7MM **Privately
Held**
Web: www.bakertilly.com
SIC: **8721** Certified public accountant
PA: Baker Tilly Us, Llp
205 N Mich Ave Ste 2800
312 729-8000

PRODUCTS & SVCS

(P-17705)

BAKER TILLY US LLP

Also Called: Baker Tilly California
18500 Von Karman Ave Fl 10, Irvine
(92612-0527)
PHONE..................................949 222-2999
Thomas Bennett, *Mng Pt*
EMP: 545
SALES (corp-wide): 178.7MM **Privately Held**
Web: www.bakertilly.com
SIC: 8721 Certified public accountant
PA: Baker Tilly Us, Llp
   205 N Mich Ave Ste 2800
   312 729-8000

(P-17706)

BAKER TILLY US LLP

3655 Nobel Dr Ste 300, San Diego
(92122-1050)
PHONE..................................858 597-4100
Vanessa Liguzinski, *Brnch Mgr*
EMP: 545
SALES (corp-wide): 178.7MM **Privately Held**
Web: www.bakertilly.com
SIC: 8721 Certified public accountant
PA: Baker Tilly Us, Llp
   205 N Mich Ave Ste 2800
   312 729-8000

(P-17707)

BRAULT

Also Called: Emergency Groups' Office
180 Via Verde Ste 100, San Dimas
(91773-3993)
PHONE..................................626 447-0296
EMP: 200 EST: 2015
SALES (est): 10.21MM **Privately Held**
Web: www.brault.us
SIC: 8721 Billing and bookkeeping service

(P-17708)

CALIFORNIA BUSINESS BUREAU INC (PA)

Also Called: Medical Billing Services
1711 S Mountain Ave, Monrovia
(91016-4256)
P.O. Box 5010 (91017-7110)
PHONE..................................626 303-1515
Michael J Sigal, *Pr*
EMP: 132 EST: 1973
SQ FT: 24,000
SALES (est): 9.8MM
SALES (corp-wide): 9.8MM **Privately Held**
Web: www.cbbinc.com
SIC: 8721 Billing and bookkeeping service

(P-17709)

CALIFORNIA STATE UNIV LONG BCH

Also Called: Bursar's Office
1250 N Bellflower Blvd Bh155, Long Beach
(90840-0004)
PHONE..................................562 985-1764
Randy Nielson, *Supervisor*
EMP: 172
SALES (corp-wide): 534.4MM **Privately Held**
Web: www.csulb.edu
SIC: 8721 8221 9411 Accounting, auditing, and bookkeeping; University; Administration of educational programs
HQ: California State University, Long Beach
   1250 N Bellflower Blvd
   Long Beach CA 90840
   562 985-4111

(P-17710)

CAST & CREW LLC (PA)

Also Called: Cast and Crew Entrmt Svcs
2300 W Empire Ave Ste 500, Burbank
(91504-5399)
PHONE..................................818 570-6180
Eric Belcher, *Pr*
Sally Knutson, *
Shardell Cavaliere, *LIFE SERVCS**
Andrew Patterson, *
EMP: 195 EST: 1976
SQ FT: 12,000
SALES (est): 8.22MM
SALES (corp-wide): 8.22MM **Privately Held**
Web: www.castandcrew.com
SIC: 8721 Payroll accounting service

(P-17711)

CERIDIAN LLC

Also Called: Ceridian
1515 W 190th St Ste 100, Gardena
(90248-4913)
PHONE..................................310 719-7481
Chris Byers, *Brnch Mgr*
EMP: 98
SALES (corp-wide): 89.59MM **Privately Held**
Web: www.dayforce.com
SIC: 8721 Payroll accounting service
PA: Ceridian Corporation
   3311 E Old Shakopee Rd
   952 853-8100

(P-17712)

CLIFTONLARSONALLEN LLP

Also Called: Nsbn
1925 Century Park E 16th Fl, Los Angeles
(90067-2701)
PHONE..................................310 273-2501
Randy Wells, *Brnch Mgr*
EMP: 91
SALES (corp-wide): 966.83MM **Privately Held**
Web: www.claconnect.com
SIC: 8721 Accounting services, except auditing
PA: Cliftonlarsonallen Llp
   220 S 6th St Ste 300
   612 376-4500

(P-17713)

COMPUTERIZED MGT SVCS INC

Also Called: CMS
4100 Guardian St Ste 205, Simi Valley
(93063-6721)
P.O. Box 190 (93062-0190)
PHONE..................................805 522-5940
J Daryl Favale, *Pr*
EMP: 100 EST: 1985
SQ FT: 7,500
SALES (est): 579.98K
SALES (corp-wide): 679.11MM **Privately Held**
Web: www.cmsmanagement.net
SIC: 8721 Billing and bookkeeping service
HQ: Xifin, Inc.
   12225 El Camino Real
   San Diego CA 92130
   858 793-5700

(P-17714)

CONSIDINE CNSDINE AN ACCNTNCY

8989 Rio San Diego Dr Ste 250, San Diego
(92108-1604)
PHONE..................................619 231-1977
Perry S Wright, *CEO*
Timothy Considine, *
Don Bonk, *

Jerry Hotz, *
Charles E Considine, *
EMP: 117 EST: 1946
SQ FT: 20,000
SALES (est): 1.86MM **Privately Held**
Web: www.cccpa.com
SIC: 8721 Certified public accountant

(P-17715)

COUNTY OF LOS ANGELES

Also Called: Internal Services Department
1100 N Eastern Ave, Los Angeles
(90063-3200)
PHONE..................................323 267-2136
Scott Minnix, *Dir*
EMP: 1800
Web: www.lacounty.gov
SIC: 8721 Accounting, auditing, and bookkeeping
PA: County Of Los Angeles
   500 W Temple St Ste 437
   213 974-1101

(P-17716)

DELOITTE & TOUCHE LLP

555 W 5th St Ste 2700, Los Angeles
(90013-1024)
PHONE..................................213 688-0800
Byron David, *Brnch Mgr*
EMP: 1000
Web: www.deloitte.com
SIC: 8721 Accounting services, except auditing
HQ: Deloitte & Touche Llp
   30 Rockefeller Plz
   New York NY 10112
   212 492-4000

(P-17717)

DELOITTE & TOUCHE LLP

695 Town Center Dr Ste 1200, Costa Mesa
(92626-7188)
PHONE..................................714 436-7419
Bob Grant, *Mgr*
EMP: 215
Web: www.deloitte.com
SIC: 8721 7291 Accounting services, except auditing; Tax return preparation services
HQ: Deloitte & Touche Llp
   30 Rockefeller Plz
   New York NY 10112
   212 492-4000

(P-17718)

DELOITTE & TOUCHE LLP

12830 El Camino Real Ste 600, San Diego
(92130-2978)
PHONE..................................619 232-6500
Cathy Jennings, *Mgr*
EMP: 1731
Web: www.deloitte.com
SIC: 8721 7291 Certified public accountant; Tax return preparation services
HQ: Deloitte & Touche Llp
   30 Rockefeller Plz
   New York NY 10112
   212 492-4000

(P-17719)

DELOITTE TAX LLP

555 W 5th St Ste 2700, Los Angeles
(90013-1024)
PHONE..................................404 885-6754
EMP: 104
Web: www.deloitte.com
SIC: 8721 Auditing services
HQ: Deloitte Tax Llp
   30 Rockefeller Plz
   New York NY 10112
   212 492-4000

(P-17720)

DUFFY KRUSPODIN LLP

21600 Oxnard St Ste 2000, Woodland Hills
(91367-4969)
PHONE..................................818 385-0585
Tim Duffy, *Owner*
EMP: 158 EST: 2013
SALES (est): 6MM **Privately Held**
Web: www.dkllpcpa.com
SIC: 8721 Certified public accountant

(P-17721)

EGO INC

Also Called: Emergency Groups Office
180 Via Verde Ste 100, San Dimas
(91773-3993)
PHONE..................................626 447-0296
Andrea Brault, *Pr*
Del Brault, *
Jane Brault, *
James Blakeman, *
EMP: 150 EST: 1990
SQ FT: 8,500
SALES (est): 24.04MM **Privately Held**
Web: www.brault.us
SIC: 8721 Billing and bookkeeping service

(P-17722)

EIDE BAILLY LLP

10681 Foothill Blvd Ste 300, Rancho Cucamonga (91730-3831)
PHONE..................................909 466-4410
Dave Stende, *Mng Pt*
EMP: 300
SALES (corp-wide): 537.56MM **Privately Held**
Web: www.eidebailly.com
SIC: 8721 Certified public accountant
PA: Eide Bailly Llp
   4310 17th Ave S
   701 239-8500

(P-17723)

ENTERTAINMENT PARTNERS INC (PA)

2950 N Hollywood Way, Burbank
(91505-1072)
PHONE..................................818 955-6000
Mark Goldstein, *CEO*
George Vaughan, *
EMP: 295 EST: 1992
SQ FT: 38,000
SALES (est): 26.01MM **Privately Held**
Web: www.ep.com
SIC: 8721 Payroll accounting service

(P-17724)

ERNST & YOUNG LLP

Also Called: Ey
18101 Von Karman Ave Ste 1700, Irvine
(92612-0181)
PHONE..................................949 794-2300
Linda Minx, *Off Mgr*
EMP: 450
Web: www.ey.com
SIC: 8721 8742 Certified public accountant; Business management consultant
HQ: Ernst & Young Llp
   1 Manhattan W
   New York NY 10001
   703 747-0049

(P-17725)

ERNST & YOUNG LLP

Also Called: Ey
4365 Executive Dr Ste 1600, San Diego
(92121-2101)
PHONE..................................858 535-7200
Michael J Hartnett, *Mgr*
EMP: 164

Web: www.ey.com
SIC: 8721 8742 7291 Certified public
    accountant; Business management
    consultant; Tax return preparation services
HQ: Ernst & Young Llp
    1 Manhattan W
    New York NY 10001
    703 747-0049

(P-17726)
ERNST & YOUNG LLP
Also Called: Ey
2931 Townsgate Rd Ste 100, Westlake
Village (91361-5874)
PHONE..............................805 778-7000
Brian Ladin, *Brnch Mgr*
EMP: 89
Web: www.ey.com
SIC: 8721 8742 8748 Certified public
    accountant; Business management
    consultant; Business consulting, nec
HQ: Ernst & Young Llp
    1 Manhattan W
    New York NY 10001
    703 747-0049

(P-17727)
ERNST & YOUNG LLP
Also Called: Ey
725 S Figueroa St Ste 200, Los Angeles
(90017-5403)
PHONE..............................213 977-3200
Jeff Kaufman, *Mgr*
EMP: 1000
Web: www.ey.com
SIC: 8721 8742 7291 Certified public
    accountant; Business management
    consultant; Tax return preparation services
HQ: Ernst & Young Llp
    1 Manhattan W
    New York NY 10001
    703 747-0049

(P-17728)
FILM PAYROLL SERVICES INC
(PA)
Also Called: Quantos Payroll
500 S Sepulveda Blvd Fl 4, Los Angeles
(90049-3550)
PHONE..............................310 440-9600
Gregory Pickert, *CEO*
EMP: 100 EST: 1978
SQ FT: 5,000
SALES (est): 2.53MM Privately Held
Web: www.mediaservices.com
SIC: 8721 Payroll accounting service

(P-17729)
GATTO POPE WALWICK LLP
3131 Camino Del Rio N Ste 1200, San
Diego (92108-5742)
PHONE..............................619 282-7366
Charlie Pope, *Mng Pt*
Daniel Gatto, *Pt*
Kirk Walwick, *Pt*
Thomas Mcfadden, *Pt*
EMP: 83 EST: 1983
SALES (est): 2.06MM Privately Held
Web: www.gpwcpas.com
SIC: 8721 8111 Certified public accountant;
    General practice attorney, lawyer

(P-17730)
GREEN HASSON & JANKS LLP
700 S Flower St Ste 3300, Los Angeles
(90017-4221)
PHONE..............................310 873-1600
Leon Janks, *Pt*
William Cline, *
EMP: 120 EST: 1953

SALES (est): 7.97MM Privately Held
Web: www.ghjadvisors.com
SIC: 8721 Certified public accountant

(P-17731)
GURSEY SCHNEIDER & CO LLC
(PA)
1888 Century Park E Ste 900, Los Angeles
(90067-1735)
PHONE..............................310 552-0960
Donald Gursey, *
David Blumenthal, *
Robert Watts, *
Rosanna Purzycki, *
EMP: 98 EST: 1964
SQ FT: 12,000
SALES (est): 179.49K
SALES (corp-wide): 179.49K Privately
Held
Web: www.gursey.com
SIC: 8721 Certified public accountant

(P-17732)
HAGEN STREIFF NEWTON &
OSHIRO ACCOUNTANTS PC
4667 Macarthur Blvd Ste 400, Newport
Beach (92660-1874)
PHONE..............................949 390-7647
EMP: 99
SIC: 8721 Calculating and statistical service

(P-17733)
HOLTHOUSE CARLIN VAN
TRIGT LLP (PA)
Also Called: H C V T
11444 W Olympic Blvd Fl 11, Los Angeles
(90064-1500)
PHONE..............................310 566-1900
Philip Holthouse, *Mng Pt*
James Carlin, *
John Van Trigt, *
Zach Shuman, *
Blake Christian, *
EMP: 110 EST: 1991
SALES (est): 36.22MM Privately Held
Web: www.hcvt.com
SIC: 8721 Certified public accountant

(P-17734)
HOTTA LIESENBERG SAITO LLP
970 W 190th St Ste 900, Torrance
(90502-1053)
PHONE..............................424 246-2000
George Liesenberg, *Prin*
EMP: 75 EST: 2010
SALES (est): 2.7MM Privately Held
Web: www.hls-global.com
SIC: 8721 Certified public accountant

(P-17735)
INFINEON TECH AMERICAS
CORP
Interntnal Rctfr/Ccunting Dept
222 Kansas St, El Segundo (90245-4315)
PHONE..............................310 726-8000
Michael Mcgee, *Mgr*
EMP: 699
SALES (corp-wide): 16.7B Privately Held
Web: www-blue.infineon.com
SIC: 8721 3674 Accounting, auditing, and
    bookkeeping; Semiconductors and related
    devices
HQ: Infineon Technologies Americas Corp.
    101 N Pacific Coast Hwy
    El Segundo CA 90245
    310 726-8200

(P-17736)
JS HELD LLC
4667 Macarthur Blvd Ste 400, Newport
Beach (92660-1874)
PHONE..............................949 390-7647
EMP: 99
SALES (corp-wide): 200MM Privately
Held
Web: www.jsheld.com
SIC: 8721 Calculating and statistical service
PA: J.S. Held Llc
    50 Jercho Qdrngle Ste 117
    516 621-2900

(P-17737)
KBKG INC
225 S Lake Ave Ste 400, Pasadena
(91101-3010)
PHONE..............................626 449-4225
Gian Pazzia, *CEO*
Gregory A Kniss, *Ch Bd*
EMP: 194 EST: 2001
SALES (est): 3.23MM Privately Held
Web: www.kbkg.com
SIC: 8721 Certified public accountant

(P-17738)
KPMG LLP
4464 Jasmine Ave, Culver City
(90232-3429)
PHONE..............................703 286-8175
Daniel Smith, *Mgr*
EMP: 99
SALES (corp-wide): 1.34B Privately Held
Web: www.kpmg.com
SIC: 8721 Certified public accountant
PA: Kpmg Llp
    345 Park Ave
    212 758-9700

(P-17739)
KPMG LLP
20 Pacifica Ste 700, Irvine (92618-3391)
PHONE..............................949 885-5400
EMP: 120
SALES (corp-wide): 1.34B Privately Held
Web: www.home.kpmg
SIC: 8721 Certified public accountant
PA: Kpmg Llp
    345 Park Ave
    212 758-9700

(P-17740)
KROST (PA)
Also Called: Krost Bumgarten Kniss Guerrero
225 S Lake Ave Ste 400, Pasadena
(91101-3010)
PHONE..............................626 449-4225
Richard B Krost, *CEO*
Gregory Kniss, *
EMP: 170 EST: 1930
SALES (est): 7.16MM
SALES (corp-wide): 7.16MM Privately
Held
Web: www.krostcpas.com
SIC: 8721 Accounting services, except
    auditing

(P-17741)
LANCE SOLL & LUNGHARD
LLP
203 N Brea Blvd Ste 203, Brea
(92821-4056)
PHONE..............................714 672-0022
Ronald Stumpf, *Pr*
Gregory N Lewis, *
Edward J Leiber, *
Sherry Radmore, *
Yen Nguyen, *
EMP: 100 EST: 1968

SQ FT: 7,000
SALES (est): 930.64K Privately Held
Web: www.lslcpas.com
SIC: 8721 Certified public accountant

(P-17742)
LLP MOSS ADAMS
2040 Main St Ste 900, Irvine (92614-8213)
PHONE..............................949 221-4000
Roger Weninger, *Brnch Mgr*
EMP: 102
SALES (corp-wide): 317.2MM Privately
Held
Web: www.mossadams.com
SIC: 8721 Certified public accountant
PA: Moss Adams Llp
    999 3rd Ave Ste 2800
    206 302-6800

(P-17743)
LLP MOSS ADAMS
21700 Oxnard St Ste 300, Woodland Hills
(91367-7561)
PHONE..............................310 477-0450
Rod Green, *Pt*
EMP: 150
SALES (corp-wide): 317.2MM Privately
Held
Web: www.mossadams.com
SIC: 8721 Certified public accountant
PA: Moss Adams Llp
    999 3rd Ave Ste 2800
    206 302-6800

(P-17744)
LLP MOSS ADAMS
4747 Executive Dr Ste 1300, San Diego
(92121-3114)
PHONE..............................858 627-1400
Laura Roos, *Pt*
EMP: 76
SALES (corp-wide): 317.2MM Privately
Held
Web: www.mossadams.com
SIC: 8721 Certified public accountant
PA: Moss Adams Llp
    999 3rd Ave Ste 2800
    206 302-6800

(P-17745)
MARCUM LLP
600 Anton Blvd Ste 1600, Costa Mesa
(92626-7652)
PHONE..............................949 236-5600
Philip Wilson, *Mgr*
EMP: 79
SALES (corp-wide): 379.94MM Privately
Held
Web: www.marcumllp.com
SIC: 8721 Certified public accountant
PA: Marcum Llp
    730 3rd Ave Fl 11
    212 485-5500

(P-17746)
MILLER KAPLAN ARASE LLP
(PA)
Also Called: Cahn, Jsph/Miller Kaplan Arase
4123 Lankershim Blvd, North Hollywood
(91602-2828)
PHONE..............................818 769-2010
EMP: 129 EST: 1940
SALES (est): 17.38MM
SALES (corp-wide): 17.38MM Privately
Held
Web: www.millerkaplan.com
SIC: 8721 Certified public accountant

PRODUCTS & SVCS

(P-17747)
NASIF HICKS HARRIS & CO LLP
Also Called: Harris, Jeffery P
104 W Anapamu St Ste B, Santa Barbara
(93101-3126)
PHONE..............................805 966-1521
William Nasif, Pt
Jeffrey Hicks, Pt
Steven Hicks, Pt
EMP: 75 EST: 1988
SQ FT: 2,400
SALES (est): 2.47MM Privately Held
Web: www.nhhco.com
SIC: 8721 Certified public accountant

(P-17748)
NEW TALCO ENTERPRISES LLC
Also Called: Caps Payroll
2300 W Empire Ave, Burbank
(91504-3341)
PHONE..............................310 280-0755
Doug Sylvester, CEO
Frank Devito, *
David Lee, CIO*
Fran Lucci-pannozzo, CMO
Anne Plechner, *
EMP: 114 EST: 2010
SALES (est): 2.31MM
SALES (corp-wide): 8.22MM Privately Held
Web: www.castandcrew.com
SIC: 8721 Payroll accounting service
PA: Cast & Crew Llc
2300 W Empire Ave Fl-5
818 570-6180

(P-17749)
OMEGA ACCOUNTING SOLUTIONS INC
15101 Alton Pkwy Ste 450, Irvine
(92618-2300)
PHONE..............................949 348-2433
Jay Woods, Prin
EMP: 151 EST: 2008
SALES (est): 2.3MM Privately Held
Web: www.omega-accounting.com
SIC: 8721 Accounting, auditing, and bookkeeping

(P-17750)
PHYSICIAN SUPPORT SYSTEMS INC (DH)
1131 W 6th St Ste 300, Ontario
(91762-1118)
PHONE..............................717 653-5340
Douglas Estock, Pr
EMP: 400 EST: 1991
SALES (est): 481.36K
SALES (corp-wide): 308.95B Publicly Held
Web: www.pssbilling.com
SIC: 8721 Billing and bookkeeping service
HQ: Ndchealth Corporation
1564 Northeast Expy Ne
Brookhaven GA 30329
404 728-2000

(P-17751)
PHYSICIANS CHOICE LLC
5950 Canoga Ave Ste 300, Woodland Hills
(91367-5041)
P.O. Box 4419 (91365-4419)
PHONE..............................818 340-9988
John Uphold, CEO
John D Uphold, *
Jonathan Sturm, *
Michelle Reckleff, *
EMP: 80 EST: 1999
SQ FT: 10,000
SALES (est): 2.02MM Privately Held

Web: www.physchoice.com
SIC: 8721 Billing and bookkeeping service

(P-17752)
PRICEWATERHOUSECOOPERS LLP
601 S Figueroa St Ste 900, Los Angeles
(90017-5743)
PHONE..............................213 356-6000
EMP: 111
SQ FT: 400
SALES (corp-wide): 6.79B Privately Held
Web: www.pwc.com
SIC: 8721 Certified public accountant
HQ: Pricewaterhousecoopers Llp
300 Madison Ave
New York NY 10017
646 471-3000

(P-17753)
RBZ LLP
11766 Wilshire Blvd Fl 9, Los Angeles
(90025-6548)
PHONE..............................310 478-4148
EMP: 150
Web: www.armanino.com
SIC: 8721 Certified public accountant

(P-17754)
SIGNATURE ANALYTICS LLC
10120 Pacific Heights Blvd Ste 110, San
Diego (92121-4210)
PHONE..............................888 284-3842
EMP: 87 EST: 2016
SALES (est): 1.1MM Privately Held
Web: www.signatureanalytics.com
SIC: 8721 Accounting, auditing, and bookkeeping

(P-17755)
SINGERLEWAK LLP (PA)
Also Called: Singerlewak
10960 Wilshire Blvd, Los Angeles
(90024-3702)
PHONE..............................310 477-3924
Jim Pitrat, Mng Pt
Jim Pitrat Mng Pttnr, Prin
Norman Greenbaum, Pt
William D Simon, Pt
David Free, Pt
◆ EMP: 120 EST: 1959
SALES (est): 12.23MM
SALES (corp-wide): 12.23MM Privately Held
Web: www.singerlewak.com
SIC: 8721 8742 Certified public accountant;
Business management consultant

(P-17756)
TEAM COMPANIES LLC (PA)
Also Called: Team Services
2300 W Empire Ave Ste 500, Burbank
(91504-5399)
PHONE..............................818 558-3261
Greg Smith, Pr
An De Vooght, *
Geoffrey Matus, *
EMP: 90 EST: 1992
SALES (est): 22.8MM
SALES (corp-wide): 22.8MM Privately Held
Web: www.theteamcompanies.com
SIC: 8721 Payroll accounting service

(P-17757)
UNIVERSITY CALIFORNIA IRVINE
Also Called: UCI Division Plastic Surgery
200 S Manchester Ave Ste 650, Orange
(92868-3224)

PHONE..............................714 456-6655
Gregory Evans, Brnch Mgr
EMP: 82
SALES (corp-wide): 534.4MM Privately Held
Web: www.uciplasticsurgery.com
SIC: 8721 8221 9411 Accounting, auditing,
and bookkeeping; University;
Administration of educational programs
HQ: University Of California, Irvine
510 Aldrich Hall
Irvine CA 92697
949 824-5011

(P-17758)
UNIVERSITY CALIFORNIA IRVINE
Also Called: Accounting and Fiscal Services
120 Theory Ste 200, Irvine (92617-3210)
PHONE..............................949 824-6828
Griselda Duran Optns, Mgr
EMP: 71
SALES (corp-wide): 534.4MM Privately Held
Web: www.uci.edu
SIC: 8721 Accounting, auditing, and bookkeeping
HQ: University Of California, Irvine
510 Aldrich Hall
Irvine CA 92697
949 824-5011

(P-17759)
WINDES INC (PA)
3780 Kilroy Airport Way Ste 600, Long
Beach (90806-6825)
P.O. Box 87 (90801-0087)
PHONE..............................562 435-1191
John L Dicarlo, CEO
Scott J Dionne, *
EMP: 100 EST: 1926
SQ FT: 26,560
SALES (est): 21.23MM
SALES (corp-wide): 21.23MM Privately Held
Web: www.windes.com
SIC: 8721 Certified public accountant

(P-17760)
WRIGHT FORD YOUNG & CO
16140 Sand Canyon Ave, Irvine
(92618-3715)
PHONE..............................949 910-2727
EMP: 96 EST: 2019
SALES (est): 2.26MM Privately Held
Web: www.cpa-wfy.com
SIC: 8721 Certified public accountant

8731 Commercial Physical Research

(P-17761)
ACEA BIOSCIENCES INC
6779 Mesa Ridge Rd Ste 100, San Diego
(92121-2996)
PHONE..............................858 724-0928
Xiao Xu, Pr
Xiaobo Wang, *
▲ EMP: 85 EST: 2001
SALES (est): 3.96MM
SALES (corp-wide): 6.83B Publicly Held
Web: explore.agilent.com
SIC: 8731 Biotechnical research, commercial
PA: Agilent Technologies, Inc.
5301 Stevens Creek Blvd
800 227-9770

(P-17762)
AGENDIA INC
22 Morgan, Irvine (92618-2022)
PHONE..............................949 540-6300
Mark R Straley, CEO
Brian Dow, CFO
Kurt Schmidt, CFO
Glen Fredenberg, CFO
Neil M Barth, Chief Medical Officer
EMP: 107 EST: 2008
SALES (est): 27.96MM
SALES (corp-wide): 57.36MM Privately Held
Web: www.agendia.com
SIC: 8731 Biotechnical research, commercial
PA: Agendia N.V.
Radarweg 60
204621500

(P-17763)
AGOURON PHARMACEUTICALS INC
3550 General Atomics Ct Bldg 9, San Diego
(92121-1122)
PHONE..............................858 455-3200
Peter Johnson, Pr
EMP: 130
SALES (corp-wide): 58.5B Publicly Held
Web: www.agi.org
SIC: 8731 5122 Biotechnical research,
commercial; Pharmaceuticals
HQ: Agouron Pharmaceuticals, Inc.
10777 Science Center Drv
San Diego CA 92121
858 622-3000

(P-17764)
AGOURON PHARMACEUTICALS INC
3301 N Torrey Pines Ct, La Jolla
(92037-1022)
PHONE..............................858 622-3000
Evaristo Cruz, Mgr
EMP: 359
SALES (corp-wide): 58.5B Publicly Held
Web: www.agi.org
SIC: 8731 Biotechnical research, commercial
HQ: Agouron Pharmaceuticals, Inc.
10777 Science Center Drv
San Diego CA 92121
858 622-3000

(P-17765)
AINOS INC (PA)
Also Called: VELDONA
8880 Rio San Diego Dr Ste 800, San Diego
(92108-1642)
PHONE..............................858 869-2986
Chun-hsien Tsai, Ch Bd
Christopher Hsin-liang Lee, CFO
Lawrence K Lin, Ofcr
EMP: 46 EST: 1984
SALES (est): 122.11K
SALES (corp-wide): 122.11K Publicly Held
Web: www.amarbio.com
SIC: 8731 2834 Biotechnical research,
commercial; Pharmaceutical preparations

(P-17766)
ANSUN BIOPHARMA INC
Also Called: Ansun
10045 Mesa Rim Rd, San Diego
(92121-2913)
PHONE..............................858 452-2631
Nancy Chang, CEO
George Wang, *
Stanley Lewis, CMO*
EMP: 25 EST: 2003
SQ FT: 12,000

SALES (est): 5.8MM **Privately Held**
Web: www.ansunbiopharma.com
SIC: **8731** 2834 Biotechnical research,
commercial; Druggists' preparations
(pharmaceuticals)

(P-17767)
APPLIED RESEARCH ASSOC INC
10833 Valley View St Ste 250, Cypress
(90630-5060)
PHONE..................................505 881-8074
Robert H Sues, *Brnch Mgr*
EMP: 99
SALES (corp-wide): 418.64MM **Privately Held**
Web: www.ara.com
SIC: **8731** Commercial physical research
HQ: Applied Research Associates, Inc.
4300 San Mteo Blvd Ne Ste
Albuquerque NM 87110
505 883-3636

(P-17768)
AQUANEERING LLC
Also Called: Aquaneering
340 Rancheros Dr Ste 180, San Marcos
(92069-2980)
PHONE..................................858 578-2028
Sandeep Patel, *Managing Member*
EMP: 30 EST: 1984
SALES (est): 8.07MM **Privately Held**
Web: www.aquaneering.com
SIC: **8731** 3589 Biotechnical research,
commercial; Water filters and softeners,
household type

(P-17769)
ARCHIMDES TECH GROUP HLDNGS LL
5660 Eastgate Dr, San Diego (92121-2816)
PHONE..................................858 642-9170
David Gerson, *
Scott Tierney, *
EMP: 71 EST: 1998
SQ FT: 20,000
SALES (est): 520.52K **Privately Held**
SIC: **8731** Environmental research

(P-17770)
ARCTURUS THERAPEUTICS INC
10628 Science Center Dr Ste 250, San
Diego (92121-1132)
PHONE..................................858 900-2660
Joseph Payne, *Pr*
Andrew Sassine, *
Steve Hughes, *COO*
Lance Kurata, *CLO*
EMP: 150 EST: 2013
SALES (est): 42.71MM
SALES (corp-wide): 166.8MM **Publicly Held**
Web: www.arctursrx.com
SIC: **8731** Biotechnical research, commercial
PA: Arcturus Therapeutics Holdings Inc.
10628 Scnce Ctr Dr Ste 25
858 900-2660

(P-17771)
ASTUTE MEDICAL INC
Also Called: Astute
3550 General Atomics Ct Bldg 02/620, San
Diego (92121-1122)
PHONE..................................858 792-3544
Paul Mcpherson, *CEO*
EMP: 87 EST: 2007
SALES (est): 9.56MM
SALES (corp-wide): 7.5MM **Privately Held**
Web: www.astutemedical.corn

SIC: **8731** Medical research, commercial
HQ: Biomerieux Sa
376 Chemin De L'orme
Marcy-L'etoile ARA 69280
478872000

(P-17772)
AVERY CORP
207 N Goode Ave Fl 6, Glendale
(91203-1364)
PHONE..................................626 304-2000
Dean Scarborough, *Pr*
EMP: 200 EST: 1968
SALES (est): 1.17MM
SALES (corp-wide): 8.36B **Publicly Held**
Web: www.averydennison.com
SIC: **8731** Biological research
PA: Avery Dennison Corporation
8080 Norton Pkwy
440 534-6000

(P-17773)
AXONICS INC (PA)
26 Technology Dr, Irvine (92618-2380)
PHONE..................................949 396-6322
Raymond W Cohen, *CEO*
Michael H Carrel, *Ch Bd*
Danny L Dearen, *Pr*
Rinda Sama, *COO*
Karen Noblett, *CMO*
EMP: 774 EST: 2013
SQ FT: 25,548
SALES (est): 366.38MM
SALES (corp-wide): 366.38MM **Privately Held**
Web: www.axonics.com
SIC: **8731** Biotechnical research, commercial

(P-17774)
BIOAGILYTIX LABS LLC
9050 Camino Santa Fe, San Diego
(92121-3203)
PHONE..................................858 652-4600
EMP: 574
SALES (corp-wide): 246.19MM **Privately Held**
Web: www.bioagilytix.com
SIC: **8731** Biotechnical research, commercial
HQ: Bioagilytix Labs, Llc
2300 Englert Dr Ste G
Durham NC 27713

(P-17775)
BIODURO LLC
72 Fairbanks, Irvine (92618-1668)
PHONE..................................858 529-6600
Kent M Payne, *Brnch Mgr*
EMP: 204
Web: www.bioduro-sundia.com
SIC: **8731** Biotechnical research, commercial
PA: Bioduro Llc
11011 Torreyana Rd

(P-17776)
BIODURO LLC (PA)
Also Called: Bioduro-Sundia
11011 Torreyana Rd, San Diego
(92121-1104)
PHONE..................................858 529-6600
Kent M Payne, *CEO*
Teo Nee Chuan, *
EMP: 40 EST: 2005
SALES (est): 53.39MM **Privately Held**
Web: www.bioduro-sundia.com
SIC: **8731** 2834 Biotechnical research,
commercial; Medicines, capsuled or
ampuled

(P-17777)
BIOLEGEND INC (HQ)
8999 Biolegend Way, San Diego
(92121-2284)
PHONE..................................858 455-9588
Gene Lay, *Pr*
Kent Johnson, *
◆ EMP: 99 EST: 2002
SQ FT: 75,000
SALES (est): 49.11MM
SALES (corp-wide): 2.75B **Publicly Held**
Web: www.biolegend.com
SIC: **8731** Biotechnical research, commercial
PA: Revvity, Inc.
77 4th Ave
781 663-6900

(P-17778)
BIOQUIP PRODUCTS INC
2321 E Gladwick St, Rancho Dominguez
(90220-6209)
PHONE..................................310 667-8800
▲ EMP: 30 EST: 1947
SALES (est): 2.65MM **Privately Held**
Web: www.bioquip.com
SIC: **8731** 3821 Biological research;
Laboratory apparatus and furniture

(P-17779)
BIOSPACE INC
Also Called: Inbody
13850 Cerritos Corporate Dr Ste C, Cerritos
(90703-2467)
PHONE..................................323 932-6503
Ki Chul Cha, *Pr*
Hak Hee Yun, *
▲ EMP: 86 EST: 2000
SQ FT: 35,319
SALES (est): 9.29MM **Privately Held**
Web: www.inbody.com
SIC: **8731** 3821 Energy research; Calibration
tapes, for physical testing machines
PA: Shenzhen Longgang District Baolong
Kangxing Fruit Firm
No.419-420, Chishi Gang Xiaoqu
Tongfu Road, Longxin Community, B

(P-17780)
BOUNDLESS BIO INC
Also Called: Boundless
9880 Campus Point Dr Ste 120, San Diego
(92121-1564)
PHONE..................................858 766-9912
Zachary D Hornby, *Pr*
Jonathan E Lim, *
Jami Rubin, *CFO*
Jessica Oien, *CLO*
Klaus Wagner, *CMO*
EMP: 72 EST: 2018
SQ FT: 28,700
SALES (est): 10.86MM **Privately Held**
Web: www.boundlessbio.com
SIC: **8731** 5122 Biotechnical research,
commercial; Biotherapeutics

(P-17781)
CIBUS GLOBAL LTD
6455 Nancy Ridge Dr, San Diego
(92121-2249)
PHONE..................................858 450-0008
Peter Beetham, *Pr*
Rory Riggs, *
Gerhard Prante, *
Greg Gocal, *CSO*
Jim Hinrichs, *CFO*
EMP: 134 EST: 2001
SQ FT: 53,000
SALES (est): 668.2K **Privately Held**
Web: www.cibus.com

SIC: **8731** Biotechnical research, commercial

(P-17782)
COI PHARMACEUTICALS INC
11099 N Torrey Pines Rd Ste 290, La Jolla
(92037-1029)
PHONE..................................858 750-4700
Jay Lichter, *CEO*
EMP: 25 EST: 2013
SALES (est): 4.94MM **Privately Held**
Web: www.avalonbioventures.com
SIC: **8731** 2834 Biological research;
Pharmaceutical preparations

(P-17783)
CRL TECHNOLOGIES INC
543 W Graaf Ave # B, Ridgecrest
(93555-2529)
PHONE..................................760 495-3000
Carlos M Velez, *Brnch Mgr*
EMP: 71
Web: www.crltechnologies.com
SIC: **8731** Commercial physical research
PA: Crl Technologies, Inc
9426 Ferry Landing Ct

(P-17784)
DISNEY RESEARCH PITTSBURGH
532 Paula Ave, Glendale (91201-2328)
PHONE..................................412 623-1800
Jessica K Hodgins, *Dir*
EMP: 142 EST: 2011
SALES (est): 456.8K
SALES (corp-wide): 91.36B **Publicly Held**
SIC: **8731** Commercial research laboratory
HQ: Walt Disney Imagineering Research &
Development, Inc.
1401 Flower St
Glendale CA 91201
818 544-6500

(P-17785)
DUPONT DISPLAYS INC
600 Ward Dr Ste C, Santa Barbara
(93111-2300)
PHONE..................................805 562-5400
Steve Quindlen, *Brnch Mgr*
EMP: 135
SALES (corp-wide): 17.23B **Publicly Held**
Web: www.dupont.com
SIC: **8731** Commercial physical research
HQ: Dupont Displays, Inc.
974 Centre Rd
Wilmington DE 19805

(P-17786)
EBIOSCIENCE INC
Also Called: Affymetrix
10255 Science Center Dr, San Diego
(92121-1117)
PHONE..................................858 642-2058
EMP: 200
Web: www.thermofisher.com
SIC: **8731** Biotechnical research, commercial

(P-17787)
ENVIRONMENTAL SCIENCE ASSOC
Also Called: ESA
633 W 5th St, Los Angeles (90071-2005)
PHONE..................................213 599-4300
Melissa Gross, *Mgr*
EMP: 150
SALES (corp-wide): 47.32MM **Privately Held**
Web: www.esassoc.com
SIC: **8731** 8748 Environmental research;
Environmental consultant

PA: Environmental Science Associates
575 Market St
415 896-5900

(P-17788)
FLUXERGY INC (PA)
Also Called: Carter Laboratories
30 Fairbanks, Irvine (92618-1623)
PHONE.....................949 305-4201
Tej Patel, Pr
Ryan Revilla, *
Jonathan Tu, *
EMP: 34 EST: 2013
SALES (est): 10.44MM
SALES (corp-wide): 10.44MM Privately Held
Web: www.fluxergy.com
SIC: 8731 3841 Biotechnical research, commercial; Diagnostic apparatus, medical

(P-17789)
GENERAL ATOMICS
16969 Mesamint St, San Diego (92127-2407)
PHONE.....................858 676-7100
Anthony Navarra, Co-Vice President
EMP: 99
Web: www.ga.com
SIC: 8731 Commercial physical research
HQ: General Atomics
3550 General Atomics Ct
San Diego CA 92121
858 455-2810

(P-17790)
GENERAL ATOMICS
Also Called: General Atomics Energy Pdts
4949 Greencraig Ln, San Diego (92123-1675)
PHONE.....................858 455-4000
Joel Ennis, Genl Mgr
EMP: 170
Web: www.ga.com
SIC: 8731 7371 3823 Commercial physical research; Custom computer programming services; Process control instruments
HQ: General Atomics
3550 General Atomics Ct
San Diego CA 92121
858 455-2810

(P-17791)
GENERAL ATOMICS
Also Called: Shipping and Receiving
3483 Dunhill St, San Diego (92121-1200)
P.O. Box 85608 (92186-5608)
PHONE.....................858 455-4141
Jene Spence, Mgr
EMP: 88
Web: www.ga.com
SIC: 8731 Commercial physical research
HQ: General Atomics
3550 General Atomics Ct
San Diego CA 92121
858 455-2810

(P-17792)
GENTEX CORPORATION
Also Called: Western Operations
9859 7th St, Rancho Cucamonga (91730-5244)
PHONE.....................909 481-7667
Robert Mccay, Brnch Mgr
EMP: 90
SALES (corp-wide): 83.71MM Privately Held
Web: www.gentexcorp.com
SIC: 8731 3845 3841 Commercial research laboratory; Electromedical equipment; Surgical and medical instruments

PA: Gentex Corporation
324 Main St
570 282-3550

(P-17793)
HALOZYME INC
Also Called: Halozyme Therapeutics
12390 El Camino Real Ste 150, San Diego (92130-3190)
PHONE.....................858 794-8889
Helen I Torley, CEO
Harry J Leonhardt, Sec
Laureen Stelzer, CFO
EMP: 216 EST: 1998
SALES (est): 5.34MM
SALES (corp-wide): 829.25MM Publicly Held
Web: www.halozyme.com
SIC: 8731 Biotechnical research, commercial
PA: Halozyme Therapeutics, Inc.
12390 El Camino Real
858 794-8889

(P-17794)
HGST INC
3355 Michelson Dr, Irvine (92612-0684)
PHONE.....................949 448-0385
Michael Cordano, Brnch Mgr
EMP: 330
SALES (corp-wide): 13B Publicly Held
Web: www.westerndigital.com
SIC: 8731 Commercial physical research
HQ: Hgst, Inc.
5601 Great Oaks Pkwy
San Jose CA 95119
408 717-6000

(P-17795)
HII FLEET SUPPORT GROUP LLC
9444 Balboa Ave Ste 400, San Diego (92123-4378)
PHONE.....................858 522-6319
Michelle Wurl, Dir
EMP: 229
SIC: 8731 8711 Commercial physical research; Engineering services
HQ: Hii Fleet Support Group Llc
5701 Cleveland St
Virginia Beach VA 23462
757 463-6666

(P-17796)
INOVA DIAGNOSTICS INC (HQ)
Also Called: Werfen
9900 Old Grove Rd, San Diego (92131-1638)
PHONE.....................858 586-9900
Carlos Pascual, CEO
Javier Gomez, *
▲ EMP: 285 EST: 1987
SQ FT: 81,000
SALES (est): 37.29MM Privately Held
Web: www.werfen.com
SIC: 8731 2835 Medical research, commercial; In vitro diagnostics
PA: Werfen S.A.
Plaza Europa, 21 - 23

(P-17797)
INTRI-PLEX TECHNOLOGIES INC
751 S Kellogg Ave, Goleta (93117-3806)
PHONE.....................805 845-9600
David Dexter, CEO
EMP: 34 EST: 1989
SALES (est): 658.94K Privately Held
Web: www.intriplex.com
SIC: 8731 3599 Commercial physical research; Machine shop, jobbing and repair

(P-17798)
INVASIX INC
Also Called: Inmode Aesthetic Solutions
17 Hughes, Irvine (92618-1902)
PHONE.....................855 411-2639
Moshe Mizrahy, CEO
Shakil Lakhani, *
Yair Malca, *
EMP: 99 EST: 2008
SALES (est): 11.55MM Privately Held
Web: www.inmodemd.com
SIC: 8731 5047 Medical research, commercial; Electro-medical equipment

(P-17799)
INVIZYNE TECHNOLOGIES INC (PA)
750 Royal Oaks Dr Ste 106, Monrovia (91016-6357)
PHONE.....................626 415-1488
Michael Heltzen, CEO
Mo Hayat, Ch Bd
Fouad Nawaz, VP Fin
Tyler Korman, Research Vice President
Paul Opgenorth, VP
EMP: 27 EST: 2014
SALES (est): 3.87MM
SALES (corp-wide): 3.87MM Publicly Held
Web: www.invizyne.com
SIC: 8731 2836 Biotechnical research, commercial; Biological products, except diagnostic

(P-17800)
ISE CORPORATION
Also Called: I S E
12302 Kerran St, Poway (92064-6884)
PHONE.....................858 413-1720
▲ EMP: 140
SIC: 8731 3621 Commercial physical research; Electric motor and generator parts

(P-17801)
ISOTIS ORTHOBIOLOGICS INC
2 Goodyear Ste A, Irvine (92618-2052)
PHONE.....................949 595-8710
Keith Valentine, CEO
Peter J Arduini, *
Christian S Schade, *
▲ EMP: 150 EST: 1990
SALES (est): 4.24MM
SALES (corp-wide): 746.64MM Privately Held
Web: www.seaspine.com
SIC: 8731 5047 Biotechnical research, commercial; Surgical equipment and supplies
PA: Orthofix Medical Inc.
3451 Plano Pkwy
214 937-2000

(P-17802)
KITE PHARMA INC (HQ)
Also Called: Kite, A Gilead Company
2400 Broadway Ste 100, Santa Monica (90404-3058)
PHONE.....................310 824-9999
Christi Shaw, CEO
Robin L Washington, *
Cindy Perettie, *
EMP: 92 EST: 2009
SQ FT: 20,000
SALES (est): 120.5MM
SALES (corp-wide): 27.12B Publicly Held
Web: www.kitepharma.com
SIC: 8731 2836 Biotechnical research, commercial; Biological products, except diagnostic
PA: Gilead Sciences, Inc.
333 Lakeside Dr

650 574-3000

(P-17803)
LEIDOS INC
Also Called: Saic
10260 Campus Point Dr Bldg C, San Diego (92121-1522)
PHONE.....................703 676-4300
Jere Drummond, Dir
EMP: 97
Web: www.leidos.com
SIC: 8731 7373 Commercial physical research; Systems software development services
HQ: Leidos, Inc.
1750 Presidents St
Reston VA 20190
855 953-4367

(P-17804)
LEIDOS INC
4161 Campus Point Ct Stop Em3, San Diego (92121-1513)
PHONE.....................858 826-9416
Paul Chang, Mgr
EMP: 109
Web: www.leidos.com
SIC: 8731 Commercial physical research
HQ: Leidos, Inc.
1750 Presidents St
Reston VA 20190
855 953-4367

(P-17805)
LEIDOS INC
Also Called: Reveal Imaging
2985 Scott St, Vista (92081-8339)
PHONE.....................858 826-9090
EMP: 130
Web: www.leidos.com
SIC: 8731 3829 3826 Commercial physical research; Measuring and controlling devices, nec; Analytical instruments
HQ: Leidos, Inc.
1750 Presidents St
Reston VA 20190
855 953-4367

(P-17806)
LEIDOS INC
Also Called: Saic
Naval Air Station, San Diego (92135)
PHONE.....................858 826-6000
EMP: 66
Web: www.leidos.com
SIC: 8731 7373 8742 3679 Commercial physical research; Systems engineering, computer related; Training and development consultant; Recording and playback apparatus, including phonograph
HQ: Leidos, Inc.
1750 Presidents St
Reston VA 20190
855 953-4367

(P-17807)
LEIDOS ENGRG & SCIENCES LLC
1330 30th St Ste A, San Diego (92154-3471)
PHONE.....................619 542-3130
Karen Parizeau, Mgr
EMP: 129
SIC: 8731 Natural resource research
HQ: Leidos Engineering & Sciences, Llc
9737 Washingtonian Blvd
Gaithersburg MD 20878
301 240-7000

(P-17808)
MARAVAI LF SCNCES HOLDINGS LLC (HQ)
10770 Wateridge Cir Ste 100, San Diego (92121-5801)
PHONE................................650 697-3600
Eric Tardif, *Pr*
EMP: 148 **EST:** 2014
SALES (est): 50.97MM
SALES (corp-wide): 288.94MM **Publicly Held**
Web: www.maravai.com
SIC: 8731 Commercial physical research
PA: Maravai Lifesciences Holdings, Inc.
10770 Wtridge Cir Ste 200
858 546-0004

(P-17809)
MEMORIAL HEALTHTEC LABRATORIES
9920 Talbert Ave, Fountain Valley (92708-5153)
PHONE................................714 962-4677
Marcia Manker, *Mgr*
EMP: 211
Web: www.memorialcare.org
SIC: 8731 Commercial physical research
HQ: Memorial Healthtec Labratories Inc
2865 Atlantic Ave Ste 203
Long Beach CA 90806

(P-17810)
MOTECH AMERICAS LLC
Also Called: GE Energy
1300 Valley Vista Dr Ste 207, Diamond Bar (91765-3940)
PHONE................................302 451-7500
▲ **EMP:** 320
Web: www.motech-americas.com
SIC: 8731 3674 Energy research; Solar cells

(P-17811)
NANTCELL INC
9920 Jefferson Blvd, Culver City (90232-3506)
PHONE................................562 397-3639
Richard Adcock, *CEO*
EMP: 432 **EST:** 2014
SALES (est): 427.87K **Publicly Held**
Web: www.immunitybio.com
SIC: 8731 Biotechnical research, commercial
PA: Immunitybio, Inc.
3530 John Hopkins Ct

(P-17812)
NAVIGATE BIOPHARMA SVCS INC
1890 Rutherford Rd, Carlsbad (92008-7344)
PHONE................................000 992-4909
Kevin Zou, *CEO*
EMP: 180 **EST:** 2016
SALES (est): 24.83MM **Privately Held**
Web: www.navigatebp.com
SIC: 8731 Biotechnical research, commercial
HQ: Novartis Finance Corporation
1 Health Plz
East Hanover NJ 07936

(P-17813)
NORTHROP GRMMN SPCE & MSSN SYS
Space Technology Sector
862 E Hospitality Ln, San Bernardino (92408-3530)
PHONE................................909 382-6800
FAX: 909 382-6249
EMP: 200

SIC: 8731 7373 Commercial physical research; Computer integrated systems design
HQ: Northrop Grumman Space & Mission Systems Corp.
6379 San Ignacio Ave
San Jose CA 95119
703 280-2900

(P-17814)
NOVARTIS INST FOR FNCTNAL GNMI
Also Called: Nibr
10675 John J Hopkins Dr, San Diego (92121-1127)
PHONE................................858 812-1500
Hans Seidel, *Pr*
Timothy Smith, *
Karl Olsen, *
Robert Downs, *
Daniel Vasella Md, *Prin*
EMP: 234 **EST:** 1998
SALES (est): 49.86MM **Privately Held**
Web: www.novartis.com
SIC: 8731 Biotechnical research, commercial

(P-17815)
NOYMED CORP
1101 N Pacific Ave Ste 303, Glendale (91202-4376)
PHONE................................800 224-2090
Armen Margaryan, *CEO*
Tatevik Simonyan, *
EMP: 130 **EST:** 2020
SALES (est): 8MM **Privately Held**
Web: www.noymed.com
SIC: 8731 Commercial physical research

(P-17816)
ONE LAMBDA INC (HQ)
22801 Roscoe Blvd, West Hills (91304-3200)
PHONE................................747 494-1000
Seth H Hoogasian, *CEO*
George M Ayoub, *
Don Arii, *
James Keegan, *
Emiko Terasaki, *Corporate Secretary*
EMP: 94 **EST:** 1984
SQ FT: 53,000
SALES (est): 42.33MM
SALES (corp-wide): 42.86B **Publicly Held**
Web: www.onelambda.com
SIC: 8731 Biotechnical research, commercial
PA: Thermo Fisher Scientific Inc.
168 3rd Ave
781 622-1000

(P-17817)
OPTO-KNOWLEDGE SYSTEMS INC
Also Called: Optoknowledge
19805 Hamilton Ave, Torrance (90502-1341)
PHONE................................310 756-0520
Christopher Holmes Parker, *Prin*
Ilana Gat, *
Joel Gat, *
EMP: 29 **EST:** 1991
SQ FT: 14,000
SALES (est): 5.74MM **Privately Held**
Web: www.oksi.ai
SIC: 8731 3827 Engineering laboratory, except testing; Optical instruments and lenses

(P-17818)
PROSCIENTO INC (PA)
6160 Cornerstone Ct E Ste 200, San Diego (92121-3720)

PHONE................................619 427-1300
Marcus Hompesch, *CEO*
Linda Morrow, *COO*
Markus Hofmann, *CFO*
Christian Weyer, *Chief Development Officer*
EMP: 166 **EST:** 2002
SQ FT: 20,000
SALES (est): 23.16MM
SALES (corp-wide): 23.16MM **Privately Held**
Web: www.prosciento.com
SIC: 8731 Biotechnical research, commercial

(P-17819)
QNAP INC
168 University Pkwy, Pomona (91768-4300)
PHONE................................909 598-6933
Ming-chi Chang, *Pr*
EMP: 82 **EST:** 2009
SALES (est): 3.15MM **Privately Held**
Web: www.qnap.com
SIC: 8731 Biotechnical research, commercial
PA: Qnap Systems, Inc.
2f, No. 22, Zhongxing Rd.

(P-17820)
REVEAL BIOSCIENCES INC
80 Empire Dr, Lake Forest (92630-2244)
PHONE................................858 274-3663
Claire Weston, *Pr*
EMP: 25 **EST:** 2012
SALES (est): 2.24MM **Privately Held**
Web: www.revealbio.com
SIC: 8731 2835 Biotechnical research, commercial; Cytology and histology diagnostic agents

(P-17821)
SEMINIS INC (DH)
2700 Camino Del Sol, Oxnard (93030-7967)
PHONE................................805 485-7317
Bruno Ferrari, *Pr*
Oscar J Velasco Senior, *Area Vice President*
Charles E Green, *
Enrique Lopez, *
Jorge B Gutierrez, *
◆ **EMP:** 300 **EST:** 1995
SALES (est): 13.66MM
SALES (corp-wide): 51.78B **Privately Held**
Web: www.seminis.com
SIC: 8731 8742 2099 Agricultural research; Productivity improvement consultant; Food preparations, nec
HQ: Monsanto Technology Llc.
800 North Lindbergh Blvd
Saint Louis MO 63167
314 694-1000

(P-17822)
SEQUENOM INC (DH)
Also Called: Sequenom Ctr For Mlclar Mdcine
3595 John Hopkins Ct, San Diego (92121-1121)
PHONE................................858 202-9000
Dirk Van Den Boom, *Pr*
Carolyn D Beaver, *
Daniel S Grosu, *CMO*
Jeffrey D Linton, *
Robert J Lozuk, *Senior Vice President Commercial*
EMP: 80 **EST:** 1994
SALES (est): 22.5MM
SALES (corp-wide): 12.18B **Publicly Held**
Web: womenshealth.labcorp.com
SIC: 8731 Biological research
HQ: Laboratory Corporation Of America Holdings
358 S Main St

Burlington NC 27215

(P-17823)
SPREADTRUM CMMNCATIONS USA INC
Also Called: Spreadtrum
10180 Telesis Ct Ste 500, San Diego (92121-2787)
PHONE................................858 546-0895
EMP: 70 **EST:** 2003
SALES (est): 9.74MM **Privately Held**
SIC: 8731 Electronic research
HQ: Spreadtrum Communications (Shanghai) Co., Ltd.
Building 1, Spreadtrum Center, Lane 2288, Zuchongzhi Road, China
Shanghai SH 20120

(P-17824)
TAE LIFE SCIENCES US LLC
19571 Pauling, Foothill Ranch (92610-2619)
P.O. Box 7010 (92688-7010)
PHONE................................949 344-6112
Bruce Bauer, *Managing Member*
Anna Theriault, *
EMP: 90 **EST:** 2017
SALES (est): 1.92MM **Privately Held**
Web: www.taelifesciences.com
SIC: 8731 Biotechnical research, commercial

(P-17825)
TAE TECHNOLOGIES INC (PA)
Also Called: Tae Technologies
19631 Pauling, Foothill Ranch (92610-2607)
P.O. Box 7010 (92688-7010)
PHONE................................949 830-2117
Michl Binderbauer, *CEO*
Mark J Lewis, *Pr*
EMP: 155 **EST:** 2002
SALES (est): 45.87MM
SALES (corp-wide): 45.87MM **Privately Held**
Web: www.tae.com
SIC: 8731 Energy research

(P-17826)
TANVEX BIOPHARMA USA INC (PA)
Also Called: L J B
10394 Pacific Center Ct, San Diego (92121-4340)
PHONE................................858 210-4100
Allen Chao, *CEO*
Chi-chuan Chen, *Pr*
EMP: 100 **EST:** 1984
SALES (est): 22.98MM
SALES (corp-wide): 22.98MM **Privately Held**
Web: www.tanvex.com
SIC: 8731 Biotechnical research, commercial

(P-17827)
TELEDYNE SCENTIFIC IMAGING LLC
Also Called: Teledyne Judson Technologies
5212 Verdugo Way, Camarillo (93012-8662)
PHONE................................805 373-4979
James Beletic, *Pr*
EMP: 85
SQ FT: 54,295
SALES (corp-wide): 5.64B **Publicly Held**
Web: www.teledyne-si.com
SIC: 8731 Commercial physical research
HQ: Teledyne Scientific & Imaging, Llc
1049 Camino Dos Rios
Thousand Oaks CA 91360

PRODUCTS & SVCS

(P-17828)

TELEDYNE SCENTIFIC IMAGING LLC (HQ)

Also Called: Teledyne Scientific Company
1049 Camino Dos Rios, Thousand Oaks
(91360-2362)
PHONE..............................805 373-4545
Aldo Pichelli Presidnet, *Prin*
James Beletic, *IMAGING SENSORS**
Berinder Brar, *SCIENTIFIC**
EMP: 125 **EST:** 1962
SQ FT: 161,000
SALES (est): 40.19MM
SALES (corp-wide): 5.64B **Publicly Held**
Web: www.teledyneimaging.com
SIC: 8731 8732 8733 Commercial physical
research; Commercial nonphysical research
; Noncommercial research organizations
PA: Teledyne Technologies Inc
1049 Camino Dos Rios
805 373-4545

(P-17829)

THE SALK INSTITUTE FOR BIOLOGICAL STUDIES SAN DIEGO CALIFORNIA

Also Called: Salk Institute, The
10010 N Torrey Pines Rd, La Jolla
(92037-1002)
P.O. Box 85800 (92186-5800)
PHONE..............................858 453-4100
EMP: 1100 **EST:** 1960
SALES (est): 173.65MM **Privately Held**
Web: www.salk.edu
SIC: 8731 Commercial physical research

(P-17830)

TISSUE-GROWN CORPORATION

15245 W Telegraph Rd, Santa Paula
(93060-3039)
PHONE..............................805 525-1975
Carolyn Sluis, *Pr*
◆ **EMP:** 85 **EST:** 1986
SQ FT: 10,500
SALES (est): 2MM **Privately Held**
Web: www.tissuegrown.com
SIC: 8731 Biotechnical research, commercial

(P-17831)

TNK THERAPEUTICS INC (HQ)

9380 Judicial Dr, San Diego (92121-3830)
PHONE..............................858 210-3700
Henry Ji, *CEO*
EMP: 94 **EST:** 2015
SALES (est): 292.09K
SALES (corp-wide): 62.84MM **Publicly Held**
Web: www.sorrentotherapeutics.com
SIC: 8731 Medical research, commercial
PA: Sorrento Therapeutics, Inc.
4955 Directors Pl
858 203-4100

(P-17832)

TREELINE BIOSCIENCES INC

11180 Roselle St, San Diego (92121-1211)
PHONE..............................858 766-5725
EMP: 70
SALES (corp-wide): 68.51MM **Privately
Held**
Web: www.treeline.bio
SIC: 8731 Commercial physical research
PA: Treeline Biosciences, Inc.
500 Arsenal St Fl 2
857 228-0050

(P-17833)

TRILINK BIOTECHNOLOGIES LLC

10770 Wateridge Cir Ste 200, San Diego
(92121-5801)
PHONE..............................800 863-6801
Richard Hogrefe, *Pr*
Terry Beck, ***
Chris Perez, ***
EMP: 159 **EST:** 1996
SQ FT: 40,000
SALES (est): 34.94MM
SALES (corp-wide): 288.94MM **Publicly
Held**
Web: www.trilinkbiotech.com
SIC: 8731 8748 Biotechnical research,
commercial; Test development and
evaluation service
PA: Maravai Lifesciences Holdings, Inc.
10770 Wtridge Cir Ste 200
858 546-0004

(P-17834)

TRUVIAN SCIENCES INC

10300 Campus Point Dr Ste 190, San Diego
(92121-1504)
PHONE..............................858 251-3646
Jeff Hawkins, *CEO*
Conner Hargrave, ***
Dena Marrinucci, ***
Katherine Atkinson, *CCO**
Ria Francisco, ***
EMP: 74 **EST:** 2015
SQ FT: 1,500
SALES (est): 9.94MM **Privately Held**
Web: www.truvianhealth.com
SIC: 8731 Biotechnical research, commercial

(P-17835)

TURNING POINT THERAPEUTICS INC

10300 Campus Point Dr Ste 100, San Diego
(92121-1504)
PHONE..............................858 926-5251
Athena Countouriotis, *Pr*
Andrew Partridge, *CCO*
Annette North, *Ex VP*
Brian Baker, *VP Fin*
EMP: 87 **EST:** 2013
SALES (est): 30.83MM
SALES (corp-wide): 45.01B **Publicly Held**
Web: www.bms.com
SIC: 8731 Biotechnical research, commercial
PA: Bristol-Myers Squibb Company
Route 206/Prvince Line Rd
609 252-4621

(P-17836)

UNIVERSITY CALIFORNIA IRVINE

Also Called: Henry Samueli School Engrg
2220 Engineering Gtwy, Irvine
(92697-0001)
PHONE..............................949 824-2819
Doctor G P Li, *Dir*
EMP: 430
SALES (corp-wide): 534.4MM **Privately
Held**
Web: www.uci.edu
SIC: 8731 8221 9411 Electronic research;
University; Administration of educational
programs
HQ: University Of California, Irvine
510 Aldrich Hall
Irvine CA 92697
949 824-5011

(P-17837)

UNIVERSITY CALIFORNIA IRVINE

Also Called: Cancer Immnlogy Intrvtal McRsc
843 Health Sciences Rd, Irvine
(92617-3058)

PHONE..............................949 824-3359
EMP: 102
SALES (corp-wide): 534.4MM **Privately
Held**
Web: www.uci.edu
SIC: 8731 Commercial physical research
HQ: University Of California, Irvine
510 Aldrich Hall
Irvine CA 92697
949 824-5011

(P-17838)

VENTYX BIOSCIENCES INC (PA)

12790 El Camino Real Ste 200, San Diego
(92130-2008)
PHONE..............................760 593-4832
Raju S Mohan, *Pr*
Sheila Gujrathi, *Ex Ch Bd*
Matthew Moore, *COO*
Roy M Gonzales, *Interim Chief Financial
Officer*
John M Nuss, *CSO*
EMP: 75 **EST:** 2018
SQ FT: 35,016
Web: www.ventyxbio.com
SIC: 8731 Commercial physical research

(P-17839)

VIRIDOS INC

250 W Schrimpf Rd, Calipatria
(92233-9745)
PHONE..............................858 754-2900
EMP: 101
Web: www.viridos.com
SIC: 8731 Biotechnical research, commercial
HQ: Viridos, Inc.
11149 N Torrey Pines Rd
La Jolla CA 92037

(P-17840)

WILDCAT DISCOVERY TECH INC

6255 Ferris Sq Ste A, San Diego
(92121-3232)
PHONE..............................858 550-1980
Mark Gresser, *CEO*
Mark Grasser, *Pr*
Steven Kaye, *Prin*
Jon Jacobs, *VP*
Laura Marion, *CFO*
EMP: 59 **EST:** 2006
SALES (est): 11.44MM **Privately Held**
Web: www.wildcatdiscovery.com
SIC: 8731 2819 Biotechnical research,
commercial; Industrial inorganic chemicals,
nec

8732 Commercial Nonphysical Research

(P-17841)

CHASE GROUP LLC

Also Called: Simi Vly Care & Rehabilitation
5270 E Los Angeles Ave, Simi Valley
(93063-4137)
PHONE..............................805 522-9155
Phil Chase, *Mgr*
EMP: 295
Web: www.chasegroup.us
SIC: 8732 8742 Research services, except
laboratory; Management consulting services
PA: The Chase Group Llc
5374 Long Shadow Ct

(P-17842)

CORNERSTONE RESEARCH INC

555 W 5th St Ste 3800, Los Angeles
(90013-3016)
PHONE..............................213 553-2500
Richard Dalbeck, *VP*

EMP: 81
SALES (corp-wide): 38.17MM **Privately
Held**
Web: www.cornerstone.com
SIC: 8732 Market analysis, business, and
economic research
PA: Cornerstone Research, Inc.
1000 Coleman Ave Ste 25
650 853-1660

(P-17843)

DAVIS RESEARCH LLC

26610 Agoura Rd Ste 240, Calabasas
(91302-3857)
PHONE..............................818 591-2408
William A Davis Iii, *Managing Member*
EMP: 150 **EST:** 1970
SALES (est): 5.91MM **Privately Held**
Web: www.davisresearch.com
SIC: 8732 Market analysis or research

(P-17844)

GENERAL ATOMICS (HQ)

3550 General Atomics Ct, San Diego
(92121-1194)
P.O. Box 85608 (92186-5608)
PHONE..............................858 455-2810
J Neal Blue, *Pr*
Linden Blue, ***
Liam Kelly, ***
Robert S Forney, ***
Jeffrey Quintenz, ***
▲ **EMP:** 2015 **EST:** 1955
SQ FT: 1,000,000
SALES (est): 506.15MM **Privately Held**
Web: www.ga.com
SIC: 8732 Commercial sociological and
educational research
PA: General Atomic Technologies
Corporation
3550 General Atomics Ct

(P-17845)

HENKEL US OPERATIONS CORP

14000 Jamboree Rd, Irvine (92606-1730)
PHONE..............................714 368-8000
Jim Heaton, *Brnch Mgr*
EMP: 83
SALES (corp-wide): 23.39B **Privately Held**
Web: www.henkel-northamerica.com
SIC: 8732 Business research service
HQ: Henkel Us Operations Corporation
1 Henkel Way
Rocky Hill CT 06067
860 571-5100

(P-17846)

HI LLC

Also Called: Kernel
10361 Jefferson Blvd, Culver City
(90232-3511)
PHONE..............................757 655-4113
Bryan Johnson, *Managing Member*
EMP: 90 **EST:** 2016
SQ FT: 3,500
SALES (est): 2.73MM **Privately Held**
SIC: 8732 Business research service

(P-17847)

HIGH DSERT PRTNR IN ACDMIC EXC

Also Called: NORTON SCIENCE AND
LANGUAGE AC
17500 Mana Rd, Apple Valley
(92307-2181)
PHONE..............................760 946-5414
Lisa Lamb, *CEO*
Teresa Dowd, ***
EMP: 350 **EST:** 1992
SQ FT: 35,000

SALES (est): 45.02MM **Privately Held**
Web: www.lewiscenter.org
SIC: 8732 Commercial nonphysical research

(P-17848)
HONDA R&D AMERICAS LLC
Also Called: Honda
1900 Harpers Way, Torrance (90501-1521)
PHONE.....................310 781-5500
▲ EMP: 1537
Web: www.hondaresearch.com
SIC: 8732 Market analysis or research

(P-17849)
HRL LABORATORIES LLC
Also Called: Hughes Research Laboratories
3011 Malibu Canyon Rd, Malibu
(90265-4797)
PHONE.....................310 317-5000
Penrose Albright, *Pr*
Roger Gronwald, *
◆ EMP: 647 EST: 1997
SQ FT: 250,000
SALES (est): 106.52MM **Privately Held**
Web: www.hrl.com
SIC: 8732 Commercial sociological and
educational research

(P-17850)
INFORMA RESEARCH
SERVICES INC (HQ)
26565 Agoura Rd Ste 300, Calabasas
(91302-1942)
PHONE.....................818 880-8877
Michael E Adler, *Pr*
Charles A Miwa, *
Lori Jomsky, *
EMP: 193 EST: 1993
SQ FT: 16,000
SALES (est): 11.98MM
SALES (corp-wide): 3.98B **Privately Held**
Web: www.informaconnect.com
SIC: 8732 Market analysis or research
PA: Informa Plc
5 Howick Place
208 052-0400

(P-17851)
INSTANTLY INC
Also Called: Usamp
16501 Ventura Blvd Ste 300, Encino
(91436-2067)
PHONE.....................866 872-4006
EMP: 200
SIC: 8732 Market analysis or research

(P-17852)
INTERVIEWING SERVICE AMER
LLC (PA)
Also Called: ISA
1900 Avenue Of The Stars, Los Angeles
(90067-4301)
PHONE.....................818 989-1044
Michael Halberstam, *Ch*
Tony Kretzmer, *
John Fitzpatrick, *
Vicky Agalsoff, *
EMP: 250 EST: 1982
SALES (est): 6.55MM
SALES (corp-wide): 6.55MM **Privately
Held**
Web: www.mysoapbox.com
SIC: 8732 Market analysis or research

(P-17853)
IQVIA INC (PA)
Also Called: SK&a
2601 Main St Ste 650, Irvine (92614-4228)
PHONE.....................866 267-4479

David Escalante Junior, *Pr*
Al M Cosentino, *
Jaqueline Aguilera, *
Albert Chang, *
EMP: 87 EST: 1998
SQ FT: 12,000
SALES (est): 11.15MM
SALES (corp-wide): 11.15MM **Privately
Held**
Web: www.onekeydata.com
SIC: 8732 Market analysis or research

(P-17854)
LUTH RESEARCH INC (PA)
Also Called: Surveysavvy.com
404 Camino Del Rio S Ste 505, San Diego
(92108-3588)
P.O. Box 12557 (92112-3557)
PHONE.....................619 234-5884
Roseanne Luth, *Pr*
Charles Rosen, *
EMP: 305 EST: 1977
SALES (est): 5.78MM
SALES (corp-wide): 5.78MM **Privately
Held**
Web: www.luthresearch.com
SIC: 8732 Market analysis or research

(P-17855)
MATERIAL HOLDINGS LLC (PA)
Also Called: Lrw Group
1900 Avenue Of The Stars Ste 1600, Los
Angeles (90067-4412)
PHONE.....................310 553-0550
David Sackman, *Ch*
Arnold Fishman, *
Cathy Lindquist, *
EMP: 140 EST: 1973
SQ FT: 24,560
SALES (est): 53.1MM
SALES (corp-wide): 53.1MM **Privately
Held**
Web: www.lrwonline.com
SIC: 8732 Market analysis or research

(P-17856)
NATIONAL RESEARCH GROUP
INC
Also Called: National Research Group
12101 Bluff Creek Dr, Los Angeles
(90094-2627)
PHONE.....................323 406-6200
Jon Penn, *CEO*
Jeff Hall, *
James Mcnamara, *Ex VP*
Jenny Swisher, *
Ray Ydoyaga, *
EMP: 278 EST: 1977
SALES (est): 10.22MM **Privately Held**
Web: www.nrgmr.com
SIC: 8732 Market analysis or research

(P-17857)
NITTO DENKO TECHNICAL
CORP
Also Called: Nitto
501 Via Del Monte, Oceanside
(92058-1251)
PHONE.....................760 435-7011
Kenji Matsumoto, *Pr*
EMP: 99 EST: 1985
SALES (est): 16.11MM **Privately Held**
Web: www.ndtcorp.com
SIC: 8732 3089 3462 Research services,
except laboratory; Automotive parts, plastic;
Automotive and internal combustion engine
forgings
PA: Nitto Denko Corporation
4-20, Ofukacho, Kita-Ku

(P-17858)
PALLADIUM VALLEY GLOBAL
INC ✪
3857 Birch St Ste 9017, Newport Beach
(92660-2616)
PHONE.....................949 723-9613
Jason Wilhite, *Ex Dir*
EMP: 75 EST: 2023
SALES (est): 231.17K **Privately Held**
SIC: 8732 Merger, acquisition, and
reorganization research

(P-17859)
PROSEARCH STRATEGIES LLC
3250 Wilshire Blvd Ste 301, Los Angeles
(90010-1451)
PHONE.....................877 447-7291
Julia Kim Hasenzahl, *CEO*
EMP: 140 EST: 2005
SALES (est): 24.79MM **Privately Held**
Web: www.prosearchstrategies.com
SIC: 8732 Research services, except
laboratory

(P-17860)
QUINTILES PACIFIC
INCORPORATED
10201 Wateridge Cir Ste 300, San Diego
(92121-5800)
PHONE.....................858 552-3400
Kevin Keim, *Brnch Mgr*
EMP: 371
SIC: 8732 Market analysis or research
HQ: Quintiles Pacific Incorporated
448 E Middlefield Rd
Mountain View CA
650 567-2000

(P-17861)
SCIENTFIC APPLCTONS RES
ASSOC
Also Called: Sara
33159 Camino Capistrano Ste B, San Juan
Capistrano (92675-4827)
PHONE.....................714 224-4410
Ruth Craig, *Mgr*
EMP: 82
Web: www.sara.com
SIC: 8732 Market analysis, business, and
economic research
PA: Scientific Applications & Research
Associates, Inc.
6300 Gateway Dr

(P-17862)
STREAMELEMENTS INC (PA)
11400 W Olympic Blvd, Los Angeles
(90064-1550)
PHONE.....................323 928-7848
Udi Hoffmann, *CFO*
EMP: 98 EST: 2017
SALES (est): 1.96MM
SALES (corp-wide): 1.96MM **Privately
Held**
SIC: 8732 Commercial nonphysical research

(P-17863)
TRENDSOURCE INC
Also Called: Examine Your Practice
4891 Pacific Hwy Ste 200, San Diego
(92110-4026)
PHONE.....................619 718-7467
Rodney Moll, *Ch Bd*
Rodney Moll, *Ch*
Neil A Wykes, *
Bob Post, *
EMP: 143 EST: 1989
SQ FT: 7,500
SALES (est): 4.47MM **Privately Held**

Web: www.trendsource.com
SIC: 8732 Market analysis or research

(P-17864)
ZEFR INC
Also Called: Movieclips.com
4101 Redwood Ave, Los Angeles
(90066-5603)
PHONE.....................310 392-3555
Rich Raddon, *CEO*
Toby Byrne, *
EMP: 437 EST: 2010
SALES (est): 15.82MM **Privately Held**
Web: www.zefr.com
SIC: 8732 7371 Market analysis, business,
and economic research; Software
programming applications

8733 Noncommercial
Research Organizations

(P-17865)
AEROSPACE CORPORATION
200 S Los Robles Ave Ste 150, Pasadena
(91101-4614)
PHONE.....................626 873-7700
Matthew Hart, *Brnch Mgr*
EMP: 116
SALES (corp-wide): 1.3B **Privately Held**
Web: www.aerospace.org
SIC: 8733 8711 8731 Scientific research
agency; Engineering services; Commercial
physical research
PA: The Aerospace Corporation
14745 Lee Rd
310 336-5000

(P-17866)
AMERICAN REGENT INC
536 Vanguard Way, Brea (92821-3932)
PHONE.....................714 989-5058
Donald F Hodgson, *Brnch Mgr*
EMP: 40
Web: www.americanregent.com
SIC: 8733 2834 Noncommercial research
organizations; Pharmaceutical preparations
HQ: American Regent, Inc.
5 Ramsey Rd
Shirley NY 11967
631 924-4000

(P-17867)
BRENTWOOD BMDICAL RES
INST INC
11301 Wilshire Blvd Bldg 114, Los Angeles
(90073-1003)
P.O. Box 25027 (90025-0027)
PHONE.....................310 312-1554
Kenneth Hickman, *CEO*
Thoyd Ellis, *
EMP: 130 EST: 1988
SQ FT: 1,500
SALES (est): 1MM **Privately Held**
Web: www.brentwoodresearch.org
SIC: 8733 Medical research

(P-17868)
CALIFORNIA INSTITUTE FOR
BIOMEDICAL RESEARCH
Also Called: California Institute For
11119 N Torrey Pines Rd, La Jolla
(92037-1046)
PHONE.....................858 242-1000
EMP: 110
Web: www.calibr.org
SIC: 8733 Medical research

(P-17869)
CALIFORNIA INSTITUTE TECH
Also Called: Jet Propulsion Laboratory
4800 Oak Grove Dr, Pasadena
(91109-8001)
PHONE..............................818 354-9154
Michael Watkins, *Dir*
EMP: 6000
SALES (corp-wide): 3.63B Privately Held
Web: www.caltech.edu
SIC: 8733 Research institute
PA: California Institute Of Technology
1200 E California Blvd
626 395-6811

(P-17870)
CARNEGIE INSTITUTION WASH
Also Called: Observatories of The Carnegie
813 Santa Barbara St, Pasadena
(91101-1232)
PHONE..............................626 577-1122
Wendy L Freedman, *Dir*
EMP: 100
SQ FT: 24,075
SALES (corp-wide): 129.09MM Privately
Held
Web: obs.carnegiescience.edu
SIC: 8733 7999 Scientific research agency;
Observation tower operation
PA: Carnegie Institution Of Washington
1530 P St Nw
202 387-6400

(P-17871)
CHILDRENS INST LOS
ANGELES (PA)
2121 W Temple St, Los Angeles
(90026-4915)
PHONE..............................213 385-5100
Bradley Myslinski, *Pr*
Martine Singer, *
Eugene Straub, *
EMP: 150 EST: 2011
SALES (est): 392.05K
SALES (corp-wide): 392.05K Privately
Held
Web: www.childrensinstitute.org
SIC: 8733 Noncommercial research
organizations

(P-17872)
DOHENY EYE INSTITUTE (PA)
150 N Orange Grove Blvd, Pasadena
(91103-3534)
PHONE..............................323 342-7120
EMP: 100 EST: 1947
SALES (est): 25.49MM
SALES (corp-wide): 25.49MM Privately
Held
Web: www.doheny.org
SIC: 8733 Medical research

(P-17873)
DXTERITY DIAGNOSTICS INC
(PA)
19500 S Rancho Way Ste 116, Compton
(90220-6017)
PHONE..............................310 537-7857
Doctor Bob Terbrueggen, *CEO*
Bill Coty, *
Jim Healy, *
Aviva Jacobs, *
Brett Swansiger, *Chief Commercialization
Officer*
EMP: 39 EST: 2006
SQ FT: 14,000
SALES (est): 12.89MM Privately Held
Web: www.dxterity.com

SIC: 8733 8071 2835 Medical research;
Medical laboratories; Diagnostic substances

(P-17874)
HISAMITSU PHARMACEUTICAL
CO INC
2730 Loker Ave W, Carlsbad (92010-6603)
PHONE..............................760 931-1756
EMP: 626
SIC: 8733 Medical research

(P-17875)
HOUSE RESEARCH INSTITUTE
2100 W 3rd St, Los Angeles (90057-1944)
PHONE..............................213 353-7012
EMP: 160
Web: www.hifla.org
SIC: 8733 Medical research

(P-17876)
INSTITUTE FOR DEFENSE
ANALYSES
Center For Communications RES
4320 Westerra Ct, San Diego (92121-1969)
PHONE..............................858 622-5439
Joe Buhler, *Mgr*
EMP: 170
SALES (corp-wide): 312.67MM Privately
Held
Web: www.ida.org
SIC: 8733 Research institute
PA: Institute For Defense Analyses Inc
730 E Glebe Rd
703 845-2000

(P-17877)
J CRAIG VENTER INSTITUTE
INC (PA)
4120 Capricorn Ln, La Jolla (92037-3498)
PHONE..............................301 795-7000
J Craig Venter, *CEO*
Karen Nelson, *
Reid Adler, *
Kathleen L Mattis, *
Robert Friedman, *
EMP: 275 EST: 1993
SQ FT: 125,000
SALES (est): 25.45MM
SALES (corp-wide): 25.45MM Privately
Held
Web: www.jcvi.org
SIC: 8733 8731 Research institute;
Biological research

(P-17878)
JWCH INSTITUTE INC
6912 Ajax Ave, Bell (90201-4057)
PHONE..............................323 562-5813
Annabel Munoz, *Mgr*
EMP: 178
SALES (corp-wide): 112.81MM Privately
Held
Web: www.jwchinstitute.org
SIC: 8733 Noncommercial research
organizations
PA: Jwch Institute, Inc.
5650 Jillson St
323 477-1171

(P-17879)
JWCH INSTITUTE INC
12360 Firestone Blvd, Norwalk
(90650-4324)
PHONE..............................562 281-0306
Oyamendan Itohan, *COO*
EMP: 178
SALES (corp-wide): 112.81MM Privately
Held
Web: www.jwchinstitute.org

SIC: 8733 Noncommercial research
organizations
PA: Jwch Institute, Inc.
5650 Jillson St
323 477-1171

(P-17880)
LA JOLLA INST FOR
IMMUNOLOGY
Also Called: La Jolla Inst For Allrgy Immnl
9420 Athena Cir, La Jolla (92037-1387)
PHONE..............................858 752-6500
Erica Ollmann Saphire, *Pr*
Stephen Wilson Ph.d., *Ex VP*
Michael Dollar, *CFO*
Eric Zwisler, *Ch Bd*
Skip Carpowich, *CFO*
EMP: 400 EST: 1988
SQ FT: 87,000
SALES (est): 92.27MM Privately Held
Web: www.lji.org
SIC: 8733 8731 Medical research;
Biotechnical research, commercial

(P-17881)
LUNDQUIST INSTITUTE FOR
BIOMEDICAL INNOVATION AT
HARBOR-UCLA MEDICAL
CENTER
Also Called: LA BIOMED
1124 W Carson St, Torrance (90502-2006)
PHONE..............................877 452-2674
EMP: 800 EST: 1952
SALES (est): 91.63MM Privately Held
Web: www.lundquist.org
SIC: 8733 Medical research

(P-17882)
MIND RESEARCH INSTITUTE
Also Called: Music Intllgnce Neuro Dev Inst
5281 California Ave Ste 300, Irvine
(92617-3219)
PHONE..............................949 345-8700
Brett Woudenberg, *CEO*
Matthew Peterson Crdo, *Prin*
Josephine Garrett, *CFO*
EMP: 160 EST: 2000
SALES (est): 18.12MM Privately Held
Web: www.mindresearch.org
SIC: 8733 Medical research

(P-17883)
NANOCOMPOSIX LLC
4878 Ronson Ct Ste J, San Diego
(92111-1806)
PHONE..............................858 565-4227
Steven Oldenburg, *Pr*
EMP: 90 EST: 2004
SQ FT: 16,000
SALES (est): 14MM
SALES (corp-wide): 30.48MM Privately
Held
Web: www.nanocomposix.com
SIC: 8733 Scientific research agency
PA: Fortis Life Sciences, Llc
222 Berkeley St Fl 18

(P-17884)
NANTCELL INC
2040 E Mariposa Ave, El Segundo
(90245-5027)
PHONE..............................310 883-1300
Patrick Soon-shiong, *CEO*
EMP: 248 EST: 2014
SALES (est): 10.15MM
SALES (corp-wide): 158.26K Publicly
Held
SIC: 8733 Bacteriological research
PA: Nantworks, Llc
9920 Jefferson Blvd

310 883-1300

(P-17885)
PERATON TECHNOLOGY SVCS
INC
2750 Womble Rd Ste 202, San Diego
(92106-6114)
PHONE..............................571 313-6000
John Curtis, *CEO*
EMP: 24
SQ FT: 10,000
SALES (corp-wide): 2.28B Privately Held
Web: www.perspecta.com
SIC: 8733 3812 7372 8711 Economic
research, noncommercial; Defense
systems and equipment; Application
computer software; Professional engineer
HQ: Peraton Technology Services Inc.
12975 Worldgate Dr
Herndon VA 20170
571 313-6000

(P-17886)
RANCHO RESEARCH INSTITUTE
Also Called: RRI
7601 Imperial Hwy, Downey (90242-3456)
P.O. Box 3500 (90242-3500)
PHONE..............................562 401-8111
Julia Laplount, *CEO*
Yaga Szlachcic, *
EMP: 175 EST: 1956
SQ FT: 15,000
SALES (est): 11.07MM Privately Held
Web: www.ranchoresearch.org
SIC: 8733 Educational research agency

(P-17887)
SAFE LIFE CORPORATION
Also Called: Trisoyn
12250 El Camino Real, San Diego
(92130-3076)
PHONE..............................858 794-3208
Richard Jaffe, *CEO*
John Metz, *
Pierre Jean Messier, *Vice Chairman*
EMP: 80 EST: 2006
SALES (est): 2.17MM Privately Held
Web: www.sellmax.com
SIC: 8733 Biotechnical research,
noncommercial

(P-17888)
SANFORD BRNHAM PRBYS
MED DSCVE (PA)
Also Called: SBP
10901 N Torrey Pines Rd, La Jolla
(92037-1005)
PHONE..............................858 795-5000
C Randal Mills, *CEO*
Kristiina Vuori, *
Robin Ryan, *
Gary Chessum, *
EMP: 966 EST: 1976
SQ FT: 397,000
SALES (est): 122.42MM
SALES (corp-wide): 122.42MM Privately
Held
Web: www.sbpdiscovery.org
SIC: 8733 Research institute

(P-17889)
SCIENCELL RESEARCH LABS
INC
1610 Faraday Ave, Carlsbad (92008-7313)
PHONE..............................760 602-8549
James Shen, *Pr*
Yong Juan Yu, *
Jim Shen, *
EMP: 40 EST: 1990

SQ FT: 9,000
SALES (est): 5.76MM **Privately Held**
Web: www.sciencellonline.com
SIC: 8733 8731 2836 Medical research; Commercial physical research; Biological products, except diagnostic

(P-17890)
SCRIPPS RESEARCH INSTITUTE
Also Called: Calibr A Division Scripps RES
11119 N Torrey Pines Rd Ste 100, La Jolla (92037-1012)
PHONE.................858 242-1000
EMP: 99
Web: www.scripps.edu
SIC: 8733 Medical research
PA: The Scripps Research Institute
10550 N Torrey Pines Rd

(P-17891)
SOUTHERN CAL INST FOR RES EDCA
Also Called: S C I R E
5901 E 7th St 151, Long Beach (90822-5201)
P.O. Box 15298 (90815-0298)
PHONE.................562 826-8139
Timothy R Morgan, *Pr*
Moti Kashyap Md, *Treas*
EMP: 80 **EST:** 1989
SALES (est): 3.4MM **Privately Held**
Web: www.scire-lb.org
SIC: 8733 Medical research

(P-17892)
THE RAND CORPORATION (PA)
Also Called: RAND
1776 Main St, Santa Monica (90401-3297)
P.O. Box 2138 (90407-2138)
PHONE.................310 393-0411
EMP: 900 **EST:** 1948
SALES (est): 467.2MM
SALES (corp-wide): 467.2MM **Privately Held**
Web: www.rand.org
SIC: 8733 8732 8742 Noncommercial research organizations; Commercial nonphysical research; Management consulting services

(P-17893)
UNITED STTES DEPT ENRGY BRKLEY
Also Called: Lawrence Berkeley National Lab
555 W Imperial Hwy, Brea (92821-4802)
PHONE.................510 486-7089
EMP: 154
Web: www.lbl.gov
SIC: 8733 9611 Noncommercial research organizations; Energy development and conservation agency, government
HQ: United States Department Of Energy
Berkeley Office
1 Cyclotron Rd
Berkeley CA 94720
510 486-5784

(P-17894)
UNIVERSITY CAL SAN DIEGO
Also Called: Health Services Research Ctr
5440 Morehouse Dr Ste 2600, San Diego (92121-6708)
PHONE.................858 622-1771
Theodore Ganiats, *Ex Dir*
EMP: 100
SALES (corp-wide): 534.4MM **Privately Held**
Web: www.ucsd.edu

SIC: 8733 8221 9411 Noncommercial research organizations; University; Administration of educational programs
HQ: University Of California, San Diego
9500 Gilman Dr
La Jolla CA 92093
858 534-2230

(P-17895)
VIACYTE INC
5580 Morehouse Dr Ste 100, San Diego (92121-1755)
PHONE.................858 455-3708
Paul K Laikind, *Pr*
Allan Robins, *VP*
Howard Foyt, *VP*
Anthony Gringeri, *Chief Development Officer*
EMP: 55 **EST:** 1999
SALES (est): 18.04MM **Privately Held**
Web: www.vrtx.com
SIC: 8733 2836 Medical research; Biological products, except diagnostic

(P-17896)
VITAL RESEARCH LLC
6300 Wilshire Blvd Ste 860, Los Angeles (90048-5202)
PHONE.................323 951-1670
EMP: 91 **EST:** 1982
SQ FT: 1,600
SALES (est): 1.84MM **Privately Held**
Web: www.vitalresearch.com
SIC: 8733 7361 8732 Noncommercial research organizations; Employment agencies; Market analysis or research

(P-17897)
WILLOW LABORATORIES INC
Also Called: Nutu
15750 Alton Pkwy, Irvine (92618-3825)
PHONE.................949 679-6100
Gerry Hammarth, *CFO*
EMP: 80 **EST:** 1998
SALES (est): 12.91MM **Publicly Held**
Web: www.willowlaboratories.com
SIC: 8733 Biotechnical research, noncommercial
PA: Masimo Corporation
52 Discovery

8734 Testing Laboratories

(P-17898)
911 HEALTH INC
701 Santa Monica Blvd Ste 300, Santa Monica (90401-2624)
PHONE.................310 560-8509
Steve Farzam, *COO*
EMP: 99
SALES (est): 6.35MM **Privately Held**
Web: www.911health.com
SIC: 8734 Testing laboratories

(P-17899)
AIRCRAFT XRAY LABORATORIES INC
5216 Pacific Blvd, Huntington Park (90255-2529)
PHONE.................323 587-4141
Gary G Newton, *CEO*
James Newton, *
Sandi Spelic, *
Justin Guzman, *
EMP: 80 **EST:** 1938
SQ FT: 60,000
SALES (est): 8.08MM **Privately Held**
Web: www.aircraftxray.com

SIC: 8734 7384 3471 Testing laboratories; Photograph developing and retouching; Plating and polishing

(P-17900)
ALCON VISION LLC
20521 Lake Forest Dr, Lake Forest (92630-7741)
PHONE.................949 505-6890
EMP: 553
Web: www.alcon.com
SIC: 8734 Testing laboratories
HQ: Alcon Vision, Llc
6201 South Fwy
Fort Worth TX 76134
817 293-0450

(P-17901)
ALS GROUP USA CORP
Also Called: Bioscreen Testing Services
3904 Del Amo Blvd, Torrance (90503-2160)
PHONE.................310 214-0043
Ranil Fernando, *Genl Mgr*
EMP: 70
SIC: 8734 8731 Testing laboratories; Commercial physical research
HQ: Als Group Usa, Corp.
10450 Stncliff Rd Ste 210
Houston TX 77099
281 530-5656

(P-17902)
ANALYSTS INC
Also Called: Analysts Maintenance and Labs
3401 Jack Northrop Ave, Hawthorne (90250-4428)
P.O. Box 2955 (90509-2955)
PHONE.................800 424-0099
EMP: 148
Web: www.oil-testing.com
SIC: 8734 Product testing laboratory, safety or performance

(P-17903)
ANALYTICAL PACE SERVICES LLC
4100 Atlas Ct, Bakersfield (93308-4510)
PHONE.................800 878-4911
Stuart Buttram, *Brnch Mgr*
EMP: 104
SALES (corp-wide): 64.88MM **Privately Held**
Web: www.pacelabs.com
SIC: 8734 Water testing laboratory
HQ: Pace Analytical Services, Llc
2665 Long Lake Rd Ste 300
Roseville MN 55113

(P-17904)
APTIM CORP
18100 Von Karman Ave # 450, Irvine (92612-0169)
PHONE.................949 261-6441
EMP: 502
SALES (corp-wide): 2.2B **Privately Held**
SIC: 8734 Pollution testing
HQ: Aptim Corp.
10001 Woodloch Forest Dr # 450
The Woodlands TX 70802
832 823-2700

(P-17905)
BABCOCK LABORATORIES INC
Also Called: E. S. Babcock & Sons
6100 Quail Valley Ct, Riverside (92507-0704)
P.O. Box 432 (92502-0432)
PHONE.................951 653-3351
Allison Mackenzie, *CEO*
Marianna Etcheverria, *

Lawrence Chrystal, *
EMP: 70 **EST:** 1978
SQ FT: 20,000
SALES (est): 11.1MM **Privately Held**
Web: www.babcocklabs.com
SIC: 8734 Water testing laboratory

(P-17906)
CALIFORNIA LAB SCIENCES LLC
Also Called: West Pacific Medical Lab
10200 Pioneer Blvd Ste 500, Santa Fe Springs (90670-6008)
PHONE.................562 758-6900
EMP: 300 **EST:** 2009
SALES (est): 3.47MM **Privately Held**
Web: www.westpaclab.com
SIC: 8734 Testing laboratories

(P-17907)
CATALENT SAN DIEGO INC
7330 Carroll Rd Ste 200, San Diego (92121-2364)
PHONE.................858 805-6383
Timothy Scott, *Pr*
Bryan Knox, *OF PHARMACEUTICS**
Jason Everett, *
EMP: 120 **EST:** 1999
SQ FT: 6,600
SALES (est): 22.99MM **Privately Held**
Web: catalent.dejobs.org
SIC: 8734 8731 Testing laboratories; Commercial research laboratory
HQ: Catalent Pharma Solutions, Inc.
14 Schoolhouse Rd
Somerset NJ 08873

(P-17908)
CERTIFIED LABORATORIES LLC
3125 N Damon Way, Burbank (91505-1016)
PHONE.................818 845-0070
Doug Shepard, *Mgr*
EMP: 1500
SALES (corp-wide): 80.43MM **Privately Held**
Web: www.certified-laboratories.com
SIC: 8734 Food testing service
PA: Certified Laboratories, Llc
65 Marcus Dr
516 576-1400

(P-17909)
COLOR DESIGN LABORATORY INC (PA)
Also Called: Color Design Labs
9533 Irondale Ave, Chatsworth (91311-5007)
PHONE.................818 341-5100
Gilberto Amparo, *CEO*
Maria Amparo, *
Maria Gonzalez, *
▲ **EMP:** 100 **EST:** 2010
SALES (est): 11MM **Privately Held**
Web: www.colordesignlaboratory.com
SIC: 8734 Testing laboratories

(P-17910)
CONSUMER SAFETY ANALYTICS LLC
Also Called: Cannasafe
7027 Hayvenhurst Ave, Van Nuys (91406-3802)
PHONE.................818 922-2416
Aaron Riley, *Prin*
Antonio Frazier, *Prin*
Bosco Ramirez, *Prin*
EMP: 99 **EST:** 2017
SALES (est): 2.32MM **Privately Held**

SIC: 8734 Testing laboratories

(P-17911)
COUNTY OF LOS ANGELES
Also Called: Hertzbrg-Dvis Frnsic Scnce Ctr
1800 Paseo Rancho Castilla, Los Angeles
(90032-4210)
PHONE....................323 267-6167
Joseph Hourigan, *Brnch Mgr*
EMP: 122
Web: www.lacounty.gov
SIC: 8734 8731 Forensic laboratory;
Commercial physical research
PA: County Of Los Angeles
500 W Temple St Ste 437
213 974-1101

(P-17912)
DICKSON TESTING CO INC (DH)
11126 Palmer Ave, South Gate
(90280-7492)
PHONE....................562 862-8378
Robert Lyddon, *Pr*
Jim Scanell, *
EMP: 80 EST: 1970
SQ FT: 40,000
SALES (est): 10.82MM
SALES (corp-wide): 364.48B Publicly
Held
Web: www.dicksontesting.com
SIC: 8734 Metallurgical testing laboratory
HQ: Precision Castparts Corp.
5885 Meadows Rd Ste 620
Lake Oswego OR 97035
503 946-4800

(P-17913)
ELEMENT MATERIALS (DH)
15062 Bolsa Chica St, Huntington Beach
(92649-1023)
PHONE....................714 892-1961
Charles Noall, *Pr*
Pete Regan, *
Jo Wetz, *
Jeff Joyce, *
Eelco Niermeijer, *
▲ EMP: 80 EST: 1997
SQ FT: 4,500
SALES (est): 25.02MM Privately Held
Web: www.element.com
SIC: 8734 Metallurgical testing laboratory
HQ: Element Materials Technology Group
Us Holdings Inc.
15062 Bolsa Chica St
Huntington Beach CA 92649
714 892-1961

(P-17914)
ELEMENT MTRLS TECH HB INC
Also Called: Element Rancho Dominguez
18100 S Wilmington Ave, Compton
(90220-5909)
PHONE....................310 632-8500
Chuck Gee, *Genl Mgr*
EMP: 86
Web: www.element.com
SIC: 8734 Metallurgical testing laboratory
HQ: Element Materials Technology
Huntington Beach Llc
15062 Bolsa Chica Rd
Huntington Beach CA 92649
714 892-1961

(P-17915)
ELLISON INSTITUTE LLC (PA)
Also Called: Ellison Institute Technology
12414 Exposition Blvd, Los Angeles
(90064-1016)
PHONE....................310 228-6400
Paul Marinelli, *CEO*

Jason Bowman, *
EMP: 105 EST: 2019
SQ FT: 80,000
SALES (est): 10.43MM
SALES (corp-wide): 10.43MM Privately
Held
Web: www.eit.org
SIC: 8734 Testing laboratories

(P-17916)
EUROFINS EATON ANALYTICAL LLC (DH)
750 Royal Oaks Dr Ste 100, Monrovia
(91016-6359)
PHONE....................626 386-1100
Wilson Hershey, *Ch*
Bosco Ramirez, *
Andrew Eaton, *
Yongtao Bruce Li, *Dir*
EMP: 93 EST: 2012
SALES (est): 24.27MM
SALES (corp-wide): 336.21K Privately
Held
Web: www.eurofinsus.com
SIC: 8734 Testing laboratories
HQ: Eurofins Lancaster Laboratories, Llc
2425 New Holland Pike
Lancaster PA 17601
717 656-2300

(P-17917)
FORENSIC ANALYTICAL SPC INC
Also Called: Forensic Analytical
20535 Belshaw Ave, Carson (90746-3505)
PHONE....................310 763-2374
Bruce White, *Prin*
EMP: 94
SALES (corp-wide): 4.72MM Privately
Held
Web: www.facs.com
SIC: 8734 8748 8731 8071 Forensic
laboratory; Environmental consultant;
Commercial physical research; Medical
laboratories
PA: Forensic Analytical Specialties
Incorporated
3777 Depot Rd Ste 409
510 887-8828

(P-17918)
HYUNDAI AMER TECHNICAL CTR INC
Also Called: Hyundai America/Tech Center
12610 Eastend Ave, Chino (91710-3006)
PHONE....................909 627-3525
Scott Kin, *Mgr*
EMP: 113
SQ FT: 19,620
Web: www.hatci.com
SIC: 8734 8711 Product testing laboratories;
Mechanical engineering
HQ: Hyundai America Technical Center
Incorporated
6800 Geddes Rd
Ypsilanti MI 48198
734 337-2500

(P-17919)
INTERTEK USA INC
Also Called: Intertek Pharmaceutical Svcs
10420 Wateridge Cir, San Diego
(92121-5773)
PHONE....................858 558-2599
Arron Xu, *Mgr*
EMP: 100
SALES (corp-wide): 4.15B Privately Held
Web: www.intertek.com
SIC: 8734 Testing laboratories
HQ: Intertek Usa Inc.
200 Westlake Park Blvd # 1010

Houston TX 77079
713 543-3600

(P-17920)
MICHELSON LABORATORIES INC (PA)
6280 Chalet Dr, Commerce (90040-3704)
PHONE....................562 928-0553
Grant Michelson, *Pr*
Jack E Michelson, *
EMP: 70 EST: 1970
SQ FT: 20,000
SALES (est): 10.48MM
SALES (corp-wide): 10.48MM Privately
Held
Web: www.michelsonlab.com
SIC: 8734 Food testing service

(P-17921)
MILLENNIUM HEALTH LLC
16981 Via Tazon Ste F, San Diego
(92127-1645)
PHONE....................877 451-3534
Jennifer Strickland, *CEO*
Howard Appel, *
David Cohen, *
Martin Price, *
Janna Sipes, *Regional COMP*
EMP: 258 EST: 2007
SALES (est): 56.01MM Privately Held
Web: www.millenniumhealth.com
SIC: 8734 Testing laboratories

(P-17922)
NATIONAL GENETICS INSTITUTE
2440 S Sepulveda Blvd Ste 235, Los
Angeles (90064-1748)
PHONE....................310 996-6610
Mike Aicher, *CEO*
Geri Cox, *
EMP: 200 EST: 1991
SQ FT: 35,000
SALES (est): 4.79MM
SALES (corp-wide): 12.18B Publicly Held
Web: plasma.labcorp.com
SIC: 8734 Testing laboratories
HQ: Laboratory Corporation Of America
Holdings
358 S Main St
Burlington NC 27215

(P-17923)
PHAMATECH INCORPORATED
15175 Innovation Dr, San Diego
(92128-3401)
PHONE....................888 635-5840
Tuan Pham, *CEO*
Tuan H Pham, *
▲ EMP: 200 EST: 1991
SQ FT: 50,000
SALES (est): 10.44MM Privately Held
Web: www.phamatech.com
SIC: 8734 5047 Forensic laboratory; Medical
laboratory equipment

(P-17924)
QUALICON DIAGNOSTICS LLC
941 Avenida Acaso, Camarillo
(93012-8700)
PHONE....................805 388-2383
Steven Nason, *CEO*
EMP: 278 EST: 2016
SALES (est): 1.71MM
SALES (corp-wide): 5.1B Privately Held
Web: www.hygiena.com
SIC: 8734 Food testing service
HQ: Hygiena Llc
941 Avenida Acaso
Camarillo CA 93012
805 388-8007

(P-17925)
SCANTIBODIES LABORATORY INC (PA)
9336 Abraham Way, Santee (92071-2861)
PHONE....................619 258-9300
Thomas L Cantor, *CEO*
John Van Duzer, *
▲ EMP: 240 EST: 1976
SQ FT: 60,500
SALES (est): 24.96MM
SALES (corp-wide): 24.96MM Privately
Held
Web: www.scantibodies.com
SIC: 8734 Testing laboratories

(P-17926)
SHOGUN LABS INC (PA)
340 S Lemon Ave # 1085, Walnut
(91789-2706)
PHONE....................317 676-2719
Finbarr Taylor, *CEO*
EMP: 146 EST: 2015
SALES (est): 2.08MM
SALES (corp-wide): 2.08MM Privately
Held
Web: www.getshogun.com
SIC: 8734 Testing laboratories

(P-17927)
TANDEX TEST LABS INC
15849 Business Center Dr, Irwindale
(91706-2053)
PHONE....................626 962-7166
Brian Peale, *Pr*
Charles T Goolsby, *
EMP: 49 EST: 1980
SQ FT: 15,000
SALES (est): 9.37MM Privately Held
Web: www.tandexlabs.com
SIC: 8734 3674 Testing laboratories; Hybrid
integrated circuits

(P-17928)
TWINING INC (PA)
Also Called: Twining Laboratories
4811 Airport Plaza Dr, Long Beach
(90815-1371)
PHONE....................562 426-3355
Edward Butch M Twining Junior, *CEO*
Brian Kramer, *
Robert M Ryan, *
Boris Stein D Sc, *VP*
Linas Vitkus, *
EMP: 81 EST: 1959
SALES (est): 24.71MM
SALES (corp-wide): 24.71MM Privately
Held
Web: www.twininginc.com
SIC: 8734 Testing laboratories

(P-17929)
WECK ANLYTICAL ENVMTL SVCS INC
Also Called: Weck Laboratories
14859 Clark Ave, City Of Industry
(91745-1379)
PHONE....................626 336-2139
Alfredo Pierri, *Pr*
Alfredo E Pierri, *
Cecilia G Pierri, *
EMP: 74 EST: 1964
SQ FT: 27,000
SALES (est): 10.82MM Privately Held
Web: www.wecklabs.com
SIC: 8734 Testing laboratories

(P-17930)
WESTPAC LABS INC
10200 Pioneer Blvd # 500, Santa Fe
Springs (90670-6000)

PHONE..............................562 906-5227
EMP: 452
SALES (est): 53MM Privately Held
Web: www.westpaclab.com
SIC: 8734 8071 Testing laboratories;
Pathological laboratory

(P-17931)
XCOM LABS INC
9450 Carroll Park Dr, San Diego
(92121-5201)
PHONE..............................858 987-9266
Paul E Jacobs, *Prin*
Derek Aberle, *
Matt Grob, *
EMP: 70 EST: 2019
SALES (est): 4.39MM Privately Held
Web: www.globalstar.com
SIC: 8734 Testing laboratories

8741 Management Services

(P-17932)
360 HEALTH PLAN INC
Also Called: 360 Clinic
13800 Arizona St Ste 104, Westminster
(92683-3951)
PHONE..............................800 446-8888
Vince Pien, *CEO*
David Ngo, *CFO*
Mike Lee, *COO*
EMP: 200 EST: 2020
SALES (est): 1.78MM Privately Held
Web: www.360clinic.md
SIC: 8741 Hospital management

(P-17933)
360 SUPPORT SERVICES
306 S Myrtle Ave, Monrovia (91016-2849)
P.O. Box 801238 (91380-1238)
PHONE..............................866 360-6468
Kelly Martinez, *CEO*
Ola Ostlund, *
Renee Fields, *
EMP: 72 EST: 2016
SALES (est): 425.46K Privately Held
SIC: 8741 7349 Nursing and personal care
facility management; Building cleaning
service

(P-17934)
ACTIVCARE LIVING INC (PA)
10603 Rancho Bernardo Rd, San Diego
(92123)
PHONE..............................858 565-4424
William Major Chance, *CEO*
D Kevin Moriarty, *VP*
Frank A Virgadamo, *
B Renee Barnard, *
Todd A Shetter, *
EMP: 100 EST: 1979
SQ FT: 9,000
SALES (est): 29.14MM
SALES (corp-wide): 29.14MM Privately
Held
Web: www.activcareliving.com
SIC: 8741 Nursing and personal care facility
management

(P-17935)
AEG MANAGEMENT LACC LLC
Also Called: Los Angeles Convention Center
1201 S Figueroa St, Los Angeles
(90015-1308)
PHONE..............................213 741-1151
Brad Gessner, *Sr VP*
Greg Rosicky, *
Carisa Malanum, *
Ellen Schwartz, *

Keith Hilsgen, *
EMP: 220 EST: 2013
SALES (est): 302.15K Privately Held
Web: www.lacclink.com
SIC: 8741 Business management
HQ: Aeg Facilities, Llc
800 W Olympic Blvd Ste 30
Los Angeles CA 90015
213 763-7700

(P-17936)
AJIT HEALTHCARE INC
316 S Westlake Ave, Los Angeles
(90057-2906)
PHONE..............................213 484-0510
Jasvant N Modi, *Pr*
Sagar Parikh, *Prin*
EMP: 80 EST: 2004
SALES (est): 2.37MM Privately Held
Web: www.wlchospital.com
SIC: 8741 Nursing and personal care facility
management

(P-17937)
**ALLEGIS RESIDENTIAL SVCS
INC**
Also Called: Aspm-Sandiego
9340 Hazard Way Ste B2, San Diego
(92123-1228)
PHONE..............................858 430-5700
Karen Martinez, *CEO*
Jorge Martinez, *
Steve Howe, *
EMP: 80 EST: 1971
SQ FT: 4,000
SALES (est): 3.75MM Privately Held
Web: www.aspm-sandiego.com
SIC: 8741 Business management
PA: S.H.E. Manages Properties, Inc.
9340 Hazard Way Ste B2

(P-17938)
**ALLZONE MANAGEMENT SVCS
INC**
Also Called: Allzone Management Solutions
3795 La Crescenta Ave Ste 200, Glendale
(91208-1072)
PHONE..............................213 291-8879
Jonathan Rodrigues, *Pr*
EMP: 500 EST: 2011
SALES (est): 1.32MM Privately Held
Web: www.allzonems.com
SIC: 8741 Management services

(P-17939)
ALTER MANAGEMENT LLC
Also Called: Alter Health Group
34232 Pacific Coast Hwy Ste D, Dana Point
(92629-3856)
PHONE..............................949 629-0214
Michael Castanon, *Prin*
EMP: 100 EST: 2018
SALES (est): 7.11MM Privately Held
SIC: 8741 Management services

(P-17940)
**ALTURA MANAGEMENT
SERVICES LLC**
1401 N Montebello Blvd, Montebello
(90640-2584)
PHONE..............................323 768-2898
Jose Esparza, *CFO*
EMP: 375 EST: 2015
SALES (est): 3.09MM Privately Held
Web: www.alturamso.com
SIC: 8741 Management services

(P-17941)
**AMERICAN INTGRTED
RSOURCES INC**
Also Called: Air Demolition and Envmtl
2341 N Pacific St, Orange (92865-2601)
PHONE..............................714 921-4100
Thomas C Stevens, *CEO*
EMP: 80 EST: 2013
SALES (est): 9.95MM Privately Held
Web: www.american-integrated.com
SIC: 8741 Construction management

(P-17942)
**AMERICAN MANAGEMENT
SVCS W LLC**
1240 Bethel Ln, Santa Maria (93458-8386)
PHONE..............................805 352-1921
EMP: 330
SALES (corp-wide): 5.34MM Privately
Held
Web: www.hollandamerica.com
SIC: 8741 Management services
PA: American Management Services West
Llc
11235 Se 6th St
206 215-9700

(P-17943)
**AMERICAN MZHOU DNGPO
GROUP INC**
4520 Maine Ave, Baldwin Park
(91706-2671)
PHONE..............................626 820-9239
Gang Wang, *CEO*
Xiaoteng Fu, *
Di Liang, *CFO*
EMP: 100 EST: 2012
SALES (est): 2.31MM Privately Held
SIC: 8741 Restaurant management

(P-17944)
**ANSER ADVISORY
MANAGEMENT LLC (HQ)**
1820 E 1st St Ste 410, Santa Ana
(92705-8311)
PHONE..............................714 276-1135
Sudhir Damle, *Pr*
Eric Slaasted, *
Melanie Estes, *
Hemalata Damle, *
Gary Cooley, *
EMP: 140 EST: 2012
SQ FT: 6,000
SALES (est): 10.33MM Privately Held
Web: www.dhsconsulting.com
SIC: 8741 Construction management
PA: Accenture Public Limited Company
7 Grand Canal

(P-17945)
APCN-ACO INC
223 N Garfield Ave Ste 208, Monterey Park
(91754-1700)
PHONE..............................626 288-7988
EMP: 100 EST: 2016
SALES (est): 312.98K Publicly Held
SIC: 8741 Management services
PA: Astrana Health, Inc.
1668 S Garfield Ave Fl 2

(P-17946)
APPLECARE MEDICAL MGT LLC
18 Centerpointe Dr Ste 100, La Palma
(90623-1028)
P.O. Box 6014 (90702-6014)
PHONE..............................714 443-4507
Vinod Jivrajka, *Prin*
EMP: 108 EST: 2010
SALES (est): 11.57MM

SALES (corp-wide): 371.62B Publicly
Held
Web: www.optum.com
SIC: 8741 Nursing and personal care facility
management
PA: Unitedhealth Group Incorporated
9900 Bren Rd E
800 328-5979

(P-17947)
**ASSET MANAGEMENT TR SVCS
LLC**
Also Called: A Mediation & Resolution Ctr
1455 Frazee Rd Ste 500, San Diego
(92108-4350)
PHONE..............................858 457-2202
Steven K Dony, *Managing Member*
Rochelle O'donnell Juarez, *Managing
Member*
EMP: 72 EST: 1983
SALES (est): 1.8MM Privately Held
Web: amediationresoluti.wixsite.com
SIC: 8741 Financial management for
business

(P-17948)
**AWI MANAGEMENT
CORPORATION**
1800 E Lakeshore Dr, Lake Elsinore
(92530-4469)
PHONE..............................951 674-8200
Angelica Chaidez, *Brnch Mgr*
EMP: 120
SALES (corp-wide): 4.23MM Privately
Held
Web: www.awimc.com
SIC: 8741 Business management
PA: Awi Management Corporation
120 Center St
530 745-6170

(P-17949)
AZUL HOSPITALITY GROUP INC
800 W Ivy St Ste D, San Diego
(92101-1771)
PHONE..............................619 223-4200
Alvaro Fraile, *CEO*
Douglas Leiber, *
Mark Crisci, *
EMP: 197 EST: 2007
SALES (est): 9.51MM Privately Held
Web: www.azulhospitalitygroup.com
SIC: 8741 Business management

(P-17950)
**BEECH STREET CORPORATION
(HQ)**
25550 Commercentre Dr Ste 200, Lake
Forest (92630-8893)
PHONE..............................949 672-1000
William Fickling Junior, *Ch*
William Hale, *
Norm Werthwein, *
Rick Markus, *
Jon Bird, *
EMP: 350 EST: 1951
SQ FT: 60,000
SALES (est): 6.91MM
SALES (corp-wide): 961.52MM Publicly
Held
SIC: 8741 Administrative management
PA: Multiplan Corporation
640 5th Ave Fl 12
212 380-7500

(P-17951)
**BELLWETHER ASSET MGT INC
(PA)**
Also Called: Bellwether

200 N Pacific Coast Hwy Ste 1400, El
Segundo (90245-5640)
PHONE......................310 525-3022
Dennis Grzeskowiak, *CEO*
EMP: 71 **EST:** 2013
SALES (est): 14.36MM
SALES (corp-wide): 14.36MM **Privately
Held**
Web: www.bellwetherco.com
SIC: 8741 Financial management for
business

(P-17952)
BJS RESTAURANT
OPERATIONS CO
Also Called: BJ's Restaurant & Brewhouse
7755 Center Ave Ste 300, Huntington
Beach (92647-3084)
PHONE......................714 500-2440
EMP: 258 **EST:** 2017
SALES (est): 1.62MM
SALES (corp-wide): 1.33B **Publicly Held**
SIC: 8741 Restaurant management
PA: Bj's Restaurants, Inc.
7755 Center Ave Ste 300
714 500-2400

(P-17953)
BON APPETIT MANAGEMENT
CO
Also Called: Bon Appetit
1200 Getty Center Dr, Los Angeles
(90049-1657)
PHONE......................310 440-6052
EMP: 183
SALES (corp-wide): 39.16B **Privately Held**
Web: www.bamco.com
SIC: 8741 Management services
HQ: Bon Appetit Management Co.
201 Rdwood Shres Pkwy Ste
Redwood City CA 94065
650 798-8000

(P-17954)
BON APPETIT MANAGEMENT
CO
1050 N Mills Ave, Claremont (91711-3908)
PHONE......................909 607-2788
EMP: 164
SALES (corp-wide): 39.16B **Privately Held**
Web: www.bamco.com
SIC: 8741 Management services
HQ: Bon Appetit Management Co.
201 Rdwood Shres Pkwy Ste
Redwood City CA 94065
650 798-8000

(P-17955)
BON APPETIT MANAGEMENT
CO
Also Called: Getty Center
1200 Getty Center Dr Ste 100, Los Angeles
(90049-1677)
PHONE......................310 440-6209
Javier Ramirez, *Mgr*
EMP: 229
SALES (corp-wide): 39.16B **Privately Held**
Web: www.getty.edu
SIC: 8741 Restaurant management
HQ: Bon Appetit Management Co.
201 Rdwood Shres Pkwy Ste
Redwood City CA 94065
650 798-8000

(P-17956)
BRIDGE GROUP HH INC
5090 Shoreham Pl Ste 109, San Diego
(92122-5934)
PHONE......................858 455-5000

Jeff Mongonia, *CEO*
Jeff Reynolds, *CFO*
April Collins, *COO*
Marsha Lambert, *CCO*
Andrea Goodwin, *Ex VP*
EMP: 126 **EST:** 2016
SALES (est): 3.9MM **Privately Held**
Web: www.bridgehh.com
SIC: 8741 Nursing and personal care facility
management

(P-17957)
CAL STATE LA UNIV AUX SVCS
INC
Also Called: UNIVERSITY COMMERCIAL
SERVICES
5151 State University Dr, Los Angeles
(90032-4226)
PHONE......................323 343-2531
Tariq Marji, *Ex Dir*
▲ **EMP:** 600 **EST:** 1954
SQ FT: 108,000
SALES (est): 34.08MM **Privately Held**
Web: www.calstatela.edu
SIC: 8741 5942 5651 5812 Business
management; College book stores; Unisex
clothing stores; Cafeteria

(P-17958)
CAMARILLO HEALTHCARE
CENTER
205 Granada St, Camarillo (93010-7715)
PHONE......................805 482-9805
Erica Olsen, *Admn*
Angie Chavz, *Admn*
EMP: 253 **EST:** 2007
SALES (est): 1.76MM
SALES (corp-wide): 3.73B **Publicly Held**
Web: www.camarillohealthcare.com
SIC: 8741 Nursing and personal care facility
management
PA: The Ensign Group Inc
29222 Rncho Vejo Rd Ste 1
949 487-9500

(P-17959)
CAPITAL GROUP COMPANIES
INC (PA)
Also Called: Capital Group, The
333 S Hope St Fl 53, Los Angeles
(90071-1418)
PHONE......................213 486-9200
Tim Armour, *Ch*
Jody Jonsson, *Vice Chairman**
Rob Klausner, *
Matt O'connor, *Distributor*
EMP: 800 **EST:** 1931
SQ FT: 106,000
SALES (est): 7.25B
SALES (corp-wide): 7.25B **Privately Held**
Web: www.capitalgroup.com
SIC: 8741 6722 6091 6282 Management
services; Mutual fund sales, on own account
; Nondeposit trust facilities; Investment
advice

(P-17960)
CAREMORE MEDICAL
MANAGEMENT COMPANY A
CALIFORNIA LIMITED
PARTNERSHIP
Also Called: Caremore AP
12900 Park Plaza Dr Ste 150, Cerritos
(90703-9329)
PHONE......................562 741-4300
EMP: 900
SIC: 8741 5047 Business management;
Medical equipment and supplies

(P-17961)
CGP MAINTENANCE CNSTR
SVCS INC
8614 Siesta Rd, Santee (92071-4537)
PHONE......................858 454-7326
Jim Robinson, *Pr*
EMP: 70 **EST:** 1982
SQ FT: 3,000
SALES (est): 11.33MM **Privately Held**
Web: www.cgpconstruction.com
SIC: 8741 Construction management

(P-17962)
CHAN FAMILY PARTNERSHIP LP
801 S Grand Ave Apt 1811, Los Angeles
(90017-4673)
PHONE......................626 322-7132
Ann Chan, *Pt*
EMP: 100 **EST:** 2017
SALES (est): 329.81K **Privately Held**
SIC: 8741 Restaurant management

(P-17963)
CHANCELLOR HEALTH CARE
INC
Also Called: Chancellor Place
24350 Jackson Ave, Murrieta (92562-1905)
PHONE......................951 696-5753
Jennifer Benner, *Admn*
EMP: 86
Web: www.chancellorhealthcare.com
SIC: 8741 8051 Nursing and personal care
facility management; Skilled nursing care
facilities
PA: Chancellor Health Care, Inc.
115 Johnson St

(P-17964)
CHANCELLOR HEALTH CARE
INC
Also Called: Chancellor Place
6500 Butterfield Ranch Rd, Chino Hills
(91709-6379)
PHONE......................909 606-2553
Michelle Augsburger, *Pr*
EMP: 110
Web: www.chancellorhealthcare.com
SIC: 8741 8051 Nursing and personal care
facility management; Skilled nursing care
facilities
PA: Chancellor Health Care, Inc.
115 Johnson St

(P-17965)
CIK POWER DISTRIBUTORS LLC
240 W Grove Ave, Orange (92865-3204)
PHONE......................714 938-0297
Chris A Christopher, *Managing Member*
Stephen G Carter, *
Robert M Tulley, *
EMP: 84 **EST:** 2005
SALES (est): 22.8MM **Privately Held**
Web: www.cikpower.com
SIC: 8741 Construction management

(P-17966)
CITY OF HOPE (PA)
Also Called: Beckman RES Inst of The Cy
Hop
1500 Duarte Rd, Duarte (91010-3012)
PHONE......................626 256-4673
TOLL FREE: 800
EMP: 260 **EST:** 1929
SALES (est): 330.02MM
SALES (corp-wide): 330.02MM **Privately
Held**
Web: www.cityofhope.org

SIC: 8741 8399 Hospital management; Fund
raising organization, non-fee basis

(P-17967)
CITY OF MENIFEE
29844 Haun Rd, Menifee (92586-6539)
PHONE......................951 672-6777
Kathy Benett, *City Clerk**
EMP: 90 **EST:** 2008
SALES (est): 142.99MM **Privately Held**
Web: www.cityofmenifee.us
SIC: 8741 Personnel management

(P-17968)
COLLECTIVE MGT GROUP LLC
Also Called: Collective Management Group
8383 Wilshire Blvd Ste 1050, Beverly Hills
(90211-2415)
PHONE......................323 655-8585
Reza Izad, *
Gary Binkow, *
Jordan Berliant, *
Jordan Toplitzky, *
EMP: 206 **EST:** 1999
SQ FT: 15,000
SALES (est): 2.04MM **Privately Held**
SIC: 8741 Management services

(P-17969)
CORVEL CORPORATION
1920 Main St Ste 900, Irvine (92614-7228)
PHONE......................503 222-3144
EMP: 120
Web: www.corvel.com
SIC: 8741 Nursing and personal care facility
management
PA: Corvel Corporation
5128 Apche Plume Rd Ste 4

(P-17970)
CORVEL CORPORATION
Also Called: Corvel
1100 W Town And Country Rd Ste 400,
Orange (92868-4645)
PHONE......................714 385-8500
Laurie Wright, *Brnch Mgr*
EMP: 147
Web: www.corvel.com
SIC: 8741 Management services
PA: Corvel Corporation
5128 Apche Plume Rd Ste 4

(P-17971)
COUNTRY VILLA SERVICE
CORP (PA)
Also Called: Country Villa Health Services
2400 E Katella Ave Ste 800, Anaheim
(92806-5955)
PHONE......................310 574-3733
Stephen Reissman, *CEO*
Diane Reissman, *
Cheryl Petterson, *
EMP: 80 **EST:** 1972
SQ FT: 24,000
SALES (est): 28.62MM
SALES (corp-wide): 28.62MM **Privately
Held**
Web: www.evictionlawyer.com
SIC: 8741 Nursing and personal care facility
management

(P-17972)
COUNTRY VILLA SERVICE CORP
Also Called: Country Villa E Convalescent
2415 S Western Ave, Los Angeles
(90018-2608)
PHONE......................323 734-1101
Phadra Johnson, *Mgr*
EMP: 102
SALES (corp-wide): 28.62MM **Privately
Held**

Web: www.evictionlawyer.com
SIC: 8741 8051 8011 8059 Nursing and
personal care facility management; Skilled
nursing care facilities; Clinic, operated by
physicians; Convalescent home
PA: Country Villa Service Corp.
2400 E Katella Ave # 800
310 574-3733

(P-17973)
COUNTRY VILLA SERVICE CORP
3233 W Pico Blvd, Los Angeles
(90019-3698)
PHONE..................323 734-9122
Mike Demchuck, *Mgr*
EMP: 102
SALES (corp-wide): 28.62MM **Privately
Held**
Web: www.evictionlawyer.com
SIC: 8741 8051 Nursing and personal care
facility management; Skilled nursing care
facilities
PA: Country Villa Service Corp.
2400 E Katella Ave # 800
310 574-3733

(P-17974)
COUNTRY VILLA SERVICE CORP
3002 Rowena Ave, Los Angeles
(90039-2005)
PHONE..................323 666-1544
Stephen Rissman, *Pr*
EMP: 103
SALES (corp-wide): 28.62MM **Privately
Held**
Web: www.evictionlawyer.com
SIC: 8741 8051 Nursing and personal care
facility management; Skilled nursing care
facilities
PA: Country Villa Service Corp.
2400 E Katella Ave # 800
310 574-3733

(P-17975)
COUNTRY VILLA SERVICE CORP
1730 Grand Ave, Long Beach (90804-2011)
PHONE..................562 597-8817
EMP: 102
SALES (corp-wide): 28.62MM **Privately
Held**
Web: www.evictionlawyer.com
SIC: 8741 Nursing and personal care facility
management
PA: Country Villa Service Corp.
2400 E Katella Ave # 800
310 574-3733

(P-17976)
COUNTRY VILLA SERVICE CORP
615 W Duarte Rd, Monrovia (91016-4436)
PHONE..................626 358-4547
Sam Chia, *Brnch Mgr*
EMP: 102
SALES (corp-wide): 28.62MM **Privately
Held**
Web: www.evictionlawyer.com
SIC: 8741 Management services
PA: Country Villa Service Corp.
2400 E Katella Ave # 800
310 574-3733

(P-17977)
COUNTY OF LOS ANGELES
Also Called: Internal Services Department
9150 Imperial Hwy, Downey (90242-2835)
PHONE..................562 940-2907
Dave Chittenten, *Dir*
EMP: 111
Web: probation.lacounty.gov

SIC: 8741 9199 Administrative management;
General government administration
PA: County Of Los Angeles
500 W Temple St Ste 437
213 974-1101

(P-17978)
CURATIVE INC
Also Called: Curative Labs
605 E Huntington Dr Ste 207, Monrovia
(91016-6353)
PHONE..................650 713-8928
EMP: 289 EST: 2020
SALES (est): 36.09MM **Privately Held**
Web: www.curative.com
SIC: 8741 Management services

(P-17979)
D I F GROUP INC
Also Called: Manufacture
2201 Yates Ave, Commerce (90040-1913)
PHONE..................323 231-8800
Angie Kim, *CEO*
EMP: 23 EST: 2010
SALES (est): 1.58MM **Privately Held**
SIC: 8741 3161 Management services;
Clothing and apparel carrying cases

(P-17980)
**DAICEL AMERICA HOLDINGS
INC**
21515 Hawthorne Blvd Ste 600, Torrance
(90503-6532)
PHONE..................480 798-6737
Kenichi Tanaka, *Brnch Mgr*
EMP: 338
Web: www.daicelamerica.com
SIC: 8741 Administrative management
HQ: Daicel America Holdings, Inc.
1 Parker Plz 400 Kelby St
Fort Lee NJ 07024
201 461-4466

(P-17981)
ENTEGRIS INC
4175 Santa Fe Rd, San Luis Obispo
(93401-8159)
PHONE..................805 541-9299
EMP: 88
SALES (corp-wide): 3.52B **Publicly Held**
Web: www.entegris.com
SIC: 8741 3674 Management services;
Semiconductors and related devices
PA: Entegris, Inc.
129 Concord Rd
978 436-6500

(P 17082)
**EPIC MANAGEMENT SERVICES
LLC (PA)**
1615 Orange Tree Ln, Redlands
(92374-2804)
P.O. Box 19020 (92423-9020)
PHONE..................909 799-1818
John D Goodman, *Pr*
Don J Stuckey, *
EMP: 77 EST: 1995
SALES (est): 23.26MM **Privately Held**
Web: www.epicmanagementlp.com
SIC: 8741 Nursing and personal care facility
management

(P-17983)
**EVOLUTION HOSPITALITY LLC
(HQ)**
1211 Puerta Del Sol Ste 170, San Clemente
(92673-6353)
PHONE..................949 325-1350
John Murphy, *Pr*

William Loughran, *
Matt Raine, *
EMP: 77 EST: 2010
SALES (est): 12.94MM
SALES (corp-wide): 819.71MM **Privately
Held**
Web: www.evolutionhospitality.com
SIC: 8741 7011 Hotel or motel management;
Hotels and motels
PA: Aimbridge Hospitality, Llc
5301 Headquarters Dr
972 952-0200

(P-17984)
FAR EAST NATIONAL BANK
977 N Broadway Ste 306, Los Angeles
(90012-1786)
P.O. Box Po Box 54198 (90099-0001)
PHONE..................213 687-1300
EMP: 354
SIC: 8741 6021 Management services;
National commercial banks

(P-17985)
**FIRSTSRVICE RSIDENTIAL CAL
LLC**
3415 S Sepulveda Blvd Ste 720, Los
Angeles (90034-6983)
PHONE..................213 213-0886
Gregg Evangelho, *Brnch Mgr*
EMP: 110
SALES (corp-wide): 4.33B **Privately Held**
Web: www.fsresidential.com
SIC: 8741 6531 Business management;
Real estate managers
HQ: Firstservice Residential California, Llc
15241 Laguna Canyon Rd
Irvine CA 92618
949 448-6000

(P-17986)
FRONT LINE MGT GROUP INC
1100 Glendon Ave Ste 2000, Los Angeles
(90024-3524)
PHONE..................310 209-3100
Irving Azoff, *Pr*
EMP: 71 EST: 2004
SALES (est): 2.36MM **Publicly Held**
SIC: 8741 Management services
HQ: Flmg Holdings Corp.
9348 Civic Center Dr
Beverly Hills CA 90210
310 867-7000

(P-17987)
FUJITEC AMERICA INC
12170 Mora Dr Ste 1, Santa Fe Springs
(90670-7039)
PHONE..................310 464-8270
Timothy Mooney, *Mgr*
EMP: 105
Web: www.fujitecamerica.com
SIC: 8741 1796 Business management;
Elevator installation and conversion
HQ: Fujitec America Inc
7258 Innovation Way
Mason OH 45040
513 755-6100

(P-17988)
**GHP MANAGEMENT
CORPORATION**
270 N Canon Dr, Beverly Hills
(90210-5323)
PHONE..................310 432-1441
Geoffrey H Palmer, *Brnch Mgr*
EMP: 223
SALES (corp-wide): 15.48MM **Privately
Held**
Web: www.ghpmgmt.com

SIC: 8741 Business management
PA: Ghp Management Corporation
1082 W 7th St
213 213-0190

(P-17989)
GRIMMWAY ENTERPRISES INC
Grimmway Fresh Processing
14141 Di Giorgio Rd, Arvin (93203-9518)
P.O. Box 81498 (93380-1498)
PHONE..................661 854-6200
Jeff Meger, *Pr*
EMP: 181
SALES (corp-wide): 577.4MM **Privately
Held**
Web: www.grimmway.com
SIC: 8741 2099 2037 Management services;
Food preparations, nec; Frozen fruits and
vegetables
PA: Grimmway Enterprises, Inc.
12064 Buena Vista Blvd
800 301-3101

(P-17990)
**HARBOR-UCLA MED
FOUNDATION INC (PA)**
Also Called: Harbor Ucla Med Foundation
21840 Normandie Ave Ste 100, Torrance
(90502-2046)
PHONE..................310 222-5015
Chester Choi, *CEO*
EMP: 100 EST: 1967
SQ FT: 45,000
SALES (est): 2.41MM **Privately Held**
Web: www.harbor-ucla.org
SIC: 8741 Hospital management

(P-17991)
HOTEL MANAGERS GROUP LLC
Also Called: Hotel Managers Group
11590 W Bernardo Ct Ste 211, San Diego
(92127-1624)
PHONE..................858 673-1534
Joel Biggs, *Managing Member*
Charles W Giacomini, *Managing Member*
Michelle Demayo, *
EMP: 400 EST: 1996
SALES (est): 3.6MM **Privately Held**
Web: www.hotelmanagersgroup.com
SIC: 8741 7011 7041 Hotel or motel
management; Hotels and motels;
Membership-basis organization hotels

(P-17992)
**IKEA PURCHASING SVCS US
INC**
600 N San Fernando Blvd, Burbank
(91502-1021)
PHONE..................818 841-3500
Chris Maynard, *Mgr*
EMP: 104
Web: www.ikea.com
SIC: 8741 8721 5712 Administrative
management; Accounting, auditing, and
bookkeeping; Furniture stores
HQ: Ikea Purchasing Services (Us) Inc.
7810 Katy Fwy
Houston TX 77024

(P-17993)
**INLAND CNTIES REGIONAL CTR
INC**
Also Called: Inland Regional Center
1500 Iowa Ave Ste 100, Riverside
(92507-2165)
PHONE..................951 826-2600
Lavina Johnson, *Brnch Mgr*
EMP: 224
SALES (corp-wide): 853.46MM **Privately
Held**

Web: www.inlandrc.org
SIC: 8741 Management services
PA: Inland Counties Regional Center, Inc.
1365 S Waterman Ave
909 890-3000

(P-17994)
J2 CLOUD SERVICES LLC
700 S Flower St Ste 1500, Los Angeles
(90017-4202)
PHONE.....................844 804-1234
Scott Turicchi, *CEO*
EMP: 300 EST: 1995
SALES (est): 2.22MM
SALES (corp-wide): 362.56MM **Publicly Held**
SIC: 8741 Management services
PA: Consensus Cloud Solutions, Inc.
700 S Flower St Fl 15
323 860-9200

(P-17995)
JC RESORTS LLC
Also Called: Encinitas Ranch Golf Course
4154 Maryland St, San Diego (92103-2330)
PHONE.....................760 944-1936
Rod Landville, *Mgr*
EMP: 329
Web: www.jcgolf.com
SIC: 8741 7992 Hotel or motel management;
Public golf courses
PA: Jc Resorts Llc
533 Coast Blvd S

(P-17996)
JC RESORTS LLC
Also Called: Rancho Bernardo Inn
17550 Bernardo Oaks Dr, San Diego
(92128-2112)
PHONE.....................855 574-5356
Jhon Gates, *Brnch Mgr*
EMP: 219
Web: www.jcresorts.com
SIC: 8741 7991 5813 5812 Hotel or motel
management; Physical fitness facilities;
Drinking places; Eating places
PA: Jc Resorts Llc
533 Coast Blvd S

(P-17997)
JC RESORTS LLC
Also Called: Surf Sand Hotel
1555 S Coast Hwy, Laguna Beach
(92651-3226)
PHONE.....................949 376-2779
Blaise Bartell, *Brnch Mgr*
EMP: 642
Web: www.surfandsandresort.com
SIC: 8741 5813 5812 7011 Hotel or motel
management; Drinking places; Eating
places; Hotels
PA: Jc Resorts Llc
533 Coast Blvd S

(P-17998)
JPL MANAGEMENT LLC
Also Called: Jpl Management
6427 W Sunset Blvd # 101, Los Angeles
(90028-7314)
PHONE.....................310 844-3662
Julian Ledesma, *CEO*
EMP: 72 EST: 2018
SALES (est): 2.49MM **Privately Held**
SIC: 8741 8748 Management services;
Business consulting, nec

(P-17999)
JUVENILE JUSTICE DIVISION CAL
Also Called: Ventura Yuth Crrctional Fcilty

3100 Wright Rd, Camarillo (93010-8307)
PHONE.....................805 485-7951
Vivian Craford, *Superintnt*
EMP: 886
SALES (corp-wide): 534.4MM **Privately Held**
SIC: 8741 9223 Office management; House
of correction, government
HQ: Juvenile Justice Division, California
1515 S St Ste 502s
Sacramento CA 95811

(P-18000)
KA MANAGEMENT II INC
Also Called: Emeryville Chevron
5820 Oberlin Dr Ste 201, San Diego
(92121-3743)
PHONE.....................858 404-6080
Kayvon Agahnia, *CEO*
Kambiz Agahnia, *
Ken Assi, *CIO**
EMP: 90 EST: 2015
SALES (est): 4.47MM **Privately Held**
SIC: 8741 Financial management for
business

(P-18001)
KEIRO SERVICES
Also Called: Keiro Senior Health Care
420 E 3rd St Ste 1000, Los Angeles
(90033)
PHONE.....................213 873-5700
Shawn Miyake, *CEO*
EMP: 500 EST: 1984
SQ FT: 26,000
SALES (est): 1.59MM **Privately Held**
Web: www.keiro.org
SIC: 8741 Nursing and personal care facility
management

(P-18002)
LA 1000 SANTA FE LLC
1000 S Santa Fe Ave, Los Angeles
(90021-1741)
PHONE.....................213 205-1000
EMP: 210 EST: 2019
SALES (est): 2.15MM **Privately Held**
SIC: 8741 Hotel or motel management

(P-18003)
LAKESIDE SYSTEMS INC
Also Called: Lakeside Medical Systems
8510 Balboa Blvd Ste 150, Northridge
(91325-5810)
PHONE.....................866 654-3471
Richard Merkin, *CEO*
EMP: 700 EST: 1991
SQ FT: 20,000
SALES (est): 4.01MM
SALES (corp-wide): 48.79MM **Privately Held**
SIC: 8741 8742 6411 Management services;
Management consulting services;
Insurance agents, brokers, and service
PA: Heritage Provider Network Inc
8510 Balboa Blvd Ste 285
818 654-3461

(P-18004)
LEGACY PRTNERS RESIDENTIAL INC
5141 California Ave Ste 100, Irvine
(92617-3050)
PHONE.....................949 930-6600
Deborah Dodd, *Brnch Mgr*
EMP: 205
SALES (corp-wide): 14.02MM **Privately Held**
Web: www.legacypartners.com

SIC: 8741 Management services
PA: Legacy Partners Residential, Inc.
950 Tower Ln Ste 900
650 571-2250

(P-18005)
LEWIS MANAGEMENT CORP
1154 N Mountain Ave, Upland
(91786-3633)
PHONE.....................909 985-0971
John M Goodman, *CEO*
EMP: 86 EST: 2017
SALES (est): 7.43MM **Privately Held**
Web: www.lewisgroupofcompanies.com
SIC: 8741 Management services

(P-18006)
LEXXIOM INC
99 N San Antonio Ave Ste 330, Upland
(91786-7415)
PHONE.....................909 581-7313
Robert Lemelin, *Pr*
Brian Lemelin, *
Leo Lemelin, *
EMP: 360 EST: 2000
SALES (est): 6.71MM **Privately Held**
Web: www.lexxiom.com
SIC: 8741 Administrative management

(P-18007)
LION-VALLEN LTD PARTNERSHIP
22 Area Aven A Bldg #2234, Camp
Pendleton (92055)
P.O. Box 555045 (92055-5045)
PHONE.....................760 385-4885
EMP: 95
SALES (corp-wide): 18.69MM **Privately Held**
SIC: 8741 Management services
HQ: Lion-Vallen Limited Partnership
7200 Poe Ave Ste 400
Dayton OH 45414

(P-18008)
LIVINGSTON MEM VNA HLTH CORP
Also Called: Livingston Mem Vsting Nrse Ass
1996 Eastman Ave Ste 101, Ventura
(93003-7789)
PHONE.....................805 642-0239
Lanyard K Dial Md, *Pr*
Judy Hecox, *
Charles Hair Md, *Ch Bd*
Jeffrey Paul, *
EMP: 292 EST: 1947
SQ FT: 12,600
SALES (est): 15.8MM **Privately Held**
Web: www.lmvna.org
SIC: 8741 8082 Hospital management;
Home health care services

(P-18009)
LOS ANGELES RAMS LLC
Also Called: La Rams Football Club
10271 W Pico Blvd, Los Angeles
(90064-2606)
P.O. Box 69216 (90069-0216)
PHONE.....................310 277-4700
John Shaw, *Prin*
EMP: 91
SALES (corp-wide): 1.23MM **Privately Held**
Web: www.therams.com
SIC: 8741 7941 Administrative management;
Football club
PA: The Los Angeles Rams Llc
29899 Agoura Rd
314 982-7267

(P-18010)
MARINER HEALTH CARE INC
Also Called: Palm Springs Health Care Ctr
277 S Sunrise Way, Palm Springs
(92262-6792)
PHONE.....................760 327-8541
Darrin Tharp, *Admn*
EMP: 123
SALES (corp-wide): 497.49MM **Privately Held**
Web: www.marinerhealthcare.com
SIC: 8741 8322 Nursing and personal care
facility management; Rehabilitation services
PA: Mariner Health Care, Inc.
3060 Mrcer Univ Dr Ste 20
678 443-7000

(P-18011)
MEDICAL NETWORK INC
Also Called: MBC Systems
1809 E Dyer Rd Ste 311, Santa Ana
(92705-5740)
PHONE.....................949 863-0022
David Conrad, *Pr*
Michael Weinstein, *Ch*
EMP: 80 EST: 1993
SQ FT: 3,500
SALES (est): 9.98MM **Privately Held**
Web: www.mbcsystems.com
SIC: 8741 Hospital management

(P-18012)
MIG MANAGEMENT SERVICES LLC
660 Newport Center Dr Ste 1300, Newport
Beach (92660-6492)
PHONE.....................949 474-5800
EMP: 80 EST: 2010
SALES (est): 1.32MM
SALES (corp-wide): 11.6MM **Privately Held**
Web: www.migcap.com
SIC: 8741 Management services
PA: Mig Capital, Llc
660 Nwport Ctr Dr Ste 13
949 474-5800

(P-18013)
MIKE ROVNER CONSTRUCTION INC
22600 Lambert St, Lake Forest
(92630-6201)
PHONE.....................949 458-1562
Mike Rovner, *Brnch Mgr*
EMP: 141
Web: www.rovnerconstruction.com
SIC: 8741 1522 1521 Construction
management; Residential construction, nec
; Single-family housing construction
PA: Mike Rovner Construction, Inc.
5400 Tech Cir

(P-18014)
MONTAGE HOTELS & RESORTS LLC
Also Called: Montage Laguna Beach
30801 Coast Hwy, Laguna Beach
(92651-4221)
PHONE.....................949 715-6000
Alan Fuerstman, *CEO*
EMP: 600
SALES (corp-wide): 153.78MM **Privately Held**
Web: www.montage.com
SIC: 8741 7011 5813 5812 Hotel or motel
management; Hotels; Drinking places;
Eating places
PA: Montage Hotels & Resorts, Llc
3 Ada Pkwy Ste 100

949 715-5002

(P-18015)
MOVEMENT FOR LIFE INC
Also Called: Pt Harmony
408 Higuera St Ste 200, San Luis Obispo
(93401-6135)
PHONE..............................805 788-0805
Kelly Sanders, *Pr*
James E Glinn Junior, *Managing Member*
EMP: 320 **EST:** 2014
SALES (est): 4.77MM **Privately Held**
Web: www.movementforlife.com
SIC: 8741 Management services

(P-18016)
MTC FINANCIAL INC
Also Called: Trustee Corps
17100 Gillette Ave, Irvine (92612)
PHONE..............................949 252-8300
Rande Johnsen, *CEO*
EMP: 90 **EST:** 1992
SALES (est): 9.11MM **Privately Held**
Web: www.trusteecorps.com
SIC: 8741 Management services

(P-18017)
NAVIGANT CYMETRIX
CORPORATION
1515 W 190th St Ste 350, Gardena
(90248-4910)
PHONE..............................424 201-6300
Jeff Macdonald, *Brnch Mgr*
EMP: 73
SALES (corp-wide): 587.29MM **Privately Held**
Web: www.navigantcymetrix.com
SIC: 8741 Management services
HQ: Navigant Cymetrix Corporation
1 Park Plz Ste 1050
Irvine CA 92614
714 361-6800

(P-18018)
NAVIGANT CYMETRIX
CORPORATION
10920 Via Frontera Ste 500, San Diego
(92127-1733)
PHONE..............................858 217-1800
Jeff Macdonald, *Brnch Mgr*
EMP: 73
SALES (corp-wide): 587.29MM **Privately Held**
Web: www.navigantcymetrix.com
SIC: 8741 Management services
HQ: Navigant Cymetrix Corporation
1 Park Plz Ste 1050
Irvine CA 92614
714 361-6800

(P-18019)
NAVIGATORS MANAGEMENT
CO INC
19100 Von Karman Ave, Irvine
(92612-1539)
PHONE..............................949 255-4860
EMP: 166
SIC: 8741 Management services
HQ: Navigators Management Company, Inc.
6 International Dr # 100
Port Chester NY 10573
412 995-2255

(P-18020)
NELSON BROS PROPERTY MGT
INC
Also Called: Nelson Brothers Property MGT
16b Journey Ste 200, Aliso Viejo
(92656-3317)

PHONE..............................949 916-7300
Patrick Nelson, *Pr*
EMP: 134 **EST:** 2007
SALES (est): 2.56MM **Privately Held**
Web: www.nelson-brotherscm.com
SIC: 8741 Management services

(P-18021)
NETWORK MANAGEMENT
GROUP INC (PA)
1100 S Flower St Ste 3110, Los Angeles
(90015-2287)
PHONE..............................323 263-2632
John Park, *Pr*
EMP: 160 **EST:** 1997
SQ FT: 2,039
SALES (est): 1.22MM
SALES (corp-wide): 1.22MM **Privately Held**
Web: www.socialworkmanager.org
SIC: 8741 8742 Business management;
Management consulting services

(P-18022)
NETWORK MEDICAL
MANAGEMENT INC
1668 S Garfield Ave Ste 100, Alhambra
(91801-5474)
PHONE..............................626 282-0288
Gary Augusta, *Pr*
Hing Ang, *COO*
Mihir Shah, *CFO*
Adrian Vazquez Md, *Co-Chief Medical Officer*
EMP: 130 **EST:** 1994
SQ FT: 14,000
SALES (est): 15.03MM **Publicly Held**
Web: www.bbbs.org
SIC: 8741 Hospital management
PA: Astrana Health, Inc.
1668 S Garfield Ave Fl 2

(P-18023)
NORTH AMERICAN CLIENT
SVCS INC (PA)
25910 Acero Ste 350, Mission Viejo
(92691-7908)
PHONE..............................949 240-2423
Darian Dahl, *Pr*
Jonathan Sloey, *
Jeffrey Daly, *
John L Sorensen, *
Timothy J Paulsen, *
▲ **EMP:** 175 **EST:** 1989
SALES (est): 48.37MM **Privately Held**
Web: www.naclientservices.com
SIC: 8741 Nursing and personal care facility management

(P-18024)
NORTH AMERICAN MED MGT
CAL INC (DH)
Also Called: Optum
3990 Concours Ste 500, Ontario
(91764-7983)
PHONE..............................909 605-8000
Jung Lee, *Pr*
Jared Campbell, *
Paul Lim, *CMO*
EMP: 75 **EST:** 1995
SALES (est): 20.97MM
SALES (corp-wide): 371.62B **Publicly Held**
Web: www.nammcal.com
SIC: 8741 Nursing and personal care facility management
HQ: Namm Holdings, Inc.
3281 E Guasti Rd Ste 700
Ontario CA 91761

(P-18025)
ONNI PROPERTIES LLC
Also Called: Level Furnished Living
888 S Olive St, Los Angeles (90014-3006)
PHONE..............................213 568-0278
Javier Sepeda, *Genl Mgr*
EMP: 206
SALES (corp-wide): 26.81MM **Privately Held**
Web: www.stayinglevel.com
SIC: 8741 Business management
PA: Onni Properties Llc
5055 N 32nd St
602 595-4810

(P-18026)
OREQ CORPORATION
Also Called: Orchem Division
42306 Remington Ave, Temecula
(92590-2512)
PHONE..............................951 296-5076
Jess L Hetzner, *CEO*
Ron Hetzner, *
▲ **EMP:** 82 **EST:** 1999
SALES (est): 12.76MM **Privately Held**
Web: www.oreqcorp.com
SIC: 8741 5941 5091 Business management; Water sport equipment; Spa equipment and supplies

(P-18027)
OVG FACILITIES LLC
Also Called: Fredericksburg Convention Ctr
1100 Glendon Ave Ste 2100, Los Angeles
(90024-3592)
PHONE..............................757 323-9380
Doug Higgons, *Prin*
EMP: 75 **EST:** 2019
SALES (est): 4.02MM **Privately Held**
Web: www.oakviewgroup.com
SIC: 8741 Management services

(P-18028)
PACIFIC GARDENS MED CTR
LLC
21530 Pioneer Blvd, Hawaiian Gardens
(90716-2608)
PHONE..............................562 860-0401
EMP: 250 **EST:** 2017
SALES (est): 21.65MM **Privately Held**
SIC: 8741 Hospital management

(P-18029)
PACIFIC LIFE FUND ADVISORS
LLC
Pacific Asset Management
700 Newport Contor Dr, Newport Beach
(92660-6307)
PHONE..............................949 260-9000
Rex Olson, *Prin*
EMP: 435
SALES (corp-wide): 12.84B **Privately Held**
Web: www.aristotlepacific.com
SIC: 8741 Financial management for business
HQ: Pacific Life Fund Advisors Llc
700 Newport Center Drive
Newport Beach CA 92660

(P-18030)
PACIFIC VENTURES LTD
Also Called: Jacmar Companies, The
2200 W Valley Blvd, Alhambra
(91803-1928)
PHONE..............................626 576-0737
William H Tilley, *CEO*
Jim Dalpozzo, *
Randy Hill, *
EMP: 250 **EST:** 1976

SQ FT: 20,000
SALES (est): 665.02K **Privately Held**
SIC: 8741 6722 Restaurant management; Management investment, open-end

(P-18031)
PARSONS CONSTRUCTORS INC
Also Called: PARSONS
100 W Walnut St, Pasadena (91103-3697)
PHONE..............................626 440-2000
Chuck Harrington, *CEO*
Robert Camp, *
EMP: 118 **EST:** 1978
SALES (est): 6.33MM
SALES (corp-wide): 5.44B **Publicly Held**
Web: www.parsons.com
SIC: 8741 8711 Management services; Engineering services
PA: The Parsons Corporation
14291 Pk Madow Dr Ste 100
703 988-8500

(P-18032)
PREMIER HLTHCARE
SOLUTIONS INC
Also Called: Premier IMS Insurance Services
12225 El Camino Real, San Diego
(92130-2084)
PHONE..............................858 569-8629
Susan Devore, *Brnch Mgr*
EMP: 275
SALES (corp-wide): 1.35B **Publicly Held**
Web: www.premierinc.com
SIC: 8741 Management services
HQ: Premier Healthcare Solutions, Inc.
13034 Ballantyne Corp Pl
Charlotte NC 28277
704 357-0022

(P-18033)
PRIDE RESOURCE PARTNERS
LLC
4499 Ruffin Rd Ste 250, San Diego
(92123-4323)
P.O. Box 633075 (92163)
PHONE..............................858 430-6630
Joe Maak, *CEO*
EMP: 105 **EST:** 2015
SQ FT: 4,000
SALES (est): 17.38MM **Privately Held**
Web: www.priderp.com
SIC: 8741 7389 8742 4924 Management services; Relocation service; Human resource consulting services; Natural gas distribution

(P-18034)
PRIMARY CARE ASSOD MED
GROUP I
3998 Vista Way Ste B, Oceanside
(92056-4514)
PHONE..............................760 724-1033
Jeannette Brody, *Mgr*
EMP: 112
SALES (corp-wide): 1.49MM **Privately Held**
SIC: 8741 Administrative management
PA: Primary Care Associated Medical Group, Inc.
1635 Lake San Marcos Dr
760 471-7505

(P-18035)
PRIMARY CARE ASSOD MED
GROUP I (PA)
1635 Lake San Marcos Dr Ste 201, San Marcos (92078-4698)
PHONE..............................760 471-7505
Robert Mongeon, *Pr*

EMP: 70 EST: 1992
SALES (est): 1.49MM
SALES (corp-wide): 1.49MM **Privately Held**
SIC: 8741 Administrative management

(P-18036)
PRIMARY PROVIDER MGT CO INC (HQ)
Also Called: Ppmc
2115 Compton Ave Ste 301, Corona (92881-7272)
PHONE..............................951 280-7700
Robert Dukes Md, *CEO*
Robert Dukes, *CEO*
Maureen B Tyson, *
EMP: 90 EST: 1983
SQ FT: 23,500
SALES (est): 4.47MM
SALES (corp-wide): 4.32B **Publicly Held**
SIC: 8741 Business management
PA: Agilon Health, Inc.
6210 E Hwy 290 Ste 450
562 256-3800

(P-18037)
PROACTIVE RISK MANAGEMENT INC
22617 Hawthorne Blvd, Torrance (90505-2510)
PHONE..............................213 840-8856
Benoit Grenier, *CEO*
EMP: 100 EST: 2014
SALES (est): 1.16MM **Privately Held**
Web: www.parminc.com
SIC: 8741 Business management

(P-18038)
PROFESSIONAL COMMUNITY MGT CAL
Also Called: Pcm
23081 Via Campo Verde, Aliso Viejo (92656)
PHONE..............................949 380-0725
Richard Lee, *Bmch Mgr*
EMP: 78
SALES (corp-wide): 17.24MM **Privately Held**
Web: www.pcminternet.com
SIC: 8741 6519 Business management; Real property lessors, nec
PA: Professional Community Management Of California, Inc.
27051 Twne Cntre Dr Ste 2
800 369-7260

(P-18039)
PROSPECT MEDICAL GROUP INC (HQ)
1920 E 17th St Ste 200, Santa Ana (92705-8626)
PHONE..............................714 796-5900
Jacob Y Terner Md, *Pr*
Mitchell Lew Md, *CEO*
Mike Heather, *
Stewart Kahn, *
EMP: 350 EST: 1986
SQ FT: 2,420
SALES (est): 11.92MM
SALES (corp-wide): 3.91B **Privately Held**
Web: www.prospectmedical.com
SIC: 8741 Hospital management
PA: Prospect Medical Holdings, Inc.
3415 S Sepulveda Blvd
310 943-4500

(P-18040)
PROSPECT MEDICAL SYSTEMS INC (HQ)

Also Called: Genesis Health Care
600 City Pkwy W Ste 800, Orange (92868-2948)
PHONE..............................714 667-8156
Mitchell Lew Md, *CEO*
Brice Keyser Senior, *Dir Fin*
EMP: 127 EST: 1996
SALES (est): 46.62MM
SALES (corp-wide): 3.91B **Privately Held**
Web: www.prospectmedical.com
SIC: 8741 Hospital management
PA: Prospect Medical Holdings, Inc.
3415 S Sepulveda Blvd
310 943-4500

(P-18041)
PROVIDENT FINANCIAL MANAGEMENT
3130 Wilshire Blvd Ste 600, Santa Monica (90403-2349)
P.O. Box 4084 (90411-4084)
PHONE..............................310 282-0477
Ivan Axelrod, *Mng Pt*
Barry Siegel, *
EMP: 95 EST: 1981
SQ FT: 34,000
SALES (est): 2.61MM **Privately Held**
Web: www.providentfm.com
SIC: 8741 Financial management for business

(P-18042)
QTC
924 Overland Ct, San Dimas (91773-1742)
PHONE..............................909 978-3531
EMP: 102 EST: 2018
SALES (est): 3.1MM **Privately Held**
Web: www.qtcm.com
SIC: 8741 Management services

(P-18043)
RAYMOND GROUP (PA)
Also Called: Orange Cnty George M Raymond N
520 W Walnut Ave, Orange (92868-5008)
PHONE..............................714 771-7670
Travis Winsor, *CEO*
James Watson, *
Mary Raymond, *
Tom Obrien, *
Michael Potter, *
EMP: 95 EST: 1955
SQ FT: 20,000
SALES (est): 36.98MM
SALES (corp-wide): 36.98MM **Privately Held**
Web: www.raymondgroup.com
SIC: 8741 Construction management

(P-18044)
RELOCITY INC
10250 Constellation Blvd Ste 100, Los Angeles (90067-6272)
PHONE..............................323 207-9160
Klaus Siegmann, *CEO*
EMP: 120 EST: 2016
SQ FT: 800
SALES (est): 3.8MM **Privately Held**
Web: www.relocity.com
SIC: 8741 Management services

(P-18045)
RENOVO SOLUTIONS LLC (PA)
4 Executive Cir Ste 185, Irvine (92614-6791)
PHONE..............................714 599-7969
Joseph Happ, *CIO*
Donald K Carson, *OF WEST COAST*
Haresh Saitiani, *
Fernando Castorena, *

EMP: 297 EST: 2009
SQ FT: 5,400
SALES (est): 20.04MM
SALES (corp-wide): 20.04MM **Privately Held**
Web: www.renovo1.com
SIC: 8741 Hospital management

(P-18046)
RHS CORP
Also Called: REDLANDS COMMUNITY HOSPITAL
350 Terracina Blvd, Redlands (92373-4850)
PHONE..............................909 335-5500
James R Holmes, *Pr*
EMP: 1450 EST: 1985
SQ FT: 265,000
SALES (est): 595.74K **Privately Held**
Web: www.redlandshospital.org
SIC: 8741 Hospital management

(P-18047)
ROCKPORT ADM SVCS LLC (PA)
Also Called: Rockport Healthcare Services
5900 Wilshire Blvd Ste 1600, Los Angeles (90036-5016)
PHONE..............................323 330-6500
Vincent S Hambright, *CEO*
Brad Gibson, *
Michael Wasserman, *CMO*
EMP: 75 EST: 2010
SALES (est): 41.08MM **Privately Held**
SIC: 8741 Administrative management

(P-18048)
SAGA KAPITAL GROUP INC
108 Saybrook, Irvine (92620-7307)
PHONE..............................714 294-4132
Ashish Kapoor, *CEO*
EMP: 75 EST: 2019
SALES (est): 2.71MM **Privately Held**
Web: www.sagakgi.com
SIC: 8741 Business management

(P-18049)
SCIENCE INC
450 S Melrose Dr, Vista (92081-6674)
PHONE..............................310 395-3432
Greg Gilman, *Pr*
EMP: 91 EST: 2015
SALES (est): 3.7MM **Privately Held**
Web: www.science-inc.com
SIC: 8741 Management services

(P-18050)
SCRIPPS CLINIC MED GROUP INC
12395 El Camino Real Ste 112, San Diego (92130-3084)
PHONE..............................858 554-9000
Doctor Hugh Greenway, *CEO*
EMP: 183 EST: 1999
SALES (est): 4.26MM
SALES (corp-wide): 4.14B **Privately Held**
Web: www.scrippsclinicmedicalgroup.com
SIC: 8741 Management services
PA: Scripps Health
10140 Cmpus Pt Dr Cpa 415
800 727-4777

(P-18051)
SETHI MANAGEMENT INC
6156 Innovation Way, Carlsbad (92009-1728)
P.O. Box 235927 (92023-5927)
PHONE..............................760 692-5288
Jeetander Sethi, *CEO*
EMP: 154 EST: 2009
SALES (est): 40MM **Privately Held**

Web: www.sethimanagement.com
SIC: 8741 Business management

(P-18052)
SMILE BRANDS GROUP INC (PA)
Also Called: Bright Now Dental
100 Spectrum Center Dr Ste 1500, Irvine (92618-4984)
PHONE..............................714 668-1300
Steven C Bilt, *CEO*
Stan Andrakowicz, *
Robert C Crim, *CDO*
George Suda, *CIO*
Cheryl Dore, *Chief Human Resource Officer*
EMP: 90 EST: 1978
SQ FT: 15,000
SALES (est): 582.07MM
SALES (corp-wide): 582.07MM **Privately Held**
Web: www.smilebrands.com
SIC: 8741 8021 Management services; Dental clinics and offices

(P-18053)
SMITH BROADCASTING GROUP INC (PA)
2315 Red Rose Way, Santa Barbara (93109-1259)
PHONE..............................805 965-0400
Debrah Egar, *Ex Sec*
David A Fitz, *
EMP: 165 EST: 1985
SALES (est): 4.14MM
SALES (corp-wide): 4.14MM **Privately Held**
SIC: 8741 8742 Business management; Management consulting services

(P-18054)
SNF MANAGEMENT
1901 Avenue Of The Stars, Los Angeles (90067-6001)
PHONE..............................310 385-1090
Lee Samson, *Pr*
EMP: 122 EST: 2010
SALES (est): 9.87MM **Privately Held**
Web: www.windsorcares.com
SIC: 8741 Management services

(P-18055)
SODEXO MANAGEMENT INC
16200 Sand Canyon Ave, Irvine (92618-3714)
PHONE..............................949 753-2042
Howard Hays, *Brnch Mgr*
EMP: 1807
SALES (corp-wide): 246.43MM **Privately Held**
Web: www.sodexo.com
SIC: 8741 Management services
HQ: Sodexo Management Inc.
915 Meeting St
Rockville MD 20852

(P-18056)
SODEXO MANAGEMENT INC
13729 Earlham Dr, Whittier (90602-1478)
PHONE..............................650 506-4814
Eric Herttua, *Mgr*
EMP: 2108
SALES (corp-wide): 246.43MM **Privately Held**
Web: www.sodexo.com
SIC: 8741 6552 Management services; Subdividers and developers, nec
HQ: Sodexo Management Inc.
915 Meeting St
Rockville MD 20852

(P-18057)
SOLPAC CONSTRUCTION INC
Also Called: Soltek Pacific Construction Co
2424 Congress St, San Diego
(92110-2819)
PHONE...................619 296-6247
Stephen Thompson, *CEO*
Brandon Richie, *
John Myers, *
Kevin Cammall, *
Robert Thompson, *
EMP: 130 **EST:** 2005
SQ FT: 12,291
SALES (est): 177.75MM **Privately Held**
Web: www.soltekpacific.com
SIC: 8741 1542 1611 Construction
management; Commercial and office
building contractors; General contractor,
highway and street construction

(P-18058)
SOUTH COAST PLAZA SECURITY
695 Town Center Dr Ste 50, Costa Mesa
(92626-1924)
PHONE...................714 435-2180
Craig Farrow, *Mgr*
EMP: 120 **EST:** 1989
SALES (est): 2.65MM **Privately Held**
Web: www.southcoastplaza.com
SIC: 8741 Management services

(P-18059)
SOUTHERN IMPLANTS INC
5 Holland Ste 209, Irvine (92618-2576)
PHONE...................949 273-8505
Michael Kehoe, *Pr*
Michael Nealon, *
EMP: 125 **EST:** 2007
SALES (est): 1.34MM **Privately Held**
Web: www.southernimplants.us
SIC: 8741 Management services

(P-18060)
SUNAMERICA INVESTMENTS INC (DH)
Also Called: SunAmerica
1 Sun America Ctr Fl 37, Los Angeles
(90067-6103)
PHONE...................310 772-6000
Eli Broad, *Pr*
EMP: 80 **EST:** 1978
SQ FT: 76,000
SALES (est): 3.58MM
SALES (corp-wide): 46.8B **Publicly Held**
SIC: 8741 6211 6282 7311 Administrative
management; Security brokers and dealers;
Investment advisory service; Advertising
agencies
HQ: Sunamerica Inc.
1 Sun America Ctr Fl 38
Los Angeles CA 90067
310 772-6000

(P-18061)
SUNROAD ASSET MANAGEMENT INC
4445 Eastgate Mall Ste 400, San Diego
(92121-1979)
PHONE...................858 362-8500
Dan Feldman, *Pr*
EMP: 176 **EST:** 1986
SALES (est): 1.46MM **Privately Held**
Web: www.sunroadenterprises.com
SIC: 8741 Business management
PA: Sunroad Holding Corporation
8620 Spctrum Ctr Blvd Ste

(P-18062)
SYLMARK INC (PA)
Also Called: Sylmark Group
7821 Orion Ave Ste 200, Van Nuys
(91406-2032)
PHONE...................818 217-2000
Peter Spiegel, *Pr*
Steven Ober, *
Mark Funk, *
EMP: 90 **EST:** 1998
SALES (est): 3.71MM
SALES (corp-wide): 3.71MM **Privately Held**
Web: www.sylmark.com
SIC: 8741 Management services

(P-18063)
TCT MOBILE INC
189 Technology Dr, Irvine (92618-2402)
PHONE...................949 892-2990
Xin Zhang, *Pr*
Juanjuan Feng, *
Qian Wen, *
EMP: 100 **EST:** 2008
SALES (est): 933.46K
SALES (corp-wide): 293.57K **Privately Held**
Web: us.alcatelmobile.com
SIC: 8741 8711 7389 8721 Management
services; Engineering services; Financial
services; Accounting, auditing, and
bookkeeping
HQ: Tcl Communication Technology
Holdings Limited
C/O: Conyers Trust Company
(Cayman) Limited
George Town GR CAYMAN

(P-18064)
TEAM GROUP LLC
4076 Flat Rock Dr, Riverside (92505-5858)
PHONE...................951 688-8593
EMP: 78 **EST:** 2018
SALES (est): 1.89MM
SALES (corp-wide): 3.32MM **Privately Held**
Web: www.teamcorpint.com
SIC: 8741 Management services
PA: Total Educational Activity Model Corp
4076 Flat Rock Dr
951 977-9690

(P-18065)
TELACU INDUSTRIES INC
1175 N Del Rio Pl, Ontario (91764-4505)
PHONE...................323 721-1655
EMP: 174
SALES (corp-wide): 11.23MM **Privately Held**
Web: www.telacu.com
SIC: 8741 Construction management
HQ: Telacu Industries, Inc.
5400 E Olympic Blvd # 300
Commerce CA 90022
323 721-1655

(P-18066)
TRAFFIC MANAGEMENT INC
Also Called: TRAFFIC MANAGEMENT, INC.
1244 S Claudina St, Anaheim (92805-6232)
PHONE...................562 264-2353
Christopher Spano, *Prin*
EMP: 72
Web: www.trafficmanagement.com
SIC: 8741 Business management
PA: Traffic Management, Llc
4900 Arprt Plz Dr Ste 300

(P-18067)
TRANSCOSMOS OMNICONNECT LLC
879 W 190th St Ste 1050, Gardena
(90248-4224)
PHONE...................310 630-0072
EMP: 100 **EST:** 2019
SALES (est): 1.37MM
SALES (corp-wide): 23.83MM **Privately Held**
SIC: 8741 Management services
PA: Trans Cosmos America, Inc.
879 W 190th St Ste 410
310 630-0072

(P-18068)
TRICOM MANAGEMENT LLC
Also Called: United Owners Services
4025 E La Palma Ave Ste 101, Anaheim
(92807-1764)
PHONE...................714 630-2029
Woody Cary, *Pr*
EMP: 200 **EST:** 1979
SQ FT: 9,000
SALES (est): 8.69MM **Privately Held**
Web: www.tricommanagement.com
SIC: 8741 7389 Management services; Time-
share condominium exchange

(P-18069)
TRILAR MANAGEMENT GROUP
1025 S Gilbert St, Hemet (92543-7090)
PHONE...................951 925-2021
Susan A York, *Brnch Mgr*
EMP: 127
SALES (corp-wide): 10.04MM **Privately Held**
Web: www.trilar.com
SIC: 8741 Business management
PA: Trilar Management Group
2225 Faraday Ave Ste A
760 603-3205

(P-18070)
TRIPALINK CORP
600 Wilshire Blvd Ste 1540, Los Angeles
(90005-3983)
PHONE...................323 717-9139
Donghal Li, *Prin*
EMP: 180 **EST:** 2016
SALES (est): 16.07MM **Privately Held**
Web: www.tripalink.com
SIC: 8741 Management services

(P-18071)
TROON GOLF LLC
Also Called: Indian Wells Golf Resort
44500 Indian Wells Ln, Indian Wells
(92210-8746)
PHONE...................760 346-4653
Rich Carter, *Genl Mgr*
EMP: 130
Web: www.indianwellsgolfresort.com
SIC: 8741 7997 Management services;
Country club, membership
PA: Troon Golf, L.L.C.
15044 N Scttsdale Rd Ste

(P-18072)
TWENTY4SEVEN HOTELS CORP
520 Newport Center Dr Ste 520, Newport
Beach (92660-7087)
PHONE...................949 734-6400
David Wani, *CEO*
Drew Hardy, *
EMP: 500 **EST:** 2002
SQ FT: 15,000
SALES (est): 15.69MM **Privately Held**
Web: www.247hotels.com

SIC: 8741 Hotel or motel management

(P-18073)
VENBROOK GROUP LLC (PA)
6320 Canoga Ave Fl 12, Woodland Hills
(91367-2584)
PHONE...................818 598-8900
Jason D Turner, *CEO*
Jack Reddy, *Chief Human Resource Officer*
Juan Aguilar, *
Brooke Norton Lais, *CMO*
EMP: 170 **EST:** 2006
SALES (est): 110.95MM **Privately Held**
Web: www.venbrook.com
SIC: 8741 Management services

(P-18074)
VENTURA MEDICAL MANAGEMENT LLC
2601 E Main St, Ventura (93003-2801)
PHONE...................805 477-6220
EMP: 325 **EST:** 2002
SALES (est): 2.74MM **Privately Held**
Web: www.ventura.org
SIC: 8741 Hospital management

(P-18075)
VILLAGE MANAGEMENT SVCS INC
24351 El Toro Rd, Laguna Woods
(92637-4901)
PHONE...................949 597-4360
EMP: 123 **EST:** 2016
SALES (est): 2.38MM **Privately Held**
Web: www.lagunawoodsvillage.com
SIC: 8741 Management services

(P-18076)
VPM MANAGEMENT INC
2400 Main St Ste 201, Irvine (92614-6271)
PHONE...................949 863-1500
Philip H Mcnamee, *CEO*
Scott J Barker, *Managing Member*
Steve Tomlin, *
Mark Ellis, *
EMP: 150 **EST:** 1997
SALES (est): 4.34MM **Privately Held**
Web: www.vpmmanagement.com
SIC: 8741 Management services

(P-18077)
WARMINGTON MR 14 ASSOC LLC
Also Called: Warmington
3090 Pullman St, Costa Mesa
(92626-5901)
PHONE...................714 557-5511
EMP: 80 **EST:** 2013
SALES (est): 8.82MM **Privately Held**
Web: www.homesbywarmington.com
SIC: 8741 Business management

(P-18078)
WARNER BROS DISTRIBUTING INC
Warner Bros. Pictures Domestic
4000 Warner Blvd Bldg 154, Burbank
(91522-0001)
PHONE...................818 954-6000
Dan Fellman, *Brnch Mgr*
EMP: 418
SIC: 8741 7822 Management services;
Distribution, exclusive of production: motion
picture
HQ: Warner Bros. Distributing Inc.
4000 Warner Blvd
Burbank CA 91522

PRODUCTS & SVCS

(P-18079)
WESTERN NATIONAL CONTRACTORS
8 Executive Cir, Irvine (92614-6746)
PHONE.................(949) 862-6200
Michael Hayde, *CEO*
Jeffrey R Scott, *
John Townsend, *
Randy Avery, *
Larry Johnson, *
EMP: 88 **EST:** 2004
SALES (est): 3.81MM **Privately Held**
Web: www.wng.com
SIC: 8741 Construction management

(P-18080)
WESTREC PROPERTIES INC
16633 Ventura Blvd Fl 6, Encino
(91436-1826)
PHONE.................818 907-0400
Michael M Sachs, *Pr*
EMP: 477 **EST:** 1990
SALES (est): 654.52K **Privately Held**
SIC: 8741 Administrative management
PA: Westrec Financial, Inc.
　　16633 Ventura Blvd Fl 6

(P-18081)
WHISKEY GIRL
702 5th Ave, San Diego (92101-6918)
PHONE.................619 236-1616
Jerry Lopez, *Genl Mgr*
EMP: 152 **EST:** 2011
SALES (est): 717.52K
SALES (corp-wide): 1.6MM **Privately Held**
Web: www.whiskeygirl.com
SIC: 8741 5813 Restaurant management;
　　Night clubs
PA: Buffalo Joe's, L. P.
　　1620 5th Ave Ste 770
　　619 235-6796

(P-18082)
WOLF & RAVEN LLC
206 W 4th St Ste 439, Santa Ana
(92701-4679)
PHONE.................800 431-6471
Josue B Vazquez, *CEO*
EMP: 99 **EST:** 2021
SALES (est): 2.2MM **Privately Held**
SIC: 8741 8742 Business management;
　　Business management consultant

(P-18083)
ZA MANAGEMENT
101 N Robertson Blvd, Beverly Hills
(90211-2146)
PHONE.................310 271-2200
Alexander Zaks, *CEO*
EMP: 90 **EST:** 2001
SALES (est): 2.42MM **Privately Held**
SIC: 8741 Management services

8742 Management Consulting Services

(P-18084)
AA BLOCKS LLC
9823 Pacific Heights Blvd Ste F, San Diego
(92121-4705)
PHONE.................858 523-8231
Branden G Lee, *Mgr*
EMP: 92 **EST:** 2017
SALES (est): 1.79MM **Privately Held**
Web: www.aablocks.com
SIC: 8742 Business management consultant

(P-18085)
ACCENTURE FEDERAL SERVICES LLC
Also Called: Accenture National SEC Svcs
1615 Murray Canyon Rd Ste 400, San
Diego (92108-4318)
PHONE.................619 574-2400
Jim Wangler, *Brnch Mgr*
EMP: 1486
Web: www.accenture.com
SIC: 8742 7361 8711 7373 Business
　　management consultant; Employment
　　agencies; Engineering services; Computer
　　integrated systems design
HQ: Accenture Federal Services Llc
　　800 N Glebe Rd Ste 300
　　Arlington VA 22203
　　703 947-2000

(P-18086)
ADVANTAGE MEDIA SERVICES INC
Also Called: AMS Fulfillment
28545 Livingston Ave, Valencia
(91355-4166)
PHONE.................661 775-0611
EMP: 70
SALES (corp-wide): 56.03MM **Privately
Held**
Web: www.amsfulfillment.com
SIC: 8742 Marketing consulting services
PA: Advantage Media Services, Inc.
　　29010 Commerce Center Dr
　　661 775-0611

(P-18087)
ALAN B WHITSON COMPANY INC
1507 W Alton Ave, Santa Ana
(92704-7219)
P.O. Box 9229 (92728-9229)
PHONE.................949 955-1200
Alan B Whitson, *Pr*
EMP: 750 **EST:** 1990
SQ FT: 18,000
SALES (est): 691.66K **Privately Held**
SIC: 8742 1389 5411 Corporation organizing
　　consultant; Servicing oil and gas wells;
　　Convenience stores, chain

(P-18088)
ALTRUIST CORP
3030 La Cienega Blvd, Culver City
(90232-7315)
PHONE.................949 370-5096
EMP: 271 **EST:** 2008
SALES (est): 13.03MM **Privately Held**
Web: www.altruist.com
SIC: 8742 Financial consultant

(P-18089)
ALVAREZ MRSAL BUS CNSLTING LLC
Also Called: ALVAREZ & MARSAL
BUSINESS CONSULTING LLC
2029 Century Park E, Los Angeles
(90002-3076)
PHONE.................310 975-2600
Dora Alverez, *Prin*
EMP: 334
SALES (corp-wide): 1.22B **Privately Held**
Web: www.alvarezandmarsal.com
SIC: 8742 Management consulting services
PA: Alvarez & Marsal Corporate
　　Performance Improvement, Llc
　　600 Madison Ave Fl 8
　　212 759-4433

(P-18090)
AMCO FOODS INC
601 E Glenoaks Blvd Ste 108, Glendale
(91207-1760)
PHONE.................818 247-4716
Bobken Amirian, *Pr*
Nick Amirian, *
Brian Polthow, *
Nareg Amirian, *
EMP: 475 **EST:** 1999
SALES (est): 1.4MM **Privately Held**
SIC: 8742 Business management consultant

(P-18091)
AMPM SYSTEMS INC
16520 Harbor Blvd Ste E, Fountain Valley
(92708-1360)
PHONE.................949 629-7800
Hirbod Davari, *Prin*
EMP: 75
SALES (est): 368.34K **Privately Held**
SIC: 8742 Management information systems
　　consultant

(P-18092)
AMTEX SUPPLY HOLDINGS INC
736 Inland Center Dr, San Bernardino
(92408-1806)
PHONE.................909 985-8918
EMP: 120
SALES (corp-wide): 8.22MM **Privately
Held**
SIC: 8742 Management consulting services
PA: Amtex Supply Holdings, Inc.
　　544 Lakeview Pkwy Ste 300
　　800 766-6676

(P-18093)
ANTHOS GROUP INC
705 N Douglas St, El Segundo
(90245-2830)
PHONE.................888 778-2986
Shan Umer, *Pr*
EMP: 25 **EST:** 2019
SALES (est): 911.55K **Privately Held**
Web: www.tidl.com
SIC: 8742 5047 2834 6111 Manufacturing
　　management consultant; Medical
　　equipment and supplies; Pharmaceutical
　　preparations; Export/Import Bank

(P-18094)
APA INCORPORATED
405 S Beverly Dr, Beverly Hills
(90212-4416)
P.O. Box 45 (90213-0045)
PHONE.................310 888-4200
Kat Cafeler, *Pr*
EMP: 83 **EST:** 2008
SALES (est): 1.74MM **Privately Held**
Web: www.apawood.org
SIC: 8742 Business management consultant

(P-18095)
APN BUSINESS RESOURCES INC
21418 Osborne St, Canoga Park
(91304-1520)
PHONE.................818 717-9980
Michael Noori, *CEO*
Khosrow Noori, *
EMP: 85 **EST:** 2011
SALES (est): 536.61K **Privately Held**
SIC: 8742 8748 Business planning and
　　organizing services; Business consulting,
　　nec

(P-18096)
ARTEMIS CONSULTING LLC
Also Called: Artemis Consulting
1012 W Washington St, San Diego
(92103-1808)
PHONE.................619 573-6328
Adam Svoboda, *Managing Member*
▲ **EMP:** 81 **EST:** 2005
SALES (est): 11.71MM **Privately Held**
Web: www.consultartemis.com
SIC: 8742 8741 8748 Management
　　engineering; Administrative management;
　　Systems analysis and engineering
　　consulting services

(P-18097)
ASSET MKTG SYSTEMS INSUR SVCS
Also Called: AMS
15050 Avenue Of Science Ste 100, San
Diego (92128-3418)
PHONE.................888 303-8755
Mike Botkin, *CEO*
Dee Costa, *Pr*
Jeff Stemler, *Ex VP*
Louise Kinard Erdman, *CFO*
EMP: 70 **EST:** 2003
SQ FT: 19,000
SALES (est): 8.63MM **Privately Held**
Web: www.assetmarketingsystems.com
SIC: 8742 Marketing consulting services

(P-18098)
AUNT RUBYS LLC
1014 E Carson St, Long Beach
(90807-3636)
PHONE.................562 326-6783
Todd Dotson, *Prin*
EMP: 50 **EST:** 2017
SALES (est): 439.41K **Privately Held**
SIC: 8742 7381 2771 8322 Corporation
　　organizing consultant; Security guard
　　service; Greeting cards; Adult day care
　　center

(P-18099)
AVASANT LLC (PA)
1960 E Grand Ave Ste 1050, El Segundo
(90245-5096)
PHONE.................310 643-3030
Kevin Parikh, *Managing Member*
Robert Randolph, *
EMP: 80 **EST:** 2006
SQ FT: 6,000
SALES (est): 4.82MM
SALES (corp-wide): 4.82MM **Privately
Held**
Web: www.avasant.com
SIC: 8742 Marketing consulting services

(P-18100)
AVETA HEALTH SOLUTION INC
3990 Concours Ste 500, Ontario
(91764-7983)
PHONE.................909 605-8000
Tim O'rourke, *Pr*
Rod St Clair, *Chief Medical Officer**
Marcia Anderson, *
Carol Hairston, *Health Service Vice
President**
EMP: 239 **EST:** 2010
SALES (est): 237.68K
SALES (corp-wide): 1.8MM **Privately Held**
SIC: 8742 Hospital and health services
　　consultant
HQ: Innovacare Services Company Llc
　　425 W Colonial Dr
　　Orlando FL 32804

(P-18101)
BAMKO LLC (HQ)
Also Called: Bamko Promotional Items
10925 Weyburn Ave, Los Angeles
(90024-2808)
PHONE.................................310 470-5859
Jake Himelstein, *CEO*
EMP: 567 EST: 2016
SALES (est): 55.07MM
SALES (corp-wide): 543.3MM **Publicly
Held**
Web: www.bamko.net
SIC: **8742** 7336 Merchandising consultant;
Package design
PA: Superior Group Of Companies, Inc.
200 Central Ave Ste 2000
727 397-9611

(P-18102)
BASKETBALL MARKETING CO INC
Also Called: and 1
101 Enterprise Ste 100, Aliso Viejo
(92656-2604)
PHONE.................................610 249-2255
Kevin Wulff, *Pr*
▲ EMP: 113 EST: 2006
SALES (est): 401.02K
SALES (corp-wide): 2.82B **Publicly Held**
SIC: **8742** Marketing consulting services
HQ: American Sporting Goods Corp
101 Enterprise Ste 200
Aliso Viejo CA 92656
949 267-2800

(P-18103)
BDS CONNECTED SOLUTIONS LLC
25962 Atlantic Ocean Dr, Lake Forest
(92630)
PHONE.................................800 234-4237
EMP: 174
SALES (corp-wide): 187.07MM **Privately
Held**
Web: www.bdssolutions.com
SIC: **8742** Marketing consulting services
HQ: Bds Connected Solutions, Llc
3802 Corporex Park Dr
Tampa FL 33619
949 472-6700

(P-18104)
BEACON RESOURCES LLC
17300 Red Hill Ave, Irvine (92614-5643)
PHONE.................................949 955-1773
Mike Kelly, *
EMP: 225 EST: 2010
SALES (est): 070.91K
SALES (corp-wide): 166.95MM **Privately
Held**
Web: www.addisongroup.com
SIC: **8742** Business planning and organizing
services
HQ: David M. Lewis Company, Llc
1201 Dove St
Newport Beach CA 92660

(P-18105)
BLACKSTONE CONSULTING INC (PA)
Also Called: BCI Alabama
11726 San Vicente Blvd Ste 550, Los
Angeles (90049-5089)
PHONE.................................310 826-4389
Ronald Joseph Blackstone, *Pr*
EMP: 71 EST: 1993
SQ FT: 1,500
SALES (est): 50.86MM **Privately Held**
Web: www.blackstone-consulting.com

SIC: **8742** Management consulting services

(P-18106)
BLANCHARD TRAINING AND DEV INC (PA)
Also Called: Ken Blanchard Companies, The
125 State Pl, Escondido (92029-1323)
PHONE.................................760 489-5005
Thomas J Mckee, *CEO*
Howard Farfel, *
Deborah K Blanchard, *
Scott Blanchard, *
▼ EMP: 200 EST: 1978
SALES (est): 61.26MM
SALES (corp-wide): 61.26MM **Privately
Held**
Web: www.blanchard.com
SIC: **8742** Training and development
consultant

(P-18107)
BON APPETIT MANAGEMENT CO
1259 E Colton Ave, Redlands (92374-3755)
PHONE.................................909 748-8970
Bret Martin, *Genl Mgr*
EMP: 237
SALES (corp-wide): 39.16B **Privately Held**
Web: www.bamco.com
SIC: **8742** Administrative services consultant
HQ: Bon Appetit Management Co.
201 Rdwood Shres Pkwy Ste
Redwood City CA 94065
650 798-8000

(P-18108)
BRANDED GROUP INC
Also Called: Facilities MGT & Coml RPS Svcs
222 S Harbor Blvd Ste 500, Anaheim
(92805-3712)
PHONE.................................323 940-1444
Mike Kurland, *CEO*
Kiira Esposito, *
Jerry Jonathan Thomas Iii, *Pr*
EMP: 218 EST: 2014
SQ FT: 13,372
SALES (est): 11.89MM **Privately Held**
Web: www.branded-group.com
SIC: **8742** 8741 Maintenance management
consultant; Construction management

(P-18109)
BRETT DINOVI & ASSOCIATES LLC
23046 Avenida De La Carlota Ste 600,
Laguna Hills (92653-1537)
PHONE.................................609 200-0123
EMP: 113
SALES (corp-wide): 8.96MM **Privately
Held**
Web: www.brettdassociates.com
SIC: **8742** Management consulting services
PA: Brett Dinovi & Associates Llc
3000 Atrium Way Ste 430
609 200-0123

(P-18110)
BRETT DINOVI & ASSOCIATES LLC
3200 E Guasti Rd Ste 100, Ontario
(91761-8661)
PHONE.................................609 200-0123
EMP: 113
SALES (corp-wide): 8.96MM **Privately
Held**
Web: www.brettdassociates.com
SIC: **8742** Management consulting services
PA: Brett Dinovi & Associates Llc
3000 Atrium Way Ste 430

---

609 200-0123

(P-18111)
BRIDGWTER CONSULTING GROUP INC
18881 Von Karman Ave Ste 1450, Irvine
(92612-8558)
PHONE.................................949 535-1755
Mark Montgomery, *CEO*
EMP: 90 EST: 2015
SQ FT: 1,600
SALES (est): 3.62MM **Privately Held**
Web: www.bridgewcg.com
SIC: **8742** 7379 Management consulting
services; Online services technology
consultants

(P-18112)
BSW CONSULTANTS INC
9532 Zion Cir, Huntington Beach
(92646-5363)
PHONE.................................949 279-3063
Brenna S Walraven, *Pr*
EMP: 1457 EST: 2014
SALES (est): 224.7K
SALES (corp-wide): 700MM **Privately
Held**
Web:
www.corporatesustainabilitystrategies.com
SIC: **8742** Business management consultant
PA: Legence Holdings Llc
1601 Las Plumas Ave
408 347-3400

(P-18113)
CAPTAIN MARKETING INC
3577 N Figueroa St, Los Angeles
(90065-2445)
PHONE.................................310 402-9709
EMP: 73
SALES (corp-wide): 940.62K **Privately
Held**
Web: www.captainmarketing.com
SIC: **8742** Marketing consulting services
PA: Captain Marketing, Inc.
337 Ne Emerson Ave
888 297-9977

(P-18114)
CATALYST SPEECH LLC
Also Called: Catalyst Spech Lngage Pthology
835 Milan Ave, South Pasadena
(91030-2812)
PHONE.................................213 346-9945
Ji Soo Kim, *CEO*
EMP: 186 EST: 2015
SALES (est): 351.15K
SALES (corp-wide): 105.05MM **Privately
Held**
SIC: **8742** Hospital and health services
consultant
PA: Pediatric Therapy Services, Llc
184 High St Ste 701
800 337-5965

(P-18115)
CHASE GROUP LLC
Also Called: Center At Parkwest, The
6740 Wilbur Ave, Reseda (91335-5179)
PHONE.................................818 708-3533
Phil Chase, *Brnch Mgr*
EMP: 295
Web: www.chasegroup.us
SIC: **8742** 8049 Management consulting
services; Nurses and other medical
assistants
PA: The Chase Group Llc
5374 Long Shadow Ct

(P-18116)
CITY OF IRVINE
Also Called: Dept of Public Works
6427 Oak Cyn, Irvine (92618-5202)
P.O. Box 19575 (92623-9575)
PHONE.................................949 724-7600
Allison Hart, *Mgr*
EMP: 147
SALES (corp-wide): 873.9MM **Privately
Held**
Web: www.cityofirvine.org
SIC: **8742** 9111 8748 7349 Public utilities
consultant; Mayors' office; Business
consulting, nec; Building maintenance
services, nec
PA: City Of Irvine
1 Civic Center Plaza
949 724-6000

(P-18117)
CITY OF RIVERSIDE
5901 Payton Ave, Riverside (92504-1003)
PHONE.................................951 826-5485
David Wright, *Dir*
EMP: 107
Web: www.riversideca.gov
SIC: **8742** Business planning and organizing
services
PA: City Of Riverside
3900 Main St 7 Fl
951 826-5311

(P-18118)
CO-PRODUCTION INTL INC
8716 Sherwood Ter, San Diego
(92154-7718)
PHONE.................................619 429-4344
Enrique Esparza, *Pr*
Jaime Edgar Esparza, *
EMP: 2300 EST: 1997
SALES (est): 8.3MM **Privately Held**
Web: www.co-production.net
SIC: **8742** Marketing consulting services
PA: Co-Production De Tijuana, S.A. De
C.V.
Blvd. Carretera Libre Antiguo Camino
Tijuana

(P-18119)
COCKRAM CONSTRUCTION INC
16340 Roscoe Blvd, Van Nuys
(91406-1217)
PHONE.................................818 650-0999
David Judd, *Pr*
Malcolm W Batten, *
Robert Sirgiovanni, *
Louis E Sciuto, *
Rene Alicea, *
EMP: 315 EST: 2000
SALES (est): 10.64MM **Privately Held**
Web: www.cockram.com
SIC: **8742** 8741 1541 Construction project
management consultant; Construction
management; Food products manufacturing
or packing plant construction
HQ: Kajima Cockram International Pty Ltd
L 2 110 Cubitt St
Cremorne VIC 3121

(P-18120)
CONSUMER RESOURCE NETWORK LLC
Also Called: Launchpad Communications
4420 E Miraloma Ave Ste J, Anaheim
(92807-1839)
PHONE.................................800 291-4794
EMP: 340 EST: 1995
SALES (est): 942.35K **Privately Held**
SIC: **8742** Marketing consulting services

(P-18121)
COVARIO INC
9255 Towne Centre Dr Ste 600, San Diego (92121-3039)
PHONE..............................858 397-1500
EMP: 96
SIC: 8742 Marketing consulting services

(P-18122)
CPE HR INC
9000 W Sunset Blvd Ste 900, West Hollywood (90069-5804)
PHONE..............................310 270-9800
Harold Walt, *CEO*
Faith Branvold, *
Grace Drulias, *
EMP: 90 EST: 1982
SALES (est): 3.23MM **Privately Held**
Web: www.cpehr.com
SIC: 8742 Human resource consulting services

(P-18123)
CROWN GOLF PROPERTIES LP
Also Called: Tustin Ranch Golf Club
12442 Tustin Ranch Rd, Tustin (92782-1000)
PHONE..............................714 730-1611
Steve Plummer, *Mgr*
EMP: 214
SALES (corp-wide): 24.85MM **Privately Held**
Web: www.tustinranchgolf.com
SIC: 8742 7997 7992 Business management consultant; Membership sports and recreation clubs; Public golf courses
PA: Crown Golf Properties, Lp
222 N La Salle St # 2000
312 395-7701

(P-18124)
CROWNE COLD STORAGE LLC
786 Road 188, Delano (93215-9508)
PHONE..............................661 725-6458
Cliff Woolley, *Managing Member*
EMP: 50 EST: 2014
SALES (est): 2.33MM **Privately Held**
SIC: 8742 2033 Business management consultant; Apple sauce: packaged in cans, jars, etc.

(P-18125)
DCW DCW INC
20500 Denker Ave, Torrance (90501-1645)
PHONE..............................310 858-1050
Mevlut Matteo Kirisci, *Mng Pt*
EMP: 75 EST: 2021
SALES (est): 945.76K **Privately Held**
SIC: 8742 Distribution channels consultant

(P-18126)
DENKEN SOLUTIONS INC
9170 Irvine Center Dr Ste 200, Irvine (92618-4614)
PHONE..............................949 630-5263
Rajendra Maddula, *CEO*
Eddie Gallardo, *
Rajendra Maddula, *Dir*
EMP: 250 EST: 2010
SQ FT: 4,000
SALES (est): 7.45MM **Privately Held**
Web: www.denkensolutions.com
SIC: 8742 8748 7371 7361 Management consulting services; Systems analysis and engineering consulting services; Computer software systems analysis and design, custom; Employment agencies

(P-18127)
DIAGNOSTIC HEALTH CORPORATION
Also Called: Diagnostic Health Los Angeles
6801 Park Ter, Los Angeles (90045-1543)
PHONE..............................310 665-7180
Janet Bateman, *Prin*
EMP: 192
SALES (corp-wide): 1.81B **Privately Held**
SIC: 8742 Hospital and health services consultant
HQ: Diagnostic Health Corporation
22 Inverness Pkwy Ste 425
Birmingham AL 35242

(P-18128)
DOPPLER AUTOMOTIVE INC
1515 W 190th St Ste 440, Gardena (90248-4374)
PHONE..............................310 765-4100
David Stokols, *CEO*
George Lewis, *CFO*
EMP: 100 EST: 2019
SALES (est): 11MM **Privately Held**
Web: www.dopplerdrives.com
SIC: 8742 Marketing consulting services

(P-18129)
DOWLING ADVISORY GROUP
3579 E Foothill Blvd Ste 651, Pasadena (91107-3119)
PHONE..............................626 319-1369
James Dowling, *Owner*
EMP: 100 EST: 2010
SALES (est): 597.33K **Privately Held**
Web: www.dowlingadvisorygroup.com
SIC: 8742 Business management consultant

(P-18130)
EASTERN GOLDFIELDS INC
1660 Hotel Cir N Ste 207, San Diego (92108-2803)
PHONE..............................619 497-2555
Michael Mcchesney, *CEO*
EMP: 218 EST: 1998
SALES (est): 439.72K **Privately Held**
Web: www.easterngoldfields.com
SIC: 8742 Management consulting services

(P-18131)
EGNITE INC
Also Called: Egnite Health, Inc.
65 Enterprise Pmb 455, Aliso Viejo (92656-2705)
PHONE..............................949 594-2330
Joel Portice, *Pr*
Mike Dobbles, *
Rahul Sharma Senior Medical, *Adviser*
Jessica Neufeld, *
Kahla Verhoef, *CPO**
EMP: 90 EST: 2020
SALES (est): 4.52MM **Privately Held**
Web: www.egnitehealth.com
SIC: 8742 8011 Hospital and health services consultant; Cardiologist and cardio-vascular specialist

(P-18132)
EXULT INC
121 Innovation Dr Ste 200, Irvine (92612)
P.O. Box 6300 (92658-6300)
PHONE..............................949 856-8800
James C Madden V, *Ch Bd*
Kevin Campbell, *
John Adams, *
Stephen M Unterberger, *Executive Business Model Operations Vice President**
Robert E Ball, *CPO**
EMP: 2424 EST: 1998
SQ FT: 22,000

SALES (est): 3.43MM
SALES (corp-wide): 3.41B **Publicly Held**
Web: www.exult.net
SIC: 8742 Human resource consulting services
HQ: Alight (Us), Llc
200 E Rndolph St Lowr Ll3
Chicago IL 60601
312 381-1000

(P-18133)
FAIRWAY TECHNOLOGIES LLC (PA)
4370 La Jolla Village Dr Ste 500, San Diego (92122-1251)
PHONE..............................858 454-4471
Brett Humphrey, *CEO*
EMP: 90 EST: 2002
SALES (est): 4.64MM
SALES (corp-wide): 4.64MM **Privately Held**
Web: www.accenture.com
SIC: 8742 Business management consultant

(P-18134)
FDSI LOGISTICS LLC
Also Called: Fdsi Logistics
27680 Avenue Mentry # 2, Valencia (91355-1200)
PHONE..............................818 971-3300
David Kolchins, *VP*
Dee Weller, *
John Hudson, *
EMP: 75 EST: 2000
SALES (est): 6.24MM
SALES (corp-wide): 226.83B **Publicly Held**
SIC: 8742 4731 Transportation consultant; Freight transportation arrangement
PA: Cardinal Health, Inc.
7000 Cardinal Pl
614 757-5000

(P-18135)
FERRY INTERNATIONAL LLC
Also Called: Tom Ferry Coaching
6 Hutton Centre Dr Ste 700, Santa Ana (92707-5735)
PHONE..............................888 866-3377
EMP: 74 EST: 2018
SALES (est): 5.18MM **Privately Held**
Web: www.tomferry.com
SIC: 8742 Management consulting services

(P-18136)
FINANCIAL TECH SLTONS INTL INC
Also Called: Ftsi
406 E Huntington Dr Ste 100, Monrovia (91016-3662)
PHONE..............................818 241-9571
Susan Baird Napier, *CEO*
Susan Baird Napier, *Pr*
John De La Pena, *
EMP: 140 EST: 2000
SALES (est): 21.97MM **Privately Held**
Web: www.ftsius.com
SIC: 8742 Banking and finance consultant

(P-18137)
FIRST CAPITOL CONSULTING INC
Also Called: Trusaic
520 S Grand Ave, Los Angeles (90071-2600)
PHONE..............................213 382-1115
Robert Sheen, *Pr*
EMP: 73 EST: 1999
SALES (est): 2.16MM **Privately Held**

Web: www.trusaic.com
SIC: 8742 Management consulting services

(P-18138)
FISHERIES RESOURCE VLNTR CORPS
109 Stanford Ln, Seal Beach (90740-2533)
PHONE..............................562 596-9261
Thomas J Walsh, *Pr*
EMP: 113 EST: 2011
SALES (est): 280.58K **Privately Held**
Web: www.frvc.org
SIC: 8742 Business planning and organizing services

(P-18139)
FOUNDATION PROPERTY MGT INC
Also Called: RETIREMENT HOUSING
911 N Studebaker Rd Ste 100, Long Beach (90815-4980)
PHONE..............................562 257-5100
Laverne R Joseph, *CEO*
Robert Amberg, *Sr VP*
Stuart Hartman, *VP*
Deborah Stouff, *Sec*
Cheryl Howell, *Sec*
EMP: 111 EST: 1981
SQ FT: 24,000
SALES (est): 14.53MM
SALES (corp-wide): 106.87MM **Privately Held**
Web: www.rhf.org
SIC: 8742 Business planning and organizing services
PA: Retirement Housing Foundation Inc
911 N Stdbaker Rd Ste 100
562 257-5100

(P-18140)
GANZ USA LLC
16525 Sherman Way Ste C5, Van Nuys (91406-3753)
PHONE..............................818 901-0077
Marilyn Smith, *Brnch Mgr*
EMP: 99
SIC: 8742 5199 Management consulting services; Gifts and novelties
HQ: Ganz U.S.A., Llc
3855 Shallowford Rd # 220
Marietta GA 30062

(P-18141)
GAVIN DE BECKER & ASSOC GP LLC
Also Called: Gavin De Becker & Associates
350 N Glendale Ave Ste 517, Glendale (91206-3794)
PHONE..............................818 505-0177
Gavin De Becker, *Managing Member*
Michael La Fever, *
EMP: 180 EST: 1979
SQ FT: 1,600
SALES (est): 39.15MM **Privately Held**
Web: www.gdba.com
SIC: 8742 Business management consultant

(P-18142)
GCORP CONSULTING
2831 Camino Del Rio S Ste 311, San Diego (92108-3829)
PHONE..............................619 587-3160
Alba Graham, *CEO*
James Graham, *
EMP: 147 EST: 2011
SALES (est): 2.41MM **Privately Held**
Web: www.gcorpconsulting.com

▲ = Import ▼ = Export
◆ = Import/Export

SIC: 8742 8711 7379 8243 Management consulting services; Engineering services; Online services technology consultants; Software training, computer

(P-18143)
GLP CAPITAL PARTNERS LP
100 Wilshire Blvd Ste 1400, Santa Monica (90401-1196)
PHONE..................310 356-0880
Adam Burnes, *Prin*
EMP: 86 EST: 2019
SALES (est): 8.33MM **Privately Held**
Web: www.gcp.com
SIC: 8742 Business management consultant

(P-18144)
GOETZMAN GROUP INC
21333 Oxnard St Ste 200, Woodland Hills (91367-5194)
PHONE..................818 595-1112
Greg Goetzman, *Pr*
EMP: 90 EST: 1998
SALES (est): 5.59MM **Privately Held**
Web: www.goetzmangroup.com
SIC: 8742 8721 Management consulting services; Accounting, auditing, and bookkeeping

(P-18145)
GREENHOUSE AGENCY INC
4100 Birch St Ste 500, Newport Beach (92660-2273)
PHONE..................949 752-7542
Sean Roche, *Prin*
EMP: 113 EST: 2012
SALES (est): 3.51MM **Privately Held**
Web: www.greenhouseagency.com
SIC: 8742 Marketing consulting services

(P-18146)
HATCHBEAUTY AGENCY LLC (PA)
355 S Grand Ave Ste 1450, Los Angeles (90071-3152)
PHONE..................310 396-7070
Tracy Holland, *Managing Member*
◆ EMP: 30 EST: 2008
SALES (est): 4.87MM **Privately Held**
SIC: 8742 2844 5122 Marketing consulting services; Perfumes, cosmetics and other toilet preparations; Cosmetics, perfumes, and hair products

(P-18147)
HEALTHCARE FINANCE DIRECT LLC
1707 Eye St Ste 300, Bakersfield (93301-5208)
PHONE..................661 616-4400
Tyler Johnson, *CEO*
Mark Weighall, *CFO*
EMP: 84 EST: 2009
SALES (est): 7.15MM **Privately Held**
Web: www.gohfd.com
SIC: 8742 Financial consultant

(P-18148)
HEALTHTRIO LLC
21255 Burbank Blvd, Woodland Hills (91367-6610)
PHONE..................520 571-1988
John Bradley, *Brnch Mgr*
EMP: 75
SALES (corp-wide): 43.05MM **Privately Held**
Web: www.healthtrio.com

SIC: 8742 7371 Management consulting services; Custom computer programming services
HQ: Healthtrio Llc
201 Columbine St Ste 300
Denver CO 80206

(P-18149)
HR&A ADVISORS INC
700 S Flower St Ste 2995, Los Angeles (90017-4217)
PHONE..................310 581-0900
George Bogakos, *Brnch Mgr*
EMP: 75
Web: www.hraadvisors.com
SIC: 8742 Business management consultant
PA: Hr&A Advisors, Inc.
99 Hudson St Rm 3l

(P-18150)
IMPACT TECH INC (HQ)
223 E De La Guerra St, Santa Barbara (93101-2206)
PHONE..................805 324-6021
David Yovanno, *CEO*
Scott Brazin, *CMO**
EMP: 309 EST: 2007
SQ FT: 8,000
SALES (est): 50.47MM **Privately Held**
Web: www.impact.com
SIC: 8742 Marketing consulting services
PA: Estalea (Pty) Ltd
Office 202 Santyger Office Park, 313
Durban Rd

(P-18151)
INDEPENDENT FINCL GROUP LLC
12671 High Bluff Dr Ste 200, San Diego (92130-3018)
PHONE..................858 436-3180
EMP: 209 EST: 2003
SALES (est): 5.71MM **Privately Held**
Web: www.ifgsd.com
SIC: 8742 Financial consultant

(P-18152)
INFORMATION FORECAST INC
Also Called: Infocast
22144 Clarendon St Ste 280, Woodland Hills (91367-6321)
PHONE..................818 888-4445
William A Meyer, *Pr*
Bill Meyer, *
Carin Ralph, *
EMP: 30 EST: 1986
SALES (est): 4.9MM **Privately Held**
Web: www.infocastinc.com
SIC: 8742 2721 Public utilities consultant; Magazines: publishing only, not printed on site

(P-18153)
INFOSPAN
18301 Von Karman Ave Ste 1000, Irvine (92612-0198)
PHONE..................714 856-2655
Farooq Bajwa, *Pr*
EMP: 721
SALES (corp-wide): 1.81MM **Privately Held**
SIC: 8742 Management consulting services
PA: Infospan
31878 Del Obspo St Ste 11
949 260-9990

(P-18154)
INTELITY INC
16501 Ventura Blvd, Encino (91436-2007)
PHONE..................310 596-8160

Steve Proctor, *CEO*
EMP: 126 EST: 2014
SALES (est): 3.33MM **Privately Held**
Web: www.intelity.com
SIC: 8742 General management consultant

(P-18155)
JACK NADEL INC (PA)
Also Called: Jack Nadel International
5820 Uplander Way, Culver City (90230-6608)
P.O. Box 8342 (91109)
PHONE..................310 815-2600
Craig Nadel, *CEO*
Jack Nadel, *
Debbie Abergel, *
Craig Reese, *
Steve Widdicombe, *
◆ EMP: 70 EST: 1953
SQ FT: 30,000
SALES (est): 31.57MM
SALES (corp-wide): 31.57MM **Privately Held**
Web: www.nadel.com
SIC: 8742 5199 Marketing consulting services; Advertising specialties

(P-18156)
KINGS GARDEN LLC
Also Called: Kings Garden Royal Deliveries
3540 N Anza Rd, Palm Springs (92262-1606)
PHONE..................760 275-4969
Lauri Kibby, *Managing Member*
Michael King, *Managing Member*
EMP: 180 EST: 2018
SALES (est): 3.53MM **Privately Held**
Web: www.kingsgarden.com
SIC: 8742 Marketing consulting services

(P-18157)
KORN FERRY (US) (HQ)
Also Called: Hay Group
1900 Avenue Of The Stars Ste 2600, Los Angeles (90067-4507)
PHONE..................310 552-1834
EMP: 250 EST: 1963
SALES (est): 72.79MM
SALES (corp-wide): 2.8B **Publicly Held**
SIC: 8742 Human resource consulting services
PA: Korn Ferry
1900 Ave Of The Stars Ste
310 552-1834

(P-18158)
KPC GROUP INC (PA)
0 Kpo Pkwy # 301, Corona (02870 7102)
PHONE..................951 782-8812
Michael O'brien, *Pr*
EMP: 167 EST: 2006
SALES (est): 354.46MM **Privately Held**
Web: www.thekpcgroup.com
SIC: 8742 Financial consultant

(P-18159)
KVC GROUP LLC
Also Called: National Credit Partners
1551 N Tustin Ave Ste 550, Santa Ana (92705-8637)
PHONE..................855 438-0377
Kim Vo, *Managing Member*
EMP: 75 EST: 2018
SALES (est): 1.46MM **Privately Held**
Web: www.corporatefinanceliability.com
SIC: 8742 Marketing consulting services

(P-18160)
LBA INC
Also Called: Lba Realty

3333 Michelson Dr Ste 230, Irvine (92612-8803)
PHONE..................949 833-0400
Perry Schonfeid, *Brnch Mgr*
EMP: 73
Web: www.lbarealty.com
SIC: 8742 Real estate consultant
PA: Lba Inc.
3347 Michelson Dr Ste 200

(P-18161)
LOLLICUP FRANCHISING LLC
6185 Kimball Ave, Chino (91708-9126)
PHONE..................626 965-8882
Alan Yu, *Prin*
EMP: 243 EST: 2009
SALES (est): 437.44K
SALES (corp-wide): 405.65MM **Publicly Held**
Web: www.lollicupfresh.com
SIC: 8742 5149 Food and beverage consultant; Coffee and tea
PA: Karat Packaging Inc.
6185 Kimball Ave
626 965-8882

(P-18162)
LOTUS WORKFORCE LLC
Also Called: Human Capital Select, LLC
5930 Cornerstone Ct W Ste 300, San Diego (92121-3772)
PHONE..................480 264-0773
Martha White, *Pr*
EMP: 534 EST: 2012
SALES (est): 502K **Privately Held**
Web: www.ayahealthcare.com
SIC: 8742 Human resource consulting services
PA: Aya Healthcare, Inc.
5930 Crnrstone Ct W Ste 3

(P-18163)
LPL HOLDINGS INC (HQ)
Also Called: Lpl Holdings
4707 Executive Dr, San Diego (92121-3091)
PHONE..................858 450-9606
Mark Casady, *Ch*
EMP: 208 EST: 1989
SALES (est): 568.06MM **Publicly Held**
Web: www.lpl.com
SIC: 8742 Financial consultant
PA: Lpl Financial Holdings Inc.
4707 Executive Dr

(P-18164)
M F SALTA CO INC (PA)
Also Called: Atlas Advertising
20 Executive Park Ste 150, Irvine (92614-4732)
PHONE..................562 421-2512
Mike Salta, *Pr*
James Smith, *
EMP: 70 EST: 1959
SALES (est): 782.47K
SALES (corp-wide): 782.47K **Privately Held**
SIC: 8742 Management consulting services

(P-18165)
MANAGEMENT TRUST ASSN INC
12607 Hiddencreek Way Ste R, Cerritos (90703-2146)
PHONE..................562 926-3372
Christie Alviso, *Admn*
EMP: 94
Web: www.managementtrust.com
SIC: 8742 8741 Management consulting services; Business management
PA: The Management Trust Association Inc
15661 Red Hl Ave Ste 201

(PA)=Parent Co (HQ)=Headquarters
✪ = New Business established in last 2 years

(P-18166)
MAPP DIGITAL US LLC
4660 La Jolla Village Dr Ste 100, San Diego
(92122-2604)
PHONE....................619 342-4340
Steve Warren, *CEO*
Jonah Sulak, *
Cody Kase, *
Eric Hinkle, *
Juhan Lee, *
EMP: 308 **EST:** 2000
SALES (est): 50MM **Privately Held**
Web: www.mapp.com
SIC: 8742 Marketing consulting services
PA: Marlin Equity Partners, Llc
1301 Manhattan Ave

(P-18167)
MATT CONSTRUCTION CORPORATION (PA)
9814 Norwalk Blvd Ste 100, Santa Fe
Springs (90670-2997)
PHONE....................562 903-2277
Paul J Matt, *CEO*
Steve F Matt, *
Alan B Matt, *
EMP: 109 **EST:** 1991
SQ FT: 21,000
SALES (est): 29.2MM **Privately Held**
Web: www.mattconstruction.com
SIC: 8742 Construction project management
consultant

(P-18168)
MEDICAL MANAGEMENT CONS INC
Also Called: MMC
6046 Cornerstone Ct W, San Diego
(92121-4758)
PHONE....................858 587-0609
Mister Rahmani, *Mgr*
EMP: 4950
SALES (corp-wide): 18.24MM **Privately
Held**
Web: www.mmchr.com
SIC: 8742 Hospital and health services
consultant
PA: Medical Management Consultants, Inc.
8150 Beverly Blvd
310 659-3835

(P-18169)
MEDICAL RECORD ASSOCIATES INC
600 Corporate Pointe, Culver City
(90230-7600)
PHONE....................617 698-4411
Charlie Sopanelo, *Owner*
EMP: 140 **EST:** 1986
SALES (est): 2.36MM **Privately Held**
Web: www.mrahis.com
SIC: 8742 8741 7334 Industry specialist
consultants; Hospital management;
Photocopying and duplicating services

(P-18170)
MENTOR MDIA USA SUP CHAIN MGT
865 S Washington Ave, San Bernardino
(92408-2237)
PHONE....................909 930-0800
Kok Khoon Lim, *CEO*
▲ **EMP:** 80 **EST:** 2008
SALES (est): 1.64MM **Privately Held**
Web: www.mentormedia.com
SIC: 8742 8741 Business planning and
organizing services; Business management
HQ: Mentor Media Ltd
47 Jalan Buroh

Singapore 61949

(P-18171)
METROSTUDY INC
Also Called: Zonda Intelligence
4000 Macarthur Blvd Ste 400, Newport
Beach (92660-2543)
PHONE....................714 619-7800
Jeff Meyers, *CEO*
Melissa Billiter, *
EMP: 121 **EST:** 2013
SALES (est): 2.57MM
SALES (corp-wide): 179.03MM **Privately
Held**
Web: www.zondahome.com
SIC: 8742 7379 Real estate consultant;
Computer related consulting services
HQ: Hanley Wood Market Intelligence
555 Anton Blvd Ste 950
Costa Mesa CA 92626

(P-18172)
MICHAELSON CONNOR & BOUL (PA)
5312 Bolsa Ave, Huntington Beach
(92649-1051)
PHONE....................714 230-3600
Joan Heid, *Pr*
Michael Ryan, *
Firmin Boul, *
EMP: 100 **EST:** 1994
SQ FT: 12,500
SALES (est): 3.44MM **Privately Held**
Web: www.mcbreo.com
SIC: 8742 Real estate consultant

(P-18173)
MORRIS & WILLNER PARTNERS
Also Called: Mw Partners
1503 S Coast Dr, Costa Mesa
(92626-1534)
PHONE....................949 705-0682
Divya Pyreddy, *CEO*
EMP: 100 **EST:** 2010
SALES (est): 11.79MM **Privately Held**
Web: www.mwpartners.net
SIC: 8742 Management consulting services

(P-18174)
MUTH MACHINE WORKS
4510 Rutile St, Riverside (92509-2649)
PHONE....................951 685-1521
Dwayne Gleason, *Mgr*
EMP: 80
SALES (corp-wide): 23.6MM **Privately
Held**
SIC: 8742 Manufacturing management
consultant
HQ: Muth Machine Works
8042 Katella Ave
Stanton CA 90680

(P-18175)
NAN MCKAY AND ASSOCIATES INC
1810 Gillespie Way Ste 202, El Cajon
(92020-0920)
PHONE....................619 258-1855
Nan Mckay, *Pr*
James Mckay, *VP*
John Mckay, *CEO*
Raymond Adair, *
Dorian Jenkins, *
EMP: 58 **EST:** 1980
SQ FT: 14,000
SALES (est): 18.73MM **Privately Held**
Web: www.nanmckay.com

SIC: 8742 7371 2731 Training and
development consultant; Computer
software development; Textbooks:
publishing and printing

(P-18176)
NATIONAL CLEARING CORPORATION (PA)
Also Called: J B Oxford & Co
9665 Wilshire Blvd, Beverly Hills
(90212-2340)
PHONE....................310 385-2165
Christopher Garrett, *Pr*
EMP: 70 **EST:** 2003
SQ FT: 20,400
SALES (est): 496.46K
SALES (corp-wide): 496.46K **Privately
Held**
SIC: 8742 Financial consultant

(P-18177)
NATIONAL TOUR INTGRTED RSRCES
23141 Arroyo Vis Ste 100, Rcho Sta Marg
(92688-2613)
PHONE....................949 215-6330
Johnny R Capels, *Pr*
EMP: 23 **EST:** 2009
SQ FT: 6,000
SALES (est): 2.51MM **Privately Held**
Web: www.nationaltourintegrated.com
SIC: 8742 3448 Marketing consulting
services; Prefabricated metal buildings and
components

(P-18178)
NATIONSBENEFITS LLC
1540 Scenic Ave, Costa Mesa
(92626-1408)
PHONE....................877 439-2665
EMP: 809
SALES (corp-wide): 125.57MM **Privately
Held**
Web: www.nationsbenefits.com
SIC: 8742 6371 6411 Management
consulting services; Pension, health, and
welfare funds; Insurance agents, brokers,
and service
PA: Nationsbenefits, Llc
1700 N University Dr
877 439-2665

(P-18179)
NBC CONSULTING INC
Also Called: Pacific Health and Welness
2110 Artesia Blvd Ste 323, Redondo Beach
(90278-3073)
PHONE....................310 798-5000
Neal M Bychek, *Pr*
Robin Bychek, *
EMP: 100 **EST:** 2004
SALES (est): 785.95K **Privately Held**
Web: www.nbc-consulting.com
SIC: 8742 Hospital and health services
consultant

(P-18180)
NCOMPASS INTERNATIONAL LLC
Also Called: Ncompass International
12101 Crenshaw Blvd Ste 800, Hawthorne
(90250-3458)
PHONE....................323 785-1700
Donna Direnzo Graves, *Pr*
Kae Erickson, *
EMP: 138 **EST:** 2003
SALES (est): 8.86MM **Privately Held**
Web: www.ncompassonline.com

SIC: 8742 Marketing consulting services

(P-18181)
NEARDATA INC
Also Called: Neardata Systems
1361 Foothill Blvd, La Canada Flintridge
(91011-2121)
PHONE....................818 249-2469
Samuel S Chilingurian, *Pr*
EMP: 76 **EST:** 2005
SALES (est): 4.03MM **Privately Held**
Web: www.neardata.net
SIC: 8742 7371 Management consulting
services; Computer software development

(P-18182)
NISSAN NORTH AMERICA INC
18501 S Figueroa St, Gardena
(90248-4504)
P.O. Box 2814 (90509-2814)
PHONE....................310 768-3700
Minoru Nakamura, *Pr*
EMP: 10350 **EST:** 1990
SALES (est): 5.12MM **Privately Held**
SIC: 8742 3711 5012 6159 Management
consulting services; Motor vehicles and car
bodies; Automobiles and other motor
vehicles; Equipment and vehicle finance
leasing companies
PA: Nissan Motor Co., Ltd.
1-1-1, Takashima, Nishi-Ku

(P-18183)
NORTH HIGHLAND COMPANY LLC
4640 Lankershim Blvd Ste 305, North
Hollywood (91602-1848)
PHONE....................818 509-5100
John Depoma, *Brnch Mgr*
EMP: 85
Web: www.northhighland.com
SIC: 8742 Business management consultant
PA: The North Highland Company Llc
3333 Piedmont Rd Ste 1000

(P-18184)
NORTHGATE GONZALEZ INC
425 S Soto St, Los Angeles (90033-4315)
PHONE....................323 262-0595
Estela Gonz Lez De Ortiz, *Prin*
EMP: 438
SALES (corp-wide): 217.82MM **Privately
Held**
Web: www.northgatemarket.com
SIC: 8742 5411 Marketing consulting
services; Grocery stores
PA: Northgate Gonzalez, Inc.
1201 N Magnolia Ave
714 778-3784

(P-18185)
NUSANO INC
28575 Livingston Ave, Valencia
(91355-4166)
PHONE....................424 270-9600
Chris Lowe, *CEO*
Scott Holbrook, *Ch Bd*
Alexandre Gibim, *COO*
EMP: 95 **EST:** 2015
SALES (est): 9.95MM **Privately Held**
Web: www.nusano.com
SIC: 8742 Management consulting services

(P-18186)
NVE INC
912 N La Cienega Blvd 2nd Fl, Los Angeles
(90069-4848)
PHONE....................323 512-8400
Brett Nathan Hyman, *CEO*
EMP: 100 **EST:** 2005

SALES (est): 8.67MM **Privately Held**
Web: www.experiencenve.com
SIC: **8742** Marketing consulting services

(P-18187)
ONLINE MARKETING GROUP LLC
Also Called: Zoek
530 Technology Dr Ste 100, Irvine
(92618-1350)
PHONE................................888 737-9635
Samuel Riemer, *CEO*
Doug Powell, *
EMP: **106** EST: **2015**
SALES (est): 7.7MM **Privately Held**
Web: www.gozoek.com
SIC: **8742** Marketing consulting services

(P-18188)
ONYX GLOBAL HR LLC (PA)
110 Pine Ave Ste 920, Long Beach
(90802-4455)
P.O. Box 5673 (92863-5673)
PHONE................................866 715-4806
EMP: **163** EST: **2008**
SQ FT: 1,000
SALES (est): 7.3MM **Privately Held**
Web: www.onyxglobalhr.com
SIC: **8742** Human resource consulting services

(P-18189)
OPERAM INC
1041 N Formosa Ave 500, West Hollywood
(90046-6703)
PHONE................................855 673-7261
Johnny Wong, *Prin*
EMP: **84** EST: **2015**
SQ FT: 23,000
SALES (est): 9.44MM **Privately Held**
Web: www.operam.com
SIC: **8742** Marketing consulting services

(P-18190)
PANDORA MARKETING LLC
Also Called: Timeshare Compliance
26970 Aliso Viejo Pkwy Ste 150, Aliso Viejo
(92656-2621)
PHONE................................800 705-6856
EMP: **75** EST: **2016**
SALES (est): 8.53MM **Privately Held**
Web: www.timesharecompliance.com
SIC: **8742** Marketing consulting services

(P-18191)
PATHOLOGY INC
19951 Mariner Ave Ste 150, Torrance
(90503-1738)
PHONE................................310 769-0561
EMP: **356**
Web: www.pathologyinc.com
SIC: **0742** **0071** Hospital and health services consultant; Medical laboratories

(P-18192)
PLUG CONNECTION LLC
3742 Blue Bird Canyon Rd, Vista
(92084-7432)
PHONE................................760 631-0992
Ken Altman, *Managing Member*
EMP: **106** EST: **2016**
SALES (est): 583.3K **Privately Held**
Web: www.plugconnection.com
SIC: **8742** Business management consultant

(P-18193)
PMCS GROUP INC
2600 E Pacific Coast Hwy Ste 160, Long
Beach (90804-1532)

PHONE................................562 498-0808
Walid Azar, *Pr*
Violene Azar, *
Walid Azar, *VP*
EMP: **100** EST: **2005**
SALES (est): 5.12MM **Privately Held**
Web: www.pmcsgroup.net
SIC: **8742** Construction project management consultant

(P-18194)
POWER DIGITAL MARKETING INC (PA)
2251 San Diego Ave Ste A250, San Diego
(92110-2984)
PHONE................................619 501-1211
Grayson Lafrenz, *CEO*
Sasha Dagayev, *Ex VP*
Corey Eulas, *CSO*
EMP: **340** EST: **2012**
SALES (est): 30.49MM
SALES (corp-wide): 30.49MM **Privately Held**
Web: www.powerdigitalmarketing.com
SIC: **8742** Marketing consulting services

(P-18195)
POWERSOURCE TALENT LLC
12655 W Jefferson Blvd Ste 400, Los
Angeles (90066-7008)
PHONE................................424 835-0878
EMP: **101** EST: **2017**
SALES (est): 3.4MM **Privately Held**
Web: www.powersourcetalent.com
SIC: **8742** Management consulting services

(P-18196)
PRO SAFETY & RESCUE INC
3700 Pegasus Dr Ste 200, Bakersfield
(93308-6805)
PHONE................................888 269-5095
Sarah Pierce, *Pr*
Jessie Pierce, *TRESR*
EMP: **70** EST: **2014**
SALES (est): 4.83MM **Privately Held**
Web: www.prosafetyandrescue.com
SIC: **8742** **8999** Training and development consultant; Search and rescue service

(P-18197)
PWC STRATEGY& (US) LLC
601 S Figueroa St Ste 900, Los Angeles
(90017-5743)
PHONE................................213 356-6000
EMP: **113**
SALES (corp-wide): 6.79B **Privately Held**
Web: www.pwc.com
SIC: **8742** Management consulting services
HQ: Pwc Strategy& (Us) Llc
101 Park Ave 18th Fl
New York NY 10178

(P-18198)
Q SQUARED SOLUTIONS LLC
Also Called: Q2 Solutions
27027 Tourney Rd Ste2e, Valencia
(91355-5386)
PHONE................................661 964-6635
EMP: **88**
Web: www.q2labsolutions.com
SIC: **8742** Management consulting services
HQ: Q Squared Solutions Llc
2400 Ellis Rd
Durham NC

(P-18199)
RALIS SERVICES CORP
Also Called: Ralis
1 City Blvd W Ste 600, Orange
(92868-3639)

PHONE................................844 347-2547
Delbert O Meeks, *CEO*
Mike Chiang, *
EMP: **150** EST: **2014**
SALES (est): 6MM **Privately Held**
Web: www.ralisservices.com
SIC: **8742** **7371** **8721** Human resource consulting services; Custom computer programming services; Accounting services, except auditing

(P-18200)
RALPH BRENNAN REST GROUP LLC
Also Called: Red Fish Grill
1590 S Disneyland Dr, Anaheim
(92802-2319)
PHONE................................714 776-5200
Kiki Lungquist, *Brnch Mgr*
EMP: **143**
Web: www.neworleans-food.com
SIC: **8742** Restaurant and food services consultants
PA: The Ralph Brennan Restaurant Group Llc
550 Bienville St

(P-18201)
RED PEAK GROUP LLC
23975 Park Sorrento Ste 410, Calabasas
(91302-4031)
PHONE................................818 222-7762
EMP: **90** EST: **2009**
SALES (est): 665.27K **Privately Held**
SIC: **8742** Marketing consulting services

(P-18202)
RMD GROUP INC
2311 E South St, Long Beach (90805-4424)
PHONE................................562 866-9288
Ralph Holguin, *Pr*
EMP: **300** EST: **2008**
SALES (est): 8.32MM **Privately Held**
Web: www.rmdgroupinc.com
SIC: **8742** Marketing consulting services

(P-18203)
ROCKY POINT INVESTMENTS LLC (HQ)
Also Called: Creative Channel Services LLC
6601 Center Dr W Ste 400, Los Angeles
(90045-1577)
PHONE................................310 482-6500
Andy Restivo, *CEO*
George Plumb, *
Hanoz Gandhi, *
Michael Butler, *
EMP: **105** EST: **1995**
SALES (est): 8.45MM
SALES (corp-wide): 14.69B **Publicly Held**
SIC: **0742** Marketing consulting services
PA: Omnicom Group Inc.
280 Park Ave
212 415-3600

(P-18204)
SABAN BRANDS LLC (HQ)
10100 Santa Monica Blvd Ste 500, Los
Angeles (90067-4121)
PHONE................................310 557-5230
Elie Dekel, *Managing Member*
William Kehoe, *Managing Member*
Nina Leong, *Managing Member*
Kirk Bloomgarden, *Managing Member*
Rami Yanni, *Managing Member*
EMP: **88** EST: **2010**
SQ FT: 605,000
SALES (est): 2.25MM
SALES (corp-wide): 30.44MM **Privately Held**

Web: www.saban.com
SIC: **8742** General management consultant
PA: Global Reach 18, Inc.
10100 Santa Monica Blvd
310 203-5850

(P-18205)
SCORPION DESIGN LLC (PA)
Also Called: Scorpion
27750 Entertainment Dr, Valencia
(91355-1091)
PHONE................................661 702-0100
Rustin Kretz, *CEO*
Daniel Street, *
Mikel Chertudi, *
Raj Ramanan, *
EMP: **585** EST: **2003**
SQ FT: 100,000
SALES (est): 98.02MM
SALES (corp-wide): 98.02MM **Privately Held**
Web: www.scorpion.co
SIC: **8742** Marketing consulting services

(P-18206)
SEEK CAPITAL LLC
Also Called: Seek Government Funds
6420 Wilshire Blvd, Los Angeles
(90048-5502)
PHONE................................855 978-6106
Roy Ferman, *CEO*
EMP: **75** EST: **2014**
SALES (est): 7.21MM **Privately Held**
Web: www.seekcapital.com
SIC: **8742** Management consulting services

(P-18207)
SENDLANE INC
10620 Treena St Ste 250, San Diego
(92131-1141)
PHONE................................301 520-3812
EMP: **75** EST: **2018**
SALES (est): 2.27MM **Privately Held**
Web: www.sendlane.com
SIC: **8742** Marketing consulting services

(P-18208)
SHEIN TECHNOLOGY LLC (PA)
777 S Alameda St Fl 2, Los Angeles
(90021-1657)
PHONE................................213 628-4008
EMP: **500** EST: **2021**
SALES (est): 3.31MM
SALES (corp-wide): 3.31MM **Privately Held**
SIC: **8742** Management consulting services

(P-18209)
SHELL OIL COMPANY
Also Called: Shell
511 N Brookhurst St, Anaheim
(92801-5231)
P.O. Box 4848 (92803-4848)
PHONE................................714 991-9200
Roger Underwood, *Brnch Mgr*
EMP: **125**
SALES (corp-wide): 316.62B **Privately Held**
Web: www.shell.com
SIC: **8742** Industry specialist consultants
HQ: Shell Usa, Inc.
150 N Dairy Ashford Rd
Houston TX 77079
832 337-2000

(P-18210)
SIMPSON SMPSON MGT CNSLTING IN
718 S Date Ave Ste A1, Alhambra
(91803-1412)

PHONE..................626 282-4000
Hamid Taheri, *Admn*
Carl P Simpson, *
EMP: 74 **EST:** 2001
SQ FT: 2,000
SALES (est): 1.95MM **Privately Held**
Web: www.ssmci.net
SIC: 8742 Business management consultant

(P-18211)
SITE HELPERS LLC
25232 Steinbeck Ave, Stevenson Ranch
(91381-1240)
PHONE..................877 217-5395
Danika Weber, *Managing Member*
EMP: 100 **EST:** 2021
SALES (est): 291.53K **Privately Held**
SIC: 8742 7389 Marketing consulting
    services; Business services, nec

(P-18212)
SL BLUE GARDEN CORP
2251 Las Palmas Dr, Carlsbad
(92011-1527)
PHONE..................626 633-2672
Brandon Phan, *CEO*
Susan Luo, *
EMP: 126 **EST:** 2014
SALES (est): 517.77K **Privately Held**
SIC: 8742 Management consulting services

(P-18213)
SMART CIRCLE
INTERNATIONAL LLC (PA)
Also Called: Smart Circle, The
4490 Von Karman Ave, Newport Beach
(92660-2008)
PHONE..................949 587-9207
Michael Meryash, *CEO*
George Graffy, *
Jigna Patel, *
Paul Sunny, *
EMP: 90 **EST:** 2007
SQ FT: 10,700
SALES (est): 327.12MM **Privately Held**
Web: www.smartcircle.com
SIC: 8742 Marketing consulting services

(P-18214)
SMG HOLDINGS LLC
Also Called: Palm Springs Convention Center
277 N Avenida Caballeros, Palm Springs
(92262-6440)
PHONE..................760 325-6611
Jim Dunn, *Brnch Mgr*
EMP: 84
SALES (corp-wide): 1.13B **Privately Held**
Web: www.asmglobal.com
SIC: 8742 7389 Business management
    consultant; Convention and show services
HQ: Smg Holdings, Llc
    800 W Olympic Blvd Fl 3
    Los Angeles CA 90015

(P-18215)
SMITH-EMERY INTERNATIONAL
INC (PA)
791 E Washington Blvd Fl 3, Los Angeles
(90021-3043)
PHONE..................213 741-8500
James E Patridge, *Pr*
Helen Choe, *
EMP: 222 **EST:** 1976
SQ FT: 32,380
SALES (est): 29.55MM **Privately Held**
Web: www.smithemeryinternational.com
SIC: 8742 Management consulting services

(P-18216)
SOCIALCOM INC (PA)
Also Called: Audiencex
73 Market St, Venice (90291-3603)
PHONE..................310 289-4477
EMP: 91 **EST:** 2013
SALES (est): 387.67MM
SALES (corp-wide): 387.67MM **Privately
Held**
Web: www.audiencex.com
SIC: 8742 Marketing consulting services

(P-18217)
SODEXO MANAGEMENT INC
450 World Way, Los Angeles (90045-5812)
PHONE..................310 646-3738
EMP: 1882
SALES (corp-wide): 246.43MM **Privately
Held**
Web: www.sodexo.com
SIC: 8742 Food and beverage consultant
HQ: Sodexo Management Inc.
    915 Meeting St
    Rockville MD 20852

(P-18218)
SPOTIFY USA INC
555 Mateo St, Los Angeles (90013-2647)
PHONE..................213 505-3040
EMP: 246
SALES (corp-wide): 2.67MM **Privately
Held**
SIC: 8742 Management consulting services
HQ: Spotify Usa Inc.
    150 Greenwich St Fl 62
    New York NY 10007

(P-18219)
SQA SERVICES INC
Also Called: Sqa Services
425 Via Corta Ste 203, Palos Verdes
Estates (90274-1358)
P.O. Box 5220 (90274-9672)
PHONE..................800 333-6180
Michael Guymon, *Pr*
Jim Mckay, *Ch*
Gerard Pearce, *
EMP: 267 **EST:** 1995
SQ FT: 8,000
SALES (est): 26.55MM **Privately Held**
Web: www.sqaservices.com
SIC: 8742 Quality assurance consultant

(P-18220)
ST MARYS MEDICAL CENTER
Also Called: ST MARY'S MEDICAL CENTER
1050 Linden Ave, Long Beach
(90813-3393)
PHONE..................562 491-9230
Suzan Konel, *Brnch Mgr*
EMP: 3489
SALES (corp-wide): 19.17B **Publicly Held**
Web: www.paleyinstitute.org
SIC: 8742 Hospital and health services
    consultant
HQ: St. Mary's Medical Center, Inc.
    901 45th St
    West Palm Beach FL 33407
    561 844-6300

(P-18221)
STONE CANYON INDS
HOLDINGS LLC (PA)
1875 Century Park E Ste 320, Los Angeles
(90067-2539)
PHONE..................424 316-2061
James Fordyce, *CEO*
Michael C Salvator, *COO*
Michael Neumann, *Pr*
EMP: 48 **EST:** 2018

SALES (est): 3.82B
SALES (corp-wide): 3.82B **Privately Held**
Web: www.scihinc.com
SIC: 8742 2899 Industrial consultant; Heat
    treating salts

(P-18222)
SULLIVNCRTSMNROE INSUR
SVCS LL (PA)
Also Called: Nationwide
1920 Main St Ste 600, Irvine (92614-7226)
P.O. Box 19763 (92623-9763)
PHONE..................800 427-3253
John Monroe, *CEO*
David Kummer, *
Shawn Kraatz, *
Jeannine Coronado, *
William Curtis, *
EMP: 103 **EST:** 1987
SQ FT: 22,000
SALES (est): 11.61MM
SALES (corp-wide): 11.61MM **Privately
Held**
Web: www.sullivancurtismonroe.com
SIC: 8742 6411 Management consulting
    services; Insurance brokers, nec

(P-18223)
SUN PACIFIC MARKETING
COOP INC
33502 Lerdo Hwy, Bakersfield
(93308-9438)
PHONE..................213 612-9957
Berne H Evans Iii, *Brnch Mgr*
EMP: 395
SALES (corp-wide): 24.27MM **Privately Held**
Web: www.sunpacific.com
SIC: 8742 Marketing consulting services
PA: Sun Pacific Marketing Cooperative, Inc.
    1095 E Green St
    213 612-9957

(P-18224)
T G T ENTERPRISES INC
Also Called: Anderson
12650 Danielson Ct, Poway (92064-6822)
PHONE..................858 413-0300
Randy Dale, *CEO*
Scott Hopkins, *Ex VP*
Todd Stoker, *COO*
EMP: 145 **EST:** 1976
SQ FT: 77,000
SALES (est): 21.68MM **Privately Held**
Web: www.andersondd.com
SIC: 8742 2759 7311 Marketing consulting
    services; Commercial printing, nec;
    Advertising agencies

(P-18225)
TECHNICAL MICRO CONS INC
(PA)
Also Called: Technology Management
Concepts
807 N Park View Dr Ste 150, El Segundo
(90245-4932)
PHONE..................310 559-3982
Jennifer Harris, *Pr*
EMP: 25 **EST:** 1985
SQ FT: 3,000
SALES (est): 4.76MM
SALES (corp-wide): 4.76MM **Privately
Held**
Web: www.abouttmc.com
SIC: 8742 7372 5734 Management
    information systems consultant;
    Prepackaged software; Software, business
    and non-game

(P-18226)
TECHNOLOGY ASSOCIATES EC
INC
3129 Tiger Run Ct Ste 206, Carlsbad
(92010-6512)
PHONE..................760 765-5275
Walter Oleski, *CEO*
EMP: 74 **EST:** 2010
SALES (est): 4.62MM **Privately Held**
Web: www.taec.net
SIC: 8742 General management consultant

(P-18227)
TECOLOTE RESEARCH INC
Also Called: Santa Barbara Group
5266 Hollister Ave Ste 301, Santa Barbara
(93111-2089)
PHONE..................805 964-6963
James Suttle, *Brnch Mgr*
EMP: 141
SALES (corp-wide): 39.02MM **Privately
Held**
Web: www.socalpianoacademy.com
SIC: 8742 Marketing consulting services
PA: Tecolote Research, Inc.
    420 S Fairview Ave # 201
    805 571-6366

(P-18228)
TECOLOTE RESEARCH INC
2120 E Grand Ave Ste 200, El Segundo
(90245-5024)
PHONE..................310 640-4700
James Takayesu, *Pr*
EMP: 89
SALES (corp-wide): 39.02MM **Privately
Held**
Web: www.tecolote.com
SIC: 8742 8731 Management consulting
    services; Commercial physical research
PA: Tecolote Research, Inc.
    420 S Fairview Ave # 201
    805 571-6366

(P-18229)
TELESECTOR RESOURCES
GROUP INC
Also Called: Verizon
5010 Azusa Canyon Rd, Baldwin Park
(91706-1830)
PHONE..................626 813-4538
Nancy Cano, *Mgr*
EMP: 431
SALES (corp-wide): 133.97B **Publicly
Held**
SIC: 8742 Management consulting services
HQ: Telesector Resources Group, Inc.
    140 West St
    New York NY 10007
    212 395-1000

(P-18230)
TELESTAR INTERNATIONAL
CORP
Also Called: Telestar Material
5536 Balboa Blvd, Encino (91316-1505)
PHONE..................818 582-3018
Frank Liu, *Pr*
Charlie Fu, *
Karen Liu, *
EMP: 46 **EST:** 1976
SALES (est): 2.25MM **Privately Held**
SIC: 8742 3861 3663 Marketing consulting
    services; Photographic equipment and
    supplies; Antennas, transmitting and
    communications

▲ = Import ▼ = Export
◆ = Import/Export

(P-18231)
TELUS HEALTH (US) LTD
27715 Jefferson Ave Ste 103, Temecula
(92590-2636)
PHONE.....................888 577-3784
EMP: 155
SALES (corp-wide): 518.71MM **Privately Held**
Web: www.telus.com
SIC: **8742** Human resource consulting services
HQ: Telus Health (Us) Ltd.
250 Royall St Ste 210 W
Canton MA 02021

(P-18232)
TORRID MERCHANDISING INC
18501 San Jose Ave, City Of Industry
(91748-1330)
PHONE.....................626 667-1002
Lisa Harper, *CEO*
Tim Martin, *
Chinwe Abaelu, *
Elizabeth Munoz, *Chief Creative Officer**
▲ EMP: 418 EST: 2015
SALES (est): 5.69MM **Publicly Held**
SIC: **8742** 5621 Merchandising consultant; Ready-to-wear apparel, women's
HQ: Torrid Holdings Inc.
18501 E San Jose Ave
City Of Industry CA 91748
626 667-1002

(P-18233)
TOTAL RECON SOLUTIONS INC
27 Oakbrook, Trabuco Canyon
(92679-4741)
PHONE.....................949 584-8417
Santiago Rydelski, *CEO*
EMP: 90 EST: 2011
SALES (est): 2.06MM **Privately Held**
SIC: **8742** Management consulting services

(P-18234)
TRI-AD ACTUARIES INC
Also Called: Tri-Ad
221 W Crest St Ste 300, Escondido
(92025-1737)
PHONE.....................760 743-7555
Thad Hamilton, *CEO*
Curtis Hamilton, *
Judy Simons, *
Thad Hamilton, *VP*
Robert Krier, *
EMP: 117 EST: 1973
SQ FT: 17,500
SALES (est): 4.96MM **Privately Held**
Web: www.tri-ad.com
SIC: **8742** 6411 Human resource consulting services; Pension and retirement plan consultants

(P-18235)
TRINAMIX INC (PA)
35 Amoret Dr, Irvine (92602-0770)
PHONE.....................408 507-3583
Amit Sharma, *CEO*
Molly Chakraborty, *Pr*
Sandeep Goyal, *CFO*
EMP: 289 EST: 2008
SALES (est): 2.03MM
SALES (corp-wide): 2.03MM **Privately Held**
Web: www.trinamix.com
SIC: **8742** 7379 7361 Management consulting services; Computer related consulting services; Labor contractors (employment agency)

(P-18236)
UNITED TALENT AGENCY LLC
Also Called: UNITED TALENT AGENCY, LLC
1880 Century Park E Ste 711, Los Angeles
(90067-1618)
PHONE.....................310 385-2800
Grant Ledger, *Owner*
EMP: 81
SALES (corp-wide): 34.87MM **Privately Held**
Web: www.xcastlabs.com
SIC: **8742** Management consulting services
PA: United Talent Agency Holdings, Inc.
888 7th Ave Ste 922
310 273-6700

(P-18237)
UPSTREM INC
1253 University Ave Ste 1003, San Diego
(92103-3391)
PHONE.....................858 229-2979
Jacob Risman, *CEO*
Steven Maman, *
EMP: 70 EST: 2018
SQ FT: 1,500
SALES (est): 18MM **Privately Held**
Web: www.upstrem.com
SIC: **8742** Sales (including sales management) consultant

(P-18238)
VISTANCIA MARKETING LLC
Also Called: Shea Homes Ltd Prtnershp
655 Brea Canyon Rd, Walnut (91789-3078)
PHONE.....................909 594-9500
John Francisshea, *Prin*
EMP: 92 EST: 2003
SALES (est): 927.29K
SALES (corp-wide): 2.1B **Privately Held**
Web: www.jfshea.com
SIC: **8742** Marketing consulting services
HQ: Shea Homes Limited Partnership, A California Limited Partnership
655 Brea Canyon Rd
Walnut CA 91789

(P-18239)
WASSERMAN MEDIA GROUP LLC (PA)
Also Called: Wasserman
10900 Wilshire Blvd Ste 1200, Los Angeles
(90024-6548)
PHONE.....................310 407-0200
Casey Wasserman, *Managing Member*
Tim Chadwick, *COO*
Dean Christopher, *CFO*
EMP: 115 EST: 2003
SQ FT: 40,000
SALES (est): 116.26MM
SALES (corp-wide): 116.26MM **Privately Held**
Web: www.wmgllc.com
SIC: **8742** Marketing consulting services

(P-18240)
WATTS HEALTH SYSTEMS INC (PA)
3405 W Imperial Hwy, Inglewood
(90303-2219)
PHONE.....................310 424-2220
Clyde W Oden, *Pr*
EMP: 700 EST: 1983
SALES (est): 847.89K
SALES (corp-wide): 847.89K **Privately Held**
Web: www.wattshealthsystems.com
SIC: **8742** Hospital and health services consultant

(P-18241)
WELLMADE INC
Also Called: Polagram
800 E 12th St, Los Angeles (90021-2198)
PHONE.....................213 221-1123
Jin Kim, *Pr*
EMP: 100 EST: 2018
SALES (est): 759.18K **Privately Held**
Web: www.wellmadeusa.com
SIC: **8742** Business management consultant

(P-18242)
WILLIS NORTH AMERICA INC
Also Called: Willis Insurance Services Cal
18101 Von Karman Ave Ste 600, Irvine
(92612-0158)
PHONE.....................909 476-3300
Bryan Fitzpatrick, *Prin*
EMP: 236
Web: www.wtwco.com
SIC: **8742** Management consulting services
HQ: Willis North America Inc.
200 Liberty St Fl 7
New York NY 10281
212 915-8888

(P-18243)
WILSHIRE ADVISORS LLC (PA)
1299 Ocean Ave Ste 600, Santa Monica
(90401-1021)
PHONE.....................310 451-3051
Andy Stewart, *CEO*
Emily Brown, *
Scott Condron, *
Josh Emmanuel, *CIO**
Leah Emkin, *CCO**
EMP: 210 EST: 1972
SQ FT: 57,530
SALES (est): 45.88MM
SALES (corp-wide): 45.88MM **Privately Held**
Web: www.wilshire.com
SIC: **8742** Financial consultant

(P-18244)
WPROMOTE LLC (PA)
101 Continental Blvd Fl 1, El Segundo
(90245-4516)
PHONE.....................310 421-4844
Michael Mothner, *Pr*
Paul Rappoport, *
Michael Block, *
Paul Dumais, *
Michael Stone, *CRO**
EMP: 104 EST: 2004
SALES (est): 48.59MM
SALES (corp-wide): 48.59MM **Privately Held**
Web: www.wpromote.com
SIC: **8742** Marketing consulting services

(P-18245)
YMARKETING LLC
4000 Macarthur Blvd Ste 350, Newport
Beach (92660-2517)
PHONE.....................714 545-2550
Ryan Lash, *CEO*
Brian Yun, *COO*
Jennifer Jee, *Chief Relations Officer*
EMP: 70 EST: 2007
SALES (est): 4.81MM
SALES (corp-wide): 38.29MM **Privately Held**
SIC: **8742** Marketing consulting services
HQ: The Sandbox Group Llc
200 E Randolph St # 3450
Chicago IL 60601
312 803-1900

(P-18246)
YOUNG & RUBICAM LLC
1735 Irvine Center Dr, Irvine (92618)
PHONE.....................949 224-6300
David Murphy, *Pr*
EMP: 300
SALES (corp-wide): 18.5B **Privately Held**
Web: www.vml.com
SIC: **8742** Marketing consulting services
HQ: Young & Rubicam Llc
175 Greenwich St Fl 28
New York NY 10007
212 210-3017

(P-18247)
YOUR PRACTICE ONLINE LLC (PA)
4590 Macarthur Blvd Ste 500, Newport
Beach (92660-2028)
PHONE.....................877 388-8569
Doctor Prem Lobo, *Managing Member*
EMP: 109 EST: 2004
SALES (est): 288.84K **Privately Held**
Web: www.yourpracticeonline.net
SIC: **8742** Marketing consulting services

(P-18248)
ZENLEADS INC
Also Called: Apollo.io
440 N Barranca Ave # 4750, Covina
(91723-1722)
PHONE.....................415 640-9303
Timothy Tianyuan Zheng, *CEO*
Malvin Hoxhallari, *
EMP: 500 EST: 2016
SALES (est): 28.42MM **Privately Held**
Web: www.apollo.io
SIC: **8742** Marketing consulting services

(P-18249)
ZIPRECRUITER INC (PA)
Also Called: ZIPRECRUITER
604 Arizona Ave, Santa Monica
(90401-1610)
PHONE.....................877 252-1062
Ian Siegel, *Ch Bd*
David Travers, *Pr*
Timothy Yarbrough, *CFO*
Qasim Saifee, *COO*
Ryan Sakamoto, *CLO*
EMP: 1150 EST: 2010
SQ FT: 60,000
SALES (est): 645.72MM **Publicly Held**
Web: www.ziprecruiter.com
SIC: **8742** 7371 Human resource consulting services; Custom computer programming services

8743 Public Relations Services

(P-18250)
BERK COMMUNICATIONS INC
329 N Wetherly Dr Ste 203, Beverly Hills
(90211-1675)
PHONE.....................310 734-5525
EMP: 73
Web: www.berkcommunications.com
SIC: **8743** Public relations and publicity
HQ: Berk Communications, Inc.
1250 Broadway Fl 3
New York NY 10001
212 889-0440

(P-18251)
BRAND AMP LLC
1945 Placentia Ave Ste C, Costa Mesa
(92627-6274)

PHONE..............................949 438-1060
Todd Brooks, *Managing Member*
Karen Schaefer, *
EMP: 74 EST: 2012
SQ FT: 16,069
SALES (est): 9.6MM Privately Held
Web: www.thebrandamp.com
SIC: 8743 8742 Public relations and publicity
; Marketing consulting services

(P-18252)
CALIBRE INTERNATIONAL LLC
Also Called: High Caliber Line
6250 N Irwindale Ave, Irwindale
(91702-3208)
PHONE..............................626 969-4660
Catherine Oas, *
◆ **EMP: 165 EST: 1998**
SQ FT: 100,000
SALES (est): 25.26MM Privately Held
Web: www.highcaliberline.com
SIC: 8743 2759 Promotion service;
Promotional printing

(P-18253)
COALITION TECHNOLOGIES LLC
445 S Figueroa St Ste 3100, Los Angeles
(90071-1635)
PHONE..............................310 827-3890
Joel Gross, *CEO*
EMP: 143 EST: 2009
SALES (est): 2.33MM Privately Held
Web: www.coalitiontechnologies.com
SIC: 8743 8243 7372 7371 Public relations
services; Software training, computer;
Business oriented computer software;
Computer software development

(P-18254)
HAVAS FORMULA LLC
1215 Cushman Ave, San Diego
(92110-3904)
PHONE..............................619 234-0345
Michael A Olguin, *Pr*
Alexis Mccance, *Sr VP*
Tara Reid, *
EMP: 100 EST: 2014
SQ FT: 2,700
SALES (est): 21.68MM Privately Held
Web: www.havasformula.com
SIC: 8743 Public relations and publicity
HQ: Havas
29-30
Puteaux IDF 92800
158478000

(P-18255)
MAGIC WORKFORCE SOLUTIONS LLC
9100 Wilshire Blvd Ste 700e, Beverly Hills
(90212-3423)
PHONE..............................310 246-6153
Earvin Johnson, *CEO*
Eric Holoman, *
Kawanna Brown, *
EMP: 2021 EST: 2007
SALES (est): 532.05K
SALES (corp-wide): 24.92MM Privately Held
Web: www.magicjohnson.com
SIC: 8743 Promotion service
PA: Magic Johnson Enterprises, Inc.
9100 Wlshire Blvd Ste 700
310 247-2033

8744 Facilities Support Services

(P-18256)
ADVANCED CLEANUP TECH INC
Also Called: Acti
230 E C St, Wilmington (90744-6612)
PHONE..............................310 763-1423
Ruben Garcia, *CEO*
EMP: 260 EST: 1992
SALES (est): 8.99MM Privately Held
Web: www.advancedcleanup.com
SIC: 8744 Environmental remediation

(P-18257)
AMERITAC INC (PA)
24 Toscana Way W, Rancho Mirage
(92270-1978)
P.O. Box 2550 (92270-1088)
PHONE..............................925 989-2942
Isiah Harris, *Pr*
Lawrence Stevens, *
EMP: 80 EST: 1994
SQ FT: 2,024
SALES (est): 3.26MM Privately Held
Web: www.ameritac.net
SIC: 8744 Base maintenance (providing
personnel on continuing basis)

(P-18258)
ARGUS MANAGEMENT COMPANY LLC
Also Called: Argus Medical Management
5150 E Pacific Coast Hwy Ste 500, Long
Beach (90804-3328)
PHONE..............................562 299-5200
Robert Lugliani, *
Peter Ferrera, *
Barry Allswang, *
Mansoor Shah, *
EMP: 300 EST: 1995
SQ FT: 2,500
SALES (est): 23.01MM Privately Held
Web: www.argusmso.com
SIC: 8744 Facilities support services

(P-18259)
CAMSTON WRATHER LLC
2856 Whiptail Loop, Carlsbad (92010-6708)
PHONE..............................858 525-9999
Dirk Wray, *CEO*
Aaron Kamenash, *CIO**
Jason Price, *
EMP: 250 EST: 2014
SQ FT: 1,000
SALES (est): 5.85MM Privately Held
Web: www.camstonwrather.com
SIC: 8744 8711 1629 1041 Environmental
remediation; Mining engineer; Land
reclamation; Placer gold mining

(P-18260)
CHUGACH GOVERNMENT SVCS INC
9466 Black Mountain Rd Ste 240, San
Diego (92126-6500)
PHONE..............................858 578-0276
Kevin Terry, *Mgr*
EMP: 487
SALES (corp-wide): 1.06B Privately Held
Web: www.chugach.com
SIC: 8744 Facilities support services
HQ: Chugach Government Services, Inc.
3800 Cntrpint Dr Ste 1200
Anchorage AK 99503

(P-18261)
DEPARTMENT MILITARY CALIFORNIA
Also Called: CA Arng 115th Rsg
11300 Lexington Dr Bldg 1000, Los
Alamitos (90720-5002)
PHONE..............................562 795-2065
Chi Huynh, *Brnch Mgr*
EMP: 500
**SALES (corp-wide): 534.4MM Privately
Held**
Web: calguard.ca.gov
SIC: 8744 Facilities support services
HQ: Department Of Military California
10601 Bear Hollow Dr
Rancho Cordova CA 95670

(P-18262)
INDYNE INC
1036 California Blvd Bldg 11013,
Vandenberg Afb (93437-6202)
PHONE..............................805 606-7225
Kenneth A Cinal, *Brnch Mgr*
EMP: 297
**SALES (corp-wide): 45.03MM Privately
Held**
Web: www.indyneinc.com
SIC: 8744 Base maintenance (providing
personnel on continuing basis)
PA: Indyne, Inc.
46561 Expedition Dr 100
703 903-6900

(P-18263)
INNOVATIVE CNSTR SOLUTIONS
575 Anton Blvd Ste 850, Costa Mesa
(92626-7023)
PHONE..............................714 893-6366
Hirad Emadi, *Pr*
John R White, *
EMP: 105 EST: 1999
SQ FT: 2,000
SALES (est): 112.42MM Privately Held
Web: www.icsinc.tv
SIC: 8744 1795 Environmental remediation;
Demolition, buildings and other structures

(P-18264)
M & E TECHNICAL SERVICES L L C
Also Called: Mets//
3601 Bayview Dr, Manhattan Beach
(90266-3225)
PHONE..............................256 964-6486
EMP: 100
Web: www.metechservices.com
SIC: 8744 4225 4731 7539 Facilities support
services; General warehousing and storage
; Freight transportation arrangement;
Automotive repair shops, nec

(P-18265)
OLYMPUS BUILDING SERVICES INC
Also Called: OLYMPUS BUILDING
SERVICES INC
441 La Moree Rd, San Marcos
(92078-5017)
PHONE..............................760 750-4629
Anthony Hipple, *Brnch Mgr*
EMP: 920
**SALES (corp-wide): 620.83MM Privately
Held**
Web: www.olympusinc.com
SIC: 8744 Facilities support services
HQ: Olympus Building Services, Llc
1430 E Missouri Ave B205
Phoenix AZ 85014
480 284-8018

(P-18266)
PONDER ENVIRONMENTAL SVCS INC
19484 Broken Ct, Shafter (93263-3146)
PHONE..............................661 589-7771
Curtis Fox, *Mgr*
EMP: 25
**SALES (corp-wide): 16.11MM Privately
Held**
Web:
www.ponderenvironmentalservices.com
SIC: 8744 4959 2899 Environmental
remediation; Environmental cleanup
services; Fuel tank or engine cleaning
chemicals
PA: Ponder Environmental Services, Inc.
4563 E 2nd St
707 748-7775

(P-18267)
PRO ENERGY SERVICES GROUP LLC
2060 Aldergrove Ave, Escondido
(92029-1901)
PHONE..............................760 744-7077
Gavin Necochea, *CEO*
EMP: 465 EST: 2012
SALES (est): 18.96MM Privately Held
Web: www.proeservices.com
SIC: 8744 Facilities support services

(P-18268)
TECHFLOW INC (PA)
Also Called: Techflow Scntfic A Div Tchflow
9889 Willow Creek Rd Ste 100, San Diego
(92131-1119)
PHONE..............................858 412-8000
Robert Baum, *CEO*
Mark Carter, *
Lorie Atoe, *
EMP: 104 EST: 1995
SQ FT: 19,000
SALES (est): 22.52MM
**SALES (corp-wide): 22.52MM Privately
Held**
Web: www.techflow.com
SIC: 8744 8711 8748 Facilities support
services; Engineering services; Systems
analysis and engineering consulting
services

(P-18269)
ULTURA INC
Also Called: Ultura
3605 Long Beach Blvd Ste 201, Long Beach
(90807-4024)
PHONE..............................562 661-4999
EMP: 128
SIC: 8744 3399 Environmental remediation;
Iron ore recovery from open hearth slag

(P-18270)
VALIANT GOVERNMENT SVCS LLC
540 Perdew Ave Ste B, Ridgecrest
(93555-2596)
PHONE..............................760 499-1400
Roger Stuart, *Mgr*
EMP: 446
**SALES (corp-wide): 560.35MM Privately
Held**
Web: www.onevaliant.com
SIC: 8744 Facilities support services
HQ: Valiant Government Services Llc
225 Ray Ave Ste 300
Fayetteville NC 28301

(P-18271)
WORKCARE INC
300 S Harbor Blvd Ste 600, Anaheim
(92805-3718)
PHONE....................714 978-7488
Doctor Peter P Greaney, *CEO*
William E Nixon, *
Paula Sandrock, *
Mason D Harrell Iii, *Chief Medical Officer*
EMP: 181 **EST:** 1997
SQ FT: 11,000
SALES (est): 22.35MM **Privately Held**
Web: www.workcare.com
SIC: 8744 8011 Facilities support services;
Offices and clinics of medical doctors

8748 Business Consulting, Nec

(P-18272)
3E COMPANY ENV EC N ENG (PA)
Also Called: 3e
3207 Grey Hawk Ct, Carlsbad
(92010-6662)
PHONE....................760 602-8700
Gregory Gartland, *CEO*
Justin Byron, *
Audrey Jean, *
EMP: 102 **EST:** 1985
SQ FT: 38,139
SALES (est): 48.54MM **Privately Held**
Web: www.3eco.com
SIC: 8748 8731 8711 Environmental
consultant; Environmental research;
Consulting engineer

(P-18273)
ACCENT COMPUTER SOLUTIONS LLC
8438 Red Oak St, Rancho Cucamonga
(91730-3815)
PHONE....................909 825-2772
Marlin J Kaufman, *CEO*
Debbie Kaufman, *Sec*
EMP: 70 **EST:** 1987
SQ FT: 4,000
SALES (est): 9.54MM **Privately Held**
Web: www.vc3.com
SIC: 8748 1623 Systems engineering
consultant, ex. computer or professional;
Cable laying construction
PA: Vc3, Inc.
1301 Gervais St Ste 1800

(P-18274)
ACTIVATE INC
8383 Wilshire Blvd Ste 240, Beverly Hills
(90211-2445)
PHONE....................212 598-4625
EMP: 76
SALES (corp-wide): 2.29MM **Privately Held**
Web: www.vacuactivus.com
SIC: 8748 Business consulting, nec
PA: Activate Inc.
11 Madison Sq N Fl 18
212 316-4444

(P-18275)
ADVANCED STRILIZATION PDTS INC
33 Technology Dr, Irvine (92618-2346)
PHONE....................888 783-7723
Chad Rohrer, *Pr*
EMP: 424 **EST:** 2018
SALES (est): 10.45MM
SALES (corp-wide): 6.07B **Publicly Held**

Web: www.asp.com
SIC: 8748 Business consulting, nec
PA: Fortive Corporation
6920 Seaway Blvd
425 446-5000

(P-18276)
AECOM TECHNICAL SERVICES INC (HQ)
300 S Grand Ave Fl 9, Los Angeles
(90071-3135)
PHONE....................213 593-8100
Timothy H Keener, *CEO*
▲ **EMP:** 100 **EST:** 1970
SQ FT: 43,000
SALES (est): 271.74MM
SALES (corp-wide): 16.11B **Publicly Held**
Web: www.aecom.com
SIC: 8748 4953 8742 8711 Environmental
consultant; Refuse systems; Industry
specialist consultants; Engineering services
PA: Aecom
13355 Noel Rd Ste 400
972 788-1000

(P-18277)
AECOM USA INC
999 W Town And Country Rd, Orange
(92868-4713)
PHONE....................714 567-2501
Bruce Toro, *Mgr*
EMP: 122
SALES (corp-wide): 16.11B **Publicly Held**
SIC: 8748 Business consulting, nec
HQ: Aecom Usa, Inc.
605 3rd Ave
New York NY 10158
212 973-2900

(P-18278)
AECOM USA INC
300 S Grand Ave Ste 900, Los Angeles
(90071-3135)
PHONE....................213 593-8000
Frederick Werner, *Brnch Mgr*
EMP: 122
SALES (corp-wide): 16.11B **Publicly Held**
Web: www.aecom.com
SIC: 8748 Business consulting, nec
HQ: Aecom Usa, Inc.
605 3rd Ave
New York NY 10158
212 973-2900

(P-18279)
AECOM USA INC
515 S Figueroa St Ste 400, Los Angeles
(90071-3323)
PHONE....................213 330-7200
EMP: 102
SALES (corp-wide): 16.11B **Publicly Held**
Web: www.aecom.com
SIC: 8748 Business consulting, nec
HQ: Aecom Usa, Inc.
605 3rd Ave
New York NY 10158
212 973-2900

(P-18280)
AECOM USA INC
401 W A St Ste 1200, San Diego
(92101-7905)
PHONE....................858 947-7144
Frederick William Werner, *Brnch Mgr*
EMP: 122
SALES (corp-wide): 16.11B **Publicly Held**
SIC: 8748 8741 Business consulting, nec;
Construction management
HQ: Aecom Usa, Inc.
605 3rd Ave

New York NY 10158
212 973-2900

(P-18281)
ALIANTEL INC
1940 W Corporate Way, Anaheim
(92801-5373)
PHONE....................714 829-1650
Suresh Sachdeva, *CEO*
John Kelly, *
EMP: 90 **EST:** 1996
SALES (est): 1.24MM **Privately Held**
SIC: 8748 7389 Telecommunications
consultant; Telephone services

(P-18282)
ALLIANT INSURANCE SERVICES INC (PA)
Also Called: Nationwide
18100 Von Karman Ave Ste 1000, Irvine
(92612-7196)
P.O. Box 6450 (92658)
PHONE....................949 756-0271
Greg Zimmer, *CEO*
Ilene Anders, *CFO*
Peter Carpenter, *COO*
Diana Kiehl, *CAO*
Kevin Wintermute, *Ex VP*
EMP: 175 **EST:** 1997
SALES (est): 1.15B
SALES (corp-wide): 1.15B **Privately Held**
Web: www.alliant.com
SIC: 8748 6411 Business consulting, nec;
Insurance agents, nec

(P-18283)
ALLIANT INSURANCE SERVICES INC
Also Called: Nationwide
701 B St Fl 6, San Diego (92101-8156)
PHONE....................619 238-1828
Robert Campbell, *Mgr*
EMP: 75
SALES (corp-wide): 1.15B **Privately Held**
Web: www.alliant.com
SIC: 8748 6411 Business consulting, nec;
Insurance agents and brokers
PA: Alliant Insurance Services, Inc.
18100 Von Krman Ave Fl 10
949 756-0271

(P-18284)
ANCHOR CNSLING EDCATN SLTONS L
19200 Von Karman Ave Ste 600, Irvine
(92612-8516)
PHONE....................213 505-6322
Guillermo Valdez Ii, *CEO*
EMP: 70 **EST:** 2015
SALES (est): 2.69MM **Privately Held**
Web: www.anchorcounseling.solutions
SIC: 8748 7389 Educational consultant;
Business Activities at Non-Commercial Site

(P-18285)
ANKURA CONSULTING GROUP LLC
633 W 5th St Fl 28, Los Angeles
(90071-3502)
PHONE....................213 223-2109
Shannon Nolan, *Prin*
EMP: 102
SALES (corp-wide): 110MM **Privately Held**
Web: www.ankura.com
SIC: 8748 Business consulting, nec
HQ: Ankura Consulting Group, Llc
485 Lexington Ave Fl 10
New York NY 10017
212 818-1555

(P-18286)
APTIM CORP
1230 Columbia St Ste 1200, San Diego
(92101-8517)
PHONE....................619 239-1690
EMP: 260
SALES (corp-wide): 2.2B **Privately Held**
SIC: 8748 Environmental consultant
HQ: Aptim Corp.
10001 Woodloch Forest Dr # 450
The Woodlands TX 70802
832 823-2700

(P-18287)
ATI RESTORATION LLC
8444 Miralani Dr Ste 200, San Diego
(92126-4389)
PHONE....................858 530-2400
Eric Gotsom, *Brnch Mgr*
EMP: 242
Web: www.atirestoration.com
SIC: 8748 Environmental consultant
PA: Ati Restoration, Llc
3360 E La Palma Ave

(P-18288)
BE SMITH INC
12400 High Bluff Dr Ste 100, San Diego
(92130-3077)
PHONE....................913 341-9116
John Doug Smith, *CEO*
Lisa Carr, *
Colleen Chapp, *
Brian Christianson, *
Mark Madden, *
EMP: 271 **EST:** 1980
SALES (est): 3.71MM
SALES (corp-wide): 3.79B **Publicly Held**
Web: www.besmith.com
SIC: 8748 Business consulting, nec
PA: Amn Healthcare Services, Inc.
2999 Olympus Blvd Ste 500
866 871-8519

(P-18289)
BEHAVIORAL SCIENCE TECHNOLOGY INC (PA)
Also Called: Dekra Insight
1000 Town Center Dr Ste 600, Oxnard
(93036-1132)
PHONE....................805 646-0166
EMP: 104 **EST:** 1981
SALES (est): 6.79MM
SALES (corp-wide): 6.79MM **Privately Held**
SIC: 8748 Safety training service

(P-18290)
BEYONDSOFT CONSULTING INC
19009 S Laurel Park Rd Spc 6, Compton
(90220-6054)
PHONE....................310 532-2822
EMP: 120
Web: www.beyondsoft.com
SIC: 8748 Business consulting, nec
HQ: Beyondsoft Consulting, Inc.
10700 Northup Way Ste 120
Bellevue WA 98004
425 332-4520

(P-18291)
BON SUISSE INC
392 W Walnut Ave, Fullerton (92832-2351)
PHONE....................714 578-0001
EMP: 30
Web: www.bonsuisse.com

SIC: 8748 5149 2052 Agricultural consultant; Bakery products; Cones, ice cream
PA: Bon Suisse Inc.
11860 Cmnty Rd Ste 100

(P-18292)
BRIDGE SMS RETAIL SOLUTIONS
16520 Harbor Blvd Ste E, Fountain Valley (92708-1360)
PHONE..............................949 629-7800
Hirbod Davari, CEO
EMP: 78 EST: 2013
SALES (est): 10MM Privately Held
Web: www.bridgesmsrs.com
SIC: 8748 Business consulting, nec

(P-18293)
BROADBAND TELECOM INC
515 S Flower St Fl 36, Los Angeles (90071-2221)
PHONE..............................818 450-5714
EMP: 191
SALES (corp-wide): 9.29MM Privately Held
Web: www.broadbandtele.net
SIC: 8748 Telecommunications consultant
HQ: Broadband Telecom, Inc.
100 Qntin Rsvelt Blvd Ste
Garden City NY 11530
718 713-8417

(P-18294)
BY REFERRAL ONLY INC
2035 Corte Del Nogal Ste 200, Carlsbad (92011-1445)
PHONE..............................760 707-1300
Joseph F Stumpf, Pr
EMP: 100 EST: 1991
SALES (est): 2.63MM Privately Held
Web: www.byreferralonly.com
SIC: 8748 Educational consultant

(P-18295)
C M E CORP
1051 S East St, Anaheim (92805-5749)
PHONE..............................714 632-6939
EMP: 222
SALES (corp-wide): 26.2MM Privately Held
Web: www.cmecorp.com
SIC: 8748 Business consulting, nec
PA: C. M. E. Corp.
1206 Jefferson Blvd
800 338-2372

(P-18296)
C&B HOLDING CO INC (PA)
3000 Belle Terrace, Bakersfield (93304-4104)
PHONE..............................661 633-1451
John A Braun, Pr
EMP: 307 EST: 2000
SALES (est): 47.75MM
SALES (corp-wide): 47.75MM Privately Held
SIC: 8748 1731 Business consulting, nec; General electrical contractor

(P-18297)
CAL SOUTHERN ASSN GOVERNMENTS (PA)
Also Called: S C A G
900 Wilshire Blvd Ste 1700, Los Angeles (90017-4729)
PHONE..............................213 236-1800
Hasan Ikhrata, Ex Dir
Basil Panas, *
EMP: 116 EST: 1965

SQ FT: 50,000
SALES (est): 15.54MM
SALES (corp-wide): 15.54MM Privately Held
Web: scag.ca.gov
SIC: 8748 Urban planning and consulting services

(P-18298)
CASK NX LLC
Also Called: Cask
8910 University Center Ln Ste 400, San Diego (92121)
P.O. Box 927170 (92192)
PHONE..............................858 232-8900
Jason Rosenfeld, CEO
Mark Larsen, *
Jayson Rosenfeld, *
Craig Amundsen, *
Kent Moddelmog, *
EMP: 200 EST: 2018
SALES (est): 22.69MM Privately Held
Web: www.casknx.com
SIC: 8748 Business consulting, nec

(P-18299)
CDSNET LLC
Also Called: Fmsinfoserv
6053 W Century Blvd, Los Angeles (90045-6430)
PHONE..............................310 981-9500
Michael Griffus, Pr
Francis G Homan, CFO
EMP: 494 EST: 2006
SALES (est): 429.51K
SALES (corp-wide): 4.23MM Privately Held
SIC: 8748 Business consulting, nec
HQ: Keolis Transit America, Inc.
53 State St Fl 11
Boston MA 02109

(P-18300)
CENTER FOR SUSTAINABLE ENERGY
3980 Sherman St Ste 170, San Diego (92110-4314)
PHONE..............................858 244-1177
Michael Akavan, Bd *
Mary Mcgroarty, Ch Bd
Lawrence E Goldenhersh, *
Michael Akavan Former, BD
Nick Leibham, Vice Chairman*
EMP: 87 EST: 2001
SALES (est): 274.17MM Privately Held
Web: www.energycenter.org
SIC: 8748 Energy conservation consultant

(P-18301)
CHAMBERS GROUP INC (PA)
5 Hutton Centre Dr Ste 750, Santa Ana (92707-8720)
PHONE..............................949 261-5414
EMP: 80 EST: 1978
SALES (est): 10.2MM Privately Held
Web: www.chambersgroupinc.com
SIC: 8748 Environmental consultant

(P-18302)
CHANNELWAVE SOFTWARE INC
27081 Aliso Creek Rd, Aliso Viejo (92656-5365)
PHONE..............................949 448-4500
Rob Hagen, Mgr
EMP: 83
Web: www.channelwave.com
SIC: 8748 8742 Business consulting, nec; Management consulting services
HQ: Channelwave Software, Inc.
1 Kendall Sq Bldg 200

Cambridge MA 02139

(P-18303)
CITY OF NORCO
Also Called: Successor Agcy To Nrco Cmnty R
2870 Clark Ave, Norco (92860-1903)
PHONE..............................951 270-5617
Greg Newton, Mayor
EMP: 100
SALES (corp-wide): 51.08MM Privately Held
Web: www.norco.ca.us
SIC: 8748 Urban planning and consulting services
PA: City Of Norco
2870 Clark Ave
951 270-5617

(P-18304)
CLEARESULT OPERATING LLC
807 N Park View Dr # 150, El Segundo (90245-4932)
PHONE..............................508 836-9500
Kimberly Simpson, Brnch Mgr
EMP: 77
SALES (corp-wide): 499.94MM Privately Held
Web: www.clearesult.com
SIC: 8748 Energy conservation consultant
HQ: Clearesult Operating, Llc
6504 Brdge Pt Pkwy Ste 42
Austin TX 78730
512 327-9200

(P-18305)
CRYSTALVIEW TECHNOLOGY CORP
32 Mauchly Ste C, Irvine (92618-2336)
PHONE..............................949 788-0738
Frances Chiang, Pr
En Fu Chiang, *
EMP: 300 EST: 1993
SQ FT: 2,400
SALES (est): 1.12MM Privately Held
SIC: 8748 7373 Systems engineering consultant, ex. computer or professional; Computer integrated systems design

(P-18306)
EDGE MORTGAGE ADVISORY CO LLC
2125 E Katella Ave Ste 350, Anaheim (92806-6025)
PHONE..............................714 564-5800
Doug Speaker, *
EMP: 88 EST: 2009
SALES (est): 9.89MM Privately Held
Web: www.incenterdiligence.com
SIC: 8748 Business consulting, nec

(P-18307)
ENVIRONMENTAL RESOLUTIONS INC
Also Called: Cardno Eri
25371 Commercentre Dr Ste 250, Lake Forest (92630-8867)
PHONE..............................949 457-8950
Steve M Zigan, CEO
Robert L Kroeger, VP
EMP: 300 EST: 1989
SQ FT: 14,100
SALES (est): 3.1MM Privately Held
Web: www.erinj.com
SIC: 8748 8744 Environmental consultant; Environmental remediation
HQ: Cardno Usa, Inc.
8310 S Valley Hwy Ste 300
Englewood CO 80112

(P-18308)
ENVIRONMENTAL SCIENCE ASSOC
9191 Towne Centre Dr Ste 340, San Diego (92122-1274)
PHONE..............................858 638-0900
Ralene Cavataio, Brnch Mgr
EMP: 92
SALES (corp-wide): 47.32MM Privately Held
Web: www.esassoc.com
SIC: 8748 Environmental consultant
PA: Environmental Science Associates
575 Market St
415 896-5900

(P-18309)
FRYMAN MANAGEMENT INC
18 Goodyear Ste 105, Irvine (92618-3749)
PHONE..............................949 481-5211
Ross Fryman, Pr
EMP: 88 EST: 2014
SALES (est): 4.96MM Privately Held
Web: www.frymanmanagement.com
SIC: 8748 Traffic consultant

(P-18310)
GARRAD HASSAN AMERICA INC (DH)
Also Called: GL
9665 Chesapeake Dr Ste 435, San Diego (92123-1378)
PHONE..............................858 836-3370
Carole Barbeau, CEO
EMP: 70 EST: 2002
SQ FT: 1,380
SALES (est): 1.23MM Privately Held
Web: www.dnv.com
SIC: 8748 Energy conservation consultant
HQ: Garrad Hassan Group Limited
One Linear Park, Avon Street
Bristol BS2 0

(P-18311)
GATEB CONSULTING INC
815 Hampton Dr Unit 1b, Venice (90291-5702)
PHONE..............................310 526-8323
Sarah Iskander, CEO
EMP: 90 EST: 2013
SALES (est): 546.57K Privately Held
Web: www.gateb.com
SIC: 8748 Business consulting, nec

(P-18312)
GEOCON CONSULTANTS INC (PA)
Also Called: Geocon
6960 Flanders Dr, San Diego (92121-3992)
PHONE..............................858 558-6900
Michael Chapin, CEO
Joe Vettel, *
John Hoobs, *
John Juhrend, *
Neal Berliner, *
EMP: 85 EST: 1987
SQ FT: 10,000
SALES (est): 22.47MM Privately Held
Web: www.geoconinc.com
SIC: 8748 8711 Environmental consultant; Engineering services

(P-18313)
GEOLOGICS CORPORATION
25375 Orchard Village Rd Ste 102, Valencia (91355-3000)
PHONE..............................661 259-5767
Fernando Arroyo, Mgr
EMP: 182

Web: www.geologics.com
SIC: 8748 8711 7379 Systems analysis and engineering consulting services; Consulting engineer; Computer related consulting services
PA: Geologics Corporation
5500 Cherokee Ave Ste 400

(P-18314)
GOLDMAN DATA LLC
2156 N Shaffer St, Orange (92865-3407)
PHONE.............................714 283-5889
EMP: 87
SALES (corp-wide): 1.51MM Privately Held
Web: www.goldmandata.com
SIC: 8748 Business consulting, nec
PA: Goldman Data, Llc
1407 N Batavia St Ste 106

(P-18315)
GREATER LOS ANGLES CNTY VCTOR
12545 Florence Ave, Santa Fe Springs (90670-3919)
PHONE.............................562 944-7976
Trucmai Nguyen-dever, *Mgr*
EMP: 132 EST: 2019
SALES (est): 2.3MM Privately Held
Web: www.glamosquito.org
SIC: 8748 Environmental consultant

(P-18316)
GUARDIAN GROUP INTL LLC (HQ)
2350 W 205th St, Torrance (90501-1436)
PHONE.............................310 320-0320
Henry W Bauer, *Pr*
Todd Bauer, *Ex VP*
EMP: 132 EST: 1991
SQ FT: 7,000
SALES (est): 6.1MM
SALES (corp-wide): 17.45MM Privately Held
Web: www.guardiangroup.com
SIC: 8748 Business consulting, nec
PA: Young & Associates, Inc.
815 N Main St
423 968-1743

(P-18317)
HALEY & ALDRICH INC
5333 Mission Center Rd Ste 300, San Diego (92108-1350)
PHONE.............................619 280-9210
Anita Broughton, *Brnch Mgr*
EMP: 79
SALES (corp-wide): 70.95MM Privately Held
Web: www.haleyaldrich.com
SIC: 8748 8711 Environmental consultant; Engineering services
PA: Haley & Aldrich, Inc.
70 Blanchard Rd Ste 204
781 685-2115

(P-18318)
HIGHER GROUND EDUCATION INC (PA)
10 Orchard Ste 200, Lake Forest (92630-8309)
PHONE.............................949 836-9401
Ramandeep Grin, *CEO*
Ramandeep Girn, *CEO*
Guy Barnett, *VP*
EMP: 337 EST: 2016
SALES (est): 37.31MM
SALES (corp-wide): 37.31MM Privately Held

Web: www.tohigherground.com
SIC: 8748 8299 Business consulting, nec; Educational services

(P-18319)
HQE SYSTEMS INC
27348 Via Industria, Temecula (92590-3699)
PHONE.............................800 967-3036
Qais Alkurdi, *CEO*
Henry Hernandez, *
EMP: 65 EST: 2014
SALES (est): 16.2MM Privately Held
Web: www.hqesystems.com
SIC: 8748 7629 3669 3571 Systems analysis and engineering consulting services; Telecommunication equipment repair (except telephones); Emergency alarms; Electronic computers

(P-18320)
IACCESS TECHNOLOGIES INC (PA)
1251 E Dyer Rd Ste 160, Santa Ana (92705-5655)
P.O. Box 53545 (92619-3545)
PHONE.............................714 922-9158
Hasan I Ramlaoui, *CEO*
Max Todorov, *Dir Fin*
EMP: 48 EST: 2003
SALES (est): 10.77MM
SALES (corp-wide): 10.77MM Privately Held
Web: www.iaccesstech.com
SIC: 8748 3812 3699 3728 Business consulting, nec; Aircraft/aerospace flight instruments and guidance systems; Flight simulators (training aids), electronic; Refueling equipment for use in flight, airplane

(P-18321)
IBASET INC (PA)
26812 Vista Ter, Lake Forest (92630-8115)
PHONE.............................949 598-5200
Ladeira Poonian, *Ch Bd*
Naveen Poonian, *
Daniel De Haas, *
EMP: 34 EST: 2015
SQ FT: 28,000
SALES (est): 11.03MM
SALES (corp-wide): 11.03MM Privately Held
Web: www.ibaset.com
SIC: 8748 7371 7372 Business consulting, nec; Custom computer programming services; Application computer software

(P-18322)
ICF JONES & STOKES INC
525 B St Ste 1700, San Diego (92101-4478)
PHONE.............................858 578-8964
Tevon Muto, *Brnch Mgr*
EMP: 91
SALES (corp-wide): 1.96B Publicly Held
Web: www.icf.com
SIC: 8748 Environmental consultant
HQ: Icf Jones & Stokes, Inc
1902 Reston Metro Plz
Reston VA 20190
703 934-3000

(P-18323)
IN MONTROSE WTR SSTNBLITY SVCS
Also Called: Mwss
4 Park Plz Ste 790, Irvine (92614-5262)
PHONE.............................949 988-3500
Vijay Manthripragada, *Pr*

Jose Revuelta, *
Nasym Afsari, *
Allan Dicks, *
EMP: 90 EST: 2019
SALES (est): 2.1MM
SALES (corp-wide): 624.21MM Publicly Held
Web: www.montrose-env.com
SIC: 8748 8744 Environmental consultant; Environmental remediation
PA: Montrose Environmental Group, Inc.
5120 Northshore Dr
501 602-7008

(P-18324)
IRVINE TECHNOLOGY CORPORATION
2850 Redhill Ave Ste 230, Santa Ana (92705-5550)
PHONE.............................714 445-2624
Nicole Mcmackin, *Pr*
Janet Thornby, *
Michael Rose, *
Kevin Orlando, *
EMP: 160 EST: 2000
SALES (est): 6.84MM Privately Held
Web: www.irvinetechcorp.com
SIC: 8748 7363 7371 7379 Business consulting, nec; Temporary help service; Software programming applications; Computer related consulting services

(P-18325)
IVY ENTERPRISES INC
5564 E 61st St, Commerce (90040-3406)
PHONE.............................323 887-8661
Jane Kim, *Mgr*
EMP: 440
Web: www.kissusa.com
SIC: 8748 Business consulting, nec
HQ: Ivy Enterprises, Inc.
25 Harbor Park Dr
Port Washington NY 11050

(P-18326)
JAG PROFESSIONAL SERVICES INC
2008 Walnut Ave, Manhattan Beach (90266-2841)
P.O. Box 3007 (90245-8107)
PHONE.............................310 945-5648
Judith Hinkley, *CEO*
EMP: 126 EST: 2001
SQ FT: 1,000
SALES (est): 944.36K Privately Held
Web: www.jagprof.com
SIC: 8748 Business consulting, nec

(P-18327)
JOHNSON JOHNSON INNOVATION LLC
Also Called: Jlabs
3210 Merryfield Row, San Diego (92121-1126)
PHONE.............................858 242-1504
Tom Heyman, *Pr*
EMP: 421 EST: 2016
SALES (est): 13.36MM
SALES (corp-wide): 85.16B Publicly Held
Web: www.jnj.com
SIC: 8748 Test development and evaluation service
PA: Johnson & Johnson
1 Johnson & Johnson Plz
732 524-0400

(P-18328)
KARMAN TOPCO LP (PA)
18100 Von Karman Ave Ste 1000, Irvine (92612-7196)

PHONE.............................949 797-2900
EMP: 115 EST: 2014
SALES (est): 4.71B
SALES (corp-wide): 4.71B Publicly Held
SIC: 8748 Business consulting, nec

(P-18329)
KINKISHARYO INTERNATIONAL
2825 E Avenue P, Palmdale (93550-2177)
PHONE.............................661 265-1647
EMP: 79 EST: 2014
SALES (est): 1.31MM Privately Held
Web: www.kinkisharyo.com
SIC: 8748 Business consulting, nec
HQ: Kinkisharyo International, L.L.C.
1960 E Grand Ave Ste 1210
El Segundo CA 90245
424 276-1803

(P-18330)
KROS-WISE
435 E Carmel St, San Marcos (92078-4362)
PHONE.............................619 607-2899
Lily Aragon, *Pr*
EMP: 150 EST: 2004
SALES (est): 10.92MM Privately Held
Web: www.kros-wise.com
SIC: 8748 Business consulting, nec

(P-18331)
LAND DESIGN CONSULTANTS INC
2700 E Foothill Blvd Ste 200, Pasadena (91107-3443)
PHONE.............................626 578-7000
Robert Sims, *Pr*
Steve Hunter, *
Larry Mar, *
EMP: 70 EST: 1992
SALES (est): 1.75MM Privately Held
Web: www.ldcla.com
SIC: 8748 8711 8713 Urban planning and consulting services; Civil engineering; Surveying services

(P-18332)
LSA ASSOCIATES INC (PA)
Also Called: L S A
3210 El Camino Real Ste 100, Irvine (92602-1366)
PHONE.............................949 553-0666
Les Card, *CEO*
Rob Mccann, *Pr*
James Baum, *
EMP: 110 EST: 1974
SALES (est): 24.02MM
SALES (corp-wide): 24.02MM Privately Held
Web: www.lsa.net
SIC: 8748 Environmental consultant

(P-18333)
LUSIVE DECOR
Also Called: Luxe Light and Home
3400 Medford St, Los Angeles (90063-2530)
PHONE.............................323 227-9207
Jason Kai Cooper, *CEO*
EMP: 90 EST: 2006
SALES (est): 9.63MM Privately Held
Web: www.lusive.com
SIC: 8748 3646 Lighting consultant; Ceiling systems, luminous

(P-18334)
MARSH CONSULTING GROUP
2626 Summer Ranch Rd, Paso Robles (93446-8473)
PHONE.............................239 433-5500

Brad Heinrichs, *Pr*
EMP: 70 **EST:** 2005
SALES (est): 797.12K
SALES (corp-wide): 6.98MM **Privately Held**
Web: www.mcgteam.com
SIC: 8748 Business consulting, nec
PA: Foster & Foster Consulting Actuaries, Inc.
  13420 Parker Commons Blvd
  239 433-5500

(P-18335)
MIDNIGHT SUN ENTERPRISES INC
Also Called: Spearmint Rhino Gentlemens CLB
19900 Normandie Ave, Torrance (90502-1113)
PHONE.....................310 532-2427
Kathy Vercher, *Prin*
EMP: 86 **EST:** 2008
SALES (est): 672.63K **Privately Held**
Web: www.rhinotorrance.com
SIC: 8748 Business consulting, nec

(P-18336)
MSLA MANAGEMENT LLC
1294 E Colorado Blvd, Pasadena (91106-1901)
PHONE.....................626 824-6020
Michael Lambert, *CEO*
Sahniah Siciarz-lambert, *Pr*
Robert Worth Oberrender, *
EMP: 612 **EST:** 2016
SALES (est): 3.67MM
SALES (corp-wide): 371.62B **Publicly Held**
SIC: 8748 Business consulting, nec
HQ: Optumserve Health Services, Inc.
  328 Front St S
  La Crosse WI 54601
  866 284-8788

(P-18337)
NETFORTRIS ACQUISITION CO INC
11954 S La Cienega Blvd, Hawthorne (90250-3465)
PHONE.....................877 366-2548
Grant Evans, *CEO*
EMP: 80
SALES (corp-wide): 247.28MM **Privately Held**
Web: www.sangoma.com
SIC: 8748 Telecommunications consultant
HQ: Netfortris Acquisition Co., Inc.
  5340 Legacy Dr
  Plano TX 75024
  877 366-2548

(P-18338)
NETFORTRIS ACQUISITION CO INC
200 Corporate Pointe Ste 300, Culver City (90230-7631)
PHONE.....................310 861-4300
Chris Vuillaume, *Brnch Mgr*
EMP: 80
SALES (corp-wide): 247.28MM **Privately Held**
Web: www.sangoma.com
SIC: 8748 Telecommunications consultant
HQ: Netfortris Acquisition Co., Inc.
  5340 Legacy Dr
  Plano TX 75024
  877 366-2548

(P-18339)
NETWORK SLTONS PRVIDER USA INC
1240 Rosecrans Ave, Manhattan Beach (90266-2555)
PHONE.....................213 985-2173
Phillip Walker, *CEO*
EMP: 33 **EST:** 2011
SQ FT: 8,000
SALES (est): 1.89MM **Privately Held**
Web: www.networksolutionsprovider.com
SIC: 8748 7379 3571 4813 Telecommunications consultant; Online services technology consultants; Computers, digital, analog or hybrid; Internet connectivity services

(P-18340)
NEXGENIX INC (PA)
2 Peters Canyon Rd Ste 200, Irvine (92606-1798)
PHONE.....................714 665-6240
Rick Dutta, *CEO*
Don Ganguly, *Ch Bd*
Mark Iwanowski, *COO*
Ravi Renduchintala, *VP*
EMP: 258 **EST:** 1990
SQ FT: 14,264
SALES (est): 1.65MM **Privately Held**
SIC: 8748 7371 4813 Systems analysis or design; Computer software development; Online service providers

(P-18341)
NINJIO LLC
880 Hampshire Rd Ste B, Westlake Village (91361-2836)
PHONE.....................805 864-1992
Tim Acker, *CRO*
EMP: 79 **EST:** 2017
SALES (est): 2.96MM **Privately Held**
Web: www.ninjiopeople.com
SIC: 8748 Business consulting, nec

(P-18342)
NINYO MORE GTCHNCAL ENVMTL SCN (PA)
5710 Ruffin Rd, San Diego (92123-1013)
PHONE.....................858 576-1000
Avram Ninyo, *CEO*
EMP: 80 **EST:** 1986
SQ FT: 24,000
SALES (est): 46.06MM
SALES (corp-wide): 46.06MM **Privately Held**
Web: www.ninyoandmoore.com
SIC: 8748 Environmental consultant

(P-18343)
NORTH LA COUNTY REGIONAL CTR (PA)
9200 Oakdale Ave Ste 100, Chatsworth (91311-6505)
PHONE.....................818 778-1900
George Stevens, *Dir*
Ellen Stein, *
EMP: 280 **EST:** 1974
SQ FT: 57,000
SALES (est): 645.13MM **Privately Held**
Web: www.nlacrc.org
SIC: 8748 Test development and evaluation service

(P-18344)
OCEAN PARK COMMUNITY CENTER
Turning Point
1447 16th St, Santa Monica (90404-2715)

PHONE.....................310 828-6717
Patricia Bauman, *Dir*
EMP: 130
SALES (corp-wide): 83.33MM **Privately Held**
Web: www.thepeopleconcern.org
SIC: 8748 Urban planning and consulting services
PA: The People Concern
  2116 Arlngton Ave Ste 100
  323 334-9000

(P-18345)
OPENPOPCOM INC (PA)
165 Newall, Irvine (92618-1031)
PHONE.....................714 249-7044
Sun Jong Baek, *Pr*
EMP: 75 **EST:** 1999
SALES (est): 1.1MM
SALES (corp-wide): 1.1MM **Privately Held**
Web: www.perfectdomain.com
SIC: 8748 Telecommunications consultant

(P-18346)
PATRIOT WASTEWATER LLC
314 W Freedom Ave, Orange (92865-2647)
PHONE.....................714 921-4545
Richard Yukihiro, *Mgr*
EMP: 93 **EST:** 2015
SALES (est): 305.98K
SALES (corp-wide): 709.33MM **Privately Held**
Web: www.patriotenvironmental.com
SIC: 8748 Environmental consultant
HQ: Patriot Environmental Services, Inc.
  1250 E 23rd St
  Signal Hill CA 90755
  800 624-9136

(P-18347)
PCS LINK INC
Also Called: Greenwood & Hall
12424 Wilshire Blvd Ste 1030, Los Angeles (90025-1031)
PHONE.....................949 655-5000
EMP: 310 **EST:** 1997
SALES (est): 9.55MM **Privately Held**
SIC: 8748 Communications consulting

(P-18348)
PRO-SPECTUS INC
13223 Black Mountain Rd Ste 1271, San Diego (92129-2698)
PHONE.....................877 877-0096
Charmie Chirgwin, *Pr*
EMP: 83 **EST:** 2011
SALES (est): 713.04K **Privately Held**
Web: www.pro-spectus.com
SIC: 8748 Business consulting, nec

(P-18349)
PROFIT RECOVERY PARTNERS LLC
Also Called: P R P
3501 W Sunflower Ave Ste 100, Santa Ana (92704-6918)
PHONE.....................949 851-2777
Bill Carpou, *
Teresa Madden, *
Edward Lyon, *
Marty Bozarth, *
EMP: 75 **EST:** 1997
SALES (est): 9.92MM **Privately Held**
Web: www.prpllc.com
SIC: 8748 Business consulting, nec

(P-18350)
PROJECT DESIGN CONSULTANTS LLC

Also Called: PDC A Bowman Company
701 B St Ste 800, San Diego (92101-8162)
PHONE.....................619 235-6471
Gregory M Shields, *CEO*
William R Dick, *
Debby Reece, *
EMP: 92 **EST:** 1976
SQ FT: 22,000
SALES (est): 4.41MM **Publicly Held**
Web: www.projectdesign.com
SIC: 8748 8711 8713 Urban planning and consulting services; Civil engineering; Surveying services
PA: Bowman Consulting Group Ltd.
  12355 Snrise Vly Dr Ste 5

(P-18351)
PSI SERVICES LLC (PA)
Also Called: PSI
611 N Brand Blvd Ste 10, Glendale (91203-3290)
PHONE.....................818 847-6180
EMP: 80 **EST:** 2001
SALES (est): 49.92MM
SALES (corp-wide): 49.92MM **Privately Held**
Web: www.psiexams.com
SIC: 8748 Testing services

(P-18352)
RECON ENVIRONMENTAL INC (PA)
Also Called: Recon
3111 Camino Del Rio N Ste 600, San Diego (92108-5726)
PHONE.....................619 308-9333
Robert Hobbs, *Pr*
Michael Page, *
Lee Sherwood, *
Jennifer Campos, *
Charles Bull, *
EMP: 82 **EST:** 1977
SALES (est): 8.06MM
SALES (corp-wide): 8.06MM **Privately Held**
Web: www.recon-us.com
SIC: 8748 Environmental consultant

(P-18353)
RINCON CONSULTANTS INC
1530 Monterey St Ste D, San Luis Obispo (93401-2969)
PHONE.....................805 547-0900
John Rickenvach, *Mgr*
EMP: 238
Web: www.rinconconsultants.com
SIC: 8748 Environmental consultant
PA: Rincon Consultants, Inc.
  180 N Ashwood Ave

(P-18354)
SANYO NORTH AMERICA CORP
Also Called: Sanyo Fisher Company
2055 Sanyo Ave, San Diego (92154-6234)
PHONE.....................619 661-1134
◆ **EMP:** 400
SIC: 8748 3632 Business consulting, nec; Household refrigerators and freezers

(P-18355)
SBT HEALTH INC
Also Called: Solution Based Trtmnt & Detox
25819 Jefferson Ave Ste 110, Murrieta (92562-6965)
PHONE.....................951 813-2597
Samuel G Lockhart, *Admn*
EMP: 102 **EST:** 2016
SALES (est): 1.43MM **Privately Held**
SIC: 8748 Business consulting, nec

(P-18356)
SIERRA MONOLITHICS INC (HQ)
103 W Torrance Blvd, Redondo Beach
(90277-3633)
PHONE...........................310 698-1000
Charles Harper, *CEO*
Javed Patel, *Pr*
Trevor Roots, *CFO*
EMP: 27 **EST:** 1986
SQ FT: 15,000
SALES (est): 4.63MM
SALES (corp-wide): 868.76MM **Publicly Held**
Web: www.jarietech.com
SIC: 8748 8731 3812 Communications consulting; Electronic research; Radar systems and equipment
PA: Semtech Corporation
200 Flynn Rd
805 498-2111

(P-18357)
SLR INTERNATIONAL CORPORATION
20 Corporate Park Ste 200, Irvine
(92606-3111)
PHONE...........................949 553-8417
Rebecca Hjelm, *Brnch Mgr*
EMP: 681
SALES (corp-wide): 10.95MM **Privately Held**
Web: www.slrconsulting.com
SIC: 8748 Environmental consultant
HQ: Slr International Corporation
22118 20th Ave Se Ste G20
Bothell WA 98021
425 402-8800

(P-18358)
SOURCE 44 LLC
Also Called: Source Intelligence
4660 La Jolla Village Dr Ste 100, San Diego
(92122-4604)
PHONE...........................877 916-6337
Glenn Trout, *CEO*
Matt Thorn, *
Lina Ramos, *
Jennifer Kraus, *
Dan Dague, *Chief Development Officer*
EMP: 130 **EST:** 2009
SALES (est): 3.99MM
SALES (corp-wide): 4.52MM **Privately Held**
Web: www.sourceintelligence.com
SIC: 8748 7371 Environmental consultant; Computer software development
PA: Pg Source Acquisition, Inc.
4660 La Jolla Village Dr # 1
877 916-6337

(P-18359)
SOUTH CAST A QLTY MGT DST BLDG (PA)
Also Called: A Q M D
21865 Copley Dr, Diamond Bar
(91765-4178)
P.O. Box 4940 (91765)
PHONE...........................909 396-2000
Raymond E Robinson, *CEO*
Barry R Wallerstein, *
EMP: 720 **EST:** 1955
SQ FT: 350
SALES (est): 449.02MM
SALES (corp-wide): 449.02MM **Privately Held**
Web: www.aqmd.gov
SIC: 8748 Environmental consultant

(P-18360)
SYNAPSE FINANCIAL TECH INC
21255 Burbank Blvd Ste 120, Woodland Hills (91367-6669)
PHONE...........................901 942-8167
Sankaet Pathak, *CEO*
Jack Doan, *PEOPLE CULTURE*
Derek Drennan, *Chief Customer Officer*
EMP: 93 **EST:** 2016
SALES (est): 5.78MM **Privately Held**
Web: www.synapsefi.com
SIC: 8748 Business consulting, nec

(P-18361)
T-FORCE INC (PA)
Also Called: T-Force
4695 Macarthur Ct, Newport Beach
(92660-1882)
PHONE...........................949 208-1527
Raid Al-khawaldeh, *Pr*
EMP: 98 **EST:** 2004
SALES (est): 3.75MM
SALES (corp-wide): 3.75MM **Privately Held**
Web: www.tforcelogistics.com
SIC: 8748 7379 Telecommunications consultant; Online services technology consultants

(P-18362)
TANGOE-PL INC
9920 Pacific Heights Blvd Ste 200, San Diego (92121-4331)
P.O. Box 509088 (92150-9088)
EMP: 235
SIC: 8748 Telecommunications consultant

(P-18363)
TEAM RISK MGT STRATEGIES LLC
Also Called: Trust Employee ADM & MGT
3131 Camino Del Rio N Ste 650, San Diego (92108-5751)
PHONE...........................877 767-8728
Rachel Green, *CEO*
Josh Greenberg, *
Anchi Chern, *
Joe Sofia, *CRO*
Baui Senkfor, *
EMP: 2500 **EST:** 2003
SALES (est): 19.29MM **Privately Held**
Web: www.teamemployer.com
SIC: 8748 Employee programs administration

(P-18364)
TRC SOLUTIONS INC (HQ)
Also Called: Alton Geoscience
9685 Research Dr Ste 100, Irvine
(92618-4657)
PHONE...........................949 753-0101
Christopher P Vincze, *CEO*
Thomas W Bennet Junior, *CFO*
John Cowdery, *
Martin H Dodd, *
Ed Wiegele, *
EMP: 125 **EST:** 1981
SQ FT: 47,000
SALES (est): 9.69MM
SALES (corp-wide): 1.27B **Privately Held**
SIC: 8748 8711 Environmental consultant; Engineering services
PA: Trc Companies, Inc.
21 Griffin Rd N
860 298-9692

(P-18365)
VENTEGRA INC A CAL BENEFT CORP
450 N Brand Blvd Ste 600, Glendale
(91203-2349)

PHONE...........................858 551-8111
Robert Taketomo, *Pr*
Mariana Ritchie, *
Don Schoenly, *
Mike Gannon, *
Michele Yoon, *
EMP: 85 **EST:** 2004
SALES (est): 3.64MM **Privately Held**
Web: www.ventegra.com
SIC: 8748 Business consulting, nec

(P-18366)
VERIDIAM ALLIED SWISS
4645 North Ave, Oceanside (92056-3593)
PHONE...........................760 941-1702
Thomas Cresante, *Owner*
EMP: 72 **EST:** 2007
SALES (est): 957.14K
SALES (corp-wide): 98MM **Privately Held**
Web: www.veridiam.com
SIC: 8748 Business consulting, nec
HQ: Veridiam, Inc.
1717 N Cuyamaca St
El Cajon CA 92020
619 448-1000

(P-18367)
VETERANS EZ INFO INC
Also Called: Veterans EZ Info
1901 1st Ave Ste 192, San Diego
(92101-2356)
PHONE...........................866 839-1329
James Miner, *Ch Bd*
Phonprapha Miner, *
EMP: 138 **EST:** 2012
SQ FT: 1,200
SALES (est): 3.74MM **Privately Held**
Web: www.vetsez.com
SIC: 8748 7371 7373 Business consulting, nec; Computer software development; Computer systems analysis and design

(P-18368)
VINCULUMS SERVICES LLC
Also Called: Vinculums
10 Pasteur Ste 100, Irvine (92618-3823)
PHONE...........................949 783-3552
Paul Foster, *CEO*
Lisa Di Giovanna, *
Brian Woodward, *
Norm Alexander, *
EMP: 220 **EST:** 2005
SQ FT: 8,000
SALES (est): 8.56MM
SALES (corp-wide): 195.73MM **Privately Held**
Web: www.qualtekservices.com
SIC: 8748 Telecommunications consultant
HQ: Qualtek Llc
475 Sntry Pkwy E Ste 1000
Blue Bell PA 19422
404 004-4500

(P-18369)
VOLT TELECOM GROUP INC
Also Called: Volt Telecom Group
218 Helicopter Cir, Corona (92880)
PHONE...........................951 493-8900
Frank D'alessio, *CEO*
EMP: 260
SALES (corp-wide): 885.39MM **Privately Held**
Web: www.volt.com
SIC: 8748 Telecommunications consultant
HQ: Volt Telecommunications Group, Inc.
1455 Lincoln Pkwy E
Atlanta GA 30346
212 704-2400

(P-18370)
WARNER BROS CONSUMER PDTS INC (DH)
4001 W Olive Ave, Burbank (91505-4272)
PHONE...........................818 954-7980
Brad Globe, *Pr*
Dan Romanelli, *Pr*
Randy Blotky, *Sr VP*
John Schulman, *Sec*
▲ **EMP:** 112 **EST:** 2003
SALES (est): 4.23MM **Publicly Held**
SIC: 8748 5961 Business consulting, nec; Novelty merchandise, mail order
HQ: Warner Bros. Entertainment Inc.
4000 Warner Blvd
Burbank CA 91522
818 954-6000

(P-18371)
WEST COAST CONSULTING LLC
9233 Research Dr Ste 200, Irvine
(92618-4294)
PHONE...........................949 250-4102
EMP: 125 **EST:** 1997
SALES (est): 3.39MM **Privately Held**
Web: www.westcoastllc.com
SIC: 8748 Business consulting, nec

8999 Services, Nec

(P-18372)
DATA TRACE INFO SVCS LLC (HQ)
4 First American Way, Santa Ana
(92707-5913)
PHONE...........................714 250-6700
EMP: 100 **EST:** 2000
SALES (est): 5.31MM **Publicly Held**
Web: www.datatracetitle.com
SIC: 8999 Information bureau
PA: First American Financial Corporation
1 First American Way

(P-18373)
ESSENSE
Also Called: Maxus USA
6300 Wilshire Blvd Ste 720, Los Angeles
(90048-5206)
PHONE...........................323 202-4650
EMP: 600 **EST:** 2015
SALES (est): 242.78K
SALES (corp-wide): 18.5B **Privately Held**
SIC: 8999 Communication services
HQ: Maxus Communications Llc
498 Fashion Ave
New York NY 10018
212 297-8300

(P-18374)
HEALTHCARE SERVICES GROUP INC
5199 E Pacific Coast Hwy Ste 402, Long Beach (90804-3378)
PHONE...........................562 494-7939
Mike Hammond, *Prin*
EMP: 1198
SALES (corp-wide): 1.76B **Publicly Held**
Web: www.hcsgcorp.com
SIC: 8999 Artists and artists' studios
PA: Healthcare Services Group Inc
3220 Tillman Dr Ste 300
215 639-4274

(P-18375)
MGM AND UA SERVICES COMPANY
245 N Beverly Dr, Beverly Hills
(90210-5319)

PHONE..................310 449-3000
Gary Barber, *Pr*
EMP: 560 **EST:** 1994
SALES (est): 3.51MM **Publicly Held**
Web: www.mgm.com
SIC: 8999 Artists and artists' studios
HQ: Metro-Goldwyn-Mayer, Inc.
      245 N Beverly Dr
      Beverly Hills CA 90210

(P-18376)
OVERSEAS SERVICE CORPORATION
Also Called: Ocean Service
8221 Arjons Dr Ste B2, San Diego
(92126-6319)
PHONE..................858 408-0751
Paul Hogan, *Pr*
EMP: 232
SALES (corp-wide): 10.17MM **Privately Held**
Web: www.oscweb.com
SIC: 8999 Actuarial consultant
PA: Overseas Service Corporation
      1100 Nrthpint Pkwy Ste 20
      561 683-4090

(P-18377)
PACE LITHOGRAPHERS INC
Also Called: Pace Marketing Communications
18030 Cortney Ct, City Of Industry
(91748-1202)
PHONE..................626 913-2108
Robert Bennitt, *Pr*
Robert Bennitt, *Pr*
Carl Bennitt Junior, *VP Opers*
Carl Bennitt Senior Sales, *Prin*
EMP: 35 **EST:** 1970
SQ FT: 27,000
SALES (est): 2.24MM **Privately Held**
Web: www.engagepace.com
SIC: 8999 2752 Communication services; Commercial printing, lithographic

(P-18378)
RIVERSIDE CNTY FLOOD CTRL WTR
1995 Market St, Riverside (92501-1719)
PHONE..................951 955-1200
Jason Uhley, *Prin*
EMP: 210 **EST:** 1945
SALES (est): 87.05MM **Privately Held**
Web: www.rcflood.org
SIC: 8999 Natural resource preservation service

(P-18379)
RUBIO ARTS CORPORATION
1313 S Harbor Blvd, Anaheim
(92802-2309)
PHONE..................407 849-1643
David Johnson, *Brnch Mgr*
EMP: 111
SALES (corp-wide): 2.27MM **Privately Held**
SIC: 8999 Artist
PA: Rubio Arts Corporation
      8100 Chancellor Dr # 100
      407 849-1643

(P-18380)
WEAPON X SECURITY INC
297 Country Club Dr, Simi Valley
(93065-6632)
P.O. Box 940835 (93094-0835)
PHONE..................818 818-9950
Mish Marie, *CEO*
Sayed Sadat, *
EMP: 80 **EST:** 2018
SALES (est): 962.55K **Privately Held**

Web: www.weaponxsecurity.com
SIC: 8999 1731 7381 Personal services; Safety and security specialization; Security guard service

(P-18381)
WESTAMERICA COMMUNICATIONS INC
26012 Atlantic Ocean Dr, Lake Forest
(92630-8843)
PHONE..................949 340-8942
Douglas Grant, *CEO*
EMP: 83 **EST:** 1975
SALES (est): 3.98MM **Privately Held**
Web: www.mywestamerica.com
SIC: 8999 Communication services

9111 Executive Offices

(P-18382)
CITY OF CERRITOS
Also Called: Cerritos Ctr For Prfrmg Arts
18125 Bloomfield Ave, Cerritos
(90703-8577)
PHONE..................562 916-8500
TOLL FREE: 800
Dianne Cheney, *Ex Dir*
EMP: 113
SALES (corp-wide): 102.55MM **Privately Held**
Web: www.cerritoscenter.com
SIC: 9111 7922 Executive offices, Local government; Legitimate live theater producers
PA: City Of Cerritos
      18125 S Bloomfield Ave
      562 860-0311

(P-18383)
CITY OF CULVER CITY
Also Called: Transportation Department
4343 Duquesne Ave, Culver City
(90232-2944)
PHONE..................310 253-6525
Steven Cunningham, *Mgr*
EMP: 91
SALES (corp-wide): 183.7MM **Privately Held**
Web: www.culvercity.org
SIC: 9111 8611 Executive offices, state and local; Business associations
PA: City Of Culver City
      9770 Culver Blvd
      310 253-5640

(P-18384)
LOS ANGLES CNTY MSEUM NTRAL HS (PA)
900 Exposition Blvd, Los Angeles
(90007-4057)
PHONE..................213 763-3466
Lori Bettison-varga, *Pr*
Egbert Gutierrez, *
EMP: 210 **EST:** 1913
SQ FT: 450,000
SALES (est): 64.34MM
SALES (corp-wide): 64.34MM **Privately Held**
Web: www.nhm.org
SIC: 9111 8399 8412 County supervisors' and executives' office; Fund raising organization, non-fee basis; Museums and art galleries

---

9131 Executive And Legislative Combined

(P-18385)
SAN PSQUAL BAND MSSION INDIANS (PA)
16400 Kumeyaay Way, Valley Center
(92082-6796)
P.O. Box 365 (92082-0365)
PHONE..................760 749-3200
Allen Lawson, *Ch*
EMP: 99 **EST:** 1971
Web:
www.sanpasqualbandofmissionindians.org
SIC: 9131 6733 Indian Reservation; Trusts, nec

9199 General Government, Nec

(P-18386)
CALIFORNIA DEPT OF PUB HLTH
681 S Parker St Ste 200, Orange
(92868-4719)
PHONE..................714 567-2906
Jacqueline Lincer, *Brnch Mgr*
EMP: 204
SALES (corp-wide): 534.4MM **Privately Held**
Web: cdph.ca.gov
SIC: 9199 8051 General government administration, State government; Extended care facility
HQ: The California Department Of Public Health
      1615 Capitol Ave
      Sacramento CA 95814
      916 558-1784

(P-18387)
COUNTY OF ORANGE
Also Called: Public Fclities Resources Dept
1300 S Grand Ave Ste B, Santa Ana
(92705-4434)
PHONE..................714 567-7444
Manny Apodaca, *Brnch Mgr*
EMP: 43
SALES (corp-wide): 5.63B **Privately Held**
Web: www.ocgov.com
SIC: 9199 2759 General government administration; Commercial printing, nec
PA: County Of Orange
      400 W. Civic Center Dr
      714 834-6200

(P-18388)
COUNTY OF SAN DIEGO
5560 Overland Ave Ste 410, San Diego
(92123-1204)
PHONE..................858 505-6100
Danielle Enriquez, *CFO*
EMP: 87
SQ FT: 10,000
Web: www.sandiegocounty.gov
SIC: 9199 6531 General government administration; Real estate brokers and agents
PA: County Of San Diego
      1600 Pacific Hwy Ste 209
      619 531-5880

9221 Police Protection

(P-18389)
SAN DIEGO UNIFIED PORT DST
Also Called: San Diego Unified Hbr Police
3380 N Harbor Dr, San Diego (92101-1023)
PHONE..................619 686-6585
Betty Kelepecz, *Brnch Mgr*
EMP: 105
SALES (corp-wide): 202.99MM **Privately Held**
Web: www.portofsandiego.org
SIC: 9221 4491 Police protection; Marine cargo handling
PA: San Diego Unified Port District
      3165 Pacific Hwy
      619 686-6200

9222 Legal Counsel And Prosecution

(P-18390)
COUNTY OF LOS ANGELES
Also Called: District Attorney
42011 4th St W Ste 3530, Lancaster
(93534-7196)
PHONE..................661 974-7700
Steve Cooley, *Admn*
EMP: 91
Web: www.lacounty.gov
SIC: 9222 8111 District attorneys' office; General practice attorney, lawyer
PA: County Of Los Angeles
      500 W Temple St Ste 437
      213 974-1101

9431 Administration Of Public Health Programs

(P-18391)
CITY OF LONG BEACH
Also Called: Long Bch Dept Hlth & Humn Svcs
2525 Grand Ave, Long Beach
(90815-1765)
PHONE..................562 570-4000
Ronald Arias, *Dir*
EMP: 124
SQ FT: 56,733
Web: www.longbeach.gov
SIC: 9431 8322 Administration of public health programs, Local government; Individual and family services
PA: City Of Long Beach
      1800 E Wardlow Rd
      562 570-6450

(P-18392)
COUNTY OF LOS ANGELES
Also Called: Department of Mental Health
510 S Vermont Ave Fl 1, Los Angeles
(90020-1991)
PHONE..................213 738-4601
Richard Kushi, *Brnch Mgr*
EMP: 91
Web: www.lacounty.gov
SIC: 9431 8093 Mental health agency administration, government; Mental health clinic, outpatient
PA: County Of Los Angeles
      500 W Temple St Ste 437
      213 974-1101

(P-18393)
COUNTY OF RIVERSIDE
Also Called: Children & Families Commission
585 Technology Ct, Riverside (92507-2192)

▲ = Import ▼ = Export
◆ = Import/Export

PHONE.....................951 248-0014
Harry Freedman, *Mgr*
EMP: 83
SALES (corp-wide): 5.07B **Privately Held**
Web: www.first5riverside.org
SIC: 9431 8322 Child health program
administration, government; Parole office
PA: County Of Riverside
4080 Lemon St Fl 11
951 955-1110

(P-18394)
KAISER FOUNDATION HOSPITALS
Also Called: Baldwin Park Laboratory
1011 Baldwin Park Blvd, Baldwin Park
(91706-5806)
PHONE.....................626 851-5144
Robert J Thomas, *Branch Chief*
EMP: 87
SALES (corp-wide): 70.8B **Privately Held**
Web: healthy.kaiserpermanente.org
SIC: 9431 8731 Administration of public
health programs; Commercial research
laboratory
HQ: Kaiser Foundation Hospitals Inc
1 Kaiser Plz
Oakland CA 94612
510 271-6611

(P-18395)
REGIONAL CTR ORANGE CNTY INC (PA)
Also Called: Development Disabilities Ctr
1525 N Tustin Ave, Santa Ana
(92705-8621)
P.O. Box 22010 (92702-2010)
PHONE.....................714 796-5100
William J Bowman, *Ex Dir*
EMP: 309 **EST:** 1977
SQ FT: 41,128
Web: www.rcocdd.com
SIC: 9431 8322 Mental health agency
administration, government; Individual and
family services

9441 Administration Of Social And Manpower Programs

(P-18396)
CALIFORNIA DEPT SOCIAL SVCS
Also Called: Community Care Licensing
3737 Main St Ste 700, Riverside
(92501-3349)
PHONE.....................951 782-4200
Robert Gonzales, *Brnch Mgr*
EMP: 70
SALES (corp-wide): 534.4MM **Privately Held**
Web: www.ca.gov
SIC: 9441 8322 Administration of social and
manpower programs; Offender self-help
agency
HQ: California Dept Of Social Services
744 P St
Sacramento CA 95814

(P-18397)
COUNTY OF KERN
Also Called: Employers Training Resource
1600 E Belle Ter Ste 5, Bakersfield
(93307-3872)
PHONE.....................661 336-6871
Verna Lewis, *Ex Dir*
EMP: 76
Web: www.kerncounty.com

SIC: 9441 8331 Administration of social and
manpower programs; Job training and
related services
PA: County Of Kern
1115 Truxtun Ave Rm 505
661 868-3690

(P-18398)
COUNTY OF RIVERSIDE
Also Called: Community Health Agency
4065 County Circle Dr, Riverside
(92503-3410)
P.O. Box 7849 (92513-7849)
PHONE.....................951 358-5000
Gary Feldman, *Asst Dir*
EMP: 131
SALES (corp-wide): 5.07B **Privately Held**
Web: www.rivco.org
SIC: 9441 8621 Public welfare
administration: nonoperating, government;
Health association
PA: County Of Riverside
4080 Lemon St Fl 11
951 955-1110

9512 Land, Mineral, And Wildlife Conservation

(P-18399)
CITY OF CULVER CITY
Also Called: Culver City Parks & Recreation
4117 Overland Ave, Culver City
(90230-3733)
P.O. Box 507 (90232-0507)
PHONE.....................310 253-6650
W Vincent Mctaggart, *Brnch Mgr*
EMP: 71
SQ FT: 57,787
SALES (corp-wide): 183.7MM **Privately Held**
Web: www.culvercity.org
SIC: 9512 8748 Recreational program
administration, government; Business
consulting, nec
PA: City Of Culver City
9770 Culver Blvd
310 253-5640

9621 Regulation, Administration Of Transportation

(P-18400)
CITY OF LOS ANGELES
Harbor Dept- Port Los Angeles
425 S Palos Verdes St, San Pedro
(90731-3309)
P.O. Box 151 (90733-0151)
PHONE.....................310 732-3734
Geraldine Knatz, *Ex Dir*
EMP: 650
SALES (corp-wide): 9.82B **Privately Held**
Web: www.lacity.gov
SIC: 9621 8721 Water vessels and port
regulating agencies; Accounting services,
except auditing
PA: City Of Los Angeles
200 N Spring St Ste 303
213 978-0600

9641 Regulation Of Agricultural Marketing

(P-18401)
CALIFORNIA DEPT FD AGRICULTURE

Also Called: Del Mar Fair Grounds
2260 Jimmy Durante Blvd, Del Mar
(92014-2216)
PHONE.....................858 755-1161
Carlene Moore, *CEO*
EMP: 758
SALES (corp-wide): 534.4MM **Privately Held**
Web: www.sdfair5k.com
SIC: 9641 7948 Food inspection agency,
government; Racing, including track
operation
HQ: California Department Of Food And
Agriculture
1220 N St Fl 4 Ste 400
Sacramento CA 95814

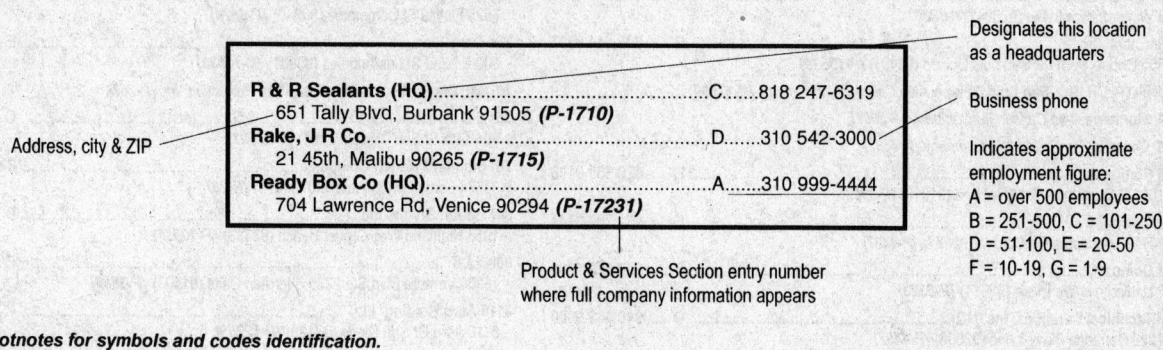

Address, city & ZIP

R & R Sealants (HQ) ....C......818 247-6319
651 Tally Blvd, Burbank 91505 **(P-1710)**
Rake, J R Co ....D......310 542-3000
21 45th, Malibu 90265 **(P-1715)**
Ready Box Co (HQ) ....A......310 999-4444
704 Lawrence Rd, Venice 90294 **(P-17231)**

Designates this location as a headquarters

Business phone

Indicates approximate employment figure:
A = over 500 employees
B = 251-500, C = 101-250
D = 51-100, E = 20-50
F = 10-19, G = 1-9

Product & Services Section entry number where full company information appears

See footnotes for symbols and codes identification.
- Companies listed alphabetically.
- Complete physical or mailing address.

---

10 Day Parts Inc .... E 951 279-4810
20109 Paseo Del Prado Walnut (91789) **(P-4033)**

10x Hvac of Ca LLC ....D 760 343-7488
31170 Reserve Dr Thousand Palms (92276) **(P-724)**

1111 6th Ave LLC ....D 312 283-3683
1111 6th Ave Ste 102 San Diego (92101) **(P-14431)**

1115 Bakersfield Mhrc, Bakersfield *Also Called: Crestwood Behavioral Hlth Inc* **(P-15847)**

1154 San Diego Mhrc, San Diego *Also Called: Crestwood Behavioral Hlth Inc* **(P-15848)**

1167 Fallbrook Mhrc, Fallbrook *Also Called: Crestwood Behavioral Hlth Inc* **(P-15849)**

1170 Lompoc Mhrc, Lompoc *Also Called: Crestwood Behavioral Hlth Inc* **(P-17143)**

1221 Ocean Ave Apartments, Santa Monica *Also Called: Irvine APT Communities LP* **(P-12354)**

123 Home Care, Pasadena *Also Called: Confido LLC* **(P-16381)**

1260 Bb Property LLC ....B 805 969-2261
1260 Channel Dr Santa Barbara (93108) **(P-12750)**

1334 Partners LP ....D 310 546-5656
1330 Park View Ave Manhattan Beach (90266) **(P-15111)**

174 Power Global, Irvine *Also Called: Hanwha Enrgy USA Holdings Corp* **(P-6826)**

180 Snacks Inc .... E 714 238-1192
1173 N Armando St Anaheim (92806) **(P-1499)**

180la LLC ....C 310 382-1400
12777 W Jefferson Blvd Los Angeles (90066) **(P-13192)**

1835 Columbia Street LP ....D 619 564-3993
1835 Columbia St San Diego (92101) **(P-12751)**

1855 S Hbr Blvd Drv Hldngs LLC ....C 714 750-1811
1855 S Harbor Blvd Anaheim (92802) **(P-12752)**

1928 Jewelry Company, Burbank *Also Called: Mel Bernie and Company Inc* **(P-10550)**

1nteger LLC ....C 424 320-2977
10351 Santa Monica Blvd Ste 405 Los Angeles (90025) **(P-13637)**

1on1 LLC ....E ... 310 998-7473
8730 Wilshire Blvd Ste 350 Beverly Hills (90211) **(P-13868)**

1st Century Bancshares Inc ....D 310 270-9500
1075 Century Park E Ste 1400 Los Angeles (90007) **(P-11742)**

1st Meridian Medical Transport, San Diego *Also Called: First Meridian Care Svcs Inc* **(P-16390)**

1st Team Real Estate, Tustin *Also Called: First Team RE - Orange Cnty* **(P-12452)**

2.95 Guys, Poway *Also Called: Smoothreads Inc* **(P-2267)**

20/20 Mobile Corp ....D 909 587-2973
3380 La Sierra Ave Riverside (92503) **(P-9379)**

20/20 Plumbing & Heating Inc ....C 760 535-3101
674 Rancheros Dr San Marcos (92069) **(P-725)**

20/20 Plumbing & Heating Inc (PA) ....D 951 396-2020
7343 Orangewood Dr Ste B Riverside (92504) **(P-726)**

20th Century Fox Studio, Los Angeles *Also Called: Fox Net Inc* **(P-14829)**

20th Century Studios Inc ....C 888 223-4369
10201 W Pico Blvd Los Angeles (90064) **(P-14915)**

211 LA COUNTY, San Gabriel *Also Called: Informtion Rfrral Fdrtion of L* **(P-13176)**

21515 Hawthorne Owner LLC ....D 310 406-3730
21535 Hawthorne Blvd Ste 100 Torrance (90503) **(P-17320)**

21st Century Insurance, Woodland Hills *Also Called: 21st Century Life Insurance Co* **(P-12165)**

21st Century Lf & Hlth Co Inc (PA) .... C 818 887-4436
21600 Oxnard St Ste 1500 Woodland Hills (91367) **(P-12055)**

21st Century Life Insurance Co (DH) ....A 877 310-5687
6301 Owensmouth Ave Ste 700 Woodland Hills (91367) **(P-12165)**

2253 Apparel LLC (PA) ....D 323 837-9800
1708 Aeros Way Montebello (90640) **(P-10700)**

24 Hour Fitness, Carlsbad *Also Called: 24 Hour Fitness Usa LLC* **(P-15041)**

24 Hour Fitness Usa LLC (HQ) ....C 925 543-3100
1265 Laurel Tree Ln Ste 200 Carlsbad (92011) **(P-15041)**

24 Hour Fitness Worldwide Inc ....A 925 543-3100
1265 Laurel Tree Ln Ste 200 Carlsbad (92011) **(P-15042)**

24-Hour Med Staffing Svcs LLC ....C 909 895-8960
1370 Valley Vista Dr Ste 280 Diamond Bar (91765) **(P-13480)**

29 Palms Enterprises Corp ....A 760 775-5566
46200 Harrison Pl Coachella (92236) **(P-15190)**

2h Construction Inc ....D 562 424-5567
2653 Walnut Ave Signal Hill (90755) **(P-513)**

2nd Source Wire & Cable, Walnut *Also Called: 2nd Source Wire & Cable Inc* **(P-4508)**

2nd Source Wire & Cable Inc ....D 714 482-2866
20445 E Walnut Dr N Walnut (91789) **(P-4508)**

3-D Precision Machine Inc ....E 951 296-5449
42132 Remington Ave Temecula (92590) **(P-6055)**

3-V Fastener Co Inc ....D 949 888-7700
630 E Lambert Rd Brea (92821) **(P-5117)**

313 Acquisition LLC ....A 801 234-6374
1111 Citrus St Ste 1 Riverside (92507) **(P-14372)**

360 Clinic, Westminster *Also Called: 360 Health Plan Inc* **(P-17932)**

360 Health Plan Inc ....C 800 446-8888
13800 Arizona St Ste 104 Westminster (92683) **(P-17932)**

360 Support Services ....D 866 360-6468
306 S Myrtle Ave Monrovia (91016) **(P-17933)**

365 Delivery Inc ....D 818 815-5005
440 E Huntington Dr Ste 300 Arcadia (91006) **(P-8886)**

365 Hlthcare Staffing Svcs Inc ....D 310 436-3650
25550 Hawthorne Blvd Ste 211 Torrance (90505) **(P-16523)**

365 Home Care ....D 310 908-5179
10225 Austin Dr Ste 208 Spring Valley (91978) **(P-16349)**

3d Instruments LLC ....D 714 399-9200
4990 E Hunter Ave Anaheim (92807) **(P-7844)**

3d Machine Co Inc ....E 714 777-8985
4790 E Wesley Dr Anaheim (92807) **(P-6056)**

3d/International Inc ....C 661 250-2020
20724 Centre Pointe Pkwy Unit 1 Santa Clarita (91350) **(P-3596)**

3dna Corp (PA) ....C 213 992-4809
750 W 7th St Ste 201 Los Angeles (90017) **(P-13638)**

3e, Carlsbad *Also Called: 3E Company Env Ec n Eng* **(P-18272)**

3E Company Env Ec n Eng (PA) ....C 760 602-8700
3207 Grey Hawk Ct Carlsbad (92010) **(P-18272)**

Employee Codes: A=Over 500 employees, B=251-500
C=101-250, D=51-100, E=20-50, F=10-19, G=1-9

2025 Southern California
Business Directory and Buyers Guide

© Mergent Inc. 1-800-342-5647

917

3h Communication Systems Inc .... E 949 529-1583
3 Winterbranch Irvine (92604) *(P-9380)*

3i Infotech Inc .... E 805 544-8327
555 Chorro St Ste B San Luis Obispo (93405) *(P-13639)*

3I INFOTECH INC, San Luis Obispo *Also Called: 3i Infotech Inc (P-13639)*

3M, Monrovia *Also Called: 3M Company (P-3907)*

3M, Corona *Also Called: 3M Company (P-4487)*

3M Company .... E 626 358-0136
1601 S Shamrock Ave Monrovia (91016) *(P-3907)*

3M Company .... E 951 737-3441
18750 Minnesota Rd Corona (92881) *(P-4487)*

3M Company .... B 949 863-1360
2111 Mcgaw Ave Irvine (92614) *(P-8323)*

3M Technical Ceramics Inc (HQ) .... D 949 862-9600
1922 Barranca Pkwy Irvine (92606) *(P-4497)*

3M Technical Ceramics Inc .... E 949 756-0642
17466 Daimler St Irvine (92614) *(P-4498)*

3M Unitek, Monrovia *Also Called: 3M Unitek Corporation (P-8324)*

3M Unitek Corporation .... B 626 445-7960
2724 Peck Rd Monrovia (91016) *(P-8324)*

3m/Pharmaceuticals, Northridge *Also Called: Kindeva Drug Delivery LP (P-3438)*

3s Sign Services Inc .... E 714 683-1120
1320 N Red Gum St Anaheim (92806) *(P-8588)*

4 Earth Farms LLC (PA) .... B 323 201-5800
5555 E Olympic Blvd Los Angeles (90022) *(P-10884)*

4 Flight, Rancho Cucamonga *Also Called: Safran Cabin Inc (P-7558)*

4 Over, Glendale *Also Called: 4 Over LLC (P-3111)*

4 Over LLC (HQ) .... E 818 246-1170
1225 Los Angeles St Glendale (91204) *(P-3111)*

4 What Its Worth Inc (PA) .... E 323 728-4503
5815 Smithway St Commerce (90040) *(P-2003)*

4 Wheel Parts Wholesalers LLC .... C 310 900-7725
400 W Artesia Blvd Compton (90220) *(P-9809)*

402 Shoes Inc .... E 323 655-5437
402 N La Cienega Blvd West Hollywood (90048) *(P-2145)*

48forty Solutions LLC .... B 909 371-0101
14966 Whittram Ave Fontana (92335) *(P-9917)*

4excelsior, Anaheim *Also Called: Excelsior Nutrition Inc (P-3316)*

4g Wireless Inc (PA) .... D 949 748-6100
775 Laguna Canyon Rd Laguna Beach (92651) *(P-9381)*

4inkjets, Signal Hill *Also Called: Ld Products Inc (P-2630)*

4l Technologies Inc .... A 817 538-0974
325 Weakley St Calexico (92231) *(P-5659)*

4liberty Inc .... D 619 400-1000
7675 Dagget St Ste 200 San Diego (92111) *(P-876)*

5 Arches LLC .... D 949 387-8092
19800 Macarthur Blvd Irvine (92612) *(P-11938)*

5 Design Inc (PA) .... D 323 308-3558
6161 Santa Monica Blvd Ste 208 Los Angeles (90038) *(P-17664)*

5 Star Jobs .... D 562 788-7391
12025 Garfield Ave South Gate (90280) *(P-13481)*

5 Star Service Inc .... E 323 647-7777
18723 Via Princessa Santa Clarita (91387) *(P-14726)*

5.11 Tactical Series, Costa Mesa *Also Called: 511 Inc (P-11502)*

511 Inc (DH) .... E 866 451-1726
3150 Bristol St Ste 300 Costa Mesa (92626) *(P-11502)*

51st St & 8th Ave Corp .... C 619 424-4000
4000 Coronado Bay Rd Coronado (92118) *(P-12753)*

5design, Los Angeles *Also Called: 5 Design Inc (P-17664)*

5e Boron Americas LLC .... E 442 292-2120
27555 Hector Rd Newberry Springs (92365) *(P-380)*

5th Axis Inc (PA) .... C 858 505-0432
7140 Engineer Rd San Diego (92111) *(P-6057)*

6417 Selma Hotel LLC .... C 323 844-6417
6417 Selma Ave Los Angeles (90028) *(P-12754)*

6500 Hllister Ave Partners LLC .... D 805 722-1362
6500 Hollister Ave Goleta (93117) *(P-12277)*

7 Diamonds Clothing, Tustin *Also Called: M & S Trading Inc (P-10687)*

7 Up / R C Bottling Co, Vernon *Also Called: American Bottling Company (P-1601)*

716 Management Inc .... D 818 471-4956
3900 W Alameda Ave # 120 Burbank (91505) *(P-441)*

71yrs Inc (PA) .... D 310 639-0390
6525 Flotilla St Commerce (90040) *(P-6674)*

75s Corp .... E 323 234-7708
800 E 62nd St Los Angeles (90001) *(P-10533)*

76, San Diego *Also Called: Cosco Fire Protection Inc (P-767)*

7th & C Investments LLC .... C 619 233-7327
404 14th St San Diego (92101) *(P-12697)*

7th Standard Ranch Company .... B 661 399-0416
33374 Lerdo Hwy Bakersfield (93308) *(P-28)*

805 Beach Breaks Inc .... D 408 896-4854
1053 Highland Way Grover Beach (93433) *(P-10991)*

80lv LLC .... E 818 435-6613
15260 Ventura Blvd Ste 2230 Sherman Oaks (91403) *(P-2880)*

8110 Aero Holding LLC .... C 858 277-8888
8110 Aero Dr San Diego (92123) *(P-12755)*

860, Shameless, Hot Wire, Los Angeles *Also Called: JT Design Studio Inc (P-2109)*

88 Special Sweet Inc .... D 909 525-7055
10488 Hickson St El Monte (91731) *(P-2762)*

89908 Inc .... E 949 221-0023
15651 Mosher Ave Tustin (92780) *(P-7214)*

901 West Olympic Blvd Ltd Prtn .... C 213 443-9200
901 W Olympic Blvd Los Angeles (90015) *(P-12756)*

911 Health Inc .... D 310 560-8509
701 Santa Monica Blvd Ste 300 Santa Monica (90401) *(P-17898)*

911 Restoration Entps Inc .... C 832 887-2582
6932 Gross Ave West Hills (91307) *(P-13351)*

99 Cents Only Stores, Tustin *Also Called: 99 Cents Only Stores LLC (P-11107)*

99 Cents Only Stores LLC (HQ) .... B 323 980-8145
1730 Flight Way Tustin (92782) *(P-11107)*

99 Ranch Market, Chino *Also Called: Tawa Supermarket Inc (P-99)*

99 Ranch Market, Buena Park *Also Called: Tawa Supermarket Ihc (P-1403)*

A & A Ready Mix Concrete, Newport Beach *Also Called: Lebata Inc (P-4444)*

A & A Ready Mixed Concrete Inc (PA) .... E 949 253-2800
4621 Teller Ave Ste 130 Newport Beach (92660) *(P-4425)*

A & B Aerospace Inc .... E 626 334-2976
612 S Ayon Ave Azusa (91702) *(P-6058)*

A & B Equipment, Corona *Also Called: Boudreau Pipeline Corporation (P-664)*

A & D Fire Protection Inc .... D 619 258-7697
7130 Convoy Ct San Diego (92111) *(P-727)*

A & H Communications Inc .... C 949 250-4555
15 Chrysler Irvine (92618) *(P-657)*

A & I Color Laboratory, Burbank *Also Called: Jake Hey Incorporated (P-14429)*

A & J Manufacturing Company .... E 714 544-9570
70 Icon Foothill Ranch (92610) *(P-5167)*

A & M Electronics Inc .... E 661 257-3680
25018 Avenue Kearny Valencia (91355) *(P-6702)*

A & M Engineering Inc .... D 626 813-2020
15854 Salvatiera St Irwindale (91706) *(P-6059)*

A & P Towing-Metropro Rd Svcs, Costa Mesa *Also Called: Metropro Road Services Inc (P-14718)*

A & R, Carson *Also Called: A & R Engineering Co Inc (P-6060)*

A & R Engineering Co Inc .... D 310 603-9060
1053 E Bedmar St Carson (90746) *(P-6060)*

A & S Mold and Die Corp .... D 818 341-5393
9705 Eton Ave Chatsworth (91311) *(P-4034)*

A & S Technologies, Northridge *Also Called: Ikano Communications Inc (P-14138)*

A A A Automobile Club So Cal, Los Angeles *Also Called: Automobile Club Southern Cal (P-12176)*

A A A Automobile Club So Cal, Irvine *Also Called: Automobile Club Southern Cal (P-12177)*

A A A Automobile Club So Cal, Oceanside *Also Called: Automobile Club Southern Cal (P-17429)*

A A A Automobile Club So Cal, Hemet *Also Called: Automobile Club Southern Cal (P-17433)*

A A A Automobile Club So Cal, Long Beach *Also Called: Automobile Club Southern Cal (P-17436)*

A A A Automobile Club So Cal, Pasadena *Also Called: Automobile Club Southern Cal (P-17445)*

A A A Automobile Club So Cal, Inglewood *Also Called: Automobile Club Southern Cal (P-17447)*

A A A Automobile Club So Cal, Valencia *Also Called: Automobile Club Southern Cal (P-17449)*

A A A Automobile Club So Cal, Laguna Hills *Also Called: Automobile Club Southern Cal (P-17457)*

Mergent email: customerrelations@mergent.com
918

2025 Southern California
Business Directory and Buyers Guide

(P-0000) Products & Services Section entry number
(PA)=Parent Co (HQ)=Headquarters (DH)=Div Headquarters

A A A Partitions, Los Angeles *Also Called: King Wire Partitions Inc (P-5098)*

A A C N, Aliso Viejo *Also Called: American Assn Crtcal Care Nrse (P-16849)*

A A E Aerospace & Coml Tech, Huntington Beach *Also Called: American Automated Engrg Inc (P-7666)*

A A Gonzalez Inc .... D 818 367-2242
13264 Ralston Ave Rancho Cascades (91342) *(P-993)*

A A P, Gardena *Also Called: American Aircraft Products Inc (P-4946)*

A and G Inc (HQ).. A 714 765-0400
11296 Harrel St Jurupa Valley (91752) *(P-2004)*

A B, Sylmar *Also Called: Advanced Bionics LLC (P-8249)*

A B C Design Rugs, Los Angeles *Also Called: ABC Carpet Co Inc (P-11519)*

A B M, Irvine *Also Called: ABM Facility Services LLC (P-17476)*

A B S, Diamond Bar *Also Called: Magnell Associate Inc (P-10015)*

A B S, Huntington Beach *Also Called: Applied Business Software Inc (P-13882)*

A Better Life Recovery LLC .... B 866 278-8804
30310 Rancho Viejo Rd San Juan Capistrano (92675) *(P-13640)*

A Breast Pump and More, Carlsbad *Also Called: Hygeia II Medical Group Inc (P-8384)*

A Buchalter Professional Corp (PA)............................... C 213 891-0700
1000 Wilshire Blvd Ste 1500 Los Angeles (90017) *(P-16630)*

A C I Communications, Calabasas *Also Called: Able Cable Inc (P-14727)*

A C M, Santa Ana *Also Called: Advanced Clnroom McRclean Corp (P-13352)*

A C T, Hawthorne *Also Called: All Cartage Transportation Inc (P-8988)*

A Clark/Mccarthy Joint Venture .... A 714 429-9779
18201 Von Karman Ave Ste 800 Irvine (92612) *(P-387)*

A Commom Thread, Los Angeles *Also Called: Dda Holdings Inc (P-2090)*

A D G, San Diego *Also Called: Affinity Development Group Inc (P-17424)*

A D S, Los Angeles *Also Called: Advanced Digital Services Inc (P-14804)*

A Dentons Innovation Wirthlin, Los Angeles *Also Called: Dentons US LLP (P-16671)*

A Development Stage Company, Beverly Hills *Also Called: Stratos Renewables Corporation (P-3737)*

A Division Continental Can Co, Santa Ana *Also Called: Altium Packaging LP (P-3992)*

A E M, Hawthorne *Also Called: Nmsp Inc (P-7277)*

A F C, Rancho Dominguez *Also Called: Advanced Fresh Concepts Corp (P-12676)*

A Fab, Lake Forest *Also Called: American Deburring Inc (P-6079)*

A Filml Inc .... D 213 977-8600
4024 Radford Ave Studio City (91604) *(P-14880)*

A G Hacienda Incorporated .... B 661 792-2418
32794 Sherwood Ave Mc Farland (93250) *(P-8887)*

A J Parent Company Inc (PA).. D 714 521-1100
6910 Aragon Cir Ste 6 Buena Park (90620) *(P-14432)*

A Lighting By Design, La Habra *Also Called: Albd Electric and Cable (P-881)*

A M Cabinets Inc (PA).. D 310 532-1919
239 E Gardena Blvd Gardena (90248) *(P-2504)*

A M I Encn-Trzana Rgnal Med Ce, Tarzana *Also Called: AMI-Hti Trzana Encino Jint Vnt (P-15910)*

A M I/Coast Magnetics Inc .... E 323 936-6188
5333 W Washington Blvd Los Angeles (90016) *(P-6922)*

A M Ortega Construction Inc (PA)................................. C 619 390-1988
10125 Channel Rd Lakeside (92040) *(P-877)*

A Mediation & Resolution Ctr, San Diego *Also Called: Asset Management Tr Svcs LLC (P-17947)*

A O Reed & Co LLC .... B 858 565-4131
4777 Ruffner St San Diego (92111) *(P-720)*

A P R Consulting Inc .... A 714 544-3696
17852 17th St Ste 206 Tustin (92780) *(P-14192)*

A P R Inc .... C 805 379-3400
100 E Thousand Oaks Blvd Ste 240 Thousand Oaks (91360) *(P-13586)*

A P S, Santa Clarita *Also Called: Applied Polytech Systems Inc (P-2403)*

A P V Crepaco, Lake Forest *Also Called: SPX Flow Us LLC (P-4928)*

A Plus International Inc (PA)... D 909 591-5168
5138 Eucalyptus Ave Chino (91710) *(P-10057)*

A Plus Label Inc .... E 714 229-9811
3215 W Warner Ave Santa Ana (92704) *(P-2763)*

A Preman Roofing, San Diego *Also Called: A Preman Roofing Inc (P-1071)*

A Preman Roofing Inc .... D 619 276-1700
875 34th St San Diego (92102) *(P-1071)*

A Q M D, Diamond Bar *Also Called: South Cast A Qlty MGT Dst Bldg (P-18359)*

A Q Pharmaceuticals Inc .... E 714 903-1000
11555 Monarch St Ste C Garden Grove (92841) *(P-3335)*

A R C O, La Palma *Also Called: Atlantic Richfield Company (P-11473)*

A R P, Santa Paula *Also Called: Automotive Racing Products Inc (P-4754)*

A R P, Ventura *Also Called: Automotive Racing Products Inc (P-4755)*

A R Santex LLC (PA)... E 888 622-7098
6790 Embarcadero Ln Ste 100 Carlsbad (92011) *(P-13641)*

A Rudin Inc (PA)... D 323 589-5547
6062 Alcoa Ave Vernon (90058) *(P-2439)*

A Rudin Designs, Vernon *Also Called: A Rudin Inc (P-2439)*

A S I, Valencia *Also Called: Advanced Semiconductor Inc (P-6794)*

A S I, Valencia *Also Called: Asi Semiconductor Inc (P-6802)*

A S I American, Corona *Also Called: Spangler Industries Inc (P-3938)*

A S P, Irvine *Also Called: Advanced Sterlization (P-8078)*

A Shoc Beverage LLC .... E 949 490-1612
844 Production Pl Newport Beach (92663) *(P-1424)*

A Speedcast Co, San Diego *Also Called: Ultisat Inc (P-14115)*

A Steris Company, Ontario *Also Called: Isomedix Operations Inc (P-8278)*

A SUNRISE HORIZON, Covina *Also Called: West Covina Foster Family Agcy (P-12269)*

A T A, Paso Robles *Also Called: Applied Technologies Assoc Inc (P-8032)*

A T S, Burbank *Also Called: Accratronics Seals LLC (P-6962)*

A Transportation, Tarzana *Also Called: Airey Enterprises LLC (P-10485)*

A V Nursing Care Center, Lancaster *Also Called: Antelope Vly Retirement HM Inc (P-15832)*

A W Chang Corporation (PA).. E 310 764-2000
6945 Atlantic Ave Long Beach (90805) *(P-10660)*

A-1 Delivery Co .... D 909 444-1220
1777 S Vintage Ave Ontario (91761) *(P-8888)*

A-1 Enterprises Inc .... E 714 630-3390
2831 E La Cresta Ave Anaheim (92806) *(P-1193)*

A-1 Fence, Anaheim *Also Called: A-1 Enterprises Inc (P-1193)*

A-1 Metal Products Inc .... E 323 721-3334
2707 Supply Ave Commerce (90040) *(P-4936)*

A-1 Pomona Linen, Paramount *Also Called: Braun Linen Service (P-13115)*

A-A Mortgage Opportunities LP .... A 888 469-0810
1 Baxter Way Westlake Village (91362) *(P-11880)*

A-Aztec Rents & Sells Inc (PA)....................................... C 310 347-3010
2665 Columbia St Torrance (90503) *(P-2233)*

A-G Sod Farms Inc .... D 951 687-7581
2900 Adams St Ste C120 Riverside (92504) *(P-51)*

A-Info Inc .... E 949 346-7326
60 Tesla Irvine (92618) *(P-7397)*

A-List, Vernon *Also Called: Just For Wraps Inc (P-2110)*

A-Mark, El Segundo *Also Called: A-Mark Precious Metals Inc (P-10544)*

A-Mark Precious Metals Inc (PA).................................... C 310 587-1477
2121 Rosecrans Ave Ste 6300 El Segundo (90245) *(P-10544)*

A-Team Delivers LLC .... D 858 254-8401
12127 Mall Blvd Ste A322 Victorville (92392) *(P-8889)*

A-W Engineering Company Inc .... E 562 945-1041
8528 Dice Rd Santa Fe Springs (90670) *(P-5168)*

A-Z Bus Sales Inc (PA).. C 951 781-7188
1900 S Riverside Ave Colton (92324) *(P-9795)*

A-Z Industries Div, Los Angeles *Also Called: Aero Shade Co Inc (P-11526)*

A-Z Mfg Inc .... E 714 444-4446
3101 W Segerstrom Ave Santa Ana (92704) *(P-6061)*

A.B.C. Carpet & Home, Los Angeles *Also Called: ABC Home Furnishings Inc (P-11510)*

A.J. Metal Manufacturing, Corona *Also Called: Aqua Performance Inc (P-10509)*

A&A Concrete Supply, Newport Beach *Also Called: A & A Ready Mixed Concrete Inc (P-4425)*

A&A Fulfillment Center, Vernon *Also Called: A&A Global Imports LLC (P-4035)*

A&A Global Imports LLC (PA).. D 888 315-2453
1801 E 41st St Vernon (90058) *(P-4035)*

A&A Jewelry Supply, Los Angeles *Also Called: Adfa Incorporated (P-5306)*

A&R Tarpaulins Inc .... E 909 829-4444
16246 Valley Blvd Fontana (92335) *(P-2232)*

A2z Color Graphics, Van Nuys *Also Called: Investment Enterprises Inc (P-3148)*

AA Blocks LLC .... D 858 523-8231
9823 Pacific Heights Blvd Ste F San Diego (92121) *(P-18084)*

Aa Equipment, Montclair *Also Called: Cascade Turf LLC (P-10361)*

Aa Leasing, Los Angeles *Also Called: Vahe Enterprises Inc (P-7213)*

AAA, Santa Maria *Also Called: Automobile Club Southern Cal (P-12179)*

AAA, La Mesa *Also Called: Automobile Club Southern Cal (P-12180)*

Employee Codes: A=Over 500 employees, B=251-500
C=101-250, D=51-100, E=20-50, F=10-19, G=1-9

2025 Southern California
Business Directory and Buyers Guide

© Mergent Inc. 1-800-342-5647

919

A
L
P
H
A
B
E
T
I
C

AAA, Chino *Also Called: Automobile Club Southern Cal (P-17426)*

AAA, San Diego *Also Called: Automobile Club Southern Cal (P-17427)*

AAA, San Diego *Also Called: Automobile Club Southern Cal (P-17428)*

AAA, Escondido *Also Called: Automobile Club Southern Cal (P-17430)*

AAA, San Diego *Also Called: Automobile Club Southern Cal (P-17431)*

AAA, Artesia *Also Called: Automobile Club Southern Cal (P-17437)*

AAA, West Hollywood *Also Called: Automobile Club Southern Cal (P-17438)*

AAA, Bakersfield *Also Called: Automobile Club Southern Cal (P-17439)*

AAA, Torrance *Also Called: Automobile Club Southern Cal (P-17440)*

AAA, Glendora *Also Called: Automobile Club Southern Cal (P-17441)*

AAA, Northridge *Also Called: Automobile Club Southern Cal (P-17442)*

AAA, Downey *Also Called: Automobile Club Southern Cal (P-17443)*

AAA, Manhattan Beach *Also Called: Automobile Club Southern Cal (P-17444)*

AAA, Woodland Hills *Also Called: Automobile Club Southern Cal (P-17446)*

AAA, Whittier *Also Called: Automobile Club Southern Cal (P-17448)*

AAA, San Luis Obispo *Also Called: Automobile Club Southern Cal (P-17450)*

AAA, Thousand Oaks *Also Called: Automobile Club Southern Cal (P-17453)*

AAA, Anaheim *Also Called: Automobile Club Southern Cal (P-17454)*

AAA, San Clemente *Also Called: Automobile Club Southern Cal (P-17456)*

AAA Auto Club, Costa Mesa *Also Called: Automobile Club Southern Cal (P-12178)*

AAA Elctrcal Cmmunications Inc (PA)..................................... C 800 892-4784
25007 Anza Dr Valencia (91355) *(P-878)*

AAA Facility Services, Valencia *Also Called: AAA Elctrcal Cmmunications Inc (P-878)*

AAA Flag & Banner, Los Angeles *Also Called: AAA Flag & Banner Mfg Co Inc (P-11673)*

AAA Flag & Banner Mfg Co Inc (PA)....................................... C 310 836-3200
8937 National Blvd Los Angeles (90034) *(P-11673)*

AAA Imaging & Supplies Inc .... E 714 431-0570
2313 S Susan St Santa Ana (92704) *(P-9964)*

AAA Imaging Solutions, Santa Ana *Also Called: AAA Imaging & Supplies Inc (P-9964)*

AAA Pallet, Mentone *Also Called: Power Pt Inc (P-5533)*

AAA Plating & Inspection Inc .... D 323 979-8930
424 E Dixon St Compton (90222) *(P-5224)*

AAC, Irvine *Also Called: American Audio Component Inc (P-6965)*

Aadlen Bros Auto Wrecking Inc (PA)...................................... D 323 875-1400
11590 Tuxford St Sun Valley (91352) *(P-10534)*

Aall Care In Home Services, San Diego *Also Called: Faith Jones & Associates Inc (P-16389)*

Aalto Scientific Ltd .... E 800 748-6674
1959 Kellogg Ave Carlsbad (92008) *(P-8071)*

AAM, Anaheim *Also Called: Anaheim Arena Management LLC (P-15016)*

Aamp of America, Chino *Also Called: Aamp of Florida Inc (P-10040)*

Aamp of Florida Inc .... E 805 338-6800
7166 Bickmore Ave # 2 Chino (91708) *(P-10040)*

Aap Division, Inglewood *Also Called: Engineered Magnetics Inc (P-6373)*

AAR Manufacturing Inc .... C 714 634-8807
2220 E Cerritos Ave Anaheim (92806) *(P-4906)*

Aardvark Clay & Supplies Inc (PA).. E 714 541-4157
1400 E Pomona St Santa Ana (92705) *(P-8557)*

Aaren Scientific Inc (DH) .... D 909 937-1033
9010 Hellman Ave Rancho Cucamonga (91730) *(P-7993)*

Aaron Corporation .... C 323 235-5959
2645 Industry Way Lynwood (90262) *(P-2079)*

Aaron Thomas, Garden Grove *Also Called: Aaron Thomas Company Inc (P-14433)*

Aaron Thomas Company Inc (PA)... C 714 894-4468
7421 Chapman Ave Garden Grove (92841) *(P-14433)*

AB Cellular Holding LLC .... A 562 468-6846
1452 Edinger Ave Tustin (92780) *(P-9425)*

Abacus Data Systems Inc (PA)... C 858 452-4280
2010 Jimmy Durante Blvd Ste 130 Del Mar (92014) *(P-13642)*

Abacus Powder Coating .... E 626 443-7556
1829 Tyler Ave South El Monte (91733) *(P-5305)*

Abacusnext, Del Mar *Also Called: Abacus Data Systems Inc (P-13642)*

Abad Foam Inc .... E 714 994-2223
6560 Caballero Blvd Buena Park (90620) *(P-3991)*

Abbey Carpet, National City *Also Called: Sids Carpet Barn (P-9906)*

Abbey-Properties LLC (PA).. D 562 435-2100
12447 Lewis St Ste 203 Garden Grove (92840) *(P-12278)*

Abbott Laboratories .... E 818 493-2388
15900 Valley View Ct Sylmar (91342) *(P-3336)*

Abbott Technologies Inc .... E 818 504-0644
8203 Vineland Ave Sun Valley (91352) *(P-6280)*

Abbott Vascular, Murrieta *Also Called: Abbott Vascular Inc (P-8073)*

Abbott Vascular Inc .... B 951 941-2400
26531 Ynez Rd Temecula (92591) *(P-3337)*

Abbott Vascular Inc .... A 951 914-2400
42301 Zevo Dr Ste D Temecula (92590) *(P-8072)*

Abbott Vascular Inc .... A 408 845-3186
30590 Cochise Cir Murrieta (92563) *(P-8073)*

Abbyson Living Corp .... C 805 465-5500
26500 Agoura Rd Ste 102 Calabasas (91302) *(P-9864)*

ABC, Burbank *Also Called: ABC Cable Networks Group (P-9474)*

ABC - Clio Inc (HQ) .... C 805 968-1911
75 Aero Camino Goleta (93117) *(P-2881)*

ABC Bus Inc .... D 714 444-5888
1485 Dale Way Costa Mesa (92626) *(P-9796)*

ABC Cable Networks Group (HQ) .... C 818 460-7477
500 S Buena Vista St Burbank (91521) *(P-9474)*

ABC Carpet Co Inc (PA).. D 212 473-3000
11111 Santa Monica Blvd Los Angeles (90025) *(P-11519)*

ABC Custom Wood Shutters Inc .... E 949 595-0300
20561 Pascal Way Lake Forest (92630) *(P-2294)*

ABC Family, Burbank *Also Called: ABC Family Worldwide Inc (P-14803)*

ABC Family Worldwide Inc (HQ).. B 818 560-1000
500 S Buena Vista St Burbank (91521) *(P-14803)*

ABC Home Furnishings Inc (PA).. A 212 473-3000
11111 Santa Monica Blvd Los Angeles (90025) *(P-11510)*

ABC Home Health Care Llc .... C 858 455-5000
5090 Shoreham Pl Ste 209 San Diego (92122) *(P-16350)*

ABC Imaging of Washington .... E 949 419-3728
17240 Red Hill Ave Irvine (92614) *(P-3112)*

ABC Recovery Center Inc .... D 760 342-6616
44359 Palm St Indio (92201) *(P-16437)*

ABC School Equipment Inc .... D 951 817-2200
1451 E 6th St Corona (92879) *(P-10117)*

ABC Sheet Metal, Anaheim *Also Called: Steeldyne Industries (P-5039)*

ABC Signature Studios Inc .... D 818 560-1000
500 S Buena Vista St Burbank (91521) *(P-9491)*

ABC Valencia, Corona *Also Called: Amerisourcebergen Drug Corp (P-10612)*

ABC-Clio, Goleta *Also Called: ABC - Clio Inc (P-2881)*

Abco Insulation, Azusa *Also Called: Oj Insulation LP (P-1017)*

Abel Automatics LLC .... E 805 388-3721
165 N Aviador St Camarillo (93010) *(P-5102)*

Abel Reels, Camarillo *Also Called: Abel Automatics LLC (P-5102)*

Aberdeen, Santa Fe Springs *Also Called: Source Code LLC (P-5868)*

Abex Display Systems Inc (PA).. C 800 537-0231
355 Parkside Dr San Fernando (91340) *(P-2651)*

Abex Exhibit Systems, San Fernando *Also Called: Abex Display Systems Inc (P-2651)*

Abhe & Svoboda Inc .... D 619 659-1320
880 Tavern Rd Alpine (91901) *(P-514)*

ABI Document Support Services, Loma Linda *Also Called: ABI Document Support Svcs LLC (P-14434)*

ABI Document Support Svcs LLC .... D 909 793-0613
10459 Mountain View Ave Ste E Loma Linda (92354) *(P-14434)*

Ability, Carson *Also Called: American Fruits & Flavors LLC (P-1663)*

Ability Counts Inc (PA)... D 951 734-6595
775 Trademark Cir Ste 101 Corona (92879) *(P-17043)*

Abl Space Systems Company .... D 424 321-6060
224 Oregon St El Segundo (90245) *(P-7640)*

Able Building Maintenance, Tustin *Also Called: Crown Building Maintenance Co (P-13368)*

Able Cable Inc (PA).. C 818 223-3600
5115 Douglas Fir Rd Ste A Calabasas (91302) *(P-14727)*

Able Card Corporation, Irwindale *Also Called: Million Corporation (P-3155)*

Able Design and Fabrication, Rancho Dominguez *Also Called: Adf Incorporated (P-5058)*

Able Engineering Services, Los Angeles *Also Called: Crown Energy Services Inc (P-13370)*

Able Freight Services LLC .... D 310 568-8883
5140 W 104th St Inglewood (90304) *(P-9245)*

Able Freight Services LLC (PA)... D 310 568-8883
5340 W 104th St Los Angeles (90045) *(P-9246)*

Able Health Group LLC .... D 760 610-2093
41990 Cook St Ste 2004 Palm Desert (92211) *(P-16524)*

Able Industrial Products Inc (PA) .... E 909 930-1585
2006 S Baker Ave Ontario (91761) *(P-3878)*

Able Patrol & Guard, San Diego *Also Called: Locator Services Inc (P-14315)*

Able Sheet Metal Inc (PA) .... E 323 269-2181
614 N Ford Blvd Los Angeles (90022) *(P-4937)*

ABM Facility Services LLC .... A 949 330-1555
152 Technology Dr Irvine (92618) *(P-17476)*

ABM Onsite Services Inc .... A 949 863-9100
3337 Michelson Dr Ste Cn7 Irvine (92612) *(P-14266)*

ABM Parking Services Inc .... A 213 284-7600
1150 S Olive St Fl 19 Los Angeles (90015) *(P-14654)*

Abode Communities LLC .... C 213 629-2702
1149 S Hill St Fl 7 Los Angeles (90015) *(P-12378)*

Above & Beyond Balloons Inc .... E 949 586-8470
1 Wrigley Unit A Irvine (92618) *(P-8655)*

Above and Beyond, Irvine *Also Called: Above & Beyond Balloons Inc (P-8655)*

Abraxis Bioscience LLC (DH) .... C 800 564-0216
11755 Wilshire Blvd Fl 20 Los Angeles (90025) *(P-3338)*

Abrazar Inc .... C 714 893-3581
7101 Wyoming St Westminster (92683) *(P-16860)*

Abrazar Elderly Assistance, Westminster *Also Called: Abrazar Inc (P-16860)*

Abrisa Industrial Glass Inc (HQ) .... D 805 525-4902
200 Hallock Dr Santa Paula (93060) *(P-7994)*

Abrisa Technologies .... E 805 525-4902
200 Hallock Dr Santa Paula (93060) *(P-7995)*

ABS By Allen Schwartz, Encino *Also Called: Aquarius Rags LLC (P-2058)*

ABS Computer Technologies, Whittier *Also Called: Magnell Associate Inc (P-9086)*

ABS Computer Technologies, City Of Industry *Also Called: Magnell Associate Inc (P-10016)*

ABS Consulting Inc .... D 714 734-4242
420 Exchange Ste 200 Irvine (92602) *(P-17477)*

ABS Group, Irvine *Also Called: ABS Consulting Inc (P-17477)*

Absen Inc .... E 909 480-0129
20311 Valley Blvd Ste J Walnut (91789) *(P-6791)*

Absolute Graphic Tech USA Inc .... E 909 597-1133
235 Jason Ct Corona (92879) *(P-6339)*

Absolute Packaging Inc .... E 714 630-3020
1201 N Miller St Anaheim (92806) *(P-2701)*

Absolute Pro Music, Los Angeles *Also Called: Absolute Usa Inc (P-6521)*

Absolute Return Portfolio .... A 800 800-7646
700 Newport Center Dr Newport Beach (92660) *(P-12623)*

Absolute Screenprint Inc .... C 714 529-2120
333 Cliffwood Park St Brea (92821) *(P-2256)*

Absolute Technologies, Anaheim *Also Called: D & D Gear Incorporated (P-7459)*

Absolute Usa Inc .... E 213 744-0044
1800 E Washington Blvd Los Angeles (90021) *(P-6521)*

Absolutely Zero Corporation .... B 949 269-3300
1 City Blvd W Ste 1000 Orange (92868) *(P-12379)*

AC Irrigation Holdco LLC .... C 661 368-3550
4700 Stockdale Hwy Bakersfield (93309) *(P-100)*

AC Pro Inc (PA) .... C 951 360-7849
11700 Inductry Ave Fontana (92337) *(P-10328)*

AC Products Inc .... E 714 630-7311
9930 Painter Ave Whittier (90605) *(P-3757)*

AC Tech, Garden Grove *Also Called: Advanced Chemistry & Technology Inc (P-3758)*

AC&a Enterprises LLC (HQ) .... E 949 716-3511
25671 Commercentre Dr Lake Forest (92630) *(P-7376)*

Academic Cap & Gown, Chatsworth *Also Called: Academic Ch Choir Gwns Mfg Inc (P-2184)*

Academic Ch Choir Gwns Mfg Inc .... E 818 886-8697
8944 Mason Ave Chatsworth (91311) *(P-2184)*

Academy Mpic Arts & Sciences (PA) .... D 310 247-3000
8949 Wilshire Blvd Beverly Hills (90211) *(P-17292)*

Academy of Cosmetology, Santa Barbara *Also Called: Santa Brbara Cmnty College Dst (P-16841)*

Acadia, San Diego *Also Called: Acadia Pharmaceuticals Inc (P-3339)*

ACADIA HEALTHCARE, Riverside *Also Called: Vista Behavioral Health Inc (P-16280)*

Acadia Pharmaceuticals Inc (PA) .... A 858 558-2871
12830 El Camino Real Ste 400 San Diego (92130) *(P-3339)*

Acapulco Mxican Rest Escondido, Escondido *Also Called: Acapulco Restaurants Inc (P-11546)*

Acapulco Mxican Rest Y Cantina, Moreno Valley *Also Called: Acapulco Restaurants Inc (P-11547)*

Acapulco Restaurants Inc .... D 562 346-1200
1541 E Valley Pkwy Escondido (92027) *(P-11546)*

Acapulco Restaurants Inc .... D 951 653-8809
12625 Frederick St Ste T Moreno Valley (92553) *(P-11547)*

Accel Therapies Inc .... D 855 443-3822
1845 W Orangewood Ave Ste 101 Orange (92868) *(P-16438)*

Accelerated Memory Prod Inc .... E 714 460-9800
1317 E Edinger Ave Santa Ana (92705) *(P-6792)*

Accent Ceilings, City Of Industry *Also Called: Adams-Campbell Company Ltd (P-4938)*

Accent Computer Solutions LLC .... D 909 825-2772
8438 Red Oak St Rancho Cucamonga (91730) *(P-18273)*

Accentcare Inc .... A 858 576-7410
5050 Murphy Canyon Rd Ste 200 San Diego (92123) *(P-16351)*

Accentcare HM Hlth El Cntro In .... B 760 352-4022
2344 S 2nd St Ste A El Centro (92243) *(P-16352)*

Accentcare Home Hlth Yuma Inc .... B 909 605-7000
1455 Auto Center Dr Ste 125 Ontario (91761) *(P-16353)*

Accenture Federal Services LLC .... A 619 574-2400
1615 Murray Canyon Rd Ste 400 San Diego (92108) *(P-18085)*

Accenture National SEC Svcs, San Diego *Also Called: Accenture Federal Services LLC (P-18085)*

Access Biologicals, Vista *Also Called: Grifols Usa LLC (P-3578)*

Access Books .... C 310 920-1694
1800 Century Park E Ste 600 Los Angeles (90067) *(P-2882)*

Access Business Group LLC .... B 714 562-6200
5600 Beach Blvd Buena Park (90621) *(P-11004)*

Access Business Group LLC .... B 714 562-7914
5609 River Way Buena Park (90621) *(P-11005)*

Access Business Group LLC .... B 808 422-9482
12825 Leffingwell Ave Santa Fe Springs (90670) *(P-11006)*

Access Dental Centers, Orange *Also Called: Access Dental Plan (P-15514)*

Access Dental Plan (PA) .... D 916 922-5000
530 S Main St Orange (92868) *(P-15514)*

Access Info Holdings LLC .... A 909 459-1417
12135 Davis St Moreno Valley (92557) *(P-9132)*

Access Logistics, Santa Fe Springs *Also Called: Access Business Group LLC (P-11006)*

Access Nurses Inc .... D 858 458-4400
5935 Cornerstone Ct W Ste 300 San Diego (92121) *(P-13482)*

Access Overlay, San Diego *Also Called: Lpl Financial Holdings Inc (P-11974)*

ACCESS PARATRANSIT, El Monte *Also Called: Access Services (P-8746)*

Access Services .... D 213 270-6000
3449 Santa Anita Ave El Monte (91731) *(P-8746)*

Acclara Holdings Group Inc .... C 714 571-5000
770 The City Dr S Orange (92868) *(P-17700)*

Acclarent Inc .... B 650 687-5888
31 Technology Dr Ste 200 Irvine (92618) *(P-8074)*

Acco, Pasadena *Also Called: Acco Engineered Systems Inc (P-729)*

Acco Engineered Systems Inc (PA) .... A 818 244-6571
888 E Walnut St Pasadena (91101) *(P-729)*

Accor Corp .... C 310 278-5444
8555 Beverly Blvd Los Angeles (90048) *(P-11548)*

Accountble Hlth Care IPA A Pro .... C 562 435-3333
2525 Cherry Ave Ste 225 Signal Hill (90755) *(P-16525)*

Accounting and Fiscal Services, Irvine *Also Called: University California Irvine (P-17768)*

Accounts Payable Department, Ontario *Also Called: Vantiva Sup Chain Slutions Inc (P-14913)*

Accratronics Seals LLC .... D 818 843-1500
2211 Kenmere Ave Burbank (91504) *(P-6962)*

Accredited Debt Relief, San Diego *Also Called: Beyond Finance LLC (P-13168)*

Accredited Fms Inc .... B 818 435-4200
5955 De Soto Ave Ste 136 Woodland Hills (91367) *(P-16354)*

Accredited Home Care, Woodland Hills *Also Called: Barry & Taffy Inc (P-16367)*

Accredited Home Care, Woodland Hills *Also Called: Berger Inc (P-16368)*

Accredited Nursing Care, Pasadena *Also Called: Accredited Nursing Services (P-15560)*

Accredited Nursing Care, Costa Mesa *Also Called: Accredited Nursing Services (P-16355)*

Accredited Nursing Care, San Diego *Also Called: Accredited Nursing Services (P-16356)*

Accredited Nursing Care, Woodland Hills *Also Called: Dunn & Berger Inc (P-16385)*

Accredited Nursing Services .... C 626 573-1234
80 S Lake Ave Ste 630 Pasadena (91101) *(P-15560)*

Accredited Nursing Services .... C 714 973-1234
950 S Coast Dr Ste 215 Costa Mesa (92626) *(P-16355)*

A
L
P
H
A
B
E
T
I
C

Employee Codes: A=Over 500 employees, B=251-500
C=101-250, D=51-100, E=20-50, F=10-19, G=1-9

2025 Southern California
Business Directory and Buyers Guide

© Mergent Inc. 1-800-342-5647
921

Accredited Nursing Services .... C 818 986-1234
3570 Camino Del Rio N Ste 108 San Diego (92108) *(P-16356)*

Accriva Dgnostics Holdings Inc (DH)................ B 858 404-8203
6260 Sequence Dr San Diego (92121) *(P-8075)*

Accton Manufacturing & Svc Inc (HQ)............... D 949 679-8029
20 Mason Irvine (92618) *(P-9983)*

Accu-Seal Sencorpwhite Inc .... E
225 Bingham Dr Ste B San Marcos (92069) *(P-5785)*

Accu-Sembly Inc .... D 626 357-3447
1835 Huntington Dr Duarte (91010) *(P-6703)*

Accu-Tech Laser Processing Inc .... E 760 744-6692
1175 Linda Vista Dr San Marcos (92078) *(P-6062)*

Accunex Inc .... E 818 882-5858
20700 Lassen St Chatsworth (91311) *(P-17478)*

Accurate Air Engineering, Cerritos *Also Called: Atlas Copco Compressors LLC (P-5755)*

Accurate Background LLC (PA)..................... B 800 784-3911
200 Spectrum Center Dr Ste 1100 Irvine (92618) *(P-14166)*

Accurate Circuit Engrg Inc .... D 714 546-2162
3019 Kilson Dr Santa Ana (92707) *(P-6704)*

Accurate Electronics, Chatsworth *Also Called: Accunex Inc (P-17478)*

Accurate Emplyment Scrning LLC .... C 847 255-1852
200 Spectrum Center Dr Ste 1100 Irvine (92618) *(P-14267)*

Accurate Engineering Inc .... E 818 768-3919
8710 Telfair Ave Sun Valley (91352) *(P-6705)*

Accurate Grinding and Mfg Corp .... E 951 479-0909
807 E Parkridge Ave Corona (92879) *(P-7377)*

Accurate Laminated Pdts Inc .... E 714 632-2773
1826 Dawns Way Fullerton (92831) *(P-2336)*

Accurate Plating Company .... E 323 268-8567
2811 Alcazar St Los Angeles (90033) *(P-5225)*

Accurate Steel Treating Inc .... E 562 927-6528
10008 Miller Way South Gate (90280) *(P-4694)*

Accurate Technology, Long Beach *Also Called: Gledhill/Lyons Inc (P-7484)*

Accuride International Inc (PA)................... E 562 903-0200
12311 Shoemaker Ave Santa Fe Springs (90670) *(P-4749)*

Accutek Packaging Equipment Co (PA).............. E 760 734-4177
2980 Scott St Vista (92081) *(P-5786)*

Accuturn Corporation .... E 951 656-6621
7189 Old 215 Frontage Rd Ste 101 Moreno Valley (92553) *(P-7684)*

Acd LLC (DH)..................................... E 949 261-7533
2321 Pullman St Santa Ana (92705) *(P-4907)*

Ace, Anaheim *Also Called: Anaheim Custom Extruders Inc (P-4050)*

Ace, Santa Ana *Also Called: Accurate Circuit Engrg Inc (P-6704)*

Ace Boiler, Santa Ana *Also Called: Ajax Boiler Inc (P-4908)*

Ace Cash Express, Riverside *Also Called: Populus Financial Group Inc (P-11842)*

Ace Clearwater Enterprises Inc .... E 310 538-5380
1614 Kona Dr Compton (90220) *(P-5564)*

Ace Clearwater Enterprises Inc (PA).............. D 310 323-2140
19815 Magellan Dr Torrance (90502) *(P-7398)*

Ace Commercial Inc .... E 562 946-6664
10310 Pioneer Blvd Ste 1 Santa Fe Springs (90670) *(P-2958)*

Ace Duraflo Pipe Restoration, Santa Ana *Also Called: Pipe Restoration Inc (P-819)*

Ace Fence Company, La Puente *Also Called: AZ Construction Inc (P-390)*

Ace Hardware, Baldwin Park *Also Called: Nichols Lumber & Hardware Co (P-9926)*

Ace Machine Shop Inc .... D 310 608-2277
11200 Wright Rd Lynwood (90262) *(P-6063)*

Ace Sushi, Torrance *Also Called: Asiana Cuisine Enterprises Inc (P-1741)*

Ace Wireless & Trading Inc .... B 949 748-5700
3031 Orange Ave Ste B Santa Ana (92707) *(P-10227)*

Acea Biosciences Inc .... D 858 724-0928
6779 Mesa Ridge Rd Ste 100 San Diego (92121) *(P-17761)*

Acg Ecopack, Ontario *Also Called: Advanced Color Graphics (P-2959)*

Ach Mechanical Contractors Inc .... D 909 307-2850
411 Business Center Ct Redlands (92373) *(P-730)*

Achates Power Inc .... D 858 535-9920
4060 Sorrento Valley Blvd Ste A San Diego (92121) *(P-7215)*

Aci International (PA)........................... D 310 889-3400
844 Moraga Dr Los Angeles (90049) *(P-10732)*

Aci Jet, Santa Ana *Also Called: Aviation Consultants Inc (P-9191)*

Aci Medical LLC .... E 760 744-4400
1857 Diamond St Ste A San Marcos (92078) *(P-8076)*

Acker Stone Industries Inc (DH).................. E 951 674-0047
13296 Temescal Canyon Rd Corona (92883) *(P-4378)*

Acme Auto Headlining, Long Beach *Also Called: Acme Headlining Co (P-7216)*

Acme Cryogenics Inc .... E 805 981-4500
531 Sandy Cir Oxnard (93036) *(P-5686)*

Acme Headlining Co .... D 562 432-0281
550 W 16th St Long Beach (90813) *(P-7216)*

Acme Portable Machines Inc .... E 626 610-1888
1330 Mountain View Cir Azusa (91702) *(P-5838)*

Acme Staffing, El Centro *Also Called: I N C Builders Inc (P-13600)*

Acme Vial, Paso Robles *Also Called: Acme Vial & Glass Co (P-4320)*

Acme Vial & Glass Co .... E 805 239-2666
1601 Commerce Way Paso Robles (93446) *(P-4320)*

Acon Laboratories Inc (PA)...................... E 858 875-8000
9440 Carroll Park Dr San Diego (92121) *(P-3528)*

Acorn Engineering Company (PA)................... A 800 488-8999
15125 Proctor Ave City Of Industry (91746) *(P-3788)*

Acorn Paper Products Co., Los Angeles *Also Called: Oak Paper Products Co LLC (P-10595)*

Acorn-Gencon Plastics LLC .... D 909 591-8461
13818 Oaks Ave Chino (91710) *(P-4036)*

Acorns, Irvine *Also Called: Acorns Grow Incorporated (P-12644)*

Acorns Grow Incorporated (PA).................... D 949 251-0095
5300 California Ave Irvine (92617) *(P-12644)*

Acosta Remainco Inc .... C 714 988-1500
480 Apollo St Ste C Brea (92821) *(P-10740)*

Acosta Sales & Marketing, Brea *Also Called: Acosta Remainco Inc (P-10740)*

Acpt, Huntington Beach *Also Called: Advanced Cmpsite Pdts Tech Inc (P-4037)*

Acralight International, Santa Ana *Also Called: International Skylights (P-4316)*

Acrl, Chatsworth *Also Called: Advanced Cosmetic RES Labs Inc (P-8656)*

Acrobat Staffing, San Diego *Also Called: SE Scher Corporation (P-13569)*

Acromil LLC .... D 951 808-9929
1168 Sherborn St Corona (92879) *(P-7399)*

Acromil LLC (HQ)................................ C 626 964-2522
18421 Railroad St City Of Industry (91748) *(P-7400)*

Acromil Corporation (PA)........................ C 626 964-2522
18421 Railroad St City Of Industry (91748) *(P-7401)*

Acrontos Manufacturing Inc .... E 714 850-9133
1641 E Saint Gertrude Pl Santa Ana (92705) *(P-5169)*

ACS, Los Angeles *Also Called: Authorized Cellular Service (P-14728)*

ACS Communications Inc .... C 310 767-2145
680 Knox St Ste 150 Torrance (90502) *(P-879)*

Acss, Beaumont *Also Called: Anderson Chrnesky Strl Stl Inc (P-4816)*

Act 1 Group Inc (PA)............................ D 310 750-3400
1999 W 190th St Torrance (90504) *(P-13483)*

Act Fulfillment Inc (PA)........................ C 909 930-9083
3155 Universe Dr Mira Loma (91752) *(P-9045)*

Actavis LLC .... D 909 270-1400
311 Bonnie Cir Corona (92878) *(P-3340)*

Acti, Wilmington *Also Called: Advanced Cleanup Tech Inc (P-18256)*

Action, Ontario *Also Called: Action Embroidery Corp (P-2270)*

Action Bag & Cover Inc .... D 714 965-7777
18401 Mount Langley St Fountain Valley (92708) *(P-2227)*

Action Cleaning Corporation .... E 619 233-1881
1668 Newton Ave San Diego (92113) *(P-14752)*

Action Crash Parts, Santa Fe Springs *Also Called: Global Trade Alliance Inc (P-11447)*

Action Embroidery Corp (PA)..................... C 909 983-1359
1315 Brooks St Ontario (91762) *(P-2270)*

Action Hlth Care Prsnnel Svcs .... C 562 799-5523
3020 Old Ranch Pkwy Ste 300 Seal Beach (90740) *(P-16357)*

Action Messenger Service, Los Angeles *Also Called: Peach Inc (P-9010)*

Action Property Management, Irvine *Also Called: Action Property Management Inc (P-12373)*

Action Property Management Inc (PA)............. D 949 450-0202
2603 Main St Ste 500 Irvine (92614) *(P-12373)*

Action Property Management Inc .... D 800 400-2284
530 S Hewitt St Los Angeles (90013) *(P-17321)*

Action Roofing, Santa Barbara *Also Called: Action Roofing Company LLC (P-1072)*

Action Roofing Company LLC .... D 805 966-3696
534 E Ortega St Santa Barbara (93103) *(P-1072)*

Action Stamping Inc .... E 626 914-7466
119 Explorer St Pomona (91768) *(P-5170)*

Activate Inc .... D 212 598-4625
  8383 Wilshire Blvd Ste 240 Beverly Hills (90211) *(P-18274)*

Activcare Living Inc (PA) .... C 858 565-4424
  10603 Rancho Bernardo Rd San Diego (92123) *(P-17934)*

Active Window Products .... D 323 245-5185
  5431 W San Fernando Rd Los Angeles (90039) *(P-4883)*

Activeon Inc (PA) .... E 858 798-3300
  10905 Technology Pl San Diego (92127) *(P-6522)*

Activision Blizzard, Santa Monica Also Called: Activision Blizzard Inc (P-13869)

Activision Blizzard Inc (HQ) .... B 310 255-2000
  2701 Olympic Blvd Bldg B Santa Monica (90404) *(P-13869)*

Activision Blizzard Inc .... D 949 955-1380
  3 Blizzard Irvine (92606) *(P-13870)*

Actron Manufacturing Inc .... D 951 371-0885
  1841 Railroad St Corona (92878) *(P-4750)*

Acufast Aircraft Products Inc .... E 818 365-7077
  12445 Gladstone Ave Sylmar (91342) *(P-7402)*

Acuity Brands Lighting Inc .... C 818 362-9465
  12881 Bradley Ave Sylmar (91342) *(P-10165)*

Acuprint, Los Angeles Also Called: Ink & Color Inc (P-3017)

Acushnet Company .... B 760 804-6500
  2819 Loker Ave E Carlsbad (92010) *(P-8498)*

Acute Psychiatric Hospital, Rosemead Also Called: Success Healthcare 1 LLC (P-15483)

Acutus Medical, Carlsbad Also Called: Acutus Medical Inc (P-8077)

Acutus Medical Inc .... C 442 232-6080
  2210 Faraday Ave Ste 100 Carlsbad (92008) *(P-8077)*

Ad Art Company, Los Angeles Also Called: RJ Acquisition Corp (P-3171)

Ad Populum LLC (PA) .... D 619 818-7644
  1234 6th St Apt 410 Santa Monica (90401) *(P-13193)*

Ad/S Companies, Corona Also Called: Architectural Design Signs Inc (P-8590)

Adactive Media Ca Inc .... D 818 465-7500
  14724 Ventura Blvd Ste 1110 Sherman Oaks (91403) *(P-13258)*

Adam Nutrition, Irvine Also Called: International Vitamin Corp (P-3426)

Adam Nutrition Inc .... C 951 361-1120
  11010 Hopkins St Ste B Jurupa Valley (91752) *(P-3341)*

Adams and Brooks Inc .... C 909 880-2305
  4345 Hallmark Pkwy San Bernardino (92407) *(P-1500)*

Adams Business Media, Palm Springs Also Called: Adams Trade Press LP (P-2841)

Adams Comm & Engrg Tech Inc .... C 301 861-5000
  1875 Century Park E Ste 1130 Los Angeles (90067) *(P-14193)*

Adams Rite Aerospace Inc (DH) .... D 714 278-6500
  4141 N Palm St Fullerton (92835) *(P-7403)*

Adams Steel, Anaheim Also Called: Self Serve Auto Dismantlers (P-10541)

Adams Trade Press LP (PA) .... E 760 318-7000
  420 S Palm Canyon Dr Palm Springs (92262) *(P-2841)*

Adams-Campbell Company Ltd (PA) .... D 626 330-3425
  15343 Proctor Ave City Of Industry (91745) *(P-4938)*

Adapt Automation Inc .... E 714 662-4454
  1661 Palm St Ste A Santa Ana (92701) *(P-5651)*

Adaptamed LLC .... C 877 478-7773
  6699 Alvarado Rd Ste 2301 San Diego (92120) *(P-13643)*

Adaptive Aerospace Corporation .... E 661 300-0616
  501 Bailey Ave Tehachapi (93561) *(P-7404)*

Adaptive Digital Systems Inc .... E 949 955-3116
  20322 Sw Acacia St Ste 200 Newport Beach (92660) *(P-6592)*

Adat ARI El .... C 818 766-4992
  12020 Burbank Blvd Valley Village (91607) *(P-16800)*

Adat ARI El Day School, Valley Village Also Called: Adat ARI El (P-16800)

ADC Aerospace, Buena Park Also Called: Alloy Die Casting Co (P-4643)

Adcolony Inc .... D 650 625-1262
  11400 W Olympic Blvd # 1200 Los Angeles (90064) *(P-13644)*

Adcom Interactive Media Inc .... D 800 296-7104
  6320 Canoga Ave Ste 200 Woodland Hills (91367) *(P-14194)*

Adconion Media Inc (PA) .... C 310 382-5521
  3301 Exposition Blvd Fl 1 Santa Monica (90404) *(P-13194)*

Adconion Media Group, Santa Monica Also Called: Adconion Media Inc (P-13194)

Adcraft Labels, Anaheim Also Called: Adcraft Products Co Inc (P-3113)

Adcraft Products Co Inc .... E 714 776-1230
  1230 S Sherman St Anaheim (92805) *(P-3113)*

Add-On Cmpt Peripherals Inc .... C 949 546-8200
  15775 Gateway Cir Tustin (92780) *(P-5898)*

Add-On Cmpt Peripherals LLC .... D 949 546-8200
  15775 Gateway Cir Tustin (92780) *(P-5872)*

Addiction Treatment Tech LLC .... D 818 437-5609
  120 Birmingham Dr Ste 200 Cardiff (92007) *(P-16439)*

Addink Turf, Riverside Also Called: A-G Sod Farms Inc (P-51)

Addition Manufacturing Technologies CA Inc ...... E 760 597-5220
  1391 Specialty Dr Ste A Vista (92081) *(P-5555)*

Addon Networks, Tustin Also Called: Add-On Cmpt Peripherals LLC (P-5872)

Adecco Employment Services .... C 949 586-2342
  25301 Cabot Rd Ste 214 Aliso Viejo (92653) *(P-13587)*

Adecco Staffing, Chula Vista Also Called: Ado Staffing Inc (P-13588)

Adelfi Credit Union .... C 714 671-5700
  135 S State College Blvd Ste 500 Brea (92821) *(P-11822)*

Adept Fasteners Inc (PA) .... C 661 257-6600
  27949 Hancock Pkwy Valencia (91355) *(P-7405)*

Adept Process Services Inc .... E 619 434-3194
  609 Anita St Chula Vista (91911) *(P-7615)*

Adesa Corporation LLC .... C 619 661-5565
  2175 Cactus Rd San Diego (92154) *(P-9797)*

Adesso Inc .... C 909 839-2929
  20659 Valley Blvd Walnut (91789) *(P-9984)*

Adexa Inc (PA) .... E 310 642-2100
  5777 W Century Blvd Ste 1100 Los Angeles (90045) *(P-13871)*

Adf Incorporated .... E 310 669-9700
  1550 W Mahalo Pl Rancho Dominguez (90220) *(P-5058)*

Adfa Incorporated .... E 213 627-8004
  319 W 6th St Los Angeles (90014) *(P-5306)*

ADI, Compton Also Called: American Dawn Inc (P-1965)

ADI, Valencia Also Called: Aerospace Dynamics Intl Inc (P-7413)

ADI, San Bernardino Also Called: Aviation & Defense Inc (P-9190)

Adicio Inc .... D 760 602-9502
  5857 Owens Ave Ste 300 Carlsbad (92008) *(P-9426)*

Adient Aerospace LLC (PA) .... C 949 514-1851
  2850 Skyway Dr Santa Maria (93455) *(P-9184)*

Adj Products LLC (PA) .... C 323 582-2650
  6122 S Eastern Ave Los Angeles (90040) *(P-10166)*

ADM Works, Santa Ana Also Called: Advanced Digital Mfg LLC (P-7406)

Admar Corporation .... C 714 953-9600
  1551 N Tustin Ave Ste 300 Santa Ana (92705) *(P-12068)*

Admedia, Woodland Hills Also Called: Adcom Interactive Media Inc (P-14194)

ADMINISTRATIVE OFFICES, Upland Also Called: Inland Vly DRG Alchol Rcvery S (P-16480)

Administrative Svcs Coop Inc .... C 310 715-1968
  2129 W Rosecrans Ave Gardena (90249) *(P-8857)*

Adminsure Inc .... C 909 718-1200
  3380 Shelby St Ontario (91764) *(P-12166)*

Ado Staffing Inc .... C 619 691-3659
  850 Lagoon Dr Bldg 99a Chula Vista (91910) *(P-13588)*

Adonis Inc .... E 951 432-3960
  475 N Sheridan St Corona (92878) *(P-3628)*

Adopt-A-Beach, Costa Mesa Also Called: Adopt-A-Highway Maintenance (P-606)

Adopt-A-Highway Maintenance .... C 800 200-0003
  3158 Red Hill Ave Ste 200 Costa Mesa (92626) *(P-606)*

ADP, Irvine Also Called: Automatic Data Processing Inc (P-14122)

ADP, San Dimas Also Called: Automatic Data Processing Inc (P-14123)

Adrenaline Lacrosse Inc .... E 888 768-8479
  24 21st St San Diego (92102) *(P-11503)*

Adriennes Gourmet Foods .... D 805 964-6848
  849 Ward Dr Santa Barbara (93111) *(P-1474)*

ADS Techonlogy, Walnut Also Called: Adesso Inc (P-9984)

ADT LLC .... C 951 782-6900
  1120 Palmyrita Ave Ste 280 Riverside (92507) *(P-14373)*

ADT LLC .... C 951 824-7205
  1808 Commercenter W Ste E San Bernardino (92408) *(P-14374)*

ADT LLC .... D 714 450-6461
  731 E Ball Rd Anaheim (92805) *(P-14375)*

ADT LLC .... C 626 593-1020
  475 N Muller St Anaheim (92801) *(P-14376)*

ADT LLC .... C 818 373-6200
  26074 Avenue Hall Ste 1 Valencia (91355) *(P-14377)*

ADT LLC .... C 818 464-5001
  9201 Oakdale Ave Ste 100 Chatsworth (91311) *(P-14378)*

A
L
P
H
A
B
E
T
I
C

Employee Codes: A=Over 500 employees, B=251-500
C=101-250, D=51-100, E=20-50, F=10-19, G=1-9

2025 Southern California
Business Directory and Buyers Guide

© Mergent Inc. 1-800-342-5647

923

ADT Security Services, San Bernardino *Also Called: ADT LLC (P-14374)*

Adtech Optics, City Of Industry *Also Called: Adtech Photonics Inc (P-6793)*

Adtech Photonics Inc .... E 626 956-1000
18007 Cortney Ct City Of Industry (91748) *(P-6793)*

Adult Video News, Chatsworth *Also Called: Avn Media Network Inc (P-2883)*

Advance Adapters Inc .... E 805 238-7000
4320 Aerotech Center Way Paso Robles (93446) *(P-7217)*

Advance Adapters LLC .... E 805 238-7000
4320 Aerotech Center Way Paso Robles (93446) *(P-7218)*

Advance Beverage Co Inc .... D 661 833-3783
5200 District Blvd Bakersfield (93313) *(P-11038)*

Advance Disposal Company, Hesperia *Also Called: Best Way Disposal Co Inc (P-9732)*

Advance Paper Box Company .... C 323 750-2550
6100 S Gramercy Pl Los Angeles (90047) *(P-2652)*

Advance Plastics, National City *Also Called: B and P Plastics Inc (P-4058)*

Advanced Air, Hawthorne *Also Called: Advanced Air LLC (P-9178)*

Advanced Air LLC .... C 310 644-3344
12101 Crenshaw Blvd Ste 100 Hawthorne (90250) *(P-9178)*

Advanced Aircraft Seal, Riverside *Also Called: Sphere Alliance Inc (P-3293)*

Advanced Biohealing.com, San Diego *Also Called: Shire Rgenerative Medicine Inc (P-3501)*

Advanced Bionics LLC (HQ) .... B 661 362-1400
12740 San Fernando Rd Sylmar (91342) *(P-8249)*

Advanced Bionics Corporation (HQ) .... C 661 362-1400
28515 Westinghouse Pl Valencia (91355) *(P-8250)*

Advanced Chemical Technology .... E 800 527-9607
3540 E 26th St Vernon (90058) *(P-3226)*

Advanced Chemical Technology, Vernon *Also Called: Advanced Chemical Technology (P-3226)*

Advanced Chemical Trnspt Inc .... C 951 790-7989
600 Iowa St Redlands (92373) *(P-8890)*

Advanced Chemistry & Technology Inc .... D 714 373-8118
7341 Anaconda Ave Garden Grove (92841) *(P-3758)*

Advanced Circuits Inc .... E 818 345-1993
17067 Cantara St Van Nuys (91406) *(P-6706)*

Advanced Cleanup Tech Inc .... B 310 763-1423
230 E C St Wilmington (90744) *(P-18256)*

Advanced Clnroom McRclean Corp .... C 714 751-1152
3250 S Susan St Ste A Santa Ana (92704) *(P-13352)*

Advanced Clutch Technology Inc .... E 661 940-7555
206 E Avenue K4 Lancaster (93535) *(P-7219)*

Advanced Cmpsite Pdts Tech Inc .... E 714 895-5544
15602 Chemical Ln Huntington Beach (92649) *(P-4037)*

Advanced Color Graphics .... D 909 930-1500
1921 S Business Pkwy Ontario (91761) *(P-2959)*

Advanced Cosmetic RES Labs Inc .... E 818 709-9945
20550 Prairie St Chatsworth (91311) *(P-8656)*

Advanced Cutting Tools Inc .... E 714 842-9376
17741 Metzler Ln Huntington Beach (92647) *(P-4733)*

Advanced Digital Mfg LLC .... E 714 245-0536
1343 E Wilshire Ave Santa Ana (92705) *(P-7406)*

Advanced Digital Services Inc (PA) .... D 323 962-8585
948 N Cahuenga Blvd Los Angeles (90038) *(P-14804)*

Advanced Electromagnetics Inc .... E 619 449-9492
1320 Air Wing Rd Ste 101 San Diego (92154) *(P-7845)*

Advanced Electronic Solutions, Irvine *Also Called: Patric Communications Inc (P-949)*

Advanced Equipment Corporation (PA) .... E 714 635-5350
2401 W Commonwealth Ave Fullerton (92833) *(P-2576)*

Advanced Flow Engineering Inc (PA) .... E 951 493-7155
252 Granite St Corona (92879) *(P-7220)*

Advanced Fresh Cncpts Frnchise .... D 310 604-3200
19700 Mariner Ave Torrance (90503) *(P-1700)*

Advanced Fresh Concepts Corp (PA) .... E 310 604-3630
19205 S Laurel Park Rd Rancho Dominguez (90220) *(P-12676)*

Advanced Grund Systems Engrg L (HQ) .... E 562 906-9300
10805 Painter Ave Santa Fe Springs (90670) *(P-7378)*

Advanced Image Direct, Fullerton *Also Called: Real Estate Image Inc (P-13305)*

Advanced Image Direct LLC .... E 714 502-3900
1415 S Acacia Ave Fullerton (92831) *(P-13298)*

Advanced Industrial Services, Bakersfield *Also Called: CL Knox Inc (P-326)*

Advanced Industrial Svcs Cal, Paramount *Also Called: Advanced Industrial Svcs Inc (P-858)*

Advanced Industrial Svcs Inc .... D 562 940-8305
7831 Alondra Blvd Paramount (90723) *(P-858)*

Advanced Innvtive Rcvery Tech .... E 949 273-8100
3401 Space Center Ct Ste 811b Jurupa Valley (91752) *(P-2477)*

Advanced Instruments, Pomona *Also Called: Analytical Industries Inc (P-7848)*

Advanced Joining Technologies Inc .... E 949 756-8091
3030 Red Hill Ave Santa Ana (92705) *(P-6064)*

Advanced Machining Tooling Inc .... E 858 486-9050
13535 Danielson St Poway (92064) *(P-5565)*

Advanced Materials Inc (HQ) .... E 310 537-5444
20211 S Susana Rd Compton (90221) *(P-4038)*

Advanced McHning Solutions Inc .... E 619 671-3055
3523 Main St Ste 606 Chula Vista (91911) *(P-6065)*

Advanced Med Prsonnel Svcs Inc .... D 386 756-4395
12400 High Bluff Dr Ste 100 San Diego (92130) *(P-13484)*

Advanced Medical Analysis LLC .... D 626 301-0126
1941 Walker Ave Monrovia (91016) *(P-16303)*

Advanced Metal Mfg Inc .... E 805 322-4161
49 Strathearn Pl Simi Valley (93065) *(P-4939)*

Advanced Micro Instruments Inc .... E 714 848-5533
225 Paularino Ave Costa Mesa (92626) *(P-8030)*

Advanced Motion Controls, Camarillo *Also Called: Barta - Schoenewald Inc (P-6314)*

Advanced Mp Technology LLC (DH) .... C 800 492-3113
27271 Las Ramblas Ste 300 Mission Viejo (92691) *(P-10228)*

Advanced Mtls Joining Corp (PA) .... E 626 449-2696
2858 E Walnut St Pasadena (91107) *(P-7407)*

Advanced Multimodal Dist Inc .... C 800 838-3058
14822 Central Ave Chino (91710) *(P-9357)*

Advanced Office, Irvine *Also Called: Integrus LLC (P-9974)*

Advanced Photonix, Camarillo *Also Called: OSI Optoelectronics Inc (P-6863)*

Advanced Protection Inds LLC .... C 800 662-1711
25341 Commercentre Dr Lake Forest (92630) *(P-14379)*

Advanced Semiconductor Inc .... D 818 982-1200
24955 Avenue Kearny Valencia (91355) *(P-6794)*

Advanced Sterlization (HQ) .... C 800 595-0200
33 Technology Dr Irvine (92618) *(P-8078)*

Advanced Strilization Pdts Inc .... B 888 783-7723
33 Technology Dr Irvine (92618) *(P-18275)*

Advanced Strztion Pdts Lgstic, Fontana *Also Called: Advanced Strztion Pdts Svcs I (P-9046)*

Advanced Strztion Pdts Svcs I .... D 909 350-6987
13135 Napa St Fontana (92335) *(P-9046)*

Advanced Structural Tech Inc .... C 805 204-9133
950 Richmond Ave Oxnard (93030) *(P-5140)*

Advanced Technology Center, Burbank *Also Called: Burbank Dental Laboratory Inc (P-16341)*

Advanced Technology Co, Pasadena *Also Called: Advanced Mtls Joining Corp (P-7407)*

Advanced Uv Inc (PA) .... E 562 407-0299
16350 Manning Way Cerritos (90703) *(P-5994)*

Advanced Vision Science Inc .... E 805 683-3851
5743 Thornwood Dr Goleta (93117) *(P-8403)*

Advanced Waveguide Tech .... E 949 297-3564
29 Musick Irvine (92618) *(P-6963)*

Advanced Web Offset Inc .... D 760 727-1700
2260 Oak Ridge Way Vista (92081) *(P-3114)*

Advancment Through Oprtnty Knwl .... D 323 730-9400
1200 W 37th Pl Los Angeles (90007) *(P-16861)*

Advanstar Communications Inc .... D 714 513-8400
2525 Main St Ste 300 Irvine (92614) *(P-2842)*

Advanstar Communications Inc .... E 310 857-7500
2901 28th St Ste 100 Santa Monica (90405) *(P-14435)*

Advanstar Communications Inc (DH) .... C 310 857-7500
2501 Colorado Ave Ste 280 Santa Monica (90404) *(P-14436)*

Advanstar Global, Santa Monica *Also Called: Advanstar Communications Inc (P-14436)*

Advantage Adhesives Inc .... E 909 204-4990
1420 S Vintage Ave Ontario (91761) *(P-3759)*

Advantage Ford, Pasadena *Also Called: Advantage Ford Lincoln Mercury (P-11312)*

Advantage Ford Lincoln Mercury .... D 626 305-9188
260 California Ter Pasadena (91105) *(P-11312)*

Advantage Mailing LLC (PA) .... C 714 538-3881
1600 N Kraemer Blvd Anaheim (92806) *(P-13299)*

Advantage Mailing Service, Anaheim *Also Called: Advantage Mailing LLC (P-13299)*

Advantage Manufacturing Inc .... E 714 505-1166
616 S Santa Fe St Santa Ana (92705) *(P-10167)*

Advantage Media Services Inc .... C 661 705-7588
28220 Industry Dr Valencia (91355) *(P-9047)*

Advantage Media Services Inc (PA) .... D **661 775-0611**
29010 Commerce Center Dr Valencia (91355) *(P-9352)*

Advantage Media Services Inc .... D 661 775-0611
28545 Livingston Ave Valencia (91355) *(P-18086)*

Advantage Resourcing Amer Inc .... C 562 465-0099
11005 Firestone Blvd Ste 105 Norwalk (90650) *(P-13485)*

Advantest Test Solutions Inc .... D 949 523-6900
26211 Enterprise Way Lake Forest (92630) *(P-6795)*

Advent Resources Inc .... D 310 241-1500
235 W 7th St San Pedro (90731) *(P-13645)*

ADVENTIST HEALTH, Montebello *Also Called: Beverly Community Hosp Assn (P-15926)*

Adventist Health Bakersfield, Bakersfield *Also Called: San Joaquin Community Hospital (P-16170)*

Adventist Health Delano .... C 661 721-5337
1205 Garces Hwy Ste 208 Delano (93215) *(P-15892)*

Adventist Health Delano (HQ) .... A **661 725-4800**
1401 Garces Hwy Delano (93215) *(P-15893)*

Adventist Health Med Tehachapi (PA) .... C **661 750-4848**
305 S Robinson St Tehachapi (93561) *(P-15894)*

Adventist Hlth Systm/West Corp .... B 661 316-6000
3001 Sillect Ave Bakersfield (93308) *(P-15895)*

Adventist Media Center Inc (PA) .... C **805 955-7777**
11291 Pierce St Riverside (92505) *(P-14952)*

Adventure City Inc .... D 714 821-3311
1238 S Beach Blvd Anaheim (92804) *(P-15191)*

Adviceperiod .... D 424 281-3600
2121 Avenue Of The Stars Ste 2400 Los Angeles (90067) *(P-12013)*

Advisorsquare, Culver City *Also Called: Liveoffice LLC (P-13968)*

Advisys Inc .... E 949 250-0794
3 Corporate Park Ste 240 Irvine (92606) *(P-13872)*

Advocacy For Rspect Chice - Lo (PA) .... D **562 597-7716**
4519 E Stearns St Long Beach (90815) *(P-17044)*

Adwest, Anaheim *Also Called: Adwest Technologies Inc (P-5766)*

Adwest Technologies Inc (HQ) .... E **714 632-8595**
4222 E La Palma Ave Anaheim (92807) *(P-5766)*

AEC, Brea *Also Called: Aerospace Engineering LLC (P-7415)*

AEC - Able Engineering Company Inc .... C 805 685-2262
600 Pine Ave Goleta (93117) *(P-4815)*

Aecom Services Inc (HQ) .... C **213 593-8000**
300 S Grand Ave Ste 900 Los Angeles (90071) *(P-17665)*

Aecom Technical Services Inc (HQ) .... D **213 593-8100**
300 S Grand Ave Fl 9 Los Angeles (90071) *(P-18276)*

Aecom Usa Inc .... C 714 567-2501
999 W Town And Country Rd Orange (92868) *(P-18277)*

Aecom Usa Inc .... C 213 593-8000
300 S Grand Ave Ste 900 Los Angeles (90071) *(P-18278)*

Aecom Usa Inc .... C 213 330-7200
515 S Figueroa St Ste 400 Los Angeles (90071) *(P-18279)*

Aecom Usa Inc .... C 858 947-7144
401 W A St Ste 1200 San Diego (92101) *(P-18280)*

AEG Management Lacc LLC .... C 213 741-1151
1201 S Figueroa St Los Angeles (90015) *(P-17935)*

AEG Presents, Los Angeles *Also Called: AEG Presents LLC (P-14953)*

AEG Presents LLC (DH) .... C **323 930-5700**
425 W 11th St Los Angeles (90015) *(P-14953)*

AEG Worldwide, Los Angeles *Also Called: Anschutz Entrmt Group Inc (P-14985)*

Aegis Biodefense, San Diego *Also Called: Aegis Life Inc (P-3342)*

Aegis Life Inc .... E 650 666-5287
3033 Science Park Rd Ste 270 San Diego (92121) *(P-3342)*

Aegis of Granada Hills, Granada Hills *Also Called: Aegis Senior Communities LLC (P-16358)*

Aegis of Laguna Niguel, Laguna Niguel *Also Called: Aegis Senior Communities LLC (P-17118)*

Aegis of Ventura, Ventura *Also Called: Aegis Senior Communities LLC (P-16359)*

Aegis SEC & Investigations Inc .... C 310 838-2787
10866 Washington Blvd Ste 308 Culver City (90232) *(P-14268)*

Aegis Senior Communities LLC .... C 818 363-3373
10801 Lindley Ave Granada Hills (91344) *(P-16358)*

Aegis Senior Communities LLC .... D 805 650-1114
4964 Telegraph Rd Ventura (93003) *(P-16359)*

Aegis Senior Communities LLC .... C 949 496-8080
32170 Niguel Rd Laguna Niguel (92677) *(P-17118)*

Aem, Camarillo *Also Called: Applied Enterprise MGT Corp (P-13657)*

Aemi, San Diego *Also Called: Advanced Electromagnetics Inc (P-7845)*

Aemi Holdings LLC .... D 858 481-0210
6610 Cobra Way San Diego (92121) *(P-6300)*

Aer Logistics, Brea *Also Called: Aer Technologies Inc (P-14753)*

Aer Technologies Inc .... B 714 871-7357
650 Columbia St Brea (92821) *(P-14753)*

Aera Energy LLC .... C 661 334-3100
19590 7th Standard Rd Mc Kittrick (93251) *(P-263)*

Aera Energy LLC .... A 661 665-5000
10000 Ming Ave Bakersfield (93389) *(P-264)*

Aera Energy Services Company .... C 661 665-4400
59231 Main Camp Rd Mc Kittrick (93251) *(P-285)*

Aera Energy Services Company .... D 661 665-3200
29235 Highway 33 Maricopa (93252) *(P-286)*

Aera Energy Services Company (HQ) .... A **661 665-5000**
10000 Ming Ave Bakersfield (93311) *(P-287)*

Aera Energy South Midway, Maricopa *Also Called: Aera Energy Services Company (P-286)*

Aero ARC .... E 310 324-3400
16634 S Figueroa St Gardena (90248) *(P-4940)*

Aero Bending Company .... D 661 948-2363
560 Auto Center Dr Ste A Palmdale (93551) *(P-4941)*

Aero Chip Inc .... E 562 404-6300
13563 Freeway Dr Santa Fe Springs (90670) *(P-6066)*

Aero Dynamic Machining Inc .... D 714 379-1073
7472 Chapman Ave Garden Grove (92841) *(P-6067)*

Aero Engineering, Valencia *Also Called: Aero Engineering & Mfg Co LLC (P-7408)*

Aero Engineering & Mfg Co LLC .... D 661 295-0875
28217 Avenue Crocker Valencia (91355) *(P-7408)*

Aero Industries LLC .... B 805 688-6734
139 Industrial Way Buellton (93427) *(P-6068)*

Aero Mechanism Precision Inc .... E 818 886-1855
21700 Marilla St Chatsworth (91311) *(P-6069)*

Aero Pacific Corporation .... C 714 961-9200
20445 E Walnut Dr N Walnut (91789) *(P-7409)*

Aero Performance, Corona *Also Called: Irwin Aviation Inc (P-7504)*

Aero Port Services Inc (PA) .... A **310 623-8230**
216 W Florence Ave Inglewood (90301) *(P-14380)*

Aero Precision Engineering .... E 310 642-9747
11300 Hindry Ave Los Angeles (90045) *(P-4942)*

Aero Shade Co Inc (PA) .... E **323 938-2314**
8404 W 3rd St Los Angeles (90048) *(P-11526)*

Aero Technologies Inc (PA) .... C **323 745-2376**
16233 Vanowen St Van Nuys (91406) *(P-9179)*

Aero Worx, Torrance *Also Called: Aeroworx Inc (P-14754)*

Aero-Craft Hydraulics Inc .... E 951 736-4690
392 N Smith Ave Corona (92878) *(P-7410)*

Aero-Electric Connector Inc (PA) .... B **310 618-3737**
2280 W 208th St Torrance (90501) *(P-6410)*

Aero k .... E 626 350 5125
2040 E Dyer Rd Santa Ana (92705) *(P-6070)*

Aeroantenna Technology Inc .... C 818 993-3842
20732 Lassen St Chatsworth (91311) *(P-7685)*

Aerocraft Heat Treating Co Inc .... D 562 674-2400
15701 Minnesota Ave Paramount (90723) *(P-4695)*

Aerodynamic Engineering Inc .... E 714 891-2651
15495 Graham St Huntington Beach (92649) *(P-6071)*

Aerodyne Prcsion Machining Inc .... E 714 891-1311
5471 Argosy Ave Huntington Beach (92649) *(P-6072)*

Aerofit LLC .... C 714 521-5060
1425 S Acacia Ave Fullerton (92831) *(P-5423)*

Aeroflex Incorporated .... C 800 843-1553
15375 Barranca Pkwy Ste F106 Irvine (92618) *(P-6796)*

Aeroflite Enterprises Inc .... D 714 773-4251
261 Gemini Ave Brea (92821) *(P-6941)*

Aerofoam Industries Inc .... D 951 245-4429
31855 Corydon St Lake Elsinore (92530) *(P-2535)*

Employee Codes: A=Over 500 employees, B=251-500
C=101-250, D=51-100, E=20-50, F=10-19, G=1-9

2025 Southern California
Business Directory and Buyers Guide

© Mergent Inc. 1-800-342-5647

925

Aerojet Rcketdyne Holdings Inc (HQ).................... D 310 252-8100
222 N Pacific Coast Hwy Ste 500 El Segundo (90245) *(P-7686)*

Aerojet Rocketdyne, Canoga Park *Also Called: Aerojet Rocketdyne De Inc (P-3724)*

Aerojet Rocketdyne De Inc (DH).................... B 818 586-1000
8900 De Soto Ave Canoga Park (91304) *(P-3724)*

Aerojet Rocketdyne De Inc.................... C 818 586-9629
8495 Carla Ln West Hills (91304) *(P-3725)*

Aerojet Rocketdyne De Inc.................... C 818 586-1000
9001 Lurline Ave Chatsworth (91311) *(P-3726)*

Aerojet Rocketdyne De Inc.................... B 818 586-1000
6633 Canoga Ave Canoga Park (91303) *(P-7379)*

Aerojet Rocketdyne De Inc.................... A 310 414-0110
222 N Pacific Coast Hwy Ste 50 El Segundo (90245) *(P-7687)*

Aerol Co, Rancho Dominguez *Also Called: Aerol Co Inc (P-4663)*

Aerol Co Inc.................... E 310 762-2660
19560 S Rancho Way Rancho Dominguez (90220) *(P-4663)*

Aeronet Worldwide Inc.................... C 310 787-6960
850 W Artesia Blvd Compton (90220) *(P-9247)*

Aeroshear Aviation Svcs Inc (PA).................... E 818 779-1650
7701 Woodley Ave 200 Van Nuys (91406) *(P-7411)*

Aerospace Corporation.................... C 626 873-7700
200 S Los Robles Ave Ste 150 Pasadena (91101) *(P-17865)*

Aerospace Dynamics Intl Inc.................... B 661 310-6986
25575 Rye Canyon Rd Santa Clarita (91355) *(P-7412)*

Aerospace Dynamics Intl Inc (DH).................... C 661 257-3535
25540 Rye Canyon Rd Valencia (91355) *(P-7413)*

Aerospace Engineering LLC.................... E 714 641-5884
2141 S Standard Ave Santa Ana (92707) *(P-7414)*

Aerospace Engineering LLC (PA).................... D 714 996-8178
2632 Saturn St Brea (92821) *(P-7415)*

Aerospace Engrg Support Corp.................... E 310 297-4050
645 Hawaii St El Segundo (90245) *(P-7416)*

Aerospace Fasteners Group, Santa Ana *Also Called: SPS Technologies LLC (P-8576)*

Aerospace Parts Holdings Inc.................... A 949 877-3630
3150 E Miraloma Ave Anaheim (92806) *(P-7417)*

Aerospace Systems, Redondo Beach *Also Called: Northrop Grumman Systems Corp (P-7366)*

Aerotec Alloys Inc.................... E 562 809-1378
10632 Alondra Blvd Norwalk (90650) *(P-4642)*

Aerotech News and Review Inc (PA).................... E 661 945-5634
220 E Avenue K4 Ste 4 Lancaster (93535) *(P-2843)*

Aerotek Inc.................... A 805 604-3000
2751 Park View Ct Ste 221 Oxnard (93036) *(P-6073)*

Aerotransporte De Carge Union.................... B 310 649-0069
5625 W Imperial Hwy Los Angeles (90045) *(P-9155)*

Aerounion, Los Angeles *Also Called: Aerotransporte De Carge Union (P-9155)*

Aerovironment Inc.................... E 626 357-9983
825 S Myrtle Ave Monrovia (91016) *(P-7324)*

Aerovironment Inc.................... E 626 357-9983
1610 S Magnolia Ave Monrovia (91016) *(P-7325)*

Aerovironment Inc.................... E 626 357-9983
222 E Huntington Dr Ste 118 Monrovia (91016) *(P-7326)*

Aerovironment Inc.................... D 805 520-8350
900 Innovators Way Simi Valley (93065) *(P-7327)*

Aeroworx Inc.................... E 310 891-0300
2565 W 237th St Torrance (90505) *(P-14754)*

AES, Long Beach *Also Called: AES Alamitos LLC (P-9573)*

AES Alamitos LLC.................... D 562 493-7891
690 N Studebaker Rd Long Beach (90803) *(P-9573)*

Aethercomm Inc.................... C 760 208-6002
3205 Lionshead Ave Carlsbad (92010) *(P-6593)*

Afc Distribution Corp.................... C 310 604-3630
19205 S Laurel Park Rd Rancho Dominguez (90220) *(P-10741)*

Afcfc, Torrance *Also Called: Advanced Fresh Cncpts Frnchise (P-1700)*

Afco, Alhambra *Also Called: Alhambra Foundry Company Ltd (P-4556)*

Afe Power, Corona *Also Called: Advanced Flow Engineering Inc (P-7220)*

Aferin LLC.................... E 562 903-1500
9808 Alburtis Ave Santa Fe Springs (90670) *(P-5873)*

Affinity Auto Programs Inc.................... B 858 643-9324
10251 Vista Sorrento Pkwy Ste 300 San Diego (92121) *(P-14437)*

Affinity Development Group Inc.................... C 858 643-9324
10590 W Ocean Air Dr Ste 300 San Diego (92130) *(P-17424)*

Affinity Group, Ventura *Also Called: Agi Holding Corp (P-15112)*

Affymetrix, San Diego *Also Called: Ebioscience Inc (P-17786)*

Affymetrix Inc.................... D 858 642-2058
5893 Oberlin Dr San Diego (92121) *(P-7936)*

Afm & Sg-Ftra Intllctual Prprt.................... D 818 255-7980
4705 Laurel Canyon Blvd Ste 400 Valley Village (91607) *(P-14438)*

AFP, City Of Industry *Also Called: Alum-A-Fold Pacific Inc (P-4589)*

Afr Apparel International Inc.................... D 818 773-5000
25365 Prado De La Felicidad Calabasas (91302) *(P-2146)*

African Women Rising.................... C 415 278-1784
801 Cold Springs Rd Santa Barbara (93108) *(P-17322)*

Aftco Mfg Co Inc.................... D 949 660-8757
2400 S Garnsey St Santa Ana (92707) *(P-10508)*

After-Party2 Inc (DH).................... C 310 202-0011
901 W Hillcrest Blvd Inglewood (90301) *(P-13446)*

After-Party6 Inc.................... C 310 966-4900
901 W Hillcrest Blvd Inglewood (90301) *(P-13447)*

AG Adriano Goldschmied Inc (PA).................... E 323 357-1111
2741 Seminole Ave Ste A South Gate (90280) *(P-1990)*

AG Jeans, South Gate *Also Called: AG Adriano Goldschmied Inc (P-1990)*

AG Millworks, Ventura *Also Called: Art Glass Etc Inc (P-2297)*

AG Rx (PA).................... D 805 487-0696
751 S Rose Ave Oxnard (93030) *(P-11068)*

AG Seal Beach LLC.................... C 562 592-2477
3000 N Gate Rd Seal Beach (90740) *(P-15561)*

Ag-Wise Enterprises Inc (PA).................... C 661 325-1567
5100 California Ave Ste 209 Bakersfield (93309) *(P-140)*

Age Incorporated.................... E 562 483-7300
14831 Spring Ave Santa Fe Springs (90670) *(P-6301)*

Agency For Performing Arts Inc (PA).................... D 310 557-9049
405 S Beverly Dr Ste 500 Beverly Hills (90212) *(P-14954)*

Agencycom LLC.................... B 415 817-3800
5353 Grosvenor Blvd Los Angeles (90066) *(P-13873)*

Agendia Inc.................... C 949 540-6300
22 Morgan Irvine (92618) *(P-17762)*

Agent Franchise LLC.................... C 949 930-5025
9518 9th St Ste C2 Rancho Cucamonga (91730) *(P-12056)*

Agents West Inc.................... E 949 614-0293
6 Hughes Ste 210 Irvine (92618) *(P-7108)*

Agi Cargo LLC.................... A 310 646-2446
6181 W Imperial Hwy Los Angeles (90045) *(P-9185)*

Agi Cargo LLC.................... A 310 342-0136
6851 W Imperial Hwy Los Angeles (90045) *(P-9186)*

Agi Ground Inc.................... A 310 215-4902
300 World Way Los Angeles (90045) *(P-9187)*

Agi Holding Corp (PA).................... D 805 667-4100
2575 Vista Del Mar Dr Ventura (93001) *(P-15112)*

Agia Affinity, Oxnard *Also Called: AGIA Inc (P-12167)*

AGIA Inc (PA).................... C 805 566-9191
300 E Esplanade Dr Ste 2010 Oxnard (93036) *(P-12167)*

Agile, Corona *Also Called: Agile Sourcing Partners Inc (P-9677)*

Agile Sourcing Partners Inc.................... C 951 279-4154
2385 Railroad St Corona (92878) *(P-9677)*

Agilent Technologies, Carpinteria *Also Called: Agilent Technologies Inc (P-7896)*

Agilent Technologies Inc.................... E 858 373-6300
11011 N Torrey Pines Rd La Jolla (92037) *(P-7894)*

Agilent Technologies Inc.................... E 805 566-6655
1170 Mark Ave Carpinteria (93013) *(P-7895)*

Agilent Technologies Inc.................... E 805 566-1405
6392 Via Real Carpinteria (93013) *(P-7896)*

Agileone, Torrance *Also Called: Act 1 Group Inc (P-13483)*

Agilex Flavors & Fragrances, Commerce *Also Called: Key Essentials Inc (P-1686)*

Agility Holdings Inc (DH).................... D 714 617-6300
310 Commerce Ste 250 Irvine (92602) *(P-9248)*

Agility Logistics, Irvine *Also Called: Agility Holdings Inc (P-9248)*

Agility Logistics Corp (DH).................... D 714 617-6300
310 Commerce Ste 250 Irvine (92602) *(P-9249)*

Agl, Temecula *Also Called: Artificial Grass Liquidators (P-8660)*

AGM California Inc.................... C 661 328-0118
1400 Easton Dr Ste 144 Bakersfield (93309) *(P-9475)*

Agoura Hills Renaissance Hotel, Agoura Hills *Also Called: Davidson Hotel Partners Lp* **(P-12806)**

Agouron Pharmaceuticals Inc (HQ).............................**E 858 622-3000**
10777 Science Center Dr San Diego (92121) *(P-3343)*

Agouron Pharmaceuticals Inc ....C 858 455-3200
3550 General Atomics Ct Bldg 9 San Diego (92121) *(P-17763)*

Agouron Pharmaceuticals Inc ....B 858 622-3000
3301 N Torrey Pines Ct La Jolla (92037) *(P-17764)*

Agreserves Inc ....C 661 391-9000
15443 Beech Ave Wasco (93280) *(P-38)*

Agri Service Inc ....E 760 295-6255
2141 Oceanside Blvd Oceanside (92054) *(P-9726)*

Agri-Empire ....C 951 654-7311
630 W 7th St San Jacinto (92583) *(P-10885)*

Agron Inc (PA)...D 310 473-7223
2440 S Sepulveda Blvd Ste 201 Los Angeles (90064) *(P-2156)*

AGS Usa LLC ....C 323 588-2200
1210 Rexford Ave Pasadena (91107) *(P-2057)*

Agse, Santa Fe Springs *Also Called: Advanced Grund Systems Engrg L* **(P-7378)**

Agt, Corona *Also Called: Absolute Graphic Tech USA Inc* **(P-6339)**

Agua Caliente Casino & Resort, Rancho Mirage *Also Called: Agua Clnte Band Chilla Indians* **(P-12757)**

Agua Clnte Band Chilla Indians ....A 760 321-2000
32250 Bob Hope Dr Rancho Mirage (92270) *(P-12757)*

Agua Clnte Band Chilla Indians ....A 800 854-1279
401 E Amado Rd Palm Springs (92262) *(P-12758)*

Agua Clnte Band Chilla Indians (PA) ....B 760 699-6800
5401 Dinah Shore Dr Palm Springs (92264) *(P-17425)*

Ahf-Ducommun Incorporated (HQ) ....C 310 380-5390
268 E Gardena Blvd Gardena (90248) *(P-7418)*

Ahg Inc ....B 703 596-0111
340 S Lemon Ave 6633 Walnut (91789) *(P-13160)*

Ahi Investment Inc (DH) ....E 818 979-0030
675 Glenoaks Blvd San Fernando (91340) *(P-11108)*

Ahm Gemch Inc ....C 626 579-7777
1701 Santa Anita Ave El Monte (91733) *(P-15896)*

Ahmc, Anaheim *Also Called: Ahmc Anheim Rgional Med Ctr LP* **(P-15898)**

Ahmc Anheim Rgional Med Ctr LP ....B 714 774-1450
1111 W La Palma Ave Anaheim (92801) *(P-15897)*

Ahmc Anheim Rgional Med Ctr LP ....B 714 999-3847
1211 W La Palma Ave Anaheim (92801) *(P-15898)*

Ahmc Anheim Rgional Med Ctr LP ....A 714 774-1450
1111 W La Palma Ave Anaheim (92801) *(P-15899)*

Ahmc Anheim Rgional Med Ctr LP (HQ) ....B 714 774-1450
1111 W La Palma Ave Anaheim (92801) *(P-16281)*

Ahmc Garfield Medical Ctr LP ....C 626 573-2222
525 N Garfield Ave Monterey Park (91754) *(P-15562)*

Ahmc Healthcare Inc (PA)...C 626 943-7526
506 W Valley Blvd Ste 300 San Gabriel (91776) *(P-15900)*

Ahmc Healthcare Inc ....C 626 579-7777
1701 Santa Anita Ave South El Monte (91733) *(P-15901)*

Ahmc Healthcare Inc ....C 626 248-3452
506 W Valley Blvd Ste 300 San Gabriel (91776) *(P-16526)*

Ahmc Healthcare Inc ....C 626 570-9000
900 3 Atlantic Blvd Monterey Park (91754) *(P-16527)*

Ahmc Whittier Hosp Med Ctr LP ....A 562 945-3561
9080 Colima Rd Whittier (90605) *(P-15902)*

Ahs Trinity Group Inc (PA)...E 818 508-2105
11041 Vanowen St North Hollywood (91605) *(P-2185)*

Ahw, Long Beach *Also Called: Aircraft Hardware West* **(P-10484)**

Aids Project La, Los Angeles *Also Called: Aids Project Los Angeles* **(P-16862)**

Aids Project Los Angeles (PA)..D 213 201-1600
611 S Kingsley Dr Los Angeles (90005) *(P-16862)*

AIG Direct Insurance Svcs Inc ....B 858 309-3000
9640 Granite Ridge Dr Ste 200 San Diego (92123) *(P-12168)*

Aii Beauty, Commerce *Also Called: American Intl Inds Inc* **(P-3630)**

Ailo Logistics ....A 310 707-1120
435 E Weber Ave Compton (90222) *(P-8891)*

Aimloan.com, A Direct Lender, San Diego *Also Called: American Internet Mortgage Inc* **(P-11882)**

Ainos Inc (PA)..E 858 869-2986
8880 Rio San Diego Dr Ste 800 San Diego (92108) *(P-17765)*

Aio Acquisition Inc (HQ)..D 800 333-3795
3200 E Guasti Rd Ste 300 Ontario (91761) *(P-2901)*

Air & Gas Tech Inc ....E 619 955-5980
11433 Woodside Ave Santee (92071) *(P-7616)*

Air 88 Inc ....E 858 277-1453
3753 John J Montgomery Dr San Diego (92123) *(P-9188)*

Air Cabin Engineering Inc ....E 714 637-4111
231 W Blueridge Ave Orange (92865) *(P-7419)*

Air Combat Systems, Palmdale *Also Called: Northrop Grumman Systems Corp* **(P-7365)**

Air Demolition and Envmtl, Orange *Also Called: American Intgrted Rsources Inc* **(P-17941)**

Air Electro Inc (PA)...C 818 407-5400
9452 De Soto Ave Chatsworth (91311) *(P-10229)*

Air Fayre USA Inc ....C 310 808-1061
1720 W 135th St Gardena (90249) *(P-11549)*

Air Flow Research, Valencia *Also Called: Air Flow Research Heads Inc* **(P-7221)**

Air Flow Research Heads Inc ....E 661 257-8124
28611 Industry Dr Valencia (91355) *(P-7221)*

Air Force Village West Inc ....B 951 697-2000
17050 Arnold Dr Riverside (92518) *(P-15563)*

Air Frame Mfg & Supply Co Inc ....E 661 257-7728
26135 Technology Dr Valencia (91355) *(P-10483)*

Air Frame Mfg. & Supply Co., Valencia *Also Called: Air Frame Mfg & Supply Co Inc* **(P-10483)**

Air Gap International, Placentia *Also Called: Altinex Inc* **(P-6595)**

Air Group Leasing Inc ....B 310 684-4095
1111 E Watson Center Rd Ste C Carson (90745) *(P-9250)*

Air Liquid Healthcare ....E 909 899-4633
12460 Arrow Rte Rancho Cucamonga (91739) *(P-3210)*

Air Liquide Electronics US LP ....A 310 549-7079
1502 W Anaheim St Wilmington (90744) *(P-3211)*

Air Liquide Electronics US LP ....A 713 624-8000
1831 Carnegie Ave Santa Ana (92705) *(P-17479)*

Air Louvers Inc ....E 800 554-6077
6285 Randolph St Commerce (90040) *(P-4884)*

Air Lquide Globl E C Solutions, Santa Ana *Also Called: Air Liquide Electronics US LP* **(P-17479)**

Air New Zealand Limited ....D 310 648-7000
222 N Pacific Coast Hwy Ste 900 El Segundo (90245) *(P-9156)*

Air Products, Vernon *Also Called: Evonik Corporation* **(P-3797)**

Air Products and Chemicals Inc ....D 760 931-9555
1969 Palomar Oaks Way Carlsbad (92011) *(P-3212)*

Air-TEC, Carson *Also Called: Clay Dunn Enterprises Inc* **(P-764)**

Air-Tro Air Conditioning & Htg, Monrovia *Also Called: Air-Tro Incorporated* **(P-731)**

Air-Tro Incorporated ....D 626 357-3535
1630 S Myrtle Ave Monrovia (91016) *(P-731)*

Air-Vol Block Inc ....E 805 543-1314
1 Suburban Rd San Luis Obispo (93401) *(P-4369)*

Aira Tech, Carlsbad *Also Called: Aira Tech Corp* **(P-13874)**

Aira Tech Corp ....C 800 835-1934
3451 Via Montebello Ste 192 Pmb 214 Carlsbad (92009) *(P-13874)*

Airborne Components, Carson *Also Called: Stanford Mu Corporation* **(P-7673)**

Airborne Systems N Amer CA Inc ....C 714 662-1400
3100 W Segerstrom Ave Santa Ana (92704) *(P-2271)*

Airborne Technologies, Camarillo *Also Called: Airborne Technologies Inc* **(P-7420)**

Airborne Technologies Inc ....C 805 389-3700
999 Avenida Acaso Camarillo (93012) *(P-7420)*

Aircarbon, Huntington Beach *Also Called: Newlight Technologies Inc* **(P-4180)**

Aircraft Hardware West ....E 562 961-9324
2180 Temple Ave Long Beach (90804) *(P-10484)*

Aircraft Spruce & Specialty, Corona *Also Called: Irwin International Inc* **(P-11487)**

Aircraft Xray Laboratories Inc ....D 323 587-4141
5216 Pacific Blvd Huntington Park (90255) *(P-17899)*

Airdraulics Inc ....E 818 982-1400
13261 Saticoy St North Hollywood (91605) *(P-14701)*

Airdyne Refrigeration, Cerritos *Also Called: ARI Industries Inc* **(P-5968)**

Airdyne Refrigeration, Cerritos *Also Called: Refrigerator Manufacturers LLC* **(P-5982)**

Aireloom, Rancho Cucamonga *Also Called: ES Kluft & Company Inc* **(P-2482)**

Airey Enterprises LLC ....C 818 530-3362
5530 Corbin Ave Ste 325 Tarzana (91356) *(P-10485)*

Airframer R, Torrance *Also Called: Sonic Industries Inc* **(P-17633)**

Employee Codes: A=Over 500 employees, B=251-500
C=101-250, D=51-100, E=20-50, F=10-19, G=1-9

2025 Southern California
Business Directory and Buyers Guide

© Mergent Inc. 1-800-342-5647
927

Airgas, Long Beach *Also Called: Airgas Inc (P-3213)*

Airgas Inc .... E 510 429-4216
3737 Worsham Ave Long Beach (90808) *(P-3213)*

Airgas Usa LLC .... E 562 945-1383
8832 Dice Rd Santa Fe Springs (90670) *(P-3214)*

Airgas Usa LLC .... E 562 906-8700
9756 Santa Fe Springs Rd Santa Fe Springs (90670) *(P-3215)*

Airgas Usa LLC .... A 562 497-1991
3737 Worsham Ave Long Beach (90808) *(P-10365)*

Airo Industries Company .... E 818 838-1008
429 Jessie St San Fernando (91340) *(P-2536)*

Airport Connection Inc .... C 805 389-8196
95 Dawson Dr Camarillo (93012) *(P-8747)*

Airport Honda, Los Angeles *Also Called: Noarus Investments Inc (P-11388)*

Airport Marina Ford, Los Angeles *Also Called: Fox Hills Auto Inc (P-11351)*

Airport Terminal MGT Inc .... B 310 988-1492
6851 W Imperial Hwy Los Angeles (90045) *(P-9189)*

Airport Terminal Services, Los Angeles *Also Called: Agi Ground Inc (P-9187)*

Airtech Advanced Mtls Group, Huntington Beach *Also Called: Airtech International Inc (P-7421)*

Airtech International Inc (PA) .... C 714 899-8100
5700 Skylab Rd Huntington Beach (92647) *(P-7421)*

Airx Utility Surveyors Inc (PA) .... D 760 480-2347
785 E Mission Rd # 100 San Marcos (92069) *(P-658)*

Ais Construction Company .... D 805 928-9467
7015 Vista Del Rincon Dr Ventura (93001) *(P-515)*

Aisling Industries, Calexico *Also Called: Creation Tech Calexico Inc (P-6721)*

AITA Clutch Inc .... E 323 585-4140
960 S Santa Fe Ave Compton (90221) *(P-7222)*

Aitech Defense Systems Inc .... D 818 700-2000
19756 Prairie St Chatsworth (91311) *(P-7109)*

Aitech Rugged Group Inc (PA) .... E 818 700-2000
19756 Prairie St Chatsworth (91311) *(P-7110)*

AJ Kirkwood & Associates Inc .... B 714 505-1977
4300 N Harbor Blvd Fullerton (92835) *(P-880)*

Ajax Boiler Inc .... D 714 437-9050
2701 S Harbor Blvd Santa Ana (92704) *(P-4908)*

Ajilon LLC .... C 949 955-0100
4590 Macarthur Blvd Newport Beach (92660) *(P-14195)*

Ajinomoto Althea Inc (HQ) .... E 858 882-0123
11040 Roselle St San Diego (92121) *(P-8079)*

Ajinomoto Bio-Pharma Services, San Diego *Also Called: Ajinomoto Althea Inc (P-8079)*

Ajinomoto Foods North Amer Inc (DH) .... D 909 477-4700
4200 Concours Ste 100 Ontario (91764) *(P-1383)*

Ajinomoto Foods North Amer Inc .... C 909 477-4700
4200 Concours Ste 100 Ontario (91764) *(P-1384)*

Ajit Healthcare Inc .... D 213 484-0510
316 S Westlake Ave Los Angeles (90057) *(P-17936)*

Akcea Therapeutics, Carlsbad *Also Called: Akcea Therapeutics Inc (P-3344)*

Akcea Therapeutics Inc (HQ) .... D 617 207-0202
2850 Gazelle Ct Carlsbad (92010) *(P-3344)*

Aker International Inc .... E 619 423-5182
2248 Main St Ste 4 Chula Vista (91911) *(P-4308)*

Aker Leather Products, Chula Vista *Also Called: Aker International Inc (P-4308)*

Akerman LLP .... D 213 688-9500
633 W 5th St Los Angeles (90071) *(P-16631)*

Akh Company Inc .... D 909 748-5016
1647 W Redlands Blvd Ste C Redlands (92373) *(P-11437)*

Akh Company Inc .... D 951 924-5356
23316 Sunnymead Blvd Moreno Valley (92553) *(P-11438)*

Akh Company Inc .... D 818 691-1978
7120 Laurel Canyon Blvd North Hollywood (91605) *(P-14702)*

Akkodis Inc .... C 818 546-2848
801 N Brand Blvd Ste 250 Glendale (91203) *(P-13646)*

Akra Plastic Products Inc .... E 909 930-1999
1504 E Cedar St Ontario (91761) *(P-4039)*

Aks, Amy K Su, Garden Grove *Also Called: Bodywaves Inc (P-2168)*

Akua Behavioral Health Inc (PA) .... C 949 777-2283
20271 Sw Birch St Ste 200 Newport Beach (92660) *(P-16282)*

Akua Mind & Body, Newport Beach *Also Called: Akua Behavioral Health Inc (P-16282)*

Al Asher & Sons Inc .... E 800 896-2480
5301 Valley Blvd Los Angeles (90032) *(P-11313)*

Al Global Corporation (HQ) .... E 619 934-3980
2400 Boswell Rd Chula Vista (91914) *(P-11653)*

Al Industries, Santa Ana *Also Called: Acrontos Manufacturing Inc (P-5169)*

Al Shellco LLC (HQ) .... C 570 296-6444
9330 Scranton Rd Ste 600 San Diego (92121) *(P-6523)*

Alabama Metal Industries Corp .... E 909 350-9280
11093 Beech Ave Fontana (92337) *(P-5059)*

Alabbasi, Perris *Also Called: Mamco Inc (P-634)*

Alaco Ladder Company .... E 909 591-7561
5167 G St Chino (91710) *(P-2408)*

Alaco Ladder Company, Chino *Also Called: B E & P Enterprises LLC (P-2409)*

Aladdin Bail Bonds, Carlsbad *Also Called: Triton Management Services LLC (P-14615)*

Aladdin Bail Bonds, Carlsbad *Also Called: Two Jinn Inc (P-14616)*

Alakor Healthcare LLC .... C 626 408-9800
323 S Heliotrope Ave Monrovia (91016) *(P-15903)*

ALAMITOS BELMONT REHABILITATIO, Long Beach *Also Called: Alamitos-Belmont Rehab Inc (P-15564)*

Alamitos Intermediate School, Garden Grove *Also Called: Garden Grove Unified Schl Dst (P-16807)*

Alamitos W Convalescent Hosp, Los Alamitos *Also Called: Katella Properties (P-15685)*

Alamitos-Belmont Rehab Inc .... C 562 434-8421
3901 E 4th St Long Beach (90814) *(P-15564)*

Alamo Rings, Cypress *Also Called: Eno Brands Inc (P-11639)*

Alan B Whitson Company Inc .... A 949 955-1200
1507 W Alton Ave Santa Ana (92704) *(P-18087)*

Alan Gordon Enterprises Inc .... E 323 466-3561
5625 Melrose Ave Los Angeles (90038) *(P-14881)*

Alan Johnson Prfmce Engrg Inc .... E 805 922-1202
1097 Foxen Canyon Rd Santa Maria (93454) *(P-7164)*

Alan Smith Pool Plastering Inc .... D 714 628-9494
227 W Carleton Ave Orange (92867) *(P-994)*

Alanic International Corp .... E 855 525-2642
8730 Wilshire Blvd Ph Beverly Hills (90211) *(P-1964)*

Alard Machine Products, Gardena *Also Called: GT Precision Inc (P-5108)*

Alarin Aircraft Hinge Inc .... E 323 725-1666
6231 Randolph St Commerce (90040) *(P-4751)*

Alastin Skincare Inc .... C 844 858-7546
5999 Avenida Encinas Carlsbad (92008) *(P-3629)*

Alatus Aerosystems .... D 626 498-7376
9301 Mason Ave Chatsworth (91311) *(P-7422)*

Alatus Aerosystems .... D 714 732-0559
9301 Mason Ave Chatsworth (91311) *(P-7423)*

Albany Farms Inc .... E 213 330-6573
625 Fair Oaks Ave Ste 125 South Pasadena (91030) *(P-1736)*

Albd Electric and Cable .... D 949 440-1216
1031 S Leslie St La Habra (90631) *(P-881)*

Albert & Mackenzie, Agoura Hills *Also Called: Albert & Mackenzie LLP (P-16632)*

Albert & Mackenzie LLP (PA) .... D 818 575-9876
28216 Dorothy Dr Ste 200 Agoura Hills (91301) *(P-16632)*

Albert A Webb Associates (PA) .... C 951 686-1070
3788 Mccray St Riverside (92506) *(P-17480)*

Albertson's Distribution Ctr, Irvine *Also Called: Albertsons LLC (P-9048)*

Albertsons 6514, Riverside *Also Called: Albertsons LLC (P-11271)*

Albertsons 6798, Lake Elsinore *Also Called: Albertsons LLC (P-11272)*

Albertsons LLC .... D 949 855-2465
9300 Toledo Way Irvine (92618) *(P-9048)*

Albertsons LLC .... D 951 656-6603
8938 Trautwein Rd Ste A Riverside (92508) *(P-11271)*

Albertsons LLC .... E 951 245-4461
30901 Riverside Dr Lake Elsinore (92530) *(P-11272)*

Albireo Energy, Poway *Also Called: Electronic Control Systems LLC (P-913)*

Alcast Mfg Inc .... E 310 542-3581
2910 Fisk Ln Redondo Beach (90278) *(P-4655)*

Alcast Mfg Inc (PA) .... E 310 542-3581
7355 E Slauson Ave Commerce (90040) *(P-4664)*

Alcatel-Lucent, Newbury Park *Also Called: Nokia of America Corporation (P-6589)*

Alcatel-Lucent Enterprise USA, Thousand Oaks *Also Called: Ale USA Inc (P-6594)*

Alcatraz Brewing Company, Orange *Also Called: Tavistock Restaurants LLC (P-11620)*

Alchem Plastics Inc .... C 714 523-2260
14263 Gannet St La Mirada (90638) *(P-3963)*

Alchemy, Los Angeles *Also Called: Our Alchemy LLC (P-14928)*

Alco Designs, Gardena *Also Called: Vege-Mist Inc (P-5991)*

Alco Engrg & Tooling Corp .... E 714 556-6060
3001 Oak St Santa Ana (92707) *(P-6074)*

Alco Metal Fab, Santa Ana *Also Called: Alco Engrg & Tooling Corp (P-6074)*

Alco Plating Corp (PA).. E 213 749-7561
1400 Long Beach Ave Los Angeles (90021) *(P-5226)*

Alcon, Irvine *Also Called: Alcon Lensx Inc (P-8080)*

Alcon Lensx Inc (DH)... D 949 753-1393
15800 Alton Pkwy Irvine (92618) *(P-8080)*

Alcon Research Ltd .... D 949 387-2142
15800 Alton Pkwy Irvine (92618) *(P-8081)*

ALCON RESEARCH, LTD., Irvine *Also Called: Alcon Research Ltd (P-8081)*

Alcon Surgical, Irvine *Also Called: Alcon Vision LLC (P-8083)*

Alcon Vision LLC .... B 949 753-6218
24514 Sunshine Dr Laguna Niguel (92677) *(P-8082)*

Alcon Vision LLC .... A 949 753-6488
15800 Alton Pkwy Irvine (92618) *(P-8083)*

Alcon Vision LLC .... A 949 505-6890
20521 Lake Forest Dr Lake Forest (92630) *(P-17900)*

Alcone Marketing Group Inc (HQ) .... D 949 595-5322
4 Studebaker Irvine (92618) *(P-13195)*

Aldila Golf Corp .... C 858 513-1801
13450 Stowe Dr Poway (92064) *(P-8499)*

Aldila Golf Corp (DH)... D 858 513-1801
1945 Kellogg Ave Carlsbad (92008) *(P-8500)*

Aldila Materials Tech Corp (DH)......................... E 858 486-6970
13450 Stowe Dr Poway (92064) *(P-3787)*

Aldon Inc .... D
1333 E 223rd St Carson (90745) *(P-12591)*

Aldon Ter Convalsent Hosptial, Los Angeles *Also Called: Longwood Management Corp (P-15866)*

Aldridge Pite LLP .... B 858 750-7700
4375 Jutland Dr Ste 200 San Diego (92117) *(P-16633)*

Ale USA Inc .... A 818 880-3500
2000 Corporate Center Dr Thousand Oaks (91320) *(P-6594)*

Alegacy, Santa Fe Springs *Also Called: Alegacy Fdsrvice Pdts Group In (P-2609)*

Alegacy Fdsrvice Pdts Group In .... D 562 320-3100
12683 Corral Pl Santa Fe Springs (90670) *(P-2609)*

Aleratec Inc .... E
21722 Lassen St Chatsworth (91311) *(P-5839)*

Alere Inc .... D 858 805-2000
9975 Summers Ridge Rd San Diego (92121) *(P-3529)*

Alere San Diego Inc (DH).................................. D 858 805-2000
9942 Mesa Rim Rd San Diego (92121) *(P-3530)*

Alere San Diego Inc .... B 858 805-2000
828 Towne Center Dr Pomona (91767) *(P-3531)*

Alere San Diego Inc .... B 909 482-0840
829 Towne Center Dr Pomona (91767) *(P-3532)*

Alert Plating, Sun Valley *Also Called: Alert Plating Company (P-5227)*

Alert Plating Company .... E 818 771-9304
9939 Glenoaks Blvd Sun Valley (91352) *(P-5227)*

Alesmith Brewing Company, San Diego *Also Called: Jdz Inc (P 1544)*

Alex and Jane, Maywood *Also Called: KSM Garment Inc (P-2043)*

Alexander Dennis Incorporated .... A 951 244-9429
31566 Railroad Canyon Rd Ste 3 Canyon Lake (92587) *(P-9798)*

Alexander Henry Fabrics Inc .... E 818 562-8200
1951 N Ontario St Burbank (91505) *(P-10661)*

Alexander's Moving & Storage, Tustin *Also Called: Stanley G Alexander Inc (P-8974)*

Alexandra Lzano Immrgtion Law .... C 323 524-9944
5800 S Eastern Ave Ste 270 Commerce (90040) *(P-16634)*

Alexs Tile Works Inc .... E 805 967-5308
5920 Matthews St Goleta (93117) *(P-1036)*

Alfa Scientific Designs Inc .... D 858 513-3888
13200 Gregg St Poway (92064) *(P-3533)*

Alflex, Compton *Also Called: Southwire Inc (P-4593)*

Alfred Louie Incorporated .... E 661 831-2520
4501 Shepard St Bakersfield (93313) *(P-1737)*

Alfred Music Publishing, Van Nuys *Also Called: The Full Void 2 Inc (P-2897)*

Alg Inc .... D 424 258-8026
120 Broadway Ste 200 Santa Monica (90401) *(P-2902)*

Alger International, Los Angeles *Also Called: Alger-Triton Inc (P-6436)*

Alger Precision Machining LLC .... C 909 986-4591
724 S Bon View Ave Ontario (91761) *(P-5103)*

Alger-Triton Inc .... E 310 229-9500
5600 W Jefferson Blvd Los Angeles (90016) *(P-6436)*

Algorithmic Objective Corp .... E 858 249-9580
8910 University Center Ln Ste 400 San Diego (92122) *(P-13647)*

Algotive, San Diego *Also Called: Algorithmic Objective Corp (P-13647)*

Alhambra Foundry Company Ltd .... E 626 289-4294
1147 S Meridian Ave Alhambra (91803) *(P-4556)*

Alhambra Hospital Med Ctr LP .... C 626 570-1606
100 S Raymond Ave Alhambra (91801) *(P-15904)*

Alhambra Motors Inc .... C 626 576-1114
1400 W Main St Alhambra (91801) *(P-11314)*

Aliantel Inc .... D 714 829-1650
1940 W Corporate Way Anaheim (92801) *(P-18281)*

Alice G Fink-Painter, Santa Fe Springs *Also Called: Spec Tool Company (P-7566)*

Alicorns, Valencia *Also Called: Medical Brkthrugh Mssage Chirs (P-8699)*

Align Aerospace LLC (PA).................................. B 818 727-7800
9401 De Soto Ave Chatsworth (91311) *(P-7424)*

Align Precision - Anaheim Inc (DH).................... D 714 961-9200
7100 Belgrave Ave Garden Grove (92841) *(P-7425)*

Alignment Health, Orange *Also Called: Alignment Healthcare Inc (P-12070)*

Alignment Health Plan .... D 323 728-7232
1100 W Town And Country Rd Ste 1600 Orange (92868) *(P-12069)*

Alignment Healthcare Inc (PA)............................ C 844 310-2247
1100 W Town And Country Rd Ste 1600 Orange (92868) *(P-12070)*

Alin Party Supply Co .... E 951 682-7441
6493 Magnolia Ave Riverside (92506) *(P-11649)*

Aliquantum International Inc .... E 909 773-0880
1131 W 6th St Ste 260b Ontario (91762) *(P-8481)*

Alisal Guest Ranch, Solvang *Also Called: Alisal Properties (P-13099)*

Alisal Properties (PA).. C 805 688-6411
1054 Alisal Rd Solvang (93463) *(P-13099)*

Aliso Creek Apts, Aliso Viejo *Also Called: Sares Rgis Group Rsdential Inc (P-12365)*

Aliso Rdge Behavioral Hlth LLC .... D 949 415-9218
200 Freedom Ln Aliso Viejo (92656) *(P-16261)*

Aliso Ridge Behavioral Health, Aliso Viejo *Also Called: Aliso Rdge Behavioral Hlth LLC (P-16261)*

Aliso Viejo Medical Offices, Aliso Viejo *Also Called: Kaiser Foundation Hospitals (P-15339)*

Alj, Camarillo *Also Called: Gc International Inc (P-4674)*

All About Printing, Canoga Park *Also Called: Barrys Printing Inc (P-2968)*

All About Produce Company .... C 805 543-9000
712 Fiero Ln Ste 30 San Luis Obispo (93401) *(P-10886)*

All Access Apparel Inc (PA).............................. C 323 889-4300
1515 Gage Rd Montebello (90640) *(P-2162)*

All Access Rental, Santa Ana *Also Called: County of Orange (P-13434)*

All Access Stging Prdctons Inc (PA).................. E 310 784-2464
1320 Storm Pkwy Torrance (90501) *(P-6488)*

All American Asphalt .... C 951 736-7617
1776 All American Way Corona (92879) *(P-607)*

All American Pipe Bending, Santa Ana *Also Called: Saf-T-Co Supply (P-6434)*

All American Print Supply Co .... E 714 616-5834
17511 Valley View Ave Cerritos (90703) *(P-5899)*

All American Racers Inc .... C 714 540-1771
2334 S Broadway Santa Ana (92707) *(P-7628)*

All Amrcan Injction Mlding Svc, Temecula *Also Called: TST Molding LLC (P-4265)*

All Care Medical Group Inc .... D 408 278-3550
31 Crescent Street Huntington Park (90255) *(P-15234)*

All Cartage Transportation Inc (PA).................... D 310 970-0600
12621 Chadron Ave Hawthorne (90250) *(P-8988)*

All Counties Courier .... C 714 599-9300
1900 S State College Blvd Ste 450 Anaheim (92806) *(P-8998)*

All Manufacturers Inc .... C 951 280-4200
1831 Commerce St Ste 101 Corona (92878) *(P-8084)*

All Metals Processing of San Diego Inc .... C 714 828-8238
8401 Standustrial St Stanton (90680) *(P-5228)*

Employee Codes: A=Over 500 employees, B=251-500
C=101-250, D=51-100, E=20-50, F=10-19, G=1-9

2025 Southern California
Business Directory and Buyers Guide

© Mergent Inc. 1-800-342-5647

929

All Mtals Proc Orange Cnty LLC .... C 714 828-8238
8401 Standustrial St Stanton (90680) *(P-5229)*

All New Stamping Co .... C 626 443-8813
10801 Lower Azusa Rd El Monte (91731) *(P-5171)*

All One God Faith Inc (PA)...................... C **844 937-2551**
1335 Park Center Dr Vista (92081) *(P-3589)*

All One God Faith Inc .... D 760 599-4010
1225 Park Center Dr Ste D Vista (92081) *(P-3590)*

All Power Manufacturing Co .... C 562 802-2640
13141 Molette St Santa Fe Springs (90670) *(P-7426)*

All Pro Bail Bonds, Vista Also Called: All-Pro Bail Bonds Inc *(P-14439)*

All Star Precision .... E 909 944-8373
8739 Lion St Rancho Cucamonga (91730) *(P-6075)*

All State Association Inc .... C 877 425-2558
11487 San Fernando Rd San Fernando (91340) *(P-17277)*

All Strong Industry (usa) Inc (PA)................ E **909 598-6494**
326 Paseo Tesoro Walnut (91789) *(P-2599)*

All Swiss Turning .... E 818 466-3076
7745 Alabama Ave Ste 13 Canoga Park (91304) *(P-6076)*

All Tmperatures Controlled Inc .... D 818 882-1478
9720 Topanga Canyon Pl Chatsworth (91311) *(P-732)*

All Valley Home Care, San Diego Also Called: All Valley Home Hlth Care Inc *(P-16360)*

All Valley Home Hlth Care Inc .... D 619 276-8001
3665 Ruffin Rd Ste 103 San Diego (92123) *(P-16360)*

All Valley Washer Service Inc .... D 818 787-1100
15008 Delano St Van Nuys (91411) *(P-13128)*

All Wall Inc .... D 760 600-5108
46150 Commerce St Ste 102 Indio (92201) *(P-995)*

All-Power Plastcs Div Dial, Los Angeles Also Called: Dial Industries Inc *(P-4102)*

All-Pro Bail Bonds Inc .... D 760 512-1969
530 Hacienda Dr Ste 104d Vista (92081) *(P-14439)*

All-Rite Leasing Company Inc .... B 714 957-1822
950 S Coast Dr Ste 110 Costa Mesa (92626) *(P-13353)*

All-Ways Metal Inc .... E 310 217-1177
401 E Alondra Blvd Gardena (90248) *(P-4943)*

Allan Aircraft Supply Co LLC .... E 818 765-4992
11643 Vanowen St North Hollywood (91605) *(P-5383)*

Allan Company, Baldwin Park Also Called: Cedarwood-Young Company *(P-9738)*

Allan Company, Baldwin Park Also Called: Cedarwood-Young Company *(P-10537)*

Allblack Co Inc .... E 562 946-2955
8155 Byron Rd Whittier (90606) *(P-5230)*

Allcare Nursing Services Inc .... D 626 432-1999
3675 Huntington Dr Ste 228 Pasadena (91107) *(P-16361)*

Allclear Aerospace & Def Inc .... E 619 660-6220
757 Main St # 102 Chula Vista (91911) *(P-7427)*

Allclear Aerospace & Def Inc .... D 805 446-2700
1283 Flynn Rd Camarillo (93012) *(P-7428)*

Allclear Inc .... E 424 316-1596
200 N Pacific Coast Hwy Ste 1350 El Segundo (90245) *(P-7328)*

Allegion Access Tech LLC .... E 909 628-9272
15750 Jurupa Ave Fontana (92337) *(P-4734)*

Allegion Access Tech LLC .... E 858 431-5940
8380 Camino Santa Fe Ste 100 San Diego (92121) *(P-4735)*

Allegis Residential Svcs Inc .... D 858 430-5700
9340 Hazard Way Ste B2 San Diego (92123) *(P-17937)*

Allegretto Vineyard Resort, Paso Robles Also Called: Ayres - Paso Robles LP *(P-12765)*

Allen Associates, Santa Barbara Also Called: Dennis Allen Associates *(P-398)*

Allen Engineering Contractor Inc .... C 909 478-5500
1655 Riverview Dr San Bernardino (92408) *(P-17481)*

Allen Gwynn Chevrolet, Glendale Also Called: Allen Gwynn Chevrolet Inc *(P-11315)*

Allen Gwynn Chevrolet Inc .... D 818 240-0000
1400 S Brand Blvd Glendale (91204) *(P-11315)*

Allen Lund Company LLC (HQ)................ D **800 777-6142**
4529 Angeles Crest Hwy La Canada Flintridge (91011) *(P-9251)*

Allen Matkins, Los Angeles Also Called: Allen Mtkins Leck Gmble Mllory *(P-16635)*

Allen Mtkins Leck Gmble Mllory (PA)........... C **213 622-5555**
865 S Figueroa St Ste 2800 Los Angeles (90017) *(P-16635)*

Allergan, Irvine Also Called: Allergan Spclty Thrpeutics Inc *(P-3346)*

Allergan Sales LLC (DH)...................... A **862 261-7000**
2525 Dupont Dr Irvine (92612) *(P-3345)*

Allergan Spclty Thrpeutics Inc .... A 714 246-4500
2525 Dupont Dr Irvine (92612) *(P-3346)*

Allergan Usa Inc (DH)...................... D **714 427-1900**
18581 Teller Ave Irvine (92612) *(P-3347)*

Allermed Laboratories Inc .... E 858 292-1060
7203 Convoy Ct San Diego (92111) *(P-3308)*

Alliance, Irvine Also Called: Alliance Healthcare Svcs Inc *(P-16304)*

Alliance Air Products Llc (DH)................ E **619 428-9688**
2285 Michael Faraday Dr Ste 15 San Diego (92154) *(P-5964)*

Alliance Air Products Llc .... A 619 664-0027
9565 Heinrich Hertz Dr Ste 1 San Diego (92154) *(P-5965)*

Alliance Childrens Services .... C 661 863-0350
1001 Tower Way Ste 110 Bakersfield (93309) *(P-17119)*

Alliance Display & Packaging, Burbank Also Called: Westrock Rkt LLC *(P-2694)*

Alliance Healthcare Svcs Inc (DH)............ C **800 544-3215**
18201 Von Karman Ave Ste 600 Irvine (92612) *(P-16304)*

Alliance Insptn MGT Holdg Inc (PA)........... A **562 495-8853**
330 Golden Shore Ste 400 Long Beach (90802) *(P-14711)*

Alliance Medical Products Inc (DH)............ E **949 768-4690**
9342 Jeronimo Rd Irvine (92618) *(P-8085)*

Alliance Medical Products Inc .... E 949 664-9616
9292 Jeronimo Rd Irvine (92618) *(P-8086)*

Alliance Metal Products Inc .... C 818 709-1204
20844 Plummer St Chatsworth (91311) *(P-4944)*

Alliance Ready Mix Inc .... E 805 556-3015
310 James Way Ste 210 Pismo Beach (93449) *(P-4426)*

Alliance Spacesystems, Los Alamitos Also Called: Vanguard Space Tech Inc *(P-7586)*

Alliance Spacesystems LLC .... C 714 226-1400
4398 Corporate Center Dr Los Alamitos (90720) *(P-6337)*

Alliance Title, Glendale Also Called: Wfg National Title Insur Co *(P-12563)*

Alliancebernstein LP .... C 310 286-6000
1999 Avenue Of The Stars Ste 2150 Los Angeles (90067) *(P-12624)*

Alliant Asset MGT Co LLC (HQ)................ D **818 668-2805**
26050 Mureau Rd Fl 2 Calabasas (91302) *(P-12380)*

Alliant Insurance Services Inc (PA)........... C **949 756-0271**
18100 Von Karman Ave Ste 1000 Irvine (92612) *(P-18282)*

Alliant Insurance Services Inc .... D 619 238-1828
701 B St Fl 6 San Diego (92101) *(P-18283)*

Alliant Tchsystems Oprtons LLC .... E 818 887-8195
9401 Corbin Ave Northridge (91324) *(P-7688)*

Alliant Tchsystems Oprtons LLC .... B 818 887-8195
9401 Corbin Ave Northridge (91324) *(P-7689)*

Allianz Global Investors of America LP .... A 949 219-2200
680 Newport Center Dr Ste 250 Newport Beach (92660) *(P-12014)*

Allianz Globl Investors US LLC .... C 949 219-2638
680 Newport Center Dr Ste 250 Newport Beach (92660) *(P-12015)*

Allianz Globl Risks US Insur (DH)............ C **818 260-7500**
2350 W Empire Ave Ste 200 Burbank (91504) *(P-12115)*

Allianz Insurance Company, Burbank Also Called: Allianz Globl Risks US Insur *(P-12115)*

Allianz Sweeper Company C
5405 Industrial Pkwy San Bernardino (92407) *(P-7165)*

Allied Artists International, City Of Industry Also Called: Allied Entertainment Group Inc *(P-14805)*

Allied Bio Medical, Ventura Also Called: Implantech Associates Inc *(P-8274)*

Allied Company Holdings Inc .... C 661 510-6533
28311 Constellation Rd Santa Clarita (91355) *(P-11039)*

Allied Company Holdings Inc (PA)............ D **818 493-6400**
13235 Golden State Rd Sylmar (91342) *(P-11040)*

Allied Components Intl .... E 949 356-1780
2372 Morse Ave Irvine (92614) *(P-6923)*

Allied Entertainment Group Inc (PA)........... B **626 330-0600**
273 W Allen Ave City Of Industry (91746) *(P-14805)*

Allied Harbor Aerospace Fas, Corona Also Called: All Manufacturers Inc *(P-8084)*

Allied High Tech Products Inc .... D 310 635-2466
16207 Carmenita Rd Cerritos (90703) *(P-10424)*

Allied International, Valencia Also Called: Allied International LLC *(P-10300)*

Allied International LLC .... E 818 364-2333
28955 Avenue Sherman Valencia (91355) *(P-10300)*

Allied Lube Inc .... C 949 651-8814
3087 Edinger Ave Tustin (92780) *(P-14685)*

Allied Mdular Bldg Systems Inc (PA)........... E **714 516-1188**
642 W Nicolas Ave Orange (92868) *(P-5074)*

Mergent email: customerrelations@mergent.com
930

2025 Southern California
Business Directory and Buyers Guide

(P-0000) Products & Services Section entry number
(PA)=Parent Co (HQ)=Headquarters (DH)=Div Headquarters

Allied Mechanical Products, Ontario *Also Called: Tower Industries Inc (P-6254)*

Allied Mechanical Products, Ontario *Also Called: Tower Mechanical Products Inc (P-7820)*

Allied Protection Services Inc .... C 310 330-8314
24303 Berendo Ave Harbor City (90710) *(P-14269)*

Allied Signal Aerospace, Torrance *Also Called: Alliedsignal Arospc Svc Corp (P-4684)*

Allied Steel Co Inc .... D 951 241-7000
1027 Palmyrita Ave Riverside (92507) *(P-1147)*

Allied Trench Shoring Service, Newport Beach *Also Called: Traffic Control Service Inc (P-13476)*

Allied Universal, Irvine *Also Called: Universal Services America LP (P-14361)*

Allied Universal Event Svcs, Huntington Beach *Also Called: Staff Pro Inc (P-14422)*

Allied Universal Security Svcs, Irvine *Also Called: Universal Protection Svc LP (P-14360)*

Allied Universal Services, Santa Ana *Also Called: Staff Pro Inc (P-14423)*

Allied West Paper Corp .... D 909 349-0710
11101 Etiwanda Ave Unit 100 Fontana (92337) *(P-2620)*

Allied Wheel Components Inc .... E 800 529-4335
12300 Edison Way Garden Grove (92841) *(P-7223)*

Alliedsignal Arospc Svc Corp (HQ)... D 310 323-9500
2525 W 190th St Torrance (90504) *(P-4684)*

Allison-Kaufman Co .... D 818 373-5100
7640 Haskell Ave Van Nuys (91406) *(P-8448)*

Alloy Die Casting Co (PA)... C 714 521-9800
6550 Caballero Blvd Buena Park (90620) *(P-4643)*

Allstate, Los Angeles *Also Called: Allstate Financial Svcs LLC (P-12169)*

Allstate Financial Svcs LLC .... D 323 981-8520
5161 Pomona Blvd Ste 212 Los Angeles (90022) *(P-12169)*

Allstate Floral Inc .... C 562 926-2989
15928 Commerce Way Cerritos (90703) *(P-12170)*

Allstate Imaging Inc (PA).. D 818 678-4550
21621 Nordhoff St Chatsworth (91311) *(P-9970)*

Alltec Integrated Mfg Inc .... E 805 595-3500
2240 S Thornburg St Santa Maria (93455) *(P-4040)*

Alltech Industries Inc .... E 323 450-2168
301 E Pomona Blvd Monterey Park (91755) *(P-882)*

Allzone Management Solutions, Glendale *Also Called: Allzone Management Svcs Inc (P-17938)*

Allzone Management Svcs Inc .... B 213 291-8879
3795 La Crescenta Ave Ste 200 Glendale (91208) *(P-17938)*

Alma Rosa Winery Vineyards LLC .... E 805 688-9090
1607 Mission Dr Ste 300 Solvang (93463) *(P-1558)*

Almavia of Camarillo, Camarillo *Also Called: Elder Care Alliance Camarillo (P-15625)*

Alna Envelope Company, Pomona *Also Called: Inland Envelope Company (P-2750)*

Alogent, Carlsbad *Also Called: Alogent Holdings Inc (P-13648)*

Alogent Holdings Inc .... D 760 410-9000
5868 Owens Ave Ste 200 Carlsbad (92008) *(P-13648)*

Alor International Ltd .... E 858 454-0011
11722 Sorrento Valley Rd San Diego (92121) *(P-8449)*

Alorica Customer Care Inc .... D 619 298-7103
8885 Rio San Diego Dr Ste 107 San Diego (92108) *(P-14440)*

Alorica Customer Care Inc .... C 941 906-9000
5161 California Ave Ste 100 Irvine (92617) *(P-14441)*

Alorica Inc (PA)... D 866 256-7422
5161 California Ave Ste 100 Irvine (92617) *(P-14442)*

Alpargatas Usa Inc .... F 646 277-7171
513 Boccaccio Ave Venice (90291) *(P-4283)*

Alpase, Chino *Also Called: Tst Inc (P-4588)*

Alpha & Omega Pavers, Calimesa *Also Called: Paver Decor Masonry Inc (P-642)*

Alpha Aviation Components Inc (PA).. E 818 894-8801
16772 Schoenborn St North Hills (91343) *(P-6077)*

Alpha Corporation of Tennessee .... C 951 657-5161
19991 Seaton Ave Perris (92570) *(P-3256)*

Alpha Dental of Utah Inc .... E 562 467-7759
12898 Towne Center Dr Cerritos (90703) *(P-8325)*

Alpha Materials Inc .... E 951 788-5150
6170 20th St Riverside (92509) *(P-4427)*

Alpha Mechanical Inc .... C 858 278-3500
4990 Greencraig Ln Ste A San Diego (92123) *(P-733)*

Alpha Mechanical Heating & Air Conditioning Inc .... C 858 279-1300
4885 Greencraig Ln San Diego (92123) *(P-734)*

Alpha Polishing Corporation (PA)... D 323 263-7593
1313 Mirasol St Los Angeles (90023) *(P-5231)*

Alpha Professional Resources, Thousand Oaks *Also Called: A P R Inc (P-13586)*

Alpha Project For Homeless .... C 760 630-9922
993 Postal Way Vista (92083) *(P-16863)*

Alpha Technics Inc .... C 949 250-6578
24024 Humphries Rd Tecate (91980) *(P-7846)*

Alpha-Owens Corning, Perris *Also Called: Alpha Corporation of Tennessee (P-3256)*

Alphabold Inc .... D 909 979-1425
2011 Palomar Airport Rd Ste 305 Carlsbad (92011) *(P-14196)*

Alphacoat Finishing LLC .... E 949 748-7796
9350 Cabot Dr San Diego (92126) *(P-5307)*

Alphaeon Corporation .... C 949 284-4555
17901 Von Karman Ave Ste 150 Irvine (92614) *(P-10058)*

Alphatec, Carlsbad *Also Called: Alphatec Holdings Inc (P-8087)*

Alphatec Holdings Inc (PA)... B 760 431-9286
1950 Camino Vida Roble Carlsbad (92008) *(P-8087)*

Alphatec Spine Inc (HQ).. C 760 431-9286
1950 Camino Vida Roble Carlsbad (92008) *(P-8251)*

Alphatech General Inc .... D 626 337-4640
4750 Littlejohn St Baldwin Park (91706) *(P-14755)*

Alpine Convalescent Center Inc .... D 619 659-3120
2120 Alpine Blvd Alpine (91901) *(P-16440)*

Alpine Inn Restaurant, Torrance *Also Called: Alpine Village (P-12279)*

Alpine Special Treatment Ctr, Alpine *Also Called: Alpine Convalescent Center Inc (P-16440)*

Alpine Village .... C 310 327-4384
23670 Hawthorne Blvd Ste 208 Torrance (90505) *(P-12279)*

Alpinestars USA .... D 310 891-0222
2780 W 237th St Torrance (90505) *(P-2033)*

Alpinestars USA, Torrance *Also Called: Alpinestars USA (P-2033)*

Alquest Technologies Inc .... D 909 392-9209
1687 Curtiss Ct La Verne (91750) *(P-14184)*

Als Garden Art Inc (PA).. B 909 424-0221
311 W Citrus St Colton (92324) *(P-4499)*

Als Group Inc .... E 909 622-7555
1788 W 2nd St Pomona (91766) *(P-10366)*

Als Group Usa Corp .... D 310 214-0043
3904 Del Amo Blvd Torrance (90503) *(P-17901)*

Alstyle AP & Activewear MGT Co (HQ)...................................... A 714 765-0400
1501 E Cerritos Ave Anaheim (92805) *(P-10701)*

Alstyle Apparel, Jurupa Valley *Also Called: A and G Inc (P-2004)*

Alstyle Apparel LLC .... A 714 765-0400
1501 E Cerritos Ave Anaheim (92805) *(P-1869)*

Alta Healthcare System LLC (HQ).. C 323 267-0477
4081 E Olympic Blvd Los Angeles (90023) *(P-15905)*

Alta Hllywood Cmnty Hosp Van N .... A 818 787-1511
14433 Emelita St Van Nuys (91401) *(P-16262)*

Alta Hospitals System LLC .... A 714 619-7700
14662 Newport Ave Tustin (92780) *(P-15906)*

Alta Med Health Services, El Monte *Also Called: Altamed Health Services Corp (P-16528)*

Alta One Fcu, Ridgecrest *Also Called: Altaone Federal Credit Union (P-11790)*

Alta-Dena Certified Dairy LLC (DH)... B 626 964-6401
17037 E Valley Blvd City Of Industry (91744) *(P-09)*

Altadena Town and Country Club .... D 626 345-9088
2290 Country Club Dr Altadena (91001) *(P-15113)*

Altair Lighting, Compton *Also Called: Jimway Inc (P-6505)*

Altamed Adhc Golden Age, Lynwood *Also Called: Altamed Health Services Corp (P-15238)*

Altamed Health Services Corp .... B 323 728-0411
5425 Pomona Blvd Los Angeles (90022) *(P-15235)*

Altamed Health Services Corp .... C 323 269-0421
2219 E 1st St Los Angeles (90033) *(P-15236)*

Altamed Health Services Corp .... D 562 923-9414
1500 Hughes Way Ste A150 Long Beach (90810) *(P-15237)*

Altamed Health Services Corp .... C 310 632-0415
3820 Martin Luther King Jr Blvd Lynwood (90262) *(P-15238)*

Altamed Health Services Corp .... C 323 980-4466
5427 Whittier Blvd Los Angeles (90022) *(P-15239)*

Altamed Health Services Corp .... D 714 426-5400
2720 S Bristol St Santa Ana (92704) *(P-15240)*

Altamed Health Services Corp (PA).. C 323 725-8751
2040 Camfield Ave Los Angeles (90040) *(P-15241)*

Altamed Health Services Corp .... D 626 453-8466
10418 Valley Blvd Ste B El Monte (91731) *(P-16528)*

A
L
P
H
A
B
E
T
I
C

Employee Codes: A=Over 500 employees, B=251-500
C=101-250, D=51-100, E=20-50, F=10-19, G=1-9

2025 Southern California
Business Directory and Buyers Guide

© Mergent Inc. 1-800-342-5647

931

Altamed Health Services Corp .... C 323 562-6700
8627 Atlantic Ave South Gate (90280) *(P-16529)*

Altamed Health Services Corp .... C 323 307-0400
3945 Whittier Blvd Los Angeles (90023) *(P-16530)*

Altamed Health Services Corp .... C 562 949-8717
9436 Slauson Ave Pico Rivera (90660) *(P-16531)*

Altamed Med & Dntl Group Bell, South Gate Also Called: Altamed Health Services Corp *(P-16529)*

Altamed Med Dntl Grp Whttier W, Los Angeles Also Called: Altamed Health Services Corp *(P-16530)*

Altametrics, Costa Mesa Also Called: Altametrics LLC *(P-9985)*

Altametrics LLC .... C 800 676-1281
3191 Red Hill Ave Ste 100 Costa Mesa (92626) *(P-9985)*

Altaone Federal Credit Union (PA) .... C 760 371-7000
701 S China Lake Blvd Ridgecrest (93555) *(P-11790)*

Altec Inc .... E 661 679-4177
1127 Carrier Parkway Ave Bakersfield (93308) *(P-5486)*

Altec Products Inc (PA) .... D 949 727-1248
23422 Mill Creek Dr Ste 225 Laguna Hills (92653) *(P-14443)*

Altech Services Inc .... B 888 725-8324
400 Continental Blvd Fl 6 El Segundo (90245) *(P-13589)*

Altegra Health, Los Angeles Also Called: The Coding Source LLC *(P-16847)*

Alter Health Group, Dana Point Also Called: Alter Management LLC *(P-17939)*

Alter Management LLC .... D 949 629-0214
34232 Pacific Coast Hwy Ste D Dana Point (92629) *(P-17939)*

Alternative Ira Services LLC .... D 877 936-7175
15303 Ventura Blvd Ste 1060 Sherman Oaks (91403) *(P-14444)*

Alteryx, Irvine Also Called: Alteryx Inc *(P-14070)*

Alteryx Inc (PA) .... E 888 836-4274
3347 Michelson Dr Ste 400 Irvine (92612) *(P-14070)*

Altinex Inc .... E 714 990-0877
500 S Jefferson St Placentia (92870) *(P-6595)*

Altium Inc (DH) .... D 858 864-1500
4225 Executive Sq Ste 800 La Jolla (92037) *(P-13649)*

Altium Holdings LLC .... A 951 340-9390
12165 Madera Way Riverside (92503) *(P-4041)*

Altium Packaging .... D 626 856-2100
4516 Azusa Canyon Rd Irwindale (91706) *(P-4042)*

ALTIUM PACKAGING, Irwindale Also Called: Altium Packaging *(P-4042)*

Altium Packaging LLC .... D 310 952-8736
1500 E 223rd St Carson (90745) *(P-3981)*

Altium Packaging LLC .... D 888 425-7343
1070 Samuelson St City Of Industry (91748) *(P-4043)*

Altium Packaging LP .... E 714 241-6640
1217 E Saint Gertrude Pl Santa Ana (92707) *(P-3992)*

Altium Packaging LP .... E 909 590-7334
14312 Central Ave Chino (91710) *(P-4044)*

Altman Flowers, Fallbrook Also Called: Altman Specialty Plants LLC *(P-11079)*

Altman Plants, Vista Also Called: Altman Specialty Plants LLC *(P-11080)*

Altman Specialty Plants LLC .... B 800 348-4881
2575 Olive Hill Rd Fallbrook (92028) *(P-11079)*

Altman Specialty Plants LLC (PA) .... A 800 348-4881
3742 Blue Bird Canyon Rd Vista (92084) *(P-11080)*

Alto Lucero Transitional Care, Santa Barbara Also Called: Compass Health Inc *(P-15602)*

Alton Geoscience, Irvine Also Called: TRC Solutions Inc *(P-18364)*

Altour International Inc (PA) .... D 310 571-6000
12100 W Olympic Blvd Ste 300 Los Angeles (90064) *(P-9216)*

Altour International Inc .... D 818 464-9200
21800 Burbank Blvd Ste 120 Woodland Hills (91367) *(P-9217)*

Altour International Inc .... B 310 571-6000
10635 Santa Monica Blvd Ste 200 Los Angeles (90025) *(P-9218)*

Altour Travel Master, Los Angeles Also Called: Altour International Inc *(P-9218)*

Altro Usa Inc .... E 562 944-8292
12648 Clark St Santa Fe Springs (90670) *(P-8653)*

Altruist Corp .... B 949 370-5096
3030 La Cienega Blvd Culver City (90232) *(P-18088)*

Alts Tool & Machine Inc .... D 619 562-6653
10926 Woodside Ave N Santee (92071) *(P-6078)*

Altumind Inc .... E 858 382-3956
10620 Treena St Ste 230 San Diego (92131) *(P-13875)*

Altura Holdings LLC .... B 714 948-8400
1335 S Acacia Ave Fullerton (92831) *(P-12625)*

Altura Management Services LLC .... B 323 768-2898
1401 N Montebello Blvd Montebello (90640) *(P-17940)*

Alturdyne Power Systems Inc .... E 619 343-3204
1405 N Johnson Ave El Cajon (92020) *(P-5454)*

Alum-A-Fold Pacific Inc .... E 562 699-4550
3730 Capitol Ave City Of Industry (90601) *(P-4589)*

Alum-Alloy Co Inc .... E 909 986-0410
603 S Hope Ave Ontario (91761) *(P-5152)*

Alumax Building Products, Sun City Also Called: Omnimax International LLC *(P-4897)*

Alumen-8, Oceanside Also Called: Amerillum LLC *(P-6490)*

Aluminum Casting Company, Ontario Also Called: Employee Owned PCF Cast Pdts I *(P-4673)*

Aluminum Die Casting Co Inc .... D 951 681-3900
10775 San Sevaine Way Jurupa Valley (91752) *(P-4644)*

Aluminum Precision Pdts Inc (PA) .... A 714 546-8125
3333 W Warner Ave Santa Ana (92704) *(P-4575)*

Aluminum Precision Pdts Inc .... C 805 488-4401
1001 Mcwane Blvd Oxnard (93033) *(P-10123)*

Alumistar Inc .... E 562 633-6673
520 S Palmetto Ave Ontario (91762) *(P-4665)*

Alva Manufacturing Inc .... E 714 237-0925
236 E Orangethorpe Ave Placentia (92870) *(P-7429)*

Alvarado Hospital LLC (DH) .... C 619 287-3270
6655 Alvarado Rd San Diego (92120) *(P-15907)*

Alvarado Hospital Med Ctr Inc .... A 619 287-3270
6655 Alvarado Rd San Diego (92120) *(P-15908)*

Alvarado Manufacturing Co Inc .... C 909 591-8431
12660 Colony Ct Chino (91710) *(P-8031)*

Alvarado Parkway Institute, La Mesa Also Called: Bh-SD Opco LLC *(P-16446)*

Alvarado Parkway Institute, La Mesa Also Called: Helix Healthcare Inc *(P-16477)*

Alvardo Contracting, Wasco Also Called: Juan Carlos Alvardo *(P-139)*

ALVAREZ & MARSAL BUSINESS CONSULTING LLC, Los Angeles Also Called: Alvarez Mrsal Bus Cnsltng LLC *(P-18089)*

Alvarez Mrsal Bus Cnsltng LLC .... B 310 975-2600
2029 Century Park E Los Angeles (90002) *(P-18089)*

Alvaria Inc .... C 408 595-5002
101 Academy Ste 130 Irvine (92617) *(P-13650)*

Always Best Care Desert Cities, Indian Wells Also Called: Bjz LLC *(P-16369)*

Always Best Care Temecula Vly, Temecula Also Called: James Rebecca Prouty Entps Inc *(P-16399)*

Always Right Home Care, Northridge Also Called: Tiffany Homecare Inc *(P-16425)*

Alyn Industries Inc .... D 818 988-7696
16028 Arminta St Van Nuys (91406) *(P-6964)*

Am-Pac Tire Dist Inc (DH) .... D 805 581-1311
51 Moreland Rd Simi Valley (93065) *(P-11439)*

Am-PM Sewer & Drain Cleaning, San Diego Also Called: Bill Howe Plumbing Inc *(P-750)*

Am-Touch Dental, Valencia Also Called: American Med & Hosp Sup Co Inc *(P-10059)*

Am/PM Mini Market, La Palma Also Called: Prestige Stations Inc *(P-11280)*

AMA Plastics .... B 951 734-5600
1100 Citrus St Riverside (92507) *(P-4045)*

Amada America Inc .... D 714 739-2111
100 S Puente St Brea (92821) *(P-5308)*

Amada America Inc (HQ) .... D 714 739-2111
7025 Firestone Blvd Buena Park (90621) *(P-10367)*

Amada Enterprises Inc .... C 323 757-1881
12619 Avalon Blvd Los Angeles (90061) *(P-15565)*

Amada Senior Care .... D 949 284-8036
901 Calle Amanecer Ste 350 San Clemente (92673) *(P-16362)*

Amada Weld Tech Inc (HQ) .... E 626 303-5676
1820 S Myrtle Ave Monrovia (91016) *(P-5642)*

Amada Weld Tech Inc .... A 626 303-5676
245 E El Norte St Monrovia (91016) *(P-8088)*

Amag Technology Inc (DH) .... E 310 518-2380
2205 W 126th St Ste B Hawthorne (90250) *(P-5900)*

Amanecer Cmnty Cnsling Svc A N .... D 213 481-7464
1200 Wilshire Blvd Ste 200 Los Angeles (90017) *(P-16441)*

Amare Global LP .... E 888 898-8551
17872 Gillette Ave Ste 100 Irvine (92614) *(P-3348)*

Mergent email: customerrelations@mergent.com
932

2025 Southern California
Business Directory and Buyers Guide

(P-0000) Products & Services Section entry number
(PA)=Parent Co (HQ)=Headquarters (DH)=Div Headquarters

Amass Brands Inc .... E 619 204-2560
860 E Stowell Rd Santa Maria (93454) *(P-3309)*

Amatix, Sun Valley *Also Called: Marfred Industries* *(P-2681)*

Amawaterways LLC (PA).................................... C 800 626-0126
4500 Park Granada Ste 200 Calabasas (91302) *(P-9219)*

Amaya Curiel Corporation .... A 619 661-1230
9775 Marconi Dr Ste G San Diego (92154) *(P-470)*

Amaya Curiel Y CIA S.A., San Diego *Also Called: Amaya Curiel Corporation* *(P-470)*

Amays Bakery & Noodle Co Inc (PA)................ D 213 626-2713
837 E Commercial St Los Angeles (90012) *(P-1475)*

Amazing Coachella Inc .... D 760 398-0151
85810 Peter Rabbit Ln Coachella (92236) *(P-7)*

Amazing Steel, Montclair *Also Called: Mitchell Fabrication* *(P-4857)*

Amazon Processing LLC .... C 858 565-1135
4619 Viewridge Ave Ste C San Diego (92123) *(P-14121)*

Amazon Studios LLC .... C 818 804-0884
9336 Washington Blvd Culver City (90232) *(P-13651)*

Amber Chemical Inc .... E 661 325-2072
5201 Boylan St Bakersfield (93308) *(P-3227)*

Amber Holding Inc .... E 603 324-3000
1601 Cloverfield Blvd Ste 600s Santa Monica (90404) *(P-13876)*

Amber Steel Co., Rialto *Also Called: H Wayne Lewis Inc (P-5095)*

Amberwood Convalescent Hosp .... D 323 254-3407
6071 York Blvd Los Angeles (90042) *(P-15830)*

Ambiance Transportation LLC .... D 818 955-5757
6901 San Fernando Rd Glendale (91201) *(P-9358)*

Ambit Biosciences Corporation .... D 858 334-2100
10201 Wateridge Cir Ste 200 San Diego (92121) *(P-3349)*

Ambrit Engineering Corporation .... D 714 557-1074
2640 Halladay St Santa Ana (92705) *(P-5566)*

Ambrit Industries Inc .... E 818 243-1224
432 Magnolia Ave Glendale (91204) *(P-5556)*

Ambrx, La Jolla *Also Called: Ambrx Biopharma Inc (P-3555)*

Ambrx Inc (PA).. D **858 875-2400**
10975 N Torrey Pines Rd Ste 100 La Jolla (92037) *(P-3350)*

Ambrx Biopharma Inc .... D 858 875-2400
10975 N Torrey Pines Rd La Jolla (92037) *(P-3555)*

Ambulnz Health LLC .... B 877 311-5555
12531 Vanowen St North Hollywood (91605) *(P-8809)*

AMC, Stanton *Also Called: All Metals Processing of San Diego Inc (P-5228)*

AMC Machining Inc .... E 805 238-5452
1540 Commerce Way Paso Robles (93446) *(P-5090)*

AMC Networks Inc .... D 310 998-9300
2425 Olympic Blvd Ste 5050w Santa Monica (90404) *(P-9523)*

Amco Foods Inc .... B 818 247-4716
601 E Glenoaks Blvd Ste 108 Glendale (91207) *(P-18090)*

Amcor Flexibles Healthcare, Commerce *Also Called: Amcor Flexibles LLC (P-2703)*

Amcor Flexibles LLC .... A 323 721-6777
5416 Union Pacific Ave Commerce (90022) *(P-2703)*

Amcor Industries Inc .... E 323 585-2852
6131 Knott Ave Buena Park (90620) *(P-7224)*

AMD International Tech LLC .... E 909 985-8300
1725 S Campus Ave Ontario (91761) *(P-4945)*

AME Unmanned Air Systems Inc .... D 805 541-4448
125 Venture Dr Ste 110 San Luis Obispo (93401) *(P-17482)*

AME-Gyu Co Ltd .... A 310 214-9572
20000 Mariner Ave Ste 500 Torrance (90503) *(P-12592)*

Ameditech Inc .... C 858 535-1968
9940 Mesa Rim Rd San Diego (92121) *(P-8089)*

Amen Clinics Inc A Med Corp (PA).................... D **888 564-2700**
959 S Coast Dr Costa Mesa (92626) *(P-15242)*

Ameresco Solar LLC .... B 888 967-6527
42261 Zevo Dr Temecula (92590) *(P-17483)*

Amergence Technology Inc .... E 909 859-8400
295 Brea Canyon Rd Walnut (91789) *(P-5687)*

Ameri-Kleen .... E 805 546-0706
1023 E Grand Ave Arroyo Grande (93420) *(P-13354)*

Ameri-Kleen Building Services, Arroyo Grande *Also Called: Ameri-Kleen (P-13354)*

American Academic Hlth Sys LLC .... A 310 414-7200
222 N Pacific Coast Hwy Ste 900 El Segundo (90245) *(P-12593)*

American Aircraft Products Inc .... D 310 532-7434
15411 S Broadway Gardena (90248) *(P-4946)*

American Airlines Inc .... C 310 646-4553
400 World Way Ste F Los Angeles (90045) *(P-9157)*

American Airlines/Eagle, Long Beach *Also Called: Piedmont Airlines Inc (P-9163)*

American Apparel, Los Angeles *Also Called: App Winddown LLC (P-2187)*

American Arium .... E 949 623-7090
17791 Fitch Irvine (92614) *(P-6797)*

American Assets Inc .... C 619 255-9944
2799 Adrian St San Diego (92110) *(P-12280)*

American Assn Crtcal Care Nrse .... C 949 362-2000
27071 Aliso Creek Rd Aliso Viejo (92656) *(P-16849)*

American Assod Roofg Distrs, Monterey Park *Also Called: Oakcroft Associates Inc (P-10354)*

American Audio Component Inc .... E 909 596-3788
20 Fairbanks Ste 198 Irvine (92618) *(P-6965)*

American Automated Engrg Inc .... C 714 898-9951
5382 Argosy Ave Huntington Beach (92649) *(P-7666)*

American Bath Factory, Corona *Also Called: Le Elegant Bath Inc (P-4030)*

American Beech Solar LLC .... D 949 398-3915
18575 Jamboree Rd Ste 850 Irvine (92612) *(P-735)*

American Beef Packers Inc .... C 909 628-4888
13677 Yorba Ave Chino (91710) *(P-137)*

American Best Car Parts, Anaheim *Also Called: American Fabrication Corp (P-7225)*

American Bottling Company .... D 951 341-7500
1188 Mt Vernon Ave Riverside (92507) *(P-1600)*

American Bottling Company .... C 323 268-7779
3220 E 26th St Vernon (90058) *(P-1601)*

American Bottling Company .... D 818 898-1471
1166 Arroyo St San Fernando (91340) *(P-1602)*

American Bottling Company .... D 661 323-7921
230 E 18th St Bakersfield (93305) *(P-1603)*

American Bottling Company .... D 805 928-1001
618 Hanson Way Santa Maria (93458) *(P-1604)*

American Bottling Company .... C 714 974-8560
1166 Arroyo St Orange (92865) *(P-1605)*

American Building Supply, Rialto *Also Called: Jeld-Wen Inc (P-9924)*

American Business Bank .... C 310 808-1200
970 W 190th St Ste 850 Torrance (90502) *(P-11743)*

American Business Bank .... C 909 919-2040
3633 Inland Empire Blvd Ste 720 Ontario (91764) *(P-11744)*

American Circuit Tech Inc (PA).......................... E **714 777-2480**
5330 E Hunter Ave Anaheim (92807) *(P-6707)*

American Cmpus Communities Inc .... D 949 854-0900
62600 Arroyo Dr Irvine (92617) *(P-13096)*

American Compaction Eqp Inc .... E 949 661-2921
29380 Hunco Way Lake Elsinore (92530) *(P-5487)*

American Condenser, Gardena *Also Called: American Condenser & Coil LLC (P-5966)*

American Condenser & Coil LLC .... D 310 327-8600
1628 W 139th St Gardena (90249) *(P-5966)*

American Consumer Products LLC .... D 323 289-6610
120 E 8th St Ste 908 Los Angeles (90014) *(P-3789)*

American Contrs Indemnity Co (DH).................. C **213 330-1309**
801 S Figueroa St Ste 700 Los Angeles (90017) *(P-12144)*

American Copak Corporation .... C 818 576-1000
9175 Eton Ave Chatsworth (91311) *(P-14445)*

American Cover Design 26 Inc .... E 323 582-8666
2131 E 52nd St Vernon (90058) *(P-1946)*

American Dawn Inc (PA).................................... D **800 821-2221**
401 W Artesia Blvd Compton (90220) *(P-1965)*

American De Rosa Lamparts LLC .... D 800 777-4440
10650 4th St Rancho Cucamonga (91730) *(P-471)*

American Deburring Inc .... E 949 457-9790
20742 Linear Ln Lake Forest (92630) *(P-6079)*

American Development Corp (PA)........................ D **562 989-3730**
3605 Long Beach Blvd Ste 410 Long Beach (90807) *(P-12381)*

American Die Casting Inc .... E 909 356-7768
14576 Fontlee Ln Fontana (92335) *(P-4656)*

American Dj Group of Companies, Commerce *Also Called: D J American Supply Inc (P-10557)*

American Eagle Protective Svcs, Inglewood *Also Called: American Egle Prtctive Svcs In (P-14270)*

American Egle Prtctive Svcs In .... D 310 412-0019
425 W Kelso St Inglewood (90301) *(P-14270)*

Employee Codes: A=Over 500 employees, B=251-500
C=101-250, D=51-100, E=20-50, F=10-19, G=1-9

2025 Southern California
Business Directory and Buyers Guide

© Mergent Inc. 1-800-342-5647

933

American Electronics, Carson *Also Called: Ducommun Labarge Tech Inc (P-7469)*

American Etching & Mfg .... E 323 875-3910
13730 Desmond St Pacoima (91331) *(P-5309)*

American Fabrication, Bakersfield *Also Called: Russell Fabrication Corp (P-5438)*

American Fabrication Corp (PA)............................... D 714 632-1709
2891 E Via Martens Anaheim (92806) *(P-7225)*

American Faucet Coatings Corp .... E 760 598-5895
1333 Keystone Way Vista (92081) *(P-9888)*

American Financial Network Inc (PA)....................... C 714 831-4000
10 Pointe Dr Ste 330 Brea (92821) *(P-11881)*

American First Credit Union (PA)............................. D 562 691-1112
6 Pointe Dr Ste 400 Brea (92821) *(P-11791)*

American Fish and Seafood, Los Angeles *Also Called: Prospect Enterprises Inc (P-10858)*

American Fleet & Ret Graphics .... E 909 937-7570
2091 Del Rio Way Ontario (91761) *(P-8589)*

American Foam & Packaging, Gardena *Also Called: Amfoam Inc (P-3993)*

American Foam Fiber & Sups Inc (PA)...................... E 626 969-7268
255 S 7th Ave Ste A City Of Industry (91746) *(P-1966)*

American Food Ingredients Inc .... E 760 967-6287
4021 Avenida De La Plata Ste 501 Oceanside (92056) *(P-1364)*

American Foothill Pubg Co Inc .... E 818 352-7878
10009 Commerce Ave Tujunga (91042) *(P-3115)*

American Fruits & Flavors LLC (HQ)......................... C 818 899-9574
10725 Sutter Ave Pacoima (91331) *(P-1660)*

American Fruits & Flavors LLC .... E 909 291-2620
9345 Santa Anita Ave Rancho Cucamonga (91730) *(P-1661)*

American Fruits & Flavors LLC .... D 213 624-1831
400 S Central Ave Los Angeles (90013) *(P-1662)*

American Fruits & Flavors LLC .... D 310 522-1844
22560 Lucerne St Carson (90745) *(P-1663)*

American Fruits & Flavors LLC .... E 323 881-8321
3001 Sierra Pine Ave Vernon (90058) *(P-1664)*

American Fruits & Flavors LLC .... E 562 320-2802
13530 Rosecrans Ave Santa Fe Springs (90670) *(P-1665)*

American Fruits & Flavors LLC .... E 818 899-9574
1527 Knowles Ave Los Angeles (90063) *(P-1666)*

American Fruits & Flavors LLC .... E 818 899-9574
1565 Knowles Ave Los Angeles (90063) *(P-1667)*

American Fruits & Flavors LLC .... B 818 899-9574
510 Park Ave San Fernando (91340) *(P-13167)*

American Funds Distrs Inc (DH)............................... C 213 486-9200
333 S Hope St Ste Levb Los Angeles (90071) *(P-12626)*

American Funds Service Company (DH).................... B 949 975-5000
6455 Irvine Center Dr Irvine (92618) *(P-12038)*

American Furniture Alliance, Corona *Also Called: Widly Inc (P-2496)*

American Future Tech Corp .... C 888 462-3899
529 Baldwin Park Blvd City Of Industry (91746) *(P-9986)*

American Garment Sewing, Pasadena *Also Called: AGS Usa LLC (P-2057)*

American Golf Construction, Canoga Park *Also Called: American Landscape Inc (P-146)*

American Golf Corporation (HQ)............................... C 310 664-4000
909 N Pacific Coast Hwy Ste 650 El Segundo (90245) *(P-15114)*

American Green Lights, San Diego *Also Called: American Green Lights LLC (P-9667)*

American Green Lights LLC .... E 858 547-8837
10755 Scripps Poway Pkwy Ste 419 San Diego (92131) *(P-9667)*

American Grip Inc .... E 818 768-8922
8468 Kewen Ave Sun Valley (91352) *(P-6489)*

American Guard Services Inc (PA)............................ B 310 645-6200
1125 W 190th St Gardena (90248) *(P-14271)*

American Handgunner and Guns, Escondido *Also Called: Publishers Development Corp (P-2872)*

American Health Connection .... A 424 226-0420
8484 Wilshire Blvd Ste 501 Beverly Hills (90211) *(P-14446)*

American Healthcare Reit Inc (PA)........................... D 949 270-9200
18191 Von Karman Ave Ste 300 Irvine (92612) *(P-12682)*

American Heritage, Irvine *Also Called: American Heritage Lf Insur Co (P-12171)*

American Heritage Lf Insur Co .... D 800 753-9227
400 Exchange Ste 210 Irvine (92602) *(P-12171)*

American Hlthcare Systems Corp (PA)...................... B 818 646-9933
505 N Brand Blvd Ste 1110 Glendale (91203) *(P-15909)*

American Honda, Torrance *Also Called: American Honda Motor Co Inc (P-9799)*

AMERICAN HONDA, Torrance *Also Called: American Honda Finance Corp (P-11847)*

American Honda Finance Corp (DH)......................... C 310 972-2239
1919 Torrance Blvd Torrance (90501) *(P-11847)*

American Honda Motor Co Inc (HQ).......................... A 310 783-2000
1919 Torrance Blvd Torrance (90501) *(P-9799)*

American Honda Protection Prod .... D 310 972-2200
20800 Madrona Ave Torrance (90503) *(P-11848)*

American Household Company, Los Angeles *Also Called: Housewares International Inc (P-4135)*

American HX Auto Trade Inc .... D 909 484-1010
4845 Via Del Cerro Yorba Linda (92887) *(P-7166)*

American Industrial Manufacturing Services Inc .... C 951 698-3379
41673 Corning Pl Murrieta (92562) *(P-7087)*

American Industrial Source Inc .... D 800 661-0622
15759 Strathern St Ste 1 Van Nuys (91406) *(P-10425)*

American Integrity Corp .... E 760 247-1082
13510 Central Rd Apple Valley (92308) *(P-4046)*

American International Inds, Los Angeles *Also Called: Glamour Industries Co (P-10624)*

American Internet Mortgage Inc .... C 888 411-4246
4121 Camino Del Rio S Ste 200 San Diego (92108) *(P-11882)*

American Intgrted Rsources Inc .... D 714 921-4100
2341 N Pacific St Orange (92865) *(P-17941)*

American Intl Inds Inc .... A 323 728-2999
2220 Gaspar Ave Commerce (90040) *(P-3630)*

American Justice Solutions Inc .... D 949 369-6210
25910 Acero Ste 100 Mission Viejo (92691) *(P-16850)*

American Kal Enterprises Inc (PA)............................ D 626 338-7308
4265 Puente Ave Baldwin Park (91706) *(P-10301)*

American Koyu Corporation .... C 626 793-0669
1733 S Anaheim Blvd Anaheim (92805) *(P-12759)*

American Lab and Systems, Los Angeles *Also Called: Mjw Inc (P-5737)*

American Landscape Inc .... C 818 999-2041
7013 Owensmouth Ave Canoga Park (91303) *(P-146)*

American Landscape MGT Inc (PA)........................... C 818 999-2041
7013 Owensmouth Ave Canoga Park (91303) *(P-147)*

American Landscape MGT Inc .... D 805 647-5077
1607 Los Angeles Ave Ste I Ventura (93004) *(P-197)*

American Legal Copy - Oc LLC .... D 415 777-4449
655 W Broadway Ste 200 San Diego (92101) *(P-13309)*

American Management Svcs W LLC .... B 805 352-1921
1240 Bethel Ln Santa Maria (93458) *(P-17942)*

American Marble, Vista *Also Called: Kammerer Enterprises Inc (P-4474)*

American Med & Hosp Sup Co Inc .... E 661 294-1213
28703 Industry Dr Valencia (91355) *(P-10059)*

American Med Rspnse Inland Emp (HQ)..................... D 951 782-5200
879 Marlborough Ave Riverside (92507) *(P-8810)*

American Medical Response, Palm Springs *Also Called: American Medical Response Inc (P-8811)*

American Medical Response Inc .... C 760 883-5000
1111 Montalvo Way Palm Springs (92262) *(P-8811)*

American Medical Tech Inc .... D 949 553-0359
750 The City Dr S Orange (92868) *(P-10060)*

American Metal, Pomona *Also Called: American Mtal Mfg Resource Inc (P-7380)*

American Mortgage Network, Chula Vista *Also Called: Amnet Esop Corporation (P-11883)*

American Mtal Mfg Resource Inc .... E 909 620-4500
1989 W Holt Ave Pomona (91768) *(P-7380)*

American Multimedia TV USA .... D 626 466-1038
530 S Lake Ave Unit 368 Pasadena (91101) *(P-9492)*

American Mutual Fund .... C 213 486-9200
333 S Hope St Fl 51 Los Angeles (90071) *(P-12627)*

American Mzhou Dngpo Group Inc .... D 626 820-9239
4520 Maine Ave Baldwin Park (91706) *(P-17943)*

American Nail Plate Ltg Inc .... D 909 982-1807
9044 Del Mar Ave Montclair (91763) *(P-6437)*

American Nat Red Cross - Blood, Long Beach *Also Called: American National Red Cross (P-16866)*

American Nat Red Crss-Blood Sv, Pomona *Also Called: American National Red Cross (P-16864)*

American National Mfg Inc .... D 951 273-7888
252 Mariah Cir Corona (92879) *(P-2478)*

American National Red Cross .... C 909 859-7006
100 Red Cross Cir Pomona (91765) *(P-16864)*

Mergent email: customerrelations@mergent.com
934

2025 Southern California
Business Directory and Buyers Guide

(P-0000) Products & Services Section entry number
(PA)=Parent Co (HQ)=Headquarters (DH)=Div Headquarters

American National Red Cross .... D 310 445-9900
1450 S Central Ave Los Angeles (90021) *(P-16865)*

American National Red Cross .... D 562 595-6341
3150 E 29th St Long Beach (90806) *(P-16866)*

American Paper & Plastics LLC .... C 626 444-0000
550 S 7th Ave City Of Industry (91746) *(P-11109)*

American Paper & Provisions, City Of Industry *Also Called: American Paper & Plastics LLC*
(P-11109)

American PCF Prtrs College Inc .... E 949 250-3212
675 N Main St Orange (92868) *(P-2960)*

American Peptide Company Inc .... D 408 733-7604
1271 Avenida Chelsea Vista (92081) *(P-3556)*

American Plant Services Inc (PA).................... E 562 630-1773
6242 N Paramount Blvd Long Beach (90805) *(P-4509)*

American Plastic Products Inc .... D 818 504-1073
9243 Glenoaks Blvd Sun Valley (91352) *(P-4047)*

American Power SEC Svc Inc .... D 866 974-9994
1451 Rimpau Ave Ste 207 Corona (92879) *(P-14272)*

American Precision Assembly, Huntington Beach *Also Called: American Precision Hydraulics*
(P-5557)

American Precision Hydraulics .... E 714 903-8610
5601 Research Dr Huntington Beach (92649) *(P-5557)*

American Private Duty Inc .... D 818 386-6358
13111 Ventura Blvd Ste 100 Studio City (91604) *(P-16363)*

American Prof Ambulance Corp .... D 818 996-2200
16945 Sherman Way Van Nuys (91406) *(P-8812)*

American Protection Group Inc (PA).................... C 818 279-2433
8741 Van Nuys Blvd Ste 202 Panorama City (91402) *(P-14273)*

American Prprty-Mnagement Corp .... A 619 232-3121
326 Broadway San Diego (92101) *(P-12760)*

American Prtctive Svcs Invstgt .... C 626 705-8600
12471 Balsam Rd Victorville (92395) *(P-14274)*

American Quality Tools, Riverside *Also Called: American Quality Tools Inc (P-5604)*

American Quality Tools Inc .... E 951 280-4700
12650 Magnolia Ave Ste B Riverside (92503) *(P-5604)*

American Quilting Company Inc .... E 323 233-2500
1540 Calzona St Los Angeles (90023) *(P-2245)*

American Rag Compagnie .... D 323 935-3154
150 S La Brea Ave Los Angeles (90036) *(P-11490)*

American Range Corporation .... C 818 897-0808
13592 Desmond St Pacoima (91331) *(P-4947)*

American Ready Mix, Escondido *Also Called: Superior Ready Mix Concrete LP (P-4464)*

American Recovery Service Inc (DH).................... C 805 379-8500
555 Saint Charles Dr Ste 100 Thousand Oaks (91360) *(P-13276)*

American Red Cross, Los Angeles *Also Called: American Red Cross Los Angles (P-16867)*

American Red Cross, San Diego *Also Called: American Red Cross San Dg-Mpri (P-16868)*

American Red Cross Los Angles (PA).................... C 310 445-9900
1320 Newton St Los Angeles (90021) *(P-16867)*

American Red Cross San Dg-Mpri (PA).................... D 858 309-1200
3950 Calle Fortunada San Diego (92123) *(P-16868)*

American Regent Inc .... E 714 989-5058
538 Vanguard Way Brea (92821) *(P-17866)*

American Reliable Insurance Co .... A 714 937-2300
333 S Anita Dr Ste 980 Orange (92868) *(P-12116)*

American Reliance Inc .... E 626 443-6818
789 N Fair Oaks Ave Pasadena (91103) *(P-5840)*

American Retirement Corp .... C 310 399-3227
2107 Ocean Ave Santa Monica (90405) *(P-15566)*

American Rigging & Supply, San Diego *Also Called: Carpenter Group (P-10428)*

American Rim Supply Inc .... E 760 431-3666
1955 Kellogg Ave Carlsbad (92008) *(P-7226)*

American Rotary Broom Co Inc .... E 909 629-9117
688 New York Dr Pomona (91768) *(P-8583)*

American Sanitary Supply Inc .... D 714 632-3010
3800 E Miraloma Ave Anaheim (92806) *(P-10471)*

American Scale Co Inc .... E 800 773-7225
21326 E Arrow Hwy Covina (91724) *(P-9987)*

American Scence Tech As T Corp .... D 310 773-1978
2372 Morse Ave Ste 571 Irvine (92614) *(P-7329)*

American Security Bank .... D 949 440-5200
1401 Dove St Ste 100 Newport Beach (92660) *(P-11745)*

American Security Force Inc .... D 323 722-8585
5430 E Olympic Blvd Commerce (90022) *(P-14381)*

American Security Products Co .... C 951 685-9680
11925 Pacific Ave Fontana (92337) *(P-5440)*

American Sheet Metal, El Cajon *Also Called: Asm Construction Inc (P-4954)*

American Soc Cmpsers Athors Pb .... C 323 883-1000
7920 W Sunset Blvd Ste 300 Los Angeles (90046) *(P-2903)*

American Soccer Company Inc (PA).................... C 310 830-6161
726 E Anaheim St Wilmington (90744) *(P-11504)*

American Solar LLC .... E 323 250-1307
8484 Wilshire Blvd Ste 630 Beverly Hills (90211) *(P-4808)*

American Solar Direct Inc .... C 424 214-6700
11766 Wilshire Blvd Ste 500 Los Angeles (90025) *(P-883)*

American Spclty Hlth Group Inc .... B 858 754-2000
10221 Wateridge Cir Ste 201 San Diego (92121) *(P-12071)*

American Spclty Hlth Plans Cal .... B 619 297-8100
10221 Wateridge Cir San Diego (92121) *(P-12172)*

American States Water Company (PA).................... A 909 394-3600
630 E Foothill Blvd San Dimas (91773) *(P-9682)*

American Sunrise Inc .... D 858 610-4766
12646 Carmel Country Rd Unit 153 San Diego (92130) *(P-13652)*

American Suzuki Motor Corporation .... B 714 996-7040
3251 E Imperial Hwy Brea (92821) *(P-11316)*

American Technical Svcs Inc .... D 951 372-9664
20384 Via Mantua Porter Ranch (91326) *(P-17484)*

American Textile Maint Co .... D 213 749-4433
1705 Hooper Ave Los Angeles (90021) *(P-13112)*

American Textile Maint Co .... C 323 735-1661
1664 W Washington Blvd Los Angeles (90007) *(P-13113)*

American Textile Maint Co .... D 562 424-1607
2201 E Carson St Long Beach (90807) *(P-13138)*

American Tire Depot, Pomona *Also Called: Atv Canter LLC (P-11440)*

American Tooth Industries .... D 805 487-9868
1200 Stellar Dr Oxnard (93033) *(P-10061)*

American Transportation Co LLC .... D 818 660-2343
635 W Colorado St Ste 108a Glendale (91204) *(P-9359)*

American Traveler Inc .... E 909 466-4000
9509 Feron Blvd Rancho Cucamonga (91730) *(P-4290)*

American Turn-Key Fabricators, Rancho Cucamonga *Also Called: Romeros Engineering Inc*
(P-6221)

American Two-Way, North Hollywood *Also Called: Emergency Technologies Inc (P-14397)*

American Untd HM Care Crp-Priv, Studio City *Also Called: American Private Duty Inc*
(P-16363)

American Vanguard Corporation (PA).................... D 949 260-1200
4695 Macarthur Ct Newport Beach (92660) *(P-3750)*

American Vision Baths, Simi Valley *Also Called: American Vision Windows Inc (P-14756)*

American Vision Windows Inc .... C 805 582-1833
2125 N Madera Rd Ste A Simi Valley (93065) *(P-14756)*

American Woodmark Corporation .... B 714 449-2200
400 E Orangethorpe Ave Anaheim (92801) *(P-2337)*

American Wrecking Inc .... D 626 350-8303
2459 Lee Ave South El Monte (91733) *(P-1178)*

American Yeast Corporation .... E 661 834-1050
5455 District Blvd Bakersfield (93313) *(P-1738)*

American Zabin Intl Inc .... E 213 746-3770
3933 S Hill St Los Angeles (90037) *(P-3116)*

American Zinc Enterprises, Walnut *Also Called: Sea Shield Marine Products Inc (P-4653)*

Americantours Intl LLC (HQ).................... C 310 641-9953
6053 W Century Blvd Ste 700 Los Angeles (90045) *(P-9220)*

Americare Hlth Retirement Inc .... C 760 744-4484
1550 Security Pl Ofc San Marcos (92078) *(P-12281)*

Americare Home Health Inc .... D 818 881-0005
16501 Sherman Way Ste 225 Van Nuys (91406) *(P-16364)*

Americas Finest Carpet Company, Chula Vista *Also Called: Home Carpet Investment Inc*
(P-1068)

Americas Gold Inc .... E 213 688-4904
650 S Hill St Ste 224 Los Angeles (90014) *(P-8450)*

Americas Gold - Amrcas Damonds, Los Angeles *Also Called: Americas Gold Inc (P-8450)*

Americas Printer.com, Buena Park *Also Called: A J Parent Company Inc (P-14432)*

Americas Regional Division, San Diego *Also Called: Synergy Health Ast LLC (P-8233)*

Americas Styrenics LLC .... D 424 488-3757
305 Crenshaw Blvd Torrance (90503) *(P-3257)*

Employee Codes: A=Over 500 employees, B=251-500
C=101-250, D=51-100, E=20-50, F=10-19, G=1-9

2025 Southern California
Business Directory and Buyers Guide

© Mergent Inc. 1-800-342-5647
935

A
L
P
H
A
B
E
T
I
C

Americh Corporation (PA)......................C 818 982-1711
13222 Saticoy St North Hollywood (91605) *(P-8252)*

Americhip, Gardena *Also Called: Americhip Inc (P-2961)*

Americhip Inc (PA)..............................E 310 323-3697
19032 S Vermont Ave Gardena (90248) *(P-2961)*

Americold Logistics LLC.....................C 909 937-2200
5401 Santa Ana St Ontario (91761) *(P-9034)*

Americold Logistics LLC.....................D 909 390-4950
700 Malaga St Ontario (91761) *(P-9035)*

Americold Realty, Ontario *Also Called: Americold Logistics LLC (P-9035)*

Americor Financial, Irvine *Also Called: Americor Funding LLC (P-14447)*

Americor Funding LLC (PA)..................C 888 211-2660
18200 Von Karman Ave Fl 6 Irvine (92612) *(P-14447)*

Ameriflex Inc.....................................D 951 737-5557
2390 Railroad St Corona (92878) *(P-5424)*

Ameriflight LLC..................................D 818 847-0000
4700 W Empire Ave Burbank (91505) *(P-9158)*

Amerihome Mortgage, Westlake Village *Also Called: Amerihome Mortgage Company LLC (P-11958)*

Amerihome Mortgage Company LLC......A 888 469-0810
1 Baxter Way Ste 300 Westlake Village (91362) *(P-11958)*

Amerillum LLC...................................D 760 727-7675
3728 Maritime Way Oceanside (92056) *(P-6490)*

Ameripark LLC...................................B 949 279-7525
17165 Von Karman Ave Ste 110 Irvine (92614) *(P-14655)*

Ameripec Inc.....................................C 714 690-9191
6965 Aragon Cir Buena Park (90620) *(P-1606)*

Ameripharma, Orange *Also Called: Harpers Pharmacy Inc (P-3418)*

Ameripride Services LLC.....................C 323 587-3941
5950 Alcoa Ave Los Angeles (90058) *(P-13114)*

Amerisourcebergen Drug Corp...............C 951 371-2000
1851 California Ave Corona (92881) *(P-10612)*

Amerisourcebergen Drug Corp...............C 484 222-9726
500 N State College Blvd Ste 900 Orange (92868) *(P-10613)*

Amerit Fleet Solutions Inc..................A 909 357-0100
15325 Manila St Fontana (92337) *(P-14712)*

Ameritac Inc (PA)..............................D 925 989-2942
24 Toscana Way W Rancho Mirage (92270) *(P-18257)*

Ameritex International, Los Angeles *Also Called: Amtex California Inc (P-2203)*

Ameron International Corp....................C 425 258-2616
1020 B St Fillmore (93015) *(P-4379)*

Ameron International Corp....................D 805 524-0223
1020 B St Fillmore (93015) *(P-4380)*

Ameron Protective Coatings, Fillmore *Also Called: Ameron International Corp (P-4379)*

Ames Construction Inc.........................B 951 356-1275
391 N Main St Ste 302 Corona (92878) *(P-11511)*

Ames Industrial, Los Angeles *Also Called: Ames Rubber Mfg Co Inc (P-3908)*

Ames Rubber Mfg Co Inc.....................E 818 240-9313
4516 Brazil St Los Angeles (90039) *(P-3908)*

Ametek Ameron LLC (HQ)....................D 626 856-0101
4750 Littlejohn St Baldwin Park (91706) *(P-7847)*

Ametek HCC, Rosemead *Also Called: Hermetic Seal Corporation (P-7005)*

Ametek Intellipower, Orange *Also Called: Intellipower Inc (P-10254)*

Ametek Programmable Power, San Diego *Also Called: Ametek Programmable Power Inc (P-7897)*

Ametek Programmable Power Inc (HQ)....B 858 450-0085
9250 Brown Deer Rd San Diego (92121) *(P-7897)*

Ametek-Ameron, Baldwin Park *Also Called: Alphatech General Inc (P-14755)*

AMF Anaheim LLC..............................C 714 363-9206
2100 E Orangewood Ave Anaheim (92806) *(P-4948)*

AMF Support Surfaces Inc (DH).............C 951 549-6800
1691 N Delilah St Corona (92879) *(P-2479)*

Amfoam Inc (PA)................................E 310 327-4003
15110 S Broadway Gardena (90248) *(P-3993)*

Amgen, Thousand Oaks *Also Called: Amgen Inc (P-3557)*

Amgen Inc...C 805 447-1000
1840 De Havilland Dr Newbury Park (91320) *(P-3351)*

Amgen Inc (PA)..................................A 805 447-1000
1 Amgen Center Dr Thousand Oaks (91320) *(P-3557)*

Amgen Manufacturing Limited..............E 787 656-2000
1 Amgen Center Dr Newbury Park (91320) *(P-8657)*

Amgen USA Inc (HQ)...........................D 805 447-1000
1 Amgen Center Dr Thousand Oaks (91320) *(P-3352)*

Amgraph, Ontario *Also Called: American Fleet & Ret Graphics (P-8589)*

AMI, Costa Mesa *Also Called: Advanced Micro Instruments Inc (P-8030)*

AMI-Hti Trzana Encino Jint Vnt.............C 818 881-0800
18321 Clark St Tarzana (91356) *(P-15910)*

Amiad Filtration Systems, Oxnard *Also Called: Amiad USA Inc (P-5996)*

Amiad USA Inc...................................E 805 988-3323
1251 Maulhardt Ave Oxnard (93030) *(P-5995)*

Amiad USA Inc...................................E 805 988-3323
1251 Maulhardt Ave Oxnard (93030) *(P-5996)*

Amico Fontana, Fontana *Also Called: Alabama Metal Industries Corp (P-5059)*

Amigo Baby Inc..................................D 805 901-1237
1901 N Rice Ave Ste 325 Oxnard (93030) *(P-16869)*

Aminco International USA Inc...............E 949 457-3261
20571 Crescent Bay Dr Lake Forest (92630) *(P-8451)*

Amiri, Los Angeles *Also Called: Atelier Luxury Group LLC (P-2257)*

Amisub of California Inc (DH)...............A 818 881-0800
18321 Clark St Tarzana (91356) *(P-15911)*

Amity Foundation, Los Angeles *Also Called: Epidaurus (P-12657)*

Amk Foodservices Inc.........................C 805 544-7600
830 Capitolio Way San Luis Obispo (93401) *(P-10742)*

Amko Service Company.......................D 760 246-3600
17909 Adelanto Rd Adelanto (92301) *(P-14757)*

Amkom Design Group Inc....................E 760 295-1957
2598 Fortune Way Ste J Vista (92081) *(P-14448)*

Amn Healthcare Inc (HQ).....................B 858 792-0711
12400 High Bluff Dr Ste 100 San Diego (92130) *(P-15243)*

Amnet Esop Corporation.....................C 877 354-1110
347 Third Ave Fl 2 Chula Vista (91910) *(P-11883)*

Amnet Mortgage LLC..........................A 858 909-1200
10421 Wateridge Cir Ste 250 San Diego (92121) *(P-11884)*

AMO Usa Inc......................................C 714 247-8200
1700 E Saint Andrew Pl Santa Ana (92705) *(P-8090)*

Amonix Inc..C 562 344-4750
1709 Apollo Ct Seal Beach (90740) *(P-6798)*

Amoretti, Oxnard *Also Called: Noushig Inc (P-1462)*

AMP, Santa Ana *Also Called: Accelerated Memory Prod Inc (P-6792)*

AMP Plus Inc.....................................D 323 231-2600
2042 E Vernon Ave Los Angeles (90058) *(P-6483)*

AMP Research, Tustin *Also Called: 89908 Inc (P-7214)*

AMP Research, Brea *Also Called: Lund Motion Products Inc (P-7267)*

Ampac Usa Inc...................................E 435 291-0961
5255 State St 5275 Montclair (91763) *(P-5997)*

Ampam Parks Mechanical Inc (PA).........A 310 835-1532
17036 Avalon Blvd Carson (90746) *(P-736)*

Ampco Airport Parking, Los Angeles *Also Called: ABM Parking Services Inc (P-14654)*

Ampco Contracting Inc.......................C 949 955-2255
17991 Cowan Irvine (92614) *(P-9785)*

AMPHASTAR, Rancho Cucamonga *Also Called: Amphastar Pharmaceuticals Inc (P-3353)*

Amphastar Pharmaceuticals Inc (PA)......C 909 980-9484
11570 6th St Rancho Cucamonga (91730) *(P-3353)*

Amphion, Rancho Cucamonga *Also Called: Executive Safe and SEC Corp (P-5447)*

Amplifier Technologies Inc (HQ)...........E 323 278-0001
901 S Greenwood Ave Montebello (90640) *(P-6596)*

AMpm Maintenance Corporation............E 424 230-1300
1010 E 14th St Los Angeles (90021) *(P-1967)*

Ampm Systems Inc.............................D 949 629-7800
16520 Harbor Blvd Ste E Fountain Valley (92708) *(P-18091)*

Ampronix LLC....................................D 949 273-8000
15 Whatney Irvine (92618) *(P-8368)*

Ampure Charging Systems Inc (PA).........D 626 415-4000
1333 S Mayflower Ave Ste 100 Monrovia (91016) *(P-9810)*

Amrapur Overseas Incorporated (PA)......E 714 893-8808
1560 E 6th St Ste 101 Corona (92879) *(P-1968)*

Amrel, Pasadena *Also Called: American Reliance Inc (P-5840)*

Amrep Inc...B 770 422-2071
1555 S Cucamonga Ave Ontario (91761) *(P-3597)*

Amrep Manufacturing Co LLC...............B 877 468-9278
1555 S Cucamonga Ave Ontario (91761) *(P-5688)*

Mergent email: customerrelations@mergent.com
936

2025 Southern California
Business Directory and Buyers Guide

(P-0000) Products & Services Section entry number
(PA)=Parent Co (HQ)=Headquarters (DH)=Div Headquarters

Amro Fabricating Corporation (PA) .... C 626 579-2200
1430 Amro Way South El Monte (91733) *(P-7430)*

Amron, Vista *Also Called: Amron International Inc (P-8501)*

Amron International Inc (PA) .... D 760 208-6500
1380 Aspen Way Vista (92081) *(P-8501)*

AMS, Anaheim *Also Called: Walnut Investment Corp (P-9933)*

AMS, San Diego *Also Called: Asset Mktg Systems Insur Svcs (P-18097)*

AMS American Mech Svcs MD Inc .... C 714 888-6820
2116 E Walnut Ave Fullerton (92831) *(P-737)*

AMS Fulfillment, Valencia *Also Called: Advantage Media Services Inc (P-9352)*

AMS Fulfillment, Valencia *Also Called: Advantage Media Services Inc (P-9047)*

AMS Fulfillment, Valencia *Also Called: Advantage Media Services Inc (P-18086)*

AMS Plastics Inc .... B 951 734-5600
1100 Citrus St Riverside (92507) *(P-4048)*

AMS Plastics Inc (PA) .... E 619 713-2000
20109 Paseo Del Prado Walnut (91789) *(P-4049)*

Amsafe Bridport, Buena Park *Also Called: Bridport Erie Aviation Inc (P-14758)*

Amsco US Inc .... C 562 630-0333
15341 Texaco Ave Paramount (90723) *(P-6966)*

Amscope, Irvine *Also Called: United Scope LLC (P-8027)*

Amsec, Fontana *Also Called: American Security Products Co (P-5440)*

Amtek, Poway *Also Called: United Security Products Inc (P-7157)*

Amtex California Inc .... E 323 859-2200
113 S Utah St Los Angeles (90033) *(P-2203)*

Amtex Supply Holdings Inc .... C 909 985-8918
736 Inland Center Dr San Bernardino (92408) *(P-18092)*

Amtrend Corporation .... D 714 630-2070
1458 Manhattan Ave Fullerton (92831) *(P-2556)*

Amtv USA, Pasadena *Also Called: American Multimedia TV USA (P-9492)*

Amvac Chemical Corporation (HQ) .... E 323 264-3910
4695 Macarthur Ct Ste 1200 Newport Beach (92660) *(P-3751)*

Amwear USA Inc .... E 800 858-6755
250 Benjamin Dr Corona (92879) *(P-1974)*

Amwest Funding Corp .... C 714 831-3333
6 Pointe Dr Ste 300 Brea (92821) *(P-11864)*

Amylin Ohio LLC .... A 858 552-2200
9360 Towne Centre Dr San Diego (92121) *(P-3354)*

An Open Check, Costa Mesa *Also Called: North American Acceptance Corp (P-11859)*

Ana Global LLC (PA) .... D 619 482-9990
2360 Marconi Ct San Diego (92154) *(P-2497)*

Anabella Hotel The, Anaheim *Also Called: Fjs Inc (P-12825)*

Anaco Inc .... C 951 372-2732
311 Corporate Terrace Cir Corona (92879) *(P-5805)*

Anacom General Corporation .... E 714 774-8484
1240 S Claudina St Anaheim (92805) *(P-6524)*

Anacom Medtek, Anaheim *Also Called: Anacom General Corporation (P-6524)*

Anaheim - 1855 S Hbr Blvd Owne .... D 714 750-1811
1855 S Harbor Blvd Anaheim (92802) *(P-12761)*

Anaheim Arena Management LLC .... A 714 704-2400
2695 E Katella Ave Anaheim (92806) *(P-15016)*

Anaheim Automation Inc .... E 714 992-6990
4985 E Landon Dr Anaheim (92807) *(P-6340)*

Anaheim Custom Extruders Inc .... E 714 693-8508
1360 N Mccan St Anaheim (92806) *(P-4050)*

Anaheim Ducks Hockey Club LLC (PA) .... D 714 940-2900
2695 E Katella Ave Anaheim (92806) *(P-15017)*

Anaheim Extrusion Co Inc .... D 714 630-3111
1330 N Kraemer Blvd Anaheim (92806) *(P-4595)*

Anaheim Global Medical Center .... A 714 533-6220
1025 S Anaheim Blvd Anaheim (92805) *(P-15912)*

Anaheim Healthcare Center, Anaheim *Also Called: Anaheim Healthcare Center LLC (P-15567)*

Anaheim Healthcare Center LLC .... C 714 816-0540
501 S Beach Blvd Anaheim (92804) *(P-15567)*

Anaheim Inn, Anaheim *Also Called: Best Western Stovalls Inn (P-12773)*

Anaheim Majestic Garden Hotel, Anaheim *Also Called: Ken Real Estate Lease Ltd (P-12883)*

Anaheim Plant, Anaheim *Also Called: Stepan Company (P-3294)*

Anaheim Warehouse 125, Anaheim *Also Called: Paragon Industries Inc (P-11249)*

Analog, La Verne *Also Called: Micro Analog Inc (P-6850)*

Analysts Inc .... C 800 424-0099
3401 Jack Northrop Ave Hawthorne (90250) *(P-17902)*

Analysts Maintenance and Labs, Hawthorne *Also Called: Analysts Inc (P-17902)*

Analytic Endodontics, Orange *Also Called: Sybron Dental Specialties Inc (P-8358)*

Analytical Industries Inc .... E 909 392-6900
2855 Metropolitan Pl Pomona (91767) *(P-7848)*

Analytical Pace Services LLC .... C 800 878-4911
4100 Atlas Ct Bakersfield (93308) *(P-17903)*

Anamex Corporation (PA) .... E 714 779-7055
250 S Peralta Way Anaheim (92807) *(P-13653)*

Anaplex Corporation .... E 714 522-4481
15547 Garfield Ave Paramount (90723) *(P-5232)*

ANAPTYSBIO, San Diego *Also Called: Anaptysbio Inc (P-3355)*

Anaptysbio Inc (PA) .... C 858 362-6295
10770 Wateridge Cir Ste 210 San Diego (92121) *(P-3355)*

Anatex, Van Nuys *Also Called: Anatex Enterprises Inc (P-10517)*

Anatex Enterprises Inc .... E 818 908-1888
15911 Arminta St Van Nuys (91406) *(P-10517)*

Anatomic Global Inc .... C 800 874-7237
1241 Old Temescal Rd Ste 103 Corona (92881) *(P-2206)*

Anaya Brothers Cutting LLC .... D 323 582-5758
3130 Leonis Blvd Vernon (90058) *(P-2186)*

Anc Technology Inc .... D 805 530-3958
10195 Stockton Rd Moorpark (93021) *(P-6708)*

Ancca Corporation .... D 949 553-0084
7 Goddard Irvine (92618) *(P-996)*

Anchen Pharmaceuticals Inc .... C 949 639-8100
5 Goodyear Irvine (92618) *(P-3356)*

Anchor Audio Inc (PA) .... E 760 827-7100
5931 Darwin Ct Carlsbad (92008) *(P-6525)*

Anchor Blue, Corona *Also Called: Hub Distributing Inc (P-11489)*

Anchor Cnsling Edcatn Sltons L .... D 213 505-6322
19200 Von Karman Ave Ste 600 Irvine (92612) *(P-18284)*

Anchor General Insur Agcy Inc .... C 858 527-3600
10256 Meanley Dr San Diego (92131) *(P-12173)*

Anchor Loans LP .... C 310 395-0010
1 Baxter Way # 220 Westlake Village (91362) *(P-11885)*

Anchor Nationwide Loans, Westlake Village *Also Called: Anchor Loans LP (P-11885)*

Anchored Prints .... E 714 929-9317
1199 N Grove St Anaheim (92806) *(P-2962)*

Anco, San Bernardino *Also Called: Anco International Inc (P-5384)*

Anco International Inc .... E 909 887-2521
19851 Cajon Blvd San Bernardino (92407) *(P-5384)*

Ancon Marine LLC .... C 562 326-5900
2735 Rose Ave Signal Hill (90755) *(P-8892)*

Ancon Services, Signal Hill *Also Called: Ancon Marine LLC (P-8892)*

Ancora Software Inc (PA) .... E 888 476-4839
402 W Broadway Ste 400 San Diego (92101) *(P-13877)*

Ancra International LLC (HQ) .... C 626 765-4800
601 S Vincent Ave Azusa (91702) *(P-5524)*

Ancra International LLC .... C 626 765-4810
601 S Vincent Ave Azusa (91702) *(P-5525)*

and 1, Aliso Viejo *Also Called: Basketball Marketing Co Inc (P-18102)*

and Syndicated Productions Inc .... D 818 308-5200
3500 W Olive Ave Ste 1000 Burbank (91505) *(P-14806)*

Andanov Music, Burbank *Also Called: Hollywood Records Inc (P-6576)*

Andari, El Monte *Also Called: Andari Fashion Inc (P-2005)*

Andari Fashion Inc .... C 626 575-2759
9626 Telstar Ave El Monte (91731) *(P-2005)*

Andaz Sandiego, San Diego *Also Called: Hyatt Corporation (P-12864)*

Anderco Inc .... E 714 446-9508
540 Airpark Dr Fullerton (92833) *(P-2295)*

Andersen Commercial Plbg Inc .... C 909 599-5950
1608 Yeager Ave La Verne (91750) *(P-738)*

Andersen Industries Inc .... E 760 246-8766
17079 Muskrat Ave Adelanto (92301) *(P-7313)*

Andersen Tax LLC .... C 213 593-2300
400 S Hope St Ste 2000 Los Angeles (90071) *(P-13161)*

Anderson, Poway *Also Called: T G T Enterprises Inc (P-18224)*

Anderson & Howard Electric Inc .... C 949 250-4555
15 Chrysler Irvine (92618) *(P-884)*

A L P H A B E T I C

Employee Codes: A=Over 500 employees, B=251-500
C=101-250, D=51-100, E=20-50, F=10-19, G=1-9

2025 Southern California
Business Directory and Buyers Guide

© Mergent Inc. 1-800-342-5647

937

Anderson Assoc Staffing Corp (PA)...........C 323 930-3170
8200 Wilshire Blvd Ste 200 Beverly Hills (90211) *(P-13590)*

Anderson Burton Cnstr Inc (PA)...........D 805 481-5096
121 Nevada St Arroyo Grande (93420) *(P-516)*

Anderson Chrnesky Strl Stl Inc...........D 951 769-5700
353 Risco Cir Beaumont (92223) *(P-4816)*

Anderson Howard, Irvine *Also Called: Anderson & Howard Electric Inc (P-884)*

Anderson Kayne Capital...........B 800 231-7414
1800 Avenue Of The Stars Ste 200 # 3rd Los Angeles (90067) *(P-12016)*

Anderson La Inc...........D 323 460-4115
3550 Tyburn St Los Angeles (90065) *(P-2963)*

Anderson Plbg Htg A Condition, El Cajon *Also Called: Walter Anderson Plumbing Inc (P-851)*

Anderson Printing, Los Angeles *Also Called: Anderson La Inc (P-2963)*

Anderson Real Estate, Los Angeles *Also Called: Topa Property Group Inc (P-12321)*

Andrew Alexander Inc...........D 323 752-0066
1306 S Alameda St Compton (90221) *(P-4276)*

Andrew L Youngquist Cnstr Inc...........D 949 862-5611
3187 Red Hill Ave Ste 200 Costa Mesa (92626) *(P-517)*

Andrew Lauren Company Inc...........C 949 861-4222
15225 Alton Pkwy Unit 300 Irvine (92618) *(P-14449)*

Andrews International Inc...........B 310 575-4844
11601 Wilshire Blvd Ste 500 Los Angeles (90025) *(P-14275)*

Andrews International Inc (HQ)...........A 818 487-4060
455 N Moss St Burbank (91502) *(P-14276)*

Androp Packaging Inc...........E 909 605-8842
4400 E Francis St Ontario (91761) *(P-2653)*

Anduril Industries Inc...........E 949 891-1607
2910 S Tech Center Dr Santa Ana (92705) *(P-7690)*

Anduril Industries Inc (PA)...........A 949 891-1607
1400 Anduril Costa Mesa (92626) *(P-7691)*

Andwin Corporation (PA)...........D 818 999-2828
167 W Cochran St Simi Valley (93065) *(P-10588)*

Andwin Scientific, Simi Valley *Also Called: Andwin Corporation (P-10588)*

Andy Anand Chocolates, Chino *Also Called: Hira Paris Inc (P-1505)*

Anemostat Products, Carson *Also Called: Mestek Inc (P-5978)*

Anesthsia Med Group Snta Brbar...........D 805 682-7751
514 W Pueblo St Fl 2 Santa Barbara (93105) *(P-15244)*

Anesthsia Med Group Snta Brbar, Santa Barbara *Also Called: Anesthsia Med Group Snta Brbar (P-15244)*

Angel City Public Hse & Brewry...........E 562 983-6880
216 S Alameda St Los Angeles (90012) *(P-1530)*

Angeles Mesa YWCA Chldren Lrng, Los Angeles *Also Called: Young Wns Chrstn Assn Grter Lo (P-17411)*

Angell & Giroux Inc...........D 323 269-8596
2727 Alcazar St Los Angeles (90033) *(P-2520)*

Angelo Gordon & Co LP...........A 310 777-5440
2000 Avenue Of The Stars Ste 1020 Los Angeles (90067) *(P-12017)*

Angels Baseball LP (PA)...........A 714 940-2000
2000 E Gene Autry Way Anaheim (92806) *(P-15018)*

Angels In Motion LLC...........D 909 590-9102
13768 Roswell Ave Chino (91710) *(P-16365)*

Angelus Block Co Inc (PA)...........E 714 637-8594
11374 Tuxford St Sun Valley (91352) *(P-4370)*

Angelus Machine Corp Intl...........E 323 583-2171
4900 Pacific Blvd Vernon (90058) *(P-5558)*

Anheuser-Busch, Pomona *Also Called: Anheuser-Busch LLC (P-1531)*

Anheuser-Busch, Santa Fe Springs *Also Called: Anheuser-Busch LLC (P-1532)*

Anheuser-Busch, Carson *Also Called: Anheuser-Busch LLC (P-1533)*

Anheuser-Busch, San Diego *Also Called: Anheuser-Busch LLC (P-1534)*

Anheuser-Busch, Van Nuys *Also Called: Anheuser-Busch LLC (P-14450)*

Anheuser-Busch LLC...........C 951 782-3935
2800 S Reservoir St Pomona (91766) *(P-1531)*

Anheuser-Busch LLC...........E 562 699-3424
12065 Pike St Santa Fe Springs (90670) *(P-1532)*

Anheuser-Busch LLC...........E 310 761-4600
20499 S Reeves Ave Carson (90810) *(P-1533)*

Anheuser-Busch LLC...........D 858 581-7000
5959 Santa Fe St San Diego (92109) *(P-1534)*

Anheuser-Busch LLC...........C 805 381-4700
15800 Roscoe Blvd Van Nuys (91406) *(P-14450)*

Anillo Industries, Orange *Also Called: Anillo Industries LLC (P-5118)*

Anillo Industries, Orange *Also Called: Hightower Plating & Mfg Co LLC (P-5266)*

Anillo Industries LLC...........E 714 637-7000
2090 N Glassell St Orange (92865) *(P-5118)*

Anitas Mexican Foods Corp (PA)...........D 909 884-8706
3454 N Mike Daley Dr San Bernardino (92407) *(P-1721)*

Anitas Mexican Foods Corp...........E 909 884-8706
3392 N Mike Daley Dr San Bernardino (92407) *(P-1722)*

Anitsa Inc...........C 213 237-0533
6032 Shull St Bell Gardens (90201) *(P-13110)*

Anixter Inc...........D 800 854-2088
7140 Opportunity Rd San Diego (92111) *(P-10168)*

Anjana Software Solutions Inc...........D 805 583-0121
1445 E Los Angeles Ave Ste 305 Simi Valley (93065) *(P-13654)*

Ankura Consulting Group LLC...........C 213 223-2109
633 W 5th St Fl 28 Los Angeles (90071) *(P-18285)*

Annandale Golf Club...........C 626 796-6125
1 N San Rafael Ave Pasadena (91105) *(P-15115)*

Annas Linens, Costa Mesa *Also Called: Annas Linens Inc (P-11527)*

Annas Linens Inc...........A 714 850-0504
3550 Hyland Ave Costa Mesa (92626) *(P-11527)*

Annie Golf Club, Goleta *Also Called: Glen Annie Golf Club (P-15081)*

Anns Trading Company Inc...........E 323 585-4702
5333 S Downey Rd Vernon (90058) *(P-11110)*

Anodizing Industries Inc...........E 323 227-4916
5222 Alhambra Ave Los Angeles (90032) *(P-5233)*

Anodyne Inc...........E 714 549-3321
2230 S Susan St Santa Ana (92704) *(P-5234)*

Anoroc, Compton *Also Called: Anoroc Precision Shtmtl Inc (P-4949)*

Anoroc Precision Shtmtl Inc...........E 310 515-6015
19122 S Santa Fe Ave Compton (90221) *(P-4949)*

Anp Lighting, Montclair *Also Called: American Nail Plate Ltg Inc (P-6437)*

Anre Tech, Altadena *Also Called: Anre Technologies Inc (P-13655)*

Anre Technologies Inc...........C 818 627-5433
741 W Woodbury Rd Altadena (91001) *(P-13655)*

Ansar Gallery Inc...........C 949 220-0000
2505 El Camino Rd Tustin (92782) *(P-10743)*

Anschutz Entrmt Group Inc (HQ)...........C 213 763-7700
800 W Olympic Blvd Ste 305 Los Angeles (90015) *(P-14985)*

Anschutz Film Group LLC (HQ)...........E 310 887-1000
10201 W Pico Blvd # 52 Los Angeles (90064) *(P-8420)*

Anschutz Sthern Cal Spt Cmplex...........C 310 630-2000
18400 Avalon Blvd Ste 100 Carson (90746) *(P-15192)*

Ansell Sndel Med Solutions LLC...........E 818 534-2500
9301 Oakdale Ave Ste 300 Chatsworth (91311) *(P-8253)*

Anser Advisory Management LLC (HQ)...........C 714 276-1135
1820 E 1st St Ste 410 Santa Ana (92705) *(P-17944)*

Ansun, San Diego *Also Called: Ansun Biopharma Inc (P-17766)*

Ansun Biopharma Inc...........E 858 452-2631
10045 Mesa Rim Rd San Diego (92121) *(P-17766)*

Answer Financial Inc (HQ)...........C 818 644-4000
15910 Ventura Blvd Fl 6 Encino (91436) *(P-14451)*

Antaky Quilting Company, Los Angeles *Also Called: American Quilting Company Inc (P-2245)*

Antcom, Torrance *Also Called: Antcom Corporation (P-6597)*

Antcom Corporation...........E 310 782-1076
367 Van Ness Way Ste 602 Torrance (90501) *(P-6597)*

Antelope Valley Care Center, Lancaster *Also Called: Pacs Group Inc (P-15733)*

Antelope Valley Health Care Di (PA)...........A 661 949-5000
1600 W Avenue J Lancaster (93534) *(P-15913)*

Antelope Valley Hlth Care Dst...........C 661 949-5936
44335 Lowtree Ave Lancaster (93534) *(P-15914)*

Antelope Valley Hlth Care Dst, Lancaster *Also Called: Antelope Valley Hospital Inc (P-15915)*

Antelope Valley Home Care, Lancaster *Also Called: Antelope Valley Hlth Care Dst (P-15914)*

Antelope Valley Hospital, Lancaster *Also Called: Kaiser Foundation Hospitals (P-16045)*

Antelope Valley Hospital Inc...........B 661 726-6180
1600 W Avenue J Lancaster (93534) *(P-15245)*

Antelope Valley Hospital Inc...........C 661 949-5000
44335 Lowtree Ave Lancaster (93534) *(P-15915)*

Antelope Valley Hospital Inc...........C 661 726-6050
44105 15th St W Ste 100 Lancaster (93534) *(P-15916)*

Mergent email: customerrelations@mergent.com
938

2025 Southern California
Business Directory and Buyers Guide

(P-0000) Products & Services Section entry number
(PA)=Parent Co (HQ)=Headquarters (DH)=Div Headquarters

Antelope Valley Lincoln, Lancaster *Also Called: Johnson Ford (P-11367)*

Antelope Valley Newspapers Inc .... E 661 940-1000
44939 10th St W Lancaster (93534) *(P-2779)*

Antelope Valley Press, Lancaster *Also Called: Antelope Valley Newspapers Inc (P-2779)*

Antelope Vly Cntry CLB Imprv .... C 661 947-3142
39800 Country Club Dr Palmdale (93551) *(P-15116)*

Antelope Vly Convalecnt Hosp, Lancaster *Also Called: Antelope Vly Retirement HM Inc (P-15831)*

Antelope Vly Retirement HM Inc .... C 661 949-5584
44523 15th St W Lancaster (93534) *(P-15568)*

Antelope Vly Retirement HM Inc .... C 661 948-7501
44445 15th St W Lancaster (93534) *(P-15831)*

Antelope Vly Retirement HM Inc .... C 661 949-5524
44567 15th St W Lancaster (93534) *(P-15832)*

Antelope Vly Retirement Manor, Lancaster *Also Called: Antelope Vly Retirement HM Inc (P-15568)*

Antelope Vly Schl Trnsp Agcy .... C 661 952-3106
670 W Avenue L8 Lancaster (93534) *(P-8866)*

Antenna Audio Inc (PA) .... A 203 523-0320
555 W 5th St Ste 3725 Los Angeles (90013) *(P-9238)*

Antenna International, Los Angeles *Also Called: Antenna Audio Inc (P-9238)*

Antex Knitting Mills, Los Angeles *Also Called: Tenenblatt Corporation (P-1927)*

Antex Knitting Mills, Los Angeles *Also Called: Matchmaster Dyg & Finshg Inc (P-1942)*

Antex Knitting Mills, Los Angeles *Also Called: Guru Knits Inc (P-2037)*

Anthony Inc (DH) .... A 818 365-9451
12391 Montero Ave Sylmar (91342) *(P-5967)*

Anthony California Inc (PA) .... E 909 627-0351
14485 Monte Vista Ave Chino (91710) *(P-6438)*

Anthony International, Sylmar *Also Called: Anthony Inc (P-5967)*

Anthony Vineyards Inc .... D 760 391-5488
52301 Enterprise Way Coachella (92236) *(P-29)*

Anthos Group Inc .... E 888 778-2986
705 N Douglas St El Segundo (90245) *(P-18093)*

Anti-Recidivism Coalition .... D 213 955-5885
1320 E 7th St Los Angeles (90021) *(P-17210)*

Antique Apparatus Company, Torrance *Also Called: Rock-Ola Manufacturing Corp (P-6551)*

Antis Roofg Waterproofing LLC .... C 949 461-9222
2649 Campus Dr Irvine (92612) *(P-1194)*

Antis Roofing, Irvine *Also Called: Antis Roofg Waterproofing LLC (P-1194)*

Anvil Cases Inc .... C 626 968-4100
1242 E Edna Pl Unit B Covina (91724) *(P-4291)*

Anvil Iron, Gardena *Also Called: Anvil Steel Corporation (P-1148)*

Anvil Steel Corporation .... D 310 329-5811
134 W 168th St Gardena (90248) *(P-1148)*

Anydata Corporation .... D 949 900-6040
5405 Alton Pkwy Irvine (92604) *(P-6598)*

Anywhere Integrated Svcs LLC .... B 818 291-4400
801 N Brand Blvd Glendale (91203) *(P-12553)*

Ao, Orange *Also Called: Architects Orange Inc (P-17666)*

Aoc LLC .... D 951 657-5161
19991 Seaton Ave Perris (92570) *(P-1958)*

AOC California Plant, Perris *Also Called: Aoc LLC (P-1958)*

AOC USA, Pico Rivera *Also Called: Lubricating Specialties Company (P-3857)*

Aoclsc Inc .... E 562 776-4000
3365 E Slauson Ave Vernon (90058) *(P-3847)*

Aoclsc Inc .... C 813 248-1988
8015 Paramount Blvd Pico Rivera (90660) *(P-3848)*

Aocusa, Vernon *Also Called: Aoclsc Inc (P-3847)*

Aocusa, Pico Rivera *Also Called: Aoclsc Inc (P-3848)*

AOE International Inc .... E
20611 Belshaw Ave Carson (90746) *(P-3357)*

Aos, Torrance *Also Called: Finest Hour Holdings Inc (P-8267)*

AP Labs Inc (PA) .... E 800 822-7522
9477 Waples St Ste 150 San Diego (92121) *(P-5841)*

AP Parpro Inc .... E 619 498-9004
2700 S Fairview St Santa Ana (92704) *(P-6341)*

AP Precision Metals Inc .... E 619 628-0003
1185 Park Center Dr Vista (92081) *(P-4950)*

APA Incorporated .... D 310 888-4200
405 S Beverly Dr Beverly Hills (90212) *(P-18094)*

Apcn-Aco Inc .... D 626 288-7988
223 N Garfield Ave Ste 208 Monterey Park (91754) *(P-17945)*

Apct Anaheim, Orange *Also Called: Cirtech Inc (P-14472)*

Apct Orange County, Placentia *Also Called: Cartel Electronics LLC (P-6714)*

Apeel Sciences, Goleta *Also Called: Apeel Technology Inc (P-103)*

Apeel Technology Inc (PA) .... B 805 203-0146
71 S Los Carneros Rd Goleta (93117) *(P-103)*

Apeiro Technologies, Irvine *Also Called: It Division Inc (P-16843)*

Apem Inc (HQ) .... E 978 372-1602
970 Park Center Dr Vista (92081) *(P-5901)*

Apem Inc .... D 760 598-2518
970 Park Center Dr Vista (92081) *(P-6967)*

Aperio, Vista *Also Called: Leica Biosystems Imaging Inc (P-7964)*

Aperto Property Management Inc .... B 626 965-1961
17351 Main St La Puente (91744) *(P-12332)*

Apex Bulk Commodities, Adelanto *Also Called: Apex Bulk Commodities Inc (P-8893)*

Apex Bulk Commodities Inc (PA) .... C 760 246-6077
12531 Violet Rd Ste A Adelanto (92301) *(P-8893)*

Apex Design Tech., Corona *Also Called: Btl Machine (P-6100)*

Apex Design Technology, Anaheim *Also Called: Apex Technology Holdings Inc (P-7692)*

Apex Holding Co .... D 818 876-0161
23901 Calabasas Rd Ste 2090 Calabasas (91302) *(P-11027)*

Apex Logistics Intl Inc (DH) .... C 310 665-0288
18554 S Susana Rd East Rancho Domingue (90221) *(P-9252)*

Apex Mechanical Systems Inc .... D 858 536-8700
7440 Trade St Ste A San Diego (92121) *(P-739)*

Apex Precision Technologies Inc .... E 317 821-1000
23622 Calabasas Rd Ste 323 Calabasas (91302) *(P-7227)*

Apex Technology Holdings Inc .... A 321 270-3630
2850 E Coronado St Anaheim (92806) *(P-7692)*

Apex USA, East Rancho Domingue *Also Called: Apex Logistics Intl Inc (P-9252)*

Apffels Coffee, Santa Fe Springs *Also Called: Apffels Coffee Inc (P-1714)*

Apffels Coffee Inc .... E 562 309-0400
12115 Pacific St Santa Fe Springs (90670) *(P-1714)*

Apg, Panorama City *Also Called: American Protection Group Inc (P-14273)*

API Group Life Safety USA LLC .... D 562 279-0770
3720 Industry Ave Ste 107 Lakewood (90712) *(P-740)*

Apic Corporation .... D 310 642-7975
5800 Uplander Way Culver City (90230) *(P-6799)*

Apical Industries Inc .... D 760 724-5300
3030 Enterprise Ct Ste A Vista (92081) *(P-10486)*

APM Manufacturing .... C 714 453-0100
341 W Blueridge Ave Orange (92865) *(P-7330)*

APM Terminals Pacific LLC .... B 310 221-4000
2500 Navy Way Pier 400 San Pedro (90731) *(P-9253)*

APn Business Resources Inc .... D 818 717-9980
21418 Osborne St Canoga Park (91304) *(P-18095)*

Apogee Electronics, Santa Monica *Also Called: Apogee Electronics Corporation (P-6526)*

Apogee Electronics Corporation .... E 310 584-9394
1715 Berkeley St Santa Monica (90404) *(P-6526)*

Apollo Interactive LLC (PA) .... D 310 836-9777
139 Illinois St El Segundo (90245) *(P-13196)*

Apollo Printing & Graphics, Anaheim *Also Called: Tajen Graphics Inc (P-3087)*

Apollo.io, Covina *Also Called: Zenleads Inc (P-18248)*

Apon Industries Corp C
10005 Marconi Dr Ste 2 San Diego (92154) *(P-4051)*

Apotheka Systems Inc .... E 844 777-4455
14040 Panay Way Marina Del Rey (90292) *(P-13878)*

App Wholesale LLC .... B 323 980-8315
3686 E Olympic Blvd Los Angeles (90023) *(P-10927)*

App Winddown LLC (HQ) C
747 Warehouse St Los Angeles (90021) *(P-2187)*

Apparel House USA, Gardena *Also Called: Stanzino Inc (P-1887)*

Apparel Newsgroup, The, Los Angeles *Also Called: Mnm Corporation (P-2865)*

Apparel Prod Svcs Globl LLC (PA) .... E 818 700-3700
8954 Lurline Ave Chatsworth (91311) *(P-2080)*

Apperson Inc (PA) .... D 562 356-3333
17315 Studebaker Rd Ste 211 Cerritos (90703) *(P-3190)*

Appfolio, Santa Barbara *Also Called: Appfolio Inc (P-13879)*

Employee Codes: A=Over 500 employees, B=251-500
C=101-250, D=51-100, E=20-50, F=10-19, G=1-9

2025 Southern California
Business Directory and Buyers Guide

© Mergent Inc. 1-800-342-5647

939

Appfolio Inc (PA)...B 805 364-6093
70 Castilian Dr Santa Barbara (93117) *(P-13879)*

Appfolio Inc ....C 866 648-1536
2305 Historic Decatur Rd San Diego (92106) *(P-13880)*

Apple Farm Collections-Slo Inc (PA)....................B 805 544-2040
2015 Monterey St San Luis Obispo (93401) *(P-11550)*

Apple Graphics Inc ....E 626 301-4287
3550 Tyburn St Los Angeles (90065) *(P-2964)*

Apple Store Glendale Galleria, Glendale Also Called: Glendale Associates Ltd *(P-12294)*

Applecare Medical MGT LLC ....C 714 443-4507
18 Centerpointe Dr Ste 100 La Palma (90623) *(P-17946)*

Appleone Employment Services, Glendale Also Called: AppleOne Inc *(P-13486)*

Appleone Employment Services, Glendale Also Called: AppleOne Inc *(P-13487)*

AppleOne Inc ....C 818 240-8688
325 W Broadway Glendale (91204) *(P-13486)*

AppleOne Inc (HQ)...C 818 240-8688
327 W Broadway Glendale (91204) *(P-13487)*

Applied Biosystems, Carlsbad Also Called: Applied Biosystems LLC *(P-13881)*

Applied Biosystems LLC (DH)..............................C
5791 Van Allen Way Carlsbad (92008) *(P-13881)*

Applied Business Software Inc ....D 562 426-2188
7755 Center Ave Huntington Beach (92647) *(P-13882)*

Applied Cardiac Systems Inc ....D 949 855-9366
1 Hughes Ste A Irvine (92618) *(P-8091)*

Applied Cmpsite Structures Inc (HQ)....................D 714 990-6300
1195 Columbia St Brea (92821) *(P-7431)*

Applied Coatings & Linings ....E 626 280-6354
3224 Rosemead Blvd El Monte (91731) *(P-5310)*

Applied Companies ....E 661 257-0090
28020 Avenue Stanford Santa Clarita (91355) *(P-17485)*

Applied Computer Solutions (DH).........................D 714 861-2200
110 Progress Irvine (92618) *(P-13656)*

Applied Enterprise MGT Corp ....C 805 484-1909
760 Paseo Camarillo Ste 101 Camarillo (93010) *(P-13657)*

Applied Instrument Tech Inc ....E 909 204-3700
2121 Aviation Dr Upland (91786) *(P-7937)*

Applied Manufacturing LLC ....A 949 713-8000
22872 Avenida Empresa Rancho Santa Margari (92688) *(P-8092)*

Applied Medical Corporation (PA)..........................C 949 713-8000
22872 Avenida Empresa Rancho Santa Margari (92688) *(P-8093)*

Applied Medical Dist Corp ....A 949 713-8000
22872 Avenida Empresa Rcho Sta Marg (92688) *(P-8094)*

Applied Medical Distribution, Rancho Santa Margari Also Called: Applied Medical Resources Corp *(P-8096)*

Applied Medical Resources ....E 949 459-1042
30152 Esperanza Rcho Sta Marg (92688) *(P-8095)*

Applied Medical Resources, Rancho Santa Margari Also Called: Applied Medical Corporation *(P-8093)*

Applied Medical Resources Corp (HQ).....................E 949 713-8000
22872 Avenida Empresa Rancho Santa Margari (92688) *(P-8096)*

Applied Membranes Inc ....C 760 727-3711
2450 Business Park Dr Vista (92081) *(P-5998)*

Applied Mlecular Evolution Inc (HQ)......................E 858 597-4990
10300 Campus Point Dr Ste 200 San Diego (92121) *(P-3358)*

Applied Polytech Systems Inc ....E 818 504-9261
26000 Springbrook Ave Ste 102 Santa Clarita (91350) *(P-2403)*

Applied Powdercoat Inc ....E 805 981-1991
3101 Camino Del Sol Oxnard (93030) *(P-5311)*

Applied Research Assoc Inc ....D 505 881-8074
10833 Valley View St Ste 250 Cypress (90630) *(P-17767)*

Applied Statistics & MGT Inc ....D 951 699-4600
32848 Wolf Store Rd Ste A Temecula (92592) *(P-13883)*

Applied Technologies Assoc Inc (HQ)....................C 805 239-9100
3025 Buena Vista Dr Paso Robles (93446) *(P-8032)*

Apprentice Jrnymen Trning Tr F ....C 310 604-0892
7850 Haskell Ave Van Nuys (91406) *(P-17045)*

Approved Aeronautics LLC ....E 951 200-3730
9130 Pulsar Ct Corona (92883) *(P-7432)*

Appstar Financial, San Diego Also Called: Amazon Processing LLC *(P-14121)*

APR Engineering Inc ....E 562 983-3800
1812 W 9th St Long Beach (90813) *(P-7596)*

Apricorn LLC ....E 858 513-2000
12191 Kirkham Rd Poway (92064) *(P-5902)*

APS Global, Chatsworth Also Called: Apparel Prod Svcs Globl LLC *(P-2080)*

APS Marine, Chula Vista Also Called: Adept Process Services Inc *(P-7615)*

APT Electronics, Anaheim Also Called: APT Electronics Inc *(P-6709)*

APT Electronics Inc ....C 714 687-6760
241 N Crescent Way Anaheim (92801) *(P-6709)*

APT Metal Fabricators Inc ....E 818 896-7478
11164 Bradley Ave Pacoima (91331) *(P-5172)*

Aptco LLC (PA)...D 661 792-2107
31381 Pond Rd Bldg 2 Mc Farland (93250) *(P-3258)*

Aptim Corp ....A 949 261-6441
18100 Von Karman Ave # 450 Irvine (92612) *(P-17904)*

Aptim Corp ....B 619 239-1690
1230 Columbia St Ste 1200 San Diego (92101) *(P-18286)*

Aptim Federal Services LLC ....B 619 239-1690
1230 Columbia St Ste 1200 San Diego (92101) *(P-388)*

Aptiv Services Us LLC ....B 818 661-6667
5137 Clareton Dr Ste 220 Agoura Hills (91301) *(P-7228)*

Aputure Imaging Industries ....E 626 295-6133
1715 N Gower St Los Angeles (90028) *(P-4323)*

Apw Knox-Seeman Warehouse Inc (HQ)................D 310 604-4373
1073 E Artesia Blvd Carson (90746) *(P-9811)*

Aq Lighting Group, Santa Clarita Also Called: Aq Lighting Group Texas Inc *(P-10169)*

Aq Lighting Group Texas Inc ....E 818 534-5300
28486 Westinghouse Pl Ste 120 Santa Clarita (91355) *(P-10169)*

Aqi, Ontario Also Called: Aliquantum International Inc *(P-8481)*

Aqua Performance Inc ....E 951 340-2056
425 N Smith Ave Corona (92880) *(P-10509)*

Aqua Pro Properties Vii LP ....B 310 516-9911
2000 W 135th St Gardena (90249) *(P-5689)*

Aqua Products Inc (DH)..E 973 857-2700
2882 Whiptail Loop Ste 100 Carlsbad (92010) *(P-5999)*

Aquafine Corporation (HQ)....................................D 661 257-4770
29010 Avenue Paine Valencia (91355) *(P-6000)*

Aquahydrate Inc ....E 310 559-5058
5870 W Jefferson Blvd Ste D Los Angeles (90016) *(P-1607)*

Aquamar Inc ....C 909 481-4700
10888 7th St Rancho Cucamonga (91730) *(P-1694)*

Aquamor LLC (PA)...D 951 541-9517
42188 Rio Nedo Temecula (92590) *(P-6001)*

Aquaneering, San Marcos Also Called: Aquaneering LLC *(P-17768)*

Aquaneering LLC ....E 858 578-2028
340 Rancheros Dr Ste 180 San Marcos (92069) *(P-17768)*

Aquarium of Pacific (PA).......................................C 562 590-3100
100 Aquarium Way Long Beach (90802) *(P-17269)*

Aquarius Rags LLC (PA).......................................D 213 895-4400
15821 Ventura Blvd Ste 270 Encino (91436) *(P-2058)*

Aquastar Pool Productions, Ventura Also Called: Aquastar Pool Products Inc *(P-5726)*

Aquastar Pool Products Inc ....E 877 768-2717
2340 Palma Dr Ste 104 Ventura (93003) *(P-5726)*

Aquatec International Inc ....D 949 225-2200
17422 Pullman St Irvine (92614) *(P-5727)*

Aquatec Water Systems, Irvine Also Called: Aquatec International Inc *(P-5727)*

Aquatic Co ....C 714 993-1220
8101 E Kaiser Blvd Ste 200 Anaheim (92808) *(P-4023)*

Aquatic Co ....B 714 993-1220
1700 N Delilah St Corona (92879) *(P-4024)*

Aqueos Corporation (PA).......................................E 805 364-0570
418 Chapala St Ste E Santa Barbara (93101) *(P-5503)*

Aqueos Corporation ....C 805 676-4330
2550 Eastman Ave Ventura (93003) *(P-5504)*

Aqueous Technologies Corp ....E 909 944-7771
1678 N Maple St Corona (92878) *(P-6002)*

Aquire, Norwalk Also Called: Aquirecorps Norwalk Auto Auctn *(P-9800)*

Aquirecorps Norwalk Auto Auctn ....C 562 864-7464
12405 Rosecrans Ave Norwalk (90650) *(P-9800)*

AR Tech Aerospace, Fontana Also Called: A&R Tarpaulins Inc *(P-2232)*

Araca Merchandise LP ....D 818 743-5400
459 Park Ave San Fernando (91340) *(P-3117)*

Araco Enterprises LLC .... B 818 767-0675
9189 De Garmo Ave Sun Valley (91352) *(P-9727)*

Arakelian Enterprises Inc .... C 818 768-2644
11121 Pendleton St Sun Valley (91352) *(P-8894)*

Arakelian Enterprises Inc .... B 626 336-3636
15045 Salt Lake Ave City Of Industry (91746) *(P-9728)*

Arakelian Enterprises Inc (PA) .... C 626 336-3636
14048 Valley Blvd City Of Industry (91746) *(P-9729)*

Arakelian Enterprises Inc .... C 951 342-3300
687 Iowa Ave Riverside (92507) *(P-9730)*

Aramark, Los Angeles Also Called: Aramark Facility Services LLC (P-13355)

Aramark Facility Services LLC .... C 213 740-8968
941 W 35th St Los Angeles (90007) *(P-13355)*

Aranda Tooling LLC .... D 714 379-6565
13950 Yorba Ave Chino (91710) *(P-6080)*

Ararat Convalescent Hospital, Los Angeles Also Called: Ararat Home Los Angeles Inc
(P-15834)

Ararat Home Los Angeles Inc .... C 818 837-1800
15099 Mission Hills Rd Mission Hills (91345) *(P-15833)*

Ararat Home Los Angeles Inc .... C 323 256-8012
2373 Colorado Blvd Los Angeles (90041) *(P-15834)*

Ararat Nursing Facility, Mission Hills Also Called: Ararat Home Los Angeles Inc (P-15833)

Araya Construction Inc .... D 760 758-3454
2870 S Santa Fe Ave San Marcos (92069) *(P-13356)*

Arb Inc (HQ) .... C 949 598-9242
26000 Commercentre Dr Lake Forest (92630) *(P-659)*

Arb Inc .... B 619 295-2754
2130 La Mirada Dr Vista (92081) *(P-708)*

ARB Industrial, Lake Forest Also Called: Arb Inc (P-659)

Arbiter Systems Incorporated (PA) .... E 805 237-3831
1324 Vendels Cir Ste 121 Paso Robles (93446) *(P-7898)*

Arbonne International LLC (DH) .... E 949 770-2610
21 Technology Dr Irvine (92618) *(P-11674)*

Arbonne International Dist Inc .... E 800 272-6663
9400 Jeronimo Rd Irvine (92618) *(P-11675)*

Arbor Glen Care Center, Glendora Also Called: Harbor Glen Care Center (P-15671)

Arbor Glen Care Center, Glendora Also Called: Ensign San Dimas LLC (P-15850)

Arbor Hills Nursing Center, La Mesa Also Called: Life Gnerations Healthcare LLC (P-15698)

Arbormed Inc (PA) .... C 714 689-1500
725 W Town And Country Rd Orange (92868) *(P-16532)*

Arbors, The, San Diego Also Called: G&L Penasquitos Inc (P-16946)

ARC, Torrance Also Called: Good Sports Plus Ltd (P-13739)

ARC - Imperial Valley .... E 760 768-1944
340 E 1st St Calexico (92231) *(P-16442)*

ARC - SD E Cnty Training Ctrs, El Cajon Also Called: ARC of San Diego (P-17212)

ARC Document Solutions LLC .... B 951 445-4480
41521 Date St Apt 101 Murrieta (92562) *(P-13310)*

ARC ENTERPRISES, San Diego Also Called: ARC of San Diego (P-17211)

ARC Los Angeles & Orange Cnty (PA) .... D 562 803-4606
12049 Woodruff Ave Downey (90241) *(P-17046)*

ARC of San Diego (PA) .... C 619 685-1175
3030 Market St San Diego (92102) *(P-17211)*

ARC of San Diego .... C 619 448-2415
1855 John Towers Ave El Cajon (92020) *(P-17212)*

ARC of San Diego .... A 760 740-6800
1336 Rancheros Dr Ste 100 San Marcos (92069) *(P-17213)*

ARC Products, San Diego Also Called: Ssco Manufacturing Inc (P-5649)

Arcadia Convalescent Hosp Inc .... D 818 352-4438
10158 Sunland Blvd Sunland (91040) *(P-15569)*

Arcadia Convalescent Hosp Inc (PA) .... C 626 445-2170
1601 S Baldwin Ave Arcadia (91007) *(P-15835)*

Arcadia Gardens MGT Corp .... D 626 574-8571
720 W Camino Real Ave Arcadia (91007) *(P-15806)*

Arcadia Health Care Center, Arcadia Also Called: Arcadia Convalescent Hosp Inc (P-15835)

Arcadia Norcal, Los Angeles Also Called: Arcadia Products LLC (P-4614)

Arcadia Products LLC (HQ) .... C 323 771-9819
2301 E Vernon Ave Los Angeles (90023) *(P-4614)*

Arch Health Partners, Poway Also Called: Palomar Health Medical Group (P-16120)

Arch Med Sltons - Escndido LLC .... C 760 432-9785
950 Borra Pl Escondido (92029) *(P-8097)*

Arch Motorcycle Company Inc .... E 970 443-1380
3216 W El Segundo Blvd Hawthorne (90250) *(P-11481)*

Archimdes Tech Group Hldngs LL .... D 858 642-9170
5660 Eastgate Dr San Diego (92121) *(P-17769)*

Archipelago Inc .... C 213 743-9200
1548 18th St Santa Monica (90404) *(P-3631)*

Archipelago Botanicals, Santa Monica Also Called: Archipelago Inc (P-3631)

Archipelago Development Inc .... D 858 699-6272
Rancho Santa Fe (92067) *(P-12564)*

Archipelago Lighting Inc .... D 909 627-5333
4615 State St Montclair (91763) *(P-10170)*

Architctral Mllwk Snta Barbara .... E 805 965-7011
8 N Nopal St Santa Barbara (93103) *(P-2296)*

Architects Orange Inc .... C 714 639-9860
144 N Orange St Orange (92866) *(P-17666)*

Architectural Design Signs Inc (PA) .... D 951 278-0680
1160 Railroad St Corona (92882) *(P-8590)*

Architectural Enterprises Inc .... E 323 268-4000
5821 Randolph St Commerce (90040) *(P-5091)*

Architectural Mtls USA Inc .... D 888 219-2126
4025 Camino Del Rio S Ste 300 San Diego (92108) *(P-17667)*

Architectural Window Shades, Pasadena Also Called: Roberson Construction (P-2606)

Architectural Woodworking Co .... D 626 570-4125
582 Monterey Pass Rd Monterey Park (91754) *(P-1044)*

Arciero Brothers Inc .... C 714 238-6600
5614 E La Palma Ave Anaheim (92807) *(P-1101)*

Arconic Fastening Systems, Carson Also Called: Huck International Inc (P-5129)

Arconic Fastening Systems, City Of Industry Also Called: Valley-Todeco Inc (P-5139)

Arcs Commercial Mortgage, Calabasas Also Called: Arcs Commercial Mortgage Co LP
(P-11886)

Arcs Commercial Mortgage Co LP (DH) .... C 818 676-3274
26901 Agoura Rd Ste 200 Calabasas (91301) *(P-11886)*

Arctic Glacier USA Inc .... C 310 638-0321
17011 Central Ave Carson (90746) *(P-1730)*

Arcticom Group Rfrgn LLC .... B 916 484-3190
3675 De Forest Cir Jurupa Valley (91752) *(P-14723)*

Arctiq, Irvine Also Called: Dyntek Inc (P-14215)

ARCTURUS, San Diego Also Called: Arcturus Thrptics Holdings Inc (P-3359)

Arcturus Therapeutics Inc .... C 858 900-2660
10628 Science Center Dr Ste 250 San Diego (92121) *(P-17770)*

Arcturus Thrptics Holdings Inc (PA) .... E 858 900-2660
10628 Science Center Dr Ste 250 San Diego (92121) *(P-3359)*

Arcules Inc .... D 949 439-0053
17875 Von Karman Ave Ste 450 Irvine (92614) *(P-14382)*

Ardcore Senior Living .... B 714 974-2226
525 S Anaheim Hills Rd Anaheim (92807) *(P-17120)*

Ardea Biosciences Inc .... E 858 625-0787
9390 Towne Centre Dr Ste 100 San Diego (92121) *(P-3360)*

Arden Engineering Inc .... C 714 998-6410
1878 N Main St Orange (92865) *(P-7433)*

Arden Realty Inc .... B 310 966-2600
11601 Wilshire Blvd Fl 5 Los Angeles (90025) *(P-12282)*

Ardent Companies Inc .... D 661 633-1465
4842 Airport Dr Bakersfield (93308) *(P-885)*

Ardmore Home Design Inc (PA) .... E 626 803-7769
918 S Stimson Ave City Of Industry (91745) *(P-2440)*

Ardwin Freight, Burbank Also Called: Ardwin Inc (P-8932)

Ardwin Inc .... C 818 767-7777
2940 N Hollywood Way Burbank (91505) *(P-8932)*

Are/Cal-Sd Region No 62 LLC .... D 626 578-0777
26 N Euclid Ave Pasadena (91101) *(P-12698)*

Arecont Vision Costar LLC .... D 818 937-0700
1801 Highland Ave Duarte (91010) *(P-14383)*

Arecont Vision LLC .... C 818 937-0700
425 E Colorado St Fl 7 Glendale (91205) *(P-6367)*

Aremac Associates Inc .... E 626 303-8795
2004 S Myrtle Ave Monrovia (91016) *(P-6081)*

Aremac Heat Treating Inc .... E 626 333-3898
330 S 9th Ave City Of Industry (91746) *(P-4696)*

Arena Painting Contractors Inc .... D 310 316-2446
525 E Alondra Blvd Gardena (90248) *(P-859)*

A
L
P
H
A
B
E
T
I
C

Employee Codes: A=Over 500 employees, B=251-500
C=101-250, D=51-100, E=20-50, F=10-19, G=1-9

2025 Southern California
Business Directory and Buyers Guide

© Mergent Inc. 1-800-342-5647
941

Ares, Los Angeles *Also Called: Ares Management Corporation (P-12628)*

Ares Management Corporation (PA) .... C 310 201-4100
1800 Avenue Of The Stars Ste 1400 Los Angeles (90067) *(P-12628)*

Arete Associates (PA) .... C 818 885-2200
9301 Corbin Ave Ste 2000 Northridge (91324) *(P-7693)*

Arete Associates, Northridge *Also Called: Arete Associates (P-7693)*

Arevalo Tortilleria Inc .... E 323 888-1711
3033 Supply Ave Commerce (90040) *(P-1739)*

Arevalo Tortilleria Inc (PA) .... D 323 888-1711
1537 W Mines Ave Montebello (90640) *(P-1740)*

Arey Jones Eductl Solutions, San Diego *Also Called: Broadway Typewriter Co Inc (P-9993)*

Argee, Santee *Also Called: Argee Mfg Co San Diego Inc (P-4052)*

Argee Mfg Co San Diego Inc .... D 619 449-5050
9550 Pathway St Santee (92071) *(P-4052)*

Argen Corporation (PA) .... C 858 455-7900
8515 Miralani Dr San Diego (92126) *(P-4579)*

Argo Spring Mfg Co Inc .... D 800 252-2740
13930 Shoemaker Ave Norwalk (90650) *(P-5378)*

Argon St Inc .... D 703 270-6927
6696 Mesa Ridge Rd Ste A San Diego (92121) *(P-7694)*

Argonaut Mfg Svcs Inc .... D 888 834-8892
2841 Loker Ave E Carlsbad (92010) *(P-10062)*

Arguello Inc .... E 805 567-1632
17100 Calle Mariposa Reina Goleta (93117) *(P-294)*

Argus Management Company LLC .... B 562 299-5200
5150 E Pacific Coast Hwy Ste 500 Long Beach (90804) *(P-18258)*

Argus Medical Management, Long Beach *Also Called: Argus Management Company LLC (P-18258)*

ARI Industries Inc .... D 714 993-3700
17018 Edwards Rd Cerritos (90703) *(P-5968)*

Aria Group Incorporated .... D 949 475-2915
17395 Daimler St Irvine (92614) *(P-17486)*

Aries Beef LLC .... E 818 526-4855
17 W Magnolia Blvd Burbank (91502) *(P-1254)*

Arium, Irvine *Also Called: American Arium (P-6797)*

Ariza Cheese Co Inc .... E 562 630-4144
7602 Jackson St Paramount (90723) *(P-1284)*

Ariza Global Foods Inc .... E 562 630-4144
7602 Jackson St Paramount (90723) *(P-1285)*

Arizona Channel Isla .... D 480 788-0755
300 W 9th St Oxnard (93030) *(P-15193)*

Arizona Pipeline Company (PA) .... B 760 244-8212
17372 Lilac St Hesperia (92345) *(P-660)*

Arizona Pipeline Company .... C 951 270-3100
1745 Sampson Ave Corona (92879) *(P-661)*

Arizona Portland Cement, Glendora *Also Called: Calportland Company (P-4352)*

Arjo Inc .... C 714 412-1170
17502 Fabrica Way Cerritos (90703) *(P-10063)*

Ark Animal Health Inc .... E 858 203-4100
4955 Directors Pl San Diego (92121) *(P-3558)*

Arkebauer Properties, Irvine *Also Called: Western National Prpts LLC (P-458)*

Arkema Coating Resins, Torrance *Also Called: Arkema Inc (P-3207)*

Arkema Inc .... E 310 214-5327
19206 Hawthorne Blvd Torrance (90503) *(P-3207)*

Arktura LLC (HQ) .... E 310 532-1050
966 Sandhill Ave Carson (90746) *(P-2499)*

ARLO, Carlsbad *Also Called: Arlo Technologies Inc (P-6527)*

Arlo Technologies Inc (PA) .... D 408 890-3900
2200 Faraday Ave Ste 150 Carlsbad (92008) *(P-6527)*

Arlon Graphics LLC (HQ) .... C 714 985-6300
200 Boysenberry Ln Placentia (92870) *(P-3944)*

Arlon LLC .... C 714 540-2811
2811 S Harbor Blvd Santa Ana (92704) *(P-4053)*

Arm Inc .... A 858 453-1900
5375 Mira Sorrento Pl Ste 540 San Diego (92121) *(P-6800)*

Armand Hmmer Mseum of Art Cltr .... C 310 443-7000
10899 Wilshire Blvd Los Angeles (90024) *(P-17248)*

Armani Trade LLC .... E 310 849-0067
21255 Burbank Blvd Ste 120 Woodland Hills (91367) *(P-11111)*

Armanino LLP .... B 310 478-4148
11766 Wilshire Blvd Fl 9 Los Angeles (90025) *(P-17701)*

Armanino LLP .... D 310 822-8552
2101 E El Segundo Blvd Ste 400 El Segundo (90245) *(P-17702)*

Armata Pharmaceuticals, Los Angeles *Also Called: Armata Pharmaceuticals Inc (P-3559)*

Armata Pharmaceuticals Inc (PA) .... E 310 665-2928
5005 Mcconnell Ave Los Angeles (90066) *(P-3559)*

Armc, Colton *Also Called: Arrowhead Regional Medical Ctr (P-15917)*

Armed Services YMCA of USA .... C 858 751-5755
3293 Santo Rd San Diego (92124) *(P-17323)*

Armed/Xctive Prtction Armed Un, Harbor City *Also Called: Allied Protection Services Inc (P-14269)*

Armen Living, Valencia *Also Called: Legacy Commercial Holdings Inc (P-2429)*

Arminak Solutions LLC .... E 626 802-7332
475 N Sheridan St Corona (92878) *(P-8658)*

Armlogi Holding Corp (PA) .... C 888 691-2911
20301 E Walnut Dr N Walnut (91789) *(P-9049)*

Armor Dermalogics LLC .... E 714 202-6424
9151 Atlanta Ave Unit 5864 Huntington Beach (92615) *(P-1291)*

Armorcast Products Company Inc .... E 909 390-1365
500 S Dupont Ave Ontario (91761) *(P-4054)*

Armorcast Products Company Inc (DH) .... C 818 982-3600
9140 Lurline Ave Chatsworth (91311) *(P-4951)*

Armtec Defense Products Co (DH) .... B 760 398-0143
85901 Avenue 53 Coachella (92236) *(P-5356)*

Armtec Defense Technologies, Coachella *Also Called: Armtec Defense Products Co (P-5356)*

Army of Happy LLC .... E 704 517-9890
4580 Euclid Ave San Diego (92115) *(P-1989)*

Arnco .... E 323 249-7500
5141 Firestone Pl South Gate (90280) *(P-3303)*

Arnies Supply Service Ltd (PA) .... E 323 263-1696
1541 N Ditman Ave Los Angeles (90063) *(P-2385)*

Arnold & Porter, Los Angeles *Also Called: Arnold Porter Kaye Scholer LLP (P-16636)*

Arnold Magnetics, Camarillo *Also Called: Arnold Magnetics Corporation (P-6281)*

Arnold Magnetics Corporation .... D 805 484-4221
841 Avenida Acaso Ste A Camarillo (93012) *(P-6281)*

Arnold Porter Kaye Scholer LLP .... C 213 243-4000
777 S Figueroa St Ste 4400 Los Angeles (90017) *(P-16636)*

Arnold-Gonsalves Engrg Inc .... E 909 465-1579
5731 Chino Ave Chino (91710) *(P-6082)*

Aroma Housewares, San Diego *Also Called: Mirama Enterprises Inc (P-6387)*

Arosa, Los Angeles *Also Called: Livhome Inc (P-16402)*

Around The Clock Care, Bakersfield *Also Called: Vasinda Investments Inc (P-13629)*

Arq, Costa Mesa *Also Called: Arq LLC (P-17487)*

Arq LLC .... D
555 Anton Blvd Costa Mesa (92626) *(P-17487)*

Arrietta Incorporated .... E 626 334-0302
429 N Azusa Ave Azusa (91702) *(P-11273)*

Arrival Communications Inc (DH) .... D 661 716-2100
1800 19th St Bakersfield (93301) *(P-14452)*

Arriver Holdco Inc .... A 858 587-1121
5775 Morehouse Dr San Diego (92121) *(P-7088)*

Arrk North America Inc .... C 858 552-1587
4660 La Jolla Village Dr Ste 100 San Diego (92122) *(P-4952)*

Arrow Engineering .... E 626 960-2806
4946 Azusa Canyon Rd Irwindale (91706) *(P-6083)*

Arrow Screw Products Inc .... E 805 928-2269
941 W Mccoy Ln Santa Maria (93455) *(P-6084)*

Arrow Transit Mix .... E 661 945-7600
507 E Avenue L12 Lancaster (93535) *(P-4428)*

Arrowhead, Pasadena *Also Called: Arrowhead Pharmaceuticals Inc (P-3361)*

Arrowhead Brass & Plumbing LLC .... D 800 332-4267
5147 Alhambra Ave Los Angeles (90032) *(P-741)*

Arrowhead Central Credit Union (PA) .... B 866 212-4333
8686 Haven Ave Rancho Cucamonga (91730) *(P-11792)*

ARROWHEAD CREDIT UNION, Rancho Cucamonga *Also Called: Arrowhead Central Credit Union (P-11792)*

Arrowhead Gen Insur Agcy Inc (HQ) .... C 619 881-8600
701 B St Ste 2100 San Diego (92101) *(P-12117)*

Arrowhead Pharmaceuticals Inc (PA) .... C 626 304-3400
177 E Colorado Blvd Ste 700 Pasadena (91105) *(P-3361)*

Arrowhead Products, Los Alamitos *Also Called: Arrowhead Products Corporation (P-7434)*

Mergent email: customerrelations@mergent.com
942

2025 Southern California
Business Directory and Buyers Guide

(P-0000) Products & Services Section entry number
(PA)=Parent Co (HQ)=Headquarters (DH)=Div Headquarters

Arrowhead Products Corporation .... A 714 822-2513
4411 Katella Ave Los Alamitos (90720) *(P-7434)*

Arrowhead Regional Medical Ctr .... A 909 580-1000
400 N Pepper Ave Colton (92324) *(P-15917)*

Arrowhead Water, Orange *Also Called: Bluetriton Brands Inc (P-10932)*

Arroyo Grande Care Center, Arroyo Grande *Also Called: Compass Health Inc (P-15600)*

Arroyo Grande Community Hospital .... B 805 473-7626
345 S Halcyon Rd Arroyo Grande (93420) *(P-15918)*

Arroyo Vista Family Health Ctr, Los Angeles *Also Called: Arroyo Vsta Fmly Hlth Fndation (P-15246)*

Arroyo Vsta Fmly Hlth Fndation .... D 323 224-2188
2411 N Broadway Los Angeles (90031) *(P-15246)*

ARS, Burbank *Also Called: Hutchinson Arospc & Indust Inc (P-7490)*

ARS, Los Angeles *Also Called: Asian Rehabilitation Svc Inc (P-17047)*

ARS National Services Inc (PA).......... C 800 456-5053
201 W Grand Ave Escondido (92025) *(P-13277)*

Arsi of California, Thousand Oaks *Also Called: American Recovery Service Inc (P-13276)*

Art Autism Related Therapy LLC .... D 909 304-1039
10134 6th St Ste I Rancho Cucamonga (91730) *(P-16443)*

Art Glass Etc Inc .... E 805 644-4494
3111 Golf Course Dr Ventura (93003) *(P-2297)*

Artboxx Framing Inc .... E 310 604-6933
555 W Victoria St Compton (90220) *(P-8659)*

Artcrafters Cabinets .... E 818 752-8960
5446 Cleon Ave North Hollywood (91601) *(P-2338)*

Arte De Mexico, North Hollywood *Also Called: Arte De Mexico Inc (P-6452)*

Arte De Mexico Inc (PA).......... D 818 753-4559
1000 Chestnut St Burbank (91506) *(P-2521)*

Arte De Mexico Inc .... D 818 753-4510
5506 Riverton Ave North Hollywood (91601) *(P-6452)*

Artemis Consulting, San Diego *Also Called: Artemis Consulting LLC (P-18096)*

Artemis Consulting LLC .... D 619 573-6328
1012 W Washington St San Diego (92103) *(P-18096)*

Artemis Inst For Clncal RES LL .... D 858 278-3647
770 Washington St Ste 300 San Diego (92103) *(P-15530)*

Artesia Christian Home Inc .... C 562 865-5218
11614 183rd St Artesia (90701) *(P-15836)*

Artesia Palms Care Center, Artesia *Also Called: Pacs Group Inc (P-15731)*

Artesia Sawdust Products Inc .... E 909 947-5983
13434 S Ontario Ave Ontario (91761) *(P-2285)*

Arthur Dogswell LLC (PA).......... E 888 559-8833
11301 W Olympic Blvd Ste 520 Los Angeles (90064) *(P-1416)*

Arthur Loussararian MD, Mission Viejo *Also Called: Mission Internal Med Group Inc (P-15390)*

Arthurmade Plastics Inc .... D 323 721-7325
2131 Garfield Ave City Of Commerce (90040) *(P-4055)*

Artic Sentinel Inc .... D 310 227-8230
1700 E Walnut Ave Ste 200 El Segundo (90245) *(P-13658)*

Artifacts International, Chula Vista *Also Called: Califrnia Furn Collections Inc (P-2500)*

Artificial Grass Liquidators .... E 951 677-3377
42505 Rio Nedo Temecula (92590) *(P-8660)*

Artimex Iron Inc .... C 619 444-3155
315 Cypress Ln El Cajon (92020) *(P-1149)*

Artisan Entertainment Inc .... A 310 449-9200
2700 Colorado Ave Ste 200 Santa Monica (90404) *(P-14807)*

Artisan House Inc .... E 818 767-7476
8238 Lankershim Blvd North Hollywood (91605) *(P-5441)*

ARTISAN HOUSE, INC, North Hollywood *Also Called: Artisan House Inc (P-5441)*

Artisan Nameplate Awards Corp .... E 714 556-6222
2730 S Shannon St Santa Ana (92704) *(P-3118)*

Artisan Screen Printing Inc .... C 626 815-2700
1055 W 5th St Azusa (91702) *(P-3119)*

Artisan Vehicle Systems Inc .... D 805 402-6856
742 Pancho Rd Camarillo (93012) *(P-7167)*

Artissimo Designs LLC (HQ).......... E 310 906-3700
2100 E Grand Ave Ste 400 El Segundo (90245) *(P-2764)*

Artistic Coverings, Cerritos *Also Called: Sports Venue Padding Inc (P-4019)*

Artistic Welding .... D 310 515-4922
505 E Gardena Blvd Gardena (90248) *(P-4953)*

Artiva, Chino *Also Called: Artiva USA Inc (P-6439)*

Artiva, Santa Fe Springs *Also Called: Artiva USA Inc (P-6440)*

Artiva Biotherapeutics Inc .... D 858 267-4467
5505 Morehouse Dr Ste 100 San Diego (92121) *(P-3560)*

Artiva USA Inc (PA).......... E 909 628-1388
13901 Magnolia Ave Chino (91710) *(P-6439)*

Artiva USA Inc .... E 562 298-8968
12866 Ann St Ste 1 Santa Fe Springs (90670) *(P-6440)*

Artkive .... E 310 975-9809
16225 Huston St Encino (91436) *(P-13884)*

Artkive, Van Nuys *Also Called: Kive Company (P-13961)*

Arto Brick / California Pavers .... E 310 768-8500
15209 S Broadway Gardena (90248) *(P-4360)*

Arto Brick and Cal Pavers, Gardena *Also Called: Arto Brick / California Pavers (P-4360)*

Arts & Crafts Press, San Diego *Also Called: Rush Press Inc (P-3078)*

Arts Elegance Inc .... E 626 793-4794
154 W Bellevue Dr Pasadena (91105) *(P-8452)*

Artsons Manufacturing Company .... E 323 773-3469
11121 Garfield Ave South Gate (90280) *(P-4510)*

Arup North America Limited .... B 310 578-4182
12777 W Jefferson Blvd Ste 300 Los Angeles (90066) *(P-17488)*

Arvato Services, Valencia *Also Called: Bertelsmann Inc (P-2884)*

Arvato USA LLC .... C 502 356-8063
2053 E Jay St Ontario (91764) *(P-14453)*

Arvin Post Acute, Arvin *Also Called: Pacs Group Inc (P-15735)*

Arvinyl Laminates LP .... D 951 371-7800
233 N Sherman Ave Corona (92882) *(P-3945)*

Aryzta Sweet Life, Santa Ana *Also Called: The Sweet Life Enterprises Inc (P-1409)*

Asa, Oxnard *Also Called: Advanced Structural Tech Inc (P-5140)*

Asab Inc (DH).......... C 818 551-7300
500 N Brand Blvd Fl 3 Glendale (91203) *(P-13339)*

Asacrete Inc .... C 818 398-3400
7117 Valjean Ave Van Nuys (91406) *(P-1102)*

Asai, Glendale *Also Called: Passport Technology Usa Inc (P-14781)*

Asbury, La Mirada *Also Called: Orange Courier Inc (P-14564)*

Asbury Environmental Services (PA).......... D 310 886-3400
1300 S Santa Fe Ave Compton (90221) *(P-8895)*

ASC, Valencia *Also Called: ASC Process Systems Inc (P-5690)*

ASC Engineered Solutions LLC .... D 800 766-0076
2867 Vail Ave Commerce (90040) *(P-5425)*

ASC Engineered Solutions LLC .... D 909 418-3233
551 N Loop Dr Ontario (91761) *(P-5426)*

ASC Group Inc .... B 818 896-1101
12243 Branford St Sun Valley (91352) *(P-6801)*

ASC Process Systems Inc (PA).......... C 818 833-0088
28402 Livingston Ave Valencia (91355) *(P-5690)*

Ascap, Los Angeles *Also Called: American Soc Cmpsers Athors Pb (P-2903)*

Ascend Healthcare, Los Angeles *Also Called: Ascend Healthcare LLC (P-17121)*

Ascend Healthcare LLC .... D 310 598-1840
11515 W Washington Blvd Los Angeles (90066) *(P-17121)*

Ascender Software Inc .... C 877 561-7501
8885 Rio San Diego Dr Ste 270 San Diego (92108) *(P-13885)*

Ascent Aerospace .... D 586 726-0500
1395 S Lyon St Santa Ana (92705) *(P-7695)*

Ascent Health Services LLC .... D 719 250-0824
27101 Puerta Real Ste 450 Mission Viejo (92691) *(P-15570)*

Ascent Manufacturing LLC .... E 714 540-6414
2545 W Via Palma Anaheim (92801) *(P-5173)*

Asco Sintering Co .... E 323 725-3550
2750 Garfield Ave Commerce (90040) *(P-4752)*

Ascot Hotel LP .... C 310 476-6411
170 N Church Ln Los Angeles (90049) *(P-12762)*

Aseptic Technology, Yorba Linda *Also Called: Aseptic Technology LLC (P-1348)*

Aseptic Technology LLC .... C 714 694-0168
24855 Corbit Pl Yorba Linda (92887) *(P-1348)*

Ash & Violet, Commerce *Also Called: Trixxi Clothing Company Inc (P-2075)*

Ash Holdings LLC .... D 909 793-2609
1620 W Fern Ave Redlands (92373) *(P-15571)*

Ashley & Vance Engineering Inc .... D 805 545-0010
1229 Carmel St San Luis Obispo (93401) *(P-17489)*

Ashley Furniture, Redlands *Also Called: Ashley Furniture Inds LLC (P-9050)*

Ashley Furniture Inds LLC .... B 909 825-4900
2250 W Lugonia Ave Redlands (92374) *(P-9050)*

Employee Codes: A=Over 500 employees, B=251-500
C=101-250, D=51-100, E=20-50, F=10-19, G=1-9

2025 Southern California
Business Directory and Buyers Guide

© Mergent Inc. 1-800-342-5647
943

Ashtel Dental, Ontario *Also Called: Ashtel Studios Inc (P-8363)*

Ashtel Studios Inc .... E 909 434-0911
1610 E Philadelphia St Ontario (91761) *(P-8363)*

Ashunya Inc .... D 714 385-1900
642 N Eckhoff St Orange (92868) *(P-13659)*

Ashworth Inc .... A 760 438-6610
2765 Loker Ave W Carlsbad (92010) *(P-2006)*

Ashworth Studio, Carlsbad *Also Called: Ashworth Inc (P-2006)*

ASI Hastings Inc .... C 619 590-9300
4870 Viewridge Ave Ste 200 San Diego (92123) *(P-742)*

Asi Heating, Air and Solar, San Diego *Also Called: ASI Hastings Inc (P-742)*

Asi Semiconductor Inc .... E 818 982-1200
24955 Avenue Kearny Valencia (91355) *(P-6802)*

Asia-Pacific California Inc .... E 626 281-8500
1710 S Del Mar Ave San Gabriel (91776) *(P-2780)*

Asian European Products Inc .... C 949 553-3900
18071 Fitch Fl 250 Irvine (92614) *(P-9812)*

Asian Pacific Family Center, Rosemead *Also Called: Pacific Clinics (P-15418)*

Asian Rehabilitation Svc Inc .... C 213 680-3790
312 N Spring St Ste B30 Los Angeles (90012) *(P-17047)*

Asiana Cuisine Enterprises Inc .... A 310 327-2223
22771 S Western Ave Ste 100 Torrance (90501) *(P-1741)*

Asics America Corporation (HQ) .... **C 949 453-8888**
7755 Irvine Center Dr Ste 400 Irvine (92618) *(P-10733)*

Asics Tiger, Irvine *Also Called: Asics America Corporation (P-10733)*

Asm Construction Inc .... E 619 449-1966
1947 John Towers Ave El Cajon (92020) *(P-4954)*

Asmb LLC .... D 949 347-7100
2021 Arizona Ave Santa Monica (90404) *(P-15572)*

Asml Us Inc .... B 760 443-6244
1 Viper Way Ste A Vista (92081) *(P-5691)*

Asml Us LLC .... B 858 385-6500
17075 Thornmint Ct San Diego (92127) *(P-5692)*

ASML US, Inc., Vista *Also Called: Asml Us Inc (P-5691)*

Asp Henry Holdings Inc .... A 310 955-9200
999 N Pacific Coast Hwy Ste 800 El Segundo (90245) *(P-12594)*

Aspen Medical Products LLC .... D 949 681-0200
6481 Oak Cyn Irvine (92618) *(P-8098)*

Aspen Surgery Center, Simi Valley *Also Called: Simi Vly Hosp & Hlth Care Svcs (P-16200)*

Asphalt Fabric and Engrg Inc .... D 562 997-4129
2683 Lime Ave Signal Hill (90755) *(P-8502)*

Aspire Bakeries Holdco LLC (HQ) .... **C 844 992-7747**
6701 Center Dr W Ste 850 Los Angeles (90045) *(P-1476)*

Aspire Bakeries LLC (DH) .... **C 844 992-7747**
6701 Center Dr W Ste 850 Los Angeles (90045) *(P-1477)*

Aspire Bakeries LLC .... B 818 904-8230
15963 Strathern St Van Nuys (91406) *(P-1478)*

Aspire Bakeries LLC .... C 714 478-4656
357 W Santa Ana Ave Bloomington (92316) *(P-1479)*

Aspire Bakeries LLC .... C 909 472-3500
1220 S Baker Ave Ontario (91761) *(P-10928)*

Aspire Bakeries LLC .... C 661 832-0409
6501 District Blvd Bakersfield (93313) *(P-10929)*

Aspirez Inc .... D 714 485-8104
1440 N Harbor Blvd Ste 900 Fullerton (92835) *(P-13660)*

Aspm-Sandiego, San Diego *Also Called: Allegis Residential Svcs Inc (P-17937)*

Aspyr, Costa Mesa *Also Called: Aspyr Holdings LLC (P-15043)*

Aspyr Holdings LLC .... B 714 651-1840
270 Baker St Ste 300 Costa Mesa (92626) *(P-15043)*

Assa Abloy AB .... A 949 672-4003
19701 Da Vinci Lake Forest (92610) *(P-7084)*

Assa Abloy ACC Door Cntrls Gro .... C 805 642-2600
4226 Transport St Ventura (93003) *(P-4753)*

Asset Management Tr Svcs LLC .... D 858 457-2202
1455 Frazee Rd Ste 500 San Diego (92108) *(P-17947)*

Asset Mktg Systems Insur Svcs .... D 888 303-8755
15050 Avenue Of Science Ste 100 San Diego (92128) *(P-18097)*

ASSICIATED STUDENTS, San Luis Obispo *Also Called: Associated Students Inc (P-16870)*

Assign Corporation .... C 818 247-7100
200 N Maryland Ave Ste 204 Glendale (91206) *(P-14197)*

Assisted Home Care, Northridge *Also Called: Assisted Home Recovery Inc (P-13488)*

Assisted Home Care, Thousand Oaks *Also Called: Staff Assistance Inc (P-13574)*

Assisted Home Recovery Inc (PA) .... **C 818 894-8117**
8550 Balboa Blvd Lbby Northridge (91325) *(P-13488)*

Associate Mech Contrs Inc .... C 760 294-3517
622 S Vinewood St Escondido (92029) *(P-743)*

Associated Desert Newspaper (DH) .... E 760 337-3400
205 N 8th St El Centro (92243) *(P-2781)*

Associated Desert Shoppers Inc (DH) .... D 760 346-1729
73400 Highway 111 Palm Desert (92260) *(P-2904)*

Associated Group, Los Angeles *Also Called: Associted Ldscp Display Group In (P-14454)*

Associated Intl Insur Co, Woodland Hills *Also Called: Markel Corp (P-12228)*

Associated Microbreweries Inc .... D 858 587-2739
9675 Scranton Rd San Diego (92121) *(P-1535)*

Associated Microbreweries Inc .... E 858 273-2739
5985 Santa Fe St San Diego (92109) *(P-1536)*

Associated Microbreweries Inc .... D 619 234-2739
1157 Columbia St San Diego (92101) *(P-1537)*

Associated Microbreweries Inc .... D 714 546-2739
901 S Coast Dr Ste A Costa Mesa (92626) *(P-1538)*

Associated Plating Company .... E 562 946-5525
9636 Ann St Santa Fe Springs (90670) *(P-5235)*

Associated Ready Mix Con Inc .... D 818 504-3100
8946 Bradley Ave Sun Valley (91352) *(P-4429)*

ASSOCIATED READY MIX CONCRETE, INC., Sun Valley *Also Called: Associated Ready Mix Con Inc (P-4429)*

Associated Ready Mixed Con Inc (PA) .... **E 949 253-2800**
4621 Teller Ave Ste 130 Newport Beach (92660) *(P-4430)*

Associated Students Inc (PA) .... **D 805 756-1281**
University Union Bldg 65 San Luis Obispo (93407) *(P-16870)*

Associated Students UCLA .... C 310 825-2787
308 Westwood Plz Ste 118 Los Angeles (90095) *(P-2782)*

Associated Students UCLA .... D 310 825-9451
650 Charles Young Dr S Rm 23120 Los Angeles (90095) *(P-15247)*

Associated Students UCLA .... C 310 206-8282
11000 Kinross Ave Ave Ste 245 Los Angeles (90095) *(P-16831)*

Associated Students UCLA .... C 310 794-0242
924 Westwood Blvd Los Angeles (90024) *(P-17214)*

Associated Students UCLA (PA) .... **B 310 794-8836**
308 Westwood Plz Los Angeles (90095) *(P-17215)*

Associated Third Party Administrators Inc .... B
222 N Pacific Coast Hwy Ste 2000 El Segundo (90245) *(P-12158)*

Associates First Capital Corp .... C 818 248-7055
3634 5th Ave Glendale (91214) *(P-11849)*

Associted Fgn Exch Holdings Inc (HQ) .... **D 818 386-2702**
21045 Califa St Woodland Hills (91367) *(P-11837)*

Associted Ldscp Dsplay Group In .... D 714 558-6100
1005 Mateo St Los Angeles (90021) *(P-14454)*

Associted McRbrwries Ltd A Cal .... E 858 273-2739
5985 Santa Fe St San Diego (92109) *(P-1539)*

AST Sportswear Inc (PA) .... **D 714 223-2030**
2701 E Imperial Hwy Brea (92821) *(P-2163)*

AST Sportswear Inc .... B 714 223-2030
Anaheim (92817) *(P-13300)*

Astea International Inc .... E 949 784-5000
8 Hughes Irvine (92618) *(P-13886)*

Astella, Jurupa Valley *Also Called: March Products Inc (P-8698)*

Asteres Inc (PA) .... **E 858 777-8600**
10650 Treena St Ste 105 San Diego (92131) *(P-5957)*

Astiva Health Inc .... D 858 707-5111
765 The City Dr S Ste 200 Orange (92868) *(P-16533)*

Astor Manufacturing .... E 661 645-5585
779 Anita St Ste B Chula Vista (91911) *(P-7435)*

Astra Oil Company Inc .... C 714 969-6569
301 Main St Ste 201 Huntington Beach (92648) *(P-11028)*

Astrion .... B 805 644-2191
4125 Market St Ste 12 Ventura (93003) *(P-17490)*

Astro Aluminum Treating Co .... D 562 923-4344
11040 Palmer Ave South Gate (90280) *(P-4697)*

Astro Chrome and Polsg Corp .... E 818 781-1463
8136 Lankershim Blvd North Hollywood (91605) *(P-5312)*

Astro Mechanical Contractors Inc .... D 619 442-9686
603 S Marshall Ave El Cajon (92020) *(P-744)*

Astro News, Lancaster *Also Called: Aerotech News and Review Inc (P-2843)*

Astro Seal Inc .... E 951 787-6670
827 Palmyrita Ave Ste B Riverside (92507) *(P-6968)*

Astro Spar Inc .... E 626 839-7858
3130 E Miraloma Ave Anaheim (92806) *(P-7436)*

Astrobotic Technology Inc .... D 888 488-8455
1570 Sabovich St Mojave (93501) *(P-7641)*

Astrochef LLC .... D 213 627-9860
1111 Mateo St Los Angeles (90021) *(P-1385)*

Astron Corporation .... E 949 458-7277
9 Autry Irvine (92618) *(P-6924)*

Astronic .... C 949 454-1180
2 Orion Aliso Viejo (92656) *(P-6710)*

Astronics Test Systems Inc (HQ)................... **C 800 722-2528**
2652 Mcgaw Ave Irvine (92614) *(P-7899)*

Astrophysics Inc (PA).................................. **C 909 598-5488**
21481 Ferrero City Of Industry (91789) *(P-8364)*

Asturies Manufacturing Co Inc .... E 951 270-1766
310 Cessna Cir Corona (92878) *(P-7437)*

Astute, San Diego *Also Called: Astute Medical Inc (P-17771)*

Astute Medical Inc .... D 858 792-3544
3550 General Atomics Ct Bldg 02/620 San Diego (92121) *(P-17771)*

Asucla Publications, Los Angeles *Also Called: Associated Students UCLA (P-2782)*

Asylum Research, Santa Barbara *Also Called: Oxford Instrs Asylum RES Inc (P-7970)*

At & T Wireless Service, Tustin *Also Called: AB Cellular Holding LLC (P-9425)*

At Apollo Technologies LLC .... E 949 888-0573
31441 Santa Margarita Pkwy Ste A219 Rcho Sta Marg (92688) *(P-3790)*

At Work, Tustin *Also Called: B2 Services Llc (P-13490)*

AT&T, San Diego *Also Called: New Cingular Wireless Svcs Inc (P-9405)*

AT&T Enterprises LLC .... D 949 581-1600
24321 Avenida De La Carlota Ste H3 Laguna Hills (92653) *(P-9382)*

AT&T Enterprises LLC .... B 714 284-2878
Rm 620 Anaheim (92805) *(P-9383)*

AT&T Enterprises LLC .... C 714 940-9976
2400 E Katella Ave Anaheim (92806) *(P-9384)*

AT&T Mobility LLC .... B 562 468-6142
12900 Park Plaza Dr Cerritos (90703) *(P-9385)*

Atara Bio, Thousand Oaks *Also Called: Atara Biotherapeutics Inc (P-3561)*

Atara Biotherapeutics Inc (PA)..................... **C 805 623-4211**
2380 Conejo Spectrum St Ste 200 Thousand Oaks (91320) *(P-3561)*

Atascadero State Hospital, Atascadero *Also Called: Califrnia Dept State Hospitals (P-16270)*

Atec Spine, Carlsbad *Also Called: Alphatec Spine Inc (P-8251)*

Atelier Luxury Group LLC .... E 310 751-2444
1330 Channing St Los Angeles (90021) *(P-2257)*

Ateliere Creative Tech Inc .... E 800 921-4252
315 S Beverly Dr Ste 315 Beverly Hills (90212) *(P-13887)*

Ateliere Crtive Tech Hldg Corp .... E 855 466-9696
315 S Beverly Dr Ste 315 Beverly Hills (90212) *(P-5903)*

Aten Technology Inc .... D 949 453-0702
15365 Barranca Pkwy Irvine (92618) *(P-9988)*

Atg - Designing Mobility Inc (DH).................. **E 562 921-0258**
11075 Knott Ave Ste B Cypress (90630) *(P-10064)*

Athas Capital Group Inc .... C 877 877-1477
27001 Agoura Rd Ste 100 Agoura Hills (91301) *(P-11939)*

Athens Disposal Company Inc (PA)................ **B 626 336-3636**
14048 Valley Blvd La Puente (91746) *(P-9731)*

Athens Environmental Services, Sun Valley *Also Called: Araco Enterprises LLC (P-9727)*

Athens Services, Sun Valley *Also Called: Arakelian Enterprises Inc (P-8894)*

Athens Services, City Of Industry *Also Called: Arakelian Enterprises Inc (P-9728)*

Athens Services, City Of Industry *Also Called: Arakelian Enterprises Inc (P-9729)*

Atherton Baptist Homes .... C 626 863-1710
214 S Atlantic Blvd Alhambra (91801) *(P-15573)*

Athleisure Inc .... E 858 866-0108
3126 Micaion Blvd Ste B San Diego (92109) *(P-11505)*

ATI, Anaheim *Also Called: ATI Restoration LLC (P-1195)*

ATI Forged Products, Irvine *Also Called: Chen-Tech Industries Inc (P-8130)*

ATI Restoration LLC .... C 951 682-9200
1175 Hall Ave Riverside (92509) *(P-389)*

ATI Restoration LLC (PA)............................. **C 714 283-9990**
3360 E La Palma Ave Anaheim (92806) *(P-1195)*

ATI Restoration LLC .... C 858 530-2400
8444 Miralani Dr Ste 200 San Diego (92126) *(P-18287)*

ATI Rstrtion Spring Vly CA Inc .... C 619 466-9876
2709 Via Orange Way Ste A Spring Valley (91978) *(P-1196)*

ATI Systems International Inc .... A 858 715-8484
8807 Complex Dr San Diego (92123) *(P-14277)*

ATI Windows, Riverside *Also Called: San Joaquin Window Inc (P-4901)*

Atk, San Diego *Also Called: Composite Optics Incorporated (P-7668)*

Atk Arspace Strctres Test Fclt, San Diego *Also Called: Atk Space Systems LLC (P-7697)*

Atk Audiotek, Valencia *Also Called: Sound River Corporation (P-962)*

Atk Launch Systems LLC .... B 858 592-2509
16707 Via Del Campo Ct San Diego (92127) *(P-7696)*

Atk Space Systems LLC .... D 858 487-0970
16707 Via Del Campo Ct San Diego (92127) *(P-7697)*

Atk Space Systems LLC .... C 858 530-3047
7130 Miramar Rd Ste 100b San Diego (92121) *(P-7698)*

Atk Space Systems LLC .... D 858 621-5700
7130 Miramar Rd Ste 100b San Diego (92121) *(P-7699)*

Atk Space Systems LLC .... D 805 685-2262
600 Pine Ave Goleta (93117) *(P-7700)*

Atk Space Systems LLC (DH)........................ E 323 722-0222
6033 Bandini Blvd Commerce (90040) *(P-7701)*

Atk Space Systems LLC .... D 310 343-3799
1960 E Grand Ave Ste 1150 El Segundo (90245) *(P-7702)*

Atk Space Systems LLC .... D 626 351-0205
370 N Halstead St Pasadena (91107) *(P-7703)*

Atkinson Andelson Loya, Cerritos *Also Called: Atkinson Andlson Loya Ruud Rom (P-16637)*

Atkinson Andlson Loya Ruud Rom (PA)........... **C 562 653-3200**
12800 Center Court Dr S Ste 300 Cerritos (90703) *(P-16637)*

Atkinson Construction Inc .... B 303 410-2540
611 Anton Blvd Costa Mesa (92626) *(P-608)*

Atlantic Box & Carton Company, Pico Rivera *Also Called: Jkv Inc (P-2678)*

Atlantic Diving Equipment, Santa Ana *Also Called: Xs Scuba Inc (P-8555)*

Atlantic Express of California, Long Beach *Also Called: Atlantic Express Trnsp (P-8813)*

Atlantic Express Trnsp .... B 562 997-6868
2450 Long Beach Blvd Long Beach (90806) *(P-8813)*

Atlantic Mem Healthcare Ctr, Long Beach *Also Called: Atlantic Mem Hlthcare Assoc In (P-15574)*

Atlantic Mem Hlthcare Assoc In (HQ)............. D 562 424-8101
2750 Atlantic Ave Long Beach (90806) *(P-15574)*

Atlantic Mem Hlthcare Assoc In .... D 562 494-3311
3801 E Anaheim St Long Beach (90804) *(P-15575)*

Atlantic Pacific Automotive, Jurupa Valley *Also Called: Highline Aftermarket LLC (P-9828)*

Atlantic Representations Inc .... E 562 903-9550
10018 Santa Fe Springs Rd Santa Fe Springs (90670) *(P-2463)*

Atlantic Richfield Company (DH)..................... A 800 333-3991
4 Centerpointe Dr La Palma (90623) *(P-11473)*

Atlantis Computing Inc .... E 650 917-9471
900 Glenneyre St Laguna Beach (92651) *(P-13888)*

Atlantis Seafood LLC .... D 626 626-4900
10501 Valley Blvd Ste 1820 El Monte (91731) *(P-1701)*

Atlas Advertising, Irvine *Also Called: M F Salta Co Inc (P-18164)*

Atlas Carpet Mills Inc .... C 323 724-7930
3201 S Susan St Santa Ana (92704) *(P-1947)*

Atlas Construction Supply Inc (PA)................. **D 858 277-2100**
4640 Brinnell St San Diego (92111) *(P-9936)*

Atlas Construction Supply Inc .... E 714 441-9500
7550 Stage Rd Buena Park (90621) *(P-9937)*

Atlas Copco, Santa Maria *Also Called: Atlas Copco Mafi-Trench Co LLC (P-5767)*

Atlas Copco Compressors LLC .... E 562 484-6370
16207 Carmenita Rd Cerritos (90703) *(P-5755)*

Atlas Copco Mafi-Trench Co LLC (DH)............ **C 805 928-5757**
3037 Industrial Pkwy Santa Maria (93455) *(P-5767)*

Atlas Galvanizing LLC .... E 323 587-6247
2639 Leonis Blvd Vernon (90058) *(P-5313)*

Atlas General Insur Svcs LLC .... C 858 529-6700
6165 Greenwich Dr Ste 200 San Diego (92122) *(P-12174)*

Atlas Hospitality Group .... D 949 622-3400
1901 Main St Ste 175 Irvine (92614) *(P-12382)*

Atlas Hotels Inc .... A 619 291-2232
500 Hotel Cir N San Diego (92108) *(P-12763)*

Atlas Lithium Corporation .... D 833 661-7900
433 N Camden Dr Ste 810 Beverly Hills (90210) *(P-384)*

Atlas Mechanical Inc (PA)....................................... D 858 554-0700
8260 Camino Santa Fe Ste B San Diego (92121) *(P-745)*

Atlas Pacific Corporation (PA)................................. E 909 421-1200
2803 Industrial Dr Bloomington (92316) *(P-10535)*

Atlas Roofing Corporation .... E 626 334-5358
2335 Roll Dr Ste 4121 San Diego (92154) *(P-3994)*

Atlas Survival Shelters LLC .... E 323 727-7084
7407 Telegraph Rd Montebello (90640) *(P-2464)*

Atmospheric-Greenscreen, Los Angeles *Also Called: Greenscreen (P-171)*

Atomica Corp .... C 805 681-2807
75 Robin Hill Rd Goleta (93117) *(P-6803)*

Atpa, El Segundo *Also Called: Associated Third Party Administrators Inc (P-12158)*

Atr Sales Inc .... E 714 432-8411
110 E Garry Ave Santa Ana (92707) *(P-5806)*

Atra-Flex, Santa Ana *Also Called: Atr Sales Inc (P-5806)*

Atrium Hotel, Irvine *Also Called: Golden Hotels Ltd Partnership (P-12828)*

Ats Systems, Rancho Santa Margari *Also Called: Ats Workholding Llc (P-5605)*

Ats Workholding Llc (PA).................................... E 800 321-1833
30222 Esperanza Rancho Santa Margari (92688) *(P-5605)*

Attainment Holdco LLC .... C 310 954-1578
840 Apollo St El Segundo (90245) *(P-17293)*

Atterdag Village of Solvang, Solvang *Also Called: Solvang Lutheran Home Inc (P-15781)*

Attn Inc .... C 323 413-2878
5700 Wilshire Blvd Ste 375 Los Angeles (90036) *(P-13259)*

Attollo Engineering, Camarillo *Also Called: Attollo Engineering LLC (P-6804)*

Attollo Engineering LLC .... D 805 384-8046
160 Camino Ruiz Camarillo (93012) *(P-6804)*

Attorney Network Services, Los Angeles *Also Called: Attorney Network Services Inc (P-13489)*

Attorney Network Services Inc .... D 213 430-0440
725 S Figueroa St Ste 3065 Los Angeles (90017) *(P-13489)*

Attorney Recovery Systems Inc (PA)........................ D 818 774-1420
18757 Burbank Blvd Ste 300 Tarzana (91356) *(P-13278)*

Atv Canter LLC (PA)... D 562 977-8565
2875 Pomona Blvd Pomona (91768) *(P-11440)*

Atx Networks (san Diego) Corp (DH)....................... E 858 546-5050
2800 Whiptail Loop Ste 6 Carlsbad (92010) *(P-6599)*

Atx Networks San Diego, Carlsbad *Also Called: Atx Networks (san Diego) Corp (P-6599)*

Atyr Pharma, San Diego *Also Called: Atyr Pharma Inc (P-3562)*

Atyr Pharma Inc (PA)... D 858 731-8389
10240 Sorrento Valley Rd Ste 300 San Diego (92121) *(P-3562)*

Auction.com, Irvine *Also Called: Auctioncom Inc (P-12383)*

Auction.com, Irvine *Also Called: Auctioncom LLC (P-12384)*

Auctioncom Inc .... C 800 499-6199
1 Mauchly Ste 27 Irvine (92618) *(P-12383)*

Auctioncom LLC (PA)... C 949 859-2777
1 Mauchly Irvine (92618) *(P-12384)*

Audacy Inc .... C 323 569-1070
5670 Wilshire Blvd Ste 200 Los Angeles (90036) *(P-9476)*

Audiencex, Venice *Also Called: Socialcom Inc (P-18216)*

Audio Images, Irvine *Also Called: Henrys Adio Vsual Slutions Inc (P-6542)*

Audio Video Color Corporation .... C 424 213-7500
17707 S Santa Fe Ave E Rncho Dmngz (90221) *(P-2704)*

Auditboard Inc (PA)... D 877 769-5444
12900 Park Plaza Dr Ste 200 Cerritos (90703) *(P-13661)*

Augerscope Inc .... E
10375 Wilshire Blvd Apt 1b Los Angeles (90024) *(P-4736)*

Augora Hills 8 Cinema Center, Agoura Hills *Also Called: Weststar Cinemas Inc (P-14945)*

August Accessories, Thousand Oaks *Also Called: August Hat Company Inc (P-2157)*

August Hat Company Inc (PA)............................... E 805 983-4651
2021 Calle Yucca Thousand Oaks (91360) *(P-2157)*

Augustine Casino, Coachella *Also Called: Augustine Gaming MGT Corp (P-13662)*

Augustine Gaming MGT Corp .... D 760 391-9500
84001 Avenue 54 Coachella (92236) *(P-13662)*

Aunt Rubys LLC .... E 562 326-6783
1014 E Carson St Long Beach (90807) *(P-18098)*

Auptix and Flock Freight, Encinitas *Also Called: Flock Freight Inc (P-9282)*

Aurasound Inc .... D 949 829-4000
1801 E Edinger Ave Ste 190 Santa Ana (92705) *(P-6528)*

Aurelio Felix Barreto III .... C 951 354-9528
169 Radio Rd Corona (92879) *(P-11506)*

Aurident Incorporated .... E 714 870-1851
610 S State College Blvd Fullerton (92831) *(P-8326)*

Aurora, Pico Rivera *Also Called: Aurora World Inc (P-10518)*

Aurora - San Diego LLC (DH) .... D 858 487-3200
11878 Avenue Of Industry San Diego (92128) *(P-16263)*

Aurora Behavioral Health Care .... D 818 515-4735
2900 E Del Mar Blvd Pasadena (91107) *(P-16264)*

AURORA BEHAVIORAL HEALTH CARE, Pasadena *Also Called: Aurora Behavioral Health Care (P-16264)*

Aurora Chrtr Oak - Los Angles .... C 626 966-1632
1161 E Covina Blvd Covina (91724) *(P-16265)*

Aurora Las Encinas LLC .... C 626 795-9901
2900 E Del Mar Blvd Pasadena (91107) *(P-16266)*

Aurora Las Encinas Hospital, Pasadena *Also Called: Aurora Las Encinas LLC (P-16266)*

Aurora World Inc .... C 562 205-1222
8820 Mercury Ln Pico Rivera (90660) *(P-10518)*

Ausgar Technologies Inc .... C 855 428-7427
10721 Treena St Ste 100 San Diego (92131) *(P-17491)*

Auspex Pharmaceuticals Inc .... E 858 558-2400
3333 N Torrey Pines Ct Ste 400 La Jolla (92037) *(P-3362)*

Austin Commercial LP .... D 619 446-5637
402 W Broadway Ste 400 San Diego (92101) *(P-518)*

Austin Commercial LP .... D 310 421-0269
5901 W Century Blvd Ste 600 Los Angeles (90045) *(P-519)*

Austin Sidley CA LLP .... C 213 896-6000
350 S Grand Ave Los Angeles (90071) *(P-16638)*

Austin Veum Rbbins Prtners Inc (PA)...................... D 619 231-1960
501 W Broadway Ste A San Diego (92101) *(P-17668)*

Authentic Entertainment .... D 747 529-8800
5200 Lankershim Blvd Ste 200 North Hollywood (91601) *(P-14955)*

Authorized Cellular Service .... D 310 466-4144
8808 S Sepulveda Blvd Los Angeles (90045) *(P-14728)*

Autism Otrach Southern Cal LLC .... D 619 795-9925
3110 Camino Del Rio S Ste 307 San Diego (92108) *(P-16871)*

Autism Spctrm Intrvntions LLC .... C 562 972-4846
713 W Commonwealth Ave Ste A Fullerton (92832) *(P-16872)*

Auto Club Enterprises (PA).................................. A 714 850-5111
3333 Fairview Rd Costa Mesa (92626) *(P-12057)*

Auto Club Enterprises .... B 310 914-8500
8761 Santa Monica Blvd West Hollywood (90069) *(P-12058)*

Auto Edge Solutions, Pacoima *Also Called: Moc Products Company Inc (P-3815)*

Auto Insurance Specialists LLC (DH)....................... C 562 345-6247
17785 Center Court Dr N Ste 110 Cerritos (90703) *(P-12175)*

Auto Motive Power Inc .... C 800 894-7104
11643 Telegraph Rd Santa Fe Springs (90670) *(P-7229)*

Auto Pride, Anaheim *Also Called: Cal-State Auto Parts Inc (P-9818)*

Auto Trend Products, Vernon *Also Called: Punch Press Products Inc (P-5594)*

Auto Value, San Bernardino *Also Called: Metropolitan Automotive Warehouse (P-9834)*

Autocrib Inc .... C 714 274-0400
2882 Dow Ave Tustin (92780) *(P-14455)*

Autograph Collection Hotels, Pismo Beach *Also Called: Vpb Operating Co LLC (P-13067)*

Autoliv Akr Fcilty -Casa Whse, San Diego *Also Called: Autoliv Asp Inc (P-2272)*

Autoliv Asp Inc .... E 619 662-8018
9355 Airway Rd San Diego (92154) *(P-2272)*

Autoliv Safety Technology Inc .... A 619 662-8000
2475 Paseo De Las Americas Ste A San Diego (92154) *(P-2273)*

Automatic Data Processing Inc .... C 949 751-0360
3972 Barranca Pkwy Ste J610 Irvine (92606) *(P-14122)*

Automatic Data Processing Inc .... C 800 225-5237
400 W Covina Blvd San Dimas (91773) *(P-14123)*

Automatic Screw Mch Pdts Co, Brea *Also Called: Nelson Stud Welding Inc (P-10452)*

Automation Holdco Inc .... D 858 967-8650
10815 Rancho Bernardo Rd Ste 102 San Diego (92127) *(P-14071)*

Automation Plating Corporation .... E 323 245-4951
927 Thompson Ave Glendale (91201) *(P-5236)*

Mergent email: customerrelations@mergent.com
946

2025 Southern California
Business Directory and Buyers Guide

(P-0000) Products & Services Section entry number
(PA)=Parent Co (HQ)=Headquarters (DH)=Div Headquarters

Automax Styling Inc .... E 951 530-1876
16833 Krameria Ave Riverside (92504) *(P-7230)*

Automobile Club Southern Cal (PA) .... C 213 741-3686
2601 S Figueroa St Los Angeles (90007) *(P-12176)*

Automobile Club Southern Cal .... C 714 973-1211
13331 Jamboree Rd Irvine (92602) *(P-12177)*

Automobile Club Southern Cal .... C 714 885-1343
3333 Fairview Rd Costa Mesa (92626) *(P-12178)*

Automobile Club Southern Cal .... C 805 922-5731
2033b S Broadway Santa Maria (93454) *(P-12179)*

Automobile Club Southern Cal .... C 619 464-7001
8765 Fletcher Pkwy La Mesa (91942) *(P-12180)*

Automobile Club Southern Cal .... C 909 591-9451
5402 Philadelphia St Ste A Chino (91710) *(P-17426)*

Automobile Club Southern Cal .... C 858 483-4960
4973 Clairemont Dr Ste C San Diego (92117) *(P-17427)*

Automobile Club Southern Cal .... C 619 233-1000
2440 Hotel Cir N Ste 100 San Diego (92108) *(P-17428)*

Automobile Club Southern Cal .... D 760 433-6261
3330 Vista Way Oceanside (92056) *(P-17429)*

Automobile Club Southern Cal .... C 760 745-2124
800 La Terraza Blvd Escondido (92025) *(P-17430)*

Automobile Club Southern Cal .... D 858 486-0786
12630 Sabre Springs Pkwy Ste 301 San Diego (92128) *(P-17431)*

Automobile Club Southern Cal .... C 951 684-4250
3700 Central Ave Riverside (92506) *(P-17432)*

Automobile Club Southern Cal .... D 951 652-6202
450 W Stetson Ave Hemet (92543) *(P-17433)*

Automobile Club Southern Cal .... D 951 808-9624
1170 El Camino Ave Corona (92879) *(P-17434)*

Automobile Club Southern Cal .... C 310 453-1909
2730 Santa Monica Blvd Santa Monica (90404) *(P-17435)*

Automobile Club Southern Cal .... D 562 425-8350
4800 Airport Plaza Dr Ste 100 Long Beach (90815) *(P-17436)*

Automobile Club Southern Cal .... D 562 924-6636
18642 Gridley Rd Artesia (90701) *(P-17437)*

Automobile Club Southern Cal .... C 323 525-0018
8761 Santa Monica Blvd West Hollywood (90069) *(P-17438)*

Automobile Club Southern Cal .... D 661 327-4661
1500 Commercial Way Bakersfield (93309) *(P-17439)*

Automobile Club Southern Cal .... C 310 325-3111
23001 Hawthorne Blvd Torrance (90505) *(P-17440)*

Automobile Club Southern Cal .... D 626 963-8531
1301s S Grand Ave Glendora (91740) *(P-17441)*

Automobile Club Southern Cal .... D 818 993-1616
9440 Reseda Blvd Northridge (91324) *(P-17442)*

Automobile Club Southern Cal .... D 562 904-5970
8223 Firestone Blvd Downey (90241) *(P-17443)*

Automobile Club Southern Cal .... C 310 376-0521
700 S Aviation Blvd Manhattan Beach (90266) *(P-17444)*

Automobile Club Southern Cal .... D 626 795-0601
801 E Union St Pasadena (91101) *(P-17445)*

Automobile Club Southern Cal .... D 818 883-2660
22708 Victory Blvd Woodland Hills (91367) *(P-17446)*

Automobile Club Southern Cal .... D 310 673 5170
1234 Centinela Ave Inglewood (90302) *(P-17447)*

Automobile Club Southern Cal .... D 562 698-3721
16041 Whittier Blvd Whittier (90603) *(P-17448)*

Automobile Club Southern Cal .... C 661 259-6222
23770 Valencia Blvd Ste 100 Valencia (91355) *(P-17449)*

Automobile Club Southern Cal .... D 805 543-6454
1445 Calle Joaquin San Luis Obispo (93405) *(P-17450)*

Automobile Club Southern Cal .... C 805 682-5811
3712 State St Santa Barbara (93105) *(P-17451)*

Automobile Club Southern Cal .... D 805 735-2731
525 W Central Ave Lompoc (93436) *(P-17452)*

Automobile Club Southern Cal .... D 805 497-0911
100 E Wilbur Rd Thousand Oaks (91360) *(P-17453)*

Automobile Club Southern Cal .... C 714 774-2392
420 N Euclid St Anaheim (92801) *(P-17454)*

Automobile Club Southern Cal .... D 949 476-8880
3880 Birch St Newport Beach (92660) *(P-17455)*

Automobile Club Southern Cal .... D 949 489-5572
638 Camino De Los Mares Ste E100 San Clemente (92673) *(P-17456)*

Automobile Club Southern Cal .... D 949 951-1400
25181 Paseo De Alicia Laguna Hills (92653) *(P-17457)*

Automotive Aftermarket Inc .... D 310 793-0046
15912 Hawthorne Blvd Lawndale (90260) *(P-9813)*

Automotive Racing Products Inc .... D 805 525-1497
1760 E Lemonwood Dr Santa Paula (93060) *(P-4754)*

Automotive Racing Products Inc (PA) .... D 805 339-2200
1863 Eastman Ave Ventura (93003) *(P-4755)*

Automotive Tstg & Dev Svcs Inc (PA) .... C 909 390-1100
400 Etiwanda Ave Ontario (91761) *(P-14713)*

Autonation Finance, Irvine *Also Called: Cig Financial LLC (P-11852)*

Autonation Ford Valencia, Valencia *Also Called: Magic Acquisition Corp (P-11376)*

Autonomous Defense Tech Corp .... E 805 616-2030
2889 W 5th St Ste 111 Oxnard (93030) *(P-14384)*

Autonomous Medical Devices Inc (PA) .... E 657 660-6800
3511 W Sunflower Ave Santa Ana (92704) *(P-7938)*

Autonomous Medical Devices Inc .... E 310 641-2700
10524 S La Cienega Blvd Inglewood (90304) *(P-7939)*

Autosplice, San Diego *Also Called: Autosplice Parent Inc (P-6411)*

Autosplice Parent Inc (PA) .... C 858 535-0077
10431 Wateridge Cir Ste 110 San Diego (92121) *(P-6411)*

Autostore Integrator, Valencia *Also Called: Sdi Industries Inc (P-5518)*

Autovitals Inc .... D 866 949-2848
4141 Jutland Dr Ste 300 San Diego (92117) *(P-14198)*

Autry Museum, Los Angeles *Also Called: Autry Museum of American West (P-17249)*

Autry Museum of American West .... C 323 667-2000
4700 Western Heritage Way Los Angeles (90027) *(P-17249)*

Autumn Hills Convalescent Home, Glendale *Also Called: Mariner Health Care Inc (P-15714)*

Auxilary of Mssion Hosp Mssion .... A 949 364-1400
27700 Medical Center Rd Mission Viejo (92691) *(P-15919)*

Ava Enterprises Inc (PA) .... D 805 988-0192
3451 Lunar Ct Oxnard (93030) *(P-10214)*

Avadyne Health, San Diego *Also Called: H & R Accounts Inc (P-13741)*

Avalon Apparel LLC .... D 323 440-4344
1901 W Center St Colton (92324) *(P-2059)*

Avalon Apparel LLC (PA) .... C 323 581-3511
2520 W 6th St Los Angeles (90057) *(P-2060)*

Avalon At Newport LLC .... D 949 719-4082
23 Corporate Plaza Dr Ste 190 Newport Beach (92660) *(P-15807)*

Avalon Building Maint Inc .... B 714 693-2407
1832 Commercenter Cir San Bernardino (92408) *(P-13357)*

Avalon Communications, Hawthorne *Also Called: Technology Training Corp (P-3088)*

Avalon Hotel, Beverly Hills *Also Called: Honeymoon Real Estate LP (P-12853)*

Avalon Medical Dev Corp .... D 310 510-0700
100 Falls Canyon Rd Avalon (90704) *(P-15920)*

Avalon Shutters Inc .... D 909 937-4900
3407 N Perris Blvd Perris (92571) *(P-2298)*

Avalon Transportation Co, Culver City *Also Called: Virgin Fish Inc (P-8853)*

Avamar Technologies Inc .... D 949 743-5100
135 Technology Dr Irvine (92618) *(P-13663)*

Avanir Pharmaceuticals Inc (DH) .... D 949 389-6700
30 Enterprise Ste 200 Aliso Viejo (92656) *(P-3383)*

Avanquest North America LLC (HQ) .... D 818 591-9600
23801 Calabasas Rd Ste 2005 Calabasas (91302) *(P-13664)*

Avante Health Solutions, San Clemente *Also Called: Pacific Medical Group Inc (P-10099)*

Avantgarde Senior Living .... C 818 881-0055
5645 Lindley Ave Tarzana (91356) *(P-17122)*

Avantus Aerospace Inc .... E 562 633-6626
14957 Gwenchris Ct Paramount (90723) *(P-4756)*

Avantus Aerospace Inc (DH) .... C 661 295-8620
29101 The Old Rd Valencia (91355) *(P-7438)*

Avasant LLC (PA) .... D 310 643-3030
1960 E Grand Ave Ste 1050 El Segundo (90245) *(P-18099)*

Avatar Machine LLC .... E 714 434-2737
18100 Mount Washington St Fountain Valley (92708) *(P-6085)*

Avatar Technology Inc .... E 909 598-7696
339 Cheryl Ln City Of Industry (91789) *(P-9989)*

Avco Financial, Glendale *Also Called: Associates First Capital Corp (P-11849)*

Avd, Newport Beach *Also Called: American Vanguard Corporation (P-3750)*

Avenue Medical Equipment Inc .... E 949 680-7444
38062 Encanto Rd Murrieta (92563) *(P-10065)*

Avenue of Arts Wyndham Hotel, Costa Mesa *Also Called: Rosanna Inc (P-13001)*

Aveox Inc .... E 805 915-0200
2265 Ward Ave Ste A Simi Valley (93065) *(P-6368)*

Avery Corp .... C 626 304-2000
207 N Goode Ave Fl 6 Glendale (91203) *(P-17772)*

Avery Dennison Corporation .... C 626 304-2000
2900 Bradley St Pasadena (91107) *(P-2715)*

Avery Dennison Corporation .... D 909 987-4631
11195 Eucalyptus St Rancho Cucamonga (91730) *(P-2716)*

Avery Dennison Corporation .... B 714 674-8500
50 Pointe Dr Brea (92821) *(P-2717)*

Avery Dennison Foundation .... E 626 304-2000
207 N Goode Ave Ste 500 Glendale (91203) *(P-2718)*

Avery Dennison Office Products Co Inc .... A
50 Pointe Dr Brea (92821) *(P-2755)*

Avery Dnnson Ret Info Svcs LLC (HQ) .... D 626 304-2000
207 N Goode Ave Fl 6 Glendale (91203) *(P-2756)*

Avery Group Inc .... B 310 217-1070
8941 Dalton Ave Los Angeles (90047) *(P-11665)*

Avery Products Corporation (DH) .... C 714 674-8500
50 Pointe Dr Brea (92821) *(P-2757)*

Avery Products Corporation .... C 619 671-1022
6987 Calle De Linea Ste 101 San Diego (92154) *(P-2758)*

Aveta Health Solution Inc .... C 909 605-8000
3990 Concours Ste 500 Ontario (91764) *(P-18100)*

Aveva Software LLC .... C 760 268-7700
5850 El Camino Real Carlsbad (92008) *(P-13665)*

Aveva Software LLC (DH) .... B 949 727-3200
26561 Rancho Pkwy S Lake Forest (92630) *(P-14072)*

Aviar Golf Club, Carlsbad *Also Called: Four Seasons Resort Aviara (P-15080)*

Aviara Fsrc Associates Limited .... A 760 603-6800
7100 Aviara Resort Dr Carlsbad (92011) *(P-12764)*

Aviation & Defense Inc .... C 909 382-3487
255 S Leland Norton Way San Bernardino (92408) *(P-9190)*

Aviation Consultants Inc .... D 949 201-2550
19301 Campus Dr Santa Ana (92707) *(P-9191)*

Aviation Consultants Inc .... D 805 596-0212
4900 Wing Way Paso Robles (93446) *(P-9192)*

Aviation Design Group Inc .... E 818 350-1900
9060 Winnetka Ave Northridge (91324) *(P-7439)*

Aviation Equipment Processing, Costa Mesa *Also Called: Flare Group (P-7474)*

Aviation Maintenance Group Inc .... D 714 469-0515
8352 Kimball Ave Hngr 3 Chino (91708) *(P-9193)*

Avibank, North Hollywood *Also Called: Avibank Mfg Inc (P-7440)*

Avibank Mfg Inc .... D 661 257-2329
25323 Rye Canyon Rd Valencia (91355) *(P-4757)*

Avibank Mfg Inc (DH) .... C 818 392-2100
11500 Sherman Way North Hollywood (91605) *(P-7440)*

Avid, Norco *Also Called: Avid Idntification Systems Inc (P-6805)*

Avid, Burbank *Also Called: Avid Technology Inc (P-8421)*

Avid Bioservices, Tustin *Also Called: Avid Bioservices Inc (P-3364)*

Avid Bioservices, Tustin *Also Called: Pphm Inc (P-10646)*

Avid Bioservices Inc (PA) .... C 714 508-6100
14191 Myford Rd Tustin (92780) *(P-3364)*

Avid Bioservices Inc .... D 714 508-6000
14272 Franklin Ave Ste 115 Tustin (92780) *(P-3365)*

Avid Bioservices Inc .... E 714 508-6166
14282 Franklin Ave Tustin (92780) *(P-3366)*

Avid Idntification Systems Inc (PA) .... D 951 371-7505
3185 Hamner Ave Norco (92860) *(P-6805)*

Avid Technology Inc .... D 818 557-2520
101 S 1st St Ste 200 Burbank (91502) *(P-8421)*

Avidex Industries LLC .... D 949 428-6333
20382 Hermana Cir Lake Forest (92630) *(P-14199)*

AVIDITY BIOSCIENCES, San Diego *Also Called: Avidity Biosciences Inc (P-3367)*

Avidity Biosciences Inc (PA) .... E 858 401-7900
10578 Science Center Dr Ste 125 San Diego (92121) *(P-3367)*

Avient Colorants USA LLC .... D 909 606-1325
14355 Ramona Ave Chino (91710) *(P-3727)*

Avilas Garden Art (PA) .... D 909 350-4546
14608 Merrill Ave Fontana (92335) *(P-4381)*

Avion Graphics Inc .... E 949 472-0438
27192 Burbank Foothill Ranch (92610) *(P-2965)*

Avis Roto Die Co .... E 323 255-7070
1560 N San Fernando Rd Los Angeles (90065) *(P-5567)*

AVITA MEDICAL, Valencia *Also Called: Avita Medical Americas LLC (P-10066)*

Avita Medical Americas LLC .... C 661 367-9170
28159 Avenue Stanford Ste 220 Valencia (91355) *(P-10066)*

Avitex Inc (PA) .... C 818 994-6487
20362 Plummer St Chatsworth (91311) *(P-1870)*

AVIVA FAMILY & CHILDREN'S SERV, Los Angeles *Also Called: Hamburger Home (P-17157)*

Aviva Family & Childrens Svcs (PA) .... D 323 876-0550
1701 Camino Palmero St Los Angeles (90046) *(P-16873)*

Avjet Corporation (DH) .... D 818 841-6190
4301 W Empire Ave Burbank (91505) *(P-9180)*

Avmc, Lancaster *Also Called: Antelope Valley Health Care Di (P-15913)*

Avn Media Network Inc .... E 818 718-5788
9400 Penfield Ave Chatsworth (91311) *(P-2883)*

Avocado Packer & Shipper, Murrieta *Also Called: West Pak Avocado Inc (P-122)*

Avr Global Tech, Escondido *Also Called: Avr Global Technologies Inc (P-6969)*

Avr Global Technologies Inc (PA) .... C 949 391-1180
500 La Terraza Blvd Ste 150 Escondido (92025) *(P-6969)*

Avt Inc .... E 951 737-1057
341 Bonnie Cir Ste 102 Corona (92880) *(P-5961)*

AVX Filters Corporation .... D 818 767-6770
11144 Penrose St Sun Valley (91352) *(P-5812)*

AW Die Engraving Inc .... E 714 521-7910
8550 Roland St Buena Park (90621) *(P-5568)*

Award Metals, Jurupa Valley *Also Called: Pacific Award Metals Inc (P-5013)*

Award Metals, Baldwin Park *Also Called: Pacific Award Metals Inc (P-5014)*

Award-Superstars .... D 619 593-4300
1530 Hilton Head Rd Ste 201 El Cajon (92019) *(P-12385)*

Aware Products LLC .... C 818 206-6700
9250 Mason Ave Chatsworth (91311) *(P-3632)*

Awe, San Diego *Also Called: Herring Networks Inc (P-9507)*

Awesome Products Inc (PA) .... C 714 562-8873
6370 Altura Blvd Buena Park (90620) *(P-3598)*

Awhap Acquisition Corp .... C 888 611-4328
28358 Constellation Rd Ste 698 Valencia (91355) *(P-746)*

AWI Management Corporation .... C 951 674-8200
1800 E Lakeshore Dr Lake Elsinore (92530) *(P-17948)*

Awnings.com, Cerritos *Also Called: Eide Industries Inc (P-2237)*

Awo, Vista *Also Called: Advanced Web Offset Inc (P-3114)*

Awr, San Dimas *Also Called: American States Water Company (P-9682)*

Axelacare Holdings Inc .... B 714 522-8802
12604 Hiddencreek Way Ste C Cerritos (90703) *(P-16366)*

Axelgaard, Fallbrook *Also Called: Axelgaard Manufacturing Co (P-8369)*

Axelgaard Manufacturing, Fallbrook *Also Called: Axelgaard Manufacturing Co (P-8370)*

Axelgaard Manufacturing Co (PA) .... D 760 723-7554
520 Industrial Way Fallbrook (92028) *(P-8369)*

Axelgaard Manufacturing Co .... E 760 723-7554
329 W Aviation Rd Fallbrook (92028) *(P-8370)*

Axelliant LLC .... D 424 535-1100
2640 Main St Irvine (92614) *(P-11538)*

Axeon Water Technologies .... D 760 723-5417
40980 County Center Dr Ste 100 Temecula (92591) *(P-6003)*

Axiom Label & Packaging, Compton *Also Called: Resource Label Group LLC (P-3109)*

Axiom Label Group, Compton *Also Called: Kmr Label LLC (P-3107)*

Axiom Materials Inc .... E 949 623-4400
2320 Pullman St Santa Ana (92705) *(P-3760)*

Axiom Medical Incorporated .... E 310 533-9020
19320 Van Ness Ave Torrance (90501) *(P-8099)*

Axiom Memory Solutions Inc .... D 949 581-1450
16 Goodyear Ste 120 Irvine (92618) *(P-9990)*

Axium Packaging LLC .... A 909 969-0766
5701 Clark St Ontario (91761) *(P-4056)*

Axon Networks Inc (PA) .... D 949 310-4429
15420 Laguna Canyon Rd Ste 150 Irvine (92618) *(P-13666)*

2025 Southern California
Business Directory and Buyers Guide
(P-0000) Products & Services Section entry number
(PA)=Parent Co (HQ)=Headquarters (DH)=Div Headquarters

Axonics Inc (PA) .... A 949 396-6322
26 Technology Dr Irvine (92618) *(P-17773)*

Axxis Arms, Perris *Also Called: Axxis Corporation (P-6086)*

Axxis Corporation .... E 951 436-9921
1535 Nandina Ave Perris (92571) *(P-6086)*

Aya Healthcare Inc (PA) .... C 858 458-4410
5930 Cornerstone Ct W Ste 300 San Diego (92121) *(P-13591)*

Aya Living Inc .... C 619 446-6469
1450 Frazee Rd San Diego (92108) *(P-16874)*

Aya Locums Services Inc .... A 866 687-7390
5930 Cornerstone Ct W Ste 300 San Diego (92121) *(P-16534)*

Ayo Food, Delano *Also Called: Ayo Foods LLC (P-1324)*

Ayo Foods LLC .... E 661 345-5457
927 Main St Delano (93215) *(P-1324)*

Ayres - Paso Robles LP .... C 714 850-0409
2700 Buena Vista Dr Paso Robles (93446) *(P-12765)*

AZ Construction Inc (PA) .... C 626 333-0727
727 Glendora Ave La Puente (91744) *(P-390)*

AZ Displays Inc .... E 949 831-5000
2410 Birch St Vista (92081) *(P-6970)*

AZ Manufacturing, Santa Ana *Also Called: A-Z Mfg Inc (P-6061)*

Aza Industries Inc (PA) .... E 760 560-0440
1410 Vantage Ct Vista (92081) *(P-8503)*

Azaa Investments Inc (PA) .... E 858 569-8111
6602 Convoy Ct Ste 200 San Diego (92111) *(P-7168)*

Azalea Systems Corp Inc .... E 951 547-5910
820 E Parkridge Ave Corona (92879) *(P-2966)*

Azimc Investments Inc .... C 818 678-1200
8901 Canoga Ave Canoga Park (91304) *(P-9814)*

Azira LLC .... C 606 889-7680
80 S Lake Ave Ste 719 Pasadena (91101) *(P-13197)*

Azitex Knitting Mills, Los Angeles *Also Called: Azitex Trading Corp (P-1928)*

Azitex Trading Corp .... D 213 745-7072
1850 E 15th St Los Angeles (90021) *(P-1928)*

Aztec Landscaping Inc (PA) .... C 619 464-3303
7980 Lemon Grove Way Lemon Grove (91945) *(P-198)*

Aztec Manufacturing Inc (PA) .... E 858 513-4350
13821 Danielson St Poway (92064) *(P-5119)*

Aztec Tents, Torrance *Also Called: A-Aztec Rents & Sells Inc (P-2233)*

Aztec Washer Company, Poway *Also Called: Aztec Manufacturing Inc (P-5119)*

Azteca Landscape .... D 951 369-9210
4073 Mennes Ave Riverside (92509) *(P-148)*

Aztecs Telecom, Corona *Also Called: Aztecs Telecom Inc (P-14456)*

Aztecs Telecom Inc .... D 714 373-1560
1353 Walker Ln Corona (92879) *(P-14456)*

Azul Hospitality Group Inc .... C 619 223-4200
800 W Ivy St Ste D San Diego (92101) *(P-17949)*

Azumex Corp .... E 619 710-8855
2320 Paseo De Las Americas San Diego (92154) *(P-1497)*

Azure Microdynamics Inc .... D 949 699-3344
19652 Descartes Foothill Ranch (92610) *(P-6087)*

Azusa Lights & Water Dept, Azusa *Also Called: City of Azusa (P-9683)*

Azusa Rock LLC .... E 619 440-2363
3605 Dehesa Rd El Cajon (92019) *(P-371)*

B & B Nurseries Inc .... C 951 352-8383
9505 Cleveland Ave Riverside (92503) *(P-11081)*

B & B Pipe and Tool Co (PA) .... E 562 424-0704
3035 Walnut Ave Long Beach (90807) *(P-317)*

B & B Pipe and Tool Co .... E 661 323-8208
2301 Parker Ln Bakersfield (93308) *(P-6088)*

B & B Plastics Recyclers Inc (PA) .... E 909 829-3606
3040 N Locust Ave Rialto (92377) *(P-10536)*

B & B Specialties Inc (PA) .... D 714 985-3000
4321 E La Palma Ave Anaheim (92807) *(P-4758)*

B & B Specialties Inc .... D 714 985-3075
4321 E La Palma Ave Anaheim (92807) *(P-10302)*

B & C Nutritional Products Inc .... D 714 238-7225
2995 E Miraloma Ave Anaheim (92806) *(P-3310)*

B & E Manufacturing Co Inc .... E 714 898-2269
12151 Monarch St Garden Grove (92841) *(P-7441)*

B & G House of Printing, Gardena *Also Called: Matsuda House Printing Inc (P-3042)*

B & M Contractors Inc .... D 805 581-5480
4473 Cochran St Simi Valley (93063) *(P-1103)*

B & S Plastics Inc .... C 805 981-0262
2200 Sturgis Rd Oxnard (93030) *(P-4057)*

B & W, Carlsbad *Also Called: Equity International Inc (P-10243)*

B & W Tile Co Inc (PA) .... E 310 538-9579
14600 S Western Ave Gardena (90249) *(P-11520)*

B & W Tile Manufacturing, Gardena *Also Called: B & W Tile Co Inc (P-11520)*

B and P Plastics Inc .... E 619 477-1893
225 W 30th St National City (91950) *(P-4058)*

B and Z Printing Inc .... E 714 892-2000
1300 E Wakeham Ave # B Santa Ana (92705) *(P-2967)*

B B Blu, Los Angeles *Also Called: Treivush Industries Inc (P-2140)*

B B G Management Group (PA) .... E 909 797-9581
12164 California St Yucaipa (92399) *(P-10840)*

B B S I, San Diego *Also Called: Barrett Business Services Inc (P-13491)*

B Braun Medical Inc .... D 909 906-7575
1151 Mildred St Ste B Ontario (91761) *(P-8100)*

B Braun US Phrm Mfg LLC .... A 610 691-5400
2525 Mcgaw Ave Irvine (92614) *(P-8101)*

B C I, San Diego *Also Called: Brehm Communications Inc (P-2973)*

B C S, Canoga Park *Also Called: Buyers Consultation Svc Inc (P-10235)*

B E & P Enterprises LLC (PA) .... E 909 591-7561
5167 G St Chino (91710) *(P-2409)*

B E B E, Los Angeles *Also Called: Bebe Studio Inc (P-11528)*

B F, Riverside *Also Called: Brenner-Fiedler & Assoc Inc (P-8035)*

B F I Labels, Yorba Linda *Also Called: Beckers Fabrication Inc (P-2719)*

B J Bindery Inc .... D 714 835-7342
833 S Grand Ave Santa Ana (92705) *(P-3201)*

B Jacqueline and Assoc Inc .... D 626 844-1400
1192 N Lake Ave Pasadena (91104) *(P-13667)*

B L S Limousine Service, Los Angeles *Also Called: Bls Lmsine Svc Los Angeles Inc (P-8814)*

B M S, Poway *Also Called: Broadcast Microwave Svcs LLC (P-6602)*

B M W of Riverside, Riverside *Also Called: David A Campbell Corporation (P-11332)*

B P W, Santa Fe Springs *Also Called: Brown-Pacific Inc (P-4512)*

B Riley Financial Inc (PA) .... D 310 966-1444
11100 Santa Monica Blvd Ste 800 Los Angeles (90025) *(P-14457)*

B T I, City Of Industry *Also Called: Battery Technology Inc (P-7072)*

B Young Enterprises Inc .... D 858 748-0935
12254 Iavelli Way Poway (92064) *(P-2339)*

B-Metal Holding Company Inc .... E 951 367-1510
12790 Holly St Riverside (92509) *(P-4511)*

B-Reel Films Inc .... E 917 388-3836
8383 Wilshire Blvd Ste 1000 Beverly Hills (90211) *(P-5842)*

B-Spring Valley LLC .... D 619 797-3991
9009 Campo Rd Spring Valley (91977) *(P-15576)*

B. Riley, Los Angeles *Also Called: B Riley Financial Inc (P-14457)*

B/E Aerospace Inc .... C 714 896-9001
7155 Fenwick Ln Westminster (92683) *(P-7442)*

B/E Aerospace Macrolink .... E 714 777-8800
1500 N Kellogg Dr Anaheim (92807) *(P-7443)*

B&B Industrial Services Inc (PA) .... B 909 428-3167
14549 Manzanita Dr Fontana (92335) *(P-980)*

B&B Manufacturing Co (PA) .... C 661 257-2161
27940 Beale Ct Santa Clarita (91355) *(P-6089)*

B&C Liquidating Corp (HQ) .... C 626 799-7000
3475 E Foothill Blvd Ste 100 Pasadena (91107) *(P-12181)*

B&D Investment Partners Inc (PA) .... E
20950 Centre Pointe Pkwy Santa Clarita (91350) *(P-3599)*

B2 Services Llc .... D 714 363-3481
17291 Irvine Blvd Ste 258 Tustin (92780) *(P-13490)*

B2b Payroll Services, Cypress *Also Called: B2b Staffing Services Inc (P-13592)*

B2b Staffing Services Inc .... B 714 243-4104
4501 Cerritos Ave Ste 201 Cypress (90630) *(P-13592)*

Ba Holdings Inc (DH) .... E 951 684-5110
3016 Kansas Ave Bldg 1 Riverside (92507) *(P-4909)*

Baatz Enterprises Inc .... E 323 660-4866
2223 W San Bernardino Rd West Covina (91790) *(P-7169)*

Babcock Enterprises Inc .... E 805 736-1455
5175 E Highway 246 Lompoc (93436) *(P-30)*

Employee Codes: A=Over 500 employees, B=251-500
C=101-250, D=51-100, E=20-50, F=10-19, G=1-9

2025 Southern California
Business Directory and Buyers Guide

© Mergent Inc. 1-800-342-5647

949

ALPHABETIC

Babcock Laboratories Inc .... D 951 653-3351
6100 Quail Valley Ct Riverside (92507) *(P-17905)*

Babcock Vineyards, Lompoc *Also Called: Babcock Enterprises Inc (P-30)*

Baby Phat, Commerce *Also Called: BP Clothing LLC (P-10702)*

Babyfirst Americas LLC .... D 310 442-9853
10390 Santa Monica Blvd Ste 310 Los Angeles (90025) *(P-13668)*

Babylon International LLC .... E 323 433-4104
16520 Bake Pkwy Ste 230 Irvine (92618) *(P-1871)*

Babylon Security Services Inc .... D 818 766-8122
6032 One Half Vineland Ave North Hollywood (91606) *(P-14278)*

Bacara Resorts and Spa, Santa Barbara *Also Called: Bcra Resort Services Inc (P-12769)*

Bace Manufacturing Inc (HQ)............................. **A 714 630-6002**
3125 E Coronado St Anaheim (92806) *(P-4059)*

Bachem Americas Inc .... E 888 422-2436
1271 Avenida Chelsea Vista (92081) *(P-3368)*

Bachem Americas Inc .... E 424 347-5600
3131 Fujita St Torrance (90505) *(P-3369)*

Bachem Americas Inc .... E 310 539-4171
3031 Fujita St Torrance (90505) *(P-3563)*

Bachem Americas Inc .... E 310 784-4440
3152 Kashiwa St Torrance (90505) *(P-3564)*

Bachem Americas Inc (DH) .... **E 310 784-4440**
3132 Kashiwa St Torrance (90505) *(P-3565)*

Bachem California, Torrance *Also Called: Bachem Americas Inc (P-3565)*

Bachem Vista BSD, Vista *Also Called: Bachem Americas Inc (P-3368)*

Backbone Capital Advisors LLC .... D 818 769-8016
4084 Camellia Ave Studio City (91604) *(P-12699)*

Bae Systems, San Diego *Also Called: Bae Systems Info Elctrnic Syst (P-7900)*

Bae Systems Info Elctrnic Syst .... A 858 592-5000
10920 Technology Pl San Diego (92127) *(P-7900)*

Bae Systems Land Armaments LP .... E 619 455-0213
1650 Industrial Blvd Chula Vista (91911) *(P-7704)*

Bae Systems Maritime Engineering & Services Inc .... B 619 238-1000
7330 Engineer Rd Ste A San Diego (92111) *(P-17492)*

Bae Systems National Security Solutions Inc .... A 858 592-5000
10920 Technology Pl San Diego (92127) *(P-7901)*

Bae Systems San Dego Ship Repr .... A 619 238-1000
2205 Belt St San Diego (92113) *(P-7597)*

Bae Systems Tech Sltons Svcs I .... D 858 278-3042
9650 Chesapeake Dr San Diego (92123) *(P-7705)*

Bagcraftpapercon III LLC .... C 626 961-6766
515 Turnbull Canyon Rd City Of Industry (91745) *(P-2728)*

Baghouse and Indus Shtmtl Svcs, Corona *Also Called: MS Industrial Shtmtl Inc (P-5010)*

Bagmasters, Corona *Also Called: CTA Manufacturing Inc (P-2228)*

Bahare .... C 516 472-1457
11769 W Sunset Blvd Los Angeles (90049) *(P-13669)*

Bahia Resort Hotels, San Diego *Also Called: Bh Partnership LP (P-12775)*

Baja Designs, San Marcos *Also Called: Bestop Baja LLC (P-9816)*

Baja Fresh, Chino Hills *Also Called: Gateway Fresh LLC (P-12599)*

Baja Fresh Supermarket .... B 760 843-7730
14827 Seventh St Victorville (92395) *(P-96)*

Bakbone Software Inc (HQ).............................. **D 858 450-9009**
9540 Towne Centre Dr Ste 100 San Diego (92121) *(P-13670)*

Baked In The Sun .... C 760 591-9045
2560 Progress St Vista (92081) *(P-1435)*

Bakell LLC .... D 800 292-2137
824 Lytle St Redlands (92374) *(P-472)*

Bakemark, Pico Rivera *Also Called: Bakemark USA LLC (P-10930)*

Bakemark USA LLC (PA)................................... **C 562 949-1054**
7351 Crider Ave Pico Rivera (90660) *(P-10930)*

Baker & Hostetler LLP .... C 310 820-8800
1900 Avenue Of The Stars Los Angeles (90067) *(P-16639)*

Baker & Hostetler LLP .... D 714 754-6600
600 Anton Blvd Ste 900 Costa Mesa (92626) *(P-16640)*

Baker & McKenzie LLP .... C 310 201-4728
10250 Constellation Blvd Ste 1850 Los Angeles (90067) *(P-16641)*

Baker & Taylor LLC .... C 858 457-2500
10350 Barnes Canyon Rd Ste 100 San Diego (92121) *(P-11074)*

Baker & Taylor Holdings LLC .... A 858 457-2500
10350 Barnes Canyon Rd San Diego (92121) *(P-9991)*

Baker & Taylor Marketing Svc, San Diego *Also Called: Baker & Taylor Holdings LLC (P-9991)*

Baker Commodities Inc .... E 323 318-8260
3001 Sierra Pine Ave Vernon (90058) *(P-1521)*

Baker Commodities Inc (PA).............................. **C 323 268-2801**
4020 Bandini Blvd Vernon (90058) *(P-1522)*

Baker Electric & Renewables LLC .... A 760 745-2001
1298 Pacific Oaks Pl Escondido (92029) *(P-886)*

Baker Tilly California, Irvine *Also Called: Baker Tilly Us LLP (P-17705)*

Baker Tilly Us LLP .... B 818 981-2600
6320 Canoga Ave Woodland Hills (91367) *(P-17703)*

Baker Tilly Us LLP .... A 310 826-4474
11150 Santa Monica Blvd Ste 600 Los Angeles (90025) *(P-17704)*

Baker Tilly Us LLP .... A 949 222-2999
18500 Von Karman Ave Fl 10 Irvine (92612) *(P-17705)*

Baker Tilly Us LLP .... A 858 597-4100
3655 Nobel Dr Ste 300 San Diego (92122) *(P-17706)*

Bakers Kneaded LLC .... E 310 819-8700
148 W 132nd St Ste D Los Angeles (90061) *(P-1436)*

Bakersfeld Bhvral Hlthcare Hos .... C 661 398-1800
5201 White Ln Bakersfield (93309) *(P-16267)*

Bakersfield Hlthcare Wllness CN .... D 661 872-2121
2211 Mount Vernon Ave Bakersfield (93306) *(P-15577)*

Bakersfield Mem Hosp Foundation .... D 661 327-4647
420 34th St Bakersfield (93301) *(P-15921)*

Bakersfield Country Club .... D 661 871-4000
4200 Country Club Dr Bakersfield (93306) *(P-15117)*

Bakersfield District Office, Bakersfield *Also Called: State Compensation Insur Fund (P-12137)*

Bakersfield Family Medical Ctr, Bakersfield *Also Called: Bakersfield Family Medical Group Inc (P-15248)*

Bakersfield Family Medical Group Inc (PA)......... **D 661 327-4411**
4580 California Ave Bakersfield (93309) *(P-15248)*

Bakersfield Heart Hospital, Bakersfield *Also Called: Adventist Hlth Systm/West Corp (P-15895)*

Bakersfield Machine Co Inc .... D 661 709-1992
5605 North Chester Ave Ext Bakersfield (93308) *(P-6090)*

Bakersfield Mazda, Bakersfield *Also Called: Cjm Automotive Group Inc (P-11327)*

Bakersfield Memorial Hospital .... A 661 327-1792
420 34th St Bakersfield (93301) *(P-15922)*

Bakersfield Post Acute, Bakersfield *Also Called: Pacs Group Inc (P-15734)*

Bakersfield Respite Homecare, Bakersfield *Also Called: Maxim Healthcare Services Inc (P-13608)*

Bakersfield Shingles Wholesale Inc .... D 661 327-3727
4 P St Bakersfield (93304) *(P-9960)*

Bakersfield Westwind Corp .... C 661 327-2121
1810 Westwind Dr Bakersfield (93301) *(P-12386)*

Bakersfieldidence Opco LLC .... D 661 399-2472
5151 Knudsen Dr Bakersfield (93308) *(P-15578)*

Bakery Ex Southern Cal LLC .... D 714 446-9470
1910 W Malvern Ave Fullerton (92833) *(P-10931)*

Bal Seal Engineering LLC (DH)........................... **C 949 460-2100**
19650 Pauling Foothill Ranch (92610) *(P-5392)*

Balaji Trading Inc .... D 909 444-7999
4850 Eucalyptus Ave Chino (91710) *(P-6581)*

Balance Foods Inc .... E 323 838-5555
5743 Smithway St Ste 103 Commerce (90040) *(P-10841)*

Balboa Bay Club Inc (HQ)................................. **B 949 645-5000**
1221 W Coast Hwy Newport Beach (92663) *(P-15118)*

Balboa Capital Corporation (DH)........................ **C 949 756-0800**
575 Anton Blvd Ste 1200 Costa Mesa (92626) *(P-11865)*

Balboa Manufacturing Co LLC (PA)..................... **E 858 715-0060**
4909 Murphy Canyon Rd Ste 310 San Diego (92123) *(P-1911)*

Balboa Nphrology Med Group Inc .... C 858 810-8000
4225 Executive Sq Ste 450 La Jolla (92037) *(P-15249)*

Balboa Water Group LLC (HQ)........................... **D 714 384-0384**
2020 Piper Ranch Rd Ste 150 San Diego (92154) *(P-6342)*

Balda C Brewer Inc (DH)................................... **D 909 212-0290**
4501 E Wall St Ontario (91761) *(P-5569)*

Balda HK Plastics Inc .... E 760 757-1100
3229 Roymar Rd Oceanside (92058) *(P-5104)*

Balda Precision Inc (DH)................................... **D 760 757-1100**
3233 Roymar Rd Oceanside (92058) *(P-5105)*

Baldwin Brass, Lake Forest *Also Called: Baldwin Hardware Corporation (P-4759)*

Baldwin Hardware Corporation (DH)........................A 949 672-4000
19701 Da Vinci Lake Forest (92610) *(P-4759)*

Baldwin Hospitality LLC ....D 626 446-2988
14635 Baldwin Park Towne Ctr Baldwin Park (91706) *(P-12766)*

Baldwin Park Laboratory, Baldwin Park *Also Called: Kaiser Foundation Hospitals (P-18394)*

Baldwin Park Unified Schl Dst ....D 626 337-2711
13529 Francisquito Ave Baldwin Park (91706) *(P-16801)*

Baldwin Pk Unified Schl Dst Chl, Baldwin Park *Also Called: Baldwin Park Unified Schl Dst (P-16801)*

Balfour Beatty Cnstr LLC ....D 858 635-7400
13520 Evening Creek Dr N Ste 270 San Diego (92128) *(P-520)*

Bali Construction Inc ....D 626 442-8003
9852 Joe Vargas Way South El Monte (91733) *(P-662)*

Ball TEC, Los Angeles *Also Called: Micro Surface Engr Inc (P-4718)*

Ballard & Tighe Publishers, Brea *Also Called: Educational Ideas Incorporated (P-2889)*

Ballard Rehabilitation Hospital, San Bernardino *Also Called: Robert Ballard Rehab Hospital (P-15556)*

Ballard Spahr LLP ....D 424 204-4400
2029 Century Park E Ste 1400 Los Angeles (90002) *(P-16642)*

Bally Total Fitness, Norwalk *Also Called: Bally Total Fitness Corporation (P-15044)*

Bally Total Fitness Corporation ....A 562 484-2000
12440 Imperial Hwy Ste 300 Norwalk (90650) *(P-15044)*

Balt Usa LLC ....D 949 788-1443
29 Parker Ste 100 Irvine (92618) *(P-10067)*

Baltic Ltvian Unvrsal Elec LLC ....E 818 879-5200
5706 Corsa Ave Westlake Village (91362) *(P-6529)*

Bamko, Los Angeles *Also Called: Bamko Inc (P-13256)*

Bamko LLC (HQ)...**A 310 470-5859**
10925 Weyburn Ave Los Angeles (90024) *(P-18101)*

Bamko Inc ....C 310 470-5859
11620 Wilshire Blvd Ste 610 Los Angeles (90025) *(P-13256)*

Bamko Promotional Items, Los Angeles *Also Called: Bamko LLC (P-18101)*

Bana Home Loan Servicing ....A 213 345-7975
31303 Agoura Rd Westlake Village (91361) *(P-11704)*

Banamex USA Bancorp (DH)................................**C 310 203-3440**
787 W 5th St Los Angeles (90071) *(P-12590)*

Banc of California Inc ....A 310 887-8500
9701 Wilshire Blvd Ste 700 Beverly Hills (90212) *(P-11705)*

Banc of California Inc (PA)................................**C 855 361-2262**
11611 San Vicente Blvd Ste 500 Los Angeles (90049) *(P-11706)*

Bancorp, Los Angeles *Also Called: Cathay General Bancorp (P-11752)*

Bandai Namco, Irvine *Also Called: Bandai Namco Entrmt Amer Inc (P-10519)*

Bandai Namco Entrmt Amer Inc ....C 408 235-2000
23 Odyssey Irvine (92618) *(P-10519)*

Bandai Nmco Toys Cllctbles AME (DH).....................**D 949 271-6000**
23 Odyssey Irvine (92618) *(P-8482)*

Bandel Mfg Inc ....E 818 246-7493
4459 Alger St Los Angeles (90039) *(P-5174)*

Bandlock Corporation ....D 909 947-7500
1734 S Vineyard Ave Ontario (91761) *(P-4060)*

Bandy Manufacturing LLC ....D 818 846-9020
3420 N San Fernando Blvd Burbank (91504) *(P-7444)*

Bandy Ranch Floral Corp ....C 805 757-9905
2755 Dos Aarons Way Ste B Vista (92081) *(P-11082)*

Bang Printing, Palmdale *Also Called: D & J Printing Inc (P-2997)*

Bangkit (usa) Inc ....D 626 672-0888
10511 Valley Blvd El Monte (91731) *(P-10577)*

Banh Hoi Minh Phung, Westminster *Also Called: Minh Phung Incorporated (P-10961)*

Bank of Hope (HQ)..**C 213 639-1700**
3200 Wilshire Blvd Ste 1400 Los Angeles (90010) *(P-11707)*

Bank of Manhattan ....C 310 606-8000
2141 Rosecrans Ave Ste 1100 El Segundo (90245) *(P-11782)*

Bankcard Services (PA)....................................**C 213 365-1122**
21281 S Western Ave Torrance (90501) *(P-14458)*

Bankcard Services, Torrance *Also Called: Credit Card Services Inc (P-14485)*

Bankcard USA Merchant Srvc ....D 818 597-7000
5701 Lindero Canyon Rd Westlake Village (91362) *(P-14459)*

Bankruptcy Management Cons, El Segundo *Also Called: BMC Group Inc (P-16647)*

Banks Pest Control ....C 661 323-7858
7440 District Blvd Ste A Bakersfield (93313) *(P-13342)*

Banks Power Products, Azusa *Also Called: Gale Banks Engineering (P-5468)*

Banner Mattress Inc ....D 909 835-4200
1501 E Cooley Dr Ste B Colton (92324) *(P-2480)*

Bapko Metal Inc ....D 714 639-9380
721 S Parker St Ste 300 Orange (92868) *(P-1150)*

Bar Code Specialties Inc ....E 877 411-2633
12272 Monarch St Garden Grove (92841) *(P-5904)*

Barber Volkeswagen, Ventura *Also Called: R E Barber-Ford (P-11398)*

Barber Welding and Mfg Co ....E 562 928-2570
7171 Scout Ave Bell Gardens (90201) *(P-6091)*

Barber-Webb Company Inc (PA)..........................**E 541 488-4821**
12912 Lakeland Rd Santa Fe Springs (90670) *(P-4061)*

Barbour & Floyd Medical Assoc, Lynwood *Also Called: South Cntl Hlth Rhblttion Prgr (P-16504)*

Barco Uniforms Inc ....**B 310 323-7315**
350 W Rosecrans Ave Gardena (90248) *(P-1975)*

Bardex Corporation (PA)..................................**D 805 964-7747**
6338 Lindmar Dr Goleta (93117) *(P-5505)*

Bargain Rent-A-Car ....C 562 865-7447
18800 Studebaker Rd Cerritos (90703) *(P-11317)*

Barkens Hardchrome Inc ....E 310 632-2000
239 E Greenleaf Blvd Compton (90220) *(P-5693)*

Barker Management Incorporated ....D 619 236-8130
438 3rd Ave Apt 312 San Diego (92101) *(P-12333)*

Barksdale Inc (DH)..**D 323 583-6243**
3211 Fruitland Ave Los Angeles (90058) *(P-8033)*

Barlow Group (PA)..**C 213 250-4200**
2000 Stadium Way Los Angeles (90026) *(P-16283)*

Barlow Respiratory Hospital ....A 562 698-0811
12401 Washington Blvd Whittier (90602) *(P-16284)*

Barlow Respiratory Hospital (PA)..........................**C 213 250-4200**
2000 Stadium Way Los Angeles (90026) *(P-16285)*

BARLOW RESPITORY HOSPITAL, Los Angeles *Also Called: Barlow Group (P-16283)*

Barnes & Thornburg LLP ....C 310 284-3880
2029 Century Park E Ste 300 Los Angeles (90067) *(P-16643)*

Barnes Plastics, Gardena *Also Called: Barnes Plastics Inc (P-4062)*

Barnes Plastics Inc ....E 310 329-6301
18903 Anelo Ave Gardena (90248) *(P-4062)*

Barnett Performance Products, Ventura *Also Called: Barnett Tool & Engineering (P-7629)*

Barnett Tool & Engineering ....D 805 642-9435
2238 Palma Dr Ventura (93003) *(P-7629)*

Barney & Barney Inc ....C 800 321-4696
9171 Towne Centre Dr Ste 500 San Diego (92122) *(P-12182)*

Barnhart Inc ....B 858 635-7400
10620 Treena St Ste 300 San Diego (92131) *(P-521)*

Barona Resort & Casino ....A 619 443-2300
1932 Wildcat Canyon Rd Lakeside (92040) *(P-12767)*

Barr Engineering Inc ....D 562 944-1722
19 Castano Rcho Sta Marg (92688) *(P-747)*

Barr, Ronald J MD /UCI Med Gro, Orange *Also Called: University California Irvine (P-15502)*

Barranca Diamond Products, Torrance *Also Called: Barranca Holdings Ltd (P-5606)*

Barranca Holdings Ltd ....C 310 523-5867
22815 Frampton Ave Torrance (90501) *(P-5606)*

Barranca Medical Offices, Irvine *Also Called: Kaiser Foundation Hospitals (P-16057)*

Barrett Business Services Inc ....A 858 314-1100
8880 Rio San Diego Dr Ste 800 San Diego (92108) *(P-13491)*

Barrett Business Services Inc ....A 909 890-3633
862 E Hospitality Ln San Bernardino (92408) *(P-13492)*

Barrett Business Services Inc ....A 805 987-0331
815 Camarillo Springs Rd Ste C Camarillo (93012) *(P-13493)*

Barrette Outdoor Living Inc ....E 800 336-2383
1151 Palmyrita Ave Riverside (92507) *(P-4532)*

Barrington Associates, Los Angeles *Also Called: Wells Fargo Securities LLC (P-11741)*

Barry & Taffy Inc ....A 818 986-1234
5955 De Soto Ave Ste 160 Woodland Hills (91367) *(P-16367)*

Barry Avenue Plating Co Inc ....D 310 478-0078
2210 Barry Ave Los Angeles (90064) *(P-5237)*

Barry Controls Aerospace, Burbank *Also Called: Hutchinson Arospc & Indust Inc (P-3915)*

Barry D. Payne and Associates, Long Beach *Also Called: Mangan Inc (P-17581)*

Barrys Printing Inc ....E 818 998-8600
9005 Eton Ave Ste D Canoga Park (91304) *(P-2968)*

Employee Codes: A=Over 500 employees, B=251-500
C=101-250, D=51-100, E=20-50, F=10-19, G=1-9

2025 Southern California
Business Directory and Buyers Guide

© Mergent Inc. 1-800-342-5647

951

Barrys Security Services Inc (PA).................... C 951 789-7575
16739 Van Buren Blvd Riverside (92504) *(P-14279)*

Barstow Community Hospital, Barstow *Also Called: Hospital of Barstow Inc (P-16026)*

Barta - Schoenewald Inc (PA)........................ C 805 389-1935
3805 Calle Tecate Camarillo (93012) *(P-6314)*

Bartco Lighting Inc .... D 714 230-3200
5761 Research Dr Huntington Beach (92649) *(P-10171)*

Bartell Hotels .... D 619 291-6700
1960 Harbor Island Dr San Diego (92101) *(P-12768)*

Barton Perreira LLC .... E 949 305-5360
459 Wald Irvine (92618) *(P-8404)*

Basaw Manufacturing, North Hollywood *Also Called: Basaw Manufacturing Inc (P-2383)*

Basaw Manufacturing Inc (PA)........................ E 818 765-6650
11323 Hartland St North Hollywood (91605) *(P-2383)*

Base Lite Corporation .... E 909 444-2776
12260 Eastend Ave Chino (91710) *(P-6441)*

Baselite, Chino *Also Called: Base Lite Corporation (P-6441)*

Basepoint Analytics LLC .... B 760 602-4971
703 Palomar Airport Rd Ste 350 Carlsbad (92011) *(P-13291)*

BASF Corporation .... C 714 921-1430
138 E Meats Ave Orange (92865) *(P-3728)*

BASF Corporation .... E 714 521-6085
6700 8th St Buena Park (90620) *(P-3729)*

BASF Enzymes LLC (DH) .... D 858 431-8520
3550 John Hopkins Ct San Diego (92121) *(P-3730)*

Basic Agency, San Diego *Also Called: Thinkbasic Inc (P-13336)*

Basic Electronics Inc .... E 714 530-2400
11371 Monarch St Garden Grove (92841) *(P-6971)*

Basic Energy Services Inc .... E 661 588-3800
6710 Stewart Way Bakersfield (93308) *(P-318)*

Basic Industries Intl Inc (PA)......................... E 951 226-1500
10850 Wilshire Blvd Ste 760 Los Angeles (90024) *(P-4910)*

Basin Marine Inc .... E 949 673-0360
829 Harbor Island Dr Ste A Newport Beach (92660) *(P-7617)*

Basin Marine Shipyard, Newport Beach *Also Called: Basin Marine Inc (P-7617)*

Basket Basics, Carson *Also Called: Kole Imports (P-11126)*

Basketball Marketing Co Inc .... C 610 249-2255
101 Enterprise Ste 100 Aliso Viejo (92656) *(P-18102)*

Basmat Inc (PA).. D 310 325-2063
1531 240th St Harbor City (90710) *(P-4955)*

Bassani Exhaust, Anaheim *Also Called: Bassani Manufacturing (P-5427)*

Bassani Manufacturing .... E 714 630-1821
2900 E La Jolla St Anaheim (92806) *(P-5427)*

Batchmaster Software, Irvine *Also Called: Eworkplace Manufacturing Inc (P-10003)*

Batia Infotech .... C 855 776-7763
3101 Ocean Park Blvd Ste 100 Pmb 187 Santa Monica (90405) *(P-13671)*

Battery Technology Inc (PA)........................... D 626 336-6878
16651 E Johnson Dr City Of Industry (91745) *(P-7072)*

Battery-Biz Inc .... D 800 848-6782
1380 Flynn Rd Camarillo (93012) *(P-7089)*

Battle-Tested Strategies LLC .... D 661 802-6509
650 Commerce Ave Ste E Palmdale (93551) *(P-8999)*

Bau Furniture Mfg Inc .... D 949 643-2729
21 Kelly Ln Ladera Ranch (92694) *(P-2419)*

Baumann Engineering .... D 909 621-4181
212 S Cambridge Ave Claremont (91711) *(P-6092)*

Bausch & Lomb Surgical Div, Irvine *Also Called: Eyeonics Inc (P-8407)*

Bavarian Nordic Inc .... E 919 600-1260
6275 Nancy Ridge Dr Ste 110 San Diego (92121) *(P-2759)*

Baxalta US Inc .... A 818 240-5600
4501 Colorado Blvd Los Angeles (90039) *(P-3370)*

Baxalta US Inc .... A 805 498-8664
1700 Rancho Conejo Blvd Thousand Oaks (91320) *(P-8102)*

Baxalta US Inc .... C 949 474-6301
17511 Armstrong Ave Irvine (92614) *(P-14460)*

Baxter Healthcare Corporation .... C 949 474-6301
17511 Armstrong Ave Irvine (92614) *(P-8103)*

Baxter Healthcare Corporation .... D 805 372-3000
1 Baxter Way Ste 100 Westlake Village (91362) *(P-10614)*

Baxter Medication Delivery, Irvine *Also Called: Baxter Healthcare Corporation (P-8103)*

Bay Area Community Med Group, Los Angeles *Also Called: Santa Monica Bay Physicians He (P-15446)*

Bay Cities Container Corp (PA)....................... D 562 948-3751
5138 Industry Ave Pico Rivera (90660) *(P-2654)*

Bay Cities Container Corp .... E 562 551-2946
9206 Santa Fe Springs Rd Santa Fe Springs (90670) *(P-2705)*

Bay Cities Metal Products, Gardena *Also Called: Bay Cities Tin Shop Inc (P-4956)*

Bay Cities Packaging & Design, Pico Rivera *Also Called: Bay Cities Container Corp (P-2654)*

Bay Cities Tin Shop Inc .... C 310 660-0351
301 E Alondra Blvd Gardena (90248) *(P-4956)*

Bay City Equipment Inds Inc .... D 619 938-8200
13625 Danielson St Poway (92064) *(P-10172)*

Bay City Marine Inc (PA)............................... E 619 477-3991
1625 Cleveland Ave National City (91950) *(P-4817)*

Bay City Television Inc (PA)........................... D 858 279-6666
8253 Ronson Rd San Diego (92111) *(P-9493)*

Bay Clubs Company LLC .... C 310 643-6878
2250 Park Pl Thousand Oaks (91362) *(P-15119)*

Bay Clubs Company LLC .... B 858 509-9933
12000 Carmel Country Rd San Diego (92130) *(P-15120)*

Bay Sheet Metal Inc .... E 619 401-9270
9343 Bond Ave Ste C El Cajon (92021) *(P-4957)*

Bay Valley Mortgage, La Mirada *Also Called: Bay-Valley Mortgage Group (P-11940)*

Bay-Valley Mortgage Group .... D 714 367-5125
15020 La Mirada Blvd La Mirada (90638) *(P-11940)*

Bayless Manufacturing LLC .... C 661 257-3373
26140 Avenue Hall Valencia (91355) *(P-6093)*

Baymark Health Services La Inc .... C 310 761-4762
11682 Atlantic Ave Lynwood (90262) *(P-16535)*

Baymarr Constructors Inc .... C 661 395-1676
6950 Mcdivitt Dr Bakersfield (93313) *(P-1104)*

Bayshore Healthcare Inc .... C 805 544-5100
3033 Augusta St San Luis Obispo (93401) *(P-15579)*

Bayside Care Center, Morro Bay *Also Called: Compass Health Inc (P-15599)*

Bayside Healthcare Inc .... C 619 426-8611
553 F St Chula Vista (91910) *(P-15580)*

Baywa RE Epc LLC .... E 949 398-3915
17901 Von Karman Ave Ste 1050 Irvine (92614) *(P-6806)*

Bazic Product, El Monte *Also Called: Bangkit (usa) Inc (P-10577)*

Bazz Houston Co, Garden Grove *Also Called: Houston Bazz Co (P-5192)*

Bb Co Inc .... E 213 550-1158
1753 E 21st St Los Angeles (90058) *(P-2081)*

Bbcn Bank .... A 213 251-2222
3731 Wilshire Blvd Los Angeles (90010) *(P-11708)*

Bbeautiful LLC .... E 626 610-2332
1361 Mountain View Cir Azusa (91702) *(P-3633)*

Bbk Performance Inc .... D 951 296-1771
27427 Bostik Ct Temecula (92590) *(P-9815)*

Bbm Fairway Inc (PA).................................... C
3520 Challenger St Torrance (90503) *(P-2844)*

Bbsi Camarillo, Camarillo *Also Called: Barrett Business Services Inc (P-13493)*

Bcc Dissolution Inc .... E 323 583-3444
2929 S Santa Fe Ave Los Angeles (90058) *(P-5428)*

Bcd Food Inc .... E 310 323-1200
320 W Carob St Compton (90220) *(P-1742)*

Bcd Tofu House, Los Angeles *Also Called: Wilshire Kingsley Inc (P-12331)*

BCI Alabama, Los Angeles *Also Called: Blackstone Consulting Inc (P-18105)*

BCM Customer Service .... D 858 679-5757
12155 Kirkham Rd Poway (92064) *(P-748)*

Bcp Systems Inc .... D 714 202-3900
1560 S Sinclair St Anaheim (92806) *(P-14185)*

Bcra Resort Services Inc .... C 805 571-3176
8301 Hollister Ave Santa Barbara (93117) *(P-12769)*

Bd Carefusion, San Diego *Also Called: Carefusion Corporation (P-8374)*

BD&j PC .... C 855 906-3699
9701 Wilshire Blvd Ste 630 Beverly Hills (90212) *(P-16644)*

Bdc Distribution Center, Redlands *Also Called: Becton Dickinson and Company (P-7943)*

Bdc Epoxy Systems Inc .... E 562 944-6177
12903 Sunshine Ave Santa Fe Springs (90670) *(P-3259)*

Bdfco Inc .... D 714 228-2900
1926 Kauai Dr Costa Mesa (92626) *(P-6675)*

Mergent email: customerrelations@mergent.com
952

2025 Southern California
Business Directory and Buyers Guide

(P-0000) Products & Services Section entry number
(PA)=Parent Co (HQ)=Headquarters (DH)=Div Headquarters

Bdi Inc .... D 626 442-8948
9917 Gidley St Unit A El Monte (91731) *(P-10426)*

BDR Industries Inc (PA).. D 661 940-8554
820 E Avenue L12 Lancaster (93535) *(P-9524)*

BDS Connected Solutions LLC .... C 800 234-4237
25962 Atlantic Ocean Dr Lake Forest (92630) *(P-18103)*

Be Beauty, Garden Grove *Also Called: Cali Chem Inc (P-3637)*

Be Bop Clothing .... B 323 846-0121
5833 Avalon Blvd Los Angeles (90003) *(P-2082)*

BE Smith Inc .... B 913 341-9116
12400 High Bluff Dr Ste 100 San Diego (92130) *(P-18288)*

Be Structured Tech Group Inc .... D 323 331-9452
500 S Grand Ave Ste 2200 Los Angeles (90071) *(P-14200)*

Beach Area Family Health Ctr, San Diego *Also Called: Family Hlth Ctrs San Diego Inc (P-15311)*

Beach Cities Health District .... C 310 374-3426
1200 Del Amo St Redondo Beach (90277) *(P-17216)*

Beach Creek Post-Acute, Anaheim *Also Called: Oceanside Harbor Holdings LLC (P-15727)*

Beach House Group, El Segundo *Also Called: Beach House Group LLC (P-8661)*

Beach House Group LLC .... D 310 356-6180
222 N Pacific Coast Hwy Fl 10 El Segundo (90245) *(P-8661)*

Beach News, Encinitas *Also Called: Coast News Inc (P-2790)*

Beach Reporter, Rllng Hls Est *Also Called: National Media Inc (P-2817)*

Beach State, Moorpark *Also Called: Picnic Time Inc (P-8716)*

Beachbody, El Segundo *Also Called: Beachbody LLC (P-13260)*

Beachbody LLC (HQ)... B 310 883-9000
400 Continental Blvd Ste 400 El Segundo (90245) *(P-13260)*

Beachbody Company Inc (PA).. D 310 883-9000
400 Continental Blvd Ste 400 El Segundo (90245) *(P-13261)*

Beachbody Company, The, El Segundo *Also Called: Beachbody Company Inc (P-13261)*

Beacon Electric Supply .... D 858 279-9770
9630 Chesapeake Dr San Diego (92123) *(P-10173)*

Beacon Pacific Inc .... C 714 288-1974
675 N Batavia St Orange (92868) *(P-9956)*

Beacon Resources LLC .... C 949 955-1773
17300 Red Hill Ave Irvine (92614) *(P-18104)*

Beador Construction Co Inc .... D 951 674-7352
2900 Bristol St Costa Mesa (92626) *(P-609)*

Beam Global (PA).. C 858 799-4583
5660 Eastgate Dr San Diego (92121) *(P-6807)*

Bear Communications Inc .... D 619 263-2159
8290 Vickers St Ste D San Diego (92111) *(P-10230)*

Bear Communications Inc .... D 310 854-2327
8584 Venice Blvd Los Angeles (90034) *(P-10231)*

Bear Mountain, Big Bear Lake *Also Called: Snow Summit LLC (P-13028)*

Bear Valley Springs Assn .... C 661 821-5537
29541 Rollingoak Dr Tehachapi (93561) *(P-17324)*

Bear Vly Cmnty Healthcare Dst (PA)................................ C 909 866-6501
41870 Garstin Dr Big Bear Lake (92315) *(P-15923)*

Bearcom Wireless Worldwide, San Diego *Also Called: Bear Communications Inc (P-10230)*

Bearcom Wireless Worldwide, Los Angeles *Also Called: Bear Communications Inc (P-10231)*

Bearsaver, Ontario *Also Called: Compumeric Engineering Inc (P-4971)*

Beating Wall Street Inc (PA).. C 818 332-9696
20121 Ventura Blvd Ste 305 Woodland Hills (91364) *(P-12018)*

Beats By Dre, Culver City *Also Called: Beats Electronics LLC (P-6530)*

Beats Electronics LLC .... B 424 326-4679
8600 Hayden Pl Culver City (90232) *(P-6530)*

Beauchamp Distributing Company .... D 310 639-5320
1911 S Santa Fe Ave Compton (90221) *(P-11041)*

Beaumont Juice LLC .... D 951 769-7171
550 B St Beaumont (92223) *(P-1349)*

Beaumont Nielsen Marine Inc .... E 619 223-2628
2420 Shelter Island Dr San Diego (92106) *(P-14461)*

Beaumont Unfied Schl Dst Pub F .... B 951 845-6580
126 W Fifth St Beaumont (92223) *(P-16802)*

Beauty & Health International .... E 714 903-9730
7541 Anthony Ave Garden Grove (92841) *(P-3371)*

Beauty 21 Cosmetics Inc .... C 909 945-2220
2021 S Archibald Ave Ontario (91761) *(P-10615)*

Beauty Barrage LLC .... C 949 771-3399
4340 Von Karman Ave Ste 240 Newport Beach (92660) *(P-13146)*

Beauty Health Company (PA)... B 800 603-4996
2165 E Spring St Long Beach (90806) *(P-8104)*

Beauty Tent Inc .... E 323 717-7131
1131 N Kenmore Ave Apt 6 Los Angeles (90029) *(P-8662)*

Beaver Medical Clinic, Highland *Also Called: Beaver Medical Group LP (P-15251)*

Beaver Medical Clinic Inc (PA).. C 909 793-3311
1615 Orange Tree Ln Redlands (92374) *(P-15250)*

Beaver Medical Group LP (HQ).. C 909 425-3321
7000 Boulder Ave Highland (92346) *(P-15251)*

Beazer, Brea *Also Called: Beazer Mortgage Corporation (P-459)*

Beazer Mortgage Corporation .... D 714 480-1635
1800 E Imperial Hwy Ste 200 Brea (92821) *(P-459)*

Bebe Studio Inc .... C 213 362-2323
10250 Santa Monica Blvd Ste 6 Los Angeles (90067) *(P-11528)*

Becca, Anaheim *Also Called: The Lunada Bay Corporation (P-2172)*

Becker Automotive Design USA, Oxnard *Also Called: Becker Automotive Designs Inc (P-7170)*

Becker Automotive Designs Inc .... E 805 487-5227
1711 Ives Ave Oxnard (93033) *(P-7170)*

Becker Specialty Corporation .... D 909 356-1095
15310 Arrow Blvd Fontana (92335) *(P-6925)*

Beckers Fabrication Inc .... E 714 692-1600
22465 La Palma Ave Yorba Linda (92887) *(P-2719)*

Beckman Coulter Inc .... C 760 438-9151
2470 Faraday Ave Carlsbad (92010) *(P-7940)*

Beckman Coulter Inc .... C 818 970-2161
250 S Kraemer Blvd Brea (92821) *(P-8105)*

Beckman Coulter Inc (HQ).. A 714 993-5321
250 S Kraemer Blvd Brea (92821) *(P-7941)*

Beckman Instruments Inc .... D 626 309-0110
8733 Scott St Rosemead (91770) *(P-7942)*

Beckman RES Inst of The Cy Hop .... C 626 359-8111
1500 Duarte Rd Duarte (91010) *(P-15252)*

Beckman RES Inst of The Cy Hop, Duarte *Also Called: City of Hope (P-17966)*

BECKMAN RESEARCH INSTITUTE OF, Duarte *Also Called: Beckman RES Inst of The Cy Hop (P-15252)*

BECKMAN RESEARCH INSTITUTE OF, Duarte *Also Called: City Hope Medical Foundation (P-15278)*

Becton Dickinson and Company .... D 909 748-7300
2200 W San Bernardino Ave Redlands (92374) *(P-7943)*

Becton Dickinson and Company .... D 888 876-4287
3750 Torrey View Ct San Diego (92130) *(P-8106)*

Becton Dickinson and Company .... E 858 617-2000
3750 Torrey View Ct San Diego (92130) *(P-8107)*

Bed Time Originals, El Segundo *Also Called: Lambs & Ivy Inc (P-2214)*

Bedrock Company .... D 951 273-1931
2970 Myers St Riverside (92503) *(P-1105)*

Bedrosian's Tile, Sylmar *Also Called: Paragon Industries Inc (P-1042)*

Bee Wire & Cable Inc .... E 909 923-5800
2850 E Spruce St Ontario (91761) *(P-5400)*

Beech Street Corporation (HQ).. B 949 672-1000
25550 Commercentre Dr Ste 200 Lake Forest (92630) *(P-17950)*

Beecher Carlson Holdings Inc .... D 818 598-4200
21650 Oxnard St Ste 1600 Woodland Hills (91367) *(P-12183)*

Beemak Plastics LLC .... D 800 421-4393
1515 S Harris Ct Anaheim (92806) *(P-4063)*

Beemak-Idl Display Products, Anaheim *Also Called: Beemak Plastics LLC (P-4063)*

Bega, Carpinteria *Also Called: Bega North America Inc (P-6491)*

Bega North America Inc .... D 805 684-0533
1000 Bega Way Carpinteria (93013) *(P-6491)*

Behavioral Health Works Inc .... D 800 249-1266
1301 E Orangewood Ave Anaheim (92805) *(P-16444)*

Behavioral Learning Center Inc .... C 818 308-6226
13400 Riverside Dr Ste 209 Sherman Oaks (91423) *(P-16875)*

Behavioral Medicine Center, Redlands *Also Called: Loma Linda University Med Ctr (P-16080)*

Behavioral Science Technology Inc (PA).......................... C 805 646-0166
1000 Town Center Dr Ste 600 Oxnard (93036) *(P-18289)*

Behr Holdings, Santa Ana *Also Called: Behr Sales Inc (P-3705)*

Behr Holdings Corporation (HQ)...................................... E 714 545-7101
3400 W Segerstrom Ave Santa Ana (92704) *(P-3703)*

Employee Codes: A=Over 500 employees, B=251-500
C=101-250, D=51-100, E=20-50, F=10-19, G=1-9

2025 Southern California
Business Directory and Buyers Guide

© Mergent Inc. 1-800-342-5647
953

A
L
P
H
A
B
E
T
I
C

Behr Paint Company, Santa Ana *Also Called: Behr Process LLC (P-3704)*

Behr Process LLC (DH)..A **714 545-7101**
1801 E Saint Andrew Pl Santa Ana (92705) *(P-3704)*

Behr Sales Inc (HQ)..C **714 545-7101**
3400 W Segerstrom Ave Santa Ana (92704) *(P-3705)*

Behringer Harvard Wilshire Blv ....D 310 475-8711
10740 Wilshire Blvd Los Angeles (90024) *(P-12770)*

BEI Industrial Encoders, Thousand Oaks *Also Called: Carros Sensors Systems Co LLC (P-8038)*

BEI Industrial Encoders, Thousand Oaks *Also Called: Sensata Technologies Inc (P-14250)*

BEI North America LLC (DH)...C **805 716-0642**
1461 Lawrence Dr Thousand Oaks (91320) *(P-8034)*

Bel Tren Vlla Cnvalescent Hosp, Bellflower *Also Called: Life Care Centers America Inc (P-15694)*

Bel Vista Healthcare Center, Long Beach *Also Called: Villa De La Mar Inc (P-15890)*

Bel-Air Bay Club Ltd ....C 310 230-4700
16801 Pacific Coast Hwy Pacific Palisades (90272) *(P-15121)*

Bel-Air Country Club ....C 310 472-9563
10768 Bellagio Rd Los Angeles (90077) *(P-15122)*

Belching Beaver Brewery ....C 760 599-5832
1334 Rocky Point Dr Oceanside (92056) *(P-11611)*

Belco Packaging Systems Inc ....E 626 357-9566
910 S Mountain Ave Monrovia (91016) *(P-5787)*

Belden Inc ....A 310 639-9473
1048 E Burgrove St Carson (90746) *(P-4625)*

Belding Golf Bag Company, The, Oxnard *Also Called: Illah Sports Inc (P-8526)*

Belhome Inc ....E 310 618-8437
560 Alaska Ave Torrance (90503) *(P-5643)*

Belinda, Vernon *Also Called: New Pride Corporation (P-10717)*

Belkin, El Segundo *Also Called: Belkin Inc (P-6531)*

Belkin Inc ....A 800 223-5546
555 S Aviation Blvd El Segundo (90245) *(P-6531)*

Belkin Components, El Segundo *Also Called: Belkin International Inc (P-5905)*

Belkin International Inc (DH)..B 310 751-5100
555 S Aviation Blvd Ste 180 El Segundo (90245) *(P-5905)*

Bell Foundry Co (PA)...E 323 564-5701
5310 Southern Ave South Gate (90280) *(P-8504)*

Bell Gardens Bicycle Club Inc ....A 562 806-4646
888 Bicycle Casino Dr Bell Gardens (90201) *(P-15194)*

Bell Sports Inc (HQ)..D **469 417-6600**
16752 Armstrong Ave Irvine (92606) *(P-8505)*

Bell Villa Care Associates LLC ....D 562 925-4252
9028 Rose St Bellflower (90706) *(P-15581)*

Bella Collina San Clemente ....D 949 498-6604
200 Avenida La Pata San Clemente (92673) *(P-15123)*

Bella Terra Nursery Inc ....D 619 585-1118
302 Hollister St San Diego (92154) *(P-11083)*

Bella Vsta Trnstional Care Ctr, San Luis Obispo *Also Called: Bayshore Healthcare Inc (P-15579)*

Bellami Hair, Chatsworth *Also Called: Bellami Hair LLC (P-13147)*

Bellami Hair LLC ....D 844 235-5264
21123 Nordhoff St Chatsworth (91311) *(P-13147)*

Bellflower Dental Group, Bellflower *Also Called: Peter Wylan DDS (P-15525)*

Bellflower Medical Center, Los Angeles *Also Called: Jupiter Bellflower Doctors Hospital (P-16031)*

Bellissimo Distribution LLC ....E 760 292-9100
1389 Park Center Dr Vista (92081) *(P-1337)*

Bellota US Corp ....C 951 737-6515
22440 Temescal Canyon Rd Corona (92883) *(P-12629)*

Bellows Mfg & RES Inc ....E 818 838-1333
864 Arroyo St San Fernando (91340) *(P-4818)*

Bellrock Media Inc (PA) ....E 310 315-2727
11500 W Olympic Blvd Ste 400 Los Angeles (90064) *(P-13672)*

Bellwether, El Segundo *Also Called: Bellwether Asset MGT Inc (P-17951)*

Bellwether Asset MGT Inc (PA)..D **310 525-3022**
200 N Pacific Coast Hwy Ste 1400 El Segundo (90245) *(P-17951)*

Belmond El Encanto, Santa Barbara *Also Called: El Encanto Inc (P-12820)*

Belshire, Foothill Ranch *Also Called: Belshire Trnsp Svcs Inc (P-8896)*

Belshire Trnsp Svcs Inc ....C 949 460-5200
25971 Towne Centre Dr Foothill Ranch (92610) *(P-8896)*

Belvedere Hotel Partnership ....B 310 551-2888
9882 Santa Monica Blvd Beverly Hills (90212) *(P-12771)*

Belvedere Partnership ....B 310 551-2888
9882 Santa Monica Blvd Beverly Hills (90212) *(P-12772)*

Bemco Inc (PA) ....E **805 583-4970**
2255 Union Pl Simi Valley (93065) *(P-7944)*

Bemus Landscape Inc ....B 714 557-7910
951 Calle Negocio Ste D San Clemente (92673) *(P-709)*

Ben F Smith Inc ....C 858 271-4320
8655 Miramar Pl Ste B San Diego (92121) *(P-1106)*

Ben Group Inc ....B 310 342-1500
14724 Ventura Blvd Ste 1200 Sherman Oaks (91403) *(P-13673)*

Bench 2 Bench Technologies, Fullerton *Also Called: Winonics Inc (P-6789)*

Bench Depot, Rancho Cucamonga *Also Called: Benchpro Inc (P-9865)*

Benchmark, Moorpark *Also Called: Benchmark Elec Mfg Sltons Mrpa (P-6711)*

Benchmark Contractors, Santa Monica *Also Called: Morley Builders Inc (P-494)*

Benchmark Elec Mfg Sltons Mrpa ....A 805 532-2800
200 Science Dr Moorpark (93021) *(P-6711)*

Benchmark Elec Phoenix ....B 619 397-2402
1659 Gailes Blvd San Diego (92154) *(P-6712)*

Benchmark Landscape Svcs Inc ....C 858 513-7190
12575 Stowe Dr Poway (92064) *(P-149)*

Benchmark Secure Technology, Santa Ana *Also Called: Secure Comm Systems Inc (P-6658)*

Benchpro Inc ....C 619 478-9400
13463 Windy Grove Dr Rancho Cucamonga (91739) *(P-9865)*

Bend-Tek Inc (PA)..E **714 210-8966**
2205 S Yale St Santa Ana (92704) *(P-4958)*

Bender Ccp Inc ....E 619 232-5719
757 Main St Unit 102 Chula Vista (91911) *(P-6094)*

Bender Ccp Inc (PA)..C 323 232-2371
2150 E 37th St Vernon (90058) *(P-6095)*

Bender Ready Mix Inc ....E 714 560-0744
516 S Santa Fe St Santa Ana (92705) *(P-4431)*

Bender Ready Mix Concrete, Santa Ana *Also Called: Bender Ready Mix Inc (P-4431)*

Bender US, Vernon *Also Called: Bender Ccp Inc (P-6095)*

Bendpak Inc (PA)...D **805 933-9970**
30440 Agoura Rd Agoura Hills (91301) *(P-5694)*

Beneficial State Bank ....D 323 264-3310
3626 E 1st St Los Angeles (90063) *(P-11746)*

Benefit Programs ADM, City Of Industry *Also Called: Management Applied Prgrm Inc (P-14142)*

Benefitmall, Woodland Hills *Also Called: Centerstone Insur & Fincl Svcs (P-12193)*

Benefits Prgram Adminsitration ....D 562 463-5000
13191 Concords Pkwy N Ste 205 City Of Industry (91746) *(P-12655)*

Benefitvision Inc ....D 818 348-3100
5550 Topanga Canyon Blvd Woodland Hills (91367) *(P-17048)*

Benetrac, San Diego *Also Called: Paychex Benefit Tech Inc (P-9453)*

Benevolence Food Products LLC ....E 888 832-3738
2761 Saturn St Ste D Brea (92821) *(P-1743)*

Benihana 24, Encino *Also Called: Benihana Inc (P-11551)*

Benihana Inc ....D 818 788-7121
16226 Ventura Blvd Encino (91436) *(P-11551)*

Benjamin Moore Authorized Ret, Corona *Also Called: Ganahl Lumber Company (P-11155)*

Bennett Entps A Cal Ldscp Cntg ....D 310 534-3543
25889 Belle Porte Ave Harbor City (90710) *(P-150)*

Bennett Landscape, Harbor City *Also Called: Bennett Entps A Cal Ldscp Cntg (P-150)*

Bennion Deville Fine Homes Inc ....B 760 674-3452
74850 Us Highway 111 Indian Wells (92210) *(P-12387)*

Benny Enterprises Inc ....E 619 592-4455
1100 N Johnson Ave Ste 110 El Cajon (92020) *(P-11042)*

Benrich Service Company Inc (PA) ....E **714 241-0284**
3190 Airport Loop Dr Ste G Costa Mesa (92626) *(P-14462)*

Bens Asphalt & Maint Co Inc ....D 951 248-1103
2537 Rubidoux Blvd Riverside (92509) *(P-610)*

Bent Manufacturing Co Inc ....D 714 842-0600
17311 Nichols Ln Huntington Beach (92647) *(P-4064)*

Bent Manufacturing Company, Huntington Beach *Also Called: Bent Manufacturing Co Inc (P-4064)*

Bentley Mills, City Of Industry *Also Called: Bentley Mills Inc (P-1948)*

Bentley Mills Inc (PA)..C **626 333-4585**
14641 Don Julian Rd City Of Industry (91746) *(P-1948)*

Bento Box Entertainment LLC .... B 818 333-7700
   5161 Lankershim Blvd Ste 120 North Hollywood (91601) *(P-14808)*

Benz - One Complete Operation, Tehachapi *Also Called: Pjbs Holdings Inc (P-9755)*

Beranek LLC .... E 310 328-9094
   2340 W 205th St Torrance (90501) *(P-6096)*

Berenice 2 AM Corp .... E 858 255-8693
   8008 Girard Ave Ste 150 La Jolla (92037) *(P-1313)*

Berg Lacquer Co (PA)..................................... D 323 261-8114
   3150 E Pico Blvd Los Angeles (90023) *(P-11106)*

Bergandi Machinery Company, Ontario *Also Called: Bmci Inc (P-5652)*

Bergelectric Corp (PA)................................... D 760 638-2374
   3182 Lionshead Ave Carlsbad (92010) *(P-887)*

Bergelectric Corp .... A 760 746-1003
   3182 Lionshead Ave Carlsbad (92010) *(P-888)*

Bergelectric Corp .... C 760 746-1003
   2210 Meyers Ave Escondido (92029) *(P-889)*

Bergelectric Corp .... D 760 291-8100
   955 Borra Pl Escondido (92029) *(P-890)*

Bergelectric Corp .... D 949 250-7005
   15776 Gateway Cir Tustin (92780) *(P-891)*

Bergensons Property Svcs Inc .... A 760 631-5111
   3605 Ocean Ranch Blvd Ste 200 Oceanside (92056) *(P-13358)*

Berger Inc .... A 818 986-1234
   5955 De Soto Ave Ste 160 Woodland Hills (91367) *(P-16368)*

Berger Bros Inc .... B 626 334-2699
   154 N Aspan Ave Azusa (91702) *(P-997)*

Berger Kahn A Law Corporation (PA)....................... D 949 474-1880
   1 Park Plz Ste 340 Irvine (92614) *(P-16645)*

Bergman Kprs LLC (PA).................................... C 714 924-7000
   2850 Saturn St Ste 100 Brea (92821) *(P-522)*

Bergsen Inc .... E 562 236-9787
   12241 Florence Ave Santa Fe Springs (90670) *(P-10124)*

Bericap, Ontario *Also Called: Bericap LLC (P-4065)*

Bericap LLC .... D 909 390-5518
   1671 Champagne Ave Ste B Ontario (91761) *(P-4065)*

Berk Communications Inc .... D 310 734-5525
   329 N Wetherly Dr Ste 203 Beverly Hills (90211) *(P-18250)*

Berkeley E Convalescent Hosp .... C 310 829-5377
   2021 Arizona Ave Santa Monica (90404) *(P-15837)*

Berkeley E Convalescent Hosp, Santa Monica *Also Called: Berkeley E Convalescent Hosp (P-15837)*

Berkeley Farms LLC .... B 510 265-8600
   17637 E Valley Blvd City Of Industry (91744) *(P-1325)*

Berkley East Healthcare Center, Santa Monica *Also Called: Asmb LLC (P-15572)*

Berkshire Hthway HM Svcs Cal P .... C 619 302-8082
   2365 Northside Dr Ste 200 San Diego (92108) *(P-11887)*

Berkshire Hthway Hmsrvces Trot, Lancaster *Also Called: V Troth Inc (P-12546)*

Bermingham Cntrls Inc A Cal Co (PA)...................... E 562 860-0463
   11144 Business Cir Cerritos (90703) *(P-5359)*

Bernardo Hts Healthcare Inc .... B 858 673-0101
   11895 Avenue Of Industry San Diego (92128) *(P-15838)*

Bernards Builders Inc .... B 818 898-1521
   555 1st St San Fernando (91340) *(P-442)*

Bernel Inc .... C 714 778-6070
   501 W Southern Ave Orange (92865) *(P-749)*

Bernell Hydraulics Inc (PA).............................. E 909 899-1751
   8821 Etiwanda Ave Rancho Cucamonga (91739) *(P-6049)*

Berney-Karp Inc .... D 323 260-7122
   3350 E 26th St Vernon (90058) *(P-4366)*

Bernstein, Los Angeles *Also Called: Alliancebernstein LP (P-12624)*

Berry Global Inc .... C 909 465-9055
   14000 Monte Vista Ave Chino (91710) *(P-4066)*

Berry Global Inc .... D 714 777-5200
   4875 E Hunter Ave Anaheim (92807) *(P-4067)*

Berry Global Films LLC .... C 909 517-2872
   14000 Monte Vista Ave Chino (91710) *(P-3946)*

Berry Petroleum Company LLC .... D 661 769-8820
   28700 Hovey Hills Rd Taft (93268) *(P-265)*

Berry Petroleum Company LLC (HQ)......................... E 661 616-3900
   11117 River Run Blvd Bakersfield (93311) *(P-266)*

Berry Petroleum Company LLC .... D 661 255-6066
   25121 Sierra Hwy Newhall (91321) *(P-267)*

Bert W Salas Inc .... C 619 562-7711
   11203 Highway 67 Lakeside (92040) *(P-17493)*

Bert-Co, Ontario *Also Called: Bert-Co Industries Inc (P-2969)*

Bert-Co Industries Inc .... C 323 669-5700
   2150 S Parco Ave Ontario (91761) *(P-2969)*

Bertelsmann Inc .... A 661 702-2700
   29011 Commerce Center Dr Valencia (91355) *(P-2884)*

Best Contracting Services Inc (PA)....................... B 310 328-9176
   19027 S Hamilton Ave Gardena (90248) *(P-1073)*

Best Data Products Inc .... D 818 534-1414
   7801 Alabama Ave Canoga Park (91304) *(P-5906)*

Best Financial, The, Signal Hill *Also Called: First American Team Realty Inc (P-12443)*

Best Formulations, City Of Industry *Also Called: Best Formulations LLC (P-1744)*

Best Formulations LLC (HQ).............................. E 626 912-9998
   17758 Rowland St City Of Industry (91748) *(P-1744)*

Best Formulations LLC .... C 626 912-9998
   938 Radecki Ct City Of Industry (91748) *(P-1745)*

Best Formulations LLC .... C 626 912-9998
   17775 Rowland St City Of Industry (91748) *(P-3372)*

Best Friends Animal Society .... C 818 643-3989
   1845 Pontius Ave Los Angeles (90025) *(P-17458)*

Best Interiors Inc (PA)................................. C 714 490-7999
   2100 E Via Burton Anaheim (92806) *(P-998)*

Best Interiors Inc .... D 858 715-3760
   4395 Murphy Canyon Rd San Diego (92123) *(P-999)*

BEST OPPORTUNITIES, Apple Valley *Also Called: BEST Opportunities Inc (P-17049)*

BEST Opportunities Inc .... C 760 628-0111
   22450 Headquarters Ave Apple Valley (92307) *(P-17049)*

Best Overnight Express, Irwindale *Also Called: Best Overnite Express Inc (P-8933)*

Best Overnite Express Inc (PA).......................... D 626 256-6340
   406 Live Oak Ave Irwindale (91706) *(P-8933)*

Best Redwood, San Diego *Also Called: Rtmex Inc (P-2292)*

Best Signs Inc (PA).................................... E 760 320-3042
   1550 S Gene Autry Trl Palm Springs (92264) *(P-14463)*

Best Way Disposal Co Inc .... D 760 244-9773
   17105 Mesa St Hesperia (92345) *(P-9732)*

Best Way Marble, Los Angeles *Also Called: Best-Way Marble & Tile Co Inc (P-4471)*

Best Western, Santa Barbara *Also Called: Encina Pepper Tree Joint Ventr (P-12821)*

Best Western, Santa Barbara *Also Called: Encina Pepper Tree Joint Ventr (P-12822)*

Best Western Bayside Inn, San Diego *Also Called: Tic Hotels Inc (P-13052)*

Best Western Golden Sails Ht, Torrance *Also Called: Long Beach Golden Sails Inc (P-12905)*

Best Western Stovalls Inn (PA)......................... D 714 956-4430
   1110 W Katella Ave Anaheim (92802) *(P-12773)*

Best Wstn Fireside Inn By Sea, Cambria *Also Called: Moonstone Bch Innvstors A Cal (P-12929)*

Best-Way Distributing Co, Sylmar *Also Called: Allied Company Holdings Inc (P-11040)*

Best-Way Marble & Tile Co Inc .... E 323 266-6794
   5037 Telegraph Rd Los Angeles (90022) *(P-4471)*

Bestforms Inc .... E 805 388-0503
   1135 Avenida Acaso Camarillo (93012) *(P-3191)*

Bestop Baja LLC .... C 760 560-2252
   2950 Norman Strasse Rd San Marcos (92069) *(P-9816)*

Bestpack Packaging Systems, Ontario *Also Called: Future Commodities Intl Inc (P-5789)*

Bestway Foods, Valencia *Also Called: Bestway Sandwiches Inc (P-1437)*

Bestway Sandwiches Inc (PA)............................ E 818 361-1800
   28209 Avenue Stanford Valencia (91355) *(P-1437)*

Bestwestren Inn of Chicago, Newport Coast *Also Called: Inn of Chicago Associates Ltd (P-12875)*

Beta Bionics Inc .... E 949 297-6635
   11 Hughes Irvine (92618) *(P-8371)*

Beta Offshore, Long Beach *Also Called: Beta Operating Company LLC (P-268)*

Beta Operating Company LLC .... D 562 628-1526
   111 W Ocean Blvd Long Beach (90802) *(P-268)*

Bethar Corporation C
   17625 Railroad St City Of Industry (91748) *(P-12595)*

Bethlehem Construction Inc .... D 661 758-1001
   425 J St Wasco (93280) *(P-473)*

Betta Assets Inc .... D 818 990-7733
   17141 Ventura Blvd Ste 205 Encino (91316) *(P-12388)*

Better Bakery Co, Ventura *Also Called: Better Bakery LLC (P-1480)*

Better Bakery LLC .... C 661 294-9882
444 E Santa Clara St Ventura (93001) *(P-1480)*

Better Beverages Inc (PA) .... **E 562 924-8321**
10624 Midway Ave Cerritos (90703) *(P-1668)*

Better Mens Clothes, Los Angeles *Also Called: Hirsh Inc (P-335)*

Better Nutritionals LLC .... D 310 356-9019
3380 Horseless Carriage Rd Norco (92860) *(P-1292)*

Better Nutritionals LLC .... D 310 356-9019
3350 Horseless Carriage Rd Norco (92860) *(P-1293)*

Better Nutritionals LLC .... E 310 356-9019
17120 S Figueroa St Ste B Gardena (90248) *(P-1294)*

Better Nutritionals LLC (PA) .... D 310 356-9019
3390 Horseless Carriage Dr Norco (92860) *(P-1295)*

Betts Company .... E 909 427-9988
10007 Elm Ave Fontana (92335) *(P-5393)*

Betts Truck Parts, Fontana *Also Called: Betts Company (P-5393)*

Betty Ford Center (HQ) .... C 760 773-4100
39000 Bob Hope Dr Rancho Mirage (92270) *(P-16445)*

Beveragefactory.com, San Diego *Also Called: Cydea Inc (P-1563)*

Beverages & More Inc .... C 949 643-3020
28011 Greenfield Dr Laguna Niguel (92677) *(P-1608)*

Beverages & More Inc .... C 714 891-1242
6820 Katella Ave Cypress (90630) *(P-10338)*

Beverages & More Inc .... C 714 990-2060
875 E Birch St Ste A Brea (92821) *(P-11625)*

Beverages & More Inc .... C 714 279-8131
2000 N Tustin St Orange (92865) *(P-11626)*

Beverly Center, Los Angeles *Also Called: La Cienega Associates (P-12476)*

Beverly Community Hosp Assn .... B 323 889-2452
101 E Beverly Blvd Ste 104 Montebello (90640) *(P-15924)*

Beverly Community Hosp Assn .... B 323 725-1519
1920 W Whittier Blvd Montebello (90640) *(P-15925)*

Beverly Community Hosp Assn (HQ) .... **B 323 726-1222**
309 W Beverly Blvd Montebello (90640) *(P-15926)*

Beverly Furniture, Pomona *Also Called: Rbf Lifestyle Holdings LLC (P-2516)*

Beverly Hills BMW, Los Angeles *Also Called: FAA Beverly Hills Inc (P-11345)*

Beverly Hills Hotel, Beverly Hills *Also Called: Sajahtera Inc (P-13009)*

Beverly Hills Luxury Hotel LLC .... B 310 274-9999
1801 Century Park E Ste 1200 Los Angeles (90067) *(P-12774)*

Beverly Hills Plaza Hotel, Los Angeles *Also Called: Donald T Sterling Corporation (P-12815)*

Beverly Hlls Cncierge Hlth Ctr, Beverly Hills *Also Called: Beverly Hlls Onclogy Med Group (P-16286)*

Beverly Hlls Onclogy Med Group .... D 310 432-8900
8900 Wilshire Blvd Beverly Hills (90211) *(P-16286)*

Beverly Hlls Rhbltation Centre, Los Angeles *Also Called: Pacs Group Inc (P-15732)*

Beverly West Health Care Inc .... D 323 938-2451
1020 S Fairfax Ave Los Angeles (90019) *(P-15582)*

Bevmo, Laguna Niguel *Also Called: Beverages & More Inc (P-1608)*

Bevpack, Van Nuys *Also Called: Power Brands Consulting LLC (P-1550)*

Bexel, Van Nuys *Also Called: Nep Bexel Inc (P-14897)*

Bey-Berk International (PA) .... E 818 773-7534
9145 Deering Ave Chatsworth (91311) *(P-5442)*

Beyond Finance LLC .... A 800 282-7186
9525 Towne Centre Dr Ste 100 San Diego (92121) *(P-13168)*

Beyond Meat and Company, Anaheim *Also Called: Caballero & Sons Inc (P-12011)*

Beyondsoft Consulting Inc .... C 310 532-2822
19009 S Laurel Park Rd Spc 6 Compton (90220) *(P-18290)*

Bezel, San Luis Obispo *Also Called: Phase 2 Cellars LLC (P-1581)*

BF Suma Pharmaceuticals Inc .... E 626 285-8366
5001 Earle Ave Rosemead (91770) *(P-3373)*

Bfg Supply Co LLC .... C 909 591-0461
2552 Shenandoah Way San Bernardino (92407) *(P-11069)*

BFI Waste Systems N Amer Inc .... D 323 321-1722
9200 Glenoaks Blvd Sun Valley (91352) *(P-9733)*

Bfp, Brea *Also Called: Benevolence Food Products LLC (P-1743)*

Bgk Equities Inc (HQ) .... D 505 982-2184
2000 Avenue Of The Stars Ste 550 Los Angeles (90067) *(P-12389)*

Bh Partnership LP (PA) .... **B 858 539-7635**
998 W Mission Bay Dr San Diego (92109) *(P-12775)*

Bh-SD Opco LLC (PA) .... **D 619 465-4411**
7050 Parkway Dr La Mesa (91942) *(P-16446)*

Bh-Tech Inc .... A 858 694-0900
5425 Oberlin Dr Ste 207 San Diego (92121) *(P-4068)*

Bhc Alhambra Hospital, Rosemead *Also Called: Bhc Alhambra Hospital Inc (P-16536)*

Bhc Alhambra Hospital Inc .... B 626 286-1191
4619 Rosemead Blvd Rosemead (91770) *(P-16536)*

Bhc Industries, Compton *Also Called: Barkens Hardchrome Inc (P-5693)*

BHC Industries Inc .... E 310 632-2000
239 E Greenleaf Blvd Compton (90220) *(P-5238)*

Bi Nutraceuticals Inc .... C 310 669-2100
2384 E Pacifica Pl Rancho Dominguez (90220) *(P-1669)*

Bi Technologies Corporation (HQ) .... **B 714 447-2300**
120 S State College Blvd Ste 175 Brea (92821) *(P-6972)*

Bi-Search International Inc .... E 714 258-4500
17550 Gillette Ave Irvine (92614) *(P-6973)*

Bicara Ltd .... B 310 316-6222
318 Avenue I Ste 65 Redondo Beach (90277) *(P-10865)*

Bicycle Club Casino, Bell Gardens *Also Called: Bell Gardens Bicycle Club Inc (P-15194)*

Bien Air, Irvine *Also Called: Bien Air Usa Inc (P-8327)*

Bien Air Usa Inc .... D 949 477-6050
8861 Research Dr Ste 100 Irvine (92618) *(P-8327)*

Big Bear Grizzly & Big Bear Lf, Big Bear Lake *Also Called: Hi-Desert Publishing Company (P-11671)*

Big Brand Tire & Service .... D 951 679-6266
26920 Newport Rd Menifee (92584) *(P-3862)*

Big Brand Tire & Svc - Menifee, Menifee *Also Called: Big Brand Tire & Service (P-3862)*

Big Canyon Country Club .... C 949 644-5404
1 Big Canyon Dr Newport Beach (92660) *(P-15124)*

Big Dog Sportswear, Los Angeles *Also Called: Walking Company Holdings Inc (P-11498)*

Big Eight, Lancaster *Also Called: City of Lancaster (P-15102)*

BIG Enterprises .... E 626 448-1449
9702 Rush St El Monte (91733) *(P-5075)*

Big Horn Wealth Management Inc .... D 951 273-7900
2577 Research Dr Corona (92882) *(P-2970)*

Big Lgue Dreams Consulting LLC .... C 760 324-5600
33700 Date Palm Dr Cathedral City (92234) *(P-13100)*

Big Lgue Dreams Consulting LLC .... C 619 846-8855
2155 Trumble Rd Perris (92571) *(P-15019)*

Big Lgue Dreams Consulting LLC .... C 626 839-1100
2100 S Azusa Ave West Covina (91792) *(P-15020)*

Big Nickel, Palm Desert *Also Called: Daniels Inc (P-2911)*

Big Star, South Gate *Also Called: Koos Manufacturing Inc (P-14524)*

Big Strike, Los Angeles *Also Called: Tlmf Inc (P-2073)*

Big T Industries, Lake Forest *Also Called: Big Train Inc (P-1314)*

Big Train Inc .... C 949 340-8800
25392 Commercentre Dr Lake Forest (92630) *(P-1314)*

Big Tree Furniture & Inds Inc (PA) .... **E 310 894-7500**
760 S Vail Ave Montebello (90640) *(P-2420)*

Bigge Group .... C 714 523-4092
14511 Industry Cir La Mirada (90638) *(P-13431)*

Bighorn Golf Club Charities .... C 760 773-2468
255 Palowet Dr Palm Desert (92260) *(P-15125)*

Bijan, Beverly Hills *Also Called: Fashion World Incorporated (P-10683)*

Bikes Online Inc .... D 650 272-3378
2711 Loker Ave W Carlsbad (92010) *(P-10510)*

Bill Howe Plumbing Inc .... D 800 245-5469
9210 Sky Park Ct Ste 200 San Diego (92123) *(P-750)*

Bilt-Well Roofing & Mtl Co, Los Angeles *Also Called: Sbb Roofing Inc (P-1095)*

Bimeda Inc .... C 626 815-1680
5539 Ayon Ave Irwindale (91706) *(P-3374)*

Binder Metal Products Inc .... D 800 233-0896
14909 S Broadway Gardena (90248) *(P-5175)*

Binding Site Inc (HQ) .... **D 858 453-9177**
6730 Mesa Ridge Rd San Diego (92121) *(P-10068)*

Binex, Torrance *Also Called: Binex Line Corp (P-9254)*

Binex Line Corp (PA) .... **D 310 416-8600**
19515 S Vermont Ave Torrance (90502) *(P-9254)*

Bio Hazard Inc .... E 213 625-2116
6019 Randolph St Commerce (90040) *(P-11112)*

Bio-Med Services Inc .... D 909 235-4400
3300 E Guasti Rd Ontario (91761) *(P-15927)*

Bio-Medical Devices Inc	E	949 752-9642
17171 Daimler St Irvine (92614) *(P-8108)*		
Bio-Medical Devices Intl Inc	E	949 752-9642
17171 Daimler St Irvine (92614) *(P-8109)*		
Bio-Medics Inc	C	909 883-9501
371 W Highland Ave San Bernardino (92405) *(P-16537)*		
Bio-Nutritional RES Group Inc	C	714 427-6990
6 Morgan Ste 100 Irvine (92618) *(P-1296)*		
Bio-RAD Laboratories Inc	C	949 598-1200
9500 Jeronimo Rd Irvine (92618) *(P-3311)*		
Bioagilytix Labs LLC	A	858 652-4600
9050 Camino Santa Fe San Diego (92121) *(P-17774)*		
Bioatla, San Diego *Also Called: Bioatla Inc (P-3566)*		
Bioatla Inc	D	858 558-0708
11085 Torreyana Rd San Diego (92121) *(P-3566)*		
Biocell Laboratories Inc	E	310 537-3300
2001 E University Dr Rancho Dominguez (90220) *(P-3534)*		
Biodefensor Corporation		888 899-2956
13448 Manhasset Rd Ste 3 Apple Valley (92308) *(P-10329)*		
Biodot Inc (HQ)	D	949 440-3685
2852 Alton Pkwy Irvine (92606) *(P-7849)*		
Bioduro LLC	B	858 529-6600
72 Fairbanks Irvine (92618) *(P-17775)*		
Bioduro LLC (PA)	E	858 529-6600
11011 Torreyana Rd San Diego (92121) *(P-17776)*		
Bioduro-Sundia, San Diego *Also Called: Bioduro LLC (P-17776)*		
Biofilm Inc	D	760 727-9030
3225 Executive Rdg Vista (92081) *(P-8110)*		
Biogeneral Inc	E	858 453-4451
9925 Mesa Rim Rd San Diego (92121) *(P-8111)*		
Biolase, Lake Forest *Also Called: Biolase Inc (P-8328)*		
Biolase Inc (PA)	D	
27042 Towne Centre Dr Ste 270 Lake Forest (92610) *(P-8328)*		
Biolase Inc	D	949 361-1200
4225 Prado Rd Ste 102 Corona (92880) *(P-8329)*		
Biolegend Inc (HQ)	D	858 455-9588
8999 Biolegend Way San Diego (92121) *(P-17777)*		
Biomed California Inc	D	310 665-1121
721 S Glasgow Ave Ste C Inglewood (90301) *(P-3375)*		
Biomed Realty, San Diego *Also Called: Biomed Realty Trust Inc (P-12683)*		
Biomed Realty Trust (PA)	B	858 207-2513
4570 Executive Dr Ste 400 San Diego (92121) *(P-12683)*		
Biomet Inc	E	949 453-3200
181 Technology Dr Irvine (92618) *(P-8254)*		
Bionano Genomics, San Diego *Also Called: Bionano Genomics Inc (P-7945)*		
Bionano Genomics Inc (PA)	D	858 888-7600
9540 Towne Centre Dr Ste 100 San Diego (92121) *(P-7945)*		
Bioness Inc	C	661 362-4850
25103 Rye Canyon Loop Valencia (91355) *(P-8372)*		
Bionime USA Corporation	E	909 781-6969
1450 E Spruce St Ste B Ontario (91761) *(P-10069)*		
Biopac Systems Inc	E	805 685-0066
42 Aero Camino Goleta (93117) *(P-7946)*		
Bioquip Products Inc	E	310 667-8800
2321 E Gladwick St Rancho Dominguez (90220) *(P-17778)*		
Biorepository, Valencia *Also Called: Q Squared Solutions LLC (P-16330)*		
Biorx Laboratories, Commerce *Also Called: Biorx Pharmaceuticals Inc (P-3376)*		
Biorx Pharmaceuticals Inc	E	323 725-3100
6320 Chalet Dr Commerce (90040) *(P-3376)*		
Bioscience Research Reagents, Temecula *Also Called: EMD Millipore Corporation (P-3572)*		
Bioscreen Testing Services, Torrance *Also Called: Als Group Usa Corp (P-17901)*		
Bioseal	E	714 528-4695
167 W Orangethorpe Ave Placentia (92870) *(P-8112)*		
Biosense Webster Inc (HQ)	C	909 839-8500
31 Technology Dr Ste 200 Irvine (92618) *(P-8373)*		
Biosero (PA)	E	858 880-7376
4770 Ruffner St San Diego (92111) *(P-13674)*		
Bioserv Corporation	E	917 817-1326
9380 Judicial Dr San Diego (92121) *(P-3535)*		
Bioserve, San Diego *Also Called: Bioserv Corporation (P-3535)*		

Biosite Inc	D	510 683-9063
9975 Summers Ridge Rd San Diego (92121) *(P-10070)*		
Biosource International	E	805 659-5759
5791 Van Allen Way Carlsbad (92008) *(P-3536)*		
Biospace Inc	D	323 932-6503
13850 Cerritos Corporate Dr Ste C Cerritos (90703) *(P-17779)*		
Biotheranostics Inc (HQ)	E	877 886-6739
9640 Towne Centre Dr Ste 200 San Diego (92121) *(P-16305)*		
Biotix	E	858 875-5479
6995 Calle De Linea Ste 106 San Diego (92154) *(P-474)*		
Biotix (HQ)	E	858 875-7696
10636 Scripps Summit Ct Ste 130 San Diego (92131) *(P-3731)*		
Biotone Professional Products, San Diego *Also Called: Natural Thoughts Incorporated (P-3671)*		
Biovia, San Diego *Also Called: Dassault Systemes Biovia Corp (P-13912)*		
Bioxp, San Diego *Also Called: Telesis Bio Inc (P-7983)*		
Birch Ptrick Convalescent Cntr, Chula Vista *Also Called: Sharp Healthcare (P-16193)*		
Birchwood Lighting Inc	E	714 550-7118
3340 E La Palma Ave Anaheim (92806) *(P-6492)*		
Bird B Gone LLC	D	949 472-3122
1921 E Edinger Ave Santa Ana (92705) *(P-3961)*		
Birdwell Beach Britches, Irvine *Also Called: Birdwell Enterprises Inc (P-2007)*		
Birdwell Enterprises Inc	E	714 557-7040
8801 Research Dr Irvine (92618) *(P-2007)*		
Birmingham Fastener & Sup Inc	E	562 944-9549
12748 Florence Ave Santa Fe Springs (90670) *(P-4760)*		
Bis Computer Solutions Inc (PA)	E	818 248-4282
5500 Alta Canyada Rd La Canada Flintridge (91011) *(P-13675)*		
Bisco Industries Inc (HQ)	D	800 323-1232
5065 E Hunter Ave Anaheim (92807) *(P-10232)*		
Biscomerica Corp	B	909 877-5997
565 West Slover Ave Rialto (92377) *(P-1481)*		
Bish Inc	E	619 660-6220
2820 Via Orange Way Ste G Spring Valley (91978) *(P-7445)*		
Bitcentral, Newport Beach *Also Called: Bitcentral Inc (P-10233)*		
Bitcentral Inc	D	949 253-9000
4340 Von Karman Ave Ste 410 Newport Beach (92660) *(P-10233)*		
Bitchin Inc (PA)	E	760 224-7447
6211 Yarrow Dr Ste C Carlsbad (92011) *(P-1746)*		
Bitchin Sauce, Carlsbad *Also Called: Bitchin Inc (P-1746)*		
Bitchin Sauce LLC	D	737 248-2446
4509 Adams St Carlsbad (92008) *(P-1747)*		
Bitchin' Sauce, Carlsbad *Also Called: Bitchin Sauce LLC (P-1747)*		
Bitcoin Ira, Sherman Oaks *Also Called: Alternative Ira Services LLC (P-14444)*		
Bitmax	E	323 978-7878
6600 W Sunset Blvd Los Angeles (90028) *(P-13889)*		
Bittree Incorporated	E	818 500-8142
600 W Elk Ave Glendale (91204) *(P-6600)*		
Bivar, Irvine *Also Called: Bivar Inc (P-6974)*		
Bivar Inc	E	949 951-8808
4 Thomas Irvine (92618) *(P-6974)*		
BIW Connector Systems, Irvine *Also Called: ITT Cannon LLC (P-6351)*		
Bixby Land Company	C	949 336-7000
1501 Quail St Ste 200 Newport Beach (92660) *(P-12390)*		
Bixolon America Inc	E	858 764-4580
2575 W 237th St Torrance (90505) *(P-5907)*		
BJ Liquidation Inc	D	626 961-7221
428 Turnbull Canyon Rd City Of Industry (91745) *(P-2441)*		
BJ's Restaurant & Brewhouse, Huntington Beach *Also Called: BJs Restaurant Operations Co (P-17952)*		
Bjb Enterprises Inc	E	714 734-8450
14791 Franklin Ave Tustin (92780) *(P-3260)*		
BJs Restaurant Operations Co	B	714 500-2440
7755 Center Ave Ste 300 Huntington Beach (92647) *(P-17952)*		
BJS&t Enterprises Inc	E	619 448-7795
1702 N Magnolia Ave El Cajon (92020) *(P-5314)*		
Bjz LLC	C	760 851-0740
45150 Club Dr Indian Wells (92210) *(P-16369)*		
Bkf Engineers/Ags	D	949 526-8400
4675 Macarthur Ct Ste 400 Newport Beach (92660) *(P-17494)*		

Employee Codes: A=Over 500 employees, B=251-500
C=101-250, D=51-100, E=20-49, F=10-19, G=1-9

2025 Southern California
Business Directory and Buyers Guide

© Mergent Inc. 1-800-342-5647

957

ALPHABETIC

BKF ENGINEERS/AGS, Newport Beach Also Called: Bkf Engineers/Ags *(P-17494)*

BKM Diablo 227 LLC .... D 602 688-6409
1701 Quail St Ste 100 Newport Beach (92660) *(P-12391)*

BKM Total Office of Texas, Santa Fe Springs Also Called: New Tangram LLC *(P-9877)*

Black & Decker, El Toro Also Called: Black & Decker Corporation *(P-5633)*

Black & Decker Corporation .... E 949 672-4000
19701 Da Vinci El Toro (92610) *(P-5633)*

Black Box Distribution LLC .... D 760 268-1174
371 2nd St Ste 1 Encinitas (92024) *(P-8506)*

Black Box Inc .... D 760 804-3300
371 2nd St Ste 1 Encinitas (92024) *(P-10678)*

Black Box Network Services, Los Angeles Also Called: Scottel Voice & Data Inc *(P-14731)*

Black Diamond Blade Company (PA).............................. E **800 949-9014**
234 E O St Colton (92324) *(P-5488)*

Black Dot Wireless LLC .... D 949 502-3800
23456 Madero Ste 210 Mission Viejo (92691) *(P-9386)*

Black Jack Farms, Santa Maria Also Called: Blackjack Frms De La Csta Cntl *(P-75)*

Black Knight Infoserv LLC .... B 904 854-5100
2500 Redhill Ave Ste 100 Santa Ana (92705) *(P-14124)*

Black Knight Patrol Inc .... D 213 985-6499
505 S Pacific Ave Ste 201 San Pedro (90731) *(P-14280)*

Black N Gold, Paramount Also Called: Kum Kang Trading USA Inc *(P-3667)*

Black Oxide, Anaheim Also Called: Black Oxide Industries Inc *(P-5239)*

Black Oxide Industries Inc .... E 714 870-9610
1745 N Orangethorpe Park Ste A Anaheim (92801) *(P-5239)*

Black Stallion Industries, Santa Fe Springs Also Called: Revco Industries Inc *(P-10459)*

Blackbaud Internet Solutions, San Diego Also Called: Kintera Inc *(P-13960)*

Blackburn Alton Invstments LLC .... E 714 731-2000
700 E Alton Ave Santa Ana (92705) *(P-3120)*

Blackjack Frms De La Csta Cntl .... C 805 347-1333
2385 A St Santa Maria (93455) *(P-75)*

Blackline, Woodland Hills Also Called: Blackline Inc *(P-13890)*

Blackline Inc (PA) .... A **818 223-9008**
21300 Victory Blvd Fl 12 Woodland Hills (91367) *(P-13890)*

Blackrock Logistics, Fontana Also Called: Blackrock Logistics Inc *(P-9255)*

Blackrock Logistics Inc .... C 909 259-5357
14601 Slover Ave Fontana (92337) *(P-9255)*

Blackstone Consulting Inc (PA) .... D 310 826-4389
11726 San Vicente Blvd Ste 550 Los Angeles (90049) *(P-18105)*

Blakely Sokoloff Taylor & Zafman LLP .... C 310 207-3800
12400 Wilshire Blvd Ste 700 Los Angeles (90025) *(P-16646)*

Blanchard Training and Dev Inc (PA) .... C **760 489-5005**
125 State Pl Escondido (92029) *(P-18106)*

Blaze Solutions Inc .... D 415 964-5689
155 N Riverview Dr Anaheim (92808) *(P-13676)*

Blc Residential Care Inc .... D 310 722-7541
1455 W 112th St Los Angeles (90047) *(P-16876)*

Blc Wc Inc (PA) .... C **562 926-1452**
13260 Moore St Cerritos (90703) *(P-3121)*

Bleau Consulting Inc (PA) .... D **619 263-5550**
555 Raven St San Diego (92102) *(P-2505)*

Blenders Eyewear, San Diego Also Called: Blenders Eyewear LLC *(P-8405)*

Blenders Eyewear LLC .... D 858 490-2178
4683 Cass St San Diego (92109) *(P-8405)*

Blh Construction Company .... C 818 905-3837
20750 Ventura Blvd Ste 155 Woodland Hills (91364) *(P-443)*

Bligh Pacific, Santa Fe Springs Also Called: Bligh Roof Co *(P-1074)*

Bligh Roof Co .... D 562 944-9753
11043 Forest Pl Santa Fe Springs (90670) *(P-1074)*

Blind Squirrel Games Inc .... E 714 460-0860
7545 Irvine Center Dr Ste 150 Irvine (92618) *(P-13891)*

Bliss Holdings LLC .... E 626 506-8696
745 S Vinewood St Escondido (92029) *(P-6493)*

Bliss World LLC .... D 323 500-0921
6250 Hollywood Blvd Fl 4 Los Angeles (90028) *(P-15045)*

Blisslights Inc .... E 888 868-4603
2449 Cades Way Vista (92081) *(P-7111)*

Blitz Rocks Inc .... E 310 883-5183
750 B St Ste 3300 San Diego (92101) *(P-13892)*

Blizzard Entertainment Inc (DH).. D **949 955-1380**
1 Blizzard Irvine (92618) *(P-13893)*

Blk International LLC .... E 424 282-3443
12410 Clark St Santa Fe Springs (90670) *(P-1609)*

Block Tops Inc (PA).. E **714 978-5080**
1321 S Sunkist St Anaheim (92806) *(P-2557)*

Blockade Medical, Irvine Also Called: Balt Usa LLC *(P-10067)*

Blockaire, Glendale Also Called: Assign Corporation *(P-14197)*

Blois Construction Inc .... C 805 485-0011
3201 Sturgis Rd Oxnard (93030) *(P-663)*

Blood Bnk San Brnrdino Rvrside, San Bernardino Also Called: Lifestream Blood Bank *(P-16582)*

Bloomers Metal Stampings Inc .... E 661 257-2955
28615 Braxton Ave Valencia (91355) *(P-5176)*

Bloomfield Bakers ....A 626 610-2253
10711 Bloomfield St Los Alamitos (90720) *(P-1482)*

Bloomfield Bakers, Los Alamitos Also Called: Bloomfield Bakers *(P-1482)*

Bloomios Inc .... E 805 222-6330
201 W Montecito St Santa Barbara (93101) *(P-8663)*

Blow Molded Products, Riverside Also Called: Plastic Technologies Inc *(P-4201)*

Blow Molded Products Inc .... E 951 360-6055
4720 Felspar St Riverside (92509) *(P-4069)*

Blower-Dempsay Corporation (PA)................................... C **714 481-3800**
4042 W Garry Ave Santa Ana (92704) *(P-2655)*

Bls Lmsine Svc Los Angeles Inc .... B 323 644-7166
2860 Fletcher Dr Los Angeles (90039) *(P-8814)*

BLT, Los Angeles Also Called: BLT & Associates Inc *(P-13321)*

BLT & Associates Inc .... C 323 860-4000
6430 W Sunset Blvd Ste 800 Los Angeles (90028) *(P-13321)*

BLT Cmmnctions LLC A Ltd Lblty .... C 323 860-4000
6430 W Sunset Blvd Ste 800 Los Angeles (90028) *(P-13262)*

Blue Bay Industries, Encino Also Called: Sayari Shahrzad *(P-10695)*

Blue Beacon of Wheeler Ridge, Arvin Also Called: Blue Beacon USA LP *(P-14704)*

Blue Beacon USA LP .... C 661 858-2090
5831 Santa Elena Dr Arvin (93203) *(P-14704)*

Blue Chip Stamps Inc ....A 626 585-6700
301 E Colorado Blvd Ste 300 Pasadena (91101) *(P-10125)*

Blue Desert International Inc .... D 951 273-7575
510 N Sheridan St Ste A Corona (92878) *(P-6004)*

Blue Microphone, Westlake Village Also Called: Baltic Ltvian Unvrsal Elec LLC *(P-6529)*

Blue Nalu Inc .... E 858 703-8703
6060 Nancy Ridge Dr Ste 100 San Diego (92121) *(P-1702)*

Blue Ocean Marine LLC .... E 805 658-2628
2060 Knoll Dr Ste 100 Ventura (93003) *(P-9153)*

Blue Pacific Flavors Inc .... E 626 934-0099
1354 Marion Ct City Of Industry (91745) *(P-1670)*

Blue Ribbon Draperies Inc .... E 562 425-4637
7341 Adams St Ste A Paramount (90723) *(P-11521)*

Blue Ridge Home Fashions Inc .... E 626 960-6069
15761 Tapia St Irwindale (91706) *(P-10662)*

Blue Shield Cal Lf Hlth Insur ....A 619 686-4200
2275 Rio Bonito Way Ste 250 San Diego (92108) *(P-12072)*

Blue Shield of California, Ontario Also Called: California Physicians Service *(P-12073)*

Blue Shield of California, Long Beach Also Called: California Physicians Service *(P-12074)*

Blue Shield of California, Woodland Hills Also Called: California Physicians Service *(P-12075)*

Blue Sky The Clor Imgntion LLC .... D 714 389-7700
410 Exchange Ste 250 Irvine (92602) *(P-10578)*

Blue Sphere Inc .... E 714 953-7555
10869 Portal Dr Los Alamitos (90720) *(P-1976)*

Blue Squirrel Inc .... D 858 268-0717
8295 Aero Pl San Diego (92123) *(P-6676)*

Blue Star Education, Garden Grove Also Called: Teacher Created Resources Inc *(P-2896)*

Blue Star Steel Inc ....E 619 448-5520
12122 Industry Rd Lakeside (92040) *(P-4819)*

Blue-White Industries Ltd (PA)... D **714 893-8529**
5300 Business Dr Huntington Beach (92649) *(P-7887)*

Bluebeam Inc (PA) .... C **626 788-4100**
443 S Raymond Ave Pasadena (91105) *(P-13677)*

Bluebird Office Supplies, Los Angeles Also Called: Image Source Inc *(P-10581)*

Bluefield Associates Inc .... E 909 476-6027
5430 Brooks St Montclair (91763) *(P-3634)*

Bluelab Corporation Usa Inc .... E 909 599-1940
437 S Cataract Ave San Dimas (91773) *(P-5813)*

Bluemark Inc ....C 323 230-0770
27909 Hancock Pkwy Valencia (91355) *(P-11113)*

Bluenalu, San Diego *Also Called: Blue Nalu Inc (P-1702)*

Bluetriton Brands Inc ....C 714 532-6220
619 N Main St Orange (92868) *(P-10932)*

Bluewater Wear, Santa Ana *Also Called: Aftco Mfg Co Inc (P-10508)*

Blufi Lending Corporation C
9909 Mira Mesa Blvd Ste 160 San Diego (92131) *(P-11888)*

Blumenthal Distributing Inc (PA)...................C **909 930-2000**
1901 S Archibald Ave Ontario (91761) *(P-9866)*

Bluprint Clothing Corp ....D 323 780-4347
4851 S Santa Fe Ave Vernon (90058) *(P-2034)*

Blyth/Wndsor Cntry Pk Hlthcare ....D 310 385-1090
3232 E Artesia Blvd Long Beach (90805) *(P-15808)*

Blythe Global Advisors LLC ....D 949 757-4180
19800 Macarthur Blvd Ste 1180 Irvine (92612) *(P-12019)*

Blytheco Inc (PA)......................................E **949 583-9500**
530 Technology Dr Ste 100 Irvine (92618) *(P-14201)*

Bm Extrusion Inc ....E 951 782-9020
1575 Omaha Ct Riverside (92507) *(P-4070)*

BMC ....E 310 321-5555
300 Continental Blvd Ste 570 El Segundo (90245) *(P-13894)*

BMC Group Inc ....D 310 321-5555
300 Continental Blvd Ste 570 El Segundo (90245) *(P-16647)*

BMC Industries, Bakersfield *Also Called: Bakersfield Machine Co Inc (P-6090)*

Bmci Inc ....E 951 361-8000
1689 S Parco Ave Ontario (91761) *(P-5652)*

Bmi, Temecula *Also Called: Bomatic Inc (P-4071)*

Bmp, Riverside *Also Called: Blow Molded Products Inc (P-4069)*

Bmp, Glendale *Also Called: Bunim-Murray Productions (P-14810)*

Bms Healthcare Inc ....C 562 942-7019
8925 Mines Ave Pico Rivera (90660) *(P-16538)*

BMw Precision Machining Inc ....E 760 439-6813
2379 Industry St Oceanside (92054) *(P-6097)*

Bni Publications Inc ....E 760 734-1113
990 Park Center Dr Ste E Vista (92081) *(P-11631)*

Bnk Petroleum (us) Inc ....E 805 484-3613
925 Broadbeck Dr Ste 220 Newbury Park (91320) *(P-295)*

Bnl Technologies Inc ....E 310 320-7272
22301 S Western Ave Ste 101 Torrance (90501) *(P-5874)*

BOa Inc ....E 714 256-8960
580 W Lambert Rd Ste L Brea (92821) *(P-2008)*

Boardriders Wholesale LLC ....E 949 916-3060
6201 Oak Cyn Ste 100 Irvine (92618) *(P-2083)*

Boardwalk Solutions, Gardena *Also Called: Ocean Direct LLC (P-1710)*

Bob Baker Chrysler-Plymouth, Carlsbad *Also Called: Bob Baker Volkswagen (P-11318)*

Bob Baker Volkswagen ....D 760 438-2200
5500 Paseo Del Norte Carlsbad (92008) *(P-11318)*

Bob Hope Health Center, Woodland Hills *Also Called: Motion Picture and TV Fund (P-16102)*

Bob Siemon Designs Inc ....D 714 549-0678
3501 W Segerstrom Ave Santa Ana (92704) *(P-8569)*

Bob Stall Chevrolet ....C 619 460-1311
7601 Alvarado Rd La Mesa (91942) *(P-11319)*

Bobbi Boss, Cerritos *Also Called: Midway International Inc (P 11120)*

Bobboi Natural Gelato, La Jolla *Also Called: Berenice 2 AM Corp (P-1313)*

Bobit Business Media Inc ....C 310 533-2400
21250 Hawthorne Blvd Ste 360 Torrance (90503) *(P-2845)*

Bobrick Washroom Equipment Inc (HQ)............D **818 764-1000**
6901 Tujunga Ave North Hollywood (91605) *(P-2577)*

Bobster Eyewear, San Diego *Also Called: Balboa Manufacturing Co LLC (P-1911)*

Bocchi Laboratories, Santa Clarita *Also Called: Bright Innovation Labs (P-3636)*

Bodycote Thermal Proc Inc ....E 562 946-1717
9921 Romandel Ave Santa Fe Springs (90670) *(P-4698)*

Bodycote Thermal Proc Inc ....E 714 893-6561
515 W Apra St Compton (90220) *(P-4699)*

Bodycote Thermal Proc Inc ....D 323 583-1231
3370 Benedict Way Huntington Park (90255) *(P-5240)*

Bodycote Usa Inc ....A 323 264-0111
2900 S Sunol Dr Vernon (90058) *(P-4700)*

Bodykore Inc ....E 949 325-3088
7466 Orangewood Ave Garden Grove (92841) *(P-10511)*

Bodywaves Inc (PA)...................................E **714 898-9900**
12362 Knott St Garden Grove (92841) *(P-2168)*

Boeing, El Segundo *Also Called: Boeing Satellite Systems Inc (P-6601)*

Boeing, Long Beach *Also Called: Boeing Company (P-7331)*

Boeing, Carson *Also Called: Boeing Company (P-7332)*

Boeing, Long Beach *Also Called: Boeing Company (P-7333)*

Boeing, San Diego *Also Called: Boeing Company (P-7334)*

Boeing, El Segundo *Also Called: Boeing Satellite Systems Inc (P-7336)*

Boeing, Huntington Beach *Also Called: Boeing Company (P-7642)*

Boeing Company ....A 562 496-1000
4000 N Lakewood Blvd Long Beach (90808) *(P-7331)*

Boeing Company ....C 310 522-2809
2220 E Carson St Carson (90810) *(P-7332)*

Boeing Company ....A 562 593-5511
4060 N Lakewood Blvd Long Beach (90808) *(P-7333)*

Boeing Company ....A 619 545-8382
Bldg-1454 Receiving San Diego (92135) *(P-7334)*

Boeing Company ....B 714 896-3311
14441 Astronautics Ln Huntington Beach (92647) *(P-7642)*

Boeing Company, The, El Segundo *Also Called: Boeing Stllite Systems Intl In (P-10487)*

Boeing Intllctual Prprty Lcnsi ....C 562 797-2020
14441 Astronautics Ln Huntington Beach (92647) *(P-7335)*

Boeing Satellite Systems Inc (HQ).................E **310 791-7450**
900 N Pacific Coast Hwy El Segundo (90245) *(P-6601)*

Boeing Satellite Systems Inc ....A 310 568-2735
2300 E Imperial Hwy El Segundo (90245) *(P-7336)*

Boeing Stllite Systems Intl In (HQ).................E **310 364-4000**
2260 E Imperial Hwy El Segundo (90245) *(P-10487)*

Boerner Truck Center, Huntington Park *Also Called: Fred M Boerner Motor Co (P-11445)*

Boiling Crab Operations LLC ....B 714 636-4885
5811 Mcfadden Ave Huntington Beach (92649) *(P-11552)*

Boiling Crab, The, Huntington Beach *Also Called: Boiling Crab Operations LLC (P-11552)*

Boiling Point Rest S CA Inc ....B 626 551-5181
13668 Valley Blvd Unit C2 City Of Industry (91746) *(P-13494)*

Boiling Point Rest W Grove, City Of Industry *Also Called: Boiling Point Rest S CA Inc (P-13494)*

Boise Cascade, Riverside *Also Called: Boise Cascade Company (P-11149)*

Boise Cascade Company ....D 951 343-3000
7145 Arlington Ave Riverside (92503) *(P-11149)*

Boldyn Networks US Services LL ....B 877 999-7070
121 Innovation Dr Ste 200 Irvine (92617) *(P-9427)*

Boldyn Ntwrks US Oprations LLC ....C 949 515-1500
121 Innovation Dr Ste 200 Irvine (92617) *(P-9428)*

Bolide International, San Dimas *Also Called: Bolide Technology Group Inc (P-14385)*

Bolide Technology Group Inc ....D 909 305-8889
468 S San Dimas Ave San Dimas (91773) *(P-14385)*

Bolt Brewery, La Mesa *Also Called: Prost LLC (P-1551)*

Bolt Medical Inc ....D 949 287-3207
2131 Faraday Ave Carlsbad (92008) *(P-8113)*

Bolthouse Farms ....A 661 366-7205
3200 E Brundage Ln Bakersfield (93304) *(P-8)*

Bolthouse Farms, Bakersfield *Also Called: Wm Bolthouse Farms Inc (P-1382)*

Bomatic Inc (DH)..F **909 947-3900**
43225 Business Park Dr Temecula (92590) *(P-4071)*

Bomatic Inc ....D 909 947-3900
2181 E Francis St Ontario (91761) *(P-4072)*

Bomel Construction Co Inc ....C 909 923-3319
939 E Francis St Ontario (91761) *(P-523)*

Bon Appetit, Los Angeles *Also Called: Bon Appetit Management Co (P-17953)*

Bon Appetit Management Co ....C 310 440-6052
1200 Getty Center Dr Los Angeles (90049) *(P-17953)*

Bon Appetit Management Co ....C 909 607-2788
1050 N Mills Ave Claremont (91711) *(P-17954)*

Bon Appetit Management Co ....C 310 440-6209
1200 Getty Center Dr Ste 100 Los Angeles (90049) *(P-17955)*

Bon Appetit Management Co ....C 909 748-8970
1259 E Colton Ave Redlands (92374) *(P-18107)*

Bon Suisse Inc ....E 714 578-0001
392 W Walnut Ave Fullerton (92832) *(P-18291)*

Bonded Carpet, San Diego *Also Called: Bonded Inc (P-13134)*

Employee Codes: A=Over 500 employees, B=251-500
C=101-250, D=51-100, E=20-50, F=10-19, G=1-9

2025 Southern California
Business Directory and Buyers Guide

© Mergent Inc. 1-800-342-5647

959

Bonded Fiberloft Inc .... B 323 726-7820
2748 Tanager Ave Commerce (90040) *(P-1872)*

Bonded Inc (PA) .... D 858 576-8400
7590 Carroll Rd San Diego (92121) *(P-13134)*

Bonert's Slice of Pie, Santa Ana *Also Called: Bonerts Incorporated (P-1493)*

Bonerts Incorporated .... E 714 540-3535
3144 W Adams St Santa Ana (92704) *(P-1493)*

Boneso Brothers Cnstr Inc .... D 805 227-4450
1446 Spring St Paso Robles (93446) *(P-751)*

Bonita Golf Club, Bonita *Also Called: Crockett & Coinc (P-15075)*

Bonita Medical Offices, Bonita *Also Called: Kaiser Foundation Hospitals (P-16054)*

Bonne Brdges Mller Okefe Nchol (PA) .... D 213 480-1900
355 S Grand Ave Ste 1750 Los Angeles (90071) *(P-16648)*

Bonterra Psomas, Santa Ana *Also Called: Psomas (P-17699)*

Boochcraft, Chula Vista *Also Called: Boochery Inc (P-1596)*

Boochery Inc .... D 619 207-0530
684 Anita St Ste F Chula Vista (91911) *(P-1596)*

Book Binders, Los Angeles *Also Called: Kater-Crafts Incorporated (P-3202)*

Boom Industrial Inc .... D 909 495-3555
2010 Wright Ave La Verne (91750) *(P-5695)*

Boone Printing & Graphics Inc .... D 805 683-2349
70 S Kellogg Ave Ste 8 Goleta (93117) *(P-2971)*

Boost Mobile LLC .... A 949 451-1563
6316 Irvine Blvd Irvine (92620) *(P-14464)*

Booth Mitchel & Strange LLP .... D 805 400-0703
979 Osos St Ste C1 San Luis Obispo (93401) *(P-16649)*

Boozak Inc .... E 951 245-6045
508 Chaney St Ste A Lake Elsinore (92530) *(P-4959)*

Boral Industries, Oceanside *Also Called: Royal Westlake Roofing LLC (P-1094)*

Borbon Incorporated .... C 714 994-0170
2560 W Woodland Dr Anaheim (92801) *(P-860)*

Bordeaux, Vernon *Also Called: Heather By Bordeaux Inc (P-2100)*

Border X Brewing LLC .... E 619 501-0503
2181 Logan Ave San Diego (92113) *(P-11612)*

Borderview Y M C A, San Diego *Also Called: YMCA of San Diego County (P-17385)*

Borg Produce Sales, Los Angeles *Also Called: Pacific Trellis Fruit LLC (P-10913)*

Borg Produce Sales LLC .... C 213 624-2674
1601 E Olympic Blvd Ste 100 Los Angeles (90021) *(P-10887)*

Borin Manufacturing Inc .... E 310 822-1000
5741 Buckingham Pkwy Ste B Culver City (90230) *(P-5728)*

Borrego Cmnty Hlth Foundation (PA) .... C 855 436-1234
587 Palm Canyon Dr Ste 208 Borrego Springs (92004) *(P-15253)*

Borrego Cmnty Hlth Foundation .... C 760 466-1080
1121 E Washington Ave Escondido (92025) *(P-15254)*

Borrego Cmnty Hlth Foundation .... C 951 487-8506
651 N State St Ste 5 San Jacinto (92583) *(P-15255)*

Borrego Cmnty Hlth Foundation .... C 760 251-0044
11750 Cholla Dr Ste B Desert Hot Springs (92240) *(P-15256)*

Borrego Health, San Jacinto *Also Called: Borrego Cmnty Hlth Foundation (P-15255)*

BORREGO MEDICAL CENTER, Borrego Springs *Also Called: Borrego Cmnty Hlth Foundation (P-15253)*

Boskovich Farms Inc .... C 805 987-1443
4224 Pleasant Valley Rd Camarillo (93012) *(P-9)*

Boskovich Farms Inc (PA) .... C 805 487-2299
711 Diaz Ave Oxnard (93030) *(P-104)*

Boskovich Fresh Cut LLC .... C 805 487-2299
711 Diaz Ave Oxnard (93030) *(P-10888)*

Boss, Commerce *Also Called: Norstar Office Products Inc (P-2512)*

Boss Audio Systems, Oxnard *Also Called: Ava Enterprises Inc (P-10214)*

Boss Litho Inc .... E 626 912-7088
1544 Hauser Blvd Los Angeles (90019) *(P-2972)*

Bostik Inc .... E 951 296-6425
27460 Bostik Ct Temecula (92590) *(P-3761)*

Boston Scientific - Valencia, Valencia *Also Called: Boston Scientific Corporation (P-8114)*

Boston Scientific Corporation .... E 800 678-2575
25155 Rye Canyon Loop Valencia (91355) *(P-8114)*

Boston Scntfic Nrmdlation Corp (HQ) .... B 661 949-4310
25155 Rye Canyon Loop Valencia (91355) *(P-8255)*

Bostonia Medical Offices, El Cajon *Also Called: Kaiser Foundation Hospitals (P-16052)*

Boswell Properties Inc .... B 626 583-3000
101 W Walnut St Pasadena (91103) *(P-102)*

Botanx LLC .... E 714 854-1601
3357 E Miraloma Ave Ste 156 Anaheim (92806) *(P-3635)*

Bottaia Wines LP .... E 951 252-1799
35601 Rancho California Rd Temecula (92591) *(P-1559)*

Bottle Coatings, Sun Valley *Also Called: Sundial Powder Coatings Inc (P-5349)*

Bottlemate Inc (PA) .... E 323 887-9009
2095 Leo Ave Commerce (90040) *(P-4073)*

Bottling Group LLC .... D 951 697-3200
6659 Sycamore Canyon Blvd Riverside (92507) *(P-1610)*

Boudraux Prcsion McHining Corp .... E 714 894-4523
11762 Western Ave Ste G Stanton (90680) *(P-6098)*

Boudreau Pipeline Corporation .... B 951 493-6780
463 N Smith Ave Corona (92878) *(P-664)*

Boughts Inc .... E 619 895-7246
5927 Balfour Ct Carlsbad (92008) *(P-14202)*

BOULDER CREEK POST ACUTE, Poway *Also Called: Pomerado Operations LLC (P-15756)*

Boulevard Automotive Group (PA) .... D 562 492-1000
2850 Cherry Ave Signal Hill (90755) *(P-11320)*

Boulevard Collision Center, Signal Hill *Also Called: Boulevard Automotive Group (P-11320)*

Boulevard Labs Inc .... C 323 310-2093
626 Wilshire Blvd Ste 410 Los Angeles (90005) *(P-13678)*

Boundless, San Diego *Also Called: Boundless Bio Inc (P-17780)*

Boundless Bio Inc .... D 858 766-9912
9880 Campus Point Dr Ste 120 San Diego (92121) *(P-17780)*

Bouqs Company .... D 888 320-2687
4094 Glencoe Ave Marina Del Rey (90292) *(P-11084)*

Bourns, Riverside *Also Called: Bourns Inc (P-6926)*

Bourns Inc (PA) .... C 951 781-5500
1200 Columbia Ave Riverside (92507) *(P-6926)*

Bourns Inc .... E 951 781-5690
1200 Columbia Ave Riverside (92507) *(P-7902)*

BOWERS MUSEUM, Santa Ana *Also Called: Charles W Bowers Museum Corp (P-17252)*

Bowman Pipeline Contractors, Bakersfield *Also Called: Southwest Contractors (P-696)*

Bowman Plating Co Inc .... C 310 639-4343
2631 E 126th St Compton (90222) *(P-5241)*

Bowman-Field Inc .... D 310 638-8519
2800 Martin Luther King Jr Blvd Lynwood (90262) *(P-5242)*

Boxes R Us Inc .... D 626 820-5410
15051 Don Julian Rd City Of Industry (91746) *(P-2656)*

BOY SCOUTS OF AMERICA, Los Angeles *Also Called: Greater Los Angles Area Cncil (P-17347)*

BOY'S & GIRL'S CLUB OF BAKERSF, Bakersfield *Also Called: Boys Girls Clubs of Kern Cnty (P-17326)*

Boyd and Associates (PA) .... C 818 752-1888
2191 E Thompson Blvd Ventura (93001) *(P-14281)*

Boyd Chatsworth Inc .... D 818 998-1477
9959 Canoga Ave Chatsworth (91311) *(P-8256)*

Boyd Coddington Wheels, La Habra *Also Called: NRG Motorsports Inc (P-7280)*

Boyd Construction, Yorba Linda *Also Called: Boyd Corporation (P-4820)*

Boyd Corporation (PA) .... E 714 533-2375
5832 Ohio St Yorba Linda (92886) *(P-4820)*

Boyd Dental Corporation .... C 909 890-0421
362 E Vanderbilt Way San Bernardino (92408) *(P-15515)*

Boyd Flotation Inc .... E 314 997-5222
7551 Cherry Ave Fontana (92336) *(P-11512)*

Boyd Specialties LLC .... D 909 219-5120
1016 E Cooley Dr Ste N Colton (92324) *(P-1255)*

Boyd Specialty Sleep, Fontana *Also Called: Boyd Flotation Inc (P-11512)*

Boyle Engineering Corporation .... B 949 476-3300
999 W Town And Country Rd Orange (92868) *(P-17495)*

Boys & Girls Club, Goleta *Also Called: United Bys Grls Clubs Snta BRB (P-17371)*

BOYS & GIRLS CLUBS OF HUNTINGT, Fountain Valley *Also Called: Boys Grls Clubs Huntington Vly (P-17329)*

Boys & Girls Clubs South Cnty .... D 619 424-2266
847 Encina Ave Imperial Beach (91932) *(P-17325)*

Boys Girls Clubs of Kern Cnty .... B 661 325-3730
801 Niles St Bakersfield (93305) *(P-17326)*

Boys Girls Clubs Santa Monica, Santa Monica *Also Called: Boys Grls CLB Snta Monica Inc (P-17328)*

Boys Grls CLB Brbank Grter E V .... D 818 842-9333
300 E Angeleno Ave Burbank (91502) *(P-17327)*

Mergent email: customerrelations@mergent.com
960

2025 Southern California
Business Directory and Buyers Guide

(P-0000) Products & Services Section entry number
(PA)=Parent Co (HQ)=Headquarters (DH)=Div Headquarters

Boys Grls CLB Snta Monica Inc .... D 310 361-8500
1220 Lincoln Blvd Santa Monica (90401) *(P-17328)*

Boys Grls Clubs Grdn Grove Inc (PA) .... C 714 530-0430
10540 Chapman Ave Garden Grove (92840) *(P-16851)*

Boys Grls Clubs Huntington Vly (PA) .... D 714 531-2582
16582 Brookhurst St Fountain Valley (92708) *(P-17329)*

Boys Republic (PA) .... C 909 902-6690
1907 Boys Republic Dr Chino Hills (91709) *(P-17123)*

BP, San Diego *Also Called: Qualcomm Technologies Inc (P-6881)*

BP Clothing LLC C
3424 Garfield Ave Commerce (90040) *(P-10702)*

Bpi Records, Commerce *Also Called: Bridge Publications Inc (P-2885)*

Bpo Management Services Inc (PA) .... D 714 972-2670
8175 E Kaiser Blvd # 100 Anaheim (92808) *(P-13679)*

Bpoms/Hro Inc (HQ) .... D 714 974-2670
8175 E Kaiser Blvd # 100 Anaheim (92808) *(P-13895)*

BQE Software Inc .... D 310 602-4020
3825 Del Amo Blvd Torrance (90503) *(P-13896)*

BR Building Resources Co .... C 626 963-4880
2247 Lindsay Way Glendora (91740) *(P-524)*

Bradford Soap Mexico Inc .... B 760 768-4539
1778 Zinetta Rd Ste G Calexico (92231) *(P-3591)*

Bradley Court, Chula Vista *Also Called: Healthcare Management Systems Inc (P-15675)*

Bradley Manufacturing Co Inc .... E 562 923-5556
9368 Stewart And Gray Rd Downey (90241) *(P-4074)*

Bradley's Plastic Bag Co, Downey *Also Called: Bradley Manufacturing Co Inc (P-4074)*

Bradshaw Home, Rancho Cucamonga *Also Called: Bradshaw International Inc (P-9889)*

Bradshaw International Inc (PA) .... B 909 476-3884
9409 Buffalo Ave Rancho Cucamonga (91730) *(P-9889)*

Brady Company/San Diego Inc .... B 619 462-2600
8100 Center St La Mesa (91942) *(P-1000)*

Brady Socal Incorporated .... D 619 462-2600
8100 Center St La Mesa (91942) *(P-1001)*

Braemar Country Club, Tarzana *Also Called: Braemar Country Club Inc (P-15126)*

Braemar Country Club Inc .... C 323 873-6880
4001 Reseda Blvd Tarzana (91356) *(P-15126)*

Braemar Partnership .... B 858 488-1081
3999 Mission Blvd San Diego (92109) *(P-12776)*

Braga Fresh Family Farms Inc .... C 760 353-1155
817 W Hackleman Rd El Centro (92243) *(P-76)*

Braga Fresh Imperial, El Centro *Also Called: Braga Fresh Family Farms Inc (P-76)*

Bragel International Inc .... E 909 598-8808
3383 Pomona Blvd Pomona (91768) *(P-2153)*

Bragg Crane, Fontana *Also Called: Bragg Investment Company Inc (P-13432)*

Bragg Crane & Rigging, Long Beach *Also Called: Bragg Investment Company Inc (P-13433)*

Bragg Investment Company Inc .... C 805 485-2106
1930 Lockwood St Oxnard (93036) *(P-9817)*

Bragg Investment Company Inc .... C 909 350-3738
13188 Dahlia St Fontana (92337) *(P-13432)*

Bragg Investment Company Inc (PA) .... B 562 984-2400
6251 N Paramount Blvd Long Beach (00806) *(P-13433)*

Braille Institute, Los Angeles *Also Called: Braille Institute America Inc (P-16877)*

Braille Institute America Inc (PA) .... C 323 663-1111
741 N Vermont Ave Los Angeles (90029) *(P-16877)*

Brain Corporation .... C 858 689-7600
10182 Telesis Ct Ste 100 San Diego (92121) *(P-13680)*

Brainstorm Corporation .... C 888 370-8882
1600 Proforma Ave Ontario (91761) *(P-9992)*

Brake &Tlre Depot, Santa Ana *Also Called: Brake Depot Systems Inc (P-14686)*

Brake Depot Systems Inc .... B 714 835-4833
1205 E 1st St Santa Ana (92701) *(P-14686)*

Branan Medical Corporation (PA) .... E 949 598-7166
9940 Mesa Rim Rd San Diego (92121) *(P-8115)*

Branch Medical Center, San Diego *Also Called: United States Dept of Navy (P-15496)*

Brand Amp LLC .... D 949 438-1060
1945 Placentia Ave Ste C Costa Mesa (92627) *(P-18251)*

Brand New Day, Long Beach *Also Called: Universal Care Inc (P-16516)*

Branded Entrmt Netwrk Inc (PA) .... C 310 342-1500
14724 Ventura Blvd Ste 1200 Sherman Oaks (91403) *(P-13318)*

Branded Group Inc .... C 323 940-1444
222 S Harbor Blvd Ste 500 Anaheim (92805) *(P-18108)*

Brandes Inv Partners Inc (PA) .... C 858 755-0239
11988 El Camino Real Ste 300 San Diego (92130) *(P-12020)*

Brandes Investment Partners LP .... C 858 755-0239
4275 Executive Sq Ste 500 La Jolla (92037) *(P-12021)*

Brands Republic Inc .... E 302 401-1195
10333 Rush St South El Monte (91733) *(P-6393)*

Branlyn Prominence Inc .... C 760 843-5655
13334 Amargosa Rd Victorville (92392) *(P-16370)*

Branlyn Prominence Inc (PA) .... D 909 476-9030
9213 Archibald Ave Rancho Cucamonga (91730) *(P-16371)*

Brantner and Associates Inc (DH) .... C 619 456-6827
1700 Gillespie Way El Cajon (92020) *(P-6942)*

Brasstech Inc .... C 714 796-9278
1301 E Wilshire Ave Santa Ana (92705) *(P-4801)*

Brasstech Inc (HQ) .... D 949 417-5207
2001 Carnegie Ave Santa Ana (92705) *(P-4802)*

Brault .... C 626 447-0296
180 Via Verde Ste 100 San Dimas (91773) *(P-17707)*

Braun Linen Service (PA) .... C 909 623-2678
16514 Garfield Ave Paramount (90723) *(P-13115)*

Brava, Pomona *Also Called: Bragel International Inc (P-2153)*

Bravo Highline LLC .... E 562 484-5100
3101 Ocean Park Blvd Ste 100 Santa Monica (90405) *(P-8507)*

Bravo Sports .... E 858 408-0083
4370 Jutland Dr San Diego (92117) *(P-8508)*

Bravo Sports .... E 562 457-8916
9043 Siempre Viva Rd San Diego (92154) *(P-8509)*

Bravo Sports (HQ) .... D 562 484-5100
12801 Carmenita Rd Santa Fe Springs (90670) *(P-8510)*

Bravo Support, Los Angeles *Also Called: S Bravo Systems Inc (P-4925)*

Brawley Union High School Dist (PA) .... D 760 312-6068
480 N Imperial Ave Brawley (92227) *(P-16803)*

Brax Company Inc .... E 760 749-2209
31248 Valley Center Rd Valley Center (92082) *(P-1142)*

Braxton Caribbean Mfg Co Inc .... D 714 508-3570
2641 Walnut Ave Tustin (92780) *(P-5177)*

Bread Bar, El Segundo *Also Called: El Segundo Bread Bar LLC (P-1444)*

Break Media, Beverly Hills *Also Called: Nextpoint Inc (P-9451)*

Breakthru Beverage Cal LLC (HQ) .... B 800 331-2829
6550 E Washington Blvd Commerce (90040) *(P-11054)*

Breathe Technologies Inc .... E 949 988-7700
15091 Bake Pkwy Irvine (92618) *(P-8257)*

Brecht BMW, Escondido *Also Called: Brecht Enterprises Inc (P-11321)*

Brecht Enterprises Inc .... D 760 745-3000
1555 Auto Park Way Escondido (92029) *(P-11321)*

Bree Engineering Corp .... E 760 510-4950
1750 Marilyn Ln San Marcos (92069) *(P-6975)*

Breeze Air Conditioning LLC .... D 760 346-0855
75145 Saint Charles Pl Ste A Palm Desert (92211) *(P-752)*

Breg Inc (HQ) .... C 760 599-3000
2382 Faraday Ave Ste 300 Carlsbad (92008) *(P-8116)*

Brehm Communications Inc (PA) .... E 858 451-6200
16644 W Bernardo Dr Ste 300 San Diego (92127) *(P-2973)*

Breitburn Energy Holdings LLC .... E 213 225-5900
707 Wilshire Blvd Ste 4600 Los Angeles (90017) *(P-296)*

Breitburn Energy Partners LP .... A 213 225-5900
707 Wilshire Blvd Ste 4600 Los Angeles (90017) *(P-269)*

Brek Manufacturing Co .... C 310 329-7638
1513 W 132nd St Gardena (90249) *(P-6099)*

Brennan International Trnspt, Long Beach *Also Called: Vanguard Lgistics Svcs USA Inc (P-9349)*

Brenner-Fiedler & Assoc Inc (PA) .... E 562 404-2721
4059 Flat Rock Dr Riverside (92505) *(P-8035)*

Brenntag Pacific Inc (DH) .... D 562 903-9626
10747 Patterson Pl Santa Fe Springs (90670) *(P-11007)*

Brent-Wood Products Inc .... E 800 400-7335
17071 Hercules St Hesperia (92345) *(P-2410)*

Brentwood Appliances Inc .... E 323 266-4600
3088 E 46th St Vernon (90058) *(P-6399)*

Brentwood Bmdical RES Inst Inc .... C 310 312-1554
11301 Wilshire Blvd Bldg 114 Los Angeles (90073) *(P-17867)*

Employee Codes: A=Over 500 employees, B=251-500
C=101-250, D=51-100, E=20-50, F=10-19, G=1-9

2025 Southern California
Business Directory and Buyers Guide

© Mergent Inc. 1-800-342-5647
961

Brentwood Builders, Burbank *Also Called: 716 Management Inc (P-441)*

BRENTWOOD COUNTRY CLUB, Los Angeles *Also Called: Brentwood Country Club Los Angeles (P-15127)*

Brentwood Country Club Los Angeles .... D 310 451-8011
　590 S Burlingame Ave Los Angeles (90049) *(P-15127)*

BRENTWOOD HEALTH CARE CENTER, Santa Monica *Also Called: Coastal Health Care Inc (P-15592)*

Brentwood Home LLC (PA) .... C 562 949-3759
　621 Burning Tree Rd Fullerton (92833) *(P-2481)*

Brentwood Originals, Long Beach *Also Called: Brentwood Originals Inc (P-2207)*

Brentwood Originals Inc (PA) .... E 310 637-6804
　3780 Kilroy Airport Way Ste 540 Long Beach (90806) *(P-2207)*

Brer Affiliates LLC (DH) .... C 949 794-7900
　18500 Von Karman Ave Ste 400 Irvine (92612) *(P-12677)*

Brethren Hillcrest Homes .... C 909 593-4917
　2705 Mountain View Dr Ofc La Verne (91750) *(P-15583)*

Bretkeri Corporation .... E 858 292-4919
　8316 Clairemont Mesa Blvd Ste 105 San Diego (92111) *(P-3122)*

Brett Dinovi & Associates LLC .... C 609 200-0123
　23046 Avenida De La Carlota Ste 600 Laguna Hills (92653) *(P-18109)*

Brett Dinovi & Associates LLC .... C 609 200-0123
　3200 E Guasti Rd Ste 100 Ontario (91761) *(P-18110)*

Breville, Torrance *Also Called: Breville Usa Inc (P-6400)*

Breville Usa Inc .... E 310 755-3000
　19400 S Western Ave Torrance (90501) *(P-6400)*

Brewer Crane & Rigging, Lakeside *Also Called: LLC Brewer Crane (P-13441)*

Brian Guy Electric Ltg Svcs Co, Moorpark *Also Called: Insparation Inc (P-3661)*

Bridge Group Hh Inc .... C 858 455-5000
　5090 Shoreham Pl Ste 109 San Diego (92122) *(P-17956)*

Bridge Home Health LLC .... C 858 277-5200
　5090 Shoreham Pl Ste 109 San Diego (92122) *(P-16372)*

Bridge Metals, Los Angeles *Also Called: Zia Aamir (P-4882)*

Bridge Publications Inc (PA) .... E 323 888-6200
　5600 E Olympic Blvd Commerce (90022) *(P-2885)*

Bridge SMS Retail Solutions .... D 949 629-7800
　16520 Harbor Blvd Ste E Fountain Valley (92708) *(P-18292)*

Bridgestone Americas .... E 909 770-8523
　14521 Hawthorne Ave Fontana (92335) *(P-14681)*

Bridgestone Americas Inc .... E 858 874-3109
　3690 Murphy Canyon Rd San Diego (92123) *(P-3863)*

Bridgestone Hosepower LLC .... E 562 699-9500
　2865 Pellissier Pl City Of Industry (90601) *(P-10427)*

Bridgewave Communications Inc .... E 408 567-6900
　17034 Camino San Bernardo San Diego (92127) *(P-4626)*

Bridgewest Group, The, San Diego *Also Called: Bridgewest Ventures LLC (P-12645)*

Bridgewest Ventures LLC (PA) .... A 858 529-6600
　7310 Miramar Rd Ste 500 San Diego (92126) *(P-12645)*

Bridgford Marketing Company (DH) .... D 714 526-5533
　1308 N Patt St Anaheim (92801) *(P-10866)*

Bridgwter Consulting Group Inc .... D 949 535-1755
　18881 Von Karman Ave Ste 1450 Irvine (92612) *(P-18111)*

Bridport Erie Aviation Inc .... E 714 634-8801
　6900 Orangethorpe Ave Buena Park (90620) *(P-14758)*

Brierwood Terrace Ventura Inc .... D 805 642-4101
　4904 Telegraph Rd Ventura (93003) *(P-15839)*

Briggs Electric Inc (PA) .... D 714 544-2500
　14381 Franklin Ave Tustin (92780) *(P-892)*

Bright Event Rentals, Torrance *Also Called: Bright Event Rentals LLC (P-13448)*

Bright Event Rentals LLC (PA) .... C 310 202-0011
　1640 W 190th St Ste A Torrance (90501) *(P-13448)*

Bright Glow, Covina *Also Called: Bright Glow Candle Company Inc (P-8664)*

Bright Glow Candle Company Inc (PA) .... E 909 469-4733
　20591 E Via Verde St Covina (91724) *(P-8664)*

Bright Health Physicians (PA) .... C 562 947-8478
　15725 Whittier Blvd Ste 500 Whittier (90603) *(P-15257)*

Bright Innovation Labs .... C 661 252-3807
　26421 Ruether Ave Santa Clarita (91350) *(P-3636)*

Bright Now Dental, Irvine *Also Called: Smile Brands Group Inc (P-18052)*

Brightcloud Inc .... C 858 652-4803
　4370 La Jolla Village Dr Ste 820 San Diego (92122) *(P-14386)*

Brighten Corp .... E 626 231-6238
　328 S Atlantic Blvd Ste 201 Monterey Park (91754) *(P-6494)*

Brighton Convalescent LLC .... D 626 798-9124
　1836 N Fair Oaks Ave Pasadena (91103) *(P-15840)*

Brighton Convalescent Center, Pasadena *Also Called: Brighton Convalescent LLC (P-15840)*

Brighton Place Spring Valley, Spring Valley *Also Called: B-Spring Valley LLC (P-15576)*

Brightstar Care Oxnard Cmrllo, Oxnard *Also Called: Tripod Inc (P-13627)*

Brightview Companies LLC .... C 714 437-1586
　11555 Coley River Cir Fountain Valley (92708) *(P-151)*

Brightview Golf Maint Inc .... C 805 968-6400
　405 Glen Annie Rd Santa Barbara (93117) *(P-152)*

Brightview Landscape Dev Inc .... B 858 458-9900
　8450 Miramar Pl San Diego (92121) *(P-153)*

Brightview Landscape Dev Inc .... C 714 546-7975
　2000 S Yale St Santa Ana (92704) *(P-753)*

Brightview Landscape Dev Inc .... D 818 838-4700
　13691 Vaughn St San Fernando (91340) *(P-754)*

Brightview Landscape Svcs Inc .... C 858 458-1900
　8500 Miramar Pl San Diego (92121) *(P-154)*

Brightview Landscape Svcs Inc .... C 909 946-3196
　8726 Calabash Ave Fontana (92335) *(P-155)*

Brightview Landscape Svcs Inc .... C 805 642-9300
　6464 Hollister Ave Ste 8 Goleta (93117) *(P-156)*

Brightview Landscape Svcs Inc .... B 714 546-7843
　1960 S Yale St Santa Ana (92704) *(P-157)*

Brightview Landscape Svcs Inc .... C 714 546-7843
　32202 Paseo Adelanto San Juan Capistrano (92675) *(P-158)*

Brightview Landscape Svcs Inc .... B 310 327-8700
　17813 S Main St Ste 105 Gardena (90248) *(P-159)*

Brightview Landscapes LLC .... C 760 598-7065
　2180 La Mirada Dr Vista (92081) *(P-199)*

Brightview Tree Company .... D 760 955-2560
　Apple Valley (92307) *(P-160)*

Brightview Tree Company .... D 818 951-5500
　9500 Foothill Blvd Sunland (91040) *(P-249)*

Brightview Tree Company .... D 714 546-7975
　3200 W Telegraph Rd Fillmore (93015) *(P-250)*

Briles Aerospace LLC .... D 424 320-3817
　1559 W 135th St Gardena (90249) *(P-5120)*

Brilliant Corners Teri Enomoto .... D 213 232-0134
　527 W 7th St Rm 1100 Los Angeles (90014) *(P-17459)*

Brilliant Solutions, Irvine *Also Called: Meguiars Inc (P-3613)*

Brillstein Entrmt Partners LLC (HQ) .... D 310 205-5100
　9150 Wilshire Blvd Ste 350 Beverly Hills (90212) *(P-14809)*

Brillstein Grey Entertainment, Beverly Hills *Also Called: Brillstein Entrmt Partners LLC (P-14809)*

Brimes International, San Diego *Also Called: Cali Resources Inc (P-6978)*

Brinderson LLC (DH) .... C 714 466-7100
　18841 S Broadwick St Compton (90220) *(P-17496)*

Brink's, Garden Grove *Also Called: Brinks Incorporated (P-14282)*

Brinks Incorporated .... C 714 903-9272
　7191 Patterson Dr Garden Grove (92841) *(P-14282)*

Brio Water Technology Inc .... E 800 781-1680
　768 Turnbull Canyon Rd Hacienda Heights (91745) *(P-10339)*

Brisam Lax (de) LLC .... D 310 649-5151
　9901 S La Cienega Blvd Los Angeles (90045) *(P-12777)*

Bristol Farms (HQ) .... D 310 233-4700
　915 E 230th St Carson (90745) *(P-1748)*

Bristol Industries LLC .... C 714 990-4121
　630 E Lambert Rd Brea (92821) *(P-5121)*

Bristol Omega Inc .... E 909 794-6862
　9441 Opal Ave Ste 2 Mentone (92359) *(P-2558)*

Bristolite, Santa Ana *Also Called: Sundown Liquidating Corp (P-4318)*

Brite Media LLC .... B 818 826-5790
　16027 Ventura Blvd Ste 210 Encino (91436) *(P-13263)*

Brite Promotions, Encino *Also Called: Brite Media LLC (P-13263)*

Briteworks, Covina *Also Called: Briteworks Inc (P-13359)*

Briteworks Inc .... D 626 337-0099
　620 N Commercial Ave Covina (91723) *(P-13359)*

Brithinee Electric .... D 909 825-7971
　620 S Rancho Ave Colton (92324) *(P-10174)*

Brittany House LLC ....C 562 421-4717
5401 E Centralia St Long Beach (90808) *(P-17124)*

Brixen & Sons Inc ....E 714 566-1444
2100 S Fairview St Santa Ana (92704) *(P-3123)*

Brixton LLC ....D 866 264-4245
3821 Ocean Ranch Blvd Oceanside (92056) *(P-10679)*

Brm Manufacturing, Los Angeles Also Called: Brush Research Mfg Co Inc *(P-8584)*

Broadata Communications Inc ....E 310 530-1416
2545 W 237th St Ste K Torrance (90505) *(P-4627)*

Broadband Telecom Inc ....C 818 450-5714
515 S Flower St Fl 36 Los Angeles (90071) *(P-18293)*

Broadcast Microwave Svcs LLC (PA).........................**C .. 858 391-3050**
13475 Danielson St Ste 130 Poway (92064) *(P-6602)*

Broadcom Corporation ....C 858 385-8800
16340 W Bernardo Dr Bldg A San Diego (92127) *(P-6808)*

Broadcom Corporation ....C 949 926-5000
15101 Alton Pkwy Irvine (92618) *(P-6809)*

Broadcom Corporation ....D 714 376-5029
15191 Alton Pkwy Irvine (92618) *(P-6810)*

Broadcom Limited Bldg 2, Irvine Also Called: Broadcom Corporation *(P-6810)*

Broadley-James Corporation (PA).............................**D .. 949 829-5555**
19 Thomas Irvine (92618) *(P-7947)*

Broadreach Capitl Partners LLC ....A 310 691-5760
6430 W Sunset Blvd Ste 504 Los Angeles (90028) *(P-12700)*

Broadview Networks Inc ....C 818 939-0015
7731 Hayvenhurst Ave Van Nuys (91406) *(P-9429)*

Broadway AC Htg & Shtmtl ....E 818 781-1477
7855 Burnet Ave Van Nuys (91405) *(P-4960)*

Broadway Auto Parts, Santa Ana Also Called: United Syatt America Corp *(P-11472)*

Broadway Manor Care Center, Glendale Also Called: Longwood Management Corp *(P-15871)*

Broadway Sheet Metal, Van Nuys Also Called: Broadway AC Htg & Shtmtl *(P-4960)*

Broadway Typewriter Co Inc ....D 800 998-9199
1055 6th Ave Ste 101 San Diego (92101) *(P-9993)*

Brochure Holders 4u, Santa Ana Also Called: Clear-Ad Inc *(P-4090)*

Broco, Ontario Also Called: Broco Inc *(P-5644)*

Broco Inc ....E 909 483-3222
400 S Rockefeller Ave Ontario (91761) *(P-5644)*

Bromack, Los Angeles Also Called: LA Cabinet & Millwork Inc *(P-2569)*

Bromack Company ....E 323 227-5000
3005 Humboldt St Los Angeles (90031) *(P-2340)*

Bromic Heating Pty Limited ....D 855 552-7432
7595 Irvine Center Dr Ste 100 Irvine (92618) *(P-755)*

Bronze-Way Plating Corporation (PA).........................**E .. 323 266-6933**
3301 E 14th St Los Angeles (90023) *(P-5243)*

Brook & Whittle Limited ....E 714 634-3466
1177 N Grove St Anaheim (92806) *(P-3124)*

Brookdale Clairemont, San Diego Also Called: Emeritus Corporation *(P-15627)*

Brookfeld Sthland Holdings LLC ....C 714 427-6868
3200 Park Center Dr Ste 1000 Costa Mesa (92626) *(P-391)*

Brookfield Residential, Costa Mesa Also Called: Brookfeld Sthland Holdings LLC *(P-391)*

Brooks Restaurant Group Inc (PA)............................**E .. 559 485-0520**
220 Five Cities Dr Pismo Beach (93449) *(P-10744)*

Brothers Desserts, Santa Ana Also Called: Brothers Intl Desserts *(P-1315)*

Brothers Intl Desserts (PA)......................................**C .. 949 655-0080**
3400 W Segerstrom Ave Santa Ana (92704) *(P-1315)*

Brotherwise Games, Hawthorne Also Called: Marina Graphic Center Inc *(P-3040)*

Brotman Medical Center Inc ....B 310 836-7000
3828 Delmas Ter Culver City (90232) *(P-15928)*

Brower Hale, Laguna Hills Also Called: Valley Insurance Service Inc *(P-12264)*

Brown-Pacific Inc ....E 562 921-3471
13639 Bora Dr Santa Fe Springs (90670) *(P-4512)*

Brownco Construction, Anaheim Also Called: Brownco Construction Co Inc *(P-392)*

Brownco Construction Co Inc ....D 714 935-9600
1000 E Katella Ave Anaheim (92805) *(P-392)*

Browne Child Development Ctr, Oceanside Also Called: Marine Corps Community Svcs *(P-17094)*

Brownstone Companies Inc ....A 310 297-3600
2629 Manhattan Beach Blvd 100 Redondo Beach (90278) *(P-10234)*

Brownstone Security, Redondo Beach Also Called: Brownstone Companies Inc *(P-10234)*

Browntrout, El Segundo Also Called: Browntrout Publishers Inc *(P-3125)*

Browntrout Publishers Inc (PA)................................**E .. 310 607-9010**
201 Continental Blvd Ste 200 El Segundo (90245) *(P-3125)*

Brownwood Furniture Inc ....C 909 945-5613
9805 6th St Ste 104 Rancho Cucamonga (91730) *(P-2421)*

Bruck Lighting Systems, Irvine Also Called: Ledra Brands Inc *(P-9898)*

Brunton Enterprises Inc ....C 562 945-0013
8815 Sorensen Ave Santa Fe Springs (90670) *(P-4821)*

Brusco Tug & Barge Inc ....C 805 986-1600
170 E Port Hueneme Rd Port Hueneme (93041) *(P-9150)*

Brush Research Mfg Co Inc ....C 323 261-2193
4642 Floral Dr Los Angeles (90022) *(P-8584)*

Brutoco Engineering, Covina Also Called: Brutoco Engineering & Construction Inc *(P-611)*

Brutoco Engineering & Construction Inc C
1272 Center Court Dr Ste 101 Covina (91724) *(P-611)*

Bryan Cave Lighton Paisner LLP ....D 310 576-2100
120 Broadway Ste 300 Santa Monica (90401) *(P-16650)*

Bryant Elementary School, Garden Grove Also Called: Garden Grove Unified Schl Dst *(P-17091)*

Bryant Rubber Corp (PA)..**E .. 310 530-2530**
1580 W Carson St Long Beach (90810) *(P-3879)*

Bryant Rubber Corp ....C 310 530-2530
1083 W 251st St. Bellflower (90706) *(P-3880)*

Brymax Construction Svcs Inc ....D 949 200-9619
7436 Lorge Cir Huntington Beach (92647) *(P-756)*

Bsh Home Appliances Corp (DH)...............................**C .. 949 440-7100**
1901 Main St Ste 600 Irvine (92614) *(P-14729)*

Bstg, Los Angeles Also Called: Be Structured Tech Group Inc *(P-14200)*

Bstz, Los Angeles Also Called: Blakely Sokoloff Taylor & Zafman LLP *(P-16646)*

Bsw Consultants Inc ....A 949 279-3063
9532 Zion Cir Huntington Beach (92646) *(P-18112)*

Bsw Roofing Contractors, Bakersfield Also Called: Bakersfield Shingles Wholesale Inc *(P-9960)*

BT Infonet, El Segundo Also Called: Infonet Services Corporation *(P-9445)*

Btg Textiles, Montebello Also Called: Btg Textiles Inc *(P-11666)*

Btg Textiles Inc ....E 323 586-9488
710 Union St Montebello (90640) *(P-11666)*

Btl Machine ....D 951 808-9929
1168 Sherborn St Corona (92879) *(P-6100)*

BTS Trading Inc ....E 213 800-6755
2052 E Vernon Ave Vernon (90058) *(P-1873)*

Bubbles Baking Company ....E 818 786-1700
15215 Keswick St Van Nuys (91405) *(P-1438)*

Bubbles Baking Company, Van Nuys Also Called: Danish Baking Co Inc *(P-1440)*

Buchanan Street Partners LP ....D 949 721-1414
3501 Jamboree Rd Ste 4200 Newport Beach (92660) *(P-12392)*

Buchbinder, Jay Industries, Compton Also Called: Jbi LLC *(P-2470)*

Buddha Teas, Carlsbad Also Called: Living Wellness Partners LLC *(P-1809)*

Buddy Bar Casting LLC ....C 562 861-9664
10801 Sessler St South Gate (90280) *(P-4666)*

Buddy Group Inc ....C 949 468-0042
7 Studebaker Irvine (92618) *(P-13681)*

Budget Enterprises Llc ....E 949 697-9544
23042 Mill Creek Dr Laguna Hills (92653) *(P-4312)*

Buds Ice Cream San Francisco, City Of Industry Also Called: Berkeley Farms LLC *(P-1325)*

Buena Ventura Care Center Inc ....D 818 247-4476
1505 Colby Dr Glendale (91205) *(P-15841)*

Buena Vista Care Center, Santa Barbara Also Called: Covenant Care California LLC *(P-15614)*

Buena Vista Food Products Inc (DH)..........................**C .. 626 815-8859**
823 W 8th St Azusa (91702) *(P-10933)*

Buena Vista Manor, Duarte Also Called: Humangood Socal *(P-17165)*

Buena Vista MGT Svcs LLC ....C 619 450-4300
2045 1st Ave San Diego (92101) *(P-16373)*

Buena Vista Television (DH).......................................**C .. 818 560-1878**
500 S Buena Vista St Burbank (91521) *(P-14426)*

Buena Vista TV Advg Sls, Burbank Also Called: Buena Vista Television *(P-14426)*

Buenaventura 6, Ventura Also Called: Weststar Cinemas Inc *(P-14947)*

Buff and Shine Mfg Inc ....E 310 886-5111
2139 E Del Amo Blvd Rancho Dominguez (90220) *(P-4481)*

Buffalo, Chatsworth Also Called: Piege Co *(P-10722)*

Employee Codes: A=Over 500 employees, B=251-500
C=101-250, D=51-100, E=20-50, F=10-19, G=1-9

2025 Southern California
Business Directory and Buyers Guide

© Mergent Inc. 1-800-342-5647
963

Buffalo Market, Los Angeles *Also Called: Buffalo Market Inc (P-10745)*

Buffalo Market Inc .... C 650 337-0078
1439 N Highland Ave Los Angeles (90028) *(P-10745)*

Buffalo Wild Wings, Beverly Hills *Also Called: BW Hotel LLC (P-11553)*

Buffini & Company (PA) .... C 760 827-2100
6349 Palomar Oaks Ct Carlsbad (92011) *(P-17050)*

Bugatti Newport Beach, Irvine *Also Called: Newport Beach Auto Group LLC (P-14696)*

Builders Fence Company Inc (PA) .... E 818 768-5500
8937 San Fernando Rd Sun Valley (91352) *(P-9918)*

Building Elctronic Contrls Inc (PA) .... E 909 305-1600
2246 Lindsay Way Glendora (91740) *(P-893)*

Building News, Vista *Also Called: Bni Publications Inc (P-11631)*

Buk Optics Inc .... E 714 384-9620
3600 W Moore Ave Santa Ana (92704) *(P-7996)*

Bumble Bee Foods LLC .... E 562 483-7474
13100 Arctic Cir Santa Fe Springs (90670) *(P-1695)*

Bumble Bee Seafoods LP .... C 858 715-4000
280 10th Ave San Diego (92101) *(P-1696)*

Bump.me, La Jolla *Also Called: Eventscom Inc (P-13929)*

Bunim-Murray Productions .... C 818 756-5100
1015 Grandview Ave Glendale (91201) *(P-14810)*

Bunker Corp (PA) .... D 949 361-3935
1131 Via Callejon San Clemente (92673) *(P-7231)*

Bunzl, Anaheim *Also Called: Bunzl Distribution Cal LLC (P-10589)*

Bunzl Agrclture Group Chstrfel, Oxnard *Also Called: Cool-Pak LLC (P-4092)*

Bunzl Distribution Cal LLC (DH) .... D 714 688-1900
3310 E Miraloma Ave Anaheim (92806) *(P-10589)*

Burbank Airport Mariott Hotel, Burbank *Also Called: PHF II Burbank LLC (P-12973)*

Burbank Dental Laboratory Inc .... C 818 841-2256
2101 Floyd St Burbank (91504) *(P-16341)*

Burbank Leader, Glendale *Also Called: California Community News LLC (P-2783)*

Burbank Steel Treating Inc .... E 818 842-0975
415 S Varney St Burbank (91502) *(P-4701)*

Burbank Water & Power, Burbank *Also Called: City of Burbank (P-9669)*

Burger King, Ontario *Also Called: Ta Operating LLC (P-11603)*

Burke, Los Angeles *Also Called: Burke Williams & Sorensen LLP (P-16651)*

Burke Engineering Co .... D 626 579-6763
9700 Factorial Way El Monte (91733) *(P-10315)*

Burke Williams & Sorensen LLP (PA) .... D 213 236-0600
444 S Flower St Ste 2400 Los Angeles (90071) *(P-16651)*

Burleigh Point LLC .... C 949 428-3200
5600 Argosy Ave Ste 100 Huntington Beach (92649) *(P-12393)*

Burleigh Point, Ltd., Huntington Beach *Also Called: Burleigh Point LLC (P-12393)*

Burlingame Industries Inc .... C 909 355-7000
2352 N Locust Ave Rialto (92377) *(P-4500)*

Burlingame Industries Inc (PA) .... D 909 355-7000
3546 N Riverside Ave Rialto (92377) *(P-13107)*

Burlington Convalescent Hosp (PA) .... D 213 381-5585
845 S Burlington Ave Los Angeles (90057) *(P-15584)*

Burlington Convalescent Hosp .... C 323 295-7737
3737 Don Felipe Dr Los Angeles (90008) *(P-15585)*

Burnett & Son Meat Co Inc .... D 626 357-2165
1420 S Myrtle Ave Monrovia (91016) *(P-1238)*

Burnett Fine Foods, Monrovia *Also Called: Burnett & Son Meat Co Inc (P-1238)*

Burnham Bnefits Insur Svcs LLC .... D 310 370-5000
15901 Red Hill Ave Tustin (92780) *(P-12184)*

Burnham Bnefits Insur Svcs LLC (PA) .... D 805 772-7965
2211 Michelson Dr Ste 1200 Irvine (92612) *(P-12185)*

Burnham Risk Insurance, Tustin *Also Called: Burnham Bnefits Insur Svcs LLC (P-12184)*

Burnham Wgb Insur Solutions, Tustin *Also Called: Wood Gutmann Bogart Insur Brks (P-12274)*

Burns & McDonnell Inc .... D 714 256-1595
145 S State College Blvd Ste 600 Brea (92821) *(P-17497)*

Burns and Sons Trucking Inc .... D 619 460-5394
9210 Olive Dr Spring Valley (91977) *(P-8897)*

Burns Environmental Svcs Inc .... E 800 577-4009
19360 Rinaldi St Ste 381 Northridge (91326) *(P-3600)*

Burrtec, Fontana *Also Called: Burrtec Waste Industries Inc (P-9734)*

Burrtec Waste Industries Inc (HQ) .... C 909 429-4200
9890 Cherry Ave Fontana (92335) *(P-9734)*

Bursar's Office, Long Beach *Also Called: California State Univ Long Bch (P-17709)*

Burtech Pipeline Incorporated .... D 760 634-2822
1325 Pipeline Dr Vista (92081) *(P-665)*

Burtech Plumbing, Vista *Also Called: Burtech Pipeline Incorporated (P-665)*

Burton James, City Of Industry *Also Called: BJ Liquidation Inc (P-2441)*

Burton Way Hotels LLC .... D 310 273-2222
300 S Doheny Dr Los Angeles (90048) *(P-12778)*

Burton Way Htels Ltd A Cal Ltd .... C 818 575-3000
2 Dole Dr Westlake Village (91362) *(P-12779)*

Burton-Way House Ltd A CA .... C 310 273-2222
300 S Doheny Dr Los Angeles (90048) *(P-12780)*

Busa Servicing Inc (PA) .... C 310 203-3400
787 W 5th St Los Angeles (90071) *(P-11747)*

Business Department, Murrieta *Also Called: Southwest Healthcare Sys Aux (P-16211)*

Business Information Systems, La Canada Flintridge *Also Called: Bis Computer Solutions Inc (P-13675)*

Business Office, Irvine *Also Called: St Joseph Hospital of Orange (P-16215)*

Buslink Media, Baldwin Park *Also Called: Global Silicon Electronics Inc (P-5878)*

Butler America Holdings Inc .... C 805 243-0061
1125 S Oxnard Blvd Oxnard (93030) *(P-13495)*

Butler America Holdings Inc .... C 909 417-3660
8647 Haven Ave Ste 100 Rancho Cucamonga (91730) *(P-13496)*

Butler America Holdings Inc .... C 951 563-0020
12625 Frederick St Ste E2 Moreno Valley (92553) *(P-13497)*

Butler Home Products LLC .... C 909 476-3884
9409 Buffalo Ave Rancho Cucamonga (91730) *(P-8585)*

Butler International Inc (PA) .... C 805 882-2200
3820 State St Ste A Santa Barbara (93105) *(P-13498)*

Butler Service Group Inc (HQ) .... D 201 891-5312
3820 State St Ste A Santa Barbara (93105) *(P-13593)*

Buy Fresh Produce Inc .... D 323 796-0127
6636 E 26th St Commerce (90040) *(P-10889)*

Buyefficient LLC .... C 949 382-3129
903 Calle Amanecer Ste 200 San Clemente (92673) *(P-10041)*

Buyers Consultation Svc Inc (PA) .... D 818 341-4820
8735 Remmet Ave Canoga Park (91304) *(P-10235)*

BV General Inc .... D 818 244-2323
413 E Cypress St Glendale (91205) *(P-12334)*

BW Hotel LLC .... A 310 275-5200
9500 Wilshire Blvd Beverly Hills (90212) *(P-11553)*

By Referral Only Inc .... D 760 707-1300
2035 Corte Del Nogal Ste 200 Carlsbad (92011) *(P-18294)*

By The Blue Sea LLC .... B 310 458-0030
1 Pico Blvd Santa Monica (90405) *(P-12781)*

Bycor General Contractors, San Diego *Also Called: Bycor General Contractors Inc (P-525)*

Bycor General Contractors Inc .... D 858 587-1901
6490 Marindustry Dr San Diego (92121) *(P-525)*

Byd Motors LLC (DH) .... E 213 748-3980
888 E Walnut St Fl 2 Pasadena (91101) *(P-7232)*

Byer California .... C 323 780-7615
1201 Rio Vista Ave Los Angeles (90023) *(P-1912)*

Byrnes & Kiefer Co .... D 714 554-4000
501 Airpark Dr Fullerton (92833) *(P-1671)*

Bzya Corporation .... B 949 656-3220
3790 Keri Way Fallbrook (92028) *(P-13360)*

C & B Delivery Service .... D 909 623-4708
1405 E Franklin Ave Pomona (91766) *(P-9051)*

C & D Aerospace, Garden Grove *Also Called: Safran Cabin Inc (P-7554)*

C & D Wax Inc .... C 858 292-5954
9353 Waxie Way San Diego (92123) *(P-12283)*

C & F Foods Inc .... B 626 723-1000
12400 Wilshire Blvd Ste 1180 Los Angeles (90025) *(P-1749)*

C & G Mercury Plastics, Sylmar *Also Called: C & G Plastics (P-4075)*

C & G Plastics .... E 818 837-3773
12729 Foothill Blvd Sylmar (91342) *(P-4075)*

C & H Machine Inc .... D 760 746-6459
943 S Andreasen Dr Escondido (92029) *(P-6101)*

C & H Meat Company, Vernon *Also Called: Eastland Corporation (P-10868)*

C & H Travel & Tours Inc (HQ) .... C 323 933-2288
4751 Wilshire Blvd Ste 201 Los Angeles (90010) *(P-9221)*

Mergent email: customerrelations@mergent.com
964

2025 Southern California
Business Directory and Buyers Guide

(P-0000) Products & Services Section entry number
(PA)=Parent Co (HQ)=Headquarters (DH)=Div Headquarters

C & J Metal Prducts, Paramount *Also Called: Jeffrey Fabrication LLC (P-4994)*

C & L Refrigeration Corp .... C 800 901-4822
4111 N Palm St Fullerton (92835) *(P-757)*

C & R Molds Inc .... E 805 658-7098
2737 Palma Dr Ventura (93003) *(P-4076)*

C A A, Los Angeles *Also Called: Creative Artsts Agcy Hldngs LL (P-14958)*

C A Buchen Corp .... E 818 767-5408
9231 Glenoaks Blvd Sun Valley (91352) *(P-4822)*

C A S, Ontario *Also Called: Certified Aviation Svcs LLC (P-9194)*

C A Schroeder Inc (PA) .... E 818 365-9561
1318 1st St San Fernando (91340) *(P-4490)*

C and H International, Los Angeles *Also Called: C & H Travel & Tours Inc (P-9221)*

C B Coast Newport Properties .... A 949 644-1600
840 Newport Center Dr Ste 100 Newport Beach (92660) *(P-12394)*

C B M, Santa Ana *Also Called: Custom Built Machinery Inc (P-17508)*

C B S, San Marcos *Also Called: Winchster Intrcnnect CM CA Inc (P-4640)*

C Brewer Company, Ontario *Also Called: Balda C Brewer Inc (P-5569)*

C C M P, Anaheim *Also Called: Copper Clad Mltilayer Pdts Inc (P-6720)*

C D C, Costa Mesa *Also Called: Creative Design Consultants (P-14483)*

C D Listening Bar Inc .... A 949 225-1170
17822 Gillette Ave Ste A Irvine (92614) *(P-10555)*

C D Lyon Construction Inc (PA) .... D 805 653-0173
380 W Stanley Ave Ventura (93001) *(P-17498)*

C D R, Oxnard *Also Called: Child Dev Rsrces of Vntura CNT (P-16887)*

C D S, Canyon Country *Also Called: Commercial Display Systems LLC (P-5970)*

C D Video, Santa Ana *Also Called: CD Video Manufacturing Inc (P-7103)*

C E D, Orange *Also Called: County Whl Elc Co Los Angeles (P-10178)*

C Enterprises, Inc., San Diego *Also Called: Exce LP (P-5919)*

C F I, Los Angeles *Also Called: Commodity Forwarders Inc (P-9265)*

C G Systems LLC .... E 714 632-8882
1470 N Hundley St Anaheim (92806) *(P-894)*

C I Container Line, Monterey Park *Also Called: Carmichael International Svc (P-9258)*

C I G A, Glendale *Also Called: Califrnia Insur Guarantee Assn (P-12187)*

C J Foods, Los Angeles *Also Called: CJ America Inc (P-10937)*

C L A, Van Nuys *Also Called: Clay Lacy Aviation Inc (P-9195)*

C L E, Downey *Also Called: Can Lines Engineering Inc (P-5788)*

C M Automotive Systems Inc (PA) .... E 909 869-7912
5646 W Mission Blvd Ontario (91762) *(P-5756)*

C M C Steel Fabricators Inc .... E 909 899-9993
1455 Auto Center Dr Ste 200 Ontario (91761) *(P-5401)*

C M E Corp .... E 714 632-6939
1051 S East St Anaheim (92805) *(P-18295)*

C M I, Corona *Also Called: Corona Magnetics Inc (P-6927)*

C Magazine, Santa Monica *Also Called: C Publishing LLC (P-2905)*

C N B Commercial Banking Ctr, La Jolla *Also Called: City National Bank (P-11725)*

C N B Commercial Banking Ctr, Riverside *Also Called: City National Bank (P-11727)*

C N B Commercial Banking Ctr, Ontario *Also Called: City National Bank (P-11728)*

C N B Real Estate Group, Los Angeles *Also Called: City National Bank (P-11722)*

C N P Signs & Graphics, El Cajon *Also Called: California Neon Products (P-8591)*

C P I, Simi Valley *Also Called: Chatsworth Products Inc (P-5443)*

C P S Express .... C 951 685-1041
4375 E Lowell St Ste G Ontario (91761) *(P-8898)*

C Publishing LLC .... E 310 393-3800
1543 7th St Ste 202 Santa Monica (90401) *(P-2905)*

C R Laurence Co Inc (HQ) .... B 323 588-1281
2503 E Vernon Ave Los Angeles (90058) *(P-7233)*

C S C, Garden Grove *Also Called: Container Supply Company Incorporated (P-4720)*

C S C, Poway *Also Called: Advanced Machining Tooling Inc (P-5565)*

C S C, Northridge *Also Called: Contemporary Services Corp (P-14288)*

C S I, Santa Fe Springs *Also Called: Csi Electrical Contractors Inc (P-907)*

C S I, Santa Ana *Also Called: Color Science Inc (P-3723)*

C S S, Bakersfield *Also Called: Construction Specialty Svc Inc (P-669)*

C S T, Thousand Oaks *Also Called: Custom Sensors & Tech Inc (P-6988)*

C T and F Inc .... D 562 927-2339
7228 Scout Ave Bell Gardens (90201) *(P-895)*

C T I, Rancho Cucamonga *Also Called: Collection Technology Inc (P-13281)*

C T L Printing Inds Inc .... E 714 635-2980
1741 W Lincoln Ave Ste A Anaheim (92801) *(P-3126)*

C W Cole & Company Inc .... E 626 443-2473
2560 Rosemead Blvd South El Monte (91733) *(P-6453)*

C W Driver Incorporated .... C 619 696-5100
7588 Metropolitan Dr San Diego (92108) *(P-526)*

C W Hotels Ltd .... C 310 395-9700
1740 Ocean Ave Santa Monica (90401) *(P-12782)*

C W S, San Diego *Also Called: Communction Wirg Spcalists Inc (P-901)*

C-28, Corona *Also Called: Aurelio Felix Barreto III (P-11506)*

C-Cure, Huntington Beach *Also Called: Custom Building Products LLC (P-3762)*

C-Cure, Ontario *Also Called: Western States Wholesale Inc (P-4377)*

C-Pak Industries Inc .... E 909 880-6017
4925 Hallmark Pkwy San Bernardino (92407) *(P-4077)*

C-Thru Sunrooms, Ontario *Also Called: Stell Industries Inc (P-5088)*

C. W. DRIVER, INCORPORATED, San Diego *Also Called: C W Driver Incorporated (P-526)*

C&B Holding Co Inc (PA) .... B 661 633-1451
3000 Belle Terrace Bakersfield (93304) *(P-18296)*

C&C Jewelry Mfg Inc .... D 213 623-6800
323 W 8th St Fl 4 Los Angeles (90014) *(P-10545)*

C&D Aerodesign, San Diego *Also Called: Safran Cabin Inc (P-7556)*

C&D Zodiac Aerospace .... E 714 891-0683
7330 Lincoln Way Garden Grove (92841) *(P-7446)*

C&J Well Services LLC .... A 661 589-5220
3752 Allen Rd Bakersfield (93314) *(P-319)*

C&K Form Fabrication Inc .... E 909 825-1882
370 N 9th St Colton (92324) *(P-5092)*

C&O Manufacturing Company Inc .... D 562 692-7525
9640 Beverly Rd Pico Rivera (90660) *(P-4961)*

C&W Facility Services Inc .... A 805 267-7123
3011 Townsgate Rd Ste 410 Westlake Village (91361) *(P-13361)*

C2 Financial Corporation .... C 858 220-2112
703 Sunset Ct San Diego (92109) *(P-12022)*

C4 Litho LLC .... E 714 259-1073
27020 Daisy Cir Yorba Linda (92887) *(P-2974)*

CA Arng 115th Rsg, Los Alamitos *Also Called: Department Military California (P-18261)*

CA Department Development Svc, Cathedral City *Also Called: Califrnia Dept Dvlpmental Svcs (P-16540)*

CA Landscape and Design, Upland *Also Called: California Ldscp & Design Inc (P-201)*

CA Signs, Pacoima *Also Called: California Signs Inc (P-8592)*

CA Station Management Inc .... C 909 245-6251
3200 E Guasti Rd Ste 100 Ontario (91761) *(P-666)*

Ca'del Sole, Toluca Lake *Also Called: Tre Venezie Inc (P-11605)*

Ca75 Atk, San Diego *Also Called: Northrop Grmman Innvtion Syste (P-7748)*

Caballero & Sons Inc .... E 562 368-1644
5753 E Santa Ana Canyon Rd Ste G-380 Anaheim (92807) *(P-12011)*

Cabazon Band Mission Indians .... A 760 342-5000
84245 Indio Springs Dr Indio (92203) *(P-12783)*

Cabe Brothers .... D 562 595-7411
2895 Long Beach Blvd Long Beach (90806) *(P-11322)*

Cabe Toyota, Long Beach *Also Called: Cabe Brothers (P-11322)*

Cabin Editing Company LLC .... D 310 752-0520
1754 14th St Santa Monica (90404) *(P-14811)*

Cabinets 2000 LLC .... C 562 868-0909
11100 Firestone Blvd Norwalk (90650) *(P-2341)*

Cabinets By Prcision Works Inc .... E 760 342-1133
81101 Indio Blvd Ste D22 Indio (92201) *(P-2342)*

Cableconn, San Diego *Also Called: Cableconn Industries Inc (P-10175)*

Cableconn Industries Inc .... D 858 571-7111
7198 Convoy Ct San Diego (92111) *(P-10175)*

Cabrillo Crdolgy Med Group Inc .... D 805 983-0922
2241 Wankel Way Ste C Oxnard (93030) *(P-15258)*

Cabrillo Hoist, Fontana *Also Called: Engel Holdings Inc (P-536)*

Caci Enterprise Solutions LLC .... B 619 881-6000
1455 Frazee Rd Ste 700 San Diego (92108) *(P-14073)*

Cacique, La Puente *Also Called: Cacique Distributors US (P-10826)*

Cacique, La Puente *Also Called: Cacique Foods LLC (P-10827)*

Cacique Distributors US .... C 626 961-3399
14923 Proctor Ave La Puente (91746) *(P-10826)*

Cacique Foods LLC .... C 626 961-3399
14923 Proctor Ave La Puente (91746) *(P-10827)*

Employee Codes: A=Over 500 employees, B=251-500
C=101-250, D=51-100, E=20-50, F=10-19, G=1-9

2025 Southern California
Business Directory and Buyers Guide

© Mergent Inc. 1-800-342-5647

965

A
L
P
H
A
B
E
T
I
C

Caco-Pacific Corporation (PA)..............................C 626 331-3361
813 N Cummings Rd Covina (91724) *(P-5570)*

Cadence Aerospace, Anaheim *Also Called: Aerospace Parts Holdings Inc (P-7417)*

Cadence Aerospace, LLC, Anaheim *Also Called: Verus Aerospace LLC (P-7588)*

Cadillac Motor Div Area ....C 805 373-9575
30930 Russell Ranch Rd Westlake Village (91362) *(P-11323)*

Caelus Corporation ....E 949 877-7170
26226 Enterprise Ct Lake Forest (92630) *(P-320)*

Caelux Corporation ....E 626 502-7033
404 N Halstead St Pasadena (91107) *(P-6811)*

Caer Inc ....E 415 879-9864
8070 Melrose Ave Los Angeles (90046) *(P-1338)*

Caerus Marketing Group LLC ....D 800 792-1015
409 Santa Monica Blvd Ste 2a Santa Monica (90401) *(P-16374)*

Caes Mission Systems LLC ....E 858 812-7300
4820 Eastgate Mall Ste 200 San Diego (92121) *(P-6976)*

Caes Systems LLC ....C 858 560-1301
9404 Chesapeake Dr San Diego (92123) *(P-7706)*

Caesars Entrtnment Oprting Inc ....A 760 751-3100
777 Harrahs Rincon Way Valley Center (92082) *(P-15195)*

Cafe Champagne, Temecula *Also Called: Thornton Winery (P-1589)*

Caffe DAmore Inc C
1916 S Tubeway Ave Commerce (90040) *(P-1715)*

Cafvina Coffee & Tea, Garden Grove *Also Called: Quoc Viet Foods (P-1838)*

Cageco Inc ....E 800 605-4859
16225 Beaver Rd Adelanto (92301) *(P-5472)*

Cahn, Jsph/Miller Kaplan Arase, North Hollywood *Also Called: Miller Kaplan Arase LLP (P-17746)*

Cahuilla Creek Casino, Anza *Also Called: Cahuilla Creek Rest & Casino (P-15196)*

Cahuilla Creek Rest & Casino ....C 951 763-1200
52702 Us Highway 371 Anza (92539) *(P-15196)*

Cai, Orange *Also Called: Califrnia Anlytical Instrs Inc (P-7850)*

Cai, Corona *Also Called: Combustion Associates Inc (P-9575)*

Caine & Weiner, Sherman Oaks *Also Called: Caine & Weiner Company Inc (P-13279)*

Caine & Weiner Company Inc (PA) ....D 818 226-6000
5805 Sepulveda Blvd Fl 4 Sherman Oaks (91411) *(P-13279)*

Caitac Garment Processing Inc ....B 310 217-9888
14725 S Broadway Gardena (90248) *(P-1931)*

Cake Mortgage Corp ....D 818 812-5150
9200 Oakdale Ave Ste 501 Chatsworth (91311) *(P-11889)*

Cal Coffee Shop, Lakewood *Also Called: Nationwide Theatres Corp (P-15015)*

Cal LLC Powerflex Systems ....E 650 469-3392
15445 Innovation Dr San Diego (92128) *(P-6315)*

Cal Mutual Inc ....D 888 700-4650
34077 Temecula Creek Rd Temecula (92592) *(P-11890)*

Cal Pac Sheet Metal, Santa Ana *Also Called: Cal Pac Sheet Metal Inc (P-4962)*

Cal Pac Sheet Metal Inc ....E 714 979-2733
2720 S Main St Ste B Santa Ana (92707) *(P-4962)*

Cal Pipe Manufacturing Inc (PA) ....E 562 803-4388
12160 Woodruff Ave Downey (90241) *(P-5429)*

Cal Plate (PA) ....D 562 403-3000
17110 Jersey Ave Artesia (90701) *(P-5660)*

Cal Rehab, Carlsbad *Also Called: Physical Rhbltation Netwrk LLC (P-15552)*

Cal Simba Inc (PA) ....E 805 240-1177
1283 Flynn Rd Camarillo (93012) *(P-8463)*

Cal Southern Assn Governments (PA) ....C 213 236-1800
900 Wilshire Blvd Ste 1700 Los Angeles (90017) *(P-18297)*

Cal Southern Braiding Inc ....D 562 927-5531
7450 Scout Ave Bell Gardens (90201) *(P-6977)*

Cal Southern Graphics Corp (HQ) ....D 310 559-3600
9655 De Soto Ave Chatsworth (91311) *(P-2975)*

Cal Southern Med Ctr Inc ....D 818 650-6700
14550 Haynes St Van Nuys (91411) *(P-15259)*

Cal Southern Sound Image Inc (PA) ....D 760 737-3900
2425 Auto Park Way Escondido (92029) *(P-10236)*

Cal Southern United Food ....C 714 220-2297
6425 Katella Ave Ste 100 Cypress (90630) *(P-12159)*

Cal State La Univ Aux Svcs Inc ....A 323 343-2531
5151 State University Dr Los Angeles (90032) *(P-17957)*

Cal Tape & Label, Anaheim *Also Called: C T L Printing Inds Inc (P-3126)*

Cal Tech Precision Inc ....D 714 992-4130
1830 N Lemon St Anaheim (92801) *(P-7447)*

Cal Treehouse Almonds LLC ....C 661 725-6334
2115 Road 144 Delano (93215) *(P-105)*

Cal West Designs, La Habra *Also Called: K S Designs Inc (P-8612)*

Cal West Enterprises, San Diego *Also Called: Wamc Company Inc (P-12370)*

Cal Western Foreclosure Svcs, El Cajon *Also Called: EC Closing Corp (P-11899)*

Cal-A-Vie, Vista *Also Called: Spa Havens LP (P-15063)*

Cal-Aurum, Huntington Beach *Also Called: Cal-Aurum Industries (P-5244)*

Cal-Aurum Industries ....E 714 898-0996
15632 Container Ln Huntington Beach (92649) *(P-5244)*

Cal-AZ Sales & Marketing, Placentia *Also Called: Fruth Custom Plastics Inc (P-4120)*

Cal-Coast Pkg & Crating Inc ....E 310 518-7215
2040 E 220th St Carson (90810) *(P-2384)*

Cal-Comp Electronics (usa) Co Ltd ....B 858 587-6900
9877 Waples St San Diego (92121) *(P-6343)*

Cal-Comp USA (san Diego) Inc ....C 858 587-6900
1940 Camino Vida Roble Carlsbad (92008) *(P-6713)*

Cal-Draulics, Corona *Also Called: Johnson Caldraul Inc (P-7508)*

Cal-June Inc (PA) ....E 323 877-4164
5238 Vineland Ave North Hollywood (91601) *(P-4761)*

Cal-Med Ambulance, South El Monte *Also Called: California Med Response Inc (P-8815)*

Cal-Monarch, Corona *Also Called: California Wire Products Corp (P-5402)*

Cal-Organic Farms, Lamont *Also Called: Grimmway Enterprises Inc (P-10906)*

Cal-State Auto Parts Inc (PA) ....C 714 630-5950
1361 N Red Gum St Anaheim (92806) *(P-9818)*

Cal-State Steel Corporation ....C 310 632-2772
1397 Lynnmere Dr Thousand Oaks (91360) *(P-1151)*

Cal-Tron Plating Inc ....E 562 945-1181
11919 Rivera Rd Santa Fe Springs (90670) *(P-5245)*

Cal-West Nurseries Inc ....C 951 270-0667
138 North Dr Norco (92860) *(P-200)*

Calabasas Memory Care Cmnty, Calabasas *Also Called: Silverado Senior Living Inc (P-15777)*

Calamigos Guest Rnch & Bch CLB, Malibu *Also Called: Malibu Conference Center Inc (P-12303)*

Calamp, Irvine *Also Called: Calamp Corp (P-13897)*

Calamp Corp (PA) ....C 949 600-5600
15635 Alton Pkwy Ste 250 Irvine (92618) *(P-13897)*

Calance, Anaheim *Also Called: Partners Information Tech (P-14241)*

Calavo, Santa Paula *Also Called: Calavo Growers Inc (P-1750)*

Calavo Growers Inc (PA) ....C 805 525-1245
1141 Cummings Rd Ste A Santa Paula (93060) *(P-1750)*

Calbee America Incorporated ....D 310 370-2500
3625 Del Amo Blvd Ste 235 Torrance (90503) *(P-10842)*

Calbiotech Export Inc ....E 619 660-6162
1935 Cordell Ct El Cajon (92020) *(P-8117)*

Caldera Medical Inc (PA) ....D 818 879-6555
4360 Park Terrace Dr Ste 140 Westlake Village (91361) *(P-8118)*

Calderon Drywall Contrs Inc ....D 714 696-2977
1931 E Meats Ave Trlr 127 Orange (92865) *(P-1002)*

Caldesso LLC ....D 909 888-2882
439 S Stoddard Ave San Bernardino (92401) *(P-11676)*

Caldyn, Chatsworth *Also Called: California Dynamics Corp (P-8036)*

Calenergy LLC ....B 402 231-1527
7030 Gentry Rd Calipatria (92233) *(P-896)*

Calex, Northridge *Also Called: Valley Hospital Medical Center Foundation (P-16252)*

Calex Engineering Inc ....D 661 254-1866
23651 Pine St Newhall (91321) *(P-1170)*

Calex Engineering Co., Newhall *Also Called: Calex Engineering Inc (P-1170)*

Cali Chem Inc ....E 714 265-3740
14271 Corporate Dr Ste B Garden Grove (92843) *(P-3637)*

Cali Resources Inc ....E 619 661-5741
2310 Michael Faraday Dr San Diego (92154) *(P-6978)*

Cali-Fame Los Angeles Inc ....D 310 747-5263
20934 S Santa Fe Ave Carson (90810) *(P-2158)*

Caliber Bodyworks Texas LLC ....D 714 665-3905
5 Auto Center Dr Tustin (92782) *(P-14672)*

Caliber Collision, Tustin *Also Called: Caliber Bodyworks Texas LLC (P-14672)*

Caliber Home Loans Inc .... D 805 983-0904
1500 Ventura Blvd Oxnard (93036) *(P-11891)*

Calibr A Division Scripps RES, La Jolla *Also Called: Scripps Research Institute (P-17890)*

Calibre International LLC .... C 626 969-4660
6250 N Irwindale Ave Irwindale (91702) *(P-18252)*

Calico, Irvine *Also Called: Calico Building Services Inc (P-13362)*

Calico Building Services Inc .... C 949 380-8707
15550 Rockfield Blvd Ste C Irvine (92618) *(P-13362)*

Calidad Inc .... E 909 947-3937
1730 S Balboa Ave Ontario (91761) *(P-4667)*

Calient Technologies, Goleta *Also Called: Calient Technologies Inc (P-6582)*

Calient Technologies Inc (PA) .... E 805 695-4800
120 Cremona Dr Ste 160 Goleta (93117) *(P-6582)*

Caliente Farms, Delano *Also Called: M Caratan Disc Inc (P-35)*

California Air Tools Inc .... E 866 409-4581
8560 Siempre Viva Rd San Diego (92154) *(P-5634)*

California Amforge, Azusa *Also Called: California Amforge Corporation (P-4513)*

California Amforge Corporation .... C 626 334-4931
750 N Vernon Ave Azusa (91702) *(P-4513)*

California Assn Realtors Inc (PA) .... C 213 739-8200
525 S Virgil Ave Los Angeles (90020) *(P-17278)*

California Baking Company .... B 619 591-8289
681 Anita St Chula Vista (91911) *(P-10934)*

California Bank & Trust .... A 858 793-7400
11622 El Camino Real San Diego (92130) *(P-11748)*

California Basic, Montebello *Also Called: Mias Fashion Mfg Co Inc (P-10716)*

California Blue Apparel Inc .... E 213 745-5400
245 W 28th St Los Angeles (90007) *(P-2061)*

CALIFORNIA BOTANIC GARDEN, Claremont *Also Called: Rancho Santa Ana Botanic Grdn (P-17271)*

California Box Company (PA) .... D 562 921-1223
13901 Carmenita Rd Santa Fe Springs (90670) *(P-2657)*

California Box II .... D 909 944-9202
8949 Toronto Ave Rancho Cucamonga (91730) *(P-10590)*

California Bread Co., Chula Vista *Also Called: California Baking Company (P-10934)*

California Business Bureau Inc (PA) .... C 626 303-1515
1711 S Mountain Ave Monrovia (91016) *(P-17708)*

California Cancer Specialists Medical Group Inc .... B 626 775-3200
1333 S Mayflower Ave Ste 200 Monrovia (91016) *(P-17294)*

California Candy, South El Monte *Also Called: California Snack Foods Inc (P-1501)*

California Center Bank, Los Angeles *Also Called: Bbcn Bank (P-11708)*

California Chassis Inc .... C 714 666-8511
3356 E La Palma Ave Anaheim (92806) *(P-4963)*

California Childrens Academy .... C 323 263-3846
233 N Breed St Los Angeles (90033) *(P-17078)*

California Choice, Orange *Also Called: Choic Admini Insur Servi (P-12195)*

California Churros Corporation .... B 909 370-4777
751 Via Lata Colton (92324) *(P-1439)*

California City San Bernardino (PA) .... B 909 384-7272
290 N D St San Bernardino (92401) *(P-16652)*

California Closet Co, Huntington Beach *Also Called: California Closet Company Inc (P-1197)*

California Closet Company Inc .... C 714 899-4905
5921 Skylab Rd Huntington Beach (92647) *(P-1197)*

California Club .... C 213 622-1391
538 S Flower St Los Angeles (90071) *(P-17330)*

California Coast Credit Union (PA) .... D 858 495-1600
9201 Spectrum Center Blvd Ste 300 San Diego (92123) *(P-11823)*

California Combining Corp .... E 323 589-5727
5607 S Santa Fe Ave Vernon (90058) *(P-1959)*

California Commerce Club Inc .... A 323 721-2100
6131 Telegraph Rd Commerce (90040) *(P-12784)*

California Community News LLC .... D 818 843-8700
221 N Brand Blvd Fl 2 Glendale (91203) *(P-2783)*

California Community News LLC (DH) .... B 626 388-1017
2000 E 8th St Los Angeles (90021) *(P-2784)*

California Control Solutions, Anaheim *Also Called: George T Hall Co Inc (P-10333)*

California Costume Int'l, Los Angeles *Also Called: Califrnia Cstume Cllctions Inc (P-2188)*

California Credit Union .... D 858 769-7369
503 Telegraph Canyon Rd Chula Vista (91910) *(P-11793)*

California Credit Union (PA) .... C 818 291-6700
701 N Brand Blvd Fl 7 Glendale (91203) *(P-11824)*

California Cryobank LLC (DH) .... D 310 496-5691
11915 La Grange Ave Los Angeles (90025) *(P-16539)*

California Cstm Frt & Flavors, Irwindale *Also Called: Califrnia Cstm Frits Flvors LL (P-1672)*

California Dairies Inc .... D 562 809-2595
11709 Artesia Blvd Artesia (90701) *(P-1326)*

California Dept Fd Agriculture .... A 858 755-1161
2260 Jimmy Durante Blvd Del Mar (92014) *(P-18401)*

California Dept of Pub Hlth .... C 714 567-2906
681 S Parker St Ste 200 Orange (92868) *(P-18386)*

California Dept Social Svcs .... D 951 782-4200
3737 Main St Ste 700 Riverside (92501) *(P-18396)*

California Die Casting Inc .... E 909 947-9947
1820 S Grove Ave Ontario (91761) *(P-4657)*

California Digital Inc (PA) .... D 310 217-0500
6 Saddleback Rd Rolling Hills (90274) *(P-5908)*

California Dynamics Corp (PA) .... E 323 223-3882
20500 Prairie St Chatsworth (91311) *(P-8036)*

California Dynasty, Los Angeles *Also Called: MGT Industries Inc (P-2121)*

California Endowment (PA) .... D 213 928-8800
1000 N Alameda St Los Angeles (90012) *(P-17217)*

California Exotic Novlt LLC .... D 909 606-1950
1455 E Francis St Ontario (91761) *(P-8665)*

California Fair Plan Assn .... D 213 487-0111
725 S Figueroa St Ste 3900 Los Angeles (90017) *(P-12186)*

California Faucets Inc (PA) .... E 800 822-8855
5271 Argosy Ave Huntington Beach (92649) *(P-4803)*

California Faucets Inc .... E 657 400-1639
5231 Argosy Ave Huntington Beach (92649) *(P-4804)*

California Fine Wire Co (PA) .... E 805 489-5144
338 S 4th St Grover Beach (93433) *(P-4628)*

California Flexrake Corp .... E 626 443-4026
9620 Gidley St Temple City (91780) *(P-4737)*

California Friends Homes .... B 714 530-9100
12151 Dale Ave Stanton (90680) *(P-17125)*

California Gasket and Rbr Corp (PA) .... E 714 202-8500
533 W Collins Ave Orange (92867) *(P-3909)*

California Gate Entry Systems, Anaheim *Also Called: C G Systems LLC (P-894)*

California Glass & Mirror Div, Santa Ana *Also Called: Twed-Dells Inc (P-4349)*

California Graphics, Chatsworth *Also Called: Cal Southern Graphics Corp (P-2975)*

California Industrial Fabrics .... E 619 661-7166
2325 Marconi Ct San Diego (92154) *(P-1898)*

California Institute For, La Jolla *Also Called: California Institute For Biomedical Research (P-17868)*

California Institute For Biomedical Research .... C 858 242-1000
11119 N Torrey Pines Rd La Jolla (92037) *(P-17868)*

California Institute Tech .... A 818 354-9154
4800 Oak Grove Dr Pasadena (91109) *(P-17869)*

California Insulated Wire & .... D 818 569-4930
3050 N California St Burbank (91504) *(P-4629)*

California Internet LP (PA) .... C 805 225-4638
251 Camarillo Ranch Rd Camarillo (93012) *(P-9430)*

California Lab Sciences LLC .... B 562 758-6900
10200 Pioneer Blvd Ste 500 Santa Fe Springs (90670) *(P-17906)*

California Ldscp & Design Inc .... C 909 949-1601
273 N Benson Ave Upland (91786) *(P-201)*

California Marine Cleaning Inc (PA) .... C 619 231-8788
2049 Main St San Diego (92113) *(P-9735)*

California Marketing, San Diego *Also Called: Mabie Marketing Group Inc (P-14534)*

California Med Caregiver Svcs, Canoga Park *Also Called: Calmedcasvs Inc (P-16543)*

California Med Response Inc .... D 562 968-1818
1557 Santa Anita Ave South El Monte (91733) *(P-8815)*

California Mfg Tech Consulting .... D 310 263-3060
3760 Kilroy Airport Way Ste 450 Long Beach (90806) *(P-17499)*

California Neon Products .... D 619 283-2191
9944 Blossom Valley Rd El Cajon (92021) *(P-8591)*

California Newspaper Service, Los Angeles *Also Called: California Newsppr Svc Bur Inc (P-2785)*

California Newsppr Svc Bur Inc .... E 213 229-5500
915 E 1st St Los Angeles (90012) *(P-2785)*

California Offset Printers Inc (PA) .... D 818 291-1100
5075 Brooks St Montclair (91763) *(P-2976)*

A
L
P
H
A
B
E
T
I
C

Employee Codes: A=Over 500 employees, B=251-500
C=101-250, D=51-100, E=20-50, F=10-19, G=1-9

2025 Southern California
Business Directory and Buyers Guide

© Mergent Inc. 1-800-342-5647
967

California Physicians Service .... D 909 974-5201
3401 Centre Lake Dr Ste 400 Ontario (91761) *(P-12073)*

California Physicians Service .... D 310 744-2668
3840 Kilroy Airport Way Long Beach (90806) *(P-12074)*

California Physicians Service .... C 818 598-8000
6300 Canoga Ave Ste A Woodland Hills (91367) *(P-12075)*

California Plasteck, Ontario *Also Called: Paramount Panels Inc (P-4192)*

California Plastics, Riverside *Also Called: Altium Holdings LLC (P-4041)*

California Plastix Inc .... E 909 629-8288
1319 E 3rd St Pomona (91766) *(P-2729)*

California Pools, Coachella *Also Called: Teserra (P-1228)*

California Portland Cement, Mojave *Also Called: Calportland Company (P-4353)*

California Poultry, Los Angeles *Also Called: Western Supreme Inc (P-1282)*

California Premium Incentives, Lake Forest *Also Called: Aminco International USA Inc (P-8451)*

California Rain, Los Angeles *Also Called: California Rain Company Inc (P-10703)*

California Rain Company Inc .... D 213 623-6061
1213 E 14th St Los Angeles (90021) *(P-10703)*

California RE Assn Inc .... D 213 739-8200
525 S Virgil Ave Los Angeles (90020) *(P-17279)*

California Real Estate, Los Angeles *Also Called: California RE Assn Inc (P-17279)*

California Republic Bank .... B 949 270-9700
18400 Von Karman Ave Ste 1100 Irvine (92612) *(P-11749)*

California Resources Corp (PA) .... **D 888 848-4754**
1 World Trade Ctr Ste 1500 Long Beach (90831) *(P-270)*

California Resources Prod Corp (HQ) .... **C 661 869-8000**
27200 Tourney Rd Ste 200 Santa Clarita (91355) *(P-271)*

California Resources Prod Corp .... E 661 869-8000
4900 W Lokern Rd Mc Kittrick (93251) *(P-272)*

California Respiratory Care .... D 818 379-9999
16055 Ventura Blvd # 715 Encino (91436) *(P-3791)*

California Ribbon Carbn Co Inc .... D 323 724-9100
8420 Quinn St Downey (90241) *(P-8561)*

California Screw Products Corp .... D 562 633-6626
14950 Gwenchris Ct Paramount (90723) *(P-4762)*

California Semiconductor Tech .... C 310 579-2939
429 Santa Monica Blvd Santa Monica (90401) *(P-17500)*

California Sensor Corporation .... E 760 438-0525
2075 Corte Del Nogal Ste P Carlsbad (92011) *(P-8037)*

California Sheet Metal, El Cajon *Also Called: California Shtmtl Works Inc (P-475)*

California Shtmtl Works Inc .... D 619 562-7010
1020 N Marshall Ave El Cajon (92020) *(P-475)*

California Signs Inc .... E 818 899-1888
10280 Glenoaks Blvd Pacoima (91331) *(P-8592)*

California Silica Products LLC .... D 909 947-0028
12808 Rancho Rd Adelanto (92301) *(P-3228)*

California Skateparks .... C 909 949-1601
285 N Benson Ave Upland (91786) *(P-161)*

California Snack Foods Inc .... E 626 444-4508
2131 Tyler Ave South El Monte (91733) *(P-1501)*

California Specialty Farms, Los Angeles *Also Called: Worldwide Specialties Inc (P-1866)*

California Spirits Company LLC .... E 619 677-7066
2946 Norman Strasse Rd San Marcos (92069) *(P-1611)*

California Sportservice Inc .... A 619 795-5000
100 Park Blvd San Diego (92101) *(P-15021)*

California State Univ Long Bch .... C 562 985-1764
1250 N Bellflower Blvd Bh155 Long Beach (90840) *(P-17709)*

California Steel and Tube .... C 626 968-5511
16049 Stephens St City Of Industry (91745) *(P-10126)*

California Steel Inds Inc (HQ) .... **C 909 350-6300**
14000 San Bernardino Ave Fontana (92335) *(P-4514)*

California Steel Inds Inc .... B 909 350-6300
1 California Steel Way Fontana (92335) *(P-4547)*

California Steel Services, San Bernardino *Also Called: California Steel Services Inc (P-10127)*

California Steel Services Inc .... E 909 796-2222
1212 S Mountain View Ave San Bernardino (92408) *(P-10127)*

California Strl Concepts Inc .... D 661 257-6903
28358 Constellation Rd Ste 660 Valencia (91355) *(P-527)*

California Sulphur Company .... E 562 437-0768
2250 E Pacific Coast Hwy Wilmington (90744) *(P-3229)*

California Tool & Engineering, Jurupa Valley *Also Called: Cte California Tl & Engrg Inc (P-5610)*

California Traffic Control .... D 562 595-7575
3333 Cherry Ave Long Beach (90807) *(P-14465)*

California Traffic Ctrl Svcs, Long Beach *Also Called: California Traffic Control (P-14465)*

California Transit Inc .... D 323 234-8750
1900 S Alameda St Vernon (90058) *(P-8748)*

California Trusframe LLC .... C 951 657-7491
23447 Cajalco Rd Perris (92570) *(P-2373)*

California Trusframe LLC (HQ) .... **D 951 350-4880**
23665 Cajalco Rd Perris (92570) *(P-2374)*

California Truss Company (PA) .... **D 951 657-7491**
23665 Cajalco Rd Perris (92570) *(P-2375)*

California Waste Services LLC .... C 310 538-5998
621 W 152nd St Gardena (90247) *(P-9736)*

California Wire Products Corp .... E 951 371-7730
1316 Railroad St Corona (92882) *(P-5402)*

California Woodworking Inc .... E 805 982-9090
1726 Ives Ave Oxnard (93033) *(P-2343)*

Californian, The, San Diego *Also Called: North County Times (P-2820)*

Califrnia Anlytical Instrs Inc .... D 714 974-5560
1312 W Grove Ave Orange (92865) *(P-7850)*

Califrnia Assn Hlth Edcatn Lnk .... D 760 955-3536
17800 Us Highway 18 Apple Valley (92307) *(P-17295)*

Califrnia Auto Dalers Exch LLC .... B 714 996-2400
1320 N Tustin Ave Anaheim (92807) *(P-9801)*

Califrnia Crtive Solutions Inc (PA) .... **D 458 208-4131**
13475 Danielson St Ste 230 Poway (92064) *(P-14203)*

Califrnia Cstm Frits Flvors LL (PA) .... **E 626 736-4130**
15800 Tapia St Irwindale (91706) *(P-1672)*

Califrnia Cstume Cllctions Inc (PA) .... **B 323 262-8383**
210 S Anderson St Los Angeles (90033) *(P-2188)*

Califrnia Ctr For Arts Escndid .... C 760 839-4138
340 N Escondido Blvd Escondido (92025) *(P-17250)*

Califrnia Dept Dvlpmental Svcs .... B 760 770-6248
696 Ramon Cathedral City (92234) *(P-16540)*

Califrnia Dept Dvlpmental Svcs .... A 714 957-5151
2501 Harbor Blvd Costa Mesa (92626) *(P-17051)*

Califrnia Dept State Hospitals .... A 714 957-5000
2501 Harbor Blvd Costa Mesa (92626) *(P-16268)*

Califrnia Dept State Hospitals .... A 909 425-7000
3102 E Highland Ave Patton (92369) *(P-16269)*

Califrnia Dept State Hospitals .... A 805 468-2000
10333 El Camino Real Atascadero (93422) *(P-16270)*

Califrnia Dluxe Wndows Inds In (PA) .... **E 818 349-5566**
20735 Superior St Chatsworth (91311) *(P-2299)*

Califrnia Dsgners Chice Cstm C .... E 805 987-5820
547 Constitution Ave Ste F Camarillo (93012) *(P-2344)*

Califrnia Frnsic Med Group Inc .... D 858 694-4690
2801 Meadow Lark Dr San Diego (92123) *(P-16541)*

Califrnia Frnsic Med Group Inc .... D 805 654-3343
800 S Victoria Ave Ventura (93009) *(P-16542)*

Califrnia Furn Collections Inc .... C 619 621-2455
150 Reed Ct Ste A Chula Vista (91911) *(P-2500)*

Califrnia Grnhse Frm II Ltd PR .... D 949 715-3987
17712 Adobe Rd Bakersfield (93307) *(P-14466)*

Califrnia Hosp Med Ctr Fndtion .... A 213 742-5867
1401 S Grand Ave Los Angeles (90015) *(P-15929)*

Califrnia Insur Guarantee Assn .... C 818 844-4300
330 N Brand Blvd Ste 500 Glendale (91203) *(P-12187)*

Califrnia Nutritional Pdts Inc .... D 760 625-3884
64405 Lincoln St Mecca (92254) *(P-1410)*

Califrnia Nwspapers Ltd Partnr (DH) .... B 626 962-8811
605 E Huntington Dr Ste 100 Monrovia (91016) *(P-2786)*

Califrnia Nwspapers Ltd Partnr .... B 909 987-6397
3200 E Guasti Rd Ste 100 Ontario (91761) *(P-2787)*

Califrnia Nwspapers Ltd Partnr .... B 909 793-3221
19 E Citrus Ave Ste 102 Redlands (92373) *(P-2788)*

Califrnia Rhblitation Inst LLC .... A 424 363-1003
2070 Century Park E Los Angeles (90067) *(P-15930)*

Califrnia Rsrces Elk Hills LLC .... B 661 412-0000
27200 Tourney Rd Ste 200 Santa Clarita (91355) *(P-297)*

Mergent email: customerrelations@mergent.com
968

2025 Southern California
Business Directory and Buyers Guide

(P-0000) Products & Services Section entry number
(PA)=Parent Co (HQ)=Headquarters (DH)=Div Headquarters

Califrnia Scnce Ctr Foundation .... B 213 744-2545
700 Exposition Park Dr Los Angeles (90037) *(P-17251)*

Califrnia Sthland Prvate SEC L .... C 714 367-4005
1818 S State College Blvd Anaheim (92806) *(P-14283)*

Califrnia Trade Converters Inc .... E 818 899-1455
9816 Variel Ave Chatsworth (91311) *(P-2640)*

Calimesa Operations LLC .... C 909 795-2421
13542 2nd St Yucaipa (92399) *(P-15586)*

CALIMESA POST ACUTE, Yucaipa Also Called: Calimesa Operations LLC *(P-15586)*

Call To Action Partners Llc .... C 310 996-7200
11601 Wilshire Blvd Fl 23 Los Angeles (90025) *(P-12701)*

Call-The-Car .... C 855 282-6968
2589 E Washington Blvd Pasadena (91107) *(P-8816)*

Callaway Vineyard & Winery .... D 951 676-4001
32720 Rancho California Rd Temecula (92591) *(P-1560)*

Calmat Co .... B 661 858-2673
16101 Hwy 156 Maricopa (93252) *(P-372)*

Calmedcasvs Inc .... D 818 888-0700
6507 Winnetka Ave Canoga Park (91306) *(P-16543)*

Calmet Inc (PA) .... C 323 721-8120
7202 Petterson Ln Paramount (90723) *(P-9737)*

Calmont Engrg & Elec Corp (PA) .... E 714 549-0336
420 E Alton Ave Santa Ana (92707) *(P-4630)*

Calmont Wire & Cable, Santa Ana Also Called: Calmont Engrg & Elec Corp *(P-4630)*

Calnetix Technologies LLC (HQ) .... D 562 293-1660
16323 Shoemaker Ave Cerritos (90703) *(P-6316)*

Calpaco Papers Inc (PA) .... C 323 767-2600
3155 Universe Dr Jurupa Valley (91752) *(P-2765)*

Calpine Energy Solutions LLC (DH) .... C 877 273-6772
401 W A St Ste 500 San Diego (92101) *(P-9668)*

Calpipe Industries LLC .... E 562 803-4388
923 Calpipe Rd Santa Paula (93060) *(P-4515)*

Calpipe Security Bollards, Downey Also Called: Cal Pipe Manufacturing Inc *(P-5429)*

Calportland .... D 760 343-3403
2025 E Financial Way Glendora (91741) *(P-4432)*

Calportland Company .... D 760 245-5321
19409 National Trails Hwy Oro Grande (92368) *(P-4351)*

Calportland Company (DH) .... D 626 852-6200
2025 E Financial Way Glendora (91741) *(P-4352)*

Calportland Company .... C 661 824-2401
9350 Oak Creek Rd Mojave (93501) *(P-4353)*

Calsemi, Santa Monica Also Called: California Semiconductor Tech *(P-17500)*

Calsense, Carlsbad Also Called: California Sensor Corporation *(P-8037)*

Calvary Church Santa Ana Inc .... C 714 973-4800
1010 N Tustin Ave Santa Ana (92705) *(P-17079)*

Calvillo Construction Corp .... E 310 985-3911
1133 Brooks St Ste C Ontario (91762) *(P-393)*

Calvin Dubois .... D 909 222-6662
9057 Arrow Rte Rancho Cucamonga (91730) *(P-758)*

Calwax LLC (DH) .... E 626 969-4334
16511 Knott Ave La Mirada (90638) *(P-11008)*

Calwest Mfg and Lsk Suspension, Fontana Also Called: Lamer Street Kreations Corp *(P-17577)*

CAM, Fullerton Also Called: Consolidated Aerospace Mfg LLC *(P-7709)*

CAM Properties Inc .... D 714 844-2200
26415 Summit Cir Santa Clarita (91350) *(P-202)*

Camarillo Family YMCA, Camarillo Also Called: Channel Islnds Yung MNS Chrstn *(P-17336)*

Camarillo Healthcare Center .... B 805 482-9805
205 Granada St Camarillo (93010) *(P-17958)*

Camber Operating Company Inc .... B 864 438-0000
393 Cheryl Ln City Of Industry (91789) *(P-7171)*

Cambium Business Group Inc (PA) .... C 714 670-1171
6950 Noritsu Ave Buena Park (90620) *(P-9867)*

Cambria Pines Lodge, Cambria Also Called: Pacific Cambria Inc *(P-12957)*

Cambridge Equities LP .... E 858 350-2300
9922 Jefferson Blvd Culver City (90232) *(P-3567)*

Cambridge Sierra Holdings LLC .... B 909 370-4411
1350 Reche Canyon Rd Colton (92324) *(P-15587)*

Cambro, Huntington Beach Also Called: Cambro Manufacturing Company *(P-4080)*

Cambro Manufacturing, Huntington Beach Also Called: Cambro Manufacturing Company *(P-4079)*

Cambro Manufacturing Company .... C 714 848-1555
7601 Clay Ave Huntington Beach (92648) *(P-4078)*

Cambro Manufacturing Company .... D 714 848-1555
5801 Skylab Rd Huntington Beach (92647) *(P-4079)*

Cambro Manufacturing Company (PA) .... B 714 848-1555
5801 Skylab Rd Huntington Beach (92647) *(P-4080)*

Cambro Manufacturing Company .... C 909 354-8962
21558 Ferrero City Of Industry (91789) *(P-8666)*

Camden Development Inc .... C 949 427-4674
27261 Las Ramblas Mission Viejo (92691) *(P-12395)*

Camellia Gardens Care Center, Pasadena Also Called: Highland Hlthcare Cmllia Grdns *(P-15677)*

Camelot Theatres, Palm Springs Also Called: Metropolitan Theatres Corp *(P-14942)*

Camera Ready Cars, Fountain Valley Also Called: Gaffoglio Fmly Mtlcrafters Inc *(P-4333)*

Cameron Health Inc .... D 949 940-4000
905 Calle Amanecer Ste 300 San Clemente (92673) *(P-10071)*

Cameron Intrstate Pipeline LLC .... C 619 696-3110
488 8th Ave San Diego (92101) *(P-667)*

Cameron Surface Systems, Bakersfield Also Called: Cameron West Coast Inc *(P-10345)*

Cameron Technologies Us LLC .... E 562 222-8440
4040 Capitol Ave Whittier (90601) *(P-7851)*

Cameron Welding, Stanton Also Called: Cameron Welding Supply *(P-14737)*

Cameron Welding Supply (PA) .... E 714 530-9353
11061 Dale Ave Stanton (90680) *(P-14737)*

Cameron West Coast Inc .... D
4315 Yeager Way Bakersfield (93313) *(P-10345)*

Cameron's Measurement Systems, Whittier Also Called: Cameron Technologies Us LLC *(P-7851)*

Camfil Farr Inc .... E 973 616-7300
3625 Del Amo Blvd Ste 260 Torrance (90503) *(P-5768)*

Camino Real Foods Inc (PA) .... C 323 585-6599
2638 E Vernon Ave Los Angeles (90058) *(P-1751)*

Camino Real Kitchens, Los Angeles Also Called: Camino Real Foods Inc *(P-1751)*

Camino Ruiz Suite 235, San Diego Also Called: Operation Samahan Inc *(P-15414)*

Camp Glenn Rocky, San Dimas Also Called: County of Los Angeles *(P-16927)*

Camp Pendleton Hospital, Oceanside Also Called: Marine Corps United States *(P-16296)*

Campbell Certified Inc .... E 760 722-9353
1629 Ord Way Oceanside (92056) *(P-4823)*

Campbell Engineering, Lake Forest Also Called: Campbell Engineering Inc *(P-5607)*

Campbell Engineering Inc .... E 949 859-3306
20412 Barents Sea Cir Lake Forest (92630) *(P-5607)*

Campbell Membrane Tech Inc .... E 619 938-2481
1168 N Johnson Ave El Cajon (92020) *(P-5814)*

Campbell-Ewald Company .... D 310 358-4800
1840 Century Park E Ste 1600 Los Angeles (90067) *(P-13198)*

Campbell-Ewald-West, Los Angeles Also Called: Campbell-Ewald Company *(P-13198)*

Campo Band Missions Indians .... B 619 938-6000
1800 Golden Acorn Way Campo (91906) *(P-15099)*

Campus By The Sea, Avalon Also Called: Intervrsity Chrstn Fllwshp/Usa *(P-13103)*

Campus Images, Anaheim Also Called: University Frames Inc *(P-2418)*

Camstar International Inc .... D 909 931-2540
479 Ballena Dr Diamond Bar (91765) *(P-14387)*

Camston Wrather LLC .... C 858 525-9999
2856 Whiptail Loop Carlsbad (92010) *(P-18259)*

Camtech, Irvine Also Called: Computer Assisted Mfg Tech LLC *(P-6108)*

Can Lines Engineering Inc (PA) .... D 562 861-2996
9839 Downey Norwalk Rd Downey (90241) *(P-5788)*

Canadas Finest Foods Inc .... D 951 296-1040
26090 Ynez Rd Temecula (92591) *(P-1374)*

Canari, San Marcos Also Called: Leemarc Industries LLC *(P-2019)*

Canary Medical USA LLC .... D 760 448-5066
2710 Loker Ave W Ste 350 Carlsbad (92010) *(P-8119)*

Cancer Center of Santa Barbara .... D 805 898-2182
2410 Fletcher Ave Ste 104 Santa Barbara (93105) *(P-15260)*

Cancer Immnlogy Intrvtal McRsc, Irvine Also Called: University California Irvine *(P-17837)*

Candle Lamp Holdings LLC .... B 951 682-9600
949 S Coast Dr Ste 650 Costa Mesa (92626) *(P-6402)*

Candy Cane Inn, Anaheim Also Called: Cinderella Motel *(P-12794)*

Canine Caviar, Riverside Also Called: Canine Caviar Pet Foods Inc *(P-1425)*

Employee Codes: A=Over 500 employees, B=251-500
C=101-250, D=51-100, E=20-50, F=10-19, G=1-9

2025 Southern California
Business Directory and Buyers Guide

© Mergent Inc. 1-800-342-5647

969

ALPHABETIC

Canine Caviar Pet Foods Inc ....E 714 223-1800
4131 Tigris Way Riverside (92503) *(P-1425)*

Cannasafe, Van Nuys *Also Called: Consumer Safety Analytics LLC (P-17910)*

Cannon Gasket Inc ....E 909 355-1547
7784 Edison Ave Fontana (92336) *(P-3881)*

Canoga Perkins Corporation (HQ)..................D 818 718-6300
20600 Prairie St Chatsworth (91311) *(P-6677)*

Canon, Ventura *Also Called: Canon Solutions America Inc (P-9972)*

Canon Business Solutions-West Inc ....B 310 217-3000
110 W Walnut St Gardena (90248) *(P-9971)*

Canon Medical Systems USA Inc (DH)..........B 714 730-5000
2441 Michelle Dr Tustin (92780) *(P-10072)*

Canon Recruiting Group LLC ....B 661 252-7400
27651 Lincoln Pl Ste 250 Santa Clarita (91387) *(P-13499)*

Canon Solutions America Inc ....E 844 443-4636
6435 Ventura Blvd Ste C007 Ventura (93003) *(P-9972)*

Canon USA Inc ....B 949 753-4000
15955 Alton Pkwy Irvine (92618) *(P-9965)*

Canoo, Torrance *Also Called: Canoo Inc (P-7234)*

Canoo Inc (PA)..E 424 271-2144
19951 Mariner Ave Torrance (90503) *(P-7234)*

Canopy Energy, Van Nuys *Also Called: Energy Enterprises USA Inc (P-777)*

Canteen Vending, Garden Grove *Also Called: Compass Group Usa Inc (P-13453)*

Canterbury, The, Pls Vrds Pnsl *Also Called: Episcopal Communities & Servic (P-15648)*

Canton Food Co Inc ....C 213 688-7707
750 S Alameda St Los Angeles (90021) *(P-10746)*

Canvas Concepts, San Diego *Also Called: Masterpiece Artist Canvas LLC (P-1884)*

Canvas Concepts Inc ....E 619 424-3428
649 Anita St Ste A2 Chula Vista (91911) *(P-2234)*

Canvas Specialty Inc ....E
1309 S Eastern Ave Commerce (90040) *(P-2235)*

Canvas Worldwide LLC ....C 424 303-4300
12015 Bluff Creek Dr Playa Vista (90094) *(P-13264)*

Canyon Composites Incorporated ....E 714 991-8181
1548 N Gemini Pl Anaheim (92801) *(P-7448)*

Canyon Engineering Pdts Inc ....D 661 294-0084
28909 Avenue Williams Valencia (91355) *(P-7449)*

Canyon Graphics Inc ....D 858 646-0444
3738 Ruffin Rd San Diego (92123) *(P-2300)*

Canyon Hills Club, Anaheim *Also Called: Ardcore Senior Living (P-17120)*

Canyon Plastics LLC ....D 800 350-6325
28455 Livingston Ave Valencia (91355) *(P-4081)*

Canyon Ridge Hospital Inc ....B 909 590-3700
5353 G St Chino (91710) *(P-16271)*

Canyon Rock & Asphalt, San Diego *Also Called: Superior Ready Mix Concrete LP (P-4458)*

Cap Diagnostics LLC ....C 714 966-1221
15545 Sand Canyon Ave Irvine (92618) *(P-16306)*

Cap-Mpt (PA)..C 213 473-8600
333 S Hope St Fl 8 Los Angeles (90071) *(P-12145)*

Cap-Mpt, Los Angeles *Also Called: Coopertive Amrcn Physcians Inc (P-17297)*

Capable Transport Inc ....D 310 697-0198
3528 Torrance Blvd Ste 220 Torrance (90503) *(P-9256)*

Capax Technologies Inc ....E 661 257-7666
24842 Avenue Tibbitts Valencia (91355) *(P-6369)*

Capc Adult Services, Whittier *Also Called: Whittier Union High Schl Dist (P-16830)*

Cape Robbin Inc ....E 626 810-8080
1943 W Mission Blvd Pomona (91766) *(P-10734)*

Capillary Biomedical Inc ....E 949 317-1701
2 Wrigley Ste 101 Irvine (92618) *(P-7948)*

Capistrano Volkswagen, San Juan Capistrano *Also Called: Mission Volkswagen Inc (P-11380)*

Capital Brands Distribution L (PA).................D 800 523-5993
11601 Wilshire Blvd Ste 2300 Los Angeles (90025) *(P-6394)*

Capital Commercial Property, Culver City *Also Called: Property Management Assoc Inc (P-12513)*

Capital Cooking, Carson *Also Called: Capital Cooking Equipment Inc (P-4809)*

Capital Cooking Equipment Inc ....E 562 903-1168
1025 E Bedmar St Carson (90746) *(P-4809)*

Capital Drywall LP ....C 909 599-6818
333 S Grand Ave Ste 4070 Los Angeles (90071) *(P-1003)*

Capital Group, Irvine *Also Called: American Funds Service Company (P-12038)*

Capital Group Companies Inc (PA)................A 213 486-9200
333 S Hope St Fl 53 Los Angeles (90071) *(P-17959)*

Capital Group, The, Los Angeles *Also Called: Capital Group Companies Inc (P-17959)*

Capital Guardian Trust Company (HQ) ....D 213 486-9200
333 S Hope St Fl 52 Los Angeles (90071) *(P-12656)*

Capital Invstmnts Vntures Corp (PA).............C 949 858-0647
30151 Tomas Rcho Sta Marg (92688) *(P-17296)*

Capital Mortgage Services, Ventura *Also Called: E&S Financial Group Inc (P-11898)*

Capital Network Funding Svcs, Los Angeles *Also Called: Capnet Financial Services Inc (P-11876)*

Capital Ready Mix Inc ....E 818 771-1122
11311 Pendleton St Sun Valley (91352) *(P-4433)*

Capital Research and MGT Co (HQ) ....B 213 486-9200
333 S Hope St Fl 55 Los Angeles (90071) *(P-12023)*

Capital Westward, Cerritos *Also Called: Bermingham Cntrls Inc A Cal Co (P-5359)*

Capitalsource Bank ....C 714 989-4600
130 S State College Blvd Brea (92821) *(P-11750)*

Capitalsource Inc ....A 213 443-7700
633 W 5th St 33rd Fl Los Angeles (90071) *(P-11875)*

Capitol Distribution Co LLC (PA)...................E 562 404-4321
12836 Alondra Blvd Cerritos (90703) *(P-10935)*

Capitol Food Company, Cerritos *Also Called: Capitol Distribution Co LLC (P-10935)*

Capitol Records, Los Angeles *Also Called: Medholdings of Newnan LLC (P-14542)*

Capitol Steel Fabricators Inc ....E 323 721-5460
3522 Greenwood Ave Commerce (90040) *(P-4824)*

Capitol-Emi Music Inc ....A 323 462-6252
1750b Vine St Los Angeles (90028) *(P-6572)*

Caplugs, Rancho Dominguez *Also Called: Caplugs Inc (P-4082)*

Caplugs Inc ....D 310 537-2300
18704 S Ferris Pl Rancho Dominguez (90220) *(P-4082)*

Capna Fabrication ....E 888 416-6777
9801 Independence Ave Chatsworth (91311) *(P-5668)*

Capna Systems, Chatsworth *Also Called: Capna Fabrication (P-5668)*

Capnet Financial Services Inc (PA)................D 877 980-0558
11901 Santa Monica Blvd Ste 338 Los Angeles (90025) *(P-11876)*

Capo Industries Division, El Cajon *Also Called: Senior Operations LLC (P-6233)*

Capri Tools, Pomona *Also Called: Als Group Inc (P-10366)*

Capricor ....E 310 423-2104
8700 Beverly Blvd West Hollywood (90048) *(P-3377)*

Capricor Inc ....D 310 358-3200
10865 Road To The Cure Ste 150 San Diego (92121) *(P-16544)*

Caps Payroll, Burbank *Also Called: New Talco Enterprises LLC (P-17748)*

CAPSBC, San Bernardino *Also Called: Community Action Prtnr San Brn (P-17221)*

Capstone, Van Nuys *Also Called: Capstone Dstr Spport Svcs Corp (P-5455)*

Capstone Dstr Spport Svcs Corp (PA)...........C 818 734-5300
16640 Stagg St Van Nuys (91406) *(P-5455)*

Capstone Fire Management Inc (PA).............E 760 839-2290
2240 Auto Park Way Escondido (92029) *(P-5815)*

Capstone Logistics, Moreno Valley *Also Called: Capstone Logistics LLC (P-9360)*

Capstone Logistics LLC ....C 770 414-1929
12661 Aldi Pl Moreno Valley (92555) *(P-9360)*

Capsule Manufacturing Inc ....D 949 245-4151
1399 N Miller St Anaheim (92806) *(P-321)*

Capsule Mfg, Anaheim *Also Called: Capsule Manufacturing Inc (P-321)*

Captain Marketing Inc ....D 310 402-9709
3577 N Figueroa St Los Angeles (90065) *(P-18113)*

Captek Midco Inc ....D 760 734-6800
2710 Progress St Vista (92081) *(P-3378)*

Captek Pharma, La Mirada *Also Called: Captek Softgel Intl Inc (P-3380)*

Captek Softgel Intl Inc (DH)..........................B 562 921-9511
16218 Arthur St Cerritos (90703) *(P-3379)*

Captek Softgel Intl Inc ....E 657 325-0412
14535 Industry Cir La Mirada (90638) *(P-3380)*

Captiva Software Corporation (DH)................D 858 320-1000
10145 Pacific Heights Blvd San Diego (92121) *(P-14074)*

Captive-Aire Systems Inc ....E 310 876-8505
1123 Washington Ave Santa Monica (90403) *(P-4964)*

Car Sound Exhaust System Inc ....C 949 888-1625
1901 Corporate Centre Dr Oceanside (92056) *(P-3230)*

2025 Southern California
Business Directory and Buyers Guide

Car Sound Exhaust System Inc .... E 949 858-5900
30142 Avenida De Las Bandera Rcho Sta Marg (92688) *(P-7235)*

Car Sound Exhaust System Inc .... E 949 858-5900
23201 Antonio Pkwy Rcho Sta Marg (92688) *(P-7236)*

Car Wash Partners Inc .... C 661 377-1020
2619 Mount Vernon Ave Bakersfield (93306) *(P-14705)*

Car Wash Partners Inc .... D 661 231-3689
5375 Olive Dr Bakersfield (93308) *(P-14706)*

CAR WASH PARTNERS INC., Bakersfield *Also Called: Car Wash Partners Inc (P-14706)*

CAR WASH PARTNERS, INC., Bakersfield *Also Called: Car Wash Partners Inc (P-14705)*

Cara Communications LLC .... D 310 442-5600
12233 W Olympic Blvd Ste 170 Los Angeles (90064) *(P-14882)*

Caran Precision Engineering & Manufacturing Corp (PA) .... D 714 447-5400
2830 Orbiter St Brea (92821) *(P-5178)*

Caravan Canopy, Cerritos *Also Called: Caravan Canopy Intl Inc (P-2236)*

Caravan Canopy Intl Inc .... D 714 367-3000
17510-17512 Studebaker Rd Cerritos (90703) *(P-2236)*

Carberry LLC .... E 562 264-5078
3645 Long Beach Blvd Long Beach (90807) *(P-8667)*

Carberry LLC (HQ) .... E 800 564-0842
17130 Muskrat Ave Ste B Adelanto (92301) *(P-8668)*

Carbomer Inc 858 552-0992
6324 Ferris Sq Ste B San Diego (92121) *(P-3231)*

Carbon 38 Inc .... D 888 723-5838
2866 Westbrook Ave Los Angeles (90046) *(P-2084)*

Carbon Activated Corporation (PA) .... E 310 885-4555
2250 S Central Ave Compton (90220) *(P-3232)*

Carbon By Design LLC .... D 760 643-1300
1491 Poinsettia Ave Ste 136 Vista (92081) *(P-7450)*

Carbon California Company LLC .... E 805 933-1901
270 Quail Ct Ste 201 Santa Paula (93060) *(P-273)*

Carbro Company, Lawndale *Also Called: Curry Company LLC (P-5611)*

Cardenas Markets LLC .... C 909 923-7426
1621 E Francis St Ontario (91761) *(P-1386)*

Cardiac Noninvasive Laboratory, Los Angeles *Also Called: Cedars-Sinai Medical Center (P-15266)*

Cardiac Unit, Anaheim *Also Called: Ahmc Anheim Rgional Med Ctr LP (P-15897)*

CARDIFF ONCOLOGY, San Diego *Also Called: Cardiff Oncology Inc (P-3381)*

Cardiff Oncology Inc .... E 858 952-7570
11055 Flintkote Ave San Diego (92121) *(P-3381)*

Cardiff Transportation, Palm Desert *Also Called: Gary Cardiff Enterprises Inc (P-8828)*

Cardinal C G, Moreno Valley *Also Called: Cardinal Glass Industries Inc (P-4313)*

Cardinal Glass Industries Inc .... C 951 485-9007
24100 Cardinal Ave Moreno Valley (92551) *(P-4313)*

Cardinal Industrial Finishes (PA) .... D 626 444-9274
1329 Potrero Ave Ca South El Monte (91733) *(P-3706)*

Cardinal Paint and Powder Inc .... C 626 937-6767
15010 Don Julian Rd City Of Industry (91746) *(P-3707)*

Cardinal Paint and Powder Inc .... D 626 444-9274
1329 Potrero Ave South El Monte (91733) *(P-3708)*

Cardinal Point Captains, San Diego *Also Called: Cardinal Point Captains Inc (P-13594)*

Cardinal Point Captains Inc .... D 760 438-7361
5005 Texas St Ste 104 San Diego (92108) *(P-13594)*

Cardinal Transportation, Gardena *Also Called: First Student Inc (P-8880)*

Cardionet Inc .... D 619 243-7500
750 B St Ste 1400 San Diego (92101) *(P-15261)*

CARDIONET, INC., San Diego *Also Called: Cardionet Inc (P-15261)*

Cardiovascular Systems, Tustin *Also Called: Terumo Americas Holding Inc (P-7984)*

Cardno Eri, Lake Forest *Also Called: Environmental Resolutions Inc (P-18307)*

Cardona Manufacturing Corp .... E 818 841-8358
1869 N Victory Pl Burbank (91504) *(P-7451)*

Cardservice International Inc (DH) .... B
5898 Condor Dr # 220 Moorpark (93021) *(P-14467)*

Care 1st Health Plan (PA) .... C 323 889-6638
601 Potrero Grande Dr Fl 2 Monterey Park (91755) *(P-12059)*

Care A Van Transport, Carlsbad *Also Called: CAV Inc (P-8818)*

Care Ambulance, Redlands *Also Called: Care Medical Trnsp Inc (P-8817)*

Care Ambulance, Orange *Also Called: Lifestar Response of Alabama (P-8834)*

Care Choice Health Systems Inc .... C 760 798-4508
1151 S Santa Fe Ave Vista (92083) *(P-15842)*

Care Choice Home Care, Vista *Also Called: Care Choice Health Systems Inc (P-15842)*

Care Fusion Products, San Diego *Also Called: Becton Dickinson and Company (P-8106)*

Care Medical Trnsp Inc .... C 858 653-4520
1801 Orange Tree Ln Ste 100 Redlands (92374) *(P-8817)*

Care Solace, Cardiff *Also Called: Addiction Treatment Tech LLC (P-16439)*

Care Stffng Professionals Inc .... D 909 906-2060
2151 E Convention Center Way Ste 204 Ontario (91764) *(P-13595)*

Care Unlimited Health Svcs Inc .... D 626 332-3767
1025 W Arrow Hwy Ste 103 Glendora (91740) *(P-16375)*

Carecredit LLC .... C 800 300-3046
555 Anton Blvd Ste 700 Costa Mesa (92626) *(P-14468)*

Career Engagement Group LLC .... D 212 235-1470
30025 Alicia Pkwy Laguna Niguel (92677) *(P-13682)*

Career Group Inc (PA) .... A 310 277-8188
10100 Santa Monica Blvd Ste 900 Los Angeles (90067) *(P-13500)*

Career Strategies Tmpry Inc .... C 714 824-6840
575 Anton Blvd Ste 630 Costa Mesa (92626) *(P-13501)*

Career Strategies Tmpry Inc .... C 818 883-0440
21031 Ventura Blvd Ste 1005 Woodland Hills (91364) *(P-13502)*

Career Strategies Tmpry Inc .... C 760 564-5959
78060 Calle Estado La Quinta (92253) *(P-13503)*

Career Strategies Tmpry Inc .... C 909 230-4504
9267 Haven Ave Ste 225 Rancho Cucamonga (91730) *(P-13504)*

Career Tech Circuit Services, Chatsworth *Also Called: Circuit Services Llc (P-6717)*

Carefree Communities, Newbury Park *Also Called: Carefree Communities Inc (P-12375)*

Carefree Communities Inc .... C 805 498-2612
1251 Old Conejo Rd Newbury Park (91320) *(P-12375)*

Carefusion 207 Inc .... B 760 778-7200
1100 Bird Center Dr Palm Springs (92262) *(P-8120)*

Carefusion 213 LLC (DH) .... B 800 523-0502
3750 Torrey View Ct San Diego (92130) *(P-8121)*

Carefusion Corporation .... D 858 617-4271
10020 Pacific Mesa Blvd Bldg A San Diego (92121) *(P-8122)*

Carefusion Corporation .... E 760 778-7200
1100 Bird Center Dr Palm Springs (92262) *(P-8123)*

Carefusion Corporation .... D 800 231-2466
22745 Savi Ranch Pkwy Yorba Linda (92887) *(P-8124)*

Carefusion Corporation (HQ) .... B 858 617-2000
3750 Torrey View Ct San Diego (92130) *(P-8374)*

Carefusion Solutions LLC (DH) .... A 858 617-2100
3750 Torrey View Ct San Diego (92130) *(P-8125)*

Careismatic Brands LLC (DH) .... C 818 671-2128
15301 Ventura Blvd Sherman Oaks (91403) *(P-4282)*

Carelon Bhavioral Hlth Cal Inc .... A 800 228-1286
12898 Towne Center Dr Cerritos (90703) *(P-12188)*

Carelon Health California Inc (HQ) .... C 562 622-2950
12900 Park Plaza Dr Ste 150 Cerritos (90703) *(P-12060)*

Carelon Med Benefits MGT Inc .... A 847 310-0366
505 N Brand Blvd Glendale (91203) *(P-12061)*

Caremark Rx Inc .... D 909 822-1164
1851 N Riverside Ave Rialto (92376) *(P-15262)*

Caremore AP, Cerritos *Also Called: Caremore Medical Management Company A California Limited Partnership (P-17960)*

Caremore Health Plan, Cerritos *Also Called: Carelon Health California Inc (P-12060)*

Caremore Medical Group .... D 714 529-3971
420 W Central Ave Ste A Brea (92821) *(P-15263)*

Caremore Medical Management Company A California Limited Par .... A 562 741-4300
12900 Park Plaza Dr Ste 150 Cerritos (90703) *(P-17960)*

Cares, San Diego *Also Called: Center For Atism RES Evltion S (P-16449)*

Cargill, Fullerton *Also Called: Cargill Incorporated (P-3312)*

Cargill Incorporated .... E 714 449-6708
600 N Gilbert St Fullerton (92833) *(P-3312)*

Cargill Meat Solutions Corp .... D 909 476-3120
10602 N Trademark Pkwy Ste 500 Rancho Cucamonga (91730) *(P-1239)*

Cargill Meat Solutions Corp .... E 562 345-5240
13034 Excelsior Dr Norwalk (90650) *(P-1240)*

Cargill Meat Solutions Corp .... C 515 735-9800
3501 E Vernon Ave Vernon (90058) *(P-1752)*

Cargo Service Center, Los Angeles *Also Called: Swissport Cargo Services LP (P-9210)*

Cargo Solution Brokerage LLC .... C 909 350-1644
14769 San Bernardino Ave Fontana (92335) *(P-8899)*

Employee Codes: A=Over 500 employees, B=251-500
C=101-250, D=51-100, E=20-50, F=10-19, G=1-9

2025 Southern California
Business Directory and Buyers Guide

© Mergent Inc. 1-800-342-5647

971

Cargo Solution Express Inc (PA) .... C 800 582-5104
14587 Valley Blvd # 89 Fontana (92335) *(P-8934)*

Cargomatic Inc (PA) .... C 866 513-2343
211 E Ocean Blvd Ste 350 Long Beach (90802) *(P-9257)*

Carick Lending, Encino *Also Called: Betta Assets Inc (P-12388)*

Cariloha, Rancho Cucamonga *Also Called: South Bay International Inc (P-2492)*

Carinet, San Diego *Also Called: Fortitude Technology Inc (P-9433)*

Carl Warren & Company LLC (HQ) .... C 657 622-4200
175 N Riverview Dr Pmb A Anaheim (92808) *(P-12189)*

Carl Zeiss Meditec Prod LLC .... D 877 644-4657
1040 S Vintage Ave Ste A Ontario (91761) *(P-7997)*

Carl Zeiss Meditec,, Rancho Cucamonga *Also Called: Aaren Scientific Inc (P-7993)*

Carla Senter .... E 310 366-7295
515 E Alondra Blvd Gardena (90248) *(P-4965)*

Carley (PA) .... C 310 325-8474
1502 W 228th St Torrance (90501) *(P-4324)*

Carlisle Construction Mtls LLC .... D 909 591-7425
5635 Schaefer Ave Chino (91710) *(P-9957)*

Carlsbad By The Sea, Carlsbad *Also Called: Front Porch Communities & Svcs (P-17154)*

Carlsbad Firefighters Assn .... D 760 729-3730
2560 Orion Way Carlsbad (92010) *(P-17460)*

Carlsbad Premium Outlets, Carlsbad *Also Called: Premium Outlet Partners LP (P-12313)*

Carlsbad Tech, Carlsbad *Also Called: Carlsbad Technology Inc (P-3382)*

Carlsbad Tech, Carlsbad *Also Called: Carlsbad Technology Inc (P-3383)*

Carlsbad Technology Inc .... D 760 431-8284
5923 Balfour Ct Carlsbad (92008) *(P-3382)*

Carlsbad Technology Inc (DH) .... E 760 431-8284
5922 Farnsworth Ct Ste 101 Carlsbad (92008) *(P-3383)*

Carlstar Group LLC .... D 909 829-1703
10730 Production Ave Fontana (92337) *(P-7237)*

Carlton Forge Works, Paramount *Also Called: Carlton Forge Works LLC (P-5153)*

Carlton Forge Works LLC .... B 562 633-1131
7743 Adams St Paramount (90723) *(P-5153)*

Carmax Inc .... C 951 387-3887
25560 Madison Ave Murrieta (92562) *(P-11435)*

Carmel Mtn Rhab Healthcare Ctr, San Diego *Also Called: Bernardo Hts Healthcare Inc (P-15838)*

Carmel Partners LLC .... C 916 479-5286
530 Wilshire Blvd Ste 203 Santa Monica (90401) *(P-12630)*

Carmi Flavors, Commerce *Also Called: Carmi Flvr & Fragrance Co Inc (P-1673)*

Carmi Flvr & Fragrance Co Inc (PA) .... E 323 888-9240
6030 Scott Way Commerce (90040) *(P-1673)*

Carmichael International Svc (DH) .... D 213 353-0800
1200 Corporate Center Dr Ste 200 Monterey Park (91754) *(P-9258)*

Carmike Cinemas, Thousand Oaks *Also Called: Carmike Cinemas LLC (P-14929)*

Carmike Cinemas LLC .... C 805 494-4702
166 W Hillcrest Dr Thousand Oaks (91360) *(P-14929)*

Carnegie Agency Inc .... D 805 445-1470
2535 W Hillcrest Dr Newbury Park (91320) *(P-12190)*

Carnegie General Insur Agcy, Newbury Park *Also Called: Carnegie Agency Inc (P-12190)*

Carnegie Institution Wash .... D 626 577-1122
813 Santa Barbara St Pasadena (91101) *(P-17870)*

Carnegie Mortgage LLC .... B 949 379-7000
15480 Laguna Canyon Rd Ste 100 Irvine (92618) *(P-11941)*

Carnevale & Lohr Inc .... E 562 927-8311
6521 Clara St Bell Gardens (90201) *(P-4472)*

Carol Anderson Inc (PA) .... E 310 638-3333
18700 S Laurel Park Rd Rancho Dominguez (90220) *(P-2062)*

Carol Anderson By Invitation, Rancho Dominguez *Also Called: Carol Anderson Inc (P-2062)*

Carol Cole Company .... C 888 360-9171
1325 Sycamore Ave Ste A Vista (92081) *(P-8126)*

Carol Electric Company Inc .... D 562 431-1870
3822 Cerritos Ave Los Alamitos (90720) *(P-897)*

Carolense Entrmt Group LLC .... D 405 493-1120
506 S Spring St Los Angeles (90013) *(P-8422)*

Carolina Lquid Chmistries Corp .... E 336 722-8910
510 W Central Ave Ste C Brea (92821) *(P-8127)*

Carolyn E Wylie Ctr For Chldre .... D 951 683-5193
4164 Brockton Ave Riverside (92501) *(P-16878)*

Carousel Child Care Corp .... C 310 216-6641
8333 Airport Blvd Los Angeles (90045) *(P-17080)*

Carpenter Zuckerman & Rowley .... C 310 273-1230
8827 W Olympic Blvd Beverly Hills (90211) *(P-16653)*

Carpenter Co .... E 951 354-7550
7809 Lincoln Ave Riverside (92504) *(P-3995)*

Carpenter E R Co, Riverside *Also Called: Carpenter Co (P-3995)*

Carpenter Group .... E 619 233-5625
2380 Main St San Diego (92113) *(P-10428)*

Carpenters Southwest ADM Corp .... C 805 688-5581
376 Avenue Of The Flags Buellton (93427) *(P-11554)*

Carpenters Southwest ADM Corp (PA) .... D 213 386-8590
533 S Fremont Ave Los Angeles (90071) *(P-12785)*

Carr Corporation (PA) .... E 310 587-1113
1547 11th St Santa Monica (90401) *(P-8365)*

Carr Management Inc .... D 951 277-4800
22324 Temescal Canyon Rd Corona (92883) *(P-4083)*

Carrara Marble Co Amer Inc (PA) .... D 626 961-6010
15939 Phoenix Dr City Of Industry (91745) *(P-9938)*

Carriage Carpet Mills, Cypress *Also Called: Shaw Industries Group Inc (P-1956)*

Carrico Pediatric Therapy Inc .... D 562 607-1937
1301 W Arrow Hwy San Dimas (91773) *(P-16447)*

Carrington Mortgage Svcs LLC .... D 909 226-7963
10370 Commerce Center Dr Ste 140 Rancho Cucamonga (91730) *(P-11959)*

Carrington Mrtg Holdings LLC .... C 888 267-0584
1600 S Douglass Rd Ste 110 Anaheim (92806) *(P-11892)*

Carroll Fulmer Logistics Corp .... C 626 435-9940
13773 Algranti Ave Sylmar (91342) *(P-9259)*

Carroll Metal Works Inc .... D 619 477-9125
740 W 16th St National City (91950) *(P-4825)*

Carroll Shelby Licensing Inc .... D 310 914-1843
7927 Garden Grove Blvd Garden Grove (92841) *(P-9052)*

Carros Americas, Inc., Westlake Village *Also Called: Carros Sensors Americas LLC (P-6979)*

Carros Sensors Americas LLC .... C 805 267-7176
2945 Townsgate Rd Ste 200 Westlake Village (91361) *(P-6979)*

Carros Sensors Systems Co LLC (DH) .... C 805 968-0782
1461 Lawrence Dr Thousand Oaks (91320) *(P-8038)*

CARS, San Diego *Also Called: Charitble Adult Rides Svcs Inc (P-17461)*

Carson Industries LLC .... A 951 788-9720
2434 Rubidoux Blvd Riverside (92509) *(P-4084)*

Carson Kurtzman Consultants (DH) .... C 310 823-9000
2335 Alaska Ave El Segundo (90245) *(P-16654)*

Carson Operating Company LLC .... D 310 830-9200
2 Civic Plaza Dr Carson (90745) *(P-12786)*

Carson Trailer Inc (PA) .... D 310 835-0876
14831 S Maple Ave Gardena (90248) *(P-11486)*

Carson Trailer Sales, Gardena *Also Called: Carson Trailer Inc (P-11486)*

Cartel Electronics LLC .... D 714 993-0270
1900 Petra Ln Ste C Placentia (92870) *(P-6714)*

Cartel Industries, Irvine *Also Called: Cartel Industries LLC (P-4966)*

Cartel Industries LLC .... E 949 474-3200
17152 Armstrong Ave Irvine (92614) *(P-4966)*

Cartel Marketing Inc .... C 818 483-1130
6345 Balboa Blvd Encino (91316) *(P-12191)*

Carter Laboratories, Irvine *Also Called: Fluxergy Inc (P-17788)*

Carters Metal Fabricators Inc .... E 626 815-4225
935 W 5th St Azusa (91702) *(P-2522)*

Carton Design, Pico Rivera *Also Called: CD Container Inc (P-2658)*

Carttronics LLC (HQ) .... E 888 696-2278
90 Icon Foothill Ranch (92610) *(P-7112)*

Cartwright Trmt Pest Ctrl Inc .... E 619 442-9613
1376 Broadway El Cajon (92021) *(P-13343)*

Carvin Corp .... C 858 487-1600
16262 W Bernardo Dr San Diego (92127) *(P-11544)*

Carvin Guitars & Pro Sound, San Diego *Also Called: Carvin Corp (P-11544)*

Cas Medical Systems Inc (HQ) .... D 203 488-6056
1 Edwards Way Irvine (92614) *(P-8128)*

Casa Clina Ctrs For Rhbltation, Pomona *Also Called: Casa Clina Hosp Ctrs For Hlthc (P-15931)*

Casa Clina Hosp Ctrs For Hlthc .... C 626 334-8735
910 E Alosta Ave Azusa (91702) *(P-15537)*

Casa Clina Hosp Ctrs For Hlthc (HQ) .... B 909 596-7733
255 E Bonita Ave Pomona (91767) *(P-15931)*

2025 Southern California
Business Directory and Buyers Guide

Casa Clina Hosp Ctrs For Hlthc .... C 760 248-6245
11981 Midway Ave Lucerne Valley (92356) *(P-16879)*

Casa Clina Hosp Ctrs For Hlthc, Pomona *Also Called: Casa Colina Inc (P-16880)*

Casa Colina Inc (PA) .... A 909 596-7733
255 E Bonita Ave Pomona (91767) *(P-16880)*

Casa De Amparo (PA) .... D 760 754-5500
325 Buena Creek Rd San Marcos (92069) *(P-17126)*

Casa De Hermandad (PA) .... E 310 477-8272
1639 11th St Santa Monica (90404) *(P-8511)*

Casa De Las Campanas Inc (PA) .... D 858 451-9152
18655 W Bernardo Dr San Diego (92127) *(P-17127)*

Casa De Manana, La Jolla *Also Called: Front Porch Communities & Svcs (P-12342)*

Casa Dorinda, Santa Barbara *Also Called: Montecito Retirement Assn (P-15723)*

Casa Herrera Inc (PA) .... D 909 392-3930
2655 Pine St Pomona (91767) *(P-5669)*

CASA PACIFICA, Camarillo *Also Called: Casa Pcfica Ctrs For Chldren F (P-16881)*

Casa Palmera LLC .... D 888 481-4481
14750 El Camino Real Del Mar (92014) *(P-16448)*

Casa Pcfica Ctrs For Chldren F (PA) .... C 805 482-3260
1722 S Lewis Rd Camarillo (93012) *(P-16881)*

Casa Raphael, Vista *Also Called: Alpha Project For Homeless (P-16863)*

Casa-Pacifica Inc .... B 951 658-3369
2200 W Acacia Ave Ofc Hemet (92545) *(P-17128)*

Casa-Pacifica Inc .... B 951 766-5116
2400 W Acacia Ave Hemet (92545) *(P-17129)*

Cascade Pump Company .... D 562 946-1414
10107 Norwalk Blvd Santa Fe Springs (90670) *(P-5729)*

Cascade Thermal Solutions LLC (PA) .... E 619 562-8852
1890 Cordell Ct Ste 102 El Cajon (92020) *(P-759)*

Cascade Turf LLC .... D 909 626-8586
4811 Brooks St Montclair (91763) *(P-10361)*

Casco Mfg, San Fernando *Also Called: C A Schroeder Inc (P-4490)*

Caseworx, Redlands *Also Called: Caseworx Inc (P-2506)*

Caseworx Inc (PA) .... E 909 799-9550
1130 Research Dr Redlands (92374) *(P-2506)*

Casey Company (PA) .... C 562 436-9685
180 E Ocean Blvd Ste 1010 Long Beach (90802) *(P-11029)*

Cash It Here, Santa Ana *Also Called: Continental Currency Svcs Inc (P-11838)*

Cashcall Inc .... A 949 752-4600
1 City Blvd W Ste 102 Orange (92868) *(P-11850)*

Casing Specialties Inc .... E 661 399-5522
12454 Snow Rd Bakersfield (93314) *(P-322)*

Cask, San Diego *Also Called: Cask Nx LLC (P-18298)*

Cask Nx LLC .... C 858 232-8900
8910 University Center Ln Ste 400 San Diego (92121) *(P-18298)*

Casper Company .... C 619 589-6001
3825 Bancroft Dr Spring Valley (91977) *(P-1107)*

Cass, El Cajon *Also Called: Cass Construction Inc (P-668)*

Cass Construction Inc (PA) .... B 619 590-0929
1100 Wagner Dr El Cajon (92020) *(P-668)*

Cast & Crew LLC (PA) .... C 818 570-6180
2300 W Empire Ave Ste 500 Burbank (91504) *(P-17710)*

Cast and Crew Entrmt Svcs, Burbank *Also Called: Cast & Crew LLC (P-17710)*

Cast Partner Inc .... E 323 876-9000
4658 W Washington Blvd Los Angeles (90016) *(P-4685)*

Cast Parts Inc .... C 626 937-3444
16800 Chestnut St City Of Industry (91748) *(P-4562)*

Cast Parts Inc (HQ) .... C 909 595-2252
4200 Valley Blvd Walnut (91789) *(P-4563)*

Cast-Rite Corporation .... D 310 532-2080
515 E Airline Way Gardena (90248) *(P-5571)*

Cast-Rite International Inc (PA) .... D 310 532-2080
515 E Airline Way Gardena (90248) *(P-4686)*

Castaic Truck Stop Inc .... E 661 295-1374
31611 Castaic Rd Castaic (91384) *(P-3823)*

Castaway Restaurant, The, Burbank *Also Called: Specialty Restaurants Corp (P-11601)*

Castle & Cooke Investments Inc .... C 310 208-3636
1 Dole Dr Westlake Village (91362) *(P-528)*

Castle Harlan Partners III LP .... A 661 863-0305
3801 California Ave Bakersfield (93309) *(P-11555)*

Castle Importing Inc .... E 909 428-9200
14550 Miller Ave Fontana (92336) *(P-11556)*

Castle Industries Inc of California .... E 909 390-0899
4056 Easy St El Monte (91731) *(P-4967)*

Castle Metals Aerospace, Paramount *Also Called: Transtar Metals Corp (P-10163)*

Castle Press .... E 800 794-0858
1128 N Gilbert St Anaheim (92801) *(P-3204)*

Caston Inc .... D 909 381-1619
354 S Allen St San Bernardino (92408) *(P-1004)*

Castro Construction LLC .... E 689 220-9145
18375 Ventura Blvd Tarzana (91356) *(P-323)*

Casualway Home & Garden, Oxnard *Also Called: Casualway Usa LLC (P-2465)*

Casualway Usa LLC .... D 805 660-7408
1623 Lola Way Oxnard (93030) *(P-2465)*

Catalent Pharma Solutions Inc .... C 858 805-6383
7330 Carroll Rd Ste 200 San Diego (92121) *(P-3384)*

Catalent Pharma Solutions Inc .... D 877 587-1835
8926 Ware Ct San Diego (92121) *(P-3385)*

Catalent San Diego Inc .... C 858 805-6383
7330 Carroll Rd Ste 200 San Diego (92121) *(P-17907)*

Catalina Carpet Mills Inc (PA) .... E 562 926-5811
14418 Best Ave Santa Fe Springs (90670) *(P-1949)*

Catalina Channel Express Inc (HQ) .... C 310 519-7971
385 E Swinford St San Pedro (90731) *(P-9139)*

Catalina Express Cruises, San Pedro *Also Called: Catalina Channel Express Inc (P-9139)*

Catalina Home, Santa Fe Springs *Also Called: Catalina Carpet Mills Inc (P-1949)*

CATALINA ISLÁND MEDICAL CENTER, Avalon *Also Called: Avalon Medical Dev Corp (P-15920)*

Catalina Yachts Inc (PA) .... E 818 884-7700
2259 Ward Ave Simi Valley (93065) *(P-7618)*

Catalyst Spech Lngage Pthology, South Pasadena *Also Called: Catalyst Speech LLC (P-18114)*

Catalyst Speech LLC .... C 213 346-9945
835 Milan Ave South Pasadena (91030) *(P-18114)*

Catalytic Solutions Inc (HQ) .... E 805 486-4649
1700 Fiske Pl Oxnard (93033) *(P-7833)*

Catamaran Resort Hotel, San Diego *Also Called: Braemar Partnership (P-12776)*

Catapult Communications Corp (DH) .... E 818 871-1800
26601 Agoura Rd Calabasas (91302) *(P-13898)*

Catawba County Schools, Camarillo *Also Called: Microsemi Communications Inc (P-6851)*

Caterpillar, San Diego *Also Called: Hawthorne Machinery Co (P-10376)*

Caterpillar Authorized Dealer, Santa Maria *Also Called: Quinn Company (P-10355)*

Caterpillar Authorized Dealer, Oxnard *Also Called: Quinn Company (P-10356)*

Caterpillar Authorized Dealer, Bakersfield *Also Called: Quinn Company (P-10357)*

Caterpillar Authorized Dealer, City Of Industry *Also Called: Quinn Shepherd Machinery (P-10358)*

Caterpillar Authorized Dealer, San Diego *Also Called: Hawthorne Rent-It Service (P-13438)*

Cathay Bank (HQ) .... C 626 279-3698
777 N Broadway Los Angeles (90012) *(P-11751)*

Cathay General Bancorp (PA) .... C 213 625-4700
777 N Broadway Los Angeles (90012) *(P-11752)*

Catholic Charities, Ventura *Also Called: Catholic Chrties Snta Clara CN (P-16882)*

Catholic Chrties Snta Clara CN .... D 805 643-4694
303 N Ventura Ave Ste A Ventura (93001) *(P-16882)*

Catholic Hlthcare W Sthern Cal (HQ) .... C 562 491-9000
1050 Linden Ave Long Beach (90813) *(P-15932)*

Catholic Resource Center, West Covina *Also Called: Saint Jseph Communications Inc (P-14854)*

Cathy Ireland Home, Chino *Also Called: Omnia Leather Motion Inc (P-2219)*

Catridge Return Center, Calexico *Also Called: 4l Technologies Inc (P-5659)*

Cats U S A Pest Control, North Hollywood *Also Called: Cats USA Inc (P-13344)*

Cats USA Inc .... D 818 506-1000
5683 Whitnall Hwy North Hollywood (91601) *(P-13344)*

Causal Iq .... C 805 367-6348
2945 Townsgate Rd 350 Westlake Village (91361) *(P-13199)*

Causeway Capital MGT LLC (PA) .... D 310 231-6100
11111 Santa Monica Blvd Fl 15 Los Angeles (90025) *(P-12631)*

CAV Inc .... D 760 729-5199
5931 Sea Lion Pl Ste 110 Carlsbad (92010) *(P-8818)*

Cavalier Inn Inc .... D 805 927-4688
9415 Hearst Dr San Simeon (93452) *(P-12787)*

Employee Codes: A=Over 500 employees, B=251-500
C=101-250, D=51-100, E=20-50, F=10-19, G=1-9

2025 Southern California
Business Directory and Buyers Guide

© Mergent Inc. 1-800-342-5647

973

Cavalier Oceanfront Resort, San Simeon *Also Called: Cavalier Inn Inc (P-12787)*

Cavanaugh Machine Works Inc .... E 562 437-1126
1540 Santa Fe Ave Long Beach (90813) *(P-6102)*

Cavco Industries Inc .... E 951 688-5353
7007 Jurupa Ave Riverside (92504) *(P-2396)*

Cavins Oil Well Tools, Signal Hill *Also Called: Dawson Enterprises (P-5508)*

Cavotec Dabico US Inc .... E 714 947-0005
5665 Corporate Ave Cypress (90630) *(P-7452)*

Cavotec Inet US Inc .... D 714 947-0005
5665 Corporate Ave Cypress (90630) *(P-5489)*

CAW Cowie Inc (PA) .... E 212 396-9007
7 Ginger Root Ln Rancho Palos Verdes (90275) *(P-14469)*

Caylent Inc (PA) .... C 800 215-9124
4521 Campus Dr Ste 344 Irvine (92612) *(P-14204)*

CB Controls, Jurupa Valley *Also Called: Christian Brothers Mechanical Services Inc (P-761)*

CB Richard Ellis Strgc Prtners .... D 213 683-4200
515 S Flower St Ste 3100 Los Angeles (90071) *(P-12284)*

CB Tang MD Incorporated .... D 562 437-0831
1250 Pacific Ave Long Beach (90813) *(P-15264)*

Cbabr Inc (PA) .... D 951 640-7056
31620 Railroad Canyon Rd Ste A Canyon Lake (92587) *(P-12396)*

Cbd Living Water .... E 800 940-3660
1343 Versante Cir Corona (92881) *(P-8669)*

Cbec, San Diego *Also Called: Clear Blue Energy Corp (P-6495)*

Cbes, Irvine *Also Called: Accurate Emplyment Scrning LLC (P-14267)*

Cbiz Life Insur Solutions Inc .... B 858 444-3100
13500 Evening Creek Dr N Ste 450 San Diego (92128) *(P-12192)*

Cbj LP .... D 818 676-1750
11150 Santa Monica Blvd Ste 350 Los Angeles (90025) *(P-2846)*

Cbj LP .... E 323 549-5225
11150 Santa Monica Blvd Los Angeles.(90025) *(P-2847)*

Cbj LP .... E 949 833-8373
18500 Von Karman Ave Ste 150 Irvine (92612) *(P-2848)*

Cbj LP .... E 858 277-6359
4909 Murphy Canyon Rd Ste 200 San Diego (92123) *(P-2849)*

Cbol Corporation .... C 818 704-8200
19850 Plummer St Chatsworth (91311) *(P-10237)*

Cbr Electric Inc .... C 949 455-0331
22 Rancho Cir Lake Forest (92630) *(P-898)*

Cbre, El Segundo *Also Called: Cbre Foundation Inc (P-12398)*

Cbre, Newport Beach *Also Called: Cbre Globl Value Investors LLC (P-12400)*

Cbre Inc .... C 858 546-4600
4301 La Jolla Village Dr # 3000 San Diego (92122) *(P-12397)*

Cbre Foundation Inc .... D 949 809-3744
2221 Rosecrans Ave Ste 100 El Segundo (90245) *(P-12398)*

Cbre Globl Value Investors LLC (DH) .... C 213 683-4200
601 S Figueroa St Ste 49 Los Angeles (90017) *(P-12399)*

Cbre Globl Value Investors LLC .... C 949 725-8500
3501 Jamboree Rd Ste 100 Newport Beach (92660) *(P-12400)*

Cbre Partner Inc .... D 213 613-3333
400 S Hope St Fl 25 Los Angeles (90071) *(P-12401)*

CBS, Studio City *Also Called: CBS Broadcasting Inc (P-9494)*

CBS Broadcasting Inc .... D 818 655-8500
4024 Radford Ave Bldg 4 Studio City (91604) *(P-9494)*

CBS Fasteners LLC .... E 714 779-6368
1345 N Brasher St Anaheim (92807) *(P-5122)*

CBS Studio Center, Studio City *Also Called: Radford Studio Center LLC (P-14974)*

CBS Studios Inc .... B 661 964-6020
27420 Avenue Scott Ste A Santa Clarita (91355) *(P-9495)*

CBS Studios Inc .... C 818 655-5160
4024 Radford Ave Studio City (91604) *(P-14812)*

CCC Property Holdings LLC .... C 310 609-1957
7223 Alondra Blvd Paramount (90723) *(P-12596)*

Cce .... E 213 744-8909
1334 S Central Ave Los Angeles (90021) *(P-1612)*

CCH Incorporated .... A 310 800-9800
2050 W 190th St Torrance (90504) *(P-14125)*

CCI, Vernon *Also Called: Cherokee Chemical Co Inc (P-11011)*

CCI Industries Inc (PA) .... E 714 662-3879
350 Fischer Ave Ste A Costa Mesa (92626) *(P-4085)*

CCL Label Inc .... D 909 608-2655
576 College Commerce Way Upland (91786) *(P-3127)*

CCL Label (delaware) Inc .... B 909 608-2260
576 College Commerce Way Upland (91786) *(P-3128)*

CCL Tube Inc (HQ) .... D 310 635-4444
2250 E 220th St Carson (90810) *(P-4086)*

CCM Assembly & Mfg Inc (PA) .... E 760 560-1310
2275 Michael Faraday Dr Ste 6 San Diego (92154) *(P-6980)*

CCM Enterprises (PA) .... D 619 562-2605
10848 Wheatlands Ave Santee (92071) *(P-2559)*

Cco Holdings LLC .... C 714 509-5861
2684 N Tustin St Orange (92865) *(P-9525)*

Cco Holdings LLC .... C 626 500-1214
3106 San Gabriel Blvd Rosemead (91770) *(P-9526)*

Cco Holdings LLC .... C 310 589-3008
23841 Malibu Rd Malibu (90265) *(P-9527)*

Cco Holdings LLC .... C 562 239-2761
12319 Norwalk Blvd Norwalk (90650) *(P-9528)*

Cco Holdings LLC .... C 626 513-0204
1151 N Azusa Ave Azusa (91702) *(P-9529)*

Cco Holdings LLC .... C 562 228-1262
2310 N Bellflower Blvd Long Beach (90815) *(P-9530)*

Cco Holdings LLC .... C 760 810-4076
21898 Us Highway 18 Apple Valley (92307) *(P-9531)*

Cco Holdings LLC .... C 909 742-8273
26827 Baseline St Highland (92346) *(P-9532)*

Cco Holdings LLC .... C 805 904-1047
1128 W Branch St Arroyo Grande (93420) *(P-9533)*

Cco Holdings LLC .... C 805 400-1002
1131 Creston Rd Paso Robles (93446) *(P-9534)*

Cco Holdings LLC .... C 805 232-5887
51 W Main St Ste F Ventura (93001) *(P-9535)*

Ccpu, San Diego *Also Called: Continuous Computing Corp (P-5843)*

CCS Global Tech, Poway *Also Called: Califrnia Crtive Solutions Inc (P-14203)*

Ccsd, San Diego *Also Called: Cal-Comp Electronics (usa) Co Ltd (P-6343)*

Ccts, Santa Ana *Also Called: Satellite Management Co (P-12527)*

CD Container Inc .... D 562 948-1910
7343 Paramount Blvd Pico Rivera (90660) *(P-2658)*

CD Digital, Rancho Cucamonga *Also Called: Digital Flex Media Inc (P-6574)*

CD Video Manufacturing Inc .... D 714 265-0770
12650 Westminster Ave Santa Ana (92706) *(P-7103)*

Cdcf III PCF Lndmark Scrmnto L .... C 310 552-7211
515 S Flower St 44th Fl Los Angeles (90071) *(P-12285)*

CDI, Reseda *Also Called: Child Development Institute (P-16888)*

CDI Torque Products, City Of Industry *Also Called: Consolidated Devices Inc (P-11257)*

CDM, Newport Beach *Also Called: CDM Company Inc (P-8670)*

CDM Company Inc .... E 949 644-2820
12 Corporate Plaza Dr Ste 200 Newport Beach (92660) *(P-8670)*

CDM Constructors Inc .... D 909 579-3500
9220 Cleveland Ave Ste 100 Rancho Cucamonga (91730) *(P-17501)*

Cdr Graphics Inc (PA) .... E 310 474-7600
1207 E Washington Blvd Los Angeles (90021) *(P-2977)*

CDS Moving Equipment Inc (PA) .... D 310 631-1100
375 W Manville St Rancho Dominguez (90220) *(P-10368)*

Cds Packing Solutions, Rancho Dominguez *Also Called: CDS Moving Equipment Inc (P-10368)*

Cdsnet LLC .... B 310 981-9500
6053 W Century Blvd Los Angeles (90045) *(P-18299)*

Cdti, Oxnard *Also Called: Cdti Advanced Materials Inc (P-3233)*

Cdti Advanced Materials Inc (PA) .... E 805 639-9458
1641 Fiske Pl Oxnard (93033) *(P-3233)*

Cdw, Anaheim *Also Called: Consolidated Design West Inc (P-13323)*

CECILLA GONZALEZ DE AL HOYA CA, Los Angeles *Also Called: White Memorial Medical Center (P-16259)*

Ceco, Oxnard *Also Called: Component Equipment Coinc (P-6943)*

Cedar Holdings LLC .... D 909 862-0611
7534 Palm Ave Highland (92346) *(P-15588)*

Cedar Mountain Post Acute, Yucaipa *Also Called: Cedar Operations LLC (P-15589)*

Cedar Operations LLC .... C 909 790-2273
11970 4th St Yucaipa (92399) *(P-15589)*

Mergent email: customerrelations@mergent.com
974

2025 Southern California
Business Directory and Buyers Guide

(P-0000) Products & Services Section entry number
(PA)=Parent Co (HQ)=Headquarters (DH)=Div Headquarters

Cedar Snai Bomanufacturing Ctr, West Hollywood *Also Called: Cedars-Sinai Medical Center* *(P-16307)*

Cedarlane Foods, Carson *Also Called: Cedarlane Natural Foods Inc (P-1753)*

Cedarlane Natural Foods Inc (PA) .... D 310 886-7720
717 E Artesia Blvd Ste A Carson (90746) *(P-1753)*

Cedars Surgical Research Ctr, West Hollywood *Also Called: Cedars-Sinai Medical Center* *(P-15951)*

Cedars-Sinai Home Care, Los Angeles *Also Called: Cedars-Sinai Medical Center (P-15943)*

Cedars-Sinai Marina Hospital .... A 310 673-4660
555 E Hardy St Inglewood (90301) *(P-15933)*

Cedars-Sinai Marina Hospital .... A 310 823-8911
4650 Lincoln Blvd Marina Del Rey (90292) *(P-15934)*

Cedars-Sinai Marina Hospital .... A 310 448-7800
4640 Admiralty Way Ste 650 Marina Del Rey (90292) *(P-15935)*

Cedars-Sinai Medical Center .... D 310 423-4208
8720 Beverly Blvd Lowr Level Los Angeles (90048) *(P-15265)*

Cedars-Sinai Medical Center .... B 310 423-3849
127 S San Vicente Blvd Rm 3417 Los Angeles (90048) *(P-15266)*

Cedars-Sinai Medical Center .... D 310 423-7900
8631 W 3rd St # 800-E Los Angeles (90048) *(P-15267)*

Cedars-Sinai Medical Center .... C 310 423-2587
8730 Alden Dr 220 Los Angeles (90048) *(P-15936)*

Cedars-Sinai Medical Center .... C 310 423-8965
8723 Alden Dr Los Angeles (90048) *(P-15937)*

Cedars-Sinai Medical Center .... C 310 659-3732
110 N George Burns Rd Los Angeles (90048) *(P-15938)*

Cedars-Sinai Medical Center .... C 310 423-5841
8700 Beverly Blvd Ste 8211 Los Angeles (90048) *(P-15939)*

Cedars-Sinai Medical Center .... C 310 423-5147
8700 Beverly Blvd Ste 2216 Los Angeles (90048) *(P-15940)*

Cedars-Sinai Medical Center .... C 310 423-9310
310 N San Vicente Blvd West Hollywood (90048) *(P-15941)*

Cedars-Sinai Medical Center .... C 310 967-1884
99 N La Cienega Blvd Ste Mezz Beverly Hills (90211) *(P-15942)*

Cedars-Sinai Medical Center .... A 310 423-3277
8635 W 3rd St Ste 1165w Los Angeles (90048) *(P-15943)*

Cedars-Sinai Medical Center .... B 310 423-9520
444 S San Vicente Blvd Ste 1001 Los Angeles (90048) *(P-15944)*

Cedars-Sinai Medical Center .... A 310 967-1900
4100 W 190th St Torrance (90504) *(P-15945)*

Cedars-Sinai Medical Center .... A 310 385-3400
250 N Robertson Blvd # 101 Beverly Hills (90211) *(P-15946)*

Cedars-Sinai Medical Center .... D 310 423-5468
8797 Beverly Blvd Ste 220 West Hollywood (90048) *(P-15947)*

Cedars-Sinai Medical Center .... C 310 423-6451
8727 W 3rd St Los Angeles (90048) *(P-15948)*

Cedars-Sinai Medical Center .... C 310 423-8780
8700 Beverly Blvd Ste 1103 West Hollywood (90048) *(P-15949)*

Cedars-Sinai Medical Center .... B 310 824-3664
8635 W 3rd St Ste 1195 Los Angeles (90048) *(P-15950)*

Cedars-Sinai Medical Center .... C 310 855-7701
8700 Beverly Blvd # 4018 West Hollywood (90048) *(P-15951)*

Cedars-Sinai Medical Center .... C 814 758-5466
8687 Melrose Ave Ste B227 West Hollywood (90069) *(P-16307)*

Cedarwood-Young Company (PA) .... C 626 962-4047
14620 Joanbridge St Baldwin Park (91706) *(P-9738)*

Cedarwood-Young Company .... D 626 962-4047
14618 Arrow Hwy Baldwin Park (91706) *(P-10537)*

Cee Baileys Aircraft Plastics, Montebello *Also Called: Desser Tire & Rubber Co LLC* *(P-10490)*

Celebrity Casinos Inc .... B 310 631-3838
123 E Artesia Blvd Compton (90220) *(P-12788)*

Celebrity Pink, Montebello *Also Called: 2253 Apparel LLC (P-10700)*

Celestial Lighting, Santa Fe Springs *Also Called: Shimada Enterprises Inc (P-6516)*

Celestial-Saturn Parent Inc (PA) .... C 949 214-1000
40 Pacifica Irvine (92618) *(P-13292)*

Celestica Aerospace Tech Corp .... C 512 310-7540
895 S Rockefeller Ave Ste 102 Ontario (91761) *(P-6715)*

Celestica LLC .... D 760 357-4880
280 Campillo St Ste G Calexico (92231) *(P-6412)*

Celestica-Aerospace, Ontario *Also Called: Celestica Aerospace Tech Corp (P-6715)*

Celex Solutions, Brea *Also Called: Contract Services Group Inc (P-13366)*

Celgene Corporation .... E 858 795-4961
10300 Campus Point Dr Ste 100 San Diego (92121) *(P-3386)*

Celgene Signal Research, San Diego *Also Called: Celgene Corporation (P-3386)*

Cell-Crete, Monrovia *Also Called: Cell-Crete Corporation (P-1108)*

Cell-Crete Corporation (PA) .... D 626 357-3500
135 Railroad Ave Monrovia (91016) *(P-1108)*

Cellco Partnership .... D 951 205-4170
20 City Blvd W Orange (92868) *(P-9387)*

Cellco Partnership .... D 949 472-0700
23718 El Toro Rd Ste A Lake Forest (92630) *(P-9388)*

Cellco Partnership .... D 714 258-8870
2687 Park Ave Tustin (92782) *(P-9389)*

Cellco Partnership .... D 714 564-0050
691 S Main St Ste 80 Orange (92868) *(P-9390)*

Cellco Partnership .... D 310 603-0101
237 E Compton Blvd Compton (90220) *(P-9391)*

Cellco Partnership .... D 661 296-7585
26445 Bouquet Canyon Rd Santa Clarita (91350) *(P-9392)*

Cellco Partnership .... D 323 662-0009
2921 Los Feliz Blvd Los Angeles (90039) *(P-9393)*

Cellco Partnership .... D 562 244-8814
11902 Gem St Norwalk (90650) *(P-9394)*

Cellco Partnership .... D 661 765-5397
407 Kern St Taft (93268) *(P-9395)*

Cellco Partnership .... D 760 568-5542
71800 Highway 111 Ste A110 Rancho Mirage (92270) *(P-9396)*

Cellco Partnership .... D 760 642-0430
258 N El Camino Real Ste A Encinitas (92024) *(P-9397)*

Cellco Partnership .... D 909 591-9740
3825 Grand Ave Chino (91710) *(P-9398)*

Cello Jeans, Commerce *Also Called: Hidden Jeans Inc (P-1881)*

Celtic Bank Corporation .... C 951 303-3330
32605 Temecula Pkwy Ste 204 Temecula (92592) *(P-11851)*

Celtic Commercial Finance, Irvine *Also Called: Celtic Leasing Corp (P-13449)*

Celtic Leasing Corp .... D 949 263-3880
4 Park Plz Ste 300 Irvine (92614) *(P-13449)*

Cem, Santee *Also Called: Air & Gas Tech Inc (P-7616)*

Cemco LLC (DH) .... D 800 775-2362
13191 Crossroads Pkwy N Ste 325 City Of Industry (91746) *(P-4968)*

Cemco Steel, City Of Industry *Also Called: Cemco LLC (P-4968)*

Cement Cutting Inc .... D 619 296-9592
3610 Hancock St Frnt San Diego (92110) *(P-1109)*

Cemex Cement Inc .... C 760 381-7616
25220 Black Mountain Quarry Rd Apple Valley (92307) *(P-4434)*

Cemex Cement Inc .... C 626 969-1747
1201 W Gladstone St Azusa (91702) *(P-9939)*

Cemex Construction Mtls Inc (DH) .... E 909 974-5500
3990 Concours Ste 200 Ontario (91764) *(P-9940)*

Cemex Materials LLC .... D 909 825-1500
1205 S Rancho Ave Colton (92324) *(P-4435)*

Cencal Health, Santa Barbara *Also Called: Santa Brbara San Luis Obspo RG (P-12066)*

Cencora Inc .... D 610 727-7000
1368 Metropolitan Dr Orange (92868) *(P-10616)*

Center At Parkwest, The, Reseda *Also Called: Chase Group Llc (P-18115)*

Center Automotive Inc .... D 818 907-9995
5201 Van Nuys Blvd Sherman Oaks (91401) *(P-11324)*

Center B M W, Sherman Oaks *Also Called: Center Automotive Inc (P-11324)*

Center For Achievement Center, Bakersfield *Also Called: New Advnces For Pple With Dsbl* *(P-17237)*

Center For Atism RES Evltion S .... D 858 444-8823
8787 Complex Dr Ste 300 San Diego (92123) *(P-16449)*

Center For Discovery, Irvine *Also Called: Discovery Practice MGT Inc (P-16469)*

Center For Sustainable Energy .... D 858 244-1177
3980 Sherman St Ste 170 San Diego (92110) *(P-18300)*

Center Street Lending Corp .... D 949 244-1090
18201 Von Karman Ave Irvine (92612) *(P-11942)*

Center Thtre Group Los Angeles (PA) .... C 213 972-7344
601 W Temple St Los Angeles (90012) *(P-14956)*

Centerfield Media, Los Angeles *Also Called: Qology Direct LLC (P-14580)*

Centerline, Fontana *Also Called: STC Netcom Inc (P-966)*

Centerline Industrial Inc .... E 858 505-0838
2530 Southport Way Ste D National City (91950) *(P-10369)*

Centerline Wood Products .... D 760 246-4530
15447 Anacapa Rd Ste 102 Victorville (92392) *(P-10556)*

Centerpoint Mfg Co Inc .... E 818 842-2147
2625 N San Fernando Blvd Burbank (91504) *(P-6103)*

Centerstone Insur & Fincl Svcs .... C 818 348-1200
21550 Oxnard St Woodland Hills (91367) *(P-12193)*

Centerwell Health Services Inc .... C 858 565-2499
9444 Balboa Ave Ste 290 San Diego (92123) *(P-16376)*

Centex Insurance Agency, Woodland Hills *Also Called: Westwood Insurance Agency LLC (P-12271)*

Centinela Frman Rgonal Med Ctr, Inglewood *Also Called: Cedars-Sinai Marina Hospital (P-15933)*

Centinela Frman Rgonal Med Ctr, Marina Del Rey *Also Called: Cedars-Sinai Marina Hospital (P-15934)*

Centinela Frman Rgonal Med Ctr, Marina Del Rey *Also Called: Cedars-Sinai Marina Hospital (P-15935)*

Centinela Hospital Medical Center, Inglewood *Also Called: Prime Healthcare Centinela LLC (P-16140)*

Centinela Skld Nrng Wlns Cntr, Inglewood *Also Called: West Cntinela Vly Care Ctr Inc (P-15800)*

Centinela Sklled Nrsing Wllnes .... D 310 674-3216
950 S Flower St Inglewood (90301) *(P-15590)*

Centon, Aliso Viejo *Also Called: Centon Electronics Inc (P-5875)*

Centon Electronics Inc (PA) .... D 949 855-9111
27 Journey Ste 100 Aliso Viejo (92656) *(P-5875)*

Central California Power .... E 661 589-2870
19487 Broken Ct Shafter (93263) *(P-14687)*

Central Cardiology Med Clinic .... C 661 395-0000
2901 Sillect Ave Ste 100 Bakersfield (93308) *(P-15268)*

Central Coast Agriculture Inc (PA) .... E 805 694-8594
8701 Santa Rosa Rd Buellton (93427) *(P-77)*

Central Coast Distributing LLC .... D 805 922-2108
815 S Blosser Rd Santa Maria (93458) *(P-11043)*

Central Coast Printing, San Luis Obispo *Also Called: David B Anderson (P-2999)*

Central Health Plan Cal Inc .... C 866 314-2427
200 Oceangate Ste 100 Long Beach (90802) *(P-16377)*

Central Prcss 4140, Los Angeles *Also Called: US Foods Inc (P-10988)*

Central Purchasing LLC (HQ) .... B 800 444-3353
26677 Agoura Rd Calabasas (91302) *(P-10429)*

Central Shop, Los Angeles *Also Called: Los Angeles Unified School Dst (P-13387)*

Central States Logistics Inc .... D 661 295-7222
28338 Constellation Rd Ste 940 Valencia (91355) *(P-8900)*

Central Tent, Santa Clarita *Also Called: Framement Inc (P-2238)*

Centre For Neuro Skills (PA) .... B 661 872-3408
5215 Ashe Rd Bakersfield (93313) *(P-16450)*

Centrescapes Inc .... D 909 392-3303
165 Gentry St Pomona (91767) *(P-162)*

Centric Brands Inc .... E 951 797-5077
48650 Seminole Dr Ste 170 Cabazon (92230) *(P-1874)*

Centric Brands Inc .... E 760 603-8520
5630 Paseo Del Norte Ste 144 Carlsbad (92008) *(P-1875)*

CENTRIC BRANDS INC., Carlsbad *Also Called: Centric Brands Inc (P-1875)*

Centro De Salud De La Comuni .... B 619 477-0165
1420 E Plaza Blvd Ste E4 National City (91950) *(P-16883)*

Centro De Slud De La Cmndad De .... B 619 662-4118
2400 E 8th St National City (91950) *(P-15269)*

Centro De Slud De La Cmndad De .... B 619 662-4100
316 25th St San Diego (92102) *(P-15270)*

Centro De Slud De La Cmndad De .... B 619 205-6341
4004 Beyer Blvd San Ysidro (92173) *(P-16451)*

Centro De Slud De La Cmndad De .... B 619 336-2300
1136 D Ave National City (91950) *(P-16452)*

Centro De Slud De La Cmndad De (PA) .... D 619 428-4463
1601 Precision Park Ln San Diego (92173) *(P-16453)*

Centro De Slud De La Cmndad De .... B 619 662-4161
1180 Third Ave Ste C2 Chula Vista (91911) *(P-16545)*

Centron Industries Inc .... E 310 324-6443
441 W Victoria St Gardena (90248) *(P-6603)*

Centurion Group Inc (PA) .... C 760 471-8536
365 S Rancho Santa Fe Rd # 3rd San Marcos (92078) *(P-11960)*

Centurion Group, The, Los Angeles *Also Called: Mulholland SEC & Patrol Inc (P-14318)*

Century 21, El Cajon *Also Called: Award-Superstars (P-12385)*

Century 21, South Gate *Also Called: Century 21 A Better Svc Rlty (P-12402)*

Century 21, Redlands *Also Called: Lois Lauer Realty (P-12479)*

Century 21 A Better Svc Rlty .... D 562 806-1000
5831 Firestone Blvd Ste J South Gate (90280) *(P-12402)*

Century 21 Crest, Sunland *Also Called: EAM Enterprises Inc (P-12434)*

Century 8, North Hollywood *Also Called: Century Theatres Inc (P-14949)*

Century Blinds Inc .... D 951 734-3762
300 S Promenade Ave Corona (92879) *(P-2600)*

Century Downtown 10, Ventura *Also Called: Century Theatres Inc (P-14948)*

Century Electronics, Newbury Park *Also Called: Perillo Industries Inc (P-10278)*

Century Gaming Management Inc .... A 310 330-2800
3883 W Century Blvd Inglewood (90303) *(P-12789)*

Century Hlth Staffing Svcs Inc .... C 661 322-0606
1701 Westwind Dr Ste 101 Bakersfield (93301) *(P-13505)*

Century National, Westlake Village *Also Called: Kramer-Wilson Company Inc (P-12122)*

Century Pacific Realty Corp .... C 310 729-9922
10345 W Olympic Blvd Los Angeles (90064) *(P-12565)*

Century Pk Capitl Partners LLC (PA) .... C 310 867-2210
880 Apollo St Ste 300 El Segundo (90245) *(P-12646)*

Century Precision Engrg Inc .... E 310 538-0015
2141 W 139th St Gardena (90249) *(P-6104)*

Century Snacks LLC .... B 323 278-9578
5560 E Slauson Ave Commerce (90040) *(P-10843)*

Century Spring, Commerce *Also Called: Matthew Warren Inc (P-5395)*

Century Theatres Inc .... C 714 373-4573
7777 Edinger Ave Ste 170 Huntington Beach (92647) *(P-14930)*

Century Theatres Inc .... B 805 641-6555
555 E Main St Ventura (93001) *(P-14948)*

Century Theatres Inc .... B 818 508-1943
12827 Victory Blvd North Hollywood (91606) *(P-14949)*

Century West LLC .... D 818 432-5800
4245 Lankershim Blvd North Hollywood (91602) *(P-11325)*

Century West Concrete Inc .... B 951 712-4065
9782 Indiana Ave Riverside (92503) *(P-1110)*

Century West Plumbing, Westlake Village *Also Called: Sdg Enterprises (P-835)*

Century Wire & Cable Inc .... D 800 999-5566
5701 S Eastern Ave Commerce (90040) *(P-4631)*

Century-National Insurance Co (DH) .... B 818 760-0880
16650 Sherman Way Ste 200 Van Nuys (91406) *(P-12194)*

Cenveo Worldwide Limited .... B 626 369-4921
705 Baldwin Park Blvd City Of Industry (91746) *(P-10579)*

Ceradyne Esk LLC .... E 714 549-0421
3169 Red Hill Ave M Costa Mesa (92626) *(P-4501)*

Ceramic Decorating Company Inc .... E 323 268-5135
4651 Sheila St Commerce (90040) *(P-14470)*

Ceramic Tile Art Inc .... D 818 767-9088
11601 Pendleton St Sun Valley (91352) *(P-1037)*

Cerecons, Anaheim *Also Called: Unlimited Innovations Inc (P-14060)*

Ceridian, Fountain Valley *Also Called: Ceridian Tax Service Inc (P-13162)*

Ceridian, Gardena *Also Called: Ceridian LLC (P-17711)*

Ceridian LLC .... D 310 719-7481
1515 W 190th St Ste 100 Gardena (90248) *(P-17711)*

Ceridian Tax Service Inc .... B 714 963-1311
17390 Brookhurst St Fountain Valley (92708) *(P-13162)*

Cerna Healthcare LLC .... C 949 298-3200
2151 Michelson Dr Ste 225 Irvine (92612) *(P-16546)*

Cerritos Ctr For Prfrmg Arts, Cerritos *Also Called: City of Cerritos (P-18382)*

Certance LLC (HQ) .... B 949 856-7800
141 Innovation Dr Irvine (92617) *(P-5876)*

Certified Alloy Products Inc .... C 562 595-6621
3245 Cherry Ave Long Beach (90807) *(P-4582)*

Certified Archtctral Fbrction, Los Angeles *Also Called: Certified Enameling Inc (P-5315)*

Certified Aviation Svcs LLC (PA) .... D 909 605-0380
3237 E Guasti Rd Ste 120 Ontario (91761) *(P-9194)*

Certified Enameling Inc (PA) .... D 323 264-4403
3342 Emery St Los Angeles (90023) *(P-5315)*

Mergent email: customerrelations@mergent.com
976

2025 Southern California
Business Directory and Buyers Guide

(P-0000) Products & Services Section entry number
(PA)=Parent Co (HQ)=Headquarters (DH)=Div Headquarters

Certified Frt Logistics Inc (PA)..................C 800 592-5906
1344 White Ct Santa Maria (93458) *(P-8935)*

Certified Laboratories LLC ....A 818 845-0070
3125 N Damon Way Burbank (91505) *(P-17908)*

Certified Steel Treating Corp ....E 323 583-8711
2454 E 58th St Vernon (90058) *(P-5246)*

Certified Thermoplastics Inc ....E 661 222-3006
26381 Ferry Ct Santa Clarita (91350) *(P-4087)*

Certified Thermoplastics LLC, Santa Clarita *Also Called: Certified Thermoplastics Inc (P-4087)*

Certified Tire & Svc Ctrs Inc ....E 951 656-6466
23920 Alessandro Blvd Ste A Moreno Valley (92553) *(P-11441)*

Certified Transportation, Santa Ana *Also Called: Certified Trnsp Svcs Inc (P-8862)*

Certified Trnsp Svcs Inc ....D 714 835-8676
1038 N Custer St Santa Ana (92701) *(P-8862)*

Certified Wtr Dmage Rstrtion E ....E 800 417-1776
5319 University Dr Irvine (92612) *(P-13363)*

Certis USA LLC ....E 661 758-8471
720 5th St Wasco (93280) *(P-3752)*

Cesar Chavez Center, San Diego *Also Called: San Diego Cmnty College Dst (P-16824)*

Cetera Financial Group Inc (PA)..................C 866 489-3100
655 W Broadway Ste 1680 San Diego (92101) *(P-14471)*

Ceva Freight LLC ....C 310 972-5500
19600 S Western Ave Torrance (90501) *(P-9260)*

Ceva Logistics LLC ....B 310 223-6500
19600 S Western Ave Torrance (90501) *(P-9261)*

Ceva Ocean Line, Torrance *Also Called: Ceva Freight LLC (P-9260)*

Cevians LLC (PA)..................D 714 619-5135
3193 Red Hill Ave Costa Mesa (92626) *(P-4314)*

Cexi, Oxnard *Also Called: Cryogenic Experts Inc (P-5698)*

Cfhc, Los Angeles *Also Called: Essential Access Health (P-17225)*

Cflute Corp ....C 562 404-6221
13220 Molette St Santa Fe Springs (90670) *(P-2659)*

Cfp Fire Protection Inc ....D 949 727-3277
153 Technology Dr Ste 200 Irvine (92618) *(P-760)*

Cfr Rinkens LLC (DH) ....D 310 639-7725
444 W Ocean Blvd Ste 1200 Long Beach (90802) *(P-9262)*

Cfr Rinknes, Long Beach *Also Called: Cfr Rinkens LLC (P-9262)*

CFS, Apple Valley *Also Called: Consolidated Frt Systems LLC (P-5526)*

Cfwf Inc ....C 310 221-6280
842 Flint Ave Wilmington (90744) *(P-1703)*

Cg Oncology, Irvine *Also Called: Cg Oncology Inc (P-3568)*

Cg Oncology Inc ....D 949 409-3700
400 Spectrum Center Dr Ste 2040 Irvine (92618) *(P-3568)*

CGB, Gardena *Also Called: Pulp Studio Incorporated (P-13334)*

Cgm Inc ....E 818 609-7088
19611 Ventura Blvd Ste 211 Tarzana (91356) *(P-8464)*

Cgm Findings, Tarzana *Also Called: Cgm Inc (P-8464)*

Cgp Maintenance Cnstr Svcs Inc ....D 858 454-7326
8614 Siesta Rd Santee (92071) *(P-17961)*

Cll Laboratories Inc (PA)..................E 310 510-0273
1243 W 130th St Gardena (90247) *(P-3387)*

Ch Products, Vista *Also Called: Apem Inc (P-6967)*

Cha Health Systems Inc (PA)..................A 213 487-3211
3731 Wilshire Blvd Ste 850 Los Angeles (90010) *(P-15271)*

Cha Hollywood Medical Ctr LP ....A 213 413-3000
4636 Fountain Ave Los Angeles (90029) *(P-15591)*

Cha La Mirada LLC ....C 714 739-8500
14299 Firestone Blvd La Mirada (90638) *(P-12790)*

Cha Renetative Medicine, Los Angeles *Also Called: Cha Health Systems Inc (P-15271)*

Chad, Anaheim *Also Called: Chad Industries Incorporated (P-6716)*

Chad Industries Incorporated ....E 714 938-0080
1565 S Sinclair St Anaheim (92806) *(P-6716)*

Challenger Sheet Metal Inc ....D 619 596-8040
9353 Abraham Way Ste A Santee (92071) *(P-1075)*

Cham-Cal Engineering Co ....D 714 898-9721
12722 Western Ave Garden Grove (92841) *(P-4331)*

Chambers Group Inc (PA)..................D 949 261-5414
5 Hutton Centre Dr Ste 750 Santa Ana (92707) *(P-18301)*

Chameleon Beverage Company Inc (PA)..................D 323 724-8223
6444 E 26th St Commerce (90040) *(P-1613)*

Champion Home Builders Inc ....C 951 256-4617
299 N Smith Ave Corona (92878) *(P-394)*

Champion Investment Corp ....D 917 712-7807
12809 Oakfield Way Poway (92064) *(P-12791)*

Championx LLC ....E 661 834-0454
6321 District Blvd Bakersfield (93313) *(P-3234)*

Chan Family Partnership LP ....D 626 322-7132
801 S Grand Ave Apt 1811 Los Angeles (90017) *(P-17962)*

Chancellor Health Care Inc ....D 951 696-5753
24350 Jackson Ave Murrieta (92562) *(P-17963)*

Chancellor Health Care Inc ....C 909 606-2553
6500 Butterfield Ranch Rd Chino Hills (91709) *(P-17964)*

Chancellor Oil Tools Inc ....E 661 324-2213
3521 Gulf St Bakersfield (93308) *(P-5506)*

Chancellor Place, Murrieta *Also Called: Chancellor Health Care Inc (P-17963)*

Chancellor Place, Chino Hills *Also Called: Chancellor Health Care Inc (P-17964)*

Chandler Packaging A Transpak Company ....D 858 292-5674
7595 Raytheon Rd San Diego (92111) *(P-9353)*

Change Lending LLC ....D 949 769-3526
32 Discovery Ste 160 Irvine (92618) *(P-11893)*

Change Lending LLC ....D 858 500-3060
6265 Greenwich Dr Ste 215 San Diego (92122) *(P-11943)*

Channel Islands Post Acute, Santa Barbara *Also Called: Powers Park Healthcare Inc (P-15757)*

Channel Islnds Yung MNS Chrstn ....D 805 963-8775
301 W Figueroa St Santa Barbara (93101) *(P-17331)*

Channel Islnds Yung MNS Chrstn ....D 805 736-3483
201 W College Ave Lompoc (93436) *(P-17332)*

Channel Islnds Yung MNS Chrstn ....D 805 687-7727
36 Hitchcock Way Santa Barbara (93105) *(P-17333)*

Channel Islnds Yung MNS Chrstn ....D 805 969-3288
591 Santa Rosa Ln Santa Barbara (93108) *(P-17334)*

Channel Islnds Yung MNS Chrstn ....D 805 686-2037
900 N Refugio Rd Santa Ynez (93460) *(P-17335)*

Channel Islnds Yung MNS Chrstn ....D 805 484-0423
3111 Village Park Dr Camarillo (93012) *(P-17336)*

Channel Islnds Yung MNS Chrstn ....D 805 484-0423
3760 Telegraph Rd Ventura (93003) *(P-17337)*

Channel Technologies Group, Santa Barbara *Also Called: International Tranducer Corp (P-7917)*

Channel Technologies Group LLC ....A
879 Ward Dr Santa Barbara (93111) *(P-7707)*

Channel Vision Technology, Laguna Hills *Also Called: Djh Enterprises (P-6608)*

Channelwave Software Inc ....D 949 448-4500
27081 Aliso Creek Rd Aliso Viejo (92656) *(P-18302)*

Chaparral Motorsports, San Bernardino *Also Called: Ocelot Engineering Inc (P-11484)*

Chapman Academic Center, Palmdale *Also Called: Chapman University (P-16832)*

Chapman Family Health, Orange *Also Called: Chapman Global Medical Ctr Inc (P-15952)*

Chapman Global Medical Ctr Inc ....B 714 633-0011
2601 E Chapman Ave Orange (92869) *(P-15952)*

Chapman Golf Development LLC ....D 760 564-8723
78505 Avenue 52 La Quinta (92253) *(P-15072)*

Chapman University ....C 661 267-2001
39115 Trade Center Dr # 203 Palmdale (93551) *(P-16832)*

Chapmn/Lnard Stdio Eqp Cnada I (PA)..................C 323 877-5309
12950 Raymer St North Hollywood (91605) *(P-14883)*

Chapter Seven Lending, Orange *Also Called: Cashcall Inc (P-11850)*

Charades, Walnut *Also Called: Diamond Collection LLC (P-2192)*

Charades LLC ....C 626 435-0077
20579 Valley Blvd Walnut (91789) *(P-2189)*

Chargers Football Company LLC (PA)..................D 714 540-7100
One Chargers Way El Segundo (90245) *(P-15022)*

Chargie LLC ....D 310 621-0024
3947 Landmark St Culver City (90232) *(P-6317)*

Charitble Adult Rides Svcs Inc ....D 858 300-2900
4669 Murphy Canyon Rd Ste 100 San Diego (92123) *(P-17461)*

Charles & Cynthia Eberly Inc ....D 323 937-6468
8383 Wilshire Blvd Ste 906 Beverly Hills (90211) *(P-12335)*

Charles Dunn RE Svcs Inc (PA)..................D 213 270-6200
800 W 6th St Ste 600 Los Angeles (90017) *(P-12403)*

Charles Komar & Sons Inc ....B 951 934-1377
11850 Riverside Dr Jurupa Valley (91752) *(P-2147)*

Employee Codes: A=Over 500 employees, B=251-500
C=101-250, D=51-100, E=20-50, F=10-19, G=1-9

2025 Southern California
Business Directory and Buyers Guide

© Mergent Inc. 1-800-342-5647
977

A L P H A B E T I C

Charles Meisner Inc .... E 909 946-8216
201 Sierra Pl Ste A Upland (91786) *(P-5572)*

Charles Rver Labs Cell Sltons (HQ) .... D 877 310-0717
8500 Balboa Blvd Ste 130 Northridge (91325) *(P-16547)*

Charles Schwab, San Diego *Also Called: Charles Schwab Corporation (P-11961)*

Charles Schwab, Temecula *Also Called: Charles Schwab Corporation (P-11962)*

Charles Schwab, Beverly Hills *Also Called: Charles Schwab Corporation (P-11963)*

Charles Schwab, San Diego *Also Called: Charles Schwab Corporation (P-12647)*

Charles Schwab Corporation .... D 800 435-4000
7510 Hazard Center Dr Ste 407 San Diego (92108) *(P-11961)*

Charles Schwab Corporation .... C 800 435-4000
27580 Ynez Rd Ste A Temecula (92591) *(P-11962)*

Charles Schwab Corporation .... D 800 435-4000
9757 Wilshire Blvd Beverly Hills (90212) *(P-11963)*

Charles Schwab Corporation .... D 800 435-4000
10920 Via Frontera Ste 100 San Diego (92127) *(P-12647)*

Charles W Bowers Museum Corp .... D 714 567-3600
2002 N Main St Santa Ana (92706) *(P-17252)*

Charlies Specialties Inc .... D 724 346-2350
501 Airpark Dr Fullerton (92833) *(P-1483)*

Charmaine Plastics Inc .... D 714 630-8117
2941 E La Jolla St Anaheim (92806) *(P-4088)*

Charming Trim & Packaging .... A 415 302-7021
5889 Rickenbacker Rd Commerce (90040) *(P-10663)*

Chart Sequal Technologies Inc .... D 858 202-3100
12230 World Trade Dr Ste 100 San Diego (92128) *(P-8129)*

Charter Communications, Long Beach *Also Called: Cco Holdings LLC (P-9530)*

Charter Communications, Ventura *Also Called: Cco Holdings LLC (P-9535)*

Chase Group Llc .... B 805 522-9155
5270 E Los Angeles Ave Simi Valley (93063) *(P-17841)*

Chase Group Llc .... B 818 708-3533
6740 Wilbur Ave Reseda (91335) *(P-18115)*

Chateau Lk San Mrcos Hmwners A .... D 760 471-0083
1502 Circa Del Lago San Marcos (92078) *(P-12336)*

Chatmeter Inc .... D 619 300-1050
225 Broadway Ste 2200 San Diego (92101) *(P-13899)*

Chatsworth Park Hlth Care Ctr, Chatsworth *Also Called: Cpcc Inc (P-15846)*

Chatsworth Products Inc (PA) .... E 818 735-6100
4175 Guardian St Simi Valley (93063) *(P-5443)*

Chavers Gasket Corporation .... E 949 472-8118
23325 Del Lago Dr Laguna Hills (92653) *(P-3882)*

CHC, Hollywood *Also Called: Covenant House California (P-17140)*

Che Snior Psychlogical Svcs PC .... D 888 307-0893
4929 Wilshire Blvd Ste 510 Los Angeles (90010) *(P-15538)*

Checkworks Inc .... D 626 333-1444
315 Cloverleaf Dr Ste J Baldwin Park (91706) *(P-3197)*

Cheesecake Factory Bakery Inc .... B 818 871-3000
26950 Agoura Rd Calabasas Hills (91301) *(P-11557)*

Cheesecake Factory Inc (PA) .... B 818 871-3000
26901 Malibu Hills Rd Calabasas Hills (91301) *(P-11558)*

CHEESECAKE FACTORY, THE, Calabasas Hills *Also Called: Cheesecake Factory Inc (P-11558)*

Chef Merito LLC (PA) .... E 818 787-0100
7915 Sepulveda Blvd Van Nuys (91405) *(P-1754)*

Chef Works Inc .... B 858 643-5600
12325 Kerran St # A Poway (92064) *(P-10680)*

Chefmaster .... E 714 554-4000
501 Airpark Dr Fullerton (92833) *(P-1755)*

Chem Arrow Corp .... E 626 358-2255
13643 Live Oak Ln Irwindale (91706) *(P-3849)*

Chem-Mark of Orange County, Cerritos *Also Called: Better Beverages Inc (P-1668)*

Chem-Tronics, El Cajon *Also Called: GKN Aerospace Chem-Tronics Inc (P-7386)*

Chemat Technology Inc .... E 818 727-9786
9036 Winnetka Ave Northridge (91324) *(P-7823)*

Chemat Vision, Northridge *Also Called: Chemat Technology Inc (P-7823)*

Chembridge Corporation (PA) .... B 858 451-7400
11199 Sorrento Valley Rd Ste 206 San Diego (92121) *(P-11009)*

Chemco Products Company, Paramount *Also Called: LMC Enterprises (P-3610)*

Chemdiv Inc .... E 858 794-4860
12730 High Bluff Dr San Diego (92130) *(P-3792)*

Chemeor Inc .... E 626 966-3808
727 Arrow Grand Cir Covina (91722) *(P-3624)*

Chemi-Source Inc .... E 760 477-8177
2665 Vista Pacific Dr Oceanside (92056) *(P-10617)*

Chemical Diversity Labs, San Diego *Also Called: Chemdiv Inc (P-3792)*

Chemical Guys, Torrance *Also Called: Smart LLC (P-4241)*

Chemical Methods Assoc LLC (DH) .... E 714 898-8781
17707 Valley View Ave Cerritos (90703) *(P-6005)*

Chemlogics Group LLC .... E 805 591-3314
7305 Morro Rd Ste 200 Atascadero (93422) *(P-3732)*

Chemseal, Pacoima *Also Called: Flamemaster Corporation (P-3766)*

Chemsil Silicones Inc .... E 818 700-0302
21900 Marilla St Chatsworth (91311) *(P-11010)*

Chemtainer Industries, Compton *Also Called: County Plastics Corp (P-4094)*

Chemtec Chemical Company, Chatsworth *Also Called: Vijall Inc (P-11024)*

Chemtool Incorporated .... C 661 823-7190
1300 Goodrick Dr Tehachapi (93561) *(P-3850)*

Chemtreat Inc .... D 804 935-2000
8885 Rehco Rd San Diego (92121) *(P-3793)*

Chen Dvid MD Dgnstc Med Group .... D 626 288-8029
208 N Garfield Ave Monterey Park (91754) *(P-15272)*

Chen-Tech Industries Inc (DH) .... E 949 855-6716
9 Wrigley Irvine (92618) *(P-8130)*

Cheque Guard Inc .... D 818 563-9335
512 S Verdugo Dr Burbank (91502) *(P-13683)*

Cherokee Chemical Co Inc (PA) .... E 323 265-1112
3540 E 26th St Vernon (90058) *(P-11011)*

Cherokee Uniform, Sherman Oaks *Also Called: Careismatic Brands LLC (P-4282)*

Cherokee Uniforms, Sherman Oaks *Also Called: Strategic Distribution L P (P-2002)*

Cherry City Electric, City Of Industry *Also Called: Morrow-Meadows Corporation (P-942)*

Chester Paul Company, Anaheim *Also Called: Welbilt Fdsrvice Companies LLC (P-5992)*

Chevelle Classics Parts & ACC, Seal Beach *Also Called: Original Parts Group Inc (P-11450)*

Chevron, El Segundo *Also Called: Chevron Corporation (P-11474)*

Chevron Corporation .... A 310 615-5000
324 W El Segundo Blvd El Segundo (90245) *(P-11474)*

Chevron Mining Inc .... C 760 856-7625
67750 Bailey Rd Mountain Pass (92366) *(P-258)*

CHG Foundation .... B 619 422-0422
740 Bay Blvd Chula Vista (91910) *(P-17462)*

Chicago Brothers, Vernon *Also Called: Overhill Farms Inc (P-1830)*

Chicago Title, Santa Barbara *Also Called: Chicago Title Insurance Co (P-12149)*

Chicago Title Insurance Co (HQ) .... C 805 565-6900
4050 Calle Real Santa Barbara (93110) *(P-12149)*

Chicken of Sea International, El Segundo *Also Called: Tri-Union Seafoods LLC (P-10864)*

Child & Family Center .... C 661 259-9439
21545 Centre Pointe Pkwy Santa Clarita (91350) *(P-16884)*

Child and Family Guidance Ctr (PA) .... C 818 739-5140
9650 Zelzah Ave Northridge (91325) *(P-16454)*

Child Care Resource Center Inc (PA) .... C 818 717-1000
20001 Prairie St Chatsworth (91311) *(P-16885)*

Child Care Resource Center Inc .... C 661 723-3246
250 Grand Cypress Ave Ste 601 Palmdale (93551) *(P-16886)*

Child Care Resource Center Inc .... C 818 837-0097
454 S Kalisher St San Fernando (91340) *(P-17081)*

Child Dev Rsrces of Vntura CNT (PA) .... C 805 485-7878
221 Ventura Blvd Oxnard (93036) *(P-16887)*

Child Development Assoc Inc .... C 619 422-7115
380 Telegraph Canyon Rd Chula Vista (91910) *(P-17082)*

Child Development Incorporated .... B 714 842-4064
17341 Jacquelyn Ln Huntington Beach (92647) *(P-12404)*

Child Development Incorporated .... B 949 854-5060
5151 Amalfi Dr Irvine (92603) *(P-17083)*

Child Development Institute .... D 818 888-4559
18050 Vanowen St Reseda (91335) *(P-16888)*

Child Guidance Center Inc .... C 714 953-4455
600 W Santa Ana Blvd Santa Ana (92701) *(P-16455)*

Child Help Head Start Center, Beaumont *Also Called: Childhelp Inc (P-17130)*

Child Support Services, Commerce *Also Called: County of Los Angeles (P-16912)*

Childhelp Inc .... C 951 845-6737
14700 Manzanita Rd Beaumont (92223) *(P-17130)*

Mergent email: customerrelations@mergent.com
978

2025 Southern California
Business Directory and Buyers Guide

(P-0000) Products & Services Section entry number
(PA)=Parent Co (HQ)=Headquarters (DH)=Div Headquarters

CHILDNET, Long Beach *Also Called: Childnet Youth & Fmly Svcs Inc (P-16889)*

Childnet Youth & Fmly Svcs Inc (PA)..............................C 562 498-5500
3545 Long Beach Blvd Ste 200 Long Beach (90807) *(P-16889)*

Children & Families Commission, Riverside *Also Called: County of Riverside (P-18393)*

Children & Family Svcs Dept, Los Angeles *Also Called: County of Los Angeles (P-16910)*

Children & Family Svcs Dept, Santa Fe Springs *Also Called: County of Los Angeles (P-16913)*

CHILDREN, YOUTH & FAMILY COLLA, Los Angeles *Also Called: Advancment Thrugh Oprtnty Knwl (P-16861)*

Children's Hospital, San Diego *Also Called: Rady Childrens Hosp & Hlth Ctr (P-16156)*

Childrens Associated Med Group, San Diego *Also Called: Childrens Spclsts of San Dego (P-15276)*

Childrens Bureau Southern Cal (PA)..............................C 213 342-0100
1910 Magnolia Ave Los Angeles (90007) *(P-16890)*

Childrens Clnic Srving Chldren......................................B 562 264-4638
701 E 28th St Ste 200 Long Beach (90806) *(P-15273)*

Childrens Co, Chula Vista *Also Called: Child Development Assoc Inc (P-17082)*

Childrens Healthcare Cal...B 714 997-3000
455 S Main St Orange (92868) *(P-15274)*

Childrens Healthcare Cal (PA).......................................A 714 997-3000
1201 W La Veta Ave Orange (92868) *(P-16287)*

Childrens Hospital Los Angeles.....................................B 323 361-2751
4661 W Sunset Blvd Los Angeles (90027) *(P-15953)*

Childrens Hospital Los Angeles (PA)...........................A 323 660-2450
4650 W Sunset Blvd Los Angeles (90027) *(P-16288)*

Childrens Hospital Orange Cnty....................................A 949 365-2416
455 S Main St Orange (92868) *(P-15954)*

Childrens Hospital Orange Cnty....................................C 949 387-2586
980 Roosevelt Irvine (92620) *(P-15955)*

Childrens Hospital Orange Cnty....................................B 714 638-5990
10602 Chapman Ave Ste 200 Garden Grove (92840) *(P-15956)*

Childrens Hospital Orange Cnty....................................C 949 769-6473
15785 Laguna Canyon Rd Ste 120 Irvine (92618) *(P-15957)*

Childrens Hospital Orange Cnty (PA)...........................A 714 509-8300
1201 W La Veta Ave Orange (92868) *(P-15958)*

Childrens Hospital Orange Cnty....................................B 949 631-2062
500 Superior Ave Newport Beach (92663) *(P-17084)*

Childrens Inst Los Angeles...A 213 383-2765
679 S New Hampshire Ave Los Angeles (90005) *(P-16891)*

Childrens Inst Los Angeles (PA)...................................C 213 385-5100
2121 W Temple St Los Angeles (90026) *(P-17871)*

Childrens Institute Inc (PA)..C 213 385-5100
2121 W Temple St Los Angeles (90026) *(P-16892)*

Childrens Law Center Cal (PA)......................................D 323 980-8700
101 Centre Plaza Dr Monterey Park (91754) *(P-16655)*

Childrens Oncology Group..C 626 241-1500
1333 S Mayflower Ave Ste 260 Monrovia (91016) *(P-15275)*

Childrens Spclsts of San Dego (PA).............................B 858 576-1700
3020 Childrens Way San Diego (92123) *(P-15276)*

Chili's, Santa Maria *Also Called: Impo International LLC (P-4285)*

Chilicon Power LLC (PA)..E 310 800-1396
15415 W Sunset Blvd Ste 102 Pacific Palisades (90272) *(P-7903)*

Chinatown Service Center (PA).....................................D 213 808-1701
767 N Hill St Ste 400 Los Angeles (90012) *(P-17052)*

Chinese Consumer Yellow Pages, Rosemead *Also Called: Chinese Overseas Mktg Svc Corp (P-2906)*

Chinese Overseas Mktg Svc Corp (PA).........................D 626 280-8588
3940 Rosemead Blvd Rosemead (91770) *(P-2906)*

Chino Medical Group Inc...D 909 591-6446
5475 Walnut Ave Chino (91710) *(P-15277)*

Chino Valley Medical Center, Chino *Also Called: Veritas Health Services Inc (P-16255)*

Chino Valley YMCA, Chino *Also Called: West End Yung MNS Christn Assn (P-17377)*

Chipton-Ross Inc...D 310 414-7800
420 Culver Blvd Playa Del Rey (90293) *(P-7337)*

Chiro Inc (PA)...C 909 879-1160
1834 Business Center Dr San Bernardino (92408) *(P-10472)*

Chirotech Inc...C 619 528-0040
9265 Sky Park Ct Ste 200 San Diego (92123) *(P-15534)*

Chirotouch, San Diego *Also Called: Chirotech Inc (P-15534)*

Chlor Alkali Products & Vinyls, Santa Fe Springs *Also Called: Olin Chlor Alkali Logistics (P-3209)*

Choc, Orange *Also Called: Childrens Hospital Orange Cnty (P-15958)*

Choc Childern's, Garden Grove *Also Called: Childrens Hospital Orange Cnty (P-15956)*

CHOC CHILDREN'S, Orange *Also Called: Childrens Healthcare Cal (P-16287)*

Choc Mission, Orange *Also Called: Childrens Hospital Orange Cnty (P-15954)*

Chocolates A La Carte Inc...C 661 257-3700
24836 Avenue Rockefeller Valencia (91355) *(P-1502)*

Chocolates and Health, La Verne *Also Called: Vitawest Nutraceuticals Inc (P-1310)*

Choic Admini Insur Servi...B 714 542-4200
721 S Parker St Ste 200 Orange (92868) *(P-12195)*

Choice Foodservices Inc..C 818 504-8213
8134 Lankershim Blvd North Hollywood (91605) *(P-10747)*

Choice Lithographics, Buena Park *Also Called: Cyu Lithographics Inc (P-2996)*

Choicepoint, Irvine *Also Called: Lexisnexis Risk Assets Inc (P-12226)*

Choon Inc (PA)...E 213 225-2500
1443 E 4th St Los Angeles (90033) *(P-2063)*

Chop Stop Inc...D 818 369-7350
601 N Glendale Ave Glendale (91206) *(P-11559)*

Chopra Global LLC..D 760 494-1604
6451 El Camino Real Ste A Carlsbad (92009) *(P-15046)*

Choura Events...D 310 320-6200
540 Hawaii Ave Torrance (90503) *(P-13450)*

Choura Venue Services...D 562 426-0555
4101 E Willow St Long Beach (90815) *(P-11560)*

Choura Vnue Svcs At Carson Ctr, Long Beach *Also Called: Choura Venue Services (P-11560)*

Chownow Inc (PA)..D 888 707-2469
3585 Hayden Ave Culver City (90232) *(P-13900)*

Chris Putrimas..E 877 434-1666
1930 E Carson St Ste 102 Carson (90810) *(P-8671)*

Chrislie Formulations, Azusa *Also Called: Bbeautiful LLC (P-3633)*

Christan Community Theatre..D 619 588-0206
1545 Pioneer Way El Cajon (92020) *(P-16852)*

Christian Arcadia School...D 626 574-8229
1900 S Santa Anita Ave Arcadia (91006) *(P-16804)*

Christian Bros Flrg Interiors, Lakeside *Also Called: Christian Bros Flrg Intrors In (P-11522)*

Christian Bros Flrg Intrors In..D 619 443-9500
12086 Woodside Ave Lakeside (92040) *(P-11522)*

Christian Brothers Mechanical Services Inc....................C 951 361-2247
11140 Thurston Ln Jurupa Valley (91752) *(P-761)*

Christian Community Credit Un (PA)..............................D 626 915-7551
255 N Lone Hill Ave San Dimas (91773) *(P-11825)*

Christian Schl Soc of Arcadia, Arcadia *Also Called: Christian Arcadia School (P-16804)*

CHRISTIAN YOUTH THEATER, El Cajon *Also Called: Christan Community Theatre (P-16852)*

Christie Digital Systems Inc (HQ).................................D 714 236-8610
10550 Camden Dr Cypress (90630) *(P-8423)*

Christie Parker & Hale LLP (PA)...................................C 626 795-9900
655 N Central Ave Ste 2300 Glendale (91203) *(P-16656)*

Chroma Systems Solutions Inc......................................E 949 600-6400
25612 Commercentre Dr Lake Forest (92630) *(P-7904)*

Chromacode Inc..E 442 244-4369
2330 Faraday Ave Ste 100 Carlsbad (92008) *(P-13684)*

Chromadex, Los Angeles *Also Called: Chromadex Corporation (P-3313)*

Chromadex Corporation (PA)...E 310 388-6706
10900 Wilshire Blvd Ste 600 Los Angeles (90024) *(P-3313)*

Chromal Plating & Grinding, Los Angeles *Also Called: Chromal Plating Company (P-5247)*

Chromal Plating Company..E 323 222-0119
1748 Workman St Los Angeles (90031) *(P-5247)*

Chromalloy Component Svcs Inc....................................E 858 877-2800
7007 Consolidated Way San Diego (92121) *(P-7381)*

Chromalloy Gas Turbine LLC...D 760 768-3723
1749 Stergios Rd Ste 2 Calexico (92231) *(P-7382)*

Chromalloy San Diego Corp...C 858 877-2800
7007 Consolidated Way San Diego (92121) *(P-14759)*

Chromalloy Southwest, Calexico *Also Called: Chromalloy Gas Turbine LLC (P-7382)*

Chromatic Inc Lithographers..E 818 242-5785
127 Concord St Glendale (91203) *(P-2978)*

Chromavision Medical Systems, San Juan Capistrano *Also Called: Clarient Inc (P-16308)*

Chrome Hearts, Los Angeles *Also Called: Chrome Hearts LLC (P-2178)*

Chrome Hearts LLC (PA)...E 323 957-7544
915 N Mansfield Ave Los Angeles (90038) *(P-2178)*

Employee Codes: A=Over 500 employees, B=251-500
C=101-250, D=51-100, E=20-50, F=10-19, G=1-9

2025 Southern California
Business Directory and Buyers Guide

© Mergent Inc. 1-800-342-5647
979

A L P H A B E T I C

Chrome Nickel Plating, Lynwood *Also Called: Bowman-Field Inc (P-5242)*

Chrome River Technologies Inc .... C 888 781-0088
5757 Wilshire Blvd Ste 270 Los Angeles (90036) *(P-13685)*

Chrome Tech Inc .... C 714 543-4092
2310 Cape Cod Way Santa Ana (92703) *(P-5248)*

Chromium Dental II LLC .... C 949 733-3111
1524 Brookhollow Dr Santa Ana (92705) *(P-15516)*

Chromologic, Monrovia *Also Called: Chromologic LLC (P-8131)*

Chromologic LLC .... E 626 381-9974
1225 S Shamrock Ave Monrovia (91016) *(P-8131)*

Chronic Tacos, Aliso Viejo *Also Called: Chronic Tacos Enterprises (P-11561)*

Chronic Tacos Enterprises .... C 949 680-4602
95 Enterprise Ste 320 Aliso Viejo (92656) *(P-11561)*

Chronomite Laboratories Inc .... E 310 534-2300
17451 Hurley St City Of Industry (91744) *(P-7834)*

Chua & Sons Co Inc .... E 323 588-8044
3300 E 50th St Vernon (90058) *(P-1905)*

Chubb, Los Angeles *Also Called: Pacific Indemnity Company (P-12242)*

Chubby Gorilla Inc (PA) .... E **844 365-5218**
4320 N Harbor Blvd Fullerton (92835) *(P-4089)*

Chugach Government Svcs Inc .... B 858 578-0276
9466 Black Mountain Rd Ste 240 San Diego (92126) *(P-18260)*

Church & Larsen Inc .... C 626 303-8741
16103 Avenida Padilla Irwindale (91702) *(P-1005)*

Churm Publishing Inc (PA) .... E **714 796-7000**
1451 Quail St Ste 201 Newport Beach (92660) *(P-2789)*

Chuze Fitness, Anaheim *Also Called: Rachas Inc (P-15059)*

Ciao, Camarillo *Also Called: Ciao Wireless Inc (P-6981)*

Ciao Wireless Inc .... D 805 389-3224
4000 Via Pescador Camarillo (93012) *(P-6981)*

Ciasons Industrial Inc .... E 714 259-0838
1615 Boyd St Santa Ana (92705) *(P-3883)*

Cibaria International Inc .... E 951 823-8490
705 Columbia Ave Riverside (92507) *(P-10936)*

Cibus, San Diego *Also Called: Cibus Inc (P-3753)*

Cibus Inc .... C 858 450-0008
6455 Nancy Ridge Dr San Diego (92121) *(P-3753)*

Cibus Global Ltd .... C 858 450-0008
6455 Nancy Ridge Dr San Diego (92121) *(P-17781)*

Cicoil LLC .... C 661 295-1295
28606 Livingston Ave Valencia (91355) *(P-10238)*

Cicon Engineering Inc (PA) .... C **818 909-6060**
6633 Odessa Ave Van Nuys (91406) *(P-6982)*

Cidara, San Diego *Also Called: Cidara Therapeutics Inc (P-3569)*

Cidara Therapeutics Inc (PA) .... D **858 752-6170**
6310 Nancy Ridge Dr Ste 101 San Diego (92121) *(P-3569)*

Cig Financial LLC .... D 877 244-4442
6 Executive Cir Ste 100 Irvine (92614) *(P-11852)*

Cigna, Glendale *Also Called: Cigna Behavioral Health of Cal (P-12076)*

Cigna, Glendale *Also Called: Cigna Healthcare Cal Inc (P-12077)*

Cigna Behavioral Health of Cal .... C 800 753-0540
450 N Brand Blvd Ste 500 Glendale (91203) *(P-12076)*

Cigna Healthcare Cal Inc (DH) .... B **818 500-6262**
400 N Brand Blvd Ste 400 Glendale (91203) *(P-12077)*

Cii, Santee *Also Called: Compucraft Industries Inc (P-7455)*

Cik Power Distributors LLC .... D 714 938-0297
240 W Grove Ave Orange (92865) *(P-17965)*

Cilajet LLC .... E 310 320-8000
16425 Ishida Ave Gardena (90248) *(P-3601)*

Cim Group LP (PA) .... D **323 860-4900**
4700 Wilshire Blvd Ste 1 Los Angeles (90010) *(P-12792)*

Cim Services, Compton *Also Called: Circle Industrial Mfg Corp (P-5797)*

Cim/H & H Hotel LP .... B 323 856-1200
1755 N Highland Ave Los Angeles (90028) *(P-12793)*

Cimarron Group, The, Los Angeles *Also Called: Cimarron Partner Associates LLC (P-13200)*

Cimarron Partner Associates LLC .... C 323 337-0300
6855 Santa Monica Blvd Los Angeles (90038) *(P-13200)*

Cimc Intermodal Equipment, South Gate *Also Called: Cimc Intermodal Equipment LLC (P-7314)*

Cimc Intermodal Equipment LLC (HQ) .... D **562 904-8600**
10530 Sessler St South Gate (90280) *(P-7314)*

Cincom, Riverside *Also Called: Cincom Systems Inc (P-13686)*

Cincom Systems Inc (PA) .... B **513 612-2300**
871 Marlborough Ave Riverside (92507) *(P-13686)*

Cinderella Motel .... D 559 432-0118
1747 S Harbor Blvd Anaheim (92802) *(P-12794)*

Cinema Secrets Inc .... D 818 846-0579
6639 Odessa Ave Van Nuys (91406) *(P-11677)*

Cingular Wireless, Cerritos *Also Called: AT&T Mobility LLC (P-9385)*

Cinnabar .... C 818 842-8190
4571 Electronics Pl Los Angeles (90039) *(P-13322)*

Cintas, Santa Ana *Also Called: Cintas Sales Corporation (P-13116)*

Cintas Corporation .... D 714 646-2550
4320 E Miraloma Ave Anaheim (92807) *(P-11507)*

Cintas Fire, Anaheim *Also Called: Cintas Corporation (P-11507)*

Cintas Sales Corporation .... D 714 957-2852
2618 Oak St Santa Ana (92707) *(P-13116)*

Cinton LLC .... E 714 961-8808
620 Richfield Rd Placentia (92870) *(P-2720)*

Circle Industrial Mfg Corp (PA) .... E **310 638-5101**
1613 W El Segundo Blvd Compton (90222) *(P-5797)*

Circle W Enterprises Inc .... E 661 257-2400
27737 Avenue Hopkins Valencia (91355) *(P-5403)*

Circor Aerospace Inc (DH) .... C **951 270-6200**
2301 Wardlow Cir Corona (92878) *(P-5360)*

Circuit Services Llc .... E 818 701-5391
9134 Independence Ave Chatsworth (91311) *(P-6717)*

Circulating Air Inc (PA) .... D **818 764-0530**
7337 Varna Ave North Hollywood (91605) *(P-762)*

Circulating Air Inc .... D 661 942-2048
1109 W Columbia Way Lancaster (93534) *(P-763)*

Ciri - Stroup Inc .... C 949 488-3104
25135 Park Lantern Dana Point (92629) *(P-13169)*

Cirks Construction Inc .... D 877 632-6717
507 W Blueridge Ave Orange (92865) *(P-529)*

Cirpa Radiology Management, El Segundo *Also Called: Radiology Partners Inc (P-15429)*

Cirrus Asset Management Inc (PA) .... D **818 222-4840**
20720 Ventura Blvd Ste 300 Woodland Hills (91364) *(P-12405)*

Cirrus Enterprises LLC .... D 310 204-6159
18027 Bishop Ave Carson (90746) *(P-10995)*

Cirrus Property MGT Svcs, Woodland Hills *Also Called: Cirrus Asset Management Inc (P-12405)*

Cirtech Inc .... E 714 921-0860
250 E Emerson Ave Orange (92865) *(P-14472)*

Cisco & Brothers Designs, Pasadena *Also Called: Cisco Bros Corp (P-2442)*

Cisco Bros Corp (PA) .... C **323 778-8612**
474 S Arroyo Pkwy Pasadena (91105) *(P-2442)*

CIT Bank NA (HQ) .... C **626 859-5400**
75 N Fair Oaks Ave Ste C Pasadena (91103) *(P-11709)*

CIT Bank NA .... D 310 820-9650
12401 Wilshire Blvd Los Angeles (90025) *(P-11753)*

CIT Bank NA .... D 323 838-6881
7320 Firestone Blvd Ste 101 Downey (90241) *(P-11754)*

CIT Bank NA .... D 310 394-1640
401 Wilshire Blvd Santa Monica (90401) *(P-11755)*

CIT Bank NA .... D 310 559-7222
10784 Jefferson Blvd Culver City (90230) *(P-11756)*

CIT Bank NA .... D 858 454-8800
888 Prospect St Ste 140 La Jolla (92037) *(P-11757)*

Citadel Panda Express Inc .... C 626 799-9898
899 El Centro St Ste 201 South Pasadena (91030) *(P-11562)*

Citibank, Long Beach *Also Called: Citibank FSB (P-11710)*

Citibank FSB .... A 562 999-3453
1 World Trade Ctr Ste 100 Long Beach (90831) *(P-11710)*

Citifinancial, City Of Industry *Also Called: Citifinancial Credit Company (P-11853)*

Citifinancial Credit Company .... C 626 712-8780
2655 Del Vista Dr City Of Industry (91745) *(P-11853)*

Citiguard Inc .... B 800 613-5903
22736 Vanowen St Ste 300 West Hills (91307) *(P-14284)*

Citivest Inc .... D 949 705-0420
4350 Von Karman Ave Ste 200 Newport Beach (92660) *(P-12406)*

Citizen Watch America, Torrance *Also Called: Citizen Watch Company of America Inc (P-10546)*

Mergent email: customerrelations@mergent.com
980

2025 Southern California
Business Directory and Buyers Guide

(P-0000) Products & Services Section entry number
(PA)=Parent Co (HQ)=Headquarters (DH)=Div Headquarters

Citizen Watch Company of America Inc (HQ)	C	800 321-1023
1000 W 190th St Torrance (90502) *(P-10546)*		
Citizens Business Bank (HQ)	C	909 980-4030
701 N Haven Ave Ste 280 Ontario (91764) *(P-11758)*		
Citizens Choice Health Plan, Orange Also Called: Alignment Health Plan *(P-12069)*		
Citizens of Humanity LLC (PA)	C	323 923-1240
5715 Bickett St Huntington Park (90255) *(P-2085)*		
Citrix Online Group, Goleta Also Called: Citrix Online LLC *(P-13687)*		
Citrix Online LLC	B	805 690-6400
7414 Hollister Ave Goleta (93117) *(P-13687)*		
Citrix Online Svc Prvder Group	C	805 690-6400
7414 Hollister Ave Goleta (93117) *(P-14205)*		
Citrus Ford, Ontario Also Called: Citrus Motors Ontario Inc *(P-11326)*		
Citrus Motors Ontario Inc (PA)	C	909 390-0930
1375 S Woodruff Way Ontario (91761) *(P-11326)*		
Citrus North Venture LLC	D	256 428-2000
6591 Collins Dr Ste E11 Moorpark (93021) *(P-12795)*		
Citrus Restaurant LLC	C	858 277-8888
8110 Aero Dr San Diego (92123) *(P-11563)*		
CITRUS VALLEY HEALTH PARTNERS, INC., Covina Also Called: Citrus Vly Hlth Partners Inc *(P-16548)*		
Citrus Vly Hlth Care Partners, Glendora Also Called: Emanate Health *(P-15991)*		
Citrus Vly Hlth Partners Inc	A	626 732-3100
1325 N Grand Ave Ste 300 Covina (91724) *(P-16548)*		
Citrusbyte LLC	E	888 969-2983
21550 Oxnard St Ste 300 # 11 Woodland Hills (91367) *(P-13688)*		
City Chevrolet of San Diego	C	619 276-6171
2111 Morena Blvd San Diego (92110) *(P-14688)*		
City Chevrolet of Volkswagen, San Diego Also Called: City Chevrolet of San Diego *(P-14688)*		
City Hope Medical Foundation	A	626 256-4673
1500 Duarte Rd Duarte (91010) *(P-15278)*		
City Hope National Medical Ctr (HQ)	B	626 553-8061
1500 Duarte Rd Duarte (91010) *(P-15959)*		
City National Bank	C	818 487-1040
4605 Lankershim Blvd Ste 150 North Hollywood (91602) *(P-11711)*		
City National Bank	D	818 487-7530
12515 Ventura Blvd Studio City (91604) *(P-11712)*		
City National Bank	D	424 280-8000
1315 Lincoln Blvd Ste 110 Santa Monica (90401) *(P-11713)*		
City National Bank	D	562 624-8600
100 Oceangate Ste 1000 Long Beach (90802) *(P-11714)*		
City National Bank	C	626 432-7100
89 S Lake Ave Pasadena (91101) *(P-11715)*		
City National Bank	C	323 634-7200
8641 Wilshire Blvd Ste 101 Beverly Hills (90211) *(P-11716)*		
City National Bank	D	310 855-7960
11677 San Vicente Blvd Ste 103 Los Angeles (90049) *(P-11717)*		
City National Bank	D	310 888-6800
9229 W Sunset Blvd Ste 100 Los Angeles (90069) *(P-11718)*		
City National Bank	C	310 888-6150
400 N Roxbury Dr Beverly Hills (90210) *(P-11719)*		
City National Bank	C	818 905-4100
16133 Ventura Blvd Ste 100 Encino (91436) *(P-11720)*		
City National Bank	D	310 297-6606
2100 Park Pl Ste 150 El Segundo (90245) *(P-11721)*		
City National Bank	B	310 888-6500
555 S Flower St Ste 2500 Los Angeles (90071) *(P-11722)*		
City National Bank	D	661 291-3160
24200 Magic Mountain Pkwy Ste 140 Valencia (91355) *(P-11723)*		
City National Bank	D	805 981-2700
500 E Esplanade Dr Fl 2 Oxnard (93036) *(P-11724)*		
City National Bank	D	858 642-4950
4275 Executive Sq Ste 101 La Jolla (92037) *(P-11725)*		
City National Bank	C	858 875-2030
501 W Broadway Ste 100 San Diego (92101) *(P-11726)*		
City National Bank	C	951 276-8800
3484 Central Ave Riverside (92506) *(P-11727)*		
City National Bank	D	909 476-7999
3633 Inland Empire Blvd Ste 100 Ontario (91764) *(P-11728)*		
City National Bank (DH)	B	310 888-6000
555 S Flower St Ste 2500 Los Angeles (90071) *(P-11729)*		
City National Bank	C	949 223-4000
18111 Von Karman Ave Ste 100 Irvine (92612) *(P-11730)*		
City National Corporation	A	
555 S Flower St Los Angeles (90071) *(P-11731)*		
City National Rochdale LLC	C	310 888-6000
400 N Roxbury Dr Ste 400 Beverly Hills (90210) *(P-12024)*		
City National Securities Inc	B	310 888-6393
400 N Roxbury Dr Ste 400 Beverly Hills (90210) *(P-11732)*		
City Net, Long Beach Also Called: Kingdom Causes Inc *(P-16968)*		
City of Anaheim	D	714 254-0125
201 S Anaheim Blvd Anaheim (92805) *(P-9790)*		
City of Azusa	D	626 969-4408
729 N Azusa Ave Azusa (91702) *(P-9683)*		
City of Bakersfield	C	661 852-7300
1001 Truxtun Ave Bakersfield (93301) *(P-16893)*		
City of Burbank	B	818 238-3550
164 W Magnolia Blvd Burbank (91502) *(P-9669)*		
City of Burbank	D	818 238-3838
124 S Lake St Burbank (91502) *(P-14689)*		
City of Cerritos	C	562 916-8500
18125 Bloomfield Ave Cerritos (90703) *(P-18382)*		
City of Coronado	C	619 522-7380
101 B Ave Coronado (92118) *(P-9670)*		
City of Culver City	D	310 253-6525
4343 Duquesne Ave Culver City (90232) *(P-18383)*		
City of Culver City	D	310 253-6650
4117 Overland Ave Culver City (90230) *(P-18399)*		
City of Delano	E	661 721-3352
1107 Lytle Ave Delano (93215) *(P-6006)*		
City of Downey	C	562 861-8211
8435 Firestone Blvd Downey (90241) *(P-14957)*		
City of Downey	D	562 803-4982
12334 Bellflower Blvd Downey (90242) *(P-15128)*		
City of Glendale	D	818 548-3980
634 Bekins Way Glendale (91201) *(P-9574)*		
City of Glendale	D	818 548-2011
800 Air Way Glendale (91201) *(P-9684)*		
City of Glendale	D	818 548-3945
633 E Broadway Ste 205 Glendale (91206) *(P-17502)*		
City of Hope	D	951 898-2828
320 W 6th St Corona (92882) *(P-15279)*		
City of Hope	C	213 202-5735
1500 Duarte Rd Duarte (91010) *(P-17218)*		
City of Hope (PA)	B	626 256-4673
1500 Duarte Rd Duarte (91010) *(P-17966)*		
City of Hope Corona, Duarte Also Called: City Hope National Medical Ctr *(P-15959)*		
City of Huntington Beach	D	714 846-4450
16782 Graham St Huntington Beach (92649) *(P-15073)*		
City of Industry, Chino Also Called: Balaji Trading Inc *(P-6581)*		
City of Irvine	C	949 724-7600
6427 Oak Cyn Irvine (92618) *(P-18116)*		
City of Lancaster	C	661 723-6071
43011 10th St W Lancaster (93534) *(P-15102)*		
City of Long Beach	D	562 570-2000
2400 E Spring St Long Beach (90806) *(P-9674)*		
City of Long Beach	C	562 570-4000
2525 Grand Ave Long Beach (90815) *(P-18391)*		
City of Los Angeles	A	310 732-3734
425 S Palos Verdes St San Pedro (90731) *(P-18400)*		
City of Menifee	D	951 672-6777
29844 Haun Rd Menifee (92586) *(P-17967)*		
City of Norco	D	951 270-5617
2870 Clark Ave Norco (92860) *(P-18303)*		
City of Riverside	C	951 351-6140
5950 Acorn St Riverside (92504) *(P-6007)*		
City of Riverside	C	951 826-5485
5901 Payton Ave Riverside (92504) *(P-18117)*		
City of San Diego	C	619 527-7482
2781 Caminito Chollas San Diego (92105) *(P-612)*		
City of San Diego	C	619 758-2310
2392 Kincaid Rd San Diego (92101) *(P-7949)*		

Employee Codes: A=Over 500 employees, B=251-500
C=101-250, D=51-100, E=20-50, F=10-19, G=1-9

2025 Southern California
Business Directory and Buyers Guide

© Mergent Inc. 1-800-342-5647

981

ALPHABETIC

City of San Diego .... C 619 795-5000
100 Park Blvd San Diego (92101) *(P-15023)*

City of Santa Ana .... D 714 647-6545
1000 E Santa Ana Blvd Ste 107 Santa Ana (92701) *(P-17053)*

City of Santa Monica .... C 310 826-6712
1228 S Bundy Dr Los Angeles (90025) *(P-6008)*

City Orange Police Assn Inc .... C 714 457-5340
1107 N Batavia St Orange (92867) *(P-17280)*

CITY RESCUE MISSION, San Diego Also Called: San Diego Rescue Mission Inc *(P-17241)*

City Snta Mnica Wtr Trtmnt Pla, Los Angeles Also Called: City of Santa Monica *(P-6008)*

City Steel Heat Treating, Orange Also Called: Thermal-Vac Technology Inc *(P-4715)*

City Triangles, Los Angeles Also Called: Jodi Kristopher LLC *(P-2066)*

City Wire Cloth, Fontana Also Called: Daniel Gerard Worldwide Inc *(P-10132)*

City-Wide Electronic Systems Inc .... D 619 444-0219
440 Highland Ave El Cajon (92020) *(P-899)*

Civco, Rcho Sta Marg Also Called: Capital Invstmnts Vntures Corp *(P-17296)*

CIVIC THEATRE, San Diego Also Called: San Diego Theatres Inc *(P-12315)*

CJ Advisors Inc .... E 714 956-3388
6900 8th St Buena Park (90620) *(P-6105)*

CJ America, La Palma Also Called: CJ Foods Inc *(P-1756)*

CJ America Inc (HQ) .... D 213 338-2700
300 S Grand Ave Ste 1100 Los Angeles (90071) *(P-10937)*

CJ Berry Well Services MGT LLC .... A 661 589-5220
3752 Allen Rd Bakersfield (93314) *(P-324)*

CJ Foods Inc (HQ) .... D 714 367-7200
4 Centerpointe Dr Ste 100 La Palma (90623) *(P-1756)*

CJ Foods Mfg Beaumont LLC .... D 951 916-9300
415 Nicholas Rd Beaumont (92223) *(P-8672)*

CJ Logistics America LLC .... C 909 605-7233
12350 Philadelphia Ave Eastvale (91752) *(P-8901)*

CJ Logistics America LLC .... D 909 363-4354
1895 Marigold Ave Redlands (92374) *(P-8936)*

CJ Logistics America LLC .... D 951 436-7131
17789 Harvill Ave Perris (92570) *(P-9053)*

CJ Logistics America LLC .... C 540 377-2302
5690 Industrial Pkwy San Bernardino (92407) *(P-9263)*

CJd Construction Svcs Inc .... E 626 335-1116
503 E Route 66 Glendora (91740) *(P-325)*

Cji Process Systems Inc .... D 562 777-0614
12000 Clark St Santa Fe Springs (90670) *(P-4911)*

Cjm Automotive Group Inc .... D 661 832-3000
3101 Cattle Dr Bakersfield (93313) *(P-11327)*

CK Manufacturing & Trading Inc .... E 949 529-3400
3 Holland Irvine (92618) *(P-2560)*

Cks Solution Incorporated .... E 714 292-6307
556 Vanguard Way Ste C Brea (92821) *(P-6983)*

CL Knox Inc .... D 661 837-0477
34933 Imperial Ave Bakersfield (93308) *(P-326)*

CL Solutions LLC .... D 714 597-6499
1900 S Susan St Santa Ana (92704) *(P-4315)*

Cla-Val Co, Costa Mesa Also Called: Griswold Industries *(P-4675)*

Claremont Club, The, Claremont Also Called: Claremont Tennis Club *(P-15129)*

Claremont Tennis Club .... C 909 625-9515
1777 Monte Vista Ave Claremont (91711) *(P-15129)*

Claremont Toyota, Claremont Also Called: R&C Motor Corporation *(P-14698)*

Clarendon Specialty Fas Inc .... D 714 842-2603
2180 Temple Ave Long Beach (90804) *(P-10303)*

Clariant Corporation .... E 909 825-1793
926 S 8th St Colton (92324) *(P-2721)*

Clarient Inc .... C 949 445-7300
33171 Paseo Cerveza San Juan Capistrano (92675) *(P-16308)*

Clarion Hotel, Anaheim Also Called: Comfort California Inc *(P-12798)*

Clarios LLC .... E 951 222-0284
2100 Chicago Ave Riverside (92507) *(P-2537)*

Clarios LLC .... E 760 200-5225
39312 Leopard St Ste A Palm Desert (92211) *(P-2538)*

Clarios LLC .... E 805 522-5555
4100 Guardian St Simi Valley (93063) *(P-2539)*

Clariphy Communications Inc (DH) .... D 949 861-3074
15485 Sand Canyon Ave Irvine (92618) *(P-6812)*

Clarity Design Inc .... E 858 746-3500
13000 Gregg St Ste B Poway (92064) *(P-6718)*

Clark - Pacific Corporation .... E 626 962-8755
9367 Holly Rd Adelanto (92301) *(P-4382)*

Clark - Pacific Corporation .... E 909 823-1433
4684 Ontario Mills Pkwy Ste 200 Ontario (91764) *(P-4383)*

Clark Cnstr Group - Cal Inc .... B 714 754-0764
18201 Von Karman Ave Ste 800 Irvine (92612) *(P-476)*

Clark Cnstr Group - Cal LP .... B 714 429-9779
18201 Von Karman Ave Ste 800 Irvine (92612) *(P-530)*

Clark Steel Fabricators Inc .... E 619 390-1502
12610 Vigilante Rd Lakeside (92040) *(P-5060)*

Clarkdietrich Building Systems, Riverside Also Called: Clarkwestern Dietrich Building
(P-4969)

Clarkson Law Firm PC .... D 213 788-4050
22525 Pacific Coast Hwy Ste 102 Malibu (90265) *(P-16657)*

Clarkwestern Dietrich Building .... E 951 360-3500
6510 General Rd Riverside (92509) *(P-4969)*

Clary Corporation .... E 626 359-4486
150 E Huntington Dr Monrovia (91016) *(P-6984)*

Classe Party Rentals, Rancho Cucamonga Also Called: Sunn America Inc *(P-13473)*

Classic Bev Southern Cal LLC .... B 626 934-3700
120 Puente Ave City Of Industry (91746) *(P-11044)*

Classic Camaro Inc .... C 714 847-6887
18460 Gothard St Huntington Beach (92648) *(P-11442)*

Classic Components, Torrance Also Called: I C Class Components Corp *(P-10251)*

Classic Containers Inc .... B 909 930-3610
1700 S Hellman Ave Ontario (91761) *(P-3982)*

Classic Firebird, Huntington Beach Also Called: Classic Camaro Inc *(P-11442)*

Classic Installs Inc .... D 951 678-9906
41755 Elm St Murrieta (92562) *(P-1187)*

Classic Litho & Design Inc .... E 310 224-5200
340 Maple Ave Torrance (90503) *(P-2979)*

Classic Party Rentals, Inglewood Also Called: After-Party2 Inc *(P-13446)*

Classic Party Rentals, Inglewood Also Called: After-Party6 Inc *(P-13447)*

Classic Party Rentals, Inglewood Also Called: Classic Party Rentals Inc *(P-13451)*

Classic Party Rentals Inc .... A 310 966-4900
901 W Hillcrest Blvd Inglewood (90301) *(P-13451)*

Classic Tents .... E 310 328-5060
19119 S Reyes Ave Compton (90221) *(P-5969)*

Classic Tents, Compton Also Called: Classic Tents *(P-5969)*

Classic Tents, Torrance Also Called: Classic/Prime Inc *(P-13452)*

Classic Wire Cut Company Inc .... C 661 257-0558
28210 Constellation Rd Valencia (91355) *(P-6106)*

Classic/Prime Inc .... D 310 328-5060
540 Hawaii Ave Torrance (90503) *(P-13452)*

Classy, San Diego Also Called: Classy Inc *(P-13901)*

Classy Inc .... C 619 961-1892
350 10th Ave Ste 1300 San Diego (92101) *(P-13901)*

Clauss Construction .... D 619 390-4940
9911 Maine Ave Lakeside (92040) *(P-1179)*

Clave, San Clemente Also Called: Icu Medical Inc *(P-8166)*

Clay Corona Company (PA) .... E 951 277-2667
22079 Knabe Rd Corona (92883) *(P-531)*

Clay Dunn Enterprises Inc .... C 310 549-1698
1606 E Carson St Carson (90745) *(P-764)*

Clay Lacy Aviation Inc (PA) .... B 818 989-2900
7435 Valjean Ave Van Nuys (91406) *(P-9195)*

Clayton Industries, City Of Industry Also Called: Clayton Manufacturing Company *(P-5816)*

Clayton Manufacturing Company (PA) .... C 626 443-9381
17477 Hurley St City Of Industry (91744) *(P-5816)*

Clayton Manufacturing Inc (HQ) .... D 626 443-9381
17477 Hurley St City Of Industry (91744) *(P-5817)*

CLC Work Gear, Commerce Also Called: Custom Leathercraft Mfg LLC *(P-4309)*

Clean Cut Technologies, Anaheim Also Called: Oliver Healthcare Packaging Co *(P-10386)*

Clean Cut Technologies LLC .... D 714 864-3500
1145 N Ocean Cir Anaheim (92806) *(P-3996)*

Clean Energy .... A 949 437-1000
4675 Macarthur Ct Ste 800 Newport Beach (92660) *(P-9644)*

Clean Energy Fuels Corp (PA) .... D 949 437-1000
4675 Macarthur Ct Ste 800 Newport Beach (92660) *(P-9675)*

Clean Water Technology Inc (HQ)............................E 310 380-4648
13008 S Western Ave Gardena (90249) *(P-6009)*

Clean Wave Management Inc ....E 949 370-0740
1291 Puerta Del Sol San Clemente (92673) *(P-5748)*

Cleanstreet LLC ....C 800 225-7316
1918 W 169th St Gardena (90247) *(P-9786)*

Clear Behavioral Health, Torrance Also Called: Clear Recovery Center *(P-16456)*

Clear Blue Energy Corp ....D 858 451-1549
17150 Via Del Campo Ste 203 San Diego (92127) *(P-6495)*

Clear Channel Entertainment, Beverly Hills Also Called: Live Nation Worldwide Inc *(P-14994)*

Clear Channel Radio Sales, Los Angeles Also Called: Katz Millennium Sls & Mktg Inc *(P-6621)*

Clear Image Printing Inc ....E 818 547-4684
12744 San Fernando Rd Sylmar (91342) *(P-2980)*

Clear Recovery Center ....D 310 318-2122
18119 Prairie Ave Ste 102 Torrance (90504) *(P-16456)*

Clear View Sanitarium, Gardena Also Called: Clear View Sanitarium Inc *(P-15843)*

Clear View Sanitarium Inc ....C 310 538-2323
15823 S Western Ave Gardena (90247) *(P-15843)*

Clear View Windows & Doors Inc ....D 661 257-5050
28106 Avenue Crocker Santa Clarita (91355) *(P-1045)*

Clear-Ad Inc ....E 866 627-9718
2410 W 3rd St Santa Ana (92703) *(P-4090)*

Clearesult Operating LLC ....D 508 836-9500
807 N Park View Dr # 150 El Segundo (90245) *(P-18304)*

Clearlake Capital Group LP (PA).............................B 310 400-8800
233 Wilshire Blvd Ste 800 Santa Monica (90401) *(P-12632)*

Clearlake Capital Partners ....A 310 400-8800
233 Wilshire Blvd Ste 800 Santa Monica (90401) *(P-13902)*

Clearlake Cpitl Partners IV LP ....C 310 400-8800
233 Wilshire Blvd Ste 800 Santa Monica (90401) *(P-12633)*

Clearpath Lending ....C 949 502-3577
15635 Alton Pkwy Ste 300 Irvine (92618) *(P-11944)*

Clearpath Lending, Irvine Also Called: Clearpath Lending *(P-11944)*

Clearpoint Neuro, Solana Beach Also Called: Clearpoint Neuro Inc *(P-8132)*

Clearpoint Neuro Inc (PA)..D 888 287-9109
120 S Sierra Ave Ste 100 Solana Beach (92075) *(P-8132)*

Clearview Capital LLC ....A 310 806-9555
12100 Wilshire Blvd Ste 800 Los Angeles (90025) *(P-12702)*

Clearwater Living, Newport Beach Also Called: Csl Berkshire Operating Co LLC *(P-12416)*

Cleatech LLC ....E 714 754-6668
2106 N Glassell St Orange (92865) *(P-7824)*

Clegg Industries Inc ....C 310 225-3800
19032 S Vermont Ave Gardena (90248) *(P-8593)*

Clegg Promo, Gardena Also Called: Clegg Industries Inc *(P-8593)*

Clemson Distribution Inc (PA).................................E 909 595-2770
20722 Currier Rd City Of Industry (91789) *(P-10828)*

Cleveland Tramrail So Calif, Corona Also Called: General Conveyor Inc *(P-14768)*

Cli, Indio Also Called: Commercial Lighting Inds Inc *(P-10176)*

Clickup, San Diego Also Called: Mango Technologies Inc *(P-13766)*

Cliff View Terrace Inc ....D 805 682-7443
623 N Junipero St Santa Barbara (93105) *(P-17131)*

Cliffdale Manufacturing LLC ....C 818 341-3344
20409 Prairie St Chatsworth (91311) *(P-7887)*

Cliftonlarsonallen LLP ....D 310 273-2501
1925 Century Park E 16th Fl Los Angeles (90067) *(P-17712)*

Clima-Tech Inc ....D 909 613-5513
1820 Town And Country Dr Norco (92860) *(P-14724)*

Clinic Inc ....D 323 730-1920
3834 S Western Ave Los Angeles (90062) *(P-15280)*

Clinica Sierra Vista ....D 661 845-3717
8787 Hall Rd Lamont (93241) *(P-15281)*

Clinica Sierra Vista (PA)..D 661 635-3050
1430 Truxtun Ave Ste 400 Bakersfield (93301) *(P-15282)*

Clinica Srra Vsta Adult Mntal, Lamont Also Called: Clinica Sierra Vista *(P-15281)*

Clinical Research, Rancho Mirage Also Called: Eisenhower Medical Center *(P-16313)*

Clinical Translational RES Ctr, Los Angeles Also Called: Cedars-Sinai Medical Center *(P-15937)*

Clinicomp International Inc (PA)..............................D 858 546-8202
9655 Towne Centre Dr San Diego (92121) *(P-14075)*

Clinics On Demand Inc ....D 310 709-7355
1001 Gayley Ave Unit 24673 Los Angeles (90024) *(P-16378)*

Cliniqa, San Marcos Also Called: Cliniqa Corporation *(P-3570)*

Cliniqa Corporation (HQ)..E 760 744-1900
495 Enterprise St San Marcos (92078) *(P-3570)*

Cliniqa Corporation ....D 760 744-1900
258 La Moree Rd San Marcos (92078) *(P-3571)*

Clipboard Health, Covina Also Called: Twomagnets LLC *(P-13579)*

Clipper Windpower, Carpinteria Also Called: Clipper Windpower PLC *(P-5456)*

Clipper Windpower PLC ....A 805 690-3275
6305 Carpinteria Ave Ste 300 Carpinteria (93013) *(P-5456)*

Cliq Inc ....D 714 361-1900
2900 Bristol St Ste F Costa Mesa (92626) *(P-14473)*

Clique Brands Inc ....E 310 623-6916
750 N San Vicente Blvd Ste 800 West Hollywood (90069) *(P-2850)*

Clockparts, Culver City Also Called: Innovation Specialties *(P-14515)*

Clorox, Redlands Also Called: Clorox Manufacturing Company *(P-3602)*

Clorox Manufacturing Company ....E 909 307-2756
2300 W San Bernardino Ave Redlands (92374) *(P-3602)*

Closet Factory Inc (PA)...C 310 516-7000
12800 S Bdwy Los Angeles (90061) *(P-1198)*

Closet World Inc ....D 626 855-0846
14438 Don Julian Rd City Of Industry (91746) *(P-1046)*

Closet World, The, City Of Industry Also Called: Home Organizers Inc *(P-1052)*

Clothing Illustrated Inc (PA).....................................E 213 403-9950
836 Traction Ave Los Angeles (90013) *(P-2086)*

Clothng/Pparel/Uniform/ppe Mfg, Vernon Also Called: David Grment Ctng Fsing Svc In *(P-2089)*

Cloud Automation Division, Aliso Viejo Also Called: Quest Software Inc *(P-14015)*

Cloud Creations Inc ....D 800 951-7651
301 N Lake Ave Ste 600 Pasadena (91101) *(P-14206)*

Cloud Nine Comforts, Los Angeles Also Called: Universal Cushion Company Inc *(P-2225)*

Cloudbeds, San Diego Also Called: Digital Arbitrage Dist Inc *(P-13915)*

Cloudcover, Irvine Also Called: Cloudcover Iot Inc *(P-13903)*

Cloudcover Iot Inc (PA)...E 888 511-2022
14 Goodyear Ste 125b Irvine (92618) *(P-13903)*

Cloudradiant Corp (PA)...C 408 256-1527
12 Fuchsia Lake Forest (92630) *(P-11114)*

Cloudstaff LLC ....B 888 551-5339
26895 Aliso Creek Rd # B-209 Aliso Viejo (92656) *(P-13170)*

Cloudvirga Inc ....D 949 799-2643
5291 California Ave Ste 300 Irvine (92617) *(P-13904)*

Clougherty Packing LLC (DH)...................................B 323 583-4621
3049 E Vernon Ave Los Angeles (90058) *(P-1241)*

Clover Envmtl Solutions LLC ....E 760 357-9277
315 Weakley St Bldg 3 Calexico (92231) *(P-8424)*

Clover Envmtl Solutions LLC ....A 815 431-8100
9414 Eton Ave Chatsworth (91311) *(P-10430)*

Clover Imaging, Calexico Also Called: Clover Envmtl Solutions LLC *(P-8424)*

Clovis Skilled Care LLC ....D 559 299-2591
1817 Avenida Del Diablo Escondido (92029) *(P-144T4)*

CLP Inc (PA)...E 619 444-3105
1546 E Main St El Cajon (92021) *(P-14738)*

Cls Landscape Management, Montclair Also Called: Cls Landscape Management Inc *(P-244)*

Cls Landscape Management Inc ....B 909 628-3005
4329 State St Ste B Montclair (91763) *(P-244)*

Cls Trnsprttion Los Angles LLC (HQ).......................C 310 414-8189
600 S Allied Way El Segundo (90245) *(P-8819)*

Club Speed LLC (PA)...E 951 817-7073
300 Spectrum Center Dr Irvine (92618) *(P-13905)*

CM Laundry LLC ....D 310 436-6170
14919 S Figueroa St Gardena (90248) *(P-13143)*

CMA Dish Machines, Cerritos Also Called: Chemical Methods Assoc LLC *(P-6005)*

Cmb Laboratory, Cypress Also Called: Consoldted Med Bo-Analysis Inc *(P-16309)*

CMC, Goleta Also Called: CMC Rescue Inc *(P-11678)*

CMC Rebar West ....C 858 737-7700
7326 Mission Gorge Rd San Diego (92120) *(P-477)*

CMC Rebar West ....D 714 692-7082
10840 Norwalk Blvd Santa Fe Springs (90670) *(P-478)*

CMC Rebar West ....C 909 713-1130
5425 Industrial Pkwy San Bernardino (92407) *(P-10128)*

Employee Codes: A=Over 500 employees, B=251-500
C=101-250, D=51-100, E=20-50, F=10-19, G=1-9

2025 Southern California
Business Directory and Buyers Guide

© Mergent Inc. 1-800-342-5647

983

CMC Rescue Inc .... D 805 562-9120
6740 Cortona Dr Goleta (93117) *(P-11678)*

CMC Steel California, San Bernardino *Also Called: Tamco (P-4527)*

CMC Steel Us LLC .... E 909 646-7827
5425 Industrial Pkwy San Bernardino (92407) *(P-5093)*

Cmf Inc .... D 714 637-2409
1317 W Grove Ave Orange (92865) *(P-1076)*

CMI, Irvine *Also Called: Cooper Microelectronics Inc (P-6815)*

CMI, San Clemente *Also Called: Composite Manufacturing Inc (P-8134)*

CMI Integrated Tech Inc .... E
11250 Playa Ct Culver City (90230) *(P-6318)*

Cmk Manufacturing LLC .... E
10375 Wilshire Blvd Apt 2h Los Angeles (90024) *(P-1899)*

Cmre Financial Services Inc .... B 714 528-3200
3075 E Imperial Hwy Ste 200 Brea (92821) *(P-13280)*

CMS, Simi Valley *Also Called: Computerized Mgt Svcs Inc (P-17713)*

CMS Products LLC .... E 714 424-5520
29620 Skyline Dr Tehachapi (93561) *(P-5909)*

CMTC, Long Beach *Also Called: California Mfg Tech Consulting (P-17499)*

CN Publishing Group, Irvine *Also Called: Cycle News Inc (P-2792)*

Cnc Worldwide Inc (PA) .... D 310 670-7121
2805 E Ana St Compton (90221) *(P-9264)*

Cnet Express .... C 949 357-5475
15134 Indiana Ave Apt 38 Paramount (90723) *(P-8902)*

Cni Thl Propco Fe LLC .... D 661 325-9700
5101 California Ave Bakersfield (93309) *(P-12796)*

Co Ltd, All Nippon Airways, Torrance *Also Called: Nippon Express (P-9318)*

Co-Op Solutions, Rancho Cucamonga *Also Called: CU Cooperative Systems LLC (P-11827)*

Co-Production Intl Inc .... A 619 429-4344
8716 Sherwood Ter San Diego (92154) *(P-18118)*

Coach Usa Inc .... D 626 357-7912
5640 Peck Rd Arcadia (91006) *(P-8863)*

Coachella Valley Water Dst, Palm Desert *Also Called: Coachlla Vly Wtr Dst Pub Fclti (P-9686)*

Coachella Vly Rescue Mission .... D 760 347-3512
82873 Via Venecia Indio (92201) *(P-16894)*

Coachlla Vly Wtr Dst Pub Fclti .... C 760 398-2651
75525 Hovley Ln E Palm Desert (92260) *(P-9685)*

Coachlla Vly Wtr Dst Pub Fclti (PA) .... C 760 398-2651
75515 Hovley Ln E Palm Desert (92211) *(P-9686)*

Coalition For Family Harmony .... D 805 983-6014
1000 Town Center Dr Oxnard (93036) *(P-16895)*

Coalition Technologies LLC .... C 310 827-3890
445 S Figueroa St Ste 3100 Los Angeles (90071) *(P-18253)*

Coast Aerospace, Placentia *Also Called: Coast Aerospace Mfg Inc (P-5573)*

Coast Aerospace Mfg Inc .... E 714 893-8066
950 Richfield Rd Placentia (92870) *(P-5573)*

Coast Aluminum, Santa Fe Springs *Also Called: Coast Aluminum Inc (P-10129)*

Coast Aluminum Inc (PA) .... C 562 946-6061
10628 Fulton Wells Ave Santa Fe Springs (90670) *(P-10129)*

Coast Autonomous Inc (PA) .... E 626 838-2469
23 E Colorado Blvd Ste 203 Pasadena (91105) *(P-7238)*

Coast Citrus Distributors (PA) .... D 619 661-7950
7597 Bristow Ct San Diego (92154) *(P-10890)*

Coast Composites LLC .... E 949 455-0665
7 Burroughs Irvine (92618) *(P-6107)*

Coast Composites LLC (PA) .... D 949 455-0665
5 Burroughs Irvine (92618) *(P-7453)*

Coast Custom Cable, Carson *Also Called: Belden Inc (P-4625)*

Coast Flagstone Co .... D 310 829-4010
1810 Colorado Ave Santa Monica (90404) *(P-4473)*

Coast Group Financial, San Marcos *Also Called: Centurion Group Inc (P-11960)*

Coast Health Plan Gold .... B 888 301-1228
711 E Daily Dr Ste 106 Camarillo (93010) *(P-16549)*

Coast Home Loans, Riverside *Also Called: Secure Choice Lending (P-11878)*

Coast Index 965, Newbury Park *Also Called: Coast Index Co Inc (P-2760)*

Coast Index Co Inc .... D 805 499-6844
850 Lawrence Dr Newbury Park (91320) *(P-2760)*

Coast Iron & Steel Co .... E 562 946-4421
12300 Lakeland Rd Santa Fe Springs (90670) *(P-1152)*

Coast Magnetics, Los Angeles *Also Called: A M I/Coast Magnetics Inc (P-6922)*

Coast News Inc .... E 760 436-9737
531 Encinitas Blvd Ste 204 Encinitas (92024) *(P-2790)*

Coast Packing Company .... D 323 277-7700
3275 E Vernon Ave Vernon (90058) *(P-1525)*

Coast Plating Inc (PA) .... E 323 770-0240
128 W 154th St Gardena (90248) *(P-5249)*

Coast Plz Dctors Hosp A Cal Lt (DH) .... D 562 868-3751
13100 Studebaker Rd Norwalk (90650) *(P-15960)*

Coast Produce Company (PA) .... C 213 955-4900
1791 Bay St Los Angeles (90021) *(P-10891)*

Coast Rock Products Inc .... E 805 925-2505
1625 E Donovan Rd Santa Maria (93454) *(P-9941)*

Coast Sheet Metal Inc .... E 949 645-2224
990 W 17th St Costa Mesa (92627) *(P-4970)*

Coast Sign Display, Anaheim *Also Called: Coast Sign Incorporated (P-8594)*

Coast Sign Incorporated .... C 714 520-9144
1500 W Embassy St Anaheim (92802) *(P-8594)*

Coast To Coast Circuits Inc (PA) .... E 714 891-9441
5331 Mcfadden Ave Huntington Beach (92649) *(P-6719)*

Coast To Coast Cmpt Pdts Inc (PA) .... C 805 244-9500
4277 Valley Fair St Simi Valley (93063) *(P-11539)*

Coast To Coast Met Finshg Corp .... E 626 282-2122
401 S Raymond Ave Alhambra (91803) *(P-5250)*

Coast Tropical, San Diego *Also Called: Coast Citrus Distributors (P-10890)*

Coast Wire & Plastic Tech LLC .... A 310 639-9473
1048 E Burgrove St Carson (90746) *(P-7113)*

Coastal Alliance Holdings Inc .... C 562 370-1000
1650 Ximeno Ave Ste 120 Long Beach (90804) *(P-12407)*

Coastal Building Services Inc .... B 714 775-2855
1433 W Central Park Ave N Anaheim (92802) *(P-13364)*

Coastal Cmnty Senior Care LLC .... C 562 596-4884
5500 E Atherton St Ste 216 Long Beach (90815) *(P-16379)*

Coastal Cocktails Inc (PA) .... E 949 250-8951
1920 E Deere Ave Ste 100 Santa Ana (92705) *(P-10938)*

Coastal Community Hospital, Santa Ana *Also Called: Health Resources Corp (P-16014)*

Coastal Connections .... E 805 644-5051
2085 Sperry Ave Ste B Ventura (93003) *(P-6583)*

Coastal Health Care Inc .... D 310 828-5596
1321 Franklin St Santa Monica (90404) *(P-15592)*

Coastal International, Tustin *Also Called: Coastal Intl Holdings LLC (P-14475)*

Coastal Intl Holdings LLC .... B 714 635-1200
2832 Walnut Ave Ste B Tustin (92780) *(P-14475)*

Coastal Pacific Fd Distrs Inc .... D 909 947-2066
1520 E Mission Blvd Ste B Ontario (91761) *(P-9054)*

Coastal Pacific Foods, Ontario *Also Called: Coastal Pacific Fd Distrs Inc (P-9054)*

Coastal Rdtion Onclogy Med Gro .... D 805 494-4483
1240 S Westlake Blvd Ste 103 Westlake Village (91361) *(P-15283)*

Coastal Tag & Label Inc .... D 562 946-4318
13233 Barton Cir Whittier (90605) *(P-3129)*

Coastal The, Sherman Oaks *Also Called: Coastal Tile Inc (P-1038)*

Coastal Tile Inc .... D 818 988-6134
13226 Moorpark St Apt 104 Sherman Oaks (91423) *(P-1038)*

Coastal View Halthcare Ctr LLC .... D 805 642-4101
4904 Telegraph Rd Ventura (93003) *(P-15593)*

Coastal View Healthcare Center, Ventura *Also Called: Coastal View Halthcare Ctr LLC (P-15593)*

Coastal Wood Products, City Of Industry *Also Called: McConnell Cabinets Inc (P-2354)*

Coasthills Credit Union (PA) .... D 805 733-7600
1075 E Betteravia Rd Santa Maria (93454) *(P-11826)*

Coastline Cnstr & Awng Co Inc .... D 714 891-9798
5742 Research Dr Huntington Beach (92649) *(P-395)*

Coastline Equipment, Oxnard *Also Called: Bragg Investment Company Inc (P-9817)*

Coastline International .... C 888 748-7177
1207 Bangor St San Diego (92106) *(P-8375)*

Coastline Metal Finishing Corp .... D 714 895-9099
7061 Patterson Dr Garden Grove (92841) *(P-5251)*

Coatinc United States Inc .... E 619 638-7261
325 W Washington St Ste 2340 San Diego (92103) *(P-3794)*

Coatings Resource, Huntington Beach *Also Called: Laird Coatings Corporation (P-3716)*

Cobalt Construction Company .... D 805 577-6222
2259 Ward Ave Ste 200 Simi Valley (93065) *(P-444)*

2025 Southern California
Business Directory and Buyers Guide

Cobalt Southwest Company, Simi Valley *Also Called: Cobalt Construction Company (P-444)*

Cobham, San Diego *Also Called: Remec Defense & Space Inc (P-7801)*

Cobrapro, Orange *Also Called: Word & Brown Insurance Administrators Inc (P-12275)*

Coca-Cola, Ontario *Also Called: Coca-Cola Company (P-1614)*

Coca-Cola, Victorville *Also Called: Reyes Coca-Cola Bottling LLC (P-1641)*

Coca-Cola, Santa Maria *Also Called: Reyes Coca-Cola Bottling LLC (P-1642)*

Coca-Cola, Ventura *Also Called: Reyes Coca-Cola Bottling LLC (P-1643)*

Coca-Cola, Los Angeles *Also Called: Reyes Coca-Cola Bottling LLC (P-1646)*

Coca-Cola, Orange *Also Called: Reyes Coca-Cola Bottling LLC (P-1647)*

Coca-Cola, Irvine *Also Called: Reyes Coca-Cola Bottling LLC (P-1648)*

Coca-Cola, Coachella *Also Called: Reyes Coca-Cola Bottling LLC (P-1649)*

Coca-Cola, Fontana *Also Called: Reyes Coca-Cola Bottling LLC (P-1650)*

Coca-Cola, San Diego *Also Called: Reyes Coca-Cola Bottling LLC (P-1651)*

Coca-Cola, Downey *Also Called: Reyes Coca-Cola Bottling LLC (P-1652)*

Coca-Cola, Sylmar *Also Called: Reyes Coca-Cola Bottling LLC (P-10974)*

Coca-Cola Company .... D 909 975-5200
   1650 S Vintage Ave Ontario (91761) *(P-1614)*

Cockram Construction Inc .... B 818 650-0999
   16340 Roscoe Blvd Van Nuys (91406) *(P-18119)*

Cod USA Inc .... E 949 381-7367
   25954 Commercentre Dr Lake Forest (92630) *(P-2540)*

Coda Mexico, San Diego *Also Called: Eleanor Rigby Leather Co (P-4310)*

Codan US, Santa Ana *Also Called: Codan US Corporation (P-4091)*

Codan US Corporation .... D 714 545-2111
   3501 W Sunflower Ave Santa Ana (92704) *(P-4091)*

Codazen, Irvine *Also Called: Codazen Inc (P-13689)*

Codazen Inc .... D 949 916-6266
   60 Bunsen Irvine (92618) *(P-13689)*

Coffee Bean & Tea Leaf, The, Los Angeles *Also Called: International Coffee & Tea LLC (P-11577)*

Coffman Specialties Inc (PA) .... C **858 536-3100**
   9685 Via Excelencia Ste 200 San Diego (92126) *(P-1111)*

Cognella Inc .... D 858 552-1120
   320 S Cedros Ave Ste 400 Solana Beach (92075) *(P-2907)*

Cognizant Trizetto .... D 949 719-2200
   567 San Nicolas Dr Ste 360 Newport Beach (92660) *(P-14207)*

Cognizant Trztto Sftwr Group I .... C 714 481-0396
   3631 S Harbor Blvd Ste 200 Santa Ana (92704) *(P-14076)*

Coherent Aerospace & Def Inc .... D 714 247-7100
   14192 Chambers Rd Tustin (92780) *(P-7998)*

Coherent Aerospace & Defense Inc (HQ) .... C **951 926-2994**
   36570 Briggs Rd Murrieta (92563) *(P-7708)*

Cohu, Poway *Also Called: Cohu Inc (P-7905)*

Cohu Inc (PA) .... C **858 848-8100**
   12367 Crosthwaite Cir Poway (92064) *(P-7905)*

Cohu Interface Solutions LLC (HQ) .... D **858 848-8000**
   12367 Crosthwaite Cir Poway (92064) *(P-7906)*

Coi Ceramics Inc .... E 858 621-5700
   7130 Miramar Rd Ste 100b San Diego (92121) *(P-7454)*

Coi Pharmaceuticals Inc .... E 858 750-4700
   11099 N Torrey Pines Rd Ste 290 La Jolla (92037) *(P-17782)*

Coi Rubber Products Inc .... B 626 965-9966
   19255 San Jose Ave Unit D-1 City Of Industry (91748) *(P-3910)*

Coic, San Diego *Also Called: Coi Ceramics Inc (P-7454)*

Colbi Technologies Inc .... E 714 505-9544
   13891 Newport Ave Ste 150 Tustin (92780) *(P-2908)*

Colbrit Manufacturing Co Inc .... E 818 709-3608
   9666 Owensmouth Ave Ste G Chatsworth (91311) *(P-5574)*

Coldwater Care Center LLC .... C 818 766-6105
   12750 Riverside Dr North Hollywood (91607) *(P-15594)*

Coldwell Banker, Bakersfield *Also Called: Bakersfield Westwind Corp (P-12386)*

Coldwell Banker, Canyon Lake *Also Called: Cbabr Inc (P-12396)*

Coldwell Banker, Mission Viejo *Also Called: Coldwell Banker Residential (P-12408)*

Coldwell Banker, Newport Beach *Also Called: Coldwell Bnkr Rsdntial Rfrral (P-12409)*

Coldwell Banker, Mission Viejo *Also Called: Coldwell Bnkr Rsdntial Rfrral (P-12410)*

Coldwell Banker, Bakersfield *Also Called: Preferred Brokers Inc (P-12507)*

Coldwell Banker Coastl Alliance, Long Beach *Also Called: Coastal Alliance Holdings Inc (P-12407)*

Coldwell Banker Residential (DH) .... D 949 837-5700
   27742 Vista Del Lago Ste 1 Mission Viejo (92692) *(P-12408)*

Coldwell Bnkr Rsdntial Rfrral .... A 949 673-8700
   201 Marine Ave Newport Beach (92662) *(P-12409)*

Coldwell Bnkr Rsdntial Rfrral (DH) .... B 949 367-1800
   27271 Las Ramblas Mission Viejo (92691) *(P-12410)*

Coldwell Bnkr Rsdntial Rfrral, Newport Beach *Also Called: C B Coast Newport Properties (P-12394)*

Cole Instrument Corp .... D 714 556-3100
   2650 S Croddy Way Santa Ana (92704) *(P-6319)*

Cole Lighting, South El Monte *Also Called: C W Cole & Company Inc (P-6453)*

Cole, Norman Anne, Anaheim *Also Called: House Seven Gables RE Inc (P-12465)*

Colin Cowie Lifestyle, Rancho Palos Verdes *Also Called: CAW Cowie Inc (P-14469)*

Collection Technology Inc .... D 800 743-4284
   10801 6th St Ste 200 Rancho Cucamonga (91730) *(P-13281)*

Collective Management Group, Beverly Hills *Also Called: Collective MGT Group LLC (P-17968)*

Collective MGT Group LLC .... C 323 655-8585
   8383 Wilshire Blvd Ste 1050 Beverly Hills (90211) *(P-17968)*

Collectors Universe, Santa Ana *Also Called: Collectors Universe Inc (P-14760)*

Collectors Universe Inc (PA) .... C **949 567-1234**
   1600 E Saint Andrew Pl Santa Ana (92705) *(P-14760)*

College Hospital Inc (PA) .... B **562 924-9581**
   10802 College Pl Cerritos (90703) *(P-16272)*

COLLEGE HOSPITAL CERRITOS, Costa Mesa *Also Called: College Hospital Costa Mesa Mso Inc (P-15961)*

College Hospital Cerritos, Cerritos *Also Called: College Hospital Inc (P-16272)*

College Hospital Costa Mesa Mso Inc (HQ) .... D **949 642-2734**
   301 Victoria St Costa Mesa (92627) *(P-15961)*

College Park Realty Inc (PA) .... D **562 594-6753**
   10791 Los Alamitos Blvd Los Alamitos (90720) *(P-12411)*

Collins & Collins .... D 626 243-1100
   790 E Colorado Blvd Ste 600 Pasadena (91101) *(P-12286)*

Collins Aerospace, Chula Vista *Also Called: Rohr Inc (P-7548)*

Collins Company, Ontario *Also Called: Warren Collins and Assoc Inc (P-723)*

Collins Technologies, Brea *Also Called: Curtiss-Wright Flow Ctrl Corp (P-5365)*

Collwood Ter Stellar Care Inc .... D 619 287-2920
   4518 54th St San Diego (92115) *(P-17132)*

Colmol Inc .... E 858 693-7575
   8517 Production Ave San Diego (92121) *(P-3130)*

Colombo Construction Co Inc .... D 661 316-0100
   3211 Rio Mirada Dr Bakersfield (93308) *(P-532)*

Colonel Lee's Enterprises, Vernon *Also Called: T & T Foods Inc (P-1346)*

Colonial Care Center, Long Beach *Also Called: Longwood Management Corp (P-15869)*

Colonial Enterprises Inc .... E 909 822-8700
   690 Knox St Ste 200 Torrance (90502) *(P-3638)*

Colonial Gardens Nursing Home, Pico Rivera *Also Called: Rivera Sanatarium Inc (P-15761)*

Colonial Home Textiles, Corona *Also Called: Amrapur Overseas Incorporated (P-1968)*

Colonnas Shipyard West LLC .... E 757 545-2414
   2890 Faivre St Ste 150 Chula Vista (91911) *(P-7598)*

Colony Dstrssed Cr Spcial Stto, Los Angeles *Also Called: Cdcf III PCF Lndmark Scrmnto L (P-12285)*

Colony Palms Hotel LLC .... D 760 969-1800
   572 N Indian Canyon Dr Palm Springs (92262) *(P-12797)*

Color Inc .... E 818 240-1350
   1600 Flower St Glendale (91201) *(P-2981)*

Color Concepts, Canoga Park *Also Called: Rte Enterprises Inc (P-872)*

Color Design Laboratory Inc (PA) .... D **818 341-5100**
   9533 Irondale Ave Chatsworth (91311) *(P-17909)*

Color Design Labs, Chatsworth *Also Called: Color Design Laboratory Inc (P-17909)*

Color Laser R&D, Chatsworth *Also Called: Clover Envmtl Solutions LLC (P-10430)*

Color ME Cotton, Los Angeles *Also Called: Jd/Cmc Inc (P-2105)*

Color Science Inc .... E 714 434-1033
   1230 E Glenwood Pl Santa Ana (92707) *(P-3723)*

Color West Inc .... C 818 840-8881
   2228 N Hollywood Way Burbank (91505) *(P-2982)*

Color West Printing & Packg, Burbank *Also Called: Color West Inc (P-2982)*

Colorado Farms LLC .... C 805 389-0401
   400 Camarillo Ranch Rd Ste 107 Camarillo (93012) *(P-78)*

Employee Codes: A=Over 500 employees, B=251-500
C=101-250, D=51-100, E=20-50, F=10-19, G=1-9

2025 Southern California
Business Directory and Buyers Guide

© Mergent Inc. 1-800-342-5647

985

Colorado River Adventures Inc (PA)...................... C 760 663-3737
2715 Parker Dam Rd Earp (92242) *(P-13108)*

COLORADO RIVER MEDICAL CENTER, Needles *Also Called: Community Hlthcare Partner Inc (P-15286)*

Colorama Paints, Los Angeles *Also Called: Ennis Traffic Safety Solutions (P-3712)*

Colorama Wholesale Nursery, Azusa *Also Called: Richard Wilson Wellington (P-68)*

Coloredge .... D 818 842-1121
3520 W Valhalla Dr Burbank (91505) *(P-14428)*

Colorescience Inc .... C 866 426-5673
2141 Palomar Airport Rd Ste 200 Carlsbad (92011) *(P-10618)*

Colorfx Inc .... E 818 767-7671
11050 Randall St Sun Valley (91352) *(P-2983)*

Colorgraphics, Los Angeles *Also Called: Madisn/Grham Clor Graphics Inc (P-3037)*

Colormax Industries Inc (PA)...................... E 213 748-6600
1627 Paloma St Los Angeles (90021) *(P-1876)*

Colornet Press, Van Nuys *Also Called: Niknejad Inc (P-3050)*

Colors Pizza, Oceanside *Also Called: Sadie Rose Baking Co (P-10977)*

Colosseum Athletics, Compton *Also Called: Colosseum Athletics Corp (P-10681)*

Colosseum Athletics Corp .... D 310 538-8991
2400 S Wilmington Ave Compton (90220) *(P-10681)*

Colour Concepts Inc C
1225 Los Angeles St Glendale (91204) *(P-2984)*

Colsa Corporation .... D 619 553-0031
2727 Camino Del Rio S Ste 340 San Diego (92108) *(P-13690)*

Colt Services Inc .... D 858 271-9910
9655 Via Excelencia San Diego (92126) *(P-13135)*

Columbia Aluminum Products LLC .... D 323 728-7361
1150 W Rincon St Corona (92878) *(P-4826)*

Columbia Pictures, Culver City *Also Called: Columbia Pictures Inds Inc (P-14814)*

Columbia Pictures Inds Inc .... D 818 655-5820
4024 Radford Ave Studio City (91604) *(P-14813)*

Columbia Pictures Inds Inc (DH) .... C 310 244-4000
10202 Washington Blvd Culver City (90232) *(P-14814)*

Columbia Showcase & Cab Co Inc .... C 818 765-9710
11034 Sherman Way Ste A Sun Valley (91352) *(P-2561)*

Columbia Spclty A Trstar Indus, Long Beach *Also Called: Tristar Industrial LLC (P-10469)*

Columbia Specialty Company Inc .... D 562 634-6425
5875 Obispo Ave Long Beach (90805) *(P-10431)*

Columbia Steel Inc .... D 909 874-8840
2175 N Linden Ave Rialto (92377) *(P-4827)*

Columbia TV Advertiser Sls, Culver City *Also Called: Sony Pictures Television Inc (P-14859)*

Com Dev Usa LLC .... D 424 456-8000
2333 Utah Ave El Segundo (90245) *(P-10488)*

Comac America Corporation .... E 760 616-9614
4350 Von Karman Ave Ste 400 Newport Beach (92660) *(P-7338)*

Comav LLC .... C 760 523-5100
18260 Phantom W Victorville (92394) *(P-9196)*

Comav LLC (PA)...................... E 760 523-5100
18499 Phantom St Ste 17 Victorville (92394) *(P-10489)*

Comav Aviation, Victorville *Also Called: Comav LLC (P-9196)*

Comav Technical Services LLC .... C 760 530-2400
18438 Readiness St Victorville (92394) *(P-9197)*

Combustion Associates Inc .... E 951 272-6999
555 Monica Cir Corona (92878) *(P-9575)*

Comcast, Ontario *Also Called: Comcast Corporation (P-9536)*

Comcast Corporation .... D 909 890-0886
1205 S Dupont Ave Ontario (91761) *(P-9536)*

Comco Inc .... E 818 333-8500
2151 N Lincoln St Burbank (91504) *(P-6010)*

Come Land Maint Svc Co Inc .... A 818 567-2455
1419 N San Fernando Blvd Ste 250 Burbank (91504) *(P-13365)*

Comedy Club Oxnard LLC .... D 805 535-5400
591 Collection Blvd Oxnard (93036) *(P-15130)*

Comet Electric Inc .... C 818 340-0965
21625 Prairie St Chatsworth (91311) *(P-900)*

Comet Medical, Ventura *Also Called: Peter Brasseler Holdings LLC (P-10102)*

Comfort California Inc .... C 714 750-3131
616 W Convention Way Anaheim (92802) *(P-12798)*

Comfort Industries Inc .... E 562 692-8288
301 W Las Tunas Dr San Gabriel (91776) *(P-1900)*

Comfort Inn, Santa Ana *Also Called: Ocean Sands Hotel (P-12945)*

Command Gard Srvces Wsa Srvces, Gardena *Also Called: United Facility Solutions Inc (P-14357)*

Command Guard Services, Torrance *Also Called: Resource Collection Inc (P-13413)*

Command Packaging, Los Angeles *Also Called: Revoltion Cnsmr Sltions CA LLC (P-11139)*

Commander Packaging West Inc .... E 714 921-9350
602 S Rockefeller Ave Ste D Ontario (91761) *(P-2660)*

Commerce, Commerce *Also Called: Alarin Aircraft Hinge Inc (P-4751)*

Commerce Casino, Commerce *Also Called: California Commerce Club Inc (P-12784)*

Commerce Coating Services Inc .... D 310 345-1979
20725 S Western Ave Ste 144 Torrance (90501) *(P-3709)*

Commerce On Demand LLC .... D 562 360-4819
7121 Telegraph Rd Montebello (90640) *(P-8673)*

Commercial Cstm Sting Uphl Inc .... D 714 850-0520
12601 Western Ave Garden Grove (92841) *(P-2610)*

Commercial Display Systems LLC .... E 818 361-8160
17341 Sierra Hwy Canyon Country (91351) *(P-5970)*

Commercial Due Diligence Svcs, Irvine *Also Called: First Amercn Prof RE Svcs Inc (P-12442)*

Commercial Intr Resources Inc .... D 562 926-5885
6077 Rickenbacker Rd Commerce (90040) *(P-2443)*

Commercial Inv MGT Group, Los Angeles *Also Called: Cim Group LP (P-12792)*

Commercial Lbr & Pallet Co Inc (PA)...................... C 626 968-0631
135 Long Ln City Of Industry (91746) *(P-2386)*

Commercial Lighting Inds Inc .... D 800 755-0155
81161 Indio Blvd Indio (92201) *(P-10176)*

Commercial Metal Forming, Orange *Also Called: Commercial Metal Forming Inc (P-4912)*

Commercial Metal Forming Inc .... E 714 532-6321
341 W Collins Ave Orange (92867) *(P-4912)*

Commercial Protective Services, Gardena *Also Called: Construction Protective Services Inc (P-14287)*

Commercial Protective Svcs Inc .... A 310 515-5290
17215 Studebaker Rd Ste 205 Cerritos (90703) *(P-14285)*

Commercial RE Exch Inc .... C 888 273-0423
5510 Lincoln Blvd Ste 400 Playa Vista (90094) *(P-12412)*

Commercial Shtmtl Works Inc .... E 213 748-7321
1800 S San Pedro St Los Angeles (90015) *(P-4828)*

Commercial Truck Eqp Co LLC .... D 562 803-4466
12351 Bellflower Blvd Downey (90242) *(P-7197)*

Commercial Truck Equipment Co, Downey *Also Called: Commercial Truck Eqp Co LLC (P-7197)*

Commercial Wood Products Company .... C 760 246-4530
10019 Yucca Rd Adelanto (92301) *(P-1047)*

Commodity Forwarders Inc (DH)...................... C 310 348-8855
11101 S La Cienega Blvd Los Angeles (90045) *(P-9265)*

Commodity Resource Envmtl Inc .... E 661 824-2416
11847 United St Mojave (93501) *(P-4580)*

Commodity Rsource Enviromeal, Mojave *Also Called: Commodity Resource Envmtl Inc (P-4580)*

Commodity Sales Co .... C 323 980-5463
517 S Clarence St Los Angeles (90033) *(P-1276)*

Common Grounds Holdings LLC .... D 760 206-7861
6790 Embarcadero Ln Ste 100 Carlsbad (92011) *(P-12413)*

Commonwealth Land Title, Irvine *Also Called: Commonwealth Land Title Insur (P-12554)*

Commonwealth Land Title, Temecula *Also Called: Commonwealth Land Title Insur (P-12555)*

Commonwealth Land Title Insur .... C 949 460-4500
6 Executive Cir Ste 100 Irvine (92614) *(P-12554)*

Commonwealth Land Title Insur .... C 951 296-6289
41637 Margarita Rd Ste 101 Temecula (92591) *(P-12555)*

Communction Systms-Wst/Lnkabit, San Diego *Also Called: L3 Technologies Inc (P-6625)*

Communction Wirg Spcalists Inc .... D 858 278-4545
8909 Complex Dr Ste F San Diego (92123) *(P-901)*

Communication Tech Svcs LLC .... B 508 382-2700
1590 S Milliken Ave Ste H Ontario (91761) *(P-902)*

Communications Supply Corp .... D 714 670-7711
6251 Knott Ave Buena Park (90620) *(P-9561)*

Community & Senior Svcs, Lancaster *Also Called: County of Los Angeles (P-16915)*

Community Action Partnership .... D 805 541-4122
3970 Short St San Luis Obispo (93401) *(P-16896)*

Community Action Partnr Kern .... D 661 336-5300
1611 1st St Bakersfield (93304) *(P-17133)*

Mergent email: customerrelations@mergent.com
986

2025 Southern California
Business Directory and Buyers Guide

(P-0000) Products & Services Section entry number
(PA)=Parent Co (HQ)=Headquarters (DH)=Div Headquarters

Community Action Partnr Kern .... D 661 835-5405
315 Stine Rd Bakersfield (93309) *(P-17219)*

Community Action Partnr Kern .... D 760 371-1469
814 N Norma St Ridgecrest (93555) *(P-17220)*

Community Action Prtnr Ornge C .... C 714 897-6670
11870 Monarch St Garden Grove (92841) *(P-16897)*

Community Action Prtnr Rvrside, Riverside Also Called: County of Riverside *(P-16928)*

Community Action Prtnr San Brn .... D 909 723-1500
696 S Tippecanoe Ave San Bernardino (92408) *(P-17221)*

Community Action Prtnr San Lui .... C 805 544-2478
705 Grand Ave San Luis Obispo (93401) *(P-16457)*

Community Action Prtnr San Lui .... C 805 541-2272
805 Fiero Ln Ste A San Luis Obispo (93401) *(P-17085)*

Community Action Prtnr San Lui (PA) .... D 805 544-4355
1030 Southwood Dr San Luis Obispo (93401) *(P-17086)*

Community Bank .... B 626 577-1700
460 Sierra Madre Villa Ave Pasadena (91107) *(P-11759)*

Community Care Center .... D 619 465-0702
8665 La Mesa Blvd La Mesa (91942) *(P-15595)*

Community Care Licensing, Riverside Also Called: California Dept Social Svcs *(P-18396)*

Community Care On Palm Rvrside .... D 951 686-9001
4768 Palm Ave Riverside (92501) *(P-15596)*

Community Cnvlscent Hosp Mntcl, Montclair Also Called: US Skillserve Inc *(P-15790)*

Community Corp Santa Monica .... C 310 394-8487
1410 2nd St Ste 200 Santa Monica (90401) *(P-12337)*

Community Day School, Beaumont Also Called: Beaumont Unified Schl Dst Pub F *(P-16802)*

Community Dev Inst Head Start .... B 858 668-2985
12988 Bowron Rd Poway (92064) *(P-17087)*

Community Food Connection .... D 858 751-4613
14047 Twin Peaks Rd Poway (92064) *(P-16898)*

Community Health Agency, Moreno Valley Also Called: County of Riverside *(P-15296)*

Community Health Agency, Riverside Also Called: County of Riverside *(P-18398)*

Community Health Center, Bakersfield Also Called: Omni Family Health *(P-15411)*

Community Health Group .... C 800 224-7766
2420 Fenton St Ste 100 Chula Vista (91914) *(P-15284)*

Community Health Systems Inc .... C 951 571-2300
21801 Alessandro Blvd Moreno Valley (92553) *(P-15285)*

Community Hlth Plan Off MGT Ca, Alhambra Also Called: County of Los Angeles *(P-12078)*

Community Hlthcare Partner Inc .... D 760 326-4531
1401 Bailey Ave Needles (92363) *(P-15286)*

Community Hosp San Bernardino (DH) .... B 909 887-6333
1805 Medical Center Dr San Bernardino (92411) *(P-15962)*

Community Hospital, Long Beach Also Called: Community Hospital Long Beach *(P-15963)*

Community Hospital Long Beach .... A 562 494-0600
1760 Termino Ave Ste 105 Long Beach (90804) *(P-15963)*

Community Interface Services .... D 760 729-3866
981 Vale Terrace Dr Vista (92084) *(P-16899)*

Community Media Corporation (PA) .... E 714 220-0292
15005 S Vermont Ave Gardena (90247) *(P-2791)*

Community Memorial Health Sys .... C 805 646-1401
1306 Maricopa Hwy Ojai (93023) *(P-15964)*

Community Memorial Health Sys (PA) .... A 805 652-5011
147 N Brent St Ventura (93003) *(P-15965)*

Community Memorial Hospital, Ventura Also Called: Community Memorial Health Sys *(P-15965)*

Community Partners (PA) .... C 213 346-3200
1000 N Alameda St Ste 240 Los Angeles (90012) *(P-17222)*

Community Patrol Inc .... D 657 247-4744
1420 E Edinger Ave Ste 213 Santa Ana (92705) *(P-14286)*

Community Support Options Inc .... C 661 758-5331
1401 Poso Dr Wasco (93280) *(P-16900)*

Community TV Southern Cal, Burbank Also Called: Public Mdia Group Southern Cal *(P-9514)*

Community West Bancshares .... C 805 692-5821
445 Pine Ave Goleta (93117) *(P-11760)*

Compaction American, Lake Elsinore Also Called: American Compaction Eqp Inc *(P-5487)*

Companion Medical Inc .... D 858 522-0252
11011 Via Frontera Ste D San Diego (92127) *(P-8133)*

Compas Health, Templeton Also Called: Compass Health Inc *(P-15597)*

Compass Flooring, Santa Fe Springs Also Called: Altro Usa Inc *(P-8653)*

Compass Group Usa Inc .... C 714 899-2520
12640 Knott St Garden Grove (92841) *(P-13453)*

Compass Health Inc .... C 805 434-3035
290 Heather Ct Templeton (93465) *(P-15597)*

Compass Health Inc .... C 805 543-0210
1425 Woodside Dr San Luis Obispo (93401) *(P-15598)*

Compass Health Inc .... C 805 772-7372
1405 Teresa Dr Morro Bay (93442) *(P-15599)*

Compass Health Inc .... C 805 489-8137
1212 Farroll Ave Arroyo Grande (93420) *(P-15600)*

Compass Health Inc .... C 805 466-9254
10805 El Camino Real Atascadero (93422) *(P-15601)*

Compass Health Inc .... C 805 687-6651
3880 Via Lucero Santa Barbara (93110) *(P-15602)*

Compass Health Inc .... C 805 474-7260
222 S Elm St Arroyo Grande (93420) *(P-17134)*

Compass Water Solutions Inc (HQ) .... E 949 222-5777
15542 Mosher Ave Tustin (92780) *(P-6011)*

Compass365, Glendale Also Called: General Networks Corporation *(P-14222)*

Compatico Inc .... E 616 940-1772
1901 S Archibald Ave Ontario (91761) *(P-2562)*

Competent Care Inc .... D 714 545-4818
2900 Bristol St Ste D107 Costa Mesa (92626) *(P-16380)*

Competent Care HM Hlth Nursing, Costa Mesa Also Called: Competent Care Inc *(P-16380)*

Competition Clutch Inc .... E 800 809-6598
1570 Lakeview Loop Anaheim (92807) *(P-9819)*

Competrol A Western Pump Co, San Diego Also Called: Western Pump Inc *(P-14801)*

Compex Legal Services, Torrance Also Called: Compex Legal Services Inc *(P-16658)*

Compex Legal Services Inc (PA) .... C 310 782-1801
325 Maple Ave Torrance (90503) *(P-16658)*

Complete Aquatic Systems, Gardena Also Called: Wally & Pat Enterprises *(P-8739)*

Complete Clothing Company (PA) .... E 213 892-1188
4950 E 49th St Vernon (90058) *(P-2064)*

Complete Coach Works .... C 800 300-3751
42882 Ivy St Murrieta (92562) *(P-14714)*

Complete Logistics Company .... D 619 661-9610
1207 Air Wing Rd San Diego (92154) *(P-8937)*

Complete Truck Body Repair Inc .... E 323 445-2675
1217 N Alameda St Compton (90222) *(P-7198)*

Completely Fresh Foods Inc .... C 323 722-9136
4401 S Downey Rd Vernon (90058) *(P-10939)*

Completes Plus, Lawndale Also Called: Automotive Aftermarket Inc *(P-9813)*

Compliance Poster, Monrovia Also Called: Global Compliance Inc *(P-2917)*

Complyright Dist Svcs Inc .... E 805 981-0992
3451 Jupiter Ct Oxnard (93030) *(P-3192)*

Component Equipment Coinc .... E 805 988-8004
3050 Camino Del Sol Oxnard (93030) *(P-6943)*

Composite Manufacturing Inc .... E 949 361-7580
970 Calle Amanecer Ste D San Clemente (92673) *(P-8134)*

Composite Optics Incorporated .... A 937 490-4145
7130 Miramar Rd Ste 100b San Diego (92121) *(P-7668)*

Composite Technology Corp .... C 949 428-8500
2026 Mcgaw Ave Irvine (92614) *(P-6370)*

Composites Horizons LLC (DH) .... C 626 331-0861
1629 W Industrial Park St Covina (91722) *(P-3261)*

Comppro, San Diego Also Called: Rf Industries Ltd *(P-6958)*

Comprehensive Blood Cancer Ctr, Bakersfield Also Called: Ravi Patel MD Inc *(P-15434)*

Comprehensive Cancer Centers Inc .... C 323 966-3400
8201 Beverly Blvd Los Angeles (90048) *(P-16458)*

Comprehensive Dist Svcs Inc .... C 310 523-1546
18726 S Western Ave Ste 300 Gardena (90248) *(P-9361)*

Compton Service Center, Compton Also Called: Southern California Edison Co *(P-9626)*

COMPTON TRAINING CENTER, Van Nuys Also Called: Apprentice Jrnymen Trning Tr F *(P-17045)*

Compton Unified School Dst .... D 310 898-6470
1104 E 148th St Compton (90220) *(P-16805)*

Compu Aire Inc .... C 562 945-8971
8167 Byron Rd Whittier (90606) *(P-5971)*

Compucase Corporation .... A 626 336-6588
16720 Chestnut St Ste C City Of Industry (91748) *(P-5877)*

Compucraft Industries Inc .... E 619 448-0787
8787 Olive Ln Santee (92071) *(P-7455)*

Employee Codes: A=Over 500 employees, B=251-500
C=101-250, D=51-100, E=20-50, F=10-19, G=1-9

2025 Southern California
Business Directory and Buyers Guide

© Mergent Inc. 1-800-342-5647
987

Compugroup Medical Inc .... E 949 789-0500
25b Technology Dr Ste 200 Irvine (92618) *(P-13906)*

Compulink Business Systems Inc (PA).............. C 805 446-2050
1100 Business Center Cir Newbury Park (91320) *(P-13907)*

Compulink Healthcare Solutions, Newbury Park *Also Called: Compulink Business Systems Inc (P-13907)*

Compulink Management Ctr Inc (PA).............. C 562 988-1688
3443 Long Beach Blvd Long Beach (90807) *(P-13691)*

Compumeric Engineering Inc .... E 909 605-7666
1390 S Milliken Ave Ontario (91761) *(P-4971)*

Compushare Inc .... C 714 427-1000
3 Hutton Centre Dr Ste 700 Santa Ana (92707) *(P-14126)*

Computational Systems Inc .... D 661 832-5306
4301 Resnik Ct Bakersfield (93313) *(P-7852)*

Computer Assisted Mfg Tech LLC .... E 949 263-8911
8710 Research Dr 8750 Irvine (92618) *(P-6108)*

Computer Metal Products Corp .... D 805 520-6966
370 E Easy St Simi Valley (93065) *(P-4972)*

Computer Service Company .... E 951 738-1444
210 N Delilah St Corona (92879) *(P-6678)*

Computer Tech Resources Inc .... C 714 665-6507
16 Technology Dr Ste 202 Irvine (92618) *(P-14077)*

Computerized Mgt Svcs Inc .... D 805 522-5940
4100 Guardian St Ste 205 Simi Valley (93063) *(P-17713)*

Computerized Security Systems, Costa Mesa *Also Called: Winfield Locks Inc (P-4796)*

Computershare Inc .... C 800 522-6645
2335 Alaska Ave El Segundo (90245) *(P-12039)*

Computerworks Technologies, Burbank *Also Called: Global Service Resources Inc (P-13738)*

Computrition Inc (HQ)............................. D 818 961-3999
8521 Fallbrook Ave Ste 100 Canoga Park (91304) *(P-13692)*

Con-Tech Plastics, Brea *Also Called: Ramtec Associates Inc (P-4217)*

Conam Management Corporation (PA).......... C 858 614-7200
3990 Ruffin Rd Ste 100 San Diego (92123) *(P-12414)*

Conamco SA De CV .... D 760 586-4356
3008 Palm Hill Dr Vista (92084) *(P-8330)*

Concept Packaging Group, Ontario *Also Called: Southland Container Corp (P-2690)*

Concept Technology Inc .... B 949 851-6550
2941 W Macarthur Blvd Ste 136 Santa Ana (92704) *(P-17503)*

Concept Technology Inc (PA).................... D 949 854-7047
895 Dove St 3rd Fl Newport Beach (92660) *(P-17504)*

Concepts & Wood, Huntington Park *Also Called: Plycraft Industries Inc (P-2371)*

Concise Fabricators, San Diego *Also Called: Concise Fabricators Inc (P-4973)*

Concise Fabricators Inc .... E 520 746-3226
7550 Panasonic Way San Diego (92154) *(P-4973)*

CONCISYS .... E 858 292-5888
5452 Oberlin Dr San Diego (92121) *(P-7907)*

Conco Cement Co, Fontana *Also Called: Gonsalves & Santucci Inc (P-1117)*

Concord Document Services Inc (PA).......... E 213 745-3175
1407 W 11th St Los Angeles (90015) *(P-13311)*

Concord Foods Inc (HQ).......................... D 909 975-2000
300 Baldwin Park Blvd City Of Industry (91746) *(P-10748)*

Concorse Ht At Los Angles Arpr, Los Angeles *Also Called: Humnit Hotel At Lax LLC (P-12858)*

Concrete Construction, San Diego *Also Called: Ben F Smith Inc (P-1106)*

Concrete Holding Co Cal Inc .... A 818 788-4228
15821 Ventura Blvd Ste 475 Encino (91436) *(P-4436)*

Concrete Tie, Compton *Also Called: Concrete Tie Industries Inc (P-9942)*

Concrete Tie Industries Inc (PA)................ D 310 628-2328
130 E Oris St Compton (90222) *(P-9942)*

Concurrent Holdings LLC .... A 310 473-3065
11150 Santa Monica Blvd Ste 825 Los Angeles (90025) *(P-6371)*

Condon-Johnson & Assoc Inc .... D 858 530-9165
3434 Grove St Lemon Grove (91945) *(P-445)*

Condor, Baldwin Park *Also Called: Condor Outdoor Products Inc (P-8512)*

Condor Outdoor Products Inc (PA)............. E 626 358-3270
5268 Rivergrade Rd Baldwin Park (91706) *(P-8512)*

Condor Productions LLC .... D 310 449-3000
245 N Beverly Dr Beverly Hills (90210) *(P-14884)*

Conduit Lngage Specialists Inc .... D 859 299-3178
22720 Ventura Blvd Ste 100 Woodland Hills (91364) *(P-14476)*

Conesys Inc .... D 310 212-0065
548 Amapola Ave Torrance (90501) *(P-6944)*

Conexant Holdings Inc .... A 415 983-2706
4000 Macarthur Blvd Newport Beach (92660) *(P-6813)*

Conexant Systems LLC (HQ).................... E 949 483-4600
1901 Main St Ste 300 Irvine (92614) *(P-6814)*

Conexis Bnfits Admnstrators LP (HQ).......... C 714 835-5006
721 S Parker St Ste 300 Orange (92868) *(P-12196)*

Confab, Van Nuys *Also Called: Consolidated Fabricators Corp (P-4913)*

Confido LLC .... A 310 361-8558
1055 E Colorado Blvd Pasadena (91106) *(P-16381)*

Confie, Huntington Beach *Also Called: Confie Holding II Co (P-12197)*

Confie Holding II Co (PA)........................ C 714 252-2500
7711 Center Ave Ste 200 Huntington Beach (92647) *(P-12197)*

Confluent Medical Tech Inc .... C 949 448-7056
27752 El Lazo Laguna Niguel (92677) *(P-8135)*

Confluent Medical Tech Inc .... D 949 448-7056
27721 La Paz Rd Laguna Niguel (92677) *(P-8136)*

Congatec Inc .... E 858 457-2600
6262 Ferris Sq San Diego (92121) *(P-5910)*

Conglas, Bakersfield *Also Called: Consolidated Fibrgls Pdts Co (P-4491)*

Conleys Greenhouse Mfg & Sales, Montclair *Also Called: John L Conley Inc (P-5080)*

Connect Computers, Anaheim *Also Called: General Procurement Inc (P-10007)*

Connectec Company Inc (PA).................... D 949 252-1077
1701 Reynolds Ave Irvine (92614) *(P-6413)*

Connecticut Ctr Plastic Surg .... D 760 779-9595
73260 El Paseo Ste 2b Palm Desert (92260) *(P-11672)*

Connell Processing Inc (PA)..................... E 818 845-7661
3094 N Avon St Burbank (91504) *(P-5252)*

Connexity Inc (DH)................................ C 310 571-1235
2120 Colorado Ave Ste 400 Santa Monica (90404) *(P-9431)*

Conquer Nation Inc .... C 310 651-5555
2651 E 12th St Los Angeles (90023) *(P-2190)*

Conquer Nation Staffing, Los Angeles *Also Called: Conquer Nation Inc (P-2190)*

Conquest Industries Inc .... E 562 906-1111
12740 Lakeland Rd Santa Fe Springs (90670) *(P-10130)*

Conquistador International LLC .... D 424 249-9304
21200 Oxnard St Ste 492 Woodland Hills (91367) *(P-10619)*

Conrad Los Angeles, Los Angeles *Also Called: Core/Related Gala Retail LLC (P-12799)*

Consensus Cloud Solutions Inc (PA).......... D 323 860-9200
700 S Flower St Fl 15 Los Angeles (90017) *(P-13908)*

Conservation Corps Long Beach .... C 562 986-1249
340 Nieto Ave Long Beach (90814) *(P-17054)*

Conserve Construction, Westlake Village *Also Called: Sperber Ldscp Companies LLC (P-194)*

Conserve Landcare LLC .... D 760 343-1433
72265 Manufacturing Rd Thousand Palms (92276) *(P-163)*

Considine Cnsdine An Accntncy .... C 619 231-1977
8989 Rio San Diego Dr Ste 250 San Diego (92108) *(P-17714)*

Consoldted Fire Protection LLC (HQ).......... A 949 727-3277
153 Technology Dr Ste 200 Irvine (92618) *(P-14477)*

Consoldted Med Bo-Analysis Inc (PA)........ D 714 657-7369
10700 Walker St Cypress (90630) *(P-16309)*

Consoldted Precision Pdts Corp .... D 805 488-6451
705 Industrial Way Port Hueneme (93041) *(P-4668)*

Consoldted Precision Pdts Corp .... D 909 595-2252
4200 West Valley Blvd Pomona (91769) *(P-4669)*

Consolidated Aerospace Mfg LLC .... D 714 989-2802
630 E Lambert Rd Brea (92821) *(P-4763)*

Consolidated Aerospace Mfg LLC (HQ)....... E 714 989-2797
1425 S Acacia Ave Fullerton (92831) *(P-7709)*

Consolidated Color Corporation .... E 562 420-7714
12316 Carson St Hawaiian Gardens (90716) *(P-3710)*

Consolidated Design West Inc .... E 714 999-1476
1345 S Lewis St Anaheim (92805) *(P-13323)*

Consolidated Devices Inc (HQ)................. E 626 965-0668
19220 San Jose Ave City Of Industry (91748) *(P-11257)*

Consolidated Fabricators Corp (PA).......... C 800 635-8335
14620 Arminta St Van Nuys (91402) *(P-4913)*

Consolidated Fibrgls Pdts Co .... D 661 323-6026
3801 Standard St Bakersfield (93308) *(P-4491)*

Consolidated Foundries Inc .... C 323 773-2363
8333 Wilcox Ave Cudahy (90201) *(P-4670)*

Mergent email: customerrelations@mergent.com
988

2025 Southern California
Business Directory and Buyers Guide

(P-0000) Products & Services Section entry number
(PA)=Parent Co (HQ)=Headquarters (DH)=Div Headquarters

Consolidated Frt Systems LLC .... E 310 424-9924
24407 Shoshone Rd Apple Valley (92307) *(P-5526)*

Consolidated Graphics Inc .... C 323 460-4115
3550 Tyburn St Los Angeles (90065) *(P-3131)*

Consolidated Plastics Corp (PA) .... **E 909 393-8222**
14954 La Palma Dr Chino (91710) *(P-10996)*

Consolidated Svc Distrs Inc .... D 908 687-5800
777 S Central Ave Los Angeles (90021) *(P-10844)*

Constrction Instlltion Mint Gr, Anaheim Also Called: Kesa Incorporated *(P-14410)*

Construction, Gardena Also Called: Best Contracting Services Inc *(P-1073)*

Construction Protective Services Inc (PA) .... **A 800 257-5512**
436 W Walnut St Gardena (90248) *(P-14287)*

Construction Specialty Svc Inc .... D 661 864-7573
4550 Buck Owens Blvd Bakersfield (93308) *(P-669)*

Consumer Loan Dept, Tustin Also Called: Schoolsfirst Federal Credit Un *(P-11814)*

Consumer Resource Network LLC .... B 800 291-4794
4420 E Miraloma Ave Ste J Anaheim (92807) *(P-18120)*

Consumer Safety Analytics LLC .... D 818 922-2416
7027 Hayvenhurst Ave Van Nuys (91406) *(P-17910)*

Container Supply Company Incorporated .... C 714 892-8321
12571 Western Ave Garden Grove (92841) *(P-4720)*

Contemporary Services Corp (PA) .... **B 818 885-5150**
17101 Superior St Northridge (91325) *(P-14288)*

Contemporary Services Corp .... B 310 320-8418
369 Van Ness Way Ste 702 Torrance (90501) *(P-14388)*

Contessa Liquidating Co Inc C
222 W 6th St Fl 8 San Pedro (90731) *(P-10818)*

Contessa Premium Foods, Vernon Also Called: F I O Imports Inc *(P-1772)*

Contessa Premium Foods Inc .... C 310 832-8000
5980 Alcoa Ave Vernon (90058) *(P-10819)*

Continental Acrylics, Compton Also Called: Plaskolite West LLC *(P-3287)*

Continental Airlines, Los Angeles Also Called: United Airlines Inc *(P-9168)*

Continental Bdr Specialty Corp (PA) .... **C 310 324-8227**
407 W Compton Blvd Gardena (90248) *(P-3198)*

Continental Colorcraft, Monterey Park Also Called: Graphic Color Systems Inc *(P-3008)*

Continental Controls Corp .... E 858 453-9880
7710 Kenamar Ct San Diego (92121) *(P-7853)*

Continental Currency Svcs Inc (PA) .... **D 714 667-6699**
1108 E 17th St Santa Ana (92701) *(P-11838)*

Continental Data Graphics, Long Beach Also Called: Continental Graphics Corp *(P-2985)*

Continental Data Graphics, El Segundo Also Called: Continental Graphics Corp *(P-2986)*

Continental Data Graphics, Rancho Cucamonga Also Called: Continental Graphics Corp *(P-2989)*

Continental Data Graphics, Long Beach Also Called: Continental Graphics Corp *(P-13324)*

Continental Engineering Svcs, San Diego Also Called: Continental Graphics Corp *(P-2988)*

Continental Exch Solutions Inc .... D 562 345-2100
7001 Village Dr Ste 200 Buena Park (90621) *(P-14478)*

Continental Forge Company LLC .... D 310 603-1014
412 E El Segundo Blvd Compton (90222) *(P-5154)*

Continental Graphics Corp .... D 714 503-4200
4000 N Lakewood Blvd Long Beach (90000) *(P-2905)*

Continental Graphics Corp .... D 310 662-2307
222 N Pacific Coast Hwy Ste 300 El Segundo (90245) *(P-2986)*

Continental Graphics Corp .... D 714 827-1752
4060 N Lakewood Blvd Bldg 801 Long Beach (90808) *(P-2987)*

Continental Graphics Corp .... D 858 552-6520
6910 Carroll Rd San Diego (92121) *(P-2988)*

Continental Graphics Corp .... D 909 758-9800
9302 Pittsburgh Ave Ste 100 Rancho Cucamonga (91730) *(P-2989)*

Continental Graphics Corp (HQ) .... **C 714 503-4200**
4060 N Lakewood Blvd Bldg 801 Long Beach (90808) *(P-13324)*

Continental Heat Treating Inc .... D 562 944-8808
10643 Norwalk Blvd Santa Fe Springs (90670) *(P-4702)*

Continental Industries, Anaheim Also Called: International West Inc *(P-4992)*

Continental Maritime Inds Inc .... B 619 234-8851
1995 Bay Front St San Diego (92113) *(P-7599)*

Continental Vitamin Co Inc .... D 323 581-0176
4510 S Boyle Ave Vernon (90058) *(P-3388)*

Continental Data Graphics, Long Beach Also Called: Continental Graphics Corp *(P-2987)*

Continuous Computing Corp .... C 858 882-8800
10431 Wateridge Cir Ste 110 San Diego (92121) *(P-5843)*

Contra Costa Electric Inc .... C 661 322-4036
3208 Landco Dr Bakersfield (93308) *(P-903)*

Contract Furn & Ancillary Pdts, Commerce Also Called: 71yrs Inc *(P-6674)*

Contract Labeling Service Inc .... E 909 937-0344
13885 Ramona Ave Chino (91710) *(P-14479)*

Contract Resources, Commerce Also Called: Commercial Intr Resources Inc *(P-2443)*

Contract Services Group Inc .... C 714 582-1800
480 Capricorn St Brea (92821) *(P-13366)*

Contractor, Anaheim Also Called: Sunset Signs and Printing Inc *(P-8642)*

Contractors Cargo Company (PA) .... **D 310 609-1957**
7233 Alondra Blvd Paramount (90723) *(P-8938)*

Contractors Cargo Company, Paramount Also Called: CCC Property Holdings LLC *(P-12596)*

Contractors Flrg Svc Cal Inc .... C 714 556-6100
3403 W Macarthur Blvd Santa Ana (92704) *(P-9890)*

Contractors Rigging & Erectors, Paramount Also Called: Contractors Cargo Company *(P-8938)*

Contractors Wardrobe, Valencia Also Called: Contractors Wardrobe Inc *(P-2301)*

Contractors Wardrobe Inc (PA) .... **C 661 257-1177**
26121 Avenue Hall Valencia (91355) *(P-2301)*

Control Air Conditioning Corporation .... B 714 777-8600
5200 E La Palma Ave Anaheim (92807) *(P-765)*

Control Air Enterprises LLC .... B 760 744-2727
1390 Armorlite Dr San Marcos (92069) *(P-14725)*

Control Switches Intl Inc .... E 562 498-7331
2425 Mira Mar Ave Long Beach (90815) *(P-6344)*

Control Systems Intl Inc .... D 949 238-4150
35 Parker Irvine (92618) *(P-5507)*

Controlmyspa, San Diego Also Called: Balboa Water Group LLC *(P-6342)*

Convaid Products LLC .... D 310 618-0111
2830 California St Torrance (90503) *(P-10073)*

Convention Center, San Diego Also Called: San Dego Cnvntion Ctr Corp Inc *(P-14588)*

Converse Inc .... D 310 451-0314
1437 3rd Street Promenade 39 Santa Monica (90401) *(P-10735)*

Conversion Technology Co Inc (PA) .... **E 805 378-0033**
5360 N Commerce Ave Moorpark (93021) *(P-8558)*

Conversionpoint Holdings Inc .... D 888 706-6764
840 Newport Center Dr Ste 450 Newport Beach (92660) *(P-13909)*

Conveyor Concepts, Los Angeles Also Called: Machine Building Spc Inc *(P-5680)*

Conveyor Service & Electric .... E 562 777-1221
9550 Ann St Santa Fe Springs (90670) *(P-5516)*

Cook and Cook Incorporated .... E 714 680-6669
1000 E Elm Ave Fullerton (92831) *(P-4914)*

Cook King, La Mirada Also Called: Stainless Stl Fabricators Inc *(P-10406)*

Cookingcom Inc .... C 310 664-1283
1960 E Grand Ave Ste 60 El Segundo (90245) *(P-11529)*

Cooksey Tlen Gage Dffy Woog A (PA) .... **D 714 431-1100**
535 Anton Blvd Fl 10 Costa Mesa (92626) *(P-16659)*

Cool Curtain CCI, Costa Mesa Also Called: CCI Industries Inc *(P-4085)*

Cool Things, Santa Ana Also Called: Ecoolthing Corp *(P-5445)*

Cool-Pak LLC .... D 805 981-2434
401 N Rice Ave Oxnard (93030) *(P-4092)*

Coola LLC .... D 760 940-2125
6023 Innovation Way Ste 110 Carlsbad (92009) *(P-3639)*

Coola Suncare, Carlsbad Also Called: Coola LLC *(P-3639)*

Coolhaus, Culver City Also Called: Farchitecture Bb LLC *(P-1317)*

Cooljet Systems, Placentia Also Called: Mkt Innovations *(P-6182)*

Coolsys Coml Indus Sltions Inc (DH) .... **C 714 510-9609**
145 S State College Blvd Ste 200 Brea (92821) *(P-766)*

Coop, Irvine Also Called: Coop Home Goods LLC *(P-2208)*

Coop Home Goods LLC .... E 888 316-1886
9 Executive Cir Irvine (92614) *(P-2208)*

Cooper Crouse-Hinds LLC .... E 951 241-8766
3350 Enterprise Dr Bloomington (92316) *(P-7114)*

Cooper Interconnect, Bloomington Also Called: Cooper Crouse-Hinds LLC *(P-7114)*

Cooper Interconnect Inc .... D 617 389-7080
13039 Crossroads Pkwy S City Of Industry (91746) *(P-6985)*

Cooper Lighting, Bloomington Also Called: Cooper Lighting LLC *(P-6496)*

Cooper Lighting LLC .... D 760 357-4760
285 Rood Rd Ste 101 Calexico (92231) *(P-904)*

A L P H A B E T I C

Employee Codes: A=Over 500 employees, B=251-500
C=101-250, D=51-100, E=20-50, F=10-19, G=1-9

2025 Southern California
Business Directory and Buyers Guide

© Mergent Inc. 1-800-342-5647

989

Cooper Lighting LLC .... A 909 605-6615
  3350 Enterprise Dr Bloomington (92316) *(P-6496)*

Cooper Microelectronics Inc .... E 949 553-8352
  1671 Reynolds Ave Irvine (92614) *(P-6815)*

Coopertive Amrcn Physcians Inc (PA).......... D 213 473-8600
  333 S Hope St Fl 8 Los Angeles (90071) *(P-17297)*

Cop Communications, Montclair *Also Called: California Offset Printers Inc (P-2976)*

Cop Shopper, San Diego *Also Called: Krasnes Inc (P-2181)*

Copley Family YMCA, San Diego *Also Called: YMCA of San Diego County (P-17388)*

Copley Newspapers, La Jolla *Also Called: The Copley Press Inc (P-14427)*

Coppel, Calexico *Also Called: Coppel Corporation (P-9868)*

Coppel Corporation .... D 760 357-3707
  503 Scaroni Ave Calexico (92231) *(P-9868)*

Copper Clad Mltilayer Pdts Inc .... E 714 237-1388
  1150 N Hawk Cir Anaheim (92807) *(P-6720)*

Coppersmith Global Logistics, El Segundo *Also Called: L E Coppersmith Inc (P-9303)*

Copypage, Los Angeles *Also Called: CP Document Technologies LLC (P-10239)*

Cor Medica, Irvine *Also Called: Cor Medica Technology (P-15287)*

Cor Medica Technology .... E 949 353-4554
  188 Technology Dr Ste F Irvine (92618) *(P-15287)*

Corbell Products, Bloomington *Also Called: Westco Industries Inc (P-4880)*

Corbett Vineyards LLC .... E 805 782-9463
  2195 Corbett Canyon Rd Arroyo Grande (93420) *(P-1561)*

Cordelia Lighting Inc .... C 310 886-3490
  20101 S Santa Fe Ave Compton (90221) *(P-10177)*

Cordial .... D 619 501-5548
  402 W Broadway Ste 700 San Diego (92101) *(P-13693)*

Cordial Experience Inc .... D 619 793-9787
  402 W Broadway Ste 700 San Diego (92101) *(P-13694)*

Cordova Industries, Sylmar *Also Called: International Academy of Fin (P-3734)*

CORE, Los Angeles *Also Called: Core Cmnty Orgnzed Rlief Effor (P-16901)*

Core Bts Inc .... C 818 766-2400
  5250 Lankershim Blvd Ste 620 North Hollywood (91601) *(P-14078)*

Core Cmnty Orgnzed Rlief Effor .... B 323 934-4400
  910 N Hill St Los Angeles (90012) *(P-16901)*

Core Holdings Inc .... C 714 969-2342
  17291 Irvine Blvd Ste 404 Tustin (92780) *(P-16382)*

Core Med Staff .... D 213 382-5550
  3946 Wilshire Blvd Los Angeles (90010) *(P-15288)*

Core Realty Holdings MGT Inc .... D 949 863-1031
  1600 Dove St Ste 450 Newport Beach (92660) *(P-12415)*

Core Systems, Poway *Also Called: Rugged Systems Inc (P-5866)*

Core-Mark International Inc .... C 323 583-6531
  2311 E 48th St Vernon (90058) *(P-10940)*

Core-Mark International Inc .... C 661 366-2673
  200 Coremark Ct Bakersfield (93307) *(P-10941)*

Core/Related Gala Retail LLC .... D 213 349-8585
  100 S Grand Ave Los Angeles (90012) *(P-12799)*

Corecare I I I .... C 714 256-8000
  800 Morningside Dr Fullerton (92835) *(P-17135)*

Coredux USA LLC .... D 858 642-0713
  6721 Cobra Way San Diego (92121) *(P-6109)*

Corelation Inc .... C 619 876-5074
  2305 Historic Decatur Rd Ste 300 San Diego (92106) *(P-13695)*

Corelis Inc .... E 562 926-6727
  13100 Alondra Blvd Ste 102 Cerritos (90703) *(P-6986)*

Corelogic Credco, Irvine *Also Called: Corelogic Credco LLC (P-13293)*

Corelogic Credco LLC (DH)......................... C 800 255-0792
  40 Pacifica Ste 900 Irvine (92618) *(P-13293)*

Corelogic Credco LLC .... B 619 938-7028
  2385 Northside Dr San Diego (92108) *(P-13294)*

Corelogic Dorado, Irvine *Also Called: Dorado Network Systems Corp (P-13917)*

Coresite LLC .... C 213 327-1231
  624 S Grand Ave Ste 1800 Los Angeles (90023) *(P-12684)*

Coreslab Structures La Inc .... C 951 943-9119
  150 W Placentia Ave Perris (92571) *(P-4384)*

Corkys Pest Control Inc .... D 760 432-8801
  150 Vallecitos De Oro San Marcos (92069) *(P-13345)*

Corn Maiden Foods Inc .... D 310 784-0400
  24201 Frampton Ave Harbor City (90710) *(P-1339)*

Cornerstone, Valencia *Also Called: Cornerstone Display Group Inc (P-8595)*

Cornerstone, Santa Monica *Also Called: Cornerstone Ondemand Inc (P-13910)*

Cornerstone Concrete Inc .... D 951 279-2221
  255 Benjamin Dr Corona (92879) *(P-1112)*

Cornerstone Display Group Inc .... E 661 705-1700
  28340 Avenue Crocker Valencia (91355) *(P-8595)*

Cornerstone Ondemand Inc (HQ).................. C 310 752-0200
  1601 Cloverfield Blvd Ste 620s Santa Monica (90404) *(P-13910)*

Cornerstone Protective Svcs .... C 888 848-4791
  1327 Crenshaw Blvd Torrance (90501) *(P-14289)*

Cornerstone Research Inc .... D 213 553-2500
  555 W 5th St Ste 3800 Los Angeles (90013) *(P-17842)*

Cornerstone Southern Cal .... D 714 998-3574
  1950 E 17th St Ste 150 Santa Ana (92705) *(P-16289)*

Corningware Corelle & More, Riverside *Also Called: Snapware Corporation (P-4242)*

Cornucopia Tool & Plastics Inc .... E 805 238-7660
  448 Sherwood Rd Paso Robles (93446) *(P-4093)*

Coromega Company Inc .... E 760 599-6088
  2525 Commerce Way Vista (92081) *(P-11304)*

Coron-Rnge Fods Intrmdate Hldn, Fullerton *Also Called: Vanlaw Food Products Inc (P-1373)*

Corona - Cllege Hts Ornge Lmon .... B 951 359-6451
  8000 Lincoln Ave Riverside (92504) *(P-106)*

Corona Clipper Inc .... D 800 847-7863
  22440 Temescal Canyon Rd Ste 102 Corona (92883) *(P-10304)*

Corona Magnetics Inc .... C 951 735-7558
  201 Corporate Terrace St Corona (92879) *(P-6927)*

Corona Millworks Company (PA)..................... D 909 606-3288
  5572 Edison Ave Chino (91710) *(P-2345)*

Corona Regional Med Ctr Hosp, Corona *Also Called: Uhs-Corona Inc (P-16238)*

Corona Regional Med Ctr LLC .... C 951 737-4343
  800 S Main St Corona (92882) *(P-15289)*

Corona Rgnal Med Ctr Rhbltion, Corona *Also Called: Uhs-Corona Inc (P-16514)*

Corona Tools, Corona *Also Called: Corona Clipper Inc (P-10304)*

Coronado Brewing Company Inc (PA)............. E 619 437-4452
  170 Orange Ave Coronado (92118) *(P-11613)*

Coronado Hospital, Coronado *Also Called: Sharp Coronado Hospital & Healthcare Center (P-16192)*

Coronado Manufacturing LLC .... E 818 768-5010
  8991 Glenoaks Blvd Sun Valley (91352) *(P-7456)*

Coronado Stone Products, Perris *Also Called: Creative Stone Mfg Inc (P-4385)*

Coronet Lighting, Beverly Hills *Also Called: Dasol Inc (P-6403)*

Corovan Corporation (PA).............................. C 858 762-8100
  12302 Kerran St Poway (92064) *(P-8989)*

Corovan Moving & Storage Co (HQ)............... D 858 748-1100
  12302 Kerran St Poway (92064) *(P-8990)*

Corp., R.g Barry, Fontana *Also Called: DSV Solutions LLC (P-9273)*

Corpinfo Services, Santa Monica *Also Called: K-Micro Inc (P-10013)*

Corporate Alnce Strategies Inc .... C 877 777-7487
  3410 La Sierra Ave Ste F244 Riverside (92503) *(P-14389)*

Corporate Graphics Intl Inc .... D 323 826-3440
  4909 Alcoa Ave Vernon (90058) *(P-2990)*

Corporate Graphics West, Vernon *Also Called: Corporate Graphics Intl Inc (P-2990)*

Corporate Impressions La Inc .... E 818 761-9295
  10742 Burbank Blvd North Hollywood (91601) *(P-3132)*

Corporate Real Estate Advisors, San Diego *Also Called: Cushman & Wakefield Cal Inc (P-12424)*

Corptax LLC .... C 818 316-2400
  21550 Oxnard St Ste 700 Woodland Hills (91367) *(P-13696)*

Correctivesolutions, Mission Viejo *Also Called: American Justice Solutions Inc (P-16850)*

Corridor Capital LLC (PA).............................. C 310 442-7000
  12400 Wilshire Blvd Ste 645 Los Angeles (90025) *(P-12703)*

Corrpro Companies Inc .... E 562 944-1636
  23309 La Palma Ave Yorba Linda (92887) *(P-4574)*

Corru Kraft Buena Pk Div 5058, Buena Park *Also Called: Orora Packaging Solutions (P-10597)*

Corrugados De Baja California .... A 619 662-8672
  2475 Paseo De Las A San Diego (92154) *(P-2661)*

Corsair Elec Connectors Inc .... C 949 833-0273
  17100 Murphy Ave Irvine (92614) *(P-6945)*

Cortica Healthcare Inc .... D 858 304-6440
  7090 Miratech Dr San Diego (92121) *(P-16550)*

Corvel, Orange *Also Called: Corvel Corporation (P-17970)*

Corvel Corporation .... C 503 222-3144
1920 Main St Ste 900 Irvine (92614) *(P-17969)*

Corvel Corporation .... C 714 385-8500
1100 W Town And Country Rd Ste 400 Orange (92868) *(P-17970)*

Corwin Press Inc .... E 805 499-9734
2455 Teller Rd Newbury Park (91320) *(P-2909)*

Cosco Fire Protection Inc .... D 858 444-2000
4990 Greencraig Ln San Diego (92123) *(P-767)*

Cosco Home & Office Products, Ontario *Also Called: Dorel Juvenile Group Inc (P-4108)*

Cosmedx Science Inc .... E 951 371-0509
3550 Vine St Ste 210 Riverside (92507) *(P-3389)*

Cosmetic Group Usa Inc .... C 818 767-2889
12708 Branford St Pacoima (91331) *(P-3640)*

Cosmetic Laboratories America, Chatsworth *Also Called: Cosmetic Laboratories of America LLC (P-11679)*

Cosmetic Laboratories of America LLC .... B 818 717-6140
20245 Sunburst St Chatsworth (91311) *(P-11679)*

Cosmetic Laboratories-America, Chatsworth *Also Called: Kdc/One Chatsworth Inc (P-3663)*

Cosmetic Technologies LLC .... D 805 376-9960
2585 Azurite Cir Newbury Park (91320) *(P-3641)*

Cosmo Fiber Corporation (PA) .... **E 626 256-6098**
1802 Santo Domingo Ave Duarte (91010) *(P-3133)*

Cosmo International Corp .... D 310 271-1100
9200 W Sunset Blvd Ste 401 West Hollywood (90069) *(P-3642)*

Cosmo International Fragrances, West Hollywood *Also Called: Cosmo International Corp (P-3642)*

Cosmodyne LLC .... E 562 795-5990
3010 Old Ranch Pkwy Ste 300 Seal Beach (90740) *(P-5696)*

Cosmos Food Co Inc .... E 323 221-9142
17501 Mondino Dr Rowland Heights (91748) *(P-1757)*

Cosrich Group Inc .... E 818 686-2500
12243 Branford St Sun Valley (91352) *(P-3643)*

COSTA COFFEE, Carlsbad *Also Called: La Costa Coffee Roasting Co (P-11306)*

Costa Del Sol Healthcare, Los Angeles *Also Called: East Los Angles Healthcare LLC (P-15624)*

Costa Mesa Country Club, Costa Mesa *Also Called: Mesa Verde Partners (P-15092)*

Costco, Montebello *Also Called: Costco Wholesale Corporation (P-11270)*

Costco Auto Program, San Diego *Also Called: Affinity Auto Programs Inc (P-14437)*

Costco Wholesale Corporation .... A 951 361-3606
11600 Riverside Dr Ste A Jurupa Valley (91752) *(P-9055)*

Costco Wholesale Corporation .... C 323 890-1904
1345 N Montebello Blvd Montebello (90640) *(P-11270)*

Cottage Childrens Medical Ctr, Santa Barbara *Also Called: Santa Brbara Cttage Hosp Fndti (P-16175)*

Cottage Health .... C 805 688-6432
2050 Viborg Rd Solvang (93463) *(P-15966)*

Cottage Health System, Santa Barbara *Also Called: Goleta Valley Cottage Hosp Aux (P-16008)*

Cotterman Company, Bakersfield *Also Called: Material Control Inc (P-5452)*

Cotton Heritage, Commerce *Also Called: Roochi Traders Incorporated (P-10694)*

Cotton Links LLC .... E 714 444-4700
2990 Grace Ln Costa Mesa (92626) *(P-1981)*

Cottrell Paul Enterprises LLC (PA) .... **C 661 212-2357**
16654 Soledad Canyon Rd Ste 233 Santa Clarita (91387) *(P-14290)*

Cougar Biotechnology Inc .... D 310 943-8040
10990 Wilshire Blvd Ste 1200 Los Angeles (90024) *(P-3390)*

Council On Aging - Sthern Cal .... D 714 479-0107
2 Executive Cir Ste 175 Irvine (92614) *(P-16902)*

Counseling and Research Assoc (PA) .... **C 310 715-2020**
108 W Victoria St Gardena (90248) *(P-17136)*

Country Archer Jerky, San Bernardino *Also Called: S&E Gourmet Cuts Inc (P-10850)*

Country Club Fashions Inc .... E 323 965-2707
6083 W Pico Blvd Los Angeles (90035) *(P-11491)*

Country Floral Supply Inc (PA) .... **D 805 520-8026**
3802 Weatherly Cir Westlake Village (91361) *(P-11085)*

Country Furnishings, Westlake Village *Also Called: Country Floral Supply Inc (P-11085)*

Country Hills Health Care Inc .... C 619 441-8745
1580 Broadway El Cajon (92021) *(P-15603)*

Country Hills Post Acute, El Cajon *Also Called: Country Hills Health Care Inc (P-15603)*

Country Oaks Care Center Inc .... D 805 922-6657
830 E Chapel St Santa Maria (93454) *(P-15604)*

Country Villa E Convalescent, Los Angeles *Also Called: Country Villa Service Corp (P-17972)*

Country Villa Health Services, Anaheim *Also Called: Country Villa Service Corp (P-17971)*

Country Villa Nursing Ctr Inc .... C 213 484-9730
340 S Alvarado St Los Angeles (90001) *(P-15605)*

Country Villa Service Corp .... C 760 340-0053
39950 Vista Del Sol Rancho Mirage (92270) *(P-14480)*

Country Villa Service Corp .... C 626 445-2421
400 W Huntington Dr Arcadia (91007) *(P-15606)*

Country Villa Service Corp .... C 310 537-2500
3611 E Imperial Hwy Lynwood (90262) *(P-15607)*

Country Villa Service Corp .... C 818 246-5516
1208 S Central Ave Glendale (91204) *(P-15608)*

Country Villa Service Corp .... C 626 285-2165
112 E Broadway San Gabriel (91776) *(P-15844)*

Country Villa Service Corp .... C 562 598-2477
3000 N Gate Rd Seal Beach (90740) *(P-16903)*

Country Villa Service Corp (PA) .... **D 310 574-3733**
2400 E Katella Ave Ste 800 Anaheim (92806) *(P-17971)*

Country Villa Service Corp .... C 323 734-1101
2415 S Western Ave Los Angeles (90018) *(P-17972)*

Country Villa Service Corp .... C 323 734-9122
3233 W Pico Blvd Los Angeles (90019) *(P-17973)*

Country Villa Service Corp .... C 323 666-1544
3002 Rowena Ave Los Angeles (90039) *(P-17974)*

Country Villa Service Corp .... C 562 597-8817
1730 Grand Ave Long Beach (90804) *(P-17975)*

Country Villa Service Corp .... C 626 358-4547
615 W Duarte Rd Monrovia (91016) *(P-17976)*

Country Villa Terrace (PA) .... **D 323 653-3980**
6050 W Pico Blvd Los Angeles (90035) *(P-15845)*

Country Vlla Convalescent Hosp, Los Angeles *Also Called: Country Villa Terrace (P-15845)*

Country Vlla Mar Vsta Nrsing C, Los Angeles *Also Called: Rrt Enterprises LP (P-15767)*

Country Vlla Nrsing Rhblttion, Los Angeles *Also Called: Country Villa Nursing Ctr Inc (P-15605)*

Country Vlla Rncho Mrage Hlthc .... C 760 340-0053
39950 Vista Del Sol Rancho Mirage (92270) *(P-16904)*

Countrywide, Glendale *Also Called: Countrywide Home Loans Inc (P-11894)*

Countrywide, Westlake Village *Also Called: Countrywide Home Loans Inc (P-11895)*

Countrywide Home Loans Inc .... A 818 550-8700
801 N Brand Blvd Ste 750 Glendale (91203) *(P-11894)*

Countrywide Home Loans Inc (HQ) .... **A**
31303 Agoura Rd Westlake Village (91361) *(P-11895)*

County Clothing Company, Irvine *Also Called: Snowmass Apparel Inc (P-10728)*

County Ford North Inc (PA) .... **C 760 945-9900**
450 W Vista Way Vista (92083) *(P-11328)*

County General Hospital, San Luis Obispo *Also Called: County of San Luis Obispo (P-15972)*

County Los Angles Prbtion Dept, Pomona *Also Called: County of Los Angeles (P-16918)*

County of Imperial .... D 760 482-4120
202 N 8th St El Centro (92243) *(P-16459)*

County of Imperial .... D 760 482-4441
935 Broadway Ave El Centro (92243) *(P-16551)*

County of Kern .... A 661 326-2054
1700 Mount Vernon Ave Bakersfield (93306) *(P-15967)*

County of Kern .... D 661 336-6871
1600 E Belle Ter Ste 5 Bakersfield (93307) *(P-18397)*

County of Los Angeles .... E 626 968-3312
14959 Proctor Ave La Puente (91746) *(P-5490)*

County of Los Angeles .... E 310 456-8014
3637 Winter Canyon Rd Malibu (90265) *(P-5491)*

County of Los Angeles .... C 562 945-2581
9402 Greenleaf Ave Whittier (90605) *(P-8867)*

County of Los Angeles .... D 626 458-1707
1537 Alcazar St Los Angeles (90033) *(P-9056)*

County of Los Angeles .... D 213 367-3176
6801 E 2nd St Long Beach (90803) *(P-9687)*

County of Los Angeles .... B 626 458-4000
900 S Fremont Ave Alhambra (91803) *(P-9688)*

County of Los Angeles .... D 626 299-5300
1000 S Fremont Ave Unit 4 Alhambra (91803) *(P-12078)*

A L P H A B E T I C

County of Los Angeles .... D 562 985-4687
6300 E State University Dr Ste 104 Long Beach (90815) *(P-12651)*

County of Los Angeles .... D 818 340-2633
7326 Jordan Ave Canoga Park (91303) *(P-13101)*

County of Los Angeles .... B 213 922-6210
1 Gateway Plz Los Angeles (90012) *(P-13325)*

County of Los Angeles .... A 562 940-4324
1100 N Eastern Ave Los Angeles (90063) *(P-13697)*

County of Los Angeles .... D 562 462-2094
12400 Imperial Hwy Norwalk (90650) *(P-14127)*

County of Los Angeles .... C 213 974-0515
320 W Temple St Fl 9 Los Angeles (90012) *(P-14167)*

County of Los Angeles .... D 323 267-2771
1100 N Eastern Ave Los Angeles (90063) *(P-14481)*

County of Los Angeles .... C 909 231-0549
1875 Fairplex Dr Pomona (91768) *(P-15074)*

County of Los Angeles .... D 213 744-3919
2829 S Grand Ave Los Angeles (90007) *(P-15290)*

County of Los Angeles .... D 626 968-3711
15930 Central Ave Ste 100 La Puente (91744) *(P-15291)*

County of Los Angeles .... D 562 804-8111
10005 Flower St Bellflower (90706) *(P-15292)*

County of Los Angeles .... A 323 226-7131
1900 Zonal Ave Los Angeles (90033) *(P-15293)*

County of Los Angeles .... C 323 226-6021
1100 N Mission Rd Rm 236 Los Angeles (90033) *(P-15968)*

County of Los Angeles .... D 213 473-6100
450 Bauchet St Los Angeles (90012) *(P-15969)*

County of Los Angeles .... C 310 222-2401
1000 W Carson St 8th Fl Palos Verdes Peninsu (90274) *(P-15970)*

County of Los Angeles .... C 310 668-4545
12025 Wilmington Ave Los Angeles (90059) *(P-15971)*

County of Los Angeles .... C 661 223-8700
30500 Arrastre Canyon Rd Acton (93510) *(P-16290)*

County of Los Angeles .... C 323 226-3468
1240 N Mission Rd Los Angeles (90033) *(P-16291)*

County of Los Angeles .... D 213 974-7284
515 E 6th St Los Angeles (90021) *(P-16292)*

County of Los Angeles .... C 661 223-8700
38200 Lake Hughes Rd Castaic (91384) *(P-16293)*

County of Los Angeles .... D 562 402-0688
17707 Studebaker Rd Artesia (90703) *(P-16460)*

County of Los Angeles .... D 323 769-7800
5205 Melrose Ave Los Angeles (90038) *(P-16461)*

County of Los Angeles .... B 562 401-7088
7601 Imperial Hwy Downey (90242) *(P-16462)*

County of Los Angeles .... B 323 897-6187
5850 S Main St Los Angeles (90003) *(P-16463)*

County of Los Angeles .... D 562 861-0316
5525 Imperial Hwy South Gate (90280) *(P-16552)*

County of Los Angeles .... D 213 974-2811
210 W Temple St Fl 19 Los Angeles (90012) *(P-16660)*

County of Los Angeles .... C 213 974-3812
210 W Temple St Rm 18-1144 Los Angeles (90012) *(P-16661)*

County of Los Angeles .... D 805 237-3110
530 12th St 1st Fl Paso Robles (93446) *(P-16905)*

County of Los Angeles .... D 626 356-5281
300 E Walnut St Dept 200 Pasadena (91101) *(P-16906)*

County of Los Angeles .... D 213 974-9331
320 W Temple St Ste 1101 Los Angeles (90012) *(P-16907)*

County of Los Angeles .... D 562 908-3119
8240 Broadway Ave Whittier (90606) *(P-16908)*

County of Los Angeles .... D 323 226-8511
1601 Eastlake Ave Los Angeles (90033) *(P-16909)*

County of Los Angeles .... D 213 351-5600
510 S Vermont Ave Fl 1 Los Angeles (90020) *(P-16910)*

County of Los Angeles .... D 661 940-4181
5300 W Avenue I Lancaster (93536) *(P-16911)*

County of Los Angeles .... C 323 889-3405
5770 S Eastern Ave 4th Fl Commerce (90040) *(P-16912)*

County of Los Angeles .... D 562 903-5000
10355 Slusher Dr Santa Fe Springs (90670) *(P-16913)*

County of Los Angeles .... D 562 497-3500
4060 Watson Plaza Dr Lakewood (90712) *(P-16914)*

County of Los Angeles .... D 661 948-2320
777 W Jackman St Lancaster (93534) *(P-16915)*

County of Los Angeles .... D 562 940-2470
9150 Imperial Hwy Downey (90242) *(P-16916)*

County of Los Angeles .... D 562 940-6856
7285 Quill Dr Downey (90242) *(P-16917)*

County of Los Angeles .... D 909 469-4500
1660 W Mission Blvd Pomona (91766) *(P-16918)*

County of Los Angeles .... D 310 266-3711
1725 Main St Rm 125 Santa Monica (90401) *(P-16919)*

County of Los Angeles .... D 818 374-2000
14414 Delano St Van Nuys (91401) *(P-16920)*

County of Los Angeles .... C 323 780-2185
4849 Civic Center Way Los Angeles (90022) *(P-16921)*

County of Los Angeles .... D 213 351-7257
501 Shatto Pl Ste 301 Los Angeles (90020) *(P-16922)*

County of Los Angeles .... D 323 586-6469
8526 Grape St Los Angeles (90001) *(P-16923)*

County of Los Angeles .... D 310 603-7311
200 W Compton Blvd Ste 300 Compton (90220) *(P-16924)*

County of Los Angeles .... D 626 356-5281
199 N Euclid Ave Pasadena (91101) *(P-16925)*

County of Los Angeles .... D 626 308-5542
200 W Woodward Ave Alhambra (91801) *(P-16926)*

County of Los Angeles .... C 909 599-2391
1900 Sycamore Canyon Rd San Dimas (91773) *(P-16927)*

County of Los Angeles .... D 323 226-8611
1605 Eastlake Ave Los Angeles (90033) *(P-17137)*

County of Los Angeles .... D 818 364-2011
16350 Filbert St Sylmar (91342) *(P-17138)*

County of Los Angeles .... D 626 291-2200
9668 Valley Blvd Ste 104 Rosemead (91770) *(P-17223)*

County of Los Angeles .... C 213 240-8412
313 N Figueroa St 9th Fl Los Angeles (90012) *(P-17298)*

County of Los Angeles .... C 661 723-6088
44933 Fern Ave Lancaster (93534) *(P-17505)*

County of Los Angeles .... D 626 337-1277
14747 Ramona Blvd Baldwin Park (91706) *(P-17506)*

County of Los Angeles .... A 323 267-2136
1100 N Eastern Ave Los Angeles (90063) *(P-17715)*

County of Los Angeles .... C 323 267-6167
1800 Paseo Rancho Castilla Los Angeles (90032) *(P-17911)*

County of Los Angeles .... C 562 940-2907
9150 Imperial Hwy Downey (90242) *(P-17977)*

County of Los Angeles .... D 661 974-7700
42011 4th St W Ste 3530 Lancaster (93534) *(P-18390)*

County of Los Angeles .... D 213 738-4601
510 S Vermont Ave Fl 1 Los Angeles (90020) *(P-18392)*

County of Orange .... C 949 252-5006
3160 Airway Ave Costa Mesa (92626) *(P-9198)*

County of Orange .... D 714 647-1552
1631 E Wilshire Ave Santa Ana (92705) *(P-13434)*

County of Orange .... D 714 834-6021
405 W 5th St Ofc Santa Ana (92701) *(P-15809)*

County of Orange .... E 714 567-7444
1300 S Grand Ave Ste B Santa Ana (92705) *(P-18387)*

County of Riverside .... D 951 955-4800
3450 14th St Riverside (92501) *(P-396)*

County of Riverside .... C 951 955-0840
5256 Mission Blvd Riverside (92509) *(P-15294)*

County of Riverside .... A 951 486-4000
26520 Cactus Ave Moreno Valley (92555) *(P-15295)*

County of Riverside .... A 951 486-4000
26520 Cactus Ave Moreno Valley (92555) *(P-15296)*

County of Riverside .... C 951 955-6000
4075 Main St Riverside (92501) *(P-16662)*

County of Riverside .... D 951 955-4900
2038 Iowa Ave Ste 102 Riverside (92507) *(P-16928)*

County of Riverside .... D 951 955-3434
1325 Spruce St Ste 400 Riverside (92507) *(P-17055)*

County of Riverside .... C 951 683-7691
4500 Glenwood Dr Ste A Riverside (92501) *(P-17338)*

County of Riverside .... D 951 248-0014
585 Technology Ct Riverside (92507) *(P-18393)*

County of Riverside .... C 951 358-5000
4065 County Circle Dr Riverside (92503) *(P-18398)*

County of San Diego .... C 858 694-2960
5510 Overland Ave Ste 410 San Diego (92123) *(P-14482)*

County of San Diego .... D 619 956-2800
9065 Edgemoor Dr Santee (92071) *(P-15609)*

County of San Diego .... B 619 692-8200
3853 Rosecrans St San Diego (92110) *(P-16273)*

County of San Diego .... D 619 531-4040
330 W Broadway Ste 1020 San Diego (92101) *(P-16663)*

County of San Diego .... B 619 515-8202
330 W Broadway Ste 1100 San Diego (92101) *(P-16929)*

County of San Diego .... C 619 338-2558
1255 Imperial Ave Ste 433 San Diego (92101) *(P-17139)*

County of San Diego .... D 858 505-6100
5560 Overland Ave Ste 410 San Diego (92123) *(P-18388)*

County of San Luis Obispo .... C 805 781-4753
2180 Johnson Ave San Luis Obispo (93401) *(P-15972)*

County of Ventura .... C 805 654-2561
800 S Victoria Ave Ventura (93009) *(P-16930)*

County of Ventura .... D 805 652-6000
3291 Loma Vista Rd Ventura (93003) *(P-16931)*

County Plastics Corp .... E 310 635-5400
135 E Stanley St Compton (90220) *(P-4094)*

County Rvrside Wrkfrce Dev Div, Riverside *Also Called: County of Riverside (P-17055)*

County Ventura Human Resources, Ventura *Also Called: County of Ventura (P-16930)*

County Whl Elc Co Los Angeles .... D 714 633-3801
560 N Main St Orange (92868) *(P-10178)*

Countywide Mech Systems LLC .... C 619 449-9900
1400 N Johnson Ave Ste 114 El Cajon (92020) *(P-768)*

Courtesy Chevrolet Center .... C 619 297-4321
750 Camino Del Rio N San Diego (92108) *(P-11329)*

Courtney Inc (PA)..................................... **D 949 222-2050**
16781 Millikan Ave Irvine (92606) *(P-1199)*

Courtside Cellars LLC (PA)........................... **E 805 782-0500**
4910 Edna Rd San Luis Obispo (93401) *(P-1562)*

Courtyard By Marriott, Baldwin Park *Also Called: Baldwin Hospitality LLC (P-12766)*

Courtyard By Marriott Irvine, Irvine *Also Called: Courtyard Management Corp (P-12800)*

Courtyard By Mrrott Los Angles, Monrovia *Also Called: Sage Hospitality Resources LLC (P-13007)*

Courtyard Management Corp .... D 949 453-1033
7955 Irvine Center Dr Irvine (92618) *(P-12800)*

Courtyard Marriott Mission Vly, San Diego *Also Called: Mbp Land LLC (P-12920)*

Courtyard Oxnard .... D 805 988-3600
600 E Esplanade Dr Oxnard (93036) *(P-12801)*

Courtyard San Dego Mssion Vlly, San Diego *Also Called: Mhf Mv Operating VI LLC (P-12924)*

Couts Heating & Cooling Inc .... C 951 278-5560
1693 Rimpau Ave Corona (92881) *(P-769)*

Covalent Cbd, San Diego *Also Called: Green Star Labs Inc (P-3317)*

Covanta Long Bch Rnwble Enrgy .... D 562 436-0636
118 Pier S Ave Long Beach (90802) *(P-9739)*

Covario Inc .... D 858 397-1500
9255 Towne Centre Dr Ste 600 San Diego (92121) *(P-18121)*

Cove Bar and Grill, The, Carlsbad *Also Called: Grand Pacific Resorts Inc (P-12458)*

Covenant Care California LLC .... D 714 554-9700
1929 N Fairview St Santa Ana (92706) *(P-15610)*

Covenant Care California LLC .... D 323 589-5941
6425 Miles Ave Huntington Park (90255) *(P-15611)*

Covenant Care California LLC .... D 562 427-7493
2725 Pacific Ave Long Beach (90806) *(P-15612)*

Covenant Care California LLC .... D 805 488-3696
5225 S J St Oxnard (93033) *(P-15613)*

Covenant Care California LLC .... D 805 964-4871
160 S Patterson Ave Santa Barbara (93111) *(P-15614)*

Covenant Care La Jolla LLC .... C 858 453-5810
2552 Torrey Pines Rd Ste 1 La Jolla (92037) *(P-15615)*

Covenant Care LLC (PA)............................. **B 949 349-1200**
120 Vantis Dr Ste 200 Aliso Viejo (92656) *(P-15616)*

Covenant House California .... C 323 461-3131
1325 N Western Ave Hollywood (90027) *(P-17140)*

Covenant Living At Mt Miguel, Spring Valley *Also Called: Covenant Living West (P-17141)*

Covenant Living At Samarkand, Santa Barbara *Also Called: Covenant Living West (P-17142)*

Covenant Living West .... D 619 931-1114
325 Kempton St Spring Valley (91977) *(P-17141)*

Covenant Living West .... D 805 687-0701
2550 Treasure Dr Santa Barbara (93105) *(P-17142)*

COVENANT RETIREMENT COMMUNITIES, Santa Barbara *Also Called: Covenant Rtirement Communities (P-15617)*

Covenant Rtirement Communities .... D 805 687-0701
2550 Treasure Dr Santa Barbara (93105) *(P-15617)*

Covenant Transport, Pomona *Also Called: Covenant Transport Inc (P-8939)*

Covenant Transport Inc .... A 909 469-0130
1300 E Franklin Ave Pomona (91766) *(P-8939)*

Coventry Court Health Center .... C 714 636-2800
2040 S Euclid St Anaheim (92802) *(P-15618)*

Coverking, Anaheim *Also Called: Shrin LLC (P-9848)*

Covid Clinic, Huntington Beach *Also Called: Rume Medical Group Inc (P-15440)*

Covidien Holding Inc .... C 760 603-5020
2101 Faraday Ave Carlsbad (92008) *(P-8137)*

Covidien Holding Inc .... C 619 690-8500
2475 Paseo De Las Americas Ste A San Diego (92154) *(P-8138)*

Covidien Kenmex, San Diego *Also Called: Covidien Holding Inc (P-8138)*

Covidien LP .... C 949 837-3700
9775 Toledo Way Irvine (92618) *(P-8139)*

Covina Rehabilitation Center .... C 626 967-3874
261 W Badillo St Covina (91723) *(P-15619)*

Covina Service Center, San Dimas *Also Called: Southern California Edison Co (P-9631)*

Covington & Burling LLP .... C 424 332-4800
1999 Avenue Of The Stars Ste 3500 Los Angeles (90067) *(P-16664)*

Coway Usa Inc .... E 213 486-1600
4221 Wilshire Blvd Ste 210 Los Angeles (90010) *(P-11680)*

Cowboy Direct Response .... E 714 824-3780
130 E Alton Ave Santa Ana (92707) *(P-8596)*

Cowelco .... E 562 432-5766
1634 W 14th St Long Beach (90813) *(P-4974)*

Cowelco Steel Contractors, Long Beach *Also Called: Cowelco (P-4974)*

Cox Castle & Nicholson LLP (PA).................... **C 310 284-2200**
2029 Century Park E Ste 2100 Los Angeles (90067) *(P-16665)*

Cox Castle, Los Angeles *Also Called: Cox Castle & Nicholson LLP (P-16665)*

Cox Communications, San Diego *Also Called: Cox Communications Inc (P-9537)*

Cox Communications, El Cajon *Also Called: Cox Communications Inc (P-9538)*

Cox Communications, Foothill Ranch *Also Called: Cox Communications Inc (P-9539)*

Cox Communications Inc .... B 858 715-4500
1535 Euclid Ave San Diego (92105) *(P-9537)*

Cox Communications Inc .... D 619 592-4011
1985 Gillespie Way El Cajon (92020) *(P-9538)*

Cox Communications Inc .... A 949 216-9765
20 Icon Foothill Ranch (92610) *(P-9539)*

Cox Communications Cal LLC .... B 619 262-1122
5159 Federal Blvd San Diego (92105) *(P-9540)*

Cox Enterprises LLC .... D 858 822-8587
325 W 3rd Ave Ste 101 Escondido (92025) *(P-16383)*

Cox Petroleum Transport, Cudahy *Also Called: HF Cox Inc (P-8916)*

Coy Industries Inc .... D 310 603-2970
2970 E Maria St E Rncho Dmngz (90221) *(P-4975)*

Coyle Reproductions Inc (PA)....................... **C 866 269-5373**
2850 Orbiter St Brea (92821) *(P-2991)*

CP Document Technologies LLC (PA)................ **D 213 617-4040**
800 W 6th St Ste 1400 Los Angeles (90017) *(P-10239)*

CP Document Technologies LLC .... E 310 575-6640
11835 W Olympic Blvd Ste 145 Los Angeles (90064) *(P-13312)*

CP Manufacturing, San Diego *Also Called: CP Manufacturing Inc (P-5697)*

CP Manufacturing Inc (HQ).......................... **C 619 477-3175**
6795 Calle De Linea San Diego (92154) *(P-5697)*

Cp-Carrillo Inc (DH)................................. **C 949 567-9000**
1902 Mcgaw Ave Irvine (92614) *(P-6041)*

Cp-Carrillo Inc .... E 949 567-9000
17401 Armstrong Ave Irvine (92614) *(P-6042)*

Employee Codes: A=Over 500 employees, B=251-500
C=101-250, D=51-100, E=20-50, F=10-19, G=1-9

2025 Southern California
Business Directory and Buyers Guide

© Mergent Inc. 1-800-342-5647

993

Cpaperless LLC .... E 949 510-3365
605 1/2 Orchid Ave Corona Del Mar (92625) *(P-6573)*

Cpcc Inc .... D 818 882-3200
10610 Owensmouth Ave Chatsworth (91311) *(P-15846)*

Cpd Industries .... E 909 465-5596
4665 State St Montclair (91763) *(P-4095)*

Cpe Hr Inc .... D 310 270-9800
9000 W Sunset Blvd Ste 900 West Hollywood (90069) *(P-18122)*

Cph Monarch Hotel LLC .... A 949 234-3200
1 Monarch Beach Resort Dana Point (92629) *(P-12802)*

CPI Malibu Division .... D 805 383-1829
3623 Old Conejo Rd Ste 205 Newbury Park (91320) *(P-6604)*

CPI Satcom & Antenna Tech Inc .... B 310 539-6704
3111 Fujita St Torrance (90505) *(P-6605)*

Cpl Holdings LLC .... C 310 348-6800
12181 Bluff Creek Dr Ste 250 Playa Vista (90094) *(P-11266)*

Cpp - Pomona, Pomona *Also Called: Consolidted Precision Pdts Corp (P-4669)*

Cpp Cudahy, Cudahy *Also Called: Consolidated Foundries Inc (P-4670)*

Cpp Rancho Cucamonga, Rancho Cucamonga *Also Called: Pac-Rancho Inc (P-4569)*

Cpp-Azusa, Azusa *Also Called: Magparts (P-4676)*

Cpp-City of Industry, City Of Industry *Also Called: Cast Parts Inc (P-4562)*

Cpp-Pomona, Walnut *Also Called: Cast Parts Inc (P-4563)*

Cpp-Port Hueneme, Port Hueneme *Also Called: Pac Foundries Inc (P-4683)*

Cpp/Belwin Inc .... D 818 891-5999
16320 Roscoe Blvd Ste 100 Van Nuys (91406) *(P-2886)*

CPS Security, Cerritos *Also Called: Commercial Protective Svcs Inc (P-14285)*

Cputer Inc .... D 844 394-1538
2110 Artesia Blvd Redondo Beach (90278) *(P-14208)*

Cq Press Fairfax Co, Thousand Oaks *Also Called: Sage Publications Inc (P-2895)*

Cr & A Custom, Los Angeles *Also Called: CR & A Custom Apparel Inc (P-3134)*

CR & A Custom Apparel Inc .... E 213 749-4440
312 W Pico Blvd Los Angeles (90015) *(P-3134)*

CR&r Incorporated .... C 951 634-8079
1706 Goetz Rd Perris (92570) *(P-9740)*

Craft, San Diego *Also Called: Elco Rfrgn Solutions LLC (P-5975)*

Craft Labor & Support Svcs LLC .... C 619 336-9977
1545 Tidelands Ave Ste C National City (91950) *(P-7600)*

Craftech, Anaheim *Also Called: Sp Craftech I LLC (P-4246)*

Craftech Metal Forming Inc .... E 951 940-6444
24100 Water Ave Ste B Perris (92570) *(P-4829)*

Craftsman Lath and Plaster Inc .... B 951 685-9922
8325 63rd St Riverside (92509) *(P-1048)*

Craftsman Unity LLC .... C 714 776-8995
2273 E Via Burton Anaheim (92806) *(P-4738)*

Crafttech, Anaheim *Also Called: Charmaine Plastics Inc (P-4088)*

Craftwood Industries Inc .... E 616 796-1209
222 Shelbourne Irvine (92620) *(P-2523)*

Crafty Apes LLC (PA) .... A 310 837-3900
127 Lomita St El Segundo (90245) *(P-14815)*

Craig Kackert Design Tech, Simi Valley *Also Called: Jaxx Manufacturing Inc (P-7016)*

Craig Manufacturing Company (PA) .... D 323 726-7355
8129 Slauson Ave Montebello (90640) *(P-7239)*

Craig Tools Inc .... E 310 322-0614
142 Lomita St El Segundo (90245) *(P-5608)*

Cramer-Decker Industries (PA) .... E 714 566-3800
1300 E Wakeham Ave Ste A Santa Ana (92705) *(P-10074)*

Crane Aerospace Inc .... D 818 526-2600
3000 Winona Ave Burbank (91504) *(P-7457)*

Crane Co .... C 562 426-2531
3201 Walnut Ave Long Beach (90755) *(P-5372)*

CRANE CO., Long Beach *Also Called: Crane Co (P-5372)*

Crane Instrmnttion Smpling Inc .... D 951 270-6200
2301 Wardlow Cir Corona (92878) *(P-5361)*

Craneveyor Corp (PA) .... D 626 442-1524
1524 Potrero Ave El Monte (91733) *(P-5521)*

Crate Modular Inc .... D 310 405-0829
3025 E Dominguez St Carson (90810) *(P-5076)*

Cratex, Encinitas *Also Called: Cratex Manufacturing Co Inc (P-4482)*

Cratex Manufacturing Co Inc .... D 760 942-2877
328 Encinitas Blvd Ste 200 Encinitas (92024) *(P-4482)*

Crave Foods, Los Angeles *Also Called: Crave Foods Inc (P-1387)*

Crave Foods Inc .... E 562 900-7272
2043 Imperial St Los Angeles (90021) *(P-1387)*

Crawford Associates .... E 760 922-6804
2635 E Chanslor Way Blythe (92225) *(P-1113)*

Crazy Industries .... E 619 270-9090
8675 Avenida Costa Norte San Diego (92154) *(P-8513)*

CRC Health Corporate .... A 714 542-3581
2101 E 1st St Santa Ana (92705) *(P-16464)*

CRC Health Group Inc .... D 760 744-2104
1560 Capalina Clinic San Marcos (92069) *(P-16465)*

CRC Health Group Inc .... C 951 784-8010
1021 W La Cadena Dr Riverside (92501) *(P-16466)*

Crd Mfg Inc .... E 714 871-3300
615 Fee Ana St Placentia (92870) *(P-4764)*

Creation Tech Calexico Inc (HQ) .... E
1778 Zinetta Rd Ste F Calexico (92231) *(P-6721)*

Creative Age Publications Inc .... E 818 782-7328
15975 High Knoll Rd Encino (91436) *(P-2851)*

Creative Artsts Agcy Hldngs LL (DH) .... A 424 288-2000
2000 Avenue Of The Stars Ste 100 Los Angeles (90067) *(P-14958)*

Creative Channel Services LLC, Los Angeles *Also Called: Rocky Point Investments LLC (P-18203)*

Creative Costuming & Designs, Huntington Beach *Also Called: Creative Costuming Designs Inc (P-1877)*

Creative Costuming Designs Inc .... E 714 895-0982
15402 Electronic Ln Huntington Beach (92649) *(P-1877)*

Creative Design Consultants (PA) .... D 714 641-4868
2915 Red Hill Ave Ste G201 Costa Mesa (92626) *(P-14483)*

Creative Design Industries .... C 619 710-2525
2587 Otay Center Dr San Diego (92154) *(P-1982)*

Creative Foods LLC .... E 858 748-0070
12622 Poway Rd # A Poway (92064) *(P-1758)*

Creative Inflatables, South El Monte *Also Called: Promotnal Design Concepts Inc (P-3930)*

Creative Machine Technology, Corona *Also Called: Cremach Tech Inc (P-5539)*

Creative Machine Technology, Corona *Also Called: Cremach Tech Inc (P-5540)*

Creative Maintenance Systems .... D 949 852-2871
1340 Reynolds Ave Ste 111 Irvine (92614) *(P-13367)*

Creative Outdoor Distrs USA, Lake Forest *Also Called: Cod USA Inc (P-2540)*

Creative Park Productions LLC .... C 818 622-3702
100 Universal City Plz Universal City (91608) *(P-14916)*

Creative Pathways Inc .... E 310 530-1965
20815 Higgins Ct Torrance (90501) *(P-5645)*

Creative Press, Anaheim *Also Called: Creative Press LLC (P-2992)*

Creative Press LLC (PA) .... E 714 774-5060
1350 S Caldwell Cir Anaheim (92805) *(P-2992)*

Creative Press LLC .... E 714 774-5060
1600 E Ball Rd Anaheim (92805) *(P-2993)*

Creative Solutions Svcs LLC .... C 646 495-1558
1745 N Vista St Los Angeles (90046) *(P-13506)*

Creative Stone Mfg Inc (PA) .... C 800 847-8663
342 W Perry St Perris (92571) *(P-4385)*

Creative Teaching Press Inc (PA) .... D 714 799-2100
11145 Knott Ave Cypress (90630) *(P-2887)*

Creatoriq, Pasadena *Also Called: Socialedge Inc (P-13827)*

Creatorup Inc .... D 323 300-4725
525 S Hewitt St Los Angeles (90013) *(P-14816)*

Credibility Corp .... A 310 456-8271
22761 Pacific Coast Hwy Malibu (90265) *(P-14484)*

Credit Card Services Inc (PA) .... D 213 365-1122
21281 S Western Ave Torrance (90501) *(P-14485)*

Credit Union Southern Cal (PA) .... D 562 698-8326
8101 E Kaiser Blvd Ste 300 Anaheim (92808) *(P-11794)*

Cremach Tech Inc .... C 951 735-3194
400 E Parkridge Ave Corona (92879) *(P-5539)*

Cremach Tech Inc (DH) .... E 951 735-3194
369 Meyer Cir Corona (92879) *(P-5540)*

Crenshaw Chrstn Ctr Ch Los Ang (PA) .... B 323 758-3777
7901 S Vermont Ave Los Angeles (90044) *(P-17413)*

Crenshaw Die and Mfg Corp .... D 949 475-5505
7432 Prince Dr Huntington Beach (92647) *(P-5575)*

Crenshaw Nursing, Los Angeles *Also Called: Longwood Management Corp (P-15705)*

Crescent Inc ...... E 714 992-6030
670 S Jefferson St Placentia (92870) *(P-2994)*

Crescent Healthcare Inc (HQ) ...... C 714 520-6300
11980 Telegraph Rd Ste 100 Santa Fe Springs (90670) *(P-16384)*

Crescenta-Canada YMCA ...... C 818 352-3255
6840 Foothill Blvd Tujunga (91042) *(P-17339)*

Crescenta-Canada YMCA (PA) ...... C 818 790-0123
1930 Foothill Blvd La Canada (91011) *(P-17340)*

Crescentone Inc (HQ) ...... C 310 563-7000
200 Continental Blvd Fl 3 El Segundo (90245) *(P-13698)*

Cresco Manufacturing Inc ...... E 714 525-2326
1614 N Orangethorpe Way Anaheim (92801) *(P-6110)*

Crescomfg.com, Anaheim *Also Called: Cresco Manufacturing Inc (P-6110)*

Crest Beverage LLC ...... B 858 452-2300
1348 47th St San Diego (92102) *(P-11045)*

Crest Beverage Company Inc ...... C 858 452-2300
3840 Via De La Valle Ste 300 Del Mar (92014) *(P-11046)*

Crest Chevrolet, San Bernardino *Also Called: Harbill Inc (P-11359)*

Crest Coating Inc ...... D 714 635-7090
1361 S Allec St Anaheim (92805) *(P-5316)*

Crest R E O & Relocation, La Crescenta *Also Called: EAM Enterprises Inc (P-12435)*

Crest Steel, Riverside *Also Called: Crest Steel Corporation (P-10131)*

Crest Steel Corporation ...... D 951 727-2600
6580 General Rd Riverside (92509) *(P-10131)*

Crestec Los Angeles, Long Beach *Also Called: Crestec Usa Inc (P-2995)*

Crestec Usa Inc ...... E 310 327-9000
2410 Mira Mar Ave Long Beach (90815) *(P-2995)*

Crestline Hotels & Resorts Inc (HQ) ...... C 213 629-1200
120 S Los Angeles St 11 Los Angeles (90012) *(P-12803)*

Crestmont Capital LLC ...... C 949 537-3882
1422 Edinger Ave Ste 210 Tustin (92780) *(P-12704)*

Creston Village, Paso Robles *Also Called: Emeritus Corporation (P-12339)*

Crestview Landscape Inc ...... D 818 962-7771
13949 Ventura Blvd Sherman Oaks (91423) *(P-164)*

Crestwood Behavioral Hlth Inc ...... D 661 363-8127
6700 Eucalyptus Dr Ste A Bakersfield (93306) *(P-15847)*

Crestwood Behavioral Hlth Inc ...... C 619 481-6790
5550 University Ave Ste A San Diego (92105) *(P-15848)*

Crestwood Behavioral Hlth Inc ...... C 760 451-4165
624 E Elder St Fallbrook (92028) *(P-15849)*

Crestwood Behavioral Hlth Inc ...... D 805 308-8720
303 S C St Lompoc (93436) *(P-17143)*

Creu LLC ...... E 909 483-4888
12750 Baltic Ct Rancho Cucamonga (91739) *(P-4096)*

Crevier Classics LLC ...... B 714 835-3171
1500 Auto Mall Dr Santa Ana (92705) *(P-11330)*

Crew Builders Inc ...... C 619 587-2033
8130 Commercial St La Mesa (91942) *(P-533)*

Crew Knitwear LLC ...... D 323 526-3888
2155 E 7th St Ste 125 Los Angeles (90023) *(P-1913)*

Crew Knitwear LLC (PA) ...... D 323 526-3888
660 S Myers St Los Angeles (90023) *(P-2087)*

Crexi, Playa Vista *Also Called: Commercial RE Exch Inc (P-12412)*

Crh Management, Newport Beach *Also Called: Core Realty Holdings MGT Inc (P-12415)*

Cri 2000 LP (PA) ...... E 619 542-1975
2245 San Diego Ave Ste 125 San Diego (92110) *(P-2411)*

Cri Help Drug Rehabilitation, North Hollywood *Also Called: Cri-Help Inc (P-17144)*

Cri Sub 1 (DH) ...... E 310 537-1657
1715 S Anderson Ave Compton (90220) *(P-2507)*

Cri-Help Inc (PA) ...... D 818 985-8323
11027 Burbank Blvd North Hollywood (91601) *(P-17144)*

Crinetics, San Diego *Also Called: Crinetics Pharmaceuticals Inc (P-3391)*

Crinetics Pharmaceuticals Inc (PA) ...... D 858 450-6464
6055 Lusk Blvd San Diego (92121) *(P-3391)*

Crislu Corp ...... E 310 322-3444
20916 Higgins Ct Torrance (90501) *(P-8453)*

Crissair Inc ...... C 661 367-3300
28909 Avenue Williams Valencia (91355) *(P-6050)*

Cristek, Anaheim *Also Called: Cristek Interconnects LLC (P-6946)*

Cristek Interconnects LLC (DH) ...... C 714 696-5200
5395 E Hunter Ave Anaheim (92807) *(P-6946)*

Critchfeld Mech Inc Sthern Cal ...... D 949 390-2900
15391 Springdale St Huntington Beach (92649) *(P-770)*

Criterion Machine Works ...... E
765 W 16th St Costa Mesa (92627) *(P-5609)*

Criticalpoint Capital LLC ...... D 909 987-9533
9433 Hyssop Dr Rancho Cucamonga (91730) *(P-3304)*

CRITTENTON SERVICES FOR CHILDR, Fullerton *Also Called: Florence Crttnton Svcs Ornge C (P-17153)*

Crl, Los Angeles *Also Called: C R Laurence Co Inc (P-7233)*

Crl Technologies Inc ...... D 760 495-3000
543 W Graaf Ave # B Ridgecrest (93555) *(P-17783)*

Crmls LLC ...... C 909 859-2040
15325 Fairfield Ranch Rd Ste 200 Chino Hills (91709) *(P-12287)*

Crockett & Coinc ...... D 619 267-1103
5540 Sweetwater Rd Bonita (91902) *(P-15075)*

Crockett Graphics Inc (PA) ...... D 805 987-8577
980 Avenida Acaso Camarillo (93012) *(P-2662)*

Crosby Fruit Products, Fontana *Also Called: Refresco Beverages US Inc (P-1355)*

Crosno Construction Inc ...... E 805 343-7437
819 Sheridan Rd Arroyo Grande (93420) *(P-4830)*

Crosscountry Mortgage LLC ...... C 858 735-0255
4655 Executive Dr Ste 300 San Diego (92121) *(P-11896)*

Crossfield Products Corp (PA) ...... E 310 886-9100
3000 E Harcourt St Compton (90221) *(P-3262)*

Crossing Guard Company ...... A 310 202-8284
10440 Pioneer Blvd Ste 5 Santa Fe Springs (90670) *(P-14291)*

Crossrads Adult Day Hlth Care, Rancho Cucamonga *Also Called: Horrigan Enterprises Inc (P-16953)*

Crossrads Chrstn Schols Corona ...... C 951 278-3199
2380 Fullerton Ave Corona (92881) *(P-16853)*

Crosstown Elec & Data Inc ...... D 626 813-6693
5454 Diaz St Baldwin Park (91706) *(P-905)*

Crothall Services Group ...... A 714 562-9275
14710 Northam St La Mirada (90638) *(P-14761)*

Crowdstrike Inc ...... C 888 512-8906
400 Continental Blvd Ste 275 El Segundo (90245) *(P-14209)*

Crowdstrike Inc ...... C 888 512-8906
15440 Laguna Canyon Rd Ste 250 Irvine (92618) *(P-14210)*

Crowdstrike Inc ...... C 888 512-8906
15441 Laguna Canyon Rd, Ste 260 Irvine (92618) *(P-14211)*

Crowell & Moring LLP ...... C 949 263-8400
3 Park Plz Ste 2000 Irvine (92614) *(P-16666)*

Crowell & Moring LLP ...... C 213 622-4750
515 S Flower St Ste 4000 Los Angeles (90071) *(P-16667)*

Crower Cams, San Diego *Also Called: Crower Engrg & Sls Co Inc (P-7240)*

Crower Engrg & Sls Co Inc ...... D 619 661-6477
6180 Business Center Ct San Diego (92154) *(P-7240)*

Crowley Marine Services Inc ...... B 310 732-6500
86 Berth 300 S Harbor Blvd San Pedro (90731) *(P-9266)*

Crown Dolt, Aliso Viejo *Also Called: HJ Supply Distribution Services LLC (P-10308)*

Crown Building Maintenance Co ...... B 714 434-9494
14201 Franklin Ave Tustin (92780) *(P-13368)*

Crown Building Maintenance Co ...... B 858 560-5785
5482 Complex St Ste 108 San Diego (92123) *(P-13369)*

Crown Discount Tools, Sylmar *Also Called: TMW Corporation (P-7580)*

Crown Energy Services Inc ...... A 213 765-7800
2601 S Figueroa St Bldg 1 Los Angeles (90007) *(P-13370)*

Crown Equipment Corporation ...... E 909 923-8357
4250 Greystone Dr Ontario (91761) *(P-5527)*

Crown Equipment Corporation ...... E 626 968-0556
1300 Palomares St La Verne (91750) *(P-5528)*

Crown Equipment Corporation ...... D 310 952-6600
4061 Via Oro Ave Long Beach (90810) *(P-5529)*

Crown Fence Co ...... D 562 864-5177
12070 Telegraph Rd Ste 340 Santa Fe Springs (90670) *(P-1200)*

Crown Golf Properties LP ...... C 714 730-1611
12442 Tustin Ranch Rd Tustin (92782) *(P-18123)*

Crown Lift Trucks, Ontario *Also Called: Crown Equipment Corporation (P-5527)*

Crown Lift Trucks, La Verne *Also Called: Crown Equipment Corporation (P-5528)*

A
L
P
H
A
B
E
T
I
C

Employee Codes: A=Over 500 employees, B=251-500
C=101-250, D=51-100, E=20-50, F=10-19, G=1-9

2025 Southern California
Business Directory and Buyers Guide

© Mergent Inc. 1-800-342-5647
995

Crown Lift Trucks, Long Beach *Also Called: Crown Equipment Corporation (P-5529)*

Crown Paper Converting, Ontario *Also Called: Crown Paper Converting Inc (P-2621)*

Crown Paper Converting Inc .... E 909 923-5226
1380 S Bon View Ave Ontario (91761) *(P-2621)*

Crown Plaza La Harbor Hotel, San Pedro *Also Called: Spf Capital Real Estate LLC (P-13033)*

Crown Poly Inc .... C 323 585-5522
5700 Bickett St Huntington Park (90255) *(P-2730)*

Crown Printers, San Bernardino *Also Called: Shorett Printing Inc (P-3175)*

Crown Technical Systems (PA) .... C 951 332-4170
13470 Philadelphia Ave Fontana (92337) *(P-6302)*

Crown Vly Precision Machining, Irwindale *Also Called: Sinecera Inc (P-14598)*

Crownair Aviation, San Diego *Also Called: Air 88 Inc (P-9188)*

Crowne Cold Storage LLC .... E 661 725-6458
786 Road 188 Delano (93215) *(P-18124)*

Crowne Plaza Ventura Beach, Ventura *Also Called: Ventura Hsptality Partners LLC (P-13065)*

Crowne Plz Los Angeles Hbr Ht, Long Beach *Also Called: Nhca Inc (P-12938)*

Crowntonka California Inc .... E 909 230-6720
6514 E 26th St Commerce (90040) *(P-5972)*

CRST Expedited Inc .... B 909 563-5606
9032 Merrill Ave Chino (91708) *(P-8940)*

CRST Expedited Inc .... B 909 563-5606
1219 E Elm St Ontario (91761) *(P-8941)*

Crumbl Cookies .... D 949 519-0791
23702 El Toro Rd Ste B Lake Forest (92630) *(P-1484)*

Crunchyroll LLC (DH) .... D 972 355-7300
10202 Washington Blvd Culver City (90232) *(P-14817)*

Crush Master Grinding Corp .... E 909 595-2249
755 Penarth Ave Walnut (91789) *(P-6111)*

Crydom Inc (DH) .... E 619 210-1590
2320 Paseo De Las Americas Ste 201 San Diego (92154) *(P-6345)*

Cryogenic Experts, Oxnard *Also Called: Acme Cryogenics Inc (P-5686)*

Cryogenic Experts Inc .... E 805 981-4500
531 Sandy Cir Oxnard (93036) *(P-5698)*

Cryogenic Industries, Murrieta *Also Called: Hexco International (P-5704)*

Cryogenic Industries Inc .... C 951 677-2060
25720 Jefferson Ave Murrieta (92562) *(P-6395)*

Cryostar USA, Whittier *Also Called: Messer LLC (P-3218)*

Cryostar USA LLC .... D 562 903-1290
13117 Meyer Rd Whittier (90605) *(P-5730)*

Cryoworks Inc .... D 951 360-0920
3309 Grapevine St Mira Loma (91752) *(P-5430)*

Cryst Mark Inc A Swan Techno C .... E 818 240-7520
613 Justin Ave Glendale (91201) *(P-5699)*

Crystal, Riverside *Also Called: Crystal PCF Win & Door Sys LLC (P-4885)*

Crystal Art Gallery, Vernon *Also Called: Rggd Inc (P-10567)*

Crystal Casino & Hotel, Compton *Also Called: Celebrity Casinos Inc (P-12788)*

Crystal Cathedral Ministries (PA) .... C 714 622-2900
12901 Lewis St Garden Grove (92840) *(P-17414)*

Crystal Creamery Inc .... D 209 576-3479
1629 Carlotti Dr Santa Maria (93454) *(P-10829)*

Crystal Engineering Corp .... E 805 595-5477
708 Fiero Ln Ste 9 San Luis Obispo (93401) *(P-7854)*

Crystal Geyser Water Company .... E 661 323-6296
1233 E California Ave Bakersfield (93307) *(P-1615)*

Crystal Geyser Water Company .... E 661 321-0896
2351 E Brundage Ln Ste A Bakersfield (93307) *(P-1616)*

Crystal Mark, Glendale *Also Called: Cryst Mark Inc A Swan Techno C (P-5699)*

Crystal Organic Farms LLC .... D 661 845-5200
10000 Stockdale Hwy Ste 200 Bakersfield (93311) *(P-79)*

Crystal PCF Win & Door Sys LLC .... C 951 779-9300
1850 Atlanta Ave Riverside (92507) *(P-4885)*

Crystal Stairs Inc (PA) .... B 323 299-8998
5110 W Goldleaf Cir Ste 150 Los Angeles (90056) *(P-16932)*

Crystal Tip, Irvine *Also Called: Westside Resources Inc (P-8361)*

Crystalview Technology Corp .... B 949 788-0738
32 Mauchly Ste C Irvine (92618) *(P-18305)*

Cs Electronics, Irvine *Also Called: Cs Systems Inc (P-5911)*

Cs Systems Inc .... E 949 475-9100
16781 Noyes Ave Irvine (92606) *(P-5911)*

CSC Serviceworks Inc .... D 626 389-0169
14426 Bonelli St City Of Industry (91746) *(P-13129)*

CSCU, Santa Maria *Also Called: Coasthills Credit Union (P-11826)*

Cshg Holdings, Temecula *Also Called: Hines Growers Inc (P-57)*

Csi Electrical Contractors Inc .... B 661 723-0869
41769 11th St W Ste B Palmdale (93551) *(P-906)*

Csi Electrical Contractors Inc (HQ) .... C 562 946-0700
10623 Fulton Wells Ave Santa Fe Springs (90670) *(P-907)*

Csi Electrical Contractors Inc .... B 760 227-0577
310 Via Vera Cruz Ste 106 San Marcos (92078) *(P-908)*

Csi Vegas, Santa Clarita *Also Called: CBS Studios Inc (P-9495)*

Csl Berkshire Operating Co LLC .... D 949 333-8580
5000 Birch St Ste 400 Newport Beach (92660) *(P-12416)*

CSM Metal Fabricating & Engrg, Los Angeles *Also Called: Commercial Shtmtl Works Inc (P-4828)*

CTA Fixtures Inc .... D 909 390-6744
5721 Santa Ana St Ste B Ontario (91761) *(P-2578)*

CTA Manufacturing Inc .... E 951 280-2400
1160 California Ave Corona (92881) *(P-2228)*

Ctac Research 60901, Irwindale *Also Called: Southern California Edison Co (P-9634)*

Ctbla Inc .... D 323 276-1933
1740 Albion St Los Angeles (90031) *(P-7199)*

Ctc Global, Irvine *Also Called: Ctc Global Corporation (P-6414)*

Ctc Global Corporation (PA) .... C 949 428-8500
2026 Mcgaw Ave Irvine (92614) *(P-6414)*

Ctc Group Inc (DH) .... C 310 540-0500
21333 Hawthorne Blvd Torrance (90503) *(P-12804)*

Cte California TI & Engrg Inc .... E
7801 Bolero Dr Jurupa Valley (92509) *(P-5610)*

Ctek Inc .... E 310 241-2973
2425 Golden Hill Rd Ste 106 Paso Robles (93446) *(P-9562)*

Ctf, Perris *Also Called: California Trusframe LLC (P-2374)*

Ctg, Santa Barbara *Also Called: Channel Technologies Group LLC (P-7707)*

CTI Foods Azusa LLC .... C 626 633-1609
1120 W Foothill Blvd Azusa (91702) *(P-1256)*

Ctour Holiday LLC .... B 323 261-8811
222 E Huntington Dr Ste 105 Monrovia (91016) *(P-15197)*

Ctr For Autism Rltd Disorders .... D 209 618-1253
21600 Oxnard St Ste 1800 Woodland Hills (91367) *(P-15539)*

CTS Cement Manufacturing Corp (PA) .... E 714 379-8260
12442 Knott St Garden Grove (92841) *(P-4354)*

CU Cooperative Systems LLC (PA) .... B 909 948-2500
9692 Haven Ave Ste 300 Rancho Cucamonga (91730) *(P-11827)*

CU Direct Corporation (PA) .... C 833 908-0121
2855 E Guasti Rd Ste 500 Ontario (91761) *(P-13699)*

Cubework, City Of Industry *Also Called: Cubeworkcom Inc (P-12417)*

Cubeworkcom Inc (PA) .... C 909 991-6669
900 Turnbull Canyon Rd City Of Industry (91745) *(P-12417)*

Cubic, San Diego *Also Called: Cubic Corporation (P-7710)*

Cubic, San Diego *Also Called: Cubic Trnsp Systems Inc (P-13700)*

Cubic Corporation (HQ) .... A 858 277-6780
9233 Balboa Ave San Diego (92123) *(P-7710)*

Cubic Corporation .... A 858 277-6780
9233 Balboa Ave San Diego (92123) *(P-14079)*

Cubic Defense Applications Inc (DH) .... A 858 776-5664
9233 Balboa Ave San Diego (92123) *(P-7115)*

Cubic Defense Applications Inc .... A 858 277-6780
4285 Ponderosa Ave San Diego (92123) *(P-7116)*

Cubic Defense Applications Inc .... C 858 505-2870
9233 Balboa Ave San Diego (92123) *(P-7117)*

Cubic Defense Systems, San Diego *Also Called: Cubic Corporation (P-14079)*

Cubic Ground Training, San Diego *Also Called: Cubic Defense Applications Inc (P-7115)*

Cubic Secure Communications I .... B 858 505-2000
9233 Balboa Ave San Diego (92123) *(P-9399)*

Cubic Trnsp Systems Inc (DH) .... A 858 268-3100
9233 Balboa Ave San Diego (92123) *(P-13700)*

Cucamonga Valley Water Dst .... D 909 987-2591
10440 Ashford St Rancho Cucamonga (91730) *(P-9689)*

Cudahy Medical Offices, Cudahy *Also Called: Kaiser Foundation Hospitals (P-16032)*

Cudc, Ontario *Also Called: CU Direct Corporation (P-13699)*

Mergent email: customerrelations@mergent.com
996

2025 Southern California
Business Directory and Buyers Guide

(P-0000) Products & Services Section entry number
(PA)=Parent Co (HQ)=Headquarters (DH)=Div Headquarters

Culinary Brands Inc (PA).................................... E 626 289-3000
3280 E 44th St Vernon (90058) *(P-1388)*

Culinary Hispanic Foods Inc .... A 619 955-6101
805 Bow St Chula Vista (91914) *(P-10942)*

Culinary International LLC (PA) .... C 626 289-3000
3280 E 44th St Vernon (90058) *(P-1759)*

Culinary Specialties, San Marcos *Also Called: Culinary Specialties Inc (P-1760)*

Culinary Specialties Inc .... D 760 744-8220
1231 Linda Vista Dr San Marcos (92078) *(P-1760)*

Culver City Parks & Recreation, Culver City *Also Called: City of Culver City (P-18399)*

Culver Personnel Agencies Inc .... C 888 600-5733
445 Marine View Ave Ste 101 Del Mar (92014) *(P-13507)*

Culver Personnel Services, Del Mar *Also Called: Culver Personnel Agencies Inc (P-13507)*

Culver West Health Center LLC .... D 310 390-9506
4035 Grand View Blvd Los Angeles (90066) *(P-15620)*

Cummings Resources LLC .... E 951 248-1130
1495 Columbia Ave Riverside (92507) *(P-8597)*

Cummings Resources LLC .... E 951 248-1130
330 W Citrus St Colton (92324) *(P-8598)*

Cummings Transportation, Bakersfield *Also Called: Cummings Vacuum Service Inc (P-327)*

Cummings Vacuum Service Inc .... D 661 746-1786
112 El Paso Rd Bakersfield (93314) *(P-327)*

Cummins, Irvine *Also Called: Cummins Pacific LLC (P-5466)*

Cummins Aerospace, Anaheim *Also Called: Cummins Aerospace LLC (P-7711)*

Cummins Aerospace LLC (PA) .... E 714 879-2800
2320 E Orangethorpe Ave Anaheim (92806) *(P-7711)*

Cummins Pacific LLC (HQ) .... D 949 253-6000
1939 Deere Ave Irvine (92606) *(P-5466)*

Cunico Corporation .... E 562 733-4600
1910 W 16th St Long Beach (90813) *(P-5431)*

Curation Foods Inc (HQ) .... D 800 454-1355
2811 Airpark Dr Santa Maria (93455) *(P-1761)*

Curative Inc .... B 650 713-8928
605 E Huntington Dr Ste 207 Monrovia (91016) *(P-17978)*

Curative Labs, Monrovia *Also Called: Curative Inc (P-17978)*

Curative-Korva LLC .... D 424 645-7575
605 E Huntington Dr Monrovia (91016) *(P-16310)*

Curio Home Goods, Van Nuys *Also Called: Munchkin Inc (P-3983)*

Curiosity Ink Media LLC .... D 561 287-5776
478 Ellis St Pasadena (91105) *(P-10432)*

Curology Inc .... B 617 959-2480
5717 Pacific Center Blvd Ste 200 San Diego (92121) *(P-15297)*

Current Home, Hemet *Also Called: Current Home Inc (P-1188)*

Current Home Inc .... D 866 454-6073
7100 W Florida Ave Hemet (92545) *(P-1188)*

Currie Enterprises .... D 714 528-6957
382 N Smith Ave Corona (92878) *(P-7241)*

Curry Company LLC .... E 310 643-8400
15724 Condon Ave Lawndale (90260) *(P-5611)*

Curtco Robb Media LLC (PA) .... E 310 589-7700
29100 Heathercliff Rd Ste 200 Malibu (90265) *(P-2852)*

Curtin Maritime Corp .... B 562 983-7257
725 Pier T Ave Long Beach (90802) *(P-710)*

Curtis Winery, Los Olivos *Also Called: Firestone Vineyard LP (P-1569)*

Curtiss-Wrght Cntrls Elctrnic (DH) .... C 661 257-4430
28965 Avenue Penn Santa Clarita (91355) *(P-6346)*

Curtiss-Wrght Cntrls Elctrnic .... C 661 257-4430
28965 Avenue Penn Santa Clarita (91355) *(P-17507)*

Curtiss-Wrght Cntrls Elctrnic, Santa Clarita *Also Called: Curtiss-Wrght Cntrls Elctmic (P-6346)*

Curtiss-Wrght Cntrls Intgrted .... D 714 982-1860
210 Ranger Ave Brea (92821) *(P-8258)*

Curtiss-Wright Controls Inc .... E 818 503-0998
6940 Farmdale Ave North Hollywood (91605) *(P-7458)*

Curtiss-Wright Corporation .... D 619 482-3405
1675 Brandywine Ave Ste F Chula Vista (91911) *(P-5362)*

Curtiss-Wright Corporation .... D 661 257-4430
28965 Avenue Penn Santa Clarita (91355) *(P-5363)*

Curtiss-Wright Corporation .... D 619 656-4740
1675 Brandywine Ave Ste E Chula Vista (91911) *(P-14762)*

Curtiss-Wright Flow Control .... C 626 851-3100
28965 Avenue Penn Valencia (91355) *(P-5364)*

Curtiss-Wright Flow Ctrl Corp .... E 949 271-7500
2950 E Birch St Brea (92821) *(P-5365)*

Curtiss-Wright Flow Ctrl Corp (DH) .... D 714 528-1365
2950 E Birch St Brea (92821) *(P-5385)*

Curvature LLC (DH) .... B 800 230-6638
7418 Hollister Ave Ste 110 Santa Barbara (93117) *(P-9994)*

Cushman & Wakefield, Ontario *Also Called: Cushman & Wakefield Cal Inc (P-12425)*

Cushman & Wakefield Cal Inc .... B 310 556-1805
10250 Constellation Blvd Ste 2200 Los Angeles (90067) *(P-12418)*

Cushman & Wakefield Cal Inc .... B 562 276-1400
3760 Kilroy Airport Way Long Beach (90806) *(P-12419)*

Cushman & Wakefield Cal Inc .... B 714 591-0451
7281 Garden Grove Blvd Ste G Garden Grove (92841) *(P-12420)*

Cushman & Wakefield Cal Inc .... A 949 474-4004
18111 Von Karman Ave Ste 1000 Irvine (92612) *(P-12421)*

Cushman & Wakefield Cal Inc .... B 805 418-5811
3011 Townsgate Rd Westlake Village (91361) *(P-12422)*

Cushman & Wakefield Cal Inc .... B 805 322-7244
770 Paseo Camarillo 315 Camarillo (93010) *(P-12423)*

Cushman & Wakefield Cal Inc .... A 858 452-6500
12830 El Camino Real Ste 100 San Diego (92130) *(P-12424)*

Cushman & Wakefield Cal Inc .... B 909 483-0077
3800 Concours Ste 300 Ontario (91764) *(P-12425)*

Cushman & Wakefield Cal Inc .... B 909 980-3781
901 Via Piemonte Ste 200 Ontario (91764) *(P-12426)*

Cushman & Wakefield California, Garden Grove *Also Called: Cushman & Wakefield Cal Inc (P-12420)*

Cushman Realty Corporation .... C 213 627-4700
601 S Figueroa St Ste 4700 Los Angeles (90017) *(P-12427)*

Cushman Winery Corporation .... E 805 688-9339
6905 Foxen Canyon Rd Los Olivos (93441) *(P-11055)*

Custom Aviation Supply, Chatsworth *Also Called: Custom Control Sensors LLC (P-6303)*

Custom Building Products LLC (DH) .... D 800 272-8786
7711 Center Ave Ste 500 Huntington Beach (92647) *(P-3762)*

Custom Building Products LLC .... C 323 582-0846
6511 Salt Lake Ave Bell (90201) *(P-3763)*

Custom Building Products LLC .... D 661 393-0422
1900 Norris Rd Bakersfield (93308) *(P-10433)*

Custom Built Machinery Inc .... E 714 424-9250
2614 S Hickory St Santa Ana (92707) *(P-17508)*

Custom Chemical Formulators, Santa Fe Springs *Also Called: Morgan Gallacher Inc (P-3614)*

Custom Chrome, South El Monte *Also Called: Custom Chrome Manufacturing (P-9820)*

Custom Chrome Manufacturing .... B 408 825-5000
9228 Rush St South El Monte (91733) *(P-9820)*

Custom Comfort Mattress Co, Orange *Also Called: Custom Comfort Mattress Co Inc (P-9869)*

Custom Comfort Mattress Co Inc (PA) .... D 714 693-6161
581 N Batavia St Orange (92868) *(P-9869)*

Custom Control Sensors LLC (PA) .... C 818 341-4610
21111 Plummer St Chatsworth (91311) *(P-6303)*

Custom Fibreglass Mfg Co .... C 562 432-5454
1711 Harbor Ave Long Beach (90813) *(P-7675)*

Custom Flavors, San Clemente *Also Called: Custom Ingredients Inc (P-1674)*

Custom Foods, Santa Fe Springs *Also Called: J & J Processing Inc (P-1684)*

Custom Furniture Designs, LLC, Chino *Also Called: Royal Custom Designs LLC (P-2459)*

Custom Goods LLC .... D 310 241-6700
809 E 236th St Carson (90745) *(P-9057)*

Custom Goods LLC .... D 310 241-6700
907 E 236th St Carson (90745) *(P-9058)*

Custom Hardtops, Long Beach *Also Called: Custom Fibreglass Mfg Co (P-7675)*

Custom Hotel, Los Angeles *Also Called: Playa Proper Jv LLC (P-12975)*

Custom Hotel LLC .... C 310 645-0400
8639 Lincoln Blvd Los Angeles (90045) *(P-12805)*

Custom Ingredients Inc (PA) .... E 949 276-7995
160 Calle Iglesia Ste 102 San Clemente (92672) *(P-1674)*

Custom Lawn Services, Canoga Park *Also Called: American Landscape MGT Inc (P-147)*

Custom Lawn Services, Ventura *Also Called: American Landscape MGT Inc (P-197)*

Custom Leathercraft Mfg LLC .... D
5701 S Eastern Ave Commerce (90040) *(P-4309)*

Employee Codes: A=Over 500 employees, B=251-500
C=101-250, D=51-100, E=20-50, F=10-19, G=1-9

2025 Southern California
Business Directory and Buyers Guide

© Mergent Inc. 1-800-342-5647

997

Custom Logos Inc .... E 858 277-1886
7889 Clairemont Mesa Blvd San Diego (92111) *(P-1932)*

Custom Magnetics Cal Inc .... E 909 620-3877
15142 Vista Del Rio Ave Chino (91710) *(P-6282)*

Custom Metal Fabricators, Orange *Also Called: Cmf Inc (P-1076)*

Custom Molded Devices, Simi Valley *Also Called: Poly-Tainer Inc (P-3988)*

Custom Packaging Design, Montclair *Also Called: Cpd Industries (P-4095)*

Custom Pipe & Fabrication Inc (HQ)................... D 800 553-3058
10560 Fern Ave Stanton (90680) *(P-5432)*

Custom Power LLC .... D 714 962-7600
10910 Talbert Ave Fountain Valley (92708) *(P-10179)*

Custom Quilting Inc .... E 714 731-7271
2832 Walnut Ave Ste D Tustin (92780) *(P-2209)*

Custom Sensors & Tech Inc .... B 805 716-0322
2475 Paseo De Las Americas San Diego (92154) *(P-6987)*

Custom Sensors & Tech Inc (HQ)..................... A 805 716-0322
1461 Lawrence Dr Thousand Oaks (91320) *(P-6988)*

Custom Truck One Source LP .... E 316 627-2608
4500 State Rd Bakersfield (93308) *(P-7200)*

Custom Vinyls, Fontana *Also Called: Patrick Industries Inc (P-9950)*

Customer Loan Depot, Irvine *Also Called: Loandepotcom LLC (P-11919)*

Customfab Inc .... C 714 891-9119
7345 Orangewood Ave Garden Grove (92841) *(P-4277)*

Customripe Avocado Company, Escondido *Also Called: Henry Avocado Corporation (P-49)*

Customzed Svcs Admnstrtors Inc .... C 858 810-2004
9797 Aero Dr Ste 300 San Diego (92123) *(P-12198)*

Cut and Sew Co Inc .... C 714 981-7244
1939 S Susan St Santa Ana (92704) *(P-1914)*

Cut N Clean Greens, Oxnard *Also Called: San Miguel Produce Inc (P-13)*

Cutting Edge Creative LLC .... D 562 907-7007
9944 Flower St Bellflower (90706) *(P-2579)*

Cutting Edge Supply, Colton *Also Called: Black Diamond Blade Company (P-5488)*

Cutwater Spirits LLC (HQ)............................... D 858 672-3848
9750 Distribution Ave San Diego (92121) *(P-3795)*

Cv Sciences Inc (PA)..................................... E 866 290-2157
9530 Padgett St Ste 107 San Diego (92126) *(P-3392)*

Cvc Specialties, Vernon *Also Called: Continental Vitamin Co Inc (P-3388)*

CVRM, Indio *Also Called: Coachella Vly Rescue Mission (P-16894)*

Cw Industries Inc (PA).................................... E 562 432-5421
1735 Santa Fe Ave Long Beach (90813) *(P-14739)*

Cw Network LLC (HQ)..................................... C 818 977-2500
3300 W Olive Ave Fl 3 Burbank (91505) *(P-9496)*

Cwbc, Goleta *Also Called: Community West Bancshares (P-11760)*

Cwdre, Irvine *Also Called: Certified Wtr Dmage Rstrtion E (P-13363)*

Cwi Steel Technologies Corporation .... E 949 476-7600
2415 Campus Dr Ste 100 Irvine (92612) *(P-4570)*

Cwp, Adelanto *Also Called: Commercial Wood Products Company (P-1047)*

Cwp Cabinets Inc .... C 760 246-4530
15447 Anacapa Rd Ste 102 Victorville (92392) *(P-1049)*

CWT, Gardena *Also Called: Clean Water Technology Inc (P-6009)*

Cwtv, Burbank *Also Called: Cw Network LLC (P-9496)*

Cyber Medical Imaging Inc .... E 888 937-9729
11300 W Olympic Blvd Ste 710 Los Angeles (90064) *(P-8331)*

Cyber-Pro Systems Inc .... C 562 256-3800
2121 S Towne Centre Pl Ste 200 Anaheim (92806) *(P-14128)*

Cybercoders Inc .... C 949 885-5151
101 Progress Irvine (92618) *(P-13508)*

Cybernet Manufacturing Inc .... A 949 600-8000
5 Holland Ste 201 Irvine (92618) *(P-5844)*

Cyberpolicy Inc .... C 877 626-9991
19584 Pine Valley Ave Porter Ranch (91326) *(P-12199)*

Cyberscientific, Irvine *Also Called: Cybercoders Inc (P-13508)*

Cycle News Inc (PA)....................................... E 949 863-7082
17771 Mitchell N Irvine (92614) *(P-2792)*

Cydea Inc .... E 800 710-9939
8510 Miralani Dr San Diego (92126) *(P-1563)*

Cydwoq Inc .... E 818 848-8307
2102 Kenmere Ave Burbank (91504) *(P-4280)*

Cygnet Stmping Fabg Inc A Swan (PA)............... E 818 240-7574
613 Justin Ave Glendale (91201) *(P-5179)*

Cylinder Division, Corona *Also Called: Parker-Hannifin Corporation (P-6052)*

Cymbiotika LLC (PA)...................................... E 770 910-4945
5825 Oberlin Dr Ste 5 San Diego (92121) *(P-3393)*

Cymbiotika LLC .... D 949 652-8177
8885 Rehco Rd San Diego (92121) *(P-3394)*

Cymer LLC (HQ)... A 858 385-7300
17075 Thornmint Ct San Diego (92127) *(P-7118)*

Cynergy Prof Systems LLC .... E 800 776-7978
23187 La Cadena Dr Ste 102 Laguna Hills (92653) *(P-10240)*

Cypress Creek Holdings LLC .... D 310 581-6299
3402 Pico Blvd Ste 215 Santa Monica (90405) *(P-9576)*

Cypress Creek Rnwbles Hldngs L (HQ)............... B 310 581-6299
3402 Pico Blvd Santa Monica (90405) *(P-9577)*

Cypress Equity Investments LLC .... D 310 207-1699
233 Wilshire Blvd Ste 325 Santa Monica (90401) *(P-12025)*

Cypress Pnt-Rrowhead Gen Insur .... D 619 681-0560
2365 Northside Dr Ste 450 San Diego (92108) *(P-12200)*

Cypress Private Security LP .... D 562 222-4197
9926 Pioneer Blvd Ste 106 Santa Fe Springs (90670) *(P-14292)*

Cys Knship Sneca Tstin Wrprund, Santa Ana *Also Called: Seneca Family of Agencies (P-12253)*

Cytec Engineered Materials Inc .... C 714 630-9400
645 N Cypress St Orange (92867) *(P-3796)*

Cytec Engineered Materials Inc .... C 714 632-1174
1440 N Kraemer Blvd Anaheim (92806) *(P-4671)*

Cyu Lithographics Inc .... E 888 878-9898
6951 Oran Cir Buena Park (90621) *(P-2996)*

Czinger Vehicles, Torrance *Also Called: Czv Inc (P-7172)*

Czv Inc .... D 424 603-1450
19601 Hamilton Ave Torrance (90502) *(P-7172)*

D - Link, Irvine *Also Called: D-Link Systems Incorporated (P-9995)*

D & D Cremations Service, Vernon *Also Called: D & D Services Inc (P-1523)*

D & D Gear Incorporated .... C 714 692-6570
4890 E La Palma Ave Anaheim (92807) *(P-7459)*

D & D Saw Works Inc C
1445 Engineer St Ste 110 Vista (92081) *(P-10434)*

D & D Services Inc .... E 323 261-4176
4105 Bandini Blvd Vernon (90058) *(P-1523)*

D & D Tool & Supply, Vista *Also Called: D & D Saw Works Inc (P-10434)*

D & J Printing Inc .... D 661 265-1995
600 W Technology Dr Palmdale (93551) *(P-2997)*

D & K Engineering (HQ).................................. D 760 840-2214
16990 Goldentop Rd San Diego (92127) *(P-7888)*

D & M Steel Inc .... E 818 896-2070
13020 Pierce St Pacoima (91331) *(P-4831)*

D & R Screen Printing Inc .... E 562 458-6443
7314 Pierce Ave Whittier (90602) *(P-2998)*

D A C, Carpinteria *Also Called: Dac International Inc (P-5541)*

D A C, Carpinteria *Also Called: Development Associates Contrls (P-5542)*

D and J Marketing Inc .... E 310 538-1583
580 W 184th St Gardena (90248) *(P-2258)*

D B Specialty Farms, Santa Maria *Also Called: Darensberries LLC (P-15)*

D C Shower Doors Inc .... C 661 257-1177
26121 Avenue Hall Valencia (91355) *(P-8942)*

D D N, Chatsworth *Also Called: Datadirect Networks Inc (P-13702)*

D E X, Camarillo *Also Called: Data Exchange Corporation (P-9997)*

D F Stauffer Biscuit Co Inc .... E 714 546-6855
4041 W Garry Ave Santa Ana (92704) *(P-1485)*

D G A, Los Angeles *Also Called: Directors Guild America Inc (P-14885)*

D G X, E Rncho Dmngz *Also Called: Dependable Global Express Inc (P-9269)*

D I F Group Inc .... E 323 231-8800
2201 Yates Ave Commerce (90040) *(P-17979)*

D J American Supply Inc .... C 323 582-2650
6122 S Eastern Ave Commerce (90040) *(P-10557)*

D K Environmental, Vernon *Also Called: Demenno/Kerdoon Holdings (P-3852)*

D Longo Inc .... B 626 580-6000
3534 Peck Rd El Monte (91731) *(P-11331)*

D Mills Grnding Machining Inc .... C 951 697-6847
1738 N Neville St Orange (92865) *(P-6112)*

D R I, Irvine *Also Called: Dri Commercial Corporation (P-1078)*

Mergent email: customerrelations@mergent.com
998

2025 Southern California
Business Directory and Buyers Guide

(P-0000) Products & Services Section entry number
(PA)=Parent Co (HQ)=Headquarters (DH)=Div Headquarters

D S I, Brea *Also Called: Delivery Solutions Inc (P-8903)*

D S T Macdonald, Valencia *Also Called: Whi Solutions Inc (P-10039)*

D V S Mdia Srvces/Intelestream, Burbank *Also Called: Dvs Media Services (P-13313)*

D W Mack Co Inc .... E 626 969-1817
900 W 8th St Azusa (91702) *(P-3884)*

D X Communications Inc .... E 323 256-3000
8160 Van Nuys Blvd Panorama City (91402) *(P-6606)*

D-Link Systems Incorporated .... C 714 885-6000
14420 Myford Rd Ste 100 Irvine (92606) *(P-9995)*

D-Mac Inc .... E 714 808-3918
1105 E Discovery Ln Anaheim (92801) *(P-2397)*

D'Andrea Graphics, Cypress *Also Called: DAndrea Vsual Cmmncations LLC (P-13326)*

D'Veal Family and Youth Svcs, Pasadena *Also Called: DVeal Corporation (P-17224)*

D&A Endeavors Inc .... D 310 390-7540
11400 W Olympic Blvd Los Angeles (90064) *(P-1201)*

D&D Wholesale Distributors LLC .... D 626 333-2111
777 Baldwin Park Blvd City Of Industry (91746) *(P-10892)*

D&E Propogators, Encinitas *Also Called: Dramm and Echter Inc (P-53)*

D3 Equipment, El Cajon *Also Called: Denardi Machinery Inc (P-10346)*

D3 Go, Encino *Also Called: D3publisher of America Inc (P-13911)*

D3publisher of America Inc .... D 310 268-0820
15910 Ventura Blvd Ste 800 Encino (91436) *(P-13911)*

Da Vinci Schools Fund .... C 310 725-5800
201 N Douglas St El Segundo (90245) *(P-14486)*

Dab Inc .... D 562 623-4773
13415 Marquardt Ave Santa Fe Springs (90670) *(P-6442)*

Dac International Inc .... E 805 684-8307
6390 Rose Ln Carpinteria (93013) *(P-5541)*

Dacha Enterprises Inc .... D 951 273-7777
1915 Elise Cir Corona (92879) *(P-4097)*

Dacor (DH) .... **D 626 799-1000**
14425 Clark Ave City Of Industry (91745) *(P-11530)*

Dae Shin Usa Inc .... D 714 578-9900
610 N Gilbert St Fullerton (92833) *(P-1891)*

Daicel America Holdings Inc .... B 480 798-6737
21515 Hawthorne Blvd Ste 600 Torrance (90503) *(P-17980)*

Daico Industries Inc .... D 310 507-3242
1070 E 233rd St Carson (90745) *(P-6989)*

Daikin Comfort Tech Dist Inc .... B 713 861-2500
525 Park Ave San Fernando (91340) *(P-10330)*

Daikin Comfort Tech Dist Inc .... B 626 210-4595
20035 E Walnut Dr N Walnut (91789) *(P-12288)*

Daikin Comfort Tech Dist Inc .... B 909 946-0632
5160 Richton St Ste A Montclair (91763) *(P-17509)*

Daikin Comfort Tech Mfg LP .... B 760 955-7770
15024 Anacapa Rd Victorville (92392) *(P-5973)*

Dailey & Associates .... D 323 490-3847
8687 Melrose Ave Ste G300 West Hollywood (90069) *(P-13201)*

Daily Journal Corporation (PA) .... **D 213 229-5300**
915 E 1st St Los Angeles (90012) *(P-2793)*

Daily Manufacturing, San Bernardino *Also Called: Ten Days Manufacturing (P-10467)*

Daily Transcript, Laguna Niguel *Also Called: San Diego Daily Transcript (P-2636)*

Dairy Farmers America Inc .... E 805 653-0042
4375 N Ventura Ave Ventura (93001) *(P-1327)*

Daisy Publishing Company Inc .... D 661 295-1910
25233 Anza Dr Santa Clarita (91355) *(P-2910)*

Dakine Equipment LLC .... E 424 276-3618
19400 Harborgate Way Torrance (90501) *(P-2088)*

Dako North America Inc .... B 805 566-6655
6392 Via Real Carpinteria (93013) *(P-10620)*

Dalton Trucking Inc (PA) .... **C 909 823-0663**
13560 Whittram Ave Fontana (92335) *(P-9059)*

Damac, Costa Mesa *Also Called: Bdfco Inc (P-6675)*

Damar Plastics, El Cajon *Also Called: Damar Plastics Manufacturing Inc (P-4098)*

Damar Plastics Manufacturing Inc .... E 619 283-2300
1035 Pioneer Way Ste 160 El Cajon (92020) *(P-4098)*

Dameron Alloy Foundries (PA) .... D 310 631-5165
6330 Gateway Dr Ste B Cypress (90630) *(P-4571)*

Damo Clothing Company, Los Angeles *Also Called: Damo Textile Inc (P-10704)*

Damo Textile Inc .... E 213 741-1323
12121 Wilshire Blvd Ste 1120 Los Angeles (90025) *(P-10704)*

Dan Gurneys All Amercn Racers, Santa Ana *Also Called: All American Racers Inc (P-7628)*

Dan-Loc Bolt & Gasket, Carson *Also Called: Dan-Loc Group LLC (P-3885)*

Dan-Loc Group LLC .... D 310 538-2822
20444 Tillman Ave Carson (90746) *(P-3885)*

Dana Creath Designs Ltd .... E 714 662-0111
3030 Kilson Dr Santa Ana (92707) *(P-6497)*

Dana Innovations (PA) .... **C 949 492-7777**
991 Calle Amanecer San Clemente (92673) *(P-6532)*

Danchuk Manufacturing Inc .... D 714 540-4363
3211 Halladay St Santa Ana (92705) *(P-7242)*

Danco, Ontario *Also Called: Danco Anodizing Inc (P-5254)*

Danco Anodizing Inc (PA) .... E 626 445-3303
44 La Porte St Arcadia (91006) *(P-5253)*

Danco Anodizing Inc .... C 909 923-0562
1750 E Monticello Ct Ontario (91761) *(P-5254)*

Danco Metal Surfacing, Arcadia *Also Called: Danco Anodizing Inc (P-5253)*

DAndrea Vsual Cmmncations LLC .... D 714 947-8444
6100 Gateway Dr Cypress (90630) *(P-13326)*

Dane Elec Corp USA (HQ) .... **E 949 450-2900**
17520 Von Karman Ave Irvine (92614) *(P-9996)*

Daniel Gerard Worldwide Inc .... D 951 361-1111
13055 Jurupa Ave Fontana (92337) *(P-10132)*

Daniels Inc (PA) .... **E 801 621-3355**
74745 Leslie Ave Palm Desert (92260) *(P-2911)*

Danish Baking Co Inc .... D 818 786-1700
15215 Keswick St Van Nuys (91405) *(P-1440)*

Danish Care Center, Atascadero *Also Called: Compass Health Inc (P-15601)*

Danmer Custom Shutters, Van Nuys *Also Called: Danmer Inc (P-2302)*

Danmer Inc .... C 516 670-5125
8000 Woodley Ave Van Nuys (91406) *(P-2302)*

Danning Gill Damnd Kollitz LLP .... D 310 277-0077
1901 Avenue Of The Stars Ste 450 Los Angeles (90067) *(P-16668)*

Danny Letner Inc .... C 714 633-0030
1490 N Glassell St Orange (92867) *(P-1077)*

Danny Ryan Precision Contg Inc .... D 949 642-6664
16782 Millikan Ave Irvine (92606) *(P-1180)*

Danone Us LLC .... E 949 474-9670
3500 Barranca Pkwy Ste 240 Irvine (92606) *(P-1316)*

Danrich Welding Co Inc .... E 562 634-4811
155 N Eucla Ave San Dimas (91773) *(P-4976)*

Dansereau Health Products .... E 951 549-1400
1581 Commerce St Corona (92878) *(P-8332)*

Daou Vineyards, Paso Robles *Also Called: Daou Vineyards LLC (P-1564)*

Daou Vineyards LLC .... E 805 226-5460
2740 Hidden Mountain Rd Paso Robles (93446) *(P-1564)*

Dar-Ken Inc .... E 760 246-4010
10515 Rancho Rd Adelanto (92301) *(P-3886)*

Darensberries LLC .... C 805 937-8000
714 S Blosser Rd Santa Maria (93458) *(P-15)*

Dark Horse Services .... C 949 779-0219
12955 Glenoaks Blvd Sylmar (91342) *(P-14390)*

Darling Ingredients Inc .... E 323 583-6311
2626 E 25th St Los Angeles (90058) *(P-1524)*

Darmark Corporation .... D 858 679-3970
13225 Gregg St Poway (92064) *(P-6113)*

Darnell-Rose Inc .... E 626 912-1688
1205 Via Roma Colton (92324) *(P-4765)*

DART, Ridgecrest *Also Called: Desert Area Resources Training (P-11627)*

Dart Aerospace, Vista *Also Called: Apical Industries Inc (P-10486)*

Dart Container Corp California (PA) .... **B 951 735-8115**
150 S Maple Center Corona (92880) *(P-3997)*

Dart Entities, Commerce *Also Called: Dart International A Corp (P-9060)*

Dart International A Corp (HQ) .... C 323 264-8746
1430 S Eastman Ave Commerce (90023) *(P-9060)*

Dart Warehouse Corporation (HQ) .... B 323 264-1011
1430 S Eastman Ave Commerce (90023) *(P-9061)*

Dasco Engineering Corp .... C 310 326-2277
24747 Crenshaw Blvd Torrance (90505) *(P-7460)*

Dasol Inc .... C 310 327-6700
9004 Meredith Pl Beverly Hills (90210) *(P-6403)*

Employee Codes: A=Over 500 employees, B=251-500
C=101-250, D=51-100, E=20-50, F=10-19, G=1-9

2025 Southern California
Business Directory and Buyers Guide

© Mergent Inc. 1-800-342-5647
999

A
L
P
H
A
B
E
T
I
C

Dassault Systemes Biovia Corp (DH)........................E 858 799-5000
5005 Wateridge Vista Dr San Diego (92121) *(P-13912)*

Data 911, Poway *Also Called: Hubb Systems LLC (P-14085)*

Data Aire Inc (HQ)..D 800 347-2473
230 W Blueridge Ave Orange (92865) *(P-5974)*

Data Council LLC...D 904 512-3200
15310 Barranca Pkwy Ste 100 Irvine (92618) *(P-14487)*

Data Device Corporation ....E 858 503-3300
13000 Gregg St Ste C Poway (92064) *(P-6816)*

Data Display Products, El Segundo *Also Called: Display Products Inc (P-6818)*

Data Exchange, Camarillo *Also Called: Dex Corporation (P-17513)*

Data Exchange Corporation (PA)........................B 805 388-1711
3600 Via Pescador Camarillo (93012) *(P-9997)*

Data Lights Rigging LLC..................................E 818 786-0536
7508 Tyrone Ave Van Nuys (91405) *(P-6304)*

Data Processing Design Inc ....E 714 695-1000
1409 Glenneyre St Ste B Laguna Beach (92651) *(P-13701)*

Data Trace Info Svcs LLC (HQ)..........................D 714 250-6700
4 First American Way Santa Ana (92707) *(P-18372)*

Datadirect Networks Inc (PA)............................C 818 700-7600
9351 Deering Ave Chatsworth (91311) *(P-13702)*

Datadivider, Carlsbad *Also Called: Exois Inc (P-14218)*

Datallegro Inc..D 949 680-3000
85 Enterprise Ste 200 Aliso Viejo (92656) *(P-9998)*

Datatronics, Menifee *Also Called: Datatronics Romoland Inc (P-6283)*

Datatronics Romoland Inc ....D 951 928-7700
28151 Us Highway 74 Menifee (92585) *(P-6283)*

Datron Advanced Tech Inc ....C 805 579-2966
200 W Los Angeles Ave Simi Valley (93065) *(P-7461)*

Dauntless Industries Inc ....E 626 966-4494
806 N Grand Ave Covina (91724) *(P-5576)*

Dauntless Molds, Covina *Also Called: Dauntless Industries Inc (P-5576)*

Davalan Fresh, Los Angeles *Also Called: Davalan Sales Inc (P-10893)*

Davalan Sales Inc ....C 213 623-2500
1601 E Olympic Blvd Ste 325 Los Angeles (90021) *(P-10893)*

Dave Inc (PA)...B 844 857-3283
1265 S Cochran Ave Los Angeles (90019) *(P-13913)*

Dave Whipple Sheet Metal Inc ....E 619 562-6962
1077 N Cuyamaca St El Cajon (92020) *(P-4977)*

Dave Williams Plbg & Elec Inc ....C 760 296-1397
75140 Saint Charles Pl Ste C Palm Desert (92211) *(P-771)*

David & Goliath LLC ....C 310 445-5200
909 N Pacific Coast Hwy Ste 700 El Segundo (90245) *(P-13202)*

DAVID & MARGARET YOUTH AND FAM, La Verne *Also Called: David and Margaret Home Inc (P-17145)*

David A Campbell Corporation ....C 951 785-4444
3060 Adams St Riverside (92504) *(P-11332)*

David and Margaret Home Inc ....C 909 596-5921
1350 3rd St La Verne (91750) *(P-17145)*

David B Anderson ....E 805 489-0661
174 Suburban Rd Ste 100 San Luis Obispo (93401) *(P-2999)*

David Engineering & Manufacturing Inc ....E 951 735-5200
1230 Quarry St Corona (92879) *(P-5577)*

David Engineering & Mfg, Corona *Also Called: David Engineering & Mfg Inc (P-5180)*

David Engineering & Mfg Inc ....E 951 735-5200
1230 Quarry St Corona (92879) *(P-5180)*

David Grment Ctng Fsing Svc In ....E 323 216-1574
5008 S Boyle Ave Vernon (90058) *(P-2089)*

David H Fell & Co Inc (PA)...............................E 323 722-9992
6009 Bandini Blvd Los Angeles (90040) *(P-4583)*

David Kopf Instruments ....E 818 352-3274
7324 Elmo St Tujunga (91042) *(P-8140)*

David Morse & Assoc., Glendale *Also Called: Dma Claims Management Inc (P-12204)*

David Morse & Associates, Glendale *Also Called: Dma Claims Inc (P-12203)*

David Shield Security Inc ....D 310 849-4950
23945 Calabasas Rd Ste 102 Calabasas (91302) *(P-14293)*

David Wilson's Villa Ford, Orange *Also Called: Villa Ford Inc (P-11427)*

David-Kleis II LLC ....D 951 845-3125
1665 E Eighth St Beaumont (92223) *(P-16553)*

Davidson Hotel Partners Lp ....A 818 707-1220
30100 Agoura Rd Agoura Hills (91301) *(P-12806)*

Davis Research LLC ....C 818 591-2408
26610 Agoura Rd Ste 240 Calabasas (91302) *(P-17843)*

Davis Wire Corporation (HQ)............................C 626 969-7651
5555 Irwindale Ave Irwindale (91706) *(P-4533)*

Davis Wright Tremaine LLP ....C 213 633-6800
865 S Figueroa St Ste 2400 Los Angeles (90017) *(P-16669)*

Daviselen Advertising Inc (PA)..........................C 213 688-7000
865 S Figueroa St Ste 1200 Los Angeles (90017) *(P-13203)*

Davita Inc ....B 949 930-4400
15271 Laguna Canyon Rd Irvine (92618) *(P-16434)*

Davita Magan Management (DH).........................C 626 331-6411
420 W Rowland St Covina (91723) *(P-15298)*

Dawn Food Products Inc ....C 714 258-1223
15601 Mosher Ave Ste 230 Tustin (92780) *(P-1441)*

Dawn Sign Press Inc ....E 858 625-0600
6130 Nancy Ridge Dr San Diego (92121) *(P-2888)*

Dawson Enterprises (PA).................................E 562 424-8564
2853 Cherry Ave Signal Hill (90755) *(P-5508)*

Day Care Center, San Luis Obispo *Also Called: Community Action Prtnr San Lui (P-17085)*

Day Designer, Irvine *Also Called: Blue Sky The Clor Imgntion LLC (P-10578)*

Daybreak, San Diego *Also Called: Daybreak Game Company LLC (P-13703)*

Daybreak Game Company LLC ....B 858 239-0500
13500 Evening Creek Dr N Ste 300 San Diego (92128) *(P-13703)*

Daylight Defense LLC ....C 858 432-7500
16465 Via Esprillo Ste 100 San Diego (92127) *(P-8376)*

Daylight Solutions Inc (DH)..............................D 858 432-7500
16465 Via Esprillo Ste 100 San Diego (92127) *(P-6817)*

Daymark Properties Realty, San Diego *Also Called: Daymark Realty Advisors Inc (P-12428)*

Daymark Realty Advisors Inc ....B 714 975-2999
750 B St Ste 2620 San Diego (92101) *(P-12428)*

Days Inn, Glendale *Also Called: JP Allen Extended Stay (P-12879)*

Days Inn, Encinitas *Also Called: Trigild International Inc (P-13056)*

Dayton Dmh Inc ....C 858 350-4400
121 Spinnaker Ct Del Mar (92014) *(P-12374)*

Dayton Rogers of California Inc ....C 763 784-7714
13630 Saticoy St Van Nuys (91402) *(P-5181)*

Dayton Superior Corporation ....E 951 782-9517
6001 20th St Riverside (92509) *(P-4534)*

Daz, Los Angeles *Also Called: Daz Systems LLC (P-13704)*

Daz Systems LLC ....B 310 640-1300
1003 E 4th Pl Ste 800 Los Angeles (90013) *(P-13704)*

Dazpak Flexible Packaging, City Of Industry *Also Called: Signature Flexible Packg LLC (P-3779)*

Dbi, Cypress *Also Called: Hilti US Manufacturing Inc (P-4747)*

DC, Huntington Beach *Also Called: DC Shoes LLC (P-2009)*

DC Partners Inc (PA).....................................E 714 558-9444
1356 N Santiago St Santa Ana (92701) *(P-4672)*

DC Shoes LLC (HQ)......................................D 714 889-4206
5600 Argosy Ave Ste 100 Huntington Beach (92649) *(P-2009)*

Dcc General Engrg Contrs Inc ....D 760 480-7400
2180 Meyers Ave Escondido (92029) *(P-4386)*

Dcec Holdings Inc ....C 562 802-3488
13259 166th St Cerritos (90703) *(P-6384)*

DCH Acura of Temecula ....D 877 847-9532
26705 Ynez Rd Temecula (92591) *(P-11333)*

DCH California Motors Inc ....D 805 988-7900
1631 Auto Center Dr Oxnard (93036) *(P-11334)*

DCH Gardena Honda ....C 310 515-5700
15541 S Western Ave Gardena (90249) *(P-11335)*

DCI Hollow Metal On Demand, Fontana *Also Called: Door Components Inc (P-4886)*

Dcii North America LLC (HQ).............................D 714 817-7000
200 S Kraemer Blvd Bldg E Brea (92821) *(P-8333)*

Dcli, Huntington Beach *Also Called: Direct Chassislink Inc (P-13455)*

Dcor, Oxnard *Also Called: Dcor LLC (P-298)*

Dcor LLC (PA)..D 805 535-2000
1000 Town Center Dr Fl 6 Oxnard (93036) *(P-298)*

DCS Corporation ....C 760 384-5600
137 W Drummond Ave Ste C Ridgecrest (93555) *(P-17510)*

Dcw Dcw Inc ....D 310 324-3147
20500 Denker Ave Torrance (90501) *(P-9267)*

Dcw Dcw Inc .... D 310 858-1050
20500 Denker Ave Torrance (90501) *(P-18125)*

Dcx-Chol Enterprises Inc (PA)........................... D 310 516-1692
12831 S Figueroa St Los Angeles (90061) *(P-6990)*

Dda Holdings Inc .... E 213 624-5200
834 S Broadway Ste 600 Los Angeles (90014) *(P-2090)*

DDB Wrldwide Cmmnctons Group L .... C 310 907-1500
340 Main St Venice (90291) *(P-13204)*

Ddh Enterprise Inc (PA)..................................... D 760 599-0171
2220 Oak Ridge Way Vista (92081) *(P-6415)*

De Leon Enterprises, Sun Valley *Also Called: De Leon Entps Elec Spclist Inc (P-6722)*

De Leon Entps Elec Spclist Inc .... E 818 252-6690
11934 Allegheny St Sun Valley (91352) *(P-6722)*

De Menno-Kerdoon Trading Co (HQ)................. C 310 537-7100
2000 N Alameda St Compton (90222) *(P-3824)*

De Vries International Inc (PA)............................ E 949 252-1212
17671 Armstrong Ave Irvine (92614) *(P-328)*

De Well Container Shipping Inc .... D 310 735-8600
5553 Bandini Blvd Unit A Bell (90201) *(P-9268)*

Dealership Auto Dtail Rstrtons, Monrovia *Also Called: Executive Auto Reconditioning (P-14708)*

Dean Hesketh Company Inc .... E 714 236-2138
2551 W La Palma Ave Anaheim (92801) *(P-3135)*

Dean Socal LLC .... C 951 734-3950
17637 E Valley Blvd City Of Industry (91744) *(P-1328)*

Deanco Healthcare LLC .... A 818 787-2222
14850 Roscoe Blvd Panorama City (91402) *(P-15973)*

Deasy Penner Podley .... C 626 408-1280
30 N Baldwin Ave Sierra Madre (91024) *(P-12429)*

Debisys Inc (PA)... D 949 699-1401
27442 Portola Pkwy Ste 150 Foothill Ranch (92610) *(P-11839)*

Dec, Santa Ana *Also Called: Dynasty Electronic Company LLC (P-6723)*

Deca International Corp .... E 714 367-5900
10700 Norwalk Blvd Santa Fe Springs (90670) *(P-7712)*

Decatur Electronics Inc (DH)............................. D 888 428-4315
15890 Bernardo Center Dr San Diego (92127) *(P-7713)*

Decco Castings Inc .... E 818 416-0068
1410 Hill St El Cajon (92020) *(P-4687)*

Deccofelt Corporation .... E 626 963-8511
555 S Vermont Ave Glendora (91741) *(P-1969)*

Decipher Corp .... D 888 975-4540
6925 Lusk Blvd Ste 200 San Diego (92121) *(P-16311)*

Decision Ready, Irvine *Also Called: Decision Ready Solutions Inc (P-11897)*

Decision Ready Solutions Inc .... E 949 400-1126
400 Spectrum Center Dr Ste 2050 Irvine (92618) *(P-11897)*

Decisionlogic LLC .... E 858 586-0202
13500 Evening Creek Dr N Ste 600 San Diego (92128) *(P-13914)*

DECKERS, Goleta *Also Called: Deckers Outdoor Corporation (P-2191)*

Deckers Outdoor Corporation (PA)..................... A 805 967-7611
250 Coromar Dr Goleta (93117) *(P-2191)*

Deco Enterprises Inc .... D 323 726-2575
2917 Vail Ave Commerce (90040) *(P-6454)*

Deco Lighting, Commerce *Also Called: Deco Enterprises Inc (P-6454)*

Decore-Ative Spc NC LLC (PA)........................... A 626 254-9191
2772 Peck Rd Monrovia (91010) *(P-2303)*

Decore-Ative Spc NC LLC .... C 626 960-7731
4414 Azusa Canyon Rd Irwindale (91706) *(P-2304)*

Decra, Corona *Also Called: Decra Roofing Systems Inc (P-4978)*

Decra Roofing Systems Inc (DH)........................ D 951 272-8180
1230 Railroad St Corona (92882) *(P-4978)*

Decurion Corporation (PA).................................. D 310 659-9432
120 N Robertson Blvd Fl 3 Los Angeles (90048) *(P-14931)*

Dedicted Dfned Beneft Svcs LLC .... C 415 931-1990
550 N Brand Blvd Ste 1610 Glendale (91203) *(P-12201)*

Dee Engineering Inc .... E 909 947-5616
6918 Ed Perkic St Riverside (92504) *(P-7243)*

Deepsea Power & Light Inc .... E 858 576-1261
4033 Ruffin Rd San Diego (92123) *(P-6498)*

Deering Banjo Company Inc .... E 619 464-8252
3733 Kenora Dr Spring Valley (91977) *(P-11545)*

Defense Solutions, Santa Clarita *Also Called: Curtiss-Wright Corporation (P-5363)*

Defense Specialist, The, Los Angeles *Also Called: Defense Specialists LLC (P-16670)*

Defense Specialists LLC .... D 818 270-7162
924 W Washington Blvd Los Angeles (90015) *(P-16670)*

Defenseweb Technologies Inc .... D 858 272-8505
10188 Telesis Ct Ste 300 San Diego (92121) *(P-14212)*

Dei Headquarters Inc .... B 760 598-6200
3002 Wintergreen Dr Carlsbad (92008) *(P-6679)*

Dei Holdings Inc (HQ).. E 760 598-6200
5541 Fermi Ct Carlsbad (92008) *(P-6680)*

Dek Industry Inc .... C 909 941-8810
807 Palmyrita Ave Riverside (92507) *(P-5700)*

Dekra Insight, Oxnard *Also Called: Behavioral Science Technology Inc (P-18289)*

Dekra-Lite Industries Inc .... D 714 436-0705
3102 W Alton Ave Santa Ana (92704) *(P-14488)*

Del AMO Hospital, Torrance *Also Called: Del AMO Hospital Inc (P-16467)*

Del AMO Hospital Inc .... B 310 530-1151
23700 Camino Del Sol Torrance (90505) *(P-16467)*

Del Mar Country Club Inc .... D 858 759-5500
6001 Clubhouse Dr Rancho Santa Fe (92067) *(P-15131)*

Del Mar Die Casting Co, Gardena *Also Called: Del Mar Industries (P-4658)*

Del Mar Fair Grounds, Del Mar *Also Called: California Dept Fd Agriculture (P-18401)*

Del Mar Fairgrounds .... C 858 792-4288
2260 Jimmy Durante Blvd Del Mar (92014) *(P-13171)*

Del Mar Holding LLC .... A 313 659-7300
1022 Bay Marina Dr # 10 National City (91950) *(P-10867)*

Del Mar Industries (PA)...................................... D 323 321-0600
12901 S Western Ave Gardena (90249) *(P-4658)*

Del Mar Seafoods Inc .... C 805 850-0421
1449 Spinnaker Dr Ventura (93001) *(P-10852)*

Del Mar Thoroughbred Club .... B 858 755-1141
2260 Jimmy Durante Blvd Del Mar (92014) *(P-15038)*

Del Monte Fresh Produce Co .... D 562 777-1127
10730 Patterson Pl Santa Fe Springs (90670) *(P-10894)*

Del Real LLC (PA).. D 951 681-0395
11041 Inland Ave Jurupa Valley (91752) *(P-1389)*

Del Real Foods, Jurupa Valley *Also Called: Del Real LLC (P-1389)*

Del Rio Convalescent, Bell Gardens *Also Called: Del Rio Sanitarium Inc (P-15621)*

Del Rio Sanitarium Inc .... C 562 927-6586
7002 Gage Ave Bell Gardens (90201) *(P-15621)*

Del Rosa Villa, San Bernardino *Also Called: Del Rosa Villaidence Opco LLC (P-15810)*

Del Rosa Villaidence Opco LLC .... C 909 885-3261
2018 Del Rosa Ave San Bernardino (92404) *(P-15810)*

Del Taco, Lake Forest *Also Called: Del Taco Restaurants Inc (P-11564)*

Del Taco Restaurants Inc (PA)............................ C 949 462-9300
25521 Commercentre Dr Ste 200 Lake Forest (92630) *(P-11564)*

Del West Engineering Inc (PA)............................ C 661 295-5700
28128 Livingston Ave Valencia (91355) *(P-7244)*

Del West USA, Valencia *Also Called: Del West Engineering Inc (P-7244)*

Delafield Corporation (PA).................................. C 626 303-0740
1520 Flower Ave Duarte (91010) *(P-6114)*

Delafield Fluid Technology, Duarte *Also Called: Delafield Corporation (P-6114)*

Delafoil Holdings Inc (PA).................................. C 949 752-4580
18500 Von Karman Ave Ste 450 Irvine (92612) *(P-4979)*

Delamo Manufacturing Inc .... D 323 936-3566
7171 Telegraph Rd Montebello (90640) *(P-4099)*

Delano Dst Sklled Nrsing Fclty, Delano *Also Called: North Kern S Tulare Hosp Dst (P-16106)*

Delano Growers Grape Products .... D 661 725-3255
32351 Bassett Ave Delano (93215) *(P-1675)*

Delano Regional Medical Center, Delano *Also Called: Adventist Health Delano (P-15892)*

Delano Regional Medical Center, Delano *Also Called: Adventist Health Delano (P-15893)*

Delano Waste Water Treatment, Delano *Also Called: City of Delano (P-6006)*

Delaware Ancra International, Azusa *Also Called: Ancra International LLC (P-5524)*

Delaware Systems Technology, San Bernardino *Also Called: Systems Technology Inc (P-5793)*

Delfin Design & Mfg Inc .... E 949 888-4644
15672 Producer Ln Huntington Beach (92649) *(P-4100)*

Deliver-It, Anaheim *Also Called: Di Overnite LLC (P-9001)*

Deliverr Inc .... B 213 534-8686
307 S Wilson Ave Apt 6 Pasadena (91106) *(P-10749)*

Employee Codes: A=Over 500 employees, B=251-500
C=101-250, D=51-100, E=20-50, F=10-19, G=1-9

2025 Southern California
Business Directory and Buyers Guide

© Mergent Inc. 1-800-342-5647

1001

Delivery Solutions Inc .... D 800 335-6557
595 Tamarack Ave Ste D Brea (92821) *(P-8903)*

Delkin Devices, Poway *Also Called: Delkin Devices Inc (P-5912)*

Delkin Devices Inc (PA) .... D 858 391-1234
13350 Kirkham Way Poway (92064) *(P-5912)*

Dellarobbia Inc (PA) .... E 949 251-9532
119 Waterworks Way Irvine (92618) *(P-2444)*

Deloitte & Touche LLP .... A 213 688-0800
555 W 5th St Ste 2700 Los Angeles (90013) *(P-17716)*

Deloitte & Touche LLP .... C 714 436-7419
695 Town Center Dr Ste 1200 Costa Mesa (92626) *(P-17717)*

Deloitte & Touche LLP .... A 619 232-6500
12830 El Camino Real Ste 600 San Diego (92130) *(P-17718)*

Deloitte Tax LLP .... C 404 885-6754
555 W 5th St Ste 2700 Los Angeles (90013) *(P-17719)*

Delori Foods, City Of Industry *Also Called: Delori-Nutifood Products Inc (P-1762)*

Delori-Nutifood Products Inc .... E 626 965-3006
17043 Green Dr City Of Industry (91745) *(P-1762)*

Delphi Display Systems Inc .... D 714 825-3400
3550 Hyland Ave Costa Mesa (92626) *(P-5913)*

Delphic Enterprises Inc .... D 661 254-2000
23026 Soledad Canyon Rd Santa Clarita (91350) *(P-127)*

Delstar Holding Corp .... E 619 258-1503
9225 Isaac St Santee (92071) *(P-3947)*

Delstar Technologies Inc .... E 619 258-1503
1306 Fayette St El Cajon (92020) *(P-3948)*

Delta Computer Consulting .... C 310 541-9440
25550 Hawthorne Blvd Ste 106 Torrance (90505) *(P-14213)*

Delta Dental, San Diego *Also Called: Delta Dental of California (P-12079)*

Delta Dental of California .... C 619 683-2549
1450 Frazee Rd Ste 200 San Diego (92108) *(P-12079)*

Delta Design Inc (HQ) .... B 858 848-8000
12367 Crosthwaite Cir Poway (92064) *(P-5818)*

Delta Design (littleton) Inc .... A 858 848-8100
12367 Crosthwaite Cir Poway (92064) *(P-7908)*

Delta Fabrication Inc .... D 818 407-4000
9600 De Soto Ave Chatsworth (91311) *(P-6115)*

Delta Floral Distributors Inc .... C 323 751-8116
6810 West Blvd Los Angeles (90043) *(P-11086)*

Delta Galil USA Inc .... B 213 488-4859
777 S Alameda St Fl 3 Los Angeles (90021) *(P-2148)*

Delta Galil USA Inc .... B 949 296-0380
16912 Von Karman Ave Irvine (92606) *(P-10705)*

Delta Group Electronics, San Diego *Also Called: Delta Group Electronics Inc (P-6991)*

Delta Group Electronics Inc .... D 858 569-1681
10180 Scripps Ranch Blvd San Diego (92131) *(P-6991)*

Delta Hi-Tech .... C 818 407-4000
9600 De Soto Ave Chatsworth (91311) *(P-6116)*

Delta Microwave LLC .... D 805 751-1100
300 Del Norte Blvd Oxnard (93030) *(P-6992)*

Delta Pacific Activewear Inc .... D 714 871-9281
331 S Hale Ave Fullerton (92831) *(P-1915)*

Delta Packaging Products, Los Angeles *Also Called: E & S Paper Co (P-10591)*

Delta Printing Solutions Inc .... C 661 257-0584
28210 Avenue Stanford Valencia (91355) *(P-3000)*

Delta Scientific Corporation (PA) .... C 661 575-1100
40355 Delta Ln Palmdale (93551) *(P-14391)*

Delta Tau Data Systems Inc Cal (HQ) .... C 818 998-2095
21314 Lassen St Chatsworth (91311) *(P-5819)*

Delta-T Group Inc .... C 619 543-0556
4420 Hotel Circle Ct Ste 205 San Diego (92108) *(P-13509)*

Deltronic Corporation .... D 714 545-5800
3900 W Segerstrom Ave Santa Ana (92704) *(P-7999)*

Deluxe Building Products, Pomona *Also Called: Wcs Equipment Holdings LLC (P-4573)*

Deluxe Nms Inc .... C 310 760-8500
4499 Glencoe Ave Marina Del Rey (90292) *(P-14917)*

Demand Cnc, Irvine *Also Called: Synventive Engineering Inc (P-5561)*

Demcon Concrete Contractor, Poway *Also Called: Demcon Concrete Contrs Inc (P-1114)*

Demcon Concrete Contrs Inc .... D 858 748-5090
13795 Blaisdell Pl Ste 202 Poway (92064) *(P-1114)*

Demenno-Kerdoon, South Gate *Also Called: Demenno/Kerdoon Holdings (P-3851)*

Demenno/Kerdoon Holdings (DH) .... D 562 231-1550
9302 Garfield Ave South Gate (90280) *(P-3851)*

Demenno/Kerdoon Holdings .... E 323 268-3387
3650 E 26th St Vernon (90058) *(P-3852)*

Demler Brothers LLC .... D 760 789-2457
25818 Highway 78 Ramona (92065) *(P-93)*

Dempsey Construction Inc .... D 760 918-6900
1835 Aston Ave Carlsbad (92008) *(P-397)*

Den-Mat Corporation .... C 800 445-0345
21515 Vanowen St Ste 200 Canoga Park (91303) *(P-3644)*

Den-Mat Corporation (DH) .... B 805 922-8491
236 S Bdwy Orcutt (93455) *(P-3645)*

Dena Corp .... D 415 375-3170
360 N Pacific Coast Hwy El Segundo (90245) *(P-13705)*

Denardi Machinery Inc .... C 619 749-0039
1475 Pioneer Way El Cajon (92020) *(P-10346)*

Dendreon Pharmaceuticals LLC (HQ) .... E 562 252-7500
1700 Saturn Way Seal Beach (90740) *(P-3395)*

Denim-Tech LLC .... D 323 277-8998
375 E 2nd St Apt 604 Los Angeles (90012) *(P-5963)*

Denken Solutions Inc .... C 949 630-5263
9170 Irvine Center Dr Ste 200 Irvine (92618) *(P-18126)*

Denmac Industries Inc .... E 562 634-2714
7616 Rosecrans Ave Paramount (90723) *(P-5317)*

Dennis & Leen, Los Angeles *Also Called: EC Group Inc (P-9870)*

Dennis Allen Associates (PA) .... D 805 884-8777
201 N Milpas St Santa Barbara (93103) *(P-398)*

Dennis DiGiorgio .... E 714 408-7527
333 City Blvd W Ste 1700 Orange (92868) *(P-4332)*

Dennis Foland Inc (PA) .... E 909 930-9900
1500 S Hellman Ave Ontario (91761) *(P-10558)*

Dennis M McCoy & Sons Inc .... D 818 874-3872
32107 Lindero Canyon Rd Ste 212 Westlake Village (91361) *(P-613)*

Dennison Division, Brea *Also Called: Avery Dennison Office Products Co Inc (P-2755)*

Dennison Inc .... E 626 965-8917
17901 Railroad St City Of Industry (91748) *(P-5061)*

Denso Pdts & Svcs Americas Inc .... C 951 698-3379
41673 Corning Pl Murrieta (92562) *(P-7245)*

Denso Pdts & Svcs Americas Inc (DH) .... B 310 834-6352
3900 Via Oro Ave Long Beach (90810) *(P-9821)*

Denso Wireless Systems America Inc .... C 760 734-4600
2251 Rutherford Rd # 100 Carlsbad (92008) *(P-6607)*

Dentalville, Bell *Also Called: Leonid M Glsman DDS A Dntl Cor (P-15520)*

Dentons US LLP .... C 213 623-9300
601 S Figueroa St Ste 2500 Los Angeles (90017) *(P-16671)*

Department Children Fmly Svcs, Los Angeles *Also Called: County of Los Angeles (P-16922)*

Department Military California .... B 562 795-2065
11300 Lexington Dr Bldg 1000 Los Alamitos (90720) *(P-18261)*

Department of Arprts of The Cy .... A 855 463-5252
1 World Way Los Angeles (90045) *(P-9199)*

Department of Dermatology, Irvine *Also Called: University California Irvine (P-16340)*

Department of Health Services, Los Angeles *Also Called: County of Los Angeles (P-16291)*

Department of Mental Health, Los Angeles *Also Called: County of Los Angeles (P-14167)*

Department of Mental Health, Los Angeles *Also Called: County of Los Angeles (P-18392)*

Department of Public Works, Alhambra *Also Called: County of Los Angeles (P-9688)*

Department of Social Services, Paso Robles *Also Called: County of Los Angeles (P-16905)*

Dependable Companies .... C 800 548-8608
2555 E Olympic Blvd Los Angeles (90023) *(P-8943)*

Dependable Disposal and Recycl, Spring Valley *Also Called: Burns and Sons Trucking Inc (P-8897)*

Dependable Global Express Inc (PA) .... C 310 537-2000
19201 S Susana Rd E Rncho Dmngz (90221) *(P-9269)*

Dependable Highway Express Inc (PA) .... B 323 526-2200
2555 E Olympic Blvd Los Angeles (90023) *(P-8944)*

Dependable Highway Express Inc .... C 310 522-4111
800 E 230th St Carson (90745) *(P-8945)*

Dependable Highway Express Inc .... C 909 923-0065
1351 S Campus Ave Ontario (91761) *(P-8946)*

Dependable Supply Chain Svcs, Los Angeles *Also Called: Dependable Highway Express Inc (P-8944)*

Mergent email: customerrelations@mergent.com
1002

2025 Southern California
Business Directory and Buyers Guide

(P-0000) Products & Services Section entry number
(PA)=Parent Co (HQ)=Headquarters (DH)=Div Headquarters

Dependble Break Rm Sltions Inc .... D 909 982-5933
1431 W 9th St Ste B Upland (91786) *(P-10042)*

Depo Auto Parts, Fontana *Also Called: Maxzone Vehicle Lighting Corp (P-9832)*

Dept Children and Family Svcs, Lakewood *Also Called: County of Los Angeles (P-16914)*

Dept of Public Works, Irvine *Also Called: City of Irvine (P-18116)*

Depuy, San Diego *Also Called: Medical Device Bus Svcs Inc (P-8283)*

Derek and Constance Lee Corp (PA) .... D 909 595-8831
19355 San Jose Ave City Of Industry (91748) *(P-1257)*

Dermal Group, The, Carson *Also Called: Dermalogica LLC (P-3646)*

Dermalogica LLC (HQ) .... C 310 900-4000
1535 Beachey Pl Carson (90746) *(P-3646)*

Dermtech Inc (PA) .... C 866 450-4223
12340 El Camino Real San Diego (92130) *(P-3537)*

DES PERES HOSPITAL, INC., Indio *Also Called: John F Kennedy Mem Hosp Aux (P-16030)*

Desco, Chino *Also Called: Desco Industries Inc (P-6372)*

Desco Industries Inc (PA) .... D 909 627-8178
3651 Walnut Ave Chino (91710) *(P-6372)*

Desert Area Resources Training (PA) .... D 760 375-9787
201 E Ridgecrest Blvd Ridgecrest (93555) *(P-11627)*

Desert Grafics, Palm Springs *Also Called: Desert Publications Inc (P-2853)*

Desert Haven Enterprises .... A 661 948-8402
43437 Copeland Cir Lancaster (93535) *(P-203)*

DESERT HORIZONS COUNTRY CLUB, Indian Wells *Also Called: Dhccnp (P-15132)*

Desert Hot Springs Spa Hotel, Desert Hot Springs *Also Called: Desert Hot Sprng Real Prpts In (P-12289)*

Desert Hot Sprng Real Prpts In .... D 760 329-6000
10805 Palm Dr Desert Hot Springs (92240) *(P-12289)*

Desert Inn & Suites, Anaheim *Also Called: SAI Management Co Inc (P-13008)*

Desert Knlls Convalescent Hosp, Victorville *Also Called: Knolls Convalescent Hosp Inc (P-15686)*

Desert Mechanical Inc .... A 702 873-7333
15870 Olden St Rancho Cascades (91342) *(P-772)*

Desert Medical Group Inc (PA) .... C 760 320-8814
275 N El Cielo Rd Ste D-402 Palm Springs (92262) *(P-15299)*

Desert Mountain Fics, Victorville *Also Called: Victor Cmnty Support Svcs Inc (P-16519)*

Desert Oasis Healthcare, Palm Springs *Also Called: Desert Medical Group Inc (P-15299)*

Desert Orthpd Ctr A Med Group (PA) .... D 760 568-2684
39000 Bob Hope Dr Ste W301 Rancho Mirage (92270) *(P-15300)*

Desert Publications Inc (PA) .... E 760 325-2333
303 N Indian Canyon Dr Palm Springs (92262) *(P-2853)*

Desert Regional Med Ctr Inc (HQ) .... A 760 323-6511
1150 N Indian Canyon Dr Palm Springs (92262) *(P-15974)*

Desert Snds Unfied Schl Dst SC .... D 760 777-4200
47950 Dune Palms Rd La Quinta (92253) *(P-17088)*

Desert Sun Publishing Co (DH) .... C 760 322-8889
750 N Gene Autry Trl Palm Springs (92262) *(P-2794)*

Desert Sun The, Palm Springs *Also Called: Desert Sun Publishing Co (P-2794)*

Desert Valley Date LLC .... D 760 398-0999
86740 Industrial Way Coachella (92236) *(P-10943)*

Desert Valley Hospital Inc (DH) .... C 760 241-8000
16850 Bear Valley Rd Victorville (92395) *(P-15975)*

Desert Valley Industries, Palm Desert *Also Called: Desertarc (P-16933)*

Desert Valley Med Group Inc (DH) .... B 760 241-8000
16850 Bear Valley Rd Victorville (92392) *(P-15301)*

Desert Valley Medical Group, Victorville *Also Called: Desert Valley Med Group Inc (P-15301)*

Desert Water Agency Fing Corp .... D 760 323-4971
1200 S Gene Autry Trl Palm Springs (92264) *(P-9690)*

Desert Willow Golf Course, Palm Desert *Also Called: Desert Willow Golf Resort Inc (P-15076)*

Desert Willow Golf Resort Inc .... C 760 346-0015
38995 Desert Willow Dr Palm Desert (92260) *(P-15076)*

Desertarc .... B 760 346-1611
73255 Country Club Dr Palm Desert (92260) *(P-16933)*

Design International Group Inc .... E 626 369-2289
755 Epperson Dr City Of Industry (91748) *(P-10520)*

Design Made Easy, Los Angeles *Also Called: Emser Tile LLC (P-9945)*

Design Masonry Inc .... D 661 252-2784
20703 Santa Clara St Canyon Country (91351) *(P-981)*

Design People Inc .... D 800 969-5799
1700 E Walnut Ave Ste 400 El Segundo (90245) *(P-14129)*

Design Science Inc .... E 562 442-4779
444 W Ocean Blvd Ste 800 Long Beach (90802) *(P-13706)*

DESIGN THERAPEUTICS, Carlsbad *Also Called: Design Therapeutics Inc (P-3396)*

Design Therapeutics Inc .... C 858 293-4900
6005 Hidden Valley Rd Ste 110 Carlsbad (92011) *(P-3396)*

Design Todays Inc (PA) .... E 213 745-3091
11707 Cetona Way Porter Ranch (91326) *(P-2091)*

Design West Technologies Inc .... D 714 731-0201
2701 Dow Ave Tustin (92780) *(P-4101)*

Designed Metal Connections Inc .... E 310 323-6200
623 E Artesia Blvd Carson (90746) *(P-5106)*

Designed Metal Connections Inc (DH) .... B 310 323-6200
14800 S Figueroa St Gardena (90248) *(P-7462)*

Designory, Long Beach *Also Called: Designory Inc (P-13327)*

Designory Inc (HQ) .... C 562 624-0200
211 E Ocean Blvd Ste 100 Long Beach (90802) *(P-13327)*

Designworks/Usa Inc .... D 805 499-9590
2201 Corporate Center Dr Newbury Park (91320) *(P-17511)*

Deskmakers Inc .... E 323 264-2260
6525 Flotilla St Commerce (90040) *(P-2508)*

Desksite, Irvine *Also Called: Qdos Inc (P-14011)*

Desmond Ventures Inc .... C 949 474-0400
17451 Von Karman Ave Irvine (92614) *(P-3764)*

Desser Holding Company LLC (HQ) .... E 323 721-4900
6900 W Acco St Montebello (90640) *(P-12597)*

Desser Tire & Rubber Co, Montebello *Also Called: Desser Tire & Rubber Co LLC (P-3864)*

Desser Tire & Rubber Co LLC .... E 323 837-1497
6900 W Acco St Montebello (90640) *(P-10490)*

Desser Tire & Rubber Co LLC (DH) .... E 323 721-4900
6900 W Acco St Montebello (90640) *(P-3864)*

Desser Tire & Rubber Co., Montebello *Also Called: Desser Holding Company LLC (P-12597)*

Dessert Cancer Care, Yucca Valley *Also Called: Eisenhower Medical Center (P-15304)*

Destination Residences LLC .... A 760 346-4647
45750 San Luis Rey Ave Palm Desert (92260) *(P-12807)*

Destination Residences LLC .... A 858 550-1000
9700 N Torrey Pines Rd La Jolla (92037) *(P-13172)*

Detoronics Corp .... E 626 579-7130
13071 Rosecrans Ave Santa Fe Springs (90670) *(P-6947)*

Detroit Diesel Corporation .... D 562 929-7016
10645 Studebaker Rd 2nd Fl Downey (90241) *(P-5467)*

Deutsch La Inc .... D 310 862-3000
12901 W Jefferson Blvd Los Angeles (90066) *(P-13205)*

Deutsche Bank National Tr Co .... D 714 247-6054
1761 E Saint Andrew Pl Santa Ana (92705) *(P-11835)*

Deutsche Bank National Tr Co .... D 310 788-6200
1999 Avenue Of The Stars Ste 3750 Los Angeles (90067) *(P-11845)*

Deva, Tustin *Also Called: Distribution Electrnics Vlued (P-7119)*

Devax Inc .... E 949 461-0450
13900 Alton Pkwy Ste 125 Irvine (92618) *(P-8141)*

Developers Surety Indemnity Co (DH) .... D 949 263-3300
17771 Cowan Ste 100 Irvine (92614) *(P-12146)*

Developers Surety Indemnity Co, Irvine *Also Called: Insco Insurance Services Inc (P-12221)*

Developlus Inc .... C 951 738-8595
1575 Magnolia Ave Corona (92879) *(P-8674)*

Development Associates Contrls .... E 805 684-8307
6390 Rose Ln Carpinteria (93013) *(P-5542)*

Development Disabilities Ctr, Santa Ana *Also Called: Regional Ctr Orange Cnty Inc (P-18395)*

Development Resource Cons Inc (PA) .... D 714 685-6860
160 S Old Springs Rd Ste 210 Anaheim (92808) *(P-17512)*

Development Services, Lancaster *Also Called: Lancaster Cmnty Svcs Fndtion I (P-14693)*

Develpmntal Svcs Continuum Inc .... D 619 460-7333
7944 Golden Ave Lemon Grove (91945) *(P-17146)*

Devereux California Center, Goleta *Also Called: Devereux Foundation (P-16468)*

Devereux Foundation .... B 805 968-2525
7055 Seaway Dr Goleta (93117) *(P-16468)*

Devil Mountain Whl Nurs LLC .... D 949 496-9356
29001 Ortega Hwy San Juan Capistrano (92675) *(P-52)*

Dewitt Stern Group Inc .... C 818 933-2700
5990 Sepulveda Blvd Ste 550 Van Nuys (91411) *(P-12202)*

Dex Corporation .... C 805 388-1711
3600 Via Pescador Camarillo (93012) *(P-17513)*

Employee Codes: A=Over 500 employees, B=251-500
C=101-250, D=51-100, E=20-50, F=10-19, G=1-9

2025 Southern California
Business Directory and Buyers Guide

© Mergent Inc. 1-800-342-5647
1003

ALPHABETIC

Dex-O-Tex Division, Compton *Also Called: Crossfield Products Corp (P-3262)*

Dexcom, San Diego *Also Called: Dexcom Inc (P-8142)*

Dexcom Inc (PA)... A 858 200-0200
6340 Sequence Dr San Diego (92121) *(P-8142)*

Dext Company, Santa Monica *Also Called: Reconserve Inc (P-1432)*

Dexter Axle Company .... E 760 744-1610
135 Sunshine Ln San Marcos (92069) *(P-7315)*

Dexyp, Glendale *Also Called: Yellowpagescom LLC (P-14637)*

Df One Operator LLC .... D 310 961-9739
11 Via Santanella Rancho Mirage (92270) *(P-14489)*

Dfa Dairy Brands Fluid LLC .... B 800 395-7004
17851 Railroad St City Of Industry (91748) *(P-90)*

Dfds International Corporation .... D 310 414-1516
898 N Pacific Coast Hwy 6th Fl El Segundo (90245) *(P-9270)*

Dfds Transport US, El Segundo *Also Called: Dfds International Corporation (P-9270)*

Dfm Dietary Food Management, Canoga Park *Also Called: Computrition Inc (P-13692)*

Dg Brands Inc .... D 323 268-0220
5548 Lindbergh Ln Bell (90201) *(P-10706)*

DG Performance Spc Inc .... D 714 961-8850
4100 E La Palma Ave Anaheim (92807) *(P-7682)*

Dg-Displays LLC .... E 877 358-5976
355 Parkside Dr San Fernando (91340) *(P-8599)*

Dgl Holdings Inc .... E 714 630-7840
3850 E Miraloma Ave Anaheim (92806) *(P-5123)*

Dgwb Inc .... D 714 881-2300
217 N Main St Ste 200 Santa Ana (92701) *(P-13206)*

Dgwb Advg & Communications, Santa Ana *Also Called: Dgwb Inc (P-13206)*

Dha America Inc .... D 858 925-3246
5403 Harvest Run Dr San Diego (92130) *(P-5404)*

Dharma Ventures Group Inc (PA) .... B 661 294-4200
24700 Avenue Rockefeller Valencia (91355) *(P-11681)*

Dhb Delivery LLC .... D 626 588-7562
1134 N Chestnut Ln Azusa (91702) *(P-9000)*

Dhccnp .... D 760 340-4646
44900 Desert Horizons Dr Indian Wells (92210) *(P-15132)*

Dhe, Ontario *Also Called: Dependable Highway Express Inc (P-8946)*

Dhv Industries Inc .... D 661 392-8948
3451 Pegasus Dr Bakersfield (93308) *(P-10435)*

Dhx-Dependable Hawaiian Ex Inc (PA) .... C 310 537-2000
19201 S Susana Rd Compton (90221) *(P-9271)*

Di Overnite LLC .... D 877 997-7447
1900 S State College Blvd Ste 450 Anaheim (92806) *(P-9001)*

Di Vizio Lab, Los Angeles *Also Called: Cedars-Sinai Medical Center (P-15938)*

Diagnostic Health Corporation .... C 310 665-7180
6801 Park Ter Los Angeles (90045) *(P-18127)*

Diagnostic Health Los Angeles, Los Angeles *Also Called: Diagnostic Health Corporation (P-18127)*

Diagnostic Labs & Rdlgy, North Hollywood *Also Called: Kan-Di-Ki LLC (P-16321)*

Diagnostic Medical Group, Monterey Park *Also Called: Chen Dvid MD Dgnstc Med Group (P-15272)*

Diagnstic Intrvntnal Srgcal CT .... D 310 574-0400
13160 Mindanao Way Ste 150 Marina Del Rey (90292) *(P-15302)*

Diakont, Oceanside *Also Called: Diakont Advanced Tech Inc (P-9966)*

Diakont Advanced Tech Inc .... E 858 551-5551
1662 Ord Way Oceanside (92056) *(P-9966)*

Dial Communications, Camarillo *Also Called: Dial Security Inc (P-14392)*

Dial Global Digital, Culver City *Also Called: Triton Media Group LLC (P-9490)*

Dial Industries Inc .... D 323 263-6878
3616 Noakes St Los Angeles (90023) *(P-4102)*

Dial Industries Inc (PA) .... D 323 263-6878
3628 Noakes St Los Angeles (90023) *(P-4103)*

Dial Precision Inc .... D 760 947-3557
17235 Darwin Ave Hesperia (92345) *(P-6117)*

Dial Security Inc (PA) .... C 805 389-6700
760 W Ventura Blvd Camarillo (93010) *(P-14392)*

Diality Inc .... D 949 916-5851
181 Technology Dr Ste 150 Irvine (92618) *(P-8143)*

Diamond Bar Imports Inc .... D 626 935-1700
17525 Gale Ave City Of Industry (91748) *(P-11336)*

Diamond Baseball Company Inc .... E 949 409-9300
121 Waterworks Way Ste 150 Irvine (92618) *(P-8514)*

Diamond Collection LLC .... E 626 435-0077
20579 Valley Blvd Walnut (91789) *(P-2192)*

Diamond Contract Services Inc .... B 818 565-3554
11432 Vanowen St North Hollywood (91605) *(P-13371)*

Diamond Environmental Services, San Marcos *Also Called: Diamond Environmental Svcs LP (P-13454)*

Diamond Environmental Svcs LP .... D 760 744-7191
807 E Mission Rd San Marcos (92069) *(P-13454)*

Diamond Goldenwest Corporation (PA) .... C 714 542-9000
15732 Tustin Village Way Tustin (92780) *(P-11638)*

Diamond Ground Products Inc .... E 805 498-3837
2651 Lavery Ct Newbury Park (91320) *(P-5646)*

Diamond Honda, City Of Industry *Also Called: Diamond Bar Imports Inc (P-11336)*

Diamond Mattress Company Inc (PA) .... E 310 638-0363
3112 E Las Hermanas St Compton (90221) *(P-11513)*

Diamond Mattress Nf, Compton *Also Called: Diamond Mattress Company Inc (P-11513)*

Diamond Multimedia, Canoga Park *Also Called: Best Data Products Inc (P-5906)*

Diamond Resorts Intl Inc .... D 702 823-7000
2800 S Palm Canyon Dr Palm Springs (92264) *(P-12808)*

Diamond Resorts LLC .... D 760 866-1800
2800 S Palm Canyon Dr Palm Springs (92264) *(P-12809)*

Diamond Ridge Corporation .... C 909 949-0605
121 S Mountain Ave Upland (91786) *(P-12430)*

Diamond Sports, Irvine *Also Called: Diamond Baseball Company Inc (P-8514)*

Diamond Wipes, Chino *Also Called: Diamond Wipes Intl Inc (P-3649)*

Diamond Wipes Intl Inc .... C 909 230-9888
4200 E Mission Blvd Ontario (91761) *(P-3647)*

Diamond Wipes Intl Inc .... D 909 230-9888
13775 Ramona Ave Chino (91710) *(P-3648)*

Diamond Wipes Intl Inc (PA) .... D 909 230-9888
4651 Schaefer Ave Chino (91710) *(P-3649)*

Diamondrock San Dego Tnant LLC .... B 619 239-4500
400 W Broadway San Diego (92101) *(P-12810)*

Diana Did-It Designs Inc .... E 970 226-5062
20579 Valley Blvd Walnut (91789) *(P-2193)*

Dianas Mexican Food Pdts Inc .... D 626 444-0555
2905 Durfee Ave El Monte (91732) *(P-1763)*

Dianas Mexican Food Pdts Inc (PA) .... E 562 926-5802
16330 Pioneer Blvd Norwalk (90650) *(P-1764)*

Dianas Mexican Food Pdts Inc .... E 310 834-4886
300 E Sepulveda Blvd Carson (90745) *(P-11274)*

Diasorin Molecular LLC .... C 562 240-6500
11331 Valley View St Cypress (90630) *(P-3538)*

Diba Fashions Inc .... D 323 232-3775
472 N Bowling Green Way Los Angeles (90049) *(P-14490)*

Dibella, Oceanside *Also Called: Dibella Baking Company Inc (P-1486)*

Dibella Baking Company Inc .... D 951 797-4144
3524 Seagate Way Ste 110 Oceanside (92056) *(P-1486)*

Dicaperl Corporation (DH) .... D 610 667-6640
23705 Crenshaw Blvd Ste 101 Torrance (90505) *(P-385)*

Dick Dewese Chevrolet Inc .... C 909 793-2681
800 Alabama St Redlands (92374) *(P-11337)*

Dickeys Barbecue Pit, Tustin *Also Called: Dickeys Barbecue Rest Inc (P-11565)*

Dickeys Barbecue Rest Inc .... E 714 602-3874
17245 17th St Tustin (92780) *(P-11565)*

Dickson Testing Co Inc (DH) .... D 562 862-8378
11126 Palmer Ave South Gate (90280) *(P-17912)*

Didi Hirsch Psychiatric Svc (PA) .... C 310 390-6612
4760 Sepulveda Blvd Culver City (90230) *(P-16934)*

Didi Hrsch Cmnty Mntal Hlth Ct, Culver City *Also Called: Didi Hirsch Psychiatric Svc (P-16934)*

Different Rules LLC .... D 858 571-2121
9357 Spectrum Center Blvd San Diego (92123) *(P-11566)*

Dig Corporation .... E 760 727-0914
1210 Activity Dr Vista (92081) *(P-5473)*

Digirad Imaging Solutions Inc .... D 800 947-6134
13100 Gregg St Ste A Poway (92064) *(P-13430)*

Digital Arbitrage Dist Inc (PA) .... E 888 392-9478
3033 5th Ave Ste 100 San Diego (92103) *(P-13915)*

Digital Domain, Venice *Also Called: Power Studios Inc (P-14848)*

Digital Domain 30 Inc (PA) .... B 213 797-3100
12641 Beatrice St Los Angeles (90066) *(P-14818)*

Mergent email: customerrelations@mergent.com
1004

2025 Southern California
Business Directory and Buyers Guide

(P-0000) Products & Services Section entry number
(PA)=Parent Co (HQ)=Headquarters (DH)=Div Headquarters

Digital Domain Media Group Inc .... A
12641 Beatrice St Los Angeles (90066) (P-13328)

Digital Film Labs, Los Angeles Also Called: Point360 (P-14902)

Digital Flex Media Inc .... D 909 484-8440
11150 White Birch Dr Rancho Cucamonga (91730) (P-6574)

Digital Force Technologies, San Diego Also Called: Raytheon Dgital Force Tech LLC (P-7800)

Digital Insight Corporation .... D 818 879-1010
5601 Lindero Canyon Rd Ste 100 Westlake Village (91362) (P-14168)

Digital Label Solutions LLC .... E 714 982-5000
1177 N Grove St Anaheim (92806) (P-2766)

Digital Marketing, San Diego Also Called: Stn Digital LLC (P-13247)

Digital Payment Services, Westlake Village Also Called: Input 1 LLC (P-11868)

Digital Periph Solutions Inc .... E 714 998-3440
160 S Old Springs Rd Ste 220 Anaheim (92808) (P-6533)

Digital Printing Systems Inc (PA) .... D 626 815-1888
2350 Panorama Ter Los Angeles (90039) (P-3001)

Digital Room Holdings Inc (HQ) .... D 310 575-4440
8000 Haskell Ave Van Nuys (91406) (P-3136)

Digital Signal Power Mfg, San Bernardino Also Called: DSPM Inc (P-6928)

Digital Supercolor Inc .... D 949 622-0010
Irvine (92606) (P-3002)

Digital Surgery Systems Inc .... E 805 978-5400
125 Cremona Dr Pmb 110 Goleta (93117) (P-8144)

Digitalmojo Inc .... D 800 413-5916
3111 Camino Del Rio N Ste 400 San Diego (92108) (P-9432)

Digitalpro Inc (PA) .... E 858 874-7750
13257 Kirkham Way Poway (92064) (P-3003)

Digitaria, San Diego Also Called: Mirum Inc (P-13331)

Digitas Inc .... C 617 867-1000
13031 W Jefferson Blvd Ste 800 Los Angeles (90094) (P-13207)

Digitaslbi, Los Angeles Also Called: Digitas Inc (P-13207)

Digitran, Rancho Cucamonga Also Called: Electro Switch Corp (P-6305)

Dignified Home Loans LLC .... D 818 421-7753
1 Baxter Way Ste 120 Westlake Village (91362) (P-11945)

Dignity Health .... B 805 739-3000
1400 E Church St Santa Maria (93454) (P-15976)

Dignity Health .... C 805 389-5800
2309 Antonio Ave Camarillo (93010) (P-15977)

Dignity Health .... A 805 988-2500
1600 N Rose Ave Oxnard (93030) (P-15978)

Dignity Health .... C 661 663-6000
400 Old River Rd Bakersfield (93311) (P-15979)

Dignity Health .... B 805 988-2868
200 Oceangate Long Beach (90802) (P-15980)

Dignity Health .... A 818 885-8500
18300 Roscoe Blvd Northridge (91325) (P-15981)

Dignity Health .... C 562 491-9000
1050 Linden Ave Long Beach (90813) (P-15982)

Dilbeck Inc (PA) .... D 818 790-6774
1030 Foothill Blvd La Canada (91011) (P-12431)

Dilbeck Realtors, La Canada Also Called: Dilbeck Inc (P-12431)

Diligent Delivery Systems, Valencia Also Called: Central States Logistics Inc (P-8900)

Dillon Companies Inc .... C 951 352-8353
4250 Van Buren Blvd Riverside (92503) (P-11275)

Dimensions In Screen Printing, Irvine Also Called: Tomorrows Look Inc (P-1936)

Dimic Steel Tech Inc .... E 909 946-6767
145 N 8th Ave Upland (91786) (P-4980)

Dincloud Inc .... D 310 929-1101
27520 Hawthorne Blvd Ste 185 Rlling Hls Est (90274) (P-13916)

DINE BRANDS GLOBAL, Pasadena Also Called: Dine Brands Global Inc (P-11567)

Dine Brands Global Inc (PA) .... B 818 240-6055
10 W Walnut St Fl 5 Pasadena (91103) (P-11567)

Ding Sticks, Huntington Beach Also Called: Sandra Gruca (P-7292)

Dioz Group, The, Beverly Hills Also Called: Alanic International Corp (P-1964)

Diplomatic Security Services, Rancho Cucamonga Also Called: Harrison Iyke (P-14405)

Diplomatic Security Svcs LLC .... D 909 463-8409
7581 Etiwanda Ave Rancho Cucamonga (91739) (P-14294)

Direct Chassislink Inc .... B 657 216-5846
7777 Center Ave Ste 325 Huntington Beach (92647) (P-13455)

Direct Chemicals, Huntington Beach Also Called: Home & Body Company (P-3802)

Direct Drive Systems Inc .... D 714 872-5500
621 Burning Tree Rd Fullerton (92833) (P-6320)

Direct Medical Supply Inc .... C 949 823-9565
5 Knowles Irvine (92603) (P-10075)

Directors Guild America Inc (PA) .... C 310 289-2000
7920 W Sunset Blvd Los Angeles (90046) (P-14885)

Directv, El Segundo Also Called: Directv Group Holdings LLC (P-9400)

Directv, El Segundo Also Called: Directv Group Inc (P-9546)

Directv Inc .... B 888 388-4249
2260 E Imperial Hwy El Segundo (90245) (P-9541)

Directv Enterprises LLC .... A 310 535-5000
2230 E Imperial Hwy El Segundo (90245) (P-9542)

Directv Group Holdings LLC (HQ) .... C 424 432-5554
2260 E Imperial Hwy El Segundo (90245) (P-9400)

Directv Group Holdings LLC .... A 661 632-6562
715 E Avenue L8 Ste 101 Lancaster (93535) (P-9543)

Directv Group Holdings LLC .... A 760 375-8300
140 Station Ave Ridgecrest (93555) (P-9544)

Directv Group Holdings LLC .... A 805 207-6675
360 Cortez Cir Camarillo (93012) (P-9545)

Directv Group Inc (DH) .... C 310 964-5000
2260 E Imperial Hwy El Segundo (90245) (P-9546)

Directv Holdings LLC (DH) .... D 310 964-5000
2230 E Imperial Hwy El Segundo (90245) (P-9547)

Directv International Inc .... A 310 964-6460
2230 E Imperial Hwy Fl 10 El Segundo (90245) (P-9548)

Disaster Rstrtion Prfssnals In .... D 310 301-8030
1517 W 130th St Gardena (90249) (P-399)

Discount Tire, Ventura Also Called: Southern Cal Disc Tire Co Inc (P-11456)

Discount Tire, Escondido Also Called: Southern Cal Disc Tire Co Inc (P-11457)

Discount Tire, San Marcos Also Called: Southern Cal Disc Tire Co Inc (P-11458)

Discount Tire, Escondido Also Called: Southern Cal Disc Tire Co Inc (P-11459)

Discount Tire, Solana Beach Also Called: Southern Cal Disc Tire Co Inc (P-11460)

Discount Tire, Poway Also Called: Southern Cal Disc Tire Co Inc (P-11461)

Discount Tire, Oceanside Also Called: Southern Cal Disc Tire Co Inc (P-11462)

Discount Tire, Hemet Also Called: Southern Cal Disc Tire Co Inc (P-11463)

Discount Tire, Encinitas Also Called: Southern Cal Disc Tire Co Inc (P-11464)

Discount Tire, San Diego Also Called: Southern Cal Disc Tire Co Inc (P-11465)

Discount Tire, Huntington Beach Also Called: Southern Cal Disc Tire Co Inc (P-11466)

Discount Tire, Carson Also Called: Southern Cal Disc Tire Co Inc (P-11467)

Discount Tire, Glendora Also Called: Southern Cal Disc Tire Co Inc (P-11468)

Discount Tire Center 025, North Hollywood Also Called: Akh Company Inc (P-14702)

Discount Tire Center 038, Redlands Also Called: Akh Company Inc (P-11437)

Discount Tire Center 077, Moreno Valley Also Called: Akh Company Inc (P-11438)

Discounted Wheel Warehouse, Santa Ana Also Called: Wheel and Tire Club Inc (P-4529)

Discovery Communications Inc (PA) .... B 310 975-5906
10100 Santa Monica Blvd Ste 1500 Los Angeles (90067) (P-9563)

Discovery Health Services LLC .... B 858 459-0785
5726 La Jolla Blvd Ste 104 La Jolla (92037) (P-16554)

Discovery Medical Staffing, La Jolla Also Called: Discovery Health Services LLC (P-16554)

Discovery Opco LLC .... C 844 933-3627
41 Discovery Irvine (92618) (P-13707)

Discovery Practice MGT Inc .... A 714 828-1800
18401 Von Karman Ave Ste 500 Irvine (92612) (P-16469)

Discovery Scnce Ctr Ornge Cnty .... C 866 552-2823
2500 N Main St Santa Ana (92705) (P-17253)

Discus Dental LLC .... C 310 845-8600
1700 S Baker Ave Ontario (91761) (P-10076)

Disguise Inc (HQ) .... D 858 391-3600
12120 Kear Pl Poway (92064) (P-2194)

Dish For All Inc .... E 760 690-3869
148 S Escondido Blvd Escondido (92025) (P-14722)

Disney, Anaheim Also Called: Walt Dsney Imgnring RES Dev In (P-2202)

Disney, Burbank Also Called: Disney Enterprises Inc (P-9477)

Disney, Anaheim Also Called: Disney Enterprises Inc (P-12811)

Disney, Anaheim Also Called: Disney Enterprises Inc (P-14819)

Disney, Anaheim Also Called: Disney Enterprises Inc (P-14820)

Disney, Glendale Also Called: Disney Enterprises Inc (P-14821)

A
L
P
H
A
B
E
T
I
C

Employee Codes: A=Over 500 employees, B=251-500
C=101-250, D=51-100, E=20-50, F=10-19, G=1-9

2025 Southern California
Business Directory and Buyers Guide

© Mergent Inc. 1-800-342-5647
1005

Disney, Burbank *Also Called: Disney Incorporated (P-14822)*

Disney, Burbank *Also Called: Walt Disney Music Company (P-14870)*

Disney, Glendale *Also Called: Walt Disney Pictures (P-14871)*

Disney, Burbank *Also Called: Walt Disney Records Direct (P-14872)*

Disney, Glendale *Also Called: Walt Dsney Imgnring RES Dev In (P-14914)*

Disney, Burbank *Also Called: Walt Disney Company (P-15110)*

Disney, Burbank *Also Called: Disney Regional Entrmt Inc (P-15198)*

Disney Editions, Burbank *Also Called: Disney Publishing Worldwide (P-2854)*

Disney Enterprises Inc (DH)..............................A 818 560-1000
500 S Buena Vista St Burbank (91521) *(P-9477)*

Disney Enterprises Inc ....A 714 778-6600
1150 W Magic Way Anaheim (92802) *(P-12811)*

Disney Enterprises Inc ....D 407 397-6000
1313 S Harbor Blvd Anaheim (92802) *(P-14819)*

Disney Enterprises Inc ....C 714 781-1651
700 W Ball Rd Anaheim (92802) *(P-14820)*

Disney Enterprises Inc ....C 818 553-4103
1101 Flower St Glendale (91201) *(P-14821)*

Disney Financial Services, Burbank *Also Called: Twdc Enterprises 18 Corp (P-9520)*

Disney Incorporated (DH)...................................C 818 560-1000
500 S Buena Vista St Burbank (91521) *(P-14822)*

Disney Interactive Studios, Burbank *Also Called: Disney Interactive Studios Inc (P-13708)*

Disney Interactive Studios Inc ....B 818 553-5000
681 W Buena Vista St Burbank (91521) *(P-13708)*

Disney Interactive Studios Inc ....B 818 560-1000
601 Circle Seven Dr Glendale (91201) *(P-13709)*

Disney Networks Group LLC (DH)......................D 310 369-1000
10201 W Pico Blvd Bldg 101 Los Angeles (90064) *(P-9497)*

Disney Publishing Worldwide (DH)......................D 212 633-4400
500 S Buena Vista St Burbank (91521) *(P-2854)*

Disney Regional Entrmt Inc (DH)........................C 818 560-1000
500 S Buena Vista St Burbank (91521) *(P-15198)*

Disney Research Pittsburgh ....C 412 623-1800
532 Paula Ave Glendale (91201) *(P-17784)*

Disneyland, Anaheim *Also Called: Disneyland International (P-12812)*

Disneyland, Anaheim *Also Called: Disneyland International (P-15103)*

Disneyland International ....A 714 956-6746
1580 S Disneyland Dr Anaheim (92802) *(P-12812)*

Disneyland International (DH).............................C 714 781-4565
1313 S Harbor Blvd Anaheim (92802) *(P-15103)*

Disneys Grnd Clifornian Ht Spa, Anaheim *Also Called: Wco Hotels Inc (P-13072)*

Disorderly Kids, Los Angeles *Also Called: Avalon Apparel LLC (P-2060)*

Dispatch Trucking LLC (PA).................................D 909 355-5531
14032 Santa Ana Ave Fontana (92337) *(P-9272)*

Dispensing Dynamics Intl Inc (PA).......................D 626 961-3691
1940 Diamond St San Marcos (92078) *(P-4104)*

Display Fabrication Group Inc ....E 714 373-2100
1231 N Miller St Ste 100 Anaheim (92806) *(P-2274)*

Display Products Inc ....E 310 640-0442
445 S Douglas St El Segundo (90245) *(P-6818)*

Disposable Waste System, Santa Ana *Also Called: Jwc Environmental Inc (P-6018)*

Distillery, Manhattan Beach *Also Called: Distillery Tech Inc (P-13710)*

Distillery Tech Inc ....C 310 776-6234
1500 Rosecrans Ave Ste 500 Manhattan Beach (90266) *(P-13710)*

Distinct Indulgence Inc ....E 818 546-1700
5018 Lante St Baldwin Park (91706) *(P-1442)*

Distinctive Inds Texas Inc ....E 323 889-5766
9419 Ann St Santa Fe Springs (90670) *(P-2179)*

Distinctive Industries ....B 800 421-9777
10618 Shoemaker Ave Santa Fe Springs (90670) *(P-2259)*

Distinctive Plastics Inc ....D 760 599-9100
1385 Decision St Vista (92081) *(P-4105)*

Distribution Alternatives Inc ....D 909 746-5600
10621 6th St Rancho Cucamonga (91730) *(P-9062)*

Distribution Alternatives Inc ....D 909 770-8900
1979 Renaissance Pkwy Rialto (92376) *(P-10621)*

Distribution Electrnics Vlued ....E 714 368-1717
2651 Dow Ave Tustin (92780) *(P-7119)*

District Attorney, Lancaster *Also Called: County of Los Angeles (P-18390)*

District Attys Off - Cntl Tral, Los Angeles *Also Called: County of Los Angeles (P-16661)*

Distro Worldwide LLC ....E 818 849-0953
3400 S Main St Los Angeles (90007) *(P-1983)*

Divergent 3d, Torrance *Also Called: Divergent Technologies Inc (P-17514)*

Divergent Technologies Inc (PA).........................B 424 542-2158
19601 Hamilton Ave Torrance (90502) *(P-17514)*

Diverscape Inc ....D 951 245-1686
21730 Bundy Canyon Rd Wildomar (92595) *(P-204)*

Diverse Journeys Inc (PA)..................................D 310 643-7403
525 S Douglas St Ste 210 El Segundo (90245) *(P-16935)*

Diversfied Tchncal Systems Inc (HQ)...................E 562 493-0158
1720 Apollo Ct Seal Beach (90740) *(P-7909)*

Diversified Direct, La Mirada *Also Called: Diversified Mailing Incorporated (P-13301)*

Diversified Landscape Co, Wildomar *Also Called: Diverscape Inc (P-204)*

Diversified Mailing Incorporated ....C 714 994-6245
14407 Alondra Blvd La Mirada (90638) *(P-13301)*

Diversified Metal Works, Orange *Also Called: Rika Corporation (P-1163)*

Diversified Minerals Inc ....E 805 247-1069
1100 Mountain View Ave Ste F Oxnard (93030) *(P-4437)*

Diversified Plastics Inc ....E 760 598-5333
1333 Keystone Way Vista (92081) *(P-4106)*

Diversified Printers Inc ....D 714 994-3400
12834 Maxwell Dr Tustin (92782) *(P-2912)*

Diversified Prj Svcs Intl Inc (PA).........................D 661 371-2800
5351 Olive Dr Ste 100 Bakersfield (93308) *(P-17515)*

Diversified Silicone, Santa Fe Springs *Also Called: Rogers Corporation (P-3933)*

Diversified Tool & Die ....E 760 598-9100
2585 Birch St Vista (92081) *(P-5182)*

Diversified Utility Svcs Inc ....B 661 325-3212
3105 Unicorn Rd Bakersfield (93308) *(P-670)*

Diversity Bus Solutions Inc ....C 909 395-0243
3532 Old Archibald Ranch Rd Ontario (91761) *(P-13510)*

Divine Pasta Company ....E 818 559-7440
140 W Providencia Ave Burbank (91502) *(P-1765)*

Divine Pasta Company, Burbank *Also Called: Palermo Family LP (P-1832)*

Diving Unlimited Int., San Diego *Also Called: Diving Unlimited Intl Inc (P-8515)*

Diving Unlimited Intl Inc ....D 619 236-1203
1148 Delevan Dr San Diego (92102) *(P-8515)*

Division 1, Los Angeles *Also Called: Los Angles Cnty Mtro Trnsp Aut (P-8765)*

Division 7, Venice *Also Called: Los Angles Cnty Mtro Trnsp Aut (P-8772)*

Dixieline Lumber Company LLC ....B 951 224-8491
2625 Durahart St Riverside (92507) *(P-11150)*

Dixieline Lumber Company LLC (DH)....................D 619 224-4120
3250 Sports Arena Blvd San Diego (92110) *(P-11151)*

Dixieline Probuild, San Diego *Also Called: Dixieline Lumber Company LLC (P-11151)*

Djh Enterprises ....E 714 424-6500
23011 Moulton Pkwy Ste B6 Laguna Hills (92653) *(P-6608)*

Dji Technology Inc ....C 818 235-0789
17301 Edwards Rd Cerritos (90703) *(P-8425)*

DJM Suspension, Gardena *Also Called: D and J Marketing Inc (P-2258)*

Djo LLC (HQ)...D 800 321-9549
5919 Sea Otter Pl Ste 200 Carlsbad (92010) *(P-8259)*

Dkn Hotel LLC (PA)..B 714 427-4320
42 Corporate Park Ste 200 Irvine (92606) *(P-12813)*

DL Horton Enterprises Inc ....D 323 777-1700
12705 Daphne Ave Hawthorne (90250) *(P-6118)*

Dl Imaging, Santa Ana *Also Called: Dekra-Lite Industries Inc (P-14488)*

DL Long Landscaping Inc ....D 909 628-5531
5475 G St Chino (91710) *(P-165)*

Dla Piper LLP (us) ....D 310 595-3000
2000 Avenue Of The Stars Ste 400n Los Angeles (90067) *(P-16672)*

Dlf Logistics, Los Angeles *Also Called: Dlf Logistics LLC (P-8904)*

Dlf Logistics LLC ....D 626 387-3797
1019 S Rimpau Blvd Los Angeles (90019) *(P-8904)*

Dlr Group Inc (HQ)..C 213 800-9400
700 S Flower St Ste 2200 Los Angeles (90017) *(P-17669)*

Dm Luxury LLC ....C 858 366-9721
875 Prospect St Ste 300 La Jolla (92037) *(P-3137)*

Dma Claims Inc ....C 877 880-3616
330 N Brand Blvd Ste 230 Glendale (91203) *(P-12203)*

Mergent email: customerrelations@mergent.com
1006

2025 Southern California
Business Directory and Buyers Guide

(P-0000) Products & Services Section entry number
(PA)=Parent Co (HQ)=Headquarters (DH)=Div Headquarters

Dma Claims Management Inc .... D 323 342-6800
330 N Brand Blvd Ste 230 Glendale (91203) *(P-12204)*

DMA Enterprises Inc (PA) .... E 805 520-2468
2255 Union Pl Simi Valley (93065) *(P-8675)*

Dmbm LLC .... E 714 321-6032
2445 E 12th St Ste C Los Angeles (90021) *(P-2092)*

DMC, Carson *Also Called: Designed Metal Connections Inc (P-5106)*

DMC Power Inc (PA) .... E 310 323-1616
623 E Artesia Blvd Carson (90746) *(P-6416)*

Dmf Inc .... D 323 934-7779
1118 E 223rd St Unit 1 Carson (90745) *(P-6443)*

Dmf Lighting, Carson *Also Called: Dmf Inc (P-6443)*

Dmi, Rancho Cascades *Also Called: Desert Mechanical Inc (P-772)*

Dmi Ready Mix, Oxnard *Also Called: Diversified Minerals Inc (P-4437)*

DMS, Anaheim *Also Called: DMS Facility Services Inc (P-13372)*

DMS Facility Services Inc .... A 949 975-1366
2861 E Coronado St Anaheim (92806) *(P-13372)*

DMS Facility Services LLC .... A 949 975-1366
2861 E Coronado St Anaheim (92806) *(P-17516)*

DMS Facility Services LLC .... A 858 560-4191
5735 Kearny Villa Rd Ste 108 San Diego (92123) *(P-17517)*

Dn Tanks Inc .... C 619 440-8181
351 Cypress Ln El Cajon (92020) *(P-7679)*

Dna Motor Inc .... E 626 965-8898
801 Sentous Ave City Of Industry (91744) *(P-11443)*

Dna Motoring, City Of Industry *Also Called: Dna Motor Inc (P-11443)*

Dna Specialty Inc .... D 310 767-4070
200 W Artesia Blvd Compton (90220) *(P-9822)*

DNam Apparel Industries LLC .... E 323 859-0114
4938 Triggs St Commerce (90022) *(P-2093)*

Dneg North America Inc (PA) .... D 323 461-7887
5750 Hannum Ave Ste 100 Culver City (90230) *(P-14886)*

Dnib Unwind Inc .... C 213 617-2717
333 S Grand Ave Ste 4070 Los Angeles (90071) *(P-3397)*

Do It Best, Pasadena *Also Called: George L Throop Co (P-11258)*

Dockside Machine & Ship Repair, Wilmington *Also Called: Marine Technical Services Inc (P-14538)*

Docmagic Inc .... D 800 649-1362
1800 W 213th St Torrance (90501) *(P-14491)*

Doctor On Demand Inc .... D 310 988-2882
9454 Wilshire Blvd Ste 803 Beverly Hills (90212) *(P-16555)*

Doctors Hospital W Covina Inc .... C 626 338-3481
725 S Orange Ave West Covina (91790) *(P-15983)*

Document Systems, Torrance *Also Called: Docmagic Inc (P-14491)*

Docupace Technologies LLC (PA) .... C 310 445-7722
400 Corporate Pointe Ste 300 Culver City (90230) *(P-13711)*

Docusource Inc .... D 562 447-2600
13100 Alondra Blvd Ste 108 Cerritos (90703) *(P-11682)*

Dodger Stadium, Los Angeles *Also Called: Fox BSB Holdco Inc (P-15026)*

DOE & Ingalls Cal Oper LLC .... E 951 801-7175
1060 Citrus St Riverside (92507) *(P-7950)*

Dogswell, Los Angeles *Also Called: Arthur Dogswell LLC (P-1416)*

Doheny Eye Institute (PA) .... D 323 342-7120
150 N Orange Grove Blvd Pasadena (91103) *(P-17872)*

Dole Holding Company LLC .... A 818 879-6600
1 Dole Dr Westlake Village (91362) *(P-47)*

Dole Packaged Foods LLC (HQ) .... A 800 232-8888
1 Baxter Way Westlake Village (91362) *(P-1375)*

Dollar Shave Club Inc (HQ) .... C 310 975-6528
13335 Maxella Ave Marina Del Rey (90292) *(P-5543)*

Dolores Canning Co Inc .... E 323 263-9155
1020 N Eastern Ave Los Angeles (90063) *(P-1340)*

Dolphin Bay Hotel & Residences, Shell Beach *Also Called: Dolphin Bay Ht & Residence Inc (P-12814)*

Dolphin Bay Ht & Residence Inc .... D 805 773-4300
2727 Shell Beach Rd Shell Beach (93449) *(P-12814)*

Dolphin Hkg Ltd (PA) .... D 310 215-3356
1125 W Hillcrest Blvd Inglewood (90301) *(P-11115)*

Dolphin International, Inglewood *Also Called: Dolphin Hkg Ltd (P-11115)*

Dolphin Medical Inc (HQ) .... D 800 448-6506
12525 Chadron Ave Hawthorne (90250) *(P-8377)*

Dominator Radiology Systems, San Diego *Also Called: DR Systems Inc (P-16312)*

Dominguez Law Group PC .... D 213 388-7788
3250 Wilshire Blvd Ste 2200 Los Angeles (90010) *(P-16673)*

Don Alderson Associates Inc .... E 310 837-5141
3327 La Cienega Pl Los Angeles (90016) *(P-2501)*

Don Lee Farms, Inglewood *Also Called: Goodman Food Products Inc (P-1785)*

Don Miguel Foods, Orange *Also Called: Don Miguel Mexican Foods Inc (P-1390)*

Don Miguel Mexican Foods Inc (HQ) .... E 714 385-4500
333 S Anita Dr Ste 1000 Orange (92868) *(P-1390)*

Donahue Schrber Rlty Group Inc (PA) .... D 714 545-1400
200 Baker St Ste 100 Costa Mesa (92626) *(P-12432)*

Donahue Schriber Rlty Group LP (PA) .... D 714 545-1400
200 Baker St Ste 100 Costa Mesa (92626) *(P-12290)*

Donald J Schefflers Cnstr, Azusa *Also Called: Heidi Corporation (P-1120)*

Donald T Sterling Corporation .... D 310 275-5575
10300 Wilshire Blvd Los Angeles (90024) *(P-12815)*

Donaldson Company Inc .... E 661 295-0800
26235 Technology Dr Valencia (91355) *(P-7246)*

Doncasters Gce Integrated, Chula Vista *Also Called: Integrated Energy Technologies Inc (P-5750)*

Donco & Sons Inc .... E 714 779-0099
2871 E Blue Star St Anaheim (92806) *(P-909)*

Donco Associates & Sons, Anaheim *Also Called: Donco & Sons Inc (P-909)*

Donoco Industries Inc .... E 714 893-7889
5642 Research Dr Ste B Huntington Beach (92649) *(P-4325)*

Dool Fna Inc .... C 562 483-4100
16624 Edwards Rd Cerritos (90703) *(P-1892)*

Door Components Inc .... C 909 770-5700
7980 Redwood Ave Fontana (92336) *(P-4886)*

Door Doctor, Anaheim *Also Called: R & S Ovrhd Doors So-Cal Inc (P-14786)*

Doorking, Inglewood *Also Called: Doorking Inc (P-7120)*

Doorking Inc (PA) .... C 310 645-0023
120 S Glasgow Ave Inglewood (90301) *(P-7120)*

Doose Landscape Incorporated .... D 760 591-4500
785 E Mission Rd San Marcos (92069) *(P-205)*

Doppler Automotive Inc .... D 310 765-4100
1515 W 190th St Ste 440 Gardena (90248) *(P-18128)*

Dorado Network Systems Corp .... C 650 227-7300
40 Pacifica Irvine (92618) *(P-13917)*

Dorado Pkg, North Hollywood *Also Called: Corporate Impressions La Inc (P-3132)*

Dorel Home Furnishings Inc .... C 909 390-5705
5400 Shea Center Dr Ontario (91761) *(P-2422)*

Dorel Juvenile Group Inc .... C 909 428-0295
9950 Calabash Ave Fontana (92335) *(P-4107)*

Dorel Juvenile Group Inc .... C 909 390-5705
5400 Shea Center Dr Ontario (91761) *(P-4108)*

Doremi, Burbank *Also Called: Doremi Labs Inc (P-6534)*

Doremi Labs Inc .... E 818 562-1101
1020 Chestnut St Burbank (91506) *(P-6534)*

Dos Gringos, Vista *Also Called: Gringo Ventures LLC (P-11088)*

DOT Blue Safes Corporation .... E 909 445-8888
2707 N Garey Ave Pomona (91767) *(P-5444)*

DOT Printer Inc (PA) .... D 949 474-1100
2424 Mcgaw Ave Irvine (92614) *(P-3004)*

Doty Bros Equipment Co (HQ) .... D 562 864-6566
11232 Firestone Blvd Norwalk (90650) *(P-671)*

Double Eagle Trnsp Corp .... C 760 956-3770
12135 Scarbrough Ct Oak Hills (92344) *(P-8947)*

Doubleco Incorporated .... D 909 481-0799
9444 9th St Rancho Cucamonga (91730) *(P-5124)*

Doubletree By Hilton, San Diego *Also Called: Gringteam Inc (P-12836)*

Doubletree By Hilton Carson, Carson *Also Called: Carson Operating Company LLC (P-12786)*

Doubletree Golf Resort, San Diego *Also Called: Gringteam Inc (P-12837)*

Doubletree Hotel, Torrance *Also Called: Ctc Group Inc (P-12804)*

Doubletree Hotel, Irvine *Also Called: Spectrum Hotel Group LLC (P-13032)*

Doubletree Hotel Boston, Los Angeles *Also Called: L-O Bedford Operating LLC (P-12891)*

Doubletree Ht San Diego Dwntwn, San Diego *Also Called: Harbor View Hotel Ventures LLC (P-12842)*

Doubltree Palm Sprng Golf Rsor, Cathedral City *Also Called: T Alliance One - Palm Sprng LLC (P-15224)*

Employee Codes: A=Over 500 employees, B=251-500
C=101-250, D=51-100, E=20-50, F=10-19, G=1-9

2025 Southern California
Business Directory and Buyers Guide

© Mergent Inc. 1-800-342-5647

1007

Doubltree Stes By Hlton Anheim, Anaheim *Also Called: Orangewood LLC (P-12954)*

Doubltree Stes By Hlton Snta M, Santa Monica *Also Called: Santa Monica Hotel Owner LLC (P-13016)*

Doug Mockett & Company Inc .... D 310 318-2491
1915 Abalone Ave Torrance (90501) *(P-2423)*

Doughpro, Perris *Also Called: Stearns Product Dev Corp (P-5835)*

Douglas Fir Holdings LLC .... C 714 842-5551
8382 Newman Ave Huntington Beach (92647) *(P-15622)*

Douglas Furniture of California LLC .... A 310 749-0003
809 Tyburn Rd Palos Verdes Estates (90274) *(P-2466)*

Douglas Steel Supply Inc (PA) .... D 323 587-7676
4804 Laurel Canyon Blvd Valley Village (91607) *(P-10133)*

DOUGLAS STEEL SUPPLY CO., Valley Village *Also Called: Douglas Steel Supply Inc (P-10133)*

Douglas Technologies Group Inc .... E 760 758-5560
42092 Winchester Rd Ste B Temecula (92590) *(P-7247)*

Douglas Wheel, Temecula *Also Called: Douglas Technologies Group Inc (P-7247)*

Douglass Truck Bodies Inc .... E 661 327-0258
231 21st St Bakersfield (93301) *(P-7201)*

Doval Industries Inc .... D 323 226-0335
3961 N Mission Rd Los Angeles (90031) *(P-4766)*

Doval Industries Co, Los Angeles *Also Called: Doval Industries Inc (P-4766)*

Dow Company Foundation .... C 909 476-4127
11266 Jersey Blvd Rancho Cucamonga (91730) *(P-3263)*

Dow Hydraulic Systems Inc .... D 909 596-6602
2895 Metropolitan Pl Pomona (91767) *(P-6119)*

Dow-Elco Inc .... E 323 723-1288
1313 W Olympic Blvd Montebello (90640) *(P-6284)*

Dow-Key Microwave, Ventura *Also Called: Dow-Key Microwave Corporation (P-6347)*

Dow-Key Microwave Corporation .... C 805 650-0260
4822 Mcgrath St Ventura (93003) *(P-6347)*

Dowell Schlumberger, Bakersfield *Also Called: Schlumberger Technology Corp (P-363)*

Dowling Advisory Group .... D 626 319-1369
3579 E Foothill Blvd Ste 651 Pasadena (91107) *(P-18129)*

Downey Care Center, Downey *Also Called: Ensign Group Inc (P-15638)*

Downey Civic Theatre, Downey *Also Called: City of Downey (P-14957)*

Downey Community Health Center .... C 562 862-6506
8425 Iowa St Downey (90241) *(P-15623)*

Downey Grinding Co .... E 562 803-5556
12323 Bellflower Blvd Downey (90242) *(P-5544)*

Downey Regional Medical Center, Downey *Also Called: Pih Health Hospital - Whitti (P-16133)*

Downhole Stabilization Inc .... E 661 631-1044
3515 Thomas Way Bakersfield (93308) *(P-5509)*

Downtown Diversion Inc .... D 818 252-0019
9081 Tujunga Ave Sun Valley (91352) *(P-9741)*

Downtown Edit, Los Angeles *Also Called: Daviselen Advertising Inc (P-13203)*

Dozuki, San Luis Obispo *Also Called: Dzkicorp Inc (P-13714)*

Dpa Components International, Simi Valley *Also Called: Dpa Labs Inc (P-6819)*

Dpa Labs Inc .... E 805 581-9200
2251 Ward Ave Simi Valley (93065) *(P-6819)*

Dpi Direct, Poway *Also Called: Digitalpro Inc (P-3003)*

DPI Labs Inc .... E 909 392-5777
1350 Arrow Hwy La Verne (91750) *(P-7463)*

Dpi Specialty Foods West Inc .... B 909 975-1019
930 S Rockefeller Ave Ontario (91761) *(P-10750)*

Dpi West, Ontario *Also Called: Dpi Specialty Foods West Inc (P-10750)*

Dpp 2020 Inc (DH) .... E 951 845-3161
533 E Third St Beaumont (92223) *(P-4109)*

Dpp Real Estate, Sierra Madre *Also Called: Deasy Penner Podley (P-12429)*

Dpr Construction A Gen Partnr .... C 858 646-0757
5010 Shoreham Pl Ste 100 San Diego (92122) *(P-534)*

Dpr Construction A Gen Partnr .... C 626 463-1265
88 W Colorado Blvd Ste 301 Pasadena (91105) *(P-535)*

DR Horton Inc .... D 818 334-1955
8501 Fallbrook Ave Ste 270 West Hills (91304) *(P-460)*

Dr Pepper Snapple Group, Riverside *Also Called: American Bottling Company (P-1600)*

Dr Smoothie Brands LLC .... E 714 449-9787
1730 Raymer Ave Fullerton (92833) *(P-1676)*

Dr Squatch LLC .... C 631 229-7068
4065 Glencoe Ave Apt 300b Marina Del Rey (90292) *(P-3650)*

DR Systems Inc .... C 858 625-3344
10140 Mesa Rim Rd San Diego (92121) *(P-16312)*

Dr. Bronners Magic Soaps, Vista *Also Called: All One God Faith Inc (P-3589)*

Dr. Bronners Magic Soaps, Vista *Also Called: All One God Faith Inc (P-3590)*

Dr. Fresh, La Palma *Also Called: Ranir LLC (P-3488)*

Dragon Herbs, Los Angeles *Also Called: Ron Teeguarden Enterprises Inc (P-3329)*

Dragon Trade Intl Corp .... C 619 816-6062
1205 Highland Ave National City (91950) *(P-10215)*

Dramm and Echter Inc .... D 760 436-0188
1150 Quail Gardens Dr Encinitas (92024) *(P-53)*

Drapery Affair, Paramount *Also Called: Blue Ribbon Draperies Inc (P-11521)*

Drata Inc .... C 858 754-8811
4660 La Jolla Village Dr Ste 100 San Diego (92122) *(P-14214)*

Dray Alliance Inc .... D 844 767-6776
111 W Ocean Blvd Ste 1000 Long Beach (90802) *(P-13712)*

Dream Big Childrens Center .... D 626 239-0138
612 S Myrtle Ave Monrovia (91016) *(P-17089)*

Dream Hollywood, Los Angeles *Also Called: 6417 Selma Hotel LLC (P-12754)*

Dream Mortgage Group, Brea *Also Called: Emet Lending Group Inc (P-11900)*

Dreamfields California LLC .... B 310 691-9739
65000 Two Bunch Palms Trl Desert Hot Springs (92240) *(P-2706)*

Dreamgear LLC .... E 310 222-5522
20001 S Western Ave Torrance (90501) *(P-8483)*

Dreamgirl International, Bell *Also Called: Dg Brands Inc (P-10706)*

Dreamhost.com, Los Angeles *Also Called: New Dream Network LLC (P-9450)*

Dreamstart Labs Inc .... E 408 914-1234
2907 Shelter Island Dr Ste 105 San Diego (92106) *(P-13918)*

Dreamteam Logistics LLC .... D 818 300-7785
8605 Santa Monica Blvd West Hollywood (90069) *(P-9362)*

Dreamworks Animation Pubg LLC .... A 818 695-5000
1000 Flower St Glendale (91201) *(P-14823)*

Drees Wood Products Inc .... D 562 633-7337
14020 Orange Ave Paramount (90723) *(P-2346)*

Dreier's Nursing Care Center, Glendale *Also Called: Ksm Healthcare Inc (P-15688)*

Dresser-Rand Company .... E 310 223-0600
18502 Dominguez Hill Dr Rancho Dominguez (90220) *(P-5757)*

Drew Chain Security Corp .... D 626 457-8626
55 S Raymond Ave Ste 303 Alhambra (91801) *(P-14295)*

Drew Ford .... C 619 464-7777
8970 La Mesa Blvd La Mesa (91942) *(P-11338)*

Drew Hyundai, La Mesa *Also Called: Drew Ford (P-11338)*

Dri Commercial Corporation .... C 949 266-1900
2081 Business Center Dr Ste 195 Irvine (92612) *(P-1078)*

Dri Companies .... B 949 266-1900
2081 Business Center Dr Ste 195 Irvine (92612) *(P-1079)*

Driftwood Health Care Ctr, Torrance *Also Called: Mariner Health Care Inc (P-15711)*

Drillmec Inc .... D 281 885-0777
8140 Rosecrans Ave Paramount (90723) *(P-299)*

Drinkpak LLC .... A 833 376-5725
21375 Needham Ranch Pkwy Santa Clarita (91321) *(P-1617)*

Driscoll Inc .... E 619 226-2500
2500 Shelter Island Dr San Diego (92106) *(P-7619)*

Driscoll Boat Works, San Diego *Also Called: Driscoll Inc (P-7619)*

Drive Devilbiss Healthcare, Rialto *Also Called: Medical Depot Inc (P-8189)*

Driveshaftpro .... E 714 893-4585
7532 Anthony Ave Garden Grove (92841) *(P-7248)*

Dropzone Waterpark .... C 951 210-1600
2165 Trumble Rd Perris (92571) *(P-15199)*

Drs Daylight Defense, San Diego *Also Called: Daylight Defense LLC (P-8376)*

Drs Daylight Solutions, San Diego *Also Called: Daylight Solutions Inc (P-6817)*

Drs Network & Imaging Systems, Cypress *Also Called: Drs Ntwork Imaging Systems LLC (P-6820)*

Drs Ntwork Imaging Systems LLC .... D 714 220-3800
10600 Valley View St Cypress (90630) *(P-6820)*

Drywater Inc .... E 844 434-0829
3901 Westerly Pl Ste 111 Newport Beach (92660) *(P-1677)*

Ds Fibertech Corp .... E 619 562-7001
11015 Mission Park Ct Santee (92071) *(P-5798)*

Ds Lakeshore, Costa Mesa *Also Called: Donahue Schriber Rlty Group LP (P-12290)*

Mergent email: customerrelations@mergent.com
1008   2025 Southern California
Business Directory and Buyers Guide   (P-0000) Products & Services Section entry number
(PA)=Parent Co (HQ)=Headquarters (DH)=Div Headquarters

Ds Lakeshore LP .... D 916 286-5231
200 Baker St Ste 100 Costa Mesa (92626) *(P-17341)*

DSA Phototech LLC .... E 866 868-1602
2321 E Gladwick St Rancho Dominguez (90220) *(P-6455)*

DSA Signage, Rancho Dominguez Also Called: DSA Phototech LLC *(P-6455)*

Dsca, Long Beach Also Called: Denso Pdts & Svcs Americas Inc *(P-9821)*

Dsd Trucking Inc .... D 310 338-3395
2411 Santa Fe Ave Redondo Beach (90278) *(P-9200)*

DSI Process Systems LLC .... C 314 382-1525
7595 Reynolds Cir Huntington Beach (92647) *(P-10370)*

DSM&t Co Inc .... C 909 357-7960
10609 Business Dr Fontana (92337) *(P-7090)*

DSPM Inc .... E 714 970-2304
439 S Stoddard Ave San Bernardino (92401) *(P-6928)*

Dss, Calabasas Also Called: David Shield Security Inc *(P-14293)*

DSV, Fontana Also Called: DSV Solutions LLC *(P-9275)*

DSV Solutions LLC .... D 732 850-8000
6681 River Run Riverside (92507) *(P-9133)*

DSV Solutions LLC .... C 909 349-6100
13230 San Bernardino Ave Fontana (92335) *(P-9273)*

DSV Solutions LLC .... D 909 390-4563
1670 Etiwanda Ave Ste A Ontario (91761) *(P-9274)*

DSV Solutions LLC .... D 909 829-5804
13032 Slover Ave Ste 200 Fontana (92337) *(P-9275)*

DSV Solutions LLC .... D 714 630-0110
3454 E Miraloma Ave Anaheim (92806) *(P-9276)*

Dt Club Hotel Santa Ana, Santa Ana Also Called: Jhc Investment Inc *(P-12878)*

DT Mattson Enterprises Inc .... E 951 849-9781
201 W Lincoln St Banning (92220) *(P-8484)*

Dt123 (PA) .... E 213 488-1230
13035 Hartsook St Sherman Oaks (91423) *(P-3205)*

Dtiq Holdings Inc .... C 323 576-1400
1755 N Main St Los Angeles (90031) *(P-14393)*

Dtrs Santa Monica LLC .... B 310 458-6700
1700 Ocean Ave Santa Monica (90401) *(P-12816)*

Dts Inc (DH) .... C 818 436-1000
5220 Las Virgenes Rd Calabasas (91302) *(P-14887)*

Dtt, Los Angeles Also Called: Dtiq Holdings Inc *(P-14393)*

Dtwusa, Hacienda Heights Also Called: Brio Water Technology Inc *(P-10339)*

Dtx, Corona Also Called: Dart Container Corp California *(P-3997)*

Dtz, Westlake Village Also Called: C&W Facility Services Inc *(P-13361)*

Dual Diagnosis Trtmnt Ctr Inc (PA) .... C 949 276-5553
1211 Puerta Del Sol Ste 200 San Clemente (92673) *(P-16470)*

Dual Diagnosis Trtmnt Ctr Inc .... C 949 324-4531
69640 Highway 111 Rancho Mirage (92270) *(P-16556)*

Duarte Manor, Los Angeles Also Called: Emp III Inc *(P-12705)*

Dubnoff Ctr For Child Dev Edct (PA) .... D 818 755-4950
10526 Dubnoff Way North Hollywood (91606) *(P-16806)*

Duckor Mtzger Wynne A Prof Law .... E 619 209-3000
101 W Broadway Ste 1700 San Diego (92101) *(P-16674)*

DUCOMMUN, Costa Mesa Also Called: Ducommun Incorporated *(P-7407)*

Ducommun Aerostructures Inc (HQ) .... B 310 380-5390
600 Anton Blvd Ste 1100 Costa Mesa (92626) *(P-7383)*

Ducommun Aerostructures Inc .... C 714 637-4401
1885 N Batavia St Orange (92865) *(P-7384)*

Ducommun Aerostructures Inc .... E 626 358-3211
801 Royal Oaks Dr Monrovia (91016) *(P-7464)*

Ducommun Aerostructures Inc .... D 310 513-7200
23301 Wilmington Ave Carson (90745) *(P-7465)*

Ducommun Aerostructures Inc .... E 760 246-4191
4001 El Mirage Rd Adelanto (92301) *(P-7466)*

Ducommun Arostructures-Gardena, Gardena Also Called: Ahf-Ducommun Incorporated
(P-7418)

Ducommun Incorporated (PA) .... C 657 335-3665
600 Anton Blvd Ste 1100 Costa Mesa (92626) *(P-7467)*

Ducommun Incorporated .... E 626 358-3211
801 Royal Oaks Dr Monrovia (91016) *(P-7468)*

Ducommun Labarge Tech Inc (HQ) .... C 310 513-7200
23301 Wilmington Ave Carson (90745) *(P-7469)*

Dudek Inc (PA) .... D 760 942-5147
605 3rd St Encinitas (92024) *(P-17518)*

Dudleys Bakery Inc .... E 760 765-0488
30218 Highway 78 Santa Ysabel (92070) *(P-11294)*

Duffy Kruspodin LLP .... C 818 385-0585
21600 Oxnard St Ste 2000 Woodland Hills (91367) *(P-17720)*

Duhig and Co Inc .... E
5071 Telegraph Rd Los Angeles (90022) *(P-10436)*

Duhig Stainless, Los Angeles Also Called: Duhig and Co Inc *(P-10436)*

Duke Pacific Inc .... D 909 591-0191
13950 Monte Vista Ave Chino (91710) *(P-1080)*

Dulcich Inc .... B 310 835-4343
605 Flint Ave Wilmington (90744) *(P-10853)*

Duncan Carter Corporation (PA) .... D 805 964-9749
5427 Hollister Ave Santa Barbara (93111) *(P-8466)*

Duncan McIntosh Company Inc (PA) .... E 949 660-6150
18475 Bandilier Cir Fountain Valley (92708) *(P-2855)*

Dunkel Bros. Machinery Moving, La Mirada Also Called: MEI Rigging & Crating LLC *(P-5709)*

Dunn & Berger Inc .... B 818 986-1234
5955 De Soto Ave Ste 160 Woodland Hills (91367) *(P-16385)*

Dunn-Dwrds Pints Wallcoverings, Commerce Also Called: Dunn-Edwards Corporation
(P-11254)

Dunn-Edwards Corporation (DH) .... C 888 337-2468
6119 E Washington Blvd Commerce (90040) *(P-11254)*

Dupaco Inc .... E 760 758-4550
4144 Avenida De La Plata Ste B Oceanside (92056) *(P-8145)*

Dupont Displays Inc .... C 805 562-5400
600 Ward Dr Ste C Santa Barbara (93111) *(P-17785)*

Dupree Inc .... E 909 597-4889
14395 Ramona Ave Chino (91710) *(P-5125)*

Dur-Red Products .... E 323 771-9000
5634 Costa Dr Chino Hills (91709) *(P-4981)*

Dura Coat Products Inc (PA) .... D 951 341-6500
5361 Via Ricardo Riverside (92509) *(P-5318)*

Dura Technologies Inc .... C 909 877-8477
2720 S Willow Ave Ste A Bloomington (92316) *(P-3711)*

Durabag Company Inc .... D 714 259-8811
1432 Santa Fe Dr Tustin (92780) *(P-2731)*

Duraco Express, Walnut Also Called: Essentra International LLC *(P-3765)*

Durago, Rancho Dominguez Also Called: Iap West Inc *(P-9830)*

Duramax Building Products, Montebello Also Called: US Polymers Inc *(P-4267)*

Duray, Vernon Also Called: J F Duncan Industries Inc *(P-6016)*

Durham School Services L P .... C 818 880-4257
4029 Las Virgenes Rd Calabasas (91302) *(P-8868)*

Durham School Services L P .... C 310 767-5820
723 S Alameda St Compton (90220) *(P-8869)*

Durham School Services L P .... C 562 408-1206
8555 Flower Ave Paramount (90723) *(P-8870)*

Durham School Services L P .... A 626 573-3769
2713 River Ave Rosemead (91770) *(P-8871)*

Durham School Services L P .... C 909 899-1809
12999 Victoria St Rancho Cucamonga (91739) *(P-8872)*

Durham School Services L P .... C 805 483-6076
3151 W 5th St Ste A Oxnard (93030) *(P-8873)*

Durham School Services L P .... C 949 376-0376
2003 Laguna Canyon Rd Laguna Beach (92651) *(P-8874)*

Durham School Services L P .... B 714 542-8989
2818 W 5th St Santa Ana (92703) *(P-8875)*

Durkan Patterned Carpets Inc .... C 310 838-2898
3633 Lenawee Ave # 120 Los Angeles (90016) *(P-1950)*

Dutek Incorporated .... E 760 566-8888
2228 Oak Ridge Way Vista (92081) *(P-7121)*

Dux Dental Products, Orange Also Called: Dux Industries Inc *(P-8334)*

Dux Industries Inc .... D 805 488-1122
1717 W Collins Ave Orange (92867) *(P-8334)*

Dv Custom Farming LLC .... D 661 858-2888
2101 Mettler Frontage Rd E Bakersfield (93307) *(P-80)*

DVeal Corporation .... C 626 296-8900
2750 E Washington Blvd Ste 230 Pasadena (91107) *(P-17224)*

Dvele Inc .... E 909 796-2561
25525 Redlands Blvd Loma Linda (92354) *(P-2398)*

Dvele Omega Corporation .... D 909 796-2561
25525 Redlands Blvd Loma Linda (92354) *(P-2399)*

A
L
P
H
A
B
E
T
I
C

Employee Codes: A=Over 500 employees, B=251-500
C=101-250, D=51-100, E=20-50, F=10-19, G=1-9

2025 Southern California
Business Directory and Buyers Guide

© Mergent Inc. 1-800-342-5647

1009

Dvm Insurance Agency, Brea *Also Called: Veterinary Pet Insurance Services Inc (P-12266)*

Dvs Media Services (PA)................................... E 818 841-6750
   2625 W Olive Ave Burbank (91505) *(P-13313)*

Dw and Bb Consulting Inc .... D 818 896-9899
   11381 Bradley Ave Pacoima (91331) *(P-7669)*

DWA, Palm Springs *Also Called: Desert Water Agency Fing Corp (P-9690)*

Dwa Holdings LLC (DH)................................... D 818 695-5000
   1000 Flower St Glendale (91201) *(P-14824)*

Dwi Enterprises .... E 714 842-2236
   11081 Winners Cir Ste 100 Los Alamitos (90720) *(P-6535)*

Dxterity Diagnostics Inc (PA).......................... E 310 537-7857
   19500 S Rancho Way Ste 116 Compton (90220) *(P-17873)*

Dyk, El Cajon *Also Called: Dn Tanks Inc (P-7679)*

Dyk Incorporated (HQ)...................................... E 619 440-8181
   351 Cypress Ln El Cajon (92020) *(P-7680)*

Dyk Prestressed Tanks, El Cajon *Also Called: Dyk Incorporated (P-7680)*

Dymax Service, Cerritos *Also Called: Resa Service LLC (P-9601)*

Dynabook Americas Inc (HQ)............................ B 949 583-3000
   5241 California Ave Ste 100 Irvine (92617) *(P-5845)*

Dynacast LLC .... C 949 707-1211
   25952 Commercentre Dr Lake Forest (92630) *(P-4659)*

Dynacast, LLC, Lake Forest *Also Called: Dynacast LLC (P-4659)*

Dynaco Equipment Co, Pismo Beach *Also Called: Brooks Restaurant Group Inc (P-10744)*

Dynaflex Products (PA).................................... D 323 724-1555
   6466 Gayhart St Commerce (90040) *(P-7202)*

Dynalectric Company .... B 619 328-4007
   1111 Pioneer Way El Cajon (92020) *(P-910)*

Dynamet Incorporated .... E 714 375-3150
   16052 Beach Blvd Ste 221 Huntington Beach (92647) *(P-4617)*

Dynamic Auto Images Inc .... B 714 771-3400
   2860 Michelle Ste 140 Irvine (92606) *(P-14707)*

Dynamic Cooking Systems Inc .... A 714 372-7000
   695 Town Center Dr Ste 180 Costa Mesa (92626) *(P-6012)*

Dynamic Detail, Irvine *Also Called: Dynamic Auto Images Inc (P-14707)*

Dynamic Fabrication Inc .... E 714 662-2440
   890 Mariner St Brea (92821) *(P-7470)*

DYNAMIC HOME CARE, Sherman Oaks *Also Called: Dynamic Home Care Service Inc (P-16386)*

Dynamic Home Care Service Inc (PA)................ D 818 981-4446
   14260 Ventura Blvd Ste 301 Sherman Oaks (91423) *(P-16386)*

Dynamic Plumbing Systems Inc .... B 951 343-1200
   5920 Winterhaven Ave Riverside (92504) *(P-773)*

Dynamic Resources Inc .... D 619 268-3070
   7894 Dagget St Ste 202e San Diego (92111) *(P-2622)*

Dynamic Sciences Intl Inc .... E 818 226-6262
   9400 Lurline Ave Unit B Chatsworth (91311) *(P-6609)*

Dynamics O&P, Los Angeles *Also Called: Dynamics Orthtics Prsthtics In (P-8260)*

Dynamics Orthtics Prsthtics In .... E 213 383-9212
   1830 W Olympic Blvd Ste 123 Los Angeles (90006) *(P-8260)*

Dynamo Aviation Inc .... D 818 785-9561
   9601 Mason Ave # A Chatsworth (91311) *(P-4982)*

Dynasty Electronic Company LLC .... D 714 550-1197
   1790 E Mcfadden Ave Ste 105 Santa Ana (92705) *(P-6723)*

Dynasty Marketplace Inc .... C 804 837-0119
   716 Hampton Dr Venice (90291) *(P-13713)*

Dynatrac Products LLC .... E 714 596-4461
   7392 Count Cir Huntington Beach (92647) *(P-7249)*

Dyntek Inc (DH) .... C 949 271-6700
   5241 California Ave Ste 150 Irvine (92617) *(P-14215)*

Dytran Instruments Inc .... C 818 700-7818
   21592 Marilla St Chatsworth (91311) *(P-6993)*

Dzkicorp Inc .... D 805 464-0573
   762 Higuera St Ste 216 San Luis Obispo (93401) *(P-13714)*

E & B Ntral Resources Mgt Corp (PA)............... D 661 387-8500
   1608 Norris Rd Bakersfield (93308) *(P-300)*

E & B Ntral Resources MGT Corp .... E 661 766-2501
   1848 Perkins Rd New Cuyama (93254) *(P-301)*

E & C Fashion Inc .... B 323 262-0099
   1420 Esperanza St Los Angeles (90023) *(P-14492)*

E & S International Entps Inc (PA)..................... C 818 887-0700
   7801 Hayvenhurst Ave Van Nuys (91406) *(P-10216)*

E & S Paper Co .... E 310 538-8700
   14110 S Broadway Los Angeles (90061) *(P-10591)*

E & S Ring Management Corp .... D 310 670-5983
   6300 Green Valley Cir Culver City (90230) *(P-12433)*

E Appliance Repair and Hvac, Santa Clarita *Also Called: 5 Star Service Inc (P-14726)*

E B Bradley Co (PA).. E 323 585-9917
   5602 Bickett St Vernon (90058) *(P-10305)*

E C R M C, El Centro *Also Called: El Centro Rgnal Med Ctr Fndtio (P-15989)*

E D Q Inc .... E 714 546-6010
   2920 Halladay St Santa Ana (92705) *(P-7855)*

E Entertainment Television Inc .... A 323 954-2400
   5750 Wilshire Blvd Ste 500 Los Angeles (90036) *(P-9549)*

E Film Digital Labratories, Los Angeles *Also Called: Efilm LLC (P-14825)*

E J Harrison & Sons Inc .... C 805 647-1414
   1589 Lirio Ave Ventura (93004) *(P-9742)*

E J Lauren LLC .... E 562 803-1113
   2690 Pellissier Pl City Of Industry (90601) *(P-2445)*

E M D, Los Angeles *Also Called: Capitol-Emi Music Inc (P-6572)*

E M E Inc .... C 310 639-1621
   500 E Pine St Compton (90222) *(P-5255)*

E M S, Santa Ana *Also Called: Sandberg Industries Inc (P-7047)*

E Management Services LLC .... D 818 835-9525
   20010 Ventura Blvd Woodland Hills (91364) *(P-10622)*

E O C, Compton *Also Called: Cri Sub 1 (P-2507)*

E O C Health Services, San Luis Obispo *Also Called: Community Action Prtnr San Lui (P-16457)*

E O S International, Carlsbad *Also Called: Electronic Online Systems International (P-14080)*

E P I, Irvine *Also Called: Asian European Products Inc (P-9812)*

E P I, San Diego *Also Called: Engineering Partners Inc (P-17523)*

E R C Company, E Rncho Dmngz *Also Called: Coy Industries Inc (P-4975)*

E R G International, Oxnard *Also Called: Ergonom Corporation (P-2611)*

E R I T Inc (PA)... D 760 433-6024
   251 Airport Rd Oceanside (92058) *(P-17147)*

E S 3, San Diego *Also Called: Enginring Sftwr Sys Sltons Inc (P-17524)*

E S I, San Dimas *Also Called: Edgebanding Services Inc (P-10997)*

E S T, Carlsbad *Also Called: Electro Surface Tech Inc (P-6724)*

E Sales, Garden Grove *Also Called: Elasco Inc (P-3265)*

E V G, Anaheim *Also Called: Emergency Vehicle Group Inc (P-11342)*

E Vasquez Distributors Inc .... E 805 487-8458
   4524 E Pleasant Valley Rd Oxnard (93033) *(P-2387)*

E Z Buy & E Z Sell Recycl Corp (DH)................. C 310 886-7808
   4954 Van Nuys Blvd Ste 201 Sherman Oaks (91403) *(P-2795)*

E Z Staffing Inc (PA)....................................... B 818 845-2500
   200 N Maryland Ave Ste 303 Glendale (91206) *(P-13511)*

E-Band Communications LLC .... E 858 408-0660
   82 Coromar Dr Goleta (93117) *(P-6610)*

E-Scepter, City Of Industry *Also Called: Sceptre Inc (P-7049)*

E-Times Corporation (PA)................................ B 213 452-6720
   601 S Figueroa St Ste 5000 Los Angeles (90017) *(P-14169)*

E-Z Lok Division, Gardena *Also Called: Tool Components Inc (P-10161)*

E-Z Mix Inc (PA)... E 818 768-0568
   11450 Tuxford St Sun Valley (91352) *(P-4438)*

E. S. Babcock & Sons, Riverside *Also Called: Babcock Laboratories Inc (P-17905)*

E.V. Roberts, Carson *Also Called: Cirrus Enterprises LLC (P-10995)*

E/G Electro-Graph, Vista *Also Called: Plansee USA LLC (P-6868)*

E&S Financial Group Inc .... D 805 644-1621
   700 E Main St Ventura (93001) *(P-11898)*

Eagle Dominion Energy Corp .... E 270 366-4817
   3020 W Olive Ave Burbank (91505) *(P-302)*

Eagle Dominion Trust, Burbank *Also Called: Eagle Dominion Energy Corp (P-302)*

Eagle Eye SEC Solutions Inc .... D 800 372-8142
   1045 Bay Blvd Ste B Chula Vista (91911) *(P-14296)*

Eagle Labs, Rancho Cucamonga *Also Called: Eagle Labs LLC (P-8146)*

Eagle Labs LLC .... D 909 481-0011
   10201a Trademark St Ste A Rancho Cucamonga (91730) *(P-8146)*

Eagle Med Packg Sterilization, Paso Robles *Also Called: Eagle Med Pckg Strlization Inc (P-14493)*

Eagle Med Pckg Strlization Inc .... E 805 238-7401
   2921 Union Rd Ste A Paso Robles (93446) *(P-14493)*

Eagle One Golf Products, Anaheim *Also Called: Golf Supply House Usa Inc* *(P-8519)*

Eagle Paving LLC .... D 858 486-6400
13915 Danielson St Ste 201 Poway (92064) *(P-614)*

Eagle Roofing Products, Rialto *Also Called: Burlingame Industries Inc* *(P-13107)*

Eagle Roofing Products Co, Rialto *Also Called: Burlingame Industries Inc* *(P-4500)*

Eagle Security Services Inc .... C 310 642-0656
12903 S Normandie Ave Gardena (90249) *(P-14297)*

Eagle Topco LP .... A 949 585-4329
18200 Von Karman Ave Irvine (92612) *(P-13919)*

Eagle Vnes Vnyrds Golf CLB LLC .... D 707 257-4470
1733 S Anaheim Blvd Anaheim (92805) *(P-15077)*

Eagleware Manufacturing Co Inc .... E 562 320-3100
12683 Corral Pl Santa Fe Springs (90670) *(P-5183)*

EAM Enterprises Inc .... D 818 951-6464
8307 Foothill Blvd Sunland (91040) *(P-12434)*

EAM Enterprises Inc (PA) .... D **818 248-9100**
4005 Foothill Blvd La Crescenta (91214) *(P-12435)*

Eappraiseit LLC .... C 800 281-6200
12395 First American Way Poway (92064) *(P-12436)*

Earle M Jorgensen Company .... D 323 567-1122
350 S Grand Ave Ste 5100 Los Angeles (90071) *(P-10134)*

Earle M Jorgensen Company (HQ) .... C 323 567-1122
10650 Alameda St Lynwood (90262) *(P-10135)*

Early Childhood Education, La Quinta *Also Called: Desert Snds Unfied Schl Dst SC* *(P-17088)*

Early Childhood Resources, San Diego *Also Called: Ecr4kids LP* *(P-2541)*

Early Learning Center, Los Angeles *Also Called: California Childrens Academy* *(P-17078)*

Earth Island LLC (HQ) .... E **818 725-2820**
9201 Owensmouth Ave Chatsworth (91311) *(P-1766)*

Earthlite, Vista *Also Called: Earthlite LLC* *(P-2467)*

Earthlite LLC (DH) .... D 760 599-1112
990 Joshua Way Vista (92081) *(P-2467)*

Earthrise Nutritionals LLC .... E 760 348-5027
113 E Hoober Rd Calipatria (92233) *(P-1767)*

Earthrise Nutritionals LLC (HQ) .... E **949 623-0980**
3333 Michelson Dr Ste 300 Irvine (92612) *(P-3398)*

Ease Entertainment Services LP .... D 310 469-7300
8383 Wilshire Blvd Ste 90 Beverly Hills (90211) *(P-14986)*

East Cast Repr Fabrication LLC .... E 619 591-9577
280 Trousdale Dr Ste E Chula Vista (91910) *(P-4832)*

East Los Angles Dctors Hosp In .... B
4060 Whittier Blvd Los Angeles (90023) *(P-15984)*

East Los Angles Healthcare LLC (HQ) .... D **323 268-0106**
1016 S Record Ave Los Angeles (90023) *(P-15624)*

East Los Angles Rmrkble Ctzens .... D 323 223-3079
3839 Selig Pl Los Angeles (90031) *(P-16936)*

East Valley Glendora Hosp LLC .... B 626 852-5000
150 W Route 66 Glendora (91740) *(P-15985)*

East Valley Tourist Dev Auth .... A 760 342-5000
84245 Indio Springs Dr Indio (92203) *(P-15200)*

East West, Pasadena *Also Called: East West Bancorp Inc* *(P-11761)*

East West Bancorp Inc (PA) .... B **626 768-6000**
135 N Los Robles Ave Fl 7 Pasadena (91101) *(P-11761)*

East West Bank (HQ) .... B 626 768-6000
135 N Los Robles Ave Ste 100 Pasadena (91101) *(P-11762)*

East West Tea Company LLC .... C 310 275-9891
1616 Preuss Rd Los Angeles (90035) *(P-1411)*

Eastbiz Corporation .... C 310 212-7134
3501 Jack Northrop Ave Hawthorne (90250) *(P-15201)*

Easterday Building Maintenance, Anaheim *Also Called: Hunter Easterday Corporation* *(P-13377)*

Eastern District Office, El Cajon *Also Called: San Diego Gas & Electric Co* *(P-9608)*

Eastern Goldfields Inc .... C 619 497-2555
1660 Hotel Cir N Ste 207 San Diego (92108) *(P-18130)*

Eastern Los Angles Rgnal Ctr F (PA) .... C **626 299-4700**
1000 S Fremont Ave Unit 23 Alhambra (91803) *(P-16937)*

Eastern Mncpl Wtr Dst Fclties .... A 951 928-3777
2270 Trumble Rd Perris (92572) *(P-9691)*

Eastern Municipal Water Dst .... C 951 657-7469
19750 Evans Rd Perris (92571) *(P-9692)*

Eastern Municipal Water Dst (PA) .... B **951 928-3777**
2270 Trumble Rd Perris (92572) *(P-9693)*

Eastern Sports, Thousand Oaks *Also Called: Easton Hockey Inc* *(P-8516)*

Eastern Staffing LLC .... B 805 882-2200
301 Mentor Dr # 210 Santa Barbara (93111) *(P-13512)*

Easterncctv (usa) LLC .... D 626 961-8999
525 Parriott Pl W City Of Industry (91745) *(P-14394)*

Eastland Corporation .... E 323 261-5388
3017 Bandini Blvd Vernon (90058) *(P-10868)*

Eastman Music Company (PA) .... E **909 868-1777**
2158 Pomona Blvd Pomona (91768) *(P-10559)*

Eastmans Guitars, Pomona *Also Called: Eastman Music Company* *(P-10559)*

Easton Bell Sports, Irvine *Also Called: Bell Sports Inc* *(P-8505)*

Easton Diamond Sports LLC .... D 800 632-7866
112 S Lakeview Canyon Rd Westlake Village (91362) *(P-10512)*

Easton Hockey Inc .... A 818 782-6445
3500 Willow Ln Thousand Oaks (91361) *(P-8516)*

Eastridge Workforce Solutions, San Diego *Also Called: Eplica Corporate Services Inc* *(P-13515)*

Eastridge Workforce Solutions, San Diego *Also Called: Teg Staffing Inc* *(P-13576)*

Eastridge Workforce Solutions, San Diego *Also Called: Eplica Inc* *(P-13596)*

Eastwestproto Inc .... B 888 535-5728
6605 E Washington Blvd Commerce (90040) *(P-8820)*

Easy Care Mso LLC .... B 562 676-9600
3780 Kilroy Airport Way Ste 530 Long Beach (90806) *(P-16557)*

Easy Fuel, Aliso Viejo *Also Called: Efuel LLC* *(P-11030)*

Easy Reach Supply LLC .... E 601 582-7866
3737 Capitol Ave City Of Industry (90601) *(P-8586)*

Easyflex, Santa Ana *Also Called: Easyflex Inc* *(P-4516)*

Easyflex Inc .... E 888 577-8999
2700 N Main St Ste 800 Santa Ana (92705) *(P-4516)*

Eat Like A Woman, Burbank *Also Called: Staness Jonekos Entps Inc* *(P-1857)*

Eatgud, Los Angeles *Also Called: Pensieve Foods* *(P-1837)*

Eaton, Irvine *Also Called: Eaton Aerospace LLC* *(P-7714)*

Eaton Aerospace LLC .... E 949 452-9500
9650 Jeronimo Rd Irvine (92618) *(P-7714)*

Eaton Aerospace LLC .... B 818 409-0200
4690 Colorado Blvd Los Angeles (90039) *(P-10180)*

Eaton Electrical Inc .... C 951 685-5788
13201 Dahlia St Fontana (92337) *(P-6348)*

Ebara Mixers Inc .... E 760 246-3430
9351 Industrial Way Adelanto (92301) *(P-5670)*

Ebatts.com, Camarillo *Also Called: Battery-Biz Inc* *(P-7089)*

Ebc Inc (PA) .... D 310 753-6407
219 Manhattan Beach Blvd Ste 3 Manhattan Beach (90266) *(P-400)*

Eberhard .... C 818 782-4604
15220 Raymer St Van Nuys (91405) *(P-1081)*

Eberine Enterprises Inc .... E 323 587-1111
3360 Fruitland Ave Los Angeles (90058) *(P-1716)*

Ebioscience Inc .... C 858 642-2058
10255 Science Center Dr San Diego (92121) *(P-17786)*

Ebs General Engineering Inc .... D 951 279-6869
1345 Quarry St Ste 101 Corona (92879) *(P-615)*

EC Closing Corp .... D 800 546-1531
525 E Main St El Cajon (92020) *(P-11899)*

EC Design LLC .... E 310 220-2362
4860 W 147th St Hawthorne (90250) *(P-11635)*

EC Group Inc (PA) .... D 310 815-2700
5960 Bowcroft St Los Angeles (90016) *(P-9870)*

ECB Corp (PA) .... D **714 385-8900**
6400 Artesia Blvd Buena Park (90620) *(P-774)*

Eccu, Brea *Also Called: Adelfi Credit Union* *(P-11822)*

Echelon Fine Printing, Vernon *Also Called: The Ligature Inc* *(P-3089)*

Echo Bridge Home Entertainment, Los Angeles *Also Called: Platinum Disc LLC* *(P-10566)*

Eci Water Ski Products Inc .... E 951 940-9999
224 Malbert St Perris (92570) *(P-11630)*

Eckert Zegler Isotope Pdts (HQ) .... E **661 309-1010**
24937 Avenue Tibbitts Valencia (91355) *(P-8039)*

Eckert Zegler Isotope Pdts Inc .... E 661 309-1010
1800 N Keystone St Burbank (91504) *(P-8040)*

Ecko Print & Packaging, Ontario *Also Called: Ecko Products Group LLC* *(P-2663)*

Ecko Products Group LLC .... E 909 628-5678
740 S Milliken Ave Ste C Ontario (91761) *(P-2663)*

A L P H A B E T I C

Eclipse Berry Farms LLC .... D 310 207-7879
11812 San Vicente Blvd Ste 250 Los Angeles (90049) *(P-16)*

Eclipse Lighting & Electrical .... D 714 871-9366
935 E Discovery Ln Anaheim (92801) *(P-911)*

Eclipse Prtg & Graphics LLC .... E 909 390-2452
9145 Milliken Ave Rancho Cucamonga (91730) *(P-3005)*

Ecmd Inc .... E 909 980-1775
10863 Jersey Blvd 100 Rancho Cucamonga (91730) *(P-2305)*

Ecmm Services Inc .... C 714 988-9388
1320 Valley Vista Dr # 204 Diamond Bar (91765) *(P-8562)*

Eco Services Operations Corp .... D 310 885-6719
20720 S Wilmington Ave Long Beach (90810) *(P-3235)*

Ecoatm LLC (DH).................... C 858 999-3200
10121 Barnes Canyon Rd San Diego (92121) *(P-6700)*

Ecobat California RE LLC .... B 626 937-3201
720 S 7th Ave City Of Industry (91746) *(P-9743)*

Ecology Recycling Services LLC .... C 909 370-1318
785 E M St Colton (92324) *(P-9744)*

Econo Air, Placentia Also Called: Mddr Inc *(P-802)*

Econolite Control Products Inc (PA).................... C 714 630-3700
1250 N Tustin Ave Anaheim (92807) *(P-6681)*

Ecoolthing Corp .... E 714 368-4791
1321 E Saint Gertrude Pl Ste A Santa Ana (92705) *(P-5445)*

Ecosense Lighting Inc (PA).................... D 855 632-6736
837 N Spring St Ste 103 Los Angeles (90012) *(P-10181)*

Ecosense Lighting Inc .... C 714 823-1014
14811 Myford Rd Tustin (92780) *(P-10182)*

Ecosheld Pest Sltons Phnix LLC .... C 310 295-9511
9037 Owensmouth Ave Canoga Park (91304) *(P-13346)*

Ecosmart Technologies Inc .... E 770 667-0006
1585 W Mission Blvd Pomona (91766) *(P-3754)*

Ecotrak, Irvine Also Called: Ecotrak LLC *(P-13715)*

Ecotrak LLC .... D 888 219-0000
18004 Sky Park Cir Ste 100 Irvine (92614) *(P-13715)*

Ecowater Systems, Vista Also Called: Yanchewski & Wardell Entps Inc *(P-6038)*

Ecowise Inc .... E 626 759-3997
13538 Excelsior Dr Unit B Santa Fe Springs (90670) *(P-3264)*

Ecr4kids LP .... E 619 323-2005
5630 Kearny Mesa Rd Ste B San Diego (92111) *(P-2541)*

Ectron Corporation .... E 858 278-0600
9340 Hazard Way Ste B2 San Diego,(92123) *(P-6611)*

Ed Hardy, Commerce Also Called: DNam Apparel Industries LLC *(P-2093)*

Edata Solutions Inc .... A 510 574-5380
17100 Pioneer Blvd Artesia (90701) *(P-14130)*

Edco Disposal Corporation (PA).................... C 619 287-7555
2755 California Ave Signal Hill (90755) *(P-9745)*

Edco Plastics Inc .... E 714 772-1986
2110 E Winston Rd Anaheim (92806) *(P-4110)*

Edelbrock LLC .... E 310 781-2290
501 Amapola Ave Torrance (90501) *(P-7250)*

Edelbrock Foundry Corp .... E 951 654-6677
1320 S Buena Vista St San Jacinto (92583) *(P-4645)*

Edf Renewables Inc (PA).................... C 858 521-3300
15445 Innovation Dr San Diego (92128) *(P-9578)*

Edgate Holdings Inc .... E 858 712-9341
4655 Cass St San Diego (92109) *(P-13920)*

Edge Autonomy Bend LLC (HQ).................... E 541 678-0515
831 Buckley Rd San Luis Obispo (93401) *(P-7643)*

Edge Autonomy Slo LLC .... E 805 544-0932
831 Buckley Rd San Luis Obispo (93401) *(P-7715)*

Edge Mortgage Advisory Co LLC .... D 714 564-5800
2125 E Katella Ave Ste 350 Anaheim (92806) *(P-18306)*

Edge Solutions Consulting Inc (PA).................... E 818 591-3500
5126 Clareton Dr Ste 160 Agoura Hills (91301) *(P-5846)*

Edge Systems, Long Beach Also Called: Hydrafacial LLC *(P-8164)*

Edgebanding Services Inc (PA).................... D 909 599-2336
828 W Cienega Ave San Dimas (91773) *(P-10997)*

Edgecast Inc .... A 310 396-7400
13031 W Jefferson Blvd Ste 900 Los Angeles (90094) *(P-14216)*

Edgemine Inc .... C 323 267-8222
1801 E 50th St Los Angeles (90058) *(P-10707)*

Edgewave Inc .... D 800 782-3762
4225 Executive Sq Ste 1600 La Jolla (92037) *(P-13921)*

Edgewood Partners Insur Ctr .... B 949 263-0606
4675 Macarthur Ct Newport Beach (92660) *(P-12205)*

Edgeworth Integration LLC .... D 805 915-0211
2360 Shasta Way Ste F Simi Valley (93065) *(P-14395)*

Edi Ideas, Fountain Valley Also Called: Freightgate Inc *(P-13935)*

Edison Capital .... C 909 594-3789
18101 Von Karman Ave Ste 1700 Irvine (92612) *(P-9579)*

Edison Energy LLC .... C 949 491-1633
18500 Von Karman Ave Ste 260 Irvine (92612) *(P-9580)*

Edison International (PA).................... A 626 302-2222
2244 Walnut Grove Ave Rosemead (91770) *(P-9581)*

Edison Mission, Rosemead Also Called: Edison Mission Energy *(P-9582)*

Edison Mission Energy (PA).................... D 626 302-5778
2244 Walnut Grove Ave Rosemead (91770) *(P-9582)*

Edison Mssion Midwest Holdings .... A 626 302-2222
2244 Walnut Grove Ave Rosemead (91770) *(P-9583)*

Edison Price Lighting Inc (PA).................... C 718 685-0700
5424 E Slauson Ave Commerce (90040) *(P-6456)*

Edje-Enterprises .... D 951 245-7070
18500 Pasadena St Ste B Lake Elsinore (92530) *(P-1082)*

Edmund A Gray Co (PA).................... D 213 625-0376
2277 E 15th St Los Angeles (90021) *(P-5433)*

Edmund A Gray Co .... E 213 625-2725
1901 Imperial St Los Angeles (90021) *(P-9063)*

Edmunds Holding Company (PA).................... A 310 309-6300
2401 Colorado Ave Santa Monica (90404) *(P-14170)*

Edmunds.com, Santa Monica Also Called: Edmunds Holding Company *(P-14170)*

Edmundscom Inc (HQ).................... A 310 309-6300
2401 Colorado Ave Ste P1 Santa Monica (90404) *(P-13265)*

EDN Aviation Inc .... E 818 988-8826
6720 Valjean Ave Van Nuys (91406) *(P-14763)*

Edna H Pagel Inc .... D 323 234-2200
2050 E 38th St Vernon (90058) *(P-479)*

Edo Communications and Countermeasures Systems Inc .... D 818 464-2475
7821 Orion Ave Van Nuys (91406) *(P-7716)*

Edris Plastics Mfg Inc .... E 323 581-7000
4560 Pacific Blvd Vernon (90058) *(P-4111)*

Edro Engineering LLC (DH).................... E 909 594-5751
20500 Carrey Rd Walnut (91789) *(P-5578)*

Edsi .... C 760 731-3501
700 Ammunition Rd Bldg 103 Fallbrook (92028) *(P-17519)*

Education Ln Ctr Alexandria Ci, San Diego Also Called: Goal Financial LLC *(P-11906)*

Educational Ideas Incorporated .... E 714 990-4332
950 W Central Ave Brea (92821) *(P-2889)*

Edward G Chester Adult Center, Compton Also Called: Compton Unified School Dst *(P-16805)*

Edward Thomas Companies .... C 714 782-7500
640 W Katella Ave Anaheim (92802) *(P-12817)*

Edward Thomas Hospitality Corp .... B 310 458-0030
1 Pico Blvd Santa Monica (90405) *(P-12818)*

Edwards, Irvine Also Called: Edwards Lifesciences Corp *(P-8263)*

Edwards, Irvine Also Called: Edwards Lifesciences US Inc *(P-8378)*

Edwards Assoc Cmmnications Inc (PA).................... C 805 658-2626
2277 Knoll Dr Ste A Ventura (93003) *(P-2722)*

Edwards Cinemas University, Irvine Also Called: Edwards Theatres Circuit Inc *(P-14938)*

Edwards Label, Ventura Also Called: Edwards Assoc Cmmnications Inc *(P-2722)*

Edwards Life Sciences Cardio V, Irvine Also Called: Edwards Lifesciences Corp *(P-8261)*

Edwards Lifesciences Corp .... D 949 250-2500
17221 Red Hill Ave Irvine (92614) *(P-8261)*

Edwards Lifesciences Corp .... E 949 553-0611
1212 Alton Pkwy Irvine (92606) *(P-8262)*

Edwards Lifesciences Corp (PA).................... A 949 250-2500
1 Edwards Way Irvine (92614) *(P-8263)*

Edwards Lifesciences LLC (HQ).................... A 949 250-2500
1 Edwards Way Irvine (92614) *(P-3399)*

Edwards Lifesciences US Inc (HQ).................... D 949 250-2500
1 Edwards Way Irvine (92614) *(P-8378)*

Edwards Theatres Inc .... C 949 582-4078
27741 Crown Valley Pkwy Ste 301 Mission Viejo (92691) *(P-14932)*

Edwards Theatres Inc .... C 844 462-7342
1950 Foothill Blvd La Verne (91750) *(P-14933)*

Edwards Theatres Inc (DH).................................. C 949 640-4600
300 Newport Center Dr Newport Beach (92660) *(P-14934)*

Edwards Theatres Circuit Inc .... C 619 660-3460
2951 Jamacha Rd El Cajon (92019) *(P-14935)*

Edwards Theatres Circuit Inc .... C 951 296-0144
40750 Winchester Rd Temecula (92591) *(P-14936)*

Edwards Theatres Circuit Inc .... C 714 428-0962
901 S Coast Dr Costa Mesa (92626) *(P-14937)*

Edwards Theatres Circuit Inc .... C 949 854-8811
4245 Campus Dr Irvine (92612) *(P-14938)*

Edwards Theatres Circuit, Inc., Newport Beach *Also Called: Edwards Theatres Inc (P-14934)*

Eeco, Los Angeles *Also Called: Elevator Equipment Corporation (P-10371)*

Eeco Switch, Brea *Also Called: Transico Inc (P-7062)*

Eeg 3 LLC (DH).. C
6080 Center Dr Ste 1200 Los Angeles (90045) *(P-6612)*

Eeg Glider Inc (HQ).. C 310 437-6000
1561 E Orangethorpe Ave Fullerton (92831) *(P-9564)*

Eema Industries Inc .... E 323 904-0200
5461 W Jefferson Blvd Los Angeles (90016) *(P-6499)*

Eess, Chula Vista *Also Called: Eagle Eye SEC Solutions Inc (P-14296)*

Eevelle LLC .... E 760 434-2231
5928 Balfour Ct Carlsbad (92008) *(P-2275)*

Efaxcom (DH)... D 323 817-3207
6922 Hollywood Blvd Fl 5 Los Angeles (90028) *(P-5914)*

Efaxcom .... E 805 692-0064
5385 Hollister Ave Ste 208 Santa Barbara (93111) *(P-5915)*

Efilm LLC .... C 323 463-7041
1144 N Las Palmas Ave Los Angeles (90038) *(P-14825)*

Efuel LLC .... D 949 330-7145
65 Enterprise 3rd Fl Aliso Viejo (92656) *(P-11030)*

Egge Machine Company Inc (PA).......................... E 562 945-3419
8403 Allport Ave Santa Fe Springs (90670) *(P-9823)*

Eggleston Youth Centers Inc (PA)........................ D 626 480-8107
256 W Badillo St Covina (91723) *(P-16938)*

Eggs Unlimited, Irvine *Also Called: Eggs Unlimited LLC (P-10834)*

Eggs Unlimited LLC .... D 888 554-3977
17875 Von Karman Ave Ste 450 Irvine (92614) *(P-10834)*

Egl Holdco Inc .... A 800 678-7423
18200 Von Karman Ave Ste 1000 Irvine (92612) *(P-13922)*

Egnite Inc .... D 949 594-2330
65 Enterprise Pmb 455 Aliso Viejo (92656) *(P-18131)*

Egnite Health, Inc., Aliso Viejo *Also Called: Egnite Inc (P-18131)*

Ego Inc .... C 626 447-0296
180 Via Verde Ste 100 San Dimas (91773) *(P-17721)*

Egr Incorporated (DH)... E 800 757-7075
4000 Greystone Dr Ontario (91761) *(P-7251)*

Egs Financial Care Inc (DH).................................. B 877 217-4423
5 Park Plz Ste 1100 Irvine (92614) *(P-13282)*

Eharmony Inc (HQ).. C 424 258-1199
3583 Hayden Ave Culver City (90232) *(P-13173)*

Eharmony.com, Culver City *Also Called: Eharmony Inc (P-13173)*

Ehmcke Sheet Metal Corp .... D 619 477-6484
840 W 19th St National City (91950) *(P-1083)*

Ehp Administrators, Chatsworth *Also Called: Electronic Health Plans Inc (P-16558)*

Eibach Inc .... D 951 256-8300
264 Mariah Cir Corona (92879) *(P-5379)*

Eibach Springs, Inc., Corona *Also Called: Eibach Inc (P-5379)*

Eichleay Inc .... C 562 256-8600
500 N State College Blvd Orange (92868) *(P-17520)*

Eide Bailly LLP .... B 909 466-4410
10681 Foothill Blvd Ste 300 Rancho Cucamonga (91730) *(P-17722)*

Eide Industries Inc .... D 562 402-8335
16215 Piuma Ave Cerritos (90703) *(P-2237)*

Eighteenth Meridian Inc .... B 714 706-3643
200 Spectrum Center Dr Ste 300 Irvine (92618) *(P-13716)*

Einstein Dental, San Diego *Also Called: Einstein Industries Inc (P-13717)*

Einstein Industries Inc .... C 858 459-1182
6825 Flanders Dr San Diego (92121) *(P-13717)*

Einstein Noah Rest Group Inc .... C 714 847-4609
16304 Beach Blvd Westminster (92683) *(P-1286)*

Eisenberg Village, Reseda *Also Called: Los Angles Jewish HM For Aging (P-15707)*

EISENHOWER HEALTH, Rancho Mirage *Also Called: Eisenhower Medical Center (P-15988)*

Eisenhower Health Services, Rancho Mirage *Also Called: Eisenhower Medical Center (P-16387)*

Eisenhower Medical Center .... C 760 836-0232
34450 Gateway Dr Palm Desert (92211) *(P-15303)*

Eisenhower Medical Center .... D 760 228-9900
57475 29 Palms Hwy Ste 104 Yucca Valley (92284) *(P-15304)*

Eisenhower Medical Center .... C 760 610-7200
45280 Seeley Dr La Quinta (92253) *(P-15986)*

Eisenhower Medical Center .... C 760 325-6621
555 E Tachevah Dr Palm Springs (92262) *(P-15987)*

Eisenhower Medical Center (PA)........................... A 760 340-3911
39000 Bob Hope Dr Rancho Mirage (92270) *(P-15988)*

Eisenhower Medical Center .... C 760 773-1364
39000 Bob Hope Dr Frnt Rancho Mirage (92270) *(P-16313)*

Eisenhower Medical Center .... C 760 773-1888
39000 Bob Hope Dr Ste 102 Rancho Mirage (92270) *(P-16387)*

Eisenhower-Memory-Care-center, Palm Desert *Also Called: Eisenhower Medical Center (P-15303)*

Eisner Pediatric Fmly Med Ctr, Los Angeles *Also Called: Pediatric and Family Med Ctr (P-15420)*

Eiu of California, Bakersfield *Also Called: Electrical & Instrumentation Unlimited of California Inc (P-912)*

Ejay Filtration Inc .... E 951 683-0805
3036 Durahart St Riverside (92507) *(P-5405)*

Ejl, City Of Industry *Also Called: E J Lauren LLC (P-2445)*

Ekedal Concrete Inc .... D 949 729-8082
19600 Fairchild Ste 123 Irvine (92612) *(P-1115)*

Eknowledge Group Inc .... E 951 256-4076
160 W Foothill Pkwy Ste 105 Corona (92882) *(P-13923)*

EL ARCA, Los Angeles *Also Called: East Los Angles Rmrkble Ctzens (P-16936)*

El Aviso Magazine .... E 323 586-9199
4850 Gage Ave Bell (90201) *(P-11075)*

El Caballero Country Club .... C 818 654-3000
18300 Tarzana Dr Tarzana (91356) *(P-15133)*

El Cajon Ford, El Cajon *Also Called: El Cajon Motors (P-14650)*

El Cajon Medical Offices, El Cajon *Also Called: Kaiser Foundation Hospitals (P-15342)*

El Cajon Motors (PA)... D 619 579-8888
1595 E Main St El Cajon (92021) *(P-14650)*

El Centro Motors .... D 760 336-2100
1520 Ford Dr El Centro (92243) *(P-11339)*

El Centro Rgnal Med Ctr Fndtio (PA).................... A 760 339-7100
1415 Ross Ave El Centro (92243) *(P-15989)*

El Clasificado (PA)... E 323 837-4095
11205 Imperial Hwy Norwalk (90650) *(P-2796)*

El Dorado Enterprises Inc .... A 310 719-9800
1000 W Redondo Beach Blvd Gardena (90247) *(P-12819)*

El Encanto Inc .... C 805 845-5800
800 Alvarado Pl Santa Barbara (93103) *(P-12820)*

El Gallito Market Inc .... E 626 442-1190
12242 Valley Blvd El Monte (91732) *(P-1768)*

El Guapo Spices Inc (PA)...................................... D 213 312-1300
6200 E Slauson Ave Commerce (90040) *(P-10944)*

El Guapo Spices and Herbs Pkg, Commerce *Also Called: El Guapo Spices Inc (P-10944)*

El Indio Mexican Restaurant, San Diego *Also Called: El Indio Shops Incorporated (P-1297)*

El Indio Shops Incorporated .... D 619 299-0333
3695 India St San Diego (92103) *(P-1297)*

El Latino Newspaper, Chula Vista *Also Called: Latina & Associates Inc (P-2812)*

El Metate Inc .... C 949 646-9362
817 W 19th St Costa Mesa (92627) *(P-1443)*

El Metate Market, Costa Mesa *Also Called: El Metate Inc (P-1443)*

El Monte Automotive Group Inc .... C 626 580-6200
3530 Peck Rd El Monte (91731) *(P-11340)*

El Monte Automotive Group LLC .... D 626 444-0321
3464 Peck Rd El Monte (91731) *(P-11341)*

El Monte Rents Inc (HQ).. C 562 404-9300
12818 Firestone Blvd Santa Fe Springs (90670) *(P-14653)*

Employee Codes: A=Over 500 employees, B=251-500
C=101-250, D=51-100, E=20-50, F=10-19, G=1-9

2025 Southern California
Business Directory and Buyers Guide

© Mergent Inc. 1-800-342-5647

1013

ALPHABETIC

El Monte Rv, Santa Fe Springs *Also Called: El Monte Rents Inc (P-14653)*

El Nido Family Centers (PA) .... C 818 830-3646
10200 Sepulveda Blvd Ste 350 Mission Hills (91345) *(P-16939)*

El Pollo Loco, Costa Mesa *Also Called: El Pollo Loco Holdings Inc (P-11568)*

El Pollo Loco, Cypress *Also Called: WKS Restaurant Corporation (P-11610)*

El Pollo Loco Holdings Inc (PA) .... C 714 599-5000
3535 Harbor Blvd Ste 100 Costa Mesa (92626) *(P-11568)*

El Prado Golf Course LP .... D 909 597-1751
6555 Pine Ave Chino (91708) *(P-15078)*

El Primo Foods Inc .... C 626 289-5054
608 Monterey Pass Rd Monterey Park (91754) *(P-10820)*

El Rancho Vista Hlth Care Ctr, Pico Rivera *Also Called: Mariner Health Care Inc (P-15715)*

El Segundo Bread Bar LLC .... E 310 615-9898
701 E El Segundo Blvd El Segundo (90245) *(P-1444)*

El Tigre Inc .... C 619 429-8212
2909 Coronado Ave San Diego (92154) *(P-11276)*

El Tigre Warehouse 2, San Diego *Also Called: El Tigre Inc (P-11276)*

El Torito Franchising Company, Cypress *Also Called: Real Mex Foods Inc (P-10767)*

Elasco Inc .... D 714 373-4767
11377 Markon Dr Garden Grove (92841) *(P-3265)*

Elasco Urethane Inc .... E 714 895-7031
11377 Markon Dr Garden Grove (92841) *(P-3266)*

Elation Lighting Inc .... D 323 582-3322
6122 S Eastern Ave Commerce (90040) *(P-6500)*

Elation Professional, Commerce *Also Called: Elation Lighting Inc (P-6500)*

Elavon Inc .... B 865 403-7000
700 S Western Ave Los Angeles (90005) *(P-14171)*

Elco Lighting, Los Angeles *Also Called: AMP Plus Inc (P-6483)*

Elco Rfrgn Solutions LLC .... A 858 888-9447
2554 Commercial St San Diego (92113) *(P-5975)*

Elder Care Alliance Camarillo .... D 510 769-2700
2500 Ponderosa Dr N Camarillo (93010) *(P-15625)*

Eldorado Care Center LP .... B 619 440-1211
510 E Washington Ave El Cajon (92020) *(P-15626)*

Eldorado Country Club .... C 760 346-8081
46000 E Eldorado Dr Indian Wells (92210) *(P-15134)*

Eldorado National Cal Inc (HQ) .... E 909 591-9557
9670 Galena St Riverside (92509) *(P-7173)*

Eldorado Stone LLC (DH) .... E 800 925-1491
3817 Ocean Ranch Blvd Ste 114 Oceanside (92056) *(P-4387)*

Eldorado Stone LLC .... A 951 601-3838
24100 Orange Ave Perris (92570) *(P-9943)*

Eleanor Rigby Leather Co .... D 619 356-5590
4660 La Jolla Village Dr Ste 500 Pmb 50054 San Diego (92122) *(P-4310)*

Electra Craft, Westlake Village *Also Called: Toller Enterprises Inc (P-11478)*

Electra Owners Assoc .... C 619 236-3310
700 W E St San Diego (92101) *(P-17281)*

Electrasem Corp .... D 951 371-6140
372 Elizabeth Ln Corona (92878) *(P-7835)*

Electric, San Clemente *Also Called: Electric Visual Evolution LLC (P-8406)*

Electric Designs, Gardena *Also Called: Gloria Lance Inc (P-2036)*

Electric Gate Store Inc .... C 818 504-2300
15342 Chatsworth St Mission Hills (91345) *(P-7122)*

Electric Motors, Santa Ana *Also Called: Advantage Manufacturing Inc (P-10167)*

Electric Solidus LLC .... E 917 692-7764
26565 Agoura Rd Ste 200 Calabasas (91302) *(P-2913)*

Electric Visual Evolution LLC (PA) .... E 949 940-9125
950 Calle Amanecer Ste 101 San Clemente (92673) *(P-8406)*

Electrical & Instrumentation Unlimited of California Inc C
6950 District Blvd Bakersfield (93313) *(P-912)*

Electrical Products Rep, Irvine *Also Called: Agents West Inc (P-7108)*

Electrical Rebuilders Sls Inc .... D 323 249-7545
7603 Willow Glen Rd Los Angeles (90046) *(P-7091)*

Electro Adapter Inc .... D 818 998-1198
20640 Nordhoff St Chatsworth (91311) *(P-6417)*

Electro Kinetics Division, Simi Valley *Also Called: Pacific Scientific Company (P-7790)*

Electro Machine & Engrg Co, Compton *Also Called: E M E Inc (P-5255)*

Electro Surface Tech Inc .... E 760 431-8306
2281 Las Palmas Dr # 101 Carlsbad (92011) *(P-6724)*

Electro Switch Corp .... D 909 581-0855
10410 Trademark St Rancho Cucamonga (91730) *(P-6305)*

Electro-Tech Machining Div, Long Beach *Also Called: Kbr Inc (P-6338)*

Electro-Tech Products, Glendora *Also Called: Electro-Tech Products Inc (P-6994)*

Electro-Tech Products Inc .... E 909 592-1434
2001 E Gladstone St Ste A Glendora (91740) *(P-6994)*

Electrocube Inc (PA) .... E 909 595-1821
3366 Pomona Blvd Pomona (91768) *(P-6995)*

Electrode Technologies Inc .... E 714 549-3771
3110 W Harvard St Ste 14 Santa Ana (92704) *(P-5256)*

Electrofilm Mfg Co LLC .... D 661 257-2242
28150 Industry Dr Valencia (91355) *(P-5373)*

Electrolizing Inc .... E 213 749-7876
1947 Hooper Ave Los Angeles (90011) *(P-5257)*

Electrolurgy Inc .... D 949 250-4494
1121 Duryea Ave Irvine (92614) *(P-5258)*

Electromed Inc .... D 805 523-7500
4590 Ish Dr Simi Valley (93063) *(P-10077)*

Electron Devices, Torrance *Also Called: Stellant Systems Inc (P-7813)*

Electronic Clearing House Inc (HQ) .... D 805 419-8700
730 Paseo Camarillo Camarillo (93010) *(P-13924)*

Electronic Commerce, Newport Beach *Also Called: Electronic Commerce LLC (P-11877)*

Electronic Commerce LLC .... D 800 770-5520
4100 Newport Place Dr Ste 500 Newport Beach (92660) *(P-11877)*

Electronic Control Systems LLC .... C 858 513-1911
12575 Kirkham Ct Ste 1 Poway (92064) *(P-913)*

Electronic Hardware Limited (PA) .... E 818 982-6100
13257 Saticoy St North Hollywood (91605) *(P-10241)*

Electronic Health Plans Inc .... D 818 734-4700
9131 Oakdale Ave Ste 150 Chatsworth (91311) *(P-16558)*

Electronic Online Systems International .... D 760 431-8400
2292 Faraday Ave Frnt Carlsbad (92008) *(P-14080)*

Electronic Precision Spc Inc .... E 714 256-8950
545 Mercury Ln Brea (92821) *(P-5259)*

Electronic Source Company, Van Nuys *Also Called: Alyn Industries Inc (P-6964)*

Electronic Surfc Mounted Inds .... E 858 455-1710
6731 Cobra Way San Diego (92121) *(P-6725)*

Electronic Waveform Lab Inc .... E 714 843-0463
5702 Bolsa Ave Huntington Beach (92649) *(P-8147)*

Eleganza Tiles Inc (PA) .... D 714 224-1700
3125 E Coronado St Anaheim (92806) *(P-1039)*

Element Anheim Rsort Cnvntion, Anaheim *Also Called: Singod Investors Vi LLC (P-3247)*

Element Materials (DH) .... D 714 892-1961
15062 Bolsa Chica St Huntington Beach (92649) *(P-17913)*

Element Mtrls Tech HB Inc .... D 310 632-8500
18100 S Wilmington Ave Compton (90220) *(P-17914)*

Element Rancho Dominguez, Compton *Also Called: Element Mtrls Tech HB Inc (P-17914)*

Elementis Specialties Inc .... D 760 257-9112
31763 Mountain View Rd Newberry Springs (92365) *(P-3236)*

Elements Food Group Inc .... D 909 983-2011
5560 Brooks St Montclair (91763) *(P-1487)*

Elevated Resources Inc (PA) .... C 949 419-6632
3990 Westerly Pl Ste 270 Newport Beach (92660) *(P-14131)*

Elevator Equipment Corporation (PA) .... D 323 245-0147
4035 Goodwin Ave Los Angeles (90039) *(P-10371)*

Eleven Western Builders Inc (PA) .... D 760 796-6346
2862 Executive Pl Escondido (92029) *(P-401)*

Elicc Americas Corporation .... C 760 233-0066
13475 Danielson St Ste 250 Poway (92064) *(P-1164)*

Eliel & Co .... E 760 877-8469
2215 La Mirada Dr Vista (92081) *(P-10682)*

Eliel Cycling, Vista *Also Called: Eliel & Co (P-10682)*

Elijah Textiles Inc .... D 310 666-3443
1251 E Olympic Blvd Ste 108 Los Angeles (90021) *(P-9891)*

Elim Bedding Town, Walnut *Also Called: Tae Sook Chung (P-9909)*

Elite, Culver City *Also Called: West Publishing Corporation (P-14117)*

Elite Craftsman (PA) .... C 562 989-3511
2763 Saint Louis Ave Long Beach (90755) *(P-13373)*

Elite Electric .... D 951 681-5811
9415 Bellegrave Ave Riverside (92509) *(P-914)*

Elite Enfrcment SEC Sltons Inc .... C 866 354-8308
29970 Technology Dr Ste 117d Murrieta (92563) *(P-14298)*

Elite Intractive Solutions Inc .... E ... 310 740-5426
1200 W 7th Ave Ste L1-180 Los Angeles (90017) *(P-14396)*

Elite Leather LLC .... D 909 548-8600
1620 5th Ave Ste 400 San Diego (92101) *(P-2446)*

Elite Lighting .... C 323 888-1973
5424 E Slauson Ave Commerce (90040) *(P-6501)*

Elite Lighting, Commerce Also Called: Elite Lighting *(P-6501)*

Elite Metal Finishing LLC (PA)........................ C **805 983-4320**
540 Spectrum Cir Oxnard (93030) *(P-5260)*

Elite Mfg Corp .... C 888 354-8356
12143 Altamar Pl Santa Fe Springs (90670) *(P-2524)*

Elite Modern, Santa Fe Springs Also Called: Elite Mfg Corp *(P-2524)*

Elite Screens Inc .... E 877 511-1211
12282 Knott St Garden Grove (92841) *(P-8426)*

Elite Show Services Inc .... A 619 574-1589
2878 Camino Del Rio S Ste 260 San Diego (92108) *(P-14299)*

Elite Stone Group Inc ....E 909 629-6988
1205 S Dupont Ave Ontario (91761) *(P-2347)*

Elitra Pharmaceuticals ....D 858 410-3030
3510 Dunhill St Ste A San Diego (92121) *(P-3400)*

Elixir Industries .... D 949 860-5000
24800 Chrisanta Dr Ste 210 Mission Viejo (92691) *(P-5184)*

Elizabeth Glaser Pedia ....B 310 231-0400
16130 Ventura Blvd Ste 250 Encino (91436) *(P-16559)*

Elizabeth Glser Pdtric Aids FN .... B 310 593-0047
2950 31st St Ste 125 Santa Monica (90405) *(P-17342)*

Elizabeth Hospice Inc (PA) .... C **760 737-2050**
800 W Valley Pkwy Escondido (92025) *(P-16388)*

Elizabeth Shutters, Colton Also Called: Elizabeth Shutters Inc *(P-4887)*

Elizabeth Shutters Inc .... E 909 825-1531
525 S Rancho Ave Colton (92324) *(P-4887)*

Elk, Shafter Also Called: Elk Corporation of Texas *(P-4388)*

Elk Corporation of Texas .... C 661 391-3900
6200 Zerker Rd Shafter (93263) *(P-4388)*

Elkay Plastics Co Inc (PA)............................. D **323 722-7073**
6000 Sheila St Commerce (90040) *(P-10998)*

Elkins Kalt Wntraub Rben Grtsi .... D 310 746-4431
10345 W Olympic Blvd Los Angeles (90064) *(P-16675)*

Ellie Mae Inc ....B 818 223-2000
24025 Park Sorrento Ste 210 Calabasas (91302) *(P-13718)*

ELLIE MAE, INC., Calabasas Also Called: Ellie Mae Inc *(P-13718)*

Elliotts Designs Inc .... E 310 631-4931
2473 E Rancho Del Amo Pl Compton (90220) *(P-2468)*

Ellis Building Contractors, Manhattan Beach Also Called: Ebc Inc *(P-400)*

Ellis Grge Cpllone Obrien Anng .... D 310 274-7100
2121 Avenue Of The Stars Fl 30 Los Angeles (90067) *(P-16676)*

Ellison Educational Eqp Inc (PA) .... E **949 598-8822**
25671 Commercentre Dr Lake Forest (92630) *(P-5658)*

Ellison Institute LLC (PA) .... C **310 228-6400**
12414 Exposition Blvd Los Angeles (90064) *(P-17915)*

Ellison Technologies Inc .... C 562 949-9311
9912 Pioneer Blvd Santa Fe Springs (90670) *(P-10372)*

Ellisson Institute Technology, Los Angeles Also Called: Ellison Institute LLC *(P-17915)*

Elljay Acoustics Inc .... D 714 961-1173
511 Cameron St Placentia (92870) *(P-1006)*

Elmco Group, City Of Industry Also Called: Elmco Sales Inc *(P-10316)*

Elmco Sales Inc (PA)......................................D **626 855-4831**
15070 Proctor Ave City Of Industry (91746) *(P-10316)*

Elrob LLC, Garden Grove Also Called: Winchester Interconnect EC LLC *(P-10298)*

Elsevier, San Diego Also Called: Elsevier Inc *(P-2914)*

Elsevier Academic Press, San Diego Also Called: Elsevier Inc *(P-2915)*

Elsevier Inc .... D 619 231-6616
10620 Treena St San Diego (92131) *(P-2914)*

Elsevier Inc .... E 619 231-6616
525 B St San Diego (92101) *(P-2915)*

Eltron International, Agoura Hills Also Called: Zebra Technologies Corporation *(P-5956)*

Elum, San Diego Also Called: Elum Designs Inc *(P-3006)*

Elum Designs Inc .... E 858 650-3586
8969 Kenamar Dr Ste 113 San Diego (92121) *(P-3006)*

Ely Co Inc ....E 310 539-5831
3046 Kashiwa St Torrance (90505) *(P-6120)*

Elysium Jennings LLC ....C ... 661 679-1700
1600 Norris Rd Bakersfield (93308) *(P-288)*

Ema, City Of Industry Also Called: Engineering Model Assoc Inc *(P-4112)*

Emanate Health .... C 626 912-5282
1722 Desire Ave Ste 206 Rowland Heights (91748) *(P-15305)*

Emanate Health .... A 626 962-4011
1115 S Sunset Ave West Covina (91790) *(P-15990)*

Emanate Health .... B 626 857-3477
427 W Carroll Ave Glendora (91741) *(P-15991)*

Emanate Health (PA)...................................... A **626 331-7331**
210 W San Bernardino Rd Covina (91722) *(P-15992)*

Emanate Health, Rowland Heights Also Called: Emanate Health *(P-15305)*

Emanate Health, West Covina Also Called: Emanate Health Medical Center *(P-15993)*

Emanate Health Medical Center (PA)................. A **626 962-4011**
1115 S Sunset Ave West Covina (91790) *(P-15993)*

Emanate Health Medical Center .... A 626 858-8515
140 W College St Covina (91723) *(P-15994)*

Emanate Health Medical Center .... B 626 963-8411
1115 S Sunset Ave West Covina (91790) *(P-15995)*

Emanate Health Medical Center .... A 626 331-7331
210 W San Bernardino Rd Covina (91723) *(P-15996)*

Emanate Hlth Fthill Prsbt Hosp (PA)................ D **626 857-3145**
250 S Grand Ave Glendora (91741) *(P-15997)*

Emanate Hlth Intr-Cmmnity Hosp, Covina Also Called: Emanate Health *(P-15992)*

Embassy Suites, San Diego Also Called: Sunstone Top Gun Lessee Inc *(P-13045)*

Embassy Suites, Temecula Also Called: Windsor Capital Group Inc *(P-13082)*

Embassy Suites, Brea Also Called: Windsor Capital Group Inc *(P-13085)*

Embassy Suites Arcadia, Santa Monica Also Called: Windsor Capital Group Inc *(P-13086)*

Embassy Suites El Paso, Santa Monica Also Called: Windsor Capital Group Inc *(P-13090)*

Embassy Suites Lompoc, Santa Monica Also Called: Windsor Capital Group Inc *(P-13087)*

Embedded Designs Inc .... E 858 673-6050
16120 W Bernardo Dr Ste A San Diego (92127) *(P-7856)*

Embedded Systems Inc .... E 805 624-6030
2250a Union Pl Simi Valley (93065) *(P-6349)*

Embee Plating, Santa Ana Also Called: Embee Processing LLC *(P-17521)*

Embee Processing LLC .... B 714 546-9842
2158 S Hathaway St Santa Ana (92705) *(P-17521)*

Emcor Facilities Services Inc ....C 949 475-6020
2 Cromwell Irvine (92618) *(P-7889)*

Emcor Group Inc .... D 714 993-9500
3233 Enterprise St Brea (92821) *(P-775)*

Emcor Services Mesa Energy, Irvine Also Called: Mesa Energy Systems Inc *(P-805)*

Emcor Svcs Intgrated Solutions .... C 513 679-3325
2 Cromwell Irvine (92618) *(P-776)*

Emcore, Alhambra Also Called: Emcore Corporation *(P-6821)*

Emcore Corporation (PA)................................. C **626 293-3400**
2015 Chestnut St Alhambra (91803) *(P-6821)*

EMD Millipore Corporation .... D 951 676-8080
28820 Single Oak Dr Temecula (92590) *(P-3572)*

EMD Millipore Corporation .... D 951 676-8080
28835 Single Oak Dr Temecula (92590) *(P-7951)*

EMD Millipore Corporation .... E 760 788-9692
26578 Old Julian Hwy Ramona (92065) *(P-7952)*

Eme Fan & Motor, La Verne Also Called: Sunon Inc *(P-5778)*

Emerald Connect LLC (HQ)............................ D **800 233-2834**
15050 Avenue Of Science Ste 200 San Diego (92128) *(P-14132)*

Emerald Health Services, El Segundo Also Called: Tempus LLC *(P-13577)*

Emerald Landscape Services Inc, Santa Clarita Also Called: CAM Properties Inc *(P-202)*

Emerald X LLC .... E 949 226-5754
31910 Del Obispo St Ste 200 San Juan Capistrano (92675) *(P-2856)*

Emergency Ambulance Svc Inc .... D 714 990-1331
3200 E Birch St Ste A Brea (92821) *(P-8821)*

Emergency Dept Dignity Hlth, Arroyo Grande Also Called: Arroyo Grande Community Hospital *(P-15918)*

Emergency Groups Office, San Dimas Also Called: Ego Inc *(P-17721)*

Emergency Groups' Office, San Dimas Also Called: Brault *(P-17707)*

Emergency Technologies Inc .... D 818 765-4421
7345 Varna Ave North Hollywood (91605) *(P-14397)*

Emergency Vehicle Group Inc .... E 714 238-0110
2883 E Coronado St Ste A Anaheim (92806) *(P-11342)*

Employee Codes: A=Over 500 employees, B=251-500
C=101-250, D=51-100, E=20-50, F=10-19, G=1-9

2025 Southern California
Business Directory and Buyers Guide

© Mergent Inc. 1-800-342-5647

1015

Emergent Group Inc (DH)..D 818 394-2800
10939 Pendleton St Sun Valley (91352) *(P-8264)*

Emeritus At Casa Glendale, Glendale *Also Called: Emeritus Corporation (P-15631)*

Emeritus At San Dimas, San Dimas *Also Called: Emeritus Corporation (P-15630)*

Emeritus At Villa Colima, Walnut *Also Called: Emeritus Corporation (P-15632)*

Emeritus Corporation ....C 760 741-3055
1351 E Washington Ave Escondido (92027) *(P-12338)*

Emeritus Corporation ....C 805 239-1313
1919 Creston Rd Ofc Paso Robles (93446) *(P-12339)*

Emeritus Corporation ....C 858 292-8044
5219 Clairemont Mesa Blvd San Diego (92117) *(P-15627)*

Emeritus Corporation ....C 951 744-9861
1001 N Lyon Ave Hemet (92545) *(P-15628)*

Emeritus Corporation ....C 909 420-0153
22325 Barton Rd Grand Terrace (92313) *(P-15629)*

Emeritus Corporation ....C 909 394-0304
1740 S San Dimas Ave San Dimas (91773) *(P-15630)*

Emeritus Corporation ....C 818 246-7457
426 Piedmont Ave Glendale (91206) *(P-15631)*

Emeritus Corporation ....C 909 595-5030
19850 Colima Rd Walnut (91789) *(P-15632)*

Emeritus Corporation ....C 714 639-3590
142 S Prospect St Orange (92869) *(P-15633)*

Emeritus Corporation ....C 714 441-0644
411 E Commonwealth Ave Fullerton (92832) *(P-15634)*

Emeryville Chevron, San Diego *Also Called: Ka Management II Inc (P-18000)*

Emet Lending Group Inc ....D 714 933-9800
2601 Saturn St Ste 200 Brea (92821) *(P-11900)*

Emida Technologies, Foothill Ranch *Also Called: Debisys Inc (P-11839)*

Emids Tech Private Ltd Corp ....A 805 304-5986
6320 Canoga Ave Woodland Hills (91367) *(P-13719)*

EMJ Corporate, Lynwood *Also Called: Earle M Jorgensen Company (P-10135)*

Emp III Inc ....D 323 231-4174
1755 Mrtn Lthr Kng Jr Blv Los Angeles (90058) *(P-12705)*

Empcc Inc ....B 888 278-8200
1682 Langley Ave Fl 2 Irvine (92614) *(P-861)*

Emperors Cllege Clnic Trdtnal, Santa Monica *Also Called: Emperors Cllege Trdtnal Orntal (P-15540)*

Emperors Cllege Trdtnal Orntal ....D 310 453-8383
1807 Wilshire Blvd Ste B Santa Monica (90403) *(P-15540)*

Empi Inc ....D 714 446-9606
301 E Orangethorpe Ave Anaheim (92801) *(P-9824)*

Empire Cls Wrldwide Chffred Sv, El Segundo *Also Called: Cls Trnsprttion Los Angles LLC (P-8819)*

Empire Community Painting, Irvine *Also Called: Empcc Inc (P-861)*

Empire Container Corporation ....D 310 537-8190
1161 E Walnut St Carson (90746) *(P-2664)*

Empire Demolition Inc ....D 909 393-8300
137 N Joy St Corona (92879) *(P-1181)*

Empire Med Transportations LLC ....D 877 473-6029
1433 W Linden St Ste M Riverside (92507) *(P-9277)*

Empire Oil Co ....C 909 877-0226
2756 S Riverside Ave Bloomington (92316) *(P-11031)*

Empire Products Inc ....D 909 399-3355
5061 Brooks St Montclair (91763) *(P-4810)*

Empire Transportation Inc ....B 562 529-2676
8800 Park St Bellflower (90706) *(P-8861)*

Empirical Systems Arospc Inc (PA)...........................C 805 474-5900
3580 Sueldo St San Luis Obispo (93401) *(P-7339)*

Employee Owned PCF Cast Pdts I ....E 562 633-6673
520 S Palmetto Ave Ontario (91762) *(P-4673)*

Employer Defense Group ....E 949 200-0137
2390 E Orangewood Ave Ste 520 Anaheim (92806) *(P-7717)*

Employers Training Resource, Bakersfield *Also Called: County of Kern (P-18397)*

Employment Intake Training Ctr, Los Angeles *Also Called: Swissport Usa Inc (P-9211)*

Employnet Inc ....A 909 458-0961
123 E 9th St Ste 103 Upland (91786) *(P-13513)*

Empower Our Youth ....D 323 203-5436
6767 W Sunset Blvd Ste 8-188 Los Angeles (90028) *(P-12652)*

Empower Rf, Inglewood *Also Called: Empower Rf Systems Inc (P-6613)*

Empower Rf Systems Inc (PA)...................................D 310 412-8100
316 W Florence Ave Inglewood (90301) *(P-6613)*

Emser International LLC (PA).....................................D 323 650-2000
8431 Santa Monica Blvd Los Angeles (90069) *(P-9944)*

Emser Tile LLC ....E 661 837-4400
4546 Stine Rd Bakersfield (93313) *(P-11152)*

Emser Tile LLC ....E 951 296-3671
42092 Winchester Rd Temecula (92590) *(P-11153)*

Emser Tile LLC (PA)..B 323 650-2000
8431 Santa Monica Blvd Los Angeles (90069) *(P-9945)*

Emsoc, Orange *Also Called: Joshua A Siembieda MD PC (P-13601)*

Emtek Products, Irwindale *Also Called: Emtek Products Group LLC (P-10306)*

Emtek Products Group LLC (HQ)...............................C 626 961-0413
12801 Schabarum Ave Irwindale (91706) *(P-10306)*

Emtek Products Group LLC ....A 626 369-4718
600 Baldwin Park Blvd City Of Industry (91746) *(P-10307)*

Emulex Corporation (DH)...C
5300 California Ave Irvine (92617) *(P-5916)*

En Pointe Technologies Sls LLC ....C 310 337-6151
200 N Pacific Coast Hwy Ste 1050 El Segundo (90245) *(P-9999)*

Enagic Usa Inc (PA)..D 310 542-7700
4115 Spencer St Torrance (90503) *(P-11667)*

Enbio Corp ....C 818 953-9976
150 E Olive Ave Ste 114 Burbank (91502) *(P-14764)*

Enbiz International, Lake Forest *Also Called: Cloudradiant Corp (P-11114)*

Enc, Riverside *Also Called: Eldorado National Cal Inc (P-7173)*

Enchannel Medical Ltd ....E 949 694-6802
555 Corporate Dr Ste 165 Ladera Ranch (92694) *(P-8148)*

Encina Pepper Tree Joint Ventr (PA)...........................D 805 687-5511
3850 State St Santa Barbara (93105) *(P-12821)*

Encina Pepper Tree Joint Ventr ....D 805 682-7277
2220 Bath St Santa Barbara (93105) *(P-12822)*

Encinitas Ford, Encinitas *Also Called: Wayne Gossett Ford Inc (P-11432)*

Encinitas Ranch Golf Course, San Diego *Also Called: JC Resorts LLC (P-17995)*

Encino Financial Center, Encino *Also Called: Lowe Enterprises Rlty Svcs Inc (P-12481)*

Encino Office 24, Encino *Also Called: City National Bank (P-11720)*

Enclarity Inc ....B 949 797-7160
16815 Von Karman Ave Ste 125 Irvine (92606) *(P-14133)*

Encompass Health Corporation ....C 714 832-9200
15120 Kensington Park Dr Tustin (92782) *(P-16471)*

Encompass Health Corporation ....D 626 445-4714
614 W Duarte Rd Arcadia (91007) *(P-16472)*

Encompass Health Corporation ....D 661 323-5500
5001 Commerce Dr Bakersfield (93309) *(P-17148)*

Encore, San Diego *Also Called: Encore Capital Group Inc (P-11866)*

Encore Capital Group Inc (PA)...................................A 877 445-4581
350 Camino De La Reina Ste 100 San Diego (92108) *(P-11866)*

Encore Cases Inc ....E 818 768-8803
8600 Tamarack Ave Sun Valley (91352) *(P-4292)*

Encore Image, Torrance *Also Called: Encore Image Group Inc (P-8601)*

Encore Image Inc ....E 909 986-4632
303 W Main St Ontario (91762) *(P-8600)*

Encore Image Group Inc (PA)....................................D 310 534-7500
1445 Sepulveda Blvd Torrance (90501) *(P-8601)*

Encore Plastics, Huntington Beach *Also Called: Donoco Industries Inc (P-4325)*

Encore Seats Inc ....E 949 559-0930
5511 Skylab Rd Huntington Beach (92647) *(P-7471)*

Encore Semi Inc ....D 858 225-4993
7310 Miramar Rd Ste 410 San Diego (92126) *(P-17522)*

Encore Senior Living III LLC ....D 760 243-2271
13815 Rodeo Dr Ofc Victorville (92395) *(P-17149)*

Encorr Sheets LLC ....E 626 523-4661
5171 E Francis St Ontario (91761) *(P-2767)*

Encrypted Access Corporation ....C 714 371-4125
1730 Redhill Ave Irvine (92697) *(P-5917)*

Endeavor Group Holdings Inc (PA)............................D 310 285-9000
9601 Wilshire Blvd Fl 3 Beverly Hills (90210) *(P-15024)*

Endologix, Irvine *Also Called: Endologix Inc (P-8149)*

Endologix Inc (PA)..C 949 595-7200
2 Musick Irvine (92618) *(P-8149)*

Mergent email: customerrelations@mergent.com
1016

2025 Southern California
Business Directory and Buyers Guide

(P-0000) Products & Services Section entry number
(PA)=Parent Co (HQ)=Headquarters (DH)=Div Headquarters

Endologix Canada LLC .... D 949 595-7200
2 Musick Irvine (92618) *(P-8150)*

Endpak Packaging Inc .... D 562 801-0281
9101 Perkins St Pico Rivera (90660) *(P-2743)*

Endress & Hauser Conducta Inc .... E 800 835-5474
4123 E La Palma Ave St200 Anaheim (92807) *(P-7953)*

Endress+hser Optcal Analis Inc .... E 909 477-2329
11027 Arrow Rte Rancho Cucamonga (91730) *(P-7954)*

Endresshauser Conducta, Anaheim *Also Called: Endress & Hauser Conducta Inc (P-7953)*

Endura Healthcare Inc .... C 949 487-9500
29222 Rancho Viejo Rd Ste 127 San Juan Capistrano (92675) *(P-15635)*

Energetic Lighting, Chino *Also Called: Yankon Industries Inc (P-6482)*

Energy Club, Pacoima *Also Called: Energy Club Inc (P-10845)*

Energy Club Inc .... D
12950 Pierce St Pacoima (91331) *(P-10845)*

Energy Enterprises USA Inc (PA) .... D 424 339-0005
6842 Van Nuys Blvd Ste 800 Van Nuys (91405) *(P-777)*

Energy Link Indus Svcs Inc .... E 661 765-4444
11439 S Enos Ln Bakersfield (93311) *(P-6121)*

Energy Solutions (us) LLC .... B 310 669-5300
20851 S Santa Fe Ave Long Beach (90810) *(P-3237)*

Energy Suspension, San Clemente *Also Called: Bunker Corp (P-7231)*

Energy Vault Inc (HQ) .... E 805 852-0000
4360 Park Terrace Dr Ste 100 Westlake Village (91361) *(P-7073)*

Energy Watch .... D 661 324-0930
3555 Landco Dr Bakersfield (93308) *(P-915)*

Enerpro Inc .... E 805 683-2114
99 Aero Camino Goleta (93117) *(P-10242)*

Enersys .... E 909 464-8251
5580 Edison Ave Chino (91710) *(P-7074)*

Enertron Technologies Inc .... E 800 537-7649
3525 Del Mar Heights Rd San Diego (92130) *(P-6457)*

Enevate, Irvine *Also Called: Enevate Corporation (P-7075)*

Enevate Corporation .... D 949 243-0399
101 Theory Ste 200 Irvine (92617) *(P-7075)*

Engel & Gray Inc .... E 805 925-2771
745 W Betteravia Rd Ste A Santa Maria (93455) *(P-329)*

Engel Holdings Inc .... C 866 950-9862
14754 Ceres Ave Fontana (92335) *(P-536)*

Engel Volkers Beverly Hills .... D 310 777-7510
340 N Camden Dr Beverly Hills (90210) *(P-12437)*

Engineered Food Systems .... E 714 921-9913
2490 Anselmo Dr Corona (92879) *(P-6013)*

Engineered Magnetics Inc .... E 310 649-9000
10524 S La Cienega Blvd Inglewood (90304) *(P-6373)*

Engineering Division, Lancaster *Also Called: County of Los Angeles (P-17505)*

Engineering Jk Aerospace & Def .... E 714 499-9092
23231 La Palma Ave Yorba Linda (92887) *(P-7472)*

Engineering Model Assoc Inc (PA) .... E 626 912-7011
1020 Wallace Way City Of Industry (91748) *(P-4112)*

Engineering Partners Inc .... D 858 824-1761
10150 Meanley Dr Ste 200 San Diego (92131) *(P-17523)*

Engineering Public Works, Glendale *Also Called: City of Glendale (P-17502)*

Enginring Sftwr Sys Sltons Inc (PA) .... D 619 338-0380
600 B St San Diego (92101) *(P-17524)*

Engstrom Lipscomb and Lack A (PA) .... D 310 552-3800
10100 Santa Monica Blvd Los Angeles (90067) *(P-16677)*

Enhanced Vision Systems Inc (HQ) .... D 800 440-9476
15301 Springdale St Huntington Beach (92649) *(P-8000)*

Enjoy Haircare, Oceanside *Also Called: USP Inc (P-3694)*

Enkeboll Design, Carson *Also Called: The Enkeboll Co (P-2331)*

Enki Health and RES Systems .... D 626 961-8971
160 S 7th Ave La Puente (91746) *(P-15306)*

Enki Health and RES Systems .... D 626 227-7001
3208 Rosemead Blvd Ste 100 El Monte (91731) *(P-16473)*

Enki Health Care, La Puente *Also Called: Enki Health and RES Systems (P-15306)*

Enlyte, San Diego *Also Called: Mitchell International Inc (P-14094)*

Ennis Traffic Safety Solutions .... E 323 758-1147
6624 Stanford Ave Los Angeles (90001) *(P-3712)*

Enniss Inc .... E 619 561-1101
12535 Vigilante Rd Lakeside (92040) *(P-374)*

Eno Brands Inc .... E 714 220-1318
6481 Global Dr Cypress (90630) *(P-11639)*

Enoah Isolutions Inc .... D 805 285-3418
2955 E Hillcrest Dr Ste 124 Westlake Village (91362) *(P-13720)*

Enrich Enterprises Inc .... E 310 515-5055
3925 E Vernon St Long Beach (90815) *(P-2246)*

Enron Wind Corp .... A 661 822-6835
13000 Jameson Rd Tehachapi (93561) *(P-9584)*

Enron Wind Systems .... A 661 822-6835
13000 Jameson Rd Tehachapi (93561) *(P-9585)*

Ens Security, City Of Industry *Also Called: Easterncctv (usa) LLC (P-14394)*

Ensemble Communications Inc .... C 858 458-1400
2223 Avenida De La Playa La Jolla (92037) *(P-6614)*

ENSIGN, Palm Springs *Also Called: Ensign Palm I LLC (P-15644)*

ENSIGN, Whittier *Also Called: Ensign Whittier East LLC (P-15647)*

ENSIGN, San Diego *Also Called: La Jolla Skilled Inc (P-15689)*

ENSIGN, Upland *Also Called: Upland Community Care Inc (P-15789)*

Ensign Group Inc .... D 949 487-9500
32232 Paseo Adelanto Ste 100 San Juan Capistrano (92675) *(P-15636)*

Ensign Group Inc .... D 949 642-0387
340 Victoria St Costa Mesa (92627) *(P-15637)*

Ensign Group Inc .... A 562 923-9301
13007 Paramount Blvd Downey (90242) *(P-15638)*

Ensign Group Inc .... A 818 893-6385
9541 Van Nuys Blvd Panorama City (91402) *(P-15639)*

Ensign Group Inc .... B 562 947-7817
10426 Bogardus Ave Whittier (90603) *(P-15640)*

Ensign Group Inc .... B 626 607-2400
4800 Delta Ave Rosemead (91770) *(P-15641)*

Ensign Group Inc .... C 760 746-0303
201 N Fig St Escondido (92025) *(P-15642)*

Ensign Group Inc .... C 909 886-4731
4343 N Sierra Way San Bernardino (92407) *(P-15643)*

Ensign Group Inc .... B 805 925-8713
1405 E Main St Santa Maria (93454) *(P-17150)*

Ensign Palm I LLC .... C 760 323-2638
2990 E Ramon Rd Palm Springs (92264) *(P-15644)*

Ensign San Dimas LLC .... C 626 963-7531
1033 E Arrow Hwy Glendora (91740) *(P-15850)*

Ensign Services Inc .... D 949 487-9500
29222 Rancho Viejo Rd Ste 127 San Juan Capistrano (92675) *(P-15645)*

Ensign Southland LLC .... D 949 487-9500
29222 Rancho Viejo Rd Ste 127 San Juan Capistrano (92675) *(P-15646)*

Ensign Whittier East LLC .... C 562 947-7817
10426 Bogardus Ave Whittier (90603) *(P-15647)*

Ensign-Bickford Arospc Def Co .... C 805 292-4000
14370 White Sage Rd Moorpark (93021) *(P-7718)*

Entech Instruments Inc .... D 805 527-5939
2207 Agate Ct Simi Valley (93065) *(P-7955)*

Entegris Inc .... D 805 541-9299
4175 Santa Fe Rd San Luis Obispo (93401) *(P-17981)*

Entegris Gp Inc .... C 805 541-9299
4175 Santa Fe Rd San Luis Obispo (93401) *(P-5820)*

Enterprise Bank & Trust .... C 858 432-7000
11939 Rancho Bernardo Rd Ste 200 San Diego (92128) *(P-11763)*

Enterprise Bank & Trust .... C 562 345-9092
17785 Center Court Dr N # 750 Cerritos (90703) *(P-11764)*

Enterprise Rent-A-Car, Orange *Also Called: Enterprise Rnt--car Los Angles (P-14644)*

Enterprise Rnt--car Los Angles (DH) .... D 657 221-4400
333 City Blvd W Ste 1000 Orange (92868) *(P-14644)*

Enterprise Security Inc (PA) .... D 714 630-9100
22860 Savi Ranch Pkwy Yorba Linda (92887) *(P-14398)*

Enterprise Security Solutions, Yorba Linda *Also Called: Enterprise Security Inc (P-14398)*

Enterprises Industries Inc .... C 818 989-6103
7500 Tyrone Ave Van Nuys (91405) *(P-5185)*

Entertainment Partners Inc (PA) .... B 818 955-6000
2950 N Hollywood Way Burbank (91505) *(P-17723)*

Entrance Tech, El Monte *Also Called: Santoshi Corporation (P-5292)*

Entravsion Communications Corp (PA) .... C 310 447-3870
2425 Olympic Blvd Ste 6000w Santa Monica (90404) *(P-9498)*

Entravsion Communications Corp .... D 323 900-6100
5700 Wilshire Blvd Ste 250 Los Angeles (90036) *(P-9499)*

Employee Codes: A=Over 500 employees, B=251-500
C=101-250, D=51-100, E=20-50, F=10-19, G=1-9

2025 Southern California
Business Directory and Buyers Guide

© Mergent Inc. 1-800-342-5647
1017

Entrepeneur Magazine, Santa Ana *Also Called: Entrepreneur Media LLC (P-2857)*

Entrepreneur Media LLC (PA)...................................... D 949 261-2325
1651 E 4th St Ste 125 Santa Ana (92701) *(P-2857)*

Entrepreneurial Capital Corp .... C 949 809-3900
4100 Newport Place Dr Ste 400 Newport Beach (92660) *(P-12291)*

Envelopments Inc .... E 714 569-3300
13091 Sandhurst Pl Santa Ana (92705) *(P-2623)*

Envion LLC .... D 818 217-2500
14724 Ventura Blvd Fl 200 Sherman Oaks (91403) *(P-5769)*

Envirochem Technologies, Atascadero *Also Called: Chemlogics Group LLC (P-3732)*

Envirofabrics, Los Angeles *Also Called: Roshan Trading Inc (P-1903)*

Envirogenics Systems Company .... D 818 573-9220
9255 Telstar Ave El Monte (91731) *(P-711)*

Enviroguard, Montclair *Also Called: Expo Power Systems Inc (P-10183)*

Environmental Construction Inc .... D 818 449-8920
21550 Oxnard St Ste 1060 Woodland Hills (91367) *(P-537)*

Environmental Industries, Fillmore *Also Called: Brightview Tree Company (P-250)*

Environmental Resolutions Inc .... B 949 457-8950
25371 Commercentre Dr Ste 250 Lake Forest (92630) *(P-18307)*

Environmental Science Assoc .... C 213 599-4300
633 W 5th St Los Angeles (90071) *(P-17787)*

Environmental Science Assoc .... D 858 638-0900
9191 Towne Centre Dr Ste 340 San Diego (92122) *(P-18308)*

Environmental Systems Research Institute Inc (PA)......... A 909 793-2853
380 New York St Redlands (92373) *(P-10000)*

Envision Plastics, Chino *Also Called: Envision Plastics Industries LLC (P-4113)*

Envision Plastics Industries LLC .... E 909 590-7334
14312 Central Ave Chino (91710) *(P-4113)*

Envista, Brea *Also Called: Envista Holdings Corporation (P-8335)*

Envista Holdings Corporation (PA)............................... D 714 817-7000
200 S Kraemer Blvd Bldg E Brea (92821) *(P-8335)*

Envveno Medical Corporation .... E 949 261-2900
70 Doppler Irvine (92618) *(P-8151)*

Eos, Paso Robles *Also Called: Eos Estate Winery (P-1565)*

Eos Estate Winery .... E 805 239-2562
2300 Airport Rd Paso Robles (93446) *(P-1565)*

Eoy, Los Angeles *Also Called: Empower Our Youth (P-12652)*

EPC Power Corp (PA)... C 858 748-5590
13250 Gregg St Ste A2 Poway (92064) *(P-6374)*

Ephesoft Inc .... D 949 335-5335
8707 Research Dr Irvine (92618) *(P-10001)*

Epic Management Services LLC (PA)............................. D 909 799-1818
1615 Orange Tree Ln Redlands (92374) *(P-17982)*

Epic Sciences Inc .... D 858 356-6610
9381 Judicial Dr Ste 200 San Diego (92121) *(P-16314)*

Epic Technologies LLC (HQ).. A 908 707-4085
9340 Owensmouth Ave Chatsworth (91311) *(P-6584)*

Epic Wings, San Diego *Also Called: Sacco Restaurants Inc (P-11598)*

Epica Medical Innovations LLC .... E 949 238-6323
901 Calle Amanecer Ste 150 San Clemente (92673) *(P-8152)*

EPICENTRE, San Diego *Also Called: Harmonium Inc (P-17092)*

Epicuren Discovery .... D 949 588-5807
31 Journey Ste 100 Aliso Viejo (92656) *(P-3539)*

Epidaurus .... B 213 743-9075
3745 S Grand Ave Los Angeles (90007) *(P-12657)*

Epilogue and Arrested, Los Angeles *Also Called: Rhapsody Clothing Inc (P-2129)*

Epirus Inc .... E 310 620-8678
19145 Gramercy Pl Torrance (90501) *(P-13925)*

Episcopal Communities & Servic .... D 310 544-2204
5801 Crestridge Rd Pls Vrds Pnsl (90275) *(P-15648)*

Episource LLC .... A 714 452-1961
500 W 190th St Ste 400 Gardena (90248) *(P-12206)*

Epitec Inc .... A 760 650-2515
515 Olive Ave Vista (92083) *(P-13721)*

Epl, Commerce *Also Called: Edison Price Lighting Inc (P-6456)*

Eplastics, San Diego *Also Called: Plastics Family Holdings Inc (P-3954)*

Eplica Inc .... C 562 977-4300
17785 Center Court Dr N Cerritos (90703) *(P-13514)*

Eplica Inc (PA).. C 619 260-2000
2385 Northside Dr Ste 250 San Diego (92108) *(P-13596)*

Eplica Corporate Services Inc .... A 619 282-1400
2385 Northside Dr Ste 250 San Diego (92108) *(P-13515)*

Epmar Corporation .... E 562 946-8781
9930 Painter Ave Whittier (90605) *(P-3713)*

Epoca Yocool, South Gate *Also Called: Win Soon Inc (P-1336)*

Epoch.com, Santa Monica *Also Called: Epochcom LLC (P-14134)*

Epochcom LLC .... C 310 664-5700
3110 Main St Ste 220 Santa Monica (90405) *(P-14134)*

Epsilon Electronics Inc (PA).. D 323 722-3333
1550 S Maple Ave Montebello (90640) *(P-10217)*

Epsilon Plastics Inc .... D 310 609-1320
3100 E Harcourt St Compton (90221) *(P-11116)*

Epsilon Systems Sltons Mssion .... D 619 702-1700
9242 Lightwave Ave Ste 100 San Diego (92123) *(P-17525)*

Epsilon Systems Solutions Inc .... C 619 474-3252
2101 Haffley Ave # A National City (91950) *(P-17282)*

Epsilon Systems Solutions Inc (PA)............................. D 619 702-1700
9444 Balboa Ave Ste 100 San Diego (92123) *(P-17526)*

Epson America Inc (DH).. A 800 463-7766
3131 Katella Ave Los Alamitos (90720) *(P-5918)*

Epson Electronics America Inc (DH)............................. E 408 922-0200
3131 Katella Ave Los Alamitos (90720) *(P-6822)*

Epstein Becker & Green PC .... D 415 398-3500
1925 Century Park E Ste 500 Los Angeles (90067) *(P-16678)*

Epstein Becker & Green PC .... C 310 556-8861
1875 Century Park E Ste 500 Los Angeles (90067) *(P-16679)*

Epworth Morehouse Cowles, Chino *Also Called: Morehouse-Cowles LLC (P-5711)*

Equal Exchange Inc .... D 619 335-6259
2920 Norman Strasse Rd San Marcos (92069) *(P-1717)*

Equator LLC (HQ)... C 310 469-9500
6060 Center Dr Ste 500 Los Angeles (90045) *(P-13722)*

Equator Business Solutions, Los Angeles *Also Called: Equator LLC (P-13722)*

Equillium Inc (PA)... E 858 412-1200
2223 Avenida De La Playa Ste 105 La Jolla (92037) *(P-3401)*

Equimine .... E 877 204-9040
26457 Rancho Pkwy S Lake Forest (92630) *(P-13926)*

Equine Comfort Products, Simi Valley *Also Called: Eurow and OReilly Corp (P-11118)*

Equinox Fitness Club, Los Angeles *Also Called: Equinox-76th Street Inc (P-15049)*

Equinox Fitness Club, Irvine *Also Called: Equinox-76th Street Inc (P-15050)*

Equinox-76th Street Inc .... D 310 727-9543
5400 W Rosecrans Ave Ste Uppr Hawthorne (90250) *(P-15047)*

Equinox-76th Street Inc .... C 310 479-5200
1835 S Sepulveda Blvd Los Angeles (90025) *(P-15048)*

Equinox-76th Street Inc .... D 310 552-0420
10250 Santa Monica Blvd Los Angeles (90067) *(P-15049)*

Equinox-76th Street Inc .... D 949 296-1700
19540 Jamboree Rd Irvine (92612) *(P-15050)*

Equinox-76th Street Inc .... D 949 975-8400
1980 Main St Fl 4 Irvine (92614) *(P-15541)*

Equipment & Tool Institute, Irvine *Also Called: Innova Electronics Corporation (P-7263)*

Equipment Brokers Unlimited, Cerritos *Also Called: Docusource Inc (P-11682)*

Equipment Depot Inc .... C 562 949-1000
16748 Boyle Ave Fontana (92337) *(P-10373)*

Equipment Design & Mfg Inc .... D 909 594-2229
119 Explorer St Pomona (91768) *(P-4983)*

Equity Concept Inc .... D 714 374-8859
16902 Bolsa Chica St Ste 203 Huntington Beach (92649) *(P-12438)*

Equity Fund Advisors Inc .... C 602 716-8803
11995 El Camino Real San Diego (92130) *(P-12685)*

Equity International Inc .... A 978 664-2712
5541 Fermi Ct Carlsbad (92008) *(P-10243)*

Equity Smart Home Loans Inc .... D 626 864-8774
1499 Huntington Dr Ste 500 South Pasadena (91030) *(P-11901)*

Equity Title Company (DH).. D 818 291-4400
801 N Brand Blvd Ste 400 Glendale (91203) *(P-12556)*

Equus Products Inc .... E 714 424-6779
17352 Von Karman Ave Irvine (92614) *(P-7910)*

ERA Real Estate, Beverly Hills *Also Called: Nelson Shelton & Associates (P-12495)*

Erasca, San Diego *Also Called: Erasca Inc (P-3402)*

Erasca Inc .... C 858 465-6511
3115 Merryfield Row Ste 300 San Diego (92121) *(P-3402)*

Mergent email: customerrelations@mergent.com
1018

2025 Southern California
Business Directory and Buyers Guide

(P-0000) Products & Services Section entry number
(PA)=Parent Co (HQ)=Headquarters (DH)=Div Headquarters

Ereplacements LLC .... E 714 361-2652
16885 W Bernardo Dr Ste 370 San Diego (92127) *(P-7076)*

Erg International, Oxnard *Also Called: Ergonom Corporation (P-2612)*

Ergocraft Contract Solutions .... E
6055 E Washington Blvd Ste 500 Commerce (90040) *(P-2525)*

Ergocraft Office Furniture, Commerce *Also Called: Ergocraft Contract Solutions (P-2525)*

Ergomotion Inc (PA) .... D 888 550-3746
6790 Navigator Way Goleta (93117) *(P-13723)*

Ergonom Corporation (PA) .... D 805 981-9978
361 Bernoulli Cir Oxnard (93030) *(P-2611)*

Ergonom Corporation .... D 805 981-9978
390 Lombard St Oxnard (93030) *(P-2612)*

Erickson-Hall Construction Co (PA) .... D 760 796-7700
500 Corporate Dr Escondido (92029) *(P-538)*

Erin Condren, Hawthorne *Also Called: EC Design LLC (P-11635)*

Ernest Packaging (PA) .... C 800 233-7788
5777 Smithway St Commerce (90040) *(P-11117)*

Ernest Paper, Commerce *Also Called: Ernest Packaging (P-11117)*

Ernie Ball, San Luis Obispo *Also Called: Ernie Ball Inc (P-8467)*

Ernie Ball Inc (PA) .... E 805 544-7726
4117 Earthwood Ln San Luis Obispo (93401) *(P-8467)*

Ernst & Young LLP .... B 949 794-2300
18101 Von Karman Ave Ste 1700 Irvine (92612) *(P-17724)*

Ernst & Young LLP .... C 858 535-7200
4365 Executive Dr Ste 1600 San Diego (92121) *(P-17725)*

Ernst & Young LLP .... D 805 778-7000
2931 Townsgate Rd Ste 100 Westlake Village (91361) *(P-17726)*

Ernst & Young LLP .... A 213 977-3200
725 S Figueroa St Ste 200 Los Angeles (90017) *(P-17727)*

Eroad Inc .... D 503 305-2255
15110 Avenue Of Science Ste 100 San Diego (92128) *(P-6321)*

Eros Stx Global Corporation .... A 818 524-7000
3900 W Alameda Ave Fl 32 Burbank (91505) *(P-14951)*

Erp, Rancho Dominguez *Also Called: Expanded Rubber & Plastics Corp (P-4114)*

Erp Integrated Solutions LLC .... D 562 425-7800
5000 Airport Plaza Dr Ste 230 Long Beach (90815) *(P-13724)*

Erwin Street Medical Offices, Woodland Hills *Also Called: Kaiser Foundation Hospitals (P-16034)*

Es Engineering Services LLC .... D 949 988-3500
4 Park Plz Ste 790 Irvine (92614) *(P-17527)*

ES Kluft & Company Inc (DH) .... C 909 373-4211
11096 Jersey Blvd Ste 101 Rancho Cucamonga (91730) *(P-2482)*

ESA, Los Angeles *Also Called: Environmental Science Assoc (P-17787)*

Esaero, San Luis Obispo *Also Called: Empirical Systems Arospc Inc (P-7339)*

Esaloncom LLC .... C 866 550-2424
1910 E Maple Ave El Segundo (90245) *(P-13148)*

Escalade Sports, San Diego *Also Called: Indian Industries Inc (P-8527)*

Eschat .... D 805 541-5044
3450 Broad St Ste 106 San Luis Obispo (93401) *(P-9401)*

Esco Technologies Inc .... D 805 604-3875
501 Del Norte Blvd Oxnard (93030) *(P-6682)*

Escondido Medical Offices, Escondido *Also Called: Kaiser Foundation Hospitals (P-15343)*

Escondido Memory Care Cmnty, Escondido *Also Called: Silverado Senior Living Inc (P-15775)*

Escondido Motors LLC .... D 760 745-5000
1101 W 9th Ave Escondido (92025) *(P-11343)*

Escondido Post Acute Rehab, Escondido *Also Called: Mek Escondido LLC (P-15719)*

Ese, El Segundo *Also Called: Mod-Electronics Inc (P-8447)*

Ese, Los Angeles *Also Called: ESE INC (P-11012)*

ESE INC .... E 213 614-0102
1163 E 12th St Los Angeles (90021) *(P-11012)*

Eset LLC (HQ) .... C 619 876-5400
655 W Broadway Ste 700 San Diego (92101) *(P-10002)*

Eset North America, San Diego *Also Called: Eset LLC (P-10002)*

Esi Motion, Simi Valley *Also Called: Embedded Systems Inc (P-6349)*

Esign Emcee, Moorpark *Also Called: Topaz Systems Inc (P-5952)*

Eska Inc .... E 323 846-3700
1370 Mirasol St Los Angeles (90023) *(P-2094)*

Esl, Burbank *Also Called: Esl Gaming America Inc (P-14987)*

Esl Gaming America Inc (DH) .... D 213 235-7079
3111 Winona Ave Unit 105 Burbank (91506) *(P-14987)*

Esl Power Systems Inc .... D 800 922-4188
2800 Palisades Dr Corona (92878) *(P-6418)*

ESM Aerospace Inc .... E 818 841-3653
1203 W Isabel St Burbank (91506) *(P-4984)*

Esmi, San Diego *Also Called: Electronic Surfc Mounted Inds (P-6725)*

Esmond Natural Inc .... E 626 337-1588
5316 Irwindale Ave Irwindale (91706) *(P-3314)*

Esparza Enterprises Inc .... A 760 344-2031
251 W Main St Ste G&F Brawley (92227) *(P-141)*

Esparza Enterprises Inc .... A 661 631-0347
500 Workman St Bakersfield (93307) *(P-8948)*

Esparza Enterprises Inc .... A 760 398-0349
51335 Cesar Chavez St Ste 112 Coachella (92236) *(P-13516)*

Esparza Enterprises Inc .... A 661 631-0347
222 S Union Ave Bakersfield (93307) *(P-13517)*

Especial T Hvac Shtmtl Fttngs .... E 909 869-9150
1239 E Franklin Ave Pomona (91766) *(P-10331)*

Especializados Del Aire, San Diego *Also Called: Alliance Air Products Llc (P-5964)*

Espelette Beverly Hills, Los Angeles *Also Called: Oasis West Realty LLC (P-12649)*

Esperanzas Tortilleria .... E 760 743-5908
750 Rock Springs Rd Escondido (92025) *(P-1769)*

Esri, Redlands *Also Called: Environmental Systems Research Institute Inc (P-10000)*

Ess LLC .... D 888 303-6424
5227 Dantes View Dr Agoura Hills (91301) *(P-778)*

Essence of America .... E 312 805-9365
1855 1st Ave Ste 103 San Diego (92101) *(P-16940)*

Essense .... A 323 202-4650
6300 Wilshire Blvd Ste 720 Los Angeles (90048) *(P-18373)*

Essential Access Health (PA) .... D 213 386-5614
3600 Wilshire Blvd Ste 600 Los Angeles (90010) *(P-17225)*

Essentra International LLC .... A 708 315-7498
21303 Ferrero Walnut (91789) *(P-3765)*

Essex Electronics Inc .... E 805 684-7601
1130 Mark Ave Carpinteria (93013) *(P-6823)*

Essex Industries, Huntington Beach *Also Called: Momeni Engineering LLC (P-6185)*

Essex Properties LLC .... D 949 798-8100
18012 Sky Park Cir Ste 100 Irvine (92614) *(P-12439)*

Estates At Trump Nat Golf CLB .... C 310 265-5000
1 Trump National Dr Rancho Palos Verdes (90275) *(P-15079)*

Estech Digital, Los Angeles *Also Called: Techture Inc (P-2946)*

Esterline Mason, Rancho Cascades *Also Called: Janco Corporation (P-7014)*

Estes, City Of Industry *Also Called: Estes Express Lines (P-8949)*

Estes Express Lines .... C 626 333-9090
13327 Temple Ave City Of Industry (91746) *(P-8949)*

Estes Express Lines .... C 909 427-9850
10736 Cherry Ave Fontana (92337) *(P-8950)*

Estes Express Lines .... D 619 425-4040
120 Press Ln Chula Vista (91910) *(P-8951)*

Estify Inc .... E 801 341 1011
5023 Parkway Calabasas Calabasas (91302) *(P-13927)*

Estrella Inc .... C 562 925-6418
6712 Alamitos Cir Huntington Beach (92648) *(P-15649)*

Et Whitehall Seascape LLC .... C 310 581-5533
1910 Ocean Way Santa Monica (90405) *(P-12823)*

Etap, Irvine *Also Called: Operation Technology Inc (P-13789)*

Etchandy Farms LLC .... D 805 983-4700
4324 E Vineyard Ave Oxnard (93036) *(P-17)*

Etekcity, Anaheim *Also Called: Etekcity Corporation (P-10218)*

Etekcity Corporation .... C 855 686-3835
1202 N Miller St Unit A Anaheim (92806) *(P-10218)*

Etherwan Systems Inc .... D 714 779-3800
2301 E Winston Rd Anaheim (92806) *(P-14217)*

Ethicon Inc .... B 949 581-5799
33 Technology Dr Irvine (92618) *(P-8265)*

Ethos Seafood Group LLC .... D 312 858-3474
18531 S Broadwick St Rancho Dominguez (90220) *(P-1704)*

Ethosenergy Field Services LLC (DH) .... E 310 639-3523
10455 Slusher Dr # 12 Santa Fe Springs (90670) *(P-330)*

Employee Codes: A=Over 500 employees, B=251-500
C=101-250, D=51-100, E=20-50, F=10-19, G=1-9

2025 Southern California
Business Directory and Buyers Guide

© Mergent Inc. 1-800-342-5647

1019

Eti B Si Professional, Commerce *Also Called: Eti Sound Systems Inc (P-6536)*

Eti Sound Systems Inc .... E 323 835-6660
5300 Harbor St Commerce (90040) *(P-6536)*

Eti Systems .... D 310 684-3664
1800 Century Park E Ste 600 Los Angeles (90067) *(P-7857)*

Etnies, Lake Forest *Also Called: Sole Technology Inc (P-4289)*

Etrade 24 Inc .... E 818 712-0574
16600 Calneva Dr Encino (91436) *(P-1970)*

Ets Express, Oxnard *Also Called: Ets Express LLC (P-5319)*

Ets Express LLC (DH).. E 805 278-7771
420 Lombard St Oxnard (93030) *(P-5319)*

Eturns Inc .... E 949 265-2626
19700 Fairchild Ste 290 Irvine (92612) *(P-13928)*

Eugene Burger Management Corp .... D 661 273-4447
1020 E Avenue R Ofc Palmdale (93550) *(P-12340)*

Euro Coffee, Los Angeles *Also Called: Eberine Enterprises Inc (P-1716)*

Euro Motorparts Group, Anaheim *Also Called: Empi Inc (P-9824)*

Euroamerican Propagators LLC .... B 760 731-6029
32149 Aquaduct Rd Bonsall (92003) *(P-54)*

Eurocraft Archtectural Met Inc .... E 323 771-1323
5619 Watcher St Bell Gardens (90201) *(P-5062)*

Eurodrip USA Inc .... D 559 674-2670
7545 Carroll Rd San Diego (92121) *(P-10362)*

Eurofins Eaton Analytical LLC (DH)........................ D 626 386-1100
750 Royal Oaks Dr Ste 100 Monrovia (91016) *(P-17916)*

Euroline Steel Windows .... D 877 590-2741
22600 Savi Ranch Pkwy Ste E Yorba Linda (92887) *(P-4888)*

Euroline Steel Windows & Doors, Yorba Linda *Also Called: Euroline Steel Windows (P-4888)*

Euronext Hair Collection, Commerce *Also Called: West Bay Imports Inc (P-11148)*

Europa Auto Imports Inc .... C 858 569-6900
4750 Kearny Mesa Rd San Diego (92111) *(P-11344)*

Europa Village, Temecula *Also Called: Europa Village LLC (P-1566)*

Europa Village LLC .... C 951 506-1818
33475 La Serena Way Temecula (92591) *(P-1566)*

Europcar, Los Angeles *Also Called: Fox Rent A Car Inc (P-14646)*

European Wholesale Counter .... C 619 562-0565
10051 Prospect Ave Santee (92071) *(P-2563)*

Europro Inc .... D 661 588-5666
6023 Coffee Rd Bakersfield (93308) *(P-13174)*

Eurotec Seating, La Habra *Also Called: Orbo Corporation (P-2550)*

Eurotec Seating Incorporated .... E 562 806-6171
1000 S Euclid St La Habra (90631) *(P-2542)*

Eurotech Luxury Shower Doors, Laguna Hills *Also Called: Eurotech Showers Inc (P-4025)*

Eurotech Showers Inc .... E 949 716-4099
23552 Commerce Center Dr Ste B Laguna Hills (92653) *(P-4025)*

Eurow and OReilly Corp .... E 800 747-7452
51 Moreland Rd Simi Valley (93065) *(P-11118)*

Ev Charging Solutions Inc .... D 866 300-3827
11800 Clark St Arcadia (91006) *(P-7092)*

Ev Connect Inc .... D 888 780-0062
26521 Rancho Pkwy S Lake Forest (92630) *(P-916)*

Ev R Inc .... E 323 312-5400
3400 Slauson Ave Maywood (90270) *(P-2095)*

Ev Ray Inc .... E 818 346-5381
6400 Variel Ave Woodland Hills (91367) *(P-9892)*

Ev3 Neurovascular, Irvine *Also Called: Micro Therapeutics Inc (P-8199)*

Evans Hydro, Compton *Also Called: Evans Hydro Inc (P-14765)*

Evans Hydro Inc .... E 310 608-5801
18128 S Santa Fe Ave Compton (90221) *(P-14765)*

Evans Industries Inc .... D 626 912-1688
17915 Railroad St City Of Industry (91748) *(P-5446)*

Evans Manufacturing LLC (HQ)............................. C 714 379-6100
7422 Chapman Ave Garden Grove (92841) *(P-8602)*

Evans Manufacturing, Inc., Garden Grove *Also Called: Evans Manufacturing LLC (P-8602)*

Eve, Lakewood *Also Called: Eve Hair Inc (P-11119)*

Eve Hair Inc (PA) .... E 562 377-1020
3935 Paramount Blvd Lakewood (90712) *(P-11119)*

Event Intelligence Group .... D 310 237-5375
4140 Jackson Ave Culver City (90232) *(P-14399)*

Eventscom Inc .... E 858 257-2300
811 Prospect St La Jolla (92037) *(P-13929)*

Ever Blue, Los Angeles *Also Called: California Blue Apparel Inc (P-2061)*

Ever Increasing Faith Ministry, Los Angeles *Also Called: Crenshaw Chrstn Ctr Ch Los Ang (P-17413)*

Ever-Pac, Riverside *Also Called: Jmc Closing Co LLC (P-6153)*

Everbrands Inc .... E 855 595-2999
11791 Monarch St Garden Grove (92841) *(P-3651)*

Everbridge Inc (PA) .... C 818 230-9700
155 N Lake Ave Ste 900 Pasadena (91101) *(P-13930)*

Everde Growers, Fallbrook *Also Called: Treesap Farms LLC (P-88)*

Evergreen At Lakeport LLC .... D 661 871-3133
6212 Tudor Way Bakersfield (93306) *(P-15650)*

Evergreen Environmental Svcs, Gardena *Also Called: Evergreen Oil Inc (P-3854)*

Evergreen Fullerton Healthcare, Fullerton *Also Called: Fullerton Hlthcare Wllness CNT (P-15659)*

Evergreen Health Care LLC .... A 661 854-4475
323 Campus Dr Arvin (93203) *(P-15651)*

Evergreen Healthcare Center, Bakersfield *Also Called: Evergreen At Lakeport LLC (P-15650)*

Evergreen Holdings Inc .... C 949 757-7770
18952 Macarthur Blvd Ste 410 Irvine (92612) *(P-3853)*

Evergreen Industries Inc (DH)................................ D 323 583-1331
2254 E 49th St Vernon (90058) *(P-7825)*

Evergreen Lighting, Pomona *Also Called: Yawitz Inc (P-6451)*

Evergreen Oil Inc (HQ)... E 949 757-7770
18025 S Broadway Gardena (90248) *(P-3854)*

Evergreen Scientific, Vernon *Also Called: Evergreen Industries Inc (P-7825)*

Evergreen Solar Services, Agoura Hills *Also Called: Ess LLC (P-778)*

Everidge Inc .... E 909 605-6419
8886 White Oak Ave Rancho Cucamonga (91730) *(P-5976)*

Evernote Corporation (PA) .... B 650 216-7700
4231 Balboa Ave # 1008 San Diego (92117) *(P-13725)*

Everpark Inc .... C 310 987-6922
3470 Wilshire Blvd Ste 940 Los Angeles (90010) *(P-14656)*

Everson Spice Company Inc .... E 562 595-4785
2667 Gundry Ave Long Beach (90755) *(P-1770)*

Everytable, Los Angeles *Also Called: Everytable Pbc (P-1771)*

Everytable Pbc .... E 323 296-0311
3650 W Martin Luther King Jr Blvd Los Angeles (90008) *(P-1771)*

Evgo Montgomery Co, Los Angeles *Also Called: Evgo Services LLC (P-11475)*

Evgo Services LLC .... B 310 954-2900
11835 W Olympic Blvd Ste 900e Los Angeles (90064) *(P-11475)*

Evkii Inc .... E 760 721-5200
624 Garrison St Ste1-2 Oceanside (92054) *(P-11295)*

Evocative Inc .... D 888 365-2656
26 Centerpointe Dr La Palma (90623) *(P-13931)*

Evolife Scientific Llc .... E 888 750-0310
3150 Long Beach Blvd Long Beach (90807) *(P-3315)*

Evolus, Newport Beach *Also Called: Evolus Inc (P-3403)*

Evolus Inc (PA) .... B 949 284-4555
520 Newport Center Dr Ste 1200 Newport Beach (92660) *(P-3403)*

Evolution Design Lab Inc .... E 626 960-8388
144 W Colorado Blvd Pasadena (91105) *(P-4284)*

Evolution Fresh Inc .... C 800 794-9986
11655 Jersey Blvd Ste A Rancho Cucamonga (91730) *(P-10895)*

Evolution Hospitality LLC .... B 562 435-3511
1126 Queens Hwy Long Beach (90802) *(P-12824)*

Evolution Hospitality LLC (HQ)............................... D 949 325-1350
1211 Puerta Del Sol Ste 170 San Clemente (92673) *(P-17983)*

Evolution Industries, Walnut *Also Called: Crush Master Grinding Corp (P-6111)*

Evolution Juice, Rancho Cucamonga *Also Called: Evolution Fresh Inc (P-10895)*

Evolve Growth Initiatives LLC .... C 424 281-5000
820 Moraga Dr Los Angeles (90049) *(P-17151)*

Evolve Treatment Centers, Los Angeles *Also Called: Evolve Growth Initiatives LLC (P-17151)*

Evonik Corporation .... D 323 264-0311
3305 E 26th St Vernon (90058) *(P-3797)*

Evoq Properties Inc .... D 213 988-8890
1318 E 7th St Ste 200 Los Angeles (90021) *(P-12440)*

Evoqua Water Technologies LLC .... E 213 748-8511
1441 E Washington Blvd Los Angeles (90021) *(P-11683)*

Evoralight, Costa Mesa *Also Called: Flexfire Leds Inc (P-6458)*

Evriholder, Brea *Also Called: Evriholder Products LLC (P-9893)*

Mergent email: customerrelations@mergent.com
1020

2025 Southern California
Business Directory and Buyers Guide

(P-0000) Products & Services Section entry number
(PA)=Parent Co (HQ)=Headquarters (DH)=Div Headquarters

Evriholder Products LLC (PA)...................D 714 490-7878
975 W Imperial Hwy Ste 100 Brea (92821) *(P-9893)*

Evy of California Inc ....C 213 746-4647
2042 Garfield Ave Commerce (90040) *(P-2164)*

Ew Corprtion Indus Fabricators (PA)...........D 760 337-0020
1002 E Main St El Centro (92243) *(P-4833)*

EW Scripps Company ....A 619 237-1010
4600 Air Way San Diego (92102) *(P-9500)*

Eworkplace Manufacturing Inc ....C 949 583-1646
9861 Irvine Center Dr Irvine (92618) *(P-10003)*

Exactax Inc (PA)...D 714 284-4802
1100 E Orangethorpe Ave Ste 100 Anaheim (92801) *(P-13163)*

Exagen Inc ....C 505 272-7966
1261 Liberty Way Ste C Vista (92081) *(P-16315)*

Examine Your Practice, San Diego *Also Called: Trendsource Inc (P-17863)*

Examone, San Diego *Also Called: Examone World Wide Inc (P-16316)*

Examone World Wide Inc ....D 619 299-3926
7480 Mission Valley Rd Ste 101 San Diego (92108) *(P-16316)*

Excalibur Extrusion Inc ....E 714 528-8834
110 E Crowther Ave Placentia (92870) *(P-3973)*

Excalibur International, Long Beach *Also Called: A W Chang Corporation (P-10660)*

Excalibur Well Services Corp ....C 661 589-5338
22034 Rosedale Hwy Bakersfield (93314) *(P-289)*

Exce LP ....D 858 549-6340
16868 Via Del Campo Ct Ste 200 San Diego (92127) *(P-5919)*

Excel Bridge Manufacturing Co., Santa Fe Springs *Also Called: Excel Sheet Metal Inc (P-4985)*

Excel Cabinets Inc ....E 951 279-4545
225 Jason Ct Corona (92879) *(P-2348)*

Excel Contractors Inc ....D 661 942-6944
348 E Avenue K8 Ste B Lancaster (93535) *(P-402)*

Excel Landscape Inc ....C 951 735-9650
710 Rimpau Ave Ste 108 Corona (92879) *(P-206)*

Excel Manufacturing Inc ....E 661 257-1900
20409 Prairie St Chatsworth (91311) *(P-6122)*

Excel Mdular Scaffold Lsg Corp ....A 760 598-0050
2555 Birch St Vista (92081) *(P-1202)*

Excel Paving Co, Long Beach *Also Called: Palp Inc (P-641)*

Excel Picture Frames Inc ....E 323 231-0244
647 E 59th St Los Angeles (90001) *(P-14766)*

Excel Sheet Metal Inc (PA)...........................D 562 944-0701
12001 Shoemaker Ave Santa Fe Springs (90670) *(P-4985)*

Excell Staffing & SEC Svcs, El Cajon *Also Called: Xl Staffing Inc (P-13585)*

Excelline Food Products LLC ....E 818 701-7710
833 N Hollywood Way Burbank (91505) *(P-1391)*

Excello Circuits Inc ....D 714 993-0560
5330 E Hunter Ave Anaheim (92807) *(P-6726)*

Excellon Acquisition LLC (HQ) ....E 310 668-7700
16130 Gundry Ave Paramount (90723) *(P-5701)*

Excellon Automation Co, Paramount *Also Called: Excellon Acquisition LLC (P-5701)*

Excelsior Nutrition Inc ....D 657 999-5188
1206 N Miller St Unit D Anaheim (92806) *(P-3316)*

Exceptional Chld Foundation (PA) ....C 310 204-3300
5350 Machado Ln Culver City (90230) *(P-17056)*

Exceptional Chld Foundation ....C 213 748-3556
1430 Venice Blvd Los Angeles (90006) *(P-17057)*

Exceptional Chld Foundation ....C 310 915-6606
11124 Fairbanks Way Culver City (90230) *(P-17343)*

Executive Auto Reconditioning ....E 626 416-3322
522 E Duarte Rd Monrovia (91016) *(P-14708)*

Executive Car Leasing Company (PA)...............D 800 800-3932
7807 Santa Monica Blvd West Hollywood (90046) *(P-14651)*

Executive Landscape Inc ....C 760 731-9036
2131 Huffstatler St Fallbrook (92028) *(P-166)*

Executive Network Entps Inc (PA) ....D 310 447-2759
13440 Beach Ave Marina Del Rey (90292) *(P-8822)*

Executive Network Entps Inc ....A 310 457-8822
1224 21st St Apt E Santa Monica (90404) *(P-8823)*

Executive Personnel Services ....B 714 310-9506
1526 Brookhollow Dr Ste 83 Santa Ana (92705) *(P-13518)*

Executive Safe and SEC Corp ....E 909 947-7020
10722 Edison Ct Rancho Cucamonga (91730) *(P-5447)*

Exemplis LLC (PA) ....E 714 995-4800
6415 Katella Ave Cypress (90630) *(P-2526)*

Exemplis LLC ....C 714 995-4800
6280 Artesia Blvd Buena Park (90620) *(P-2527)*

Exemplis LLC ....E 714 898-5500
6280 Artesia Blvd Buena Park (90620) *(P-2528)*

Exer, Simi Valley *Also Called: Providnce Facey Med Foundation (P-15531)*

Exeter Packers Inc ....C 626 993-6245
1095 E Green St Pasadena (91106) *(P-43)*

Exeter Packers Inc ....C 661 399-0416
33374 Lerdo Hwy Bakersfield (93308) *(P-9036)*

Exhaust Tech, Commerce *Also Called: Dynaflex Products (P-7202)*

Exigent Sensors LLC ....E 949 439-1321
11441 Markon Dr Garden Grove (92841) *(P-6683)*

Exile LLC ....D 310 450-2255
4203 Redwood Ave Los Angeles (90066) *(P-14888)*

Exiton Inc ....E 562 699-1122
12226 Coast Dr Whittier (90601) *(P-8603)*

Exois Inc ....C 408 777-6630
2567 Ingleton Ave Carlsbad (92009) *(P-14218)*

Expak Logistics, Los Angeles *Also Called: Kxp Carrier Services LLC (P-9006)*

Expanded Rubber & Plastics Corp ....E 310 324-6692
19200 S Laurel Park Rd Rancho Dominguez (90220) *(P-4114)*

Expeditors International, Hawthorne *Also Called: Expeditors Intl Wash Inc (P-9279)*

Expeditors Intl Ocean Inc ....D 310 343-6200
5200 W Century Blvd Fl 6 Los Angeles (90045) *(P-9278)*

Expeditors Intl Wash Inc ....D 310 343-6200
12200 Wilkie Ave # 100 Hawthorne (90250) *(P-9279)*

Expeditors Intl Wash Inc ....B 310 343-6200
19701 Hamilton Ave Torrance (90502) *(P-9280)*

Experian, Costa Mesa *Also Called: Experian Info Solutions Inc (P-13295)*

Experian Employer Services Inc ....C 866 997-0422
475 Anton Blvd Costa Mesa (92626) *(P-13519)*

Experian Info Solutions Inc (DH) ....A 714 830-7000
475 Anton Blvd Costa Mesa (92626) *(P-13295)*

Experian Marketing, Costa Mesa *Also Called: Experian Mktg Solutions LLC (P-13296)*

Experian Mktg Solutions LLC ....A 714 830-7000
475 Anton Blvd Costa Mesa (92626) *(P-13296)*

Expert Assembly Services Inc ....E 714 258-8880
14312 Chambers Rd Ste B Tustin (92780) *(P-6727)*

Expert Ems, Tustin *Also Called: Expert Assembly Services Inc (P-6727)*

Exploding Kittens LLC ....E 310 788-8699
101 S La Brea Ave Ste A Los Angeles (90036) *(P-8485)*

Expo Builders Supply, San Diego *Also Called: Expo Industries Inc (P-9919)*

Expo Dyeing & Finishing Inc ....C 714 220-9583
8898 Los Coyotes Ct Unit 320 Buena Park (90621) *(P-1940)*

Expo Industries Inc ....D 858 566-3110
7455 Carroll Rd San Diego (92121) *(P-9919)*

Expo Power Systems Inc ....E 800 506-9884
5534 Olive St Montclair (91763) *(P-10183)*

Express, San Diego *Also Called: Express Business Systems Inc (P-3138)*

Express Business Systems Inc ....E 858 549-9828
9155 Trade Pl San Diego (92126) *(P-3138)*

Exprooo Capital Lending ....D 714 429-1025
3134 Airway Ave Costa Mesa (92020) *(P-11902)*

Express Contractors Inc ....D 951 360-6500
3810 Wacker Dr Jurupa Valley (91752) *(P-13136)*

Express Group Incorporated (PA).....................D 310 474-5999
10801 National Blvd Ste 104 Los Angeles (90064) *(P-9002)*

Express Hotels, Burbank *Also Called: OH So Original Inc (P-12947)*

Express Imaging Services Inc ....D 888 846-8804
1805 W 208th St Ste 202 Torrance (90501) *(P-9134)*

Express Manufacturing Inc (PA).......................B 714 979-2228
3519 W Warner Ave Santa Ana (92704) *(P-6996)*

Expressmed, Carlsbad *Also Called: Mooreford Inc (P-10093)*

Exquisite Dental Technology ....D 626 237-0107
4816 Temple City Blvd Temple City (91780) *(P-16317)*

Extension Services, Long Beach *Also Called: County of Los Angeles (P-12651)*

Extensions Plus, Tarzana *Also Called: Extensions Plus Inc (P-10473)*

Extensions Plus Inc ....E 818 881-5611
5428 Reseda Blvd Tarzana (91356) *(P-10473)*

Employee Codes: A=Over 500 employees, B=251-500
C=101-250, D=51-100, E=20-50, F=10-19, G=1-9

2025 Southern California
Business Directory and Buyers Guide

© Mergent Inc. 1-800-342-5647
1021

Extron Electronics, Anaheim *Also Called: Rgb Systems Inc (P-5949)*

Extrumed Inc (DH) .... E **951 547-7400**
547 Trm Cir Corona (92879) *(P-4115)*

Exult Inc .... A 949 856-8800
121 Innovation Dr Ste 200 Irvine (92612) *(P-18132)*

Exxel Outdoors Inc .... C 626 369-7278
343 Baldwin Park Blvd City Of Industry (91746) *(P-2276)*

Exxon, Goleta *Also Called: Exxon Mobil Corporation (P-11476)*

Exxon Mobil Corporation .... E 805 961-4093
12000 Calle Real Goleta (93117) *(P-11476)*

Ey, Irvine *Also Called: Ernst & Young LLP (P-17724)*

Ey, San Diego *Also Called: Ernst & Young LLP (P-17725)*

Ey, Westlake Village *Also Called: Ernst & Young LLP (P-17726)*

Ey, Los Angeles *Also Called: Ernst & Young LLP (P-17727)*

Eye Care Center, The, Fullerton *Also Called: Marshall B Ketchum University (P-16833)*

Eye Exam of California, San Diego *Also Called: James G Meyers & Associates (P-15535)*

Eyeline Studios, Los Angeles *Also Called: Scanlinevfx La LLC (P-14856)*

Eyeonics Inc .... E 949 788-6000
32 Discovery Irvine (92618) *(P-8407)*

Eyeshadow, Los Angeles *Also Called: Stony Apparel Corp (P-2054)*

EZ Lube LLC .... D 951 766-1996
532 W Florida Ave Hemet (92543) *(P-3855)*

EZ Lube LLC .... C 714 966-1647
3599 Harbor Blvd Costa Mesa (92626) *(P-14715)*

EZ Lube LLC .... C 310 821-2517
13421 Washington Blvd Marina Del Rey (90292) *(P-14716)*

EZ Lube- Costco, Marina Del Rey *Also Called: EZ Lube LLC (P-14716)*

Ezcaretech Usa Inc .... B 424 558-3191
21081 S Western Ave Ste 130 Torrance (90501) *(P-11120)*

Ezviz Inc .... C 855 693-9849
18639 Railroad St City Of Industry (91748) *(P-14400)*

F & A Federal Credit Union .... D 213 268-1226
2625 Corporate Pl Monterey Park (91754) *(P-11795)*

F & E Arcft Mint Los Angles LL .... B 310 338-0063
531 Main St Ste 672 El Segundo (90245) *(P-9201)*

F & L Industrial Solutions, Poway *Also Called: Motion Industries Inc (P-10451)*

F C I, Anaheim *Also Called: Fci Lender Services Inc (P-13283)*

F E E, Rcho Sta Marg *Also Called: Fakouri Electrical Engrg Inc (P-14186)*

F Gavina & Sons Inc .... B 323 582-0671
2700 Fruitland Ave Vernon (90058) *(P-1718)*

F I N, Granada Hills *Also Called: Financial Info Netwrk Inc (P-13731)*

F I O Imports Inc .... C 323 263-5100
5980 Alcoa Ave Vernon (90058) *(P-1772)*

F I T, Compton *Also Called: Fastener Innovation Tech Inc (P-5107)*

F Korbel & Bros .... E 661 854-6137
15401 Bear Mountain Winery Rd Arvin (93203) *(P-1567)*

F M H, Irvine *Also Called: Fmh Aerospace Corp (P-7478)*

F M I, Santa Ana *Also Called: Flexible Manufacturing LLC (P-6948)*

F M P, Downey *Also Called: Florence Meat Packing Co Inc (P-11572)*

F M Tarbell Co (HQ) .... C **714 972-0988**
1403 N Tustin Ave Ste 380 Santa Ana (92705) *(P-12441)*

F O X, Los Angeles *Also Called: Fox Sports Inc (P-9503)*

F R T International Inc .... D 310 329-5700
14439 S Avalon Blvd Gardena (90248) *(P-9064)*

F R T International Inc (PA) .... D **310 604-8208**
1700 N Alameda St Compton (90222) *(P-9065)*

F R T International Inc .... D 909 390-4892
5750 E Francis St Ontario (91761) *(P-9281)*

F T I, Long Beach *Also Called: Fundamental Tech Intl Inc (P-7858)*

F-J-E Inc .... E 562 437-7466
546 W Esther St Long Beach (90813) *(P-2564)*

F&M Bank, Long Beach *Also Called: Farmers Merchants Bnk Long Bch (P-11765)*

FAA Beverly Hills Inc .... D 323 801-1430
5070 Wilshire Blvd Los Angeles (90036) *(P-11345)*

Fab Services West Inc .... D 909 350-7500
10007 Elm Ave Fontana (92335) *(P-5094)*

Fabco Steel Fabrication Inc .... E 909 350-1535
14688 San Bernardino Ave Fontana (92335) *(P-4834)*

Fabcon, Santa Ana *Also Called: Fabrication Concepts Corporation (P-4986)*

Fabcon, Valencia *Also Called: Bayless Manufacturing LLC (P-6093)*

Faber Enterprises Inc .... C 310 323-6200
14800 S Figueroa St Gardena (90248) *(P-5374)*

Fabri Cote, Los Angeles *Also Called: Rdmm Legacy Inc (P-10672)*

Fabric8labs Inc .... D 858 215-1142
11075 Roselle St San Diego (92121) *(P-5661)*

Fabrica Fine Carpet, Santa Ana *Also Called: Fabrica International Inc (P-1951)*

Fabrica International Inc .... C 949 261-7181
3201 S Susan St Santa Ana (92704) *(P-1951)*

Fabricated Components Corp .... C 714 974-8590
130 W Bristol Ln Orange (92865) *(P-6728)*

Fabrication Concepts Corporation .... C 714 881-2000
1800 E Saint Andrew Pl Santa Ana (92705) *(P-4986)*

Fabrication Tech Inds Inc .... D 619 477-4141
2200 Haffley Ave National City (91950) *(P-4835)*

Fabricmate, Ventura *Also Called: Fabricmate Systems Inc (P-1893)*

Fabricmate Systems Inc .... E 805 642-7470
2781 Golf Course Dr Unit A Ventura (93003) *(P-1893)*

Fabtex Inc .... C 714 538-0877
615 S State College Blvd Fullerton (92831) *(P-1894)*

Facefirst LLC .... E 805 482-8428
31416 Agoura Rd Ste 250 Westlake Village (91361) *(P-13932)*

Facilitec West, Covina *Also Called: Stavros Enterprises Inc (P-14793)*

Facilities MGT & Coml RPS Svcs, Anaheim *Also Called: Branded Group Inc (P-18108)*

Facilities Resource Group, Ontario *Also Called: Maintenance Resource Inc (P-491)*

Facter Direct Ltd .... B 323 634-1999
4751 Wilshire Blvd Ste 140 Los Angeles (90010) *(P-14494)*

Factory One Studio Inc .... D 323 752-1670
6700 Avalon Blvd Ste 101 Los Angeles (90003) *(P-1878)*

Factron Test Fixtures, Poway *Also Called: Cohu Interface Solutions LLC (P-7906)*

Fahetas LLC (PA) .... D **949 280-1983**
1419 N Tustin St Ste A Orange (92867) *(P-11569)*

Fair Financial Corp (PA) .... D **800 584-5000**
1540 2nd St Ste 200 Santa Monica (90401) *(P-13726)*

Fair Price Carpets, Riverside *Also Called: Fairprice Enterprises Inc (P-11523)*

Fairbanks Ranch Cntry CLB Inc .... C 858 259-8811
15150 San Dieguito Rd Rancho Santa Fe (92067) *(P-15135)*

Fairfax Office 11, Beverly Hills *Also Called: City National Bank (P-11716)*

Fairfield Development Inc (PA) .... C **858 457-2123**
5355 Mira Sorrento Pl Ste 100 San Diego (92121) *(P-446)*

Fairfield Properties, San Diego *Also Called: Ffrt Residential LLC (P-12341)*

Fairmont Designs, Buena Park *Also Called: Cambium Business Group Inc (P-9867)*

Fairmont Miramar Hotel, Santa Monica *Also Called: Ocean Avenue LLC (P-12944)*

Fairplex Enterprises Inc .... C 909 623-3111
1101 W Mckinley Ave Pomona (91768) *(P-15202)*

Fairplex Rv Park, Pomona *Also Called: Los Angeles County Fair Assn (P-15210)*

Fairprice Enterprises Inc .... D 951 684-8578
1070 Center St Riverside (92507) *(P-11523)*

Fairview Developmental Center, Costa Mesa *Also Called: Califrnia Dept State Hospitals (P-16268)*

Fairview Developmental Center, Costa Mesa *Also Called: Califrnia Dept Dvlpmental Svcs (P-17051)*

Fairway Injection Molds Inc .... D 909 595-2201
20109 Paseo Del Prado Walnut (91789) *(P-5579)*

Fairway Technologies LLC (PA) .... D **858 454-4471**
4370 La Jolla Village Dr Ste 500 San Diego (92122) *(P-18133)*

Fairwinds-West Hills, West Hills *Also Called: Leisure Care LLC (P-15813)*

Faith Electric LLC .... C 909 767-2682
1980 Orange Tree Ln Ste 106 Redlands (92374) *(P-917)*

Faith Jones & Associates Inc (PA) .... D **619 297-9601**
7801 Mission Center Ct Ste 106 San Diego (92108) *(P-16389)*

Fakouri Electrical Engrg Inc .... D 949 888-2400
30001 Comercio Rcho Sta Marg (92688) *(P-14186)*

Falck Mobile Health Corp .... B 323 720-1578
212 S Atlantic Blvd Ste 102 Los Angeles (90022) *(P-8824)*

Falck Mobile Health Corp .... B 714 828-7750
8932 Katella Ave Ste 201 Anaheim (92804) *(P-8825)*

Falcon Aerospace Holdings LLC .... A 661 775-7200
27727 Avenue Scott Valencia (91355) *(P-10491)*

Falken Tire, Rancho Cucamonga *Also Called: Sumitomo Rubber North Amer Inc (P-9860)*

Mergent email: customerrelations@mergent.com
1022

2025 Southern California
Business Directory and Buyers Guide

(P-0000) Products & Services Section entry number
(PA)=Parent Co (HQ)=Headquarters (DH)=Div Headquarters

Falken Tire Holdings Inc .... D 800 723-2553
8656 Haven Ave Rancho Cucamonga (91730) *(P-9855)*

Falken Tires, Rancho Cucamonga Also Called: Falken Tire Holdings Inc *(P-9855)*

Falkner Winery Inc .... D 951 676-6741
40620 Calle Contento Temecula (92591) *(P-1568)*

Fallas Discount Stores, Gardena Also Called: J & M Sales Inc *(P-11497)*

Fallbrook Bonsall Village News, Temecula Also Called: Village News Inc *(P-2835)*

Fallbrook Industries Inc .... E 760 728-7229
323 Industrial Way Ste 1 Fallbrook (92028) *(P-5186)*

Falltech, Compton Also Called: Andrew Alexander Inc *(P-4276)*

Fam LLC (PA) .... D 323 888-7755
5553 Bandini Blvd B Bell (90201) *(P-1901)*

Fam Brands, Bell Also Called: Fam LLC *(P-1901)*

Fam Ppe LLC .... C 323 888-7755
5553 Bandini Blvd B Bell (90201) *(P-10560)*

Family Assistance Program .... C 760 843-0701
15075 Seventh St Victorville (92395) *(P-16941)*

Family Care Network Inc (PA) .... D 805 503-6240
1255 Kendall Rd San Luis Obispo (93401) *(P-17090)*

Family Health Center San Diego, Spring Valley Also Called: Family Hlth Ctrs San Diego Inc *(P-15310)*

Family Health Program, Long Beach Also Called: Optumcare Management LLC *(P-16597)*

Family Hlth Ctrs San Diego Inc .... B 619 515-2526
1845 Logan Ave San Diego (92113) *(P-15307)*

Family Hlth Ctrs San Diego Inc .... B 619 515-2435
2391 Island Ave San Diego (92102) *(P-15308)*

Family Hlth Ctrs San Diego Inc .... B 619 515-2400
5379 El Cajon Blvd San Diego (92115) *(P-15309)*

Family Hlth Ctrs San Diego Inc .... B 619 515-2555
8788 Jamacha Rd Spring Valley (91977) *(P-15310)*

Family Hlth Ctrs San Diego Inc .... B 619 515-2444
3705 Mission Blvd San Diego (92109) *(P-15311)*

Family Hlth Ctrs San Diego Inc .... B 619 515-2300
1809 National Ave San Diego (92113) *(P-15517)*

Family Hlth Ctrs San Diego Inc .... B 619 515-2550
7592 Broadway Lemon Grove (91945) *(P-16560)*

Family Loompya Corporation .... E 619 477-2125
2626 Southport Way Ste F National City (91950) *(P-1773)*

Family Svc Agcy Snta Brbara CN .... D 805 965-1001
123 W Gutierrez St Santa Barbara (93101) *(P-16942)*

Family Ties Home Care LLC .... D 818 565-9147
1350 Lafitte Dr Oak Park (91377) *(P-15851)*

Family Tree Produce Inc .... C 714 693-5688
5510 E La Palma Ave Anaheim (92807) *(P-10896)*

Family Zone Inc .... D 844 723-3932
10803 Thornmint Rd Ste 100 San Diego (92127) *(P-13727)*

Fancy Life Enterprises LLC (PA) .... C 619 560-9890
8030 La Mesa Blvd Pmb 3039 La Mesa (91942) *(P-14826)*

Fancy Life Studios, La Mesa Also Called: Fancy Life Enterprises LLC *(P-14826)*

Fandango Inc (HQ) .... D 310 954-0278
12200 W Olympic Blvd Ste 400 Los Angeles (90064) *(P-14959)*

Fandangonow, Los Angeles Also Called: Fandango Inc *(P-14959)*

Fantasy Activewear Inc (PA) .... E 213 705-4111
5383 Alcoa Ave Vernon (90058) *(P-1916)*

Fantasy Cookie Company, Sylmar Also Called: Fantasy Cookie Corporation *(P-1488)*

Fantasy Cookie Corporation (PA) .... E 818 361-6901
12322 Gladstone Ave Sylmar (91342) *(P-1488)*

Fantasy Dyeing & Finishing Inc .... E 323 983-9988
5383 Alcoa Ave Vernon (90058) *(P-1917)*

Fantasy Manufacturing, Vernon Also Called: Fantasy Activewear Inc *(P-1916)*

Fantasy Springs Resort Casino, Indio Also Called: East Valley Tourist Dev Auth *(P-15200)*

Fantom Drives, Torrance Also Called: Bnl Technologies Inc *(P-5874)*

Fanuc America Corporation .... D 949 595-2700
25951 Commercentre Dr Lake Forest (92630) *(P-5702)*

Fanuc Robotics West, Lake Forest Also Called: Fanuc America Corporation *(P-5702)*

Far East National Bank .... B 213 687-1300
977 N Broadway Ste 306 Los Angeles (90012) *(P-17984)*

Far West Inc .... D 909 884-4781
467 E Gilbert St San Bernardino (92404) *(P-15652)*

Far West Bond Services Cal Inc (PA) .... B 818 704-1111
5230 Las Virgenes Rd Calabasas (91302) *(P-12147)*

Far West Meats, Highland Also Called: Raemica Inc *(P-1268)*

Farchitecture Bb LLC .... E 917 701-2777
8588 Washington Blvd Culver City (90232) *(P-1317)*

Farley Interlocking Pav Stones, Palm Desert Also Called: Farley Paving Stone Co Inc *(P-4389)*

Farley Paving Stone Co Inc .... D 760 773-3960
39301 Badger St Palm Desert (92211) *(P-4389)*

Farmdale, San Bernardino Also Called: Farmdale Creamery LLC *(P-1329)*

Farmdale Creamery LLC .... D 909 888-4938
1049 W Base Line St San Bernardino (92411) *(P-1329)*

Farmers Group Inc (HQ) .... A 323 932-3200
6301 Owensmouth Ave Woodland Hills (91367) *(P-12207)*

Farmers Group Inc 401 K Sav Pl .... D 323 932-3200
4680 Wilshire Blvd Los Angeles (90010) *(P-12208)*

Farmers Insur Group Fdral Cr U (PA) .... D 323 209-6000
2255 N Ontario St Ste 320 Burbank (91504) *(P-11796)*

Farmers Insurance .... C 626 288-0870
113 Avondale Ave Monterey Park (91754) *(P-12209)*

Farmers Insurance .... C 661 257-0844
27433 Tourney Rd Ste 170 Valencia (91355) *(P-12210)*

Farmers Insurance .... C 951 681-1068
3600 Lime St Ste 122 Riverside (92501) *(P-12211)*

Farmers Insurance, Burbank Also Called: Farmers Insur Group Fdral Cr U *(P-11796)*

Farmers Insurance, Woodland Hills Also Called: Farmers Group Inc *(P-12207)*

Farmers Insurance, Los Angeles Also Called: Farmers Group Inc 401 K Sav Pl *(P-12208)*

Farmers Insurance, Woodland Hills Also Called: Farmers Insurance Exchange *(P-12212)*

Farmers Insurance Exchange (DH) .... A 888 327-6335
6301 Owensmouth Ave Woodland Hills (91367) *(P-12212)*

Farmers Merchants Bnk Long Bch (HQ) .... C 562 437-0011
302 Pine Ave Long Beach (90802) *(P-11765)*

Farstone Technology Inc .... C 949 336-4321
184 Technology Dr Ste 205 Irvine (92618) *(P-7104)*

Farwest Insulation Contracting .... D 310 634-2800
2741 Yates Ave Commerce (90040) *(P-1007)*

Fashion Logistics Inc .... C 424 201-4100
20550 Denker Ave Torrance (90501) *(P-9066)*

Fashion World Incorporated .... C 310 273-6544
420 N Rodeo Dr Beverly Hills (90210) *(P-10683)*

Fast Track Energy Drink LLc .... E 310 281-2045
8447 Wilshire Blvd Ste 401 Beverly Hills (90211) *(P-1618)*

Fast Undercar, Ventura Also Called: Parts Authority LLC *(P-9837)*

Fastclick Inc .... A 805 689-9839
530 E Montecito St Santa Barbara (93103) *(P-13273)*

Fastclick.com, Santa Barbara Also Called: Fastclick Inc *(P-13273)*

Fastcor, Anaheim Also Called: Bisco Industries Inc *(P-10232)*

Fastec Imaging Corporation .... E 858 592-2342
17150 Via Del Campo Ste 301 San Diego (92127) *(P-8427)*

Fastech, Buena Park Also Called: Fueling and Service Tech Inc *(P-10374)*

Fastener Dist Holdings LLC .... E 213 620-9950
5200 Sheila St Commerce (90040) *(P-7340)*

Fastener Dist Holdings LLC (HQ) .... D 213 620-9950
5200 Sheila St Commerce (90040) *(P-10437)*

Fastener Innovation Tech Inc .... D 310 538-1111
10000 O Ousana Rd Compton (90221) *(P-3107)*

Fastener Technology Corp .... C 818 764-6467
7415 Fulton Ave North Hollywood (91605) *(P-10438)*

Fatco Holdings LLC .... D 714 250-3000
1 First American Way Santa Ana (92707) *(P-12040)*

Fattail Inc (HQ) .... E 818 615-0380
23586 Calabasas Rd Ste 102 Calabasas (91302) *(P-13728)*

Faze Clan, Culver City Also Called: Faze Holdings Inc *(P-15204)*

Faze Clan Inc .... B 818 688-6373
9950 Jefferson Blvd Culver City (90232) *(P-15203)*

Faze Holdings Inc .... C 818 688-6373
9950 Jefferson Blvd Ste 3 Culver City (90232) *(P-15204)*

FB Corporation .... B 626 300-0880
1211 E Valley Blvd Alhambra (91801) *(P-11766)*

Fci Lender Services Inc .... C 800 931-2424
8180 E Kaiser Blvd Anaheim (92808) *(P-13283)*

Fcp Inc (PA) .... D 951 678-4571
23100 Wildomar Trl Wildomar (92595) *(P-5077)*

Employee Codes: A=Over 500 employees, B=251-500
C=101-250, D=51-100, E=20-50, F=10-19, G=1-9

2025 Southern California
Business Directory and Buyers Guide

© Mergent Inc. 1-800-342-5647

1023

Fdh Aero, Commerce *Also Called: Fastener Dist Holdings LLC (P-7340)*

FDS Manufacturing Company (PA).................................D 909 591-1733
2200 S Reservoir St Pomona (91766) *(P-2768)*

FDS Manufacturing Company Svcs, Pomona *Also Called: Federated Diversified Sls Inc (P-2707)*

Fdsi Logistics, Valencia *Also Called: Fdsi Logistics LLC (P-18134)*

Fdsi Logistics LLC ....D 818 971-3300
27680 Avenue Mentry # 2 Valencia (91355) *(P-18134)*

Fear of God LLC ....E 213 235-7985
558 S Alameda St Los Angeles (90013) *(P-2010)*

Feathersoft Inc ....E 925 230-0740
600 N Mountain Ave Ste C100 Upland (91786) *(P-6575)*

Federal Dfenders San Diego Inc (PA).........................D 619 234-8467
225 Broadway Ste 900 San Diego (92101) *(P-16680)*

Federal Express Corporation ....D 800 463-3339
3333 S Grand Ave Los Angeles (90007) *(P-9174)*

Federal Heath Sign Company LLC ....C 760 941-0715
3609 Ocean Ranch Blvd Ste 204 Oceanside (92056) *(P-8604)*

Federal Home Loan Mrtg Corp ....A 213 337-4200
444 S Flower St Fl 44 Los Angeles (90071) *(P-11903)*

Federal Industries Inc ....E 310 297-4040
645 Hawaii St El Segundo (90245) *(P-5386)*

Federal Manufacturing Corp ....E 818 341-9825
9825 De Soto Ave Chatsworth (91311) *(P-5126)*

Federal Rsrve Bnk San Frncisco ....A 213 683-2300
950 S Grand Ave Fl 1 Los Angeles (90015) *(P-11703)*

Federated Diversified Sls Inc ....D 909 591-1733
2200 S Reservoir St Pomona (91766) *(P-2707)*

Fedex, Los Angeles *Also Called: Federal Express Corporation (P-9174)*

Fei-Zyfer Inc (HQ)...E 714 933-4000
7321 Lincoln Way Garden Grove (92841) *(P-6615)*

Feihe International Inc (PA).................................A 626 757-8885
2275 Huntington Dr Pmb 278 San Marino (91108) *(P-1298)*

Feit Electric, Pico Rivera *Also Called: Feit Electric Company Inc (P-6444)*

Feit Electric Company Inc (PA).................................C 562 463-2852
4901 Gregg Rd Pico Rivera (90660) *(P-6444)*

Felbro Inc ....C 323 263-8686
3666 E Olympic Blvd Los Angeles (90023) *(P-2580)*

Feld Care Therapy Inc ....D 818 926-9057
100 E Thousand Oaks Blvd Thousand Oaks (91360) *(P-16474)*

Feldcare Connects, Thousand Oaks *Also Called: Feld Care Therapy Inc (P-16474)*

Felix Chevrolet, Los Angeles *Also Called: Felix Chevrolet LP (P-11346)*

Felix Chevrolet LP (PA)...C 213 748-6141
714 W Olympic Blvd Ste 1124 Los Angeles (90015) *(P-11346)*

Felix Schoeller North Amer Inc ....E 315 298-8425
1260 N Lakeview Ave Anaheim (92807) *(P-2723)*

Fellow, Venice *Also Called: Fellow Industries Inc (P-6396)*

Fellow Industries Inc ....E 415 649-0361
1342 1/2 Abbot Kinney Blvd Venice (90291) *(P-6396)*

Fema Electronics Corporation ....E 714 825-0140
22 Corporate Park Irvine (92606) *(P-6997)*

Fencecorp Inc ....D 760 721-2101
3045 Industry St Oceanside (92054) *(P-1203)*

Fencecorp Inc (HQ)...C 951 686-3170
18440 Van Buren Blvd Riverside (92508) *(P-1204)*

Fenceworks LLC (PA)...C 951 788-5620
870 Main St Riverside (92501) *(P-1205)*

Fender Digital LLC ....D 323 462-2198
1575 N Gower St Ste 170 Los Angeles (90028) *(P-13729)*

Fender Musical Instrs Corp ....A 480 596-9690
311 Cessna Cir Corona (92878) *(P-8468)*

Fenderscape Incorporated ....C 562 988-2228
1446 E Hill St Signal Hill (90755) *(P-167)*

Fenico Precision Castings Inc ....D 562 634-5000
7805 Madison St Paramount (90723) *(P-4688)*

Fennemore Craig PC ....D 619 794-0050
600 B St Ste 1700 San Diego (92101) *(P-16681)*

Fennemore Craig PC ....D 619 794-0050
550 E Hospitality Ln Ste 300 San Bernardino (92408) *(P-16682)*

Fennemore Craig, P.C., San Diego *Also Called: Fennemore Craig PC (P-16681)*

Fennemore Craig, P.C., San Bernardino *Also Called: Fennemore Craig PC (P-16682)*

Ferco Color Inc (PA)...E 909 930-0773
5498 Vine St Chino (91710) *(P-3267)*

Ferco Plastic Products, Chino *Also Called: Ferco Color Inc (P-3267)*

Fergadis Enterprises, Bell *Also Called: Perrin Bernard Supowitz LLC (P-10607)*

Ferguson Fire Fabrication Inc (DH).........................D 909 517-3085
2750 S Towne Ave Pomona (91766) *(P-10317)*

Ferra Aerospace Inc ....E 918 787-2220
940 E Orangethorpe Ave Ste A Anaheim (92801) *(P-7473)*

Ferraco Inc (HQ)...E 562 988-2414
2933 Long Beach Blvd Long Beach (90806) *(P-8266)*

Ferrante Paul Cstm Lmps & Shds, West Hollywood *Also Called: Paul Ferrante Inc (P-8710)*

Ferreira Construction Co Inc ....A 909 606-5900
10370 Commerce Center Dr Ste 200 Rancho Cucamonga (91730) *(P-403)*

Ferry International LLC ....D 888 866-3377
6 Hutton Centre Dr Ste 700 Santa Ana (92707) *(P-18135)*

Fetish Group Inc (PA)...E 323 587-7873
1013 S Los Angeles St Ste 700 Los Angeles (90015) *(P-2011)*

Ffd II, San Diego *Also Called: Fairfield Development Inc (P-446)*

FFF Enterprises Inc (PA)...B 951 296-2500
44000 Winchester Rd Temecula (92590) *(P-10623)*

Ffi, Irvine *Also Called: First Foundation Inc (P-11767)*

Ffna, Irvine *Also Called: Frontech N Fujitsu Amer Inc (P-13733)*

Ffrt Residential LLC ....C 858 457-2123
5510 Morehouse Dr Ste 200 San Diego (92121) *(P-12341)*

Ffs Tech Inc ....D 323 965-9300
6000 Venice Blvd Los Angeles (90034) *(P-17528)*

Fgr 1 LLC ....E 800 653-3517
3191 Red Hill Ave Ste 100 Costa Mesa (92626) *(P-11570)*

Fgs Packing Services, Valencia *Also Called: Fruit Growers Supply Company (P-2666)*

Fhc, South Gate *Also Called: Frameless Hardware Company LLC (P-4768)*

Fht Printing, Fullerton *Also Called: Advanced Image Direct LLC (P-13298)*

Fi, El Segundo *Also Called: Federal Industries Inc (P-5386)*

Fiber Care Baths Inc ....B 760 246-0019
9832 Yucca Rd Ste A Adelanto (92301) *(P-4026)*

Fiber Optic Technologies, Torrance *Also Called: ACS Communications Inc (P-879)*

Fiberoptic Systems Inc ....E 805 579-6600
60 Moreland Rd Ste A Simi Valley (93065) *(P-4632)*

Fibreform Electronics Inc ....E 714 898-9641
5341 Argosy Ave Huntington Beach (92649) *(P-6123)*

Fibreform Precision Machining, Huntington Beach *Also Called: Fibreform Electronics Inc (P-6123)*

Fidelis Security LLC ....D 240 650-2041
871 Marlborough Ave Ste 100 Riverside (92507) *(P-13730)*

Fidelity Nat Title Insur Co NY ....A 805 370-1400
950 Hampshire Rd Westlake Village (91361) *(P-12557)*

Fidelity National, Westlake Village *Also Called: Fidelity Nat Title Insur Co NY (P-12557)*

Field Fresh Foods Incorporated ....A 310 719-8422
14805 S San Pedro St Gardena (90248) *(P-10897)*

Field Manufacturing Corp (PA).................................E 310 781-9292
1751 Torrance Blvd Ste N Torrance (90501) *(P-2581)*

Field Time Target Training LLC ....E 714 677-2841
8230 Electric Ave Stanton (90680) *(P-5354)*

Fieldpiece, Orange *Also Called: Fieldpiece Instruments Inc (P-7911)*

Fieldpiece Instruments Inc (PA).................................E 714 634-1844
1636 W Collins Ave Orange (92867) *(P-7911)*

Fieldstone Communities Inc (PA).................................C 949 790-5400
16 Technology Dr Ste 125 Irvine (92618) *(P-461)*

Fiesta Concession, Vernon *Also Called: Mahar Manufacturing Corp (P-8476)*

Fiesta De Reyes, San Diego *Also Called: Old Town Fmly Hospitality Corp (P-12950)*

Fiesta Ford Inc ....C 760 775-7777
79015 Avenue 40 Indio (92203) *(P-11347)*

Fiesta Ford Lincoln-Mercury, Indio *Also Called: Fiesta Ford Inc (P-11347)*

Fiesta Mexican Foods Inc ....E 760 344-3580
979 G St Brawley (92227) *(P-1445)*

Fifth Season LLC ....C 862 432-3068
11355 W Olympic Blvd Ste 1000w Los Angeles (90064) *(P-14889)*

Figs, Santa Monica *Also Called: Figs Inc (P-1994)*

Figs Inc ....B 424 300-8330
2834 Colorado Ave Ste 100 Santa Monica (90404) *(P-1994)*

Mergent email: customerrelations@mergent.com
1024

2025 Southern California
Business Directory and Buyers Guide

(P-0000) Products & Services Section entry number
(PA)=Parent Co (HQ)=Headquarters (DH)=Div Headquarters

Figueroa Hotel, Los Angeles *Also Called: New Figueroa Hotel Inc (P-12936)*

Figure 8, Torrance *Also Called: Nothing To Wear Inc (P-2051)*

Filenet Corporation .... A 800 345-3638
3565 Harbor Blvd Costa Mesa (92626) *(P-14081)*

Film Department Lmu .... D 310 258-5465
1 Lmu Dr Los Angeles (90045) *(P-14890)*

Film Payroll Services Inc (PA) .... D 310 440-9600
500 S Sepulveda Blvd Fl 4 Los Angeles (90049) *(P-17728)*

Film Roman Llc .... C 818 748-4000
6320 Canoga Ave Ste 450 Woodland Hills (91367) *(P-14827)*

Filml.a, Studio City *Also Called: A Filml Inc (P-14880)*

Filmtools Inc (PA) .... E 323 467-1116
1015 N Hollywood Way Burbank (91505) *(P-11646)*

Filtec, Torrance *Also Called: Industrial Dynamics Co Ltd (P-5705)*

Filter Concepts Incorporated .... E 714 545-7003
22895 Eastpark Dr Yorba Linda (92887) *(P-6929)*

Filter Pump Industries, Sun Valley *Also Called: Penguin Pumps Incorporated (P-5739)*

Filyn Corporation .... C 714 632-0225
2950 E La Jolla St Anaheim (92806) *(P-8826)*

Final Touch Apparel, Los Angeles *Also Called: Final Touch Apparel Inc (P-10708)*

Final Touch Apparel Inc .... E 323 484-9621
116 E 32nd St Los Angeles (90011) *(P-10708)*

Financial Info Netwrk Inc .... E 818 782-0331
11164 Bertrand Ave Granada Hills (91344) *(P-13731)*

Financial Partners Credit Un (PA) .... D 562 904-3000
7800 Imperial Hwy Downey (90242) *(P-11797)*

Financial Partners Credit Un, Downey *Also Called: Financial Partners Credit Un (P-11797)*

Financial Statement Svcs Inc (PA) .... C 714 436-3326
3300 S Fairview St Santa Ana (92704) *(P-13302)*

Financial Tech Sltons Intl Inc .... C 818 241-9571
406 E Huntington Dr Ste 100 Monrovia (91016) *(P-18136)*

Find It Parts Inc .... D 888 312-8812
11858 La Grange Ave Los Angeles (90025) *(P-9825)*

Finditparts, Los Angeles *Also Called: Find It Parts Inc (P-9825)*

Fine Line Circuits & Tech Inc .... E 714 529-2942
594 Apollo St Ste A Brea (92821) *(P-6729)*

Fineline Architectural Mllwk, Costa Mesa *Also Called: Fineline Woodworking Inc (P-2306)*

Fineline Settings LLC .... E 845 369-6100
2041 S Turner Ave Unit 30 Ontario (91761) *(P-2700)*

Fineline Woodworking Inc .... D 714 540-5468
1139 Baker St Costa Mesa (92626) *(P-2306)*

Finesse, South Pasadena *Also Called: Finesse Apparel Inc (P-2096)*

Finesse Apparel Inc .... E 213 747-7077
815 Fairview Ave Unit 101 South Pasadena (91030) *(P-2096)*

Finest Hour Holdings Inc .... E 310 533-9966
3203 Kashiwa St Torrance (90505) *(P-8267)*

Finis LLC .... D 949 250-4929
3347 Michelson Dr Ste 100 Irvine (92612) *(P-5920)*

Finish Carpentry, Escondido *Also Called: Taylor Trim & Supply Inc (P-1062)*

Finishing Touch Millwork, Carlsbad *Also Called: Finishing Touch Moulding Inc (P-2349)*

Finishing Touch Moulding Inc .... D 760 444-1019
6190 Corte Del Cedro Carlsbad (92011) *(P-2349)*

Finleys Tree & Landcare Inc .... C 310 326-9818
1209 W 228th St Torrance (90502) *(P-168)*

Fiore Stone Inc .... E 909 424-0221
1814 Commercenter W Ste E San Bernardino (92408) *(P-4390)*

Firan Tech Group USA Corp (HQ) .... D 818 407-4024
20750 Marilla St Chatsworth (91311) *(P-7719)*

Fire Insurance Exchange (PA) .... A 323 932-3200
6301 Owensmouth Ave Woodland Hills (91367) *(P-12213)*

Fire Protection Group Amer Inc .... E 323 732-4200
3712 W Jefferson Blvd Los Angeles (90016) *(P-17529)*

Fire Sprnklr Fire Alarm Dsign, San Diego *Also Called: Symons Fire Protection Inc (P-14424)*

Fireblast, Murrieta *Also Called: Fireblast Global Inc (P-5821)*

Fireblast Global Inc .... E 951 277-8319
41633 Eastman Dr Murrieta (92562) *(P-5821)*

Firefighters First Credit Un (PA) .... C 323 254-1700
1520 W Colorado Blvd Pasadena (91105) *(P-11798)*

Firestarter Entertainment LLC .... D 805 907-6428
4304 Wildwest Cir Moorpark (93021) *(P-14988)*

Firestone, Ontario *Also Called: Ramona Auto Services Inc (P-11454)*

Firestone Cmplete Auto Care 79, San Diego *Also Called: Bridgestone Americas Inc (P-3863)*

Firestone Vineyard LP .... D 805 688-3940
5000 Zaca Station Rd Los Olivos (93441) *(P-1569)*

Firestone Walker Inc .... D 805 226-8514
1332 Vendels Cir Paso Robles (93446) *(P-1540)*

Firestone Walker Inc (PA) .... C 805 225-5911
1400 Ramada Dr Paso Robles (93446) *(P-1541)*

Firestone Walker Inc .... D 805 254-4205
620 Mcmurray Rd Buellton (93427) *(P-1542)*

Firestone Walker Brewing Co, Paso Robles *Also Called: Firestone Walker Inc (P-1541)*

Firestone Walker Brewing Co, Buellton *Also Called: Firestone Walker Inc (P-1542)*

Firmenich .... D 714 535-2871
424 S Atchison St Anaheim (92805) *(P-3733)*

Firmenich, Anaheim *Also Called: Firmenich Incorporated (P-3798)*

Firmenich Incorporated .... C 714 535-2871
424 S Atchison St Anaheim (92805) *(P-3798)*

Firmenich Incorporated .... D 858 646-8323
10636 Scripps Summit Ct San Diego (92131) *(P-3799)*

First 5 La .... C 213 482-5920
750 N Alameda St Ste 300 Los Angeles (90012) *(P-16943)*

First Allied, San Diego *Also Called: First Allied Securities Inc (P-11964)*

First Allied Securities Inc (HQ) .... D 619 702-9600
655 W Broadway Fl 11 San Diego (92101) *(P-11964)*

First Amercn Prof RE Svcs Inc (HQ) .... C 714 250-1400
200 Commerce Irvine (92602) *(P-12442)*

First American, Santa Ana *Also Called: First American Financial Corp (P-12150)*

First American Financial Corp (PA) .... A 714 250-3000
1 First American Way Santa Ana (92707) *(P-12150)*

First American Mortgage Svcs .... B 714 250-4210
3 First American Way Santa Ana (92707) *(P-12151)*

First American Mortgage Svcs, Santa Ana *Also Called: First American Title Insur Co (P-12152)*

First American Team Realty Inc (PA) .... C 562 427-7765
2501 Cherry Ave Ste 100 Signal Hill (90755) *(P-12443)*

First American Title Company .... A 714 250-3109
1 First American Way Santa Ana (92707) *(P-12558)*

First American Title Insur Co (HQ) .... B 800 854-3643
1 First American Way Santa Ana (92707) *(P-12152)*

First Bank and Trust .... D 562 595-8775
4040 Atlantic Ave Long Beach (90807) *(P-11733)*

First Capitol Consulting Inc .... D 213 382-1115
520 S Grand Ave Los Angeles (90071) *(P-18137)*

First Class Foods, Hawthorne *Also Called: Firstclass Foods - Trojan Inc (P-1242)*

First Community Bancorp .... D 858 756-3023
5900 La Place Ct Ste 200 Carlsbad (92008) *(P-11734)*

First Entertainment Credit Un (PA) .... D 323 851-3673
6735 Forest Lawn Dr Ste 100 Los Angeles (90068) *(P-11799)*

First Financial Federal Cr Un .... C 800 537-8491
650 Sierra Madre Villa Ave Ste 300 Pasadena (91107) *(P-11800)*

First Finish Inc .... E 310 631-6717
11126 Wright Rd Lynwood (90262) *(P-1879)*

First Fire Systems, Los Angeles *Also Called: Ffs Tech Inc (P-17528)*

First Foundation Inc (PA) .... C 949 202-4160
18101 Von Karman Ave Ste 700 Irvine (92612) *(P-11767)*

First Group, Inglewood *Also Called: First Transit Inc (P-8750)*

First Legal Network .... C 213 250-1111
1517 Beverly Blvd Los Angeles (90026) *(P-7912)*

First Meridian Care Svcs Inc .... D 858 529-1886
4545 Murphy Canyon Rd Ste 204 San Diego (92123) *(P-16390)*

First Mortgage Corporation .... B 909 595-1996
1131 W 6th St Ste 300 Ontario (91762) *(P-11904)*

First Reprographic, Los Angeles *Also Called: Lasr Inc (P-13314)*

First Student, Baldwin Park *Also Called: First Student Inc (P-8879)*

First Student Inc .... D 855 870-8747
16332 Construction Cir W Irvine (92606) *(P-8876)*

First Student Inc .... C 909 383-1640
234 S I St San Bernardino (92410) *(P-8877)*

First Student Inc .... D 951 736-3234
300 S Buena Vista Ave Corona (92882) *(P-8878)*

Employee Codes: A=Over 500 employees, B=251-500
C=101-250, D=51-100, E=20-50, F=10-19, G=1-9

2025 Southern California
Business Directory and Buyers Guide

© Mergent Inc. 1-800-342-5647

1025

A L P H A B E T I C

First Student Inc .... C 855 870-8747
5127 Heintz St Baldwin Park (91706) *(P-8879)*

First Student Inc .... A 310 769-2400
14800 S Avalon Blvd Gardena (90248) *(P-8880)*

First Team RE - Orange Cnty .... D 562 346-5088
42 64th Pl Long Beach (90803) *(P-12444)*

First Team RE - Orange Cnty .... D 562 424-2004
3626 Long Beach Blvd Long Beach (90807) *(P-12445)*

First Team RE - Orange Cnty .... D 714 974-9191
8028 E Santa Ana Canyon Rd Anaheim (92808) *(P-12446)*

First Team RE - Orange Cnty .... C 949 389-0004
26711 Aliso Creek Rd Ste 200a Aliso Viejo (92656) *(P-12447)*

First Team RE - Orange Cnty (PA) .... C 949 988-3000
108 Pacifica Ste 300 Irvine (92618) *(P-12448)*

First Team RE - Orange Cnty .... D 562 596-9911
12501 Seal Beach Blvd Ste 100 Seal Beach (90740) *(P-12449)*

First Team RE - Orange Cnty .... C 714 485-7984
4040 Barranca Pkwy Ste 100 Irvine (92604) *(P-12450)*

First Team RE - Orange Cnty .... C 949 240-7979
32451 Golden Lantern Ste 210 Laguna Niguel (92677) *(P-12451)*

First Team RE - Orange Cnty .... B 714 544-5456
17240 17th St Tustin (92780) *(P-12452)*

First Team RE - Orange Cnty .... D 951 270-2800
200 S Main St Ste 100 Corona (92879) *(P-12453)*

First Team Real Estate, Anaheim *Also Called: First Team RE - Orange Cnty (P-12446)*

First Team Real Estate, Aliso Viejo *Also Called: First Team RE - Orange Cnty (P-12447)*

First Team Real Estate, Irvine *Also Called: First Team RE - Orange Cnty (P-12450)*

First Team Walk-In Realty, Irvine *Also Called: First Team RE - Orange Cnty (P-12448)*

First Transit Inc .... D 626 307-7842
4337 Rowland Ave El Monte (91731) *(P-8749)*

First Transit Inc .... D 310 216-9584
1213 W Arbor Vitae St Inglewood (90301) *(P-8750)*

First Transit Inc .... D 323 222-0010
15730 S Figueroa St Gardena (90248) *(P-8751)*

First Transit Inc .... C 805 544-2730
29 Prado Rd San Luis Obispo (93401) *(P-8752)*

First Transit Inc .... D 909 948-3474
9421 Feron Blvd Ste 101 Rancho Cucamonga (91730) *(P-8753)*

First Transit Inc .... D 714 644-9828
1717 E Via Burton Anaheim (92806) *(P-8754)*

Firstat Nursing Services Inc .... C 619 220-7600
411 Camino Del Rio S Ste 100 San Diego (92108) *(P-16391)*

Firstclass Foods - Trojan Inc .... C 310 676-2500
12500 Inglewood Ave Hawthorne (90250) *(P-1242)*

Firstsrvice Rsidential Cal LLC (HQ) .... C 949 448-6000
15241 Laguna Canyon Rd Irvine (92618) *(P-12454)*

Firstsrvice Rsidential Cal LLC .... C 213 213-0886
3415 S Sepulveda Blvd Ste 720 Los Angeles (90034) *(P-17985)*

Fisa, Laguna Beach *Also Called: Flavor Infusion LLC (P-1679)*

Fischer Mold Incorporated .... D 951 279-1140
393 Meyer Cir Corona (92879) *(P-4116)*

Fish & Richardson PC .... C 858 678-5070
12390 El Camino Real San Diego (92130) *(P-16683)*

Fish Bowl, Woodland Hills *Also Called: Second Generation Inc (P-2131)*

Fish House Foods Inc .... C 760 597-1270
1263 Linda Vista Dr San Marcos (92078) *(P-1705)*

Fish House Partners One LLC .... D 323 460-4170
5955 Melrose Ave Los Angeles (90038) *(P-11571)*

Fishel Company .... C 858 658-0830
5878 Autoport Mall San Diego (92121) *(P-918)*

Fisher & Paykel, Costa Mesa *Also Called: Dynamic Cooking Systems Inc (P-6012)*

Fisher & Paykel Healthcare Inc .... C 949 453-4000
17400 Laguna Canyon Rd Ste 300 Irvine (92618) *(P-10078)*

Fisher & Phillips LLP .... C 949 851-2424
2050 Main St Ste 1000 Irvine (92614) *(P-16684)*

Fisher Printing Inc (PA) .... C 714 998-9200
2257 N Pacific St Orange (92865) *(P-3007)*

Fisher Ranch LLC .... D 760 922-4151
10610 Ice Plant Rd Blythe (92225) *(P-107)*

Fisheries Resource Vlntr Corps .... C 562 596-9261
109 Stanford Ln Seal Beach (90740) *(P-18138)*

Fishermans Pride Prcessors Inc .... B 323 232-1980
4510 S Alameda St Vernon (90058) *(P-1706)*

Fisk Electric Company .... C 818 884-1166
15870 Olden St Rancho Cascades (91342) *(P-919)*

Fisker, La Palma *Also Called: Fisker Inc (P-7175)*

Fisker Automotive Inc .... D
3080 Airway Ave Costa Mesa (92626) *(P-7174)*

Fisker Inc (PA) .... E 833 434-7537
14 Centerpointe Dr La Palma (90623) *(P-7175)*

Fit-Line Inc .... E 714 549-9091
2901 S Tech Center Dr Santa Ana (92705) *(P-4117)*

Fit-Line Global, Santa Ana *Also Called: Fit-Line Inc (P-4117)*

Fitbit LLC .... C 415 513-1000
15255 Innovation Dr Ste 200 San Diego (92128) *(P-8041)*

Fitness Warehouse LLC (PA) .... E 858 578-7676
9990 Alesmith Ct Ste 130 San Diego (92126) *(P-8517)*

Fitparts, Gardena *Also Called: Getpart La Inc (P-4125)*

Fitzgerald Formliners, Santa Ana *Also Called: Prime Forming & Cnstr Sups Inc (P-4414)*

FIVE ACRES, Altadena *Also Called: Five Acres - The Bys Grls Aid (P-17152)*

Five Acres - The Bys Grls Aid .... B 626 798-6793
760 Mountain View St Altadena (91001) *(P-17152)*

Five Star Food Containers Inc .... D 626 437-6219
250 Eastgate Rd Barstow (92311) *(P-3998)*

Five Star Gourmet Foods Inc (PA) .... C 909 390-0032
3880 Ebony St Ontario (91761) *(P-1774)*

Five Star Labor, Torrance *Also Called: Golden Arrow Construction Inc (P-406)*

Five Star Plastering Inc .... D 949 683-5091
23022 La Cadena Dr Ste 200 Laguna Hills (92653) *(P-1008)*

Five Star Qulty Care-CA II LLC (DH) .... D 805 492-2444
93 W Avenida De Los Arboles Thousand Oaks (91360) *(P-15653)*

Five Star Senior Living Inc .... C 760 479-1818
1350 S El Camino Real Encinitas (92024) *(P-15654)*

Five Star Senior Living Inc .... C 858 673-6300
16925 Hierba Dr San Diego (92128) *(P-15655)*

Five Star Senior Living Inc .... D 949 642-8044
466 Flagship Rd Newport Beach (92663) *(P-15656)*

Fivesixtwo Inc, Long Beach *Also Called: Traffic Management Pdts Inc (P-14056)*

Fixd Construction Co., Ontario *Also Called: Nhs Western Division Inc (P-422)*

FJ Willert Contracting Co .... C 619 421-1980
1869 Nirvana Ave Chula Vista (91911) *(P-539)*

Fjs Inc .... C 714 905-1050
888 S Disneyland Dr Ste 400 Anaheim (92802) *(P-12825)*

Fkc-Lake Shore, Rancho Cascades *Also Called: Frontier-Kemper Constructors Inc (P-713)*

Flagship Airport Services Inc .... D 310 328-8221
1830 W 208th St Torrance (90501) *(P-13374)*

Flagship Credit Acceptance LLC .... D 949 748-7172
7525 Irvine Center Dr Irvine (92618) *(P-14495)*

Flagship Health Care Center, Newport Beach *Also Called: Five Star Senior Living Inc (P-15656)*

Flame and Wax Inc .... C 949 752-4000
2900 Mccabe Way Irvine (92614) *(P-8676)*

Flamemaster Corporation .... E 818 890-1401
13576 Desmond St Pacoima (91331) *(P-3766)*

Flanders Pointe Apts, Tustin *Also Called: Steadfast Management Co Inc (P-12367)*

Flare Group .... E 714 549-0202
1571 Macarthur Blvd Costa Mesa (92626) *(P-5261)*

Flare Group .... E 714 850-2080
1571 Macarthur Blvd Costa Mesa (92626) *(P-7474)*

Flatiron West Inc .... C 909 597-8413
16341 Chino Corona Rd Chino (91708) *(P-651)*

Flavor House Inc .... E 760 246-9131
16378 Koala Rd Adelanto (92301) *(P-1678)*

Flavor Infusion LLC .... E 949 715-4369
332 Forest Ave Ste 19 Laguna Beach (92651) *(P-1679)*

Flavor Producers, West Hills *Also Called: Flavor Producers LLC (P-1680)*

Flavor Producers LLC (PA) .... E 661 257-3400
8521 Fallbrook Ave Ste 380 West Hills (91304) *(P-1680)*

Fleet Management Solutions Inc .... E 800 500-6009
310 Commerce Ste 100 Irvine (92602) *(P-6616)*

Fleetwood Continental Inc .... D 310 609-1477
19451 S Susana Rd Compton (90221) *(P-4679)*

Mergent email: customerrelations@mergent.com
1026

2025 Southern California
Business Directory and Buyers Guide

(P-0000) Products & Services Section entry number
(PA)=Parent Co (HQ)=Headquarters (DH)=Div Headquarters

Fleetwood Fibre LLC .... C 626 968-8503
15250 Don Julian Rd City Of Industry (91745) *(P-2665)*

Fleetwood Fibre Pkg & Graphics, City Of Industry *Also Called: Fleetwood Fibre LLC (P-2665)*

Fleetwood Homes, Riverside *Also Called: Cavco Industries Inc (P-2396)*

Fleetwood Homes, Riverside *Also Called: Fleetwood Homes California Inc (P-2400)*

Fleetwood Homes, Riverside *Also Called: Fleetwood Motor Homes-Califinc (P-14767)*

Fleetwood Homes California Inc (DH) .... C 951 351-2494
7007 Jurupa Ave Riverside (92504) *(P-2400)*

Fleetwood Motor Homes-Califinc .... C 951 274-2000
2350 Fleetwood Dr Riverside (92509) *(P-14767)*

Fleetwood Travel Trlrs Ind Inc (DH) .... C 951 354-3000
3125 Myers St Riverside (92503) *(P-7676)*

Fleetwood Windows and Doors, Corona *Also Called: McDavis and Gumbys Inc (P-9925)*

Fleming Metal Fabricators .... E 323 723-8203
874 Camino De Los Mares San Clemente (92673) *(P-7203)*

Fletcher Bldg Holdings USA Inc (DH) .... D 951 272-8180
1230 Railroad St Corona (92882) *(P-4987)*

Fletcher Coating, Orange *Also Called: Fletcher Coating Co (P-5320)*

Fletcher Coating Co .... E 714 637-4763
426 W Fletcher Ave Orange (92865) *(P-5320)*

Flex Company .... E 424 209-2711
318 Lincoln Blvd Ste 204 Venice (90291) *(P-3911)*

Flexco Inc .... E 562 927-2525
6855 Suva St Bell Gardens (90201) *(P-7475)*

Flexcon Company Inc .... E 909 465-0408
12840 Reservoir St Chino (91710) *(P-3949)*

Flexfire Leds Inc .... E 925 273-9080
3554 Business Park Dr Ste F Costa Mesa (92626) *(P-6458)*

Flexible Manufacturing LLC .... D 714 259-7996
1719 S Grand Ave Santa Ana (92705) *(P-6948)*

Flexible Metal Inc .... C 734 516-3017
1685 Brandywine Ave Chula Vista (91911) *(P-5434)*

Flexible Video Systems, Marina Del Rey *Also Called: Sewer Rodding Equipment Co (P-6031)*

Flexicare Incorporated .... E 949 450-9399
15281 Barranca Pkwy Ste D Irvine (92618) *(P-8379)*

Flexline Incorporated .... E 562 921-4141
3727 S Meyler St San Pedro (90731) *(P-3206)*

Flexrake, Temple City *Also Called: California Flexrake Corp (P-4737)*

Flight Environments Inc .... E
570 Linne Rd Ste 100 Paso Robles (93446) *(P-7476)*

Flight Line Products Inc .... E 661 775-8366
28732 Witherspoon Pkwy Valencia (91355) *(P-7477)*

Flight Microwave Corporation .... E 310 607-9819
410 S Douglas St El Segundo (90245) *(P-5703)*

Flight Suits .... D 619 440-2700
1900 Weld Blvd Ste 140 El Cajon (92020) *(P-2180)*

Flightways Manufacturing, Valencia *Also Called: Flight Line Products Inc (P-7477)*

Flint Energy Services Inc .... C 213 593-8000
1999 Avenue Of The Stars Ste 2600 Los Angeles (90067) *(P-17530)*

Flixbus Inc .... C 925 577-4164
12575 Beatrice St Los Angeles (90066) *(P-8827)*

Flo Dynamics, Compton *Also Called: Norco Industries Inc (P-5830)*

Flo Kino Inc .... C 818 767-6528
2040 N Hollywood Way Burbank (91505) *(P-0459)*

Flo-CHI, Los Angeles *Also Called: Lindsey & Sons (P-14530)*

Flo-Kem, Compton *Also Called: LMC Enterprises (P-3611)*

Flo-Kem Inc .... E 310 632-7124
19402 S Susana Rd Compton (90221) *(P-3603)*

Floaties Swim School, Poway *Also Called: Floaties Swim School LLC (P-15205)*

Floaties Swim School LLC .... D 877 277-7946
13180 Poway Rd Poway (92064) *(P-15205)*

Flock Freight Inc .... C 855 744-7585
701 S Coast Highway 101 Encinitas (92024) *(P-9282)*

Flood Ranch Company .... E 805 937-3616
6600 Foxen Canyon Rd Santa Maria (93454) *(P-1570)*

Flora Gold Corporation (PA) .... A 949 252-1908
3165 Red Hill Ave Ste 201 Costa Mesa (92626) *(P-8677)*

Floral Gift HM Decor Intl Inc .... E 818 849-8832
3200 Golf Course Dr Ste B Ventura (93003) *(P-55)*

Florence Crttnton Svcs Ornge C .... B 714 680-9000
801 E Chapman Ave Ste 203 Fullerton (92831) *(P-17153)*

Florence Filter Corporation .... D 310 637-1137
530 W Manville St Compton (90220) *(P-10332)*

Florence Meat Packing Co Inc .... E 562 401-0760
9840 Everest St Downey (90242) *(P-11572)*

Flotron .... E 760 727-2700
2630 Progress St Vista (92081) *(P-5580)*

Flowers Bakeries Sls Socal LLC .... E 702 281-4797
10625 Poplar Ave Fontana (92337) *(P-1446)*

Flowers Bkg Co Henderson LLC .... D 818 884-8970
21540 Blythe St Canoga Park (91304) *(P-1447)*

Flowers Bkg Co Henderson LLC .... D 310 695-9846
3800 W Century Blvd Inglewood (90303) *(P-1448)*

Flowers Bkg Co Henderson LLC .... D 702 281-4797
7311 Doig Dr Garden Grove (92841) *(P-1449)*

Flowline Inc .... E 562 598-3015
10500 Humbolt St Los Alamitos (90720) *(P-8042)*

Flowline Liquid Intelligence, Los Alamitos *Also Called: Flowline Inc (P-8042)*

Flowserve Corporation .... D 951 296-2464
27455 Tierra Alta Way Ste C Temecula (92590) *(P-5731)*

Flowserve Corporation .... B 323 584-1890
2300 E Vernon Ave Stop 76 Vernon (90058) *(P-5732)*

Flowserve Corporation .... D 310 667-4220
1909 E Cashdan St Compton (90220) *(P-5733)*

Fluid Line Technology Corp .... E 818 998-8848
4590 Ish Dr Simi Valley (93063) *(P-8153)*

Fluidmaster Inc (PA) .... D 949 728-2000
30800 Rancho Viejo Rd San Juan Capistrano (92675) *(P-4118)*

Fluidra North America LLC (HQ) .... D 760 599-9600
2882 Whiptail Loop Ste 100 Carlsbad (92010) *(P-6014)*

Fluids Manufacturing Inc .... C 818 264-4657
11941 Vose St North Hollywood (91605) *(P-10992)*

Fluor Corporation .... D 949 349-2000
3 Polaris Way Aliso Viejo (92656) *(P-17531)*

Fluor Daniel, Aliso Viejo *Also Called: Fluor Plant Services Intl Inc (P-17532)*

Fluor Daniel Construction Co (DH) .... B 949 349-2000
3 Polaris Way Aliso Viejo (92656) *(P-652)*

FLUOR DANIEL INTERCONTINENTAL, Aliso Viejo *Also Called: Fluor Daniel Construction Co (P-652)*

Fluor Fltron Blfour Btty Drgdo .... D 949 420-5000
5901 W Century Blvd Los Angeles (90045) *(P-9363)*

Fluor Plant Services Intl Inc .... D 949 349-2000
1 Enterprise Aliso Viejo (92656) *(P-17532)*

Fluorescent Supply Co Inc .... E 909 948-8878
9120 Center Ave Rancho Cucamonga (91730) *(P-6460)*

Flux Power Holdings Inc (PA) .... C 877 505-3589
2685 S Melrose Dr Vista (92081) *(P-7077)*

Fluxergy Inc (PA) .... E 949 305-4201
30 Fairbanks Irvine (92618) *(P-17788)*

Fly On My Jet, Los Angeles *Also Called: Forrest Group LLC (P-8755)*

Flyer Defense LLC .... D 310 324-5650
151 W 135th St Los Angeles (90061) *(P-7176)*

Flying Colors, Walnut *Also Called: Jakks Pacific Inc (P-8490)*

Flying Machine Factory, Compton *Also Called: Fmf Racing (P-7630)*

Flynt, Larry Publishing, Beverly Hills *Also Called: L F P Inc (P-2863)*

FMC Financial Group (PA) .... D 949 226-0360
4675 Macarthur Ct Ste 1250 Newport Beach (92660) *(P-12214)*

FMC Metals, Los Angeles *Also Called: 75s Corp (P-10533)*

Fmf Racing .... C 310 631-4363
18033 S Santa Fe Ave Compton (90221) *(P-7630)*

Fmh Aerospace Corp .... D 714 751-1000
17072 Daimler St Irvine (92614) *(P-7478)*

FMI, Chula Vista *Also Called: Flexible Metal Inc (P-5434)*

FMI International West 2, San Pedro *Also Called: Toll Global Fwdg Scs USA Inc (P-9344)*

Fmsinfoserv, Los Angeles *Also Called: Cdsnet LLC (P-18299)*

FN Logistics Llc .... A 213 625-5900
12588 Florence Ave Santa Fe Springs (90670) *(P-8991)*

FNS, Torrance *Also Called: Fns Inc (P-9283)*

Fns Inc (PA) .... D 661 615-2300
1545 Francisco St Torrance (90501) *(P-9283)*

Fntech .... D 714 429-7833
3000 W Segerstrom Ave Santa Ana (92704) *(P-14496)*

Employee Codes: A=Over 500 employees, B=251-500
C=101-250, D=51-100, E=20-50, F=10-19, G=1-9

2025 Southern California
Business Directory and Buyers Guide

© Mergent Inc. 1-800-342-5647
1027

Foam Depot, City Of Industry *Also Called: American Foam Fiber & Sups Inc (P-1966)*

Foam Factory Inc .... E 310 603-9808
17515 S Santa Fe Ave Compton (90221) *(P-3999)*

Foam Molders and Specialties .... E 562 924-7757
20004 State Rd Cerritos (90703) *(P-4000)*

Foam Molders and Specialties (PA) .... **E 562 924-7757**
11110 Business Cir Cerritos (90703) *(P-4001)*

Foam Specialties, Cerritos *Also Called: Foam Molders and Specialties (P-4001)*

Foam-Craft Inc .... C 714 459-9971
2441 Cypress Way Fullerton (92831) *(P-4002)*

Foamex, San Bernardino *Also Called: Foamex LP (P-4003)*

Foamex LP .... E 909 824-8981
1400 E Victoria Ave San Bernardino (92408) *(P-4003)*

Foamex LP .... C 323 774-5600
19201 S Reyes Ave Compton (90221) *(P-9067)*

Foampro Manufacturing, Santa Ana *Also Called: Foampro Mfg Inc (P-8587)*

Foampro Mfg Inc .... D 949 252-0112
1438 Ritchey St Santa Ana (92705) *(P-8587)*

Focus Diagnostics, Cypress *Also Called: Focus Diagnostics Inc (P-16318)*

Focus Diagnostics Inc .... B 714 220-1900
11331 Valley View St Ste 150 Cypress (90630) *(P-16318)*

Focus Features LLC (DH) .... D 310 315-1722
1540 2nd St Ste 200 Santa Monica (90401) *(P-14828)*

Focus Industries Inc .... D 949 830-1350
25301 Commercentre Dr Lake Forest (92630) *(P-6461)*

Focus Landscape, Lake Forest *Also Called: Focus Industries Inc (P-6461)*

Focus On Intervention LLC .... B 858 578-0769
12612 Rue Sienne Nord San Diego (92131) *(P-17058)*

Focus-Gramercy Film Music, Santa Monica *Also Called: Focus Features LLC (P-14828)*

Foh Group Inc (PA) .... E
6255 W Sunset Blvd Ste 2212 Los Angeles (90028) *(P-2154)*

Folding Cartons, Camarillo *Also Called: Crockett Graphics Inc (P-2662)*

Foley Fmly Wines Holdings Inc .... D 805 450-7225
90 Easy St Buellton (93427) *(P-1571)*

Follow Your Heart, Chatsworth *Also Called: Earth Island LLC (P-1766)*

Fontana Paper Mills Inc .... D 909 823-4100
13733 Valley Blvd Fontana (92335) *(P-3840)*

Fontana Resources At Work .... E 909 428-3833
9460 Sierra Ave Fontana (92335) *(P-17059)*

Fontana Steel, Ontario *Also Called: C M C Steel Fabricators Inc (P-5401)*

Fontana Water Company, El Monte *Also Called: San Gabriel Valley Water Co (P-9716)*

Food 4 Less, Riverside *Also Called: Dillon Companies Inc (P-11275)*

Food 4 Less, Paso Robles *Also Called: Paq Inc (P-11477)*

Food For Life Baking Co Inc (PA) .... **D 951 279-5090**
2991 Doherty St Corona (92879) *(P-1450)*

Food Pharma, Santa Fe Springs *Also Called: Food Technology and Design LLC (P-1503)*

Food Sales West Inc .... D 714 966-2900
235 Baker St Costa Mesa (92626) *(P-10751)*

Food Technology and Design LLC (PA) .... **E 562 944-7821**
10012 Painter Ave Santa Fe Springs (90670) *(P-1503)*

Foodology LLC .... D 818 252-1888
8920 Norris Ave Sun Valley (91352) *(P-1775)*

Foods On Fly LLC .... E 858 404-0642
7004 Carroll Rd San Diego (92121) *(P-1776)*

Fooma America Inc .... E 310 921-0717
12735 Stanhill Dr La Mirada (90638) *(P-5653)*

Foote Axle & Forge LLC .... E 323 268-4151
250 W Duarte Rd Ste A Monrovia (91016) *(P-7252)*

Foothill / Estrn Trnsp Crrdor .... D 949 754-3400
125 Pacifica Ste 100 Irvine (92618) *(P-616)*

Foothill Family Service .... C 626 246-1240
3629 Santa Anita Ave Ste 201 El Monte (91731) *(P-16944)*

Foothill Family Service .... C 626 795-6907
2500 E Foothill Blvd Ste 300 Pasadena (91107) *(P-16945)*

Foothill Packing Inc .... B 805 925-7900
2255 S Broadway Santa Maria (93454) *(P-10752)*

Foothill Presbyterian Hospital, Glendora *Also Called: Emanate Hlth Fthill Prsbt Hosp (P-15997)*

Foothill Regional Medical Ctr .... C 310 943-4500
14662 Newport Ave Tustin (92780) *(P-15998)*

Foothill Regional Medical Ctr, Tustin *Also Called: Alta Hospitals System LLC (P-15906)*

Foothill Transit West Covina, Arcadia *Also Called: Coach Usa Inc (P-8863)*

Foothill Vctonal Opportunities, Pasadena *Also Called: Fvo Solutions Inc (P-5321)*

For Cali Productions LLC .... B 323 956-9500
5555 Melrose Ave Bldg 213 Los Angeles (90038) *(P-14891)*

Forbes Industries Div .... C 909 923-4559
1933 E Locust St Ontario (91761) *(P-2613)*

Force Protection Systems, Van Nuys *Also Called: Edo Communications and Countermeasures Systems Inc (P-7716)*

Ford, Irvine *Also Called: Ford Motor Company (P-11348)*

Ford, Santa Monica *Also Called: Ford of Santa Monica Inc (P-11349)*

Ford, Simi Valley *Also Called: Ford of Simi Valley Inc (P-11350)*

Ford, Upland *Also Called: Park Place Ford LLC (P-11393)*

Ford, Irvine *Also Called: Ford Motor Land Dev Corp (P-12292)*

Ford Lincoln Mercury, El Centro *Also Called: El Centro Motors (P-11339)*

Ford Motor Company .... D 949 341-5800
3 Glen Bell Way Ste 200 Irvine (92618) *(P-11348)*

Ford Motor Land Dev Corp .... C 949 242-6606
3 Glen Bell Way Ste 100 Irvine (92618) *(P-12292)*

Ford of Santa Monica Inc .... D 310 451-1588
1402 Santa Monica Blvd Santa Monica (90404) *(P-11349)*

Ford of Simi Valley Inc .... D 805 583-0333
2440 1st St Simi Valley (93065) *(P-11350)*

Forecast 3d, Carlsbad *Also Called: Product Slingshot Inc (P-5593)*

Foreign Trade Corporation .... C 805 823-8400
685 Cochran St Ste 200 Simi Valley (93065) *(P-10244)*

Foremay Inc (PA) .... **E 408 228-3468**
225 S Lake Ave Ste 300 Pasadena (91101) *(P-13732)*

Forensic Analytical, Carson *Also Called: Forensic Analytical Spc Inc (P-17917)*

Forensic Analytical Spc Inc .... D 310 763-2374
20535 Belshaw Ave Carson (90746) *(P-17917)*

Forensic Toxicology Associates, Chatsworth *Also Called: Pacific Toxicology Labs (P-16326)*

Foreside Management Company .... B 949 966-1933
26023 Acero Ste 100 Mission Viejo (92691) *(P-16392)*

Forespar, Rcho Sta Marg *Also Called: Light Composite Corporation (P-4777)*

Forespar Products Corp .... D 949 858-8820
22322 Gilberto Rancho Santa Margari (92688) *(P-4767)*

Forest Home Inc .... C 909 389-2300
40000 Valley Of The Falls Dr Forest Falls (92339) *(P-13102)*

Forest Home Ministries, Forest Falls *Also Called: Forest Home Inc (P-13102)*

Forest Lawn Co .... C 818 241-4151
1712 S Glendale Ave Glendale (91205) *(P-12583)*

Forest Lawn Mem Parks Mortuary, Glendale *Also Called: Forest Lawn Memorial-Park Assn (P-11669)*

Forest Lawn Memorial-Park Assn (PA) .... B 323 254-3131
1712 S Glendale Ave Glendale (91205) *(P-11669)*

Forest Lawn Mortuary .... B 760 329-8737
66272 Pierson Blvd Desert Hot Springs (92240) *(P-13155)*

Forged Metals Inc .... C 909 350-9260
10685 Beech Ave Fontana (92337) *(P-5141)*

Forgiato, Sun Valley *Also Called: Forgiato Inc (P-7253)*

Forgiato Inc .... D 818 771-9779
11915 Wicks St Sun Valley (91352) *(P-7253)*

Foria International Inc .... C 626 912-8836
18689 Arenth Ave City Of Industry (91748) *(P-10684)*

Form Grind Corporation .... E 949 858-7000
30062 Aventura Rcho Sta Marg (92688) *(P-6124)*

Form Products, Rcho Sta Marg *Also Called: Form Grind Corporation (P-6124)*

Formed Lighting, Chatsworth *Also Called: Lf Illumination LLC (P-6466)*

Former Luna Subsidiary Inc (HQ) .... **D 805 987-0146**
Camarillo (93012) *(P-6824)*

Formerly Known As LLC .... D 310 551-3500
40 E Verdugo Ave Burbank (91502) *(P-13208)*

Formex LLC .... E 858 529-6600
9601 Jeronimo Rd Irvine (92618) *(P-3404)*

Formosa Meat Company Inc .... E 909 987-0470
10646 Fulton Ct Rancho Cucamonga (91730) *(P-1258)*

Forms and Surfaces Inc .... D 805 684-8626
6395 Cindy Ln Carpinteria (93013) *(P-5063)*

Mergent email: customerrelations@mergent.com
1028

2025 Southern California
Business Directory and Buyers Guide

(P-0000) Products & Services Section entry number
(PA)=Parent Co (HQ)=Headquarters (DH)=Div Headquarters

Forms and Surfaces Company LLC .... C 805 684-8626
  6395 Cindy Ln Carpinteria (93013) *(P-4391)*

Formula Plastics Inc .... B 866 307-1362
  451 Tecate Rd Ste 2b Tecate (91980) *(P-4119)*

Fornaca Inc (PA) .... C 866 308-9461
  2400 National City Blvd National City (91950) *(P-11444)*

Forrest Group LLC (PA) .... D 619 808-9798
  1422 N Curson Ave Apt 9 Los Angeles (90046) *(P-8755)*

Forrest Machining LLC .... C 661 257-0231
  27756 Avenue Mentry Valencia (91355) *(P-7479)*

Forrestmachining.com, Valencia Also Called: Forrest Machining LLC (P-7479)

Fort Hill Construction (PA) .... D 323 656-7425
  12711 Ventura Blvd Ste 390 Studio City (91604) *(P-404)*

Fortanasce & Associates, Murrieta Also Called: Michael G Frtnsce Physcl Thrap (P-15551)

Forterra Pipe & Precast LLC .... E 858 715-5600
  9229 Harris Plant Rd San Diego (92145) *(P-4392)*

Forterra Pipe & Precast LLC .... E 951 523-7039
  26380 Palomar Rd Sun City (92585) *(P-4393)*

Fortiss LLC .... C 323 415-4900
  888 Bicycle Casino Dr Bell Gardens (90201) *(P-15206)*

Fortitude Technology Inc .... D 858 974-5080
  8929 Complex Dr Ste A San Diego (92123) *(P-9433)*

Fortner Eng & Mfg Inc .... E 818 240-7740
  2927 N Ontario St Burbank (91504) *(P-6125)*

Fortress Inc .... E 909 593-8600
  1721 Wright Ave La Verne (91750) *(P-2509)*

Fortress Holding Group LLC .... D 714 202-8710
  5500 E Santa Ana Canyon Rd Ste 220 Anaheim (92807) *(P-12598)*

Fortuna Enterprises LP .... B 310 410-4000
  5711 W Century Blvd Los Angeles (90045) *(P-12826)*

Fortune Casuals LLC (PA) .... D 310 733-2100
  10119 Jefferson Blvd Culver City (90232) *(P-2035)*

Fortune Dynamic Inc .... D 909 979-8318
  21923 Ferrero City Of Industry (91789) *(P-10736)*

Fortune Manufacturing Inc .... E 909 591-1547
  13849 Magnolia Ave Chino (91710) *(P-6126)*

Fortune Swimwear LLC (HQ) .... E 310 733-2130
  2340 E Olympic Blvd Ste A Los Angeles (90021) *(P-1918)*

Forty-Niner Shops Inc .... A 562 985-5093
  6049 E 7th St Long Beach (90840) *(P-11632)*

Forward .... E 310 962-2522
  13020 Pacific Promenade Los Angeles (90094) *(P-5807)*

Forward Slope Incorporated (PA) .... D 619 299-4400
  2020 Camino Del Rio N Ste 400 San Diego (92108) *(P-17533)*

Forward Slope., San Diego Also Called: Forward Slope Incorporated (P-17533)

Foshay Electric Co Inc .... D 858 277-7676
  950 Industrial Blvd Chula Vista (91911) *(P-920)*

Foster Poultry Farms .... B 310 223-1499
  1805 N Santa Fe Ave Compton (90221) *(P-1277)*

FOSTER POULTRY FARMS, Compton Also Called: Foster Poultry Farms (P-1277)

Foster Print, Santa Ana Also Called: Blackburn Alton Invstments LLC (P-3120)

Fotis and Son Imports Inc (PA) .... E 714 894-9022
  15451 Electronic Ln Huntington Beach (92649) *(P-5671)*

Foto Kem Film & Video, Burbank Also Called: Foto-Kem Industries Inc (P-14892)

Foto-Kem Industries Inc (PA) .... C 818 846-3102
  2801 W Alameda Ave Burbank (91505) *(P-14892)*

Foundation 9 Entertainment Inc (PA) .... C 949 698-1500
  30211 Avenida De Las Bandera Ste 200 Rancho Santa Margari (92688) *(P-13933)*

Foundation Ai, Irvine Also Called: Foundation Inc (P-13934)

Foundation Building Materials, Santa Ana Also Called: Foundation Building Mtls Inc (P-9920)

Foundation Building Mtls Inc (HQ) .... B 714 380-3127
  2520 Redhill Ave Santa Ana (92705) *(P-9920)*

Foundation Inc .... E 310 294-8955
  19800 Macarthur Blvd Ste 300 Irvine (92612) *(P-13934)*

Foundation Laboratory, Pomona Also Called: Latara Enterprise Inc (P-16322)

Foundation Pile Inc .... D 909 350-1584
  8375 Almeria Ave Fontana (92335) *(P-712)*

Foundation Property MGT Inc .... C 562 257-5100
  911 N Studebaker Rd Ste 100 Long Beach (90815) *(P-18139)*

Foundry Service & Supplies Inc .... E 909 284-5000
  2029 S Parco Ave Ontario (91761) *(P-4502)*

Fountain Valley Post Acute, Fountain Valley Also Called: Pacs Group Inc (P-15745)

Fountain View Cnvalescent Hosp, Los Angeles Also Called: Genesis Healthcare LLC (P-15854)

Fountain Vly Rgnal Hosp Med CT .... A 714 966-7200
  17100 Euclid St Fountain Valley (92708) *(P-15999)*

Fountains At The Carlotta, The, Palm Desert Also Called: Watermark Rtrment Cmmnties Inc (P-15799)

Fountains At The Sea Bluffs, Dana Point Also Called: Watermark Rtrment Cmmnties Inc (P-12371)

Four Pnts By Shrton La Intl Ar, Los Angeles Also Called: Irp Lax Hotel LLC (P-12877)

Four Points Bakersfield, Bakersfield Also Called: Cni Thl Propco Fe LLC (P-12796)

Four Seasons Design Inc (PA) .... E 619 761-5151
  2451 Britannia Blvd San Diego (92154) *(P-2260)*

Four Seasons Hotel, Los Angeles Also Called: Burton-Way House Ltd A CA (P-12780)

Four Seasons Hotels Limited, Los Angeles Also Called: Burton Way Hotels LLC (P-12778)

Four Seasons Ht Westlake Vlg, Westlake Village Also Called: Burton Way Htels Ltd A Cal Ltd (P-12779)

Four Seasons Resort Aviara .... D 760 603-6900
  7447 Batiquitos Dr Carlsbad (92011) *(P-15080)*

Four Ssons Rsort Santa Barbara, Santa Barbara Also Called: 1260 Bb Property LLC (P-12750)

Four Star Chemical, Los Angeles Also Called: Starco Enterprises Inc (P-5720)

Four Wheel Parts Wholesalers, Compton Also Called: Transamerican Dissolution LLC (P-11471)

Foursquare International, Los Angeles Also Called: Interntnal Ch of Frsqare Gospl (P-17416)

Fourthfloor Fashion Talent, Los Angeles Also Called: Career Group Inc (P-13500)

Foutains Executive Course, Escondido Also Called: Welk Group Inc (P-15098)

Fovell Enterprises Inc .... E 951 734-6275
  1852 Pomona Rd Corona (92878) *(P-8605)*

Fox, Los Angeles Also Called: Twenteth Cntury Fox HM Entrmt (P-14922)

Fox, Los Angeles Also Called: Twentieth Cntury Fox Intl Corp (P-14924)

Fox Inc (DH) .... A 310 369-1000
  10201 W Pico Blvd Los Angeles (90064) *(P-9501)*

Fox Baseball Holdings Inc .... A 323 224-1500
  1000 Vin Scully Ave Los Angeles (90012) *(P-15025)*

Fox Broadcasting Company LLC (HQ) .... C 310 369-1000
  10201 W Pico Blvd Bldg 1003220 Los Angeles (90064) *(P-9502)*

Fox BSB Holdco Inc (HQ) .... C 323 224-1500
  1000 Vin Scully Ave Los Angeles (90012) *(P-15026)*

Fox Electronics, Laguna Hills Also Called: Fox Enterprises LLC (P-6998)

Fox Enterprises LLC (HQ) .... E 239 693-0099
  24422 Avenida De La Carlota Ste 290 Laguna Hills (92653) *(P-6998)*

Fox Family Channel, Burbank Also Called: International Fmly Entrmt Inc (P-9553)

Fox Films Entertainment, Los Angeles Also Called: Twentieth Cntury Fox Film Corp (P-14864)

Fox Head Inc (HQ) .... B 949 757-9500
  16752 Armstrong Ave Irvine (92606) *(P-10709)*

Fox Hills Auto Inc (PA) .... C 310 649-3673
  5880 W Centinela Ave Los Angeles (90045) *(P-11351)*

Fox Interactive Media Inc .... C 310 969-7000
  6100 Center Dr Ste 800 Los Angeles (90045) *(P-9434)*

Fox Net Inc .... A 310 369-1000
  10201 W Pico Blvd Los Angeles (90064) *(P-14829)*

Fox Network Center, Los Angeles Also Called: Disney Networks Group LLC (P-9497)

Fox Racing, Irvine Also Called: Fox Head Inc (P-10709)

Fox Rent A Car Inc .... D 909 635-6390
  1776 E Holt Blvd Ontario (91761) *(P-14645)*

Fox Rent A Car Inc .... C 310 342-5155
  5500 W Century Blvd Los Angeles (90045) *(P-14646)*

Fox Rent A Car Inc .... D 310 342-5155
  325 Baker St Costa Mesa (92626) *(P-14647)*

Fox Sports Inc (DH) .... C 310 369-1000
  10201 W Pico Blvd Los Angeles (90035) *(P-9503)*

Fox Television Center, Los Angeles Also Called: Fox Television Stations Inc (P-9504)

Fox Television Stations Inc (HQ) .... B 310 584-2000
  1999 S Bundy Dr Los Angeles (90025) *(P-9504)*

Fox Transportation Inc (PA) .... D 909 291-4646
  8610 Helms Ave Rancho Cucamonga (91730) *(P-8905)*

Fox Transportation Inc .... C 310 971-0867
  18408 S Laurel Park Rd Compton (90220) *(P-8992)*

Employee Codes: A=Over 500 employees, B=251-500
C=101-250, D=51-100, E=20-50, F=10-19, G=1-9

2025 Southern California
Business Directory and Buyers Guide

© Mergent Inc. 1-800-342-5647
1029

A
L
P
H
A
B
E
T
I
C

Fox US Productions 27 Inc .... A 310 727-2550
1600 Rosecrans Ave Bldg 5a Manhattan Beach (90266) *(P-9505)*

Foxen Canyon Winery & Vineyard, Santa Maria *Also Called: Foxen Vineyard Inc (P-1572)*

Foxen Vineyard Inc .... E 805 937-4251
7600 Foxen Canyon Rd Santa Maria (93454) *(P-1572)*

Foxfury Lighting Solution, Oceanside *Also Called: Foxfury LLC (P-6502)*

Foxfury LLC .... E 760 945-4231
3544 Seagate Way Oceanside (92056) *(P-6502)*

Foxlink International Inc (HQ) .... E 714 256-1777
3010 Saturn St Ste 200 Brea (92821) *(P-6419)*

Fpc Inc .... E 323 468-5778
1017 N Las Palmas Ave Los Angeles (90038) *(P-8428)*

Fpk Investigaions, Valencia *Also Called: Fpk Security Inc (P-14300)*

Fpk Security Inc .... B 661 702-9091
28348 Constellation Rd Ste 880 Valencia (91355) *(P-14300)*

Fragile Handle With Care, San Diego *Also Called: Chandler Packaging A Transpak Company (P-9353)*

Fralock, Valencia *Also Called: Lockwood Industries LLC (P-6846)*

Frameless Hardware Company LLC .... E 888 295-4531
4361 Firestone Blvd South Gate (90280) *(P-4768)*

Frametent Inc .... E 661 290-3375
26480 Summit Cir Santa Clarita (91350) *(P-2238)*

FRANK D LANTERMAN REGIONAL CEN, Los Angeles *Also Called: Los Angles Cnty Dvlpmntal Svcs (P-16583)*

Frank S Smith Masonry Inc .... D 909 468-0525
2830 Pomona Blvd Pomona (91768) *(P-982)*

Frank Toyata & Scion, National City *Also Called: Fornaca Inc (P-11444)*

Frankies Bikinis, Venice *Also Called: Frankies Bikinis LLC (P-2169)*

Frankies Bikinis LLC .... E 323 354-4133
4030 Del Rey Ave Venice (90292) *(P-2169)*

FRANKLIN WIRELESS, San Diego *Also Called: Franklin Wireless Corp (P-6585)*

Franklin Wireless Corp .... D 858 623-0000
3940 Ruffin Rd Ste C San Diego (92123) *(P-6585)*

Franklins Inds San Diego Inc .... E 858 486-9399
12135 Dearborn Pl Poway (92064) *(P-6127)*

Franz Family Bakeries, Los Angeles *Also Called: United States Bakery (P-1468)*

Frazee Industries Inc .... A 858 626-3600
6625 Miramar Rd San Diego (92121) *(P-3714)*

Frazee Paint & Wallcovering, San Diego *Also Called: Frazee Industries Inc (P-3714)*

Frazier Aviation Inc .... E 818 898-1998
445 N Fox St San Fernando (91340) *(P-7480)*

Fred M Boerner Motor Co (PA)................. D 323 560-3882
3620 E Florence Ave Huntington Park (90255) *(P-11445)*

Fred R Rippy Inc .... E 562 698-9801
12450 Whittier Blvd Whittier (90602) *(P-5187)*

Freddie Mac, Los Angeles *Also Called: Federal Home Loan Mrtg Corp (P-11903)*

Frederick Pump Company, Valley Center *Also Called: Brax Company Inc (P-1142)*

Fredericka Manor Care Center, Chula Vista *Also Called: Front Porch Communities & Svcs (P-15658)*

FREDERICKA MANOR CARE CENTER, Glendale *Also Called: Front Prch Cmmnties Oprting Gr (P-15853)*

Fredericks.com, Los Angeles *Also Called: Foh Group Inc (P-2154)*

Fredericksburg Convention Ctr, Los Angeles *Also Called: Ovg Facilities LLC (P-18027)*

Free Conferencing Corporation .... C 562 437-1411
4300 E Pacific Coast Hwy Long Beach (90804) *(P-9435)*

Freeberg Indus Fbrication Corp .... D 760 737-7614
2874 Progress Pl Escondido (92029) *(P-4836)*

Freeberg Industrial, Escondido *Also Called: Freeberg Indus Fbrication Corp (P-4836)*

Freeconferencecall.com, Long Beach *Also Called: Free Conferencing Corporation (P-9435)*

Freedom Communications Inc .... A 714 796-7000
625 N Grand Ave Santa Ana (92701) *(P-2797)*

Freedom Designs Inc .... C 805 582-0077
2241 N Madera Rd Simi Valley (93065) *(P-8268)*

Freedom Forever, Temecula *Also Called: Freedom Forever LLC (P-779)*

Freedom Forever, Temecula *Also Called: Freedom Solar Services (P-780)*

Freedom Forever LLC (PA).........................D 888 557-6431
43445 Business Park Dr Ste 104 Temecula (92590) *(P-779)*

Freedom Newspapers, Santa Ana *Also Called: Freedom Communications Inc (P-2797)*

Freedom Photonics LLC .... E 805 967-4900
41 Aero Camino Santa Barbara (93117) *(P-7123)*

Freedom Prfmce Exhaust Inc .... E 951 898-4733
1255 Railroad St Corona (92882) *(P-11446)*

Freedom Properties, Hemet *Also Called: Casa-Pacifica Inc (P-17128)*

Freedom Properties Village, Hemet *Also Called: Casa-Pacifica Inc (P-17129)*

Freedom Properties-Hemet LLC .... C 949 489-0430
27122b Paseo Espada Ste 1024 San Juan Capistrano (92675) *(P-12293)*

Freedom Solar Services .... C 888 557-6431
43445 Business Park Dr Ste 110 Temecula (92590) *(P-780)*

Freedom Village Healthcare Ctr .... C 949 472-4733
23442 El Toro Rd Bldg 2 Lake Forest (92630) *(P-15657)*

Freeman, Anaheim *Also Called: Freeman Expositions LLC (P-14497)*

Freeman Company, Anaheim *Also Called: Freeman Expositions LLC (P-14498)*

Freeman Expositions LLC .... C 714 254-3400
2170 S Towne Centre Pl Ste 100 Anaheim (92806) *(P-14497)*

Freeman Expositions LLC .... C 858 320-7800
2170 S Towne Centre Pl Ste 100 Anaheim (92806) *(P-14498)*

Freeport-Mcmoran Oil & Gas LLC .... C 661 322-7600
1200 Discovery Dr Ste 500 Bakersfield (93309) *(P-303)*

Freeport-Mcmoran Oil & Gas LLC .... D 323 298-2200
5640 S Fairfax Ave Los Angeles (90056) *(P-304)*

Freeport-Mcmoran Oil & Gas LLC .... E 805 567-1601
760 W Hueneme Rd Oxnard (93033) *(P-305)*

Freestyle, Santa Fe Springs *Also Called: Freestyle Sales Co Ltd Partnr (P-11647)*

Freestyle Sales Co Ltd Partnr .... D 323 660-3460
12231 Florence Ave Santa Fe Springs (90670) *(P-11647)*

Freeway Insurance (PA)............................ C 714 252-2500
7711 Center Ave Ste 200 Huntington Beach (92647) *(P-12215)*

Freightgate Inc .... E 714 799-2833
10055 Slater Ave Ste 231 Fountain Valley (92708) *(P-13935)*

Fremantle Media, Burbank *Also Called: Prdctions N Fremantle Amer Inc (P-14971)*

Fremarc Designs, City Of Industry *Also Called: Fremarc Industries Inc (P-2424)*

Fremarc Industries Inc (PA) .... D 626 965-0802
18810 San Jose Ave City Of Industry (91748) *(P-2424)*

Fremont Office, Irvine *Also Called: Western Digital Corporation (P-5893)*

French Hospital Medical Center (DH) .... B 805 543-5353
1911 Johnson Ave San Luis Obispo (93401) *(P-16000)*

Fresgo LLC .... D 626 389-3500
55 S Madison Ave Pasadena (91101) *(P-8906)*

Fresh & Ready, San Fernando *Also Called: Lehman Foods Inc (P-1806)*

Fresh & Ready Foods LLC (PA) .... D 818 837-7600
1145 Arroyo St Ste B San Fernando (91340) *(P-1777)*

Fresh Griller, Costa Mesa *Also Called: Fgr 1 LLC (P-11570)*

Fresh Start Bakeries, Ontario *Also Called: Aspire Bakeries LLC (P-10928)*

Fresh Start Bakeries Inc .... A 714 256-8900
145 S State College Blvd Ste 200 Brea (92821) *(P-1451)*

Fresh Start Bakeries N Amer, Brea *Also Called: Fresh Start Bakeries Inc (P-1451)*

Fresh Venture Farms LLC .... D 805 754-4449
1181 S Wolff Rd Oxnard (93033) *(P-10)*

Fresh Venture Foods LLC .... C 805 928-3374
1205 Craig Dr Santa Maria (93458) *(P-5672)*

Freshpoint Inc .... C 626 855-1400
155 N Orange Ave City Of Industry (91744) *(P-10898)*

Freshpoint Las Vegas, City Of Industry *Also Called: Freshpoint Inc (P-10898)*

Freshpoint Southern Cal Inc .... C 626 855-1400
155 N Orange Ave City Of Industry (91744) *(P-10899)*

Freshpoint Southern California, City Of Industry *Also Called: Freshpoint Southern Cal Inc (P-10899)*

Freshrealm Inc (PA).................................. C 800 264-1297
1330 Calle Avanzado San Clemente (92673) *(P-1778)*

Freshway Farms LLC .... C 805 349-7170
2165 W Main St Santa Maria (93458) *(P-18)*

Freudenberg Medical LLC .... C 626 814-9684
5050 Rivergrade Rd Baldwin Park (91706) *(P-8154)*

Freudenberg Medical LLC .... D 805 576-5308
6385 Rose Ln Ste A Carpinteria (93013) *(P-8269)*

Freudenberg Medical LLC .... E 805 684-3304
1009 Cindy Ln Carpinteria (93013) *(P-8270)*

Freudenberg Medical LLC (DH).................. C 805 684-3304
1110 Mark Ave Carpinteria (93013) *(P-8271)*

Freudenberg-Nok General Partnr .... C 714 834-0602
2041 E Wilshire Ave Santa Ana (92705) *(P-3887)*

Mergent email: customerrelations@mergent.com
1030

2025 Southern California
Business Directory and Buyers Guide

(P-0000) Products & Services Section entry number
(PA)=Parent Co (HQ)=Headquarters (DH)=Div Headquarters

Freund Baking, Los Angeles *Also Called: Oakhurst Industries Inc (P-10967)*

Frick Paper Company LLC .... C 714 787-4900
2164 N Batavia St Orange (92865) *(P-10592)*

Friedas Inc .... D 714 826-6100
1765 W Penhall Way Anaheim (92801) *(P-10900)*

Friedas Specialty Produce, Anaheim *Also Called: Friedas Inc (P-10900)*

Friendly Hlls Cntry CLB Fndtio .... C 562 698-0331
8500 Villaverde Dr Whittier (90605) *(P-15136)*

Friends Group Express Inc .... D 909 346-6814
14520 Village Dr Apt 1013 Fontana (92337) *(P-8952)*

Friends of Cultural Center Inc .... D 760 346-6505
73000 Fred Waring Dr Palm Desert (92260) *(P-14960)*

Fringe Studio LLC .... E 310 390-9900
6029 W Slauson Ave Culver City (90230) *(P-2624)*

Frisco Baking Company, Los Angeles *Also Called: Frisco Baking Company Inc (P-1452)*

Frisco Baking Company Inc .... C 323 225-6111
621 W Avenue 26 Los Angeles (90065) *(P-1452)*

Frito-Lay, Bakersfield *Also Called: Frito-Lay North America Inc (P-10846)*

Frito-Lay, Rancho Cucamonga *Also Called: Frito-Lay North America Inc (P-10847)*

Frito-Lay, Rancho Cucamonga *Also Called: Frito-Lay North America Inc (P-10848)*

Frito-Lay North America Inc .... C 661 328-6034
28801 Highway 58 Bakersfield (93314) *(P-10846)*

Frito-Lay North America Inc .... E 909 941-6218
9846 4th St Rancho Cucamonga (91730) *(P-10847)*

Frito-Lay North America Inc .... B 909 941-6214
9535 Archibald Ave Rancho Cucamonga (91730) *(P-10848)*

Frize Corporation .... D 800 834-2127
16605 Gale Ave City Of Industry (91745) *(P-480)*

Front Line MGT Group Inc .... D 310 209-3100
1100 Glendon Ave Ste 2000 Los Angeles (90024) *(P-17986)*

Front Porch Communities & Svcs .... C 858 454-2151
849 Coast Blvd La Jolla (92037) *(P-12342)*

Front Porch Communities & Svcs .... C 619 427-2777
111 Third Ave Chula Vista (91910) *(P-15658)*

Front Porch Communities & Svcs .... C 805 687-0793
3775 Modoc Rd Santa Barbara (93105) *(P-15852)*

Front Porch Communities & Svcs .... C 760 729-4983
2855 Carlsbad Blvd Carlsbad (92008) *(P-17154)*

Front Porch Communities & Svcs .... C 323 661-1128
1055 N Kingsley Dr Los Angeles (90029) *(P-17155)*

Front Prch Cmmnties Oprting Gr .... C 800 233-3709
800 N Brand Blvd Fl 19 Glendale (91203) *(P-15853)*

Frontech N Fujitsu Amer Inc (DH) .... C 877 766-7545
36 Technology Dr Ste 150 Irvine (92618) *(P-13733)*

Frontier California Inc .... B 818 365-0542
510 Park Ave San Fernando (91340) *(P-9436)*

Frontier California Inc .... B 760 342-0500
83793 Doctor Carreon Blvd Indio (92201) *(P-9437)*

Frontier California Inc .... B 805 372-6000
1 Wellpoint Way Westlake Village (91362) *(P-9438)*

Frontier California Inc .... B 805 925-0000
200 W Church St Santa Maria (93458) *(P-9439)*

Frontier California Inc .... B 714 375-6713
7352 Slater Ave Huntington Beach (92647) *(P-9440)*

Frontier Engrg & Mfg Tech Inc (PA) .... E 310 767-1227
800 W 16th St Long Beach (90813) *(P-6128)*

Frontier Logistics Services, Gardena *Also Called: F R T International Inc (P-9064)*

Frontier Logistics Services, Compton *Also Called: F R T International Inc (P-9065)*

Frontier Logistics Services, Ontario *Also Called: F R T International Inc (P-9281)*

Frontier Mechanical Inc .... D 661 589-6203
6309 Seven Seas Ave Bakersfield (93308) *(P-781)*

Frontier Plumbing, Bakersfield *Also Called: Frontier Mechanical Inc (P-781)*

Frontier Technologies, Long Beach *Also Called: Frontier Engrg & Mfg Tech Inc (P-6128)*

Frontier-Kemper Constructors Inc (HQ) .... D 818 362-2062
15900 Olden St Rancho Cascades (91342) *(P-713)*

Frontwave Credit Union (PA) .... C 760 430-7511
1278 Rocky Point Dr Oceanside (92056) *(P-11801)*

Frozen Bean Inc .... E 855 837-6936
9238 Bally Ct Rancho Cucamonga (91730) *(P-1681)*

Fruit Growers Supply Company (PA) .... E 888 997-4855
27770 Entertainment Dr Ste 120 Valencia (91355) *(P-2666)*

Fruit Growers Supply Company .... D 909 390-0190
225 S Wineville Ave Ontario (91761) *(P-10901)*

Fruth Custom Plastics Inc .... D 714 993-9955
701 Richfield Rd Placentia (92870) *(P-4120)*

Fry Reglet Corporation (PA) .... D 800 237-9773
14013 Marquardt Ave Santa Fe Springs (90670) *(P-4596)*

Fry Steel Company .... C 562 802-2721
13325 Molette St Santa Fe Springs (90670) *(P-10136)*

Fryman Management Inc .... D 949 481-5211
18 Goodyear Ste 105 Irvine (92618) *(P-18309)*

Fs - Precision Tech Co LLC .... D 310 638-0595
3025 E Victoria St Compton (90221) *(P-4689)*

FS Commercial Landscape Inc (PA) .... D 951 360-7070
5151 Pedley Rd Riverside (92509) *(P-169)*

Fsc, Rancho Cucamonga *Also Called: Fluorescent Supply Co Inc (P-6460)*

FSI Coating Technologies Inc .... E 949 540-1140
45 Parker Ste 100 Irvine (92618) *(P-3715)*

Fssi, Santa Ana *Also Called: Financial Statement Svcs Inc (P-13302)*

Ft 2 Inc .... C 714 765-5555
1211 N Miller St Anaheim (92806) *(P-10561)*

Ft Textiles, Fullerton *Also Called: Fabtex Inc (P-1894)*

Ft3 Tactical, Stanton *Also Called: Field Time Target Training LLC (P-5354)*

Ftdi West Inc .... D 909 473-1111
3375 Enterprise Dr Bloomington (92316) *(P-9068)*

Ftg Aerospace Inc (DH) .... E 818 407-4024
20740 Marilla St Chatsworth (91311) *(P-4660)*

Ftg Circuits Inc (DH) .... D 818 407-4024
20750 Marilla St Chatsworth (91311) *(P-6730)*

Fti Consulting Inc .... D 213 689-1200
350 S Grand Ave Ste 3000 Los Angeles (90071) *(P-17534)*

Ftr Associates Inc .... E 562 945-7504
11862 Burke St Santa Fe Springs (90670) *(P-5188)*

Ftsi, Monrovia *Also Called: Financial Tech Sltons Intl Inc (P-18136)*

Fuel50, Laguna Niguel *Also Called: Career Engagement Group LLC (P-13682)*

Fueling and Service Tech Inc .... D 714 523-0194
7050 Village Dr Ste D Buena Park (90621) *(P-10374)*

Fuji Food Products Inc (PA) .... D 562 404-2590
14420 Bloomfield Ave Santa Fe Springs (90670) *(P-1779)*

Fuji Food Products Inc .... C 619 268-3118
8660 Miramar Rd Ste N San Diego (92126) *(P-1780)*

Fuji Natural Foods Inc (HQ) .... D 909 947-1008
13500 S Hamner Ave Ontario (91761) *(P-1781)*

Fujifilm Dsynth Btchnlgies Cal .... E 914 789-8100
2430 Conejo Spectrum St Thousand Oaks (91320) *(P-3573)*

Fujifilm Dsynth Btchnlgies USA .... C 805 699-5579
2430 Conejo Spectrum St Thousand Oaks (91320) *(P-3574)*

Fujifilm Irvine Scientific Inc (DH) .... E 949 261-7800
1830 E Warner Ave Santa Ana (92705) *(P-3575)*

Fujifilm Rcrding Media USA Inc .... D 310 536-0800
6200 Phyllis Dr Cypress (90630) *(P-8429)*

Fujitec America Inc .... C 310 464-8270
12170 Mora Dr Ste 1 Santa Fe Springs (90670) *(P-17987)*

Fulcrum Microsystems Inc .... D 818 871-8100
26630 Agoura Rd Calabasas (91302) *(P-6825)*

Fulgent Genetics Inc .... A 626 350-0537
4373 Santa Anita Ave El Monte (91731) *(P-9069)*

Fulgent Receiving, El Monte *Also Called: Fulgent Genetics Inc (P-9069)*

Fulham Co Inc .... E 323 779-2980
12705 S Van Ness Ave Hawthorne (90250) *(P-6285)*

Full Scale Logistics LLC .... D 805 279-6799
2722 Rocky Point Ct Thousand Oaks (91362) *(P-9364)*

Full Stack Finance .... D 800 941-0356
2701 Ocean Park Blvd Ste 210 Santa Monica (90405) *(P-12706)*

Full-Swing Golf Inc .... E 858 675-1100
1905 Aston Ave Ste 100 Carlsbad (92008) *(P-10513)*

Fulldeck, Los Angeles *Also Called: SD&a Teleservices Inc (P-14591)*

Fullerton College Bookstore, Fullerton *Also Called: North Ornge Cnty Cmnty Cllege (P-11633)*

Fullerton Hlthcare Wllness CNT .... C 714 992-5701
2222 N Harbor Blvd Fullerton (92835) *(P-15659)*

Fullmer Construction .... C 909 947-9467
1725 S Grove Ave Ontario (91761) *(P-481)*

Employee Codes: A=Over 500 employees, B=251-500
C=101-250, D=51-100, E=20-50, F=10-19, G=1-9

2025 Southern California
Business Directory and Buyers Guide

© Mergent Inc. 1-800-342-5647

1031

Fulwider and Patton LLP .... D 310 824-5555
111 W Ocean Blvd Ste 1510 Long Beach (90802) *(P-16685)*

Fun Furnishings, Rancho Cucamonga *Also Called: G & M Mattress and Foam Corporation*
(P-2483)

Fun Properties Inc .... D 310 787-4500
2645 Maricopa St Torrance (90503) *(P-4739)*

Funai Corporation Inc (DH) .... E 310 787-3000
12489 Lakeland Rd Santa Fe Springs (90670) *(P-6537)*

Funai Corporation Inc .... D 201 727-4560
19900 Van Ness Ave Torrance (90501) *(P-6538)*

Funai Electric Co., Torrance *Also Called: Funai Corporation Inc (P-6538)*

Fundamental Tech Intl Inc .... E 562 595-0661
2900 E 29th St Long Beach (90806) *(P-7858)*

Funimation Entertainment, Culver City *Also Called: Crunchyroll LLC (P-14817)*

Funnelcloudsales .... D 661 284-6032
21758 Placeritos Blvd Santa Clarita (91321) *(P-9003)*

Furniture America Cal Inc (PA) .... E 866 923-8500
680 S Lemon Ave City Of Industry (91789) *(P-9871)*

Furniture Factory Holding LLC (HQ) .... C 918 427-0241
11111 Santa Monica Blvd Los Angeles (90025) *(P-14499)*

Furniture of America, City Of Industry *Also Called: Furniture America Cal Inc (P-9871)*

Furniture Technics Inc .... E 562 802-0261
2900 Supply Ave Commerce (90040) *(P-2425)*

Furniture Techniques, Commerce *Also Called: Furniture Technics Inc (P-2425)*

Furniture Technologies Inc .... E 760 246-9180
17227 Columbus St Adelanto (92301) *(P-2288)*

Furst, Marina Del Rey *Also Called: Lf Sportswear Inc (P-2046)*

Fuscoe Engineering Inc (PA) .... D 949 474-1960
15535 Sand Canyon Ave Irvine (92618) *(P-17535)*

Fusefx, North Hollywood *Also Called: Fusefx LLC (P-14893)*

Fusefx LLC .... B 818 237-5052
5161 Lankershim Blvd North Hollywood (91601) *(P-14893)*

Fusion Biotec LLC .... E 949 264-3437
160 S Cypress St Ste 400 Orange (92866) *(P-8155)*

Fusion Product Mfg Inc .... D 619 819-5521
24024 Humphries Rd Bldg 1 Tecate (91980) *(P-5581)*

Fusion Sign & Design Inc .... E 562 946-7545
12226 Coast Dr Whittier (90601) *(P-8606)*

Fusionzone Automotive Inc .... C 888 576-1136
1011 Swarthmore Ave Ste T-10 Pacific Palisades (90272) *(P-14219)*

Futek Advanced Sensor Tech, Irvine *Also Called: Futek Advanced Sensor Tech Inc (P-7859)*

Futek Advanced Sensor Tech Inc .... C 949 465-0900
10 Thomas Irvine (92618) *(P-7859)*

Future Commodities Intl Inc .... E 888 588-2378
1425 S Campus Ave Ontario (91761) *(P-5789)*

Future Energy Corporation .... D 760 477-9700
4120 Avenida De La Plata Oceanside (92056) *(P-1009)*

Future Foam, Fullerton *Also Called: Future Foam Inc (P-4005)*

Future Foam Inc .... E 714 871-2344
2451 Cypress Way Fullerton (92831) *(P-4004)*

Future Foam Inc .... C 714 459-9971
2441 Cypress Way Fullerton (92831) *(P-4005)*

Futuristics Machine Inc .... E 858 450-0644
7014 Carroll Rd San Diego (92121) *(P-6129)*

Fvo Solutions Inc .... D 626 449-0218
789 N Fair Oaks Ave Pasadena (91103) *(P-5321)*

Fx Networks LLC .... C 310 369-1000
10201 W Pico Blvd Bldg 103 Los Angeles (90064) *(P-9550)*

Fxc Corporation .... D 714 557-8032
3050 Red Hill Ave Costa Mesa (92626) *(P-2277)*

Fxp Technologies, Brea *Also Called: S&B Industry Inc (P-4233)*

Fziomed Inc (PA) .... E 805 546-0610
231 Bonetti Dr San Luis Obispo (93401) *(P-8156)*

G - L Veneer Co Inc (PA) .... D 323 582-5203
2224 E Slauson Ave Huntington Park (90255) *(P-2369)*

G & G Door Products Inc .... E 714 228-2008
7600 Stage Rd Buena Park (90621) *(P-11154)*

G & G Quality Case Co Inc .... D 323 233-2482
2025 E 25th St Vernon (90058) *(P-4293)*

G & I Industries, Baldwin Park *Also Called: G & I Islas Industries Inc (P-5673)*

G & I Islas Industries Inc (PA) .... E 626 960-5020
12860 Schabarum Ave Baldwin Park (91706) *(P-5673)*

G & M Mattress and Foam Corporation .... D 909 593-1000
10606 7th St Rancho Cucamonga (91730) *(P-2483)*

G A Systems, Orange *Also Called: SA Serving Lines Inc (P-5032)*

G B Remanufacturing Inc .... D 562 272-7333
2040 E Cherry Industrial Cir Long Beach (90805) *(P-4121)*

G C Pallets Inc .... E 909 357-8515
5490 26th St Riverside (92509) *(P-2388)*

G E Aviation, Victorville *Also Called: General Electric Company (P-7354)*

G F I, Vernon *Also Called: Good Fellas Industries Inc (P-11531)*

G Girl Clothing, Vernon *Also Called: LAT LLC (P-2116)*

G Global Alpha, San Diego *Also Called: G-Global Inc (P-9826)*

G Kagan and Sons Inc (PA) .... E 323 583-1400
3957 S Hill St Los Angeles (90037) *(P-1880)*

G M I, Anaheim *Also Called: Gear Manufacturing Inc (P-7481)*

G M I, San Diego *Also Called: Guard Management Inc (P-14304)*

G M S, Carlsbad *Also Called: Global Microwave Systems Inc (P-6617)*

G M S, Rancho Cucamonga *Also Called: General Micro Systems Inc (P-10006)*

G P H Medical Services, Beverly Hills *Also Called: GPh Medical & Legal Services (P-15668)*

G P Resources, Compton *Also Called: General Petroleum LLC (P-11032)*

G P S, Taft *Also Called: General Production Svc Cal Inc (P-672)*

G R C, Chatsworth *Also Called: General Ribbon Corp (P-8563)*

G R Leonard & Co Inc .... E 847 797-8101
181 N Vermont Ave Glendora (91741) *(P-2916)*

G S N, Santa Monica *Also Called: Game Show Network Music LLC (P-9551)*

G S T, Cerritos *Also Called: Golden Star Technology Inc (P-11540)*

G T C, Whittier *Also Called: General Transistor Corporation (P-10245)*

G Tech Construction .... C 858 224-2909
1291 Simpson Way Escondido (92029) *(P-447)*

G V Industries Inc .... E 619 474-3013
1346 Cleveland Ave National City (91950) *(P-6130)*

G W Surfaces (PA) .... D 805 642-5004
2432 Palma Dr Ventura (93003) *(P-1206)*

G-2 Graphic Service Inc .... D 818 623-3100
5510 Cleon Ave North Hollywood (91601) *(P-3139)*

G-G Distribution & Dev Co Inc .... C 661 257-5700
28545 Livingston Ave Valencia (91355) *(P-5387)*

G-Global Inc (PA) .... C 619 661-6292
2695 Customhouse Ct San Diego (92154) *(P-9826)*

G-M Enterprises, Corona *Also Called: Jhawar Industries LLC (P-5801)*

G/G Industries, Valencia *Also Called: G-G Distribution & Dev Co Inc (P-5387)*

G/M Business Interiors, San Diego *Also Called: Goforth & Marti (P-9872)*

G/M Business Interiors, Riverside *Also Called: Goforth & Marti (P-9873)*

G&L Penasquitos Inc .... A 858 538-0802
10584 Rancho Carmel Dr San Diego (92128) *(P-16946)*

G2 Software Systems Inc .... C 619 222-8025
4025 Hancock St Ste 105 San Diego (92110) *(P-13734)*

G4s Government Services, Anaheim *Also Called: G4s Justice Services LLC (P-14401)*

G4s Justice Services LLC .... D 800 589-6003
1290 N Hancock St Ste 103 Anaheim (92807) *(P-14401)*

GA Gertmenian and Sons LLC (PA) .... C 213 250-7777
300 W Avenue 33 Los Angeles (90031) *(P-9894)*

Ga-Asi, Poway *Also Called: General Atmics Arntcal Systems (P-7349)*

Gable House Inc .... D 310 378-2265
1611 S Pacific Coast Hwy Ste 306 Redondo Beach (90277) *(P-15011)*

Gable House Bowl, Redondo Beach *Also Called: Gable House Inc (P-15011)*

Gabriel Container (PA) .... C 562 699-1051
8844 Millergrove Dr Santa Fe Springs (90670) *(P-2667)*

GAF Materials, Shafter *Also Called: Standard Bldg Solutions Inc (P-1097)*

Gaffoglio Fmly Mtlcrafters Inc (PA) .... C 714 444-2000
11161 Slater Ave Fountain Valley (92708) *(P-4333)*

Gaikai Inc .... D
65 Enterprise Aliso Viejo (92656) *(P-13936)*

Gail Materials Inc .... E 951 667-6106
10060 Dawson Canyon Rd Corona (92883) *(P-375)*

Gaines Manufacturing Inc .... E 858 486-7100
12200 Kirkham Rd Poway (92064) *(P-4988)*

Mergent email: customerrelations@mergent.com
1032

2025 Southern California
Business Directory and Buyers Guide

(P-0000) Products & Services Section entry number
(PA)=Parent Co (HQ)=Headquarters (DH)=Div Headquarters

Gaju Market, Los Angeles *Also Called: Gaju Market Corporation (P-11121)*

Gaju Market Corporation .... C 213 382-9444
450 S Western Ave Los Angeles (90020) *(P-11121)*

Galassos Bakery (PA) .... C 951 360-1211
10820 San Sevaine Way Mira Loma (91752) *(P-1453)*

Galaxy Bearing Company, Valencia *Also Called: Galaxy Die and Engineering Inc (P-4680)*

Galaxy Die and Engineering Inc .... E 661 775-9301
24910 Avenue Tibbitts Valencia (91355) *(P-4680)*

Gale Banks Engineering .... C 626 969-9600
546 S Duggan Ave Azusa (91702) *(P-5468)*

Gale/Triangle Inc (PA) .... D 562 741-1300
12816 Shoemaker Ave Santa Fe Springs (90670) *(P-8907)*

Gallagher Rental Inc .... E 714 690-1559
15701 Heron Ave La Mirada (90638) *(P-6503)*

Gallegos United, Huntington Beach *Also Called: Grupo Gallegos (P-13210)*

Galleher, Santa Fe Springs *Also Called: Galleher LLC (P-9895)*

Galleher LLC (PA) .... C 562 944-8885
9303 Greenleaf Ave Santa Fe Springs (90670) *(P-9895)*

Gallo Vineyards Inc .... C 209 394-6281
5595 Creston Rd Paso Robles (93446) *(P-1573)*

Galpin Ford, North Hills *Also Called: Galpin Motors Inc (P-11352)*

Galpin Motors Inc (PA) .... B 818 787-3800
15505 Roscoe Blvd North Hills (91343) *(P-11352)*

Galpin Motors Inc .... D 323 957-3333
1763 Ivar Ave Los Angeles (90028) *(P-14648)*

Galt, San Diego *Also Called: Global A Lgistics Training Inc (P-7722)*

Gama Contracting Services Inc .... C 626 442-7200
1835 Floradale Ave South El Monte (91733) *(P-10347)*

Gambol Industries Inc .... E 562 901-2470
1880 Century Park E Ste 950 Los Angeles (90067) *(P-7620)*

Gamco, North Hollywood *Also Called: Bobrick Washroom Equipment Inc (P-2577)*

Game Show Network Music LLC (DH) .... C 310 255-6800
2150 Colorado Ave Ste 100 Santa Monica (90404) *(P-9551)*

Gameday Mens Health Llc .... D 858 252-9202
2753 Jefferson St Ste 204 Carlsbad (92008) *(P-16561)*

Gamemine LLC .... E 310 310-3105
439 Carroll Canal Venice (90291) *(P-13937)*

Gameworks Entertainment LLC (PA) .... A 206 521-0952
9737 Lurline Ave Chatsworth (91311) *(P-11573)*

Gamma, Vernon *Also Called: Rotax Incorporated (P-2130)*

Gamma Aerospace LLC .... E 310 532-1480
1461 S Balboa Ave Ontario (91761) *(P-6131)*

Gamma Scientific Inc .... E 858 635-9008
9925 Carroll Canyon Rd San Diego (92131) *(P-8043)*

Gan, Irvine *Also Called: Gan Limited (P-13735)*

Gan Limited (PA) .... A 833 565-0550
400 Spectrum Center Dr Ste 1900 Irvine (92618) *(P-13735)*

Ganahl Lumber Company .... D 951 278-4000
150 W Blaine St Corona (92878) *(P-11155)*

Gans Digital, Los Angeles *Also Called: Gans Ink and Supply Co Inc (P-3784)*

Gans Ink and Supply Co Inc (PA) .... E 323 264 2200
1441 Boyd St Los Angeles (90033) *(P-3784)*

Gantner Instruments Inc .... E 888 512-5788
402 W Broadway Ste 400 San Diego (92101) *(P-8044)*

Ganz USA LLC .... D 818 901-0077
16525 Sherman Way Ste C5 Van Nuys (91406) *(P-18140)*

Gar Enterprises .... E 909 985-4575
1396 W 9th St Upland (91786) *(P-6999)*

Gar Enterprises (PA) .... D 626 574-1175
418 E Live Oak Ave Arcadia (91006) *(P-10004)*

Gar Laboratories Inc .... C 951 788-0700
1844 Massachusetts Ave Riverside (92507) *(P-3652)*

Garage Team Mazda, Costa Mesa *Also Called: Team Garage LLC (P-13249)*

Garda CL West Inc (HQ) .... B 213 383-3611
1612 W Pico Blvd Los Angeles (90015) *(P-14301)*

Gardaworld .... D 909 468-2229
20325 E Walnut Dr N City Of Industry (91789) *(P-14302)*

Garden Crest Cnvlscent Hosp In .... D 323 663-8281
909 Lucile Ave Los Angeles (90026) *(P-15660)*

GARDEN CREST RETIREMENT RESIDE, Los Angeles *Also Called: Garden Crest Cnvlscent Hosp In (P-15660)*

Garden Grove Advanced Imaging .... C 310 445-2800
1510 Cotner Ave Los Angeles (90025) *(P-15312)*

Garden Grove Hospital, Garden Grove *Also Called: Kenneth Corp (P-16060)*

Garden Grove Medical Investors (HQ) .... D 714 534-1041
12332 Garden Grove Blvd Garden Grove (92843) *(P-15661)*

Garden Grove Rehabilitation, Garden Grove *Also Called: Garden Grove Medical Investors (P-15661)*

Garden Grove Unified Schl Dst .... D 714 663-6101
12381 Dale St Garden Grove (92841) *(P-16807)*

Garden Grove Unified Schl Dst .... C 714 663-6437
8371 Orangewood Ave Garden Grove (92841) *(P-17091)*

Gardena Honda, Gardena *Also Called: DCH Gardena Honda (P-11335)*

Gardena Hospital LP .... A 310 532-4200
1145 W Redondo Beach Blvd Gardena (90247) *(P-16001)*

Gardena Medical Offices, Gardena *Also Called: Kaiser Foundation Hospitals (P-16033)*

Gardena Valley News Inc .... E 310 329-6351
15005 S Vermont Ave Gardena (90247) *(P-2798)*

Gardens Regional Hosp Med Ctr, Hawaiian Gardens *Also Called: Gardens Regional Hospital and Medical Center Incorporated (P-16002)*

Gardens Regional Hospital and Medical Center Incorporated .... B 877 877-1104
21530 Pioneer Blvd Hawaiian Gardens (90716) *(P-16002)*

Gardner Logistics, Chino *Also Called: CRST Expedited Inc (P-8940)*

Garfield Imaging Center Inc .... C 626 572-0912
555 N Garfield Ave Monterey Park (91754) *(P-15313)*

Garich Inc (PA) .... B 858 453-1331
841 Quails Trail Rd Vista (92081) *(P-13520)*

Garich Inc .... B 951 302-4750
504 E Alvarado St Ste 201 Fallbrook (92028) *(P-13521)*

Garich Inc .... B 951 699-2899
27540 Ynez Rd Temecula (92591) *(P-13597)*

Garlic Company (PA) .... D 661 393-4212
18602 Zerker Rd Shafter (93263) *(P-4)*

Garmin International Inc .... B 909 444-5000
135 S State College Blvd Ste 110 Brea (92821) *(P-7720)*

Garmon Corporation (PA) .... D 888 628-8783
27461 Via Industria Temecula (92590) *(P-1426)*

Garner Holt Productions, Redlands *Also Called: Garner Holt Productions Inc (P-5847)*

Garner Holt Productions Inc .... E 909 799-3030
1255 Research Dr Redlands (92374) *(P-5847)*

Garrad Hassan America Inc (DH) .... D 858 836-3370
9665 Chesapeake Dr Ste 435 San Diego (92123) *(P-18310)*

Garrett J Gentry Gen Engrg Inc .... D 909 693-3391
1297 W 9th St Upland (91786) *(P-17536)*

Garrett Transportation I Inc (HQ) .... E 973 455-2000
2525 W 190th St Torrance (90504) *(P-7385)*

Garris Plastering, Orange *Also Called: Padilla Construction Company (P-1022)*

Garrison Manufacturing Inc .... E 714 549-4880
3320 S Yale St Santa Ana (92704) *(P-7254)*

Garvey Nut & Candy, Pico Rivera *Also Called: Genesis Foods Corporation (P-1504)*

Gary Bale Redi-Mix Con Inc .... D 949 786-9441
16131 Construction Cir W Irvine (92606) *(P-4439)*

Gary Cardiff Enterprises Inc .... D 760 568-1403
75255 Sheryl Ave Palm Desert (92211) *(P-8828)*

GARY MANUFACTURING, National City *Also Called: Gmi Inc (P-2229)*

Gary Manufacturing Inc .... E 619 429-4479
2626 Southport Way Ste E National City (91950) *(P-4122)*

Gary Steel Division, Santa Fe Springs *Also Called: Kloeckner Metals Corporation (P-10143)*

Gas Company, The, Downey *Also Called: Southern California Gas Co (P-9659)*

Gas Company, The, Los Angeles *Also Called: Southern California Gas Co (P-9664)*

Gasket Manufacturing Co .... E 310 217-5600
8427 Secura Way Santa Fe Springs (90670) *(P-3888)*

Gasketfab Division, Lakewood *Also Called: Industrial Gasket and Sup Co (P-3891)*

Gate City Beverage Distrs (PA) .... B 909 799-0281
2505 Steele Rd San Bernardino (92408) *(P-11047)*

Gate Three Healthcare LLC .... C 949 587-9000
24962 Calle Aragon Laguna Hills (92637) *(P-15662)*

Gateb Consulting Inc .... D 310 526-8323
815 Hampton Dr Unit 1b Venice (90291) *(P-18311)*

Gatehouse Media LLC .... E 760 241-7744
13891 Park Ave Victorville (92392) *(P-2799)*

Employee Codes: A=Over 500 employees, B=251-500
C=101-250, D=51-100, E=20-50, F=10-19, G=1-9

2025 Southern California
Business Directory and Buyers Guide

© Mergent Inc. 1-800-342-5647
1033

Gatekeeper Systems Inc (PA).................................... D **888 808-9433**
90 Icon Foothill Ranch (92610) *(P-7124)*

Gateway, Poway Also Called: *Gateway Inc (P-5848)*

Gateway, Irvine Also Called: *Gateway Inc (P-5849)*

Gateway, Los Angeles Also Called: *County of Los Angeles (P-13325)*

Gateway Inc .... E 858 451-9933
12750 Gateway Park Rd # 124 Poway (92064) *(P-5848)*

Gateway Inc (DH).. C **949 471-7000**
7565 Irvine Center Dr Ste 150 Irvine (92618) *(P-5849)*

Gateway Fresh LLC .... C 951 378-5439
3660 Grand Ave Ste A Chino Hills (91709) *(P-12599)*

Gateway Genomics LLC .... D 858 886-7250
11436 Sorrento Valley Rd San Diego (92121) *(P-3540)*

Gateway Home Realty, Brea Also Called: *American Financial Network Inc (P-11881)*

Gateway Logistics Tech LLC .... C 732 750-9000
11400 W Olympic Blvd Los Angeles (90064) *(P-8908)*

Gateway Mattress Co Inc .... D 323 725-1923
624 S Vail Ave Montebello (90640) *(P-2484)*

Gateway US Retail Inc .... E 949 471-7000
7565 Irvine Center Dr Irvine (92618) *(P-5850)*

Gateways Hosp Mental Hlth Ctr (PA)................. C **323 644-2000**
1891 Effie St Los Angeles (90026) *(P-16274)*

Gatto Pope Walwick LLP .... D 619 282-7366
3131 Camino Del Rio N Ste 1200 San Diego (92108) *(P-17729)*

Gavia, Vernon Also Called: *F Gavina & Sons Inc (P-1718)*

Gavial Engineering & Mfg Inc .... E 805 614-0060
1435 W Mccoy Ln Santa Maria (93455) *(P-6731)*

Gavin De Becker & Assoc GP LLC .... C 818 505-0177
350 N Glendale Ave Ste 517 Glendale (91206) *(P-18141)*

Gavin De Becker & Associates, Glendale Also Called: *Gavin De Becker & Assoc GP LLC (P-18141)*

Gaytan Foods LLC .... D 626 330-4553
15430 Proctor Ave City Of Industry (91745) *(P-1259)*

Gaze USA Inc .... E 213 622-0022
2011 E 25th St Vernon (90058) *(P-2097)*

Gazelle Transportation LLC .... C 661 322-8868
34915 Gazelle Ct Bakersfield (93308) *(P-8909)*

Gb007 Inc .... D 858 684-1300
3013 Science Park Rd San Diego (92121) *(P-3576)*

Gbc Concrete Masnry Cnstr Inc .... C 951 245-2355
561 Birch St Lake Elsinore (92530) *(P-983)*

GBF Enterprises Inc .... E 714 979-7131
2709 Halladay St Santa Ana (92705) *(P-6132)*

Gbl Systems Corporation .... E 805 987-4345
760 Paseo Camarillo Ste 401 Camarillo (93010) *(P-14082)*

Gbm, Alhambra Also Called: *Gracing Brand Management Inc (P-2170)*

GBS Linens Inc (PA).. D **714 778-6448**
305 N Muller St Anaheim (92801) *(P-13117)*

GBS Party Linens, Anaheim Also Called: *GBS Linens Inc (P-13117)*

GBT Inc .... C 626 854-9338
17358 Railroad St City Of Industry (91748) *(P-10005)*

Gc International Inc (PA)..................................... E **805 389-4631**
4671 Calle Carga Camarillo (93012) *(P-4674)*

Gciu Employer Retirement Fund, City Of Industry Also Called: *Benefits Prgram Adminsitration (P-12655)*

Gcl W, Los Angeles Also Called: *Garda CL West Inc (P-14301)*

Gcn Supply LLC .... E 909 643-4603
9070 Bridgeport Pl Rancho Cucamonga (91730) *(P-5078)*

Gcorp Consulting .... C 619 587-3160
2831 Camino Del Rio S Ste 311 San Diego (92108) *(P-18142)*

GCR Tires & Service 185, Fontana Also Called: *Bridgestone Americas (P-14681)*

GD Heil Inc .... C 714 687-9100
1031 Segovia Cir Placentia (92870) *(P-1182)*

Gdr Group Inc .... D 949 453-8818
3 Park Plz Ste 1700 Irvine (92614) *(P-14220)*

GE Energy, Diamond Bar Also Called: *Motech Americas LLC (P-17810)*

GE Renewables North Amer LLC .... C 661 823-6423
13681 Chantico Rd Tehachapi (93561) *(P-5457)*

GE Water & Process Tech, Avila Beach Also Called: *Veolia Wts Usa Inc (P-3822)*

Gear Manufacturing Inc .... E 714 792-2895
3701 E Miraloma Ave Anaheim (92806) *(P-7481)*

Gear Technology, Rancho Cucamonga Also Called: *Marino Enterprises Inc (P-7518)*

Gear Vendors, El Cajon Also Called: *Gear Vendors Inc (P-7255)*

Gear Vendors Inc .... E 619 562-0060
1717 N Magnolia Ave El Cajon (92020) *(P-7255)*

Gearment, Huntington Beach Also Called: *Gearment Inc (P-1941)*

Gearment Inc (PA).. C **866 236-5476**
14801 Able Ln Ste 102 Huntington Beach (92647) *(P-1941)*

Gedney Foods Company .... C 952 448-2612
12243 Branford St Sun Valley (91352) *(P-1367)*

Geek Squad, Cerritos Also Called: *Geek Squad Inc (P-14221)*

Geek Squad Inc .... D 562 402-1555
12989 Park Plaza Dr Cerritos (90703) *(P-14221)*

Geeriraj Inc .... E 760 244-6149
7042 Santa Fe Ave E Ste A1 Hesperia (92345) *(P-6732)*

Gehr Group, Commerce Also Called: *Gehr Industries Inc (P-4633)*

Gehr Industries Inc (HQ)..................................... C **323 728-5558**
5701 S Eastern Ave Commerce (90040) *(P-4633)*

Gehry Partners LLP .... C 310 482-3000
12541 Beatrice St Los Angeles (90066) *(P-17670)*

Gehry Technologies Inc .... D 310 862-1200
12181 Bluff Creek Dr Los Angeles (90094) *(P-13736)*

Gel Industries Inc .... C 714 639-8191
810 N Lemon St Orange (92867) *(P-5155)*

Gelfand Rennert & Feldman LLP (DH)................ C **310 553-1707**
1880 Century Park E Ste 1600 Los Angeles (90067) *(P-14500)*

Gelsons Markets .... D 310 306-3192
13455 Maxella Ave Marina Del Rey (90292) *(P-11277)*

Geltman Industries, Vernon Also Called: *Rezex Corporation (P-1945)*

Gem, Palmdale Also Called: *Golden Empire Mortgage Inc (P-11909)*

Gem Medical Management, Tustin Also Called: *Professnal Rgistry Netwrk Corp (P-13558)*

Gem Mortgage, Bakersfield Also Called: *Golden Empire Mortgage Inc (P-11908)*

Gem-Pack Berries LLC .... C 949 861-4919
14271 Jeffrey Rd Unit 315 Irvine (92620) *(P-19)*

Gemalto Cogent Inc (HQ)................................... D **626 325-9600**
2964 Bradley St Pasadena (91107) *(P-14083)*

Gemini Film & Bag Inc (PA)................................. E **323 582-0901**
3574 Fruitland Ave Maywood (90270) *(P-4123)*

Gemini Industries Inc .... D 949 250-4011
2311 Pullman St Santa Ana (92705) *(P-4584)*

Gemini Plastics, Maywood Also Called: *Gemini Film & Bag Inc (P-4123)*

Gemini-Rosemont Realty LLC .... D 505 992-5100
2000 Avenue Of The Stars Ste 550 Los Angeles (90067) *(P-12455)*

Gemmm Corporation (PA).................................. D **805 496-0555**
2860 E Thousand Oaks Blvd Thousand Oaks (91362) *(P-12456)*

Gemological Institute Amer Inc (PA).................. A **760 603-4000**
5345 Armada Dr Carlsbad (92008) *(P-16845)*

Gemological Institute America, Carlsbad Also Called: *Gemological Institute Amer Inc (P-16845)*

Gemtech Inds Good Earth Mfg .... E 714 848-2517
2737 S Garnsey St Santa Ana (92707) *(P-5322)*

Gemtech International, Santa Ana Also Called: *Gemtech Inds Good Earth Mfg (P-5322)*

Gen-Probe Incorporated .... D 858 410-8000
10210 Genetic Center Dr San Diego (92121) *(P-3541)*

Gen-Probe Sales & Service Inc .... D 858 410-8000
10210 Genetic Center Dr San Diego (92121) *(P-8380)*

GENASYS, San Diego Also Called: *Genasys Inc (P-13938)*

Genasys Inc (PA).. D **858 676-1112**
16262 W Bernardo Dr San Diego (92127) *(P-13938)*

Genbody America LLC .... E 949 561-0664
3420 De Forest Cir Jurupa Valley (91752) *(P-8157)*

Genea Energy Partners Inc .... C 714 694-0536
19100 Von Karman Ave Ste 550 Irvine (92612) *(P-14084)*

Genentech Inc .... A 760 231-2440
1 Antibody Way Oceanside (92056) *(P-3405)*

General AC & Plbg, Thousand Palms Also Called: *10x Hvac of Ca LLC (P-724)*

General Acute Care Hospital, Los Angeles Also Called: *Pih Health Good Samaritan Hosp (P-16132)*

General Acute Care Hospital, Whittier Also Called: *Pih Health Whittier Hospital (P-16134)*

General Atmics Arntcal Systems .... D 858 455-3358
11906 Tech Center Ct Poway (92064) *(P-7341)*

General Atmics Arntcal Systems .... B 858 964-6700
13330 Evening Creek Dr N San Diego (92128) *(P-7342)*

General Atmics Arntcal Systems .... B 858 312-4247
13550 Stowe Dr Poway (92064) *(P-7343)*

General Atmics Arntcal Systems .... B 858 455-3000
12220 Parkway Centre Dr Poway (92064) *(P-7344)*

General Atmics Arntcal Systems .... A 858 762-6700
16761 Via Del Campo Ct San Diego (92127) *(P-7345)*

General Atmics Arntcal Systems .... D 858 312-2810
14102 Stowe Dr Ste A47 Poway (92064) *(P-7346)*

General Atmics Arntcal Systems .... B 858 455-2810
3550 General Atomics Ct San Diego (92121) *(P-7347)*

General Atmics Arntcal Systems .... B 858 762-6700
12365 Crosthwaite Cir Poway (92064) *(P-7348)*

General Atmics Arntcal Systems (DH) .... **B 858 312-2810**
14200 Kirkham Way Poway (92064) *(P-7349)*

General Atomic Aeron .... C 760 388-8208
73 El Mirage Airport Rd Ste B Adelanto (92301) *(P-7350)*

General Atomic Aeron .... C 858 455-4560
14040 Danielson St Poway (92064) *(P-7351)*

General Atomic Aeron .... B 858 312-3428
13950 Stowe Dr Poway (92064) *(P-7352)*

General Atomic Aeron .... B 858 312-2543
14115 Stowe Dr Poway (92064) *(P-7353)*

General Atomics .... D 858 676-7100
16969 Mesamint St San Diego (92127) *(P-17789)*

General Atomics .... C 858 455-4000
4949 Greencraig Ln San Diego (92123) *(P-17790)*

General Atomics .... D 858 455-4141
3483 Dunhill St San Diego (92121) *(P-17791)*

General Atomics (HQ) .... **A 858 455-2810**
3550 General Atomics Ct San Diego (92121) *(P-17844)*

General Atomics, San Diego *Also Called: General Atmics Arntcal Systems (P-7347)*

General Atomics, Adelanto *Also Called: General Atomic Aeron (P-7350)*

General Atomics Electronic Systems Inc .... B 858 522-8495
4949 Greencraig Ln San Diego (92123) *(P-6917)*

General Atomics Energy Pdts, San Diego *Also Called: General Atomics (P-17790)*

General Coatings Corporation .... D 858 587-1277
600 W Freedom Ave Orange (92865) *(P-862)*

General Coatings Corporation (PA) .... **C 858 587-1277**
6711 Nancy Ridge Dr San Diego (92121) *(P-863)*

General Coatings Corporation .... D 909 204-4150
1230 Carbide Dr Corona (92881) *(P-864)*

General Cold Stg 4145, Bell Gardens *Also Called: US Foods Inc (P-10987)*

General Container .... D 714 562-8700
235 Radio Rd Corona (92879) *(P-2668)*

General Contracting, San Marcos *Also Called: MB Builders Inc (P-418)*

General Contractor, Irvine *Also Called: Uprite Construction Corp (P-511)*

General Contractor, Duarte *Also Called: Png Builders (P-573)*

General Conveyor Inc .... E 951 734-3460
13385 Estelle St Corona (92879) *(P-14768)*

General Dynamics Mission .... D 619 671-5400
7603 Saint Andrews Ave Ste H San Diego (92154) *(P-6350)*

GENERAL DYNAMICS OTS (CALIFORNIA), INC., San Diego *Also Called: General Dynamics Ots Cal Inc (P-7482)*

General Dynamics Ots Cal Inc .... C 619 671-5411
7603 Saint Andrews Ave Ste H San Diego (92154) *(P-7482)*

General Electric Company .... E 760 530-5200
18000 Phantom St Victorville (92394) *(P-7354)*

General Forming Corporation .... E 310 326-0624
640 Alaska Ave Torrance (90503) *(P-7721)*

General Industrial Repair .... E 323 278-0873
6865 Washington Blvd Montebello (90640) *(P-6133)*

General Lgstics Systems US Inc .... C 562 577-6037
12300 Bell Ranch Dr Santa Fe Springs (90670) *(P-8910)*

General Lgstics Systems US Inc .... C 951 677-3972
24305 Prielipp Rd Wildomar (92595) *(P-8911)*

General Micro Systems Inc (PA) .... **D 909 980-4863**
8358 Maple Pl Rancho Cucamonga (91730) *(P-10006)*

General Mills, Carson *Also Called: General Mills Inc (P-1330)*

General Mills, Vernon *Also Called: General Mills Inc (P-1405)*

General Mills Inc .... D 310 605-6108
1055 Sandhill Ave Carson (90746) *(P-1330)*

General Mills Inc .... E 323 584-3433
4309 Fruitland Ave Vernon (90058) *(P-1405)*

General Monitors Inc (DH) .... **C 949 581-4464**
16782 Von Karman Ave Ste 14 Irvine (92606) *(P-6684)*

General Motors, Torrance *Also Called: General Motors LLC (P-11353)*

General Motors LLC .... E 313 556-5000
3050 Lomita Blvd Ste 237 Torrance (90505) *(P-11353)*

General Networks Corporation .... D 818 249-1962
3524 Ocean View Blvd Glendale (91208) *(P-14222)*

General Pavement Management Inc .... D 805 933-0909
850 Lawrence Dr Ste 100 Thousand Oaks (91320) *(P-1116)*

General Petroleum LLC (HQ) .... **C 562 983-7300**
19501 S Santa Fe Ave Compton (90221) *(P-11032)*

General Photonics, Chino *Also Called: General Photonics Corp (P-6586)*

General Photonics Corp .... D 909 590-5473
14351 Pipeline Ave Chino (91710) *(P-6586)*

General Plastics, Sun Valley *Also Called: Plastic Services and Products (P-4009)*

General Plating, Los Angeles *Also Called: Alpha Polishing Corporation (P-5231)*

General Power Systems, Anaheim *Also Called: General Power Systems Inc (P-7000)*

General Power Systems Inc .... E 714 956-9321
955 E Ball Rd Anaheim (92805) *(P-7000)*

General Procurement Inc (PA) .... **D 949 679-7960**
1964 W Corporate Way Anaheim (92801) *(P-10007)*

General Produce, Vernon *Also Called: V & L Produce Inc (P-10921)*

General Production Svc Cal Inc .... C 661 765-5330
1333 Kern St Taft (93268) *(P-672)*

General Ribbon Corp .... B 818 709-1234
5775 E Los Angeles Ave Ste 230 Chatsworth (91311) *(P-8563)*

General Sealants .... C 626 961-0211
300 Turnbull Canyon Rd City Of Industry (91745) *(P-3767)*

General Switchgear Inc .... E
14729 Spring Ave Santa Fe Springs (90670) *(P-6306)*

General Tool Inc .... D 949 261-2322
2025 Alton Pkwy Irvine (92606) *(P-10439)*

General Transistor Corporation (PA) .... **E 310 578-7344**
12449 Putnam St Whittier (90602) *(P-10245)*

General Undgrd Fire Prtction I .... C 714 632-8646
701 W Grove Ave Orange (92865) *(P-782)*

General Veneer Mfg Co .... E 323 564-2661
8652 Otis St South Gate (90280) *(P-2370)*

General Wax & Candle Co, North Hollywood *Also Called: General Wax Co Inc (P-8678)*

General Wax Co Inc (PA) .... **D 818 765-5800**
6863 Beck Ave North Hollywood (91605) *(P-8678)*

Generate Life Sciences Co, Los Angeles *Also Called: California Cryobank LLC (P-16539)*

Generation Construction Inc .... C 909 923-2077
15650 El Prado Rd Chino (91710) *(P-405)*

Generational Properties Inc .... B 323 583-3163
3141 E 44th St Vernon (90058) *(P-9070)*

Generis Holdings I P (PA) .... **C 661 366-7209**
7200 E Brundage Ln Bakersfield (93307) *(P-11)*

Genes Plating Works Inc (PA) .... **E 323 269-8748**
3498 E 14th St Los Angeles (90023) *(P-5262)*

Genesis Foods Corporation .... D 323 890-5890
8825 Mercury Ln Pico Rivera (90660) *(P-1504)*

Genesis Health Care, Orange *Also Called: Prospect Medical Systems Inc (P-18040)*

Genesis Healthcare LLC .... A 805 922-3558
425 Barcellus Ave Santa Maria (93454) *(P-15663)*

Genesis Healthcare LLC .... B 310 370-3594
20900 Earl St Ste 100 Torrance (90503) *(P-15664)*

Genesis Healthcare LLC .... A 323 461-9961
5310 Fountain Ave Los Angeles (90029) *(P-15854)*

Genesis Tech Partners LLC .... C 800 950-2647
21540 Plummer St Ste A Chatsworth (91311) *(P-14769)*

Genetronics Inc .... E 858 597-6006
11494 Sorrento Valley Rd Ste A San Diego (92121) *(P-7826)*

Genex (DH) .... **C 424 672-9500**
800 Corporate Pointe Ste 100 Culver City (90230) *(P-13737)*

Genica Corporation .... B 855 433-5747
43195 Business Park Dr Temecula (92590) *(P-10008)*

Employee Codes: A=Over 500 employees, B=251-500
C=101-250, D=51-100, E=20-50, F=10-19, G=1-9

2025 Southern California
Business Directory and Buyers Guide

© Mergent Inc. 1-800-342-5647
1035

Genius Products Inc .... C 310 453-1222
3301 Exposition Blvd Ste 100 Santa Monica (90404) *(P-10562)*

Genius Products Nt Inc .... C 510 671-0219
556 N Diamond Bar Blvd Ste 101 Diamond Bar (91765) *(P-1619)*

Genlabs (PA) .... **C ... 909 591-8451**
5568 Schaefer Ave Chino (91710) *(P-3592)*

Genmark, Carlsbad *Also Called: Genmark Diagnostics Inc (P-8158)*

Genmark Diagnostics Inc (DH) .... **A 760 448-4300**
5964 La Place Ct Ste 100 Carlsbad (92008) *(P-8158)*

Genomics Inst of Nvrtis RES FN .... D 858 812-1805
10675 John J Hopkins Dr San Diego (92121) *(P-3406)*

Genon Holdings LLC .... D 805 984-5215
393 Harbor Blvd Oxnard (93035) *(P-9586)*

Gensler, Newport Beach *Also Called: M Arthur Gensler Jr Assoc Inc (P-17683)*

Gensler and Associates, Los Angeles *Also Called: M Arthur Gensler Jr Assoc Inc (P-17682)*

Gentex Corporation .... D 909 481-7667
9859 7th St Rancho Cucamonga (91730) *(P-17792)*

Gentiva Hospice .... D 661 324-1232
5001 E Commercecenter Dr Ste 140 Bakersfield (93309) *(P-15811)*

Genuine Parts Distributors, Ontario *Also Called: Tracy Industries Inc (P-5470)*

Genvivo Inc .... E 626 441-6695
1981 E Locust St Ontario (91761) *(P-3407)*

Genzyme Corporation .... D 626 471-9922
655 E Huntington Dr Monrovia (91016) *(P-3408)*

Genzyme Genetics, Monrovia *Also Called: Genzyme Corporation (P-3408)*

Geo Drilling Fluids Inc (PA) .... E 661 325-5919
1431 Union Ave Bakersfield (93305) *(P-11013)*

Geo Guidance Drilling Svcs Inc (PA) .... E 661 833-9999
200 Old Yard Dr Bakersfield (93307) *(P-290)*

Geo Plastics .... E 323 277-8106
2200 E 52nd St Vernon (90058) *(P-4124)*

Geo Sales-Courtesy Chevrolet, San Diego *Also Called: Courtesy Chevrolet Center (P-11329)*

Geocon, San Diego *Also Called: Geocon Consultants Inc (P-18312)*

Geocon Consultants Inc (PA) .... D 858 558-6900
6960 Flanders Dr San Diego (92121) *(P-18312)*

Geocon Incorporated .... D 858 558-6900
6960 Flanders Dr San Diego (92121) *(P-17537)*

Geolinks, Camarillo *Also Called: California Internet LP (P-9430)*

Geologics Corporation .... C 661 259-5767
25375 Orchard Village Rd Ste 102 Valencia (91355) *(P-18313)*

Georg Fischer LLC (DH) .... **D 714 731-8800**
9271 Jeronimo Rd Irvine (92618) *(P-10137)*

Georg Fischer Piping, Irvine *Also Called: Georg Fischer LLC (P-10137)*

Georg Fischer Signet LLC .... D 626 571-2770
5462 Irwindale Ave Ste A Baldwin Park (91706) *(P-7860)*

George Chevrolet .... D 562 925-2500
17000 Lakewood Blvd Bellflower (90706) *(P-11354)*

George Chevrolet, Bellflower *Also Called: George Chevrolet (P-11354)*

George Fischer Inc (HQ) .... **C ... 626 571-2770**
5462 Irwindale Ave Ste A Baldwin Park (91706) *(P-6134)*

George G Sharp Inc .... D 619 425-4211
1065 Bay Blvd Ste D Chula Vista (91911) *(P-17538)*

George Industries (HQ) .... **E 323 264-6660**
4116 Whiteside St Los Angeles (90063) *(P-5263)*

George Jue Mfg Co Inc .... D 562 634-8181
8140 Rosecrans Ave Paramount (90723) *(P-5635)*

George L Throop Co .... E 626 796-0285
444 N Fair Oaks Ave Pasadena (91103) *(P-11258)*

George P Johnson Company .... E 310 965-4300
18500 Crenshaw Blvd Torrance (90504) *(P-8607)*

George T Hall Co Inc (PA) .... **E ... 909 825-9751**
1605 E Gene Autry Way Anaheim (92805) *(P-10333)*

Georgetown Mortgage, Rancho Cucamonga *Also Called: Lower LLC (P-11922)*

Georgia-Pacific, Santa Fe Springs *Also Called: Georgia-Pacific LLC (P-10593)*

Georgia-Pacific, La Mirada *Also Called: Georgia-Pacific LLC (P-11684)*

Georgia-Pacific LLC .... B 562 861-6226
9206 Santa Fe Springs Rd Santa Fe Springs (90670) *(P-10593)*

Georgia-Pacific LLC .... E 562 926-8888
15500 Valley View Ave La Mirada (90638) *(P-11684)*

Gerald J Alexander MD .... D 714 634-4567
280 S Main St Ste 200 Orange (92868) *(P-15314)*

Gerdau Ameristeel, San Bernardino *Also Called: CMC Steel Us LLC (P-5093)*

Gerdau Rancho Cucamonga, Newport Beach *Also Called: Tamco (P-5101)*

Gerhardt Gear Co Inc .... E 818 842-6700
133 E Santa Anita Ave Burbank (91502) *(P-7256)*

Geri-Care Inc .... D 310 320-0961
21521 S Vermont Ave Torrance (90502) *(P-15665)*

Geri-Care II Inc .... C 310 328-0812
22035 S Vermont Ave Torrance (90502) *(P-15855)*

German Machine Products, Gardena *Also Called: German Machined Products Inc (P-6135)*

German Machined Products Inc .... E 310 532-4480
1415 W 178th St Gardena (90248) *(P-6135)*

Gersh Agency LLC (PA) .... **D ... 310 274-6611**
9465 Wilshire Blvd Fl 6 Beverly Hills (90212) *(P-14961)*

Ges, Huntington Beach *Also Called: Global Exprnce Specialists Inc (P-14502)*

GES Sheet Metal Inc .... D 909 598-3332
14531 Fontlee Ln Fontana (92335) *(P-1084)*

Get Primped, Los Angeles *Also Called: Distro Worldwide LLC (P-1983)*

Get-A-Lift Handicap Bus Trnsp, Bakersfield *Also Called: Golden Empire Transit District (P-8756)*

Getac Inc .... D 949 681-2900
15495 Sand Canyon Ave Ste 350 Irvine (92618) *(P-10009)*

Getac North America, Irvine *Also Called: Getac Inc (P-10009)*

Getmedlegal, San Dimas *Also Called: Legal Solutions Holdings Inc (P-16728)*

Getpart La Inc .... E 424 331-9599
13705 Cimarron Ave Gardena (90249) *(P-4125)*

Getty Center, Los Angeles *Also Called: Bon Appetit Management Co (P-17955)*

Getty Images Inc .... D 323 202-4200
6300 Wilshire Blvd Ste 1600 Los Angeles (90048) *(P-13319)*

Getty Publications, Los Angeles *Also Called: The J Paul Getty Trust (P-17268)*

Gettyone Image Bank, Los Angeles *Also Called: Getty Images Inc (P-13319)*

Gff Inc .... D 323 232-6255
145 Willow Ave City Of Industry (91746) *(P-1368)*

GFS Capital Holdings .... B 714 720-3918
6499 Havenwood Cir Ste 720 Huntington Beach (92648) *(P-11905)*

GFS Home Loans, Pasadena *Also Called: Right Start Mortgage Inc (P-11932)*

Ggg Demolition Inc (PA) .... **D ... 714 699-9350**
1130 W Trenton Ave Orange (92867) *(P-1183)*

Ggtw LLC .... E 619 423-3388
1470 Bay Blvd Chula Vista (91911) *(P-3800)*

Gh Group Inc .... C 562 264-5078
3645 Long Beach Blvd Long Beach (90807) *(P-12600)*

Ghost Management Group LLC .... C 949 870-1400
41 Discovery Irvine (92618) *(P-13266)*

Ghost Vfx, Burbank *Also Called: Streamland Media LLC (P-14905)*

Ghp Management Corporation .... C 310 432-1441
270 N Canon Dr Beverly Hills (90210) *(P-17988)*

Giant Inland Empire Rv Ctr Inc (PA) .... **C ... 909 981-0444**
9150 Benson Ave Montclair (91763) *(P-11479)*

Giant Mgllan Tlscope Orgnztion, Pasadena *Also Called: Gmto Corporation (P-8001)*

Giant Rv, Montclair *Also Called: Giant Inland Empire Rv Ctr Inc (P-11479)*

Giant Sportz Paintball Park, Bellflower *Also Called: Hollywood Sports Park LLC (P-14510)*

Gibbs Giden Locher .... D 310 552-3400
1880 Century Park E Ste 1200 Los Angeles (90067) *(P-16686)*

Gibo/Kodama Chairs, Garden Grove *Also Called: Intra Storage Systems Inc (P-5448)*

Gibraltar, Jurupa Valley *Also Called: Pacific Award Metals Inc (P-9959)*

Gibraltar Cnvalescent Hosp Inc .... D 626 443-9425
2720 Nevada Ave El Monte (91733) *(P-15856)*

Gibraltar Plastic Pdts Corp .... E 818 365-9318
12885 Foothill Blvd Sylmar (91342) *(P-4126)*

Gibson Dunn & Crutcher LLP (PA) .... **B ... 213 229-7000**
333 S Grand Ave Los Angeles (90071) *(P-16687)*

Gibson Dunn & Crutcher LLP .... C 310 552-8500
2029 Century Park E Ste 4000 Los Angeles (90002) *(P-16688)*

Gibson Dunn & Crutcher LLP .... C 949 451-3800
3161 Michelson Dr Ste 1200 Irvine (92612) *(P-16689)*

Gibson & Barnes, El Cajon *Also Called: Flight Suits (P-2180)*

Gibson & Schaefer Inc (PA) .... **E ... 619 352-3535**
1126 Rock Wood Rd Heber (92249) *(P-4440)*

Gibson Exhaust Systems, Corona *Also Called: Gibson Performance Corporation (P-7257)*

Mergent email: customerrelations@mergent.com
1036

2025 Southern California
Business Directory and Buyers Guide

(P-0000) Products & Services Section entry number
(PA)=Parent Co (HQ)=Headquarters (DH)=Div Headquarters

Gibson Homeware, Commerce *Also Called: Gibson Overseas Inc (P-9896)*

Gibson Overseas Inc (PA)............................B 323 832-8900
2410 Yates Ave Commerce (90040) *(P-9896)*

Gibson Performance Corporation ....D 951 372-1220
1270 Webb Cir Corona (92879) *(P-7257)*

Giddens Industries Inc (DH)..........................C
3130 E Miraloma Ave Anaheim (92806) *(P-7483)*

Gifting Group LLC ....D 951 296-0310
42210 Zevo Dr Temecula (92590) *(P-11122)*

Gigabyte Technology, City Of Industry *Also Called: GBT Inc (P-10005)*

Gigastone America, Irvine *Also Called: Dane Elec Corp USA (P-9996)*

Gilbert Klly Crwley Jnnett LLP (PA)...................D 213 615-7000
550 S Hope St Ste 2200 Los Angeles (90071) *(P-16690)*

Gilbert Martin Wdwkg Co Inc (PA)....................E 800 268-5669
2345 Britannia Blvd San Diego (92154) *(P-2498)*

Gildan USA Inc ....E 909 485-1475
28200 Highway 189 Lake Arrowhead (92352) *(P-1908)*

GILDAN USA INC., Lake Arrowhead *Also Called: Gildan USA Inc (P-1908)*

Gilead Palo Alto Inc ....C 909 394-4000
550 Cliffside Dr San Dimas (91773) *(P-3409)*

Gilead Palo Alto Inc ....C 760 945-7701
4049 Avenida De La Plata Oceanside (92056) *(P-3410)*

Gilead Sciences Inc ....D 650 522-2771
1800 Wheeler St La Verne (91750) *(P-3411)*

Gilead Scientist, San Dimas *Also Called: Gilead Palo Alto Inc (P-3409)*

Gill Corporation (PA).................................C 626 443-6094
4056 Easy St El Monte (91731) *(P-4127)*

Gils Distributing Service ....C 213 627-0539
718 E 8th St Los Angeles (90021) *(P-13274)*

Giovanni Cosmetics Inc ....D 310 952-9960
2064 E University Dr Rancho Dominguez (90220) *(P-3653)*

Giovanni Hair Care & Cosmetics, Rancho Dominguez *Also Called: Giovanni Cosmetics Inc (P-3653)*

Gipson Hffman Pncone A Prof Co ....D 310 556-4660
1901 Avenue Of The Stars Ste 1100 Los Angeles (90067) *(P-16691)*

Girard Food Service, City Of Industry *Also Called: Gff Inc (P-1368)*

Girardi Keese (PA)...................................D 213 977-0211
1126 Wilshire Blvd Los Angeles (90017) *(P-16692)*

GIRL SCOUTS, Ventura *Also Called: Girl Scuts Clfrnias Cntl Coast (P-17344)*

GIRL SCOUTS SAN DIEGO, San Diego *Also Called: Girl Scuts San Dg-Mprial Cncil (P-17346)*

Girl Scuts Clfrnias Cntl Coast ....D 831 633-4877
1500 Palma Dr # 110 Ventura (93003) *(P-17344)*

Girl Scuts Greater Los Angeles (PA)..................C 626 677-2265
423 N La Brea Ave Inglewood (90302) *(P-17345)*

Girl Scuts San Dg-Mprial Cncil (PA)..................D 619 610-0751
1231 Upas St San Diego (92103) *(P-17346)*

GIRLS REPUBLIC, Chino Hills *Also Called: Boys Republic (P-17123)*

Giroux, Los Angeles *Also Called: Giroux Glass Inc (P-1165)*

Giroux Glass Inc (PA)................................C 213 747-7406
850 W Washington Blvd Ste 200 Los Angeles (90015) *(P-1165)*

Giuliano-Pagano Corporation ....D 310 537-7700
1264 E Walnut St Carson (90746) *(P-1454)*

Giuliano's Bakery, Carson *Also Called: Giuliano-Pagano Corporation (P-1454)*

Giumarra Agricom Intl LLC ....A 760 480-8502
15651 Old Milky Way Escondido (92027) *(P-10902)*

Giumarra Bros Fruit Co Inc (PA)......................D 213 627-2900
1601 E Olympic Blvd Ste 400 Los Angeles (90021) *(P-10903)*

Giumarra International Berry, Los Angeles *Also Called: Giumarra Bros Fruit Co Inc (P-10903)*

Giumarra Vineyards Corporation ....B 661 395-7071
11220 Edison Hwy Bakersfield (93307) *(P-31)*

Giumarra Vineyards Corporation (PA).................B 661 395-7000
11220 Edison Hwy Edison (93220) *(P-32)*

Giumarra Vineyards Corporation ....C 661 395-7000
11220 Edison Hwy Bakersfield (93307) *(P-1574)*

Given Imaging Los Angeles LLC ....C 310 641-8492
5860 Uplander Way Culver City (90230) *(P-8381)*

Giving Keys Inc ....E 213 935-8791
836 Traction Ave Los Angeles (90013) *(P-8454)*

GK Management Co Inc (PA)..........................C 310 204-2050
5150 Overland Ave Culver City (90230) *(P-12457)*

Gkk Corporation (PA).................................D 949 250-1500
2355 Main St Ste 220 Irvine (92614) *(P-17671)*

Gkkworks, Irvine *Also Called: Gkk Corporation (P-17671)*

GKN Aerospace ....C 714 653-7531
12122 Western Ave Garden Grove (92841) *(P-7355)*

GKN Aerospace Chem-Tronics Inc (DH)...............A 619 258-5000
1150 W Bradley Ave El Cajon (92020) *(P-7386)*

GKN Arspace Trnsprncy Systems ....B 714 893-7531
12122 Western Ave Garden Grove (92841) *(P-4128)*

Gky Dental Arts Inc (PA).............................D 310 214-8007
4212 Artesia Blvd Torrance (90504) *(P-16342)*

GL, San Diego *Also Called: Garrad Hassan America Inc (P-18310)*

GL Nemirow Inc ....D 818 562-9433
2550 N Hollywood Way Ste 502 Burbank (91505) *(P-13209)*

GL Woodworking Inc ....D 949 515-2192
14341 Franklin Ave Tustin (92780) *(P-2307)*

Glacier Foods Division, Westlake Village *Also Called: Dole Packaged Foods LLC (P-1375)*

Glad-A-Way Gardens Inc ....C 805 938-0569
2669 E Clark Ave Santa Maria (93455) *(P-56)*

Glam and Glits Nail Design Inc ....D 661 393-4800
8700 Swigert Ct Unit 209 Bakersfield (93311) *(P-3654)*

Glamour Industries Co ....D 213 687-8600
100 Wilshire Blvd Ste 700 Santa Monica (90401) *(P-10474)*

Glamour Industries Co (PA)..........................C 323 728-2999
2220 Gaspar Ave Los Angeles (90040) *(P-10624)*

Glare Technology Usa Inc ....C 909 437-6999
30898 Wealth St Murrieta (92563) *(P-14402)*

Glas Werk Inc ....E 949 766-1296
29710 Avenida De Las Bandera Rancho Santa Margari (92688) *(P-4326)*

Glaser Weil Fink Jacobs (PA).........................C 310 553-3000
10250 Constellation Blvd Fl 19 Los Angeles (90067) *(P-16693)*

Glaspro, Santa Fe Springs *Also Called: GP Merger Sub Inc (P-4335)*

Glass House Group, Long Beach *Also Called: Gh Group Inc (P-12600)*

Glasswerks Group, South Gate *Also Called: Glasswerks La Inc (P-4334)*

Glasswerks La Inc (HQ)..............................B 888 789-7810
8600 Rheem Ave South Gate (90280) *(P-4334)*

Glaukos Corporation (PA)............................C 949 367-9600
1 Glaukos Way Aliso Viejo (92656) *(P-8159)*

GLAZA, Los Angeles *Also Called: Greater Los Angeles Zoo Assn (P-17227)*

Gleason Industrial Pdts Inc ....C 574 533-1141
10474 Santa Monica Blvd Ste 400 Los Angeles (90025) *(P-5530)*

Gledhill/Lyons Inc ....E 714 502-0274
2511 Termino Ave Long Beach (90815) *(P-7484)*

Glen Annie Golf Club ....D 805 968-6400
405 Glen Annie Rd Goleta (93117) *(P-15081)*

Glen Ivy Hot Springs ....C 714 990-2090
1001 Brea Mall Brea (92821) *(P-13175)*

Glenair Inc (PA)....................................B 818 247-6000
1211 Air Way Glendale (91201) *(P-6420)*

Glendale Adventist Medical Ctr (HQ)..................A 818 409-8000
1509 Wilson Ter Glendale (91206) *(P-16003)*

Glendale Associates Ltd ....D 818 246-6737
100 W Broadway Ste 100 Glendale (91210) *(P-12294)*

Glendale Medical Offices, Glendale *Also Called: Kaiser Foundation Hospitals (P-15363)*

Glendale Mem Hlth Foundation ....D 818 502-2375
1420 S Central Ave Glendale (91204) *(P-16004)*

Glendale Memorial Breast Ctr, Glendale *Also Called: Glendale Memorial Health Corp (P-16005)*

Glendale Memorial Center, Glendale *Also Called: Glendale Memorial Health Corporation (P-16006)*

Glendale Memorial Health Corp ....A 818 502-2323
222 W Eulalia St Glendale (91204) *(P-16005)*

Glendale Memorial Health Corporation ....A 818 502-1900
1420 S Central Ave Glendale (91204) *(P-16006)*

GLENDALE YMCA SWIM SCHOOL, Glendale *Also Called: Young MNS Chrstn Assn Glndale (P-17403)*

Glendee Corp (PA)..................................E 805 523-2422
5390 Gabbert Rd Moorpark (93021) *(P-6136)*

Glendora Country Club ....D 626 335-4051
2400 Country Club Drive Glendora (91741) *(P-15137)*

Glendora Oaks Bhvral Hlth Hosp, Glendora *Also Called: East Valley Glendora Hosp LLC (P-15985)*

Employee Codes: A=Over 500 employees, B=251-500
C=101-250, D=51-100, E=20-50, F=10-19, G=1-9

2025 Southern California
Business Directory and Buyers Guide

© Mergent Inc. 1-800-342-5647

1037

Glenn A Rick Engrg & Dev Co (PA)................C 619 291-0708
5620 Friars Rd San Diego (92110) *(P-17539)*

Glenoaks Convalescent Hospital ....D 818 240-4300
409 W Glenoaks Blvd Glendale (91202) *(P-16007)*

Glenoaks Food Inc ....E 818 768-9091
11030 Randall St Sun Valley (91352) *(P-1278)*

Glentek Inc ....D 310 322-3026
208 Standard St El Segundo (90245) *(P-6322)*

Glenwood Surgical Center LP ....D .,.... 951 689-2647
8945 Magnolia Ave Ste 200 Riverside (92503) *(P-15315)*

Glidewell Laboratories, Newport Beach Also Called: James R Gldwell Dntl Crmics In
(P-16343)

Glimmer Healthcare Inc ....C 626 442-5721
11900 Ramona Blvd El Monte (91732) *(P-15666)*

Global A Lgistics Training Inc ....E 760 688-0365
3860 Calle Fortunada Ste 100 San Diego (92123) *(P-7722)*

Global Care Travel, San Diego Also Called: Customzed Svcs Admnstrtors Inc *(P-12198)*

Global Cash Card Inc ....C 949 751-0360
3972 Barranca Pkwy Ste J610 Irvine (92606) *(P-13939)*

Global Casuals Inc ....E 310 817-2828
18505 S Broadway Gardena (90248) *(P-2012)*

Global Compliance Inc ....E 626 303-6855
438 W Chestnut Ave Ste A Monrovia (91016) *(P-2917)*

Global Customer Services Inc ....D 760 995-7949
17373 Lilac St Hesperia (92345) *(P-14501)*

Global Eagle, Fullerton Also Called: Eeg Glider Inc *(P-9564)*

Global Elastomeric Pdts Inc ....D 661 831-5380
5551 District Blvd Bakersfield (93313) *(P-5510)*

Global Environmental Pdts Inc ....D 909 713-1600
5405 Industrial Pkwy San Bernardino (92407) *(P-7177)*

Global Exprnce Specialists Inc ....C 619 498-6300
18504 Beach Blvd Unit 511 Huntington Beach (92648) *(P-14502)*

Global Fabricators, Shafter Also Called: McM Fabricators Inc *(P-4851)*

Global Gaming League, Los Angeles Also Called: Professnal Intrctive Entrmt In *(P-14973)*

Global Impact Inv Partners LLC ....E 310 592-2000
1410 Westwood Blvd Apt 260 Los Angeles (90024) *(P-1455)*

Global Innovation Partner, Los Angeles Also Called: Cbre Globl Value Investors LLC
(P-12399)

Global Integrated Logistics, Irvine Also Called: Agility Logistics Corp *(P-9249)*

GLOBAL LAB SUPPLY, Orange Also Called: Cleatech LLC *(P-7824)*

Global Language Solutions LLC ....D 949 798-1400
19800 Macarthur Blvd Irvine (92612) *(P-14503)*

Global Link Sourcing Inc ....D 951 698-1977
41690 Corporate Center Ct Murrieta (92562) *(P-2708)*

Global Mail Inc ....C 310 735-0800
921 W Artesia Blvd Compton (90220) *(P-9284)*

Global Metal Solutions Inc ....E 949 872-2995
2150 Mcgaw Ave Irvine (92614) *(P-5264)*

Global Microwave Systems Inc ....E 760 496-0046
1916 Palomar Oaks Way Ste 100 Carlsbad (92008) *(P-6617)*

Global Nature Foods, Bell Also Called: H & T Seafood Inc *(P-10855)*

Global Packaging Solutions Inc ....B 619 710-2661
6259 Progressive Dr Ste 200 San Diego (92154) *(P-2669)*

Global Paratransit Inc ....B 310 715-7550
400 W Compton Blvd Gardena (90248) *(P-8829)*

Global Pcci (gpc) (PA).................................C 757 637-9000
2465 Campus Dr Ste 100 Irvine (92612) *(P-5189)*

Global Plastics Inc ....C 951 657-5466
145 Malbert St Perris (92570) *(P-10538)*

Global Plumbing & Fire Supply ....C 818 550-8444
723 Sonora Ave Glendale (91201) *(P-10318)*

Global Rental Co Inc ....C 909 469-5160
1253 Price Ave Pomona (91767) *(P-13435)*

Global Service Resources Inc ....D 800 679-7658
711 S Victory Blvd Burbank (91502) *(P-13738)*

Global Silicon Electronics Inc ....E 626 336-1888
440 Cloverleaf Dr Baldwin Park (91706) *(P-5878)*

Global Solutions Integration ....D 949 307-1849
26632 Towne Centre Dr Ste 300 Foothill Ranch (92610) *(P-17540)*

Global Sweeping Solutions, San Bernardino Also Called: Global Environmental Pdts Inc
(P-7177)

Global Trade Alliance Inc ....C 562 944-6422
13642 Orden Dr Santa Fe Springs (90670) *(P-11447)*

Global Travel Collection LLC ....D 310 271-9566
345 N Maple Dr Beverly Hills (90210) *(P-9222)*

Global Truss, Vernon Also Called: Global Truss America LLC *(P-4597)*

Global Truss America LLC ....D 323 415-6225
4295 Charter St Vernon (90058) *(P-4597)*

Globe Iron Foundry Inc ....D 323 723-8983
5649 Randolph St Commerce (90040) *(P-4557)*

Globe Shoes, Carson Also Called: Osata Enterprises Inc *(P-10737)*

Globecast America Incorporated ....C 310 845-3900
2 Dole Dr Westlake Village (91362) *(P-9552)*

Gloria Lance Inc (PA)..................................D 310 767-4400
15616 S Broadway Gardena (90248) *(P-2036)*

Glovis America Inc (HQ)...............................C 714 427-0944
18191 Von Karman Ave Ste 500 Irvine (92612) *(P-9285)*

Glp Capital Partners LP ....D 310 356-0880
100 Wilshire Blvd Ste 1400 Santa Monica (90401) *(P-18143)*

Glysens Incorporated ....E 858 638-7708
3931 Sorrento Valley Blvd Ste 110 San Diego (92121) *(P-8160)*

Gma Cover Corp C
1170 Somera Rd Los Angeles (90077) *(P-2239)*

Gmi Inc ....E 619 429-4479
2626 Southport Way Ste E National City (91950) *(P-2229)*

GMI Building Services Inc ....C 858 279-6262
8001 Vickers St San Diego (92111) *(P-13375)*

Gmp Laboratories America Inc (PA)................D 714 630-2467
2931 E La Jolla St Anaheim (92806) *(P-3412)*

Gmp Labratories of America, Anaheim Also Called: Gmp Laboratories America Inc *(P-3412)*

Gms Elevator Services, San Dimas Also Called: Gms Elevator Services Inc *(P-5514)*

Gms Elevator Services Inc ....E 909 599-3904
401 Borrego Ct San Dimas (91773) *(P-5514)*

Gmto Corporation ....D 626 204-0500
300 N Lake Ave Fl 14 Pasadena (91101) *(P-8001)*

Go-Staff Inc ....A 760 730-8520
9878 Complex Dr Oceanside (92054) *(P-13522)*

Go-Staff Inc ....A 657 242-9350
240 W Lincoln Ave Anaheim (92805) *(P-13523)*

Goal Financial LLC ....C 619 684-7600
401 W A St Ste 1300 San Diego (92101) *(P-11906)*

Goetzman Group Inc ....D 818 595-1112
21333 Oxnard St Ste 200 Woodland Hills (91367) *(P-18144)*

Goforth & Marti (PA)...................................B 800 686-6583
110 W A St Ste 140 San Diego (92101) *(P-9872)*

Goforth & Marti ....D 951 684-0870
1099 W La Cadena Dr Riverside (92501) *(P-9873)*

Gofund.me, San Diego Also Called: Gofundme Giving Fund *(P-17226)*

Gofundme Giving Fund ....D 650 260-3436
3223 Greyling Dr San Diego (92123) *(P-17226)*

Goglanian, Santa Ana Also Called: Goglanian Bakeries Inc *(P-10945)*

Goglanian Bakeries Inc (HQ)........................B 714 338-1145
3401 W Segerstrom Ave Santa Ana (92704) *(P-10945)*

Gohz Inc ....E 800 603-1219
23555 Golden Springs Dr Ste K1 Diamond Bar (91765) *(P-6323)*

Gold Coast Baking Company LLC (PA)............D 818 575-7280
21250 Califa St Ste 104 Woodland Hills (91367) *(P-1456)*

Gold Coast Baking Company LLC ....E 714 545-2253
1590 E Saint Gertrude Pl Santa Ana (92705) *(P-1457)*

Gold Coast Health Plan, Camarillo Also Called: Ventura Cnty Md-Cal Mnged Care *(P-16626)*

Gold Coast Ingredients Inc ....D 323 724-8935
2429 Yates Ave Commerce (90040) *(P-1782)*

Gold Coast Tours, Brea Also Called: Hot Dogger Tours Inc *(P-8864)*

Gold Crest Industries Inc ....E 909 930-9069
1018 E Acacia St Ontario (91761) *(P-2230)*

Gold Cross Ambulance, Los Angeles Also Called: Schaefer Ambulance Service Inc *(P-8848)*

Gold Parent LP ....A 310 954-0444
11111 Santa Monica Blvd Ste 2000 Los Angeles (90025) *(P-11965)*

Gold Peak Industries (north America) Inc ....E 858 674-6099
11245 W Bernardo Ct Ste 104 San Diego (92127) *(P-7078)*

Gold Prospectors Assn Amer, Murrieta Also Called: Gold Prospectors Assn Amer LLC
(P-2858)

Mergent email: customerrelations@mergent.com
1038

2025 Southern California
Business Directory and Buyers Guide

(P-0000) Products & Services Section entry number
(PA)=Parent Co (HQ)=Headquarters (DH)=Div Headquarters

Gold Prospectors Assn Amer LLC .... E 951 699-4749
25819 Jefferson Ave Ste 110 Murrieta (92562) *(P-2858)*

Gold Star Foods Inc (HQ) .... D 909 843-9600
3781 E Airport Dr Ontario (91761) *(P-1783)*

Gold's Gym, West Hollywood Also Called: Rsg Group USA Inc *(P-12611)*

Goldak Inc .... E 818 240-2666
15835 Monte St Ste 104 Sylmar (91342) *(P-7723)*

Goldberg and Solovy Foods Inc, Vernon Also Called: Palisades Ranch Inc *(P-10764)*

Goldco, Calabasas Also Called: Goldco Direct LLC *(P-10547)*

Goldco Direct LLC .... D 818 343-0186
24025 Park Sorrento Ste 210 Calabasas (91302) *(P-10547)*

Golden Acorn Casino & Trvl Ctr, Campo Also Called: Campo Band Missions Indians *(P-15099)*

Golden Arrow Construction Inc .... C 310 523-9056
21213b Hawthorne Blvd Pmb 5402 Torrance (90503) *(P-406)*

Golden Bolt LLC .... D 818 626-8261
9361 Canoga Ave Chatsworth (91311) *(P-5127)*

Golden Brands, Huntington Beach Also Called: Harbor Distributing LLc *(P-11049)*

Golden Care Inc .... D 818 763-6275
6120 Vineland Ave North Hollywood (91606) *(P-15857)*

Golden Day Pre-School, Los Angeles Also Called: Golden Day Schools Inc *(P-16808)*

Golden Day Schools Inc .... D 323 296-6280
4508 Crenshaw Blvd Los Angeles (90043) *(P-16808)*

Golden Door, San Marcos Also Called: Golden Door Properties LLC *(P-12827)*

Golden Door Properties LLC .... C 760 744-5777
777 Deer Springs Rd San Marcos (92069) *(P-12827)*

Golden Eagle, San Diego Also Called: Golden Eagle Insurance Corp *(P-12118)*

Golden Eagle Insurance Corp (DH) .... C 619 744-6000
525 B St Ste 1300 San Diego (92101) *(P-12118)*

Golden Empire Con Pdts Inc .... D 661 833-4490
8261 Mccutchen Rd Bakersfield (93311) *(P-4394)*

Golden Empire Mortgage Inc (PA) .... D 661 328-1600
2130 Chester Ave Bakersfield (93301) *(P-11907)*

Golden Empire Mortgage Inc (PA) .... D 661 328-1600
1200 Discovery Dr Ste 300 Bakersfield (93309) *(P-11908)*

Golden Empire Mortgage Inc .... B 661 949-3388
41331 12th St W Ste 102 Palmdale (93551) *(P-11909)*

Golden Empire Transit District (PA) .... C 661 869-2438
1830 Golden State Ave Bakersfield (93301) *(P-8756)*

Golden Hotels Ltd Partnership .... C 949 833-2770
18700 Macarthur Blvd Irvine (92612) *(P-12828)*

Golden Hour Data Systems Inc .... C 858 768-2500
10052 Mesa Ridge Ct Ste 200 San Diego (92121) *(P-9286)*

Golden International .... A 213 628-1388
424 S Los Angeles St Ste 2 Los Angeles (90013) *(P-12707)*

Golden Kraft Inc .... B 562 926-8888
15500 Valley View Ave La Mirada (90638) *(P-2769)*

Golden Mattress Co Inc .... D 323 887-1888
11680 Wright Rd Lynwood (90262) *(P-2485)*

Golden Pacific, Pomona Also Called: Travelers Choice Travelware *(P-4302)*

Golden Pacific Seafoods Inc .... F 714 589-8888
700 S Raymond Ave Fullerton (92831) *(P-5674)*

Golden Queen Mining Co LLC .... C 661 824-4300
2818 Silver Queen Rd Mojave (93501) *(P-253)*

Golden Specialty Foods LLC .... E 562 802-2537
14605 Best Ave Norwalk (90650) *(P-1784)*

Golden Star Technology Inc (PA) .... D 562 345-8700
12881 166th St Cerritos (90703) *(P-11540)*

Golden State Care Center, Baldwin Park Also Called: Golden State Habilitation Conv *(P-15667)*

Golden State Drilling Inc .... D 661 589-0730
3500 Fruitvale Ave Bakersfield (93308) *(P-291)*

Golden State Engineering Inc .... C 562 634-3125
15338 Garfield Ave Paramount (90723) *(P-5654)*

Golden State Fence Co., Riverside Also Called: Fenceworks LLC *(P-1205)*

Golden State Foods, Irvine Also Called: Golden State Foods Corp *(P-1682)*

Golden State Foods Corp .... B 626 465-7500
640 S 6th Ave City Of Industry (91746) *(P-1392)*

Golden State Foods Corp (PA) .... E 949 247-8000
18301 Von Karman Ave Ste 1100 Irvine (92612) *(P-1682)*

Golden State Habilitation Conv (PA) .... C 626 962-3274
1758 Big Dalton Ave Baldwin Park (91706) *(P-15667)*

Golden State Health Ctrs Inc .... C 310 451-9706
1340 15th St Santa Monica (90404) *(P-15858)*

Golden State Medical Sup Inc .... C 805 477-9866
5187 Camino Ruiz Camarillo (93012) *(P-10079)*

Golden State Mutl Lf Insur Co (PA) .... D 713 526-4361
1999 W Adams Blvd Los Angeles (90018) *(P-12041)*

Golden State Phone & Wireless .... D 805 545-5400
138 W Branch St Ste B Arroyo Grande (93420) *(P-9402)*

Golden Supreme Inc .... E 562 903-1063
12304 Mccann Dr Santa Fe Springs (90670) *(P-8679)*

Golden Temple, Los Angeles Also Called: East West Tea Company LLC *(P-1411)*

Golden West Casino, Bakersfield Also Called: Golden West Partners Inc *(P-12829)*

Golden West K-9, Pacoima Also Called: Golden West Security *(P-14303)*

Golden West Machine Inc .... E 562 903-1111
9930 Jordan Cir Santa Fe Springs (90670) *(P-6137)*

Golden West Packg Group LLC (PA) .... B 888 501-5893
15250 Don Julian Rd City Of Industry (91745) *(P-2670)*

Golden West Partners Inc .... C 661 324-6936
1001 S Union Ave Bakersfield (93307) *(P-12829)*

Golden West Security .... C 818 897-5965
12502 Van Nuys Blvd Ste 215 Pacoima (91331) *(P-14303)*

Golden West Shutters, Lake Forest Also Called: ABC Custom Wood Shutters Inc *(P-2294)*

Golden West Technology .... D 714 738-3775
1180 E Valencia Dr Fullerton (92831) *(P-6733)*

Goldencorr Sheets LLC .... C 626 369-6446
13890 Nelson Ave City Of Industry (91746) *(P-2671)*

Goldenwood Truss Corporation .... D 805 659-2520
11032 Nardo St Ventura (93004) *(P-2376)*

Goldfax, Laguna Beach Also Called: Data Processing Design Inc *(P-13701)*

Goldman Data LLC .... D 714 283-5889
2156 N Shaffer St Orange (92865) *(P-18314)*

Goldman Sachs, Los Angeles Also Called: Goldman Sachs & Co LLC *(P-11966)*

Goldman Sachs & Co LLC .... C 310 407-5700
2121 Avenue Of The Stars Ste 2600 Los Angeles (90067) *(P-11966)*

Goldrich & Kest Industries LLC (PA) .... A 310 204-2050
5150 Overland Ave Culver City (90230) *(P-12566)*

Goldrich Kest Hirsch Stern LLC (PA) .... C 310 204-2050
5150 Overland Ave Culver City (90230) *(P-12567)*

Golds Gym, Northridge Also Called: Musclebound Inc *(P-15057)*

Goldsign, Huntington Park Also Called: Citizens of Humanity LLC *(P-2085)*

Goldstar Asphalt Products, Perris Also Called: Npg Inc *(P-3838)*

Goldstar Asphalt Products Inc .... E 951 940-1610
1354 Jet Way Perris (92571) *(P-3837)*

Goleta Valley Cottage Hosp Aux .... B 805 681-6468
351 S Patterson Ave Santa Barbara (93111) *(P-16008)*

Golf Buddy, Santa Fe Springs Also Called: Deca International Corp *(P-7712)*

Golf Management Operating LLC .... A 760 777-4839
50200 Avenida Vista Bonita La Quinta (92253) *(P-15082)*

Golf Sales West, Oxnard Also Called: Golf Sales West Inc *(P-8518)*

Golf Sales West Inc .... E 805 988-3363
1901 Eastman Ave Oxnard (93030) *(P-8518)*

Golf Supply House Usa Inc .... D 714 983-0050
1340 N Jefferson St Anaheim (92807) *(P-8519)*

Gomen Furniture Mfg Inc .... E 310 635-4894
11612 Wright Rd Lynwood (90262) *(P-2447)*

Gonsalves & Santucci Inc .... B 909 350-0474
13052 Dahlia St Fontana (92337) *(P-1117)*

Gooch and Housego Cal LLC .... D 805 529-3324
5390 Kazuko Ct Moorpark (93021) *(P-8002)*

Good American LLC (PA) .... E 213 357-5100
1601 Vine St Los Angeles (90028) *(P-2098)*

Good Culture LLC .... E 949 545-9945
22 Corporate Park Irvine (92606) *(P-1331)*

Good Fellas Industries Inc .... D 323 924-9495
4400 Bandini Blvd Vernon (90058) *(P-11531)*

Good Health Inc .... C 714 961-7930
410 Cloverleaf Dr Baldwin Park (91706) *(P-16562)*

Good Neighbor Pharmacy, Orange Also Called: Amerisourcebergen Drug Corp *(P-10613)*

Employee Codes: A=Over 500 employees, B=251-500
C=101-250, D=51-100, E=20-50, F=10-19, G=1-9

2025 Southern California
Business Directory and Buyers Guide

© Mergent Inc. 1-800-342-5647

1039

Good Shepherd Cemetery, Huntington Beach *Also Called: Roman Cthlic Diocese of Orange* *(P-12586)*

Good Shepherd Lutheran HM of W .... C 805 526-2482
2949 Alamo St Simi Valley (93063) *(P-17156)*

Good Smrtan Hosp A Cal Ltd Prt .... B 661 903-9555
901 Olive Dr Bakersfield (93308) *(P-16009)*

Good Sports Plus Ltd .... B 310 671-4400
370 Amapola Ave Ste 208 Torrance (90501) *(P-13739)*

Good Tree, Montebello *Also Called: Commerce On Demand LLC (P-8673)*

Good Worldwide LLC .... E 323 206-6495
6380 Wilshire Blvd # 15 Los Angeles (90048) *(P-2918)*

Good-West Rubber Corp (PA) .... **C 909 987-1774**
9615 Feron Blvd Rancho Cucamonga (91730) *(P-3912)*

Gooden Center .... D 626 356-0078
191 N El Molino Ave Pasadena (91101) *(P-16294)*

Goodfellow Corporation .... D 909 874-2700
590 Crane St Lake Elsinore (92530) *(P-10348)*

Goodman Food Products Inc (PA) .... **C 310 674-3180**
200 E Beach Ave Fl 1 Inglewood (90302) *(P-1785)*

Goodrich Corporation .... D 562 944-4441
9920 Freeman Ave Santa Fe Springs (90670) *(P-7485)*

Goodrich Corporation .... C 714 984-1461
3355 E La Palma Ave Anaheim (92806) *(P-7486)*

GOODRX, Santa Monica *Also Called: Goodrx Holdings Inc (P-14135)*

Goodrx Holdings Inc (PA) .... **C 855 268-2822**
2701 Olympic Blvd Santa Monica (90404) *(P-14135)*

Goodwill Central Coast .... C 805 544-0542
880 Industrial Way San Luis Obispo (93401) *(P-11628)*

Goodwill Inds Orange Cnty Cal .... D 714 881-3986
5880 Edinger Ave Huntington Beach (92649) *(P-17060)*

Goodwill Inds San Diego Cnty .... D 760 806-7670
3841 Plaza Dr Ste 902 Oceanside (92056) *(P-17463)*

Goodwill Inds San Luis Obispo, San Luis Obispo *Also Called: Goodwill Central Coast* *(P-11628)*

Goodwill Inds Southern Cal (PA) .... A 323 223-1211
342 N San Fernando Rd Los Angeles (90031) *(P-11267)*

Goodwill Industries, Huntington Beach *Also Called: Goodwill Inds Orange Cnty Cal (P-17060)*

Goodwill Industries, Oceanside *Also Called: Goodwill Inds San Diego Cnty (P-17463)*

Goodwill Sthern Los Angles CNT (PA) .... D 562 435-3411
800 W Pacific Coast Hwy Long Beach (90806) *(P-14504)*

Goodwin Ammonia Company LLC .... D 714 894-0531
12361 Monarch St Garden Grove (92841) *(P-3593)*

Goodyear, Moreno Valley *Also Called: Certified Tire & Svc Ctrs Inc (P-11441)*

Goodyear Rbr Co Southern Cal, Rancho Cucamonga *Also Called: Good-West Rubber Corp* *(P-3912)*

Google International LLC (DH) .... **D 650 253-0000**
35018 Avenue D Yucaipa (92399) *(P-9441)*

Goproto, San Diego *Also Called: Higgs Fletcher & Mack Llp (P-16701)*

Gordian Medical Inc .... B 714 556-0200
750 The City Dr S Orange (92868) *(P-10080)*

Gordon Rees Scully Mansukhani .... C 213 576-5000
633 W 5th St 52nd Fl Los Angeles (90071) *(P-16694)*

Gordon Rees Scully Mansukhani .... C 619 696-6700
101 W Broadway Ste 1600 San Diego (92101) *(P-16695)*

Gores Group LLC (PA) .... D 310 209-3010
9800 Wilshire Blvd Beverly Hills (90212) *(P-11967)*

Gorilla Automotive Products, Buena Park *Also Called: Amcor Industries Inc (P-7224)*

Gorlitz Sewer & Drain Inc .... E 562 944-3060
10132 Norwalk Blvd Santa Fe Springs (90670) *(P-6015)*

Gosch Ford Lincoln Mercury, Hemet *Also Called: Jack Gosch Ford Inc (P-11364)*

Gosecure Inc (PA) .... **C 301 442-3432**
13220 Evening Creek Dr S Ste 107 San Diego (92128) *(P-11541)*

Gossamer Bio Inc (PA) .... **E 858 684-1300**
3013 Science Park Rd Ste 200 San Diego (92121) *(P-3413)*

Gothic Ground Management, Santa Clarita *Also Called: Gothic Landscaping Inc (P-207)*

Gothic Grounds Mgmt, Valencia *Also Called: Gothic Landscaping Inc (P-170)*

Gothic Landscaping Inc .... C 661 257-5085
27413 Tourney Rd Ste 200 Valencia (91355) *(P-170)*

Gothic Landscaping Inc (PA) .... **C 661 678-1400**
27413 Tourney Rd Santa Clarita (91355) *(P-207)*

Gottstein Corporation .... C 661 322-8934
3500 Chester Ave Bakersfield (93301) *(P-10349)*

Goudy Honda, Alhambra *Also Called: Alhambra Motors Inc (P-11314)*

Gould & Bass Company Inc .... E 909 623-6793
1431 W 2nd St Pomona (91766) *(P-7913)*

Gould Electric Inc .... C 858 486-1727
12975 Brookprinter Pl Ste 280 Poway (92064) *(P-921)*

Gourmet Foods Inc (PA) .... **D 310 632-3300**
2910 E Harcourt St Compton (90221) *(P-10753)*

Gourmet India Food Company LLC .... D 562 698-9763
12220 Rivera Rd Ste A Whittier (90606) *(P-10946)*

Gourmet Specialties Inc .... D 323 587-1734
2120 E 25th St Vernon (90058) *(P-10904)*

Governmentjobscom Inc (PA) .... **D 877 204-4442**
2120 Park Pl Ste 100 El Segundo (90245) *(P-13940)*

GP Batteries, San Diego *Also Called: Gold Peak Industries (north America) Inc (P-7078)*

GP Color Imaging Group, North Hollywood *Also Called: Wes Go Inc (P-3187)*

GP Merger Sub Inc .... D 562 946-7722
9401 Ann St Santa Fe Springs (90670) *(P-4335)*

Gpc, Irvine *Also Called: Global Pcci (gpc) (P-5189)*

GPde Slva Spces Incrporation (PA) .... **D 562 407-2643**
8531 Loch Lomond Dr Pico Rivera (90660) *(P-1786)*

GPh Medical & Legal Services (PA) .... **C 213 207-2700**
468 N Camden Dr Beverly Hills (90210) *(P-15668)*

Gpi Ca-Niii Inc .... D 626 305-3000
1434 Buena Vista St Duarte (91010) *(P-11355)*

GPM, Thousand Oaks *Also Called: General Pavement Management Inc (P-1116)*

Gps Associates Inc .... E 949 408-3162
1803 Carnegie Ave Santa Ana (92705) *(P-3604)*

Gps Painting Wallcovering Inc .... C 714 730-8904
1307 E Saint Gertrude Pl Ste C Santa Ana (92705) *(P-865)*

Gr8 Care Inc .... D 626 337-7229
14518 Los Angeles St Baldwin Park (91706) *(P-15669)*

Grabit Interactive Inc .... E 844 472-2488
14724 Ventura Blvd Sherman Oaks (91403) *(P-13267)*

Grace Communications Inc (PA) .... **E 213 628-4384**
210 S Spring St Los Angeles (90012) *(P-2800)*

Gracek Jewelry, Newport Coast *Also Called: Krystal Ventures LLC (P-8455)*

Gracelight Community Health .... D 323 780-4510
4618 Fountain Ave Los Angeles (90029) *(P-15316)*

Gracelight Community Health .... D 323 644-6180
4618 Fountain Ave Los Angeles (90029) *(P-15317)*

Gracing Brand Management Inc .... B 626 297-2472
1108 W Valley Blvd Ste 660 Alhambra (91803) *(P-2170)*

Graco Childrens Products Inc .... B 770 418-7200
17182 Nevada St Victorville (92394) *(P-2469)*

Gradient Engineers Inc .... C 949 477-0555
17781 Cowan Ste 140 Irvine (92614) *(P-17541)*

Graffiti Shield Inc .... E 714 575-1100
2940 E La Palma Ave Ste D Anaheim (92806) *(P-3950)*

Graham Webb International Inc (HQ) .... **D 760 918-3600**
6109 De Soto Ave Woodland Hills (91367) *(P-3655)*

Granatelli Motor Sports Inc .... E 805 486-6644
1000 Yarnell Pl Oxnard (93033) *(P-7258)*

GRANCELL VILLAGE, Reseda *Also Called: Los Angles Jewish HM For Aging (P-15708)*

Grand Del Mar, San Diego *Also Called: Grand Del Mar Resort LP (P-12830)*

Grand Del Mar Resort LP .... A 858 314-2000
5300 Grand Del Mar Ct San Diego (92130) *(P-12830)*

Grand General, Rancho Dominguez *Also Called: Grand General Accessories LLC (P-6286)*

Grand General Accessories LLC .... E 310 631-2589
1965 E Vista Bella Way Rancho Dominguez (90220) *(P-6286)*

Grand Pacific Carlsbad Ht LP .... B 760 827-2400
5480 Grand Pacific Dr Carlsbad (92008) *(P-12831)*

Grand Pacific Resorts Inc (PA) .... **C 760 431-8500**
5900 Pasteur Ct Ste 200 Carlsbad (92008) *(P-12458)*

Grand Pacific Resorts Inc .... A 760 431-8500
5900 Pasteur Ct Ste 200 Carlsbad (92008) *(P-12832)*

Grand Pacific Resorts Svcs LP .... C 760 431-8500
5900 Pasteur Ct Ste 200 Carlsbad (92008) *(P-12833)*

Grand Slam Tennis Program, Pacific Palisades *Also Called: Riviera Country Club Inc* *(P-15217)*

2025 Southern California
Business Directory and Buyers Guide

Grand Textile, Cerritos *Also Called: Dool Fna Inc (P-1892)*

Grand Vista Hotel, Simi Valley *Also Called: Simi West Inc (P-13024)*

Grandall Distributing LLC .... E 818 242-6640
321 El Bonito Ave Glendale (91204) *(P-14505)*

Grandcare Health Services LLC (PA).................... C 866 554-2447
3452 E Foothill Blvd Ste 700 Pasadena (91107) *(P-16393)*

Grani Installation Inc (PA)....................................... D 714 898-0441
5411 Commercial Dr Huntington Beach (92649) *(P-540)*

Granite Construction Company .... B 760 775-7500
38000 Monroe St Indio (92203) *(P-617)*

Granite Construction Company .... C 805 964-9951
5335 Debbie Rd Santa Barbara (93111) *(P-618)*

Granite Construction Inc .... D 805 667-8210
213 Columbia Way Lancaster (93535) *(P-619)*

Granite Gold Inc .... D 858 499-8933
12780 Danielson Ct Ste A Poway (92064) *(P-3605)*

Granite Solutions Groupe Inc (PA)......................... C 415 963-3999
26565 Agoura Rd Ste 200 Calabasas (91302) *(P-13524)*

Granitize Aviation Intl, South Gate *Also Called: Granitize Products Inc (P-3606)*

Granitize Products Inc .... D 562 923-5438
11022 Vulcan St South Gate (90280) *(P-3606)*

Granlund Candies, Yucaipa *Also Called: B B G Management Group (P-10840)*

Grant & Weber (PA).. D 818 878-7700
26610 Agoura Rd Ste 209 Calabasas (91302) *(P-13284)*

Grant & Weber Travel, Calabasas *Also Called: Grant & Weber (P-13284)*

Grant Piston Rings, Anaheim *Also Called: Rtr Industries LLC (P-6046)*

Graphic Business Solutions Inc .... E 619 258-4081
1912 John Towers Ave El Cajon (92020) *(P-10580)*

Graphic Color Systems Inc .... D 323 283-3000
1166 W Garvey Ave Monterey Park (91754) *(P-3008)*

Graphic Ink Corp .... E 714 901-2805
5382 Industrial Dr Huntington Beach (92649) *(P-13329)*

Graphic Ink and Graphic Ink, Huntington Beach *Also Called: Graphic Ink Corp (P-13329)*

Graphic Packaging Intl LLC .... D 949 250-0900
1600 Barranca Pkwy Irvine (92606) *(P-11123)*

Graphic Prints Inc .... E 310 870-1239
904 Silver Spur Rd Ste 415 Rolling Hills Estate (90274) *(P-2261)*

Graphic Research Inc .... E 818 886-7340
3339 Durham Ct Burbank (91504) *(P-6734)*

Graphic Trends Incorporated .... E 562 531-2339
7301 Adams St Paramount (90723) *(P-3140)*

Graphic Visions Inc .... E 818 845-8393
7119 Fair Ave North Hollywood (91605) *(P-3009)*

Graphics 2000 LLC .... D 714 879-1188
1600 E Valencia Dr Fullerton (92831) *(P-3141)*

Graphiq LLC .... C 805 335-2433
101a Innovation Pl Santa Barbara (93108) *(P-2919)*

Graphtec, Irvine *Also Called: Graphtec America Inc (P-7861)*

Graphtec America Inc (DH)...................................... E 949 770-6010
17462 Armstrong Ave Irvine (92614) *(P-7861)*

Grasshopper House Partners LLC .... C 310 589-2880
6428 Meadows Ct Malibu (90265) *(P-16947)*

Gray Construction Inc .... C 714 491-1315
2070 N Tustin Ave Santa Ana (92705) *(P-407)*

GRAY WC, Santa Ana *Also Called: Gray West Construction Inc (P-482)*

Gray West Construction Inc .... C 714 491-1317
2070 N Tustin Ave Santa Ana (92705) *(P-482)*

Graybar, Diamond Bar *Also Called: Graybar Electric Company Inc (P-10184)*

Graybar Electric Company Inc .... C 909 451-4300
1370 Valley Vista Dr Ste 100 Diamond Bar (91765) *(P-10184)*

Graybar Electric Company Inc .... D 858 578-8606
8606 Miralani Dr San Diego (92126) *(P-10185)*

Graybill Medical Group Inc (PA).............................. C 866 228-2236
225 E 2nd Ave Escondido (92025) *(P-15318)*

Graycon Inc .... D 626 961-9640
232 S 8th Ave City Of Industry (91746) *(P-783)*

Grease Company, The, Vernon *Also Called: Baker Commodities Inc (P-1522)*

Great Amercn Seafood Import Co, Carson *Also Called: Southwind Foods LLC (P-1698)*

Great American Cstm Insur Svcs .... B 213 430-4300
725 S Figueroa St Ste 3400 Los Angeles (90017) *(P-12119)*

Great American Custom, Los Angeles *Also Called: Great American Cstm Insur Svcs (P-12119)*

Great American Packaging .... E 323 582-2247
4361 S Soto St Vernon (90058) *(P-2732)*

Great Amrcn Logistics Dist Inc .... D 562 229-3601
13565 Larwin Cir Santa Fe Springs (90670) *(P-8993)*

Great Atlantic News LLC .... C 770 863-9000
1575 N Main St Orange (92867) *(P-11076)*

Great Eastern Entertainment Co .... E 310 638-5058
610 W Carob St Compton (90220) *(P-2920)*

Great Pacific Elbow LLC .... E 909 606-5551
13900 Sycamore Way Chino (91710) *(P-4989)*

Great Pacific Elbow Company, Chino *Also Called: Great Pacific Elbow LLC (P-4989)*

Great Pacific Patagonia, Ventura *Also Called: Patagonia Inc (P-2023)*

Great River Food, City Of Industry *Also Called: Derek and Constance Lee Corp (P-1257)*

Great Western Distributing Svc, Los Angeles *Also Called: Gils Distributing Service (P-13274)*

Great Western Malting Co .... D 360 991-0888
995 Joshua Way Ste B Vista (92081) *(P-1557)*

Great Western Packaging LLC .... D 818 464-3800
8230 Haskell Ave 8240 Van Nuys (91406) *(P-3142)*

Great Western Sales Inc .... D 310 323-7900
8737 Dice Rd Santa Fe Springs (90670) *(P-10319)*

Great Wolf Rsorts Holdings Inc .... C 888 960-9653
12681 Harbor Blvd Garden Grove (92840) *(P-12834)*

Greatbatch Medical, San Diego *Also Called: Integer Holdings Corporation (P-8171)*

Greatcall Inc .... A 800 733-6632
10945 Vista Sorrento Pkwy Ste 120 San Diego (92130) *(P-11685)*

Greater Alarm Company (DH)................................... D 949 474-0555
3750 Schaufele Ave Ste 200 Long Beach (90808) *(P-14403)*

Greater Los Angeles Zoo Assn .... D 323 644-4200
5333 Zoo Dr Los Angeles (90027) *(P-17227)*

Greater Los Angles Area Cncil (PA)......................... D 213 413-4400
2333 Scout Way Los Angeles (90026) *(P-17347)*

Greater Los Angles Cnty Vctor .... C 562 944-7976
12545 Florence Ave Santa Fe Springs (90670) *(P-18315)*

Greater Los Angles Vtrans RES .... D 310 312-1554
11301 Wilshire Blvd Bldg 114 Los Angeles (90073) *(P-12653)*

Greater San Diego AC Co Inc .... C 619 469-7818
3883 Ruffin Rd Ste C San Diego (92123) *(P-784)*

Greater Valley Med Group Inc .... C 818 781-7097
14600 Sherman Way Ste 300 Van Nuys (91405) *(P-16475)*

Greater Valley Med Group Inc (PA).......................... D 818 838-4500
11600 Indian Hills Rd 300 Mission Hills (91345) *(P-16476)*

Greatwide Dedicated Transport, Vernon *Also Called: Greatwide Logistics Svcs LLC (P-9287)*

Greatwide Logistics Svcs LLC .... D 323 268-7100
4310 Bandini Blvd Vernon (90058) *(P-9287)*

Grech Motors LLC (PA).. E 951 688-8347
6915 Arlington Ave Riverside (92504) *(P-14749)*

Greco and Sons, Vista *Also Called: Bellissimo Distribution LLC (P-1337)*

Greco Los Angeles, City Of Industry *Also Called: Concord Foods Inc (P-10748)*

Green Acres Lodge, Rosemead *Also Called: Longwood Management Corp (P-15703)*

Green Convergence (PA)... D 661 294-9495
28476 Westinghouse Pl Valencia (91355) *(P-10320)*

Green Dragon, Los Angeles *Also Called: Cmk Manufacturing LLC (P-1099)*

Green Energy Innovations, Buena Park *Also Called: Stadia Inc (P-960)*

Green Farms Inc .... D 858 831-7701
2652 Long Beach Ave Los Angeles (90058) *(P-10905)*

Green Hasson & Janks LLP .... C 310 873-1600
700 S Flower St Ste 3300 Los Angeles (90017) *(P-17730)*

Green Hills Software, Santa Barbara *Also Called: Green Hills Software LLC (P-13941)*

Green Hills Software LLC (HQ)................................. C 805 965-6044
30 W Sola St Santa Barbara (93101) *(P-13941)*

Green Line Rail Eqp Maint, Lawndale *Also Called: Los Angles Cnty Mtro Trnsp Aut (P-8762)*

Green River Golf Corporation .... D 714 970-8411
5215 Green River Rd Corona (92878) *(P-15083)*

Green River Golf Course, Corona *Also Called: Green River Golf Corporation (P-15083)*

Green Star Labs Inc .... E 619 489-9020
4075 Ruffin Rd San Diego (92123) *(P-3317)*

Green Thumb International Inc .... D 818 340-6400
21812 Sherman Way Canoga Park (91303) *(P-11087)*

Employee Codes: A=Over 500 employees, B=251-500
C=101-250, D=51-100, E=20-50, F=10-19, G=1-9

2025 Southern California
Business Directory and Buyers Guide

© Mergent Inc. 1-800-342-5647
1041

ALPHABETIC

Green Thumb International Inc .... D 661 259-1071
23734 Newhall Ave Newhall (91321) *(P-11259)*

Green Thumb Nurseries, Newhall *Also Called: Green Thumb International Inc (P-11259)*

Green Tomato Grill, Orange *Also Called: Fahetas LLC (P-11569)*

Green-N-Clean Ex Car Wash Inc .... D 949 749-4977
28622 Oso Pkwy Pmb C Rcho Sta Marg (92688) *(P-14709)*

Greenball Corp (PA) .... E 714 782-3060
222 S Harbor Blvd Ste 700 Anaheim (92805) *(P-9856)*

Greenberg Glsker Flds Clman Mc .... C 310 553-3610
2049 Century Park E Ste 2600 Los Angeles (90067) *(P-16696)*

Greenberg Traurig, Irvine *Also Called: Greenberg Traurig LLP (P-16697)*

Greenberg Traurig LLP .... D 949 732-6500
18565 Jamboree Rd Ste 500 Irvine (92612) *(P-16697)*

Greenberg Traurig LLP .... D 310 586-7708
1840 Century Park E Ste 1900 Los Angeles (90067) *(P-16698)*

Greenbox, Los Angeles *Also Called: Greenbox Loans Inc (P-11785)*

Greenbox Art and Culture, San Diego *Also Called: No Boundaries Inc (P-3051)*

Greenbox Loans Inc .... D 800 919-1086
3250 Wilshire Blvd Ste 1900 Los Angeles (90010) *(P-11785)*

Greenbrier Rail, San Bernardino *Also Called: Meridian Rail Acquisition (P-9370)*

Greenbrier Rail Services, San Bernardino *Also Called: Gunderson Rail Services LLC (P-9365)*

Greene Group Industries, Oceanside *Also Called: Southwest Greene Intl Inc (P-5213)*

Greenheart, Arroyo Grande *Also Called: Greenheart Farms Inc (P-81)*

Greenheart Farms Inc .... B 805 481-2234
902 Zenon Way Arroyo Grande (93420) *(P-81)*

Greenhedge Escrow .... C 310 640-3040
2015 Manhattan Beach Blvd Redondo Beach (90278) *(P-12559)*

Greenhouse Agency Inc .... C 949 752-7542
4100 Birch St Ste 500 Newport Beach (92660) *(P-18145)*

Greenlots, Los Angeles *Also Called: Zeco Systems Inc (P-11026)*

Greenpath Recovery Recycl Svcs, Colton *Also Called: Greenpath Recovery West Inc (P-10539)*

Greenpath Recovery West Inc .... D 909 954-0686
330 W Citrus St Ste 250 Colton (92324) *(P-10539)*

Greenpower Motor Company Inc .... D 909 308-0960
8885 Haven Ave Ste 200 Rancho Cucamonga (91730) *(P-7178)*

Greens Group Inc .... C 949 829-4902
16530 Bake Pkwy Ste 200 Irvine (92618) *(P-12835)*

Greenscreen .... E 310 837-0526
725 S Figueroa St Ste 1825 Los Angeles (90017) *(P-171)*

Greenshine New Energy LLC .... D 949 609-9636
23661 Birtcher Dr Lake Forest (92630) *(P-6504)*

Greensoft Technology Inc .... C 323 254-5961
155 S El Molino Ave Ste 100 Pasadena (91101) *(P-14136)*

Greenwich Biosciences LLC (DH) .... E 760 795-2200
5750 Fleet St Ste 200 Carlsbad (92008) *(P-3414)*

Greenwich Biosciences, Inc., Carlsbad *Also Called: Greenwich Biosciences LLC (P-3414)*

Greenwlds Atbody Frmeworks Inc .... D 619 477-2600
2850 Erie St San Diego (92117) *(P-14673)*

Greenwood & Hall, Los Angeles *Also Called: Pcs Link Inc (P-18347)*

Greenwood Hall Inc .... C 310 905-8300
6230 Wilshire Blvd Ste 136 Los Angeles (90048) *(P-16854)*

Grefco Dicaperl, Torrance *Also Called: Dicaperl Corporation (P-385)*

Gregg Drilling LLC .... C 562 427-6899
2726 Walnut Ave Signal Hill (90755) *(P-1143)*

Gregg Drilling & Testing Inc (PA) .... D 562 427-6899
2726 Walnut Ave Signal Hill (90755) *(P-1207)*

Gregg Electric Inc .... C 909 983-1794
608 W Emporia St Ontario (91762) *(P-922)*

Gregory Consulting Inc (PA) .... C 805 642-0111
6350 Leland St Ventura (93003) *(P-11356)*

Greif Inc .... E 323 724-7500
6001 S Eastern Ave Commerce (90040) *(P-2394)*

Greif Inc .... D 909 350-2112
8250 Almeria Ave Fontana (92335) *(P-4728)*

Greka, Santa Maria *Also Called: Greka Integrated Inc (P-306)*

Greka Integrated Inc .... C 805 347-8700
1700 Sinton Rd Santa Maria (93458) *(P-306)*

Gremlin Inc .... D 408 214-9885
440 N Barranca Ave Ste 3101 Walnut (91789) *(P-13942)*

Gremlin Software, Inc., Walnut *Also Called: Gremlin Inc (P-13942)*

Greneker Solutions, Los Angeles *Also Called: Pacific Manufacturing MGT Inc (P-2586)*

Gresean Industries Inc .... E
6320 Caballero Blvd Buena Park (90620) *(P-1050)*

Greyhound Lines Inc .... D 213 629-8400
1716 E 7th St Los Angeles (90021) *(P-8858)*

Greystar, Newport Beach *Also Called: Greystar Management Svcs LP (P-12460)*

Greystar Management Svcs LP .... C 818 596-2180
6320 Canoga Ave Ste 1512 Woodland Hills (91367) *(P-12459)*

Greystar Management Svcs LP .... A 949 705-0010
620 Newport Center Dr 15th Fl Newport Beach (92660) *(P-12460)*

Greystar Rs Group LLC .... C 818 841-2441
1200 W Riverside Dr Burbank (91506) *(P-12295)*

Griffith Company .... B 661 392-6640
1128 Carrier Parkway Ave Bakersfield (93308) *(P-620)*

Griffith Company (PA) .... C 714 984-5500
3050 E Birch St Brea (92821) *(P-621)*

Griffith Park Healthcare Ctr, Glendale *Also Called: Griffith Pk Rhbltation Ctr LLC (P-15670)*

Griffith Pk Rhbltation Ctr LLC .... D 818 845-8507
201 Allen Ave Glendale (91201) *(P-15670)*

Grifols Bio Supplies Inc .... C 760 651-4042
980 Park Center Dr Ste F Vista (92081) *(P-16563)*

Grifols Biologicals LLC (DH) .... D 323 225-2221
5555 Valley Blvd Los Angeles (90032) *(P-3577)*

Grifols Usa LLC .... D 760 931-8444
995 Park Center Dr Vista (92081) *(P-3578)*

Grifols Usa LLC .... A 626 435-2600
13111 Temple Ave City Of Industry (91746) *(P-10081)*

Grifols Wrldwide Oprtons USA I .... D 626 435-2600
13111 Temple Ave City Of Industry (91746) *(P-16564)*

Griley Air Freight, Los Angeles *Also Called: Southern Counties Terminals (P-8924)*

Grimmway Enterprises Inc .... C 661 399-0844
6301 Zerker Rd Shafter (93263) *(P-82)*

Grimmway Enterprises Inc .... B 661 393-3320
6101 Zerker Rd Shafter (93263) *(P-108)*

Grimmway Enterprises Inc .... B 661 854-6250
830 Sycamore Rd Arvin (93203) *(P-109)*

Grimmway Enterprises Inc .... B 661 854-6200
11412 Malaga Rd Arvin (93203) *(P-110)*

Grimmway Enterprises Inc .... C 661 845-5200
6900 Mountain View Rd Bakersfield (93307) *(P-111)*

Grimmway Enterprises Inc .... B 661 854-6240
12020 Malaga Rd Arvin (93203) *(P-483)*

Grimmway Enterprises Inc .... D 307 302-0090
11646 Malaga Rd Arvin (93203) *(P-8912)*

Grimmway Enterprises Inc .... B 661 845-3758
12000 Main St Lamont (93241) *(P-10906)*

Grimmway Enterprises Inc .... D 760 344-0204
2171 W Bannister Rd Brawley (92227) *(P-14690)*

Grimmway Enterprises Inc .... C 661 854-6200
14141 Di Giorgio Rd Arvin (93203) *(P-17989)*

Grimmway Farms, Arvin *Also Called: Grimmway Enterprises Inc (P-110)*

Grimmway Farms, Bakersfield *Also Called: Grimmway Enterprises Inc (P-111)*

Grimmway Frozen Foods, Arvin *Also Called: Grimmway Enterprises Inc (P-109)*

Grindr LLC .... C 310 776-6680
750 N San Vicente Blvd West Hollywood (90069) *(P-13740)*

Gringo Ventures LLC .... B 760 477-7999
3260 Corporate Vw Vista (92081) *(P-11088)*

Gringteam Inc .... B 619 297-5466
7450 Hazard Center Dr San Diego (92108) *(P-12836)*

Gringteam Inc .... C 858 485-4145
800 W Ivy St Ste D San Diego (92101) *(P-12837)*

Gripp, Temecula *Also Called: Bbk Performance Inc (P-9815)*

Griswold Controls, Irvine *Also Called: Griswold Controls LLC (P-5388)*

Griswold Controls LLC (PA) .... D 949 559-6000
1700 Barranca Pkwy Irvine (92606) *(P-5388)*

Griswold Industries (PA) .... B 949 722-4800
1701 Placentia Ave Costa Mesa (92627) *(P-4675)*

Griswold Pump Company .... E 909 422-1700
22069 Van Buren St Grand Terrace (92313) *(P-5734)*

Mergent email: customerrelations@mergent.com
1042
2025 Southern California
Business Directory and Buyers Guide
(P-0000) Products & Services Section entry number
(PA)=Parent Co (HQ)=Headquarters (DH)=Div Headquarters

Gro-Power Inc .... E 909 393-3744
15065 Telephone Ave Chino (91710) *(P-3744)*

Grolink, Oxnard *Also Called: Grolink Plant Company Inc (P-11089)*

Grolink Plant Company Inc (PA) .... C 805 984-7958
4107 W Gonzales Rd Oxnard (93036) *(P-11089)*

Grossmont Home Hlth & Hospice, La Mesa *Also Called: Grossmont Hospital Corporation*
(P-16011)

Grossmont Hospital Corporation (HQ) .... A 619 740-6000
5555 Grossmont Center Dr La Mesa (91942) *(P-16010)*

Grossmont Hospital Corporation .... B 619 667-1900
8881 Fletcher Pkwy Ste 105 La Mesa (91942) *(P-16011)*

Grosvenor Inv MGT US Inc .... D 310 265-0297
2308 Chelsea Rd Palos Verdes Estates (90274) *(P-12216)*

Ground Control Business MGT (DH) .... E 310 315-6200
2049 Century Park E Ste 1400 Los Angeles (90067) *(P-1895)*

Ground Force One, Redondo Beach *Also Called: Cputer Inc (P-14208)*

Ground Hog Inc .... E 909 478-5700
1470 Victoria Ct San Bernardino (92408) *(P-5492)*

Groundwork Coffee, North Hollywood *Also Called: Groundwork Coffee Roasters LLC*
(P-1719)

Groundwork Coffee Roasters LLC .... C 818 506-6020
5457 Cleon Ave North Hollywood (91601) *(P-1719)*

Groundwork Open Source Inc .... D 415 992-4500
23332 Mill Creek Dr Ste 155 Laguna Hills (92653) *(P-14172)*

Group Five, Whittier *Also Called: Russ Bassett Corp (P-2434)*

Group H Engineering .... E 818 999-0999
2030 Vista Ave Sierra Madre (91024) *(P-331)*

Grove Diagnstc Imaging Ctr Inc .... C 909 982-8638
8805 Haven Ave Ste 120 Rancho Cucamonga (91730) *(P-15319)*

Grove Lumber & Bldg Sups Inc (PA) .... C 909 947-0277
27126 Watson Rd Menifee (92585) *(P-9921)*

Grover Manufacturing, South El Monte *Also Called: Grover Smith Mfg Corp (P-5735)*

Grover Products Co .... D 323 263-9981
3424 E Olympic Blvd Los Angeles (90023) *(P-7259)*

Grover Smith Mfg Corp .... E 323 724-3444
9717 Factorial Way South El Monte (91733) *(P-5735)*

Grow More Inc .... D 310 515-1700
15600 New Century Dr Gardena (90248) *(P-3755)*

Grubb & Ellis Company .... A 714 667-8252
1551 N Tustin Ave Ste 300 Santa Ana (92705) *(P-12461)*

Grubb & Ellis Management Services Inc .... A 412 201-8200
1551 N Tustin Ave Ste 300 Santa Ana (92705) *(P-12462)*

Grubb & Nadler Inc .... E 760 728-0040
1719 Rainbow Valley Blvd Fallbrook (92028) *(P-259)*

Gruber Systems Inc .... E 661 257-0464
29071 The Old Rd Valencia (91355) *(P-5582)*

Gruen Assoc Archtects Planners, Los Angeles *Also Called: Gruen Associates Inc (P-17672)*

Gruen Associates Inc .... D 323 937-4270
6330 San Vicente Blvd Ste 200 Los Angeles (90048) *(P-17672)*

Gruma Corporation .... D 909 980-3566
11559 Jersey Blvd Ste A Rancho Cucamonga (91730) *(P-1723)*

Gruma Corporation .... B 323 803-1100
5505 E Olympic Blvd Commerce (90022) *(P-1724)*

Grupo Gallegos .... D 562 256-3600
300 Pacific Coast Hwy Ste 200 Huntington Beach (92648) *(P-13210)*

Grupoex, La Mirada *Also Called: Mejico Express Inc (P-9175)*

Gryphon, Chula Vista *Also Called: Gryphon Marine LLC (P-17542)*

Gryphon Marine LLC .... D 619 407-4010
694 Moss St Chula Vista (91911) *(P-17542)*

Gs Brothers Inc (PA) .... C 310 833-1369
20331 Main St Carson (90745) *(P-208)*

Gsa Des Plaines LLC .... D 310 557-5100
10100 Santa Monica Blvd Ste 2600 Los Angeles (90067) *(P-12708)*

Gsico, Foothill Ranch *Also Called: Global Solutions Integration (P-17540)*

Gsp Metal Finishing Inc .... E 818 744-1328
16520 S Figueroa St Gardena (90248) *(P-5265)*

Gst Industries, Inc., Northridge *Also Called: Aviation Design Group Inc (P-7439)*

Gt Diamond, Irvine *Also Called: General Tool Inc (P-10439)*

GT Precision Inc .... C 310 323-4374
1629 W 132nd St Gardena (90249) *(P-5108)*

GT Styling Corp .... E 714 644-9214
2830 E Via Martens Anaheim (92806) *(P-4129)*

Gtl, Los Angeles *Also Called: Public Communications Svcs Inc (P-9455)*

Gtran Inc (PA) .... E 805 445-4500
829 Flynn Rd Camarillo (93012) *(P-7001)*

Gts Living Foods LLC (PA) .... A 323 581-7787
4415 Bandini Blvd Los Angeles (90058) *(P-1620)*

Gtt International Inc .... E 951 788-8729
1615 Eastridge Ave Riverside (92507) *(P-9897)*

Guadalupe Cooling Company Inc .... D 805 343-2331
2040 Guadalupe Rd Guadalupe (93434) *(P-112)*

Guadalupe Union School Dst (PA) .... C 805 343-2114
4465 9th St Guadalupe (93434) *(P-16809)*

Guarachi Wine Partners Inc .... D 818 225-5100
27001 Agoura Rd Ste 285 Calabasas (91301) *(P-11056)*

Guaranteed Rate Inc .... C 760 310-6008
1455 Frazee Rd Ste 500 San Diego (92108) *(P-11910)*

Guaranteed Rate Inc .... C 805 550-6933
1065 Higuera St Ste 100 San Luis Obispo (93401) *(P-11911)*

Guaranteed Rate Inc .... C 424 354-5344
230 Commerce Irvine (92602) *(P-11912)*

Guard Management Inc .... C 858 279-8282
8001 Vickers St San Diego (92111) *(P-14304)*

Guard Systems District 1, Monterey Park *Also Called: Guard-Systems Inc (P-14306)*

Guard-Systems Inc .... A 909 947-5400
1910 S Archibald Ave Ste M2 Ontario (91761) *(P-14305)*

Guard-Systems Inc .... A 323 881-6715
1190 Monterey Pass Rd Monterey Park (91754) *(P-14306)*

Guardian Group Intl LLC (HQ) .... C 310 320-0320
2350 W 205th St Torrance (90501) *(P-18316)*

Guardian Integrated SEC Inc (PA) .... C 800 400-3167
9701 Topanga Canyon Pl Chatsworth (91311) *(P-14404)*

Guardian Intl Solutions .... D 323 528-6555
3415 S Sepulveda Blvd Ste 1100 Los Angeles (90034) *(P-14307)*

Guardian Life Insur Co Amer .... D 626 792-1935
975 San Pasqual St Pasadena (91106) *(P-12042)*

Guardian Life Insur Co Amer .... D 213 624-2002
510 W 6th St Ste 815 Los Angeles (90014) *(P-12043)*

Guardian Solutions, Orange *Also Called: Lres Corporation (P-12482)*

Guardian Title Company .... D 949 495-9306
300 Commerce Irvine (92602) *(P-12560)*

Guardsmark LLC (DH) .... D 714 619-9700
1551 N Tustin Ave Ste 650 Santa Ana (92705) *(P-14308)*

Guayaki Sstnble Rnfrest Pdts I (PA) .... C 888 482-9254
215 Rose Ave Venice (90291) *(P-10947)*

Guayaki Yerba Mate, Venice *Also Called: Guayaki Sstnble Rnfrest Pdts I (P-10947)*

Guckenheimer Enterprises Inc .... D 760 414-3659
4010 Ocean Ranch Blvd Oceanside (92056) *(P-3415)*

Guelaguetza, Los Angeles *Also Called: Pbf & E LLC (P-11595)*

Guess (PA) .... A 213 765-3100
1444 S Alameda St Los Angeles (90021) *(P-2149)*

GUESS?, Los Angeles *Also Called: Guess Inc (P-2149)*

Guesty Inc (PA) .... D 415 244-0277
440 N Barranca Ave Pmb 9720 Covina (91723) *(P-12838)*

Guggenheim Prtners Inv MGT LLC .... A 310 576-1270
100 Wilshire Blvd 5th Fl Santa Monica (90401) *(P-12634)*

Guhring Inc .... E 714 841-3582
15581 Computer Ln Huntington Beach (92649) *(P-5612)*

Guidance Software Inc (HQ) .... C 626 229-9191
1055 E Colorado Blvd Ste 400 Pasadena (91106) *(P-13943)*

Guild Mortgage, San Diego *Also Called: Guild Mortgage Company LLC (P-12658)*

Guild Mortgage Company LLC (HQ) .... C 800 365-4441
5887 Copley Dr San Diego (92111) *(P-12658)*

Guinn Corporation .... D 661 325-6109
6533 Rosedale Hwy Bakersfield (93308) *(P-1171)*

Guitar Center Holdings Inc .... D 661 222-7521
24961 Pico Canyon Rd Stevenson Ranch (91381) *(P-14770)*

Gulf Development, Torrance *Also Called: Signtronix Inc (P-8637)*

Gulfstream, Van Nuys *Also Called: Gulfstream Aerospace Corp GA (P-7357)*

Gulfstream Aerospace Corp GA .... C 562 907-9300
9818 Mina Ave Whittier (90605) *(P-7356)*

A
L
P
H
A
B
E
T
I
C

Employee Codes: A=Over 500 employees, B=251-500
C=101-250, D=51-100, E=20-50, F=10-19, G=1-9

2025 Southern California
Business Directory and Buyers Guide

© Mergent Inc. 1-800-342-5647

1043

Gulfstream Aerospace Corp GA .... B 805 236-5755
16644 Roscoe Blvd Van Nuys (91406) *(P-7357)*

Gulfstream Aerospace Corp GA .... A 562 420-1818
4150 E Donald Douglas Dr Long Beach (90808) *(P-7358)*

Gumbiner Savett Inc .... D 310 828-9798
1723 Cloverfield Blvd Santa Monica (90404) *(P-12296)*

Gumbiner Svett Fnkel Fnglson R, Santa Monica *Also Called: Gumbiner Savett Inc (P-12296)*

Gumgum Sports Inc .... E 310 400-0396
1314 7th St Fl 4 Santa Monica (90401) *(P-13944)*

Gunderson Rail Services LLC .... C 909 478-0541
1475 Cooley Ct San Bernardino (92408) *(P-9365)*

Gunjoy Inc .... E 714 289-0055
22895 Eastpark Dr Yorba Linda (92887) *(P-7002)*

Gursey Schneider & Co LLC (PA) .... D 310 552-0960
1888 Century Park E Ste 900 Los Angeles (90067) *(P-17731)*

Guru Denim LLC (DH) .... C 323 266-3072
500 W 190th St Ste 300 Gardena (90248) *(P-11488)*

Guru Knits Inc .... D 323 235-9424
225 W 38th St Los Angeles (90037) *(P-2037)*

Gurucul Solutions LLC .... D 213 291-6888
222 N Pacific Coast Hwy Ste 1322 El Segundo (90245) *(P-11542)*

Gurunanda, Buena Park *Also Called: Gurunanda LLC (P-11014)*

Gurunanda LLC (PA) .... D 714 256-4050
6645 Caballero Blvd Buena Park (90620) *(P-11014)*

Guthy-Renker Direct, Santa Monica *Also Called: Guthy-Renker LLC (P-10563)*

Guthy-Renker LLC .... D 310 581-6250
3340 Ocean Park Blvd Fl 2 Santa Monica (90405) *(P-10563)*

Guy Yocom Construction Inc (PA) .... C 951 284-3456
3299 Horseless Carriage Dr Ste H Norco (92860) *(P-1118)*

Guys Patio Inc .... E 844 968-7485
845 N Elm St Orange (92867) *(P-14735)*

Guzman Grading and Paving Corp .... D 909 428-5960
14030 Rose Ave Fontana (92337) *(P-13456)*

Gvs Italy .... D 424 382-4343
8616 La Tijera Blvd Ste 512 Los Angeles (90045) *(P-10138)*

GW Reed Printing Inc .... E 909 947-0599
4071 Greystone Dr Ontario (91761) *(P-3010)*

Gxo Logistics Supply Chain Inc .... A 336 309-6201
3520 S Cactus Ave Bloomington (92316) *(P-9071)*

Gxo Logistics Supply Chain Inc .... D 951 512-1201
2163 S Riverside Ave Colton (92324) *(P-9072)*

Gxo Logistics Supply Chain Inc .... D 909 838-5631
7140 Cajon Blvd San Bernardino (92407) *(P-9288)*

Gxo Logistics Supply Chain Inc .... D 909 253-5356
2615 E 3rd St San Bernardino (92415) *(P-9289)*

Gxo Logistics Supply Chain Inc .... C 336 989-0537
2401 Chain Dr Simi Valley (93065) *(P-9290)*

Gymnastics Center, Carlsbad *Also Called: YMCA of San Diego County (P-17384)*

Gyre Therapeutics Inc (PA) .... B 650 266-8674
12730 High Bluff Dr Ste 250 San Diego (92130) *(P-3416)*

H & A Transmissions Inc .... E 909 941-9020
8727 Rochester Ave Rancho Cucamonga (91730) *(P-14684)*

H & H LLC (PA) .... D 805 925-2036
1131 S Russell Ave Santa Maria (93458) *(P-12839)*

H & H Agency Inc (PA) .... D 949 260-8840
1403 N Tustin Ave Ste 280 Santa Ana (92705) *(P-12217)*

H & H Manufacturing, Pomona *Also Called: Holland & Herring Mfg Inc (P-6142)*

H & H Specialties Inc .... E 626 575-0776
14850 Don Julian Rd Ste B City Of Industry (91746) *(P-8680)*

H & H Truck Terminal, Victorville *Also Called: Hartwick & Hand Inc (P-8914)*

H & L Forge Company, Montebello *Also Called: H & L Tooth Company (P-5493)*

H & L Tooth Company (PA) .... D 323 721-5146
1540 S Greenwood Ave Montebello (90640) *(P-5493)*

H & N Fish Co., Vernon *Also Called: H & N Foods International Inc (P-10854)*

H & N Foods International Inc (HQ) .... C 323 586-9300
5580 S Alameda St Vernon (90058) *(P-10854)*

H & R Accounts Inc .... C 619 819-8844
3131 Camino Del Rio N Ste 1500 San Diego (92108) *(P-13741)*

H & T Seafood Inc .... E 323 526-0888
5598 Lindbergh Ln Bell (90201) *(P-10855)*

H and H Drug Stores Inc .... D 909 890-9700
114 E Airport Dr San Bernardino (92408) *(P-10082)*

H and H Drug Stores Inc (HQ) .... D 818 956-6691
3604 San Fernando Rd Glendale (91204) *(P-10083)*

H C I, Riverside *Also Called: Hci LLC (P-673)*

H C Olsen Cnstr Co Inc .... D 626 359-8900
710 Los Angeles Ave Monrovia (91016) *(P-484)*

H C V T, Los Angeles *Also Called: Holthouse Carlin Van Trigt LLP (P-17733)*

H Co Computer Products (PA) .... E 949 833-3222
16812 Hale Ave Irvine (92606) *(P-5879)*

H D Smith LLC .... D 310 641-1885
1370 E Victoria St Carson (90746) *(P-10625)*

H G Group Inc .... B 805 486-6463
4225 Saviers Rd Oxnard (93033) *(P-13164)*

H J Harkins Company Inc .... E 805 929-1333
1400 W Grand Ave Ste F Grover Beach (93433) *(P-3417)*

H K Prcision Turning Machining, Oceanside *Also Called: Balda HK Plastics Inc (P-5104)*

H L Moe Co Inc (PA) .... C 818 572-2100
526 Commercial St Glendale (91203) *(P-785)*

H M C, Chula Vista *Also Called: Heartland Meat Company Inc (P-10871)*

H M E, Carlsbad *Also Called: HM Electronics Inc (P-10250)*

H M F, Anaheim *Also Called: Hitech Metal Fabrication Corp (P-4837)*

H Rauvel Inc .... C 562 989-3333
501 W Walnut St Compton (90220) *(P-8953)*

H Rauvel Inc (PA) .... D 310 604-0060
1710 E Sepulveda Blvd Carson (90745) *(P-9073)*

H Roberts Construction .... D 562 590-4825
2165 W Gaylord St Long Beach (90813) *(P-5079)*

H T V, Studio City *Also Called: High Technology Video Inc (P-14832)*

H W Hunter Inc (PA) .... D 661 948-8411
1130 Auto Mall Dr Lancaster (93534) *(P-11357)*

H Wayne Lewis Inc .... E 909 874-2213
312 S Willow Ave Rialto (92376) *(P-5095)*

H&M Fashion Usa Inc .... C 909 990-7815
4413 Patterson Ave Perris (92571) *(P-2195)*

H2go Car Wash, Rcho Sta Marg *Also Called: Green-N-Clean Ex Car Wash Inc (P-14709)*

H2o Innovation Operation Maint, Vista *Also Called: H2o Innovation USA Holding Inc (P-10321)*

H2o Innovation USA Holding Inc .... A 760 639-4400
1048 La Mirada Ct Vista (92081) *(P-10321)*

H2o Leak Pros, Orange *Also Called: Alan Smith Pool Plastering Inc (P-994)*

H2v By Burke Williams, Inglewood *Also Called: Hunter Vaughan LLC (P-3659)*

Haas Automation Inc (PA) .... A 805 278-1800
2800 Sturgis Rd Oxnard (93030) *(P-5545)*

Haberfelde Ford (PA) .... C 661 328-3600
2001 Oak St Bakersfield (93301) *(P-11358)*

Hacienda Golf Club .... D 562 694-1081
718 East Rd La Habra Heights (90631) *(P-15138)*

Hadley Date Gardens Inc .... D 760 347-3044
47382 Madison St Indio (92201) *(P-48)*

Hadley Fruit Orchards Inc (PA) .... E 951 849-5255
48980 Seminole Dr Cabazon (92230) *(P-11654)*

Hadrian, Torrance *Also Called: Hadrian Automation Inc (P-6618)*

Hadrian Automation Inc .... D 503 807-4490
19501 S Western Ave Torrance (90502) *(P-6618)*

Hadronex Inc (PA) .... E 760 291-1980
2110 Enterprise St Escondido (92029) *(P-9725)*

Haea, Fountain Valley *Also Called: Hyundai Autoever America LLC (P-14187)*

Haemonetics Manufacturing Inc (HQ) .... E 626 339-7388
1630 W Industrial Park St Covina (91722) *(P-8161)*

Hagen Streiff Newton & Oshiro Accountants PC .... D 949 390-7647
4667 Macarthur Blvd Ste 400 Newport Beach (92660) *(P-17732)*

Hagen-Renaker Inc (PA) .... D 909 599-2341
914 W Cienega Ave San Dimas (91773) *(P-4367)*

Haight, Los Angeles *Also Called: Haight Brown & Bonesteel LLP (P-16699)*

Haight Brown & Bonesteel LLP (PA) .... D 213 542-8000
555 S Flower St Ste 4500 Los Angeles (90071) *(P-16699)*

Hain Celestial Group Inc .... C 323 859-0553
5630 Rickenbacker Rd Bell (90201) *(P-3656)*

Hakes Sash & Door Inc .... C 951 674-2414
31945 Corydon St Lake Elsinore (92530) *(P-1051)*

Hal Hays Construction Inc (PA) .... C 951 788-0703
4181 Latham St Riverside (92501) *(P-485)*

Mergent email: customerrelations@mergent.com
1044

2025 Southern California
Business Directory and Buyers Guide

(P-0000) Products & Services Section entry number
(PA)=Parent Co (HQ)=Headquarters (DH)=Div Headquarters

Halcore Group Inc .... E 626 575-0880
10941 Weaver Ave South El Monte (91733) *(P-7179)*

Hales Engineering Coinc .... E
18 Wood Rd Camarillo (93010) *(P-6138)*

Halex Corporation (DH) .... E **909 629-6219**
4200 Santa Ana St Ste A Ontario (91761) *(P-4740)*

Haley & Aldrich Inc .... D 619 280-9210
5333 Mission Center Rd Ste 300 San Diego (92108) *(P-18317)*

Haley Bros, Riverside *Also Called: T M Cobb Company (P-2328)*

Haley Bros Inc (HQ) .... D **714 670-2112**
6291 Orangethorpe Ave Buena Park (90620) *(P-2308)*

Haley Bros Inc .... C 800 854-5951
1575 Riverview Dr San Bernardino (92408) *(P-2309)*

Haliburton International Foods Inc .... B 909 428-8520
3855 Jurupa St Ontario (91761) *(P-1787)*

Hall Ambulance Service Inc .... D 661 322-8741
2001 O St # O Bakersfield (93301) *(P-8830)*

Halliburton Company .... D 661 393-8111
34722 7th Standard Rd Bakersfield (93314) *(P-332)*

Hallmark Channel, Studio City *Also Called: Hallmark Media US LLC (P-9506)*

Hallmark Lighting, Commerce *Also Called: Hallmark Lighting LLC (P-6462)*

Hallmark Lighting LLC .... D 818 885-5010
1945 S Tubeway Ave Commerce (90040) *(P-6462)*

Hallmark Media US LLC (DH) .... D 818 755-2400
12700 Ventura Blvd Ste 100 Studio City (91604) *(P-9506)*

Hallmark Metals Inc .... E 626 335-1263
600 W Foothill Blvd Glendora (91741) *(P-4990)*

Hallmark Southwest, Loma Linda *Also Called: Dvele Omega Corporation (P-2399)*

Halozyme, San Diego *Also Called: Halozyme Therapeutics Inc (P-3579)*

Halozyme Inc .... C 858 794-8889
12390 El Camino Real Ste 150 San Diego (92130) *(P-17793)*

Halozyme Therapeutics, San Diego *Also Called: Halozyme Inc (P-17793)*

Halozyme Therapeutics Inc (PA) .... D **858 794-8889**
12390 El Camino Real San Diego (92130) *(P-3579)*

Hamann Construction .... D 619 440-7424
1000 Pioneer Way El Cajon (92020) *(P-541)*

Hamblin's Auto & Body Shop, Riverside *Also Called: Hamblins Bdy Pnt Frame Sp Inc (P-14691)*

Hamblins Bdy Pnt Frame Sp Inc .... D 951 689-8440
7590 Cypress Ave Riverside (92503) *(P-14691)*

Hamburger Home (PA) .... D **323 876-0550**
7120 Franklin Ave Los Angeles (90046) *(P-17157)*

Hamilton Metalcraft Inc .... E 626 795-4811
848 N Fair Oaks Ave Pasadena (91103) *(P-4991)*

Hamilton Sundstrand Corp .... C 909 593-5300
960 Overland Ct San Dimas (91773) *(P-7956)*

Hamilton Sundstrand Spc Systms .... D 909 288-5300
960 Overland Ct San Dimas (91773) *(P-8045)*

HAMMER MUSEUM, Los Angeles *Also Called: Armand Hmmer Mseum of Art Cltr (P-17248)*

Hammitt Inc .... D 310 292-5200
2101 Pacific Coast Hwy Hermosa Beach (90254) *(P-4294)*

Hammond Inc Which Will Do Bus .... E 925 381-5392
404 S Coast Hwy Oceanside (92054) *(P-1597)*

Hamo Construction .... F 818 415-3334
3650 Altura Ave La Crescenta (91214) *(P-333)*

Hampton Inn, Foothill Ranch *Also Called: Stonebridge Rlty Advisors Inc (P-13038)*

Hampton Products Intl Corp (PA) .... C **800 562-5625**
50 Icon Foothill Ranch (92610) *(P-4769)*

Hamrock Inc .... C 562 944-0255
3019 Wilshire Blvd Santa Monica (90403) *(P-4535)*

Hana Commercial Finance LLC .... D 213 240-1234
1000 Wilshire Blvd Ste 570 Los Angeles (90017) *(P-11867)*

Hana Financial Inc (PA) .... D 213 240-1234
1000 Wilshire Blvd Ste 2000 Los Angeles (90017) *(P-13457)*

Hancor Inc .... D 661 366-1520
140 Vineland Rd Bakersfield (93307) *(P-3974)*

Handbill Printers, Corona *Also Called: Azalea Systems Corp Inc (P-2966)*

Handbill Printers, Corona *Also Called: Handbill Printers LP (P-3011)*

Handbill Printers LP .... E 951 547-5910
820 E Parkridge Ave Corona (92879) *(P-3011)*

Handlery Hotels, San Diego *Also Called: Handlery Hotels Inc (P-12840)*

Handlery Hotels Inc .... C 415 781-4550
950 Hotel Cir N San Diego (92108) *(P-12840)*

Handpiece Parts & Products Inc .... E 714 997-4331
707 W Angus Ave Orange (92868) *(P-8336)*

Hanford Hotels Inc .... C 714 557-3000
3131 Bristol St Costa Mesa (92626) *(P-12841)*

Hanger Prsthtics Orthtics W In .... D 213 250-7850
1127 Wilshire Blvd Ste 310 Los Angeles (90017) *(P-8272)*

Hanjin Global Logistics, Gardena *Also Called: Hanjin Transportation Co Ltd (P-9291)*

Hanjin Shipping Co Ltd .... A 201 291-4600
301 Hanjin Rd Long Beach (90802) *(P-9154)*

Hanjin Transportation Co Ltd .... C 310 522-5030
15913 S Main St Gardena (90248) *(P-9291)*

Hanken Cono Assad & Co Inc .... C 619 575-3100
1504 Oro Vista Rd Apt 145 San Diego (92154) *(P-12463)*

Hankey Group, Los Angeles *Also Called: Nowcom LLC (P-14236)*

Hanks Inc .... D 909 350-8365
13866 Slover Ave Fontana (92337) *(P-8913)*

Hanley Wood Media (HQ) .... E **202 736-3300**
4000 Macarthur Blvd Ste 400 Newport Beach (92660) *(P-2921)*

Hanmar LLC (PA) .... E **818 890-2802**
11441 Bradley Ave Pacoima (91331) *(P-5190)*

Hanna Fuji Sushi, Santa Fe Springs *Also Called: Nikko Enterprise Corporation (P-1709)*

Hannahmax Baking Inc .... C 310 380-6778
14601 S Main St Gardena (90248) *(P-1458)*

Hannam Chain Super 1 Market, Los Angeles *Also Called: Hannam Chain USA Inc (P-10043)*

Hannam Chain USA Inc (PA) .... C 213 382-2922
2740 W Olympic Blvd Los Angeles (90006) *(P-10043)*

Hannspree North America Inc .... D 909 992-5025
13223 Black Mountain Rd San Diego (92129) *(P-7003)*

Hanover Accessories Corp C
6049 E Slauson Ave Commerce (90040) *(P-3199)*

Hansen Engineering Co .... D 310 534-3870
24020 Frampton Ave Harbor City (90710) *(P-6139)*

Hansen Engineering Co .... E 310 534-3870
24050 Frampton Ave Harbor City (90710) *(P-7487)*

Hansens Welding Inc .... E 310 329-6888
358 W 168th St Gardena (90248) *(P-14740)*

Hanson Distributing Company (PA) .... C **626 224-9800**
975 W 8th St Azusa (91702) *(P-9827)*

Hanson Lab Solutions LLC .... E 805 498-3121
747 Calle Plano Camarillo (93012) *(P-7827)*

Hanson Roof Tile Inc .... B 888 509-4787
10651 Elm Ave Fontana (92337) *(P-4395)*

Hanson Tank, Los Angeles *Also Called: Roy E Hanson Jr Mfg (P-4924)*

Hanson Truss Inc .... B 909 591-9256
13950 Yorba Ave Chino (91710) *(P-2377)*

Hanwha Enrgy USA Holdings Corp (HQ) .... E **949 748-5996**
400 Spectrum Center Dr Ste 1400 Irvine (92618) *(P-6826)*

Hanwha Q Cells Usa Inc .... E 706 671-3077
300 Spectrum Center Dr Ste 500 Irvine (92618) *(P-6827)*

Hanwha Q Cells USA Corp .... D 949 748-5996
300 Spectrum Center Dr Ste 1250 Irvine (92618) *(P-9587)*

Happy Money, Costa Mesa *Also Called: Payoff Inc (P-11861)*

Happy Money Inc .... B 949 430-0630
21515 Hawthorne Blvd Ste 200 Torrance (90503) *(P-11840)*

Happy Planner, The, Cypress *Also Called: ME & My Big Ideas LLC (P-10523)*

Har-Bro LLC (HQ) .... D **562 528-8000**
2750 Signal Pkwy Signal Hill (90755) *(P-542)*

Haralambos Beverage Co .... B 562 347-4300
26717 Palmetto Ave Redlands (92374) *(P-11048)*

Harari Inc (PA) .... E **323 734-5302**
9646 Brighton Way Los Angeles (90016) *(P-2038)*

Harbill Inc .... D 909 883-8833
909 W 21st St San Bernardino (92405) *(P-11359)*

Harbinger Motors Inc .... C 714 684-1067
12821 Knott St Ste A Garden Grove (92841) *(P-7180)*

Harbor Area Security Training, San Pedro *Also Called: Black Knight Patrol Inc (P-14280)*

Harbor Distributing LLc (HQ) .... C **714 933-2400**
5901 Bolsa Ave Huntington Beach (92647) *(P-11049)*

Employee Codes: A=Over 500 employees, B=251-500
C=101-250, D=51-100, E=20-50, F=10-19, G=1-9

2025 Southern California
Business Directory and Buyers Guide

© Mergent Inc. 1-800-342-5647

1045

Harbor Dvlpmntal Dsblties Fndt .... C 310 540-1711
  21231 Hawthorne Blvd Torrance (90503) *(P-17228)*

Harbor Freight Tools, Calabasas Also Called: Central Purchasing LLC *(P-10429)*

Harbor Furniture Mfg Inc (PA)...................... E 323 636-1201
  15817 Whitepost Ln La Mirada (90638) *(P-2448)*

Harbor Glen Care Center .... C 626 963-7531
  1033 E Arrow Hwy Glendora (91740) *(P-15671)*

Harbor Green Grain LP .... E 310 991-8089
  13181 Crossroads Pkwy N Ste 200 City Of Industry (91746) *(P-1427)*

Harbor Health Care Inc .... C 562 866-7054
  9461 Flower St Bellflower (90706) *(P-17158)*

Harbor Health Systems LLC .... A 949 273-7020
  3501 Jamboree Rd Ste 540 Newport Beach (92660) *(P-16565)*

Harbor House, La Mirada Also Called: Harbor Furniture Mfg Inc *(P-2448)*

Harbor Industrial, Wilmington Also Called: Harbor Industrial Svcs Corp *(P-13436)*

Harbor Industrial Svcs Corp .... D 310 522-1193
  211 N Marine Ave Wilmington (90744) *(P-13436)*

Harbor Pipe and Steel Inc .... C 951 369-3990
  1495 Columbia Ave Bldg 10 Riverside (92507) *(P-10139)*

Harbor Post Accute Care Center, Torrance Also Called: Geri-Care Inc *(P-15665)*

Harbor Regional Center, Torrance Also Called: Harbor Dvlpmntal Dsblties Fndt *(P-17228)*

Harbor Truck Bodies Inc .... D 714 996-0411
  255 Voyager Ave Brea (92821) *(P-7204)*

Harbor Truck Body, Brea Also Called: Harbor Truck Bodies Inc *(P-7204)*

Harbor Ucla Med Foundation, Torrance Also Called: Harbor-Ucla Med Foundation Inc *(P-17990)*

Harbor View Hotel Ventures LLC .... D 619 239-6800
  1646 Front St San Diego (92101) *(P-12842)*

Harbor View House, San Pedro Also Called: Healthview Inc *(P-17161)*

Harbor-Ucla Med Foundation Inc .... B 310 533-0413
  21602 S Vermont Ave Torrance (90502) *(P-16435)*

Harbor-Ucla Med Foundation Inc (PA) .... D 310 222-5015
  21840 Normandie Ave Ste 100 Torrance (90502) *(P-17990)*

Harcon Precision Metals Inc .... E 619 423-5544
  1790 Dornoch Ct Chula Vista (91910) *(P-5494)*

Harcourt Trade Publishers, San Diego Also Called: Houghton Mifflin Harcourt Pubg *(P-2890)*

Hard Rock Hotel, San Diego Also Called: T-12 Three LLC *(P-13050)*

Hardwood Flrg Liquidators Inc (PA).................. D 323 201-4200
  7227 Telegraph Rd Montebello (90640) *(P-2289)*

Hardy & Harper Inc .... C 714 444-1851
  32 Rancho Cir Lake Forest (92630) *(P-622)*

Hardy Diagnostics (PA)................................... B 805 346-2766
  1430 W Mccoy Ln Santa Maria (93455) *(P-10084)*

Hardy Frames Inc .... D 951 245-9525
  250 Klug Cir Corona (92878) *(P-4517)*

Hardy Process Solutions .... E 858 278-2900
  10075 Mesa Rim Rd San Diego (92121) *(P-7862)*

Hardy Process Solutions, San Diego Also Called: Hardy Process Solutions *(P-7862)*

Hardy Window Company (PA)........................... C 714 996-1807
  1639 E Miraloma Ave Placentia (92870) *(P-9922)*

Haringa Inc (PA).. D 800 499-9991
  14422 Best Ave Santa Fe Springs (90670) *(P-14506)*

Harkham Industries Inc (PA)........................... E 323 586-4600
  857 S San Pedro St Ste 300 Los Angeles (90014) *(P-2039)*

Harland Brewing Co LLC .... E 858 800-4566
  10115 Carroll Canyon Rd San Diego (92131) *(P-11614)*

Harman Envelopes, North Hollywood Also Called: Harman Press Inc *(P-3012)*

Harman International Inds Inc .... B 818 893-8411
  8500 Balboa Blvd Northridge (91325) *(P-10246)*

Harman Press Inc .... E 818 432-0570
  6840 Vineland Ave North Hollywood (91605) *(P-3012)*

Harman Professional, Northridge Also Called: Harman Professional Inc *(P-6541)*

Harman Professional Inc .... C 844 776-4899
  14780 Bar Harbor Rd Fontana (92336) *(P-6539)*

Harman Professional Inc .... C 951 242-2927
  24950 Grove View Rd Moreno Valley (92551) *(P-6540)*

Harman Professional Inc (DH)......................... B 818 893-8411
  8500 Balboa Blvd Northridge (91329) *(P-6541)*

Harman-Kardon, Northridge Also Called: Harman-Kardon Incorporated *(P-10219)*

Harman-Kardon Incorporated .... B 818 841-4600
  8500 Balboa Blvd Northridge (91325) *(P-10219)*

Harmonium Inc (PA)....................................... C 858 684-3080
  5440 Morehouse Dr Ste 1000 San Diego (92121) *(P-17092)*

Harper Federal Cnstr LLC .... D 619 543-1296
  14130 Biscayne Pl Poway (92064) *(P-623)*

Harpers Pharmacy Inc .... C 877 778-3773
  132 S Anita Dr Ste 210 Orange (92868) *(P-3418)*

Harpo Entertainment Group, Van Nuys Also Called: Harpo Productions Inc *(P-14830)*

Harpo Productions Inc .... C 312 633-1000
  7619 N Patriot Way Van Nuys (91405) *(P-14830)*

Harrah's, Valley Center Also Called: Caesars Entrtnment Oprting Inc *(P-15195)*

Harrahs Resort Southern Cal, Valley Center Also Called: Hcal LLC *(P-12847)*

Harrell Holdings (PA)...................................... C 661 322-5627
  1707 Eye St Ste 102 Bakersfield (93301) *(P-2801)*

Harrington Industrial Plas LLC (PA).................. D 909 597-8641
  14480 Yorba Ave Chino (91710) *(P-10322)*

Harris, Van Nuys Also Called: L3harris Technologies Inc *(P-7732)*

Harris, Los Angeles Also Called: L3harris Technologies Inc *(P-7733)*

Harris & Huri Trnsp Svcs LLC .... D 909 791-0531
  9520 Palo Alto St Rancho Cucamonga (91730) *(P-9366)*

Harris & Ruth Painting Contg (PA).................... D 626 960-4004
  28408 Lorna Ave West Covina (91790) *(P-866)*

Harris Freeman & Co Inc (PA).......................... B 714 765-7525
  3110 E Miraloma Ave Anaheim (92806) *(P-10948)*

Harris Industries Inc (PA)................................ E 714 898-8048
  5181 Argosy Ave Huntington Beach (92649) *(P-2724)*

Harris Tea Company, Anaheim Also Called: Harris Freeman & Co Inc *(P-10948)*

Harris, Jeffery P, Santa Barbara Also Called: Nasif Hicks Harris & Co LLP *(P-17747)*

Harrison Iyke .... D 909 463-8409
  7611 Etiwanda Ave Rancho Cucamonga (91739) *(P-14405)*

Harrison, E J & Sons Recycling, Ventura Also Called: E J Harrison & Sons Inc *(P-9742)*

Harry's Berries, Oxnard Also Called: Iwamoto & Gean Farm *(P-12)*

Harry's Dye & Wash, Anaheim Also Called: Harrys Dye and Wash Inc *(P-1933)*

Harrys Dye and Wash Inc .... E 714 446-0300
  1015 E Orangethorpe Ave Anaheim (92801) *(P-1933)*

Hart & Cooley Inc .... E 951 332-5132
  10855 Philadelphia Ave Ste B Jurupa Valley (91752) *(P-5064)*

HART & COOLEY, INC., Jurupa Valley Also Called: Hart & Cooley Inc *(P-5064)*

Hartman Slicer Div, Santa Fe Springs Also Called: United Bakery Equipment Co Inc *(P-5794)*

Hartmark Cab Design & Mfg Inc .... E 909 591-9153
  3575 Grapevine St Jurupa Valley (91752) *(P-1208)*

Hartmark Cabinet Design, Jurupa Valley Also Called: Hartmark Cab Design & Mfg Inc *(P-1208)*

Hartwell Corporation (DH)................................ C 714 993-4200
  900 Richfield Rd Placentia (92870) *(P-4770)*

Hartwick & Hand Inc (PA)................................ D 760 245-1666
  16953 N D St Victorville (92394) *(P-8914)*

Hartzell Aerospace, Valencia Also Called: Electrofilm Mfg Co LLC *(P-5373)*

Harvard Card Systems, City Of Industry Also Called: Harvard Label LLC *(P-2625)*

Harvard Label LLC .... C 626 333-8881
  111 Baldwin Park Blvd City Of Industry (91746) *(P-2625)*

Harvest Farms Inc .... D 661 945-3636
  45000 Yucca Ave Lancaster (93534) *(P-1393)*

Harvest Food Distributors, National City Also Called: Harvest Meat Company Inc *(P-10870)*

Harvest Landscape Entps Inc (PA).................... C 714 693-8100
  8030 E Crystal Dr Anaheim (92807) *(P-172)*

Harvest Landscape Maintenance, Anaheim Also Called: Harvest Landscape Entps Inc *(P-172)*

Harvest Management Sub LLC .... A 805 543-0187
  1299 Briarwood Dr San Luis Obispo (93401) *(P-12343)*

Harvest Meat Company Inc .... D 619 477-0185
  1022 Bay Marina Dr Ste 106 National City (91950) *(P-10869)*

Harvest Meat Company Inc (HQ)...................... D 619 477-0185
  1000 Bay Marina Dr National City (91950) *(P-10870)*

HARVEST MEAT COMPANY, INC., National City Also Called: Harvest Meat Company Inc *(P-10869)*

Harvey General Contracting, San Diego Also Called: Harvey USA LLC *(P-543)*

Harvey Performance Company LLC .... D 661 467-0440
  28231 Avenue Crocker Ste 90 Valencia (91355) *(P-10375)*

Harvey USA LLC .... C 858 769-4000
  9455 Ridgehaven Ct Ste 200 San Diego (92123) *(P-543)*

Mergent email: customerrelations@mergent.com
1046

2025 Southern California
Business Directory and Buyers Guide

(P-0000) Products & Services Section entry number
(PA)=Parent Co (HQ)=Headquarters (DH)=Div Headquarters

Harwil, Oxnard *Also Called: Harwil Precision Products (P-7004)*

Harwil Precision Products .... E 805 988-6800
541 Kinetic Dr Oxnard (93030) *(P-7004)*

Hasa Inc (PA) .... D 661 259-5848
23119 Drayton St Saugus (91350) *(P-3208)*

Hasco, Placentia *Also Called: Hartwell Corporation (P-4770)*

Haskel International LLC (HQ) .... C 818 843-4000
100 E Graham Pl Burbank (91502) *(P-5736)*

Haskon, Div of, Brea *Also Called: Kirkhill Inc (P-3894)*

Hatchbeauty, Los Angeles *Also Called: Hatchbeauty Products LLC (P-10626)*

Hatchbeauty Agency LLC (PA) .... E 310 396-7070
355 S Grand Ave Ste 1450 Los Angeles (90071) *(P-18146)*

Hatchbeauty Products LLC (PA) .... D 310 396-7070
355 S Grand Ave Los Angeles (90071) *(P-10626)*

Hathaway Children and Family, Pacoima *Also Called: Hathawy-Sycmres Child Fmly Svc (P-16948)*

Hathaway LLC .... E 661 393-2004
4205 Atlas Ct Bakersfield (93308) *(P-274)*

Hathaway-Sycmres Child Fmly Svc .... C 626 395-7100
12502 Van Nuys Blvd Ste 120 Pacoima (91331) *(P-16948)*

Hathaway-Sycmres Child Fmly Svc .... C 323 733-0322
3741 Stocker St Ste 101 View Park (90008) *(P-16949)*

Hathaway-Sycmres Child Fmly Svc .... C 323 257-9600
840 N Avenue 66 Los Angeles (90042) *(P-17159)*

Haulaway Storage Cntrs Inc .... A 800 826-9040
11292 Western Ave Stanton (90680) *(P-9074)*

Hayaianas, Venice *Also Called: Alpargatas Usa Inc (P-4283)*

Havas Edge LLC (DH) .... D 760 929-0041
1525 Faraday Ave Ste 250 Carlsbad (92008) *(P-13211)*

Havas Formula LLC .... D 619 234-0345
1215 Cushman Ave San Diego (92110) *(P-18254)*

Havasu Landing Casino (PA) .... D 760 858-5380
1 Main St Needles (92363) *(P-12843)*

Hawaiian Gardens Casino .... A 562 860-5887
11871 Carson St Hawaiian Gardens (90716) *(P-12844)*

Hawaiian Gardens Casino .... A 562 860-5887
11871 Carson St Hawaiian Gardens (90716) *(P-15207)*

Hawaiian Hotels & Resorts Inc .... C 805 480-0052
2830 Borchard Rd Newbury Park (91320) *(P-12845)*

Hawker Pacific Aerospace .... B 818 765-6201
11240 Sherman Way Sun Valley (91352) *(P-14771)*

Hawkins Brown USA Inc .... B 310 600-2695
3415 S Sepulveda Blvd Los Angeles (90034) *(P-17673)*

Hawthorne Cat, San Diego *Also Called: Hawthorne Machinery Co (P-13437)*

Hawthorne Lift Systems, Coachella *Also Called: Naumann/Hobbs Mtl Hdlg Corp II (P-10353)*

Hawthorne Lowe's, Hawthorne *Also Called: Lowes Home Centers LLC (P-11244)*

Hawthorne Machinery Co .... C 858 674-7000
16945 Camino San Bernardo San Diego (92127) *(P-10376)*

Hawthorne Machinery Co (PA) .... C 858 674-7000
16945 Camino San Bernardo San Diego (92127) *(P-13437)*

Hawthorne Rent-It Service (HQ) .... D 858 674-7000
16945 Camino San Bernardo San Diego (92127) *(P-13438)*

Hay Group, Los Angeles *Also Called: Korn Ferry (us) (P-18157)*

Hayday Farms Inc .... D 760 922-4713
15500 S Commercial St Blythe (92225) *(P-5)*

Hayes Welding Inc (PA) .... D 760 246-4878
12522 Violet Rd Adelanto (92301) *(P-14741)*

Haymarket Worldwide Inc .... E 949 417-6700
17030 Red Hill Ave Irvine (92614) *(P-2859)*

Haynes & Boone LLP .... D 949 202-3000
600 Anton Blvd Ste 700 Costa Mesa (92626) *(P-16700)*

Haynes Building Service LLC .... C 626 359-6100
16027 Arrow Hwy Ste I Baldwin Park (91706) *(P-13376)*

Haynes Family Programs Inc .... C 909 593-2581
233 Baseline Rd La Verne (91750) *(P-17160)*

Hazard Construction, Lakeside *Also Called: Hazard Construction Company (P-653)*

Hazard Construction Company .... D 858 587-3600
10529 Vine St Ste 1 Lakeside (92040) *(P-653)*

Hazens Investment LLC .... B 310 642-1111
6101 W Century Blvd Los Angeles (90045) *(P-12846)*

HB Parkco Construction Inc (PA) .... B 714 567-4752
24795 State Highway 74 Perris (92570) *(P-1119)*

Hba Incorporated .... D 714 635-8602
512 E Vermont Ave Anaheim (92805) *(P-984)*

Hba International, Santa Monica *Also Called: Hirsch/Bedner Intl Inc (P-14509)*

Hc West LLC .... B 858 277-3473
7130 Convoy Ct San Diego (92111) *(P-7125)*

HCA HEALTHCARE, Riverside *Also Called: Riverside Cmnty Hlth Systems (P-16161)*

Hcal LLC .... D 760 751-3100
777 S Resort Dr Valley Center (92082) *(P-12847)*

HCC Surety Group, Los Angeles *Also Called: American Contrs Indemnity Co (P-12144)*

Hci, San Marcos *Also Called: Hughes Circuits Inc (P-6737)*

Hci LLC (HQ) .... B 951 520-4200
6830 Airport Dr Riverside (92504) *(P-673)*

Hco Holding I Corporation (HQ) .... D 323 583-5000
999 N Pacific Coast Hwy Ste 800 El Segundo (90245) *(P-12601)*

Hco Holding II Corporation .... A 310 955-9200
999 N Pacific Coast Hwy Ste 800 El Segundo (90245) *(P-3841)*

Hcr Manorcare Med Svcs Fla LLC .... C 949 587-9000
24962 Calle Aragon Aliso Viejo (92653) *(P-15672)*

Hct Group, Santa Monica *Also Called: Hct Packaging Inc (P-14507)*

Hct Packaging Inc (PA) .... C 310 260-7680
2800 28th St Ste 240 Santa Monica (90405) *(P-14507)*

Hd Supply Distribution Services LLC .... A 949 643-4700
26940 Aliso Viejo Pkwy Aliso Viejo (92656) *(P-10308)*

Hd Window Fashions Inc (DH) .... B 213 749-6333
1818 Oak St Los Angeles (90015) *(P-2601)*

Hdc, Tustin *Also Called: Healthcare Design & Cnstr LLC (P-544)*

Hdmc Holdings LLC .... D 760 366-3711
6601 White Feather Rd Joshua Tree (92252) *(P-16012)*

Hdp Holdings, San Diego *Also Called: Wd-40 Company (P-3836)*

Hdz Brothers Inc .... E 714 953-4010
1924 E Mcfadden Ave Santa Ana (92705) *(P-3889)*

Head Office Banking 1, Beverly Hills *Also Called: City National Bank (P-11719)*

Headlight Health Inc .... C 503 961-4406
5060 Shoreham Pl Ste 330 San Diego (92122) *(P-16566)*

Headwaters Incorporated .... E 909 627-9066
1345 Philadelphia St Pomona (91766) *(P-4396)*

Heal Bay .... D 310 451-1500
1444 9th St Santa Monica (90401) *(P-17348)*

Health & Human Services, San Diego *Also Called: County of San Diego (P-16273)*

Health & Human Services- Aging, Santee *Also Called: County of San Diego (P-15609)*

Health & Human Svcs, San Diego *Also Called: County of San Diego (P-17139)*

Health Advocates, Chatsworth *Also Called: Health Advocates LLC (P-13285)*

Health Advocates LLC .... B 818 995-9500
21540 Plummer St Ste B Chatsworth (91311) *(P-13285)*

Health Dept, Los Angeles *Also Called: County of Los Angeles (P-16463)*

Health Fitness America, Irvine *Also Called: Equinox-76th Street Inc (P-15541)*

Health Investment Corporation .... A 714 669-2085
14642 Newport Ave Ste 388 Tustin (92780) *(P-16013)*

Health Net LLC (HQ) .... C 818 676-6000
21650 Oxnard St Woodland Hills (91367) *(P-12080)*

Health Net LLC .... C 661 321-3904
6013 Niles St Bakersfield (93306) *(P-12081)*

Health Net Inc .... A 818 676-6000
21650 Oxnard St Woodland Hills (91367) *(P-12082)*

Health Resources Corp .... B 714 754-5454
2701 S Bristol St Santa Ana (92704) *(P-16014)*

Health Services Dept, Los Angeles *Also Called: County of Los Angeles (P-15968)*

Health Services Dept, Palos Verdes Peninsu *Also Called: County of Los Angeles (P-15970)*

Health Services Research Ctr, San Diego *Also Called: University Cal San Diego (P-17894)*

Health Services, Dept of, La Puente *Also Called: County of Los Angeles (P-15291)*

Health Services, Dept of, Bellflower *Also Called: County of Los Angeles (P-15292)*

Health Services, Dept of, Los Angeles *Also Called: County of Los Angeles (P-15293)*

Health Services, Dept of, Los Angeles *Also Called: County of Los Angeles (P-15971)*

Health Services, Dept of, Acton *Also Called: County of Los Angeles (P-16290)*

Health Services, Dept of, Castaic *Also Called: County of Los Angeles (P-16293)*

Health Services, Dept of, Los Angeles *Also Called: County of Los Angeles (P-16461)*

Health Services, Dept of, Downey *Also Called: County of Los Angeles (P-16462)*

Health Smart Clinic, Long Beach *Also Called: Healthsmart Pacific Inc (P-15320)*

Health System Medical Network, Beverly Hills *Also Called: Cedars-Sinai Medical Center (P-15946)*

Healthcare, Oxnard *Also Called: Amigo Baby Inc (P-16869)*

Healthcare Center Orange Cnty, Buena Park *Also Called: Rehabittion Ctr of Ornge Cnty (P-15760)*

Healthcare Ctr of Downey LLC .... C 562 869-0978
12023 Lakewood Blvd Downey (90242) *(P-15673)*

Healthcare Design & Cnstr LLC .... D 714 245-0144
18302 Irvine Blvd Ste 120 Tustin (92780) *(P-544)*

Healthcare Finance Direct LLC .... D 661 616-4400
1707 Eye St Ste 300 Bakersfield (93301) *(P-18147)*

Healthcare Investments Inc .... C 310 323-3194
1140 W Rosecrans Ave Gardena (90247) *(P-15674)*

Healthcare Management Systems Inc .... C 619 521-9641
900 Lane Ave Ste 190 Chula Vista (91914) *(P-15675)*

Healthcare Partners, Van Nuys *Also Called: Greater Valley Med Group Inc (P-16475)*

Healthcare Partners Med Group, El Segundo *Also Called: Optumcare Management LLC (P-15415)*

Healthcare Resource Group .... C 562 945-7224
6571 Altura Blvd Ste 200 Buena Park (90620) *(P-13598)*

Healthcare Services Group Inc .... A 562 494-7939
5199 E Pacific Coast Hwy Ste 402 Long Beach (90804) *(P-18374)*

Healthpoint Capital LLC (PA)... C 212 935-7780
9920 Pacific Heights Blvd Ste 150 San Diego (92121) *(P-12709)*

Healthsmart MGT Svcs Orgnztion .... D 714 947-8600
10855 Business Center Dr Ste C Cypress (90630) *(P-12218)*

Healthsmart Mso, Cypress *Also Called: Healthsmart MGT Svcs Orgnztion (P-12218)*

Healthsmart Pacific Inc .... B 562 595-1911
2683 Pacific Ave Long Beach (90806) *(P-15320)*

Healthsmart Pacific Inc (PA) .... A 562 595-1911
5150 E Pacific Coast Hwy Ste 200 Long Beach (90804) *(P-16015)*

HealthSouth, Oxnard *Also Called: N S C Channel Islands Inc (P-15398)*

HealthSouth, Tustin *Also Called: Encompass Health Corporation (P-16471)*

HealthSouth, Bakersfield *Also Called: Encompass Health Corporation (P-17148)*

Healthsuth Glnwood Srgical Ctr, Riverside *Also Called: Glenwood Surgical Center LP (P-15315)*

Healthtrio LLC .... D 520 571-1988
21255 Burbank Blvd Woodland Hills (91367) *(P-18148)*

Healthview Inc (PA)... C 310 638-4113
921 S Beacon St San Pedro (90731) *(P-17161)*

Healthy Medical Solutions Inc .... D 818 974-1980
5943 Rhodes Ave Valley Village (91607) *(P-16567)*

Heart Rate Inc .... E 714 850-9716
2619 Oak St Santa Ana (92707) *(P-8520)*

Heartland Express, Fontana *Also Called: Heartland Express Inc Iowa (P-8954)*

Heartland Express Inc Iowa .... A 319 626-3600
10131 Redwood Ave Fontana (92335) *(P-8954)*

Heartland Farms, City Of Industry *Also Called: Sbm Dairies Inc (P-1653)*

Heartland Label Printers LLC .... A 909 243-7151
9817 7th St Ste 703 Rancho Cucamonga (91730) *(P-3143)*

Heartland Meat Company Inc .... D 619 407-3668
3461 Main St Chula Vista (91911) *(P-10871)*

Hearts Delight .... E 805 648-7123
4035 N Ventura Ave Ventura (93001) *(P-2099)*

Heat Transfer Pdts Group LLC .... C 909 786-3669
1933 S Vineyard Ave Ontario (91761) *(P-10334)*

Heater Designs Inc .... E 909 421-0971
2211 S Vista Ave Bloomington (92316) *(P-5799)*

Heather By Bordeaux Inc .... E 213 622-0555
5983 Malburg Way Vernon (90058) *(P-2100)*

Heatherfield Foods Inc .... E 877 460-3060
1150 Brooks St Ontario (91762) *(P-1243)*

Heaviland Enterprises Inc .... C 858 412-1576
8710 Miramar Pl San Diego (92121) *(P-173)*

Heaviland Enterprises Inc (PA)... D 760 598-7065
2180 La Mirada Dr Vista (92081) *(P-209)*

Heavy Civil - Gen Engrg Cnstr, Chatsworth *Also Called: Maloof Naman Builders (P-10352)*

Heavy Equipment Rentals, Corona *Also Called: Porter Hire Ltd (P-13467)*

Heavy Load Transfer LLC .... D 310 816-0260
4811 Airport Plaza Dr Long Beach (90815) *(P-8915)*

Heavy Metal Steel, San Diego *Also Called: Heavy Metal Steel Company Inc (P-1153)*

Heavy Metal Steel Company Inc .... E 858 433-4800
12130 Lomica Dr San Diego (92128) *(P-1153)*

Hec Asset Management Inc .... D 661 587-2250
29341 Kimberlina Rd Wasco (93280) *(P-10044)*

Hec Inc .... B 818 879-7414
30961 Agoura Rd Ste 311 Westlake Village (91361) *(P-10247)*

Heck Cellars, Arvin *Also Called: F Korbel & Bros (P-1567)*

Hedman Hedders, Whittier *Also Called: Hedman Manufacturing (P-7260)*

Hedman Manufacturing (PA).. E 562 204-1031
12438 Putnam St Whittier (90602) *(P-7260)*

Hee Environmental Engineering LLC .... E 760 530-1409
16605 Koala Rd Adelanto (92301) *(P-4130)*

Hehr International Inc .... C 323 663-1261
Los Angeles (90039) *(P-4889)*

Hehr International Polymers, Los Angeles *Also Called: Hehr International Inc (P-4889)*

HEI Hospitality LLC .... C 818 887-4800
21850 Oxnard St Woodland Hills (91367) *(P-12848)*

HEI Long Beach LLC .... C 562 983-3400
701 W Ocean Blvd Long Beach (90831) *(P-12849)*

Heidi Corporation .... D 626 333-6317
727 N Vernon Ave Azusa (91702) *(P-1120)*

Heil Construction Inc .... D 626 303-7141
701 S Myrtle Ave Monrovia (91016) *(P-486)*

Heimark Distributing, Santa Fe Springs *Also Called: Triangle Distributing Co (P-11053)*

Helendale Lckheed Plant Prtcti, Helendale *Also Called: Lockheed Martin Corporation (P-7738)*

Helical Products, Santa Maria *Also Called: Matthew Warren Inc (P-5381)*

Helical Products Company Inc .... C 805 928-3851
901 W Mccoy Ln Santa Maria (93455) *(P-5808)*

Helicopter Tech Co Ltd Partnr .... E 310 523-2750
12902 S Broadway Los Angeles (90061) *(P-7488)*

Helicopter Technology Company, Los Angeles *Also Called: Helicopter Tech Co Ltd Partnr (P-7488)*

Helix Electric Inc .... A 562 941-7200
13100 Alondra Blvd Ste 108 Cerritos (90703) *(P-923)*

Helix Electric Inc (PA)... C 858 535-0505
6795 Flanders Dr San Diego (92121) *(P-924)*

Helix Healthcare Inc .... B 619 465-4411
7050 Parkway Dr La Mesa (91942) *(P-16477)*

Helix Mechanical Inc .... C 619 440-1518
1100 N Magnolia Ave Ste L El Cajon (92020) *(P-786)*

Helix Medical, Carpinteria *Also Called: Freudenberg Medical LLC (P-8271)*

Helix Renewables, San Diego *Also Called: Helix Electric Inc (P-924)*

Hellas Construction Inc .... B 760 891-8090
5135 Avenida Encinas Ste A Carlsbad (92008) *(P-714)*

Hellmuth Obata & Kassabaum Inc .... D 310 838-9555
757 S Alameda St Los Angeles (90021) *(P-17674)*

Helloworld Travel Svcs USA Inc .... D 310 535-1005
6171 W Century Blvd Ste 160 Los Angeles (90045) *(P-9223)*

Hells Kitchen Geothermal LLC .... E 760 604-0433
124 W 9th St Ste 101 Imperial (92251) *(P-3238)*

Helm Management Co (PA).. D 619 589-6222
4668 Nebo Dr Ste A La Mesa (91941) *(P-12464)*

Helm, The, La Mesa *Also Called: Helm Management Co (P-12464)*

Helmet House LLC (PA)... D 800 421-7247
26855 Malibu Hills Rd Calabasas Hills (91301) *(P-10685)*

Help Children World Foundation .... B 818 706-9848
26500 Agoura Rd Ste 657 Calabasas (91302) *(P-16950)*

Help Group West (PA)... C 818 781-0360
13130 Burbank Blvd Sherman Oaks (91401) *(P-16478)*

Help Unlimited, Ojai *Also Called: Help Unlmted Personnel Svc Inc (P-16394)*

Help Unlmted Personnel Svc Inc .... A 805 962-4646
3202 E Ojai Ave Ojai (93023) *(P-16394)*

Heluna Health, City Of Industry *Also Called: Public Hlth Fndation Entps Inc (P-17360)*

Hely & Weber Orthopedic, Santa Paula *Also Called: Weber Orthopedic LP (P-8319)*

Hemacare Corporation, Northridge *Also Called: Charles Rver Labs Cell Sltons (P-16547)*

Hemet Hills Post Acute, Hemet *Also Called: Pacs Group Inc (P-15738)*

Hemet Ready Mix, Hemet *Also Called: Superior Ready Mix Concrete LP (P-4462)*

Mergent email: customerrelations@mergent.com
1048

2025 Southern California
Business Directory and Buyers Guide

(P-0000) Products & Services Section entry number
(PA)=Parent Co (HQ)=Headquarters (DH)=Div Headquarters

Hemet Unified School District .... D 951 765-5100
2075 W Acacia Ave Hemet (92545) *(P-16810)*

Hemet Unified School District .... D 951 765-6287
985 N Cawston Ave Hemet (92545) *(P-16811)*

Hemet Valley Medical Center, Hemet *Also Called: Hemet Valley Medical Center-Education*
(P-16016)

Hemet Valley Medical Center-Education .... A 951 652-2811
1117 E Devonshire Ave Hemet (92543) *(P-16016)*

Hemodialysis Inc .... D 626 792-0548
806 S Fair Oaks Ave Pasadena (91105) *(P-15321)*

Hemodialysis Inc .... D 818 365-6961
14901 Rinaldi St Ste 100 Mission Hills (91345) *(P-16436)*

Hemosure Inc .... E 888 436-6787
5358 Irwindale Ave Baldwin Park (91706) *(P-3801)*

Hemp Industries .... E 619 458-9090
3717 El Cajon Blvd San Diego (92105) *(P-8681)*

Henkel Chemical Management LLC .... C 888 943-6535
14000 Jamboree Rd Irvine (92606) *(P-3768)*

Henkel Electronic Mtls LLC, Irvine *Also Called: Henkel Chemical Management LLC (P-3768)*

Henkel US Operations Corp .... E 818 435-0889
21551 Prairie St Chatsworth (91311) *(P-3625)*

Henkel US Operations Corp .... C 562 297-6840
20021 S Susana Rd Compton (90221) *(P-3626)*

Henkel US Operations Corp .... E 626 321-4100
5800 Bristol Pkwy Culver City (90230) *(P-3657)*

Henkel US Operations Corp .... E 203 655-8911
12155 Paine Pl Poway (92064) *(P-3658)*

Henkel US Operations Corp .... D 626 968-6511
15051 Don Julian Rd City Of Industry (91746) *(P-3769)*

Henkel US Operations Corp .... D 424 308-0505
5800 Bristol Pkwy Culver City (90230) *(P-11015)*

Henkel US Operations Corp .... D 714 368-8000
14000 Jamboree Rd Irvine (92606) *(P-17845)*

Henkels & McCoy Inc .... B 909 517-3011
2840 Ficus St Pomona (91766) *(P-674)*

Henry Avocado Corporation (HQ) .... D 760 745-6632
2208 Harmony Grove Rd Escondido (92029) *(P-49)*

Henry Building Products, El Segundo *Also Called: Henry Company LLC (P-3842)*

Henry Company LLC (HQ) .... D 310 955-9200
999 N Pacific Coast Hwy Ste 800 El Segundo (90245) *(P-3842)*

Henry Mayo Diagnostic Imaging, Valencia *Also Called: Henry Mayo Newhall Mem Hosp*
(P-15322)

Henry Mayo Newhall Mem Hosp .... D 661 253-8400
23845 Mcbean Pkwy Valencia (91355) *(P-15322)*

Henry Mayo Newhall Mem Hosp (PA) .... A 661 253-8000
23845 Mcbean Pkwy Valencia (91355) *(P-16017)*

Henry Mayo Newhall Mem Hosp .... C 661 253-8227
23845 Mcbean Pkwy Santa Clarita (91355) *(P-16568)*

Henry Mayo Nwhall Mem Hlth Fnd .... A 661 253-8000
23845 Mcbean Pkwy Valencia (91355) *(P-16018)*

Henry Samueli School Engrg, Irvine *Also Called: University California Irvine (P-17836)*

Henry Schein Orthodontics, Carlsbad *Also Called: Ortho Organizers Inc (P-8347)*

HENRYMAYO NEWHALL MEMORIAL HOS, Valencia *Also Called: Henry Mayo Nwhall Mem*
Hlth Fnd (P-16018)

Henrys Adio Visual Slutions Inc .... E 714 258-7238
18002 Cowan Irvine (92614) *(P-6542)*

Hensel Phelps, Irvine *Also Called: Hensel Phelps Construction Co (P-545)*

Hensel Phelps Construction Co .... D 626 636-4449
18850 Von Karman Ave Ste 100 Irvine (92612) *(P-545)*

Hepa Corporation .... D 714 630-5700
3071 E Coronado St Anaheim (92806) *(P-5770)*

Hera Technologies LLC .... E 951 751-6191
1055 E Francis St Ontario (91761) *(P-6140)*

Heraeus Prcous Mtls N Amer LLC (DH) .... C 562 921-7464
15524 Carmenita Rd Santa Fe Springs (90670) *(P-4585)*

Herald Christian Health Center (PA) .... D 626 286-8700
3401 Aero Jet Ave El Monte (91731) *(P-15323)*

Herbalife Manufacturing LLC (DH) .... D 866 866-4744
800 W Olympic Blvd Ste 406 Los Angeles (90015) *(P-1683)*

Herbert Malarkey Roofing Co .... D 562 806-8000
9301 Garfield Ave South Gate (90280) *(P-1085)*

Herca Construction Services, Perris *Also Called: Herca Telecomm Services Inc (P-10350)*

Herca Telecomm Services Inc .... D 951 940-5941
18610 Beck St Perris (92570) *(P-10350)*

Heritage Auctions Inc .... D 310 300-8390
9478 W Olympic Blvd Beverly Hills (90212) *(P-14508)*

Heritage California Aco, Northridge *Also Called: Regal Medical Group Inc (P-17305)*

Heritage Container Inc .... D 951 360-1900
4777 Felspar St Riverside (92509) *(P-2672)*

Heritage Distributing Company (PA) .... E 323 838-1225
5743 Smithway St Ste 105 Commerce (90040) *(P-1332)*

Heritage Foods, Santa Ana *Also Called: Stremicks Heritage Foods LLC (P-1335)*

Heritage Gardens Hlth Care Ctr, Loma Linda *Also Called: Heritage Health Care Inc (P-15676)*

Heritage Golf Group LLC .... C 661 254-4401
27330 Tourney Rd Valencia (91355) *(P-15084)*

Heritage Golf Group LLC .... D 949 369-6226
990 Avenida Talega San Clemente (92673) *(P-15085)*

Heritage Health Care, Lancaster *Also Called: High Dsert Med Corp A Med Grou (P-15324)*

Heritage Health Care Inc .... C 909 796-0216
25271 Barton Rd Loma Linda (92354) *(P-15676)*

Heritage Leather Company Inc .... E 323 983-0420
4011 E 52nd St Maywood (90270) *(P-4278)*

Heritage Medical Group .... B 760 956-1286
12370 Hesperia Rd Ste 6 Victorville (92395) *(P-16569)*

HERITAGE MEDICAL GROUP, Victorville *Also Called: Heritage Medical Group (P-16569)*

Heritage Oaks Bancorp .... B 805 369-5200
1222 Vine St Paso Robles (93446) *(P-11768)*

Heritage Oaks Bank .... C 805 239-5200
1222 Vine St Paso Robles (93446) *(P-11769)*

Heritage Paper Co (HQ) .... D 714 540-9737
2400 S Grand Ave Santa Ana (92705) *(P-2673)*

Heritage Pointe, Rancho Cucamonga *Also Called: National Community Renaissance*
(P-12360)

HERITAGE POINTE, Mission Viejo *Also Called: Jewish HM For The Aging Ornge (P-15684)*

Heritage Security Services, Temecula *Also Called: Richman Management Corporation*
(P-14334)

Herman Weissker Inc (HQ) .... C 951 826-8800
1645 Brown Ave Riverside (92509) *(P-675)*

Hermetic Seal Corporation (DH) .... C 626 443-8931
4232 Temple City Blvd Rosemead (91770) *(P-7005)*

Hermetics Material Solutions, Santa Ana *Also Called: IJ Research Inc (P-7006)*

Heron Therapeutics, San Diego *Also Called: Heron Therapeutics Inc (P-3419)*

Heron Therapeutics Inc (PA) .... C 858 251-4400
4242 Campus Point Ct Ste 200 San Diego (92121) *(P-3419)*

Herring Networks Inc .... C 858 270-6900
4757 Morena Blvd San Diego (92117) *(P-9507)*

Hertzbrg-Dvis Frnsic Scnce Ctr, Los Angeles *Also Called: County of Los Angeles (P-17911)*

Herzog & Company .... D 818 762-4640
4640 Lankershim Blvd Ste 400 North Hollywood (91602) *(P-14831)*

Herzog Contracting Corp .... D 562 595-7414
3760 Kilroy Airport Way Ste 120 Long Beach (90806) *(P-715)*

Herzog Contracting Corp .... D 619 849-6990
2155 Hancock St San Diego (92110) *(P-1209)*

Hesperia Holding Inc .... D 760 244-8787
9700 E Ave I Hesperia (92345) *(P-2370)*

Hesperia Unified School Dst .... D 760 948-1051
11176 G Ave Hesperia (92345) *(P-1788)*

Hesperia Usd Food Service, Hesperia *Also Called: Hesperia Unified School Dst (P-1788)*

Hestan Commercial Corporation .... C 714 869-2380
3375 E La Palma Ave Anaheim (92806) *(P-6401)*

Hetherington Engineering (PA) .... C 760 931-1917
4333 Apache St Oceanside (92056) *(P-17543)*

Hexagon Agility Inc .... E 949 236-5520
3335 Susan St Ste 100 Costa Mesa (92626) *(P-284)*

Hexagon Mfg Intelligence Inc .... D 760 994-1401
3536 Seagate Way Ste 100 Oceanside (92056) *(P-7914)*

Hexco International .... C 951 677-2081
25720 Jefferson Ave Murrieta (92562) *(P-5704)*

Hexoden Holdings Inc (PA) .... D 858 201-3412
1219 Linda Vista Dr San Marcos (92078) *(P-8682)*

Hexpol Compounding CA Inc (DH) .... D 626 961-0311
2500 E Thompson St Long Beach (90805) *(P-3913)*

Employee Codes: A=Over 500 employees, B=251-500
C=101-250, D=51-100, E=20-50, F=10-19, G=1-9

2025 Southern California
Business Directory and Buyers Guide

© Mergent Inc. 1-800-342-5647
1049

HF Cox Inc .... B 323 587-2359
8330 Atlantic Ave Cudahy (90201) *(P-8916)*

Hf Group Inc (PA)... E 310 605-0755
203 W Artesia Blvd Compton (90220) *(P-8430)*

HG Fenton Company .... C 619 400-0120
7577 Mission Valley Rd Ste 200 San Diego (92108) *(P-12344)*

HG Fenton Property Company (PA)................... C 619 400-0120
7577 Mission Valley Rd Ste 200 San Diego (92108) *(P-12376)*

Hgst Inc .... B 949 448-0385
3355 Michelson Dr Irvine (92612) *(P-17794)*

Hhi, Lake Forest *Also Called: Assa Abloy AB (P-7084)*

HI LLC .... D 757 655-4113
10361 Jefferson Blvd Culver City (90232) *(P-17846)*

HI Pro Inc .... C 442 205-0063
57019 Yucca Trl Ste D Yucca Valley (92284) *(P-8955)*

HI Rel Connectors Inc .... B 909 626-1820
760 Wharton Dr Claremont (91711) *(P-6421)*

HI Tech Electronic Mfg Corp .... D 858 657-0908
1938 Avenida Del Oro Oceanside (92056) *(P-6735)*

HI Tech Honeycomb Inc .... C 858 974-1600
9355 Ruffin Ct San Diego (92123) *(P-5191)*

Hi-Desert Medical Center, Joshua Tree *Also Called: Hdmc Holdings LLC (P-16012)*

Hi-Desert Publishing Company .... E 909 795-8145
35154 Yucaipa Blvd Yucaipa (92399) *(P-2802)*

Hi-Desert Publishing Company .... E 909 336-3555
28200 Highway 189 Bldg O-1 Lake Arrowhead (92352) *(P-2803)*

Hi-Desert Publishing Company (HQ).................. D 760 365-3315
56445 29 Palms Hwy Yucca Valley (92284) *(P-2804)*

Hi-Desert Publishing Company .... E 909 866-3456
42007 Fox Farm Rd Ste 3b Big Bear Lake (92315) *(P-11671)*

Hi-Grade Materials Co .... D 661 533-3100
6500 E Avenue T Littlerock (93543) *(P-4441)*

Hi-Lite Manufacturing Co Inc .... D 909 465-1999
13450 Monte Vista Ave Chino (91710) *(P-6463)*

Hi-Plas, Mira Loma *Also Called: Highland Plastics Inc (P-4132)*

Hi-Precision Grinding, Santa Ana *Also Called: Deltronic Corporation (P-7999)*

Hi-Rel Plastics & Molding Corp .... E 951 354-0258
7575 Jurupa Ave Riverside (92504) *(P-4131)*

Hi-Shear Corporation (DH)................................. A 310 326-8110
2600 Skypark Dr Torrance (90505) *(P-5128)*

Hi-Tech Iron Works, Commerce *Also Called: Architectural Enterprises Inc (P-5091)*

Hi-Tech Labels Incorporated .... E 714 670-2150
8530 Roland St Buena Park (90621) *(P-6141)*

Hi-Tech Products, Buena Park *Also Called: Hi-Tech Labels Incorporated (P-6141)*

Hi-Temp Insulation Inc .... B 805 484-2774
4700 Calle Alto Camarillo (93012) *(P-1010)*

Hi-Torque Publications, Santa Clarita *Also Called: Daisy Publishing Company Inc (P-2910)*

Hi-Way Safety, Chino *Also Called: Myers & Sons Hi-Way Safety Inc (P-8618)*

Hiatus, Los Angeles *Also Called: Crew Knitwear LLC (P-2087)*

Hibernia Woolen Mills, Manhattan Beach *Also Called: Stanton Carpet Corp (P-1957)*

Hid Global Corporation .... D 949 732-2000
15370 Barranca Pkwy Irvine (92618) *(P-7915)*

Hidden Jeans Inc .... E 213 746-4223
7210 Dominion Cir Commerce (90040) *(P-1881)*

Hidden Villa Ranch, Fullerton *Also Called: Hidden Villa Ranch Produce Inc (P-10835)*

Hidden Villa Ranch Produce Inc (HQ) .... B 714 680-3447
310 N Harbor Blvd Ste 205 Fullerton (92832) *(P-10835)*

Hideaway .... C 760 777-7400
80440 Hideaway Club Ct La Quinta (92253) *(P-11574)*

Hideaway, La Quinta *Also Called: Hideaway Club (P-15139)*

Hideaway Club .... A 760 777-7400
80440 Hideaway Club Ct La Quinta (92253) *(P-15139)*

Higgs Fletcher & Mack Llp .... C 619 236-1551
401 W A St Ste 2600 San Diego (92101) *(P-16701)*

High Caliber Line, Irwindale *Also Called: Calibre International LLC (P-18252)*

High Dsert Med Corp A Med Grou (PA)............. C 661 945-5984
43839 15th St W Lancaster (93534) *(P-15324)*

High Dsert Prtnr In Acdmic Exc .... B 760 946-5414
17500 Mana Rd Apple Valley (92307) *(P-17847)*

High Performance Logistics LLC .... D 702 300-4880
7227 Central Ave Riverside (92504) *(P-8917)*

High Performance Seals, Garden Grove *Also Called: Saint-Gobain Prfmce Plas Corp (P-3292)*

High Road Craft Ice Cream Inc (PA)................... E 678 701-7623
12243 Branford St Sun Valley (91352) *(P-1318)*

High Tech Pet Products .... D 805 644-1797
2111 Portola Rd # A Ventura (93003) *(P-10248)*

High Technology Video Inc .... D 323 969-8822
10900 Ventura Blvd Studio City (91604) *(P-14832)*

Highbury Defense Group LLC .... D 619 316-7979
2725 Congress St Ste 1m San Diego (92110) *(P-17544)*

Higher Ground Education Inc (PA)..................... B 949 836-9401
10 Orchard Ste 200 Lake Forest (92630) *(P-18318)*

Higher Talent, Los Angeles *Also Called: Creative Solutions Svcs LLC (P-13506)*

Highland Hlthcare Cmllia Grdns .... C 626 798-6777
1920 N Fair Oaks Ave Pasadena (91103) *(P-15677)*

Highland Lumber Sales Inc .... E 714 778-2293
300 E Santa Ana St Anaheim (92805) *(P-2310)*

Highland Palms Healthcare Ctr, Highland *Also Called: Cedar Holdings LLC (P-15588)*

Highland Pk Sklled Nrsing Wlln .... D 323 254-6125
5125 Monte Vista St Los Angeles (90042) *(P-15678)*

Highland Plastics Inc .... C 951 360-9587
3650 Dulles Dr Mira Loma (91752) *(P-4132)*

Highline Aftermarket LLC .... D 951 361-0331
10385 San Sevaine Way Ste B Jurupa Valley (91752) *(P-9828)*

Highmark, Huntington Beach *Also Called: Highmark Smart Reliable Seating Inc (P-2529)*

Highmark Smart Reliable Seating Inc .... C 714 903-2257
5559 Mcfadden Ave Huntington Beach (92649) *(P-2529)*

Hightower Metal Products LLC .... D 714 637-7000
2090 N Glassell St Orange (92865) *(P-5583)*

Hightower Plating & Mfg Co LLC .... E 714 637-9110
2090 N Glassell St Orange (92865) *(P-5266)*

Highways Magazine, Oxnard *Also Called: TI Enterprises LLC (P-2877)*

Hii Fleet Support Group LLC .... C 619 474-8820
131 W 33rd St Ste 100a National City (91950) *(P-17545)*

Hii Fleet Support Group LLC .... C 858 522-6319
9444 Balboa Ave Ste 400 San Diego (92123) *(P-17795)*

Hii San Diego Shipyard Inc .... B 619 234-8851
1995 Bay Front St San Diego (92101) *(P-7601)*

Hikma Pharmaceuticals USA Inc .... E 760 683-0901
2325 Camino Vida Roble Ste B Carlsbad (92011) *(P-3420)*

Hikvision USA Inc (HQ)...................................... C 909 895-0400
18639 Railroad St City Of Industry (91748) *(P-14406)*

Hill Brothers Chemical, Brea *Also Called: Hill Brothers Chemical Company (P-11016)*

Hill Brothers Chemical Company (PA)................ C 714 998-8800
3000 E Birch St Ste 108 Brea (92821) *(P-11016)*

Hill Farrer & Burrill .... D 213 620-0460
300 S Grand Ave Fl 37 Los Angeles (90071) *(P-16702)*

Hill Phoenix Inc .... D 909 592-8830
14680 Monte Vista Ave Chino (91710) *(P-10340)*

Hillcrest, La Verne *Also Called: Brethren Hillcrest Homes (P-15583)*

Hillcrest Contracting Inc .... D 951 273-9600
1467 Circle City Dr Corona (92879) *(P-624)*

Hillcrest Country Club .... C 310 553-8911
10000 W Pico Blvd Los Angeles (90064) *(P-15140)*

Hillcrest Manor Sanitarium, National City *Also Called: Imaginative Horizons Inc (P-15680)*

Hiller Companies LLC .... E 858 899-5008
7070 Convoy Ct San Diego (92111) *(P-4681)*

Hiller Marine, San Diego *Also Called: Hiller Companies LLC (P-4681)*

Hills Wldg & Engrg Contr Inc .... D 661 746-5400
22038 Stockdale Hwy Bakersfield (93314) *(P-334)*

Hillsdale Group LP .... C 818 623-2170
12750 Riverside Dr North Hollywood (91607) *(P-15859)*

Hillside Capital Inc .... C 650 367-2011
6222 Fallbrook Ave Woodland Hills (91367) *(P-6619)*

Hillside Entps - AR C Long Bch, Long Beach *Also Called: Advocacy For Rspect Chice - Lo (P-17044)*

Hillside House .... D 805 687-0788
1235 Veronica Springs Rd Santa Barbara (93105) *(P-15812)*

Hillsides .... B 323 254-2274
940 Avenue 64 Pasadena (91105) *(P-16951)*

Hillview Mental Health Ctr Inc .... D 818 896-1161
12450 Van Nuys Blvd Ste 200 Pacoima (91331) *(P-16479)*

Hilti US Manufacturing Inc .... E 714 230-7410
6601 Darin Way Cypress (90630) *(P-4747)*

Hilton, Los Angeles *Also Called: Fortuna Enterprises LP (P-12826)*

Hilton, Anaheim *Also Called: Makar Anaheim LLC (P-12912)*

Hilton, Long Beach *Also Called: Merritt Hospitality LLC (P-12922)*

Hilton, San Bernardino *Also Called: San Bernardino Hilton (P-13010)*

Hilton, Huntington Beach *Also Called: Waterfront Hotel LLC (P-13071)*

Hilton, San Diego *Also Called: Ww San Diego Harbor Island LLC (P-13094)*

Hilton Garden Inn Calabasas, Calabasas *Also Called: T M Mian & Associates Inc (P-13049)*

Hilton Grdn Inn San Dego Dwntw, San Diego *Also Called: M4dev LLC (P-12910)*

Hilton Hotels, Long Beach *Also Called: HEI Long Beach LLC (P-12849)*

Hilton Los Angeles Culver City, Culver City *Also Called: Woodbine Lgacy/Playa Owner LLC (P-13092)*

Hilton Los Angls/Nversal Cy Ht, Universal City *Also Called: Sun Hill Properties Inc (P-13040)*

Hilton Resort In Palm Spring, Palm Springs *Also Called: Walters Family Partnership (P-13070)*

Hilton San Diego Airport/Hrbr, San Diego *Also Called: Bartell Hotels (P-12768)*

Hilton San Diego/Del Mar, Del Mar *Also Called: Sunstone Durante LLC (P-13041)*

Hines Growers Inc .... A 800 554-4065
27368 Via Industria Ste 201 Temecula (92590) *(P-57)*

Hines Horticulture Inc (PA) .... B 949 559-4444
12621 Jeffery Rd Irvine (92620) *(P-58)*

Hines Nurseries, Irvine *Also Called: Hines Horticulture Inc (P-58)*

Hino Motors Mfg USA Inc .... D 951 727-0286
4550 Wineville Ave Jurupa Valley (91752) *(P-9829)*

Hinoichi Tofu, Garden Grove *Also Called: House Foods America Corp (P-1790)*

Hip Hop Royalty, Santa Ana *Also Called: Tailgate Printing Inc (P-3086)*

Hira Paris Inc .... C 909 634-3900
3811 Schaefer Ave Ste B Chino (91710) *(P-1505)*

Hirel Connectors, Claremont *Also Called: HI Rel Connectors Inc (P-6421)*

Hirsch Electronics LLC .... D 949 250-3888
1900 Carnegie Ave Ste B Santa Ana (92705) *(P-10249)*

Hirsch/Bedner Intl Inc (PA) .... D 310 829-9087
3216 Nebraska Ave Santa Monica (90404) *(P-14509)*

Hirsch3667 Corp .... C 310 641-6690
5700 Hannum Ave Ste 250 Culver City (90230) *(P-12602)*

Hirsh Inc .... E 213 622-9441
860 S Los Angeles St # 900 Los Angeles (90014) *(P-335)*

Hisamitsu Pharmaceutical Co Inc .... A 760 931-1756
2730 Loker Ave W Carlsbad (92010) *(P-17874)*

Historic Mission Inn Corp .... B 951 784-0300
3649 Mission Inn Ave Riverside (92501) *(P-12850)*

Historical Properties Inc (PA) .... D 619 230-8417
311 Island Ave San Diego (92101) *(P-12851)*

Historynet, Beverly Hills *Also Called: World History Group LLC (P-2879)*

Hitachi Astemo Americas Inc .... C 951 340-0702
1235 Graphite Dr Corona (92881) *(P-7261)*

Hitachi Automotive Systems .... D 310 212-0200
6200 Gateway Dr Cypress (90630) *(P-6324)*

Hitachi Solutions America Ltd (DH) .... E 040 242 1300
100 Spectrum Center Dr Ste 350 Irvine (92618) *(P-10010)*

Hitachi Transport System (america) Ltd .... B 310 787-3420
21061 S Western Ave Ste 300 Torrance (90501) *(P-0202)*

Hitech Metal Fabrication Corp .... D 714 635-3505
1705 S Claudina Way Anaheim (92805) *(P-4837)*

Hitem, Oceanside *Also Called: HI Tech Electronic Mfg Corp (P-6735)*

Hitex Dyeing & Finishing Inc .... E 626 363-0160
355 Vineland Ave City Of Industry (91746) *(P-2278)*

Hitt Companies .... E 714 979-1405
3231 W Macarthur Blvd Santa Ana (92704) *(P-3914)*

Hitt Contracting Inc .... C 424 326-1042
3733 Motor Ave Ste 200 Los Angeles (90034) *(P-546)*

Hitt Marking Devices I D Tech, Santa Ana *Also Called: Hitt Companies (P-3914)*

Hiv Neural Behavioral Center .... D 619 543-5000
150 W Washington St La Jolla (92093) *(P-15325)*

Hixson Metal Finishing .... D 800 900-9798
829 Production Pl Newport Beach (92663) *(P-5267)*

HK Canning Inc (PA) .... E 805 652-1392
130 N Garden St Ventura (93001) *(P-1350)*

HK Precision Turning Machining, Oceanside *Also Called: Balda Precision Inc (P-5105)*

Hkf Inc (PA) .... D 323 225-1318
5983 Smithway St Commerce (90040) *(P-10335)*

HM Electronics Inc (PA) .... B 858 535-6000
2848 Whiptail Loop Carlsbad (92010) *(P-10250)*

HMC Architects, Ontario *Also Called: HMC Group (P-17675)*

HMC Assets LLC .... C 310 535-9293
2015 Manhattan Beach Blvd Ste 200 Redondo Beach (90278) *(P-12120)*

HMC Group (HQ) .... C 909 989-9979
3546 Concours Ontario (91764) *(P-17675)*

Hmr Building Systems LLC .... D 951 749-4700
620 Newport Center Dr Fl 12 Newport Beach (92660) *(P-2286)*

HMS, Vista *Also Called: HMS Construction Inc (P-17546)*

HMS Construction Inc (PA) .... D 760 727-9808
2885 Scott St Vista (92081) *(P-17546)*

Hmt Electric Inc .... D 858 458-9771
2340 Meyers Ave Escondido (92029) *(P-925)*

Hnc Parent Inc (PA) .... D 310 955-9200
999 N Pacific Coast Hwy Ste 800 El Segundo (90245) *(P-3843)*

Hntb Corporation .... C 714 460-1600
6 Hutton Centre Dr Ste 500 Santa Ana (92707) *(P-17547)*

Hntb Gerwick Water Solutions .... C 714 460-1600
200 Sandpointe Ave Santa Ana (92707) *(P-17548)*

Hoag Clinic .... A 949 764-1888
1 Hoag Dr Newport Beach (92663) *(P-16019)*

HOAG CORPORATE HEALTH, Newport Beach *Also Called: Hoag Clinic (P-16019)*

Hoag Family Cancer Institute .... C 949 764-7777
1190 Baker St Costa Mesa (92626) *(P-16020)*

Hoag Hospital Irvine .... D 949 764-4624
16200 Sand Canyon Ave Irvine (92618) *(P-16021)*

Hoag Memorial Hospital Presbt (PA) .... A 949 764-4624
1 Hoag Dr Newport Beach (92658) *(P-16022)*

Hoag Orthopedic Institute LLC .... C 949 515-0708
22 Corporate Plaza Dr Ste 150 Newport Beach (92660) *(P-16023)*

Hoag Orthpd Inst Srgery Ctr -, Newport Beach *Also Called: Hoag Orthopedic Institute LLC (P-16023)*

Hob Entertainment LLC (DH) .... C 323 769-4600
7060 Hollywood Blvd Los Angeles (90028) *(P-14989)*

Hob Entertainment LLC .... C 714 520-2310
400 W Disney Way Ste 337 Anaheim (92802) *(P-14990)*

Hob Entertainment LLC .... D 619 299-2583
1055 5th Ave San Diego (92101) *(P-14991)*

Hobie Cat Company (PA) .... C 760 758-9100
4925 Oceanside Blvd Oceanside (92056) *(P-7621)*

Hobie Cat Company II LLC .... C 760 758-9100
4925 Oceanside Blvd Oceanside (92056) *(P-8521)*

Hochiki, Buena Park *Also Called: Hochiki America Corporation (P-10186)*

Hochiki America Corporation (HQ) .... D 714 522-2246
7051 Village Dr Ste 100 Buena Park (90621) *(P-10186)*

Hodge Products Inc .... E 800 778-2217
7365 Mission Gorge Rd Ste F San Diego (92120) *(P-4771)*

Hoehn Company Inc .... D 760 438-1818
5454 Paseo Del Norte Carlsbad (92008) *(P-11360)*

Hoehn Honda, Carlsbad *Also Called: Hoehn Company Inc (P-11360)*

Hoffman Plastic Compounds Inc .... D 323 636-3346
16616 Garfield Ave Paramount (90723) *(P-3268)*

Hoffy, Vernon *Also Called: Square H Brands Inc (P-1271)*

Hogue Bros Inc .... E 805 239-1440
550 Linne Rd Paso Robles (93446) *(P-2290)*

Hogue Grips, Paso Robles *Also Called: Hogue Bros Inc (P-2290)*

Hoist Fitness, Poway *Also Called: Hoist Fitness Systems Inc (P-8522)*

Hoist Fitness Systems, San Diego *Also Called: Fitness Warehouse LLC (P-8517)*

Hoist Fitness Systems Inc .... D 858 578-7676
11900 Community Rd Poway (92064) *(P-8522)*

Hokey Pokey La, Santa Monica *Also Called: Hokey Pokey LLC (P-10830)*

Hokey Pokey LLC .... E 213 361-2503
1235 24th St Unit 4 Santa Monica (90404) *(P-10830)*

Hokto Kinoko Company .... D 323 526-1155
130 S Myers St Los Angeles (90033) *(P-72)*

Holbrook Construction Inc .... D 714 523-1150
9814 Norwalk Blvd Ste 200 Santa Fe Springs (90670) *(P-547)*

Holcim Solutions & Pdts US LLC .... E 714 898-0025
12271 Monarch St Garden Grove (92841) *(P-3269)*

Holdrite, Poway *Also Called: Securus Inc (P-5071)*

Holguin & Holguin Inc .... E 626 815-0168
968 W Foothill Blvd Azusa (91702) *(P-2543)*

Holiday Foliage, San Diego *Also Called: Holiday Foliage Inc (P-8683)*

Holiday Foliage Inc .... E 619 661-9094
2592 Otay Center Dr San Diego (92154) *(P-8683)*

Holiday Inn, Los Angeles *Also Called: Brisam Lax (de) LLC (P-12777)*

Holiday Inn, North Hollywood *Also Called: Marcus Hotels Inc (P-12914)*

Holiday Inn, Bakersfield *Also Called: Newport Hospitality Group Inc (P-12937)*

Holiday Inn, Los Angeles *Also Called: Packard Realty Inc (P-12964)*

Holiday Inn, Los Angeles *Also Called: Remington Hotel Corporation (P-12989)*

Holiday Inn, North Hollywood *Also Called: Rio Vista Development Co Inc (P-12994)*

Holiday Inn, Santa Ana *Also Called: S W K Properties LLC (P-13005)*

Holiday Inn, Los Angeles *Also Called: Seattle Arprt Hospitality LLC (P-13019)*

Holiday Inn, Lebec *Also Called: Six Continents Hotels Inc (P-13025)*

Holiday Inn, Buena Park *Also Called: Uniwell Corporation (P-13059)*

Holiday Inn, Torrance *Also Called: V Todays Inc (P-13063)*

Holiday Inn, Victorville *Also Called: Victorvlle Trsure Holdings LLC (P-13066)*

Holiday Inn, Long Beach *Also Called: Yhb Long Beach LLC (P-13095)*

Holiday Inn Express, San Diego *Also Called: Win Time Ltd (P-13081)*

Holiday Inn La Mirada, La Mirada *Also Called: Cha La Mirada LLC (P-12790)*

Holiday Manor Care Center, Canoga Park *Also Called: Sela Healthcare Inc (P-15773)*

Holiday Manor Care Center, Upland *Also Called: Sela Healthcare Inc (P-15774)*

Holiday Transportation, Van Nuys *Also Called: Rwh Inc (P-4455)*

Holiday Tree Farms Inc .... C 323 276-1900
329 Van Norman Rd Montebello (90640) *(P-251)*

Holland & Herring Mfg Inc .... E 909 469-4700
661 E Monterey Ave Pomona (91767) *(P-6142)*

Holland & Knight LLP .... C 213 896-2400
400 S Hope St Ste 800 Los Angeles (90071) *(P-16703)*

Holland Electronics, Ventura *Also Called: Holland Electronics LLC (P-6949)*

Holland Electronics LLC .... E 888 628-5411
2935 Golf Course Dr Ventura (93003) *(P-6949)*

Hollandia Dairy Inc (PA) .... C 760 744-3222
622 E Mission Rd San Marcos (92069) *(P-91)*

Hollandia Oxnard .... C 805 886-1272
6135 N Rose Ave Oxnard (93036) *(P-10907)*

HOLLENBECK HOME FOR THE AGED, Newhall *Also Called: Hollenbeck Palms (P-17162)*

Hollenbeck Palms .... C 323 263-6195
24431 Lyons Ave Apt 336 Newhall (91321) *(P-17162)*

Holliday Trucking Inc .... D 888 273-2200
2300 W Base Line St San Bernardino (92410) *(P-4442)*

Holliday Trucking Inc (PA) .... D 909 982-1553
1401 N Benson Ave Upland (91786) *(P-4443)*

Hollingshead Management, Los Angeles *Also Called: Proland Property Managment LLC (P-12512)*

Hollywood Bed & Spring Mfg, Commerce *Also Called: Hollywood Bed Spring Mfg Inc (P-4772)*

Hollywood Bed Spring Mfg Inc (PA) .... D 323 887-9500
5959 Corvette St Commerce (90040) *(P-4772)*

Hollywood Bowl, Los Angeles *Also Called: Los Angeles Philharmonic Assn (P-14996)*

Hollywood Chairs (PA) .... E 760 471-6600
120 W Grand Ave Ste 102 Escondido (92025) *(P-2426)*

Hollywood Cmnty Hosp Hollywood, Los Angeles *Also Called: Hollywood Cmnty Hosp Med Ctr I (P-16024)*

Hollywood Cmnty Hosp Med Ctr I .... C 323 462-2271
6245 De Longpre Ave Los Angeles (90028) *(P-16024)*

Hollywood Medical Center LP .... A 213 413-3000
1300 N Vermont Ave Los Angeles (90027) *(P-16025)*

Hollywood Park Casino, Inglewood *Also Called: Century Gaming Management Inc (P-12789)*

Hollywood Park Casino Co Inc .... C 310 330-2800
3883 W Century Blvd Inglewood (90303) *(P-12852)*

Hollywood Presbyterian Med Ctr, Los Angeles *Also Called: Hollywood Medical Center LP (P-16025)*

Hollywood Records Inc .... E 818 560-5670
500 S Buena Vista St Burbank (91521) *(P-6576)*

Hollywood Ribbon Industries Inc .... B 323 266-0670
9000 Rochester Ave Rancho Cucamonga (91730) *(P-1906)*

Hollywood Rntals Prod Svcs LLC (PA) .... D 818 407-7800
5300 Melrose Ave Los Angeles (90038) *(P-14894)*

Hollywood Roosevelt Hotel, Los Angeles *Also Called: Roosevelt Hotel LLC (P-13000)*

Hollywood Sports Park LLC .... D 562 867-9600
9030 Somerset Blvd Bellflower (90706) *(P-14510)*

Holmes & Narver Inc (HQ) .... C 714 567-2400
999 W Town And Country Rd Orange (92868) *(P-17549)*

Holmes Body Shop Riverside, Riverside *Also Called: Holmes Body Shop-Alhambra Inc (P-14674)*

Holmes Body Shop-Alhambra Inc .... D 951 734-9920
3860 Buchanan St Riverside (92503) *(P-14674)*

Hologic Inc .... E 858 410-8792
9393 Waples St San Diego (92121) *(P-8382)*

Hologic Inc .... B 858 410-8000
10210 Genetic Center Dr San Diego (92121) *(P-8383)*

Holt Integrated Circuits, Aliso Viejo *Also Called: W G Holt Inc (P-6913)*

Holthouse Carlin Van Trigt LLP (PA) .... C 310 566-1900
11444 W Olympic Blvd Fl 11 Los Angeles (90064) *(P-17733)*

Holy Cross Cemetary, San Diego *Also Called: Roman Cthlic Bshp of San Diego (P-12525)*

Holy Cross Renal Center, Mission Hills *Also Called: Hemodialysis Inc (P-16436)*

Holy Sepulcher Cemetery, Orange *Also Called: Roman Cthlic Diocese of Orange (P-12587)*

Holzheus El Rancho Market Inc .... D 805 688-4300
2886 Mission Dr Solvang (93463) *(P-11278)*

Home & Body Company (PA) .... B 714 842-8000
5800 Skylab Rd Huntington Beach (92647) *(P-3802)*

Home Brew Mart Inc .... B 858 790-6900
9045 Carroll Way San Diego (92121) *(P-1543)*

Home Carpet Investment Inc (PA) .... D 619 262-8040
730 Design Ct Ste 401 Chula Vista (91911) *(P-1068)*

Home Comfort USA, Anaheim *Also Called: Ken Starr Inc (P-793)*

Home Decor Wholesaler, City Of Industry *Also Called: Pacific Heritg HM Fashion Inc (P-9904)*

Home Depot USA Inc .... C 714 522-8651
14659 Alondra Blvd Ste B La Mirada (90638) *(P-9075)*

Home Depot USA Inc .... C 909 483-8115
8535 Oakwood Pl Ste B Rancho Cucamonga (91730) *(P-9076)*

Home Depot USA Inc .... C 951 361-1235
11650 Venture Dr Mira Loma (91752) *(P-9077)*

Home Depot USA Inc .... D 858 859-4143
13250 Gregg St Ste A2 Poway (92064) *(P-9078)*

Home Depot USA Inc .... B 805 389-9918
401 W Ventura Blvd Camarillo (93010) *(P-11156)*

Home Depot USA Inc .... B 805 983-0653
401 W Esplanade Dr Oxnard (93036) *(P-11157)*

Home Depot USA Inc .... B 323 292-1397
1830 W Slauson Ave Los Angeles (90047) *(P-11158)*

Home Depot USA Inc .... D 323 342-9495
2055 N Figueroa St Los Angeles (90065) *(P-11159)*

Home Depot USA Inc .... C 562 272-8055
6400 Alondra Blvd Paramount (90723) *(P-11160)*

Home Depot USA Inc .... D 626 813-7131
3200 Puente Ave Baldwin Park (91706) *(P-11161)*

Home Depot USA Inc .... B 626 256-0580
1625 S Mountain Ave Monrovia (91016) *(P-11162)*

Home Depot USA Inc .... D 760 375-4614
575 N China Lake Blvd Ridgecrest (93555) *(P-11163)*

Home Depot USA Inc .... C 562 776-2200
7121 Firestone Blvd Downey (90241) *(P-11164)*

Home Depot USA Inc .... B 818 780-5448
16800 Roscoe Blvd Van Nuys (91406) *(P-11165)*

Home Depot USA Inc .... C 323 587-5520
3040 E Slauson Ave Huntington Park (90255) *(P-11166)*

Home Depot USA Inc .... D 310 677-1944
3363 W Century Blvd Inglewood (90303) *(P-11167)*

Home Depot USA Inc .... B 310 835-7547
110 E Sepulveda Blvd Carson (90745) *(P-11168)*

Home Depot USA Inc .... C 562 789-4121
12322 Washington Blvd Whittier (90606) *(P-11169)*

Home Depot USA Inc .... C 310 644-9600
14603 Ocean Gate Ave Hawthorne (90250) *(P-11170)*

Home Depot USA Inc .... B 323 727-9600
7015 Telegraph Rd Los Angeles (90040) *(P-11171)*

Home Depot USA Inc .... B 310 822-3330
12975 W Jefferson Blvd Los Angeles (90066) *(P-11172)*

Home Depot USA Inc .... C 818 365-7662
12960 Foothill Blvd San Fernando (91340) *(P-11173)*

Home Depot USA Inc .... B 661 252-7800
20642 Golden Triangle Rd Santa Clarita (91351) *(P-11174)*

Home Depot USA Inc .... C 562 595-9200
2450 Cherry Ave Long Beach (90755) *(P-11175)*

Home Depot USA Inc .... B 951 358-1370
3323 Madison St Riverside (92504) *(P-11176)*

Home Depot USA Inc .... C 951 727-0324
6140 Hamner Ave Mira Loma (91752) *(P-11177)*

Home Depot USA Inc .... D 951 485-5400
15975 Perris Blvd Moreno Valley (92551) *(P-11178)*

Home Depot USA Inc .... C 951 698-1555
25100 Madison Ave Murrieta (92562) *(P-11179)*

Home Depot USA Inc .... C 951 808-0327
1355 E Ontario Ave Corona (92881) *(P-11180)*

Home Depot USA Inc .... C 619 589-2999
7530 Broadway Lemon Grove (91945) *(P-11181)*

Home Depot USA Inc .... B 760 955-2999
15150 Bear Valley Rd Victorville (92395) *(P-11182)*

Home Depot USA Inc .... B 909 393-5205
14549 Ramona Ave Chino (91710) *(P-11183)*

Home Depot USA Inc .... D 909 948-9200
11884 Foothill Blvd Rancho Cucamonga (91730) *(P-11184)*

Home Depot USA Inc .... C 619 263-1533
355 Marketplace Ave San Diego (92113) *(P-11185)*

Home Depot USA Inc .... C 760 233-1285
1475 E Valley Pkwy Escondido (92027) *(P-11186)*

Home Depot USA Inc .... C 619 421-0639
1320 Eastlake Pkwy Chula Vista (91915) *(P-11187)*

Home Depot USA Inc .... C 619 401-6610
298 Fletcher Pkwy El Cajon (92020) *(P-11188)*

Home Depot USA Inc .... C 909 748-0505
1151 W Lugonia Ave Redlands (92374) *(P-11189)*

Home Depot USA Inc .... C 949 646-4220
2300 Harbor Blvd Ste F Costa Mesa (92626) *(P-11190)*

Home Depot USA Inc .... C 949 609-0221
20021 Lake Forest Dr Lake Forest (92630) *(P-11191)*

Home Depot USA Inc .... C 949 364-1900
27952 Hillcrest Mission Viejo (92692) *(P-11192)*

Home Depot USA Inc .... D 949 831-3698
27401 La Paz Rd Laguna Niguel (92677) *(P-11193)*

Home Depot USA Inc .... D 714 459-4909
625 S Placentia Ave Fullerton (92831) *(P-11194)*

Home Depot USA Inc .... D 714 921-1215
1095 N Pullman St Anaheim (92807) *(P-11195)*

Home Depot USA Inc .... D 562 690-6006
600 S Harbor Blvd La Habra (90631) *(P-11196)*

Home Depot USA Inc .... C 714 966-8551
3500 W Macarthur Blvd Santa Ana (92704) *(P-11197)*

Home Depot USA Inc .... C 714 538-9600
435 W Katella Ave Orange (92867) *(P-11198)*

Home Depot USA Inc .... C 714 539-0319
10801 Garden Grove Blvd Garden Grove (92843) *(P-11199)*

Home Depot USA Inc .... D 714 259-1030
1750 E Edinger Ave Santa Ana (92705) *(P-11200)*

Home Depot, The, La Mirada *Also Called: Home Depot USA Inc (P-9075)*

Home Depot, The, Rancho Cucamonga *Also Called: Home Depot USA Inc (P-9076)*

Home Depot, The, Mira Loma *Also Called: Home Depot USA Inc (P-9077)*

Home Depot, The, Poway *Also Called: Home Depot USA Inc (P-9078)*

Home Depot, The, Camarillo *Also Called: Home Depot USA Inc (P-11156)*

Home Depot, The, Oxnard *Also Called: Home Depot USA Inc (P-11157)*

Home Depot, The, Los Angeles *Also Called: Home Depot USA Inc (P-11158)*

Home Depot, The, Los Angeles *Also Called: Home Depot USA Inc (P-11159)*

Home Depot, The, Paramount *Also Called: Home Depot USA Inc (P-11160)*

Home Depot, The, Baldwin Park *Also Called: Home Depot USA Inc (P-11161)*

Home Depot, The, Monrovia *Also Called: Home Depot USA Inc (P-11162)*

Home Depot, The, Ridgecrest *Also Called: Home Depot USA Inc (P-11163)*

Home Depot, The, Downey *Also Called: Home Depot USA Inc (P-11164)*

Home Depot, The, Van Nuys *Also Called: Home Depot USA Inc (P-11165)*

Home Depot, The, Huntington Park *Also Called: Home Depot USA Inc (P-11166)*

Home Depot, The, Inglewood *Also Called: Home Depot USA Inc (P-11167)*

Home Depot, The, Carson *Also Called: Home Depot USA Inc (P-11168)*

Home Depot, The, Whittier *Also Called: Home Depot USA Inc (P-11169)*

Home Depot, The, Hawthorne *Also Called: Home Depot USA Inc (P-11170)*

Home Depot, The, Los Angeles *Also Called: Home Depot USA Inc (P-11171)*

Home Depot, The, Los Angeles *Also Called: Home Depot USA Inc (P-11172)*

Home Depot, The, San Fernando *Also Called: Home Depot USA Inc (P-11173)*

Home Depot, The, Santa Clarita *Also Called: Home Depot USA Inc (P-11174)*

Home Depot, The, Long Beach *Also Called: Home Depot USA Inc (P-11175)*

Home Depot, The, Riverside *Also Called: Home Depot USA Inc (P-11176)*

Home Depot, The, Mira Loma *Also Called: Home Depot USA Inc (P-11177)*

Home Depot, The, Moreno Valley *Also Called: Home Depot USA Inc (P-11178)*

Home Depot, The, Murrieta *Also Called: Home Depot USA Inc (P-11179)*

Home Depot, The, Corona *Also Called: Home Depot USA Inc (P-11180)*

Home Depot, The, Lemon Grove *Also Called: Home Depot USA Inc (P-11181)*

Home Depot, The, Victorville *Also Called: Home Depot USA Inc (P-11182)*

Home Depot, The, Chino *Also Called: Home Depot USA Inc (P-11183)*

Home Depot, The, Rancho Cucamonga *Also Called: Home Depot USA Inc (P-11184)*

Home Depot, The, San Diego *Also Called: Home Depot USA Inc (P-11185)*

Home Depot, The, Escondido *Also Called: Home Depot USA Inc (P-11186)*

Home Depot, The, Chula Vista *Also Called: Home Depot USA Inc (P-11187)*

Home Depot, The, El Cajon *Also Called: Home Depot USA Inc (P-11188)*

Home Depot, The, Redlands *Also Called: Home Depot USA Inc (P-11189)*

Home Depot, The, Costa Mesa *Also Called: Home Depot USA Inc (P-11190)*

Home Depot, The, Lake Forest *Also Called: Home Depot USA Inc (P-11191)*

Home Depot, The, Mission Viejo *Also Called: Home Depot USA Inc (P-11192)*

Home Depot, The, Laguna Niguel *Also Called: Home Depot USA Inc (P-11193)*

Home Depot, The, Fullerton *Also Called: Home Depot USA Inc (P-11194)*

Home Depot, The, Anaheim *Also Called: Home Depot USA Inc (P-11195)*

Home Depot, The, La Habra *Also Called: Home Depot USA Inc (P-11196)*

Home Depot, The, Santa Ana *Also Called: Home Depot USA Inc (P-11197)*

Home Depot, The, Orange *Also Called: Home Depot USA Inc (P-11198)*

Home Depot, The, Garden Grove *Also Called: Home Depot USA Inc (P-11199)*

Home Depot, The, Santa Ana *Also Called: Home Depot USA Inc (P-11200)*

Home Entertainment Div, Los Angeles *Also Called: Fox Inc (P-9501)*

Home Express Delivery Svc LLC .... A 949 715-9844
1405 E Franklin Ave Pomona (91766) *(P-9293)*

Home Guiding Hands Corporation (PA)................. B 619 938-2850
1908 Friendship Dr El Cajon (92020) *(P-17163)*

Home Helpers of North County, Escondido *Also Called: Cox Enterprises LLC (P-16383)*

Home Instead Senior Care, Victorville *Also Called: Branlyn Prominence Inc (P-16370)*

Home Instead Senior Care, Rancho Cucamonga *Also Called: Branlyn Prominence Inc (P-16371)*

Home Instead Senior Care, Long Beach *Also Called: Coastal Cmnty Senior Care LLC (P-16379)*

Home Junction Inc .... D 858 777-9533
1 Venture Ste 300 Irvine (92618) *(P-13742)*

Home Organizers Inc .... A 562 699-9945
3860 Capitol Ave City Of Industry (90601) *(P-1052)*

Home Security and HM Ctrl Svcs, Anaheim *Also Called: ADT LLC (P-14376)*

Home-Flex, Valencia *Also Called: Valencia Pipe Company (P-3980)*

Homeboy Bakery, Los Angeles *Also Called: Homeboy Industries (P-16952)*

Homeboy Industries (PA)............................... B 323 526-1254
130 Bruno St Los Angeles (90012) *(P-16952)*

Homebridge Financial Svcs Inc .... A 818 981-0606
15301 Ventura Blvd Ste D300 Sherman Oaks (91403) *(P-11946)*

Homeland Housewares LLC ....D 310 996-7200
10900 Wilshire Blvd Ste 900 Los Angeles (90024) *(P-10220)*

Homeowners Association, Helendale *Also Called: Silver Lakes Association (P-17367)*

Homestead Sheet Metal .... E 619 469-4373
9031 Memory Ln Spring Valley (91977) *(P-4838)*

Homestore Apartments & Rentals, Westlake Village *Also Called: Move Sales Inc (P-12492)*

Homewatch Caregivers, Carlsbad *Also Called: North Coast Home Care Inc (P-16408)*

Employee Codes: A=Over 500 employees, B=251-500
C=101-250, D=51-100, E=20-50, F=10-19, G=1-9

2025 Southern California
Business Directory and Buyers Guide

© Mergent Inc. 1-800-342-5647
1053

A
L
P
H
A
B
E
T
I
C

Homewatch Caregivers, Los Angeles *Also Called: South Bay Senior Services Inc (P-16421)*

Homewood Suites, San Diego *Also Called: SD Hotel Circle LLC (P-13018)*

Homexpress Mortgage Corp .... C 714 944-3022
1936 E Deere Ave Ste 200 Santa Ana (92705) *(P-11913)*

Honda, Torrance *Also Called: Honda R&D Americas LLC (P-17848)*

Honda R&D Americas LLC .... A 310 781-5500
1900 Harpers Way Torrance (90501) *(P-17848)*

Honda World Westminster .... C 714 890-8900
13600 Beach Blvd Westminster (92683) *(P-11361)*

Honest, Los Angeles *Also Called: Honest Company Inc (P-2150)*

Honest Company Inc (PA) .... C 310 917-9199
12130 Millennium Ste 500 Los Angeles (90094) *(P-2150)*

Honest Kitchen Inc .... D 619 544-0018
1785 Hancock St Ste 100 San Diego (92110) *(P-1417)*

Honey, Los Angeles *Also Called: Honey Science LLC (P-13743)*

Honey Bennetts Farm .... E 805 521-1375
3176 Honey Ln Fillmore (93015) *(P-1789)*

Honey Isabells Inc .... E 800 708-8485
539 N Glenoaks Blvd Ste 207b Burbank (91502) *(P-95)*

Honey Punch, Los Angeles *Also Called: Klk Forte Industry Inc (P-2113)*

Honey Science LLC .... C 949 795-1695
963 E 4th St Ste 100 Los Angeles (90013) *(P-13743)*

Honeybee Robotics LLC .... D 510 207-4555
398 W Washington Blvd Ste 200 Pasadena (91103) *(P-5822)*

Honeybee Robotics LLC .... D 303 774-7613
2408 Lincoln Ave Altadena (91001) *(P-5823)*

Honeymoon Real Estate LP .... D 310 277-5221
9400 W Olympic Blvd Beverly Hills (90212) *(P-12853)*

Honeyville Inc .... D 909 980-9500
11600 Dayton Dr Rancho Cucamonga (91730) *(P-9033)*

Honeywell, Torrance *Also Called: Honeywell International Inc (P-7387)*

Honeywell, San Diego *Also Called: Honeywell International Inc (P-7836)*

Honeywell Authorized Dealer, Riverside *Also Called: 20/20 Plumbing & Heating Inc (P-726)*

Honeywell Authorized Dealer, Chatsworth *Also Called: All Tmperatures Controlled Inc (P-732)*

Honeywell Authorized Dealer, San Diego *Also Called: Atlas Mechanical Inc (P-745)*

Honeywell Authorized Dealer, Fullerton *Also Called: C & L Refrigeration Corp (P-757)*

Honeywell Authorized Dealer, North Hollywood *Also Called: Circulating Air Inc (P-762)*

Honeywell Authorized Dealer, Anaheim *Also Called: Control Air Conditioning Corporation (P-765)*

Honeywell Authorized Dealer, San Diego *Also Called: Greater San Diego AC Co Inc (P-784)*

Honeywell Authorized Dealer, Corona *Also Called: LDI Mechanical Inc (P-795)*

Honeywell Authorized Dealer, Corona *Also Called: Multi Mechanical Inc (P-808)*

Honeywell Authorized Dealer, San Diego *Also Called: Pacific Rim Mech Contrs Inc (P-815)*

Honeywell Authorized Dealer, Paramount *Also Called: Reliable Energy Management Inc (P-829)*

Honeywell Authorized Dealer, Santa Fe Springs *Also Called: Western Allied Corporation (P-853)*

Honeywell Authorized Dealer, Santa Clarita *Also Called: Tri-Signal Integration Inc (P-974)*

Honeywell International Inc .... A 310 323-9500
2525 W 190th St Torrance (90504) *(P-7387)*

Honeywell International Inc .... C 619 671-5612
2055 Dublin Dr San Diego (92154) *(P-7836)*

Honeywell Safety Pdts USA Inc .... C 619 661-8383
7828 Waterville Rd San Diego (92154) *(P-7388)*

Honeywell SEC Americas LLC .... D 949 737-7800
2955 Red Hill Ave Ste 100 Costa Mesa (92626) *(P-6685)*

Honk Technologies Inc .... C 800 979-3162
2251 Barry Ave Los Angeles (90064) *(P-14137)*

Honor Life, Vista *Also Called: Rayzist Photomask Inc (P-8566)*

Honor Plastics, Pomona *Also Called: Performnce Engineered Pdts Inc (P-4195)*

Honor Rancho Station, Valencia *Also Called: Southern California Gas Co (P-9652)*

Hood Manufacturing Inc .... D 714 979-7681
2621 S Birch St Santa Ana (92707) *(P-4133)*

Hook It Up .... E 714 600-0100
1513 S Grand Ave Santa Ana (92705) *(P-1867)*

Hoosier Inc .... D 951 272-3070
1152 California Ave Corona (92881) *(P-4134)*

Hoover Containers Inc .... D 909 444-9454
19570 San Jose Ave City Of Industry (91748) *(P-2674)*

Hoover Treated Wood Pdts Inc .... E 661 833-0429
5601 District Blvd Bakersfield (93313) *(P-2406)*

Hoover Treated Wood Pdts Plant, Bakersfield *Also Called: Hoover Treated Wood Pdts Inc (P-2406)*

Hope Hse For Mltple Hndcpped I (PA) .... D 626 443-1313
4215 Peck Rd El Monte (91732) *(P-17164)*

Hopkins Labratory Co, Irwindale *Also Called: Esmond Natural Inc (P-3314)*

Horiba Americas Holding Inc (HQ) .... A 949 250-4811
9755 Research Dr Irvine (92618) *(P-7957)*

Horiba Automotive Test Systems, Irvine *Also Called: Horiba Instruments Inc (P-7958)*

Horiba Instruments Inc (DH) .... C 949 250-4811
9755 Research Dr Irvine (92618) *(P-7958)*

Horiba International Corp .... A 949 250-4811
9755 Research Dr Irvine (92618) *(P-8046)*

Horiba Medical, Irvine *Also Called: Horibaabx Inc (P-10085)*

Horibaabx Inc .... C 949 453-0500
34 Bunsen Irvine (92618) *(P-10085)*

Horizon Communication, Irvine *Also Called: Horizon Communication Tech Inc (P-9565)*

Horizon Communication Tech Inc .... D 714 982-3900
13700 Alton Pkwy Ste 154-278 Irvine (92618) *(P-9565)*

Horizon Hobby LLC .... D 909 390-9595
4710 E Guasti Rd Ste A Ontario (91761) *(P-10521)*

Horizon Media Inc .... B 310 282-0909
1888 Century Park E Ste 700 Los Angeles (90067) *(P-13212)*

HORIZON MEDIA, INC., Los Angeles *Also Called: Horizon Media Inc (P-13212)*

Horizon Solar Power, Hemet *Also Called: Lpsh Holdings Inc (P-798)*

Horizon Well Logging Inc .... E 805 733-0972
711 Saint Andrews Way Lompoc (93436) *(P-336)*

Hornblower Yachts LLC .... C 310 301-9900
13755 Fiji Way Marina Del Rey (90292) *(P-9224)*

Hornet Acquisitionco LLC .... C 714 984-1461
3355 E La Palma Ave Anaheim (92806) *(P-7489)*

Horrigan Cole Enterprises, Murrieta *Also Called: National Mentor Holdings Inc (P-17183)*

Horrigan Enterprises Inc .... C 909 481-9663
7945 Cartilla Ave Rancho Cucamonga (91730) *(P-16953)*

Horsemen Inc .... D 714 847-4243
16911 Algonquin St Huntington Beach (92649) *(P-14309)*

Horton Grand Hotel, San Diego *Also Called: Historical Properties Inc (P-12851)*

Hose Power USA, City Of Industry *Also Called: Bridgestone Hosepower LLC (P-10427)*

Hospital of Barstow Inc (DH) .... D 760 256-1761
820 E Mountain View St Barstow (92311) *(P-16026)*

Hospitler Order of St John Go .... B 323 731-0641
2468 S St Andrews Pl Los Angeles (90018) *(P-17415)*

Host Healthcare Inc .... A 858 999-3579
4225 Executive Sq Ste 1500 La Jolla (92037) *(P-13599)*

Hot Dogger Tours Inc .... C 714 449-6888
105 Gemini Ave Brea (92821) *(P-8864)*

Hot Topic Inc (DH) .... A 800 892-8674
18305 San Jose Ave City Of Industry (91748) *(P-11508)*

Hotel Angeleno, Los Angeles *Also Called: Ascot Hotel LP (P-12762)*

Hotel Associates Palm Springs, La Quinta *Also Called: Msr Desert Resort LP (P-11591)*

Hotel Bel-Air .... B 310 472-1211
701 Stone Canyon Rd Los Angeles (90077) *(P-12854)*

Hotel Bel-Air, Los Angeles *Also Called: Kava Holdings Inc (P-12882)*

Hotel Casa Del Mar, Santa Monica *Also Called: Et Whitehall Seascape LLC (P-12823)*

Hotel Circle Property LLC .... B 619 291-7131
500 Hotel Cir N San Diego (92108) *(P-12855)*

Hotel Company, El Segundo *Also Called: Uhg Lax Prop Llc (P-13057)*

Hotel Del Coronado, Coronado *Also Called: Ksl Resorts Hotel Del Coronado (P-12889)*

Hotel Fullerton Anaheim, The, Fullerton *Also Called: Huoyen International Inc (P-12860)*

Hotel Hanford, The, Costa Mesa *Also Called: Hanford Hotels Inc (P-12841)*

Hotel Indigo Los Angles Dwntwn, Los Angeles *Also Called: Metropolis Hotel MGT LLC (P-12923)*

Hotel June, The, Los Angeles *Also Called: Custom Hotel LLC (P-12805)*

Hotel Managers Group, San Diego *Also Called: Hotel Managers Group Llc (P-17991)*

Hotel Managers Group Llc .... B 858 673-1534
11590 W Bernardo Ct Ste 211 San Diego (92127) *(P-17991)*

Hotel Maya, Long Beach *Also Called: Queensbay Hotel LLC (P-12980)*

Hotel Palomar, Los Angeles *Also Called: Behringer Harvard Wilshire Blv (P-12770)*

Mergent email: customerrelations@mergent.com
1054

2025 Southern California
Business Directory and Buyers Guide

(P-0000) Products & Services Section entry number
(PA)=Parent Co (HQ)=Headquarters (DH)=Div Headquarters

Hotel Shangri-La .... D 310 394-2791
11400 W Olympic Blvd Los Angeles (90064) *(P-12856)*

Hotlix (PA) .... **E 805 473-0596**
966 Griffin St Grover Beach (93433) *(P-1506)*

Hotlix Candy, Grover Beach *Also Called: Hotlix (P-1506)*

Hotta Liesenberg Saito LLP .... D 424 246-2000
970 W 190th St Ste 900 Torrance (90502) *(P-17734)*

Houalla Enterprises Ltd .... D 949 515-4350
2610 Avon St Newport Beach (92663) *(P-548)*

Houghton Mifflin Harcourt Pubg .... E 617 351-5000
525 B St Ste 1900 San Diego (92101) *(P-2890)*

Houlihan Lokey Inc (PA) .... **B 310 788-5200**
10250 Constellation Blvd Fl 5 Los Angeles (90067) *(P-12026)*

House Ear, Los Angeles *Also Called: House Ear Clinic Inc (P-15326)*

House Ear Clinic Inc (PA) .... D 213 483-9930
1245 Wilshire Blvd Ste 812 Los Angeles (90017) *(P-15326)*

House Foods America Corp (HQ) .... **E 714 901-4350**
7351 Orangewood Ave Garden Grove (92841) *(P-1790)*

House of Blues, Los Angeles *Also Called: Hob Entertainment LLC (P-14989)*

House of Blues Anaheim, Anaheim *Also Called: Hob Entertainment LLC (P-14990)*

House of Blues Concerts Inc (DH) .... **C 323 769-4977**
6255 W Sunset Blvd Fl 16 Los Angeles (90028) *(P-14992)*

House of Magnets, El Cajon *Also Called: Graphic Business Solutions Inc (P-10580)*

House Research Institute .... C 213 353-7012
2100 W 3rd St Los Angeles (90057) *(P-17875)*

House Seven Gables RE Inc .... D 714 282-0306
5753 E Santa Ana Canyon Rd Ste P Anaheim (92807) *(P-12465)*

House Seven Gables RE Inc .... D 714 974-7000
5481 E Santa Ana Canyon Rd Anaheim (92807) *(P-12466)*

Housewares International .... E 323 581-3000
1933 S Broadway Ste 867 Los Angeles (90007) *(P-4135)*

Houston Bazz Co .... D 714 898-2666
12700 Western Ave Garden Grove (92841) *(P-5192)*

Houston Fearless 76, Compton *Also Called: Hf Group Inc (P-8430)*

Houwelings Camarillo Inc .... B 805 250-1600
645 Laguna Rd Camarillo (93012) *(P-73)*

Howard Johnson, Anaheim *Also Called: Northwest Hotel Corporation (P-12940)*

Howard Roofing Company Inc .... D 909 622-5598
245 N Mountain View Ave Pomona (91767) *(P-1086)*

Howards Mbs Inc .... D 202 570-4074
23909 Sylvan St Woodland Hills (91367) *(P-12219)*

Howmedica Osteonics Corp .... C 800 621-6104
6885 Flanders Dr Ste G San Diego (92121) *(P-8273)*

Howmet Aerospace Inc .... B 212 836-2674
3016 Lomita Blvd Torrance (90505) *(P-4576)*

Howmet Aerospace Inc .... C 323 728-3901
1550 Gage Rd Montebello (90640) *(P-4590)*

Howmet Aerospace Inc, Montebello *Also Called: Howmet Aerospace Inc (P-4590)*

Howmet Corporation .... A 310 847-8152
900 E Watson Center Rd Carson (90745) *(P-4564)*

Howmet Fastening Systems, Simi Valley *Also Called: Howmet Globl Fstning Systems I (P-10440)*

Howmet Globl Fstning Systems I .... D 714 871-1550
800 S State College Blvd Fullerton (92831) *(P-4565)*

Howmet Globl Fstning Systems I (HQ) .... **C 805 426-2270**
3990a Heritage Oak Ct Simi Valley (93063) *(P-10440)*

Hoya Corporation .... E 858 309-6050
4255 Ruffin Rd San Diego (92123) *(P-8003)*

Hoya Holdings Inc .... C 626 739-5200
425 E Huntington Dr Monrovia (91016) *(P-8004)*

Hoya San Diego, San Diego *Also Called: Hoya Corporation (P-8003)*

HP, San Diego *Also Called: HP Inc (P-5851)*

HP Communications Inc (PA) .... **D 951 572-1200**
13341 Temescal Canyon Rd Corona (92883) *(P-676)*

HP Communications Inc .... D 951 579-8339
15453 Olde Highway 80 El Cajon (92021) *(P-677)*

HP Communications Inc .... D 951 457-0133
1931 Mateo St Los Angeles (90021) *(P-678)*

HP Inc .... B 858 924-5117
16399 W Bernardo Dr Bldg 61 San Diego (92127) *(P-5851)*

HP It Services Incorporated .... E 714 844-7737
1506 W Flower Ave Fullerton (92833) *(P-5921)*

HP Lq Investment LP .... B 760 564-4111
49499 Eisenhower Dr La Quinta (92253) *(P-12857)*

Hpa-USA, Compton *Also Called: Hydroprocessing Associates LLC (P-14512)*

Hpcwire, San Diego *Also Called: Tabor Communications Inc (P-2944)*

Hpi Architecture .... C 858 203-4999
12636 High Bluff Dr Ste 100 San Diego (92130) *(P-17676)*

Hpi Liquidations Inc .... C 858 391-7302
13100 Danielson St Poway (92064) *(P-2675)*

Hpi Racing, Lake Forest *Also Called: SMC Products Inc (P-10529)*

Hpp Food Services, Wilmington *Also Called: Icpk Corporation (P-10754)*

Hps Mechanical Inc (PA) .... C 661 397-2121
3100 E Belle Ter Bakersfield (93307) *(P-787)*

Hqe Systems Inc .... D 800 967-3036
27348 Via Industria Temecula (92590) *(P-18319)*

HR&a Advisors Inc .... D 310 581-0900
700 S Flower St Ste 2995 Los Angeles (90017) *(P-18149)*

Hrd Aero Systems Inc (PA) .... **C 661 295-0670**
25555 Avenue Stanford Valencia (91355) *(P-14772)*

Hre Performance Wheels, Vista *Also Called: Phoenix Wheel Company Inc (P-9838)*

Hrl Laboratories LLC .... A 310 317-5000
3011 Malibu Canyon Rd Malibu (90265) *(P-17849)*

Hrn Services Inc .... D 323 951-1450
520 N Brand Blvd Ste 200 Glendale (91203) *(P-13525)*

Hsa & Associates Inc .... D 626 521-9931
301 N Lake Ave Ste 500 Pasadena (91101) *(P-17550)*

HSA BELL GARDENS LAUP, Bell *Also Called: Human Services Association (P-16954)*

Hsb Holdings Inc .... E 951 214-6590
14050 Day St Moreno Valley (92553) *(P-3865)*

Hsiao & Montano Inc .... E 626 588-2528
809 W Santa Anita Ave San Gabriel (91776) *(P-4295)*

Hsssi, San Dimas *Also Called: Hamilton Sundstrand Spc Systms (P-8045)*

Htl Manufacturing Div, Simi Valley *Also Called: Meggitt Safety Systems Inc (P-7526)*

Htpghnl, Ontario *Also Called: Heat Transfer Pdts Group LLC (P-10334)*

Hub City, Fullerton *Also Called: Hub Group Los Angeles LLC (P-9294)*

Hub Distributing Inc (HQ) .... **B 951 340-3149**
1260 Corona Pointe Ct Corona (92879) *(P-11489)*

Hub Group Los Angeles LLC .... D 714 449-6300
1400 N Harbor Blvd Ste 300 Fullerton (92835) *(P-9294)*

Hub Group Trucking Inc .... B 909 770-8950
13867 Valley Blvd Fontana (92335) *(P-8918)*

Hub Television Networks LLC .... D 818 531-3600
2950 N Hollywood Way Ste 100 Burbank (91505) *(P-9508)*

Hubb Systems LLC .... D 510 865-9100
12305 Crosthwaite Cir Poway (92064) *(P-14085)*

Huck International Inc .... C 310 830-8200
900 E Watson Center Rd Carson (90745) *(P-5129)*

Hudson H Clude Cmplete Hlth Ct, Los Angeles *Also Called: County of Los Angeles (P-15290)*

Hudson Pacific Properties Inc (PA) .... **D 310 445-5700**
11001 Wilshire Blvd Ste 1000 Los Angeles (90025) *(P-12088)*

Hudson Printing, Carlsbad *Also Called: Hudson Printing Inc (P-3144)*

Hudson Printing Inc .... E 760 602-1260
2780 Loker Ave W Carlsbad (92010) *(P-3144)*

Hueston Hennigan LLP .... D 213 788-4340
523 W 6th St Ste 400 Los Angeles (90014) *(P-16704)*

Hughes Bros Aircrafters Inc .... E 323 773-4541
11010 Garfield Pl South Gate (90280) *(P-5584)*

Hughes Circuits Inc .... C 760 744-0300
540 S Pacific St San Marcos (92078) *(P-6736)*

Hughes Circuits Inc (PA) .... **D 760 744-0300**
546 S Pacific St San Marcos (92078) *(P-6737)*

Hughes Research Laboratories, Malibu *Also Called: Hrl Laboratories LLC (P-17849)*

Hugo Venture Solutions Corp .... E 805 684-0935
6325 Carpinteria Ave Carpinteria (93013) *(P-6143)*

Huhtamaki Inc .... C 323 269-0151
4209 Noakes St Commerce (90023) *(P-4006)*

Hulu LLC (HQ) .... **C 310 571-4700**
2500 Broadway Ste 200 Santa Monica (90404) *(P-9442)*

Hulu LLC .... A 888 631-4858
12312 W Olympic Blvd Los Angeles (90064) *(P-9443)*

A
L
P
H
A
B
E
T
I
C

Human Capital Select, LLC, San Diego *Also Called: Lotus Workforce LLC (P-18162)*

Human Dsgns Prsthtic Orthtic L, Long Beach *Also Called: Ferraco Inc (P-8266)*

Human Resources, Anaheim *Also Called: L3harris Interstate Elec Corp (P-7922)*

Human Resources Department, Covina *Also Called: Emanate Health Medical Center (P-15994)*

Human Resources Services, Los Angeles *Also Called: Los Angeles World Airports (P-9203)*

Human Services Association (PA) .... D 562 806-5400
6800 Florence Ave Bell (90201) *(P-16954)*

Humangood (PA) .... C 602 906-4024
1900 Huntington Dr Duarte (91010) *(P-15860)*

Humangood Norcal .... B 661 834-0620
1401 New Stine Rd Bakersfield (93309) *(P-15861)*

Humangood Norcal .... C 909 793-1233
900 Salem Dr Redlands (92373) *(P-15862)*

Humangood Socal .... C 626 357-1632
1763 Royal Oaks Dr Ofc Duarte (91010) *(P-12345)*

Humangood Socal .... C 818 244-7219
1230 E Windsor Rd Ofc Glendale (91205) *(P-12346)*

Humangood Socal .... C 949 854-9500
19191 Harvard Ave Ofc Irvine (92612) *(P-12347)*

Humangood Socal .... C 626 359-8141
802 Buena Vista St Duarte (91010) *(P-17165)*

Humangood Socal .... B 760 747-4306
710 W 13th Ave Escondido (92025) *(P-17166)*

Humangood Socal .... B 858 454-4201
7450 Olivetas Ave Ofc La Jolla (92037) *(P-17167)*

Humnit Hotel At Lax LLC .... D 424 702-1234
6225 W Century Blvd Los Angeles (90045) *(P-12858)*

Hungry Heart Media Inc .... C 323 951-0010
5450 W Washington Blvd Los Angeles (90016) *(P-14833)*

Hunnington Dialysis Center, Pasadena *Also Called: Hemodialysis Inc (P-15321)*

Hunsaker & Assoc Irvine Inc (PA) .... D 949 583-1010
3 Hughes Irvine (92618) *(P-17551)*

Hunsaker & Assoc Irvine Inc .... B 951 352-7200
2900 Adams St Ste A15 Riverside (92504) *(P-17552)*

Hunsaker & Associates, Irvine *Also Called: Hunsaker & Assoc Irvine Inc (P-17551)*

Hunter, San Marcos *Also Called: Hunter Industries Incorporated (P-9791)*

Hunter Dodge Chrysler Jeep Ram, Lancaster *Also Called: H W Hunter Inc (P-11357)*

Hunter Douglas Fabrication Co .... D 858 679-7500
12975 Brookprinter Pl Ste 210 Poway (92064) *(P-14511)*

Hunter Douglas Inc .... B 858 679-7500
9900 Gidley St El Monte (91731) *(P-2602)*

Hunter Easterday Corporation .... C 714 238-3400
1475 N Hundley St Anaheim (92806) *(P-13377)*

Hunter Industries Incorporated (PA) .... C 760 744-5240
1940 Diamond St San Marcos (92078) *(P-9791)*

Hunter Vaughan LLC .... C 626 534-7050
450 N Oak St Inglewood (90302) *(P-3659)*

Huntington Bch Senior Hsing LP .... C 714 842-4006
18765 Florida St Huntington Beach (92648) *(P-12348)*

Huntington Beach Ford, Huntington Beach *Also Called: York Enterprises South Inc (P-11434)*

Huntington Beach Hospital, Huntington Beach *Also Called: Prime Hlthcare Hntngtn Bch LL (P-16142)*

Huntington Beach Union High .... C 714 478-7684
7180 Yorktown Ave Huntington Beach (92648) *(P-13526)*

Huntington Care LLC .... C 877 405-6990
3452 E Foothill Blvd Ste 760 Pasadena (91107) *(P-16395)*

Huntington Extended Care Ctr, Pasadena *Also Called: Pasadena Hospital Assn Ltd (P-15750)*

Huntington Gardens, Huntington Beach *Also Called: Huntington Bch Senior Hsing LP (P-12348)*

Huntington Health Physicians .... D 626 397-8300
100 W California Blvd Pasadena (91105) *(P-16570)*

Huntington Home Care, Pasadena *Also Called: Huntington Care LLC (P-16395)*

Huntington Hotel Company .... D 858 756-1131
5951 Linea Del Cielo Rancho Santa Fe (92067) *(P-12859)*

Huntington Industries Inc .... C 323 772-5575
12520 Chadron Ave Hawthorne (90250) *(P-2449)*

Huntington Ingalls Industries .... E 858 522-6000
9444 Balboa Ave Ste 400 San Diego (92123) *(P-8684)*

Huntington Lib Art Msums Btnca .... B 626 405-2100
1151 Oxford Rd San Marino (91108) *(P-16842)*

Huntington Medical Foundation .... C 626 795-4210
10 Congress St Ste 208 Pasadena (91105) *(P-15327)*

Huntington Medical Foundation .... C 626 792-3141
65 N Madison Ave Ste 800 Pasadena (91101) *(P-16027)*

HUNTINGTON MEMORIAL HOSPITAL, Pasadena *Also Called: Pasadena Hospital Assn Ltd (P-16128)*

Huntington Memory Care Cmnty, Alhambra *Also Called: Silverado Senior Living Inc (P-15776)*

Huntington Park Nursing Center, Huntington Park *Also Called: Covenant Care California LLC (P-15611)*

Huntington Vly Healthcare Ctr, Huntington Beach *Also Called: Douglas Fir Holdings LLC (P-15622)*

HUNTINGTON, THE, San Marino *Also Called: Huntington Lib Art Msums Btnca (P-16842)*

Huntley Hotel Santa Monica Bch, Santa Monica *Also Called: Second Street Corporation (P-13020)*

Huntsman, Los Angeles *Also Called: Huntsman Advanced Materials AM (P-3270)*

Huntsman Advanced Materials AM .... C 818 265-7221
5121 W San Fernando Rd Los Angeles (90039) *(P-3270)*

Huoyen International Inc .... D 714 635-9000
1500 S Raymond Ave Fullerton (92831) *(P-12860)*

Hurley, Costa Mesa *Also Called: Hurley International LLC (P-2013)*

Hurley International LLC (PA) .... C 855 655-2515
3080 Bristol St Costa Mesa (92626) *(P-2013)*

Husks Unlimited (PA) .... E 619 476-8301
9925 Airway Rd # C San Diego (92154) *(P-1791)*

Husky Injction Mlding Systems .... D 714 545-8200
3505 Cadillac Ave Ste N4 Costa Mesa (92626) *(P-4136)*

Husky Injction Mlding Systems .... D 805 523-9593
5245 Maureen Ln Moorpark (93021) *(P-4137)*

Hussmann Corporation .... B 909 590-4910
13770 Ramona Ave Chino (91710) *(P-5977)*

Hustler Casino, Gardena *Also Called: El Dorado Enterprises Inc (P-12819)*

Hutchinson Arospc & Indust Inc .... C 818 843-1000
4510 W Vanowen St Burbank (91505) *(P-3915)*

Hutchinson Arospc & Indust Inc .... C 818 843-1000
4510 W Vanowen St Burbank (91505) *(P-7490)*

Hutchinson Seal Corporation (DH) .... C 248 375-4190
11634 Patton Rd Downey (90241) *(P-3890)*

Huxtable's, Vernon *Also Called: Huxtables Kitchen Inc (P-11575)*

Huxtables Kitchen Inc .... D 323 923-2900
2100 E 49th St Vernon (90058) *(P-11575)*

HV Randall Foods LLC (PA) .... C 323 261-6565
2900 Ayers Ave Vernon (90058) *(P-10872)*

Hvac Installation and Repair, Los Angeles *Also Called: Precise Air Systems Inc (P-822)*

Hvantage Technologies Inc (PA) .... D 818 661-6301
22048 Sherman Way Ste 306 Canoga Park (91303) *(P-13744)*

Hwave .... D 714 843-0463
5702 Bolsa Ave Huntington Beach (92649) *(P-16571)*

Hwe Mechanical, Bakersfield *Also Called: Hills Wldg & Engrg Contr Inc (P-334)*

Hy-Tech Tile Inc .... C 951 788-0550
1130 Palmyrita Ave Ste 350 Riverside (92507) *(P-1069)*

Hyatt Corp As Agt Brcp Hef Ht .... D 760 603-6851
7100 Aviara Resort Dr Carlsbad (92011) *(P-12861)*

Hyatt Corporation .... D 858 453-0018
3777 La Jolla Village Dr San Diego (92122) *(P-12862)*

Hyatt Corporation .... C 619 232-1234
1 Market Pl San Diego (92101) *(P-12863)*

Hyatt Corporation .... D 619 849-1234
600 F St San Diego (92101) *(P-12864)*

Hyatt Corporation .... B 760 341-1000
44600 Indian Wells Ln Indian Wells (92210) *(P-12865)*

Hyatt Corporation .... D 949 975-1234
17900 Jamboree Rd Irvine (92614) *(P-12866)*

Hyatt Corporation .... B 949 729-1234
1107 Jamboree Rd Newport Beach (92660) *(P-12867)*

Hyatt Corporation .... B 562 432-0161
200 S Pine Ave Long Beach (90802) *(P-12868)*

Hyatt Corporation .... C 323 656-1234
8401 W Sunset Blvd Los Angeles (90069) *(P-12869)*

Hyatt Corporation .... B 312 750-1234
6225 W Century Blvd Los Angeles (90045) *(P-12870)*

Mergent email: customerrelations@mergent.com
1056

2025 Southern California
Business Directory and Buyers Guide

(P-0000) Products & Services Section entry number
(PA)=Parent Co (HQ)=Headquarters (DH)=Div Headquarters

Hyatt Die Cast and Engineering Corporation - South (PA)..................D 714 826-7550
4656 Lincoln Ave Cypress (90630) *(P-4646)*

Hyatt Die Cast Engrg Corp - S .... E 714 622-2131
12250 Industry St Garden Grove (92841) *(P-4647)*

Hyatt Equities LLC .... D 562 436-1047
285 Bay St Long Beach (90802) *(P-12871)*

Hyatt Grand Champion Resort, Indian Wells *Also Called: Hyatt Corporation (P-12865)*

Hyatt Hotel, Carlsbad *Also Called: Hyatt Corp As Agt Brcp Hef Ht (P-12861)*

Hyatt Hotel, Irvine *Also Called: Hyatt Corporation (P-12866)*

Hyatt Hotel, Newport Beach *Also Called: Hyatt Corporation (P-12867)*

Hyatt Hotel, Long Beach *Also Called: Hyatt Corporation (P-12868)*

Hyatt Hotel, Los Angeles *Also Called: Hyatt Corporation (P-12869)*

Hyatt Hotel, Long Beach *Also Called: Hyatt Equities LLC (P-12871)*

Hyatt Hotel, Palm Springs *Also Called: Hyatt Hotels Management Corp (P-12872)*

Hyatt Hotels Management Corp .... C 760 322-9000
285 N Palm Canyon Dr Palm Springs (92262) *(P-12872)*

Hyatt Los Angeles Airport, Los Angeles *Also Called: Hyatt Corporation (P-12870)*

Hyatt Regency Century Plaza .... A 310 228-1234
2025 Avenue Of The Stars Los Angeles (90067) *(P-12873)*

Hyatt Regency Lajolla, San Diego *Also Called: Hyatt Corporation (P-12862)*

Hyatt Rgency Suites Palm Sprng, Palm Springs *Also Called: Rbd Hotel Palm Springs LLC*
(P-12986)

Hyatt Westlake, Westlake Village *Also Called: Swvp Westlake LLC (P-13046)*

Hybrid Promotions, Cypress *Also Called: Hybrid Promotions LLC (P-10686)*

Hybrid Promotions LLC (PA)... C 714 952-3866
10700 Valley View St Cypress (90630) *(P-10686)*

Hycor, Garden Grove *Also Called: Hycor Biomedical LLC (P-8162)*

Hycor Biomedical LLC .... C 714 933-3000
7272 Chapman Ave Ste A Garden Grove (92841) *(P-8162)*

Hyde Pk Rehabilitation Ctr LLC .... D 323 753-1354
6520 West Blvd Los Angeles (90043) *(P-15679)*

Hydra-Electric Company (PA).. C 818 843-6211
3151 N Kenwood St Burbank (91505) *(P-6307)*

Hydrafacial Company, The, Long Beach *Also Called: Hydrafacial LLC (P-8163)*

Hydrafacial LLC (HQ)... C 800 603-4996
3600 E Burnett St Long Beach (90815) *(P-8163)*

Hydrafacial LLC .... E 562 391-2052
3600 E Burnett St Long Beach (90815) *(P-8164)*

Hydraflow .... B 714 773-2600
1881 W Malvern Ave Fullerton (92833) *(P-7491)*

Hydraflow, Fullerton *Also Called: Hydraflow (P-7491)*

Hydralic Systems Cmponents Inc .... E 760 744-9350
725 N Twin Oaks Valley Rd San Marcos (92069) *(P-14773)*

Hydranautics (DH) .... B 760 901-2500
401 Jones Rd Oceanside (92058) *(P-3803)*

Hydraulics International Inc (PA)... B 818 998-1231
20961 Knapp St Chatsworth (91311) *(P-7492)*

Hydro Extrusion Usa LLC .... B 626 964-3411
18111 Railroad St City Of Industry (91748) *(P-4598)*

Hydro Quip, Corona *Also Called: Blue Desert International Inc (P-6004)*

Hydro Systems Inc (PA)... D 661 775-0686
29132 Avenue Paine Valencia (91355) *(P-4798)*

Hydro-Aire Inc (HQ)... D 818 526-2600
3000 Winona Ave Burbank (91504) *(P-7493)*

Hydro-Aire Aerospace Corp .... C 818 526-2600
3000 Winona Ave Burbank (91504) *(P-7494)*

Hydro-Dig Inc .... D 714 772-9947
700 E Sycamore St Anaheim (92805) *(P-174)*

Hydro-Pressure Systems, North Hollywood *Also Called: Woods Maintenance Services Inc*
(P-1236)

Hydrochempsc, Bakersfield *Also Called: PSC Industrial Outsourcing LP (P-361)*

Hydroform USA Incorporated .... C 310 632-6353
2848 E 208th St Carson (90810) *(P-7495)*

Hydromach Inc .... E 818 341-0915
20400 Prairie St Chatsworth (91311) *(P-7670)*

Hydroprocessing Associates LLC .... D 310 667-6456
19122 S Santa Fe Ave Compton (90221) *(P-14512)*

Hydrotech Construction Group, Newport Beach *Also Called: Citivest Inc (P-12406)*

Hygeia II Medical Group Inc .... E 714 515-7571
6241 Yarrow Dr Ste A Carlsbad (92011) *(P-8384)*

Hygenia, Camarillo *Also Called: Medical Packaging Corporation (P-8284)*

Hyland's Homeopathic, Los Angeles *Also Called: Hylands Consumer Health Inc (P-3421)*

Hylands Consumer Health Inc (PA)... B 310 768-0700
13301 S Main St Los Angeles (90061) *(P-3421)*

Hyper Ice Inc (PA)... E 949 565-4994
525 Technology Dr Ste 100 Irvine (92618) *(P-8523)*

Hyperbaric Technologies Inc .... D 619 336-2022
3224 Hoover Ave National City (91950) *(P-8385)*

Hyperfly Inc .... E 760 300-0909
8390 Miramar Pl Ste D San Diego (92121) *(P-8524)*

Hyperice, Irvine *Also Called: Hyper Ice Inc (P-8523)*

Hyperion Healing LLC .... D 818 626-9078
20660 Bahama St Chatsworth (91311) *(P-15542)*

Hyperion Motors LLC .... E 714 363-5858
1032 W Taft Ave Orange (92865) *(P-6051)*

Hyponex Corporation .... C 909 597-2811
12273 Brown Ave Jurupa Valley (92509) *(P-3745)*

Hyspan, Chula Vista *Also Called: Hyspan Precision Products Inc (P-5809)*

Hyspan Precision Products Inc (PA)... D 619 421-1355
1685 Brandywine Ave Chula Vista (91911) *(P-5809)*

Hytron Mfg Co Inc .... E 714 903-6701
15582 Chemical Ln Huntington Beach (92649) *(P-6144)*

Hyundai ABS Funding LLC .... C 949 732-2697
3161 Michelson Dr Irvine (92612) *(P-11968)*

Hyundai Amer Technical Ctr Inc .... C 734 337-2500
101 Peters Canyon Rd Irvine (92606) *(P-17553)*

Hyundai Amer Technical Ctr Inc .... C 909 627-3525
12610 Eastend Ave Chino (91710) *(P-17918)*

Hyundai America/Tech Center, Chino *Also Called: Hyundai Amer Technical Ctr Inc (P-17918)*

Hyundai Autoever America LLC .... A 714 965-3000
10550 Talbert Ave 3rd Fl Fountain Valley (92708) *(P-14187)*

Hyundai Motor America (HQ)... B 714 965-3000
10550 Talbert Ave Fountain Valley (92708) *(P-9802)*

Hyundai Protection Plan Inc .... B 949 468-4000
3161 Michelson Dr Ste 1900 Irvine (92612) *(P-11854)*

Hyundai Translead (HQ)... D 619 574-1500
8880 Rio San Diego Dr Ste 600 San Diego (92108) *(P-4915)*

I A C, Irvine *Also Called: Irvine APT Communities LP (P-12350)*

I and E Cabinets Inc .... E 818 933-6480
14660 Raymer St Van Nuys (91405) *(P-2350)*

I Brands LLC .... C 424 336-5216
2617 N Sepulveda Blvd Manhattan Beach (90266) *(P-10363)*

I C C, Anaheim *Also Called: Interntnal Cnnctors Cable Corp (P-6587)*

I C Class Components Corp (PA) .... D 310 539-5500
23605 Telo Ave Torrance (90505) *(P-10251)*

I C S, Ventura *Also Called: Instrument Control Services (P-337)*

I C W, San Diego *Also Called: Insurance Company of West (P-12222)*

I Copy Inc .... E 562 921-0202
11266 Monarch St Ste B Garden Grove (92841) *(P-6145)*

I D Brand LLC .... E 949 422-7057
3185 Airway Ave Ste A Costa Mesa (92626) *(P-2262)*

I D Property Corporation .... C 213 625-0100
1001 Wilshire Blvd Ste 100 Los Angeles (90017) *(P-12467)*

I I D, Imperial *Also Called: Imperial Irrigation District (P-9500)*

I J S, San Dimas *Also Called: Industrial Janitor Service (P-13378)*

I M S Electonics Recycling, Poway *Also Called: IMS Electronics Recycling Inc (P-9746)*

I N C Builders Inc .... B 760 352-4200
1560 Ocotillo Dr Ste L El Centro (92243) *(P-13600)*

I P S, Mentone *Also Called: International Paving Svcs Inc (P-626)*

I Pwlc Inc .... D 760 630-0231
408 Olive Ave Vista (92083) *(P-175)*

I S E, Poway *Also Called: ISE Corporation (P-17800)*

I T P, Brea *Also Called: Industrial Threaded Pdts Inc (P-10309)*

I V C, Newport Beach *Also Called: International Vitamin Corporat (P-3427)*

I-Coat Company LLC .... E 562 941-9989
12020 Mora Dr Ste 2 Santa Fe Springs (90670) *(P-8005)*

I-Flow LLC .... A 800 448-3569
43 Discovery Ste 100 Irvine (92618) *(P-8165)*

I.V. League Medical, Camarillo *Also Called: Western Mfg & Distrg LLC (P-7639)*

Employee Codes: A=Over 500 employees, B=251-500
C=101-250, D=51-100, E=20-50, F=10-19, G=1-9

2025 Southern California
Business Directory and Buyers Guide

© Mergent Inc. 1-800-342-5647
1057

I/O Magic Corporation .... E 949 707-4800
4 Marconi Irvine (92618) *(P-5852)*

I/Omagic Corporation (PA) .... E 949 707-4800
20512 Crescent Bay Dr Lake Forest (92630) *(P-5880)*

I3dnet LLC .... A 800 482-6910
7 N Fair Oaks Ave Pasadena (91103) *(P-14086)*

Iaba, Culver City *Also Called: Institute For Applied Bhvior A (P-15545)*

Iaba, Camarillo *Also Called: Institute For Applied Bhvior A (P-15546)*

Iaccess Technologies Inc (PA) .... E 714 922-9158
1251 E Dyer Rd Ste 160 Santa Ana (92705) *(P-18320)*

IaMplus LLC .... D 323 210-3852
809 N Cahuenga Blvd Los Angeles (90038) *(P-6375)*

IaMplus Electronics Inc (PA) .... E 323 210-3852
809 N Cahuenga Blvd Los Angeles (90038) *(P-13945)*

Iap West Inc .... D 310 667-9720
20036 S Via Baron Rancho Dominguez (90220) *(P-9830)*

Ibackup.com, Calabasas *Also Called: Idrive Inc (P-14223)*

Ibaset Inc (PA) .... E 949 598-5200
26812 Vista Ter Lake Forest (92630) *(P-18321)*

Ibaset Federal Services LLC (PA) .... D 949 598-5200
27442 Portola Pkwy Ste 300 Foothill Ranch (92610) *(P-13745)*

Ibe Digital, Garden Grove *Also Called: I Copy Inc (P-6145)*

Ibftech Inc .... D 424 217-8010
343 Main St El Segundo (90245) *(P-13527)*

IBM, Glendale *Also Called: International Bus Mchs Corp (P-5855)*

Ibuypower, City Of Industry *Also Called: American Future Tech Corp (P-9986)*

Icann, Los Angeles *Also Called: Internet Corp For Assgned Nmes (P-14089)*

ICC, Riverside *Also Called: Inland Cc Inc (P-1121)*

Ice Currency Services USA, Los Angeles *Also Called: Lenlyn Ltd Which Will Do Bus I (P-11841)*

Ice Management Systems Inc .... E 951 676-2751
27449 Colt Ct Temecula (92590) *(P-7496)*

Icf Jones & Stokes Inc .... D 858 578-8964
525 B St Ste 1700 San Diego (92101) *(P-18322)*

Icl Systems Inc .... D 877 425-8725
19782 Macarthur Blvd Ste 260 Irvine (92612) *(P-14087)*

Icon Media Direct Inc (PA) .... D 818 995-6400
5910 Lemona Ave Van Nuys (91411) *(P-13213)*

Iconn Inc .... D 800 286-6742
8909 Irvine Center Dr Irvine (92618) *(P-6308)*

Iconn Engineering LLC .... E 714 696-8826
6882 Preakness Dr Huntington Beach (92648) *(P-5394)*

Iconn Technologies, Irvine *Also Called: Iconn Inc (P-6308)*

ICP West, Buena Park *Also Called: Interntional Color Posters Inc (P-3147)*

Icpk Corporation .... D 310 830-8020
1130 W C St Wilmington (90744) *(P-10754)*

Icu Medical Inc (PA) .... A 949 366-2183
951 Calle Amanecer San Clemente (92673) *(P-8166)*

Icw Group Holdings Inc (PA) .... D 858 350-2400
15025 Innovation Dr San Diego (92128) *(P-12121)*

ID Analytics LLC .... C 858 312-6200
10089 Willow Creek Rd Ste 120 San Diego (92131) *(P-13746)*

ID Matters LLC .... E 323 822-4800
7060 Hollywood Blvd 8th Fl Los Angeles (90028) *(P-2860)*

ID Supply .... E 949 287-9200
3183 Red Hill Ave Costa Mesa (92626) *(P-3145)*

ID&c, Brea *Also Called: Avery Products Corporation (P-2757)*

Ida Classic Inc (PA) .... C 818 773-9042
9530 De Soto Ave Chatsworth (91311) *(P-3660)*

Idea Tooling and Engrg Inc .... D 310 608-7488
13915 S Main St Los Angeles (90061) *(P-5585)*

Ideal Day Program H73485, Los Angeles *Also Called: Ideal Program Services Inc (P-13528)*

Ideal Mattress Company Inc .... E 619 595-0003
1901 Main St San Diego (92113) *(P-2486)*

Ideal Products Inc .... E 951 727-8600
4025 Garner Rd Riverside (92501) *(P-2565)*

Ideal Program Services Inc .... D 323 296-2255
3970 W Martin Luther King Jr Blvd Los Angeles (90008) *(P-13528)*

Idealab (HQ) .... D 626 356-3654
130 W Union St Pasadena (91103) *(P-11362)*

Idealab Holdings LLC (PA) .... A 626 585-6900
130 W Union St Pasadena (91103) *(P-12710)*

Idemia America Corp .... C 310 884-7900
3150 E Ana St Compton (90221) *(P-4138)*

Identigraphix Inc .... E 909 468-4741
19866 Quiroz Ct Walnut (91789) *(P-13330)*

Identity Intlligence Group LLC .... C 626 522-7993
43454 Business Park Dr Temecula (92590) *(P-14407)*

Ideon, Buena Park *Also Called: Exemplis LLC (P-2528)*

Idex Health & Science LLC .... D 760 438-2131
2051 Palomar Airport Rd Ste 200 Carlsbad (92011) *(P-8006)*

Idiq, Temecula *Also Called: Identity Intlligence Group LLC (P-14407)*

Idirect Home Loans, San Diego *Also Called: Iserve Residential Lending LLC (P-11915)*

Idrive Inc .... D 818 594-5972
26115 Mureau Rd Ste A Calabasas (91302) *(P-14223)*

IDS Inc .... D 866 297-5757
20300 Ventura Blvd Ste 200 Woodland Hills (91364) *(P-9225)*

IDS Technology, Woodland Hills *Also Called: IDS Inc (P-9225)*

Idx Los Angeles LLC .... C 909 212-8333
5005 E Philadelphia St Ontario (91761) *(P-2582)*

Ie Construction, Ontario *Also Called: Integrated Energy Group LLC (P-790)*

IEC, Commerce *Also Called: Interstate Electric Co Inc (P-10045)*

Iecp, Oxnard *Also Called: Inclusive Edcatn Cmnty Prtnr I (P-16812)*

Iee, Sylmar *Also Called: Industrial Elctrnic Engners In (P-5923)*

Ieee Computer Society, Los Alamitos *Also Called: Institute of Elec Elec Engners (P-17283)*

Iehp, Rancho Cucamonga *Also Called: Inland Empire Health Plan (P-12062)*

Ies, San Diego *Also Called: Ies Commercial Inc (P-625)*

Ies Commercial Inc .... C 858 210-4900
6885 Flanders Dr Ste A San Diego (92121) *(P-625)*

Ies Engineering, Bakersfield *Also Called: Innovative Engrg Systems Inc (P-17557)*

Ifco Systems Us LLC .... D 909 484-4332
8950 Rochester Ave Ste 150 Rancho Cucamonga (91730) *(P-2389)*

Ifiber Optix Inc .... E 714 665-9796
14450 Chambers Rd Tustin (92780) *(P-4327)*

Ifit Inc .... A 909 335-2888
2220 Almond Ave Redlands (92374) *(P-8525)*

Igenomix Usa Inc .... E 818 919-1657
383 Van Ness Ave Ste 1605 Torrance (90501) *(P-8167)*

Ignite Health LLC (PA) .... D 949 861-3200
7535 Irvine Center Dr Ste 200 Irvine (92618) *(P-13214)*

Ignited LLC (PA) .... C 310 773-3100
111 Penn St El Segundo (90245) *(P-13215)*

Ignition Creative LLC .... C 310 315-6300
1201 W 5th St Ste T1100 Los Angeles (90017) *(P-14834)*

Ihealth Manufacturing Inc .... D 216 785-0107
15715 Arrow Hwy Irwindale (91706) *(P-10086)*

Iherb LLC (PA) .... A 951 616-3600
17400 Laguna Canyon Rd Ste 400 Irvine (92618) *(P-11305)*

Iherb House Brands, Irvine *Also Called: Iherb LLC (P-11305)*

Ihg Management (maryland) LLC .... D 213 688-7777
900 Wilshire Blvd Los Angeles (90017) *(P-12874)*

Ii-VI Aerospace & Defense Inc, Murrieta *Also Called: Coherent Aerospace & Defense Inc (P-7708)*

IJ Research Inc .... E 714 546-8522
2919 S Tech Center Dr Santa Ana (92705) *(P-7006)*

Ikano Communications Inc (PA) .... D 801 924-0900
9221 Corbin Ave Ste 260 Northridge (91324) *(P-14138)*

IKEA Purchasing Svcs US Inc .... C 818 841-3500
600 N San Fernando Blvd Burbank (91502) *(P-17992)*

Ikhana Aircraft Services, Murrieta *Also Called: Ikhana Group LLC (P-7497)*

Ikhana Group LLC .... C 951 600-0009
37260 Sky Canyon Dr Hngr 20 Murrieta (92563) *(P-7497)*

Ikonick LLC .... E 516 680-7765
705 W 9th St Apt 1404 Los Angeles (90015) *(P-3013)*

IL Fornaio (america) LLC .... C 714 752-7052
16932 Valley View Ave Ste A La Mirada (90638) *(P-11576)*

Ilco Industries, Compton *Also Called: Ilco Industries Inc (P-5435)*

Ilco Industries Inc .... E 310 631-8655
1308 W Mahalo Pl Compton (90220) *(P-5435)*

Ilingo2com Inc .... D 800 311-8331
800 Los Vallecitos Blvd Ste N San Marcos (92069) *(P-15328)*

Illah Sports Inc .... E 805 240-7790
1610 Fiske Pl Oxnard (93033) *(P-8526)*

Illume Agriculture LLC .... C 661 587-5198
9100 Ming Ave Ste 200 Bakersfield (93311) *(P-142)*

Illumina, San Diego *Also Called: Illumina Inc (P-7960)*

Illumina Inc .... E 800 809-4566
9885 Towne Centre Dr San Diego (92121) *(P-7959)*

Illumina Inc (PA) .... B 858 202-4500
5200 Illumina Way San Diego (92122) *(P-7960)*

Illumnate Educatn Holdings Inc (PA) .... E 949 656-3133
6531 Irvine Center Dr Ste 100 Irvine (92618) *(P-13946)*

Ilts California, Vista *Also Called: International Lottery & Totalizator Systems Inc (P-13753)*

Ilts Delaware, Vista *Also Called: Interntnal Lttery Ttlztor Syst (P-13754)*

Im-Logstics An Ingram McRo Div, Irvine *Also Called: Ingram Micro Inc (P-10011)*

Image Apparel For Business Inc .... E 714 541-5247
1618 E Edinger Ave Santa Ana (92705) *(P-1995)*

Image Business Forms, El Segundo *Also Called: Ibftech Inc (P-13527)*

Image IV Systems Inc (PA) .... D 818 841-0756
512 S Varney St Burbank (91502) *(P-9973)*

Image Options .... D 949 586-7665
80 Icon Foothill Ranch (92610) *(P-13275)*

Image Options Painting & Dctg, Foothill Ranch *Also Called: Image Options (P-13275)*

Image Solutions, Torrance *Also Called: Image Solutions Apparel Inc (P-1996)*

Image Solutions Apparel Inc .... C 310 464-8991
19571 Magellan Dr Torrance (90502) *(P-1996)*

Image Source Inc (PA) .... C 310 477-0700
2110 Pontius Ave Los Angeles (90025) *(P-10581)*

Image Transfer, Valencia *Also Called: D C Shower Doors Inc (P-8942)*

Image X, Goleta *Also Called: Image-X Enterprises Inc (P-13747)*

Image-X Enterprises Inc .... E 805 964-3535
6464 Hollister Ave Ste 7g Goleta (93117) *(P-13747)*

Imageworks, Culver City *Also Called: Sony Pictures Imageworks Inc (P-14156)*

Imagic .... D 818 333-1670
2810 N Lima St Burbank (91504) *(P-3014)*

Imaginative Horizons Inc .... D 619 477-1176
1889 National City Blvd National City (91950) *(P-15680)*

Imagine This, Irvine *Also Called: Shye West Inc (P-8631)*

Imaging Hlthcare Spcalists LLC .... C 619 229-2299
6386 Alvarado Ct San Diego (92120) *(P-15329)*

IMC, Canoga Park *Also Called: Azimc Investments Inc (P-9814)*

IMC, Los Angeles *Also Called: International Medical Corps (P-16961)*

IMC Logistics LLC .... C 844 903-4737
550 W. Artesia Blvd Compton (90220) *(P-8956)*

IMC Networks Corp (PA) .... E 949 465-3000
25531 Commercentre Dr Ste 200 Lake Forest (92630) *(P-5895)*

Imcsd, San Diego *Also Called: Integrated Microwave Corp (P-7009)*

Imeg Consultants Corp .... D 714 490-5555
222 S Harbor Blvd Ste 800 Anaheim (92805) *(P-17554)*

Imerys Minerals California Inc (HQ) .... D ..... 805 736-¡221
2500 San Miguelito Rd Lompoc (93436) *(P-386)*

Imhoff & Associates PC .... D 310 691-2200
12424 Wilshire Blvd Ste 770 Los Angeles (90025) *(P-16705)*

IMI CCI, Rcho Sta Marg *Also Called: IMI Critical Engineering LLC (P-5366)*

IMI Critical Engineering LLC (DH) .... B 949 858-1877
22591 Avenida Empresa Rcho Sta Marg (92688) *(P-5366)*

IMMDEF, Los Angeles *Also Called: Immigrant Defenders Law Center (P-16706)*

Immigrant Defenders Law Center .... D 213 634-0999
634 S Spring St Fl 10 Los Angeles (90014) *(P-16706)*

Immortals LLC .... D 310 554-8267
6100 Center Dr Ste 1050 Los Angeles (90045) *(P-15027)*

Immunalysis, Pomona *Also Called: Alere San Diego Inc (P-3532)*

Immunalysis Corporation .... D 909 482-0840
829 Towne Center Dr Pomona (91767) *(P-16319)*

Immunitybio, San Diego *Also Called: Immunitybio Inc (P-3580)*

Immunitybio Inc (PA) .... D 844 696-5235
3530 John Hopkins Ct San Diego (92121) *(P-3580)*

Imobile, San Dimas *Also Called: Imobile LLC (P-9403)*

Imobile LLC .... C 909 599-8322
875 W Arrow Hwy San Dimas (91773) *(P-9403)*

Impac International, Ontario *Also Called: LLC Walker West (P-2585)*

Impac Mortgage, Irvine *Also Called: Impac Mortgage Corp (P-11914)*

Impac Mortgage Corp .... B 949 475-3600
19500 Jamboree Rd Ste 100 Irvine (92612) *(P-11914)*

Impac Secured Assets Corp .... D 949 475-3600
19500 Jamboree Rd Irvine (92612) *(P-12659)*

Impact Bearing, San Clemente *Also Called: Clean Wave Management Inc (P-5748)*

Impact Components, San Diego *Also Called: Impact Components A California Limited Partnership (P-10252)*

Impact Components A California Limited Partnership .... E 858 634-4800
6010 Cornerstone Ct W Ste 200 San Diego (92121) *(P-10252)*

Impact LLC .... E 714 546-6000
7121 Magnolia Ave Riverside (92504) *(P-7007)*

Impact Printing & Graphics .... E 909 614-1678
15150 Sierra Bonita Ln Chino (91710) *(P-3015)*

Impact Tech Inc (HQ) .... B 805 324-6021
223 E De La Guerra St Santa Barbara (93101) *(P-18150)*

Impco, Santa Ana *Also Called: Impco Technologies Inc (P-7262)*

Impco Technologies Inc (HQ) .... C 714 656-1200
3030 S Susan St Santa Ana (92704) *(P-7262)*

Imperfect Foods Inc (HQ) .... D 510 595-6683
351 Cheryl Ln Walnut (91789) *(P-1792)*

Imperfect Produce, Walnut *Also Called: Imperfect Foods Inc (P-1792)*

Imperial Bag & Paper Co LLC .... D 800 834-6248
550 S 7th Ave City Of Industry (91746) *(P-10594)*

Imperial Cal Products Inc .... E 714 990-9100
425 Apollo St Brea (92821) *(P-5193)*

Imperial Capital Bancorp Inc (PA) .... C 858 551-0511
10618 Edenoaks St San Diego (92131) *(P-11770)*

Imperial Capital Group LLC (PA) .... D 310 246-3700
2000 Avenue Of The Stars Ste 900s Los Angeles (90067) *(P-12711)*

Imperial Capital LLC (PA) .... D 310 246-3700
10100 Santa Monica Blvd Ste 2400 Los Angeles (90067) *(P-11969)*

Imperial Care Center, Studio City *Also Called: Longwood Management Corp (P-15867)*

Imperial Coml Cooking Eqp, Corona *Also Called: Spenuzza Inc (P-6034)*

Imperial Convalescent, La Mirada *Also Called: Life Care Centers America Inc (P-15693)*

Imperial County Mental Health, El Centro *Also Called: County of Imperial (P-16459)*

Imperial Crest Healthcare Ctr, Hawthorne *Also Called: Longwood Management Corp (P-15706)*

Imperial Irrigation District (PA) .... A 800 303-7756
333 E Barioni Blvd Imperial (92251) *(P-9588)*

Imperial Irrigation District .... C 760 398-5811
81600 58th Ave La Quinta (92253) *(P-9678)*

Imperial Marking Systems, Cerritos *Also Called: Blc Wc Inc (P-3121)*

Imperial Rubber Products Inc .... E 909 393-0528
5691 Gates St Chino (91710) *(P-5662)*

Imperial Toy LLC (PA) .... C 818 536-6500
16641 Roscoe Pl North Hills (91343) *(P-8486)*

Imperial Valley Foods Inc .... B 760 203-1896
1961 Buchanan Ave Calexico (92231) *(P-1376)*

Imperial Valley Press, El Centro *Also Called: Associated Desert Newspaper (P-2781)*

Imperial Western Products Inc A California Corporation (HQ) .... E 760 398-0815
86600 Avenue 54 Coachella (92236) *(P-10993)*

Imperials Sand Dunes, Brea *Also Called: Worldwide Envmtl Pdts Inc (P-7885)*

Implant Direct, Thousand Oaks *Also Called: Implant Direct Sybron Mfg LLC (P-8338)*

Implant Direct Sybron Intl LLC (HQ) .... D 818 444-3000
3050 E Hillcrest Dr Ste 100 Westlake Village (91362) *(P-8337)*

Implant Direct Sybron Mfg LLC .... C 818 444-3300
3050 E Hillcrest Dr Thousand Oaks (91362) *(P-8338)*

Implantech Associates Inc .... E 805 289-1665
6025 Nicolle St Ste B Ventura (93003) *(P-8274)*

Impo International LLC .... E 805 922-7753
3510 Black Rd Santa Maria (93455) *(P-4285)*

Import, Vernon *Also Called: Brentwood Appliances Inc (P-6399)*

Import Direct, Van Nuys *Also Called: E & S International Entps Inc (P-10216)*

Impresa Aerospace LLC .... C 310 354-1200
344 W 157th St Gardena (90248) *(P-7498)*

Impress Communications LLC .... D 818 701-8800
9320 Lurline Ave Chatsworth (91311) *(P-3016)*

Impressions Vanity Company (PA) .... E 844 881-0790
17353 Derian Ave Irvine (92614) *(P-11532)*

A
L
P
H
A
B
E
T
I
C

Employee Codes: A=Over 500 employees, B=251-500
C=101-250, D=51-100, E=20-50, F=10-19, G=1-9

2025 Southern California
Business Directory and Buyers Guide

© Mergent Inc. 1-800-342-5647

1059

Imprimisrx, Carlsbad *Also Called: Imprimisrx LLC (P-3422)*

Imprimisrx LLC .... C 844 446-6979
1000 Aviara Dr Ste 220 Carlsbad (92011) *(P-3422)*

Impulse Amusement, Sun Valley *Also Called: Impulse Industries Inc (P-5962)*

Impulse Industries Inc .... E 818 767-4258
9281 Borden Ave Sun Valley (91352) *(P-5962)*

Impulse Space Inc .... E 949 315-5540
2651 Manhattan Beach Blvd Redondo Beach (90278) *(P-7644)*

Imri, Aliso Viejo *Also Called: Information MGT Resources Inc (P-14088)*

IMS, South El Monte *Also Called: Interntnal Mdction Systems Ltd (P-3428)*

IMS, Chula Vista *Also Called: Integrated Marine Services Inc (P-7602)*

IMS Electronics Recycling Inc .... C 858 679-1555
12455 Kerran St Ste 300 Poway (92064) *(P-9746)*

IMS Recycling Services, San Diego *Also Called: IMS Recycling Services Inc (P-9747)*

IMS Recycling Services Inc (PA) .... D 619 231-2521
2697 Main St San Diego (92113) *(P-9747)*

IMS-Ess, Temecula *Also Called: Ice Management Systems Inc (P-7496)*

IMT Analytical, Goleta *Also Called: Atomica Corp (P-6803)*

In Montrose Wtr Sstnblity Svcs .... D 949 988-3500
4 Park Plz Ste 790 Irvine (92614) *(P-18323)*

In Stepps Inc .... D 949 474-1493
10 Skypark Circle, Suite 110 Irvine (92614) *(P-15543)*

In-Line Construction, Ramona *Also Called: In-Line Fence & Railing Co Inc (P-1210)*

In-Line Fence & Railing Co Inc .... E 760 789-0282
1307 Walnut St Ramona (92065) *(P-1210)*

In-Roads Creative Programs .... B 909 989-9944
9057 Arrow Rte Ste 120 Rancho Cucamonga (91730) *(P-16955)*

In-Roads Creative Programs .... B 909 947-9142
1951 E Saint Andrews Dr Ontario (91761) *(P-16956)*

Inari Medical, Irvine *Also Called: Inari Medical Inc (P-8168)*

Inari Medical Inc (PA) .... A 877 923-4747
6001 Oak Cyn Ste 100 Irvine (92618) *(P-8168)*

Inbody, Cerritos *Also Called: Biospace Inc (P-17779)*

Inc Polycarbon, Valencia *Also Called: Sgl Technic LLC (P-4489)*

Inca One Corporation .... E 310 808-0001
1632 1/2 W 134th St Gardena (90249) *(P-6918)*

Incipio Group, Irvine *Also Called: Incipio Technologies Inc (P-5922)*

Incipio Technologies Inc (PA) .... E 888 893-1638
190 Newport Ctr Dr Ste 150 Irvine (92612) *(P-5922)*

Incircle LLC .... A 800 843-7477
44000 Winchester Rd Temecula (92590) *(P-14513)*

Inclinator of California, San Fernando *Also Called: TL Shield & Associates Inc (P-5515)*

Inclusion Services, Whittier *Also Called: Inclusion Services LLC (P-16957)*

Inclusion Services LLC .... C 562 945-2000
7255 Greenleaf Ave Ste 20 Whittier (90602) *(P-16957)*

Inclusive Edcatn Cmnty Prtnr I .... B 805 985-4808
2323 Roosevelt Blvd Apt 3 Oxnard (93035) *(P-16812)*

Incomnet Communications Corp .... D 949 251-8000
2801 Main St Irvine (92614) *(P-9444)*

Incora, Valencia *Also Called: Wesco Aircraft Hardware Corp (P-10506)*

Incotec, Mojave *Also Called: Innovative Coatings Technology Corporation (P-5324)*

Indel Engineering Inc .... E 562 594-0995
6400 E Marina Dr Long Beach (90803) *(P-7622)*

Indemnity Company California (DH) .... D 949 263-3300
17771 Cowan Ste 100 Irvine (92614) *(P-12220)*

Independence Park, Downey *Also Called: City of Downey (P-15128)*

Independent, Santa Barbara *Also Called: Santa Barbara Independent Inc (P-2826)*

Independent Energy Solutions Inc .... E 760 752-9706
663 S Rancho Santa Fe Rd Ste 682 San Marcos (92078) *(P-4811)*

Independent Fincl Group LLC .... C 858 436-3180
12671 High Bluff Dr Ste 200 San Diego (92130) *(P-18151)*

Independent Forge Company .... E 714 997-7337
692 N Batavia St Orange (92868) *(P-5142)*

Independent Options Inc .... C 858 598-5260
5095 Murphy Canyon Rd San Diego (92123) *(P-17168)*

Independent Options Inc .... D 714 738-4991
2625 Sherwood Ave Fullerton (92831) *(P-17169)*

Indepndnt Asstd Lvng & Memory, Arcadia *Also Called: Arcadia Gardens MGT Corp (P-15806)*

Index Fresh Inc (PA) .... D 909 877-0999
1250 Corona Pointe Ct Ste 401 Corona (92879) *(P-10908)*

India Tea Importers, Commerce *Also Called: Interntional Tea Importers Inc (P-1793)*

Indian Health Council Inc (PA) .... D 760 749-1410
50100 Golsh Rd Valley Center (92082) *(P-15330)*

Indian Industries Inc .... E 800 467-1421
7756 Saint Andrews Ave Ste 115 San Diego (92154) *(P-8527)*

Indian Summer, Rancho Cucamonga *Also Called: Mizkan America Inc (P-1817)*

Indian Wells Golf Resort, Indian Wells *Also Called: Troon Golf LLC (P-18071)*

INDIE, Aliso Viejo *Also Called: Indie Semiconductor Inc (P-6828)*

Indie Semiconductor Inc (PA) .... E 949 608-0854
32 Journey Ste 100 Aliso Viejo (92656) *(P-6828)*

Indio Products Inc .... E 323 720-9117
5331 E Slauson Ave Commerce (90040) *(P-3804)*

Indio Products Inc (PA) .... C 323 720-1188
12910 Mulberry Dr Unit A Whittier (90602) *(P-10118)*

Indorama Vntres Sstnble Sltion .... E 951 727-8318
11591 Etiwanda Ave Fontana (92337) *(P-3271)*

Indu-Electric North Amer Inc (PA) .... E 310 578-2144
27756 Avenue Hopkins Valencia (91355) *(P-5810)*

Induction Technology Corp .... E 760 246-7333
22060 Bear Valley Rd Apple Valley (92308) *(P-5800)*

Indus Technology Inc .... C 619 299-2555
2243 San Diego Ave Ste 200 San Diego (92110) *(P-17555)*

Induspac California Inc .... E 909 390-4422
1550 Champagne Ave Ontario (91761) *(P-3272)*

Industrial Coml Systems Inc .... C 760 300-4094
1165 Joshua Way Vista (92081) *(P-788)*

Industrial Components Div, Simi Valley *Also Called: Rexnord Industries LLC (P-5684)*

Industrial Dynamics Co Ltd (PA) .... C 310 325-5633
3100 Fujita St Torrance (90505) *(P-5705)*

Industrial Elctrnic Engners In .... D 818 787-0311
13170 Telfair Ave Sylmar (91342) *(P-5923)*

Industrial Fire Sprnklr Co Inc .... E 619 266-6030
3845 Imperial Ave San Diego (92113) *(P-5824)*

Industrial Gasket and Sup Co .... E 310 530-1771
2702 Dashwood St Lakewood (90712) *(P-3891)*

Industrial Janitor Service .... D 818 782-5658
221 N San Dimas Ave Ste 217 San Dimas (91773) *(P-13378)*

Industrial Media Inc (PA) .... C 310 777-1940
6007 Sepulveda Blvd Van Nuys (91411) *(P-14895)*

Industrial Medical Support Inc .... A 877 878-9185
3320 E Airport Way Long Beach (90806) *(P-16572)*

Industrial Metal Supply Co, Irvine *Also Called: Norman Industrial Mtls Inc (P-10147)*

Industrial Metal Supply Co, Sun Valley *Also Called: Norman Industrial Mtls Inc (P-10148)*

Industrial Minerals Company, Bakersfield *Also Called: Geo Drilling Fluids Inc (P-11013)*

Industrial Parts Depot LLC (HQ) .... D 310 530-1900
1550 Charles Willard St Carson (90746) *(P-10377)*

Industrial Stitchtech Inc .... C 818 361-6319
520 Library St San Fernando (91340) *(P-14514)*

Industrial Strength Corp .... E 760 795-1068
6115 Corte Del Cedro Carlsbad (92011) *(P-10548)*

Industrial Tctnics Brings Corp (DH) .... C 310 537-3750
18301 S Santa Fe Ave E Rncho Dmngz (90221) *(P-5749)*

Industrial Threaded Pdts Inc (PA) .... E 562 802-4626
515 N Puente St Brea (92821) *(P-10309)*

Industrial Tools Inc .... E 805 483-1111
1800 Avenue Of The Stars Los Angeles (90067) *(P-5706)*

Industrial Tube Company, Valencia *Also Called: Industrial Tube Company LLC (P-5375)*

Industrial Tube Company LLC .... D 661 295-4000
28150 Industry Dr Valencia (91355) *(P-5375)*

Industrial Valco Inc (PA) .... E 310 635-0711
3135 E Ana St Compton (90221) *(P-10441)*

Industry Entrmt Partners .... D 323 954-9000
955 Carrillo Dr Ste 300 Los Angeles (90048) *(P-14962)*

Industry Station, City Of Industry *Also Called: Southern California Gas Co (P-9661)*

Indyme Solutions LLC .... E 858 268-0717
8295 Aero Pl Ste 260 San Diego (92123) *(P-6686)*

Indyne Inc .... B 805 606-7225
1036 California Blvd Bldg 11013 Vandenberg Afb (93437) *(P-18262)*

Ineos, Carson *Also Called: Ineos Polypropylene LLC (P-3274)*

Ineos Composites Us LLC .... D 323 767-1300
6608 E 26th St Los Angeles (90040) *(P-3273)*

Mergent email: customerrelations@mergent.com
1060

2025 Southern California
Business Directory and Buyers Guide

(P-0000) Products & Services Section entry number
(PA)=Parent Co (HQ)=Headquarters (DH)=Div Headquarters

Ineos Polypropylene LLC .... E 310 847-8523
2384 E 223rd St Carson (90810) *(P-3274)*

Inertech, Monterey Park *Also Called: Inertech Supply Inc (P-3892)*

Inertech Supply Inc .... D 626 282-2000
641 Monterey Pass Rd Monterey Park (91754) *(P-3892)*

Inet, Cypress *Also Called: Inet Airport Systems Inc (P-7499)*

Inet Airport Systems Inc .... E 714 888-2700
5665 Corporate Ave Cypress (90630) *(P-7499)*

Infab LLC .... D 805 987-5255
1040 Avenida Acaso Camarillo (93012) *(P-8275)*

Infineon Tech Americas Corp .... A 951 375-6008
41915 Business Park Dr Temecula (92590) *(P-5924)*

Infineon Tech Americas Corp (HQ) .... A 310 726-8200
101 N Pacific Coast Hwy El Segundo (90245) *(P-6829)*

Infineon Tech Americas Corp .... E 310 726-8000
233 Kansas St El Segundo (90245) *(P-6830)*

Infineon Tech Americas Corp .... C 310 252-7116
1521 E Grand Ave El Segundo (90245) *(P-6831)*

Infineon Tech Americas Corp .... A 310 726-8000
222 Kansas St El Segundo (90245) *(P-17735)*

Infinite Electronics Inc (HQ) .... E 949 261-1920
17792 Fitch Irvine (92614) *(P-7008)*

Infinite Electronics Intl Inc (DH) .... D 949 261-1920
17792 Fitch Irvine (92614) *(P-6950)*

Infinite Electronics Intl Inc .... E 949 261-1920
17802 Fitch Irvine (92614) *(P-6951)*

Infinite Optics Inc .... E 714 557-2299
1712 Newport Cir Ste F Santa Ana (92705) *(P-8007)*

Infinity Aerospace Inc (PA) .... E 818 998-9811
9060 Winnetka Ave Northridge (91324) *(P-7500)*

Infinity Drywall Contg Inc .... C 714 634-2255
237 Glider Cir Corona (92878) *(P-1011)*

Infinity Plumbing Designs Inc .... B 951 737-4436
9182 Stellar Ct Corona (92883) *(P-789)*

Infinity Watch Corporation .... E 626 289-9878
21078 Commerce Point Dr Walnut (91789) *(P-8608)*

Inflight Entrmt & Connectivity, Irvine *Also Called: Thales Avionics Inc (P-7576)*

Infocast, Woodland Hills *Also Called: Information Forecast Inc (P-18152)*

Infocrossing LLC .... D 714 986-8722
6320 Canoga Ave Ste 600 Woodland Hills (91367) *(P-14139)*

Infogen Labs Inc .... D 323 816-4813
25350 Magic Mountain Pkwy Ste 300 Valencia (91355) *(P-14224)*

Infomagnus LLC .... D 714 810-3430
5882 Bolsa Ave Ste 210 Huntington Beach (92649) *(P-13748)*

Infonet Services Corporation (DH) .... A 310 335-2600
2160 E Grand Ave El Segundo (90245) *(P-9445)*

Infor (us) LLC .... E 678 319-8000
26250 Enterprise Way Ste 220 Lake Forest (92630) *(P-13947)*

Informa Business Media Inc .... E 949 252-1146
16815 Von Karman Ave # 150 Irvine (92606) *(P-2922)*

Informa Research Services Inc (HQ) .... C 818 880-8877
26565 Agoura Rd Ste 300 Calabasas (91302) *(P-17850)*

Information Forecast Inc .... E 818 888-4445
22144 Clarendon St Ste 280 Woodland Hills (91367) *(P-18152)*

Information MGT Resources Inc (PA) .... C 949 215-8889
85 Argonaut Ste 215 Aliso Viejo (92656) *(P-14088)*

Information Systems, Orange *Also Called: St Joseph Hospital of Orange (P-16218)*

Informtion Rfrral Fdrtion of L .... D 626 350-1841
526 W Las Tunas Dr San Gabriel (91776) *(P-13176)*

Infosend Inc (PA) .... E 714 993-2690
4240 E La Palma Ave Anaheim (92807) *(P-13340)*

Infospan .... A 714 856-2655
18301 Von Karman Ave Ste 1000 Irvine (92612) *(P-18153)*

Infusion Care, Long Beach *Also Called: Long Beach Medical Center (P-16084)*

Ingardia Bros Produce Inc .... C 949 645-1365
700 S Hathaway St Santa Ana (92705) *(P-10909)*

Ingenium Technologies Corp .... D 858 227-4422
5665 Oberlin Dr Ste 202 San Diego (92121) *(P-17556)*

Ingenue Inc .... D 323 726-8084
1111 W Olympic Blvd Montebello (90640) *(P-1279)*

Ingla Rubber Products, Bellflower *Also Called: Bryant Rubber Corp (P-3880)*

Inglewood Health Care Center, Inglewood *Also Called: Mariner Health Care Inc (P-15712)*

Inglewood Park Cemetery (PA) .... C 310 412-6500
720 E Florence Ave Inglewood (90301) *(P-12584)*

Ingram Micro Inc (HQ) .... A 714 566-1000
3351 Michelson Dr Ste 100 Irvine (92612) *(P-10011)*

Inhibrx, La Jolla *Also Called: Inhibrx Inc (P-3581)*

Inhibrx Inc (HQ) .... C 858 795-4220
11025 N Torrey Pines Rd Ste 200 La Jolla (92037) *(P-3581)*

Inhibrx Biosciences Inc .... C 858 795-4220
11025 N Torrey Pines Rd Ste 140 La Jolla (92037) *(P-3582)*

Inhouseit Inc .... D 949 660-5655
400 Exchange Ste 100 Irvine (92602) *(P-14188)*

Initiative Media North America, Los Angeles *Also Called: Mediabrands Worldwide Inc (P-13225)*

Injen Technology Company Ltd .... E 909 839-0706
244 Pioneer Pl Pomona (91768) *(P-10336)*

Ink & Color Inc .... E 310 280-6060
5920 Bowcroft St Los Angeles (90016) *(P-3017)*

Ink Fx Corporation .... E 909 673-1950
513 S La Serena Dr Covina (91723) *(P-3146)*

Ink Spot Inc .... E 626 338-4500
9737 Bell Ranch Dr Santa Fe Springs (90670) *(P-3018)*

Ink Systems Inc (PA) .... D 323 720-4000
2311 S Eastern Ave Commerce (90040) *(P-3785)*

Inkwright LLC .... E 714 892-3300
5822 Research Dr Huntington Beach (92649) *(P-3019)*

Inland Cc Inc .... C 909 355-1318
7010 Wyndham Hill Dr Riverside (92506) *(P-1121)*

Inland Chrstn HM Fundation Inc .... C 909 395-9322
1950 S Mountain Ave Ofc Ontario (91762) *(P-15681)*

Inland Cnties Regional Ctr Inc (PA) .... C 909 890-3000
1365 S Waterman Ave San Bernardino (92408) *(P-16958)*

Inland Cnties Regional Ctr Inc .... C 951 826-2600
1500 Iowa Ave Ste 100 Riverside (92507) *(P-17993)*

Inland Cold Storage .... E 951 369-0230
2356 Fleetwood Dr Riverside (92509) *(P-1707)*

Inland Empire 66ers Bsbal CLB .... C 909 888-9922
280 Se St San Bernardino (92401) *(P-15028)*

Inland Empire Chptr-Ssction Cr .... D 512 478-9000
2210 E Route 66 Glendora (91740) *(P-17464)*

Inland Empire Foods Inc (PA) .... E 951 682-8222
5425 Wilson St Riverside (92509) *(P-1365)*

Inland Empire Health Plan (PA) .... A 909 890-2000
10801 6th St Ste 120 Rancho Cucamonga (91730) *(P-12062)*

Inland Empire Health Plan .... A 866 228-4347
805 W 2nd St Ste C San Bernardino (92410) *(P-12083)*

Inland Empire Heart Institute, San Bernardino *Also Called: St Bernardine Med Ctr Aux Inc (P-16213)*

Inland Empire Magazine, Temecula *Also Called: Inland Empire Media Group Inc (P-2861)*

Inland Empire Media Group Inc .... E 951 682-3026
36095 Monte De Oro Rd Temecula (92592) *(P-2861)*

Inland Empire Utlties Agcy A M (PA) .... D 909 993-1600
6075 Kimball Ave Chino (91708) *(P-9694)*

Inland Envelope Company .... D 909 622-2016
150 N Park Ave Pomona (91768) *(P-2750)*

Inland Eye Inst Med Group Inc (PA) .... D 909 825-3425
1900 E Washington St Colton (92324) *(P-15331)*

Inland Group, Anaheim *Also Called: Inland Litho LLC (P-3020)*

Inland Kenworth Inc (HQ) .... C 909 823-9955
9730 Cherry Ave Fontana (92335) *(P-9803)*

Inland Litho LLC .... D 714 993-6000
4305 E La Palma Ave Anaheim (92807) *(P-3020)*

Inland Powder Coating Corp .... C 909 947-1122
1656 S Bon View Ave Ste F Ontario (91761) *(P-5323)*

Inland Regional Center, San Bernardino *Also Called: Inland Cnties Regional Ctr Inc (P-16958)*

Inland Regional Center, Riverside *Also Called: Inland Cnties Regional Ctr Inc (P-17993)*

Inland Truss Inc (PA) .... D 951 300-1758
275 W Rider St Perris (92571) *(P-2379)*

Inland Valley Care & Rehab Ctr, Pomona *Also Called: Inland Valley Partners LLC (P-15544)*

Inland Valley Daily Bulletin, Monrovia *Also Called: Califrnia Nwspapers Ltd Partnr (P-2786)*

Inland Valley Daily Bulletin, Ontario *Also Called: Califrnia Nwspapers Ltd Partnr (P-2787)*

Employee Codes: A=Over 500 employees, B=251-500
C=101-250, D=51-100, E=20-50, F=10-19, G=1-9

2025 Southern California
Business Directory and Buyers Guide

© Mergent Inc. 1-800-342-5647

1061

A
L
P
H
A
B
E
T
I
C

Inland Valley Partners LLC .... C 909 623-7100
250 W Artesia St Pomona (91768) *(P-15544)*

Inland Vly DRG Alchol Rcvery S (PA)............... D **909 932-1069**
1260 E Arrow Hwy Upland (91786) *(P-16480)*

Inland Vly Rgional Med Ctr Inc .... B 951 677-1111
36485 Inland Valley Dr Wildomar (92595) *(P-16028)*

Inline Plastics Inc .... E 909 923-1033
1950 S Baker Ave Ontario (91761) *(P-4139)*

Inlog Inc .... D 949 212-3867
6765 Westminster Blvd Ste 424 Westminster (92683) *(P-9295)*

Inmode .... D 949 387-5711
17 Hughes Irvine (92618) *(P-15332)*

Inmode Aesthetic Solutions, Irvine *Also Called: Invasix Inc (P-17798)*

Inmotion Entrmt Group LLC .... C 904 332-0459
3225 N Harbor Dr San Diego (92101) *(P-14993)*

Inn At Mssion San Juan Cpstran, San Juan Capistrano *Also Called: Marriott International Inc (P-12917)*

Inn of Chicago Associates Ltd .... C 312 787-3100
1 Del Mar Newport Coast (92657) *(P-12875)*

Innercool Therapies, San Diego *Also Called: Philips North America LLC (P-10222)*

Inners Tasks LLC .... E 951 225-9696
27708 Jefferson Ave Ste 201 Temecula (92590) *(P-5853)*

Innocoll Biotherapeutics NA .... D 484 406-5200
5163 Lakeview Canyon Rd Westlake Village (91362) *(P-3423)*

Innocor West LLC .... A 909 307-3737
300 S Tippecanoe Ave 310 San Bernardino (92408) *(P-3916)*

Innophase, San Diego *Also Called: Innophase Inc (P-6832)*

Innophase Inc .... D 619 541-8280
5880 Oberlin Dr Ste 600 San Diego (92121) *(P-6832)*

Innov8v, Irvine *Also Called: Innovative Tech & Engrg Inc (P-5925)*

Innova Electronics Corporation .... E 714 241-6800
17352 Von Karman Ave Irvine (92614) *(P-7263)*

Innovasystems Intl LLC .... C 619 955-5890
850 Beech St Unit 1006 San Diego (92101) *(P-13749)*

Innovation Specialties .... C 888 827-2387
11869 Teale St Ste 302 Culver City (90230) *(P-14515)*

Innovations Building Svcs LLC .... D 323 787-6068
402 S Orange Ave Apt D Monterey Park (91755) *(P-13379)*

Innovative Casework Mfg Inc .... E 714 890-9100
12261 Industry St Garden Grove (92841) *(P-8685)*

Innovative Cleaning Svcs Inc .... B 949 251-9188
44 Waterworks Way Irvine (92618) *(P-13380)*

Innovative Cnstr Solutions .... C 714 893-6366
575 Anton Blvd Ste 850 Costa Mesa (92626) *(P-18263)*

Innovative Coatings Technology Corporation .... C 661 824-8101
1347 Poole St 106 Mojave (93501) *(P-5324)*

Innovative Communities Inc (PA) .... D **760 690-5225**
1282 Pacific Oaks Pl Escondido (92029) *(P-408)*

Innovative Data Solutions, El Segundo *Also Called: Powerdms Inc (P-14008)*

Innovative Dialysis Partners Inc .... B 562 495-8075
1 World Trade Ctr Ste 2500 Long Beach (90831) *(P-11686)*

Innovative Engrg Systems Inc (PA) .... D
8800 Crippen St Bakersfield (93311) *(P-17557)*

Innovative Integration Inc .... E 805 520-3300
741 Flynn Rd Camarillo (93012) *(P-7863)*

Innovative Metal Inds Inc .... D 909 796-6200
1330 Riverview Dr San Bernardino (92408) *(P-5096)*

Innovative Placements Inc .... C 800 322-9796
12400 High Bluff Dr Ste 100 San Diego (92130) *(P-13529)*

Innovative Skin Care, Burbank *Also Called: Science of Skincare LLC (P-10650)*

Innovative Stamping Inc .... E 310 537-6996
2068 E Gladwick St Compton (90220) *(P-5194)*

Innovative Systems, Compton *Also Called: Innovative Stamping Inc (P-5194)*

Innovative Tech & Engrg Inc .... E 949 955-2501
2691 Richter Ave Ste 124 Irvine (92606) *(P-5925)*

Innovel Solutions Inc .... A 619 497-1123
960 Sherman St San Diego (92110) *(P-9296)*

Innovive LLC (PA) .... E **858 309-6620**
10019 Waples Ct San Diego (92121) *(P-5406)*

Innovtive Artsts Tlent Ltrary (PA) .... D **310 656-0400**
1505 10th St Santa Monica (90401) *(P-14963)*

Inogen, Goleta *Also Called: Inogen Inc (P-8169)*

Inogen Inc (PA) .... C **805 562-0500**
859 Ward Dr Ste 200 Goleta (93111) *(P-8169)*

Inova Diagnostics Inc .... C 858 586-9900
9889 Willow Creek Rd San Diego (92131) *(P-3424)*

Inova Diagnostics Inc .... C 858 586-9900
9675 Businesspark Ave San Diego (92131) *(P-3542)*

Inova Diagnostics Inc (HQ) .... B 858 586-9900
9900 Old Grove Rd San Diego (92131) *(P-17796)*

Inova Labs Inc .... D 866 647-0691
9001 Spectrum Center Blvd Ste 200 San Diego (92123) *(P-8170)*

Inovativ Inc .... E 626 969-5300
1500 W Mckinley St Azusa (91702) *(P-4577)*

Input 1 LLC .... C 888 882-2554
1 Baxter Way Ste 270 Westlake Village (91362) *(P-11868)*

Insco Dico Group , The, Irvine *Also Called: Developers Surety Indemnity Co (P-12146)*

Insco Insurance Services Inc (DH) .... D **949 263-3415**
17771 Cowan Ste 100 Irvine (92614) *(P-12221)*

Inseego, San Diego *Also Called: Inseego Corp (P-13750)*

Inseego Corp (PA) .... D **858 812-3400**
9710 Scranton Rd Ste 200 San Diego (92121) *(P-13750)*

Insignia/Esg Ht Partners Inc (DH) .... B **310 765-2600**
11150 Santa Monica Blvd Ste 220 Los Angeles (90025) *(P-12297)*

Insite Digestive Health Care .... E 626 817-2900
21250 Hawthorne Blvd Torrance (90503) *(P-15333)*

Insomniac Games Inc (PA) .... D **818 729-2400**
2255 N Ontario St Ste 550 Burbank (91504) *(P-8487)*

Insparation Inc .... E 805 553-0820
11950 Hertz Ave Moorpark (93021) *(P-3661)*

Inspectorate America Corp .... C 800 424-0099
3401 Jack Northrop Ave Hawthorne (90250) *(P-14516)*

INSPECTORATE AMERICA CORPORATION, Hawthorne *Also Called: Inspectorate America Corp (P-14516)*

Inspira, Vernon *Also Called: Offline Inc (P-1999)*

Inspire Energy, Santa Monica *Also Called: Inspire Energy Holdings LLC (P-9589)*

Inspire Energy Holdings LLC .... C 866 403-2620
3402 Pico Blvd Ste 300 Santa Monica (90405) *(P-9589)*

Inspired Flight, San Luis Obispo *Also Called: Inspired Flight Tech Inc (P-4773)*

Inspired Flight Tech Inc .... E 805 776-3640
225 Suburban Rd Ste A San Luis Obispo (93401) *(P-4773)*

Insta Graphic Systems, Cerritos *Also Called: Insta-Lettering Machine Co (P-1919)*

Insta-Lettering Machine Co (PA) .... D **562 404-3000**
13925 166th St Cerritos (90703) *(P-1919)*

Instacure Healing Products .... E 818 222-9600
235 N Moorpark Rd Unit 2022 Thousand Oaks (91360) *(P-3425)*

Instant Tuck Inc .... E 310 955-8824
9663 Santa Monica Blvd Beverly Hills (90210) *(P-2210)*

Instant Web LLC .... C 562 658-2020
7300 Flores St Downey (90242) *(P-3021)*

Instantly Inc .... C 866 872-4006
16501 Ventura Blvd Ste 300 Encino (91436) *(P-17851)*

Institute For Applied Bhvior A (PA) .... C **310 649-0499**
5601 W Slauson Ave Culver City (90230) *(P-15545)*

Institute For Applied Bhvior A .... D 805 987-5886
2310 E Ponderosa Dr Ste 1 Camarillo (93010) *(P-15546)*

Institute For Applied Bhvior A .... D 818 341-1933
9221 Corbin Ave Northridge (91324) *(P-15547)*

Institute For Bhvoral Hlth Inc .... B 909 289-1041
1905 Business Center Dr Ste 100 San Bernardino (92408) *(P-16481)*

Institute For Defense Analyses .... C 858 622-5439
4320 Westerra Ct San Diego (92121) *(P-17876)*

Institute of Elec Elec Engners .... D 714 821-8380
10662 Los Vaqueros Cir Los Alamitos (90720) *(P-17283)*

Instride, El Segundo *Also Called: Attainment Holdco LLC (P-17293)*

Instrument Bearing Factory USA .... E 818 989-5052
19360 Rinaldi St Northridge (91326) *(P-5130)*

Instrument Control Services .... E 805 642-1999
6085 King Dr Unit 100 Ventura (93003) *(P-337)*

Instrumentl Inc .... E 909 258-9291
440 N Barranca Ave Covina (91723) *(P-13948)*

Instruments Incorporated .... E 858 571-1111
7263 Engineer Rd Ste G San Diego (92111) *(P-7126)*

Mergent email: customerrelations@mergent.com
1062

2025 Southern California
Business Directory and Buyers Guide

(P-0000) Products & Services Section entry number
(PA)=Parent Co (HQ)=Headquarters (DH)=Div Headquarters

Insua Graphics Incorporated .... E 818 767-7007
9121 Glenoaks Blvd Sun Valley (91352) *(P-3022)*

Insul-Therm, Commerce *Also Called: Insul-Therm International Inc (P-9958)*

Insul-Therm International Inc (PA) .... E 323 728-0558
6651 E 26th St Commerce (90040) *(P-9958)*

Insulectro (PA) .... D 949 587-3200
20362 Windrow Dr Lake Forest (92630) *(P-10253)*

Insultech, Santa Ana *Also Called: Insultech LLC (P-3805)*

Insultech LLC (PA) .... E 714 384-0506
3530 W Garry Ave Santa Ana (92704) *(P-3805)*

Insurance Company of West (HQ) .... D 858 350-2400
15025 Innovation Dr San Diego (92128) *(P-12222)*

Insure Express Insurance Svc, Encino *Also Called: Cartel Marketing Inc (P-12191)*

Integer Holdings Corporation .... E 619 498-9448
8830 Siempre Viva Rd Ste 100 San Diego (92101) *(P-8171)*

Integra Lfscnces Holdings Corp .... E 609 529-9748
5955 Pacific Center Blvd San Diego (92121) *(P-8172)*

Integra Lifesciences, Carlsbad *Also Called: Seaspine Inc (P-8300)*

Integra Technologies Inc .... E 310 606-0855
321 Coral Cir El Segundo (90245) *(P-6833)*

Integral Aerospace LLC .... C 949 250-3123
2040 E Dyer Rd Santa Ana (92705) *(P-7501)*

Integral Senior Living, Carlsbad *Also Called: Isl Employees Inc (P-17170)*

Integral Senior Living LLC (PA) .... C 760 547-2863
2333 State St Ste 300 Carlsbad (92008) *(P-12349)*

Integrated Communications Inc .... E 310 851-8066
208 N Broadway Santa Ana (92701) *(P-3023)*

Integrated Energy Group LLC .... E 605 381-7859
3929 E Guasti Rd Ste F Ontario (91761) *(P-790)*

Integrated Energy Technologies Inc .... C 619 421-1151
1478 Santa Sierra Dr Chula Vista (91913) *(P-5750)*

Integrated Food Service, Gardena *Also Called: Lets Do Lunch (P-1807)*

INTEGRATED HEALTHCARE DELIVERY, Whittier *Also Called: Pih Health Inc (P-16130)*

INTEGRATED HEALTHCARE DELIVERY, Downey *Also Called: Pih Health Downey Hospital (P-16131)*

Integrated Intermodal Svcs Inc .... D 909 355-4100
8600 Banana Ave Fontana (92335) *(P-14225)*

Integrated Magnetics, Culver City *Also Called: Magnet Sales & Mfg Co Inc (P-4364)*

Integrated Magnetics Inc .... E 310 391-7213
11250 Playa Ct Culver City (90230) *(P-6325)*

Integrated Marine Services Inc .... D 619 429-0300
2320 Main St Chula Vista (91911) *(P-7602)*

Integrated Mfg Solutions LLC .... E 760 599-4300
2590 Pioneer Ave Ste C Vista (92081) *(P-8686)*

Integrated Microwave Corp .... D 858 259-2600
11353 Sorrento Valley Rd San Diego (92121) *(P-7009)*

Integrated Parcel Network .... B 714 278-6100
11135 Rush St Ste A South El Monte (91733) *(P-9004)*

Integrated Procurement Tech (PA) .... D 805 682-0842
7230 Hollister Ave Goleta (93117) *(P-10492)*

Integrated Sign Associates, El Cajon *Also Called: Integrted Sign Assoc A Cal Cor (P-8609)*

Integrated Technical Services, Anaheim *Also Called: L3harris Interstate Elec Corp (P-7923)*

Integrity Hlthcare Sltions Inc .... D 760 432-9811
5625 Ruffin Rd San Diego (92123) *(P-16396)*

Integrity Rebar Placers .... C 951 696-6843
1345 Nandina Ave Perris (92571) *(P-1154)*

Integrted Crygnic Slutions LLC .... E 951 234-0899
2835 Progress Pl Escondido (92029) *(P-5707)*

Integrted Sign Assoc A Cal Cor .... E 619 579-2229
1160 Pioneer Way Ste M El Cajon (92020) *(P-8609)*

Integrus LLC .... D 949 538-9211
14370 Myford Rd Ste 100 Irvine (92606) *(P-9974)*

Intelex Systems Inc .... D 818 992-2969
21900 Burbank Blvd Ste 3087 Woodland Hills (91367) *(P-13751)*

Intelity Inc .... C 310 596-8160
16501 Ventura Blvd Encino (91436) *(P-18154)*

Intell Set, Long Beach *Also Called: Intelsat US LLC (P-9566)*

Intellective, Irvine *Also Called: Vegatek Corporation (P-13858)*

Intellectyx, Pasadena *Also Called: Intellectyx Inc (P-13752)*

Intellectyx Inc .... D 720 256-7540
680 E Colorado Blvd Ste 180 Pasadena (91101) *(P-13752)*

Intellgard Inventory Solutions, San Diego *Also Called: Intelliguard Group LLC (P-8047)*

Intelligent Beauty LLC .... A 310 683-0940
2301 Rosecrans Ave Ste 4110 El Segundo (90245) *(P-11687)*

Intelligent Blends LLC .... E 858 888-7937
5330 Eastgate Mall San Diego (92121) *(P-1412)*

Intelligent Cmpt Solutions Inc (PA) .... E 818 998-5805
8968 Fullbright Ave Chatsworth (91311) *(P-7916)*

Intelligent Technologies LLC .... C 858 458-1500
9454 Waples St San Diego (92121) *(P-6376)*

Intelliguard Group LLC .... E 760 448-9500
12220 World Trade Dr Ste 210 San Diego (92128) *(P-8047)*

Intelliloan, Costa Mesa *Also Called: Metropolitan Home Mortgage Inc (P-11923)*

Intellipower Inc .... D 714 921-1580
1746 N Saint Thomas Cir Orange (92865) *(P-10254)*

Intellisense Systems Inc .... C 310 320-1827
21041 S Western Ave Torrance (90501) *(P-7724)*

Intelsat US LLC .... C 310 525-5500
1600 Forbes Way Long Beach (90810) *(P-9566)*

Intense Lighting LLC .... D 714 630-9877
3340 E La Palma Ave Anaheim (92806) *(P-6464)*

Inter Community Hospital, Covina *Also Called: Emanate Health Medical Center (P-15996)*

Inter-Con Security Systems Inc (PA) .... A 626 535-2200
210 S De Lacey Ave Pasadena (91105) *(P-14310)*

Interactive Display Solutions, Irvine *Also Called: Interctive Dsplay Slutions Inc (P-7011)*

Interactive Films LLC .... D 310 988-0643
12049 Jefferson Blvd Culver City (90230) *(P-10522)*

Interactive Media Holdings Inc .... C 949 861-8888
2722 Michelson Dr Ste 100 Irvine (92612) *(P-13216)*

Intercare Therapy Inc .... C 323 866-1880
4221 Wilshire Blvd Ste 300a Los Angeles (90010) *(P-15548)*

Intercntnntal Los Angles Dwntw, Los Angeles *Also Called: Ihg Management (maryland) LLC (P-12874)*

Intercommunity Care Center, Long Beach *Also Called: Intercommunity Care Ctrs Inc (P-15682)*

Intercommunity Care Ctrs Inc .... C 562 427-8915
2626 Grand Ave Long Beach (90815) *(P-15682)*

Interconnect Solutions Co LLC (PA) .... D 714 556-7007
17595 Mount Herrmann St Fountain Valley (92708) *(P-6377)*

Interconnect Solutions Co LLC .... D 661 295-0020
25358 Avenue Stanford Valencia (91355) *(P-7010)*

Interconnect Systems Intl LLC (DH) .... D 805 482-2870
741 Flynn Rd Camarillo (93012) *(P-6834)*

Interconnect Systems, Inc., Camarillo *Also Called: Interconnect Systems Intl LLC (P-6834)*

Intercontinental Art, Compton *Also Called: Artboxx Framing Inc (P-8659)*

Intercontinental San Diego, San Diego *Also Called: Lfs Development LLC (P-12898)*

Interctive Dsplay Slutions Inc .... E 949 727-1959
490 Wald Irvine (92618) *(P-7011)*

Interdent Service Corporation .... D 951 682-1720
3630 Central Ave Riverside (92506) *(P-15518)*

Interdigital Inc .... D 858 210-4800
9276 Scranton Rd Ste 300 San Diego (92121) *(P-6620)*

INTERDIGITAL, INC., San Diego *Also Called: Interdigital Inc (P-6620)*

Interface Associates, Laguna Niguel *Also Called: Confluent Medical Tech Inc (P-8135)*

Interface Associates Inc .... C 949 448-7056
27721 La Paz Rd Laguna Niguel (92677) *(P-8173)*

Interface Catheter Solutions, Laguna Niguel *Also Called: Interface Associates Inc (P-8173)*

INTERFACE CHILDREN FAMILY SERV, Camarillo *Also Called: Interface Community (P-16959)*

Interface Community (PA) .... D 805 485-6114
4001 Mission Oaks Blvd Ste I Camarillo (93012) *(P-16959)*

Interface Rehab Inc .... A 714 646-8300
774 S Placentia Ave Ste 200 Placentia (92870) *(P-15549)*

Interfaceflor LLC .... D 213 741-2139
1111 S Grand Ave Ste 103 Los Angeles (90015) *(P-1952)*

INTERFAITH COMMUNITY SERVICES, Escondido *Also Called: Interfaith Community Svcs Inc (P-16960)*

Interfaith Community Svcs Inc .... D 760 489-6380
250 N Ash St Escondido (92025) *(P-16960)*

Interglobal Waste MGT Inc .... D 805 388-1588
820 Calle Plano Camarillo (93012) *(P-7961)*

INTERGROUP, Los Angeles *Also Called: Portsmouth Square Inc (P-12577)*

Employee Codes: A=Over 500 employees, B=251-500
C=101-250, D=51-100, E=20-50, F=10-19, G=1-9

2025 Southern California
Business Directory and Buyers Guide

© Mergent Inc. 1-800-342-5647

1063

Interhealth Services Inc (HQ)..................... C 562 698-0811
12401 Washington Blvd Whittier (90602) *(P-16397)*

Interim Healthcare Inc .... C 951 684-6111
7000 Indiana Ave Ste 107 Riverside (92506) *(P-16398)*

Interim Services, Riverside *Also Called: Interim Healthcare Inc (P-16398)*

Interior Electric Incorporated .... D 714 771-9098
747 N Main St Orange (92868) *(P-926)*

Interior Experts Gen Bldrs Inc .... C 909 203-4922
4534 Carter Ct Chino (91710) *(P-549)*

Interior Rmoval Specialist Inc .... C 323 357-6900
8990 Atlantic Ave South Gate (90280) *(P-1184)*

Interior Specialists Inc .... B 909 983-5386
15822 Bernardo Center Dr Ste 1 San Diego (92127) *(P-14517)*

Interlink Inc .... D 714 905-7700
3845 E Coronado St Anaheim (92807) *(P-3024)*

Interlink Securities Corp .... D 818 992-6700
20750 Ventura Blvd Ste 300 Woodland Hills (91364) *(P-11970)*

Intermountain Specialty Eqp, La Palma *Also Called: Isec Incorporated (P-1053)*

Internal Revenue Service .... D 714 512-2818
2400 E Katella Ave Ste 800 Anaheim (92806) *(P-13165)*

Internal Services, Los Angeles *Also Called: County of Los Angeles (P-13697)*

Internal Services Department, Los Angeles *Also Called: County of Los Angeles (P-17715)*

Internal Services Department, Downey *Also Called: County of Los Angeles (P-17977)*

Internal Services Dept, Los Angeles *Also Called: County of Los Angeles (P-14481)*

International Academy of Fin (PA).............. E 818 361-7724
13177 Foothill Blvd Sylmar (91342) *(P-3734)*

International Bus Mchs Corp .... E 714 472-2237
600 Anton Blvd Ste 400 Costa Mesa (92626) *(P-5854)*

International Bus Mchs Corp .... A 818 553-8100
400 N Brand Blvd Fl 7 Glendale (91203) *(P-5855)*

INTERNATIONAL CHILDREN'S CHARI, Calabasas *Also Called: Help Children World Foundation (P-16950)*

International Coatings, Cerritos *Also Called: International Coatings Co Inc (P-3770)*

International Coatings Co Inc (PA).............. E 562 926-1010
13929 166th St Cerritos (90703) *(P-3770)*

International Coffee & Tea LLC (HQ)........... D 310 237-2326
550 S Hope St Ste 2100 Los Angeles (90071) *(P-11577)*

International Component Tech, Santa Ana *Also Called: Nivek Industries Inc (P-6424)*

International Consulting Unltd .... E 714 449-3318
13045 Park St Santa Fe Springs (90670) *(P-4548)*

International Die Casting Inc .... E 310 324-2278
515 E Airline Way Gardena (90248) *(P-4690)*

International E-Z Up Inc (PA)....................... D 800 742-3363
1900 2nd St Norco (92860) *(P-2240)*

International Energy Services USA Inc .... C 310 257-8222
3445 Kashiwa St Torrance (90505) *(P-17558)*

International Energy Svcs Co, Torrance *Also Called: International Energy Services USA Inc (P-17558)*

International Fmly Entrmt Inc (DH).............. C 818 560-1000
3800 W Alameda Ave Burbank (91505) *(P-9553)*

International Gourmet, City Of Industry *Also Called: Mercado Latino Inc (P-10760)*

International Iron Products, San Diego *Also Called: Price Industries Inc (P-4522)*

International Lottery & Totalizator Systems Inc .... E 760 598-1655
2310 Cousteau Ct Vista (92081) *(P-13753)*

International Medical Corps (PA)................. A 310 826-7800
12400 Wilshire Blvd Ste 1500 Los Angeles (90025) *(P-16961)*

International Merchandising, Beverly Hills *Also Called: Wme Img LLC (P-15037)*

International Mfg Tech Inc (DH)................... D 619 544-7741
2798 Harbor Dr San Diego (92113) *(P-4518)*

International Paper, Santa Fe Springs *Also Called: International Paper Company (P-2627)*

International Paper, Carson *Also Called: International Paper Company (P-2628)*

International Paper, Compton *Also Called: International Paper Company (P-2629)*

International Paper, Ontario *Also Called: New-Indy Containerboard LLC (P-2631)*

International Paper, Santa Fe Springs *Also Called: International Paper Company (P-2676)*

International Paper Company .... C 714 776-6060
601 E Ball Rd Anaheim (92805) *(P-2626)*

International Paper Company .... D 562 692-9465
9211 Norwalk Blvd Santa Fe Springs (90670) *(P-2627)*

International Paper Company .... D 310 549-5525
1350 E 223rd St Carson (90745) *(P-2628)*

International Paper Company .... E 310 639-2310
19615 S Susana Rd Compton (90221) *(P-2629)*

International Paper Company .... E 323 946-6100
11211 Greenstone Ave Santa Fe Springs (90670) *(P-2676)*

International Paving Svcs Inc .... D 909 794-2101
1199 Opal Ave Mentone (92359) *(P-626)*

International Plating Svc LLC (PA).............. E 619 454-2135
4045 Bonita Rd Ste 309 Bonita (91902) *(P-5268)*

International Processing Corp (DH).............. E 310 458-1574
233 Wilshire Blvd Ste 310 Santa Monica (90401) *(P-1428)*

International Research Labs, Moorpark *Also Called: Lifetech Resources LLC (P-10629)*

International Rite-Way Pdts, Ontario *Also Called: AMD International Tech LLC (P-4945)*

International Rubber Pdts Inc (HQ).............. D 909 947-1244
1035 Calle Amanecer San Clemente (92673) *(P-3917)*

International Seal Company, Santa Ana *Also Called: Freudenberg-Nok General Partnr (P-3887)*

International Skylights .... C 800 325-4355
1831 Ritchey St Santa Ana (92705) *(P-4316)*

International Technidyne Corp (DH)............. C 858 263-2300
6260 Sequence Dr San Diego (92121) *(P-8174)*

International Tranducer Corp .... C 805 683-2575
869 Ward Dr Santa Barbara (93111) *(P-7917)*

International Trnsp Svc LLC (PA)................ C 562 435-7781
1281 Pier G Way Long Beach (90802) *(P-9141)*

International Vitamin Corp .... C 949 664-5500
1 Park Plz Ste 800 Irvine (92614) *(P-3426)*

International Vitamin Corporat (PA)............. D 949 664-5500
4695 Macarthur Ct Ste 1400 Newport Beach (92660) *(P-3427)*

International West Inc .... E 714 632-9190
1025 N Armando St Anaheim (92806) *(P-4992)*

International Wind Inc (PA).......................... E 562 240-3963
137 N Joy St Corona (92879) *(P-7389)*

International Wood Products, San Diego *Also Called: Jeld-Wen Inc (P-2311)*

Internet Brands, El Segundo *Also Called: Mh Sub I LLC (P-13226)*

Internet Corp For Assgned Nmes (PA)........ C 310 823-9358
12025 Waterfront Dr Ste 300 Los Angeles (90094) *(P-14089)*

Internet Machines Corporation (PA)............ D 818 575-2100
30501 Agoura Rd Ste 203 Agoura Hills (91301) *(P-5926)*

Interntional Color Posters Inc .... E 949 768-1005
8081 Orangethorpe Ave Buena Park (90621) *(P-3147)*

Interntional Tea Importers Inc (PA)............. E 562 801-9600
2140 Davie Ave Commerce (90040) *(P-1793)*

Interntional Tech Systems Corp .... E 714 761-8886
10721 Walker St Cypress (90630) *(P-10255)*

Interntional Un Oper Engineers .... B 619 295-3186
3935 Normal St San Diego (92103) *(P-17311)*

Interntional Un Oper Engineers .... A 909 307-8700
1647 W Lugonia Ave Redlands (92374) *(P-17312)*

Interntnal Ch of Frsqare Gospl (PA)............ D 714 701-1818
1910 W Sunset Blvd Los Angeles (90026) *(P-17416)*

Interntnal Cnnctors Cable Corp .... C 888 275-4422
1270 N Hancock St Anaheim (92807) *(P-6587)*

Interntnal Fndtion For Krea Un .... B 213 550-2182
3435 Wilshire Blvd Ste 480 Los Angeles (90010) *(P-17229)*

Interntnal Lttery Ttlztor Syst .... E 760 598-1655
2310 Cousteau Ct Vista (92081) *(P-13754)*

Interntnl Mdction Systems Ltd .... A 626 442-6757
1886 Santa Anita Ave South El Monte (91733) *(P-3428)*

Interntnal Ntrtn Wllness Hldng, Corona *Also Called: Inw Living Ecology Opco LLC (P-1507)*

Interntonal Thermoproducts Div, Santee *Also Called: Ds Fibertech Corp (P-5798)*

Interocean Industries Inc .... E 858 292-0808
9201 Isaac St Ste C Santee (92071) *(P-7725)*

Interocean Systems, Santee *Also Called: Interocean Industries Inc (P-7725)*

Interocean Systems LLC .... E 858 565-8400
9201 Isaac St Ste C Santee (92071) *(P-7726)*

Interpore Cross Intl Inc (DH)....................... D 949 453-3200
181 Technology Dr Irvine (92618) *(P-8276)*

Interscan Corporation .... E 805 823-8301
4590 Ish Dr Ste 110 Simi Valley (93063) *(P-7890)*

Interspace Battery Inc (PA)......................... E 626 813-1234
2009 W San Bernardino Rd West Covina (91790) *(P-4618)*

Interstate Electric Co Inc .... D 800 225-5432
  2240 Yates Ave Commerce (90040) *(P-10045)*

Interstate Foods Inc .... C 310 635-2442
  310 S Long Beach Blvd Compton (90221) *(P-10836)*

Interstate Hotels Resorts Inc .... D 805 966-2285
  901 E Cabrillo Blvd Santa Barbara (93103) *(P-12876)*

Interstate Meat Co Inc .... E 323 838-9400
  6114 Scott Way Commerce (90040) *(P-5675)*

Interstate Rhbltation Svcs LLC .... C 818 244-5656
  333 E Glenoaks Blvd Ste 204 Glendale (91207) *(P-16482)*

Interstate Steel Center Co Inc .... E 323 583-0855
  7001 S Alameda St Los Angeles (90001) *(P-4519)*

Intertek Pharmaceutical Svcs, San Diego Also Called: Intertek USA Inc (P-17919)

Intertek USA Inc .... D 858 558-2599
  10420 Wateridge Cir San Diego (92121) *(P-17919)*

Intertrade Industries Ltd .... D 714 894-5566
  14600 Hoover St Westminster (92683) *(P-4140)*

Intertrend Communications Inc .... D 562 733-1888
  228 E Broadway Long Beach (90802) *(P-13217)*

Interviewing Service Amer LLC (PA) .... C 818 989-1044
  1900 Avenue Of The Stars Los Angeles (90067) *(P-17852)*

Intervrsity Chrstn Fllwshp/Usa .... B 310 510-0015
  Gallager&Apos;S Cove Avalon (90704) *(P-13103)*

Intex Properties S Bay Corp (PA) .... D 310 549-5400
  4001 Via Oro Ave Ste 210 Long Beach (90810) *(P-10514)*

INTEX RECREATION, Long Beach Also Called: Intex Recreation Corp (P-9874)

Intex Recreation Corp .... D 310 549-5400
  4001 Via Oro Ave Long Beach (90810) *(P-9874)*

Intex Recreation Corp .... C 310 549-5400
  1665 Hughes Way Long Beach (90810) *(P-12298)*

INTEX RECREATION CORP, Long Beach Also Called: Intex Recreation Corp (P-12298)

Intimo Industry, Vernon Also Called: Pjy LLC (P-1885)

Intouch Health, Goleta Also Called: Intouch Technologies Inc (P-17230)

Intouch Technologies Inc (HQ) .... D 805 562-8686
  7402 Hollister Ave Goleta (93117) *(P-17230)*

Intra Aerospace LLC .... E 909 476-0343
  10671 Civic Center Dr Rancho Cucamonga (91730) *(P-6146)*

Intra Storage Systems Inc .... E 714 373-2346
  7100 Honold Cir Garden Grove (92841) *(P-5448)*

Intrepid Inv Bankers LLC .... A 310 478-9000
  11755 Wilshire Blvd Ste 2200 Los Angeles (90025) *(P-12712)*

Intri-Plex Technologies Inc (HQ) .... C 805 683-3414
  751 S Kellogg Ave Goleta (93117) *(P-6147)*

Intri-Plex Technologies Inc .... E 805 845-9600
  751 S Kellogg Ave Goleta (93117) *(P-17797)*

Intuit Inc .... E 818 436-7800
  21650 Oxnard St Ste 2200 Woodland Hills (91367) *(P-13949)*

Intuit Inc .... B 858 780-2846
  7535 Torrey Santa Fe Rd San Diego (92129) *(P-13950)*

Intuit Inc .... B 858 215-8000
  7545 Torrey Santa Fe Rd San Diego (92129) *(P-13951)*

Invapharm Inc (PA) .... E 909 757-1818
  1320 W Mission Blvd Ontario (91762) *(P-12012)*

Invasix Inc .... D 855 411-2639
  17 Hughes Irvine (92618) *(P-17798)*

Inveco Inc .... E 949 378-3850
  440 Fair Dr Ste 200 Costa Mesa (92626) *(P-5269)*

Invenios, Santa Barbara Also Called: Picosys Incorporated (P-5619)

Invenios LLC .... D 805 962-3333
  320 N Nopal St Santa Barbara (93103) *(P-4336)*

Invenlux Corporation .... E 626 277-4163
  168 Mason Way Ste B5 City Of Industry (91746) *(P-6835)*

Invensys Climate Controls, Long Beach Also Called: Schneider Elc Buildings LLC (P-7148)

Inventure Capital Corporation (PA) ...... A 213 262-6903
  429 Santa Monica Blvd Ste 450 Santa Monica (90401) *(P-12713)*

Inveserve Corporation .... D 626 458-3435
  812 W Las Tunas Dr San Gabriel (91776) *(P-12468)*

Investment Enterprises Inc (PA) .... E 818 464-3800
  8230 Haskell Ave Ste 8240 Van Nuys (91406) *(P-3148)*

Investors Business Daily Inc (HQ) .... C 800 831-2525
  5900 Wilshire Blvd Ste 2950 Los Angeles (90036) *(P-2805)*

Invision Networking LLC .... C 949 309-3441
  333 City Blvd W Ste 1700 Orange (92868) *(P-14226)*

Invitation Homes Inc .... D 805 372-2900
  680 E Colorado Blvd Pasadena (91101) *(P-12469)*

Invitrogen Ip Holdings Inc .... D 760 603-7200
  5791 Van Allen Way Carlsbad (92008) *(P-7962)*

Invizyne Technologies Inc (PA) .... E 626 415-1488
  750 Royal Oaks Dr Ste 106 Monrovia (91016) *(P-17799)*

Inw Living Ecology Opco LLC (HQ) .... E 951 371-4982
  240 Crouse Dr Corona (92879) *(P-1507)*

Inwesco Incorporated (HQ) .... D 626 334-7115
  746 N Coney Ave Azusa (91702) *(P-4536)*

INX International Ink Co .... E 562 404-5664
  13821 Marquardt Ave Santa Fe Springs (90670) *(P-3806)*

INX Prints Inc .... D 949 660-9190
  1802 Kettering Irvine (92614) *(P-1938)*

Iogear, Irvine Also Called: Aten Technology Inc (P-9988)

Ionis, Carlsbad Also Called: Ionis Pharmaceuticals Inc (P-3431)

Ionis Pharmaceuticals Inc .... D 760 603-3567
  2282 Faraday Ave Carlsbad (92008) *(P-3429)*

Ionis Pharmaceuticals Inc .... D 760 931-9200
  1896 Rutherford Rd Carlsbad (92008) *(P-3430)*

Ionis Pharmaceuticals Inc (PA) .... A 760 931-9200
  2855 Gazelle Ct Carlsbad (92010) *(P-3431)*

Ipayment Inc .... C 213 387-1353
  3325 Wilshire Blvd Ste 535 Los Angeles (90010) *(P-14518)*

IPC Cal Flex Inc .... E 714 952-0373
  13337 South St # 307 Cerritos (90703) *(P-6738)*

IPC Healthcare Inc (DH) .... C 888 447-2362
  4605 Lankershim Blvd Ste 617 North Hollywood (91602) *(P-15334)*

Ipd, Carson Also Called: Industrial Parts Depot LLC (P-10377)

Ipi Travel, San Diego Also Called: Innovative Placements Inc (P-13529)

Ipitek, Carlsbad Also Called: Ipitek Inc (P-927)

Ipitek Inc .... C 760 438-1010
  2461 Impala Dr Carlsbad (92010) *(P-927)*

Ipr Software, Encino Also Called: Ipr Software Inc (P-13952)

Ipr Software Inc .... E 310 499-0544
  16501 Ventura Blvd Ste 424 Encino (91436) *(P-13952)*

Ips Corporation (HQ) .... C 310 898-3300
  455 W Victoria St Compton (90220) *(P-3771)*

Ips Group Inc (PA) .... E 858 404-0607
  7737 Kenamar Ct San Diego (92121) *(P-7891)*

Ips Industries Inc .... D 562 623-2555
  12641 166th St Cerritos (90703) *(P-4141)*

Ipt, Goleta Also Called: Integrated Procurement Tech (P-10492)

Iq Cosmetics, El Segundo Also Called: Intelligent Beauty LLC (P-11687)

Iq Power Tools, Perris Also Called: Jpl Global LLC (P-10351)

Iq-Analog Corporation .... E 858 200-0388
  12348 High Bluff Dr Ste 110 San Diego (92130) *(P-6836)*

Iqair North America Inc .... E 877 715-4247
  14351 Firestone Blvd La Mirada (90638) *(P-5771)*

Iqd Frequency Products Inc .... E 408 250-1435
  592 N Tercero Cir Palm Springs (92262) *(P-7012)*

Iqms LLC (HQ) .... C 805 227-1122
  2231 Wisteria Ln Paso Robles (93446) *(P-13953)*

Iqvia Inc (PA) .... D 866 267-4479
  2601 Main St Ste 650 Irvine (92614) *(P-17853)*

Irell & Manella LLP .... B 949 760-0991
  840 Newport Center Dr Ste 400 Newport Beach (92660) *(P-16707)*

Irell & Manella LLP (PA) .... C 310 277-1010
  1800 Avenue Of The Stars Ste 900 Los Angeles (90067) *(P-16708)*

Iris Group Inc .... C 760 431-1103
  1675 Faraday Ave Carlsbad (92008) *(P-3149)*

Iris Technology Corporation .... D 949 975-8410
  2811 Mcgaw Ave Ste A Irvine (92614) *(P-17559)*

Irise (PA) .... D 800 556-0399
  2381 Rosecrans Ave Ste 100 El Segundo (90245) *(P-13755)*

Irish Communication Company (DH) ...... D 626 288-6170
  2649 Stingle Ave Rosemead (91770) *(P-679)*

Irish Construction (HQ) .... C 626 288-8530
  2641 River Ave Rosemead (91770) *(P-680)*

Employee Codes: A=Over 500 employees, B=251-500
C=101-250, D=51-100, E=20-50, F=10-19, G=1-9

2025 Southern California
Business Directory and Buyers Guide

© Mergent Inc. 1-800-342-5647

1065

ALPHABETIC

Irish Interiors Inc .... C 562 344-1700
5511 Skylab Rd Ste 101 Huntington Beach (92647) *(P-7502)*

Irish Interiors Inc (HQ)......................... **C 949 559-0930**
5511 Skylab Rd Ste 101 Huntington Beach (92647) *(P-7503)*

Irish International .... C 949 559-0930
5511 Skylab Rd Huntington Beach (92647) *(P-7390)*

Irisys Inc .... D 858 623-1520
6828 Nancy Ridge Dr Ste 100 San Diego (92121) *(P-10627)*

Iron Beds of America, Los Angeles *Also Called: Wesley Allen Inc (P-2476)*

Iron Grip Barbell Company Inc .... D 714 850-6900
11377 Markon Dr Garden Grove (92841) *(P-8528)*

Iron Mountain Info MGT LLC .... D 818 848-9766
441 N Oak St Inglewood (90302) *(P-9297)*

Ironman Inc .... E 818 341-0980
20555 Superior St Chatsworth (91311) *(P-14742)*

Ironman Renewal LLC .... D 951 735-3710
2535 Anselmo Dr Corona (92879) *(P-14692)*

Ironwood Electric Inc .... E 714 630-2350
13 Ashton Mission Viejo (92692) *(P-7127)*

Irp, San Clemente *Also Called: International Rubber Pdts Inc (P-3917)*

Irp Lax Hotel LLC .... C 310 645-4600
9750 Airport Blvd Los Angeles (90045) *(P-12877)*

Irriscape Construction Inc .... D 951 694-6936
20182 Carancho Rd Temecula (92590) *(P-210)*

Irvine APT Communities LP (HQ)............... **C 949 720-5600**
110 Innovation Dr Irvine (92617) *(P-12350)*

Irvine APT Communities LP .... B 714 505-7181
100 Robinson Dr Tustin (92782) *(P-12351)*

Irvine APT Communities LP .... C 714 537-8500
13212 Magnolia St Ofc Garden Grove (92844) *(P-12352)*

Irvine APT Communities LP .... C 714 937-8900
299 N State College Blvd Orange (92868) *(P-12353)*

Irvine APT Communities LP .... C 310 255-1221
1221 Ocean Ave Santa Monica (90401) *(P-12354)*

Irvine APT Communities LP .... C 949 854-4942
146 Berkeley Irvine (92612) *(P-12470)*

Irvine Biomedical Inc .... C 949 851-3053
2375 Morse Ave Irvine (92614) *(P-8175)*

Irvine Company Office Property, Newport Beach *Also Called: Irvine Eastgate Office II LLC (P-12687)*

Irvine Eastgate Office II LLC .... A 949 720-2000
550 Newport Center Dr Newport Beach (92660) *(P-12687)*

Irvine Electronics LLC .... D 949 250-0315
1601 Alton Pkwy Ste A Irvine (92606) *(P-6739)*

Irvine Electronics Inc, Irvine *Also Called: Irvine Electronics LLC (P-6739)*

Irvine Medical Center, Orange *Also Called: University California Irvine (P-16245)*

Irvine Ranch Water District (PA).............. C 949 453-5300
15600 Sand Canyon Ave Irvine (92618) *(P-9695)*

Irvine Ranch Water District .... C 949 453-5300
3512 Michelson Dr Irvine (92612) *(P-9696)*

Irvine Regional Hospital, Anaheim *Also Called: Tenet Healthsystem Medical Inc (P-16227)*

Irvine Scientific, Santa Ana *Also Called: Fujifilm Irvine Scientific Inc (P-3575)*

Irvine Sensors, Costa Mesa *Also Called: Isc8 Inc (P-7128)*

Irvine Sensors Corporation .... E 714 444-8700
3000 Airway Ave Ste A1 Costa Mesa (92626) *(P-6837)*

Irvine Technology Corporation .... C 714 445-2624
2850 Redhill Ave Ste 230 Santa Ana (92705) *(P-18324)*

Irwin Aviation Inc .... E 951 372-9555
225 Airport Cir Corona (92878) *(P-7504)*

Irwin Industries Inc .... A 704 457-5117
2301 Rosecrans Ave Ste 3185 El Segundo (90245) *(P-716)*

Irwin International Inc (PA)....................... D 951 372-9555
225 Airport Cir Corona (92880) *(P-11487)*

ISA, Los Angeles *Also Called: Interviewing Service Amer LLC (P-17852)*

Isaac Fair Corporation .... D 858 369-8000
3661 Valley Centre Dr San Diego (92130) *(P-13756)*

Isabell's Honey Farm, Burbank *Also Called: Honey Isabells Inc (P-95)*

Isabelle Handbag Inc .... E 323 277-9888
3155 Bandini Blvd Unit A Vernon (90058) *(P-4303)*

Isc8 Inc .... E 714 549-8211
151 Kalmus Dr Ste A203 Costa Mesa (92626) *(P-7128)*

ISE Corporation .... C 858 413-1720
12302 Kerran St Poway (92064) *(P-17800)*

Isec Incorporated .... C 858 279-9085
10105 Carroll Canyon Rd San Diego (92131) *(P-487)*

Isec Incorporated .... C 858 279-9085
5735 Kearny Villa Rd Ste 105 San Diego (92123) *(P-7828)*

Isec Incorporated .... C 714 761-5151
20 Centerpointe Dr Ste 140 La Palma (90623) *(P-1053)*

Isec Incorporated .... D 805 375-6957
2363 Teller Rd Ste 106 Newbury Park (91320) *(P-1054)*

Iserve Residential Lending LLC .... C 858 486-4169
10815 Rancho Bernardo Rd San Diego (92127) *(P-11915)*

Isiqalo LLC .... B 714 683-2820
5610 Daniels St Chino (91710) *(P-1920)*

Isl Employees Inc .... D 760 547-2863
2333 State St Ste 300 Carlsbad (92008) *(P-17170)*

Island Powder Coating .... E 626 279-2460
1830 Tyler Ave South El Monte (91733) *(P-5325)*

Isolatek International, San Bernardino *Also Called: Usmpc Buyer Inc (P-4496)*

Isolutecom Inc (PA).............................. **E 805 498-6259**
9 Northam Ave Newbury Park (91320) *(P-13954)*

Isomedix Operations Inc .... D 951 694-9340
43425 Business Park Dr Temecula (92590) *(P-8277)*

Isomedix Operations Inc .... E 909 390-9942
1000 Sarah Pl Ontario (91761) *(P-8278)*

Isotis Orthobiologics Inc .... C 949 595-8710
2 Goodyear Ste A Irvine (92618) *(P-17801)*

Isotope Products Lab, Valencia *Also Called: Eckert Zegler Isotope Pdts Inc (P-8039)*

Isound, Torrance *Also Called: Dreamgear LLC (P-8483)*

Isovac Engineering Inc .... E 818 552-6200
614 Justin Ave Glendale (91201) *(P-14519)*

Issac, Tustin *Also Called: Trellborg Sling Sltions US Inc (P-8240)*

Issac Medical Inc .... B 805 239-4284
2761 Walnut Ave Tustin (92780) *(P-8176)*

Ista Pharmaceuticals Inc .... B 949 788-6000
50 Technology Dr Irvine (92618) *(P-3432)*

Istarusa Group .... E 888 989-1189
727 Phillips Rowland Heights (91748) *(P-5856)*

ISU Petasys Corp .... D 818 833-5800
12930 Bradley Ave Sylmar (91342) *(P-6740)*

Isuzu North America Corp (HQ)................. **C 714 935-9300**
1400 S Douglass Rd Ste 100 Anaheim (92806) *(P-11363)*

Isuzu Truck Services, Santa Ana *Also Called: Toms Truck Center Inc (P-11420)*

It Campus, Vernon *Also Called: It Jeans Inc (P-2101)*

It Division Inc .... C 678 648-2709
9170 Irvine Center Dr Ste 200 Irvine (92618) *(P-16843)*

It Is Written, Riverside *Also Called: Adventist Media Center Inc (P-14952)*

It Jeans Inc .... E 323 588-2156
2425 E 38th St Vernon (90058) *(P-2101)*

It's Delish, North Hollywood *Also Called: Mave Enterprises Inc (P-1509)*

Itc, San Diego *Also Called: International Technidyne Corp (P-8174)*

Itc Nexus Holding Company, San Diego *Also Called: Accriva Dgnostics Holdings Inc (P-8075)*

Itc Sftware Slutions Group LLC (PA).......... **B 877 248-2774**
201 Sandpointe Ave Ste 305 Santa Ana (92707) *(P-13955)*

Itc Solutions & Services Group, Santa Ana *Also Called: Itc Sftware Slutions Group LLC (P-13955)*

ITD Arizona Inc .... D 323 722-8542
6737 E Washington Blvd Commerce (90040) *(P-9857)*

Itech, San Diego *Also Called: Intelligent Technologies LLC (P-6376)*

Itek Services Inc .... D 949 770-4835
25501 Arctic Ocean Dr Lake Forest (92630) *(P-14227)*

Itochu Aviation Inc (DH).......................... **E 310 640-2770**
222 N Pacific Coast Hwy Ste 2200 El Segundo (90245) *(P-10493)*

Itrex Group USA Corporation .... B 213 436-7785
120 Vantis Dr Ste 545 Aliso Viejo (92656) *(P-13757)*

Itsco, Cypress *Also Called: Interntional Tech Systems Corp (P-10255)*

ITT Aerospace Controls LLC (HQ)............. **D 315 568-7258**
28150 Industry Dr Valencia (91355) *(P-7505)*

ITT Aerospace Controls LLC .... B 661 295-4000
28150 Industry Dr Valencia (91355) *(P-7506)*

ITT Cannon LLC .... C 714 557-4700
56 Technology Dr Irvine (92618) *(P-6351)*

ITT LLC .... D 562 908-4144
3951 Capitol Ave City Of Industry (90601) *(P-6352)*

ITW Space Bag, San Diego *Also Called: New West Products Inc (P-4178)*

Ivar's Displays, Ontario *Also Called: Ivars Display (P-2566)*

Ivars Display (PA) .... D **909 923-2761**
2314 E Locust Ct Ontario (91761) *(P-2566)*

Ivigen, Torrance *Also Called: Igenomix Usa Inc (P-8167)*

Ivy Enterprises Inc .... B 323 887-8661
5564 E 61st St Commerce (90040) *(P-18325)*

Iwamoto & Gean Farm .... D 805 659-4568
2064 Olga St Oxnard (93036) *(P-12)*

Iwco Direct - Downey, Downey *Also Called: Instant Web LLC (P-3021)*

Iwcus, Walnut *Also Called: Infinity Watch Corporation (P-8608)*

Iwerks Entertainment Inc .... D 661 678-1800
25040 Avenue Tibbitts Ste F Valencia (91355) *(P-7129)*

Iworks, Commerce *Also Called: Iworks Us Inc (P-6404)*

Iworks Us Inc .... D 323 278-8363
2501 S Malt Ave Commerce (90040) *(P-6404)*

Ixi Technology, Yorba Linda *Also Called: Ixi Technology Inc (P-5857)*

Ixi Technology Inc .... E 714 221-5000
22705 Savi Ranch Pkwy Ste 200 Yorba Linda (92887) *(P-5857)*

Ixia (HQ) .... C **818 871-1800**
26601 Agoura Rd Calabasas (91302) *(P-7918)*

Ixia .... E 818 871-1800
26701 Agoura Rd Calabasas (91302) *(P-7919)*

Ixia Communications, Calabasas *Also Called: Ixia (P-7919)*

Ixys Intgrted Crcits Div AV In .... A 949 831-4622
145 Columbia Aliso Viejo (92656) *(P-6838)*

Ixys Long Beach Inc (DH) .... E **562 296-6584**
2500 Mira Mar Ave Long Beach (90815) *(P-6839)*

Iyuno USA Inc (HQ) .... D **310 388-8800**
2901 W Alameda Ave Burbank (91505) *(P-14835)*

Izola, San Diego *Also Called: Tallgrass Pictures LLC (P-1467)*

J - T E C H .... C 310 533-6700
548 Amapola Ave Torrance (90501) *(P-6952)*

J & D Laboratories Inc .... B 760 734-6800
2710 Progress St Vista (92081) *(P-3318)*

J & F Design Inc .... D 323 526-4444
2042 Garfield Ave Commerce (90040) *(P-2102)*

J & J Processing Inc .... E 562 926-2333
14715 Anson Ave Santa Fe Springs (90670) *(P-1684)*

J & J Snack Foods Corp Cal (HQ) .... D **323 581-0171**
5353 S Downey Rd Los Angeles (90058) *(P-1489)*

J & L Cstm Plstic Extrsons Inc .... E 626 442-0711
850 Lawson St City Of Industry (91748) *(P-4142)*

J & L Vineyards .... D 559 268-1627
1850 Ramada Dr Ste 3 Paso Robles (93446) *(P-33)*

J & M Products Inc .... D 818 837-0205
1647 Truman St San Fernando (91340) *(P-4774)*

J & M Realty Company (PA) .... C **949 261-2727**
41 Corporate Park Ste 240 Irvine (92606) *(P-12471)*

J & M Richman Corporation .... E 800 422-9646
1501 Beach St Montebello (90640) *(P-2247)*

J & M Sales Inc .... A 310 324-9962
15001 S Figueroa St Gardena (90248) *(P-11497)*

J & R Concrete Products Inc .... E 951 943-5855
440 W Markham St Perris (92571) *(P-4397)*

J & S Inc .... E 310 719-7144
229 E Gardena Blvd Gardena (90248) *(P-6148)*

J A English II Inc .... E 760 598-5333
1333 Keystone Way Vista (92081) *(P-4143)*

J and K Manufacturing Inc .... E 562 630-8417
14701 Garfield Ave Paramount (90723) *(P-6149)*

J and L Industries, El Segundo *Also Called: Aerospace Engrg Support Corp (P-7416)*

J B, Chatsworth *Also Called: J B Whl Roofg Bldg Sups Inc (P-11201)*

J B A, Pasadena *Also Called: B Jacqueline and Assoc Inc (P-13667)*

J B Oxford & Co, Beverly Hills *Also Called: National Clearing Corporation (P-18176)*

J B Whl Roofg Bldg Sups Inc (DH) .... D 818 998-0440
21524 Nordhoff St Chatsworth (91311) *(P-11201)*

J B3d, Orange *Also Called: John Bishop Design Inc (P-8610)*

J C Ford Company (HQ) .... E 714 871-7361
901 S Leslie St La Habra (90631) *(P-5676)*

J C Sales, Los Angeles *Also Called: Shims Bargain Inc (P-11143)*

J C Trimming Company Inc .... D 323 235-4458
3800 S Hill St Los Angeles (90037) *(P-2065)*

J Craig Venter Institute Inc (PA) .... B 301 795-7000
4120 Capricorn Ln La Jolla (92037) *(P-17877)*

J Deluca Fish Company Inc .... E 310 221-6500
505 E Harry Bridges Blvd Wilmington (90744) *(P-1708)*

J F Duncan Industries Inc (PA) .... E **562 862-4269**
4380 Ayers Ave Vernon (90058) *(P-6016)*

J F I, Los Angeles *Also Called: Jet Fleet International Corp (P-13178)*

J G Boswell Company .... A 661 327-7721
21101 Bear Mountain Blvd Bakersfield (93311) *(P-1)*

J G Boswell Company .... B 661 764-9000
36889 Highway 58 Buttonwillow (93206) *(P-39)*

J Ginger Masonry LP (PA) .... B **951 688-5050**
8188 Lincoln Ave Ste 100 Riverside (92504) *(P-985)*

J H Textiles Inc .... E 323 585-4124
2301 E 55th St Vernon (90058) *(P-1971)*

J Hellman Frozen Foods Inc (PA) .... E **213 243-9105**
1601 E Olympic Blvd Ste 200 Los Angeles (90021) *(P-1377)*

J I Machine Company Inc .... E 858 695-1787
9720 Distribution Ave San Diego (92121) *(P-6150)*

J L Cooper Electronics Inc .... E 310 322-9990
142 Arena St El Segundo (90245) *(P-7013)*

J L F/Lone Meadow, San Diego *Also Called: J L Furnishings LLC (P-2544)*

J L Fisher Inc .... D 818 846-8366
1000 W Isabel St Burbank (91506) *(P-13458)*

J L Furnishings LLC .... B 310 605-6600
1620 5th Ave Ste 400 San Diego (92101) *(P-2544)*

J L M C Inc .... E 909 947-2980
1944 S Bon View Ave Ontario (91761) *(P-4839)*

J L Shepherd and Assoc Inc .... E 818 898-2361
1010 Arroyo St San Fernando (91340) *(P-8048)*

J La, The, Los Angeles *Also Called: Westside Jewish Cmnty Ctr Inc (P-17247)*

J Lohr Winery Corporation .... E 805 239-8900
6169 Airport Rd Paso Robles (93446) *(P-1575)*

J M Smucker Company .... E 805 487-5483
800 Commercial Ave Oxnard (93030) *(P-1351)*

J M V B Inc .... D 714 288-9797
12118 Severn Way Riverside (92503) *(P-867)*

J Miller Canvas LLC .... E 714 641-0052
2429 S Birch St Santa Ana (92707) *(P-1960)*

J Miller Co Inc .... E 818 837-0181
11537 Bradley Ave San Fernando (91340) *(P-3893)*

J P Allen Co, Riverside *Also Called: James Allen Productions LLC (P-14918)*

J P H Consulting Inc .... C 323 934-5660
4515 Huntington Dr S Los Angeles (90032) *(P-15683)*

J P Sportswear, Lynwood *Also Called: Aaron Corporation (P-2079)*

J R Industries, Westlake Village *Also Called: Jri Inc (P-10258)*

J Robert Scott Inc .... C 310 680-4300
722 N La Cienega Blvd West Hollywood (90069) *(P-10664)*

J T Walker Industries Inc .... A 909 481-1909
9322 Hyssop Dr Rancho Cucamonga (91730) *(P-4890)*

J Talley Corporation (PA) .... D 951 654-2123
989 W 7th St San Jacinto (92582) *(P-5065)*

J W Floor Covering Inc (PA) .... C **858 536-8565**
9881 Carroll Centre Rd San Diego (92126) *(P-1070)*

J-M Manufacturing Company Inc .... E 951 657-7400
23711 Rider St Perris (92570) *(P-3275)*

J-M Manufacturing Company Inc .... D 909 822-3009
10990 Hemlock Ave Fontana (92337) *(P-3276)*

J-M Manufacturing Company Inc (PA) .... C **310 693-8200**
5200 W Century Blvd Los Angeles (90045) *(P-3975)*

J. W. Floor Covering, San Diego *Also Called: J W Floor Covering Inc (P-1070)*

J&E Conveyor Services, Lake Elsinore *Also Called: Jose Perez (P-5517)*

J&G Berry Farms LLC .... C 831 750-9408
720 Rosemary Rd Santa Maria (93454) *(P-20)*

Employee Codes: A=Over 500 employees, B=251-500
C=101-250, D=51-100, E=20-50, F=10-19, G=1-9

2025 Southern California
Business Directory and Buyers Guide

© Mergent Inc. 1-800-342-5647

1067

ALPHABETIC

J&M Keystone, Inc., Spring Valley *Also Called: ATI Rstrtion Spring Vly CA Inc (P-1196)*

J&R Taylor Brothers Assoc Inc .... D 626 334-9301
16321 Arrow Hwy Irwindale (91706) *(P-1418)*

J&S Goodwin Inc (HQ)... D 714 956-4040
5753 E Santa Ana Canyon Rd Ste G-355 Anaheim (92807) *(P-5531)*

J&S Machine Works, Sylmar *Also Called: Kay & James Inc (P-6158)*

J2 Cloud Services LLC .... B 844 804-1234
700 S Flower St Ste 1500 Los Angeles (90017) *(P-17994)*

J2 Global Communications, Santa Barbara *Also Called: Efaxcom (P-5915)*

J2m Test Solutions Inc .... D 571 333-0291
13225 Gregg St Poway (92064) *(P-7920)*

Jab Foods, Santa Clarita *Also Called: Jeckys Best Inc (P-10821)*

Jabil Chad Automation, Anaheim *Also Called: Jabil Inc (P-6741)*

Jabil Inc .... E 714 938-0080
1565 S Sinclair St Anaheim (92806) *(P-6741)*

Jack Gosch Ford Inc .... D 951 658-3181
150 Carriage Cir Hemet (92545) *(P-11364)*

Jack In Box Inc (PA) .... A 858 571-2121
9357 Spectrum Center Blvd San Diego (92123) *(P-11578)*

Jack In The Box, San Diego *Also Called: Different Rules LLC (P-11566)*

Jack In The Box, San Diego *Also Called: Jack In Box Inc (P-11578)*

Jack Jones Trucking Inc .... D 909 456-2500
1090 E Belmont St Ontario (91761) *(P-8957)*

Jack Nadel Inc (PA) .... D 310 815-2600
5820 Uplander Way Culver City (90230) *(P-18155)*

Jack Nadel International, Culver City *Also Called: Jack Nadel Inc (P-18155)*

Jack Pwell Chrysler - Ddge Inc .... D 760 745-2880
1625 Auto Park Way Escondido (92029) *(P-11365)*

Jack Pwell Chrysler Ddge Jeep, Escondido *Also Called: Jack Pwell Chrysler - Ddge Inc (P-11365)*

Jack Rubin & Sons Inc (PA) .... E 310 635-5407
13103 S Alameda St Compton (90222) *(P-10140)*

Jackie Robinson Family YMCA, San Diego *Also Called: YMCA of San Diego County (P-17392)*

Jackoway Tyrman Wrthmer Asten .... D 310 553-0305
1925 Century Park E 2nd Fl Los Angeles (90067) *(P-16709)*

Jacks Candy, Los Angeles *Also Called: Consolidated Svc Distrs Inc (P-10844)*

JACKSAM CORP BLACKOUT, Newport Beach *Also Called: Jacksam Corporation (P-5790)*

Jacksam Corporation .... E 800 605-3580
4440 Von Karman Ave Ste 220 Newport Beach (92660) *(P-5790)*

Jackson & Blanc .... C 858 831-7900
7929 Arjons Dr San Diego (92126) *(P-791)*

Jackson Engineering Co Inc .... E 818 886-9567
9411 Winnetka Ave # A Chatsworth (91311) *(P-6287)*

Jacmar Companies LLC .... C 626 430-9082
12761 Schabarum Ave Baldwin Park (91706) *(P-11579)*

Jacmar Companies, The, Alhambra *Also Called: Pacific Ventures Ltd (P-18030)*

Jaco Engineering .... E 714 991-1680
879 S East St Anaheim (92805) *(P-6151)*

Jacobs Civil Inc .... C 310 847-2500
1500 Hughes Way Ste B400 Long Beach (90810) *(P-17560)*

Jacobs Engineering Company .... A 626 449-2171
1111 S Arroyo Pkwy Pasadena (91105) *(P-17561)*

Jacobs Engineering Group Inc .... D 949 224-7500
2600 Michelson Dr Ste 500 Irvine (92612) *(P-17562)*

Jacobs Engineering Group Inc .... D 626 578-3500
1111 S Arroyo Pkwy Pasadena (91105) *(P-17563)*

Jacobs Engineering Inc (DH) .... C 626 578-3500
155 N Lake Ave Pasadena (91101) *(P-17564)*

Jacobs International Ltd Inc .... B 626 578-3500
155 N Lake Ave Ste 800 Pasadena (91101) *(P-17565)*

Jacobs Med Ctr At Uc San Diego, La Jolla *Also Called: Uc San Diego Hlth Accntble Care (P-16235)*

Jacobs Project Management Co .... D 949 224-7695
2600 Michelson Dr Ste 500 Irvine (92612) *(P-17566)*

Jacobson Plastics Inc .... D 562 433-4911
1401 Freeman Ave Long Beach (90804) *(P-4144)*

Jacobsson Engrg Cnstr Inc .... D 760 345-8700
72310 Varner Rd Thousand Palms (92276) *(P-627)*

Jacuzzi Brands LLC .... E 909 606-1416
14525 Monte Vista Ave Chino (91710) *(P-8687)*

Jacuzzi Inc (DH).. C 909 606-7733
17872 Gillette Ave Ste 300 Irvine (92614) *(P-6017)*

Jacuzzi Outdoor Products, Irvine *Also Called: Jacuzzi Inc (P-6017)*

Jacuzzi Products Co (DH).. C 909 606-1416
13925 City Center Dr Ste 200 Chino Hills (91709) *(P-4027)*

Jacuzzi Products Co .... B 909 548-7732
14525 Monte Vista Ave Chino (91710) *(P-4028)*

Jada Group Inc .... D 626 810-8382
18521 Railroad St City Of Industry (91748) *(P-8488)*

Jada Toys, City Of Industry *Also Called: Jada Group Inc (P-8488)*

Jade Inc .... D 818 365-7137
11126 Sepulveda Blvd Ste B Mission Hills (91345) *(P-1012)*

Jade Gilbert Dental Corp .... C 805 583-5700
1197 E Los Angeles Ave Ste E Simi Valley (93065) *(P-15519)*

Jade Products, Brea *Also Called: Jade Range LLC (P-6385)*

Jade Range LLC .... C 714 961-2400
2650 Orbiter St Brea (92821) *(P-6385)*

Jae Electronics Inc (HQ) .... E 949 753-2600
142 Technology Dr Ste 100 Irvine (92618) *(P-10256)*

Jafra Cosmetics, Westlake Village *Also Called: Jafra Cosmetics Intl Inc (P-11688)*

Jafra Cosmetics Intl Inc (DH) .... D 805 449-3000
1 Baxter Way Ste 150 Westlake Village (91362) *(P-11688)*

Jag Professional Services Inc .... C 310 945-5648
2008 Walnut Ave Manhattan Beach (90266) *(P-18326)*

Jaguar Energy LLC (PA)... E 949 706-7060
2404 Colony Plz Newport Beach (92660) *(P-338)*

Jake Hey Incorporated .... C 323 856-5280
257 S Lake St Burbank (91502) *(P-14429)*

Jakks, Santa Monica *Also Called: Jakks Pacific Inc (P-8489)*

Jakks Pacific Inc (PA).. D 424 268-9444
2951 28th St Santa Monica (90405) *(P-8489)*

Jakks Pacific Inc .... E 909 594-7771
21749 Baker Pkwy Walnut (91789) *(P-8490)*

Jakov Dulcich and Sons LLC .... C 661 792-6360
31956 Peterson Rd Mc Farland (93250) *(P-34)*

Jal Avionet USA (HQ)... E 310 606-1000
300 Continental Blvd # 190 El Segundo (90245) *(P-10012)*

Jam City Inc .... D 804 920-8760
2255 N Ontario St Burbank (91504) *(P-13956)*

Jamboree Management, Laguna Hills *Also Called: Jamboree Realty Corp (P-12472)*

Jamboree Realty Corp (PA).. C 949 380-0300
22982 Mill Creek Dr Laguna Hills (92653) *(P-12472)*

James Allen Productions LLC .... D 951 944-2564
11801 Pierce St Riverside (92505) *(P-14918)*

James G Meyers & Associates .... E 858 622-2165
4353 La Jolla Village Dr Ste 180 San Diego (92122) *(P-15535)*

James H Cowan & Associates Inc .... D 310 457-2574
5126 Clareton Dr Ste 200 Agoura Hills (91301) *(P-211)*

James Hardie Building Pdts Inc .... D 949 348-1800
26300 La Alameda Ste 400 Mission Viejo (92691) *(P-4355)*

James Hardie Building Pdts Inc .... D 909 355-6500
10901 Elm Ave Fontana (92337) *(P-9923)*

James Hardie Trading Co Inc .... C 949 582-2378
26300 La Alameda Ste 400 Mission Viejo (92691) *(P-3844)*

James Jones Company .... A 909 418-2558
1470 S Vintage Ave Ontario (91761) *(P-5367)*

James Litho, Rancho Cucamonga *Also Called: Eclipse Prtg & Graphics LLC (P-3005)*

James Metals, Riverside *Also Called: Harbor Pipe and Steel Inc (P-10139)*

James R Gldwell Dntl Crmics In (PA)....................................... A 800 854-7256
4141 Macarthur Blvd Newport Beach (92660) *(P-16343)*

James Rebecca Prouty Entps Inc .... D 951 292-9777
43980 Margarita Rd Ste 102 Temecula (92592) *(P-16399)*

James Tobin Cellars Inc .... E 805 239-2204
8950 Union Rd Paso Robles (93446) *(P-1576)*

Jameson Inn, North Hollywood *Also Called: Park Management Group LLC (P-12968)*

Jan-Al Cases, Los Angeles *Also Called: Jan-Al Innerprizes Inc (P-4296)*

Jan-Al Innerprizes Inc .... E 323 260-7212
3339 Union Pacific Ave Los Angeles (90023) *(P-4296)*

Jan-Kens Enameling Company Inc .... E 626 358-1849
715 E Cypress Ave Monrovia (91016) *(P-5326)*

Mergent email: customerrelations@mergent.com
1068

2025 Southern California
Business Directory and Buyers Guide

(P-0000) Products & Services Section entry number
(PA)=Parent Co (HQ)=Headquarters (DH)=Div Headquarters

Janco Corporation .... C 818 361-3366
  13955 Balboa Blvd Rancho Cascades (91342) *(P-7014)*

Jandy Pool Products, Carlsbad *Also Called: Zodiac Pool Systems LLC (P-6040)*

Janin .... C 323 564-0995
  10031 Hunt Ave South Gate (90280) *(P-2103)*

Jano Graphics, Oxnard *Also Called: National Graphics LLC (P-3048)*

Jans Enterprises Corporation .... E 626 575-2000
  4181 Temple City Blvd Ste A El Monte (91731) *(P-10949)*

Jansen Ornamental Supply Co .... E 626 442-0271
  10926 Schmidt Rd El Monte (91733) *(P-5066)*

Janssen Research & Dev LLC .... C 858 450-2000
  3210 Merryfield Row San Diego (92121) *(P-3433)*

Janus Et Cie (PA) .... C 800 245-2687
  12310 Greenstone Ave Santa Fe Springs (90670) *(P-9875)*

Janux, San Diego *Also Called: Janux Therapeutics Inc (P-3434)*

Janux Therapeutics Inc .... D 858 751-4493
  10955 Vista Sorrento Pkwy Ste 200 San Diego (92130) *(P-3434)*

Jariet Technologies Inc .... E 310 698-1000
  103 W Torrance Blvd Redondo Beach (90277) *(P-7727)*

Jarrow Formulas Inc (PA) .... D 310 204-6936
  15233 Ventura Blvd Fl 900 Sherman Oaks (91403) *(P-10628)*

Jarrow Industries LLC (PA) .... D 562 906-1919
  12246 Hawkins St Santa Fe Springs (90670) *(P-3435)*

Jason Incorporated .... E 562 921-9821
  13006 Philadelphia St Ste 305 Whittier (90601) *(P-4483)*

Jason Markk Inc (PA) .... E 213 687-7060
  15325 Blackburn Ave Norwalk (90650) *(P-3607)*

Jason Tool and Engineering Inc .... E 714 895-5067
  7101 Honold Cir Garden Grove (92841) *(P-4145)*

Jason's Natural, Bell *Also Called: Hain Celestial Group Inc (P-3656)*

Jasper Electronics .... E 714 917-0749
  1580 N Kellogg Dr Anaheim (92807) *(P-7015)*

Javo Beverage Company Inc .... D 760 560-5286
  1311 Specialty Dr Vista (92081) *(P-1685)*

Jaxx Manufacturing Inc .... E 805 526-4979
  1912 Angus Ave Simi Valley (93063) *(P-7016)*

Jay's Catering, Garden Grove *Also Called: Mastroianni Family Entps Ltd (P-13179)*

Jaya Apparel Group LLC (PA) .... D 323 584-3500
  2761 Fruitland Ave Fl 2 Los Angeles (90058) *(P-2104)*

Jayco/Mmi Inc .... E 951 738-2000
  1351 Pico St Corona (92881) *(P-7017)*

Jayone Foods Inc .... E 562 633-7400
  7212 Alondra Blvd Paramount (90723) *(P-1794)*

Jazz Semiconductor, Newport Beach *Also Called: Newport Fab LLC (P-6860)*

Jazzercise, Carlsbad *Also Called: Jazzercise Inc (P-15051)*

Jazzercise Inc (PA) .... D 760 476-1750
  2460 Impala Dr Carlsbad (92010) *(P-15051)*

JB Bostick LLC (PA) .... D 714 238-2121
  2870 E La Cresta Ave Anaheim (92806) *(P-628)*

JB Dental Supply Co Inc (PA) .... C 310 202-8855
  17000 Kingsview Ave Carson (90746) *(P-10087)*

JB Plastics Inc .... E 714 541-8500
  1921 E Edinger Ave Santa Ana (92705) *(P-4146)*

Jbi LLC .... E 310 537-2910
  18521 S Santa Fe Ave Compton (90221) *(P-2470)*

Jbi LLC (PA) .... C 310 886-8034
  2650 E El Presidio St Long Beach (90810) *(P-2614)*

Jbi Interiors, Long Beach *Also Called: Jbi LLC (P-2614)*

Jbs Case Ready, Riverside *Also Called: Swift Beef Company (P-1273)*

JBW Precision Inc .... E 805 499-1973
  2650 Lavery Ct Newbury Park (91320) *(P-4993)*

JC Ford, La Habra *Also Called: J C Ford Company (P-5676)*

JC Industries, Los Angeles *Also Called: J C Trimming Company Inc (P-2065)*

JC Penney, San Bernardino *Also Called: Penney Opco LLC (P-9098)*

JC Penney, Thousand Oaks *Also Called: Penney Opco LLC (P-11262)*

JC Penney, Arcadia *Also Called: Penney Opco LLC (P-11263)*

JC Penney 1505, West Covina *Also Called: Penney Opco LLC (P-11264)*

JC Resorts LLC .... B 760 944-1936
  4154 Maryland St San Diego (92103) *(P-17995)*

JC Resorts LLC .... C 855 574-5356
  17550 Bernardo Oaks Dr San Diego (92128) *(P-17996)*

JC Resorts LLC .... A 949 376-2779
  1555 S Coast Hwy Laguna Beach (92651) *(P-17997)*

JC Sales, Commerce *Also Called: Shims Bargain Inc (P-500)*

JC Supply & Manufacturing, Ontario *Also Called: Lightcap Industries Inc (P-4846)*

JC Weight Loss Centres Inc (PA) .... C 760 696-4000
  5770 Fleet St Carlsbad (92008) *(P-13177)*

JC Window Fashions, Whittier *Also Called: JC Window Fashions Inc (P-2603)*

JC Window Fashions Inc .... E 909 364-8888
  2438 Peck Rd Whittier (90601) *(P-2603)*

Jc's Pie Pops, Chatsworth *Also Called: We The Pie People LLC (P-1321)*

Jci Metal Products (PA) .... D 619 229-8206
  6540 Federal Blvd Lemon Grove (91945) *(P-4840)*

Jcm Engineering Corp .... D 909 923-3730
  2690 E Cedar St Ontario (91761) *(P-10494)*

Jcr Aircraft Deburring LLC .... D 714 870-4427
  221 Foundation Ave La Habra (90631) *(P-5270)*

Jcr Deburring, La Habra *Also Called: Jcr Aircraft Deburring LLC (P-5270)*

JD Processing Inc .... E 714 972-8161
  2220 Cape Cod Way Santa Ana (92703) *(P-5271)*

Jd/Cmc Inc .... E 818 767-2260
  2834 E 11th St Los Angeles (90023) *(P-2105)*

Jdh Pacific Inc (PA) .... E 562 926-8088
  1818 E Orangethorpe Ave Fullerton (92831) *(P-4558)*

Jdi Distribution, Redlands *Also Called: Bakell LLC (P-472)*

Jdz Inc .... D 858 549-9888
  9990 Alesmith Ct San Diego (92126) *(P-1544)*

Jeanne Jugan, A Residence, San Pedro *Also Called: Little Ssters of The Poor Los (P-15700)*

Jeb Holdings Corp .... E 951 296-9900
  42033 Rio Nedo Temecula (92590) *(P-4634)*

Jeb Holdings Corp (PA) .... D 951 659-2183
  54125 Maranatha Dr Idyllwild (92549) *(P-10257)*

Jeckys Best Inc .... E 661 259-1313
  26450 Summit Cir Santa Clarita (91350) *(P-10821)*

Jeep Chrysler Ddge Ram Ontario, Ontario *Also Called: Jeep Chrysler of Ontario (P-11366)*

Jeep Chrysler of Ontario .... D 909 390-9898
  1202 Auto Center Dr Ontario (91761) *(P-11366)*

Jeep Gear, Irvine *Also Called: Alcone Marketing Group Inc (P-13195)*

Jeeva Corporation .... D 909 238-4073
  750 E E St Unit B Ontario (91764) *(P-928)*

Jeffer Mngels Btlr Mtchell LLP (PA) .... C 310 203-8080
  1900 Avenue Of The Stars Fl 7 Los Angeles (90067) *(P-16710)*

Jeffrey Court, Norco *Also Called: Jeffrey Court Inc (P-1040)*

Jeffrey Court Inc .... D 951 340-3383
  620 Parkridge Ave Norco (92860) *(P-1040)*

Jeffrey Fabrication LLC .... E 562 634-3101
  6323 Alondra Blvd Paramount (90723) *(P-4994)*

Jeffries Global Inc .... D 888 255-3488
  8484 Wilshire Blvd Ste 605 Beverly Hills (90211) *(P-1211)*

Jeld-Wen Inc .... C 800 468-3667
  3760 Convoy St Ste 111 San Diego (92111) *(P-2311)*

Jold Won Ino .... C 909 079-0700
  120 S Cedar Ave Rialto (92376) *(P-9924)*

Jelenko, San Diego *Also Called: Argen Corporation (P-4579)*

Jellco Container Inc .... D 714 666-2728
  1151 N Tustin Ave Anaheim (92807) *(P-2677)*

Jellypop, Pasadena *Also Called: Evolution Design Lab Inc (P-4284)*

Jenco Productions LLC (PA) .... C 909 381-9453
  401 S J St San Bernardino (92410) *(P-14520)*

Jeneric/Pentron Incorporated (HQ) .... C 203 265-7397
  1717 W Collins Ave Orange (92867) *(P-8339)*

Jenny Craig, Carlsbad *Also Called: JC Weight Loss Centres Inc (P-13177)*

Jensen Enterprises Inc .... B 909 357-7264
  14221 San Bernardino Ave Fontana (92335) *(P-4398)*

Jensen Meat Company Inc .... D 619 754-6400
  2550 Britannia Blvd Ste 101 San Diego (92154) *(P-10873)*

Jensen Precast, Fontana *Also Called: Jensen Enterprises Inc (P-4398)*

Jerde Partnership Intl, Los Angeles *Also Called: The Jerde Partnership Inc (P-17694)*

Jerry Leigh Entertainment AP, Van Nuys *Also Called: Leigh Jerry California Inc (P-2166)*

Jerry Melton & Sons Cnstr, Taft *Also Called: Jerry Melton & Sons Cnstr Inc (P-339)*

A
L
P
H
A
B
E
T
I
C

Employee Codes: A=Over 500 employees, B=251-500
C=101-250, D=51-100, E=20-50, F=10-19, G=1-9

2025 Southern California
Business Directory and Buyers Guide

© Mergent Inc. 1-800-342-5647
1069

Jerry Melton & Sons Cnstr Inc .... D 661 765-5546
100 Jamison Ln Taft (93268) *(P-339)*

Jessie Lord, Torrance *Also Called: Jessie Lord Bakery LLC (P-11296)*

Jessie Lord Bakery LLC .... E 310 533-6010
21100 S Western Ave Torrance (90501) *(P-11296)*

Jet Air Fbo LLC .... E 619 448-5991
681 Kenney St El Cajon (92020) *(P-7507)*

Jet Cutting Solutions Inc .... E 909 948-2424
10853 Bell Ct Rancho Cucamonga (91730) *(P-6152)*

Jet Delivery Inc (PA) .... D 800 716-7177
2169 Wright Ave La Verne (91750) *(P-9005)*

Jet Fleet International Corp .... E 310 440-3820
2370 Westwood Blvd Ste K Los Angeles (90064) *(P-13178)*

Jet Plastics (PA) .... E 323 268-6706
941 N Eastern Ave Los Angeles (90063) *(P-4147)*

Jet Products, San Diego *Also Called: Senior Operations LLC (P-6234)*

Jet Propulsion Laboratory, Pasadena *Also Called: California Institute Tech (P-17869)*

Jet Sets, North Hollywood *Also Called: M Gaw Inc (P-1215)*

Jetfax, Los Angeles *Also Called: Efaxcom (P-5914)*

Jetro Cash and Carry Entps LLC .... D 619 233-0200
1709 Main St San Diego (92113) *(P-10874)*

Jetro Holdings LLC .... C 213 516-0301
1611 E Washington Blvd Los Angeles (90021) *(P-10046)*

Jetro Holdings LLC .... B 858 564-0466
7466 Carroll Rd Ste 100 San Diego (92121) *(P-10047)*

Jetzero Inc (PA) .... E 949 474-8222
4150 E Donald Douglas Dr Long Beach (90808) *(P-7359)*

Jewelry Exchange, The, Tustin *Also Called: Diamond Goldenwest Corporation (P-11638)*

Jewish Cmnty Fndtion Los Angle (PA) .... C 323 761-8700
6505 Wilshire Blvd Ste 1150 Los Angeles (90048) *(P-17349)*

Jewish Community Center, Long Beach *Also Called: Jewish Community Ctr Long Bch (P-16962)*

Jewish Community Ctr Long Bch .... C 562 426-7601
3801 E Willow St Long Beach (90815) *(P-16962)*

Jewish Family Service, San Diego *Also Called: Jewish Family Svc San Diego (P-16964)*

Jewish Family Svc Los Angeles .... C 323 937-5900
330 N Fairfax Ave Los Angeles (90036) *(P-16963)*

Jewish Family Svc San Diego (PA) .... C 858 637-3000
8804 Balboa Ave San Diego (92123) *(P-16964)*

Jewish HM For The Aging Ornge .... C 949 364-9685
27356 Bellogente Mission Viejo (92691) *(P-15684)*

Jewish Journal, The, Los Angeles *Also Called: Tribe Mdia Corp A Cal Nnprfit (P-2834)*

Jewish Synagogue, Los Angeles *Also Called: Temple Israel of Hollywood (P-13159)*

Jezowski & Markel Contrs Inc .... C 714 978-2222
749 N Poplar St Orange (92868) *(P-1122)*

Jf Fixtures & Design, Long Beach *Also Called: F-J-E Inc (P-2564)*

JF Shea Construction Inc (HQ) .... C 909 594-9500
655 Brea Canyon Rd Walnut (91789) *(P-409)*

Jfc International Inc .... C 323 721-6900
7140 Bandini Blvd Commerce (90040) *(P-10950)*

Jfc International Inc (HQ) .... C 323 721-6100
7101 E Slauson Ave Commerce (90040) *(P-10951)*

Jfe Shoji America Holdings Inc (DH) .... D 562 637-3500
301 E Ocean Blvd Ste 1750 Long Beach (90802) *(P-10141)*

Jff Uniforms, Torrance *Also Called: Just For Fun Inc (P-1985)*

JFK Memorial Hospital Inc .... C 760 347-6191
47111 Monroe St Indio (92201) *(P-16029)*

JG Plastics Group LLC .... E 714 751-4266
335 Fischer Ave Costa Mesa (92626) *(P-4148)*

Jh Biotech, Ventura *Also Called: Jh Biotech Inc (P-3749)*

Jh Biotech Inc (PA) .... E 805 650-8933
4951 Olivas Park Dr Ventura (93003) *(P-3749)*

Jh Design Group .... D 213 747-5700
940 W Washington Blvd Los Angeles (90015) *(P-2014)*

Jhawar Industries LLC .... E 951 340-4646
525 Klug Cir Corona (92878) *(P-5801)*

Jhc Investment Inc .... D 714 751-2400
7 Hutton Centre Dr Santa Ana (92707) *(P-12878)*

Jiffy Lube, Tustin *Also Called: Allied Lube Inc (P-14685)*

Jim Burke Ford, Bakersfield *Also Called: Haberfelde Ford (P-11358)*

Jim ONeal Distributing Inc .... E 805 426-3300
799 Camarillo Springs Rd Camarillo (93012) *(P-11482)*

Jim-Buoy, North Hollywood *Also Called: Cal-June Inc (P-4761)*

Jim's Machining, Camarillo *Also Called: Thiessen Products Inc (P-6248)*

Jimenes Food Inc .... E 562 602-2505
7046 Jackson St Paramount (90723) *(P-1795)*

Jimenez Nursery Inc .... D 805 684-7955
3800 Via Real Carpinteria (93013) *(P-212)*

Jimenez Nursery and Landscapes, Carpinteria *Also Called: Jimenez Nursery Inc (P-212)*

Jims Supply Co Inc (PA) .... D 661 616-6977
3500 Buck Owens Blvd Bakersfield (93308) *(P-10142)*

Jimway Inc .... D 310 886-3718
20101 S Santa Fe Ave Compton (90221) *(P-6505)*

Jipcob Inc .... C 661 859-1111
3709 Rosedale Hwy Bakersfield (93308) *(P-11580)*

JIT Manufacturing Inc .... E 805 238-5000
1610 Commerce Way Paso Robles (93446) *(P-8177)*

Jitterbug, San Diego *Also Called: Greatcall Inc (P-11685)*

Jj Acquisitions LLC .... E 818 772-0100
8501 Fallbrook Ave Ste 370 West Hills (91304) *(P-3918)*

JJ Mac Intyre Co Inc (PA) .... C 951 898-4300
4160 Temescal Canyon Rd Ste 601 Corona (92883) *(P-13286)*

Jk Imaging Ltd .... D 310 755-6848
14067 Stage Rd Santa Fe Springs (90670) *(P-9967)*

JKL Components Corporation .... E 818 896-0019
13343 Paxton St Pacoima (91331) *(P-6484)*

Jkv Inc .... E 562 948-3000
8343 Loch Lomond Dr Pico Rivera (90660) *(P-2678)*

JI Design Enterprises Inc .... D 714 479-0240
37407 Industry Way Murrieta (92563) *(P-1984)*

JI Racing.com, Murrieta *Also Called: JI Design Enterprises Inc (P-1984)*

Jlabs, San Diego *Also Called: Johnson Johnson Innovation LLC (P-18327)*

Jlcooper, El Segundo *Also Called: J L Cooper Electronics Inc (P-7013)*

Jlg Industries Inc .... E 951 358-1915
7820 Lincoln Ave Riverside (92504) *(P-5495)*

Jlg Serviceplus, Riverside *Also Called: Jlg Industries Inc (P-5495)*

JLJ Rebar Extreme Inc .... E 909 381-9177
1532 Wall Ave San Bernardino (92404) *(P-5097)*

Jlm & Mag Associates Inc .... D 562 869-3343
9204 Lakewood Blvd Downey (90240) *(P-13149)*

JM Eagle, Perris *Also Called: J-M Manufacturing Company Inc (P-3275)*

JM Eagle, Los Angeles *Also Called: J-M Manufacturing Company Inc (P-3975)*

JM Eagle, Los Angeles *Also Called: Pw Eagle Inc (P-3978)*

JM Huber Micropowders Inc .... E 714 994-7855
16024 Phoebe Ave La Mirada (90638) *(P-3239)*

Jmbm, Los Angeles *Also Called: Jeffer Mngels Btlr Mtchell LLP (P-16710)*

Jmc Closing Co LLC .... E 951 278-9900
1499 Palmyrita Ave Riverside (92507) *(P-6153)*

Jme Inc (PA) .... D 201 896-8600
527 Park Ave San Fernando (91340) *(P-10187)*

Jmg Security Systems Inc .... D 714 545-8882
17150 Newhope St Ste 109 Fountain Valley (92708) *(P-929)*

Jmh Engineering and Cnstr .... D 562 317-1700
2825 Temple Ave Signal Hill (90755) *(P-410)*

JMJ Enterprises Inc .... C 818 343-5151
5973 Reseda Blvd Tarzana (91356) *(P-11581)*

Jmmca Inc (PA) .... D 619 448-2711
850 W Bradley Ave El Cajon (92020) *(P-5143)*

JMS Interiors Inc .... D 619 749-5098
10735 Prospect Ave Santee (92071) *(P-14521)*

Jmw Truss and Components, San Diego *Also Called: Trademark Construction Co Inc (P-7101)*

JNJ Apparel Inc .... E 323 584-9700
18788 Fairfield Rd Porter Ranch (91326) *(P-2106)*

Job Options Incorporated .... A 909 890-4612
1110 S Washington Ave San Bernardino (92408) *(P-13144)*

Jobbers Meat Packing Co LLC .... C 323 585-6328
3336 Fruitland Ave Vernon (90058) *(P-1244)*

Jobot LLC .... A 949 688-2000
3101 W Coast Hwy Ste 200 Newport Beach (92663) *(P-13530)*

Mergent email: customerrelations@mergent.com
1070

2025 Southern California
Business Directory and Buyers Guide

(P-0000) Products & Services Section entry number
(PA)=Parent Co (HQ)=Headquarters (DH)=Div Headquarters

Jodi Kristopher LLC (PA).................... D 323 890-8000
1950 Naomi Ave Los Angeles (90011) *(P-2066)*

Jody of California, Los Angeles *Also Called: Private Brand Mdsg Corp (P-2069)*

Joe & Mary Mottino YMCA, Encinitas *Also Called: YMCA of San Diego County (P-17397)*

Joe Blasco Cosmetics, Palm Springs *Also Called: Joe Blasco Enterprises Inc (P-8688)*

Joe Blasco Enterprises Inc................ E 323 467-4949
1285 N Valdivia Way # A Palm Springs (92262) *(P-8688)*

Joe Heger Farms LLC........................... C 760 353-5111
1625 Drew Rd El Centro (92243) *(P-83)*

Joe Wells Enterprises Inc.................... E
1500 S Sunkist St Ste D Anaheim (92806) *(P-2015)*

Joe's Auto Parks, Los Angeles *Also Called: L and R Auto Parks Inc (P-14657)*

Joe's Dsert Hlls Prmium Otlets, Cabazon *Also Called: Centric Brands Inc (P-1874)*

Joes Plastics, Vernon *Also Called: Joes Plastics Inc (P-3277)*

Joes Plastics Inc................................. E 323 771-8433
5725 District Blvd Vernon (90058) *(P-3277)*

Johanson Technology Inc..................... C 805 575-0124
4001 Calle Tecate Camarillo (93012) *(P-6919)*

Johasee Rebar, Corona *Also Called: Johasee Rebar Inc (P-4841)*

Johasee Rebar Inc.............................. E 661 589-0972
26365 Earthmover Cir Corona (92883) *(P-4841)*

John Alden Life Insurance Co.............. C 818 595-7600
20950 Warner Center Ln Ste A Woodland Hills (91367) *(P-12044)*

John Bean Technologies Corp............. D 951 222-2300
1660 Iowa Ave Ste 100 Riverside (92507) *(P-5677)*

John Bishop Design Inc...................... E 714 744-2300
731 N Main St Orange (92868) *(P-8610)*

John Collins Co Inc............................ D 818 227-2190
5155 Cedarwood Rd Bonita (91902) *(P-12355)*

John Deere Authorized Dealer, Colton *Also Called: A-Z Bus Sales Inc (P-9795)*

John Deere Authorized Dealer, Poway *Also Called: Bay City Equipment Inds Inc (P-10172)*

John Deere Authorized Dealer, City Of Industry *Also Called: Valley Power Systems Inc (P-10413)*

John Digiovanni DDS Ms.................... D 949 640-0202
1401 Avocado Ave Newport Beach (92660) *(P-15335)*

John F Kennedy Mem Hosp Aux.......... A 760 347-6191
47111 Monroe St Indio (92201) *(P-16030)*

John Hancock, Los Angeles *Also Called: John Hancock Life Insur Co USA (P-12223)*

John Hancock, San Diego *Also Called: John Hancock Life Insur Co USA (P-12224)*

John Hancock Life Insur Co USA......... B 949 254-1440
5000 Birch St Ste 120 Newport Beach (92660) *(P-12045)*

John Hancock Life Insur Co USA (DH)... A 213 689-0813
865 S Figueroa St Ste 3320 Los Angeles (90017) *(P-12223)*

John Hancock Life Insur Co USA......... B 858 292-1667
10180 Telesis Ct San Diego (92121) *(P-12224)*

John Jory Corporation (PA)................. B 714 279-7901
2180 N Glassell St Orange (92865) *(P-1013)*

John L Conley Inc.............................. D 909 627-0981
4344 Mission Blvd Montclair (91763) *(P-5080)*

John List Corporation......................... E 818 882-7848
9732 Cozycroft Ave Chatsworth (91311) *(P-5639)*

John M Frank Construction Inc............ D 714 210-3600
913 E 4th St Santa Ana (92701) *(P-550)*

John M Frank Service Group, Santa Ana *Also Called: John M Frank Construction Inc (P-550)*

John M Phillips LLC............................ E 661 327-3118
2800 Gibson St Bakersfield (93308) *(P-340)*

John M Phillips Oil Field Eqp, Bakersfield *Also Called: John M Phillips LLC (P-340)*

JOHN TILLMAN COMPANY (DH).......... D 310 764-0110
1300 W Artesia Blvd Compton (90220) *(P-10378)*

John Wayne Airport, Costa Mesa *Also Called: County of Orange (P-9198)*

John's Incredible Pizza Co, Bakersfield *Also Called: Jipcob Inc (P-11580)*

Johnny Was LLC................................ D 310 656-0600
395 Santa Monica Pl Ste 124 Santa Monica (90401) *(P-10710)*

Johnny Was Showroom, Los Angeles *Also Called: Jwc Studio Inc (P-2067)*

Johns Manville Corporation................. D 323 568-2220
4301 Firestone Blvd South Gate (90280) *(P-4492)*

Johnson & Johnson............................ B 909 839-8650
15715 Arrow Hwy Irwindale (91706) *(P-8279)*

Johnson & Johnson Vision, Irvine *Also Called: Johnson Jhnson Srgcal Vsion In (P-8386)*

Johnson Caldraul Inc.......................... E 951 340-1067
220 N Delilah St Ste 101 Corona (92879) *(P-7508)*

Johnson Cntrls Fire Prtction L............. C 858 633-9100
3568 Ruffin Rd San Diego (92123) *(P-6687)*

Johnson Cntrls SEC Sltions LLC.......... D 561 988-3600
3870 Murphy Canyon Rd Ste 140 San Diego (92123) *(P-14408)*

Johnson Contrls Authorized Dlr, Montebello *Also Called: Johnstone Supply Inc (P-11537)*

Johnson Controls............................... C 562 405-3817
12728 Shoemaker Ave Santa Fe Springs (90670) *(P-14409)*

Johnson Controls, Riverside *Also Called: Clarios LLC (P-2537)*

Johnson Controls, Palm Desert *Also Called: Clarios LLC (P-2538)*

Johnson Controls, Simi Valley *Also Called: Clarios LLC (P-2539)*

Johnson Controls, Whittier *Also Called: Johnson Controls Inc (P-2545)*

Johnson Controls, Cypress *Also Called: Johnson Controls Inc (P-2546)*

Johnson Controls Inc.......................... E 562 698-8301
12393 Slauson Ave Whittier (90606) *(P-2545)*

Johnson Controls Inc.......................... C 562 594-3200
5770 Warland Dr Ste A Cypress (90630) *(P-2546)*

Johnson doc Enterprises..................... E 818 764-1543
11933 Vose St North Hollywood (91605) *(P-3919)*

Johnson Fain, Los Angeles *Also Called: Johnson Fain Inc (P-17677)*

Johnson Fain Inc................................ D 323 224-6000
1201 N Broadway Los Angeles (90012) *(P-17677)*

Johnson Ford (PA).............................. C 661 206-2597
1155 Auto Mall Dr Lancaster (93534) *(P-11367)*

Johnson Jhnson Srgcal Vsion In (HQ)... B 949 581-5799
31 Technology Dr Bldg 29a Irvine (92618) *(P-8386)*

Johnson Johnson Innovation LLC......... B 858 242-1504
3210 Merryfield Row San Diego (92121) *(P-18327)*

Johnson Laminating Coating Inc.......... D 310 635-4929
20631 Annalee Ave Carson (90746) *(P-3964)*

Johnson Manufacturing Inc................. E 714 903-0393
15201 Connector Ln Huntington Beach (92649) *(P-6154)*

Johnson Matthey Inc.......................... C 858 716-2400
12205 World Trade Dr San Diego (92128) *(P-4586)*

Johnson Outdoors Inc......................... D 619 402-1023
1166 Fesler St Ste A El Cajon (92020) *(P-8529)*

Johnson Racing, Santa Maria *Also Called: Alan Johnson Prfmce Engrg Inc (P-7164)*

Johnson Wilshire Inc.......................... E 562 777-0088
17343 Freedom Way City Of Industry (91748) *(P-8280)*

Johnson-Peltier.................................. D 562 944-3408
12021 Shoemaker Ave Santa Fe Springs (90670) *(P-930)*

Johnson-Peltier, Santa Fe Springs *Also Called: Johnson-Peltier (P-930)*

Johnston International Corporation....... E 714 542-4487
14272 Chambers Rd Tustin (92780) *(P-5825)*

Johnstone Supply Inc......................... D 323 722-2859
8040 Slauson Ave Montebello (90640) *(P-11537)*

Joico Laboratories Inc........................ E 626 321-4100
5800 Bristol Pkwy Culver City (90230) *(P-3662)*

Joimax Inc.. E 949 859-3472
140 Technology Dr Ste 150 Irvine (92618) *(P-8178)*

Jolly Roger Games, Commerce *Also Called: Ultra Pro International LLC (P-10530)*

Jolly Roger Inn, Anaheim *Also Called: Edward Thomas Companies (P-12817)*

Jolyn Clothing Company LLC.............. E 714 794-2149
16390 Pacific Coast Hwy Ste 201 Huntington Beach (92649) *(P-2107)*

Jomar Table Linens Inc....................... D 909 390-1444
4000 E Airport Dr Ste A Ontario (91761) *(P-2211)*

Jon Brooks Inc (PA)........................... D 626 330-0631
14400 Lomitas Ave City Of Industry (91746) *(P-4488)*

Jon Davler Inc................................... E 626 941-6558
9440 Gidley St Temple City (91780) *(P-11689)*

Jon-Lin Foods, Colton *Also Called: Jon-Lin Frozen Foods (P-10822)*

Jon-Lin Frozen Foods (PA).................. D 909 825-8542
1620 N 8th St Colton (92324) *(P-10822)*

Jonathan Beach Club, Santa Monica *Also Called: Jonathan Club (P-15141)*

Jonathan Club................................... D 310 393-9245
850 Palisades Beach Rd Santa Monica (90403) *(P-15141)*

Jonathan Club (PA)............................ C 213 624-0881
545 S Figueroa St Los Angeles (90071) *(P-17350)*

Jonathan Engnred Slutions Corp (HQ)... E 714 665-4400
250 Commerce Ste 100 Irvine (92602) *(P-4775)*

A L P H A B E T I C

Employee Codes: A=Over 500 employees, B=251-500
C=101-250, D=51-100, E=20-50, F=10-19, G=1-9

2025 Southern California
Business Directory and Buyers Guide

© Mergent Inc. 1-800-342-5647
1071

Jonathan Martin, Los Angeles *Also Called: Harkham Industries Inc (P-2039)*

Jondo Ltd (HQ)..D 714 279-2300
 22700 Savi Ranch Pkwy Yorba Linda (92887) *(P-8431)*

Jones Brothers Cnstr Corp (PA)..................................D 310 470-1885
 1601 Cloverfield Blvd Santa Monica (90404) *(P-551)*

Jones Day ....C 213 489-3939
 555 S Flower St Fl 50 Los Angeles (90071) *(P-16711)*

Jones Sign Co Inc ....C 858 569-1400
 9474 Chesapeake Dr Ste 902 San Diego (92123) *(P-8611)*

Jones Signs Co Inc ....C 858 569-1400
 9025 Balboa Ave Ste 150 San Diego (92123) *(P-10048)*

Joni and Friends Foundation (PA)................................D 818 707-5664
 30009 Ladyface Ct Agoura (91301) *(P-16965)*

Jonset LLC ....D 949 551-5151
 16251 Construction Cir W Irvine (92606) *(P-9787)*

Joong-Ang Daily News Cal Inc ....D 858 573-1111
 7750 Dagget St Ste 208 San Diego (92111) *(P-2806)*

Joong-Ang Daily News Cal Inc, Los Angeles *Also Called: Joongangilbo Usa Inc (P-2807)*

JOONG-ANG DAILY NEWS CALIFORNIA, INC., San Diego *Also Called: Joong-Ang Daily News Cal Inc (P-2806)*

Joongangilbo Usa Inc (DH)..C 213 368-2512
 690 Wilshire Pl Los Angeles (90005) *(P-2807)*

Jordache Enterprises Inc ....C 714 978-1901
 20 City Blvd W Orange (92868) *(P-12299)*

Jordano's Food Service, Santa Barbara *Also Called: Jordanos Inc (P-11050)*

Jordanos Inc (PA)..C 805 964-0611
 550 S Patterson Ave Santa Barbara (93111) *(P-11050)*

Jose Perez ....E 920 318-6527
 41403 Stork Ct Lake Elsinore (92532) *(P-5517)*

Joseph Manufacturing Co Inc ....D 626 334-1471
 411 N Aerojet Dr Azusa (91702) *(P-2547)*

Joshua A Siembieda MD PC ....D 714 543-8911
 1310 W Stewart Dr Ste 212 Orange (92868) *(P-13601)*

Joslyn Sunbank Company LLC ....B 805 238-2840
 1740 Commerce Way Paso Robles (93446) *(P-6953)*

Jourducci Inc ....C 626 791-9400
 841 W Foothill Blvd Azusa (91702) *(P-13137)*

Jowett Garments Factory Inc ....E 626 350-0515
 10359 Rush St South El Monte (91733) *(P-2108)*

Jowett Group, South El Monte *Also Called: Jowett Garments Factory Inc (P-2108)*

Joybird, Los Angeles *Also Called: Stitch Industries Inc (P-2460)*

JP Allen Extended Stay (PA).......................................D 818 956-0202
 450 Pioneer Dr Glendale (91203) *(P-12879)*

JP Products LLC ....E 310 237-6237
 2054 Davie Ave Commerce (90040) *(P-2427)*

Jpl Global LLC ....E 888 274-7744
 4635 Wade Ave Perris (92571) *(P-10351)*

Jpl Management, Los Angeles *Also Called: Jpl Management LLC (P-17998)*

Jpl Management LLC ....D 310 844-3662
 6427 W Sunset Blvd # 101 Los Angeles (90028) *(P-17998)*

JR Construction Inc ....D 858 505-4760
 8123 Engineer Rd San Diego (92111) *(P-411)*

JR Filanc Cnstr Co Inc (PA).......................................D 760 941-7130
 740 N Andreasen Dr Escondido (92029) *(P-681)*

JR Machine Company Inc ....E 562 903-9477
 13245 Florence Ave Santa Fe Springs (90670) *(P-6155)*

Jri Inc ....E 818 706-2424
 31280 La Baya Dr Westlake Village (91362) *(P-10258)*

Js Apparel Inc ....D 310 631-6333
 1751 E Del Amo Blvd Carson (90746) *(P-2016)*

JS Held LLC ....D 949 390-7647
 4667 Macarthur Blvd Ste 400 Newport Beach (92660) *(P-17736)*

Jsl Foods Inc (PA)..D 323 223-2484
 3550 Pasadena Ave Los Angeles (90031) *(P-1796)*

Jsl Technologies Inc ....B 805 985-7700
 1701 Pacific Ave Ste 270 Oxnard (93033) *(P-17567)*

Jsn Industries Inc ....D 949 458-0050
 9700 Jeronimo Rd Irvine (92618) *(P-4149)*

Jsn Packaging Products Inc ....D 949 458-0050
 9700 Jeronimo Rd Irvine (92618) *(P-3962)*

JT Design Studio Inc (PA)...E 213 891-1500
 860 S Los Angeles St Ste 912 Los Angeles (90014) *(P-2109)*

Jt Resources Inc ....C 661 367-6827
 26372 Ruether Ave Santa Clarita (91350) *(P-13531)*

JT Wimsatt Contg Co Inc (PA).....................................B 661 775-8090
 28064 Avenue Stanford Unit B Valencia (91355) *(P-1123)*

Jt3 LLC ....A 661 277-4900
 190 S Wolfe Ave Bldg 1260 Edwards (93524) *(P-17568)*

Jtb Americas Ltd (HQ)..D 310 406-3121
 3625 Del Amo Blvd Ste 260 Torrance (90503) *(P-9226)*

Jti Elctrcal Instrmntation LLC ....D 661 393-5535
 3901 Fanucchi Way Unit 201 Shafter (93263) *(P-9590)*

Jts Modular Inc ....E 661 835-9270
 7001 Mcdivitt Dr Ste B Bakersfield (93313) *(P-5081)*

Juan Carlos Alvardo ....D 661 758-6128
 1301 Willow Pl Wasco (93280) *(P-139)*

Juanita F Wade ....E 310 519-1208
 435 N Harbor Blvd Ste B1 San Pedro (90731) *(P-2279)*

Juanitas Foods ....C 310 834-5339
 645 George De La Torre Jr Ave Wilmington (90744) *(P-1341)*

Judco Manufacturing Inc (PA).....................................C 310 534-0959
 1429 240th St Harbor City (90710) *(P-6422)*

Judith Von Hopf Inc ....E 909 481-1884
 1525 W 13th St Ste H Upland (91786) *(P-2567)*

Judson Studios Inc ....E 323 255-0131
 200 S Avenue 66 Los Angeles (90042) *(P-4337)*

Judy Ann, Culver City *Also Called: Fortune Casuals LLC (P-2035)*

Judy Ann of California Inc ....C 213 623-9233
 1936 Mateo St Los Angeles (90021) *(P-2040)*

Judy O Productions Inc ....E 323 938-8513
 4858 W Pico Blvd Ste 331 Los Angeles (90019) *(P-2891)*

Juengermann Inc ....E 805 644-7165
 1899 Palma Dr Ste A Ventura (93003) *(P-5380)*

Juice Division, Pacoima *Also Called: American Fruits & Flavors LLC (P-1660)*

Juicy Couture Inc ....C 888 824-8826
 1580 Jesse St Los Angeles (90021) *(P-1896)*

Juicy Whip Inc (PA)...E 909 392-7500
 1668 Curtiss Ct La Verne (91750) *(P-5678)*

Jumper Media, La Jolla *Also Called: Jumper Media LLC (P-2923)*

Jumper Media LLC ....D 831 333-6202
 1719 Alta La Jolla Dr La Jolla (92037) *(P-2923)*

June Group LLC ....D 858 450-4290
 10089 Willow Creek Rd San Diego (92131) *(P-13602)*

Jungle Jumps, Pacoima *Also Called: Twin Peak Industries Inc (P-8550)*

Jungo Inc ....D 619 727-4600
 3033 5th Ave San Diego (92103) *(P-13758)*

Jungotv LLC ....D 650 207-6227
 1800 Vine St Los Angeles (90028) *(P-2924)*

Jupiter Bellflower Doctors Hospital ....B
 3699 Wilshire Blvd Ste 540 Los Angeles (90010) *(P-16031)*

Jurny Inc ....E 888 875-8769
 6600 W Sunset Blvd Los Angeles (90028) *(P-13957)*

Jurupa Community Services Dst ....D 951 685-7073
 11201 Harrel St Riverside (92509) *(P-9697)*

Jurupa Hills Post Acute, Riverside *Also Called: Mt Rubidouxidence Opco LLC (P-15725)*

Just For Fun Inc ....E 310 320-1327
 557 Van Ness Ave Torrance (90501) *(P-1985)*

Just For Wraps Inc (PA)..C 213 239-0503
 4871 S Santa Fe Ave Vernon (90058) *(P-2110)*

Justanswer LLC ....C 800 785-2305
 440 N Barranca Ave # 7508 Covina (91723) *(P-9446)*

Justenough Software Corp Inc (HQ)............................E 949 706-5400
 15440 Laguna Canyon Rd Ste 100 Irvine (92618) *(P-13958)*

Justice Bros Dist Co Inc ....E 626 359-9174
 2734 Huntington Dr Duarte (91010) *(P-3627)*

Justice Bros-J B Car Care Pdts, Duarte *Also Called: Justice Bros Dist Co Inc (P-3627)*

Justin, El Monte *Also Called: Justin Inc (P-6288)*

Justin Inc ....E 626 444-4516
 2663 Lee Ave El Monte (91733) *(P-6288)*

Justman Packaging & Display (PA)..............................D 323 728-8888
 5819 Telegraph Rd Commerce (90040) *(P-10049)*

Juvenile Justice Division Cal ....A 805 485-7951
 3100 Wright Rd Camarillo (93010) *(P-17999)*

Jvckenwood USA Corporation (HQ) .... C 310 639-9000
4001 Worsham Ave Long Beach (90808) *(P-10259)*

Jvr Sheetmetal Fabrication Inc .... E 714 841-2464
7101 Patterson Dr Garden Grove (92841) *(P-7360)*

JW Fulfillment Lax Inc .... D 909 578-9228
4039 State St Montclair (91763) *(P-9298)*

JW Marriott Le Merigot, Santa Monica *Also Called: C W Hotels Ltd (P-12782)*

Jwc Environmental Inc .... D 714 662-5329
2600 S Garnsey St Santa Ana (92707) *(P-6018)*

Jwc Environmental Inc (DH) .... E 949 833-3888
2850 Redhill Ave Ste 125 Santa Ana (92705) *(P-10379)*

Jwc Studio Inc (PA) .... E 323 231-8222
2423 E 23rd St Los Angeles (90058) *(P-2067)*

Jwch Institute Inc .... C 562 867-7999
14371 Clark Ave Bellflower (90706) *(P-16573)*

Jwch Institute Inc .... C 562 862-1000
8530 Firestone Blvd Downey (90241) *(P-16574)*

Jwch Institute Inc .... C 310 223-1035
3591 E Imperial Hwy Lynwood (90262) *(P-16966)*

Jwch Institute Inc .... C 323 562-5813
6912 Ajax Ave Bell (90201) *(P-17878)*

Jwch Institute Inc .... C 562 281-0306
12360 Firestone Blvd Norwalk (90650) *(P-17879)*

Jwch Medical Center, Lynwood *Also Called: Jwch Institute Inc (P-16966)*

K & D Graphics .... E 714 639-8900
1432 N Main St Ste C Orange (92867) *(P-2745)*

K & D Graphics Prtg & Packg, Orange *Also Called: K & D Graphics (P-2745)*

K & J Wire Products Corp .... E 714 816-0360
1220 N Lance Ln Anaheim (92806) *(P-5067)*

K & N Engineering Inc (PA) .... A 951 826-4000
1455 Citrus St Riverside (92507) *(P-7631)*

K & P Janitorial Services .... D 310 540-8878
412 S Pacific Coast Hwy Ste 200 Redondo Beach (90277) *(P-13381)*

K & S Air Conditioning Inc .... C 714 685-0077
143 E Meats Ave Orange (92865) *(P-792)*

K & S Enterprises, Adelanto *Also Called: Dar-Ken Inc (P-3886)*

K & Z Cabinet Co Inc .... D 909 947-3567
1450 S Grove Ave Ontario (91761) *(P-2351)*

K A R Construction Inc .... D 909 988-5054
1306 Brooks St Ontario (91762) *(P-412)*

K B Socks Inc (DH) .... D 310 670-3235
550 N Oak St Inglewood (90302) *(P-1909)*

K Bell, Inglewood *Also Called: K B Socks Inc (P-1909)*

K C C, El Segundo *Also Called: Carson Kurtzman Consultants (P-16654)*

K C Restoration Co Inc .... E 310 280-0597
1514 W 130th St Gardena (90249) *(P-341)*

K E, Irvine *Also Called: Kite Electric Incorporated (P-932)*

K E S, San Diego *Also Called: Koam Engineering Systems Inc (P-14090)*

K I C, San Diego *Also Called: Embedded Designs Inc (P-7856)*

K L Electronic Inc .... E 714 751-5611
3083 S Harbor Blvd Santa Ana (92704) *(P-6742)*

K M I, Dana Point *Also Called: Kanstul Musical Instrs Inc (P-8469)*

K Motors Inc .... C 619 270-3000
965 Arnele Ave El Cajon (92020) *(P-11436)*

K P B S, San Diego *Also Called: San Diego State University (P-16834)*

K S Designs Inc .... E 562 929-3973
901 S Cypress St La Habra (90631) *(P-8612)*

K S Fabrication & Machine Inc .... C 661 617-1700
6205 District Blvd Bakersfield (93313) *(P-682)*

K S I, Bakersfield *Also Called: KS Industries LP (P-684)*

K S S C - F M, Los Angeles *Also Called: Entravsion Communications Corp (P-9499)*

K Squared Metals, Lake Elsinore *Also Called: Boozak Inc (P-4959)*

K T Lucky Co Inc .... D 626 579-7272
10925 Schmidt Rd El Monte (91733) *(P-10952)*

K Too .... E 213 747-7766
800 E 12th St Ste 117 Los Angeles (90021) *(P-2041)*

K Tube Technologies, Poway *Also Called: K-Tube Corporation (P-4549)*

K-1 Packaging Group .... C 626 964-9384
2001 W Mission Blvd Pomona (91766) *(P-3025)*

K-1 Packaging Group, Pomona *Also Called: K-1 Packaging Group (P-3025)*

K-1 Packaging Group LLC (PA) .... D 626 964-9384
17989 Arenth Ave City Of Industry (91748) *(P-3026)*

K-Jack Engineering Co Inc .... D 310 327-8389
5672 Buckingham Dr Huntington Beach (92649) *(P-2583)*

K-Micro Inc .... D 310 442-3200
1618 Stanford St Santa Monica (90404) *(P-10013)*

K-Swiss, Glendale *Also Called: K-Swiss Inc (P-3868)*

K-Swiss Inc .... E 951 361-7501
12450 Philadelphia Ave Eastvale (91752) *(P-3867)*

K-Swiss Inc (DH) .... E 323 675-2700
101 N Brand Blvd Ste 1700 Glendale (91203) *(P-3868)*

K-Swiss Sales Corp .... C 323 675-2700
101 N Brand Blvd Glendale (91203) *(P-3869)*

K-Tech Machine Inc .... C 800 274-9424
1377 Armorlite Dr San Marcos (92069) *(P-6156)*

K-Tek, Vista *Also Called: M Klemme Technology Corp (P-6543)*

K-Too, Los Angeles *Also Called: K Too (P-2041)*

K-Tube Corporation .... D 858 513-9229
13400 Kirkham Way Frnt Poway (92064) *(P-4549)*

K-V Engineering Inc .... D 714 229-9977
2411 W 1st St Santa Ana (92703) *(P-5546)*

K.G.S.electronics, Upland *Also Called: Gar Enterprises (P-6999)*

K&B Electric LLC .... C 951 808-9501
290 Corporate Terrace Cir Ste 200 Corona (92879) *(P-17569)*

K&B Engineering, Corona *Also Called: K&B Electric LLC (P-17569)*

K&L Gates LLP .... D 310 552-5000
10100 Santa Monica Blvd Ste 700 Los Angeles (90067) *(P-16712)*

K&N, Riverside *Also Called: K & N Engineering Inc (P-7631)*

K&S, Orange *Also Called: K & S Air Conditioning Inc (P-792)*

K2 Space Corporation .... D 312 307-8930
960 Knox St Bldg A Torrance (90502) *(P-7645)*

K31, Laguna Beach *Also Called: K31 Road Engineering LLC (P-8689)*

K31 Road Engineering LLC .... E 305 928-1968
1968 S Coast Hwy Pmb 593 Laguna Beach (92651) *(P-8689)*

Ka Management II Inc .... D 858 404-6080
5820 Oberlin Dr Ste 201 San Diego (92121) *(P-18000)*

Kaar Drect Mail Flfillment LLC .... E 619 382-3670
1225 Exposition Way Ste 160 San Diego (92154) *(P-2808)*

Kafco Sales Company .... E 323 588-7141
2300 E 37th St Vernon (90058) *(P-10380)*

Kaga (usa) Inc .... E 714 540-2697
2620 S Susan St Santa Ana (92704) *(P-5195)*

Kagan Trim Center, Los Angeles *Also Called: G Kagan and Sons Inc (P-1880)*

Kai USA Ltd .... E 323 589-2600
6031 Malburg Way Vernon (90058) *(P-4729)*

Kainalu Blue Inc .... E 760 806-6400
4675 North Ave Oceanside (92056) *(P-4493)*

Kair Harbor Express LLC (PA) .... D 562 432-6800
2200 Technology Pl Long Beach (90810) *(P-9079)*

Kaiser Air Conditioning, Oxnard *Also Called: Kaiser Air Conditioning and Sheet Metal Inc (P-1087)*

Kaiser Air Conditioning and Sheet Metal Inc .... E 805 988-1800
600 Pacific Ave Oxnard (93030) *(P-1087)*

Kaiser Aluminum Corporation .... D 323 726-0011
6250 Bandini Blvd Commerce (90040) *(P-4599)*

Kaiser Fndtion Hlth Plan GA In .... B 951 270-1200
1850 California Ave Corona (92881) *(P-12084)*

Kaiser Foundation Health Plan, Corona *Also Called: Kaiser Fndtion Hlth Plan GA In (P-12084)*

Kaiser Foundation Health Plan, Temecula *Also Called: Kaiser Foundation Hospitals (P-12085)*

Kaiser Foundation Health Plan, Fontana *Also Called: Kaiser Foundation Hospitals (P-12087)*

Kaiser Foundation Health Plan, Downey *Also Called: Kaiser Foundation Hospitals (P-12089)*

Kaiser Foundation Health Plan, North Hollywood *Also Called: Kaiser Foundation Hospitals (P-12090)*

Kaiser Foundation Health Plan, San Diego *Also Called: Southern Cal Prmnnte Med Group (P-12110)*

Kaiser Foundation Health Plan, Victorville *Also Called: Kaiser Foundation Hospitals (P-15345)*

Kaiser Foundation Health Plan, Corona *Also Called: Kaiser Foundation Hospitals (P-16575)*

Kaiser Foundation Hospitals .... C 323 264-4310
3355 E 26th St Vernon (90058) *(P-11514)*

Employee Codes: A=Over 500 employees, B=251-500
C=101-250, D=51-100, E=20-50, F=10-19, G=1-9

2025 Southern California
Business Directory and Buyers Guide

© Mergent Inc. 1-800-342-5647
1073

Kaiser Foundation Hospitals .... D 866 984-7483
27309 Madison Ave Temecula (92590) *(P-12085)*

Kaiser Foundation Hospitals .... D 888 750-0036
3750 Grand Ave Chino (91710) *(P-12086)*

Kaiser Foundation Hospitals .... B 909 427-3910
9961 Sierra Ave Fontana (92335) *(P-12087)*

Kaiser Foundation Hospitals .... C 866 340-5974
12470 Whittier Blvd Whittier (90602) *(P-12088)*

Kaiser Foundation Hospitals .... C 562 622-4190
12200 Bellflower Blvd Downey (90242) *(P-12089)*

Kaiser Foundation Hospitals .... C 818 503-7082
11666 Sherman Way North Hollywood (91605) *(P-12090)*

Kaiser Foundation Hospitals .... D 866 319-4269
1249 S Sunset Ave West Covina (91790) *(P-12091)*

Kaiser Foundation Hospitals .... A 626 851-1011
1011 Baldwin Park Blvd Baldwin Park (91706) *(P-12092)*

Kaiser Foundation Hospitals .... C 949 932-5000
6640 Alton Pkwy Irvine (92618) *(P-12660)*

Kaiser Foundation Hospitals .... A 619 528-5888
4647 Zion Ave San Diego (92120) *(P-12661)*

Kaiser Foundation Hospitals .... D 714 830-6500
3401 S Harbor Blvd Santa Ana (92704) *(P-15336)*

Kaiser Foundation Hospitals .... C 714 562-3420
5 Centerpointe Dr La Palma (90623) *(P-15337)*

Kaiser Foundation Hospitals .... D 714 279-4675
411 N Lakeview Ave Anaheim (92807) *(P-15338)*

Kaiser Foundation Hospitals .... D 949 425-3150
24502 Pacific Park Dr Aliso Viejo (92656) *(P-15339)*

Kaiser Foundation Hospitals .... C 714 741-3448
12100 Euclid St Garden Grove (92840) *(P-15340)*

Kaiser Foundation Hospitals .... C 619 528-5000
780 Shadowridge Dr Vista (92083) *(P-15341)*

Kaiser Foundation Hospitals .... D 619 528-5000
250 Travelodge Dr El Cajon (92020) *(P-15342)*

Kaiser Foundation Hospitals .... C 619 528-5000
732 N Broadway Escondido (92025) *(P-15343)*

Kaiser Foundation Hospitals .... C 888 750-0036
1301 California St Redlands (92374) *(P-15344)*

Kaiser Foundation Hospitals .... D 888 750-0036
14011 Park Ave Victorville (92392) *(P-15345)*

Kaiser Foundation Hospitals .... C 909 724-5000
2295 S Vineyard Ave Ontario (91761) *(P-15346)*

Kaiser Foundation Hospitals .... A 909 427-5000
9961 Sierra Ave Fontana (92335) *(P-15347)*

Kaiser Foundation Hospitals .... C 951 353-3790
10800 Magnolia Ave Riverside (92505) *(P-15348)*

Kaiser Foundation Hospitals .... A 951 353-2000
10800 Magnolia Ave Riverside (92505) *(P-15349)*

Kaiser Foundation Hospitals .... A 951 243-0811
27300 Iris Ave Moreno Valley (92555) *(P-15350)*

Kaiser Foundation Hospitals .... C 818 375-4023
13652 Cantara St Panorama City (91402) *(P-15351)*

Kaiser Foundation Hospitals .... C 323 857-2000
6041 Cadillac Ave Los Angeles (90034) *(P-15352)*

Kaiser Foundation Hospitals .... A 323 857-2000
6041 Cadillac Ave Los Angeles (90034) *(P-15353)*

Kaiser Foundation Hospitals .... A 818 375-2000
13651 Willard St Panorama City (91402) *(P-15354)*

Kaiser Foundation Hospitals .... D 800 823-4040
9449 Imperial Hwy Downey (90242) *(P-15355)*

Kaiser Foundation Hospitals .... C 661 398-5011
3501 Stockdale Hwy Bakersfield (93309) *(P-15356)*

Kaiser Foundation Hospitals .... D 661 334-2020
5055 California Ave Ste 110 Bakersfield (93309) *(P-15357)*

Kaiser Foundation Hospitals .... C 310 922-8916
1011 Baldwin Park Blvd Baldwin Park (91706) *(P-15358)*

Kaiser Foundation Hospitals .... C 817 372-8201
9521 Dalen St Downey (90242) *(P-15359)*

Kaiser Foundation Hospitals .... D 310 915-5000
12001 W Washington Blvd Los Angeles (90066) *(P-15360)*

Kaiser Foundation Hospitals .... A 310 325-5111
25825 Vermont Ave Harbor City (90710) *(P-15361)*

Kaiser Foundation Hospitals .... C 323 783-7955
1550 N Edgemont St Los Angeles (90027) *(P-15362)*

Kaiser Foundation Hospitals .... C 818 552-3000
444 W Glenoaks Blvd Glendale (91202) *(P-15363)*

Kaiser Foundation Hospitals .... C 626 440-5639
3280 E Foothill Blvd Pasadena (91107) *(P-15364)*

Kaiser Foundation Hospitals .... D 833 574-2273
5300 Mcconnell Ave Los Angeles (90066) *(P-15365)*

Kaiser Foundation Hospitals .... B 323 783-8306
1515 N Vermont Ave Fl 3 Los Angeles (90027) *(P-15366)*

Kaiser Foundation Hospitals .... C 661 222-2323
27107 Tourney Rd Santa Clarita (91355) *(P-15367)*

Kaiser Foundation Hospitals .... D 310 419-3303
110 N La Brea Ave Inglewood (90301) *(P-15368)*

Kaiser Foundation Hospitals .... C 323 562-6400
7825 Atlantic Ave Cudahy (90201) *(P-16032)*

Kaiser Foundation Hospitals .... C 310 517-2956
15446 S Western Ave Gardena (90249) *(P-16033)*

Kaiser Foundation Hospitals .... D 818 592-3100
5601 De Soto Ave Woodland Hills (91367) *(P-16034)*

Kaiser Foundation Hospitals .... D 833 574-2273
20000 Rinaldi St Porter Ranch (91326) *(P-16035)*

Kaiser Foundation Hospitals .... C 661 412-6777
8800 Ming Ave Bakersfield (93311) *(P-16036)*

Kaiser Foundation Hospitals .... B 626 440-5659
1055 E Colorado Blvd Ste 100 Pasadena (91106) *(P-16037)*

Kaiser Foundation Hospitals .... C 888 750-0036
250 W San Jose Ave Claremont (91711) *(P-16038)*

Kaiser Foundation Hospitals .... A 818 719-2000
5601 De Soto Ave Woodland Hills (91367) *(P-16039)*

Kaiser Foundation Hospitals .... B 661 726-2500
43112 15th St W Lancaster (93534) *(P-16040)*

Kaiser Foundation Hospitals .... B 562 657-9000
9333 Imperial Hwy Downey (90241) *(P-16041)*

Kaiser Foundation Hospitals .... C 310 937-4311
400 S Sepulveda Blvd Manhattan Beach (90266) *(P-16042)*

Kaiser Foundation Hospitals .... C 323 783-4011
4733 W Sunset Blvd Fl 2 Los Angeles (90027) *(P-16043)*

Kaiser Foundation Hospitals .... C 909 394-2530
1255 W Arrow Hwy San Dimas (91773) *(P-16044)*

Kaiser Foundation Hospitals .... D 661 949-5000
1600 W Avenue J Lancaster (93534) *(P-16045)*

Kaiser Foundation Hospitals .... D 951 352-0292
3951 Van Buren Blvd Riverside (92503) *(P-16046)*

Kaiser Foundation Hospitals .... C 951 353-2000
36450 Inland Valley Dr Ste 204 Wildomar (92595) *(P-16047)*

Kaiser Foundation Hospitals .... C 909 386-5500
325 W Hospitality Ln Ste 312 San Bernardino (92408) *(P-16048)*

Kaiser Foundation Hospitals .... C 619 528-2583
4405 Vandever Ave Fl 5 San Diego (92120) *(P-16049)*

Kaiser Foundation Hospitals .... C 858 573-1504
9455 Clairemont Mesa Blvd San Diego (92123) *(P-16050)*

Kaiser Foundation Hospitals .... C 619 528-5000
8080 Parkway Dr La Mesa (91942) *(P-16051)*

Kaiser Foundation Hospitals .... C 619 528-5000
1630 E Main St El Cajon (92021) *(P-16052)*

Kaiser Foundation Hospitals .... D 442 385-7000
360 Rush Dr San Marcos (92078) *(P-16053)*

Kaiser Foundation Hospitals .... D 619 409-6405
3955 Bonita Rd Bonita (91902) *(P-16054)*

Kaiser Foundation Hospitals .... A 714 644-2000
3440 E La Palma Ave Anaheim (92806) *(P-16055)*

Kaiser Foundation Hospitals .... C 714 967-4700
1900 E 4th St Santa Ana (92705) *(P-16056)*

Kaiser Foundation Hospitals .... C 949 262-5780
6 Willard Irvine (92604) *(P-16057)*

Kaiser Foundation Hospitals .... C 951 353-4000
12620 Prescott Ave Tustin (92782) *(P-16058)*

Kaiser Foundation Hospitals .... C 213 580-7200
765 W College St Los Angeles (90012) *(P-16275)*

Kaiser Foundation Hospitals .... D 833 574-2273
22750 Wildomar Trl Wildomar (92595) *(P-16320)*

Mergent email: customerrelations@mergent.com
1074

2025 Southern California
Business Directory and Buyers Guide

(P-0000) Products & Services Section entry number
(PA)=Parent Co (HQ)=Headquarters (DH)=Div Headquarters

Kaiser Foundation Hospitals .... C 310 513-6707
23621 Main St Carson (90745) *(P-16483)*

Kaiser Foundation Hospitals .... D 866 984-7483
2055 Kellogg Ave Corona (92879) *(P-16575)*

Kaiser Foundation Hospitals .... D 626 851-5144
1011 Baldwin Park Blvd Baldwin Park (91706) *(P-18394)*

Kaiser Mental Health Center, Los Angeles *Also Called: Kaiser Foundation Hospitals (P-16275)*

Kaiser Ontario Surgical Center .... D 909 724-5000
2295 S Vineyard Ave Ste A Ontario (91761) *(P-16576)*

Kaiser Permanente, Chino *Also Called: Kaiser Foundation Hospitals (P-12086)*

Kaiser Permanente, Whittier *Also Called: Kaiser Foundation Hospitals (P-12088)*

Kaiser Permanente, West Covina *Also Called: Kaiser Foundation Hospitals (P-12091)*

Kaiser Permanente, Baldwin Park *Also Called: Kaiser Foundation Hospitals (P-12092)*

Kaiser Permanente, San Diego *Also Called: Kaiser Foundation Hospitals (P-12661)*

Kaiser Permanente, Santa Ana *Also Called: Kaiser Foundation Hospitals (P-15336)*

Kaiser Permanente, Garden Grove *Also Called: Kaiser Foundation Hospitals (P-15340)*

Kaiser Permanente, Vista *Also Called: Kaiser Foundation Hospitals (P-15341)*

Kaiser Permanente, Redlands *Also Called: Kaiser Foundation Hospitals (P-15344)*

Kaiser Permanente, Fontana *Also Called: Kaiser Foundation Hospitals (P-15347)*

Kaiser Permanente, Panorama City *Also Called: Kaiser Foundation Hospitals (P-15354)*

Kaiser Permanente, Bakersfield *Also Called: Kaiser Foundation Hospitals (P-15357)*

Kaiser Permanente, Los Angeles *Also Called: Kaiser Foundation Hospitals (P-15360)*

Kaiser Permanente, Harbor City *Also Called: Kaiser Foundation Hospitals (P-15361)*

Kaiser Permanente, Los Angeles *Also Called: Kaiser Foundation Hospitals (P-15366)*

Kaiser Permanente, Santa Clarita *Also Called: Kaiser Foundation Hospitals (P-15367)*

Kaiser Permanente, Inglewood *Also Called: Kaiser Foundation Hospitals (P-15368)*

Kaiser Permanente, San Diego *Also Called: Southern Cal Prmnnte Med Group (P-15477)*

Kaiser Permanente, Bakersfield *Also Called: Kaiser Foundation Hospitals (P-16036)*

Kaiser Permanente, Pasadena *Also Called: Kaiser Foundation Hospitals (P-16037)*

Kaiser Permanente, Claremont *Also Called: Kaiser Foundation Hospitals (P-16038)*

Kaiser Permanente, Woodland Hills *Also Called: Kaiser Foundation Hospitals (P-16039)*

Kaiser Permanente, Lancaster *Also Called: Kaiser Foundation Hospitals (P-16040)*

Kaiser Permanente, San Dimas *Also Called: Kaiser Foundation Hospitals (P-16044)*

Kaiser Permanente, Riverside *Also Called: Kaiser Foundation Hospitals (P-16046)*

Kaiser Permanente, San Diego *Also Called: Kaiser Foundation Hospitals (P-16049)*

Kaiser Permanente, San Diego *Also Called: Kaiser Foundation Hospitals (P-16050)*

Kaiser Permanente, Santa Ana *Also Called: Kaiser Foundation Hospitals (P-16056)*

Kaiser Permanente, Tustin *Also Called: Kaiser Foundation Hospitals (P-16058)*

Kaiser Permanente, Downey *Also Called: Southern Cal Prmnnte Med Group (P-16204)*

Kaiser Permanente, Wildomar *Also Called: Kaiser Foundation Hospitals (P-16320)*

Kaiser Permanente, Carson *Also Called: Kaiser Foundation Hospitals (P-16483)*

Kaiser Prmnente Downey Med Ctr, Downey *Also Called: Kaiser Foundation Hospitals (P-16041)*

Kaiser Prmnnte Brnard J Tyson .... C 888 576-3348
98 S Los Robles Ave Pasadena (91101) *(P-16577)*

Kaiser Prmnnte Mreno Vly Med C, Moreno Valley *Also Called: Kaiser Foundation Hospitals (P-15350)*

Kaiser Prmnnte Nat Fclties Svc, Vernon *Also Called: Kaiser Foundation Hospitals (P-11514)*

Kaiser Prmnnte Ornge Cnty-Nhei, Anaheim *Also Called: Kaiser Foundation Hospitals (P-16055)*

Kaiser Prmnnte Psadena Med Off, Pasadena *Also Called: Kaiser Foundation Hospitals (P-15364)*

Kaiser Prmnnte San Mrcos Med C, San Marcos *Also Called: Kaiser Foundation Hospitals (P-16053)*

Kaiser Prmnnte Schl Anesthesia .... D 626 564-3016
100 S Los Robles Ste 501 Pasadena (91101) *(P-15369)*

Kaiser Prmnnte W Los Angles Me, Los Angeles *Also Called: Kaiser Foundation Hospitals (P-15353)*

Kaizen Syndicate LLC .... C 858 309-2028
10413 Magical Waters Ct Spring Valley (91978) *(P-14228)*

Kakuichi America Inc .... D 310 539-1590
23540 Telo Ave Torrance (90505) *(P-3976)*

Kal-Cameron Manufacturing Corp (HQ)........... D 626 338-7308
4265 Puente Ave Baldwin Park (91706) *(P-4741)*

Kaleidioscope Stadium Cinema, Mission Viejo *Also Called: Edwards Theatres Inc (P-14932)*

Kam Sang Company Inc .... D 714 523-2800
14419 Firestone Blvd La Mirada (90638) *(P-12880)*

Kamm Industries Inc .... E 800 317-6253
43352 Business Park Dr Temecula (92590) *(P-2263)*

Kammerer Enterprises Inc .... D 760 560-0550
1280 N Melrose Dr Vista (92083) *(P-4474)*

Kan-Di-Ki LLC (HQ)................................. **D 818 549-1880**
12612 Raymer St North Hollywood (91605) *(P-16321)*

Kana Pipeline Inc .... D 714 986-1400
12620 Magnolia Ave Riverside (92503) *(P-683)*

Kanan Baking Company, Woodland Hills *Also Called: Gold Coast Baking Company LLC (P-1456)*

Kandy Kiss of California Inc .... D
14761 Califa St Van Nuys (91411) *(P-2042)*

Kanex .... E 714 332-1681
9377 Haven Ave Rancho Cucamonga (91730) *(P-7130)*

Kaney Foods, San Luis Obispo *Also Called: Amk Foodservices Inc (P-10742)*

Kang Family Partners LLC .... C 805 688-1000
555 Mcmurray Rd Buellton (93427) *(P-12881)*

Kanstul Musical Instrs Inc .... E 714 563-1000
23772 Perth Bay Dana Point (92629) *(P-8469)*

Kap Manufacturing Inc .... E 909 599-2525
327 W Allen Ave San Dimas (91773) *(P-6157)*

Kap Medical .... E 951 340-4360
1395 Pico St Corona (92881) *(P-8049)*

Kapan - Kent Company Inc .... E 760 631-1716
3540 Seagate Way Ste 100 Oceanside (92056) *(P-2264)*

Kaplan Indus Car Wash Sups Inc .... E 562 921-5544
13875 Mica St Santa Fe Springs (90670) *(P-10475)*

Kaplan Industries Mfg, Santa Fe Springs *Also Called: Kaplan Indus Car Wash Sups Inc (P-10475)*

KARAT, Chino *Also Called: Karat Packaging Inc (P-4150)*

Karat Packaging Inc (PA)............................ E 626 965-8882
6185 Kimball Ave Chino (91708) *(P-4150)*

Karem Aircraft Inc .... E 949 859-4444
1 Capital Dr Lake Forest (92630) *(P-7509)*

Karen Kane Inc (PA)................................. **C 323 588-0000**
2275 E 37th St Vernon (90058) *(P-10711)*

Kareo PM, Corona Del Mar *Also Called: Tebra Technologies Inc (P-13840)*

Kargo Global Inc .... C 212 979-9000
1437 4th St Ste 200 Santa Monica (90401) *(P-13268)*

Karl Storz Endscpy-America Inc (HQ).............. **C 424 218-8100**
2151 E Grand Ave El Segundo (90245) *(P-8179)*

Karl Storz Endscpy-America Inc .... D 800 964-5563
1 N Los Carneros Dr Goleta (93117) *(P-8180)*

Karl Storz Imaging Inc (HQ)....................... **B 805 968-5563**
1 S Los Carneros Rd Goleta (93117) *(P-8050)*

Karl Storz Imaging Inc .... E 805 968-5563
32 Aero Camino Goleta (93117) *(P-8181)*

Karl Storz Intgrated Solutions, El Segundo *Also Called: Karl Storz Endscpy-America Inc (P-8179)*

Karl Strauss Brewery & Rest, San Diego *Also Called: Associated Microbreweries Inc (P-1537)*

Karl Strauss Brewery Garden, San Diego *Also Called: Associated Microbreweries Inc (P-1536)*

Karl Strauss Brewing Company (PA)................ E 858 273-2739
5985 Santa Fe St San Diego (92109) *(P-1545)*

Karl Strauss Brewing Company, San Diego *Also Called: Associted McRbrwries Ltd A Cal (P-1539)*

Karma Automotive Inc .... A 855 565-2762
9950 Jeronimo Rd Irvine (92618) *(P-7181)*

Karma Automotive LLC, Irvine *Also Called: Karma Automotive Inc (P-7181)*

Karman Missile & Space Systems, South El Monte *Also Called: Amro Fabricating Corporation (P-7430)*

Karman Topco LP (PA)............................... **C 949 797-2900**
18100 Von Karman Ave Ste 1000 Irvine (92612) *(P-18328)*

Karoun Cheese, San Fernando *Also Called: Karoun Dairies Inc (P-1287)*

Karoun Dairies Inc (PA)............................. **E 818 767-7000**
13023 Arroyo St San Fernando (91340) *(P-1287)*

Kas Engineering Inc (PA)............................ **E 310 450-8925**
1714 14th St Santa Monica (90404) *(P-4151)*

Katch Inc .... E 626 369-0958
520 Hofgaarden St City Of Industry (91744) *(P-4842)*

Katch LLC .... D 310 219-6200
2381 Rosecrans Ave Ste 400 El Segundo (90245) *(P-13218)*

Employee Codes: A=Over 500 employees, B=251-500
C=101-250, D=51-100, E=20-50, F=10-19, G=1-9

2025 Southern California
Business Directory and Buyers Guide

© Mergent Inc. 1-800-342-5647
1075

Kate Farms Inc .... C 805 845-2446
  101 Innovation Pl Santa Barbara (93108) *(P-1797)*

Kate Smrvlle Skin Hlth Experts, El Segundo *Also Called: Kate Somerville Skincare LLC*
(P-3436)

Kate Somerville Skincare LLC (HQ)................................ D 323 655-7546
  2121 Park Pl Ste 100 El Segundo (90245) *(P-3436)*

Katella Properties .... D 562 704-8695
  10140 Grayling Ave Whittier (90603) *(P-12300)*

Katella Properties .... D 562 596-5561
  3902 Katella Ave Los Alamitos (90720) *(P-15685)*

Kater-Crafts Incorporated .... E 562 692-0665
  3205 Weldon Ave Los Angeles (90065) *(P-3202)*

Katerra Construction LLC .... A 720 449-3909
  1950 W Corporate Way Anaheim (92801) *(P-413)*

Katten Muchin Rosenman LLP .... C 310 788-4400
  2121 Avenue Of The Stars Los Angeles (90067) *(P-16713)*

Katz Millennium Sls & Mktg Inc .... C 323 966-5066
  5700 Wilshire Blvd Ste 100 Los Angeles (90036) *(P-6621)*

Katzkin Leather Inc (PA).. C 323 725-1243
  6868 W Acco St Montebello (90640) *(P-11124)*

Kava Holdings Inc (DH)... C 310 472-1211
  701 Stone Canyon Rd Los Angeles (90077) *(P-12882)*

Kavlico Corporation (DH).. A 805 523-2000
  1461 Lawrence Dr Thousand Oaks (91320) *(P-7018)*

Kawasaki Motors Corp USA (HQ)............................... B 949 837-4683
  26972 Burbank Foothill Ranch (92610) *(P-11483)*

Kawneer Company Inc .... D 951 410-4779
  925 Marlborough Ave Riverside (92507) *(P-4891)*

Kay & James Inc .... D 818 998-0357
  14062 Balboa Blvd Sylmar (91342) *(P-6158)*

Kaydan Logistics LLC .... D 951 961-9000
  45562 Ponderosa Ct Temecula (92592) *(P-9367)*

Kaylas Cake Corporation .... E 714 869-1522
  1311 S Gilbert St Fullerton (92833) *(P-11297)*

Kayo Clothing Company, Lynwood *Also Called: Kayo of California (P-2111)*

Kayo of California (PA).. E 323 233-6107
  11854 Alameda St Lynwood (90262) *(P-2111)*

KB Delta Inc .... E 310 530-1539
  3155 Fujita St Torrance (90505) *(P-5196)*

KB Delta Comprsr Valve Parts, Torrance *Also Called: KB Delta Inc (P-5196)*

KB Home (PA)... D 310 231-4000
  10990 Wilshire Blvd Fl 7 Los Angeles (90024) *(P-462)*

KB Home Grater Los Angeles Inc (HQ)........................ D 310 231-4000
  10990 Wilshire Blvd Ste 700 Los Angeles (90024) *(P-414)*

KB Home Grater Los Angeles Inc .... C 951 691-5300
  36310 Inland Valley Dr Wildomar (92595) *(P-415)*

KB Sheetmetal Fabrication Inc .... E 714 979-1780
  17371 Mount Wynne Cir # B Fountain Valley (92708) *(P-4995)*

Kba Engineering LLC .... D 661 323-0487
  2157 Mohawk St Bakersfield (93308) *(P-5511)*

Kbkg Inc .... C 626 449-4225
  225 S Lake Ave Ste 400 Pasadena (91101) *(P-17737)*

Kbm Building Services, San Diego *Also Called: Kbm Fclity Sltons Holdings LLC (P-13382)*

Kbm Fclity Sltons Holdings LLC .... B 858 467-0202
  7976 Engineer Rd Ste 200 San Diego (92111) *(P-13382)*

Kbr Inc .... E 562 436-9281
  2000 W Gaylord St Long Beach (90813) *(P-6338)*

Kc Hilites Inc .... E 928 635-2607
  13637 Cimarron Ave Gardena (90249) *(P-6485)*

Kc Pharmaceuticals Inc (PA) .... D 909 598-9499
  3420 Pomona Blvd Pomona (91768) *(P-3437)*

Kc Services, Anaheim *Also Called: Korean Community Services Inc (P-16295)*

Kca Electronics Inc .... C 714 239-2433
  223 N Crescent Way Anaheim (92801) *(P-6743)*

Kcb Towers Inc .... D 909 862-0322
  27260 Meines St Highland (92346) *(P-1155)*

Kdc Inc (HQ).. C 714 828-7000
  4462 Corporate Center Dr Los Alamitos (90720) *(P-931)*

Kdc Systems, Los Alamitos *Also Called: Kdc Inc (P-931)*

Kdc/One Chatsworth Inc .... C 818 709-1345
  20320 Prairie St Chatsworth (91311) *(P-3663)*

Kdc/One Chatsworth Inc (DH).................................. D 818 709-1345
  20245 Sunburst St Chatsworth (91311) *(P-3664)*

Kdg Construction Consulting, Glendale *Also Called: Kennard Development Group (P-448)*

Kds Construction, Orange *Also Called: Cirks Construction Inc (P-529)*

Keating Dental Arts Inc .... C 949 955-2100
  16881 Hale Ave Ste A Irvine (92606) *(P-16344)*

Keating Dental Lab, Irvine *Also Called: Keating Dental Arts Inc (P-16344)*

Kec Engineering .... C 951 734-3010
  26320 Lester Cir Corona (92883) *(P-629)*

Kechika, Rcho Sta Marg *Also Called: Point Conception Inc (P-2127)*

Keck Hospital of Usc .... A 800 872-2273
  1500 San Pablo St Los Angeles (90033) *(P-16059)*

Kedren Acute Psychtric Hosp Cm, Los Angeles *Also Called: Kedren Community Hlth Ctr Inc*
(P-16276)

Kedren Community Hlth Ctr Inc (PA)........................... B 323 233-0425
  4211 Avalon Blvd Los Angeles (90011) *(P-16276)*

Kedren Community Hlth Ctr Inc .... C 323 524-0634
  3800 S Figueroa St Los Angeles (90037) *(P-16967)*

Keefe Plumbing Services, Glendale *Also Called: H L Moe Co Inc (P-785)*

Keenan & Associates (HQ)...................................... B 310 212-3344
  2355 Crenshaw Blvd Ste 200 Torrance (90501) *(P-12225)*

Keesal Young Logan A Prof Corp (PA).......................... D 562 436-2000
  400 Oceangate Long Beach (90802) *(P-16714)*

Keiro Senior Health Care, Los Angeles *Also Called: Keiro Services (P-18001)*

Keiro Services .... B 213 873-5700
  420 E 3rd St Ste 1000 Los Angeles (90033) *(P-18001)*

Keith Co, Pico Rivera *Also Called: W P Keith Co Inc (P-5804)*

Kelco, Oxnard *Also Called: Kim Laube & Company Inc (P-3666)*

Kelcourt Plastics Inc (DH)....................................... D 949 361-0774
  1000 Calle Recodo San Clemente (92673) *(P-4152)*

Keller North America Inc .... D 805 933-1331
  1780 E Lemonwood Dr Santa Paula (93060) *(P-1212)*

Keller Williams Realtors, Beverly Hills *Also Called: Keller Wllams Rlty Bvrly Hills (P-12473)*

Keller Williams Realtors, Corona *Also Called: Pro Group Inc (P-12508)*

Keller Wllams Rlty Bvrly Hills .... D 310 432-6400
  439 N Canon Dr Ste 300 Beverly Hills (90210) *(P-12473)*

Kellermyer Bergensons Svcs LLC (PA)......................... E 760 631-5111
  3605 Ocean Ranch Blvd Ste 200 Oceanside (92056) *(P-6019)*

Kelley Blue Book Co Inc (DH)................................... D 949 770-7704
  195 Technology Dr Irvine (92618) *(P-2862)*

Kelly Services, Costa Mesa *Also Called: Southern Home Care Svcs Inc (P-13623)*

Kelly Spicers Inc (HQ)... C 562 698-1199
  12310 Slauson Ave Santa Fe Springs (90670) *(P-10576)*

Kelly Spicers Packaging North, Santa Fe Springs *Also Called: Kelly Spicers Inc (P-10576)*

Kelly Thomas MD Ucsd Hlth Care .... D 619 543-2885
  200 W Arbor Dr San Diego (92103) *(P-16578)*

Kelmscott Communications LLC .... B 949 475-1900
  2485 Da Vinci Irvine (92614) *(P-3027)*

Kelpac Medical, San Clemente *Also Called: Kelcourt Plastics Inc (P-4152)*

Kelpien Health Care, Montebello *Also Called: Beverly Community Hosp Assn (P-15925)*

Kemac Technology Inc .... E 626 334-1519
  503 S Vincent Ave Azusa (91702) *(P-6159)*

Kemira Water Solutions Inc .... E 909 350-5678
  14000 San Bernardino Ave Fontana (92335) *(P-3240)*

Kemira Water Solutions Inc .... E 909 350-5678
  14000 San Bernardino Ave Fontana (92335) *(P-3807)*

Kemiron Pacific, Fontana *Also Called: Kemira Water Solutions Inc (P-3807)*

Kempton Machine Works Inc .... E 714 990-0596
  4070 E Leaverton Ct Anaheim (92807) *(P-5613)*

Ken Blanchard Companies, The, Escondido *Also Called: Blanchard Training and Dev Inc*
(P-18106)

Ken Grody Ford, Carlsbad *Also Called: Ted Ford Jones Inc (P-11417)*

Ken Grody Ford, Buena Park *Also Called: Ted Ford Jones Inc (P-14700)*

Ken Grody Ford - Redlands, Redlands *Also Called: Ken Grody Redlands LLC (P-11368)*

Ken Grody Redlands LLC .... D 909 793-3211
  1121 W Colton Ave Redlands (92374) *(P-11368)*

Ken Real Estate Lease Ltd .... D 714 778-1700
  900 S Disneyland Dr Anaheim (92802) *(P-12883)*

Ken Starr Inc .... D 714 632-8789
  1120 N Tustin Ave Anaheim (92807) *(P-793)*

Ken's Spray Equipment, Inc., Compton *Also Called: Kens Spray Equipment LLC (P-5328)*

Kenai Drilling Limited .... C 661 587-0117
2651 Patton Way Bakersfield (93308) *(P-1144)*

Kenco Group Inc .... C 800 758-3289
6509 Kimball Ave Chino (91708) *(P-9080)*

KENCO GROUP, INC., Chino *Also Called: Kenco Group Inc (P-9080)*

Kendal Floral Supply LLC (PA)............................. D 888 828-9875
1960 Kellogg Ave Carlsbad (92008) *(P-11090)*

Kendal North Bouquet Co, Carlsbad *Also Called: Kendal Floral Supply LLC (P-11090)*

Kennard Development Group .... D 818 241-0800
1025 N Brand Blvd Ste 300 Glendale (91202) *(P-448)*

Kennedy Athletics, Carson *Also Called: Cali-Fame Los Angeles Inc (P-2158)*

Kennedy Name Plate Co .... E 323 585-0121
4501 Pacific Blvd Vernon (90058) *(P-5327)*

Kennedy-Wilson Inc (PA)..................................... C 310 887-6400
151 El Camino Dr Beverly Hills (90212) *(P-12474)*

Kenneth Corp .... A 714 537-5160
12601 Garden Grove Blvd Garden Grove (92843) *(P-16060)*

KENNETH NORRIS CANCER HOSPITAL, Los Angeles *Also Called: Tenet Health Systems Norris (P-16226)*

Kenny The Printer, Orange *Also Called: American PCF Prtrs College Inc (P-2960)*

Kens Spray Equipment LLC .... C 310 635-9995
1900 W Walnut St Compton (90220) *(P-5328)*

Kentina, Temecula *Also Called: Sft Realty Galway Downs LLC (P-12528)*

Kenvue Brands LLC .... C 310 642-1150
5760 W 96th St Los Angeles (90045) *(P-3665)*

Kenwait Die Casting Company, Sun Valley *Also Called: Kenwalt Die Casting Corp (P-4648)*

Kenwalt Die Casting Corp .... E 818 768-5800
8719 Bradley Ave Sun Valley (91352) *(P-4648)*

Keolis Transit America Inc .... C 818 616-5254
14663 Keswick St Van Nuys (91405) *(P-8757)*

Keolis Transit America Inc .... D 661 341-3910
660 W Avenue L Lancaster (93534) *(P-8758)*

Kepner Plas Fabricators Inc .... E 562 543-4472
3131 Lomita Blvd Torrance (90505) *(P-4153)*

Kerlan-Jobe Orthopedic Clinic (PA) .... D 310 665-7200
6801 Park Ter Ste 500 Los Angeles (90045) *(P-15370)*

Kerleylegacy63 Inc .... D 714 630-7286
3000-3010 La Jolla St Anaheim (92806) *(P-6160)*

Kern County Hospital Authority (PA).................. A 661 326-2102
1700 Mount Vernon Ave Bakersfield (93306) *(P-16061)*

Kern County Hospital Authority .... B 661 843-7980
1902 B St Bakersfield (93301) *(P-16484)*

Kern Direct Marketing, Woodland Hills *Also Called: Kern Organization Inc (P-13219)*

Kern Energy, Bakersfield *Also Called: Kern Oil & Refining Co (P-3825)*

Kern Engineering, Chino *Also Called: R Kern Engineering & Mfg Corp (P-6957)*

Kern Family Helathcare, Bakersfield *Also Called: Kern Health Systems Inc (P-15371)*

Kern Health Systems Inc .... D 661 664-5000
2900 Buck Owens Blvd Bakersfield (93308) *(P-15371)*

Kern Oil & Refining Co (HQ)................................ C 661 845-0761
7724 E Panama Ln Bakersfield (93307) *(P-3825)*

Kern Organization Inc .... D 818 703-8775
20955 Warner Center Ln Woodland Hills (91367) *(P-13219)*

Korn Rdlgy Imaging Systems Inc .... D 001 322-9958
4100 Truxtun Ave Ste 306 Bakersfield (93309) *(P-15372)*

Kern Regional Center (PA)................................... C 661 327-8531
3200 N Sillect Ave Bakersfield (93308) *(P-17231)*

Kern Ridge Growers LLC .... B 661 854-3141
25429 Barbara St Arvin (93203) *(P-113)*

Kern River Transitional Care, Bakersfield *Also Called: Bakersfieldidence Opco LLC (P-15578)*

Kern Steel Fabrication Inc (PA)........................... D 661 327-9588
627 Williams St Bakersfield (93305) *(P-4843)*

Kern Valley Hosp Foundation (PA)...................... B 760 379-2681
6412 Laurel Ave Lake Isabella (93240) *(P-11621)*

KERN VALLEY HOSPITAL, Lake Isabella *Also Called: Kern Valley Hosp Foundation (P-11621)*

Kern Valley Sun, Lake Isabella *Also Called: Wick Communications Co (P-2839)*

Kernel, Culver City *Also Called: HI LLC (P-17846)*

Kernridge Division, Mc Kittrick *Also Called: Aera Energy LLC (P-263)*

Kerr Corporation (HQ).. C 714 516-7400
1717 W Collins Ave Orange (92867) *(P-8340)*

Kerry Inc .... D 760 396-2116
64405 Lincoln St Mecca (92254) *(P-1299)*

Kerv Interactive, Sherman Oaks *Also Called: Grabit Interactive Inc (P-13267)*

Kesa Incorporated .... E 714 956-2827
960 E Discovery Ln Anaheim (92801) *(P-14410)*

Kettenbach LP .... E 877 532-2123
16052 Beach Blvd Ste 221 Huntington Beach (92647) *(P-8341)*

Kettenburg Marine Corporation .... C 619 224-8211
2810 Carleton St San Diego (92106) *(P-10495)*

Kevcon Inc .... D 760 432-0307
10679 Westview Pkwy San Diego (92126) *(P-488)*

Kevin Whaley .... E 619 596-4000
9565 Pathway St Santee (92071) *(P-5407)*

Kevita, Oxnard *Also Called: Kevita Inc (P-1621)*

Kevita Inc (HQ)... D 805 200-2250
2220 Celsius Ave Ste A Oxnard (93030) *(P-1621)*

Key Code Media Inc (PA)...................................... E 818 303-3900
270 S Flower St Burbank (91502) *(P-5858)*

Key Container, South Gate *Also Called: Liberty Container Company (P-2679)*

Key Essentials Inc .... D
1916 S Tubeway Ave Commerce (90040) *(P-1686)*

Key-Bak, Ontario *Also Called: West Coast Chain Mfg Co (P-7161)*

Keyes Lexus, Van Nuys *Also Called: Keylex Inc (P-11370)*

Keyes Motors Inc (PA).. D 818 782-0122
5855 Van Nuys Blvd Van Nuys (91401) *(P-11369)*

Keyes Toyota, Van Nuys *Also Called: Keyes Motors Inc (P-11369)*

Keylex Inc (PA)... D 818 379-4000
5905 Van Nuys Blvd Van Nuys (91401) *(P-11370)*

Keyline Sales Inc .... E 562 904-3910
9768 Firestone Blvd Downey (90241) *(P-10323)*

Keystone, Van Nuys *Also Called: Keystone Towing Inc (P-14717)*

Keystone Automotive Warehouse .... D 951 277-5237
15640 Cantu Galleano Ranch Rd Eastvale (91752) *(P-9831)*

KEYSTONE AUTOMOTIVE WAREHOUSE, Eastvale *Also Called: Keystone Automotive Warehouse (P-9831)*

Keystone Dental Inc .... E 781 328-3324
5 Holland Ste 209 Irvine (92618) *(P-8342)*

Keystone Dental Inc .... E 781 328-3382
13645 Alton Pkwy Ste A Irvine (92618) *(P-8343)*

Keystone Educatn & Youth Svcs, Riverside *Also Called: Keystone NPS LLC (P-17232)*

Keystone Ford Inc (PA)... C 562 868-0825
12000 Firestone Blvd Norwalk (90650) *(P-11371)*

Keystone NPS LLC .... C 951 785-0504
9994 County Farm Rd Riverside (92503) *(P-17232)*

Keystone NPS LLC (DH)....................................... D 909 633-6354
11980 Mount Vernon Ave Grand Terrace (92313) *(P-17233)*

Keystone Schools-Ramona, Grand Terrace *Also Called: Keystone NPS LLC (P-17233)*

Keystone Towing Inc .... D 818 782-1996
7817 Woodley Ave Van Nuys (91406) *(P-14717)*

Keyt Television, Santa Barbara *Also Called: Smith Broadcasting Group Inc (P-9517)*

Kgs Electronics, Arcadia *Also Called: Car Enterprises (P-10004)*

Kgtv, San Diego *Also Called: EW Scripps Company (P-9500)*

Kharon, Los Angeles *Also Called: 1nteger LLC (P-13637)*

Khw Enterprises Inc .... D 562 236-8440
8550 Chetle Ave Ste A Whittier (90606) *(P-11125)*

Kia Design Center America, Irvine *Also Called: Hyundai Amer Technical Ctr Inc (P-17553)*

Kiara Sky Professional Nails, Bakersfield *Also Called: Glam and Glits Nail Design Inc (P-3654)*

Kids Empire, West Hollywood *Also Called: Kids Empire USA LLC (P-15208)*

Kids Empire USA LLC .... D 424 527-1039
8605 Santa Monica Blvd West Hollywood (90069) *(P-15208)*

Kids Healthy Foods LLC .... E 949 260-4950
2030 Main St Ste 1300 Irvine (92614) *(P-10953)*

Kids Line LLC .... C 310 660-0110
10541 Humbolt St Los Alamitos (90720) *(P-2212)*

KIDSPACE, Pasadena *Also Called: Kidspce A Prticipatory Museum (P-17254)*

Kidspce A Prticipatory Museum .... D 626 449-9144
480 N Arroyo Blvd Pasadena (91103) *(P-17254)*

Kieran Label Corp .... E 619 449-4457
2321 Siempre Viva Ct Ste 101 San Diego (92154) *(P-3150)*

Employee Codes: A=Over 500 employees, B=251-500
C=101-250, D=51-100, E=20-50, F=10-19, G=1-9

2025 Southern California
Business Directory and Buyers Guide

© Mergent Inc. 1-800-342-5647

1077

Kiewit Corporation	D 858 208-4285	
12700 Stowe Dr Ste 180 Poway (92064) *(P-552)*		

Kiewit Corporation .... D 907 222-9350
10704 Shoemaker Ave Santa Fe Springs (90670) *(P-17570)*

Kiewit Infrastructure West Co .... C 562 946-1816
10704 Shoemaker Ave Santa Fe Springs (90670) *(P-630)*

Kifm Smooth Jazz 981 Inc .... C 619 297-3698
1615 Murray Canyon Rd San Diego (92108) *(P-9478)*

Kifuki USA Co Inc (HQ) .... D 626 334-8090
15547 1st St Irwindale (91706) *(P-1280)*

Kik, Santa Fe Springs *Also Called: Kik-Socal Inc (P-3608)*

Kik Custom Products, Torrance *Also Called: Prestone Products Corporation (P-3818)*

Kik Pool Additives Inc .... C 909 390-9912
5160 E Airport Dr Ontario (91761) *(P-3808)*

Kik-Socal Inc .... A 562 946-6427
9028 Dice Rd Santa Fe Springs (90670) *(P-3608)*

Killion Industries Inc (PA) .... D 760 727-5102
1380 Poinsettia Ave Vista (92081) *(P-2568)*

Kilovac, Carpinteria *Also Called: Te Connectivity Corporation (P-6363)*

Kim & Cami Productions Inc .... E 323 584-1300
2950 Leonis Blvd Vernon (90058) *(P-2112)*

Kim Laube & Company Inc .... E 805 240-1300
2221 Statham Blvd Oxnard (93033) *(P-3666)*

Kim Lighting & Mfg, City Of Industry *Also Called: Kim Lighting Inc (P-6506)*

Kim Lighting Inc .... A 626 968-5666
16555 Gale Ave City Of Industry (91745) *(P-6506)*

Kimball Tirey & St John LLP (PA) .... D 619 234-1690
7676 Hazard Center Dr Ste 900 San Diego (92108) *(P-16715)*

Kimberly Machine Inc .... E 714 539-0151
12822 Joy St Garden Grove (92840) *(P-6161)*

Kimco Facility Services LLC .... A 404 487-1165
3605 Ocean Ranch Blvd Oceanside (92056) *(P-13383)*

Kimco Services, Oceanside *Also Called: Kimco Facility Services LLC (P-13383)*

Kimco Services, Ontario *Also Called: Kimco Staffing Services Inc (P-13532)*

Kimco Staffing Services Inc .... A 909 390-9881
4295 Jurupa St Ste 107 Ontario (91761) *(P-13532)*

Kimco Staffing Services Inc .... A 951 686-3800
1770 Iowa Ave Ste 160 Riverside (92507) *(P-13533)*

Kimco Staffing Services Inc .... B 310 622-1616
3415 S Sepulveda Blvd Ste 1100 Los Angeles (90034) *(P-13534)*

Kimco Staffing Solutions, Riverside *Also Called: Kimco Staffing Services Inc (P-13533)*

Kimlor Innovative HM Fashions, Santa Ana *Also Called: Kimlor Mills Inc (P-9876)*

Kimlor Mills Inc .... D 803 531-2037
18142 Blue Ridge Dr Santa Ana (92705) *(P-9876)*

Kimpton Hotel & Rest Group LLC .... C 323 852-6000
6317 Wilshire Blvd Los Angeles (90048) *(P-12884)*

Kinamed Inc .... E 805 384-2748
820 Flynn Rd Camarillo (93012) *(P-8281)*

Kincaid Industries Inc .... D 760 343-5457
31065 Plantation Dr Thousand Palms (92276) *(P-794)*

Kinder Mrgan Enrgy Partners LP .... D 909 873-5100
2319 S Riverside Ave Bloomington (92316) *(P-9215)*

Kindersystems Inc .... D 760 975-9750
101 State Pl Ste Q Escondido (92029) *(P-14229)*

Kindeva Drug Delivery LP .... B 818 341-1300
19901 Nordhoff St Northridge (91324) *(P-3438)*

Kindred, San Diego *Also Called: Kindred Healthcare LLC (P-16064)*

Kindred Healthcare LLC .... C 562 531-3110
16453 Colorado Ave Paramount (90723) *(P-16062)*

Kindred Healthcare LLC .... B 951 436-3535
2224 Medical Center Dr Perris (92571) *(P-16063)*

Kindred Healthcare LLC .... D 619 546-9653
1503 30th St San Diego (92102) *(P-16064)*

Kindred Healthcare LLC .... D 714 564-7800
1901 College Ave Santa Ana (92706) *(P-16065)*

KINDRED HOSPITAL - RANCHO, Rancho Cucamonga *Also Called: Knd Development 55 LLC (P-16066)*

Kindred Hospital La Mirada, La Mirada *Also Called: Southern Cal Spcialty Care LLC (P-16210)*

Kindred Hospital La Mirata, West Covina *Also Called: Southern Cal Spcialty Care Inc (P-16208)*

Kindred Hospital Paramount, Paramount *Also Called: Kindred Healthcare LLC (P-16062)*

Kindred Hospital Santa Ana, Santa Ana *Also Called: Kindred Healthcare LLC (P-16065)*

Kindred Hospital Santa Ana, Santa Ana *Also Called: Southern Cal Spcialty Care Inc (P-16209)*

Kindred Litho Incorporated .... E 909 944-4015
10833 Bell Ct Rancho Cucamonga (91730) *(P-3028)*

Kinecta, Manhattan Beach *Also Called: Kinecta Federal Credit Union (P-11802)*

Kinecta Federal Credit Union (PA) .... C 310 643-5400
1440 Rosecrans Ave Manhattan Beach (90266) *(P-11802)*

Kinema Fitness Inc .... D 866 608-5704
2450 Colorado Ave Ste 100e Santa Monica (90404) *(P-15209)*

Kinemetrics Inc (DH) .... D 626 795-2220
222 Vista Ave Pasadena (91107) *(P-17571)*

Kineticom Inc (PA) .... D 619 330-3100
333 H St Chula Vista (91910) *(P-13535)*

King & Spalding LLP .... D 213 443-4355
633 W 5th St Ste 1600 Los Angeles (90071) *(P-16716)*

King Bros Enterprises LLC .... C 661 257-3262
29101 The Old Rd Valencia (91355) *(P-4029)*

King Bros Industries C
29101 The Old Rd Valencia (91355) *(P-4154)*

King Equipment LLC .... D 909 986-5300
1690 Ashley Way Colton (92324) *(P-13439)*

King Graphics, San Diego *Also Called: Colmol Inc (P-3130)*

King Henrys Inc .... E 818 536-3692
29124 Hancock Pkwy 1 Valencia (91355) *(P-1725)*

King Holding Corporation .... A 586 254-3900
360 N Crescent Dr Beverly Hills (90210) *(P-5131)*

King Instrument Company Inc .... E 714 891-0008
12700 Pala Dr Garden Grove (92841) *(P-7864)*

King Nutronics LLC .... E 818 887-5460
6421 Independence Ave Woodland Hills (91367) *(P-7865)*

King Nutronics Corporation, Woodland Hills *Also Called: King Nutronics LLC (P-7865)*

King Plastics Inc .... D 714 997-7540
840 N Elm St Orange (92867) *(P-4155)*

King Relocation Services, Santa Fe Springs *Also Called: Van King & Storage Inc (P-8982)*

King Shock Technology Inc .... D 719 394-3754
12472 Edison Way Garden Grove (92841) *(P-7264)*

King Supply Company LLC .... D 714 670-8980
6340 Valley View St Buena Park (90620) *(P-1213)*

King Taco Restaurant Inc (PA) .... D 323 266-3585
3421 E 14th St Los Angeles (90023) *(P-11582)*

King Ventures .... C 805 544-4444
285 Bridge St San Luis Obispo (93401) *(P-12568)*

King Wire Partitions Inc .... E 323 256-4848
6044 N Figueroa St Los Angeles (90042) *(P-5098)*

Kingcom(us) LLC (DH) .... E 424 744-5697
3100 Ocean Park Blvd Santa Monica (90405) *(P-13959)*

Kingdom Causes Inc .... C 714 904-0167
4508 Atlantic Ave Ste 292 Long Beach (90807) *(P-16968)*

Kingman Industries, Tustin *Also Called: Johnston International Corporation (P-5825)*

Kings & Convicts Bp LLC .... C 619 255-7213
2215 India St San Diego (92101) *(P-1546)*

Kings & Convicts Bp LLC .... C 619 295-2337
5401 Linda Vista Rd Ste 406 San Diego (92110) *(P-1547)*

Kings Garden LLC .... C 760 275-4969
3540 N Anza Rd Palm Springs (92262) *(P-18156)*

Kings Garden Royal Deliveries, Palm Springs *Also Called: Kings Garden LLC (P-18156)*

Kings Hawaiian Bakery, Gardena *Also Called: Kings Hawaiian Bakery W Inc (P-11583)*

Kings Hawaiian Bakery W Inc (HQ) .... E 310 533-3250
1411 W 190th St Gardena (90248) *(P-11583)*

Kings Oil Tools Inc (PA) .... E 805 238-9311
2235 Spring St Paso Robles (93446) *(P-13440)*

Kings Seafood Company LLC .... A 714 793-1177
7691 Edinger Ave Huntington Beach (92647) *(P-10856)*

Kingsley Manor, Los Angeles *Also Called: Front Porch Communities & Svcs (P-17155)*

Kingson Mold & Machine Inc .... E 714 871-0221
1350 Titan Way Brea (92821) *(P-5586)*

Kingston Technology Company .... A 310 729-3394
17600 Newhope St Fountain Valley (92708) *(P-5881)*

Kingston Technology Company Inc (HQ) .... A 714 435-2600
17600 Newhope St Fountain Valley (92708) *(P-10014)*

Mergent email: customerrelations@mergent.com
1078

2025 Southern California
Business Directory and Buyers Guide

(P-0000) Products & Services Section entry number
(PA)=Parent Co (HQ)=Headquarters (DH)=Div Headquarters

Kingston Technology Corp (PA) .... B 714 435-2600
17600 Newhope St Fountain Valley (92708) *(P-5927)*

Kingswood Capital MGT LLC (PA) .... C 424 744-8238
11111 Santa Monica Blvd Ste 1700 Los Angeles (90025) *(P-12648)*

Kinkisharyo (usa) Inc .... C 424 276-1803
300 Continental Blvd Ste 300 El Segundo (90245) *(P-7627)*

Kinkisharyo International .... D 661 265-1647
2825 E Avenue P Palmdale (93550) *(P-18329)*

Kino Flo Lighting Systems, Burbank *Also Called: Nomoflo Enterprises Inc (P-6468)*

Kinsta Inc .... D 310 736-9306
8605 Santa Monica Blvd # 92581 West Hollywood (90069) *(P-13759)*

Kintera Inc (HQ) .... C 858 795-3000
9605 Scranton Rd Ste 200 San Diego (92121) *(P-13960)*

Kintetsu Enterprises Co Amer (HQ) .... C 310 782-9300
21241 S Western Ave Ste 100 Torrance (90501) *(P-12885)*

Kintetsu Enterprises Co Amer, Torrance *Also Called: Kintetsu Enterprises Co Amer (P-12885)*

Kirk Containers, City Of Commerce *Also Called: Arthurmade Plastics Inc (P-4055)*

Kirkhill Inc .... A 714 529-4901
300 E Cypress St Brea (92821) *(P-3894)*

Kirkhill Inc .... D 562 803-1117
1451 S Carlos Ave Ontario (91761) *(P-3920)*

Kirkhill Inc (HQ) .... D 714 529-4901
300 E Cypress St Brea (92821) *(P-7510)*

Kirkhill Manufacturing Company, Ontario *Also Called: KMC Acquisition LLC (P-3922)*

Kirkhill Rubber Company .... D 562 803-1117
2500 E Thompson St Long Beach (90805) *(P-3921)*

Kirkland & Ellis LLP .... B 213 680-8400
333 S Hope St Ste 3000 Los Angeles (90071) *(P-16717)*

Kirkland & Ellis LLP .... C 310 552-4200
2049 Century Park E Ste 3700 Los Angeles (90067) *(P-16718)*

Kirkland & Ellis LLP .... C 213 680-8400
555 S Flower St Ste 3700 Los Angeles (90071) *(P-16719)*

Kirkwood Collection, Beverly Hills *Also Called: Kirkwood Collection Inc (P-12886)*

Kirkwood Collection Inc .... D 424 532-1160
301 N Canon Dr Ste 302 Beverly Hills (90210) *(P-12886)*

Kirschenman Enterprises Sls LP .... C 661 366-5736
12826 Edison Hwy Edison (93220) *(P-14522)*

Kisca, Los Angeles *Also Called: Komarov Enterprises Inc (P-2076)*

Kisco Senior Living LLC .... C 714 997-5355
620 S Glassell St Orange (92866) *(P-12356)*

Kiss Packaging Systems, Vista *Also Called: Accutek Packaging Equipment Co (P-5786)*

Kitch Engineering Inc .... E 818 897-7133
12320 Montague St Pacoima (91331) *(P-6162)*

Kitchen and Rail, Arroyo Grande *Also Called: Corbett Vineyards LLC (P-1561)*

Kitchen Cuts LLC .... D 323 560-7415
6045 District Blvd Maywood (90270) *(P-1260)*

Kitchen United, Pasadena *Also Called: Fresgo LLC (P-8906)*

Kitcor Corporation .... E 323 875-2820
9959 Glenoaks Blvd Sun Valley (91352) *(P-5197)*

Kite Electric Incorporated .... C 949 380-7471
2 Thomas Irvine (92618) *(P-932)*

Kite Pharma Inc (HQ) .... D 310 824-9999
2400 Broadway Ste 100 Santa Monica (90404) *(P-17802)*

Kite, A Gilead Company, Santa Monica *Also Called: Kite Pharma Inc (P-17802)*

Kitson Landscape MGT Inc .... D 805 681-9460
5787 Thornwood Dr Goleta (93117) *(P-213)*

Kittrich Corporation (PA) .... C 714 736-1000
1585 W Mission Blvd Pomona (91766) *(P-2604)*

Kittyhawk Inc (PA) .... E 714 895-5024
11651 Monarch St Garden Grove (92841) *(P-4703)*

Kittyhawk Products, Garden Grove *Also Called: Kpi Services Inc (P-4705)*

Kittyhawk Products CA LLC .... E 714 895-5024
11651 Monarch St Garden Grove (92841) *(P-4704)*

Kive Company .... E 747 212-0337
15800 Arminta St Van Nuys (91406) *(P-13961)*

Kjos Music, San Diego *Also Called: Neil A Kjos Music Company (P-2928)*

Kkw Trucking Inc (PA) .... A 909 869-1200
3100 Pomona Blvd Pomona (91768) *(P-9081)*

Klax Radio Station, Los Angeles *Also Called: Spanish Brdcstg Sys of Cal (P-9489)*

Klein Electronics, Escondido *Also Called: Klein Electronics Inc (P-10260)*

Klein Electronics Inc .... E 760 781-3220
349 N Vinewood St Escondido (92029) *(P-10260)*

Kleinfelder, San Diego *Also Called: Kleinfelder Inc (P-17572)*

Kleinfelder Inc (HQ) .... C 619 831-4600
770 1st Ave Ste 400 San Diego (92101) *(P-17572)*

Kleinfelder Group Inc (PA) .... C 619 831-4600
770 1st Ave Ste 400 San Diego (92101) *(P-17573)*

Kleintob Inc .... D 805 527-3389
2691 Tapo Canyon Rd Ste B Simi Valley (93063) *(P-13150)*

Klentysoft Inc .... C 707 518-9640
440 N Barranca Ave # 2331 Covina (91723) *(P-13962)*

Klientboost LLC .... C 657 203-7866
2787 Bristol St Ste 100 Costa Mesa (92626) *(P-13220)*

Klk Forte Industry Inc (PA) .... E 323 415-9181
1535 Rio Vista Ave Los Angeles (90023) *(P-2113)*

Kllm Transport Services LLC .... D 909 350-9600
5361 Santa Ana St Ontario (91761) *(P-8958)*

Klm Laboratories Inc .... D 661 295-2600
28280 Alta Vista Ave Valencia (91355) *(P-10088)*

Klm Orthotic, Valencia *Also Called: Klm Laboratories Inc (P-10088)*

Kloeckner Metals Corporation .... D 562 906-2020
9804 Norwalk Blvd # A Santa Fe Springs (90670) *(P-10143)*

Klune Industries Inc (DH) .... B 818 503-8100
7323 Coldwater Canyon Ave North Hollywood (91605) *(P-7511)*

KMC Acquisition LLC (PA) .... E 562 396-0121
1451 S Carlos Ave Ontario (91761) *(P-3922)*

Kme Fire, Fontana *Also Called: Kovatch Mobile Equipment Corp (P-7182)*

Kmp Numatech Pacific, Pomona *Also Called: Numatech West (kmp) LLC (P-2682)*

Kmr Label LLC .... E 310 603-8910
1360 W Walnut Pkwy Compton (90220) *(P-3107)*

Knd Development 55 LLC .... D 909 581-6400
10841 White Oak Ave Rancho Cucamonga (91730) *(P-16066)*

Knight Law Group LLP .... C 424 355-1155
10250 Constellation Blvd Ste 2500 Los Angeles (90067) *(P-16720)*

Knight LLC (HQ) .... D 949 595-4800
15340 Barranca Pkwy Irvine (92618) *(P-5826)*

Knit Generation Group Inc .... E 213 221-5081
3818 S Broadway Los Angeles (90037) *(P-1882)*

Knobbe Martens Olson Bear LLP (PA) .... B 949 760-0404
2040 Main St Fl 14 Irvine (92614) *(P-16721)*

Knobbe Martens Olson Bear LLP .... D 858 707-4000
12790 El Camino Real Ste 100 San Diego (92130) *(P-16722)*

Knolls Convalescent Hosp Inc (PA) .... C 760 245-5361
16890 Green Tree Blvd Victorville (92395) *(P-15686)*

Knolls West Enterprise .... C 760 245-0107
16890 Green Tree Blvd Victorville (92395) *(P-15687)*

Knolls West Residential Care, Victorville *Also Called: Knolls West Enterprise (P-15687)*

Knott's Berry Farm, Buena Park *Also Called: Knotts Berry Farm LLC (P-15104)*

Knott's Berry Farm Hotel, Buena Park *Also Called: Knotts Berry Farm LLC (P-12887)*

Knotts Berry Farm LLC .... D 714 995-1111
7675 Crescent Ave Buena Park (90620) *(P-12887)*

Knotts Berry Farm LLC (HQ) .... B 714 827-1776
8039 Beach Blvd Buena Park (90620) *(P-15104)*

Knox Attorney Service Inc (PA) .... C 619 233-9700
1550 Hotel Cir N Ste 440 San Diego (92108) *(P-14523)*

Knox Services, San Diego *Also Called: Knox Attorney Service Inc (P-14523)*

Kns Industrial Supply, Santa Fe Springs *Also Called: International Consulting Unltd (P-4548)*

Koam Engineering Systems Inc .... C 858 292-0922
7807 Convoy Ct Ste 200 San Diego (92111) *(P-14090)*

Kobelco Compressors Amer Inc (DH) .... B 951 739-3030
1450 W Rincon St Corona (92880) *(P-5758)*

Kobelco Compressors Amer Inc .... D 951 739-3030
301 N Smith Ave Corona (92878) *(P-5759)*

Kobert & Company Inc .... D 323 725-1000
6131 Garfield Ave Commerce (90040) *(P-10188)*

Kobis Windows & Doors Mfg Inc .... E 818 764-6400
7326 Laurel Canyon Blvd North Hollywood (91605) *(P-2352)*

Kodella LLC .... C 844 563-3552
17922 Fitch Ste 200 Irvine (92614) *(P-14230)*

Kofax Limited (PA) .... A 949 783-1000
15211 Laguna Canyon Rd Irvine (92618) *(P-13963)*

Kole Imports .... D 310 834-0004
  24600 Main St Carson (90745) *(P-11126)*

Koll Construction LP .... D 949 833-3030
  4343 Von Karman Ave Ste 150 Newport Beach (92660) *(P-553)*

Kollmorgen Corporation .... D 805 696-1236
  33 S La Patera Ln Santa Barbara (93117) *(P-6326)*

Koloa Pacific Construction Inc .... C 858 486-7800
  12700 Stowe Dr Ste 260 Poway (92064) *(P-416)*

Komar Apparel Supply, Los Angeles *Also Called: Mdc Interior Solutions LLC (P-2198)*

Komar Distribution Services, Jurupa Valley *Also Called: Charles Komar & Sons Inc (P-2147)*

Komarov Enterprises Inc .... D 213 244-7000
  10939 Venice Blvd Los Angeles (90034) *(P-2076)*

Kona Bay Hotel, Manhattan Beach *Also Called: Oka & Oka Hawaii LLC (P-12949)*

Kona Kai Resort Hotel, San Diego *Also Called: Westgroup Kona Kai LLC (P-15187)*

Konami, Hawthorne *Also Called: Konami Digital Entrmt Inc (P-13964)*

Konami Digital Entrmt Inc (DH) .... **E 310 220-8100**
  1 Konami Way Hawthorne (90250) *(P-13964)*

Kone Inc .... E 714 890-7080
  1540 Scenic Ave # 100 Costa Mesa (92626) *(P-14774)*

Konecranes Inc .... E 562 903-1371
  10310 Pioneer Blvd Ste 2 Santa Fe Springs (90670) *(P-5522)*

Konecranes Inc .... E 909 930-0108
  1620 S Carlos Ave Ontario (91761) *(P-5523)*

Konigsberg Instruments Inc .... E 626 775-6500
  1017 S Mountain Ave Monrovia (91016) *(P-8182)*

Kooji Intl Minority Educatn .... D 951 313-7403
  6896 Magnolia Ave Riverside (92506) *(P-17351)*

Koos Manufacturing Inc .... A 323 249-1000
  2741 Seminole Ave South Gate (90280) *(P-14524)*

Kor Realty Group LLC (PA) .... **D 323 930-3700**
  1212 S Flower St Fl 5 Los Angeles (90015) *(P-12475)*

Koral Activewear, Santa Monica *Also Called: Koral LLC (P-2017)*

Koral Industries LLC (PA) .... **E 323 585-5343**
  1334 3rd Street Promenade Ste 200 Santa Monica (90401) *(P-2114)*

Koral LLC .... E 323 391-1060
  1334 3rd Street Promenade Ste 200 Santa Monica (90401) *(P-2017)*

Koral Los Angeles, Santa Monica *Also Called: Koral Industries LLC (P-2114)*

Korden Inc .... E 909 988-8979
  601 S Milliken Ave Ste H Ontario (91761) *(P-2530)*

Kore1 Inc .... D 949 706-6990
  36 Discovery Irvine (92618) *(P-14231)*

Kore1 LLC .... C 949 706-6990
  36 Discovery Irvine (92618) *(P-13536)*

Korea Times, Los Angeles *Also Called: The Korea Times Los Angeles Inc (P-2832)*

Korean Air, Los Angeles *Also Called: Korean Air Lines Co Ltd (P-9159)*

Korean Air, Los Angeles *Also Called: Korean Airlines Co Ltd (P-9243)*

Korean Air Lines Co Ltd .... C 310 646-4866
  380 World Way Ste S4 Los Angeles (90045) *(P-9159)*

Korean Airlines Co Ltd .... C 310 410-2000
  6101 W Imperial Hwy Los Angeles (90045) *(P-9160)*

Korean Airlines Co Ltd .... B 213 484-5700
  900 Wilshire Blvd Ste 1100 Los Angeles (90017) *(P-9243)*

Korean Arln Crgo Reservations, Los Angeles *Also Called: Korean Airlines Co Ltd (P-9160)*

Korean Community Services Inc .... C 714 527-6561
  451 W Lincoln Ave Ste 100 Anaheim (92805) *(P-16295)*

Korn Ferry (PA) .... **C 310 552-1834**
  1900 Avenue Of The Stars Ste 1500 Los Angeles (90067) *(P-13537)*

Korn Ferry, Los Angeles *Also Called: Korn Ferry (P-13537)*

Korn Ferry (us) (HQ) .... **C 310 552-1834**
  1900 Avenue Of The Stars Ste 2600 Los Angeles (90067) *(P-18157)*

Koros USA Inc .... E 805 529-0825
  610 Flinn Ave Moorpark (93021) *(P-8183)*

Kosakura Associates, Irvine *Also Called: CK Manufacturing & Trading Inc (P-2560)*

Kovatch Mobile Equipment Corp .... E 951 685-1224
  14562 Manzanita Dr Fontana (92335) *(P-7182)*

Kovin Corporation Inc .... E 858 558-0100
  9240 Mira Este Ct San Diego (92126) *(P-3029)*

Kpc Global Medical Centers Inc (DH) .... **C 714 953-3500**
  1117 E Devonshire Ave Hemet (92543) *(P-16067)*

Kpc Group Inc (PA) .... **C 951 782-8812**
  9 Kpc Pkwy # 301 Corona (92879) *(P-18158)*

Kpff Inc .... D 949 252-1022
  18500 Von Karman Ave Ste 1000 Irvine (92612) *(P-17574)*

Kpi Services Inc .... E 714 895-5024
  11651 Monarch St Garden Grove (92841) *(P-4705)*

Kpmg, Los Angeles *Also Called: Kpmg New York Foundation Inc (P-17352)*

Kpmg LLP .... D 703 286-8175
  4464 Jasmine Ave Culver City (90232) *(P-17738)*

Kpmg LLP .... C 949 885-5400
  20 Pacifica Ste 700 Irvine (92618) *(P-17739)*

Kpmg New York Foundation Inc .... C 212 758-9700
  550 S Hope St Ste 1500 Los Angeles (90071) *(P-17352)*

Kprs, Brea *Also Called: Kprs Construction Services Inc (P-554)*

Kprs Construction Services Inc (PA) .... **D 714 672-0800**
  2850 Saturn St Ste 110 Brea (92821) *(P-554)*

Kpwr Radio LLC .... C 562 745-2300
  9550 Firestone Blvd Ste 105 Downey (90241) *(P-14525)*

Kraco Enterprises LLC .... C 310 639-0666
  505 E Euclid Ave Compton (90222) *(P-11448)*

Kraft Foods, Fullerton *Also Called: Kraft Heinz Foods Company (P-1352)*

Kraft Heinz Foods Company .... E 949 250-4080
  2450 White Rd Irvine (92614) *(P-1342)*

Kraft Heinz Foods Company .... E 714 870-8235
  1500 E Walnut Ave Fullerton (92831) *(P-1352)*

Kramer-Wilson Company Inc (PA) .... **C 818 760-0880**
  340 N Westlake Blvd Ste 210 Westlake Village (91362) *(P-12122)*

Krasnes Inc .... D 619 232-2066
  2222 Commercial St San Diego (92113) *(P-2181)*

KRATOS, San Diego *Also Called: Kratos Def & SEC Solutions Inc (P-7646)*

Kratos Def & SEC Solutions Inc (PA) ...... **C 858 812-7300**
  10680 Treena St Ste 600 San Diego (92131) *(P-7646)*

Kratos Public Safety & Security Solutions Inc ... D 858 812-7300
  4820 Eastgate Mall Ste 200 San Diego (92121) *(P-14411)*

Kratos Tech Trning Sltions Inc (HQ) .... D 858 812-7300
  10680 Treena St Ste 600 San Diego (92131) *(P-17575)*

KRC Orange, Orange *Also Called: Kisco Senior Living LLC (P-12356)*

Krca License LLC .... C 818 840-1400
  1845 W Empire Ave Burbank (91504) *(P-9479)*

Kretek International Inc (DH) .... **D 805 531-8888**
  5449 Endeavour Ct Moorpark (93021) *(P-11104)*

Krg Technologies Inc (PA) .... **B 661 257-9967**
  25000 Avenue Stanford Ste 243 Valencia (91355) *(P-13760)*

Krieger Speciality Pdts LLC (DH) .... **D 562 695-0645**
  4880 Gregg Rd Pico Rivera (90660) *(P-4892)*

Krieger Steel Products, Pico Rivera *Also Called: Krieger Speciality Pdts LLC (P-4892)*

Krikorian Premiere Theatre LLC .... D 714 826-7469
  8290 La Palma Ave Buena Park (90620) *(P-14939)*

Krikorian Premiere Theatre LLC .... D 760 945-7469
  25 Main St Vista (92083) *(P-14940)*

Krikorian Premiere Theatre LLC .... D 562 205-3456
  8540 Whittier Blvd Pico Rivera (90660) *(P-14941)*

Kroger Co .... B 859 630-6959
  2201 S Wilmington Ave Compton (90220) *(P-9082)*

Kros-Wise .... C 619 607-2899
  435 E Carmel St San Marcos (92078) *(P-18330)*

Krost (PA) .... **C 626 449-4225**
  225 S Lake Ave Ste 400 Pasadena (91101) *(P-17740)*

Krost Bumgarten Kniss Guerrero, Pasadena *Also Called: Krost (P-17740)*

Krueger International Inc .... E 949 748-7000
  16510 Bake Pkwy Ste 100 Irvine (92618) *(P-2548)*

Kruse and Son Inc .... E 626 358-4536
  235 Kruse Ave Monrovia (91016) *(P-1261)*

Kruse Pet Holdings LLC (PA) .... **E 559 302-4880**
  1609 W Highway 246 Buellton (93427) *(P-1419)*

Kryler Corp .... E 714 871-9611
  1217 E Ash Ave Fullerton (92831) *(P-5272)*

Krystal Enterprises, Riverside *Also Called: Krystal Infinity LLC (P-7205)*

Krystal Infinity LLC .... B
  6915 Arlington Ave Riverside (92504) *(P-7205)*

Krystal Ventures LLC .... E 213 507-2215
  17 Shell Bch Newport Coast (92657) *(P-8455)*

KS Fabrication & Machine, Bakersfield *Also Called: K S Fabrication & Machine Inc (P-682)*

Mergent email: customerrelations@mergent.com
1080

2025 Southern California
Business Directory and Buyers Guide

(P-0000) Products & Services Section entry number
(PA)=Parent Co (HQ)=Headquarters (DH)=Div Headquarters

KS Industries LP (PA) .... A 661 617-1700
6205 District Blvd Bakersfield (93313) *(P-684)*

Ksby Communications LLC .... D 805 541-6666
1772 Calle Joaquin San Luis Obispo (93405) *(P-9509)*

Ksl Rancho Mirage Operating Co Inc .... B 760 568-2727
41000 Bob Hope Dr Rancho Mirage (92270) *(P-12888)*

Ksl Recreation Management Operations LLC ..... A 760 564-8000
50905 Avenida Bermudas La Quinta (92253) *(P-15086)*

Ksl Resorts Hotel Del Coronado .... C 619 435-6611
1500 Orange Ave Coronado (92118) *(P-12889)*

KSM Garment Inc .... E 323 585-8811
5613 Maywood Ave Maywood (90270) *(P-2043)*

Ksm Healthcare Inc .... D 818 242-1183
1400 W Glenoaks Blvd Glendale (91201) *(P-15688)*

Ktb Software LLC .... D 505 306-0390
11101 W Olympic Blvd Los Angeles (90064) *(P-13761)*

Ktgy Architecture Planning, Irvine *Also Called: Ktgy Group Inc (P-17678)*

Ktgy Group Inc (PA) .... D 949 851-2133
17911 Von Karman Ave Ste 200 Irvine (92614) *(P-17678)*

Kti Incorporated .... D 909 434-1888
3011 N Laurel Ave Rialto (92377) *(P-4399)*

Kts Kitchens Inc .... C 310 764-0850
1065 E Walnut St Ste C Carson (90746) *(P-1798)*

Kubota Industrial Equipment .... C 817 756-1171
3401 Del Amo Blvd Torrance (90503) *(P-10050)*

Kuehne + Nagel Inc .... C 909 574-2300
9425 Nevada St Redlands (92374) *(P-9299)*

Kuehne + Nagel Inc .... B 310 641-5500
20000 S Western Ave Torrance (90501) *(P-9300)*

Kui Co Inc .... E 949 369-7949
266 Calle Pintoresco San Clemente (92672) *(P-4156)*

Kulicke & Soffa Industries, Santa Ana *Also Called: Kulicke Sffa Wedge Bonding Inc (P-7131)*

Kulicke Sffa Wedge Bonding Inc .... C 949 660-0440
1821 E Dyer Rd Ste 200 Santa Ana (92705) *(P-7131)*

Kulr Technology Corporation .... D 408 663-5247
4863 Shawline St Ste B San Diego (92111) *(P-6840)*

Kum Kang Trading USA Inc .... E 562 531-6111
6433 Alondra Blvd Paramount (90723) *(P-3667)*

Kumar Industries .... E 909 591-0722
4775 Chino Ave Chino (91710) *(P-4844)*

Kura Oncology Inc (PA) .... E 858 500-8800
12730 High Bluff Dr Ste 400 San Diego (92130) *(P-3439)*

Kurz Transfer Products LP .... D 951 738-9521
415 N Smith Ave Corona (92878) *(P-8690)*

Kuster Co Oil Well Services .... E 562 595-0661
2900 E 29th St Long Beach (90806) *(P-342)*

Kuster Company, Long Beach *Also Called: Kuster Co Oil Well Services (P-342)*

Kustom Kanopies Inc .... E 801 399-3400
210 Senior Cir Lompoc (93436) *(P-489)*

Kut From The Kloth, City Of Industry *Also Called: Swatfame Inc (P-10730)*

Kvc Group LLC .... D 855 438-0377
1551 N Tustin Ave Ste 550 Santa Ana (92705) *(P-18159)*

Kvcr, TV & FM, San Bernardino *Also Called: San Brnrdino Cmnty College Dst (P-9488)*

Kvr Investment Group Inc .... D 818 896-1102
12113 Branford St Sun Valley (91352) *(P-5700)*

Kw International Inc .... D 310 354-6944
1457 Glenn Curtiss St Carson (90746) *(P-9301)*

Kw International Inc .... D 310 747-1380
18511 S Broadwick St Rancho Dominguez (90220) *(P-9302)*

Kwdz Manufacturing LLC (PA) .... D 323 526-3526
337 S Anderson St Los Angeles (90033) *(P-2165)*

Kwikset Corporation .... A 949 672-4000
19701 Da Vinci Foothill Ranch (92610) *(P-4776)*

Kxp Carrier Services LLC .... C 424 320-5300
11777 San Vicente Blvd Los Angeles (90049) *(P-9006)*

Kyoceara, Costa Mesa *Also Called: Kyocera Tycom Corporation (P-5547)*

Kyocera America Inc .... E 858 576-2600
8611 Balboa Ave San Diego (92123) *(P-6841)*

Kyocera Dcment Solutions W LLC .... C 800 996-9591
14101 Alton Pkwy Irvine (92618) *(P-9975)*

Kyocera International Inc (HQ) .... D 858 576-2600
8611 Balboa Ave San Diego (92123) *(P-6842)*

Kyocera Medical Tech Inc .... E 909 557-2360
1289 Bryn Mawr Ave Ste A Redlands (92374) *(P-8282)*

Kyocera Precision Tools, Orange *Also Called: Kyocera SGS Precision Tls Inc (P-5614)*

Kyocera SGS Precision Tls Inc .... D 888 848-9266
1814 W Collins Ave Orange (92867) *(P-5614)*

Kyocera Sld Laser Inc .... E 310 808-4542
111 Castilian Dr Goleta (93117) *(P-7132)*

Kyocera Tycom Corporation .... B 714 428-3600
3565 Cadillac Ave Costa Mesa (92626) *(P-5547)*

Kyolic, Mission Viejo *Also Called: Wakunaga of America Co Ltd (P-3522)*

Kyoto Grand Hotel and Gardens, Los Angeles *Also Called: Crestline Hotels & Resorts Inc (P-12803)*

Kyowa Kirin Inc .... E 858 952-7000
9420 Athena Cir La Jolla (92037) *(P-3440)*

Kyriba Corp (PA) .... E 858 210-3560
4435 Eastgate Mall Ste 200 San Diego (92121) *(P-13965)*

Kythera Biopharmaceuticals Inc .... C 818 587-4500
30930 Russell Ranch Rd Fl 3 Westlake Village (91362) *(P-3441)*

L & H Mold & Engineering Inc (PA) .... E 909 930-1547
140 Atlantic St Pomona (91768) *(P-4157)*

L & H Molds, Pomona *Also Called: L & H Mold & Engineering Inc (P-4157)*

L & L Distributors, Los Angeles *Also Called: L&L Manufacturing Co Inc (P-2115)*

L & L Printers Carlsbad LLC .... E 760 477-0321
6200 Yarrow Dr Carlsbad (92011) *(P-3030)*

L & M Machining Corporation .... D 714 414-0923
550 S Melrose St Placentia (92870) *(P-6954)*

L & O Aliso Viejo LLC .... C 949 643-6700
50 Enterprise Aliso Viejo (92656) *(P-12890)*

L & R Distributors Inc .... B 909 980-3807
9292 9th St Rancho Cucamonga (91730) *(P-10665)*

L & S Stone and Fireplace Shop, San Marcos *Also Called: L&S Stone LLC (P-4475)*

L & T Meat Co .... D 323 262-2815
3050 E 11th St Los Angeles (90023) *(P-10875)*

L & T Precision LLC .... C 858 513-7874
12105 Kirkham Rd Poway (92064) *(P-4996)*

L A Air Inc .... C 310 215-8245
5933 W Century Blvd # 500 Los Angeles (90045) *(P-9161)*

L A Cstm AP & Promotions Inc (PA) .... E 562 595-1770
2680 Temple Ave Long Beach (90806) *(P-2018)*

L A Gauge Company Inc .... D 818 767-7193
7440 San Fernando Rd Sun Valley (91352) *(P-6163)*

L A Girl, Ontario *Also Called: Beauty 21 Cosmetics Inc (P-10615)*

L A Glo Inc .... E 323 932-0091
1451 Hi Point St Los Angeles (90035) *(P-2068)*

L A H S A, Los Angeles *Also Called: Los Angeles Homeless Svcs Auth (P-16974)*

L A Lighting, El Monte *Also Called: Los Angeles Ltg Mfg Co Inc (P-10190)*

L A P F C U, Van Nuys *Also Called: Los Angeles Police Credit Un (P-11829)*

L A Party Rents Inc .... D 818 989-4300
13520 Saticoy St Van Nuys (91402) *(P-13459)*

L A Philharmonic, Los Angeles *Also Called: Los Angeles Philharmonic Assn (P-14997)*

L A Press, Los Angeles *Also Called: LA Printing & Graphics Inc (P-3031)*

L A Propoint Inc .... E 818 767-6800
10870 La Tuna Canyon Rd Sun Valley (91352) *(P-5449)*

L A Supply Co .... E 949 470-9900
4241 E Brickell St Ontario (91761) *(P-3151)*

L and R Auto Parks Inc .... C 213 784-3018
707 Wilshire Blvd Ste 4300 Los Angeles (90017) *(P-14657)*

L C Miller Company .... E 323 268-3611
717 Monterey Pass Rd Monterey Park (91754) *(P-5802)*

L C Pringle Sales Inc (PA) .... E 714 892-1524
12020 Western Ave Garden Grove (92841) *(P-2605)*

L E Coppersmith Inc (HQ) .... D 310 607-8000
525 S Douglas St Ste 100 El Segundo (90245) *(P-9303)*

L F P Inc (PA) .... D 323 651-3525
8484 Wilshire Blvd Ste 900 Beverly Hills (90211) *(P-2863)*

L J B, San Diego *Also Called: Tanvex Biopharma Usa Inc (P-17826)*

L M I, Ontario *Also Called: Larry Mthvin Installations Inc (P-4338)*

L M S, Irvine *Also Called: Ovation Tech Inc (P-14240)*

L M Scofield Company (DH) .... E 323 720-3000
12767 Imperial Hwy Santa Fe Springs (90670) *(P-3809)*

Employee Codes: A=Over 500 employees, B=251-500
C=101-250, D=51-100, E=20-50, F=10-19, G=1-9

2025 Southern California
Business Directory and Buyers Guide

© Mergent Inc. 1-800-342-5647
1081

L S A, Irvine *Also Called: Lsa Associates Inc (P-18332)*

L Space, Irvine *Also Called: Lspace America LLC (P-1922)*

L Spark .... E 805 626-0511
1140 Kendall Rd Ste A San Luis Obispo (93401) *(P-8456)*

L-3 Interstate Electronics, Anaheim *Also Called: L3harris Interstate Elec Corp (P-7924)*

L-3 Telemetry & Rf Products, San Diego *Also Called: L3 Technologies Inc (P-6623)*

L-Com, Irvine *Also Called: Infinite Electronics Inc (P-7008)*

L-O Bedford Operating LLC .... C 781 275-5500
11755 Wilshire Blvd Ste 1350 Los Angeles (90025) *(P-12891)*

L-O Coronado Hotel Inc .... D 619 435-6611
1500 Orange Ave Coronado (92118) *(P-12892)*

L.A. Care Health Plan, Los Angeles *Also Called: Local Inttive Hlth Auth For Lo (P-12096)*

L.A. Cold Storage, Los Angeles *Also Called: Standard-Southern Corporation (P-9043)*

L.A. GAY & LESBIAN CENTER, Los Angeles *Also Called: Los Angeles Lgbt Center (P-17235)*

L.A. Inflight Service Company, Gardena *Also Called: World Svc Wst/La Inflght Svc L (P-9213)*

L.A. Sleeve, Santa Fe Springs *Also Called: Los Angeles Sleeve Co Inc (P-7266)*

L.A.cO., Whittier *Also Called: Los Angles Cnty Snttion Dstrct (P-9788)*

L.H. Dottie Co, Commerce *Also Called: Kobert & Company Inc (P-10188)*

L'Auberge Del Mar, Del Mar *Also Called: Lhoberge Lessee Inc (P-12902)*

L'Ermitage Hotel, Beverly Hills *Also Called: Raffles Lrmitage Beverly Hills (P-12983)*

L&L Manufacturing Co Inc .... B
12400 Wilshire Blvd Ste 360 Los Angeles (90025) *(P-2115)*

L&S Stone LLC (DH).. E 760 736-3232
1370 Grand Ave Ste B San Marcos (92078) *(P-4475)*

L&T Staffing Inc .... B 323 727-9056
2122 W Whittier Blvd Montebello (90640) *(P-13538)*

L3 Maripro Inc .... D 805 683-3881
1522 Cook Pl Goleta (93117) *(P-17576)*

L3 Technologies Inc .... D 818 367-0111
15825 Roxford St Sylmar (91342) *(P-6622)*

L3 Technologies Inc .... B 858 279-0411
9020 Balboa Ave San Diego (92123) *(P-6623)*

L3 Technologies Inc .... D 858 552-9716
10180 Barnes Canyon Rd San Diego (92121) *(P-6624)*

L3 Technologies Inc .... B 858 552-9500
9020 Balboa Ave San Diego (92123) *(P-6625)*

L3 Technologies Inc .... D 805 683-3881
7414 Hollister Ave Goleta (93117) *(P-6626)*

L3 Technologies Inc .... C 714 758-4222
602 E Vermont Ave Anaheim (92805) *(P-6627)*

L3 Technologies Inc .... E 714 956-9200
901 E Ball Rd Anaheim (92805) *(P-7728)*

L3 Technologies Inc .... C 760 431-6800
5957 Landau Ct Carlsbad (92008) *(P-7729)*

L3 Technologies Inc .... D 805 584-1717
200 W Los Angeles Ave Simi Valley (93065) *(P-7730)*

L3 Technologies Inc .... C 818 367-0111
28022 Industry Dr Valencia (91355) *(P-7731)*

L3harris Interstate Elec Corp .... D 714 758-3395
604 E Vermont Ave Anaheim (92805) *(P-6628)*

L3harris Interstate Elec Corp .... D 858 552-9500
3033 Science Park Rd San Diego (92121) *(P-7921)*

L3harris Interstate Elec Corp .... D 714 758-0500
708 E Vermont Ave Anaheim (92805) *(P-7922)*

L3harris Interstate Elec Corp .... D 714 758-0500
600 E Vermont Ave Anaheim (92805) *(P-7923)*

L3harris Interstate Elec Corp (DH).............................. B 714 758-0500
602 E Vermont Ave Anaheim (92805) *(P-7924)*

L3harris Interstate Elec Corp .... C 714 758-0500
707 E Vermont Ave A Anaheim (92805) *(P-10261)*

L3harris Technologies Inc .... B 818 901-2523
7821 Orion Ave Van Nuys (91406) *(P-7732)*

L3harris Technologies Inc .... E 310 481-6000
12121 Wilshire Blvd Ste 910 Los Angeles (90025) *(P-7733)*

L3harris Technologies Inc .... C 626 305-6230
1400 S Shamrock Ave Monrovia (91016) *(P-7734)*

La 1000 Santa Fe LLC .... C 213 205-1000
1000 S Santa Fe Ave Los Angeles (90021) *(P-18002)*

La Apparel, Los Angeles *Also Called: Los Angeles Apparel Inc (P-2196)*

La Apparel, Los Angeles *Also Called: Los Angeles Apparel Inc (P-2197)*

La Asccion Ncnal Pro Prsnas My .... A 213 202-5900
1452 W Temple St Ste 100 Los Angeles (90026) *(P-16969)*

La Barca Tortilleria Inc .... E 323 268-1744
3047 Whittier Blvd Los Angeles (90023) *(P-1799)*

LA BIOMED, Torrance *Also Called: Lundquist Institute For Biomedical Innovation At Harbor-Ucla Medical Center (P-17881)*

La Bonita, Norwalk *Also Called: Dianas Mexican Food Pdts Inc (P-1764)*

La Boxing Franchise Corp .... C 714 668-0911
1241 E Dyer Rd Ste 100 Santa Ana (92705) *(P-15052)*

LA Cabinet & Millwork Inc .... E 323 227-5000
3005 Humboldt St Los Angeles (90031) *(P-2569)*

La Canada Flintridge Cntry CLB .... D 818 790-0611
5500 Godbey Dr La Canada (91011) *(P-15142)*

La Capital, Los Angeles *Also Called: Los Angeles Capital MGT LLC (P-12635)*

La Casa Mhrc, Long Beach *Also Called: Telecare Corporation (P-16512)*

La Cienega Associates .... D 310 854-0071
8500 Beverly Blvd Ste 501 Los Angeles (90048) *(P-12476)*

La Clippers LLC .... B 213 742-7500
3930 W Century Blvd Inglewood (90303) *(P-15029)*

La Colonial Mexican Foods, Monterey Park *Also Called: La Colonial Tortilla Pdts Inc (P-1800)*

La Colonial Tortilla Pdts Inc .... C 626 289-3647
543 Monterey Pass Rd Monterey Park (91754) *(P-1800)*

La Costa Coffee Roasting Co (PA) .... E 760 438-8160
6965 El Camino Real Ste 208 Carlsbad (92009) *(P-11306)*

La Costa Glen, Carlsbad *Also Called: La Costa Glen Crlsbad Ccrc LLC (P-13539)*

La Costa Glen Crlsbad Ccrc LLC (PA)............................ D 760 704-6400
1940 Levante St Carlsbad (92009) *(P-13539)*

La Costa Resort & Spa, Carlsbad *Also Called: Lc Trs Inc (P-12897)*

La County Museum of Art, Los Angeles *Also Called: Museum Associates (P-17256)*

La County Probation, Whittier *Also Called: County of Los Angeles (P-16908)*

La Cumbre Country Club .... D 805 687-2421
4015 Via Laguna Santa Barbara (93110) *(P-15143)*

La Dye & Print Inc .... E 310 327-3200
13416 Estrella Ave Gardena (90248) *(P-10712)*

LA Envelope Incorporated .... E 323 838-9300
1053 S Vail Ave Montebello (90640) *(P-2751)*

La Espanola Meats Inc .... E 310 539-0455
25020 Doble Ave Harbor City (90710) *(P-1262)*

La Fe Tortilleria Factory, San Marcos *Also Called: La Fe Tortilleria Inc (P-1801)*

La Fe Tortilleria Inc (PA) .... E 760 752-8350
1512 Linda Vista Dr San Marcos (92078) *(P-1801)*

La Flora Del Sur, Los Angeles *Also Called: Walker Foods Inc (P-1363)*

La Folltte Jhnson De Haas Fsle (PA)............................. C 213 426-3600
701 N Brand Blvd Ste 600 Glendale (91203) *(P-16723)*

La Fortaleza Inc .... D 323 261-1211
525 N Ford Blvd Los Angeles (90022) *(P-1802)*

LA Gem and Jewelry Design (PA) .... E 213 488-1290
659 S Broadway Fl 7 Los Angeles (90014) *(P-8457)*

LA Gem and Jewelry Design .... D 213 488-1290
3232 E Washington Blvd Los Angeles (90058) *(P-8458)*

La Gloria Foods Corp (PA).. D 323 262-0410
3455 E 1st St Los Angeles (90063) *(P-1803)*

La Gloria Tortilleria, Los Angeles *Also Called: La Gloria Foods Corp (P-1803)*

La Habra Stucco, Riverside *Also Called: Parex Usa Inc (P-11250)*

La Jolla Bch & Tennis CLB Inc .... B 858 459-8271
8110 Camino Del Oro La Jolla (92037) *(P-12893)*

La Jolla Bch & Tennis CLB Inc (PA).............................. C 858 454-7126
2000 Spindrift Dr La Jolla (92037) *(P-15144)*

La Jolla Cove Ht Mtl Aprtmnts .... D 858 459-2621
1155 Coast Blvd La Jolla (92037) *(P-12894)*

La Jolla Cove Motel, La Jolla *Also Called: La Jolla Cove Ht Mtl Aprtmnts (P-12894)*

La Jolla Csmtc Srgery Cntre In .... D 858 452-1981
9850 Genesee Ave Ste 130 La Jolla (92037) *(P-15373)*

La Jolla Group Inc (PA) .... B 949 428-2800
14350 Myford Rd Irvine (92606) *(P-14526)*

La Jolla Inst For Allrgy Immnl, La Jolla *Also Called: La Jolla Inst For Immunology (P-17880)*

La Jolla Inst For Immunology .... B 858 752-6500
9420 Athena Cir La Jolla (92037) *(P-17880)*

La Jolla Nrsing Rhbltation Ctr, La Jolla *Also Called: Covenant Care La Jolla LLC (P-15615)*

LA JOLLA PLAYHOUSE, La Jolla *Also Called: Theater Arts Fndtion San Dego (P-17369)*

La Jolla Skilled Inc .... B 858 625-8700
3884 Nobel Dr San Diego (92122) **(P-15689)**

La Jolla Station, Anaheim *Also Called: Southern California Gas Co (P-9663)*

La Jolla YMCA, La Jolla *Also Called: YMCA of San Diego County (P-17383)*

La La Land Production & Design .... E 323 406-9223
1701 S Santa Fe Ave Los Angeles (90021) **(P-4279)**

La Linen Inc .... E 213 745-4004
1760 E 15th St Los Angeles (90021) **(P-11533)**

LA MAESTRA COMMUNITY HEALTH CE, San Diego *Also Called: La Maestra Family Clinic Inc (P-15374)*

La Maestra Family Clinic Inc (PA) .... C 619 584-1612
4060 Fairmount Ave San Diego (92105) **(P-15374)**

La Mamba LLC .... E 323 526-3526
150 N Myers St Los Angeles (90033) **(P-2044)**

La Mesa Disposal, Signal Hill *Also Called: Edco Disposal Corporation (P-9745)*

La Mesa Medical Offices, La Mesa *Also Called: Kaiser Foundation Hospitals (P-16051)*

La Mesa R V Center Inc (PA) .... C 858 874-8000
7430 Copley Park Pl San Diego (92111) **(P-11480)**

LA Metropolitan Medical Center .... A 323 730-7300
2231 Southwest Dr Los Angeles (90043) **(P-16068)**

La Mexicana LLC .... E 323 277-3660
6535 Caballero Blvd Unit A Buena Park (90620) **(P-1394)**

La Mousse, Gardena *Also Called: La Mousse Desserts Inc (P-1395)*

La Mousse Desserts Inc .... E 310 478-6051
18211 S Broadway Gardena (90248) **(P-1395)**

La Opinion LP (HQ) .... D 213 891-9191
915 Wilshire Blvd Ste 915 Los Angeles (90017) **(P-2809)**

La Opinion LP .... B 213 896-2222
210 E Washington Blvd Los Angeles (90015) **(P-2810)**

La Palm Furnitures & ACC Inc (PA) .... E 310 217-2700
1650 W Artesia Blvd Gardena (90248) **(P-2248)**

La Palma Hospital Medical Center .... B 714 670-7400
7901 Walker St La Palma (90623) **(P-16069)**

La Palma Intercommunity Hosp, La Palma *Also Called: La Palma Hospital Medical Center (P-16069)*

La Palma Medical Offices, La Palma *Also Called: Kaiser Foundation Hospitals (P-15337)*

La Peer Health Systems, Beverly Hills *Also Called: La Peer Surgery Center LLC (P-15375)*

La Peer Surgery Center LLC .... D 310 360-9119
8920 Wilshire Blvd Ste 101 Beverly Hills (90211) **(P-15375)**

LA Pillow & Fiber Inc .... D 323 724-7969
7633 Bequette Ave Pico Rivera (90660) **(P-2213)**

LA Printing & Graphics Inc .... E 310 527-4526
13951 S Main St Los Angeles (90061) **(P-3031)**

La Provence Inc .... D 760 736-3299
1370 W San Marcos Blvd Ste 130 San Marcos (92078) **(P-10954)**

La Provence Bakery, San Marcos *Also Called: La Provence Inc (P-10954)*

La Quinta Brewing Company LLC .... D 760 200-2597
74714 Technology Dr Palm Desert (92211) **(P-1548)**

La Quinta Cliff House, La Quinta *Also Called: TS Enterprises Inc (P-11606)*

La Quinta Resort & Club, La Quinta *Also Called: HP Lq Investment LP (P-12857)*

La Rams Football Club, Los Angeles *Also Called: Los Angeles Rams LLC (P-18009)*

La Rancherita Tortilleria Deli, Santa Ana *Also Called: MRS Foods Incorporated (P-1821)*

La Rocks, Los Angeles *Also Called: LA Gem and Jewelry Design (P-8457)*

La Rocque Better Roofs Inc .... D 909 476-2699
9077 Arrow Rte Ste 100 Rancho Cucamonga (91730) **(P-1088)**

La Sentinel Newspaper, Los Angeles *Also Called: Los Angeles Sentinel Inc (P-2813)*

LA Spas Inc .... C 714 630-1150
1325 N Blue Gum St Anaheim (92806) **(P-8691)**

LA Specialty Produce Co (PA) .... B 562 741-2200
13527 Orden Dr Santa Fe Springs (90670) **(P-10910)**

La Sports Arena, Los Angeles *Also Called: Los Angeles Mem Coliseum Comm (P-17465)*

LA Sports Properties Inc .... C 213 742-7500
1212 S Flower St Fl 5 Los Angeles (90015) **(P-15030)**

La Times .... E 213 237-2279
202 W 1st St Ste 500 Los Angeles (90012) **(P-2811)**

La Tolteca Mexican Foods, Azusa *Also Called: Arrietta Incorporated (P-11273)*

LA Triumph Inc .... E 562 404-7657
13336 Alondra Blvd Cerritos (90703) **(P-1997)**

LA Turbine (HQ) .... D 661 294-8290
28557 Industry Dr Valencia (91355) **(P-5458)**

La Verne Cinema 12, La Verne *Also Called: Edwards Theatres Inc (P-14933)*

La Verne Nursery Inc .... D 805 521-0111
3653 Center St Piru (93040) **(P-59)**

La Vida Del Mar Associates, Solana Beach *Also Called: Senior Resource Group LLC (P-12366)*

La Workout Inc .... C 805 482-8884
500 Paseo Camarillo Camarillo (93010) **(P-15053)**

La Workout Camarillo West, Camarillo *Also Called: La Workout Inc (P-15053)*

La Xpress Air & Heating Svcs .... D 310 856-9678
6400 E Washington Blvd Ste 121 Commerce (90040) **(P-2925)**

La's Totally Awesome, Buena Park *Also Called: Awesome Products Inc (P-3598)*

Laaco Ltd (HQ) .... C 213 622-1254
4469 Admiralty Way Marina Del Rey (90292) **(P-12377)**

Lab Clean Inc .... E 714 689-0063
3627 Briggeman Dr Los Alamitos (90720) **(P-3609)**

Lab Health Medical, Anaheim *Also Called: Teco Diagnostics (P-3554)*

Labarge/Stc Inc .... E 281 207-1400
600 Anton Blvd Costa Mesa (92626) **(P-6843)**

Label House, Ontario *Also Called: L A Supply Co (P-3151)*

Label Impressions, Anaheim *Also Called: Brook & Whittle Limited (P-3124)*

Label Impressions Inc .... E 714 634-3466
1831 W Sequoia Ave Orange (92868) **(P-3152)**

Label Shoppe, The, City Of Industry *Also Called: Labels-R-Us Inc (P-11629)*

Label-Aire, Fullerton *Also Called: Label-Aire Inc (P-5791)*

Label-Aire Inc (PA) .... D 714 449-5155
550 Burning Tree Rd Fullerton (92833) **(P-5791)**

Labels-R-Us Inc .... E 626 333-4001
1121 Fullerton Rd City Of Industry (91748) **(P-11629)**

Labeltex Mills Inc (PA) .... C 323 582-0228
5301 S Santa Fe Ave Vernon (90058) **(P-8572)**

Labeltronix LLC (HQ) .... D 800 429-4321
2419 E Winston Rd Anaheim (92806) **(P-3153)**

Labonita Diana's Mexican Food, Carson *Also Called: Dianas Mexican Food Pdts Inc (P-11274)*

Labor Law Center Inc .... E 800 745-9970
3501 W Garry Ave Santa Ana (92704) **(P-3032)**

Laborlawcenter.com, Santa Ana *Also Called: Labor Law Center Inc (P-3032)*

Labrucherie Produce LLC .... E 760 352-2170
1407 S La Brucherie Rd El Centro (92243) **(P-1804)**

Labs.dental, Santa Ana *Also Called: Chromium Dental II LLC (P-15516)*

Lac & Usc Medical Center .... C 323 409-2345
2051 Marengo St Los Angeles (90033) **(P-15376)**

Lac Usc Medical Center C
1200 N State St Rm 5250 Los Angeles (90089) **(P-16070)**

Lacera, Pasadena *Also Called: Los Angles Cnty Emplyees Rtrme (P-12160)*

Lacerta Group LLC .... D 508 339-3312
20650 Prairie St Chatsworth (91311) **(P-2709)**

Laclede Inc .... E 310 605-4280
2103 E University Dr Rancho Dominguez (90220) **(P-8344)**

Laclede Research Center, Rancho Dominguez *Also Called: Laclede Inc (P-8344)*

Lacmnta, Los Angeles *Also Called: Los Angles Cnty Mtro Trnsp Aut (P-8771)*

LAdesserts Inc .... E 323 588-2522
1433 E Gage Ave Los Angeles (90001) **(P-11261)**

Ladwp, Los Angeles *Also Called: Los Angeles Dept Wtr & Pwr (P-9699)*

Laetitia Vineyard & Winery Inc .... D 805 481-1772
453 Laetitia Vineyard Dr Arroyo Grande (93420) **(P-1577)**

Laetitia Winery, Arroyo Grande *Also Called: Laetitia Vineyard & Winery Inc (P-1577)*

Laguna Blanca School (PA) .... D 805 687-2461
4125 Paloma Dr Santa Barbara (93110) **(P-16813)**

Laguna Clay Company, City Of Industry *Also Called: Jon Brooks Inc (P-4488)*

Laguna Cookie Company Inc .... D 714 546-6855
4041 W Garry Ave Santa Ana (92704) **(P-1490)**

Laguna Home Health Svcs LLC .... C 949 707-5023
25411 Cabot Rd Ste 205 Laguna Hills (92653) **(P-16400)**

Laguna Playhouse (PA) .... C 949 497-2787
606 Laguna Canyon Rd Laguna Beach (92651) **(P-14964)**

Laguna Woods Village .... A 949 597-4267
24351 El Toro Rd Laguna Woods (92637) **(P-12477)**

Laird Coatings Corporation .... D 714 894-5252
15541 Commerce Ln Huntington Beach (92649) **(P-3716)**

Employee Codes: A=Over 500 employees, B=251-500
C=101-250, D=51-100, E=20-50, F=10-19, G=1-9

2025 Southern California
Business Directory and Buyers Guide

© Mergent Inc. 1-800-342-5647
1083

A L P H A B E T I C

Laird R & F Products Inc (DH)..................E 760 916-9410
2091 Rutherford Rd Carlsbad (92008) *(P-7735)*

Lake Arrwhead Rsort Oprtor Inc (HQ)..........C 909 336-1511
27984 Hwy 189 Lake Arrowhead (92352) *(P-12895)*

Lake Chevrolet....................................C 951 674-3116
31201 Auto Center Dr Lake Elsinore (92530) *(P-11372)*

Lake Elsnore Dntl Spcalty Care, Vista *Also Called: Vista Community Clinic (P-15533)*

Lake Frest No II Mstr Hmwners................D 949 586-0860
24752 Toledo Ln Lake Forest (92630) *(P-17353)*

Lake Mission Viejo Association................D 949 770-1313
22555 Olympiad Rd Mission Viejo (92692) *(P-17354)*

Lakes Country Club Assn Inc (PA)............C 760 568-4321
161 Old Ranch Rd Palm Desert (92211) *(P-15145)*

Lakes Country Club, The, Palm Desert *Also Called: Lakes Country Club Assn Inc (P-15145)*

Lakeshirts LLC....................................E 805 239-1290
1400 Railroad St Ste 104 Paso Robles (93446) *(P-2249)*

Lakeside Golf Club................................D 818 984-0601
4500 W Lakeside Dr Burbank (91505) *(P-15087)*

Lakeside Medical Systems, Northridge *Also Called: Lakeside Systems Inc (P-18003)*

Lakeside Systems Inc..........................A 866 654-3471
8510 Balboa Blvd Ste 150 Northridge (91325) *(P-18003)*

Lakeview Medical Offices, Anaheim *Also Called: Kaiser Foundation Hospitals (P-15338)*

Lakewood Healthcare Center, Downey *Also Called: Healthcare Ctr of Downey LLC (P-15673)*

Lakewood Park Health Ctr Inc (PA)..........B 562 869-0978
12023 Lakewood Blvd Downey (90242) *(P-14527)*

Lakewood Regional Med Ctr Inc................A 562 531-2550
3700 South St Lakewood (90712) *(P-16071)*

Lakewood Regional Medical Ctr, Lakewood *Also Called: Tenet Healthsystem Medical Inc (P-15487)*

Lakewood Regional Medical Ctr, Lakewood *Also Called: Lakewood Regional Med Ctr Inc (P-16071)*

Lakin Tire of Calif, Santa Fe Springs *Also Called: Lakin Tire West Incorporated (P-9858)*

Lakin Tire West Incorporated (PA)............C 562 802-2752
15305 Spring Ave Santa Fe Springs (90670) *(P-9858)*

Lamar Jhnson Collaborative Inc................C 424 361-3960
8590 National Blvd Culver City (90232) *(P-17679)*

Lambda Research Optics Inc..................D 714 327-0600
1695 Macarthur Blvd Costa Mesa (92626) *(P-7963)*

Lambs & Ivy Inc..................................E 310 322-3800
2042 E Maple Ave El Segundo (90245) *(P-2214)*

Lamer Street Kreations Corp..................E 909 305-4824
13815 Arrow Blvd Fontana (92335) *(P-17577)*

Laminated Shim Company Inc..................E 951 273-3900
1691 California Ave Corona (92881) *(P-5450)*

Laminating Company of America, Lake Forest *Also Called: Tri-Star Laminates Inc (P-6779)*

Lamont Community Health Center, Bakersfield *Also Called: Clinica Sierra Vista (P-15282)*

Lamp Inc..C 213 488-9559
2116 Arlington Ave Lbby Los Angeles (90018) *(P-17171)*

Lamp Community, Los Angeles *Also Called: Lamp Inc (P-17171)*

Lamps Plus Inc..................................E 805 642-9007
4723 Telephone Rd Ventura (93003) *(P-6465)*

Lamsco West Inc................................D 661 295-8620
29101 The Old Rd Santa Clarita (91355) *(P-4158)*

Lancaster Cmnty Svcs Fndtion I............C 661 723-6230
46008 7th St W Lancaster (93534) *(P-14693)*

Lancaster Crdlgy Med Group Inc (PA)......D 661 726-3058
43847 Heaton Ave Ste B Lancaster (93534) *(P-15377)*

Lancaster Hospital Corporation................A 661 948-4781
38600 Medical Center Dr Palmdale (93551) *(P-16072)*

Lance Soll & Lunghard LLP................D 714 672-0022
203 N Brea Blvd Ste 203 Brea (92821) *(P-17741)*

Land Design Consultants Inc..................D 626 578-7000
2700 E Foothill Blvd Ste 200 Pasadena (91107) *(P-18331)*

Land Disposition Company, Irvine *Also Called: NRLL LLC (P-12726)*

Landcare USA LLC................................D 760 747-1174
770 Metcalf St Escondido (92025) *(P-214)*

Landcare USA LLC................................D 858 453-1755
5248 Governor Dr San Diego (92122) *(P-215)*

Landcare USA LLC................................D 949 559-7771
216 N Clara St Santa Ana (92703) *(P-216)*

Landforce Corporation............................C 760 843-7839
17201 N D St Victorville (92394) *(P-8959)*

Landing Gear, Los Angeles *Also Called: Judy Ann of California Inc (P-2040)*

Landjet (PA)......................................C 909 873-4636
1090 Hall Ave Jurupa Valley (92509) *(P-8831)*

Landmark Distribution LLC......................D 805 965-3058
34 E Sola St Santa Barbara (93101) *(P-9368)*

Landmark Dividend, El Segundo *Also Called: Landmark Dividend LLC (P-12478)*

Landmark Dividend LLC (PA)..................D 323 306-2683
400 Continental Blvd Ste 500 El Segundo (90245) *(P-12478)*

Landmark Electronics Inc......................E 626 967-2857
990 N Amelia Ave San Dimas (91773) *(P-7019)*

Landmark Event Staffing........................A 714 293-4248
4790 Irvine Blvd Ste 105 Irvine (92620) *(P-14311)*

Landmark Health LLC..........................C 619 274-8200
3131 Camino Del Rio N San Diego (92108) *(P-16579)*

Landmark Medical Center, Pomona *Also Called: Landmark Medical Services Inc (P-16277)*

Landmark Medical Services Inc................D 909 593-2585
2030 N Garey Ave Pomona (91767) *(P-16277)*

Landmark Mfg Inc................................E 760 941-6626
4112 Avenida De La Plata Oceanside (92056) *(P-6164)*

Landmark Motor Cycle ACC, Oceanside *Also Called: Landmark Mfg Inc (P-6164)*

Landor Associates, Irvine *Also Called: Young & Rubicam LLC (P-13255)*

Landsberg Flflment Sltons Div, Fontana *Also Called: Orora Packaging Solutions (P-10601)*

Landsberg Los Angeles Div 1001, Montebello *Also Called: Orora Packaging Solutions (P-10598)*

Landsberg Orange Cnty Div 1025, Buena Park *Also Called: Orora Packaging Solutions (P-10604)*

Landsberg Snta Brbara Div 1046, Oxnard *Also Called: Orora Packaging Solutions (P-10600)*

Landscape Center, Riverside *Also Called: B & B Nurseries Inc (P-11081)*

Landscape Communications......................E 714 979-5276
14771 Plaza Dr Ste A Tustin (92780) *(P-2864)*

Landscape Contract National, Tustin *Also Called: Landscape Communications Inc (P-2864)*

Landscape Development Inc (PA)............B 661 295-1970
28447 Witherspoon Pkwy Valencia (91355) *(P-217)*

Landscape Development Inc..................C 951 371-9370
1290 Carbide Dr Corona (92881) *(P-218)*

Landstar Global Logistics Inc..................D 909 266-0096
2313 E Philadelphia St Ste D Ontario (91761) *(P-8960)*

Langer Juice Company Inc......................C 626 336-3100
400 S Stimson Ave City Of Industry (91745) *(P-10955)*

Langer Juice Company Inc (PA)..............C 626 336-3100
16195 Stephens St City Of Industry (91745) *(P-11307)*

Langer Juice Company Inc......................B 626 336-3100
16185 Stephens St City Of Industry (91744) *(P-1378)*

Langers Juice, City Of Industry *Also Called: Langer Juice Company Inc (P-11307)*

Langham Huntington Hotel & Spa, Pasadena *Also Called: Pacific Huntington Hotel Corp (P-12960)*

Langlois Company................................E 951 360-3900
10810 San Sevaine Way Jurupa Valley (91752) *(P-1414)*

Langlois Fancy Frozen Foods Inc............E 949 497-1741
2975 Laguna Canyon Rd Laguna Beach (92651) *(P-1396)*

Langlois Flour Company, Jurupa Valley *Also Called: Langlois Company (P-1414)*

Lani, Irvine *Also Called: Loan Administration Netwrk Inc (P-13541)*

Lanic Aerospace, Rancho Cucamonga *Also Called: Lanic Engineering Inc (P-7512)*

Lanic Engineering (PA)..........................E 877 763-0411
12144 6th St Rancho Cucamonga (91730) *(P-7512)*

Lantz Security Systems Inc....................C 805 496-5775
101 N Westlake Blvd Ste 200 Westlake Village (91362) *(P-14312)*

Lao-Hmong Security Agency Inc..............D 714 533-6776
10682 Trask Ave Garden Grove (92843) *(P-14313)*

Largo Concrete Inc............................C 619 356-2142
591 Camino De La Reina Ste 620 San Diego (92108) *(P-417)*

Largo Concrete Inc............................C 909 981-7844
1690 W Foothill Blvd Ste B Upland (91786) *(P-1124)*

Largo Concrete Inc (PA)........................D 714 731-3600
2741 Walnut Ave Ste 110 Tustin (92780) *(P-1125)*

Laritech Inc......................................C 805 529-5000
5898 Condor Dr Moorpark (93021) *(P-6744)*

Lark Ellen Farm, Ojai *Also Called: Pure Simple Foods LLC (P-497)*

Mergent email: customerrelations@mergent.com
1084   2025 Southern California
Business Directory and Buyers Guide   (P-0000) Products & Services Section entry number
(PA)=Parent Co (HQ)=Headquarters (DH)=Div Headquarters

Larry Jacinto Construction Inc .... D 909 794-2151
9555 N Wabash Ave Redlands (92374) *(P-631)*

Larry Jacinto Farming Inc .... D 909 794-2276
9555 N Wabash Ave Redlands (92374) *(P-143)*

Larry Mthvin Installations Inc (HQ)............C 909 563-1700
501 Kettering Dr Ontario (91761) *(P-4338)*

Larry Spun Products Inc .... E 323 881-6300
1533 S Downey Rd Los Angeles (90023) *(P-5198)*

Larsen Supply Co (PA)................................ D 562 698-0731
12055 Slauson Ave Santa Fe Springs (90670) *(P-10324)*

Larson Al Boat Shop .... D 310 514-4100
1046 S Seaside Ave San Pedro (90731) *(P-7603)*

Larson Picture Frames, Santa Fe Springs *Also Called: Larson-Juhl US LLC (P-2412)*

Larson-Juhl US LLC .... E 562 946-6873
12206 Bell Ranch Dr Santa Fe Springs (90670) *(P-2412)*

Las Brisas, San Luis Obispo *Also Called: Harvest Management Sub LLC (P-12343)*

Las Colinas Post Acute, Ontario *Also Called: Ontarioidence Opco LLC (P-15817)*

Las Posas Berry Farms LLC .... D 805 483-1000
730 S A St Oxnard (93030) *(P-21)*

Las Posas Country Club 805 482-4518
955 Fairway Dr Camarillo (93010) *(P-15146)*

Las Vegas / LA Express Inc (PA)................C 909 972-3100
1000 S Cucamonga Ave Ontario (91761) *(P-8961)*

Las Villas De Carlsbad, Oceanside *Also Called: Villas De Crlsbad Ltd A Cal Lt (P-17205)*

Las Villas Del Norte .... C 760 741-1047
1325 Las Villas Way Escondido (92026) *(P-17172)*

Las Virgenes Municipal Wtr Dst .... C 818 251-2100
4232 Las Virgenes Rd Lbby Calabasas (91302) *(P-9698)*

Lasco, Santa Fe Springs *Also Called: Larsen Supply Co (P-10324)*

Laser Electric Inc 760 658-6626
650 Opper St Escondido (92029) *(P-933)*

Laser Industries Inc .... D 714 532-3271
1351 Manhattan Ave Fullerton (92831) *(P-6165)*

Laser Operations LLC .... E 818 986-0000
15632 Roxford St Rancho Cascades (91342) *(P-6844)*

Laser Technologies, San Fernando *Also Called: Laser Technologies & Services LLC (P-8432)*

Laser Technologies & Services LLC .... D
1175 Aviation Pl San Fernando (91340) *(P-8432)*

Lasercare, Irvine *Also Called: Lasercare Technologies Inc (P-8564)*

Lasercare Technologies Inc (PA)................E 310 202-4200
14370 Myford Rd Ste 100 Irvine (92606) *(P-8564)*

Laserfiche Document Imaging, Long Beach *Also Called: Compulink Management Ctr Inc (P-13691)*

Lasergraphics Inc .... E 949 753-8282
20 Ada Irvine (92618) *(P-5928)*

Lasergraphics General Business, Irvine *Also Called: Lasergraphics Inc (P-5928)*

Laseta Organica, Escondido *Also Called: Mountain Meadow Mushrooms Inc (P-74)*

Lash Construction Inc .... D 805 963-3553
721 Carpinteria St Santa Barbara (93103) *(P-17578)*

Lasr Inc .... C 877 591-9979
1517 Beverly Blvd Los Angeles (90026) *(P-13314)*

Lassonde Pappas and Co Inc .... E 909 923-4041
1755 E Acacia St Ontario (91761) *(P-1805)*

LAT LLC .... F 323 233-3017
2618 Fruitland Ave Vernon (90058) *(P-2116)*

Latara Enterprise Inc (PA)..........................C 909 623-9301
1716 W Holt Ave Pomona (91768) *(P-16322)*

Lateral Link Group Inc .... D 310 405-0092
940 E 2nd St Apt 2 Los Angeles (90012) *(P-13540)*

Latexco West, Santa Fe Springs *Also Called: Sleepcomp West LLC (P-4017)*

Latham & Watkins LLP .... C 858 523-5400
12670 High Bluff Dr Ste 100 San Diego (92130) *(P-16724)*

Latham & Watkins LLP .... B 714 540-1235
650 Town Center Dr Ste 2000 Costa Mesa (92626) *(P-16725)*

Latham & Watkins LLP (PA).........................A 213 485-1234
555 W 5th St Ste 300 Los Angeles (90013) *(P-16726)*

Latigo Inc .... E 323 583-8000
4371 E 49th St Vernon (90058) *(P-1921)*

Latina & Associates Inc (PA).......................E 619 426-1491
1031 Bay Blvd Chula Vista (91911) *(P-2812)*

Launchpad Communications, Anaheim *Also Called: Consumer Resource Network LLC (P-18120)*

Lauras House .... D 949 361-3775
33 Journey Ste 150 Aliso Viejo (92656) *(P-16970)*

Lauren Anthony & Co Inc .... E 619 590-1141
11425 Woodside Ave Ste B Santee (92071) *(P-2428)*

Laurence-Hovenier Inc .... C 951 736-2990
179 N Maple St Corona (92878) *(P-1055)*

Lav Hotel Corp .... C 858 454-0771
1132 Prospect St La Jolla (92037) *(P-12896)*

Lava Scs LLC .... D 909 437-7881
218 Machlin Ct Walnut (91789) *(P-9083)*

Lavash Corporation of America .... E 323 663-5249
2835 Newell St Los Angeles (90039) *(P-1459)*

Lavi Industries LLC (PA).............................D 877 275-5284
27810 Avenue Hopkins Valencia (91355) *(P-5068)*

Law Offces Les Zeve A Prof Cor .... C 714 848-7920
30 Corporate Park Ste 450 Irvine (92606) *(P-16727)*

Law Offices Juan J. Dominguez, Los Angeles *Also Called: Dominguez Law Group PC (P-16673)*

Law School Financial Inc .... C 626 243-1800
175 S Lake Ave Unit 200 Pasadena (91101) *(P-11846)*

Law School Loans, Pasadena *Also Called: Law School Financial Inc (P-11846)*

Lawrence Berkeley National Lab, Brea *Also Called: United Sttes Dept Enrgy Brkley (P-17893)*

Lawrence Equipment, El Monte *Also Called: Lawrence Equipment Leasing Inc (P-5679)*

Lawrence Equipment Leasing Inc (PA)...........C 626 442-2894
2034 Peck Rd El Monte (91733) *(P-5679)*

Lawrence Fmly Jwish Cmnty Ctrs (PA)............C 858 362-1144
4126 Executive Dr La Jolla (92037) *(P-17234)*

Lawrence Roll Up Doors Inc (PA)..................E 626 962-4163
4525 Littlejohn St Baldwin Park (91706) *(P-4893)*

Lawrence Welk Desert Oasis, Cathedral City *Also Called: Whv Resort Group Inc (P-13080)*

Lawrys Restaurants II Inc .... C 323 664-0228
2980 Los Feliz Blvd Los Angeles (90039) *(P-11584)*

Lawrys Restaurants II Inc .... D 310 652-2827
100 N La Cienega Blvd Beverly Hills (90211) *(P-11585)*

Lawyers Title Escrow, Newport Beach *Also Called: Lawyers Title Insurance Corp (P-12154)*

Lawyers Title Insurance Corp .... A 805 484-2701
2751 Park View Ct Oxnard (93036) *(P-12153)*

Lawyers Title Insurance Corp .... B 949 223-5575
5000 Birch St Newport Beach (92660) *(P-12154)*

Lawyers Title Insurance Corp .... A 949 223-5575
18551 Von Karman Ave Ste 100 Irvine (92612) *(P-12155)*

Layfield USA Corporation (DH)......................D 619 562-1200
10038 Marathon Pkwy Lakeside (92040) *(P-1214)*

Laymon Candy Co Inc .... E 909 825-4408
276 Commercial Rd San Bernardino (92408) *(P-10849)*

Laz Karp Associates LLC .... C 323 464-4190
1400 Ivar Ave Los Angeles (90028) *(P-14658)*

Lazy Acres Natural Market .... D 619 847-8443
422 W Washington St San Diego (92103) *(P-10956)*

Lb Beadeis LLC .... E 562 726-1700
70 Atlantic Ave Long Beach (90802) *(P-1508)*

Lb3 Enterprises Inc .... D 619 579-6161
12485 Highway 67 # 3 Lakeside (92040) *(P-632)*

Lba Inc .... D 949 833-0400
3333 Michelson Dr Ste 230 Irvine (92612) *(P-18160)*

Lba Realty, Irvine *Also Called: Lba Inc (P-18160)*

Lbct LLC .... D 562 951-6000
1171 Pier F Ave Long Beach (90802) *(P-9142)*

Lbf Travel Inc .... B 858 429-7599
4545 Murphy Canyon Rd Ste 210 San Diego (92123) *(P-9227)*

Lbi - USA, Chatsworth *Also Called: Lehrer Brllnprfktion Werks Inc (P-4160)*

Lbi Media Holdings Inc (HQ)........................C 818 563-5722
1845 W Empire Ave Burbank (91504) *(P-9480)*

Lbi Radio License LLC .... C 818 563-5722
1845 W Empire Ave Burbank (91504) *(P-9481)*

Lbs Financial Credit Union (PA)....................C 562 598-9007
5505 Garden Grove Blvd Ste 500 Westminster (92683) *(P-11828)*

Lc Trs Inc .... A 760 438-9111
2100 Costa Del Mar Rd Carlsbad (92009) *(P-12897)*

Employee Codes: A=Over 500 employees, B=251-500
C=101-250, D=51-100, E=20-50, F=10-19, G=1-9

2025 Southern California
Business Directory and Buyers Guide

© Mergent Inc. 1-800-342-5647
1085

A
L
P
H
A
B
E
T
I
C

LCD&d, Chatsworth *Also Called: Lighting Control & Design Inc (P-6509)*

Lcs Janitorial Services LLC .... C 619 488-7434
311 F St Ste 207 Chula Vista (91910) *(P-13384)*

Ld Acquisition Company 16 LLC .... D 310 294-8160
400 Continental Blvd Ste 500 El Segundo (90245) *(P-12714)*

Ld Products Inc .... C 888 321-2552
2501 E 28th St Signal Hill (90755) *(P-2630)*

LDI Mechanical Inc (PA).. C 951 340-9685
1587 E Bentley Dr Corona (92879) *(P-795)*

Le Elegant Bath Inc .... C 951 734-0238
13405 Estelle St Corona (92879) *(P-4030)*

Le Parc Suite Hotel, West Hollywood *Also Called: Ols Hotels & Resorts LLC (P-12951)*

Leach Grain & Milling Co Inc .... E 562 869-4451
8131 Pivot St Downey (90241) *(P-11070)*

Leach International Corp (DH) .... B 714 736-7537
6900 Orangethorpe Ave Buena Park (90620) *(P-7513)*

Leadcrunch, San Diego *Also Called: Leadcrunch Inc (P-13966)*

Leadcrunch Inc (PA) .... E 888 708-6649
750 B St Ste 1630 San Diego (92101) *(P-13966)*

Leader Drug Store, Torrance *Also Called: Little Company Mary Hospital (P-16074)*

Leader Emergency Vehicles, South El Monte *Also Called: Leader Industries Inc (P-8832)*

Leader Industries Inc .... C 626 575-0880
10941 Weaver Ave South El Monte (91733) *(P-8832)*

Leading Edge Aviation Svcs Inc .... A 714 556-0576
5251 California Ave Ste 170 Irvine (92617) *(P-868)*

Leading Edge Logistix LLC .... C 951 870-6801
29436 Tremont Dr Menifee (92584) *(P-9369)*

Leading Industry Inc .... D 805 385-4100
1151 Pacific Ave Oxnard (93033) *(P-4159)*

Leads360 LLC .... E 888 843-1777
207 Hindry Ave Inglewood (90301) *(P-13967)*

Leaf Group, Santa Monica *Also Called: Leaf Group Ltd (P-14140)*

Leaf Group Ltd (HQ) .... C 310 394-6400
1655 26th St Santa Monica (90404) *(P-14140)*

Leal, Jennifer A, Pasadena *Also Called: Collins & Collins (P-12286)*

Lear Capital Inc .... D 310 571-0190
1990 S Bundy Dr Ste 600 Los Angeles (90025) *(P-11971)*

Learjet Inc .... E 818 894-8241
16750 Schoenborn St North Hills (91343) *(P-7361)*

Learning Ovations Inc .... E 734 904-1459
16 Coltrane Ct Irvine (92617) *(P-16855)*

Learning Tree Pre-School, Tujunga *Also Called: Crescenta-Canada YMCA (P-17339)*

Leather Pro Inc .... E 818 833-8822
12900 Bradley Ave Sylmar (91342) *(P-4305)*

Lebata Inc .... E 949 253-2800
4621 Teller Ave Ste 130 Newport Beach (92660) *(P-4444)*

Lecangs LLC (PA)... B 925 968-5094
728 W Rider St Perris (92571) *(P-9304)*

Leda Corporation .... E 714 841-7821
7080 Kearny Dr Huntington Beach (92648) *(P-7671)*

Leda Multimedia, Chino *Also Called: Shop4techcom (P-5887)*

Ledconn, Brea *Also Called: Ledconn Corp (P-6507)*

Ledconn Corp .... E 714 256-2111
301 Thor Pl Brea (92821) *(P-6507)*

Ledcor CMI Inc .... D 602 595-3017
6405 Mira Mesa Blvd Ste 100 San Diego (92121) *(P-490)*

Ledra Brands Inc .... C 714 259-9959
88 Maxwell Irvine (92618) *(P-9898)*

Ledtronics Inc (PA).. E 310 534-1505
23105 Kashiwa Ct Torrance (90505) *(P-6845)*

Ledvance LLC .... E 909 923-3003
1651 S Archibald Ave Ontario (91761) *(P-6405)*

Lee Burkhart Liu Inc .... D 310 829-2249
5510 Lincoln Blvd # 250 Playa Vista (90094) *(P-17680)*

Lee Kum Kee (usa) Foods Inc (PA)............................ D 626 709-1888
14455 Don Julian Rd City Of Industry (91746) *(P-1369)*

Lee Kum Kee (usa) Inc (DH)..................................... E 626 709-1888
14841 Don Julian Rd City Of Industry (91746) *(P-10957)*

Lee Mar Aquarium & Pet Sups, Vista *Also Called: Lee-Mar Aquarium & Pet Sups (P-11127)*

Lee Pharmaceuticals .... D 626 442-3141
1434 Santa Anita Ave South El Monte (91733) *(P-3668)*

Lee Ray Sandblasting, Santa Fe Springs *Also Called: Cji Process Systems Inc (P-4911)*

Lee Thomas Inc (PA).. E 310 532-7560
13800 S Figueroa St Los Angeles (90061) *(P-2117)*

Lee-Mar Aquarium & Pet Sups .... D 760 727-1300
2459 Dogwood Way Vista (92081) *(P-11127)*

Lee's Enterprise, Chatsworth *Also Called: Molnar Engineering Inc (P-6184)*

Lee's Kitchen, City Of Industry *Also Called: Lee Kum Kee (usa) Inc (P-10957)*

Leebe, Los Angeles *Also Called: Leebe Apparel Inc (P-2045)*

Leebe Apparel Inc .... E 323 897-5585
3499 S Main St Los Angeles (90007) *(P-2045)*

Leed Electric Inc .... C 562 270-9500
13138 Arctic Cir Santa Fe Springs (90670) *(P-934)*

Leemarc Industries LLC .... D 760 598-0505
340 Rancheros Dr Ste 172 San Marcos (92069) *(P-2019)*

Leeper's Stair Products, Corona *Also Called: Leepers Wood Turning Co Inc (P-2312)*

Leepers Wood Turning Co Inc (PA)............................ E 562 422-6525
341 Bonnie Cir Ste 104 Corona (92878) *(P-2312)*

Lees Maintenance Service Inc .... B 818 988-6644
14740 Keswick St Van Nuys (91405) *(P-13385)*

Lefiell, Santa Fe Springs *Also Called: Lefiell Manufacturing Company (P-7514)*

Lefiell Manufacturing Company .... C 562 921-3411
13700 Firestone Blvd Santa Fe Springs (90670) *(P-7514)*

Leftbank Art, La Mirada *Also Called: Outlook Resources Inc (P-2254)*

Lefty Production Co LLC .... E 323 515-9266
318 W 9th St Ste 1010 Los Angeles (90015) *(P-2118)*

Legacy Commercial Holdings Inc .... E 818 767-6626
28939 Avenue Williams Valencia (91355) *(P-2429)*

Legacy Epoch LLC .... D 844 673-7305
21011 Warner Center Ln Ste A Woodland Hills (91367) *(P-1429)*

Legacy Farms LLC .... D 714 736-1800
1765 W Penhall Way Anaheim (92801) *(P-10911)*

Legacy Healthcare Center LLC .... D 626 798-0558
1570 N Fair Oaks Ave Pasadena (91103) *(P-16580)*

Legacy Prtners Residential Inc .... C 949 930-6600
5141 California Ave Ste 100 Irvine (92617) *(P-18004)*

Legacy Reinforcing Steel LLC .... D 619 646-0205
1057 Tierra Del Rey Ste F Chula Vista (91910) *(P-1156)*

Legal Enterprise, Calabasas *Also Called: Litigtion Rsrces of America-CA (P-14531)*

Legal Solutions Holdings Inc .... C 800 244-3495
955 Overland Ct Ste 200 San Dimas (91773) *(P-16728)*

Legal Vision Group LLC .... E 310 945-5550
2030 Paddock Ln Norco (92860) *(P-3033)*

LEGALZOOM, Glendale *Also Called: Legalzoomcom Inc (P-14141)*

Legalzoomcom Inc (PA).. B 323 962-8600
101 N Brand Blvd Fl 11 Glendale (91203) *(P-14141)*

Legendary Foods LLC .... E 888 698-1708
2601 Colorado Ave Santa Monica (90404) *(P-11293)*

Legendary Headwear, San Diego *Also Called: Legendary Holdings Inc (P-2159)*

Legendary Holdings Inc .... E 619 872-6100
2295 Paseo De Las Americas Ste 19 San Diego (92154) *(P-2159)*

Leggett & Platt Incorporated .... D 909 937-1010
1050 S Dupont Ave Ontario (91761) *(P-2487)*

Leggett & Platt 0768, Poway *Also Called: Valley Metals LLC (P-4555)*

Legion Creative Group .... E 323 498-1100
500 N Brand Blvd Ste 1800 Glendale (91203) *(P-3154)*

Legoland California LLC .... B 760 450-3661
1 Legoland Dr Carlsbad (92008) *(P-15105)*

Legoland California Resort, Carlsbad *Also Called: Legoland California LLC (P-15105)*

Leham Millet West, Santa Ana *Also Called: Lehman Millet Incorporated (P-3543)*

Lehman Foods Inc .... E 818 837-7600
1145 Arroyo St Ste B San Fernando (91340) *(P-1806)*

Lehman Millet Incorporated .... E 714 850-7900
3 Macarthur Pl Ste 700 Santa Ana (92707) *(P-3543)*

Lehrer Brllnprfktion Werks Inc .... D 818 407-1890
20801 Nordhoff St Chatsworth (91311) *(P-4160)*

Lei AG Seattle, Los Angeles *Also Called: Lowe Enterprises Inc (P-12907)*

Leica Biosystems Imaging Inc (HQ)........................... C 760 539-1100
1360 Park Center Dr Vista (92081) *(P-7964)*

LEICHTAG ASSISTED LIVING, Encinitas *Also Called: San Diego Hebrew Homes (P-15768)*

Leidos Inc .... D 703 676-4300
10260 Campus Point Dr Bldg C San Diego (92121) *(P-17803)*

Mergent email: customerrelations@mergent.com
1086

2025 Southern California
Business Directory and Buyers Guide

(P-0000) Products & Services Section entry number
(PA)=Parent Co (HQ)=Headquarters (DH)=Div Headquarters

Leidos Inc .... C 858 826-9416
4161 Campus Point Ct Stop Em3 San Diego (92121) *(P-17804)*

Leidos Inc .... C 858 826-9090
2985 Scott St Vista (92081) *(P-17805)*

Leidos Inc .... D 858 826-6000
Naval Air Station San Diego (92135) *(P-17806)*

Leidos Engrg & Sciences LLC .... C 619 542-3130
1330 30th St Ste A San Diego (92154) *(P-17807)*

Leidos Government Services Inc .... C 323 721-6979
500 N Via Val Verde Montebello (90640) *(P-14232)*

Leigh Jerry California Inc (PA) .... C 818 909-6200
7860 Nelson Rd Van Nuys (91402) *(P-2166)*

Leighton & Associates, Irvine *Also Called: Gradient Engineers Inc (P-17541)*

Leighton Group Inc .... C 760 776-4192
75450 Gerald Ford Dr Ste 301 Palm Desert (92211) *(P-17299)*

Leiner Health Products, Carson *Also Called: Leiner Health Products Inc (P-3442)*

Leiner Health Products, Garden Grove *Also Called: Leiner Health Products Inc (P-3443)*

Leiner Health Products Inc (DH) .... C 631 200-2000
901 E 233rd St Carson (90745) *(P-3442)*

Leiner Health Products Inc .... C 714 898-9936
7366 Orangewood Ave Garden Grove (92841) *(P-3443)*

Leisure Care LLC .... C 818 713-0900
8138 Woodlake Ave West Hills (91304) *(P-15813)*

Leisure Care LLC .... C 626 447-0106
601 Sunset Blvd Arcadia (91007) *(P-17173)*

Leisure Care LLC .... C 714 974-1616
380 S Anaheim Hills Rd Ofc Anaheim (92807) *(P-17174)*

Leisure Glen Convalescent Ctr, Glendale *Also Called: Buena Ventura Care Center Inc (P-15841)*

Leisure Vale Retirement Hotel, Glendale *Also Called: BV General Inc (P-12334)*

Leisure World Pharmacy, Seal Beach *Also Called: Tenet Healthsystem Medical Inc (P-15489)*

Leisure World Resales, Laguna Hills *Also Called: Professional Cmnty MGT Cal Inc (P-12510)*

Lejon Tulliani, Corona *Also Called: Shirinian-Shaw Inc (P-2183)*

Lekos Dye & Finishing Inc (PA) .... D 310 763-0900
3131 E Harcourt St Compton (90221) *(P-1902)*

Lemon Grove Care Rhbltttion Ctr, Lemon Grove *Also Called: Lemon Grove Health Assoc LLC (P-15690)*

Lemon Grove Health Assoc LLC .... B 619 463-0294
8351 Broadway Lemon Grove (91945) *(P-15690)*

Lenders Investment Corp .... D 714 540-4747
18101 Von Karman Ave Ste 400 Irvine (92612) *(P-11916)*

Lending Enterprise, South Pasadena *Also Called: Equity Smart Home Loans Inc (P-11901)*

Lendingusa LLC .... D 800 994-6177
15303 Ventura Blvd Ste 850 Sherman Oaks (91403) *(P-14528)*

Lendsure Mortgage Corp .... B 888 707-7811
12230 World Trade Dr Ste 250 San Diego (92128) *(P-11917)*

Lenlyn Ltd Which Will Do Bus I (HQ) .... D 310 417-3432
5777 W Century Blvd Los Angeles (90045) *(P-11841)*

Lennar Corporation .... D 949 349-8000
15131 Alton Pkwy Ste 190 Irvine (92618) *(P-463)*

Lennar Multi Family Community, Aliso Viejo *Also Called: LMC Hllywood Hghland Hldngs LL (P-555)*

Lenntek Corporation .... E 310 534-2738
1610 Lockness Pl Torrance (90501) *(P-6629)*

Lenore John & Co (PA) .... C 619 232-6136
1250 Delevan Dr San Diego (92102) *(P-10958)*

Leo Hoffman Chevrolet Inc (PA) .... D 626 968-8411
17300 E Gale Ave City Of Industry (91748) *(P-11373)*

Leoben Company .... E 951 284-9653
16692 Burke Ln Huntington Beach (92647) *(P-8692)*

Leoch Battery Corporation (DH) .... D 949 588-5853
20322 Valencia Cir Lake Forest (92630) *(P-6327)*

Leon Krous Drilling Inc .... E 818 833-4654
9300 Borden Ave Sun Valley (91352) *(P-292)*

Leonard Craft Co LLC .... D 714 549-0678
1815 Ritchey St Ste B Santa Ana (92705) *(P-8459)*

Leonard Green & Partners LP (PA) .... D 310 954-0444
11111 Santa Monica Blvd Ste 2000 Los Angeles (90025) *(P-11972)*

Leonard Roofing Inc .... C 951 506-3811
43280 Business Park Dr Ste 107 Temecula (92590) *(P-1089)*

Leonard's Guide, Glendora *Also Called: G R Leonard & Co Inc (P-2916)*

Leonards Carpet Service Inc (PA) .... D 714 630-1930
1121 N Red Gum St Anaheim (92806) *(P-2570)*

Leonards Molded Products Inc .... E 661 253-2227
25031 Anza Dr Valencia (91355) *(P-3923)*

Leonesse Cellars, Temecula *Also Called: Temecula Valley Winery MGT LLC (P-1586)*

Leonesse Cellars LLC .... E 951 302-7601
38311 De Portola Rd Temecula (92592) *(P-1578)*

Leonid M Glsman DDS A Dntl Cor .... C 323 560-4514
5021 Florence Ave Bell (90201) *(P-15520)*

Leport Educational Inst Inc .... B 914 374-8860
1 Technology Dr Bldg A Irvine (92618) *(P-17093)*

Leport Montessori Academy, Yorba Linda *Also Called: Mulberry Child Care Ctrs Inc (P-17100)*

Leport Schools, Irvine *Also Called: Leport Educational Inst Inc (P-17093)*

Lereta LLC (PA) .... B 626 543-1765
901 Corporate Center Dr Pomona (91768) *(P-11973)*

Lereta LLC .... C 626 332-1942
10760 4th St Rancho Cucamonga (91730) *(P-12301)*

LEROY HAYNES CENTER, La Verne *Also Called: Haynes Family Programs Inc (P-17160)*

Lester Lithograph Inc .... E 714 491-3981
1128 N Gilbert St Anaheim (92801) *(P-3034)*

Lestonnac Preschool, Tustin *Also Called: Tustin Unified School District (P-16827)*

Letner Roofing Company, Orange *Also Called: Danny Letner Inc (P-1077)*

Lets Do Lunch .... B 310 523-3664
310 W Alondra Blvd Gardena (90248) *(P-1807)*

Level 99, Gardena *Also Called: Phoenix Textile Inc (P-10721)*

Level Furnished Living, Los Angeles *Also Called: Onni Properties LLC (P-18025)*

Level One Protection Inc .... C 949 514-4182
5861 Pine Ave Chino Hills (91709) *(P-14314)*

Levity Live, Oxnard *Also Called: Comedy Club Oxnard LLC (P-15130)*

Levity of Brea LLC .... D 714 482-0700
180 S Brea Blvd Brea (92821) *(P-11615)*

Levlad LLC .... C 818 882-2951
9200 Mason Ave Chatsworth (91311) *(P-10089)*

Lewis Brsbois Bsgard Smith LLP .... D 714 545-9200
650 Town Center Dr Ste 1400 Costa Mesa (92626) *(P-16729)*

Lewis Brsbois Bsgard Smith LLP (PA) ...... A 213 250-1800
633 W 5th St Ste 4000 Los Angeles (90071) *(P-16730)*

Lewis Brsbois Bsgard Smith LLP .... C 619 233-1006
701 B St Ste 1900 San Diego (92101) *(P-16731)*

Lewis Companies (PA) .... C 909 985-0971
1156 N Mountain Ave Upland (91786) *(P-464)*

Lewis Group of Companies .... B 909 985-0971
1156 N Mountain Ave Upland (91785) *(P-12569)*

Lewis Lifetime Tools, Poway *Also Called: Richmond Engineering Co Inc (P-233)*

Lewis Management Corp .... D 909 985-0971
1154 N Mountain Ave Upland (91786) *(P-18005)*

Lexani, Corona *Also Called: Lexani Wheel Corporation (P-4520)*

Lexani Wheel Corporation .... E 951 808-4220
1121 Olympic Dr Corona (92881) *(P-4520)*

Lexicon Marketing, Los Angeles *Also Called: Lexicon Marketing (usa) Inc (P-10119)*

Lexicon Marketing (usa) Inc (PA) .... D 323 782-8282
640 S San Vicente Blvd Los Angeles (90048) *(P-10119)*

Lexington, North Hollywood *Also Called: Lexington Acquisition Inc (P-4845)*

Lexington Acquisition Inc .... C 818 768-5768
11125 Vanowen St North Hollywood (91605) *(P-4845)*

Lexisnexis Risk Assets Inc .... D 949 222-0028
2112 Business Center Dr Ste 150 Irvine (92614) *(P-12226)*

Lexor Inc .... D 714 444-4144
7400 Hazard Ave Westminster (92683) *(P-8693)*

Lexus of Cerritos, Cerritos *Also Called: Bargain Rent-A-Car (P-11317)*

Lexus Santa Monica, Santa Monica *Also Called: Volkswagen Santa Monica Inc (P-11430)*

Lexxiom Inc .... B 909 581-7313
99 N San Antonio Ave Ste 330 Upland (91786) *(P-18006)*

Ley Grand Foods Corporation .... E 626 336-2244
287 S 6th Ave La Puente (91746) *(P-1808)*

Lf Illumination LLC .... D 818 885-1335
9200 Deering Ave Chatsworth (91311) *(P-6466)*

Lf Sportswear Inc (PA) .... E 310 437-4100
13336 Beach Ave Marina Del Rey (90292) *(P-2046)*

Lfp Broadcasting LLC (PA) .... D 323 852-5020
8484 Wilshire Blvd Ste 900 Beverly Hills (90211) *(P-14919)*

Employee Codes: A=Over 500 employees, B=251-500
C=101-250, D=51-100, E=20-50, F=10-19, G=1-9

2025 Southern California
Business Directory and Buyers Guide

© Mergent Inc. 1-800-342-5647

1087

Lfp Ecommerce LLC .... D 314 428-5069
210 N Sunset Ave West Covina (91790) *(P-14529)*

Lfs Development LLC .... C 619 501-5400
901 Bayfront Ct Ste 1 San Diego (92101) *(P-12898)*

Lg Nanoh2o LLC .... E 424 218-4000
21250 Hawthorne Blvd Ste 330 Torrance (90503) *(P-3810)*

Lg Nanoh2o, Inc., Torrance *Also Called: Lg Nanoh2o LLC (P-3810)*

Lg-Ericsson USA Inc .... E 877 828-2673
20 Mason Irvine (92618) *(P-6588)*

LGarde Inc .... E 714 259-0771
15181 Woodlawn Ave Tustin (92780) *(P-5882)*

Lgg Industrial Inc .... D 562 802-7782
15500 Blackburn Ave Norwalk (90650) *(P-3895)*

Lh Indian Wells Operating LLC .... C 760 341-2200
4500 Indian Wells Ln Indian Wells (92210) *(P-12899)*

Lh Universal Operating LLC .... B 818 980-1212
333 Universal Hollywood Dr Universal City (91608) *(P-12900)*

Lho Mssion Bay Rsie Lessee Inc .... B 619 276-4010
1775 E Mission Bay Dr San Diego (92109) *(P-12901)*

Lhoberge Lessee Inc .... C 858 259-1515
1540 Camino Del Mar Del Mar (92014) *(P-12902)*

Lhv Power Corporation (PA) .... E 619 258-7700
10221 Buena Vista Ave Ste A Santee (92071) *(P-7020)*

Liberman Broadcasting Inc (PA) .... D 818 729-5300
1845 W Empire Ave Burbank (91504) *(P-9482)*

Liberty Ambulance LLC .... C 562 741-6230
9770 Candida St San Diego (92126) *(P-8833)*

Liberty Container Company .... C 323 564-4211
4224 Santa Ana St South Gate (90280) *(P-2679)*

Liberty Dental Plan Cal Inc .... B 949 223-0007
340 Commerce Ste 100 Irvine (92602) *(P-12093)*

Liberty Dental Plan Corp (PA) .... D 888 703-6999
340 Commerce Ste 100 Irvine (92602) *(P-12094)*

Liberty Diversified Intl Inc .... C 858 391-7302
13100 Danielson St Poway (92064) *(P-2584)*

Liberty Film, Commerce *Also Called: Liberty Packg & Extruding Inc (P-2733)*

Liberty Landscaping Inc (PA) .... C 951 683-2999
5212 El Rivino Rd Riverside (92509) *(P-219)*

Liberty Packaging, Poway *Also Called: Liberty Diversified Intl Inc (P-2584)*

Liberty Packg & Extruding Inc .... E 323 722-5124
3015 Supply Ave Commerce (90040) *(P-2733)*

Liberty Photo Products, San Clemente *Also Called: Liberty Synergistics Inc (P-10442)*

Liberty Residential Svcs Inc .... D 858 500-0852
12700 Stowe Dr Ste 110 Poway (92064) *(P-16401)*

Liberty School, Paso Robles *Also Called: Treana Winery LLC (P-1591)*

Liberty Synergistics Inc .... D 949 361-1100
1041 Calle Trepadora San Clemente (92673) *(P-10442)*

Liberty Vegetable Oil Company .... E 562 921-3567
15760 Ventura Blvd Encino (91436) *(P-1526)*

Licher Direct Mail Inc .... E 626 795-3333
980 Seco St Pasadena (91103) *(P-3035)*

Lidlaw Educational Services, Rancho Cucamonga *Also Called: Durham School Services L P (P-8872)*

Lief Labs, Valencia *Also Called: Lief Organics LLC (P-1300)*

Lief Organics LLC (PA) .... E 661 775-2500
28903 Avenue Paine Valencia (91355) *(P-1300)*

Life Alert, Encino *Also Called: Life Alert Emrgncy Rsponse Inc (P-14412)*

Life Alert Emrgncy Rsponse Inc (PA) .... C 800 247-0000
16027 Ventura Blvd Ste 400 Encino (91436) *(P-14412)*

Life Care Center of La Habra, La Habra *Also Called: Life Care Centers America Inc (P-15697)*

Life Care Center of Norwalk, Norwalk *Also Called: Life Care Centers America Inc (P-15695)*

Life Care Centers America Inc .... C 760 252-2515
27555 Rimrock Rd Barstow (92311) *(P-15691)*

Life Care Centers America Inc .... C 760 741-6109
1980 Felicita Rd Escondido (92025) *(P-15692)*

Life Care Centers America Inc .... C 562 943-7156
11926 La Mirada Blvd La Mirada (90638) *(P-15693)*

Life Care Centers America Inc .... C 562 867-1761
16910 Woodruff Ave Bellflower (90706) *(P-15694)*

Life Care Centers America Inc .... D 562 921-6624
12350 Rosecrans Ave Norwalk (90650) *(P-15695)*

Life Care Centers America Inc .... C 562 947-8691
12200 La Mirada Blvd La Mirada (90638) *(P-15696)*

Life Care Centers America Inc .... B 562 690-0852
1233 W La Habra Blvd La Habra (90631) *(P-15697)*

Life Care Centers America Inc .... C 760 724-8222
304 N Melrose Dr Vista (92083) *(P-15863)*

Life Care Centers of Escondido, Escondido *Also Called: Life Care Centers America Inc (P-15692)*

Life Cycle Engineering Inc .... C 619 785-5990
7510 Airway Rd Ste 2 San Diego (92154) *(P-13386)*

Life Gnerations Healthcare LLC .... D 619 460-2330
7800 Parkway Dr La Mesa (91942) *(P-15698)*

Life Gnerations Healthcare LLC .... D 619 449-5555
8778 Cuyamaca St Santee (92071) *(P-15864)*

Life Is Life LLC .... E 310 584-7541
2611 Cottonwood Ave Moreno Valley (92553) *(P-1288)*

Life Plans, Irvine *Also Called: Burnham Bnefits Insur Svcs LLC (P-12185)*

Life Science Outsourcing Inc .... D 714 672-1090
830 Challenger St Brea (92821) *(P-8184)*

Life Steps Foundation Inc .... D 562 436-0751
500 E 4th St Long Beach (90802) *(P-16971)*

Life Steps Foundation Inc .... D 805 549-0150
1107 Johnson Ave San Luis Obispo (93401) *(P-16972)*

Life Steps Foundation Inc .... D 805 349-9810
2255 S Depot St Santa Maria (93455) *(P-16973)*

Life Technologies, Carlsbad *Also Called: Life Technologies Corporation (P-7965)*

Life Technologies Corporation (HQ) .... C 760 603-7200
5781 Van Allen Way Carlsbad (92008) *(P-3544)*

Life Technologies Corporation .... B 760 918-0135
5791 Van Allen Way Carlsbad (92008) *(P-7965)*

Life Technologies Corporation .... E 760 918-4259
5791 Van Allen Way Carlsbad (92008) *(P-7966)*

Life Time Inc .... D 858 459-0281
1055 Wall St La Jolla (92037) *(P-15054)*

Life Time Inc .... C 949 492-1515
111 Avenida Vista Montana San Clemente (92672) *(P-15055)*

Life Time Fitness, San Clemente *Also Called: Life Time Inc (P-15055)*

Life Time Fitness Inc .... C 949 238-2700
28221 Crown Valley Pkwy Laguna Niguel (92677) *(P-16581)*

LIFE TIME FITNESS, INC., Laguna Niguel *Also Called: Life Time Fitness Inc (P-16581)*

Lifecare Assurance Company .... C 818 887-4436
21600 Oxnard St Fl 16 Woodland Hills (91367) *(P-12063)*

Lifecare Assurance Company, Woodland Hills *Also Called: 21st Century Lf & Hlth Co Inc (P-12055)*

Lifeline Ambulance, Commerce *Also Called: Eastwestproto Inc (P-8820)*

Lifemd, Huntington Beach *Also Called: Lifemd Inc (P-15378)*

Lifemd Inc .... D 800 852-1575
5882 Bolsa Ave Ste 100 Huntington Beach (92649) *(P-15378)*

Lifeproof, San Diego *Also Called: Otter Products LLC (P-10276)*

Liferay, Diamond Bar *Also Called: Liferay Inc (P-14091)*

Liferay Inc (PA) .... A 877 543-3729
1400 Montefino Ave Ste 100 Diamond Bar (91765) *(P-14091)*

Lifescript, Newport Beach *Also Called: Lifescript Inc (P-14173)*

Lifescript Inc .... C 949 454-0422
4000 Macarthur Blvd Ste 800 Newport Beach (92660) *(P-14173)*

Lifestar Response of Alabama .... C 800 449-4911
1517 W Braden Ct Orange (92868) *(P-8834)*

Lifestream Blood Bank (HQ) .... C 909 885-6503
384 W Orange Show Rd San Bernardino (92412) *(P-16582)*

Lifetech Resources LLC .... D 805 944-1199
700 Science Dr Moorpark (93021) *(P-10629)*

Lifetime Entrmt Svcs LLC .... B 310 556-7500
2049 Century Park E Ste 840 Los Angeles (90067) *(P-9510)*

Lifetime Memory Products Inc .... E 949 794-9000
2505 Da Vinci Ste A Irvine (92614) *(P-6745)*

Lifetime TV Network, Los Angeles *Also Called: Lifetime Entrmt Svcs LLC (P-9510)*

Lifoam Industries LLC .... E 714 891-5035
15671 Industry Ln Huntington Beach (92649) *(P-2680)*

Lift By Encore, Huntington Beach *Also Called: Encore Seats Inc (P-7471)*

Lift By Encore, Huntington Beach *Also Called: Irish Interiors Inc (P-7503)*

Mergent email: customerrelations@mergent.com
1088

2025 Southern California
Business Directory and Buyers Guide

(P-0000) Products & Services Section entry number
(PA)=Parent Co (HQ)=Headquarters (DH)=Div Headquarters

Lift It, Pomona Also Called: Lift-It Manufacturing Co Inc (P-1963)

Lift-It Manufacturing Co Inc .... E 909 469-2251
1603 W 2nd St Pomona (91766) *(P-1963)*

Light Composite Corporation .... E 949 858-8820
22322 Gilberto Rcho Sta Marg (92688) *(P-4777)*

Light Composites Inc .... E 619 339-0638
12170 Paine Pl Poway (92064) *(P-7362)*

Light Helmets, Carlsbad Also Called: Safer Sports Inc (P-8538)

Light Vast Inc .... E 800 358-0499
1202 Monte Vista Ave Ste 1 Upland (91786) *(P-6508)*

Lightcap Industries Inc .... E 909 930-3772
1612 S Cucamonga Ave Ontario (91761) *(P-4846)*

Lightform, Carpinteria Also Called: Forms and Surfaces Company LLC (P-4391)

Lighthouse Healthcare Ctr LLC .... D 323 564-4461
2222 Santa Ana S Los Angeles (90059) *(P-15699)*

Lighting Control & Design Inc .... E 323 226-0000
9144 Deering Ave Chatsworth (91311) *(P-6509)*

Lighting Technologies Intl LLC .... C 626 480-0755
13700 Live Oak Ave Baldwin Park (91706) *(P-10189)*

Lightpointe Communications Inc .... E 858 834-4083
8515 Arjons Dr Ste G San Diego (92126) *(P-10262)*

Lightpointe Wireless, San Diego Also Called: Lightpointe Communications Inc (P-10262)

Lights of America Inc (PA) .... B 909 594-7883
13602 12th St Ste B Chino (91710) *(P-6445)*

Lightstone Dt La LLC .... B 310 669-9252
1260 S Figueroa St Los Angeles (90015) *(P-12903)*

Lightthipe Substation, Long Beach Also Called: Southern California Edison Co (P-9629)

Lightworks Optics Inc .... D 714 247-7100
14192 Chambers Rd Tustin (92780) *(P-8008)*

Limoneira, Santa Paula Also Called: Limoneira Company (P-114)

Limoneira Company (PA) .... D 805 525-5541
1141 Cummings Rd Santa Paula (93060) *(P-114)*

Limos By Tiffany Inc .... E 951 657-2680
23129 Cajalco Rd Perris (92570) *(P-7206)*

Lincoln Training Center, South El Monte Also Called: Lincoln Trning Ctr Rhbltion W (P-17061)

Lincoln Trning Ctr Rhbltion W .... D 626 442-0621
2643 Loma Ave South El Monte (91733) *(P-17061)*

Linda Loma Univ Hlth Care (HQ) .... C 909 558-2806
11370 Anderson St Ste 3900 Loma Linda (92354) *(P-16073)*

LINDA VISTA HEALTH CARE CENTER, San Diego Also Called: San Diego Family Care (P-15444)

Lindbergh Child Care Center, Lynwood Also Called: Lynwood Unified School Dst (P-16816)

Linde Inc .... E 909 390-0283
5705 E Airport Dr Ontario (91761) *(P-3216)*

Lindsey & Sons .... D 657 306-5369
1226 E 76th St Los Angeles (90001) *(P-14530)*

Lindsey Manufacturing Co .... C 626 969-3471
760 N Georgia Ave Azusa (91702) *(P-5156)*

Lindsey Systems, Azusa Also Called: Lindsey Manufacturing Co (P-5156)

Line Hotel, The, Los Angeles Also Called: Sydell Hotels LLC (P-13048)

Lineago, Vernon Also Called: American Fruits & Flavors LLC (P-1664)

Linear Industries Ltd (PA) .... E 626 303-1130
1850 Enterprise Way Monrovia (91016) *(P-10443)*

Linen Lovers, Ontario Also Called: Jomar Table Linens Inc (P-2211)

Linen Salvage Et Cie LLC .... E 323 904-3100
1073 Stearns Dr Los Angeles (90035) *(P-11534)*

Liner Law, Los Angeles Also Called: Liner LLP (P-16732)

Liner LLP .... C 310 500-3500
1100 Glendon Ave 14th Los Angeles (90024) *(P-16732)*

Linewize, San Diego Also Called: Family Zone Inc (P-13727)

Linfinity Microelectronics, Garden Grove Also Called: Microsemi Corp - Anlog Mxed Sg (P-6852)

Ling's, South El Monte Also Called: Out of Shell LLC (P-1829)

LINKS SIGN LANGUAGE INTERPRETI, Long Beach Also Called: Goodwill Sthern Los Angles CNT (P-14504)

Linksoul LLC .... E 760 231-7069
530 S Coast Hwy Oceanside (92054) *(P-1883)*

Linksys LLC .... C 408 526-4000
120 Theory Irvine (92617) *(P-10263)*

Linksys LLC .... C 310 751-5100
121 Theory Ste 150 Irvine (92617) *(P-10264)*

Linksys Usa Inc .... D 949 270-8500
121 Theory Irvine (92617) *(P-10265)*

Linn's Main Bin, Cambria Also Called: Linns Fruit Bin Inc (P-11291)

Linnco LLC .... A 661 616-3900
5201 Truxtun Ave Bakersfield (93309) *(P-307)*

Linns Fruit Bin Inc (PA) .... E 805 927-1499
2535 Village Ln Ste A Cambria (93428) *(P-11291)*

Linzer Products, San Fernando Also Called: Ahi Investment Inc (P-11108)

Lion Shield Protection Inc .... D 949 334-7905
93 Plateau Aliso Viejo (92656) *(P-935)*

Lion-Vallen Ltd Partnership .... D 760 385-4885
22 Area Aven A Bldg #2234 Camp Pendleton (92055) *(P-18007)*

Lions Gate Films Inc .... C 310 449-9200
2700 Colorado Ave Santa Monica (90404) *(P-14836)*

Lionsgate Productions Inc .... C 310 255-3937
2700 Colorado Ave Ste 200 Santa Monica (90404) *(P-14920)*

Lionsgate Studios Corp (PA) .... A 877 848-3866
2700 Colorado Ave Santa Monica (90404) *(P-14837)*

Lip Service, Burbank Also Called: The Original Cult Inc (P-2138)

Lippert Components Mfg Inc .... E 909 628-5557
1021 Walnut Ave Pomona (91766) *(P-4339)*

Liquid Advertising Inc .... D 310 450-2653
138 Eucalyptus Dr El Segundo (90245) *(P-13221)*

Liquid Death Mountain Water .... E 818 521-5500
1447 2nd St Ste 200 Santa Monica (90401) *(P-1622)*

Liquid Graphics Inc .... C 949 486-3588
2701 S Harbor Blvd Unit A Santa Ana (92704) *(P-2020)*

Liquid Investments Inc (PA) .... C 858 509-8510
3840 Via De La Valle Ste 300 Del Mar (92014) *(P-11051)*

Liquidarcade, El Segundo Also Called: Liquid Advertising Inc (P-13221)

Lisa Factory Inc .... D 213 536-5326
144 N Swall Dr Beverly Hills (90211) *(P-1986)*

Lisi Aerospace .... E 310 326-8110
2600 Skypark Dr Torrance (90505) *(P-8185)*

Lisi Aerospace, City Of Industry Also Called: Monadnock Company (P-4782)

Lisi Aerospace North Amer Inc .... A 310 326-8110
2602 Skypark Dr Torrance (90505) *(P-4566)*

Lite Extrusions, Gardena Also Called: Lite Extrusions Mfg Inc (P-3965)

Lite Extrusions Mfg Inc .... E 323 770-4298
15025 S Main St Gardena (90248) *(P-3965)*

Lite Solar, Long Beach Also Called: Lite Solar Corp (P-796)

Lite Solar Corp .... C 562 256-1249
3553 Atlantic Ave Long Beach (90807) *(P-796)*

Litegear, Burbank Also Called: Litegear Inc (P-6406)

Litegear Inc .... E 818 358-8542
4406 W Vanowen St Burbank (91505) *(P-6406)*

Lith-O-Roll Corporation .... E 626 579-0340
9521 Telstar Ave El Monte (91731) *(P-5663)*

Lithia, Temecula Also Called: DCH Acura of Temecula (P-11333)

Lithocraft Co, Anaheim Also Called: Man-Grove Industries Inc (P-3039)

Lithographix Inc (PA) .... B 323 770-1000
12250 Crenshaw Blvd Hawthorne (90250) *(P-3036)*

Lithonia Lighting Hydrel, Sylmar Also Called: Acuity Brands Lighting Inc (P-10165)

Litigtion Rsrces of America-CA (PA) .... D 818 878-9227
4232-1 Las Virgenes Rd Ste 100 Calabasas (91302) *(P-14531)*

Liton Lighting, Los Angeles Also Called: Eema Industries Inc (P-6499)

Little Brothers Bakery, Gardena Also Called: Little Brothers Bakery LLC (P-1460)

Little Brothers Bakery LLC .... D 310 225-3790
320 W Alondra Blvd Gardena (90248) *(P-1460)*

Little Castle Furniture Co Inc .... E 805 278-4646
301 Todd Ct Oxnard (93030) *(P-2450)*

Little Co Mary- San Pedro Hosp, San Pedro Also Called: San Pedro Peninsula Hospital (P-16171)

Little Company Mary Hospital .... A 310 540-7676
4101 Torrance Blvd Torrance (90503) *(P-16074)*

Little Company Mary Svc Area, Torrance Also Called: Little Company of Mary Health Services (P-16075)

Little Company of Mary Health Services .... A 310 540-7676
4101 Torrance Blvd Torrance (90503) *(P-16075)*

Little Ssters of The Poor Los .... D 310 548-0625
2100 S Western Ave San Pedro (90732) *(P-15700)*

Employee Codes: A=Over 500 employees, B=251-500
C=101-250, D=51-100, E=20-50, F=10-19, G=1-9

2025 Southern California
Business Directory and Buyers Guide

© Mergent Inc. 1-800-342-5647
1089

A L P H A B E T I C

Littlejohn-Reuland Corporation .... E 323 587-5255
4575 Pacific Blvd Vernon (90058) *(P-936)*

Live Fresh Corporation .... C 909 478-0895
1055 E Cooley Ave San Bernardino (92408) *(P-1379)*

Live Nation, Beverly Hills *Also Called: Live Nation Entertainment Inc (P-14532)*

Live Nation Entertainment Inc (PA) .... C 310 867-7000
9348 Civic Center Dr Lbby Beverly Hills (90210) *(P-14532)*

Live Nation Worldwide Inc .... B 310 867-7000
325 N Maple Dr Ste 100 Beverly Hills (90210) *(P-14994)*

Live Nation Worldwide Inc (HQ) .... B 310 867-7000
9348 Civic Center Dr Lbby Beverly Hills (90210) *(P-14995)*

Live Oak Rehab, San Gabriel *Also Called: Longwood Management Corp (P-15868)*

Liveoffice LLC .... E 877 253-2793
900 Corporate Pointe Culver City (90230) *(P-13968)*

Livescribe Inc .... E
930 Roosevelt Irvine (92620) *(P-5929)*

Livhome Inc (PA) .... A 800 807-5854
5670 Wilshire Blvd Ste 500 Los Angeles (90036) *(P-16402)*

Living Desert .... C 760 346-5694
47900 Portola Ave Palm Desert (92260) *(P-17270)*

LIVING OPPORTUNITIES MANAGEMENT COMPANY, Huntington Park *Also Called: Living Opportunities MGT Co (P-12357)*

Living Opportunities MGT Co .... D 323 589-5956
6900 Seville Ave Huntington Park (90255) *(P-12357)*

Living Spaces Furniture LLC .... C 760 945-6805
1900 University Dr Vista (92083) *(P-11515)*

Living Spaces Furniture LLC (PA) .... C 877 266-7300
14501 Artesia Blvd La Mirada (90638) *(P-11516)*

Living Wellness Partners LLC .... E 800 642-3754
3305 Tyler St Carlsbad (92008) *(P-1809)*

Livingston Mem Vna Hlth Corp .... B 805 642-0239
1996 Eastman Ave Ste 101 Ventura (93003) *(P-18008)*

Livingston Mem Vsting Nrse Ass, Ventura *Also Called: Livingston Mem Vna Hlth Corp (P-18008)*

Lj Smith Stair Systems, Corona *Also Called: Novo Manufacturing LLC (P-2317)*

Ljg, Irvine *Also Called: La Jolla Group Inc (P-14526)*

Lk Packaging, Commerce *Also Called: Elkay Plastics Co Inc (P-10998)*

Llamas Plastics Inc .... C 818 362-0371
12970 Bradley Ave Sylmar (91342) *(P-7515)*

LLC Bates White .... C 858 523-2150
322 8th St Del Mar (92014) *(P-16733)*

LLC Brewer Crane .... D 619 390-8252
12570 Highway 67 Lakeside (92040) *(P-13441)*

LLC Walker West .... D 800 767-9378
5500 Jurupa St Ontario (91761) *(P-2585)*

LLC Walker West .... C 909 390-4300
1555 S Vintage Ave Ontario (91761) *(P-4161)*

LLC Walker West .... D 951 685-9660
11445 Pacific Ave Fontana (92337) *(P-4997)*

LLC Woodward West .... C 661 822-7900
28400 Stallion Springs Dr Tehachapi (93561) *(P-13104)*

Lloyd Design Corporation .... D 818 768-6001
19731 Nordhoff St Northridge (91324) *(P-7265)*

Lloyd Mats, Northridge *Also Called: Lloyd Design Corporation (P-7265)*

Lloyd Staffing Inc .... B 631 777-7600
18000 Studebaker Rd Ste 700 Cerritos (90703) *(P-13603)*

LLP Mayer Brown .... B 213 229-9500
350 S Grand Ave Ste 2500 Los Angeles (90071) *(P-16734)*

LLP Moss Adams .... C 949 221-4000
2040 Main St Ste 900 Irvine (92614) *(P-17742)*

LLP Moss Adams .... C 310 477-0450
21700 Oxnard St Ste 300 Woodland Hills (91367) *(P-17743)*

LLP Moss Adams .... D 858 627-1400
4747 Executive Dr Ste 1300 San Diego (92121) *(P-17744)*

Llumc, Loma Linda *Also Called: Loma Linda University Med Ctr (P-16078)*

Lm Veterinary Enterprises Inc .... D 310 659-5287
8725 Santa Monica Blvd West Hollywood (90069) *(P-128)*

Lmb Opco LLC .... B 310 348-6800
12181 Bluff Creek Dr Ste 250 Playa Vista (90094) *(P-11947)*

LMC Enterprises (PA) .... D 562 602-2116
6401 Alondra Blvd Paramount (90723) *(P-3610)*

LMC Enterprises .... E 310 632-7124
19402 S Susana Rd Compton (90221) *(P-3611)*

LMC Hllywood Hghland Hldngs LL .... B 949 448-1600
20 Enterprise Aliso Viejo (92656) *(P-555)*

LMS .... E 909 623-8781
1462 E 9th St Pomona (91766) *(P-8694)*

Lni Custom Manufacturing Inc .... E 310 978-2000
15542 Broadway Center St Gardena (90248) *(P-5069)*

Load Delivered Logistics LLC .... C 310 822-0215
214 Main St Venice (90291) *(P-8962)*

Loan Administration Netwrk Inc .... D 949 752-5246
2082 Business Center Dr Ste 250 Irvine (92612) *(P-13541)*

Loandepot, Irvine *Also Called: Loandepot Inc (P-11918)*

Loandepot Inc (PA) .... C 888 337-6888
6561 Irvine Center Dr Irvine (92618) *(P-11918)*

Loandepotcom LLC (DH) .... A 888 337-6888
6561 Irvine Center Dr Irvine (92618) *(P-11919)*

Loandepotcom LLC .... A 760 797-6000
901 N Palm Canyon Dr Ste 107 Palm Springs (92262) *(P-11920)*

Loandepotcom LLC .... A 661 202-1700
42455 10th St W Ste 109 Lancaster (93534) *(P-11921)*

Loanmart, Van Nuys *Also Called: Wheels Financial Group LLC (P-11863)*

Locai Inc .... C 469 834-5364
2044 1st Ave Ste 200 San Diego (92101) *(P-13762)*

Local 12, San Diego *Also Called: Interntional Un Oper Engineers (P-17311)*

Local 12, Redlands *Also Called: Interntional Un Oper Engineers (P-17312)*

Local Corporation (PA) .... D 949 784-0800
7555 Irvine Center Dr Irvine (92618) *(P-13222)*

Local Inttive Hlth Auth For Lo .... B 909 620-1661
696 W Holt Ave Pomona (91768) *(P-12095)*

Local Inttive Hlth Auth For Lo (PA) .... B 213 694-1250
1200 W 7th St Los Angeles (90017) *(P-12096)*

Local Media San Diego LLC .... D 858 888-7000
6160 Cornerstone Ct E Ste 150 San Diego (92121) *(P-9483)*

Local.com, Irvine *Also Called: Local Corporation (P-13222)*

Locator Services Inc .... C 619 229-6100
4616 Mission Gorge Pl San Diego (92120) *(P-14315)*

Lock People, The, San Diego *Also Called: Hodge Products Inc (P-4771)*

Lock-Ridge Tool Company Inc .... D 909 865-8309
145 N 8th Ave Upland (91786) *(P-5199)*

Lockheed Martin, Coronado *Also Called: Lockheed Martin Corporation (P-7737)*

Lockheed Martin, Chula Vista *Also Called: Lockheed Martin Services LLC (P-17579)*

Lockheed Martin Aeronautics Co, Palmdale *Also Called: Lockheed Martin Corporation (P-7739)*

Lockheed Martin Corporation .... E 805 571-2346
346 Bollay Dr Goleta (93117) *(P-7736)*

Lockheed Martin Corporation .... C 619 437-7230
Nas North Island Coronado (92118) *(P-7737)*

Lockheed Martin Corporation .... D 760 952-4200
17452 Wheeler Rd Helendale (92342) *(P-7738)*

Lockheed Martin Corporation .... A 661 572-7428
1011 Lockheed Way Palmdale (93599) *(P-7739)*

Lockheed Martin Corporation .... C 760 386-2572
Bldg 821 South Loop Fort Irwin (92310) *(P-9084)*

Lockheed Martin Orincon Corp (HQ) .... C 858 455-5530
10325 Meanley Dr San Diego (92131) *(P-7740)*

Lockheed Martin Services LLC .... B 619 271-9831
645 Marsat Ct Ste D Chula Vista (91911) *(P-17579)*

Lockheed Martin Unmndd, San Luis Obispo *Also Called: AME Unmanned Air Systems Inc (P-17482)*

Lockton Cmpnies LLC - PCF Srie (HQ) ...... B 213 689-0500
777 S Figueroa St Ste 5200 Los Angeles (90017) *(P-12227)*

Lockton Insurance Brokers, Los Angeles *Also Called: Lockton Cmpnies LLC - PCF Srie (P-12227)*

Lockwood Industries LLC (HQ) .... C 661 702-6999
28525 Industry Dr Valencia (91355) *(P-6846)*

Locums Unlimited LLC .... A 619 550-3763
4141 Jutland Dr Ste 305 San Diego (92117) *(P-15550)*

Loeb & Loeb, Los Angeles *Also Called: Loeb & Loeb LLP (P-16735)*

Loeb & Loeb LLP (PA) .... C 310 282-2000
10100 Santa Monica Blvd Ste 2200 Los Angeles (90067) *(P-16735)*

Mergent email: customerrelations@mergent.com
1090

2025 Southern California
Business Directory and Buyers Guide

(P-0000) Products & Services Section entry number
(PA)=Parent Co (HQ)=Headquarters (DH)=Div Headquarters

Loews Coronado Bay Resort, Coronado *Also Called: 51st St & 8th Ave Corp (P-12753)*

Loews Hollywood Hotel LLC .... B 323 450-2235
1755 N Highland Ave Hollywood (90028) *(P-12904)*

Loews Santa Monica Beach Hotel, Santa Monica *Also Called: Dtrs Santa Monica LLC*
(P-12816)

Lofta .... E 858 299-8000
9225 Brown Deer Rd San Diego (92121) *(P-2215)*

Lofty Coffee Inc .... D 760 230-6747
97 N Coast Highway 101 Ste 101 Encinitas (92024) *(P-11586)*

Logicmonitor Inc (PA) .... **C 805 394-8632**
820 State St Fl 5 Santa Barbara (93101) *(P-14174)*

Logility Inc .... D 858 565-4238
4885 Greencraig Ln 200 San Diego (92123) *(P-13763)*

Login Consulting Services Inc .... D 310 607-9091
300 Continental Blvd Ste 405 El Segundo (90245) *(P-14233)*

Logisteed America Inc .... D 323 263-8100
1000 Corporate Center Dr Ste 400 Monterey Park (91754) *(P-9305)*

Logisteed Monterey Park, Monterey Park *Also Called: Logisteed America Inc (P-9305)*

Logistical Support LLC .... C 818 341-3344
20409 Prairie St Chatsworth (91311) *(P-7391)*

Logistical Support LLC .... C 818 341-3344
20409 Prairie St Chatsworth (91311) *(P-10496)*

Logistics, Bell *Also Called: De Well Container Shipping Inc (P-9268)*

Logitech Inc .... A 510 795-8500
3 Jenner Ste 180 Irvine (92618) *(P-5930)*

Logitech Inc .... B 972 947-7100
2053 E Jay St Ontario (91764) *(P-5931)*

Logix Federal Credit Union (PA) .... **C 888 718-5328**
2340 N Hollywood Way Burbank (91505) *(P-11803)*

Logix3, Irvine *Also Called: Data Council LLC (P-14487)*

Logo Expressions, Ontario *Also Called: Dennis Foland Inc (P-10558)*

Logomark Inc .... C 714 675-6100
1201 Bell Ave Tustin (92780) *(P-11128)*

Lois Lauer Realty (PA) .... **C 909 748-7000**
1998 Orange Tree Ln Redlands (92374) *(P-12479)*

Lollicup Franchising LLC .... C 626 965-8882
6185 Kimball Ave Chino (91708) *(P-18161)*

Loma Linda Broadcasting, Loma Linda *Also Called: Loma Linda University (P-14896)*

Loma Linda Community Hospital, Loma Linda *Also Called: Loma Linda University Med Ctr*
(P-16077)

Loma Linda Healthcare Sys 605, Loma Linda *Also Called: Veterans Health Administration*
(P-15507)

Loma Linda Post Acute, Loma Linda *Also Called: Pacs Group Inc (P-15737)*

Loma Linda University .... D 909 558-8611
11125 Campus St Ste 100 Loma Linda (92354) *(P-14896)*

Loma Linda University .... C 909 558-4475
11234 Anderson St Ste 2532 Loma Linda (92354) *(P-15379)*

Loma Linda University Med Ctr .... D 909 558-4000
1269 E San Bernardino Ave San Bernardino (92408) *(P-9306)*

Loma Linda University Med Ctr .... C 877 558-6248
11234 Anderson St Loma Linda (92354) *(P-15380)*

Loma Linda University Med Ctr .... D 909 558-4385
11370 Anderson St Loma Linda (92354) *(P-16076)*

Loma Linda University Med Ctr .... D 909 796-0167
25333 Barton Rd Loma Linda (92350) *(P-16077)*

Loma Linda University Med Ctr (DH) .... **A 909 558-4000**
11234 Anderson St Loma Linda (92354) *(P-16078)*

Loma Linda University Med Ctr .... D 909 558-4000
26780 Barton Rd Redlands (92373) *(P-16079)*

Loma Linda University Med Ctr .... C 909 558-9275
1710 Barton Rd Redlands (92373) *(P-16080)*

Loma Linda University Med Ctr, Loma Linda *Also Called: Loma Lnda - Inland Empire Cnsr*
(P-16081)

Loma Lnda - Inland Empire Cnsr .... C 909 558-4000
11234 Anderson St Loma Linda (92354) *(P-16081)*

Loma Lnda Univ Ansthsology Med, Loma Linda *Also Called: Loma Linda University*
(P-15379)

Loma Lnda Univ Med Ctr - Mrret .... B 951 672-1010
28062 Baxter Rd Murrieta (92563) *(P-15381)*

Loma Palisades, San Diego *Also Called: American Assets Inc (P-12280)*

Lombardy Holdings Inc (PA) .... **C 951 808-4550**
151 Kalmus Dr Ste F6 Costa Mesa (92626) *(P-685)*

Lomita Logistics LLC .... D 310 784-8485
3541 Lomita Blvd Torrance (90505) *(P-13303)*

Lompoc Family YMCA, Lompoc *Also Called: Channel Islnds Yung MNS Chrstn (P-17332)*

Lompoc Skilled Care Center, Lompoc *Also Called: Lompoc Valley Medical Center (P-16083)*

Lompoc Valley Medical Center .... C 805 735-9229
1111 E Ocean Ave Ste 2 Lompoc (93436) *(P-16082)*

Lompoc Valley Medical Center (PA) .... **B 805 737-3300**
1515 E Ocean Ave Lompoc (93436) *(P-16083)*

Lompoc-Vandenberg Afb, Lompoc *Also Called: Serco Services Inc (P-13817)*

Lonestar Sierra LLC .... C 866 575-5680
1820 W Orangewood Ave Orange (92868) *(P-10444)*

Long Bch Dept Hlth & Humn Svcs, Long Beach *Also Called: City of Long Beach (P-18391)*

Long Beach Care Center Inc .... C 562 426-6141
2615 Grand Ave Long Beach (90815) *(P-15701)*

Long Beach Golden Sails Inc .... D 562 596-1631
23545 Crenshaw Blvd Ste 100 Torrance (90505) *(P-12905)*

Long Beach Marriott, Long Beach *Also Called: Ruffin Hotel Corp of Cal (P-13003)*

Long Beach Medical Center .... B 562 933-7701
450 E Spring St Ste 11 Long Beach (90806) *(P-16084)*

Long Beach Medical Center .... B 562 933-0085
1720 Termino Ave Long Beach (90804) *(P-16085)*

Long Beach Medical Center (HQ) .... **A 562 933-2000**
2801 Atlantic Ave Fl 2 Long Beach (90806) *(P-16086)*

Long Beach Medical Clinic, Long Beach *Also Called: CB Tang MD Incorporated (P-15264)*

Long Beach Memorial Med Ctr .... B 562 933-0432
1057 Pine Ave Long Beach (90813) *(P-16087)*

LONG BEACH MEMORIAL MEDICAL CENTER, Long Beach *Also Called: Long Beach*
Memorial Med Ctr (P-16087)

Long Beach Pain Center, Long Beach *Also Called: Healthsmart Pacific Inc (P-16015)*

Long Beach Public Trnsp Co .... D 562 591-2301
1300 Gardenia Ave Long Beach (90804) *(P-8759)*

Long Beach Public Trnsp Co (PA) .... **A 562 599-8571**
1963 E Anaheim St Long Beach (90813) *(P-8760)*

Long Beach Transit, Long Beach *Also Called: Long Beach Public Trnsp Co (P-8760)*

Long Beach Unified School Dst .... C 562 426-6176
2700 Pine Ave Long Beach (90806) *(P-8881)*

Long Beach Unified School Dst .... D 562 426-5571
3038 Delta Ave Long Beach (90810) *(P-16814)*

Long Point Development LLC .... A 310 265-2800
100 Terranea Way Rancho Palos Verdes (90275) *(P-12906)*

LONGBOARD, La Jolla *Also Called: Longboard Pharmaceuticals Inc (P-3444)*

Longboard Pharmaceuticals Inc .... E 858 789-9283
4275 Executive Sq Ste 950 La Jolla (92037) *(P-3444)*

Longo Lexus, El Monte *Also Called: El Monte Automotive Group Inc (P-11340)*

Longo Scion, El Monte *Also Called: D Longo Inc (P-11331)*

Longwood Management, San Dimas *Also Called: San Dimas Retirement Center (P-12364)*

Longwood Management Corp .... D 818 360-1864
17922 San Fernando Mission Blvd Granada Hills (91344) *(P-15702)*

Longwood Management Corp .... C 626 280-2293
8101 Hill Dr Rosemead (91770) *(P-15703)*

Longwood Management Corp .... D 626 280-4820
8035 Hill Dr Rosemead (91770) *(P-15704)*

Longwood Management Corp .... C 323 933-1560
1900 S Longwood Ave Los Angeles (90016) *(P-15705)*

Longwood Management Corp .... C 310 679-1461
11834 Inglewood Ave Hawthorne (90250) *(P-15706)*

Longwood Management Corp .... D 323 737-7778
2190 W Adams Blvd Los Angeles (90018) *(P-15865)*

Longwood Management Corp .... C 213 382-8461
1240 S Hoover St Los Angeles (90006) *(P-15866)*

Longwood Management Corp .... C 818 980-8200
11429 Ventura Blvd Studio City (91604) *(P-15867)*

Longwood Management Corp .... C 626 289-3763
537 W Live Oak St San Gabriel (91776) *(P-15868)*

Longwood Management Corp .... C 562 432-5751
1913 E 5th St Long Beach (90802) *(P-15869)*

Longwood Management Corp .... C 323 735-5146
2000 W Washington Blvd Los Angeles (90018) *(P-15870)*

Longwood Management Corp .... C 818 246-7174
605 W Broadway Glendale (91204) *(P-15871)*

Employee Codes: A=Over 500 employees, B=251-500
C=101-250, D=51-100, E=20-50, F=10-19, G=1-9

2025 Southern California
Business Directory and Buyers Guide

© Mergent Inc. 1-800-342-5647
1091

Longwood Management Corp .... D 562 693-5240
7716 Pickering Ave Whittier (90602) *(P-16088)*

Longwood Management Corp .... D 818 881-7414
7836 Reseda Blvd Reseda (91335) *(P-16089)*

Longwood Management Corp .... D 310 675-9163
14110 Cordary Ave Hawthorne (90250) *(P-17175)*

Loomworks Apparel, Irvine *Also Called: Delta Galil USA Inc (P-10705)*

Looney Bins Inc (HQ)...................................... D 818 485-8200
12153 Montague St Pacoima (91331) *(P-9748)*

Loop Inc .... E 888 385-6674
115 Eucalyptus Dr El Segundo (90245) *(P-7093)*

Lopez & Associates Engineers, El Monte *Also Called: R and L Lopez Associates Inc*
(P-17617)

Lord & Sons Inc .... C 562 529-2500
10504 Pioneer Blvd Santa Fe Springs (90670) *(P-10445)*

Lorem Cytori Usa Inc .... E 858 746-8696
8659 Production Ave San Diego (92121) *(P-3445)*

Loren Electric Sign & Lighting, Whittier *Also Called: Exiton Inc (P-8603)*

Lorenzo USA, Solana Beach *Also Called: Simon Golub & Sons Inc (P-10553)*

Lorimar Winery .... E 951 240-5177
42031 Main St Ste C Temecula (92590) *(P-1579)*

Los Alamitos Medical Ctr Inc (HQ)................... A 714 826-6400
3751 Katella Ave Los Alamitos (90720) *(P-16090)*

Los Alamitos Race Course .... C 714 820-2800
4961 Katella Ave Cypress (90720) *(P-11587)*

Los Altos, City Of Industry *Also Called: Los Altos Food Products LLC (P-10831)*

Los Altos Food Products LLC .... C 626 330-6555
450 Baldwin Park Blvd City Of Industry (91746) *(P-10831)*

Los Angeles Angels of Anaheim, Anaheim *Also Called: Angels Baseball LP (P-15018)*

Los Angeles Apparel Inc (PA)......................... C 213 275-3120
1020 E 59th St Los Angeles (90001) *(P-2196)*

Los Angeles Apparel Inc .... C 213 275-3120
647 E 59th St Los Angeles (90001) *(P-2197)*

Los Angeles Apparel Inc .... C 323 561-8518
902 E 59th St Los Angeles (90001) *(P-14533)*

Los Angeles Athletic Club Inc .... C 213 625-2211
431 W 7th St Los Angeles (90014) *(P-15056)*

Los Angeles Branch, Commerce *Also Called: Jfc International Inc (P-10950)*

Los Angeles Branch, Los Angeles *Also Called: Federal Rsrve Bnk San Frncisco (P-11703)*

Los Angeles Business Journal, Los Angeles *Also Called: Cbj LP (P-2847)*

Los Angeles Capital MGT LLC (PA)................. D 310 479-9998
11150 Santa Monica Blvd Ste 200 Los Angeles (90025) *(P-12635)*

Los Angeles Chargers, El Segundo *Also Called: Chargers Football Company LLC (P-15022)*

Los Angeles City Hauling, Sun Valley *Also Called: USA Waste of California Inc (P-9770)*

Los Angeles Clippers, Los Angeles *Also Called: LA Sports Properties Inc (P-15030)*

Los Angeles Cold Storage, Los Angeles *Also Called: Standard-Southern Corporation*
(P-9042)

LOS ANGELES COMMUNITY HOSPITAL, Los Angeles *Also Called: Paraclsus Los Angles*
Cmnty Hos (P-16124)

Los Angeles Convention Center, Los Angeles *Also Called: AEG Management Lacc LLC*
(P-17935)

Los Angeles Country Club .... C 310 276-6104
10101 Wilshire Blvd Los Angeles (90024) *(P-15147)*

Los Angeles County Bar Assn (PA)................... D 213 627-2727
444 S Flower St Los Angeles (90071) *(P-17300)*

Los Angeles County Fair Assn (PA)................... D 909 623-3111
1101 W Mckinley Ave Pomona (91768) *(P-15210)*

Los Angeles County Hospital, Los Angeles *Also Called: Lac Usc Medical Center (P-16070)*

Los Angeles County Pub Works, South Gate *Also Called: County of Los Angeles (P-16552)*

Los Angeles Dept Wtr & Pwr .... A 310 524-8500
12700 Vista Del Mar Playa Del Rey (90293) *(P-9679)*

Los Angeles Dept Wtr & Pwr (HQ)................... A 213 367-1320
111 N Hope St Los Angeles (90012) *(P-9699)*

Los Angeles Dept Wtr & Pwr .... A 213 367-5706
1141 W 2nd St Bldg D Los Angeles (90012) *(P-9700)*

Los Angeles Dept Wtr & Pwr .... A 213 367-4211
1630 N Main St Los Angeles (90012) *(P-9701)*

Los Angeles Dept Wtr & Pwr .... A 323 256-8079
4030 Crenshaw Blvd Los Angeles (90008) *(P-9702)*

Los Angeles Dept Wtr & Pwr .... A 213 367-1342
11801 Sheldon St Sun Valley (91352) *(P-9703)*

Los Angeles Engineering Inc .... C 626 869-1400
633 N Barranca Ave Covina (91723) *(P-17580)*

Los Angeles Federal Credit Un (PA)................. D 818 242-8640
300 S Glendale Ave Ste 100 Glendale (91205) *(P-11804)*

LOS ANGELES FEDERAL CREDIT UNI, Glendale *Also Called: Los Angeles Federal Credit Un*
(P-11804)

Los Angeles Fiber Co, Vernon *Also Called: Marspring Corporation (P-2488)*

Los Angeles Free Clinic .... C 323 653-1990
5205 Melrose Ave Los Angeles (90038) *(P-15382)*

Los Angeles Free Clinic (PA)........................... D 323 653-8622
8405 Beverly Blvd Los Angeles (90048) *(P-15383)*

Los Angeles Freightliner, Fontana *Also Called: Los Angeles Truck Centers LLC (P-9804)*

Los Angeles Galvanizing Co .... D 323 583-2263
2518 E 53rd St Huntington Park (90255) *(P-5329)*

Los Angeles Homeless Svcs Auth .... A 213 683-3333
707 Wilshire Blvd Ste 1000 Los Angeles (90017) *(P-16974)*

LOS ANGELES LAWYER MAGAZINE, Los Angeles *Also Called: Los Angeles County Bar*
Assn (P-17300)

Los Angeles Lgbt Center (PA).......................... C 323 993-7618
1625 Schrader Blvd Los Angeles (90028) *(P-17235)*

Los Angeles Ltg Mfg Co Inc .... D 626 454-8300
10141 Olney St El Monte (91731) *(P-10190)*

Los Angeles Mem Coliseum Comm .... B 213 747-7111
3911 S Figueroa St Los Angeles (90037) *(P-17465)*

Los Angeles Mission Inc (PA).......................... D 213 629-1227
303 E 5th St Los Angeles (90013) *(P-17176)*

Los Angeles Opera Company .... B 213 972-7219
135 N Grand Ave Ste 327 Los Angeles (90012) *(P-14965)*

Los Angeles Philharmonic Assn .... A 323 850-2060
2301 N Highland Ave Los Angeles (90068) *(P-14996)*

Los Angeles Philharmonic Assn (PA)............... C 213 972-7300
151 S Grand Ave Los Angeles (90012) *(P-14997)*

Los Angeles Plant, Cypress *Also Called: Hitachi Automotive Systems (P-6324)*

Los Angeles Police Credit Un (PA)................... D 818 787-6520
16150 Sherman Way Van Nuys (91406) *(P-11829)*

Los Angeles Poultry Co Inc .... D 323 232-1619
4816 Long Beach Ave Los Angeles (90058) *(P-1281)*

Los Angeles Rams LLC (PA)............................ D 314 982-7267
29899 Agoura Rd Agoura Hills (91301) *(P-15031)*

Los Angeles Rams LLC .... D 310 277-4700
10271 W Pico Blvd Los Angeles (90064) *(P-18009)*

Los Angeles Regional Food Bank .... C 323 234-3030
1734 E 41st St Los Angeles (90058) *(P-16975)*

Los Angeles Residential Comm F .... D 661 296-8636
29890 Bouquet Canyon Rd Santa Clarita (91390) *(P-17177)*

Los Angeles Sales Office, Northridge *Also Called: Harman International Inds Inc (P-10246)*

Los Angeles Sentinel Inc .... D 323 299-3800
3800 Crenshaw Blvd Los Angeles (90008) *(P-2813)*

Los Angeles Sleeve Co Inc .... E 562 945-7578
12051 Rivera Rd Santa Fe Springs (90670) *(P-7266)*

Los Angeles Times, El Segundo *Also Called: Los Angles Tmes Cmmnctions LLC (P-2814)*

Los Angeles Truck Centers LLC .... C 909 510-4000
13800 Valley Blvd Fontana (92335) *(P-9804)*

Los Angeles Truck Centers LLC (PA)............... D 562 447-1200
2429 Peck Rd Whittier (90601) *(P-14694)*

Los Angeles Turf Club Inc (DH)....................... D 626 574-6330
285 W Huntington Dr Arcadia (91007) *(P-15039)*

Los Angeles Unified School Dst .... D 213 763-2900
1240 Naomi Ave Los Angeles (90021) *(P-13387)*

Los Angeles Unified School Dst .... C 818 346-3540
6200 Winnetka Ave Woodland Hills (91367) *(P-16815)*

Los Angeles World Airports (PA)....................... C 855 463-5252
1 World Way Los Angeles (90045) *(P-9202)*

Los Angeles World Airports .... A 424 646-5900
7301 World Way W Fl 5 Los Angeles (90045) *(P-9203)*

Los Angeles World Airports .... B 424 646-9118
5312 W 99th Pl Los Angeles (90045) *(P-9204)*

Los Angles Area Chmber Cmmerce .... D 213 580-7500
350 S Bixel St Los Angeles (90017) *(P-17284)*

Los Angles Cnty Cntl Jail Hosp, Los Angeles *Also Called: County of Los Angeles (P-15969)*

Los Angles Cnty Dvlpmntal Svcs .... C 213 383-1300
3303 Wilshire Blvd Ste 700 Los Angeles (90010) *(P-16583)*

Mergent email: customerrelations@mergent.com
1092

2025 Southern California
Business Directory and Buyers Guide

(P-0000) Products & Services Section entry number
(PA)=Parent Co (HQ)=Headquarters (DH)=Div Headquarters

Los Angles Cnty Emplyees Rtrme (PA)................................ C 626 564-6000
300 N Lake Ave Ste 720 Pasadena (91101) *(P-12160)*

Los Angles Cnty Mseum Ntrral Hs (PA)............................ C 213 763-3466
900 Exposition Blvd Los Angeles (90007) *(P-18384)*

Los Angles Cnty Mtro Trnsp Aut .... A 323 466-3876
1 Gateway Plz Fl 25 Los Angeles (90012) *(P-8761)*

Los Angles Cnty Mtro Trnsp Aut .... B 310 643-3804
14724 Aviation Blvd Lawndale (90260) *(P-8762)*

Los Angles Cnty Mtro Trnsp Aut .... A 213 922-6308
9201 Canoga Ave Chatsworth (91311) *(P-8763)*

Los Angles Cnty Mtro Trnsp Aut .... B 213 922-5887
900 Lyon St Los Angeles (90012) *(P-8764)*

Los Angles Cnty Mtro Trnsp Aut .... B 213 922-6301
1130 E 6th St Los Angeles (90021) *(P-8765)*

Los Angles Cnty Mtro Trnsp Aut .... B 213 922-6203
630 W Avenue 28 Los Angeles (90065) *(P-8766)*

Los Angles Cnty Mtro Trnsp Aut .... A 213 922-6202
1 Gateway Plz Los Angeles (90012) *(P-8767)*

Los Angles Cnty Mtro Trnsp Aut .... A 213 922-6207
8800 Santa Monica Blvd Los Angeles (90069) *(P-8768)*

Los Angles Cnty Mtro Trnsp Aut .... A 213 922-6215
11900 Branford St Sun Valley (91352) *(P-8769)*

Los Angles Cnty Mtro Trnsp Aut .... A 213 533-1506
720 E 15th St Los Angeles (90021) *(P-8770)*

Los Angles Cnty Mtro Trnsp Aut .... A 213 922-5012
470 Bauchet St Los Angeles (90012) *(P-8771)*

Los Angles Cnty Mtro Trnsp Aut .... B 310 392-8636
100 Sunset Ave Venice (90291) *(P-8772)*

Los Angles Cnty Mtro Trnsp Aut .... B 213 244-6783
818 W 7th St Ste 500 Los Angeles (90017) *(P-8773)*

Los Angles Cnty Mtro Trnsp Aut .... A 626 471-7855
1600 S California Ave Monrovia (91016) *(P-8774)*

Los Angles Cnty Mtro Trnsp Aut .... A 213 626-4455
320 S Santa Fe Ave Los Angeles (90013) *(P-8775)*

Los Angles Cnty Rncho Los Amgo .... A 562 385-7111
7601 Imperial Hwy Downey (90242) *(P-15814)*

Los Angles Cnty Snttion Dstrct (PA)................................. A 562 699-7411
1955 Workman Mill Rd Whittier (90601) *(P-9788)*

Los Angles Cnvntion Exhbtion C .... B 213 741-1151
1201 S Figueroa St Los Angeles (90015) *(P-12302)*

Los Angles Dept Cnvtion Trism, Los Angeles *Also Called: Los Angles Cnvntion Exhbtion C (P-12302)*

Los Angles Dst Off Policy Svcs, Monterey Park *Also Called: State Compensation Insur Fund (P-12136)*

Los Angles Jewish HM For Aging .... B 818 774-3000
18855 Victory Blvd Reseda (91335) *(P-15707)*

Los Angles Jewish HM For Aging (PA)............................... B 818 774-3000
7150 Tampa Ave Reseda (91335) *(P-15708)*

Los Angles Ryal Vsta Golf Crse .... D 909 595-7441
20055 Colima Rd Walnut (91789) *(P-15148)*

Los Angles Ryal Vsta Golf Crse, Walnut *Also Called: Los Angles Ryal Vsta Golf Crse (P-15148)*

Los Angles Tmes Cmmnctions LLC (PA)............................ A 213 237-5000
2300 E Imperial Hwy El Segundo (90245) *(P-2814)*

Los Cabos Mexican Foods, Santa Fe Springs *Also Called: MCI Foods Inc (P-1814)*

Los Feliz Ford Inc (PA)... D 818 502-1901
1101 S Brand Blvd Glendale (91204) *(P-11374)*

Los Palos Convalescent Hosp, San Pedro *Also Called: San Pedro Convalescent HM Inc (P-15769)*

Los Pericos Food Products LLC .... E 909 623-5625
2301 Valley Blvd Pomona (91768) *(P-1810)*

Los Robles Hospital & Med Ctr, Thousand Oaks *Also Called: Los Robles Regional Med Ctr (P-16091)*

Los Robles Regional Med Ctr .... B 805 370-4531
150 Via Merida Westlake Village (91362) *(P-15384)*

Los Robles Regional Med Ctr .... B 805 494-0880
2200 Lynn Rd Thousand Oaks (91360) *(P-15385)*

Los Robles Regional Med Ctr (DH).................................. A 805 497-2727
215 W Janss Rd Thousand Oaks (91360) *(P-16091)*

Los Serranos Golf & Cntry CLB, Chino Hills *Also Called: Los Serranos Golf Club (P-15088)*

Los Serranos Golf Club .... C 909 597-1769
15656 Yorba Ave Chino Hills (91709) *(P-15088)*

Loss and Risk Advisors, San Diego *Also Called: Barney & Barney Inc (P-12182)*

Lost Dutchmans Minings Assn (DH)................................. E 951 699-4749
43445 Business Park Dr Ste 113 Temecula (92590) *(P-254)*

Lotus Clinical Research LLC .... D 626 381-9830
100 W California Blvd Pasadena (91105) *(P-16323)*

Lotus Workforce LLC .... A 480 264-0773
5930 Cornerstone Ct W Ste 300 San Diego (92121) *(P-18162)*

Lou Ana Foods, Brea *Also Called: Ventura Foods LLC (P-1527)*

Loud Mfg, Thousand Oaks *Also Called: Midnight Manufacturing LLC (P-3319)*

Louden Madelon, Vernon *Also Called: National Corset Supply House (P-2151)*

Louidar LLC .... E 951 676-5047
33820 Rancho California Rd Temecula (92591) *(P-1580)*

Louis Sardo Upholstery Inc (PA)..................................... D 310 327-0532
512 W Rosecrans Ave Gardena (90248) *(P-2549)*

Lounge Fly, Walnut *Also Called: Loungefly LLC (P-8570)*

Loungefly LLC .... E 818 718-5600
108 S Mayo Ave Walnut (91789) *(P-8570)*

Louroe Electronics Inc .... E 818 994-6498
6955 Valjean Ave Van Nuys (91406) *(P-14413)*

Lovco Construction, Signal Hill *Also Called: Lovco Construction Inc (P-1172)*

Lovco Construction Inc .... C 562 595-1601
1300 E Burnett St Signal Hill (90755) *(P-1172)*

Love At First Bite Catering .... D 714 369-0561
18281 Gothard St Ste 108 Huntington Beach (92648) *(P-11588)*

Love Stitch, Los Angeles *Also Called: Clothing Illustrated Inc (P-2086)*

Low Cost Interlock Inc .... E 844 387-0326
2038 W Park Ave Redlands (92373) *(P-7094)*

Lowe Enterprises, Los Angeles *Also Called: Lowe Enterprises RE Group (P-12570)*

Lowe Enterprises Inc .... D 949 724-1515
300 Spectrum Center Dr Ste 1460 Irvine (92618) *(P-12480)*

Lowe Enterprises Inc (PA).. C 310 820-6661
11777 San Vicente Blvd Ste 900 Los Angeles (90049) *(P-12907)*

Lowe Enterprises Inc .... C 310 820-6661
843 2nd St Ste C Encinitas (92024) *(P-12908)*

Lowe Enterprises RE Group .... B 310 820-6661
11777 San Vicente Blvd Ste 900 Los Angeles (90049) *(P-12570)*

Lowe Enterprises Real Estate, Irvine *Also Called: Lowe Enterprises Inc (P-12480)*

Lowe Enterprises Rlty Svcs Inc .... A 818 990-9555
16133 Ventura Blvd Ste 535 Encino (91436) *(P-12481)*

Lowe's, Perris *Also Called: Lowes Home Centers LLC (P-9085)*

Lowe's, Rancho Santa Margari *Also Called: Lowes Home Centers LLC (P-11202)*

Lowe's, San Clemente *Also Called: Lowes Home Centers LLC (P-11203)*

Lowe's, Anaheim *Also Called: Lowes Home Centers LLC (P-11204)*

Lowe's, La Habra *Also Called: Lowes Home Centers LLC (P-11205)*

Lowe's, Huntington Beach *Also Called: Lowes Home Centers LLC (P-11206)*

Lowe's, Tustin *Also Called: Lowes Home Centers LLC (P-11207)*

Lowe's, Ventura *Also Called: Lowes Home Centers LLC (P-11208)*

Lowe's, Simi Valley *Also Called: Lowes Home Centers LLC (P-11209)*

Lowe's, Paso Robles *Also Called: Lowes Home Centers LLC (P-11210)*

Lowe's, Rancho Cucamonga *Also Called: Lowes Home Centers LLC (P-11211)*

Lowe's, Victorville *Also Called: Lowes Home Centers LLC (P-11212)*

Lowe's, Upland *Also Called: Lowes Home Centers LLC (P-11213)*

Lowe's, Fontana *Also Called: Lowes Home Centers LLC (P-11214)*

Lowe's, Redlands *Also Called: Lowes Home Centers LLC (P-11215)*

Lowe's, Apple Valley *Also Called: Lowes Home Centers LLC (P-11216)*

Lowe's, Ontario *Also Called: Lowes Home Centers LLC (P-11217)*

Lowe's, Menifee *Also Called: Lowes Home Centers LLC (P-11218)*

Lowe's, Riverside *Also Called: Lowes Home Centers LLC (P-11219)*

Lowe's, La Quinta *Also Called: Lowes Home Centers LLC (P-11220)*

Lowe's, Palm Springs *Also Called: Lowes Home Centers LLC (P-11221)*

Lowe's, Murrieta *Also Called: Lowes Home Centers LLC (P-11222)*

Lowe's, Moreno Valley *Also Called: Lowes Home Centers LLC (P-11223)*

Lowe's, Temecula *Also Called: Lowes Home Centers LLC (P-11224)*

Lowe's, Corona *Also Called: Lowes Home Centers LLC (P-11225)*

Lowe's, Hemet *Also Called: Lowes Home Centers LLC (P-11226)*

Lowe's, Lake Elsinore *Also Called: Lowes Home Centers LLC (P-11227)*

Lowe's, Oceanside *Also Called: Lowes Home Centers LLC (P-11228)*

Employee Codes: A=Over 500 employees, B=251-500
C=101-250, D=51-100, E=20-50, F=10-19, G=1-9

2025 Southern California
Business Directory and Buyers Guide

© Mergent Inc. 1-800-342-5647
1093

Lowe's, Vista *Also Called: Lowes Home Centers LLC (P-11229)*

Lowe's, Chula Vista *Also Called: Lowes Home Centers LLC (P-11230)*

Lowe's, Santee *Also Called: Lowes Home Centers LLC (P-11231)*

Lowe's, Escondido *Also Called: Lowes Home Centers LLC (P-11232)*

Lowe's, Chino Hills *Also Called: Lowes Home Centers LLC (P-11233)*

Lowe's, Highland *Also Called: Lowes Home Centers LLC (P-11234)*

Lowe's, San Diego *Also Called: Lowes Home Centers LLC (P-11235)*

Lowe's, Lancaster *Also Called: Lowes Home Centers LLC (P-11236)*

Lowe's, Northridge *Also Called: Lowes Home Centers LLC (P-11237)*

Lowe's, Santa Clarita *Also Called: Lowes Home Centers LLC (P-11238)*

Lowe's, El Centro *Also Called: Lowes Home Centers LLC (P-11239)*

Lowe's, Bakersfield *Also Called: Lowes Home Centers LLC (P-11240)*

Lowe's, Pacoima *Also Called: Lowes Home Centers LLC (P-11241)*

Lowe's, West Hills *Also Called: Lowes Home Centers LLC (P-11242)*

Lowe's, Burbank *Also Called: Lowes Home Centers LLC (P-11243)*

Lowe's, Pico Rivera *Also Called: Lowes Home Centers LLC (P-11245)*

Lowe's, Palmdale *Also Called: Lowes Home Centers LLC (P-11246)*

Lowe's, Torrance *Also Called: Lowes Home Centers LLC (P-11247)*

Lowe's, Norwalk *Also Called: Lowes Home Centers LLC (P-11248)*

Lower LLC .... C 909 527-3736
9587 Foothill Blvd Rancho Cucamonga (91730) *(P-11922)*

Lowermybills Inc .... C 310 348-6800
12181 Bluff Creek Dr Ste 250 Playa Vista (90094) *(P-14175)*

Lowermybills.com, Playa Vista *Also Called: Lmb Opco LLC (P-11947)*

Lowermybills.com, Playa Vista *Also Called: Lowermybills Inc (P-14175)*

Lowes Home Centers LLC .... B 951 443-2500
3984 Indian Ave Perris (92571) *(P-9085)*

Lowes Home Centers LLC .... D 949 589-5005
30481 Avenida De Las Flores Rancho Santa Margari (92688) *(P-11202)*

Lowes Home Centers LLC .... C 949 369-4644
907 Avenida Pico San Clemente (92673) *(P-11203)*

Lowes Home Centers LLC .... D 714 447-6140
1500 N Lemon St Anaheim (92801) *(P-11204)*

Lowes Home Centers LLC .... C 562 690-5122
1380 S Beach Blvd La Habra (90631) *(P-11205)*

Lowes Home Centers LLC .... D 714 907-9006
8175 Warner Ave Huntington Beach (92647) *(P-11206)*

Lowes Home Centers LLC .... C 714 913-2663
2500 Park Ave Tustin (92782) *(P-11207)*

Lowes Home Centers LLC .... C 805 675-8800
500 S Mills Rd Ventura (93003) *(P-11208)*

Lowes Home Centers LLC .... C 805 426-2780
1275 Simi Town Center Way Simi Valley (93065) *(P-11209)*

Lowes Home Centers LLC .... C 805 602-9051
2445 Golden Hill Rd Paso Robles (93446) *(P-11210)*

Lowes Home Centers LLC .... C 909 476-9697
11399 Foothill Blvd Rancho Cucamonga (91730) *(P-11211)*

Lowes Home Centers LLC .... C 760 949-9565
14333 Bear Valley Rd Victorville (92392) *(P-11212)*

Lowes Home Centers LLC .... C 909 982-4795
1659 W Foothill Blvd Upland (91786) *(P-11213)*

Lowes Home Centers LLC .... C 909 350-7900
16851 Sierra Lakes Pkwy Fontana (92336) *(P-11214)*

Lowes Home Centers LLC .... C 909 307-8883
1725 W Redlands Blvd Redlands (92373) *(P-11215)*

Lowes Home Centers LLC .... C 760 961-3000
12189 Apple Valley Rd Apple Valley (92308) *(P-11216)*

Lowes Home Centers LLC .... C 909 969-9053
2390 S Grove Ave Ontario (91761) *(P-11217)*

Lowes Home Centers LLC .... C 951 723-1930
30472 Haun Rd Menifee (92584) *(P-11218)*

Lowes Home Centers LLC .... C 951 509-5500
9851 Magnolia Ave Riverside (92503) *(P-11219)*

Lowes Home Centers LLC .... C 760 771-5566
78865 Highway 111 La Quinta (92253) *(P-11220)*

Lowes Home Centers LLC .... C 760 866-1901
5201 E Ramon Rd Palm Springs (92264) *(P-11221)*

Lowes Home Centers LLC .... D 951 461-8916
24701 Madison Ave Murrieta (92562) *(P-11222)*

Lowes Home Centers LLC .... D 951 656-1859
12400 Day St Moreno Valley (92553) *(P-11223)*

Lowes Home Centers LLC .... D 951 296-1618
40390 Winchester Rd Temecula (92591) *(P-11224)*

Lowes Home Centers LLC .... D 951 256-9004
1285 Magnolia Ave Corona (92879) *(P-11225)*

Lowes Home Centers LLC .... C 951 492-7000
350 S Sanderson Ave Hemet (92545) *(P-11226)*

Lowes Home Centers LLC .... C 951 253-6000
29335 Central Ave Lake Elsinore (92532) *(P-11227)*

Lowes Home Centers LLC .... C 760 966-7140
155 Old Grove Rd Oceanside (92057) *(P-11228)*

Lowes Home Centers LLC .... C 760 631-6255
151 Vista Village Dr Vista (92083) *(P-11229)*

Lowes Home Centers LLC .... C 619 739-9060
2225 Otay Lakes Rd Chula Vista (91915) *(P-11230)*

Lowes Home Centers LLC .... C 619 212-4100
9416 Mission Gorge Rd Santee (92071) *(P-11231)*

Lowes Home Centers LLC .... C 760 484-5113
620 W Mission Ave Escondido (92025) *(P-11232)*

Lowes Home Centers LLC .... C 909 438-9000
4777 Chino Hills Pkwy Chino Hills (91709) *(P-11233)*

Lowes Home Centers LLC .... C 909 557-9010
27847 Greenspot Rd Highland (92346) *(P-11234)*

Lowes Home Centers LLC .... C 619 584-5500
2318 Northside Dr San Diego (92108) *(P-11235)*

Lowes Home Centers LLC .... D 661 341-9000
730 W Avenue K Lancaster (93534) *(P-11236)*

Lowes Home Centers LLC .... C 818 477-9022
19601 Nordhoff St Northridge (91324) *(P-11237)*

Lowes Home Centers LLC .... C 661 678-4430
19001 Golden Valley Rd Santa Clarita (91387) *(P-11238)*

Lowes Home Centers LLC .... C 760 337-6700
2053 N Imperial Ave El Centro (92243) *(P-11239)*

Lowes Home Centers LLC .... C 661 889-9000
1601 Columbus St Bakersfield (93305) *(P-11240)*

Lowes Home Centers LLC .... D 818 686-4300
13500 Paxton St Pacoima (91331) *(P-11241)*

Lowes Home Centers LLC .... C 818 610-1960
8383 Topanga Canyon Blvd West Hills (91304) *(P-11242)*

Lowes Home Centers LLC .... C 818 557-2300
2000 W Empire Ave Burbank (91504) *(P-11243)*

Lowes Home Centers LLC .... C 323 327-4000
2800 W 120th St Hawthorne (90250) *(P-11244)*

Lowes Home Centers LLC .... B 562 942-9909
8600 Washington Blvd Pico Rivera (90660) *(P-11245)*

Lowes Home Centers LLC .... C 661 267-9888
39500 Lowes Dr Palmdale (93551) *(P-11246)*

Lowes Home Centers LLC .... C 310 787-1469
22255 S Western Ave Torrance (90501) *(P-11247)*

Lowes Home Centers LLC .... C 562 926-0826
14873 Carmenita Rd Norwalk (90650) *(P-11248)*

Lowratscom 1st Lbrty Cal State, Cerritos *Also Called: Sun West Mortgage Company Inc (P-11936)*

Lozano Caseworks Inc .... D 909 783-7530
242 W Hanna St Colton (92324) *(P-1056)*

Lozano Enterprises, Los Angeles *Also Called: La Opinion LP (P-2809)*

Lozano Plumbing Services Inc .... C 951 683-4840
3615 Presley Ave Riverside (92507) *(P-797)*

LPA Inc (PA) .... **C 949 261-1001**
5301 California Ave Ste 100 Irvine (92617) *(P-17681)*

Lpa Design Group, Inc., Irvine *Also Called: LPA Inc (P-17681)*

LPC Commercial Services Inc .... C 213 362-9080
915 Wilshire Blvd Ste 250 Los Angeles (90017) *(P-12571)*

LPC COMMERCIAL SERVICES, INC., Los Angeles *Also Called: LPC Commercial Services Inc (P-12571)*

Lpcc, Camarillo *Also Called: Las Posas Country Club (P-15146)*

Lpcc 6008, Ontario *Also Called: Leggett & Platt Incorporated (P-2487)*

Lpl Financial Holdings Inc (PA) .... **B 800 877-7210**
4707 Executive Dr San Diego (92121) *(P-11974)*

Lpl Holdings, San Diego *Also Called: Lpl Holdings Inc (P-18163)*

Lpl Holdings Inc (HQ)..................................C 858 450-9606
4707 Executive Dr San Diego (92121) *(P-18163)*

Lpsh Holdings Inc ....B 951 926-1176
3570 W Florida Ave Ste 168 Hemet (92545) *(P-798)*

Lres Corporation (PA).................................D 714 520-5737
765 The City Dr S Orange (92868) *(P-12482)*

Lrw Group, Los Angeles Also Called: Material Holdings LLC *(P-17855)*

Lsa Associates Inc (PA)...............................C 949 553-0666
3210 El Camino Real Ste 100 Irvine (92602) *(P-18332)*

Lsf9 Cypress Parent 2 LLC ....A 714 380-3127
2741 Walnut Ave Ste 200 Tustin (92780) *(P-9961)*

Lso, San Diego Also Called: Cri 2000 LP *(P-2411)*

Lspace America LLC ....D 949 750-2292
14420 Myford Rd Irvine (92606) *(P-1922)*

Ltl Pros Inc ....D 909 350-1600
13610 S Archibald Ave Ontario (91761) *(P-8963)*

Ltr, South Gate Also Called: Lunday-Thagard Company *(P-3860)*

Lubeco Inc ....E 562 602-1791
6859 Downey Ave Long Beach (90805) *(P-3856)*

Lubricating Specialties Company ....C 562 776-4000
8015 Paramount Blvd Pico Rivera (90660) *(P-3857)*

Lubrication Scientifics LLC ....E 714 557-0664
17651 Armstrong Ave Irvine (92614) *(P-5827)*

Lubrizol Global Management Inc ....E 805 239-1550
3115 Propeller Dr Paso Robles (93446) *(P-3811)*

Lucas & Lewellen Vineyards Inc (PA)..............E 805 686-9336
1645 Copenhagen Dr Solvang (93463) *(P-11057)*

Lucas Lwllen Vnyrds Tasting Rm, Solvang Also Called: Lucas & Lewellen Vineyards Inc
(P-11057)

Lucas Museum of Narrative Art ....D 831 566-9332
700 S Flower St Ste 2400 Los Angeles (90017) *(P-17255)*

Lucent Diamonds Inc ....E 424 781-7127
6303 Owensmouth Ave Fl 10 Woodland Hills (91367) *(P-8465)*

Lucite Intl Prtnr Holdings Inc ....D 760 929-0001
5441 Avenida Encinas Ste B Carlsbad (92008) *(P-8530)*

Lucix, Camarillo Also Called: Lucix Corporation *(P-7021)*

Lucix Corporation (HQ)................................D 805 987-6645
800 Avenida Acaso Ste E Camarillo (93012) *(P-7021)*

Lucky Line Products Inc ....E 858 549-6699
7890 Dunbrook Rd San Diego (92126) *(P-4778)*

Lucky Strike Entertainment Inc ....B 213 542-4880
800 W Olympic Blvd Ste 250 Los Angeles (90015) *(P-15012)*

Lucky Strike Entertainment LLC ....D 818 933-3752
6801 Hollywood Blvd Ste 143 Los Angeles (90028) *(P-15013)*

Lucky Strike Entertainment LLC ....C 248 374-3420
20 City Blvd W Ste G2 Orange (92868) *(P-15014)*

Lucky-13 Apparel, Los Alamitos Also Called: Blue Sphere Inc *(P-1976)*

Ludfords Inc ....E 909 948-0797
3038 Pleasant St Riverside (92507) *(P-1353)*

Lugano Diamonds & Jewelry Inc (HQ)..............D 949 625-7722
545 Newport Center Dr Newport Beach (92660) *(P-11640)*

Luma Comfort, Cypress Also Called: Luma Comfort LLC *(P-6397)*

Luma Comfort LLC ....E 855 963-9247
6600 Katella Ave Cypress (90630) *(P-6397)*

Lumenova Ai Inc ....E 310 694-2461
1419 Beaudry Blvd, 1419 Beaudry Blvd Glendale (91208) *(P-13969)*

Lumin, Laguna Beach Also Called: Pangaea Holdings Inc *(P-3677)*

Lumina Alliance ....D 805 781-6400
51 Zaca Ln Ste 150 San Luis Obispo (93401) *(P-16976)*

Luminance, Rancho Cucamonga Also Called: American De Rosa Lamparts LLC *(P-471)*

Luminit LLC ....E 310 320-1066
1850 W 205th St Torrance (90501) *(P-8009)*

Lumiradx Inc ....C 951 201-9384
444 S Cedros Ave Ste 101 Solana Beach (92075) *(P-13764)*

Lund Motion Products Inc ....E 888 983-2204
3172 Nasa St Brea (92821) *(P-7267)*

Lunday-Thagard Company ....B 562 928-6990
9301 Garfield Ave South Gate (90280) *(P-3845)*

Lunday-Thagard Company (HQ).......................C 562 928-7000
9302 Garfield Ave South Gate (90280) *(P-3860)*

Lundquist Institute For Biomedical Innovation At Harbor-Ucla ....A 877 452-2674
1124 W Carson St Torrance (90502) *(P-17881)*

Luppen Holdings Inc (PA).............................E 323 581-8121
3050 Leonis Blvd Vernon (90058) *(P-5200)*

Lusive Decor ....D 323 227-9207
3400 Medford St Los Angeles (90063) *(P-18333)*

Lusk Quality Machine Products ....E 661 272-0630
39457 15th St E Palmdale (93550) *(P-6166)*

Lustros Inc ....E 619 449-4800
9025 Carlton Hills Blvd Ste A Santee (92071) *(P-252)*

Lutema, San Diego Also Called: MI Technologies Inc *(P-4169)*

Luth Research Inc (PA)................................B 619 234-5884
404 Camino Del Rio S Ste 505 San Diego (92108) *(P-17854)*

Luxe Light and Home, Los Angeles Also Called: Lusive Decor *(P-18333)*

Luxfer Gas Cylinder, Riverside Also Called: Luxfer Inc *(P-7516)*

Luxfer Inc ....E 951 684-5110
1995 3rd St Riverside (92507) *(P-4600)*

Luxfer Inc ....E 951 351-4100
6825 Jurupa Ave Riverside (92504) *(P-5157)*

Luxfer Inc (DH) ....D 951 684-5110
3016 Kansas Ave Bldg 1 Riverside (92507) *(P-7516)*

Luxre Realty Inc ....D 949 498-3702
222 Avenida Del Mar San Clemente (92672) *(P-12483)*

Luxtera LLC ....C 760 448-3520
2320 Camino Vida Roble Ste 100 Carlsbad (92011) *(P-6847)*

Lymi Inc (PA)..D 844 701-0139
2263 E Vernon Ave Vernon (90058) *(P-10713)*

Lynam Industries Inc ....E 951 360-1919
13050 Santa Ana Ave Fontana (92337) *(P-4998)*

Lynam Industries Inc ....D 951 360-1919
11027 Jasmine St Fontana (92337) *(P-4999)*

Lynch Ambulance Service, Anaheim Also Called: Filyn Corporation *(P-8826)*

Lyncole Grunding Solutions LLC ....E 310 214-4000
369 Van Ness Way Torrance (90501) *(P-6423)*

Lyncole Xit Grounding, Torrance Also Called: Lyncole Grunding Solutions LLC *(P-6423)*

Lynn Products Inc ....A 310 530-5966
2645 W 237th St Torrance (90505) *(P-5932)*

Lynwood Unified School Dst ....D 310 631-7308
12120 Lindbergh Ave Lynwood (90262) *(P-16816)*

Lytx Inc (PA)..B 858 430-4000
9785 Towne Centre Dr San Diego (92121) *(P-7741)*

M & B Window Fashions, Los Angeles Also Called: Hd Window Fashions Inc *(P-2601)*

M & C, Los Angeles Also Called: Murchison & Cumming LLP *(P-16748)*

M & E Technical Services L L C ....D 256 964-6486
3601 Bayview Dr Manhattan Beach (90266) *(P-18264)*

M & G Jewelers Inc ....D 909 989-2929
10823 Edison Ct Rancho Cucamonga (91730) *(P-11641)*

M & H Electric Fabricators Inc ....E 562 926-9552
13537 Alondra Blvd Santa Fe Springs (90670) *(P-7095)*

M & M Plumbing Inc ....D 951 354-5388
6782 Columbus St Riverside (92504) *(P-799)*

M & O Perry Industries Inc ....E 951 734-9838
412 N Smith Ave Corona (92878) *(P-5792)*

M & S Acquisition Corporation (PA).................C 213 385-1515
707 Wilshire Blvd Ste 5200 Los Angeles (90017) *(P-12484)*

M & S Security Services Inc ....D 661 397-9616
2900 L St Bakersfield (93301) *(P-14316)*

M & S Trading Inc ....D 714 241-7190
15778 Gateway Cir Tustin (92780) *(P-10687)*

M A A C Project, Chula Vista Also Called: Metropltan Area Advsory Cmmtte *(P-17062)*

M A G, Santa Maria Also Called: Microwave Applications Group *(P-17587)*

M A G Engineering Mfg Co ....E
17305 Demler St Irvine (92614) *(P-4779)*

M Arthur Gensler Jr Assoc Inc ....C 213 927-3600
500 S Figueroa St Los Angeles (90071) *(P-17682)*

M Arthur Gensler Jr Assoc Inc ....D 949 863-9434
4675 Macarthur Ct Ste 100 Newport Beach (92660) *(P-17683)*

M Bar C Construction Inc ....D 760 744-4131
1770 La Costa Meadows Dr San Marcos (92078) *(P-1157)*

M C, Los Angeles Also Called: Muir-Chase Plumbing Co Inc *(P-807)*

M C C, Torrance Also Called: Medical Chemical Corporation *(P-3814)*

M C C, Brea Also Called: Mercury Casualty Company *(P-12123)*

A
L
P
H
A
B
E
T
I
C

M C E, Torrance *Also Called: Magnetic Component Engrg LLC (P-5451)*

M Caratan Disc Inc .... C 661 725-2566
33787 Cecil Ave Delano (93215) *(P-35)*

M E D Inc .... D 562 921-0464
14001 Marquardt Ave Santa Fe Springs (90670) *(P-7268)*

M E I, Santa Barbara *Also Called: Motion Engineering Inc (P-5938)*

M F G West, Adelanto *Also Called: Molded Fiber GL Companies - W (P-4174)*

M F Salta Co Inc (PA).. D 562 421-2512
20 Executive Park Ste 150 Irvine (92614) *(P-18164)*

M G Disposal, Anaheim *Also Called: M-G Disposal Service Inc (P-8919)*

M Gaw Inc .... D 818 503-7997
6910 Farmdale Ave North Hollywood (91605) *(P-1215)*

M K Products Inc .... D 949 798-1234
16882 Armstrong Ave Irvine (92606) *(P-5647)*

M K Smith Chevrolet .... C 909 628-8961
12845 Central Ave Chino (91710) *(P-11375)*

M Klemme Technology Corp .... E 760 727-0593
1384 Poinsettia Ave Ste F Vista (92081) *(P-6543)*

M L Stern & Co LLC (DH) .... C 323 658-4400
8350 Wilshire Blvd Ste 300 Beverly Hills (90211) *(P-11975)*

M M C, Covina *Also Called: Davita Magan Management Inc (P-15298)*

M M Fab Inc .... D 310 763-3800
2300 E Gladwick St Compton (90220) *(P-10666)*

M M S, Claremont *Also Called: Micro Matrix Systems (P-5203)*

M Nexon Inc .... E 213 858-5930
222 N Pacific Coast Hwy Ste 300 El Segundo (90245) *(P-13970)*

M R I, Chatsworth *Also Called: Medical Research Institute (P-10632)*

M S E, Burbank *Also Called: Matthews Studio Equipment Inc (P-8433)*

M S International Inc (PA)...................................... B 714 685-7500
2095 N Batavia St Orange (92865) *(P-9946)*

M T C, Fallbrook *Also Called: Maneri Traffic Control Inc (P-635)*

M T C, City Of Industry *Also Called: Micro-Technology Concepts Inc (P-10018)*

M T D, Santa Barbara *Also Called: Santa Barbara Metro Trnst Dst (P-8802)*

M W Reid Welding Inc .... D 619 401-5880
781 Oconner St El Cajon (92020) *(P-4847)*

M W Sausse & Co Inc (PA)....................................... D 661 257-3311
28744 Witherspoon Pkwy Valencia (91355) *(P-6353)*

M Z J, Chino Hills *Also Called: Victory Intl Group LLC (P-10531)*

M Z T, Santa Ana *Also Called: Macro-Z-Technology Company (P-633)*

M-5 Steel Mfg Inc (PA)... E 323 263-9383
1353 Philadelphia St Pomona (91766) *(P-5000)*

M-7 Consolidation Inc .... C 310 898-3456
475 W Apra St Compton (90220) *(P-9307)*

M-Aurora Worldwide (us) LP (PA)................................ C 800 888-0808
2222 Corinth Ave Los Angeles (90064) *(P-13097)*

M-G Disposal Service Inc .... D 714 238-3300
1131 N Blue Gum St Anaheim (92806) *(P-8919)*

M-H Ironworks Inc .... D
1000 S Seaward Ave Ventura (93001) *(P-10144)*

M-I LLC .... E 661 321-5400
4400 Fanucchi Way Shafter (93263) *(P-343)*

M-I Swaco, Shafter *Also Called: M-I LLC (P-343)*

M-Industrial Enterprises LLC .... E 949 413-7513
11 Via Onagro Rcho Sta Marg (92688) *(P-6167)*

M-N-Z Janitorial Services Inc .... C 323 851-4115
2109 W Burbank Blvd Burbank (91506) *(P-13388)*

M.A.g Engineering & Mfg, Irvine *Also Called: M A G Engineering Mfg Co (P-4779)*

M.C. Gill, El Monte *Also Called: Castle Industries Inc of California (P-4967)*

M&C Hotel Interests Inc .... B 310 399-9344
530 Pico Blvd Santa Monica (90405) *(P-12909)*

M&J Design Inc .... E 714 687-9918
1303 S Claudina St Anaheim (92805) *(P-2451)*

M&J Design Furniture, Anaheim *Also Called: M&J Design Inc (P-2451)*

M2 Automotive .... A 310 399-3887
1100 Colorado Ave 2nd Fl Santa Monica (90401) *(P-14675)*

M4dev LLC .... D 619 696-6300
2137 Pacific Hwy Ste A San Diego (92101) *(P-12910)*

Maas-Hansen Steel, Westminster *Also Called: Neighborhood Steel LLC (P-10146)*

Mabel Baas Inc .... E 805 520-8075
3960 Royal Ave Simi Valley (93063) *(P-5330)*

Mabie Marketing Group Inc .... C 858 279-5585
8352 Clairemont Mesa Blvd San Diego (92111) *(P-14534)*

Mac M Mc Cully Corporation .... E 805 529-0661
5316 Kazuko Ct Moorpark (93021) *(P-6328)*

Mac M McCully Co, Moorpark *Also Called: Mac M Mc Cully Corporation (P-6328)*

Macadamia Holdings LLC .... C 909 465-0246
5454 Walnut Ave Chino (91710) *(P-14535)*

Macerich Company (PA).. C 310 394-6000
401 Wilshire Blvd Ste 700 Santa Monica (90401) *(P-12688)*

Machine Building Spc Inc .... E 323 666-8289
1977 Blake Ave Los Angeles (90039) *(P-5680)*

Machine Vision Products Inc (PA)............................... E 760 438-1138
3270 Corporate Vw Ste D Vista (92081) *(P-8010)*

Mackie International Inc (PA).................................. E 951 346-0530
4193 Flat Rock Dr Ste 200 Riverside (92505) *(P-1319)*

Macom, Newport Beach *Also Called: Mindspeed Technologies LLC (P-6856)*

Macro Air Technologies, San Bernardino *Also Called: Macroair Technologies Inc (P-5772)*

Macro-Pro Inc (PA)... C 562 595-0900
2400 Grand Ave Long Beach (90815) *(P-14536)*

Macro-Z-Technology Company (PA)................................ D 714 564-1130
841 E Washington Ave Santa Ana (92701) *(P-633)*

Macroair Technologies Inc (PA)................................. E 909 890-2270
794 S Allen St San Bernardino (92408) *(P-5772)*

Macs Lift Gate Inc (PA).. E 562 529-3465
2801 E South St Long Beach (90805) *(P-8695)*

Mad Catz, San Diego *Also Called: Mad Catz Inc (P-5933)*

Mad Catz Inc .... C 858 790-5008
10680 Treena St Ste 500 San Diego (92131) *(P-5933)*

Mad Engine, Glendale *Also Called: Mad Engine Global LLC (P-1923)*

Mad Engine Global LLC (HQ)..................................... D 858 558-5270
1017 Grandview Ave Glendale (91201) *(P-1923)*

Mad Engine Global LLC .... B 858 558-5270
6740 Cobra Way Ste 100 San Diego (92121) *(P-10714)*

Made In Love Dggy Cture Thrapy .... D 805 410-0774
3946 Ceanothus Pl Calabasas (91302) *(P-8696)*

Made Media LLC .... E 866 263-6233
2337 Roscomare Rd Ste 2302 Los Angeles (90077) *(P-9567)*

Made Merch, Los Angeles *Also Called: Made Media LLC (P-9567)*

Mader News Inc .... D 818 551-5000
913 Ruberta Ave Glendale (91201) *(P-11077)*

Maderas Golf Club .... D 858 451-8100
17750 Old Coach Rd Poway (92064) *(P-15089)*

Madisn/Grham Clor Graphics Inc .... B 323 261-7171
150 N Myers St Los Angeles (90033) *(P-3037)*

Madison Inc of Oklahoma .... D 918 224-6990
18000 Studebaker Rd Cerritos (90703) *(P-4848)*

Madison Club Owners Assn .... C 760 777-9320
53035 Meriwether Way La Quinta (92253) *(P-15090)*

Madison Club, The, La Quinta *Also Called: Madison Club Owners Assn (P-15090)*

Madison Industries (HQ).. E 562 484-5099
17201 Darwin Ave Hesperia (92345) *(P-5082)*

Madn Aircraft Hinge .... E 661 257-3430
26911 Ruether Ave Ste Q Santa Clarita (91351) *(P-7363)*

Madonna Inn Inc .... C 805 543-3000
100 Madonna Rd San Luis Obispo (93405) *(P-11298)*

Maersk Whsng Dist Svcs USA LLC .... D 562 977-1820
12920 Imperial Hwy Santa Fe Springs (90670) *(P-9308)*

Maersk Whsng Dist Svcs USA LLC .... C 801 301-1732
1651 California St Ste A Redlands (92374) *(P-9309)*

Maersk Whsng Dist Svcs USA LLC (DH)............................ C 562 345-2200
2240 E Maple Ave El Segundo (90245) *(P-9310)*

Mag Aerospace Industries LLC .... B 801 400-7944
1500 Glenn Curtiss St Carson (90746) *(P-4799)*

Mag Instrument Inc (PA).. B 909 947-1006
2001 S Hellman Ave Ontario (91761) *(P-6510)*

Magdalena Ecke Family YMCA, Encinitas *Also Called: YMCA of San Diego County (P-17389)*

MAGELLAN, San Diego *Also Called: Aurora - San Diego LLC (P-16263)*

Magic 92.5, San Diego *Also Called: Local Media San Diego LLC (P-9483)*

Magic Acquisition Corp .... B 661 382-4700
23920 Creekside Rd Valencia (91355) *(P-11376)*

Mergent email: customerrelations@mergent.com
1096

2025 Southern California
Business Directory and Buyers Guide

(P-0000) Products & Services Section entry number
(PA)=Parent Co (HQ)=Headquarters (DH)=Div Headquarters

Magic Apparel & Magic Headwear, Compton *Also Called: Magic Apparel Group Inc (P-2160)*

Magic Apparel Group Inc .... E 310 223-4000
1100 W Walnut St Compton (90220) *(P-2160)*

Magic Bullet, Los Angeles *Also Called: Homeland Housewares LLC (P-10220)*

Magic Castles Inc .... D 323 851-3313
7001 Franklin Ave Los Angeles (90028) *(P-11589)*

Magic Touch Software Intl .... E 800 714-6490
950 Boardwalk Ste 200 San Marcos (92078) *(P-13971)*

Magic Workforce Solutions LLC .... A 310 246-6153
9100 Wilshire Blvd Ste 700e Beverly Hills (90212) *(P-18255)*

Magical Cruise Company Limited .... D 800 742-8939
500 S Buena Vista St Burbank (91521) *(P-9228)*

Magma, Escondido *Also Called: One Stop Systems Inc (P-5944)*

Magma Inc .... E 858 530-2511
9918 Via Pasar San Diego (92126) *(P-5934)*

Magma Products LLC .... D 562 627-0500
3940 Pixie Ave Lakewood (90712) *(P-6386)*

Magnaslow, Rcho Sta Marg *Also Called: Car Sound Exhaust System Inc (P-7235)*

Magnebit Holding Corp .... E 858 573-0727
9474 La Cuesta Dr La Mesa (91941) *(P-7925)*

Magnell Associate Inc .... B 626 271-1320
17708 Rowland St City Of Industry (91748) *(P-5859)*

Magnell Associate Inc .... B 626 271-1420
9997 Rose Hills Rd Whittier (90601) *(P-9086)*

Magnell Associate Inc (DH) .... C 800 685-3471
21688 Gateway Center Dr Ste 300 Diamond Bar (91765) *(P-10015)*

Magnell Associate Inc .... B 626 271-1580
18045 Rowland St City Of Industry (91748) *(P-10016)*

Magnesium Alloy Pdts Co Inc .... E 310 605-1440
2420 N Alameda St Compton (90222) *(P-4649)*

Magnesium Alloy Products Co LP .... E 323 636-2276
2420 N Alameda St Compton (90222) *(P-4650)*

Magnet Sales & Mfg Co Inc (HQ) .... D 310 391-7213
11250 Playa Ct Culver City (90230) *(P-4364)*

Magnetic Component Engrg LLC (PA) .... D 310 784-3100
2830 Lomita Blvd Torrance (90505) *(P-5451)*

Magnetic Sensors Corporation .... E 714 630-8380
1365 N Mccan St Anaheim (92806) *(P-7022)*

Magnetika Inc (PA) .... D 310 527-8100
2041 W 139th St Gardena (90249) *(P-10191)*

Magnit Rs Inc .... D 800 660-9544
9 Executive Cir Ste 290 Irvine (92614) *(P-13604)*

Magnolia Convalescent Hospital, Riverside *Also Called: Magnolia Rhblttion Nursing Ctr (P-15872)*

Magnolia Grdns Convalescent HM, Granada Hills *Also Called: Longwood Management Corp (P-15702)*

Magnolia Rhblttion Nursing Ctr .... C 951 688-4321
8133 Magnolia Ave Riverside (92504) *(P-15872)*

Magnuson Products LLC .... E 805 642-8833
1990 Knoll Dr Ste A Ventura (93003) *(P-7269)*

Magnuson Superchargers, Ventura *Also Called: Magnuson Products LLC (P-7269)*

Magor Mold LLC .... D 909 592-3663
420 S Lone Hill Ave San Dimas (91773) *(P-5587)*

Magparts (HQ) .... C 626 334-7897
1545 W Roosevelt St Azusa (91702) *(P-4676)*

Magtech & Power Conversion Inc .... E 714 451-0106
1146 E Ash Ave Fullerton (92831) *(P-6930)*

Magtek Inc (PA) .... C 562 546-6400
1710 Apollo Ct Seal Beach (90740) *(P-5935)*

Mahar Manufacturing Corp (PA) .... E 323 581-9988
2834 E 46th St Vernon (90058) *(P-8476)*

MAI Systems, Lake Forest *Also Called: Infor (us) LLC (P-13947)*

Mail Boxes Etc, San Diego *Also Called: UPS Store Inc (P-14623)*

Mail Handling Group Inc .... C 952 975-5000
2840 Madonna Dr Fullerton (92835) *(P-3038)*

Mail Handling Services, Fullerton *Also Called: Mail Handling Group Inc (P-3038)*

Mailers Software, Rcho Sta Marg *Also Called: Melissa Data Corporation (P-13768)*

Maimone Liquidating Corp (PA) .... D 626 286-5691
1390 E Palm St Altadena (91001) *(P-14676)*

Main Electric Supply Co LLC .... E 858 737-7000
4674 Cardin St San Diego (92111) *(P-10192)*

Main Steel LLC .... D 951 231-4949
3100 Jefferson St Riverside (92504) *(P-5273)*

Mainline, Torrance *Also Called: Mainline Equipment Inc (P-6630)*

Mainline Equipment Inc .... D 800 444-2288
20917 Higgins Ct Torrance (90501) *(P-6630)*

Mainplace Senior Living, Orange *Also Called: Pennant Group Inc (P-15753)*

MainStay Medical Limited .... D 619 261-9144
2159 India St Ste 200 San Diego (92101) *(P-15386)*

Mainstream Energy Corporation .... B 805 528-9705
775 Fiero Ln Ste 200 San Luis Obispo (93401) *(P-800)*

Maintech Incorporated .... C 714 921-8000
2401 N Glassell St Orange (92865) *(P-13765)*

Maintech Resources Inc .... E 562 804-0664
5042 Northwestern Way Westminster (92683) *(P-1189)*

Maintenace Operations Svc Ctr, National City *Also Called: National School District (P-16817)*

Maintenance & Operation Dept, Montebello *Also Called: Montebello Unified School Dst (P-13395)*

Maintenance Dept, Port Hueneme *Also Called: United States Dept of Navy (P-14798)*

Maintenance Resource Inc .... D 616 406-0004
1151 N Del Rio Pl Ontario (91764) *(P-491)*

Maintex Inc (PA) .... C 800 446-1888
13300 Nelson Ave City Of Industry (91746) *(P-3612)*

Majestic Industry Hills LLC .... A 626 810-4455
1 Industry Hills Pkwy City Of Industry (91744) *(P-12911)*

Majestic Management Co., City Of Industry *Also Called: Majestic Realty Co (P-12485)*

Majestic Realty Co (PA) .... C 562 692-9581
13191 Crossroads Pkwy N Ste 600 City Of Industry (91746) *(P-12485)*

Major Market Inc .... C 760 723-0857
845 S Main Ave Fallbrook (92028) *(P-11279)*

Major Market-Ftd Florist, Fallbrook *Also Called: Major Market Inc (P-11279)*

Makallon La Jolla Properties, Newport Beach *Also Called: Makar Properties LLC (P-12572)*

Makar Anaheim LLC .... A 714 750-4321
777 W Convention Way Anaheim (92802) *(P-12912)*

Makar Properties LLC (PA) .... D 949 255-1100
4100 Macarthur Blvd Ste 150 Newport Beach (92660) *(P-12572)*

Maker Studios LLC (DH) .... C 310 606-2182
3515 Eastham Dr Culver City (90232) *(P-14998)*

Makespace Labs Inc .... C 800 920-9440
3526 Hayden Ave Culver City (90232) *(P-9087)*

Makesy, Irvine *Also Called: Wood Candle Wick Tech Inc (P-8742)*

Makino Inc .... E 714 444-4334
17800 Newhope St Ste H Fountain Valley (92708) *(P-5615)*

Makita, La Mirada *Also Called: Makita USA Inc (P-10310)*

Makita USA Inc (HQ) .... C 714 522-8088
14930 Northam St La Mirada (90638) *(P-10310)*

Malbon Golf LLC .... E 323 433-4028
1740 Stanford St Santa Monica (90404) *(P-8531)*

Malcolm & Cisneros A Law Corp .... C 949 252-9400
2112 Business Center Dr Ste 100 Irvine (92612) *(P-16736)*

Malcolm Cisneros, Irvine *Also Called: Malcolm & Cisneros A Law Corp (P-16736)*

Malibu Conference Center Inc .... D 818 889-0440
327 Latigo Canyon Rd Malibu (90265) *(P-12303)*

Malibu Leather Inc .... C 310 985-0707
510 W 6th St Ste 1002 Los Angeles (90014) *(P-4306)*

Malibu Limousine Service, Marina Del Rey *Also Called: Executive Network Entps Inc (P-8822)*

Mallin Casual Furniture, Los Angeles *Also Called: Minson Corporation (P-2455)*

Malmberg Engineering Inc .... E 925 606-6500
655 Deep Valley Dr Ste 125 Rllng Hls Est (90274) *(P-6168)*

Maloof Naman Builders .... D 818 775-0040
9614 Cozycroft Ave Chatsworth (91311) *(P-10352)*

Malys of California Inc .... B 661 295-8317
28145 Harrison Pkwy Valencia (91355) *(P-10476)*

Mama Mellaces Old World Treats, Carlsbad *Also Called: Mfb Liquidation Inc (P-1513)*

Mamco Inc (PA) .... C 951 776-9300
764 Ramona Expy Ste C Perris (92571) *(P-634)*

Mammography Center, Lompoc *Also Called: Lompoc Valley Medical Center (P-16082)*

Mammoth Media Inc .... D 832 315-0833
1447 2nd St Santa Monica (90401) *(P-2815)*

Mammoth Water, Montebello *Also Called: Unix Packaging LLC (P-1656)*

Mamolos Cntntl Bailey Bakeries .... C 805 496-0045
2734 Townsgate Rd Westlake Village (91361) *(P-11299)*

Employee Codes: A=Over 500 employees, B=251-500
C=101-250, D=51-100, E=20-50, F=10-19, G=1-9

2025 Southern California
Business Directory and Buyers Guide

© Mergent Inc. 1-800-342-5647

1097

Man Theateres, Westlake Village *Also Called: Weststar Cinemas Inc (P-14946)*

Man-Grove Industries Inc .... D 714 630-3020
1201 N Miller St Anaheim (92806) *(P-3039)*

Managed Health, Huntington Beach *Also Called: Managed Health Network (P-12097)*

Managed Health Network .... B 714 934-5519
7755 Center Ave Ste 700 Huntington Beach (92647) *(P-12097)*

Management Applied Prgrm Inc (PA) .... D 562 463-5000
13191 Crossroads Pkwy N Ste 205 City Of Industry (91746) *(P-14142)*

Management Trust Assn Inc .... D 858 547-4373
9815 Carroll Canyon Rd Ste 103 San Diego (92131) *(P-12662)*

Management Trust Assn Inc .... D 951 694-1758
4160 Temescal Canyon Rd Ste 202 Corona (92883) *(P-12663)*

Management Trust Assn Inc .... D 562 926-3372
12607 Hiddencreek Way Ste R Cerritos (90703) *(P-18165)*

Manatt Phelps & Phillips LLP (PA) .... B 310 312-4000
2049 Century Park E Ste 1700 Los Angeles (90067) *(P-16737)*

Manchester Grand Resorts LP .... D 619 232-1234
1 Market Pl Fl 33 San Diego (92101) *(P-12913)*

Manchster Grnd Hyatt San Diego, San Diego *Also Called: Hyatt Corporation (P-12863)*

Manchster Grnd Hyatt San Diego, San Diego *Also Called: Manchester Grand Resorts LP (P-12913)*

Mandala, Vista *Also Called: Oceanside Glasstile Company (P-4361)*

Maneri Sign Co Inc .... E 310 327-6261
2722 S Fairview St Santa Ana (92704) *(P-8613)*

Maneri Traffic Control Inc .... D 951 695-5104
4949 2nd St Fallbrook (92028) *(P-635)*

Maney Aircraft, Ontario *Also Called: Maney Aircraft Inc (P-7517)*

Maney Aircraft Inc .... E 909 390-2500
1305 S Wanamaker Ave Ontario (91761) *(P-7517)*

Mangan Inc (PA) .... D 310 835-8080
3901 Via Oro Ave Long Beach (90810) *(P-17581)*

Mango Technologies Inc (PA) .... A 888 625-4258
350 10th Ave Ste 500 San Diego (92101) *(P-13766)*

Manhattan Bancorp .... C 310 606-8000
2141 Rosecrans Ave Ste 1100 El Segundo (90245) *(P-11735)*

Manhattan Beachwear LLC (PA) .... D 657 384-2110
10855 Business Center Dr Ste C Cypress (90630) *(P-2171)*

Manhattan Country Club, Manhattan Beach *Also Called: 1334 Partners LP (P-15111)*

Manhattan Stitching Co, Buena Park *Also Called: Manhattan Stitching Co Inc (P-2250)*

Manhattan Stitching Co Inc .... E 714 521-9479
8362 Artesia Blvd Ste E Buena Park (90621) *(P-2250)*

Manley Laboratories Inc .... E 909 627-4256
13880 Magnolia Ave Chino (91710) *(P-6631)*

Mann+hmmel Wtr Fluid Sltons In (DH) .... D 805 964-8003
93 S La Patera Ln Goleta (93117) *(P-6020)*

Manning Kass Ellrod Rmrez Trst (PA) .... C 213 624-6900
801 S Figueroa St 15th Fl Los Angeles (90017) *(P-16738)*

Mannkind Corporation .... B 818 661-5000
30930 Russell Ranch Rd Ste 300 Westlake Village (91362) *(P-3446)*

MANOR AT SANTA TERESITA HOSPIT, Duarte *Also Called: Santa Teresita Inc (P-16176)*

Manorcare Health Services, Aliso Viejo *Also Called: Hcr Manorcare Med Svcs Fla LLC (P-15672)*

Manson Construction Co .... D 562 983-2340
340 Golden Shore Ste 310 Long Beach (90802) *(P-717)*

Manson Western LLC .... C 424 201-8800
625 Alaska Ave Torrance (90503) *(P-2892)*

Mantels & More Corp .... E 323 869-9764
2909 Tanager Ave Commerce (90040) *(P-1041)*

Manufacture, Vernon *Also Called: BTS Trading Inc (P-1873)*

MANUFACTURE, Irvine *Also Called: Connectec Company Inc (P-6413)*

Manufacture, Commerce *Also Called: D I F Group Inc (P-17979)*

Manufactured Solutions LLC .... E 714 548-6915
9601 Janice Cir Villa Park (92861) *(P-8697)*

Manufacturer, Ventura *Also Called: Novotech Nutraceuticals Inc (P-1305)*

Manufacturer, Lake Forest *Also Called: Sonnet Technologies Inc (P-7152)*

Manufacturer and Distributor, Corona *Also Called: Approved Aeronautics LLC (P-7432)*

Manufacturers of Wood Products, Santa Barbara *Also Called: Architctral Mllwk Snta Barbara (P-2296)*

Manufacturing, Valencia *Also Called: King Henrys Inc (P-1725)*

Manufacturing, Temecula *Also Called: Marathon Finishing Systems Inc (P-5001)*

Manufacturing, Chino *Also Called: Manley Laboratories Inc (P-6631)*

Manufacturing, San Diego *Also Called: Continental Controls Corp (P-7853)*

Many LLC .... D 310 399-1515
17575 Pacific Coast Hwy Pacific Palisades (90272) *(P-13223)*

MAOF, Montebello *Also Called: Mexican Amrcn Oprtnty Fndation (P-16978)*

Mapcargo Global Logistics (PA) .... D 310 297-8300
2501 Santa Fe Ave Redondo Beach (90278) *(P-9311)*

Mapei Corporation .... D 909 475-4100
5415 Industrial Pkwy San Bernardino (92407) *(P-3278)*

Maple Dairy, Bakersfield *Also Called: Maple Dairy LP (P-92)*

Maple Dairy LP .... D 661 396-9600
15857 Bear Mountain Blvd Bakersfield (93311) *(P-92)*

Maple Imaging LLC (HQ) .... E 805 373-4545
1049 Camino Dos Rios Thousand Oaks (91360) *(P-7023)*

Mapp Digital Us LLC .... B 619 342-4340
4660 La Jolla Village Dr Ste 100 San Diego (92122) *(P-18166)*

Mapquest Holdings LLC .... B 310 256-4882
4235 Redwood Ave Los Angeles (90066) *(P-7742)*

Mar Cor Purification Inc .... E 800 633-3080
6351 Orangethorpe Ave Buena Park (90620) *(P-6021)*

Mar Engineering Company .... E 818 765-4805
7350 Greenbush Ave North Hollywood (91605) *(P-6169)*

Marathon Finishing Systems Inc .... E 310 791-5601
42355 Rio Nedo Temecula (92590) *(P-5001)*

Marathon General Inc .... D 760 738-9714
1728 Mission Rd Escondido (92029) *(P-636)*

Marathon Industries Inc .... C 661 286-1520
20950 Centre Pointe Pkwy Santa Clarita (91350) *(P-9805)*

Marathon Land Inc .... C 805 488-3585
2599 E Hueneme Rd Oxnard (93033) *(P-60)*

Marathon Truck Bodies, Santa Clarita *Also Called: Marathon Industries Inc (P-9805)*

Maravai Lf Scnces Holdings LLC (HQ) .... C 650 697-3600
10770 Wateridge Cir Ste 100 San Diego (92121) *(P-17808)*

Maravai Lfscences Holdings Inc (PA) .... E 858 546-0004
10770 Wateridge Cir Ste 200 San Diego (92121) *(P-3447)*

Maravai Lifesciences, San Diego *Also Called: Maravai Lfscences Holdings Inc (P-3447)*

Maravilla Foundation (PA) .... C 323 721-4162
5729 Union Pacific Ave Commerce (90022) *(P-17355)*

Marbleworks, Huntington Beach *Also Called: Tile & Marble Design Co Inc (P-1043)*

Marborg Industries (PA) .... C 805 963-1852
728 E Yanonali St Santa Barbara (93103) *(P-9749)*

Marborg Recovery LP .... C 805 963-1852
14470 Calle Real Goleta (93117) *(P-9750)*

Marcel Electronics Inc .... E 714 974-8590
130 W Bristol Ln Orange (92865) *(P-6746)*

March Products Inc .... D 909 622-4800
4645 Troy Ct Jurupa Valley (92509) *(P-8698)*

March Vision Care Inc .... E 310 665-0975
6701 Center Dr W Ste 790 Los Angeles (90045) *(P-8408)*

Marchem Solvay Group, Long Beach *Also Called: Energy Solutions (us) LLC (P-3237)*

Marchem Technologies LLC .... E 310 638-9352
20851 S Santa Fe Ave Carson (90810) *(P-3241)*

Marco Products, Los Angeles *Also Called: Augerscope Inc (P-4736)*

Marco's Auto Body, Altadena *Also Called: Maimone Liquidating Corp (P-14676)*

Marcoa Media LLC (PA) .... E 858 635-9627
9955 Black Mountain Rd San Diego (92126) *(P-2926)*

Marcos M Uriarte .... D 714 326-1064
28202 Cabot Rd Ste 300 Laguna Niguel (92677) *(P-801)*

Marcum LLP .... D 949 236-5600
600 Anton Blvd Ste 1600 Costa Mesa (92626) *(P-17745)*

Marcus & Millichap, Calabasas *Also Called: Marcus & Millichap Inc (P-12486)*

Marcus & Millichap Inc (PA) .... D 818 212-2250
23975 Park Sorrento Ste 400 Calabasas (91302) *(P-12486)*

Marcus Hotels Inc .... C 818 980-8000
4222 Vineland Ave North Hollywood (91602) *(P-12914)*

Mareblu Naturals, Anaheim *Also Called: 180 Snacks Inc (P-1499)*

Marflex, Vernon *Also Called: Marspring Corporation (P-1953)*

Marfred Industries .... B
12708 Branford St Sun Valley (91353) *(P-2681)*

Marge Carson Inc (PA) .... D 626 571-1111
555 W 5th St Los Angeles (90013) *(P-2452)*

Marian Medical Center .... A 805 739-3000
1400 E Church St Santa Maria (93454) *(P-16092)*

Marian Regional Medical Center, Santa Maria *Also Called: Dignity Health (P-15976)*

Marian Regional Medical Center, Santa Maria *Also Called: Marian Medical Center (P-16092)*

Marie Callender's Pie Shops, Rancho Palos Verdes *Also Called: Pie Rise Ltd (P-11596)*

Marie Callender's Pie Shops 73, Bakersfield *Also Called: Castle Harlan Partners III LP* *(P-11555)*

Marie Cllender Wholesalers Inc .... A 951 737-6760
170 E Rincon St Corona (92879) *(P-10823)*

Marie Edward Vineyards Inc .... E 661 363-5038
6901 E Brundage Ln Bakersfield (93307) *(P-5474)*

Marika LLC .... D 323 888-7755
5553 Bandini Blvd B Bell (90201) *(P-2119)*

Marina, Orange *Also Called: Marina Landscape Inc (P-220)*

Marina City Club LP A Cali .... C 310 822-0611
4333 Admiralty Way Marina Del Rey (90292) *(P-12358)*

Marina Graphic Center Inc .... C 310 970-1777
12901 Cerise Ave Hawthorne (90250) *(P-3040)*

Marina Landscape Inc .... B 714 939-6600
3707 W Garden Grove Blvd Orange (92868) *(P-220)*

Marina Landscape Maint Inc, Anaheim *Also Called: Marina Maintenance Group Inc (P-176)*

Marina Maintenance Group Inc .... B 714 939-6600
1900 S Lewis St Anaheim (92805) *(P-176)*

Marina Shipyard, Long Beach *Also Called: Indel Engineering Inc (P-7622)*

Marina Village, San Diego *Also Called: Southern Cal Pipe Trades ADM (P-12529)*

Marine & Rest Fabricators Inc .... E 619 232-7267
3768 Dalbergia St San Diego (92113) *(P-5002)*

Marine Aviation Logistics, Oceanside *Also Called: United States Marine Corps (P-10505)*

Marine Corps United States .... C 760 577-6716
Usmc Barstow (92311) *(P-5496)*

Marine Corps United States .... D 760 725-3092
Traffic Management Office Camp Pendleton (92055) *(P-9312)*

Marine Corps United States .... B 858 307-3434
11 3dmaw San Diego (92145) *(P-14537)*

Marine Corps United States .... B 760 830-6000
Air Ground Combat Ctr, #1145 Twentynine Palms (92278) *(P-16093)*

Marine Corps United States .... A 760 725-1304
Camp Pendleton Oceanside (92055) *(P-16296)*

Marine Corps Air Stn Miramar, San Diego *Also Called: Marine Corps United States (P-14537)*

Marine Corps Cmnty Svcs Dept, San Diego *Also Called: Marine Corps Community Svcs* *(P-15211)*

Marine Corps Community Svcs .... B 858 577-1061
2273 Elrod Ave San Diego (92145) *(P-15211)*

Marine Corps Community Svcs .... C 760 725-6195
Acs Mccs Attn Semper Fi Box 555020 Marine Corp Base Camp Pendleton (92055) *(P-15212)*

Marine Corps Community Svcs .... C 760 725-5187
Camp Pendleton Marine Corps Base Oceanside (92055) *(P-15521)*

Marine Corps Community Svcs .... C 760 725-2817
202860 San Jacinto Rd Oceanside (92054) *(P-17094)*

Marine Corps Community Svcs .... C 760 725-7311
Basilone Rd Bldg 51080 Camp Pendleton (92055) *(P-17095)*

Marine Fenders Intl Inc .... E 310 834-7037
452 W Valley Blvd Rialto (92376) *(P-4162)*

Marine Group Boat Works, Chula Vista *Also Called: Marine Group Boat Works LLC (P-14776)*

Marine Group Boat Works LLC .... C 619 427-6767
997 G St Chula Vista (91910) *(P-14775)*

Marine Memorial Golf Course, Camp Pendleton *Also Called: United States Marine Corps* *(P-15097)*

Marine Room Restaurant, La Jolla *Also Called: La Jolla Bch & Tennis CLB Inc (P-15144)*

Marine Technical Services Inc .... D 310 549-8030
211 N Marine Ave Wilmington (90744) *(P-14538)*

Marine Terminals Corporation .... B 310 519-2300
389 Terminal Way San Pedro (90731) *(P-9143)*

Mariner Health Care Inc .... C 760 776-7700
44610 Monterey Ave Palm Desert (92260) *(P-15709)*

Mariner Health Care Inc .... C 818 957-0850
3050 Montrose Ave La Crescenta (91214) *(P-15710)*

Mariner Health Care Inc .... C 310 371-4628
4109 Emerald St Torrance (90503) *(P-15711)*

Mariner Health Care Inc .... C 310 677-9114
100 S Hillcrest Blvd Inglewood (90301) *(P-15712)*

Mariner Health Care Inc .... D 323 665-1185
3032 Rowena Ave Los Angeles (90039) *(P-15713)*

Mariner Health Care Inc .... C 818 246-5677
430 N Glendale Ave Glendale (91206) *(P-15714)*

Mariner Health Care Inc .... C 562 942-7019
8925 Mines Ave Pico Rivera (90660) *(P-15715)*

Mariner Health Care Inc .... C 760 327-8541
277 S Sunrise Way Palm Springs (92262) *(P-18010)*

Mariner Systems Inc (PA) .... E 305 266-7255
114 C Ave Coronado (92118) *(P-14539)*

Marino Enterprises Inc .... E 909 476-0343
10671 Civic Center Dr Rancho Cucamonga (91730) *(P-7518)*

Mariposa Horticultural Entps, Irwindale *Also Called: Mariposa Landscapes Inc (P-221)*

Mariposa Landscapes Inc (PA) .... D 626 960-0196
6232 Santos Diaz St Irwindale (91702) *(P-221)*

Maripro, Goleta *Also Called: L3 Technologies Inc (P-6626)*

Maritime Telecom Netwrk Inc, Los Angeles *Also Called: Eeg 3 LLC (P-6612)*

Marjan Stone Inc .... E 619 825-6000
2758 Via Orange Way Spring Valley (91978) *(P-9947)*

Mark & Fred Enterprises .... C 714 821-1993
645 S Beach Blvd Anaheim (92804) *(P-15716)*

Mark 1 Restoration Service LLC .... D 714 283-9990
3360 E La Palma Ave Anaheim (92806) *(P-16977)*

Mark Christopher Chevrolet Inc (PA) .... C 909 321-5860
2131 E Convention Center Way Ontario (91764) *(P-11377)*

Mark Christopher Hummer, Ontario *Also Called: Mark Christopher Chevrolet Inc (P-11377)*

Mark Clemons .... C 760 361-1531
4584 Adobe Rd Twentynine Palms (92277) *(P-8964)*

Mark Company, Orange *Also Called: Santa Ana Creek Development Company (P-1134)*

Mark Land Electric Inc .... D 818 883-5110
7876 Deering Ave Canoga Park (91304) *(P-937)*

Markar & Pemko Products, Ventura *Also Called: Assa Abloy ACC Door Cntrls Gro (P-4753)*

Markel Corp .... B 818 595-0600
21600 Oxnard St Ste 900 Woodland Hills (91367) *(P-12228)*

Market Scan, Camarillo *Also Called: Market Scan Info Systems Inc (P-13767)*

Market Scan Info Systems Inc .... D 800 658-7226
815 Camarillo Springs Rd Camarillo (93012) *(P-13767)*

Markland Industries Inc (PA) .... E 714 245-2850
21 Merano Laguna Niguel (92677) *(P-7632)*

Marko Foam Products, Huntington Beach *Also Called: Marko Foam Products Inc (P-4007)*

Marko Foam Products Inc .... D 949 417-3307
7441 Vincent Cir Huntington Beach (92648) *(P-4007)*

Markwins Beauty Brands Inc (PA) .... C 909 595-8898
22067 Ferrero City Of Industry (91789) *(P-10630)*

Marlee Manufacturing Inc .... E 909 390-3222
4711 E Guasti Rd Ontario (91761) *(P-8186)*

Marlin Designs LLC .... C 949 637-7257
13845 Alton Pkwy Ste C Irvine (92618) *(P-2453)*

Marlin Equity Partners LLC (PA) .... D 310 364-0100
1301 Manhattan Ave Hermosa Beach (90254) *(P-12027)*

Marlin Equity Partners III LP (PA) .... C 310 364-0100
1301 Manhattan Ave Hermosa Beach (90254) *(P-12715)*

Marlinda Imperial Hospital, Pasadena *Also Called: Two Palms Nursing Center Inc (P-15886)*

Marlinda Management Inc (PA) .... C 310 631 6122
3351 E Imperial Hwy Lynwood (90262) *(P-15873)*

Marlora Convalescent Hospital, Long Beach *Also Called: Atlantic Mem Hlthcare Assoc In* *(P-15575)*

Marlora Investments LLC .... D 562 494-3311
3801 E Anaheim St Long Beach (90804) *(P-15717)*

Marlora Post Accute Rhbltton, Long Beach *Also Called: Marlora Investments LLC (P-15717)*

Marman Industries Inc .... D 909 392-2136
1701 Earhart La Verne (91750) *(P-5588)*

Marmol Rdzner An Archtctral Co .... D 310 826-6222
12210 Nebraska Ave Los Angeles (90025) *(P-17684)*

Marna Health Services Inc .... D 909 882-2965
4280 Cypress Dr San Bernardino (92407) *(P-15874)*

Marples Gears Inc .... E 626 570-1744
1310 Mountain View Cir Azusa (91702) *(P-5795)*

Marquez & Marquez Food PR, South Gate *Also Called: Marquez Marquez Inc (P-1726)*

Marquez Brothers Entps Inc (PA) .... C 626 330-3310
15480 Valley Blvd City Of Industry (91746) *(P-10755)*

Employee Codes: A=Over 500 employees, B=251-500
C=101-250, D=51-100, E=20-50, F=10-19, G=1-9

2025 Southern California
Business Directory and Buyers Guide

© Mergent Inc. 1-800-342-5647

1099

ALPHABETIC

Marquez Marquez Inc .... E 562 408-0960
11821 Industrial Ave South Gate (90280) *(P-1726)*

Marriott, Woodland Hills *Also Called: HEI Hospitality LLC (P-12848)*

Marriott, Lake Arrowhead *Also Called: Lake Arrwhead Rsort Oprtor Inc (P-12895)*

Marriott, Los Angeles *Also Called: Marriott International Inc (P-12915)*

Marriott, La Jolla *Also Called: Marriott International Inc (P-12916)*

Marriott, Irvine *Also Called: Marriott International Inc (P-12918)*

Marriott, Fullerton *Also Called: Merritt Hospitality LLC (P-12921)*

Marriott, Los Angeles *Also Called: Renaissance Hotel Operating Co (P-12990)*

Marriott, Palm Desert *Also Called: Residence Inn By Marriott LLC (P-12992)*

Marriott, Riverside *Also Called: Windsor Capital Group Inc (P-13083)*

Marriott, Santa Monica *Also Called: Windsor Capital Group Inc (P-13088)*

Marriott, Newport Beach *Also Called: Wj Newport LLC (P-13091)*

Marriott International Inc .... A 310 641-5700
5855 W Century Blvd Los Angeles (90045) *(P-12915)*

Marriott International Inc .... B 858 587-1414
4240 La Jolla Village Dr La Jolla (92037) *(P-12916)*

Marriott International Inc .... D 949 503-5700
31692 El Camino Real San Juan Capistrano (92675) *(P-12917)*

Marriott International Inc .... B 949 724-3606
18000 Von Karman Ave Irvine (92612) *(P-12918)*

Marriott San Dego Gslamp Qrter, San Diego *Also Called: San Diego Hotel Company LLC (P-13011)*

Marrs Printing Inc .... D 909 594-9459
860 Tucker Ln City Of Industry (91789) *(P-3041)*

Mars Air Curtains, Gardena *Also Called: Mars Air Systems LLC (P-5773)*

Mars Air Systems LLC .... D 310 532-1555
14716 S Broadway Gardena (90248) *(P-5773)*

Mars Food North America, Rancho Dominguez *Also Called: Mars Food Us LLC (P-1811)*

Mars Food Us LLC .... E 562 616-7347
6875 Pacific View Dr Los Angeles (90068) *(P-1413)*

Mars Food Us LLC (HQ) .... B 310 933-0670
2001 E Cashdan St Ste 201 Rancho Dominguez (90220) *(P-1811)*

Mars Petcare Us Inc .... E 909 887-8131
2765 Lexington Way San Bernardino (92407) *(P-1420)*

Mars Petcare Us Inc .... D 760 261-7900
13243 Nutro Way Victorville (92395) *(P-1421)*

Mars Printing and Packaging, City Of Industry *Also Called: Marrs Printing Inc (P-3041)*

Marsh, San Diego *Also Called: Marsh & McLennan Agency LLC (P-12229)*

Marsh & McLennan Agency LLC .... C 858 457-3414
9171 Towne Centre Dr Ste 500 San Diego (92122) *(P-12229)*

Marsh Consulting Group .... D 239 433-5500
2626 Summer Ranch Rd Paso Robles (93446) *(P-18334)*

Marsh Risk & Insurance Svcs .... A 213 624-5555
633 W 5th St Ste 1200 Los Angeles (90017) *(P-12230)*

Marshall Advertising and Design Inc .... E 714 545-5757
2729 Bristol St Ste 100 Costa Mesa (92626) *(P-13224)*

Marshall B Ketchum University (PA) .... C 714 463-7567
2575 Yorba Linda Blvd Fullerton (92831) *(P-16833)*

Marshall Electronics Inc (PA) .... D 310 333-0606
20608 Madrona Ave Torrance (90503) *(P-6544)*

Marshall S Ezralow & Assoc, Calabasas *Also Called: MSE Enterprises Inc (P-12493)*

Marshall, Spector MD, San Gabriel *Also Called: Providnce Facey Med Foundation (P-16605)*

Marspring Corporation (PA) .... E 323 589-5637
4920 S Boyle Ave Vernon (90058) *(P-1953)*

Marspring Corporation .... D 310 484-6849
5190 S Santa Fe Ave Vernon (90058) *(P-2488)*

Martin AC Partners Inc .... C 213 683-1900
444 S Flower St Ste 1200 Los Angeles (90071) *(P-17685)*

Martin Bros/Marcowall Inc (PA) .... C 310 532-5335
17104 S Figueroa St Gardena (90248) *(P-1014)*

Martin Chancey Corporation .... E 510 972-6300
525 Malloy Ct Corona (92878) *(P-4163)*

Martin Chevrolet .... D 323 772-6494
23505 Hawthorne Blvd Torrance (90505) *(P-11378)*

Martin Furniture, San Diego *Also Called: Gilbert Martin Wdwkg Co Inc (P-2498)*

Martin Integrated, Orange *Also Called: Martin Integrated Systems (P-1015)*

Martin Integrated Systems .... E 714 998-9100
1525 W Orange Grove Ave Ste D Orange (92868) *(P-1015)*

Martin Lther King Jr-Los Angle .... C 424 338-8000
1680 E 120th St Los Angeles (90059) *(P-16584)*

MARTIN LUTHER KING, JR. COMMUN, Los Angeles *Also Called: Martin Lther King Jr-Los Angle (P-16584)*

Martin-Brower Company LLC .... D 909 595-8764
21489 Baker Pkwy Walnut (91789) *(P-10756)*

Martin/Brattrud Inc .... D 323 770-4171
1231 W 134th St Gardena (90247) *(P-2454)*

Martinez & Turek, Rialto *Also Called: Martinez and Turek Inc (P-6170)*

Martinez and Turek Inc .... C 909 820-6800
300 S Cedar Ave Rialto (92376) *(P-6170)*

Martinez Steel Corporation .... C 909 946-0686
1500 S Haven Ave Ste 150 Ontario (91761) *(P-1158)*

Marton Precision Mfg LLC .... E 714 808-6523
1365 S Acacia Ave Fullerton (92831) *(P-7392)*

Maruchan Inc .... C 949 789-2300
1902 Deere Ave Irvine (92606) *(P-1732)*

Maruchan Inc (HQ) .... B 949 789-2300
15800 Laguna Canyon Rd Irvine (92618) *(P-1812)*

Maruichi American Corporation .... D 562 903-8600
11529 Greenstone Ave Santa Fe Springs (90670) *(P-4550)*

Marukan Vinegar U S A Inc .... E 562 630-6060
7755 Monroe St Paramount (90723) *(P-1813)*

Marvell Semiconductor Inc .... A 949 614-7700
15485 Sand Canyon Ave Irvine (92618) *(P-6848)*

Marvin Engineering Co Inc (PA) .... A 310 674-5030
261 W Beach Ave Inglewood (90302) *(P-17582)*

Marvin Group The, Inglewood *Also Called: Marvin Land Systems Inc (P-7183)*

Marvin Group, The, Inglewood *Also Called: Marvin Engineering Co Inc (P-17582)*

Marvin Land Systems Inc .... E 310 674-5030
261 W Beach Ave Inglewood (90302) *(P-7183)*

Marvin Test Solutions Inc .... D 949 263-2222
1770 Kettering Irvine (92614) *(P-7926)*

Marway Power Solutions, Santa Ana *Also Called: Marway Power Systems Inc (P-5936)*

Marway Power Systems Inc (PA) .... E 714 917-6200
1721 S Grand Ave Santa Ana (92705) *(P-5936)*

Mary Hlth of Sick Cnvlscent Nr .... D 805 498-3644
2929 Theresa Dr Newbury Park (91320) *(P-15718)*

Maryvale .... C 626 280-6510
7600 Graves Ave Rosemead (91770) *(P-17178)*

Maryvale Day Care Center .... C 626 357-1514
2502 Huntington Dr Duarte (91010) *(P-17096)*

Maryvale Edcatn Fmly Rsrce Ctr, Duarte *Also Called: Maryvale Day Care Center (P-17096)*

MASADA HOMES, Gardena *Also Called: Counseling and Research Assoc (P-17136)*

Mashburn Trnsp Svcs Inc .... C 661 763-5724
22140 Rosedale Hwy Bakersfield (93314) *(P-8965)*

Masimo, Irvine *Also Called: Masimo Corporation (P-8389)*

Masimo Americas Inc .... E 949 297-7000
52 Discovery Irvine (92618) *(P-8187)*

Masimo Consumer, Carlsbad *Also Called: Dei Holdings Inc (P-6680)*

Masimo Corporation .... E 949 297-7000
40 Parker Irvine (92618) *(P-8387)*

Masimo Corporation .... E 949 297-7000
9600 Jeronimo Rd Irvine (92618) *(P-8388)*

Masimo Corporation (PA) .... B 949 297-7000
52 Discovery Irvine (92618) *(P-8389)*

Mason Electric Co .... B 818 361-3366
13955 Balboa Blvd Rancho Cascades (91342) *(P-7519)*

Masonry Concepts Inc .... D 562 802-3700
15408 Cornet St Santa Fe Springs (90670) *(P-986)*

Masonry Group Nevada Inc .... D 951 509-5300
8188 Lincoln Ave Ste 99 Riverside (92504) *(P-987)*

Mass Systems, Baldwin Park *Also Called: Ametek Ameron LLC (P-7847)*

Mast Biosurgery, San Diego *Also Called: Mast Biosurgery USA Inc (P-8188)*

Mast Biosurgery USA Inc .... E 858 550-8050
6749 Top Gun St Ste 108 San Diego (92121) *(P-8188)*

Masten Space, Mojave *Also Called: Masten Space Systems Inc (P-7647)*

Masten Space Systems Inc .... E 888 488-8455
1570 Sabovich St 25 Mojave (93501) *(P-7647)*

Master Builders LLC .... A 909 987-1758
9060 Haven Ave Rancho Cucamonga (91730) *(P-3812)*

Mergent email: customerrelations@mergent.com
1100

2025 Southern California
Business Directory and Buyers Guide

(P-0000) Products & Services Section entry number
(PA)=Parent Co (HQ)=Headquarters (DH)=Div Headquarters

Master Lightning SEC Solutions .... D 626 337-2915
545 N Mountain Ave Ste 207 Upland (91786) *(P-14317)*

Master Machine Products, Riverside *Also Called: Metric Machining (P-6176)*

Master Research & Mfg Inc .... D 562 483-8/89
13528 Pumice St Norwalk (90650) *(P-7520)*

Master-Chef's Linen Rental, Los Angeles *Also Called: American Textile Maint Co (P-13113)*

Masterbrand Cabinets LLC .... E 951 682-1535
3700 S Riverside Ave Colton (92324) *(P-2353)*

Masterpiece Artist Canvas LLC .... E 619 710-2500
1401 Air Wing Rd San Diego (92154) *(P-1884)*

Mastey De Paris Inc .... E 661 257-4814
24841 Avenue Tibbitts Valencia (91355) *(P-3669)*

Mastroianni Family Entps Ltd .... B 310 952-1700
10581 Garden Grove Blvd Garden Grove (92843) *(P-13179)*

Matches Inc .... B 760 899-1919
1700 E Araby St Ste 64 Palm Springs (92264) *(P-3305)*

Matchmaster Dyg & Finshg Inc (PA) .... C 323 232-2061
3750 S Broadway Los Angeles (90007) *(P-1942)*

Materals MGT At St Mary Med Ct, Apple Valley *Also Called: St Mary Medical Center LLC (P-16222)*

Material Control Inc .... D 661 617-6033
6901 District Blvd Ste A Bakersfield (93313) *(P-5452)*

Material Handling Supply Inc (HQ) .... D 562 921-7715
12900 Firestone Blvd Santa Fe Springs (90670) *(P-10381)*

Material Holdings LLC (PA) .... C 310 553-0550
1900 Avenue Of The Stars Ste 1600 Los Angeles (90067) *(P-17855)*

Material Sciences Corporation .... E 562 699-4550
3730 Capitol Ave City Of Industry (90601) *(P-4591)*

Matesta Corporation .... C 949 874-6052
5620 Knott Ave Buena Park (90621) *(P-10715)*

Math Holdings Inc (PA) .... C 909 517-2200
15820 Euclid Ave Chino (91708) *(P-14540)*

Mathy Machine Inc .... E 619 448-0404
9315 Wheatlands Rd Santee (92071) *(P-6171)*

Matich Corporation (PA) .... D 909 382-7400
1596 E Harry Shepard Blvd San Bernardino (92408) *(P-637)*

Matri Kart .... E 858 609-0933
448 W Market St San Diego (92101) *(P-5860)*

Matrix, Commerce *Also Called: Matrix International Tex Inc (P-10667)*

Matrix Aviation Services Inc .... C 310 337-3037
6171 W Century Blvd Ste 100 Los Angeles (90045) *(P-9244)*

Matrix Direct Insurance Svcs, San Diego *Also Called: AIG Direct Insurance Svcs Inc (P-12168)*

Matrix International Tex Inc .... E 323 582-9100
1363 S Bonnie Beach Pl Commerce (90023) *(P-10667)*

Matrix USA Inc .... E 714 825-0404
2730 S Main St Santa Ana (92707) *(P-6747)*

Matsuda House Printing Inc .... E 310 532-1533
1825 W 169th St Ste A Gardena (90247) *(P-3042)*

Matsui International Co Inc (HQ) .... E 310 767-7812
1501 W 178th St Gardena (90248) *(P-3813)*

Matsushita International Corp (PA) .... D 949 498-1000
1141 Via Callejon San Clemente (92673) *(P-12716)*

Matt Construction Corporation (PA) .... C 562 903-2277
9814 Norwalk Blvd Ste 100 Santa Fe Springs (90670) *(P-18187)*

Mattco Forge Inc .... E 562 634-8635
7530 Jackson St Paramount (90723) *(P-5144)*

Mattel, El Segundo *Also Called: Mattel Inc (P-8477)*

Mattel, El Segundo *Also Called: Mattel Direct Import Inc (P-8491)*

Mattel Inc (PA) .... A 310 252-2000
333 Continental Blvd El Segundo (90245) *(P-8477)*

Mattel Direct Import Inc (HQ) .... E 310 252-2000
333 Continental Blvd El Segundo (90245) *(P-8491)*

Matteo LLC .... E 213 617-2813
1000 E Cesar E Chavez Ave Los Angeles (90033) *(P-2216)*

Matthew Warren Inc .... E 805 928-3851
901 W Mccoy Ln Santa Maria (93455) *(P-5381)*

Matthew Warren Inc .... D 800 237-5225
5959 Triumph St Commerce (90040) *(P-5395)*

Matthew Warren Inc .... E 714 630-7840
3850 E Miraloma Ave Anaheim (92806) *(P-8573)*

Matthews Studio Equipment Inc .... E 818 843-6715
4520 W Valerio St Burbank (91505) *(P-8433)*

Maud Booth Family Center, North Hollywood *Also Called: Volunteers of Amer Los Angeles (P-17034)*

Maurice & Maurice Engrg Inc .... E 760 949-5151
17579 Mesa St Ste B4 Hesperia (92345) *(P-4578)*

Maurice Kraiem & Company .... E 213 629-0038
228 S Beverly Dr Beverly Hills (90212) *(P-10549)*

Maury Microwave Inc (PA) .... C 909 987-4715
2900 Inland Empire Blvd Ontario (91764) *(P-10266)*

Mave Enterprises Inc .... E 818 767-4533
11555 Cantara St Ste B-E North Hollywood (91605) *(P-1509)*

Maverick Abrasives Corporation .... D 714 854-9531
4340 E Miraloma Ave Anaheim (92807) *(P-4484)*

Maverick Aerospace LLC .... D 714 578-1700
3718 Capitol Ave City Of Industry (90601) *(P-7521)*

Maverick Desk, Gardena *Also Called: New Maverick Desk Inc (P-2511)*

Maverick Hospitality Inc .... D 714 730-7717
17662 Irvine Blvd Ste 4 Tustin (92780) *(P-12919)*

Max Leon Inc (PA) .... D 626 797-6886
3100 New York Dr Ste 100 Pasadena (91107) *(P-2120)*

Max Muscle, Anaheim *Also Called: Joe Wells Enterprises Inc (P-2015)*

Max Studio.com, Pasadena *Also Called: Max Leon Inc (P-2120)*

Maxair Systems, Irvine *Also Called: Bio-Medical Devices Inc (P-8108)*

Maxim Healthcare Services Inc .... C 951 694-0100
27555 Ynez Rd Temecula (92591) *(P-13605)*

Maxim Healthcare Services Inc .... D 951 684-4148
1845 Business Center Dr Ste 112 San Bernardino (92408) *(P-13606)*

Maxim Healthcare Services Inc .... C 310 329-9115
879 W 190th St Gardena (90248) *(P-13607)*

Maxim Healthcare Services Inc .... D 661 322-3039
4540 California Ave Bakersfield (93309) *(P-13608)*

Maxim Healthcare Services Inc .... D 661 964-6350
28470 Avenue Stanford Ste 250 Valencia (91355) *(P-13609)*

Maxim Healthcare Services Inc .... D 626 962-6453
801 Corporate Center Dr Ste 210 Pomona (91768) *(P-13610)*

Maxim Healthcare Services Inc .... D 805 489-2685
104 Traffic Way Ste A Arroyo Grande (93420) *(P-13611)*

Maxim Healthcare Services Inc .... D 805 278-4593
300 E Esplanade Dr Ste 1500 Oxnard (93036) *(P-13612)*

Maxim Healthcare Services Inc .... B 866 465-5678
3580 Wilshire Blvd Ste 1000 Los Angeles (90010) *(P-16403)*

Maxim Healthcare Services Inc .... B 619 299-9350
3111 Camino Del Rio N Ste 1200 San Diego (92108) *(P-16404)*

Maxim Healthcare Services Inc .... C 760 243-3377
560 E Hospitality Ln Ste 400 San Bernardino (92408) *(P-16405)*

Maxim Lighting, City Of Industry *Also Called: Maxim Lighting Intl Inc (P-10193)*

Maxim Lighting Intl Inc .... D 626 956-4200
247 Vineland Ave City Of Industry (91746) *(P-6446)*

Maxim Lighting Intl Inc (PA) .... D 626 956-4200
253 Vineland Ave City Of Industry (91746) *(P-10193)*

Maxima Racing Oils, Santee *Also Called: South West Lubricants Inc (P-3858)*

Maxima Thrapy Spech Clinic Inc .... C 818 287-8875
3940 Laurel Canyon Blvd # 456 Studio City (91604) *(P-16585)*

Maxin, Tustin *Also Called: Core Holdings Inc (P-16382)*

Maxlinear Inc (PA) .... E 760 692-0711
5966 La Place Ct Ste 100 Carlsbad (92008) *(P-6849)*

Maxon Industries Inc .... D 562 464-0099
11921 Slauson Ave Santa Fe Springs (90670) *(P-7270)*

Maxon Lift Corp (PA) .... D 562 464-0099
11921 Slauson Ave Santa Fe Springs (90670) *(P-10382)*

Maxtrol Corporation .... E 714 245-0506
1701 E Edinger Ave Ste B6 Santa Ana (92705) *(P-6748)*

Maxus USA, Los Angeles *Also Called: Essense (P-18373)*

Maxwell, San Diego *Also Called: Maxwell Technologies Inc (P-7096)*

Maxwell Alarm Screen Mfg Inc .... E 818 773-5533
20327 Nordhoff St Chatsworth (91311) *(P-8614)*

Maxwell Sign and Decal Div, Chatsworth *Also Called: Maxwell Alarm Screen Mfg Inc (P-8614)*

Maxwell Technologies Inc .... D 858 503-3493
3912 Calle Fortunada San Diego (92123) *(P-6378)*

Employee Codes: A=Over 500 employees, B=251-500
C=101-250, D=51-100, E=20-50, F=10-19, G=1-9

2025 Southern California
Business Directory and Buyers Guide

© Mergent Inc. 1-800-342-5647

1101

A
L
P
H
A
B
E
T
I
C

Maxwell Technologies Inc (HQ).................................D 858 503-3300
6155 Cornerstone Ct E Ste 210 San Diego (92121) *(P-7096)*

Maxxon Company, City Of Industry Also Called: Dennison Inc *(P-5061)*

Maxzone Vehicle Lighting Corp (HQ).........................E 909 822-3288
15889 Slover Ave Unit A Fontana (92337) *(P-9832)*

Maya Steel Fabrications Inc...D 310 532-8830
301 E Compton Blvd Gardena (90248) *(P-4849)*

Mayer Brown & Platt, Los Angeles Also Called: LLP Mayer Brown *(P-16734)*

Mayoni Enterprises...D 818 896-0026
10320 Glenoaks Blvd Pacoima (91331) *(P-5003)*

MAYWOOD ACRES HEALTHCARE, Oxnard Also Called: Milwood Healthcare Inc *(P-12305)*

Mazda Motor of America Inc (HQ)................................B 949 727-1990
200 Spectrum Center Dr Ste 100 Irvine (92618) *(P-7184)*

Mazda North Amercn Operations, Irvine Also Called: Mazda Motor of America Inc *(P-7184)*

Mazzei Injector Company LLC.....................................E 661 363-6500
500 Rooster Dr Bakersfield (93307) *(P-6022)*

MB Builders Inc...D 760 410-1442
403 S Las Posas Rd San Marcos (92078) *(P-418)*

MB Coatings Inc..D 714 625-2118
1540 S Lewis St Anaheim (92805) *(P-14541)*

MB Herzog Electric Inc..C 562 531-2002
15709 Illinois Ave Paramount (90723) *(P-938)*

MBC Systems, Santa Ana Also Called: Medical Network Inc *(P-18011)*

Mbe, Pasadena Also Called: Ttg Engineers *(P-17653)*

Mbit Wireless Inc (PA)..C 949 205-4559
4340 Von Karman Ave Ste 140 Newport Beach (92660) *(P-9404)*

Mboc, Torrance Also Called: Mortgage Bank of California *(P-11925)*

Mbp Land LLC...A 619 291-5720
595 Hotel Cir S San Diego (92108) *(P-12920)*

Mc Cann's Engineering & Mfg Co, La Mirada Also Called: MEMC Liquidating Corporation *(P-5681)*

Mc-40 (PA)..D 323 225-4111
777 N Georgia Ave Azusa (91702) *(P-13389)*

MC&a Usa LLC..D 504 267-8145
19700 Mariner Ave Torrance (90503) *(P-419)*

McCain Manufacturing Inc...D 760 295-9290
2633 Progress St Vista (92081) *(P-4850)*

MCCALLUM THEATRE, Palm Desert Also Called: Friends of Cultural Center Inc *(P-14960)*

McCarthy Bldg Companies Inc.....................................B 949 851-8383
20401 Sw Birch St Ste 200 Newport Beach (92660) *(P-556)*

McCarthy Bldg Companies Inc.....................................D 949 851-8383
20401 Sw Birch St Ste 300 Newport Beach (92660) *(P-557)*

McCarthy Bldg Companies Inc.....................................D 949 851-8383
1113 S Bush St Orange (92868) *(P-558)*

McCarthy Bldg Companies Inc.....................................B 213 655-1100
515 S Flower St Ste 3600 Los Angeles (90071) *(P-559)*

McConnell Cabinets Inc...A 626 937-2200
13110 Louden Ln City Of Industry (91746) *(P-2354)*

McConnells Fine Ice Creams LLC................................E 805 963-8813
800 Del Norte Blvd Oxnard (93030) *(P-10832)*

McCormick Ambulance, Compton Also Called: Westmed Ambulance Inc *(P-8855)*

McCrometer Inc (HQ)...C 951 652-6811
3255 W Stetson Ave Hemet (92545) *(P-7866)*

McDavis and Gumbys Inc..C 800 736-7363
1 Fleetwood Way Corona (92879) *(P-9925)*

McDowell Craig Off Systems Inc..................................D 562 921-4441
13146 Firestone Blvd Norwalk (90650) *(P-2531)*

McDowell-Craig Office Furn, Norwalk Also Called: McDowell Craig Off Systems Inc *(P-2531)*

McElroy Metal, Adelanto Also Called: McElroy Metal Mill Inc *(P-5083)*

McElroy Metal Mill Inc...E 760 246-5545
17031 Koala Rd Adelanto (92301) *(P-5083)*

McFiebow Inc (PA)..E 310 327-7474
17025 S Main St Gardena (90248) *(P-4400)*

McFiebow Inc..E 310 327-7474
13238 S Figueroa St Los Angeles (90061) *(P-4401)*

MCI Foods Inc...C 562 977-4000
13013 Molette St Santa Fe Springs (90670) *(P-1814)*

McK Enterprises Inc..D 805 483-5292
910 Commercial Ave Oxnard (93030) *(P-1815)*

McKeever Danlee Confectionary..................................C 626 334-8964
760 N Mckeever Ave Azusa (91702) *(P-1510)*

McKenna Boiler Works Inc...E 323 221-1171
2601 Industry St Oceanside (92054) *(P-14776)*

McKenna Labs Inc (PA)...E 714 687-6888
1601 E Orangethorpe Ave Fullerton (92831) *(P-3448)*

McKenna Pomona Dodge, Pomona Also Called: Pomona Mc Kenna Motors *(P-11396)*

McKesson Corporation..C 562 463-2100
9501 Norwalk Blvd Santa Fe Springs (90670) *(P-10631)*

McKesson Drug Company, Santa Fe Springs Also Called: McKesson Corporation *(P-10631)*

McKesson Mdcl-Srgcal Top Hldng...............................B 800 300-4350
1938 W Malvern Ave Fullerton (92833) *(P-10090)*

McKinley Childrens Center Inc (PA)..............................C 909 599-1227
180 Via Verde Ste 200 San Dimas (91773) *(P-17179)*

McKinnon Publishing Company....................................A 858 571-5151
4575 Viewridge Ave San Diego (92123) *(P-9511)*

McL Fresh, Los Angeles Also Called: 4 Earth Farms LLC *(P-10884)*

McLane Foodservice Inc..C 951 867-3727
14813 Meridian Pkwy Riverside (92518) *(P-10757)*

McLane Foodservice Dist Inc.......................................C 909 912-3700
1051 Wineville Ave Ontario (91764) *(P-10758)*

McLane Foodservice Dist Inc.......................................D 909 484-6100
9408 Richmond Pl Ste A Rancho Cucamonga (91730) *(P-10759)*

McLane Inland, Ontario Also Called: McLane Foodservice Dist Inc *(P-10758)*

McLane Manufacturing Inc...D 562 633-8158
6814 Foster Bridge Blvd Bell Gardens (90201) *(P-5481)*

McLane Rancho Cucamonga, Rancho Cucamonga Also Called: McLane Foodservice Dist Inc *(P-10759)*

McLane Riverside, Riverside Also Called: McLane Foodservice Inc *(P-10757)*

MCM Construction Inc...D 909 875-0533
19010 Slover Ave Bloomington (92316) *(P-654)*

McM Fabricators Inc..C 661 589-2774
720 Commerce Way Shafter (93263) *(P-4851)*

MCM Harvesters Inc..B 805 659-6833
1585 Lirio Ave Ventura (93004) *(P-13542)*

McMahon Steel Company Inc.......................................C 619 671-9700
1880 Nirvana Ave Chula Vista (91911) *(P-4780)*

McMaster-Carr Supply Company..................................B 562 692-5911
9630 Norwalk Blvd Santa Fe Springs (90670) *(P-10446)*

McMillin Communities Inc..C 951 506-3303
41687 Temeku Dr Temecula (92591) *(P-15091)*

McMillin Companies LLC (PA)......................................D 619 477-4117
2750 Womble Rd Ste 102 San Diego (92106) *(P-12717)*

McMillin Homes, San Diego Also Called: McMillin Companies LLC *(P-12717)*

McNeilus Truck and Mfg Inc..E 909 370-2100
401 N Pepper Ave Colton (92324) *(P-7207)*

McQ, Burbank Also Called: Silver Saddle Ranch & Club Inc *(P-12579)*

MCR Printing and Packg Corp......................................C 619 488-3012
8830 Siempre Viva Rd San Diego (92154) *(P-9088)*

McStarlite, Harbor City Also Called: Basmat Inc *(P-4955)*

McWhirter Steel Inc...D 661 951-8998
42211 7th St E Lancaster (93535) *(P-4852)*

MD Care Inc..D 562 344-3400
1640 E Hill St Signal Hill (90755) *(P-12064)*

MD Care Healthplan, Signal Hill Also Called: MD Care Inc *(P-12064)*

MD Engineering Inc...E 951 736-5390
1550 Consumer Cir Corona (92878) *(P-6172)*

Md-Staff, Temecula Also Called: Applied Statistics & MGT Inc *(P-13883)*

Mdc Interior Solutions LLC..E 800 621-4006
6900 E Washington Blvd Los Angeles (90040) *(P-2198)*

Mddr Inc...C 714 792-1993
1921 Petra Ln Placentia (92870) *(P-802)*

Mdh, Monrovia Also Called: Radcal Corporation *(P-8060)*

Mdm Solutions LLC...B 800 669-6361
575 Anton Blvd Ste 300 Costa Mesa (92626) *(P-344)*

Mds Consulting (PA)...D 949 251-8821
17320 Red Hill Ave Ste 350 Irvine (92614) *(P-17583)*

ME & My Big Ideas LLC...C 240 348-5240
6261 Katella Ave Ste 150 Cypress (90630) *(P-10523)*

Meadow Lake Country Club, Escondido Also Called: Welk Group Inc *(P-15186)*

Meadowbrook Vlg Chrstn Rtrment................................C 760 746-2500
100 Holland Gln Escondido (92026) *(P-17180)*

Meadowlark Golf Course, Huntington Beach *Also Called: City of Huntington Beach (P-15073)*

Meadows Mechanical, Gardena *Also Called: Meadows Sheet Metal and AC Inc (P-5004)*

Meadows Sheet Metal and AC Inc .... E 310 615-1125
333 Crown Vista Dr Gardena (90248) *(P-5004)*

Meadows, The, Culver City *Also Called: E & S Ring Management Corp (P-12433)*

Means Engineering Inc .... D 760 931-9452
5927 Geiger Ct Carlsbad (92008) *(P-7967)*

Mearsk, San Pedro *Also Called: APM Terminals Pacific LLC (P-9253)*

Measure of Excellence Cabinets, Poway *Also Called: Kiewit Corporation (P-552)*

Measure Uas Inc .... E 714 916-6166
5862 Bolsa Ave Ste 104 Huntington Beach (92649) *(P-8051)*

Measurement Specialties Inc .... C 818 701-2750
9131 Oakdale Ave Ste 170 Chatsworth (91311) *(P-8052)*

Med Couture Inc .... E 214 231-2500
15301 Ventura Blvd Sherman Oaks (91403) *(P-1998)*

Med Source Prof Personnel, San Diego *Also Called: Med Source Ventures Inc (P-13613)*

Med Source Ventures Inc .... B 858 560-9941
3750 Convoy St Ste 155 San Diego (92111) *(P-13613)*

Med-Legal LLC .... C 626 653-5160
955 Overland Ct Ste 200 San Dimas (91773) *(P-16739)*

Med-Pharmex Inc .... C 909 593-7875
2727 Thompson Creek Rd Pomona (91767) *(P-3449)*

Medasend Biomedical Inc (PA) .... C 800 200-3581
1402 Daisy Ave Long Beach (90813) *(P-16586)*

Medata LLC (HQ) .... D 714 918-1310
5 Peters Canyon Rd Ste 250 Irvine (92606) *(P-13972)*

Medegen LLC (DH) .... E 909 390-9080
4501 E Wall St Ontario (91761) *(P-4164)*

Medegen Inc .... C 909 390-9080
930 S Wanamaker Ave Ontario (91761) *(P-4165)*

Medennium Inc (PA) .... E 949 789-9000
9 Parker Ste 150 Irvine (92618) *(P-8409)*

Medgear, Cerritos *Also Called: LA Triumph Inc (P-1997)*

Medholdings of Newnan LLC .... A 213 462-6252
1750 Vine St Los Angeles (90028) *(P-14542)*

Media Nation Enterprises LLC (PA) .... E 888 502-8222
15271 Barranca Pkwy Irvine (92618) *(P-8615)*

Media Nation USA, Irvine *Also Called: Media Nation Enterprises LLC (P-8615)*

Media Services, Los Angeles *Also Called: Oberman Tivoli & Pickert Inc (P-14101)*

Media Temple Inc .... C 877 578-4000
12655 W Jefferson Blvd # 400 Los Angeles (90066) *(P-9447)*

Mediaalpha, Los Angeles *Also Called: Mediaalpha Inc (P-13269)*

Mediaalpha Inc (PA) .... C 213 316-6256
700 S Flower St Ste 640 Los Angeles (90017) *(P-13269)*

Mediabrands Worldwide Inc .... B 323 370-8000
1840 Century Park E Los Angeles (90067) *(P-13225)*

Mediatek USA Inc .... C 408 526-1899
1 Ada Ste 200 Irvine (92618) *(P-5861)*

Mediatek USA Inc .... C 858 731-9200
10188 Telesis Ct Ste 500 San Diego (92121) *(P-10017)*

Medic 1 Ambulance Service Inc .... D 000 502 8840
1305 W Arrow Hwy Ste 206 San Dimas (91773) *(P-8835)*

Medical Billing Services, Monrovia *Also Called: California Business Bureau Inc (P-17708)*

Medical Brkthrugh Mssage Chlrs .... E 408 677-7702
24971 Avenue Stanford Valencia (91355) *(P-8699)*

Medical Center, San Bernardino *Also Called: Far West Inc (P-15652)*

Medical Center, San Diego *Also Called: University Cal San Diego (P-16241)*

Medical Center, Ventura *Also Called: County of Ventura (P-16931)*

Medical Chemical Corporation .... E 310 787-6800
19250 Van Ness Ave Torrance (90501) *(P-3814)*

Medical Data Exchange, Anaheim *Also Called: Cyber-Pro Systems Inc (P-14128)*

Medical Depot Inc .... D 877 224-0946
548 W Merrill Ave Rialto (92376) *(P-8189)*

Medical Device Bus Svcs Inc .... E 858 560-4165
5644 Kearny Mesa Rd Ste I San Diego (92111) *(P-8283)*

Medical Device Manufacturing, Brea *Also Called: Life Science Outsourcing Inc (P-8184)*

Medical Eye Services Inc .... D 714 619-4660
345 Baker St Costa Mesa (92626) *(P-12231)*

Medical Genetics, Los Angeles *Also Called: Cedars-Sinai Medical Center (P-15944)*

Medical Management Cons Inc .... A 858 587-0609
6046 Cornerstone Ct W San Diego (92121) *(P-18168)*

Medical Network Inc .... D 949 863-0022
1809 E Dyer Rd Ste 311 Santa Ana (92705) *(P-18011)*

Medical Packaging Corporation .... D 805 388-2383
941 Avenida Acaso Camarillo (93012) *(P-8284)*

Medical Record Associates Inc .... C 617 698-4411
600 Corporate Pointe Culver City (90230) *(P-18169)*

Medical Research Institute .... C 818 739-6000
21411 Prairie St Chatsworth (91311) *(P-10632)*

Medical Specialty Billing, Orange *Also Called: Acclara Holdings Group Inc (P-17700)*

Medico Professional Linen Svc, Los Angeles *Also Called: American Textile Maint Co (P-13112)*

Medieval Times Entrmt Inc (HQ) .... A 714 523-1100
7662 Beach Blvd Buena Park (90620) *(P-13109)*

Mediland Corporation .... D 562 630-9696
15 Longitude Way Corona (92881) *(P-4317)*

Medimpact Hlthcare Systems Inc (HQ) .... C 800 788-2949
10181 Scripps Gateway Ct San Diego (92131) *(P-17301)*

Medimpact Holdings Inc (PA) .... A 858 566-2727
10181 Scripps Gateway Ct San Diego (92131) *(P-12718)*

Medina Construction, Riverside *Also Called: Bens Asphalt & Maint Co Inc (P-610)*

Mediscan Diagnostic Svcs LLC .... D 818 758-4224
21050 Califa St Ste 100 Woodland Hills (91367) *(P-13543)*

Mediscan Staffing Services, Woodland Hills *Also Called: Mediscan Diagnostic Svcs LLC (P-13543)*

Medix Ambulance Service Inc (PA) .... C 949 470-8915
26021 Pala Mission Viejo (92691) *(P-8836)*

Medley Communications Inc (PA) .... C 951 245-5200
43015 Black Deer Loop Ste 203 Temecula (92590) *(P-939)*

Medlin & Sons, Whittier *Also Called: Medlin and Son Engrg Svc Inc (P-6173)*

Medlin and Son Engrg Svc Inc .... E 562 464-5889
12484 Whittier Blvd Whittier (90602) *(P-6173)*

Medlin Ramps .... E 877 463-3546
14903 Marquardt Ave Santa Fe Springs (90670) *(P-5559)*

Medline Industries LP .... E 951 296-2600
42500 Winchester Rd Temecula (92590) *(P-8285)*

Medresponse (PA) .... C 818 442-9222
7040 Hayvenhurst Ave Van Nuys (91406) *(P-8837)*

Medresponse LLC .... D 877 311-5555
9961 Baldwin Pl El Monte (91731) *(P-8838)*

Medsco Fabrication & Dist Inc .... D 323 263-0511
938 N Eastern Ave Los Angeles (90063) *(P-4853)*

Medterra Cbd LLC .... D 800 971-1288
18500 Von Karman Ave Ste 100 Irvine (92612) *(P-6)*

Medtrans Inc .... D 323 780-9500
345 S Woods Ave Los Angeles (90022) *(P-8839)*

Medtrans Inc, Los Angeles *Also Called: Medtrans Inc (P-8839)*

Medtronic, San Diego *Also Called: Medtronic Inc (P-8190)*

Medtronic, Carlsbad *Also Called: Medtronic Inc (P-8191)*

Medtronic, Irvine *Also Called: Medtronic Inc (P-8192)*

Medtronic, Northridge *Also Called: Medtronic Minimed Inc (P-8195)*

Medtronic, Irvine *Also Called: Medtronic PS Medical Inc (P-8196)*

Medtronic Inc .... E 949 708-3034
1650 Gailes Blvd San Diego (92154) *(P-8190)*

Medtronic Inc .... E 760 214-3009
2101 Faraday Ave Carlsbad (92008) *(P-8191)*

Medtronic Inc .... C 949 837-3700
9775 Toledo Way Irvine (92618) *(P-8192)*

Medtronic Inc .... A 949 474-3943
1851 E Deere Ave Santa Ana (92705) *(P-8193)*

Medtronic Ats Medical Inc .... C 949 380-9333
1851 E Deere Ave Santa Ana (92705) *(P-8194)*

Medtronic Minimed Inc (DH) .... A 800 646-4633
18000 Devonshire St Northridge (91325) *(P-8195)*

Medtronic PS Medical Inc (DH) .... C 805 571-3769
5290 California Ave # 100 Irvine (92617) *(P-8196)*

Medusind Solutions Inc (PA) .... D 949 240-8895
31103 Rancho Viejo Rd Ste 2150 San Juan Capistrano (92675) *(P-14543)*

Medway Plastics Corporation .... C 562 630-1175
2250 E Cherry Industrial Cir Long Beach (90805) *(P-4166)*

Employee Codes: A=Over 500 employees, B=251-500
C=101-250, D=51-100, E=20-50, F=10-19, G=1-9

2025 Southern California
Business Directory and Buyers Guide

© Mergent Inc. 1-800-342-5647

1103

Mega Appraisers Inc .... A 818 246-7370
14724 Ventura Blvd Ste 800 Sherman Oaks (91403) *(P-14544)*

Mega Brands America Inc (DH)........................... D **949 727-9009**
333 Continental Blvd El Segundo (90245) *(P-8492)*

Mega Toys, Commerce *Also Called: PC Woo Inc (P-10526)*

Mega Western Sales, Santa Fe Springs *Also Called: Great Western Sales Inc (P-10319)*

Meggitt (orange County) Inc (DH)....................... C **949 493-8181**
4 Marconi Irvine (92618) *(P-8053)*

Meggitt (san Diego) Inc (HQ)............................. C **858 824-8976**
6650 Top Gun St San Diego (92121) *(P-7522)*

Meggitt Arcft Braking Systems, Gardena *Also Called: Nasco Aircraft Brake Inc (P-7529)*

Meggitt Control Systems, North Hollywood *Also Called: Meggitt North Hollywood Inc (P-7525)*

Meggitt Defense Systems Inc .... B 949 465-7700
9801 Muirlands Blvd Irvine (92618) *(P-7523)*

Meggitt North Hollywood Inc .... E 818 691-6258
10092 Foxrun Rd Santa Ana (92705) *(P-7524)*

Meggitt North Hollywood Inc (DH)....................... C 818 765-8160
12838 Saticoy St North Hollywood (91605) *(P-7525)*

Meggitt Polymers & Composites, San Diego *Also Called: Meggitt (san Diego) Inc (P-7522)*

Meggitt Polymers & Composites, Simi Valley *Also Called: Meggitt-Usa Inc (P-7527)*

Meggitt Safety Systems Inc .... D 442 792-3217
11661 Sorrento Valley Rd San Diego (92121) *(P-7133)*

Meggitt Safety Systems Inc (DH)......................... C **805 584-4100**
1785 Voyager Ave Simi Valley (93063) *(P-7134)*

Meggitt Safety Systems Inc .... D 805 584-4100
1785 Voyager Ave Simi Valley (93063) *(P-7526)*

Meggitt Sensing Systems, Irvine *Also Called: Meggitt (orange County) Inc (P-8053)*

Meggitt Western Design Inc .... C 949 465-7700
9801 Muirlands Blvd Irvine (92618) *(P-7837)*

Meggitt-Usa Inc (DH).. B **805 526-5700**
1955 Surveyor Ave Simi Valley (93063) *(P-7527)*

Megiddo Global LLC .... E 844 477-7007
17101 Central Ave Ste 1c Carson (90746) *(P-8286)*

Meguiars Inc (HQ).. E **949 752-8000**
213 Technology Dr Irvine (92618) *(P-3613)*

MEI Pharma, San Diego *Also Called: MEI Pharma Inc (P-3450)*

MEI Pharma Inc .... E 858 369-7100
11455 El Camino Real Ste 250 San Diego (92130) *(P-3450)*

MEI Rigging & Crating LLC .... D 714 712-5888
14555 Alondra Blvd La Mirada (90638) *(P-5709)*

Meissner Corporation .... E 805 388-9911
1001 Flynn Rd Camarillo (93012) *(P-6931)*

Meissner Mfg Co Inc (PA)................................... D **818 678-0400**
21701 Prairie St Chatsworth (91311) *(P-6023)*

Mejico Express Inc (PA)...................................... C **714 690-8300**
14849 Firestone Blvd Fl 1 La Mirada (90638) *(P-9175)*

Mek Enterprises Inc .... D 619 527-0957
3517 Camino Del Rio S Ste 215 San Diego (92108) *(P-9354)*

Mek Escondido LLC .... C 760 747-0430
421 E Mission Ave Escondido (92025) *(P-15719)*

Mek Industries Inc .... C 858 610-9601
11491 Woodside Ave Santee (92071) *(P-13614)*

Mel Bernie and Company Inc (PA)....................... C **818 841-1928**
3000 W Empire Ave Burbank (91504) *(P-10550)*

Melano Enterprises, Oceanside *Also Called: Mellano & Co (P-11091)*

Melcast, Cerritos *Also Called: Molino Company (P-3046)*

Melco Steel Inc .... E 626 334-7875
1100 W Foothill Blvd Azusa (91702) *(P-4916)*

Melfred Borzall Inc .... E 805 614-4344
2712 Airpark Dr Santa Maria (93455) *(P-5548)*

Melin LLC .... E 323 489-3274
10 Faraday Irvine (92618) *(P-8532)*

Melissa Data Corporation (PA)............................ D **949 858-3000**
22382 Avenida Empresa Rcho Sta Marg (92688) *(P-13768)*

Melissas World Variety Produce, Vernon *Also Called: World Variety Produce Inc (P-10926)*

Mellace Family Brands Cal Inc .... E 760 448-1940
6195 El Camino Real Carlsbad (92009) *(P-1512)*

Mellano & Co .... C 760 433-9550
734 Wilshire Rd Oceanside (92057) *(P-11091)*

Mellano & Company (PA)..................................... D **213 622-0796**
766 Wall St Los Angeles (90014) *(P-11092)*

Mellano Enterprises, Los Angeles *Also Called: Mellano & Company (P-11092)*

Melles Griot Inc .... D 760 438-2254
2051 Palomar Airport Rd Carlsbad (92011) *(P-8011)*

Melimo Inc .... C 858 847-3272
131 Aberdeen Dr Cardiff By The Sea (92007) *(P-13769)*

Melmarc Products Inc .... C 714 549-2170
752 S Campus Ave Ontario (91761) *(P-2251)*

Melton Intl Tackle Inc .... E 714 978-9192
1375 S State College Blvd Anaheim (92806) *(P-11655)*

MEMC Liquidating Corporation .... C 818 637-7200
4570 Colorado Blvd La Mirada (90638) *(P-5681)*

Memco Holdings Inc .... C 310 277-0057
10390 Santa Monica Blvd Ste 210 Los Angeles (90025) *(P-12487)*

Memeged Tevuot Shemesh (PA)........................... C 866 575-1211
5550 Topanga Canyon Blvd Ste 280 Woodland Hills (91367) *(P-803)*

Memorex Products Inc .... C 562 653-2800
17777 Center Court Dr N Ste 800 Cerritos (90703) *(P-10221)*

Memorial Care Medical Centers, Fountain Valley *Also Called: Memorial Health Services (P-16094)*

MEMORIAL CARE MEDICAL CENTERS, Fountain Valley *Also Called: Orange Coast Memorial Med Ctr (P-16109)*

MEMORIAL CARE MEDICAL CENTERS, Laguna Hills *Also Called: Saddleback Memorial Med Ctr (P-16164)*

Memorial Center, Bakersfield *Also Called: Bakersfield Memorial Hospital (P-15922)*

Memorial Health Services (PA)............................ B **714 377-2900**
17360 Brookhurst St Ste 160 Fountain Valley (92708) *(P-16094)*

Memorial Healthtec Labratories .... C 714 962-4677
9920 Talbert Ave Fountain Valley (92708) *(P-17809)*

Memorial Hlth Svcs - Univ Cal (PA)..................... A 562 933-2000
2801 Atlantic Ave Long Beach (90806) *(P-16095)*

Memorial Hospital of Gardena .... B 323 268-5514
4060 Woody Blvd Los Angeles (90023) *(P-16096)*

Memorial Hospital of Gardena, Gardena *Also Called: Gardena Hospital LP (P-16001)*

Memorial Medical Center Foundation .... A 562 933-2273
2801 Atlantic Ave Long Beach (90806) *(P-17466)*

Memorial Orthpdic Srgcal Group .... D 562 424-6666
2760 Atlantic Ave Long Beach (90806) *(P-15387)*

Memorlcare Srgcal Ctr At Ornge .... C 714 369-1100
18111 Brookhurst St Ste 3200 Fountain Valley (92708) *(P-15388)*

Menifee Valley AC Inc .... D 888 785-6125
3875 Industrial Ave Hemet (92545) *(P-804)*

Menke Marketing Devices, Santa Fe Springs *Also Called: Menke Marking Devices Inc (P-10383)*

Menke Marking Devices Inc .... E 562 921-1380
10440 Pioneer Blvd Ste 4 Santa Fe Springs (90670) *(P-10383)*

Mental Health Dept of, Artesia *Also Called: County of Los Angeles (P-16460)*

Mental Health Systems Inc (PA).......................... D 858 573-2600
9465 Farnham St San Diego (92123) *(P-16485)*

Mentor California, Bakersfield *Also Called: Alliance Childrens Services (P-17119)*

Mentor Mdia USA Sup Chain MGT .... D 909 930-0800
865 S Washington Ave San Bernardino (92408) *(P-18170)*

Mentor Worldwide LLC (DH)................................. C **800 636-8678**
31 Technology Dr Ste 200 Irvine (92618) *(P-8287)*

Mentor Worldwide LLC .... B 805 681-6000
5425 Hollister Ave Santa Barbara (93111) *(P-10091)*

Meow Logistics, Walnut *Also Called: Straight Forwarding Inc (P-9339)*

Mer-Kote Products Inc .... E 714 778-2266
4125 E La Palma Ave Ste 250 Anaheim (92807) *(P-3279)*

Mer-Mar Electronics, Hesperia *Also Called: Geeriraj Inc (P-6732)*

Mercado Latino Inc .... D 310 537-1062
1420 W Walnut St Compton (90220) *(P-8700)*

Mercado Latino Inc (PA)...................................... D **626 333-6862**
245 Baldwin Park Blvd City Of Industry (91746) *(P-10760)*

Mercedes Benz of Bakersfield, Bakersfield *Also Called: Sangera Buick Inc (P-14699)*

Mercedes Benz of Escondido, Escondido *Also Called: Escondido Motors LLC (P-11343)*

Mercedes Benz of Riverside, Riverside *Also Called: Walters Auto Sales and Svc Inc (P-11431)*

Mercedes Benz of San Diego, San Diego *Also Called: Europa Auto Imports Inc (P-11344)*

Merchant of Tennis Inc .... A 909 923-3388
1625 Proforma Ave Ontario (91761) *(P-14545)*

Merchant Services, Irvine *Also Called: Universal Card Inc (P-14618)*

Mergent email: customerrelations@mergent.com
1104

2025 Southern California
Business Directory and Buyers Guide

(P-0000) Products & Services Section entry number
(PA)=Parent Co (HQ)=Headquarters (DH)=Div Headquarters

Merchants Bank California N A .... D 310 549-4350
1 Civic Plaza Dr Ste 100 Carson (90745) *(P-11771)*

Merchants Building Maint Co .... B 714 973-9272
1639 E Edinger Ave Ste C Santa Ana (92705) *(P-13390)*

Merchants Building Maint Co .... A 909 622-8260
1995 W Holt Ave Pomona (91768) *(P-13391)*

Merchants Building Maint Co .... C 323 881-8902
606 Monterey Pass Rd Ste 202 Monterey Park (91754) *(P-13392)*

Merchants Building Maint Co .... B 858 455-0163
9555 Distribution Ave Ste 102 San Diego (92121) *(P-13393)*

Merchants Building Maintenance, Santa Ana *Also Called: Merchants Building Maint Co (P-13390)*

Merchants Building Maintenance, Pomona *Also Called: Merchants Building Maint Co (P-13391)*

Merchants Landscape Services .... D 909 981-1022
8748 Industrial Ln # 1 Rancho Cucamonga (91730) *(P-177)*

Merchants Landscape Services .... D 619 778-6239
2865 Main St Ste A Chula Vista (91911) *(P-222)*

Merchants Metals, Riverside *Also Called: Merchants Metals LLC (P-4537)*

Merchants Metals LLC .... D 951 686-1888
6466 Mission Blvd Riverside (92509) *(P-4537)*

Merchsource LLC (DH) .... C **800 374-2744**
7755 Irvine Center Dr Ste 100 Irvine (92618) *(P-10524)*

Merco Manufacturing Co, Walnut *Also Called: Aero Pacific Corporation (P-7409)*

Mercury Casualty Company (HQ) .... A **323 937-1060**
555 W Imperial Hwy Brea (92821) *(P-12123)*

Mercury Computer System Inc .... E 760 494-9600
1815 Aston Ave Ste 107 Carlsbad (92008) *(P-5862)*

Mercury Defense Systems Inc .... D 714 898-8200
10855 Business Center Dr Ste A Cypress (90630) *(P-14143)*

MERCURY GENERAL, Los Angeles *Also Called: Mercury General Corporation (P-12124)*

Mercury General Corporation (PA) .... A **323 937-1060**
4484 Wilshire Blvd Los Angeles (90010) *(P-12124)*

Mercury Insurance Broker, Santa Monica *Also Called: Mercury Insurance Company (P-12129)*

Mercury Insurance Company .... A 714 255-5000
1700 Greenbriar Ln Brea (92821) *(P-12125)*

Mercury Insurance Company (HQ) .... C **323 937-1060**
555 W Imperial Hwy Brea (92821) *(P-12126)*

Mercury Insurance Company .... A 858 694-4100
9635 Granite Ridge Dr Ste 200 San Diego (92123) *(P-12127)*

Mercury Insurance Company .... A 661 291-6470
27200 Tourney Rd Ste 400 Valencia (91355) *(P-12128)*

Mercury Insurance Company .... C 310 451-4943
1433 Santa Monica Blvd Santa Monica (90404) *(P-12129)*

Mercury LLC - Rf Integrated Solutions .... C 805 388-1345
1000 Avenida Acaso Camarillo (93012) *(P-7024)*

Mercury Plastics Inc (HQ) .... B **626 961-0165**
14825 Salt Lake Ave City Of Industry (91746) *(P-2734)*

Mercury Plastics Inc .... D 323 264-2100
2939 E Washington Blvd Los Angeles (90023) *(P-3951)*

Mercury Systems, Cypress *Also Called: Mercury Defense Systems Inc (P-14143)*

Mercury Systems Inc .... C 805 388-1345
400 Del Norte Blvd Oxnard (93030) *(P-6749)*

Mercury Systems Inc .... C 805 751-1100
300 Del Norte Blvd Oxnard (93030) *(P-6750)*

Mercury Systems Inc .... D 714 898-8200
10855 Business Center Dr Ste A Cypress (90630) *(P-14144)*

Mercury Technology Group Inc .... D 949 417-0260
6430 Oak Cyn Ste 100 Irvine (92618) *(P-14145)*

Mercy Ambulance, Valley Center *Also Called: Mercy Medical Trnsp Inc (P-8840)*

Mercy For Animals Inc .... C 347 839-6464
8033 W Sunset Blvd Ste 864 Los Angeles (90046) *(P-129)*

Mercy House Living Centers .... C 714 836-7188
807 N Garfield St Santa Ana (92701) *(P-17285)*

MERCY HOUSE TRANSITIONAL LIVIN, Santa Ana *Also Called: Mercy House Living Centers (P-17285)*

Mercy Medical Trnsp Inc .... C 760 739-8026
27350 Valley Center Rd Ste A Valley Center (92082) *(P-8840)*

Meredith Baer & Associates, South Gate *Also Called: Meribear Productions Inc (P-14546)*

Merger Sub Gotham 2 LLC .... C 714 462-4603
6261 Katella Ave Ste 250 Cypress (90630) *(P-4167)*

Meribear Productions Inc .... D 310 204-5353
4100 Ardmore Ave South Gate (90280) *(P-14546)*

Merical, Anaheim *Also Called: B & C Nutritional Products Inc (P-3310)*

Merical LLC .... C 714 685-0977
447 W Freedom Ave Orange (92865) *(P-14547)*

Merical LLC .... C 714 283-9551
233 E Bristol Ln Orange (92865) *(P-14548)*

Merical LLC .... C 714 238-7225
445 W Freedom Ave Orange (92865) *(P-14549)*

Merical/Vita-Pak, Orange *Also Called: Merical LLC (P-14548)*

Meridian, San Diego *Also Called: Meridian Rack & Pinion Inc (P-9833)*

Meridian Graphics Inc .... D 949 833-3500
2652 Dow Ave Tustin (92780) *(P-3043)*

Meridian Rack & Pinion Inc .... C 888 875-0026
9980 Huennekens St Ste 200 San Diego (92121) *(P-9833)*

Meridian Rail Acquisition .... C 909 478-0541
1475 Cooley Ct San Bernardino (92408) *(P-9370)*

Meridian Vineyards, Paso Robles *Also Called: Treasury Wine Estates Americas (P-37)*

Meridianlink, Costa Mesa *Also Called: Meridianlink Inc (P-13770)*

Meridianlink Inc (PA) .... D **714 708-6950**
3560 Hyland Ave Ste 200 Costa Mesa (92626) *(P-13770)*

Merit Aluminum Inc (PA) .... C **951 735-1770**
2480 Railroad St Corona (92880) *(P-4601)*

Merit Cables Incorporated .... E 714 918-1932
830 N Poinsettia St Santa Ana (92701) *(P-8197)*

Merit Companies The, Irvine *Also Called: Firstsrvice Rsidential Cal LLC (P-12454)*

Merit Day Food Service, Pico Rivera *Also Called: Three Sons Inc (P-10883)*

Meritek Electronics Corp (PA) .... D **626 373-1728**
5160 Rivergrade Rd Baldwin Park (91706) *(P-5710)*

Merito.com, Van Nuys *Also Called: Chef Merito LLC (P-1754)*

Merle Norman Cosmetics, Los Angeles *Also Called: Merle Norman Cosmetics Inc (P-3670)*

Merle Norman Cosmetics Inc (PA) .... B **310 641-3000**
9130 Bellanca Ave Los Angeles (90045) *(P-3670)*

Merqbiz LLC .... E 855 637-7249
300 Continental Blvd Ste 640 El Segundo (90245) *(P-11656)*

Merrick Engineering Inc (PA) .... C **951 737-6040**
1275 Quarry St Corona (92879) *(P-4168)*

Merrill Lynch, Los Angeles *Also Called: Merrill Lynch Inv MGT Inc (P-11976)*

Merrill Lynch, Bakersfield *Also Called: Merrill Lynch Prce Fnner Smith (P-11977)*

Merrill Lynch, Valencia *Also Called: Merrill Lynch Prce Fnner Smith (P-11978)*

Merrill Lynch, El Segundo *Also Called: Merrill Lynch Prce Fnner Smith (P-11979)*

Merrill Lynch, Pasadena *Also Called: Merrill Lynch Prce Fnner Smith (P-11980)*

Merrill Lynch, Costa Mesa *Also Called: Merrill Lynch Prce Fnner Smith (P-11981)*

Merrill Lynch, Newport Beach *Also Called: Merrill Lynch Prce Fnner Smith (P-11982)*

Merrill Lynch, Brea *Also Called: Merrill Lynch Prce Fnner Smith (P-11983)*

Merrill Lynch, Seal Beach *Also Called: Merrill Lynch Prce Fnner Smith (P-11984)*

Merrill Lynch, San Luis Obispo *Also Called: Merrill Lynch Prce Fnner Smith (P-11985)*

Merrill Lynch, Santa Barbara *Also Called: Merrill Lynch Prce Fnner Smith (P-11986)*

Merrill Lynch, Santa Barbara *Also Called: Merrill Lynch Prce Fnner Smith (P-11987)*

Merrill Lynch, Westlake Village *Also Called: Merrill Lynch Prce Fnner Smith (P-11988)*

Merrill Lynch, Indian Wells *Also Called: Merrill Lynch Prce Fnner Smith (P-11989)*

Merrill Lynch, San Diego *Also Called: Merrill Lynch Prce Fnner Smith (P-11990)*

Merrill Lynch, La Jolla *Also Called: Merrill Lynch Prce Fnner Smith (P-11991)*

Merrill Lynch, San Diego *Also Called: Merrill Lynch Prce Fnner Smith (P-11992)*

Merrill Lynch, San Diego *Also Called: Merrill Lynch Prce Fnner Smith (P-11993)*

Merrill Lynch Carlsbad Office, Carlsbad *Also Called: Merrill Lynch Prce Fnner Smith (P-11994)*

Merrill Lynch Inv MGT Inc .... C 310 209-4000
10877 Wilshire Blvd Ste 1900 Los Angeles (90024) *(P-11976)*

Merrill Lynch Prce Fnner Smith .... C 661 326-7700
5080 California Ave Ste 102 Bakersfield (93309) *(P-11977)*

Merrill Lynch Prce Fnner Smith .... D 661 802-0764
24200 Magic Mountain Pkwy Ste 115 Valencia (91355) *(P-11978)*

Merrill Lynch Prce Fnner Smith .... D 310 536-1600
2301 Rosecrans Ave Ste 3150 El Segundo (90245) *(P-11979)*

Merrill Lynch Prce Fnner Smith .... C 800 637-7455
800 E Colorado Blvd Ste 400 Pasadena (91101) *(P-11980)*

Merrill Lynch Prce Fnner Smith .... D 714 429-2800
650 Town Center Dr # 500 Costa Mesa (92626) *(P-11981)*

Employee Codes: A=Over 500 employees, B=251-500
C=101-250, D=51-100, E=20-50, F=10-19, G=1-9

2025 Southern California
Business Directory and Buyers Guide

© Mergent Inc. 1-800-342-5647

1105

Merrill Lynch Prce Fnner Smith .... C 949 467-3760
520 Newport Center Dr Ste 1900 Newport Beach (92660) *(P-11982)*

Merrill Lynch Prce Fnner Smith .... C 714 257-4400
145 S State College Blvd Ste 300 Brea (92821) *(P-11983)*

Merrill Lynch Prce Fnner Smith .... D 562 493-1300
3010 Old Ranch Pkwy Ste 150 Seal Beach (90740) *(P-11984)*

Merrill Lynch Prce Fnner Smith .... D 805 596-2222
1020 Marsh St San Luis Obispo (93401) *(P-11985)*

Merrill Lynch Prce Fnner Smith .... C 805 695-7028
1096 Coast Village Rd Santa Barbara (93108) *(P-11986)*

Merrill Lynch Prce Fnner Smith .... C 805 963-0333
1424 State St Santa Barbara (93101) *(P-11987)*

Merrill Lynch Prce Fnner Smith .... D 805 381-2600
2815 Townsgate Rd Ste 300 Westlake Village (91361) *(P-11988)*

Merrill Lynch Prce Fnner Smith : .... C 760 862-1400
74800 Us Highway 111 Indian Wells (92210) *(P-11989)*

Merrill Lynch Prce Fnner Smith .... C 858 673-6700
11811 Bernardo Plaza Ct San Diego (92128) *(P-11990)*

Merrill Lynch Prce Fnner Smith .... C 858 456-3600
7825 Fay Ave Ste 300 La Jolla (92037) *(P-11991)*

Merrill Lynch Prce Fnner Smith .... D 858 677-1300
12830 El Camino Real Ste 300 San Diego (92130) *(P-11992)*

Merrill Lynch Prce Fnner Smith .... C 619 699-3700
701 B St Ste 2350 San Diego (92101) *(P-11993)*

Merrill Lynch Prce Fnner Smith .... D 760 930-3100
1000 Aviara Dr Ste 200 Carlsbad (92011) *(P-11994)*

Merrimans Incorporated .... E 909 795-5301
32195 Dunlap Blvd Yucaipa (92399) *(P-4854)*

Merritt Hawkins & Assoc LLC (HQ) .... C 858 792-0711
12400 High Bluff Dr Ste 100 San Diego (92130) *(P-13544)*

Merritt Hospitality LLC .... C 714 738-7800
2701 Nutwood Ave Fullerton (92831) *(P-12921)*

Merritt Hospitality LLC .... C 562 983-3400
701 W Ocean Blvd Long Beach (90831) *(P-12922)*

Merry An Cejka .... E 323 560-3949
4601 Cecilia St Cudahy (90201) *(P-6174)*

Meruelo Enterprises Inc (PA) .... A 562 745-2300
9550 Firestone Blvd Ste 105 Downey (90241) *(P-560)*

Meruelo Group, Downey *Also Called: Meruelo Group LLC (P-17584)*

Meruelo Group LLC (PA) .... D 562 745-2300
9550 Firestone Blvd Ste 105 Downey (90241) *(P-17584)*

Mesa Associates Inc .... D 909 979-6609
3670 W Temple Ave Ste 152 Pomona (91768) *(P-17585)*

Mesa Energy Systems Inc (HQ) .... C 949 460-0460
2 Cromwell Irvine (92618) *(P-805)*

Mesa Insurance Solutions Inc .... C 805 308-6308
50 Castilian Dr Goleta (93117) *(P-12232)*

Mesa Management Inc .... D 949 851-0995
1451 Quail St Ste 201 Newport Beach (92660) *(P-12488)*

Mesa Pointe Stadium 12, Costa Mesa *Also Called: Edwards Theatres Circuit Inc (P-14937)*

Mesa Verde Country Club .... C 714 549-0377
3000 Club House Rd Costa Mesa (92626) *(P-15149)*

Mesa Verde Partners .... C 714 540-7500
1701 Golf Course Dr Costa Mesa (92626) *(P-15092)*

Mesa Verde Prosecute Care, Costa Mesa *Also Called: Mesa Vrde Cnvalescent Hosp Inc (P-15720)*

Mesa Vineyard Management Inc (PA) .... D 805 434-4100
110 Gibson Rd Templeton (93465) *(P-144)*

Mesa Vrde Cnvalescent Hosp Inc .... C 949 548-5584
661 Center St Costa Mesa (92627) *(P-15720)*

Mesfin Enterprises .... B 310 615-0881
222 N Pacific Coast Hwy Ste 1570 El Segundo (90245) *(P-14092)*

Messenger Express (PA) .... C 213 614-0475
5435 Cahuenga Blvd Ste C North Hollywood (91601) *(P-9007)*

Messer LLC .... E 626 855-8366
660 Baldwin Park Blvd City Of Industry (91746) *(P-3217)*

Messer LLC .... E 562 903-1290
13117 Meyer Rd Whittier (90605) *(P-3218)*

Messer LLC .... D 310 533-8394
2535 Del Amo Blvd Torrance (90503) *(P-3219)*

Mestek Inc 310 835-7500
1220 E Watson Center Rd Carson (90745) *(P-5978)*

Mesvision, Costa Mesa *Also Called: Medical Eye Services Inc (P-12231)*

Metabolic Response Modifiers, Oceanside *Also Called: Chemi-Source Inc (P-10617)*

Metacrine, San Diego *Also Called: Metacrine Inc (P-3451)*

Metacrine Inc .... E 858 369-7800
3985 Sorrento Valley Blvd Ste C San Diego (92121) *(P-3451)*

Metagenics LLC (PA) .... C 949 366-0818
25 Enterprise Ste 200 Aliso Viejo (92656) *(P-10633)*

Metal Art of California Inc (PA) .... D 714 532-7100
640 N Cypress St Orange (92867) *(P-8616)*

Metal Chem, Chatsworth *Also Called: Metal Chem Inc (P-5274)*

Metal Chem Inc .... E 818 727-9951
21514 Nordhoff St Chatsworth (91311) *(P-5274)*

Metal Coaters California Inc .... D 909 987-4681
9123 Center Ave Rancho Cucamonga (91730) *(P-5331)*

Metal Coaters System, Rancho Cucamonga *Also Called: Metal Coaters California Inc (P-5331)*

Metal Container Corporation .... C 951 354-0444
7155 Central Ave Riverside (92504) *(P-4721)*

Metal Container Corporation .... C 951 360-4500
10980 Inland Ave Jurupa Valley (91752) *(P-4722)*

Metal Engineering Inc .... E 626 334-1819
1642 S Sacramento Ave Ontario (91761) *(P-5005)*

Metal Finishing Pntg Lab Tstg, Oxnard *Also Called: Elite Metal Finishing LLC (P-5260)*

Metal Improvement Company LLC .... E 949 855-8010
35 Argonaut Ste A1 Laguna Hills (92656) *(P-4706)*

Metal Improvement Company LLC .... D 323 585-2168
2588 Industry Way Ste A Lynwood (90262) *(P-4707)*

Metal Improvement Company LLC .... D 818 983-1952
6940 Farmdale Ave North Hollywood (91605) *(P-4708)*

Metal Improvement Company LLC .... D 818 407-6280
20751 Superior St Chatsworth (91311) *(P-4709)*

Metal Master Inc .... E 858 292-8880
4611 Overland Ave San Diego (92123) *(P-5006)*

Metal Products Engineering, Vernon *Also Called: Luppen Holdings Inc (P-5200)*

Metal Supply LLC .... D 562 634-9940
11810 Center St South Gate (90280) *(P-4855)*

Metal Surfaces Intl LLC .... C 562 927-1331
6060 Shull St Bell Gardens (90201) *(P-5275)*

Metal-Fab Services Indust Inc .... E 714 630-7771
2500 E Miraloma Way Anaheim (92806) *(P-5007)*

Metalagraphics, Moorpark *Also Called: Glendee Corp (P-6136)*

Metalite Manufacturing, Pacoima *Also Called: Hanmar LLC (P-5190)*

Metalite Manufacturing Company .... E 818 890-2802
11441 Bradley Ave Pacoima (91331) *(P-5201)*

Metalite Mfg Companys, Pacoima *Also Called: Metalite Manufacturing Company (P-5201)*

Metalore Inc .... E 310 643-0360
750 S Douglas St El Segundo (90245) *(P-6175)*

Metals USA, Brea *Also Called: Metals USA Building Pdts LP (P-4615)*

Metals USA Building Pdts LP (DH) .... A 713 946-9000
955 Columbia St Brea (92821) *(P-4615)*

Metals USA Building Pdts LP .... D 800 325-1305
1951 S Parco Ave Ste C Ontario (91761) *(P-4616)*

Metals USA Building Pdts LP .... C 714 522-7852
6450 Caballero Blvd Ste A Buena Park (90620) *(P-4856)*

Metarom USA Inc .... E 619 449-0299
1725 Gillespie Way Ste 101 El Cajon (92020) *(P-1687)*

Metcal, Cypress *Also Called: OK International Inc (P-5648)*

Metco Fourslide Manufacturing, Gardena *Also Called: Metco Manufacturing Inc (P-5202)*

Metco Manufacturing Inc .... E 310 516-6547
17540 S Denver Ave Gardena (90248) *(P-5202)*

Metcoe Skylight Specialites, Gardena *Also Called: Weiss Sheet Metal Company (P-1099)*

METHODIST HOSPITAL, Arcadia *Also Called: Usc Arcadia Hospital (P-16249)*

Methodist Hospital of S CA .... D 626 574-3755
300 W Huntington Dr Arcadia (91007) *(P-16097)*

Metric Machining (PA) .... E 909 947-9222
3263 Trade Center Dr Riverside (92507) *(P-6176)*

Metro, Los Angeles *Also Called: Los Angles Cnty Mtro Trnsp Aut (P-8761)*

Metro, Sun Valley *Also Called: Los Angles Cnty Mtro Trnsp Aut (P-8769)*

Metro, Los Angeles *Also Called: Los Angles Cnty Mtro Trnsp Aut (P-8770)*

Mergent email: customerrelations@mergent.com
1106

2025 Southern California
Business Directory and Buyers Guide

(P-0000) Products & Services Section entry number
(PA)=Parent Co (HQ)=Headquarters (DH)=Div Headquarters

Metro Bldrs & Engineers Group, Newport Beach *Also Called: Houalla Enterprises Ltd (P-548)*

Metro Ports, Long Beach *Also Called: Suderman Contg Stevedores Inc (P-9148)*

Metro Truck Body Inc .... E 310 532-5570
240 Citation Cir Corona (92878) *(P-14677)*

Metro-Goldwyn-Mayer Inc (DH) .... B **310 449-3000**
245 N Beverly Dr Beverly Hills (90210) *(P-14838)*

Metrolink, Los Angeles *Also Called: Southern Cal Rgional Rail Auth (P-8806)*

Metrolink Doc, Pomona *Also Called: Southern Cal Rgional Rail Auth (P-8805)*

Metromedia Technologies Inc .... E 818 552-6500
311 Parkside Dr San Fernando (91340) *(P-5937)*

Metropltan Area Advsory Cmmtte (PA) .... D 619 426-3595
1355 Third Ave Chula Vista (91911) *(P-17062)*

Metropltan Wtr Dst of Sthern C .... B 909 593-7474
700 Moreno Ave La Verne (91750) *(P-9704)*

Metropltan Wtr Dst of Sthern C .... D 714 577-5031
3972 Valley View Ave Yorba Linda (92886) *(P-9705)*

Metropolis Hotel MGT LLC .... C 213 683-4855
899 Francisco St Los Angeles (90017) *(P-12923)*

Metropolitan Automotive Warehouse .... A 909 885-2886
535 Tennis Court Ln San Bernardino (92408) *(P-9834)*

Metropolitan Home Mortgage Inc .... D 949 428-0161
3090 Bristol St Ste 600 Costa Mesa (92626) *(P-11923)*

Metropolitan Imports LLC .... C 646 980-5343
19560 Eagle Ridge Ln Porter Ranch (91326) *(P-14550)*

Metropolitan News Company .... E 951 369-5890
3540 12th St Riverside (92501) *(P-2816)*

Metropolitan News Company, Los Angeles *Also Called: Grace Communications Inc (P-2800)*

Metropolitan Theatres Corp .... D 760 323-3221
789 E Tahquitz Canyon Way Palm Springs (92262) *(P-14942)*

Metropolitan Waste Disposal, Paramount *Also Called: Calmet Inc (P-9737)*

Metropolitan Water Lavern, La Verne *Also Called: Metropltan Wtr Dst of Sthern C (P-9704)*

Metropro Road Services Inc .... D 714 556-7600
957 W 17th St Costa Mesa (92627) *(P-14718)*

Metrostudy Inc .... C 714 619-7800
4000 Macarthur Blvd Ste 400 Newport Beach (92660) *(P-18171)*

Mets//, Manhattan Beach *Also Called: M & E Technical Services L L C (P-18264)*

Mettler Electronics Corp .... E 714 533-2221
1333 S Claudina St Anaheim (92805) *(P-8198)*

Metwest Total Return Bond Fund .... D 800 241-4671
865 S Figueroa St Los Angeles (90017) *(P-12636)*

Meundies Inc .... B 888 552-6775
9534 Jefferson Blvd Culver City (90232) *(P-10688)*

Meus, Cypress *Also Called: Mitsubishi Electric Us Inc (P-10267)*

Mevsa, Cypress *Also Called: Mitsubshi Elc Vsual Sltons AME (P-7027)*

Mexicali Inc .... C 661 327-3861
631 18th St Bakersfield (93301) *(P-11590)*

Mexicali Restaurant, Bakersfield *Also Called: Mexicali Inc (P-11590)*

Mexican Amrcn Oprtnty Fndation (PA) .... D 323 890-9600
401 N Garfield Ave Montebello (90640) *(P-16978)*

Meyco Machine and Tool Inc .... E 714 435-1546
11579 Martens River Cir Fountain Valley (92708) *(P-5616)*

Meziere Enterprises Inc .... E 800 208-1755
220 S Hale Ave Ste A Escondido (92029) *(P-6177)*

Mf Inc .... C 213 627-2498
2010 E 15th St Los Angeles (90021) *(P-2047)*

Mfb Liquidation Inc .... E 760 448-1940
6195 El Camino Real Carlsbad (92009) *(P-1513)*

Mfcp Parker Store, Santa Ana *Also Called: Motion and Flow Ctrl Pdts Inc (P-10450)*

Mflex, Irvine *Also Called: Multi-Fineline Electronix Inc (P-6753)*

Mflex Delaware Inc .... A 949 453-6800
101 Academy Ste 250 Irvine (92617) *(P-6751)*

MGA Entertainment Inc .... A 800 222-4685
9220 Winnetka Ave Chatsworth (91311) *(P-10525)*

MGB Construction Inc .... C 951 342-0303
91 Commercial Ave Riverside (92507) *(P-420)*

Mge Underground Inc .... B 805 238-3510
2501 Golden Hill Rd Paso Robles (93446) *(P-1173)*

Mgl, Anaheim *Also Called: Michael Gerald Ltd (P-10689)*

MGM, Beverly Hills *Also Called: Metro-Goldwyn-Mayer Inc (P-14838)*

MGM and Ua Services Company .... A 310 449-3000
245 N Beverly Dr Beverly Hills (90210) *(P-18375)*

MGM Transformer Co .... D 323 726-0888
5701 Smithway St Commerce (90040) *(P-6289)*

Mgr Design International Inc .... C 805 981-6400
1950 Williams Dr Oxnard (93036) *(P-8701)*

MGT Industries Inc (PA) .... D 310 516-5900
13889 S Figueroa St Los Angeles (90061) *(P-2121)*

Mh Sub I LLC (PA) .... B 310 280-4000
909 N Pacific Coast Hwy Fl 11 El Segundo (90245) *(P-13226)*

Mhf Mv Operating VI LLC .... D 619 481-5881
595 Hotel Cir S San Diego (92108) *(P-12924)*

Mhh Holdings Inc .... C 626 744-9370
415 S Lake Ave Ste 108 Pasadena (91101) *(P-10959)*

Mhh Holdings Inc .... C 949 651-9903
5653 Alton Pkwy Irvine (92618) *(P-10960)*

Mhm Services Inc .... C 805 904-6678
230 Station Way Arroyo Grande (93420) *(P-16486)*

MHRP Resort Inc .... D 760 249-5808
24510 Highway 2 Wrightwood (92397) *(P-12925)*

MHS, San Diego *Also Called: Mental Health Systems Inc (P-16485)*

MHS Customer Services Inc .... D 858 695-2151
7586 Trade St Ste C San Diego (92121) *(P-13545)*

MI Technologies Inc .... A 619 710-2637
2215 Paseo De Las Americas Ste 30 San Diego (92154) *(P-4169)*

Mias Fashion Mfg Co Inc .... B 562 906-1060
1734 Aeros Way Montebello (90640) *(P-10716)*

Michael Baker International Inc (DH) .... B 949 472-3505
5 Hutton Centre Dr Ste 500 Santa Ana (92707) *(P-17586)*

Michael G Frtnsce Physcl Thrap .... C 626 446-7027
24630 Washington Ave Ste 200 Murrieta (92562) *(P-15551)*

Michael Gerald Ltd .... E 562 921-9611
7051 E Avenida De Santiago Anaheim (92807) *(P-10689)*

Michael Levine Inc .... D 213 622-6259
920 Maple Ave Los Angeles (90015) *(P-11650)*

Michaelson Connor & Boul (PA) .... D 714 230-3600
5312 Bolsa Ave Huntington Beach (92649) *(P-18172)*

Michelson Laboratories Inc (PA) .... D 562 928-0553
6280 Chalet Dr Commerce (90040) *(P-17920)*

MICOP, Oxnard *Also Called: Mixtec/Ndgena Cmnty Orgnzing P (P-16979)*

Micro Analog Inc .... C 909 392-8277
1861 Puddingstone Dr La Verne (91750) *(P-6850)*

Micro Matrix Systems .... E 909 626-8544
1899 Salem Ct Claremont (91711) *(P-5203)*

Micro Steel Inc .... E 818 348-8701
7850 Alabama Ave Canoga Park (91304) *(P-7672)*

Micro Surface Engr Inc (PA) .... E 323 582-7348
1550 E Slauson Ave Los Angeles (90011) *(P-4718)*

Micro Therapeutics (HQ) .... E 949 837-3700
9775 Toledo Way Irvine (92618) *(P-8199)*

Micro-Mode Products Inc .... C 619 449-3844
1870 John Towers Ave El Cajon (92020) *(P-6632)*

Micro-Pro Microfilming Svcs, Long Beach *Also Called: Macro-Pro Inc (P-14536)*

Micro-Technology Concepts Inc .... D 626 839-6800
17837 Rowland St City Of Industry (91748) *(P-10018)*

Micro/Sys Inc .... E 818 244-4600
158 W Pomona Ave Monrovia (91016) *(P-5863)*

Microblend Inc .... E 330 998-4602
543 Country Club Dr Simi Valley (93065) *(P-3717)*

Microblend Technologies, Simi Valley *Also Called: Microblend Inc (P-3717)*

Microblend Technologies Inc 480 831-0757
4333 Park Terrace Dr Westlake Village (91361) *(P-11255)*

Microcosm Inc .... E 310 539-2306
3111 Lomita Blvd Torrance (90505) *(P-7663)*

Microfabrica Inc .... E 888 964-2763
7911 Haskell Ave Van Nuys (91406) *(P-7025)*

Microfinancial Incorporated .... C 805 367-8900
2801 Townsgate Rd Westlake Village (91361) *(P-13460)*

Microlease Inc (DH) .... D 866 520-0200
6060 Sepulveda Blvd Van Nuys (91411) *(P-13461)*

Micrometals Inc (PA) .... C 714 970-9400
5615 E La Palma Ave Anaheim (92807) *(P-7026)*

Micron Instruments, Simi Valley *Also Called: Piezo-Metrics Inc (P-6867)*

Employee Codes: A=Over 500 employees, B=251-500
C=101-250, D=51-100, E=20-50, F=10-19, G=1-9

2025 Southern California
Business Directory and Buyers Guide

© Mergent Inc. 1-800-342-5647

1107

Micronova Manufacturing Inc .... E 310 784-6990
3431 Lomita Blvd Torrance (90505) *(P-2217)*

Microplate, Inglewood *Also Called: Multichrome Company Inc (P-5277)*

Microsemi, Garden Grove *Also Called: Microsemi Corp -Rf Signal Proc (P-6853)*

Microsemi Communications Inc (DH) .... **D 805 388-3700**
4721 Calle Carga Camarillo (93012) *(P-6851)*

Microsemi Corp - Anlog Mxed Sg (DH) .... **D 714 898-8121**
11861 Western Ave Garden Grove (92841) *(P-6852)*

Microsemi Corp - Santa Ana, Garden Grove *Also Called: Microsemi Corporation (P-6854)*

Microsemi Corp -Rf Signal Proc (HQ) .... E 949 380-6100
11861 Western Ave Garden Grove (92841) *(P-6853)*

Microsemi Corp-Power MGT Group .... C 714 994-6500
11861 Western Ave Garden Grove (92841) *(P-6354)*

Microsemi Corporation .... C 714 898-7112
11861 Western Ave Garden Grove (92841) *(P-6854)*

Microsoft, Irvine *Also Called: Microsoft Corporation (P-13973)*

Microsoft Corporation .... E 949 263-3000
3 Park Plz Ste 1800 Irvine (92614) *(P-13973)*

Micross Holdings Inc .... D 215 997-3200
11150 Santa Monica Blvd Ste 750 Los Angeles (90025) *(P-6855)*

Microtek Lab Inc (HQ) .... **C 310 687-5823**
13337 South St Cerritos (90703) *(P-9976)*

Microvention Inc (DH) .... **C 714 258-8000**
35 Enterprise Aliso Viejo (92656) *(P-8200)*

Microvention Terumo, Aliso Viejo *Also Called: Microvention Inc (P-8200)*

Microwave Applications Group .... E 805 928-5711
3030 Industrial Pkwy Santa Maria (93455) *(P-17587)*

Mid-Century Insurance Company .... C 323 932-7116
6303 Owensmouth Ave Fl 1 Woodland Hills (91367) *(P-12130)*

Mid-State Concrete Pdts Inc .... E 805 928-2855
1625 E Donovan Rd Ste C Santa Maria (93454) *(P-4402)*

Mid-West Fabricating Co .... E 562 698-9615
8623 Dice Rd Santa Fe Springs (90670) *(P-7271)*

Mida Industries Inc .... C 562 616-1020
6101 Obispo Ave Long Beach (90805) *(P-13394)*

Midas Express Los Angeles Inc .... C 310 609-0366
11854 Alameda St Lynwood (90262) *(P-9089)*

Midland Credit Management, San Diego *Also Called: Midland Credit Management Inc (P-11869)*

Midland Credit Management Inc .... A 877 240-2377
350 Camino De La Reina Ste 100 San Diego (92108) *(P-11869)*

Midland Industries .... D 800 821-5725
659 E Ball Rd Anaheim (92805) *(P-10447)*

Midnight Manufacturing LLC .... E 714 833-6130
2535 Conejo Spectrum St Bldg 4 Thousand Oaks (91320) *(P-3319)*

Midnight Oil Agency LLC .... B 818 295-6100
3800 W Vanowen St Ste 101 Burbank (91505) *(P-3044)*

Midnight Oil Agency, Inc., Burbank *Also Called: Midnight Oil Agency LLC (P-3044)*

Midnight Sun Enterprises Inc .... D 310 532-2427
19900 Normandie Ave Torrance (90502) *(P-18335)*

Midstream Energy Partners USA .... E 661 765-4087
9224 Tupman Rd Tupman (93276) *(P-260)*

Midway Car Rental, North Hollywood *Also Called: Midway Rent A Car Inc (P-14652)*

Midway International Inc .... D 800 826-2383
13131 166th St Cerritos (90703) *(P-11129)*

Midway Rent A Car Inc .... D 619 238-9600
2263 Pacific Hwy San Diego (92101) *(P-14649)*

Midway Rent A Car Inc .... D 818 985-9770
4201 Lankershim Blvd North Hollywood (91602) *(P-14652)*

Mig Management Services LLC .... D 949 474-5800
660 Newport Center Dr Ste 1300 Newport Beach (92660) *(P-18012)*

Mighty Green, Costa Mesa *Also Called: Inveco Inc (P-5269)*

Mikada Cabinets, Los Angeles *Also Called: Mikada Cabinets LLC (P-2355)*

Mikada Cabinets LLC .... D
11777 San Vicente Blvd Ste 777 Los Angeles (90049) *(P-2355)*

Mikawaya, Vernon *Also Called: Mochi Ice Cream Company LLC (P-1461)*

Mike Campbell & Associates Ltd .... A 626 369-3981
10907 Downey Ave Ste 203 Downey (90241) *(P-9037)*

Mike Campbell Assoc Logictics, Downey *Also Called: Mike Campbell & Associates Ltd (P-9037)*

Mike Kenney Tool Inc .... E 714 577-9262
588 Porter Way Placentia (92870) *(P-6178)*

Mike Parker Landscape, Santa Ana *Also Called: Mpl Enterprises Inc (P-224)*

Mike Rovner Construction Inc .... C 949 458-1562
22600 Lambert St Lake Forest (92630) *(P-18013)*

Mikelson Machine Shop Inc .... E 626 448-3920
2546 Merced Ave South El Monte (91733) *(P-6179)*

Mikhail Darafeev Inc (PA) .... **E 909 613-1818**
5075 Edison Ave Chino (91710) *(P-2430)*

Mil-Spec Magnetics Inc .... D 909 598-8116
169 Pacific St Pomona (91768) *(P-6932)*

Milani Cosmetics, Vernon *Also Called: New Milani Group LLC (P-10639)*

Milbank Global Securities, Los Angeles *Also Called: Milbank Tweed Hdley McCloy LLP (P-16740)*

Milbank Tweed Hdley McCloy LLP .... C 424 386-4000
2029 Century Park E Los Angeles (90002) *(P-16740)*

Mile High Valet, Dana Point *Also Called: Ciri - Stroup Inc (P-13169)*

Mile Square Golf Course .... C 714 962-5541
10401 Warner Ave Fountain Valley (92708) *(P-15093)*

Milender White Inc .... D 303 216-0420
1401 Dove St Ste 500 Newport Beach (92660) *(P-421)*

Milgard Manufacturing LLC .... C 480 763-6000
26879 Diaz Rd Temecula (92590) *(P-4170)*

Milgard Manufacturing LLC .... D 805 581-6325
355 E Easy St Simi Valley (93065) *(P-4340)*

Milgard Windows, Temecula *Also Called: Milgard Manufacturing LLC (P-4170)*

Milgard-Simi Valley, Simi Valley *Also Called: Milgard Manufacturing LLC (P-4340)*

Milken Family Foundation .... C 310 570-4800
1250 4th St Fl 1 Santa Monica (90401) *(P-17356)*

Millcraft Inc .... D 714 632-9621
2850 E White Star Ave Anaheim (92806) *(P-2313)*

Millennia Stainless Inc .... D 562 946-3545
10016 Romandel Ave Santa Fe Springs (90670) *(P-10448)*

Millennial Brands LLC .... E 925 230-0617
126 W 9th St Los Angeles (90015) *(P-4286)*

Millennial Home Lending, Chatsworth *Also Called: Cake Mortgage Corp (P-11889)*

Millennium Biltmore Hotel, Los Angeles *Also Called: Whb Corporation (P-13079)*

Millennium Fire Prtection Corp .... D 760 722-2722
2218 Faraday Ave Ste 120 Carlsbad (92008) *(P-806)*

Millennium Health LLC .... B 877 451-3534
16981 Via Tazon Ste F San Diego (92127) *(P-17921)*

Millennium Reinforcing Inc .... B 949 361-9730
1046 Calle Recodo San Clemente (92673) *(P-1159)*

Millennium Space Systems Inc (HQ) .... **E 310 683-5840**
2265 E El Segundo Blvd El Segundo (90245) *(P-6633)*

Millenworks .... D 714 426-5500
1361 Valencia Ave Tustin (92780) *(P-7185)*

Miller and Associates, Los Angeles *Also Called: Imhoff & Associates PC (P-16705)*

Miller Automotive Group Inc (HQ) .... **B 818 787-8400**
5425 Van Nuys Blvd Sherman Oaks (91401) *(P-11379)*

Miller Castings Inc (PA) .... **B 562 695-0461**
2503 Pacific Park Dr Whittier (90601) *(P-4567)*

Miller Castings Inc .... E 562 695-0461
12245 Coast Dr Whittier (90601) *(P-6180)*

Miller Children's Hospital, Long Beach *Also Called: Long Beach Medical Center (P-16086)*

MILLER CHILDREN'S HOSPITAL, Long Beach *Also Called: Memorial Medical Center Foundation (P-17466)*

Miller Environmental Inc .... C 714 385-0099
1130 W Trenton Ave Orange (92867) *(P-1185)*

Miller Gasket Co, San Fernando *Also Called: J Miller Co Inc (P-3893)*

Miller Kaplan Arase LLP (PA) .... **C 818 769-2010**
4123 Lankershim Blvd North Hollywood (91602) *(P-17746)*

Miller Marine .... E 619 791-1500
2275 Manya St San Diego (92154) *(P-7604)*

Miller Nissan, Sherman Oaks *Also Called: Miller Automotive Group Inc (P-11379)*

Millers Woodworking, Tustin *Also Called: GL Woodworking Inc (P-2307)*

Millie and Severson Inc .... D 562 493-3611
3601 Serpentine Dr Los Alamitos (90720) *(P-492)*

Million Corporation .... D 626 969-1888
1300 W Optical Dr Ste 600 Irwindale (91702) *(P-3155)*

Mergent email: customerrelations@mergent.com
1108

2025 Southern California
Business Directory and Buyers Guide

(P-0000) Products & Services Section entry number
(PA)=Parent Co (HQ)=Headquarters (DH)=Div Headquarters

Mills Corporation .... C 909 484-8300
1 Mills Cir Ste 1 Ontario (91764) *(P-12304)*

Mills Iron Works .... D 323 321-6520
14834 S Maple Ave Gardena (90248) *(P-10449)*

Millworks Etc Inc .... E 805 499-3400
2230 Statham Blvd Ste 100 Oxnard (93033) *(P-4894)*

Millworks By Design Inc .... E 818 597-1326
4525 Runway St Simi Valley (93063) *(P-2314)*

Milodon Incorporated .... E 805 577-5950
2250 Agate Ct Simi Valley (93065) *(P-7272)*

Milwaukee Hand Truck, Los Angeles *Also Called: Gleason Industrial Pdts Inc (P-5530)*

Milwood Healthcare Inc .... D 626 274-4345
2641 S C St Oxnard (93033) *(P-12305)*

Min-E-Con LLC .... D 949 250-0087
17312 Eastman Irvine (92614) *(P-6955)*

Mind Research Institute .... C 949 345-8700
5281 California Ave Ste 300 Irvine (92617) *(P-17882)*

Mindbody, San Luis Obispo *Also Called: Mindbody Inc (P-14146)*

Mindbody Inc (PA) .... C 877 755-4279
651 Tank Farm Rd San Luis Obispo (93401) *(P-14146)*

Mindera Corp .... E 858 810-6070
1221 Liberty Way Vista (92081) *(P-3583)*

Mindgruve Holdings Inc .... C 619 757-1325
627 8th Ave Ste 300 San Diego (92101) *(P-13227)*

Mindrum Precision Inc .... E 909 989-1728
10000 4th St Rancho Cucamonga (91730) *(P-7892)*

Mindrum Precision Products, Rancho Cucamonga *Also Called: Mindrum Precision Inc (P-7892)*

Mindshow Inc .... E 213 531-0277
811 W 7th St Ste 500 Los Angeles (90017) *(P-13974)*

Mindspeed Technologies LLC (HQ) .... D 949 579-3000
4000 Macarthur Blvd Newport Beach (92660) *(P-6856)*

Mindwave Software, San Diego *Also Called: Isaac Fair Corporation (P-13756)*

Mine, Los Angeles *Also Called: Edgemine Inc (P-10707)*

Ming Entertainment Group LLC .... D 949 679-2089
2082 Business Center Dr Ste 292 Irvine (92612) *(P-14999)*

Ming Tsuang Dr .... D 858 822-2464
9500 Gillman Dr Mc 0603 La Jolla (92093) *(P-15389)*

Minh Phung Incorporated .... E 714 379-0606
15216 Weststate St Westminster (92683) *(P-10961)*

Miniluxe, Los Angeles *Also Called: Miniluxe Inc (P-13151)*

Miniluxe Inc .... D 424 442-1630
11965 San Vicente Blvd Los Angeles (90049) *(P-13151)*

Minka Group, Corona *Also Called: Minka Lighting LLC (P-10194)*

Minka Lighting LLC (DH) .... D 951 735-9220
1151 Bradford Cir Corona (92882) *(P-10194)*

Minshew Brothers Stl Cnstr Inc C
12578 Vigilante Rd Lakeside (92040) *(P-493)*

Minsley Inc (PA) .... E 909 458-1100
989 S Monterey Ave Ontario (91761) *(P-1816)*

Minson Corporation .... B 323 513-1041
11701 Wilshire Blvd Ste 15a Los Angeles (90025) *(P-2455)*

Mintie Technologies, Azusa *Also Called: Mc-40 (P-13389)*

Mintz Levin Cohn Ferris GL .... D 858 314-1500
3580 Carmel Mountain Rd Ste 300 San Diego (92130) *(P-16741)*

Minus K Technology Inc .... C 310 348-9656
460 Hindry Ave Ste C Inglewood (90301) *(P-8054)*

Mir3 Inc .... D 858 724-1200
3398 Carmel Mountain Rd Ste 100 San Diego (92121) *(P-13771)*

Mira Loma Dry Depot, Jurupa Valley *Also Called: Costco Wholesale Corporation (P-9055)*

Mirada, Long Beach *Also Called: Motion Theory Inc (P-13332)*

Mirada Hlls Rehb Cnvlscent Hos, La Mirada *Also Called: Life Care Centers America Inc (P-15696)*

Miradry, Irvine *Also Called: Mist Inc (P-8288)*

Mirage Post Acute, Lancaster *Also Called: Pacs Group Inc (P-15730)*

Mirama Enterprises Inc .... D 858 587-8866
6469 Flanders Dr San Diego (92121) *(P-6387)*

Miramar Acquisition Co LLC .... C 805 900-8338
1759 S Jameson Ln Santa Barbara (93108) *(P-12719)*

Miramar Ford Truck Sales Inc .... D 619 272-5340
6066 Miramar Rd San Diego (92121) *(P-9806)*

Miramar Hotel, Santa Barbara *Also Called: Morgans Hotel Group MGT LLC (P-12930)*

Miramar Plant 33, San Diego *Also Called: Robertsons Ready Mix Ltd (P-4452)*

Miramar Transportation Inc .... D 858 693-0071
9340 Cabot Dr Ste I San Diego (92126) *(P-9313)*

Miramax LLC .... C 310 409-4321
1901 Avenue Of The Stars Ste 2000 Los Angeles (90067) *(P-14839)*

Miramonte Enterprises LLC .... C 951 658-9441
275 N San Jacinto St Hemet (92543) *(P-15721)*

Miro Technologies Inc .... C 858 677-2100
5643 Copley Dr San Diego (92111) *(P-14093)*

Mirum Inc .... C 619 237-5552
350 10th Ave Ste 1200 San Diego (92101) *(P-13331)*

Mis Sciences Corp .... C 818 847-0213
2550 N Hollywood Way Ste 404 Burbank (91505) *(P-9448)*

Misa Imports Inc .... D 562 281-6773
2343 Saybrook Ave Commerce (90040) *(P-11130)*

MISSION, Oxnard *Also Called: Mission Produce Inc (P-115)*

Mission Ambulance Inc .... D 951 272-2300
400 Ramona Ave Corona (92879) *(P-8841)*

MISSION BARGAIN CENTER, Oxnard *Also Called: Rescue Mission Alliance (P-17469)*

Mission Brewery Inc .... E 619 818-7147
8830 Rehco Rd San Diego (92121) *(P-11616)*

Mission Care Center, Rosemead *Also Called: Ensign Group Inc (P-15641)*

Mission Cloud Services Inc (PA) .... C 855 647-7466
9350 Wilshire Blvd Ste 203 Beverly Hills (90212) *(P-14234)*

Mission Community Bancorp .... C 805 782-5000
3380 S Higuera St San Luis Obispo (93401) *(P-11736)*

MISSION COMMUNITY HOSPITAL, Panorama City *Also Called: Deanco Healthcare LLC (P-15973)*

Mission Edge San Diego .... D 877 232-4541
2820 Roosevelt Rd Ste 104 San Diego (92106) *(P-17286)*

Mission Federal Credit Union .... C 858 531-5106
4250 Clairemont Mesa Blvd Ste B San Diego (92117) *(P-11805)*

Mission Federal Credit Union .... C 858 524-2850
5500 Grossmont Center Dr Ste 113 La Mesa (91942) *(P-11806)*

Mission Federal Credit Union (PA) .... D 858 546-2184
5785 Oberlin Dr Ste 312 San Diego (92121) *(P-11807)*

Mission Federal Services LLC (PA) .... C 858 524-2850
10325 Meanley Dr San Diego (92131) *(P-11808)*

Mission Foods, Rancho Cucamonga *Also Called: Gruma Corporation (P-1723)*

Mission Foods, Commerce *Also Called: Gruma Corporation (P-1724)*

Mission Healthcare, San Diego *Also Called: Mission HM Hlth San Diego LLC (P-16406)*

Mission Hills Country Club Inc .... C 760 324-9400
34600 Mission Hills Dr Rancho Mirage (92270) *(P-15150)*

Mission Hills Health Care Inc .... D 619 297-4086
726 Torrance St San Diego (92103) *(P-15722)*

Mission Hills Healthcare Ctr, San Diego *Also Called: Mission Hills Health Care Inc (P-15722)*

Mission Hills Mortgage Bankers, Irvine *Also Called: Mission Hills Mortgage Corp (P-11924)*

Mission Hills Mortgage Corp (HQ) .... C 714 972-3832
18500 Von Karman Ave Ste 1100 Irvine (92612) *(P-11924)*

Mission HM Hlth San Diego LLC .... D 619 757-2700
2365 Northside Dr Ste 200 San Diego (92108) *(P-16406)*

Mission Hosp Regional Med Ctr (PA) .... A 949 364-1400
27700 Medical Center Rd Mission Viejo (92691) *(P-16098)*

MISSION HOSPITAL, Mission Viejo *Also Called: Auxilary of Mssion Hosp Mssion (P-15919)*

MISSION HOSPITAL, Mission Viejo *Also Called: Mission Hosp Regional Med Ctr (P-16098)*

Mission Inn Hotel and Spa, The, Riverside *Also Called: Historic Mission Inn Corp (P-12850)*

Mission Internal Med Group Inc .... D 949 364-3570
26800 Crown Valley Pkwy Ste 103 Mission Viejo (92691) *(P-15390)*

Mission Internal Med Group Inc .... D 949 364-3605
27882 Forbes Rd Ste 110 Laguna Niguel (92677) *(P-15391)*

Mission Kleensweep Prod Inc .... D 323 223-1405
13644 Live Oak Ln Baldwin Park (91706) *(P-3594)*

Mission Laboratories, Baldwin Park *Also Called: Mission Kleensweep Prod Inc (P-3594)*

Mission Ldscp Companies Inc .... C 714 545-9962
16672 Millikan Ave Irvine (92606) *(P-178)*

Mission Linen & Uniform Svc, Lancaster *Also Called: Mission Linen Supply (P-13118)*

Mission Linen & Uniform Svc, Oxnard *Also Called: Mission Linen Supply (P-13119)*

Mission Linen & Uniform Svc, Santa Barbara *Also Called: Mission Linen Supply (P-13120)*

**A
L
P
H
A
B
E
T
I
C**

Mission Linen & Uniform Svc, Santa Maria *Also Called: Mission Linen Supply* *(P-13121)*

Mission Linen & Uniform Svc, Oceanside *Also Called: Mission Linen Supply* *(P-13122)*

Mission Linen & Uniform Svc, Chino *Also Called: Mission Linen Supply* *(P-13123)*

Mission Linen Supply .... D 661 948-5052
619 W Avenue I Lancaster (93534) *(P-13118)*

Mission Linen Supply .... D 805 485-6794
505 Maulhardt Ave Oxnard (93030) *(P-13119)*

Mission Linen Supply .... C 805 962-7687
712 E Montecito St Santa Barbara (93103) *(P-13120)*

Mission Linen Supply .... D 805 922-3579
602 S Western Ave Santa Maria (93458) *(P-13121)*

Mission Linen Supply .... C 760 757-9099
2727 Industry St Oceanside (92054) *(P-13122)*

Mission Linen Supply .... C 909 393-6857
5400 Alton Way Chino (91710) *(P-13123)*

Mission Medical Clinic, Pomona *Also Called: Western Univ Hlth Sciences (P-15511)*

Mission Microwave Tech LLC (PA) .... D **951 893-4925**
6060 Phyllis Dr Cypress (90630) *(P-6634)*

Mission Plastics Inc .... C 909 947-7287
1930 S Parco Ave Ontario (91761) *(P-4171)*

Mission Pools of Escondido .... C 949 588-0100
27439 Bostik Ct Temecula (92590) *(P-1216)*

Mission Pools of Lake Forest, Temecula *Also Called: Mission Pools of Escondido (P-1216)*

Mission Produce Inc (PA) .... D **805 981-3650**
2710 Camino Del Sol Oxnard (93030) *(P-115)*

Mission Rubber Company LLC .... C 951 736-1313
1660 Leeson Ln Corona (92879) *(P-5389)*

Mission Service Inc .... A 323 266-2593
1800 Avenue Of The Stars Ste 1400 Los Angeles (90067) *(P-14695)*

Mission Terrace, Santa Barbara *Also Called: Cliff View Terrace Inc (P-17131)*

Mission Valley YMCA, San Diego *Also Called: YMCA of San Diego County (P-17396)*

Mission Viejo Country Club .... C 949 582-1550
26200 Country Club Dr Mission Viejo (92691) *(P-15151)*

Mission View Health Center, San Luis Obispo *Also Called: Compass Health Inc (P-15598)*

Mission Vly Cab / Counter Tech, Poway *Also Called: B Young Enterprises Inc (P-2339)*

Mission Volkswagen Inc .... D 949 493-4511
32922 Valle Rd San Juan Capistrano (92675) *(P-11380)*

Mist Inc .... C 408 940-8700
3333 Michelson Dr Ste 650 Irvine (92612) *(P-8288)*

Misyd Corp (PA) .... D **213 742-1800**
30 Fremont Pl Los Angeles (90005) *(P-2167)*

Mitchell Fabrication .... E 909 590-0393
4564 Mission Blvd Montclair (91763) *(P-4857)*

Mitchell International Inc (PA) .... C 866 389-2069
9771 Clairemont Mesa Blvd Ste A San Diego (92124) *(P-14094)*

Mitchell Rubber Products LLC (PA) .... C **951 681-5655**
1880 Iowa Ave Ste 400 Riverside (92507) *(P-3924)*

Mitchell Silberberg Knupp LLP (PA) .... C **310 312-2000**
2049 Century Park E Fl 18 Los Angeles (90067) *(P-16742)*

Mitchell Slbrberg Knupp Fndtio, Los Angeles *Also Called: Mitchell Silberberg Knupp LLP (P-16742)*

Mitco Industries Inc (PA) .... E **909 877-0800**
2235 S Vista Ave Bloomington (92316) *(P-6181)*

Mitek, San Diego *Also Called: Mitek Systems Inc (P-13975)*

Mitek Systems Inc (PA) .... D **619 269-6800**
770 1st Ave Ste 425 San Diego (92101) *(P-13975)*

Mitratech Holdings Inc .... C 323 964-0000
5900 Wilshire Blvd Ste 1500 Los Angeles (90036) *(P-13976)*

Mitsubishi Cement Corporation .... B 562 495-0600
1150 Pier F Ave Long Beach (90802) *(P-4356)*

Mitsubishi Cement Corporation .... C 760 248-7373
5808 State Highway 18 Lucerne Valley (92356) *(P-4357)*

Mitsubishi Chemical Carbon Fiber and Composites, Inc., Irvine *Also Called: Mitsubishi Chemical Crbn Fbr (P-3772)*

Mitsubishi Chemical Crbn Fbr .... C 800 929-5471
1822 Reynolds Ave Irvine (92614) *(P-3772)*

Mitsubishi Electric Us Inc (DH) .... C 714 220-2500
5900 Katella Ave Ste A Cypress (90630) *(P-10267)*

Mitsubishi Motors Cr Amer Inc (DH) .... B **714 799-4730**
6400 Katella Ave Cypress (90630) *(P-11855)*

Mitsubshi Elc Vsual Sltons AME .... C 800 553-7278
10833 Valley View St Ste 300 Cypress (90630) *(P-7027)*

Mittal Ram .... D 310 769-6669
100 E Hillcrest Blvd Inglewood (90301) *(P-10325)*

Miva Inc .... C 858 490-2570
16870 W Bernardo Dr 100 San Diego (92127) *(P-14095)*

Miva Merchant, San Diego *Also Called: Miva Inc (P-14095)*

Mixed Nuts Inc .... E 323 587-6887
7909 Crossway Dr Pico Rivera (90660) *(P-1514)*

Mixmode Inc .... E 858 225-2352
111 W Micheltorena St Ste 300-A Santa Barbara (93101) *(P-13977)*

Mixtec/Ndgena Cmnty Orgnzing P .... D 805 483-1166
135 Magnolia Ave Oxnard (93030) *(P-16979)*

Mizkan America Inc .... D 909 484-8743
10037 8th St Rancho Cucamonga (91730) *(P-1817)*

Mj Best Videographer LLC .... C 209 208-8432
14005 S Berendo Ave Apt 3 Gardena (90247) *(P-6545)*

Mjc America Ltd (PA) .... E **888 876-5387**
20035 E Walnut Dr N Walnut (91789) *(P-6398)*

Mjw Inc .... D 323 778-8900
1328 W Slauson Ave Los Angeles (90044) *(P-5737)*

Mk Davidson Inc .... E 949 698-2963
3333 W Coast Hwy Ste 200 Newport Beach (92663) *(P-6688)*

Mk Diamond Products Inc (PA) .... D **310 539-5221**
1315 Storm Pkwy Torrance (90501) *(P-5636)*

Mk Luxury Group, Beverly Hills *Also Called: Maurice Kraiem & Company (P-10549)*

Mk Magnetics Inc .... D 760 246-6373
17030 Muskrat Ave Adelanto (92301) *(P-4538)*

Mk Manufacturing, Irvine *Also Called: M K Products Inc (P-5647)*

Mkt Innovations .... D 714 524-7668
588 Porter Way Placentia (92870) *(P-6182)*

Mkt Innovations, Placentia *Also Called: Mike Kenney Tool Inc (P-6178)*

Mktg Inc .... A 310 972-7900
5800 Bristol Pkwy Ste 500 Culver City (90230) *(P-14551)*

MKTG, INC., Culver City *Also Called: Mktg Inc (P-14551)*

ML Kishigo Mfg Co LLC .... D 949 852-1963
11250 Slater Ave Fountain Valley (92708) *(P-2199)*

ML Mortgage, Rancho Cucamonga *Also Called: ML Mortgage Corp (P-11948)*

ML Mortgage Corp .... D 909 652-0780
8270 Aspen St Rancho Cucamonga (91730) *(P-11948)*

Mlim Holdings LLC .... A 619 299-3131
350 Camino De La Reina San Diego (92108) *(P-12603)*

Mlk Community Hospital .... C 424 338-8000
1680 E 120th St Los Angeles (90059) *(P-16099)*

MMC, Los Angeles *Also Called: Marsh Risk & Insurance Svcs (P-12230)*

MMC, San Diego *Also Called: Medical Management Cons Inc (P-18168)*

Mmca, Cypress *Also Called: Mitsubishi Motors Cr Amer Inc (P-11855)*

Mmi Services Inc .... C 661 589-9366
4042 Patton Way Bakersfield (93308) *(P-345)*

Mmp Sheet Metal Inc .... E 562 691-1055
501 Commercial Way La Habra (90631) *(P-5008)*

Mmxviii Holdings Inc .... E 800 672-3974
20251 Sw Acacia St Ste 120 Newport Beach (92660) *(P-8617)*

Mnm Corporation (PA) .... E **213 627-3737**
110 E 9th St Ste A777 Los Angeles (90079) *(P-2865)*

Mnm Manufacturing Inc .... D 310 898-1099
3019 E Harcourt St Compton (90221) *(P-4895)*

MNS Engineers Inc (PA) .... D **805 692-6921**
201 N Calle Cesar Chavez Ste 300 Santa Barbara (93103) *(P-17588)*

Moark LLC .... D 850 378-2005
12005 Cabernet Dr Fontana (92337) *(P-10837)*

Mob Scene LLC .... C 323 648-7200
8447 Wilshire Blvd Ste 100 Beverly Hills (90211) *(P-13228)*

Mob Scene Creative Productions, Beverly Hills *Also Called: Mob Scene LLC (P-13228)*

Mobile Line Communications Corporation .... D
1402 Morgan Cir Tustin (92780) *(P-10268)*

Mobile Modular Management Corp .... C 800 819-1084
11450 Mission Blvd Jurupa Valley (91752) *(P-5084)*

Mobilenet Services Inc (PA) .... C **949 951-4444**
18 Morgan Ste 200 Irvine (92618) *(P-17589)*

Mobilitie Services, LLC, Irvine *Also Called: Boldyn Networks US Services LL (P-9427)*

Mobility Solutions Inc (PA) .... E 858 278-0591
7895 Convoy Ct Ste 11 San Diego (92111) *(P-10092)*

Mobilityware, Irvine *Also Called: Upstanding LLC (P-14061)*

Mobis Parts America LLC (HQ) .... D 786 515-1101
10550 Talbert Ave Fl 4 Fountain Valley (92708) *(P-9835)*

Mobis Ventures Sv, Fountain Valley *Also Called: Mobis Parts America LLC (P-9835)*

Mobisystems Inc .... C 858 350-0315
4501 Mission Bay Dr Ste 3a San Diego (92109) *(P-14096)*

Mobiz, Redlands *Also Called: Mobiz It Inc (P-940)*

Mobiz It Inc .... D 909 453-6700
1175 Idaho St Ste 103 Redlands (92374) *(P-940)*

Moc Products Company Inc (PA) .... D 818 794-3500
12306 Montague St Pacoima (91331) *(P-3815)*

Mocean, Los Angeles *Also Called: Mocean LLC (P-14147)*

Mocean LLC .... C 310 481-0808
2440 S Sepulveda Blvd Ste 150 Los Angeles (90064) *(P-14147)*

Mochi Ice Cream Company LLC (PA) .... E 323 587-5504
5563 Alcoa Ave Vernon (90058) *(P-1461)*

Mod-Electronics Inc .... E 310 322-2136
142 Sierra St El Segundo (90245) *(P-8447)*

Modalai Inc .... E 858 247-7053
10855 Sorrento Valley Rd Ste 2 San Diego (92121) *(P-6752)*

Modelo Group Inc .... E 562 446-5091
16751 Millikan Ave Irvine (92606) *(P-17590)*

Modern Campus USA Inc (PA) .... D 805 484-9400
1320 Flynn Rd Ste 100 Camarillo (93012) *(P-13772)*

Modern Candle Co Inc .... E 323 441-0104
12884 Bradley Ave Sylmar (91342) *(P-11131)*

Modern Candles, Sylmar *Also Called: Modern Candle Co Inc (P-11131)*

Modern Concepts Inc .... D 310 637-0013
3121 E Ana St E Rncho Dmngz (90221) *(P-4172)*

Modern Dev Co A Ltd Partnr .... D 949 646-6400
7900 All America City Way Paramount (90723) *(P-14552)*

Modern Embroidery Inc .... E 714 436-9960
3701 W Moore Ave Santa Ana (92704) *(P-2252)*

Modern Engine Inc .... E 818 409-9494
701 Sonora Ave Glendale (91201) *(P-6183)*

Modern Gourmet Foods, Santa Ana *Also Called: Coastal Cocktails Inc (P-10938)*

Modern Parking Inc .... C 310 821-1081
14110 Palawan Way Marina Del Rey (90292) *(P-14659)*

Modern Parking Inc .... C 818 783-3143
4955 Van Nuys Blvd Frnt Van Nuys (91403) *(P-14660)*

Modern Parking Inc .... C 619 233-0412
1025 W Laurel St Ste 105 San Diego (92101) *(P-14661)*

Modern Plating, Los Angeles *Also Called: Alco Plating Corp (P-5226)*

Modern Postcard, Carlsbad *Also Called: Iris Group Inc (P-3149)*

Modern Printing & Mailing Inc .... E 619 222-0535
3535 Enterprise St San Diego (92110) *(P-3045)*

Modern Woodworks, Canoga Park *Also Called: Modern Woodworks Inc (P-6467)*

Modern Woodworks Inc .... E 800 575-3475
7949 Deering Ave Canoga Park (91304) *(P-6467)*

Modernica, Vernon *Also Called: Modernica Inc (P-11517)*

Modernica Inc (PA) .... E 323 826-1600
2901 Saco St Vernon (90058) *(P-11517)*

Modified Plastics Inc (PA) .... E 714 546-4667
1240 E Glenwood Pl Santa Ana (92707) *(P-4173)*

Modis, Glendale *Also Called: Akkodis Inc (P-13646)*

Modivcare Solutions LLC .... C 714 503-6871
770 The City Dr S Orange (92868) *(P-9314)*

Modular Metal Fabricators Inc .... C 951 242-3154
24600 Nandina Ave Moreno Valley (92551) *(P-5009)*

Modular Wind Energy Inc .... D 562 304-6782
1709 Apollo Ct Seal Beach (90740) *(P-5459)*

Modus Advanced Inc .... D 925 960-8700
2772 Loker Ave W Carlsbad (92010) *(P-3925)*

Moelis & Company LLC .... C 310 443-2300
10100 Santa Monica Blvd Ste 1600 Los Angeles (90067) *(P-12664)*

Moeller Mfg & Sup LLC .... E 714 999-5551
630 E Lambert Rd Brea (92821) *(P-4781)*

Moffatt & Nichol .... D 657 261-2699
555 Anton Blvd Ste 400 Costa Mesa (92626) *(P-17591)*

Moffatt & Nichol, Costa Mesa *Also Called: Moffatt & Nichol (P-17591)*

Mogami, Torrance *Also Called: Marshall Electronics Inc (P-6544)*

Mogul .... E 424 245-4331
10106 Sunbrook Dr Beverly Hills (90210) *(P-7273)*

Mohawk Industries Inc .... E 909 357-1064
9687 Transportation Way Fontana (92335) *(P-1954)*

Mohawk Medical Group Inc .... D 661 324-4747
9500 Stockdale Hwy Ste 200 Bakersfield (93311) *(P-16100)*

Mohawk Western Plastics Inc .... E 909 593-7547
1496 Arrow Hwy La Verne (91750) *(P-2735)*

Mojave Foods Corporation .... C 323 890-8900
6000 E Slauson Ave Commerce (90040) *(P-1818)*

Mojave Foods Corporation (HQ) .... D 323 890-8900
6200 E Slauson Ave Los Angeles (90040) *(P-1819)*

Molded Fiber GL Companies - W .... D 760 246-4042
9400 Holly Rd Adelanto (92301) *(P-4174)*

Moldex, Culver City *Also Called: Moldex-Metric Inc (P-8289)*

Moldex-Metric Inc .... B 310 837-6500
10111 Jefferson Blvd Culver City (90232) *(P-8289)*

Molding Corporation America .... E 818 890-7877
10349 Norris Ave Pacoima (91331) *(P-4175)*

Mole-Richardson Co Ltd (PA) .... D 323 851-0111
12154 Montague St Pacoima (91331) *(P-6511)*

Moleaer Inc .... D 424 558-3567
3232 W El Segundo Blvd Hawthorne (90250) *(P-5738)*

Molecular Bio Products, San Diego *Also Called: Thermo Fisher Scientific Inc (P-7987)*

Molecular Bioproducts Inc (DH) .... C 858 453-7551
9389 Waples St San Diego (92121) *(P-7968)*

Molecular Probes Inc .... E 760 603-7200
5781 Van Allen Way Carlsbad (92008) *(P-3545)*

Molina Healthcare, Long Beach *Also Called: Molina Healthcare Inc (P-15392)*

Molina Healthcare Inc .... C 310 221-3031
1500 Hughes Way Long Beach (90810) *(P-12098)*

Molina Healthcare Inc (PA) .... A 562 435-3666
200 Oceangate Ste 100 Long Beach (90802) *(P-15392)*

Molina Healthcare Inc .... D 888 562-5442
604 Pine Ave Long Beach (90802) *(P-16587)*

Molina Healthcare Inc .... A 562 435-3666
1 Golden Shore Long Beach (90802) *(P-16588)*

Molina Healthcare Inc .... C 858 614-1580
9275 Sky Park Ct Ste 190 San Diego (92123) *(P-16589)*

Molina Healthcare California .... A 800 526-8196
200 Oceangate Ste 100 Long Beach (90802) *(P-15393)*

Molina Healthcare New York Inc .... D 888 562-5442
200 Oceangate Ste 100 Long Beach (90802) *(P-15394)*

Molina Hlthcare Cal Prtner Pla .... C 562 435-3666
200 Oceangate Ste 100 Long Beach (90802) *(P-12065)*

Molina Pathways LLC .... B 562 491-5773
200 Oceangate Ste 100 Long Beach (90802) *(P-15395)*

Molino Company .... D 323 726-1000
13712 Alondra Blvd Cerritos (90703) *(P-3046)*

Molnar Engineering Inc .... E 818 993-3495
20731 Marilla St Chatsworth (91311) *(P-6184)*

Momeni Engineering LLC .... E 714 897-9301
5451 Argosy Ave Huntington Beach (92649) *(P-6185)*

Momentous Insurance Brkg Inc .... C 818 933-2700
5990 Sepulveda Blvd Ste 550 Van Nuys (91411) *(P-12233)*

Momentum Textiles LLC (PA) .... E 949 833-8886
17811 Fitch Irvine (92614) *(P-10668)*

Momentum Textiles Wallcovering, Irvine *Also Called: Momentum Textiles LLC (P-10668)*

Monaco Baking Company, Fullerton *Also Called: Phenix Gourmet LLC (P-1491)*

Monadnock Company .... C 626 964-6581
16728 Gale Ave City Of Industry (91745) *(P-4782)*

Monarch Beach Golf Links (HQ) .... D 949 240-8247
50 Monarch Beach Resort N Dana Point (92629) *(P-15094)*

Monarch E & S Insurance Svcs .... D 559 226-0200
2540 Foothill Blvd # 101 La Crescenta (91214) *(P-12234)*

Monarch Healthcare A Medical (HQ) .... D 949 923-3200
11 Technology Dr Irvine (92618) *(P-15396)*

A
L
P
H
A
B
E
T
I
C

Employee Codes: A=Over 500 employees, B=251-500
C=101-250, D=51-100, E=20-50, F=10-19, G=1-9

2025 Southern California
Business Directory and Buyers Guide

© Mergent Inc. 1-800-342-5647

1111

Monarch Healthcare A Medical .... C 949 489-1960
675 Camino De Los Mares Ste 300 San Clemente (92673) *(P-15397)*

Monarch Hlthcare A Med Group I .... C 760 730-9448
2562 State St Carlsbad (92008) *(P-16590)*

Monarch Landscape Holdings LLC (PA).................................... C 213 816-1750
550 S Hope St Ste 1675 Los Angeles (90071) *(P-223)*

Monarch Litho Inc (PA)... E 323 727-0300
1501 Date St Montebello (90640) *(P-3047)*

Monarch Nut Company LLC .... C 661 725-6458
786 Road 188 Delano (93215) *(P-116)*

Monark LP .... D 310 769-6669
2804 W El Segundo Blvd Gardena (90249) *(P-12359)*

Mondelez Global LLC .... D 909 605-0140
5815 Clark St Ontario (91761) *(P-10962)*

Mondrian Holdings LLC ....B 323 848-6004
8440 W Sunset Blvd West Hollywood (90069) *(P-12926)*

Mondrian Hotel, Los Angeles *Also Called: Morgans Hotel Group MGT LLC (P-12931)*

Monex, Newport Beach *Also Called: Monex Deposit A Cal Ltd Partnr (P-11642)*

Monex Deposit A Cal Ltd Partnr .... D 800 444-8317
4910 Birch St Newport Beach (92660) *(P-11642)*

Monier Lifetile, Rialto *Also Called: Royal Westlake Roofing LLC (P-4420)*

Mono Engineering Corp .... E 818 772-4998
20977 Knapp St Chatsworth (91311) *(P-6186)*

Monobind Sales Inc (PA)... E 949 951-2665
100 N Pointe Dr Lake Forest (92630) *(P-8201)*

Monogram Aerospace Fas Inc .... C 323 722-4760
3423 Garfield Ave Commerce (90040) *(P-4783)*

Monogram Systems, Carson *Also Called: Mag Aerospace Industries LLC (P-4799)*

Monogram Systems, Carson *Also Called: Zodiac Wtr Waste Aero Systems (P-7595)*

Monoprice Inc .... D 877 271-2592
11701 6th St Rancho Cucamonga (91730) *(P-10564)*

Monrovia Memorial Hospital, Monrovia *Also Called: Alakor Healthcare LLC (P-15903)*

Monrovia Ranch Market, Victorville *Also Called: Baja Fresh Supermarket (P-96)*

Monrovia Service Center, Monrovia *Also Called: Southern California Edison Co (P-9638)*

Monrow, Los Angeles *Also Called: Monrow LLC (P-2048)*

Monrow LLC .... E 213 741-6007
1404 S Main St Ste C Los Angeles (90015) *(P-2048)*

Monsanto, Oxnard *Also Called: Monsanto Company (P-3756)*

Monsanto Company .... E 805 827-2341
2700 Camino Del Sol Oxnard (93030) *(P-3756)*

Monsieur Marcel, Los Angeles *Also Called: Strouk Group LLC (P-10881)*

Monster, Corona *Also Called: Monster Beverage Corporation (P-1625)*

Monster Beverage 1990 Corporation .... A 951 739-6200
1 Monster Way Corona (92879) *(P-1623)*

Monster Beverage Company .... E 866 322-4466
1990 Pomona Rd Corona (92878) *(P-1624)*

Monster Beverage Corporation (PA).. A 951 739-6200
1 Monster Way Corona (92879) *(P-1625)*

Monster Energy, Corona *Also Called: Monster Energy Company (P-10963)*

Monster Energy Company (HQ).. B 866 322-4466
1 Monster Way Corona (92879) *(P-10963)*

Monster Tool LLC .... C 760 477-1000
2470 Ash St U 2 Vista (92081) *(P-4742)*

Montage Hotels & Resorts LLC (PA).. A 949 715-5002
3 Ada Ste 100 Irvine (92618) *(P-12927)*

Montage Hotels & Resorts LLC .... A 949 715-6000
30801 Coast Hwy Laguna Beach (92651) *(P-18014)*

Montage Intl N Amer LLC .... D 800 700-7744
3 Ada Ste 100 Irvine (92618) *(P-12928)*

Montage Laguna Beach, Irvine *Also Called: Montage Hotels & Resorts LLC (P-12927)*

Montage Laguna Beach, Laguna Beach *Also Called: Montage Hotels & Resorts LLC (P-18014)*

Montclair Bronze Inc .... E 909 986-2664
2535 E 57th St Huntington Park (90255) *(P-4682)*

Montclair Hospital Medical Center, Montclair *Also Called: Prime Hlthcare Srvcs-Mntclair (P-16144)*

Monte Vista Grove Homes .... D 626 796-6135
2889 San Pasqual St Pasadena (91107) *(P-17181)*

Montebello Container, Santa Fe Springs *Also Called: Cflute Corp (P-2659)*

Montebello Plastics LLC .... E 323 728-6814
601 W Olympic Blvd Montebello (90640) *(P-3952)*

Montebello Unified School Dst .... D 323 887-2140
500 Hendricks St 2nd Fl Montebello (90640) *(P-13395)*

Montecito Country Club Inc .... D 805 969-0800
920 Summit Rd Santa Barbara (93108) *(P-15152)*

Montecito Family YMCA, Santa Barbara *Also Called: Channel Islnds Yung MNS Chrstn (P-17334)*

Montecito Retirement Assn ....B 805 969-8011
300 Hot Springs Rd Santa Barbara (93108) *(P-15723)*

Monterey Canyon LLC (PA).. D 213 741-0209
1515 E 15th St Los Angeles (90021) *(P-2122)*

Monterey Collection Services, Oceanside *Also Called: Monterey Financial Svcs Inc (P-11856)*

Monterey Financial Svcs Inc (PA)... C 760 639-3500
4095 Avenida De La Plata Oceanside (92056) *(P-11856)*

Monterey Palms Health Care Ctr, Palm Desert *Also Called: Mariner Health Care Inc (P-15709)*

Monterey Park Hospital .... C 626 570-9000
900 S Atlantic Blvd Monterey Park (91754) *(P-16101)*

Monterrey The Natural Choice, San Diego *Also Called: Mpci Holdings Inc (P-10876)*

Montesquieu Corp .... D 877 705-5669
888 W E St San Diego (92101) *(P-11058)*

Montesquieu Vins & Domaines, San Diego *Also Called: Montesquieu Corp (P-11058)*

Mony Life, Orange *Also Called: Mony Life Insurance Company (P-12235)*

Mony Life Insurance Company .... D 714 939-6669
333 S Anita Dr Ste 750 Orange (92868) *(P-12235)*

Moog Aircraft Group, Torrance *Also Called: Moog Inc (P-7744)*

Moog Inc ....B 310 533-1178
1218 W Jon St Torrance (90502) *(P-6355)*

Moog Inc .... C 818 341-5156
21339 Nordhoff St Chatsworth (91311) *(P-7743)*

Moog Inc ....B 310 533-1178
20263 S Western Ave Torrance (90501) *(P-7744)*

Moog Inc ....B 805 618-3900
7406 Hollister Ave Goleta (93117) *(P-7745)*

Moog Jon Street Warehouse, Torrance *Also Called: Moog Inc (P-6355)*

Mooney International, Chino *Also Called: Soaring America Corporation (P-7371)*

Moonstone Bch Innvstors A Cal .... C 805 927-8661
6700 Moonstone Beach Dr Cambria (93428) *(P-12929)*

Moonstone Hotel Properties, Cambria *Also Called: Moonstone Management Corp (P-12489)*

Moonstone Management Corp (PA)... C 805 927-4200
2905 Burton Dr Cambria (93428) *(P-12489)*

Moore Business Forms, Temecula *Also Called: R R Donnelley & Sons Company (P-10585)*

Moore Industries, North Hills *Also Called: Moore Industries-International Inc (P-7867)*

Moore Industries-International Inc (PA)...................................... C 818 894-7111
16650 Schoenborn St North Hills (91343) *(P-7867)*

Mooreford Inc .... D 877 822-2719
2544 Campbell Pl Ste 200 Carlsbad (92009) *(P-10093)*

Moose, El Segundo *Also Called: Moose Toys LLC (P-8478)*

Moose Toys LLC .... D 310 341-4642
737 Campus Sq W El Segundo (90245) *(P-8478)*

Mophie Inc (DH)... D 888 866-7443
15495 Sand Canyon Ave Ste 400 Irvine (92618) *(P-6635)*

Moral Welfare and Recreation, Camp Pendleton *Also Called: Marine Corps Community Svcs (P-15212)*

Moravek, Brea *Also Called: Moravek Biochemicals Inc (P-3242)*

Moravek Biochemicals Inc (PA)... E 714 990-2018
577 Mercury Ln Brea (92821) *(P-3242)*

Morehouse Foods Inc .... E 626 854-1655
760 Epperson Dr City Of Industry (91748) *(P-1370)*

Morehouse-Cowles LLC .... E 909 627-7222
13930 Magnolia Ave Chino (91710) *(P-5711)*

Morelends.com, San Diego *Also Called: Synergy One Lending Inc (P-11937)*

Moreno Valley Family Hlth Ctr, Moreno Valley *Also Called: Community Health Systems Inc (P-15285)*

Moreno Valley Snf LLC .... C 951 363-5434
26940 E Hospital Rd Moreno Valley (92555) *(P-15724)*

Morettis Design Collection Inc .... E 310 638-5555
16926 Keegan Ave Ste C Carson (90746) *(P-2431)*

Morgan Fabrics, Los Angeles *Also Called: Morgan Fabrics Corporation (P-10669)*

Morgan Fabrics Corporation (PA)... D 323 583-9981
4265 Exchange Ave Los Angeles (90058) *(P-10669)*

Mergent email: customerrelations@mergent.com
1112

2025 Southern California
Business Directory and Buyers Guide

(P-0000) Products & Services Section entry number
(PA)=Parent Co (HQ)=Headquarters (DH)=Div Headquarters

Morgan Gallacher Inc .... E 562 695-1232
8707 Millergrove Dr Santa Fe Springs (90670) *(P-3614)*

Morgan Linen Service, Los Angeles *Also Called: Morgan Services Inc (P-13124)*

Morgan Marine, Simi Valley *Also Called: Catalina Yachts Inc (P-7618)*

Morgan Polymer Seals LLC .... B 619 498-9221
3303 2475a Paseo De Las Americas San Diego (92154) *(P-5712)*

Morgan Services Inc .... D 213 485-9666
905 Yale St Los Angeles (90012) *(P-13124)*

Morgan Stanley Smith Barney, San Diego *Also Called: Morgan Stnley Smith Barney LLC (P-11997)*

Morgan Stnley Smith Barney LLC .... C 760 568-3500
74199 El Paseo Ste 201 Palm Desert (92260) *(P-11772)*

Morgan Stnley Smith Barney LLC .... C 760 438-5100
5796 Armada Dr Ste 200 Carlsbad (92008) *(P-11995)*

Morgan Stnley Smith Barney LLC .... C 212 761-4000
1225 Prospect St Ste 202 La Jolla (92037) *(P-11996)*

Morgan Stnley Smith Barney LLC .... C 619 238-1226
101 W Broadway Ste 1800 San Diego (92101) *(P-11997)*

Morgan Stnley Smith Barney LLC .... C 951 682-1181
3750 University Ave Ste 600 Riverside (92501) *(P-11998)*

Morgan Stnley Smith Barney LLC .... C 714 674-4100
10 Pointe Dr Ste 400 Brea (92821) *(P-11999)*

Morgan Stnley Smith Barney LLC .... C 213 891-3200
444 S Flower St Ste 2700 Los Angeles (90071) *(P-12000)*

Morgan Stnley Smith Barney LLC .... C 818 715-1800
21650 Oxnard St Ste 1800 Woodland Hills (91367) *(P-12001)*

Morgans Hotel Group MGT LLC .... C 805 969-2203
1555 S Jameson Ln Santa Barbara (93108) *(P-12930)*

Morgans Hotel Group MGT LLC .... C 323 650-8999
8440 W Sunset Blvd Los Angeles (90069) *(P-12931)*

Morin Corporation .... E 909 428-3747
10707 Commerce Way Fontana (92337) *(P-5085)*

Morin West, Fontana *Also Called: Morin Corporation (P-5085)*

Morley Builders Inc (PA) .... C 310 399-1600
3330 Ocean Park Blvd Santa Monica (90405) *(P-494)*

Morley Construction Company (HQ) .... D 310 399-1600
3330 Ocean Park Blvd Santa Monica (90405) *(P-1126)*

Morningside Community Assn .... D 760 328-3323
82 Mayfair Dr Rancho Mirage (92270) *(P-17357)*

Morningside of Fullerton, Fullerton *Also Called: Corecare I I I (P-17135)*

Morningstar of Mission Viejo, Mission Viejo *Also Called: Morningstar Senior MGT LLC (P-17182)*

Morningstar Senior MGT LLC .... C 949 298-3675
28570 Marguerite Pkwy Mission Viejo (92692) *(P-17182)*

Moroccanoil Inc (PA) .... C 888 700-1817
16311 Ventura Blvd Ste 1200 Encino (91436) *(P-10634)*

Morongo Band Mission Indians .... D 951 849-3080
49500 Seminole Dr Cabazon (92230) *(P-15213)*

Morongo Casino Resort Spa, Cabazon *Also Called: Morongo Band Mission Indians (P-15213)*

Morphotrak LLC (DH) .... C 714 238-2000
5515 E La Palma Ave Ste 100 Anaheim (92807) *(P-14097)*

Morroll's Metal Finishing, Compton *Also Called: Morrells Electro Plating Inc (P-5276)*

Morrells Electro Plating Inc .... E 310 639-1024
436 E Euclid Ave Compton (90222) *(P-5276)*

Morris & Willner Partners .... D 949 705-0682
1503 S Coast Dr Costa Mesa (92626) *(P-18173)*

Morris Crullo World Evangelism (PA) .... D 858 277-2200
875 Hotel Cir S # 2 San Diego (92108) *(P-17417)*

Morris Group International, City Of Industry *Also Called: Acorn Engineering Company (P-3788)*

Morris Grritano Insur Agcy Inc .... D 805 543-6887
1122 Laurel Ln San Luis Obispo (93401) *(P-12236)*

Morris Polich & Purdy LLP (PA) .... D 213 891-9100
1055 W 7th St Ste 2400 Los Angeles (90017) *(P-16743)*

Morrison & Foerster, Los Angeles *Also Called: Morrison & Foester (P-16745)*

Morrison & Foerster LLP .... B 858 720-5100
12531 High Bluff Dr Ste 100 San Diego (92130) *(P-16744)*

MORRISON & FOERSTER LLP, San Diego *Also Called: Morrison & Foerster LLP (P-16744)*

Morrison & Foester .... C 213 892-5200
707 Wilshire Blvd Los Angeles (90017) *(P-16745)*

Morrow-Meadows Corporation .... B 858 974-3650
13000 Kirkham Way Ste 101 Poway (92064) *(P-941)*

Morrow-Meadows Corporation (PA) .... A 858 974-3650
231 Benton Ct City Of Industry (91789) *(P-942)*

Morse Micro Inc .... D 949 501-7080
40 Waterworks Way Irvine (92618) *(P-6857)*

Mortech Manufacturing, Azusa *Also Called: Joseph Manufacturing Co Inc (P-2547)*

Mortex Apparel, Burbank *Also Called: Mortex Corporation (P-2021)*

Mortex Corporation C
40 E Verdugo Ave Burbank (91502) *(P-2021)*

Mortgage Bank of California .... D 310 498-2700
3555 Voyager St Ste 201 Torrance (90503) *(P-11925)*

Mortgage Works Financial, Redlands *Also Called: Mountain West Financial Inc (P-11926)*

Morton Grinding Inc .... C 661 298-0895
201 E Avenue K15 Lancaster (93535) *(P-8574)*

Morton Manufacturing, Lancaster *Also Called: Morton Grinding Inc (P-8574)*

Morton Salt Inc .... D 562 437-0071
1050 Pier F Ave Long Beach (90802) *(P-3816)*

Moseley, Goleta *Also Called: Moseley Associates Inc (P-6636)*

Moseley Associates Inc (HQ) .... D 805 968-9621
82 Coromar Dr Goleta (93117) *(P-6636)*

Moseys Production Machinists Inc (PA) .... E 714 693-4840
1550 Lakeview Loop Anaheim (92807) *(P-6187)*

Moss & Associates LLC .... C 760 385-4535
100 Wonsan Dr Oceanside (92058) *(P-14553)*

Moss & Company Inc (PA) .... D 818 305-3600
15300 Ventura Blvd Ste 405 Sherman Oaks (91403) *(P-12490)*

Moss Management Services Inc .... D 818 990-5999
15300 Ventura Blvd Ste 405 Sherman Oaks (91403) *(P-12491)*

Moss Motors Ltd (PA) .... C 805 967-4546
400 Rutherford St Goleta (93117) *(P-11449)*

Mossy Automotive Group Inc (PA) .... D 858 581-4000
4555 Mission Bay Dr San Diego (92109) *(P-11381)*

Mossy Ford Inc .... C 858 273-7500
4570 Mission Bay Dr San Diego (92109) *(P-11382)*

Mossy Nissan Inc .... D 858 565-6608
8118 Clairemont Mesa Blvd San Diego (92111) *(P-11383)*

Mossy Nissan Kearny Mesa, San Diego *Also Called: Mossy Nissan Inc (P-11383)*

Mossy Toyota, San Diego *Also Called: Mossy Automotive Group Inc (P-11381)*

Motech Americas LLC .... B 302 451-7500
1300 Valley Vista Dr Ste 207 Diamond Bar (91765) *(P-17810)*

Moteng Inc .... D 858 715-2500
12220 Parkway Centre Dr Poway (92064) *(P-10690)*

Motion and Flow Ctrl Pdts Inc .... D 714 541-2244
911 N Poinsettia St Santa Ana (92701) *(P-10450)*

Motion Engineering Inc (DH) .... D 805 696-1200
33 S La Patera Ln Santa Barbara (93117) *(P-5938)*

Motion Industries Inc .... E 858 602-1500
12550 Stowe Dr Poway (92064) *(P-10451)*

Motion Pcture Indust Pnsion HI .... C 818 769-0007
11365 Ventura Blvd Ste 300 Studio City (91604) *(P-12161)*

Motion Picture and TV Fund (PA) .... B 818 876-1777
23388 Mulholland Dr Woodland Hills (91364) *(P-16102)*

Motion Picture and TV Fund .... D 310 445-8993
2114 Pontius Ave Los Angeles (90025) *(P-17097)*

Motion Theory Inc .... C 310 396-9433
444 W Ocean Blvd Ste 1400 Long Beach (90802) *(P-13332)*

Motionloft Inc .... E 415 580-7671
13681 Newport Ave Ste 8 Tustin (92780) *(P-7969)*

Motivational Systems Inc (PA) .... D 619 474-8246
2200 Cleveland Ave National City (91950) *(P-13333)*

Motive Energy LLC (PA) .... D 714 888-2525
125 E Commercial St Ste B Anaheim (92801) *(P-10195)*

Motive Nation, Downey *Also Called: Rockview Dairies Inc (P-10975)*

Motivtnal Flfllment Lgstics Sv, Chino *Also Called: Math Holdings Inc (P-14540)*

Motor City GMC Buick Pontiac, Bakersfield *Also Called: Motor City Sales & Service (P-11384)*

Motor City Sales & Service (PA) .... C 661 836-9000
3101 Pacheco Rd Bakersfield (93313) *(P-11384)*

Motorcar Parts of America Inc (PA) .... A 310 212-7910
2929 California St Torrance (90503) *(P-7274)*

Motorola, San Diego *Also Called: Motorola Mobility LLC (P-10269)*

Motorola Mobility LLC .... D 858 455-1500
6450 Sequence Dr San Diego (92121) *(P-10269)*

Employee Codes: A=Over 500 employees, B=251-500
C=101-250, D=51-100, E=20-50, F=10-19, G=1-9

2025 Southern California
Business Directory and Buyers Guide

© Mergent Inc. 1-800-342-5647

1113

A
L
P
H
A
B
E
T
I
C

Motorola Sltons Cnnctivity Inc (HQ)..............D 951 719-2100
42555 Rio Nedo Temecula (92590) *(P-6637)*

Motors & Controls Whse Inc ....E 714 956-0480
1440 N Burton Pl Anaheim (92806) *(P-10270)*

Motorvac Technologies Inc ....E 714 558-4822
1431 Village Way Santa Ana (92705) *(P-6188)*

Moulton Animal Hospital Inc ....D 949 831-7297
27261 La Paz Rd Ste I Laguna Beach (92677) *(P-130)*

Moulton Logistics Management ....C 818 997-1800
7855 Hayvenhurst Ave Van Nuys (91406) *(P-9090)*

Moulton Nguel Wtr Dst Pub Fclt ....D 949 831-2500
26161 Gordon Rd Laguna Hills (92653) *(P-9706)*

Moulton Niguel Water District, Laguna Hills *Also Called: Moulton Nguel Wtr Dst Pub Fclt (P-9706)*

Mount Palomar Winery, Temecula *Also Called: Louidar LLC (P-1580)*

Mount San Jcnto Winter Pk Corp ....D 760 325-1449
1 Tramway Rd Palm Springs (92262) *(P-15214)*

Mountain Gear Corporation ....C 626 851-2488
4889 4th St Irwindale (91706) *(P-10691)*

Mountain High Ski Resort, Wrightwood *Also Called: MHRP Resort Inc (P-12925)*

Mountain Meadow Mushrooms Inc ....D 760 749-1201
26948 N Broadway Escondido (92026) *(P-74)*

Mountain News & Shopper, Lake Arrowhead *Also Called: Hi-Desert Publishing Company (P-2803)*

Mountain View Child Care Inc (PA)....................B 909 796-6915
1720 Mountain View Ave Loma Linda (92354) *(P-16103)*

Mountain View Child Care Inc ....C 818 252-5863
10716 La Tuna Canyon Rd Sun Valley (91352) *(P-17098)*

Mountain View Transportation, Oxnard *Also Called: AG Rx (P-11068)*

Mountain Vista Golf Course At ....D 760 200-2200
38180 Del Webb Blvd Palm Desert (92211) *(P-15215)*

Mountain Water Ice Company ....E 760 722-7611
2843 Benet Rd Oceanside (92058) *(P-9038)*

Mountain Water Ice Company Inc (PA).................D 310 638-0321
17011 Central Ave Carson (90746) *(P-1731)*

Mountain West Financial Inc (PA).......................B 909 793-1500
1255 W Colton Ave Redlands (92374) *(P-11926)*

MOUNTAINS COMMUNITY HOSPITAL, Lake Arrowhead *Also Called: Mountins Cmnty Hosp Fndtion In (P-16104)*

Mountins Cmnty Hosp Fndtion In ....C 909 336-3651
29101 Hospital Rd Lake Arrowhead (92352) *(P-16104)*

Mousepad Designs, Cerritos *Also Called: Mpd Holdings Inc (P-5940)*

Move Sales Inc (DH)......................................D 805 557-2300
30700 Russell Ranch Rd Ste 290 Westlake Village (91362) *(P-12492)*

Movement For Life Inc ....B 805 788-0805
408 Higuera St Ste 200 San Luis Obispo (93401) *(P-18015)*

Movers and Shakers LLC ....D 310 893-7051
1217 Wilshire Blvd Santa Monica (90403) *(P-13229)*

Movieclips.com, Los Angeles *Also Called: Zefr Inc (P-17864)*

Moving Image Technologies LLC ....E 714 751-7998
17760 Newhope St Ste B Fountain Valley (92708) *(P-8434)*

Moviola Digital, Burbank *Also Called: Filmtools Inc (P-11646)*

Mowbray's Tree Service, San Bernardino *Also Called: Original Mowbrays Tree Svc Inc (P-245)*

Mowery Thomason Inc ....C 714 666-1717
1225 N Red Gum St Anaheim (92806) *(P-1016)*

Moxa Americas Inc ....E 714 528-6777
601 Valencia Ave Ste 100 Brea (92823) *(P-5939)*

Moxy AC Ht Dwntwn Los Angeles, Los Angeles *Also Called: Lightstone Dt La LLC (P-12903)*

Moyes Custom Furniture Inc ....E 714 729-0234
1884 Pomona Rd Corona (92878) *(P-14736)*

Mozaik LLC ....E 562 207-1900
245 W Carl Karcher Way Anaheim (92801) *(P-2650)*

Mp Aero LLC ....D 818 901-9828
7701 Woodley Ave Van Nuys (91406) *(P-1217)*

MP Environmental Svcs Inc (PA)........................C 800 458-3036
3400 Manor St Bakersfield (93308) *(P-9751)*

Mp Materials Corp ....D 702 844-6111
67750 Bailey Rd Mountain Pass (92366) *(P-257)*

Mp Mine Operations LLC ....C 702 277-0848
67750 Bailey Rd Mountain Pass (92366) *(P-383)*

MPA, Torrance *Also Called: Motorcar Parts of America Inc (P-7274)*

Mpci Holdings Inc ....C 619 294-2222
7850 Waterville Rd San Diego (92154) *(P-10876)*

Mpd Holdings Inc ....E 213 210-2591
16200 Commerce Way Cerritos (90703) *(P-5940)*

Mpg Office Trust Inc ....D 213 626-3300
355 S Grand Ave Ste 3300 Los Angeles (90071) *(P-12689)*

Mpi Limited Inc ....D
1901 E Cooley Dr Colton (92324) *(P-12604)*

Mpl Enterprises Inc ....D 714 545-1717
2302 S Susan St Santa Ana (92704) *(P-224)*

Mpm & Associates, Van Nuys *Also Called: Mpm Building Services Inc (P-3615)*

Mpm Building Services Inc ....E 818 708-9676
7011 Hayvenhurst Ave Ste F Van Nuys (91406) *(P-3615)*

Mpo Videotronics Inc (PA)...............................D 805 499-8513
5069 Maureen Ln Moorpark (93021) *(P-8435)*

Mpower Holding Corporation (HQ).......................D 866 699-8242
515 S Flower St Fl 36 Los Angeles (90071) *(P-9449)*

Mpp Fullerton Div 6061, Fullerton *Also Called: Orora Packaging Solutions (P-10605)*

Mpp San Diego Div 6064, San Marcos *Also Called: Orora Packaging Solutions (P-10599)*

Mpressions, Anaheim *Also Called: Dean Hesketh Company Inc (P-3135)*

MPS Anzon LLC ....C 626 471-3553
11911 Clark St Arcadia (91006) *(P-8290)*

MPS Medical Inc ....E 714 672-1090
785 Challenger St Brea (92821) *(P-8202)*

Mq Power, Cypress *Also Called: Multiquip Inc (P-10196)*

Mr Bug, Anaheim *Also Called: Reels Inc (P-9844)*

Mr Clean Maintenance Systems, San Bernardino *Also Called: Chiro Inc (P-10472)*

Mr Copy Inc (DH)...D 858 573-6300
5657 Copley Dr San Diego (92111) *(P-9977)*

Mr Dj Inc ....E 213 744-0044
1800 E Washington Blvd Los Angeles (90021) *(P-6546)*

MR Mold & Engineering Corp ....E 714 996-5511
1150 Beacon St Brea (92821) *(P-5589)*

Mr Tortilla Inc ....E 818 233-8932
1112 Arroyo St San Fernando (91340) *(P-1820)*

Mrc, Smart Tech Solutions, San Diego *Also Called: Mr Copy Inc (P-9977)*

Mro Maryruth LLC ....C 424 343-6650
1171 S Robertson Blvd Ste 148 Los Angeles (90035) *(P-3320)*

Mrs Appletree's Bakery, Baldwin Park *Also Called: Distinct Indulgence Inc (P-1442)*

MRS Foods Incorporated (PA)............................E 714 554-2791
4406 W 5th St Santa Ana (92703) *(P-1821)*

Mrv, Chatsworth *Also Called: Mrv Communications Inc (P-6858)*

Mrv Communications Inc ....B 818 773-0900
20520 Nordhoff St Chatsworth (91311) *(P-6858)*

MS Aerospace Inc ....B 818 833-9095
13928 Balboa Blvd Sylmar (91342) *(P-5132)*

MS Industrial Shtmtl Inc ....C 951 272-6610
1731 Pomona Rd Corona (92878) *(P-5010)*

Msblous LLC ....D 909 929-9689
11671 Dayton Dr Rancho Cucamonga (91730) *(P-9091)*

MSC Metalworking, City Of Industry *Also Called: Rutland Tool & Supply Co (P-10460)*

MSC-La, City Of Industry *Also Called: Material Sciences Corporation (P-4591)*

Mscsoftware Corporation ....A 714 540-8900
5161 California Ave Ste 200 Irvine (92617) *(P-13978)*

MSD CAPITAL L.P., Santa Monica *Also Called: Msd Capital LP (P-12720)*

Msd Capital LP ....C 310 458-3600
100 Wilshire Blvd Ste 1450 Santa Monica (90401) *(P-12720)*

MSE Enterprises Inc (PA).................................D 818 223-3500
23622 Calabasas Rd Ste 200 Calabasas (91302) *(P-12493)*

MSI Computer Corp (HQ).................................D 626 913-0828
901 Canada Ct City Of Industry (91748) *(P-10019)*

MSI Hvac, Fontana *Also Called: AC Pro Inc (P-10328)*

MSI Orange Showroom & Dist Ctr, Orange *Also Called: M S International Inc (P-9946)*

Msla Management LLC ....A 626 824-6020
1294 E Colorado Blvd Pasadena (91106) *(P-18336)*

MSM Industries Inc ....E 951 735-0834
12660 Magnolia Ave Riverside (92503) *(P-17592)*

Msr Desert Resort LP ....A 760 564-5730
49499 Eisenhower Dr La Quinta (92253) *(P-11591)*

Msr Hotels & Resorts Inc ....C 661 325-9700
5101 California Ave Ste 204 Bakersfield (93309) *(P-12721)*

Mergent email: customerrelations@mergent.com
1114

2025 Southern California
Business Directory and Buyers Guide

(P-0000) Products & Services Section entry number
(PA)=Parent Co (HQ)=Headquarters (DH)=Div Headquarters

Msr Hotels & Resorts Inc .... C 310 543-4566
3701 Torrance Blvd Torrance (90503) *(P-12932)*

Msr Resort Lodging Tenant LLC .... A 760 564-4111
49499 Eisenhower Dr La Quinta (92253) *(P-12933)*

MSRS INC .... C 310 952-9000
945 E Church St Riverside (92507) *(P-9899)*

Mt Poso Cgnrtion A Cal Ltd PR .... E 661 663-3155
10000 Stockdale Hwy Ste 100 Bakersfield (93311) *(P-9591)*

Mt Rubidoux Convalescent Hosp, San Bernardino Also Called: Waterman Convalescent
Hosp Inc *(P-15798)*

Mt Rubidouxidence Opco LLC .... C 951 681-2200
6401 33rd St Riverside (92509) *(P-15725)*

Mt Sinai Mem Pk & Mortuary, Los Angeles Also Called: Sinai Temple *(P-13158)*

Mt Sinai Mem Pk & Mortuary, Los Angeles Also Called: Sinai Temple *(P-17419)*

Mtc Financial Inc .... D 949 252-8300
17100 Gillette Ave Irvine (92612) *(P-18016)*

Mtc Kitchen Home La, El Monte Also Called: Mutual Trading Co Inc *(P-10964)*

Mtc Transportation, Twentynine Palms Also Called: Mark Clemons *(P-8964)*

Mtc Worldwide Corp .... D 626 839-6800
17837 Rowland St City Of Industry (91748) *(P-10020)*

Mtd Kitchen Inc .... D 818 764-2254
13213 Sherman Way North Hollywood (91605) *(P-2315)*

MTI De Baja Inc .... E 951 654-2333
915 Industrial Way San Jacinto (92582) *(P-7746)*

MTI Laboratory Inc .... E 310 955-3700
201 Continental Blvd Ste 300 El Segundo (90245) *(P-6638)*

Mtil, El Segundo Also Called: MTI Laboratory Inc *(P-6638)*

Mtroiz International .... E 661 998-8013
150 S Kenmore Ave Los Angeles (90004) *(P-10271)*

MTS Solutions LLC .... E 661 589-5804
7131 Charity Ave Bakersfield (93308) *(P-3826)*

Mtv Networks, Los Angeles Also Called: Viacom Networks *(P-14869)*

Mufg Americas Leasing Corp (DH) .... D **213 488-3700**
445 S Figueroa St Ste 2700 Los Angeles (90071) *(P-13462)*

Mufg Union Bank Foundation .... A 213 236-5000
445 S Figueroa St Los Angeles (90071) *(P-11737)*

Muir Elementary School, Long Beach Also Called: Long Beach Unified School Dst *(P-16814)*

Muir-Chase Plumbing Co Inc .... D 818 500-1940
4530 Brazil St Ste 1 Los Angeles (90039) *(P-807)*

Mulberry Child Care Ctrs Inc .... D 951 688-4242
10250 Kidd St Riverside (92503) *(P-17099)*

Mulberry Child Care Ctrs Inc .... D 714 692-1111
23721 La Palma Ave Yorba Linda (92887) *(P-17100)*

Mulechain Inc .... D 888 456-8881
2901 W Coast Hwy Ste 200 Newport Beach (92663) *(P-8920)*

Mulen, Seal Beach Also Called: P2f Holdings *(P-11133)*

Mulgrew Arcft Components Inc .... D 626 256-1375
1810 S Shamrock Ave Monrovia (91016) *(P-7528)*

Mulholland Brand, Canoga Park Also Called: Mulholland Security Ctrs LLC *(P-4896)*

Mulholland Brothers .... E 510 280-5485
11840 Dorothy St Apt 301 Los Angeles (90049) *(P-9092)*

Mulholland SEC & Patrol Inc .... B 818 755-0202
11454 San Vicente Blvd Los Angeles (90049) *(P-14318)*

Mulholland Security Ctrs LLC .... D 000 502-5770
21260 Deering Ct Canoga Park (91304) *(P-4896)*

Mullen Auto Sales, Brea Also Called: Mullen Technologies Inc *(P-7186)*

Mullen Automotive Inc (PA) .... C **714 613-1900**
1405 Pioneer St Brea (92821) *(P-14148)*

Mullen Technologies Inc (PA) .... E **714 613-1900**
1405 Pioneer St Brea (92821) *(P-7186)*

Mullenlowe US Inc .... D 424 738-6600
12130 Millennium Los Angeles (90094) *(P-13230)*

Mullenlowe US Inc .... D 424 738-6500
2121 Park Pl Ste 150 El Segundo (90245) *(P-13231)*

Mullin TBG Insur Agcy Svcs LLC (DH) C
3333 Michelson Dr Ste 820 Irvine (92612) *(P-12237)*

Mullintbg, Irvine Also Called: Mullin TBG Insur Agcy Svcs LLC *(P-12237)*

Mulroses Usa Inc .... D 213 489-1761
741 S San Pedro St Los Angeles (90014) *(P-61)*

Multi Mechanical Inc .... D 714 632-7404
469 Blaine St Corona (92879) *(P-808)*

Multi Plastics, Santa Fe Springs Also Called: Multi-Plastics Inc *(P-3280)*

Multi-Fineline Electronix Inc (HQ) .... A **949 453-6800**
101 Academy Ste 250 Irvine (92617) *(P-6753)*

Multi-Plastics Inc .... E 562 692-1202
11625 Los Nietos Rd Santa Fe Springs (90670) *(P-3280)*

Multichrome Company Inc (PA) .... E 310 216-1086
1013 W Hillcrest Blvd Inglewood (90301) *(P-5277)*

Multicultural Rdo Brdcstg Inc .... C 626 844-8882
747 E Green St Pasadena (91101) *(P-9484)*

Multiquip Inc (DH) .... B 310 537-3700
6141 Katella Ave Ste 200 Cypress (90630) *(P-10196)*

Multivest, San Dimas Also Called: Webmetro *(P-14064)*

Mum Industries Inc .... D 800 729-1314
2320 Meyers Ave Escondido (92029) *(P-3281)*

Munchkin Inc (PA) .... C **800 344-2229**
7835 Gloria Ave Van Nuys (91406) *(P-3983)*

Munchkin Inc .... E 818 893-5000
27334 San Bernardino Ave Redlands (92374) *(P-3984)*

Munekata America Inc .... B 619 661-8080
2320 Paseo De Las Americas Ste 112 San Diego (92154) *(P-7028)*

Munger Tolles & Olson LLP .... C 213 683-9100
350 S Grand Ave Fl 50 Los Angeles (90071) *(P-16746)*

Munger Bros LLC .... A 661 721-0390
786 Road 188 Delano (93215) *(P-50)*

Munger Farm, Delano Also Called: Munger Bros LLC *(P-50)*

Munger Farms, Delano Also Called: Monarch Nut Company LLC *(P-116)*

Munger Tolles Olson Foundation (PA) .... B 213 683-9100
350 S Grand Ave Fl 50 Los Angeles (90071) *(P-16747)*

Murad, Los Angeles Also Called: Murad LLC *(P-3453)*

Murad LLC (HQ) .... C **310 726-0600**
2121 Park Pl Fl 1 El Segundo (90245) *(P-3452)*

Murad LLC .... C 310 906-3100
8207 W 3rd St Los Angeles (90048) *(P-3453)*

Murad LLC .... C 310 726-3300
1340 Storm Pkwy Torrance (90501) *(P-10635)*

Murad LLC .... C 310 726-0470
2141 Rosecrans Ave Ste 1151 El Segundo (90245) *(P-13152)*

Murad Spa, El Segundo Also Called: Murad LLC *(P-13152)*

Murcal, Palmdale Also Called: Murcal Inc *(P-10197)*

Murcal Inc .... E 661 272-4700
41343 12th St W Palmdale (93551) *(P-10197)*

Murchison & Cumming LLP (PA) .... D 213 623-7400
801 S Grand Ave Ste 900 Los Angeles (90017) *(P-16748)*

Murcor Inc .... C 909 623-4001
740 Corporate Center Dr Ste 100 Pomona (91768) *(P-12494)*

Muriel Siebert & Co Inc .... D 800 993-2015
9378 Wilshire Blvd Ste 300 Beverly Hills (90212) *(P-12002)*

Murray Company, E Rncho Dmngz Also Called: Murray Plumbing and Htg Corp *(P-809)*

Murray Plumbing and Htg Corp (PA) .... C 310 637-1500
18414 S Santa Fe Ave E Rncho Dmngz (90221) *(P-809)*

Murrays Iron Works Inc (PA) .... C **323 521-1100**
7355 E Slauson Ave Commerce (90040) *(P-2471)*

Murrieta Development Company Inc .... C 951 719-1680
42540 Rio Nedo Temecula (92590) *(P-686)*

Murrietta Circuits .... C 714 970-2430
5000 E Landon Dr Anaheim (92807) *(P-6754)*

Musclebound Inc .... B 818 349-0123
19835 Nordhoff St Northridge (91324) *(P-15057)*

Museum Associates .... B 323 857-6172
5905 Wilshire Blvd Los Angeles (90036) *(P-17256)*

Museum of Contemporary Art (PA) .... C 213 626-6222
250 S Grand Ave Los Angeles (90012) *(P-17257)*

Music Academy of West .... D 805 969-4726
1070 Fairway Rd Santa Barbara (93108) *(P-16856)*

Music Center, Los Angeles Also Called: Performing Arts Ctr Los Angles *(P-14970)*

Music Express Inc (PA) .... C 818 845-1502
2601 W Empire Ave Burbank (91504) *(P-8842)*

Music Intllgnce Neuro Dev Inst, Irvine Also Called: Mind Research Institute *(P-17882)*

Musick Peeler & Garrett LLP .... C **213 629-7600**
333 S Hope St Ste 2900 Los Angeles (90071) *(P-16749)*

Employee Codes: A=Over 500 employees, B=251-500
C=101-250, D=51-100, E=20-50, F=10-19, G=1-9

2025 Southern California
Business Directory and Buyers Guide

© Mergent Inc. 1-800-342-5647

1115

Musicmatch Inc .... C 858 485-4300
16935 W Bernardo Dr Ste 270 San Diego (92127) *(P-13979)*

Mutesix Group Inc .... C 800 935-6856
5800 Bristol Pkwy Ste 500 Culver City (90230) *(P-13232)*

Mutesix, An Iprospect Company, Culver City *Also Called: Mutesix Group Inc (P-13232)*

Muth Machine Works .... D 951 685-1521
4510 Rutile St Riverside (92509) *(P-18174)*

Mutiny, Los Angeles *Also Called: Trailer Park Inc (P-13250)*

Mutual Liquid Gas & Eqp Co Inc (PA)..................... E 310 515-0553
17117 S Broadway Gardena (90248) *(P-10384)*

Mutual Propane, Gardena *Also Called: Mutual Liquid Gas & Eqp Co Inc (P-10384)*

Mutual Securites Inc .... D 800 750-7862
807 Camarillo Springs Rd Camarillo (93012) *(P-14319)*

Mutual Trading Co Inc (DH) .... C 213 626-9458
4200 Shirley Ave El Monte (91731) *(P-10964)*

Mv Transportation, Newbury Park *Also Called: Mv Transportation Inc (P-8784)*

Mv Transportation Inc .... B 818 409-3387
1242 Los Angeles St Glendale (91204) *(P-8776)*

Mv Transportation Inc .... C 562 943-6776
15677 Phoebe Ave La Mirada (90638) *(P-8777)*

Mv Transportation Inc .... B 323 936-9783
5420 W Jefferson Blvd Los Angeles (90016) *(P-8778)*

Mv Transportation Inc .... B 310 638-0556
14011 S Central Ave Los Angeles (90059) *(P-8779)*

Mv Transportation Inc .... C 818 374-9145
16738 Stagg St Van Nuys (91406) *(P-8780)*

Mv Transportation Inc .... C 323 666-0856
13690 Vaughn St San Fernando (91340) *(P-8781)*

Mv Transportation Inc .... D 562 259-9911
7231 Rosecrans Ave Paramount (90723) *(P-8782)*

Mv Transportation Inc .... C 805 557-7372
265 S Rancho Rd Thousand Oaks (91361) *(P-8783)*

Mv Transportation Inc .... C 805 375-5467
670 Lawrence Dr Newbury Park (91320) *(P-8784)*

Mv Transportation Inc .... C 760 255-3330
1612 State St Barstow (92311) *(P-8785)*

Mv Transportation Inc .... B 760 400-0300
303 Via Del Norte Oceanside (92058) *(P-8786)*

Mv Transportation Inc .... C 760 520-0118
755 Norlak Ave Escondido (92025) *(P-8787)*

Mventix, Woodland Hills *Also Called: Mventix Inc (P-14554)*

Mventix Inc (PA)... D 818 337-3747
21600 Oxnard St Ste 1700 Woodland Hills (91367) *(P-14554)*

Mw Compnnts - Anheim Ideal Fas, Anaheim *Also Called: Matthew Warren Inc (P-8573)*

Mw Components - Corona, Corona *Also Called: Ameriflex Inc (P-5424)*

Mw Partners, Costa Mesa *Also Called: Morris & Willner Partners (P-18173)*

Mwd, Los Angeles *Also Called: The Metropolitan Water District of Southern California (P-9723)*

Mws Precision Wire Inds Inc .... D 818 991-8553
3000 Camino Del Sol Oxnard (93030) *(P-10145)*

Mws Wire Industries, Oxnard *Also Called: Mws Precision Wire Inds Inc (P-10145)*

Mwss, Irvine *Also Called: In Montrose Wtr Sstnblity Svcs (P-18323)*

MXF Designs Inc .... D 323 266-1451
5327 Valley Blvd Los Angeles (90032) *(P-2049)*

MY DAY COUNTS, Anaheim *Also Called: Orange Cnty Adult Achvment Ctr (P-16987)*

My Eye Media LLC .... D 818 559-7200
2211 N Hollywood Way Burbank (91505) *(P-13980)*

My Kids Dentist .... B 951 600-1062
24635 Madison Ave Ste E Murrieta (92562) *(P-15522)*

My Michelle, La Puente *Also Called: Mymichelle Company LLC (P-2050)*

My Tech USA, Corona *Also Called: Hardy Frames Inc (P-4517)*

Mycase, San Diego *Also Called: Appfolio Inc (P-13880)*

Mycelium Enterprises LLC .... E 657 251-0016
10632 Trask Ave Garden Grove (92843) *(P-3321)*

Mye Technologies Inc .... E 661 964-0217
25060 Avenue Stanford Valencia (91355) *(P-7135)*

Myers & Sons Construction LP .... C 424 227-3285
5777 W Century Blvd Ste 600 Los Angeles (90045) *(P-638)*

Myers & Sons Hi-Way Safety Inc (PA) .... D 909 591-1781
13310 5th St Chino (91710) *(P-8618)*

Myers Mixers LLC .... E 323 560-4723
8376 Salt Lake Ave Cudahy (90201) *(P-5828)*

Myevaluationscom Inc .... E 646 422-0554
11111 W Olympic Blvd Ste 401 Los Angeles (90064) *(P-13773)*

Mygrant Glass Company Inc .... E 858 455-8022
10220 Camino Santa Fe San Diego (92121) *(P-7275)*

Myhhbs Inc .... D 888 969-4427
237 N Central Ave Ste A Glendale (91203) *(P-16980)*

Mymichelle Company LLC (HQ).............................. B 626 934-4166
13077 Temple Ave La Puente (91746) *(P-2050)*

Myotek Industries Incorporated (DH)....................... D 949 502-3776
1278 Glenneyre St Ste 431 Laguna Beach (92651) *(P-7097)*

Myron L Company .... D 760 438-2021
2450 Impala Dr Carlsbad (92010) *(P-7868)*

Mytee Products Inc .... E 858 679-1191
13655 Stowe Dr Poway (92064) *(P-6024)*

Mythical Entertainment LLC .... D 818 859-7398
2121 Avenue Of The Stars Ste 1300 Los Angeles (90067) *(P-13774)*

N G I, Brea *Also Called: Nevell Group Inc (P-561)*

N H A, San Diego *Also Called: Neighborhood House Association (P-16981)*

N H Research LLC (DH)... D 949 474-3900
16601 Hale Ave Irvine (92606) *(P-7927)*

N K Cabinets Inc .... E 818 897-7909
13290 Paxton St Pacoima (91331) *(P-2356)*

N Qiagen Amercn Holdings Inc (HQ)....................... C 800 426-8157
27220 Turnberry Ln Ste 200 Valencia (91355) *(P-10636)*

N S C Channel Islands Inc .... B 805 485-1908
2300 Wankel Way Oxnard (93030) *(P-15398)*

N T S, Woodland Hills *Also Called: Network Telephone Services Inc (P-14555)*

N Trans/Sub Regional Office, Valencia *Also Called: Southern California Edison Co (P-9627)*

N-U Enterprise, Irvine *Also Called: Ancca Corporation (P-996)*

N/S Corporation (PA) .... D 310 412-7074
28309 Avenue Crocker Valencia (91355) *(P-6025)*

N2 Acquisition Company Inc .... D 714 942-3563
14440 Myford Rd Irvine (92606) *(P-12605)*

N2 Imaging Systems, Irvine *Also Called: N2 Acquisition Company Inc (P-12605)*

Nabisco, Ontario *Also Called: Mondelez Global LLC (P-10962)*

Nabors Well Services Co .... C 661 588-6140
1025 Earthmover Ct Bakersfield (93314) *(P-346)*

Nabors Well Services Co .... C 661 589-3970
7515 Rosedale Hwy Bakersfield (93308) *(P-347)*

Nabors Well Services Co .... B 661 392-7668
1954 James Rd Bakersfield (93308) *(P-348)*

Nabors Well Services Co .... D 310 639-7074
19431 S Santa Fe Ave Compton (90221) *(P-349)*

Nabors Well Services Co .... D 805 648-2731
2567 N Ventura Ave # C Ventura (93001) *(P-350)*

Nada Appraisal Guide, Costa Mesa *Also Called: National Appraisal Guides Inc (P-2927)*

Nadolife Inc .... E 619 522-0077
1025 Orange Ave Coronado (92118) *(P-4730)*

Naf, Tustin *Also Called: New American Funding LLC (P-11858)*

Nafees Memon .... D 818 997-1666
6819 Sepulveda Blvd Ste 312 Van Nuys (91405) *(P-14320)*

Nafees Mmon Cmmand Intl SEC Sv, Van Nuys *Also Called: Nafees Memon (P-14320)*

Nafhc, Santa Maria *Also Called: North American Fire Hose Corp (P-3873)*

NAFTA Distributors .... D 800 956-2382
5120 Santa Ana St Ontario (91761) *(P-10761)*

Nagles Veal Inc .... E 909 383-7075
1411 E Base Line St San Bernardino (92410) *(P-1245)*

NAI, Carlsbad *Also Called: Natural Alternatives Intl Inc (P-3322)*

Nailpro, Encino *Also Called: Creative Age Publications Inc (P-2851)*

Nakamura-Beeman Inc .... E 562 696-1400
8520 Wellsford Pl Santa Fe Springs (90670) *(P-2510)*

Nakase Brothers Whl Nurs LP (PA) .... D 949 855-4388
9441 Krepp Dr Huntington Beach (92646) *(P-11093)*

Nakase Brothers Wholesale Nurs .... C 949 855-4388
20621 Lake Forest Dr Lake Forest (92630) *(P-11094)*

NAKASE BROTHERS WHOLESALE NURSERY, Lake Forest *Also Called: Nakase Brothers Wholesale Nurs (P-11094)*

Nalco Champion, Bakersfield *Also Called: Championx LLC (P-3234)*

Nalco Water, Placentia *Also Called: Nalco Wtr Prtrtment Sltons LLC (P-6026)*

Nalco Wtr Prtrtment Sltons LLC .... E 714 792-0708
1961 Petra Ln Placentia (92870) *(P-6026)*

Mergent email: customerrelations@mergent.com
1116

2025 Southern California
Business Directory and Buyers Guide

(P-0000) Products & Services Section entry number
(PA)=Parent Co (HQ)=Headquarters (DH)=Div Headquarters

Nally & Millie, Los Angeles *Also Called: MXF Designs Inc (P-2049)*

Nalu Medical Inc .... C 760 603-8466
2320 Faraday Ave Ste 100 Carlsbad (92008) *(P-16591)*

Namar Company, Paramount *Also Called: Namar Foods (P-1366)*

Namar Foods .... E 562 531-2744
6830 Walthall Way Paramount (90723) *(P-1366)*

Namvars Inc .... D 858 792-5461
11815 Sorrento Valley Rd Ste A San Diego (92121) *(P-225)*

Nan McKay and Associates Inc .... D 619 258-1855
1810 Gillespie Way Ste 202 El Cajon (92020) *(P-18175)*

Nandi-Laksh Inc .... C 661 322-1012
901 Real Rd Bakersfield (93309) *(P-12934)*

Nano Filter Inc .... D 949 316-8866
22310 Bonita St Carson (90745) *(P-8702)*

Nanocomposix LLC .... D 858 565-4227
4878 Ronson Ct Ste J San Diego (92111) *(P-17883)*

Nanoprecision Products Inc .... E 310 597-4991
802 Calle Plano Camarillo (93012) *(P-5204)*

Nantbioscience Inc .... C 310 883-1300
9920 Jefferson Blvd Culver City (90232) *(P-10094)*

Nantcell Inc .... B 562 397-3639
9920 Jefferson Blvd Culver City (90232) *(P-17811)*

Nantcell Inc .... C 310 883-1300
2040 E Mariposa Ave El Segundo (90245) *(P-17884)*

Nantenergy LLC .... D 310 905-4866
2040 E Mariposa Ave El Segundo (90245) *(P-6329)*

Nantworks LLC (PA)... D 310 883-1300
9920 Jefferson Blvd Culver City (90232) *(P-14098)*

Napca Foundation .... A 800 799-4640
2600 W Olive Ave Ste 500 Burbank (91505) *(P-16857)*

Napd, Bakersfield *Also Called: New Advnces For Pple With Dsbl (P-17236)*

Napoleon Perdis Cosmetics Inc .... D 323 817-3611
16825 Saticoy St Van Nuys (91406) *(P-11690)*

Narayan Corporation .... E 310 719-7330
13432 Estrella Ave Gardena (90248) *(P-3985)*

Narcotics Annymous Wrld Svcs I (PA)............................. E 818 773-9999
19737 Nordhoff Pl Chatsworth (91311) *(P-2893)*

Narven Enterprises Inc .... D 619 239-2261
1430 7th Ave Ste B San Diego (92101) *(P-12935)*

Nasco Aircraft Brake Inc .... D 310 532-4430
13300 Estrella Ave Gardena (90248) *(P-7529)*

Nasco Gourmet Foods Inc .... D 714 279-2100
22720 Savi Ranch Pkwy Yorba Linda (92887) *(P-1354)*

Nasif Hicks Harris & Co LLP .... D 805 966-1521
104 W Anapamu St Ste B Santa Barbara (93101) *(P-17747)*

Nasmyth Tmf Inc .... D 818 954-9504
29102 Hancock Pkwy Valencia (91355) *(P-5278)*

Naso Industries Corporation .... E 805 650-1231
3007 Bunsen Ave Ste Q Ventura (93003) *(P-6755)*

Naso Technologies, Ventura *Also Called: Naso Industries Corporation (P-6755)*

Nassco .... E 619 929-3019
7470 Mission Valley Rd San Diego (92108) *(P-7605)*

Nassco, San Diego *Also Called: International Mfg Tech Inc (P-4518)*

Nastec International Inc .... D 818 222-0355
23875 Ventura Blvd Ste 204 Calabasas (91302) *(P-14321)*

Nasty Gal Inc (HQ)... E 213 542-3436
2049 Century Park E Ste 3400 Los Angeles (90067) *(P-11492)*

Natals Inc .... C 323 475-6033
1370 N St Andrews Pl Los Angeles (90028) *(P-3454)*

Natel Engineering, Chatsworth *Also Called: Epic Technologies LLC (P-6584)*

Natel Engineering Company LLC (PA).............................. C 818 495-8617
9340 Owensmouth Ave Chatsworth (91311) *(P-7029)*

Natel Engineering Holdings Inc .... D 818 734-6500
9340 Owensmouth Ave Chatsworth (91311) *(P-6756)*

Nathan Anthony Furniture, Vernon *Also Called: Yen-Nhai Inc (P-2462)*

National Advanced Endoscopy De .... E 818 227-2720
22134 Sherman Way Canoga Park (91303) *(P-11691)*

National Air Inc .... C 619 299-2500
2053 Kurtz St San Diego (92110) *(P-810)*

National Air and Energy, San Diego *Also Called: National Air Inc (P-810)*

National Appraisal Guides Inc .... E 714 556-8511
3186 Airway Ave Ste K Costa Mesa (92626) *(P-2927)*

National Assn For Hispanic, Los Angeles *Also Called: La Asccion Ncnal Pro Prsnas My (P-16969)*

National Attny Collection Svcs .... B 818 547-9760
700 N Brand Blvd Fl 2 Glendale (91203) *(P-16750)*

National Business Group Inc (PA).................................... D 818 221-6000
15319 Chatsworth St Mission Hills (91345) *(P-13442)*

National Cement Co Cal Inc (DH)...................................... E 818 728-5200
15821 Ventura Blvd Ste 475 Encino (91436) *(P-4445)*

National Cement Company Inc (HQ).................................. E 818 728-5200
15821 Ventura Blvd Ste 475 Encino (91436) *(P-4358)*

National Cement Company Inc .... D 323 923-4466
2626 E 26th St Vernon (90058) *(P-4446)*

National City Family Clinic, National City *Also Called: Centro De Slud De La Cmndad De (P-16452)*

National Clearing Corporation (PA)................................... D 310 385-2165
9665 Wilshire Blvd Beverly Hills (90212) *(P-18176)*

National Cmnty Renaissance Cal (PA).............................. D 909 483-2444
9692 Haven Ave Ste 100 Rancho Cucamonga (91730) *(P-12573)*

National Cmnty Renaissance Cal .... C 619 223-9222
8265 Aspen St Ste 100 Rancho Cucamonga (91730) *(P-12574)*

National Cnstr Rentals Inc (PA).. D 818 221-6000
15319 Chatsworth St Mission Hills (91345) *(P-13463)*

National Community Renaissance .... C 909 948-7579
8590 Malven Ave Rancho Cucamonga (91730) *(P-12360)*

National Corset Supply House (PA).................................. D 323 261-0265
3240 E 26th St Vernon (90058) *(P-2151)*

National Credit Partners, Santa Ana *Also Called: Kvc Group LLC (P-18159)*

National Diversified Sales Inc (HQ).................................. C 559 562-9888
21300 Victory Blvd Ste 215 Woodland Hills (91367) *(P-4176)*

National Emblem, Long Beach *Also Called: Enrich Enterprises Inc (P-2246)*

National Emblem Inc (PA)... C 310 515-5055
3925 E Vernon St Long Beach (90815) *(P-2253)*

National Financial Svcs LLC .... A 949 476-0157
19200 Von Karman Ave Ste 400 Irvine (92612) *(P-12003)*

National Fitness Testing, Los Angeles *Also Called: Young MNS Chrstn Assn Mtro Los (P-17406)*

National Genetics Institute .... C 310 996-6610
2440 S Sepulveda Blvd Ste 235 Los Angeles (90064) *(P-17922)*

National Graphics LLC .... E 805 644-9212
200 N Elevar St Oxnard (93030) *(P-3048)*

National Hot Rod Association (PA).................................... C 626 914-4761
140 Via Verde Ste 100 San Dimas (91773) *(P-15040)*

National Insurance Crime Bur .... D 818 895-2867
15545 Devonshire St Ste 309 Mission Hills (91345) *(P-12238)*

National Manufacturing Co .... A 800 346-9445
19701 Da Vinci Lake Forest (92610) *(P-4784)*

National Media Inc (HQ)... E 310 377-6877
609 Deep Valley Dr Ste 200 Rlng Hls Est (90274) *(P-2817)*

National Mentor Holdings Inc .... A 951 677-1453
30033 Technology Dr Murrieta (92563) *(P-17183)*

National Metal Stampings Inc .... D 661 945-1157
42110 8th St E Lancaster (93535) *(P-5205)*

National Monitoring Center, Lake Forest *Also Called: Advanced Protection Inds LLC (P-14379)*

National Notary Association .... C 800 876-6827
9350 De Soto Ave Chatsworth (91311) *(P-17302)*

National O Rings, Downey *Also Called: Hutchinson Seal Corporation (P-3890)*

National Packaging Products, Commerce *Also Called: Yavar Manufacturing Co Inc (P-2702)*

National Paving Company Inc .... D 951 369-1332
4361 Fort Dr Riverside (92509) *(P-639)*

National Planning Corporation .... C 800 881-7174
100 N Pacific Coast Hwy Ste 1800 El Segundo (90245) *(P-11857)*

National Rent A Fence Co., Mission Hills *Also Called: National Cnstr Rentals Inc (P-13463)*

National Research Group, Los Angeles *Also Called: National Research Group Inc (P-17856)*

National Research Group Inc .... B 323 406-6200
12101 Bluff Creek Dr Los Angeles (90094) *(P-17856)*

National Resilience Inc (PA)... E 888 737-2460
3115 Merryfield Row Ste 200 San Diego (92121) *(P-3455)*

National Retail Trnsp Inc .... D 951 243-6110
400 Harley Knox Blvd Perris (92571) *(P-8966)*

National School District .... C 619 336-7770
1400 N Ave National City (91950) *(P-16817)*

Employee Codes: A=Over 500 employees, B=251-500
C=101-250, D=51-100, E=20-50, F=10-19, G=1-9

2025 Southern California
Business Directory and Buyers Guide

© Mergent Inc. 1-800-342-5647
1117

National Security Tech LLC .... A 805 681-2432
5520 Ekwill St Ste B Goleta (93111) *(P-17593)*

National Sign & Marketing Corp .... D 909 591-4742
13580 5th St Chino (91710) *(P-8619)*

National Signal LLC .... D 714 441-7707
14489 Industry Cir La Mirada (90638) *(P-7683)*

National Stl & Shipbuilding Co (HQ)............ **B 619 544-3400**
2798 Harbor Dr San Diego (92113) *(P-7606)*

National Teleconsultants Inc .... C 818 265-4400
1830 Avenida Del Mundo Coronado (92118) *(P-17594)*

National Therapeutic Svcs Inc (PA)............. **D 866 311-0003**
3822 Campus Dr Ste 100 Newport Beach (92660) *(P-16487)*

National Tobacco Company, Santa Monica Also Called: National Tobacco Company LP
(P-11105)

National Tobacco Company LP (DH)............. **C 800 579-0975**
1315 Lincoln Blvd Santa Monica (90401) *(P-11105)*

National Tour Intgrted Rsrces .... E 949 215-6330
23141 Arroyo Vis Ste 100 Rcho Sta Marg (92688) *(P-18177)*

National Trench Safety LLC .... C 562 602-1642
13217 Laureldale Ave Downey (90242) *(P-13464)*

National Tube & Steel, Mission Hills Also Called: National Business Group Inc (P-13442)

National Wire and Cable, Los Angeles Also Called: National Wire and Cable Corporation
(P-4539)

National Wire and Cable Corporation .... C 323 225-5611
136 N San Fernando Rd Los Angeles (90031) *(P-4539)*

NationaLease, San Diego Also Called: Miramar Ford Truck Sales Inc (P-9806)

Nationbuilder, Los Angeles Also Called: 3dna Corp (P-13638)

Nationsbenefits LLC .... A 877 439-2665
1540 Scenic Ave Costa Mesa (92626) *(P-18178)*

Nationwide, San Diego Also Called: Atlas General Insur Svcs LLC (P-12174)

Nationwide, Cerritos Also Called: Auto Insurance Specialists LLC (P-12175)

Nationwide, Pasadena Also Called: B&C Liquidating Corp (P-12181)

Nationwide, Newport Beach Also Called: Edgewood Partners Insur Ctr (P-12205)

Nationwide, San Luis Obispo Also Called: Morris Grritano Insur Agcy Inc (P-12236)

Nationwide, Cypress Also Called: Pacific Pioneer Insur Group (P-12243)

Nationwide, Cerritos Also Called: Poliseek Ais Insur Sltions Inc (P-12244)

Nationwide, La Mesa Also Called: Teague Insurance Agency Inc (P-12257)

Nationwide, Tustin Also Called: Wood Gutmann Bogart Insur Brkg (P-12273)

Nationwide, Irvine Also Called: Sullivncrtsmnroe Insur Svcs LL (P-18222)

Nationwide, Irvine Also Called: Alliant Insurance Services Inc (P-18282)

Nationwide, San Diego Also Called: Alliant Insurance Services Inc (P-18283)

Nationwide Guard Services Inc .... B 909 608-1112
9327 Fairway View Pl Ste 200 Rancho Cucamonga (91730) *(P-14322)*

Nationwide Technologies Inc .... E 909 340-2770
3684 W Uva Ln San Bernardino (92407) *(P-13981)*

Nationwide Theatres Corp (HQ)................. **D 310 657-8420**
120 N Robertson Blvd Fl 3 Los Angeles (90048) *(P-14950)*

Nationwide Theatres Corp .... A 562 421-8448
2500 Carson St Lakewood (90712) *(P-15015)*

Nationwide Trans Inc (PA)........................ **D 909 355-3211**
11727 Eastend Ave Chino (91710) *(P-9315)*

Natren Inc .... D 805 371-4737
3105 Willow Ln Thousand Oaks (91361) *(P-1822)*

Natrol Inc .... C 818 739-6000
21411 Prairie St Chatsworth (91311) *(P-3456)*

Natrol LLC (PA)...................................... **C 800 262-8765**
15233 Ventura Blvd Fl 900 Sherman Oaks (91403) *(P-3457)*

Natrol LLC .... E 818 739-6000
9454 Jordan Ave Chatsworth (91311) *(P-10637)*

Natural Alternatives Intl Inc (PA)............... **C 760 736-7700**
1535 Faraday Ave Carlsbad (92008) *(P-3322)*

Natural Balance Pet Foods LLC (PA)........... **D 800 829-4493**
19425 Soledad Canyon Rd # 302 Canyon Country (91351) *(P-1430)*

Natural Balance Pet Foods LLC .... D 800 829-4493
1224 Montague Unit 1 Pacoima (91331) *(P-1431)*

Natural Envmtl Protection Co .... E 909 620-8028
750 S Reservoir St Pomona (91766) *(P-3282)*

Natural Food Mill, Corona Also Called: Food For Life Baking Co Inc (P-1450)

Natural Thoughts Incorporated .... E 619 582-0027
4757 Old Cliffs Rd San Diego (92120) *(P-3671)*

Naturalife Eco Vite Labs .... D 310 370-1563
20433 Earl St Torrance (90503) *(P-1301)*

Nature-Cide, Canoga Park Also Called: Pacific Shore Holdings Inc (P-3470)

Nature's Flavors, Orange Also Called: Newport Flavors & Fragrances (P-1688)

Natures Best .... B 714 255-4600
6 Pointe Dr Ste 300 Brea (92821) *(P-10965)*

Natures Flavors .... E 714 744-3700
833 N Elm St Orange (92867) *(P-1823)*

Natures Image Inc .... D 949 680-4400
20361 Hermana Cir Lake Forest (92630) *(P-179)*

Natures Produce .... C 323 235-4343
3305 Bandini Blvd Vernon (90058) *(P-10912)*

Natureware Inc .... D 714 251-4510
6590 Darin Way Cypress (90630) *(P-10638)*

Naturvet, Temecula Also Called: Garmon Corporation (P-1426)

Natus Inc .... D 626 355-3746
4522 Katella Ave Ste 200 Los Alamitos (90720) *(P-4297)*

Natus Medical Incorporated .... D 858 260-2590
5955 Pacific Center Blvd San Diego (92121) *(P-8390)*

Natvar, City Of Industry Also Called: Tekni-Plex Inc (P-2776)

Naumann/Hobbs Mtl Hdlg Corp II .... C 866 266-2244
86998 Avenue 52 Coachella (92236) *(P-10353)*

Nautica Opco LLC .... B 909 297-7243
950 Barrington Ave Ontario (91764) *(P-2022)*

Nautilus Seafood, Wilmington Also Called: J Deluca Fish Company Inc (P-1708)

Navajo Investments Inc (PA)...................... **D 949 863-9200**
17962 Cowan Irvine (92614) *(P-9181)*

Naval Coating Inc .... C 619 234-8366
2080 Cambridge Ave Cardiff By The Sea (92007) *(P-1218)*

Naval Facilities Engineer Comm .... D 619 532-1158
1220 Pacific Hwy San Diego (92132) *(P-17595)*

Naval Hosp Twntynine Plms Gfeb, Twentynine Palms Also Called: United States Dept of
Navy (P-16623)

Naval Medical Center, San Diego Also Called: United States Dept of Navy (P-16239)

Naval Station Child Dev Ctr, San Diego Also Called: Navy Exchange Service Command
(P-17101)

Navco Security Systems, Fullerton Also Called: North American Video Corp (P-10273)

Navcom Technology Inc (HQ)................... **D 310 381-2000**
20780 Madrona Ave Torrance (90503) *(P-6639)*

Navigage Foundation (PA)......................... **D 818 790-2522**
849 Foothill Blvd Ste 8 La Canada (91011) *(P-15726)*

Navigant Cymetrix Corporation .... D 424 201-6300
1515 W 190th St Ste 350 Gardena (90248) *(P-18017)*

Navigant Cymetrix Corporation .... D 858 217-1800
10920 Via Frontera Ste 500 San Diego (92127) *(P-18018)*

Navigate Biopharma Svcs Inc .... C 866 992-4939
1890 Rutherford Rd Carlsbad (92008) *(P-17812)*

Navigators Management Co Inc .... C 949 255-4860
19100 Von Karman Ave Irvine (92612) *(P-18019)*

Navitas Semiconductor Corp .... B 844 654-2642
3520 Challenger St Torrance (90503) *(P-12722)*

Navtrak LLC .... D 410 548-2337
20 Enterprise Ste 100 Aliso Viejo (92656) *(P-14414)*

Navy Exchange Service Command .... D 909 517-2640
4250 Eucalyptus Ave Chino (91710) *(P-9093)*

Navy Exchange Service Command .... D 619 556-7466
2375 Recreation Way San Diego (92136) *(P-17101)*

Nazzareno Electric Co Inc .... D 714 712-4744
1250 E Gene Autry Way Anaheim (92805) *(P-943)*

NBC, Universal City Also Called: NBC Subsidiary (knbc-Tv) LLC (P-9512)

NBC, Universal City Also Called: NBC Studios Inc (P-14966)

NBC 7/Channel 39, San Diego Also Called: Station Venture Operations LP (P-9518)

NBC Asset Warehouse, North Hollywood Also Called: Nbcuniversal LLC (P-9094)

NBC Consulting Inc .... D 310 798-5000
2110 Artesia Blvd Ste 323 Redondo Beach (90278) *(P-18179)*

NBC Studios Inc .... A 818 777-1000
100 Universal City Plz Fl 3 Universal City (91608) *(P-14966)*

NBC Subsidiary (knbc-Tv) LLC .... C 818 684-5746
100 Universal City Plz Bldg 2120 Universal City (91608) *(P-9512)*

NBC Universal Inc .... A
100 Universal City Plz Universal City (91608) *(P-14840)*

Nbcuniversal LLC .... C 310 989-8771
11625 Hart St North Hollywood (91605) *(P-9094)*

Nbcuniversal Media LLC .... A 818 777-1000
100 Universal City Plz Bldg 2160 Universal City (91608) *(P-9485)*

Nbcuniversal Television Dist, Universal City *Also Called: Universal Cy Stdios Prdctons L*
(P-14866)

Nbp, Claremont *Also Called: New Bedford Panoramex Corp (P-6512)*

Nbs Systems Inc (PA) .... E 217 999-3472
2477 E Orangethorpe Ave Fullerton (92831) *(P-3193)*

Nbty Manufacturing LLC .... C 714 765-8323
5115 E La Palma Ave Anaheim (92807) *(P-3458)*

NC America LLC .... E 949 447-6287
400 Spectrum Center Dr Fl 18 Irvine (92618) *(P-13775)*

NC Dynamics, Long Beach *Also Called: NC Dynamics LLC (P-6190)*

NC Dynamics Incorporated .... C 562 634-7392
6925 Downey Ave Long Beach (90805) *(P-6189)*

NC Dynamics LLC .... C 562 634-7392
3401 E 69th St Long Beach (90805) *(P-6190)*

NC Interactive LLC .... D 512 623-8700
660 Newport Center Dr Ste 800 Newport Beach (92660) *(P-14235)*

Nc4 Soltra LLC .... D 408 489-5579
21515 Hawthorne Blvd Ste 520 Torrance (90503) *(P-13982)*

Ncdi, Long Beach *Also Called: NC Dynamics Incorporated (P-6189)*

Ncompass International, Hawthorne *Also Called: Ncompass International LLC (P-18180)*

Ncompass International LLC .... C 323 785-1700
12101 Crenshaw Blvd Ste 800 Hawthorne (90250) *(P-18180)*

Ncsoft, Newport Beach *Also Called: NC Interactive LLC (P-14235)*

NDC Technologies Inc .... D 626 960-3300
5314 Irwindale Ave Irwindale (91706) *(P-8055)*

Nds, Woodland Hills *Also Called: National Diversified Sales Inc (P-4176)*

Nds Americas Inc (DH) .... D 714 434-2100
3500 Hyland Ave Costa Mesa (92626) *(P-9554)*

Ne-Mo's, Escondido *Also Called: Nemos Bakery Inc (P-1494)*

Nea Electronics Inc .... E 805 292-4010
14370 White Sage Rd Moorpark (93021) *(P-6956)*

Neal Electric Corp (HQ) .... D 858 513-2525
5928 Balfour Ct Carlsbad (92008) *(P-944)*

Neal Feay Company .... D 805 967-4521
133 S La Patera Ln Goleta (93117) *(P-4602)*

Neardata Inc .... D 818 249-2469
1361 Foothill Blvd La Canada Flintridge (91011) *(P-18181)*

Neardata Systems, La Canada Flintridge *Also Called: Neardata Inc (P-18181)*

Nearfield Systems Inc .... D 310 525-7000
19730 Magellan Dr Torrance (90502) *(P-7928)*

Neb Cal Printing, San Diego *Also Called: Kovin Corporation Inc (P-3029)*

Nec Logistics America, Rancho Dominguez *Also Called: Nippon Ex Nec Lgstics Amer Inc*
(P-8921)

Ned L Webster Concrete Cnstr .... D 805 529-1900
8800 Grimes Canyon Rd Moorpark (93021) *(P-1127)*

Nederlnder Cncrts San Dego LLC .... D 323 468-1700
6233 Hollywood Blvd Los Angeles (90028) *(P-15000)*

Neighborhood Healthcare (PA) .... D 833 867-4642
215 S Hickory St Escondido (92025) *(P-15399)*

Neighborhood Healthcare .... B 760 737-2000
460 N Elm St Escondido (92025) *(P-15400)*

Neighborhood Healthcare .... C 951 216-2200
26926 Cherry Hills Blvd Ste B Menifee (92586) *(P-15401)*

Neighborhood Healthcare .... D 619 440-2751
855 E Madison Ave El Cajon (92020) *(P-15402)*

Neighborhood Healthcare .... D 760 742-9919
28477 Lizard Rocks Rd Ste 200 Valley Center (92082) *(P-15403)*

Neighborhood Healthcare .... C 951 225-6400
41840 Enterprise Cir N Temecula (92590) *(P-16592)*

Neighborhood Healthcare .... C 619 390-9975
10039 Vine St Ste A Lakeside (92040) *(P-16593)*

Neighborhood Healthcare .... C 760 737-6903
401 E Valley Pkwy Escondido (92025) *(P-16594)*

NEIGHBORHOOD HEALTHCARE- RIVER, Escondido *Also Called: Neighborhood Healthcare*
(P-15399)

Neighborhood House Association (PA) .... B 858 715-2642
5660 Copley Dr San Diego (92111) *(P-16981)*

Neighborhood Steel LLC (HQ) .... E 714 236-8700
5555 Garden Grove Blvd Ste 250 Westminster (92683) *(P-10146)*

Neighbrhood Bus Advrtsment Ltd .... E 442 300-1803
14752 Crenshaw Blvd Gardena (90249) *(P-8703)*

Neil A Kjos Music Company (PA) .... E 858 270-9800
4382 Jutland Dr San Diego (92117) *(P-2928)*

Neill Aircraft Co .... B 562 432-7981
1260 W 15th St Long Beach (90813) *(P-7530)*

Neiman & Company, Van Nuys *Also Called: Neiman/Hoeller Inc (P-8620)*

Neiman/Hoeller Inc .... D 818 781-8600
6842 Valjean Ave Van Nuys (91406) *(P-8620)*

Nelco Products Inc .... C 714 879-4293
1100 E Kimberly Ave Anaheim (92801) *(P-3966)*

Nelgo Industries Inc .... E 760 433-6434
598 Airport Rd Oceanside (92058) *(P-6191)*

Nelgo Manufacturing, Oceanside *Also Called: Nelgo Industries Inc (P-6191)*

Nellix Inc .... E 650 213-8700
2 Musick Irvine (92618) *(P-8203)*

Nellxo LLC .... E 909 320-8501
5990 Bald Eagle Dr Fontana (92336) *(P-5206)*

Nelson Shelton & Associates .... C 310 271-2229
355 N Canon Dr Beverly Hills (90210) *(P-12495)*

Nelson Bros Property MGT Inc .... C 949 916-7300
16b Journey Ste 200 Aliso Viejo (92656) *(P-18020)*

Nelson Brothers Property MGT, Aliso Viejo *Also Called: Nelson Bros Property MGT Inc*
(P-18020)

Nelson Honda, El Monte *Also Called: El Monte Automotive Group LLC (P-11341)*

Nelson Name Plate Company (PA) .... E 323 663-3971
708 Nogales St City Of Industry (91748) *(P-5332)*

Nelson Stud Welding Inc .... C 256 353-1931
630 E Lambert Rd Brea (92821) *(P-10452)*

Nelson-Miller, City Of Industry *Also Called: Nelson Name Plate Company (P-5332)*

Nemos Bakery Inc (HQ) .... D 760 741-5725
416 N Hale Ave Escondido (92029) *(P-1494)*

Neo Tech, Chatsworth *Also Called: Natel Engineering Company LLC (P-7029)*

Neo Tech, Chatsworth *Also Called: Oncore Manufacturing LLC (P-17598)*

Neo Tech Natel Epic Oncore, Chatsworth *Also Called: Oncore Manufacturing Svcs Inc*
(P-6760)

Neogov, El Segundo *Also Called: Governmentjobscom Inc (P-13940)*

Neology, Carlsbad *Also Called: Neology Inc (P-7929)*

Neology Inc (PA) .... C 858 391-0260
1917 Palomar Oaks Way Ste 110 Carlsbad (92008) *(P-7929)*

Neomend Inc .... D 949 783-3300
60 Technology Dr Irvine (92618) *(P-8204)*

Neon Rose, San Diego *Also Called: Neon Rose Inc (P-3220)*

Neon Rose Inc .... E 619 218-6103
5158 Bristol Rd San Diego (92116) *(P-3220)*

Neonroots LLC .... C 310 907-9210
8560 W Sunset Blvd Ste 500 West Hollywood (90069) *(P-13776)*

Neopacific Holdings Inc .... E 818 786-2900
14940 Calvert St Van Nuys (91411) *(P-4177)*

Neovia Logistics Dist LP .... D 909 657-4900
5750 E Francis St Ontario (91761) *(P-9095)*

Neovia Logistics Dist LP .... D 815 552-5900
2289 E Orangethorpe Ave Fullerton (92831) *(P-9316)*

Nep Bexel Inc (HQ) .... D 818 565-4399
7850 Ruffner Ave Ste B Van Nuys (91406) *(P-14897)*

Nepco, Pomona *Also Called: Natural Envmtl Protection Co (P-3282)*

Nephrology, Los Angeles *Also Called: Cedars-Sinai Medical Center (P-15950)*

Neptune Foods, Vernon *Also Called: Fishermans Pride Prcessors Inc (P-1706)*

Nerdist Channel LLC .... E 818 333-2705
2900 W Alameda Ave Unit 1500 Burbank (91505) *(P-6640)*

Nerdist Industries, Burbank *Also Called: Nerdist Channel LLC (P-6640)*

Nerys Logistics Inc .... C 619 616-2124
9925 Airway Rd San Diego (92154) *(P-9371)*

Nest Parent Inc .... A 310 551-0101
2125 E Katella Ave Ste 250 Anaheim (92806) *(P-17596)*

Nestle Dist Ctr & Logistics, Jurupa Valley *Also Called: Nestle Usa Inc (P-1397)*

Nestle Ice Cream Company .... A 661 398-3500
7301 District Blvd Bakersfield (93313) *(P-10833)*

Employee Codes: A=Over 500 employees, B=251-500
C=101-250, D=51-100, E=20-50, F=10-19, G=1-9

2025 Southern California
Business Directory and Buyers Guide

© Mergent Inc. 1-800-342-5647

1119

ALPHABETIC

Nestle Purina Factory, Maricopa *Also Called: Nestle Purina Petcare Company (P-1423)*

Nestle Purina Petcare Company .... E 314 982-1000
800 N Brand Blvd Fl 5 Glendale (91203) *(P-1422)*

Nestle Purina Petcare Company .... C 661 769-8261
1710 Golden Cat Rd Maricopa (93252) *(P-1423)*

Nestle Usa Inc .... D 877 463-7853
3285 De Forest Cir Jurupa Valley (91752) *(P-1302)*

Nestle Usa Inc .... C 661 398-3536
7301 District Blvd Bakersfield (93313) *(P-1303)*

Nestle Usa Inc .... C 818 549-6000
800 N Brand Blvd Glendale (91203) *(P-1304)*

Nestle Usa Inc .... B 951 360-7200
3450 Dulles Dr Jurupa Valley (91752) *(P-1397)*

Net Element, Brea *Also Called: Mullen Automotive Inc (P-14148)*

Net Shapes Inc (PA) .... D 909 947-3231
1336 E Francis St Ste B Ontario (91761) *(P-4568)*

Netapp Inc .... C 818 227-5025
6320 Canoga Ave Ste 1500 Woodland Hills (91367) *(P-14099)*

Netfortris Acquisition Co Inc .... D 877 366-2548
11954 S La Cienega Blvd Hawthorne (90250) *(P-18337)*

Netfortris Acquisition Co Inc .... D 310 861-4300
200 Corporate Pointe Ste 300 Culver City (90230) *(P-18338)*

Netlist, Irvine *Also Called: Netlist Inc (P-6859)*

Netlist Inc (PA) .... D 949 435-0025
111 Academy Ste 100 Irvine (92617) *(P-6859)*

Netmarble Us Inc .... D 213 222-7712
600 Wilshire Blvd Ste 1100 Los Angeles (90005) *(P-2929)*

NETSOL, Encino *Also Called: Netsol Technologies Inc (P-13983)*

Netsol Technologies Inc (PA) .... C 818 222-9195
16000 Ventura Blvd Ste 770 Encino (91436) *(P-13983)*

Network Automation Inc .... E 213 738-1700
3530 Wilshire Blvd Ste 1800 Los Angeles (90010) *(P-13984)*

Network Capital, Irvine *Also Called: Network Capital Funding Corp (P-11927)*

Network Capital Funding Corp (PA) .... B 949 442-0060
7700 Irvine Center Dr Fl 3 Irvine (92618) *(P-11927)*

Network Intgrtion Partners Inc .... D 909 919-2800
11981 Jack Benny Dr Ste 103 Rancho Cucamonga (91739) *(P-14100)*

Network Management Group Inc (PA) .... C 323 263-2632
1100 S Flower St Ste 3110 Los Angeles (90015) *(P-18021)*

Network Medical Management Inc .... C 626 282-0288
1668 S Garfield Ave Ste 100 Alhambra (91801) *(P-18022)*

Network Sltons Prvider USA Inc .... E 213 985-2173
1240 Rosecrans Ave Manhattan Beach (90266) *(P-18339)*

Network Telephone Services Inc (PA) .... D 800 742-5687
21135 Erwin St Woodland Hills (91367) *(P-14555)*

Network Television Time Inc .... E 877 468-8899
3929 Clearford Ct Westlake Village (91361) *(P-2930)*

Networks Electronic Co LLC .... E 818 341-0440
9750 De Soto Ave Chatsworth (91311) *(P-5357)*

Netwrix Corporation .... D 888 638-9749
300 Spectrum Center Dr Ste 200 Irvine (92618) *(P-13985)*

Neubloc LLC (PA) .... D 858 674-8701
125 S Highway 101 Solana Beach (92075) *(P-13777)*

Neudesic LLC (HQ) .... C 949 754-4500
200 Spectrum Center Dr Ste 2000 Irvine (92618) *(P-13778)*

Neuintel LLC (PA) .... D 949 625-6117
20 Pacifica Ste 1000 Irvine (92618) *(P-13779)*

Neurasignal Inc .... E 877 638-7251
1109 Westwood Blvd Los Angeles (90024) *(P-8391)*

Neurelis Inc (PA) .... E 858 251-2111
3430 Carmel Mountain Rd Ste 300 San Diego (92121) *(P-3459)*

Neuro Drinks, Sherman Oaks *Also Called: Neurobrands LLC (P-10966)*

Neurobrands LLC .... C 310 393-6444
15303 Ventura Blvd Ste 675 Sherman Oaks (91403) *(P-10966)*

Neurocrine, San Diego *Also Called: Neurocrine Biosciences Inc (P-3584)*

Neurocrine Biosciences Inc (PA) .... C 858 617-7600
6027 Edgewood Bend Ct San Diego (92130) *(P-3584)*

Neuron Esb, Irvine *Also Called: Neudesic LLC (P-13778)*

Neuroptics Inc .... E 949 250-9792
9223 Research Dr Irvine (92618) *(P-8205)*

Neuroscience Gamma Knife Ctr, Thousand Oaks *Also Called: Los Robles Regional Med Ctr (P-15385)*

Neutraderm Inc .... E 818 534-3190
20660 Nordhoff St Chatsworth (91311) *(P-3672)*

Neutrogena, Los Angeles *Also Called: Kenvue Brands LLC (P-3665)*

Neutronic Stamping & Plating, Corona *Also Called: Ravlich Enterprises LLC (P-5287)*

Nevell Group Inc (PA) .... C 714 579-7501
3001 Enterprise St Ste 200 Brea (92821) *(P-561)*

Nevell Group Inc .... B 760 598-3501
3284 Grey Hawk Ct Carlsbad (92010) *(P-562)*

Nevell Group Inc San Diego, Carlsbad *Also Called: Nevell Group Inc (P-562)*

Nevins Adams Properties, Santa Barbara *Also Called: Nevins/Adams Properties Inc (P-12306)*

Nevins/Adams Properties Inc (PA) .... C 805 963-2884
920 Garden St Ste A Santa Barbara (93101) *(P-12306)*

New Advncs For Pple With Dsbl .... C 661 322-9735
4032 Jewett Ave Bakersfield (93301) *(P-17236)*

New Advncs For Pple With Dsbl .... D 661 327-0188
1120 21st St Bakersfield (93301) *(P-17237)*

New Age Electronics Inc .... C 310 549-0000
21950 Arnold Center Rd Carson (90810) *(P-9978)*

New Age Enclosures, Santa Maria *Also Called: Alltec Integrated Mfg Inc (P-4040)*

New Age Lamirada Inn, La Mirada *Also Called: Kam Sang Company Inc (P-12880)*

New Alternatives Incorporated .... A 619 863-5855
8755 Aero Dr Ste 230 San Diego (92123) *(P-16982)*

New American Funding LLC (PA) .... A 949 430-7029
14511 Myford Rd Ste 100 Tustin (92780) *(P-11858)*

New Bedford Panoramex Corp .... E 909 982-9806
1480 N Claremont Blvd Claremont (91711) *(P-6512)*

New Bi US Gaming LLC .... D 858 592-2472
10920 Via Frontera Ste 420 San Diego (92127) *(P-13986)*

New Brunswick Industries Inc .... E 619 448-4900
5656 La Jolla Blvd La Jolla (92037) *(P-6757)*

New CAM Commerce Solutions LLC .... D 714 338-0200
222 S Harbor Blvd Ste 1015 Anaheim (92805) *(P-13780)*

New Century Industries Inc .... E 562 634-9551
7231 Rosecrans Ave Paramount (90723) *(P-7276)*

New Century Mortgage, Irvine *Also Called: New Century Mortgage Corp (P-11928)*

New Century Mortgage Corp .... A 949 440-7030
18400 Von Karman Ave Ste 1000 Irvine (92612) *(P-11928)*

New Century Snacks, Commerce *Also Called: Snak Club LLC (P-1517)*

New Century Snacks LLC .... E 323 278-9578
5560 E Slauson Ave Commerce (90040) *(P-1515)*

New Chef Fashion Inc .... D 323 581-0300
3223 E 46th St Los Angeles (90058) *(P-1977)*

New Childrens Museum .... D 619 233-8792
200 W Island Ave San Diego (92101) *(P-17258)*

New Cingular Wireless Svcs Inc .... D 619 238-3638
252 Broadway San Diego (92101) *(P-9405)*

New Classic Furniture, Fontana *Also Called: New Classic HM Furnishing Inc (P-2456)*

New Classic HM Furnishing Inc (PA) .... E 909 484-7676
7351 Mcguire Ave Fontana (92336) *(P-2456)*

New Cntury Mtals Southeast Inc .... C 562 356-6804
15723 Shoemaker Ave Norwalk (90650) *(P-4619)*

New Crew Production Corp .... C 323 234-8880
1100 W 135th St Gardena (90247) *(P-14556)*

New Dimension One Spas Inc (DH) .... C 800 345-7727
1819 Aston Ave Ste 105 Carlsbad (92008) *(P-8704)*

New Directions Inc (PA) .... D 310 914-4045
11303 Wilshire Blvd Bldg 116 Los Angeles (90073) *(P-16983)*

NEW DIRECTIONS FOR VETERANS, Los Angeles *Also Called: New Directions Inc (P-16983)*

New Dream Network LLC .... D 323 375-3842
707 Wilshire Blvd Ste 5050 Los Angeles (90017) *(P-9450)*

New Fashion Products Inc .... C 310 354-0090
3600 E Olympic Blvd Los Angeles (90023) *(P-2123)*

New Figueroa Hotel Inc .... D 213 627-8971
1000 S Hope St Apt 201 Los Angeles (90015) *(P-12936)*

New First Fincl Resources LLC .... C 949 223-2160
100 Spectrum Center Dr Ste 400 Irvine (92618) *(P-12046)*

New Flyer of America Inc .... D 909 456-3566
2880 Jurupa St Ontario (91761) *(P-7187)*

New Generation Engrg Cnstr Inc .... E 424 329-3950
22815 Frampton Ave Torrance (90501) *(P-9948)*

Mergent email: customerrelations@mergent.com
1120

2025 Southern California
Business Directory and Buyers Guide

(P-0000) Products & Services Section entry number
(PA)=Parent Co (HQ)=Headquarters (DH)=Div Headquarters

New Generation Wellness Inc (PA)............................C 949 863-0340
46 Corporate Park Ste 200 Irvine (92606) *(P-3460)*

New Glaspro Inc............................E 800 776-2368
9401 Ann St Santa Fe Springs (90670) *(P-4341)*

New Green Day LLC............................E 323 566-7603
1710 E 111th St Los Angeles (90059) *(P-2619)*

New Haven Companies Inc............................D 818 686-7020
13571 Vaughn St Unit E San Fernando (91340) *(P-1972)*

NEW HORIZONS CENTER & WORKSHOP, North Hills *Also Called: New Hrzns Srving Indvdals With (P-16844)*

New Hrzns Srving Indvdals With (PA)............................D 818 894-9301
15725 Parthenia St North Hills (91343) *(P-16844)*

New Inspiration Brdcstg Co Inc (HQ)............................E 805 987-0400
4880 Santa Rosa Rd Camarillo (93012) *(P-9486)*

New Leaf Biofuel LLC............................E 619 236-8500
2285 Newton Ave San Diego (92113) *(P-3827)*

New Legend Inc............................C 855 210-2300
8613 Etiwanda Ave Rancho Cucamonga (91739) *(P-8967)*

New Maverick Desk Inc............................C 310 217-1554
15100 S Figueroa St Gardena (90248) *(P-2511)*

New Milani Group LLC (PA)............................D 323 582-9404
2035 E 49th St Vernon (90058) *(P-10639)*

New Power Inc............................D 800 980-9825
887 Marlborough Ave Riverside (92507) *(P-811)*

New Pride Corporation............................D 323 584-6608
5101 Pacific Blvd Vernon (90058) *(P-10717)*

New Pride Tire LLC............................E 310 631-7000
1511 E Orangethorpe Ave Ste D Fullerton (92831) *(P-14682)*

New Printing, Van Nuys *Also Called: Digital Room Holdings Inc (P-3136)*

New Pvcc Inc............................D 760 742-1230
15835 Pauma Valley Dr Pauma Valley (92061) *(P-15153)*

New Talco Enterprises LLC............................C 310 280-0755
2300 W Empire Ave Burbank (91504) *(P-17748)*

New Tangram LLC............................C 562 365-5000
9200 Sorensen Ave Santa Fe Springs (90670) *(P-9877)*

New Technology Plastics Inc............................E 562 941-6034
7110 Fenwick Ln Westminster (92683) *(P-3283)*

New Times Media Group, San Luis Obispo *Also Called: Slo New Times Inc (P-2829)*

New Vista Behavioral Hlth LLC............................D 949 284-0095
3 Park Plz Ste 550 Irvine (92614) *(P-15815)*

New Vista Health Services............................C 818 352-1421
8647 Fenwick St Sunland (91040) *(P-15875)*

New Vista Health Services............................C 310 477-5501
1516 Sawtelle Blvd Los Angeles (90025) *(P-15876)*

New Vsta Nrsing Rhbltation Ctr, Sunland *Also Called: New Vista Health Services (P-15875)*

New Vsta Post Acute Care Ctr W, Los Angeles *Also Called: New Vista Health Services (P-15876)*

New Wave Electric, Vista *Also Called: Nwec Nevada Inc (P-945)*

New Wave Entertainment, Burbank *Also Called: NW Entertainment Inc (P-14841)*

New Way Landscape & Tree Svcs............................C 858 505-8300
5752 Kearny Villa Rd San Diego (92123) *(P-226)*

New West Products Inc............................E 619 671-9022
7520 Airway Rd Ste 1 San Diego (92154) *(P-4178)*

New-Indy Containerboard, Ontario *Also Called: New-Indy Ontario LLC (P-2632)*

New-Indy Containerboard, Oxnard *Also Called: New-Indy Oxnard LLC (P-2633)*

New-Indy Containerboard LLC (DH)............................D 909 296-3400
3500 Porsche Way Ste 150 Ontario (91764) *(P-2631)*

New-Indy Ontario LLC............................C 909 390-1055
5100 Jurupa St Ontario (91761) *(P-2632)*

New-Indy Oxnard LLC............................C 805 986-3881
5936 Perkins Rd Oxnard (93033) *(P-2633)*

Newbasis LLC............................C 951 787-0600
2626 Kansas Ave Riverside (92507) *(P-4403)*

Newbasis West LLC............................C 951 787-0600
2626 Kansas Ave Riverside (92507) *(P-4404)*

Newberry Technical Services, Bakersfield *Also Called: Nts Inc (P-687)*

Newby Rubber Inc............................E 661 327-5137
320 Industrial St Bakersfield (93307) *(P-3926)*

Newco Auto Leasing, West Hollywood *Also Called: Executive Car Leasing Company (P-14651)*

Newcomb Spring Corp............................E 714 995-5341
8380 Cerritos Ave Stanton (90680) *(P-5396)*

Newcomb Spring of California, Stanton *Also Called: Newcomb Spring Corp (P-5396)*

Newegg.com, City Of Industry *Also Called: Magnell Associate Inc (P-5859)*

Newell Brands Inc............................E 760 246-2700
17182 Nevada St Victorville (92394) *(P-4179)*

Newhall Signal, Santa Clarita *Also Called: Signal (P-2827)*

Newlife2 (PA)............................E 805 549-8093
4855 Morabito Pl San Luis Obispo (93401) *(P-5829)*

Newlight Technologies Inc............................E 714 556-4500
14382 Astronautics Ln Huntington Beach (92647) *(P-4180)*

Newman and Sons Inc (PA)............................E 805 522-1646
2655 1st St Ste 210 Simi Valley (93065) *(P-4405)*

Newman Garrison + Partners Inc............................D 949 756-0818
3100 Bristol St Ste 400 Costa Mesa (92626) *(P-17686)*

Newmar Power LLC............................C 800 854-3906
1580 Sunflower Ave Costa Mesa (92626) *(P-6920)*

Newmeyer & Dillion LLP (PA)............................C 949 854-7000
895 Dove St Ste 500 Newport Beach (92660) *(P-16751)*

Newport, Irvine *Also Called: Newport Corporation (P-7829)*

Newport Beach Auto Group LLC............................D 888 703-7226
44 Auto Center Dr Irvine (92618) *(P-14696)*

Newport Beach Country Club, Newport Beach *Also Called: Newport Beach Country Club Inc (P-15154)*

Newport Beach Country Club Inc............................D 949 644-9550
1 Clubhouse Dr Newport Beach (92660) *(P-15154)*

Newport Beach Spaghetti, Newport Beach *Also Called: Osf International Inc (P-11593)*

Newport Beach Surgery Ctr LLC............................C 949 631-0988
361 Hospital Rd Ste 124 Newport Beach (92663) *(P-15404)*

Newport Brass, Santa Ana *Also Called: Brasstech Inc (P-4802)*

Newport Corporation (HQ)............................B 949 863-3144
1791 Deere Ave Irvine (92606) *(P-7829)*

Newport Diversified Inc............................C 562 921-4359
13963 Alondra Blvd Santa Fe Springs (90670) *(P-14557)*

Newport Diversified Inc............................C 619 448-4111
1286 Fletcher Pkwy El Cajon (92020) *(P-14558)*

Newport Electronics Inc............................D 714 540-4914
2229 S Yale St Santa Ana (92704) *(P-5713)*

Newport Energy............................E 408 230-7545
19200 Von Karman Ave Ste 400 Irvine (92612) *(P-308)*

Newport Fab LLC............................D 949 435-8000
4321 Jamboree Rd Newport Beach (92660) *(P-6860)*

Newport Flavors & Fragrances............................E 714 771-2200
833 N Elm St Orange (92867) *(P-1688)*

Newport Hospitality Group Inc............................D 661 323-1900
801 Truxtun Ave Bakersfield (93301) *(P-12937)*

Newport Laminates Inc............................E 714 545-8335
3121 W Central Ave Santa Ana (92704) *(P-4181)*

Newport Meat Company, Irvine *Also Called: Newport Meat Southern Cal Inc (P-10877)*

Newport Meat Southern Cal Inc............................C 949 399-4200
16691 Hale Ave Irvine (92606) *(P-10877)*

Newport Mesa Memory Care Cmnty, Costa Mesa *Also Called: Silverado Senior Living Inc (P-15778)*

NEWPORT SPECIALTY HOSPITAL, Tustin *Also Called: Foothill Regional Medical Ctr (P-15998)*

Newport Specialty Hospital, Los Angeles *Also Called: Tustin Hospital and Medical Center (P-16234)*

Newport Television LLC............................A 661 283-1700
2120 L St Bakersfield (93301) *(P-9513)*

News Corp - Fox, Los Angeles *Also Called: Twentieth Cntury Fox Japan Inc (P-13337)*

News Group, The, Orange *Also Called: Great Atlantic News LLC (P-11076)*

Newshire Investment, Los Angeles *Also Called: Otts Asia Moorer Devon (P-12727)*

Newton Heat Treating Co Inc............................D 626 964-6528
19235 E Walnut Dr N City Of Industry (91748) *(P-4710)*

Newvac LLC............................C 310 990-0401
9330 De Soto Ave Chatsworth (91311) *(P-6701)*

Newvac LLC............................E 747 202-7333
9330 De Soto Ave Chatsworth (91311) *(P-7030)*

Newvac Division, Chatsworth *Also Called: Newvac LLC (P-6701)*

Nex Group LLC............................D 209 317-6677
9018 Rancho Viejo Dr Bakersfield (93314) *(P-9317)*

Nexem Staffing, Santa Barbara *Also Called: Partners Prsnnel - MGT Svcs LL (P-13552)*

Employee Codes: A=Over 500 employees, B=251-500
C=101-250, D=51-100, E=20-50, F=10-19, G=1-9

2025 Southern California
Business Directory and Buyers Guide

© Mergent Inc. 1-800-342-5647
1121

ALPHABETIC

Nexgen AC & Htg LLC .... D 760 616-5870
700 N Valley St Ste K Anaheim (92801) *(P-812)*

Nexgen Air Conditioning & Plbg, Anaheim *Also Called: Nexgen AC & Htg LLC (P-812)*

Nexgen Pharma, Irvine *Also Called: New Generation Wellness Inc (P-3460)*

Nexgenix Inc (PA).. B 714 665-6240
2 Peters Canyon Rd Ste 200 Irvine (92606) *(P-18340)*

Nexgrill Industries, Chino *Also Called: Nexgrill Industries Inc (P-9900)*

Nexgrill Industries Inc (PA) .... D 909 598-8799
14050 Laurelwood Pl Chino (91710) *(P-9900)*

Nexogy Inc .... D 305 358-8952
10967 Via Frontera San Diego (92127) *(P-13987)*

Nexon America, El Segundo *Also Called: M Nexon Inc (P-13970)*

Nexstar Digital LLC .... D 310 971-9300
12777 W Jefferson Blvd Ste B100 Los Angeles (90066) *(P-13233)*

Next Day Frame Inc .... D 310 886-0851
11560 Wright Rd Lynwood (90262) *(P-2502)*

Next Freight Solutions Inc .... D 442 291-9220
2383 Utah Ave Ste 100 El Segundo (90245) *(P-8968)*

Next Generation, Commerce *Also Called: J & F Design Inc (P-2102)*

Next Intent, San Luis Obispo *Also Called: Next Intent Inc (P-6192)*

Next Intent Inc .... E 805 781-6755
865 Via Esteban San Luis Obispo (93401) *(P-6192)*

Next Point Bearing Group LLC .... E 818 988-1880
28364 Avenue Crocker Valencia (91355) *(P-5751)*

Nextclientcom Inc .... E 661 222-7755
25000 Avenue Stanford Valencia (91355) *(P-2931)*

Nextel, Irvine *Also Called: Nextel Communications Inc (P-9406)*

Nextel Communications Inc .... C 714 368-4509
330 Commerce Irvine (92602) *(P-9406)*

Nextgen Healthcare Inc (HQ) .... B 949 255-2600
18111 Von Karman Ave Ste 600 Irvine (92612) *(P-13988)*

Nextivity Inc (PA) .... E 858 485-9442
16550 W Bernardo Dr Ste 550 San Diego (92127) *(P-6641)*

Nextmod Inc .... E 909 740-3120
6361 Box Springs Blvd Riverside (92507) *(P-2401)*

Nextpoint Inc (PA) .... D 310 360-5904
8750 Wilshire Blvd Ste 200 Beverly Hills (90211) *(P-9451)*

Nexus Capital Management LP .... A 424 330-8820
11100 Santa Monica Blvd Los Angeles (90025) *(P-12723)*

Nexus Dx Inc .... E 858 410-4600
6759 Mesa Ridge Rd San Diego (92121) *(P-8206)*

Nexus Is Inc .... B 704 969-2200
27202 Turnberry Ln Ste 100 Valencia (91355) *(P-9568)*

Nexxen Inc .... D 310 382-8909
10100 Santa Monica Blvd Los Angeles (90067) *(P-13781)*

Neyenesch Printers Inc .... D 619 297-2281
2750 Kettner Blvd San Diego (92101) *(P-3049)*

Nfl Network, Culver City *Also Called: Nfl Properties LLC (P-15032)*

Nfl Properties LLC .... D 310 840-4635
10950 Washington Blvd Ste 100 Culver City (90232) *(P-15032)*

Nga 911 LLC .... C 877 899-8337
8383 Wilshire Blvd Ste 800 Beverly Hills (90211) *(P-13782)*

Ngd Systems Inc .... E 949 870-9148
3019 Wilshire Blvd Santa Monica (90403) *(P-5883)*

Ngp Motors Inc .... C 818 980-9800
5500 Lankershim Blvd North Hollywood (91601) *(P-11385)*

Nguoi Viet Newspaper, Westminster *Also Called: Nguoi Viet Vtnamese People Inc (P-2818)*

Nguoi Viet Vtnamese People Inc (PA) .... E 714 892-9414
14771 Moran St Westminster (92683) *(P-2818)*

Nhca Inc .... C 310 519-8200
2330 Grand Ave Long Beach (90815) *(P-12938)*

Nhk Laboratories Inc (PA) .... E 562 903-5835
12230 Florence Ave Santa Fe Springs (90670) *(P-3461)*

Nhk Laboratories Inc .... D 562 204-5002
10603 Norwalk Blvd Santa Fe Springs (90670) *(P-3462)*

Nhr, Irvine *Also Called: N H Research LLC (P-7927)*

Nhra, San Dimas *Also Called: National Hot Rod Association (P-15040)*

Nhs Western Division Inc .... D 909 947-9931
115 S Palm Ave Ontario (91762) *(P-422)*

Nibr, San Diego *Also Called: Novartis Inst For Fnctnal Gnmi (P-17814)*

Nic Partners, Rancho Cucamonga *Also Called: Network Intgrtion Partners Inc (P-14100)*

Nice North America LLC (DH).............................. C 760 438-7000
5919 Sea Otter Pl Ste 100 Carlsbad (92010) *(P-11692)*

Nicholas Michael Designs LLC .... C 714 562-8101
2330 Raymer Ave Fullerton (92833) *(P-2503)*

Nichols Inst Reference Labs (DH)...................... A 949 728-4000
33608 Ortega Hwy San Juan Capistrano (92675) *(P-16324)*

Nichols Lumber & Hardware Co .... D 626 960-4802
13470 Dalewood St Baldwin Park (91706) *(P-9926)*

Nick Alexander Imports .... C 800 800-6425
6333 S Alameda St Los Angeles (90001) *(P-11386)*

Nico Nat Mfg Corp .... E 323 721-1900
2624 Yates Ave Commerce (90040) *(P-2571)*

Nicolon Corporation .... B 805 968-1510
165 Castilian Dr Goleta (93117) *(P-14323)*

Niconat Manufacturing, Commerce *Also Called: Nico Nat Mfg Corp (P-2571)*

Niedwick Corporation .... E 714 771-9999
967 N Eckhoff St Orange (92867) *(P-6193)*

Niedwick Machine Co, Orange *Also Called: Niedwick Corporation (P-6193)*

Nieves Landscape Inc .... C 714 835-7332
1629 E Edinger Ave Santa Ana (92705) *(P-180)*

Nighthawk Flight Systems Inc .... E 760 727-4900
1370 Decision St Ste D Vista (92081) *(P-7747)*

Nihon Kohden America LLC (HQ)........................ C 949 580-1555
15353 Barranca Pkwy Irvine (92618) *(P-10095)*

Nijjar Realty Inc (PA).. D 626 575-0062
4900 Santa Anita Ave Ste 2c El Monte (91731) *(P-12496)*

Nike Inc .... E 949 616-4042
20001 Ellipse Foothill Ranch (92610) *(P-2161)*

Nike Usa Inc .... A 310 670-6770
222 E Redondo Beach Blvd Ste C Gardena (90248) *(P-15033)*

Nikken Global Inc (HQ).. C 949 789-2000
18301 Von Karman Ave Ste 120 Irvine (92612) *(P-10477)*

Nikkiso Acd, Santa Ana *Also Called: Acd LLC (P-4907)*

Nikkiso Cosmodyne, Seal Beach *Also Called: Cosmodyne LLC (P-5696)*

Nikkiso Cryoquip, Escondido *Also Called: Integrted Crygnic Slutions LLC (P-5707)*

Nikko Enterprise Corporation .... E 562 941-6080
13168 Sandoval St Santa Fe Springs (90670) *(P-1709)*

Niknejad Inc .... E 310 477-0407
6855 Hayvenhurst Ave Van Nuys (91406) *(P-3050)*

Nikon AM Synergy Inc .... E 310 607-0188
3550 E Carson St Long Beach (90808) *(P-4530)*

Nile Ai Inc .... E 818 689-9107
15260 Ventura Blvd Ste 1410 Sherman Oaks (91403) *(P-13989)*

Nina Mia Inc .... D 714 773-5588
826 Enterprise Way Fullerton (92831) *(P-1824)*

Ninas Mexican Foods Inc .... E 909 468-5888
20631 Valley Blvd Ste A Walnut (91789) *(P-1825)*

Ninja Jump Inc .... D 323 255-5418
3221 N San Fernando Rd Los Angeles (90065) *(P-8493)*

Ninjio Llc .... D 805 864-1992
880 Hampshire Rd Ste B Westlake Village (91361) *(P-18341)*

Ninyo More Gtchncal Envmtl Scn (PA).............. D 858 576-1000
5710 Ruffin Rd San Diego (92123) *(P-18342)*

Nippon Ex Nec Lgstics Amer Inc .... D 310 604-6100
18615 S Ferris Pl Rancho Dominguez (90220) *(P-8921)*

Nippon Express .... D 310 782-3000
21250 Hawthorne Blvd Fl 2 Torrance (90503) *(P-9318)*

Nippon Express USA Inc .... D 310 527-4237
19500 S Vermont Ave Torrance (90502) *(P-9319)*

Nippon Travel Agency Amer Inc .... D 310 768-1817
1411 W 190th St Ste 650 Gardena (90248) *(P-9229)*

Nippon Travel Agency PCF Inc (DH).................. D 310 768-0017
1411 W 190th St Ste 650 Gardena (90248) *(P-9230)*

Nipro Optics Inc .... E 949 215-1151
7 Marconi Irvine (92618) *(P-8012)*

Nis America Inc .... E 714 540-1122
4 Hutton Centre Dr Ste 650 Santa Ana (92707) *(P-13990)*

Niscayah Inc .... D 626 683-8167
751 N Todd Ave Azusa (91702) *(P-10272)*

Nissan North America Inc .... C 714 433-3700
1683 Sunflower Ave Costa Mesa (92626) *(P-9807)*

Mergent email: customerrelations@mergent.com
1122

2025 Southern California
Business Directory and Buyers Guide

(P-0000) Products & Services Section entry number
(PA)=Parent Co (HQ)=Headquarters (DH)=Div Headquarters

Nissan North America Inc .... A 310 768-3700
18501 S Figueroa St Gardena (90248) **(P-18182)**

Nissan of Tustin .... C 714 669-8282
30 Auto Center Dr Tustin (92782) **(P-11387)**

Nissho of California Inc .... B 760 727-9719
89055 64th Ave Thermal (92274) **(P-46)**

Nissho of California Inc (PA) .... C 760 727-9719
1902 S Santa Fe Ave Vista (92083) **(P-181)**

Nissin Foods USA Company Inc (DH) .... C 310 327-8478
2001 W Rosecrans Ave Gardena (90249) **(P-1733)**

Niterder Tchncal Ltg Vdeo Syst .... E 858 268-9316
12255 Crosthwaite Cir Ste A Poway (92064) **(P-6513)**

Niterider, Poway Also Called: Niterder Tchncal Ltg Vdeo Syst **(P-6513)**

Nitto, Oceanside Also Called: Nitto Denko Technical Corp **(P-17857)**

Nitto Denko Technical Corp .... D 760 435-7011
501 Via Del Monte Oceanside (92058) **(P-17857)**

Nitto Tyres, Cypress Also Called: Toyo Tire USA Corp **(P-9862)**

Nivek Industries Inc .... E 714 545-8855
230 E Dyer Rd Ste K Santa Ana (92707) **(P-6424)**

Nix Healthcare System, Los Angeles Also Called: Nix Hospitals System LLC **(P-16105)**

Nix Hospitals System LLC (HQ) .... C 210 271-1800
3415 S Sepulveda Blvd Ste 900 Los Angeles (90034) **(P-16105)**

Nixon Inc (PA) .... C 888 455-9200
2810 Whiptail Loop Ste 1 Carlsbad (92010) **(P-10551)**

Nixon Watches, Carlsbad Also Called: Nixon Inc **(P-10551)**

NL&a Collections Inc .... E 323 277-6266
6323 Maywood Ave Huntington Park (90255) **(P-6447)**

Nliven, San Diego Also Called: Defenseweb Technologies Inc **(P-14212)**

Nlyte Software Americas Ltd .... D 866 386-5983
1380 El Cajon Blvd Ste 220 El Cajon (92020) **(P-13783)**

NM Holdco Inc .... C 323 663-3971
2800 Casitas Ave Los Angeles (90039) **(P-5333)**

NMB (usa) Inc (HQ) .... E 818 709-1770
9730 Independence Ave Chatsworth (91311) **(P-5752)**

NMB Tech, Chatsworth Also Called: NMB (usa) Inc **(P-5752)**

Nmc Group Inc .... E 714 223-3525
300 E Cypress St Brea (92821) **(P-10453)**

NMN Construction Inc .... D 714 389-2104
2741 Walnut Ave Ste 110 Tustin (92780) **(P-1128)**

Nms Management Inc .... D 619 425-0440
155 W 35th St Ste A National City (91950) **(P-13396)**

Nms Properties Inc .... D 310 656-2700
10599 Wilshire Blvd Los Angeles (90024) **(P-12497)**

Nmsp Inc (DH) .... D 310 484-2322
2205 W 126th St Ste A Hawthorne (90250) **(P-7277)**

Nmsp Inc .... E 951 734-2453
1451 E 6th St Corona (92879) **(P-7278)**

NN Jaeschke Inc .... E 858 550-7900
9610 Waples St San Diego (92121) **(P-182)**

Nna Insurance Services, Chatsworth Also Called: National Notary Association **(P-17302)**

Nna Insurance Services LLC .... C 818 739-4071
9350 De Soto Ave Chatsworth (91311) **(P-12239)**

Nnn Realty Investors LLC .... B 714 667-8252
19700 Fairchild Ste 300 Irvine (92612) **(P-12724)**

No Boundaries Inc .... E 619 266-2349
789 Gateway Center Way San Diego (92102) **(P-3051)**

No Ordinary Moments Inc .... D 714 848-3900
16742 Gothard St Ste 115 Huntington Beach (92647) **(P-16407)**

No Second Thoughts Inc .... D 619 428-5992
1333 30th St Ste D San Diego (92154) **(P-1978)**

Noah's New York Bagels, Westminster Also Called: Einstein Noah Rest Group Inc **(P-1286)**

Noarus Investments Inc .... D 310 649-2440
5850 W Centinela Ave Los Angeles (90045) **(P-11388)**

Noarus Tgg .... D 714 895-5595
9444 Trask Ave Garden Grove (92844) **(P-11389)**

Nobbe Orthopedics Inc .... E 805 687-7508
3010 State St Santa Barbara (93105) **(P-2155)**

Nobel Biocare Usa LLC .... B 714 282-4800
200 S Kraemer Blvd Unit E Brea (92821) **(P-16345)**

Noble Energy, Seal Beach Also Called: Samedan Oil Corporation **(P-312)**

Noble Metals, San Diego Also Called: Johnson Matthey Inc **(P-4586)**

Noble/Utah Long Beach LLC .... C 562 436-3000
333 E Ocean Blvd Long Beach (90802) **(P-12939)**

Nobles Medical Tech Inc .... E 714 427-0398
17080 Newhope St Fountain Valley (92708) **(P-8207)**

Nogales Investors LLC .... B 310 276-7439
9229 W Sunset Blvd Ste 900 Los Angeles (90069) **(P-12725)**

Nohl Ranch Inn, Anaheim Also Called: Leisure Care LLC **(P-17174)**

Nokia of America Corporation .... E 818 880-3500
2000 Corporate Center Dr Newbury Park (91320) **(P-6589)**

Nolte, George S & Associates, San Diego Also Called: Nv5 Inc **(P-17597)**

Nomoflo Enterprises Inc .... E 818 767-6528
2840 N Hollywood Way Burbank (91505) **(P-6468)**

Nongshim, Rancho Cucamonga Also Called: Nongshim America Inc **(P-10762)**

Nongshim America Inc (HQ) .... C 909 481-3698
12155 6th St Rancho Cucamonga (91730) **(P-10762)**

Nor-Cal Beverage Co Inc .... D 714 526-8600
1226 N Olive St Anaheim (92801) **(P-14559)**

Nora Lighting Inc .... C 323 767-2600
6505 Gayhart St Commerce (90040) **(P-10198)**

Norac Pharma, Azusa Also Called: S&B Pharma Inc **(P-3330)**

Noranco Corona Division, Corona Also Called: Noranco Manufacturing (usa) Acquisition Corp **(P-5617)**

Noranco Manufacturing (usa) Acquisition Corp .... C 951 721-8400
345 Cessna Cir Ste 102 Corona (92878) **(P-5617)**

Norcal Inc .... C 714 224-3949
1400 Moonstone Brea (92821) **(P-1057)**

Norcal Beverage Co, Anaheim Also Called: Nor-Cal Beverage Co Inc **(P-14559)**

Norcal Pottery Products Inc .... C 909 390-3745
5700 E Airport Dr Ontario (91761) **(P-9901)**

Norcal Waste Services Inc .... D 626 357-8666
3514 Emery St Los Angeles (90023) **(P-9752)**

Norchem Corporation (PA) .... E 323 221-0221
5649 Alhambra Ave Los Angeles (90032) **(P-5714)**

Norco Industries Inc (PA) .... C 310 639-4000
365 W Victoria St Compton (90220) **(P-5830)**

Norco Injection Molding Inc .... D 909 393-4000
14325 Monte Vista Ave Chino (91710) **(P-4182)**

Norco Plastics, Chino Also Called: Norco Injection Molding Inc **(P-4182)**

Norco Plastics Inc .... D 909 393-4000
14325 Monte Vista Ave Chino (91710) **(P-4183)**

Nordhavn Yachts, Dana Point Also Called: Pacific Asian Enterprises Inc **(P-14566)**

Nordon Yestech, Carlsbad Also Called: Nordson Corporation **(P-5761)**

Nordson, Carlsbad Also Called: Nordson Dage Inc **(P-8366)**

Nordson Asymtek, Carlsbad Also Called: Nordson Corporation **(P-5762)**

Nordson Asymtek, Carlsbad Also Called: Nordson California Inc **(P-7105)**

Nordson Asymtek, Carlsbad Also Called: Nordson Asymtek Inc **(P-7869)**

Nordson Asymtek Inc .... C 760 431-1919
2747 Loker Ave W Carlsbad (92010) **(P-7869)**

Nordson California Inc .... D 760 918-8490
2747 Loker Ave W Carlsbad (92010) **(P-7105)**

Nordson Corporation .... D 760 419-6551
2762 Loker Ave W Carlsbad (92010) **(P-5760)**

Nordson Corporation .... D 760 431-1919
2762 Loker Ave W Carlsbad (92010) **(P-5761)**

Nordson Corporation .... C 760 431-1919
2762 Loker Ave W Carlsbad (92010) **(P-5762)**

Nordson Dage Inc .... E 440 985-4496
2762 Loker Ave W Carlsbad (92010) **(P-8366)**

Nordson March Inc .... D 925 827-1240
2762 Loker Ave W Carlsbad (92010) **(P-5763)**

Nordson Medical (ca) LLC .... D 657 215-4200
7612 Woodwind Dr Huntington Beach (92647) **(P-8208)**

Nordson Test Insptn Amrcas Inc .... E 760 918-8471
2762 Loker Ave W Carlsbad (92010) **(P-5764)**

Nordstrom, Ontario Also Called: Nordstrom Inc **(P-9096)**

Nordstrom Inc .... B 909 390-1040
1600 S Milliken Ave Ontario (91761) **(P-9096)**

Noredink Corp .... D 844 667-3346
442 N Barranca Ave Ste 153 Covina (91723) **(P-13784)**

Employee Codes: A=Over 500 employees, B=251-500
C=101-250, D=51-100, E=20-50, F=10-19, G=1-9

2025 Southern California
Business Directory and Buyers Guide

© Mergent Inc. 1-800-342-5647
1123

Norfox, City Of Industry *Also Called: Norman Fox & Co (P-11018)*

Noritsu-America Corporation (HQ)..........................C **714 521-9040**
6900 Noritsu Ave Buena Park (90620) *(P-9968)*

Norlaine Inc ....C 626 961-2471
1449 W Industrial Park St Covina (91722) *(P-8705)*

Norman Fox & Co ....E 323 973-4900
5511 S Boyle Ave Vernon (90058) *(P-11017)*

Norman Fox & Co (PA)...E **800 632-1777**
14970 Don Julian Rd City Of Industry (91746) *(P-11018)*

Norman Charter, La Palma *Also Called: Norman International Inc (P-9902)*

Norman Industrial Mtls Inc ....E 949 250-3343
2481 Alton Pkwy Irvine (92606) *(P-10147)*

Norman Industrial Mtls Inc (PA)................................C **818 729-3333**
8300 San Fernando Rd Sun Valley (91352) *(P-10148)*

Norman International, Vernon *Also Called: Norman Paper and Foam Co Inc (P-2736)*

Norman International Inc ....D 562 946-0420
28 Centerpointe Dr Ste 120 La Palma (90623) *(P-9902)*

Norman Paper and Foam Co Inc ....E 323 582-7132
4501 S Santa Fe Ave Vernon (90058) *(P-2736)*

Norman's Nursery, Carpinteria *Also Called: Normans Nursery Inc (P-62)*

Norman's Nursery, Baldwin Park *Also Called: Normans Nursery Inc (P-11096)*

Normans Nursery Inc ....C 805 684-1411
5770 Casitas Pass Rd Carpinteria (93013) *(P-62)*

Normans Nursery Inc ....C 805 684-5442
5800 Via Real Carpinteria (93013) *(P-11095)*

Normans Nursery Inc ....C 626 285-9795
20500 Ramona Blvd Baldwin Park (91706) *(P-11096)*

Norotos Inc ....C 714 662-3113
201 E Alton Ave Santa Ana (92707) *(P-6194)*

Norstar Office Products Inc (PA) ....E **323 262-1919**
5353 Jillson St Commerce (90040) *(P-2512)*

North American Acceptance Corp ....C 714 868-3195
3191 Red Hill Ave Ste 100 Costa Mesa (92626) *(P-11859)*

North American Client Svcs Inc (PA).........................C 949 240-2423
25910 Acero Ste 350 Mission Viejo (92691) *(P-18023)*

North American Fire Hose Corp ....D 805 922-7076
910 Noble Way Santa Maria (93454) *(P-3873)*

North American Med MGT Cal Inc (DH)......................D 909 605-8000
3990 Concours Ste 500 Ontario (91764) *(P-18024)*

North American Pet Products, Corona *Also Called: Pet Partners Inc (P-8714)*

North American Video Corp (PA)................................E **714 779-7499**
1335 S Acacia Ave Fullerton (92831) *(P-10273)*

North Amrcn Foam Ppr Cnverters ....E 818 255-3383
11835 Wicks St Sun Valley (91352) *(P-4008)*

North Amrcn SEC Investigations ....D 323 634-1911
550 E Carson Plaza Dr Ste 222 Carson (90746) *(P-14324)*

North Amrcn Staffing Group Inc ....D 714 599-8399
3 Pointe Dr Ste 100 Brea (92821) *(P-13546)*

North Anaheim Surgery Center, Anaheim *Also Called: Vanguard Health Systems Inc (P-15505)*

North Beam Inc ....E 860 940-4569
222 N Pacific Coast Hwy Ste 2000 El Segundo (90245) *(P-13991)*

North Cast Srgery Ctr Ltd A CA ....D 760 940-0997
3903 Waring Rd Oceanside (92056) *(P-15405)*

North Coast Home Care Inc ....D 760 260-8700
5927 Balfour Ct Ste 111 Carlsbad (92008) *(P-16408)*

North County GMC, Vista *Also Called: County Ford North Inc (P-11328)*

North County Health Prj Inc ....D 760 757-4566
605 Crouch St Bldg C Oceanside (92054) *(P-15406)*

North County Health Prj Inc ....C 760 736-6767
1130 2nd St Encinitas (92024) *(P-15407)*

North County Health Prj Inc (PA) ....C **760 736-6755**
150 Valpreda Rd Frnt San Marcos (92069) *(P-15408)*

North County Services, San Marcos *Also Called: North County Health Prj Inc (P-15408)*

North County Times ....E 951 676-4315
28441 Rancho California Rd Ste 103 Temecula (92590) *(P-2819)*

North County Times (DH) ....C **800 533-8830**
350 Camino De La Reina San Diego (92108) *(P-2820)*

North Highland Company LLC ....D 818 509-5100
4640 Lankershim Blvd Ste 305 North Hollywood (91602) *(P-18183)*

North Island Credit Union, San Diego *Also Called: North Island Financial Credit Union (P-11830)*

North Island Financial Credit Union ....B 619 656-6525
5898 Copley Dr Ste 100 San Diego (92111) *(P-11830)*

North Kern S Tulare Hosp Dst ....C 661 720-2101
1430 6th Ave Delano (93215) *(P-16106)*

North La County Regional Ctr (PA).............................B **818 778-1900**
9200 Oakdale Ave Ste 100 Chatsworth (91311) *(P-18343)*

North Orange County Svc Ctr, Fullerton *Also Called: Southern California Edison Co (P-9618)*

North Ornge Cnty Cmnty Cllege ....B 714 992-7008
330 E Chapman Ave Fullerton (92832) *(P-11633)*

North Ranch Country Club ....C 818 889-3531
4761 Valley Spring Dr Westlake Village (91362) *(P-15155)*

North Ranch Management Corp ....D 800 410-2153
9754 Deering Ave Chatsworth (91311) *(P-11535)*

North Star Acquisition Inc ....D 310 515-2200
14912 S Broadway Gardena (90248) *(P-5099)*

North Star Company, Gardena *Also Called: North Star Acquisition Inc (P-5099)*

Northbound Treatment Services, Newport Beach *Also Called: National Therapeutic Svcs Inc (P-16487)*

Northeast Newspapers Inc ....E 213 727-1117
621 W Beverly Blvd Montebello (90640) *(P-2821)*

Northeast Valley Health Corp (PA).............................D **818 898-1388**
1172 N Maclay Ave San Fernando (91340) *(P-16984)*

Northern Reg. Sub Base, Bakersfield *Also Called: Southern California Gas Co (P-9657)*

Northern Trust, Pasadena *Also Called: Northern Trust of California (inc) (P-11738)*

Northern Trust of California (inc) ....B
201 S Lake Ave Ste 600 Pasadena (91101) *(P-11738)*

Northfield Medical Inc ....C 248 268-2500
13631 Pawnee Rd Apple Valley (92308) *(P-14777)*

Northgate Gonzalez Inc ....B 323 262-0595
425 S Soto St Los Angeles (90033) *(P-18184)*

Northpoint Day Treatment Sch, Northridge *Also Called: Child and Family Guidance Ctr (P-16454)*

Northridge Hospital Med Ctr, Northridge *Also Called: Dignity Health (P-15981)*

Northridge Nursing Center, Reseda *Also Called: Longwood Management Corp (P-16089)*

Northrop Grmman Arospc Systems, Palmdale *Also Called: Northrop Grumman Corporation (P-7752)*

Northrop Grmman Def Mssion Sys, San Diego *Also Called: Northrop Grumman Systems Corp (P-7781)*

Northrop Grmman Elctrnic Syste, Azusa *Also Called: Northrop Grumman Systems Corp (P-7775)*

Northrop Grmman Innvtion Syste ....B 858 621-5700
9617 Distribution Ave San Diego (92121) *(P-7748)*

Northrop Grmman Innvtion Syste ....D 818 887-8100
9401 Corbin Ave Northridge (91324) *(P-7749)*

Northrop Grmmn Spce & Mssn Sys ....B 310 812-4321
2501 Santa Fe Ave Redondo Beach (90278) *(P-7279)*

Northrop Grmmn Spce & Mssn Sys ....C 909 382-6800
862 E Hospitality Ln San Bernardino (92408) *(P-17813)*

Northrop Grumman CMS, Woodland Hills *Also Called: Northrop Grumman Systems Corp (P-7769)*

Northrop Grumman Corporation ....D 310 332-0461
500 N Douglas St El Segundo (90245) *(P-7750)*

Northrop Grumman Corporation ....C 310 332-1000
1 Hornet Way El Segundo (90245) *(P-7751)*

Northrop Grumman Corporation ....E 661 272-7334
3520 E Avenue M Palmdale (93550) *(P-7752)*

Northrop Grumman Corporation ....E 949 260-9800
19782 Macarthur Blvd Irvine (92612) *(P-7753)*

Northrop Grumman Corporation ....A 858 967-1221
18701 Caminito Pasadero San Diego (92128) *(P-7754)*

Northrop Grumman Corporation ....E 310 864-7342
198 Willow Grove Pl Escondido (92027) *(P-7755)*

Northrop Grumman Space, San Diego *Also Called: Northrop Grumman Systems Corp (P-7758)*

Northrop Grumman Systems Corp ....C 310 812-5149
1 Space Park Blvd Redondo Beach (90278) *(P-6642)*

Northrop Grumman Systems Corp ....B 310 812-4321
1 Space Park Blvd # D1 1024 Redondo Beach (90278) *(P-7364)*

Northrop Grumman Systems Corp ....B 661 272-7000
3520 E Avenue M Palmdale (93550) *(P-7365)*

Northrop Grumman Systems Corp ....B 310 812-1089
1 Space Park Blvd Redondo Beach (90278) *(P-7366)*

Mergent email: customerrelations@mergent.com
1124

2025 Southern California
Business Directory and Buyers Guide

(P-0000) Products & Services Section entry number
(PA)=Parent Co (HQ)=Headquarters (DH)=Div Headquarters

Northrop Grumman Systems Corp .... D 858 514-9020
9326 Spectrum Center Blvd San Diego (92123) *(P-7756)*

Northrop Grumman Systems Corp .... D 858 621-7395
7130 Miramar Rd Ste 100b San Diego (92121) *(P-7757)*

Northrop Grumman Systems Corp .... D 858 514-9000
9326 Spectrum Center Blvd San Diego (92123) *(P-7758)*

Northrop Grumman Systems Corp .... C 805 684-6641
2601 Camino Del Sol Oxnard (93030) *(P-7759)*

Northrop Grumman Systems Corp .... D 760 380-4268
Building 806 Fort Irwin (92310) *(P-7760)*

Northrop Grumman Systems Corp .... D 703 713-4096
862 E Hospitality Ln San Bernardino (92408) *(P-7761)*

Northrop Grumman Systems Corp .... D 714 240-6521
600 Pine Ave Goleta (93117) *(P-7762)*

Northrop Grumman Systems Corp .... D 805 315-5728
1467 Fairway Dr Santa Maria (93455) *(P-7763)*

Northrop Grumman Systems Corp .... D 805 278-2074
2700 Camino Del Sol Oxnard (93030) *(P-7764)*

Northrop Grumman Systems Corp .... C 805 987-8831
760 Paseo Camarillo Ste 200 Camarillo (93010) *(P-7765)*

Northrop Grumman Systems Corp .... D 805 987-9739
5161 Verdugo Way Camarillo (93012) *(P-7766)*

Northrop Grumman Systems Corp .... B 310 556-4911
6411 W Imperial Hwy Los Angeles (90045) *(P-7767)*

Northrop Grumman Systems Corp .... A 818 715-4040
21240 Burbank Blvd Ms 29 Woodland Hills (91367) *(P-7768)*

Northrop Grumman Systems Corp .... B 818 715-4854
21240 Burbank Blvd Woodland Hills (91367) *(P-7769)*

Northrop Grumman Systems Corp .... C 818 715-2597
21200 Burbank Blvd Woodland Hills (91367) *(P-7770)*

Northrop Grumman Systems Corp .... B 818 887-8110
9401 Corbin Ave Northridge (91324) *(P-7771)*

Northrop Grumman Systems Corp .... C 714 240-6521
6033 Bandini Blvd Commerce (90040) *(P-7772)*

Northrop Grumman Systems Corp .... D 480 355-7716
400 Continental Blvd El Segundo (90245) *(P-7773)*

Northrop Grumman Systems Corp .... D 818 249-5252
2550 Honolulu Ave Montrose (91020) *(P-7774)*

Northrop Grumman Systems Corp .... A 626 812-1000
1100 W Hollyvale St Azusa (91702) *(P-7775)*

Northrop Grumman Systems Corp .... D 661 540-0446
3520 E Avenue M Palmdale (93550) *(P-7776)*

Northrop Grumman Systems Corp .... C 855 737-8364
1 Space Park Blvd Redondo Beach (90278) *(P-7777)*

Northrop Grumman Systems Corp .... D 310 812-4321
2477 Manhattan Beach Blvd Redondo Beach (90278) *(P-7778)*

Northrop Grumman Systems Corp .... A 626 812-1464
1111 W 3rd St Azusa (91702) *(P-7779)*

Northrop Grumman Systems Corp .... A 310 332-1000
1 Hornet Way El Segundo (90245) *(P-7780)*

Northrop Grumman Systems Corp .... A 410 765-5589
9326 Spectrum Center Blvd San Diego (92123) *(P-7781)*

Northrop Grumman Systems Corp .... B 858 592-4518
15120 Innovation Dr San Diego (92128) *(P-7782)*

Northrop Grumman Systems Corp .... B 858 618-4349
17066 Goldentop Rd San Diego (92127) *(P-7783)*

Northstar, West Hollywood *Also Called: Watt Inc (P-13864)*

Northstar Demolition and Remediation LP .... B
404 N Berry St Brea (92821) *(P-1186)*

Northstar Memorial Group LLC .... C 800 323-1342
2562 State St Carlsbad (92008) *(P-13156)*

Northwest Circuits Corp .... D 619 661-1701
8660 Avenida Costa Blanca San Diego (92154) *(P-6758)*

Northwest Excavating Inc .... D 818 349-5861
18201 Napa St Northridge (91325) *(P-13443)*

Northwest Hotel Corporation (PA) .... **C 714 776-6120**
1380 S Harbor Blvd Anaheim (92802) *(P-12940)*

Northwest Pipe Company .... D 760 246-3191
12351 Rancho Rd Adelanto (92301) *(P-4551)*

Northwest Recycler Core, Riverside *Also Called: Recycler Core Company Inc (P-9760)*

Northwestern Converting Co .... D 800 959-3402
2395 Railroad St Corona (92878) *(P-2218)*

Northwestern Inc .... E 818 786-1581
10153-1/2 Riverside Dr #250 Toluca Lake (91602) *(P-2316)*

Northwestern Mutl Fincl Netwrk (PA) .... **D 619 234-3111**
4225 Executive Sq Ste 1250 La Jolla (92037) *(P-12047)*

Northwestern Mutl Inv MGT LLC .... C 949 759-5555
610 Newport Center Dr Ste 850 Newport Beach (92660) *(P-12240)*

Northwestern Mutual Investment, Newport Beach *Also Called: Northwestern Mutl Inv MGT LLC (P-12240)*

Norton Packaging Inc .... E 323 588-6167
5800 S Boyle Ave Vernon (90058) *(P-4184)*

NORTON SCIENCE AND LANGUAGE AC, Apple Valley *Also Called: High Dsert Prtnr In Acdmic Exc (P-17847)*

Norton Smon Mseum Art At Psden .... D 626 449-6840
411 W Colorado Blvd Pasadena (91105) *(P-17259)*

Nortridge Software, Foothill Ranch *Also Called: Nortridge Software LLC (P-13785)*

Nortridge Software LLC .... D 714 263-7251
27422 Portola Pkwy Ste 360 Foothill Ranch (92610) *(P-13785)*

Nossaman Consults, Los Angeles *Also Called: Nossaman LLP (P-16752)*

Nossaman LLP (PA) .... **D 213 612-7800**
777 S Figueroa St Ste 3400 Los Angeles (90017) *(P-16752)*

Not Your Daughters Jeans, Los Angeles *Also Called: Nydj Apparel LLC (P-10718)*

Nothing To Wear Inc (PA) .... **E 310 328-0408**
630 Maple Ave Torrance (90503) *(P-2051)*

Noushig Inc .... E 805 983-2903
451 Lombard St Oxnard (93030) *(P-1462)*

Nov Inc .... E 714 978-1900
759 N Eckhoff St Orange (92868) *(P-5512)*

Nova, Huntington Park *Also Called: NL&a Collections Inc (P-6447)*

Nova Container Freight Station, Carson *Also Called: H Rauvel Inc (P-9073)*

Nova Development, Calabasas *Also Called: Avanquest North America LLC (P-13664)*

Nova Lifestyle Inc (PA) .... **E 323 888-9999**
6565 E Washington Blvd Commerce (90040) *(P-2432)*

Nova Medical Products, Carson *Also Called: Nova Ortho-Med Inc (P-10096)*

Nova Ortho-Med Inc (PA) .... **E 310 352-3600**
1470 Beachey Pl Carson (90746) *(P-10096)*

Nova Skilled Home Health Inc .... C 323 658-6232
3300 N San Fernando Blvd Ste 201 Burbank (91504) *(P-16595)*

Nova Transportation Services, Compton *Also Called: H Rauvel Inc (P-8953)*

Novacap LLC (HQ) .... **C 661 295-5920**
25111 Anza Dr Valencia (91355) *(P-10274)*

Novalogic Inc .... D 818 880-1997
27489 Agoura Rd Ste 300 Agoura Hills (91301) *(P-13786)*

Novartis Inst For Fnctnal Gnmi .... C 858 812-1500
10675 John J Hopkins Dr San Diego (92121) *(P-17814)*

Novasignal, Los Angeles *Also Called: Neurasignal Inc (P-8391)*

Novastor Corporation (PA) .... **E 805 579-6700**
29209 Canwood St Ste 200 Agoura Hills (91301) *(P-13992)*

Novo Brasil Brewing Co., Chula Vista *Also Called: Otay Lakes Brewery LLC (P-1549)*

Novo Manufacturing LLC .... D 951 479-4620
341 Bonnie Cir Ste 104 Corona (92878) *(P-2317)*

Novo Manufacturing LLC .... E 040 600-0544
25956 Commercentre Dr Lake Forest (92630) *(P-2318)*

Novolex Bagcraft Inc .... E 626 912-2481
17625 Railroad St Rowland Heights (91748) *(P-2737)*

Novotech Nutraceuticals Inc .... E 805 676-1098
4987 Olivas Park Dr Ventura (93003) *(P-1305)*

Nowcom LLC .... C 323 746-6888
4751 Wilshire Blvd Ste 115 Los Angeles (90010) *(P-14236)*

Nowdocs, Brea *Also Called: Nowdocs International Inc (P-3156)*

Nowdocs International Inc .... E 714 986-1559
3230 E Imperial Hwy Ste 302 Brea (92821) *(P-3156)*

Noymed Corp .... C 800 224-2090
1101 N Pacific Ave Ste 303 Glendale (91202) *(P-17815)*

NP Mechanical Inc .... B 951 667-4220
9129 Stellar Ct Corona (92883) *(P-813)*

Npg Inc (PA) .... **D 951 940-0200**
1354 Jet Way Perris (92571) *(P-3838)*

Npms Natural Products Mil Svcs, Gardena *Also Called: Sabater Usa Inc (P-1848)*

Nrea-TRC 711 LLC .... C 213 488-3500
711 S Hope St Los Angeles (90017) *(P-12941)*

Employee Codes: A=Over 500 employees, B=251-500
C=101-250, D=51-100, E=20-50, F=10-19, G=1-9

2025 Southern California
Business Directory and Buyers Guide

© Mergent Inc. 1-800-342-5647

1125

NRG, Oxnard *Also Called: Genon Holdings LLC (P-9586)*

NRG Motorsports Inc .... D 714 541-1173
861 E Lambert Rd La Habra (90631) *(P-7280)*

Nri Distribution, Los Angeles *Also Called: Nri Usa LLC (P-9320)*

Nri Usa LLC (PA) .... D 323 345-6456
13200 S Broadway Los Angeles (90061) *(P-9320)*

NRLL LLC .... B 949 768-7777
1 Mauchly Irvine (92618) *(P-12726)*

Nrp Holding Co Inc (PA) .... C 949 583-1000
1 Mauchly Irvine (92618) *(P-12606)*

NS Wash Systems, Valencia *Also Called: N/S Corporation (P-6025)*

Nsbn, Los Angeles *Also Called: Cliftonlarsonallen LLP (P-17712)*

NSK Prcsion Amer Snta Fe Sprng, Cerritos *Also Called: NSK Precision America Inc (P-10454)*

NSK Precision America Inc .... D 562 968-1000
13921 Bettencourt St Cerritos (90703) *(P-10454)*

Nst, San Diego *Also Called: No Second Thoughts Inc (P-1978)*

Nsv International Corp .... D 562 438-3836
1250 E 29th St Signal Hill (90755) *(P-9836)*

Nta America, Gardena *Also Called: Nippon Travel Agency Amer Inc (P-9229)*

Nta Pacific, Gardena *Also Called: Nippon Travel Agency PCF Inc (P-9230)*

NTD Architects .... D 858 565-4440
9665 Chesapeake Dr Ste 365 San Diego (92123) *(P-17687)*

NTD Architecture, San Diego *Also Called: NTD Architects (P-17687)*

Ntrust Infotech Inc .... D 562 207-1600
230 Commerce Ste 180 Irvine (92602) *(P-13993)*

Nts Inc .... B 661 588-8514
8200 Stockdale Hwy Ste M10306 Bakersfield (93311) *(P-687)*

Nu Health Products, Walnut *Also Called: Nu-Health Products Co (P-3323)*

Nu-Health Products Co .... E 909 869-0666
20875 Currier Rd Walnut (91789) *(P-3323)*

Nu-Hope Laboratories Inc .... E 818 899-7711
12640 Branford St Pacoima (91331) *(P-8209)*

Nubs Plastics Inc .... E 760 598-2525
991 Park Center Dr Vista (92081) *(P-4185)*

Nucleushealth LLC .... D 858 251-3400
13280 Evening Creek Dr S Ste 110 San Diego (92128) *(P-13787)*

Nuconic Packaging LLC .... E 323 588-9033
4889 Loma Vista Ave Vernon (90058) *(P-4186)*

Nucor Warehouse Systems Inc (HQ) .... C 323 588-4261
3851 S Santa Fe Ave Vernon (90058) *(P-4552)*

Nuera Communications Inc (DH) .... D 858 625-2400
9890 Towne Centre Dr Ste 150 San Diego (92121) *(P-9452)*

Nuface, Vista *Also Called: Carol Cole Company (P-8126)*

Numatech West (kmp) LLC .... D 909 706-3627
1201 E Lexington Ave Pomona (91766) *(P-2682)*

Numatic Engineering Inc .... E 818 768-1200
7915 Ajay Dr Sun Valley (91352) *(P-7870)*

Number Holdings Inc (PA) .... C 323 980-8145
4000 Union Pacific Ave Los Angeles (90023) *(P-11268)*

Numecent Inc .... E 949 833-2800
18565 Jamboree Rd Irvine (92612) *(P-13994)*

Numerade Labs Inc .... D 213 536-1489
1155 Rexford Ave Pasadena (91107) *(P-13788)*

Numotion, Cypress *Also Called: Atg - Designing Mobility Inc (P-10064)*

Nuphoton Technologies Inc .... E 951 696-8366
41610 Corning Pl Murrieta (92562) *(P-7136)*

Nura, Irvine *Also Called: Nura USA LLC (P-3463)*

Nura USA LLC .... E 949 946-5700
2652 White Rd Irvine (92614) *(P-3463)*

Nursechoice .... D 866 557-6050
12400 High Bluff Dr San Diego (92130) *(P-13547)*

Nursecore Management Svcs LLC .... A 805 938-7660
1010 S Broadway Ste A Santa Maria (93454) *(P-17184)*

Nursefinders, San Bernardino *Also Called: Nursefinders LLC (P-13548)*

Nursefinders, San Diego *Also Called: Nursefinders LLC (P-13549)*

Nursefinders LLC .... C 909 890-2286
1832 Commercenter Cir B San Bernardino (92408) *(P-13548)*

Nursefinders LLC (HQ) .... C 858 314-7427
12400 High Bluff Dr San Diego (92130) *(P-13549)*

Nusano Inc .... D 424 270-9600
28575 Livingston Ave Valencia (91355) *(P-18185)*

Nusil, Carpinteria *Also Called: Nusil Technology LLC (P-3927)*

Nusil Technology LLC (DH) .... B 805 684-8780
1050 Cindy Ln Carpinteria (93013) *(P-3927)*

Nuspace Inc (HQ) .... E 562 497-3200
4401 E Donald Douglas Dr Long Beach (90808) *(P-6195)*

Nutrawise, Irvine *Also Called: Nutrawise Health & Beauty LLC (P-3464)*

Nutrawise Health & Beauty LLC .... D 888 271-8976
9600 Toledo Way Irvine (92618) *(P-3464)*

Nutri Granulations, La Mirada *Also Called: JM Huber Micropowders Inc (P-3239)*

Nutrilite, Buena Park *Also Called: Access Business Group LLC (P-11005)*

Nutrition Services, San Bernardino *Also Called: San Brnrdino Cy Unified Schl Ds (P-16614)*

Nutrition Services, Hemet *Also Called: Hemet Unified School District (P-16810)*

Nutu, Irvine *Also Called: Willow Laboratories Inc (P-17897)*

Nuvasive Inc (HQ) .... D 858 909-1800
7475 Lusk Blvd San Diego (92121) *(P-8210)*

Nuvision Fincl Federal Cr Un (PA) .... C 714 375-8000
7812 Edinger Ave Ste 100 Huntington Beach (92647) *(P-11809)*

Nuvve Holding Corp (PA) .... E 619 456-5161
2488 Historic Decatur Rd Ste 200 San Diego (92106) *(P-6290)*

Nuwa Robotics Inc .... C 562 450-0100
9250 1/2 Hall Rd Downey (90241) *(P-10385)*

Nv5 Inc .... C 858 385-0500
15092 Avenue Of Science # 200 San Diego (92128) *(P-17597)*

NVE Inc .... D 323 512-8400
912 N La Cienega Blvd 2nd Fl Los Angeles (90069) *(P-18186)*

Nvno, Irvine *Also Called: Envveno Medical Corporation (P-8151)*

NW Entertainment Inc (PA) .... D 818 295-5000
2660 W Olive Ave Burbank (91505) *(P-14841)*

NW Packaging, Pomona *Also Called: NW Packaging LLC (P-11132)*

NW Packaging LLC (PA) .... D 909 706-3627
1201 E Lexington Ave Pomona (91766) *(P-11132)*

Nwec Nevada Inc .... D 760 757-0187
1232 Distribution Way Vista (92081) *(P-945)*

Nwp Services Corporation (DH) .... C 949 253-2500
535 Anton Blvd Ste 1100 Costa Mesa (92626) *(P-13995)*

Nxgn Management LLC .... E 949 255-2600
18111 Von Karman Ave Ste 600 Irvine (92612) *(P-13996)*

Nydj Apparel LLC (PA) .... D 323 581-9040
801 S Figueroa St Ste 2500 Los Angeles (90017) *(P-10718)*

Nydj Apparel LLC .... C 877 995-3267
5401 S Soto St Vernon (90058) *(P-10719)*

Nylok LLC .... E 714 635-3993
313 N Euclid Way Anaheim (92801) *(P-5133)*

Nylok Western Fastener, Anaheim *Also Called: Nylok LLC (P-5133)*

Nylon Molding, Brea *Also Called: Nmc Group Inc (P-10453)*

Nypro Healthcare Baja, Chula Vista *Also Called: Nypro Inc (P-4187)*

Nypro Inc .... D 619 498-9250
505 Main St Rm 107 Chula Vista (91911) *(P-4187)*

Nypro San Diego Inc .... D 619 482-7033
505 Main St Chula Vista (91911) *(P-4188)*

Nytron Aerospace - Mfg Systems, Yorba Linda *Also Called: Engineering Jk Aerospace & Def (P-7472)*

Nyx Cosmetics, Torrance *Also Called: Nyx Los Angeles Inc (P-3673)*

Nyx Los Angeles Inc .... C 323 869-9420
588 Crenshaw Blvd Torrance (90503) *(P-3673)*

Nzxt Inc (PA) .... B 626 385-8272
605 E Huntington Dr Ste 213 Monrovia (91016) *(P-10021)*

O & K Inc (PA) .... C 323 846-5700
2121 E 37th St Vernon (90058) *(P-10720)*

O & S California Inc .... B 619 661-1800
9731 Siempre Viva Rd Ste E San Diego (92154) *(P-7137)*

O & S Properties Inc .... D 626 579-1084
1817 Chico Ave South El Monte (91733) *(P-14778)*

O C M, Los Angeles *Also Called: Old Country Millwork Inc (P-5640)*

O M Y A, Lucerne Valley *Also Called: Omya California Inc (P-3243)*

O P F, Oxnard *Also Called: Oxnard Prcsion Fabrication Inc (P-5012)*

O P I Products Inc (HQ) .... B 818 759-8688
13034 Saticoy St North Hollywood (91605) *(P-3674)*

O.C. Metro Magazine, Newport Beach *Also Called: Churm Publishing Inc (P-2789)*

O'Connell Landscape Maint, Carson *Also Called: OConnell Landscape Maint Inc (P-227)*

O'Melveny, Los Angeles *Also Called: OMelveny & Myers LLP (P-16753)*

O'Neal U S A, Camarillo *Also Called: Jim ONeal Distributing Inc (P-11482)*

Oak Glen Post Acute, Beaumont *Also Called: Pacs Group Inc (P-15744)*

OAK GROVE CENTER, Murrieta *Also Called: Oak Grove Inst Foundation Inc (P-15409)*

Oak Grove Inst Foundation Inc (PA) .... C 951 677-5599
24275 Jefferson Ave Murrieta (92562) *(P-15409)*

Oak Grove Inst Foundation Inc .... C 951 238-6022
1251 N A St Perris (92570) *(P-16985)*

Oak Paper Products Co LLC (PA) .... C 323 268-0507
3686 E Olympic Blvd Los Angeles (90023) *(P-10595)*

Oak Springs Nursery Inc .... D 818 367-5832
13761 Eldridge Ave Sylmar (91342) *(P-9792)*

Oak Valley Hotel LLC .... D 619 297-1101
2270 Hotel Cir N San Diego (92108) *(P-12942)*

Oakcroft Associates Inc (PA) .... E 323 261-5122
750 Monterey Pass Rd Monterey Park (91754) *(P-10354)*

Oakdale Memorial Park (PA) .... D 626 335-0281
1401 S Grand Ave Glendora (91740) *(P-12585)*

Oakhurst Industries Inc (PA) .... C 323 724-3000
2050 S Tubeway Ave Los Angeles (90040) *(P-10967)*

Oakley Inc (DH) .... A 949 951-0991
1 Icon Foothill Ranch (92610) *(P-8410)*

Oakmont Country Club .... C 818 542-4260
3100 Country Club Dr Glendale (91208) *(P-15156)*

Oaktree Capital Management LP (DH) .... C 213 830-6300
333 S Grand Ave Fl 28 Los Angeles (90071) *(P-12028)*

Oaktree Holdings Inc .... A 213 830-6300
333 S Grand Ave Fl 28 Los Angeles (90071) *(P-12637)*

Oaktree Real Estate Opprtnties .... A 213 830-6300
333 S Grand Ave Fl 28 Los Angeles (90071) *(P-12638)*

Oaktree Strategic Income LLC .... A 213 830-6300
333 S Grand Ave Fl 28 Los Angeles (90071) *(P-12639)*

Oakwood Temporary Housing, Long Beach *Also Called: Worldwide Corporate Housing LP (P-13098)*

Oasis Brands Inc .... D 540 658-2830
100 S Anaheim Blvd Ste 280 Anaheim (92805) *(P-10596)*

Oasis Medical Inc (PA) .... D 909 305-5400
510-528 S Vermont Ave Glendora (91741) *(P-8411)*

Oasis West Realty LLC .... A 310 274-8066
1800 Century Park E Ste 500 Los Angeles (90067) *(P-12649)*

Oasis West Realty LLC .... C 310 860-6666
9850 Wilshire Blvd Beverly Hills (90210) *(P-12943)*

Obagi, Long Beach *Also Called: Obagi Cosmeceuticals LLC (P-10640)*

Obagi Cosmeceuticals LLC (HQ) .... D 800 636-7546
3760 Kilroy Airport Way Ste 500 Long Beach (90806) *(P-10640)*

Oberman Tivoli & Pickert Inc .... C 310 440-9600
500 S Sepulveda Blvd Ste 500 Los Angeles (90049) *(P-14101)*

OBryant Electric Inc (PA) .... C 818 407-1986
9314 Eton Ave Chatsworth (91311) *(P-946)*

OBryant Electric Inc .... E 949 341-0025
3 Banting Irvine (92618) *(P-7138)*

Observatories of The Carnegie, Pasadena *Also Called: Carnegie Institution Wash (P-17870)*

Observatory, The, Beverly Hills *Also Called: Live Nation Worldwide Inc (P 14095)*

Oc 405 Partners Joint Venture .... D 858 251-2200
3100 W Lake Center Dr Ste 200 Santa Ana (92704) *(P-655)*

Oc Direct Shower Door, Orange *Also Called: Dennis DiGiorgio (P-4332)*

OC FOOD BANK, Garden Grove *Also Called: Community Action Prtnr Ornge C (P-16897)*

Occidental Petroleum Corporation of California .... A
10889 Wilshire Blvd Los Angeles (90024) *(P-275)*

Occidental Petroleum Investment Co Inc .... A 310 208-8800
10889 Wilshire Blvd Fl 10 Los Angeles (90024) *(P-309)*

Occupational Therapy Training, Gardena *Also Called: Special Service For Groups Inc (P-17244)*

Ocdm, Tustin *Also Called: Orange County Direct Mail Inc (P-13304)*

Ocean Avenue LLC .... B 310 576-7777
101 Wilshire Blvd Santa Monica (90401) *(P-12944)*

Ocean Direct LLC (HQ) .... C 424 266-9300
13771 Gramercy Pl Gardena (90249) *(P-1710)*

Ocean Park Community Center .... C 310 828-6717
1447 16th St Santa Monica (90404) *(P-18344)*

Ocean Protecta Incorporated .... E 714 891-2628
14708 Biola Ave La Mirada (90638) *(P-7623)*

Ocean Sands Hotel .... D 714 966-5200
2620 Hotel Ter Santa Ana (92705) *(P-12945)*

Ocean Service, San Diego *Also Called: Overseas Service Corporation (P-18376)*

Ocean Technology Systems, Santa Ana *Also Called: Undersea Systems Intl Inc (P-7156)*

Ocean View Convelesent Hosp, Santa Monica *Also Called: Golden State Health Ctrs Inc (P-15858)*

Ocean's Eleven, Oceanside *Also Called: Oceans Eleven Casino (P-12946)*

Oceania Inc .... E 562 926-8886
14209 Gannet St La Mirada (90638) *(P-3953)*

Oceania International LLC .... E 949 407-8904
23661 Birtcher Dr Lake Forest (92630) *(P-4620)*

Oceans Eleven Casino .... B 760 439-6988
121 Brooks St Oceanside (92054) *(P-12946)*

Oceanscience, Poway *Also Called: Tern Design Ltd (P-7881)*

Oceanside Auto Country Inc (PA) .... C 760 438-2000
6030 Avenida Encinas Ste 200 Carlsbad (92011) *(P-11390)*

Oceanside Glasstile Company (PA) .... B 760 929-4000
2445 Grand Ave Vista (92081) *(P-4361)*

Oceanside Harbor Holdings LLC .... C 760 331-3177
645 S Beach Blvd Anaheim (92804) *(P-15727)*

Oceanwide Repairs, Long Beach *Also Called: APR Engineering Inc (P-7596)*

Oceanx LLC (PA) .... D 310 774-4088
100 N Pacific Coast Hwy Ste 1500 El Segundo (90245) *(P-14560)*

Ocelot Engineering Inc .... C 800 841-2960
555 S H St San Bernardino (92410) *(P-11484)*

Oci, Santa Fe Springs *Also Called: Office Chairs Inc (P-2513)*

Ocip, Anaheim *Also Called: Orange County Indus Plas Inc (P-10999)*

Ocm Pe Holdings LP .... A 213 830-6213
333 S Grand Ave Fl 28 Los Angeles (90071) *(P-7031)*

Ocm Real Estate Opprtnties Fun .... B 213 830-6300
333 S Grand Ave Fl 28 Los Angeles (90071) *(P-12640)*

Ocmban, Irvine *Also Called: Ocmbc Inc (P-11929)*

Ocmbc Inc (PA) .... C 949 679-7400
19000 Macarthur Blvd Ste 200 Irvine (92612) *(P-11929)*

OConnell Landscape Maint Inc .... A 800 339-1106
860 E Watson Center Rd Carson (90745) *(P-227)*

Ocpc Inc .... D 949 475-1900
2485 Da Vinci Irvine (92614) *(P-3052)*

Ocs America Inc (DH) .... E 310 417-0650
22912 Lockness Ave Torrance (90501) *(P-14561)*

Ocs Bookstore, Torrance *Also Called: Ocs America Inc (P-14561)*

Octa, Orange *Also Called: Orange Cnty Trnsp Auth Schlrsh (P-8792)*

Ocwd, Fountain Valley *Also Called: Orange County Water District (P-9708)*

Odeh Engineers, Irvine *Also Called: Wsp USA Inc (P-17663)*

Odw Logistics .... D 614 549-5000
2600 Stanford Ave Ontario (91761) *(P-9372)*

Odyssey Innovative Designs, San Gabriel *Also Called: Hsiao & Montano Inc (P-4295)*

OEM, Orange *Also Called: Premier Filters Inc (P-5833)*

Oem LLC .... E 714 449-7500
311 S Highland Ave Fullerton (92832) *(P-6196)*

Off Broadway, La Verne *Also Called: Fortress Inc (P-2509)*

Off Duty Officers Inc .... A 888 408-5900
2365 La Mirada Dr Vista (92081) *(P-14325)*

Office Chairs Inc .... D 562 802-0464
14815 Radburn Ave Santa Fe Springs (90670) *(P-2513)*

Office Master Inc .... D 909 392-5678
1110 Mildred St Ontario (91761) *(P-9878)*

Office of Inspector General, Los Angeles *Also Called: Los Angles Cnty Mtro Trnsp Aut (P-8773)*

Office Star Products, Ontario *Also Called: Blumenthal Distributing Inc (P-9866)*

OfficeMax, Downey *Also Called: OfficeMax North America Inc (P-13315)*

OfficeMax North America Inc .... C 562 927-6444
7075 Firestone Blvd Downey (90241) *(P-13315)*

Officeworks Inc .... D 951 784-2534
11801 Pierce St Fl 2 Riverside (92505) *(P-13550)*

A L P H A B E T I C

Officia Imaging Inc (PA) .... E 858 348-0831
5636 Ruffin Rd San Diego (92123) *(P-11693)*

Offline Inc (PA) .... E 213 742-9001
2931 S Alameda St Vernon (90058) *(P-1999)*

Ofs Brands Holdings Inc .... A 714 903-2257
5559 Mcfadden Ave Huntington Beach (92649) *(P-2514)*

Ogio, Carlsbad *Also Called: Ogio International Inc (P-4298)*

Ogio International Inc (HQ) .... E 801 619-4100
2180 Rutherford Rd Carlsbad (92008) *(P-4298)*

Ogio International Inc .... D 800 326-6325
508 Constitution Ave Camarillo (93012) *(P-4299)*

Ogio Powersports, Camarillo *Also Called: Ogio International Inc (P-4299)*

OH So Original Inc .... B 818 841-4770
150 E Angeleno Ave Burbank (91502) *(P-12947)*

Ohi Resort Hotels LLC .... D 714 867-5555
12021 Harbor Blvd Garden Grove (92840) *(P-12948)*

Ohline Corporation .... E 310 327-4630
1930 W 139th St Gardena (90249) *(P-2319)*

Ohmega Solenoid Co Inc .... E 562 944-7948
10912 Painter Ave Santa Fe Springs (90670) *(P-6291)*

Oil Field Services, Santa Maria *Also Called: Pacific Petroleum California Inc (P-356)*

Oil Well Service, Santa Paula *Also Called: Oil Well Service Company (P-353)*

Oil Well Service Company .... D 661 746-4809
10255 Enos Ln Shafter (93263) *(P-351)*

Oil Well Service Company (PA) .... C 562 612-0600
1241 E Burnett St Signal Hill (90755) *(P-352)*

Oil Well Service Company .... D 805 525-2103
1015 Mission Rock Rd Santa Paula (93060) *(P-353)*

Oil-Dri Corporation America .... E 661 765-7194
950 Petroleum Club Rd Taft (93268) *(P-3616)*

Oj Insulation LP (HQ) .... C 800 707-9278
600 S Vincent Ave Azusa (91702) *(P-1017)*

Ojai Health & Rehabilitation, Ojai *Also Called: Ojai Healthidence Opco LLC (P-15816)*

Ojai Healthidence Opco LLC .... D 805 646-8124
601 N Montgomery St Ojai (93023) *(P-15816)*

Ojai Raptor Center .... D 805 649-6884
370 Baldwin Rd Ojai (93023) *(P-138)*

Ojai Valley Community Hospital, Ojai *Also Called: Community Memorial Health Sys (P-15964)*

Ojai Valley Inn & Spa, Ojai *Also Called: Ovis LLC (P-12955)*

Ojai Valley School (PA) .... D 805 646-1423
723 El Paseo Rd Ojai (93023) *(P-16818)*

OK International Inc (DH) .... C 714 799-9910
10800 Valley View St Cypress (90630) *(P-5648)*

Oka & Oka Hawaii LLC .... C 808 329-1393
1756 Ruhland Ave Manhattan Beach (90266) *(P-12949)*

Okonite Company Inc .... C 805 922-6682
2900 Skyway Dr Santa Maria (93455) *(P-4635)*

Old Bbh Inc .... A 858 715-4000
280 10th Ave San Diego (92101) *(P-1263)*

Old Country Millwork Inc (PA) .... E 323 234-2940
5855 Hooper Ave Los Angeles (90001) *(P-5640)*

Old English Mil & Woodworks, Santa Clarita *Also Called: Old English Mil Woodworks Inc (P-2320)*

Old English Mil Woodworks Inc (PA) .... E 661 294-9171
27772 Avenue Scott Santa Clarita (91355) *(P-2320)*

Old Globe, San Diego *Also Called: Old Globe Theatre (P-14967)*

Old Globe Theatre .... B 619 234-5623
1363 Old Globe Way San Diego (92101) *(P-14967)*

Old Guys Rule, Ventura *Also Called: Streamline Dsgn Slkscreen Inc (P-2028)*

Old Spagetti Factory, San Marcos *Also Called: Osf International Inc (P-11592)*

Old Spaghetti Factory-Duarte, Duarte *Also Called: Osf International Inc (P-13182)*

Old Spc Inc .... E 310 533-0748
202 W 140th St Los Angeles (90061) *(P-5279)*

Old Town Fmly Hospitality Corp .... C 619 246-8010
2754 Calhoun St San Diego (92110) *(P-12950)*

Oldcast Precast (DH) .... E 951 788-9720
2434 Rubidoux Blvd Riverside (92509) *(P-4406)*

Oldcastle Infrastructure Inc .... E 951 928-8713
19940 Hansen Ave Nuevo (92567) *(P-4407)*

Oldcastle Infrastructure Inc .... E 909 428-3700
10650 Hemlock Ave Fontana (92337) *(P-4408)*

Oldcastle Infrastructure Inc .... E 951 683-8200
2512 Harmony Grove Rd Escondido (92029) *(P-4409)*

Oldcastle Prcast Enclsure Slto, Riverside *Also Called: Carson Industries LLC (P-4084)*

Olde Thompson LLC .... E 805 983-0388
2300 Celsius Ave Oxnard (93030) *(P-10968)*

Olea Kiosks Inc .... D 562 924-2644
13845 Artesia Blvd Cerritos (90703) *(P-5941)*

Olen Commercial Realty Corp .... B 949 644-6536
7 Corporate Plaza Dr Newport Beach (92660) *(P-12307)*

Olen Companies, The, Newport Beach *Also Called: Olen Residential Realty Corp (P-449)*

Olen Residential Realty, Newport Beach *Also Called: Olen Commercial Realty Corp (P-12307)*

Olen Residential Realty Corp (HQ) .... D 949 644-6536
7 Corporate Plaza Dr Newport Beach (92660) *(P-449)*

Oleumtech Corporation .... D 949 305-9009
19762 Pauling Foothill Ranch (92610) *(P-7871)*

Olin Chlor Alkali Logistics .... D 562 692-0510
11600 Pike St Santa Fe Springs (90670) *(P-3209)*

OLinn Security Incorporated .... C 760 320-5303
1027 S Palm Canyon Dr Palm Springs (92264) *(P-14326)*

Olive Avenue Productions LLC .... B 770 214-7052
4000 Warner Blvd Burbank (91522) *(P-14898)*

Olive Crest (PA) .... B 714 543-5437
2130 E 4th St Ste 200 Santa Ana (92705) *(P-17185)*

OLIVE CREST, Santa Ana *Also Called: Olive Crest (P-17185)*

Olive Hill Greenhouses Inc .... D 760 728-4596
3508 Olive Hill Rd Fallbrook (92028) *(P-63)*

Olive Refinish .... E 805 273-5072
19014 Pacific Coast Hwy Malibu (90265) *(P-3718)*

Olive View-Ucla Medical Center (PA) .... D 818 364-1555
14445 Olive View Dr Sylmar (91342) *(P-15410)*

Olivenhain Municipal Water Dst .... D 760 753-6466
1966 Olivenhain Rd Encinitas (92024) *(P-9707)*

Oliver Healthcare Packaging Co .... D 714 864-3500
1145 N Ocean Cir Anaheim (92806) *(P-10386)*

Olivet International Inc (PA) .... D 951 681-8888
11015 Hopkins St Mira Loma (91752) *(P-10565)*

Olli Salumeria Americana LLC .... D
1301 Rocky Point Dr Oceanside (92056) *(P-1246)*

Ols Hotels & Resorts LLC .... A 310 855-1115
733 N West Knoll Dr West Hollywood (90069) *(P-12951)*

Olson Company LLC (PA) .... D 562 596-4770
3010 Old Ranch Pkwy Ste 100 Seal Beach (90740) *(P-12575)*

Olson Homes, Seal Beach *Also Called: Olson Company LLC (P-12575)*

Olson Industrial Systems, Santee *Also Called: Olson Irrigation Systems (P-5475)*

Olson Irrigation Systems .... E 619 562-3100
10910 Wheatlands Ave Ste A Santee (92071) *(P-5475)*

Oltmans Construction Co (PA) .... D 562 948-4242
10005 Mission Mill Rd Whittier (90601) *(P-495)*

Oltmans Construction Co .... B 805 495-9553
270 Conejo Ridge Ave Ste 210 Thousand Oaks (91361) *(P-496)*

Olympia Convalescent Hospital .... C 213 487-3000
1100 S Alvarado St Los Angeles (90006) *(P-15877)*

Olympia Health Care LLC .... A 323 938-3161
5900 W Olympic Blvd Los Angeles (90036) *(P-16107)*

Olympia Medical Center, Los Angeles *Also Called: Olympia Health Care LLC (P-16107)*

Olympix Fitness LLC .... D 562 366-4600
4101 E Olympic Plz Long Beach (90803) *(P-15058)*

Olympus Building Services Inc .... A 760 750-4629
441 La Moree Rd San Marcos (92078) *(P-18265)*

OLYMPUS BUILDING SERVICES INC, San Marcos *Also Called: Olympus Building Services Inc (P-18265)*

Olympus Water Holdings IV LP (PA) .... E 310 739-6325
360 N Crescent Dr Bldg S Beverly Hills (90210) *(P-3617)*

Om Smart Seating, Ontario *Also Called: Office Master Inc (P-9878)*

Om Tactical, Van Nuys *Also Called: Rizzo Inc (P-8297)*

Omc-Thc Liquidating Inc .... E 858 486-8846
12131 Community Rd Poway (92064) *(P-4812)*

Omega, Bell *Also Called: Omega Moulding West LLC (P-9903)*

Omega Accounting Solutions Inc .... C 949 348-2433
15101 Alton Pkwy Ste 450 Irvine (92618) *(P-17749)*

Mergent email: customerrelations@mergent.com
1128

2025 Southern California
Business Directory and Buyers Guide

(P-0000) Products & Services Section entry number
(PA)=Parent Co (HQ)=Headquarters (DH)=Div Headquarters

Omega Ii Inc .... E 619 920-6650
3525 Main St Chula Vista (91911) *(P-4917)*

Omega Industrial Marine, Chula Vista *Also Called: Omega Ii Inc (P-4917)*

Omega Moulding West LLC .... C ....., 323 261-3510
5500 Lindbergh Ln Bell (90201) *(P-9903)*

Omega Precision .... E 562 946-2491
13040 Telegraph Rd Santa Fe Springs (90670) *(P-6197)*

Omega Products Corp (HQ) .... D 951 737-7447
1681 California Ave Corona (92881) *(P-4503)*

Omega Products Corp .... E 714 935-0900
282 S Anita Dr 3rd Fl Orange (92868) *(P-4504)*

Omega Products International, Corona *Also Called: Omega Products Corp (P-4503)*

Omega/Cinema Props Inc .... D 323 466-8201
1515 E 15th St Los Angeles (90021) *(P-14899)*

OMelveny & Myers LLP (PA) .... A 213 430-6000
400 S Hope St 18th Fl Los Angeles (90071) *(P-16753)*

OMelveny & Myers LLP .... C 310 553-6700
1999 Avenue Of The Stars Fl 8 Los Angeles (90067) *(P-16754)*

Omics Group Inc .... B 650 268-9744
5716 Corsa Ave Ste 110 Westlake Village (91362) *(P-2866)*

Omni Connection Intl Inc .... B 951 898-6232
126 Via Trevizio Corona (92879) *(P-7032)*

Omni Enclosures Inc .... E 619 579-6664
505 Raleigh Ave El Cajon (92020) *(P-2572)*

Omni Family Health (PA) .... D 661 459-1900
4900 California Ave Ste 400b Bakersfield (93309) *(P-15411)*

Omni Hotels, Rancho Mirage *Also Called: Omni Hotels Corporation (P-12952)*

Omni Hotels Corporation .... B 760 568-2727
41000 Bob Hope Dr Rancho Mirage (92270) *(P-12952)*

Omni La Costa Resort & Spa LLC (DH) .... D 760 438-3111
2100 Costa Del Mar Rd Carlsbad (92009) *(P-12953)*

Omni Metal Finishing Inc (PA) .... D 714 979-9414
11639 Coley River Cir Fountain Valley (92708) *(P-5280)*

Omni Optical Products Inc (PA) .... E 714 634-5700
17282 Eastman Irvine (92614) *(P-8056)*

Omni Optical Products Inc .... E 714 692-1400
22605 La Palma Ave Ste 505 Yorba Linda (92887) *(P-14779)*

Omni Pacific, El Cajon *Also Called: Omni Enclosures Inc (P-2572)*

Omni Resource Recovery Inc .... C 909 327-2900
1495 N 8th St Ste 150 Colton (92324) *(P-4189)*

Omni Seals, Rancho Cucamonga *Also Called: Smith International Inc (P-5513)*

Omni Seals Inc .... D 909 946-0181
11031 Jersey Blvd Ste A Rancho Cucamonga (91730) *(P-3904)*

Omni-Pak Industries, Anaheim *Also Called: Nbty Manufacturing LLC (P-3458)*

Omnia Italian Design LLC .... C 909 393-4400
4900 Edison Ave Chino (91710) *(P-9879)*

Omnia Leather Motion Inc .... C 909 393-4400
4950 Edison Ave Chino (91710) *(P-2219)*

Omniduct, Buena Park *Also Called: ECB Corp (P-774)*

Omnimax International LLC .... D 951 928-1000
28921 Us Highway 74 Sun City (92585) *(P-4897)*

Omniprint Inc .... E 949 833-0080
1923 E Deere Ave Santa Ana (92705) *(P-5942)*

Omniteam Inc .... C 562 923-9660
4380 Ayers Ave Vernon (90058) *(P-10341)*

Omnitracs Midco LLC .... E 858 651-5812
9276 Scranton Rd Ste 200 San Diego (92121) *(P-13997)*

Omnitrans .... C 909 383-1680
234 S I St San Bernardino (92410) *(P-8788)*

Omnitrans .... C 909 379-7100
4748 Arrow Hwy Montclair (91763) *(P-8789)*

Omnitrans (PA) .... C 909 379-7100
1700 W 5th St San Bernardino (92411) *(P-8790)*

Omnitrans Access, San Bernardino *Also Called: Omnitrans (P-8788)*

Omnitron Systems Tech Inc .... D 949 250-6510
38 Tesla Irvine (92618) *(P-10275)*

Omron Delta Tau, Chatsworth *Also Called: Delta Tau Data Systems Inc Cal (P-5819)*

Omya California Inc .... D 760 248-7306
7299 Crystal Creek Rd Lucerne Valley (92356) *(P-3243)*

Omya Inc .... D 760 248-5200
7299 Crystal Creek Rd Lucerne Valley (92356) *(P-3244)*

On Central Realty Inc .... B 323 543-8500
1648 Colorado Blvd Los Angeles (90041) *(P-12498)*

On Premise Products Inc .... E 619 562-1486
8021 Wing Ave El Cajon (92020) *(P-8706)*

On-Line Power Incorporated (PA) .... E 323 721-5017
14000 S Broadway Los Angeles (90061) *(P-6292)*

Onboard Systems Hoist & Winch, Anaheim *Also Called: Hornet Acquisitionco LLC (P-7489)*

Oncology Inst CA A Prof Corp (PA) .... A 323 278-4400
18000 Studebaker Rd Ste 800 Cerritos (90703) *(P-15412)*

Oncology Institute Inc (PA) .... A 562 735-3226
18000 Studebaker Rd Ste 800 Cerritos (90703) *(P-16325)*

Oncor Corp .... E 562 944-0230
13115 Barton Rd Ste G-H Whittier (90605) *(P-10641)*

ONCOR CORP, Whittier *Also Called: Oncor Corp (P-10641)*

Oncore Manufacturing LLC .... C 760 737-6777
237 Via Vera Cruz San Marcos (92078) *(P-6759)*

Oncore Manufacturing LLC (HQ) .... A 818 734-6500
9340 Owensmouth Ave Chatsworth (91311) *(P-17598)*

Oncore Manufacturing Svcs Inc .... C 510 360-2222
9340 Owensmouth Ave Chatsworth (91311) *(P-6760)*

Oncore Velocity, San Marcos *Also Called: Oncore Manufacturing LLC (P-6759)*

One & All Inc (HQ) .... C 626 449-6100
2 N Lake Ave Ste 600 Pasadena (91101) *(P-13234)*

One California Plaza, Los Angeles *Also Called: Hill Farrer & Burrill (P-16702)*

One Call Plumber Goleta .... D 805 284-0441
140 Nectarine Ave Apt 4 Goleta (93117) *(P-13180)*

One Call Plumber Santa Barbara .... D 805 364-6337
1016 Cliff Dr Apt 309 Santa Barbara (93109) *(P-814)*

One Clothing, Vernon *Also Called: O & K Inc (P-10720)*

One Events Inc .... D 310 498-5471
8581 Santa Monica Blvd West Hollywood (90069) *(P-13181)*

One Lambda Inc (HQ) .... D 747 494-1000
22801 Roscoe Blvd West Hills (91304) *(P-17816)*

One Silver Serve LLC .... D 818 995-6444
16601 Ventura Blvd Fl 4 Encino (91436) *(P-13397)*

One Step Gps LLC .... D 818 659-2031
675 Glenoaks Blvd Unit C San Fernando (91340) *(P-7784)*

One Stop Systems Inc (PA) .... E 760 745-9883
2235 Enterprise St Ste 110 Escondido (92029) *(P-5943)*

One Stop Systems Inc .... E 858 530-2511
2235 Enterprise St Ste 110 Escondido (92029) *(P-5944)*

One Structural Inc .... E 626 252-0778
19326 Ventura Blvd Ste 200 Tarzana (91356) *(P-354)*

One Sun Power Inc .... A 844 360-9600
3451 Via Montebello Ste 511 Carlsbad (92009) *(P-17599)*

One Up Manufacturing LLC .... E 310 749-8347
550 E Airline Way Gardena (90248) *(P-2641)*

One-Way Manufacturing Inc .... E 714 630-8833
1195 N Osprey Cir Anaheim (92807) *(P-5436)*

Onegeneration (PA) .... D 818 708-6625
17400 Victory Blvd Van Nuys (91406) *(P-17102)*

Onegenrtion Adult Dycare Chldc, Van Nuys *Also Called: Onegeneration (P-17102)*

Onehealth Solutions Inc .... C 858 947-6333
420 Stevens Ave Ste 200 Solana Beach (92075) *(P-14237)*

ONeil Capital Management Inc .... C 310 448-6400
12655 Beatrice St Los Angeles (90066) *(P-3108)*

Oneil Data Systems, Los Angeles *Also Called: ONeil Digital Solutions LLC (P-3053)*

ONeil Data Systems LLC .... C 310 448-6400
12655 Beatrice St Los Angeles (90066) *(P-10387)*

ONeil Digital Solutions LLC (HQ) .... C 972 881-1282
12655 Beatrice St Los Angeles (90066) *(P-3053)*

Onelegacy .... D 213 229-5600
1303 W Optical Dr Irwindale (91702) *(P-16596)*

Onesource Distributors LLC (DH) .... E 760 966-4500
3951 Oceanic Dr Oceanside (92056) *(P-7139)*

Onewest Bank, Culver City *Also Called: CIT Bank NA (P-11756)*

Onewest Bank Group LLC .... A 626 535-4870
888 E Walnut St Pasadena (91101) *(P-11786)*

Online Capital, Newport Beach *Also Called: RMR Financial LLC (P-11951)*

Online Marketing Group LLC .... C 888 737-9635
530 Technology Dr Ste 100 Irvine (92618) *(P-18187)*

Employee Codes: A=Over 500 employees, B=251-500
C=101-250, D=51-100, E=20-50, F=10-19, G=1-9

2025 Southern California
Business Directory and Buyers Guide

© Mergent Inc. 1-800-342-5647

1129

Onni Properties LLC .... C 213 568-0278
888 S Olive St Los Angeles (90014) *(P-18025)*

Onrad Inc .... D 800 848-5876
1770 Iowa Ave Ste 280 Riverside (92507) *(P-15413)*

Onrad Medical Group, Riverside *Also Called: Onrad Inc (P-15413)*

Onshore Technologies Inc .... E 310 533-4888
2771 Plaza Del Amo Ste 802-803 Torrance (90503) *(P-7033)*

Ontario Automotive LLC .... C 909 974-3800
1401 Auto Center Dr Ontario (91761) *(P-11391)*

Ontario Convention Center Corp .... C 909 937-3000
2000 E Convention Center Way Ontario (91764) *(P-14562)*

Ontario Foam Products, Ontario *Also Called: Androp Packaging Inc (P-2653)*

Ontario Mills Shopping Center, Ontario *Also Called: Mills Corporation (P-12304)*

Ontario Vineyard Medical Offs, Ontario *Also Called: Kaiser Foundation Hospitals (P-15346)*

Ontario/Montclair YMCA, Ontario *Also Called: West End Yung MNS Christn Assn (P-17376)*

Ontarioidence Opco LLC .... C 909 984-8629
800 E 5th St Ontario (91764) *(P-15817)*

Ontic Engineering and Mfg Inc (PA) .... D 818 678-6555
20400 Plummer St Chatsworth (91311) *(P-10497)*

Ontrac Logistics Inc .... D 818 504-9043
11085 Olinda St Sun Valley (91352) *(P-9008)*

Ontrac Logistics Inc .... D 804 334-5000
9774 Calabash Ave Fontana (92335) *(P-9009)*

Ontraport Inc .... D 855 668-7276
2030 Alameda Padre Serra Ste 200 Santa Barbara (93103) *(P-13998)*

Onyx Global Hr LLC (PA) .... C 866 715-4806
110 Pine Ave Ste 920 Long Beach (90802) *(P-18188)*

Onyx Industries Inc (PA) .... D 310 539-8830
1227 254th St Harbor City (90710) *(P-5109)*

Onyx Industries Inc .... D 310 851-6161
521 W Rosecrans Ave Gardena (90248) *(P-5110)*

Onyx Pharmaceuticals Inc .... A 650 266-0000
1 Amgen Center Dr Newbury Park (91320) *(P-3465)*

Onyx Power Inc .... C 714 513-1500
4011 W Carriage Dr Santa Ana (92704) *(P-6293)*

Op Games, The, Carlsbad *Also Called: USAopoly Inc (P-8497)*

Opal Service Inc (PA) .... E 714 935-0900
282 S Anita Dr Orange (92868) *(P-4505)*

OPEN America Inc .... C 562 428-9210
4300 Long Beach Blvd Ste 450 Long Beach (90807) *(P-13398)*

Open Systems Inc .... E 317 566-6662
5250 Lankershim Blvd Ste 620 North Hollywood (91601) *(P-13999)*

Openlight Photonics Inc .... E 805 880-2000
6868 Cortona Dr Ste C Goleta (93117) *(P-6861)*

Openpopcom Inc (PA) .... D 714 249-7044
165 Newall Irvine (92618) *(P-18345)*

Openworks, Long Beach *Also Called: OPEN America Inc (P-13398)*

Opera Patisserie .... D 858 536-5800
8480 Redwood Creek Ln San Diego (92126) *(P-1495)*

Opera Patisserie, San Diego *Also Called: Opera Patisserie (P-1495)*

Operam Inc .... D 855 673-7261
1041 N Formosa Ave 500 West Hollywood (90046) *(P-18189)*

Operating Engineers Funds Inc (PA) .... C 866 400-5200
100 Corson St Pasadena (91103) *(P-12665)*

Operation Samahan Inc .... C 619 477-4451
10737 Camino Ruiz Ste 235138 San Diego (92126) *(P-15414)*

Operation Technology Inc .... D 949 462-0100
17 Goodyear Ste 100 Irvine (92618) *(P-13789)*

Ophir Rf, Los Angeles *Also Called: Ophir Rf Inc (P-6643)*

Ophir Rf Inc .... E 310 306-5556
5300 Beethoven St Fl 3 Los Angeles (90066) *(P-6643)*

Ophthonix Inc .... E 760 842-5600
900 Glenneyre St Laguna Beach (92651) *(P-8412)*

Oprah Winfrey Network, Burbank *Also Called: Own LLC (P-9555)*

Opsec Spclized Protecttion Inc, Lancaster *Also Called: Opsec Specialized Protection (P-14327)*

Opsec Specialized Protection .... D 661 942-3999
44262 Division St Ste A Lancaster (93535) *(P-14327)*

Optec Displays Inc .... D 866 924-5239
1700 S De Soto Pl Ste A Ontario (91761) *(P-8621)*

Optec Laser Systems LLC .... E 858 220-1070
11622 El Camino Real Ste 100 San Diego (92130) *(P-3157)*

Opti-Forms Inc .... E 951 296-1300
42310 Winchester Rd Temecula (92590) *(P-5281)*

Optic Arts Holdings Inc .... E 213 250-6069
716 Monterey Pass Rd Monterey Park (91754) *(P-6469)*

Optical Corporation (DH) .... E 818 725-9750
9731 Topanga Canyon Pl Chatsworth (91311) *(P-8013)*

Optima Family Services Inc .... C 323 300-6066
253 N San Gabriel Blvd Pasadena (91107) *(P-16986)*

Optima Protection Plan, Santa Ana *Also Called: Optima Tax Relief LLC (P-13166)*

Optima Tax Relief LLC .... C 714 361-4636
6 Hutton Centre Dr Santa Ana (92707) *(P-13166)*

Options For All Inc .... B 858 565-9870
4250 Pacific Hwy San Diego (92110) *(P-17063)*

Optivus Proton Therapy Inc (PA) .... D 909 799-8300
1475 Victoria Ct San Bernardino (92408) *(P-8057)*

Opto 22 .... C 951 695-3000
43044 Business Park Dr Temecula (92590) *(P-7034)*

Opto Diode Corporation .... E 805 499-0335
1260 Calle Suerte Camarillo (93012) *(P-6862)*

Opto-Knowledge Systems Inc .... E 310 756-0520
19805 Hamilton Ave Torrance (90502) *(P-17817)*

Optoknowledge, Torrance *Also Called: Opto-Knowledge Systems Inc (P-17817)*

Optosigma Corporation .... E 949 851-5881
1540 Scenic Ave Costa Mesa (92626) *(P-8014)*

Optronics, Goleta *Also Called: Karl Storz Imaging Inc (P-8050)*

Optum, Ontario *Also Called: North American Med MGT Cal Inc (P-18024)*

Optumcare Management LLC (HQ) .... A 310 354-4200
2175 Park Pl El Segundo (90245) *(P-15415)*

Optumcare Management LLC .... D 310 316-0811
502 Torrance Blvd Redondo Beach (90277) *(P-15416)*

Optumcare Management LLC .... C 562 988-7000
2600 Redondo Ave Ste 405 Long Beach (90806) *(P-15417)*

Optumcare Management LLC .... D 562 429-2473
4910 Airport Plaza Dr Long Beach (90815) *(P-16597)*

Optumcare Management LLC .... D 714 964-6229
3501 S Harbor Blvd Santa Ana (92704) *(P-16598)*

Optumcare Management LLC .... D 714 995-1000
1236 N Magnolia Ave Anaheim (92801) *(P-16599)*

Optumcare Management LLC .... D 714 968-0068
19066 Magnolia St Huntington Beach (92646) *(P-16600)*

Optumcare Management LLC .... D 714 835-8501
901 W Civic Center Dr Ste 120 Santa Ana (92703) *(P-16601)*

Optumrx Inc .... B 760 804-2399
2858 Loker Ave E Ste 100 Carlsbad (92010) *(P-12099)*

Opus Bank .... A 949 250-9800
19900 Macarthur Blvd Ste 1200 Irvine (92612) *(P-11783)*

Oracle, Mission Viejo *Also Called: Oracle Corporation (P-14000)*

Oracle Corporation .... B 626 315-7513
1 Bolero Mission Viejo (92692) *(P-14000)*

Orange Bakery Inc .... C 949 454-1247
75 Parker Irvine (92618) *(P-12308)*

Orange Bang Inc .... E 818 833-1000
13115 Telfair Ave Sylmar (91342) *(P-1626)*

Orange Circle Studio Corp (PA) .... D 949 727-0800
2 Technology Dr Irvine (92618) *(P-3158)*

Orange Cnty Adult Achvment Ctr .... C 714 744-5301
225 W Carl Karcher Way Anaheim (92801) *(P-16987)*

Orange Cnty George M Raymond N, Orange *Also Called: Raymond Group (P-18043)*

Orange Cnty Globl Med Ctr Aux (DH) .... C 714 835-3555
1301 N Tustin Ave Santa Ana (92705) *(P-16108)*

Orange Cnty Hlth Auth A Pub AG .... B 714 246-8500
505 City Pkwy W Orange (92868) *(P-17303)*

Orange Cnty Name Plate Co Inc .... D 714 522-7693
13201 Arctic Cir Santa Fe Springs (90670) *(P-8622)*

Orange Cnty Ryale Cnvlscent Ho (PA) .... B 714 546-6450
1030 W Warner Ave Santa Ana (92707) *(P-15878)*

Orange Cnty Snttion Dst Fing C (PA) .... B 714 962-2411
10844 Ellis Ave Fountain Valley (92708) *(P-9753)*

Orange Cnty Trnsp Auth Schlrsh (PA) .... B 714 636-7433
550 S Main St Orange (92868) *(P-8791)*

Entry	Code	Phone
Orange Cnty Trnsp Auth Schlrsh	A	714 999-1726
600 S Main St Ste 910 Orange (92868) *(P-8792)*		
Orange Cnty Trnsp Auth Schlrsh	D	714 560-6282
11790 Cardinal Cir Garden Grove (92843) *(P-8793)*		
Orange Coast Ctr For Surgl Cr, Fountain Valley *Also Called: Memorlcare Srgcal Ctr At Ornge* *(P-15388)*		
Orange Coast Magazine, Los Angeles *Also Called: Orange Coast Magazine LLC (P-2867)*		
Orange Coast Magazine LLC	D	949 862-1133
5900 Wilshire Blvd # 10 Los Angeles (90036) *(P-2867)*		
Orange Coast Memorial Med Ctr (HQ)	A	714 378-7000
9920 Talbert Ave Fountain Valley (92708) *(P-16109)*		
Orange Coast Service Center, Westminster *Also Called: Southern California Edison Co* *(P-9616)*		
Orange Coast Title Company (PA)	D	714 558-2836
1551 N Tustin Ave Ste 300 Santa Ana (92705) *(P-14563)*		
Orange County Business Journal, Irvine *Also Called: Cbj LP (P-2848)*		
Orange County Direct Mail Inc	E	714 444-4412
2672 Dow Ave Tustin (92780) *(P-13304)*		
Orange County Erectors Inc	E	714 502-8455
517 E La Palma Ave Anaheim (92801) *(P-5086)*		
Orange County Head Start Inc (PA)	D	714 241-8920
2501 Pullman St Santa Ana (92705) *(P-17103)*		
Orange County Health Authority, Orange *Also Called: Orange Cnty Hlth Auth A Pub AG* *(P-17303)*		
Orange County Health Care Agcy	D	714 568-5683
405 W 5th St Ste 700 Santa Ana (92701) *(P-17304)*		
Orange County Indus Plas Inc (PA)	E	714 632-9450
4811 E La Palma Ave Anaheim (92807) *(P-10999)*		
Orange County Plst Co Inc	C	714 957-1971
3191 Airport Loop Dr Ste B1 Costa Mesa (92626) *(P-1018)*		
Orange County Printing, Irvine *Also Called: Kelmscott Communications LLC (P-3027)*		
Orange County Produce LLC	D	949 451-0880
210 W Walnut Ave Fullerton (92832) *(P-22)*		
Orange County Service Center, San Clemente *Also Called: San Diego Gas & Electric Co* *(P-9672)*		
Orange County Thermal Inds Inc (PA)	D	714 279-9416
1940 N Glassell St Orange (92865) *(P-1019)*		
Orange County Trnsp Auth, Orange *Also Called: Orange Cnty Trnsp Auth Schlrsh (P-8791)*		
Orange County Water District (PA)	D	714 378-3200
18700 Ward St Fountain Valley (92708) *(P-9708)*		
Orange County-Irvine Med Ctr, Irvine *Also Called: Kaiser Foundation Hospitals (P-12660)*		
Orange Countys Credit Union (PA)	C	714 755-5900
1721 E Saint Andrew Pl Santa Ana (92705) *(P-11810)*		
Orange Courier Inc	B	714 384-3600
15300 Desman Rd La Mirada (90638) *(P-14564)*		
Orange Hlthcare Wllness Cntre	C	714 633-3568
920 W La Veta Ave Orange (92868) *(P-15728)*		
Orange Logic LLC	D	949 396-2233
4199 Campus Dr Ste 550 Irvine (92612) *(P-13790)*		
Orange Treeidence Opco LLC	C	951 785-6060
4000 Harrison St Riverside (92503) *(P-15818)*		
Orange Woodworks Inc	E	714 997-2600
1215 N Parker St Orange (92867) *(P-2321)*		
Orangewood Foundation	D	714 619-0200
1575 E 17th St Santa Ana (92705) *(P-16988)*		
Orangewood LLC	C	714 750-3000
2085 S Harbor Blvd Anaheim (92802) *(P-12954)*		
Orangtree Cnvalescent Hosp Inc	C	951 785-6060
4000 Harrison St Riverside (92503) *(P-16110)*		
Orbit Industries Inc	D	213 745-8884
7533 Garfield Ave Bell Gardens (90201) *(P-10199)*		
Orbital Sciences LLC	C	818 887-8345
1151 W Reeves Ave Ridgecrest (93555) *(P-7785)*		
Orbital Sciences LLC	C	703 406-5000
2401 E El Segundo Blvd Ste 200 El Segundo (90245) *(P-7786)*		
Orbital Sciences LLC	B	805 734-5400
Talo Rd Bldg 1555 Lompoc (93437) *(P-7787)*		
Orbital Sciences LLC	C	858 618-1847
16707 Via Del Campo Ct San Diego (92127) *(P-7788)*		
Orbitel International LLC	E	626 369-7050
15304 Valley Blvd City Of Industry (91746) *(P-3159)*		
Orbo Corporation (PA)	E	562 806-6171
1000 S Euclid St La Habra (90631) *(P-2550)*		
Orbo Manufacturing Inc	E	562 222-4535
1000 S Euclid St La Habra (90631) *(P-2265)*		
Orca Arms, Calabasas *Also Called: Orca Arms LLC (P-8533)*		
Orca Arms LLC	D	858 586-0503
26500 Agoura Rd Calabasas (91302) *(P-8533)*		
Orchard - Post Acute Care Ctr	C	562 693-7701
12385 Washington Blvd Whittier (90606) *(P-15729)*		
Orchard Medical Offices, Downey *Also Called: Kaiser Foundation Hospitals (P-15355)*		
Orchem Division, Temecula *Also Called: Oreq Corporation (P-18026)*		
Orchid MPS	D	714 549-9203
3233 W Harvard St Santa Ana (92704) *(P-8211)*		
Orchid Orthopedis, Arcadia *Also Called: MPS Anzon LLC (P-8290)*		
Orco Block & Hardscape (PA)	D	714 527-2239
11100 Beach Blvd Stanton (90680) *(P-4371)*		
Ordermark Inc	C	833 673-3762
12045 Waterfront Dr Ste 400 # 3 Playa Vista (90094) *(P-14149)*		
Oreco Duct Systems Inc	C	626 337-8832
5119 Azusa Canyon Rd Baldwin Park (91706) *(P-5011)*		
Oregon PCF Bldg Pdts Maple Inc	C	909 627-4043
2401 E Philadelphia St Ontario (91761) *(P-9927)*		
Orepac Millwork Products, Ontario *Also Called: Oregon PCF Bldg Pdts Maple Inc (P-9927)*		
Oreq Corporation	D	951 296-5076
42306 Remington Ave Temecula (92590) *(P-18026)*		
Orexigen, La Jolla *Also Called: Orexigen Therapeutics Inc (P-3466)*		
Orexigen Therapeutics Inc	D	858 875-8600
3344 N Torrey Pines Ct Ste 200 La Jolla (92037) *(P-3466)*		
Orgain LLC	E	888 881-4246
16631 Millikan Ave Irvine (92606) *(P-3324)*		
Organic, Rancho Dominguez *Also Called: Organic By Nature Inc (P-3325)*		
Organic By Nature Inc (PA)	E	562 901-0177
2610 Homestead Pl Rancho Dominguez (90220) *(P-3325)*		
Organic Milling Inc (PA)	D	800 638-8686
505 W Allen Ave San Dimas (91773) *(P-1826)*		
Organic Milling Corporation	E	909 599-0961
505 W Allen Ave San Dimas (91773) *(P-1827)*		
Origin LLC	E	818 848-1648
119 E Graham Pl Burbank (91502) *(P-8707)*		
Original Mowbrays Tree Svc Inc	C	
686 E Mill St San Bernardino (92408) *(P-245)*		
Original Parts Group Inc (PA)	D	562 594-1000
1770 Saturn Way Seal Beach (90740) *(P-11450)*		
Original Pennysaver, The, Brea *Also Called: Pennysaver USA Publishing LLC (P-2934)*		
Orion Construction Corporation	D	760 597-9660
2185 La Mirada Dr Vista (92081) *(P-688)*		
Orion Indemnity Company	D	213 742-8700
714 W Olympic Blvd Ste 800 Los Angeles (90015) *(P-12131)*		
Orion Ornamental Iron Inc	E	818 752-0688
6918 Tujunga Ave North Hollywood (91605) *(P-4785)*		
Orion Pictures Corporation	A	310 449-3000
245 N Beverly Dr Beverly Hills (90210) *(P-14842)*		
Orion Plastics Corporation	D	310 223-0370
700 W Carob St Compton (90220) *(P-3284)*		
Orion Tech, City Of Industry *Also Called: Compucase Corporation (P-5877)*		
Orlandini Entps Pcf Die Cast	C	323 725-1332
6155 S Eastern Ave Commerce (90040) *(P-4691)*		
Orlando Precision, Huntington Beach *Also Called: Orlando Spring Corp (P-5397)*		
Orlando Spring Corp	E	562 594-8411
5341 Argosy Ave Huntington Beach (92649) *(P-5397)*		
Orly International Inc (PA)	D	818 994-1001
7710 Haskell Ave Van Nuys (91406) *(P-3675)*		
Ormat Nevada Inc	C	760 353-8200
947 Dogwood Rd Heber (92249) *(P-9592)*		
ORMAT NEVADA, INC., Heber *Also Called: Ormat Nevada Inc (P-9592)*		
Ormat Technologies Inc	E	760 337-8872
855 Dogwood Rd Heber (92249) *(P-9593)*		
Ormco Corporation	E	909 962-5705
200 S Kraemer Blvd Brea (92821) *(P-8345)*		
Ormco Corporation (HQ)	D	714 516-7400
1717 W Collins Ave Orange (92867) *(P-8346)*		

Employee Codes: A=Over 500 employees, B=251-500
C=101-250, D=51-100, E=20-50, F=10-19, G=1-9

2025 Southern California
Business Directory and Buyers Guide

© Mergent Inc. 1-800-342-5647
1131

Ormond Beach LP .... D 805 496-4948
1259 E Thousand Oaks Blvd Thousand Oaks (91362) *(P-12309)*

Oro Grande Cement Plant, Oro Grande Also Called: Calportland Company *(P-4351)*

Orora North America, Buena Park Also Called: Orora Packaging Solutions *(P-10603)*

Orora Packaging Solutions .... C 714 562-6002
6200 Caballero Blvd Buena Park (90620) *(P-10597)*

Orora Packaging Solutions .... C 323 832-2000
1640 S Greenwood Ave Montebello (90640) *(P-10598)*

Orora Packaging Solutions .... E 760 510-7170
664 N Twin Oaks Valley Rd San Marcos (92069) *(P-10599)*

Orora Packaging Solutions .... E 805 278-5040
2146 Eastman Ave Oxnard (93030) *(P-10600)*

Orora Packaging Solutions .... E 909 770-5400
13397 Marlay Ave Fontana (92337) *(P-10601)*

Orora Packaging Solutions .... E 626 284-9524
3201 W Mission Rd Alhambra (91803) *(P-10602)*

Orora Packaging Solutions (HQ) .... D 714 562-6000
6600 Valley View St Buena Park (90620) *(P-10603)*

Orora Packaging Solutions .... E 714 525-4900
7001 Village Dr Ste 155 Buena Park (90621) *(P-10604)*

Orora Packaging Solutions .... D 714 278-6000
1901 E Rosslynn Ave Fullerton (92831) *(P-10605)*

Orora Visual LLC .... D 714 879-2400
1600 E Valencia Dr Fullerton (92831) *(P-3160)*

Orthalliance Inc .... A 310 792-1300
21535 Hawthorne Blvd Ste 200 Torrance (90503) *(P-17238)*

Orthalliances, Torrance Also Called: Orthalliance Inc *(P-17238)*

Ortho Organizers Inc .... C 760 448-8600
1822 Aston Ave Carlsbad (92008) *(P-8347)*

Ortho-Clinical Diagnostics Inc .... E 714 639-2323
612 W Katella Ave Ste B Orange (92867) *(P-3546)*

Orthodental International Inc .... D 760 357-8070
280 Campillo St Ste J Calexico (92231) *(P-8348)*

Orthodyne Electronics Corporation (HQ) .... C 949 660-0440
16700 Red Hill Ave Irvine (92606) *(P-7140)*

Orthopaedic Hospital (PA) .... C 213 742-1000
403 W Adams Blvd Los Angeles (90007) *(P-16111)*

Orthopaedic Inst For Children, Los Angeles Also Called: Orthopaedic Hospital *(P-16111)*

Orthopaedic Specialty Inst, Orange Also Called: Gerald J Alexander MD *(P-15314)*

Orthopedics Department, Los Angeles Also Called: Southern Cal Prmnnte Med Group *(P-15471)*

Orthowest, Laguna Hills Also Called: South Cnty Orthpd Spclsts A ME *(P-15458)*

Osata Enterprises Inc .... D 888 445-6237
18105 Bishop Ave Carson (90746) *(P-10737)*

Osca-Arcosa, San Diego Also Called: O & S California Inc *(P-7137)*

Osf International Inc .... C 760 471-0155
111 N Twin Oaks Valley Rd San Marcos (92069) *(P-11592)*

Osf International Inc .... D 949 675-8654
2110 Newport Blvd Newport Beach (92663) *(P-11593)*

Osf International Inc .... D 626 358-2115
1431 Buena Vista St Duarte (91010) *(P-13182)*

Oshyn Inc .... D 213 483-1770
10601 Walker St Cypress (90630) *(P-13791)*

OSI Digital Inc (PA) .... E 818 992-2700
26745 Malibu Hills Rd Agoura Hills (91301) *(P-14238)*

OSI Electronics Inc (HQ) .... D 310 978-0516
12533 Chadron Ave Hawthorne (90250) *(P-6761)*

OSI Industries LLC .... B 951 684-4500
1155 Mt Vernon Ave Riverside (92507) *(P-1828)*

OSI Optoelectronics Inc .... E 805 087-0146
1240 Avenida Acaso Camarillo (93012) *(P-6863)*

OSI Optoelectronics Inc (HQ) .... D 310 978-0516
12525 Chadron Ave Hawthorne (90250) *(P-6864)*

OSI Staffing Inc .... D 562 261-5753
10913 La Reina Ave Ste B Downey (90241) *(P-13551)*

OSI Systems Inc (PA) .... A 310 978-0516
12525 Chadron Ave Hawthorne (90250) *(P-6865)*

Osr Enterprises Inc .... E 805 925-1831
1910 E Stowell Rd Santa Maria (93454) *(P-14001)*

Osram Sylvania Inc .... D 858 748-5077
13350 Gregg St Ste 101 Poway (92064) *(P-6407)*

Osram Sylvania Inc .... D 909 923-3003
1651 S Archibald Ave Ontario (91761) *(P-9097)*

Oss, Escondido Also Called: One Stop Systems Inc *(P-5943)*

Ossur Americas Inc .... C 949 382-3883
19762 Pauling Foothill Ranch (92610) *(P-8291)*

Ossur Americas Inc (HQ) .... D 800 233-6263
200 Spectrum Center Dr Ste 700 Irvine (92618) *(P-8292)*

Ost Crane Service, Ventura Also Called: Ost Trucks and Cranes Inc *(P-14565)*

Ost Trucks and Cranes Inc .... D 805 643-9963
2951 N Ventura Ave Ventura (93001) *(P-14565)*

OTasty Foods Inc .... D 626 330-1229
160 S Hacienda Blvd City Of Industry (91745) *(P-10763)*

Otay Lakes Brewery LLC .... E 619 768-0172
901 Lane Ave Ste 100 Chula Vista (91914) *(P-1549)*

Otay River Constructors LLC .... C 619 397-7500
860 Harold Pl Chula Vista (91914) *(P-640)*

Otay Water District .... C 619 670-2222
2554 Sweetwater Springs Blvd Spring Valley (91978) *(P-9709)*

Otis Elevator Company .... C 818 241-2828
512 Paula Ave Ste A Glendale (91201) *(P-10388)*

Otis Elevator Company .... D 858 560-5881
3949 Viewridge Ave San Diego (92123) *(P-10389)*

Otonomy, San Diego Also Called: Otonomy Inc *(P-3467)*

Otonomy Inc .... D 619 323-2200
4796 Executive Dr San Diego (92121) *(P-3467)*

Otter Products LLC .... C 888 533-0735
15110 Avenue Of Science San Diego (92128) *(P-10276)*

Otto Instrument Service Inc (PA) .... E 909 930-5800
1441 Valencia Pl Ontario (91761) *(P-7531)*

Otts Asia Moorer Devon .... C 323 603-6959
10015 Baring Cross St Los Angeles (90044) *(P-12727)*

Our Alchemy LLC .... D 310 893-6289
5900 Wilshire Blvd Fl 18 Los Angeles (90036) *(P-14928)*

Our House, Victorville Also Called: Family Assistance Program *(P-16941)*

Out of Shell LLC .... C 626 401-1923
9658 Remer St South El Monte (91733) *(P-1829)*

Outdate Rx LLC .... D 855 688-3283
1125 Research Dr Redlands (92374) *(P-10642)*

Outdoor Dimensions LLC .... C 714 578-9555
5325 E Hunter Ave Anaheim (92807) *(P-2413)*

Outdoor Products, Los Angeles Also Called: Outdoor Rcrtion Group Hldngs L *(P-2231)*

Outdoor Rcrtion Group Hldngs L (PA) .... E 323 226-0830
3450 Mount Vernon Dr Los Angeles (90008) *(P-2231)*

Outfront Media LLC .... E 323 222-7171
1731 Workman St Los Angeles (90031) *(P-13257)*

Outlook Amusements Inc .... C 818 433-3800
3746 Foothill Blvd La Crescenta (91214) *(P-14239)*

Outlook Resources Inc .... D 562 623-9328
14930 Alondra Blvd La Mirada (90638) *(P-2254)*

Outsource Manufacturing Inc .... D 760 795-1295
2460 Ash St Vista (92081) *(P-6866)*

Outsource Utility Contr LLC .... A 714 238-9263
970 W 190th St Torrance (90502) *(P-9594)*

Ovation Home Loans, Irvine Also Called: Carnegie Mortgage LLC *(P-11941)*

Ovation Tech Inc .... C 949 271-0054
17551 Von Karman Ave Irvine (92614) *(P-14240)*

Overair Inc .... E 949 503-7503
3001 S Susan St Santa Ana (92704) *(P-7367)*

Overhill Farms Inc (DH) .... C 323 582-9977
2727 E Vernon Ave Vernon (90058) *(P-1830)*

Overseas Service Corporation .... C 858 408-0751
8221 Arjons Dr Ste B2 San Diego (92126) *(P-18376)*

Ovg Facilities LLC .... D 757 323-9380
1100 Glendon Ave Ste 2100 Los Angeles (90024) *(P-18027)*

Ovis LLC .... A 805 646-5511
905 Country Club Rd Ojai (93023) *(P-12955)*

OVS, Ojai Also Called: Ojai Valley School *(P-16818)*

Owb Packers LLC .... D 760 351-2700
57 Shank Rd Brawley (92227) *(P-1247)*

Owen Oil Tools LP .... D 661 637-1380
5001 Standard St Bakersfield (93308) *(P-355)*

Owen Trailers Inc .... E 951 361-4557
9020 Jurupa Rd Riverside (92509) *(P-7316)*

Owens & Minor Distribution Inc .... B 805 524-0243
452 Sespe Ave Fillmore (93015) *(P-10097)*

Owens Corning, Compton *Also Called: Owens Corning Sales LLC (P-3846)*

Owens Corning Sales LLC .... C 310 631-1062
1501 N Tamarind Ave Compton (90222) *(P-3846)*

Owl Education and Training Inc .... C 949 797-2000
2465 Campus Dr Irvine (92612) *(P-17064)*

Own LLC .... C 323 602-5500
4000 Warner Blvd Burbank (91522) *(P-9555)*

Owsla Touring LLC .... E 818 385-1933
16000 Ventura Blvd Ste 600 Encino (91436) *(P-2932)*

Oxerra Americas LLC .... D 323 269-7311
3700 E Olympic Blvd Los Angeles (90023) *(P-3222)*

Oxford Instrs Asylum RES Inc (HQ)................... D 805 696-6466
7416 Hollister Ave Santa Barbara (93117) *(P-7970)*

Oxford Nanoimaging Inc .... D 858 999-8860
11045 Roselle St Ste 3 San Diego (92121) *(P-7971)*

Oxford Palace Hotel LLC .... D 213 382-7756
745 S Oxford Ave Los Angeles (90005) *(P-12956)*

Oxnard 2 Warehouse, Oxnard *Also Called: Sunrise Growers Inc (P-1858)*

Oxnard Pallet Company, Oxnard *Also Called: E Vasquez Distributors Inc (P-2387)*

Oxnard Police Department .... B 805 385-8300
251 S C St Oxnard (93030) *(P-17358)*

Oxnard Prcsion Fabrication Inc .... E 805 985-0447
2200 Teal Club Rd Oxnard (93030) *(P-5012)*

OXY, Los Angeles *Also Called: Occidental Petroleum Corporation of California (P-275)*

Oxyheal Health Group Inc .... C 619 336-2022
3224 Hoover Ave National City (91950) *(P-14780)*

Oxystrap International Inc .... E 800 699-6901
8705 Complex Dr San Diego (92123) *(P-3928)*

Oz North Coast Y M C A, Oceanside *Also Called: YMCA of San Diego County (P-17400)*

Oz San Diego, San Diego *Also Called: YMCA of San Diego County (P-17395)*

P & L Development LLC .... C 323 567-2482
11865 Alameda St Lynwood (90262) *(P-3468)*

P & R Paper Supply Co Inc .... C 619 671-2400
1350 Piper Ranch Rd San Diego (92154) *(P-2770)*

P & R Paper Supply Co Inc (HQ) .... D 909 389-1807
1898 E Colton Ave Redlands (92374) *(P-10606)*

P A C E, Los Angeles *Also Called: Pacific Asian Cnsrtium In Empl (P-17065)*

P A P, Anaheim *Also Called: Precision Anodizing & Pltg Inc (P-5285)*

P A X Industries, Costa Mesa *Also Called: Tk Pax Inc (P-3876)*

P C A Electronics Inc .... E 818 892-0761
16799 Schoenborn St North Hills (91343) *(P-10277)*

P C M, Banning *Also Called: Professional Cmnty MGT Cal Inc (P-12509)*

P C S C, Torrance *Also Called: Proprietary Controls Systems (P-8059)*

P H S, Northridge *Also Called: Progressive Health Care System (P-15424)*

P J J Enterprises Inc .... C 619 232-6136
1250 Delevan Dr San Diego (92102) *(P-13465)*

P K Metal, Los Angeles *Also Called: P Kay Metal Inc (P-4621)*

P Kay Metal Inc (PA) .... E 323 585-5058
2448 E 25th St Los Angeles (90058) *(P-4621)*

P L C Lighting, Chatsworth *Also Called: PLC Imports Inc (P-10201)*

P L M, Los Angeles *Also Called: Prudential Lighting Corp (P-6471)*

P M C, Cypress *Also Called: Plastic Molded Components Inc (P-4200)*

P M D Holding Corp .... B 949 595-4777
26672 Towne Centre Dr Ste 310 El Toro (92610) *(P-10098)*

P M I, San Diego *Also Called: Pacific Maritime Inds Corp (P-4858)*

P P I, Corona *Also Called: Preprocration Plastics Inc (P-4208)*

P P I, Santa Fe Springs *Also Called: Premiere Packaging Inds Inc (P-11135)*

P R L, City Of Industry *Also Called: Prl Glass Systems Inc (P-4344)*

P R P, Santa Ana *Also Called: Profit Recovery Partners LLC (P-18349)*

P S E Boilers, Santa Fe Springs *Also Called: Pacific Steam Equipment Inc (P-4918)*

P S I, Beaumont *Also Called: Precision Stampings Inc (P-6426)*

P T I, Torrance *Also Called: Plasma Technology Incorporated (P-5338)*

P T I, Santa Ana *Also Called: Parpro Technologies Inc (P-6762)*

P T P, Carson *Also Called: Pacific Toll Processing Inc (P-9356)*

P-Americas LLC .... E 805 641-4200
4375 N Ventura Ave Ventura (93001) *(P-1627)*

P.S. Services, Anaheim *Also Called: 3s Sign Services Inc (P-8588)*

P&O Stg-Carson 4150, Carson *Also Called: US Foods Inc (P-10989)*

P2f Holdings .... D 562 296-1055
1760 Apollo Ct Seal Beach (90740) *(P-11133)*

P2s LP .... C 562 497-2999
4660 La Jolla Village Dr Ste 600 San Diego (92122) *(P-17600)*

Paamco, Newport Beach *Also Called: Pacific Altrntive Asset MGT LL (P-12029)*

Pabco Building Products LLC .... C 323 581-6113
4460 Pacific Blvd Vernon (90058) *(P-4467)*

Pabco Paper, Vernon *Also Called: Pabco Building Products LLC (P-4467)*

Pac Fill Inc .... E 818 409-0117
5471 W San Fernando Rd Los Angeles (90039) *(P-1333)*

Pac Foundries Inc .... C 805 986-1308
705 Industrial Way Port Hueneme (93041) *(P-4683)*

Pac West Land Care Inc .... C 760 630-0231
408 Olive Ave Vista (92083) *(P-183)*

Pac-Dent Inc .... E 909 839-0888
670 Endeavor Cir Brea (92821) *(P-8349)*

Pac-Rancho Inc (HQ)... C 909 987-4721
11000 Jersey Blvd Rancho Cucamonga (91730) *(P-4569)*

Pac-Refco Inc .... E 760 956-8600
2230 Ottawa Rd Ste A Apple Valley (92307) *(P-5979)*

Pace Lithographers Inc .... E 626 913-2108
18030 Cortney Ct City Of Industry (91748) *(P-18377)*

Pace Marketing Communications, City Of Industry *Also Called: Pace Lithographers Inc (P-18377)*

Pace Punches Inc .... D 949 428-2750
297 Goddard Irvine (92618) *(P-5590)*

Pacer, Commerce *Also Called: Xpo Cartage Inc (P-8931)*

Pacer Print .... E 888 305-3144
4101 Guardian St Simi Valley (93063) *(P-3054)*

Pacer Technology (HQ)....................................... C 909 987-0550
3281 E Guasti Rd Ste 260 Ontario (91761) *(P-3773)*

Pacesetter Inc .... B 818 493-2715
13150 Telfair Ave Sylmar (91342) *(P-8392)*

Pacesetter Inc .... B 323 773-0591
4946 Florence Ave Bell (90201) *(P-8393)*

Pacesetter Inc (DH) .... A 818 362-6822
15900 Valley View Ct Sylmar (91342) *(P-8394)*

Pachulski Stang Zehl Jones LLP (PA)................. D 310 277-6910
10100 Santa Monica Blvd Ste 1100 Los Angeles (90067) *(P-16755)*

Pacifcare Hlth Plan Admnstrtor (DH)................. B 714 825-5200
3120 W Lake Center Dr Santa Ana (92704) *(P-12100)*

Pacific Advnced Cvil Engrg Inc (PA)................... D 714 481-7300
17520 Newhope St Ste 200 Fountain Valley (92708) *(P-17601)*

Pacific Aggregates Inc .... D 951 245-2460
28251 Lake St Lake Elsinore (92530) *(P-4447)*

Pacific Alloy Casting Company Inc .... C 562 928-1387
5900 Firestone Blvd Fl 1 South Gate (90280) *(P-4559)*

Pacific Altrntive Asset MGT LL (HQ) .... D 949 261-4900
660 Newport Center Dr Ste 930 Newport Beach (92660) *(P-12029)*

Pacific American Fish Co Inc (PA)...................... C 323 319-1551
5525 S Santa Fe Ave Vernon (90058) *(P-1697)*

Pacific Aquascape Inc .... D 714 843-5734
17520 Newhope St Ste 120 Fountain Valley (92708) *(P-1219)*

Pacific Archctural Mllwk Inc .... E 562 905-9282
1435 Pioneer St Brea (92821) *(P-2322)*

Pacific Archctural Mllwk Inc .... D 714 525-2059
101 E Commwl Ave Ste A Fullerton (92832) *(P-2323)*

Pacific Archctural Mllwk Inc .... D 562 905-3200
1031 S Leslie St La Habra (90631) *(P-2324)*

Pacific Artglass Corporation .... E 310 516-7828
125 W 157th St Gardena (90248) *(P-4342)*

Pacific Asian Cnsrtium In Empl (PA) .... C 213 353-3982
1055 Wilshire Blvd Ste 1475 Los Angeles (90017) *(P-17065)*

Pacific Asian Enterprises Inc (PA)..................... E 949 496-4848
25001 Dana Dr Dana Point (92629) *(P-14566)*

Pacific Asset Holding LLC .... C 949 219-3011
700 Newport Center Dr Newport Beach (92660) *(P-12048)*

Employee Codes: A=Over 500 employees, B=251-500
C=101-250, D=51-100, E=20-50, F=10-19, G=1-9

2025 Southern California
Business Directory and Buyers Guide

© Mergent Inc. 1-800-342-5647
1133

Pacific Athletic Wear Inc .... D 714 751-8006
7340 Lampson Ave Garden Grove (92841) *(P-2124)*

Pacific Aviation Corporation (HQ) .... C 310 646-4015
201 Continental Blvd Ste 220 El Segundo (90245) *(P-9205)*

Pacific Aviation LLC (PA) .... A 310 322-6290
201 Continental Blvd Ste 220 El Segundo (90245) *(P-9162)*

Pacific Award Metals Inc .... E 360 694-9530
10302 Birtcher Dr Jurupa Valley (91752) *(P-5013)*

Pacific Award Metals Inc (HQ) .... D 626 814-4410
1450 Virginia Ave Baldwin Park (91706) *(P-5014)*

Pacific Award Metals Inc .... D 909 390-9880
10302 Birtcher Dr Jurupa Valley (91752) *(P-9959)*

Pacific Barcode Inc .... E 951 587-8717
27531 Enterprise Cir W Ste 201c Temecula (92590) *(P-5664)*

Pacific Bell Telephone Company .... A 310 515-2898
3847 Cardiff Ave Culver City (90232) *(P-9407)*

Pacific Biotech Inc .... E 858 552-1100
10165 Mckellar Ct San Diego (92121) *(P-3547)*

Pacific Building Care Inc (HQ) .... C 949 261-1234
3001 Red Hill Ave Bldg 6 Costa Mesa (92626) *(P-13399)*

Pacific Building Group (PA) .... D 858 552-0600
9752 Aspen Creek Ct Ste 100 San Diego (92126) *(P-563)*

Pacific Building Group .... D 858 552-0600
13541 Stoney Creek Rd San Diego (92129) *(P-1020)*

Pacific Cambria Inc .... D 805 927-6114
2905 Burton Dr Cambria (93428) *(P-12957)*

Pacific Cast Cnstr Wtrproofing .... E 760 298-3170
390 Oak Ave Ste A Carlsbad (92008) *(P-423)*

Pacific Cast Fther Cushion LLC (HQ) .... C 562 801-9995
7600 Industry Ave Pico Rivera (90660) *(P-2220)*

Pacific Cast Products, Ontario Also Called: Alumistar Inc *(P-4665)*

Pacific Chemical, Buena Park Also Called: Pacific Chemical Dist Corp *(P-9135)*

Pacific Chemical Dist Corp (HQ) .... D 714 521-7161
6250 Caballero Blvd Buena Park (90620) *(P-9135)*

Pacific City Hotel LLC .... B 714 698-6100
21080 Pacific Coast Hwy Huntington Beach (92648) *(P-12958)*

Pacific Clay Products Inc .... C 661 857-1401
14741 Lake St Lake Elsinore (92530) *(P-9949)*

Pacific Clinics .... D 626 287-2988
9353 Valley Blvd Ste C Rosemead (91770) *(P-15418)*

Pacific Clinics .... A 626 254-5000
800 S Santa Anita Ave Arcadia (91006) *(P-16989)*

Pacific Clinics Head Start .... C 626 254-5000
171 N Altadena Dr Pasadena (91107) *(P-17104)*

Pacific Coachworks Inc .... C 951 686-7294
3411 N Perris Blvd Bldg 1 Perris (92571) *(P-7677)*

Pacific Coast Bach Label Inc .... E 213 612-0314
3015 S Grand Ave Los Angeles (90007) *(P-1943)*

Pacific Coast Bolt, Santa Fe Springs Also Called: Birmingham Fastener & Sup Inc *(P-4760)*

Pacific Coast Cabling Inc (PA) .... D 818 407-1911
20717 Prairie St Chatsworth (91311) *(P-947)*

Pacific Coast Entertainment .... B 714 841-6455
7601 Woodwind Dr Huntington Beach (92647) *(P-13183)*

Pacific Coast Entertainment, Huntington Beach Also Called: Pacific Coast Entertainment *(P-13183)*

Pacific Coast Feather Cushion, Pico Rivera Also Called: Pacific Cast Fther Cushion LLC *(P-2220)*

Pacific Coast Lacquer, Los Angeles Also Called: Berg Lacquer Co *(P-11106)*

Pacific Coast Lighting, Ventura Also Called: Lamps Plus Inc *(P-6465)*

Pacific Coast Mfg Inc .... D 909 627-7040
5270 Edison Ave Chino (91710) *(P-6388)*

Pacific Coast Tree Experts .... C 805 506-1211
21525 Strathern St Canoga Park (91304) *(P-246)*

Pacific Communications, Irvine Also Called: Allergan Usa Inc *(P-3347)*

Pacific Compensation Insur Co .... C 818 575-8500
3011 Townsgate Rd Ste 120 Westlake Village (91361) *(P-12241)*

Pacific Concept Laundry, Los Angeles Also Called: E & C Fashion Inc *(P-14492)*

Pacific Consolidated Inds LLC .... D 951 479-0860
12201 Magnolia Ave Riverside (92503) *(P-5831)*

Pacific Contntl Textiles Inc .... D 310 639-1500
2880 E Ana St Compton (90221) *(P-1944)*

Pacific Contours Corporation .... D 714 693-1260
5340 E Hunter Ave Anaheim (92807) *(P-7532)*

Pacific Couriers, South El Monte Also Called: Integrated Parcel Network *(P-9004)*

Pacific Defense, El Segundo Also Called: Pacific Defense Strategies Inc *(P-7789)*

Pacific Defense Strategies Inc (PA) .... E 310 722-6050
400 Continental Blvd Ste 100 El Segundo (90245) *(P-7789)*

Pacific Dental Services LLC (PA) .... B 714 845-8500
17000 Red Hill Ave Irvine (92614) *(P-15523)*

Pacific Die Casting, Commerce Also Called: Orlandini Entps Pcf Die Cast *(P-4691)*

Pacific Die Casting Corp .... C 323 725-1308
6155 S Eastern Ave Commerce (90040) *(P-4651)*

Pacific Diversified Capital Co .... E 619 696-2000
101 Ash St San Diego (92101) *(P-8058)*

Pacific Dntl Svcs Holdg Co Inc .... C 714 845-8500
17000 Red Hill Ave Irvine (92614) *(P-15524)*

Pacific Drayage Services LLC .... C 833 334-4622
550 W Artesia Blvd Compton (90220) *(P-8969)*

Pacific Echo Inc .... D 310 539-1822
23540 Telo Ave Torrance (90505) *(P-10455)*

Pacific Erth Rsrces Ltd A Cal .... D 209 892-3000
315 Hueneme Rd Camarillo (93012) *(P-64)*

Pacific Erth Rsrces Ltd A Cal (PA) .... D 805 986-8277
305 Hueneme Rd Camarillo (93012) *(P-65)*

Pacific Event Productions Inc (PA) .... D 858 458-9908
6989 Corte Santa Fe San Diego (92121) *(P-13184)*

Pacific Fire Safety, Pomona Also Called: Ferguson Fire Fabrication Inc *(P-10317)*

Pacific Foam, Ontario Also Called: Induspac California Inc *(P-3272)*

Pacific Forge Inc .... D 909 390-0701
10641 Etiwanda Ave Fontana (92337) *(P-5145)*

Pacific Gardens Med Ctr LLC .... C 562 860-0401
21530 Pioneer Blvd Hawaiian Gardens (90716) *(P-18028)*

Pacific Gas and Electric Co .... C 760 326-2615
145453 National Trails Hway Needles (92363) *(P-9595)*

Pacific Gas and Electric Co .... C 760 253-2925
35863 Fairview Rd Hinkley (92347) *(P-9596)*

Pacific Gas and Electric Co .... B 805 545-4562
4340 Old Santa Fe Rd San Luis Obispo (93401) *(P-9597)*

Pacific Gas and Electric Co .... A 805 506-5280
9 Mi Nw Of Avila Bch Avila Beach (93424) *(P-9598)*

Pacific Gas and Electric Co .... C 805 546-5267
800 Price Canyon Rd Pismo Beach (93449) *(P-9599)*

Pacific Gas and Electric Co .... D 805 434-4418
160 Cow Meadow Pl Templeton (93465) *(P-9600)*

Pacific Glass, Gardena Also Called: Pacific Artglass Corporation *(P-4342)*

Pacific Golf & Country Club .... D 949 498-6604
200 Avenida La Pata San Clemente (92673) *(P-15157)*

Pacific Green Landscape Inc (PA) .... C 619 390-1546
8834 Winter Gardens Blvd Lakeside (92040) *(P-184)*

Pacific Handy Cutter Inc (DH) .... E 714 662-1033
170 Technology Dr Irvine (92618) *(P-4743)*

Pacific Haven Convalescent HM .... D 714 534-1942
12072 Trask Ave Garden Grove (92843) *(P-15879)*

Pacific Health and Welness, Redondo Beach Also Called: NBC Consulting Inc *(P-18179)*

Pacific Health Corporation .... A 714 838-9600
14642 Newport Ave Tustin (92780) *(P-16112)*

Pacific Heritg HM Fashion Inc .... E 909 598-5200
901 Lawson St City Of Industry (91748) *(P-9904)*

Pacific Hospitality Design Inc .... E 323 278-7998
2620 S Malt Ave Commerce (90040) *(P-2551)*

Pacific Hotel Management Inc .... C 949 608-1091
4545 Macarthur Blvd Newport Beach (92660) *(P-12959)*

Pacific Huntington Hotel Corp .... A 626 568-3900
1401 S Oak Knoll Ave Pasadena (91106) *(P-12960)*

Pacific Hydrotech Corporation .... C 951 943-8803
314 E 3rd St Perris (92570) *(P-17602)*

Pacific Indemnity Company .... B 213 622-2334
555 S Flower St Ste 300 Los Angeles (90071) *(P-12242)*

Pacific Insulation, Commerce Also Called: Farwest Insulation Contracting *(P-1007)*

Pacific Integrated Mfg Inc .... C 619 921-3464
4364 Bonita Rd Ste 454 Bonita (91902) *(P-8212)*

Pacific Investment MGT Co LLC (DH) .... C 949 720-6000
650 Newport Center Dr Newport Beach (92660) *(P-12641)*

Pacific Life & Annuity Company .... A 949 219-3011
700 Newport Center Dr Newport Beach (92660) *(P-12049)*

Pacific Life Fund Advisors LLC .... B 949 260-9000
700 Newport Center Dr Newport Beach (92660) *(P-18029)*

Pacific Life Global Funding .... D 949 219-3011
700 Newport Center Dr Newport Beach (92660) *(P-11870)*

Pacific Life Insurance Company .... D 949 219-5200
45 Enterprise # 4 Aliso Viejo (92656) *(P-12050)*

Pacific Lock Company (PA) .... **E 661 294-3707**
25605 Hercules St Valencia (91355) *(P-4786)*

PACIFIC LODGE BOY'S HOME, Woodland Hills Also Called: Pacific Lodge Youth Svcs Inc *(P-17186)*

Pacific Lodge Youth Svcs Inc .... C 818 347-1577
4900 Serrania Ave Woodland Hills (91364) *(P-17186)*

Pacific Logistics Corp (PA) .... **C 562 478-4700**
7255 Rosemead Blvd Pico Rivera (90660) *(P-9321)*

Pacific Ltg & Standards Co .... E 310 603-9344
2815 Los Flores Blvd Lynwood (90262) *(P-6470)*

Pacific Magnetics, Chula Vista Also Called: Pacmag Inc *(P-7035)*

Pacific Manufacturing MGT Inc .... D 323 263-9000
3110 E 12th St Los Angeles (90023) *(P-2586)*

Pacific Marine Sheet Metal Corporation .... C 858 869-8900
2650 Jamacha Rd Ste 147 Pmb El Cajon (92019) *(P-5015)*

Pacific Maritime Group Inc .... D 562 590-8188
1512 Pier C St Long Beach (90813) *(P-9151)*

Pacific Maritime Inds Corp .... C 619 575-8141
1790 Dornoch Ct San Diego (92154) *(P-4858)*

Pacific Medical Group Inc .... D 866 282-6834
212 Avenida Fabricante San Clemente (92672) *(P-10099)*

Pacific Metal Products, Los Angeles Also Called: Basic Industries Intl Inc *(P-4910)*

Pacific Metal Stampings Inc .... E 661 257-7656
28415 Witherspoon Pkwy Valencia (91355) *(P-5207)*

Pacific Miniatures, Fullerton Also Called: Pacmin Incorporated *(P-8709)*

Pacific Monarch Resorts Inc (PA) .... **D 949 609-2400**
4000 Macarthur Blvd Ste 600 Newport Beach (92660) *(P-12499)*

Pacific Monarch Resorts Inc .... D 949 248-2944
34630 Pacific Coast Hwy Capistrano Beach (92624) *(P-12961)*

Pacific National Security Inc .... C 310 842-7073
3719 Robertson Blvd Culver City (90232) *(P-14328)*

Pacific Natural Spices, Commerce Also Called: Pacific Spice Company Inc *(P-1831)*

Pacific Outdoor Living, Sun Valley Also Called: Pacific Pavingstone Inc *(P-1129)*

Pacific Packaging McHy LLC .... E 951 393-2200
200 River Rd Corona (92878) *(P-5682)*

Pacific Panel Products, Irwindale Also Called: Pacific Panel Products Corp *(P-2414)*

Pacific Panel Products Corp .... E 626 851-0444
15601 Arrow Hwy Irwindale (91706) *(P-2414)*

Pacific Paper, Rancho Cucamonga Also Called: Pacific Pprbd Converting LLC *(P-2771)*

Pacific Park, Santa Monica Also Called: Santa Monica Amusements LLC *(P-15108)*

Pacific Parts International, Canoga Park Also Called: Richard Huetter Inc *(P-9845)*

Pacific Pavingstone Inc .... C 818 244-4000
8309 Tujunga Ave Unit 201 Sun Valley (91352) *(P-1129)*

Pacific Petroleum California Inc .... B 805 925-1947
1615 E Betteravia Rd Ste A Santa Maria (93454) *(P-356)*

Pacific Pharma Inc .... A 714 246-4600
18600 Von Karman Ave Irvine (92612) *(P-3469)*

Pacific Pioneer Insur Group (PA) .... **D 714 228-7888**
6363 Katella Ave Cypress (90630) *(P-12243)*

Pacific Piston Ring Co Inc .... D 310 836-3322
3620 Eastham Dr Culver City (90232) *(P-6043)*

Pacific Place Retirement, Oceanside Also Called: S L Start and Associates LLC *(P-17193)*

Pacific Plas Injection Molding, Vista Also Called: Diversified Plastics Inc *(P-4106)*

Pacific Plastics Inc .... D 714 990-9050
111 S Berry St Brea (92821) *(P-3977)*

Pacific Plating, Sun Valley Also Called: Kvr Investment Group Inc *(P-5708)*

Pacific Plms Conference Resort, City Of Industry Also Called: Majestic Industry Hills LLC *(P-12911)*

Pacific Plstcs-Njction Molding, Vista Also Called: J A English II Inc *(P-4143)*

Pacific Power Systems Integration Inc .... E 562 281-0500
14729 Spring Ave Santa Fe Springs (90670) *(P-10200)*

Pacific Pprbd Converting LLC (PA) .... **E 909 476-6466**
8865 Utica Ave Ste A Rancho Cucamonga (91730) *(P-2771)*

Pacific Precision Inc .... E 909 392-5610
1318 Palomares St La Verne (91750) *(P-5111)*

Pacific Precision Metals Inc .... C 951 226-1500
1100 E Orangethorpe Ave Ste 253 Anaheim (92801) *(P-5208)*

Pacific Precision Products, Irvine Also Called: Pacific Precision Products Mfg Inc *(P-7533)*

Pacific Precision Products Mfg Inc .... E 949 727-3844
9671 Irvine Ctr Dr Koll Ctr Ii Bldg 6 Irvine (92618) *(P-7533)*

Pacific Premier Bancorp Inc .... B 951 274-2400
3403 10th St Ste 100 Riverside (92501) *(P-11773)*

Pacific Premier Bancorp Inc .... C 951 272-3590
102 E 6th St Ste 100 Corona (92879) *(P-11774)*

Pacific Premier Bancorp Inc (PA) .... **C 949 864-8000**
17901 Von Karman Ave Ste 1200 Irvine (92614) *(P-11775)*

Pacific Press, Anaheim Also Called: Wasser Filtration Inc *(P-5836)*

Pacific Prime Meats LLC .... D 310 523-3664
3501 E Vernon Ave Vernon (90058) *(P-1248)*

Pacific Process Systems Inc (PA) .... D 661 321-9681
7401 Rosedale Hwy Bakersfield (93308) *(P-357)*

Pacific Quality Packaging Corp .... D 714 257-1234
660 Neptune Ave Brea (92821) *(P-2683)*

Pacific Refrigerator Company, Apple Valley Also Called: Pac-Refco Inc *(P-5979)*

Pacific Rim Mech Contrs Inc (PA) .... **B 858 974-6500**
9125 Rehco Rd San Diego (92121) *(P-815)*

Pacific Rim Mech Contrs Inc .... C 714 285-2600
1701 E Edinger Ave Ste F2 Santa Ana (92705) *(P-816)*

Pacific Scientific Company (DH) .... **E 805 526-5700**
1785 Voyager Ave Simi Valley (93063) *(P-7790)*

Pacific Sd/Pcfic Arbor Nrsries, Camarillo Also Called: Pacific Erth Rsrces Ltd A Cal *(P-65)*

Pacific Seafood of Los Angeles, Wilmington Also Called: Dulcich Inc *(P-10853)*

Pacific Seismic Products Inc .... E 661 942-4499
233 E Avenue H8 Lancaster (93535) *(P-5368)*

Pacific Select Distrs Inc .... D 949 219-3011
700 Newport Center Dr Fl 4 Newport Beach (92660) *(P-12004)*

Pacific Ship Repr Fbrction Inc (PA) .... **B 619 232-3200**
1625 Rigel St San Diego (92113) *(P-7607)*

Pacific Shore Holdings Inc .... E 818 998-0996
8236 Remmet Ave Canoga Park (91304) *(P-3470)*

Pacific Sky Supply Inc .... D 818 768-3700
8230 San Fernando Rd Sun Valley (91352) *(P-7534)*

Pacific Sod, Camarillo Also Called: Pacific Erth Rsrces Ltd A Cal *(P-64)*

Pacific Spice Company Inc .... C 323 726-9190
6430 E Slauson Ave Commerce (90040) *(P-1831)*

Pacific Steam Equipment Inc .... E 562 906-9292
11748 Slauson Ave Santa Fe Springs (90670) *(P-4918)*

Pacific Steel Group .... B 858 449-7219
2755 S Willow Ave Bloomington (92316) *(P-10149)*

PACIFIC STEEL GROUP, Bloomington Also Called: Pacific Steel Group *(P-10149)*

Pacific Steel Group LLC (PA) .... **C 858 251-1100**
4805 Murphy Canyon Rd San Diego (92123) *(P-5100)*

Pacific Sthwest Structures Inc .... C 619 469-2323
7845 Lemon Grove Way Ste A Lemon Grove (91945) *(P-1130)*

Pacific Stone Design Inc .... E 714 836-5757
1201 E Wakeham Ave Santa Ana (92705) *(P-4410)*

Pacific Strucframe LLC .... D 951 405-8536
1600 Chicago Ave Ste R11 Riverside (92507) *(P-1090)*

Pacific Structures, Venice Also Called: Pacific Structures Sc Inc *(P-1131)*

Pacific Structures Sc Inc (PA) .... **C 415 970-5434**
1212 Abbot Kinney Blvd Apt A Venice (90291) *(P-1131)*

Pacific Supply, Orange Also Called: Beacon Pacific Inc *(P-9956)*

Pacific Systems Interiors Inc .... C 310 436-6820
190 E Arrow Hwy Ste D San Dimas (91773) *(P-1021)*

Pacific Tank & Cnstr Inc .... E 805 237-2929
17995 E Highway 46 Shandon (93461) *(P-4919)*

Pacific Tech Solutions LLC .... D 949 830-1623
15530 Rockfield Blvd Ste B4 Irvine (92618) *(P-13792)*

Pacific Toll Processing Inc .... E 310 952-4992
24724 Wilmington Ave Carson (90745) *(P-9356)*

Pacific Toxicology Labs .... D 818 598-3110
9348 De Soto Ave Chatsworth (91311) *(P-16326)*

Pacific Transformer Corp .... D 714 779-0450
5399 E Hunter Ave Anaheim (92807) *(P-6294)*

Employee Codes: A=Over 500 employees, B=251-500
C=101-250, D=51-100, E=20-50, F=10-19, G=1-9

2025 Southern California
Business Directory and Buyers Guide

© Mergent Inc. 1-800-342-5647

1135

A
L
P
H
A
B
E
T
I
C

Pacific Trellis Fruit LLC (PA) .... C 323 859-9600
2301 E 7th St Ste C200 Los Angeles (90023) *(P-10913)*

Pacific Trust Bank .... C 949 236-5211
18500 Von Karman Ave Ste 1100 Irvine (92612) *(P-11787)*

Pacific Urethanes, Ontario *Also Called: Pacific Urethanes LLC (P-2221)*

Pacific Urethanes LLC .... C 909 390-8400
1671 Champagne Ave Ste A Ontario (91761) *(P-2221)*

Pacific Ventures Ltd .... C 626 576-0737
2200 W Valley Blvd Alhambra (91803) *(P-18030)*

Pacific Vial Mfg Inc .... E 323 721-7004
2738 Supply Ave Commerce (90040) *(P-4321)*

Pacific Wave Systems Inc .... D 714 893-0152
2525 W 190th St Torrance (90504) *(P-6644)*

Pacific West, Anaheim *Also Called: Pacific West Litho Inc (P-3055)*

Pacific West Litho Inc .... D 714 579-0868
3291 E Miraloma Ave Anaheim (92806) *(P-3055)*

Pacific West Tree Service, Vista *Also Called: Pac West Land Care Inc (P-183)*

Pacific Western Bank .... B 858 756-3023
6110 El Tordo Rancho Santa Fe (92067) *(P-11739)*

Pacific Wire Products Inc .... E 818 755-6400
10725 Vanowen St North Hollywood (91605) *(P-5408)*

Pacific World Corporation (PA) .... D 949 598-2400
757 S Alameda St Ste 280 Los Angeles (90021) *(P-3676)*

Pacifica Beauty LLC .... D 844 332-8440
1090 Eugenia Pl Ste 200 Carpinteria (93013) *(P-8708)*

Pacifica Companies, San Diego *Also Called: Pacifica Companies LLC (P-12690)*

Pacifica Companies LLC (PA) .... A **619 296-9000**
1775 Hancock St Ste 200 San Diego (92110) *(P-12690)*

Pacifica Foods LLC .... C 951 371-3123
1581 N Main St Orange (92867) *(P-1371)*

Pacifica Hospital of Valley, Sun Valley *Also Called: Pacifica of Valley Corporation (P-16113)*

Pacifica Hosts Inc .... C 310 670-9000
6225 W Century Blvd Los Angeles (90045) *(P-12962)*

Pacifica Hosts Inc .... C 858 792-8200
717 S Highway 101 Solana Beach (92075) *(P-12963)*

Pacifica International, Carpinteria *Also Called: Pacifica Beauty LLC (P-8708)*

Pacifica of Valley Corporation .... A 818 767-3310
9449 San Fernando Rd Sun Valley (91352) *(P-16113)*

Pacifica Services Inc .... D 626 405-0131
106 S Mentor Ave Ste 200 Pasadena (91106) *(P-17603)*

Pacificare, Santa Ana *Also Called: Pacifcare Hlth Plan Admnstrtor (P-12100)*

Pacificare Health Systems, Cypress *Also Called: Uhc of California (P-12114)*

Pacificare Health Systems, Cypress *Also Called: Pacificare Health Systems LLC (P-16409)*

Pacificare Health Systems LLC (HQ) .... A **714 952-1121**
5995 Plaza Dr Cypress (90630) *(P-16409)*

Pacira Pharmaceuticals Inc .... D 858 625-2424
10578 Science Center Dr San Diego (92121) *(P-3471)*

Paciugo .... E 714 536-5388
122 Main St Ste 122 Huntington Beach (92648) *(P-4731)*

Pack West Machinery, Corona *Also Called: Pacific Packaging McHy LLC (P-5682)*

Packaging Corporation America .... D 323 263-7581
4240 Bandini Blvd Vernon (90058) *(P-2684)*

Packaging Corporation America .... C 562 927-7741
9700 E Frontage Rd Ste 20 South Gate (90280) *(P-2685)*

Packaging Corporation America .... E 909 888-7008
879 E Rialto Ave San Bernardino (92408) *(P-2686)*

Packaging Manufacturing Inc .... C 619 498-9199
2285 Michael Faraday Dr Ste 12 San Diego (92154) *(P-3056)*

Packaging Spectrum, Los Angeles *Also Called: Advance Paper Box Company (P-2652)*

Packaging Systems Inc .... E 661 253-5700
26435 Summit Cir Santa Clarita (91350) *(P-3774)*

Packard Realty Inc .... C 310 649-5151
9901 S La Cienega Blvd Los Angeles (90045) *(P-12964)*

Packers Bar M, Los Angeles *Also Called: Serv-Rite Meat Company Inc (P-1250)*

Packline USA LLC .... E 909 392-8000
9555 Hyssop Dr Rancho Cucamonga (91730) *(P-4322)*

Paclo, Pico Rivera *Also Called: Pacific Logistics Corp (P-9321)*

Pacmag Inc .... E 619 872-0343
87 Georgina St Chula Vista (91910) *(P-7035)*

Pacmet Aerospace, Corona *Also Called: Pacmet Aerospace LLC (P-5469)*

Pacmet Aerospace LLC .... D 909 218-8889
224 Glider Cir Corona (92878) *(P-5469)*

Pacmin Incorporated (PA) .... D **714 447-4478**
2021 Raymer Ave Fullerton (92833) *(P-8709)*

Pacobond Inc .... E 818 768-5002
9344 Glenoaks Blvd Sun Valley (91352) *(P-2744)*

Pacon Inc .... C 626 814-4654
4249 Puente Ave Baldwin Park (91706) *(P-2634)*

Pacs Group Inc .... C 661 948-7501
44445 15th St W Lancaster (93534) *(P-15730)*

Pacs Group Inc .... C 562 865-0271
11900 Artesia Blvd Artesia (90701) *(P-15731)*

Pacs Group Inc .... C 323 782-1500
580 S San Vicente Blvd Los Angeles (90048) *(P-15732)*

Pacs Group Inc .... C 661 949-5524
44567 15th St W Lancaster (93534) *(P-15733)*

Pacs Group Inc .... C 661 873-9267
6212 Tudor Way Bakersfield (93306) *(P-15734)*

Pacs Group Inc .... C 661 854-4475
323 Campus Dr Arvin (93203) *(P-15735)*

Pacs Group Inc .... B 562 422-9219
3232 E Artesia Blvd Long Beach (90805) *(P-15736)*

Pacs Group Inc .... D 909 478-7894
25393 Cole St Loma Linda (92354) *(P-15737)*

Pacs Group Inc .... C 951 925-9171
1717 W Stetson Ave Hemet (92545) *(P-15738)*

Pacs Group Inc .... C 951 849-4723
3476 W Wilson St Banning (92220) *(P-15739)*

Pacs Group Inc .... C 951 658-9441
275 N San Jacinto St Hemet (92543) *(P-15740)*

Pacs Group Inc .... C 951 845-1606
5800 W Wilson St Banning (92220) *(P-15741)*

Pacs Group Inc .... C 760 341-0261
74350 Country Club Dr Palm Desert (92260) *(P-15742)*

Pacs Group Inc .... C 951 845-3125
1665 E Eighth St Beaumont (92223) *(P-15743)*

Pacs Group Inc .... C 951 845-3194
9246 Avenida Miravilla Beaumont (92223) *(P-15744)*

Pacs Group Inc .... C 714 241-9800
11680 Warner Ave Fountain Valley (92708) *(P-15745)*

Pactiv LLC .... C 661 392-4000
2024 Norris Rd Bakersfield (93308) *(P-4190)*

Pactrack Inc .... D 213 201-5856
11135 Rush St Ste A South El Monte (91733) *(P-9322)*

Pacwest Air Filter LLC .... E 951 698-2228
26550 Adams Ave Murrieta (92562) *(P-5774)*

Pacwest Bancorp .... B 310 887-8500
9701 Wilshire Blvd Ste 700 Beverly Hills (90212) *(P-11740)*

Padilla Construction Company .... C 714 685-8500
1620 N Brian St Orange (92867) *(P-1022)*

Padres LP .... A 619 795-5000
100 Park Blvd Petco Park San Diego (92101) *(P-15034)*

Pafco, Vernon *Also Called: Pacific American Fish Co Inc (P-1697)*

Page Private School .... D 323 272-3429
419 S Robertson Blvd Beverly Hills (90211) *(P-16819)*

Paige LLC (HQ) .... C **310 733-2100**
10119 Jefferson Blvd Culver City (90232) *(P-2052)*

Paige Premium Denim, Culver City *Also Called: Paige LLC (P-2052)*

Paisano Publications LLC (PA) .... D **818 889-8740**
28210 Dorothy Dr Agoura Hills (91301) *(P-2868)*

Paisano Publications Inc .... D 818 889-8740
28210 Dorothy Dr Agoura Hills (91301) *(P-2869)*

Pak West Paper & Packaging, Santa Ana *Also Called: Blower-Dempsay Corporation (P-2655)*

Paklab, Chino *Also Called: Universal Packg Systems Inc (P-3693)*

Paklab, Chino *Also Called: Universal Packg Systems Inc (P-9125)*

Pala Casino, Pala *Also Called: Pala Casino Spa & Resort (P-12965)*

Pala Casino Spa & Resort .... A 760 510-5100
11154 Highway 76 Pala (92059) *(P-12965)*

Paladar Mfg Inc .... D 760 775-4222
53973 Polk St Coachella (92236) *(P-8470)*

Palermo Family LP (PA) .... E **213 542-3300**
140 W Providencia Ave Burbank (91502) *(P-1832)*

Palette Life Sciences Inc (PA)..................D 805 869-7020
27 E Cota St Ste 402 Santa Barbara (93101) *(P-3326)*

Palfinger Liftgates LLC ....D 888 774-5844
15939 Piuma Ave Cerritos (90703) *(P-10390)*

Pali Adventures, Running Springs Also Called: Pali Camp *(P-13105)*

Pali Camp ....C 909 867-5743
30778 Hwy 18 Running Springs (92382) *(P-13105)*

Palisades Beach Club, Los Angeles Also Called: Fortune Swimwear LLC *(P-1918)*

Palisades Ranch Inc ....B 323 581-6161
5925 Alcoa Ave Vernon (90058) *(P-10764)*

Pall Corporation ....C 858 455-7264
4116 Sorrento Valley Blvd San Diego (92121) *(P-5832)*

Palladium Valley Global Inc ....D 949 723-9613
3857 Birch St Ste 9017 Newport Beach (92660) *(P-17858)*

Pallet Masters Inc ....D 323 758-1713
655 E Florence Ave Los Angeles (90001) *(P-2390)*

Palm Canyon Resort, Palm Springs Also Called: Diamond Resorts Intl Inc *(P-12808)*

Palm Canyon Resort & Spa, Palm Springs Also Called: Diamond Resorts LLC *(P-12809)*

Palm Desert Community Assn, Palm Desert Also Called: Sun City Palm Dsert Cmnty Assn *(P-17368)*

Palm Desert Greens Association ....D 760 346-8005
73750 Country Club Dr Palm Desert (92260) *(P-17359)*

PALM GROVE HEALTHCARE, Beaumont Also Called: David-Kleis II LLC *(P-16553)*

Palm Springs Art Museum Inc ....D 760 322-4800
101 N Museum Dr Palm Springs (92262) *(P-17260)*

Palm Springs Convention Center, Palm Springs Also Called: Smg Holdings LLC *(P-18214)*

Palm Springs Disposal Services ....D 760 327-1351
4690 E Mesquite Ave Palm Springs (92264) *(P-9754)*

Palm Springs Health Care Ctr, Palm Springs Also Called: Mariner Health Care Inc *(P-18010)*

Palm Springs Motors Inc ....C 760 699-6695
69-200a Highway 111 Cathedral City (92234) *(P-11392)*

Palm Springs Renaissance, Palm Springs Also Called: Remington Hotel Corporation *(P-12988)*

Palm Sprng Ford Lncoln Mercury, Cathedral City Also Called: Palm Springs Motors Inc *(P-11392)*

Palm Ter Hlthcare Rhblttion Ct, Laguna Hills Also Called: Gate Three Healthcare LLC *(P-15662)*

Palmcrest Grand Care Ctr Inc ....D 562 595-4551
3501 Cedar Ave Long Beach (90807) *(P-15746)*

Palmcrest Medallion Convalesc ....D 562 595-4336
3355 Pacific Pl Long Beach (90806) *(P-15747)*

Palmdale Regional Medical Ctr, Palmdale Also Called: Lancaster Hospital Corporation *(P-16072)*

Palmdale Water District (PA) ....D 661 947-4111
2029 E Avenue Q Palmdale (93550) *(P-9710)*

Palmieri Tyler Wner Wlhelm Wld ....D 949 851-9400
1900 Main St Ste 700 Irvine (92614) *(P-16756)*

Palo Verde Health Care Dst ....C 760 922-4115
250 N 1st St Blythe (92225) *(P-16114)*

Palo Verde Hospital, Blythe Also Called: Palo Verde Health Care Dst *(P-16114)*

Palo Verde Hospital Assn ....C 760 922-4115
250 N 1st St Blythe (92225) *(P-16115)*

Palo Verde Irrigation District ....D 760 922-3144
180 W 14th Ave Blythe (92225) *(P-9793)*

Palomar Health ....D 858 675-5210
152255 Innovation Dr San Diego (92128) *(P-16116)*

Palomar Health (PA) ....C 442 281-5000
2125 Citracado Pkwy Ste 300 Escondido (92029) *(P-16117)*

Palomar Health ....A 760 739-3000
15615 Pomerado Rd Poway (92064) *(P-16118)*

Palomar Health ....C 858 613-4000
15615 Pomerado Rd Poway (92064) *(P-16119)*

Palomar Health ....C 760 740-6311
800 W Valley Pkwy Ste 201 Escondido (92025) *(P-16297)*

Palomar Health Medical Group (HQ) ....C 858 675-3100
15611 Pomerado Rd Ste 575 Poway (92064) *(P-16120)*

Palomar Health Technology Inc ....C 442 281-5000
2140 Enterprise St Escondido (92029) *(P-16121)*

Palomar Medical Center ....B 858 613-4000
15615 Pomerado Rd Poway (92064) *(P-16122)*

Palomar Medical Center, Escondido Also Called: Palomar Health *(P-16117)*

Palomar Medical Center, Poway Also Called: Palomar Health *(P-16118)*

PALOMAR MEDICAL CENTER, Poway Also Called: Palomar Medical Center *(P-16122)*

Palomar Products Inc ....D 949 766-5300
23042 Arroyo Vis Rcho Sta Marg (92688) *(P-6689)*

Palomar Tech Companies (PA) ....D 760 931-3600
6305 El Camino Real Carlsbad (92009) *(P-7141)*

Palomar Technologies Inc (PA) ....E 760 931-3600
6305 El Camino Real Carlsbad (92009) *(P-5715)*

Palomar Vista Healthcare Ctr, Escondido Also Called: Ensign Group Inc *(P-15642)*

Palos Verdes Building Corp (PA) ....C 951 371-8090
1675 Sampson Ave Corona (92879) *(P-7079)*

Palos Verdes Golf & Cntry CLB, Palos Verdes Peninsu Also Called: Palos Verdes Golf Club *(P-11617)*

Palos Verdes Golf Club ....D 310 375-2759
3301 Via Campesina Palos Verdes Peninsu (90274) *(P-11617)*

Palp Inc ....C 562 599-5841
2230 Lemon Ave Long Beach (90806) *(P-641)*

Palyon Medical Corporation ....E
28432 Constellation Rd Valencia (91355) *(P-8395)*

Pamc Ltd (PA) ....A 213 624-8411
531 W College St Los Angeles (90012) *(P-16123)*

Pamc Health Foundation, Los Angeles Also Called: Pamc Ltd *(P-16123)*

Pamco, Sun Valley Also Called: Precision Arcft Machining Inc *(P-6204)*

Pampa Regional Medical Center, Ontario Also Called: Prime Hlthcare Svcs - Pmpa LLC *(P-16146)*

Pampanga Food Company Inc ....E 714 773-0537
1835 N Orangethorpe Park Ste A Anaheim (92801) *(P-1264)*

Pan American Bank Fsb ....B 949 224-1917
18191 Von Karman Ave Ste 300 Irvine (92612) *(P-11788)*

Pan Pacific Petroleum Co Inc (PA) ....D 562 928-0100
9302 Garfield Ave South Gate (90280) *(P-8970)*

Pan Pacific San Diego, San Diego Also Called: Pan Pcfic Htels Rsrts Amer Inc *(P-12966)*

Pan Pcfic Htels Rsrts Amer Inc ....C 619 239-4500
400 W Broadway San Diego (92101) *(P-12966)*

Pan-Pacific Mechanical, Fountain Valley Also Called: Pan-Pacific Mechanical LLC *(P-818)*

Pan-Pacific Mechanical LLC ....B 858 764-2464
11622 El Camino Real Ste 100 San Diego (92130) *(P-817)*

Pan-Pacific Mechanical LLC (PA) ....C 949 474-9170
18250 Euclid St Fountain Valley (92708) *(P-818)*

Pan-Pacific Plumbing & Mech, San Diego Also Called: Pan-Pacific Mechanical LLC *(P-817)*

Panaroma Gardens, Panorama City Also Called: Ensign Group Inc *(P-15639)*

Panasonic Avionics Corporation (DH) ....B 949 672-2000
3347 Michelson Dr Ste 100 Irvine (92612) *(P-17604)*

Panasonic Disc Manufacturing Corporation of America ....C 310 783-4800
20000 Mariner Ave Ste 200 Torrance (90503) *(P-6577)*

Panattoni Development Co Inc (PA) ....D 916 381-1561
2442 Dupont Dr Irvine (92612) *(P-12576)*

Panavision Group, Woodland Hills Also Called: Panavision Inc *(P-13466)*

Panavision Hollywood, Los Angeles Also Called: Panavision Inc *(P-8436)*

Panavision Inc ....E 323 464-3800
6735 Selma Ave Los Angeles (90028) *(P-8436)*

Panavision Inc (PA) ....A 818 316-1000
6101 Variel Ave Woodland Hills (91367) *(P-13466)*

Panavision International LP (HQ) ....B 818 316-1080
6101 Variel Ave Woodland Hills (91367) *(P-8437)*

Pancan, Manhattan Beach Also Called: Pancrtic Cncer Action Ntwrk In *(P-16602)*

Pancrtic Cncer Action Ntwrk In (PA) ....D 310 725-0025
1500 Rosecrans Ave Ste 200 Manhattan Beach (90266) *(P-16602)*

Panda Express, South Pasadena Also Called: Citadel Panda Express Inc *(P-11562)*

Panda Express, Rosemead Also Called: Panda Systems Inc *(P-11594)*

Panda Systems Inc ....C 626 799-9898
1683 Walnut Grove Ave Rosemead (91770) *(P-11594)*

Pandora Marketing LLC ....D 800 705-6856
26970 Aliso Viejo Pkwy Ste 150 Aliso Viejo (92656) *(P-18190)*

Pandora Media LLC ....B 424 653-6803
3000 Ocean Park Blvd Ste 3050 Santa Monica (90405) *(P-9487)*

Panel Products, Long Beach Also Called: Simulator PDT Solutions LLC *(P-7811)*

Pangaea Holdings Inc ....E 402 704-7546
1968 S Coast Hwy Pmb 3080 Laguna Beach (92651) *(P-3677)*

Pango Group Inc ....D 818 502-0400
6100 San Fernando Rd Glendale (91201) *(P-12500)*

Employee Codes: A=Over 500 employees, B=251-500
C=101-250, D=51-100, E=20-50, F=10-19, G=1-9

2025 Southern California
Business Directory and Buyers Guide

© Mergent Inc. 1-800-342-5647

1137

Pankl Aerospace Systems .... D 562 207-6300
  16615 Edwards Rd Cerritos (90703) *(P-4692)*

Pankl Engine Systems Inc .... E 949 428-8788
  1902 Mcgaw Ave Irvine (92614) *(P-7281)*

Panoramic Doors LLC .... D 760 722-1300
  3265 Production Ave Ste A Oceanside (92058) *(P-9928)*

Panrosa Enterprises Inc .... D 951 339-5888
  550 Monica Cir Corona (92878) *(P-3595)*

Papa Cantella's Sausage Plant, Vernon *Also Called: Papa Cantellas Incorporated (P-1265)*

Papa Cantellas Incorporated ....D 323 584-7272
  3341 E 50th St Vernon (90058) *(P-1265)*

Papaya .... E 310 740-6774
  14140 Ventura Blvd Ste 209 Sherman Oaks (91423) *(P-14002)*

Pape Material Handling Inc .... D 562 692-9311
  2600 Peck Rd City Of Industry (90601) *(P-5532)*

Pape Material Handling Inc .... C 562 463-8000
  2615 Pellissier Pl City Of Industry (90601) *(P-10391)*

Paper Company, The, City Of Industry *Also Called: Imperial Bag & Paper Co LLC (P-10594)*

Paper Mart Indus & Ret Packg, Orange *Also Called: Frick Paper Company LLC (P-10592)*

Paper Surce Converting Mfg Inc .... E 323 583-3800
  4800 S Santa Fe Ave Vernon (90058) *(P-2635)*

Papi, Glendale *Also Called: Glenair Inc (P-6420)*

Paq Inc .... C 805 227-1660
  1465 Creston Rd Paso Robles (93446) *(P-11477)*

PAR SERVICES, Culver City *Also Called: Exceptional Chld Foundation (P-17056)*

Par Services, Los Angeles *Also Called: Exceptional Chld Foundation (P-17057)*

Par Western Line Contrs LLC .... A 760 737-0925
  11276 5th St Ste 100 Rancho Cucamonga (91730) *(P-14567)*

Para Plate, Cerritos *Also Called: Para-Plate & Plastics Co Inc (P-5665)*

Para Tech Coating, Laguna Hills *Also Called: Metal Improvement Company LLC (P-4706)*

Para-Plate & Plastics Co Inc .... E 562 404-3434
  15910 Shoemaker Ave Cerritos (90703) *(P-5665)*

Parachute Home Inc .... C 310 903-0353
  3525 Eastham Dr Culver City (90232) *(P-2222)*

Paraclsus Los Angles Cmnty Hos .... C 323 267-0477
  4081 E Olympic Blvd Los Angeles (90023) *(P-16124)*

Paradigm, Beverly Hills *Also Called: Paradigm Music LLC (P-14968)*

Paradigm Industries Inc .... D 310 965-1900
  2522 E 37th St Vernon (90058) *(P-14568)*

Paradigm Music LLC (PA) .... **D 310 288-8000**
  360 N Crescent Dr Beverly Hills (90210) *(P-14968)*

Paradigm Packaging East LLC .... E 909 985-2750
  9595 Utica Ave Rancho Cucamonga (91730) *(P-4191)*

Paradigm Packaging West, Rancho Cucamonga *Also Called: Paradigm Packaging East LLC (P-4191)*

Paradigm Talent Agency LLC .... D 310 288-8000
  6725 W Sunset Blvd Los Angeles (90028) *(P-14969)*

Paradise Electric Inc .... C 619 449-4141
  697 Greenfield Dr El Cajon (92021) *(P-948)*

Paradise Lessee Inc .... B 858 274-4630
  1404 Vacation Rd San Diego (92109) *(P-12967)*

Paradise Point Resort, San Diego *Also Called: Westgroup San Diego Associates (P-13076)*

Paradise Point Resort & Spa, San Diego *Also Called: Paradise Lessee Inc (P-12967)*

Paradise Valley Hospital (PA) .... **A 619 470-4100**
  2400 E 4th St National City (91950) *(P-16125)*

Paradise Valley Hospital .... B 619 472-7474
  180 Otay Lakes Rd Ste 100 Bonita (91902) *(P-16126)*

Paradise Valley Manor, National City *Also Called: Sterling Care Inc (P-15783)*

Paragon Building Products Inc (PA) .... **E 951 549-1155**
  2191 5th St Ste 111 Norco (92860) *(P-4411)*

Paragon Industries Inc .... E 818 833-0550
  16450 Foothill Blvd Ste 100 Sylmar (91342) *(P-1042)*

Paragon Industries Inc .... D 714 778-1800
  1515 E Winston Rd Anaheim (92805) *(P-11249)*

Paragon Laboratories, Torrance *Also Called: Naturalife Eco Vite Labs (P-1301)*

Paragon Plastics Co Div, Chino *Also Called: Consolidated Plastics Corp (P-10996)*

Paragon Services Engineering, San Diego *Also Called: San Diego Services LLC (P-17625)*

Paragon Svcs Jntr Ornge Cnty L .... D 858 654-0150
  1111 6th Ave Ste 316 San Diego (92101) *(P-13400)*

Parallel 6 Inc (PA) .... **E 619 452-1750**
  1455 Frazee Rd Ste 900 San Diego (92108) *(P-13793)*

Paramont Metal & Supply Co, Paramount *Also Called: George Jue Mfg Co Inc (P-5635)*

Paramount Asphalt, Paramount *Also Called: Paramount Petroleum Corp (P-3828)*

Paramount Citrus, Delano *Also Called: Wonderful Company LLC (P-45)*

Paramount Citrus Packing Co, Delano *Also Called: Wonderful Citrus Packing LLC (P-123)*

Paramount Dairy Inc .... C 562 361-1800
  15255 Texaco Ave Paramount (90723) *(P-1334)*

Paramount Farms, Los Angeles *Also Called: Wonderful Pstchios Almonds LLC (P-1519)*

Paramount Machine Co Inc .... E 909 484-3600
  10824 Edison Ct Rancho Cucamonga (91730) *(P-6198)*

Paramount Metal & Supply Inc .... E 562 634-8180
  8140 Rosecrans Ave Paramount (90723) *(P-5070)*

Paramount Panels Inc (PA) .... **E 909 947-8008**
  1531 E Cedar St Ontario (91761) *(P-4192)*

Paramount Petroleum Corp (DH) .... **C 562 531-2060**
  14700 Downey Ave Paramount (90723) *(P-3828)*

Paramount Pictures Corporation (HQ) .... **A 323 956-5000**
  5555 Melrose Ave Los Angeles (90038) *(P-14843)*

Paramount Properties, Beverly Hills *Also Called: Rodeo Realty Inc (P-12524)*

Paramount Studios, Los Angeles *Also Called: Paramount Pictures Corporation (P-14843)*

Paramount Swap Meet, Paramount *Also Called: Modern Dev Co A Ltd Partnr (P-14552)*

Paramout Farms, Lost Hills *Also Called: Roll Properties Intl Inc (P-12733)*

Parcell Steel, Corona *Also Called: Parcell Steel Corp (P-4859)*

Parcell Steel Corp .... C 951 471-3200
  26365 Earthmover Cir Corona (92883) *(P-4859)*

Parco LLC (DH) .... **C 909 947-2200**
  1801 S Archibald Ave Ontario (91761) *(P-3896)*

Pardee Tree Nursery .... D 760 630-5400
  30970 Via Puerta Del Sol Oceanside (92057) *(P-11097)*

Parentsquare Inc .... D 888 496-3168
  6144 Calle Real Ste 200a Goleta (93117) *(P-14003)*

Parex Usa Inc (DH) .... **E 714 778-2266**
  2150 Eastridge Ave Riverside (92507) *(P-4506)*

Parex Usa Inc .... E 951 653-3549
  2150 Eastridge Ave Riverside (92507) *(P-11250)*

Paris Precision LLC .... C 805 239-2500
  1650 Ramada Dr Paso Robles (93446) *(P-5016)*

Parisa Lingerie & Swim Wear, Calabasas *Also Called: Afr Apparel International Inc (P-2146)*

Park Cleaners Inc (PA) .... **D 626 281-5942**
  419 Mcgroarty St San Gabriel (91776) *(P-13125)*

Park Engineering and Mfg Co .... E 714 521-4660
  6430 Roland St Buena Park (90621) *(P-6199)*

Park Landscape Maint 1-2-3-4, Rcho Sta Marg *Also Called: Park West Landscape Maint Inc (P-229)*

Park Management Group LLC .... A 404 350-9990
  1825 Gillespie Wy Ste 101 North Hollywood (91601) *(P-12968)*

Park Marino Convalescent Ctr .... C 626 463-4105
  2585 E Washington Blvd Pasadena (91107) *(P-15880)*

Park Newport Apartments, Newport Beach *Also Called: Park Newport Ltd (P-12361)*

Park Newport Ltd (PA) .... **D 949 644-1900**
  1 Park Newport Newport Beach (92660) *(P-12361)*

Park Place Ford LLC .... D 909 946-5555
  555 W Foothill Blvd Upland (91786) *(P-11393)*

Park Regency Inc .... D 818 363-6116
  10146 Balboa Blvd Granada Hills (91344) *(P-12501)*

Park Regency Club Apts, Downey *Also Called: PRC Multi-Family LLC (P-12362)*

Park Uniform Rentals, San Gabriel *Also Called: Park Cleaners Inc (P-13125)*

Park West Landscape Inc .... D 310 363-4100
  13105 Crenshaw Blvd Hawthorne (90250) *(P-228)*

Park West Landscape Maint Inc (PA) .... **B 949 546-8300**
  22421 Gilberto Ste A Rcho Sta Marg (92688) *(P-229)*

Parkco Building Company .... D 714 444-1441
  24795 State Highway 74 Perris (92570) *(P-564)*

Parker Aerospace, Irvine *Also Called: Parker-Hannifin Corporation (P-7535)*

Parker Boiler Co, Commerce *Also Called: Sid E Parker Boiler Mfg Co Inc (P-4926)*

Parker Meggitt, Simi Valley *Also Called: Meggitt Safety Systems Inc (P-7134)*

Parker Service Center, Buena Park *Also Called: Parker-Hannifin Corporation (P-3874)*

Parker Station, Calabasas *Also Called: Guarachi Wine Partners Inc (P-11056)*

Parker-Hannifin Corporation .... D 714 522-8840
  8460 Kass Dr Buena Park (90621) *(P-3874)*

Parker-Hannifin Corporation .... D 562 404-1938
14087 Borate St Santa Fe Springs (90670) *(P-4920)*

Parker-Hannifin Corporation .... D 951 280-3800
221 Helicopter Cir Corona (92878) *(P-6052)*

Parker-Hannifin Corporation .... C 619 661-7000
7664 Panasonic Way San Diego (92154) *(P-6053)*

Parker-Hannifin Corporation .... C 310 608-5600
19610 S Rancho Way Rancho Dominguez (90220) *(P-6933)*

Parker-Hannifin Corporation .... C 949 833-3000
16666 Von Karman Ave Irvine (92606) *(P-7393)*

Parker-Hannifin Corporation .... C 949 833-3000
14300 Alton Pkwy Irvine (92618) *(P-7535)*

Parker-Hannifin Corporation .... E 805 484-8533
3800 Calle Tecate Camarillo (93012) *(P-7536)*

Parker-Hannifin Corporation .... C 949 465-4519
14300 Alton Pkwy Irvine (92618) *(P-10392)*

Parkhouse Tire, San Diego *Also Called: Parkhouse Tire Service Inc (P-11451)*

Parkhouse Tire, Bell Gardens *Also Called: Parkhouse Tire Service Inc (P-11452)*

Parkhouse Tire Service Inc .... E 858 565-8473
4660 Ruffner St San Diego (92111) *(P-11451)*

Parkhouse Tire Service Inc (PA) .... D 562 928-0421
6006 Shull St Bell Gardens (90201) *(P-11452)*

Parking Company of America .... D 562 862-2118
3165 Garfield Ave Commerce (90040) *(P-14662)*

Parking Concepts Inc .... C 714 543-5725
1020 W Civic Center Dr Santa Ana (92703) *(P-14663)*

Parking Concepts Inc .... C 626 577-8963
33 E Green St Pasadena (91105) *(P-14664)*

Parking Concepts Inc .... C 213 746-5764
1801 Georgia St Los Angeles (90015) *(P-14665)*

Parking Concepts Inc .... D 310 821-1081
14110 Palawan Way Venice (90292) *(P-14666)*

Parking Concepts Inc .... D 310 208-1611
1036 Broxton Ave Los Angeles (90024) *(P-14667)*

Parking Network Inc .... C 213 613-1500
1625 W Olympic Blvd Ste 1010 Los Angeles (90015) *(P-1220)*

Parkinson Enterprises Inc .... D 714 626-0275
135 S State College Blvd Ste 625 Brea (92821) *(P-2515)*

Parks & Recreation Dept, Canoga Park *Also Called: County of Los Angeles (P-13101)*

Parks and Recreation Dept, Pomona *Also Called: County of Los Angeles (P-15074)*

Parkside Health & Wellness Ctr, El Cajon *Also Called: Parkside Healthcare Inc (P-15819)*

Parkside Healthcare Inc .... D 619 442-7744
444 W Lexington Ave El Cajon (92020) *(P-15819)*

Parkview Cmnty Hosp Med Ctr .... A 951 354-7404
3865 Jackson St Riverside (92503) *(P-16127)*

Parkview Jlian Cnvlescent Hosp .... C 661 831-9150
1801 Julian Ave Bakersfield (93304) *(P-15748)*

Parkview Julian LLC .... C 661 831-9150
1801 Julian Ave Bakersfield (93304) *(P-15749)*

Parkview Julian Healthcare Ctr, Bakersfield *Also Called: Parkview Julian LLC (P-15749)*

Parkway Bowl, El Cajon *Also Called: Newport Diversified Inc (P-14558)*

Parkwood Landscape Maint Inc .... D 818 988-9677
16443 Hart St Van Nuys (91406) *(P-230)*

Parmela Creamery, Moreno Valley *Also Called: Life Is Life LLC (P-1288)*

Parpro Technologies Inc .... C 714 545 8886
2700 S Fairview St Santa Ana (92704) *(P-6762)*

Parquet By Dian .... D 310 527-3779
16601 S Main St Gardena (90248) *(P-2291)*

Parrot Communications Intl Inc .... E 818 567-4700
25461 Rye Canyon Rd Valencia (91355) *(P-2933)*

Parrot Media Network, Valencia *Also Called: Parrot Communications Intl Inc (P-2933)*

PARSONS, Pasadena *Also Called: Parsons Constructors Inc (P-18031)*

Parsons Constructors Inc .... C 626 440-2000
100 W Walnut St Pasadena (91103) *(P-18031)*

Parsons Engrg Science Inc (DH) .... B 626 440-2000
100 W Walnut St Pasadena (91124) *(P-17605)*

Parsons Government Svcs Inc .... B 619 685-0085
525 B St Ste 1600 San Diego (92101) *(P-17606)*

Parsons Intl Cayman Islands .... A 626 440-6000
100 W Walnut St Pasadena (91124) *(P-17607)*

Parsons Service Corporation .... A 626 440-2000
100 W Walnut St Pasadena (91124) *(P-17608)*

Parter Medical Products Inc .... C 310 327-4417
17015 Kingsview Ave Carson (90746) *(P-10100)*

Partner Concepts Inc .... D 805 745-7199
811 Camino Viejo Santa Barbara (93108) *(P-2870)*

Partner Printing, Glendale *Also Called: Colour Concepts Inc (P-2984)*

Partners Capital Group, Santa Ana *Also Called: Partners Capital Group Inc (P-14569)*

Partners Capital Group Inc (PA) .... D 949 916-3900
201 Sandpointe Ave Ste 500 Santa Ana (92707) *(P-14569)*

Partners Federal Credit Union (PA) .... D 800 948-6677
100 N First St Ste 400 Burbank (91502) *(P-11811)*

Partners Information Tech (HQ) .... D 714 736-4487
888 S Disneyland Dr Ste 500 Anaheim (92802) *(P-14241)*

Partners Prsnnel - MGT Svcs LL .... A 805 689-8191
3820 State St Ste B Santa Barbara (93105) *(P-13552)*

Partnership Staffing Solutions, Santa Clarita *Also Called: Partnership Staffing Svcs Inc (P-13553)*

Partnership Staffing Svcs Inc .... A 661 542-7074
19431 Soledad Canyon Rd A3 Santa Clarita (91351) *(P-13553)*

Partnrship Prmnt Ptro Chnse En, Long Beach *Also Called: Tidelands Oil Production Inc (P-278)*

Parts Authority LLC .... C 805 676-3410
4277 Transport St Ventura (93003) *(P-9837)*

Parylene Coating Services Inc .... E 281 391-7665
35 Argonaut Aliso Viejo (92656) *(P-5334)*

Pasadena Branch, Pasadena *Also Called: City National Bank (P-11715)*

Pasadena Center Operating Co .... C 626 795-9311
300 E Green St Pasadena (91101) *(P-14570)*

Pasadena Convention Center, Pasadena *Also Called: Pasadena Center Operating Co (P-14570)*

Pasadena Hospital Assn Ltd .... B 626 397-3322
716 S Fair Oaks Ave Pasadena (91105) *(P-15750)*

Pasadena Hospital Assn Ltd (PA) .... A 626 397-5000
100 W California Blvd Pasadena (91105) *(P-16128)*

Pasadena Hotel Dev Ventr LP .... D 626 449-4000
303 Cordova St Pasadena (91101) *(P-12969)*

Pasadena Humane Society .... D 626 792-7151
361 S Raymond Ave Pasadena (91105) *(P-17467)*

Pasadena Madows Nursing Ctr LP .... D 626 796-1103
150 Bellefontaine St Pasadena (91105) *(P-15751)*

Pasadena Newspapers Inc (PA) .... C 626 578-6300
605 E Huntington Dr Ste 100 Monrovia (91016) *(P-2822)*

Pasadena Star-News, Monrovia *Also Called: Pasadena Newspapers Inc (P-2822)*

Pasco, Buena Park *Also Called: Yeager Enterprises Corp (P-4486)*

Pasea Hotel & Spa, Huntington Beach *Also Called: Pacific City Hotel LLC (P-12958)*

Pash Portfolio Inc .... C 310 888-8738
1453 3rd Street Promenade Ste 400 Santa Monica (90401) *(P-14844)*

Paso Robles Tank Inc (HQ) .... D 805 227-1641
825 26th St Paso Robles (93446) *(P-4521)*

Pass, Orange *Also Called: Prototype & Short-Run Svcs Inc (P-5210)*

Passages, Malibu *Also Called: Grasshopper House Partners LLC (P-16947)*

Passport Food Group LLC .... C 909 627-7312
2539 E Philadelphia St Ontario (91761) *(P-1833)*

Passport Foods (svc) LLC .... C 909 627-7312
2539 E Philadelphia St Ontario (91761) *(P-1834)*

Passport Technology Usa Inc .... E 818 957-5471
400 N Brand Blvd Ste 800 Glendale (91203) *(P-14781)*

Password Enterprise Inc .... E 562 988-8889
3200 E 29th St Long Beach (90806) *(P-11657)*

Passy-Muir Inc (PA) .... E 949 833-8255
17992 Mitchell S Ste 200 Irvine (92614) *(P-8293)*

Pasta Mia, Fullerton *Also Called: Nina Mia Inc (P-1824)*

Pasta Piccinini Inc .... E 626 798-0841
950 N Fair Oaks Ave Pasadena (91103) *(P-10969)*

Pat V Mack Inc .... D 619 930-5473
2305 Historic Decatur Rd Ste 100 San Diego (92106) *(P-14102)*

Patagonia Inc (HQ) .... B 805 643-8616
259 W Santa Clara St Ventura (93001) *(P-2023)*

Patagonia Works (PA) .... B 805 643-8616
259 W Santa Clara St Ventura (93001) *(P-11509)*

Employee Codes: A=Over 500 employees, B=251-500
C=101-250, D=51-100, E=20-50, F=10-19, G=1-9

2025 Southern California
Business Directory and Buyers Guide

© Mergent Inc. 1-800-342-5647
1139

Path .... A 323 644-2216
   340 N Madison Ave Los Angeles (90004) *(P-16990)*

Pathnostics, Irvine *Also Called: Cap Diagnostics LLC (P-16306)*

Pathology Inc .... B 310 769-0561
   19951 Mariner Ave Ste 150 Torrance (90503) *(P-18191)*

Pathstone Family Office LLC .... D 888 750-7284
   1900 Avenue Of The Stars Ste 970 Los Angeles (90067) *(P-12502)*

Pathstone Federal Street, Los Angeles *Also Called: Pathstone Family Office LLC (P-12502)*

Pathward National Association .... C 949 756-2600
   1301 Dove St Ste 1000 Newport Beach (92660) *(P-11860)*

Patient Business Services, San Diego *Also Called: Palomar Health (P-16116)*

Patient Safety Technologies Inc .... E 949 387-2277
   15440 Laguna Canyon Rd Ste 150 Irvine (92618) *(P-8294)*

Patientfi LLC .... D 949 441-5484
   530 Technology Dr Ste 350 Irvine (92618) *(P-13794)*

Patientpop Inc .... D 844 487-8399
   214 Wilshire Blvd Santa Monica (90401) *(P-14004)*

Patina V, Covina *Also Called: Norlaine Inc (P-8705)*

Patio Guys, Orange *Also Called: Guys Patio Inc (P-14735)*

Patio Industries, Ontario *Also Called: Western States Wholesale Inc (P-4376)*

Patric Communications Inc (PA) .... D 619 579-2898
   15215 Alton Pkwy Ste 200 Irvine (92618) *(P-949)*

Patrick Industries Inc .... E 909 350-4440
   13414 Slover Ave Fontana (92337) *(P-9950)*

Patriot Brokerage Inc .... D 910 227-4142
   7840 Foothill Blvd Ste H Sunland (91040) *(P-9323)*

Patriot Logistics Services LLC .... D 443 994-9660
   1520 Independence Way Vista (92084) *(P-9373)*

Patriot Products, Irwindale *Also Called: Pertronix Inc (P-7098)*

Patriot Wastewater LLC .... D 714 921-4545
   314 W Freedom Ave Orange (92865) *(P-18346)*

Patrol and Security Services, Los Angeles *Also Called: Guardian Intl Solutions (P-14307)*

Patron Solutions LLC .... C 949 823-1700
   5171 California Ave Ste 200 Irvine (92617) *(P-14005)*

Patterson Kincaid LLC .... E 323 584-3559
   5175 S Soto St Vernon (90058) *(P-2125)*

Patton State Hospital, Patton *Also Called: Califrnia Dept State Hospitals (P-16269)*

Pauba Valley Elem. School, Temecula *Also Called: Temecula Vly Unified Schl Dst (P-16826)*

Paul Ferrante Inc .... E 310 854-4412
   8464 Melrose Pl West Hollywood (90069) *(P-8710)*

Paul Hastings LLP (PA) .... A 213 683-6000
   515 S Flower St Fl 25 Los Angeles (90071) *(P-16757)*

Paul Hastings LLP .... C 858 458-3000
   4747 Executive Dr Ste 1200 San Diego (92121) *(P-16758)*

Paul Mitchell, Santa Clarita *Also Called: Paul Mitchell John Systems (P-10643)*

Paul Mitchell John Systems (PA) .... D 800 793-8790
   20705 Centre Pointe Pkwy Santa Clarita (91350) *(P-10643)*

Paul R Briles Inc .... A 310 323-6222
   1700 W 132nd St Gardena (90249) *(P-5134)*

Paul-Munroe Entertech Division, Brea *Also Called: Curtiss-Wright Flow Ctrl Corp (P-5385)*

Paulson Manufacturing Corp (PA) .... D 951 676-2451
   46752 Rainbow Canyon Rd Temecula (92592) *(P-8295)*

Pauma Band of Mission Indians .... B 760 742-2177
   777 Pauma Reservation Rd Pauma Valley (92061) *(P-12970)*

Pavement Recycling Systems Inc .... D 661 948-5599
   48028 90th St W Lancaster (93536) *(P-3839)*

Pavement Recycling Systems Inc (PA) .... C 951 682-1091
   10240 San Sevaine Way Jurupa Valley (91752) *(P-10540)*

Paver Decor Masonry Inc .... E 909 795-8474
   987 Calimesa Blvd Calimesa (92320) *(P-642)*

Pavilion At Ocean Point, The, San Diego *Also Called: Point Loma Rhblitation Ctr LLC (P-15755)*

Pavilion Surgery Center, Orange *Also Called: Pavilion Surgery Center LLC (P-15419)*

Pavilion Surgery Center LLC .... D 714 744-8850
   1140 W La Veta Ave Ste 300 Orange (92868) *(P-15419)*

Pavletich Elc Cmmnications Inc (PA) .... D 661 589-9473
   6308 Seven Seas Ave Bakersfield (93308) *(P-950)*

Pavletich Electric, Bakersfield *Also Called: Pavletich Elc Cmmnications Inc (P-950)*

Paw, Chatsworth *Also Called: Performance Automotive Whl Inc (P-11659)*

Paychex Benefit Tech Inc .... C 800 322-7292
   2385 Northside Dr Ste 100 San Diego (92108) *(P-9453)*

Paydarfar Industries Inc .... D 949 481-3267
   26054 Acero Mission Viejo (92691) *(P-10022)*

Payden & Rygel (PA) .... C 213 625-1900
   333 S Grand Ave Ste 4000 Los Angeles (90071) *(P-12030)*

Payment Cloud LLC .... D 800 988-2215
   16501 Ventura Blvd Ste 300 Encino (91436) *(P-14150)*

Paymentcloud, Encino *Also Called: Payment Cloud LLC (P-14150)*

Payne Magnetics Corporation .... D 626 332-6207
   854 W Front St Covina (91722) *(P-6934)*

Payoff, Torrance *Also Called: Happy Money Inc (P-11840)*

Payoff Inc .... D 949 430-0630
   3200 Park Center Dr Ste 800 Costa Mesa (92626) *(P-11861)*

Pb Fasteners, Gardena *Also Called: Paul R Briles Inc (P-5134)*

Pb Fasteners, Gardena *Also Called: SPS Technologies LLC (P-10465)*

Pbc Companies, Anaheim *Also Called: Peterson Brothers Cnstr Inc (P-1133)*

Pbc Pavers Inc .... D 714 278-0488
   2929 E White Star Ave Anaheim (92806) *(P-869)*

Pbf & E LLC .... E 213 427-0340
   3014 W Olympic Blvd Los Angeles (90006) *(P-11595)*

Pbi, Calabasas *Also Called: Picore Bristain Initiative Inc (P-14329)*

PC Cleaner, Pasadena *Also Called: Realdefense LLC (P-14416)*

PC Mechanical Inc .... E 805 925-2888
   2803 Industrial Pkwy Santa Maria (93455) *(P-358)*

PC Specialists Inc (HQ) .... C 858 566-1900
   11860 Community Rd Ste 160 Poway (92064) *(P-10023)*

PC Vaughan Mfg Corp .... D 805 278-2555
   1278 Mercantile St Oxnard (93030) *(P-4193)*

PC Woo Inc (PA) .... D 323 887-8138
   6443 E Slauson Ave Commerce (90040) *(P-10526)*

PCA Aerospace Inc .... E 714 901-5209
   15282 Newsboy Cir Huntington Beach (92649) *(P-7537)*

PCA Aerospace Inc (PA) .... D 714 841-1750
   17800 Gothard St Huntington Beach (92647) *(P-7538)*

PCA Med, Commerce *Also Called: Pcam LLC (P-14668)*

PCA/Los Angeles 349, Vernon *Also Called: Packaging Corporation America (P-2684)*

PCA/South Gate 378, South Gate *Also Called: Packaging Corporation America (P-2685)*

Pcam LLC .... D 562 862-2118
   3165 Garfield Ave Commerce (90040) *(P-14668)*

Pcamp, Commerce *Also Called: Parking Company of America (P-14662)*

PCB BANK (HQ) .... C 213 210-2000
   3701 Wilshire Blvd Ste 900 Los Angeles (90010) *(P-11776)*

Pcb Fabrication Facility, San Marcos *Also Called: Hughes Circuits Inc (P-6736)*

Pcbc Holdco Inc .... E 562 944-9549
   12748 Florence Ave Santa Fe Springs (90670) *(P-10456)*

PCC Aerostructures, North Hollywood *Also Called: Klune Industries Inc (P-7511)*

PCC Network Solutions, Chatsworth *Also Called: Pacific Coast Cabling Inc (P-947)*

PCC Rollmet Inc .... D 949 221-5333
   1822 Deere Ave Irvine (92606) *(P-4581)*

PCI, Riverside *Also Called: Pacific Consolidated Inds LLC (P-5831)*

PCI, San Diego *Also Called: Project Concern International (P-16997)*

PCI Care Venture I .... D 661 949-2177
   43454 30th St W Ofc Lancaster (93536) *(P-15752)*

PCI Industries Inc .... E 323 728-0004
   6501 Potello St Commerce (90040) *(P-5017)*

PCI Industries Inc .... E 323 889-6770
   700 S Vail Ave Montebello (90640) *(P-5018)*

PCI Industries Inc .... E 323 889-6770
   700 S Vail Ave Montebello (90640) *(P-8711)*

PCI Industries Inc .... E 323 728-0004
   6490 Fleet St Commerce (90040) *(P-8712)*

PCL Construction Services Inc .... D 858 657-3400
   4690 Executive Dr Ste 100 San Diego (92121) *(P-565)*

PCL Construction Services Inc .... C 818 246-3481
   655 N Central Ave Ste 1600 Glendale (91203) *(P-566)*

PCL Industrial Services Inc .... B 661 832-3995
   1500 S Union Ave Bakersfield (93307) *(P-567)*

Pcm, Laguna Woods *Also Called: Professional Cmnty MGT Cal Inc (P-12511)*

Pcm, Aliso Viejo *Also Called: Professional Community MGT Cal (P-18038)*

Pcm Inc (HQ) .... A 310 354-5600
   200 N Pacific Coast Hwy Ste 1050 El Segundo (90245) *(P-11658)*

Pcn3 Inc .... D 562 493-4124
11082 Winners Cir Ste B Los Alamitos (90720) *(P-568)*

Pcs Link Inc .... B 949 655-5000
12424 Wilshire Blvd Ste 1030 Los Angeles (90025) *(P-18347)*

Pcs Mobile Solutions LLC .... D 323 567-2490
3534 Tweedy Blvd South Gate (90280) *(P-9454)*

Pcs Property Managment LLC .... C 310 231-1000
11859 Wilshire Blvd Ste 600 Los Angeles (90025) *(P-12503)*

Pct, Compton *Also Called: Pacific Contntl Textiles Inc (P-1944)*

Pcv Murcor Real Estate Svcs, Pomona *Also Called: Murcor Inc (P-12494)*

Pcx Aerosystems - Santa Ana, Santa Ana *Also Called: Integral Aerospace LLC (P-7501)*

Pd Group .... E 760 674-3028
41945 Boardwalk Ste L Palm Desert (92211) *(P-8623)*

PDC A Bowman Company, San Diego *Also Called: Project Design Consultants LLC (P-18350)*

Pdc-Identicard, Valencia *Also Called: Precision Dynamics Corporation (P-2725)*

Pdf Print Communications Inc (PA)............................... D 562 426-6978
2630 E 28th St Long Beach (90755) *(P-3057)*

Pdma Ventures Inc .... E 714 777-8770
22951 La Palma Ave Yorba Linda (92887) *(P-8350)*

Pds, Compton *Also Called: Pacific Drayage Services LLC (P-8969)*

Pds, Irvine *Also Called: Pacific Dental Services LLC (P-15523)*

Pds Defense Inc .... B 214 647-9600
3100 S Harbor Blvd Ste 135 Santa Ana (92704) *(P-13554)*

Pdu Lad Corporation (PA)... E 626 442-7711
11165 Valley Spring Ln North Hollywood (91602) *(P-5335)*

Pe Facility Solutions LLC (PA)...................................... D 858 467-0202
4217 Ponderosa Ave Ste A San Diego (92123) *(P-13401)*

Pea Soup Andersen's Restaurant, Buellton *Also Called: Carpenters Southwest ADM Corp (P-11554)*

Peabody Engineering, Corona *Also Called: Peabody Engineering & Sup Inc (P-5716)*

Peabody Engineering & Sup Inc .... E 951 734-7711
13435 Estelle St Corona (92879) *(P-5716)*

Peach Inc .... C 323 654-2333
1311 N Highland Ave Los Angeles (90028) *(P-9010)*

Peaches, Sherman Oaks *Also Called: Med Couture Inc (P-1998)*

Pearson Dental Supplies Inc (PA)................................. C 818 362-2600
13161 Telfair Ave Sylmar (91342) *(P-10101)*

Pearson Ford Co (PA).. C 877 743-0421
5900 Sycamore Canyon Blvd Riverside (92507) *(P-11394)*

Pearson Surgical Supply Co, Sylmar *Also Called: Pearson Dental Supplies Inc (P-10101)*

PEC, Torrance *Also Called: Products Engineering Corp (P-4745)*

PEC Tool, Torrance *Also Called: Fun Properties Inc (P-4739)*

Pecc, San Diego *Also Called: Precision Engine Controls Corp (P-5460)*

Pechanga Development Corp .... A 951 695-4655
45000 Pechanga Pkwy Temecula (92592) *(P-12971)*

Pechanga Resort & Casino, Temecula *Also Called: Pechanga Development Corp (P-12971)*

Pechanga Resorts Incorporated .... D 888 732-4264
45000 Pechanga Pkwy Temecula (92592) *(P-12972)*

Pecific Grinding, Fullerton *Also Called: Kryler Corp (P-5272)*

Peck Jones Construction, Santa Monica *Also Called: Jones Brothers Cnstr Corp (P-551)*

Pecs, Rancho Cucamonga *Also Called: Professnal Elec Cnstr Svcs Inc (P-954)*

Pedavena Mould and Die Co Inc .... E 310 327-2814
12464 Mccann Dr Santa Fe Springs (90670) *(P-6200)*

Pedi, San Diego *Also Called: Providien Injection Molding Inc (P-4213)*

Pedi Center, Bakersfield *Also Called: Dignity Health (P-15979)*

Pediatric and Family Med Ctr .... C 213 342-3325
1530 S Olive St Los Angeles (90015) *(P-15420)*

Pediatric Cancer Research, Orange *Also Called: Childrens Healthcare Cal (P-15274)*

Pediatric Therapy Network .... C 310 328-0276
1815 W 213th St Ste 100 Torrance (90501) *(P-16488)*

Peei, Los Angeles *Also Called: Playboy Enterprises Intl Inc (P-2936)*

Peerigon Medical Distribution, El Toro *Also Called: P M D Holding Corp (P-10098)*

Peerless Building Maint Co, Chatsworth *Also Called: Tuttle Family Enterprises Inc (P-13424)*

Peerless Injection Molding LLC .... E 714 689-1920
14321 Corp Dr Garden Grove (92843) *(P-4194)*

Peerless Maintenance Svc Inc .... B 714 871-3380
1100 S Euclid St La Habra (90631) *(P-13402)*

Peerless Materials Company .... E 323 266-0313
4442 E 26th St Vernon (90058) *(P-3618)*

Pegasus Building Svcs Co Inc .... B 858 444-2290
7966 Arjons Dr Ste A San Diego (92126) *(P-13403)*

Pegasus Elite Aviation Inc .... C 818 742-6666
7943 Woodley Ave Van Nuys (91406) *(P-9182)*

Pegasus Foods, Los Angeles *Also Called: Astrochef LLC (P-1385)*

Pegasus HM Hlth Care A Cal Cor .... D 818 551-1932
505 N Brand Blvd Ste 1000 Glendale (91203) *(P-16410)*

Pegasus Home Health Services, Glendale *Also Called: Pegasus HM Hlth Care A Cal Cor (P-16410)*

Pegasus Interprint Inc .... E 800 926-9873
7111 Hayvenhurst Ave Van Nuys (91406) *(P-3058)*

Pegasus Maritime Inc .... D 714 728-8565
505 N Brand Blvd Ste 210 Glendale (91203) *(P-9324)*

Pegasus One, Fullerton *Also Called: Aspirez Inc (P-13660)*

Pegasus Squire Inc .... D 866 208-6837
12021 Wilshire Blvd Ste 770 Los Angeles (90025) *(P-14242)*

Peggs Company Inc (PA).. C 800 242-8416
4851 Felspar St Riverside (92509) *(P-14782)*

Peking Noodle Co Inc .... E 323 223-0897
1514 N San Fernando Rd Los Angeles (90065) *(P-1734)*

Pelco By Schneider Electric, Chino *Also Called: Schneider Electric Usa Inc (P-9108)*

Pelican, Torrance *Also Called: Pelican Products Inc (P-6514)*

Pelican Products Inc (PA).. C 310 326-4700
23215 Early Ave Torrance (90505) *(P-6514)*

Pelomar Family YMCA, Encinitas *Also Called: YMCA of San Diego County (P-17386)*

Peltek Holdings Inc .... E 949 855-8010
35 Argonaut Ste A1 Laguna Hills (92656) *(P-5336)*

Pem, Buena Park *Also Called: Park Engineering and Mfg Co (P-6199)*

Pemko Manufacturing Co .... C 800 283-9988
4226 Transport St Ventura (93003) *(P-4898)*

Pen Manufacturing, Anaheim *Also Called: Pen Manufacturing LLC (P-6201)*

Pen Manufacturing LLC .... E 714 992-0950
1808 N American St Anaheim (92801) *(P-6201)*

Pendry San Diego, San Diego *Also Called: Rgc Gaslamp LLC (P-12993)*

Penfield & Smith, Santa Barbara *Also Called: Penfield & Smith Engineers Inc (P-17609)*

Penfield & Smith Engineers Inc .... D 805 963-9532
111 E Victoria St Santa Barbara (93101) *(P-17609)*

Pengcheng Aluminum Enterprise Inc USA .... E 909 598-7933
19605 E Walnut Dr N Walnut (91789) *(P-4603)*

Penguin Natural Foods Inc .... E 323 488-6000
5659 Mansfield Way Bell (90201) *(P-1835)*

Penguin Natural Foods Inc (PA)..................................... E 323 727-7980
4400 Alcoa Ave Vernon (90058) *(P-1836)*

Penguin Pumps Incorporated .... E 818 504-2391
7932 Ajay Dr Sun Valley (91352) *(P-5739)*

Penhall Company .... D 858 550-1111
5775 Eastgate Dr San Diego (92121) *(P-1221)*

Penhall Holding Company .... D 714 772-6450
1801 W Penhall Way Anaheim (92801) *(P-1132)*

Penhall San Diego 202, San Diego *Also Called: Penhall Company (P-1221)*

Peninsula Beverly Hill's, Beverly Hills *Also Called: Belvedere Hotel Partnership (P-12771)*

Peninsula Beverly Hills, The, Beverly Hills *Also Called: Belvedere Partnership (P-12772)*

Peninsula Family YMCA Sunshine, San Diego *Also Called: YMCA of San Diego County (P-17391)*

Penn Elcom Inc (HQ).. E 714 230-6200
7465 Lampson Ave Garden Grove (92841) *(P-10311)*

Penn Elcom Hardware, Garden Grove *Also Called: Penn Elcom Inc (P-10311)*

Pennant Group Inc .... C 714 978-2534
1800 W Culver Ave Orange (92868) *(P-15753)*

Penney Lawn Service Inc .... D 661 587-4788
4000 Allen Rd Bakersfield (93314) *(P-231)*

Penney Opco LLC .... D 972 431-2618
5959 Palm Ave San Bernardino (92407) *(P-9098)*

Penney Opco LLC .... D 805 497-6811
280 W Hillcrest Dr Thousand Oaks (91360) *(P-11262)*

Penney Opco LLC .... C 626 445-6454
400 S Baldwin Ave Lowr Arcadia (91007) *(P-11263)*

Penney Opco LLC .... C 626 960-3711
1203 Plaza Dr West Covina (91790) *(P-11264)*

Pennoyer-Dodge Co .... E 818 547-2100
6650 San Fernando Rd Glendale (91201) *(P-5618)*

Employee Codes: A=Over 500 employees, B=251-500
C=101-250, D=51-100, E=20-50, F=10-19, G=1-9

2025 Southern California
Business Directory and Buyers Guide

© Mergent Inc. 1-800-342-5647

1141

ALPHABETIC

Penny & Giles Drive Technology, Brea *Also Called: Curtiss-Wrght Cntrls Intgrted (P-8258)*

Penny Lane Centers (PA)... B 818 892-3423
15305 Rayen St North Hills (91343) *(P-17239)*

Penny Lawn Service, Bakersfield *Also Called: Penney Lawn Service Inc (P-231)*

Pennymac, Agoura Hills *Also Called: Private Nat Mrtg Accptance LLC (P-11931)*

Pennymac Corp .... A 818 878-8416
3043 Townsgate Rd Westlake Village (91361) *(P-11949)*

Pennysaver USA Publishing LLC .... A 866 640-3900
2830 Orbiter St Brea (92821) *(P-2934)*

Pensieve Foods .... E 323 938-8666
1782 Industrial Way Los Angeles (90023) *(P-1837)*

Penske, West Covina *Also Called: Penske Motor Group LLC (P-14639)*

Penske Ford Chula Vista, Chula Vista *Also Called: Rp Automotive II Inc (P-14642)*

Penske Honda Ontario, Ontario *Also Called: Ontario Automotive LLC (P-11391)*

Penske Motor Group LLC .... B 626 859-1200
2010 E Garvey Ave S West Covina (91791) *(P-14639)*

Penske Transportation MGT LLC .... C 844 847-9518
2280 Wardlow Cir Corona (92878) *(P-14640)*

Pentacon Inc .... B 818 727-8000
21123 Nordhoff St Chatsworth (91311) *(P-10457)*

Pentair Equipment Protection, San Diego *Also Called: Schroff Inc (P-14730)*

Pentair Water Treatment, Costa Mesa *Also Called: Shurflo LLC (P-5744)*

Pentel of America Ltd (DH).................................... C **310 320-3831**
2715 Columbia St Torrance (90503) *(P-10582)*

Pentrate Metal Processing .... E 323 269-2121
3517 E Olympic Blvd Los Angeles (90023) *(P-5282)*

Penwal Industries Inc .... D 909 466-1555
10611 Acacia St Rancho Cucamonga (91730) *(P-569)*

People Pets and Vets LLC .... C 909 453-4213
10986 Sierra Ave Ste 400 Fontana (92337) *(P-131)*

People Pets and Vets LLC .... C 909 329-2860
16055 Sierra Lakes Pkwy Ste 100 Fontana (92336) *(P-132)*

People Concern .... C 310 874-2806
526 S San Pedro St Los Angeles (90013) *(P-16991)*

People Concern .... C 310 450-0650
1751 Cloverfield Blvd Santa Monica (90404) *(P-16992)*

People Concern .... C 310 883-1222
1751 Cloverfield Blvd Santa Monica (90404) *(P-16993)*

People Creating Success Inc .... D 805 644-9480
380 Arneill Rd Camarillo (93010) *(P-15421)*

People Creating Success Inc .... D 661 225-9700
1607 E Palmdale Blvd Ste H Palmdale (93550) *(P-16994)*

People Creating Success Inc .... D 805 692-5290
5350 Hollister Ave Ste I Santa Barbara (93111) *(P-16995)*

PEOPLE'S CARE INC., Victorville *Also Called: Peoples Care Inc (P-16411)*

PEOPLE'S CARE INC., Santa Fe Springs *Also Called: Peoples Care Inc (P-17105)*

Peoples Care Inc .... C 760 962-1900
13901 Amargosa Rd Ste 101 Victorville (92392) *(P-16411)*

Peoples Care Inc .... C 562 320-0174
12215 Telegraph Rd Ste 208 Santa Fe Springs (90670) *(P-17105)*

Pep Creations, San Diego *Also Called: Pacific Event Productions Inc (P-13184)*

Pep West, Inc., San Diego *Also Called: Schroff Inc (P-5743)*

Pepitastore, El Segundo *Also Called: Scalefast Inc (P-9457)*

Peppermint Ridge (PA).. D **951 273-7320**
825 Magnolia Ave Corona (92879) *(P-17187)*

Pepsi-Cola, Mojave *Also Called: Pepsi-Cola Metro Btlg Co Inc (P-1629)*

Pepsi-Cola, San Fernando *Also Called: Pepsi-Cola Metro Btlg Co Inc (P-1630)*

Pepsi-Cola, Buena Park *Also Called: Pepsi-Cola Metro Btlg Co Inc (P-1632)*

Pepsi-Cola, Carson *Also Called: Pepsi-Cola Metro Btlg Co Inc (P-1635)*

Pepsi-Cola, Riverside *Also Called: Pepsi-Cola Metro Btlg Co Inc (P-10342)*

Pepsi-Cola Bottling Group .... D 661 635-1100
215 E 21st St Bakersfield (93305) *(P-1628)*

Pepsi-Cola Metro Btlg Co Inc .... E 661 824-2051
2471 Nadeau St Mojave (93501) *(P-1629)*

Pepsi-Cola Metro Btlg Co Inc .... D 818 898-3829
1200 Arroyo St San Fernando (91340) *(P-1630)*

Pepsi-Cola Metro Btlg Co Inc .... D 949 643-5700
27717 Aliso Creek Rd Aliso Viejo (92656) *(P-1631)*

Pepsi-Cola Metro Btlg Co Inc .... C 714 522-9635
6261 Caballero Blvd Buena Park (90620) *(P-1632)*

Pepsi-Cola Metro Btlg Co Inc .... D 805 739-2160
2345 Thompson Way Santa Maria (93455) *(P-1633)*

Pepsi-Cola Metro Btlg Co Inc .... D 858 560-6735
10057 Marathon Pkwy Lakeside (92040) *(P-1634)*

Pepsi-Cola Metro Btlg Co Inc .... C 310 327-4222
19700 Figueroa St Carson (90745) *(P-1635)*

Pepsi-Cola Metro Btlg Co Inc .... E 951 697-3200
6659 Sycamore Canyon Blvd Riverside (92507) *(P-10342)*

Pepsico .... E 562 818-9429
1650 E Central Ave San Bernardino (92408) *(P-1636)*

Pepsico, Riverside *Also Called: Bottling Group LLC (P-1610)*

Pepsico, Ventura *Also Called: P-Americas LLC (P-1627)*

Pepsico, Bakersfield *Also Called: Pepsi-Cola Bottling Group (P-1628)*

Pepsico, Aliso Viejo *Also Called: Pepsi-Cola Metro Btlg Co Inc (P-1631)*

Pepsico, Santa Maria *Also Called: Pepsi-Cola Metro Btlg Co Inc (P-1633)*

Pepsico, Lakeside *Also Called: Pepsi-Cola Metro Btlg Co Inc (P-1634)*

Pepsico, Baldwin Park *Also Called: Pepsico Inc (P-1637)*

Pepsico Inc .... E 626 338-5531
4416 Azusa Canyon Rd Baldwin Park (91706) *(P-1637)*

Pepsico Beverage Sales LLC .... B 818 361-0685
1200 Arroyo St San Fernando (91340) *(P-9099)*

Pepsico Beverage Sales LLC .... C 949 362-2860
27717 Aliso Creek Rd Aliso Viejo (92656) *(P-9100)*

Pepsico Beverage Sales LLC .... B 714 228-9719
6261 Caballero Blvd Buena Park (90620) *(P-9101)*

Peraton Technology Svcs Inc .... E 571 313-6000
2750 Womble Rd Ste 202 San Diego (92106) *(P-17885)*

Perera Cnstr & Design Inc .... E 909 484-6350
2890 Inland Empire Blvd Ste 102 Ontario (91764) *(P-256)*

Perfect Banner, The, Aliso Viejo *Also Called: Perfect Impression Inc (P-14571)*

Perfect Bar LLC .... C 866 628-8548
10505 Roselle St Ste 102 San Diego (92121) *(P-10970)*

Perfect Choice Mfrs Inc .... E 714 792-0322
17819 Gillette Ave Irvine (92614) *(P-8713)*

Perfect Impression Inc .... E 949 305-0797
27111 Aliso Creek Rd Ste 145 Aliso Viejo (92656) *(P-14571)*

Perfect Snacks, San Diego *Also Called: Perfect Bar LLC (P-10970)*

Perfection Pet Brands, Buellton *Also Called: Kruse Pet Holdings LLC (P-1419)*

Performance Automotive Whl Inc (PA).................. D **805 499-8973**
20235 Nordhoff St Chatsworth (91311) *(P-11659)*

Performance Building Services .... C 949 364-4364
22642 Lambert St Ste 409 Lake Forest (92630) *(P-13404)*

Performance Cleanroom Services, Lake Forest *Also Called: Performance Building Services (P-13404)*

Performance Composites Inc .... C 310 328-6661
1418 S Alameda St Compton (90221) *(P-4328)*

Performance Contracting Inc .... D 913 310-7120
4955 E Landon Dr Anaheim (92807) *(P-1190)*

Performance Forge Inc .... E 323 722-3460
7401 Telegraph Rd Montebello (90640) *(P-5146)*

Performance Machine, La Palma *Also Called: Performance Machine Inc (P-7633)*

Performance Machine Inc .... C 714 523-3000
6892 Marlin Cir La Palma (90623) *(P-7633)*

Performance Machine Tech Inc .... E 661 294-8617
25141 Avenue Stanford Valencia (91355) *(P-6202)*

Performance Materials Corp (HQ)......................... D **805 482-1722**
1150 Calle Suerte Camarillo (93012) *(P-3285)*

Performance Motorsports Inc .... B 714 898-9763
5100 Campus Dr Ste 100 Newport Beach (92660) *(P-6044)*

Performance Nissan, Duarte *Also Called: Gpi Ca-Niii Inc (P-11355)*

Performance Plastics, San Diego *Also Called: Rock West Composites Inc (P-3290)*

Performance Plastics Inc .... D 714 343-3928
7919 Saint Andrews Ave San Diego (92154) *(P-7539)*

Performance Powder Inc .... E 714 632-0600
2940 E La Jolla St Ste A Anaheim (92806) *(P-5337)*

Performance Sheets LLC .... C 626 333-0195
440 Baldwin Park Blvd City Of Industry (91746) *(P-1091)*

Performance Team, El Segundo *Also Called: Maersk Whsng Dist Svcs USA LLC (P-9310)*

Performance Team Freight, Santa Fe Springs *Also Called: Maersk Whsng Dist Svcs USA LLC (P-9308)*

Performing Arts Ctr Los Angles .... C 213 972-7512
135 N Grand Ave Ste 314 Los Angeles (90012) *(P-14970)*

Performnce Engineered Pdts Inc .... E 909 594-7487
3270 Pomona Blvd Pomona (91768) *(P-4195)*

Perillo Industries Inc .... E 805 498-9838
2150 Anchor Ct Ste A Newbury Park (91320) *(P-10278)*

Perkowitz & Ruth Architects, Long Beach *Also Called: Rdc-S111 Inc (P-17688)*

Perlman Clinic .... C 858 554-1212
3900 5th Ave Ste 110 San Diego (92103) *(P-15422)*

Permanente Medical Group Inc .... A 310 325-5111
25825 Vermont Ave Harbor City (90710) *(P-15423)*

Permaswage USA, Gardena *Also Called: Designed Metal Connections Inc (P-7462)*

Pernod Ricard Usa LLC .... D 949 242-6800
3333 Michelson Dr Ste 925 Irvine (92612) *(P-11059)*

Perricone Juices, Beaumont *Also Called: Beaumont Juice LLC (P-1349)*

Perrin Bernard Supowitz LLC (HQ)................................ D 323 981-2800
5496 Lindbergh Ln Bell (90201) *(P-10607)*

Perrin Craft, San Marcos *Also Called: Dispensing Dynamics Intl Inc (P-4104)*

Perris Disposal Company, Perris *Also Called: CR&r Incorporated (P-9740)*

Perris Valley Cmnty Hosp LLC .... C 909 581-6400
10841 White Oak Ave Rancho Cucamonga (91730) *(P-16129)*

Perry Coast Construction Inc .... C 951 774-0677
3811 Wacker Dr Jurupa Valley (91752) *(P-570)*

Perry Ford, Poway *Also Called: Perry Ford of Poway LLC (P-11395)*

Perry Ford of Poway LLC .... D 858 748-1400
12740 Poway Rd Poway (92064) *(P-11395)*

Perry Industries, Corona *Also Called: M & O Perry Industries Inc (P-5792)*

Perseption, Vernon *Also Called: W & W Concept Inc (P-2142)*

Person & Covey Inc .... E 818 937-5000
616 Allen Ave Glendale (91201) *(P-3678)*

Personnel Concepts, Ontario *Also Called: Aio Acquisition Inc (P-2901)*

Personnel Plus Inc .... C 562 712-5490
12052 Imperial Hwy Ste 200 Norwalk (90650) *(P-13615)*

Pertronix Inc .... E 909 599-5955
15601 Cypress Ave Unit B Irwindale (91706) *(P-7098)*

Pertronix LLC .... E 909 599-5955
440 E Arrow Hwy San Dimas (91773) *(P-7838)*

Pertronix Performance Brands, San Dimas *Also Called: Pertronix LLC (P-7838)*

Pet Partners Inc (PA)... C 951 279-9888
450 N Sheridan St Corona (92878) *(P-8714)*

Petco Park, San Diego *Also Called: City of San Diego (P-15023)*

Pete's, Oxnard *Also Called: Hollandia Oxnard (P-10907)*

Peter Brasseler Holdings LLC .... D 805 658-2643
4837 Mcgrath St Ventura (93003) *(P-8213)*

Peter Brasseler Holdings LLC .... D 805 650-5209
4837 Mcgrath St Ste J Ventura (93003) *(P-10102)*

Peter Cohen Companies, Los Angeles *Also Called: Piet Retief Inc (P-2126)*

Peter Rabbit Farms, Coachella *Also Called: Amazing Coachella Inc (P-7)*

Peter Wylan DDS .... D 562 925-3765
10318 Rosecrans Ave Bellflower (90706) *(P-15525)*

Petersen-Dean Inc .... C 714 629-9670
2210 S Dupont Dr Anaheim (92806) *(P-1092)*

Petersendean, Anaheim *Also Called: Petersen-Dean Inc (P-1092)*

Peterson Bros Construction, Anaheim *Also Called: Pbc Pavers Inc (P-869)*

Peterson Brothers Cnstr Inc .... A 714 278-0488
2929 E White Star Ave Anaheim (92806) *(P-1133)*

Peterson's Spices, Pico Rivera *Also Called: GPde Slva Spces Incrporation (P-1786)*

Petes Road Service Inc (PA)... D 714 446-1207
2230 E Orangethorpe Ave Fullerton (92831) *(P-9859)*

Petit Ermitage, West Hollywood *Also Called: Valadon Hotel LLC (P-13064)*

Petro-Lud Inc .... E 661 747-4779
12625 Jomani Dr Ste 104 Bakersfield (93312) *(P-293)*

Petrochem, Long Beach *Also Called: Petrochem Insulation Inc (P-1023)*

Petrochem Insulation Inc .... C 310 638-6663
3117 E South St Long Beach (90805) *(P-1023)*

Petrol Advertising Inc .... D 323 644-3720
443 N Varney St Burbank (91502) *(P-13235)*

Petrosian Esthetic Entps LLC .... C 818 391-8231
2919 W Burbank Blvd Burbank (91505) *(P-13153)*

Petvisor, San Diego *Also Called: Locai Inc (P-13762)*

Pexco Aerospace Inc .... E 714 894-9922
5451 Argosy Ave Huntington Beach (92649) *(P-3286)*

Pezeme, Los Angeles *Also Called: Choon Inc (P-2063)*

Pf Candle Co, Commerce *Also Called: Pommes Frites Candle Co (P-8717)*

Pfeiler Psomas, Los Angeles *Also Called: Psomas (P-17698)*

Pfenex, San Diego *Also Called: Pfenex Inc (P-3472)*

Pfenex Inc .... D 858 352-4400
10790 Roselle St San Diego (92121) *(P-3472)*

Pff Bancorp Inc (PA).. A 213 683-6393
2058 N Mills Ave Pmb 139 Claremont (91711) *(P-11789)*

Pfizer, San Diego *Also Called: Pfizer Inc (P-3473)*

Pfizer, San Diego *Also Called: Pfizer Inc (P-3474)*

Pfizer Inc .... D 858 622-3000
10777 Science Center Dr San Diego (92121) *(P-3473)*

Pfizer Inc .... D 858 622-3001
10646 Science Center Dr San Diego (92121) *(P-3474)*

Pfp, Chula Vista *Also Called: Precision Fiber Products Inc (P-4636)*

Pg Usa LLC .... D 310 954-1040
5150 W Goldleaf Cir Los Angeles (90056) *(P-11269)*

PG&e, Needles *Also Called: Pacific Gas and Electric Co (P-9595)*

PG&e, Hinkley *Also Called: Pacific Gas and Electric Co (P-9596)*

PG&e, San Luis Obispo *Also Called: Pacific Gas and Electric Co (P-9597)*

PG&e, Avila Beach *Also Called: Pacific Gas and Electric Co (P-9598)*

PG&e, Pismo Beach *Also Called: Pacific Gas and Electric Co (P-9599)*

PG&e, Templeton *Also Called: Pacific Gas and Electric Co (P-9600)*

Pga West By Wldorf Astoria MGT, La Quinta *Also Called: Msr Resort Lodging Tenant LLC (P-12933)*

Pgac Corp (PA).. D 858 560-8213
9630 Ridgehaven Ct Ste B San Diego (92123) *(P-2710)*

Pgi, San Diego *Also Called: Pgac Corp (P-2710)*

Pgi, City Of Industry *Also Called: Pgi Pacific Graphics Intl (P-3059)*

Pgi Pacific Graphics Intl .... E 626 336-7707
14938 Nelson Ave City Of Industry (91744) *(P-3059)*

PH Design, Commerce *Also Called: Pacific Hospitality Design Inc (P-2551)*

Phamatech Incorporated .... C 888 635-5840
15175 Innovation Dr San Diego (92128) *(P-17923)*

Phaostron Instr Electronic Co .... D 626 969-6801
717 N Coney Ave Azusa (91702) *(P-6309)*

Phaostron Instr Electronic Co, Azusa *Also Called: Phaostron Instr Electronic Co (P-6309)*

Pharma Pac, Grover Beach *Also Called: H J Harkins Company Inc (P-3417)*

Pharmaceutic Litho Label Inc .... D 805 285-5162
3990 Royal Ave Simi Valley (93063) *(P-3475)*

Pharmachem Laboratories LLC .... E 714 630-6000
2929 E White Star Ave Anaheim (92806) *(P-1306)*

PHARMACHEM LABORATORIES, LLC, Anaheim *Also Called: Pharmachem Laboratories LLC (P-1306)*

Pharmaco-Kinesis Corporation .... E 310 641-2700
10604 S La Cienega Blvd Inglewood (90304) *(P-8214)*

Pharmatek, San Diego *Also Called: Catalent Pharma Solutions Inc (P-3384)*

Pharmavite LLC (DH)... B 818 221-6200
8531 Fallbrook Ave West Hills (91304) *(P-3327)*

Pharmerica Corporation .... A 951 683-4165
833 Marlborough Ave Riverside (92507) *(P-10644)*

Pharmion Corporation .... E 858 335-5744
12481 High Bluff Dr Ste 200 San Diego (92130) *(P-3476)*

Phase 2 Cellars LLC .... E 805 782-0300
4910 Edna Rd San Luis Obispo (93401) *(P-1581)*

PHC, Irvine *Also Called: Pacific Handy Cutter Inc (P-4743)*

PHC, Irvine *Also Called: PHC Merger Inc (P-4744)*

PHC Merger Inc .... E 714 662-1033
17819 Gillette Ave Irvine (92614) *(P-4744)*

PHC Sharp Holdings Inc (HQ)... E 714 662-1033
17819 Gillette Ave Irvine (92614) *(P-4732)*

Phenix Enterprises Inc (PA)... E 909 469-0411
1785 Mount Vernon Ave Pomona (91768) *(P-7208)*

Phenix Gourmet LLC .... C 562 404-5028
4225 N Palm St Fullerton (92835) *(P-1491)*

Phenix Truck Bodies and Eqp, Pomona *Also Called: Phenix Enterprises Inc (P-7208)*

Employee Codes: A=Over 500 employees, B=251-500
C=101-250, D=51-100, E=20-50, F=10-19, G=1-9

2025 Southern California
Business Directory and Buyers Guide

© Mergent Inc. 1-800-342-5647
1143

Phenomenex Inc (HQ)..C 310 212-0555
411 Madrid Ave Torrance (90501) *(P-7972)*

PHF II Burbank LLC ....C 818 843-6000
2500 N Hollywood Way Burbank (91505) *(P-12973)*

Phg Engineering Services LLC ....D 714 283-8288
27481 Ganso Mission Viejo (92691) *(P-17610)*

PHH, Hemet Also Called: Kpc Global Medical Centers Inc *(P-16067)*

Phiaro Incorporated ....E 949 727-1261
9016 Research Dr Irvine (92618) *(P-8715)*

Phibro Animal Health Corp ....D 562 698-8036
8851 Dice Rd Santa Fe Springs (90670) *(P-3817)*

Phibro-Tech Inc ....E 562 698-8036
8851 Dice Rd Santa Fe Springs (90670) *(P-3245)*

Phifer Incorporated ....D 626 968-0438
14408 Nelson Ave City Of Industry (91744) *(P-5409)*

Phifer Western, City Of Industry Also Called: Phifer Incorporated *(P-5409)*

Philadelphia Gear, Santa Fe Springs Also Called: Timken Gears & Services Inc *(P-5150)*

Philatron International (PA)......................................D 562 802-0452
15315 Cornet St Santa Fe Springs (90670) *(P-7142)*

Philippe Charriol USA, San Diego Also Called: Alor International Ltd *(P-8449)*

Philips ....D 916 337-8008
3721 Valley Centre Dr Ste 500 San Diego (92130) *(P-6547)*

Philips Image Gded Thrapy Corp (DH)....................B 800 228-4728
3721 Valley Centre Dr Ste 500 San Diego (92130) *(P-8396)*

Philips North America LLC ....C 909 574-1800
11201 Iberia St Ste A Jurupa Valley (91752) *(P-6448)*

Philips North America LLC ....D 858 677-6390
3721 Valley Centre Dr San Diego (92130) *(P-10222)*

Phillips 66 Co Carbon Group ....E 805 489-4050
2555 Willow Rd Arroyo Grande (93420) *(P-5717)*

Phillips Industries, Santa Fe Springs Also Called: R A Phillips Industries Inc *(P-7287)*

Phillps-Mdisize Costa Mesa LLC ....C 949 477-9495
3545 Harbor Blvd Costa Mesa (92626) *(P-8215)*

Philmont Management Inc ....D 213 380-0159
3450 Wilshire Blvd Ste 850 Los Angeles (90010) *(P-571)*

Phoenix Cars LLC ....E 909 987-0815
1500 Lakeview Loop Anaheim (92807) *(P-7188)*

Phoenix Cpitl Group Hldngs LLC ....E 303 749-0074
18575 Jamboree Rd Ste 830 Irvine (92612) *(P-310)*

Phoenix Engineering Co Inc ....D 310 532-1134
2480 Armacost Ave Los Angeles (90064) *(P-13616)*

Phoenix Houses Los Angeles Inc ....D 818 686-3000
11600 Eldridge Ave Lake View Terrace (91342) *(P-16489)*

Phoenix Marketing Services Inc ....D 909 399-4000
651 Wharton Dr Claremont (91711) *(P-3060)*

Phoenix Motor Inc (DH)..E 909 987-0815
1500 Lakeview Loop Anaheim (92807) *(P-7282)*

Phoenix Motorcars, Anaheim Also Called: Phoenix Cars LLC *(P-7188)*

Phoenix Motorcars, Anaheim Also Called: Phoenix Motor Inc *(P-7282)*

Phoenix Personnel, Los Angeles Also Called: Phoenix Engineering Co Inc *(P-13616)*

Phoenix Textile Inc (PA)..D 310 715-7090
14600 S Broadway Gardena (90248) *(P-10721)*

Phoenix Wheel Company Inc ....E 760 598-1960
2611 Commerce Way Ste D Vista (92081) *(P-9838)*

Phone & Wireless, Arroyo Grande Also Called: Golden State Phone & Wireless *(P-9402)*

Phone Check Solutions LLC ....B 310 365-1855
16027 Ventura Blvd Ste 605 Encino (91436) *(P-13795)*

Phone Ware Inc ....B 858 530-8550
8902 Activity Rd Ste A San Diego (92126) *(P-14572)*

Phonesuit Inc ....E 310 774-0282
1431 7th St Ste 201 Santa Monica (90401) *(P-6645)*

Phorus Inc ....D 310 995-2521
5220 Las Virgenes Rd Calabasas (91302) *(P-14900)*

Photo Fabricators Inc ....D 818 781-1010
7648 Burnet Ave Van Nuys (91405) *(P-6763)*

Photo Research, Chatsworth Also Called: Photo Research Inc *(P-8015)*

Photo Research Inc ....E 818 341-5151
9731 Topanga Canyon Pl Chatsworth (91311) *(P-8015)*

Photo-Sonics Inc (PA)..E 818 842-2141
9131 Independence Ave Chatsworth (91311) *(P-8438)*

Photon Research Associates Inc ....C 858 455-9741
9985 Pacific Heights Blvd Ste 200 San Diego (92121) *(P-17611)*

Photonics Division, Carlsbad Also Called: L3 Technologies Inc *(P-7729)*

Photronics California, Burbank Also Called: Photronics Inc *(P-8439)*

Photronics Inc (DH)..B 203 740-5653
2428 N Ontario St Burbank (91504) *(P-8439)*

Photronics Inc ....C 760 294-1896
1760 Arroyo Gln Escondido (92026) *(P-8440)*

Phs / Mwa ....C 951 695-1008
42374 Avenida Alvarado # A Temecula (92590) *(P-9206)*

Phs Staffing, Seal Beach Also Called: Premier Healthcare Svcs LLC *(P-16412)*

Phs/Mwa Aviation Services, Temecula Also Called: Phs / Mwa *(P-9206)*

Physical Rhbltation Netwrk LLC (PA)......................D 760 931-8310
2035 Corte Del Nogal Ste 200 Carlsbad (92011) *(P-15552)*

Physician Office Support Svcs, Torrance Also Called: Torrance Health Assn Inc *(P-16229)*

Physician Sales & Service, Fullerton Also Called: McKesson Mdcl-Srgcal Top Hldng *(P-10090)*

Physician Support Systems Inc (DH)........................B 717 653-5340
1131 W 6th St Ste 300 Ontario (91762) *(P-17750)*

Physicians Choice LLC ....D 818 340-9988
5950 Canoga Ave Ste 300 Woodland Hills (91367) *(P-17751)*

Physicians Formula Inc (DH)..................................D 626 334-3395
22067 Ferrero City Of Industry (91789) *(P-3679)*

Physicians Formula Cosmt Inc ....D 626 334-3395
22067 Ferrero City Of Industry (91789) *(P-3680)*

Physicians Referral Service, Lancaster Also Called: Lancaster Crdlgy Med Group Inc *(P-15377)*

Piazza Trucking, South Gate Also Called: Samuel J Piazza & Son Inc *(P-8994)*

Picnic At Ascot Inc ....E 310 674-3098
3237 W 131st St Hawthorne (90250) *(P-2395)*

Picnic Time Inc ....D 805 529-7400
5131 Maureen Ln Moorpark (93021) *(P-8716)*

Pico Cleaners Inc (PA)..D 310 274-2431
9150 W Pico Blvd Los Angeles (90035) *(P-13132)*

Pico Pica Foods, Wilmington Also Called: Juanitas Foods *(P-1341)*

Picore Bristain Initiative Inc ....D 818 888-3659
23679 Calabasas Rd # 215 Calabasas (91302) *(P-14329)*

Picosys Incorporated ....D 805 962-3333
320 N Nopal St Santa Barbara (93103) *(P-5619)*

Pictsweet Company ....B 805 928-4414
732 Hanson Way Santa Maria (93458) *(P-1398)*

Pie Rise Ltd ....E 310 832-4559
29051 S Western Ave Rancho Palos Verdes (90275) *(P-11596)*

Piedmont Airlines Inc ....C 562 421-1806
4100 E Donald Douglas Dr Long Beach (90808) *(P-9163)*

Piedmont Plastics, La Mirada Also Called: Regal-Piedmont Plastics LLC *(P-11001)*

Piege Co (PA)..D 818 727-9100
20120 Plummer St Chatsworth (91311) *(P-10722)*

Piercan Usa Inc ....D 760 599-4543
160 Bosstick Blvd San Marcos (92069) *(P-1929)*

Pierce Brothers (DH)..D 818 763-9121
10621 Victory Blvd North Hollywood (91606) *(P-13157)*

Pierre Landscape Inc ....C 626 587-2121
5455 2nd St Irwindale (91706) *(P-185)*

Piet Retief Inc ....E 323 732-8312
1914 6th Ave Los Angeles (90018) *(P-2126)*

Piezo-Metrics Inc (PA)..E 805 522-4676
4584 Runway St Simi Valley (93063) *(P-6867)*

Pigeon and Poodle, City Of Industry Also Called: Ardmore Home Design Inc *(P-2440)*

Pih Health Inc (PA)..A 562 698-0811
12401 Washington Blvd Whittier (90602) *(P-16130)*

Pih Health Downey Hospital (HQ)............................B 562 698-0811
11500 Brookshire Ave Downey (90241) *(P-16131)*

Pih Health Good Samaritan Hosp (HQ)....................A 213 977-2121
1225 Wilshire Blvd Los Angeles (90017) *(P-16132)*

Pih Health Hospital - Whitti ....A 562 904-5482
11500 Brookshire Ave Downey (90241) *(P-16133)*

Pih Health Whittier Hospital (HQ)............................A 562 698-0811
12401 Washington Blvd Whittier (90602) *(P-16134)*

Pilatus Unmanned, Huntington Beach Also Called: Measure Uas Inc *(P-8051)*

Pilgrim Operations LLC ....B 818 478-4500
12020 Chandler Blvd Ste 200 North Hollywood (91607) *(P-9969)*

Mergent email: customerrelations@mergent.com
1144

2025 Southern California
Business Directory and Buyers Guide

(P-0000) Products & Services Section entry number
(PA)=Parent Co (HQ)=Headquarters (DH)=Div Headquarters

Pilgrim Place In Claremont (PA).................................C 909 399-5500
625 Mayflower Rd Claremont (91711) *(P-15881)*

Pilgrim Studios Inc...D 818 728-8800
12020 Chandler Blvd Ste 200 North Hollywood (91607) *(P-14845)*

Pillsbury, Glendale *Also Called: Pillsbury Company LLC (P-1406)*

Pillsbury, Los Angeles *Also Called: Pillsbury Wnthrop Shaw Pttman (P-16759)*

Pillsbury Company LLC.................................E 818 522-3952
220 S Kenwood St Ste 202 Glendale (91205) *(P-1406)*

Pillsbury Wnthrop Shaw Pttman.......................C 213 488-7100
725 S Figueroa St Ste 2800 Los Angeles (90017) *(P-16759)*

Pilot Freight Services, San Diego *Also Called: Miramar Transportation Inc (P-9313)*

Pimco, Newport Beach *Also Called: Pacific Investment MGT Co LLC (P-12641)*

Pin Concepts, Sun Valley *Also Called: Pincraft Inc (P-8571)*

Pincraft Inc...E 818 248-0077
7933 Ajay Dr Sun Valley (91352) *(P-8571)*

Pindler, Moorpark *Also Called: Pindler & Pindler Inc (P-10670)*

Pindler & Pindler Inc (PA)..............................D 805 531-9090
11910 Poindexter Ave Moorpark (93021) *(P-10670)*

Pine Grove Hospital Corp...............................C 818 348-0500
9449 San Fernando Rd Sun Valley (91352) *(P-16278)*

Pinky Los Angeles, Burbank *Also Called: Vesture Group Incorporated (P-2175)*

PINNACLE COMMUNICATION SERVICE, Glendale *Also Called: Pinnacle Networking Svcs Inc (P-951)*

Pinnacle Escrow Company, Porter Ranch *Also Called: Pinnacle Estate Properties Inc (P-12504)*

Pinnacle Estate Properties Inc (PA).....................C 818 993-4707
20065 Rinaldi St Ste 210 Porter Ranch (91326) *(P-12504)*

Pinnacle Networking Svcs Inc...........................C 818 241-6009
730 Fairmont Ave Glendale (91203) *(P-951)*

Pinnacle Plastic Containers, Oxnard *Also Called: Leading Industry Inc (P-4159)*

Pinnacle Precision Shtmtl Corp.........................D 714 777-3129
5410 E La Palma Ave Anaheim (92807) *(P-5019)*

Pinnacle Precision Shtmtl Corp (HQ)...................D 714 777-3129
5410 E La Palma Ave Anaheim (92807) *(P-5020)*

Pinnacle Rvrside Hspitality LP..........................C 951 784-8000
3400 Market St Riverside (92501) *(P-12974)*

Pinnacle Travel Services LLC..........................C 310 414-1787
390 N Pacific Coast Hwy El Segundo (90245) *(P-9231)*

Pinnacle Veterinary Center, Santa Clarita *Also Called: Delphic Enterprises Inc (P-127)*

Pinnpack Capital Holdings LLC.........................C 805 385-4100
1151 Pacific Ave Oxnard (93033) *(P-4196)*

Pinnpack Packaging, Oxnard *Also Called: Pinnpack Capital Holdings LLC (P-4196)*

Pioneer Broach Company (PA)..........................E 323 728-1263
6434 Telegraph Rd Commerce (90040) *(P-5620)*

Pioneer Circuits Inc....................................B 714 641-3132
3021 S Shannon St Santa Ana (92704) *(P-6764)*

Pioneer Custom Elec Pdts Corp........................D 562 944-9626
10640 Springdale Ave Santa Fe Springs (90670) *(P-6295)*

Pioneer H.S. LLC, San Diego *Also Called: Pioneer Healthcare Svcs LLC (P-13555)*

Pioneer Healthcare Svcs LLC...........................B 800 683-1209
6255 Ferris Sq # F San Diego (92121) *(P-13555)*

Pioneer Magnetics Inc...................................C 310 829-6751
1745 Berkeley St Santa Monica (90404) *(P-7036)*

Pioneer North America Inc.............................C 310 952-2000
2050 W 190th St Ste 100 Torrance (90504) *(P-10223)*

Pioneer Packing Inc (PA)...............................E 714 540-9751
2430 S Grand Ave Santa Ana (92705) *(P-10608)*

Pioneer Photo Albums Inc (PA)........................C 818 882-2161
9801 Deering Ave Chatsworth (91311) *(P-3200)*

Pioneer Sands LLC.....................................E 949 728-0171
31302 Ortega Hwy San Juan Capistrano (92675) *(P-377)*

Pioneer Sands LLC.....................................E 661 746-5789
9952 Enos Lane Bakersfield (93314) *(P-378)*

Pioneer Speakers Inc....................................A 310 952-2000
2050 W 190th St Ste 100 Torrance (90504) *(P-6548)*

Pioneer Theatres Inc...................................C 310 532-8183
2500 Redondo Beach Blvd Torrance (90504) *(P-11292)*

Pioneers Mem Healthcare Dst (PA).....................A 760 351-3333
207 W Legion Rd Brawley (92227) *(P-16135)*

Pioneers Memorial Hospital, Brawley *Also Called: Pioneers Mem Healthcare Dst (P-16135)*

PIP Printing, Mission Viejo *Also Called: Postal Instant Press Inc (P-3063)*

Pipe Restoration Inc....................................D 714 564-7600
2926 W Pendleton Ave Santa Ana (92704) *(P-819)*

Pipeline, Rolling Hills Estate *Also Called: Graphic Prints Inc (P-2261)*

Pipeline Health LLC (PA)...............................D 310 379-2134
898 N Pacific Coast Hwy Ste 700 El Segundo (90245) *(P-16136)*

Pipline, Oxnard *Also Called: West Coast Wldg & Piping Inc (P-14747)*

Pircher Nichols & Meeks (PA)...........................D 310 201-0132
1925 Century Park E Ste 1700 Los Angeles (90067) *(P-16760)*

Pitts & Bachmann Realtors Inc.........................D 805 969-5005
1482 E Valley Rd Ste 44 Santa Barbara (93108) *(P-12505)*

Pitts & Bachmann Realtors Inc.........................D 805 963-1391
1436 State St Santa Barbara (93101) *(P-12506)*

Piveg Inc..C 858 436-3070
3525 Del Mar Heights Rd Ste 1069 San Diego (92130) *(P-10765)*

Pivot Interiors Inc......................................C 949 988-5400
3200 Park Center Dr Ste 100 Costa Mesa (92626) *(P-952)*

Pixar..B 510 922-4075
500 N Buena Vista St Burbank (91505) *(P-14573)*

Pixomondo LLC...A 310 394-0555
10202 Washington Blvd Culver City (90232) *(P-14901)*

Pixster Photobooth LLC.................................C 888 668-5524
4901 Morena Blvd Ste 810 San Diego (92117) *(P-13145)*

Pj Printers Inc..E 714 779-8484
1530 Lakeview Loop Anaheim (92807) *(P-3061)*

Pjbs Holdings Inc (PA).................................D 661 822-5273
1401 Goodrick Dr Tehachapi (93561) *(P-9755)*

Pjy LLC...E 323 583-7737
3251 Leonis Blvd Vernon (90058) *(P-1885)*

Pkl Services Inc..C 858 679-1755
14265 Danielson St Poway (92064) *(P-14783)*

Pl Development, Lynwood *Also Called: P & L Development LLC (P-3468)*

Pl Machine Corporation.................................E 714 892-1100
10716 Reagan St Los Alamitos (90720) *(P-6203)*

Placentia Linda Hospital, Placentia *Also Called: Tenet Healthsystem Medical Inc (P-16302)*

Plainfield Companies, Brea *Also Called: Plainfield Molding Inc (P-4197)*

Plainfield Molding Inc...................................D 815 436-7806
135 S State College Blvd Ste 200 Brea (92821) *(P-4197)*

Plainfield Stamping-Illinois, Brea *Also Called: Plainfield Tool and Engineering Inc (P-4198)*

Plainfield Tool and Engineering Inc......................B 815 436-5671
135 South College Blvd Ste 200 Brea (92821) *(P-4198)*

Plan Member Financial Corp.............................D 800 874-6910
6187 Carpinteria Ave Carpinteria (93013) *(P-12031)*

Planet DDS, Irvine *Also Called: Planet DDS Inc (P-14006)*

Planet DDS Inc (PA)...................................E 800 861-5098
17872 Gillette Ave Ste 250 Irvine (92614) *(P-14006)*

Planet Green, Chatsworth *Also Called: Planet Green Cartridges Inc (P-8565)*

Planet Green Cartridges Inc............................D 818 725-2596
20724 Lassen St Chatsworth (91311) *(P-8565)*

Planet Innovation Inc...................................E 949 238-1200
2720 Loker Ave W Ste P Carlsbad (92010) *(P-8216)*

Planetizen, Los Angeles *Also Called: Planetizen Inc (P-2935)*

Planetizen Inc...E 877 260-7526
3530 Wilshire Blvd Ste 1285 Los Angeles (90010) *(P-2935)*

Planmember Services, Carpinteria *Also Called: Plan Member Financial Corp (P-12031)*

Planned Parenthood Los Angeles (PA)...................D 213 284-3200
400 W 30th St Los Angeles (90007) *(P-16490)*

Planned Prnthood of PCF Sthwes.......................D 619 881-4500
1964 Via Ctr Vista (92081) *(P-16491)*

Planned Prnthood of PCF Sthwes.......................D 619 881-4652
4501 Mission Bay Dr Ste 1c San Diego (92109) *(P-16492)*

Planned Prnthood of PCF Sthwes (PA)..................D 619 881-4500
1075 Camino Del Rio S Ste 100 San Diego (92108) *(P-16493)*

Plansee USA LLC.......................................D 760 438-9090
1491 Poinsettia Ave Ste 138 Vista (92081) *(P-6868)*

Plant 16, Van Nuys *Also Called: Weststar Cinemas Inc (P-14944)*

Plant 2, Harbor City *Also Called: Hansen Engineering Co (P-7487)*

Plantel Nurseries Inc..................................B 805 934-4300
3990 Foxen Canyon Rd Santa Maria (93454) *(P-66)*

Plantronics Inc..D 714 897-0808
12082 Western Ave Garden Grove (92841) *(P-5864)*

Employee Codes: A=Over 500 employees, B=251-500
C=101-250, D=51-100, E=20-50, F=10-19, G=1-9

2025 Southern California
Business Directory and Buyers Guide

© Mergent Inc. 1-800-342-5647

1145

A L P H A B E T I C

Plas-Tal Manufacturing Co, Santa Fe Springs *Also Called: Brunton Enterprises Inc (P-4821)*

Plascor Inc .... C 951 328-1010
972 Columbia Ave Riverside (92507) *(P-3986)*

Plaskolite West LLC .... E 310 637-2103
2225 E Del Amo Blvd Compton (90220) *(P-3287)*

Plasma Rggedized Solutions Inc .... E 714 893-6063
5452 Business Dr Huntington Beach (92649) *(P-5283)*

Plasma Technology Incorporated (PA)............... D 310 320-3373
1754 Crenshaw Blvd Torrance (90501) *(P-5338)*

Plastic and Metal Center Inc .... E 949 770-0610
23162 La Cadena Dr Laguna Hills (92653) *(P-4199)*

Plastic Dress-Up, North Hollywood *Also Called: Pdu Lad Corporation (P-5335)*

Plastic Molded Components Inc .... E 714 229-0133
5920 Lakeshore Dr Cypress (90630) *(P-4200)*

Plastic Processing Co, Gardena *Also Called: Narayan Corporation (P-3985)*

Plastic Sales, Long Beach *Also Called: Plastic Sales Southern Inc (P-11000)*

Plastic Sales Southern Inc .... E 714 375-7900
425 Havana Ave Long Beach (90814) *(P-11000)*

Plastic Services and Products .... A 818 896-1101
12243 Branford St Sun Valley (91352) *(P-4009)*

Plastic Technologies Inc .... E 951 360-6055
4720 Felspar St Riverside (92509) *(P-4201)*

Plasticolor, Fullerton *Also Called: Plasticolor Molded Pdts Inc (P-11453)*

Plasticolor Molded Pdts Inc (PA)...................... C 714 525-3880
801 S Acacia Ave Fullerton (92831) *(P-11453)*

Plastics Development Corp .... E 949 492-0217
960 Calle Negocio San Clemente (92673) *(P-4202)*

Plastics Family Holdings Inc .... D 858 560-1551
5535 Ruffin Rd San Diego (92123) *(P-3954)*

Plastics Plus Technology Inc .... E 909 747-0555
1495 Research Dr Redlands (92374) *(P-4203)*

Plastics Research Corporation .... D 909 391-9050
1400 S Campus Ave Ontario (91761) *(P-3967)*

Plastifab Inc .... E 909 596-1927
1425 Palomares St La Verne (91750) *(P-3968)*

Plastifab/Leed Plastics, La Verne *Also Called: Plastifab Inc (P-3968)*

Plastopan, Los Angeles *Also Called: Plastopan Industries Inc (P-2696)*

Plastopan Industries Inc (PA)............................ E 323 231-2225
812 E 59th St Los Angeles (90001) *(P-2696)*

Plastpro 2000 Inc (PA).. C 310 693-8600
5200 W Century Blvd Los Angeles (90045) *(P-4204)*

Plastpro Doors, Los Angeles *Also Called: Plastpro 2000 Inc (P-4204)*

Plateronics Processing, Chatsworth *Also Called: Plateronics Processing Inc (P-5284)*

Plateronics Processing Inc .... E 818 341-2191
9164 Independence Ave Chatsworth (91311) *(P-5284)*

Platform Science Inc (PA).................................. C 844 475-8724
9560 Towne Centre Dr # 200 San Diego (92121) *(P-13796)*

Plating, Chatsworth *Also Called: Electro Adapter Inc (P-6417)*

Platinum, Fullerton *Also Called: Ultra Wheel Company (P-7304)*

Platinum Capital Group (PA)............................. D 310 406-3505
3500 N Sepulveda Blvd Ste E Manhattan Beach (90266) *(P-11930)*

Platinum Clg Indianapolis LLC .... B 310 584-8000
1522 2nd St Santa Monica (90401) *(P-13405)*

Platinum Construction Inc .... D 714 527-0700
865 S East St Anaheim (92805) *(P-572)*

Platinum Disc LLC .... D 608 784-6620
10203 Santa Monica Blvd Fl 5 Los Angeles (90067) *(P-10566)*

Platinum Distribution, Yorba Linda *Also Called: Nasco Gourmet Foods Inc (P-1354)*

Platinum Empire Group Inc .... C 310 821-5888
2430 Amsler St Ste B Torrance (90505) *(P-13617)*

Platinum Group Companies Inc (PA).................. C 818 721-3800
22560 La Quilla Dr Chatsworth (91311) *(P-12607)*

Platinum Healthcare Staffing, Torrance *Also Called: Platinum Empire Group Inc (P-13617)*

Platinum Landscape Inc .... C 760 200-3673
42575 Melanie Pl Ste C Palm Desert (92211) *(P-186)*

Platinum Performance Inc (HQ)........................ E 800 553-2400
90 Thomas Rd Buellton (93427) *(P-10645)*

Platinum Performance Inc .... D 800 553-2400
760 Mcmurray Rd Buellton (93427) *(P-14678)*

Platinum Roofing Inc .... D 408 280-5028
11500 W Olympic Blvd Ste 530 Los Angeles (90064) *(P-1093)*

Platinum Visual Systems, Corona *Also Called: ABC School Equipment Inc (P-10117)*

Plaxicon Co, Rancho Cucamonga *Also Called: Plaxicon Holding Corporation (P-3987)*

Plaxicon Holding Corporation .... B 909 944-6868
10660 Acacia St Rancho Cucamonga (91730) *(P-3987)*

Play Versus Inc .... C 949 636-4193
2236 S Barrington Ave Ste A Los Angeles (90064) *(P-17468)*

Playa Proper Jv LLC .... D 310 645-0400
8639 Lincoln Blvd Los Angeles (90045) *(P-12975)*

Playboy, Los Angeles *Also Called: Playboy Enterprises Inc (P-11694)*

Playboy Enterprises Inc .... D 310 424-1800
10960 Wilshire Blvd Fl 22 Los Angeles (90024) *(P-2871)*

Playboy Enterprises Inc (HQ)............................ D 310 424-1800
10960 Wilshire Blvd Fl 22 Los Angeles (90024) *(P-11694)*

Playboy Enterprises Intl Inc .... D 310 424-1800
10960 Wilshire Blvd Ste 2200 Los Angeles (90024) *(P-2936)*

Playboy Entrmt Group Inc (DH)........................ C 323 276-4000
2300 W Empire Ave Burbank (91504) *(P-14846)*

Players West Amusements Inc (PA).................. E 805 983-1400
2360 Sturgis Rd Ste A Oxnard (93030) *(P-15100)*

Playhaven LLC .... D 310 308-9668
1447 2nd St Ste 200 Santa Monica (90401) *(P-13797)*

Playvs, Los Angeles *Also Called: Play Versus Inc (P-17468)*

Plaza Bank .... D 949 502-4300
18200 Von Karman Ave Ste 500 Irvine (92612) *(P-11784)*

Plaza De La Raza Child Dev Svc (PA)................ D 562 776-1301
13300 Crossroads Pkwy N Ste 440 La Puente (91746) *(P-17106)*

Plaza De La Raza Child Develop .... D 323 224-1788
225 N Avenue 25 Los Angeles (90031) *(P-17107)*

Plaza De La Raza Child Develop .... D 562 695-1070
6411 Norwalk Blvd Whittier (90606) *(P-17108)*

Plaza Home Mortgage Inc .... D 858 346-1208
9808 Scranton Rd San Diego (92121) *(P-12005)*

Plaza Tower 1, Costa Mesa *Also Called: Regus Business Centre LLC (P-14584)*

PLC Imports Inc .... E 818 349-1600
9667 Owensmouth Ave Ste 201 Chatsworth (91311) *(P-10201)*

PLD Enterprises Inc .... D 213 626-4444
440 Stanford Ave Los Angeles (90013) *(P-10857)*

Pleasant Hawaiian Holiday, Westlake Village *Also Called: Pleasant Holidays LLC (P-9232)*

Pleasant Holidays LLC (HQ).............................. B 818 991-3390
2404 Townsgate Rd Westlake Village (91361) *(P-9232)*

Plenums Plus LLC .... D 619 422-5515
67 Brisbane St Chula Vista (91910) *(P-5021)*

Plg Law Group, Encino *Also Called: Price Law Group A Prof Corp (P-16762)*

Plh Products Inc .... B 714 739-6622
10541 Calle Lee Ste 119 Los Alamitos (90720) *(P-2404)*

Plott Family Care Centers, Riverside *Also Called: Orangtree Cnvalescent Hosp Inc (P-16110)*

Pls Diabetic Shoe Company Inc .... E 818 734-7080
21500 Osborne St Canoga Park (91304) *(P-3870)*

Plt Enterprises Inc .... D 805 389-5335
809 Calle Plano Camarillo (93012) *(P-6425)*

Pluckys Dump Rental LLC .... E 323 540-3510
10136 Bowman Ave South Gate (90280) *(P-4921)*

Plug Connection Inc .... D 760 631-0992
2627 Ramona Dr Vista (92084) *(P-67)*

Plug Connection LLC .... C 760 631-0992
3742 Blue Bird Canyon Rd Vista (92084) *(P-18192)*

Plugg ME LNc .... E 949 705-4472
18100 Von Karman Ave Ste 850 Irvine (92612) *(P-14007)*

Plum Healthcare Group LLC .... C 760 471-0388
100 E San Marcos Blvd Ste 200 San Marcos (92069) *(P-15754)*

Plumbing Master, Riverside *Also Called: Lozano Plumbing Services Inc (P-797)*

Plumbing Piping & Cnstr Inc .... D 714 821-0490
5950 Lakeshore Dr Cypress (90630) *(P-820)*

Plumbing Solution Specialist, Laguna Niguel *Also Called: Marcos M Uriarte (P-801)*

Plumbing World, Long Beach *Also Called: Columbia Specialty Company Inc (P-10431)*

Plump Engineering Inc .... D 714 385-1835
914 E Katella Ave Anaheim (92805) *(P-17612)*

Plural Publishing Inc .... E 858 492-1555
9177 Aero Dr San Diego (92123) *(P-2894)*

Plus Products, Adelanto *Also Called: Carberry LLC (P-8668)*

Mergent email: customerrelations@mergent.com
1146

2025 Southern California
Business Directory and Buyers Guide

(P-0000) Products & Services Section entry number
(PA)=Parent Co (HQ)=Headquarters (DH)=Div Headquarters

Plycraft Industries Inc .... C 323 587-8101
2100 E Slauson Ave Huntington Park (90255) *(P-2371)*

Plymouth Village, Redlands *Also Called: Humangood Norcal (P-15862)*

Plz Corp .... E 805 498-4531
840 Tourmaline Dr Newbury Park (91320) *(P-3221)*

Plz Corp .... C 951 683-2912
2375 3rd St Riverside (92507) *(P-3681)*

Plz Corp .... D 909 393-9475
14425 Yorba Ave Chino (91710) *(P-3682)*

Plz Corp .... D 951 683-2912
2321 3rd St Riverside (92507) *(P-3683)*

PM Corporate Group Inc (PA) .... **D 800 343-3139**
2285 Michael Faraday Dr Ste 12 San Diego (92154) *(P-3062)*

PM Packaging, San Diego *Also Called: PM Corporate Group Inc (P-3062)*

PM Realty Group LP .... D 949 390-5500
3 Park Plz Ste 450 Irvine (92614) *(P-12310)*

Pmc Inc (HQ) .... **D 818 896-1101**
12243 Branford St Sun Valley (91352) *(P-7540)*

Pmc Inc .... C 714 967-7230
3816 E La Palma Ave Anaheim (92807) *(P-14574)*

PMC Capital Partners LLC .... A 818 896-1101
12243 Branford St Sun Valley (91352) *(P-12728)*

PMC Global Inc (PA) .... **D 818 896-1101**
12243 Branford St Sun Valley (91352) *(P-4010)*

PMC Leaders In Chemicals Inc (HQ) ...... **C 818 896-1101**
12243 Branford St Sun Valley (91352) *(P-4011)*

PMC Southwest LLC, Jurupa Valley *Also Called: Arcticom Group Rfrgn LLC (P-14723)*

Pmcs Group Inc .... D 562 498-0808
2600 E Pacific Coast Hwy Ste 160 Long Beach (90804) *(P-18193)*

Pmp Forge, El Cajon *Also Called: Jmmca Inc (P-5143)*

Pmr Precision Mfg & Rbr Co Inc .... E 909 605-7525
1330 Etiwanda Ave Ontario (91761) *(P-3929)*

Pmt Crdit Risk Trnsf Tr 2015-1 .... C 818 224-7028
3043 Townsgate Rd Westlake Village (91361) *(P-12666)*

Pmt Crdit Risk Trnsf Tr 2015-2 .... C 818 224-7442
3043 Townsgate Rd Westlake Village (91361) *(P-12667)*

Pmt Crdit Risk Trnsf Tr 2019-2 .... C 818 224-7028
3043 Townsgate Rd Westlake Village (91361) *(P-12668)*

Pmt Crdit Risk Trnsf Tr 2019-3 .... C 818 224-7028
3043 Townsgate Rd Westlake Village (91361) *(P-12669)*

Pmt Crdit Risk Trnsf Tr 2020-1 .... C 818 224-7028
3043 Townsgate Rd Westlake Village (91361) *(P-12670)*

Pmt Crdit Risk Trnsf Tr 2020-2 .... C 818 224-7028
3043 Townsgate Rd Westlake Village (91361) *(P-12671)*

Pmt Issuer Trust - Fmsr .... C 818 224-7028
3043 Townsgate Rd Westlake Village (91361) *(P-12691)*

PNa Construction Tech Inc .... E 661 326-1700
301 Espee St Ste E Bakersfield (93301) *(P-5022)*

PNC Proactive Nthrn Cont LLC .... E 909 390-5624
602 S Rockefeller Ave Ste A Ontario (91761) *(P-2687)*

Pneudraulics Inc .... B 909 980-5366
8575 Helms Ave Rancho Cucamonga (91730) *(P-7791)*

Png Builders .... D 626 256-9539
2392 S Bateman Ave Duarte (91010) *(P-573)*

Pnmac Cmsr Issuer Trust .... A 818 740-2271
3043 Townsgate Rd Westlake Village (91361) *(P-12072)*

Pocino Foods Company .... D 626 968-8000
14250 Lomitas Ave City Of Industry (91746) *(P-1266)*

Point Conception Inc .... E 949 589-6890
23121 Arroyo Vis Ste A Rcho Sta Marg (92688) *(P-2127)*

Point Loma Rhblitation Ctr LLC .... C 619 308-3200
3202 Duke St San Diego (92110) *(P-15755)*

Point360 .... D 818 556-5700
1133 N Hollywood Way Burbank (91505) *(P-14847)*

Point360 (PA) .... D 818 565-1400
2701 Media Center Dr Los Angeles (90065) *(P-14902)*

Pointdirect Transport Inc .... D 909 371-0837
19083 Mermack Ave Lake Elsinore (92532) *(P-8971)*

Pointe At Lantern Crest, The, Santee *Also Called: Santee Senior Retirement Com (P-17006)*

Polagram, Los Angeles *Also Called: Wellmade Inc (P-18241)*

Polar Air Cargo LP .... B 310 568-4551
100 Oceangate Fl 15 Long Beach (90802) *(P-9164)*

Polar Power, Gardena *Also Called: Polar Power Inc (P-7099)*

Polar Power Inc .... D 310 830-9153
249 E Gardena Blvd Gardena (90248) *(P-7099)*

Polar Tankers Inc (DH) .... **D 562 388-1400**
300 Oceangate Long Beach (90802) *(P-9136)*

Polar Tankers Inc .... C 310 519-8260
60 Berth San Pedro (90731) *(P-9137)*

Polaris E-Commerce Inc .... E 714 907-0582
1941 E Occidental St Santa Ana (92705) *(P-5740)*

Polaris Music, Los Angeles *Also Called: Eti Systems (P-7857)*

Poliseek Ais Insur Sltions Inc .... D 866 480-7335
17785 Center Court Dr N Ste 250 Cerritos (90703) *(P-12244)*

Pollstar LLC .... D 559 271-7900
1100 Glendon Ave Ste 2100 Los Angeles (90024) *(P-2937)*

Pollstar.com, Los Angeles *Also Called: Pollstar LLC (P-2937)*

Polsinelli LLP, Los Angeles *Also Called: Polsinelli PC (P-16761)*

Polsinelli PC .... D 310 556-1801
2049 Century Park E Ste 2300 Los Angeles (90067) *(P-16761)*

Poly Pak America Inc .... D 323 264-2400
2939 E Washington Blvd Los Angeles (90023) *(P-3955)*

Poly-Tainer Inc (PA) .... **C 805 526-3424**
450 W Los Angeles Ave Simi Valley (93065) *(P-3988)*

Polyalloys Injected Metals Inc .... D 310 715-9800
14000 Avalon Blvd Los Angeles (90061) *(P-5501)*

Polycell Packaging Corporation .... E 562 483-6000
12851 Midway Pl Cerritos (90703) *(P-11134)*

Polycycle Solutions LLC .... D 626 856-2100
4516 Azusa Canyon Rd Irwindale (91706) *(P-3989)*

Polyfet Rf Devices Inc .... E 805 484-9582
1110 Avenida Acaso Camarillo (93012) *(P-6869)*

Polymer Coating Services, Aliso Viejo *Also Called: Parylene Coating Services Inc (P-5334)*

Polymer Logistics Inc .... D 951 567-2900
1725 Sierra Ridge Dr Riverside (92507) *(P-4205)*

Polypeptide Laboratories Inc (DH) .... **E 310 782-3569**
365 Maple Ave Torrance (90503) *(P-16327)*

Polypeptide Labs San Diego LLC .... D 858 408-0808
9395 Cabot Dr San Diego (92126) *(P-3477)*

Polytechnic School .... B 626 792-2147
1030 E California Blvd Pasadena (91106) *(P-16820)*

Pom Medical LLC .... D 805 306-2105
5456 Endeavour Ct Moorpark (93021) *(P-10103)*

Poma Holding Company Inc .... C 909 877-2441
571 W Slover Ave Bloomington (92316) *(P-11033)*

Pomerado Hospital, Poway *Also Called: Palomar Health (P-16119)*

Pomerado Operations LLC .... D 858 487-6242
12696 Monte Vista Rd Poway (92064) *(P-15756)*

Pommes Frites Candle Co .... E 213 488-2016
7300 E Slauson Ave Commerce (90040) *(P-8717)*

Pomona Box Co, La Habra *Also Called: Votaw Wood Products Inc (P-2393)*

Pomona Mc Kenna Motors .... C 909 620-7370
25 Rio Rancho Rd Pomona (91766) *(P-11396)*

Pomona Quality Foam LLC .... D 909 628-7844
1279 Philadelphia St Pomona (91766) *(P-4012)*

Pomona Valley Hospital Med Ctr (PA) ...... **A 909 865-9500**
1798 N Garey Ave Pomona (91767) *(P-16137)*

Ponder Environmental Svcs Inc .... E 661 589-7771
19484 Broken Ct Shafter (93263) *(P-18266)*

Ponto Nursery .... D 760 724-6003
2545 Ramona Dr Vista (92084) *(P-11098)*

Poor Richard's Press, San Luis Obispo *Also Called: Prpco (P-3072)*

Poor Richards Press, San Luis Obispo *Also Called: Ws Packaging-Blake Printery (P-3103)*

Pop Chips, E Rncho Dmngz *Also Called: Sonora Mills Foods Inc (P-1853)*

Pop Mart, Glendale *Also Called: Pop Mart Americas Inc (P-11644)*

Pop Mart Americas Inc .... D 415 640-8197
500 N Brand Blvd Ste 2000 Glendale (91203) *(P-11644)*

Pope Mortgage & Associates Inc .... D 909 466-5380
2980 Inland Empire Blvd Unit 100 Ontario (91764) *(P-11950)*

Popla International Inc .... E 909 923-6899
1740 S Sacramento Ave Ontario (91761) *(P-1415)*

Populus Financial Group Inc .... C 951 509-3506
6302 Van Buren Blvd Riverside (92503) *(P-11842)*

Employee Codes: A=Over 500 employees, B=251-500
C=101-250, D=51-100, E=20-50, F=10-19, G=1-9

2025 Southern California
Business Directory and Buyers Guide

© Mergent Inc. 1-800-342-5647

1147

ALPHABETIC

Port Logistics Group Inc .... C 310 669-2551
19801 S Santa Fe Ave Compton (90221) *(P-9325)*

PORT LOGISTICS GROUP, INC., Compton *Also Called: Port Logistics Group Inc (P-9325)*

Port of Long Beach .... A 562 283-7000
415 W Ocean Blvd Long Beach (90802) *(P-9144)*

Port of Los Angeles .... C 310 732-3508
425 S Palos Verdes St San Pedro (90731) *(P-9145)*

Port of San Diego, San Diego *Also Called: San Diego Unified Port Dst (P-9146)*

Port Priority Corp .... C 845 746-4300
855 W Valley Blvd Bloomington (92316) *(P-9326)*

Porteous Enterprises Inc (DH) .... C 310 549-9180
1040 E Watson Center Rd Carson (90745) *(P-10312)*

Porter Boiler Service Inc .... E 562 426-2528
1166 E 23rd St Signal Hill (90755) *(P-14784)*

Porter Hire Ltd .... E 951 674-9999
13013 Temescal Canyon Rd Corona (92883) *(P-13467)*

Porter Valley Catering, Northridge *Also Called: Porter Valley Country Club Inc (P-15158)*

Porter Valley Country Club Inc .... C 818 360-1071
19216 Singing Hills Dr Northridge (91326) *(P-15158)*

Portermatt Electric Inc .... D 714 596-8788
5431 Production Dr Huntington Beach (92649) *(P-953)*

Porto Vista Hotel, San Diego *Also Called: 1835 Columbia Street LP (P-12751)*

Portofino Inn & Suites Anaheim .... A 714 782-7600
1831 S Harbor Blvd Anaheim (92802) *(P-12976)*

Portos Bakery & Cafe, Burbank *Also Called: Portos Bakery Burbank Inc (P-11300)*

Portos Bakery Burbank Inc .... E 818 846-9100
3614 W Magnolia Blvd Burbank (91505) *(P-11300)*

Portsmouth Square Inc .... C 310 889-2500
1516 S Bundy Dr Ste 200 Los Angeles (90025) *(P-12577)*

Posca Brothers Dental Lab Inc .... D 562 427-1811
641 W Willow St Long Beach (90806) *(P-16346)*

POSEIDA, San Diego *Also Called: Poseida Therapeutics Inc (P-3585)*

Poseida Therapeutics Inc (PA) .... B 858 779-3100
9390 Towne Centre Dr Ste 200 San Diego (92121) *(P-3585)*

Posh'n Bae, Woodland Hills *Also Called: Conquistador International LLC (P-10619)*

Positioning Universal Inc .... D 619 639-0235
7071 Convoy Ct Ste 300 San Diego (92111) *(P-14243)*

Positive Behavior Steps, San Dimas *Also Called: Positive Behavior Steps Corp (P-16494)*

Positive Behavior Steps Corp .... D 626 940-5180
675 Cliffside Dr San Dimas (91773) *(P-16494)*

Post Alarm Systems (PA) .... D 626 446-7159
47 E Saint Joseph St Arcadia (91006) *(P-14415)*

Post Alarm Systems Patrol Svcs, Arcadia *Also Called: Post Alarm Systems (P-14415)*

Post Group Inc (PA) .... C 323 462-2300
1415 N Cahuenga Blvd Los Angeles (90028) *(P-14903)*

Post Group Production Suites, Los Angeles *Also Called: Post Group Inc (P-14903)*

Postaer Rubin and Associates .... C 312 644-3636
2525 Colorado Ave Ste 100 Santa Monica (90404) *(P-13236)*

Postal Instant Press Inc (HQ) .... E 949 348-5000
26722 Plaza Mission Viejo (92691) *(P-3063)*

Potential Industries Inc (PA) .... C 310 549-5901
720 East E St Wilmington (90744) *(P-9756)*

Poundex Associates Corporation .... D 909 444-5878
21490 Baker Pkwy City Of Industry (91789) *(P-9880)*

Poway Homecare, San Diego *Also Called: Maxim Healthcare Services Inc (P-16404)*

Poway Toyota, Poway *Also Called: Poway Toyota Scion Inc (P-11397)*

Poway Toyota Scion Inc .... C 858 486-2900
13631 Poway Rd Poway (92064) *(P-11397)*

Powder Coating, South El Monte *Also Called: Island Powder Coating (P-5325)*

Powder Painting By Sundial, Sun Valley *Also Called: Sundial Industries Inc (P-5348)*

Powdercoat Services LLC .... E 714 533-2251
1747 W Lincoln Ave Ste K Anaheim (92801) *(P-5339)*

Powell Works, La Puente *Also Called: Powell Works Inc (P-10393)*

Powell Works Inc .... B 909 861-6699
17807 Maclaren St Ste B La Puente (91744) *(P-10393)*

Power Acoustik Electronics, Montebello *Also Called: Epsilon Electronics Inc (P-10217)*

Power Brands Consulting LLC .... E 818 989-9646
5805 Sepulveda Blvd Ste 501 Van Nuys (91411) *(P-1550)*

Power Crunch, Irvine *Also Called: Bio-Nutritional RES Group Inc (P-1296)*

Power Digital Marketing Inc (PA) .... B 619 501-1211
2251 San Diego Ave Ste A250 San Diego (92110) *(P-18194)*

Power Fasteners Inc .... E 323 232-4362
650 E 60th St Los Angeles (90001) *(P-5135)*

Power Generation Entps Inc .... C 818 484-8550
26764 Oak Ave Canyon Country (91351) *(P-10394)*

Power Plant, Glendale *Also Called: City of Glendale (P-9574)*

Power Pt Inc (PA) .... E 951 490-4149
1500 Crafton Ave Bldg 100 Mentone (92359) *(P-5533)*

Power Pt Inc .... E 714 826-7407
9292 Nancy St Cypress (90630) *(P-5534)*

Power Services, Los Angeles *Also Called: On-Line Power Incorporated (P-6292)*

Power Studios Inc .... C 310 314-2800
300 Rose Ave Venice (90291) *(P-14848)*

Power Systems West LLC .... C 208 869-0483
13625 Danielson St Poway (92064) *(P-10202)*

Powerdms Inc .... D 407 992-6000
2120 Park Pl El Segundo (90245) *(P-14008)*

Powered By Fulfillment Inc .... D 626 825-9841
20880 Krameria Ave Riverside (92518) *(P-9039)*

Powers Park Healthcare Inc .... D 805 687-6651
3880 Via Lucero Santa Barbara (93110) *(P-15757)*

Powersource Talent LLC .... C 424 835-0878
12655 W Jefferson Blvd Ste 400 Los Angeles (90066) *(P-18195)*

Ppc Enterprises Inc .... C 951 354-5402
5920 Rickenbacker Ave Riverside (92504) *(P-821)*

Ppd Holding LLC (PA) .... D 310 733-2100
10119 Jefferson Blvd Culver City (90232) *(P-2000)*

PPG Aerospace, Valencia *Also Called: PRC - Desoto International Inc (P-3775)*

PPG Aerospace, Mojave *Also Called: PRC - Desoto International Inc (P-3776)*

PPG Aerospace, Sylmar *Also Called: Sierracin/Sylmar Corporation (P-4239)*

PPG Industries Inc .... E 661 824-4532
11601 United St Mojave (93501) *(P-3719)*

Pphm Inc .... D 714 508-6100
14282 Franklin Ave Tustin (92780) *(P-10646)*

Ppmc, Corona *Also Called: Primary Provider MGT Co Inc (P-18036)*

Pponext West Inc .... B 888 446-6098
1501 Hughes Way Ste 400 Long Beach (90810) *(P-16603)*

Pps Parking Inc .... A 949 223-8707
1800 E Garry Ave Ste 107 Santa Ana (92705) *(P-13185)*

Ppst Inc (PA) .... E 800 421-1921
17692 Fitch Irvine (92614) *(P-7037)*

PQ LLC .... C 323 326-1100
8401 Quartz Ave South Gate (90280) *(P-3246)*

PR Construction Inc .... D 714 637-7848
1995 N Batavia St Orange (92865) *(P-574)*

Prager University Foundation .... D 833 772-4378
15021 Ventura Blvd Ste 552 Sherman Oaks (91403) *(P-14849)*

Pramira Inc .... C 800 678-1169
404 N Berry St Brea (92821) *(P-14244)*

Prana, Carlsbad *Also Called: Prana Living LLC (P-10692)*

Prana Living LLC (HQ) .... D 866 915-6457
3209 Lionshead Ave Carlsbad (92010) *(P-10692)*

Pratt & Whitney Eng Svcs Inc .... A 714 373-0110
11190 Valley View St Cypress (90630) *(P-7394)*

Pratt Whitney Engine Services, Cypress *Also Called: Pratt & Whitney Eng Svcs Inc (P-7394)*

PRC, Ontario *Also Called: Plastics Research Corporation (P-3967)*

PRC - Desoto International Inc (HQ) .... B 661 678-4209
24811 Avenue Rockefeller Valencia (91355) *(P-3775)*

PRC - Desoto International Inc .... C 661 824-4532
11601 United St Mojave (93501) *(P-3776)*

PRC Composites LLC (PA) .... D 909 391-2006
1400 S Campus Ave Ontario (91761) *(P-4206)*

PRC Multi-Family LLC .... C 562 803-5000
10000 Imperial Hwy Downey (90242) *(P-12362)*

Prdctions N Fremantle Amer Inc (DH) .... D 818 748-1100
2900 W Alameda Ave Unit 800 Burbank (91505) *(P-14971)*

Pre-Con Products .... D 805 527-0841
240 W Los Angeles Ave Simi Valley (93065) *(P-4412)*

Precast Innovations Inc .... E 714 921-4060
1670 N Main St Orange (92867) *(P-4413)*

Precept Advisory Group LLC (DH)...............................D 949 955-1430
130 Theory Ste 200 Irvine (92617) *(P-12245)*

Precept Group The, Irvine *Also Called: Precept Advisory Group LLC (P-12245)*

Precise Aerospace Mfg LLC ....E 951 898-0500
22951 La Palma Ave Yorba Linda (92887) *(P-4207)*

Precise Air Systems Inc ....D 818 646-9757
5467 W San Fernando Rd Los Angeles (90039) *(P-822)*

Precise Die and Finishing ....E 818 773-9337
9400 Oso Ave Chatsworth (91311) *(P-5591)*

Precise Industries Inc ....C 714 482-2333
610 Neptune Ave Brea (92821) *(P-5023)*

Precise Media Services Inc ....E 909 481-3305
888 Vintage Ave Ontario (91764) *(P-6578)*

Precise Plastic Products, Yorba Linda *Also Called: Precise Aerospace Mfg LLC (P-4207)*

Precise-Full Service Media, Ontario *Also Called: Precise Media Services Inc (P-6578)*

Preciseq Inc ....D 310 709-6094
11601 Wilshire Blvd Ste 500 Los Angeles (90025) *(P-14245)*

Precision Aerospace Corp ....D 909 945-9604
11155 Jersey Blvd Ste A Rancho Cucamonga (91730) *(P-7541)*

Precision Anodizing & Pltg Inc ....D 714 996-1601
1601 N Miller St Anaheim (92806) *(P-5285)*

Precision Arcft Machining Inc ....E 818 768-5900
10640 Elkwood St Sun Valley (91352) *(P-6204)*

Precision Coil Spring Company ....C 626 444-0561
10107 Rose Ave El Monte (91731) *(P-5398)*

Precision Contracting, Irvine *Also Called: Danny Ryan Precision Contg Inc (P-1180)*

Precision Cutting Tools Inc ....E 562 921-7898
5572 Fresca Dr La Palma (90623) *(P-5621)*

Precision Cutting Tools LLC ....E 562 921-7898
5572 Fresca Dr La Palma (90623) *(P-5622)*

Precision Die Cutting, LLC, Chino *Also Called: Team Technologies Inc (P-5600)*

Precision Dynamics Corporation (HQ)..................C 818 897-1111
25124 Springfield Ct Ste 200 Valencia (91355) *(P-2725)*

Precision Energy Efficient Ltg, Yorba Linda *Also Called: Precision Fluorescent West Inc (P-10203)*

Precision Engine Controls Corp (DH)...................C 858 792-3217
11661 Sorrento Valley Rd San Diego (92121) *(P-5460)*

Precision Fiber Products Inc ....E 408 946-4040
642 Palomar St Chula Vista (91911) *(P-4636)*

Precision Fluorescent West Inc ....D 352 692-5900
23281 La Palma Ave Yorba Linda (92887) *(P-10203)*

Precision Frrites Ceramics Inc ....D 714 901-7622
5432 Production Dr Huntington Beach (92649) *(P-4365)*

Precision Glass & Optics, Santa Ana *Also Called: Buk Optics Inc (P-7996)*

Precision Hermetic, Redlands *Also Called: Precision Hermetic Tech Inc (P-7038)*

Precision Hermetic Tech Inc ....D 909 381-6011
1940 W Park Ave Redlands (92373) *(P-7038)*

Precision Label LLC ....E 760 757-7533
659 Benet Rd Oceanside (92058) *(P-2711)*

Precision Litho Inc ....E 760 727-9400
1185 Joshua Way Vista (92081) *(P-3064)*

Precision Machining & Fab, Anaheim *Also Called: Precision Waterjet Inc (P-6205)*

Precision Offset Inc ....D 949 752-1714
15201 Woodlawn Ave Tustin (92780) *(P-3065)*

Precision One Medical Inc ....D 760 945 7966
3923 Oceanic Dr Ste 200 Oceanside (92056) *(P-8351)*

Precision Optical, Costa Mesa *Also Called: Sellers Optical Inc (P-8021)*

Precision Pipeline LLC ....B 909 229-6858
10400 Trademark St Rancho Cucamonga (91730) *(P-689)*

Precision Plastics Packaging, Anaheim *Also Called: Interlink Inc (P-3024)*

Precision Pwdred Met Parts Inc ....E 909 595-5656
145 Atlantic St Pomona (91768) *(P-4719)*

Precision Resource Inc ....C 714 891-4439
5803 Engineer Dr Huntington Beach (92649) *(P-5209)*

Precision Resource Cal Div, Huntington Beach *Also Called: Precision Resource Inc (P-5209)*

Precision Services Group, Tustin *Also Called: Precision Offset Inc (P-3065)*

Precision Sheet Metal, Gardena *Also Called: Artistic Welding (P-4953)*

Precision Silicones, Chino *Also Called: Wacker Chemical Corporation (P-3743)*

Precision Stampings Inc (PA)..................................E 951 845-1174
500 Egan Ave Beaumont (92223) *(P-6426)*

Precision Tube Bending ....D 562 921-6723
13626 Talc St Santa Fe Springs (90670) *(P-7542)*

Precision Waterjet Inc ....E 888 538-9287
4900 E Hunter Ave Anaheim (92807) *(P-6205)*

Precision Welding Inc ....E 661 729-3436
241 Enterprise Pkwy Lancaster (93534) *(P-4860)*

Precision Wire Products Inc (PA)..........................C 323 890-9100
6150 Sheila St Commerce (90040) *(P-5410)*

Precision Works, Indio *Also Called: Cabinets By Prcision Works Inc (P-2342)*

Pred, San Diego *Also Called: Pred Technologies Usa Inc (P-7039)*

Pred Technologies Usa Inc ....D 858 999-2114
4901 Morena Blvd San Diego (92117) *(P-7039)*

Preferred Brokers Inc (PA).....................................D 661 836-2345
9100 Ming Ave Ste 100 Bakersfield (93311) *(P-12507)*

Preferred Carrier California, Chino *Also Called: Advanced Multimodal Dist Inc (P-9357)*

Preferred Employers Insur Co ....D 619 688-3900
9797 Aero Dr Ste 200 San Diego (92123) *(P-12246)*

Preferred Frzr Svcs - Lbf LLC ....D 323 263-8811
4901 Bandini Blvd Vernon (90058) *(P-9040)*

Preferred Hlthcare Rgistry Inc ....C 800 787-6787
4909 Murphy Canyon Rd Ste 210 San Diego (92123) *(P-13556)*

Preferred Printing & Packaging Inc ....E 909 923-2053
1493 E Philadelphia St Ontario (91761) *(P-2642)*

Pregel America Inc ....C 909 598-8980
116 S Brent Cir Walnut (91789) *(P-17109)*

Premere Event Services, Huntington Beach *Also Called: Love At First Bite Catering (P-11588)*

Premier Ambulance, Brea *Also Called: Premier Medical Transport Inc (P-8843)*

Premier America Credit Union (PA)........................C 818 772-4000
19867 Prairie St Lbby Chatsworth (91311) *(P-11831)*

PREMIER AMERICA WEALTH MANAGEM; Chatsworth *Also Called: Premier America Credit Union (P-11831)*

Premier Aquatic Services Llc ....D 949 716-3333
6 Journey Ste 200 Aliso Viejo (92656) *(P-15159)*

Premier Aquatics, Aliso Viejo *Also Called: Premier Aquatic Services Llc (P-15159)*

Premier Cold Storage & Pkg LLC ....C 949 444-8859
1071 E 233rd St Carson (90745) *(P-9041)*

Premier Dealer Services Inc ....D 858 810-1700
9449 Balboa Ave Ste 300 San Diego (92123) *(P-12247)*

Premier Dental Holdings Inc (PA).........................C 714 480-3000
530 S Main St Ste 600 Orange (92868) *(P-15526)*

Premier Disability Svcs LLC ....D 310 280-4000
909 N Pacific Coast Hwy Fl 11 El Segundo (90245) *(P-17240)*

Premier Filters Inc ....E 657 226-0091
952 N Elm St Orange (92867) *(P-5833)*

Premier Food Services Inc ....A 760 843-8000
14359 Amargosa Rd Ste F Victorville (92392) *(P-10766)*

Premier Fuel Delivery Service, Riverside *Also Called: Premier Fuel Distributors Inc (P-11034)*

Premier Fuel Distributors Inc ....C 760 423-3610
156 E La Cadena Dr Riverside (92507) *(P-11034)*

Premier Gear & Machining Inc ....E 951 278-5505
2360 Pomona Rd Corona (92880) *(P-5147)*

Premier Healthcare Svcs LLC (DH).......................C 626 204-7930
3030 Old Ranch Pkwy Ste 100 Seal Beach (90740) *(P-16412)*

Premier Hlthcare Solutions Inc ....B 858 569-8629
12225 El Camino Real San Diego (92130) *(P-18032)*

Premier IMS Insurance Services, San Diego *Also Called: Premier Hlthcare Solutions Inc (P-18032)*

Premier Infsion Hlthcare Svcs ....D 310 328-3897
19500 Normandie Ave Torrance (90502) *(P-16413)*

Premier Infusion Care, Torrance *Also Called: Premier Infsion Hlthcare Svcs (P-16413)*

Premier Magnetics Inc ....E 949 452-0511
20381 Barents Sea Cir Lake Forest (92630) *(P-6935)*

Premier Medical Transport Inc ....A 805 340-5191
260 N Palm St # 200 Brea (92821) *(P-8843)*

Premier Mop & Broom, Corona *Also Called: Northwestern Converting Co (P-2218)*

Premier Packaging LLC ....E 909 749-5123
10700 Business Dr Ste 100 Fontana (92337) *(P-4013)*

Premier Packaging/Assembly, Santa Fe Springs *Also Called: Haringa Inc (P-14506)*

Premier Pharmacy Service, Baldwin Park *Also Called: Good Health Inc (P-16562)*

Premier Plumbing Company, Riverside *Also Called: Ppc Enterprises Inc (P-821)*

A
L
P
H
A
B
E
T
I
C

Premier Steel Structures Inc .... E 951 356-6655
13345 Estelle St Corona (92879) *(P-4861)*

Premier Wireless Inc .... E 925 776-1070
4010 Watson Plaza Dr Ste 245 Lakewood (90712) *(P-6646)*

Premiere Customs Brokers Inc .... A 310 410-6825
5951 Skylab Rd Huntington Beach (92647) *(P-9327)*

Premiere Packaging Inds Inc .... D 562 799-9200
12202 Slauson Ave Santa Fe Springs (90670) *(P-11135)*

Premiere Packing, Shafter *Also Called: Grimmway Enterprises Inc (P-82)*

Premiere Rack Solutions Inc .... D 909 605-6300
4502 Brickell Privado St Ontario (91761) *(P-9881)*

Premiere Radio Network Inc (DH) .... C 818 377-5300
15260 Ventura Blvd Ste 400 Sherman Oaks (91403) *(P-14972)*

Premio Inc (PA) .... C 626 839-3100
918 Radecki Ct City Of Industry (91748) *(P-5865)*

Premium Outlet Partners LP .... D 805 445-8520
740 Ventura Blvd Camarillo (93010) *(P-12311)*

Premium Outlet Partners LP .... D 951 849-6641
48400 Seminole Dr Cabazon (92230) *(P-12312)*

Premium Outlet Partners LP .... D 760 804-9045
5620 Paseo Del Norte Ste 100 Carlsbad (92008) *(P-12313)*

Premium Pet Foods, Irwindale *Also Called: J&R Taylor Brothers Assoc Inc (P-1418)*

Premium Windows, Corona *Also Called: Mediland Corporation (P-4317)*

Preproduction Plastics Inc .... E 951 340-9680
210 Teller St Corona (92879) *(P-4208)*

Pres-Tek Plastics Inc (PA) .... E 909 360-1600
10700 7th St Rancho Cucamonga (91730) *(P-4209)*

Presbia, Aliso Viejo *Also Called: Presbibio LLC (P-8413)*

Presbibio LLC .... E 949 502-7010
36 Plateau Aliso Viejo (92656) *(P-8413)*

Presbyterian Inter Cmnty Hosp, Whittier *Also Called: Interhealth Services Inc (P-16397)*

Prescient Holdings Group LLC .... E 858 790-7004
10181 Scripps Gateway Ct San Diego (92131) *(P-3478)*

Prescription Solutions, Carlsbad *Also Called: Optumrx Inc (P-12099)*

Presentation Folder Inc .... E 714 289-7000
1130 N Main St Orange (92867) *(P-2746)*

Preserved Treescapes International Inc .... D 760 631-6789
180 Vallecitos De Oro San Marcos (92069) *(P-8718)*

Preserved Treescapes Intl, San Marcos *Also Called: Preserved Treescapes International Inc (P-8718)*

Presidio Components Inc .... C 858 578-9390
7169 Construction Ct San Diego (92121) *(P-10279)*

Press Colorcom, Santa Fe Springs *Also Called: Ace Commercial Inc (P-2958)*

Press Forge Company .... D 562 531-4962
7700 Jackson St Paramount (90723) *(P-5148)*

Press-Enterprise Company (PA) .... A 951 684-1200
3450 14th St Riverside (92501) *(P-2823)*

Prestige Animal Hospital North, Fontana *Also Called: People Pets and Vets LLC (P-132)*

Prestige Animal Hospital South, Fontana *Also Called: People Pets and Vets LLC (P-131)*

Prestige Asssted Lving At Lncs, Lancaster *Also Called: PCI Care Venture I (P-15752)*

Prestige Flag, San Diego *Also Called: Prestige Flag & Banner Co Inc (P-2280)*

Prestige Flag & Banner Co Inc .... D 619 497-2220
591 Camino De La Reina Ste 917 San Diego (92108) *(P-2280)*

Prestige Graphics Inc .... E 858 560-8213
9630 Ridgehaven Ct Ste B San Diego (92123) *(P-10583)*

Prestige Mold Incorporated .... D 909 980-6600
11040 Tacoma Dr Rancho Cucamonga (91730) *(P-5592)*

Prestige Stations Inc (DH) .... C 714 670-5145
4 Centerpointe Dr La Palma (90623) *(P-11280)*

Prestone Products Corporation .... E 424 271-4836
19500 Mariner Ave Torrance (90503) *(P-3818)*

Prevost Car (us) Inc .... D 951 360-2550
3384 De Forest Cir Mira Loma (91752) *(P-9839)*

PRI Medical Technologies Inc .... D 818 394-2800
10939 Pendleton St Sun Valley (91352) *(P-10104)*

Price Industries Inc .... D 858 673-4451
10883 Thornmint Rd San Diego (92127) *(P-4522)*

Price Law Group A Prof Corp (PA) .... C 818 995-4540
15760 Ventura Blvd Ste 800 Encino (91436) *(P-16762)*

Price Manufacturing Co Inc .... E 951 371-5660
372 N Smith Ave Corona (92878) *(P-5112)*

Price Pfister Brass Mfg, Lake Forest *Also Called: Price Pfister Inc (P-4805)*

Price Pfister Inc .... A 949 672-4000
19701 Da Vinci Lake Forest (92610) *(P-4805)*

Price Products Incorporated .... E 760 745-5602
106 State Pl Escondido (92029) *(P-6206)*

Pricegrabber.com, Los Angeles *Also Called: Pg Usa LLC (P-11269)*

Pricespider, Irvine *Also Called: Neuintel LLC (P-13779)*

Pricewaterhousecoopers LLP .... C 213 356-6000
601 S Figueroa St Ste 900 Los Angeles (90017) *(P-17752)*

Pride Resource Partners LLC .... C 858 430-6630
4499 Ruffin Rd Ste 250 San Diego (92123) *(P-18033)*

Primal Elements, Huntington Beach *Also Called: Primal Elements Inc (P-10647)*

Primal Elements Inc .... D 714 899-0757
18062 Redondo Cir Huntington Beach (92648) *(P-10647)*

Primapharma Inc .... E 858 259-0969
3443 Tripp Ct San Diego (92121) *(P-3479)*

Primary Care Assod Med Group I .... C 760 724-1033
3998 Vista Way Ste B Oceanside (92056) *(P-18034)*

Primary Care Assod Med Group I (PA) .... D 760 471-7505
1635 Lake San Marcos Dr Ste 201 San Marcos (92078) *(P-18035)*

Primary Color Systems Corp .... D 818 643-5944
3500 W Burbank Blvd Burbank (91505) *(P-3066)*

Primary Color Systems Corp (PA) .... B 949 660-7080
11130 Holder St Ste 210 Cypress (90630) *(P-3161)*

Primary Color Systems Corp .... D 310 841-0250
401 Coral Cir El Segundo (90245) *(P-3162)*

Primary Provider MGT Co Inc (HQ) .... D 951 280-7700
2115 Compton Ave Ste 301 Corona (92881) *(P-18036)*

Prime Administration LLC .... A 323 549-7155
357 S Curson Ave Los Angeles (90036) *(P-12692)*

Prime Converting Corporation .... E 909 476-9500
9121 Pittsburgh Ave Ste 100 Rancho Cucamonga (91730) *(P-2772)*

Prime Focus World, Culver City *Also Called: Dneg North America Inc (P-14886)*

Prime Forming & Cnstr Sups Inc .... E 714 547-6710
1500a E Chestnut Ave Santa Ana (92701) *(P-4414)*

Prime Group, Los Angeles *Also Called: Prime Administration LLC (P-12692)*

Prime Healthcare Foundation Inc (PA) .... C 909 235-4400
3480 E Guasti Rd Ontario (91761) *(P-16138)*

Prime Health Care .... D 909 394-2727
1350 W Covina Blvd San Dimas (91773) *(P-17110)*

Prime Healthcare Anaheim LLC .... A 714 827-3000
3033 W Orange Ave Anaheim (92804) *(P-16139)*

Prime Healthcare Centinela LLC .... A 310 673-4660
555 E Hardy St Inglewood (90301) *(P-16140)*

Prime Healthcare Services, Ontario *Also Called: Bio-Med Services Inc (P-15927)*

Prime Healthcare Services-Mont .... A 909 625-5411
5000 San Bernardino St Montclair (91763) *(P-16141)*

Prime Hlthcare Hntngton Bch LL .... B 714 843-5000
17772 Beach Blvd Huntington Beach (92647) *(P-16142)*

Prime Hlthcare Srvcs-Mntclair .... C 909 625-5411
5000 San Bernardino St Montclair (91763) *(P-16143)*

Prime Hlthcare Srvcs-Mntclair (DH) .... C 909 625-5411
5000 San Bernardino St Montclair (91763) *(P-16144)*

Prime Hlthcare Svcs - Encino H .... B 818 995-5000
16237 Ventura Blvd Encino (91436) *(P-16145)*

Prime Hlthcare Svcs - Pmpa LLC (DH) .... C 909 235-4400
3300 E Guasti Rd Ste 300 Ontario (91761) *(P-16146)*

Prime Hlthcare Svcs - San Dmas .... B 909 599-6811
1350 W Covina Blvd San Dimas (91773) *(P-16147)*

Prime Hlthcare Svcs - Shrman O .... B 818 981-7111
4929 Van Nuys Blvd Sherman Oaks (91403) *(P-16148)*

Prime Hospitality LLC .... D 909 975-5000
2200 E Holt Blvd Ontario (91761) *(P-12977)*

Prime Mso LLC .... D 818 937-9969
550 N Brand Blvd Ste 900 Glendale (91203) *(P-16495)*

Prime One Inc .... C 310 378-1944
22410 Hawthorne Blvd Ste 4 Torrance (90505) *(P-13557)*

Prime Plating, Sun Valley *Also Called: Schmidt Industries Inc (P-5293)*

Prime Tech Cabinets Inc .... C 949 757-4900
2215 S Standard Ave Santa Ana (92707) *(P-1058)*

Prime Wheel Corporation (PA) .... A 310 516-9126
17705 S Main St Gardena (90248) *(P-7283)*

Mergent email: customerrelations@mergent.com
1150

2025 Southern California
Business Directory and Buyers Guide

(P-0000) Products & Services Section entry number
(PA)=Parent Co (HQ)=Headquarters (DH)=Div Headquarters

Prime Wheel Corporation .... B 310 326-5080
23920 Vermont Ave Harbor City (90710) *(P-7284)*

Prime Wheel Corporation .... E 310 819-4123
17680 S Figueroa St Gardena (90248) *(P-7285)*

Prime Wheel of Figueroa, Gardena Also Called: Prime Wheel Corporation *(P-7285)*

Prime Wire & Cable Inc .... C 323 266-2010
11701 6th St Rancho Cucamonga (91730) *(P-4637)*

Primeco .... D 760 967-8278
220 Oceanside Blvd Oceanside (92054) *(P-870)*

Primetime International Inc .... D 760 399-4166
47110 Washington St Ste 103 La Quinta (92253) *(P-10914)*

Primex Clinical Labs Inc (PA) .... D 424 213-8019
16742 Stagg St Ste 120 Van Nuys (91406) *(P-16328)*

Primex Farms LLC (PA) .... E 661 758-7790
16070 Wildwood Rd Wasco (93280) *(P-1516)*

Primordial Diagnostics Inc .... E 800 462-1926
3233 Mission Oaks Blvd Ste P Camarillo (93012) *(P-7872)*

Primus Inc .... D 714 527-2261
17901 Jamestown Ln Huntington Beach (92647) *(P-8624)*

Primus Pipe and Tube Inc (DH) .... D 562 808-8000
5855 Obispo Ave Long Beach (90805) *(P-4553)*

Prince Lionheart Inc (PA) .... E 805 922-2250
2421 Westgate Rd Santa Maria (93455) *(P-4210)*

Princess Cruise Lines Ltd (HQ) .... A 661 753-0000
24305 Town Center Dr Santa Clarita (91355) *(P-9138)*

Princess Cruise Lines Ltd .... C 213 745-0314
1242 E 25th St Los Angeles (90011) *(P-9233)*

Princess Cruise Lines Ltd .... A 661 753-2197
24833 Anza Dr Santa Clarita (91380) *(P-9234)*

Princess Cruise Lines Ltd .... A 661 753-0000
24200 Magic Mountain Pkwy Santa Clarita (91355) *(P-9239)*

Princess Cruises, Santa Clarita Also Called: Princess Cruise Lines Ltd *(P-9138)*

Princess Cruises, Santa Clarita Also Called: Princess Cruise Lines Ltd *(P-9234)*

Princess Paper Inc .... E 323 588-4777
4455 Fruitland Ave Vernon (90058) *(P-2747)*

Princess Paradise, Walnut Also Called: Diana Did-It Designs Inc *(P-2193)*

Princeton Technology Inc .... E 949 851-7776
1691 Browning Irvine (92606) *(P-5945)*

Principle Plastics .... E 310 532-3411
1136 W 135th St Gardena (90247) *(P-3871)*

Prindle Decker & Amaro LLP (PA) .... D 562 436-3946
310 Golden Shore Fl 4 Long Beach (90802) *(P-16763)*

Pringle's Draperies, Garden Grove Also Called: L C Pringle Sales Inc *(P-2605)*

Print Printing, Placentia Also Called: Crescent Inc *(P-2994)*

Print Shop, San Bernardino Also Called: San Brnrdino Cmnty College Dst *(P-3174)*

Printec Ht Electronics LLC .... E 714 484-7597
501 Sally Pl Fullerton (92831) *(P-6870)*

Printegra Corp .... D 714 692-2221
23281 La Palma Ave Yorba Linda (92887) *(P-3194)*

Printing 4him, Ontario Also Called: Ultimate Print Source Inc *(P-3093)*

Printivity, San Diego Also Called: Printivity LLC *(P-3067)*

Printivity LLC .... E 877 649-5463
8840 Kenamar Dr Ste 405 San Diego (92121) *(P-3067)*

Printronix LLC (PA) .... F 714 368-2300
7700 Irvine Center Dr Ste 700 Irvine (92618) *(P-5946)*

Printrunner LLC .... E 888 296-5760
8000 Haskell Ave Van Nuys (91406) *(P-3068)*

Prints 4 Life .... E 661 942-2233
43145 Business Ctr Pkwy Lancaster (93535) *(P-3069)*

Printsafe Inc .... E 858 748-8600
11895 Community Rd Ste B Poway (92064) *(P-10024)*

Priority Building Services LLC (PA) .... D 714 255-2963
1524 W Mable St Anaheim (92802) *(P-13406)*

Priority Building Services LLC .... B 858 695-1326
7313 Carroll Rd Ste G San Diego (92121) *(P-13407)*

Priority Ctr Ending The Gnrtna .... D 714 543-4333
1940 E Deere Ave Ste 100 Santa Ana (92705) *(P-16996)*

Priority Landscape Services, Anaheim Also Called: Priority Building Services LLC *(P-13406)*

Priority Landscape Svcs LLC .... D 714 255-2940
521 Mercury Ln Brea (92821) *(P-187)*

Priority One Med Trnspt Inc (PA) .... D 909 948-4400
9327 Fairway View Pl Ste 300 Rancho Cucamonga (91730) *(P-8844)*

Prism Aerospace .... E 951 582-2850
3087 12th St Riverside (92507) *(P-5024)*

Prism Software Corporation .... E 949 855-3100
184 Technology Dr Ste 201 Irvine (92618) *(P-14009)*

Private Brand Mdsg Corp .... E 213 749-0191
214 W Olympic Blvd Los Angeles (90015) *(P-2069)*

Private Medical-Care Inc .... A 562 924-8311
12898 Towne Center Dr Cerritos (90703) *(P-12101)*

Private Nat Mrtg Accptance LLC (DH) .... A 866 549-3583
6101 Condor Dr Agoura Hills (91301) *(P-11931)*

Private Suite Lax LLC .... C 310 907-9950
6871 W Imperial Hwy Los Angeles (90045) *(P-8794)*

Privilege International Inc .... D 323 585-0777
2323 Firestone Blvd South Gate (90280) *(P-9882)*

Prl Aluminum Inc .... D 626 968-7507
14760 Don Julian Rd City Of Industry (91746) *(P-4604)*

Prl Glass Systems Inc .... D 877 775-2586
14760 Don Julian Rd City Of Industry (91746) *(P-4343)*

Prl Glass Systems Inc (PA) .... C 626 961-5890
13644 Nelson Ave City Of Industry (91746) *(P-4344)*

Prn Ambulance LLC .... B 818 810-3600
8928 Sepulveda Blvd North Hills (91343) *(P-8845)*

Prn Radio Networks, Sherman Oaks Also Called: Premiere Radio Network Inc *(P-14972)*

Pro America Premium Tools, Baldwin Park Also Called: American Kal Enterprises Inc *(P-10301)*

Pro American Premium Tools, Baldwin Park Also Called: Kal-Cameron Manufacturing Corp *(P-4741)*

Pro Building Maintenance Inc (PA) .... C 951 279-3386
149 N Maple St Ste H Corona (92878) *(P-13408)*

Pro Design Group Inc .... E 310 767-1032
438 E Alondra Blvd Gardena (90248) *(P-4211)*

Pro Detention Inc .... D 714 881-3680
2238 N Glassell St Ste E Orange (92865) *(P-4540)*

Pro Document Solutions Inc (PA) .... E 805 238-6680
1760 Commerce Way Paso Robles (93446) *(P-3070)*

Pro Energy Services Group LLC .... B 760 744-7077
2060 Aldergrove Ave Escondido (92029) *(P-18267)*

Pro Group, Irvine Also Called: Progroup *(P-3164)*

Pro Group Inc .... C 951 271-3000
4160 Temescal Canyon Rd Ste 500 Corona (92883) *(P-12508)*

Pro Loaders Inc .... C 909 355-5531
14032 Santa Ana Ave Fontana (92337) *(P-9328)*

Pro Pacific Pest Control, San Marcos Also Called: Corkys Pest Control Inc *(P-13345)*

Pro Safety & Rescue Inc .... D 888 269-5095
3700 Pegasus Dr Ste 200 Bakersfield (93308) *(P-18196)*

Pro Safety Inc .... C 562 364-7450
20503 Belshaw Ave Carson (90746) *(P-10395)*

Pro Specialties Group Inc .... D 858 541-1100
14055 Kirkham Way Poway (92064) *(P-11136)*

Pro Tooh Thermal Services .... C 951 272-5000
1954 Tandem Norco (92860) *(P-4711)*

Pro Tour Memorabilia LLC .... E 424 303-7200
700 N San Vicente Blvd Ste G606 West Hollywood (00060) *(P-2415)*

Pro Traffic Services Inc .... D 760 906-6961
321 Hunter St Ramona (92065) *(P-823)*

Pro Vote Solutions, Paso Robles Also Called: Pro Document Solutions Inc *(P-3070)*

Pro-Action Products, Van Nuys Also Called: Neopacific Holdings Inc *(P-4177)*

Pro-Cast Products Inc (PA) .... E 909 793-7602
27417 3rd St Highland (92346) *(P-4415)*

Pro-Craft Construction Inc .... C 909 790-5222
500 Iowa St Ste 100 Redlands (92373) *(P-824)*

Pro-Dex, Irvine Also Called: Pro-Dex Inc *(P-8217)*

Pro-Dex Inc (PA) .... C 949 769-3200
2361 Mcgaw Ave Irvine (92614) *(P-8217)*

Pro-Mart Industries Inc .... E 949 428-7700
17421 Von Karman Ave Irvine (92614) *(P-2223)*

Pro-Spectus Inc .... D 877 877-0096
13223 Black Mountain Rd Ste 1271 San Diego (92129) *(P-18348)*

Pro-Tek Consulting (PA) .... C 805 807-5571
21300 Victory Blvd Ste 240 Woodland Hills (91367) *(P-14246)*

Employee Codes: A=Over 500 employees, B=251-500
C=101-250, D=51-100, E=20-50, F=10-19, G=1-9

2025 Southern California
Business Directory and Buyers Guide

© Mergent Inc. 1-800-342-5647
1151

Pro-Wash Inc .... D 323 756-6000
9117 S Main St Los Angeles (90003) *(P-13130)*

Proactive Northern Container, Ontario *Also Called: PNC Proactive Nthrn Cont LLC (P-2687)*

Proactive Packg & Display LLC .... D 909 390-5624
602 S Rockefeller Ave Ste A Ontario (91761) *(P-11137)*

Proactive Risk Management Inc .... D 213 840-8856
22617 Hawthorne Blvd Torrance (90505) *(P-18037)*

Probation Department, Pasadena *Also Called: County of Los Angeles (P-16906)*

Probation Department, Los Angeles *Also Called: County of Los Angeles (P-16909)*

Probation Department, Lancaster *Also Called: County of Los Angeles (P-16911)*

Probation Department, Downey *Also Called: County of Los Angeles (P-16917)*

Probation Dept, Los Angeles *Also Called: County of Los Angeles (P-16907)*

Probation Dept, Santa Monica *Also Called: County of Los Angeles (P-16919)*

Probation Dept, Van Nuys *Also Called: County of Los Angeles (P-16920)*

Probation Dept, Los Angeles *Also Called: County of Los Angeles (P-16921)*

Probation Dept, Los Angeles *Also Called: County of Los Angeles (P-16923)*

Probation Dept, Compton *Also Called: County of Los Angeles (P-16924)*

Probation Dept, Pasadena *Also Called: County of Los Angeles (P-16925)*

Probation Dept, San Diego *Also Called: County of San Diego (P-16929)*

Probation Information Ctr Pic, Downey *Also Called: County of Los Angeles (P-16916)*

Prober & Raphael A Law Corp .... D 818 227-0100
20750 Ventura Blvd Ste 100 Woodland Hills (91364) *(P-16764)*

Prober & Raphael, ALC, Woodland Hills *Also Called: Prober & Raphael A Law Corp (P-16764)*

Probio Medicine Corp, Irvine *Also Called: Sunny Service Group LLC (P-505)*

Process Fab Inc .... C 562 921-1979
13153 Lakeland Rd Santa Fe Springs (90670) *(P-6207)*

Process Insghts - Gded Wave In .... E 919 264-9651
2121 Aviation Dr Upland (91786) *(P-7873)*

Processes By Martin Inc .... E 310 637-1855
12150 Alameda St Lynwood (90262) *(P-5340)*

Processes Unlimited, Bakersfield *Also Called: Processes Unlimited International Inc (P-17613)*

Processes Unlimited International Inc .... B 661 396-3770
5500 Ming Ave Ste 400 Bakersfield (93309) *(P-17613)*

Procisedx Inc .... E 858 382-4598
9449 Carroll Park Dr San Diego (92121) *(P-7830)*

Procopio Cory Hargreaves & Savitch LLP (PA)................ C 619 238-1900
530 B St Ste 2200 San Diego (92101) *(P-16765)*

Procore Technologies Inc (PA)..................................... A 866 477-6267
6309 Carpinteria Ave Carpinteria (93013) *(P-13798)*

Procter & Gamble, Oxnard *Also Called: Procter & Gamble Paper Pdts Co (P-2748)*

Procter & Gamble Paper Pdts Co .... A 805 485-8871
800 N Rice Ave Oxnard (93030) *(P-2748)*

Prodege LLC (PA).. D 310 294-9599
2030 E Maple Ave Ste 200 El Segundo (90245) *(P-13799)*

Producers Meat and Prov Inc .... E 619 232-7593
7651 Saint Andrews Ave San Diego (92154) *(P-10878)*

Producr-Wrters Gild Amer Pnsio (PA)......................... D 818 846-1015
2900 W Alameda Ave Unit 1100 Burbank (91505) *(P-12162)*

Product Slingshot Inc (DH)... E 760 929-9380
2221 Rutherford Rd Carlsbad (92008) *(P-5593)*

Product Solutions Inc .... E 714 545-9757
1182 N Knollwood Cir Anaheim (92801) *(P-6027)*

Production Data Inc .... E 661 327-4776
1210 33rd St Bakersfield (93301) *(P-359)*

Productive Playhouse Inc (PA)..................................... C 323 250-3445
100 N Brand Blvd Glendale (91203) *(P-14575)*

Productos Chata, Chula Vista *Also Called: Culinary Hispanic Foods Inc (P-10942)*

Products Engineering Corp .... E 310 787-4500
2645 Maricopa St Torrance (90503) *(P-4745)*

Professional Cabinet Solutions .... C 909 614-2900
2111 Eastridge Ave Riverside (92507) *(P-2357)*

Professional Cmnty MGT Cal Inc .... A 951 845-2191
850 Country Club Dr Banning (92220) *(P-12509)*

Professional Cmnty MGT Cal Inc .... D 949 597-4200
23522 Paseo De Valencia Laguna Hills (92653) *(P-12510)*

Professional Cmnty MGT Cal Inc .... D 949 206-0580
24351 El Toro Rd Laguna Woods (92637) *(P-12511)*

Professional Community MGT Cal .... D 949 380-0725
23081 Via Campo Verde Aliso Viejo (92656) *(P-18038)*

Professional Cr Reporting Inc .... C 714 556-1570
3560 Hyland Ave Costa Mesa (92626) *(P-11862)*

Professional Maint Systems, San Diego *Also Called: Professional Maint Systems Inc (P-13409)*

Professional Maint Systems Inc .... A 619 276-1150
4912 Naples St San Diego (92110) *(P-13409)*

Professional Parking .... C 949 723-4027
309 Palm St Newport Beach (92661) *(P-14669)*

Professional Plastics Inc (PA).......................................E 714 446-6500
1810 E Valencia Dr Fullerton (92831) *(P-3288)*

Professional Produce .... D 323 277-1550
2570 E 25th St Los Angeles (90058) *(P-10915)*

Professional Security Cons (PA)................................... D 310 207-7729
11454 San Vicente Blvd 2nd Fl Los Angeles (90049) *(P-14330)*

Professional Security Cons, Los Angeles *Also Called: Professional Security Cons (P-14330)*

Professional Svcs Med Group, Huntington Park *Also Called: All Care Medical Group Inc (P-15234)*

Professnal Elec Cnstr Svcs Inc .... C 909 373-4100
9112 Santa Anita Ave Rancho Cucamonga (91730) *(P-954)*

Professnal Intrctive Entrmt In .... D 310 823-4445
6080 Center Dr Ste 600 Los Angeles (90045) *(P-14973)*

Professnal Rgistry Netwrk Corp .... D 714 832-5776
17592 17th St Ste 225 Tustin (92780) *(P-13558)*

Professonal Tele Answering Svc, Chatsworth *Also Called: Seven One Inc (P-14593)*

Profile Planing Mill, Santa Ana *Also Called: Strata Forest Products Inc (P-2287)*

Profit Recovery Partners LLC .... D 949 851-2777
3501 W Sunflower Ave Ste 100 Santa Ana (92704) *(P-18349)*

Proform Inc .... D 707 752-9010
1140 S Rockefeller Ave Ontario (91761) *(P-16329)*

Proform Finishing Products LLC .... E 562 435-4465
1850 Pier B St Long Beach (90813) *(P-4468)*

Proform Interior Cnstr Inc .... D 619 881-0041
663 33rd St Ste C San Diego (92102) *(P-1222)*

Proform Labs, Ontario *Also Called: Proform Inc (P-16329)*

Prographics Inc .... E 626 287-0417
9200 Lower Azusa Rd Rosemead (91770) *(P-3071)*

Prographics Screenprinting Inc .... E 760 744-4555
1975 Diamond St San Marcos (92078) *(P-3163)*

Progression Drywall, Lancaster *Also Called: Excel Contractors Inc (P-402)*

Progressive Health Care System .... D 818 707-9603
8510 Balboa Blvd Ste 150 Northridge (91325) *(P-15424)*

Progressive Label Inc .... E 323 415-9770
2545 Yates Ave Commerce (90040) *(P-2773)*

Progressive Management Systems, West Covina *Also Called: RM Galicia Inc (P-13287)*

Progressive Manufacturing, Anaheim *Also Called: Progrssive Intgrated Solutions (P-3165)*

Progressive Marketing, Yorba Linda *Also Called: Progressive Marketing Pdts Inc (P-5087)*

Progressive Marketing Pdts Inc .... D 714 888-1700
4571 Avenida Del Este Yorba Linda (92886) *(P-5087)*

Progressive Transportation Inc .... D 310 684-2100
1210 E 223rd St Ste 328 Carson (90745) *(P-8972)*

PROGRESSIVE TRANSPORTATION, INC., Carson *Also Called: Progressive Transportation Inc (P-8972)*

Progroup .... E 949 748-5400
17622 Armstrong Ave Irvine (92614) *(P-3164)*

Progrssive Intgrated Solutions .... D 714 237-0980
3291 E Miraloma Ave Anaheim (92806) *(P-3165)*

Project Concern International (PA)................................ C 858 279-9690
5151 Murphy Canyon Rd Ste 320 San Diego (92123) *(P-16997)*

Project Design Consultants LLC .... D 619 235-6471
701 B St Ste 800 San Diego (92101) *(P-18350)*

Project Management, Rcho Sta Marg *Also Called: M-Industrial Enterprises LLC (P-6167)*

Project Skyline Intrmdate Hldg .... A 310 712-1850
360 N Crescent Dr Bldg S Beverly Hills (90210) *(P-12608)*

Project Social T LLC .... E 323 266-4500
615 S Clarence St Los Angeles (90023) *(P-2053)*

Prolabs Factory Inc .... E 818 646-3677
15001 Oxnard St Van Nuys (91411) *(P-3684)*

Prolacta Bioscience Inc .... B 626 599-9260
1800 Highland Ave Duarte (91010) *(P-1307)*

Prolacta Bioscience Inc (PA).. C 626 599-9260
757 Baldwin Park Blvd City Of Industry (91746) *(P-3586)*

Proland Property Managment LLC (PA)............................D 213 738-8175
  2510 W 7th St 2nd Fl Los Angeles (90057) *(P-12512)*

Prolifics Testing Inc ....E 925 485-9535
  24025 Park Sorrento Ste 405 Calabasas (91302) *(P-13800)*

Proline Concrete Tools Inc ....E 760 758-7240
  4645 North Ave Ste 102 Oceanside (92056) *(P-5718)*

Prologic Rdmption Slutions Inc (PA)..........................A 310 322-7774
  2121 Rosecrans Ave El Segundo (90245) *(P-14576)*

Proma Inc ....E 310 327-0035
  730 Kingshill Pl Carson (90746) *(P-8352)*

Promart Dazz, Irvine *Also Called: Pro-Mart Industries Inc (P-2223)*

Promega Biosciences LLC ....D 805 544-8524
  277 Granada Dr San Luis Obispo (93401) *(P-3328)*

Prometheus Biosciences Inc ....D 858 422-4300
  3050 Science Park Rd San Diego (92121) *(P-3480)*

Prometheus Laboratories Inc (PA)............................B 858 824-0895
  9410 Carroll Park Dr San Diego (92121) *(P-3481)*

Promises Promises Inc ....E 213 749-7725
  3121 S Grand Ave Los Angeles (90007) *(P-2070)*

Promotonal Design Concepts Inc ....D 626 579-4454
  9872 Rush St South El Monte (91733) *(P-3930)*

Promoveo Health LLC ....A 760 931-4794
  701 Palomar Airport Rd Carlsbad (92011) *(P-13237)*

Prompt Delivery Inc ....D 858 549-8000
  5757 Wilshire Blvd Ph 3 Los Angeles (90036) *(P-14577)*

Pronto Janitorial Svcs Inc ....D 562 273-5997
  12561 Persing Dr Whittier (90606) *(P-13410)*

Pronto Products Co (PA) ....E 619 661-6995
  9850 Siempre Viva Rd San Diego (92154) *(P-6028)*

Propak Logistics Inc ....D 951 934-7160
  11555 Iberia St Jurupa Valley (91752) *(P-9374)*

PROPAK LOGISTICS, INC., Jurupa Valley *Also Called: Propak Logistics Inc (P-9374)*

Propeller Health, San Diego *Also Called: Reciprocal Labs Corp (P-13805)*

Property Care Building Svc LLC ....E 626 623-6420
  126 La Porte St Ste F Arcadia (91006) *(P-13411)*

Property I D, Los Angeles *Also Called: I D Property Corporation (P-12467)*

Property Insight LLC ....A 877 747-2537
  2510 Redhill Ave Santa Ana (92705) *(P-12561)*

Property Management Assoc Inc (PA) ....C 323 295-2000
  6011 Bristol Pkwy Culver City (90230) *(P-12513)*

Proplas Technologies, Garden Grove *Also Called: Peerless Injection Molding LLC (P-4194)*

Proponent, Brea *Also Called: Proponent Inc (P-10498)*

Proponent Inc (PA) ....C 714 223-5400
  3120 Enterprise St Brea (92821) *(P-10498)*

Proprietary Controls Systems ....E 310 303-3600
  3830 Del Amo Blvd # 102 Torrance (90503) *(P-8059)*

Proprofs, Santa Monica *Also Called: Batia Infotech (P-13671)*

Propstream, Lake Forest *Also Called: Equimine (P-13926)*

Propulsion Controls Engrg (PA)..............................D 619 235-0961
  1620 Rigel St San Diego (92113) *(P-14785)*

Prorack Gas Products, Santa Ana *Also Called: Cramer-Decker Industries (P-10074)*

Pros Incorporated ....D 661 589-5400
  3400 Patton Way Bakersfield (93308) *(P-360)*

Proscape Landscape, Signal Hill *Also Called: Fenderscape Incorporated (P-167)*

Prosciento Inc (PA) ....C 619 427-1300
  6160 Cornerstone Ct E Ste 200 San Diego (92121) *(P-17818)*

Prosearch Strategies LLC ....C 877 447-7291
  3250 Wilshire Blvd Ste 301 Los Angeles (90010) *(P-17859)*

Prosites Inc ....C 888 932-3644
  38977 Sky Canyon Dr Ste 200 Murrieta (92563) *(P-14247)*

Prosoft Technology Inc (HQ)....................................D 661 716-5100
  9201 Camino Media Ste 200 Bakersfield (93311) *(P-9569)*

Prospect Enterprises Inc (PA)..................................C 213 599-5700
  625 Kohler St Los Angeles (90021) *(P-10858)*

Prospect Medical Group Inc (HQ)............................B 714 796-5900
  1920 E 17th St Ste 200 Santa Ana (92705) *(P-18039)*

Prospect Medical Holdings Inc (PA)........................C 310 943-4500
  3824 Hughes Ave Los Angeles (90034) *(P-15425)*

Prospect Medical Systems Inc (HQ)........................C 714 667-8156
  600 City Pkwy W Ste 800 Orange (92868) *(P-18040)*

Prospect Mortgage LLC ....A
  Sherman Oaks (91403) *(P-12609)*

Prost LLC ....E 619 954-4189
  8179 Center St La Mesa (91942) *(P-1551)*

Protab Laboratories (PA) ....D 949 635-1930
  25892 Towne Centre Dr Foothill Ranch (92610) *(P-3482)*

Protab Laboratories ....D 949 713-1301
  30321 Esperanza Rcho Sta Marg (92688) *(P-3483)*

Protec Arisawa America Inc ....E 760 599-4800
  2455 Ash St Vista (92081) *(P-4922)*

Protec Association Services (PA)..............................C 858 569-1080
  10180 Willow Creek Rd San Diego (92131) *(P-13412)*

Protec Building Services, San Diego *Also Called: Protec Association Services (P-13412)*

Protect-US ....C 714 721-8127
  1801 N Bellflower Blvd Long Beach (90815) *(P-14331)*

Protection One, Riverside *Also Called: ADT LLC (P-14373)*

Proto Homes LLC ....E 310 271-7544
  11301 W Olympic Blvd Los Angeles (90064) *(P-7678)*

Protocast, Chatsworth *Also Called: John List Corporation (P-5639)*

Protoform, Banning *Also Called: DT Mattson Enterprises Inc (P-8484)*

Prototype & Short-Run Svcs Inc ....E 714 449-9661
  1310 W Collins Ave Orange (92867) *(P-5210)*

Prototype Engineering and Manufacturing Inc ....E 310 532-6305
  140 E 162nd St Gardena (90248) *(P-17614)*

Prototype Express LLC ....E 714 751-3533
  3506 W Lake Center Dr Ste D Santa Ana (92704) *(P-7143)*

Prototype Industries Inc (PA)..................................E 949 680-4890
  26035 Acero Ste 100 Mission Viejo (92691) *(P-2938)*

Prototypes, Los Angeles *Also Called: Prototypes Centers For Innov (P-16998)*

Prototypes Centers For Innov ....C 213 542-3838
  1000 N Alameda St Ste 390 Los Angeles (90012) *(P-16998)*

Proulx Manufacturing Inc ....E 909 980-0662
  11433 6th St Rancho Cucamonga (91730) *(P-4212)*

Provena Foods Inc (HQ)..D 909 627-1082
  5010 Eucalyptus Ave Chino (91710) *(P-1267)*

Provenza Floors Inc (PA)..D 949 788-0900
  15541 Mosher Ave Tustin (92780) *(P-11524)*

Providence, Mission Hills *Also Called: Providence Holy Cross Medical (P-16151)*

Providence Health & Svcs - Ore ....A 818 365-8051
  15031 Rinaldi St Mission Hills (91345) *(P-16149)*

Providence Health System ....A 818 843-5111
  501 S Buena Vista St Burbank (91505) *(P-16150)*

Providence Holy Cross Med Ctr, Mission Hills *Also Called: Providence Health & Svcs - Ore (P-16149)*

Providence Holy Cross Medical (PA)........................B 818 365-8051
  15031 Rinaldi St Mission Hills (91345) *(P-16151)*

PROVIDENCE HOME HEALTH ORANGE, Anaheim *Also Called: Providence Medical Foundation (P-16152)*

PROVIDENCE HOME HEALTH ORANGE, Orange *Also Called: St Joseph Hospital of Orange (P-16214)*

PROVIDENCE HOME HEALTH ORANGE, Fullerton *Also Called: St Jude Hospital (P-16219)*

Providence Medical Foundation (DH)........................C 714 712-3308
  200 W Center Street Promenade Ste 800 Anaheim (92805) *(P-16152)*

Providence Rest Partners LLC ....D 323 460-4170
  5955 Melrose Ave Los Angeles (90038) *(P-12729)*

Providence St Johns Hlth Ctr ....B 971 268-7643
  2121 Santa Monica Blvd Santa Monica (90404) *(P-16153)*

Providence Tarzana Medical Ctr ....A 818 881-0800
  18321 Clark St Tarzana (91356) *(P-16154)*

Provident Financial Management ....D 310 282-0477
  3130 Wilshire Blvd Ste 600 Santa Monica (90403) *(P-18041)*

Providien LLC (HQ)..D 480 344-5000
  6740 Nancy Ridge Dr San Diego (92121) *(P-8218)*

Providien Injction Molding Inc ....D 760 931-1844
  6740 Nancy Ridge Dr San Diego (92121) *(P-4213)*

Providien Machining & Metals LLC ....D 818 367-3161
  12840 Bradley Ave Sylmar (91342) *(P-8219)*

Providien Machining Mtls Corp, Sylmar *Also Called: Providien Machining & Metals LLC (P-8219)*

Providien Thermoforming LLC ....E 858 850-1591
  6740 Nancy Ridge Dr San Diego (92121) *(P-3956)*

A
L
P
H
A
B
E
T
I
C

Employee Codes: A=Over 500 employees, B=251-500
C=101-250, D=51-100, E=20-50, F=10-19, G=1-9

2025 Southern California
Business Directory and Buyers Guide

© Mergent Inc. 1-800-342-5647
1153

Providien Thermoforming, Inc., San Diego *Also Called: Providien Thermoforming LLC* *(P-3956)*

Providnce Facey Med Foundation (PA) .... C 818 365-9531
15451 San Fernando Mission Blvd Mission Hills (91345) *(P-15426)*

Providnce Facey Med Foundation .... D 661 513-2100
27924 Seco Canyon Rd Santa Clarita (91350) *(P-15427)*

Providnce Facey Med Foundation .... C 818 365-9531
11165 Sepulveda Blvd Mission Hills (91345) *(P-15428)*

Providnce Facey Med Foundation .... D 805 206-2000
2655 1st St Simi Valley (93065) *(P-15531)*

Providnce Facey Med Foundation .... D 818 861-7831
191 S Buena Vista St Burbank (91505) *(P-15532)*

Providnce Facey Med Foundation .... C 818 837-5677
11211 Sepulveda Blvd Mission Hills (91345) *(P-16604)*

Providnce Facey Med Foundation .... D 626 576-0800
1237 E Main St San Gabriel (91776) *(P-16605)*

Providnce Hlth Svcs Fndtn/San .... A 818 843-5111
501 S Buena Vista St Burbank (91505) *(P-16155)*

Providnce Holy Cross Fundation, Burbank *Also Called: Providnce Hlth Svcs Fndtn/San* *(P-16155)*

Provisio Medical Inc .... E 508 740-9940
10815 Rancho Bernardo Rd Ste 110 San Diego (92127) *(P-16606)*

Provivi Inc .... D 310 828-2307
1701 Colorado Ave Santa Monica (90404) *(P-3735)*

Prowall Lath and Plaster .... D 760 480-9001
360 S Spruce St Escondido (92025) *(P-1024)*

Prp Seats, Temecula *Also Called: Kamm Industries Inc (P-2263)*

Prpco .... E 805 543-6844
2226 Beebee St San Luis Obispo (93401) *(P-3072)*

Prs Industries, Ontario *Also Called: Inland Powder Coating Corp (P-5323)*

Prsi, Jurupa Valley *Also Called: Pavement Recycling Systems Inc (P-10540)*

Prudential, Thousand Oaks *Also Called: Gemmm Corporation (P-12456)*

Prudential, Irvine *Also Called: Brer Affiliates LLC (P-12677)*

Prudential Cleanroom Services, Irvine *Also Called: Prudential Overall Supply (P-13140)*

Prudential Dust Control, Riverside *Also Called: Prudential Overall Supply (P-13139)*

Prudential Lighting Corp (PA) .... C 213 477-1694
1774 E 21st St Los Angeles (90058) *(P-6471)*

Prudential Overall Supply .... D 951 687-0440
6997 Jurupa Ave Riverside (92504) *(P-13139)*

Prudential Overall Supply (PA) .... D 949 250-4855
1661 Alton Pkwy Irvine (92606) *(P-13140)*

Prutel Joint Venture .... A 949 240-5064
1 Ritz Carlton Dr Dana Point (92629) *(P-12978)*

Pryor Products .... E 760 724-8244
1819 Peacock Blvd Oceanside (92056) *(P-8220)*

PS, Los Angeles *Also Called: Private Suite Lax LLC (P-8794)*

Psav Holdings LLC (PA) .... C 562 366-0138
111 W Ocean Blvd Ste 1110 Long Beach (90802) *(P-13468)*

Psb .... D 949 465-0772
26012 Atlantic Ocean Dr Lake Forest (92630) *(P-13238)*

PSC Environmental Services LLC .... D 323 266-6448
1601 Perrino Pl Ste D Los Angeles (90023) *(P-14578)*

PSC Industrial Outsourcing LP .... D 661 833-9991
200 Old Yard Dr Bakersfield (93307) *(P-361)*

Pscmb Repairs Inc .... E 626 448-7778
12145 Slauson Ave Santa Fe Springs (90670) *(P-6208)*

Pse Holding LLC (DH) .... B 248 377-0165
360 N Crescent Dr Beverly Hills (90210) *(P-15035)*

Psemi Corporation (DH) .... D 858 731-9400
9369 Carroll Park Dr San Diego (92121) *(P-6871)*

Psg, San Diego *Also Called: Pacific Steel Group LLC (P-5100)*

Psg California LLC (HQ) .... B 909 422-1700
22069 Van Buren St Grand Terrace (92313) *(P-5741)*

PSG Fencing Corporation .... D 951 275-9252
330 Main St Riverside (92501) *(P-1223)*

Psg Global Solutions LLC (HQ) .... A 310 405-0340
4551 Glencoe Ave Ste 150 Marina Del Rey (90292) *(P-13559)*

PSI, Glendale *Also Called: PSI Services LLC (P-18351)*

PSI Services LLC (PA) .... D 818 847-6180
611 N Brand Blvd Ste 10 Glendale (91203) *(P-18351)*

PSM Industries Inc (PA) .... D 888 663-8256
14000 Avalon Blvd Los Angeles (90061) *(P-5453)*

Psomas (PA) .... C 213 223-1400
865 S Figueroa St Ste 3200 Los Angeles (90017) *(P-17698)*

Psomas .... C 714 751-7373
5 Hutton Centre Dr Ste 300 Santa Ana (92707) *(P-17699)*

Psychic Eye Book Shops Inc (PA) .... D 818 906-8263
13435 Ventura Blvd Sherman Oaks (91423) *(P-11634)*

Psyonix LLC .... D 619 622-8772
401 W A St Ste 2400 San Diego (92101) *(P-13801)*

Pszyjw, Los Angeles *Also Called: Pachulski Stang Zehl Jones LLP (P-16755)*

Pt Gaming LLC .... A 323 260-5060
235 Oregon St El Segundo (90245) *(P-12979)*

Pt Harmony, San Luis Obispo *Also Called: Movement For Life Inc (P-18015)*

Ptb, Azusa *Also Called: Ptb Sales Inc (P-7040)*

Ptb Sales Inc (PA) .... E 626 334-0500
1361 Mountain View Cir Azusa (91702) *(P-7040)*

PTi Sand & Gravel Inc .... E 951 272-0140
14925 River Rd Eastvale (92880) *(P-376)*

Pti Technologies Inc (DH) .... C 805 604-3700
501 Del Norte Blvd Oxnard (93030) *(P-7543)*

Ptm & W Industries Inc .... E 562 946-4511
10640 Painter Ave Santa Fe Springs (90670) *(P-3969)*

Ptm Images, West Hollywood *Also Called: Pro Tour Memorabilia LLC (P-2415)*

Pts, Tustin *Also Called: Pts Advance (P-13560)*

Pts Advance .... C 949 268-4000
1775 Flight Way Ste 100 Tustin (92782) *(P-13560)*

Ptsi Managed Services Inc .... D 626 440-3118
100 W Walnut St Pasadena (91124) *(P-17615)*

Public Communications Svcs Inc .... C 310 231-1000
11859 Wilshire Blvd Ste 600 Los Angeles (90025) *(P-9455)*

Public Counsel .... D 213 385-2977
610 S Ardmore Ave Los Angeles (90005) *(P-16766)*

Public Defender Administration, Los Angeles *Also Called: County of Los Angeles (P-16660)*

Public Defender- Main Office, Riverside *Also Called: County of Riverside (P-16662)*

Public Fclties Resources Dept, Santa Ana *Also Called: County of Orange (P-18387)*

Public Health Department, El Centro *Also Called: County of Imperial (P-16551)*

Public Hlth Fndation Entps Inc .... C 562 801-2323
8666 Whittier Blvd Pico Rivera (90660) *(P-16607)*

Public Hlth Fndation Entps Inc .... C 323 733-9381
1649 W Washington Blvd Los Angeles (90007) *(P-16608)*

Public Hlth Fndation Entps Inc .... C 310 518-2835
125 E Anaheim St Wilmington (90744) *(P-16609)*

Public Hlth Fndation Entps Inc .... C 626 856-6618
12781 Shama Rd El Monte (91732) *(P-16610)*

Public Hlth Fndation Entps Inc .... C 626 856-6600
13181 Crossroads Pkwy N City Of Industry (91746) *(P-16999)*

Public Hlth Fndation Entps Inc (PA) .... C 800 201-7320
13300 Crossroads Pkwy N Ste 450 City Of Industry (91746) *(P-17360)*

Public Hlth Fndation Entps Inc .... C 323 263-0262
277 S Atlantic Blvd Los Angeles (90022) *(P-17361)*

Public Hlth Fndation Entps Inc .... C 310 320-5215
1640 W Carson St Ste G Torrance (90501) *(P-17362)*

Public Mdia Group Southern Cal (PA) .... D 714 241-4100
2900 W Alameda Ave Unit 600 Burbank (91505) *(P-9514)*

Public Service Yard, Glendale *Also Called: City of Glendale (P-9684)*

Public Services, Coronado *Also Called: City of Coronado (P-9670)*

Public Social Services, Moreno Valley *Also Called: County of Riverside (P-15295)*

Public Storage (PA) .... B 818 244-8080
701 Western Ave Glendale (91201) *(P-12693)*

Public Storage Operating Co (DH) .... B 818 244-8080
701 Western Ave Glendale (91201) *(P-12694)*

Public Utilites Emts, San Diego *Also Called: City of San Diego (P-7949)*

Public Works, San Diego *Also Called: County of San Diego (P-14482)*

Public Works Equipment, Burbank *Also Called: City of Burbank (P-14689)*

Public Works, Dept of, La Puente *Also Called: County of Los Angeles (P-5490)*

Public Works, Dept of, Malibu *Also Called: County of Los Angeles (P-5491)*

Public Works, Dept of, Los Angeles *Also Called: County of Los Angeles (P-9056)*

Publishers Development Corp .... E 858 605-0200
225 W Valley Pkwy Ste 100 Escondido (92025) *(P-2872)*

Puente Hills Chevrolet, City Of Industry *Also Called: Leo Hoffman Chevrolet Inc (P-11373)*

Puff Candy,, San Diego *Also Called: Puff Global Inc (P-14579)*

Puff Global Inc .... D 619 520-3499
402 W Broadway Ste 400 San Diego (92101) *(P-14579)*

Pull-N-Pac, Huntington Park *Also Called: Crown Poly Inc (P-2730)*

Pulltarps Manufacturing, El Cajon *Also Called: Roll-Rite LLC (P-2241)*

Pulltarps Manufacturing, El Cajon *Also Called: Transportation Equipment Inc (P-2244)*

Pulp Studio Incorporated .... D 310 815-4999
2100 W 139th St Gardena (90249) *(P-13334)*

Pulse A Yageo Company, San Diego *Also Called: Pulse Electronics Corporation (P-7041)*

Pulse Electronics Inc (HQ)............................... B 858 674-8100
15255 Innovation Dr Ste 100 San Diego (92128) *(P-6296)*

Pulse Electronics Corporation (HQ)................ E 858 674-8100
15255 Innovation Dr Ste 100 San Diego (92128) *(P-7041)*

Pulse Instruments .... E 310 515-5330
22301 S Western Ave Ste 107 Torrance (90501) *(P-7930)*

Pulse Instruments, Camarillo *Also Called: Primordial Diagnostics Inc (P-7872)*

Puma Biotechnology, Los Angeles *Also Called: Puma Biotechnology Inc (P-3484)*

Puma Biotechnology Inc (PA)........................... C 424 248-6500
10880 Wilshire Blvd Ste 2150 Los Angeles (90024) *(P-3484)*

Punch Press Products Inc .... D 323 581-7151
2035 E 51st St Vernon (90058) *(P-5594)*

Punch Studio LLC (PA)...................................... C 310 390-9900
6025 W Slauson Ave Culver City (90230) *(P-10584)*

Pupil Transportation, Whittier *Also Called: County of Los Angeles (P-8867)*

Pura Naturals Inc .... E 949 273-8100
3401 Space Center Ct Ste 811a Jurupa Valley (91752) *(P-2489)*

Pure Flo Water, Escondido *Also Called: Pure-Flo Water Co (P-1638)*

Pure Project LLC .... D 760 552-7873
1305 Hot Springs Way Vista (92081) *(P-1552)*

Pure Simple Foods LLC .... E 805 272-8448
420 Bryant Cir Ste B Ojai (93023) *(P-497)*

Pure-Flo Water Co (PA)..................................... D 619 596-4130
2169 Orange Ave Escondido (92029) *(P-1638)*

Pureformance Cables, Torrance *Also Called: Lynn Products Inc (P-5932)*

Puregear, Irwindale *Also Called: Superior Communications Inc (P-10285)*

Puretek Corporation (PA)................................... E 818 361-3316
1145 Arroyo St Ste D San Fernando (91340) *(P-3485)*

Puretek Corporation .... C 818 361-3949
7900 Nelson Rd Unit A Panorama City (91402) *(P-3486)*

Puritan Bakery Inc .... C 310 830-5451
1624 E Carson St Carson (90745) *(P-11301)*

Pusan Pipe America Inc .... B 949 655-8000
2100 Main St Ste 100 Irvine (92614) *(P-10150)*

Pvd Coatings, Huntington Beach *Also Called: California Faucets Inc (P-4803)*

Pvhmc, Pomona *Also Called: Pomona Valley Hospital Med Ctr (P-16137)*

Pvm, San Diego *Also Called: Pat V Mack Inc (P-14102)*

Pvp Advanced Eo Systems Inc (DH)............... E 714 508-2740
14312 Franklin Ave Ste 100 Tustin (92780) *(P-8016)*

Pw Eagle Inc .... A 800 621-4404
5200 W Century Blvd Los Angeles (90045) *(P-3978)*

PW Gillibrand Co Inc (PA)................................. E 805 526-2195
4537 Ish Dr Simi Valley (93063) *(P-379)*

PWC STRategy& (us) LLC .... C 213 356-6000
601 S Figueroa St Ste 900 Los Angeles (90017) *(P-18197)*

Pxise Energy Solutions LLC .... E 619 696-2944
1455 Frazee Rd Ste 150 San Diego (92108) *(P-7144)*

Pyr, San Diego *Also Called: Pyr Preservation Services (P-7608)*

Pyr Preservation Services .... E 619 338-8395
2393 Newton Ave Ste B San Diego (92113) *(P-7608)*

Pyramid Flowers Inc .... C 805 382-8070
3813 Doris Ave Oxnard (93030) *(P-11099)*

Pyramid Mold & Tool .... D 909 476-2555
10155 Sharon Cir Rancho Cucamonga (91730) *(P-5595)*

Pyramid Peak Corporation .... D 949 769-8600
1401 Avocado Ave Ste 709 Newport Beach (92660) *(P-12730)*

Pyro, Irvine *Also Called: Pyro-Comm Systems Inc (P-955)*

Pyro-Comm Systems Inc (PA)........................... C 714 902-8000
15215 Alton Pkwy Irvine (92618) *(P-955)*

Q & B Foods Inc (DH)... D 626 334-8090
15547 1st St Irwindale (91706) *(P-1372)*

Q C M Inc .... E 714 414-1173
285 Gemini Ave Brea (92821) *(P-6379)*

Q Com Inc .... E 949 833-1000
17782 Cowan Irvine (92614) *(P-6356)*

Q Microwave Inc .... D 619 258-7322
1591 Pioneer Way El Cajon (92020) *(P-7042)*

Q Squared Solutions LLC .... D 919 405-2248
28454 Livingston Ave Valencia (91355) *(P-16330)*

Q Squared Solutions LLC .... D 661 964-6635
27027 Tourney Rd Ste2e Valencia (91355) *(P-18198)*

Q Team .... E 714 228-4465
6400 Dale St Buena Park (90621) *(P-3073)*

Q Tech Corporation (PA).................................... C 310 836-7900
6161 Chip Ave Cypress (90630) *(P-10280)*

Q-See, Anaheim *Also Called: Digital Periph Solutions Inc (P-6533)*

Q2 Solutions, Valencia *Also Called: Q Squared Solutions LLC (P-18198)*

Qad, Santa Barbara *Also Called: Qad Inc (P-14010)*

Qad Inc (HQ)... C 805 566-6000
101 Innovation Pl Santa Barbara (93108) *(P-14010)*

Qantas Vctons Nwmans Vacations, Los Angeles *Also Called: Helloworld Travel Svcs USA Inc (P-9223)*

Qc Manufacturing Inc .... D 951 325-6340
26040 Ynez Rd Temecula (92591) *(P-5775)*

Qc Poultry, Montebello *Also Called: Ingenue Inc (P-1279)*

Qdoba Mexican Grill, San Diego *Also Called: Qdoba Restaurant Corporation (P-11597)*

Qdoba Restaurant Corporation (HQ)............... C 858 766-4900
350 Camino De La Reina Fl 4 San Diego (92108) *(P-11597)*

Qdos Inc .... E 949 362-8888
200 Spectrum Center Dr Ste 300 Irvine (92618) *(P-14011)*

QED Software LLC .... E 310 214-3118
211 E Ocean Blvd Long Beach (90802) *(P-14012)*

Qf Liquidation Inc (PA)...................................... C 949 930-3400
25242 Arctic Ocean Dr Lake Forest (92630) *(P-7286)*

Qfi Prv Aerospace, Torrance *Also Called: Quality Forming LLC (P-7544)*

Qg Printing Corp .... D 951 571-2500
6688 Box Springs Blvd Riverside (92507) *(P-2873)*

Qg Printing IL LLC .... C 951 571-2500
6688 Box Springs Blvd Riverside (92507) *(P-3074)*

Qlogic LLC (DH).. C 949 389-6000
15485 Sand Canyon Ave Irvine (92618) *(P-6872)*

Qmp Inc .... E 661 294-6860
25070 Avenue Tibbitts Valencia (91355) *(P-6029)*

Qnap Inc .... D 909 598-6933
168 University Pkwy Pomona (91768) *(P-17819)*

Qology Direct LLC .... C 310 341-4420
12130 Millennium Ste 600 Los Angeles (90094) *(P-14580)*

Qorvo California Inc .... E 805 480-5050
950 Lawrence Dr Newbury Park (91320) *(P-7043)*

Qorvo US, Newbury Park *Also Called: Qorvo California Inc (P-7043)*

Qpc Fiber Optic LLC .... E 949 361-8855
27612 El Lazo Laguna Niguel (92677) *(P-4638)*

Qpc Laser, Rancho Cascades *Also Called: Laser Operations LLC (P-6844)*

Qre Operating LLC .... C 213 225-5900
707 Wilshire Blvd Ste 4600 Los Angeles (90017) *(P-311)*

Qsc LLC (PA)... C 800 854-4079
1675 Macarthur Blvd Costa Mesa (92626) *(P-6549)*

Qsc Audio, Costa Mesa *Also Called: Qsc LLC (P-6549)*

Qspac Industries Inc (PA).................................. D 562 407-3868
15020 Marquardt Ave Santa Fe Springs (90670) *(P-3777)*

Qtc .... C 909 978-3531
924 Overland Ct San Dimas (91773) *(P-18042)*

Qtc Management Inc (DH)................................. D 800 682-9701
924 Overland Ct San Dimas (91773) *(P-16611)*

Qtc Mdcal Group Inc A Med Corp .... A 800 260-1515
924 Overland Ct San Dimas (91773) *(P-16612)*

Qtc Medical Group, San Dimas *Also Called: Qtc Mdcal Group Inc A Med Corp (P-16612)*

Quad Graphics, Riverside *Also Called: Qg Printing IL LLC (P-3074)*

Quad R Tech, Harbor City *Also Called: Onyx Industries Inc (P-5109)*

Employee Codes: A=Over 500 employees, B=251-500
C=101-250, D=51-100, E=20-50, F=10-19, G=1-9

2025 Southern California
Business Directory and Buyers Guide

© Mergent Inc. 1-800-342-5647

1155

Quad-C Jh Holdings Inc .... C 800 966-6662
4593 Ish Dr Ste 320 Simi Valley (93063) *(P-10105)*

Quad-C Jh Holdings Inc .... C 502 741-0421
1055 E Discovery Ln Anaheim (92801) *(P-10106)*

Quad/Graphics Inc .... D 951 689-1122
6688 Box Springs Blvd Riverside (92507) *(P-3075)*

QUAD/GRAPHICS INC., Riverside *Also Called: Quad/Graphics Inc (P-3075)*

Quadrotech Solutions Inc (PA) .... E 949 754-8000
20 Enterprise Aliso Viejo (92656) *(P-14013)*

Quake City Caps, Los Angeles *Also Called: Quake City Casuals Inc (P-10693)*

Quake City Casuals Inc .... C 213 746-0540
1800 S Flower St Los Angeles (90015) *(P-10693)*

Quaker, Whittier *Also Called: AC Products Inc (P-3757)*

Quaker City Plating .... C 562 945-3721
11729 Washington Blvd Whittier (90606) *(P-5286)*

Quaker City Plating & Silvrsm, Whittier *Also Called: Quaker City Plating (P-5286)*

QUAKER GARDENS, Stanton *Also Called: California Friends Homes (P-17125)*

Qualcomm, San Diego *Also Called: Qualcomm Incorporated (P-6647)*

Qualcomm, San Diego *Also Called: Qualcomm Incorporated (P-6648)*

Qualcomm, San Diego *Also Called: Qualcomm Incorporated (P-6649)*

Qualcomm, Carlsbad *Also Called: Qualcomm Incorporated (P-6874)*

Qualcomm, San Diego *Also Called: Qualcomm Incorporated (P-6875)*

Qualcomm, San Diego *Also Called: Qualcomm Incorporated (P-6876)*

Qualcomm, San Diego *Also Called: Qualcomm Incorporated (P-6877)*

Qualcomm, San Diego *Also Called: Qualcomm Incorporated (P-6878)*

Qualcomm, San Diego *Also Called: Qualcomm International Inc (P-12678)*

Qualcomm Datacenter Tech Inc (HQ) .... **E 858 567-1121**
5775 Morehouse Dr San Diego (92121) *(P-6873)*

Qualcomm Incorporated (PA) .... **A 858 587-1121**
5775 Morehouse Dr San Diego (92121) *(P-6647)*

Qualcomm Incorporated .... B 858 587-1121
4243 Campus Point Ct San Diego (92121) *(P-6648)*

Qualcomm Incorporated .... E 202 263-0008
5775 Morehouse Dr San Diego (92121) *(P-6649)*

Qualcomm Incorporated .... E 858 651-8481
2016 Palomar Airport Rd Ste 100 Carlsbad (92011) *(P-6874)*

Qualcomm Incorporated .... E 858 909-0316
5751 Pacific Center Blvd San Diego (92121) *(P-6875)*

Qualcomm Incorporated .... D 858 587-1121
10555 Sorrento Valley Rd San Diego (92121) *(P-6876)*

Qualcomm Incorporated .... D 858 587-1121
5525 Morehouse Dr San Diego (92121) *(P-6877)*

Qualcomm Incorporated .... C 858 587-1121
9393 Waples St Ste 150 San Diego (92121) *(P-6878)*

Qualcomm International Inc (HQ) .... **A 858 587-1121**
5775 Morehouse Dr San Diego (92121) *(P-12678)*

Qualcomm Mems Technologies Inc .... E 858 587-1121
5775 Morehouse Dr San Diego (92121) *(P-6690)*

Qualcomm Technologies Inc (HQ) .... **C 858 587-1121**
5775 Morehouse Dr San Diego (92121) *(P-6879)*

Qualcomm Technologies Inc .... E 858 587-1121
5745 Pacific Center Blvd San Diego (92121) *(P-6880)*

Qualcomm Technologies Inc .... E 858 658-3040
10350 Sorrento Valley Rd San Diego (92121) *(P-6881)*

Qualer Inc .... E 858 224-9516
9477 Waples St San Diego (92121) *(P-14014)*

Qualicon Diagnostics LLC .... B 805 388-2383
941 Avenida Acaso Camarillo (93012) *(P-17924)*

Qualis Automotive LLC .... D 859 689-7772
21046 Figueroa St Carson (90745) *(P-14697)*

Qualitas Insurance Company .... D 619 876-4355
4545 Murphy Canyon Rd Fl 3 San Diego (92123) *(P-12248)*

Qualitas Premier Insur Svcs, San Diego *Also Called: Qualitas Insurance Company (P-12248)*

Quality Aluminum Forge LLC .... C 714 639-8191
794 N Cypress St Orange (92867) *(P-5158)*

Quality Aluminum Forge LLC (HQ) .... **E 714 639-8191**
793 N Cypress St Orange (92867) *(P-5159)*

Quality Aluminum Forge Div, Orange *Also Called: Gel Industries Inc (P-5155)*

Quality Cabinet and Fixture Co (HQ) .... **E 619 266-1011**
7955 Saint Andrews Ave San Diego (92154) *(P-2358)*

Quality Controlled Mfg Inc .... D 619 443-3997
9429 Abraham Way Santee (92071) *(P-6209)*

Quality Distributor, El Cajon *Also Called: Benny Enterprises Inc (P-11042)*

Quality Fabrication Inc (PA) .... **D 818 407-5015**
4020 Garner Rd Riverside (92501) *(P-5025)*

Quality First Woodworks Inc .... C 714 632-0480
1264 N Lakeview Ave Anaheim (92807) *(P-2416)*

Quality Foam Packaging, Lake Elsinore *Also Called: Aerofoam Industries Inc (P-2535)*

Quality Foam Packaging Inc .... E 951 245-4429
31855 Corydon St Lake Elsinore (92530) *(P-4014)*

Quality Forming LLC .... D 310 539-2855
22906 Frampton Ave Torrance (90501) *(P-7544)*

Quality Heat Treating Inc .... E 818 840-8212
3305 Burton Ave Burbank (91504) *(P-4712)*

Quality Industry Repair, Santa Fe Springs *Also Called: Pscmb Repairs Inc (P-6208)*

Quality Loan Service Corp .... B 619 645-7711
2763 Camino Del Rio S San Diego (92108) *(P-12673)*

Quality Naturally Foods Inc .... E 626 854-6363
17769 Railroad St City Of Industry (91748) *(P-10971)*

Quality Naturally Foods Inc (PA) .... **E 626 854-6363**
18830 San Jose Ave City Of Industry (91748) *(P-10972)*

QUALITY NATURALLYU FOODS, INC., City Of Industry *Also Called: Quality Naturally Foods Inc (P-10971)*

Quality Production Svcs Inc .... D 310 406-3350
18711 S Broadwick St Compton (90220) *(P-1025)*

Quality Reinforcing Inc .... D 858 748-8400
13275 Gregg St Poway (92064) *(P-1160)*

Quality Service Pac Industry, Santa Fe Springs *Also Called: Qspac Industries Inc (P-3777)*

Quality Shutters Inc .... E 951 683-4939
3359 Chicago Ave Ste A Riverside (92507) *(P-2325)*

Quality Systems, San Diego *Also Called: Quality Systems Intgrated Corp (P-6766)*

Quality Systems Intgrated Corp .... C 858 536-3128
7098 Miratech Dr Ste 170 San Diego (92121) *(P-6765)*

Quality Systems Intgrated Corp (PA) .... **C 858 587-9797**
6740 Top Gun St San Diego (92121) *(P-6766)*

Quality Tech Mfg Inc .... E 909 465-9565
170 W Mindanao St Bloomington (92316) *(P-7368)*

Quality Temp Staffing, Granada Hills *Also Called: Siracusa Enterprises Inc (P-13572)*

Qualitylogic Inc .... C 208 424-1905
2245 1st St Ste 103 Simi Valley (93065) *(P-5947)*

Quallion LLC .... C 818 833-2000
12744 San Fernando Rd Ste 100 Sylmar (91342) *(P-7085)*

Qualls Stud Welding Pdts Inc .... E 562 923-7883
9459 Washburn Rd Downey (90242) *(P-10396)*

Qualstaff Resources, San Diego *Also Called: June Group LLC (P-13602)*

Qualy Pak Specialty Foods Inc .... D 310 541-3023
2208 Signal Pl San Pedro (90731) *(P-10859)*

Quantimetrix .... D 310 536-0006
2005 Manhattan Beach Blvd Redondo Beach (90278) *(P-3548)*

Quantos Payroll, Los Angeles *Also Called: Film Payroll Services Inc (P-17728)*

Quantum Automation (PA) .... **E 714 854-0800**
4400 E La Palma Ave Anaheim (92807) *(P-10204)*

Quantum Bhvioral Solutions Inc (PA) .... **D 626 531-6999**
445 S Figueroa St Ste 3100 Los Angeles (90071) *(P-15553)*

Quantum Bhvioral Solutions Inc .... D 626 531-6999
2400 E Katella Ave Ste 800 Anaheim (92806) *(P-15554)*

Quantum Corporation .... E 949 856-7800
141 Innovation Dr Ste 100 Irvine (92617) *(P-5884)*

Quantum Corporation, Irvine *Also Called: Certance LLC (P-5876)*

Quantum Design Inc (PA) .... **C 858 481-4400**
10307 Pacific Center Ct San Diego (92121) *(P-7973)*

Quantum Design International, San Diego *Also Called: Quantum Design Inc (P-7973)*

Quantum Magnetics LLC .... A 714 258-4400
1251 E Dyer Rd Ste 140 Santa Ana (92705) *(P-7974)*

Quantum Networks LLC .... E 212 993-5899
3412 Garfield Ave Commerce (90040) *(P-11660)*

Quantum Technologies, Lake Forest *Also Called: Qf Liquidation Inc (P-7286)*

Quantum World Technologies Inc .... B 805 834-0532
4281 Katella Ave Ste 102 Los Alamitos (90720) *(P-13561)*

Quarry At La Quinta Inc .... D 760 777-1100
1 Quarry Ln La Quinta (92253) *(P-15095)*

Quartic Solutions LLC .... E 858 377-8470
1427 Chalcedony St San Diego (92109) *(P-10025)*

Quartics Inc .... E 949 679-2672
15241 Laguna Canyon Rd Ste 200 Irvine (92618) *(P-6882)*

Quartus Engineering Inc (PA) .... D 858 875-6000
9689 Towne Centre Dr San Diego (92121) *(P-17616)*

Quatro Composites, Poway *Also Called: Quatro Composites LLC (P-7545)*

Quatro Composites LLC .... C 712 707-9200
13250 Gregg St Ste A1 Poway (92064) *(P-7545)*

Quechan Gaming Commission, Winterhaven *Also Called: Quechan Indian Tribe (P-15216)*

Quechan Indian Tribe .... C 760 572-2413
450 Quechan Rd Winterhaven (92283) *(P-15216)*

Queen Beach Printers Inc .... E 562 436-8201
937 Pine Ave Long Beach (90813) *(P-3076)*

Queen Mary Hotel, Long Beach *Also Called: RMS Foundation Inc (P-12999)*

Queen Mary, The, Long Beach *Also Called: Evolution Hospitality LLC (P-12824)*

Queen Mary, The, Long Beach *Also Called: Urban Commons Queensway LLC (P-13060)*

Queen of The Valley Campus, West Covina *Also Called: Emanate Health (P-15990)*

Queen of The Valley Hospital, West Covina *Also Called: Emanate Health Medical Center (P-15995)*

Queensbay Hotel LLC .... D 562 481-3910
700 Queensway Dr Long Beach (90802) *(P-12980)*

Queenscare Fmly Clnics - Estsi, Los Angeles *Also Called: Gracelight Community Health (P-15316)*

Quest, Aliso Viejo *Also Called: Quadrotech Solutions Inc (P-14013)*

Quest Dgnstics Nchls Inst Vln, Valencia *Also Called: Specialty Laboratories Inc (P-16335)*

Quest Diagnostics, San Juan Capistrano *Also Called: Quest Diagnostics Nichols Inst (P-16331)*

Quest Diagnostics, West Hills *Also Called: Unilab Corporation (P-16337)*

Quest Diagnostics Nichols Inst (HQ) .... A 949 728-4000
33608 Ortega Hwy San Juan Capistrano (92675) *(P-16331)*

Quest International, Irvine *Also Called: Quest Intl Monitor Svc Inc (P-14189)*

Quest Intl Monitor Svc Inc (PA) .... D 949 581-9900
60 Parker 65 Irvine (92618) *(P-14189)*

Quest Software Inc .... D 949 754-8000
20 Enterprise Aliso Viejo (92656) *(P-14015)*

Quest Software Inc (PA) .... A 949 754-8000
20 Enterprise Ste 100 Aliso Viejo (92656) *(P-14103)*

Quest Solution, Garden Grove *Also Called: Bar Code Specialties Inc (P-5904)*

Quick Box LLC .... C 310 436-6444
13838 S Figueroa St Los Angeles (90061) *(P-9102)*

Quick Crete Products Corp .... C 951 737-6240
731 Parkridge Ave Norco (92860) *(P-4416)*

Quick Lane, San Diego *Also Called: Mossy Ford Inc (P-11382)*

Quick Lane, Riverside *Also Called: Raceway Ford Inc (P-11399)*

Quick Lane, Hawthorne *Also Called: South Bay Ford Inc (P-11408)*

Quick Lane, Fontana *Also Called: Sunrise Ford (P-11415)*

Quickrete, Corona *Also Called: Quikrete California LLC (P-4417)*

Quidel Cardiovascular Inc .... D 858 552-1100
9975 Summers Ridge Rd San Diego (92121) *(P-14581)*

Quidel Corporation .... E 858 552-1100
10165 Mckellar Ct San Diego (92121) *(P-3549)*

Quidel Corporation (HQ) .... D 858 552-1100
9075 Summers Ridge Rd San Diego (92121) *(P-3550)*

Quidelortho Corporation (PA) .... E 858 552-1100
9975 Summers Ridge Rd San Diego (92121) *(P-3551)*

Quiel Bros Elc Sign Svc Co Inc .... E 909 885-4476
272 S I St San Bernardino (92410) *(P-8625)*

Quigley-Simpson & Hepplewhite, Los Angeles *Also Called: Quigly-Simpson Heppelwhite Inc (P-13239)*

Quigly-Simpson Heppelwhite Inc .... C 310 996-5800
11601 Wilshire Blvd Ste 710 Los Angeles (90025) *(P-13239)*

Quik Pick Express LLC .... C 310 763-3000
23610 Banning Blvd Carson (90745) *(P-9329)*

Quikrete California LLC (DH) .... E 951 277-3155
3940 Temescal Canyon Rd Corona (92883) *(P-4417)*

Quikrete Companies LLC .... E 323 875-1367
11145 Tuxford St Sun Valley (91352) *(P-4418)*

Quill Distribution Center, Ontario *Also Called: Quill LLC (P-9103)*

Quill LLC .... B 909 390-0600
1500 S Dupont Ave Ontario (91761) *(P-9103)*

Quilt In A Day Inc .... E 760 591-0929
1955 Diamond St San Marcos (92078) *(P-11661)*

Quinn Company .... D 805 925-8611
1655 Carlotti Dr Santa Maria (93454) *(P-10355)*

Quinn Company .... D 805 485-2171
801 Del Norte Blvd Oxnard (93030) *(P-10356)*

Quinn Company .... D 661 393-5800
2200 Pegasus Dr Bakersfield (93308) *(P-10357)*

Quinn Emmanuel Trial Lawyers, Los Angeles *Also Called: Quinn Emnuel Urqhart Sllvan LL (P-16767)*

Quinn Emnuel Urqhart Sllvan LL (PA) .... B 213 443-3000
865 S Figueroa St Fl 10 Los Angeles (90017) *(P-16767)*

Quinn Shepherd Machinery .... B 562 463-6000
10006 Rose Hills Rd City Of Industry (90601) *(P-10358)*

Quinstar Technology Inc .... D 310 320-1111
24085 Garnier St Torrance (90505) *(P-10281)*

Quintiles Pacific Incorporated .... B 858 552-3400
10201 Wateridge Cir Ste 300 San Diego (92121) *(P-17860)*

Quoc Viet Foods (PA) .... E 714 283-3663
12221 Monarch St Garden Grove (92841) *(P-1838)*

Quorex Pharm Inc (PA) .... E 760 602-1910
2232 Rutherford Rd Carlsbad (92008) *(P-3487)*

Qwest, Burbank *Also Called: Qwest Cybersolutions LLC (P-9456)*

Qwest Cybersolutions LLC .... C 818 729-2100
3015 Winona Ave Burbank (91504) *(P-9456)*

Qxv Programming LLC .... D 213 344-2031
6565 W Sunset Blvd Los Angeles (90028) *(P-13802)*

Qxv Software LLC .... D 626 219-0522
215 N Marengo Ave Pasadena (91101) *(P-13803)*

Qycell Corporation .... E 909 390-6644
600 Etiwanda Ave Ontario (91761) *(P-3289)*

Qyk Brands LLC .... C 833 795-7664
12101 Western Ave Garden Grove (92841) *(P-10648)*

R & B Reinforcing Steel Corp .... D 909 591-1726
13581 5th St Chino (91710) *(P-1161)*

R & B Wholesale Distrs Inc (PA) .... D 909 230-5400
2350 S Milliken Ave Ontario (91761) *(P-10224)*

R & B Wire Products Inc .... E 714 549-3355
2902 W Garry Ave Santa Ana (92704) *(P-5411)*

R & D Fasteners, Rancho Cucamonga *Also Called: Doubleco Incorporated (P-5124)*

R & D Metal Fabricators Inc .... E 714 891-4878
5250 Rancho Rd Huntington Beach (92647) *(P-5026)*

R & D Partners, San Diego *Also Called: R&D Consulting Group LLC (P-13562)*

R & D Steel Inc .... E 310 631-6183
7930 E Tarma St Long Beach (90808) *(P-4862)*

R & G Precision Machining Inc .... E 760 630-8602
2585 Jason Ct Oceanside (92056) *(P-6210)*

R & I, Ontario *Also Called: R & I Industries Inc (P-4863)*

R & I Industries Inc .... E 909 923-7747
1870 3 Taylor Ave Ontario (91701) *(P-4803)*

R & R Industries, San Clemente *Also Called: Rosen & Rosen Industries Inc (P-8536)*

R & R Industries Inc .... E 800 234-5611
204 Avenida Fabricante San Clemente (92672) *(P-2200)*

R & R Mechanical Contractors Inc .... D 619 449-9900
1400 N Johnson Ave Ste 114 El Cajon (92020) *(P-825)*

R & R Rubber Molding Inc .... E 626 575-8105
2444 Loma Ave South El Monte (91733) *(P-3931)*

R & S Automation Inc .... E 800 962-3111
283 W Bonita Ave Pomona (91767) *(P-4899)*

R & S Ovrhd Doors So-Cal Inc .... E 714 680-0600
1617 N Orangethorpe Way Anaheim (92801) *(P-14786)*

R & S Processing Co Inc .... D 562 531-0738
15712 Illinois Ave Paramount (90723) *(P-3932)*

R A Phillips Industries Inc (PA) .... E 562 781-2121
12012 Burke St Santa Fe Springs (90670) *(P-7287)*

R A Reed Electric Company (PA) .... E 323 587-2284
5503 S Boyle Ave Vernon (90058) *(P-14750)*

R and L Lopez Associates Inc (PA) .... D 626 330-5296
3649 Tyler Ave El Monte (91731) *(P-17617)*

Employee Codes: A=Over 500 employees, B=251-500
C=101-250, D=51-100, E=20-50, F=10-19, G=1-9

2025 Southern California
Business Directory and Buyers Guide

© Mergent Inc. 1-800-342-5647

1157

R B III Associates Inc .... C 760 471-5370
2386 Faraday Ave Ste 125 Carlsbad (92008) *(P-2077)*

R B R Meat Company Inc .... E 323 973-4868
5151 Alcoa Ave Vernon (90058) *(P-1249)*

R C Furniture Inc .... D 626 964-4100
1111 Jellick Ave City Of Industry (91748) *(P-2457)*

R D Abbott Co Inc .... D 562 944-5354
11958 Monarch St Garden Grove (92841) *(P-11019)*

R D Mathis Company .... E 562 426-7049
2840 Gundry Ave Signal Hill (90755) *(P-4531)*

R D Rubber Technology Corp .... E 562 941-4800
12870 Florence Ave Santa Fe Springs (90670) *(P-3905)*

R E Barber-Ford .... C 805 656-4259
3440 E Main St Ventura (93003) *(P-11398)*

R G Canning Enterprises Inc .... C 323 560-7469
4515 E 59th Pl Maywood (90270) *(P-14582)*

R H D, Corona *Also Called: Ranch House Doors Inc (P-1059)*

R H Strasbaugh (PA) .... E **805 541-6424**
825 Buckley Rd San Luis Obispo (93401) *(P-5549)*

R J Lanthier Company Inc .... D 760 738-9798
485 Corporate Dr Escondido (92029) *(P-575)*

R J Reynolds Tobacco Company .... D 858 625-8453
8380 Miramar Mall Ste 117 San Diego (92121) *(P-1868)*

R K Properties, Long Beach *Also Called: Rance King Properties Inc (P-12363)*

R Kern Engineering & Mfg Corp .... D 909 664-2440
13912 Mountain Ave Chino (91710) *(P-6957)*

R L Jones-San Diego Inc (PA) .... D **760 357-3177**
1778 Zinetta Rd Ste A Calexico (92231) *(P-9330)*

R M I, Gardena *Also Called: Rotational Molding Inc (P-4227)*

R Mc Closkey Insurance Agency .... C 949 223-8100
4001 Macarthur Blvd Ste 300 Newport Beach (92660) *(P-12249)*

R N D Enterprises, Lancaster *Also Called: BDR Industries Inc (P-9524)*

R O S, San Diego *Also Called: Remote Ocean Systems Inc (P-6515)*

R P Direct, Santa Monica *Also Called: Rubin Postaer and Associates (P-13243)*

R P S Resort Corp .... A 760 327-8311
1600 N Indian Canyon Dr Palm Springs (92262) *(P-12981)*

R Planet Earth LLC .... C 213 320-0601
3200 Fruitland Ave Vernon (90058) *(P-9757)*

R R Donnelley, San Diego *Also Called: R R Donnelley & Sons Company (P-3166)*

R R Donnelley & Sons Company .... E 619 527-4600
955 Gateway Center Way San Diego (92102) *(P-3166)*

R R Donnelley & Sons Company .... D 310 516-3100
19681 Pacific Gateway Dr Torrance (90502) *(P-3167)*

R R Donnelley & Sons Company .... D 951 296-2890
40610 County Center Dr Ste 100 Temecula (92591) *(P-10585)*

R Ranch Market .... B 714 573-1182
1112 Walnut Ave Tustin (92780) *(P-97)*

R S D, Lake Forest *Also Called: Refrigeration Supplies Distributor (P-10344)*

R T A, Riverside *Also Called: Riverside Transit Agency (P-8795)*

R V Best Inc .... E 619 448-7300
9335 Stevens Rd Santee (92071) *(P-4214)*

R W Smith & Co .... D 858 530-1800
10101 Old Grove Rd San Diego (92131) *(P-10051)*

R-Cold Inc .... D 951 436-5476
1221 S G St Perris (92570) *(P-5980)*

R&C Motor Corporation .... C 909 625-1500
601 Auto Center Dr Claremont (91711) *(P-14698)*

R&D Consulting Group LLC .... C 570 277-7066
8910 University Center Ln Ste 400 San Diego (92122) *(P-13562)*

R&D Metal, Huntington Beach *Also Called: R & D Metal Fabricators Inc (P-5026)*

R&M Supply Inc .... D 951 552-9860
420 Harley Knox Blvd Perris (92571) *(P-5482)*

R1 Concepts Inc (PA) .... E **714 777-2323**
13140 Midway Pl Cerritos (90703) *(P-9840)*

RA Industries LLC .... E 714 557-2322
900 Glenneyre St Laguna Beach (92651) *(P-6211)*

RA Snyder Properties Inc (PA) .... C **619 297-0274**
2399 Camino Del Rio S Ste 200 San Diego (92108) *(P-12514)*

Raceline Wheels, Garden Grove *Also Called: Allied Wheel Components Inc (P-7223)*

Racepak LLC .... E 949 709-5555
30402 Esperanza Rcho Sta Marg (92688) *(P-7288)*

Raceway Ford Inc .... C 951 571-9300
5900 Sycamore Canyon Blvd Riverside (92507) *(P-11399)*

Rachas Inc .... D 714 290-0636
135 N Beach Blvd Anaheim (92801) *(P-15059)*

Rackmountpro.com, La Puente *Also Called: Yang-Ming International Corp (P-14119)*

RAD Diversified Reit Inc .... D 813 723-7348
3110 E Guasti Rd Ste 300 Ontario (91761) *(P-12515)*

Radcal Corporation .... E 626 357-7921
426 W Duarte Rd Monrovia (91016) *(P-8060)*

Radford Cabinets Inc .... D 661 729-8931
216 E Avenue K8 Lancaster (93535) *(P-2433)*

Radford Studio Center LLC .... B 818 655-5000
4024 Radford Ave Studio City (91604) *(P-14974)*

Radial, Rialto *Also Called: Radial South LP (P-9104)*

Radial South LP .... A 610 491-7000
2225 Alder Ave Rialto (92377) *(P-9104)*

Radian Memory Systems Inc .... E 818 222-4080
5010 N Pkwy Ste 205 Calabasas (91302) *(P-5885)*

Radiant Services Corp (PA) .... C **310 327-6300**
651 W Knox St Gardena (90248) *(P-13111)*

Radiation Onclogy - Cdrs-Snai, Los Angeles *Also Called: Cedars-Sinai Medical Center (P-15265)*

Radiology Partners Inc (HQ) .... B **424 290-8004**
2101 E El Segundo Blvd Ste 401 El Segundo (90245) *(P-15429)*

Radiology Prtners Holdings LLC (PA) .... C **424 290-8004**
2330 Utah Ave Ste 200 El Segundo (90245) *(P-15430)*

Radiology Support Devices Inc .... E 310 518-0527
1501 W 178th St Gardena (90248) *(P-8221)*

Radison Hotel Newport Beach, Newport Beach *Also Called: Pacific Hotel Management Inc (P-12959)*

Radisson Inn, Los Angeles *Also Called: Pacifica Hosts Inc (P-12962)*

Radisson Inn, Ontario *Also Called: Prime Hospitality LLC (P-12977)*

Radisson Inn, Los Angeles *Also Called: Radlax Gateway Hotel LLC (P-12982)*

Radix, Los Angeles *Also Called: Radix Textile Inc (P-10671)*

Radix Textile Inc .... D 323 234-1667
600 E Washington Blvd Ste C2 Los Angeles (90015) *(P-10671)*

Radlax Gateway Hotel LLC .... A 310 670-9000
6225 W Century Blvd Los Angeles (90045) *(P-12982)*

Radnet, Los Angeles *Also Called: Radnet Inc (P-16332)*

Radnet Inc (PA) .... B **310 478-7808**
1510 Cotner Ave Los Angeles (90025) *(P-16332)*

Radnet Management III Inc .... D 760 346-1130
72855 Fred Waring Dr Palm Desert (92260) *(P-15431)*

Radnet Management III Inc .... D 760 243-1234
12677 Hesperia Rd Ste 190 Victorville (92395) *(P-15432)*

Radnet Management III Inc .... D 323 549-3000
8750 Wilshire Blvd Ste 100 Beverly Hills (90211) *(P-15433)*

Rady Childrens Hosp & Hlth Ctr (PA) .... A **858 576-1700**
3020 Childrens Way San Diego (92123) *(P-16156)*

Rady Chld Hospital-San Diego (HQ) .... A **858 576-1700**
3020 Childrens Way San Diego (92123) *(P-16157)*

Raemica Inc .... E 909 864-1990
7759 Victoria Ave Highland (92346) *(P-1268)*

Rafco Products Brickform, Rancho Cucamonga *Also Called: Rafco-Brickform LLC (P-5623)*

Rafco-Brickform LLC (PA) .... D **909 484-3399**
11061 Jersey Blvd Rancho Cucamonga (91730) *(P-5623)*

Raffles Lrmitage Beverly Hills .... C 310 278-3344
9291 Burton Way Beverly Hills (90210) *(P-12983)*

Raging Waters, San Dimas *Also Called: Raging Waters Group Inc (P-15106)*

Raging Waters Group Inc .... A 909 802-2200
111 Raging Waters Dr San Dimas (91773) *(P-15106)*

RAH Industries Inc (PA) .... C **661 295-5190**
24800 Avenue Rockefeller Valencia (91355) *(P-5027)*

Rahn Industries, Whittier *Also Called: Rahn Industries Incorporated (P-5981)*

Rahn Industries Incorporated (PA) .... E **562 908-0680**
2630 Pacific Park Dr Whittier (90601) *(P-5981)*

Railstech Inc .... E 267 315-2998
730 Arizona Ave Santa Monica (90401) *(P-14016)*

Rain Bird, Azusa *Also Called: Rain Bird Corporation (P-5390)*

Rain Bird Corporation .... D 626 812-3400
970 W Sierra Madre Ave Azusa (91702) *(P-4806)*

Mergent email: customerrelations@mergent.com
1158

2025 Southern California
Business Directory and Buyers Guide

(P-0000) Products & Services Section entry number
(PA)=Parent Co (HQ)=Headquarters (DH)=Div Headquarters

Rain Bird Corporation (PA) .... C 626 812-3400
970 W Sierra Madre Ave Azusa (91702) *(P-5390)*

Rain Bird Corporation .... D 619 674-4068
9491 Ridgehaven Ct San Diego (92123) *(P-5476)*

Rain Bird Golf Division, Azusa *Also Called: Rain Bird Corporation (P-4806)*

Rain For Rent, Bakersfield *Also Called: Western Oilfields Supply Co (P-13478)*

Rain For Rent, Bakersfield *Also Called: Western Oilfields Supply Co (P-13479)*

Rainbo Record Mfg Corp (PA) .... E 818 280-1100
8960 Eton Ave Canoga Park (91304) *(P-6579)*

Rainbo Records & Cassettes, Canoga Park *Also Called: Rainbo Record Mfg Corp (P-6579)*

Rainbow Disposal Co Inc (HQ) .... C 714 847-3581
17121 Nichols Ln Huntington Beach (92647) *(P-9758)*

Rainbow Refuse Recycling, Huntington Beach *Also Called: Rainbow Disposal Co Inc (P-9758)*

Raise 3d Technologies Inc .... E 949 482-2040
43 Tesla Irvine (92618) *(P-5948)*

Raj Manufacturing LLC .... E 714 838-3110
2712 Dow Ave Tustin (92780) *(P-2128)*

Rajswim, Tustin *Also Called: Raj Manufacturing LLC (P-2128)*

Rakar Incorporated .... E 805 487-2721
1680 Universe Cir Oxnard (93033) *(P-4215)*

Rakworx Inc .... C 949 215-1362
1 Mason Irvine (92618) *(P-14190)*

Ralco Holdings Inc (DH) .... C 949 440-5094
13861 Rosecrans Ave Santa Fe Springs (90670) *(P-9841)*

Ralec USA Electronic Corp, Baldwin Park *Also Called: Meritek Electronics Corp (P-5710)*

Raleigh Enterprises Inc (PA) .... C 310 899-8900
5300 Melrose Ave Los Angeles (90038) *(P-12984)*

Raleigh Holdings, Los Angeles *Also Called: Raleigh Enterprises Inc (P-12984)*

Ralis, Orange *Also Called: Ralis Services Corp (P-18199)*

Ralis Services Corp .... C 844 347-2547
1 City Blvd W Ste 600 Orange (92868) *(P-18199)*

Rally Holdings LLC .... A 817 919-6833
17771 Mitchell N Irvine (92614) *(P-9842)*

Ralph Brennan Rest Group LLC .... C 714 776-5200
1590 S Disneyland Dr Anaheim (92802) *(P-18200)*

Ralph E Ames Machine Works .... E 310 328-8523
2301 Dominguez Way Torrance (90501) *(P-6212)*

Ralph Wilson Plastics, Santa Fe Springs *Also Called: Wilsonart LLC (P-9129)*

Ralphs, Compton *Also Called: Kroger Co (P-9082)*

Ram Board Inc .... E 818 848-0400
27460 Avenue Scott Unit A Valencia (91355) *(P-8654)*

Rama Corporation .... E 951 654-7351
600 W Esplanade Ave San Jacinto (92583) *(P-5803)*

Ramada By Wyndham, Irvine *Also Called: Western National Securities (P-12549)*

Ramada Inn, San Diego *Also Called: Trigild International Inc (P-13055)*

Ramada Inn, El Cajon *Also Called: W Lodging Inc (P-13068)*

RAMCAR Batteries Inc .... E 323 726-1212
2700 Carrier Ave Commerce (90040) *(P-9843)*

Ramcast Ornamental Sup Co Inc .... E 909 469-4767
1450 E Mission Blvd Pomona (91766) *(P-10151)*

Ramcast Steel, Pomona *Also Called: Ramcast Ornamental Sup Co Inc (P-10151)*

Ramco Employment Services, Oxnard *Also Called: Ramco Enterprises LP (P-117)*

Ramco Enterprises LP .... B 805 486-9328
520 E 3rd St Ste B Oxnard (93030) *(P-117)*

Ramco Enterprises LP .... B 805 922-9888
325 Plaza Dr Ste 1 Santa Maria (93454) *(P-13563)*

Ramda Metal Specialties, Gardena *Also Called: Ramda Metal Specialties Inc (P-5028)*

Ramda Metal Specialties Inc .... E 310 538-2136
13012 Crenshaw Blvd Gardena (90249) *(P-5028)*

Ramirez Pallets Inc .... E 909 822-2066
8431 Sultana Ave Fontana (92335) *(P-2391)*

Ramko Injection Inc .... D 951 929-0360
3551 Tanya Ave Hemet (92545) *(P-4216)*

Ramko Mfg Inc .... D 951 652-3510
3500 Tanya Ave Hemet (92545) *(P-6213)*

Ramona Auto Services Inc .... D 909 986-1785
2451 S Euclid Ave Ontario (91762) *(P-11454)*

Ramona Care Inc .... C 626 442-5721
11900 Ramona Blvd El Monte (91732) *(P-15758)*

Ramona Community Services Corp (HQ) .... C 951 658-9288
890 W Stetson Ave Ste A Hemet (92543) *(P-16414)*

Ramona Nrsing Rhbilitation Ctr, El Monte *Also Called: Glimmer Healthcare Inc (P-15666)*

RAMONA NURSING & REHABILITATIO, El Monte *Also Called: Ramona Care Inc (P-15758)*

Ramona Rhbltttion Post Acute CA .... C 951 652-0011
485 W Johnston Ave Hemet (92543) *(P-16158)*

Ramona Rhbltttion Post Acute Ca, Hemet *Also Called: Ramona Rhbltttion Post Acute CA (P-16158)*

Ramona Vna & Hospice, Hemet *Also Called: Ramona Community Services Corp (P-16414)*

Ramp Engineering Inc .... E 562 531-8030
6850 Walthall Way Paramount (90723) *(P-6214)*

Rampone Industries LLC .... E 714 265-0200
168 E Liberty Ave Anaheim (92801) *(P-5412)*

Ramtec Associates Inc .... E 714 996-7477
3200 E Birch St Ste B Brea (92821) *(P-4217)*

Rance King Properties Inc (PA) .... C 562 240-1000
3737 E Broadway Long Beach (90803) *(P-12363)*

Ranch House Doors Inc .... D 951 278-2884
1527 Pomona Rd Corona (92878) *(P-1059)*

Rancho, Temecula *Also Called: Rancho Ford Inc (P-11400)*

Rancho Bellagio Post Acute, Moreno Valley *Also Called: Moreno Valley Snf LLC (P-15724)*

Rancho Bernardo Inn, San Diego *Also Called: JC Resorts LLC (P-17996)*

Rancho California Water Dst (PA) .... C 951 296-6900
42135 Winchester Rd Temecula (92590) *(P-9711)*

Rancho Del Oro Ldscp Maint Inc .... D 760 726-0215
4167 Avenida De La Plata Ste 109 Oceanside (92056) *(P-188)*

Rancho Foods Inc .... D 323 585-0503
2528 E 37th St Vernon (90058) *(P-10879)*

Rancho Ford Inc .... C 951 699-1302
26895 Ynez Rd Temecula (92591) *(P-11400)*

Rancho Laguna Farms LLC .... D 805 925-7805
2410 W Main St Santa Maria (93458) *(P-84)*

Rancho Las Palmas Resort & Spa, Rancho Mirage *Also Called: Ksl Rancho Mirage Operating Co Inc (P-12888)*

Rancho Monterey Apartments, Tustin *Also Called: Irvine APT Communities LP (P-12351)*

Rancho Physical Therapy, San Marcos *Also Called: Rancho Physical Therapy Inc (P-15555)*

Rancho Physical Therapy Inc .... C 760 752-1011
277 Rancheros Dr San Marcos (92069) *(P-15555)*

Rancho Pino Verdi, Lucerne Valley *Also Called: Casa Clina Hosp Ctrs For Hlthc (P-16879)*

Rancho Research Institute .... C 562 401-8111
7601 Imperial Hwy Downey (90242) *(P-17886)*

Rancho San Antonio Boys HM Inc (PA) .... D 818 882-6400
21000 Plummer St Chatsworth (91311) *(P-17188)*

Rancho San Diego Cinema 16, El Cajon *Also Called: Edwards Theatres Circuit Inc (P-14935)*

Rancho Santa Ana Botanic Grdn .... D 909 625-8767
1500 N College Ave Claremont (91711) *(P-17271)*

Rancho Santa Fe, Rancho Santa Fe *Also Called: Pacific Western Bank (P-11739)*

Rancho Santa Fe Association .... D 858 756-1182
5827 Viadelacumere Rancho Santa Fe (92067) *(P-15160)*

Rancho Sante Fe Golf Club, Rancho Santa Fe *Also Called: Rancho Santa Fe Association (P-15160)*

Rancho Sisquoc Winery, Santa Maria *Also Called: Flood Ranch Company (P-1570)*

Rancho Springs Medical Center, Murrieta *Also Called: Southwest Healthcare Sys Aux (P-16212)*

Rancho Vista, Vista *Also Called: Rancho Vista Health Center (P-15820)*

Rancho Vista Health Center .... D 760 941-1480
200 Grapevine Rd Apt 15 Vista (92083) *(P-15820)*

Rancho VIncia Rsort Prtners LL .... B 858 756-1123
5921 Valencia Cir Rancho Santa Fe (92067) *(P-12985)*

RAND, Santa Monica *Also Called: The Rand Corporation (P-17892)*

Randall Farms, Vernon *Also Called: Sydney & Anne Bloom Farms Inc (P-10882)*

Range WD 2 LLC .... E 951 893-6233
1751 3rd St Ste 102 Norco (92860) *(P-7839)*

Rangers Die Casting Co .... E 310 764-1800
10828 Alameda St Lynwood (90262) *(P-4652)*

Ranir LLC .... E 866 373-7374
6 Centerpointe Dr Ste 640 La Palma (90623) *(P-3488)*

Rantec Microwave Systems Inc .... E 760 744-1544
2066 Wineridge Pl Escondido (92029) *(P-6650)*

Rantec Microwave Systems Inc (PA) .... D 818 223-5000
31186 La Baya Dr Westlake Village (91362) *(P-7792)*

Employee Codes: A=Over 500 employees, B=251-500
C=101-250, D=51-100, E=20-50, F=10-19, G=1-9

2025 Southern California
Business Directory and Buyers Guide

© Mergent Inc. 1-800-342-5647
1159

ALPHABETIC *(vertical tab)*

RAP Security Inc .... D 323 560-3493
4630 Cecilia St Cudahy (90201) *(P-2587)*

Raphaels Party Rentals Inc (PA) .... C 858 444-1692
8606 Miramar Rd San Diego (92126) *(P-13469)*

Rapid Manufacturing, Anaheim *Also Called: Rapid Mfg A Cal Ltd Partnr (P-5413)*

Rapid Mfg A Cal Ltd Partnr (PA) .... C 714 974-2432
8080 E Crystal Dr Anaheim (92807) *(P-5413)*

Rapid Product Solutions Inc .... E 805 485-7234
2240 Celsius Ave Ste D Oxnard (93030) *(P-6215)*

Rapid Rack Holdings Inc .... A
1370 Valley Vista Dr Ste 100 Diamond Bar (91765) *(P-2588)*

Rapid Rack Industries Inc .... D
1370 Valley Vista Dr Ste 100 Diamond Bar (91765) *(P-2589)*

Rapiscan Systems Inc (HQ) .... C 310 978-1457
2805 Columbia St Torrance (90503) *(P-8367)*

Rapp, Los Angeles *Also Called: Rapp Worldwide Inc (P-13240)*

Rapp Worldwide Inc .... C 310 563-7200
12777 W Jefferson Blvd Bldg C Los Angeles (90066) *(P-13240)*

Rasmussen Iron Works Inc .... D 562 696-8718
12028 Philadelphia St Whittier (90601) *(P-4813)*

Raspadoxpress .... D 818 892-6969
8610 Van Nuys Blvd Panorama City (91402) *(P-2939)*

Rastaclat LLC .... E 424 287-0902
100 W Broadway Ste 3000 Long Beach (90802) *(P-8460)*

Ratpac Dimmers, Van Nuys *Also Called: Data Lights Rigging LLC (P-6304)*

Raveon Technologies Corp .... E 760 444-5995
2320 Cousteau Ct Vista (92081) *(P-6651)*

Ravi Patel MD Inc .... C 661 862-7113
6501 Truxtun Ave Bakersfield (93309) *(P-15434)*

Ravine Waterpark LLC .... C 805 237-8500
2301 Airport Rd Paso Robles (93446) *(P-15107)*

Ravine Waterpark, The, Paso Robles *Also Called: Ravine Waterpark LLC (P-15107)*

Ravlich Enterprises LLC (PA) .... E 714 964-8900
100 Business Center Dr Corona (92878) *(P-5287)*

Ravlich Enterprises LLC .... E 310 533-0748
202 W 140th St Los Angeles (90061) *(P-5288)*

Rawlings Mechanical Corp (PA) .... D 323 875-2040
11615 Pendleton St Sun Valley (91352) *(P-826)*

Rax Alar Products, Poway *Also Called: Moteng Inc (P-10690)*

Ray Products Company Inc .... E 888 776-9014
1700 Chablis Ave Ontario (91761) *(P-4218)*

Rayco Electronic Mfg Inc .... E 310 329-2660
1220 W 130th St Gardena (90247) *(P-6936)*

Raymond Group (PA) .... D 714 771-7670
520 W Walnut Ave Orange (92868) *(P-18043)*

Raymond Handling Solutions Inc (DH) .... C 562 944-8067
9939 Norwalk Blvd Santa Fe Springs (90670) *(P-10397)*

Raymond West, Santa Fe Springs *Also Called: Raymond Handling Solutions Inc (P-10397)*

Rayotek Scientific, San Diego *Also Called: Rayotek Scientific LLC (P-4345)*

Rayotek Scientific LLC .... E 858 558-3671
8845 Rehco Rd San Diego (92121) *(P-4345)*

Raypak Inc (DH) .... B 805 278-5300
2151 Eastman Ave Oxnard (93030) *(P-4814)*

Raytheon, San Diego *Also Called: Raytheon Company (P-7793)*

Raytheon, El Segundo *Also Called: Raytheon Company (P-7794)*

Raytheon, El Segundo *Also Called: Raytheon Company (P-7795)*

Raytheon, El Segundo *Also Called: Raytheon Company (P-7796)*

Raytheon, Goleta *Also Called: Raytheon Company (P-7797)*

Raytheon, El Segundo *Also Called: Raytheon Company (P-7798)*

Raytheon, El Segundo *Also Called: Raytheon Secure Information Systems LLC (P-17618)*

Raytheon Applied Sgnal Tech In .... C 310 436-7000
2000 E El Segundo Blvd El Segundo (90245) *(P-6652)*

Raytheon Applied Sgnal Tech In .... C 714 917-0255
160 N Riverview Dr Ste 300 Anaheim (92808) *(P-6691)*

Raytheon Cmmand Ctrl Sltons LL (DH) .... A 714 446-3118
1801 Hughes Dr Fullerton (92833) *(P-10282)*

Raytheon Company .... C 805 967-5511
6380 Hollister Ave Goleta (93117) *(P-7145)*

Raytheon Company .... D 858 571-6598
8650 Balboa Ave San Diego (92123) *(P-7793)*

Raytheon Company .... B 310 647-1000
2000 E El Segundo Blvd El Segundo (90245) *(P-7794)*

Raytheon Company .... E 310 647-9438
2000 E El Segundo Blvd El Segundo (90245) *(P-7795)*

Raytheon Company .... A 310 647-9438
2000 E El Segundo Blvd El Segundo (90245) *(P-7796)*

Raytheon Company .... C 805 562-4611
75 Coromar Dr Goleta (93117) *(P-7797)*

Raytheon Company .... D 310 647-1000
1921 E Mariposa Ave El Segundo (90245) *(P-7798)*

Raytheon Company .... D 714 732-0119
1801 Hughes Dr Fullerton (92833) *(P-7799)*

Raytheon Dgital Force Tech LLC (DH) .... E 858 546-1244
6779 Mesa Ridge Rd Ste 150 San Diego (92121) *(P-7800)*

Raytheon Secure Information Systems LLC .... C 310 647-9438
2000 E El Segundo Blvd El Segundo (90245) *(P-17618)*

Rayzist Photomask Inc (PA) .... D 760 727-8561
955 Park Center Dr Vista (92081) *(P-8566)*

Razor, Cerritos *Also Called: Razor USA LLC (P-7634)*

Razor USA LLC (PA) .... D 562 345-6000
12723 166th St Cerritos (90703) *(P-7634)*

Rba Builders Inc .... D 714 895-9000
16490 Harbor Blvd Ste A Fountain Valley (92708) *(P-576)*

Rbc Transport Dynamics Corp .... C 203 267-7001
3131 W Segerstrom Ave Santa Ana (92704) *(P-10458)*

Rbd Hotel Palm Springs LLC .... D 760 322-9000
285 N Palm Canyon Dr Palm Springs (92262) *(P-12986)*

Rbf Lifestyle Holdings LLC .... E 626 333-5700
1441 W 2nd St Pomona (91766) *(P-2516)*

Rbz LLP .... C 310 478-4148
11766 Wilshire Blvd Fl 9 Los Angeles (90025) *(P-17753)*

Rbz Vineyards LLC .... E 805 542-0133
2324 W Highway 46 Paso Robles (93446) *(P-1582)*

RC Construction Services, Redlands *Also Called: Robert Clapper Cnstr Svcs Inc (P-579)*

RC Maintenance Holdings Inc .... C 951 903-6303
569 Bateman Cir Corona (92878) *(P-827)*

RC Wendt Painting Inc .... C 714 960-2700
21612 Surveyor Cir Huntington Beach (92646) *(P-871)*

RCP Block & Brick Inc (PA) .... D 619 460-9101
8240 Broadway Lemon Grove (91945) *(P-4372)*

RCP Block & Brick Inc .... E 619 448-2240
8755 N Magnolia Ave Santee (92071) *(P-4373)*

RCP Block & Brick Inc .... E 619 474-1516
75 N 4th Ave Chula Vista (91910) *(P-4374)*

RCP Block & Brick Inc .... E 760 753-1164
577 N Vulcan Ave Encinitas (92024) *(P-4375)*

Rcrv Inc (PA) .... E 323 235-8070
4715 S Alameda St Vernon (90058) *(P-1991)*

Rcwd, Temecula *Also Called: Rancho California Water Dst (P-9711)*

RD Olson Construction Inc .... C 949 474-2001
400 Spectrum Center Dr Ste 1200 Irvine (92618) *(P-577)*

Rdc-S111 Inc (PA) .... D 562 628-8000
245 E 3rd St Long Beach (90802) *(P-17688)*

RDM Industries .... E 714 690-0380
14310 Gannet St La Mirada (90638) *(P-10398)*

Rdmm Legacy Inc .... E 323 232-2147
724 E 60th St Los Angeles (90001) *(P-10672)*

Re/Max, Los Alamitos *Also Called: College Park Realty Inc (P-12411)*

Re/Max, Upland *Also Called: Diamond Ridge Corporation (P-12430)*

Re/Max, Santa Clarita *Also Called: RE/Max of Valencia Inc (P-12516)*

Re/Max, Northridge *Also Called: Remax Olson & Associates Inc (P-12519)*

Re/Max, Camarillo *Also Called: Rgc Services Inc (P-12522)*

Re/Max, Ventura *Also Called: Rgc Services Inc (P-12523)*

RE/Max of Valencia Inc (PA) .... C 661 255-2650
25101 The Old Rd Santa Clarita (91381) *(P-12516)*

Reachlocal, Woodland Hills *Also Called: Reachlocal Inc (P-13241)*

Reachlocal Inc (DH) .... C 818 274-0260
21700 Oxnard St Ste 1600 Woodland Hills (91367) *(P-13241)*

Reading Entertainment Inc (HQ) .... D 213 235-2226
500 Citadel Dr Ste 300 Commerce (90040) *(P-14943)*

Ready Pac Foods, Irwindale *Also Called: Ready Pac Produce Inc (P-1840)*

Ready Pac Foods Inc (HQ).................................... **A** **626 856-8686**
4401 Foxdale St Irwindale (91706) *(P-1839)*

Ready Pac Produce Inc (DH)........................ **E** **800 800-4088**
4401 Foxdale St Irwindale (91706) *(P-1840)*

Readylink Inc .... D 760 343-7000
72030 Metroplex Dr Thousand Palms (92276) *(P-13564)*

Readylink Healthcare .... D 760 343-7000
72030 Metroplex Dr Thousand Palms (92276) *(P-13565)*

Real Estate Image Inc (PA)......................... **C** **714 502-3900**
1415 S Acacia Ave Fullerton (92831) *(P-13305)*

Real Estate Trainers Inc .... E 800 282-2352
212 Towne Centre Pl Ste 100 Anaheim (92806) *(P-16846)*

Real Marketing .... E 858 847-0335
8470 Redwood Creek Ln Ste 200 San Diego (92126) *(P-2940)*

Real Mex Foods Inc .... D 714 523-0031
5660 Katella Ave Ste 200 Cypress (90630) *(P-10767)*

Real Plating Inc .... E 909 623-2304
1245 W 2nd St Pomona (91766) *(P-5289)*

Real Seal, Escondido *Also Called: REAL Seal Co Inc (P-3897)*

REAL Seal Co Inc .... E 760 743-7263
1971 Don Lee Pl Escondido (92029) *(P-3897)*

Real Software Systems LLC (PA).................. **E** **818 313-8000**
21255 Burbank Blvd Ste 220 Woodland Hills (91367) *(P-14017)*

Real Vision Foods, Irvine *Also Called: Real Vision Foods LLC (P-1399)*

Real Vision Foods LLC .... E 253 228-5050
72 Knollglen Irvine (92614) *(P-1399)*

Realdefense LLC (PA)................................. **E** **801 895-7907**
150 S Los Robles Ave Ste 400 Pasadena (91101) *(P-14416)*

Realselect Inc .... C 661 803-5188
3063 W Chapman Ave Apt 6207 Orange (92868) *(P-12517)*

Realtruck, Anaheim *Also Called: Realtruck Enterprise Inc (P-7209)*

Realtruck Enterprise Inc .... E 956 324-5337
1747 W Lincoln Ave Ste K Anaheim (92801) *(P-7209)*

Realty Income Corporation (PA)................... **C** **858 284-5000**
11995 El Camino Real San Diego (92130) *(P-12314)*

Reapplications Inc .... D 619 230-0209
8910 University Center Ln Ste 300 San Diego (92122) *(P-13804)*

Reason Foundation .... E 310 391-2245
5737 Mesmer Ave Los Angeles (90230) *(P-14583)*

Rebar Engineering Inc .... C 562 946-2461
10706 Painter Ave Santa Fe Springs (90670) *(P-1162)*

Rebas Inc .... C 800 794-5438
12012 Burke St Santa Fe Springs (90670) *(P-10399)*

Rebco Communities Inc .... B 714 557-5511
3090 Pullman St Costa Mesa (92626) *(P-450)*

Rebecca International Inc .... E 323 973-2602
4587 E 48th St Vernon (90058) *(P-2255)*

Rebel Jeans, Los Angeles *Also Called: Be Bop Clothing (P-2082)*

Reborn Bath Solutions, Anaheim *Also Called: Reborn Cabinets LLC (P-2359)*

Reborn Cabinets LLC (PA).......................... **B** **714 630-2220**
5515 E La Palma Ave Ste 250 Anaheim (92807) *(P-2359)*

Rebound Therapeutics Corp .... E 949 305-8111
13900 Alton Pkwy Ste 120 Irvine (92618) *(P-8222)*

Rec Solar, San Luis Obispo *Also Called: Mainstream Energy Corporation (P-800)*

Rec Solar, San Luis Obispo *Also Called: Rec Solar Commercial Corp (P-828)*

Rec Solar Commercial Corp .... C 844 732-7652
3450 Broad St Ste 105 San Luis Obispo (93401) *(P-828)*

Rec Van, San Diego *Also Called: La Mesa R V Center Inc (P-11480)*

Receptos Inc .... E 858 652-5700
3033 Science Park Rd Ste 300 San Diego (92121) *(P-3489)*

RECHE CANYON REGIONAL REHAB CE, Colton *Also Called: Cambridge Sierra Holdings LLC (P-15587)*

Reciprocal Labs Corp .... D 608 251-0470
9001 Spectrum Center Blvd San Diego (92123) *(P-13805)*

Recology, Sun Valley *Also Called: Recology Los Angeles (P-9759)*

Recology Los Angeles .... B 818 767-0675
9189 De Garmo Ave Sun Valley (91352) *(P-9759)*

Recon, San Diego *Also Called: Recon Environmental Inc (P-18352)*

Recon Environmental Inc (PA)..................... D 619 308-9333
3111 Camino Del Rio N Ste 600 San Diego (92108) *(P-18352)*

Reconserve Inc (HQ).................................. E 310 458-1574
2811 Wilshire Blvd Ste 410 Santa Monica (90403) *(P-1432)*

Record Technology Inc (PA)........................ **E** **805 484-2747**
486 Dawson Dr Ste 4s Camarillo (93012) *(P-6580)*

Recovery Solutions Santa Ana, Santa Ana *Also Called: CRC Health Corporate (P-16464)*

Recp/Wndsor Port Hueneme Ventr, Port Hueneme *Also Called: Windsor Capital Group Inc (P-13084)*

Recruit 360 .... C 949 250-4420
457 Ogle St Costa Mesa (92627) *(P-13566)*

Recruitment Services Inc .... E 213 364-1960
3600 Wilshire Blvd Ste 1526 Los Angeles (90010) *(P-2874)*

Recycled Paper Products, Santa Fe Springs *Also Called: Gabriel Container (P-2667)*

Recycler Classified, Sherman Oaks *Also Called: E Z Buy & E Z Sell Recycl Corp (P-2795)*

Recycler Core Company Inc .... D 951 276-1687
2727 Kansas Ave Riverside (92507) *(P-9760)*

Red Blossom Sales Inc .... A 805 349-9404
865 Black Rd Santa Maria (93458) *(P-23)*

Red Bull Media Hse N Amer Inc .... D 310 393-4647
1630 Stewart St Ste A Santa Monica (90404) *(P-1639)*

Red Bull Media Hse N Amer Inc (HQ) .... D 310 393-4647
1740 Stewart St Santa Monica (90404) *(P-10973)*

Red Bull North America Inc (HQ) .... **D** **310 460-5356**
1630 Stewart St Santa Monica (90404) *(P-15001)*

Red Bull TV, Santa Monica *Also Called: Red Bull North America Inc (P-15001)*

Red Chamber Co (PA)................................ **B** **323 234-9000**
1912 E Vernon Ave Vernon (90058) *(P-10860)*

Red Cross, Los Angeles *Also Called: American National Red Cross (P-16865)*

Red Digital Cinema Camera Co, Foothill Ranch *Also Called: Redcom LLC (P-8441)*

Red Earth Casino .... C 760 395-1200
3089 Norm Niver Rd Thermal (92274) *(P-12987)*

Red Fish Grill, Anaheim *Also Called: Ralph Brennan Rest Group LLC (P-18200)*

Red Gate Software Inc .... E 626 993-3949
144 W Colorado Blvd Ste 200 Pasadena (91105) *(P-14018)*

Red Hill Country Club .... D 909 982-1358
8358 Red Hill Country Club Dr Rancho Cucamonga (91730) *(P-15161)*

Red Peak Group LLC .... D 818 222-7762
23975 Park Sorrento Ste 410 Calabasas (91302) *(P-18201)*

Red Pocket Inc .... D 888 993-3888
2060d E Avenida De Los Arboles Ste 288 Thousand Oaks (91362) *(P-9408)*

Red Pocket Mobile, Thousand Oaks *Also Called: Red Pocket Inc (P-9408)*

Red Rock Pallet Company .... E 530 852-7744
81153 Red Rock Rd La Quinta (92253) *(P-9331)*

Red Tail Residential LLC (PA)...................... **D** **949 399-2510**
2082 Michelson Dr Fl 4 Irvine (92612) *(P-12518)*

Redbarn Pet Products Inc (PA).................... **C** **562 495-7315**
3229 E Spring St Ste 310 Long Beach (90806) *(P-11138)*

Redbarn Premium Pet Products, Long Beach *Also Called: Redbarn Pet Products Inc (P-11138)*

Redcom LLC .... **B** **949 404-4084**
94 Icon Foothill Ranch (92610) *(P-8441)*

Redlands Community Hospital (PA) .... **D** **909 335-5500**
350 Terracina Blvd Redlands (92373) *(P-16159)*

REDLANDS COMMUNITY HOSPITAL, Redlands *Also Called: RHS Corp (P-18046)*

Redlands Country Club .... D 000 793 2661
1749 Garden St Redlands (92373) *(P-15162)*

Redlands Daily Facts, Redlands *Also Called: Califrnia Nwspapers Ltd Partnr (P-2788)*

Redlands Employment Services .... B 951 688-0083
4295 Jurupa St Ste 110 Ontario (91761) *(P-13567)*

Redlands Ford Inc .... D 909 793-3211
1121 W Colton Ave Redlands (92374) *(P-14679)*

Redlands Healthcare Center, Redlands *Also Called: Ash Holdings LLC (P-15571)*

Redlands Staffing Services, Ontario *Also Called: Redlands Employment Services (P-13567)*

Redline Detection LLC (PA)......................... **E** **714 579-6961**
828 W Taft Ave Orange (92865) *(P-8061)*

Redman Equipment & Mfg Co .... E 310 329-1134
19800 Normandie Ave Torrance (90502) *(P-14787)*

Redux Labs, El Segundo *Also Called: Design People Inc (P-14129)*

Redwood, Culver City *Also Called: Wovexx Holdings Inc (P-9572)*

Redwood Elderlink & Homelink, Escondido *Also Called: Redwood Elderlink Scph (P-17189)*

Redwood Elderlink Scph .... C 760 480-1030
710 W 13th Ave Escondido (92025) *(P-17189)*

Employee Codes: A=Over 500 employees, B=251-500
C=101-250, D=51-100, E=20-50, F=10-19, G=1-9

2025 Southern California
Business Directory and Buyers Guide

© Mergent Inc. 1-800-342-5647

1161

Redwood Family Care Netwrk Inc .... A 909 942-0218
13920 City Center Dr Chino Hills (91709) *(P-15435)*

Redwood Scientific Tech Inc .... E 310 693-5401
245 E Main St Ste 115 Alhambra (91801) *(P-3490)*

Redwood Senior Homes & Svcs, Escondido *Also Called: Humangood Socal (P-17166)*

Redwood Wellness LLC .... E 323 843-2676
1950 W Corporate Way Anaheim (92801) *(P-1973)*

Reed LLC .... E 909 287-2100
13822 Oaks Ave Chino (91710) *(P-5742)*

Reed Electric & Field Service, Vernon *Also Called: R A Reed Electric Company (P-14750)*

Reed Manufacturing, Chino *Also Called: Reed LLC (P-5742)*

Reed Smith LLP .... C 213 457-8000
355 S Grand Ave Ste 2900 Los Angeles (90071) *(P-16768)*

Reed Thomas Company Inc .... D 714 558-7691
1025 N Santiago St Santa Ana (92701) *(P-1174)*

Reedex Inc .... E 714 894-0311
15526 Commerce Ln Huntington Beach (92649) *(P-7044)*

Reef, Carlsbad *Also Called: South Cone Inc (P-10739)*

Reel Efx Inc .... E 818 762-1710
5539 Riverton Ave North Hollywood (91601) *(P-8719)*

Reel Security California Inc .... D 818 928-4737
15303 Ventura Blvd Ste 1080 Sherman Oaks (91403) *(P-14332)*

Reels Inc .... D 714 446-9606
301 E Orangethorpe Ave Anaheim (92801) *(P-9844)*

Reeve Store Equipment Company (PA) .... D 562 949-2535
9131 Bermudez St Pico Rivera (90660) *(P-2590)*

Reeves Extruded Products Inc .... D 661 854-5970
1032 Stockton Ave Arvin (93203) *(P-4219)*

Refinery, The, Burbank *Also Called: Waldberg Inc (P-13272)*

Reformation, Vernon *Also Called: Lymi Inc (P-10713)*

Refresco Beverages US Inc .... C 951 685-0481
11751 Pacific Ave Fontana (92337) *(P-1355)*

Refresco Beverages US Inc .... E 909 915-1430
499 E Mill St San Bernardino (92408) *(P-1640)*

Refriderator Manufacters LLC .... E 562 229-0500
17018 Edwards Rd Cerritos (90703) *(P-6392)*

Refrigeration Hdwr Sup Corp .... D 800 537-8300
9255 Deering Ave Chatsworth (91311) *(P-10343)*

Refrigeration Supplies Distributor (PA) .... D 949 380-7878
26021 Atlantic Ocean Dr Lake Forest (92630) *(P-10344)*

Refrigerator Manufacturers LLC .... E 562 926-2006
17018 Edwards Rd Cerritos (90703) *(P-5982)*

Refrigrated Trck Solutions LLC .... E 323 594-4500
1115 E Dominguez St Carson (90746) *(P-7317)*

Regal Medical Group Inc (PA) .... C 818 654-3400
8510 Balboa Blvd Ste 275 Northridge (91325) *(P-17305)*

Regal Technology Partners Inc .... C 714 835-1162
2921 Daimler St Santa Ana (92705) *(P-10026)*

Regal-Piedmont Plastics LLC .... E 562 404-4014
17000 Valley View Ave La Mirada (90638) *(P-11001)*

Regency Enterprises Inc (PA) .... B 818 901-0255
9261 Jordan Ave Chatsworth (91311) *(P-10205)*

Regency Group, Pasadena *Also Called: One & All Inc (P-13234)*

Regency Health Services, Covina *Also Called: Covina Rehabilitation Center (P-15619)*

Regency Inn, Costa Mesa *Also Called: US Hotel and Resort MGT Inc (P-13062)*

Regency Supply, Chatsworth *Also Called: Regency Enterprises Inc (P-10205)*

Regent, Valencia *Also Called: Regent Aerospace Corporation (P-10499)*

Regent LP (PA) .... D 310 299-4100
9720 Wilshire Blvd Fl 6 Beverly Hills (90212) *(P-12731)*

Regent Aerospace Corporation (PA) .... C 661 257-3000
28110 Harrison Pkwy Valencia (91355) *(P-10499)*

Regent Assisted Living Inc .... D 626 332-3344
150 S Grand Ave Ofc West Covina (91791) *(P-17190)*

Regent Senior Living W Covina, West Covina *Also Called: Regent Assisted Living Inc (P-17190)*

Regents of The University Cal .... D 310 267-9308
1250 16th St Santa Monica (90404) *(P-16613)*

Regents Point, Irvine *Also Called: Humangood Socal (P-12347)*

Regional Ctr Orange Cnty Inc (PA) .... B 714 796-5100
1525 N Tustin Ave Santa Ana (92705) *(P-18395)*

Regional Office, Redlands *Also Called: Southern California Gas Co (P-9648)*

Regis Contractors LP .... C 949 253-0455
18825 Bardeen Ave Irvine (92612) *(P-451)*

Regus Business Centre LLC .... C 714 371-4000
600 Anton Blvd Ste 1100 Costa Mesa (92626) *(P-14584)*

Rehababilities Inc .... C 310 473-4448
11835 W Olympic Blvd Ste 1090e Los Angeles (90064) *(P-13568)*

Rehabilitation Ctr Bakersfield, Bakersfield *Also Called: Bakersfeld Hlthcare Wllness CN (P-15577)*

Rehablition Inst Orange Cnty, Santa Ana *Also Called: Reimagine Network (P-16496)*

Rehabltion Cntre of Bvrly Hlls .... C 323 782-1500
580 S San Vicente Blvd Los Angeles (90048) *(P-15759)*

Rehablttion Ctr of Ornge Cnty .... C 714 826-2330
9021 Knott Ave Buena Park (90620) *(P-15760)*

Rehablttion Inst Sthern Cal Ri, Santa Ana *Also Called: Rio (P-16498)*

REHABWORKS AT FREEDOM VILLAGE, Lake Forest *Also Called: Freedom Village Healthcare Ctr (P-15657)*

Rehau Construction LLC .... D 951 549-9017
1250 Corona Pointe Ct Ste 301 Corona (92879) *(P-4220)*

Rehrig Pacific Company (HQ) .... C 323 262-5145
4010 E 26th St Los Angeles (90058) *(P-4221)*

Rehrig Pacific Holdings Inc (PA) .... D 323 262-5145
900 Corporate Center Dr Monterey Park (91754) *(P-4222)*

Reid Metal Finishing, Santa Ana *Also Called: Electrode Technologies Inc (P-5256)*

Reid Plastics Customer Svcs, City Of Industry *Also Called: Altium Packaging LLC (P-4043)*

Reid Products, Apple Valley *Also Called: Reid Products Inc (P-6216)*

Reid Products Inc .... E 760 240-1355
21430 Waalew Rd Apple Valley (92307) *(P-6216)*

Reimagine Network (PA) .... C 714 633-7400
1601 E Saint Andrew Pl Santa Ana (92705) *(P-16496)*

Reinhold Industries Inc (DH) .... C 562 944-3281
12827 Imperial Hwy Santa Fe Springs (90670) *(P-4223)*

Reiter Affl Companies LLC .... D 805 925-8577
124 Carmen Ln Ste A Santa Maria (93458) *(P-24)*

Reiter Affl Companies LLC .... D 805 346-1073
1755 E Stowell Rd Santa Maria (93454) *(P-85)*

Relational Center .... E 323 935-1807
2717 S Robertson Blvd Apt 1 Los Angeles (90034) *(P-14019)*

Relationedge LLC .... C 858 451-4665
10120 Pacific Heights Blvd Ste 110 San Diego (92121) *(P-14176)*

Relativity Space Inc (PA) .... B 424 393-4309
3500 E Burnett St Long Beach (90815) *(P-7664)*

Releasepoint, Claremont *Also Called: Western Feld Invstigations Inc (P-14181)*

Reliable Container Corporation .... B 562 861-6226
9206 Santa Fe Springs Rd Santa Fe Springs (90670) *(P-2688)*

Reliable Energy Management Inc .... D 562 984-5511
6829 Walthall Way Paramount (90723) *(P-829)*

Reliable Service Company, Riverside *Also Called: Rsvc Company (P-647)*

Reliable Tape Products, Vernon *Also Called: Chua & Sons Co Inc (P-1905)*

Reliable Wholesale Lumber Inc (PA) .... D 714 848-8222
7600 Redondo Cir Huntington Beach (92648) *(P-9929)*

Reliance Inc .... C 323 583-6111
2537 E 27th St Los Angeles (90058) *(P-10152)*

Reliance Inc .... D 562 944-3322
15090 Northam St La Mirada (90638) *(P-10153)*

Reliance Carpet Cushion, Huntington Park *Also Called: Reliance Upholstery Sup Co Inc (P-2224)*

Reliance Steel & Aluminum Co .... C 714 736-4800
15090 Northam St La Mirada (90638) *(P-10154)*

Reliance Steel Company, Los Angeles *Also Called: Reliance Inc (P-10152)*

Reliance Upholstery Sup Co Inc .... D 323 321-2300
4920 S Boyle Ave Huntington Park (90255) *(P-2224)*

Reliance Worldwide Corporation .... D 770 863-4005
2750 E Mission Blvd Ontario (91761) *(P-5369)*

Reliant Foodservice, Temecula *Also Called: Canadas Finest Foods Inc (P-1374)*

Reliant Funding Group, San Diego *Also Called: Reliant Services Group LLC (P-11871)*

Reliant Services Group LLC .... C 877 850-0998
9540 Towne Centre Dr Ste 100 San Diego (92121) *(P-11871)*

Relief-Mart Inc .... E 805 379-4300
28505 Canwood St Ste C Agoura Hills (91301) *(P-11695)*

Mergent email: customerrelations@mergent.com
1162

2025 Southern California
Business Directory and Buyers Guide

(P-0000) Products & Services Section entry number
(PA)=Parent Co (HQ)=Headquarters (DH)=Div Headquarters

Relocity Inc .... C 323 207-9160
  10250 Constellation Blvd Ste 100 Los Angeles (90067) *(P-18044)*

Relton Corporation .... D 800 423-1505
  317 Rolyn Pl Arcadia (91007) *(P-3819)*

REM Eye Wear, Sun Valley *Also Called: REM Optical Company Inc (P-10120)*

REM Optical Company Inc .... C 818 504-3950
  10941 La Tuna Canyon Rd Sun Valley (91352) *(P-10120)*

Remax Olson & Associates Inc .... C 818 366-3300
  11141 Tampa Ave Northridge (91326) *(P-12519)*

Remec Brdband Wrless Ntwrks LL .... C 858 312-6900
  82 Coromar Dr Goleta (93117) *(P-6653)*

Remec Broadband Wireless LLC .... C 858 312-6900
  82 Coromar Dr Goleta (93117) *(P-6654)*

Remec Defense & Space Inc .... A 858 560-1301
  9404 Chesapeake Dr San Diego (92123) *(P-7801)*

Remedy Intelligent Staffing, Aliso Viejo *Also Called: Remedytemp Inc (P-13618)*

Remedytemp Inc (DH) .... C 949 425-7600
  101 Enterprise Ste 100 Aliso Viejo (92656) *(P-13618)*

Remington Club I & II, San Diego *Also Called: Five Star Senior Living Inc (P-15655)*

Remington Hotel Corporation .... C 760 322-6000
  888 E Tahquitz Canyon Way Palm Springs (92262) *(P-12988)*

Remington Hotel Corporation .... D 310 553-6561
  1150 S Beverly Dr Los Angeles (90035) *(P-12989)*

Remn Inc .... D 951 697-8135
  3400 Central Ave Ste 330 Riverside (92506) *(P-12520)*

Remo Inc (PA) .... B 661 294-5600
  28101 Industry Dr Valencia (91355) *(P-8471)*

Remote Ocean Systems Inc (PA) .... E 858 565-8500
  9581 Ridgehaven Ct San Diego (92123) *(P-6515)*

Rempex Pharmaceuticals Inc .... E 858 875-2840
  3013 Science Park Rd 1st Fl San Diego (92121) *(P-3491)*

Remstek Corp, Temecula *Also Called: Inners Tasks LLC (P-5853)*

Renaissance Doors & Windows, Rcho Sta Marg *Also Called: Renaissnce Frnch Dors Sash Inc (P-2326)*

Renaissance Hollywood Ht & Spa, Los Angeles *Also Called: Cim/H & H Hotel LP (P-12793)*

Renaissance Hotel Clubsport, Aliso Viejo *Also Called: L & O Aliso Viejo LLC (P-12890)*

Renaissance Hotel Operating Co .... B 310 337-2800
  9620 Airport Blvd Los Angeles (90045) *(P-12990)*

Renaissance Hotel Operating Co .... A 760 773-4444
  44400 Indian Wells Ln Indian Wells (92210) *(P-12991)*

Renaissance Indian Wells, Indian Wells *Also Called: Renaissance Hotel Operating Co (P-12991)*

Renaissnce Frnch Dors Sash Inc (PA) .... C 714 578-0090
  38 Segada Rcho Sta Marg (92688) *(P-2326)*

Renal Center, Orange *Also Called: St Joseph Hospital of Orange (P-16216)*

Renkus-Heinz Inc (PA) .... D 949 588-9997
  19201 Cook St Foothill Ranch (92610) *(P-6550)*

Reno Tenco, Boron *Also Called: Rio Tinto Minerals Inc (P-261)*

Renovo Solutions LLC (PA) .... B 714 599-7969
  4 Executive Cir Ste 185 Irvine (92614) *(P-18045)*

Rent What, Compton *Also Called: Sew What Inc (P-2204)*

Rentech Inc (PA) .... E 310 571-9800
  10880 Wilshire Blvd Ste 1101 Los Angeles (90024) *(P-3861)*

Rentech Ntrgn Pasadena Spa LLC .... E 310 571-9805
  10877 Wilshire Blvd Ste 710 Los Angeles (90024) *(P-3746)*

Rentokil North America Inc .... D 714 517-9000
  1160 Sandhill Ave Carson (90746) *(P-13347)*

Rentokil North America Inc .... D 562 802-2238
  15415 Marquardt Ave Santa Fe Springs (90670) *(P-13348)*

Rentokil North America Inc .... D 714 563-2450
  311 N Crescent Way Anaheim (92801) *(P-13349)*

Rentpayment.com, Carlsbad *Also Called: Yapstone Inc (P-14636)*

Renzoni Vineyards Inc .... E 951 302-8466
  37350 De Portola Rd Temecula (92592) *(P-36)*

Reotemp Instrument Corporation (PA) .... D 858 784-0710
  10656 Roselle St San Diego (92121) *(P-7874)*

Repair Tech International, Van Nuys *Also Called: Repairtech International Inc (P-9207)*

Repairtech International Inc .... E 818 989-2681
  7850 Gloria Ave Van Nuys (91406) *(P-9207)*

Repet Inc .... C 909 594-5333
  14207 Monte Vista Ave Chino (91710) *(P-3970)*

Replacement Parts Inds Inc .... E 818 882-8611
  625 Cochran St Simi Valley (93065) *(P-8353)*

Replanet LLC .... A 951 520-1700
  800 N Haven Ave Ste 120 Ontario (91764) *(P-10400)*

Reprints Desk Inc .... D 310 477-0354
  15821 Ventura Blvd Ste 165 Encino (91436) *(P-14177)*

Republic Bag Inc (PA) .... D 951 734-9740
  580 E Harrison St Corona (92879) *(P-2738)*

Republic Fence Co Inc (PA) .... E 818 341-5323
  11309 Danube Ave Granada Hills (91344) *(P-1224)*

Republic Floor, Montebello *Also Called: Reu Distribution LLC (P-9905)*

Republic Flooring, Montebello *Also Called: Hardwood Flrg Liquidators Inc (P-2289)*

Republic Indemnity Co Amer (DH) .... C 818 990-9860
  4500 Park Granada Ste 300 Calabasas (91302) *(P-12132)*

Republic Indemnity Company Cal .... C 818 990-9860
  15821 Ventura Blvd Ste 370 Encino (91436) *(P-12133)*

Republic Nat Distrg Co LLC (PA) .... C 714 368-4615
  14402 Franklin Ave Tustin (92780) *(P-11060)*

RES-Care Inc .... D 760 775-2887
  45691 Monroe St Ste 6 Indio (92201) *(P-15821)*

RES-Care Inc .... C 951 653-1311
  22635 Alessandro Blvd Moreno Valley (92553) *(P-15822)*

RES-Care Inc .... C 909 596-5360
  2120 Foothill Blvd Ste 205 La Verne (91750) *(P-15823)*

RES-Care Inc .... D 714 662-3075
  3187 Red Hill Ave Ste 115 Costa Mesa (92626) *(P-16415)*

RES-Care Inc .... C 818 637-7727
  611 S Central Ave Glendale (91204) *(P-17191)*

Res.net, Foothill Ranch *Also Called: US Real Estate Services Inc (P-12545)*

Resa Service LLC .... C 562 567-6279
  13842 Bettencourt St Cerritos (90703) *(P-9601)*

Rescue Agency Pub Benefit LLC (PA) .... D 619 231-7555
  2437 Morena Blvd San Diego (92110) *(P-13242)*

Rescue Mission Alliance (PA) .... D 805 487-1234
  315 N A St Oxnard (93030) *(P-17469)*

Research Affiliates, Newport Beach *Also Called: Research Affiliates Capital LP (P-12032)*

Research Affiliates, Newport Beach *Also Called: Research Affiliates MGT LLC (P-12033)*

Research Affiliates Capital LP .... D 949 325-8700
  660 Newport Center Dr Newport Beach (92660) *(P-12032)*

Research Affiliates MGT LLC .... D 949 325-8700
  660 Newport Center Dr Newport Beach (92660) *(P-12033)*

Research Metal Industries Inc .... E 310 352-3200
  1970 W 139th St Gardena (90249) *(P-6217)*

Research Tool & Die Works LLC .... D 310 639-5722
  17124 Keegan Ave Carson (90746) *(P-5211)*

Resers Fine Foods Inc .... E 503 643-6431
  3285 Corporate Vw Vista (92081) *(P-5683)*

Reserve Club .... D 760 674-2222
  49400 Desert Butte Trl Indian Wells (92210) *(P-15163)*

Residence Inn By Marriott, Los Angeles *Also Called: 901 West Olympic Blvd Ltd Prtn (P-12756)*

Residence Inn By Marriott, Torrance *Also Called: Msr Hotels & Resorts Inc (P-12932)*

Residence Inn By Marriott, Los Angeles *Also Called: Sunstone Hotel Properties Inc (P-13043)*

Residence Inn By Marriott, Aliso Viejo *Also Called: Sunstone Hotel Properties Inc (P-13044)*

Residence Inn By Marriott LLC .... D 760 776-0050
  38305 Cook St Palm Desert (92211) *(P-12992)*

Resident Group Services Inc (PA) .... C 714 630-5300
  1156 N Grove St Anaheim (92806) *(P-232)*

Residential Fire Systems Inc .... D 714 666-8450
  8085 E Crystal Dr Anaheim (92807) *(P-830)*

Residential Framer, Riverside *Also Called: Silverado Framing & Cnstr (P-432)*

Residential Mortgage Ctr 39, El Segundo *Also Called: City National Bank (P-11721)*

Resilience, San Diego *Also Called: National Resilience Inc (P-3455)*

Resilience Treatment Center .... D 310 963-2065
  9663 Santa Monica Blvd Beverly Hills (90210) *(P-16497)*

Resilience Us Inc (HQ) .... E 984 202-0854
  3115 Merryfield Row Ste 200 San Diego (92121) *(P-3492)*

Resinart Corporation .... E 949 642-3665
  1621 Placentia Ave Costa Mesa (92627) *(P-4224)*

Resinart Plastics, Costa Mesa *Also Called: Resinart Corporation (P-4224)*

A
L
P
H
A
B
E
T
I
C

Resmed, Chatsworth *Also Called: Resmed Motor Technologies Inc (P-6330)*

Resmed, San Diego *Also Called: Resmed Inc (P-8223)*

Resmed Corp (HQ)... D 858 836-5000
  9001 Spectrum Center Blvd San Diego (92123) *(P-8397)*

Resmed Inc (PA)... A 858 836-5000
  9001 Spectrum Center Blvd San Diego (92123) *(P-8223)*

Resmed Motor Technologies Inc .... C 818 428-6400
  9540 De Soto Ave Chatsworth (91311) *(P-6330)*

Resort Parking Services Inc .... C 760 328-4041
  39755 Berkey Dr # B Palm Desert (92211) *(P-14670)*

Resortime.com, Carlsbad *Also Called: Grand Pacific Resorts Inc (P-12832)*

Resource Collection Inc .... E 310 219-3272
  3771 W 242nd St Ste 205 Torrance (90505) *(P-13413)*

Resource Environmental Inc .... D 562 468-7000
  13100 Alondra Blvd Ste 108 Cerritos (90703) *(P-578)*

Resource Label Group LLC .... E 310 603-8910
  1360 W Walnut Pkwy Compton (90220) *(P-3109)*

Resource Label Group LLC .... D 714 619-7100
  1511 E Edinger Ave Santa Ana (92705) *(P-3168)*

Respawn Entertainment LLC .... C 818 960-4400
  20131 Prairie St Chatsworth (91311) *(P-14850)*

Response Envelope Inc (PA)... C 909 923-5855
  1340 S Baker Ave Ontario (91761) *(P-3169)*

Response Genetics Inc .... C 323 224-3900
  1640 Marengo St Ste 7 Los Angeles (90033) *(P-3552)*

Restaurant Depot, San Diego *Also Called: Jetro Cash and Carry Entps LLC (P-10874)*

Restaurant Investment, Los Angeles *Also Called: Providence Rest Partners LLC (P-12729)*

Restaurants Bars & Food Svcs, Los Angeles *Also Called: Fish House Partners One LLC (P-11571)*

Restorixhealth, Orange *Also Called: Gordian Medical Inc (P-10080)*

Result Group Inc .... D 480 777-7130
  2603 Main St Ste 710 Irvine (92614) *(P-14104)*

Retail Opprtnity Invstmnts Prt .... D 858 677-0900
  11250 El Camino Real Ste 200 San Diego (92130) *(P-12732)*

Retail Print Media Inc .... E 424 488-6950
  2355 Crenshaw Blvd Ste 135 Torrance (90501) *(P-3170)*

Rethink Label Systems, Anaheim *Also Called: Labeltronix LLC (P-3153)*

RETIREMENT HOUSING, Long Beach *Also Called: Foundation Property MGT Inc (P-18139)*

Rettig Machine Inc .... E 909 793-7811
  301 Kansas St Redlands (92373) *(P-14743)*

Reu Distribution LLC .... A 323 201-4200
  7227 Telegraph Rd Montebello (90640) *(P-9905)*

Reuben H Fleet Science Center .... C 619 238-1233
  1875 El Prado San Diego (92101) *(P-17261)*

Reuland Electric Co (PA)... C 626 964-6411
  17969 Railroad St City Of Industry (91748) *(P-6331)*

Reuters Television La, North Hollywood *Also Called: Thomson Reuters Corporation (P-6665)*

Reva Medical Inc (PA)... E 858 966-3000
  5751 Copley Dr Ste B San Diego (92111) *(P-8296)*

Revasum Inc .... C 805 541-6424
  825 Buckley Rd San Luis Obispo (93401) *(P-6883)*

Revco Industries Inc (PA)... E 562 777-1588
  10747 Norwalk Blvd Santa Fe Springs (90670) *(P-10459)*

Revco Products .... D 714 891-6688
  7221 Acacia Ave Garden Grove (92841) *(P-14020)*

Reveal Biosciences Inc .... E 858 274-3663
  80 Empire Dr Lake Forest (92630) *(P-17820)*

Reveal Imaging, Vista *Also Called: Leidos Inc (P-17805)*

Reveal Windows & Doors, La Habra *Also Called: Pacific Archtectural Mllwk Inc (P-2324)*

Reverse Medical, Irvine *Also Called: Reverse Medical Corporation (P-8224)*

Reverse Medical Corporation .... E 949 215-0660
  13700 Alton Pkwy Ste 167 Irvine (92618) *(P-8224)*

Revlon Inc .... D 619 372-1379
  1125 Joshua Way Ste 12 Vista (92081) *(P-3685)*

Revolt, Los Angeles *Also Called: Revolt Media and Tv LLC (P-9515)*

Revolt Media and Tv LLC .... C 323 645-3000
  3336 S La Cienega Blvd Los Angeles (90016) *(P-9515)*

Revoltion Cnsmr Sltions CA LLC (DH).......................... C 323 980-0918
  3840 E 26th St Los Angeles (90058) *(P-11139)*

Rew, Riverside *Also Called: Roy E Whitehead Inc (P-1060)*

Rex Creamery, Commerce *Also Called: Heritage Distributing Company (P-1332)*

Rexford Indus Rlty & MGT Inc .... C 310 966-1690
  11620 Wilshire Blvd Ste 300 Los Angeles (90025) *(P-12521)*

Rexhall Industries Inc .... E 661 726-5470
  26857 Tannahill Ave Canyon Country (91387) *(P-7323)*

Rexnord Industries LLC .... E 805 583-5514
  2175 Union Pl Simi Valley (93065) *(P-5684)*

Rey-Crest Roofg Waterproofing .... D 323 257-9329
  3065 Verdugo Rd Los Angeles (90065) *(P-1225)*

Rey-Crest Roofg Waterproofing, Los Angeles *Also Called: Rey-Crest Roofg Waterproofing (P-1225)*

Reyes Coca-Cola Bottling LLC .... E 760 241-2653
  17220 Nutro Way Victorville (92395) *(P-1641)*

Reyes Coca-Cola Bottling LLC .... E 805 614-3702
  1000 Fairway Dr Santa Maria (93455) *(P-1642)*

Reyes Coca-Cola Bottling LLC .... E 805 644-2211
  5335 Walker St Ventura (93003) *(P-1643)*

Reyes Coca-Cola Bottling LLC .... D 661 324-6531
  4320 Ride St Bakersfield (93313) *(P-1644)*

Reyes Coca-Cola Bottling LLC .... C 323 278-2600
  666 Union St Montebello (90640) *(P-1645)*

Reyes Coca-Cola Bottling LLC .... E 213 744-8659
  1338 E 14th St Los Angeles (90021) *(P-1646)*

Reyes Coca-Cola Bottling LLC .... D 714 974-1901
  700 W Grove Ave Orange (92865) *(P-1647)*

Reyes Coca-Cola Bottling LLC (PA)................................ B 213 744-8616
  3 Park Plz Ste 600 Irvine (92614) *(P-1648)*

Reyes Coca-Cola Bottling LLC .... D 760 396-4500
  86375 Industrial Way Coachella (92236) *(P-1649)*

Reyes Coca-Cola Bottling LLC .... C 909 980-3121
  11900 Cabernet Dr Fontana (92337) *(P-1650)*

Reyes Coca-Cola Bottling LLC .... B 619 266-6300
  5255 Federal Blvd San Diego (92105) *(P-1651)*

Reyes Coca-Cola Bottling LLC .... D 562 803-8100
  8729 Cleta St Downey (90241) *(P-1652)*

Reyes Coca-Cola Bottling LLC .... D 818 362-4307
  12925 Bradley Ave Sylmar (91342) *(P-10974)*

Reynaldos Mexican Food Co LLC (PA)............................ C 562 803-3188
  3301 E Vernon Ave Vernon (90058) *(P-1841)*

Reynard Corporation .... E 949 366-8866
  1020 Calle Sombra San Clemente (92673) *(P-8017)*

Rezex Corporation .... E
  1930 E 51st St Vernon (90058) *(P-1945)*

Rf Digital Corporation .... C 949 610-0008
  1601 Pacific Coast Hwy Ste 290 Hermosa Beach (90254) *(P-6884)*

Rf Industries Ltd (PA)... D 858 549-6340
  16868 Via Del Campo Ct Ste 200 San Diego (92127) *(P-6958)*

Rf Surgical Systems LLC .... D 855 522-7027
  5927 Landau Ct Carlsbad (92008) *(P-8225)*

Rfc Wire Forms, Ontario *Also Called: Rfc Wire Forms Inc (P-5414)*

Rfc Wire Forms Inc .... D 909 467-0559
  525 Brooks St Ontario (91762) *(P-5414)*

RG Costumes & Accessories Inc .... E 626 858-9559
  726 Arrow Grand Cir Covina (91722) *(P-2201)*

Rgb Systems Inc (PA)... C 714 491-1500
  1025 E Ball Rd Ste 100 Anaheim (92805) *(P-5949)*

Rgc Gaslamp LLC .... D 619 738-7000
  550 J St San Diego (92101) *(P-12993)*

Rgc Services Inc .... C 805 484-1600
  601 E Daily Dr Ste 102 Camarillo (93010) *(P-12522)*

Rgc Services Inc (PA)... C 805 644-1242
  5720 Ralston St Ste 100 Ventura (93003) *(P-12523)*

RGF Enterprises Inc .... E 951 734-6922
  220 Citation Cir Corona (92878) *(P-5341)*

Rggd Inc (PA).. E 323 581-6617
  4950 S Santa Fe Ave Vernon (90058) *(P-10567)*

Rgis LLC .... C 714 938-0663
  1937 W Chapman Ave Orange (92868) *(P-14585)*

Rgis, Llc, Orange *Also Called: Rgis LLC (P-14585)*

Rgs Services, Anaheim *Also Called: Resident Group Services Inc (P-232)*

RH Peterson Co (PA)... C 626 369-5085
  14724 Proctor Ave City Of Industry (91746) *(P-6389)*

Rhapsody Clothing Inc .... D 213 614-8887
810 E Pico Blvd Ste 24 Los Angeles (90021) *(P-2129)*

Rhi Inc (PA) .... D 818 508-3800
5841 Lankershim Blvd North Hollywood (91601) *(P-11401)*

Rhino Building Services Inc .... C 858 455-1440
6650 Flanders Dr Ste K San Diego (92121) *(P-13414)*

Rhino Linings Corporation (PA) .... D 858 450-0441
9747 Businesspark Ave San Diego (92131) *(P-3720)*

RHS Corp .... A 909 335-5500
350 Terracina Blvd Redlands (92373) *(P-18046)*

Rhythm & Hues Studios, El Segundo *Also Called: Rhythm and Hues Inc (P-14851)*

Rhythm and Hues Inc (PA) .... D 310 448-7500
2100 E Grand Ave Ste A El Segundo (90245) *(P-14851)*

Ria Financial Services, Buena Park *Also Called: Continental Exch Solutions Inc (P-14478)*

Rialto Bioenergy Facility LLC .... C 760 436-8870
5780 Fleet St Ste 310 Carlsbad (92008) *(P-17619)*

Rialto Concrete Products, Rialto *Also Called: Kti Incorporated (P-4399)*

Ric, Santa Ana *Also Called: Rickenbacker International Corporation (P-8472)*

Rica, Calabasas *Also Called: Republic Indemnity Co Amer (P-12132)*

Rice Field Corporation .... C 626 968-6917
14500 Valley Blvd City Of Industry (91746) *(P-1269)*

Rich Products Corporation .... E 714 338-1145
3401 W Segerstrom Ave Santa Ana (92704) *(P-1496)*

Rich Products Corporation .... C 562 946-6396
12805 Busch Pl Santa Fe Springs (90670) *(P-1842)*

Richard Huetter Inc .... D 818 700-8001
21050 Osborne St Canoga Park (91304) *(P-9845)*

Richard Tyler, Alhambra *Also Called: Tyler Trafficante Inc (P-1980)*

Richard Wilson Wellington .... D 626 812-7881
1025 N Todd Ave Azusa (91702) *(P-68)*

Richards Neon Shop Inc .... E 951 279-6767
4375 Prado Rd Ste 102 Corona (92878) *(P-8626)*

Richards Wtson Grshon A Prof C (PA) .... C 213 626-8484
355 S Grand Ave 40th Fl Los Angeles (90071) *(P-16769)*

Richardson Steel Inc .... E 619 697-5892
9102 Harness St Ste A Spring Valley (91977) *(P-4864)*

Richman Management Corporation .... B 760 832-8520
35400 Bob Hope Dr Ste 107 Rancho Mirage (92270) *(P-14333)*

Richman Management Corporation .... B 909 296-6189
41743 Entp Cir N Ste 209 Temecula (92590) *(P-14334)*

Richmond Engineering Co Inc .... C 800 589-7058
15472 Markar Rd Poway (92064) *(P-233)*

Rick Engineering Company, San Diego *Also Called: Glenn A Rick Engrg & Dev Co (P-17539)*

Rick Hamm Construction Inc .... D 714 532-0815
201 W Carleton Ave Orange (92867) *(P-643)*

Rick's Hitches & Welding, El Cajon *Also Called: CLP Inc (P-14738)*

Rickenbacker International Corporation .... D 714 545-5574
3895 S Main St Santa Ana (92707) *(P-8472)*

Ricoh Electronics Inc .... C 714 259-1220
17482 Pullman St Irvine (92614) *(P-5959)*

Ricoh Electronics Inc .... C 714 566-6079
2310 Redhill Ave Santa Ana (92705) *(P-8442)*

Ricoh Prtg Systems Amer Inc (HQ) .... B 805 578-4000
2390 Ward Ave Ste A Simi Valley (93065) *(P-5950)*

Ricon Corporation .... C 818 267-3000
1135 Aviation Pl San Fernando (91340) *(P-8720)*

Ride On Transportation, San Luis Obispo *Also Called: United Crbral Plsy Assn San Lu (P-17021)*

Ridge, Corona *Also Called: Peppermint Ridge (P-17187)*

Ridge Wallet LLC .... D 818 636-2832
2448 Main St Santa Monica (90405) *(P-4307)*

Ridge Wallet, The, Santa Monica *Also Called: Ridge Wallet LLC (P-4307)*

Ridgecrest Regional Hospital (PA) .... B 760 446-3551
1081 N China Lake Blvd Ridgecrest (93555) *(P-16160)*

Ridgecrest Service Center, Ridgecrest *Also Called: Southern California Edison Co (P-9636)*

Riedon Inc (PA) C
2072 Midwick Dr Altadena (91001) *(P-6921)*

Right Angle Solutions Inc .... E 951 934-3081
6315 Pedley Rd Jurupa Valley (92509) *(P-831)*

Right Hand Manufacturing Inc .... C 619 819-5056
180 Otay Lakes Rd Ste 205 Bonita (91902) *(P-6357)*

Right Manufacturing LLC .... E 858 566-7002
7949 Stromesa Ct Ste G San Diego (92126) *(P-5437)*

Right Start Mortgage Inc (PA) .... D 855 313-9405
80 S Lake Ave Ste 520 Pasadena (91101) *(P-11932)*

Rightsourcing of Rhode Island, Irvine *Also Called: Magnit Rs Inc (P-13604)*

Rightway, Vernon *Also Called: R B R Meat Company Inc (P-1249)*

Rigos Equipment Mfg LLC .... E 626 813-6621
14501 Joanbridge St Baldwin Park (91706) *(P-5029)*

Rigos Sheet Metal, Baldwin Park *Also Called: Rigos Equipment Mfg LLC (P-5029)*

Rika Corporation .... D 949 830-9050
332 W Brenna Ln Orange (92867) *(P-1163)*

Rim of World Unified Schl Dst .... D 909 336-0330
27614 Hwy 18 Across Building I Lake Arrowhead (92352) *(P-8882)*

Rima Enterprises Inc .... D 714 893-4534
16417 Ladona Cir Huntington Beach (92649) *(P-5666)*

Rima-System, Huntington Beach *Also Called: Rima Enterprises Inc (P-5666)*

Rinaldi Convalescent Hospital .... C 818 360-1003
16553 Rinaldi St Granada Hills (91344) *(P-15882)*

Rincon Consultants Inc .... C 805 547-0900
1530 Monterey St Ste D San Luis Obispo (93401) *(P-18353)*

Rincon Engineering Tech .... E 805 684-4144
6325 Carpinteria Ave Carpinteria (93013) *(P-6218)*

Rincon Pacific LLC .... D 805 986-8806
1312 Del Norte Rd Camarillo (93010) *(P-25)*

Ring, Hawthorne *Also Called: Ring LLC (P-6297)*

Ring Container Tech LLC .... D 909 350-8416
8275 Almeria Ave Fontana (92335) *(P-3990)*

Ring LLC (HQ) .... B 310 929-7085
12515 Cerise Ave Hawthorne (90250) *(P-6297)*

Ring of Fire, Van Nuys *Also Called: Rof LLC (P-2001)*

Rio .... C 714 633-7400
1601 E Saint Andrew Pl Ste A Santa Ana (92705) *(P-16498)*

Rio Tinto Minerals Inc .... C 760 762-7121
14486 Borax Rd Boron (93516) *(P-261)*

Rio Vista Development Co Inc (PA) .... C 818 980-8000
4222 Vineland Ave North Hollywood (91602) *(P-12994)*

Riolo Transportation Inc .... B 760 729-4405
2725 Jefferson St Ste 2d Carlsbad (92008) *(P-9375)*

Riot Games, Los Angeles *Also Called: Riot Games Inc (P-14021)*

Riot Games Inc (DH) .... E 310 207-1444
12333 W Olympic Blvd Los Angeles (90064) *(P-14021)*

Riot Glass Inc .... E 800 580-2303
17941 Brookshire Ln Huntington Beach (92647) *(P-7146)*

Rip Curl Inc .... E 714 422-3617
193 Avenida La Pata San Clemente (92673) *(P-8534)*

Rip Curl Inc (DH) .... D 714 422-3600
3030 Airway Ave Costa Mesa (92626) *(P-8535)*

Rip Curl USA, Costa Mesa *Also Called: Rip Curl Inc (P-8535)*

Risco Inc .... E 951 769-2899
390 Risco Cir Beaumont (92223) *(P-5136)*

Risvolds Inc .... D 323 770-2674
1234 W El Segundo Blvd Gardena (90247) *(P-1843)*

Rite Engineering & Manufacturing Corporation ... E 562 862-2135
5832 Garfield Ave Commerce (90040) *(P-4923)*

Rite Screen, Rancho Cucamonga *Also Called: J T Walker Industries Inc (P-4890)*

Ritec, Simi Valley *Also Called: Rugged Info Tech Eqp Corp (P-5951)*

Ritual, Los Angeles *Also Called: Natals Inc (P-3454)*

Ritz Carlton Rancho Mirage, Rancho Mirage *Also Called: Ritz-Carlton Hotel Company LLC (P-12996)*

Ritz-Carlton, Dana Point *Also Called: Ritz-Carlton Hotel Company LLC (P-12995)*

Ritz-Carlton, Santa Barbara *Also Called: Ritz-Carlton Hotel Company LLC (P-12997)*

Ritz-Carlton, Marina Del Rey *Also Called: Ritz-Carlton Marina Del Rey (P-12998)*

Ritz-Carlton Hotel Company LLC .... B 949 240-5020
1 Ritz Carlton Dr Dana Point (92629) *(P-12995)*

Ritz-Carlton Hotel Company LLC .... B 760 321-8282
68900 Frank Sinatra Dr Rancho Mirage (92270) *(P-12996)*

Ritz-Carlton Hotel Company LLC .... A 805 968-0100
8301 Hollister Ave Santa Barbara (93117) *(P-12997)*

Ritz-Carlton Laguna Niguel, Dana Point *Also Called: Prutel Joint Venture (P-12978)*

Ritz-Carlton Marina Del Rey .... D 310 823-1700
4375 Admiralty Way Marina Del Rey (90292) *(P-12998)*

Employee Codes: A=Over 500 employees, B=251-500
C=101-250, D=51-100, E=20-50, F=10-19, G=1-9

2025 Southern California
Business Directory and Buyers Guide

© Mergent Inc. 1-800-342-5647

1165

River Ridge Farms Inc .... D 805 647-6880
3135 Los Angeles Ave Oxnard (93036) *(P-69)*

Rivera Sanatarium Inc .... D 562 949-2591
7246 Rosemead Blvd Pico Rivera (90660) *(P-15761)*

Riversd-San Brnrdino Cnty Indi (PA) .... D 909 864-1097
11980 Mount Vernon Ave Grand Terrace (92313) *(P-15436)*

Riversd-San Brnrdino Cnty Indi .... C 951 654-0803
607 Donna Way San Jacinto (92583) *(P-15437)*

Riverside Auto Auction, Anaheim *Also Called: Califrnia Auto Dalers Exch LLC (P-9801)*

Riverside Blltin Jrupa This We, Riverside *Also Called: Metropolitan News Company (P-2816)*

Riverside Care Inc .... C 951 683-7111
4301 Caroline Ct Riverside (92506) *(P-15762)*

Riverside Cement Holdings Company .... B 951 774-2500
1500 Rubidoux Blvd Riverside (92509) *(P-4359)*

Riverside Cmnty Hlth Systems (DH) .... A 951 788-3000
4445 Magnolia Ave 6th Fl Riverside (92501) *(P-16161)*

Riverside Cnty Flood Ctrl Wtr .... C 951 955-1200
1995 Market St Riverside (92501) *(P-18378)*

Riverside Cnty Rgional Med Ctr, Riverside *Also Called: Riverside Univ Hlth Sys Fndtio (P-16162)*

Riverside Companion Services, San Bernardino *Also Called: Maxim Healthcare Services Inc (P-13606)*

Riverside Construction Company Inc .... C 951 682-8308
4225 Garner Rd Riverside (92501) *(P-644)*

Riverside Crona Rsrce Cnsrvtio, Riverside *Also Called: County of Riverside (P-17338)*

Riverside District Office, Riverside *Also Called: State Compensation Insur Fund (P-12140)*

Riverside Equities LLC .... B 951 688-2222
8487 Magnolia Ave Riverside (92504) *(P-15763)*

Riverside Foundary, Riverside *Also Called: Oldcast Precast (P-4406)*

Riverside Marriott, Riverside *Also Called: Pinnacle Rvrside Hspitality LP (P-12974)*

Riverside Med Clnic Ptient Ctr, Riverside *Also Called: Riverside Medical Clinic Inc (P-15438)*

Riverside Medical Center, Riverside *Also Called: Kaiser Foundation Hospitals (P-15349)*

Riverside Medical Clinic Inc (PA) .... D 951 683-6370
3660 Arlington Ave Riverside (92506) *(P-15438)*

Riverside Transit Agency (PA) .... B 951 565-5000
1825 3rd St Riverside (92507) *(P-8795)*

Riverside Univ Hlth Sys Fndtio (PA) .... B 951 358-5000
4065 County Circle Dr Riverside (92503) *(P-16162)*

Riverside University Health .... B 951 486-4000
26520 Cactus Ave Moreno Valley (92555) *(P-16163)*

Riverside-San Bernardino .... C 951 849-4761
11555 1/2 Potrero Rd Banning (92220) *(P-16499)*

Riverwalk Post Acute, Riverside *Also Called: Orange Treeidence Opco LLC (P-15818)*

Riverwalk PST-Cute Rhblitation, Mission Viejo *Also Called: Rock Canyon Healthcare Inc (P-16416)*

Rivian, Irvine *Also Called: Rivian Automotive Inc (P-7189)*

Rivian Automotive Inc (PA) .... B 888 748-4261
14600 Myford Rd Irvine (92606) *(P-7189)*

Rivian Automotive LLC .... D 888 748-4261
14451 Myford Rd Tustin (92780) *(P-7190)*

Rivian Automotive LLC .... D 309 249-8777
1648 Ashley Way Colton (92324) *(P-7191)*

Riviera Country Club Inc .... D 310 454-6591
1250 Capri Dr Pacific Palisades (90272) *(P-15217)*

Riviera Finance of Texas Inc .... D 562 777-1300
10430 Pioneer Blvd Ste 1 Santa Fe Springs (90670) *(P-11872)*

Riviera Golf & Tennis Inc .... D 310 454-6591
1250 Capri Dr Pacific Palisades (90272) *(P-15164)*

Riviera Health Care Center, Pico Rivera *Also Called: Riviera Nursing & Conva (P-15764)*

Riviera Nursing & Conva .... C 562 806-2576
8203 Telegraph Rd Pico Rivera (90660) *(P-15764)*

Riviera Shores, Capistrano Beach *Also Called: Pacific Monarch Resorts Inc (P-12961)*

Riye Group LLC .... E 820 203-9215
2110 W 103rd St Los Angeles (90047) *(P-2941)*

Rize Federal Credit Union (PA) .... D 626 960-6888
12701 Schabarum Ave Baldwin Park (91706) *(P-11812)*

Rizzo Inc .... E 818 781-6891
7720 Airport Business Pkwy Van Nuys (91406) *(P-8297)*

RJ Acquisition Corp (PA) .... C 323 318-1107
3260 E 26th St Los Angeles (90058) *(P-3171)*

RJ Noble Company (PA) .... C 714 637-1550
15505 E Lincoln Ave Orange (92865) *(P-645)*

Rjn Investigations Inc .... D 951 686-7638
360 E 1st St Ste 696 Tustin (92780) *(P-14335)*

Rlh Fire Protection Inc (PA) .... D 661 322-9344
4300 Stine Rd Ste 800 Bakersfield (93313) *(P-832)*

Rlh Industries Inc .... E 714 532-1672
936 N Main St Orange (92867) *(P-6590)*

RM Galicia Inc .... C 626 813-6200
1521 W Cameron Ave Ste 100 West Covina (91790) *(P-13287)*

Rm Partners Inc .... E 714 765-5725
1439 S State College Blvd Anaheim (92806) *(P-11525)*

RMA Land Construction Inc .... D 714 985-2888
2707 Saturn St Brea (92821) *(P-234)*

Rmd Group Inc .... B 562 866-9288
2311 E South St Long Beach (90805) *(P-18202)*

RMR Financial LLC (DH) .... D 408 355-2000
610 Newport Center Dr Newport Beach (92660) *(P-11951)*

RMR Products Inc (PA) .... E 818 890-0896
11011 Glenoaks Blvd Ste 1 Pacoima (91331) *(P-4419)*

RMS Foundation Inc .... A 562 435-3511
1126 Queens Hwy Long Beach (90802) *(P-12999)*

Rnd Contractors Inc .... E 909 429-8500
14796 Jurupa Ave Ste A Fontana (92337) *(P-4865)*

Rndc, Tustin *Also Called: Republic Nat Distrg Co LLC (P-11060)*

RNS Channel Letters, Corona *Also Called: Richards Neon Shop Inc (P-8626)*

Ro Gar Mfg, El Centro *Also Called: Rogar Manufacturing Inc (P-7046)*

Road Champs Inc .... C 310 456-7799
22619 Pacific Coast Hwy Ste 250 Malibu (90265) *(P-8494)*

Road Runner Sports, San Diego *Also Called: Road Runner Sports Inc (P-11662)*

Road Runner Sports Inc (PA) .... D 858 974-4200
5549 Copley Dr San Diego (92111) *(P-11662)*

Road Vista, San Diego *Also Called: Gamma Scientific Inc (P-8043)*

Roadex America Inc .... D 310 878-9800
2132 E Dominguez St Ste B Long Beach (90810) *(P-9105)*

Roadium Open Air Market, Torrance *Also Called: Pioneer Theatres Inc (P-11292)*

Roadrunner Shuttle, Camarillo *Also Called: Airport Connection Inc (P-8747)*

Roambi, Cardiff By The Sea *Also Called: Mellmo Inc (P-13769)*

Rob Inc .... D 562 806-5589
6760 Foster Bridge Blvd Bell Gardens (90201) *(P-1992)*

Robar Enterprises Inc (PA) .... C 760 244-5456
17671 Bear Valley Rd Hesperia (92345) *(P-4448)*

Robb Curtco Media LLC .... E 310 589-7700
22741 Pacific Coast Hwy Ste 401 Malibu (90265) *(P-2875)*

Robbins Geller Rudman Dowd LLP (PA) .... B 619 231-1058
655 W Broadway Ste 1900 San Diego (92101) *(P-16770)*

Roberson Construction .... E 626 578-1936
22 Central Ct Pasadena (91105) *(P-2606)*

Robert B Diemer Trtmnt Plant, Yorba Linda *Also Called: Metropltan Wtr Dst of Sthern C (P-9705)*

Robert Ballard Rehab Hospital (HQ) .... D 909 473-1200
1760 W 16th St San Bernardino (92411) *(P-15556)*

Robert C Worth Inc .... D 661 942-6601
15846 Liggett St North Hills (91343) *(P-2360)*

Robert Clapper Cnstr Svcs Inc .... D 909 829-3688
700 New York St Redlands (92374) *(P-579)*

Robert F Chapman Inc .... D 661 940-9482
43100 Exchange Pl Lancaster (93535) *(P-5030)*

Robert H Oliva Inc .... E 818 700-1035
19863 Nordhoff St Northridge (91324) *(P-6219)*

Robert H Peterson Company, City Of Industry *Also Called: RH Peterson Co (P-6389)*

Robert Kaufman Co Inc (PA) .... C 310 538-3482
129 W 132nd St Los Angeles (90061) *(P-11651)*

Robert Kaufman Fabrics, Los Angeles *Also Called: Robert Kaufman Co Inc (P-11651)*

Robert Kinsella Inc .... D 949 453-9533
15375 Barranca Pkwy Ste G107 Irvine (92618) *(P-10768)*

Robert M Hadley Company Inc .... D 805 658-7286
4054 Transport St Ste B Ventura (93003) *(P-6937)*

Robert Michael Ltd .... B 562 758-6789
10035 Geary Ave Santa Fe Springs (90670) *(P-2458)*

Robert Moreno Insurance Svcs .... C 714 578-3318
3110 E Guasti Rd Ste 500 Ontario (91761) *(P-12250)*

Robert Rnzoni Vineyards Winery, Temecula *Also Called: Renzoni Vineyards Inc (P-36)*

Robert's Engineering, Anaheim *Also Called: Roberts Precision Engrg Inc (P-6220)*

Robert's Lumber, Bloomington *Also Called: Roberts Lumber Sales Inc (P-9930)*

Roberta, Los Angeles *Also Called: L A Glo Inc (P-2068)*

Roberts Engineers, Paramount *Also Called: Total-Western Inc (P-365)*

Roberts Lumber Sales Inc .... D 909 350-9164
2661 S Lilac Ave Bloomington (92316) *(P-9930)*

Roberts Precision Engrg Inc .... E 714 635-4485
1345 S Allec St Anaheim (92805) *(P-6220)*

Robertson Honda, North Hollywood *Also Called: Rhi Inc (P-11401)*

Robertson's, Corona *Also Called: Robertsons Rdymx Ltd A Cal Ltd (P-4449)*

Robertsons Rdymx Ltd A Cal Ltd (PA)....... D 951 493-6500
200 S Main St Ste 200 Corona (92882) *(P-4449)*

Robertsons Rdymx Ltd A Cal Ltd .... C 909 425-2930
27401 3rd St Highland (92346) *(P-4450)*

Robertsons Ready Mix Ltd .... D 760 244-7239
9635 C Ave Hesperia (92345) *(P-4451)*

Robertsons Ready Mix Ltd .... C 800 834-7557
5692 Eastgate Dr San Diego (92121) *(P-4452)*

Robertsons Ready Mix Ltd .... D 951 685-4600
1310 Simpson Way Escondido (92029) *(P-4453)*

Robertsons Ready Mix Ltd .... D 760 373-4815
7900 Moss Ave California City (93505) *(P-4454)*

Robin Red Breast Inc .... D 323 466-7800
6616 Lexington Ave Los Angeles (90038) *(P-15439)*

Robin's Jeans, Bell Gardens *Also Called: Rob Inc (P-1992)*

Robinson Helicopter Co Inc (PA)............. B 310 539-0508
2901 Airport Dr Torrance (90505) *(P-7546)*

Robinson Pharma Inc .... C 714 241-0235
3300 W Segerstrom Ave Santa Ana (92704) *(P-3493)*

Robinson Pharma Inc (PA).................... B 714 241-0235
3330 S Harbor Blvd Santa Ana (92704) *(P-3494)*

Robinson Pharma Inc .... C 714 241-0235
3701 W Warner Ave Santa Ana (92704) *(P-3495)*

Robinson Printing, Temecula *Also Called: Robinson Printing Inc (P-3172)*

Robinson Printing Inc .... E 951 296-0300
42685 Rio Nedo Temecula (92590) *(P-3172)*

Robo 3d Inc .... E 844 476-2233
5070 Santa Fe St Ste C San Diego (92109) *(P-3077)*

Robo 3d Printer, San Diego *Also Called: Robo 3d Inc (P-3077)*

Rock Canyon Healthcare Inc .... C 719 404-1000
27101 Puerta Real Ste 450 Mission Viejo (92691) *(P-16416)*

Rock Revival, Vernon *Also Called: Rcrv Inc (P-1991)*

Rock Structures-Rip Rap .... E 951 371-1112
11126 Silverton Ct Corona (92881) *(P-4494)*

Rock West Composites Inc (PA)............. D 858 537-6260
7625 Panasonic Way San Diego (92154) *(P-3290)*

Rock West Composites Inc .... E 858 537-6260
7625 Panasonic Way San Diego (92154) *(P-17620)*

Rock-Ola Manufacturing Corp .... D 310 328-1306
1445 Sepulveda Blvd Torrance (90501) *(P-6551)*

Rockblue .... D 703 314-0208
601 Foothill Rd Ojai (93023) *(P-17306)*

Rocker Industries, Huntington Beach *Also Called: Rocker Solenoid Company (P-7045)*

Rocker Solenoid Company .... D 310 534-5660
5492 Bolsa Ave Huntington Beach (92649) *(P-7045)*

Rocket Lab Usa Inc .... E 714 465-5737
4022 E Conant St Long Beach (90808) *(P-7648)*

Rocket Lab Usa Inc (PA)...................... E 714 465-5737
3881 Mcgowen St Long Beach (90808) *(P-7649)*

Rocket League, San Diego *Also Called: Psyonix LLC (P-13801)*

Rockin Jump Holdings LLC .... B 661 233-9907
1301 W Rancho Vista Blvd Ste B Palmdale (93551) *(P-15218)*

Rockin' Jump Trampoline, Palmdale *Also Called: Rockin Jump Holdings LLC (P-15218)*

Rockley Photonics Inc (HQ).................. C 626 304-9960
17252 Armstrong Ave Ste E Irvine (92614) *(P-6885)*

Rockport ADM Svcs LLC (PA)................ D 323 330-6500
5900 Wilshire Blvd Ste 1600 Los Angeles (90036) *(P-18047)*

Rockport Healthcare Services, Los Angeles *Also Called: Rockport ADM Svcs LLC (P-18047)*

Rockstar San Diego Inc .... D 760 929-0700
2200 Faraday Ave Ste 200 Carlsbad (92008) *(P-14151)*

Rockview Dairies Inc (PA)..................... C 562 927-5511
7011 Stewart And Gray Rd Downey (90241) *(P-10975)*

Rockwell Collins Inc .... D 714 929-3000
1733 Alton Pkwy Irvine (92606) *(P-7802)*

Rockwell Collins Inc .... E 714 929-3000
1733 Alton Pkwy Irvine (92606) *(P-7803)*

Rockwell Collins Inc .... E 760 768-4732
1757 Carr Rd Ste 100 Calexico (92231) *(P-7547)*

Rocky Point Investments LLC (HQ)......... C 310 482-6500
6601 Center Dr W Ste 400 Los Angeles (90045) *(P-18203)*

Rocky Point RTD, Oceanside *Also Called: Belching Beaver Brewery (P-11611)*

Rodax Distributors .... D 818 765-6400
7230 Coldwater Canyon Ave North Hollywood (91605) *(P-14852)*

Rode Microphones LLC (DH).................. C 310 328-7456
2745 Raymond Ave Signal Hill (90755) *(P-6552)*

Rodeo Realty Inc (PA)......................... D 818 349-9997
9171 Wilshire Blvd Ste 321 Beverly Hills (90210) *(P-12524)*

Rodeway Inn, San Diego *Also Called: Narven Enterprises Inc (P-12935)*

Rof LLC .... E 818 933-4000
7800 Airport Business Pkwy Van Nuys (91406) *(P-2001)*

Rogar Manufacturing Inc .... C 760 335-3700
866 E Ross Ave El Centro (92243) *(P-7046)*

Rogers Corporation .... D 562 404-8942
13937 Rosecrans Ave Santa Fe Springs (90670) *(P-3933)*

Rogers Poultry Co .... D 800 585-0802
2020 E 67th St Los Angeles (90001) *(P-10838)*

Rogers Poultry Co (PA)........................ D 323 585-0802
5050 S Santa Fe Ave Vernon (90058) *(P-10839)*

Rogerson Aircraft Corporation (PA)......... D 949 660-0666
16940 Von Karman Ave Irvine (92606) *(P-7804)*

Rogerson Kratos .... C 626 449-3090
403 S Raymond Ave Pasadena (91105) *(P-7805)*

Rohr Inc (HQ)................................... A 619 691-4111
850 Lagoon Dr Chula Vista (91910) *(P-7548)*

Rohrback Cosasco Systems Inc (DH)....... D 562 949-0123
11841 Smith Ave Santa Fe Springs (90670) *(P-7875)*

ROIC California, San Diego *Also Called: Retail Opprtnity Invstmnts Prt (P-12732)*

Rojo's, Cypress *Also Called: Simply Fresh LLC (P-1712)*

Roland Corporation US (HQ)................. C 323 890-3700
5100 S Eastern Ave Los Angeles (90040) *(P-10568)*

Roll Along Vans Inc .... E 714 528-9600
1350 E Yorba Linda Blvd Placentia (92870) *(P-7289)*

Roll Properties Intl Inc .... C 661 797-6500
13646 Highway 33 Lost Hills (93249) *(P-12733)*

Roll-Rite LLC .... E 619 449-8860
1404 N Marshall Ave El Cajon (92020) *(P-2241)*

Roller Bones, Goleta *Also Called: Skate One Corp (P-8543)*

Rolling Green Inc .... B 951 360-9294
401 W 4th St San Bernardino (92401) *(P-189)*

Rolling Hills Country Club .... D 424 903-0000
1 Chandler Ranch Rd Rolling Hills Estate (90274) *(P-15165)*

Rolling Hills Vineyard Inc .... E 310 541-5098
4213 Pascal Pl Pls Vrds Pnsl (90274) *(P-1583)*

Rolling Hlls Cntry CLB Golf Sp, Rolling Hills Estate *Also Called: Rolling Hills Country Club (P-15165)*

Rollins Leasing LLC .... D 626 913-7186
18305 Arenth Ave City Of Industry (91748) *(P-14641)*

Rollins Truck Rental-Leasing, City Of Industry *Also Called: Rollins Leasing LLC (P-14641)*

Rolls-Royce High Temperature Composites Inc ..... E 714 375-4085
5730 Katella Ave Cypress (90630) *(P-4507)*

Rolls-Royce Htc, Cypress *Also Called: Rolls-Royce High Temperature Composites Inc (P-4507)*

Roma Moulding Inc .... E 626 334-2539
6230 N Irwindale Ave Irwindale (91702) *(P-2417)*

Romac, Yorba Linda *Also Called: Romac Supply Co Inc (P-6310)*

Romac Supply Co Inc .... D 323 721-5810
17722 Neff Ranch Rd Yorba Linda (92886) *(P-6310)*

Romakk Engineering, Northridge *Also Called: Robert H Oliva Inc (P-6219)*

A
L
P
H
A
B
E
T
I
C

Employee Codes: A=Over 500 employees, B=251-500
C=101-250, D=51-100, E=20-50, F=10-19, G=1-9

2025 Southern California
Business Directory and Buyers Guide

© Mergent Inc. 1-800-342-5647

1167

Romakk Engineering, Northridge *Also Called: Vision Aerospace LLC (P-7589)*

Roman Cthlic Bshp of San Diego .... D 619 264-3127
4470 Hilltop Dr San Diego (92102) *(P-12525)*

Roman Cthlic Diocese of Orange .... D 714 847-8546
8301 Talbert Ave Huntington Beach (92646) *(P-12586)*

Roman Cthlic Diocese of Orange .... C 714 532-6551
7845 E Santiago Canyon Rd Orange (92869) *(P-12587)*

Roman Cthlic Diocese of Orange .... C 714 528-1794
801 N Bradford Ave Placentia (92870) *(P-16821)*

Roman Cthlic Diocese of Orange .... C 714 544-1533
1311 Sycamore Ave Tustin (92780) *(P-16822)*

Roman Cthlic Diocese of Orange .... C 949 766-6000
22062 Antonio Pkwy Rcho Sta Marg (92688) *(P-16823)*

Romar Innovations, Murrieta *Also Called: Romar Innovations Inc (P-7831)*

Romar Innovations Inc .... D 951 296-3480
38429 Innovation Ct Murrieta (92563) *(P-7831)*

Romero Construction, Escondido *Also Called: Romero General Cnstr Corp (P-646)*

Romero General Cnstr Corp .... C 760 715-0154
8320 Nelson Way Escondido (92026) *(P-424)*

Romero General Cnstr Corp (PA) .... D 760 489-8412
2150 N Centre City Pkwy Ste I Escondido (92026) *(P-646)*

Romeros Engineering Inc .... E 909 481-1170
9175 Milliken Ave Rancho Cucamonga (91730) *(P-6221)*

Romeros Food Products Inc (PA) .... D 562 802-1858
15155 Valley View Ave Santa Fe Springs (90670) *(P-1844)*

Romex Textiles Inc (PA) .... E 213 749-9090
2454 E 27th St Vernon (90058) *(P-10673)*

Romla Co .... E 619 946-1224
9668 Heinrich Hertz Dr Ste D San Diego (92154) *(P-5031)*

Romla Ventilator Co, San Diego *Also Called: Romla Co (P-5031)*

Ron Rick Holdings Montana LLC .... D 406 493-5606
80795 Vista Bonita Trl La Quinta (92253) *(P-12610)*

Ron Teeguarden Enterprises Inc (PA) .... E 323 556-8188
10940 Wilshire Blvd Los Angeles (90024) *(P-3329)*

Ronald Reagan Building, Los Angeles *Also Called: Ucla Health (P-16236)*

RONALD REAGAN PRESIDENTIAL LIB, Simi Valley *Also Called: Ronald Rgan Prsdntial Fndtion (P-17262)*

Ronald Reagan Ucla Medical Ctr, Los Angeles *Also Called: University Cal Los Angeles (P-16240)*

Ronald Rgan Prsdntial Fndtion .... D 805 522-2977
40 Presidential Dr Ste 200 Simi Valley (93065) *(P-17262)*

Ronan Engineering Company (PA) .... D 661 702-1344
28209 Avenue Stanford Valencia (91355) *(P-7876)*

Ronan Engnrng/Rnan Msrment Div, Valencia *Also Called: Ronan Engineering Company (P-7876)*

Roncelli Plastics Inc .... C 800 250-6516
330 W Duarte Rd Monrovia (91016) *(P-6222)*

Ronco Plastics, Tustin *Also Called: Ronco Plastics Inc (P-4225)*

Ronco Plastics Inc .... E 714 259-1385
15022 Parkway Loop Ste B Tustin (92780) *(P-4225)*

Ronford Products Inc .... E 909 622-7446
1116 E 2nd St Pomona (91766) *(P-4226)*

Ronlo Engineering Ltd .... E 805 388-3227
955 Flynn Rd Camarillo (93012) *(P-6223)*

Roochi Traders Incorporated .... D 323 722-5592
6393 E Washington Blvd Commerce (90040) *(P-10694)*

Roosevelt Hotel LLC .... C 323 466-7000
7000 Hollywood Blvd Los Angeles (90028) *(P-13000)*

Roots Fulfillment, Anaheim *Also Called: Anchored Prints (P-2962)*

Rootstrap Inc .... C 310 907-9210
8306 Wilshire Blvd Ste 249 Beverly Hills (90211) *(P-13806)*

Ropers Majeski A Prof Corp .... C 213 312-2000
445 S Figueroa St Ste 3000 Los Angeles (90071) *(P-16771)*

Rosanna Inc .... C 714 751-5100
3350 Avenue Of The Arts Costa Mesa (92626) *(P-13001)*

Roscoe Moss Company, Los Angeles *Also Called: Roscoe Moss Manufacturing Co (P-4554)*

Roscoe Moss Manufacturing Co (PA) .... D 323 261-4185
4360 Worth St Los Angeles (90063) *(P-4554)*

Rose & Shore Inc .... B 323 826-2144
5151 Alcoa Ave Vernon (90058) *(P-14586)*

Rose Art Industries, El Segundo *Also Called: Mega Brands America Inc (P-8492)*

Rose Bowl Aquatics Center .... D 626 564-0330
360 N Arroyo Blvd Pasadena (91103) *(P-15166)*

Rose Brand Wipers Inc .... D 818 505-6290
11440 Sheldon St Sun Valley (91352) *(P-14975)*

Rose Hills Company (DH) .... A 562 699-0921
3888 Workman Mill Rd Whittier (90601) *(P-12588)*

Rose Hills Holdings Corp (HQ) .... B 562 699-0921
3888 Workman Mill Rd Whittier (90601) *(P-12589)*

Rose Hills Mem Pk & Mortuary, Whittier *Also Called: Rose Hills Company (P-12588)*

Rose Hills Mem Pk & Mortuary, Whittier *Also Called: Rose Hills Holdings Corp (P-12589)*

Rose Lilla Inc .... E 888 519-8889
1050 S Cypress St La Habra (90631) *(P-8575)*

Rose Villa Healthcare Center, Bellflower *Also Called: Bell Villa Care Associates LLC (P-15581)*

Rosecrans Care Center, Gardena *Also Called: Healthcare Investments Inc (P-15674)*

Rosecrans Villa, Hawthorne *Also Called: Longwood Management Corp (P-17175)*

Rosemary Childrens Services (PA) .... C 626 844-3033
36 S Kinneloa Ave # 200 Pasadena (91107) *(P-17192)*

Rosemead Electrical Supply .... E 562 298-4190
9150 Dice Rd Santa Fe Springs (90670) *(P-7147)*

Rosemount Analytical Inc .... A 713 396-8880
2400 Barranca Pkwy Irvine (92606) *(P-6358)*

Rosen & Rosen Industries Inc .... D 949 361-9238
204 Avenida Fabricante San Clemente (92672) *(P-8536)*

Rosen Electronics, Ontario *Also Called: Rosen Electronics LLC (P-10569)*

Rosen Electronics LLC .... D 951 898-9808
2500 E Francis St Ontario (91761) *(P-10569)*

Rosendin Electric Inc .... A 714 739-1334
1730 S Anaheim Way Anaheim (92805) *(P-956)*

Rosenthal Group, The, Venice *Also Called: Trg Inc (P-12540)*

Rosewood Court, Fullerton *Also Called: Emeritus Corporation (P-15634)*

Rosewood Miramar Bch Montecito, Santa Barbara *Also Called: Miramar Acquisition Co LLC (P-12719)*

Rosewood Retirement Community, Bakersfield *Also Called: Humangood Norcal (P-15861)*

Roshan Trading Inc .... E 213 622-9904
3631 Union Pacific Ave Los Angeles (90023) *(P-1903)*

Roskam Baking Company LLC .... C 909 599-0961
505 W Allen Ave San Dimas (91773) *(P-1845)*

Roskam Baking Company LLC .... B 909 305-0185
305 S Acacia St Ste A San Dimas (91773) *(P-1846)*

Ross Bindery Inc .... C 562 623-4565
15310 Spring Ave Santa Fe Springs (90670) *(P-3203)*

Ross Name Plate Company .... E 323 725-6812
2 Red Plum Cir Monterey Park (91755) *(P-8627)*

Ross Racing Pistons .... D 310 536-0100
625 S Douglas St El Segundo (90245) *(P-6045)*

Rossin Steel Inc .... C 619 656-9200
9102 Birch St Spring Valley (91977) *(P-10155)*

Rossmoor Pastries MGT Inc .... D 562 498-2253
2325 Redondo Ave Signal Hill (90755) *(P-1463)*

Rostar Filters, Oxnard *Also Called: PC Vaughan Mfg Corp (P-4193)*

Rotary and Miission Systems, Fort Irwin *Also Called: Lockheed Martin Corporation (P-9084)*

Rotating Prcsion McHanisms Inc .... E 818 349-9774
8750 Shirley Ave Northridge (91324) *(P-6655)*

Rotational Molding Inc .... D 310 327-5401
17038 S Figueroa St Gardena (90248) *(P-4227)*

Rotax Incorporated .... E 323 589-5999
2940 Leonis Blvd Vernon (90058) *(P-2130)*

Roth Capital Partners LLC (PA) .... D 800 678-9147
888 San Clemente Dr Newport Beach (92660) *(P-12006)*

Roth Mkm, Newport Beach *Also Called: Roth Capital Partners LLC (P-12006)*

Roth Staffing Companies LP (PA) .... D 714 939-8600
450 N State College Blvd Orange (92868) *(P-13619)*

Roto Dynamics Inc .... E 714 685-0183
1925 N Lime St Orange (92865) *(P-4228)*

Roto-Rooter, Valencia *Also Called: Russell-Warner Inc (P-14788)*

Rotolo Chevrolet Inc .... C 866 756-9776
16666 S Highland Ave Fontana (92336) *(P-11402)*

Rotron Incorporated .... C 619 593-7400
474 Raleigh Ave El Cajon (92020) *(P-5776)*

Mergent email: customerrelations@mergent.com
1168

2025 Southern California
Business Directory and Buyers Guide

(P-0000) Products & Services Section entry number
(PA)=Parent Co (HQ)=Headquarters (DH)=Div Headquarters

Round 1 Bowling and Amusement, Brea *Also Called: Round One Entertainment Inc (P-15002)*

Round One Entertainment Inc (HQ)................A 714 924-7800
3070 Saturn St Ste 200 Brea (92821) *(P-15002)*

Roundabout Entertainment Inc ....D 818 842-9300
217 S Lake St Burbank (91502) *(P-14853)*

Roundtool Laboratories, Huntington Beach *Also Called: Tool Alliance Corporation (P-5627)*

Rouse Services LLC ....D 310 360-9200
8383 Wilshire Blvd Ste 900 Beverly Hills (90211) *(P-13186)*

Rove Engineering Inc ....D 760 425-0001
398 E Aurora Dr El Centro (92243) *(P-17621)*

Row House, Irvine *Also Called: Row House Franchise LLC (P-15060)*

Row House Franchise LLC ....D 949 341-5585
17877 Von Karman Ave Ste 100 Irvine (92614) *(P-15060)*

Row Management Ltd Inc ....B 310 887-3671
499 N Canon Dr Beverly Hills (90210) *(P-12526)*

Rowi Usa LLC ....D 805 356-3372
3155 Old Conejo Rd Thousand Oaks (91320) *(P-17000)*

Rowland Convalescent Hosp Inc ....D 626 967-2741
330 W Rowland St Covina (91723) *(P-15765)*

ROWLAND, THE, Covina *Also Called: Rowland Convalescent Hosp Inc (P-15765)*

Roy E Hanson Jr Mfg (PA)..............................D 213 747-7514
1600 E Washington Blvd Los Angeles (90021) *(P-4924)*

Roy E Whitehead Inc ....D 951 682-1490
2245 Via Cerro Riverside (92509) *(P-1060)*

Roy Miller Freight Lines LLC (PA).................D 714 632-5511
3165 E Coronado St Anaheim (92806) *(P-8922)*

Royal Cabinets, Pomona *Also Called: Royal Cabinets Inc (P-2361)*

Royal Cabinets, Pomona *Also Called: Royal Industries Inc (P-2362)*

Royal Cabinets Inc ....A 909 629-8565
1299 E Phillips Blvd Pomona (91766) *(P-2361)*

Royal Care Skilled Nursing Ctr, Long Beach *Also Called: Covenant Care California LLC (P-15612)*

Royal Coatings, Simi Valley *Also Called: Mabel Baas Inc (P-5330)*

Royal Crown Enterprises Inc ....C 626 854-8080
780 Epperson Dr City Of Industry (91748) *(P-10976)*

Royal Custom Designs LLC ....C 909 591-8990
13951 Monte Vista Ave Chino (91710) *(P-2459)*

Royal Equestrian Apartments, Burbank *Also Called: Greystar Rs Group LLC (P-12295)*

Royal Industries, Eastvale *Also Called: Royal Range California Inc (P-6390)*

Royal Industries Inc ....C 909 629-8565
1299 E Phillips Blvd Pomona (91766) *(P-2362)*

Royal Interpack North Amer Inc ....E 951 787-6925
475 Palmyrita Ave Riverside (92507) *(P-4229)*

Royal Oaks, Duarte *Also Called: Humangood Socal (P-12345)*

Royal Paper Box Co California (PA)...............C 323 728-7041
1105 S Maple Ave Montebello (90640) *(P-11140)*

Royal Plasticware, Gardena *Also Called: La Palm Furnitures & ACC Inc (P-2248)*

Royal Plywood Company LLC (PA).................D 562 404-2989
14171 Park Pl Cerritos (90703) *(P-9931)*

Royal Range California Inc ....D 951 360-1600
3245 Corridor Dr Eastvale (91752) *(P-6390)*

Royal Specialty Undwrt Inc ....C 818 922-6700
15303 Ventura Blvd Ste 500 Sherman Oaks (91403) *(P-12134)*

Royal Welding & Fabricating, Fullerton *Also Called: Cook and Cook Incorporated (P-4914)*

Royal West Drywall Inc ....D 951 271-4600
2008 2nd St Norco (92860) *(P-1026)*

Royal Westlake Roofing LLC ....C 760 967-0827
3093 Industry St Ste A Oceanside (92054) *(P-1094)*

Royal Westlake Roofing LLC ....E 909 822-4407
3511 N Riverside Ave Rialto (92377) *(P-4420)*

Royale Convalescent Hospital, Santa Ana *Also Called: Orange Cnty Ryale Cnvlscent Ho (P-15878)*

Royalty, Irvine *Also Called: Royalty Carpet Mills Inc (P-1955)*

Royalty Carpet Mills Inc ....A 949 474-4000
17111 Red Hill Ave Irvine (92614) *(P-1955)*

Rp Automotive II Inc ....D 619 656-2500
560 Auto Park Dr Chula Vista (91911) *(P-14642)*

Rpc Inc ....E 619 334-6244
1100 N Magnolia Ave Ste H El Cajon (92020) *(P-362)*

Rpd Hotels 18 LLC ....A 213 746-1531
1801 S La Cienega Blvd Ste 301 Los Angeles (90035) *(P-13002)*

RPI, Simi Valley *Also Called: Replacement Parts Inds Inc (P-8353)*

Rplanet Erth Los Angles Hldngs ....D 833 775-2638
5300 S Boyle Ave Vernon (90058) *(P-4230)*

RPM, Northridge *Also Called: Rotating Prcsion McHanisms Inc (P-6655)*

RPM Consolidated Services Inc (HQ)............D 714 388-3500
1901 Raymer Ave Fullerton (92833) *(P-9106)*

RPM Media, Torrance *Also Called: Retail Print Media Inc (P-3170)*

RPM Plastic Molding Inc ....E 714 630-9300
2821 E Miraloma Ave Anaheim (92806) *(P-4231)*

RPM Products Inc (PA)..................................E 949 888-8543
23201 Antonio Pkwy Rancho Santa Margari (92688) *(P-3898)*

RPM Transportation Inc (DH)........................C 714 388-3500
11660 Arroyo Ave Santa Ana (92705) *(P-8973)*

RPS Inc ....E 818 350-8088
20331 Corisco St Chatsworth (91311) *(P-5415)*

Rpsz Construction LLC ....D 314 677-5831
1201 W 5th St Ste T340 Los Angeles (90017) *(P-8537)*

Rq Construction LLC ....C 760 631-7707
1620 Faraday Ave Carlsbad (92008) *(P-498)*

Rrd Pckaging Solutions - Vista, Vista *Also Called: Precision Litho Inc (P-3064)*

RRI, Downey *Also Called: Rancho Research Institute (P-17886)*

Rrm Design Group (PA).................................D 805 439-0442
3765 S Higuera St Ste 102 San Luis Obispo (93401) *(P-17689)*

Rrt Enterprises LP ....C 323 653-1521
855 N Fairfax Ave Los Angeles (90046) *(P-15766)*

Rrt Enterprises LP (PA).................................C 310 397-2372
3966 Marcasel Ave Los Angeles (90001) *(P-15767)*

RRT ENTERPRISES LP, Los Angeles *Also Called: Rrt Enterprises LP (P-15766)*

Rsa Engineered Products LLC ....D 805 584-4150
110 W Cochran St Ste A Simi Valley (93065) *(P-7549)*

Rsg Group North America LP ....C 714 609-0572
7007 Romaine St Ste 101 West Hollywood (90038) *(P-15061)*

Rsg Group USA Inc ....A 214 574-4653
7007 Romaine St Ste 101 West Hollywood (90038) *(P-12611)*

RSI, Anaheim *Also Called: RSI Home Products LLC (P-2473)*

RSI Home Products, Anaheim *Also Called: American Woodmark Corporation (P-2337)*

RSI Home Products Inc ....C 949 720-1116
620 Newport Center Dr Ste 1030 Newport Beach (92660) *(P-2472)*

RSI Home Products LLC (HQ).........................A 714 449-2200
400 E Orangethorpe Ave Anaheim (92801) *(P-2473)*

Rsk Tool Incorporated ....E 310 537-3302
410 W Carob St Compton (90220) *(P-4232)*

Rsui Group, Sherman Oaks *Also Called: Royal Specialty Undwrt Inc (P-12134)*

Rsvc Company ....C 951 684-6578
3051 Myers St Ste B Riverside (92503) *(P-647)*

RT&d, Carson *Also Called: Research Tool & Die Works LLC (P-5211)*

RTC Aerospace, Chatsworth *Also Called: Logistical Support LLC (P-7391)*

RTC Aerospace, Chatsworth *Also Called: Cliffdale Manufacturing LLC (P-7667)*

RTC Arspace - Chtswrth Div Inc (PA)............D 818 341-3344
20409 Prairie St Chatsworth (91311) *(P-6048)*

Rte Enterprises Inc ....D 818 999-5300
21530 Roscoe Blvd Canoga Park (91304) *(P-872)*

Rti Los Angeles, Norwalk *Also Called: New Cntury Mtals Southeast Inc (P-4619)*

Rti Systems Inc ....D 213 599-8470
7635 N San Fernando Rd Burbank (91505) *(P-14417)*

Rtm Products Inc ....E 562 926-2400
13120 Arctic Cir Santa Fe Springs (90670) *(P-4523)*

Rtmex Inc ....C 619 391-9913
1202 Piper Ranch Rd San Diego (92154) *(P-2292)*

Rtr Industries LLC (PA).................................E 714 996-0050
4430 E Miraloma Ave Ste B Anaheim (92807) *(P-6046)*

Rubber Plastic & Metal Pdts, Rancho Santa Margari *Also Called: RPM Products Inc (P-3898)*

Rubber Teck Division, Long Beach *Also Called: Rubbercraft Corp Cal Ltd (P-3906)*

Rubber-Cal Inc ....E 714 772-3000
18424 Mount Langley St Fountain Valley (92708) *(P-3934)*

Rubbercraft Corp Cal Ltd (HQ).......................C 562 354-2800
3701 E Conant St Long Beach (90808) *(P-3906)*

Rubicon Gear, Corona *Also Called: Rubicon Gear Inc (P-5149)*

Rubicon Gear Inc ....D 951 356-3800
225 Citation Cir Corona (92878) *(P-5149)*

A
L
P
H
A
B
E
T
I
C

Employee Codes: A=Over 500 employees, B=251-500
C=101-250, D=51-100, E=20-49, F=10-19, G=1-9

2025 Southern California
Business Directory and Buyers Guide

© Mergent Inc. 1-800-342-5647
1169

Rubidoux Family Care Center, Riverside *Also Called: County of Riverside (P-15294)*

Rubin Postaer and Associates (PA)........................C 310 394-4000
2525 Colorado Ave Ste 100 Santa Monica (90404) *(P-13243)*

Rubio Arts Corporation ....C 407 849-1643
1313 S Harbor Blvd Anaheim (92802) *(P-18379)*

Ruby Ribbon Inc ....E 650 449-4470
4607 Lakeview Canyon Rd Pmb 405 Westlake Village (91361) *(P-10723)*

Ruby Rox, Los Angeles *Also Called: Misyd Corp (P-2167)*

Rudolph and Sletten Inc ....C 949 252-1919
2855 Michelle Ste 350 Irvine (92606) *(P-580)*

Rudolph Foods Company Inc ....C 909 388-2202
920 W Fourth St Beaumont (92223) *(P-1727)*

Ruffin Hotel Corp of Cal ....B 562 425-5210
4700 Airport Plaza Dr Long Beach (90815) *(P-13003)*

Rugby Laboratories Inc (DH) ....D 951 270-1400
311 Bonnie Cir Corona (92878) *(P-10649)*

Ruggable LLC ....B 310 295-0098
17809 S Broadway Gardena (90248) *(P-11663)*

Rugged Info Tech Eqp Corp ....D 805 577-9710
25 E Easy St Simi Valley (93065) *(P-5951)*

Rugged Systems Inc ....C 858 391-1006
13000 Danielson St Ste Q Poway (92064) *(P-5866)*

Ruggeri Marble and Granite Inc ....D 310 513-2155
25028 Vermont Ave Harbor City (90710) *(P-4476)*

Ruhs-Emergency Department, Moreno Valley *Also Called: Riverside University Health (P-16163)*

Ruiteng Internet Technology Co ....C 302 597-7438
1344 W Foothill Blvd Ste D Azusa (91702) *(P-14152)*

Ruiz Flour Tortillas, Riverside *Also Called: Ruiz Mexican Foods Inc (P-1847)*

Ruiz Mexican Foods Inc (PA)................................C 909 947-7811
1200 Marlborough Ave Ste A Riverside (92507) *(P-1847)*

Rume Medical Group Inc ....D 714 406-1887
18800 Delaware St Ste 800 Huntington Beach (92648) *(P-15440)*

Runbuggy Omi Inc ....C 888 872-8449
1377 Kettering Dr Ontario (91761) *(P-9332)*

Running Tide Technologies Inc ....D 207 835-7010
1590 Rosecrans Ave Manhattan Beach (90266) *(P-94)*

Runway Liquidation LLC (HQ) ....D 323 589-2224
2761 Fruitland Ave Vernon (90058) *(P-10724)*

Rupe's Hydraulics Sales & Svc, San Marcos *Also Called: Hydralic Systems Cmponents Inc (P-14773)*

Rush Press Inc ....E 619 296-7874
955 Gateway Center Way San Diego (92102) *(P-3078)*

Rushmore Crrspndent Lnding Svc, Irvine *Also Called: Rushmore Loan MGT Svcs LLC (P-11933)*

Rushmore Loan MGT Svcs LLC (PA) ....A 949 727-4798
15480 Laguna Canyon Rd Ste 100 Irvine (92618) *(P-11933)*

Russ August & Kabat LLP ....D 310 826-7474
12424 Wilshire Blvd Ste 1200 Los Angeles (90025) *(P-16772)*

Russ Bassett Corp ....C 562 945-2445
8189 Byron Rd Whittier (90606) *(P-2434)*

Russell Fabrication Corp ....E 661 861-8495
4940 Gilmore Ave Bakersfield (93308) *(P-5438)*

Russell Hobbs Inc ....C 909 792-8257
2301 W San Bernardino Ave Redlands (92374) *(P-499)*

Russell-Warner Inc ....E 661 257-9200
24971 Avenue Stanford Valencia (91355) *(P-14788)*

Rustic Canyon Group LLC ....D 310 998-8000
1025 Westwood Blvd Los Angeles (90024) *(P-12734)*

Rustic Canyon Partners, Los Angeles *Also Called: Rustic Canyon Group LLC (P-12734)*

Rutan & Tucker LLP (PA).......................................B 714 641-5100
18575 Jamboree Rd Ste 900 Irvine (92612) *(P-16773)*

Rutherford Co Inc (PA)...D 323 666-5284
2107 Crystal St Los Angeles (90039) *(P-1027)*

Rutland Tool & Supply Co (HQ).............................C 562 566-5000
2225 Workman Mill Rd City Of Industry (90601) *(P-10460)*

Rvl Packaging Inc ....C 818 735-5000
31330 Oak Crest Dr Westlake Village (91361) *(P-14587)*

RW Zant LLC (DH)..D 323 980-5457
1470 E 4th St Los Angeles (90033) *(P-10880)*

RW&g, Los Angeles *Also Called: Richards Wtson Grshon A Prof C (P-16769)*

Rwh Inc ....E 818 782-2350
15115 Oxnard St Van Nuys (91411) *(P-4455)*

Rx Pro Health LLC ....A 858 369-4050
12400 High Bluff Dr Ste 100 San Diego (92130) *(P-13620)*

Rxsafe, Vista *Also Called: Rxsafe LLC (P-5719)*

Rxsafe LLC ....D 760 593-7161
2453 Cades Way Bldg A Vista (92081) *(P-5719)*

RXSIGHT, Aliso Viejo *Also Called: Rxsight Inc (P-8414)*

Rxsight Inc (PA)...D 949 521-7830
100 Columbia Ste 120 Aliso Viejo (92656) *(P-8414)*

Ryan Press, Buena Park *Also Called: Q Team (P-3073)*

Ryan's Express, Torrance *Also Called: Ryans Express Trnsp Svcs Inc (P-8846)*

Ryans Express Trnsp Svcs Inc (PA) ....D 310 219-2960
19500 Mariner Ave Torrance (90503) *(P-8846)*

Rydell Chevrolet-Northridge, Northridge *Also Called: San Fernando Valley Auto LLC (P-11404)*

Rye Electric Inc ....D 949 441-0545
28202 Cabot Rd Ste 300 Laguna Niguel (92677) *(P-957)*

RYL Inc ....E 213 503-7968
2738 Supply Ave Commerce (90040) *(P-11141)*

Rynoclad Technologies Inc ....C 951 264-3441
780 E Francis St Ste M Ontario (91761) *(P-1166)*

Ryvec Inc ....E 714 520-5592
251 E Palais Rd Anaheim (92805) *(P-3223)*

S & H Cabinets and Mfg Inc ....E 909 357-0551
10860 Mulberry Ave Fontana (92337) *(P-2517)*

S & H Machine Inc ....E 626 448-5062
9928 Hayward Way South El Monte (91733) *(P-5376)*

S & H Rubber Co ....E 714 525-0277
1141 E Elm Ave Fullerton (92831) *(P-3935)*

S & M Moving Systems, Santa Fe Springs *Also Called: Van Torrance & Storage Company (P-8996)*

S & R Architectural Metals Inc ....E 714 226-0108
2609 W Woodland Dr Anaheim (92801) *(P-4866)*

S & S Bakery, Vista *Also Called: Baked In The Sun (P-1435)*

S & S Carbide Tool Inc ....E 619 670-5214
2830 Via Orange Way Ste D Spring Valley (91978) *(P-5596)*

S & S Construction Co, Beverly Hills *Also Called: Shapell Industries LLC (P-12578)*

S & W Plastic Stores Inc (PA)...............................E 909 390-0090
14270 Albers Way Chino (91710) *(P-11002)*

S & W Plastics Supply, Chino *Also Called: S & W Plastic Stores Inc (P-11002)*

S 2 K, Simi Valley *Also Called: S2k Graphics Inc (P-8628)*

S A Top-U Corporation ....E 951 916-4025
1794 Illinois Ave Perris (92571) *(P-11643)*

S B H Hotel Corporation ....B 909 889-0133
285 E Hospitality Ln San Bernardino (92408) *(P-13004)*

S Bravo Systems Inc ....E 323 888-4133
2929 Vail Ave Los Angeles (90040) *(P-4925)*

S C A, Victorville *Also Called: Comav Technical Services LLC (P-9197)*

S C A G, Los Angeles *Also Called: Cal Southern Assn Governments (P-18297)*

S C Coatings Corporation ....E 951 461-9777
41775 Elm St Ste 302 Murrieta (92562) *(P-5342)*

S C Hydraulic Engineering, Brea *Also Called: Southern Cal Hydrlic Engrg Cor (P-10404)*

S C I Industries Inc ....E
1433 Adelia Ave South El Monte (91733) *(P-7290)*

S C I R E, Long Beach *Also Called: Southern Cal Inst For RES Edca (P-17891)*

S C P M G, San Dimas *Also Called: Southern Cal Prmnnte Med Group (P-12113)*

S C P M G, Harbor City *Also Called: Permanente Medical Group Inc (P-15423)*

S C P M G, Culver City *Also Called: Southern Cal Prmnnte Med Group (P-15463)*

S C P M G, Inglewood *Also Called: Southern Cal Prmnnte Med Group (P-15464)*

S C P M G, Cudahy *Also Called: Southern Cal Prmnnte Med Group (P-15465)*

S C P M G, Woodland Hills *Also Called: Southern Cal Prmnnte Med Group (P-15466)*

S C P M G, Santa Clarita *Also Called: Southern Cal Prmnnte Med Group (P-15467)*

S C P M G, Anaheim *Also Called: Southern Cal Prmnnte Med Group (P-15473)*

S C P M G, San Juan Capistrano *Also Called: Southern Cal Prmnnte Med Group (P-15474)*

S C P M G, Santa Ana *Also Called: Southern Cal Prmnnte Med Group (P-15475)*

S C P M G, Colton *Also Called: Southern Cal Prmnnte Med Group (P-15478)*

S C P M G, El Cajon *Also Called: Southern Cal Prmnnte Med Group (P-15479)*

Mergent email: customerrelations@mergent.com
1170

2025 Southern California
Business Directory and Buyers Guide

(P-0000) Products & Services Section entry number
(PA)=Parent Co (HQ)=Headquarters (DH)=Div Headquarters

S C P M G, San Diego *Also Called: Southern Cal Prmnnte Med Group (P-15480)*

S C P M G, Escondido *Also Called: Southern Cal Prmnnte Med Group (P-15481)*

S C P M G, Fontana *Also Called: Southern Cal Prmnnte Med Group (P-16207)*

S C Village, Bellflower *Also Called: S J S Enterprise Inc (P-15219)*

S D I, Lakeside *Also Called: Standard Drywall Inc (P-1030)*

S D I, Camarillo *Also Called: Structural Diagnostics Inc (P-8065)*

S D M, Chino *Also Called: Syntech Development & Mfg Inc (P-4253)*

S E - G I Products Inc .... C 949 297-8530
20521 Teresita Way Lake Forest (92630) *(P-4900)*

S E C C Corporation (PA).. D 909 393-5419
502 N Sheridan St Corona (92878) *(P-690)*

S E O P Inc .... C 949 682-7906
1621 Alton Pkwy Ste 150 Irvine (92606) *(P-14153)*

S E Pipe Line Construction Co .... D 562 868-9771
11832 Bloomfield Ave Santa Fe Springs (90670) *(P-691)*

S G S Produce, Los Angeles *Also Called: Shapiro-Gilman-Shandler Co (P-10917)*

S J S Enterprise Inc .... C 949 489-9000
9030 Somerset Blvd Bellflower (90706) *(P-15219)*

S K Laboratories Inc .... D 714 695-9800
5420 E La Palma Ave Anaheim (92807) *(P-3496)*

S K Labs, Anaheim *Also Called: S K Laboratories Inc (P-3496)*

S L Fusco Inc (PA)... E 310 868-1010
1966 E Via Arado Rancho Dominguez (90220) *(P-5550)*

S L Start and Associates LLC .... D 760 414-9411
3500 Lake Blvd Oceanside (92056) *(P-17193)*

S R C Devices Inccustomer .... B 866 772-8668
6295 Ferris Sq Ste D San Diego (92121) *(P-6359)*

S R Machining, Norco *Also Called: S R Machining-Properties LLC (P-6225)*

S R Machining Inc .... E 951 520-9486
640 Parkridge Ave Norco (92860) *(P-6224)*

S R Machining-Properties LLC .... C 951 520-9486
640 Parkridge Ave Norco (92860) *(P-6225)*

S S, South Gate *Also Called: Shultz Steel Company LLC (P-5160)*

S S I, Long Beach *Also Called: Seal Science Inc (P-3899)*

S S I, Camarillo *Also Called: Synectic Solutions Inc (P-14257)*

S S W Mechanical Cnstr Inc .... C 760 327-1481
670 S Oleander Rd Palm Springs (92264) *(P-833)*

S W K Properties LLC .... C 714 481-6300
2726 S Grand Ave Lbby Santa Ana (92705) *(P-13005)*

S W K Properties LLC (PA).. D 213 383-9204
3807 Wilshire Blvd Ste 1226 Los Angeles (90010) *(P-13006)*

S.D.I. Media USA Inc., Burbank *Also Called: Iyuno USA Inc (P-14835)*

S&B Development Group LLC .... E 213 446-2818
1901 Avenue Of The Stars 235 Los Angeles (90067) *(P-1897)*

S&B Filters Inc (PA)... E 909 947-0015
15461 Slover Ave Ste A Fontana (92337) *(P-7291)*

S&B Industry Inc .... E 909 569-4155
105 S Puente St Brea (92821) *(P-4233)*

S&B Pharma Inc .... D 626 334-2908
405 S Motor Ave Azusa (91702) *(P-3330)*

S&E Gourmet Cuts Inc .... C 909 370-0155
1055 E Cooley Ave San Bernardino (92408) *(P-10850)*

S&H, San Diego *Also Called: Sharpmart LLC (P-3686)*

S&S Flavours, Brea *Also Called: Scisorek & Son Flavors Inc (P-1609)*

S&S Precision Mfg Inc .... E 714 754-6664
2101 S Yale St Santa Ana (92704) *(P-6226)*

S2k Graphics Inc .... E 818 885-3900
4686 Industrial St Simi Valley (93063) *(P-8628)*

SA Camp Pump and Drilling Co, Bakersfield *Also Called: SA Camp Pump Company (P-14789)*

SA Camp Pump Company .... D 661 399-2976
17876 Zerker Rd Bakersfield (93308) *(P-14789)*

SA Recycling, Orange *Also Called: SA Recycling LLC (P-9761)*

SA Recycling LLC (PA).. C 714 632-2000
2411 N Glassell St Orange (92865) *(P-9761)*

SA Serving Lines Inc .... E 714 848-7529
226 W Carleton Ave Orange (92867) *(P-5032)*

Sa-Tech, Oxnard *Also Called: Systems Application & Tech Inc (P-17640)*

Saalex Corp .... B 951 543-9259
27525 Enterprise Cir W Ste 101a Temecula (92590) *(P-13807)*

Saalex Corp (PA)... C 805 482-1070
811 Camarillo Springs Rd Ste A Camarillo (93012) *(P-17622)*

Saalex Solutions, Camarillo *Also Called: Saalex Corp (P-17622)*

Saatchi & Saatchi N Amer LLC .... C 310 437-2500
3501 Sepulveda Blvd Torrance (90505) *(P-13244)*

Saba Holding Company LLC .... C 951 277-7620
22099 Knabe Rd Corona (92883) *(P-10359)*

Sabal Capital Partners LLC .... C 949 255-1007
680 E Colorado Blvd Ste 350 Pasadena (91101) *(P-12735)*

Saban Brands LLC (HQ).. D 310 557-5230
10100 Santa Monica Blvd Ste 500 Los Angeles (90067) *(P-18204)*

Saban Capital Group LLC .... D 310 557-5100
11301 W Olympic Blvd Ste 121601 Los Angeles (90064) *(P-12612)*

SABAN COMMUNITY CLINIC, Los Angeles *Also Called: Los Angeles Free Clinic (P-15383)*

Saban Research Institute, The, Los Angeles *Also Called: Childrens Hospital Los Angeles (P-15953)*

Sabater Usa Inc (PA).. E 310 518-2227
14824 S Main St Gardena (90248) *(P-1848)*

Sabel, Vista *Also Called: Surgistar Inc (P-8231)*

Saber, Paramount *Also Called: South Coast Piering Inc (P-588)*

Sabia, San Diego *Also Called: Sabia Incorporated (P-7877)*

Sabia Incorporated (PA)... E 858 217-2200
10919 Technology Pl Ste A San Diego (92127) *(P-7877)*

Sabina Motors & Controls, Anaheim *Also Called: Motors & Controls Whse Inc (P-10270)*

Sabre Systems Inc .... D 619 528-2226
3111 Camino Del Rio N Ste 400 San Diego (92108) *(P-17623)*

Sabritec .... B 714 371-1100
1550 Scenic Ave Ste 150 Costa Mesa (92626) *(P-6959)*

Sabsaf LLC .... D 951 266-6676
17192 Murphy Ave Unit 18641 Irvine (92623) *(P-9011)*

Sabsaf Logistics, Irvine *Also Called: Sabsaf LLC (P-9011)*

Sac International Steel Inc (PA).................................. D 323 232-2467
6130 Avalon Blvd Los Angeles (90003) *(P-10156)*

Sacahn JV .... D 858 924-1110
15916 Bernardo Center Dr San Diego (92127) *(P-3829)*

Sacco Restaurants Inc .... D 858 451-9464
12075 Carmel Mountain Rd Ste 201 San Diego (92128) *(P-11598)*

Sada, North Hollywood *Also Called: Sada Systems LLC (P-14248)*

Sada Systems LLC (HQ).. C 818 766-2400
5250 Lankershim Blvd Ste 720 North Hollywood (91601) *(P-14248)*

Sadaf Foods, Los Angeles *Also Called: Soofer Co Inc (P-10980)*

Saddle Back Valley YMCA, Mission Viejo *Also Called: Young MNS Chrstn Assn Ornge CN (P-17409)*

Saddleback Memorial Med Ctr (HQ)............................ A 949 837-4500
24451 Health Center Dr Fl 1 Laguna Hills (92653) *(P-16164)*

Saddleback Valley Service Ctr, Irvine *Also Called: Southern California Edison Co (P-9620)*

Saddlemen, Compton *Also Called: Saddlemen Corporation (P-9846)*

Saddlemen Corporation .... C 310 638-1222
17801 S Susana Rd Compton (90221) *(P-9846)*

Sadie Rose Baking Co .... D 760 806-7793
2614 Temple Heights Dr Oceanside (92066) *(P-10077)*

Saehan Electronics America Inc (PA).......................... D 858 496-1500
7880 Airway Rd Ste B5g San Diego (92154) *(P-6767)*

Saeilo Manufacturing Inds, Santa Fe Springs *Also Called: SMI Ca Inc (P-8238)*

Saf-T-Co Supply .... E 714 547-9975
1300 E Normandy Pl Santa Ana (92705) *(P-6434)*

Safariland LLC .... B 909 923-7300
4700 E Airport Dr Ontario (91761) *(P-8298)*

Safc Pharma, Carlsbad *Also Called: Sigma-Aldrich Corporation (P-3820)*

Safe Haven, San Fernando *Also Called: Valeda Company LLC (P-8316)*

Safe Life Corporation .... D 858 794-3208
12250 El Camino Real San Diego (92130) *(P-17887)*

Safe Plating Inc .... D 626 810-1872
18001 Railroad St City Of Industry (91748) *(P-5290)*

Safe Publishing Company .... D 805 973-1300
400 Del Norte Blvd Oxnard (93030) *(P-3173)*

Safe Refuge .... D 562 987-5722
4510 E Pacific Coast Hwy Long Beach (90804) *(P-16500)*

Safeco Insurance Company Amer .... C 818 956-4250
330 N Brand Blvd Ste 680 Glendale (91203) *(P-12251)*

A
L
P
H
A
B
E
T
I
C

Employee Codes: A=Over 500 employees, B=251-500
C=101-250, D=51-100, E=20-50, F=10-19, G=1-9

2025 Southern California
Business Directory and Buyers Guide

© Mergent Inc. 1-800-342-5647

1171

Safeguard Envirogroup Inc .... E 626 512-7585
153 Lowell Ave Glendora (91741) *(P-7975)*

Safeguard Health Entps Inc (HQ)...................... **B 800 880-1800**
95 Enterprise Ste 100 Aliso Viejo (92656) *(P-12102)*

Safeguard On Demand Inc .... C 800 640-2327
11037 Warner Ave # 297 Fountain Valley (92708) *(P-14336)*

Safer Sports Inc .... E 760 444-0082
5670 El Camino Real Ste B Carlsbad (92008) *(P-8538)*

Safesmart Access Inc .... E 310 410-1525
13238 Florence Ave Santa Fe Springs (90670) *(P-14418)*

Safety Products Holdings LLC .... E 714 662-1033
170 Technology Dr Irvine (92618) *(P-5551)*

Safeway Inc .... A 714 990-8357
200 N Puente St Brea (92821) *(P-11670)*

Safeway Sign Company .... E 760 246-7070
9875 Yucca Rd Adelanto (92301) *(P-8629)*

Saffola Quality Foods, Ontario Also Called: Ventura Foods LLC (P-1283)

Safran, Anaheim Also Called: Morphotrak LLC (P-14097)

Safran Aerospace, Carson Also Called: Safran Usa Inc (P-6427)

Safran Cabin - Cypress, Cypress Also Called: Safran Cabin Inc (P-7553)

Safran Cabin Galleys Us Inc (HQ).................... **A 714 861-7300**
17311 Nichols Ln Huntington Beach (92647) *(P-7550)*

Safran Cabin Inc (HQ)................................ **B 714 934-0000**
5701 Bolsa Ave Huntington Beach (92647) *(P-7551)*

Safran Cabin Inc .... C 714 901-2672
12472 Industry St Garden Grove (92841) *(P-7552)*

Safran Cabin Inc .... C 562 344-4780
12240 Warland Dr Cypress (90630) *(P-7553)*

Safran Cabin Inc .... C 714 891-1906
7330 Lincoln Way Garden Grove (92841) *(P-7554)*

Safran Cabin Inc .... C 619 661-6292
2695 Customhouse Ct Ste 111 San Diego (92154) *(P-7555)*

Safran Cabin Inc .... C 619 671-0430
6754 Calle De Linea Ste 111 San Diego (92154) *(P-7556)*

Safran Cabin Inc .... C 805 922-3013
2850 Skyway Dr Santa Maria (93455) *(P-7557)*

Safran Cabin Inc .... C 909 652-9700
8595 Milliken Ave Ste 101 Rancho Cucamonga (91730) *(P-7558)*

Safran Cabin Inc .... D 714 934-0000
1500 Glenn Curtiss St Carson (90746) *(P-7559)*

Safran Cabin Tijuana S.a De Cv, San Diego Also Called: Safran Cabin Inc (P-7555)

Safran Defense & Space Inc .... D 603 296-0469
2960 Airway Ave Ste A103 Costa Mesa (92626) *(P-8018)*

Safran Defense & Space Inc .... D 805 373-9340
2665 Park Center Dr Ste A Simi Valley (93065) *(P-8019)*

Safran Pass Innovations LLC (HQ)................... **D 714 854-8600**
3151 E Imperial Hwy Brea (92821) *(P-13808)*

Safran Power Units, San Diego Also Called: Safran Pwr Units San Diego LLC (P-7395)

Safran Pwr Units San Diego LLC .... D 858 223-2228
4255 Ruffin Rd Ste 100 San Diego (92123) *(P-7395)*

Safran Seats Santa Maria LLC .... A 805 922-5995
2641 Airpark Dr Santa Maria (93455) *(P-7560)*

Safran Usa Inc .... A 310 884-7198
1500 Glenn Curtiss St Carson (90746) *(P-6427)*

SAG PRODUCERS PENSION PLAN, Burbank Also Called: Sag-Aftra Health Plan (P-12103)

Sag-Aftra Health Plan .... C 800 777-4013
3601 W Olive Ave Ste 200 Burbank (91505) *(P-12103)*

Saga Kapital Group Inc .... D 714 294-4132
108 Saybrook Irvine (92620) *(P-18048)*

Sage Goddess Inc .... E 650 733-6639
21010 Figueroa St Carson (90745) *(P-8461)*

Sage Hospitality Resources LLC .... B 626 357-5211
700 W Huntington Dr Monrovia (91016) *(P-13007)*

Sage Plastics Long Beach Corp .... D 562 423-3900
2210 E Artesia Blvd Long Beach (90805) *(P-4234)*

Sage Publications Inc (PA)........................... **C 805 499-0721**
2455 Teller Rd Thousand Oaks (91320) *(P-2895)*

Sage Software Inc .... E 949 753-1222
7595 Irvine Center Dr Ste 200 Irvine (92618) *(P-14178)*

Sage Software Holdings Inc (HQ).................... **B 866 530-7243**
6561 Irvine Center Dr Irvine (92618) *(P-14022)*

Sago Mini Inc .... D 416 731-8586
5880 W Jefferson Blvd Ste A Los Angeles (90016) *(P-13809)*

SAI Industries .... E 818 842-6144
631 Allen Ave Glendale (91201) *(P-5355)*

SAI Management Co Inc .... D 714 772-5050
1600 S Harbor Blvd Anaheim (92802) *(P-13008)*

Saic, San Diego Also Called: Science Applications Intl Corp (P-14105)

Saic, San Diego Also Called: Leidos Inc (P-17803)

Saic, San Diego Also Called: Leidos Inc (P-17806)

Saic Government Solutions, San Diego Also Called: Science Applications Intl Corp (P-14249)

Sailing Innovation (us) Inc .... A 626 965-6665
17870 Castleton St Ste 220 City Of Industry (91748) *(P-11645)*

Sails Washington Inc .... B 425 333-4114
13920 City Center Dr Ste 290 Chino Hills (91709) *(P-16417)*

Saint Cecilia School, Tustin Also Called: Roman Cthlic Diocese of Orange (P-16822)

Saint Jhns Hlth Ctr Foundation .... C 310 315-6111
2200 Santa Monica Blvd Santa Monica (90404) *(P-15441)*

Saint John's Health Center, Santa Monica Also Called: Saint Johns Health Center Foundation *(P-16165)*

Saint John's Hospital X Ray, Long Beach Also Called: Dignity Health (P-15980)

SAINT JOHN'S WELL CHILD CENTER, Los Angeles Also Called: St Johns Community Health *(P-15527)*

Saint Johns Health Center Foundation (DH)......... A 310 829-5511
2121 Santa Monica Blvd Santa Monica (90404) *(P-16165)*

SAINT JOSEPH CENTER VOLUNTEER, Venice Also Called: St Joseph Center (P-17014)

Saint Jseph Communications Inc (PA)............... E 626 331-3549
1243 E Shamwood St West Covina (91790) *(P-14854)*

Saint Mary Medical Center, Long Beach Also Called: Dignity Health (P-15982)

Saint Nine America Inc .... E 562 921-5300
10700 Norwalk Blvd Santa Fe Springs (90670) *(P-8539)*

Saint-Gobain Ceramics Plas Inc .... C 714 701-3900
4905 E Hunter Ave Anaheim (92807) *(P-3736)*

Saint-Gobain Performance Plas, San Diego Also Called: Saint-Gobain Solar Gard LLC *(P-3957)*

Saint-Gobain Prfmce Plas Corp .... C 714 893-0470
7301 Orangewood Ave Garden Grove (92841) *(P-3291)*

Saint-Gobain Prfmce Plas Corp .... D 714 630-5818
7301 Orangewood Ave Garden Grove (92841) *(P-3292)*

Saint-Gobain Solar Gard LLC (DH)................... **D 866 300-2674**
4540 Viewridge Ave San Diego (92123) *(P-3957)*

Sajahtera Inc .... A 310 276-2251
9641 Sunset Blvd Beverly Hills (90210) *(P-13009)*

Sakura Finetek USA Inc (HQ)......................... **C 310 972-7800**
1750 W 214th St Torrance (90501) *(P-10107)*

Salad Time Farms, Baldwin Park Also Called: Tanimura Antle Fresh Foods Inc (P-121)

Saleen Incorporated (PA)............................. **C 714 400-2121**
2735 Wardlow Rd Corona (92882) *(P-7192)*

Salescatcher, Orange Also Called: Salescatcher LLC (P-14023)

Salescatcher LLC .... E 714 376-6700
1570 N Batavia St Orange (92867) *(P-14023)*

SALESFORCE.COM, INC., Santa Monica Also Called: Salesforcecom Inc (P-14024)

Salesforcecom Inc .... E 310 752-7000
1442 2nd St Santa Monica (90401) *(P-14024)*

Salico Farms Inc .... C 760 344-5375
4231 Us Highway 86 Ste 4 Brawley (92227) *(P-1343)*

Salis International Inc .... E 303 384-3588
3921 Oceanic Dr Ste 802 Oceanside (92056) *(P-8559)*

Salk Institute, The, La Jolla Also Called: The Salk Institute For Biological Studies San Diego California *(P-17829)*

Salman, Brea Also Called: Parkinson Enterprises Inc (P-2515)

Salsbury Industries, Carson Also Called: Salsbury Industries Inc (P-2591)

Salsbury Industries Inc (PA)......................... **C 800 624-5269**
18300 Central Ave Carson (90746) *(P-2591)*

Salsbury Industries Inc .... D 323 846-6700
1010 E 62nd St Los Angeles (90001) *(P-2592)*

Salson Logistics Inc .... C 973 986-0200
1331 Torrance Blvd Torrance (90501) *(P-9333)*

Salvation Army (HQ)................................. **C 562 264-3600**
30840 Hawthorne Blvd Rancho Palos Verdes (90275) *(P-17001)*

Salvation Army, San Diego Also Called: Salvation Army Ray & Joan (P-15062)

Mergent email: customerrelations@mergent.com
1172
2025 Southern California
Business Directory and Buyers Guide
(P-0000) Products & Services Section entry number
(PA)=Parent Co (HQ)=Headquarters (DH)=Div Headquarters

Salvation Army Ray & Joan .... B 619 287-5762
6845 University Ave San Diego (92115) *(P-15062)*

Salvation Army Western Ttry, Rancho Palos Verdes *Also Called: Salvation Army (P-17001)*

Sam Schaffer Inc .... E 323 263-7524
3015 E Echo Hill Way Orange (92867) *(P-14790)*

Sam Sung Fixtures, Los Angeles *Also Called: Trust 1 Sales Inc (P-10056)*

Samaritan Imaging Center .... A 213 977-2140
1245 Wilshire Blvd Ste 205 Los Angeles (90017) *(P-16333)*

Same Swim LLC .... D 323 582-2588
2333 E 49th St Vernon (90058) *(P-10725)*

Samedan Oil Corporation .... B 661 319-5038
1360 Landing Ave Seal Beach (90740) *(P-312)*

Sameday Health, Venice *Also Called: Sameday Technologies Inc (P-13810)*

Sameday Technologies Inc .... C 310 697-8126
523 Victoria Ave Venice (90291) *(P-13810)*

Sample Tile and Stone Inc .... E 951 776-8562
1410 Richardson St San Bernardino (92408) *(P-4477)*

Samson Pharmaceuticals Inc .... E 323 722-3066
5635 Smithway St Commerce (90040) *(P-3497)*

Samsung Electronics Amer Inc .... C 323 374-6300
5601 E Slauson Ave Ste 200 Commerce (90040) *(P-10225)*

Samsung International Inc (DH) .... E **619 671-6001**
333 H St Ste 6000 Chula Vista (91910) *(P-10283)*

Samsung Research America Inc .... B 949 468-1143
18500 Von Karman Ave Ste 700 Irvine (92612) *(P-10027)*

Samtech Automotive Usa Inc .... E 310 638-9955
1130 E Dominguez St Carson (90746) *(P-5560)*

Samtech International, Carson *Also Called: Samtech Automotive Usa Inc (P-5560)*

Samuel Son & Co (usa) Inc .... E 951 781-7800
2345 Fleetwood Dr Riverside (92509) *(P-4605)*

Samuel Goldwyn Child Care Ctr, Los Angeles *Also Called: Motion Picture and TV Fund (P-17097)*

Samuel J Piazza & Son Inc (PA) .... D **323 357-1999**
9001 Rayo Ave South Gate (90280) *(P-8994)*

Samy's Digital Imaging, Los Angeles *Also Called: Samys Camera Inc (P-11648)*

Samys Camera Inc (PA) .... C **310 591-2100**
12636 Beatrice St Los Angeles (90066) *(P-11648)*

San Antonio Gift Shop, Los Angeles *Also Called: San Antonio Winery Inc (P-1584)*

San Antonio Regional Hospital (PA) .... A **909 985-2811**
999 San Bernardino Rd Upland (91786) *(P-16166)*

San Antonio Winery Inc (PA) .... C **323 223-1401**
737 Lamar St Los Angeles (90031) *(P-1584)*

San Bernardino Canning Co., San Bernardino *Also Called: Refresco Beverages US Inc (P-1640)*

San Bernardino Care Company .... C 909 884-4781
467 E Gilbert St San Bernardino (92404) *(P-15883)*

San Bernardino Cnty Trnsp Auth .... C 909 884-8276
1170 W 3rd St Fl 2 San Bernardino (92410) *(P-8796)*

San Bernardino County Sun, The, San Bernardino *Also Called: Sun Cmpany of San Brnrdino Cal (P-2830)*

San Bernardino Family YMCA, San Bernardino *Also Called: YMCA of East Valley (P-17380)*

San Bernardino Fics, San Bernardino *Also Called: Victor Cmnty Support Svcs Inc (P-16520)*

San Bernardino Hilton (HQ) .... C 909 889-0133
285 E Hospitality Ln San Bernardino (92408) *(P-13010)*

San Bernardino Sheet Plant, San Bernardino *Also Called: Packaging Corporation America (P-2686)*

San Brnrdino Cmnty College Dst .... D 909 888-6511
701 S Mount Vernon Ave San Bernardino (92410) *(P-3174)*

San Brnrdino Cmnty College Dst .... D 909 384-4444
701 S Mount Vernon Ave San Bernardino (92410) *(P-9488)*

San Brnrdino Cnty Prbtion Offc .... B 909 887-2544
4370 Hallmark Pkwy Ste 105 San Bernardino (92407) *(P-17002)*

San Brnrdino Cnty Rgonal Parks .... D 909 387-2583
777 E Rialto Ave San Bernardino (92415) *(P-15220)*

San Brnrdino Cy Unfied Schl Ds .... D 909 881-8000
1257 Northpark Blvd San Bernardino (92407) *(P-16614)*

San Dego Cnty Rgnal Arprt Auth (PA) .... C **619 400-2400**
3225 N Harbor Dr Fl 3 San Diego (92101) *(P-9208)*

San Dego Cnvntion Ctr Corp Inc (PA) .... B **619 782-4388**
111 W Harbor Dr San Diego (92101) *(P-14588)*

San Dego Ctr For Chldren Fndti (PA) .... D **858 277-9550**
3002 Armstrong St San Diego (92111) *(P-15884)*

San Dego Nghborhood Newspapers, Gardena *Also Called: Community Media Corporation (P-2791)*

San Dego Prcsion Machining Inc .... E 858 499-0379
9375 Ruffin Ct San Diego (92123) *(P-4524)*

San Dego Pthlgsts Med Group In .... C 619 297-4012
7592 Metropolitan Dr Ste 406 San Diego (92108) *(P-15442)*

San Dego Repertory Theatre Inc .... C 619 231-3586
79 Horton Plz San Diego (92101) *(P-14976)*

San Dego Second Chance Program .... E 619 266-2506
6145 Imperial Ave San Diego (92114) *(P-17003)*

San Dego Soc of Ntural History .... D 619 232-3821
1788 El Prado San Diego (92101) *(P-17263)*

San Dego Spt Mdcine Fmly Hlth .... D 619 229-3909
6699 Alvarado Rd Ste 2100 San Diego (92120) *(P-15443)*

San Dego Symphony Orchstra Ass .... C 619 235-0800
1245 7th Ave San Diego (92101) *(P-15003)*

San Dg-Mprial Cnties Dvlpmntal (PA) .... B **858 576-2996**
4355 Ruffin Rd Ste 220 San Diego (92123) *(P-17004)*

San Diego Ace Inc .... C 619 206-7339
5363 Sweetwater Trl San Diego (92130) *(P-4235)*

San Diego Air & Space Museum .... D 619 234-8291
2001 Pan American Plz San Diego (92101) *(P-17264)*

San Diego Arcft Interiors Inc .... E 619 474-1997
2381 Boswell Rd Chula Vista (91914) *(P-2435)*

San Diego Blood Bank (PA) .... C **619 400-8132**
3636 Gateway Center Ave Ste 100 San Diego (92102) *(P-16615)*

San Diego Blood Bnk Foundation, San Diego *Also Called: San Diego Blood Bank (P-16615)*

San Diego Business Journal, San Diego *Also Called: Cbj LP (P-2849)*

San Diego Cctv Pros, Chatsworth *Also Called: Guardian Integrated SEC Inc (P-14404)*

San Diego City College, San Diego *Also Called: San Diego Cmnty College Dst (P-16839)*

San Diego Cmnty College Dst .... C 619 388-4850
1960 National Ave San Diego (92113) *(P-16824)*

San Diego Cmnty College Dst .... C 619 388-3453
1313 Park Blvd San Diego (92101) *(P-16839)*

San Diego Cmnty College Dst .... A 619 388-2600
7250 Mesa College Dr San Diego (92111) *(P-16840)*

San Diego Composites Inc .... D 858 751-0450
9220 Activity Rd Ste 100 San Diego (92126) *(P-17624)*

San Diego Country Estates Assn .... C 760 789-3788
24157 San Vicente Rd Ramona (92065) *(P-17363)*

San Diego County Credit Union (PA) .... C **877 732-2848**
6545 Sequence Dr San Diego (92121) *(P-11813)*

San Diego County Water Auth .... C 760 480-1991
610 W 5th Ave Escondido (92025) *(P-9712)*

San Diego County Water Auth (PA) .... D **858 522-6600**
4677 Overland Ave San Diego (92123) *(P-9713)*

San Diego Daily Transcript .... D 619 232-4381
34 Emerald Gln Laguna Niguel (92677) *(P-2636)*

San Diego Data Processing Corporation Inc .... A 858 581-9600
202 C St 3rd Fl San Diego (92101) *(P-14154)*

San Diego Die Cutting Inc .... E 619 297-4453
3112 Moore Ct San Diego (92110) *(P-10609)*

San Diego District Office, San Diego *Also Called: State Compensation Insur Fund (P-12139)*

San Diego Family Care (PA) .... D **858 279-0925**
6973 Linda Vista Rd San Diego (92111) *(P-15444)*

San Diego Farms LLC .... C 760 736-4072
519 Cassou Rd San Marcos (92069) *(P-86)*

San Diego Gas & Electric Co .... C 858 547-2086
6875c Consolidated Way San Diego (92121) *(P-9107)*

San Diego Gas & Electric Co .... C 619 696-2000
1801 S Atlantic Blvd Monterey Park (91754) *(P-9602)*

San Diego Gas & Electric Co .... B 760 432-2508
2300 Harveson Pl Escondido (92029) *(P-9603)*

San Diego Gas & Electric Co .... B 858 654-6377
5488 Overland Ave San Diego (92123) *(P-9604)*

San Diego Gas & Electric Co .... C 619 699-1018
701 33rd St San Diego (92102) *(P-9605)*

San Diego Gas & Electric Co .... C 858 613-3216
10975 Technology Pl San Diego (92127) *(P-9606)*

San Diego Gas & Electric Co .... D 858 654-1289
8306 Century Park Ct # Cp42c San Diego (92123) *(P-9607)*

Employee Codes: A=Over 500 employees, B=251-500
C=101-250, D=51-100, E=20-50, F=10-19, G=1-9

2025 Southern California
Business Directory and Buyers Guide

© Mergent Inc. 1-800-342-5647
1173

A
L
P
H
A
B
E
T
I
C

San Diego Gas & Electric Co .... B 619 441-3834
104 N Johnson Ave El Cajon (92020) *(P-9608)*

San Diego Gas & Electric Co .... C 858 541-5920
5488 Overland Ave San Diego (92123) *(P-9609)*

San Diego Gas & Electric Co .... D 800 411-7343
990 Bay Blvd Chula Vista (91911) *(P-9642)*

San Diego Gas & Electric Co .... B 951 243-2241
14601 Virginia St Moreno Valley (92555) *(P-9645)*

San Diego Gas & Electric Co .... C 866 616-5565
8315 Century Park Ct Ste Cp-21d San Diego (92123) *(P-9671)*

San Diego Gas & Electric Co .... C 949 361-8090
662 Camino De Los Mares San Clemente (92673) *(P-9672)*

San Diego Gas & Electric Co (DH).......................... **B 619 696-2000**
8330 Century Park Ct San Diego (92123) *(P-9673)*

San Diego Gas & Electric Co .... C 760 438-6200
5016 Carlsbad Blvd Carlsbad (92008) *(P-9680)*

San Diego Gas & Electric Co .... B 858 654-1135
436 H St Chula Vista (91910) *(P-9681)*

San Diego Hebrew Homes (PA).............................. **C 760 942-2695**
211 Saxony Rd Encinitas (92024) *(P-15768)*

San Diego Hospice & Palliative, San Diego *Also Called: San Diego Hospice & Palliative Care Corporation (P-16418)*

San Diego Hospice & Palliative Care Corporation .... A 619 688-1600
4311 3rd Ave San Diego (92103) *(P-16418)*

San Diego Hotel Company LLC .... C 619 696-0234
660 K St San Diego (92101) *(P-13011)*

San Diego Magazine, San Diego *Also Called: San Diego Magazine Pubg Co (P-2876)*

San Diego Magazine Pubg Co .... E 619 230-9292
1230 Columbia St Ste 800 San Diego (92101) *(P-2876)*

San Diego Marriott Mission Vly, San Diego *Also Called: Ws Mmv Hotel LLC (P-13093)*

San Diego Mesa College, San Diego *Also Called: San Diego Cmnty College Dst (P-16840)*

San Diego Metro Trnst Sys .... A 619 231-1466
1255 Imperial Ave Ste 1000 San Diego (92101) *(P-8797)*

San Diego Metro Trnst Sys, San Diego *Also Called: San Diego Transit Corporation (P-8798)*

San Diego Mission Bay Resort, San Diego *Also Called: Lho Mssion Bay Rsie Lessee Inc (P-12901)*

San Diego Museum of Art .... D 619 696-1909
1450 El Prado San Diego (92112) *(P-17265)*

SAN DIEGO NATURAL HISTORY MUSE, San Diego *Also Called: San Dego Soc of Ntural History (P-17263)*

San Diego Opera Association .... C 619 232-5911
3064 Commercial St San Diego (92113) *(P-14977)*

San Diego Opera Association .... C 619 232-5911
3074 Commercial St San Diego (92113) *(P-14978)*

San Diego Padres, San Diego *Also Called: California Sportservice Inc (P-15021)*

San Diego Padres, San Diego *Also Called: Padres LP (P-15034)*

San Diego Powder Coating, El Cajon *Also Called: BJS&t Enterprises Inc (P-5314)*

San Diego Precast Concrete Inc (DH)..................... E 619 240-8000
2735 Cactus Rd San Diego (92154) *(P-4421)*

San Diego Ready Mix, San Diego *Also Called: Superior Ready Mix Concrete LP (P-11252)*

San Diego Rescue Mission Inc (PA)........................ **D 619 819-1880**
299 17th St San Diego (92101) *(P-17241)*

San Diego Saturn Retailers Inc .... D 858 373-3001
9985 Huennekens St San Diego (92121) *(P-14680)*

San Diego Services LLC .... C 858 654-0102
5415 Oberlin Dr San Diego (92121) *(P-17625)*

San Diego Sign Company Inc .... E 888 748-7446
5960 Pascal Ct Carlsbad (92008) *(P-10461)*

San Diego State Aztecs, San Diego *Also Called: San Diego State University (P-15167)*

San Diego State University .... C 619 594-4263
5302 55th St San Diego (92182) *(P-15167)*

San Diego State University .... D 619 594-1515
5200 Campanile Dr San Diego (92182) *(P-16834)*

San Diego Supercomputer Center, La Jolla *Also Called: University Cal San Diego (P-14162)*

San Diego Symphony Foundation .... C 619 235-0800
1245 7th Ave San Diego (92101) *(P-15004)*

San Diego Theatres Inc .... C 619 615-4007
233 A St Ste 900 San Diego (92101) *(P-12315)*

San Diego Transit Corporation (PA)........................ **A 619 238-0100**
100 16th St San Diego (92101) *(P-8798)*

San Diego Trolley Inc .... B 619 595-4933
1341 Commercial St San Diego (92113) *(P-8799)*

SAN DIEGO TROLLEY INC, San Diego *Also Called: San Diego Trolley Inc (P-8799)*

San Diego Unified Hbr Police, San Diego *Also Called: San Diego Unified Port Dst (P-18389)*

San Diego Unified Port Dst (PA)............................ **C 619 686-6200**
3165 Pacific Hwy San Diego (92101) *(P-9146)*

San Diego Unified Port Dst .... C 619 686-6200
1400 Tidelands Ave National City (91950) *(P-9147)*

San Diego Unified Port Dst .... C 619 686-6585
3380 N Harbor Dr San Diego (92101) *(P-18389)*

San Diego Union Tribune, The, San Diego *Also Called: San Diego Union-Tribune LLC (P-2825)*

San Diego Union-Tribune LLC .... E 619 299-3131
1920 Main St Irvine (92614) *(P-2824)*

San Diego Union-Tribune LLC (PA)........................ **A 619 299-3131**
600 B St Ste 1201 San Diego (92101) *(P-2825)*

San Diego V Inc (PA).. **D 888 308-2260**
5350 Kearny Mesa Rd San Diego (92111) *(P-11403)*

San Diego Volvo, San Diego *Also Called: San Diego V Inc (P-11403)*

San Diego Wild Animal Park, Escondido *Also Called: Zoological Society San Diego (P-17274)*

San Diego Zoo, San Diego *Also Called: Zoological Society San Diego (P-17275)*

San Diego Zoo, San Diego *Also Called: Zoological Society San Diego (P-17276)*

SAN DIEGO ZOO WILDLIFE ALLIANC, San Diego *Also Called: Zoological Society San Diego (P-17273)*

San Dieguito Printers, San Marcos *Also Called: San Dieguito Publishers Inc (P-3079)*

San Dieguito Publishers Inc .... D 760 593-5139
1880 Diamond St San Marcos (92078) *(P-3079)*

San Dimas Community Hospital, San Dimas *Also Called: Prime Hlthcare Svcs - San Dmas (P-16147)*

San Dimas Community Hospital, San Dimas *Also Called: Prime Health Care (P-17110)*

San Dimas Retirement Center (PA)........................ **D 909 599-8441**
834 W Arrow Hwy San Dimas (91773) *(P-12364)*

San Fernando City of Inc .... D 818 832-2400
10605 Balboa Blvd Ste 100 Granada Hills (91344) *(P-16501)*

San Fernando Juvenile Hall, Sylmar *Also Called: County of Los Angeles (P-17138)*

San Fernando Valley Auto LLC .... C 818 832-1600
18600 Devonshire St Northridge (91324) *(P-11404)*

San Fernando Valley Bus Jurnl, Los Angeles *Also Called: Cbj LP (P-2846)*

San Gabriel Convalescent Ctr, Rosemead *Also Called: Longwood Management Corp (P-15704)*

San Gabriel Country Club .... D 626 287-9671
350 E Hermosa Dr San Gabriel (91775) *(P-15168)*

San Gabriel Transit Inc (PA)................................ **C 626 258-1310**
3650 Rockwell Ave El Monte (91731) *(P-8800)*

San Gabriel Valley Cab Co, El Monte *Also Called: San Gabriel Transit Inc (P-8800)*

San Gabriel Valley Medical Ctr .... A 626 289-5454
438 W Las Tunas Dr San Gabriel (91778) *(P-16167)*

San Gabriel Valley Water Assn .... D 626 815-1305
725 N Azusa Ave Azusa (91702) *(P-9714)*

San Gabriel Valley Water Co .... C 909 822-2201
8440 Nuevo Ave Fontana (92335) *(P-9715)*

San Gabriel Valley Water Co (PA)........................ **C 626 448-6183**
11142 Garvey Ave El Monte (91733) *(P-9716)*

SAN GABRIEL/POMONA REGIONAL CE, Pomona *Also Called: San Gbrl/Pmona Vlleys Dvlpmnta (P-17005)*

San Gbriel Ambltory Srgery Ctr .... B 626 300-5300
207 S Santa Anita St Ste G16 San Gabriel (91776) *(P-15445)*

San Gbrl/Pmona Vlleys Dvlpmnta .... B 909 620-7722
75 Rancho Camino Dr Pomona (91766) *(P-17005)*

San Gorgonio Memorial Hospital .... A 951 845-1121
600 N Highland Springs Ave Banning (92220) *(P-16168)*

San Grgnio Mem Hosp Foundation (PA)................... **C 951 845-1121**
600 N Highland Springs Ave Banning (92220) *(P-16169)*

San Jacinto Healthcare, Hemet *Also Called: Miramonte Enterprises LLC (P-15721)*

San Jacinto Valley Post Acute, Hemet *Also Called: Pacs Group Inc (P-15740)*

San Joaquin Community Hospital (HQ)................... **A 661 395-3000**
2615 Chester Ave Bakersfield (93301) *(P-16170)*

San Joaquin Refining Co Inc .... C 661 327-4257
3500 Shell St Bakersfield (93388) *(P-3830)*

San Joaquin Window Inc .... C 909 946-3697
1455 Columbia Ave Riverside (92507) *(P-4901)*

Mergent email: customerrelations@mergent.com
1174

2025 Southern California
Business Directory and Buyers Guide

(P-0000) Products & Services Section entry number
(PA)=Parent Co (HQ)=Headquarters (DH)=Div Headquarters

San Luis Ambulance Service Inc .... C 805 543-2626
3546 S Higuera St San Luis Obispo (93401) *(P-8847)*

San Luis Obispo County YMCA .... D 805 544-7225
5785 Los Ranchos Rd San Luis Obispo (93401) *(P-17364)*

San Luis Obispo Golf Cntry CLB .... C 805 543-3400
255 Country Club Dr San Luis Obispo (93401) *(P-15169)*

San Luis Obspo Rgnal Trnst Aut .... D 805 781-4465
253 Elks Ln San Luis Obispo (93401) *(P-8801)*

San Manuel Entertainment Auth (PA) .... A 909 864-5050
777 San Manuel Blvd Highland (92346) *(P-15221)*

San Manuel Fire Dept, Highland *Also Called: San Mnuel Band Mission Indians (P-14589)*

San Marcos Mechanical, Vista *Also Called: Industrial Coml Systems Inc (P-788)*

San Miguel Produce Inc .... B 805 488-0981
600 E Hueneme Rd Oxnard (93033) *(P-13)*

San Mnuel Band Mission Indians .... C 909 425-4682
101 Pure Water Ln Highland (92346) *(P-11843)*

San Mnuel Band Mission Indians .... C 909 864-6928
26540 Indian Service Rd Highland (92346) *(P-14589)*

San Onofre Child Care Center, Camp Pendleton *Also Called: Marine Corps Community Svcs (P-17095)*

San Pedro Convalescent HM Inc .... D 310 832-6431
1430 W 6th St San Pedro (90732) *(P-15769)*

San Pedro Peninsula Hospital .... A 310 832-3311
1300 W 7th St San Pedro (90732) *(P-16171)*

San Psqual Band Mssion Indians .... C 760 291-5500
16300 Nyemii Pass Rd Valley Center (92082) *(P-13012)*

San Psqual Band Mssion Indians (PA) .... D 760 749-3200
16400 Kumeyaay Way Valley Center (92082) *(P-18385)*

San Ramon Services Inc .... D 925 901-1400
12101 Palms Blvd Los Angeles (90066) *(P-14710)*

San Val Alarm System, Thousand Palms *Also Called: San Val Corp (P-190)*

San Val Corp (PA) .... B 760 346-3999
72203 Adelaid St Thousand Palms (92276) *(P-190)*

SAN VICENTE INN & GOLF CLUB, Ramona *Also Called: San Diego Country Estates Assn (P-17363)*

San Ysidro Bb Property LLC .... C 805 368-6788
900 San Ysidro Ln Santa Barbara (93108) *(P-13013)*

San Ysidro Health, San Diego *Also Called: Centro De Slud De La Cmndad De (P-15270)*

San Ysidro Health, San Diego *Also Called: Centro De Slud De La Cmndad De (P-16453)*

San Ysidro Health Center, National City *Also Called: Centro De Slud De La Cmndad De (P-15269)*

San Ysidro Health Center, San Ysidro *Also Called: Centro De Slud De La Cmndad De (P-16451)*

San Ysidro Health Center, Chula Vista *Also Called: Centro De Slud De La Cmndad De (P-16545)*

San-Mar Construction Co Inc .... C 714 693-5400
4875 E La Palma Ave Ste 602 Anaheim (92807) *(P-581)*

SANBAG, San Bernardino *Also Called: San Bernardino Cnty Trnsp Auth (P-8796)*

Sanctary Ctrs Snta Barbara Inc .... D 805 569-2785
222 W Valerio St Santa Barbara (93101) *(P-16502)*

Sanctuary Clothing, Burbank *Also Called: Sanctuary Clothing LLC (P-11493)*

Sanctuary Clothing LLC (PA) .... E 818 505-0018
3611 N San Fernando Blvd Burbank (91505) *(P-11493)*

Sanctuary Spa, San Diego *Also Called: Bay Clubs Company LLC (P-15120)*

Sand and Sea .... D 310 458-1515
1515 Ocean Ave Santa Monica (90401) *(P-13014)*

Sand Canyon Corporation (HQ) .... D 949 727-9425
7595 Irvine Center Dr Ste 120 Irvine (92618) *(P-11952)*

Sandberg Furniture, Vernon *Also Called: Sandberg Furniture Mfg Co Inc (P-2436)*

Sandberg Furniture Mfg Co Inc (PA) .... C 323 582-0711
5705 Alcoa Ave Vernon (90058) *(P-2436)*

Sandberg Industries Inc (PA) .... D 949 660-9473
2921 Daimler St Santa Ana (92705) *(P-7047)*

Sandel, Vista *Also Called: Sandel Avionics Inc (P-7806)*

Sandel Avionics, Vista *Also Called: Sandel Avionics Inc (P-7807)*

Sandel Avionics Inc (PA) .... E 760 727-4900
1370 Decision St Ste D Vista (92081) *(P-7806)*

Sandel Avionics Inc .... C 760 727-4900
2405 Dogwood Way Vista (92081) *(P-7807)*

Sanders & Wohrman Corporation .... C 714 919-0446
709 N Poplar St Orange (92868) *(P-873)*

Sanders Composites Inc (HQ) .... E 562 354-2800
3701 E Conant St Long Beach (90808) *(P-7561)*

Sanders Composites Industries, Long Beach *Also Called: Sanders Composites Inc (P-7561)*

Sandia Plastics Inc .... E 714 901-8400
15571 Container Ln Huntington Beach (92649) *(P-4236)*

Sandm San Dego Mrriott Del Mar .... A 858 523-1700
11966 El Camino Real San Diego (92130) *(P-13015)*

Sandpiper of California Inc .... D 619 424-2222
687 Anita St Ste A Chula Vista (91911) *(P-4300)*

Sandra Gruca .... E 714 661-6464
16993 Bluewater Ln Huntington Beach (92649) *(P-7292)*

Sandusky Lee LLC .... E 661 854-5551
16125 Widmere Rd Arvin (93203) *(P-2474)*

Sanford Brnham Prbys Med Dscve (PA) .... A 858 795-5000
10901 N Torrey Pines Rd La Jolla (92037) *(P-17888)*

Sangera Buick Inc .... D 661 833-5200
5600 Gasoline Alley Dr Bakersfield (93313) *(P-14699)*

Sani-Tech West, Inc., Camarillo *Also Called: Sanisure Inc (P-3875)*

Sanisure Inc (HQ) .... D 805 389-0400
1020 Flynn Rd Camarillo (93012) *(P-3875)*

Sanitec Industries Inc .... D 818 523-1942
10700 Sherman Way Burbank (91505) *(P-9762)*

Sanittion Dstrcts Los Angles C .... A 562 908-4288
1955 Workman Mill Rd Whittier (90601) *(P-9763)*

Sanmina Corporation .... D 714 371-2800
2945 Airway Ave Costa Mesa (92626) *(P-6768)*

Sanmina Corporation .... C 714 913-2200
2950 Red Hill Ave Costa Mesa (92626) *(P-6769)*

Sansum Clinic .... D 805 681-7500
215 Pesetas Ln Santa Barbara (93110) *(P-11622)*

Santa Ana Country Club .... D 714 556-3000
20382 Newport Blvd Santa Ana (92707) *(P-15170)*

Santa Ana Creek Development Company .... D 714 685-3462
2288 N Batavia St Orange (92865) *(P-1134)*

Santa Ana District Office, Santa Ana *Also Called: State Compensation Insur Fund (P-12138)*

Santa Ana Job Training Program, Santa Ana *Also Called: City of Santa Ana (P-17053)*

Santa Ana Plating (PA) .... D 310 923-8305
1726 E Rosslynn Ave Fullerton (92831) *(P-5291)*

Santa Anita Cnvlscent Hosp Rtr .... C 626 579-0310
5522 Gracewood Ave Temple City (91780) *(P-15770)*

Santa Anita Park, Arcadia *Also Called: Los Angeles Turf Club Inc (P-15039)*

Santa Barbara Cnty Social Svcs, Santa Maria *Also Called: Santa Brbara Cttage Hosp Fndti (P-16174)*

Santa Barbara Cottage Hospital .... C 805 569-7367
400 W Pueblo St Santa Barbara (93105) *(P-16172)*

Santa Barbara Design Studio (PA) .... D 805 966-3883
1600 Pacific Ave Oxnard (93033) *(P-4368)*

Santa Barbara Family YMCA, Santa Barbara *Also Called: Channel Islnds Yung MNS Chrstn (P-17333)*

Santa Barbara Farms LLC .... C 805 736-5608
1105 Union Sugar Ave Lompoc (93436) *(P-14)*

Santa Barbara Group, Santa Barbara *Also Called: Tecolote Research Inc (P-18227)*

Santa Barbara Independent Inc .... E 805 965-5205
1715 State St Santa Barbara (93101) *(P-2826)*

Santa Barbara Infrared Inc (DH) .... D 805 965-3669
30 S Calle Cesar Chavez Ste D Santa Barbara (93103) *(P-7808)*

Santa Barbara Inn, Santa Barbara *Also Called: Interstate Hotels Resorts Inc (P-12876)*

Santa Barbara Instrument GP Inc .... E 925 463-3410
150 Castilian Dr Goleta (93117) *(P-8443)*

Santa Barbara Metro Trnst Dst (PA) .... D 805 963-3364
550 Olive St Santa Barbara (93101) *(P-8802)*

Santa Barbara Smokehouse, Santa Barbara *Also Called: SBS Acquisition Company LLC (P-10861)*

Santa Barbara Trnsp Corp .... D 661 259-7285
26501 Ruether Ave Santa Clarita (91350) *(P-8859)*

Santa Barbara Trnsp Corp .... C 760 746-0850
520 Gannon Pl Escondido (92025) *(P-8883)*

Santa Barbara Trnsp Corp .... C 661 510-0566
42138 7th St W Lancaster (93534) *(P-8884)*

Santa Barbara Trnsp Corp .... C 805 928-0402
7394 Calle Real Ste A Goleta (93117) *(P-8885)*

A
L
P
H
A
B
E
T
I
C

Employee Codes: A=Over 500 employees, B=251-500
C=101-250, D=51-100, E=20-50, F=10-19, G=1-9

2025 Southern California
Business Directory and Buyers Guide

© Mergent Inc. 1-800-342-5647
1175

Santa Barbara Zoo, Santa Barbara *Also Called: Santa Brbara Zlgcal Foundation (P-17272)*

Santa Brbara Cmnty College Dst .... B 805 683-4191
525 Anacapa St Santa Barbara (93101) *(P-16841)*

Santa Brbara Cttage Hosp Fndti .... C 805 569-7224
400 W Pueblo St Santa Barbara (93105) *(P-16173)*

Santa Brbara Cttage Hosp Fndti .... C 805 346-7135
2125 Centerpointe Pkwy Santa Maria (93455) *(P-16174)*

Santa Brbara Cttage Hosp Fndti (HQ)................................. A 805 682-7111
400 W Pueblo St Santa Barbara (93105) *(P-16175)*

Santa Brbara Med Fndtion Clnic, Santa Barbara *Also Called: Sansum Clinic (P-11622)*

Santa Brbara Mseum Ntral Hstor .... D 805 682-4711
2559 Puesta Del Sol Santa Barbara (93105) *(P-17266)*

Santa Brbara San Luis Obspo RG .... C 800 421-2560
4050 Calle Real Santa Barbara (93110) *(P-12066)*

Santa Brbara Zlgcal Foundation .... C 805 962-1673
500 Ninos Dr Santa Barbara (93103) *(P-17272)*

Santa Catalina Island Company (PA).................................. D 310 510-2000
4 Park Plz Ste 420 Irvine (92614) *(P-9240)*

Santa Clarita Health Care Ctr, Santa Clarita *Also Called: Henry Mayo Newhall Mem Hosp (P-16568)*

Santa Clarita Signs .... E 661 291-1188
26330 Diamond Pl Santa Clarita (91350) *(P-8630)*

Santa Clarita Valley Wtr Agcy .... C 661 259-2737
26521 Summit Cir Santa Clarita (91350) *(P-9717)*

Santa Clarita Water Division, Santa Clarita *Also Called: Santa Clarita Valley Wtr Agcy (P-9717)*

Santa Clrita Vly Wtr Agcy Fing .... C 661 259-2737
27234 Bouquet Canyon Rd Santa Clarita (91350) *(P-9718)*

Santa Fe Enterprises Inc .... E 562 692-7596
11654 Pike St Santa Fe Springs (90670) *(P-5597)*

Santa Fe Machine Works Inc .... E 909 350-6877
14578 Rancho Vista Dr Fontana (92335) *(P-6227)*

Santa Fe Middle School, Hemet *Also Called: Hemet Unified School District (P-16811)*

Santa Fe Pacific Pipeline, Bloomington *Also Called: Kinder Mrgan Enrgy Partners LP (P-9215)*

Santa Fe Supply Company, Santa Fe Springs *Also Called: Philatron International (P-7142)*

Santa Margarita Water District .... C 949 459-6400
26101 Antonio Pkwy Rcho Sta Marg (92688) *(P-9719)*

Santa Margarita Water District (PA).................................. D 949 459-6400
26111 Antonio Pkwy Rcho Sta Marg (92688) *(P-9720)*

Santa Margarita YMCA Garrison, Oceanside *Also Called: YMCA of San Diego County (P-17398)*

Santa Maria Tire Inc (PA)... D 805 347-4793
2170 Hutton Rd Bldg A Nipomo (93444) *(P-11455)*

Santa Maria Wisdom Center, Santa Maria *Also Called: Life Steps Foundation Inc (P-16973)*

Santa Monica City of .... C 310 458-1975
1685 Main St Santa Monica (90401) *(P-8860)*

Santa Monica Amusements LLC .... B 310 451-9641
380 Santa Monica Pier Santa Monica (90401) *(P-15108)*

Santa Monica Bay Physicians He (PA).............................. D 310 417-5900
5767 W Century Blvd Los Angeles (90045) *(P-15446)*

Santa Monica Hotel Owner LLC .... C 310 395-3332
1707 4th St Santa Monica (90401) *(P-13016)*

Santa Monica Productions, Santa Monica *Also Called: Santa Monica Studios (P-13811)*

Santa Monica Proper Hotel, Santa Monica *Also Called: Santa Monica Proper Jv LLC (P-13017)*

Santa Monica Proper Jv LLC .... C 310 620-9990
700 Wilshire Blvd Santa Monica (90401) *(P-13017)*

Santa Monica Seafood, Rancho Dominguez *Also Called: Santa Monica Seafood Company (P-1711)*

Santa Monica Seafood Company (PA)............................... D 310 886-7900
18531 S Broadwick St Rancho Dominguez (90220) *(P-1711)*

Santa Monica Studios .... D 310 453-5046
3025 Olympic Blvd Santa Monica (90404) *(P-13811)*

Santa Monica Ucla Medical Ctr, Santa Monica *Also Called: Regents of The University Cal (P-16613)*

Santa Mrgrita Cthlic High Schl, Rcho Sta Marg *Also Called: Roman Cthlic Diocese of Orange (P-16823)*

Santa Rosa Berry Farms LLC .... B 805 981-3060
3500 Camino Ave Ste 250 Oxnard (93030) *(P-26)*

Santa Teresita Inc (PA)... B 626 359-3243
819 Buena Vista St Duarte (91010) *(P-16176)*

Santa Ynez Valley Marriott, Buellton *Also Called: Kang Family Partners LLC (P-12881)*

Santa Ynez Vly Cttage Hosp Inc .... D 805 688-6431
2050 Viborg Rd Solvang (93463) *(P-16177)*

Santaluz Club Inc .... C 858 759-3120
8170 Caminito Santaluz E San Diego (92127) *(P-15171)*

Santec Inc .... E 310 542-0063
3501 Challenger St Fl 2 Torrance (90503) *(P-4807)*

Santee Senior Retirement Com .... C 619 955-0901
400 Lantern Crest Way Santee (92071) *(P-17006)*

Santex Group, Carlsbad *Also Called: A R Santex LLC (P-13641)*

Santier Inc .... D 858 271-1993
10103 Carroll Canyon Rd San Diego (92131) *(P-6886)*

Santoshi Corporation .... E 626 444-7118
2439 Seaman Ave El Monte (91733) *(P-5292)*

Sanyo Fisher Company, San Diego *Also Called: Sanyo North America Corp (P-18354)*

Sanyo Foods Corp America (DH)....................................... E 714 891-3671
11955 Monarch St Garden Grove (92841) *(P-1735)*

Sanyo Manufacturing Corporation .... D 619 661-1134
2055 Sanyo Ave San Diego (92154) *(P-6553)*

Sanyo North America Corp .... B 619 661-1134
2055 Sanyo Ave San Diego (92154) *(P-18354)*

Sapphire Chandelier LLC .... D 714 879-3660
505 Porter Way Placentia (92870) *(P-6472)*

Sapphire Clean Rooms LLC .... C 714 316-5036
2810 E Coronado St Anaheim (92806) *(P-10121)*

Sapphire Energy Inc .... D 858 768-4700
10996 Torreyana Rd Ste 280 San Diego (92121) *(P-3331)*

Sappi North America Inc .... D 714 456-0600
21700 Copley Dr Ste 165 Diamond Bar (91765) *(P-2637)*

Sapu Bioscience LLC .... E 650 635-7018
10840 Thornmint Rd Ste 118 San Diego (92127) *(P-3498)*

Saputo Cheese USA Inc .... A 562 862-7686
5611 Imperial Hwy South Gate (90280) *(P-1289)*

Sara, Cypress *Also Called: Scientfc Applctons RES Assoc (P-6380)*

Sara, San Juan Capistrano *Also Called: Scientfc Applctons RES Assoc (P-17861)*

Saratech, Mission Viejo *Also Called: Paydarfar Industries Inc (P-10022)*

Sardo Bus & Coach Upholstery, Gardena *Also Called: Louis Sardo Upholstery Inc (P-2549)*

Sares Rgis Group Rsdential Inc .... C 949 643-8922
24152 Hollyoak Aliso Viejo (92656) *(P-12365)*

Sas Manufacturing Inc .... E 951 734-1808
405 N Smith Ave Corona (92878) *(P-7048)*

Sas Safety, Cerritos *Also Called: Sas Safety Corporation (P-8299)*

Sas Safety Corporation .... D 562 427-2775
17785 Center Court Dr N Cerritos (90703) *(P-8299)*

Sas Textiles Inc .... D 323 277-5555
3100 E 44th St Vernon (90058) *(P-1930)*

Satco, El Segundo *Also Called: Satco Inc (P-2392)*

Satco Inc (PA)... C 310 322-4719
1601 E El Segundo Blvd El Segundo (90245) *(P-2392)*

Satellite Management Co (PA).. C 714 558-2411
1010 E Chestnut Ave Santa Ana (92701) *(P-12527)*

Satellite Pros, Ontario *Also Called: Jeeva Corporation (P-928)*

Satellite Security Corporation .... E 877 437-4199
6779 Mesa Ridge Rd Ste 100 San Diego (92121) *(P-6656)*

Saticoy Country Club .... D 805 647-1153
4450 Clubhouse Dr Somis (93066) *(P-15172)*

Saticoy Foods Corporation .... E 805 647-5266
554 Todd Rd Santa Paula (93060) *(P-1356)*

Saticoy Fruit Exchange, Ventura *Also Called: Saticoy Lemon Association (P-44)*

Saticoy Fruit Exchange, Santa Paula *Also Called: Saticoy Lemon Association (P-118)*

Saticoy Lemon Association .... D 805 654-6500
7560 Bristol Rd Ventura (93003) *(P-44)*

Saticoy Lemon Association (PA).. D 805 654-6500
103 N Peck Rd Santa Paula (93060) *(P-118)*

Saticoy Lemon Association .... D 805 654-6543
600 E 3rd St Oxnard (93030) *(P-17287)*

Saturn Fasteners Inc .... C 818 973-1807
425 S Varney St Burbank (91502) *(P-4787)*

Sauer Brands Inc .... D 805 597-8900
184 Suburban Rd San Luis Obispo (93401) *(P-1849)*

Saul Ewing Arnstein & Lehr LLP .... D 310 398-6100
1888 Century Park E Fl 19 Los Angeles (90067) *(P-16774)*

Saul Ewing Arnstein & Lehr LLP, Los Angeles *Also Called: Saul Ewing Arnstein & Lehr LLP (P-16774)*

Savage Machining Inc .... E 805 584-8047
2235 1st St Ste 116 Simi Valley (93065) *(P-6228)*

Savi Customs, San Diego *Also Called: Crazy Industries (P-8513)*

Savice Inc .... D 949 888-2444
30052 Tomas Rcho Sta Marg (92688) *(P-17365)*

Savitsky Stin Bcon Bcci A Cal, Los Angeles *Also Called: Ground Control Business MGT (P-1895)*

Saviynt Inc (PA) .... B 310 641-1664
1301 E El Segundo Blvd Ste D El Segundo (90245) *(P-14025)*

Saw Daily Service Inc .... E 323 564-1791
4481 Firestone Blvd South Gate (90280) *(P-10462)*

Sayari Shahrzad .... E 310 903-6368
4822 Aqueduct Ave Encino (91436) *(P-10695)*

Sazerac Company Inc .... D 310 604-8717
2202 E Del Amo Blvd Carson (90749) *(P-1598)*

Sb Waterman Holdings Inc (PA) .... C 909 883-8611
1700 N Waterman Ave San Bernardino (92404) *(P-15447)*

Sbb Roofing Inc (PA) .... C 323 254-2888
3310 Verdugo Rd Los Angeles (90065) *(P-1095)*

SBC, Irvine *Also Called: SBC Medical Group Holdings Inc (P-15448)*

SBC Medical Group Holdings Inc .... A 949 593-0250
200 Spectrum Center Dr Ste 300 Irvine (92618) *(P-15448)*

Sbcs Corporation .... C 619 420-3620
430 F St Chula Vista (91910) *(P-17007)*

SBE, Los Angeles *Also Called: Stockbridge/Sbe Holdings LLC (P-13037)*

SBE Electrical Contracting Inc .... C 714 544-5066
2817 Mcgaw Ave Irvine (92614) *(P-958)*

SBE Entertainment Group LLC (HQ) .... D 323 655-8000
2535 Las Vegas Blvd S Los Angeles (90036) *(P-11618)*

Sbhis .... D 619 427-2689
740 Bay Blvd Chula Vista (91910) *(P-452)*

Sbig Astronomical Instruments, Goleta *Also Called: Santa Barbara Instrument GP Inc (P-8443)*

Sbir, Santa Barbara *Also Called: Santa Barbara Infrared Inc (P-7808)*

Sbm Dairies Inc .... B 626 923-3000
17851 Railroad St City Of Industry (91748) *(P-1653)*

Sbnw LLC (PA) .... C 213 234-5122
5600 W Adams Blvd Los Angeles (90016) *(P-4304)*

SBP, La Jolla *Also Called: Sanford Brnham Prbys Med Dscve (P-17888)*

Sbrm Inc (PA) .... D 760 480-0208
2342 Meyers Ave Escondido (92029) *(P-13415)*

SBS Acquisition Company LLC .... D 805 966-9796
312 N Nopal St Santa Barbara (93103) *(P-10861)*

Sbsbtc, National City *Also Called: South Bay Sand Blstg Tank Clg (P-14792)*

SBT Health Inc .... C 951 813-2597
25819 Jefferson Ave Ste 110 Murrieta (92562) *(P-18355)*

SC Fuels, Orange *Also Called: Southern Counties LLC (P-11025)*

SC Liquidation Company LLC .... C 714 482-1006
566 Vanguard Way Brea (92821) *(P-2726)*

SC Wright Construction Inc .... B 619 698-6909
3838 Camino Del Rio N Ste 370 San Diego (92108) *(P-17626)*

Scaled Composites LLC .... B 661 824-4541
1624 Flight Line Mojave (93501) *(P-7369)*

Scalefast Inc (PA) .... C 310 595-4040
2100 E Grand Ave El Segundo (90245) *(P-9457)*

Scales, Covina *Also Called: American Scale Co Inc (P-9987)*

Scan Group (PA) .... B 562 308-2733
3800 Kilroy Airport Way Ste 100 Long Beach (90806) *(P-12104)*

SCAN HEALTH PLAN, Long Beach *Also Called: Senior Care Action Ntwrk Fndti (P-12105)*

Scanline Vfx Inc .... A 310 827-1555
6087 W Sunset Blvd Los Angeles (90028) *(P-14855)*

Scanlinevfx La LLC .... C 310 827-1555
6087 W Sunset Blvd Los Angeles (90028) *(P-14856)*

Scantibodies Laboratory Inc (PA) .... C 619 258-9300
9336 Abraham Way Santee (92071) *(P-17925)*

Scarborough Farms Inc .... C 805 483-9113
731 Pacific Ave Oxnard (93030) *(P-87)*

Scat Enterprises Inc .... D 310 370-5501
1400 Kingsdale Ave Ste B Redondo Beach (90278) *(P-9847)*

Scattergood Generation Plant, Playa Del Rey *Also Called: Los Angeles Dept Wtr & Pwr (P-9679)*

Scb Division, Bell Gardens *Also Called: Cal Southern Braiding Inc (P-6977)*

SCE, Rosemead *Also Called: Southern California Edison Co (P-9621)*

SCE Fcu, Baldwin Park *Also Called: Rize Federal Credit Union (P-11812)*

Scenic Studio, San Diego *Also Called: San Diego Opera Association (P-14977)*

Sceptre Inc .... E 626 369-3698
16800 Gale Ave City Of Industry (91745) *(P-7049)*

Schaefer Ambulance Service Inc .... B 323 468-1642
4627 Beverly Blvd Los Angeles (90004) *(P-8848)*

Schaeffler Group USA Inc .... E 949 234-9799
34700 Pacific Coast Hwy Ste 203 Capistrano Beach (92624) *(P-5753)*

Schaumbond Group Inc (PA) .... B 626 215-4998
225 S Lake Ave Ste 300 Pasadena (91101) *(P-12650)*

Schecter Guitar Research Inc .... E 818 767-1029
10953 Pendleton St Sun Valley (91352) *(P-8473)*

Schick Moving & Storage Co (PA) .... D 714 731-5500
2721 Michelle Dr Tustin (92780) *(P-8995)*

Schilling Paradise Corp .... C 619 449-4141
487 Vernon Way El Cajon (92020) *(P-692)*

Schindler Elevator Corporation .... C 818 336-3000
16450 Foothill Blvd Ste 200 Sylmar (91342) *(P-14791)*

Schlumberger Technology Corp .... D 661 864-4721
6120 Snow Rd Bakersfield (93308) *(P-363)*

Schmidt Fire Protection Co Inc .... D 858 279-6122
4760 Murphy Canyon Rd Ste 100 San Diego (92123) *(P-834)*

Schmidt Industries Inc .... D 818 768-9100
11321 Goss St Sun Valley (91352) *(P-5293)*

Schmitt House, El Monte *Also Called: Hope Hse For Mltple Hndcpped I (P-17164)*

Schneider Elc Buildings LLC .... C 310 900-2385
100 W Victoria St Long Beach (90805) *(P-7148)*

Schneider Electric .... E 949 713-9200
1660 Scenic Ave Costa Mesa (92626) *(P-7149)*

Schneider Electric Usa Inc .... D 909 438-2295
14725 Monte Vista Ave Chino (91710) *(P-9108)*

Schneiders Manufacturing Inc .... E 818 771-0082
11122 Penrose St Sun Valley (91352) *(P-6229)*

Scholastic Sports Inc .... D 858 496-9221
4878 Ronson Ct Ste Kl San Diego (92111) *(P-3080)*

School-Link Technologies Inc .... D 310 434-2700
1437 6th St Santa Monica (90401) *(P-13812)*

Schoolsfirst Federal Credit Un .... D 480 777-5995
15442 Del Amo Ave Tustin (92780) *(P-11814)*

Schoolsfirst Federal Credit Un (PA) .... B 714 258-4000
2115 N Broadway Santa Ana (92706) *(P-11815)*

Schrey & Sons Mold Co Inc .... E 661 294-2260
24735 Avenue Rockefeller Valencia (91355) *(P-5598)*

Schroeder Iron Corporation .... E 909 428-6471
8417 Beech Ave Fontana (92335) *(P-4867)*

Schroff Inc .... A 800 525-4682
7328 Trade St San Diego (92121) *(P-5743)*

Schroff Inc .... C 858 740-2400
7328 Trade St San Diego (92121) *(P-11142)*

Schroff Inc .... C 858 740-2400
7328 Trade St San Diego (92121) *(P-14730)*

Schurman Fine Papers .... E 714 549-0212
3333 Bristol St Costa Mesa (92626) *(P-10401)*

Schwing America Inc .... C 909 681-6430
3351 Grapevine St Bldg A Jurupa Valley (91752) *(P-5497)*

SCI, Pomona *Also Called: Structural Composites Inds LLC (P-4929)*

SCI, South El Monte *Also Called: S C I Industries Inc (P-7290)*

SCI, North Hollywood *Also Called: Pierce Brothers (P-13157)*

SCI-Pharm, Pomona *Also Called: Scientific Pharmaceuticals Inc (P-8354)*

Scico, Irvine *Also Called: Santa Catalina Island Company (P-9240)*

Scicon Technologies Corp (PA) .... E 661 295-8630
27525 Newhall Ranch Rd Ste 2 Valencia (91355) *(P-17627)*

Science Inc .... D 310 395-3432
450 S Melrose Dr Vista (92081) *(P-18049)*

Employee Codes: A=Over 500 employees, B=251-500
C=101-250, D=51-100, E=20-50, F=10-19, G=1-9

2025 Southern California
Business Directory and Buyers Guide

© Mergent Inc. 1-800-342-5647
1177

Science Applications Intl Corp .... A 858 826-3061
4015 Hancock St San Diego (92110) *(P-14105)*

Science Applications Intl Corp .... D 703 676-4300
4065 Hancock St San Diego (92110) *(P-14249)*

Science of Skincare LLC .... C 818 254-7961
3333 N San Fernando Blvd Burbank (91504) *(P-10650)*

Sciencell Research Labs Inc .... E 760 602-8549
1610 Faraday Ave Carlsbad (92008) *(P-17889)*

Scientfic Applctons RES Assoc (PA)........... D 714 224-4410
6300 Gateway Dr Cypress (90630) *(P-6380)*

Scientfic Applctons RES Assoc .... D 714 224-4410
33159 Camino Capistrano Ste B San Juan Capistrano (92675) *(P-17861)*

Scientific Cutting Tools Inc .... E 805 584-9495
220 W Los Angeles Ave Simi Valley (93065) *(P-5624)*

Scientific Pharmaceuticals Inc .... E 909 595-9922
3221 Producer Way Pomona (91768) *(P-8354)*

Scientific-Atlanta LLC .... E 619 679-6000
13112 Evening Creek Dr S San Diego (92128) *(P-7809)*

Sciforma Corporation .... E 408 899-0398
600 B St Ste 300 San Diego (92101) *(P-13813)*

Scisorek & Son Flavors Inc .... E 714 524-0550
2951 Enterprise St Brea (92821) *(P-1689)*

Sclarc, Los Angeles *Also Called: South Cntl Los Angles Rgnal CT (P-17243)*

SCMG, San Diego *Also Called: Sharp Community Medical Group (P-17307)*

Scmh, Whittier *Also Called: Southern California Material Handling Inc (P-10405)*

Scope, San Diego *Also Called: Scope Orthtics Prosthetics Inc (P-11696)*

Scope City (PA) .... E 805 522-6646
2978 Topaz Ave Simi Valley (93063) *(P-8020)*

Scope Orthtics Prosthetics Inc (DH) .... E 858 292-7448
7720 Cardinal Ct San Diego (92123) *(P-11696)*

Scopely Inc (DH)............................... C 323 400-6618
3505 Hayden Ave Culver City (90232) *(P-14026)*

Score Sports, Wilmington *Also Called: American Soccer Company Inc (P-11504)*

Scorelate Inc .... E 818 602-9176
91301 Fairview Pl Ste 2 Agoura Hills (91301) *(P-14027)*

Scorpion, Valencia *Also Called: Scorpion Design LLC (P-18205)*

Scorpion Design LLC (PA)...................... A 661 702-0100
27750 Entertainment Dr Valencia (91355) *(P-18205)*

Scosche Industries Inc .... C 805 486-4450
1550 Pacific Ave Oxnard (93033) *(P-6554)*

Scott Craft Co, Cudahy *Also Called: Merry An Cejka (P-6174)*

Scott Manufacturing Solutions, Chino *Also Called: Scott Mfg Solutions Inc (P-6381)*

Scott Mfg Solutions Inc .... C 909 594-9637
5051 Edison Ave Chino (91710) *(P-6381)*

Scott Turbon Mixer Inc., Adelanto *Also Called: Ebara Mixers Inc (P-5670)*

Scottel Voice & Data Inc .... C 310 737-7300
6100 Center Dr Ste 720 Los Angeles (90045) *(P-14731)*

Scotts Company LLC .... E 661 387-9555
742 Industrial Way Shafter (93263) *(P-3747)*

Scotts Temecula Operations LLC (DH)........... E 951 719-1700
42375 Remington Ave Temecula (92590) *(P-5483)*

Scotts- Hyponex, Jurupa Valley *Also Called: Hyponex Corporation (P-3745)*

Scottxscott Inc .... E 310 622-2775
3453 Union Pacific Ave Los Angeles (90023) *(P-14590)*

Scp Horton Owner 1 LLC .... D 310 693-4400
10850 Wilshire Blvd Ste 1050 Los Angeles (90024) *(P-12316)*

Scratchpadsaas .... C 415 707-3325
440 N Barranca Ave # 9418 Covina (91723) *(P-13814)*

Screamline Investment Corp .... C 323 201-0114
2130 S Tubeway Ave Commerce (90040) *(P-9241)*

Screen Actors Guild - American .... C 818 954-9400
3601 W Olive Ave Fl 2 Burbank (91505) *(P-12163)*

Screen Actors Guild-Producers, Burbank *Also Called: Screen Actors Guild - American (P-12163)*

Screening Systems Inc (PA).................... E 949 855-1751
36 Blackbird Ln Aliso Viejo (92656) *(P-7976)*

Screwmatic Inc .... D 626 334-7831
925 W 1st St Azusa (91702) *(P-6230)*

Scribeamerica LLC .... A 877 819-5900
840 Apollo St Ste 231 El Segundo (90245) *(P-16616)*

Scribemd LLC .... D 714 543-8911
1310 W Stewart Dr Ste 212 Orange (92868) *(P-15449)*

Scripps Clinic .... C 858 794-1250
12395 El Camino Real Ste 112 San Diego (92130) *(P-16178)*

Scripps Clinic Med Group Inc .... C 858 554-9000
12395 El Camino Real Ste 112 San Diego (92130) *(P-18050)*

Scripps Green Hospital, La Jolla *Also Called: Scripps Health (P-16183)*

Scripps Health .... D 619 294-8111
4077 5th Ave San Diego (92103) *(P-16179)*

Scripps Health .... D 858 271-9770
15004 Innovation Dr San Diego (92128) *(P-16180)*

Scripps Health .... C 760 753-6501
354 Santa Fe Dr Encinitas (92024) *(P-16181)*

Scripps Health .... C 619 691-7000
435 H St Chula Vista (91910) *(P-16182)*

Scripps Health .... B 858 455-9100
10666 N Torrey Pines Rd La Jolla (92037) *(P-16183)*

Scripps Health .... B 858 626-6150
9888 Genesee Ave La Jolla (92037) *(P-16184)*

Scripps Health .... C 858 626-4123
9888 Genesee Ave La Jolla (92037) *(P-16185)*

Scripps Health (PA)............................ A 800 727-4777
10140 Campus Point Dr San Diego (92121) *(P-16186)*

Scripps Health .... D 858 764-3000
3811 Valley Centre Dr San Diego (92130) *(P-16419)*

Scripps Health, La Jolla *Also Called: Scripps Mmral-Ximed Med Ctr LP (P-16188)*

Scripps Mem Hosp - Encinatas, Encinitas *Also Called: Scripps Health (P-16181)*

Scripps Mem Hosp - La Jolla, La Jolla *Also Called: Scripps Health (P-16185)*

Scripps Mem Hospital-La Jolla, La Jolla *Also Called: Scripps Health (P-16184)*

Scripps Mercy Hospital .... C 619 294-8111
4077 5th Ave # Mer35 San Diego (92103) *(P-16187)*

Scripps Mercy Hospital, San Diego *Also Called: Scripps Health (P-16179)*

Scripps Mercy Hospitals, Chula Vista *Also Called: Scripps Health (P-16182)*

Scripps Mmral-Ximed Med Ctr LP .... C 858 882-8350
9850 Genesee Ave Ste 900 La Jolla (92037) *(P-16188)*

Scripps Rancho Bernardo, San Diego *Also Called: Scripps Health (P-16180)*

Scripps Research Institute .... D 858 242-1000
11119 N Torrey Pines Rd Ste 100 La Jolla (92037) *(P-17890)*

Scripto-Tokai Corporation (HQ)................. D 909 930-5000
2055 S Haven Ave Ontario (91761) *(P-8721)*

Scs Engineers, Long Beach *Also Called: Stearns Conrad and Schmidt Consulting Engineers Inc (P-17637)*

Scully Leather Wear, Oxnard *Also Called: Scully Sportswear Inc (P-2182)*

Scully Sportswear Inc (PA)..................... E 805 483-6339
1701 Pacific Ave Oxnard (93033) *(P-2182)*

Scv, Santa Fe Springs *Also Called: Southern California Valve Inc (P-10464)*

Scv Facilities Services Inc .... D 310 803-4588
1907 W 75th St Los Angeles (90047) *(P-13416)*

Scw Contracting Corporation .... D 760 728-1308
2525 Old Highway 395 Fallbrook (92028) *(P-693)*

SD Hotel Circle LLC .... D 619 881-6800
2201 Hotel Cir S San Diego (92108) *(P-13018)*

SD&a Teleservices Inc (HQ)................... B
5757 W Century Blvd Ste 300 Los Angeles (90045) *(P-14591)*

SDC Technologies Inc (HQ)................... E 714 939-8300
45 Parker Ste 100 Irvine (92618) *(P-5343)*

Sdccu, San Diego *Also Called: San Diego County Credit Union (P-11813)*

Sdcraa, San Diego *Also Called: San Dego Cnty Rgnal Arprt Auth (P-9208)*

Sdg Enterprises .... D 805 777-7978
822 Hampshire Rd Ste H Westlake Village (91361) *(P-835)*

SDG&e, Monterey Park *Also Called: San Diego Gas & Electric Co (P-9602)*

SDG&e, Escondido *Also Called: San Diego Gas & Electric Co (P-9603)*

SDG&e, San Diego *Also Called: San Diego Gas & Electric Co (P-9604)*

SDG&e, San Diego *Also Called: San Diego Gas & Electric Co (P-9606)*

SDG&e, San Diego *Also Called: San Diego Gas & Electric Co (P-9607)*

SDG&e, Moreno Valley *Also Called: San Diego Gas & Electric Co (P-9645)*

SDG&E, San Diego *Also Called: San Diego Gas & Electric Co (P-9673)*

SDG&e, Chula Vista *Also Called: San Diego Gas & Electric Co (P-9681)*

SDG&ec, San Diego *Also Called: San Diego Gas & Electric Co (P-9609)*

Mergent email: customerrelations@mergent.com
1178

2025 Southern California
Business Directory and Buyers Guide

(P-0000) Products & Services Section entry number
(PA)=Parent Co (HQ)=Headquarters (DH)=Div Headquarters

Sdi, Simi Valley *Also Called: Special Devices Incorporated (P-7294)*

Sdi Industries Inc (DH)..C 818 890-6002
24307 Magic Mountain Pkwy # 443 Valencia (91355) *(P-5518)*

Sdmv LLC ....D 949 516-0088
520 Newport Center Dr Fl 2 Newport Beach (92660) *(P-12317)*

SDS Industries Inc ....C 818 492-3500
10241 Norris Ave Pacoima (91331) *(P-4902)*

SE Scher Corporation ....A 858 546-8300
2525 Camino Del Rio S Ste 200 San Diego (92108) *(P-13569)*

Sea Breeze Financial Svcs Inc ....C 949 223-9700
18191 Von Karman Ave Ste 150 Irvine (92612) *(P-11934)*

Sea Breeze Health Care Inc ....C 714 847-9671
7781 Garfield Ave Huntington Beach (92648) *(P-15771)*

Sea Breeze Mortgage Services, Irvine *Also Called: Sea Breeze Financial Svcs Inc (P-11934)*

Sea Dwelling Creatures Inc ....D 310 676-9697
5515 W 104th St Los Angeles (90045) *(P-11697)*

Sea Electric LLC ....E 424 376-3660
436 Alaska Ave Torrance (90503) *(P-6332)*

Sea Magazine, Fountain Valley *Also Called: Duncan McIntosh Company Inc (P-2855)*

Sea Shield Marine Products Inc ....E 909 594-2507
20832 Currier Rd Walnut (91789) *(P-4653)*

Seabiscuit Motorsports Inc ....E 714 898-9763
10800 Valley View St Cypress (90630) *(P-6047)*

Seaboard Envelope Co Inc ....E 626 960-4559
15601 Cypress Ave Irwindale (91706) *(P-2752)*

Seaborn Canvas, San Pedro *Also Called: Juanita F Wade (P-2279)*

Seacatch Seafoods, El Monte *Also Called: Atlantis Seafood LLC (P-1701)*

Seachrome, Long Beach *Also Called: Seachrome Corporation (P-4800)*

Seachrome Corporation ....C 310 427-8010
1906 E Dominguez St Long Beach (90810) *(P-4800)*

Seaco Technologies Inc ....E 661 326-1522
280 El Cerrito Dr Bakersfield (93305) *(P-6030)*

Seacoast Cmmerce Banc Holdings ....C 858 432-7000
11939 Rancho Bernardo Rd San Diego (92128) *(P-11777)*

Seacomp Inc (PA)...C 760 918-6722
1525 Faraday Ave Ste 200 Carlsbad (92008) *(P-6382)*

Seacrest Convalescent Hosp Inc ....D 310 833-3526
1416 W 6th St San Pedro (90732) *(P-15772)*

Seacrest Convalescent Hospital, San Pedro *Also Called: Seacrest Convalescent Hosp Inc (P-15772)*

Seah Steel America, Irvine *Also Called: Pusan Pipe America Inc (P-10150)*

Seal Bch Hlth Rhbilitation Ctr, Seal Beach *Also Called: AG Seal Beach LLC (P-15561)*

Seal Electric Inc ....C 619 449-7323
1162 Greenfield Dr El Cajon (92021) *(P-959)*

Seal For Life Industries LLC (HQ).........................E 619 671-0932
2290 Enrico Fermi Dr Ste 22 San Diego (92154) *(P-3778)*

Seal Methods Inc (PA)..D 562 944-0291
11915 Shoemaker Ave Santa Fe Springs (90670) *(P-2727)*

Seal Science Inc (HQ)...D 949 253-3130
3701 E Conant St Long Beach (90808) *(P-3899)*

Sealed Air Corporation ....E 619 421-9003
2311 Boswell Rd Ste 8 Chula Vista (91914) *(P-4015)*

Sealed Air Corporation ....C 909 594-1791
19440 Arenth Ave City Of Industry (01748) *(P 4016)*

Searing Industries, Rancho Cucamonga *Also Called: Searing Industries Inc (P-4525)*

Searing Industries Inc (PA)..................................C 909 948-3030
8901 Arrow Rte Rancho Cucamonga (91730) *(P-4525)*

Searles Valley Minerals Inc ....C 760 372-2259
80201 Trona Rd Trona (93562) *(P-381)*

Searles Valley Minerals Inc ....C 760 672-2053
13068 Main St Trona (93562) *(P-382)*

Sears, West Covina *Also Called: Sears Home Imprv Pdts Inc (P-425)*

Sears, Long Beach *Also Called: Sears Home Imprv Pdts Inc (P-426)*

Sears, Temple City *Also Called: Sears Home Imprv Pdts Inc (P-427)*

Sears, San Diego *Also Called: Innovel Solutions Inc (P-9296)*

Sears Home Imprv Pdts Inc ....C 626 671-1892
730 S Orange Ave West Covina (91790) *(P-425)*

Sears Home Imprv Pdts Inc ....C 562 485-4904
2900 N Bellflower Blvd Long Beach (90815) *(P-426)*

Sears Home Imprv Pdts Inc ....C 626 988-9134
5665 Rosemead Blvd Temple City (91780) *(P-427)*

Season Produce Co Inc ....B 213 689-0008
1601 E Olympic Blvd Ste 315 Los Angeles (90021) *(P-10916)*

Seaspace Corporation ....E 858 746-1100
9155 Brown Deer Rd San Diego (92121) *(P-6657)*

Seaspine Inc ....D 760 727-8399
5770 Armada Dr Carlsbad (92008) *(P-8300)*

Seat Planners LLC ....D 619 237-9434
311 4th Ave Apt 509 San Diego (92101) *(P-9235)*

Seating Concepts LLC ....E 619 491-3159
4229 Ponderosa Ave Ste B San Diego (92123) *(P-2552)*

Seating Resource, Azusa *Also Called: Holguin & Holguin Inc (P-2543)*

Seattle Arprt Hospitality LLC ....D 310 476-6411
170 N Church Ln Los Angeles (90049) *(P-13019)*

Seattle Trinel Prtners A Jint V ....B 206 971-8701
555 Anton Blvd Ste 1000 Costa Mesa (92626) *(P-428)*

Seaward Products Corp ....D 562 699-7997
3721 Capitol Ave City Of Industry (90601) *(P-5983)*

Seaworld Global Logistics ....B 310 742-3882
3743 Legato Ct Pomona (91766) *(P-9334)*

Sechrist Industries Inc ....A 714 579-8400
4225 E La Palma Ave Anaheim (92807) *(P-8226)*

Seco Industries, Commerce *Also Called: Specialty Enterprises Co (P-4018)*

Secom, Gardena *Also Called: Secom International (P-14106)*

Secom International (PA)......................................D 310 641-1290
15905 S Broadway Gardena (90248) *(P-14106)*

Second Generation Inc ....D
21650 Oxnard St Ste 500 Woodland Hills (91367) *(P-2131)*

Second Hrvest Fd Bnk Ornge CNT ....D 949 653-2900
8014 Marine Way Irvine (92618) *(P-17008)*

Second Image National LLC (PA)..........................C 800 229-7477
170 E Arrow Hwy San Dimas (91773) *(P-13316)*

Second Street Corporation ....C 310 394-5454
1111 2nd St Santa Monica (90403) *(P-13020)*

Sector9, San Diego *Also Called: Bravo Sports (P-8508)*

Sectran Armored Truck Service, Pico Rivera *Also Called: Sectran Security Incorporated (P-14337)*

Sectran Security Incorporated (PA)......................C 562 948-1446
7633 Industry Ave Pico Rivera (90660) *(P-14337)*

Secura Key, Chatsworth *Also Called: Soundcraft Inc (P-7153)*

Secure Choice Lending ....D 951 733-8925
1650 Spruce St Ste 100 Riverside (92507) *(P-11878)*

Secure Comm Systems Inc (HQ)...........................C 714 547-1174
1740 E Wilshire Ave Santa Ana (92705) *(P-6658)*

Secure Net Alliance ....D 818 848-4900
601 S Glenoaks Blvd Ste 409 Burbank (91502) *(P-14338)*

Secure One Data Solutions LLC ....D 562 924-7056
11090 Artesia Blvd Ste D Cerritos (90703) *(P-14155)*

Secure-Dmz, Irvine *Also Called: Eighteenth Meridian Inc (P-13716)*

Secureauth Corporation (PA)................................C 949 777-6959
49 Discovery Ste 220 Irvine (92618) *(P-13815)*

Securitas SEC Svcs USA Inc ....B 818 706-6800
4330 Park Terrace Dr Westlake Village (91361) *(P-14339)*

Securitas Technology Corp ....D 858 812-7349
7002 Convoy Ct San Diego (92111) *(P-14419)*

Securitech Security Svcs Inc ....C 213 387-5050
2733 N San Fernando Rd Los Angeles (90065) *(P-14340)*

Security and Patrol Services, Fountain Valley *Also Called: Safeguard On Demand Inc (P-14336)*

Security Company, Burbank *Also Called: Secure Net Alliance (P-14338)*

Security Front Desk, Mc Kittrick *Also Called: Aera Energy Services Company (P-285)*

Security Indust Spcialists Inc ....A 323 924-9147
477 N Oak St Inglewood (90302) *(P-14341)*

Security Indust Spcialists Inc (PA).........................D 310 215-5100
6071 Bristol Pkwy Culver City (90230) *(P-14342)*

Security Services, Commerce *Also Called: American Security Force Inc (P-14381)*

Securus Inc ....E
14284 Danielson St Poway (92064) *(P-5071)*

Secuto Music, Burbank *Also Called: Roundabout Entertainment Inc (P-14853)*

Sedgwick, Ontario *Also Called: Sedgwick CMS Holdings Inc (P-12252)*

Sedgwick CMS Holdings Inc ....A 909 477-5500
3633 Inland Empire Blvd Ontario (91764) *(P-12252)*

Employee Codes: A=Over 500 employees, B=251-500
C=101-250, D=51-100, E=20-50, F=10-19, G=1-9

2025 Southern California
Business Directory and Buyers Guide

© Mergent Inc. 1-800-342-5647

1179

Seeds of Change Inc .... C 310 764-7700
31 Mountain Laurel Trabuco Canyon (92679) (P-11071)

Seek Capital LLC .... D 855 978-6106
6420 Wilshire Blvd Los Angeles (90048) (P-18206)

Seek Government Funds, Los Angeles Also Called: Seek Capital LLC (P-18206)

Seektech, San Diego Also Called: Seescan Inc (P-5637)

Seeley Brothers, Brea Also Called: Norcal Inc (P-1057)

Seescan Inc (PA) .... C 858 244-3300
3855 Ruffin Rd San Diego (92123) (P-5637)

Sega Entertainment USA Inc .... A 310 217-9500
600 N Brand Blvd 5th Fl Glendale (91203) (P-15101)

Sega Holdings USA Inc .... A 415 701-6000
9737 Lurline Ave Chatsworth (91311) (P-8722)

Sega of America Inc (DH) .... E 949 788-0455
140 Progress Ste 100 Irvine (92618) (P-10527)

Sega of America Inc .... B 747 477-3708
2900 W Alameda Ave Burbank (91505) (P-10528)

Segway Inc .... C 603 222-6000
405 E Santa Clara St Ste 100 Arcadia (91006) (P-7635)

Seidner-Miller Inc .... C 909 305-2000
1949 Auto Centre Dr Glendora (91740) (P-11405)

Seiko Epson, Los Alamitos Also Called: Epson America Inc (P-5918)

Seirus Innovation, Poway Also Called: Seirus Innovative ACC Inc (P-8540)

Seirus Innovative ACC Inc .... D 858 513-1212
13975 Danielson St Poway (92064) (P-8540)

Seismic Productions .... D 310 407-0411
7010 Santa Monica Blvd West Hollywood (90038) (P-13245)

Seismic Software Inc (HQ) .... D 714 404-7069
12390 El Camino Real Ste 300 San Diego (92130) (P-14028)

Seiu Local 721 .... C 213 368-8660
1545 Wilshire Blvd Ste 100 Los Angeles (90017) (P-17313)

Sekai Electronics Inc (PA) .... E 949 783-5740
38 Waterworks Way Irvine (92618) (P-6659)

Sela Healthcare Inc .... B 818 341-9800
20554 Roscoe Blvd Canoga Park (91306) (P-15773)

Sela Healthcare Inc (PA) .... C 909 985-1981
867 E 11th St Upland (91786) (P-15774)

Selane Products Inc (PA) .... D 818 998-7460
9129 Lurline Ave Chatsworth (91311) (P-8355)

Select Aircargo Services Inc .... D 310 851-8500
12801 S Figueroa St Los Angeles (90061) (P-9335)

Select Data, Anaheim Also Called: Select Data Inc (P-13816)

Select Data Inc .... C 714 577-1000
4175 E La Palma Ave Ste 205 Anaheim (92807) (P-13816)

Select Home Care .... D 805 777-3855
128 Erten St Thousand Oaks (91360) (P-16420)

Select Home Warranty Ca Inc .... B 732 835-0110
222 W 6th St Ste 400 San Pedro (90731) (P-12148)

SELECT MEDICAL, Los Angeles Also Called: Califrnia Rhblitation Inst LLC (P-15930)

Select Personnel Services, Santa Barbara Also Called: Select Temporaries LLC (P-13570)

Select Staffing, Santa Barbara Also Called: Eastern Staffing LLC (P-13512)

Select Temporaries LLC (DH) .... D 805 882-2200
3820 State St Santa Barbara (93105) (P-13570)

Selectabed, Agoura Hills Also Called: Relief-Mart Inc (P-11695)

Selectra Industries Corp .... D 323 581-8500
5166 Alcoa Ave Vernon (90058) (P-2152)

Self Esteem, Montebello Also Called: All Access Apparel Inc (P-2162)

Self Realization Fellowship, Los Angeles Also Called: Self-Realization Fellowship Ch (P-17418)

Self Serve Auto Dismantlers (PA) .... C 714 630-8901
3200 E Frontera St Anaheim (92806) (P-10541)

Self-Realization Fellowship Ch (PA) .... E 323 225-2471
3880 San Rafael Ave Los Angeles (90065) (P-17418)

Sellers Optical Inc .... D 949 631-6800
320 Kalmus Dr Costa Mesa (92626) (P-8021)

Selman Chevrolet Company .... C 714 633-3521
1800 E Chapman Ave Orange (92867) (P-11406)

Selman Lchnger Edson Hsu Nwman .... D 310 445-0800
11766 Wilshire Blvd Los Angeles (90025) (P-16775)

Seltzer Cplan McMhon Vtek A La (PA) .... C 619 685-3003
750 B St Ste 2100 San Diego (92101) (P-16776)

Sema, Diamond Bar Also Called: Specilty Eqp Mkt Assn Prfmce R (P-17289)

Sema Construction Inc .... D 949 470-0500
320 Goddard Ste 150 Irvine (92618) (P-648)

Semco .... E 909 799-9666
1495 S Gage St San Bernardino (92408) (P-8062)

Semco, Vista Also Called: Systems Engineering & MGT Co (P-17641)

Semi-Kinetics Inc .... D 949 830-7364
20191 Windrow Dr Ste A Lake Forest (92630) (P-6770)

Semicoa Corporation .... D 714 979-1900
333 Mccormick Ave Costa Mesa (92626) (P-6887)

Semiconductor Process Eqp LLC .... E 661 257-0934
27963 Franklin Pkwy Valencia (91355) (P-6888)

Seminis, Oxnard Also Called: Seminis Vegetable Seeds Inc (P-11072)

Seminis Inc (DH) .... B 805 485-7317
2700 Camino Del Sol Oxnard (93030) (P-17821)

Seminis Vegetable Seeds Inc (DH) .... A 855 733-3834
2700 Camino Del Sol Oxnard (93030) (P-11072)

Sempra (PA) .... C 619 696-2000
488 8th Ave San Diego (92101) (P-9676)

Sempra Energy .... A 619 696-2000
9305 Lightwave Ave San Diego (92123) (P-9610)

Sempra Energy, San Diego Also Called: Sempra Energy (P-9610)

Sempra Energy Global Entps .... A 619 696-2000
101 Ash St San Diego (92101) (P-9611)

Sempra Energy International .... A 619 696-2000
101 Ash St San Diego (92101) (P-9612)

Sempra Energy Utilities, San Diego Also Called: Sempra Energy International (P-9612)

Sempra Global (HQ) .... D 619 696-2000
488 8th Ave San Diego (92101) (P-6298)

Semtech, Camarillo Also Called: Semtech Corporation (P-6889)

Semtech Corporation (PA) .... C 805 498-2111
200 Flynn Rd Camarillo (93012) (P-6889)

Senclub LLC .... D 626 317-8073
788 Mountain Shadows Dr Corona (92881) (P-14979)

Sendlane Inc .... D 301 520-3812
10620 Treena St Ste 250 San Diego (92131) (P-18207)

Seneca Family of Agencies .... C 714 881-8600
1801 Park Court Pl Bldg H Santa Ana (92701) (P-12253)

Seneca Family of Agencies .... C 805 434-2449
6850 Morro Rd Atascadero (93422) (P-17009)

Seneca Family of Agencies .... C 805 278-0355
2130 N Ventura Rd Oxnard (93036) (P-17010)

Senga Engineering Inc .... E 714 549-8011
1525 E Warner Ave Santa Ana (92705) (P-6231)

Senior Care Action Ntwrk Fndti .... A 562 989-5100
3800 Kilroy Airport Way Long Beach (90806) (P-12105)

Senior Flexonics, San Diego Also Called: Senior Operations LLC (P-6232)

Senior Garden APT, San Diego Also Called: Barker Management Incorporated (P-12333)

Senior Health and Activity Ctr, Los Angeles Also Called: Altamed Health Services Corp (P-15235)

Senior Nutrition Program, Los Angeles Also Called: Jewish Family Svc Los Angeles (P-16963)

Senior Operations LLC .... D 818 350-8499
28510 Industry Dr Valencia (91355) (P-5377)

Senior Operations LLC .... D 858 278-8400
9106 Balboa Ave San Diego (92123) (P-6232)

Senior Operations LLC .... D 909 627-2723
790 Greenfield Dr El Cajon (92021) (P-6233)

Senior Operations LLC .... C 858 278-8400
9106 Balboa Ave San Diego (92123) (P-6234)

Senior Operations LLC .... C 858 278-8400
9150 Balboa Ave San Diego (92123) (P-6235)

Senior Operations LLC .... B 818 260-2900
2980 N San Fernando Blvd Burbank (91504) (P-7562)

Senior Resource Group LLC .... C 858 519-0890
850 Del Mar Downs Rd Apt 338 Solana Beach (92075) (P-12366)

Sensata Technologies Inc .... D 805 716-0322
1461 Lawrence Dr Thousand Oaks (91320) (P-14250)

Sensemetrics Inc .... E 619 738-8300
750 B St Ste 1630 San Diego (92101) (P-6890)

Sensor Systems Inc .... B 818 341-5366
8929 Fullbright Ave Chatsworth (91311) (P-7810)

Mergent email: customerrelations@mergent.com
1180

2025 Southern California
Business Directory and Buyers Guide

(P-0000) Products & Services Section entry number
(PA)=Parent Co (HQ)=Headquarters (DH)=Div Headquarters

Sensorex Corporation .... D 714 895-4344
11751 Markon Dr Garden Grove (92841) *(P-7878)*

Sensoscientific LLC .... E 800 279-3101
685 Cochran St Ste 200 Simi Valley (93065) *(P-7879)*

Sentek Consulting Inc .... C 619 543-9550
2811 Nimitz Blvd Ste G San Diego (92106) *(P-14251)*

Sentek Global, San Diego Also Called: Sentek Consulting Inc *(P-14251)*

Sentinel Monitoring Corp (HQ) .... D 949 453-1550
220 Technology Dr Ste 200 Irvine (92618) *(P-14420)*

Sentinel Offender Services LLC (PA)..... D 949 453-1550
1220 N Simon Cir Anaheim (92806) *(P-14421)*

Sentinel Peak Rsources Cal LLC .... D 323 298-2200
5640 S Fairfax Ave Los Angeles (90056) *(P-313)*

Sentinel Peak Rsources Cal LLC .... D 661 395-5214
1200 Discovery Dr Ste 100 Bakersfield (93309) *(P-314)*

Sentry Life Insurance Company .... C 661 274-4018
4720 Aliso Way Oceanside (92057) *(P-12254)*

Sentynl Therapeutics Inc .... E 888 227-8725
420 Stevens Ave Ste 200 Solana Beach (92075) *(P-3499)*

Sep Group Inc .... E 858 876-4621
11374 Turtleback Ln San Diego (92127) *(P-17628)*

Separation Engineering Inc .... E 760 489-0101
931 S Andreasen Dr Ste A Escondido (92029) *(P-5834)*

Sequelae Inc .... D 801 628-0256
101 W Bdwy Fl 9 San Diego (92101) *(P-14029)*

Sequenom Inc (DH) .... **D 858 202-9000**
3595 John Hopkins Ct San Diego (92121) *(P-17822)*

Sequenom Ctr For Mlclar Mdcine .... B 858 202-9051
3595 John Hopkins Ct San Diego (92121) *(P-16334)*

Sequenom Ctr For Mlclar Mdcine, San Diego Also Called: Sequenom Inc *(P-17822)*

Sequenom Laboratories, San Diego Also Called: Sequenom Ctr For Mlclar Mdcine *(P-16334)*

Sequent Medical Inc .... D 949 830-9600
35 Enterprise Aliso Viejo (92656) *(P-8227)*

Sequoia Concepts Inc .... D 818 409-6000
28632 Roadside Dr Ste 110 Agoura Hills (91301) *(P-13288)*

Sequoia Financial Services, Agoura Hills Also Called: Sequoia Concepts Inc *(P-13288)*

Serco Inc .... C 858 569-8979
9350 Waxie Way Ste 400 San Diego (92123) *(P-17629)*

Serco Mold Inc (PA)................................ **E 626 331-0517**
2009 Wright Ave La Verne (91750) *(P-4237)*

Serco Services Inc .... D 805 736-3584
701 E North Ave Ste A Lompoc (93437) *(P-13817)*

Sercomp LLC (PA)................................... **D 805 299-0020**
5401 Tech Cir Ste 200 Moorpark (93021) *(P-8567)*

Serfin Funds Transfer (PA)...................... **D 626 457-3070**
1000 S Fremont Ave Bldg A-O Alhambra (91803) *(P-11844)*

Serpac Electronic Enclosures, La Verne Also Called: Serco Mold Inc *(P-4237)*

Serra Community Med Clinic Inc .... C 818 768-3000
9375 San Fernando Rd Sun Valley (91352) *(P-15450)*

Serra Community Medical Clinic, Sun Valley Also Called: Serra Community Med Clinic Inc *(P-15450)*

Serra Laser and Waterjet Inc .... E 714 680-6211
1740 N Orangethorpe Park Anaheim (92801) *(P-7150)*

Serra Manufacturing Corp (PA)............... **D 310 537-4560**
3039 E Las Hermanas St Compton (90221) *(P-5212)*

Serrano Industries Inc .... E 562 777-8180
9922 Tabor Pl Santa Fe Springs (90670) *(P-6236)*

Serta Simmons Bedding LLC .... E 951 807-8467
23700 Cactus Ave Moreno Valley (92553) *(P-2490)*

Serv-Rite Meat Company Inc .... D 323 227-1911
2515 N San Fernando Rd Los Angeles (90065) *(P-1250)*

Servexo .... C 323 527-9994
1411 W 190th St Ste 475 Gardena (90248) *(P-7151)*

Servexo Protective Service, Gardena Also Called: Servexo *(P-7151)*

Servi-Tek Inc .... B 858 638-7735
8765 Sparren Way San Diego (92129) *(P-13417)*

Servi-Tek Janitorial Services, San Diego Also Called: Servi-Tek Inc *(P-13417)*

Service Genius Los Angeles Inc .... D 818 200-3379
8925 Fullbright Ave Chatsworth (91311) *(P-836)*

Service Master By ARS, Gardena Also Called: Disaster Rstrtion Prfssnals In *(P-399)*

ServiceMaster By Best Pros Inc .... D 951 515-9051
6474 Western Ave Riverside (92505) *(P-13418)*

Servicetitan, Glendale Also Called: Servicetitan Inc *(P-13818)*

Servicetitan Inc (PA)................................ **A 855 899-0970**
800 N Brand Blvd Ste 100 Glendale (91203) *(P-13818)*

Servicing Solutions LLC .... D 844 907-6583
1 City Blvd W Ste 200 Orange (92868) *(P-14592)*

Servicmaster Opco Holdings LLC .... **A 951 840-0134**
13758 Amarillo Ave Chino (91710) *(P-429)*

Servicmster Cmplete Rstoration, Escondido Also Called: Sbrm Inc *(P-13415)*

Servicon Systems Inc .... A 310 970-0700
3329 Jack Northrop Ave Hawthorne (90250) *(P-13419)*

Serviz Inc .... D 818 381-4826
15303 Ventura Blvd Ste 1600 Sherman Oaks (91403) *(P-13187)*

SERVPRO, San Marcos Also Called: Araya Construction Inc *(P-13356)*

SERVPRO Encino/Sherman Oaks, Encino Also Called: One Silver Serve LLC *(P-13397)*

SERVPRO Jeffries Global, Beverly Hills Also Called: Jeffries Global Inc *(P-1211)*

SERVPRO of Beverly Hills, Los Angeles Also Called: D&A Endeavors Inc *(P-1201)*

Sesa Inc (PA)... **E 714 779-9700**
20391 Via Guadalupe Yorba Linda (92887) *(P-13335)*

Sesloc Credit Union (PA)......................... **D 805 543-1816**
3855 Broad St San Luis Obispo (93401) *(P-11832)*

Setco LLC .... C 812 424-2904
4875 E Hunter Ave Anaheim (92807) *(P-4238)*

Sethi Management Inc .... C 760 692-5288
6156 Innovation Way Carlsbad (92009) *(P-18051)*

Setschedule LLC .... C 888 222-0011
100 Spectrum Center Dr Fl 9 Irvine (92618) *(P-13819)*

Settlers Jerky Inc .... E 909 444-3999
307 Paseo Sonrisa Walnut (91789) *(P-1270)*

Sev Lasers, Burbank Also Called: Petrosian Esthetic Entps LLC *(P-13153)*

Seven Gables Real Estate, Anaheim Also Called: House Seven Gables RE Inc *(P-12466)*

Seven Licensing Company LLC .... C 323 780-8250
801 S Figueroa St Ste 2500 Los Angeles (90017) *(P-10726)*

Seven Oaks Country Club .... C 661 664-6404
2000 Grand Lakes Ave Bakersfield (93311) *(P-15173)*

Seven One Inc (PA).................................. **D 818 904-3435**
21540 Prairie St Ste E Chatsworth (91311) *(P-14593)*

Seven Sisters of New Orleans, Whittier Also Called: Indio Products Inc *(P-10118)*

Seven7 Brands, Los Angeles Also Called: Seven Licensing Company LLC *(P-10726)*

Severson Group LLC .... C 760 550-9976
950 Boardwalk Ste 202 San Marcos (92078) *(P-11599)*

Severson Group, The, San Marcos Also Called: Severson Group LLC *(P-11599)*

Seville Classics Inc (PA).......................... **C 310 533-3800**
19401 Harborgate Way Torrance (90501) *(P-11518)*

Sew What Inc .... E 310 639-6000
1978 E Gladwick St Compton (90220) *(P-2204)*

Sewer Rodding Equipment Co (PA).......... **E 310 301-9009**
3217 Carter Ave Marina Del Rey (90292) *(P-6031)*

Sewing Collection Inc (PA)...................... **E 323 264-2223**
3113 E 26th St Vernon (90058) *(P-3900)*

Sextant Wines, Paso Robles Also Called: Rbz Vineyards LLC *(P-1582)*

Sexual Recovery Institute Inc .... B 310 360-0130
1964 Westwood Blvd Ste 400 Los Angeles (90025) *(P-17011)*

Seyfarth Shaw LLP .... C 310 277-7200
2029 Century Park E Ste 3300 Los Angeles (90002) *(P-16777)*

Seymour Duncan, Santa Barbara Also Called: Duncan Carter Corporation *(P-8466)*

SF Broadcasting Wisconsin Inc .... C 310 586-2410
2425 Olympic Blvd Santa Monica (90404) *(P-9516)*

Sfadia Inc .... D 323 622-1930
8485 Artesia Blvd Ste A Buena Park (90621) *(P-960)*

Sfc, Perris Also Called: Stretch Forming Corporation *(P-5042)*

SFE, Santa Fe Springs Also Called: Santa Fe Enterprises Inc *(P-5597)*

Sfn Group Inc .... A 858 458-9200
4660 La Jolla Village Dr Ste 910 San Diego (92122) *(P-13621)*

Sfn Group Inc .... A 949 727-8500
114 Pacifica Ste 210 Irvine (92618) *(P-13622)*

Sfpp LP (DH) .... C 714 560-4400
1100 W Town And Country Rd Ste 600 Orange (92868) *(P-9214)*

Sfrlc Inc .... E 562 693-2776
12306 Washington Blvd Whittier (90606) *(P-3936)*

Sfs, Brea Also Called: Kirkhill Inc *(P-7510)*

Employee Codes: A=Over 500 employees, B=251-500
C=101-250, D=51-100, E=20-50, F=10-19, G=1-9

2025 Southern California
Business Directory and Buyers Guide

© Mergent Inc. 1-800-342-5647
1181

A
L
P
H
A
B
E
T
I
C

Sft Realty Galway Downs LLC .... D 951 232-1880
38801 Los Corralitos Rd Temecula (92592) *(P-12528)*

SGB Better Baking Co LLC .... D 818 787-9992
14528 Blythe St Van Nuys (91402) *(P-1464)*

SGB Bubbles Baking Co LLC .... D 818 786-1700
15215 Keswick St Van Nuys (91405) *(P-1465)*

Sgl Composites Inc (DH) .... D 424 329-5250
1551 W 139th St Gardena (90249) *(P-2697)*

Sgl Technic LLC (DH) .... E 661 257-0500
28176 Avenue Stanford Valencia (91355) *(P-4489)*

Sgps Inc .... D 310 538-4175
15823 S Main St Gardena (90248) *(P-8723)*

Sgry LLC .... C 805 413-7920
696 Hampshire Rd Ste 100 Westlake Village (91361) *(P-15451)*

Sgry LLC .... C 818 501-1080
16501 Ventura Blvd Ste 103 Encino (91436) *(P-16189)*

Sgt Dresser-Rand, Chula Vista *Also Called: Curtiss-Wright Corporation (P-14762)*

Shademaster Products, Santee *Also Called: R V Best Inc (P-4214)*

Shadow Hills Convalescent Home, Sunland *Also Called: Arcadia Convalescent Hosp Inc (P-15569)*

Shadow Mtn Rsort Rcquet CLB Tn, Palm Desert *Also Called: Destination Residences LLC (P-12807)*

Shady Canyon Golf Club Inc .... C 949 856-7000
100 Shady Canyon Dr Irvine (92603) *(P-15174)*

Shamir, San Diego *Also Called: Shamir Insight Inc (P-4329)*

Shamir Insight Inc .... D 858 514-8330
9938 Via Pasar San Diego (92126) *(P-4329)*

Shamrock Capital Advisors LLC .... B 310 974-6600
1100 Glendon Ave Ste 1600 Los Angeles (90024) *(P-12642)*

Shamrock Companies, The, Anaheim *Also Called: Shamrock Supply Company Inc (P-10313)*

Shamrock Foods Company .... B 951 685-6314
12400 Riverside Dr Eastvale (91752) *(P-10978)*

Shamrock Supply Company Inc (PA) .... D 714 575-1800
3366 E La Palma Ave Anaheim (92806) *(P-10313)*

Shanghai Anc Electronic Tech, Moorpark *Also Called: Anc Technology Inc (P-6708)*

Shapell Industries .... D 323 655-7330
1990 S Bundy Dr Ste 500 Los Angeles (90025) *(P-8724)*

Shapell Industries LLC (HQ) .... D 323 655-7330
8383 Wilshire Blvd Ste 700 Beverly Hills (90211) *(P-12578)*

Shapiro-Gilman-Shandler Co .... C 213 593-1200
739 Decatur St Los Angeles (90021) *(P-10917)*

Shapp International Trdg Inc .... C 818 348-3000
6000 Reseda Blvd Tarzana (91356) *(P-9932)*

Shapp Internatioonal, Tarzana *Also Called: Shapp International Trdg Inc (P-9932)*

Shara-Tex Inc .... E 323 587-7200
3338 E Slauson Ave Vernon (90058) *(P-1926)*

Sharp, Torrance *Also Called: Sharp Industries Inc (P-10402)*

Sharp Chula Vista Medical Ctr .... D 858 499-5150
8695 Spectrum Center Blvd San Diego (92123) *(P-16190)*

Sharp Chula Vista Medical Ctr .... A 619 502-5800
751 Medical Center Ct Chula Vista (91911) *(P-16191)*

Sharp Chula Vista Medical Ctr, Chula Vista *Also Called: Sharp Chula Vista Medical Ctr (P-16191)*

Sharp Community Medical Group .... C 858 499-4525
8695 Spectrum Center Blvd San Diego (92123) *(P-17307)*

Sharp Coronado Hospital & Healthcare Center .... A 619 522-3600
250 Prospect Pl Coronado (92118) *(P-16192)*

Sharp Fabric, Los Angeles *Also Called: Elijah Textiles Inc (P-9891)*

Sharp Grssmont Hosp Emrgncy Ca, La Mesa *Also Called: Team Health Holdings Inc (P-16223)*

Sharp Health Care, San Diego *Also Called: Sharp Healthcare Aco LLC (P-16196)*

Sharp Health Plan .... D a..... 858 499-8300
8520 Tech Way Ste 200 San Diego (92123) *(P-12106)*

Sharp Healthcare .... D 619 397-3088
1400 E Palomar St Chula Vista (91913) *(P-98)*

Sharp Healthcare (PA) .... A 858 499-4000
8695 Spectrum Center Blvd San Diego (92123) *(P-11623)*

Sharp Healthcare .... D 619 460-6200
8860 Center Dr Ste 450 La Mesa (91942) *(P-15452)*

Sharp Healthcare .... C 858 499-2000
751 Medical Center Ct Chula Vista (91911) *(P-16193)*

Sharp Healthcare .... C 858 939-5434
8008 Frost St Ste 106 San Diego (92123) *(P-16194)*

Sharp Healthcare Aco LLC .... C 619 688-3543
2929 Health Center Dr San Diego (92123) *(P-11624)*

Sharp Healthcare Aco LLC .... B 619 446-1575
300 Fir St San Diego (92101) *(P-16195)*

Sharp Healthcare Aco LLC .... A 858 627-5152
3554 Ruffin Rd Ste Soca San Diego (92123) *(P-16196)*

Sharp Industries Inc (PA) .... E 310 370-5990
3501 Challenger St Fl 2 Torrance (90503) *(P-10402)*

Sharp Mary Birch H .... D 858 939-3400
3003 Health Center Dr San Diego (92123) *(P-16197)*

Sharp McDonald Center .... A 858 637-6920
7989 Linda Vista Rd San Diego (92111) *(P-16298)*

Sharp Memorial Hospital (HQ) .... A 858 939-3636
7901 Frost St San Diego (92123) *(P-16198)*

Sharp Memorial Hospital .... C 858 278-4110
7850 Vista Hill Ave San Diego (92123) *(P-16279)*

Sharp Mesa Vista Hospital, San Diego *Also Called: Sharp Memorial Hospital (P-16279)*

Sharp Rees Staly Rncho Brnardo .... D 858 521-2300
16899 W Bernardo Dr San Diego (92127) *(P-15453)*

Sharp Rees-Stealy, San Diego *Also Called: Sharp Healthcare (P-16194)*

Sharp Rees-Stealy Div, San Diego *Also Called: Sharp Healthcare Aco LLC (P-16195)*

Sharp Rees-Stealy Med Group, Chula Vista *Also Called: Sharp Healthcare (P-98)*

Sharp Rees-Stealy Pharmacy, San Diego *Also Called: Sharp Healthcare Aco LLC (P-11624)*

Sharp RES-Stealy Med Group Inc .... C 619 221-9547
3555 Kenyon St Ste 200 San Diego (92110) *(P-15454)*

Sharp RES-Stealy Med Group Inc .... C 619 644-6405
7862 El Cajon Blvd Ste C La Mesa (91942) *(P-15455)*

Sharpcast, Los Angeles *Also Called: Sugarsync Inc (P-14044)*

Sharpmart LLC .... E 619 278-1473
3911 Cleveland Ave Unit 33748 San Diego (92103) *(P-3686)*

Shasta Beverages Inc .... D 714 523-2280
14405 Artesia Blvd La Mirada (90638) *(P-1654)*

Shasta Landscaping Inc .... D 760 744-6551
1340 Descanso Ave San Marcos (92069) *(P-191)*

Shaw Industries Group Inc .... E 562 430-4445
11411 Valley View St Cypress (90630) *(P-1956)*

Shawmut Design and Cnstr, Los Angeles *Also Called: Shawmut Woodworking & Sup Inc (P-582)*

Shawmut Woodworking & Sup Inc .... C 323 602-1000
11390 W Olympic Blvd Fl 2 Los Angeles (90064) *(P-582)*

Shaxon Industries Inc .... D 714 779-1140
337 W Freedom Ave Orange (92865) *(P-5886)*

Shea Convalescent Hospital, Whittier *Also Called: Longwood Management Corp (P-16088)*

Shea Homes For Active Adults, Walnut *Also Called: JF Shea Construction Inc (P-409)*

Shea Homes Ltd Prtnershp, Walnut *Also Called: Vistancia Marketing LLC (P-18238)*

Shea Properties, Aliso Viejo *Also Called: Shea Properties MGT Co Inc (P-12318)*

Shea Properties MGT Co Inc .... B 949 389-7000
130 Vantis Dr Ste 200 Aliso Viejo (92656) *(P-12318)*

Shed Media US Inc .... D 323 904-4680
3000 W Alameda Ave Burbank (91505) *(P-13270)*

Sheet Metal Engineering .... E 805 306-0390
1780 Voyager Ave Simi Valley (93063) *(P-5033)*

Sheffield Manufacturing Inc .... D 310 320-1473
9131 Glenoaks Blvd Sun Valley (91352) *(P-6237)*

Sheffield Platers Inc .... C 858 546-8484
9850 Waples St San Diego (92121) *(P-5294)*

Sheila Street Properties Inc (PA) .... D 323 838-9208
5900 Sheila St Commerce (90040) *(P-5295)*

Shein Technology LLC (PA) .... B 213 628-4008
777 S Alameda St Fl 2 Los Angeles (90021) *(P-18208)*

Shelcore Inc (PA) .... E 818 883-2400
7811 Lemona Ave Van Nuys (91405) *(P-8495)*

Shelcore Toys, Van Nuys *Also Called: Shelcore Inc (P-8495)*

Sheldon Mechanical Corporation .... D 661 286-1361
26015 Avenue Hall Santa Clarita (91355) *(P-837)*

Shell, Anaheim *Also Called: Shell Oil Company (P-18209)*

Shell Oil Company .... C 714 991-9200
511 N Brookhurst St Anaheim (92801) *(P-18209)*

Shelter Pointe Hotel & Marina, San Diego *Also Called: Shelter Pointe LLC (P-9152)*
Shelter Pointe LLC .... C 619 221-8000
  1551 Shelter Island Dr San Diego (92106) *(P-9152)*
Shen Zhen New World II LLC .... D 818 980-1212
  333 Universal Hollywood Dr Universal City (91608) *(P-13021)*
Shepard Bros Inc (PA) .... C 562 697-1366
  503 S Cypress St La Habra (90631) *(P-6032)*
Shepard-Thomason Company .... D 714 773-5539
  901 S Leslie St La Habra (90631) *(P-7293)*
Sheppard Mllin Rchter Hmpton L .... D 619 338-6500
  501 W Broadway Fl 19 San Diego (92101) *(P-16778)*
Sheppard Mllin Rchter Hmpton L .... D 858 720-8900
  12275 El Camino Real Ste 100 San Diego (92130) *(P-16779)*
Sheppard Mllin Rchter Hmpton L (PA) .... B 213 620-1780
  333 S Hope St Fl 43 Los Angeles (90071) *(P-16780)*
Sheppard Mullin, Los Angeles *Also Called: Sheppard Mllin Rchter Hmpton L (P-16780)*
Sheraton, San Diego *Also Called: 8110 Aero Holding LLC (P-12755)*
Sheraton, Anaheim *Also Called: Anaheim - 1855 S Hbr Blvd Owne (P-12761)*
Sheraton, Los Angeles *Also Called: Hazens Investment LLC (P-12846)*
Sheraton, Universal City *Also Called: Lh Universal Operating LLC (P-12900)*
Sheraton, Los Angeles *Also Called: Nrea-TRC 711 LLC (P-12941)*
Sheraton, Los Angeles *Also Called: S W K Properties LLC (P-13006)*
Sheraton, Universal City *Also Called: Shen Zhen New World II LLC (P-13021)*
Sheraton, Pomona *Also Called: Starwood Htels Rsrts Wrldwide (P-13036)*
Sheraton Carlsbad Resort & Spa, Carlsbad *Also Called: Grand Pacific Carlsbad Ht LP (P-12831)*
Sheraton Ht San Dego Mssion Vl .... D 619 260-0111
  1433 Camino Del Rio S San Diego (92108) *(P-13022)*
Sheraton Inn Bakersfield, Bakersfield *Also Called: Msr Hotels & Resorts Inc (P-12721)*
Sheraton Pasadena, Pasadena *Also Called: Pasadena Hotel Dev Ventr LP (P-12969)*
Sheraton Pk Ht At Anheim Rsort, Anaheim *Also Called: 1855 S Hbr Blvd Drv Hldngs LLC (P-12752)*
Sheraton San Diego Mission Vly, San Diego *Also Called: Sheraton Ht San Dego Mssion Vl (P-13022)*
Shercon LLC .... D
  18704 S Ferris Pl Rancho Dominguez (90220) *(P-3937)*
Shercon, Inc., Rancho Dominguez *Also Called: Shercon LLC (P-3937)*
Sherline Products, Vista *Also Called: Sherline Products Incorporated (P-5552)*
Sherline Products Incorporated .... E 760 727-5181
  3235 Executive Rdg Vista (92081) *(P-5552)*
Sherman Oaks Hospital, Sherman Oaks *Also Called: Prime Hlthcare Svcs - Shrman O (P-16148)*
Sherman Village Hlth Care Ctr, North Hollywood *Also Called: Coldwater Care Center LLC (P-15594)*
Sherman Village Hlth Care Ctr, North Hollywood *Also Called: Hillsdale Group LP (P-15859)*
Sherwood Guest Home, Lynwood *Also Called: Marlinda Management Inc (P-15873)*
Sherwood Mechanical Inc .... D 858 679-3000
  6630 Top Gun St San Diego (92121) *(P-838)*
Sherwood Oaks Post Acute, Thousand Oaks *Also Called: Westlake Oaks Healthcare LLC (P-16629)*
Sheward & Son & Sons (PA) .... E 714 556-6055
  14352 Chambers Rd Tustin (92780) *(P-2607)*
Shield AI Inc (PA) .... A 619 719-5740
  600 W Broadway Ste 250 San Diego (92101) *(P-7370)*
Shield Healthcare, Valencia *Also Called: Shield-Denver Health Care Ctr (P-10108)*
Shield Security Inc (DH) .... B 714 210-1501
  1551 N Tustin Ave Ste 650 Santa Ana (92705) *(P-14343)*
Shield Security Inc .... B 909 920-1173
  265 N Euclid Ave Upland (91786) *(P-14344)*
Shield Security Inc .... C 818 239-5800
  21110 Vanowen St Canoga Park (91303) *(P-14345)*
Shield Security Inc .... B 562 283-1100
  150 E Wardlow Rd Long Beach (90807) *(P-14346)*
Shield-Denver Health Care Ctr (HQ) .... C 661 294-4200
  27911 Franklin Pkwy Valencia (91355) *(P-10108)*
Shields, Los Angeles *Also Called: Shields For Families (P-16299)*
Shields For Families (PA) .... D 323 242-5000
  11601 S Western Ave Los Angeles (90047) *(P-16299)*
Shimada Enterprises Inc .... E 562 802-8811
  14009 Dinard Ave Santa Fe Springs (90670) *(P-6516)*

Shimadzu Medical Systems USA, Long Beach *Also Called: Shimadzu Precision Instrs Inc (P-10500)*
Shimadzu Precision Instrs Inc .... D 310 217-8855
  20101 S Vermont Ave Torrance (90502) *(P-10109)*
Shimadzu Precision Instrs Inc (DH) .... D 562 420-6226
  3645 N Lakewood Blvd Long Beach (90808) *(P-10500)*
Shimano North Amer Holdg Inc (HQ) .... C 949 951-5003
  1 Holland Irvine (92618) *(P-10515)*
Shimano North America Bicycle, Irvine *Also Called: Shimano North Amer Holdg Inc (P-10515)*
Shimmick Construction Co Inc .... C 510 777-5000
  16481 Scientific Bldg 2 Irvine (92618) *(P-430)*
Shimmick Construction Co Inc .... C 310 663-8924
  1999 Avenue Of The Stars Ste 2600 Los Angeles (90067) *(P-431)*
Shimmick Construction Co Inc (HQ) .... D 949 591-5922
  530 Technology Dr Ste 300 Irvine (92618) *(P-718)*
Shims Bargain Inc .... C 323 726-8800
  7030 E Slauson Ave Commerce (90040) *(P-500)*
Shims Bargain Inc (PA) .... D 323 881-0099
  2600 S Soto St Los Angeles (90058) *(P-11143)*
Shine Food Inc (PA) .... E 310 329-3829
  19216 Normandie Ave Torrance (90502) *(P-1344)*
Shine Food Inc .... D 310 533-6010
  21100 S Western Ave Torrance (90501) *(P-1400)*
Shining Ocean Inc .... C 253 826-3700
  10888 7th St Rancho Cucamonga (91730) *(P-10862)*
Shinwoo P&C Usa Inc (HQ) .... B 619 407-7164
  2177 Britannia Blvd Ste 203 San Diego (92154) *(P-14594)*
Ship & Shore Environmental Inc .... E 562 997-0233
  2474 N Palm Dr Signal Hill (90755) *(P-10403)*
Ship Services, San Pedro *Also Called: So Cal Ship Services (P-9140)*
SHIPERP, Long Beach *Also Called: Erp Integrated Solutions LLC (P-13724)*
Shipping and Receiving, San Diego *Also Called: General Atomics (P-17791)*
Shipping Tree LLC .... D 310 404-9502
  14339 Whittram Ave Fontana (92335) *(P-13820)*
Shire .... E 805 372-3000
  1445 Lawrence Dr Newbury Park (91320) *(P-3500)*
Shire Rgenerative Medicine Inc .... E 858 754-5396
  11095 Torreyana Rd San Diego (92121) *(P-3501)*
Shirinian-Shaw Inc .... E 951 736-1229
  1229 Railroad St Corona (92882) *(P-2183)*
Shmaze Custom Coatings, Lake Forest *Also Called: Shmaze Industries Inc (P-5344)*
Shmaze Industries Inc .... E 949 583-1448
  20792 Canada Rd Lake Forest (92630) *(P-5344)*
Shock Doctor Inc (PA) .... D 800 233-6956
  11488 Slater Ave Fountain Valley (92708) *(P-8541)*
Shock Doctor Inc .... E 657 383-4400
  11488 Slater Ave Fountain Valley (92708) *(P-8542)*
Shock Doctor Sports, Fountain Valley *Also Called: Shock Doctor Inc (P-8541)*
Shockhound, City Of Industry *Also Called: Hot Topic Inc (P-11508)*
Shoffeitt Pipeline Inc .... D 949 581-1600
  15801 Rockfield Blvd Ste L Irvine (92618) *(P-694)*
Shogun Labs Inc (PA) .... C 317 676-2719
  340 S Lemon Ave # 1085 Walnut (91789) *(P-17926)*
Shook Hardy & Bacon LLP .... C 949 475-1500
  5 Park Plz Ste 1600 Irvine (92614) *(P-16781)*
Shop4techcom .... E 909 248-2725
  13745 Seminole Dr Chino (91710) *(P-5887)*
Shopper Inc .... B 800 344-8830
  2655 Park Center Dr Ste B Simi Valley (93065) *(P-10052)*
Shopzilla.com, Santa Monica *Also Called: Connexity Inc (P-9431)*
Shore Front LLC .... E 714 612-3751
  3973 Trolley Ct Brea (92823) *(P-1850)*
Shore Hotel, Santa Monica *Also Called: Sand and Sea (P-13014)*
Shore Western Manufacturing .... E 626 357-3251
  19888 Quiroz Ct Walnut (91789) *(P-7977)*
Shorecliff Properties, Pismo Beach *Also Called: Tic Hotels Inc (P-13053)*
Shoreline Care Center, Oxnard *Also Called: Covenant Care California LLC (P-15613)*
Shores Restaurant, La Jolla *Also Called: La Jolla Bch & Tennis CLB Inc (P-12893)*
Shorett Printing Inc (PA) .... E 714 545-4689
  250 W Rialto Ave San Bernardino (92408) *(P-3175)*

ALPHABETIC

Employee Codes: A=Over 500 employees, B=251-500
C=101-250, D=51-100, E=20-50, F=10-19, G=1-9

2025 Southern California
Business Directory and Buyers Guide

© Mergent Inc. 1-800-342-5647
1183

Short Sale Agent Finder, San Diego *Also Called: Verseio Inc (P-13861)*

Shortcuts Software Inc .... E 714 622-6600
7711 Center Ave Ste 550 Huntington Beach (92647) *(P-14030)*

Show Group Production Services, Gardena *Also Called: Sgps Inc (P-8723)*

Showdogs Inc .... E 760 603-3269
168 S Pacific St San Marcos (92078) *(P-2608)*

Showershapes, Ventura *Also Called: G W Surfaces (P-1206)*

Showroom Interiors LLC .... C 323 348-1551
8905 Rex Rd Pico Rivera (90660) *(P-13470)*

Shred Labs LLC .... E 781 285-8622
8033 W Sunset Blvd # 1112 Los Angeles (90046) *(P-14031)*

Shrin LLC .... D 714 850-0303
900 E Arlee Pl Anaheim (92805) *(P-9848)*

Shriner's Hospital, Pasadena *Also Called: Shriners Hspitals For Children (P-16301)*

Shriners Hspitals For Children .... B 213 368-3302
3160 Genieva St Montrose (91020) *(P-16300)*

Shriners Hspitals For Children .... B 626 389-9300
909 S Fair Oaks Ave Pasadena (91105) *(P-16301)*

Shriners Hspitals For Children, Pasadena *Also Called: Shriners International (P-17366)*

Shriners International .... D 626 389-9300
909 S Fair Oaks Ave Pasadena (91105) *(P-17366)*

Shryne Group Inc .... A 323 614-4558
728 E Commercial St Los Angeles (90012) *(P-12613)*

Shultz Steel Company LLC .... B 323 357-3200
5321 Firestone Blvd South Gate (90280) *(P-5160)*

Shurflo LLC .... B 714 371-1550
3545 Harbor Gtwy S Ste 103 Costa Mesa (92626) *(P-5744)*

Shutters On The Beach, Santa Monica *Also Called: By The Blue Sea LLC (P-12781)*

Shutters On The Beach, Santa Monica *Also Called: Edward Thomas Hospitality Corp (P-12818)*

Shuttle Smart Inc .... C 310 338-9466
6150 W 96th St Los Angeles (90045) *(P-8803)*

Shye West Inc (PA) .... E 949 486-4598
43 Corporate Park Ste 102 Irvine (92606) *(P-8631)*

Shyft Group Inc .... D 323 276-1933
1130 S Vail Ave Montebello (90640) *(P-7193)*

Si, Fontana *Also Called: California Steel Inds Inc (P-4514)*

Si Manufacturing Inc .... E 714 956-7110
1440 S Allec St Anaheim (92805) *(P-6938)*

Sia Engineering (usa) Inc .... C 310 957-2928
7001 W Imperial Hwy Los Angeles (90045) *(P-17630)*

Sicor Inc (HQ) .... A 949 455-4700
19 Hughes Irvine (92618) *(P-3502)*

Sid E Parker Boiler Mfg Co Inc .... D 323 727-9800
5930 Bandini Blvd Commerce (90040) *(P-4926)*

Sidley Austin LLP .... D 310 284-6618
1999 Avenue Of The Stars Ste 1700 Los Angeles (90067) *(P-16782)*

Sids Carpet Barn (PA) .... E 619 477-7000
132 W 8th St National City (91950) *(P-9906)*

Siegfried Irvine, Irvine *Also Called: Alliance Medical Products Inc (P-8085)*

Siegfried Irvine, Irvine *Also Called: Alliance Medical Products Inc (P-8086)*

Siemens Energy Inc .... E 310 223-0660
18502 S Dominguez Hills Dr Rancho Dominguez (90220) *(P-5765)*

Siemens Industry Inc .... D 714 761-2200
6141 Katella Ave Cypress (90630) *(P-10206)*

Siemens Rail Automation Corp .... D 909 532-5405
9568 Archibald Ave Rancho Cucamonga (91730) *(P-6692)*

Sientra, Irvine *Also Called: Sientra Inc (P-8301)*

Sientra Inc (HQ) .... E 805 562-3500
3333 Michelson Dr Ste 650 Irvine (92612) *(P-8301)*

Sierra, Compton *Also Called: Sierra Cheese Manufacturing Company Inc (P-1290)*

Sierra Alloys Company, Irwindale *Also Called: STS Metals Inc (P-5161)*

Sierra Aluminum, Riverside *Also Called: Samuel Son & Co (usa) Inc (P-4605)*

Sierra Aluminum Company .... E 951 781-7800
2345 Fleetwood Dr Riverside (92509) *(P-4606)*

Sierra Canyon Inc .... D 818 882-8121
11052 Independence Ave Chatsworth (91311) *(P-16825)*

Sierra Canyon Day Camp, Chatsworth *Also Called: Sierra Canyon Inc (P-16825)*

Sierra Cheese Manufacturing Company Inc .... E 310 635-1216
916 S Santa Fe Ave Compton (90221) *(P-1290)*

Sierra Lathing Company Inc .... C 909 421-0211
1189 Leiske Dr Rialto (92376) *(P-1028)*

Sierra Monolithics Inc (HQ) .... E 310 698-1000
103 W Torrance Blvd Redondo Beach (90277) *(P-18356)*

Sierra Pacific Constrs Inc .... D 747 888-5000
22212 Ventura Blvd Ste 300 Woodland Hills (91364) *(P-583)*

Sierra Pacific Constructors, Woodland Hills *Also Called: Sierra Pacific Constrs Inc (P-583)*

Sierra Pacific Engrg & Pdts, Long Beach *Also Called: SPEP Acquisition Corp (P-4789)*

Sierra Precision, Anaheim *Also Called: 3d Instruments LLC (P-7844)*

Sierra Springs Apartments, San Bernardino *Also Called: Woodman Realty Inc (P-12551)*

Sierra Vista, Victorville *Also Called: Encore Senior Living III LLC (P-17149)*

Sierra Vista Hospital Inc (HQ) .... A 805 546-7600
1010 Murray Ave San Luis Obispo (93405) *(P-16199)*

Sierra Vista Regional Med Ctr, San Luis Obispo *Also Called: Sierra Vista Hospital Inc (P-16199)*

Sierracin Corporation (HQ) .... A 818 741-1656
12780 San Fernando Rd Sylmar (91342) *(P-3721)*

Sierracin/Sylmar Corporation .... A 818 362-6711
12780 San Fernando Rd Sylmar (91342) *(P-4239)*

Sigma-Aldrich Corporation .... E 760 710-6213
6211 El Camino Real Carlsbad (92009) *(P-3820)*

Sign Industries Inc .... E 909 930-0303
2101 Carrillo Privado Ontario (91761) *(P-8632)*

Sign Mart, Orange *Also Called: Metal Art of California Inc (P-8616)*

Sign-A-Rama, Palm Desert *Also Called: Pd Group (P-8623)*

Signage Solutions Corporation .... E 714 491-0299
2231 S Dupont Dr Anaheim (92806) *(P-8633)*

Signal .... E 661 259-1234
26330 Diamond Pl Ste 100 Santa Clarita (91350) *(P-2827)*

Signal 88, Ontario *Also Called: Signal 88 LLC (P-14347)*

Signal 88 LLC .... A 714 713-5306
821 S Rockefeller Ave Ontario (91761) *(P-14347)*

Signal Hill Petroleum Inc .... E 562 595-6440
2633 Cherry Ave Signal Hill (90755) *(P-315)*

Signal Pharmaceuticals LLC .... C 858 795-4700
10300 Campus Point Dr Ste 100 San Diego (92121) *(P-3503)*

Signal Products Inc (PA) .... D 213 748-0990
5600 W Adams Blvd Ste 200 Los Angeles (90016) *(P-10727)*

Signal Products/Guess Handbags, Los Angeles *Also Called: Signal Products Inc (P-10727)*

Signature Analytics LLC .... D 888 284-3842
10120 Pacific Heights Blvd Ste 110 San Diego (92121) *(P-17754)*

Signature Control Systems .... D 949 580-3640
16485 Laguna Canyon Rd Ste 130 Irvine (92618) *(P-5477)*

Signature Flexible Packg LLC (PA) .... E 909 598-7844
19310 San Jose Ave City Of Industry (91748) *(P-3779)*

Signature Fresh, City Of Industry *Also Called: Ssre Holdings LLC (P-1251)*

Signature Parking, Santa Barbara *Also Called: Signature Parking LLC (P-1226)*

Signature Parking LLC .... D 805 969-7275
924 Chapala St Ste B Santa Barbara (93101) *(P-13188)*

Signature Parking LLC .... D 805 969-7275
1482 E Valley Rd Ste 311 Santa Barbara (93108) *(P-1226)*

Signature Party Rentals, Indio *Also Called: Signature Party Rentals LLC (P-13471)*

Signature Party Rentals LLC .... C 760 863-0671
82309 Market St Indio (92201) *(P-13471)*

Signature Resolution .... D 213 622-1002
633 W 5th Ste 1000 Los Angeles (90071) *(P-14595)*

Signature Select Personnel LLC .... B 626 940-3351
138 W Bonita Ave Ste 207 San Dimas (91773) *(P-13571)*

Signco, Yorba Linda *Also Called: Sesa Inc (P-13335)*

Signet Armorlite Inc (DH) .... B 760 744-4000
5803 Newton Dr Ste A Carlsbad (92008) *(P-8415)*

Signify North America Corp .... C 732 563-3000
3350 Enterprise Dr Bloomington (92316) *(P-6473)*

Signresource LLC .... C 323 771-2098
6135 District Blvd Maywood (90270) *(P-8634)*

Signs and Services Company .... E 714 761-8200
10980 Boatman Ave Stanton (90680) *(P-8635)*

Signtech, San Diego *Also Called: Signtech Electrical Advg Inc (P-8636)*

Signtech Electrical Advg Inc .... C 619 527-6100
4444 Federal Blvd San Diego (92102) *(P-8636)*

Mergent email: customerrelations@mergent.com
1184

2025 Southern California
Business Directory and Buyers Guide

(P-0000) Products & Services Section entry number
(PA)=Parent Co (HQ)=Headquarters (DH)=Div Headquarters

Signtronix Inc .... D 310 534-7500
1445 Sepulveda Blvd Torrance (90501) *(P-8637)*

Sigue, Sylmar *Also Called: Sigue Corporation (P-14596)*

Sigue Corporation (PA).................... D 818 837-5939
13190 Telfair Ave Sylmar (91342) *(P-14596)*

Silao Tortilleria, Rowland Heights *Also Called: Silao Tortilleria Inc (P-1851)*

Silao Tortilleria Inc .... E 626 961-0761
18316 Senteno St Rowland Heights (91748) *(P-1851)*

Silc Technologies Inc .... D 626 375-1231
181 W Huntington Dr Ste 200 Monrovia (91016) *(P-6891)*

Silent Valley Club Inc .... D 951 849-4501
46305 Poppet Flats Rd Banning (92220) *(P-13023)*

Silgan, Woodland Hills *Also Called: Silgan Can Company (P-4723)*

Silgan, Woodland Hills *Also Called: Silgan Containers Corporation (P-4724)*

Silgan, Woodland Hills *Also Called: Silgan Containers Mfg Corp (P-4726)*

Silgan Can Company .... C 818 348-3700
21600 Oxnard St Ste 1600 Woodland Hills (91367) *(P-4723)*

Silgan Containers Corporation (DH) .... D 818 710-3700
21600 Oxnard St Ste 1600 Woodland Hills (91367) *(P-4724)*

Silgan Containers LLC (HQ) .... D 818 710-3700
21600 Oxnard St Ste 1600 Woodland Hills (91367) *(P-4725)*

Silgan Containers Mfg Corp (DH) .... D 818 710-3700
21600 Oxnard St Ste 1600 Woodland Hills (91367) *(P-4726)*

Silicon Processing and Trading Inc .... D 805 388-8683
322 N Aviador St Camarillo (93010) *(P-9764)*

Silicon Tech Inc .... B 949 476-1130
3009 Daimler St Santa Ana (92705) *(P-5888)*

Silicontech, Santa Ana *Also Called: Silicon Tech Inc (P-5888)*

Silk Screen Shirts Inc .... E 760 233-3900
6185 El Camino Real Carlsbad (92009) *(P-1934)*

Silla Automotive LLC .... C 800 624-1499
1217 W Artesia Blvd Compton (90220) *(P-9849)*

Silla Cooling Systems, Compton *Also Called: Silla Automotive LLC (P-9849)*

Sillcrest Nursing Home, San Bernardino *Also Called: Marna Health Services Inc (P-15874)*

Silver Creek Industries LLC .... C 951 943-5393
2830 Barrett Ave Perris (92571) *(P-584)*

Silver Hawk Freight Inc .... D 562 404-0226
16410 Bloomfield Ave Cerritos (90703) *(P-9336)*

Silver Lakes Association .... D 760 245-1606
15273 Orchard Hill Ln Helendale (92342) *(P-17367)*

Silver Rock Resort Golf Club .... D 760 777-8884
79179 Ahmanson Ln La Quinta (92253) *(P-15096)*

Silver Saddle Ranch & Club Inc .... D 818 768-8808
7635 N San Fernando Rd Burbank (91505) *(P-12579)*

Silverado Framing & Cnstr .... D 951 352-1100
3091 E La Cadena Dr Riverside (92507) *(P-432)*

Silverado Senior Living Inc .... D 760 456-5137
1500 Borden Rd Escondido (92026) *(P-15775)*

Silverado Senior Living Inc .... D 626 872-3941
1118 N Stoneman Ave Alhambra (91801) *(P-15776)*

Silverado Senior Living Inc .... D 818 746-2583
25100 Calabasas Rd Calabasas (91302) *(P-15777)*

Silverado Senior Living Inc .... D 949 945-0189
350 W Bay St Costa Mesa (92627) *(P-15778)*

Silverado Snior Lving Hldngs .... A 949 240-7200
6400 Oak Cyn Ste 200 Irvine (92618) *(P-17194)*

Silvergate San Marcos, San Marcos *Also Called: Americare Hlth Retirement Inc (P-12281)*

Silverrest, Fullerton *Also Called: Brentwood Home LLC (P-2481)*

Silverton Business Center, San Diego *Also Called: HG Fenton Property Company (P-12376)*

Silvester California, Los Angeles *Also Called: Silvestri Studio Inc (P-8725)*

Silvestri Studio Inc (PA).................... D 323 277-4420
8125 Beach St Los Angeles (90001) *(P-8725)*

Silvino Nieto .... C 909 948-0279
2990 Inland Empire Blvd Ontario (91764) *(P-14348)*

Silvino Nieto .... C 213 413-3500
1545 Wilshire Blvd Ste 302 Los Angeles (90017) *(P-14349)*

Silvus Technologies Inc (PA).................... E 310 479-3333
10990 Wilshire Blvd Ste 1500 Los Angeles (90024) *(P-6660)*

Sim Ideation, Irvine *Also Called: Specialty Interior Mfg Inc (P-9850)*

Simex-Iwerks, Valencia *Also Called: Iwerks Entertainment Inc (P-7129)*

Simi Vly Care & Rehabilitation, Simi Valley *Also Called: Chase Group Llc (P-17841)*

Simi Vly Hosp & Hlth Care Svcs .... A 805 955-6000
2750 Sycamore Dr Simi Valley (93065) *(P-16200)*

Simi Vly Hosp & Hlth Care Svcs (HQ) .... C 805 955-6000
2975 Sycamore Dr Simi Valley (93065) *(P-16201)*

Simi Vly Hosp & Hlth Care Svcs, Simi Valley *Also Called: Simi Vly Hosp & Hlth Care Svcs (P-16201)*

Simi West Inc .... C 760 346-5502
999 Enchanted Way Simi Valley (93065) *(P-13024)*

Simmons Family Corporation .... D 951 278-4563
350 W Rincon St Corona (92880) *(P-3971)*

Simon and Gladstone A Prof, Irvine *Also Called: Berger Kahn A Law Corporation (P-16645)*

Simon G Jewelry Inc .... E 818 500-8595
528 State St Glendale (91203) *(P-10552)*

Simon Golub & Sons Inc (DH).................... D
514 Via De La Valle Ste 210 Solana Beach (92075) *(P-10553)*

Simple Green, Huntington Beach *Also Called: Sunshine Makers Inc (P-3620)*

Simple Science Inc .... E 949 335-1099
1626 Ohms Way Costa Mesa (92627) *(P-14597)*

Simple Solar Industries LLC .... E 844 907-0705
661 Brea Canyon Rd Ste 1 Walnut (91789) *(P-6892)*

Simplexgrinnell, San Diego *Also Called: Johnson Cntrls Fire Prtction L (P-6687)*

Simpliphi Power Inc .... E 805 640-6700
3100 Camino Del Sol Oxnard (93030) *(P-7080)*

Simply Fresh LLC .... C 714 562-5000
11215 Knott Ave Ste A Cypress (90630) *(P-1712)*

Simpson Automotive Inc .... D 714 690-6200
6600 Auto Center Dr Buena Park (90621) *(P-11407)*

Simpson Buick Pontiac GMC, Buena Park *Also Called: Simpson Automotive Inc (P-11407)*

Simpson Industries Inc .... E 310 605-1224
20611 Belshaw Ave Carson (90746) *(P-3504)*

Simpson Labs LLC .... C 661 347-4348
24955 Avenue Kearny Valencia (91355) *(P-10979)*

Simpson Smpson MGT Cnslting In .... D 626 282-4000
718 S Date Ave Ste A1 Alhambra (91803) *(P-18210)*

Simpson Strong-Tie Company Inc .... C 714 871-8373
12246 Holly St Riverside (92509) *(P-2380)*

Simpsonsimpson Industries, Carson *Also Called: Simpson Industries Inc (P-3504)*

Sims Software, Carlsbad *Also Called: Stratcom Systems Inc (P-13833)*

Simso Tex, Compton *Also Called: Simso Tex Sublimation (P-2266)*

Simso Tex Sublimation (PA).................... E 310 885-9717
3028 E Las Hermanas St Compton (90221) *(P-2266)*

Simulator PDT Solutions LLC .... E 310 830-3331
21818 S Wilmington Ave Ste 411 Long Beach (90810) *(P-7811)*

Simulstat Incorporated .... D 858 546-4337
440 Stevens Ave Ste 200 Solana Beach (92075) *(P-14252)*

Sinai Temple .... C 323 469-6000
5950 Forest Lawn Dr Los Angeles (90068) *(P-13158)*

Sinai Temple (PA).................... B 310 474-1518
10400 Wilshire Blvd Los Angeles (90024) *(P-17419)*

Sinanian, Tarzana *Also Called: Sinanian Development Inc (P-585)*

Sinanian Development Inc .... D 818 996-9666
18980 Ventura Blvd Ste 200 Tarzana (91356) *(P-585)*

Sincere Orient Commercial Corp .... D 626 333-8882
15222 Valley Blvd City Of Industry (91746) *(P-1852)*

Sincere Orient Food Company, City Of Industry *Also Called: Sincere Orient Commercial Corp (P-1852)*

Sinecera Inc .... D 626 962-1087
5397 3rd St Irwindale (91706) *(P-14598)*

Sing Kung Corp .... E 626 358-5838
12061 Clark St Arcadia (91006) *(P-1407)*

Sing Tao Newspapers Ltd .... D 626 956-8200
17059 Green Dr City Of Industry (91745) *(P-2828)*

Sing Tao Nwspapers Los Angeles, City Of Industry *Also Called: Sing Tao Newspapers Ltd (P-2828)*

Singapore Airlines Limited .... C 310 647-1922
222 N Pacific Coast Hwy Ste 1600 El Segundo (90245) *(P-9165)*

Singer Vehicle Design LLC (PA).................... C 213 592-2728
19500 S Vermont Ave Torrance (90502) *(P-14719)*

Singerlewak, Los Angeles *Also Called: Singerlewak LLP (P-17755)*

Employee Codes: A=Over 500 employees, B=251-500
C=101-250, D=51-100, E=20-50, F=10-19, G=1-9

2025 Southern California
Business Directory and Buyers Guide

© Mergent Inc. 1-800-342-5647
1185

Singerlewak LLP (PA)...C 310 477-3924
10960 Wilshire Blvd Los Angeles (90024) *(P-17755)*

Singleton Schreiber LLP ....C 619 771-3473
591 Camino De La Reina Ste 1025 San Diego (92108) *(P-16783)*

Singlton Schrber Frless Advcac, San Diego *Also Called: Singleton Schreiber LLP (P-16783)*

Singod Investors Vi LLC ....D 714 326-7800
1600 S Clementine St Anaheim (92802) *(P-3247)*

Singular Genomics, San Diego *Also Called: Singular Genomics Systems Inc (P-7978)*

Singular Genomics Systems Inc (PA)....................C 858 333-7830
3010 Science Park Rd San Diego (92121) *(P-7978)*

Singular Genomics Systems Inc ....D 619 703-8135
10010 Mesa Rim Rd San Diego (92121) *(P-7979)*

Sir Speedy, Mission Viejo *Also Called: Sir Speedy Inc (P-3081)*

Sir Speedy, Whittier *Also Called: Ss Whittier LLC (P-3084)*

Sir Speedy Inc (HQ)...E 949 348-5000
26722 Plaza Mission Viejo (92691) *(P-3081)*

Siracusa Enterprises Inc ....D 818 831-1130
17737 Chatsworth St Ste 200 Granada Hills (91344) *(P-13572)*

SIS, Culver City *Also Called: Security Indust Spcialists Inc (P-14342)*

Siskiu, Carlsbad *Also Called: Bikes Online Inc (P-10510)*

Sisters of Nzareth Los Angeles ....D 310 839-2361
3333 Manning Ave Los Angeles (90064) *(P-17195)*

Sisters of St Joseph Orange ....A 562 430-4638
240 Ocean Ave Seal Beach (90740) *(P-17420)*

Sit On It, Buena Park *Also Called: Exemplis LLC (P-2527)*

Site 906, Sun Valley *Also Called: BFI Waste Systems N Amer Inc (P-9733)*

Site Crew Inc ....B 714 668-0100
3185 Airway Ave Ste G Costa Mesa (92626) *(P-13420)*

Site Helpers LLC ....D 877 217-5395
25232 Steinbeck Ave Stevenson Ranch (91381) *(P-18211)*

Site Sltions Cnstr Integration, Riverside *Also Called: Sitesol (P-17631)*

Sitesol ....D 562 746-5884
7372 Sycamore Canyon Blvd Riverside (92508) *(P-17631)*

Sitonit, Cypress *Also Called: Exemplis LLC (P-2526)*

Sitonit Seating Inc ....C 714 995-4800
6415 Katella Ave Cypress (90630) *(P-9883)*

Six Continents Hotels Inc ....C 661 343-3316
612 Wainwight Ct Lebec (93243) *(P-13025)*

Six Flags Magic Mountain Inc ....D 661 255-4100
26101 Magic Mountain Pkwy Valencia (91355) *(P-15109)*

Sizzix, Lake Forest *Also Called: Ellison Educational Eqp Inc (P-5658)*

Sjm Facility, Irvine *Also Called: St Jude Medical LLC (P-3508)*

SK&a, Irvine *Also Called: Iqvia Inc (P-17853)*

Skadden Arps Slate Meagher & F ....C 213 687-5000
300 S Grand Ave Ste 3400 Los Angeles (90071) *(P-16784)*

Skanska Rocky Mountain Dst, Riverside *Also Called: Skanska USA Cvil W Rcky Mtn Ds (P-719)*

Skanska USA Cvil W Cal Dst Inc (DH)...............A 951 684-5360
1995 Agua Mansa Rd Riverside (92509) *(P-649)*

Skanska USA Cvil W Rcky Mtn Ds (DH).............D 970 565-8000
1995 Agua Mansa Rd Riverside (92509) *(P-719)*

Skate One Corp ....D 805 964-1330
6860 Cortona Dr Ste B Goleta (93117) *(P-8543)*

SKB Corporation (PA)..B 714 637-1252
434 W Levers Pl Orange (92867) *(P-4240)*

Skechers, Manhattan Beach *Also Called: Skechers USA Inc (P-4288)*

Skechers Factory Outlet 335, Moreno Valley *Also Called: Skechers USA Inc (P-10738)*

Skechers USA Inc (PA)...D 310 318-3100
228 Manhattan Beach Blvd Ste 200 Manhattan Beach (90266) *(P-4288)*

Skechers USA Inc ....E 951 242-4307
29800 Eucalyptus Ave Moreno Valley (92555) *(P-10738)*

Skechers USA Inc II ....A 800 746-3411
228 Manhattan Beach Blvd Ste 200 Manhattan Beach (90266) *(P-11499)*

Skeffington Enterprises Inc ....D 714 540-1700
2200 S Yale St Santa Ana (92704) *(P-12614)*

SKF Aptitude Exchange, San Diego *Also Called: SKF Condition Monitoring Inc (P-8063)*

SKF Condition Monitoring Inc (DH)....................C 858 496-3400
9444 Balboa Ave Ste 150 San Diego (92123) *(P-8063)*

Skid Row Housing Trust, Los Angeles *Also Called: Srht Property Holding LLC (P-12532)*

Skilled Healthcare LLC (DH).................................D 949 282-5800
27442 Portola Pkwy Ste 200 Foothill Ranch (92610) *(P-15779)*

Skinmedica Inc ....B 760 929-2600
18655 Teller Ave Irvine (92612) *(P-3505)*

Skinny Minnie, Maywood *Also Called: Ev R Inc (P-2095)*

Skirball Cultural Center ....C 310 440-4500
2701 N Sepulveda Blvd Los Angeles (90049) *(P-17267)*

SKIRBALL CULTURAL CENTER, Los Angeles *Also Called: Skirball Cultural Center (P-17267)*

Skurka Aerospace Inc (DH)...................................E 805 484-8884
4600 Calle Bolero Camarillo (93012) *(P-6333)*

Sky Rider Equipment Co Inc ....E 714 632-6890
1180 N Blue Gum St Anaheim (92806) *(P-2491)*

Skyco Shading Systems Inc ....E 714 708-3038
3411 W Fordham Ave Santa Ana (92704) *(P-11536)*

Skyline Health Care Ctr, Los Angeles *Also Called: Mariner Health Care Inc (P-15713)*

SKYLINE HEALTHCARE CENTER, Los Angeles *Also Called: Skyline Hlthcare Wllness Ctr L (P-15780)*

Skyline Hlthcare Wllness Ctr L ....D 323 665-1185
3032 Rowena Ave Los Angeles (90039) *(P-15780)*

Skyline Homes Inc ....C 951 654-9321
499 W Esplanade Ave San Jacinto (92583) *(P-2402)*

Skylock Industries LLC ....D 626 334-2391
1290 W Optical Dr Azusa (91702) *(P-7563)*

Skylon, Perris *Also Called: Eci Water Ski Products Inc (P-11630)*

Skypark At Santa's Village, Skyforest *Also Called: Spsv Entertainment LLC (P-15006)*

Skypower Holdings LLC ....C 323 860-4900
4700 Wilshire Blvd Los Angeles (90010) *(P-839)*

Skytech Gaming, Ontario *Also Called: Brainstorm Corporation (P-9992)*

Skyview Capital LLC ....D 310 273-6000
2000 Avenue Of The Stars Ste 810 Los Angeles (90067) *(P-11873)*

Skyworks, Irvine *Also Called: Skyworks Solutions Inc (P-6895)*

Skyworks Solutions Inc ....D 805 480-4400
2427 W Hillcrest Dr Newbury Park (91320) *(P-6893)*

Skyworks Solutions Inc ....E 805 480-4227
730 Lawrence Dr Newbury Park (91320) *(P-6894)*

Skyworks Solutions Inc (PA)...............................A 949 231-3000
5260 California Ave Irvine (92617) *(P-6895)*

SL Blue Garden Corp ....C 626 633-2672
2251 Las Palmas Dr Carlsbad (92011) *(P-18212)*

Slater Inc ....D 909 822-6800
11045 Rose Ave Fontana (92337) *(P-720)*

Slater's 50/50, Anaheim *Also Called: Slaters 50/50 Inc (P-11600)*

Slaters 50/50 Inc ....C 714 602-8115
5801 E Camino Pinzon Anaheim (92807) *(P-11600)*

Slauson Plaza Med Group, Pico Rivera *Also Called: Altamed Health Services Corp (P-16531)*

Sleep Data Services LLC ....D 619 299-6299
5471 Kearny Villa Rd Ste 200 San Diego (92123) *(P-15456)*

Sleepcomp West LLC ....E 562 946-3222
10006 Santa Fe Springs Rd Santa Fe Springs (90670) *(P-4017)*

SLM Services, Simi Valley *Also Called: Specialized Ldscp MGT Svcs Inc (P-193)*

Slo New Times Inc ....E 805 546-8208
1010 Marsh St San Luis Obispo (93401) *(P-2829)*

Sloan Electric Corporation ....E 619 239-5174
3520 Main St San Diego (92113) *(P-10207)*

Slogcc, San Luis Obispo *Also Called: San Luis Obispo Golf Cntry CLB (P-15169)*

Slorta, San Luis Obispo *Also Called: San Luis Obspo Rgnal Trnst Aut (P-8801)*

Slr International Corporation ....A 949 553-8417
20 Corporate Park Ste 200 Irvine (92606) *(P-18357)*

Sls Hotel At Beverly Hills ....C 310 247-0400
465 S La Cienega Blvd Los Angeles (90048) *(P-13026)*

SM Tire, Nipomo *Also Called: Santa Maria Tire Inc (P-11455)*

Smac, Carlsbad *Also Called: Systems Mchs Atmtn Cmpnnts Cor (P-6362)*

Smart LLC ....E 866 822-3670
3501 Sepulveda Blvd Torrance (90505) *(P-4241)*

Smart & Final, Los Angeles *Also Called: Smart & Final Stores LLC (P-10769)*

Smart & Final, Los Angeles *Also Called: Smart & Final Stores LLC (P-10770)*

Smart & Final, Los Angeles *Also Called: Smart & Final Stores LLC (P-10771)*

Smart & Final, Los Angeles *Also Called: Smart & Final Stores LLC (P-10772)*

Smart & Final, Los Angeles *Also Called: Smart Stores Operations LLC (P-10786)*

Smart & Final Stores LLC .... B 323 725-0791
5500 Sheila St Commerce (90040) *(P-9109)*

Smart & Final Stores LLC (DH) .... D **323 869-7500**
600 Citadel Dr Los Angeles (90040) *(P-10769)*

Smart & Final Stores LLC .... D 310 559-1722
10113 Venice Blvd Los Angeles (90034) *(P-10770)*

Smart & Final Stores LLC .... C 310 207-8688
12210 Santa Monica Blvd Los Angeles (90025) *(P-10771)*

Smart & Final Stores LLC .... C 323 268-9179
2308 E 4th St Los Angeles (90033) *(P-10772)*

Smart & Final Stores LLC .... D 213 747-6697
1216 Compton Ave Los Angeles (90021) *(P-10773)*

Smart Circle International LLC (PA) .... D **949 587-9207**
4490 Von Karman Ave Newport Beach (92660) *(P-18213)*

Smart Circle, The, Newport Beach *Also Called: Smart Circle International LLC (P-18213)*

Smart Elec & Assembly Inc .... C 714 772-2651
2000 W Corporate Way Anaheim (92801) *(P-6771)*

Smart Electronics, Anaheim *Also Called: Smart Elec & Assembly Inc (P-6771)*

Smart Energy Solar Inc .... C 800 405-1978
1641 Comm St Corona (92880) *(P-840)*

Smart Energy Systems Inc .... C 909 703-9609
Michelson Dr Ste 3370 Irvine (92612) *(P-13821)*

Smart Energy USA, Corona *Also Called: Smart Energy Solar Inc (P-840)*

Smart Energy Water, Irvine *Also Called: Smart Utility Systems Inc (P-13822)*

Smart Foods LLC .... E 800 284-2250
3398 Leonis Blvd Vernon (90058) *(P-1520)*

Smart Stores Operations LLC .... B 323 725-2985
855 N Wilcox Ave Montebello (90640) *(P-10774)*

Smart Stores Operations LLC .... B 626 330-2495
15427 Amar Rd La Puente (91744) *(P-10775)*

Smart Stores Operations LLC .... B 818 368-6409
18555 Devonshire St Northridge (91324) *(P-10776)*

Smart Stores Operations LLC .... C 562 438-0450
644 Redondo Ave Long Beach (90814) *(P-10777)*

Smart Stores Operations LLC .... C 323 497-8528
615 N Pacific Coast Hwy Redondo Beach (90277) *(P-10778)*

Smart Stores Operations LLC .... C 323 855-8434
240 S Diamond Bar Blvd Diamond Bar (91765) *(P-10779)*

Smart Stores Operations LLC .... C 818 954-8631
3830 W Verdugo Ave Burbank (91505) *(P-10780)*

Smart Stores Operations LLC .... B 661 722-6210
5038 W Avenue N Palmdale (93551) *(P-10781)*

Smart Stores Operations LLC .... B 562 907-7037
13003 Whittier Blvd Whittier (90602) *(P-10782)*

Smart Stores Operations LLC .... B 626 334-5189
303 E Foothill Blvd Azusa (91702) *(P-10783)*

Smart Stores Operations LLC .... B 323 549-9586
4550 W Pico Blvd Los Angeles (90019) *(P-10784)*

Smart Stores Operations LLC .... B 909 592-2190
1005 W Arrow Hwy San Dimas (91773) *(P-10785)*

Smart Stores Operations LLC (DH) .... B **323 869-7500**
600 Citadel Dr Los Angeles (90040) *(P-10786)*

Smart Stores Operations LLC .... C 714 549-2362
1308 W Edinger Ave Santa Ana (92704) *(P-10787)*

Smart Stores Operations LLC .... B 949 581-1212
26911 Trabuco Rd Mission Viejo (92691) *(P-10788)*

Smart Stores Operations LLC .... C 858 748-0101
12339 Poway Rd Poway (92064) *(P-10789)*

Smart Stores Operations LLC .... C 619 449-2396
9870 N Magnolia Ave Santee (92071) *(P-10790)*

Smart Stores Operations LLC .... C 619 522-2014
150 B Ave Coronado (92118) *(P-10791)*

Smart Stores Operations LLC .... B 619 390-1738
13439 Camino Canada El Cajon (92021) *(P-10792)*

Smart Stores Operations LLC .... C 760 732-1480
1845 W Vista Way Vista (92083) *(P-10793)*

Smart Stores Operations LLC .... C 760 434-2449
955 Carlsbad Village Dr Carlsbad (92008) *(P-10794)*

Smart Stores Operations LLC .... C 619 668-9039
933 Sweetwater Rd Spring Valley (91977) *(P-10795)*

Smart Stores Operations LLC .... B 619 291-1842
2235 University Ave San Diego (92104) *(P-10796)*

Smart Stores Operations LLC .... C 619 589-7000
2800 Fletcher Pkwy El Cajon (92020) *(P-10797)*

Smart Stores Operations LLC .... B 858 578-7343
10740 Westview Pkwy San Diego (92126) *(P-10798)*

Smart Stores Operations LLC .... C 909 773-1813
13346 Limonite Ave Eastvale (92880) *(P-10799)*

Smart Stores Operations LLC .... C 323 869-7543
928 E Ontario Ave Corona (92881) *(P-10800)*

Smart Stores Operations LLC .... B 805 237-0323
2121 Spring St Paso Robles (93446) *(P-10801)*

Smart Stores Operations LLC .... C 805 566-2174
850 Linden Ave Carpinteria (93013) *(P-10802)*

Smart Stores Operations LLC .... C 818 889-8253
5770 Lindero Canyon Rd Westlake Village (91362) *(P-10803)*

Smart Stores Operations LLC .... B 805 647-4276
7800 Telegraph Rd Ventura (93004) *(P-10804)*

Smart Stores Operations LLC .... C 805 520-6035
5135 E Los Angeles Ave Simi Valley (93063) *(P-10805)*

Smart Utility Systems Inc .... D 909 217-3344
19900 Macarthur Blvd Ste 370 Irvine (92612) *(P-13822)*

Smartcover Systems, Escondido *Also Called: Hadronex Inc (P-9725)*

Smartdrive Systems Inc (PA) .... D **858 225-5550**
9515 Towne Centre Dr San Diego (92121) *(P-13823)*

Smarthomepro, Irvine *Also Called: Smartlabs Inc (P-11698)*

Smartlabs Inc .... D 800 762-7846
1621 Alton Pkwy Ste 100 Irvine (92606) *(P-11698)*

Smartstop Self Storage, Ladera Ranch *Also Called: Sst IV 8020 Las Vgas Blvd S LL (P-9111)*

Smbc Manubank (DH) .... C **213 489-6200**
515 S Figueroa St 4th Fl Los Angeles (90071) *(P-11778)*

SMC Grease Specialist Inc .... E 951 788-6042
1600 W Pellisier Rd Colton (92324) *(P-9765)*

SMC Networks, Inc., Irvine *Also Called: Accton Manufacturing & Svc Inc (P-9983)*

SMC Products Inc .... D 949 753-1099
22651 Lambert St Ste 105 Lake Forest (92630) *(P-10529)*

Smci, Costa Mesa *Also Called: Software Management Cons LLC (P-13828)*

Smci, Glendale *Also Called: Software Management Cons LLC (P-14254)*

Smg, Torrance *Also Called: Storm Manufacturing Group Inc (P-5370)*

Smg Holdings LLC .... D 760 325-6611
277 N Avenida Caballeros Palm Springs (92262) *(P-18214)*

Smg Management Facility, Ontario *Also Called: Ontario Convention Center Corp (P-14562)*

SMI Architectural Millwork Inc .... E 714 567-0112
2116 W Chestnut Ave Santa Ana (92703) *(P-11251)*

SMI Ca Inc .... E 562 926-9407
14340 Iseli Rd Santa Fe Springs (90670) *(P-6238)*

SMI Holdings Inc .... E 800 232-2612
28420 Witherspoon Pkwy Valencia (91355) *(P-6334)*

SMI Millwork, Santa Ana *Also Called: SMI Architectural Millwork Inc (P-11251)*

Smile Brands Group Inc (PA) .... D **714 668-1300**
100 Spectrum Center Dr Ste 1500 Irvine (92618) *(P-18052)*

Smith Broadcasting Group Inc (PA) .... C **805 965-0400**
2316 Red Rose Way Santa Barbara (03100) *(P-18053)*

Smith Broadcasting Group Inc .... B 805 882-3933
730 Miramonte Dr Santa Barbara (93109) *(P-9517)*

Smith Electric Service, Santa Maria *Also Called: Smith McHncl-Lctrical-Plumbing (P-501)*

Smith International Inc .... C 909 906-7900
11031 Jersey Blvd Ste A Rancho Cucamonga (91730) *(P-5513)*

Smith McHncl-Lctrical-Plumbing .... C 805 621-5000
1340 W Betteravia Rd Santa Maria (93455) *(P-501)*

Smith Packing Inc .... C 805 348-1817
680 S Simas Rd Santa Maria (93455) *(P-11144)*

Smith-Emery International Inc (PA) .... C **213 741-8500**
791 E Washington Blvd Fl 3 Los Angeles (90021) *(P-18215)*

Smithfield Foods, Los Angeles *Also Called: Clougherty Packing LLC (P-1241)*

Smiths Interconnect Inc .... D 805 267-0100
375 Conejo Ridge Ave Thousand Oaks (91361) *(P-7050)*

Smiths Intrcnnect Americas Inc .... B 714 371-1100
1231 E Dyer Rd Ste 235 Santa Ana (92705) *(P-7051)*

SMK, Chula Vista *Also Called: SMK Manufacturing Inc (P-5896)*

SMK Manufacturing Inc .... E 619 216-6400
1055 Tierra Del Rey Ste F Chula Vista (91910) *(P-5896)*

A
L
P
H
A
B
E
T
I
C

Sml Space Maintainers Labs, Chatsworth *Also Called: Selane Products Inc (P-8355)*

Smoke Tree Inc .... D 760 327-1221
1850 Smoke Tree Ln Palm Springs (92264) *(P-13027)*

Smoke Tree Ranch, Palm Springs *Also Called: Smoke Tree Inc (P-13027)*

Smooth-Bor Plastics, Laguna Hills *Also Called: Steward Plastics Inc (P-4250)*

Smoothreads Inc .... E 800 536-5959
13750 Stowe Dr Ste A Poway (92064) *(P-2267)*

SMS Fabrications Inc .... E 951 351-6828
11698 Warm Springs Rd Riverside (92505) *(P-5034)*

SMS Transportation Svcs Inc .... C 213 489-5367
865 S Figueroa St Ste 2750 Los Angeles (90017) *(P-8804)*

Snack It Forward LLC .... E 310 242-5517
6080 Center Dr Ste 600 Los Angeles (90045) *(P-1728)*

Snail Inc (PA) .... **E 310 988-0643**
12049 Jefferson Blvd Culver City (90230) *(P-13824)*

Snail Games, Culver City *Also Called: Snail Inc (P-13824)*

Snak Club LLC .... C 323 278-9578
5560 E Slauson Ave Commerce (90040) *(P-1517)*

Snak-King LLC (PA) .... **B 626 336-7711**
16150 Stephens St City Of Industry (91745) *(P-1729)*

Snap Inc (PA) .... **A 310 399-3339**
3000 31st St Ste C Santa Monica (90405) *(P-13825)*

Snap Inc .... D 310 745-0632
579 Toyopa Dr Pacific Palisades (90272) *(P-14032)*

SNAPCHAT, Santa Monica *Also Called: Snap Inc (P-13825)*

Snapcomms Inc .... D 805 715-0300
155 N Lake Ave Fl 9 Pasadena (91101) *(P-13826)*

Snapnrack Inc .... E 877 732-2860
775 Fiero Ln Ste 200 San Luis Obispo (93401) *(P-4788)*

Snapware Corporation .... C 951 361-3100
2325 Cottonwood Ave Riverside (92508) *(P-4242)*

Snell & Wilmer, Costa Mesa *Also Called: Snell & Wilmer LLP (P-16785)*

Snell & Wilmer LLP .... D 714 427-7000
600 Anton Blvd Ste 1400 Costa Mesa (92626) *(P-16785)*

Snf Management .... C 310 385-1090
1901 Avenue Of The Stars Los Angeles (90067) *(P-18054)*

Snow Summit LLC (PA) .... **C 909 866-5766**
880 Summit Blvd Big Bear Lake (92315) *(P-13028)*

Snow Summit Mountain Resort, Big Bear City *Also Called: Snow Summit Ski Corporation (P-15222)*

Snow Summit Ski Corporation .... D 909 585-2517
43101 Goldmine Dr Big Bear City (92314) *(P-15222)*

Snowmass Apparel Inc (PA) .... **E 949 788-0617**
15225 Alton Pkwy Irvine (92618) *(P-10728)*

Snowpure LLC .... E 949 240-2188
130 Calle Iglesia Ste A San Clemente (92672) *(P-6033)*

Snowpure Water Technologies, San Clemente *Also Called: Snowpure LLC (P-6033)*

Snowsound USA, Santa Fe Springs *Also Called: Atlantic Representations Inc (P-2463)*

Snyder Langston, Irvine *Also Called: Snyder Langston Holdings LLC (P-586)*

Snyder Langston Holdings LLC .... C 949 863-9200
17962 Cowan Irvine (92614) *(P-586)*

So Cal Graphics, San Diego *Also Called: Bretkeri Corporation (P-3122)*

So Cal Land Maintenance Inc .... D 714 231-1454
3121 E La Palma Ave Ste K Anaheim (92806) *(P-13421)*

So Cal Sandbags Inc .... D 951 277-3404
12620 Bosley Ln Corona (92883) *(P-10463)*

So Cal Ship Services .... D 310 519-8411
971 S Seaside Ave San Pedro (90731) *(P-9140)*

SO Tech/Spcl Op Tech Inc (PA) .... **E 310 202-9007**
206 Star Of India Ln Carson (90746) *(P-10674)*

So-Cal Strl Stl Fbrication Inc .... E 909 877-1299
130 S Spruce Ave Rialto (92376) *(P-4868)*

So-Cal Value Added, Camarillo *Also Called: Plt Enterprises Inc (P-6425)*

Soaptronic LLC .... E 949 465-8955
19771 Pauling Foothill Ranch (92610) *(P-3619)*

Soaring America Corporation .... E 909 270-2628
8354 Kimball Ave # F360 Chino (91708) *(P-7371)*

Soboba Band Luiseno Indians .... A 951 665-1000
22777 Soboba Rd San Jacinto (92583) *(P-14599)*

Soboba Casino, San Jacinto *Also Called: Soboba Band Luiseno Indians (P-14599)*

Soboba Indian Health Clinic, San Jacinto *Also Called: Riversd-San Brnrdino Cnty Indi (P-15437)*

Sobriety House, Long Beach *Also Called: Safe Refuge (P-16500)*

Socal Auto Supply Inc .... E 302 360-8373
21418 Osborne St Canoga Park (91304) *(P-13126)*

Socal Garment Works LLC .... E 323 300-5717
4700 S Boyle Ave Ste C Vernon (90058) *(P-1886)*

Socal Sportsnet LLC .... A 619 795-5000
100 Park Blvd San Diego (92101) *(P-15036)*

Socal Technologies LLC .... E 619 635-1128
1305 Oakdale Ave El Cajon (92021) *(P-14253)*

Socalgas, Northridge *Also Called: Southern California Gas Co (P-9658)*

Socco Plastic Coating Company .... E 909 987-4753
11251 Jersey Blvd Rancho Cucamonga (91730) *(P-5345)*

Social Advctes For Yuth San De .... C 619 283-9624
4275 El Cajon Blvd Ste 101 San Diego (92105) *(P-17012)*

Social Junky Inc .... E 213 999-1275
7874 Palmetto Ave Fontana (92336) *(P-14600)*

Social Sciences, Irvine *Also Called: University California Irvine (P-16836)*

Social Service Professionals, Los Angeles *Also Called: Rehababilities Inc (P-13568)*

Social Talkie, Gardena *Also Called: Usfi Inc (P-10815)*

Socialcom Inc (PA) .... **D 310 289-4477**
73 Market St Venice (90291) *(P-18216)*

Socialedge Inc (PA) .... **B 213 212-7079**
177 E Colorado Blvd Fl 2 Pasadena (91105) *(P-13827)*

Societal CDMO San Diego LLC .... D 858 623-1520
6828 Nancy Ridge Dr Ste 100 San Diego (92121) *(P-3506)*

Society of St Vncent De Paul C (PA) .... **D 323 226-9645**
210 N Avenue 21 Los Angeles (90031) *(P-17470)*

Soderberg Manufacturing Co Inc .... D 909 595-1291
20821 Currier Rd Walnut (91789) *(P-6486)*

Sodexo Management Inc .... A 949 753-2042
16200 Sand Canyon Ave Irvine (92618) *(P-18055)*

Sodexo Management Inc .... A 650 506-4814
13729 Earlham Dr Whittier (90602) *(P-18056)*

Sodexo Management Inc .... A 310 646-3738
450 World Way Los Angeles (90045) *(P-18217)*

Soex Group, Vernon *Also Called: Soex West Usa LLC (P-10696)*

Soex West Usa LLC .... B 323 264-8300
3294 E 26th St Vernon (90058) *(P-10696)*

Soffa Electric Inc .... E 323 728-0230
5901 Corvette St Commerce (90040) *(P-7880)*

Sofitel Los Angeles, Los Angeles *Also Called: Accor Corp (P-11548)*

Soft-Touch Tissue, Vernon *Also Called: Paper Surce Converting Mfg Inc (P-2635)*

Softscript Inc .... A 310 451-2110
2215 Campus Dr El Segundo (90245) *(P-13341)*

Softub Inc (PA) .... **D 858 602-1920**
24700 Avenue Rockefeller Valencia (91355) *(P-8726)*

Software, Encino *Also Called: Phone Check Solutions LLC (P-13795)*

Software Dynamics Incorporated .... D 818 992-3299
8501 Fallbrook Ave Ste 200 Canoga Park (91304) *(P-14107)*

Software Management Cons LLC .... C 714 662-1841
959 S Coast Dr Ste 415 Costa Mesa (92626) *(P-13828)*

Software Management Cons LLC (HQ) .... **B 818 240-3177**
500 N Brand Blvd Glendale (91203) *(P-14254)*

Soilmoisture Equipment Corp .... E 805 964-3525
601 Pine Ave Ste A Goleta (93117) *(P-8064)*

Sol-Pak Thermoforming Inc .... E 323 582-3333
3388 Fruitland Ave Vernon (90058) *(P-4243)*

Sol-Ti Inc .... D 888 765-8411
8380 Miralani Dr San Diego (92126) *(P-11308)*

Solag Disposal Co, San Juan Capistrano *Also Called: Solag Incorporated (P-9766)*

Solag Incorporated .... C 949 728-1206
31641 Ortege Hwy San Juan Capistrano (92675) *(P-9766)*

Solar Art, Laguna Hills *Also Called: Budget Enterprises Llc (P-4312)*

Solar Atmospheres Inc .... E 909 217-7400
8606 Live Oak Ave Fontana (92335) *(P-4713)*

Solar Shading Systems, Tustin *Also Called: Sheward & Son & Sons (P-2607)*

Solar Spectrum LLC .... B 844 777-6527
27368 Via Industria Ste 101 Temecula (92590) *(P-841)*

Company	Code	Phone
Solar Turbines Incorporated (HQ)	A	619 544-5352
2200 Pacific Hwy San Diego (92101) *(P-5461)*		
Solar Turbines Incorporated	E	619 544-5321
2660 Sarnen St San Diego (92154) *(P-5462)*		
Solar Turbines Incorporated	C	858 694-6110
9330 Sky Park Ct San Diego (92123) *(P-5463)*		
Solar Turbines Incorporated	D	858 715-2060
9250 Sky Park Ct A San Diego (92123) *(P-5464)*		
Solarflare Communications Inc (DH)	D	949 581-6830
7505 Irvine Center Dr Ste 100 Irvine (92618) *(P-5867)*		
Solari Enterprises Inc	C	714 282-2520
1507 W Yale Ave Orange (92867) *(P-12319)*		
Solaris Paper Inc	C	714 687-6657
505 N Euclid St Ste 630 Anaheim (92801) *(P-5960)*		
Solarreserve Inc	D	310 315-2200
520 Broadway 6th Fl Santa Monica (90401) *(P-9613)*		
Solarworld Americas LLC	D	503 844-3400
4650 Adohr Ln Camarillo (93012) *(P-10208)*		
Solatube, Vista Also Called: Solatube International Inc *(P-4903)*		
Solatube International Inc (DH)	D	888 765-2882
2210 Oak Ridge Way Vista (92081) *(P-4903)*		
Solcius LLC	C	951 772-0030
12155 Magnolia Ave Ste 12b/C Riverside (92503) *(P-842)*		
SOLCIUS LLC, Riverside Also Called: Solcius LLC *(P-842)*		
Sole Society Group Inc	C	310 220-0808
11248 Playa Ct # B Culver City (90230) *(P-4281)*		
Sole Technology Inc (PA)	D	949 460-2020
26921 Fuerte Lake Forest (92630) *(P-4289)*		
Solecta Inc (PA)	E	760 630-9643
4113 Avenida De La Plata Oceanside (92056) *(P-1961)*		
Soleo Health, Inglewood Also Called: Biomed California Inc *(P-3375)*		
Soleus International, Walnut Also Called: Mjc America Ltd *(P-6398)*		
Solevy Co LLC	D	661 622-4880
28918 Hancock Pkwy Valencia (91355) *(P-3687)*		
Solex Contracting Inc	C	951 308-1706
42146 Remington Ave Temecula (92590) *(P-695)*		
Solheim Lutheran Home	C	323 257-7518
2236 Merton Ave Los Angeles (90041) *(P-17196)*		
Solid Oak Software Inc (PA)	E	805 568-5415
319 W Mission St Santa Barbara (93101) *(P-10028)*		
Solid State Devices Inc	C	562 404-4474
14701 Firestone Blvd La Mirada (90638) *(P-6896)*		
Soligen 2006, Santa Ana Also Called: DC Partners Inc *(P-4672)*		
Solis Capital Partners LLC	D	760 309-9436
3371 Calle Tres Vistas Ste 100 Encinitas (92024) *(P-12736)*		
Solis FL Owner, Los Angeles Also Called: Truamerica Multifamily LLC *(P-12743)*		
Solo Enterprise Corp	E	626 961-3591
220 N California Ave City Of Industry (91744) *(P-6239)*		
Solo Golf, City Of Industry Also Called: Solo Enterprise Corp *(P-6239)*		
Solomon Colors Inc	E	909 873-9444
1371 Laurel Ave Rialto (92376) *(P-3224)*		
Solow	E	323 664-7772
2907 Glenview Ave Los Angeles (90039) *(P-2132)*		
Solpac Inc	C	619 296 6247
2424 Congress St San Diego (92110) *(P-587)*		
Solpac Construction Inc	C	619 296-6247
2424 Congress St San Diego (92110) *(P-18057)*		
Solrite Electric LLC	C	833 765-6682
330 Rancheros Dr Ste 116 San Marcos (92069) *(P-961)*		
Soltek Pacific, San Diego Also Called: Solpac Inc *(P-587)*		
Soltek Pacific Construction Co, San Diego Also Called: Solpac Construction Inc *(P-18057)*		
Solti, San Diego Also Called: Sol-Ti Inc *(P-11308)*		
Solugenix, Brea Also Called: Solugenix Corporation *(P-14108)*		
Solugenix Corporation (PA)	C	866 749-7658
601 Valencia Ave Ste 260 Brea (92823) *(P-14108)*		
Solut Inc	E	760 758-7240
4645 North Ave Ste 102 Oceanside (92056) *(P-2638)*		
Solution Based Trtmnt & Detox, Murrieta Also Called: SBT Health Inc *(P-18355)*		
Solutions Unlimited, Fullerton Also Called: Wilsons Art Studio Inc *(P-3189)*		
Solv Energy LLC (HQ)	C	858 251-4088
16680 W Bernardo Dr San Diego (92127) *(P-9614)*		
Solv Energy LLC	C	858 622-4040
16798 W Bernardo Dr San Diego (92128) *(P-14033)*		
Solvang Lutheran Home Inc	C	805 688-3263
636 Atterdag Rd Solvang (93463) *(P-15781)*		
Solvay America Inc	C	714 688-4403
1440 N Kraemer Blvd Anaheim (92806) *(P-3248)*		
Solvay America Inc	D	225 361-3376
645 N Cypress St Orange (92867) *(P-3249)*		
Solvay America Inc	D	562 906-3300
12801 Ann St Santa Fe Springs (90670) *(P-3250)*		
Solvay America LLC	D	713 525-4000
1191 N Hawk Cir Anaheim (92807) *(P-3251)*		
SOLVAY AMERICA, INC., Anaheim Also Called: Solvay America Inc *(P-3248)*		
SOLVAY AMERICA, INC., Orange Also Called: Solvay America Inc *(P-3249)*		
SOLVAY AMERICA, INC., Santa Fe Springs Also Called: Solvay America Inc *(P-3250)*		
Solvay Chemicals Inc	E	714 744-5610
645 N Cypress St Orange (92867) *(P-3252)*		
Solvay Composite Materials, Anaheim Also Called: Cytec Engineered Materials Inc *(P-4671)*		
Solvay Draka Inc (DH)	C	323 725-7010
6900 Elm St Commerce (90040) *(P-3958)*		
Solve All Facility Services, Oceanside Also Called: Bergensons Property Svcs Inc *(P-13358)*		
Somacis Inc	C	858 513-2200
13500 Danielson St Poway (92064) *(P-6772)*		
Someone's In The Kitchen, Tarzana Also Called: JMJ Enterprises Inc *(P-11581)*		
Somerford Place Encinitas, Encinitas Also Called: Five Star Senior Living Inc *(P-15654)*		
Son of A Barista Usa LLC	E	323 788-8718
5125 Wheeler Ridge Rd Arvin (93203) *(P-1720)*		
Sonaca North America, Vista Also Called: Versaform Corporation *(P-5054)*		
Sonance, San Clemente Also Called: Dana Innovations *(P-6532)*		
Sonar Entertainment Inc (PA)	D	424 230-7140
2834 Colorado Ave Ste 300 Santa Monica (90404) *(P-14921)*		
Sonatech LLC	C	805 683-1431
879 Ward Dr Santa Barbara (93111) *(P-17632)*		
SONENDO, Laguna Hills Also Called: Sonendo Inc *(P-8356)*		
Sonendo Inc (PA)	C	949 766-3636
26061 Merit Cir Ste 102 Laguna Hills (92653) *(P-8356)*		
Sonendo Acquisition Corp	E	858 558-3696
6235 Lusk Blvd San Diego (92121) *(P-14034)*		
Sonfarrel	E	714 630-7280
3000 E La Jolla St Anaheim (92806) *(P-4244)*		
Sonfarrel Aerospace LLC	D	714 630-7280
3010 E La Jolla St Anaheim (92806) *(P-4677)*		
Sonic Industries Inc	C	310 532-8382
20030 Normandie Ave Torrance (90502) *(P-17633)*		
Sonim Technologies Inc (PA)	E	650 378-8100
4445 Eastgate Mall Ste 200 San Diego (92121) *(P-6591)*		
Sonix, Torrance Also Called: Lenntek Corporation *(P-6629)*		
Sonnet Technologies Inc	E	949 587-3500
25 Empire Dr Ste 200 Lake Forest (92630) *(P-7152)*		
Sonoco Industrial Products Div, City Of Industry Also Called: Sonoco Products Company *(P-2643)*		
Sonoco Products Company	D	626 369-6611
166 Baldwin Park Blvd City Of Industry (91746) *(P-2643)*		
Sonoco Products Company	D	562 921-0881
12851 Leyva St Norwalk (90650) *(P-2644)*		
Sonora Bakery Inc	E	323 269-2253
4484 Whittier Blvd Los Angeles (90022) *(P-11302)*		
Sonora Mills Foods Inc (PA)	C	310 639-5333
3064 E Maria St E Rncho Dmngz (90221) *(P-1853)*		
Sonos, Goleta Also Called: Sonos Inc *(P-6555)*		
Sonos Inc (PA)	D	805 965-3001
301 Coromar Dr Goleta (93117) *(P-6555)*		
Sonrava, Orange Also Called: Premier Dental Holdings Inc *(P-15526)*		
Sonsray Inc	E	323 585-1271
23935 Madison St Torrance (90505) *(P-6240)*		
Sony Electronics Inc	C	858 942-2400
16530 Via Esprillo San Diego (92127) *(P-6556)*		
Sony Electronics Inc (DH)	A	858 942-2400
16535 Via Esprillo 1 San Diego (92127) *(P-6557)*		
Sony Media Cloud Services LLC	E	877 683-9124
10202 Washington Blvd Culver City (90232) *(P-14857)*		

ALPHABETIC

Employee Codes: A=Over 500 employees, B=251-500
C=101-250, D=51-100, E=20-50, F=10-19, G=1-9

2025 Southern California
Business Directory and Buyers Guide

© Mergent Inc. 1-800-342-5647

1189

Sony Pictures Entrmt Inc (DH)............................A 310 244-4000
10202 Washington Blvd Culver City (90232) *(P-14858)*

Sony Pictures Imageworks Inc ....A 310 840-8000
9050 Washington Blvd Culver City (90232) *(P-14156)*

Sony Pictures Studios, Culver City *Also Called: Sony Pictures Entrmt Inc (P-14858)*

Sony Pictures Television Inc (DH).......................B 310 244-7625
10202 Washington Blvd Culver City (90232) *(P-14859)*

Sony Style, San Diego *Also Called: Sony Electronics Inc (P-6556)*

Soofer Co Inc ....D 323 234-6666
2828 S Alameda St Los Angeles (90058) *(P-10980)*

Sorenson Engineering Inc (PA)..........................C 909 795-2434
32032 Dunlap Blvd Yucaipa (92399) *(P-5113)*

Sorrento Therapeutics Inc (PA)..........................D 858 203-4100
4955 Directors Pl San Diego (92121) *(P-3587)*

SOS Beauty Inc ....E 424 285-1405
9100 Wilshire Blvd Ste 500w Beverly Hills (90212) *(P-10651)*

SOS Security Incorporated ....C 310 392-9600
3000 S Robertson Blvd Ste 100 Los Angeles (90034) *(P-14350)*

Sotera Wireless Inc ....C 858 427-4620
5841 Edison Pl Ste 140 Carlsbad (92008) *(P-8398)*

Soto Company Inc ....D 949 493-9403
34275 Camino Capistrano Ste A Capistrano Beach (92624) *(P-235)*

Soto Food Service, City Of Industry *Also Called: Soto Provision Inc (P-9907)*

Soto Provision Inc ....D 626 458-4600
488 Parriott Pl W City Of Industry (91745) *(P-9907)*

Sound Image, Escondido *Also Called: Cal Southern Sound Image Inc (P-10236)*

Sound River Corporation ....D 661 705-3700
28238 Avenue Crocker Valencia (91355) *(P-962)*

Sound Seal Inc ....E 760 806-6400
4675 North Ave Oceanside (92056) *(P-4495)*

Sound United, Carlsbad *Also Called: Dei Headquarters Inc (P-6679)*

Soundcoat Company Inc ....D 631 242-2200
16901 Armstrong Ave Irvine (92606) *(P-6360)*

Soundcraft Inc ....E 818 882-0020
20301 Nordhoff St Chatsworth (91311) *(P-7153)*

Soup Bases Loaded Inc ....E 909 230-6890
2355 E Francis St Ontario (91761) *(P-1854)*

Source 44 LLC ....C 877 916-6337
4660 La Jolla Village Dr Ste 100 San Diego (92122) *(P-18358)*

Source Code LLC ....E 562 903-1500
9808 Alburtis Ave Santa Fe Springs (90670) *(P-5868)*

Source Intelligence, San Diego *Also Called: Source 44 LLC (P-18358)*

Source One Staffing LLC ....A 626 337-0560
5312 Irwindale Ave Ste 1h Baldwin Park (91706) *(P-13573)*

Source Photonics Usa Inc (PA)..........................C 818 773-9044
8521 Fallbrook Ave Ste 200 West Hills (91304) *(P-6897)*

Source Scientific LLC ....E 949 231-5096
2144 Michelson Dr Irvine (92612) *(P-8228)*

Souriau Usa Inc (DH).....................................E 805 238-2840
1740 Commerce Way Paso Robles (93446) *(P-6428)*

Souriau Usa Inc ....D 805 226-3573
1750 Commerce Way Paso Robles (93446) *(P-6429)*

SOUTH BAY CENTER FOR COMMUNITY, Wilmington *Also Called: South Bay Ctr For Counseling (P-17013)*

South Bay Ctr For Counseling ....D 310 414-2090
540 N Marine Ave Wilmington (90744) *(P-17013)*

South Bay Ford Inc (PA)..................................C 310 644-0211
5100 W Rosecrans Ave Hawthorne (90250) *(P-11408)*

South Bay Foundry Inc (HQ)..............................E 909 383-1823
895 Inland Center Dr San Bernardino (92408) *(P-4869)*

South Bay International Inc ....E 909 718-5000
8570 Hickory Ave Rancho Cucamonga (91739) *(P-2492)*

South Bay Post Acute Care, Chula Vista *Also Called: Bayside Healthcare Inc (P-15580)*

South Bay Power Plant, Chula Vista *Also Called: San Diego Gas & Electric Co (P-9642)*

South Bay Salt Works, Chula Vista *Also Called: Ggtw LLC (P-3800)*

South Bay Sand Blstg Tank Clg ....D 619 238-8338
326 W 30th St National City (91950) *(P-14792)*

South Bay Senior Services Inc ....D 310 338-8558
8929 S Sepulveda Blvd Ste 314 Los Angeles (90045) *(P-16421)*

South Bay Toyota ....C 310 323-7800
18416 S Western Ave Gardena (90248) *(P-11409)*

South Bay Welding, El Cajon *Also Called: M W Reid Welding Inc (P-4847)*

South Bay Wire & Cable Co LLC (PA)....................D 951 659-2183
54125 Maranatha Dr Idyllwild (92549) *(P-4541)*

South Baylo Acupuncture Clinic, Los Angeles *Also Called: South Baylo University (P-16503)*

South Baylo University ....C 213 999-0297
2727 W 6th St Los Angeles (90057) *(P-16503)*

South Cast A Qlty MGT Dst Bldg (PA)....................A 909 396-2000
21865 Copley Dr Diamond Bar (91765) *(P-18359)*

South Central Family Hlth Ctr ....D 323 908-4200
4425 S Central Ave Los Angeles (90011) *(P-15457)*

South Cntl Hlth Rhbltt ion Prgr ....D 310 667-4070
2620 Industry Way Lynwood (90262) *(P-16504)*

South Cntl Los Angles Rgnal CT ....C 231 744-8484
650 W Adams Blvd Los Angeles (90007) *(P-17242)*

South Cntl Los Angles Rgnal CT (PA)....................C 213 744-7000
2500 S Western Ave Los Angeles (90018) *(P-17243)*

South Cnty Lxus At Mssion Vejo ....C 949 347-3400
28242 Marguerite Pkwy Mission Viejo (92692) *(P-11410)*

South Cnty Orthpd Spclsts A ME ....D 949 586-3200
24331 El Toro Rd Ste 200 Laguna Hills (92637) *(P-15458)*

South Coast Auto Insurance, Huntington Beach *Also Called: Freeway Insurance (P-12215)*

South Coast Baking LLC (DH)............................D 949 851-9654
1711 Kettering Irvine (92614) *(P-1492)*

South Coast Baking Co., Irvine *Also Called: South Coast Baking LLC (P-1492)*

South Coast Childrens Soc Inc ....C 909 478-3377
24950 Redlands Blvd Loma Linda (92354) *(P-16505)*

South Coast Circuits LLC ....D 714 966-2108
3506 W Lake Center Dr Ste A Santa Ana (92704) *(P-6773)*

South Coast Materials Co, San Diego *Also Called: Forterra Pipe & Precast LLC (P-4392)*

South Coast Mechanical Inc ....D 714 738-6644
800 E Orangethorpe Ave Anaheim (92801) *(P-843)*

South Coast Piering Inc ....D 800 922-2488
7301 Madison St Paramount (90723) *(P-588)*

South Coast Plaza LLC ....D 714 435-2000
3333 Bristol St Ofc Costa Mesa (92626) *(P-12320)*

South Coast Plaza Mall, Costa Mesa *Also Called: South Coast Plaza LLC (P-12320)*

South Coast Plaza Security ....C 714 435-2180
695 Town Center Dr Ste 50 Costa Mesa (92626) *(P-18058)*

South Coast Stairs Inc ....E 949 858-1685
30251 Tomas Rcho Sta Marg (92688) *(P-2327)*

South Coast Trnsp & Dist Inc ....D 310 816-0280
1424 S Raymond Ave Fullerton (92831) *(P-8923)*

South Coast Westin Hotel Co ....D 714 540-2500
686 Anton Blvd Costa Mesa (92626) *(P-13029)*

South Coast Winery Inc ....E 951 587-9463
34843 Rancho California Rd Temecula (92591) *(P-1585)*

South Coast Winery Resort Spa, Temecula *Also Called: South Coast Winery Inc (P-1585)*

South Coast YMCA, Laguna Niguel *Also Called: Young MNS Chrstn Assn Orge CN (P-15189)*

South Cone Inc ....C 760 431-2300
5935 Darwin Ct Carlsbad (92008) *(P-10739)*

South Gate Engineering LLC ....C 909 628-2779
13477 Yorba Ave Chino (91710) *(P-4927)*

South Hills Country Club ....D 626 339-1231
2655 S Citrus St West Covina (91791) *(P-15175)*

South Seas Imports, Compton *Also Called: M M Fab Inc (P-10666)*

South Valley Almond Co LLC ....C 661 391-9000
15443 Beech Ave Wasco (93280) *(P-10994)*

South Valley Farms, Wasco *Also Called: South Valley Almond Co LLC (P-10994)*

South West Lubricants Inc ....D 619 449-5000
9266 Abraham Way Santee (92071) *(P-3858)*

Southbay BMW, Torrance *Also Called: Southbay European Inc (P-11411)*

Southbay European Inc ....D 310 939-7300
18800 Hawthorne Blvd Torrance (90504) *(P-11411)*

Southcoast Cabinet Inc (PA).............................E 909 594-3089
755 Pinefalls Ave Walnut (91789) *(P-2363)*

Southcoast Welding & Mfg LLC ....B 619 429-1337
2591 Faivre St Ste 1 Chula Vista (91911) *(P-14744)*

Southeast Industries, Downey *Also Called: ARC Los Angeles & Orange Cnty (P-17046)*

Southeastern Westminster, Westminster *Also Called: Southern California Edison Co (P-9619)*

Mergent email: customerrelations@mergent.com
1190

2025 Southern California
Business Directory and Buyers Guide

(P-0000) Products & Services Section entry number
(PA)=Parent Co (HQ)=Headquarters (DH)=Div Headquarters

Southern Cal Ctr For Spt Mdcin, Long Beach *Also Called: Memorial Orthpdic Srgcal Group*
(P-15387)

Southern Cal Disc Tire Co Inc .... C 805 639-0166
4640 Telephone Rd Ventura (93003) *(P-11456)*

Southern Cal Disc Tire Co Inc .... C 760 741-9805
550 N Broadway Escondido (92025) *(P-11457)*

Southern Cal Disc Tire Co Inc .... D 760 744-3526
780 Grand Ave San Marcos (92078) *(P-11458)*

Southern Cal Disc Tire Co Inc .... C 760 741-3801
209 S Escondido Blvd Escondido (92025) *(P-11459)*

Southern Cal Disc Tire Co Inc .... C 858 481-6387
685 San Rodolfo Dr Solana Beach (92075) *(P-11460)*

Southern Cal Disc Tire Co Inc .... C 858 486-3600
12651 Poway Rd Poway (92064) *(P-11461)*

Southern Cal Disc Tire Co Inc .... D 760 439-8539
1037 S Coast Hwy Oceanside (92054) *(P-11462)*

Southern Cal Disc Tire Co Inc .... C 951 929-2130
600 W Florida Ave Hemet (92543) *(P-11463)*

Southern Cal Disc Tire Co Inc .... C 760 634-2202
107 N El Camino Real Encinitas (92024) *(P-11464)*

Southern Cal Disc Tire Co Inc .... D 858 278-0661
3935 Convoy St San Diego (92111) *(P-11465)*

Southern Cal Disc Tire Co Inc .... C 714 901-8226
15672 Springdale St Huntington Beach (92649) *(P-11466)*

Southern Cal Disc Tire Co Inc .... C 310 324-2569
20741 Avalon Blvd Carson (90746) *(P-11467)*

Southern Cal Disc Tire Co Inc .... D 626 335-2883
705 S Grand Ave Glendora (91740) *(P-11468)*

Southern Cal Edson - Prvate Ch, Rosemead *Also Called: Southern California Edison Co*
(P-9625)

Southern Cal Fd Allergy Inst, Long Beach *Also Called: Transltnal Plmnary Immnlogy RE*
(P-15491)

Southern Cal Halthcare Sys Inc .... D 310 836-7000
3828 Delmas Ter Culver City (90232) *(P-16202)*

Southern Cal Halthcare Sys Inc (HQ) .... **C 310 943-4500**
3415 S Sepulveda Blvd 9th Fl Los Angeles (90034) *(P-16203)*

Southern Cal Hlth Rhblttion PR .... C 310 631-8004
2610 Industry Way Ste A Lynwood (90262) *(P-15459)*

Southern Cal Hosp At Culver Cy, Culver City *Also Called: Brotman Medical Center Inc*
(P-15928)

Southern Cal Hosp At Culver Cy, Culver City *Also Called: Southern Cal Halthcare Sys Inc*
(P-16202)

Southern Cal Hydrlic Engrg Cor .... E 714 257-4800
1130 Columbia St Brea (92821) *(P-10404)*

Southern Cal Inst For RES Edca .... D 562 826-8139
5901 E 7th St 151 Long Beach (90822) *(P-17891)*

Southern Cal Nursing Academy, Palm Desert *Also Called: Southern California Gas Co*
(P-9646)

Southern Cal Orthpd Inst LP (PA) .... **C 818 901-6600**
6815 Noble Ave Van Nuys (91405) *(P-15460)*

Southern Cal Pipe Trades ADM .... D 619 224-3125
1936 Quivira Way Bldg G San Diego (92109) *(P-12529)*

Southern Cal Pipe Trades ADM (PA) .... **D 213 385-6161**
501 Shatto Pl Ste 500 Los Angeles (90020) *(P-12674)*

Southern Cal Pipe Trades ADM, Los Angeles *Also Called: Southern Cal Pipe Trades ADM*
(P-12674)

Southern Cal Prmnnte Med Group .... C 714 734-4500
17542 17th St Ste 300 Tustin (92780) *(P-12107)*

Southern Cal Prmnnte Med Group .... C 866 984-7483
10800 Magnolia Ave Riverside (92505) *(P-12108)*

Southern Cal Prmnnte Med Group .... C 619 528-5000
6860 Avenida Encinas Carlsbad (92011) *(P-12109)*

Southern Cal Prmnnte Med Group .... B 858 974-1000
5855 Copley Dr Ste 250 San Diego (92111) *(P-12110)*

Southern Cal Prmnnte Med Group .... A 800 272-3500
13652 Cantara St Panorama City (91402) *(P-12111)*

Southern Cal Prmnnte Med Group .... B 626 960-4844
1511 W Garvey Ave N West Covina (91790) *(P-12112)*

Southern Cal Prmnnte Med Group .... C 909 394-2505
1255 W Arrow Hwy San Dimas (91773) *(P-12113)*

Southern Cal Prmnnte Med Group .... C 661 398-5085
3501 Stockdale Hwy Bakersfield (93309) *(P-15461)*

Southern Cal Prmnnte Med Group .... C 661 334-2020
5055 California Ave Bakersfield (93309) *(P-15462)*

Southern Cal Prmnnte Med Group .... C 310 737-4900
5620 Mesmer Ave Culver City (90230) *(P-15463)*

Southern Cal Prmnnte Med Group .... C 310 419-3306
110 N La Brea Ave Inglewood (90301) *(P-15464)*

Southern Cal Prmnnte Med Group .... C 323 562-6459
7825 Atlantic Ave Cudahy (90201) *(P-15465)*

Southern Cal Prmnnte Med Group .... C 818 592-3038
21263 Erwin St Woodland Hills (91367) *(P-15466)*

Southern Cal Prmnnte Med Group .... C 661 222-2150
27107 Tourney Rd Santa Clarita (91355) *(P-15467)*

Southern Cal Prmnnte Med Group .... C 323 857-2000
6041 Cadillac Ave Los Angeles (90034) *(P-15468)*

Southern Cal Prmnnte Med Group .... C 800 780-1230
25825 Vermont Ave Harbor City (90710) *(P-15469)*

Southern Cal Prmnnte Med Group .... B 323 783-5455
4841 Hollywood Blvd Los Angeles (90027) *(P-15470)*

Southern Cal Prmnnte Med Group .... C 323 783-4893
4760 W Sunset Blvd Los Angeles (90027) *(P-15471)*

Southern Cal Prmnnte Med Group .... C 714 841-7293
18081 Beach Blvd Huntington Beach (92648) *(P-15472)*

Southern Cal Prmnnte Med Group .... C 714 279-4675
411 N Lakeview Ave Anaheim (92807) *(P-15473)*

Southern Cal Prmnnte Med Group .... C 949 234-2139
30400 Camino Capistrano San Juan Capistrano (92675) *(P-15474)*

Southern Cal Prmnnte Med Group .... C 714 967-4760
1900 E 4th St Santa Ana (92705) *(P-15475)*

Southern Cal Prmnnte Med Group .... C 949 262-5780
6 Willard Irvine (92604) *(P-15476)*

Southern Cal Prmnnte Med Group .... B 619 528-5000
4647 Zion Ave San Diego (92120) *(P-15477)*

Southern Cal Prmnnte Med Group .... C 909 370-2501
789 E Cooley Dr Colton (92324) *(P-15478)*

Southern Cal Prmnnte Med Group .... C 619 528-5000
1630 E Main St El Cajon (92021) *(P-15479)*

Southern Cal Prmnnte Med Group .... C 619 516-6000
4405 Vandever Ave San Diego (92120) *(P-15480)*

Southern Cal Prmnnte Med Group .... C 760 839-7200
732 N Broadway Escondido (92025) *(P-15481)*

Southern Cal Prmnnte Med Group .... A 562 657-2200
9353 Imperial Hwy Garden Medical Bldg Flr 3 Downey (90242) *(P-16204)*

Southern Cal Prmnnte Med Group .... C 310 604-5700
3830 Martin Luther King Jr Blvd Lynwood (90262) *(P-16205)*

Southern Cal Prmnnte Med Group .... C 661 290-3100
26415 Carl Boyer Dr Santa Clarita (91350) *(P-16206)*

Southern Cal Prmnnte Med Group .... B 909 427-5000
9961 Sierra Ave Fontana (92335) *(P-16207)*

Southern Cal Prmnnte Med Group .... C 949 376-8619
23781 Maquina Mission Viejo (92691) *(P-16617)*

Southern Cal Prmnnte Med Group .... C 323 564-7911
1465 E 103rd St Los Angeles (90002) *(P-16858)*

Southern Cal Rgional Rail Auth .... C 213 808-7043
2704 N Garey Ave Pomona (91767) *(P-8805)*

Southern Cal Rgional Rail Auth (PA) .... **C 213 452-0200**
900 Wilshire Blvd Ste 1500 Los Angeles (90017) *(P-8806)*

Southern Cal Spcialty Care Inc .... C 626 339-5451
845 N Lark Ellen Ave West Covina (91791) *(P-16208)*

Southern Cal Spcialty Care Inc .... C 714 564-7800
1901 College Ave Santa Ana (92706) *(P-16209)*

Southern Cal Spcialty Care LLC (DH) .... **D 562 944-1900**
14900 Imperial Hwy La Mirada (90638) *(P-16210)*

Southern Cal Tchnical Arts Inc .... E 714 524-2626
370 E Crowther Ave Placentia (92870) *(P-6241)*

Southern California Edison Co .... D 800 336-2822
26125 Menifee Rd Romoland (92585) *(P-9615)*

Southern California Edison Co .... C 714 895-0163
7333 Bolsa Ave Westminster (92683) *(P-9616)*

Southern California Edison Co .... C 714 895-0119
7400 Fenwick Ln Westminster (92683) *(P-9617)*

Southern California Edison Co .... B 714 870-3225
1851 W Valencia Dr Fullerton (92833) *(P-9618)*

Employee Codes: A=Over 500 employees, B=251-500
C=101-250, D=51-100, E=20-50, F=10-19, G=1-9

2025 Southern California
Business Directory and Buyers Guide

© Mergent Inc. 1-800-342-5647
1191

A
L
P
H
A
B
E
T
I
C

Southern California Edison Co .... A 714 895-0420
7300 Fenwick Ln Westminster (92683) *(P-9619)*

Southern California Edison Co .... C 949 587-5416
14155 Bake Pkwy Irvine (92618) *(P-9620)*

Southern California Edison Co (HQ) .... **A 626 302-1212**
2244 Walnut Grove Ave Rosemead (91770) *(P-9621)*

Southern California Edison Co .... B 909 274-1925
2 Innovation Way Fl 1 Pomona (91768) *(P-9622)*

Southern California Edison Co .... A 909 469-0251
265 Ne End Ave Pomona (91767) *(P-9623)*

Southern California Edison Co .... D 626 302-5101
8380 Klingerman St Rosemead (91770) *(P-9624)*

Southern California Edison Co .... B 626 302-1212
2131 Walnut Grove Ave Rosemead (91770) *(P-9625)*

Southern California Edison Co .... B 310 608-5029
1924 E Cashdan St Compton (90220) *(P-9626)*

Southern California Edison Co .... C 661 607-0207
28250 Gateway Village Dr Valencia (91355) *(P-9627)*

Southern California Edison Co .... D 626 633-3070
6042 N Irwindale Ave Ste A Irwindale (91702) *(P-9628)*

Southern California Edison Co .... D 562 529-7301
6900 Orange Ave Long Beach (90805) *(P-9629)*

Southern California Edison Co .... B 626 814-4212
13025 Los Angeles St Irwindale (91706) *(P-9630)*

Southern California Edison Co .... C 909 592-3757
800 W Cienega Ave San Dimas (91773) *(P-9631)*

Southern California Edison Co .... B 562 903-3191
9901 Geary Ave Santa Fe Springs (90670) *(P-9632)*

Southern California Edison Co .... B 562 491-3803
125 Elm Ave Long Beach (90802) *(P-9633)*

Southern California Edison Co .... B 626 812-7380
6090 N Irwindale Ave Irwindale (91702) *(P-9634)*

Southern California Edison Co .... A 626 308-6193
501 S Marengo Ave Alhambra (91803) *(P-9635)*

Southern California Edison Co .... C 760 375-1821
510 S China Lake Blvd Ridgecrest (93555) *(P-9636)*

Southern California Edison Co .... D 626 543-8081
4900 Rivergrade Rd Bldg 2b1 Irwindale (91706) *(P-9637)*

Southern California Edison Co .... C 626 303-8480
1440 S California Ave Monrovia (91016) *(P-9638)*

Southern California Edison Co .... D 818 999-1880
3589 Foothill Dr Thousand Oaks (91361) *(P-9639)*

Southern California Gas, Duarte Also Called: Southern California Gas Co *(P-9651)*

Southern California Gas Co .... B 818 701-2592
9400 Oakdale Ave Chatsworth (91311) *(P-9643)*

Southern California Gas Co .... D 714 262-0091
73700 Dinah Shore Dr Ste 106 Palm Desert (92211) *(P-9646)*

Southern California Gas Co .... C 213 244-1200
25200 Trumble Rd Romoland (92585) *(P-9647)*

Southern California Gas Co .... B 909 335-7802
1981 W Lugonia Ave Redlands (92374) *(P-9648)*

Southern California Gas Co .... C 909 335-7941
155 S G St San Bernardino (92410) *(P-9649)*

Southern California Gas Co .... B 909 305-8297
1050 Overland Ct San Dimas (91773) *(P-9650)*

Southern California Gas Co .... D 626 358-4700
3318 Shadylawn Dr Duarte (91010) *(P-9651)*

Southern California Gas Co .... C 800 427-2200
23130 Valencia Blvd Valencia (91355) *(P-9652)*

Southern California Gas Co .... C 323 881-3587
333 E Main St Ste J Alhambra (91801) *(P-9653)*

Southern California Gas Co .... C 562 803-3341
6738 Bright Ave Whittier (90601) *(P-9654)*

Southern California Gas Co .... B 310 823-7945
8141 Gulana Ave Venice (90293) *(P-9655)*

Southern California Gas Co .... C 213 244-1200
1600 Corporate Center Dr Monterey Park (91754) *(P-9656)*

Southern California Gas Co .... C 661 399-4431
1510 N Chester Ave Bakersfield (93308) *(P-9657)*

Southern California Gas Co .... B 818 363-8542
12801 Tampa Ave Northridge (91326) *(P-9658)*

Southern California Gas Co .... B 562 803-7500
9240 Firestone Blvd Downey (90241) *(P-9659)*

Southern California Gas Co .... A 213 244-1200
1801 S Atlantic Blvd Monterey Park (91754) *(P-9660)*

Southern California Gas Co .... D 213 244-1200
920 S Stimson Ave City Of Industry (91745) *(P-9661)*

Southern California Gas Co .... C 714 634-7221
1 Liberty Aliso Viejo (92656) *(P-9662)*

Southern California Gas Co .... C 213 244-1200
3050 E La Jolla St Anaheim (92806) *(P-9663)*

Southern California Gas Co (HQ) .... **A 213 244-1200**
555 W 5th St Ste 14h1 Los Angeles (90013) *(P-9664)*

Southern California Gas Co .... C 714 634-3065
1919 S State College Blvd Anaheim (92806) *(P-9665)*

Southern California Gas Tower .... A 213 244-1200
555 W 5th St Los Angeles (90013) *(P-9666)*

Southern California Material Handling Inc .... C 562 949-1006
12393 Slauson Ave Whittier (90606) *(P-10405)*

Southern California Messenger, Los Angeles Also Called: Prompt Delivery Inc *(P-14577)*

Southern California Mtl Hdlg, Fontana Also Called: Equipment Depot Inc *(P-10373)*

Southern California Permanente Medical Group, Riverside Also Called: Southern Cal Prmnnte Med Group *(P-12108)*

SOUTHERN CALIFORNIA PERMANENTE MEDICAL GROUP, Carlsbad Also Called: Southern Cal Prmnnte Med Group *(P-12109)*

SOUTHERN CALIFORNIA PERMANENTE MEDICAL GROUP, Mission Viejo Also Called: Southern Cal Prmnnte Med Group *(P-16617)*

Southern California Plas Inc .... D 714 751-7084
3122 Maple St Santa Ana (92707) *(P-4245)*

Southern California Plating Co .... E 619 231-1481
3261 National Ave San Diego (92113) *(P-5296)*

Southern California Regional, Indio Also Called: Granite Construction Company *(P-617)*

Southern California Trane, Brea Also Called: Trane US Inc *(P-5988)*

Southern California Valve Inc .... D 562 404-2246
13903 Maryton Ave Santa Fe Springs (90670) *(P-10464)*

Southern Contracting Company .... C 760 744-0760
559 N Twin Oaks Valley Rd San Marcos (92069) *(P-963)*

Southern Counties LLC (DH) .... **D 714 744-7140**
1800 W Katella Ave Ste 210 Orange (92867) *(P-11025)*

Southern Counties Terminals .... D 310 642-0462
5341 W 104th St Los Angeles (90045) *(P-8924)*

Southern Electronics, Pomona Also Called: Electrocube Inc *(P-6995)*

Southern Glzers Wine Sprits Ca, Cerritos Also Called: Southern Glzers Wine Sprits LL *(P-11061)*

Southern Glzers Wine Sprits LL .... B 562 926-2000
17101 Valley View Ave Cerritos (90703) *(P-11061)*

Southern Home Care Svcs Inc .... D 714 979-7413
2900 Bristol St Ste D107 Costa Mesa (92626) *(P-13623)*

Southern Implants Inc .... C 949 273-8505
5 Holland Ste 209 Irvine (92618) *(P-18059)*

Southern Indian Health Council (PA) .... **D 619 445-1188**
4058 Willows Rd Alpine (91901) *(P-16506)*

Southern Management Corp .... C 213 312-2268
808 S Olive St Los Angeles (90014) *(P-13422)*

Southern Sierra Medical Clinic, Ridgecrest Also Called: Ridgecrest Regional Hospital *(P-16160)*

Southland Box Company .... C 323 583-2231
4201 Fruitland Ave Vernon (90058) *(P-2689)*

Southland Care, San Juan Capistrano Also Called: Ensign Southland LLC *(P-15646)*

Southland Container Corp .... B 909 937-9781
1600 Champagne Ave Ontario (91761) *(P-2690)*

Southland Envelope LLC .... C 619 449-3553
8830 Siempre Viva Rd San Diego (92154) *(P-2753)*

Southland Paving Inc .... D 760 747-6895
361 N Hale Ave Escondido (92029) *(P-1135)*

Southland Ready Mix Concrete, Escondido Also Called: Superior Ready Mix Concrete LP *(P-4460)*

Southland Rgnal Assn Rltors In (PA) .... **D 818 786-2110**
7232 Balboa Blvd Van Nuys (91406) *(P-17288)*

Southland Technology Inc .... D 858 694-0932
8053 Vickers St San Diego (92111) *(P-10029)*

Southwest Administrators Inc .... B
466 Foothill Blvd La Canada Flintridge (91011) *(P-12164)*

Southwest Airlines, Santa Ana *Also Called: Southwest Airlines Co (P-9166)*

Southwest Airlines Co .... D 949 252-5200
18601 Airport Way Ste 237 Santa Ana (92707) *(P-9166)*

Southwest Boulder & Stone Inc (PA) .... E 760 451-3333
5002 2nd St Fallbrook (92028) *(P-11699)*

Southwest Carptr Training Fund .... D 213 386-8590
533 S Fremont Ave Ste 700 Los Angeles (90071) *(P-17314)*

Southwest Concrete Products .... E 909 983-9789
519 S Benson Ave Ontario (91762) *(P-4422)*

Southwest Contractors (PA) .... E 661 588-0484
136 Allen Rd # 100 Bakersfield (93314) *(P-696)*

Southwest Convalesant, Hawthorne *Also Called: Windsor Anaheim Healthcare (P-15804)*

Southwest Data Products, San Bernardino *Also Called: Innovative Metal Inds Inc (P-5096)*

Southwest Greene Intl Inc .... D 760 639-4960
4055b Calle Platino Oceanside (92056) *(P-5213)*

Southwest Healthcare Sys Aux .... A 800 404-6627
38977 Sky Canyon Dr Ste 200 Murrieta (92563) *(P-16211)*

Southwest Healthcare Sys Aux (HQ) .... B 951 696-6000
25500 Medical Center Dr Murrieta (92562) *(P-16212)*

Southwest Landscape Inc .... D 714 545-1084
2205 S Standard Ave Santa Ana (92707) *(P-192)*

Southwest Machine & Plastic Co .... E 626 963-6919
620 W Foothill Blvd Glendora (91741) *(P-7564)*

Southwest Manufacturing Svcs, El Cajon *Also Called: Pacific Marine Sheet Metal Corporation
(P-5015)*

Southwest Material Hdlg Inc (PA) .... C 951 727-0477
3725 Nobel Ct Jurupa Valley (91752) *(P-11412)*

Southwest Offset Prtg Co Inc (PA) .... B 310 965-9154
13650 Gramercy Pl Gardena (90249) *(P-3082)*

Southwest Patrol Inc .... D 909 861-1884
1800 E Lambert Rd Ste 155 Brea (92821) *(P-14351)*

Southwest Plastics Co, Glendora *Also Called: Southwest Machine & Plastic Co (P-7564)*

Southwest Products LLC .... C 619 263-8000
8411 Siempre Viva Rd San Diego (92154) *(P-1855)*

Southwest Protective Svcs Inc .... C 760 996-1285
404 W Heil Ave El Centro (92243) *(P-14352)*

Southwest Regional Council of Carpenters, Buena Park *Also Called: Southwest Rgnal Cncil
Crpnters (P-17315)*

Southwest Rgnal Cncil Crpnters .... D 714 571-0449
7111 Firestone Blvd Buena Park (90621) *(P-17315)*

Southwest Security, El Centro *Also Called: Southwest Protective Svcs Inc (P-14352)*

Southwest Sign Company, Corona *Also Called: Fovell Enterprises Inc (P-8605)*

Southwest Sign Systems, El Centro *Also Called: Western Electrical Advg Co (P-8649)*

Southwest Specialty Contrs, Corona *Also Called: Southwest Specialty Contrs LLC (P-1096)*

Southwest Specialty Contrs LLC .... D 951 987-8008
705 E Harrison St Ste 100 Corona (92879) *(P-1096)*

Southwest Toyota Lift, Jurupa Valley *Also Called: Southwest Material Hdlg Inc (P-11412)*

Southwest Traders Incorporated (PA) .... C 951 699-7800
27565 Diaz Rd Temecula (92590) *(P-10806)*

Southwestern Industries Inc (PA) .... D 310 608-4422
2015 Homestead Pl Rancho Dominguez (90220) *(P-5553)*

Southwind Foods LLC (PA) .... C 323 262-8222
20644 S Fordyce Ave Carson (90810) *(P-1698)*

Southwire Company LLC .... D 909 989-2888
9199 Cleveland Ave Ste 100 Rancho Cucamonga (91730) *(P-4592)*

Southwire Inc .... B 310 886-8300
20250 S Alameda St Compton (90221) *(P-4593)*

Sovereign Health, Rancho Mirage *Also Called: Dual Diagnosis Trtmnt Ctr Inc (P-16556)*

Sovereign Health of California, San Clemente *Also Called: Dual Diagnosis Trtmnt Ctr Inc
(P-16470)*

Soyfoods of America .... E 626 358-3836
1091 Hamilton Rd Duarte (91010) *(P-1856)*

Sp Craftech I LLC .... E 714 630-8117
2941 E La Jolla St Anaheim (92806) *(P-4246)*

Sp Crankshaft, Irvine *Also Called: Pankl Engine Systems Inc (P-7281)*

Spa De Soleil Inc .... E 818 504-3200
10443 Arminta St Sun Valley (91352) *(P-10652)*

Spa Havens LP .... C 760 945-2055
29402 Spa Haven Way Vista (92084) *(P-15063)*

Spa Resort Casino .... A 760 883-1034
100 N Indian Canyon Dr Palm Springs (92262) *(P-13030)*

Spa Resort Casino (PA) .... D 888 999-1995
401 E Amado Rd Palm Springs (92262) *(P-13031)*

Spa Resort Casino, Palm Springs *Also Called: Agua Clnte Band Chilla Indians (P-12758)*

Space Components, Commerce *Also Called: Atk Space Systems LLC (P-7701)*

Space Components Division, San Diego *Also Called: Atk Space Systems LLC (P-7699)*

Space Exploration Tech Corp .... C 310 848-4410
731 Kelp Rd Slc-4 Vandenberg Afb (93437) *(P-7372)*

Space Exploration Tech Corp (PA) .... B 310 363-6000
1 Rocket Rd Hawthorne (90250) *(P-7650)*

Space Exploration Tech Corp .... C 310 363-6289
2980 Nimitz Rd Long Beach (90802) *(P-7651)*

Space Exploration Tech Corp .... C 714 330-8668
2700 Miner St San Pedro (90731) *(P-7652)*

Space Exploration Tech Corp .... C 323 754-1285
12520 Wilkie Ave Gardena (90249) *(P-7653)*

Space Exploration Tech Corp .... C 310 889-4968
3976 Jack Northrop Ave Hawthorne (90250) *(P-7654)*

Space Micro Inc .... C 858 332-0700
15378 Avenue Of Science Ste 200 San Diego (92128) *(P-6661)*

Space Systems Division, El Segundo *Also Called: Orbital Sciences LLC (P-7786)*

Space Vector Corporation .... E 818 734-2600
20520 Nordhoff St Chatsworth (91311) *(P-7812)*

Space-Lok Inc .... C 310 527-6150
13306 Halldale Ave Gardena (90249) *(P-7565)*

Spacestor Inc .... E 310 410-0220
16411 Carmenita Rd Cerritos (90703) *(P-2518)*

Spacex, Hawthorne *Also Called: Space Exploration Tech Corp (P-7650)*

Spacex, Long Beach *Also Called: Space Exploration Tech Corp (P-7651)*

Spacex, San Pedro *Also Called: Space Exploration Tech Corp (P-7652)*

Spacex, Hawthorne *Also Called: Space Exploration Tech Corp (P-7654)*

Spacex LLC .... A 310 970-5845
12533 Crenshaw Blvd Hawthorne (90250) *(P-7655)*

Spacex Wilkie, Gardena *Also Called: Space Exploration Tech Corp (P-7653)*

Span-O-Matic Inc .... E 714 256-4700
825 Columbia St Brea (92821) *(P-5035)*

Spangler Industries Inc .... C 951 735-5000
1711 N Delilah St Corona (92879) *(P-3938)*

Spanish Brdcstg Sys of Cal .... D 310 203-0900
7007 Nw 77th Ave Los Angeles (90064) *(P-9489)*

Spanish Hills Club LLC .... D 805 388-5000
999 Crestview Ave Camarillo (93010) *(P-15176)*

Spanish Hills Country Club (PA) .... C 805 389-1644
999 Crestview Ave Camarillo (93010) *(P-15177)*

Sparitual, Van Nuys *Also Called: Orly International Inc (P-3675)*

Spark Compass, Los Angeles *Also Called: Total Cmmnicator Solutions Inc (P-14161)*

Sparks Exhbits Envrnments Corp .... E 562 941-0101
3143 S La Cienega Blvd Los Angeles (90016) *(P-8727)*

Sparks Los Angeles, Los Angeles *Also Called: Sparks Exhbits Envrnments Corp (P-8727)*

Sparktech Software LLC .... E 818 330-9098
1419 Beaudry Blvd Glendale (91208) *(P-14035)*

Sparling Instruments LLC .... E 626 444-0571
4097 Temple City Blvd El Monte (91731) *(P-7893)*

Spartan Inc .... D 661 327-1205
3030 M St Bakersfield (93301) *(P-4870)*

Spartan Manufacturing Co .... E 714 894-1955
7081 Patterson Dr Garden Grove (92841) *(P-6242)*

Spartan Truck Company Inc .... E 818 899-1111
12266 Branford St Sun Valley (91352) *(P-7210)*

Spartech Plastics, La Mirada *Also Called: Alchem Plastics Inc (P-3963)*

Spates Fabricators, Thermal *Also Called: Spates Fabricators Inc (P-2381)*

Spates Fabricators Inc .... D 760 397-4122
85435 Middleton St Thermal (92274) *(P-2381)*

Spatial Labs Inc .... E 424 289-0275
12555 W Jefferson Blvd Ste 220 Los Angeles (90066) *(P-14036)*

Spatz Corporation .... C 805 487-2122
1600 Westar Dr Oxnard (93033) *(P-3688)*

Spatz Laboratories, Oxnard *Also Called: Spatz Corporation (P-3688)*

Spaulding Crusher Parts, Perris *Also Called: Spaulding Equipment Company (P-5502)*

Spaulding Equipment Company (PA) .... E 951 943-4531
75 Paseo Adelanto Perris (92570) *(P-5502)*

Employee Codes: A=Over 500 employees, B=251-500
C=101-250, D=51-100, E=20-50, F=10-19, G=1-9

2025 Southern California
Business Directory and Buyers Guide

© Mergent Inc. 1-800-342-5647
1193

Spc Building Services, Riverside *Also Called: J M V B Inc (P-867)*

Speakercraft LLC .... D 951 685-1759
12471 Riverside Dr Mira Loma (91752) *(P-6558)*

Spearman Aerospace Inc .... E 714 523-4751
9215 Greenleaf Ave Santa Fe Springs (90670) *(P-17634)*

Spearmint Rhino Gentlemens CLB, Torrance *Also Called: Midnight Sun Enterprises Inc*
(P-18335)

Spears Manufacturing Co .... E 818 364-1611
15860 Olden St Rancho Cascades (91342) *(P-3979)*

Spears Manufacturing Co (PA)............................... C 818 364-1611
15853 Olden St Rancho Cascades (91342) *(P-10364)*

Spec, Valencia *Also Called: Semiconductor Process Eqp LLC (P-6888)*

Spec Engineering Company Inc .... E 818 780-3045
13754 Saticoy St Panorama City (91402) *(P-6243)*

Spec Formliners Inc .... E 714 429-9500
1038 E 4th St Santa Ana (92701) *(P-4423)*

Spec Services Inc .... B 714 963-8077
10540 Talbert Ave Ste 100e Fountain Valley (92708) *(P-17635)*

Spec Tool Company .... E 323 723-9533
11805 Wakeman St Santa Fe Springs (90670) *(P-7566)*

Spec-Built Systems Inc .... D 619 661-8100
2150 Michael Faraday Dr San Diego (92154) *(P-5036)*

Special Devices Incorporated .... A 805 387-1000
2655 1st St Ste 125 Simi Valley (93065) *(P-7294)*

Special Event Audio Svcs Inc .... E 800 518-9144
35889 Shetland Hls E Fallbrook (92028) *(P-15005)*

Special Operations Tech, Carson *Also Called: SO Tech/Spcl Op Tech Inc (P-10674)*

Special Products Group, Chula Vista *Also Called: Sealed Air Corporation (P-4015)*

Special Service For Groups Inc (PA)....................... D 213 368-1888
905 E 8th St Los Angeles (90021) *(P-17066)*

Special Service For Groups Inc .... C 310 323-6887
879 W 190th St Gardena (90248) *(P-17244)*

Special Service For Groups Inc .... C 213 553-1800
520 S La Fayette Park Pl # 30 Los Angeles (90057) *(P-17245)*

Special Service For Groups Ssg, Los Angeles *Also Called: Special Service For Groups Inc*
(P-17066)

Specialist Media Group, Carlsbad *Also Called: L & L Printers Carlsbad LLC (P-3030)*

Specialists In Cstm Sftwr Inc .... E 310 315-9660
2574 Wellesley Ave Los Angeles (90064) *(P-14037)*

Speciality Labs, Fullerton *Also Called: Magtech & Power Conversion Inc (P-6930)*

Specialized Ldscp MGT Svcs Inc .... D 805 520-7590
4212 Peast Los Angeles Ave # 4211 Simi Valley (93063) *(P-193)*

Specialized Milling Corp .... E 909 357-7890
10330 Elm Ave Fontana (92337) *(P-3722)*

Specialty Brands Incorporated .... A 909 477-4851
4200 Concours Ste 100 Ontario (91764) *(P-1401)*

Specialty Coating Systems Inc .... D 909 390-8818
4435 E Airport Dr Ste 100 Ontario (91761) *(P-5346)*

Specialty Construction Inc .... D 805 543-1706
645 Clarion Ct San Luis Obispo (93401) *(P-964)*

Specialty Division, Santa Fe Springs *Also Called: Distinctive Industries (P-2259)*

Specialty Enterprises Co .... D 323 726-9721
6858 E Acco St Commerce (90040) *(P-4018)*

Specialty Fabrications Inc .... E 805 579-9730
2674 Westhills Ct Simi Valley (93065) *(P-5037)*

Specialty Finishes, Fontana *Also Called: Specialized Milling Corp (P-3722)*

Specialty Interior Mfg Inc .... E 714 296-8618
16751 Millikan Ave Irvine (92606) *(P-9850)*

Specialty Laboratories Inc (DH)........................... A 661 799-6543
27027 Tourney Rd Valencia (91355) *(P-16335)*

Specialty Minerals Inc .... C 760 248-5300
6565 Meridian Rd Lucerne Valley (92356) *(P-3253)*

Specialty Motors, Valencia *Also Called: SMI Holdings Inc (P-6334)*

Specialty Paper Mills Inc .... C 562 692-8737
8844 Millergrove Dr Santa Fe Springs (90670) *(P-2639)*

Specialty Restaurants Corp .... B 818 843-5013
1250 E Harvard Rd Burbank (91501) *(P-11601)*

Specialty Sugical Ctr Encino, Encino *Also Called: Sgry LLC (P-16189)*

Specialty Surgical of Westlake, Westlake Village *Also Called: Sgry LLC (P-15451)*

Specialty Team Plastering Inc .... C 805 966-3858
4652 Vintage Ranch Ln Santa Barbara (93110) *(P-1029)*

Specialty Textile Services LLC .... C 619 476-8750
1333 30th St Ste A San Diego (92154) *(P-10675)*

Specificmedia Inc .... D 949 861-8888
2722 Michelson Dr Ste 100 Irvine (92612) *(P-13246)*

Specilty Eqp Mkt Assn Prfmce R (PA).................. D 909 610-2030
1575 Valley Vista Dr Diamond Bar (91765) *(P-17289)*

Specimen Contracting, Sunland *Also Called: Brightview Tree Company (P-249)*

Specright Inc .... C 866 290-6952
1785 Flight Way Tustin (92782) *(P-14601)*

Spectra Color Inc .... E 951 277-0200
9116 Stellar Ct Corona (92883) *(P-3225)*

Spectra Company .... C 909 599-0760
2510 Supply St Pomona (91767) *(P-988)*

Spectra Historic Construction, Pomona *Also Called: Spectra Company (P-988)*

Spectra Industrial Electric, Carson *Also Called: Spectra Industrial Svcs Inc (P-965)*

Spectra Industrial Svcs Inc .... D 310 835-0808
21818 S Wilmington Ave Ste 402 Carson (90810) *(P-965)*

Spectra USA, Chino *Also Called: Isiqalo LLC (P-1920)*

Spectrolab Inc .... B 818 365-4611
12500 Gladstone Ave Sylmar (91342) *(P-7052)*

Spectrum Assembly Inc .... C 760 930-4000
6300 Yarrow Dr Ste 100 Carlsbad (92011) *(P-6774)*

Spectrum Bags, Cerritos *Also Called: Ips Industries Inc (P-4141)*

Spectrum Brands Hdwr HM Imprv, Foothill Ranch *Also Called: Kwikset Corporation (P-4776)*

Spectrum Clubs Inc .... A 310 727-9300
840 Apollo St Ste 100 El Segundo (90245) *(P-15064)*

Spectrum Cnstr Group Inc .... D 949 246-9749
14252 Culver Dr Ste 356 Irvine (92604) *(P-502)*

Spectrum Electronics, Carlsbad *Also Called: Spectrum Assembly Inc (P-6774)*

Spectrum Equipment LLC .... D 760 599-8849
2505 Commerce Way Vista (92081) *(P-11100)*

Spectrum Floral Service, Vista *Also Called: Spectrum Equipment LLC (P-11100)*

Spectrum Hotel Group LLC .... C 949 471-8888
90 Pacifica Irvine (92618) *(P-13032)*

Spectrum Inc .... C 310 885-4600
18617 S Broadwick St Rancho Dominguez (90220) *(P-8229)*

Spectrum Information Svcs LLC (PA)...................... D 949 752-7070
3323 Spectrum Irvine (92618) *(P-13306)*

Spectrum Intl Holdings .... A 626 333-7225
14421 Bonelli St City Of Industry (91746) *(P-2593)*

Spectrum Lab & Phrm Pdts, Gardena *Also Called: Spectrum Laboratory Pdts Inc (P-11020)*

Spectrum Laboratories, Rancho Dominguez *Also Called: Spectrum Inc (P-8229)*

Spectrum Laboratory Pdts Inc .... E 520 292-3103
14422 S San Pedro St Gardena (90248) *(P-11020)*

Spectrum Lighting, Santa Fe Springs *Also Called: Dab Inc (P-6442)*

Spectrum MGT Holdg Co LLC .... D 619 684-6106
5865 Friars Rd San Diego (92110) *(P-9556)*

Spectrum MGT Holdg Co LLC .... D 323 657-0899
3550 Wilshire Blvd Los Angeles (90010) *(P-9557)*

Spectrum Plating Company, Los Angeles *Also Called: Ravlich Enterprises LLC (P-5288)*

Spectrum Scientific Inc .... E 949 260-9900
16692 Hale Ave Ste A Irvine (92606) *(P-8022)*

Spectrum Security Services Inc (PA)...................... C 619 669-6660
13967 Campo Rd Ste 101 Jamul (91935) *(P-14353)*

Speedata Inc .... D 612 743-7960
6520 Platt Ave Ste 804 West Hills (91307) *(P-10030)*

Speedo USA, Cypress *Also Called: Speedo USA Inc (P-2024)*

Speedo USA Inc .... B 657 465-3800
6251 Katella Ave Cypress (90630) *(P-2024)*

Speedy Circuits, Huntington Beach *Also Called: Coast To Coast Circuits Inc (P-6719)*

Speedy Circuits, Anaheim *Also Called: Excello Circuits Inc (P-6726)*

Speedy Express LLC .... D 818 300-7785
4401 W Slauson Ave Ste A Los Angeles (90043) *(P-9012)*

Spencer Forrest Inc .... E
11777 San Vicente Blvd Ste 650 Los Angeles (90049) *(P-11664)*

Spenuzza Inc (HQ).. D 951 281-1830
1128 Sherborn St Corona (92879) *(P-6034)*

SPEP Acquisition Corp (PA).................................. D 310 608-0693
4041 Via Oro Ave Long Beach (90810) *(P-4789)*

Sperasoft Inc .... B 408 715-6615
1115 S Flower St Burbank (91502) *(P-13829)*

Mergent email: customerrelations@mergent.com
1194

2025 Southern California
Business Directory and Buyers Guide

(P-0000) Products & Services Section entry number
(PA)=Parent Co (HQ)=Headquarters (DH)=Div Headquarters

Sperber Ldscp Companies LLC (PA) .... C 818 437-1029
30700 Russell Ranch Rd Ste 120 Westlake Village (91362) *(P-194)*

Spf Capital Real Estate LLC .... D 310 519-8200
601 S Palos Verdes St San Pedro (90731) *(P-13033)*

Sphere Alliance Inc .... E 951 352-2400
3087 12th St Riverside (92507) *(P-3293)*

Spherion Prof Recruiting Group, San Diego *Also Called: Sfn Group Inc (P-13621)*

Spilo Worldwide, Santa Monica *Also Called: Spilo Worldwide Inc (P-10478)*

Spilo Worldwide Inc .... D 213 687-8600
100 Wilshire Blvd Ste 700 Santa Monica (90401) *(P-10478)*

Spin Products Inc .... E 909 590-7000
13878 Yorba Ave Chino (91710) *(P-4247)*

Spinal Elements, Carlsbad *Also Called: Spinal Elements Holdings Inc (P-8230)*

Spinal Elements Holdings Inc .... C 877 774-6255
3115 Melrose Dr Ste 200 Carlsbad (92010) *(P-8230)*

Spinergy Inc .... D 760 496-2121
1709 La Costa Meadows Dr San Marcos (92078) *(P-7636)*

Spiniello Companies .... C 909 629-1000
2650 Pomona Blvd Pomona (91768) *(P-697)*

Spinlaunch Inc .... C 650 516-7746
3816 Stineman Ct Long Beach (90808) *(P-7665)*

Spira Manufacturing Corp .... E 818 764-8222
650 Jessie St San Fernando (91340) *(P-3901)*

Spiral Ppr Tube & Core Co Inc .... E 562 801-9705
5200 Industry Ave Pico Rivera (90660) *(P-2698)*

Spirent Calabasas, Calabasas *Also Called: Spirent Communications Inc (P-10031)*

Spirent Communications Inc (HQ) .... B 818 676-2300
27349 Agoura Rd Calabasas (91301) *(P-10031)*

Spirit Active Wear, Los Angeles *Also Called: Spirit Clothing Company (P-2025)*

Spirit Airlines Inc .... C 800 772-7117
San Diego Intl Airport Terminal 2 E San Diego (92101) *(P-9167)*

Spirit Clothing Company (PA) .... C 213 784-0251
2211 E 37th St Los Angeles (90058) *(P-2025)*

Spirit Clothing Company .... D 213 784-5372
2137 E 37th St Vernon (90058) *(P-2026)*

Spirit Realty LP .... D 972 476-1900
11995 El Camino Real San Diego (92130) *(P-12695)*

Spm, Anaheim *Also Called: Bace Manufacturing Inc (P-4059)*

Spokeo Inc .... C 877 913-3088
556 S Fair Oaks Ave Ste 1 Pasadena (91105) *(P-9458)*

Sponges Car Wash, Los Angeles *Also Called: San Ramon Services Inc (P-14710)*

Spooners Woodworks, Poway *Also Called: Spooners Woodworks Inc (P-2573)*

Spooners Woodworks Inc .... C 858 679-9086
12460 Kirkham Ct Poway (92064) *(P-2573)*

Sport Card Co LLC .... B 800 873-7332
5830 El Camino Real Carlsbad (92008) *(P-3083)*

Sport Clips, San Diego *Also Called: Sport Clips Inc (P-13154)*

Sport Clips Inc .... A 858 273-9993
4839 Clairemont Dr Ste E San Diego (92117) *(P-13154)*

Sports Venue Padding Inc .... E 562 404-9343
14135 Artesia Blvd Cerritos (90703) *(P-4019)*

Sportsrobe Inc .... E 310 559-3999
8654 Hayden Pl Culver City (90232) *(P-2027)*

Spotify USA Inc .... C 213 505-3040
555 Mateo St Los Angeles (90013) *(P-18218)*

Spotlight 29 Casino, Coachella *Also Called: 29 Palms Enterprises Corp (P-15190)*

Spotlite Power Corporation .... E 310 838-2367
9937 Jefferson Blvd Ste 110 Culver City (90232) *(P-6474)*

Spotter Global Inc .... C 515 817-3726
1204 N Miller St Unit A Anaheim (92806) *(P-5214)*

Spray Enclosure Tech Inc .... E 909 419-7011
1427 N Linden Ave Rialto (92376) *(P-5038)*

Spray Tech, Rialto *Also Called: Spray Enclosure Tech Inc (P-5038)*

Spreadtrum, San Diego *Also Called: Spreadtrum Cmmncations USA Inc (P-17823)*

Spreadtrum Cmmncations USA Inc .... D 858 546-0895
10180 Telesis Ct Ste 500 San Diego (92121) *(P-17823)*

Spreckels Sugar Company Inc .... B 760 344-3110
395 W Keystone Rd Brawley (92227) *(P-1498)*

Spring Industries, Ventura *Also Called: Juengermann Inc (P-5380)*

Spring Senior Assisted Living, Torrance *Also Called: Genesis Healthcare LLC (P-15664)*

Spring Technologies Corp .... E 310 230-4000
10170 Culver Blvd Culver City (90232) *(P-14038)*

Spring Valley Post Acute LLC .... C 760 245-6477
14973 Hesperia Rd Victorville (92395) *(P-15782)*

Sprint, Temecula *Also Called: Sprint Communications Co LP (P-9414)*

Sprint, Los Angeles *Also Called: Sprint Corporation (P-9417)*

Sprint, South Gate *Also Called: Sprint Corporation (P-9418)*

Sprint, Irvine *Also Called: Sprint Corporation (P-9419)*

Sprint, Garden Grove *Also Called: Sprint Communications Co LP (P-9461)*

Sprint Communications Co LP .... C 562 943-8907
15582 Whittwood Ln Whittier (90603) *(P-9409)*

Sprint Communications Co LP .... C 310 216-9093
5381 W Centinela Ave Los Angeles (90045) *(P-9410)*

Sprint Communications Co LP .... C 661 951-8927
44416 Valley Central Way Lancaster (93536) *(P-9411)*

Sprint Communications Co LP .... C 310 515-0293
1270 W Redondo Beach Blvd Gardena (90247) *(P-9412)*

Sprint Communications Co LP .... C 760 941-4535
4225 Oceanside Blvd Oceanside (92056) *(P-9413)*

Sprint Communications Co LP .... C 951 303-8501
31754 Temecula Pkwy Ste A Temecula (92592) *(P-9414)*

Sprint Communications Co LP .... C 951 461-9786
23865 Clinton Keith Rd Wildomar (92595) *(P-9415)*

Sprint Communications Co LP .... C 951 340-1924
3580 Grand Oaks Corona (92881) *(P-9416)*

Sprint Communications Co LP .... C 818 755-7100
111 Universal Hollywood Dr Universal City (91608) *(P-9459)*

Sprint Communications Co LP .... C 626 339-0430
1316 N Azusa Ave Covina (91722) *(P-9460)*

Sprint Communications Co LP .... C 714 534-2107
12913 Harbor Blvd Ste Q4 Garden Grove (92840) *(P-9461)*

Sprint Communications Co LP .... C 909 382-6030
1505 E Enterprise Dr San Bernardino (92408) *(P-9462)*

Sprint Corporation .... C 213 613-4200
432 S Broadway Los Angeles (90013) *(P-9417)*

Sprint Corporation .... C 323 357-0797
4707 Firestone Blvd South Gate (90280) *(P-9418)*

Sprint Corporation .... D 949 748-3353
6591 Irvine Center Dr Ste 100 Irvine (92618) *(P-9419)*

Sprintray Inc (PA) .... D 800 914-8004
2710 Media Center Dr Los Angeles (90065) *(P-8357)*

Sproutime, Sun Valley *Also Called: Foodology LLC (P-1775)*

Sprouts Farmers Market Inc .... C 888 577-7688
280 De Berry St Colton (92324) *(P-9110)*

SPS Technologies LLC .... E 714 892-5571
12570 Knott St Garden Grove (92841) *(P-7567)*

SPS Technologies LLC .... B 714 545-9311
1224 E Warner Ave Santa Ana (92705) *(P-8576)*

SPS Technologies LLC .... B 714 371-1925
1224 E Warner Ave Santa Ana (92705) *(P-8577)*

SPS Technologies LLC .... B 310 323-6222
1700 W 132nd St Gardena (90249) *(P-10465)*

SPS Technologies LLC .... B 949 474-6000
2541 White Rd Irvine (92614) *(P-10466)*

Spsv Entertainment LLC .... D 909 744-9373
28950 State Highway 18 Skyforest (92385) *(P-15006)*

Spus7 125 Cambridgepark LP .... D 213 683-4200
515 S Flower St Ste 3100 Los Angeles (90071) *(P-12530)*

Spus7 150 Cambridgepark LP .... C 213 683-4200
515 S Flower St Ste 3100 Los Angeles (90071) *(P-12531)*

SPX Flow Us LLC .... E 949 455-8150
26561 Rancho Pkwy S Lake Forest (92630) *(P-4928)*

Spy Inc (PA) .... D 760 804-8420
1896 Rutherford Rd Carlsbad (92008) *(P-8416)*

Spyglass Pharma Inc .... E 949 284-6904
27061 Aliso Creek Rd Ste 100 Aliso Viejo (92656) *(P-3507)*

Sqa Services, Palos Verdes Estates *Also Called: Sqa Services Inc (P-18219)*

Sqa Services Inc .... B 800 333-6180
425 Via Corta Ste 203 Palos Verdes Estates (90274) *(P-18219)*

Square Enix Inc .... C 310 846-0400
999 N Pacific Coast Hwy Fl 3 El Segundo (90245) *(P-10032)*

Square H Brands Inc .... D 323 267-4600
 3615 E Vernon Ave Vernon (90058) *(P-503)*

Square H Brands Inc (PA)............................ **E 323 267-4600**
 2731 S Soto St Vernon (90058) *(P-1271)*

Srax Inc (PA).. **E 323 205-6109**
 1014 S Westlake Blvd # 14-299 Westlake Village (91361) *(P-14039)*

Sream Inc .... E 951 245-6999
 12869 Temescal Canyon Rd Ste A Corona (92883) *(P-4346)*

Srg Holdings LLC (HQ)................................. **B 858 792-9300**
 500 Stevens Ave Ste 100 Solana Beach (92075) *(P-13472)*

Srht Property Holding LLC .... C 213 683-0522
 1317 E 7th St Los Angeles (90021) *(P-12532)*

Srm Contracting & Paving, San Diego *Also Called: Superior Ready Mix Concrete LP (P-4457)*

Sroodtuo, Paramount *Also Called: Top Line Mfg Inc (P-4791)*

SRS, Camarillo *Also Called: Silicon Processing and Trading Inc (P-9764)*

SS Heritage Inn Ontario LLC .... D 909 937-5000
 3595 E Guasti Rd Ontario (91761) *(P-13034)*

Ss Whittier LLC .... E 562 698-7513
 7240 Greenleaf Ave Whittier (90602) *(P-3084)*

Ssco Manufacturing Inc .... E 619 628-1022
 8155 Mercury Ct Ste 100 San Diego (92111) *(P-5649)*

Ssdi, La Mirada *Also Called: Solid State Devices Inc (P-6896)*

Ssi, Valley Center *Also Called: Survival Systems Intl Inc (P-14795)*

Ssre Holdings LLC .... D 800 314-2098
 18901 Railroad St City Of Industry (91748) *(P-1251)*

SSS, Carlsbad *Also Called: Silk Screen Shirts Inc (P-1934)*

Sst IV 8020 Las Vgas Blvd S LL .... D 949 429-6600
 10 Terrace Rd Ladera Ranch (92694) *(P-9111)*

Sst Technologies .... E 562 803-3361
 6305 El Camino Real Carlsbad (92009) *(P-6898)*

Sst Vacuum Reflow Systems, Carlsbad *Also Called: Sst Technologies (P-6898)*

Ssw, Palm Springs *Also Called: S S W Mechanical Cnstr Inc (P-833)*

St Annes Family Services .... C 213 381-2931
 155 N Occidental Blvd Los Angeles (90026) *(P-17197)*

St Bernardine Med Ctr Aux Inc .... C 909 881-4320
 2101 N Waterman Ave San Bernardino (92404) *(P-16213)*

St George Auto Center Inc .... D 657 212-5042
 13861 Harbor Blvd Garden Grove (92843) *(P-14703)*

St George Logistics, Compton *Also Called: Tropicana Manufacturing Co Inc (P-9122)*

St Jhns Lthran Ch Bakersfield .... C 661 665-7815
 4500 Buena Vista Rd Bakersfield (93311) *(P-17421)*

St John Boutiques, Irvine *Also Called: St John Knits Intl Inc (P-2071)*

St John Knits, Anaheim *Also Called: St John Knits Inc (P-2133)*

St John Knits, Anaheim *Also Called: St John Knits Intl Inc (P-2134)*

St John Knits Inc (DH).................................. **B 877 750-1171**
 5515 E La Palma Ave Ste 100 Anaheim (92807) *(P-2133)*

St John Knits Intl Inc .... A 949 863-1171
 17421 Derian Ave Irvine (92614) *(P-2071)*

St John Knits Intl Inc (HQ)........................... **C 949 863-1171**
 5515 E La Palma Ave Anaheim (92807) *(P-2134)*

St Johns Community Health (PA)................... **C 323 541-1411**
 808 W 58th St Los Angeles (90037) *(P-15527)*

St Johns Lthran Schl Chldren C, Bakersfield *Also Called: St Jhns Lthran Ch Bakersfield (P-17421)*

St Johns Regional Medical Ctr, Oxnard *Also Called: Dignity Health (P-15978)*

St Joseph Center .... D 310 396-6468
 204 Hampton Dr Venice (90291) *(P-17014)*

St Joseph Health Per Care Svcs .... D 800 365-1110
 1315 Corona Pointe Ct Ste 201 Corona (92879) *(P-16422)*

St Joseph Hospital of Orange (DH).............. **A 714 633-9111**
 1100 W Stewart Dr Orange (92868) *(P-16214)*

St Joseph Hospital of Orange .... C 714 568-5500
 3345 Michelson Dr Ste 100 Irvine (92612) *(P-16215)*

St Joseph Hospital of Orange .... C 714 771-8037
 1100 W Stewart Dr Orange (92868) *(P-16216)*

St Joseph Hospital of Orange .... C 714 771-8222
 1310 W Stewart Dr Ste 203 Orange (92868) *(P-16217)*

St Joseph Hospital of Orange .... C 714 771-8006
 363 S Main St Ste 211 Orange (92868) *(P-16218)*

St Josephs Physical Rehab Svcs, Orange *Also Called: St Joseph Hospital of Orange (P-16217)*

St Josephs School, Placentia *Also Called: Roman Cthlic Diocese of Orange (P-16821)*

St Jseph Heritg Med Group LLC (PA)........... **C 714 633-1011**
 2212 E 4th St Ste 201 Santa Ana (92705) *(P-15482)*

St Jseph Hlth Sys HM Care Svc .... A 714 712-9500
 200 W Center Street Promenade Anaheim (92805) *(P-16423)*

St Jude Hospital (DH).................................. **A 714 871-3280**
 101 E Valencia Mesa Dr Fullerton (92835) *(P-16219)*

St Jude Medical LLC .... E 949 769-5000
 2375 Morse Ave Irvine (92614) *(P-3508)*

St Louis Rams, Agoura Hills *Also Called: Los Angeles Rams LLC (P-15031)*

St Madeleine Sophies Center .... D 619 442-5129
 2119 E Madison Ave El Cajon (92019) *(P-17067)*

St Mary Medical Center (DH)....................... **A 562 491-9000**
 1050 Linden Ave Long Beach (90813) *(P-16220)*

St Mary Medical Center LLC (HQ)................. **C 760 242-2311**
 18300 Us Highway 18 Apple Valley (92307) *(P-16221)*

St Mary Medical Center LLC .... A 760 946-8767
 16000 Kasota Rd Apple Valley (92307) *(P-16222)*

ST MARY'S MEDICAL CENTER, Long Beach *Also Called: St Marys Medical Center (P-18220)*

St Mary's School Of Nursing, Long Beach *Also Called: St Mary Medical Center (P-16220)*

St Marys Medical Center .... A 562 491-9230
 1050 Linden Ave Long Beach (90813) *(P-18220)*

St Paul Brands Inc .... E 714 903-1000
 11842 Monarch St Garden Grove (92841) *(P-3306)*

St Paul's Villa, National City *Also Called: St Pauls Episcopal Home Inc (P-17200)*

St Pauls Episcopal Home Inc .... D 619 239-2097
 2635 2nd Ave Ofc San Diego (92103) *(P-17198)*

St Pauls Episcopal Home Inc .... D 619 239-8687
 235 Nutmeg St San Diego (92103) *(P-17199)*

St Pauls Episcopal Home Inc .... D 619 232-2996
 2700 E 4th St National City (91950) *(P-17200)*

ST VINCENT DE PAUL SOCIETY OF, Los Angeles *Also Called: Society of St Vncent De Paul C (P-17470)*

St Vincent Health Care, Pasadena *Also Called: Vincent-Hayley Enterprises Inc (P-16258)*

St Worth Container LLC .... D 909 390-4550
 727 S Wanamaker Ave Ontario (91761) *(P-2691)*

St. Edna Sb-Cute Rhblttion Ctr, Santa Ana *Also Called: Covenant Care California LLC (P-15610)*

St. John's Health Center, Santa Monica *Also Called: Providence St Johns Hlth Ctr (P-16153)*

St. Johns Pleasant Valley Hosp, Camarillo *Also Called: Dignity Health (P-15977)*

STA, Thousand Palms *Also Called: Sunline Transit Agency (P-8807)*

STA Pharmaceutical US LLC .... E 609 606-6499
 6114 Nancy Ridge Dr San Diego (92121) *(P-3509)*

Staar, Lake Forest *Also Called: Staar Surgical Company (P-8417)*

Staar Surgical Company (PA)........................ **A 626 303-7902**
 25510 Commercentre Dr Lake Forest (92630) *(P-8417)*

Stability Healthcare, Pasadena *Also Called: Stability Healthcare Inc (P-13624)*

Stability Healthcare Inc .... B 626 568-1540
 87 E Green St Ste 302 Pasadena (91105) *(P-13624)*

Stable Auto Corporation .... E 415 967-2719
 124 Jupiter St Encinitas (92024) *(P-7100)*

Staco Switch, Irvine *Also Called: Staco Systems Inc (P-6311)*

Staco Systems Inc (HQ)............................... D 949 297-8700
 7 Morgan Irvine (92618) *(P-6311)*

Stadco (HQ).. D 323 227-8888
 107 S Avenue 20 Los Angeles (90031) *(P-5625)*

Staff Assistance, Thousand Oaks *Also Called: Staff Assistance Inc (P-16424)*

Staff Assistance Inc (PA)............................. **B 818 894-7879**
 72 Moody Ct Ste 100 Thousand Oaks (91360) *(P-16424)*

Staff Assistance Inc .... B 805 371-9980
 72 Moody Ct Ste 100 Thousand Oaks (91360) *(P-13574)*

Staff Pro Inc .... B 619 544-1774
 675 Convention Way San Diego (92101) *(P-14354)*

Staff Pro Inc (PA).. **A 714 230-7200**
 15272 Newsboy Cir Huntington Beach (92649) *(P-14422)*

Staff Pro Inc .... B 323 528-1929
 900 N Broadway Santa Ana (92701) *(P-14423)*

Staffing Solutions, Montebello *Also Called: L&T Staffing Inc (P-13538)*

Stainless Fixtures Inc .... E 909 622-1615
 1250 E Franklin Ave Pomona (91766) *(P-2615)*

Stainless Stl Fabricators Inc .... D 714 739-9904
15120 Desman Rd La Mirada (90638) *(P-10406)*

Stake Fastener, Chino *Also Called: Dupree Inc (P-5125)*

Stance, San Clemente *Also Called: Stance Inc (P-10729)*

Stance Inc (PA).................................... C 949 391-9030
197 Avenida La Pata San Clemente (92673) *(P-10729)*

Stand 8 Technology Services, Seal Beach *Also Called: Talent & Acquisition LLC (P-13837)*

STAND STRONG, San Luis Obispo *Also Called: Lumina Alliance (P-16976)*

Standard Armament, Glendale *Also Called: SAI Industries (P-5355)*

Standard Bldg Solutions Inc .... D 661 387-1110
6505 Zerker Rd Shafter (93263) *(P-1097)*

Standard Calibrations Inc .... D 619 477-1668
681 Anita St Ste 103 Chula Vista (91911) *(P-14732)*

Standard Chartered Bank .... D 626 639-8000
601 S Figueroa St Ste 2775 Los Angeles (90017) *(P-11779)*

Standard Drywall Inc (HQ)...................... B 619 443-7034
9831 Channel Rd Lakeside (92040) *(P-1030)*

Standard Filter Corporation (PA).............. E 866 443-3615
3801 Ocean Ranch Blvd Ste 107 Oceanside (92056) *(P-5777)*

Standard Industries, Anaheim *Also Called: Si Manufacturing Inc (P-6938)*

Standard Insurance Company .... D 714 634-8200
500 N State College Blvd Ste 1000 Orange (92868) *(P-12051)*

Standard Sales Llc (PA)........................ E 323 269-0510
2801 E 12th St Los Angeles (90023) *(P-8544)*

Standard Tool & Die Co, Los Angeles *Also Called: Stadco (P-5625)*

Standard-Southern Corporation .... C 213 624-1831
715 E 4th St Los Angeles (90013) *(P-9042)*

Standard-Southern Corporation .... C 213 624-1831
440 S Central Ave Los Angeles (90013) *(P-9043)*

Standardvision LLC .... E 323 222-3630
3370 N San Fernando Rd Ste 206 Los Angeles (90065) *(P-8638)*

Standish Precision Products, Fallbrook *Also Called: Fallbrook Industries Inc (P-5186)*

Standridge Granite Corporation .... E 562 946-6334
9437 Santa Fe Springs Rd Santa Fe Springs (90670) *(P-4478)*

Staness Jonekos Entps Inc .... E 818 606-2710
4000 W Magnolia Blvd Ste D Burbank (91505) *(P-1857)*

Stanford Advanced Materials, Lake Forest *Also Called: Oceania International LLC (P-4620)*

Stanford Crt Nrsing Cntr-Sntee, Santee *Also Called: Life Gnerations Healthcare LLC (P-15864)*

Stanford Mu Corporation .... E 310 605-2888
20725 Annalee Ave Carson (90746) *(P-7673)*

Stanford Sign & Awning Inc (PA)............ E 619 423-6200
2556 Faivre St Chula Vista (91911) *(P-8639)*

Stanley G Alexander Inc (PA).................. C 714 731-1658
2942 Dow Ave Tustin (92780) *(P-8974)*

Stanley National Hardware, Lake Forest *Also Called: National Manufacturing Co (P-4784)*

Stanley Steemer Carpet Cleaner, San Diego *Also Called: Colt Services Inc (P-13135)*

Stanley Steemer of Los Angeles, Azusa *Also Called: Jourducci Inc (P-13137)*

Stansport, Los Angeles *Also Called: Standard Sales Llc (P-8544)*

Stantec Architecture Inc .... D 626 796-9141
300 N Lake Ave Ste 400 Pasadena (91101) *(P-17690)*

Stantec Consulting Svcs Inc .... D 626 796-9141
300 N Lake Ave Ste 400 Pasadena (91101) *(P-17636)*

Stantec Consulting Svcs Inc .... C 949 923-6000
38 Technology Dr Ste 250 Irvine (92618) *(P-17691)*

Stantec Holdings Del III Inc .... B 661 396-3770
5500 Ming Ave Ste 300 Bakersfield (93309) *(P-12615)*

Stantec Oil and Gas, Bakersfield *Also Called: Stantec Holdings Del III Inc (P-12615)*

Stanton Carpet Corp .... E 562 945-8711
2209 Pine Ave Manhattan Beach (90266) *(P-1957)*

Stantru Reinforcing Steel, Fontana *Also Called: Stantru Resources Inc (P-504)*

Stantru Resources Inc .... D 909 587-1441
11175 Redwood Ave Fontana (92337) *(P-504)*

Stanzino Inc (PA)................................ E 213 746-8822
16325 S Avalon Blvd Gardena (90248) *(P-1887)*

Stanzino Inc .... C 818 602-5171
17937 Santa Rita St Encino (91316) *(P-1888)*

Star Die Casting Inc .... D 562 698-0627
12209 Slauson Ave Santa Fe Springs (90670) *(P-4790)*

Star Food Snacks, Colton *Also Called: Star Food Snacks Intl Inc (P-1272)*

Star Food Snacks Intl Inc .... D 909 825-8882
125 E Laurel St Colton (92324) *(P-1272)*

Star Ford Lincoln Mercury, Glendale *Also Called: Los Feliz Ford Inc (P-11374)*

Star Laundry Services Inc .... D 619 572-1009
3410 Main St San Diego (92113) *(P-13133)*

Star Milling Co .... D 951 657-3143
23901 Water St Perris (92570) *(P-1433)*

Star Nail International, Valencia *Also Called: Star Nail Products Inc (P-10653)*

Star Nail Products Inc .... D 661 257-3376
29120 Avenue Paine Valencia (91355) *(P-10653)*

Star of Ca LLC .... D 818 986-7827
15260 Ventura Blvd Ste 1140 Sherman Oaks (91403) *(P-16618)*

Star of Ca LLC .... D 805 466-1638
8834 Morro Rd Atascadero (93422) *(P-16619)*

Star of Ca LLC .... D 805 379-1401
501 Marin St Ste 225 Thousand Oaks (91360) *(P-16620)*

Star Plastic Design .... D 310 530-7119
25914 President Ave Harbor City (90710) *(P-4248)*

Star Pro Security Patrol Inc .... C 714 617-5056
3303 Harbor Blvd Ste B3 Costa Mesa (92626) *(P-14355)*

Star Scrap Metal Company Inc .... D 562 921-5045
1509 S Bluff Rd Montebello (90640) *(P-9767)*

Star Services, San Diego *Also Called: Star Laundry Services Inc (P-13133)*

Star Shield Solutions LLC .... D 866 662-4477
4315 Santa Ana St Ontario (91761) *(P-4249)*

Star Trac Fitness, Irvine *Also Called: Star Trac Strength Inc (P-8545)*

Star Trac Strength Inc .... B 714 669-1660
14410 Myford Rd Irvine (92606) *(P-8545)*

Star Waggons LLC .... D 818 367-5946
13334 Ralston Ave Sylmar (91342) *(P-14904)*

Starco Enterprises Inc (PA).................... D 323 266-7111
3137 E 26th St Los Angeles (90058) *(P-5720)*

Stark Awning & Canvas, Chula Vista *Also Called: Stark Mfg Co (P-2242)*

Stark Mfg Co .... E 619 425-5880
76 Broadway Chula Vista (91910) *(P-2242)*

Stark Services .... D 818 985-2003
12444 Victory Blvd Ste 300 North Hollywood (91606) *(P-14157)*

Starlight Educational Center, Westminster *Also Called: Westview Services Inc (P-17075)*

Starpint 1031 Property MGT LLC .... C 310 247-0550
450 N Roxbury Dr Ste 1050 Beverly Hills (90210) *(P-12533)*

Starrett Kinemetric Engrg Inc .... E 949 348-1213
26052 Merit Cir Ste 103 Laguna Hills (92653) *(P-5626)*

Startel Corporation (PA)........................ D 949 863-8700
16 Goodyear B-125 Irvine (92618) *(P-13830)*

Startengine Crowdfunding Inc .... D 800 317-2200
4100 W Alameda Ave Fl 3 Burbank (91505) *(P-11874)*

Starwood Hotels & Resorts, Costa Mesa *Also Called: South Coast Westin Hotel Co (P-13029)*

Starwood Hotels & Resorts, San Diego *Also Called: Starwood Htels Rsrts Wrldwide (P-13035)*

Starwood Htels Rsrts Wrldwide .... C 619 239-2200
910 Broadway Cir San Diego (92101) *(P-13035)*

Starwood Htels Rsrts Wrldwide .... C 909 622-2220
601 W Mckinley Ave Pomona (91768) *(P-13036)*

Starz Encore Group, Santa Monica *Also Called: Starz Entertainment LLC (P-14860)*

Starz Entertainment LLC (DH).................. A 720 852-7700
2700 Colorado Ave Ste 200 Santa Monica (90404) *(P-14860)*

Statco, Huntington Beach *Also Called: DSI Process Systems LLC (P-10370)*

State Bar of California .... D 805 544-7551
755 Santa Rosa St Ste 310 San Luis Obispo (93401) *(P-17308)*

State Bar of California .... D 213 765-1520
845 S Figueroa St Los Angeles (90017) *(P-17309)*

State Compensation Insur Fund .... D 888 782-8338
2901 N Ventura Rd Ste 100 Oxnard (93036) *(P-12067)*

State Compensation Insur Fund .... A 818 888-4750
21300 Victory Blvd Ste 600 Woodland Hills (91367) *(P-12135)*

State Compensation Insur Fund .... C 323 266-5000
900 Corporate Center Dr Monterey Park (91754) *(P-12136)*

State Compensation Insur Fund .... D 661 664-4000
9801 Camino Media Ste 101 Bakersfield (93311) *(P-12137)*

State Compensation Insur Fund .... C 714 565-5000
1750 E 4th St Fl 3 Santa Ana (92705) *(P-12138)*

Employee Codes: A=Over 500 employees, B=251-500
C=101-250, D=51-100, E=20-50, F=10-19, G=1-9

2025 Southern California
Business Directory and Buyers Guide

© Mergent Inc. 1-800-342-5647
1197

State Compensation Insur Fund .... C 888 782-8338
10105 Pacific Heights Blvd Ste 120 San Diego (92121) *(P-12139)*

State Compensation Insur Fund .... C 888 782-8338
6301 Day St Riverside (92507) *(P-12140)*

State Farm Insurance, Bakersfield *Also Called: State Farm Mutl Auto Insur Co (P-12255)*

State Farm Mutl Auto Insur Co .... D 309 766-2311
900 Old River Rd 400 Bakersfield (93311) *(P-12255)*

State Fish Co Inc .... C 310 547-9530
624 W 9th St Ste 100 San Pedro (90731) *(P-1713)*

State Pipe & Supply Inc .... E 909 356-5670
2180 N Locust Ave Rialto (92377) *(P-4526)*

Statek, Orange *Also Called: Statek Corporation (P-7054)*

Statek Corporation .... C 714 639-7810
1449 W Orange Grove Ave Orange (92868) *(P-7053)*

Statek Corporation (HQ) .... C 714 639-7810
512 N Main St Orange (92868) *(P-7054)*

Stater Bros Markets .... E 714 963-0949
10114 Adams Ave Huntington Beach (92646) *(P-11281)*

Stater Bros Markets .... E 714 991-5310
1131 N State College Blvd Anaheim (92806) *(P-11282)*

States Logistics Services Inc .... D 714 523-1276
7151 Cate Dr Buena Park (90621) *(P-9112)*

States Logistics Services Inc (PA) .... C 714 521-6520
5650 Dolly Ave Buena Park (90621) *(P-9337)*

Statewide Trffic Sfety Sgns In (HQ) .... E 949 553-8272
2722 S Fairview St Fl 2 Santa-Ana (92704) *(P-6693)*

Statewide Trffic Sfety Sgns In .... E 714 468-1919
2722 S Fairview St Santa Ana (92704) *(P-8640)*

Statewide Trffic Sfety Sgns In .... E 949 553-8272
1100 Main St Ste 100 Irvine (92614) *(P-8641)*

Station Venture Operations LP .... D 619 231-3939
9680 Granite Ridge Dr San Diego (92123) *(P-9518)*

Statrad - Radconnect, San Diego *Also Called: Nucleushealth LLC (P-13787)*

Staub Metals LLC .... D 562 602-2200
7747 Rosecrans Ave Paramount (90723) *(P-10157)*

Stauber, Fullerton *Also Called: Stauber Prfmce Ingredients Inc (P-3333)*

Stauber California Inc .... D 714 441-3900
4120 N Palm St Fullerton (92835) *(P-3332)*

Stauber Prfmce Ingredients Inc (HQ) .... D 714 441-3900
4120 N Palm St Fullerton (92835) *(P-3333)*

Stauber USA, Fullerton *Also Called: Stauber California Inc (P-3332)*

Stavatti Industries Ltd .... E 651 238-5369
3670 El Camino Dr San Bernardino (92404) *(P-255)*

Stavros Enterprises Inc .... E 888 463-2293
681 Arrow Grand Cir Covina (91722) *(P-14793)*

STC Netcom Inc (PA) .... D 951 685-8181
11611 Industry Ave Fontana (92337) *(P-966)*

Stci, Rancho Cucamonga *Also Called: Superior Tank Co Inc (P-4930)*

Steadfast Companies, Irvine *Also Called: Steadfast Management Co Inc (P-12534)*

Steadfast Management Co Inc .... D 714 542-2229
15520 Tustin Village Way Tustin (92780) *(P-12367)*

Steadfast Management Co Inc (PA) .... D 949 748-3000
18100 Von Karman Ave Ste 500 Irvine (92612) *(P-12534)*

Steady Platform Inc .... D 678 792-8364
5636 Fallsgrove St Los Angeles (90016) *(P-13831)*

Stealth Aerospace, Commerce *Also Called: Fastener Dist Holdings LLC (P-10437)*

Stearns Conrad and Schmidt Consulting Engineers Inc (PA) .... D 562 426-9544
3900 Kilroy Airport Way Ste 100 Long Beach (90806) *(P-17637)*

Stearns Home Loans, Costa Mesa *Also Called: Stearns Lending LLC (P-11935)*

Stearns Lending LLC .... C 714 513-7777
555 Anton Blvd Ste 300 Costa Mesa (92626) *(P-11935)*

Stearns Product Dev Corp (PA) .... D 951 657-0379
20281 Harvill Ave Perris (92570) *(P-5835)*

Stec Inc (HQ) .... B 415 222-9996
3355 Michelson Dr Ste 100 Irvine (92612) *(P-5889)*

Steel Unlimited Inc .... D 909 873-1222
4210 Riverwalk Pkwy Riverside (92505) *(P-10158)*

Steel Works Etc, Oxnard *Also Called: Millworks Etc Inc (P-4894)*

Steel-Tech Industrial Corp .... E 951 270-0144
1268 Sherborn St Corona (92879) *(P-4871)*

Steelco USA, Chino *Also Called: Wcs Equipment Holdings LLC (P-4572)*

Steelco USA, Chino *Also Called: Wcs Equipment Holdings LLC (P-5056)*

Steeldeck Inc .... E 323 290-2100
13147 S Western Ave Gardena (90249) *(P-8728)*

Steeldyne Industries .... E 714 630-6200
2871 E La Cresta Ave Anaheim (92806) *(P-5039)*

Steelhead, Los Angeles *Also Called: Deutsch La Inc (P-13205)*

Steelscape LLC .... E 909 987-4711
11200 Arrow Rte Rancho Cucamonga (91730) *(P-5347)*

Steelwave LLC .... A 310 821-1111
4553 Glencoe Ave Ste 300 Marina Del Rey (90292) *(P-12580)*

Steico, Oceanside *Also Called: Steico Industries Inc (P-5215)*

Steico Industries Inc .... C 760 438-8015
1814 Ord Way Oceanside (92056) *(P-5215)*

Stein Industries Inc (PA) .... E 714 522-4560
4005 Artesia Ave Fullerton (92833) *(P-5040)*

Stein Sam & Rose Education Ctr, San Diego *Also Called: Vista Hill Foundation (P-16859)*

Steinberg Architects, Los Angeles *Also Called: Steinberg Hart (P-17692)*

Steinberg Hart (PA) .... D 213 629-0500
818 W 7th St Ste 1100 Los Angeles (90017) *(P-17692)*

Steiny & Company, Corona *Also Called: Computer Service Company (P-6678)*

Steiny and Company Inc .... B 213 382-2331
221 N Ardmore Ave Los Angeles (90004) *(P-967)*

Stell Industries Inc .... E 951 369-8777
1951 S Parco Ave Ste B Ontario (91761) *(P-5088)*

Stellant Systems Inc (DH) .... A 310 517-6000
3100 Lomita Blvd Torrance (90505) *(P-7813)*

Stellar Exploration Inc .... E 805 459-1425
835 Airport Dr San Luis Obispo (93401) *(P-7656)*

Stellar Microelectronics Inc .... C 661 775-3500
9340 Owensmouth Ave Chatsworth (91311) *(P-6899)*

Stepan Company .... C 714 776-9870
1208 N Patt St Anaheim (92801) *(P-3294)*

Steren Electronic Solutions, San Diego *Also Called: Steren Electronics Intl LLC (P-10284)*

Steren Electronics Intl LLC (PA) .... D 800 266-3333
8445 Camino Santa Fe Ste 203 San Diego (92121) *(P-10284)*

Steril-Aire Inc .... E 818 565-1128
25060 Avenue Stanford Ste 160 Valencia (91355) *(P-6517)*

Steris, San Diego *Also Called: Steris Corporation (P-8302)*

Steris Corporation .... E 858 586-1166
9020 Activity Rd Ste D San Diego (92126) *(P-8302)*

Steris Isomedix, Temecula *Also Called: Isomedix Operations Inc (P-8277)*

Sterisyn Inc .... E 805 991-9694
11969 Challenger Ct Moorpark (93021) *(P-3510)*

Sterisyn Scientific, Moorpark *Also Called: Sterisyn Inc (P-3510)*

Sterling BMW, Newport Beach *Also Called: Sterling Motors Ltd (P-11413)*

Sterling Care Inc .... C 619 470-6700
2575 E 8th St National City (91950) *(P-15783)*

Sterling Carpets & Flooring, Anaheim *Also Called: Rm Partners Inc (P-11525)*

Sterling Motors Ltd .... D 949 645-5900
3000 W Coast Hwy Newport Beach (92663) *(P-11413)*

Sterling Pacific Meat Co., Commerce *Also Called: Interstate Meat Co Inc (P-5675)*

Sterling Plumbing Inc .... D 714 641-5480
3111 W Central Ave Santa Ana (92704) *(P-844)*

Steve P Rados Inc .... C 619 328-1360
1638 Pioneer Way El Cajon (92020) *(P-656)*

Steven Global Freight Services, Redondo Beach *Also Called: Stevens Global Logistics Inc (P-9338)*

Steven Handelman Studios Inc (PA) .... E 805 884-9070
716 N Milpas St Santa Barbara (93103) *(P-4561)*

Steven Label Corporation (PA) .... C 562 698-9971
11926 Burke St Santa Fe Springs (90670) *(P-10676)*

Stevens Global Logistics Inc (PA) .... D 800 229-7284
3700 Redondo Beach Ave Redondo Beach (90278) *(P-9338)*

Stevens Transportation Inc .... C 661 366-3286
7100 E Brundage Ln Bakersfield (93307) *(P-8975)*

Stevens Trucking, Bakersfield *Also Called: Stevens Transportation Inc (P-8975)*

Steves Plating Corporation .... C 818 842-2184
3111 N San Fernando Blvd Burbank (91504) *(P-2594)*

Steward Plastics Inc .... D 949 581-9530
23322 Del Lago Dr Laguna Hills (92653) *(P-4250)*

Mergent email: customerrelations@mergent.com
1198

2025 Southern California
Business Directory and Buyers Guide

(P-0000) Products & Services Section entry number
(PA)=Parent Co (HQ)=Headquarters (DH)=Div Headquarters

Stewart Filmscreen Corp (PA) .... C 310 784-5300
　1161 Sepulveda Blvd Torrance (90502) *(P-8444)*

Stewart Title California Inc (DH) .... C 619 692-1600
　7676 Hazard Center Dr Ste 1400 San Diego (92108) *(P-12156)*

Stewart Title California Inc .... C 818 502-2700
　525 N Brand Blvd Ste 200 Glendale (91203) *(P-12562)*

Stg Auto Group, Garden Grove Also Called: St George Auto Center Inc *(P-14703)*

Stic-Adhesive Products Co Inc .... C 323 268-2956
　3950 Medford St Los Angeles (90063) *(P-3780)*

Stila Cosmetics, Glendale Also Called: Stila Styles LLC *(P-3689)*

Stila Styles LLC (HQ) .... E 866 784-5201
　801 N Brand Blvd Ste 910 Glendale (91203) *(P-3689)*

Stillhouse LLC .... E 323 498-1111
　8201 Beverly Blvd Ste 300 Los Angeles (90048) *(P-1599)*

Stillwater Post Acute, El Cajon Also Called: Eldorado Care Center LP *(P-15626)*

Stines Machine Inc .... E 760 599-9955
　2481 Coral St Vista (92081) *(P-6244)*

Stir Foods, Orange Also Called: Pacifica Foods LLC *(P-1371)*

Stir Foods LLC .... E 714 871-9231
　1851 N Delilah St Corona (92879) *(P-1402)*

Stitch Industries Inc .... E 888 282-0842
　767 S Alameda St Ste 360 Los Angeles (90021) *(P-2460)*

Stjohn God Rtirement Care Ctr .... C 323 731-0641
　2468 S St Andrews Pl Los Angeles (90018) *(P-15784)*

Stn Digital LLC .... D 619 292-8683
　3033 Bunker Hill St San Diego (92109) *(P-13247)*

Stockbridge/Sbe Holdings LLC .... A 323 655-8000
　5900 Wilshire Blvd Ste 3100 Los Angeles (90036) *(P-13037)*

Stockdale Capital Partners LLC .... D 310 693-4400
　11601 Wilshire Blvd Ste 1750 Los Angeles (90025) *(P-12737)*

Stockdale Country Club .... D 661 832-0310
　7001 Stockdale Hwy Bakersfield (93309) *(P-15178)*

Stockdale Medical Offices, Bakersfield Also Called: Kaiser Foundation Hospitals *(P-15356)*

Stockmar Industrial, Long Beach Also Called: Elite Craftsman *(P-13373)*

Stoll Metalcraft Inc .... C 661 295-0401
　24808 Anza Dr Valencia (91355) *(P-5041)*

Stolo Cabinets Inc (PA) .... E 714 529-7303
　860 Challenger St Brea (92821) *(P-2519)*

Stolo Custom Cabinets, Brea Also Called: Stolo Cabinets Inc *(P-2519)*

Stone Brewing Co LLC .... C 619 269-2100
　2816 Historic Decatur Rd Ste 116 San Diego (92106) *(P-1553)*

Stone Brewing Co LLC .... C 760 294-7899
　1977 Citracado Pkwy Escondido (92029) *(P-1554)*

Stone Brewing Co LLC (DH) .... E 760 294-7866
　1999 Citracado Pkwy Escondido (92029) *(P-11619)*

Stone Brewing Co., Escondido Also Called: Stone Brewing Co LLC *(P-11619)*

Stone Canyon Inds Holdings LLC (PA) .... E 424 316-2061
　1875 Century Park E Ste 320 Los Angeles (90067) *(P-18221)*

Stone Canyon Industries LLC .... A 310 570-4869
　1875 Century Park E Ste 320 Los Angeles (90067) *(P-4251)*

Stone Entertainment, Costa Mesa Also Called: Volcom LLC *(P-14028)*

Stonebridge Rlty Advisors Inc .... B 949 597-8700
　27102 Towne Centre Dr Foothill Ranch (92610) *(P-13038)*

Stonecalibre LLC (PA) .... D 310 774-0014
　2049 Century Park E Ste 2550 Los Angeles (90067) *(P-12738)*

Stonehouse Restaurant, Santa Barbara Also Called: San Ysidro Bb Property LLC *(P-13013)*

Stony Apparel Corp (PA) .... C 323 981-9080
　1201 S Grand Ave Los Angeles (90015) *(P-2054)*

Stop Hop Center, Carson Also Called: Anschutz Sthern Cal Spt Cmplex *(P-15192)*

Storage Front, Newport Beach Also Called: Tenant Inc *(P-13842)*

Storage West, Marina Del Rey Also Called: Laaco Ltd *(P-12377)*

Store 3, El Cajon Also Called: Wetzels Pretzels LLC *(P-11303)*

Storm, Torrance Also Called: Storm Industries Inc *(P-5478)*

Storm Industries Inc (PA) .... D 310 534-5232
　970 W 190th St Torrance (90502) *(P-5478)*

Storm Manufacturing Group Inc .... D 310 326-8287
　23201 Normandie Ave Torrance (90501) *(P-5370)*

Str, Carlsbad Also Called: Systems & Technology RES LLC *(P-17639)*

Stradling Ycca Crlson Ruth A P (PA) .... C 949 725-4000
　660 Newport Center Dr Ste 1600 Newport Beach (92660) *(P-16786)*

Straight Forwarding Inc .... D 909 594-3400
　20275 Business Pkwy Walnut (91789) *(P-9339)*

Straight Talk Counseling Ctr, La Mirada Also Called: Straight Talk Inc *(P-17015)*

Straight Talk Inc .... D 562 943-0195
　13710 La Mirada Blvd La Mirada (90638) *(P-17015)*

Strand Art Company Inc .... E 714 777-0444
　4700 E Hunter Ave Anaheim (92807) *(P-4252)*

Strasbaugh, San Luis Obispo Also Called: R H Strasbaugh *(P-5549)*

Strat Edge, Santee Also Called: Stratedge Corporation *(P-6900)*

Strata Federal Credit Union .... D 661 327-9461
　1717 Truxtun Ave Bakersfield (93301) *(P-11816)*

Strata Forest Products Inc (PA) .... E 714 751-0800
　2600 S Susan St Santa Ana (92704) *(P-2287)*

Strata Information Group Inc (PA) .... D 619 296-0170
　3935 Harney St Ste 203 San Diego (92110) *(P-14255)*

Strata USA Llc .... E 888 878-7282
　333 City Blvd W Fl 17 Orange (92868) *(P-11668)*

Stratacare, Irvine Also Called: Stratacare Llc *(P-13832)*

Stratacare Llc .... C 949 743-1200
　17838 Gillette Ave Ste D Irvine (92614) *(P-13832)*

Stratcom Systems Inc .... E 858 481-9292
　2701 Loker Ave W Ste 130 Carlsbad (92010) *(P-13833)*

Stratedge Corporation .... E 866 424-4962
　9424 Abraham Way Santee (92071) *(P-6900)*

Strategic Distribution L P C
　15301 Ventura Blvd Sherman Oaks (91403) *(P-2002)*

Strategic Materials Inc .... E 323 415-0166
　3211 E 26th St Vernon (90058) *(P-10542)*

Strategic Operations Inc .... C 858 244-0559
　4705 Ruffin Rd San Diego (92123) *(P-14602)*

Strategic Property Management .... D 619 295-2211
　2055 3rd Ave Ste 200 San Diego (92101) *(P-12535)*

Strategic Sanitation Svcs Inc .... C 949 444-9009
　25801 Obrero Dr Ste 11 Mission Viejo (92691) *(P-11021)*

Strategy Companion Corp .... D 714 460-8398
　100 Pacifica Ste 220 Irvine (92618) *(P-14040)*

Stratgic Hlthcare Programs LLC .... C 805 963-9446
　6500 Hollister Ave Ste 210 Goleta (93117) *(P-13834)*

Stratoflex Product Division, Camarillo Also Called: Parker-Hannifin Corporation *(P-7536)*

Stratos Renewables Corporation .... E 310 402-5901
　9440 Santa Monica Blvd Ste 401 Beverly Hills (90210) *(P-3737)*

Stratus Group Duo LLC .... E 323 581-3663
　4401 S Downey Rd Vernon (90058) *(P-1655)*

Stratus Real Estate Inc .... C 626 441-5549
　435 Garfield Ave South Pasadena (91030) *(P-11953)*

Stratus Real Estate Inc .... C 310 549-7028
　1100 N Banning Blvd Apt 111 Wilmington (90744) *(P-11954)*

Stratus Realestate, South Pasadena Also Called: Stratus Real Estate Inc *(P-11953)*

Straub Distributing Co Ltd (PA) .... C 714 779-4000
　4633 E La Palma Ave Anaheim (92807) *(P-11052)*

Streamelements Inc (PA) .... D 323 928-7848
　11400 W Olympic Blvd Los Angeles (90064) *(P-17862)*

Streamland Media LLC .... D 818 855-7467
　3900 W Alameda Ave Fl 10 Burbank (91505) *(P-14905)*

Streamline Dsign Slkscreen Inc (PA) .... D 805 884 1025
　1299 S Wells Rd Ventura (93004) *(P-2028)*

Streamline Finishes Inc .... D 949 600-8964
　26429 Rancho Pkwy S Ste 140 Lake Forest (92630) *(P-589)*

Strech Plastics Incorporated .... E 951 922-2224
　900 John St Ste J Banning (92220) *(P-10501)*

Street Smart 247, El Segundo Also Called: Street Smart LLC *(P-14041)*

Street Smart LLC .... E 866 924-4644
　100 N Pacific Coast Hwy El Segundo (90245) *(P-14041)*

Stremicks Heritage Foods LLC (HQ) .... B 714 775-5000
　4002 Westminster Ave Santa Ana (92703) *(P-1335)*

Stress-O-Pedic, Ontario Also Called: Stress-O-Pedic Mattress Co Inc *(P-2493)*

Stress-O-Pedic Mattress Co Inc .... D 909 605-2010
　2060 S Wineville Ave Ste A Ontario (91761) *(P-2493)*

Stretch Forming Corporation .... D 951 443-0911
　804 S Redlands Ave Perris (92570) *(P-5042)*

Stretto Inc (PA) .... D 949 222-1212
　410 Exchange Ste 100 Irvine (92602) *(P-16787)*

ALPHABETIC

Stria, Bakersfield *Also Called: Technosocialworkcom LLC (P-14159)*

Strike Technology Inc .... E 562 437-3428
24311 Wilmington Ave Carson (90745) *(P-7055)*

Stringking Inc (PA) .... E **310 503-8901**
19100 S Vermont Ave Gardena (90248) *(P-1979)*

Stromasys Inc .... D 919 239-8450
871 Marlborough Ave Ste 100 Riverside (92507) *(P-14042)*

Strong Hand Tools, Santa Fe Springs *Also Called: Valtra Inc (P-10414)*

Strottman, Irvine *Also Called: Strottman International Inc (P-8479)*

Strottman International Inc (PA) .... E 949 623-7900
28 Executive Park Ste 200 Irvine (92614) *(P-8479)*

Strouk Group LLC .... C 323 939-7792
6333 W 3rd St Ste 150 Los Angeles (90036) *(P-10881)*

Structral Prsrvtion Systems LL .... C 714 891-9080
11800 Monarch St Garden Grove (92841) *(P-1136)*

Structural Composites Inds LLC (DH) .... E 909 594-7777
336 Enterprise Pl Pomona (91768) *(P-4929)*

Structural Diagnostics Inc .... E 805 987-7755
650 Via Alondra Camarillo (93012) *(P-8065)*

Structural Stl Fabricators Inc .... E 714 761-1695
10641 Sycamore Ave Stanton (90680) *(P-4872)*

Structurecast, Bakersfield *Also Called: Golden Empire Con Pdts Inc (P-4394)*

STS Metals Inc (PA) .... D **626 969-6711**
5467 Ayon Ave Irwindale (91706) *(P-5161)*

Stuart C. Gildred Family YMCA, Santa Ynez *Also Called: Channel Islnds Yung MNS Chrstn (P-17335)*

Stuart F Cooper Co .... C 213 747-7141
1565 E 23rd St Los Angeles (90011) *(P-3110)*

Stud Welding Products, Downey *Also Called: Qualls Stud Welding Pdts Inc (P-10396)*

Student Transportation America, Santa Clarita *Also Called: Santa Barbara Trnsp Corp (P-8859)*

Student Transportation America, Escondido *Also Called: Santa Barbara Trnsp Corp (P-8883)*

Student Transportation America, Goleta *Also Called: Santa Barbara Trnsp Corp (P-8885)*

Studio 71 LP .... C 323 370-1500
8383 Wilshire Blvd Ste 1050 Beverly Hills (90211) *(P-13271)*

Studio Depot, Pacoima *Also Called: Mole-Richardson Co Ltd (P-6511)*

Studio Designer .... D 310 896-5689
1110 N Virgil Ave Los Angeles (90029) *(P-14256)*

Studio Distribution Svcs LLC .... C 818 954-6000
4000 Warner Blvd Burbank (91522) *(P-14861)*

Studio OH, Irvine *Also Called: Orange Circle Studio Corp (P-3158)*

Studio9d8 Inc .... E 626 350-0832
9743 Alesia St South El Monte (91733) *(P-1924)*

Studykik, Santa Monica *Also Called: Caerus Marketing Group LLC (P-16374)*

Sturgeon Services Intl Inc .... B 661 322-4408
3511 Gilmore Ave Bakersfield (93308) *(P-5498)*

Sturgeon Son Grading & Pav Inc (PA) .... C **661 322-4408**
3511 Gilmore Ave Bakersfield (93308) *(P-1175)*

Stutman Treister Glatt Prof Co, Los Angeles *Also Called: Stutman Trster Glatt Prof Corp (P-16788)*

Stutman Trster Glatt Prof Corp .... D 310 228-5600
1901 Avenue Of The Stars Ste 200 Los Angeles (90067) *(P-16788)*

Stv Architects Inc .... C 213 482-9444
1055 W 7th St Ste 3150 Los Angeles (90017) *(P-17693)*

Stx Entertainment, Burbank *Also Called: Stx Financing LLC (P-14862)*

Stx Financing LLC .... C 310 742-2300
3900 W Alameda Ave Fl 32 Burbank (91505) *(P-14862)*

Style Network, Los Angeles *Also Called: E Entertainment Television Inc (P-9549)*

Styrotek Inc .... C 661 725-4957
345 Road 176 Delano (93215) *(P-4020)*

Subject, Beverly Hills *Also Called: Subject Technologies Inc (P-14043)*

Subject Technologies Inc .... E 310 243-6484
345 N Maple Dr Beverly Hills (90210) *(P-14043)*

Sublitex Inc .... E 323 582-9596
1515 E 15th St Los Angeles (90021) *(P-2072)*

Sublitex Sublimation Tech, Los Angeles *Also Called: Sublitex Inc (P-2072)*

Substance Abuse Program .... E 951 791-3350
1370 S State St Ste A Hemet (92543) *(P-6901)*

Success Healthcare 1 LLC .... A 626 288-1160
7500 Hellman Ave Rosemead (91770) *(P-15483)*

Success Strategies Inst Inc .... D 949 721-6808
6 Hutton Centre Dr Ste 700 Santa Ana (92707) *(P-17068)*

Successor Agcy To Nrco Cmnty R, Norco *Also Called: City of Norco (P-18303)*

Suderman Contg Stevedores Inc (PA) .... D **409 762-8131**
3806 Worsham Ave Long Beach (90808) *(P-9148)*

Sugar Foods, Westlake Village *Also Called: Sugar Foods LLC (P-3738)*

Sugar Foods, Westlake Village *Also Called: Sugar Foods LLC (P-10981)*

Sugar Foods LLC .... D 323 727-8290
6190 E Slauson Ave Commerce (90040) *(P-1466)*

Sugar Foods LLC (HQ) .... E **805 396-5000**
3059 Townsgate Rd Ste 101 Westlake Village (91361) *(P-3738)*

Sugar Foods LLC .... D 805 230-2591
3059 Townsgate Rd Westlake Village (91361) *(P-10981)*

Sugar Foods LLC .... C 818 768-7900
6190 E Slauson Ave Commerce (90040) *(P-14603)*

Sugarsync Inc .... E 650 571-5105
6922 Hollywood Blvd Ste 500 Los Angeles (90028) *(P-14044)*

Sui Companies, Riverside *Also Called: Steel Unlimited Inc (P-10158)*

Suissa Miller Advertising LLC .... D 310 392-9666
8687 Melrose Ave West Hollywood (90069) *(P-13248)*

Suja Juice, Oceanside *Also Called: Suja Life LLC (P-11309)*

Suja Life LLC (PA) .... E **855 879-7852**
3841 Ocean Ranch Blvd Oceanside (92056) *(P-11309)*

Sukarne, City Of Industry *Also Called: Viz Cattle Corporation (P-1252)*

Sukut Construction LLC .... D 714 540-5351
4010 W Chandler Ave Santa Ana (92704) *(P-698)*

Sukut Construction Inc .... C 714 540-5351
4010 W Chandler Ave Santa Ana (92704) *(P-1176)*

Sullins Connector Solutions, San Marcos *Also Called: Sullins Electronics Corp (P-6430)*

Sullins Electronics Corp .... D 760 744-0125
801 E Mission Rd # B San Marcos (92069) *(P-6430)*

Sullivan, San Diego *Also Called: Sullivan International Group Inc (P-9789)*

Sullivan International Group Inc .... C 619 260-1432
2750 Womble Rd Ste 100 San Diego (92106) *(P-9789)*

Sullivans Stone Factory Inc .... E 760 347-5535
83778 Avenue 45 Indio (92201) *(P-4479)*

Sullivncrtsmnroe Insur Svcs LL (PA) .... C **800 427-3253**
1920 Main St Ste 600 Irvine (92614) *(P-18222)*

Sulpizio Cardiovascular Center .... D 858 657-7000
9434 Medical Center Dr La Jolla (92037) *(P-15484)*

Sulzer Elctr-Mchncal Svcs US I .... E 909 825-7971
620 S Rancho Ave Colton (92324) *(P-14751)*

Sumaria Systems LLC .... D 805 606-4973
105 13th St Vandenberg Afb (93437) *(P-17638)*

Sumitomo Rubber North Amer Inc (HQ) .... C **909 466-1116**
8656 Haven Ave Rancho Cucamonga (91730) *(P-9860)*

Sumitronics USA Inc .... E 619 661-0450
9335 Airway Rd Ste 212 San Diego (92154) *(P-6775)*

Summer Systems Inc .... D 661 257-4419
28942 Hancock Pkwy Valencia (91355) *(P-590)*

Summerwood Winery & Inn Inc .... E 805 227-1365
2175 Arbor Rd Paso Robles (93446) *(P-13039)*

Summit Enterprises Inc .... E 858 679-2100
2471 Montecito Rd Ste A Ramona (92065) *(P-2774)*

Summit Erosion Control, Ramona *Also Called: Summit Enterprises Inc (P-2774)*

Summit Interconnect, Santa Ana *Also Called: South Coast Circuits LLC (P-6773)*

Summit Interconnect Inc (HQ) .... C **714 239-2433**
223 N Crescent Way Anaheim (92801) *(P-6776)*

Summit Interconnect - Anaheim, Anaheim *Also Called: Kca Electronics Inc (P-6743)*

Summit Interconnect Orange, Orange *Also Called: Fabricated Components Corp (P-6728)*

Summit Machine LLC .... C 909 923-2744
2880 E Philadelphia St Ontario (91761) *(P-7568)*

SUN & SAIL CLUB, Lake Forest *Also Called: Lake Frest No II Mstr Hmwners (P-17353)*

Sun Air Jets LLC .... C 805 389-9301
855 Aviation Dr Ste 200 Camarillo (93010) *(P-9183)*

Sun Badge Co .... E 909 930-1444
2248 S Baker Ave Ontario (91761) *(P-8729)*

Sun Chemical Corporation .... E 562 946-2327
12963 Park St Santa Fe Springs (90670) *(P-3786)*

Sun City Palm Dsert Cmnty Assn (PA) .... D **760 200-2100**
38180 Del Webb Blvd Palm Desert (92211) *(P-17368)*

Mergent email: customerrelations@mergent.com
1200

2025 Southern California
Business Directory and Buyers Guide

(P-0000) Products & Services Section entry number
(PA)=Parent Co (HQ)=Headquarters (DH)=Div Headquarters

Sun Cmpany of San Brnrdino Cal (HQ)............B 909 889-9666
4030 Georgia Blvd San Bernardino (92407) *(P-2830)*

Sun Coast Merchandise Corp ....C 323 720-9700
6405 Randolph St Commerce (90040) *(P-10570)*

Sun Dairy Co, Los Angeles *Also Called: Pac Fill Inc (P-1333)*

Sun Diego, San Diego *Also Called: Athleisure Inc (P-11505)*

Sun Diego Charter, National City *Also Called: Sureride Charter Inc (P-8865)*

Sun Electric LP ....D 714 210-3744
2101 S Yale St Ste B Santa Ana (92704) *(P-968)*

Sun Energy Construction, Rancho Cucamonga *Also Called: Calvin Dubois (P-758)*

Sun Express, Fontana *Also Called: Hanks Inc (P-8913)*

Sun Healthcare Group Inc (DH)......................B 949 255-7100
27442 Portola Pkwy Ste 200 Foothill Ranch (92610) *(P-15485)*

Sun Hill Properties Inc ....B 818 506-2500
555 Universal Hollywood Dr Universal City (91608) *(P-13040)*

Sun Ice USA, Riverside *Also Called: Mackie International Inc (P-1319)*

SUN MAR HEALTH CARE, Riverside *Also Called: Riverside Equities LLC (P-15763)*

Sun Pacific Cold Storage, Bakersfield *Also Called: Exeter Packers Inc (P-9036)*

Sun Pacific Farming, Bakersfield *Also Called: 7th Standard Ranch Company (P-28)*

Sun Pacific Farming, Bakersfield *Also Called: Sun Pacific Marketing Coop Inc (P-10918)*

Sun Pacific Farming Coop Inc ....D 661 399-0376
33374 Lerdo Hwy Bakersfield (93308) *(P-145)*

Sun Pacific Farms, Bakersfield *Also Called: Sun Pacific Farming Coop Inc (P-145)*

Sun Pacific Marketing Coop Inc ....B 661 847-1015
31452 Old River Rd Bakersfield (93311) *(P-10918)*

Sun Pacific Marketing Coop Inc ....B 213 612-9957
33502 Lerdo Hwy Bakersfield (93308) *(P-18223)*

Sun Pacific Shippers, Pasadena *Also Called: Exeter Packers Inc (P-43)*

Sun Plastics Inc ....E 323 888-6999
7140 E Slauson Ave Commerce (90040) *(P-2739)*

Sun Solar Energy Solutions Inc ....D 661 379-7000
12625 Jomani Dr Bakersfield (93312) *(P-845)*

Sun Stone Sales, Temecula *Also Called: Sunstone Components Group Inc (P-5216)*

Sun Valley Ltg Standards Inc ....D 661 233-2000
660 W Avenue O Palmdale (93551) *(P-6475)*

Sun Valley Products Inc (HQ).........................E 818 247-8350
4626 Sperry St Los Angeles (90039) *(P-4607)*

Sun West Mortgage Company Inc (PA)............C 833 478-6937
18303 Gridley Rd Cerritos (90703) *(P-11936)*

Sun World International Inc (PA)......................A 661 392-5000
16351 Driver Rd Bakersfield (93308) *(P-119)*

Sun-Gro Commodities Inc (PA).......................E 661 393-2612
34575 Famoso Rd Bakersfield (93308) *(P-1434)*

SunAmerica, Los Angeles *Also Called: SunAmerica Inc (P-11836)*

SunAmerica, Los Angeles *Also Called: SunAmerica Life Insurance Company (P-12052)*

SunAmerica, Los Angeles *Also Called: SunAmerica Investments Inc (P-18060)*

SunAmerica Inc (HQ).....................................A 310 772-6000
1 Sun America Ctr Fl 38 Los Angeles (90067) *(P-11836)*

SunAmerica Investments Inc (DH)..................D 310 772-6000
1 Sun America Ctr Fl 37 Los Angeles (90067) *(P-18060)*

SunAmerica Life Insurance Company ....C 310 772-6000
1 Sun America Ctr Fl 36 Los Angeles (90067) *(P-12052)*

Sunbelt Controls Inc ....D 626 610 2340
735 N Todd Ave Azusa (91702) *(P-846)*

Sunbelt Towing Inc (PA).................................D 619 297-8697
4370 Pacific Hwy San Diego (92110) *(P-14720)*

Sunco Lighting Inc ....E 844 334-9938
27811 Hancock Pkwy Ste A Valencia (91355) *(P-10209)*

Suncore Inc ....E 949 450-0054
15 Hubble Ste 200 Irvine (92618) *(P-6902)*

Sundance Creek Post Acute, Banning *Also Called: Pacs Group Inc (P-15741)*

Sundance Spas, Chino *Also Called: Jacuzzi Brands LLC (P-8687)*

Sundance Spas, Irvine *Also Called: Sundance Spas Inc (P-8730)*

Sundance Spas Inc (DH)................................D 909 606-7733
17872 Gillette Ave Ste 300 Irvine (92614) *(P-8730)*

Sundial Industries Inc ....E 818 767-4477
8421 Telfair Ave Sun Valley (91352) *(P-5348)*

Sundial Powder Coatings Inc ....E 818 767-4477
8421 Telfair Ave Sun Valley (91352) *(P-5349)*

Sundown Foods, Fontana *Also Called: Sundown Foods USA Inc (P-1357)*

Sundown Foods USA Inc ....E 909 606-6797
10891 Business Dr Fontana (92337) *(P-1357)*

Sundown Liquidating Corp (PA) ....D 714 540-8950
401 Goetz Ave Santa Ana (92707) *(P-4318)*

Suneva Medical Inc (PA)................................E 858 550-9999
5870 Pacific Center Blvd San Diego (92121) *(P-3690)*

Sunfood Corporation ....D 619 596-7979
1825 Gillespie Way El Cajon (92020) *(P-10982)*

Sunfood Superfoods, El Cajon *Also Called: Sunfood Corporation (P-10982)*

Sunfusion Energy Systems Inc ....E 800 544-0282
9020 Kenamar Dr Ste 204 San Diego (92121) *(P-7081)*

Sungard, Calabasas *Also Called: Sungard Treasury Systems Inc (P-14045)*

Sungard Treasury Systems Inc ....C 818 223-2300
23975 Park Sorrento Ste 100 Calabasas (91302) *(P-14045)*

Sungear Inc ....E 858 549-3166
8535 Arjons Dr Ste G San Diego (92126) *(P-7569)*

Sungevity, Temecula *Also Called: Solar Spectrum LLC (P-841)*

Sunkist Growers Inc (PA)...............................C 661 290-8900
27770 Entertainment Dr Valencia (91355) *(P-10919)*

Sunland Aerospace Fasteners ....D 818 485-8929
12920 Pierce St Pacoima (91331) *(P-5137)*

Sunland Ford Inc ....D 760 241-7751
15330 Palmdale Rd Victorville (92392) *(P-11414)*

Sunland Ford-Lincoln-Mercury, Victorville *Also Called: Sunland Ford Inc (P-11414)*

Sunland Shutters, Long Beach *Also Called: Ta Chen International Inc (P-10159)*

Sunline Transit Agency (PA)...........................C 760 343-3456
32505 Harry Oliver Trl Thousand Palms (92276) *(P-8807)*

Sunline Transit Agency ....C 760 972-4059
790 Vine Ave Coachella (92236) *(P-8849)*

Sunn America Inc ....E 909 944-5756
10280 Indiana Ct Rancho Cucamonga (91730) *(P-13473)*

Sunnova Energy Corporation ....C 877 757-7697
2211 Michelson Dr Irvine (92612) *(P-9640)*

Sunny Service Group LLC ....E 323 818-2625
192 Technology Dr Ste T Irvine (92618) *(P-505)*

Sunny Sky Products, Fullerton *Also Called: Dr Smoothie Brands LLC (P-1676)*

Sunny View Care Center, Los Angeles *Also Called: Longwood Management Corp (P-15870)*

Sunnygem, Wasco *Also Called: Sunnygem LLC (P-1358)*

Sunnygem LLC (PA).......................................C 661 758-0491
500 N F St Wasco (93280) *(P-1358)*

Sunon Inc (PA)..E 714 255-0208
1760 Yeager Ave La Verne (91750) *(P-5778)*

Sunopta Fruit Group Inc ....D 323 774-6000
12128 Center St South Gate (90280) *(P-1690)*

Sunopta Grains and Foods Inc ....D 323 774-6000
12128 Center St South Gate (90280) *(P-1408)*

Sunpower By Green Convergence, Valencia *Also Called: Green Convergence (P-10320)*

Sunridge Nurseries Inc ....D 661 363-8463
441 Vineland Rd Bakersfield (93307) *(P-101)*

Sunrise Ford ....C 909 822-4401
16005 Valley Blvd Fontana (92335) *(P-11415)*

Sunrise Ford, North Hollywood *Also Called: Ngp Motors Inc (P-11385)*

Sunrise Growers Inc ....A 612 619-9545
2640 Sturgis Rd Oxnard (93030) *(P-1858)*

Sunrise Growers Inc ....C 714 706-6090
701 W Kimberly Ave Ste 210 Placentia (92870) *(P-10920)*

Sunrise Med HM Hlth Care Group, Chula Vista *Also Called: Vcp-Mobility Holdings Inc (P-8317)*

Sunrise of Woodland Hills, Encino *Also Called: Sunrise Senior Living LLC (P-15785)*

Sunrise Post Acute, Banning *Also Called: Pacs Group Inc (P-15739)*

Sunrise Respiratory Care, Irvine *Also Called: Sunrise Respiratory Care Inc (P-10110)*

Sunrise Respiratory Care Inc ....C 949 398-6555
1881 Langley Ave Irvine (92614) *(P-10110)*

Sunrise Senior Living LLC ....D 818 346-9046
5501 Newcastle Ave Apt 130 Encino (91316) *(P-15785)*

Sunroad Asset Management Inc ....C 858 362-8500
4445 Eastgate Mall Ste 400 San Diego (92121) *(P-18061)*

Sunsation Inc ....E 909 542-0280
100 S Cambridge Ave Claremont (91711) *(P-1380)*

Employee Codes: A=Over 500 employees, B=251-500
C=101-250, D=51-100, E=20-50, F=10-19, G=1-9

2025 Southern California
Business Directory and Buyers Guide

© Mergent Inc. 1-800-342-5647
1201

Sunscape Eyewear Inc .... D 949 553-0590
17526 Von Karman Ave Ste A Irvine (92614) *(P-10571)*

Sunset Doheny Office 6, Los Angeles *Also Called: City National Bank (P-11718)*

Sunset Landscape Maintenance .... D 949 455-4636
27201 Burbank El Toro (92610) *(P-236)*

Sunset Manor Convalescent Hosp, El Monte *Also Called: Gibraltar Cnvalescent Hosp Inc (P-15856)*

Sunset Property Services, Irvine *Also Called: Jonset LLC (P-9787)*

Sunset Signs and Printing Inc .... E 714 255-9104
2906 E Coronado St Anaheim (92806) *(P-8642)*

Sunsets Inc .... E 310 784-3600
24511 Frampton Ave Harbor City (90710) *(P-1925)*

Sunsets Separates, Harbor City *Also Called: Sunsets Inc (P-1925)*

Sunshine, Montebello *Also Called: Sunshine Fpc Inc (P-2740)*

Sunshine Communications SE Inc .... C 619 448-7600
350 Cypress Ln Ste D El Cajon (92020) *(P-969)*

Sunshine Floral Inc .... D 805 684-1177
4595 Foothill Rd Carpinteria (93013) *(P-11101)*

Sunshine Fpc Inc .... D 323 721-8168
1600 Gage Rd Montebello (90640) *(P-2740)*

Sunshine Makers Inc (PA) .... D 562 795-6000
15922 Pacific Coast Hwy Huntington Beach (92649) *(P-3620)*

Sunshine Metal Clad Inc .... D 661 366-0575
7201 Edison Hwy Bakersfield (93307) *(P-1031)*

Sunstar Spa Covers Inc (HQ) .... E 858 602-1950
26074 Avenue Hall Ste 13 Valencia (91355) *(P-8731)*

Sunstone Components Group Inc (HQ) .... E 951 296-5010
42136 Avenida Alvarado Temecula (92590) *(P-5216)*

Sunstone Durante LLC .... C 858 792-5200
15575 Jimmy Durante Blvd Del Mar (92014) *(P-13041)*

Sunstone Hotel Properties Inc .... C 858 277-1199
3805 Murphy Canyon Rd San Diego (92123) *(P-13042)*

Sunstone Hotel Properties Inc .... C 310 228-4100
1177 S Beverly Dr Los Angeles (90035) *(P-13043)*

Sunstone Hotel Properties Inc (DH) .... C 949 330-4000
120 Vantis Dr Ste 350 Aliso Viejo (92656) *(P-13044)*

Sunstone Top Gun Lessee Inc .... C 949 330-4000
4550 La Jolla Village Dr San Diego (92122) *(P-13045)*

Sunvair, Valencia *Also Called: Sunvair Inc (P-7570)*

Sunvair Inc (HQ) .... E 661 294-3777
29145 The Old Rd Valencia (91355) *(P-7570)*

Sunvair Aerospace Group Inc (PA) .... D 661 294-3777
29145 The Old Rd Valencia (91355) *(P-14794)*

Sunwest Electric Inc .... C 714 630-8700
3064 E Mariloma Anaheim (92806) *(P-970)*

Supacolor, Hawthorne *Also Called: Supacolor Usa Inc (P-3176)*

Supacolor Usa Inc .... D 844 973-2862
12705 Daphne Ave Hawthorne (90250) *(P-3176)*

Super 8 Motel, Bakersfield *Also Called: Nandi-Laksh Inc (P-12934)*

Super Center Concepts Inc .... C 323 562-8980
7300 Atlantic Ave Cudahy (90201) *(P-11283)*

Super Center Concepts Inc .... C 323 241-6789
10211 Avalon Blvd Los Angeles (90003) *(P-11284)*

Super Center Concepts Inc .... C 323 223-3878
133 W Avenue 45 Los Angeles (90065) *(P-14604)*

Super Center Concepts Inc .... D 951 372-9485
1130 W 6th St Corona (92882) *(P-14605)*

Super Color Digital, Irvine *Also Called: Super Color Digital LLC (P-3177)*

Super Color Digital LLC (PA) .... E 949 622-0010
16761 Hale Ave Irvine (92606) *(P-3177)*

Super D Phantom Distribution, Irvine *Also Called: C D Listening Bar Inc (P-10555)*

Super Dyeing and Finishing, Santa Fe Springs *Also Called: Super Dyeing LLC (P-1935)*

Super Dyeing LLC .... D 562 692-9500
8825 Millergrove Dr Santa Fe Springs (90670) *(P-1935)*

Super Glue, Ontario *Also Called: Pacer Technology (P-3773)*

Super Struct Bldg Systems Inc .... E 760 322-2522
1251 Montalvo Way Ste F Palm Springs (92263) *(P-2532)*

Super73 Inc (PA) .... E 949 258-9245
2722 Michelson Dr Ste 125 Irvine (92612) *(P-7637)*

Superbam Inc .... E 310 845-5784
214 Main St El Segundo (90245) *(P-2942)*

Supercolor, Irvine *Also Called: Digital Supercolor Inc (P-3002)*

Supercuts, Downey *Also Called: Jlm & Mag Associates Inc (P-13149)*

Supercuts, Simi Valley *Also Called: Kleintob Inc (P-13150)*

Superior Aircraft Services Inc (HQ) .... D 636 778-2300
201 Continental Blvd Ste 220 El Segundo (90245) *(P-9209)*

Superior Awning Inc .... E 818 780-7200
14555 Titus St Panorama City (91402) *(P-2243)*

Superior Communications Inc (PA) .... C 877 522-4727
5027 Irwindale Ave Ste 900 Irwindale (91706) *(P-10285)*

Superior Construction Inc .... D 951 808-8780
265 N Joy St Corona (92879) *(P-433)*

Superior Duct Fabrication Inc .... C 909 620-8565
1683 Mount Vernon Ave Pomona (91768) *(P-5043)*

Superior Elec Mech & Plbg Inc .... B 909 357-9400
8613 Helms Ave Rancho Cucamonga (91730) *(P-971)*

Superior Equipment Solutions .... D 323 722-7900
1085 Bixby Dr City Of Industry (91745) *(P-6391)*

Superior Essex Inc .... C 909 481-4804
5250 Ontario Mills Pkwy Ste 300 Ontario (91764) *(P-4639)*

Superior Food Machinery Inc .... E 562 949-0396
8311 Sorensen Ave Santa Fe Springs (90670) *(P-5685)*

Superior Fruit LLC .... C 805 485-2519
4324 E Vineyard Ave Oxnard (93036) *(P-27)*

Superior Grocers, Los Angeles *Also Called: Super Center Concepts Inc (P-14604)*

Superior Gunite (PA) .... C 818 896-9199
12306 Van Nuys Blvd Sylmar (91342) *(P-1137)*

Superior Lithographics Inc .... D 323 263-8400
3055 Bandini Blvd Vernon (90058) *(P-3085)*

Superior Masonry Walls Ltd .... D 909 370-1800
300 W Olive St Ste A Colton (92324) *(P-989)*

Superior Metal Shapes Inc .... E 909 947-3455
4730 Eucalyptus Ave Chino (91710) *(P-4608)*

Superior Mold Co .... E 714 751-7084
3122 Maple St Santa Ana (92707) *(P-5599)*

Superior Paving Company Inc .... D 951 739-9200
1880 N Delilah St Corona (92879) *(P-650)*

Superior Press, Santa Fe Springs *Also Called: Superior Printing Inc (P-3178)*

Superior Printing Inc .... D 888 590-7998
9440 Norwalk Blvd Santa Fe Springs (90670) *(P-3178)*

Superior Quality Foods Inc .... D 909 923-4733
2355 E Francis St Ontario (91761) *(P-1345)*

Superior Ready Mix Concrete, Corona *Also Called: Superior Ready Mix Concrete LP (P-4461)*

Superior Ready Mix Concrete, Thousand Palms *Also Called: Superior Ready Mix Concrete LP (P-4463)*

Superior Ready Mix Concrete LP .... D 760 352-4341
802 E Main St El Centro (92243) *(P-4456)*

Superior Ready Mix Concrete LP .... D 619 265-0955
7192 Mission Gorge Rd San Diego (92120) *(P-4457)*

Superior Ready Mix Concrete LP .... D 619 265-0296
7500 Mission Gorge Rd San Diego (92120) *(P-4458)*

Superior Ready Mix Concrete LP .... D 619 443-7510
12494 Highway 67 Lakeside (92040) *(P-4459)*

Superior Ready Mix Concrete LP (PA) .... E 760 745-0556
1564 Mission Rd Escondido (92029) *(P-4460)*

Superior Ready Mix Concrete LP .... D 951 277-3553
24635 Temescal Canyon Rd Corona (92883) *(P-4461)*

Superior Ready Mix Concrete LP .... D 951 658-9225
1130 N State St Hemet (92543) *(P-4462)*

Superior Ready Mix Concrete LP .... D 760 343-3418
72270 Varner Rd Thousand Palms (92276) *(P-4463)*

Superior Ready Mix Concrete LP .... D 760 728-1128
1564 Mission Rd Escondido (92029) *(P-4464)*

Superior Ready Mix Concrete LP .... D 858 695-0666
9245 Camino Santa Fe San Diego (92121) *(P-11252)*

Superior Seafood Co, Los Angeles *Also Called: PLD Enterprises Inc (P-10857)*

Superior Signs & Installation (PA) .... D 562 495-3808
1700 W Anaheim St Long Beach (90813) *(P-8643)*

Superior Sod I LP .... C 909 923-5068
17821 17th St Ste 165 Tustin (92780) *(P-70)*

Superior Spring Company .... E 714 490-0881
1260 S Talt Ave Anaheim (92806) *(P-5399)*

Mergent email: customerrelations@mergent.com
1202

2025 Southern California
Business Directory and Buyers Guide

(P-0000) Products & Services Section entry number
(PA)=Parent Co (HQ)=Headquarters (DH)=Div Headquarters

Superior Super Warehouse, Cudahy *Also Called: Super Center Concepts Inc (P-11283)*

Superior Tank Co Inc (PA) .... E **909 912-0580**
9500 Lucas Ranch Rd Rancho Cucamonga (91730) *(P-4930)*

Superior Thread Rolling Co .... D 818 504-3626
12801 Wentworth St Arleta (91331) *(P-6245)*

Superior Touch, Ontario *Also Called: Superior Quality Foods Inc (P-1345)*

Superior Trailer Works .... E 909 350-0185
13700 Slover Ave Fontana (92337) *(P-5535)*

Superior Wall Systems Inc .... B 714 278-0000
1232 E Orangethorpe Ave Fullerton (92831) *(P-1032)*

Superior Warehouse, Los Angeles *Also Called: Super Center Concepts Inc (P-11284)*

Superior Window Coverings Inc .... E 818 762-6685
7683 N San Fernando Rd Burbank (91505) *(P-2205)*

Supermedia LLC .... E 562 594-5101
3131 Katella Ave Los Alamitos (90720) *(P-2943)*

Supernal LLC .... C 202 422-3275
15555 Laguna Canyon Rd Irvine (92618) *(P-4678)*

Superpak, Tustin *Also Called: Durabag Company Inc (P-2731)*

Supersprings International Inc .... E 805 745-5553
5251 6th St Carpinteria (93013) *(P-5382)*

Supervision of Shipbuilding, San Diego *Also Called: United States Dept of Navy (P-7610)*

Superwinch, San Dimas *Also Called: Superwinch LLC (P-9851)*

Superwinch LLC .... E 800 323-2031
320 W Covina Blvd San Dimas (91773) *(P-9851)*

Supplier Diversity, San Diego *Also Called: San Diego Gas & Electric Co (P-9671)*

Supplier Diversity Program, Carlsbad *Also Called: Life Technologies Corporation (P-7966)*

Support Equipment, Escondido *Also Called: C & H Machine Inc (P-6101)*

SUPPORT, TREATMENT, & EDUCATIO, Irvine *Also Called: In Stepps Inc (P-15543)*

Supra National Express Inc .... C 310 549-7105
1421 Charles Willard St Carson (90746) *(P-9340)*

Supreme Truck Bodies Cal Inc .... E 800 827-0753
22135 Alessandro Blvd Moreno Valley (92553) *(P-7211)*

Sure Grip International .... D 562 923-0724
5519 Rawlings Ave South Gate (90280) *(P-8546)*

Sureco Hlth Lf Insur Agcy Inc .... D 949 333-0263
201 Sandpointe Ave Ste 600 Santa Ana (92707) *(P-12256)*

Surecraft Supply Inc C
2875 Executive Pl Escondido (92029) *(P-1061)*

Surefire LLC .... E 714 545-9444
17680 Newhope St Ste B Fountain Valley (92708) *(P-8303)*

Surefire LLC .... E 714 545-9444
17760 Newhope St Ste A Fountain Valley (92708) *(P-8304)*

Surefire LLC .... E 714 641-0483
2110 S Anne St Santa Ana (92704) *(P-8305)*

Surefire LLC .... E 714 545-9444
18300 Mount Baldy Cir Fountain Valley (92708) *(P-8306)*

Surefire LLC .... E 714 545-9444
2121 S Yale St Santa Ana (92704) *(P-8307)*

Surefire LLC .... E 714 641-0483
2300 S Yale St Santa Ana (92704) *(P-8308)*

Surefire LLC (PA) .... C **714 545-9444**
18300 Mount Baldy Cir Fountain Valley (92708) *(P-6518)*

Sureride Charter Inc .... E 619 336-9200
522 W 8th St National City (91950) *(P-8865)*

Surf Sand Hotel, Laguna Beach *Also Called: JC Resorts LLC (P-17997)*

Surface Optics Corporation .... E 858 675-7404
11555 Rancho Bernardo Rd San Diego (92127) *(P-7931)*

Surface Pumps Inc (PA) .... D **661 393-1545**
3301 Unicorn Rd Bakersfield (93308) *(P-10407)*

Surface Technologies Corp .... E 619 564-8320
3170 Commercial St San Diego (92113) *(P-6361)*

Surfside Race Place At Del Mar, Del Mar *Also Called: Del Mar Thoroughbred Club (P-15038)*

Surgeon Worldwide Inc .... E 707 501-7962
3855 S Hill St Los Angeles (90037) *(P-4287)*

Surgistar Inc (PA) .... E **760 598-2480**
2310 La Mirada Dr Vista (92081) *(P-8231)*

Surveysavvy.com, San Diego *Also Called: Luth Research Inc (P-17854)*

Survios Inc .... E 310 736-1503
4501 Glencoe Ave Marina Del Rey (90292) *(P-14109)*

Survival Systems Intl Inc (PA) .... D **760 749-6800**
34140 Valley Center Rd Valley Center (92082) *(P-14795)*

Susan J Harris Inc .... C 619 498-8450
344 F St Ste 100 Chula Vista (91910) *(P-17201)*

Suss McRtec Phtnic Systems Inc .... D 951 817-3700
2520 Palisades Dr Corona (92882) *(P-7154)*

Suss Microtec Inc (HQ) .... C **408 940-0300**
2520 Palisades Dr Corona (92882) *(P-5721)*

Sustainable Agriculture, Trabuco Canyon *Also Called: Seeds of Change Inc (P-11071)*

Sustainable Care Company Inc .... E 310 210-7090
633 W 5th St Fl 28 Los Angeles (90071) *(P-3621)*

Suttles Plumbing & Mech Corp .... D 818 718-9779
2267 Agate Ct Simi Valley (93065) *(P-847)*

Suzhou South .... B 626 322-0101
18351 Colima Rd Ste 82 Rowland Heights (91748) *(P-5958)*

Suzuki Motor of America Inc (HQ) .... C **714 996-7040**
3251 E Imperial Hwy Brea (92821) *(P-11416)*

Suzuki USA, Brea *Also Called: Suzuki Motor of America Inc (P-11416)*

Svf Flow Controls Inc .... E 562 802-2255
5595 Fresca Dr La Palma (90623) *(P-10408)*

Svo Enterprise LLC .... E 626 406-4770
9854 Baldwin Pl El Monte (91731) *(P-2176)*

Swabplus Inc .... E 909 987-7898
9669 Hermosa Ave Rancho Cucamonga (91730) *(P-3902)*

Swagbucks, El Segundo *Also Called: Prodege LLC (P-13799)*

Swan Fence Incorporated .... E 310 669-8000
600 W Manville St Compton (90220) *(P-11253)*

Swaner Hardwood Co Inc (PA) .... D **818 953-5350**
5 W Magnolia Blvd Burbank (91502) *(P-2372)*

Swann, Santa Fe Springs *Also Called: Swann Communications USA Inc (P-10286)*

Swann Communications USA Inc .... D 562 777-2551
12636 Clark St Santa Fe Springs (90670) *(P-10286)*

Swarco McCain Inc (DH) .... C **760 727-8100**
2365 Oak Ridge Way Vista (92081) *(P-10409)*

Swarm Aero, Oxnard *Also Called: Autonomous Defense Tech Corp (P-14384)*

Swatfame Inc (PA) .... B **626 961-7928**
16425 Gale Ave City Of Industry (91745) *(P-10730)*

Sway-A-Way Inc .... E 818 700-9712
8031 Remmet Ave Canoga Park (91304) *(P-7295)*

Swds, Irvine *Also Called: Swds Holdings Inc (P-12616)*

Swds Holdings Inc .... B 800 395-5277
8659 Research Dr Irvine (92618) *(P-12616)*

Sweda, City Of Industry *Also Called: Sweda Company LLC (P-10554)*

Sweda Company LLC .... B 626 357-9999
17411 E Valley Blvd City Of Industry (91744) *(P-10554)*

Sweden & Martina Inc .... E 844 862-7846
600 Anton Blvd Ste 1134 Costa Mesa (92626) *(P-8232)*

Sweetener Products, Vernon *Also Called: Edna H Pagel Inc (P-479)*

Sweetwter Auth Emplyees Cmmtte (PA) .... C 619 420-1413
505 Garrett Ave Chula Vista (91910) *(P-9721)*

Sweis Inc (PA) .... D **310 375-0558**
20000 Mariner Ave Torrance (90503) *(P-10479)*

Swift Autonomy Inc .... E 800 547 0438
1141a Via Callejon San Clemente (92673) *(P-7373)*

Swift Beef Company .... C 951 571-2237
15555 Meridian Pkwy Riverside (92518) *(P-1273)*

Swift Engineering, San Clemente *Also Called: Swift Engineering Inc (P-7571)*

Swift Engineering Inc .... D 949 492-6608
1141a Via Callejon San Clemente (92673) *(P-7571)*

Swift Fab, Gardena *Also Called: Carla Senter (P-4965)*

Swift Leasing Co LLC .... B 909 347-0500
14392 Valley Blvd Fontana (92335) *(P-8976)*

Swift Media Entertainment Inc .... D 310 308-3694
5340 Alla Rd Ste 101 Los Angeles (90066) *(P-14606)*

Swinerton Builders, San Diego *Also Called: Solv Energy LLC (P-14033)*

Swiss Dairy, City Of Industry *Also Called: Dean Socal LLC (P-1328)*

Swiss-Micron Inc .... D 949 589-0430
22361 Gilberto Ste A Rcho Sta Marg (92688) *(P-5114)*

Swissport Cargo Services LP .... D 310 910-9541
11001 Aviation Blvd Los Angeles (90045) *(P-9210)*

Swissport Usa Inc .... D 310 345-1986
7025 W Imperial Hwy Los Angeles (90045) *(P-9211)*

Employee Codes: A=Over 500 employees, B=251-500
C=101-250, D=51-100, E=20-50, F=10-19, G=1-9

2025 Southern California
Business Directory and Buyers Guide

© Mergent Inc. 1-800-342-5647
1203

A
L
P
H
A
B
E
T
I
C

Swissport Usa Inc .... D 310 910-9560
  11001 Aviation Blvd Los Angeles (90045) *(P-9212)*

Switching Systems, Anaheim *Also Called: Xp Power Inc (P-7071)*

Swm, El Cajon *Also Called: Delstar Technologies Inc (P-3948)*

Sws, Fullerton *Also Called: Superior Wall Systems Inc (P-1032)*

Swt Stockton, Temecula *Also Called: Southwest Traders Incorporated (P-10806)*

Swvp Westlake LLC .... C 805 557-1234
  880 S Westlake Blvd Westlake Village (91361) *(P-13046)*

Swwc Utilities Inc (DH) C
  1325 N Grand Ave Ste 100 Covina (91724) *(P-9722)*

Sybron Dental Specialties Inc (PA) .... C 714 516-7400
  1717 W Collins Ave Orange (92867) *(P-8358)*

Sybron Dental Specialties Inc .... E 909 596-0276
  1332 S Lone Hill Ave Glendora (91740) *(P-8359)*

Sybron Endo, Orange *Also Called: Ormco Corporation (P-8346)*

Sycuan Casino .... A 619 445-6002
  5469 Casino Way El Cajon (92019) *(P-13047)*

Sycuan Casino (PA) .... C 619 445-6002
  5459 Casino Way El Cajon (92019) *(P-15223)*

Sycuan Resort, El Cajon *Also Called: Sycuan Tribal Development (P-11602)*

Sycuan Resort and Casino, El Cajon *Also Called: Sycuan Casino (P-15223)*

Sycuan Tribal Development .... C 619 442-3425
  1530 Hilton Head Rd Ste 210 El Cajon (92019) *(P-11602)*

Sydata Inc .... C 760 444-4368
  6494 Weathers Pl Ste 100 San Diego (92121) *(P-9463)*

Sydell Hotels LLC .... C 213 381-7411
  3515 Wilshire Blvd Los Angeles (90010) *(P-13048)*

Sydney & Anne Bloom Farms Inc .... A 323 261-6565
  2900 Ayers Ave Vernon (90058) *(P-10882)*

Sygma, Lancaster *Also Called: Sygma Network Inc (P-10807)*

Sygma Network Inc .... C 661 723-0405
  46905 47th St W Lancaster (93536) *(P-10807)*

Sylmark Group, Van Nuys *Also Called: Sylmark Inc (P-18062)*

Sylmark Inc (PA) .... D 818 217-2000
  7821 Orion Ave Ste 200 Van Nuys (91406) *(P-18062)*

Symbolic Displays Inc .... D 714 258-2811
  1917 E Saint Andrew Pl Santa Ana (92705) *(P-7572)*

Symcoat Metal Processing Inc .... E 858 451-3313
  7887 Dunbrook Rd Ste C San Diego (92126) *(P-5297)*

Symitar Systems Inc .... C 619 542-6700
  8985 Balboa Ave San Diego (92123) *(P-13835)*

Symons Fire Protection Inc .... C 619 588-6364
  9475 Chesapeake Dr Ste A San Diego (92123) *(P-14424)*

Synapse Financial Tech Inc .... D 901 942-8167
  21255 Burbank Blvd Ste 120 Woodland Hills (91367) *(P-18360)*

Synear Foods, Chatsworth *Also Called: Synear Foods Usa LLC (P-506)*

Synear Foods Usa LLC .... E 818 341-3588
  9601 Canoga Ave Chatsworth (91311) *(P-506)*

Synectic Solutions Inc (PA) .... D 805 483-4800
  771 E Daily Dr Ste 200 Camarillo (93010) *(P-14257)*

Synergetic Tech Group Inc .... E 909 305-4711
  1712 Earhart La La Verne (91750) *(P-7573)*

Synergeyes, Carlsbad *Also Called: Synergeyes Inc (P-8023)*

Synergeyes Inc (HQ) .... D 760 476-9410
  2236 Rutherford Rd Ste 115 Carlsbad (92008) *(P-8023)*

Synergy Beverages, Los Angeles *Also Called: Gts Living Foods LLC (P-1620)*

Synergy Direct Response, Santa Ana *Also Called: Cowboy Direct Response (P-8596)*

Synergy Health Ast LLC (DH) .... D 858 586-1166
  9020 Activity Rd Ste D San Diego (92126) *(P-8233)*

Synergy Microsystems Inc .... C 858 452-0020
  28965 Avenue Penn Valencia (91355) *(P-5869)*

Synergy One Lending Inc .... C 385 273-5250
  3131 Camino Del Rio N Ste 150 San Diego (92108) *(P-11937)*

Synergy Orthpd Specialists Inc .... D 858 450-7118
  4445 Eastgate Mall Ste 103 San Diego (92121) *(P-16621)*

Syneron Inc (DH) .... D 866 259-6661
  3 Goodyear Ste A Irvine (92618) *(P-8399)*

Syneron Candela, Irvine *Also Called: Syneron Inc (P-8399)*

Syng Inc (PA) .... D 770 354-0915
  120 Mildred Ave Venice (90291) *(P-6559)*

Synsus Prvate Lbel Prtners LLC .... D 713 714-0225
  980 Rancheros Dr San Marcos (92069) *(P-3622)*

Syntech Development & Mfg Inc (PA) .... E 909 465-5554
  13948 Mountain Ave Chino (91710) *(P-4253)*

Synthorx, La Jolla *Also Called: Synthorx Inc (P-3511)*

Synthorx Inc .... E 858 352-5100
  11099 N Torrey Pines Rd Ste 190 La Jolla (92037) *(P-3511)*

Syntron Bioresearch Inc .... B 760 930-2200
  2774 Loker Ave W Carlsbad (92010) *(P-3553)*

Synventive Engineering Inc .... E 312 848-8717
  3301 Michelson Dr Apt 1534 Irvine (92612) *(P-5561)*

Sypris Data Systems Inc (HQ) .... E 909 962-9400
  160 Via Verde San Dimas (91773) *(P-5890)*

Sysco, Walnut *Also Called: Sysco Los Angeles Inc (P-10808)*

Sysco, Poway *Also Called: Sysco San Diego Inc (P-10810)*

Sysco, Oxnard *Also Called: Sysco Ventura Inc (P-10811)*

Sysco Los Angeles Inc .... A 909 595-9595
  20701 Currier Rd Walnut (91789) *(P-10808)*

Sysco Riverside Inc .... B 951 601-5300
  15750 Meridian Pkwy Riverside (92518) *(P-10809)*

Sysco San Diego Inc .... B 858 513-7300
  12180 Kirkham Rd Poway (92064) *(P-10810)*

Sysco Ventura Inc .... B 805 205-7000
  3100 Sturgis Rd Oxnard (93030) *(P-10811)*

Syspro, Tustin *Also Called: Syspro Impact Software Inc (P-10033)*

Syspro Impact Software Inc .... C 714 437-1000
  1735 Flight Way Tustin (92782) *(P-10033)*

Systech, Escondido *Also Called: Systech Corporation (P-6694)*

Systech Corporation .... E 858 674-6500
  118 State Pl Ste 101 Escondido (92029) *(P-6694)*

Systech Solutions Inc (PA) .... D 818 550-9690
  500 N Brand Blvd Ste 1900 Glendale (91203) *(P-13836)*

System1 Inc (PA) .... B 310 924-6037
  4235 Redwood Ave Los Angeles (90066) *(P-14046)*

Systems & Technology RES LLC .... D 844 204-0963
  1808 Aston Ave Ste 180 Carlsbad (92008) *(P-17639)*

Systems Application & Tech Inc .... D 805 487-7373
  1000 Town Center Dr Ste 110 Oxnard (93036) *(P-17640)*

Systems Engineering & MGT Co (PA) .... E 760 727-7800
  1430 Vantage Ct Vista (92081) *(P-17641)*

Systems Mchs Atmtn Cmpnnts Cor (PA) .... C 760 929-7575
  5807 Van Allen Way Carlsbad (92008) *(P-6362)*

Systems Technology Inc .... D 909 799-9950
  1350 Riverview Dr San Bernardino (92408) *(P-5793)*

T - Y Nursery Inc .... C 760 742-2151
  15335 Highway 76 Pauma Valley (92061) *(P-11102)*

T & F Sheet Mtls Fab McHning I .... E 310 516-8548
  15607 New Century Dr Gardena (90248) *(P-5044)*

T & H Store Fixtures, Commerce *Also Called: Teichman Enterprises Inc (P-2595)*

T & J Sausage Kitchen, Anaheim *Also Called: T&J Sausage Kitchen Inc (P-1274)*

T & T Enterprises, Corona *Also Called: Thalasinos Enterprises Inc (P-10468)*

T & T Foods Inc .... E 323 588-2158
  3080 E 50th St Vernon (90058) *(P-1346)*

T Allance One - Palm Sprng LLC .... D 760 322-7000
  67967 Vista Chino Cathedral City (92234) *(P-15224)*

T and B Boots Inc .... D 805 434-9904
  72 S Main St B Templeton (93465) *(P-11500)*

T B Penick & Sons Inc .... C 858 558-1800
  13280 Evening Creek Dr S Ste 100 San Diego (92128) *(P-507)*

T C Construction Company Inc .... C 619 448-4560
  10540 Prospect Ave Santee (92071) *(P-699)*

T C P, Santa Monica *Also Called: Tennenbaum Capitl Partners LLC (P-12741)*

T E M P, Gardena *Also Called: Thermlly Engnred Mnfctred Pdts (P-4932)*

T G T Enterprises Inc .... C 858 413-0300
  12650 Danielson Ct Poway (92064) *(P-18224)*

T Hasegawa USA Inc (HQ) .... E 714 522-1900
  14017 183rd St Cerritos (90703) *(P-1691)*

T L Fabrications LP .... D 562 802-3980
  2921 E Coronado St Anaheim (92806) *(P-14745)*

T L Timmerman Cnstr Inc .... E 760 244-2532
  9845 Santa Fe Ave E Hesperia (92345) *(P-2382)*

Mergent email: customerrelations@mergent.com
1204

2025 Southern California
Business Directory and Buyers Guide

(P-0000) Products & Services Section entry number
(PA)=Parent Co (HQ)=Headquarters (DH)=Div Headquarters

T M B, San Fernando *Also Called: Jme Inc (P-10187)*

T M Cobb Company (PA)..E 951 248-2400
500 Palmyrita Ave Riverside (92507) *(P-2328)*

T M I, Gardena *Also Called: Timbucktoo Manufacturing Inc (P-6035)*

T M I, San Diego *Also Called: Toward Maximum Independence (P-17017)*

T M Mian & Associates Inc..D 818 591-2300
24150 Park Sorrento Calabasas (91302) *(P-13049)*

t McGee Electric Inc...D 909 591-6461
2390 S Reservoir St Pomona (91766) *(P-972)*

T R I, Yucaipa *Also Called: Technical Resource Industries (P-6431)*

T R L, Rancho Cucamonga *Also Called: TRL Systems Incorporated (P-975)*

T S I, Valencia *Also Called: Tape Specialty Inc (P-10289)*

T S M, Los Angeles *Also Called: Tubular Specialties Mfg Inc (P-4363)*

T-12 Three LLC...B 619 702-3000
207 5th Ave San Diego (92101) *(P-13050)*

T-Force, Newport Beach *Also Called: T-Force Inc (P-18361)*

T-Force Inc (PA)..D 949 208-1527
4695 Macarthur Ct Newport Beach (92660) *(P-18361)*

T-Rex Grilles, Corona *Also Called: T-Rex Truck Products Inc (P-5165)*

T-Rex Truck Products Inc...D 800 287-5900
2365 Railroad St Corona (92878) *(P-5165)*

T.com Ontario Fc T-9479, Ontario *Also Called: Target Corporation (P-9115)*

T/O Printing, Westlake Village *Also Called: Thousand Oaks Prtg & Spc Inc (P-14610)*

T/Q Systems Inc..E 949 455-0478
25131 Arctic Ocean Dr Lake Forest (92630) *(P-6246)*

T&J Sausage Kitchen Inc..E 714 632-8350
2831 E Miraloma Ave Anaheim (92806) *(P-1274)*

T2 Ues Inc..E 714 487-5786
5622 Research Dr Ste A Huntington Beach (92649) *(P-17642)*

T2 Utility Engineers, Huntington Beach *Also Called: T2 Ues Inc (P-17642)*

Ta Aerospace Co..C 661 702-0448
28065 Franklin Pkwy Valencia (91355) *(P-3295)*

Ta Aerospace Co (DH)..C 661 775-1100
28065 Franklin Pkwy Valencia (91355) *(P-3939)*

Ta Chen International Inc (HQ).......................................C 562 808-8000
5860 N Paramount Blvd Long Beach (90805) *(P-10159)*

Ta Division, Valencia *Also Called: Ta Aerospace Co (P-3295)*

TA Industries Inc (HQ)..E 562 466-1000
11130 Bloomfield Ave Santa Fe Springs (90670) *(P-10326)*

Ta Operating LLC..C 909 390-7800
4325 E Guasti Rd Ontario (91761) *(P-11603)*

Tabc Inc (DH)...C 562 984-3305
6375 N Paramount Blvd Long Beach (90805) *(P-7212)*

Taber Company Inc...D 714 543-7100
121 Waterworks Way Ste 100 Irvine (92618) *(P-2329)*

Tabletops Unlimited, Carson *Also Called: Tabletops Unlimited Inc (P-9908)*

Tabletops Unlimited Inc (PA)...D 310 549-6000
23000 Avalon Blvd Carson (90745) *(P-9908)*

Tabor Communications Inc..E 858 625-0070
8445 Camino Santa Fe Ste 101 San Diego (92121) *(P-2944)*

Taco Bell, Irvine *Also Called: Taco Bell Corp (P-11604)*

Taco Bell Corp (HQ)..A 949 863-4500
1 Glen Bell Way Irvine (92618) *(P-11604)*

Tactical Command Inds Inc (DH)....................................E 925 219-1097
4700 E Airport Dr Ontario (91761) *(P-6695)*

Tactical Communications Corp......................................E 805 987-4100
473 Post St Camarillo (93010) *(P-6696)*

Tactical Engrg & Analis Inc (PA)....................................D 858 573-9869
6050 Santo Rd Ste 250 San Diego (92124) *(P-14258)*

Tactsquad, Corona *Also Called: Amwear USA Inc (P-1974)*

Tad Pgs Inc...A 800 261-3779
12062 Valley View St Ste 108 Garden Grove (92845) *(P-13625)*

Tad Pgs Inc...A 571 451-2428
10805 Holder St Ste 250 Cypress (90630) *(P-13626)*

Tadin Herb & Tea Co., Vernon *Also Called: Tadin Inc (P-10983)*

Tadin Inc...D 213 406-8880
3345 E Slauson Ave Vernon (90058) *(P-10983)*

Tae Life Sciences Us LLC...D 949 344-6112
19571 Pauling Foothill Ranch (92610) *(P-17824)*

Tae Sook Chung...D 909 598-6255
21080 Golden Springs Dr Walnut (91789) *(P-9909)*

Tae Technologies, Foothill Ranch *Also Called: Tae Technologies Inc (P-17825)*

Tae Technologies Inc (PA)...C 949 830-2117
19631 Pauling Foothill Ranch (92610) *(P-17825)*

Taft Electric Company (PA)..C 805 642-0121
1694 Eastman Ave Ventura (93003) *(P-973)*

Taft Production Company..D 661 765-7194
950 Petroleum Club Rd Taft (93268) *(P-262)*

Tag Rag, Los Angeles *Also Called: Fetish Group Inc (P-2011)*

Tag Toys Inc..D 310 639-4566
1810 S Acacia Ave Compton (90220) *(P-8732)*

Tagtime Usa Inc..B 323 587-1555
4601 District Blvd Vernon (90058) *(P-2775)*

Taheem Johnson Inc...D 818 835-3785
1237 S Victoria Ave Oxnard (93035) *(P-14259)*

Tahiti Cabinets Inc..D 714 693-0618
5419 E La Palma Ave Anaheim (92807) *(P-2616)*

Tahoe Stag, Brea *Also Called: Griffith Company (P-621)*

Tailbroom Media Grop, North Hollywood *Also Called: Pilgrim Operations LLC (P-9969)*

Tailgate Printing Inc..D 714 966-3035
2930 S Fairview St Santa Ana (92704) *(P-3086)*

Taisei Construction Corporation....................................C 714 886-1530
970 W 190th St Ste 920 Torrance (90502) *(P-508)*

Tait & Associates Inc...E 714 560-8222
2131 S Dupont Dr Anaheim (92806) *(P-4931)*

Tajen Graphics Inc..E 714 527-3122
2100 W Lincoln Ave Ste B Anaheim (92801) *(P-3087)*

Takane USA Inc...C 909 923-5511
2055 S Haven Ave Ontario (91761) *(P-9113)*

Take A Break Paper...E 323 333-7773
1048 W Gardena Blvd Gardena (90247) *(P-2831)*

Takken's Comfort Shoes, Templeton *Also Called: T and B Boots Inc (P-11500)*

Tala, Santa Monica *Also Called: Inventure Capital Corporation (P-12713)*

Talbert Archtctral Panl Door I.......................................D 714 671-9700
711 S Stimson Ave City Of Industry (91745) *(P-2330)*

Talbert Medical Center, Santa Ana *Also Called: Optumcare Management LLC (P-16601)*

Talco Plastics Inc...D 562 630-1224
3270 E 70th St Long Beach (90805) *(P-4254)*

Talco Plastics Inc (PA)...D 951 531-2000
1000 W Rincon St Corona (92878) *(P-9768)*

Talega Golf Club, San Clemente *Also Called: Heritage Golf Group LLC (P-15085)*

Talent & Acquisition LLC...C 888 970-9575
3020 Old Ranch Pkwy Ste 300 Seal Beach (90740) *(P-13837)*

Talimar Systems Inc...E 714 557-4884
3105 W Alpine St Santa Ana (92704) *(P-2553)*

Talis Lending, San Diego *Also Called: Lendsure Mortgage Corp (P-11917)*

Talladium Inc (PA)...E 661 295-0900
27360 Muirfield Ln Valencia (91355) *(P-8360)*

Talley & Associates, Santa Fe Springs *Also Called: Talley LLC (P-10287)*

Talley Farms...C 805 489-2508
2900 Lopez Dr Arroyo Grande (93420) *(P-120)*

Talley LLC (DH)...C 562 906-8000
12976 Sandoval St Santa Fe Springs (90670) *(P-10287)*

Talley Metal Fabrication, San Jacinto *Also Called: J Talley Corporation (P-5065)*

Tallgrass Pictures LLC...E 619 227-2701
710 13th St Ste 300 San Diego (92101) *(P-1467)*

Talmo & Chinn Inc...E 626 443-1741
9537 Telstar Ave Ste 131 El Monte (91731) *(P-6903)*

Talsco, Garden Grove *Also Called: Jvr Sheetmetal Fabrication Inc (P-7360)*

Talsco Inc..E 714 841-2464
7101 Patterson Dr Garden Grove (92841) *(P-7574)*

Tam O'Shanter Inn, Los Angeles *Also Called: Lawrys Restaurants II Inc (P-11584)*

Tamarisk Country Club (PA)...C 760 328-2141
70240 Frank Sinatra Dr Rancho Mirage (92270) *(P-15179)*

Tamco (HQ)...E 909 899-0660
5425 Industrial Pkwy San Bernardino (92407) *(P-4527)*

Tamco...B 949 552-9714
1000 Quail St Ste 260 Newport Beach (92660) *(P-5101)*

Tammy Taylor Nails Inc...E 949 250-9287
2001 E Deere Ave Santa Ana (92705) *(P-3296)*

Employee Codes: A=Over 500 employees, B=251-500
C=101-250, D=51-100, E=20-50, F=10-19, G=1-9

2025 Southern California
Business Directory and Buyers Guide

© Mergent Inc. 1-800-342-5647
1205

**A
L
P
H
A
B
E
T
I
C**

Tampico Spice Co Incorporated .... E 323 235-3154
5901 S Central Ave # 5941 Los Angeles (90001) *(P-1859)*

Tampico Spice Company, Los Angeles *Also Called: Tampico Spice Co Incorporated (P-1859)*

Tamshell, Corona *Also Called: Tamshell Corp (P-4255)*

Tamshell Corp .... D 951 272-9395
545 Monica Cir Corona (92878) *(P-4255)*

Tamura Corporation of America (HQ) .... E 800 472-6624
277 Rancheros Dr Ste 190 San Marcos (92069) *(P-10288)*

Tandem Design Inc .... E 714 978-7272
1916 W 144th St Gardena (90249) *(P-8733)*

TANDEM DIABETES CARE, San Diego *Also Called: Tandem Diabetes Care Inc (P-8234)*

Tandem Diabetes Care Inc (PA) .... A 858 366-6900
12400 High Bluff Dr San Diego (92130) *(P-8234)*

Tandem Exhibit, Gardena *Also Called: Tandem Design Inc (P-8733)*

Tandex Test Labs Inc .... E 626 962-7166
15849 Business Center Dr Irwindale (91706) *(P-17927)*

Tangoe-PI Inc C
9920 Pacific Heights Blvd Ste 200 San Diego (92121) *(P-18362)*

Tanimura Antle Fresh Foods Inc .... A 831 424-6100
4401 Foxdale St Baldwin Park (91706) *(P-121)*

Tanimura Antle Fresh Foods Inc .... B 805 483-2358
761 Commercial Ave Oxnard (93030) *(P-9114)*

Tanvex Biopharma Usa Inc (PA) .... D 858 210-4100
10394 Pacific Center Ct San Diego (92121) *(P-17826)*

Tape Specialty Inc .... E 661 702-9030
26017 Huntington Ln Ste C Valencia (91355) *(P-10289)*

Tapestry Solutions Inc (HQ) .... C 858 503-1990
6910 Carroll Rd San Diego (92121) *(P-13838)*

Tapetech Tool Company .... A 858 268-0656
7360 Convoy Ct San Diego (92111) *(P-12739)*

Tapetech Tool Company, San Diego *Also Called: Tapetech Tool Company (P-12739)*

Tapia Brothers Co, Maywood *Also Called: Tapia Enterprises Inc (P-10812)*

Tapia Enterprises Inc (PA) .... D 323 560-7415
6067 District Blvd Maywood (90270) *(P-10812)*

Taproom Beer Co .... E 619 539-7738
2000 El Cajon Blvd San Diego (92104) *(P-1555)*

Taral Plastics, Corona *Also Called: Martin Chancey Corporation (P-4163)*

Tarantino Wholesale Fd Distrs, San Diego *Also Called: Producers Meat and Prov Inc (P-10878)*

Tarbell Financial Corporation (PA) .... D 714 972-0988
1403 N Tustin Ave Ste 380 Santa Ana (92705) *(P-11955)*

Tarbell Realtors, Santa Ana *Also Called: F M Tarbell Co (P-12441)*

Target, Fontana *Also Called: Target Corporation (P-9116)*

Target Corporation .... C 909 937-5500
1505 S Haven Ave Ontario (91761) *(P-9115)*

Target Corporation .... D 909 355-6000
14750 Miller Ave Fontana (92336) *(P-9116)*

Target Mdia Prtners Intractive, North Hollywood *Also Called: Target Mdia Prtners Intrctive (P-3179)*

Target Mdia Prtners Intrctive (HQ) .... E 323 930-3123
5200 Lankershim Blvd Ste 350 North Hollywood (91601) *(P-3179)*

Target Specialty Products, Santa Fe Springs *Also Called: Rentokil North America Inc (P-13348)*

Target Specialty Products Inc .... D 562 865-9541
15415 Marquardt Ave Santa Fe Springs (90670) *(P-11073)*

Target Technology Company LLC .... E 949 788-0909
3420 Bristol St Costa Mesa (92626) *(P-7106)*

Targus, Anaheim *Also Called: Targus International LLC (P-11145)*

Targus International LLC (HQ) .... C 714 765-5555
1211 N Miller St Anaheim (92806) *(P-11145)*

Targus US LLC .... E 714 765-5555
1211 N Miller St Anaheim (92806) *(P-4301)*

Tarsadia Hotels, Newport Beach *Also Called: Uka LLC (P-13058)*

Tarsco Holdings LLC .... C 562 869-0200
11905 Regentview Ave Downey (90241) *(P-14796)*

Tarsus Pharmaceuticals Inc .... C 949 409-9820
15440 Laguna Canyon Rd Ste 160 Irvine (92618) *(P-3588)*

Tarulli Tire Inc (PA) .... E 714 630-4722
376 Broadway Costa Mesa (92627) *(P-14683)*

Tarzana Treatment Centers Inc .... D 818 654-3815
320 E Palmdale Blvd Palmdale (93550) *(P-16507)*

Tarzana Treatment Centers Inc .... D 562 428-4111
5190 Atlantic Ave Lakewood (90805) *(P-16508)*

Tarzana Treatment Centers Inc .... C 562 218-1868
2101 Magnolia Ave Long Beach (90806) *(P-16509)*

Tarzana Treatment Centers Inc .... C 661 726-2630
44447 10th St W Lancaster (93534) *(P-16510)*

Tarzana Treatment Centers Inc (PA) .... C 818 996-1051
18646 Oxnard St Tarzana (91356) *(P-16511)*

Tarzana Treatment Ctr, Lancaster *Also Called: Tarzana Treatment Centers Inc (P-16510)*

Tarzana Trtmnt Ctrs LNG Bch O, Lakewood *Also Called: Tarzana Treatment Centers Inc (P-16508)*

Tasteful Selections LLC .... B 661 854-3998
13003 Di Giorgio Rd Arvin (93203) *(P-3)*

Tastepoint By Iff, Corona *Also Called: Tastepoint Inc (P-3739)*

Tastepoint Inc .... C 951 734-6620
790 E Harrison St Corona (92879) *(P-3739)*

Tattooed Chef Inc (PA) .... E 562 602-0822
6305 Alondra Blvd Paramount (90723) *(P-1860)*

Tatung Company America Inc (HQ) .... D 310 637-2105
2157 Mount Shasta Dr San Pedro (90732) *(P-6662)*

Tavistock Restaurants LLC .... C 714 939-8686
20 City Blvd W Ste R1 Orange (92868) *(P-11620)*

Tawa Supermarket Inc .... C 909 760-8899
4024 Grand Ave Chino (91710) *(P-99)*

Tawa Supermarket Inc (PA) .... C 714 521-8899
6281 Regio Ave Buena Park (90620) *(P-1403)*

Tax and Financial Group, Newport Beach *Also Called: R Mc Closkey Insurance Agency (P-12249)*

Tax Credit Co, The, Los Angeles *Also Called: The Tax Credit Company (P-13297)*

Tay Ho, Santa Ana *Also Called: West Lake Food Corporation (P-1253)*

Tayco Engineering Inc .... C 714 952-2240
10874 Hope St Cypress (90630) *(P-7657)*

Taylor Digital .... E 949 391-3333
101 W Avenida Vista Hermosa Ste 122 San Clemente (92672) *(P-3180)*

Taylor Graphics Inc .... E 949 752-5200
1582 Browning Irvine (92606) *(P-3181)*

Taylor Guitars, El Cajon *Also Called: Taylor-Listug Inc (P-10572)*

Taylor Morrison California LLC .... C 949 341-1200
100 Spectrum Center Dr Ste 1450 Irvine (92618) *(P-12581)*

Taylor Trim & Supply Inc .... D 760 740-2000
2342 Meyers Ave Escondido (92029) *(P-1062)*

Taylor-Dunn Manufacturing LLC (HQ) ...... D 714 956-4040
2114 W Ball Rd Anaheim (92804) *(P-5536)*

Taylor-Listug Inc (PA) .... C 619 258-1207
1980 Gillespie Way El Cajon (92020) *(P-10572)*

Taylord Products Intl Inc (PA) .... C 619 247-6544
4505 Lister St San Diego (92110) *(P-2645)*

Taylored Fmi LLC .... C 909 510-4800
1495 E Locust St Ontario (91761) *(P-9117)*

Taylored Services, Ontario *Also Called: Taylored Services LLC (P-9118)*

Taylored Services, Ontario *Also Called: Taylored Services Holdings LLC (P-9119)*

Taylored Services LLC (DH) .... D 909 510-4800
1495 E Locust St Ontario (91761) *(P-9118)*

Taylored Services Holdings LLC (DH) .... D 909 510-4800
1495 E Locust St Ontario (91761) *(P-9119)*

Taylored Svcs Parent Co Inc (PA) .... D 909 510-4800
1495 E Locust St Ontario (91761) *(P-9341)*

Taylored Transload LLC .... C 909 510-4800
1495 E Locust St Ontario (91761) *(P-9376)*

Tbs, Costa Mesa *Also Called: Transprttion Brkg Spclists Inc (P-8926)*

Tbwa Chiat/Day Inc .... B 310 305-5000
5353 Grosvenor Blvd Los Angeles (90066) *(P-14607)*

Tc Construction Company, Santee *Also Called: T C Construction Company Inc (P-699)*

Tcg Capital Management LP .... C 310 633-2900
12180 Millennium Ste 500 Playa Vista (90094) *(P-12740)*

Tcg Software Services Inc .... B 714 665-6200
320 Commerce Ste 200 Irvine (92602) *(P-13839)*

TCI Engineering Inc .... D 909 984-1773
1416 Brooks St Ontario (91762) *(P-7194)*

TCI Texarkana Inc .... D 562 808-8000
5855 Obispo Ave Long Beach (90805) *(P-4594)*

Mergent email: customerrelations@mergent.com
1206

2025 Southern California
Business Directory and Buyers Guide

(P-0000) Products & Services Section entry number
(PA)=Parent Co (HQ)=Headquarters (DH)=Div Headquarters

TCI Transportation Services .... C 909 355-8545
14561 Merrill Ave Bldg B Fontana (92335) *(P-8977)*

Tcj Manufacturing LLC .... E 213 488-8400
2744 E 11th St Los Angeles (90023) *(P-2135)*

Tcl Electronics, Irvine *Also Called: Tte Technology Inc (P-10226)*

Tcr SC Construc 1 Ltd Ptr, Costa Mesa *Also Called: Trammell Crow Residential Co (P-12369)*

TCS, Chatsworth *Also Called: Telemtry Cmmnctons Systems Inc (P-6664)*

TCS Space & Component Tech, Torrance *Also Called: Trident Space & Defense LLC (P-6907)*

Tct Mobile Inc .... D 949 892-2990
189 Technology Dr Irvine (92618) *(P-18063)*

Tcw Group Inc (PA)... **B 213 244-0000**
515 S Flower St Los Angeles (90071) *(P-12034)*

Tcw Trends Inc .... E 310 533-5177
2886 Columbia St Torrance (90503) *(P-2136)*

Tcwglobal, San Diego *Also Called: Wmbe Payrolling Inc (P-13582)*

Tdi Signs .... E 562 436-5188
13158 Arctic Cir Santa Fe Springs (90670) *(P-8644)*

Tdk Electronics Inc .... C 858 715-4200
8787 Complex Dr Ste 200 San Diego (92123) *(P-7056)*

Tdk-Lambda Americas Inc .... C 619 575-4400
401 Mile Of Cars Way Ste 325 National City (91950) *(P-10290)*

Tdmi, Gardena *Also Called: Twin Dragon Marketing Inc (P-1889)*

Tdo Software, Inc., San Diego *Also Called: Sonendo Acquisition Corp (P-14034)*

Te Connectivity Corporation .... E 805 684-4560
550 Linden Ave Carpinteria (93013) *(P-6363)*

Te Connectivity Corporation .... D 760 757-7500
3390 Alex Rd Oceanside (92058) *(P-6960)*

Te Connectivity MOG, El Cajon *Also Called: Brantner and Associates Inc (P-6942)*

Tea Tree Essentials, Rancho Santa Margari *Also Called: Forespar Products Corp (P-4767)*

Teacher Created Materials Inc .... C 714 891-2273
5301 Oceanus Dr Huntington Beach (92649) *(P-2945)*

Teacher Created Resources Inc .... C 714 230-7060
12621 Western Ave Garden Grove (92841) *(P-2896)*

Teague Insurance Agency Inc .... D 619 464-6851
7777 Alvarado Rd La Mesa (91942) *(P-12257)*

Teal Electronics Corporation (PA)... **D 858 558-9000**
10350 Sorrento Valley Rd San Diego (92121) *(P-6364)*

Tealium Inc (PA).. **C 858 779-1344**
9605 Scranton Rd Ste 600 San Diego (92121) *(P-14158)*

Team Inc .... E 310 514-2312
1515 240th St Harbor City (90710) *(P-4714)*

Team Air Inc (PA).. **E 909 823-1957**
12771 Brown Ave Riverside (92509) *(P-5984)*

Team Air Conditioning Eqp, Riverside *Also Called: Team Air Inc (P-5984)*

Team C Construction .... D 619 579-6572
1272 Greenfield Dr El Cajon (92021) *(P-1138)*

Team Companies LLC (PA).. **D 818 558-3261**
2300 W Empire Ave Ste 500 Burbank (91504) *(P-17756)*

Team Finish Inc .... D 714 671-9190
155 Arovista Cir Ste A Brea (92821) *(P-1139)*

Team Garage LLC .... D 714 913-9900
3200 Bristol St Ste 300 Costa Mesa (92626) *(P-13249)*

Team Group LLC .... D 951 688-8593
4076 Flat Rock Dr Riverside (92505) *(P-18064)*

Team Health Holdings Inc .... A 619 740-4401
5555 Grossmont Center Dr La Mesa (91942) *(P-16223)*

Team Industrial Services, Harbor City *Also Called: Team Inc (P-4714)*

Team Logic If La W Hollywood .... D 310 292-0063
751 N Formosa Ave Los Angeles (90046) *(P-17016)*

Team Manufacturing Inc .... E 310 639-0251
2625 Homestead Pl Rancho Dominguez (90220) *(P-5217)*

Team Post-Op, Irvine *Also Called: Team Post-Op Inc (P-10111)*

Team Post-Op Inc .... C 949 253-5500
17256 Red Hill Ave Irvine (92614) *(P-10111)*

Team Risk MGT Strategies LLC .... A 877 767-8728
3131 Camino Del Rio N Ste 650 San Diego (92108) *(P-18363)*

Team Select Home Care, Laguna Hills *Also Called: Laguna Home Health Svcs LLC (P-16400)*

Team Services, Burbank *Also Called: Team Companies LLC (P-17756)*

Team So-Cal Inc .... B 805 650-9946
1811 Knoll Dr Ste A Ventura (93003) *(P-15180)*

Team Technologies Inc .... D 626 334-5000
4675 Vinita Ct Chino (91710) *(P-5600)*

Team West Contracting Corp .... D 951 340-3426
2733 S Vista Ave Bloomington (92316) *(P-1227)*

Team-One Staffing Services Inc .... A 951 616-3515
16030 Ventura Blvd Ste 430 Encino (91436) *(P-13575)*

Teamone Employment, Encino *Also Called: Team-One Staffing Services Inc (P-13575)*

Teamwork Athletic Apparel, Carlsbad *Also Called: R B III Associates Inc (P-2077)*

Tearlab Corporation .... E 858 455-6006
42309 Winchester Rd Ste I Temecula (92590) *(P-8235)*

Tebra Technologies Inc (PA).. **C 888 775-2736**
1111 Bayside Dr Corona Del Mar (92625) *(P-13840)*

TEC, Rancho Dominguez *Also Called: Thermal Equipment Corporation (P-7832)*

TEC Color Craft (PA).. **E 909 392-9000**
1860 Wright Ave La Verne (91750) *(P-3182)*

TEC Color Craft Products, La Verne *Also Called: TEC Color Craft (P-3182)*

TEC Specialty Products LLC .... C 801 897-5514
1230 Rosecrans Ave Ste 520 Manhattan Beach (90266) *(P-3781)*

Tecan Sp Inc .... D 626 962-0010
14180 Live Oak Ave Baldwin Park (91706) *(P-10122)*

Tech Knowledge Associates LLC .... D 714 735-3810
1 Centerpointe Dr Ste 200 La Palma (90623) *(P-14797)*

Tech Systems Inc .... C 714 523-5404
7372 Walnut Ave Ste J Buena Park (90620) *(P-10291)*

Techflow Inc (PA)... **C 858 412-8000**
9889 Willow Creek Rd Ste 100 San Diego (92131) *(P-18268)*

Techflow Scntfic A Div Tchflow, San Diego *Also Called: Techflow Inc (P-18268)*

Techmer Pm Inc .... B 310 632-9211
18420 S Laurel Park Rd Compton (90220) *(P-3297)*

Technclor Crative Svcs USA Inc .... B 818 260-1214
8921 Lindblade St Culver City (90232) *(P-14906)*

Technclor Vdocassette Mich Inc, Camarillo *Also Called: Vantiva Scs Memphis Inc (P-14910)*

Technet Partners, Carlsbad *Also Called: Technet Partners Inc (P-14110)*

Technet Partners Inc .... C 760 683-8393
6116 Innovation Way Carlsbad (92009) *(P-14110)*

Techni Cast Corp, South Gate *Also Called: Techni-Cast Corp (P-4693)*

Techni-Cast Corp .... D 562 923-4585
11220 Garfield Ave South Gate (90280) *(P-4693)*

Techni-Tools, Moorpark *Also Called: Testequity LLC (P-14734)*

Technic Inc .... E 714 632-0200
1170 N Hawk Cir Anaheim (92807) *(P-5298)*

Technical Arts, Placentia *Also Called: Southern Cal Tchnical Arts Inc (P-6241)*

Technical Cable Concepts Inc .... E 714 835-1081
350 Lear Ave Costa Mesa (92626) *(P-7057)*

Technical Devices, Torrance *Also Called: Winther Technologies Inc (P-5650)*

Technical Devices Company, Torrance *Also Called: Belhome Inc (P-5643)*

Technical Manufacturing W LLC .... E 661 295-7226
24820 Avenue Tibbitts Valencia (91355) *(P-8734)*

Technical Micro Cons Inc (PA).. **E 310 559-3982**
807 N Park View Dr Ste 150 El Segundo (90245) *(P-18225)*

Technical Resource Industries (PA).. **E 909 446-1109**
12854 Daisy Ct Yucaipa (92399) *(P-6431)*

Technical Services, San Bernardino *Also Called: Northrop Grumman Systems Corp (P-7761)*

Technicolor, Hollywood *Also Called: Technicolor Usa Inc (P-6561)*

Technicolor, Calexico *Also Called: Vantiva Sup Chain Slutions Inc (P-14912)*

Technicolor Inc .... B 818 260-4577
2255 N Ontario St Ste 180 Burbank (91504) *(P-14430)*

Technicolor Connected USA, Lebec *Also Called: Technicolor Usa Inc (P-6560)*

Technicolor Creative Studios, Culver City *Also Called: Technclor Crative Svcs USA Inc*
(P-14906)

Technicolor Disc Services Corp (HQ).. **C 805 445-1122**
3601 Calle Tecate Ste 120 Camarillo (93012) *(P-7107)*

Technicolor Entertainment Svcs, Burbank *Also Called: Technicolor Thomson Group Inc*
(P-14907)

Technicolor Lab, Burbank *Also Called: Technicolor Inc (P-14430)*

Technicolor Thomson Group Inc (HQ).. **B**
2233 N Ontario St Ste 300 Burbank (91504) *(P-14907)*

Technicolor Usa Inc .... A 661 496-1309
4049 Industrial Parkway Dr Lebec (93243) *(P-6560)*

Employee Codes: A=Over 500 employees, B=251-500
C=101-250, D=51-100, E=20-50, F=10-19, G=1-9

2025 Southern California
Business Directory and Buyers Guide

© Mergent Inc. 1-800-342-5647
1207

Technicolor Usa Inc (HQ).. A 317 587-4287
6040 W Sunset Blvd Hollywood (90028) *(P-6561)*

Technicolor Video Services, Camarillo *Also Called: Vantiva Sup Chain Slutions Inc (P-14911)*

Technicon Design Corporation .... C 949 218-1300
30011 Ivy Glenn Dr Ste 115 Laguna Niguel (92677) *(P-14608)*

Technicote Inc .... E 951 372-0627
1587 E Bentley Dr Ste 101 Corona (92879) *(P-3782)*

Technifex Products LLC .... E 661 294-3800
25261 Rye Canyon Rd Valencia (91355) *(P-4485)*

Techniform International Corp .... C 909 877-6886
375 S Cactus Ave Rialto (92376) *(P-6247)*

Technip Usa Inc .... B 909 447-3600
555 W Arrow Hwy Claremont (91711) *(P-17643)*

Techno Coatings Inc .... D 714 774-4671
785 E Debra Ln Anaheim (92805) *(P-591)*

Techno Coatings Inc .... D 714 774-4671
795 E Debra Ln Anaheim (92805) *(P-592)*

Techno Coatings Inc (PA)... C 714 635-1130
1391 S Allec St Anaheim (92805) *(P-593)*

Techno West, Anaheim *Also Called: Techno Coatings Inc (P-593)*

Technocel, Simi Valley *Also Called: Foreign Trade Corporation (P-10244)*

Technoconcepts Inc .... E 818 988-3364
6060 Sepulveda Blvd Ste 202 Van Nuys (91411) *(P-6663)*

Technologent, Irvine *Also Called: Thomas Gallaway Corporation (P-13843)*

Technology Associates EC Inc .... D 760 765-5275
3129 Tiger Run Ct Ste 206 Carlsbad (92010) *(P-18226)*

Technology Integration Group, Poway *Also Called: PC Specialists Inc (P-10023)*

Technology Management Concepts, El Segundo *Also Called: Technical Micro Cons Inc (P-18225)*

Technology Training Corp .... D 310 644-7777
3238 W 131st St Hawthorne (90250) *(P-3088)*

Technosocialworkcom LLC .... D 661 617-6601
4300 Resnik Ct Unit 103 Bakersfield (93313) *(P-14159)*

Technossus LLC .... D 949 769-3500
5000 Birch St Newport Beach (92660) *(P-13841)*

Technovative Applications .... D 714 996-0104
3160 Enterprise St Ste A Brea (92821) *(P-7814)*

Techture Inc .... E 323 347-6209
1010 Wilshire Blvd Apt 1206 Los Angeles (90017) *(P-2946)*

Tecma Group LLC .... A 619 333-5856
6020 Progressive Ave Ste 200 San Diego (92154) *(P-14609)*

Teco Diagnostics .... D 714 693-7788
1268 N Lakeview Ave Anaheim (92807) *(P-3554)*

Tecolote Research Inc .... C 805 964-6963
5266 Hollister Ave Ste 301 Santa Barbara (93111) *(P-18227)*

Tecolote Research Inc .... D ..:... 310 640-4700
2120 E Grand Ave Ste 200 El Segundo (90245) *(P-18228)*

Tecom Industries Incorporated .... C 805 267-0100
375 Conejo Ridge Ave Thousand Oaks (91361) *(P-10292)*

Tecomet, Azusa *Also Called: Tecomet Inc (P-8236)*

Tecomet Inc .... A 626 334-1519
503 S Vincent Ave Azusa (91702) *(P-8236)*

Tecon Pacific, Ontario *Also Called: Clark - Pacific Corporation (P-4383)*

Ted Ford Jones Inc .... C 760 438-9171
5555 Paseo Del Norte Carlsbad (92008) *(P-11417)*

Ted Ford Jones Inc (PA)... C 714 521-3110
6211 Beach Blvd Buena Park (90621) *(P-14700)*

Tee Styled Inc .... E 323 983-9988
4640 E La Palma Ave Anaheim (92807) *(P-3183)*

Teg Staffing Inc .... A 800 918-1678
2385 Northside Dr Ste 250 San Diego (92108) *(P-13576)*

Tegra118 Wealth Solutions Inc (HQ).............................. D 888 800-0188
700 N San Vicente Blvd Ste G605 West Hollywood (90069) *(P-14160)*

Tei Struthers Wells, Santa Fe Springs *Also Called: Wells Struthers Corporation (P-4934)*

Teichman Enterprises Inc .... E 323 278-9000
6100 Bandini Blvd Commerce (90040) *(P-2595)*

Tek84 Inc .... D 858 676-5382
13495 Gregg St Poway (92064) *(P-8400)*

Teklam, Corona *Also Called: Simmons Family Corporation (P-3971)*

Tekni-Plex Inc .... D 909 589-4366
19555 Arenth Ave City Of Industry (91748) *(P-2776)*

Teknor Apex, City Of Industry *Also Called: Teknor Color Company (P-3299)*

Teknor Apex Company .... C 626 968-4656
420 S 6th Ave City Of Industry (91746) *(P-3298)*

Teknor Color Company .... E 626 336-7709
420 S 6th Ave City Of Industry (91746) *(P-3299)*

Tekworks Inc .... D 877 835-9675
12742 Knott St Garden Grove (92841) *(P-9464)*

Telacu Industries Inc .... C 323 721-1655
1175 N Del Rio Pl Ontario (91764) *(P-18065)*

Telair International, Anaheim *Also Called: AAR Manufacturing Inc (P-4906)*

Telecare Corporation .... D 562 630-8672
6060 N Paramount Blvd Long Beach (90805) *(P-16512)*

Telecommunication, Beverly Hills *Also Called: Nga 911 LLC (P-13782)*

Teledyne, Los Angeles *Also Called: Teledyne Technologies Inc (P-7060)*

Teledyne Analytical Instrs, City Of Industry *Also Called: Teledyne Instruments Inc (P-8068)*

Teledyne API, San Diego *Also Called: Teledyne Instruments Inc (P-8066)*

Teledyne Battery Products, Redlands *Also Called: Teledyne Technologies Inc (P-7082)*

Teledyne Controls, El Segundo *Also Called: Teledyne Technologies Inc (P-7059)*

Teledyne Controls LLC .... A 310 765-3600
501 Continental Blvd El Segundo (90245) *(P-7815)*

Teledyne Flir LLC .... C 805 964-9797
6769 Hollister Ave Goleta (93117) *(P-7816)*

Teledyne Flir Coml Systems Inc (DH)............................. B 805 964-9797
6769 Hollister Ave Goleta (93117) *(P-7980)*

Teledyne Hanson Research Inc .... E 818 882-7266
9810 Variel Ave Chatsworth (91311) *(P-7981)*

Teledyne Impulse, San Diego *Also Called: Teledyne Instruments Inc (P-6432)*

Teledyne Instruments Inc .... D 858 842-3100
9855 Carroll Canyon Rd San Diego (92131) *(P-6432)*

Teledyne Instruments Inc .... C 858 842-2600
14020 Stowe Dr Poway (92064) *(P-7817)*

Teledyne Instruments Inc .... E 818 882-7266
9810 Variel Ave Chatsworth (91311) *(P-7982)*

Teledyne Instruments Inc .... D 619 239-5959
9970 Carroll Canyon Rd Ste A San Diego (92131) *(P-8066)*

Teledyne Instruments Inc .... E 858 657-9800
9970 Carroll Canyon Rd San Diego (92131) *(P-8067)*

Teledyne Instruments Inc .... C 626 934-1500
16830 Chestnut St City Of Industry (91748) *(P-8068)*

Teledyne Judson Technologies, Camarillo *Also Called: Teledyne Scentific Imaging LLC (P-17827)*

Teledyne Lecroy Inc .... E 434 984-4500
1049 Camino Dos Rios Thousand Oaks (91360) *(P-7932)*

Teledyne Optmum Optcal Systems, Camarillo *Also Called: Teledyne Scentific Imaging LLC (P-8024)*

Teledyne Rd Instruments, Poway *Also Called: Teledyne Instruments Inc (P-7817)*

Teledyne Rd Instruments Inc .... C 858 842-2600
14020 Stowe Dr Poway (92064) *(P-7818)*

Teledyne Reson Inc .... E 805 964-6260
5212 Verdugo Way Camarillo (93012) *(P-10502)*

Teledyne Reynolds Inc .... C 310 823-5491
1001 Knox St Torrance (90502) *(P-3783)*

Teledyne Scentific Imaging LLC .... E
4153 Calle Tesoro Camarillo (93012) *(P-8024)*

Teledyne Scentific Imaging LLC .... D 805 373-4979
5212 Verdugo Way Camarillo (93012) *(P-17827)*

Teledyne Scentific Imaging LLC (HQ)............................. C 805 373-4545
1049 Camino Dos Rios Thousand Oaks (91360) *(P-17828)*

Teledyne Scientific Company, Thousand Oaks *Also Called: Teledyne Scentific Imaging LLC (P-17828)*

Teledyne Seabotix Inc .... D 619 239-5959
2877 Historic Decatur Rd Ste 100 San Diego (92106) *(P-5655)*

Teledyne Technologies, Thousand Oaks *Also Called: Teledyne Technologies Inc (P-7058)*

Teledyne Technologies Inc (PA)..................................... C 805 373-4545
1049 Camino Dos Rios Thousand Oaks (91360) *(P-7058)*

Teledyne Technologies Inc .... B 310 765-3600
501 Continental Blvd El Segundo (90245) *(P-7059)*

Teledyne Technologies Inc .... B 310 822-8229
12964 Panama St Los Angeles (90066) *(P-7060)*

Teledyne Technologies Inc .... D 909 793-3131
840 W Brockton Ave Redlands (92374) *(P-7082)*

Mergent email: customerrelations@mergent.com
1208

2025 Southern California
Business Directory and Buyers Guide

(P-0000) Products & Services Section entry number
(PA)=Parent Co (HQ)=Headquarters (DH)=Div Headquarters

Teleflora, Los Angeles *Also Called: The Wonderful Company LLC (P-1588)*			
Telemtry Cmmnctons Systems Inc	E	818 718-6248	
10020 Remmet Ave Chatsworth (91311) *(P-6664)*			
Telenet, El Segundo *Also Called: Telenet Voip Inc (P-14733)*			
Telenet Voip Inc	D	310 253-9000	
850 N Park View Dr El Segundo (90245) *(P-14733)*			
Teleperformance, Pasadena *Also Called: Tpusa - Fhcs Inc (P-14183)*			
Telescape, Los Angeles *Also Called: Truconnect Communications Inc (P-9467)*			
Telesector Resources Group Inc	B	626 813-4538	
5010 Azusa Canyon Rd Baldwin Park (91706) *(P-18229)*			
Telesign Holdings Inc (DH)	E	310 740-9700	
13274 Fiji Way Ste 600 Marina Del Rey (90292) *(P-14047)*			
Telesis Bio Inc (PA)	E	858 228-4115	
10421 Wateridge Cir Ste 200 San Diego (92121) *(P-7983)*			
Telesis Community Credit Union (PA)	D	818 885-1226	
9301 Winnetka Ave Chatsworth (91311) *(P-11817)*			
Telestar International Corp	E	818 582-3018	
5536 Balboa Blvd Encino (91316) *(P-18230)*			
Telestar Material, Encino *Also Called: Telestar International Corp (P-18230)*			
Telisimo International Corp	B	619 325-1593	
2330 Shelter Island Dr Ste 210a San Diego (92106) *(P-9465)*			
Telit Wireless Solutions Inc	C	949 461-7150	
7700 Irvine Center Dr Irvine (92618) *(P-10293)*			
Tellabs Access LLC (HQ)	E	630 798-8671	
338 Pier Ave Hermosa Beach (90254) *(P-6697)*			
Tellkamp Systems Inc (PA)	E	562 802-1621	
15523 Carmenita Rd Santa Fe Springs (90670) *(P-7840)*			
Telus Health (us) Ltd	C	888 577-3784	
27715 Jefferson Ave Ste 103 Temecula (92590) *(P-18231)*			
Temblor Brewing LLC	E	661 489-4855	
3200 Buck Owens Blvd Bakersfield (93308) *(P-1556)*			
Temco, Pomona *Also Called: C & B Delivery Service (P-9051)*			
Temco Logistics, Pomona *Also Called: Home Express Delivery Svc LLC (P-9293)*			
Temecula Homecare, Temecula *Also Called: Maxim Healthcare Services Inc (P-13605)*			
Temecula Quality Plating Inc	E	951 296-9875	
42147 Roick Dr Temecula (92590) *(P-5299)*			
Temecula Stadium Cinemas 15, Temecula *Also Called: Edwards Theatres Circuit Inc (P-14936)*			
Temecula Valley Drywall Inc	D	951 600-1742	
41228 Raintree Ct Murrieta (92562) *(P-1033)*			
Temecula Valley Hospital Inc	B	951 331-2200	
31700 Temecula Pkwy Temecula (92592) *(P-16224)*			
Temecula Valley Winery MGT LLC	D	951 699-8896	
27495 Diaz Rd Temecula (92590) *(P-1586)*			
Temecula Vly Unified Schl Dst	D	951 302-5140	
33125 Regina Dr Temecula (92592) *(P-16826)*			
Temeka Advertising Inc	D	951 277-2525	
9073 Pulsar Ct Corona (92883) *(P-2574)*			
Temeka Group, Corona *Also Called: Temeka Advertising Inc (P-2574)*			
Temeku Hills, Temecula *Also Called: McMillin Communities Inc (P-15091)*			
Temple Community Hospital, Los Angeles *Also Called: Temple Hospital Corporation (P-16225)*			
Temple Custom Jewelers LLC	E	800 988-3844	
1640 Camino Del Rio N Ste 220 San Diego (92108) *(P-8462)*			
Temple Hospital Corporation	B	213 355-3200	
242 N Hoover St Los Angeles (90004) *(P-16225)*			
Temple Israel of Hollywood (PA)	D	323 876-8330	
7300 Hollywood Blvd Los Angeles (90046) *(P-13159)*			
Temple Jdea of W San Frnndo VI	D	818 758-3800	
5429 Lindley Ave Tarzana (91356) *(P-17111)*			
Temple Judea Nursery School, Tarzana *Also Called: Temple Jdea of W San Frnndo VI (P-17111)*			
Temple Pk Cnvalescent Hosp Inc	D	213 380-2035	
2411 W Temple St Los Angeles (90026) *(P-15885)*			
Templeton Surgery Center LLC	C	805 434-3550	
1911 Johnson Ave San Luis Obispo (93401) *(P-15486)*			
Tempo Communications Inc (PA)	D	800 642-2155	
1390 Aspen Way Vista (92081) *(P-9466)*			
Tempo Industries, Irvine *Also Called: Wpmg Inc (P-6481)*			
Tempo Industries Inc	C	415 552-8074	
2137 E 55th St Vernon (90058) *(P-2494)*			

Temporary Staffing Union	A	714 728-5186	
19800 Macarthur Blvd Ste 300 Irvine (92612) *(P-17316)*			
Tempted Apparel Corp	D	323 859-2480	
4516 Loma Vista Ave Vernon (90058) *(P-2137)*			
Temptron Engineering Inc	E	818 346-4900	
7823 Deering Ave Canoga Park (91304) *(P-8069)*			
Tempus LLC	D	800 917-5055	
2041 Rosecrans Ave Ste 245 El Segundo (90245) *(P-13577)*			
Ten Days Manufacturing	D	909 871-5340	
458 Commercial Rd San Bernardino (92408) *(P-10467)*			
Ten Publishing Media LLC (PA)	C	310 531-9900	
831 S Douglas St El Segundo (90245) *(P-14908)*			
Ten Stone Wbster Prcess Tech	B	909 447-3600	
555 W Arrow Hwy Claremont (91711) *(P-17644)*			
Ten-X, Irvine *Also Called: Ten-X Finance Inc (P-12536)*			
Ten-X Finance Inc	C	949 465-8523	
15295 Alton Pkwy Irvine (92618) *(P-12536)*			
Tenant Inc	D	949 894-4500	
4920 Campus Dr Ste B Newport Beach (92660) *(P-13842)*			
Tencate Performance Composite, Camarillo *Also Called: Performance Materials Corp (P-3285)*			
Tenenblatt Corporation	C	323 232-2061	
3750 Broadway Pl Los Angeles (90007) *(P-1927)*			
TENET, Tarzana *Also Called: Amisub of California Inc (P-15911)*			
Tenet, Palm Springs *Also Called: Desert Regional Med Ctr Inc (P-15974)*			
Tenet Health Systems Norris	B	323 865-3000	
1441 Eastlake Ave Los Angeles (90089) *(P-16226)*			
Tenet Healthsystem Medical Inc	A	562 531-2550	
3700 South St Lakewood (90712) *(P-15487)*			
Tenet Healthsystem Medical Inc	B	805 546-7698	
3751 Katella Ave Los Alamitos (90720) *(P-15488)*			
Tenet Healthsystem Medical Inc	C	562 493-9581	
1661 Golden Rain Rd Seal Beach (90740) *(P-15489)*			
Tenet Healthsystem Medical Inc	B	714 428-6800	
1400 S Douglass Rd Ste 250 Anaheim (92806) *(P-16227)*			
Tenet Healthsystem Medical Inc	B	714 993-2000	
1301 N Rose Dr Placentia (92870) *(P-16302)*			
Tenet Healthsystem Medical Inc	D	310 673-4660	
555 E Hardy St Inglewood (90301) *(P-17112)*			
Tenex Health Inc	D	949 454-7500	
26902 Vista Ter Lake Forest (92630) *(P-8237)*			
Tenma America Corporation	C	619 754-2250	
333 H St Ste 5000 Chula Vista (91910) *(P-4256)*			
Tennenbaum Capitl Partners LLC (DH)	D	310 566-1000	
2951 28th St Ste 1000 Santa Monica (90405) *(P-12741)*			
Tennis Channel Inc (DH)	D	310 392-1920	
3003 Exposition Blvd Santa Monica (90404) *(P-14980)*			
Tensoriot Inc	D	909 342-2459	
625 The City Dr S Ste 485 Orange (92868) *(P-14260)*			
Tensys Medical Inc	E	858 552-1941	
12625 High Bluff Dr Ste 213 San Diego (92130) *(P-8401)*			
Teradata, San Diego *Also Called: Teradata Corporation (P-14048)*			
Teradata Corporation (PA)	A	866 548-8348	
17095 Via Del Campo San Diego (92127) *(P-14048)*			
Teradata Operations Inc (HQ)	D	937 242-4030	
17095 Via Del Campo San Diego (92127) *(P-5870)*			
Teradyne Inc		818 991-2900	
30701 Agoura Rd Agoura Hills (91301) *(P-7061)*			
TERI COMMON GROUNDS CAFE & COF, Oceanside *Also Called: E R I T Inc (P-17147)*			
Teridian Semiconductor Corp (DH)	D	714 508-8800	
6440 Oak Cyn Ste 100 Irvine (92618) *(P-6904)*			
Tern Design Ltd	E	760 754-2400	
14020 Stowe Dr Poway (92064) *(P-7881)*			
Terra Bella Nursery, San Diego *Also Called: Bella Terra Nursery Inc (P-11083)*			
Terra Furniture Inc	E		
1950 Salto Dr Hacienda Heights (91745) *(P-2461)*			
Terra Nova Technologies Inc	D	619 596-7400	
10770 Rockville St Ste A Santee (92071) *(P-5519)*			
Terra Pacific Landscape (HQ)	D	714 567-0177	
12891 Nelson St Garden Grove (92840) *(P-195)*			
Terra Universal Inc (PA)	D	714 526-0100	
800 S Raymond Ave Fullerton (92831) *(P-5779)*			

A L P H A B E T I C

Employee Codes: A=Over 500 employees, B=251-500
C=101-250, D=51-100, E=20-50, F=10-19, G=1-9

2025 Southern California
Business Directory and Buyers Guide

© Mergent Inc. 1-800-342-5647
1209

Terra Vista Management, San Diego *Also Called: Terra Vista Management Inc (P-12537)*

Terra Vista Management Inc .... B 858 581-4200
2211 Pacific Beach Dr San Diego (92109) *(P-12537)*

Terrace, The, Grand Terrace *Also Called: Emeritus Corporation (P-15629)*

Terraces At Squaw Peak, Duarte *Also Called: Humangood (P-15860)*

Terranea Resort, Rancho Palos Verdes *Also Called: Long Point Development LLC (P-12906)*

Terravant Wine, Buellton *Also Called: Terravant Wine Company LLC (P-1587)*

Terravant Wine Company LLC .... C 805 688-4245
35 Industrial Way Buellton (93427) *(P-1587)*

Terry Hines & Assoc, Burbank *Also Called: GL Nemirow Inc (P-13209)*

Terry Town Corporation .... D 619 421-5354
8851 Kerns St Ste 100 San Diego (92154) *(P-2177)*

Terumo Americas Holding Inc .... E 714 258-8001
1311 Valencia Ave Tustin (92780) *(P-7984)*

Tesancia La Jlla Ht Spa Resort, La Jolla *Also Called: Destination Residences LLC (P-13172)*

Tesca, Los Angeles *Also Called: Tesca Usa Inc (P-2268)*

Tesca Usa Inc .... E 586 991-0744
333 S Grand Ave Ste 4100 Los Angeles (90071) *(P-2268)*

Tesco Controls Inc .... D 916 395-8800
42015 Remington Ave Ste 102 Temecula (92590) *(P-7933)*

TESCO CONTROLS, INC., Temecula *Also Called: Tesco Controls Inc (P-7933)*

Teserra (PA) .... B 760 340-9000
86100 Avenue 54 Coachella (92236) *(P-1228)*

Tesoro Refining & Mktg Co LLC .... D 562 728-2215
5905 N Paramount Blvd Long Beach (90805) *(P-3831)*

Tesoro Refining & Mktg Co LLC .... C 877 837-6762
2101 E Pacific Coast Hwy Wilmington (90744) *(P-11035)*

Tessa Mia Corp .... E 877 740-5757
9565 Vassar Ave Chatsworth (91311) *(P-2364)*

Tessitura Network Inc .... B 888 643-5778
2295 Fletcher Pkwy Ste 101 El Cajon (92020) *(P-14049)*

Test-Rite Products Corp (DH) .... D 909 605-9899
1900 Burgundy Pl Ontario (91761) *(P-9910)*

Testequity, Moorpark *Also Called: Testequity Inc (P-10410)*

Testequity Inc .... D 805 498-9933
6100 Condor Dr Moorpark (93021) *(P-10410)*

Testequity LLC (HQ) .... D 805 498-9933
6100 Condor Dr Moorpark (93021) *(P-14734)*

Testronic Inc .... C 818 845-3223
111 N First St Ste 204 Burbank (91502) *(P-14909)*

Testronic Labs, Burbank *Also Called: Testronic Inc (P-14909)*

Tetra Tech, Pasadena *Also Called: Tetra Tech Inc (P-17646)*

Tetra Tech Inc .... D 949 263-0846
17885 Von Karman Ave Ste 500 Irvine (92614) *(P-17645)*

Tetra Tech Inc (PA) .... A 626 351-4664
3475 E Foothill Blvd Pasadena (91107) *(P-17646)*

Tetra Tech Ec Inc .... E 949 809-5000
17885 Von Karman Ave Ste 500 Irvine (92614) *(P-7985)*

Tetra Tech Executive Svcs Inc .... C 626 470-2400
3475 E Foothill Blvd Pasadena (91107) *(P-13578)*

Teva Parenteral Medicines Inc .... A 949 455-4700
19 Hughes Irvine (92618) *(P-3512)*

Texarkana Aluminum, Long Beach *Also Called: TCI Texarkana Inc (P-4594)*

Texas Tst Inc .... E 951 685-2155
13428 Benson Ave Chino (91710) *(P-4587)*

Texican Inc .... E 310 384-7000
21031 Ventura Blvd Ste 1000 Woodland Hills (91364) *(P-14050)*

Texollini Inc .... C 310 537-3400
2575 E El Presidio St Long Beach (90810) *(P-1962)*

Textile Unlimited Corporation (PA) .... D 310 263-7400
20917 Higgins Ct Torrance (90501) *(P-1987)*

TFC Manufacturing Inc .... D 562 426-9559
4001 Watson Plaza Dr Lakewood (90712) *(P-5045)*

Tfd Incorporated .... E 714 630-7127
39 Heritage Irvine (92604) *(P-8025)*

Tfn Architectural Signage Inc (PA) .... E 714 556-0990
527 Fee Ana St Placentia (92870) *(P-8645)*

Thaihot Investment Co US Ltd .... A 949 242-5300
18201 Von Karman Ave Ste 600 Irvine (92612) *(P-16336)*

Thalasinos Enterprises Inc .... E 951 340-0911
1220 Railroad St Corona (92882) *(P-10468)*

Thales Avionics Inc .... E 949 381-3033
48 Discovery Irvine (92618) *(P-7575)*

Thales Avionics Inc .... E 949 790-2500
51 Discovery Ste 100 Irvine (92618) *(P-7576)*

Thales Avionics Inc .... E 949 829-5808
9975 Toledo Way Irvine (92618) *(P-7577)*

Tharpe & Howell (PA) .... D 818 205-9955
15250 Ventura Blvd Fl 9 Sherman Oaks (91403) *(P-16789)*

The Alternative Copy Shop Inc .... D 805 569-2116
3887 State St Ste 12 Santa Barbara (93105) *(P-13317)*

The Bobrick Corporation (PA) .... D 818 764-1000
6901 Tujunga Ave North Hollywood (91605) *(P-2596)*

THE CANCER CENTER OF SANTA BARBARA, Santa Barbara *Also Called: Cancer Center of Santa Barbara (P-15260)*

The China Press, San Gabriel *Also Called: Asia-Pacific California Inc (P-2780)*

The Coding Source LLC .... C 866 235-7553
3415 S Sepulveda Blvd Ste 900 Los Angeles (90034) *(P-16847)*

The Copley Press Inc .... A 858 454-0411
7776 Ivanhoe Ave La Jolla (92037) *(P-14427)*

The Eberly Company, Beverly Hills *Also Called: Charles & Cynthia Eberly Inc (P-12335)*

The Enkeboll Co .... E 310 532-1400
16506 Avalon Blvd Carson (90746) *(P-2331)*

The Full Void 2 Inc .... B 818 891-5999
16320 Roscoe Blvd Ste 100 Van Nuys (91406) *(P-2897)*

The Goodwin Company, Garden Grove *Also Called: Goodwin Ammonia Company LLC (P-3593)*

The Heat Factory Inc .... E 760 893-8300
2793 Loker Ave W Carlsbad (92010) *(P-2741)*

The Hunter Spice Inc .... D 805 597-8900
184 Suburban Rd San Luis Obispo (93401) *(P-1861)*

The J Paul Getty Trust (PA) .... A 310 440-7300
1200 Getty Center Dr Ste 500 Los Angeles (90049) *(P-17268)*

The Jerde Partnership Inc .... D 310 399-1987
601 W 5th St Ste 500 Los Angeles (90071) *(P-17694)*

The Korea Times Los Angeles Inc (PA) .... C 323 692-2000
3731 Wilshire Blvd Ste 1000 Los Angeles (90010) *(P-2832)*

The Ligature Inc (HQ) .... E 323 585-6000
4909 Alcoa Ave Vernon (90058) *(P-3089)*

The Lodge At Torrey Pines Partnership L P .... B
998 W Mission Bay Dr San Diego (92109) *(P-13051)*

The Lunada Bay Corporation (PA) .... E 714 490-1313
2000 E Winston Rd Anaheim (92806) *(P-2172)*

The Metropolitan Water District of Southern California (PA) ..... A 213 217-6000
700 N Alameda St Los Angeles (90012) *(P-9723)*

The Orange County Printing Co, Irvine *Also Called: Ocpc Inc (P-3052)*

The Original Cult Inc .... D 323 260-7308
40 E Verdugo Ave Burbank (91502) *(P-2138)*

The Orthopedic Institute of .... A 213 977-2010
616 Witmer St Los Angeles (90017) *(P-15490)*

The Palace of Auburn Hills, Beverly Hills *Also Called: Pse Holding LLC (P-15035)*

The Pines Ltd .... C 619 447-1880
1423 E Washington Ave El Cajon (92019) *(P-12368)*

The Rand Corporation (PA) .... A 310 393-0411
1776 Main St Santa Monica (90401) *(P-17892)*

The Rule Group, Newport Beach *Also Called: Trg Insurance Services (P-12262)*

The Rutter Group, North Hollywood *Also Called: West Publishing Corporation (P-2900)*

The Ryland Group Inc .... A 805 367-3800
3011 Townsgate Rd Ste 200 Westlake Village (91361) *(P-465)*

The Salk Institute For Biological Studies San Diego California ..... A 858 453-4100
10010 N Torrey Pines Rd La Jolla (92037) *(P-17829)*

The San Diego Yacht Club .... C 619 221-8400
1011 Anchorage Ln San Diego (92106) *(P-15181)*

The Strand Energy Company .... B 213 225-5900
515 S Flower St Ste 4800 Los Angeles (90071) *(P-276)*

The Sweet Life Enterprises Inc .... C 949 261-7400
2350 Pullman St Santa Ana (92705) *(P-1409)*

The Tax Credit Company .... D 323 927-0750
6464 W Sunset Blvd Ste 1150 Los Angeles (90028) *(P-13297)*

The Timing Inc .... E 323 589-5577
2807 S Santa Fe Ave Vernon (90058) *(P-10731)*

The Tristaff Group, Vista *Also Called: Garich Inc (P-13520)*

The Wave, Manhattan Beach *Also Called: Wave Community Newspapers Inc (P-2837)*

The White Sheet, Palm Desert *Also Called: Associated Desert Shoppers Inc (P-2904)*

The Wonderful Company LLC (PA) .... **C** **310 966-5700**
11444 W Olympic Blvd Fl 10 Los Angeles (90064) *(P-1588)*

The/Studio .... E 213 233-1633
360 E 2nd St Ste 800 Los Angeles (90012) *(P-3184)*

Theater Arts Fndtion San Dego .... C 858 623-3366
2910 La Jolla Village Dr La Jolla (92093) *(P-17369)*

Thebouqs.com, Marina Del Rey *Also Called: Bouqs Company (P-11084)*

Theodore, Los Angeles *Also Called: Country Club Fashions Inc (P-11491)*

Theodore Robins Inc .... D 949 642-0010
2060 Harbor Blvd Costa Mesa (92627) *(P-11418)*

Theodore Robins Ford, Costa Mesa *Also Called: Theodore Robins Inc (P-11418)*

Theorem LLC, Woodland Hills *Also Called: Citrusbyte LLC (P-13688)*

Therapak LLC (DH) .... **D** **909 267-2000**
651 Wharton Dr Claremont (91711) *(P-10112)*

Therapy Specialist, Chula Vista *Also Called: Susan J Harris Inc (P-17201)*

Therapytravelers LLC .... D 888 223-8002
355 Redondo Ave Long Beach (90814) *(P-15557)*

Therm Core Products, San Bernardino *Also Called: Caldesso LLC (P-11676)*

Therm Pacific, Commerce *Also Called: Hkf Inc (P-10335)*

Thermal Dynamics, Ontario *Also Called: Thmx Holdings LLC (P-7297)*

Thermal Energy Solutions Inc .... E 661 489-4100
100 Quantico Ave Bakersfield (93307) *(P-700)*

Thermal Engineering, Cerritos *Also Called: Thermal Engrg Intl USA Inc (P-17647)*

Thermal Engrg Intl USA Inc (HQ) .... **D** **323 726-0641**
18000 Studebaker Rd Ste 400 Cerritos (90703) *(P-17647)*

Thermal Equipment Corporation .... E 310 328-6600
2146 E Gladwick St Rancho Dominguez (90220) *(P-7832)*

Thermal Rite, Commerce *Also Called: Crowntonka California Inc (P-5972)*

Thermal Solutions Mfg Inc .... E 909 796-0754
1390 S Tippecanoe Ave Ste B San Bernardino (92408) *(P-7296)*

Thermal Structures Inc (DH) .... **B** **951 736-9911**
2362 Railroad St Corona (92878) *(P-7396)*

Thermal-Vac Technology Inc .... E 714 997-2601
1221 W Struck Ave Orange (92867) *(P-4715)*

Thermalrite, Rancho Cucamonga *Also Called: Everidge Inc (P-5976)*

Thermaprint Corporation .... E 949 583-0800
11 Autry Ste B Irvine (92618) *(P-8445)*

Thermasol Steam Bath, Simi Valley *Also Called: DMA Enterprises Inc (P-8675)*

Thermech Corporation .... E 714 533-3183
1773 W Lincoln Ave Ste I Anaheim (92801) *(P-2712)*

Thermech Engineering, Anaheim *Also Called: Thermech Corporation (P-2712)*

Thermlly Engnred Mnfctred Pdts .... E 310 523-9934
543 W 135th St Gardena (90248) *(P-4932)*

Thermo Fisher Scientific, Carlsbad *Also Called: Life Technologies Corporation (P-3544)*

Thermo Fisher Scientific Inc .... E 781 622-1000
5823 Newton Dr Carlsbad (92008) *(P-7986)*

Thermo Fisher Scientific Inc .... D 858 453-7551
9389 Waples St San Diego (92121) *(P-7987)*

Thermo Fisher Scientific Inc .... D 760 603-7200
5791 Van Allen Way Carlsbad (92008) *(P-7988)*

Thermo Fisher Scntific Pag Corp (HQ) .... **C** **760 603-7200**
5791 Van Allen Way Carlsbad (92008) *(P-7989)*

Thermo Power Industries .... E 562 799-0087
10570 Humbolt St Los Alamitos (90720) *(P-1034)*

Thermo Power Industries, Los Alamitos *Also Called: Thermo Power Industries (P-1034)*

Thermo Trilogy, Wasco *Also Called: Certis USA LLC (P-3752)*

Thermobile, Santa Ana *Also Called: Hood Manufacturing Inc (P-4133)*

Thermocraft .... D 619 813-2985
2554 Commercial St San Diego (92113) *(P-5985)*

Thermodyne International Ltd .... C 909 923-9945
1841 S Business Pkwy Ontario (91761) *(P-4257)*

THETRADEDESK, Ventura *Also Called: Trade Desk Inc (P-13847)*

Thewrap .... E 424 273-4787
2260 S Centinela Ave Ste 150 Los Angeles (90064) *(P-2833)*

Thi Inc .... D 714 444-4643
1525 E Edinger Ave Santa Ana (92705) *(P-8238)*

Thi Holdings (delaware) Inc .... B 661 266-7423
2140 E Palmdale Blvd Ste O Palmdale (93550) *(P-12258)*

Thiessen Products Inc .... C 805 482-6913
555 Dawson Dr Ste A Camarillo (93012) *(P-6248)*

Thin Film Devices, Irvine *Also Called: Tfd Incorporated (P-8025)*

Thin-Lite Corporation .... E 805 987-5021
530 Constitution Ave Camarillo (93012) *(P-6519)*

Thingap, Camarillo *Also Called: Thingap Inc (P-6335)*

Thingap Inc .... E 805 477-9741
4035 Via Pescador Camarillo (93012) *(P-6335)*

Think Together .... B 562 236-3835
12016 Telegraph Rd Santa Fe Springs (90670) *(P-15065)*

Think Together .... B 626 373-2311
800 S Barranca Ave Ste 120 Covina (91723) *(P-17113)*

Think Together .... B 951 571-9944
22620 Goldencrest Dr Ste 104 Moreno Valley (92553) *(P-17114)*

Think Together .... B 909 723-1400
202 E Airport Dr Ste 200 San Bernardino (92408) *(P-17115)*

Think Together .... B 760 269-1230
17270 Bear Valley Rd Ste 103 Victorville (92395) *(P-17471)*

Thinkbasic Inc .... C 858 755-6922
350 10th Ave San Diego (92101) *(P-13336)*

Thinkcp Technologies, Irvine *Also Called: H Co Computer Products (P-5879)*

Thinkom Solutions Inc .... C 310 371-5486
4881 W 145th St Hawthorne (90250) *(P-9570)*

Third Floor North Company, Placentia *Also Called: Tfn Architectural Signage Inc (P-8645)*

Thirty Three Threads Inc (PA) .... **E** **877 486-3769**
1330 Park Center Dr Vista (92081) *(P-2029)*

Thistle Roller Co Inc .... E 323 685-5322
209 Van Norman Rd Montebello (90640) *(P-5667)*

Thmx Holdings LLC .... C 909 390-3944
4850 E Airport Dr Ontario (91761) *(P-7297)*

Thomas Gallaway Corporation (PA) .... **D** **949 517-9500**
100 Spectrum Center Dr Ste 700 Irvine (92618) *(P-13843)*

Thomas Hemmings .... D 303 489-3259
1620 5th Ave Ste 400 San Diego (92101) *(P-13844)*

Thomas James Capital Inc .... C 949 481-7026
26940 Aliso Viejo Pkwy Ste 100 Aliso Viejo (92656) *(P-12035)*

Thomas James Homes LLC .... C 949 424-2356
26880 Aliso Viejo Pkwy Ste 200 Aliso Viejo (92656) *(P-12538)*

Thomas Properties Group Inc .... C 213 613-1900
515 S Flower St Ste 600 Los Angeles (90071) *(P-12539)*

Thompco Inc .... E 805 933-8048
899 Mission Rock Rd Santa Paula (93060) *(P-10360)*

Thompson ADB Industries, Westminster *Also Called: Thompson Industries Ltd (P-7578)*

Thompson Building Materials, Fontana *Also Called: Valori Sand & Gravel Company (P-9952)*

Thompson Gundrilling Inc .... E 323 873-4045
13840 Saticoy St Van Nuys (91402) *(P-4560)*

Thompson Industries Ltd .... C 310 679-9193
7155 Fenwick Ln Westminster (92683) *(P-7578)*

Thompson Pipe Group Inc (PA) .... **E** **909 822-0200**
3011 N Laurel Ave Rialto (92377) *(P-2777)*

Thomson Industries Inc .... E 619 661-6292
2695 Customhouse Ct San Diego (92154) *(P-6249)*

Thomson Lnear Motion Optimized, San Diego *Also Called: Thomson Industries Inc (P-6249)*

Thomson Reuters Corporation .... E 310 287-2360
3280 Motor Ave Ste 200 Los Angeles (90034) *(P-2947)*

Thomson Reuters Corporation .... E 949 400-7782
163 Albert Pl Costa Mesa (92627) *(P-2948)*

Thomson Reuters Corporation .... E 877 518-2761
5161 Lankershim Blvd North Hollywood (91601) *(P-6665)*

Thornhill Companies Inc .... D 805 969-5803
132 E Carrillo St Santa Barbara (93101) *(P-11062)*

Thornton Technologies, Oceanside *Also Called: Thornton Technology Corp (P-10503)*

Thornton Technology Corp .... E 760 471-9969
2608 Temple Heights Dr Oceanside (92056) *(P-10503)*

Thornton Winery .... D 951 699-0099
32575 Rancho California Rd Temecula (92591) *(P-1589)*

Thorpe Technologies Inc (DH) .... **E** **562 903-8230**
449 W Allen Ave Ste 119 San Dimas (91773) *(P-17648)*

Thoughtful Asia Limited, Sherman Oaks *Also Called: Adactive Media Ca Inc (P-13258)*

Thousand LLC .... E 310 745-0110
915 Mateo St Ste 302 Los Angeles (90021) *(P-8547)*

Employee Codes: A=Over 500 employees, B=251-500
C=101-250, D=51-100, E=20-50, F=10-19, G=1-9

2025 Southern California
Business Directory and Buyers Guide

© Mergent Inc. 1-800-342-5647
1211

THOUSAND OAKS HEALTH CARE CENTER, Thousand Oaks *Also Called: Five Star Qúlty Care-CA II LLC* *(P-15653)*

Thousand Oaks Prtg & Spc Inc .... C 818 706-8330
5334 Sterling Center Dr Westlake Village (91361) *(P-14610)*

Thousand Oaks Service Center, Thousand Oaks *Also Called: Southern California Edison Co* *(P-9639)*

Thousand Oaks Surgical Hosp LP .... D 805 777-7750
401 Rolling Oaks Dr Thousand Oaks (91361) *(P-16228)*

Thq Inc .... A 818 591-1310
21900 Burbank Blvd Woodland Hills (91367) *(P-14051)*

Thq San Diego, Woodland Hills *Also Called: Thq Inc* *(P-14051)*

Three Sons Inc .... D 562 801-4100
5201 Industry Ave Pico Rivera (90660) *(P-10883)*

Three-D Plastics Inc (PA) .... E 323 849-1316
430 N Varney St Burbank (91502) *(P-4258)*

Three-D Traffics Works, Burbank *Also Called: Three-D Plastics Inc* *(P-4258)*

Three-Way Chevrolet Co (PA) .... C 661 847-6400
4501 Wible Rd Bakersfield (93313) *(P-11419)*

Threesixty Group, Irvine *Also Called: Merchsource LLC* *(P-10524)*

Thrio Inc .... E 858 299-7191
5230 Las Virgenes Rd Ste 210 Calabasas (91302) *(P-14052)*

Thums Long Beach Company .... C 562 624-3400
111 W Ocean Blvd Ste 800 Long Beach (90802) *(P-277)*

Thunder International Group (PA) .... D 626 723-3715
19485 E Walnut Dr N City Of Industry (91748) *(P-9342)*

Thunderbolt Manufacturing Inc .... E 714 632-0397
641 S State College Blvd Fullerton (92831) *(P-6250)*

Thursby Software Systems LLC .... E 817 478-5070
1900 Carnegie Ave Santa Ana (92705) *(P-14053)*

Thyde Inc (PA) .... C 951 817-2300
300 El Sobrante Rd Corona (92879) *(P-14611)*

Thyssenkrupp Bilstein Amer Inc .... E 858 386-5900
13225 Danielson St # 100 Poway (92064) *(P-7298)*

TI Limited LLC (PA) .... D 323 877-5991
20335 Ventura Blvd Ste 231-239 Woodland Hills (91364) *(P-14054)*

TI Wire, Walnut *Also Called: Tree Island Wire (USA) Inc* *(P-4544)*

Tianello Inc .... C 323 231-0599
138 W 38th St Los Angeles (90037) *(P-2055)*

Tianello By Steve Barraza, Los Angeles *Also Called: Tianello Inc* *(P-2055)*

Tic Hotels Inc .... D 619 238-7577
555 W Ash St San Diego (92101) *(P-13052)*

Tic Hotels Inc .... D 805 773-4671
2555 Price St Pismo Beach (93449) *(P-13053)*

Ticketmanager .... D 818 698-3616
26635 Agoura Rd Ste 200 Calabasas (91302) *(P-15225)*

Ticketmaster, Los Angeles *Also Called: Ticketmaster Corporation* *(P-15226)*

Ticketmaster, Los Angeles *Also Called: Ticketmaster Group Inc* *(P-15228)*

Ticketmaster, Beverly Hills *Also Called: Ticketmster New Vntres Hldngs* *(P-15229)*

Ticketmaster Corporation .... A 323 769-4600
7060 Hollywood Blvd Ste 2 Los Angeles (90028) *(P-15226)*

Ticketmaster Entertainment LLC .... A 800 653-8000
8800 W Sunset Blvd West Hollywood (90069) *(P-15227)*

Ticketmaster Group Inc .... A 800 745-3000
3701 Wilshire Blvd Fl 9 Los Angeles (90010) *(P-15228)*

Ticketmster New Vntres Hldngs (HQ) .... C 800 653-8000
325 N Maple Dr Beverly Hills (90210) *(P-15229)*

Ticketscom LLC (DH) .... E 714 327-5400
2100 E Grand Ave Ste 600 El Segundo (90245) *(P-14981)*

Tide Rock Holdings LLC (PA) .... C 858 204-7438
343 S Highway 101 Ste 200 Solana Beach (92075) *(P-5046)*

Tidelands Oil Production Inc .... E 562 436-9918
301 E Ocean Blvd St 300 Long Beach (90802) *(P-278)*

Tidwell Excav Acquisition Inc .... D 805 647-4707
1691 Los Angeles Ave Ventura (93004) *(P-1177)*

Tidwell Excavating, Ventura *Also Called: Tidwell Excav Acquisition Inc* *(P-1177)*

Tierra Del Sol Foundation .... D 909 626-8301
250 W 1st St Ste 120 Claremont (91711) *(P-15230)*

Tierra Del Sol Foundation (PA) .... D 818 352-1419
9919 Sunland Blvd Sunland (91040) *(P-17202)*

Tierra Del Soul, Claremont *Also Called: Tierra Del Sol Foundation* *(P-15230)*

Tierra Verde Resources Inc (PA) .... C 857 777-6190
1545 Lake Dr Encinitas (92024) *(P-237)*

Tiffany Coach Builders, Perris *Also Called: Warlock Industries* *(P-7195)*

Tiffany Coachworks, Perris *Also Called: Limos By Tiffany Inc* *(P-7206)*

Tiffany Dale Inc (PA) .... D 714 739-2700
14765 Firestone Blvd La Mirada (90638) *(P-9911)*

Tiffany Homecare Inc (PA) .... B 818 886-1602
9700 Reseda Blvd Ste 105 Northridge (91324) *(P-16425)*

Tig/M LLC .... E 818 709-8500
21020 Lassen St Chatsworth (91311) *(P-5520)*

Tiger Tanks Inc .... E 661 363-8335
3397 Edison Hwy Bakersfield (93307) *(P-7681)*

Tigerconnect Inc (PA) .... D 310 401-1820
2054 Broadway Santa Monica (90404) *(P-14261)*

Tile & Marble Design Co Inc .... E 714 847-6472
7421 Vincent Cir Huntington Beach (92648) *(P-1043)*

Tiling and Stone Counter Tops, Ontario *Also Called: Calvillo Construction Corp* *(P-393)*

Tilton Engineering Inc .... E 805 688-2353
25 Easy St Buellton (93427) *(P-7299)*

Timberlake Painting, Murrieta *Also Called: Temecula Valley Drywall Inc* *(P-1033)*

Timbucktoo Manufacturing Inc .... E 310 323-1134
1633 W 134th St Gardena (90249) *(P-6035)*

Timco, Hesperia *Also Called: T L Timmerman Cnstr Inc* *(P-2382)*

Time Warner, San Diego *Also Called: Spectrum MGT Holdg Co LLC* *(P-9556)*

Time Warner, Los Angeles *Also Called: Spectrum MGT Holdg Co LLC* *(P-9557)*

Time Warner, Burbank *Also Called: Time Warner Cable Entps LLC* *(P-9558)*

Time Warner Cable Entps LLC .... C 818 977-7840
4000 Warner Blvd Burbank (91526) *(P-9558)*

Timec, E Rncho Dmngz *Also Called: Timec Companies Inc* *(P-721)*

Timec Companies Inc .... C 310 885-4710
2997 E Maria St E Rncho Dmngz (90221) *(P-721)*

Timec Companies Inc .... E 661 322-8177
6861 Charity Ave Bakersfield (93308) *(P-5722)*

Timec Southern California, Bakersfield *Also Called: Timec Companies Inc* *(P-5722)*

Timely Prefinished Steel, Pacoima *Also Called: SDS Industries Inc* *(P-4902)*

Timemed Labeling Systems Inc (DH) .... D 818 897-1111
27770 Entertainment Dr Ste 200 Valencia (91355) *(P-3940)*

Timeshare Compliance, Aliso Viejo *Also Called: Pandora Marketing LLC* *(P-18190)*

Timevalue Software .... E 949 727-1800
22 Mauchly Irvine (92618) *(P-14055)*

Timing Fashion, Vernon *Also Called: The Timing Inc* *(P-10731)*

Timken Gears & Services Inc .... E 310 605-2600
12935 Imperial Hwy Santa Fe Springs (90670) *(P-5150)*

Tinco Sheet Metal Inc .... C 323 263-0511
958 N Eastern Ave Los Angeles (90063) *(P-1098)*

Tinker & Rasor .... E 909 890-0700
791 S Waterman Ave San Bernardino (92408) *(P-7819)*

Tiodize Co Inc .... E 714 898-4377
15701 Industry Ln Huntington Beach (92649) *(P-11036)*

Tire Pros, Simi Valley *Also Called: Am-Pac Tire Dist Inc* *(P-11439)*

Tireco Inc (PA) .... C 310 767-7990
500 W 190th St Ste 600 Gardena (90248) *(P-9861)*

Tires Warehouse LLC .... B 714 432-8851
18203 Mount Baldy Cir Fountain Valley (92708) *(P-11469)*

Tissue-Grown Corporation .... D 805 525-1975
15245 W Telegraph Rd Santa Paula (93060) *(P-17830)*

Titan, Camarillo *Also Called: Titan Metal Fabricators Inc* *(P-4873)*

Titan Metal Fabricators Inc .... D 805 487-5050
352 Balboa Cir Camarillo (93012) *(P-4873)*

Titan Oilfield Services, Bakersfield *Also Called: Titan Oilfield Services Inc* *(P-364)*

Titan Oilfield Services Inc .... D 661 861-1630
21535 Kratzmeyer Rd Bakersfield (93314) *(P-364)*

Titan Solar, Woodland Hills *Also Called: Memeged Tevuot Shemesh* *(P-803)*

Titan Wolrdwide, Cerritos *Also Called: Silver Hawk Freight Inc* *(P-9336)*

Title365 Holding Co (HQ) .... B 949 475-3752
5000 Birch St Ste 300 Newport Beach (92660) *(P-12157)*

Titleist, Carlsbad *Also Called: Acushnet Company* *(P-8498)*

Tivoli LLC .... E 714 957-6101
17110 Armstrong Ave Irvine (92614) *(P-6408)*

Mergent email: customerrelations@mergent.com
1212

2025 Southern California
Business Directory and Buyers Guide

(P-0000) Products & Services Section entry number
(PA)=Parent Co (HQ)=Headquarters (DH)=Div Headquarters

Tj Aerospace, Garden Grove *Also Called: Tj Aerospace Inc (P-7579)*

Tj Aerospace Inc .... E 714 891-3564
12601 Monarch St Garden Grove (92841) *(P-7579)*

Tjs Metal Manufacturing Inc .... E 310 604-1545
10847 Drury Ln Lynwood (90262) *(P-5072)*

Tk Elevator Corporation .... D 619 596-7220
1965 Gillespie Way Ste 101 El Cajon (92020) *(P-10411)*

Tk Pax Inc .... E 714 850-1330
1545 Macarthur Blvd Costa Mesa (92626) *(P-3876)*

Tka, La Palma *Also Called: Tech Knowledge Associates LLC (P-14797)*

Tl Enterprises LLC .... C 805 981-8393
2750 Park View Ct Ste 240 Oxnard (93036) *(P-2877)*

Tl Machine Inc .... D 714 554-4154
14272 Commerce Dr Garden Grove (92843) *(P-5115)*

TL Montgomery & Associates Inc .... C 323 583-1645
2833 Leonis Blvd Ste 205 Vernon (90058) *(P-10984)*

TL Shield & Associates Inc .... E 818 509-8228
1030 Arroyo St San Fernando (91340) *(P-5515)*

Tld Acquisition Co LLC C
505 S 7th Ave City Of Industry (91746) *(P-10985)*

Tld Distribution Co, City Of Industry *Also Called: Tld Acquisition Co LLC (P-10985)*

Tlmf Inc .... D 212 764-2334
1515 E 15th St Los Angeles (90021) *(P-2073)*

Tls Productions Inc .... E 810 220-8577
6 Venture Irvine (92618) *(P-1229)*

Tm Claims Service Inc .... D 626 568-7800
800 E Colorado Blvd Pasadena (91101) *(P-12259)*

Tm Highland Insurance Services, South Pasadena *Also Called: Tokio Marine Highland Insurance Services Inc (P-12260)*

TMI Products Inc .... C 951 272-1996
1493 E Bentley Dr Ste 102 Corona (92879) *(P-7300)*

TMI Visualogic, Corona *Also Called: TMI Products Inc (P-7300)*

TMJ Concepts, Ventura *Also Called: TMJ Solutions LLC (P-8239)*

TMJ Solutions LLC .... D 805 650-3391
6059 King Dr Ventura (93003) *(P-8239)*

TMW Corporation (PA) .... C **818 362-5665**
15148 Bledsoe St Sylmar (91342) *(P-7580)*

Tmx Aerospace .... C 562 215-4410
12821 Carmenita Rd Unit F Santa Fe Springs (90670) *(P-10160)*

Tmx Engineering and Mfg Corp .... D 714 641-5884
2141 S Standard Ave Santa Ana (92707) *(P-6251)*

Tnk Therapeutics Inc (HQ) .... D **858 210-3700**
9380 Judicial Dr San Diego (92121) *(P-17831)*

TNT Plastic Molding Inc (PA) .... D **951 808-9700**
725 E Harrison St Corona (92879) *(P-4259)*

TO HELP EVERYONE HEALTH AND WE, Los Angeles *Also Called: Clinic Inc (P-15280)*

Toad & Co, Santa Barbara *Also Called: Toad & Co International Inc (P-2139)*

Toad & Co International Inc (PA) .... E **800 865-8623**
2020 Alameda Padre Serra Ste 125 Santa Barbara (93103) *(P-2139)*

Toan D Nguyen DDS Inc .... D 909 599-3398
213 N San Dimas Ave San Dimas (91773) *(P-15528)*

TOAN D NGUYEN DDS INC, San Dimas *Also Called: Toan D Nguyen DDS Inc (P-15528)*

Tobin Lucks, West Hills *Also Called: Tobin Lucks A Prof Corp (P-16790)*

Tobin Lucks A Prof Corp (PA) .... D 818 226-3400
8511 Fallbrook Ave Ste 400 West Hills (91304) *(P-16790)*

Tobin Steel Company Inc .... D 714 541-2268
817 E Santa Ana Blvd Santa Ana (92701) *(P-4874)*

Toby Wells YMCA, San Diego *Also Called: YMCA of San Diego County (P-17382)*

Todays IV .... A 213 835-4016
404 S Figueroa St Ste 516 Los Angeles (90071) *(P-13054)*

Toesox, Vista *Also Called: Thirty Three Threads Inc (P-2029)*

Toi, Cerritos *Also Called: Oncology Institute Inc (P-16325)*

Tokio Marine Highland Insurance Services Inc (DH) .... D **626 463-6486**
899 El Centro St South Pasadena (91030) *(P-12260)*

Tokio Marine Michido, Pasadena *Also Called: Tm Claims Service Inc (P-12259)*

Tokyopop Inc (PA) .... D **323 920-5967**
4136 Del Rey Ave Marina Del Rey (90292) *(P-2898)*

Tolar Manufacturing Co Inc .... E 951 808-0081
258 Mariah Cir Corona (92879) *(P-4875)*

Toleeto Fastener International .... E 619 662-1355
1580 Jayken Way Chula Vista (91911) *(P-8578)*

Tolemar LLC .... E 657 200-3840
6412 Maple Ave Westminster (92683) *(P-6409)*

TOLL GLOBAL FORWARDING SCS (USA) INC., Jurupa Valley *Also Called: Toll Global Fwdg Scs USA Inc (P-9343)*

Toll Global Fwdg Scs USA Inc .... D 951 360-8310
3355 Dulles Dr Jurupa Valley (91752) *(P-9343)*

Toll Global Fwdg Scs USA Inc .... C 732 750-9000
400 Westmont Dr 450 San Pedro (90731) *(P-9344)*

Toller Enterprises Inc (PA) .... E **805 374-9455**
2251 Townsgate Rd Westlake Village (91361) *(P-11478)*

Tolosa Winery, San Luis Obispo *Also Called: Courtside Cellars LLC (P-1562)*

Tom Bell Chevrolet, Redlands *Also Called: Dick Dewese Chevrolet Inc (P-11337)*

Tom Dreher Sales Inc .... D 562 355-4074
2021 W 17th St Long Beach (90813) *(P-10053)*

Tom Ferry Coaching, Santa Ana *Also Called: Ferry International LLC (P-18135)*

Tom Ferry Your Coach, Santa Ana *Also Called: Success Strategies Inst Inc (P-17068)*

Tomi Engineering Inc .... D 714 556-1474
414 E Alton Ave Santa Ana (92707) *(P-6252)*

Tomorrows Look Inc .... D 949 596-8400
17462 Von Karman Ave Irvine (92614) *(P-1936)*

Toms Truck Center Inc .... C 714 835-1978
1008 E 4th St Santa Ana (92701) *(P-11420)*

Tone It Up LLC .... E 310 376-7645
1110 Manhattan Ave Manhattan Beach (90266) *(P-11310)*

Toneonel Lavash, Los Angeles *Also Called: Lavash Corporation of America (P-1459)*

Tool Alliance Corporation .... E 714 373-5864
5372 Mcfadden Ave Huntington Beach (92649) *(P-5627)*

Tool Components Inc (PA) .... E **310 323-5613**
240 E Rosecrans Ave Gardena (90248) *(P-10161)*

Tool Specialty Co, Los Angeles *Also Called: Tosco - Tool Specialty Company (P-6253)*

Tooth and Nail Winery .... E 805 369-6100
3090 Anderson Rd Paso Robles (93446) *(P-1590)*

Top Finance Company, Chatsworth *Also Called: Platinum Group Companies Inc (P-12607)*

Top Heavy Clothing Company Inc (PA) .... D **951 442-8839**
28381 Vincent Moraga Dr Temecula (92590) *(P-1988)*

Top Line Mfg Inc .... E 562 633-0605
7032 Alondra Blvd Paramount (90723) *(P-4791)*

Top Source, The, Anaheim *Also Called: Block Tops Inc (P-2557)*

Top-Shelf Fixtures LLC .... D 909 627-7423
5263 Schaefer Ave Chino (91710) *(P-5416)*

Topa Insurance Company (HQ) .... D **310 201-0451**
1800 Avenue Of The Stars Ste 1200 Los Angeles (90067) *(P-12261)*

Topa Property Group Inc (HQ) .... C **310 203-9199**
1800 Avenue Of The Stars Ste 1400 Los Angeles (90067) *(P-12321)*

Topaz Lighting Company LLC .... E 818 838-3123
225 Parkside Dr San Fernando (91340) *(P-6476)*

Topaz Systems Inc (PA) .... E **805 520-8282**
875 Patriot Dr Ste A Moorpark (93021) *(P-5952)*

Topco Sales, Simi Valley *Also Called: Wsm Investments LLC (P-12681)*

Topgolf Callaway Brands Corp (PA) .... B **760 931-1771**
2180 Rutherford Rd Carlsbad (92008) *(P-8548)*

Toppik, Los Angeles *Also Called: Spencer Forrest Inc (P-11664)*

Topson Downs, Culver City *Also Called: Topson Downs California LLC (P-11494)*

Topson Downs California Inc .... C 310 558-0300
3545 Motor Ave Los Angeles (90034) *(P-2078)*

Topson Downs California LLC (PA) .... C 310 558-0300
3840 Watseka Ave Culver City (90232) *(P-11494)*

TOPSON DOWNS OF CALIFORNIA, INC., Los Angeles *Also Called: Topson Downs California Inc (P-2078)*

Toray Membrane Usa Inc (DH) .... D **858 218-2360**
13435 Danielson St Poway (92064) *(P-3821)*

Torn & Glasser Inc .... E 909 706-4100
1845 Mount Vernon Ave Pomona (91768) *(P-1518)*

Toro Company .... C 951 688-9221
5825 Jasmine St Riverside (92504) *(P-5479)*

Toro Company .... C 619 562-2950
1588 N Marshall Ave El Cajon (92020) *(P-5480)*

Toro Engineering, Poway *Also Called: Eagle Paving LLC (P-614)*

Torrance Care Center West Inc .... C 310 370-4561
4333 Torrance Blvd Torrance (90503) *(P-15786)*

Employee Codes: A=Over 500 employees, B=251-500
C=101-250, D=51-100, E=20-50, F=10-19, G=1-9

2025 Southern California
Business Directory and Buyers Guide

© Mergent Inc. 1-800-342-5647

1213

Torrance Health Assn Inc (PA)..................A 310 325-9110
3330 Lomita Blvd Torrance (90505) *(P-16229)*

Torrance Memorial Breast Diagn, Manhattan Beach *Also Called: Torrance Memorial Medical Ctr (P-16231)*

Torrance Memorial Medical Ctr (HQ)..................A 310 325-9110
3330 Lomita Blvd Torrance (90505) *(P-16230)*

Torrance Memorial Medical Ctr..................B 310 939-7847
855 Manhattan Beach Blvd Ste 208 Manhattan Beach (90266) *(P-16231)*

Torrance Memorial Medical Ctr..................B 310 784-6316
3333 Skypark Dr Ste 200 Torrance (90505) *(P-16232)*

Torrance Memorial Medical Ctr..................B 310 784-3740
22411 Hawthorne Blvd Torrance (90505) *(P-16233)*

Torrance Refining Company LLC..................A 310 212-2800
3700 W 190th St Torrance (90504) *(P-3832)*

Torrance Steel Window Co Inc..................E 310 328-9181
1819 Abalone Ave Torrance (90501) *(P-4904)*

Torrence Aluminum Window, Redlands *Also Called: Window Enterprises Inc (P-4905)*

Torrid Merchandising Inc..................B 626 667-1002
18501 San Jose Ave City Of Industry (91748) *(P-18232)*

Tortoise Industries Inc..................E 323 258-7776
3052 Treadwell St Los Angeles (90065) *(P-5350)*

Tortoise Tube, Los Angeles *Also Called: Tortoise Industries Inc (P-5350)*

Toscana Country Club Inc..................C 760 404-1444
76009 Via Club Villa Indian Wells (92210) *(P-15182)*

Tosco - Tool Specialty Company..................E 323 232-3561
1011 E Slauson Ave Los Angeles (90011) *(P-6253)*

Toshiba, Irvine *Also Called: Toshiba Amer Elctrnic Cmpnnts (P-6562)*

Toshiba, Lake Forest *Also Called: Toshiba Amer Bus Solutions Inc (P-9979)*

Toshiba Amer Bus Solutions Inc (DH)..................B 949 462-6000
25530 Commercentre Dr Lake Forest (92630) *(P-9979)*

Toshiba Amer Elctrnic Cmpnnts (DH)..................B 949 462-7700
5231 California Ave Irvine (92617) *(P-6562)*

Toshiba Amer Info Systems Inc..................C 949 583-3000
9740 Irvine Blvd Fl 1 Irvine (92618) *(P-5871)*

Toshiba America Inc..................A 212 596-0600
5241 California Ave Ste 200 Irvine (92617) *(P-6563)*

Total Cmmnicator Solutions Inc..................D 619 277-1488
11150 Sta Monica Ste 600 Los Angeles (90025) *(P-14161)*

Total Cost Involved, Ontario *Also Called: TCI Engineering Inc (P-7194)*

Total Debt Management, Irvine *Also Called: Egs Financial Care Inc (P-13282)*

Total Garments, Westlake Village *Also Called: Hec Inc (P-10247)*

Total Health Environment LLC..................E 714 637-1010
743 W Taft Ave Orange (92865) *(P-10113)*

Total Intermodal Services Inc (PA)..................E 562 427-6300
7101 Jackson St Paramount (90723) *(P-9149)*

Total Logistics Online LLC..................D 714 526-3559
628 N Gilbert St Fullerton (92833) *(P-9345)*

Total Mont LLC..................E 562 983-1374
790 W 12th St Long Beach (90813) *(P-4347)*

Total Process Solutions LLC..................E 661 829-7910
1400 Norris Rd Bakersfield (93308) *(P-5745)*

Total Recon Solutions Inc..................D 949 584-8417
27 Oakbrook Trabuco Canyon (92679) *(P-18233)*

Total Resources Intl Inc (PA)..................E 909 594-1220
420 S Lemon Ave Walnut (91789) *(P-8309)*

Total Structures, Ventura *Also Called: Total Structures Inc (P-6520)*

Total Structures Inc..................E 805 676-3322
1696 Walter St Ventura (93003) *(P-6520)*

Total Transportation Logistics, Corona *Also Called: Total Trnsp Logistics Inc (P-8978)*

Total Trnsp Logistics Inc..................D 951 360-9521
10 Longitude Way Corona (92881) *(P-8978)*

Total Vision LLC..................C 949 652-7242
27271 Las Ramblas Ste 200a Mission Viejo (92691) *(P-15536)*

Total Warehouse, Anaheim *Also Called: Total Warehouse Inc (P-9120)*

Total Warehouse Inc..................C 714 332-3082
2895 E Miraloma Ave Anaheim (92806) *(P-9120)*

Total-Western Inc (HQ)..................E 562 220-1450
8049 Somerset Blvd Paramount (90723) *(P-365)*

Totally Bamboo, Escondido *Also Called: Hollywood Chairs (P-2426)*

Totally Kids Rhbilitation Hosp, Loma Linda *Also Called: Mountain View Child Care Inc (P-16103)*

Totally Kids Spcalty Hlth Care, Sun Valley *Also Called: Mountain View Child Care Inc (P-17098)*

Totex Manufacturing Inc..................D 310 326-2028
3050 Lomita Blvd Torrance (90505) *(P-4260)*

Totten Tubes Inc (PA)..................D 626 812-0220
500 W Danlee St Azusa (91702) *(P-10162)*

Touch International Display Enhancements Corp..................E 512 646-0310
11231 Jola Ln Garden Grove (92843) *(P-8026)*

Toughbuilt, Irvine *Also Called: Toughbuilt Industries Inc (P-4746)*

Toughbuilt Industries Inc (PA)..................B 949 528-3100
8669 Research Dr Irvine (92618) *(P-4746)*

Tour Master, Calabasas Hills *Also Called: Helmet House LLC (P-10685)*

Tourcoach Transportation, Commerce *Also Called: Screamline Investment Corp (P-9241)*

Tow Industries, West Covina *Also Called: Baatz Enterprises Inc (P-7169)*

Toward Maximum Independence (PA)..................C 858 467-0600
4740 Murphy Canyon Rd Ste 300 San Diego (92123) *(P-17017)*

Tower 26 Inc..................E 347 366-2706
8826 Bradley Ave Ste B Sun Valley (91352) *(P-8735)*

Tower Glass Inc..................D 619 596-6199
9570 Pathway St Ste A Santee (92071) *(P-1167)*

Tower Industries Inc..................C 909 947-2723
1720 S Bon View Ave Ontario (91761) *(P-6254)*

Tower Mechanical Products Inc..................C 714 947-2723
1720 S Bon View Ave Ontario (91761) *(P-7820)*

Tower Semicdtr Newport Bch Inc (DH)..................A 949 435-8000
4321 Jamboree Rd Newport Beach (92660) *(P-6905)*

Towerjazz, Newport Beach *Also Called: Tower Semicdtr Newport Bch Inc (P-6905)*

Towmaster Tire & Wheel, Anaheim *Also Called: Greenball Corp (P-9856)*

Town & Cntry Event Rentals Inc..................C 805 770-5729
3905 State St Santa Barbara (93105) *(P-13474)*

Town & Cntry Event Rentals LLC (PA)..................B 818 908-4211
7725 Airport Business Pkwy Van Nuys (91406) *(P-13475)*

TOWN & COUNTRY EVENT RENTALS, INC., Santa Barbara *Also Called: Town & Cntry Event Rentals Inc (P-13474)*

Town and Country, San Diego *Also Called: Atlas Hotels Inc (P-12763)*

Town and Country Hotel, San Diego *Also Called: Hotel Circle Property LLC (P-12855)*

Town Cntry Mnor of Chrstn Mssn..................C 714 547-7581
555 E Memory Ln Side Santa Ana (92706) *(P-15787)*

Townsend Design, Bakersfield *Also Called: Townsend Industries Inc (P-8312)*

Townsend Industries Inc..................D 661 837-1795
4401 Stine Rd Bakersfield (93313) *(P-8310)*

Townsend Industries Inc..................D 661 837-1795
4833 N Hills Dr Bakersfield (93308) *(P-8311)*

Townsend Industries Inc (DH)..................C 661 837-1795
4615 Shepard St Bakersfield (93313) *(P-8312)*

Townsteel Inc..................D 626 965-8917
17901 Railroad St City Of Industry (91748) *(P-4792)*

Toy Barn, Oxnard *Also Called: Players West Amusements Inc (P-15100)*

Toymax International Inc (HQ)..................D 310 456-7799
22619 Pacific Coast Hwy Malibu (90265) *(P-8496)*

Toyo Tire USA Corp (DH)..................D 714 236-2080
5665 Plaza Dr Ste 300 Cypress (90630) *(P-9862)*

Toyon Research Corporation (PA)..................C 805 968-6787
6800 Cortona Dr Goleta (93117) *(P-17649)*

Toyota Carlsbad, Carlsbad *Also Called: Oceanside Auto Country Inc (P-11390)*

Toyota Downtown La..................C 213 342-3646
714 W Olympic Blvd Ste 1131 Los Angeles (90015) *(P-11470)*

Toyota Logistics Services Inc (DH)..................C 310 468-4000
19001 S Western Ave Torrance (90501) *(P-11421)*

Toyota Material Hdlg Solutions, Santa Fe Springs *Also Called: Rebas Inc (P-10399)*

Toyota of Downtown L.A., Los Angeles *Also Called: Toyota Downtown La (P-11470)*

Toyota of El Cajon, El Cajon *Also Called: K Motors Inc (P-11436)*

Toyota of Glendora, Glendora *Also Called: Seidner-Miller Inc (P-11405)*

Toyota of Orange Inc..................C 714 639-6750
1400 N Tustin St Orange (92867) *(P-11422)*

Toyota of Oxnard, Oxnard *Also Called: DCH California Motors Inc (P-11334)*

Toyota of Riverside Inc..................C 951 687-1622
7870 Indiana Ave Riverside (92504) *(P-11423)*

Toyota Scion Place, Garden Grove *Also Called: Noarus Tgg (P-11389)*

Mergent email: customerrelations@mergent.com
1214

2025 Southern California
Business Directory and Buyers Guide

(P-0000) Products & Services Section entry number
(PA)=Parent Co (HQ)=Headquarters (DH)=Div Headquarters

TP USA, Claremont *Also Called: Technip Usa Inc (P-17643)*

Tp-Link Systems Inc .... C 562 528-7700
3760 Kilroy Airport Way Ste 600 Long Beach (90806) *(P-10034)*

Tp-Link Systems Inc .... C 866 225-8139
10 Mauchly Irvine (92618) *(P-13845)*

Tp-Link USA, Irvine *Also Called: Tp-Link Systems Inc (P-13845)*

Tpl Communications, Panorama City *Also Called: D X Communications Inc (P-6606)*

Tpusa - Fhcs Inc (DH) .... C 213 873-5100
215 N Marengo Ave Ste 160 Pasadena (91101) *(P-14183)*

Tpx Communications, Los Angeles *Also Called: Mpower Holding Corporation (P-9449)*

Trace3, Irvine *Also Called: Trace3 LLC (P-14111)*

Trace3 LLC (HQ) .... D 949 333-2300
7505 Irvine Center Dr Ste 100 Irvine (92618) *(P-14111)*

Trackr Inc .... D 855 981-1690
7410 Hollister Ave Santa Barbara (93117) *(P-13846)*

Tracy Industries Inc .... C 562 692-9034
3200 E Guasti Rd Ste 100 Ontario (91761) *(P-5470)*

Tracy Ryder Landscape Inc .... D 949 858-7017
22421 Gilberto Ste A Rcho Sta Marg (92688) *(P-238)*

Tracy Ryder Landscape Cnstr, Rcho Sta Marg *Also Called: Tracy Ryder Landscape Inc (P-238)*

Trade Desk Inc (PA) .... B 805 585-3434
42 N Chestnut St Ventura (93001) *(P-13847)*

Trademark Construction Co Inc (PA) .... D 760 489-5647
15916 Bernardo Center Dr San Diego (92127) *(P-7101)*

Trademark Cosmetics LLC .... E 951 683-2631
545 Columbia Ave Riverside (92507) *(P-3691)*

Trademark Plastics, Inc., Riverside *Also Called: Dek Industry Inc (P-5700)*

Tradenet Enterprise Inc .... D 888 595-3956
1580 Magnolia Ave Corona (92879) *(P-8646)*

Tradition Golf Club, La Quinta *Also Called: Chapman Golf Development LLC (P-15072)*

Traffic Control & Safety Corp .... E 858 679-7292
13755 Blaisdell Pl Poway (92064) *(P-8647)*

Traffic Control Service Inc C
4695 Macarthur Ct Ste 1100 Newport Beach (92660) *(P-13476)*

Traffic Management Inc .... D 562 264-2353
1244 S Claudina St Anaheim (92805) *(P-18066)*

Traffic Management LLC (PA) .... C 562 595-4278
4900 Airport Plaza Dr Ste 300 Long Beach (90815) *(P-14612)*

Traffic Management Pdts Inc .... A 800 763-3999
4900 Airport Plaza Dr Ste 300 Long Beach (90815) *(P-14056)*

TRAFFIC MANAGEMENT, INC., Anaheim *Also Called: Traffic Management Inc (P-18066)*

Trail Lines Inc .... D 562 758-6980
9415 Sorensen Ave Santa Fe Springs (90670) *(P-8925)*

Trailer Park Inc (PA) .... D 310 845-3000
6922 Hollywood Blvd Fl 12 Los Angeles (90028) *(P-13250)*

Train Reaction, Huntington Beach *Also Called: West Coast Trends Inc (P-8552)*

Trak Machine Tools, Rancho Dominguez *Also Called: Southwestern Industries Inc (P-5553)*

Trammell Crow Residential Co .... D 714 966-9355
949 S Coast Dr Ste 400 Costa Mesa (92626) *(P-12369)*

Trane, Walnut *Also Called: Trane US Inc (P-5986)*

Trane, San Diego *Also Called: Trane US Inc (P-5987)*

Trane US Inc .... E 626 913-7913
20450 E Walnut Dr N Walnut (91789) *(P-5986)*

Trane US Inc .... C 858 292-0833
3565 Corporate Ct Fl 1 San Diego (92123) *(P-5987)*

Trane US Inc .... D 626 913-7123
3253 E Imperial Hwy Brea (92821) *(P-5988)*

Trans-Dapt California Inc .... E 562 921-0404
12438 Putnam St Whittier (90602) *(P-7301)*

Trans-West Services Inc .... B 661 381-2900
8503 Crippen St Bakersfield (93311) *(P-14356)*

Transamerica Occidental Life Insurance Company ... A 213 742-2111
1150 S Olive St Fl 23 Los Angeles (90015) *(P-12053)*

Transamerican, Escondido *Also Called: Transamerican Direct Inc (P-13307)*

Transamerican Direct Inc .... D 760 745-5343
355 State Pl Escondido (92029) *(P-13307)*

Transamerican Dissolution LLC (HQ) .... C 310 900-5500
400 W Artesia Blvd Compton (90220) *(P-11471)*

Transcendia Inc .... E 909 944-9981
9000 9th St Ste 140 Rancho Cucamonga (91730) *(P-11003)*

Transcentra Inc .... A 310 603-0105
20500 Belshaw Ave Carson (90746) *(P-14112)*

Transcom Telecommunication Inc .... E 562 424-9616
1390 E Burnett St Ste C Signal Hill (90755) *(P-6666)*

Transcosmos Omniconnect LLC .... D 310 630-0072
879 W 190th St Ste 1050 Gardena (90248) *(P-18067)*

Transdev Services Inc .... B 619 401-4503
544 Vernon Way El Cajon (92020) *(P-8850)*

Transdev Services Inc .... A 626 357-7912
5640 Peck Rd Arcadia (91006) *(P-8851)*

Transdigm Inc .... D 323 269-9181
5000 Triggs St Commerce (90022) *(P-7581)*

Transducer Techniques LLC .... E 951 719-3965
42480 Rio Nedo Temecula (92590) *(P-8070)*

Transico Inc .... E 714 835-6000
1240 Pioneer St Ste A Brea (92821) *(P-7062)*

Transilwrap Company, Rancho Cucamonga *Also Called: Transcendia Inc (P-11003)*

Transit Air Cargo Inc .... D 714 571-0393
2204 E 4th St Santa Ana (92705) *(P-9346)*

Transitamerica Services Inc .... D 760 430-0770
1 Coaster Way Camp Pendleton (92055) *(P-8808)*

Transline Technology Inc .... E 714 533-8300
1106 S Technology Cir Anaheim (92805) *(P-6777)*

Translogic Incorporated .... E 714 890-0058
5641 Engineer Dr Huntington Beach (92649) *(P-7882)*

Transltnal Plmnary Immnlogy RE .... D 562 490-9900
701 E 28th St Ste 419 Long Beach (90806) *(P-15491)*

Transnational Computer Tech, El Segundo *Also Called: Mesfin Enterprises (P-14092)*

Transom Capital Group LLC (PA) .... E 424 293-2818
10990 Wilshire Blvd Ste 440 Los Angeles (90024) *(P-12742)*

Transom Post Midco LLC .... C 312 254-3300
100 N Pacific Coast Hwy # 17 El Segundo (90245) *(P-12617)*

Transonic Combustion Inc .... E 805 465-5145
461 Calle San Pablo Camarillo (93012) *(P-5471)*

Transpak Inc .... C 408 254-0500
2601 S Garnsey St Santa Ana (92707) *(P-14613)*

Transpak Los Angeles, Santa Ana *Also Called: Transpak Inc (P-14613)*

Transparent Products Inc .... E 661 294-9787
28064 Avenue Stanford Unit E Valencia (91355) *(P-5897)*

Transphorm Inc (DH) .... C 805 456-1300
75 Castilian Dr Ste 200 Goleta (93117) *(P-6906)*

Transportation, Lake Arrowhead *Also Called: Rim of World Unified Schl Dst (P-8882)*

Transportation Corridor Agency, Irvine *Also Called: Foothill / Estrn Trnsp Crrdor (P-616)*

Transportation Department, Long Beach *Also Called: Long Beach Unified School Dst (P-8881)*

Transportation Department, Culver City *Also Called: City of Culver City (P-18383)*

Transportation Equipment Inc .... E 619 449-8860
1404 N Marshall Ave El Cajon (92020) *(P-2244)*

Transportation Power LLC .... E 858 248-4255
2057 Aldergrove Ave Escondido (92029) *(P-7302)*

Transpower, Escondido *Also Called: Transportation Power LLC (P-7302)*

Transprttion Brkg Spclists Inc .... B 714 754-4236
3151 Airway Ave Ste F208 Costa Mesa (92626) *(P-8926)*

Transprttion Oprtion MGT Sltion .... C 858 391-0260
1917 Palomar Oaks Way Ste 110 Carlsbad (92008) *(P-14614)*

Transprttion Oprtons MGT Sltion, Irvine *Also Called: Shimmick Construction Co Inc (P-718)*

Transtar Metals Corp .... B 562 630-1400
14001 Orange Ave Paramount (90723) *(P-10163)*

Transtech Engineers Inc (PA) .... D 909 595-8599
13367 Benson Ave Chino (91710) *(P-17650)*

Transwest Truck Center LLC .... D 909 770-5170
10150 Cherry Ave Fontana (92335) *(P-11424)*

Transwestern Publishing, San Diego *Also Called: Transwestern Publishing Company LLC (P-2949)*

Transwestern Publishing Company LLC .... A 858 467-2800
8344 Clairemont Mesa Blvd San Diego (92111) *(P-2949)*

Trantronics Inc .... E 949 553-1234
1822 Langley Ave Irvine (92614) *(P-6778)*

Trashy Lingerie, West Hollywood *Also Called: 402 Shoes Inc (P-2145)*

Travel Corporation .... C 714 385-8401
5551 Katella Ave Cypress (90630) *(P-9236)*

Employee Codes: A=Over 500 employees, B=251-500
C=101-250, D=51-100, E=20-50, F=10-19, G=1-9

2025 Southern California
Business Directory and Buyers Guide

© Mergent Inc. 1-800-342-5647

1215

Travel Store (PA).. D 310 575-5540
  11601 Wilshire Blvd Ste 300 Los Angeles (90025) *(P-9237)*

Travelerhelpdesk.com, San Diego *Also Called: Lbf Travel Inc (P-9227)*

Travelers Choice Travelware .... D 909 529-7688
  2805 S Reservoir St Pomona (91766) *(P-4302)*

Travelstore, Los Angeles *Also Called: Travel Store (P-9237)*

Travere, San Diego *Also Called: Travere Therapeutics Inc (P-3513)*

Travere Therapeutics Inc (PA)............................. B 888 969-7879
  3611 Valley Centre Dr Ste 300 San Diego (92130) *(P-3513)*

TravisMathew LLC (HQ)... E 562 799-6900
  15202 Graham St Huntington Beach (92649) *(P-2030)*

Traxero North America LLC .... D 423 497-1164
  1730 E Holly Ave Ste 740 El Segundo (90245) *(P-14057)*

Traxx Corporation .... D 909 623-8032
  1201 E Lexington Ave Pomona (91766) *(P-8736)*

TRC Solutions Inc (HQ)....................................... C 949 753-0101
  9685 Research Dr Ste 100 Irvine (92618) *(P-18364)*

Tre Venezie Inc .... D 818 985-4669
  4100 Cahuenga Blvd Toluca Lake (91602) *(P-11605)*

Treana Winery LLC .... E 805 237-2932
  4280 Second Wind Way Paso Robles (93447) *(P-1591)*

Treasure Garden Inc (PA) .... E 626 814-0168
  13401 Brooks Dr Baldwin Park (91706) *(P-11260)*

Treasury Wine Estates Americas .... E 805 237-6000
  7000 E Highway 46 Paso Robles (93446) *(P-37)*

Tree House Pad & Paper Inc .... D 800 213-4184
  2341 Pomona Rd Ste 108 Corona (92878) *(P-2761)*

Tree Island Wire (usa) Inc .... C 909 595-6617
  3880 W Valley Blvd Pomona (91769) *(P-4542)*

Tree Island Wire (usa) Inc .... C 909 594-7511
  13470 Philadelphia Ave Fontana (92337) *(P-4543)*

Tree Island Wire (usa) Inc .... C 909 899-1673
  5080 Hallmark Pkwy San Bernardino (92407) *(P-5417)*

Tree Island Wire (USA) Inc (DH) .... C 909 594-7511
  3880 Valley Blvd Walnut (91789) *(P-4544)*

Tree Island Wire USA, San Bernardino *Also Called: Tree Island Wire (usa) Inc (P-5417)*

Treebeard Landscape Inc .... D 619 697-8302
  9917 Campo Rd Spring Valley (91977) *(P-196)*

Treeline Biosciences Inc .... D 858 766-5725
  11180 Roselle St San Diego (92121) *(P-17832)*

Treesap Farms LLC .... C 760 990-7770
  2500 Rainbow Valley Blvd Fallbrook (92028) *(P-88)*

Treivush Industries Inc .... D 213 745-7774
  940 W Washington Blvd Los Angeles (90015) *(P-2140)*

Trellborg Sling Sltions US Inc .... E 805 239-4284
  3077 Rollie Gates Dr Paso Robles (93446) *(P-4261)*

Trellborg Sling Sltions US Inc (DH) .... C 714 415-0280
  2761 Walnut Ave Tustin (92780) *(P-8240)*

Trelleborg Sealing Solutions .... D 805 239-4284
  3034 Propeller Dr Paso Robles (93446) *(P-8241)*

TRELLEBORG SEALING SOLUTIONS TUSTIN, INC., Paso Robles *Also Called: Trelleborg Sealing Solutions (P-8241)*

Trellis Chino, Chino *Also Called: Macadamia Holdings LLC (P-14535)*

Trellisware Technologies Inc (HQ)....................... C 858 753-1600
  10641 Scripps Summit Ct Ste 100 San Diego (92131) *(P-9420)*

Trench Plate Rental, Downey *Also Called: National Trench Safety LLC (P-13464)*

Trend Manor Furn Mfg Co Inc .... E 626 964-6493
  17047 Gale Ave City Of Industry (91745) *(P-2437)*

Trend Offset Printing, Los Alamitos *Also Called: Trend Offset Printing Services Inc (P-3090)*

Trend Offset Printing Services Inc (HQ)............... E 562 598-2446
  3701 Catalina St Los Alamitos (90720) *(P-3090)*

TREND OFFSET PRINTING SERVICES INCORPORATED, Los Alamitos *Also Called: Trend Offset Printing Svcs Inc (P-3091)*

Trend Offset Printing Svcs Inc .... B 562 598-2446
  3791 Catalina St Los Alamitos (90720) *(P-3091)*

Trend Technologies, Chino *Also Called: Trend Technologies LLC (P-5047)*

Trend Technologies LLC (DH) .... C 909 597-7861
  4626 Eucalyptus Ave Chino (91710) *(P-5047)*

Trendsource Inc .... C 619 718-7467
  4891 Pacific Hwy Ste 200 San Diego (92110) *(P-17863)*

Trepanning Specialities Inc .... E 562 633-8110
  16201 Illinois Ave Paramount (90723) *(P-6255)*

Trepanning Specialties, Paramount *Also Called: Trepanning Specialities Inc (P-6255)*

Treston IAC LLC .... E 714 990-8997
  8175 E Brookdale Ln Anaheim (92807) *(P-2617)*

Trg Inc .... D 310 396-6750
  1350 Abbot Kinney Blvd # 101 Venice (90291) *(P-12540)*

Trg Insurance Services .... C 949 474-1550
  4675 Macarthur Ct Newport Beach (92660) *(P-12262)*

Tri City Mental Health Center, Pomona *Also Called: Tri-City Mental Health Auth (P-16513)*

Tri Models Inc .... D 714 896-0823
  5191 Oceanus Dr Huntington Beach (92649) *(P-7374)*

Tri Pointe, Irvine *Also Called: Tri Pointe Homes Holdings Inc (P-454)*

Tri Pointe Homes Inc .... C 714 389-5933
  57 Furlong Irvine (92602) *(P-453)*

Tri Pointe Homes Inc .... C 949 478-8600
  5 Peters Canyon Rd Ste 100 Irvine (92606) *(P-466)*

Tri Pointe Homes Holdings Inc (HQ).................... C 949 438-1400
  3161 Michelson Dr Ste 1500 Irvine (92612) *(P-454)*

TRI POINTE HOMES, INC., Irvine *Also Called: Tri Pointe Homes Inc (P-453)*

Tri Pointe Homes, Inc., Irvine *Also Called: Tri Pointe Homes Inc (P-466)*

Tri Precision Sheetmetal Inc .... E 714 632-8838
  1104 N Armando St Anaheim (92806) *(P-5048)*

Tri Star Engineering Inc .... D 619 710-8038
  6774 Calle De Linea Ste 106 San Diego (92154) *(P-17651)*

Tri Star Spt Entrmt Group Inc .... D 615 309-0969
  9255 W Sunset Blvd Fl 2 West Hollywood (90069) *(P-15007)*

Tri-Ad, Escondido *Also Called: Tri-Ad Actuaries Inc (P-18234)*

Tri-Ad Actuaries Inc .... C 760 743-7555
  221 W Crest St Ste 300 Escondido (92025) *(P-18234)*

Tri-City Healthcare District, Oceanside *Also Called: Tri-City Medical Center (P-16622)*

Tri-City Hospital District .... B 760 931-3171
  6250 El Camino Real Carlsbad (92009) *(P-15066)*

Tri-City Medical Center (PA) .... A 760 724-8411
  4002 Vista Way Oceanside (92056) *(P-16622)*

Tri-City Mental Health Auth (PA).......................... D 909 623-6131
  2008 N Garey Ave Pomona (91767) *(P-16513)*

Tri-City Wellness Center, Carlsbad *Also Called: Tri-City Hospital District (P-15066)*

Tri-Cnties Assn For Dvlpmntlly .... C 805 543-2833
  1146 Farmhouse Ln San Luis Obispo (93401) *(P-17018)*

Tri-Counties Regional Center, San Luis Obispo *Also Called: Tri-Cnties Assn For Dvlpmntlly (P-17018)*

Tri-Dim Filter Corporation .... E 626 826-5893
  26550 Adams Ave Murrieta (92562) *(P-5780)*

Tri-Marine Fish Company LLC .... D 310 547-1144
  220 Cannery St San Pedro (90731) *(P-10863)*

Tri-Modal Dist Svcs Inc .... D 310 522-1844
  22560 Lucerne St Carson (90745) *(P-9121)*

Tri-Mountain, Irwindale *Also Called: Mountain Gear Corporation (P-10691)*

Tri-Net Technology Inc .... D 909 598-8818
  21709 Ferrero Walnut (91789) *(P-5953)*

Tri-Signal Integration Inc (PA)............................. D 818 566-8558
  28110 Avenue Stanford Unit D Santa Clarita (91355) *(P-974)*

Tri-Star Dyeing & Finshg Inc .... D 562 483-0123
  15125 Marquardt Ave Santa Fe Springs (90670) *(P-1904)*

Tri-Star Laminates Inc .... E 949 587-3200
  20322 Windrow Dr Ste 100 Lake Forest (92630) *(P-6779)*

Tri-Tech Logistics LLC .... C 855 373-7049
  1370 Brea Blvd Ste 200 Fullerton (92835) *(P-9347)*

Tri-Tech Restoration Co Inc .... D 818 565-3900
  3301 N San Fernando Blvd Burbank (91504) *(P-509)*

Tri-Tech Systems Inc (PA)................................... B 818 222-6811
  23801 Calabasas Rd Ste 2022 Calabasas (91302) *(P-13848)*

Tri-Tek Electronics, Valencia *Also Called: Interconnect Solutions Co LLC (P-7010)*

Tri-Union Seafoods LLC (DH) .... D 424 397-8556
  2150 E Grand Ave El Segundo (90245) *(P-10864)*

Tri-Valley Corporation .... E 661 864-0500
  4927 Calloway Dr Ste 101 Bakersfield (93312) *(P-279)*

Tri-West Ltd (PA).. C 562 692-9166
  12005 Pike St Santa Fe Springs (90670) *(P-9912)*

Triad Systems International, Calabasas *Also Called: Tri-Tech Systems Inc (P-13848)*

Triangle Distributing Co .... B 562 699-3424
  12065 Pike St Santa Fe Springs (90670) *(P-11053)*

Mergent email: customerrelations@mergent.com
1216

2025 Southern California
Business Directory and Buyers Guide

(P-0000) Products & Services Section entry number
(PA)=Parent Co (HQ)=Headquarters (DH)=Div Headquarters

Triangle Rock Products LLC .... C 818 553-8820
500 N Brand Blvd Ste 500 Glendale (91203) *(P-373)*

Triangle Services Inc .... C 818 350-7802
11065 Penrose St Sun Valley (91352) *(P-13423)*

Triangle West, Santa Fe Springs Also Called: Gale/Triangle Inc *(P-8907)*

Tribe Mdia Corp A Cal Nnprfit .... E 213 368-1661
3250 Wilshire Blvd Los Angeles (90010) *(P-2834)*

Tribridge Holdings LLC .... B 813 287-8887
523 W 6th St Ste 830 Los Angeles (90014) *(P-13849)*

Tricom Management LLC .... C 714 630-2029
4025 E La Palma Ave Ste 101 Anaheim (92807) *(P-18068)*

Tricom Research Inc .... D 949 250-6024
17791 Sky Park Cir Ste J Irvine (92614) *(P-6667)*

Tricom Research Inc .... D 949 250-6024
17791 Sky Park Cir Ste J Irvine (92614) *(P-6668)*

Tricon American Homes LLC .... C 844 874-2661
15771 Red Hill Ave Tustin (92780) *(P-434)*

Tricor Refining LLC .... E 661 393-7110
1134 Manor St Bakersfield (93308) *(P-3833)*

Trident Dental Labratories, Hawthorne Also Called: Trident Labs LLC *(P-16347)*

Trident Labs LLC .... C 310 915-9121
12000 Aviation Blvd Hawthorne (90250) *(P-16347)*

Trident Maritime Systems Inc .... D 619 346-3800
651 Drucker Ln San Diego (92154) *(P-7609)*

Trident Plating Inc .... E 562 906-2556
10046 Romandel Ave Santa Fe Springs (90670) *(P-5300)*

Trident Space & Defense LLC .... E 310 214-5500
19951 Mariner Ave Torrance (90503) *(P-6907)*

Trident Technologies, San Diego Also Called: Chemtreat Inc *(P-3793)*

Trigild International Inc .... C 619 295-6886
2151 Hotel Cir S San Diego (92108) *(P-13055)*

Trigild International Inc .... C 760 944-0260
133 Encinitas Blvd Encinitas (92024) *(P-13056)*

Trilar Management Group .... C 951 925-2021
1025 S Gilbert St Hemet (92543) *(P-18069)*

Trilink Biotechnologies LLC .... C 800 863-6801
10770 Wateridge Cir Ste 200 San Diego (92121) *(P-17833)*

Triller Group Inc .... C 310 893-5090
7119 W Sunset Blvd Pmb 782 Los Angeles (90046) *(P-12036)*

Trilogy Plumbing Inc .... C 714 441-2952
1525 S Sinclair St Anaheim (92806) *(P-848)*

Trim-Lok Inc (PA) .... C 714 562-0500
6855 Hermosa Cir Buena Park (90620) *(P-4262)*

Trimark Orange County, Irvine Also Called: Trimark Raygal LLC *(P-10054)*

Trimark R. W. Smith & Co., San Diego Also Called: R W Smith & Co *(P-10051)*

Trimark Raygal LLC .... C 949 474-1000
210 Commerce Irvine (92602) *(P-10054)*

Trimas Aerospace, Simi Valley Also Called: Rsa Engineered Products LLC *(P-7549)*

Trimco Finish Inc .... C 714 708-0300
3130 W Harvard St Santa Ana (92704) *(P-1063)*

Trinamix Inc (PA) .... B 408 507-3583
35 Amoret Dr Irvine (92602) *(P-18235)*

Trinidad/Benham Corp .... D 626 723-2300
12400 Wilshire Blvd Ste 1180 Los Angeles (90025) *(P-10986)*

Trinity Brdcstg Netwrk Ino .... C 714 665 3610
2442 Michelle Dr Tustin (92780) *(P-9519)*

Trinity Christn Ctr Santa Ana, Tustin Also Called: Trinity Brdcstg Netwrk Inc *(P-9519)*

Trinity Equipment Inc .... D 951 790-1652
2650 S La Cadena Dr Colton (92324) *(P-10055)*

Trinity Health Systems (PA) .... D 626 960-1971
14318 Ohio St Baldwin Park (91706) *(P-15788)*

Trinity International Inds LLC .... E 800 985-5506
1041 E 230th St Carson (90745) *(P-4263)*

Trinity Lighweight, Frazier Park Also Called: Trnlwb LLC *(P-8737)*

Trinity Sports Inc .... B 323 277-9288
2067 E 55th St Vernon (90058) *(P-2074)*

Trinity Woodworks Inc .... E 760 639-5351
2620 Temple Heights Dr Oceanside (92056) *(P-2332)*

Trinium Technologies, Long Beach Also Called: QED Software LLC *(P-14012)*

Trinus Corporation .... C 818 246-1143
35 N Lake Ave Ste 710 Pasadena (91101) *(P-13850)*

Trio, Azusa Also Called: Trio Engineered Products Inc *(P-5499)*

Trio Engineered Products Inc (HQ) .... E 626 851-3966
505 W Foothill Blvd Azusa (91702) *(P-5499)*

Trio Manufacturing, El Segundo Also Called: Trio Manufacturing Inc *(P-7582)*

Trio Manufacturing Inc .... C 310 640-6123
601 Lairport St El Segundo (90245) *(P-7582)*

Trio Metal Stamping, City Of Industry Also Called: Trio Metal Stamping Inc *(P-5049)*

Trio Metal Stamping Inc .... D 626 336-1228
15318 Proctor Ave City Of Industry (91745) *(P-5049)*

Tripalink Corp .... C 323 717-9139
600 Wilshire Blvd Ste 1540 Los Angeles (90005) *(P-18070)*

Triple A Containers Inc .... D 562 404-7433
16069 Shoemaker Ave Cerritos (90703) *(P-2692)*

Triple H Food Processors LLC .... D 951 352-5700
5821 Wilderness Ave Riverside (92504) *(P-1862)*

Triple R Transportation Inc .... D 661 725-6494
978 Rd 192 Delano (93215) *(P-8852)*

Tripod Inc .... D 805 585-2273
1545 W 5th St Ste 200 Oxnard (93030) *(P-13627)*

Trisoyn, San Diego Also Called: Safe Life Corporation *(P-17887)*

Tristaff Group, Fallbrook Also Called: Garich Inc *(P-13521)*

Tristaff Group, The, Temecula Also Called: Garich Inc *(P-13597)*

Tristar Industrial LLC .... D 562 634-6425
5875 Obispo Ave Long Beach (90805) *(P-10469)*

Tristar Insurance Group Inc (PA) .... A 562 495-6600
100 Oceangate Ste 700 Long Beach (90802) *(P-12141)*

Tristar Risk Management, Long Beach Also Called: Tristar Insurance Group Inc *(P-12141)*

Tristar Service Company Inc (HQ) .... B 562 495-6600
100 Oceangate Ste 700 Long Beach (90802) *(P-12263)*

Triton Management Services LLC .... D 760 431-9911
1000 Aviara Dr Ste 300 Carlsbad (92011) *(P-14615)*

Triton Media Group LLC .... C 661 294-9000
8935 Lindblade St Culver City (90232) *(P-9490)*

Triton Structural Concrete Inc .... C 858 866-2450
15435 Innovation Dr Ste 225 San Diego (92128) *(P-594)*

Triumph Acttion Systems - VInc .... C 661 702-7537
28150 Harrison Pkwy Valencia (91355) *(P-7583)*

Triumph Group, Valencia Also Called: Triumph Acttion Systems - VInc *(P-7583)*

Triumph Group, Calexico Also Called: Triumph Insulation Systems LLC *(P-7584)*

Triumph Insulation Systems LLC .... A 760 618-7543
1754 Carr Rd Ste 103 Calexico (92231) *(P-7584)*

Triumph Proc - Embee Div Inc .... B 714 546-9842
2158 S Hathaway St Santa Ana (92705) *(P-5301)*

Triumph Processing Inc .... C 323 563-1338
2605 Industry Way Lynwood (90262) *(P-5302)*

Triumph Structures, City Of Industry Also Called: Triumph Structures - Everett Inc *(P-7585)*

Triumph Structures - Brea, Chatsworth Also Called: Alatus Aerosystems *(P-7423)*

Triumph Structures - Everett Inc .... C 425 348-4100
17055 Gale Ave City Of Industry (91745) *(P-7585)*

Triune Enterprises Inc .... E 310 719-1600
13711 S Normandle Ave Gardena (90249) *(P-2713)*

Triune Enterprises Mfg, Gardena Also Called: Triune Enterprises Inc *(P-2713)*

Trius Therapeutics LLC .... C 858 452-0370
4747 Executive Dr Ste 1100 San Diego (92121) *(P-3514)*

Trivascular Inc (DH) .... E 707 543-8800
2 Musick Irvine (92618) *(P-8242)*

Trivascular Technologies Inc (HQ) .... C 707 543-8800
2 Musick Irvine (92618) *(P-8243)*

Triview, La Habra Also Called: Triview Glass Industries LLC *(P-4348)*

Triview Glass Industries LLC .... D 626 363-7980
279 Shawnan Ln La Habra (90631) *(P-4348)*

Triw1969 Inc .... E 619 593-3636
877 Vernon Way El Cajon (92020) *(P-4716)*

Trixxi Clothing Company Inc (PA) .... E 323 585-4200
6817 E Acco St Commerce (90040) *(P-2075)*

Triyar Sv LLC (PA) .... B 310 234-2888
10850 Wilshire Blvd Ste 1050 Los Angeles (90024) *(P-12541)*

TRL Systems Incorporated .... D 909 390-8392
9531 Milliken Ave Rancho Cucamonga (91730) *(P-975)*

Trlg Corporate Holdings LLC (PA) .... C 323 266-3072
1888 Rosecrans Ave Manhattan Beach (90266) *(P-2173)*

Employee Codes: A=Over 500 employees, B=251-500
C=101-250, D=51-100, E=20-50, F=10-19, G=1-9

2025 Southern California
Business Directory and Buyers Guide

© Mergent Inc. 1-800-342-5647

1217

A
L
P
H
A
B
E
T
I
C

Trlggc Services LLC .... C 323 266-3072
1888 Rosecrans Ave Manhattan Beach (90266) *(P-10697)*

TRM Manufacturing Inc .... C 951 256-8550
375 Trm Cir Corona (92879) *(P-3959)*

Trnlwb LLC .... A 661 245-3736
17410 Lockwood Valley Rd Frazier Park (93225) *(P-8737)*

Trojan Battery Company LLC (DH) .... C 562 236-3000
12380 Clark St Santa Fe Springs (90670) *(P-7086)*

Trojan Battery Holdings LLC .... D 800 423-6569
12380 Clark St Santa Fe Springs (90670) *(P-7083)*

Trojan Professional Svcs Inc .... D 714 816-7169
11075 Knott Ave Ste A Cypress (90630) *(P-14179)*

Trona Railway Company .... B 760 372-2312
13068 Main St Trona (93562) *(P-8744)*

Troon Golf LLC .... C 760 346-4653
44500 Indian Wells Ln Indian Wells (92210) *(P-18071)*

Troop Real Estate Inc .... C 805 402-3028
4165 E Thousand Oaks Blvd Ste 100 Westlake Village (91362) *(P-12542)*

Troop Real Estate Inc .... C 805 921-0030
586 W Main St Santa Paula (93060) *(P-12543)*

Troop Real Estate Inc (PA) .... D 805 581-3200
1308 Madera Rd Ste 8 Simi Valley (93065) *(P-12544)*

Tropical Plaza Nursery Inc .... D 714 998-4100
9642 Santiago Blvd Villa Park (92867) *(P-239)*

Tropical Preserving Co Inc .... E 213 748-5108
5 Lewiston Ct Ladera Ranch (92694) *(P-1359)*

Tropicale Foods LLC (PA) .... E 909 635-1000
1237 W State St Ontario (91762) *(P-1320)*

Tropicana Manufacturing Co Inc .... D 310 764-4395
1650 S Central Ave Compton (90220) *(P-9122)*

Tropitone Furniture Co Inc (DH) .... B 949 595-2010
5 Marconi Irvine (92618) *(P-2475)*

Troutman Ppper Hmltn Snders L .... D 949 622-2700
100 Spectrum Center Dr Ste 1500 Irvine (92618) *(P-16791)*

Troutman Sanders, Irvine *Also Called: Troutman Ppper Hmltn Snders L (P-16791)*

Trovata, Solana Beach *Also Called: Trovata Inc (P-13851)*

Trovata Inc (PA) .... D 312 914-8106
312 S Cedros Ave Ste 312 Solana Beach (92075) *(P-13851)*

Troy Lee Designs LLC (DH) .... D 951 371-5219
155 E Rincon St Corona (92879) *(P-10516)*

Troy Metal Products, Goleta *Also Called: Neal Feay Company (P-4602)*

Troy Products, Montebello *Also Called: Troy Sheet Metal Works Inc (P-5166)*

Troy Sheet Metal Works Inc (PA) .... D 323 720-4100
1024 S Vail Ave Montebello (90640) *(P-5166)*

Troy-Csl Lighting Inc .... C 626 336-4511
14508 Nelson Ave City Of Industry (91744) *(P-6449)*

Troygould PC .... D 310 553-4441
1801 Century Park E Ste 1600 Los Angeles (90067) *(P-16792)*

Trs Rentelco, Jurupa Valley *Also Called: Mobile Modular Management Corp (P-5084)*

Trs Staffing Solutions, Aliso Viejo *Also Called: Fluor Corporation (P-17531)*

Tru Form Industries, Santa Fe Springs *Also Called: Tru-Form Industries Inc (P-5218)*

Tru-Cut Inc .... E 310 630-0422
141 E 157th St Gardena (90248) *(P-5484)*

Tru-Duct Inc .... E 619 660-3858
2515 Industry St Oceanside (92054) *(P-5050)*

Tru-Form Industries Inc (PA) .... D 562 802-2041
14511 Anson Ave Santa Fe Springs (90670) *(P-5218)*

Tru-Form Plastics Inc .... E 310 327-9444
14600 Hoover St Westminster (92683) *(P-4264)*

Truaire, Santa Fe Springs *Also Called: TA Industries Inc (P-10326)*

Truamerica Multifamily LLC .... D 424 325-2750
10100 Santa Monica Blvd Ste 400 Los Angeles (90067) *(P-12743)*

Truck Underwriters Association .... A 323 932-3200
6303 Owensmouth Ave Fl 1 Woodland Hills (91367) *(P-12054)*

Truck Underwriters Association (DH) .... A 323 932-3200
4680 Wilshire Blvd Los Angeles (90010) *(P-17310)*

Truconnect Communications Inc (PA) .... C 512 919-2641
1149 S Hill St Ste 400 Los Angeles (90015) *(P-9467)*

True Air Mechanical Inc .... C 888 316-0642
1801 California Ave Corona (92881) *(P-849)*

True Cast Concrete Products, Sun Valley *Also Called: Quikrete Companies LLC (P-4418)*

True Digital Surgery, Goleta *Also Called: Digital Surgery Systems Inc (P-8144)*

True Fresh Hpp LLC .... E 949 922-8801
6535 Caballero Blvd Unit B Buena Park (90620) *(P-7841)*

True Home Heating and AC, Corona *Also Called: True Air Mechanical Inc (P-849)*

True Investments LLC .... E 949 258-9720
6535 Caballero Blvd Unit B Buena Park (90620) *(P-12744)*

True Investments LLC (PA) .... E 949 258-9720
2260 University Dr Newport Beach (92660) *(P-12745)*

True Position Technologies LLC .... D 661 294-0030
24900 Avenue Stanford Valencia (91355) *(P-6256)*

True Religion Apparel, Gardena *Also Called: Guru Denim LLC (P-11488)*

True Religion Apparel Inc (HQ) .... B 855 928-6124
500 W 190th St Ste 300 Gardena (90248) *(P-1993)*

True Religion Brand Jeans, Gardena *Also Called: True Religion Apparel Inc (P-1993)*

TRUECAR, Santa Monica *Also Called: Truecar Inc (P-13852)*

Truecar Inc (PA) .... C 800 200-2000
225 Santa Monica Blvd Fl 12 Santa Monica (90401) *(P-13852)*

Truevision 3d Surgical, Goleta *Also Called: Truevision Systems Inc (P-8244)*

Truevision Systems Inc .... E 805 963-9700
315 Bollay Dr Ste 101 Goleta (93117) *(P-8244)*

Trugreen, Escondido *Also Called: Landcare USA LLC (P-214)*

Trugreen, San Diego *Also Called: Landcare USA LLC (P-215)*

Trugreen, Santa Ana *Also Called: Landcare USA LLC (P-216)*

Truitt Oilfield Maint Corp .... B 661 871-4099
1051 James Rd Bakersfield (93308) *(P-366)*

Trulite GL Alum Solutions LLC .... D 800 877-8439
19430 San Jose Ave City Of Industry (91748) *(P-4609)*

Trumed Systems Incorporated .... E 844 878-6331
4370 La Jolla Village Dr Ste 200 San Diego (92122) *(P-5989)*

Trump Nat Golf CLB Los Angeles, Rancho Palos Verdes *Also Called: Estates At Trump Nat Golf CLB (P-15079)*

Trusaic, Los Angeles *Also Called: First Capitol Consulting Inc (P-18137)*

Trussworks International Inc .... D 714 630-2772
1275 E Franklin Ave Pomona (91766) *(P-4876)*

Trust 1 Sales Inc .... D 323 732-3300
1737 S Vermont Ave Los Angeles (90006) *(P-10056)*

Trust Automation Inc .... D 805 544-0761
125 Venture Dr Ste 110 San Luis Obispo (93401) *(P-17652)*

Trust Company of West .... A 213 244-0000
865 S Figueroa St Ste 1800 Los Angeles (90017) *(P-12007)*

Trust Employee ADM & MGT, San Diego *Also Called: Team Risk MGT Strategies LLC (P-18363)*

Trustee Corps, Irvine *Also Called: Mtc Financial Inc (P-18016)*

Truvian Sciences Inc .... D 858 251-3646
10300 Campus Point Dr Ste 190 San Diego (92121) *(P-17834)*

Tryad Service Corporation .... D 661 391-1524
5900 E Lerdo Hwy Shafter (93263) *(P-367)*

TS Enterprises Inc .... E 760 360-5991
78250 Highway 111 La Quinta (92253) *(P-11606)*

TSC Auto ID Technology America (HQ) .... C 909 468-0100
3040 Saturn St Ste 200 Brea (92821) *(P-10470)*

Tst Inc (PA) .... B 951 685-2155
13428 Benson Ave Chino (91710) *(P-4588)*

Tst Inc .... E 310 835-0115
2132 E Dominguez St Long Beach (90810) *(P-10543)*

TST Molding LLC .... E 951 296-6200
42322 Avenida Alvarado Temecula (92590) *(P-4265)*

Tst/Impreso Inc .... E 909 357-7190
10589 Business Dr Fontana (92337) *(P-3195)*

TT Elctrnics Pwr Sltons US Inc .... C 626 967-6021
1330 E Cypress St Covina (91724) *(P-7063)*

TT Electronics, Brea *Also Called: Bi Technologies Corporation (P-6972)*

TT Trucking Services, Victorville *Also Called: TT Trucking Services LLC (P-8927)*

TT Trucking Services LLC .... D 323 790-3408
12745 Jade Rd Victorville (92392) *(P-8927)*

Tte Technology Inc .... C 877 300-8837
189 Technology Dr Irvine (92618) *(P-10226)*

Ttg Engineers .... B 626 463-2800
300 N Lake Ave Fl 14 Pasadena (91101) *(P-17653)*

TTI Floor Care North Amer Inc .... D 440 996-2802
13055 Valley Blvd Fontana (92335) *(P-3877)*

Mergent email: customerrelations@mergent.com
1218

2025 Southern California
Business Directory and Buyers Guide

(P-0000) Products & Services Section entry number
(PA)=Parent Co (HQ)=Headquarters (DH)=Div Headquarters

TTI Performance Exhaust, Corona *Also Called: Tube Technologies Inc (P-7303)*

TTM, Santa Ana *Also Called: Ttm Technologies Inc (P-6781)*

Ttm Printed Circuit Group Inc (HQ) .... C 714 327-3000
2630 S Harbor Blvd Santa Ana (92704) *(P-6780)*

Ttm Technologies Inc (PA) .... B 714 327-3000
200 Sandpointe Ave Ste 400 Santa Ana (92707) *(P-6781)*

Ttm Technologies Inc .... B 714 241-0303
2630 S Harbor Blvd Santa Ana (92704) *(P-6782)*

Ttm Technologies Inc .... B 714 688-7200
3140 E Coronado St Anaheim (92806) *(P-6783)*

Ttm Technologies Inc .... C 858 874-2701
5037 Ruffner St San Diego (92111) *(P-6784)*

TTT Concrete, Lakeside *Also Called: Superior Ready Mix Concrete LP (P-4459)*

Tu Madre Romana Inc .... C 323 321-6041
13633 S Western Ave Gardena (90249) *(P-1863)*

Tu-K Industries LLC .... E 562 927-3365
5702 Firestone Pl South Gate (90280) *(P-3692)*

Tube Technologies Inc .... E 951 371-4878
1555 Consumer Cir Corona (92878) *(P-7303)*

Tube-Tainer Inc .... E 562 945-3711
8174 Byron Rd Whittier (90606) *(P-2699)*

Tubing Seal Cap Co, Anaheim *Also Called: Pacific Precision Metals Inc (P-5208)*

Tubular Specialties Mfg Inc .... D 310 515-4801
13011 S Spring St Los Angeles (90061) *(P-4363)*

Tuffer Manufacturing Co Inc .... E 714 526-3077
163 E Liberty Ave Anaheim (92801) *(P-7821)*

Tuffstuff Fitness Intl Inc .... D 909 629-1600
155 N Riverview Dr Anaheim (92808) *(P-8549)*

Tungsten Automation Corp (PA) .... B 949 783-1000
15211 Laguna Canyon Rd Irvine (92618) *(P-13853)*

Tur-Bo Jet Products Co Inc .... D 626 285-1294
5025 Earle Ave Rosemead (91770) *(P-6939)*

Turbine Repair Services LLC (PA) .... E 909 947-2256
1838 E Cedar St Ontario (91761) *(P-5465)*

Turbotax, San Diego *Also Called: Intuit Inc (P-13951)*

Turn Around Communications Inc .... C 626 443-2400
100 N Barranca St Ste 260 West Covina (91791) *(P-701)*

Turn Key Scaffold LLC .... C 619 642-0880
410 W 30th St National City (91950) *(P-1230)*

Turner Construction Company .... B 714 940-9000
1900 S State College Blvd Ste 200 Anaheim (92806) *(P-595)*

Turner Fiberfill Inc .... E 323 724-7957
1600 Date St Montebello (90640) *(P-3307)*

TURNING POINT COUNSELING, Fullerton *Also Called: Turning Point Ministries (P-17019)*

Turning Point Ministries .... D 800 998-6329
1370 Brea Blvd Ste 245 Fullerton (92835) *(P-17019)*

Turning Point Therapeutics Inc .... D 858 926-5251
10300 Campus Point Dr Ste 100 San Diego (92121) *(P-17835)*

Turtle Rock Cdc, Irvine *Also Called: Child Development Incorporated (P-17083)*

Turtleback Case, Sylmar *Also Called: Leather Pro Inc (P-4305)*

TUSIMPLE, San Diego *Also Called: Tusimple Holdings Inc (P-14114)*

Tusimple Inc .... B 520 989-7911
9191 Towne Centre Dr San Diego (92122) *(P-14113)*

Tusimple Holdings Inc (PA) .... B 619 916-3144
9191 Towne Centre Dr Ste 600 San Diego (92122) *(P-14114)*

Tustin Executive Center, Tustin *Also Called: Southern Cal Prmnnte Med Group (P-12107)*

Tustin Hospital, Tustin *Also Called: Pacific Health Corporation (P-16112)*

Tustin Hospital and Medical Center .... B 714 619-7700
3699 Wilshire Blvd Ste 540 Los Angeles (90010) *(P-16234)*

Tustin Ranch Golf Club, Tustin *Also Called: Crown Golf Properties LP (P-18123)*

Tustin Saab, Tustin *Also Called: Nissan of Tustin (P-11387)*

Tustin Unified School District .... C 714 542-4271
16791 E Main St Tustin (92780) *(P-16827)*

Tutor Perini, Sylmar *Also Called: Tutor Perini Corporation (P-596)*

Tutor Perini Corporation (PA) .... C 818 362-8391
15901 Olden St Sylmar (91342) *(P-596)*

Tutor Time Learning Ctrs LLC .... C 818 710-1677
5855 De Soto Ave Woodland Hills (91367) *(P-17116)*

Tutor Time Learning Ctrs LLC .... C 714 484-1000
5805 Corporate Ave Cypress (90630) *(P-17117)*

Tutor-Saliba Corporation (HQ) .... D 818 362-8391
15901 Olden St Rancho Cascades (91342) *(P-597)*

Tutor-Saliba Perini .... A 818 362-8391
15901 Olden St Sylmar (91342) *(P-598)*

Tuttle Click Ford, Irvine *Also Called: Tuttle-Click Ford Inc (P-11425)*

Tuttle Family Enterprises Inc .... B 818 534-2566
9510 Topanga Canyon Blvd Chatsworth (91311) *(P-13424)*

Tuttle-Click Ford Inc .... C 949 855-1704
43 Auto Center Dr Irvine (92618) *(P-11425)*

TV Ears Inc .... E 619 797-1600
2701 Via Orange Way Ste 1 Spring Valley (91978) *(P-10294)*

TW Holdings Inc .... A 858 217-8750
10805 Rancho Bernardo Rd Ste 120 San Diego (92127) *(P-15067)*

TW Security Corp (HQ) .... C 949 932-1000
5 Park Plz Ste 400 Irvine (92614) *(P-10035)*

TW Services Inc .... B 714 441-2400
1801 W Romneya Dr Ste 601 Anaheim (92801) *(P-9377)*

Twdc Enterprises 18 Corp (HQ) .... A 818 560-1000
500 S Buena Vista St Burbank (91521) *(P-9520)*

Twed-Dells Inc .... E 714 754-6900
1900 S Susan St Santa Ana (92704) *(P-4349)*

Twenteth Cntury Fox HM Entrmt (PA) .... A 310 369-1000
10201 W Pico Blvd Los Angeles (90064) *(P-14863)*

Twenteth Cntury Fox HM Entrmt .... C 310 369-1000
1440 S Sepulveda Blvd 3rd Fl Los Angeles (90025) *(P-14922)*

Twenteth Cntury Fox Intl TV In .... A 310 369-1000
10201 W Pico Blvd Los Angeles (90064) *(P-9521)*

Twentieth Century Fox Home E .... C 310 369-3900
2121 Avenue Of The Stars Ste 2500 Los Angeles (90067) *(P-14923)*

Twentieth Cntury Fox Film Corp (DH) .... D
10201 W Pico Blvd Los Angeles (90064) *(P-14864)*

Twentieth Cntury Fox Intl Corp (HQ) .... D 310 369-1000
10201 W Pico Blvd Bldg 1 Los Angeles (90064) *(P-14924)*

Twentieth Cntury Fox Japan Inc .... A 310 369-4636
10201 W Pico Blvd Los Angeles (90064) *(P-13337)*

Twenty Mile Productions LLC .... C 412 251-0767
11833 Mississippi Ave Ste 101 Los Angeles (90025) *(P-15008)*

Twenty4seven Hotels Corp .... B 949 734-6400
520 Newport Center Dr Ste 520 Newport Beach (92660) *(P-18072)*

Twin Cities Community Hosp Inc .... B 805 434-3500
1100 Las Tablas Rd Templeton (93465) *(P-15492)*

Twin Dragon Marketing Inc (PA) .... E 310 715-7070
14600 S Broadway Gardena (90248) *(P-1889)*

Twin Eagles, Inc., Cerritos *Also Called: Dcec Holdings Inc (P-6384)*

Twin Med Inc .... B
5900 Wilshire Blvd Ste 2600 Los Angeles (90036) *(P-10114)*

Twin Oaks Power LP (HQ) .... D 619 696-2034
101 Ash St Hq10b San Diego (92101) *(P-9641)*

Twin Peak Industries Inc .... E 800 259-5906
12420 Montague St Ste E Pacoima (91331) *(P-8550)*

Twining Inc (PA) .... D 562 426-3355
4011 Airport Plaza Dr Long Beach (90015) *(P-17920)*

Twining Laboratories, Long Beach *Also Called: Twining Inc (P-17928)*

Twist Tite Mfg Inc .... E 562 229-0990
13344 Cambridge St Santa Fe Springs (90670) *(P-5138)*

Two Bit Circus, Los Angeles *Also Called: Two Bit Circus Dal LLC (P-15009)*

Two Bit Circus Dal LLC .... D 323 438-9808
634 Mateo St Los Angeles (90021) *(P-15009)*

Two Jinn Inc (PA) .... D 760 431-9911
1000 Aviara Dr Ste 300 Carlsbad (92011) *(P-14616)*

Two Lads Inc (PA) .... E 323 584-0064
5001 Hampton St Vernon (90058) *(P-8579)*

Two Palms Nursing Center Inc .... C 626 796-1103
150 Bellefontaine St Pasadena (91105) *(P-15886)*

Twomagnets LLC .... A 408 837-0116
440 N Barranca Ave Pmb 5028 Covina (91723) *(P-13579)*

TWR Enterprises Inc .... C 951 279-2000
1661 Railroad St Corona (92878) *(P-1064)*

Txi Riverside Cement, Riverside *Also Called: Riverside Cement Holdings Company (P-4359)*

Tydg Enterprises Inc .... D 562 903-9030
10232 Palm Dr Santa Fe Springs (90670) *(P-12618)*

Employee Codes: A=Over 500 employees, B=251-500
C=101-250, D=51-100, E=20-50, F=10-19, G=1-9

2025 Southern California
Business Directory and Buyers Guide

© Mergent Inc. 1-800-342-5647

1219

Tyler Trafficante Inc (PA)... E 323 869-9299
700 S Palm Ave Alhambra (91803) *(P-1980)*

Typecraft Inc .... E 626 795-8093
2040 E Walnut St Pasadena (91107) *(P-3092)*

Typecraft Wood & Jones, Pasadena *Also Called: Typecraft Inc (P-3092)*

TYRA, Carlsbad *Also Called: Tyra Biosciences Inc (P-3515)*

Tyra Biosciences Inc .... E 619 728-4760
2656 State St Carlsbad (92008) *(P-3515)*

Tyte Jeans, Commerce *Also Called: 4 What Its Worth Inc (P-2003)*

Tyvak Nn-Satellite Systems Inc (DH)...................... E 949 753-1020
15330 Barranca Pkwy Irvine (92618) *(P-7658)*

U C I Distribution Plus, Pasadena *Also Called: United Couriers Inc (P-9169)*

U C L Incorporated (PA).. D 323 235-0099
620 S Hacienda Blvd City Of Industry (91745) *(P-8979)*

U C Riverside Foundation .... C 951 827-6389
900 University Ave Riverside (92521) *(P-17370)*

U C S D Medical Center, San Diego *Also Called: University Cal San Diego (P-16243)*

U C San Diego Foundation .... D 858 534-1032
9500 Gilman Dr La Jolla (92093) *(P-17472)*

U F C Pension Trust Fund, Cypress *Also Called: Cal Southern United Food (P-12159)*

U F P, San Marcos *Also Called: Unique Functional Products (P-7318)*

U Gym LLC (PA).. D 714 668-0911
1501 Quail St Ste 100 Newport Beach (92660) *(P-15068)*

U I G, Lake Forest *Also Called: United Industries Group Inc (P-17656)*

U M C, Costa Mesa *Also Called: Universal Motion Components Co Inc (P-5796)*

U S Architectural Lighting, Palmdale *Also Called: US Pole Company Inc (P-6478)*

U S C, Burbank *Also Called: Universal Switching Corp (P-6433)*

U S C, Glendale *Also Called: Usc Vrdugo Hlls Hosp Fundation (P-16251)*

U S Circuit Inc .... D 760 489-1413
2071 Wineridge Pl Escondido (92029) *(P-7064)*

U S L, San Luis Obispo *Also Called: Ultra-Stereo Labs Inc (P-7155)*

U S Medical Instruments Inc (PA)............................ E 619 661-5500
888 Prospect St Ste 100 La Jolla (92037) *(P-8245)*

U S Precision Manufacturing, Riverside *Also Called: US Precision Sheet Metal Inc (P-5051)*

U S Trust Company NA .... B 213 861-5000
515 S Flower St Ste 2700 Los Angeles (90071) *(P-12037)*

U S Weatherford L P .... C 661 589-9483
2815 Fruitvale Ave Bakersfield (93308) *(P-368)*

U S Xpress Inc .... B 760 768-6707
363 Nina Lee Rd Calexico (92231) *(P-8980)*

U T L A, Los Angeles *Also Called: United Teachers-Los Angeles (P-17318)*

U W G Southern California Div, Los Angeles *Also Called: Unified Grocers Inc (P-9123)*

U-Haul, Corona *Also Called: U-Haul Business Consultants (P-14643)*

U-Haul Business Consultants .... C 951 736-7811
314 E 6th St Corona (92879) *(P-14643)*

U-Nited Printing and Copy Ctr, Van Nuys *Also Called: Printrunner LLC (P-3068)*

U. S. Grant Hotel, San Diego *Also Called: American Prprty-Mnagement Corp (P-12760)*

U.S. Airconditioning Distrs, City Of Industry *Also Called: US Airconditioning Distributors Inc (P-10337)*

U.S. Battery Mfg Co, Corona *Also Called: Palos Verdes Building Corp (P-7079)*

U.S. Continental, Corona *Also Called: US Continental Marketing Inc (P-3623)*

U.S. Horizon Mfg, Valencia *Also Called: US Horizon Manufacturing Inc (P-4319)*

U.S. Specialty Vehicles, Yorba Linda *Also Called: American HX Auto Trade Inc (P-7166)*

U2 Science Labs Inc .... D 949 482-8540
400 Spectrum Center Dr Irvine (92618) *(P-10036)*

Ubiq, San Diego *Also Called: Ubiq Security Inc (P-10037)*

Ubiq Security Inc .... E 888 434-6674
4660 La Jolla Village Dr Ste 100 San Diego (92122) *(P-10037)*

Ubix Labs, Irvine *Also Called: U2 Science Labs Inc (P-10036)*

Ubm Canon LLC (DH)... E 310 445-4200
2901 28th St Ste 100 Santa Monica (90405) *(P-2878)*

UBS Americas Inc .... C 619 557-2400
600 W Broadway Ste 2800 San Diego (92101) *(P-12008)*

Ubtech Robotics Corp .... E 213 261-7153
767 S Alameda St Ste 250 Los Angeles (90021) *(P-5656)*

Uc Irvine Hlth Rgonal Burn Ctr, Orange *Also Called: University California Irvine (P-15498)*

Uc Irvine Medical Center, Orange *Also Called: University California Irvine (P-16244)*

Uc San Dego Hlth Accntble Care (DH)...................... C 858 657-7000
9300 Campus Point Dr La Jolla (92037) *(P-16235)*

UC SAN DIEGO, La Jolla *Also Called: U C San Diego Foundation (P-17472)*

Uce Holdings Inc .... D 213 217-4235
411 Center St Los Angeles (90012) *(P-1864)*

UCI Cancer Center, Orange *Also Called: University California Irvine (P-16246)*

UCI Construction Inc .... D 661 587-0192
3900 Fruitvale Ave Bakersfield (93308) *(P-17654)*

UCI Division Plastic Surgery, Orange *Also Called: University California Irvine (P-17757)*

UCI Family Health Center, Santa Ana *Also Called: University California Irvine (P-15499)*

UCI Halth Neuropsychiatric Ctr, Orange *Also Called: University California Irvine (P-16837)*

UCI Health Blood Donor Center, Irvine *Also Called: University California Irvine (P-16625)*

UCI Westminster Medical Center, Westminster *Also Called: University California Irvine (P-16247)*

Ucla Dept of Design Media, Los Angeles *Also Called: Associated Students UCLA (P-16831)*

Ucla Foundation .... B 310 794-3193
10889 Wilshire Blvd Ste 1100 Los Angeles (90024) *(P-12654)*

Ucla Hbr Dlysis Ctr Med Fndtio, Torrance *Also Called: Harbor-Ucla Med Foundation Inc (P-16435)*

Ucla Health .... C 310 825-9111
757 Westwood Plz Los Angeles (90095) *(P-16236)*

Ucla Health Auxiliary .... B 310 267-4327
10920 Wilshire Blvd Ste 400 Los Angeles (90024) *(P-16426)*

Ucla Healthcare .... D 310 319-4560
1821 Wilshire Blvd Fl 6 Santa Monica (90403) *(P-16237)*

Ucla Mdcn SC Phrmclgy, Los Angeles *Also Called: Associated Students UCLA (P-15247)*

UCLA STUDENT STORE, Los Angeles *Also Called: Associated Students UCLA (P-17215)*

Ucp of Orange County, Santa Ana *Also Called: United Crbral Plsy Assn Ornge (P-17020)*

Ucsd, La Jolla *Also Called: Ming Tsuang Dr (P-15389)*

Ucsd, San Diego *Also Called: Kelly Thomas MD Ucsd Hlth Care (P-16578)*

Ucsd Thornton Hospital, La Jolla *Also Called: University Cal San Diego (P-16242)*

UDC, Anaheim *Also Called: Universal Dust Cllctr Mfg Sup (P-510)*

Ues Professional Solutions Inc .... C 951 571-4081
14538 Meridian Pkwy Ste A Riverside (92518) *(P-17655)*

Ufc Gym, Newport Beach *Also Called: U Gym LLC (P-15068)*

UFO Inc .... E 323 588-5450
2110 Belgrave Ave Huntington Park (90255) *(P-4266)*

Ufp Technologies Inc .... E 714 662-0277
20211 S Susana Rd Compton (90221) *(P-4021)*

Ugm Citatah Inc (PA)... C 562 921-9549
13220 Cambridge St Santa Fe Springs (90670) *(P-9951)*

Ugmc, Santa Fe Springs *Also Called: Ugm Citatah Inc (P-9951)*

Uhc of California (DH)... A 952 936-6615
5995 Plaza Dr Cypress (90630) *(P-12114)*

Uhg Lax Prop Llc .... C 310 322-0999
1985 E Grand Ave El Segundo (90245) *(P-13057)*

Uhp Healthcare, Inglewood *Also Called: Watts Health Foundation Inc (P-15828)*

UHS, Temecula *Also Called: Temecula Valley Hospital Inc (P-16224)*

UHS, Chino *Also Called: Canyon Ridge Hospital Inc (P-16271)*

UHS Surgical Services, Sun Valley *Also Called: PRI Medical Technologies Inc (P-10104)*

Uhs-Corona Inc (HQ)... A 951 737-4343
800 S Main St Corona (92882) *(P-16238)*

Uhs-Corona Inc .... C 951 736-7200
730 Magnolia Ave Corona (92879) *(P-16514)*

Ui Medical LLC .... E 562 453-1515
1670 W Park Ave Redlands (92373) *(P-2749)*

UIC, Orange *Also Called: University California Irvine (P-15497)*

Uka LLC .... B 949 610-8000
620 Newport Center Dr Ste 1400 Newport Beach (92660) *(P-13058)*

Uke Corporation .... D 858 513-9100
13400 Danielson St Poway (92064) *(P-8551)*

Uls Express Inc .... C 310 631-0800
2850 E Del Amo Blvd Compton (90221) *(P-8928)*

Ultimate, Long Beach *Also Called: Altamed Health Services Corp (P-15237)*

Ultimate Builders Inc .... D 818 481-2627
23679 Calabasas Rd Calabasas (91302) *(P-435)*

Ultimate Demo, Pomona *Also Called: Ultimate Removal Inc (P-436)*

Ultimate Ears Consumer LLC .... C 949 502-8340
3 Jenner Ste 180 Irvine (92618) *(P-8313)*

Ultimate Landscaping MGT .... D 714 502-9711
700 E Sycamore St Anaheim (92805) *(P-240)*

Mergent email: customerrelations@mergent.com
1220

2025 Southern California
Business Directory and Buyers Guide

(P-0000) Products & Services Section entry number
(PA)=Parent Co (HQ)=Headquarters (DH)=Div Headquarters

Ultimate Metal Finishing Corp .... E 323 890-9100
6150 Sheila St Commerce (90040) *(P-5351)*

Ultimate Paper Box Company, City Of Industry *Also Called: Boxes R Us Inc (P-2656)*

Ultimate Print Source Inc .... E 909 947-5292
2070 S Hellman Ave Ontario (91761) *(P-3093)*

Ultimate Removal Inc .... C 909 524-0800
2168 Pomona Blvd Pomona (91768) *(P-436)*

Ultimate Solutions, Huntington Beach *Also Called: Sandia Plastics Inc (P-4236)*

Ultimate Sound Inc .... B 909 861-6200
1200 S Diamond Bar Blvd Ste 200 Diamond Bar (91765) *(P-6564)*

Ultimate Staffing Services, Orange *Also Called: Roth Staffing Companies LP (P-13619)*

Ultisat Inc .... A 240 243-5107
11839 Sorrento Valley Rd San Diego (92121) *(P-14115)*

Ultra Built Kitchens Inc .... E 323 232-3362
1814 E 43rd St Los Angeles (90058) *(P-2365)*

Ultra Communications Inc .... E 760 652-0011
990 Park Center Dr Ste H Vista (92081) *(P-9468)*

Ultra Mobile, Costa Mesa *Also Called: Uvnv Inc (P-9469)*

Ultra Pro International LLC .... C 323 890-2100
6049 E Slauson Ave Commerce (90040) *(P-10530)*

Ultra Wheel Company .... E 714 449-7100
586 N Gilbert St Fullerton (92833) *(P-7304)*

Ultra-Stereo Labs Inc .... E 805 549-0161
181 Bonetti Dr San Luis Obispo (93401) *(P-7155)*

Ultracare Services LLC .... D 818 266-9668
11539 Hawthorne Blvd Ste 500 Hawthorne (90250) *(P-16427)*

Ultraglas Inc .... E 818 772-7744
3392 Hampton Ct Thousand Oaks (91362) *(P-9962)*

Ultragraphics Inc .... E 818 295-3994
2800 N Naomi St Burbank (91504) *(P-13320)*

Ultramar Inc .... D 661 944-2496
9508 E Palmdale Blvd Palmdale (93591) *(P-3834)*

Ultramet .... D 818 899-0236
12173 Montague St Pacoima (91331) *(P-5303)*

Ultrasigns Electrical Advg, San Diego *Also Called: Jones Sign Co Inc (P-8611)*

Ultrasigns Electrical Advg, San Diego *Also Called: Jones Signs Co Inc (P-10048)*

Ultura, Long Beach *Also Called: Ultura Inc (P-18269)*

Ultura Inc .... C 562 661-4999
3605 Long Beach Blvd Ste 201 Long Beach (90807) *(P-18269)*

Umc Acquisition Corp (PA)......................... E 562 940-0300
9151 Imperial Hwy Downey (90242) *(P-4622)*

Umex, Downey *Also Called: Universal Mlding Extrusion Inc (P-4610)*

Umg Recordings Inc .... A 310 865-4000
2220 Colorado Ave Santa Monica (90404) *(P-12679)*

Umgd, Santa Monica *Also Called: Universal Mus Group Dist Corp (P-2950)*

Umpco Inc .... D 714 897-3531
7100 Lampson Ave Garden Grove (92841) *(P-4793)*

Ums Banking, Glendale *Also Called: United Merchant Svcs Cal Inc (P-9980)*

Un Deux Trois Inc (PA)............................. E 323 588-1067
2301 E 7th St Los Angeles (90023) *(P-2174)*

Unbroken Studios LLC .... D 310 741-2670
2120 Park Pl Ste 110 El Segundo (90245) *(P-14058)*

Uncle Ben's, Los Angeles *Also Called: Mars Food Us LLC (P-1413)*

Undersea Systems Intl Inc .... D 714 754-7848
3133 W Harvard St Santa Ana (92704) *(P-7156)*

Underwater Kinetics, Poway *Also Called: Uke Corporation (P-8551)*

Uneekor Inc .... D 888 262-6498
15770 Laguna Canyon Rd Ste 100 Irvine (92618) *(P-14059)*

Unger Fabrik LLC (PA).............................. C 626 469-8080
18525 Railroad St City Of Industry (91748) *(P-2056)*

UNI Hosiery Co Inc (PA)............................ C 213 228-0100
1911 E Olympic Blvd Los Angeles (90021) *(P-10698)*

UNI-Sport Inc .... E 310 217-4587
16933 Gramercy Pl Gardena (90247) *(P-3094)*

Unibal-Rodamco-Westfield Group .... C 310 478-4456
2049 Century Park E 41st Fl Los Angeles (90067) *(P-12322)*

Unicare Medical Transportation, Riverside *Also Called: Empire Med Transportations LLC (P-9277)*

Unicel, Chatsworth *Also Called: Meissner Mfg Co Inc (P-6023)*

Unified Field Services Corp .... E 661 325-8962
6906 Downing Ave Bakersfield (93308) *(P-280)*

Unified Grocers Inc .... C 323 232-6124
457 E Martin Luther King Jr Blvd Los Angeles (90011) *(P-9123)*

Unified Nutrimeals .... D 323 923-9335
5469 Ferguson Dr Commerce (90022) *(P-11607)*

Unifirst, Ontario *Also Called: Unifirst Corporation (P-13141)*

Unifirst Corporation .... C 909 390-8670
700 Etiwanda Ave Ste C Ontario (91761) *(P-13141)*

Unilab Corporation (HQ)............................ B 818 737-6000
8401 Fallbrook Ave West Hills (91304) *(P-16337)*

Unimark, Gardena *Also Called: Matsui International Co Inc (P-3813)*

Union Building Maintenance, Commerce *Also Called: Uniserve Facilities Svcs Corp (P-13426)*

Union Carbide Corporation .... E 310 214-5300
19206 Hawthorne Blvd Torrance (90503) *(P-2646)*

Union Pacific Lines, Long Beach *Also Called: Union Pacific Railroad Company (P-8745)*

Union Pacific Railroad Company .... B 562 490-7000
2401 E Sepulveda Blvd Long Beach (90810) *(P-8745)*

Union Sup Comsy Solutions Inc .... B 785 357-5005
2301 E Pacifica Pl Rancho Dominguez (90220) *(P-10813)*

Union Technology Corp .... E 323 266-6871
718 Monterey Pass Rd Monterey Park (91754) *(P-10295)*

Unique Carpets Ltd .... D 951 352-8125
7360 Jurupa Ave Riverside (92504) *(P-9913)*

Unique Functional Products .... C 760 744-1610
135 Sunshine Ln San Marcos (92069) *(P-7318)*

Unique Functional Products, San Marcos *Also Called: Dexter Axle Company (P-7315)*

Unique Protective Services, Santa Clarita *Also Called: Cottrell Paul Enterprises LLC (P-14290)*

Unique Sales, Vernon *Also Called: Zk Enterprises Inc (P-2032)*

Unirex Corp .... E 323 589-4000
2288 E 27th St Vernon (90058) *(P-6908)*

Unirex Technologies, Vernon *Also Called: Unirex Corp (P-6908)*

Unis LLC .... D 310 747-7388
19914 S Via Baron Rancho Dominguez (90220) *(P-9124)*

Uniserve Facilities Svcs Corp .... B 310 440-6747
1200 Getty Center Dr Los Angeles (90049) *(P-13425)*

Uniserve Facilities Svcs Corp (PA)................. B 213 533-1000
2363 S Atlantic Blvd Commerce (90040) *(P-13426)*

Unisource Solutions LLC (PA)...................... C 562 654-3500
8350 Rex Rd Pico Rivera (90660) *(P-9884)*

Unisys Corporation .... C 949 380-5000
9701 Jeronimo Rd Ste 100 Irvine (92618) *(P-13854)*

Unite Eurotherapy Inc .... D 760 585-1800
2870 Whiptail Loop Ste 100 Carlsbad (92010) *(P-10654)*

United Access LLC .... D 623 879-0800
4797 Ruffner St San Diego (92111) *(P-11700)*

United Aeronautical Corp .... E 818 764-2102
7360 Laurel Canyon Blvd North Hollywood (91605) *(P-10504)*

United Airlines Inc .... D 310 258-3319
7300 World Way W Rm 144 Los Angeles (90045) *(P-9168)*

United Amrcn Indian Invlvment (PA)................ D 213 202-3970
1125 W 6th St Ste 103 Los Angeles (90017) *(P-16515)*

United Artists Productions Inc .... C 310 449-3000
10250 Constellation Blvd Fl 19 Los Angeles (90067) *(P-14925)*

United Artists Television Corp .... B 310 449-3000
10250 Constellation Blvd Fl 27 Los Angeles (90067) *(P-14926)*

United Bakery Equipment Co Inc (PA).............. D 310 635-8121
15315 Marquardt Ave Santa Fe Springs (90670) *(P-5794)*

United Biologics .... E 949 345-7490
1642 Kaiser Ave Irvine (92614) *(P-8314)*

United Brands Company Inc .... E 619 461-5220
5930 Cornerstone Ct W Ste 170 San Diego (92121) *(P-1692)*

United Brothers Concrete Inc .... C 760 346-1013
73700 Dinah Shore Dr Palm Desert (92211) *(P-1140)*

United Bys Grls Clubs Snta BRB .... D 805 967-1612
5701 Hollister Ave Goleta (93117) *(P-17371)*

United California, Downey *Also Called: United Drill Bushing Corp (P-5628)*

United Cargo Logistics, City Of Industry *Also Called: U C L Incorporated (P-8979)*

United Carports LLC .... E 800 757-6742
7280 Sycamore Canyon Blvd Ste 1 Riverside (92508) *(P-5089)*

United Convalescent Facilities .... D 213 748-0491
230 E Adams Blvd Los Angeles (90011) *(P-15887)*

United Couriers Inc (DH).. C 213 383-3611
3280 E Foothill Blvd Pasadena (91107) *(P-9169)*

United Crbral Plsy Assn Ornge .... B 949 333-6400
1251 E Dyer Rd Ste 150 Santa Ana (92705) *(P-17020)*

United Crbral Plsy Assn San Lu .... D 805 543-2039
3620 Sacramento Dr Ste 201 San Luis Obispo (93401) *(P-17021)*

United Detector Technology, Hawthorne *Also Called: OSI Optoelectronics Inc (P-6864)*

United Drill Bushing Corp .... C 562 803-1521
12200 Woodruff Ave Downey (90241) *(P-5628)*

United Fabricare Supply Inc (PA)... D 310 537-2096
1237 W Walnut St Compton (90220) *(P-10480)*

United Facility Solutions Inc .... B 310 743-3000
19208 S Vermont Ave Ste 200 Gardena (90248) *(P-14357)*

United Farm Workers America (PA)....................................... C 661 822-5571
29700 Woodford Tehachapi Rd Keene (93531) *(P-17317)*

United Fmly Care Inc A Med Cor .... C 909 874-1679
8110 Mango Ave Ste 104 Fontana (92335) *(P-15493)*

United Gastroenterologists, Murrieta *Also Called: United Medical Doctors (P-15494)*

United Guard Security Inc .... C 909 402-0754
473 E Carnegie Dr Ste 200 San Bernardino (92408) *(P-14358)*

United Guard Security Inc .... C 714 242-4051
1100 W Town And Country Rd Ste 1250 Orange (92868) *(P-14359)*

United Imaging, Woodland Hills *Also Called: United Ribbon Company Inc (P-9981)*

United Industries Group Inc .... E 949 759-3200
11 Rancho Cir Lake Forest (92630) *(P-17656)*

United International Tech Inc .... E 818 772-9400
9207 Deering Ave Ste B Chatsworth (91311) *(P-6785)*

United Lab Services Inc .... D 951 444-0467
2479 S Vicentia Ave Corona (92882) *(P-16338)*

United Launch Alliance LLC .... B 303 269-5876
1579 Utah Ave, Bldg. 7525 Vandenberg Afb (93437) *(P-7659)*

United Medical Doctors .... C 951 566-5229
28078 Baxter Rd Ste 530 Murrieta (92563) *(P-15494)*

United Medical Imaging Inc (PA)... D 310 943-8400
10436 Santa Monica Blvd Los Angeles (90025) *(P-15495)*

United Medical Management Inc .... C 909 886-5291
1680 N Waterman Ave San Bernardino (92404) *(P-15888)*

United Merchant Svcs Cal Inc .... D 818 246-6767
750 Fairmont Ave Ste 201 Glendale (91203) *(P-9980)*

United Owners Services, Anaheim *Also Called: Tricom Management LLC (P-18068)*

United Pacific Designs, Vernon *Also Called: UPD INC (P-8480)*

United Pacific Waste .... D 562 699-7600
6500 Stanford Ave Los Angeles (90001) *(P-9769)*

United Parcel Service Inc .... D 800 828-8264
290 W Avenue L Lancaster (93534) *(P-9013)*

United Parcel Service Inc .... B 404 828-6000
16000 Arminta St Van Nuys (91406) *(P-9014)*

United Parcel Service Inc .... D 661 824-9391
1522 Sabovich St Mojave (93501) *(P-9015)*

United Parcel Service Inc .... D 800 742-5877
2800 W 227th St Torrance (90505) *(P-9016)*

United Parcel Service Inc .... C 310 217-2646
17115 S Western Ave Gardena (90247) *(P-9017)*

United Parcel Service Inc .... C 800 742-5877
16301 Trojan Way La Mirada (90638) *(P-9018)*

United Parcel Service Inc .... B 562 404-3236
13233 Moore St Cerritos (90703) *(P-9019)*

United Parcel Service Inc .... B 626 814-6216
1100 Baldwin Park Blvd Baldwin Park (91706) *(P-9020)*

United Parcel Service Inc .... A 909 974-7212
3140 Jurupa St Ontario (91761) *(P-9021)*

United Parcel Service Inc .... C 909 974-7250
3221 E Jurupa Ontario (91764) *(P-9022)*

United Parcel Service Inc .... D 760 325-1762
650 N Commercial Rd Palm Springs (92262) *(P-9023)*

United Parcel Service Inc .... D 951 749-3400
11811 Landon Dr Eastvale (91752) *(P-9024)*

United Parcel Service Inc .... C 619 482-8119
2300 Boswell Ct Chula Vista (91914) *(P-9025)*

United Parcel Service Inc .... C 858 455-8800
6060 Cornerstone Ct W San Diego (92121) *(P-9026)*

United Parcel Service Inc .... B 909 279-5111
7925 Ronson Rd San Diego (92111) *(P-9027)*

United Parcel Service Inc .... C 801 973-3400
3601 Sacramento Dr San Luis Obispo (93401) *(P-9028)*

United Parcel Service Inc .... D 805 964-7848
505 Pine Ave Goleta (93117) *(P-9029)*

United Parcel Service Inc .... C 805 922-7851
309 Cooley Ln Santa Maria (93455) *(P-9030)*

United Parcel Service Inc .... A 949 643-6634
22 Brookline Aliso Viejo (92656) *(P-9031)*

United Parcel Service Inc .... D 909 906-5700
2925 Jurupa St Ontario (91761) *(P-9170)*

United Parcel Service Inc .... C 800 742-5877
1457 E Victoria Ave San Bernardino (92408) *(P-9171)*

United Parcel Service Inc .... D 909 349-4343
10760 Tamarind Ave Bloomington (92316) *(P-9172)*

United Parcel Service Inc .... C 909 605-7740
3110 Jurupa St Ontario (91761) *(P-9173)*

United Parcel Service Inc .... C 323 260-8957
3333 S Downey Rd Los Angeles (90023) *(P-9176)*

United Parcel Service Inc .... D 951 928-5221
25283 Sherman Rd Sun City (92585) *(P-9177)*

United Paving Company, Corona *Also Called: Superior Paving Company Inc (P-650)*

United Pharma LLC .... C 714 738-8999
2317 Moore Ave Fullerton (92833) *(P-3516)*

United Precision Corp .... E 818 576-9540
20810 Plummer St Chatsworth (91311) *(P-6257)*

United Pumping Service Inc .... D 626 961-9326
14000 Valley Blvd City Of Industry (91746) *(P-8929)*

United Ribbon Company Inc .... D 818 716-1515
21201 Oxnard St Woodland Hills (91367) *(P-9981)*

United Riggers & Erectors Inc (PA)....................................... D 909 978-0400
4188 Valley Blvd Walnut (91789) *(P-1191)*

United Scope LLC (HQ)... E 714 942-3202
3210 El Camino Real Irvine (92602) *(P-8027)*

United Security Products Inc .... E 800 227-1592
12675 Danielson Ct Ste 405 Poway (92064) *(P-7157)*

United Sports Brands, Fountain Valley *Also Called: Shock Doctor Inc (P-8542)*

United States Bakery .... E 323 232-6124
457 E Martin Luther King Jr Blvd Los Angeles (90011) *(P-1468)*

United States Cold Storage Cal, Bakersfield *Also Called: United States Cold Storage Inc (P-9044)*

United States Cold Storage Inc .... D 661 832-2653
6501 District Blvd Bakersfield (93313) *(P-9044)*

United States Dept of Navy .... A 619 556-6033
32nd St Naval Sta San Diego (92136) *(P-7610)*

United States Dept of Navy .... C 805 989-1328
311 Navy Base Ventura County Port Hueneme (93042) *(P-14798)*

United States Dept of Navy .... B 858 577-9849
19871 Mitscher Way San Diego (92145) *(P-15496)*

United States Dept of Navy .... A 619 532-6400
34800 Bob Wilson Dr San Diego (92134) *(P-16239)*

United States Dept of Navy .... D 760 830-2124
1145 Sturgis Rd Twentynine Palms (92278) *(P-16623)*

United States Gypsum Company .... D 908 232-8900
401 Van Ness Ave Torrance (90501) *(P-4469)*

United States Gypsum Company .... C 760 358-3200
3810 Evan Hewes Hwy Imperial (92251) *(P-4470)*

United States Logistics Group .... E 562 989-9555
2700 Rose Ave Ste A Signal Hill (90755) *(P-7319)*

United States Luggage Co LLC .... D 562 293-4400
13300 Carmenita Rd Santa Fe Springs (90670) *(P-10573)*

United States Marine Corps .... D 760 725-3564
Marine Corps Air Stn Bldg 23122 (Camp Pendleton) Oceanside (92049) *(P-10505)*

United States Marine Corps .... B 760 725-4704
Golf Course Rd Bldg 18415 Camp Pendleton (92055) *(P-15097)*

United States Technical Svcs .... C 714 374-6300
16541 Gothard St Ste 214 Huntington Beach (92647) *(P-14262)*

United States Tile Co .... C 951 739-4613
909 Railroad St Corona (92882) *(P-4362)*

United Sttes Dept Enrgy Brkley .... C 510 486-7089
555 W Imperial Hwy Brea (92821) *(P-17893)*

Mergent email: customerrelations@mergent.com
1222

2025 Southern California
Business Directory and Buyers Guide

(P-0000) Products & Services Section entry number
(PA)=Parent Co (HQ)=Headquarters (DH)=Div Headquarters

United Sunshine American Industries Corporation .... E
2808 E Marywood Ln Orange (92867) *(P-5418)*

United Support Services Inc .... C 858 373-9500
3252 Holiday Ct Ste 110 La Jolla (92037) *(P-13855)*

United Surface Solutions LLC .... E 562 693-0202
11901 Burke St Santa Fe Springs (90670) *(P-5723)*

United Svcs Amer Federal Cr Un (PA).............................. D 858 831-8100
9999 Willow Creek Rd San Diego (92131) *(P-11818)*

United Syatt America Corp (PA).. C 714 568-1938
920 E 1st St Santa Ana (92701) *(P-11472)*

United Talent Agency LLC .... D 310 776-8160
9336 Civic Center Dr Beverly Hills (90210) *(P-14617)*

United Talent Agency LLC .... D 310 385-2800
1880 Century Park E Ste 711 Los Angeles (90067) *(P-18236)*

United Talent Agency, LLC, Beverly Hills *Also Called: United Talent Agency LLC (P-14617)*

UNITED TALENT AGENCY, LLC, Los Angeles *Also Called: United Talent Agency LLC (P-18236)*

United Teachers-Los Angeles .... D 213 487-5560
3303 Wilshire Blvd Fl 10 Los Angeles (90010) *(P-17318)*

United Therapeutics Corp .... D 858 754-2970
10578 Science Center Dr Ste 215 San Diego (92121) *(P-9571)*

United Vision Financial Inc .... C 818 285-0211
16027 Ventura Blvd Ste 200 Encino (91436) *(P-11956)*

United Way Inc (PA)... D 213 808-6220
1150 S Olive St Ste T-500 Los Angeles (90015) *(P-17246)*

UNITED WAY OF GREATER LOS ANGE, Los Angeles *Also Called: United Way Inc (P-17246)*

United Western Enterprises Inc .... E 805 389-1077
850 Flynn Rd Ste 200 Camarillo (93012) *(P-5352)*

Unity Courier Service Inc (DH).. C 323 255-9800
3231 Fletcher Dr Los Angeles (90065) *(P-9032)*

Univar Solutions USA LLC .... C 323 727-7005
2600 Garfield Ave Commerce (90040) *(P-11022)*

Universal Card Inc .... B 949 861-4000
9012 Research Dr Ste 200 Irvine (92618) *(P-14618)*

Universal Care Inc (HQ)... B 866 255-4795
200 Oceangate Ste 100 Long Beach (90802) *(P-16516)*

Universal Christian Music Pubg, Santa Monica *Also Called: Universal Music Publishing Inc (P-2951)*

Universal City Studios Lllp .... A 818 622-8477
100 Universal City Plz Universal City (91608) *(P-14865)*

Universal Cushion Company Inc (PA).................................. E 323 887-8000
1610 Mandeville Canyon Rd Los Angeles (90049) *(P-2225)*

Universal Custom Cabinets, Pacoima *Also Called: N K Cabinets Inc (P-2356)*

Universal Custom Courier, San Fernando *Also Called: Universal Mail Delivery Svc (P-13308)*

Universal Cy Stdios Prdctons L (DH).................................. E 818 777-1000
100 Universal City Plz Universal City (91608) *(P-14866)*

Universal Dust Cllctr Mfg Sup (PA).................................... D 714 630-8588
1041 N Kraemer Pl Anaheim (92806) *(P-510)*

Universal Elastic & Garment Supply Inc .... E 213 748-2995
2200 S Alameda St Vernon (90058) *(P-1907)*

Universal Framing Products, Santa Clarita *Also Called: Universal Wood Moulding Inc (P-9914)*

Universal Home Care Inc .... C 323 653-9222
151 N San Vicente Blvd Ste 200 Beverly Hills (90211) *(P-16428)*

Universal Hosiery Inc .... D 661 702-8444
28337 Constellation Rd Valencia (91355) *(P-1910)*

Universal Mail Delivery Svc (PA).. D 818 365-3144
501 S Brand Blvd # 104 San Fernando (91340) *(P-13308)*

Universal Meat Company, Rancho Cucamonga *Also Called: Formosa Meat Company Inc (P-1258)*

Universal Mlding Extrusion Inc (DH)................................... E 562 401-1015
9151 Imperial Hwy Downey (90242) *(P-4610)*

Universal Molding Company (HQ)....................................... C 310 886-1750
9151 Imperial Hwy Downey (90242) *(P-4623)*

Universal Molding Company, Downey *Also Called: Umc Acquisition Corp (P-4622)*

Universal Motion Components Co Inc .... E 714 437-9600
2920 Airway Ave Costa Mesa (92626) *(P-5796)*

Universal Mus Group Dist Corp (DH).................................. D 310 235-4700
2220 Colorado Ave Santa Monica (90404) *(P-2950)*

Universal Mus Group Dist Corp .... C 818 508-9550
111 Universal Hollywood Dr Ste 1420 Universal City (91608) *(P-14619)*

Universal Mus Investments Inc (HQ)................................... D 888 583-7176
2220 Colorado Ave Santa Monica (90404) *(P-14620)*

Universal Music Enterprises, Santa Monica *Also Called: Umg Recordings Inc (P-12679)*

Universal Music Group Inc (HQ)... D 310 865-0770
2220 Colorado Ave Santa Monica (90404) *(P-14621)*

Universal Music Publishing Inc .... D 310 235-4700
1601 Cloverfield Blvd Santa Monica (90404) *(P-2951)*

Universal Packg Systems Inc (PA)...................................... A 909 517-2442
14570 Monte Vista Ave Chino (91710) *(P-3693)*

Universal Packg Systems Inc .... C 909 517-2442
14570 Monte Vista Ave Chino (91710) *(P-9125)*

Universal Pctres HM Entrmt LLC (DH)................................ D 818 777-1000
100 Universal City Plz Bldg 1440/7 Universal City (91608) *(P-14867)*

Universal Pictures Intl, Universal City *Also Called: Nbcuniversal Media LLC (P-9485)*

Universal Plant Svcs Cal Inc .... D 310 618-1600
20545 Belshaw Ave # A Carson (90746) *(P-6258)*

Universal Plastic Mold, Baldwin Park *Also Called: Upm Inc (P-5601)*

Universal Products, Rancho Cucamonga *Also Called: Proulx Manufacturing Inc (P-4212)*

Universal Protection Svc LP (HQ).. D 866 877-1965
450 Exchange Irvine (92602) *(P-14360)*

Universal Prtnrships Licensing, Universal City *Also Called: Universal Stdios Licensing LLC (P-12680)*

Universal Punch Corp .... D 714 556-4488
4001 W Macarthur Blvd Santa Ana (92704) *(P-5562)*

Universal Services America LP .... A 714 923-3700
1815 E Wilshire Ave Ste 912 Santa Ana (92705) *(P-13427)*.

Universal Services America LP (HQ).................................... D 866 877-1965
450 Exchange Irvine (92602) *(P-14361)*

Universal Services America LP .... A 760 200-2865
77725 Enfield Ln Palm Desert (92211) *(P-14362)*

Universal Shopping Plaza A CA .... C 714 521-8899
6281 Regio Ave Buena Park (90620) *(P-12323)*

Universal Stdios Licensing LLC .... C 818 695-1273
100 Universal City Plz Universal City (91608) *(P-12680)*

Universal Studios, Universal City *Also Called: Universal City Studios Lllp (P-14865)*

Universal Studios, Universal City *Also Called: Creative Park Productions LLC (P-14916)*

Universal Studios Company LLC (DH).................................. A 818 777-1000
100 Universal City Plz North Hollywood (91608) *(P-14868)*

Universal Surveillance Systems, Rancho Cucamonga *Also Called: Universal Surveillance Systems LLC (P-7158)*

Universal Surveillance Systems LLC .... D 909 484-7870
11172 Elm Ave Rancho Cucamonga (91730) *(P-7158)*

Universal Switching Corp .... E 818 785-0200
7671 N San Fernando Rd Burbank (91505) *(P-6433)*

Universal Technical Inst Inc .... C 909 484-1929
9494 Haven Ave Rancho Cucamonga (91730) *(P-16848)*

Universal Wood Moulding Inc (PA)...................................... E 661 362-6262
21139 Centre Pointe Pkwy Santa Clarita (91350) *(P-9914)*

University Bookstore, Long Beach *Also Called: Forty-Niner Shops Inc (P-11632)*

University Business Ctr Assoc .... D 601 354-3555
5383 Hollister Ave Ste 120 Santa Barbara (93111) *(P-12324)*

University Cal Los Angeles .... A 310 825-9111
757 Westwood Plz Los Angeles (90095) *(P-16240)*

University Cal Los Angeles .... C 310 825-7852
420 Westwood Plz Rm 7702 Los Angeles (90095) *(P-16835)*

University Cal San Diego .... A 858 534-5000
10100 Hopkins Dr La Jolla (92093) *(P-14162)*

University Cal San Diego .... A 619 543-6654
200 W Arbor Dr Frnt San Diego (92103) *(P-16241)*

University Cal San Diego .... A 858 657-7000
9300 Campus Point Dr La Jolla (92037) *(P-16242)*

University Cal San Diego .... C 619 543-6170
402 Dickinson St Ste 380 San Diego (92103) *(P-16243)*

University Cal San Diego .... D 858 622-1771
5440 Morehouse Dr Ste 2600 San Diego (92121) *(P-17894)*

University California Irvine .... D 714 456-6966
101 The City Dr S Ste 313 Orange (92868) *(P-15497)*

University California Irvine .... A 714 456-6170
101 The City Dr S Bldg 1a Orange (92868) *(P-15498)*

University California Irvine .... B 714 480-2443
800 N Main St Santa Ana (92701) *(P-15499)*

Employee Codes: A=Over 500 employees, B=251-500
C=101-250, D=51-100, E=20-50, F=10-19, G=1-9

2025 Southern California
Business Directory and Buyers Guide

© Mergent Inc. 1-800-342-5647
1223

University California Irvine .... D 949 644-5245
43 Cambria Dr Corona Del Mar (92625) *(P-15500)*

University California Irvine .... D 949 646-2267
1640 Newport Blvd Ste 340 Costa Mesa (92627) *(P-15501)*

University California Irvine .... D 714 456-7890
101 The City Dr S Orange (92868) *(P-15502)*

University California Irvine .... A 714 456-6011
101 The City Dr S Orange (92868) *(P-16244)*

University California Irvine .... C 714 456-5558
200 S Manchester Ave Ste 400 Orange (92868) *(P-16245)*

University California Irvine .... A 714 456-8000
101 The City Dr S Orange (92868) *(P-16246)*

University California Irvine .... C 714 775-3066
15355 Brookhurst St Ste 102 Westminster (92683) *(P-16247)*

University California Irvine .... C 949 202-7580
B35 Rowland Hall Irvine (92697) *(P-16339)*

University California Irvine .... C 909 358-5774
118 Med Surge I Irvine (92697) *(P-16340)*

University California Irvine .... D 949 939-7106
31865 Circle Dr Laguna Beach (92651) *(P-16624)*

University California Irvine .... D 949 824-2662
106 B Student Ctr Irvine (92697) *(P-16625)*

University California Irvine .... C 949 824-7725
3151 Social Science Plz Irvine (92697) *(P-16836)*

University California Irvine .... D 714 456-2332
3800 W Chapman Ave Ste 7200 Orange (92868) *(P-16837)*

University California Irvine .... D 714 456-6655
200 S Manchester Ave Ste 650 Orange (92868) *(P-17757)*

University California Irvine .... D 949 824-6828
120 Theory Ste 200 Irvine (92617) *(P-17758)*

University California Irvine .... B 949 824-2819
2220 Engineering Gtwy Irvine (92697) *(P-17836)*

University California Irvine .... C 949 824-3359
843 Health Sciences Rd Irvine (92617) *(P-17837)*

UNIVERSITY COMMERCIAL SERVICES, Los Angeles *Also Called: Cal State La Univ Aux Svcs Inc (P-17957)*

University Credit Union .... C 310 477-6628
1500 S Sepulveda Blvd Los Angeles (90025) *(P-11819)*

University Frames Inc .... E 714 575-5100
3060 E Miraloma Ave Anaheim (92806) *(P-2418)*

University Marelich Mech Inc .... C 714 632-2600
1000 N Kraemer Pl Anaheim (92806) *(P-850)*

University Park Healthcare Ctr, Los Angeles *Also Called: United Convalescent Facilities (P-15887)*

University Readers, Solana Beach *Also Called: Cognella Inc (P-2907)*

University Southern California .... A 323 442-8500
1500 San Pablo St Los Angeles (90033) *(P-16248)*

Uniweb, Corona *Also Called: Uniweb Inc (P-2597)*

Uniweb Inc (PA) .... D 951 279-7999
222 S Promenade Ave Corona (92879) *(P-2597)*

Uniwell Corporation .... C 714 522-7000
7000 Beach Blvd Buena Park (90620) *(P-13059)*

Unix Packaging LLC (PA) .... D 213 627-5050
9 Minson Way Montebello (90640) *(P-1656)*

Unix Packaging LLC .... C 213 627-5050
5361 Alexander St Commerce (90040) *(P-11146)*

Unlimited Innovations Inc .... E 714 998-0866
180 N Rverview Dr Ste 320 Anaheim (92808) *(P-14060)*

Uns Electric Inc .... E 714 690-3660
6565 Valley View St La Palma (90623) *(P-10210)*

Unspoken Language Services Inc .... B 626 532-8096
1370 Valley Vista Dr Ste 200 Diamond Bar (91765) *(P-14622)*

UPD INC .... D 323 588-8811
4507 S Maywood Ave Vernon (90058) *(P-8480)*

Upkeep Technologies Inc .... C 323 880-0280
10880 Wilshire Blvd Ste 850 Los Angeles (90024) *(P-13856)*

Upland Community Care Inc .... B 909 985-1903
1221 E Arrow Hwy Upland (91786) *(P-15789)*

Upland Fab Inc .... E 909 986-6565
1445 Brooks St Ste L Ontario (91762) *(P-6259)*

Upm Inc .... B 626 962-4001
13245 Los Angeles St Baldwin Park (91706) *(P-5601)*

Upper Deck Company (PA) .... E 800 873-7332
5830 El Camino Real Carlsbad (92008) *(P-2952)*

Uprite Construction Corp .... D 949 877-8877
2211 Michelson Dr Ste 350 Irvine (92612) *(P-511)*

UPS, Lancaster *Also Called: United Parcel Service Inc (P-9013)*

UPS, Van Nuys *Also Called: United Parcel Service Inc (P-9014)*

UPS, Mojave *Also Called: United Parcel Service Inc (P-9015)*

UPS, Torrance *Also Called: United Parcel Service Inc (P-9016)*

UPS, Gardena *Also Called: United Parcel Service Inc (P-9017)*

UPS, La Mirada *Also Called: United Parcel Service Inc (P-9018)*

UPS, Cerritos *Also Called: United Parcel Service Inc (P-9019)*

UPS, Baldwin Park *Also Called: United Parcel Service Inc (P-9020)*

UPS, Ontario *Also Called: United Parcel Service Inc (P-9021)*

UPS, Ontario *Also Called: United Parcel Service Inc (P-9022)*

UPS, Palm Springs *Also Called: United Parcel Service Inc (P-9023)*

UPS, Eastvale *Also Called: United Parcel Service Inc (P-9024)*

UPS, Chula Vista *Also Called: United Parcel Service Inc (P-9025)*

UPS, San Diego *Also Called: United Parcel Service Inc (P-9026)*

UPS, San Diego *Also Called: United Parcel Service Inc (P-9027)*

UPS, San Luis Obispo *Also Called: United Parcel Service Inc (P-9028)*

UPS, Goleta *Also Called: United Parcel Service Inc (P-9029)*

UPS, Santa Maria *Also Called: United Parcel Service Inc (P-9030)*

UPS, Aliso Viejo *Also Called: United Parcel Service Inc (P-9031)*

UPS, Ontario *Also Called: United Parcel Service Inc (P-9170)*

UPS, San Bernardino *Also Called: United Parcel Service Inc (P-9171)*

UPS, Bloomington *Also Called: United Parcel Service Inc (P-9172)*

UPS, Ontario *Also Called: United Parcel Service Inc (P-9173)*

UPS, Los Angeles *Also Called: United Parcel Service Inc (P-9176)*

UPS, Sun City *Also Called: United Parcel Service Inc (P-9177)*

UPS Store Inc (HQ) .... B 858 455-8800
6060 Cornerstone Ct W San Diego (92121) *(P-14623)*

Upstanding LLC .... C 949 788-9900
440 Exchange Ste 100 Irvine (92602) *(P-14061)*

Upstrem Inc .... D 858 229-2979
1253 University Ave Ste 1003 San Diego (92103) *(P-18237)*

Upwind Blade Solutions Inc .... B 866 927-3142
2869 Historic Decatur Rd Ste 100 San Diego (92106) *(P-14799)*

Uqora Inc .... E 888 313-1372
4250 Executive Sq La Jolla (92037) *(P-1308)*

Urban Commons Queensway LLC .... A 562 499-1611
1126 Queens Hwy Long Beach (90802) *(P-13060)*

Urban Concepts, Vernon *Also Called: Anns Trading Company Inc (P-11110)*

Urban Corps San Diego County .... C 619 235-6884
3127 Jefferson St San Diego (92110) *(P-17372)*

Urban Decay, Newport Beach *Also Called: Urban Decay Cosmetics LLC (P-10655)*

Urban Decay Cosmetics LLC .... D 949 631-4504
833 W 16th St Newport Beach (92663) *(P-10655)*

Urban Insight Inc .... E 213 792-2000
3530 Wilshire Blvd Ste 1285 Los Angeles (90010) *(P-14116)*

Uremet Corporation .... E 657 257-4027
7012 Belgrave Ave Garden Grove (92841) *(P-3300)*

Urgent Care Center, Montclair *Also Called: Prime Hlthcare Srvcs-Mntclair (P-16143)*

URS, Long Beach *Also Called: URS Group Inc (P-17657)*

URS Group Inc .... C 562 420-2933
3995 Via Oro Ave Long Beach (90810) *(P-17657)*

US Airconditioning Distributors Inc (PA) .... C 626 854-4500
16900 Chestnut St City Of Industry (91748) *(P-10337)*

US Architectural Lighting, Palmdale *Also Called: Sun Valley Ltg Standards Inc (P-6475)*

US Armor Corporation .... E 562 207-4240
10715 Bloomfield Ave Santa Fe Springs (90670) *(P-8315)*

US Bankcard Services Inc .... D 888 888-8872
17171 Gale Ave Ste 110 City Of Industry (91745) *(P-14624)*

US Best Repair Service Inc .... C 888 750-2378
1652 Edinger Ave Ste E Tustin (92780) *(P-437)*

US Best Repairs, Tustin *Also Called: US Best Repair Service Inc (P-437)*

US Blanks LLC (PA) .... E 310 225-6774
14700 S San Pedro St Gardena (90248) *(P-3301)*

US Borax Inc .... A 760 762-7000
14486 Borax Rd Boron (93516) *(P-3254)*

US Carenet Services LLC .... C 661 945-7350
42225 10th St W Ste 2b Lancaster (93534) *(P-16429)*

US Concrete Precast, San Diego *Also Called: San Diego Precast Concrete Inc (P-4421)*

US Continental Marketing Inc (PA)........................ D 951 808-8888
310 Reed Cir Corona (92879) *(P-3623)*

US Critical, Lake Forest *Also Called: US Critical LLC (P-5891)*

US Critical LLC (PA).. E 949 916-9326
6 Orchard Ste 150 Lake Forest (92630) *(P-5891)*

US Data Management LLC (PA)............................. D 888 231-0816
535 Chapala St Santa Barbara (93101) *(P-14263)*

US Dermatology Medical Management Inc .... D 817 962-2157
1401 N Batavia St Ste 204 Orange (92867) *(P-15503)*

US Electrical Services Inc .... E 714 982-1534
1501 E Orangethorpe Ave Ste 140 Fullerton (92831) *(P-10211)*

US Elogistics Service Corp .... C 909 927-7483
1420 Tamarind Ave Rialto (92376) *(P-9126)*

US Energy Technologies Inc .... E 714 617-8800
14370 Myford Road Ste 100 Walnut (91789) *(P-6477)*

US Family Care, Rialto *Also Called: Caremark Rx Inc (P-15262)*

US Foods Inc .... C 714 670-3500
15155 Northam St La Mirada (90638) *(P-10814)*

US Foods Inc .... C 562 806-2445
8457 Eastern Ave Bell Gardens (90201) *(P-10987)*

US Foods Inc .... C 213 623-4150
636 Stanford Ave Los Angeles (90021) *(P-10988)*

US Foods Inc .... C 310 632-6265
1610 E Sepulveda Blvd Carson (90745) *(P-10989)*

US Grant Hotel Ventures LLC .... D 619 744-2007
326 Broadway San Diego (92101) *(P-13061)*

US Hanger Company LLC .... E 310 323-8030
17501 S Denver Ave Gardena (90248) *(P-4545)*

US Horizon Manufacturing Inc .... E 661 775-1675
28539 Industry Dr Valencia (91355) *(P-4319)*

US Hotel and Resort MGT Inc .... C 949 650-2988
2544 Newport Blvd Costa Mesa (92627) *(P-13062)*

US Industrial Tool & Sup Co .... E 310 464-8400
14083 S Normandie Ave Gardena (90249) *(P-5563)*

US Lighting Tech, Walnut *Also Called: US Energy Technologies Inc (P-6477)*

US Lines, Newport Beach *Also Called: US Lines LLC (P-9348)*

US Lines LLC (DH)... D 714 751-3333
3501 Jamboree Rd Ste 300 Newport Beach (92660) *(P-9348)*

US Logistics, Signal Hill *Also Called: United States Logistics Group (P-7319)*

US Motor Works LLC (PA).................................. E 562 404-0488
14722 Anson Ave Santa Fe Springs (90670) *(P-7305)*

US Pole Company Inc (PA)................................. D 800 877-6537
660 W Avenue O Palmdale (93551) *(P-6478)*

US Polo Assn - Otlets At Ornge, Orange *Also Called: Jordache Enterprises Inc (P-12299)*

US Polymers Inc (PA)....................................... D 323 728-3023
1057 S Vail Ave Montebello (90640) *(P-4267)*

US Polymers Inc .... D 323 727-6888
6010 Bandini Blvd Commerce (90040) *(P-4611)*

US Precision Sheet Metal Inc .... D 951 276-2611
4020 Garner Rd Riverside (92501) *(P-5051)*

US Radiator Corporation (PA)............................. C 323 826-0066
4423 District Blvd Vernon (90058) *(P-7306)*

US Real Estate Services Inc .... D 949 598-9920
27442 Portola Pkwy Ste 300 Foothill Ranch (92610) *(P-12545)*

US Rigging Supply Corp .... E 714 545-7444
1600 E Mcfadden Ave Santa Ana (92705) *(P-5419)*

US Security Associates, Burbank *Also Called: US Security Associates Inc (P-14364)*

US Security Associates Inc .... C 714 352-0773
2275 W 190th St Ste 100 Torrance (90504) *(P-14363)*

US Security Associates Inc .... C 818 697-1809
455 N Moss St Burbank (91502) *(P-14364)*

US Sensor Corp .... D 714 639-1000
1832 W Collins Ave Orange (92867) *(P-6909)*

US Skillserve Inc .... A 909 621-4751
9620 Fremont Ave Montclair (91763) *(P-15790)*

US Trust, Los Angeles *Also Called: U S Trust Company NA (P-12037)*

US Union Tool Inc (HQ)..................................... E 714 521-6242
1260 N Fee Ana St Anaheim (92807) *(P-5554)*

USA Enterprise Inc .... B 310 750-4246
9777 Wilshire Blvd Ste 400 Beverly Hills (90212) *(P-12746)*

USA Federal Credit Union, San Diego *Also Called: United Svcs Amer Federal Cr Un (P-11818)*

USA Industries, Orange *Also Called: United Sunshine American Industries Corporation (P-5418)*

USA Staffing Inc .... D 805 269-2677
505 Higuera St San Luis Obispo (93401) *(P-13628)*

USA Vision Systems Inc (HQ).............................. E 949 583-1519
9301 Irvine Blvd Irvine (92618) *(P-7159)*

USA Waste of California Inc .... D 818 252-3112
9081 Tujunga Ave Sun Valley (91352) *(P-9770)*

Usamp, Encino *Also Called: Instantly Inc (P-17851)*

USAopoly Inc .... D 760 431-5910
5999 Avenida Encinas Ste 150 Carlsbad (92008) *(P-8497)*

Usc Arcadia Hospital (PA).................................. A 626 898-8000
300 W Huntington Dr Arcadia (91007) *(P-16249)*

Usc University Hospital, Los Angeles *Also Called: University Southern California (P-16248)*

Usc Verdugo Hills Hospital LLC .... A 818 790-7100
1812 Verdugo Blvd Glendale (91208) *(P-16250)*

Usc Vrdugo Hlls Hosp Fundation (HQ).................... B 800 872-2273
1812 Verdugo Blvd Glendale (91208) *(P-16251)*

Uscb Inc (PA).. C 213 985-2111
355 S Grand Ave Ste 3200 Los Angeles (90071) *(P-13289)*

Uscb America, Los Angeles *Also Called: Uscb Inc (P-13289)*

Usdm Life Science, Santa Barbara *Also Called: US Data Management LLC (P-14263)*

Used Cardboard Boxes Inc .... C 323 724-2500
4032 Wilshire Blvd Ste 402 Los Angeles (90010) *(P-10610)*

Usfi Inc .... D 424 260-9210
108 W Walnut St Ste 221 Gardena (90248) *(P-10815)*

USG Ceilings Plus LLC .... E 323 724-8166
6711 E Washington Blvd Commerce (90040) *(P-5219)*

Ushio America Inc (HQ)..................................... D 714 236-8600
5440 Cerritos Ave Cypress (90630) *(P-10212)*

Usit Co, Gardena *Also Called: US Industrial Tool & Sup Co (P-5563)*

Usl Parallel Products Cal .... E 909 980-1200
12281 Arrow Rte Rancho Cucamonga (91739) *(P-3740)*

Usmpc Buyer Inc .... E 909 473-3027
4062 Georgia Blvd San Bernardino (92407) *(P-4496)*

USP Inc .... D 760 842-7700
1818 Ord Way Oceanside (92056) *(P-3694)*

USS Cal Builders Inc .... C 714 828-4882
8031 Main St Stanton (90680) *(P-599)*

UST, Aliso Viejo *Also Called: UST Global Inc (P-13857)*

UST Global Inc (HQ)... D 949 716-8757
5 Polaris Way Aliso Viejo (92656) *(P-13857)*

Usts, Huntington Beach *Also Called: United States Technical Svcs (P-14262)*

Utak Laboratories Inc .... E 661 294-3935
25020 Avenue Tibbitts Valencia (91355) *(P-3741)*

Utc, Mas, Costa Mesa *Also Called: Honeywell SEC Americas LLC (P-6685)*

Uti, Rancho Cucamonga *Also Called: Universal Technical Inst Inc (P-16848)*

Utility Refrigerator .... E 818 764-6200
12160 Sherman Way North Hollywood (91605) *(P-5990)*

Utility Traffic Services LLC .... B 562 264-2355
2845 E Spring St Long Beach (90806) *(P-17858)*

Utility Trailer California LLC (PA).......................... D 877 275-4887
15567 Valley Blvd Fontana (92335) *(P-9808)*

Utility Trailer Manufacturing (PA)......................... B 626 965-1514
17295 Railroad St Ste A City Of Industry (91748) *(P-7320)*

Utility Trailer Mfg Co .... C 909 428-8300
15567 Valley Blvd Fontana (92335) *(P-7321)*

Utility Trailer Mfg Co .... C 909 594-6026
17295 Railroad St Ste A City Of Industry (91748) *(P-7322)*

Utility Trlr Sls Southern Cal, Fontana *Also Called: Utility Trailer Mfg Co (P-7321)*

Utility Vault, Fontana *Also Called: Oldcastle Infrastructure Inc (P-4408)*

Utility Vault, Escondido *Also Called: Oldcastle Infrastructure Inc (P-4409)*

Uvnv Inc .... C 888 777-0446
1550 Scenic Ave Costa Mesa (92626) *(P-9469)*

Uwe, Camarillo *Also Called: United Western Enterprises Inc (P-5352)*

V & F Fabrication Company Inc .... E 714 265-0630
13902 Seaboard Cir Garden Grove (92843) *(P-4877)*

Employee Codes: A=Over 500 employees, B=251-500
C=101-250, D=51-100, E=20-50, F=10-19, G=1-9

2025 Southern California
Business Directory and Buyers Guide

© Mergent Inc. 1-800-342-5647

1225

A
L
P
H
A
B
E
T
I
C

V & L Produce Inc .... C 323 589-3125
2550 E 25th St Vernon (90058) *(P-10921)*

V & S Engineering Company Ltd .... E 714 898-7869
5766 Research Dr Huntington Beach (92649) *(P-6260)*

V 3, Oxnard *Also Called: V3 Printing Corporation (P-3095)*

V B I, Simi Valley *Also Called: Vanderhorst Brothers Industries Inc (P-6263)*

V M S, Glendora *Also Called: Venue Management Systems Inc (P-14365)*

V P H, Van Nuys *Also Called: Valley Presbyterian Hospital (P-16253)*

V Q Orthocare, Vista *Also Called: Vision Quest Industries Inc (P-8318)*

V Todays Inc .... C 310 781-9100
19800 S Vermont Ave Torrance (90502) *(P-13063)*

V Troth Inc .... D 661 948-4646
1801 W Avenue K Ste 101 Lancaster (93534) *(P-12546)*

V Twin Magazine, Agoura Hills *Also Called: Paisano Publications LLC (P-2868)*

V-T Industries Inc .... D 714 521-2008
9818 Firestone Blvd Downey (90241) *(P-4268)*

V-Wave Inc .... E 818 629-2164
29219 Canwood St Ste 100 Agoura Hills (91301) *(P-8246)*

V/ Twins, Agoura Hills *Also Called: Paisano Publications Inc (P-2869)*

V&H Performance LLC .... D 562 921-7461
13861 Rosecrans Ave Santa Fe Springs (90670) *(P-7638)*

V3, Oxnard *Also Called: Ventura Printing Inc (P-3098)*

V3 Printing Corporation .... D 805 981-2600
200 N Elevar St Oxnard (93030) *(P-3095)*

Vacation Interval Realty, Newport Beach *Also Called: Pacific Monarch Resorts Inc (P-12499)*

Vacco Industries (DH) .... C 626 443-7121
10350 Vacco St South El Monte (91733) *(P-5391)*

Vadnais Trenchless Svcs Inc .... D 858 550-1460
11858 Bernardo Plaza Ct Ste 100 San Diego (92128) *(P-702)*

Vagabond Inns, Los Angeles *Also Called: Rpd Hotels 18 LLC (P-13002)*

Vahe Enterprises Inc .... D 323 235-6657
750 E Slauson Ave Los Angeles (90011) *(P-7213)*

Vahi Toyota Inc (PA) .... C 760 241-6484
14612 Valley Center Dr Victorville (92395) *(P-11426)*

Val USA Manufacturer Inc .... E 626 839-8069
1050 W Central Ave Ste A Brea (92821) *(P-8738)*

Val-Pro Inc (PA) .... C 213 627-8736
748 S Alameda St Los Angeles (90021) *(P-10922)*

Valadon Hotel LLC .... D 310 854-1114
8822 Cynthia St West Hollywood (90069) *(P-13064)*

Valco Planer Works Inc .... E 323 582-6355
6131 Maywood Ave Huntington Park (90255) *(P-5602)*

Valco Precision Works, Huntington Park *Also Called: Valco Planer Works Inc (P-5602)*

Valeant Biomedicals Inc (DH) .... D 949 461-6000
1 Enterprise Aliso Viejo (92656) *(P-11023)*

Valeda Company LLC .... E 800 421-8700
13571 Vaughn St Unit E San Fernando (91340) *(P-8316)*

Valence Los Angeles, Gardena *Also Called: Coast Plating Inc (P-5249)*

Valence Lynwood, Lynwood *Also Called: Triumph Processing Inc (P-5302)*

Valencia Country Club, Valencia *Also Called: Heritage Golf Group LLC (P-15084)*

Valencia Gardens Health Care Center, Riverside *Also Called: Riverside Care Inc (P-15762)*

Valencia Pipe Company .... E 661 257-3923
28305 Livingston Ave Valencia (91355) *(P-3980)*

Valero, Wilmington *Also Called: Valero Ref Company-California (P-3835)*

Valero Ref Company-California .... A 562 491-6754
2401 E Anaheim St Wilmington (90744) *(P-3835)*

Valet Parking Service, Los Angeles *Also Called: Valet Parking Svc A Cal Partnr (P-14671)*

Valet Parking Svc A Cal Partnr (PA) .... A 323 465-5873
6933 Hollywood Blvd Los Angeles (90028) *(P-14671)*

Valet Services, Bell Gardens *Also Called: Anitsa Inc (P-13110)*

Valew Welding & Fabrication, Adelanto *Also Called: Hayes Welding Inc (P-14741)*

Valex Corp (HQ) .... D 805 658-0944
6080 Leland St Ventura (93003) *(P-5304)*

Valiant Government Svcs LLC .... B 760 499-1400
540 Perdew Ave Ste B Ridgecrest (93555) *(P-18270)*

Valiant Technical Services Inc .... D 757 628-9500
1785 Utah Ave Lompoc (93437) *(P-7611)*

Valle Vsta Cnvlescent Hosp Inc .... D 760 745-1288
1025 W 2nd Ave Escondido (92025) *(P-15889)*

Vallecitos Water District, San Marcos *Also Called: Vallecitos Water District Financing Corporation (P-9724)*

Vallecitos Water District Financing Corporation (HQ) .... D 760 744-0460
201 Vallecitos De Oro San Marcos (92069) *(P-9724)*

Valley Animal Medical Center .... A 760 342-4711
46920 Jefferson St Indio (92201) *(P-133)*

Valley Box Co Inc .... E 619 449-2882
10611 Prospect Ave Santee (92071) *(P-10611)*

Valley Bulk Inc .... D 760 843-0574
17649 Turner Rd Victorville (92394) *(P-8981)*

Valley Business Printers Inc .... D 818 362-7771
6355 Topanga Canyon Blvd Ste 225 Woodland Hills (91367) *(P-3096)*

Valley Cabinet, El Cajon *Also Called: Vcsd Inc (P-2366)*

Valley Care Olive View Med Ctr, Sylmar *Also Called: Olive View-Ucla Medical Center (P-15410)*

Valley Community Healthcare .... B 818 763-8836
6801 Coldwater Canyon Ave Ste 1b North Hollywood (91605) *(P-15504)*

Valley Detriot Diesel, Bakersfield *Also Called: Valley Power Systems Inc (P-10412)*

Valley Enerprises Inc .... E 951 789-0843
18600 Van Buren Blvd Riverside (92508) *(P-8648)*

Valley Fruit and Produce Co, Los Angeles *Also Called: Val-Pro Inc (P-10922)*

Valley Healthcare, San Bernardino *Also Called: United Medical Management Inc (P-15888)*

Valley Hospital Medical Center Foundation .... A 818 885-8500
18300 Roscoe Blvd Northridge (91325) *(P-16252)*

Valley Hunt Club .... D 626 793-7134
520 S Orange Grove Blvd Pasadena (91105) *(P-17373)*

Valley Insurance Service Inc .... C 949 707-4080
23181 Verdugo Dr Ste 100b Laguna Hills (92653) *(P-12264)*

Valley Lght Ctr For Scial Advn .... D 626 337-6200
109 W 6th St Azusa (91702) *(P-17069)*

Valley Light Industries, Azusa *Also Called: Valley Lght Ctr For Scial Advn (P-17069)*

Valley Manor Convalescent Hosp, North Hollywood *Also Called: Golden Care Inc (P-15857)*

Valley Metal Treating Inc .... E 909 623-6316
355 Se End Ave Pomona (91766) *(P-4717)*

Valley Metals LLC .... E 858 513-1300
13125 Gregg St Poway (92064) *(P-4555)*

Valley News Gardens, Gardena *Also Called: Gardena Valley News Inc (P-2798)*

Valley of Sun Cosmetics LLC .... C 310 327-9062
535 Patrice Pl Gardena (90248) *(P-10656)*

Valley of The Sun Labs, Gardena *Also Called: Valley of Sun Cosmetics LLC (P-10656)*

Valley Pacific Petro Svcs Inc .... D 661 746-7737
9521 Enos Ln Bakersfield (93314) *(P-11037)*

Valley Perforating LLC .... D 661 324-4964
3201 Gulf St Bakersfield (93308) *(P-6261)*

Valley Power Services Inc .... E 909 969-9345
425 S Hacienda Blvd City Of Industry (91745) *(P-6336)*

Valley Power Systems Inc .... C 661 325-9001
4000 Rosedale Hwy Bakersfield (93308) *(P-10412)*

Valley Power Systems Inc (PA) .... D 626 333-1243
425 S Hacienda Blvd City Of Industry (91745) *(P-10413)*

Valley Precision Met Pdts Inc .... E 661 607-0100
27771 Avenue Hopkins Valencia (91355) *(P-5052)*

Valley Precision Metal Pdts, Valencia *Also Called: Valley Precision Met Pdts Inc (P-5052)*

Valley Presbyterian Hospital .... A 818 782-6600
15107 Vanowen St Van Nuys (91405) *(P-16253)*

Valley Printers, Woodland Hills *Also Called: Valley Business Printers Inc (P-3096)*

Valley Processing, Long Beach *Also Called: Hexpol Compounding CA Inc (P-3913)*

Valley Resource Center, Hemet *Also Called: Valley Resource Center Inc (P-17070)*

Valley Resource Center Inc (PA) .... E 951 766-8659
1285 N Santa Fe St Hemet (92543) *(P-17070)*

Valley Spuds, Oxnard *Also Called: McK Enterprises Inc (P-1815)*

Valley Strong Credit Union .... D 661 833-7900
6101 Coffee Rd Bakersfield (93308) *(P-11820)*

Valley Substation, Romoland *Also Called: Southern California Edison Co (P-9615)*

Valley Tool and Machine Co Inc .... E 909 595-2205
111 Explorer St Pomona (91768) *(P-6262)*

Valley View Casino, Valley Center *Also Called: San Psqual Band Mssion Indians (P-13012)*

Valley Village .... C 818 446-0366
8727 Fenwick St Sunland (91040) *(P-15824)*

Valley Village (PA) .... D 818 587-9450
20830 Sherman Way Winnetka (91306) *(P-17022)*

Mergent email: customerrelations@mergent.com
1226

2025 Southern California
Business Directory and Buyers Guide

(P-0000) Products & Services Section entry number
(PA)=Parent Co (HQ)=Headquarters (DH)=Div Headquarters

Valley Vsta Nrsing Trnstnal CA .... C 818 763-6275
6120 Vineland Ave North Hollywood (91606) *(P-15791)*

Valley Vsta Nrsing Trnstnal Ca, North Hollywood *Also Called: Valley Vsta Nrsing Trnstnal CA (P-15791)*

Valley-HI Toyota Honda, Victorville *Also Called: Vahi Toyota Inc (P-11426)*

Valley-Todeco Inc .... C 800 992-4444
135 N Unruh Ave City Of Industry (91744) *(P-5139)*

Valleycrest Productions Ltd .... D 818 560-5391
500 S Buena Vista St Burbank (91521) *(P-9522)*

Valmont Ctngs Clwest Glvnizing, Long Beach *Also Called: Valmont Industries Inc (P-5353)*

Valmont Industries Inc .... E 310 549-2200
2226 E Dominguez St Long Beach (90810) *(P-5353)*

Valori Sand & Gravel Company .... C 909 350-3000
11027 Cherry Ave Fontana (92337) *(P-9952)*

Valtra Inc (PA) .... **E 562 949-8625**
8750 Pioneer Blvd Santa Fe Springs (90670) *(P-10414)*

Valtron Technologies Inc .... D 805 257-0333
28309 Avenue Crocker Santa Clarita (91355) *(P-14191)*

Valueoptions of California Inc, Cerritos *Also Called: Carelon Bhavioral Hlth Cal Inc (P-12188)*

Valumark, Tustin *Also Called: Logomark Inc (P-11128)*

Valverde Construction Inc .... C 562 906-1826
10936 Shoemaker Ave Santa Fe Springs (90670) *(P-703)*

Valvoline Instant Oil Change, Costa Mesa *Also Called: EZ Lube LLC (P-14715)*

Valvoline Instant Oil Change, Santa Fe Springs *Also Called: Valvoline Instant Oil Chnge Fr (P-14721)*

Valvoline Instant Oil Chnge Fr .... D 562 906-6200
9520 John St Santa Fe Springs (90670) *(P-14721)*

Van Can Company .... C 858 391-8084
13230 Evening Creek Dr S Ste 212 San Diego (92128) *(P-4727)*

Van Daele Development Corp .... C 951 354-6800
391 N Main St Corona (92878) *(P-467)*

Van Daele Homes, Corona *Also Called: Van Daele Development Corp (P-467)*

Van Daele Homes Inc .... D 951 354-2121
391 N Main St Corona (92878) *(P-455)*

Van King & Storage Inc .... D 562 921-0555
13535 Larwin Cir Santa Fe Springs (90670) *(P-8982)*

Van Torrance & Storage Company (PA) .... **D 562 567-2101**
12128 Burke St Santa Fe Springs (90670) *(P-8996)*

Vance & Hines, Santa Fe Springs *Also Called: V&H Performance LLC (P-7638)*

Vance Executive Protection, Los Angeles *Also Called: Andrews International Inc (P-14275)*

Vanderhorst Brothers Industries Inc .... D 805 583-3333
1715 Surveyor Ave Simi Valley (93063) *(P-6263)*

Vanderra Resources LLC .... B 817 439-2220
1801 Century Park E Ste 2400 Los Angeles (90067) *(P-369)*

Vanderveer Industrial Plas LLC .... E 714 579-7700
515 S Melrose St Placentia (92870) *(P-3972)*

Vanderveer Industrial Plastics, Placentia *Also Called: Vanderveer Industrial Plas LLC (P-3972)*

Vanguard Electronics Company (PA) .... **E 714 842-3330**
18292 Enterprise Ln Huntington Beach (92648) *(P-6940)*

Vanguard Health Systems Inc .... D 714 635-6272
1154 N Euclid St Anaheim (92801) *(P-15505)*

Vanguard Industries East Inc .... E 800 433-1334
2440 Impala Dr Carlsbad (92010) *(P-2281)*

Vanguard Industries West Inc (PA) .... **C 760 438-4437**
2440 Impala Dr Carlsbad (92010) *(P-2282)*

Vanguard Lgistics Svcs USA Inc (HQ) .... **D 310 847-3000**
5000 Airport Plaza Dr Ste 200 Long Beach (90815) *(P-9349)*

Vanguard Space Tech Inc .... C 858 587-4210
4398 Corporate Center Dr Los Alamitos (90720) *(P-7586)*

Vanguard Tool & Manufacturing, Rancho Cucamonga *Also Called: Vanguard Tool & Mfg Co Inc (P-5220)*

Vanguard Tool & Mfg Co Inc .... E 909 980-9392
8388 Utica Ave Rancho Cucamonga (91730) *(P-5220)*

Vanguard Univ Southern Cal .... C 714 668-6163
55 Fair Dr Costa Mesa (92626) *(P-16838)*

Vanlaw Food Products Inc (HQ) .... **D 714 870-9091**
2325 Moore Ave Fullerton (92833) *(P-1373)*

Vans Inc (DH) .... **B 714 755-4000**
1588 S Coast Dr Costa Mesa (92626) *(P-3872)*

Vans Shoes, Costa Mesa *Also Called: Vans Inc (P-3872)*

Vantage Apparel, Santa Ana *Also Called: Vantage Custom Classics Inc (P-10699)*

Vantage Associates Inc .... E 800 995-8322
1565 Macarthur Blvd Costa Mesa (92626) *(P-4031)*

Vantage Associates Inc .... D 562 968-1400
12333 Los Nietos Rd Santa Fe Springs (90670) *(P-4269)*

Vantage Associates Inc .... E 562 968-1400
1565 Macarthur Blvd Costa Mesa (92626) *(P-7587)*

Vantage Associates Inc (PA) .... **E 619 477-6940**
1565 Macarthur Blvd Costa Mesa (92626) *(P-7674)*

Vantage Custom Classics Inc .... C 714 755-1133
1815 Ritchey St Santa Ana (92705) *(P-10699)*

Vantage Led, Corona *Also Called: Tradenet Enterprise Inc (P-8646)*

Vantage Master Machine Company, Costa Mesa *Also Called: Vantage Associates Inc (P-7587)*

Vantage Point Products Corp (PA) .... **E 562 946-1718**
9234 Hall Rd Downey (90241) *(P-6565)*

Vantage Vehicle Group, Corona *Also Called: Vantage Vehicle Intl Inc (P-7102)*

Vantage Vehicle Intl Inc .... E 951 735-1200
1740 N Delilah St Corona (92879) *(P-7102)*

Vantiva Scs Memphis Inc (DH) .... **B 805 445-1122**
3601 Calle Tecate Ste 120 Camarillo (93012) *(P-14910)*

Vantiva Sup Chain Slutions Inc (HQ) .... **B 805 445-1122**
3601 Calle Tecate Ste 120 Camarillo (93012) *(P-14911)*

Vantiva Sup Chain Slutions Inc .... D 760 357-3372
461 Rood Rd Ste A Calexico (92231) *(P-14912)*

Vantiva Sup Chain Slutions Inc .... D 909 974-2016
5491 E Philadelphia St Ontario (91761) *(P-14913)*

Vapex-Genex-Precision, Los Angeles *Also Called: Electrical Rebuilders Sls Inc (P-7091)*

Vaquero Energy Incorporated .... E 661 363-7240
15545 Hermosa Rd Bakersfield (93307) *(P-281)*

Varda Space Industries Inc .... D 833 707-0020
225 S Aviation Blvd El Segundo (90245) *(P-7660)*

Variations In Stone Inc .... D 949 438-8337
360 La Perle Pl Costa Mesa (92627) *(P-990)*

Varner Bros Inc .... D 661 399-2944
1808 Roberts Ln Bakersfield (93308) *(P-9771)*

Varner Family Ltd Partnership (PA) .... **D 661 399-1163**
5900 E Lerdo Hwy Shafter (93263) *(P-12675)*

Varsity Contractors Inc .... C 949 586-8283
24155 Laguna Hills Mall Laguna Hills (92653) *(P-13428)*

Vas Engineering Inc .... E 858 569-1601
4750 Viewridge Ave San Diego (92123) *(P-7065)*

Vascular Therapies, Irvine *Also Called: Covidien LP (P-8139)*

Vasinda Investments Inc .... D 661 324-4277
5353 Truckston Ave Bakersfield (93309) *(P-13629)*

Vastek Inc .... C 925 948-5701
1230 Columbia St Ste 1180 San Diego (92101) *(P-14625)*

Vaughans Industrial Repair Inc .... E 562 633-2660
16224 Garfield Ave Paramount (90723) *(P-10415)*

Vaya Workforce Solutions LLC .... C 866 687-7390
5930 Cornerstone Ct W Ste 300 San Diego (92121) *(P-13630)*

Vbc Holdings Inc .... E 310 322-7357
134 Main St El Segundo (90245) *(P-1469)*

VCA, Los Angeles *Also Called: VCA Inc (P-11701)*

VCA Animal Hospitale Inc .... C 310 473-2951
1000 S Sepulveda Blvd Los Angeles (90025) *(P-134)*

VCA Inc (DH) .... **C 310 571-6500**
12401 W Olympic Blvd Los Angeles (90064) *(P-11701)*

VCA West Los Angles Anmal Hosp, Los Angeles *Also Called: VCA Animal Hospitals Inc (P-134)*

Vcc, Carlsbad *Also Called: Visual Communications Company LLC (P-7067)*

Vci Construction LLC (HQ) .... **D 909 946-0905**
1921 W 11th St Ste A Upland (91786) *(P-704)*

Vci Event Technology Inc .... C 714 772-2002
25172 Arctic Ocean Dr Ste 102 Lake Forest (92630) *(P-13477)*

Vcp Mobility Holdings Inc .... E 619 213-6500
745 Design Ct Ste 602 Chula Vista (91911) *(P-8317)*

Vcsd Inc .... E 619 579-6886
585 Vernon Way El Cajon (92020) *(P-2366)*

Vdp Direct LLC (PA) .... **E 858 300-4510**
5520 Ruffin Rd Ste 111 San Diego (92123) *(P-3097)*

Vector, Huntington Beach *Also Called: Vector Launch LLC (P-5358)*

Employee Codes: A=Over 500 employees, B=251-500
C=101-250, D=51-100, E=20-50, F=10-19, G=1-9

2025 Southern California
Business Directory and Buyers Guide

© Mergent Inc. 1-800-342-5647
1227

Vector Electronics & Tech Inc .... E 818 985-8208
11115 Vanowen St North Hollywood (91605) *(P-6786)*

Vector Launch LLC (PA)................................. **E 202 888-3063**
15261 Connector Ln Huntington Beach (92649) *(P-5358)*

Vector Resources Inc (PA)........................... **C 310 436-1000**
20917 Higgins Ct Torrance (90501) *(P-976)*

Vectorusa, Torrance *Also Called: Vector Resources Inc (P-976)*

Veeco Process Equipment Inc .... D 805 967-2700
112 Robin Hill Rd Goleta (93117) *(P-6264)*

Veeco Process Equipment Inc .... D 805 967-1400
112 Robin Hill Rd Goleta (93117) *(P-7990)*

Veg Fresh, Corona *Also Called: Veg-Fresh Farms LLC (P-10923)*

Veg Fresh Logistics LLC .... C 714 446-8800
1400 W Rincon St Corona (92878) *(P-9350)*

Veg-Fresh Farms LLC (PA)............................ **C 800 422-5535**
1400 W Rincon St Corona (92878) *(P-10923)*

Vegatek Corporation .... D 949 502-0090
7545 Irvine Center Dr Ste 200 Irvine (92618) *(P-13858)*

Vege - Kurl Inc .... D 818 956-5582
412 W Cypress St Glendale (91204) *(P-3695)*

Vege-Mist Inc .... D 310 353-2300
407 E Redondo Beach Blvd Gardena (90248) *(P-5991)*

Vege-Tech Company, Glendale *Also Called: Vege - Kurl Inc (P-3695)*

Velaro Incorporated .... D 800 983-5276
1234 N La Brea Ave West Hollywood (90038) *(P-11543)* .

VELDONA, San Diego *Also Called: Ainos Inc (P-17765)*

Velher LLC .... E 619 494-6310
350 10th Ave Ste 1000 San Diego (92101) *(P-7934)*

Velocity Vehicle Group, Whittier *Also Called: Los Angeles Truck Centers LLC (P-14694)*

Velvet Heart, Los Angeles *Also Called: Tcj Manufacturing LLC (P-2135)*

Venbrook Group LLC (PA)............................. **C 818 598-8900**
6320 Canoga Ave Fl 12 Woodland Hills (91367) *(P-18073)*

Venbrook Insurance Services GP .... D 818 598-8900
6320 Canoga Ave Fl 12 Woodland Hills (91367) *(P-12265)*

Venco Western Inc .... C 805 981-2400
2400 Eastman Ave Oxnard (93030) *(P-241)*

Vendor Direct Solutions LLC (PA)................ **C 213 362-5622**
515 S Figueroa St Ste 1900 Los Angeles (90071) *(P-13859)*

Vengroff Williams & Assoc Inc .... C 714 889-6200
2099 S State College Blvd Ste 600 Anaheim (92806) *(P-13290)*

Venice Family Clinic (PA)............................. **C 310 664-7703**
604 Rose Ave Venice (90291) *(P-15506)*

Ventegra Inc A Cal Beneft Corp .... D 858 551-8111
450 N Brand Blvd Ste 600 Glendale (91203) *(P-18365)*

Ventritex, Sylmar *Also Called: Pacesetter Inc (P-8394)*

Ventura Cnty Md-Cal Mnged Care .... C 888 301-1228
711 E Daily Dr Ste 106 Camarillo (93010) *(P-16626)*

Ventura Coastal LLC (PA)............................. **E 805 653-7000**
2325 Vista Del Mar Dr Ventura (93001) *(P-1381)*

Ventura Convalescent Center, Ventura *Also Called: Brierwood Terrace Ventura Inc (P-15839)*

Ventura County Credit Union (PA)................ **D 805 477-4000**
2575 Vista Del Mar Dr Ste 100 Ventura (93001) *(P-11821)*

Ventura County Lemon Coop .... D 805 385-3345
2620 Sakioka Dr Oxnard (93030) *(P-10924)*

Ventura County Medical Center .... D 805 652-6729
300 Hillmont Ave Ventura (93003) *(P-15558)*

Ventura Family YMCA, Ventura *Also Called: Channel Islnds Yung MNS Chrstn (P-17337)*

Ventura Feed and Pet Sups Inc .... E 805 648-5035
980 E Front St Ventura (93001) *(P-11501)*

Ventura Foods LLC .... E 323 262-9157
2900 Jurupa St Ontario (91761) *(P-1283)*

Ventura Foods LLC (PA)................................ **C 714 257-3700**
40 Pointe Dr Brea (92821) *(P-1527)*

Ventura Foods LLC .... D 714 257-3700
2900 Jurupa St Ontario (91761) *(P-1528)*

Ventura Harbor Boatyard Inc .... E 805 654-1433
1415 Spinnaker Dr Ventura (93001) *(P-7624)*

Ventura Hsptality Partners LLC .... C 805 648-2100
450 Harbor Blvd Ventura (93001) *(P-13065)*

Ventura Medical Management LLC .... B 805 477-6220
2601 E Main St Ventura (93003) *(P-18074)*

Ventura Pacific Co, Oxnard *Also Called: Ventura County Lemon Coop (P-10924)*

Ventura Printing Inc (PA).............................. **D 805 981-2600**
200 N Elevar St Oxnard (93030) *(P-3098)*

Ventura Transfer Company (PA)................... **D 310 549-1660**
2418 E 223rd St Long Beach (90810) *(P-8983)*

Ventura Yuth Crrctional Fcilty, Camarillo *Also Called: Juvenile Justice Division Cal (P-17999)*

Venturedyne Ltd .... D 909 793-2788
1320 W Colton Ave Redlands (92374) *(P-5781)*

Ventyx Biosciences Inc (PA)........................ **D 760 593-4832**
12790 El Camino Real Ste 200 San Diego (92130) *(P-17838)*

Venue Management Systems Inc .... A 626 445-6000
2041 E Gladstone St Ste A Glendora (91740) *(P-14365)*

Venus Alloys Inc (PA).................................. **E 714 635-8800**
1415 S Allec St Anaheim (92805) *(P-4654)*

Venus Group Inc (PA).................................. **D 949 609-1299**
25861 Wright Foothill Ranch (92610) *(P-9915)*

Venus Laboratories Inc .... D 714 891-3100
11150 Hope St Cypress (90630) *(P-3255)*

Venus Textiles, Foothill Ranch *Also Called: Venus Group Inc (P-9915)*

Veolia Wts Services Usa Inc .... D 562 942-2200
7777 Industry Ave Pico Rivera (90660) *(P-6036)*

Veolia Wts Usa Inc .... D 805 545-3743
8.5 Miles Nw Avila Beach Avila Beach (93424) *(P-3822)*

Ver Sales Inc (PA)....................................... **E 818 567-3000**
2509 N Naomi St Burbank (91504) *(P-10164)*

Vera Bradley Inc .... E 858 320-9020
4525 La Jolla Village Dr San Diego (92122) *(P-11495)*

Veratex, Chatsworth *Also Called: Avitex Inc (P-1870)*

Verdeco Recycling Inc .... E 323 537-4617
8685 Bowers Ave South Gate (90280) *(P-9772)*

Verdugo Hills Hospital Inc .... C 818 790-7100
1812 Verdugo Blvd Glendale (91208) *(P-16254)*

Verdugo Vista Healthcare Ctr, La Crescenta *Also Called: Mariner Health Care Inc (P-15710)*

Vereit Real Estate LP .... D 602 778-6000
11995 El Camino Real San Diego (92130) *(P-12696)*

Verenium Corporation .... C 858 431-8500
3550 John Hopkins Ct San Diego (92121) *(P-3742)*

Veridiam Inc (DH)... **D 619 448-1000**
1717 N Cuyamaca St El Cajon (92020) *(P-5629)*

Veridiam Allied Swiss .... D 760 941-1702
4645 North Ave Oceanside (92056) *(P-18366)*

Veris Manufacturing, Brea *Also Called: Q C M Inc (P-6379)*

Veritas Health Services Inc .... A 909 464-8600
5451 Walnut Ave Chino (91710) *(P-16255)*

Veritas Technologies LLC .... C 310 202-0757
16501 Ventura Blvd Ste 400 Encino (91436) *(P-13860)*

Verizon, Los Alamitos *Also Called: Supermedia LLC (P-2943)*

Verizon, Ontario *Also Called: Verizon New York Inc (P-9422)*

Verizon, Santa Monica *Also Called: Verizon Services Corp (P-9423)*

Verizon, Goleta *Also Called: Verizon South Inc (P-9424)*

Verizon, San Fernando *Also Called: Frontier California Inc (P-9436)*

Verizon, Indio *Also Called: Frontier California Inc (P-9437)*

Verizon, Westlake Village *Also Called: Frontier California Inc (P-9438)*

Verizon, Santa Maria *Also Called: Frontier California Inc (P-9439)*

Verizon, Huntington Beach *Also Called: Frontier California Inc (P-9440)*

Verizon, Baldwin Park *Also Called: Telesector Resources Group Inc (P-18229)*

Verizon Connect Telo Inc (DH)..................... **C 844 617-1100**
15505 Sand Canyon Ave Irvine (92618) *(P-14163)*

Verizon Media Inc (DH)................................ **D 310 907-3016**
11995 Bluff Creek Dr Los Angeles (90094) *(P-9421)*

Verizon New York Inc .... D 909 481-7897
961 N Milliken Ave Ste 101 Ontario (91764) *(P-9422)*

Verizon Services Corp .... B 310 315-1100
2530 Wilshire Blvd Fl 1 Santa Monica (90403) *(P-9423)*

Verizon South Inc .... C 805 681-8527
424 S Patterson Ave Goleta (93111) *(P-9424)*

Verizon Wireless, Laguna Beach *Also Called: 4g Wireless Inc (P-9381)*

Verizon Wireless, Orange *Also Called: Cellco Partnership (P-9387)*

Verizon Wireless, Lake Forest *Also Called: Cellco Partnership (P-9388)*

Verizon Wireless, Tustin *Also Called: Cellco Partnership (P-9389)*

Verizon Wireless, Orange *Also Called: Cellco Partnership (P-9390)*

Verizon Wireless, Compton *Also Called: Cellco Partnership (P-9391)*

Verizon Wireless, Santa Clarita *Also Called: Cellco Partnership (P-9392)*

Verizon Wireless, Los Angeles *Also Called: Cellco Partnership (P-9393)*

Verizon Wireless, Norwalk *Also Called: Cellco Partnership (P-9394)*

Verizon Wireless, Taft *Also Called: Cellco Partnership (P-9395)*

Verizon Wireless, Rancho Mirage *Also Called: Cellco Partnership (P-9396)*

Verizon Wireless, Encinitas *Also Called: Cellco Partnership (P-9397)*

Verizon Wireless, Chino *Also Called: Cellco Partnership (P-9398)*

Vermont Care Center, Torrance *Also Called: Geri-Care II Inc (P-15855)*

Vernon Central Warehouse Inc .... C 323 234-2200
2050 E 38th St Vernon (90058) *(P-8997)*

Vernon Warehouse Co, Vernon *Also Called: Vernon Central Warehouse Inc (P-8997)*

Versa Products (PA) .... C 310 353-7100
14105 Avalon Blvd Los Angeles (90061) *(P-2533)*

Versaclimber, Santa Ana *Also Called: Heart Rate Inc (P-8520)*

Versafab Corp (PA) .... E 800 421-1822
15919 S Broadway Gardena (90248) *(P-5053)*

Versaform Corporation .... D 760 599-4477
1377 Specialty Dr Vista (92081) *(P-5054)*

Versatables.com, Los Angeles *Also Called: Versa Products (P-2533)*

Verseio Inc .... D 888 373-9942
550 W B St Fl 4 San Diego (92101) *(P-13861)*

Vertechs Enterprises Inc (PA) .... E 858 578-3900
1071 Industrial Pl El Cajon (92020) *(P-4661)*

Vertex Coatings Inc .... D 909 923-5795
1291 W State St Ontario (91762) *(P-874)*

Vertex Lcd Inc .... E 714 223-7111
600 S Jefferson St Ste K Placentia (92870) *(P-7066)*

Vertex Phrmctcals San Dego LLC (HQ) .... C 858 404-6600
3215 Merryfield Row San Diego (92121) *(P-3517)*

Vertical Fiber Technologies, Montebello *Also Called: Vft Inc (P-2226)*

Vertiflex Inc .... E 442 325-5900
25155 Rye Canyon Loop Valencia (91355) *(P-8247)*

Vertiv, Irvine *Also Called: Vertiv Corporation (P-7883)*

Vertiv Corporation .... D 949 457-3600
35 Parker Irvine (92618) *(P-7883)*

Vertos Medical Inc LLC .... D 949 349-0008
95 Enterprise Ste 325 Aliso Viejo (92656) *(P-8248)*

Verus Aerospace LLC (HQ) .... D 949 877-3630
3150 E Miraloma Ave Anaheim (92806) *(P-7588)*

Verve Cloud Inc .... D 888 590-4888
10967 Via Frontera San Diego (92127) *(P-9470)*

Very Special Chocolats Inc .... C 626 334-7838
760 N Mckeever Ave Azusa (91702) *(P-1511)*

Verys, Santa Ana *Also Called: Verys LLC (P-14264)*

Verys LLC .... C 949 423-3295
1251 E Dyer Rd Ste 210 Santa Ana (92705) *(P-14264)*

Vescio Manufacturing Intl, Santa Fe Springs *Also Called: Vescio Threading Co (P-0205)*

Vescio Threading Co .... D 562 802-1868
14002 Anson Ave Santa Fe Springs (90670) *(P-6265)*

Vescom Corporation (PA) .... A 207 945-5051
1125 W 190th St Gardena (90248) *(P-14366)*

Vessels Club Restaurant, Cypress *Also Called: Los Alamitos Race Course (P-11587)*

Vest Tube LLC .... D 800 421-6370
6023 Alcoa Ave Los Angeles (90058) *(P-5641)*

Vesta, Corona *Also Called: Extrumed Inc (P-4115)*

Vesta Foodservice, Santa Fe Springs *Also Called: LA Specialty Produce Co (P-10910)*

Vesta Luxury Home Staging, Pico Rivera *Also Called: Showroom Interiors LLC (P-13470)*

Vesture Group Incorporated .... D 818 842-0200
3405 W Pacific Ave Burbank (91505) *(P-2175)*

Veterans EZ Info, San Diego *Also Called: Veterans EZ Info Inc (P-18367)*

Veterans EZ Info Inc .... C 866 839-1329
1901 1st Ave Ste 192 San Diego (92101) *(P-18367)*

Veterans Health Administration .... A 909 825-7084
11201 Benton St Loma Linda (92357) *(P-15507)*

Veterans Health Administration .... A 310 478-3711
11301 Wilshire Blvd Los Angeles (90073) *(P-15508)*

Veterans Med RES Fndtion San D .... C 858 642-3080
3350 La Jolla Village Dr Ste 151a San Diego (92161) *(P-17374)*

Veterinary Centers America VCA, Los Angeles *Also Called: Vicar Operating Inc (P-136)*

Veterinary Pet Insurance Services Inc .... B 714 989-0555
1800 E Imperial Hwy Ste 145 Brea (92821) *(P-12266)*

Veterinary Practice Assoc Inc .... C 949 833-9020
10435 Sorrento Valley Rd San Diego (92121) *(P-135)*

Veterinary Specialty Hospital, San Diego *Also Called: Veterinary Practice Assoc Inc (P-135)*

Vetronix Corporation .... C 805 966-2000
2030 Alameda Padre Serra Santa Barbara (93103) *(P-7307)*

Vets Securing America Inc .... A 310 645-6200
1125 W 190th St Gardena (90248) *(P-14367)*

Vfs Fire Protection Services, Orange *Also Called: Bernel Inc (P-749)*

Vft Inc .... E 323 728-2280
1040 S Vail Ave Montebello (90640) *(P-2226)*

Vgp Holdings LLC .... B 562 906-6200
9520 John St Santa Fe Springs (90670) *(P-9852)*

Vl Degrees Collective, Valencia *Also Called: Solevy Co LLC (P-3687)*

Vi-Star Gear Co Inc .... E 323 774-3750
7312 Jefferson St Paramount (90723) *(P-5151)*

Viacom Broadband Inc .... C 909 592-3335
802 Groveton Ave Glendora (91740) *(P-9471)*

Viacom Networks .... C 310 752-8000
1575 N Gower St Ste 100 Los Angeles (90028) *(P-14869)*

Viacyte Inc .... D 858 455-3708
5580 Morehouse Dr Ste 100 San Diego (92121) *(P-17895)*

Viant, Irvine *Also Called: Interactive Media Holdings Inc (P-13216)*

Viasat, Carlsbad *Also Called: Viasat Inc (P-6669)*

Viasat Inc (PA) .... A 760 476-2200
6155 El Camino Real Carlsbad (92009) *(P-6669)*

Vibiana, Los Angeles *Also Called: Vibiana Events LLC (P-13189)*

Vibiana Events LLC .... D 213 626-1507
214 S Main St Los Angeles (90012) *(P-13189)*

Vibra Healthcare LLC .... C 619 260-8300
555 Washington St San Diego (92103) *(P-16256)*

Vibra Hospital of San Diego, San Diego *Also Called: Vibra Healthcare LLC (P-16256)*

Vibrex, Valencia *Also Called: M W Sausse & Co Inc (P-6353)*

Vicar Operating Inc (DH) .... D 310 571-6500
12401 W Olympic Blvd Los Angeles (90064) *(P-136)*

Victor Cmnty Support Svcs Inc .... C 951 212-1770
1105 E Florida Ave Hemet (92543) *(P-16517)*

Victor Cmnty Support Svcs Inc .... C 760 987-8225
15095 Amargosa Rd Ste 201 Victorville (92394) *(P-16518)*

Victor Cmnty Support Svcs Inc .... C 760 245-4695
14360 St Andrews Dr Ste 11 Victorville (92395) *(P-16519)*

Victor Cmnty Support Svcs Inc .... C 909 890-5930
1908 Business Center Dr Ste 109 San Bernardino (92408) *(P-16520)*

Victor Treatment Centers, San Bernardino *Also Called: Victor Treatment Centers Inc (P-17203)*

Victor Treatment Centers Inc .... D 951 436-5200
1053 N D St San Bernardino (92410) *(P-17203)*

Victor Valley Global Med Ctr, Victorville *Also Called: Victor Vly Hosp Acqistion Inc (P-16257)*

Victor Vly Hosp Acqisition Inc .... D 760 245-8691
15248 Eleventh St Victorville (92395) *(P-10257)*

Victoria Care Center .... D 805 642-1736
5445 Everglades St Ventura (93003) *(P-15792)*

Victoria Care Center, Ventura *Also Called: Victoria Vntura Healthcare LLC (P-15793)*

Victoria Club .... C 951 683-5323
2521 Arroyo Dr Riverside (92506) *(P-15183)*

Victoria Place Community Assn .... D 909 981-4131
195 N Euclid Ave Upland (91786) *(P-17473)*

Victoria Vntura Healthcare LLC .... B 805 642-1736
5445 Everglades St Ventura (93003) *(P-15793)*

Victorville Daily Press, Victorville *Also Called: Gatehouse Media LLC (P-2799)*

Victorville Homecare, San Bernardino *Also Called: Maxim Healthcare Services Inc (P-16405)*

Victorvlle Trsure Holdings LLC .... D 760 245-6565
15494 Palmdale Rd Victorville (92392) *(P-13066)*

Victory Foam Inc (PA) .... D 949 474-0690
3 Holland Irvine (92618) *(P-11147)*

Victory Intl Group LLC .... C 949 407-5888
14748 Pipeline Ave Ste B Chino Hills (91709) *(P-10531)*

Employee Codes: A=Over 500 employees, B=251-500
C=101-250, D=51-100, E=20-50, F=10-19, G=1-9

2025 Southern California
Business Directory and Buyers Guide

© Mergent Inc. 1-800-342-5647
1229

Victory Koredrry, Huntington Beach Also Called: Victory Professional Pdts Inc **(P-2141)**

Victory Professional Pdts Inc .... E 714 887-0621
5601 Engineer Dr Huntington Beach (92649) **(P-2141)**

Victory Sportswear, Irwindale Also Called: Victory Sportswear Inc **(P-11652)**

Victory Sportswear Inc .... E 866 308-0798
2381 Buena Vista St Irwindale (91010) **(P-11652)**

Victory Studio, Burbank Also Called: Warner Bros Entertainment Inc **(P-14873)**

Vid, Vista Also Called: Vista Irrigation District **(P-9794)**

Vida Health Inc .... D 415 989-1017
20500 Belshaw Ave Carson (90746) **(P-13862)**

Vident .... D 714 221-6700
22705 Savi Ranch Pkwy Ste 100 Yorba Linda (92887) **(P-10115)**

Video Sensing Division, Tustin Also Called: Canon Medical Systems USA Inc **(P-10072)**

Video Vice Data Communications .... C 714 897-6300
7391 Lincoln Way Garden Grove (92841) **(P-9559)**

Videoamp Inc (PA) .... D 424 272-7774
12121 Bluff Creek Dr Playa Vista (90094) **(P-14062)**

Videocam, Lake Forest Also Called: Vci Event Technology Inc **(P-13477)**

Videssence LLC (PA) .... E 626 579-0943
10768 Lower Azusa Rd El Monte (91731) **(P-6450)**

Vie De France 108, Vernon Also Called: Vie De France Yamazaki Inc **(P-11608)**

Vie De France Yamazaki Inc .... A 323 582-1241
3046 E 50th St Vernon (90058) **(P-11608)**

View Heights Convalescent Hosp, Los Angeles Also Called: Amada Enterprises Inc **(P-15565)**

View Park Convalescent Center, Los Angeles Also Called: Burlington Convalescent Hosp **(P-15584)**

View Park Convalescent Center, Los Angeles Also Called: Burlington Convalescent Hosp **(P-15585)**

Viewsonic, Brea Also Called: Viewsonic Corporation **(P-5954)**

Viewsonic Corporation (PA) .... C 909 444-8888
10 Pointe Dr Ste 200 Brea (92821) **(P-5954)**

Vignolo Farms Inc .... D 661 746-2148
16456 Slater Ave Bakersfield (93308) **(P-2)**

Vigobyte Tape Corporation .... A 866 803-8446
2498 Roll Dr Ste 916 San Diego (92154) **(P-5892)**

Vigor Marine LLC .... D 619 474-4352
1636 Wilson Ave National City (91950) **(P-7612)**

Vigor Systems Inc .... E 866 748-4467
4660 La Jolla Village Dr Ste 500 San Diego (92122) **(P-6670)**

Vijall Inc .... E 818 700-0071
21900 Marilla St Chatsworth (91311) **(P-11024)**

Viking Office Products Inc (DH) .... B 562 490-1000
3366 E Willow St Signal Hill (90755) **(P-10586)**

Viking Products, Orange Also Called: Pro Detention Inc **(P-4540)**

Viking Products Inc .... E 949 379-5100
20 Doppler Irvine (92618) **(P-5630)**

Viking Therapeutics Inc (PA) .... E 858 704-4660
9920 Pacific Heights Blvd Ste 350 San Diego (92121) **(P-3518)**

Viktor Benes Bakeries, Westlake Village Also Called: Mamolos Cntntl Bailey Bakeries **(P-11299)**

Villa Convalescent Hosp Inc .... D 951 689-5788
8965 Magnolia Ave Riverside (92503) **(P-15794)**

VILLA CONVALESCENT HOSPITAL, Riverside Also Called: Villa Convalescent Hosp Inc **(P-15794)**

Villa De La Mar Inc .... C 562 494-5001
5001 E Anaheim St Long Beach (90804) **(P-15890)**

Villa Del Rey Retirement Inn, Escondido Also Called: Emeritus Corporation **(P-12338)**

Villa Ford Inc .... C 714 637-8222
2550 N Tustin St Orange (92865) **(P-11427)**

Villa Furniture Mfg Co .... C 714 535-7272
16440 Manning Way Cerritos (90703) **(P-2554)**

Villa International, Cerritos Also Called: Villa Furniture Mfg Co **(P-2554)**

Villa Maria Care Center, Baldwin Park Also Called: Trinity Health Systems **(P-15788)**

Villa Roma Sausage Co, Ontario Also Called: Heatherfield Foods Inc **(P-1243)**

Villa Serena Healthcare Center .... D 562 437-2797
723 E 9th St Long Beach (90813) **(P-15795)**

Villa Venetia .... C 714 540-1800
2775 Mesa Verde Dr E Costa Mesa (92626) **(P-11957)**

Village At Northridge .... C 818 514-4497
9222 Corbin Ave Northridge (91324) **(P-17204)**

Village Center Ultramar, Palmdale Also Called: Ultramar Inc **(P-3834)**

Village Gardens Apartments, Palmdale Also Called: Eugene Burger Management Corp **(P-12340)**

Village Green Foods Inc .... E 949 261-0111
1732 Kaiser Ave Irvine (92614) **(P-1865)**

Village Management Svcs Inc .... C 949 597-4360
24351 El Toro Rd Laguna Woods (92637) **(P-18075)**

Village Marine Technology, Gardena Also Called: Aqua Pro Properties Vii LP **(P-5689)**

Village News Inc .... E 760 451-3488
41740 Enterprise Cir S Temecula (92590) **(P-2835)**

Village Nurseries Whl LLC .... B 951 657-3940
20099 Santa Rosa Mine Rd Perris (92570) **(P-11103)**

Village The, San Juan Capistrano Also Called: Freedom Properties-Hemet LLC **(P-12293)**

Village West Health Center, Riverside Also Called: Air Force Village West Inc **(P-15563)**

Villas De Crisbad Ltd A Cal Lt .... D 760 434-7116
3500 Lake Blvd Oceanside (92056) **(P-17205)**

Vin Di Bona Productions, Los Angeles Also Called: Cara Communications LLC **(P-14882)**

Vincent Contractors Inc .... B 714 660-0165
4501 E La Palma Ave Ste 200 Anaheim (92807) **(P-991)**

Vincent Scaffolding, Anaheim Also Called: Vincent Contractors Inc **(P-991)**

Vincent-Hayley Enterprises Inc .... D 626 398-8182
1810 N Fair Oaks Ave Pasadena (91103) **(P-16258)**

Vinculums, Irvine Also Called: Vinculums Services LLC **(P-18368)**

Vinculums Services LLC .... C 949 783-3552
10 Pasteur Ste 100 Irvine (92618) **(P-18368)**

Vinh - Sanh Trading Corp .... D 626 968-6888
13500 Nelson Ave City Of Industry (91746) **(P-10990)**

Vintage Associates Inc .... C 760 772-3673
78755 Darby Rd Bermuda Dunes (92203) **(P-242)**

Vintage Club .... D 760 340-0500
75001 Vintage Dr W Indian Wells (92210) **(P-15184)**

Vintage Design LLC .... D 858 695-9544
8310 Juniper Creek Ln San Diego (92126) **(P-14626)**

Vintage Nursery, Bermuda Dunes Also Called: Vintage Associates Inc **(P-242)**

Vintage Production California, Santa Clarita Also Called: California Resources Prod Corp **(P-271)**

Vintage Senior Management Inc .... A 818 954-9500
2721 W Willow St Burbank (91505) **(P-17023)**

Vintage Wine Estates Inc CA .... E 805 503-9660
3070 Limestone Way Unit C Paso Robles (93446) **(P-1592)**

Vinventions Usa LLC (PA) .... C 919 460-2200
888 Prospect St La Jolla (92037) **(P-4270)**

Vinyl Technology LLC (PA) .... C 626 443-5257
200 Railroad Ave Monrovia (91016) **(P-2714)**

VIP Rubber Company Inc (PA) .... C 562 905-3456
540 S Cypress St La Habra (90631) **(P-3941)**

VIP Tours of California Inc .... D 310 216-7507
1419 E Maple Ave El Segundo (90245) **(P-9242)**

Viracta, Cardiff Also Called: Viracta Therapeutics Inc **(P-3519)**

Viracta Therapeutics Inc (PA) .... E 858 400-8470
2533 S Coast Highway 101 Ste 210 Cardiff (92007) **(P-3519)**

Virco Inc (HQ) .... E 310 533-0474
2027 Harpers Way Torrance (90501) **(P-9885)**

Virco Mfg Corporation (PA) .... D 310 533-0474
2027 Harpers Way Torrance (90501) **(P-2555)**

Virgin Fish Inc (PA) .... C 310 391-6161
1000 Corporate Pointe Ste 150 Culver City (90230) **(P-8853)**

VIRGIN GALACTIC, Tustin Also Called: Virgin Galactic Holdings Inc **(P-7661)**

Virgin Galactic Holdings Inc (PA) .... E 949 774-7640
1700 Flight Way Ste 400 Tustin (92782) **(P-7661)**

Virginia Cntry CLB of Long Bch .... C 562 427-0924
4602 N Virginia Rd Long Beach (90807) **(P-15185)**

Viridos Inc .... C 858 754-2900
250 W Schrimpf Rd Calipatria (92233) **(P-17839)**

Virtium, Rcho Sta Marg Also Called: Virtium Technology Inc **(P-6910)**

Virtium LLC .... D 949 888-2444
30052 Tomas Rcho Sta Marg (92688) **(P-10038)**

Virtium Technology Inc .... E 949 888-2444
30052 Tomas Rcho Sta Marg (92688) **(P-6910)**

Visage Imaging Inc .... D 858 345-4410
12625 High Bluff Dr Ste 205 San Diego (92130) **(P-13190)**

Mergent email: customerrelations@mergent.com
1230

2025 Southern California
Business Directory and Buyers Guide

(P-0000) Products & Services Section entry number
(PA)=Parent Co (HQ)=Headquarters (DH)=Div Headquarters

Vish Consulting Services Inc .... D 916 800-3762
9655 Granite Ridge Dr Ste 200 San Diego (92123) *(P-13580)*

Vishay Spectoral Electronics, Ontario *Also Called: Vishay Thin Film LLC (P-6911)*

Vishay Sprague Inc .... D 909 923-3313
4051 Greystone Dr Ontario (91761) *(P-10296)*

Vishay Thin Film LLC .... E 909 923-3313
4051 Greystone Dr Ontario (91761) *(P-6911)*

Vision Aerospace LLC .... E 818 700-1035
19863 Nordhoff St Northridge (91324) *(P-7589)*

Vision Engineering, Palmdale *Also Called: Vision Engrg Met Stamping Inc (P-6479)*

Vision Engrg Met Stamping Inc .... D 661 575-0933
114 Grand Cypress Ave Palmdale (93551) *(P-6479)*

Vision Envelope & Prtg Co Inc (PA) .... E 310 324-7062
13707 S Figueroa St Los Angeles (90061) *(P-2754)*

Vision Imaging Supplies Inc .... E 818 885-4515
9540 Cozycroft Ave Chatsworth (91311) *(P-8568)*

Vision Quest Industries Inc .... C 949 261-6382
1390 Decision St Ste A Vista (92081) *(P-8318)*

Vision Realty Managements, Beverly Hills *Also Called: Starpint 1031 Property MGT LLC (P-12533)*

Vision Solutions Inc (HQ) .... D 949 253-6500
15300 Barranca Pkwy Irvine (92618) *(P-13863)*

Vision Systems Inc .... D 619 258-7300
11322 Woodside Ave N Santee (92071) *(P-4612)*

Visionaire Lighting, Long Beach *Also Called: Visionaire Lighting LLC (P-6480)*

Visionaire Lighting LLC .... D 310 512-6480
3780 Kilroy Airport Way Long Beach (90806) *(P-6480)*

Visionary Contact Lens Inc .... E 714 237-1900
2940 E Miraloma Ave Anaheim (92806) *(P-8418)*

Visionary Sleep LLC .... D 909 605-2010
2060 S Wineville Ave Ste A Ontario (91761) *(P-2495)*

Visionary Vr Inc .... E 323 868-7443
409 N Plymouth Blvd Los Angeles (90004) *(P-14063)*

Visiting Angels, Chino *Also Called: Angels In Motion LLC (P-16365)*

Visiting Nrse Assn of Inland C (PA) .... A 951 413-1200
600 W Santa Ana Blvd Ste 114 Santa Ana (92701) *(P-16430)*

Visiting Nurse & Hospice Care (PA) .... D 805 965-5555
509 E Montecito St Ste 200 Santa Barbara (93103) *(P-16431)*

VISITING NURSE & HOSPICE CARE, Santa Barbara *Also Called: Visiting Nurse & Hospice Care (P-16431)*

Vista Behavioral Health Inc .... D 800 992-0901
5900 Brockton Ave Riverside (92506) *(P-16280)*

Vista Care Group LLC (PA) .... D 760 295-3900
1863 Devon Pl Vista (92084) *(P-17024)*

Vista Community Clinic (PA) .... B 760 631-5000
1000 Vale Terrace Dr Vista (92084) *(P-15533)*

Vista Del Campo, Irvine *Also Called: American Cmpus Communities Inc (P-13096)*

Vista Del Mar Child Fmly Svcs (PA) .... C 310 836-1223
3200 Motor Ave Los Angeles (90034) *(P-16828)*

Vista Del Mar Child Fmly Svcs .... B 310 836-1223
1533 Euclid St Santa Monica (90404) *(P-17206)*

Vista Del Mar Health Centers, Vista *Also Called: Life Care Centers America Inc (P-15863)*

Vista Ford Inc .... D 805 983-6511
1501 Auto Center Dr Oxnard (93036) *(P-11428)*

Vista Ford of Oxnard, Oxnard *Also Called: Vista Ford Inc (P-11428)*

Vista Gardens, Vista *Also Called: Vista Care Group LLC (P-17024)*

Vista Hill Foundation .... D 619 281-5511
6145 Decena Dr San Diego (92120) *(P-16859)*

Vista Hill Foundation .... D 619 266-0166
4125 Alpha St San Diego (92113) *(P-17025)*

Vista Hospital Riverside, Rancho Cucamonga *Also Called: Perris Valley Cmnty Hosp LLC (P-16129)*

Vista Industrial Products Inc .... C 760 599-5050
3210 Executive Rdg Vista (92081) *(P-6266)*

Vista Irrigation District .... D 760 597-3100
1391 Engineer St Vista (92083) *(P-9794)*

Vista JV Partners LLC .... B 214 738-2771
2035 Corte Del Nogal Ste 200 Carlsbad (92011) *(P-15559)*

Vista Knoll Spclzed Care Fclty, Vista *Also Called: Vista Woods Health Assoc LLC (P-15797)*

Vista Metals Corp (PA) .... C 909 823-4278
13425 Whittram Ave Fontana (92335) *(P-4613)*

Vista Pacifica Center, Jurupa Valley *Also Called: Vista Pacifica Enterprises Inc (P-15796)*

Vista Pacifica Enterprises Inc (PA) .... C 951 682-4833
3674 Pacific Ave Jurupa Valley (92509) *(P-15796)*

Vista Paint Corporation (PA) .... C 714 680-3800
2020 E Orangethorpe Ave Fullerton (92831) *(P-11256)*

Vista Real Post Acute, Beaumont *Also Called: Pacs Group Inc (P-15743)*

Vista Steel Co Inc .... E 805 653-1189
331 W Lewis St Ventura (93001) *(P-722)*

VISTA STEEL CO INC, Ventura *Also Called: Vista Steel Co Inc (P-722)*

Vista Steel Company (PA) .... E 805 964-4732
6100 Francis Botello Rd Ste C Goleta (93117) *(P-4878)*

Vista Woods Health Assoc LLC .... C 760 630-2273
2000 Westwood Rd Vista (92083) *(P-15797)*

Vistancia Marketing LLC .... D 909 594-9500
655 Brea Canyon Rd Walnut (91789) *(P-18238)*

Visterra Credit Union .... C 951 656-4411
23520 Cactus Ave Moreno Valley (92553) *(P-11833)*

Visual Communications Company LLC .... C 800 522-5546
2173 Salk Ave Ste 175 Carlsbad (92008) *(P-7067)*

Visual Information Systems Co, Chino *Also Called: National Sign & Marketing Corp (P-8619)*

Visual Pak San Diego LLC .... C 847 689-1000
2320 Paseo De Las Americas Ste 201 San Diego (92154) *(P-14627)*

VIT Products Inc .... E 760 480-6702
2063 Wineridge Pl Escondido (92029) *(P-4794)*

Vita Juice Corporation .... D 818 899-1195
10725 Sutter Ave Pacoima (91331) *(P-1360)*

Vita North America, Yorba Linda *Also Called: Vident (P-10115)*

Vita-Herb Nutriceuticals Inc .... E 714 632-3726
172 E La Jolla St Placentia (92870) *(P-11311)*

Vita-Pakt Citrus Products Co (PA) .... E 626 332-1101
10000 Stockdale Hwy Ste 390 Bakersfield (93311) *(P-1361)*

Vitacare Prescription Svcs Inc .... B 800 350-3819
2701 Olympic Blvd Santa Monica (90404) *(P-17026)*

Vitachrome Graphics, Montrose *Also Called: Vitachrome Graphics Group Inc (P-3185)*

Vitachrome Graphics Group Inc .... E 818 957-0900
3710 Park Pl Montrose (91020) *(P-3185)*

Vital Research LLC .... D 323 951-1670
6300 Wilshire Blvd Ste 860 Los Angeles (90048) *(P-17896)*

VITAMIN ANGEL, Goleta *Also Called: Vitamin Angel Alliance Inc (P-17474)*

Vitamin Angel Alliance Inc .... D 805 564-8400
6500 Hollister Ave Ste 130 Goleta (93117) *(P-17474)*

Vitamin Friends LLC .... E 310 356-9018
17120 S Figueroa St Ste B Gardena (90248) *(P-1309)*

Vitas Healthcare Corporation .... C 858 805-6254
9106 Pulsar Ct Ste D Corona (92883) *(P-15825)*

Vitas Healthcare Corporation .... C 805 437-2100
333 N Lantana St Ste 124 Camarillo (93010) *(P-15826)*

Vitatech Nutritional Sciences Inc .... B 714 832-9700
2802 Dow Ave Tustin (92780) *(P-3520)*

Vitawest Nutraceuticals Inc .... E 888 557-8012
1502 Arrow Hwy La Verne (91750) *(P-1310)*

Vitco Distributors Inc .... C 909 355-1300
715 E California St Ontario (91761) *(P-10816)*

Vitco Food Service, Ontario *Also Called: Vitco Distributors Inc (P-10816)*

Vitesse Manufacturing & Dev .... C 805 388-3700
11861 Western Ave Garden Grove (92841) *(P-6912)*

Vitesse Semiconductor, Garden Grove *Also Called: Vitesse Manufacturing & Dev (P-6912)*

Vitrek LLC (PA) .... E 858 689-2755
12169 Kirkham Rd Ste C Poway (92064) *(P-7935)*

Vitro, San Diego *Also Called: Vitrorobertson LLC (P-13251)*

Vitrorobertson LLC .... D 619 234-0408
225 Broadway San Diego (92101) *(P-13251)*

Viva Life Science Inc .... C 949 645-6100
350 Paularino Ave Costa Mesa (92626) *(P-10657)*

Vive Organic Inc .... E 877 774-9291
2554 Lincoln Blvd Ste 772 Venice (90291) *(P-1362)*

Vivometrics Inc .... E 805 667-2225
16030 Ventura Blvd Ste 470 Encino (91436) *(P-8402)*

Viz Cattle Corporation .... E 310 884-5260
17800 Castleton St Ste 435 City Of Industry (91748) *(P-1252)*

Employee Codes: A=Over 500 employees, B=251-500
C=101-250, D=51-100, E=20-50, F=10-19, G=1-9

2025 Southern California
Business Directory and Buyers Guide

© Mergent Inc. 1-800-342-5647
1231

Vizio, Irvine *Also Called: Vizio Holding Corp (P-6568)*

Vizio Inc .... C 213 746-7730
2601 S Bdwy Unit B Los Angeles (90007) *(P-6566)*

Vizio Inc (HQ) .... C **855 833-3221**
39 Tesla Irvine (92618) *(P-6567)*

Vizio Holding Corp (PA) .... E **949 428-2525**
39 Tesla Irvine (92618) *(P-6568)*

Vizualogic LLC .... C 407 509-3421
1493 E Bentley Dr Corona (92879) *(P-5724)*

Vline Industries, Simi Valley *Also Called: Computer Metal Products Corp (P-4972)*

Vm International, Riverside *Also Called: MSRS INC (P-9899)*

Vna of Greater Los Angeles Inc .... D 951 252-5314
17682 Mitchell N Ste 100 Irvine (92614) *(P-16432)*

VNA PRIVATE DUTY CARE, San Bernardino *Also Called: Vnacare (P-16433)*

Vnacare (PA) .... D 909 624-3574
412 E Vanderbilt Way Ste 100 San Bernardino (92408) *(P-16433)*

Vnaic, Santa Ana *Also Called: Visiting Nrse Assn of Inland C (P-16430)*

Vnu Business, San Juan Capistrano *Also Called: Emerald X LLC (P-2856)*

Voa, Los Angeles *Also Called: Volunteers of Amer Los Angeles (P-17035)*

Voa Plainview Head Start, Tujunga *Also Called: Volunteers of Amer Los Angeles (P-17032)*

Vocational Imprv Program Inc (PA) .... D 909 483-5924
9210 Rochester Ave Rancho Cucamonga (91730) *(P-17071)*

Vocational Visions .... C 949 837-7280
26041 Pala Mission Viejo (92691) *(P-17072)*

Voestalpine High Prfmce Mtls, Walnut *Also Called: Edro Engineering LLC (P-5578)*

Voice of San Diego .... E 619 325-0525
110 W A St Ste 650 San Diego (92101) *(P-2836)*

Volcano, San Diego *Also Called: Philips Image Gded Thrapy Corp (P-8396)*

Volcom LLC (HQ) .... C **949 646-2175**
1740 Monrovia Ave Costa Mesa (92627) *(P-14628)*

Volkswagen of Van Nuys Inc .... D 323 873-3311
300 Hitchcock Way Santa Barbara (93105) *(P-11429)*

Volkswagen Santa Monica Inc (PA) .... C **310 829-1888**
2440 Santa Monica Blvd Santa Monica (90404) *(P-11430)*

Volt Management Corp .... D 858 576-3140
7676 Hazard Center Dr Ste 1000 San Diego (92108) *(P-13631)*

Volt Management Corp .... B 800 654-2624
2411 N Glassell St Orange (92865) *(P-13632)*

Volt Management Corp .... D 714 879-9330
1400 N Harbor Blvd Ste 103 Fullerton (92835) *(P-13633)*

Volt Management Corp .... D 805 560-8658
1701 Solar Dr Oxnard (93030) *(P-13634)*

Volt Telecom Group, Corona *Also Called: Volt Telecom Group Inc (P-18369)*

Volt Telecom Group Inc .... B 951 493-8900
218 Helicopter Cir Corona (92880) *(P-18369)*

Volt Temporary Services, Orange *Also Called: Volt Management Corp (P-13632)*

Volt Workforce Solutions, San Diego *Also Called: Volt Management Corp (P-13631)*

Volt Workforce Solutions, Fullerton *Also Called: Volt Management Corp (P-13633)*

Volt Workforce Solutions, Oxnard *Also Called: Volt Management Corp (P-13634)*

Volume Services Inc .... B 323 644-6038
5333 Zoo Dr Los Angeles (90027) *(P-15231)*

Volume Services Inc .... B 619 525-5800
111 W Harbor Dr San Diego (92101) *(P-15232)*

Volunteers America Head Start, San Fernando *Also Called: Child Care Resource Center Inc (P-17081)*

Volunteers of Amer Los Angeles .... C 213 749-0362
1032 W 18th St Los Angeles (90015) *(P-17027)*

Volunteers of Amer Los Angeles .... D 818 834-9097
10896 Lehigh Ave Pacoima (91331) *(P-17028)*

Volunteers of Amer Los Angeles .... D 323 780-3770
522 N Dangler Ave Los Angeles (90022) *(P-17029)*

Volunteers of Amer Los Angeles .... C 626 337-9878
1760 W Cameron Ave Ste 104 West Covina (91790) *(P-17030)*

Volunteers of Amer Los Angeles .... D 661 290-2829
25141 Avenida Rondel Valencia (91355) *(P-17031)*

Volunteers of Amer Los Angeles .... D 818 352-5974
10819 Plainview Ave Tujunga (91042) *(P-17032)*

Volunteers of Amer Los Angeles .... C 818 769-3617
6724 Tujunga Ave North Hollywood (91606) *(P-17033)*

Volunteers of Amer Los Angeles .... C 818 506-0597
11243 Kittridge St North Hollywood (91606) *(P-17034)*

Volunteers of Amer Los Angeles .... C 213 627-8002
515 E 6th St Fl 9 Los Angeles (90021) *(P-17035)*

Volunteers of Amer Los Angeles .... D 818 834-8957
12550 Van Nuys Blvd Pacoima (91331) *(P-17036)*

Volunteers of Amer Los Angeles .... C 310 830-3404
334 Figueroa St Wilmington (90744) *(P-17037)*

Volunteers of Amer Los Angeles .... D 714 426-9834
2100 N Broadway Ste 300 Santa Ana (92706) *(P-17038)*

Volunteers of America, Los Angeles *Also Called: Volunteers of Amer Los Angeles (P-17027)*

Volunteers of America, Pacoima *Also Called: Volunteers of Amer Los Angeles (P-17028)*

Volunteers of America, Los Angeles *Also Called: Volunteers of Amer Los Angeles (P-17029)*

Volunteers of America, West Covina *Also Called: Volunteers of Amer Los Angeles (P-17030)*

Volunteers of America, Valencia *Also Called: Volunteers of Amer Los Angeles (P-17031)*

Volunteers of America, North Hollywood *Also Called: Volunteers of Amer Los Angeles (P-17033)*

Volunteers of America, Pacoima *Also Called: Volunteers of Amer Los Angeles (P-17036)*

Volunteers of America, Wilmington *Also Called: Volunteers of Amer Los Angeles (P-17037)*

Volunteers of America, Santa Ana *Also Called: Volunteers of Amer Los Angeles (P-17038)*

Voluspa, Irvine *Also Called: Flame and Wax Inc (P-8676)*

Volvo Construction Eqp & Svc, Corona *Also Called: Saba Holding Company LLC (P-10359)*

Vomar, Canoga Park *Also Called: Vomar Products Inc (P-3186)*

Vomar Products Inc .... E 818 610-5115
7800 Deering Ave Canoga Park (91304) *(P-3186)*

Vomela, Santa Fe Springs *Also Called: Vomela Specialty Company (P-3099)*

Vomela Specialty Company .... C 562 944-3853
9810 Bell Ranch Dr Santa Fe Springs (90670) *(P-3099)*

Vonnic Inc .... E 626 964-2345
16610 Gale Ave City Of Industry (91745) *(P-14425)*

Vons 2030, Stevenson Ranch *Also Called: Vons Companies Inc (P-11287)*

Vons 2111, Newhall *Also Called: Vons Companies Inc (P-11286)*

Vons 2124, Tujunga *Also Called: Vons Companies Inc (P-11285)*

Vons 2381, Corona *Also Called: Vons Companies Inc (P-11288)*

Vons 2407, Brawley *Also Called: Vons Companies Inc (P-11290)*

Vons 2560, Grover Beach *Also Called: Vons Companies Inc (P-11289)*

Vons Companies Inc .... C 818 353-4917
7789 Foothill Blvd Tujunga (91042) *(P-11285)*

Vons Companies Inc .... C 661 259-9214
24160 Lyons Ave Newhall (91321) *(P-11286)*

Vons Companies Inc .... C 661 254-3570
25850 The Old Rd Stevenson Ranch (91381) *(P-11287)*

Vons Companies Inc .... C 951 278-8284
535 N Mckinley St Corona (92879) *(P-11288)*

Vons Companies Inc .... C 805 481-2492
1758 W Grand Ave Grover Beach (93433) *(P-11289)*

Vons Companies Inc .... C 760 351-3002
475 W Main St Brawley (92227) *(P-11290)*

Vortech, Oxnard *Also Called: Vortech Engineering Inc (P-5782)*

Vortech Engineering Inc .... E 805 247-0226
1650 Pacific Ave Oxnard (93033) *(P-5782)*

Vortex Doors, Irvine *Also Called: Vortex Industries LLC (P-1065)*

Vortex Industries LLC (PA) .... E **714 434-8000**
20 Odyssey Irvine (92618) *(P-1065)*

Vortox Air Technology Inc .... E 909 621-3843
121 S Indian Hill Blvd Claremont (91711) *(P-5783)*

Votaw, Santa Fe Springs *Also Called: Votaw Precision Technologies (P-7822)*

Votaw Precision Technologies .... C 562 944-0661
13153 Lakeland Rd Santa Fe Springs (90670) *(P-7822)*

Votaw Wood Products Inc .... E 714 871-0932
301 W Imperial Hwy La Habra (90631) *(P-2393)*

Voter Prcnct Vter Rgstrtion Of, Norwalk *Also Called: County of Los Angeles (P-14127)*

Voyant Beauty, Chatsworth *Also Called: Aware Products LLC (P-3632)*

Vpb Operating Co LLC .... D 805 773-1011
147 Stimson Ave Pismo Beach (93449) *(P-13067)*

Vpet Usa LLC .... D 909 605-1668
12925b Marlay Ave Fontana (92337) *(P-4271)*

Vpm Management Inc .... C 949 863-1500
2400 Main St Ste 201 Irvine (92614) *(P-18076)*

Vps, Santa Monica *Also Called: Vitacare Prescription Svcs Inc (P-17026)*

Mergent email: customerrelations@mergent.com
1232

2025 Southern California
Business Directory and Buyers Guide

(P-0000) Products & Services Section entry number
(PA)=Parent Co (HQ)=Headquarters (DH)=Div Headquarters

Vpt Direct, Downey *Also Called: Vantage Point Products Corp (P-6565)*

Vsmpo-Tirus US Inc .... D 909 230-9020
2850 E Cedar St Ontario (91761) *(P-4624)*

VT Milcom Inc .... D 619 424-9024
1660 Logan Ave Ste 2 San Diego (92113) *(P-17659)*

Vtc Enterprises (PA) .... D 805 928-5000
2445 A St Santa Maria (93455) *(P-17073)*

Vti Instruments Corporation (HQ) .... E 949 955-1894
2031 Main St Irvine (92614) *(P-7160)*

Vtl Amplifiers Inc .... E 909 627-5944
4774 Murietta St Ste 10 Chino (91710) *(P-6569)*

Vts Industries .... D 619 337-9244
1049 Elkelton Blvd Spring Valley (91977) *(P-17375)*

Vts Sheetmetal Specialist Co .... E 714 237-1420
13831 Seaboard Cir Garden Grove (92843) *(P-5055)*

Vubiquity, Sherman Oaks *Also Called: Vubiquity Holdings Inc (P-9560)*

Vubiquity Holdings Inc (DH) .... C 818 526-5000
15301 Ventura Blvd Ste 3000 Sherman Oaks (91403) *(P-9560)*

Vulcan Materials Co .... C 760 737-3486
849 W Washington Ave Escondido (92025) *(P-4465)*

Vurger Co (usa) Corp .... E 929 318-9546
1800 Century Park E Ste 600 Los Angeles (90067) *(P-1470)*

Vvd Communications, Garden Grove *Also Called: Video Vice Data Communications (P-9559)*

Vx Logistics LLC .... D 858 868-1885
10089 Willow Creek Rd Ste 200 San Diego (92131) *(P-9378)*

Vxi Global Solutions, Los Angeles *Also Called: Vxi Global Solutions LLC (P-14629)*

Vxi Global Solutions LLC (PA) .... A 213 739-1720
515 S Figueroa St Ste 600 Los Angeles (90071) *(P-14629)*

Vytalogy Wellness LLC .... C 818 867-4440
15233 Ventura Blvd Sherman Oaks (91403) *(P-3334)*

W & F Mfg Inc .... E 818 394-6060
10635 Keswick St Sun Valley (91352) *(P-4795)*

W & W Concept Inc .... D 323 803-3090
4890 S Alameda St Vernon (90058) *(P-2142)*

W A Benjamin Electric Co .... E 213 749-7731
1615 Staunton Ave Los Angeles (90021) *(P-6312)*

W A Rasic Cnstr Co Inc (PA) .... C 562 928-6111
4150 Long Beach Blvd Long Beach (90807) *(P-705)*

W B Mason Co Inc .... E 888 926-2766
5911 E Washington Blvd Commerce (90040) *(P-11636)*

W B Powell Inc .... D 951 270-0095
630 Parkridge Ave Norco (92860) *(P-2333)*

W B Walton Enterprises Inc .... E 951 683-0930
4185 Hallmark Pkwy San Bernardino (92407) *(P-6671)*

W Brown Assoc Insur Svcs LLC .... D 949 851-2060
19000 Macarthur Blvd Ste 600 Irvine (92612) *(P-12267)*

W D Schock Corp .... E 951 277-3377
1232 E Pomona St Santa Ana (92707) *(P-7625)*

W E O'Neil Construction, Rancho Cucamonga *Also Called: WE Oneil Construction Co Cal (P-601)*

W G A, Irvine *Also Called: Western Growers Association (P-17290)*

W G Holt Inc .... D 949 859-8800
101 Columbia Aliso Viejo (92656) *(P-6913)*

W L Rubottom Co .... D 805 648-6943
320 W Lewis St Ventura (03001) *(P-2367)*

W Lodging Inc .... A 619 258-6565
1825 Gillespie Way Ste 10 El Cajon (92020) *(P-13068)*

W Los Angeles .... B 310 208-8765
930 Hilgard Ave Los Angeles (90024) *(P-13069)*

W M Lyles Co .... C 951 296-2354
42142 Roick Dr Temecula (92590) *(P-706)*

W M Lyles Co .... C 661 387-1600
2810 Unicorn Rd Bakersfield (93308) *(P-17660)*

W Machine Works Inc .... E 818 890-8049
13814 Del Sur St San Fernando (91340) *(P-6267)*

W P Keith Co Inc .... E 562 948-3636
8323 Loch Lomond Dr Pico Rivera (90660) *(P-5804)*

W Plastics Inc .... E 800 442-9727
41573 Dendy Pkwy Ste 2543 Temecula (92590) *(P-3960)*

W R Meadows Inc .... E 909 469-2606
2300 Valley Blvd Pomona (91768) *(P-4424)*

W T E, Ontario *Also Called: Wallner Expac Inc (P-5657)*

W-GL 1241 Ocbc Hldings Viii LP .... D 949 331-1323
18301 Von Karman Ave Ste 250 Irvine (92612) *(P-12619)*

W. R. Meadows Southern Cal, Pomona *Also Called: W R Meadows Inc (P-4424)*

W/S Packaging Group Inc .... E 714 992-2574
531 Airpark Dr Fullerton (92833) *(P-2778)*

Waag, Van Nuys *Also Called: Wsw Corp (P-7310)*

Wabash, Moreno Valley *Also Called: Supreme Truck Bodies Cal Inc (P-7211)*

Wabash National Trlr Ctrs Inc .... E 765 771-5300
16025 Slover Ave Fontana (92337) *(P-9853)*

Wacker Biotech US Inc .... E 858 875-4700
10390 Pacific Center Ct San Diego (92121) *(P-3521)*

Wacker Chemical Corporation .... D 909 590-8822
13910 Oaks Ave Chino (91710) *(P-3743)*

Wadco Industries Inc .... E 909 874-7800
2625 S Willow Ave Bloomington (92316) *(P-4879)*

Wadco Steel Sales, Bloomington *Also Called: Wadco Industries Inc (P-4879)*

Waddington North America Inc .... C 626 913-4022
1135 Samuelson St City Of Industry (91748) *(P-4272)*

Waev Inc (PA) .... E 714 956-4040
2114 W Ball Rd Anaheim (92804) *(P-5537)*

Wagner Die Supply Inc (PA) .... E 909 947-3044
2041 Elm Ct Ontario (91761) *(P-5603)*

Wahlco, Chino *Also Called: Wahlco Inc (P-6268)*

Wahlco Inc .... C 714 979-7300
4774 Murrietta St Ste 3 Chino (91710) *(P-6268)*

Wakool Transport .... D 626 723-3100
19130 San Jose Ave Rowland Heights (91748) *(P-5538)*

Wakunaga of America Co Ltd (HQ) .... D 949 855-2776
23501 Madero Mission Viejo (92691) *(P-3522)*

Walashek Industrial & Mar Inc .... E 619 498-1711
1428 Mckinley Ave National City (91950) *(P-7613)*

Waldberg Inc .... D 818 843-0004
3200 W Valhalla Dr Burbank (91505) *(P-13272)*

Walden House Inc .... C 626 258-0300
845 E Arrow Hwy Pomona (91767) *(P-17207)*

Walden Structures Inc .... B 909 389-9100
1000 Bristol St N # 126 Newport Beach (92660) *(P-2405)*

Waldorf Astoria Beverly Hills, Beverly Hills *Also Called: Oasis West Realty LLC (P-12943)*

Waldorf Astria Mnrc Bch Rsort, Dana Point *Also Called: Cph Monarch Hotel LLC (P-12802)*

Walker, Ontario *Also Called: Walker Spring & Stamping Corp (P-5221)*

Walker Design Inc .... E 818 252-7788
9255 San Fernando Rd Sun Valley (91352) *(P-7614)*

Walker Engineering Enterprises, Sun Valley *Also Called: Walker Design Inc (P-7614)*

Walker Foods Inc .... D 323 268-5191
237 N Mission Rd Los Angeles (90033) *(P-1363)*

Walker Products .... E 714 554-5151
14291 Commerce Dr Garden Grove (92843) *(P-7308)*

WALKER PRODUCTS, Garden Grove *Also Called: Walker Products (P-7308)*

Walker Spring & Stamping Corp .... C 909 390-4300
1555 S Vintage Ave Ontario (91761) *(P-5221)*

Walking Company Holdings Inc (PA) .... C 805 963-8727
1800 Avenue Of The Stars Ste 300 Los Angeles (90067) *(P-11498)*

Wallner Expac Inc (PA) .... D 909 481-8800
1274 S Slater Cir Ontario (91761) *(P-5657)*

Wally & Pat Enterprises .... E 310 532-2031
13530 S Budlong Ave Gardena (90247) *(P-8739)*

Walmart, Riverside *Also Called: Walmart Inc (P-9127)*

Walmart, Rialto *Also Called: Walmart Inc (P-11265)*

Walmart Inc .... C 951 320-5722
1001 Columbia Ave Riverside (92507) *(P-9127)*

Walmart Inc .... D 909 820-9912
1366 S Riverside Ave Rialto (92376) *(P-11265)*

Walnut Investment Corp .... A 714 238-9240
2940 E White Star Ave Anaheim (92806) *(P-9933)*

Walsh Construction Company .... C 951 336-7040
1260 Corona Pointe Ct Ste 201 Corona (92879) *(P-600)*

Walt Disney Company (PA) .... A 818 560-1000
500 S Buena Vista St Burbank (91521) *(P-15110)*

Walt Disney Music Company (DH) .... C 818 560-1000
500 S Buena Vista St Burbank (91521) *(P-14870)*

Employee Codes: A=Over 500 employees, B=251-500
C=101-250, D=51-100, E=20-50, F=10-19, G=1-9

2025 Southern California
Business Directory and Buyers Guide

© Mergent Inc. 1-800-342-5647
1233

A
L
P
H
A
B
E
T
I
C

Walt Disney Pictures .... B 818 409-2200
811 Sonora Ave Glendale (91201) *(P-14871)*

Walt Disney Records Direct (DH) .... A 818 560-1000
500 S Buena Vista St Burbank (91521) *(P-14872)*

Walt Dsney Imgnring RES Dev In .... E 714 781-3152
1200 N Miller St Unit D Anaheim (92806) *(P-2202)*

Walt Dsney Imgnring RES Dev In (DH) .... A 818 544-6500
1401 Flower St Glendale (91201) *(P-14914)*

Walter Anderson Plumbing Inc .... C 619 449-7646
1830 John Towers Ave El Cajon (92020) *(P-851)*

Walter Foster Publishing Inc .... E 949 380-7510
6 Orchard Ste 100 Lake Forest (92630) *(P-2899)*

Walter N Coffman Inc .... D 619 266-2642
5180 Naranja St San Diego (92114) *(P-4022)*

Walters & Wolf Glass Company .... D 909 392-1961
1975 Puddingstone Dr La Verne (91750) *(P-1168)*

Walters Auto Sales and Svc Inc .... C 888 316-4097
3213 Adams St Riverside (92504) *(P-11431)*

Walters Family Partnership .... C 760 320-6868
400 E Tahquitz Canyon Way Palm Springs (92262) *(P-13070)*

Walters Wholesale Electric Co (HQ) .... E 714 784-1900
200 N Berry St Brea (92821) *(P-10213)*

Walton Construction Inc .... D 909 267-7777
358 E Foothill Blvd Ste 100 San Dimas (91773) *(P-456)*

Walton Construction Services, San Dimas *Also Called: Walton Construction Inc (P-456)*

Walton Electric Corporation .... C 909 981-5051
755 N Central Ave Ste A Upland (91786) *(P-6698)*

Wamc Company Inc .... D 858 454-2753
7420 Clairemont Mesa Blvd San Diego (92111) *(P-12370)*

Warco, Orange *Also Called: West American Rubber Co LLC (P-3942)*

Warco, Orange *Also Called: West American Rubber Co LLC (P-3943)*

Wardlow 2 LP (PA) .... D 562 432-8066
333 S Grand Ave Ste 4070 Los Angeles (90071) *(P-14800)*

Ware Disposal Inc .... C 714 834-0234
1451 Manhattan Ave Fullerton (92831) *(P-9773)*

Ware Malcomb (PA) .... C 949 660-9128
10 Edelman Irvine (92618) *(P-17695)*

Warehouse and Receiving Center, San Bernardino *Also Called: Loma Linda University Med Ctr (P-9306)*

Warlock Industries .... E 951 657-2680
23129 Cajalco Rd Ste A Perris (92570) *(P-7195)*

Warmelin Precision Products, Hawthorne *Also Called: DL Horton Enterprises Inc (P-6118)*

Warmington, Costa Mesa *Also Called: Warmington Mr 14 Assoc LLC (P-18077)*

Warmington Homes (PA) .... C 714 434-4435
3090 Pullman St Costa Mesa (92626) *(P-468)*

Warmington Homes .... C 949 679-3100
15615 Alton Pkwy Ste 150 Irvine (92618) *(P-469)*

Warmington Homes California, Costa Mesa *Also Called: Rebco Communities Inc (P-450)*

Warmington Mr 14 Assoc LLC .... D 714 557-5511
3090 Pullman St Costa Mesa (92626) *(P-18077)*

Warmington Residential Cal Inc .... C 714 557-5511
3090 Pullman St Costa Mesa (92626) *(P-438)*

Warner Bros, Burbank *Also Called: Warner Bros Transatlantic Inc (P-14927)*

Warner Bros Consumer Pdts Inc (DH) .... C 818 954-7980
4001 W Olive Ave Burbank (91505) *(P-18370)*

Warner Bros Distributing Inc .... B 818 954-6000
4000 Warner Blvd Bldg 154 Burbank (91522) *(P-18078)*

Warner Bros Entertainment Inc (DH) .... D 818 954-6000
4000 Warner Blvd Burbank (91522) *(P-14873)*

Warner Bros Home Entrmt Inc (DH) .... D 818 954-6000
4000 Warner Blvd Bldg 160 Burbank (91522) *(P-14874)*

Warner Bros Intl TV Dist Inc .... D 818 954-6000
4000 Warner Blvd Burbank (91522) *(P-14875)*

Warner Bros Records Inc (DH) .... B 818 846-9090
777 S Santa Fe Ave Los Angeles (90021) *(P-14630)*

Warner Bros Transatlantic Inc .... C 818 977-6384
3300 W Olive Ave Ste 200 Burbank (91505) *(P-14927)*

Warner Chappell Music Inc (DH) .... C 310 441-8600
777 S Santa Fe Ave Los Angeles (90021) *(P-2953)*

Warner Food Management Co Inc .... C 818 285-2160
4917 Genesta Ave Encino (91316) *(P-11609)*

Warner Geometric Music, Los Angeles *Also Called: Warner Chappell Music Inc (P-2953)*

Warner Music Group Corp .... D 818 953-2600
777 S Santa Fe Ave Los Angeles (90021) *(P-10574)*

Warren Collins and Assoc Inc (PA) .... E 909 548-6708
300 E Eucalyptus Ave Ontario (91762) *(P-723)*

Warren E & P, Long Beach *Also Called: Warren E&P Inc (P-316)*

Warren E&P Inc .... D 214 393-9688
400 Oceangate Ste 200 Long Beach (90802) *(P-316)*

Wash Mltfmily Ldry Systems LLC (PA) .... C 800 421-6897
2200 195th St Torrance (90501) *(P-13131)*

Washington Garment Dyeing (PA) .... E 213 747-1111
1341 E Washington Blvd Los Angeles (90021) *(P-1939)*

Washington Grment Dyg Fnshg In .... E 213 747-1111
1332 E 18th St Los Angeles (90021) *(P-1937)*

Washington Inventory Service .... A 858 565-8111
9265 Sky Park Ct Ste 100 San Diego (92123) *(P-14631)*

Washington Iron Works, Gardena *Also Called: Washington Orna Ir Works Inc (P-1231)*

Washington Orna Ir Works Inc (PA) .... D 310 327-8660
17926 S Broadway Gardena (90248) *(P-1231)*

Washington Orna Ir Works Inc .... E 310 327-8660
17913 S Main St Gardena (90248) *(P-5073)*

Wassco .... C 858 679-0444
12778 Brookprinter Pl Poway (92064) *(P-10416)*

Wassco Sales, Poway *Also Called: Wassco (P-10416)*

Wasser Filtration Inc (PA) .... D 714 696-6450
1215 N Fee Ana St Anaheim (92807) *(P-5836)*

Wasserman, Los Angeles *Also Called: Wasserman Media Group LLC (P-18239)*

Wasserman Comden & Casselman (PA) .... D 323 872-0995
5567 Reseda Blvd Ste 330 Tarzana (91356) *(P-16793)*

Wasserman Media Group LLC (PA) .... C 310 407-0200
10900 Wilshire Blvd Ste 1200 Los Angeles (90024) *(P-18239)*

Waste Management, El Cajon *Also Called: Waste Management Cal Inc (P-9774)*

Waste Management, Oceanside *Also Called: Waste Management Cal Inc (P-9775)*

Waste Management, Corona *Also Called: Waste Management Cal Inc (P-9776)*

Waste Management, Palmdale *Also Called: Waste Management Cal Inc (P-9777)*

Waste Management, Simi Valley *Also Called: Waste Management Cal Inc (P-9778)*

Waste Management, Sun Valley *Also Called: Waste Management Cal Inc (P-9779)*

Waste Management, Irvine *Also Called: Waste MGT Collectn Recycl Inc (P-9780)*

Waste Management, Baldwin Park *Also Called: Waste MGT Collectn Recycl Inc (P-9781)*

Waste Management, Gardena *Also Called: Waste MGT Collectn Recycl Inc (P-9782)*

Waste Management, Moreno Valley *Also Called: Waste MGT Collectn Recycl Inc (P-9783)*

Waste Management Cal Inc .... C 619 596-5100
1001 W Bradley Ave El Cajon (92020) *(P-9774)*

Waste Management Cal Inc .... C 760 439-2824
2141 Oceanside Blvd Oceanside (92054) *(P-9775)*

Waste Management Cal Inc .... C 951 277-1740
10910 Dawson Canyon Rd Corona (92883) *(P-9776)*

Waste Management Cal Inc .... C 661 947-7197
1200 W City Ranch Rd Palmdale (93551) *(P-9777)*

Waste Management Cal Inc .... C 805 522-7023
2801 N Madera Rd Simi Valley (93065) *(P-9778)*

Waste Management Cal Inc (HQ) .... C 877 836-6526
9081 Tujunga Ave Sun Valley (91352) *(P-9779)*

Waste MGT Collectn Recycl Inc .... C 949 451-2600
16122 Construction Cir E Irvine (92606) *(P-9780)*

Waste MGT Collectn Recycl Inc .... D 626 960-7551
13940 Live Oak Ave Baldwin Park (91706) *(P-9781)*

Waste MGT Collectn Recycl Inc .... C 310 532-6511
1449 W Rosecrans Ave Gardena (90249) *(P-9782)*

Waste MGT Collectn Recycl Inc .... C 951 242-0421
17700 Indian St Moreno Valley (92551) *(P-9783)*

Wastech Controls & Engrg LLC .... D 818 998-3500
20600 Nordhoff St Chatsworth (91311) *(P-10417)*

Water & Power Department, Long Beach *Also Called: County of Los Angeles (P-9687)*

Water Purification, Rancho Dominguez *Also Called: Parker-Hannifin Corporation (P-6933)*

Water Treatment Plant, Riverside *Also Called: City of Riverside (P-6007)*

Water Works Inc .... E 858 499-0119
5490 Complex St Ste 601 San Diego (92123) *(P-6037)*

Wateranywhere, Vista *Also Called: Applied Membranes Inc (P-5998)*

Watercrest Inc .... E 909 390-3944
4850 E Airport Dr Ontario (91761) (P-4933)

Waterfront Design Group LLC .... E 213 746-5800
122 E Washington Blvd Los Angeles (90015) (P-2031)

Waterfront Hotel LLC .... B 714 845-8000
21100 Pacific Coast Hwy Huntington Beach (92648) (P-13071)

Waterman Canyon Post Acute, San Bernardino Also Called: Watermanidence Opco LLC (P-15827)

Waterman Convalescent Hosp Inc (PA)................... C 909 882-1215
1850 N Waterman Ave San Bernardino (92404) (P-15798)

Watermanidence Opco LLC .... C 909 882-1215
1850 N Waterman Ave San Bernardino (92404) (P-15827)

Watermark Rtrment Cmmnties Inc .... D 949 443-9543
25411 Sea Bluffs Dr Dana Point (92629) (P-12371)

Watermark Rtrment Cmmnties Inc .... D 760 346-5420
41505 Carlotta Dr Palm Desert (92211) (P-15799)

Waterprfing Rofg Solutions Inc .... D 310 571-0892
11041 Santa Monica Blvd Ste 306 Los Angeles (90025) (P-1232)

Watersafe Swim School, Seal Beach Also Called: Watersafe Swim School Inc (P-15233)

Watersafe Swim School Inc .... D 562 596-8608
345 10th St Seal Beach (90740) (P-15233)

Watersentinel, Temecula Also Called: Aquamor LLC (P-6001)

Waterstone Faucets, Murrieta Also Called: Waterstone Faucets LLC (P-10327)

Waterstone Faucets LLC .... C 951 304-0520
41180 Raintree Ct Murrieta (92562) (P-10327)

Waterway Plastics, Oxnard Also Called: B & S Plastics Inc (P-4057)

Watkins Manufacturing Corp .... B 760 598-6464
1325 Hot Springs Way Vista (92081) (P-4032)

Watkins Manufacturing Corp (HQ).......................... C 760 598-6464
1280 Park Center Dr Vista (92081) (P-8740)

Watkins Wellness, Vista Also Called: Watkins Manufacturing Corp (P-8740)

Watt Commercial Properties, Santa Monica Also Called: Watt Properties Inc (P-12325)

Watt Companies Inc .... D 310 789-2180
1875 Century Park E Los Angeles (90067) (P-12547)

Watt Inc .... D 310 896-8197
8605 Santa Monica Blvd Pmb 65044 West Hollywood (90069) (P-13864)

Watt Properties Inc (PA)... D 310 314-2430
2716 Ocean Park Blvd Ste 2025 Santa Monica (90405) (P-12325)

WATTS HEALTH, Los Angeles Also Called: Watts Healthcare Corporation (P-15509)

Watts Health Foundation Inc (PA)............................ B 310 424-2220
3405 W Imperial Hwy Ste 304 Inglewood (90303) (P-15828)

Watts Health Systems Inc (PA).................................. A 310 424-2220
3405 W Imperial Hwy Inglewood (90303) (P-18240)

Watts Healthcare Corporation (PA).......................... C 323 564-4331
10300 Compton Ave Los Angeles (90002) (P-15509)

Watts Labor Community Action .... C 323 563-5639
4142 Palmwood Dr Apt 11 Los Angeles (90008) (P-17039)

Wave Community Newspapers Inc (PA)................... E 323 290-3000
1007 N Sepulveda Blvd Manhattan Beach (90266) (P-2837)

Wavelengths Recovery Inc .... D 714 312-1011
703 California St Huntington Beach (92648) (P-16521)

Wavestream Corporation (HQ)................................... C 909 599-9080
545 W Terrace Dr San Dimas (91773) (P-7068)

Waxie, Ontario Also Called: Waxies Enterprises LLC (P-10401)

Waxie Sanitary Supply, San Diego Also Called: Waxies Enterprises LLC (P-10482)

Waxie Sanitary Supply, Santa Ana Also Called: Waxies Enterprises LLC (P-11702)

Waxies Enterprises LLC .... D 909 942-3100
905 Wineville Ave Ontario (91764) (P-10481)

Waxies Enterprises LLC .... D 714 545-8441
3220 S Fairview St Santa Ana (92704) (P-11702)

Waxies Enterprises LLC (DH).................................... C 800 995-4466
9353 Waxie Way San Diego (92123) (P-10482)

Wayne Gossett Ford Inc .... D 760 753-6286
1424 Encinitas Blvd Encinitas (92024) (P-11432)

Wayne Perry Inc (PA).. C 714 826-0352
8281 Commonwealth Ave Buena Park (90621) (P-1233)

Wb Music Corp (DH).. C 310 441-8600
10585 Santa Monica Blvd Ste 200 Los Angeles (90025) (P-2954)

Wbi Inc .... A 800 673-4968
8201 Woodley Ave Van Nuys (91406) (P-8446)

Wbt Group LLC .... E 323 735-1201
1401 S Shamrock Ave Monrovia (91016) (P-8741)

Wbt Industries, Monrovia Also Called: Wbt Group LLC (P-8741)

Wc Music Corp., Los Angeles Also Called: Wb Music Corp (P-2954)

Wcbm Company (PA).. E 323 262-3274
1812 W 135th St Gardena (90249) (P-8580)

Wco Hotels Inc .... A 714 635-2300
1600 S Disneyland Dr Anaheim (92802) (P-13072)

Wcp West Coast Glass LLC .... D 562 653-9797
17730 Crusader Ave Cerritos (90703) (P-4273)

Wcs Equipment Holdings LLC (HQ) .... E 909 393-8405
13568 Vintage Pl Chino (91710) (P-4572)

Wcs Equipment Holdings LLC .... D 909 993-5700
1350 E Lexington Ave Pomona (91766) (P-4573)

Wcs Equipment Holdings LLC .... D 909 393-8405
13066 14th St Chino (91710) (P-5056)

Wd-40 Company .... C 619 275-1400
9715 Businesspark Ave San Diego (92131) (P-3836)

WD-40 Company (PA)... C 619 275-1400
9715 Businesspark Ave San Diego (92131) (P-3859)

Wdm Group, San Diego Also Called: White Digital Media Inc (P-11078)

We Imagine Inc .... D 818 709-0064
9371 Canoga Ave Chatsworth (91311) (P-6787)

WE Oneil Construction Co Cal .... C 909 466-5300
9485 Haven Ave Ste 101 Rancho Cucamonga (91730) (P-601)

We Pack It All LLC .... C 626 301-9214
2745 Huntington Dr Duarte (91010) (P-14632)

We See Dragons LLC .... C 310 361-5700
1100 Glendon Ave Ste 1700 Los Angeles (90024) (P-14265)

We The Pie People LLC .... E 818 349-1880
9909 Topanga Canyon Blvd # 159 Chatsworth (91311) (P-1321)

Weapon X Security Inc .... D 818 818-9950
297 Country Club Dr Simi Valley (93065) (P-18380)

Weapons System Division, Northridge Also Called: Northrop Grumman Systems Corp (P-7771)

Weartech International Inc .... E 714 683-2430
1177 N Grove St Anaheim (92806) (P-5754)

Webb, Riverside Also Called: Albert A Webb Associates (P-17480)

Webb Del California Corp (DH)................................... B 760 772-5300
39755 Berkey Dr Palm Desert (92211) (P-12582)

Webcor Builders, San Diego Also Called: Webcor Construction LP (P-602)

Webcor Builders, Los Angeles Also Called: Webcor Construction LP (P-603)

Webcor Construction LP .... C 619 798-3891
2150 W Washington St Ste 308 San Diego (92110) (P-602)

Webcor Construction LP .... C 213 239-2800
333 S Grand Ave Ste 4400 Los Angeles (90071) (P-603)

Weber, Rancho Cucamonga Also Called: American Fruits & Flavors LLC (P-1661)

Weber Distribution, Norwalk Also Called: Weber Distribution LLC (P-9128)

Weber Distribution LLC .... D 562 404-9996
15301 Shoemaker Ave Norwalk (90650) (P-9128)

Weber Drilling Co Inc .... E 310 670-7708
4028 W 184th St Torrance (90504) (P-6269)

Weber Metals Inc (HQ).. E 562 602-0260
16706 Garfield Ave Paramount (90723) (P-5162)

Weber Metals Inc .... B 562 543-3318
233 E Manville St Compton (90220) (P-5163)

Weber Orthopedic LP (PA).. D 800 221-5465
1185 E Main St Santa Paula (93060) (P-8319)

Weber Precision Graphics, Santa Ana Also Called: Artisan Nameplate Awards Corp (P-3118)

Weber Printing Company Inc .... E 310 639-5064
1124 E Del Amo Blvd Long Beach (90807) (P-3100)

Webmetro .... D 909 599-8885
160 Via Verde Ste 1 San Dimas (91773) (P-14064)

Webtoon Entertainment Inc (PA).............................. A 323 297-3410
5700 Wilshire Blvd Ste 220 Los Angeles (90036) (P-2955)

Webx360 Inc .... D 714 896-8004
6871 Laurelton Ave Garden Grove (92845) (P-14180)

Weck Anlytical Envmtl Svcs Inc .... D 626 336-2139
14859 Clark Ave City Of Industry (91745) (P-17929)

Weck Laboratories, City Of Industry Also Called: Weck Anlytical Envmtl Svcs Inc (P-17929)

Employee Codes: A=Over 500 employees, B=251-500
C=101-250, D=51-100, E=20-50, F=10-19, G=1-9

2025 Southern California
Business Directory and Buyers Guide

© Mergent Inc. 1-800-342-5647
1235

ALPHABETIC

Weckerle Cosmetic, Torrance *Also Called: Weckerle Cosmetics Usa Inc (P-10658)*

Weckerle Cosmetics Usa Inc .... E 310 328-7000
525 Maple Ave Torrance (90503) *(P-10658)*

Wedbush Securities Inc (HQ)... B 213 688-8000
1000 Wilshire Blvd Ste 900 Los Angeles (90017) *(P-12009)*

Weddingolala, City Of Industry *Also Called: Orbitel International LLC (P-3159)*

Wedgewood Inc (PA)... D 310 640-3070
2015 Manhattan Beach Blvd Ste 100 Redondo Beach (90278) *(P-12747)*

WEI-Chuan USA Inc (PA)... C 626 225-7168
6655 Garfield Ave Bell Gardens (90201) *(P-10824)*

Weider Health and Fitness .... B 818 884-6800
21100 Erwin St Woodland Hills (91367) *(P-1693)*

Weingart Center Association .... C 213 622-6359
566 S San Pedro St Los Angeles (90013) *(P-17040)*

Weingart Center For Homeless, Los Angeles *Also Called: Weingart Center Association (P-17040)*

Weiss Sheet Metal Company .... E 310 354-2700
1715 W 135th St Gardena (90249) *(P-1099)*

Welaco, Bakersfield *Also Called: Well Analysis Corporation Inc (P-2284)*

Welbe Health LLC .... C 888 530-4415
1220 E 4th St Long Beach (90802) *(P-16627)*

Welbilt Fdsrvice Companies LLC .... B 323 245-3761
1210 N Red Gum St Anaheim (92806) *(P-5992)*

Welbilt Inc .... E 310 339-1555
3835 E Thousand Oaks Blvd Unit 315 Westlake Village (91362) *(P-370)*

WELCOME BABY, Santa Ana *Also Called: Priority Ctr Ending The Ghrtna (P-16996)*

Weld-It Co, Orange *Also Called: Sam Schaffer Inc (P-14790)*

Weld-On Adhesives, Compton *Also Called: Ips-Corporation (P-3771)*

Weldex Corporation .... B 714 761-2100
6751 Katella Ave Cypress (90630) *(P-6914)*

Weldlogic Inc .... D 805 375-1670
2651 Lavery Ct Newbury Park (91320) *(P-14746)*

Weldlogic Gas & Supply, Newbury Park *Also Called: Weldlogic Inc (P-14746)*

Weldmac Manufacturing Company .... C 619 440-2300
1451 N Johnson Ave El Cajon (92020) *(P-6270)*

Weldmac Manufacturing Company .... E 619 440-2300
1533 N Johnson Ave El Cajon (92020) *(P-6271)*

Welk Group Inc (PA)... B 760 749-3000
11400 W Olympic Blvd Ste 760 Los Angeles (90064) *(P-13073)*

Welk Group Inc .... B 760 749-3000
8860 Lawrence Welk Dr Escondido (92026) *(P-13074)*

Welk Group Inc .... C 760 749-3225
8860 Lawrence Welk Dr Escondido (92026) *(P-15098)*

Welk Group Inc .... C 760 749-0983
10333 Meadow Glen Way E Escondido (92026) *(P-15186)*

Welk Music Group, Los Angeles *Also Called: Welk Group Inc (P-13073)*

Welk Resort Center, San Marcos *Also Called: Whv Resort Group Inc (P-12550)*

Welk Resort Center, Escondido *Also Called: Welk Group Inc (P-13074)*

Well Analysis Corporation Inc (PA)................................... E 661 283-9510
5500 Woodmere Dr Bakersfield (93313) *(P-2284)*

Wella Corporation (HQ)... C 800 422-2336
4500 Park Granada # 100 Calabasas (91302) *(P-3696)*

Wella Operations US LLC .... B 818 999-5112
4500 Park Granada Ste 100 Calabasas (91302) *(P-10659)*

Wellington Crt Asssted Lving C, Arcadia *Also Called: Leisure Care LLC (P-17173)*

Wellington Foods Inc (PA)... C 951 547-7000
1930 California Ave Corona (92881) *(P-1311)*

Wellmade Inc .... D 213 221-1123
800 E 12th St Los Angeles (90021) *(P-18241)*

Wellnest Emtonal Hlth Wellness (PA)................................ C 323 373-2400
3031 S Vermont Ave Los Angeles (90007) *(P-17041)*

Wells Fargo Capital Fin LLC (DH).................................... D 310 453-7300
2450 Colorado Ave Ste 3000w Santa Monica (90404) *(P-11879)*

Wells Fargo Capital Finance Inc .... C 310 453-7300
2450 Colo Ave 3000w 3rd Fl Santa Monica (90404) *(P-14633)*

Wells Fargo Securities LLC .... A 310 479-3500
1800 Century Park E Ste 1100 Los Angeles (90067) *(P-11741)*

Wells Frgo Insur Svcs Minn Inc .... C 909 481-3802
4141 Inland Empire Blvd Ontario (91764) *(P-12268)*

Wells Struthers Corporation .... E 814 726-1000
10375 Slusher Dr Santa Fe Springs (90670) *(P-4934)*

Welltower Om Group LLC .... C 626 254-0552
301 W Huntington Dr Ste 5 Arcadia (91007) *(P-12326)*

Welovefine, Los Angeles *Also Called: Mf Inc (P-2047)*

Wems Inc (PA).. D 310 644-0251
4650 W Rosecrans Ave Hawthorne (90250) *(P-5784)*

Wems Electronics, Hawthorne *Also Called: Wems Inc (P-5784)*

Wen U Luv Liquidation LLC .... E 323 456-8821
8383 Wilshire Blvd Ste 800 Beverly Hills (90211) *(P-11496)*

Werfen, San Diego *Also Called: Inova Diagnostics Inc (P-17796)*

Wermers, San Diego *Also Called: Wermers Multi-Family Corp (P-457)*

Wermers Multi-Family Corp .... C 858 535-1475
5120 Shoreham Pl Ste 150 San Diego (92122) *(P-457)*

Wes Go Inc .... E 818 504-1200
8211 Lankershim Blvd North Hollywood (91605) *(P-3187)*

Wesanco Inc .... E 714 739-4989
14870 Desman Rd La Mirada (90638) *(P-7590)*

Wesco Aircraft, Valencia *Also Called: Falcon Aerospace Holdings LLC (P-10491)*

Wesco Aircraft Hardware Corp .... B 661 775-7200
27727 Avenue Scott Valencia (91355) *(P-10506)*

Wescom Central Credit Union (PA).................................. B 888 493-7266
123 S Marengo Ave Pasadena (91101) *(P-11834)*

Weslar Inc .... D 661 702-1362
28310 Constellation Rd Valencia (91355) *(P-1066)*

Wesley Allen Inc .... C 323 231-4275
1001 E 60th St Los Angeles (90001) *(P-2476)*

Wessco International, Los Angeles *Also Called: Wessco Intl Ltd A Cal Ltd Prtn (P-2283)*

Wessco Intl Ltd A Cal Ltd Prtn (PA)................................. D 310 477-4272
11400 W Olympic Blvd Ste 450 Los Angeles (90064) *(P-2283)*

Wessex Industries Inc .... E 562 944-5760
8619 Red Oak St Rancho Cucamonga (91730) *(P-5439)*

West American Rubber Co LLC (PA)................................. C 714 532-3355
1337 W Braden Ct Orange (92868) *(P-3942)*

West American Rubber Co LLC .... C 714 532-3355
750 N Main St Orange (92868) *(P-3943)*

West Anaheim Care Center, Anaheim *Also Called: Mark & Fred Enterprises (P-15716)*

West Anaheim Medical Center, Anaheim *Also Called: Prime Healthcare Anaheim LLC (P-16139)*

West Angeles Ch God In Chrst .... C 323 731-2567
3010 Crenshaw Blvd Los Angeles (90016) *(P-16829)*

West Angeles Christian Academy, Los Angeles *Also Called: West Angeles Ch God In Chrst (P-16829)*

West Area Opportunity Center, Santa Monica *Also Called: Casa De Hermandad (P-8511)*

West Bay Imports Inc .... E 323 720-5777
7245 Oxford Way Commerce (90040) *(P-11148)*

West Bent Bolt Division, Santa Fe Springs *Also Called: Mid-West Fabricating Co (P-7271)*

West Bond Inc (PA)... E 714 978-1551
1551 S Harris Ct Anaheim (92806) *(P-6272)*

West Cast Stl Proc Hldings LLC (PA)................................ E 909 393-8405
13568 Vintage Pl Chino (91710) *(P-4528)*

West Central Food Service, Norwalk *Also Called: West Central Produce Inc (P-10925)*

West Central Produce Inc .... B 213 629-3600
12840 Leyva St Norwalk (90650) *(P-10925)*

West Cntinela Vly Care Ctr Inc .... D 310 674-3216
950 S Flower St Inglewood (90301) *(P-15800)*

West Coast AC Co Inc .... C 619 561-8000
1155 Pioneer Way Ste 101 El Cajon (92020) *(P-852)*

West Coast Aerospace Inc (PA)....................................... D 310 518-3167
220 W E St Wilmington (90744) *(P-8581)*

West Coast Arborists Inc .... C 805 671-5092
11405 Nardo St Ventura (93004) *(P-247)*

West Coast Arborists Inc .... C 909 783-6544
21718 Walnut Ave Grand Terrace (92313) *(P-248)*

West Coast Arborists Inc .... C 858 566-4204
8163 Commercial St La Mesa (91942) *(P-439)*

West Coast Arborists Inc (PA)... D 714 991-1900
2200 E Via Burton Anaheim (92806) *(P-243)*

West Coast Button Mfg Co, Gardena *Also Called: Wcbm Company (P-8580)*

West Coast Chain Mfg Co .... E 909 923-7800
4245 Pacific Privado Ontario (91761) *(P-7161)*

West Coast Construction, Jurupa Valley *Also Called: Perry Coast Construction Inc (P-570)*

Mergent email: customerrelations@mergent.com
1236

2025 Southern California
Business Directory and Buyers Guide

(P-0000) Products & Services Section entry number
(PA)=Parent Co (HQ)=Headquarters (DH)=Div Headquarters

West Coast Consulting LLC .... C 949 250-4102
9233 Research Dr Ste 200 Irvine (92618) *(P-18371)*

West Coast Countertops Inc .... D 951 719-3670
1200 Marlborough Ave Ste B Riverside (92507) *(P-1234)*

West Coast Dental Labs LLC .... A 855 220-5600
12002 Aviation Blvd Hawthorne (90250) *(P-16348)*

West Coast Distribution Inc .... D 323 588-6508
4440 E 26th St Vernon (90058) *(P-512)*

West Coast Drywall & Co Inc .... B 951 778-3592
1610 W Linden St Riverside (92507) *(P-1035)*

West Coast Drywall & Paint, Riverside *Also Called: West Coast Drywall & Co Inc (P-1035)*

West Coast Firestopping Inc .... D 714 935-1104
1130 W Trenton Ave Orange (92867) *(P-1235)*

West Coast Furn Framers Inc .... E 760 669-5275
24006 Tahquitz Rd Apple Valley (92307) *(P-2293)*

West Coast Gasket Co .... D 714 869-0123
300 Ranger Ave Brea (92821) *(P-3903)*

West Coast Interiors Inc .... A 951 778-3592
1610 W Linden St Riverside (92507) *(P-875)*

West Coast Iron Inc .... D 619 464-8456
9302 Jamacha Rd Spring Valley (91977) *(P-1192)*

West Coast Labels, Placentia *Also Called: Cinton LLC (P-2720)*

West Coast Laboratories Inc .... E 310 527-6163
156 E 162nd St Gardena (90248) *(P-3523)*

West Coast Ltg & Enrgy Inc .... D 951 296-0680
18550 Minthorn St Lake Elsinore (92530) *(P-977)*

West Coast Manufacturing, Stanton *Also Called: West Coast Manufacturing Inc (P-5222)*

West Coast Manufacturing Inc .... E 714 897-4221
11822 Western Ave Stanton (90680) *(P-5222)*

West Coast Materials, Buena Park *Also Called: West Coast Sand and Gravel Inc (P-9953)*

West Coast Metal Stamping, Irvine *Also Called: Perfect Choice Mfrs Inc (P-8713)*

West Coast Metal Stamping Incorporated .... E 714 792-0322
550 W Crowther Ave Placentia (92870) *(P-5223)*

West Coast Mfg & Whsng, Ontario *Also Called: Idx Los Angeles LLC (P-2582)*

West Coast Milling, Lancaster *Also Called: Pavement Recycling Systems Inc (P-3839)*

West Coast Motor Sports, Perris *Also Called: West Coast Yamaha Inc (P-5811)*

West Coast Operations, Chula Vista *Also Called: East Cast Repr Fabrication LLC (P-4832)*

West Coast Painting, Riverside *Also Called: West Coast Interiors Inc (P-875)*

West Coast Physical Therapy, Laguna Niguel *Also Called: Mission Internal Med Group Inc (P-15391)*

West Coast Sales Office & Whse, Oxnard *Also Called: Amiad USA Inc (P-5995)*

West Coast Sand and Gravel Inc (PA) .... D **714 522-0282**
7282 Orangethorpe Ave Buena Park (90621) *(P-9953)*

West Coast Service Center, Ontario *Also Called: Vsmpo-Tirus US Inc (P-4624)*

West Coast Switchgear (DH) .... D **562 802-3441**
13837 Bettencourt St Cerritos (90703) *(P-6313)*

West Coast Trends Inc .... E 714 843-9288
17811 Jamestown Ln Huntington Beach (92647) *(P-8552)*

West Coast Vinyl Windows, Cerritos *Also Called: Wcp West Coast Glass LLC (P-4273)*

West Coast Wldg & Piping Inc .... D 805 246-5841
760 W Hueneme Rd Oxnard (93033) *(P-14747)*

West Coast Wood Preserving LLC .... C 661 833-0429
5801 District Blvd Bakersfield (93313) *(P-2407)*

West Coast Yamaha Inc .... E 951 943-2061
1622 Illinois Ave Perris (92571) *(P-5811)*

West Covina Foster Family Agcy .... D 626 814-9085
527 E Rowland St Ste 100 Covina (91723) *(P-12269)*

West Covina Medical Clinic Inc (PA) .... C **626 960-8614**
1500 W West Covina Pkwy Ste 100 West Covina (91790) *(P-15510)*

WEST COVINA PHYSICAL THERAPY, West Covina *Also Called: Doctors Hospital W Covina Inc (P-15983)*

West Edge, Chula Vista *Also Called: West Edge Inc (P-12548)*

West Edge Inc .... D 619 475-4095
1061 Tierra Del Rey Chula Vista (91910) *(P-12548)*

West End Yung MNS Christn Assn .... C 909 477-2780
1257 E D St Ontario (91764) *(P-17376)*

West End Yung MNS Christn Assn .... C 909 597-7445
5665 Edison Ave Chino (91710) *(P-17377)*

West Health Care, Bonita *Also Called: Paradise Valley Hospital (P-16126)*

West Health Incubator Inc .... C 858 535-7000
10350 N Torrey Pines Rd La Jolla (92037) *(P-16628)*

West Hollywood Edition .... D 310 795-7103
9040 W Sunset Blvd West Hollywood (90069) *(P-13075)*

West Lake Food Corporation (PA) .... E **714 973-2286**
301 N Sullivan St Santa Ana (92703) *(P-1253)*

West Los Angeles V A Med Ctr, Los Angeles *Also Called: Veterans Health Administration (P-15508)*

West Newport Oil Company .... E 949 631-1100
5800 W Coast Hwy Newport Beach (92663) *(P-282)*

West Pacific Medical Lab, Santa Fe Springs *Also Called: California Lab Sciences LLC (P-17906)*

West Pacific Services Inc .... C 888 401-0188
4445 Eastgate Mall Ste 200 San Diego (92121) *(P-604)*

West Pak Avocado Inc (PA) .... C **951 296-5757**
38655 Sky Canyon Dr Murrieta (92563) *(P-122)*

West Pico Foods Inc .... C 323 586-9050
5201 S Downey Rd Vernon (90058) *(P-10825)*

West Publishing Corporation .... A 800 747-3161
5161 Lankershim Blvd North Hollywood (91601) *(P-2900)*

West Publishing Corporation .... A 619 296-7862
2801 Camino Del Rio S San Diego (92108) *(P-2956)*

West Publishing Corporation .... A 424 243-2100
800 Corporate Pointe Ste 150 Culver City (90230) *(P-14117)*

West Side Rehab Corporation .... C 323 231-4174
1755 E Martin Luther King Jr Blvd Los Angeles (90069) *(P-12327)*

West Tech Contracting Inc .... D 760 233-2570
568 N Tulip St Escondido (92025) *(P-707)*

West Valley Occupational Ctr, Woodland Hills *Also Called: Los Angeles Unified School Dst (P-16815)*

West Valley Post Acute, West Hills *Also Called: West Valleyidence Opco LLC (P-15829)*

West Valleyidence Opco LLC .... D 818 348-8422
7057 Shoup Ave West Hills (91307) *(P-15829)*

West-Bag Inc .... E 323 264-0750
1161 Monterey Pass Rd Monterey Park (91754) *(P-4274)*

Westair Gases & Equipment, Bakersfield *Also Called: Westair Gases & Equipment Inc (P-10418)*

Westair Gases & Equipment Inc .... C 661 387-6800
3901 Buck Owens Blvd Bakersfield (93308) *(P-10418)*

Westamerica Communications Inc .... D 949 340-8942
26012 Atlantic Ocean Dr Lake Forest (92630) *(P-18381)*

Westbrook Ops LLC .... D 818 832-2300
24151 Ventura Blvd Ste 200 Calabasas (91302) *(P-14876)*

Westco Industries Inc .... E 909 874-8700
2625 S Willow Ave Bloomington (92316) *(P-4880)*

Westcoast Iron, Spring Valley *Also Called: West Coast Iron Inc (P-1192)*

Westech Products Inc (PA) .... E **951 279-4496**
1242 Enterprise Ct Corona (92882) *(P-8560)*

Westech Wax Products, Corona *Also Called: Westech Products Inc (P-8560)*

Westerlay Orchids, Carpinteria *Also Called: Westerlay Orchids LP (P-71)*

Westerlay Orchids LP .... C 805 684-5411
3504 Via Real Carpinteria (93013) *(P-71)*

Western Allied Corporation .... E 562 944-6341
12046 Florence Ave Santa Fe Springs (90670) *(P-853)*

Western Asset Core Plus Bond P .... C 626 844-9400
385 E Colorado Blvd Pasadena (91101) *(P-12643)*

Western Bagel Baking Corp .... E 818 887-5451
21749 Ventura Blvd Woodland Hills (91364) *(P-1471)*

Western Bagel Baking Corp (PA) .... C **818 786-5847**
7814 Sepulveda Blvd Van Nuys (91405) *(P-1472)*

Western Bay Sheet Metal Inc .... E 619 233-1753
1410 Hill St El Cajon (92020) *(P-4881)*

Western Cactus Growers Inc .... E 760 726-1710
1860 Monte Vista Dr Vista (92084) *(P-5485)*

Western Case Incorporated .... D 951 214-6380
231 E Alessandro Blvd Riverside (92508) *(P-4275)*

Western Cnc Inc .... D 760 597-7000
1001 Park Center Dr Vista (92081) *(P-6273)*

Western Convelescence, Los Angeles *Also Called: Longwood Management Corp (P-15865)*

Western Corrugated Design Inc .... E 562 695-9295
8741 Pioneer Blvd Santa Fe Springs (90670) *(P-2693)*

Western Costume Co (HQ) .... E **818 760-0900**
11041 Vanowen St North Hollywood (91605) *(P-13191)*

Employee Codes: A=Over 500 employees, B=251-500
C=101-250, D=51-100, E=20-50, F=10-19, G=1-9

2025 Southern California
Business Directory and Buyers Guide

© Mergent Inc. 1-800-342-5647
1237

Western Dental & Orthodontics, Orange *Also Called: Western Dental Services Inc* ***(P-15529)***

Western Dental Services Inc (HQ) .... **B 714 480-3000**
530 S Main St Ste 600 Orange (92868) ***(P-15529)***

Western Design, Irvine *Also Called: Meggitt Western Design Inc* ***(P-7837)***

Western Digital .... D 510 557-7553
19600 S Western Ave Torrance (90501) ***(P-7069)***

Western Digital Corporation .... E 949 672-7000
3337 Michelson Dr Irvine (92612) ***(P-5893)***

Western Division Regional Off, Long Beach *Also Called: Southern California Edison Co* ***(P-9633)***

Western Drug, Glendale *Also Called: H and H Drug Stores Inc* ***(P-10083)***

Western Drug Medical Supply, San Bernardino *Also Called: H and H Drug Stores Inc* ***(P-10082)***

Western Electrical Advg Co .... E 760 352-0471
853 S Dogwood Rd El Centro (92243) ***(P-8649)***

Western Energy Services Corp .... C 403 984-5916
3430 Getty St Bakersfield (93308) ***(P-13444)***

Western Environmental Inc .... E 760 396-0222
62150 Gene Welmas Way Mecca (92254) ***(P-7842)***

Western Equipment Mfg, Corona *Also Called: Western Equipment Mfg Inc* ***(P-5500)***

Western Equipment Mfg Inc .... E 951 284-2000
1160 Olympic Dr Corona (92881) ***(P-5500)***

Western Feld Invstigations Inc (PA) .... **D 800 999-9589**
405 W Foothill Blvd Ste 204 Claremont (91711) ***(P-14181)***

Western Filter A Division of Donaldson Company Inc .... D 661 295-0800
26235 Technology Dr Valencia (91355) ***(P-5837)***

Western Fire Protection Inc (PA) .... **D 858 513-4949**
13630 Danielson St Poway (92064) ***(P-854)***

Western Gage Corporation .... E 805 445-1410
3316 Maya Linda Ste A Camarillo (93012) ***(P-5631)***

Western General Insurance Co .... C 818 880-9070
5230 Las Virgenes Rd Ste 100 Calabasas (91302) ***(P-12270)***

Western Golf Car Mfg Inc .... D 760 671-6691
69391 Dillon Rd Desert Hot Springs (92241) ***(P-8553)***

Western Golf Car Sales Co, Desert Hot Springs *Also Called: Western Golf Car Mfg Inc* ***(P-8553)***

Western Growers Association (PA) .... **C 949 863-1000**
6501 Irvine Center Dr Irvine (92618) ***(P-17290)***

Western Highway Products, Huntington Beach *Also Called: Primus Inc* ***(P-8624)***

Western Hydrostatics Inc (PA) .... **E 951 784-2133**
1956 Keats Dr Riverside (92501) ***(P-6054)***

Western Insulfoam, Chino *Also Called: Carlisle Construction Mtls LLC* ***(P-9957)***

Western Integrated Mtls Inc (PA) .... **E 562 634-2823**
3310 E 59th St Long Beach (90805) ***(P-2334)***

Western Medical Center Aux, Santa Ana *Also Called: Orange Cnty Globl Med Ctr Aux* ***(P-16108)***

Western Methods, Santa Ana *Also Called: Western Methods Machinery Corporation* ***(P-7591)***

Western Methods Machinery Corporation .... C 949 252-6600
2344 Pullman St Santa Ana (92705) ***(P-7591)***

Western Mfg & Distrg LLC .... E 805 988-1010
835 Flynn Rd Camarillo (93012) ***(P-7639)***

Western Mill Fabricators Inc .... E 714 993-3667
670 S Jefferson St Ste B Placentia (92870) ***(P-2618)***

Western Mutual Insurance Co .... D 818 879-2142
27489 Agoura Rd Agoura Hills (91301) ***(P-12142)***

Western National Contractors .... D 949 862-6200
8 Executive Cir Irvine (92614) ***(P-18079)***

Western National Prpts LLC (PA) .... **C 949 862-6200**
8 Executive Cir Irvine (92614) ***(P-458)***

Western National Securities (PA) .... **C 949 862-6200**
8 Executive Cir Irvine (92614) ***(P-12549)***

Western Oilfields Supply Co .... D 480 895-9225
5101 Office Park Dr Ste 100 Bakersfield (93309) ***(P-13478)***

Western Oilfields Supply Co (PA) .... **C 661 399-9124**
3404 State Rd Bakersfield (93308) ***(P-13479)***

Western Operations, Rancho Cucamonga *Also Called: Gentex Corporation* ***(P-17792)***

Western Operations Center, Westlake Village *Also Called: Securitas SEC Svcs USA Inc* ***(P-14339)***

Western Outdoor News, San Clemente *Also Called: Western Outdoors Publications* ***(P-2838)***

Western Outdoors Publications (PA) .... **E 949 366-0030**
901 Calle Amanecer Ste 115 San Clemente (92673) ***(P-2838)***

Western Pacific Distrg LLC .... C 714 974-6837
341 W Meats Ave Orange (92865) ***(P-9954)***

Western Pacific Roofing Corp .... C 661 273-1336
3462 E La Campana Way Palm Springs (92262) ***(P-1100)***

Western PCF Stor Solutions Inc (PA) .... **D 909 451-0303**
300 E Arrow Hwy San Dimas (91773) ***(P-2598)***

Western Plastics Temecula, Temecula *Also Called: W Plastics Inc* ***(P-3960)***

Western Precision Aero LLC .... E 714 893-7999
11600 Monarch St Garden Grove (92841) ***(P-6274)***

Western Psychological Services, Torrance *Also Called: Manson Western LLC* ***(P-2892)***

Western Pump Inc (PA) .... **D 619 239-9988**
3235 F St San Diego (92102) ***(P-14801)***

Western Refining Inc .... D 714 708-2200
1201 Baker St Costa Mesa (92626) ***(P-10419)***

Western Refining Inc .... D 310 834-1297
22232 Wilmington Ave Carson (90745) ***(P-10420)***

Western Refining Inc .... D 323 264-8500
4357 E Cesar E Chavez Ave Los Angeles (90022) ***(P-10421)***

Western Rim Pipeline, Lakeside *Also Called: A M Ortega Construction Inc* ***(P-877)***

Western Saw, Oxnard *Also Called: Western Saw Manufacturers Inc* ***(P-4748)***

Western Saw Manufacturers Inc .... E 805 981-0999
3200 Camino Del Sol Oxnard (93030) ***(P-4748)***

Western Sign Systems, San Marcos *Also Called: Western Sign Systems Inc* ***(P-8650)***

Western Sign Systems Inc .... E 760 736-6070
261 S Pacific St San Marcos (92078) ***(P-8650)***

Western States Envelope Corp .... D 714 449-0909
2301 Raymer Ave Fullerton (92833) ***(P-3188)***

Western States Glass, Long Beach *Also Called: Total Mont LLC* ***(P-4347)***

Western States Packaging Inc .... E 818 686-6045
13276 Paxton St Pacoima (91331) ***(P-2742)***

Western States Wholesale Inc .... C 909 947-0028
1600 E Francis St Ontario (91761) ***(P-4376)***

Western States Wholesale Inc (PA) .... **D 909 947-0028**
1420 S Bon View Ave Ontario (91761) ***(P-4377)***

Western Supreme Inc .... C 213 627-3861
846 Produce Ct Los Angeles (90021) ***(P-1282)***

Western Telematic Inc .... E 949 586-9950
5 Sterling Irvine (92618) ***(P-5955)***

Western Towing, San Diego *Also Called: Sunbelt Towing Inc* ***(P-14720)***

Western Tube & Conduit Corp (HQ) .... **D 310 537-6300**
2001 E Dominguez St Long Beach (90810) ***(P-6435)***

Western Univ Hlth Sciences .... D 909 865-2565
360 E Mission Blvd Pomona (91766) ***(P-15511)***

Western Valve, Bakersfield *Also Called: Western Valve Inc* ***(P-5371)***

Western Valve Inc .... E 661 327-7660
201 Industrial St Bakersfield (93307) ***(P-5371)***

Westfall Technik, Walnut *Also Called: 10 Day Parts Inc* ***(P-4033)***

Westfall Technik, Riverside *Also Called: AMS Plastics Inc* ***(P-4048)***

Westfall Technik, Walnut *Also Called: AMS Plastics Inc* ***(P-4049)***

Westfall Technik, Walnut *Also Called: Fairway Injection Molds Inc* ***(P-5579)***

Westfield LLC (DH) .... **B 310 478-4456**
2049 Century Park E 41st Fl Los Angeles (90067) ***(P-12328)***

Westfield America Inc (HQ) .... **C 310 478-4456**
2049 Century Park E 41st Fl Los Angeles (90067) ***(P-12329)***

Westfield America Ltd Partnr .... B 310 277-3898
2049 Century Park E Ste 4100 Los Angeles (90067) ***(P-12330)***

Westgate Manufacturing, Vernon *Also Called: Westgate Mfg Inc* ***(P-7162)***

Westgate Mfg Inc .... D 323 826-9490
2462 E 28th St Vernon (90058) ***(P-7162)***

Westgroup Kona Kai LLC .... D 619 221-8000
1551 Shelter Island Dr San Diego (92106) ***(P-15187)***

Westgroup San Diego Associates .... D 858 274-4630
1404 Vacation Rd San Diego (92109) ***(P-13076)***

Westin, San Dimas *Also Called: Westin Automotive Products Inc* ***(P-2269)***

Westin, Anaheim *Also Called: Westin Anaheim Resort* ***(P-13077)***

Westin Anaheim Resort .... D 657 279-9786
1030 W Katella Ave Anaheim (92802) ***(P-13077)***

Westin Automotive Products Inc (PA) .... **E 626 960-6762**
320 W Covina Blvd San Dimas (91773) ***(P-2269)***

Westin Bonaventure Ht & Suites, Los Angeles *Also Called: Todays IV* ***(P-13054)***

Mergent email: customerrelations@mergent.com
1238
2025 Southern California
Business Directory and Buyers Guide
(P-0000) Products & Services Section entry number
(PA)=Parent Co (HQ)=Headquarters (DH)=Div Headquarters

Westin Long Beach Hotel, The, Long Beach *Also Called: Noble/Utah Long Beach LLC (P-12939)*

Westin San Diego, San Diego *Also Called: Diamondrock San Dego Tnant LLC (P-12810)*

Westlake Health Care Center .... B 805 494-1233
1101 Crenshaw Blvd Los Angeles (90019) *(P-15801)*

Westlake Oaks Healthcare LLC .... B 805 494-1233
250 Fairview Rd Thousand Oaks (91361) *(P-16629)*

Westlake Properties Inc ....C 818 889-0230
31943 Agoura Rd Westlake Village (91361) *(P-13078)*

Westlake Royal Stone LLC .... D 800 255-1727
3817 Ocean Ranch Blvd Oceanside (92056) *(P-4480)*

Westlake Village Inn, Westlake Village *Also Called: Westlake Properties Inc (P-13078)*

Westmed Ambulance Inc ....C 310 219-1779
2537 Old San Pasqual Rd Escondido (92027) *(P-8854)*

Westmed Ambulance Inc ....C 310 837-0102
2020 S Central Ave Compton (90220) *(P-8855)*

Westmed Ambulance Inc ....C 310 456-3830
3872 Las Flores Canyon Rd Malibu (90265) *(P-8856)*

WESTMED AMBULANCE, INC, Escondido *Also Called: Westmed Ambulance Inc (P-8854)*

WESTMED AMBULANCE, INC, Malibu *Also Called: Westmed Ambulance Inc (P-8856)*

Westmont Living Inc ....C 310 736-4118
11141 Washington Blvd Culver City (90232) *(P-17208)*

Westpac Labs Inc .... B 562 906-5227
10200 Pioneer Blvd # 500 Santa Fe Springs (90670) *(P-17930)*

Westpac Materials, Orange *Also Called: Western Pacific Distrg LLC (P-9954)*

Westrec Properties Inc .... B 818 907-0400
16633 Ventura Blvd Fl 6 Encino (91436) *(P-18080)*

Westridge Laboratories Inc .... E 714 259-9400
1671 E Saint Andrew Pl Santa Ana (92705) *(P-3697)*

Westrock Cp LLC .... D 951 273-7900
2577 Research Dr Corona (92882) *(P-3101)*

Westrock Rkt LLC .... D 818 729-0610
100 E Tujunga Ave Ste 102 Burbank (91502) *(P-2694)*

Westrock Rkt LLC .... E 714 978-2895
749 N Poplar St Orange (92868) *(P-2695)*

Westrux International Inc (PA) .... D **562 404-1020**
15555 Valley View Ave Santa Fe Springs (90670) *(P-11433)*

Westside Bldg San Diego LLC .... E 858 566-4343
11620 Sorrento Valley Rd San Diego (92121) *(P-9934)*

Westside Building Materials, San Diego *Also Called: Westside Bldg San Diego LLC (P-9934)*

Westside Jewish Cmnty Ctr Inc .... A 323 938-2531
5870 W Olympic Blvd Los Angeles (90036) *(P-17247)*

Westside Resources Inc .... E 800 944-3939
8850 Research Dr Irvine (92618) *(P-8361)*

Westside Security Patrol, Bakersfield *Also Called: M & S Security Services Inc (P-14316)*

Weststar Cinemas Inc .... D 818 779-0323
7876 Van Nuys Blvd Van Nuys (91402) *(P-14944)*

Weststar Cinemas Inc .... D 818 707-9987
29045 Agoura Rd Agoura Hills (91301) *(P-14945)*

Weststar Cinemas Inc ....C 805 379-8966
180 Promenade Way Ste R Westlake Village (01362) *(P-14946)*

Weststar Cinemas Inc ....C 805 658-6544
1440 Eastman Ave Ventura (93003) *(P-14947)*

Weststar Cinemas Inc ....C 661 723-0302
742 W Lancaster Blvd Lancaster (93534) *(P-14982)*

Westview Cmnty Arts Program, Anaheim *Also Called: Westview Services Inc (P-15802)*

Westview Services Inc ....D 714 956-4199
1701 S Euclid St Ste E Anaheim (92802) *(P-15802)*

Westview Services Inc ....D 714 635-2444
1655 S Euclid St Ste A Anaheim (92802) *(P-17074)*

Westview Services Inc ....D 714 418-2090
9421 Edinger Ave Westminster (92683) *(P-17075)*

Westview Services Inc ....D 626 962-0956
1515 W Cameron Ave Ste 310 West Covina (91790) *(P-17076)*

Westview Services Inc ....D 951 699-0047
27576 Commerce Center Dr Ste 103 Temecula (92590) *(P-17077)*

Westview Vocational Services, Anaheim *Also Called: Westview Services Inc (P-17074)*

Westview Vocational Services, Temecula *Also Called: Westview Services Inc (P-17077)*

Westwind Engineering Inc ....C 310 831-3454
625 Esplanade Unit 70 Redondo Beach (90277) *(P-17661)*

Westwind Equity Investors, Newport Beach *Also Called: Windjmmer Cpitl Invstors III L (P-12748)*

Westwood Building Materials Co .... E 310 643-9158
15708 Inglewood Ave Lawndale (90260) *(P-4466)*

Westwood Express Messenger Svc, Los Angeles *Also Called: Express Group Incorporated (P-9002)*

Westwood Insurance Agency LLC (HQ)...................... D 818 990-9715
6320 Canoga Ave Ste 500 Woodland Hills (91367) *(P-12271)*

Westwood Laboratories LLC (PA)............................ E 626 969-3305
710 S Ayon Ave Azusa (91702) *(P-3698)*

Westwood Laboratories LLC .... E 626 969-3305
766 S Ayon Ave Azusa (91702) *(P-3699)*

Westwood Marquis Hotel & Grdns, Los Angeles *Also Called: W Los Angeles (P-13069)*

Wet (PA)..C 818 769-6200
10847 Sherman Way Sun Valley (91352) *(P-14634)*

Wet Design, Sun Valley *Also Called: Wet (P-14634)*

Wetmore Cutting Tools, Chino *Also Called: Wetmore Tool and Engrg Co (P-5632)*

Wetmore Tool and Engrg Co .... D 909 364-1000
5091 G St Chino (91710) *(P-5632)*

Wetzel & Sons Mvg & Stor Inc .... D 818 890-0992
12400 Osborne St Pacoima (91331) *(P-8930)*

Wetzel Trucking, Pacoima *Also Called: Wetzel & Sons Mvg & Stor Inc (P-8930)*

Wetzels Pretzels LLC .... E 619 588-1074
525 Parkway Plz Unit 525 El Cajon (92020) *(P-11303)*

Wexler Corporation .... A 818 846-9381
1111 S Victory Blvd Burbank (91502) *(P-10297)*

Wexler Video, Burbank *Also Called: Wexler Corporation (P-10297)*

Weyerhaeuser Company .... D 714 523-3330
11100 Hope St Cypress (90630) *(P-9935)*

Wfb Archives Inc .... D
13500 Danielson St Poway (92064) *(P-6788)*

Wfcf Technology E2040-030, Santa Monica *Also Called: Wells Fargo Capital Finance Inc (P-14633)*

Wfg National Title Insur Co (PA).......................... D **818 476-4000**
700 N Brand Blvd Ste 1100 Glendale (91203) *(P-12563)*

Wha, Irvine *Also Called: William Hzmlhlch Archtects Inc (P-17696)*

Whalen Furniture Manufacturing, San Diego *Also Called: Whalen LLC (P-2438)*

Whalen LLC (DH)... E **619 423-9948**
1578 Air Wing Rd San Diego (92154) *(P-2438)*

Whaley, Kevin Enterprises, Santee *Also Called: Kevin Whaley (P-5407)*

Whaling Bar & Grill, La Jolla *Also Called: Lav Hotel Corp (P-12896)*

Whaling Packaging Co .... E 310 518-6021
21020 S Wilmington Ave Carson (90810) *(P-9355)*

Wham-O Inc .... D 818 963-4200
6301 Owensmouth Ave Ste 700 Woodland Hills (91367) *(P-10532)*

Wharf, The, Ventura *Also Called: Ventura Feed and Pet Sups Inc (P-11501)*

Whb Corporation .... A 213 624-1011
506 S Grand Ave Los Angeles (90071) *(P-13079)*

Wheel and Tire Club Inc .... E 800 901-6003
1909 S Susan St Ste D Santa Ana (92704) *(P-4529)*

Wheels Financial Group LLC ....C 866 422-7412
15400 Sherman Way Ste 300 Van Nuys (91406) *(P-11863)*

Whelan Security Co ....C 310 343-8628
400 Continental Blvd El Segundo (90245) *(P-14360)*

Wherewechat Online Svcs LLC .... D 302 566-1649
15442 Ventura Blvd Ste 201-275 Sherman Oaks (91403) *(P-13252)*

Whi Solutions Inc ....C 661 257-2120
28470 Avenue Stanford Ste 200 Valencia (91355) *(P-10039)*

Whiskey Girl ....C 619 236-1616
702 5th Ave San Diego (92101) *(P-18081)*

White & Case LLP .... D 213 620-7724
555 S Flower St Ste 2700 Los Angeles (90071) *(P-16794)*

White Cap 301, Santa Clarita *Also Called: White Cap Supply Group Inc (P-9963)*

White Cap Supply Group Inc .... A 661 294-7737
28255 Kelly Johnson Pkwy Santa Clarita (91355) *(P-9963)*

White Crane, Indio *Also Called: Whites Crane Service Inc (P-13445)*

White Digital Media Inc ....C 760 827-7800
3394 Carmel Mountain Rd Ste 250 San Diego (92121) *(P-11078)*

White Memorial Med Group Inc (PA)....................... D **323 987-1300**
1701 E Cesar E Chavez Ave Ste 510 Los Angeles (90033) *(P-15512)*

Employee Codes: A=Over 500 employees, B=251-500
C=101-250, D=51-100, E=20-50, F=10-19, G=1-9

2025 Southern California
Business Directory and Buyers Guide

© Mergent Inc. 1-800-342-5647
1239

White Memorial Medical Center .... A 323 260-5739
1720 E Cesar E Chavez Ave Los Angeles (90033) *(P-15513)*

White Memorial Medical Center (HQ)......................... A **323 268-5000**
1720 E Cesar E Chavez Ave Los Angeles (90033) *(P-16259)*

White Rabbit Partners Inc .... C 310 975-1450
9000 W Sunset Blvd Ste 1500 West Hollywood (90069) *(P-17209)*

White Sands of La Jolla Clinic, La Jolla *Also Called: Humangood Socal (P-17167)*

Whitefox Defense Tech Inc .... E 805 225-4506
854 Monterey St San Luis Obispo (93401) *(P-4662)*

Whites Crane Service Inc .... D 760 347-3401
45524 Towne St Indio (92201) *(P-13445)*

Whitewater Rock & Sup Co Inc .... E 760 325-2747
58645 Old Highway 60 Whitewater (92282) *(P-9955)*

Whiting Door Mfg Corp .... D 909 877-0120
301 S Milliken Ave Ontario (91761) *(P-14802)*

Whiting-Turner Contracting Co .... B 949 863-0800
250 Commerce Ste 150 Irvine (92602) *(P-605)*

Whitmor Plstic Wire Cable Corp (PA)..................... E **661 257-2400**
27737 Avenue Hopkins Santa Clarita (91355) *(P-5420)*

Whitmor Plstic Wire Cable Corp .... E 661 257-2400
28420 Avenue Stanford Valencia (91355) *(P-5421)*

Whitmor Wire and Cable, Santa Clarita *Also Called: Whitmor Plstic Wire Cable Corp (P-5420)*

Whitmor Wirenetics, Valencia *Also Called: Whitmor Plstic Wire Cable Corp (P-5421)*

Whittaker Corporation .... E 805 526-5700
1955 Surveyor Ave Fl 2 Simi Valley (93063) *(P-7592)*

Whittier Fertilizer Company .... D 562 699-3461
9441 Kruse Rd Pico Rivera (90660) *(P-3748)*

Whittier Hills Health Care Ctr, Whittier *Also Called: Ensign Group Inc (P-15640)*

Whittier Hospital Med Ctr Inc .... C 562 945-3561
9080 Colima Rd Whittier (90605) *(P-16260)*

WHITTIER HOSPITAL MEDICAL CENT, Monterey Park *Also Called: Ahmc Garfield Medical Ctr LP (P-15562)*

WHITTIER HOSPITAL MEDICAL CENT, El Monte *Also Called: Ahm Gemch Inc (P-15896)*

WHITTIER HOSPITAL MEDICAL CENT, Alhambra *Also Called: Alhambra Hospital Med Ctr LP (P-15904)*

WHITTIER HOSPITAL MEDICAL CENT, Monterey Park *Also Called: Monterey Park Hospital (P-16101)*

WHITTIER HOSPITAL MEDICAL CENT, Anaheim *Also Called: Ahmc Anheim Rgional Med Ctr LP (P-16281)*

Whittier Hospital Medical Ctr, San Gabriel *Also Called: Ahmc Healthcare Inc (P-15900)*

Whittier Service Center, Santa Fe Springs *Also Called: Southern California Edison Co (P-9632)*

Whittier Union High Schl Dist .... C 562 693-8826
7200 Greenleaf Ave Ste 170 Whittier (90602) *(P-16830)*

Who What Wear, West Hollywood *Also Called: Clique Brands Inc (P-2850)*

Wholesale Displays, Carlsbad *Also Called: San Diego Sign Company Inc (P-10461)*

Wholesale Shade, San Marcos *Also Called: Showdogs Inc (P-2608)*

Whova Inc .... C 858 227-0877
10182 Telesis Ct Ste 500 San Diego (92121) *(P-14118)*

Whv Resort Group Inc (HQ)................................... D 760 652-4913
300 Rancheros Dr Ste 310 San Marcos (92069) *(P-12550)*

Whv Resort Group Inc .... A 760 770-9755
34567 Cathedral Canyon Dr Cathedral City (92234) *(P-13080)*

Wic, El Monte *Also Called: Public Hlth Fndation Entps Inc (P-16610)*

Wic, Torrance *Also Called: Public Hlth Fndation Entps Inc (P-17362)*

Wick Communications Co .... E 760 379-3667
6404 Lake Isabella Blvd Lake Isabella (93240) *(P-2839)*

Widly Inc .... C 951 279-0900
785 E Harrison St Ste 100 Corona (92879) *(P-2496)*

Wiedenbach-Brown, Fullerton *Also Called: US Electrical Services Inc (P-10211)*

Wiens Cellars LLC .... E 951 694-9892
35055 Via Del Ponte Temecula (92592) *(P-1593)*

Wiggins Lift Co Inc .... D 805 485-7821
2571 Cortez St Oxnard (93030) *(P-10422)*

Wilbur Curtis Co Inc .... B 800 421-6150
6913 W Acco St Montebello (90640) *(P-12620)*

Wilcox Machine Co .... D 562 927-5353
7180 Scout Ave Bell Gardens (90201) *(P-6275)*

Wild Lizard, Los Angeles *Also Called: Bb Co Inc (P-2081)*

Wildcat Discovery Tech Inc .... D 858 550-1980
6255 Ferris Sq Ste A San Diego (92121) *(P-17840)*

Wilden Pump, Grand Terrace *Also Called: Psg California LLC (P-5741)*

Wildomar Medical Offices, Wildomar *Also Called: Kaiser Foundation Hospitals (P-16047)*

Will-Mann Inc .... E 714 870-0350
225 E Santa Fe Ave Fullerton (92832) *(P-5057)*

Willard Marine Inc .... D 714 666-2150
4602 North Ave Oceanside (92056) *(P-7626)*

Willdan, Anaheim *Also Called: Willdan Group Inc (P-17662)*

Willdan Group Inc (PA).. C **800 424-9144**
2401 E Katella Ave Ste 300 Anaheim (92806) *(P-17662)*

William Hzmlhlch Archtects Inc .... D 949 250-0607
200 Commerce Irvine (92602) *(P-17696)*

William Lyon Homes (HQ)...................................... D **949 833-3600**
4695 Macarthur Ct Ste 800 Newport Beach (92660) *(P-440)*

William Morris Consulting, Beverly Hills *Also Called: William Mrris Endvor Entrmt LL (P-14984)*

William Mrris Endvor Entrmt FN (DH)..................... C **310 285-9000**
9601 Wilshire Blvd Fl 3 Beverly Hills (90210) *(P-14983)*

William Mrris Endvor Entrmt LL (DH)...................... C **212 586-5100**
9601 Wilshire Blvd Beverly Hills (90210) *(P-13581)*

William Mrris Endvor Entrmt LL .... B 310 285-9000
9601 Wilshire Blvd Fl 3 Beverly Hills (90210) *(P-14984)*

William Oneil & Co Inc (PA)................................... D **310 448-6800**
12655 Beatrice St Los Angeles (90066) *(P-12010)*

Williams Aerospace & Mfg Inc (DH)....................... E **805 586-8699**
999 Avenida Acaso Camarillo (93012) *(P-10507)*

Williams Aerospace and Mfg, Chula Vista *Also Called: Allclear Aerospace & Def Inc (P-7427)*

Williams Comfort Products, Colton *Also Called: Williams Furnace Co (P-5993)*

Williams Furnace Co (DH)....................................... C **562 450-3602**
250 W Laurel St Colton (92324) *(P-5993)*

Willis Insurance Services Cal, Irvine *Also Called: Willis North America Inc (P-18242)*

Willis Machine Inc .... E 805 604-4500
11000 Alto Dr Oak View (93022) *(P-6276)*

Willis North America Inc .... C 909 476-3300
18101 Von Karman Ave Ste 600 Irvine (92612) *(P-18242)*

Willmark Cmmnties Univ Vlg Inc (PA)..................... D **858 271-0582**
9948 Hibert St Ste 210 San Diego (92131) *(P-12372)*

Willow, Vernon *Also Called: Complete Clothing Company (P-2064)*

Willow Laboratories Inc .... D 949 679-6100
15750 Alton Pkwy Irvine (92618) *(P-17897)*

Willow Springs Healthcare Ctr, Palm Desert *Also Called: Pacs Group Inc (P-15742)*

Wilmar, Vernon *Also Called: Jobbers Meat Packing Co LLC (P-1244)*

Wilorco, Carson *Also Called: Strike Technology Inc (P-7055)*

Wilsey Foods Inc .... A 714 257-3700
40 Pointe Dr Brea (92821) *(P-1529)*

Wilshire Advisors LLC (PA)..................................... C **310 451-3051**
1299 Ocean Ave Ste 600 Santa Monica (90401) *(P-18243)*

Wilshire Bancorp Inc .... A 213 387-3200
3200 Wilshire Blvd Los Angeles (90010) *(P-11780)*

Wilshire Bank .... B 213 427-1000
3200 Wilshire Blvd Ste 1400 Los Angeles (90010) *(P-11781)*

Wilshire Boulevard Temple .... D 310 457-7861
11495 Pacific Coast Hwy Malibu (90265) *(P-13106)*

Wilshire Boulevard Temple .... D 323 261-6135
4334 Whittier Blvd Los Angeles (90023) *(P-17422)*

Wilshire Country Club .... D 323 934-6050
301 N Rossmore Ave Los Angeles (90004) *(P-15188)*

Wilshire Kingsley Inc .... D 213 382-6677
3575 Wilshire Blvd Los Angeles (90010) *(P-12331)*

Wilshire Precision Pdts Inc .... E 818 765-4571
7353 Hinds Ave North Hollywood (91605) *(P-6277)*

Wilshire State Bank, Los Angeles *Also Called: Wilshire Bank (P-11781)*

Wilson Creek Winery, Temecula *Also Called: Wilson Creek Wnery Vnyards Inc (P-1594)*

Wilson Creek Wnery Vnyards Inc .... C 951 699-9463
35960 Rancho California Rd Temecula (92591) *(P-1594)*

Wilsonart LLC .... E 562 921-7426
13911 Gannet St Santa Fe Springs (90670) *(P-9129)*

Wilsons Art Studio Inc .... D 714 870-7030
501 S Acacia Ave Fullerton (92831) *(P-3189)*

Wilwood Engineering (PA)....................................... C **805 388-1188**
4700 Calle Bolero Camarillo (93012) *(P-7309)*

Mergent email: customerrelations@mergent.com
1240

2025 Southern California
Business Directory and Buyers Guide

(P-0000) Products & Services Section entry number
(PA)=Parent Co (HQ)=Headquarters (DH)=Div Headquarters

Win Soon Inc .... D 323 564-5070
4569 Firestone Blvd South Gate (90280) *(P-1336)*

Win Time Ltd (PA).. C **858 695-2300**
9335 Kearny Mesa Rd San Diego (92126) *(P-13081)*

Win-Dor Inc (PA)... C **714 576-2030**
450 Delta Ave Brea (92821) *(P-1067)*

Winc Inc .... C 855 282-5829
927 S Santa Fe Ave Los Angeles (90021) *(P-1595)*

Winchester Interconnect EC LLC .... D 714 230-6122
12691 Monarch St Garden Grove (92841) *(P-10298)*

Winchster Intrcnnect CM CA Inc .... C 800 848-4257
1810 Diamond St San Marcos (92078) *(P-4640)*

Winchster Intrcnnect Micro LLC .... C 714 637-7099
1872 N Case St Orange (92865) *(P-6961)*

Windermere RE Coachella Vly, Indian Wells *Also Called: Bennion Deville Fine Homes Inc (P-12387)*

Windes Inc (PA)... D 562 435-1191
3780 Kilroy Airport Way Ste 600 Long Beach (90806) *(P-17759)*

Windjmmer Capitl Investors III, Santa Ana *Also Called: Jwc Environmental Inc (P-10379)*

Windjmmer Cpitl Invstors III L .... A 949 706-9989
610 Newport Center Dr Ste 1100 Newport Beach (92660) *(P-12748)*

Windjmmer Cpitl Invstors IV LP .... B 919 706-9989
610 Newport Center Dr Ste 1100 Newport Beach (92660) *(P-12749)*

Window Enterprises Inc .... E 951 943-4894
430 Nevada St Redlands (92373) *(P-4905)*

Windsor Anaheim Healthcare (PA)................. C **714 826-8950**
3415 W Ball Rd Anaheim (92804) *(P-15803)*

Windsor Anaheim Healthcare .... D 310 675-3304
13922 Cerise Ave Hawthorne (90250) *(P-15804)*

Windsor Capital Group Inc .... C 951 676-5656
29345 Rancho California Rd Temecula (92591) *(P-13082)*

Windsor Capital Group Inc .... C 951 276-1200
1510 University Ave Riverside (92507) *(P-13083)*

Windsor Capital Group Inc .... D 805 986-5353
350 E Port Hueneme Rd Port Hueneme (93041) *(P-13084)*

Windsor Capital Group Inc .... C 714 990-5000
900 E Birch St Brea (92821) *(P-13085)*

Windsor Capital Group Inc .... D 310 566-1100
2800 28th St Ste 385 Santa Monica (90405) *(P-13086)*

Windsor Capital Group Inc .... D 310 566-1100
2800 28th St Ste 385 Santa Monica (90405) *(P-13087)*

Windsor Capital Group Inc .... D 209 577-3825
2800 28th St Ste 385 Santa Monica (90405) *(P-13088)*

Windsor Capital Group Inc .... D 310 566-1100
2800 28th St Ste 385 Santa Monica (90405) *(P-13089)*

Windsor Capital Group Inc .... D 310 566-1100
2800 28th St Ste 385 Santa Monica (90405) *(P-13090)*

Windsor Cypress Garden, Riverside *Also Called: Windsor Cypress Grdns Hlthcare (P-15891)*

Windsor Cypress Grdns Hlthcare .... A 951 688-3643
9025 Colorado Ave Riverside (92503) *(P-15891)*

Windsor Foods, Ontario *Also Called: Ajinomoto Foods North Amer Inc (P-1384)*

Windsor Foods, Ontario *Also Called: Windsor Quality Food Company Ltd (P-1404)*

Windsor Gardens of Long Beach, Long Beach *Also Called: Pacs Group Inc (P-15736)*

Windsor Grdns Cnvlescent Ctr A, Anaheim *Also Called: Windsor Anaheim Healthcare (P-15803)*

Windsor Manor, Glendale *Also Called: Humangood Socal (P-12346)*

Windsor Palms Care Center of Artesia, Artesia *Also Called: Windsor Twin Plms Hlthcare Ctr (P-15805)*

Windsor Quality Food Company Ltd .... A 713 843-5200
4200 Concours Ste 100 Ontario (91764) *(P-1404)*

Windsor Twin Plms Hlthcare Ctr .... C 562 865-0271
11900 Artesia Blvd Artesia (90701) *(P-15805)*

Windward Life Care, San Diego *Also Called: Buena Vista MGT Svcs LLC (P-16373)*

Wine Dept, Los Angeles *Also Called: Youngs Market Company LLC (P-11065)*

Winfield Locks Inc .... A 949 722-5400
1721 Whittier Ave Costa Mesa (92627) *(P-4796)*

Wing Hing, Los Angeles *Also Called: Wing Hing Foods LLC (P-1347)*

Wing Hing Foods LLC .... D 323 232-8899
1659 E 23rd St Los Angeles (90011) *(P-1347)*

Wing Hing Noodle Company, Ontario *Also Called: Passport Food Group LLC (P-1833)*

Wingert Grbing Brbker Jstkie L .... D 619 232-8151
1230 Columbia St Ste 400 San Diego (92101) *(P-16795)*

Winners Only Inc .... C 760 599-0300
1365 Park Center Dr Vista (92081) *(P-9886)*

Winonics Inc .... C 714 626-3755
1257 S State College Blvd Fullerton (92831) *(P-6789)*

Wintergreen Apts, San Diego *Also Called: Hanken Cono Assad & Co Inc (P-12463)*

Winterthur, Los Angeles *Also Called: Winterthur U S Holdings Inc (P-12272)*

Winterthur U S Holdings Inc .... C 213 228-0281
888 S Figueroa St Ste 570 Los Angeles (90017) *(P-12272)*

Winther Technologies Inc (PA)....................... E **310 618-8437**
560 Alaska Ave Torrance (90503) *(P-5650)*

Wintriss Engineering Corp .... E 858 550-7300
9010 Kenamar Dr Ste 101 San Diego (92121) *(P-8028)*

Wira Co, El Monte *Also Called: Jans Enterprises Corporation (P-10949)*

Wire Cut Company Inc .... E 714 994-1170
6750 Caballero Blvd Buena Park (90620) *(P-6278)*

Wire Technology Corporation .... E 310 635-6935
9527 Laurel St Los Angeles (90002) *(P-4641)*

Wireless Technology Inc .... E 805 339-9696
2064 Eastman Ave Ste 113 Ventura (93003) *(P-6570)*

Wirenetics Co, Valencia *Also Called: Circle W Enterprises Inc (P-5403)*

Wiretech Inc (PA).. D **323 722-4933**
6440 Canning St Commerce (90040) *(P-4546)*

Wirtz Quality Installations .... D 858 569-3816
7932 Armour St San Diego (92111) *(P-992)*

Wis, San Diego *Also Called: Washington Inventory Service (P-14631)*

Wise & Healthy Aging .... D 818 876-1402
23388 Mulholland Dr Stop 60 Woodland Hills (91364) *(P-17042)*

Wiser Foods Inc .... D 310 895-0888
5405 E Village Rd Unit 8219 Long Beach (90808) *(P-1657)*

Wismettac Asian Foods Inc (HQ).................... C **562 802-1900**
13409 Orden Dr Santa Fe Springs (90670) *(P-10817)*

Wismettac Fresh Fish, Santa Fe Springs *Also Called: Wismettac Asian Foods Inc (P-10817)*

Withers Bergman, San Diego *Also Called: Withers Bergman LLP (P-16796)*

Withers Bergman LLP .... B 203 974-0412
12830 El Camino Real Ste 350 San Diego (92130) *(P-16796)*

Wj Newport LLC .... C 949 476-2001
4500 Macarthur Blvd Newport Beach (92660) *(P-13091)*

WJB Bearings Inc .... E 909 598-6238
535 Brea Canyon Rd City Of Industry (91789) *(P-5164)*

WKS Restaurant Corporation (PA).................. C **562 425-1402**
5856 Corporate Ave Ste 200 Cypress (90630) *(P-11610)*

Wlcac, Los Angeles *Also Called: Watts Labor Community Action (P-17039)*

Wm Bolthouse Farms Inc (HQ)....................... A **800 467-4683**
7200 E Brundage Ln Bakersfield (93307) *(P-1382)*

WM TECHNOLOGY, Irvine *Also Called: Wm Technology Inc (P-14065)*

Wm Technology Inc (PA)................................ E **646 699-3750**
41 Discovery Irvine (92618) *(P-14065)*

Wmbe Payrolling Inc .... C 858 810-3000
3545 Aero Ct San Diego (02123) *(P-13582)*

Wme, Beverly Hills *Also Called: William Mrris Endvor Entrmt LL (P-13581)*

Wme Bi LLC .... D 877 592-2472
17075 Camino San Diego (92127) *(P-14060)*

Wme Img LLC (DH).. B **212 586-5100**
9601 Wilshire Blvd Beverly Hills (90210) *(P-15037)*

Wmk Office San Diego LLC (PA)..................... D **858 569-4700**
4780 Eastgate Mall Ste 100 San Diego (92121) *(P-9887)*

Wna City of Industry, City Of Industry *Also Called: Waddington North America Inc (P-4272)*

Wolf & Raven LLC .... D 800 431-6471
206 W 4th St Ste 439 Santa Ana (92701) *(P-18082)*

Wolfpack Inc .... E 760 736-4500
2440 Grand Ave Ste B Vista (92081) *(P-8651)*

Wolfpack Sign Group, Vista *Also Called: Wolfpack Inc (P-8651)*

Womble Bond Dickinson (us) LLP .... C 310 207-3800
400 Spectrum Center Dr Irvine (92618) *(P-16797)*

Women's Cancer Care, Cerritos *Also Called: Oncology Inst CA A Prof Corp (P-15412)*

Wonderful Agency .... A 310 966-8600
11444 W Olympic Blvd Ste 210 Los Angeles (90064) *(P-13253)*

Wonderful Citrus Cooperative .... A 661 720-2400
4050 7th Standard Rd Shafter (93263) *(P-17291)*

Employee Codes: A=Over 500 employees, B=251-500
C=101-250, D=51-100, E=20-50, F=10-19, G=1-9

2025 Southern California
Business Directory and Buyers Guide

© Mergent Inc. 1-800-342-5647

1241

Wonderful Citrus Packing LLC (HQ)............................... B 661 720-2400
  1901 S Lexington St Delano (93215) *(P-123)*

Wonderful Company LLC .... B 661 720-2400
  1901 S Lexington St Delano (93215) *(P-45)*

Wonderful Company LLC .... A 559 781-7438
  5001 California Ave Bakersfield (93309) *(P-124)*

Wonderful Company LLC .... A 661 399-4456
  6801 E Lerdo Hwy Shafter (93263) *(P-125)*

Wonderful Company LLC .... B 661 720-2609
  11444 W Olympic Blvd Ste 210 Los Angeles (90064) *(P-126)*

Wonderful Orchards LLC .... B 661 797-6400
  13646 Highway 33 Lost Hills (93249) *(P-40)*

Wonderful Orchards LLC .... C 661 797-2509
  21707 Lerdo Hwy Mc Kittrick (93251) *(P-41)*

Wonderful Orchards LLC (HQ)....................................... C 661 399-4456
  6801 E Lerdo Hwy Shafter (93263) *(P-42)*

Wonderful Pstchios Almonds LLC (HQ)......................... E 310 966-5700
  11444 W Olympic Blvd Fl 10 Los Angeles (90064) *(P-1519)*

Wonderfulpistachiosandalmonds, Lost Hills *Also Called: Wonderful Orchards LLC (P-40)*

Wonderware, Lake Forest *Also Called: Aveva Software LLC (P-14072)*

Wonderware Corporation (DH)....................................... B 949 727-3200
  26561 Rancho Pkwy S Lake Forest (92630) *(P-14067)*

Wondros, Los Angeles *Also Called: Hungry Heart Media Inc (P-14833)*

Wood Candle Wick Tech Inc .... E 310 488-5885
  9750 Irvine Blvd Ste 106 Irvine (92618) *(P-8742)*

Wood Gutmann Bogart Insur Brkg .... D 714 505-7000
  15901 Red Hill Ave Ste 100 Tustin (92780) *(P-12273)*

Wood Gutmann Bogart Insur Brks .... C 714 505-7000
  15901 Red Hill Ave Ste 100 Tustin (92780) *(P-12274)*

Woodbine Lgacy/Playa Owner LLC .... D 678 292-4962
  6161 W Centinela Ave Culver City (90230) *(P-13092)*

Woodbridge Glass Inc .... C 714 838-4444
  3441 W Macarthur Blvd Santa Ana (92704) *(P-1169)*

Woodman Realty Inc .... C 909 425-5324
  26030 Base Line St Apt 97 San Bernardino (92410) *(P-12551)*

Woodridge Press Inc .... E 949 475-1900
  2485 Da Vinci Irvine (92614) *(P-3102)*

Woodruff Convalescent Center, Huntington Beach *Also Called: Estrella Inc (P-15649)*

Woods Maintenance Services Inc .... C 818 764-2515
  7250 Coldwater Canyon Ave North Hollywood (91605) *(P-1236)*

Woodward Duarte, Duarte *Also Called: Woodward Hrt Inc (P-7593)*

Woodward Hrt Inc (HQ)... A 661 294-6000
  25200 Rye Canyon Rd Santa Clarita (91355) *(P-6365)*

Woodward Hrt Inc .... C 626 359-9211
  1700 Business Center Dr Duarte (91010) *(P-7593)*

Woodwork Pioneers Corp .... E 714 991-1017
  1757 S Claudina Way Anaheim (92805) *(P-2335)*

Woongjin Coway USA Inc., Los Angeles *Also Called: Coway Usa Inc (P-11680)*

Word & Brown Insurance Administrators Inc (PA)....... B 714 835-5006
  721 S Parker St Ste 300 Orange (92868) *(P-12275)*

Work Force Services Inc .... C 661 327-5019
  3612 Coffee Rd Ste B Bakersfield (93308) *(P-13635)*

Work Force Staffing, Bakersfield *Also Called: Work Force Services Inc (P-13635)*

Workcare Inc .... C 714 978-7488
  300 S Harbor Blvd Ste 600 Anaheim (92805) *(P-18271)*

Workforce Management Group Inc .... A 909 718-8915
  800 N Haven Ave Ste 330 Ontario (91764) *(P-13636)*

Working Nurse, Los Angeles *Also Called: Recruitment Services Inc (P-2874)*

Working With Autism Inc .... D 818 501-4240
  14724 Ventura Blvd Ste 1110 Sherman Oaks (91403) *(P-16522)*

Workrite Uniform Company Inc (DH)............................. B 805 483-0175
  1701 Lombard St Ste 200 Oxnard (93030) *(P-13142)*

Workway Inc .... C 949 553-8700
  19742 Macarthur Blvd Ste 235 Irvine (92612) *(P-13583)*

Workway Inc .... C 619 278-0012
  3111 Camino Del Rio N Ste 400 San Diego (92108) *(P-13584)*

World Class Cheerleading Inc .... E 877 923-2645
  20212 Hart St Winnetka (91306) *(P-8554)*

World Class Distribution Inc .... D 909 574-4140
  800 S Shamrock Ave Monrovia (91016) *(P-9130)*

World Gym Fitness Centers, Los Angeles *Also Called: World Gym International LLC (P-15069)*

World Gym International LLC .... D 310 557-8804
  1901 Avenue Of The Stars Ste 1100 Los Angeles (90067) *(P-15069)*

World History Group LLC .... E 703 779-8322
  9720 Wilshire Blvd Beverly Hills (90212) *(P-2879)*

World Journal La LLC (HQ).. C 323 268-4982
  1588 Corporate Center Dr Monterey Park (91754) *(P-2840)*

World Oil Corp .... C 562 928-0100
  9302 Garfield Ave South Gate (90280) *(P-283)*

World Oil Environmental Svcs, Compton *Also Called: Asbury Environmental Services (P-8895)*

World Peas Brand, Los Angeles *Also Called: Snack It Forward LLC (P-1728)*

World Private Security Inc .... C 818 894-1800
  16921 Parthenia St Ste 201 Northridge (91343) *(P-14369)*

WORLD SERVICE OFFICE, Chatsworth *Also Called: Narcotics Annonymous Wrld Svcs I (P-2893)*

World Svc Wst/La Inflght Svc L .... C 310 538-7000
  1812 W 135th St Gardena (90249) *(P-9213)*

World Trade Printing Company, Garden Grove *Also Called: Wtpc Inc (P-3104)*

World Variety Produce Inc .... B 800 588-0151
  5325 S Soto St Vernon (90058) *(P-10926)*

World Vision International (PA)...................................... C 626 303-8811
  800 W Chestnut Ave Monrovia (91016) *(P-17475)*

World Water Inc .... E 562 940-1964
  9848 Everest St Downey (90242) *(P-7884)*

World Wind & Solar, Paso Robles *Also Called: Worldwind Services LLC (P-978)*

Worldwide, Monrovia *Also Called: Worldwide Energy and Mfg USA (P-6915)*

Worldwide Aeros Corp .... D 818 344-3999
  3971 Fredonia Dr Los Angeles (90068) *(P-7375)*

Worldwide Corporate Housing LP .... B 972 392-4747
  1 World Trade Ctr Ste 2400 Long Beach (90831) *(P-13098)*

Worldwide Energy and Mfg USA (PA)........................... D 650 692-7788
  1800 S Myrtle Ave Monrovia (91016) *(P-6915)*

Worldwide Envmtl Pdts Inc (PA).................................. D 714 990-2700
  1100 Beacon St Brea (92821) *(P-7885)*

Worldwide Holdings Inc (PA).. D 213 236-4500
  725 S Figueroa St Ste 1900 Los Angeles (90017) *(P-12276)*

Worldwide Produce, Los Angeles *Also Called: Green Farms Inc (P-10905)*

Worldwide Security Assoc Inc (HQ).............................. B 310 743-3000
  10311 S La Cienega Blvd Los Angeles (90045) *(P-14370)*

Worldwide Specialties Inc .... C 323 587-2200
  2420 Modoc St Los Angeles (90021) *(P-1866)*

Worldwind Services LLC .... A 661 822-4877
  1222 Vine St Ste 301 Paso Robles (93446) *(P-978)*

Worthington Cylinder Corp .... C 909 594-7777
  336 Enterprise Pl Pomona (91768) *(P-4935)*

Wovexx Holdings Inc (DH).. D 310 424-2080
  10381 Jefferson Blvd Culver City (90232) *(P-9572)*

Wpmg Inc .... E 949 442-1601
  1961 Mcgaw Ave Irvine (92614) *(P-6481)*

Wpromote LLC (PA)... C 310 421-4844
  101 Continental Blvd Fl 1 El Segundo (90245) *(P-18244)*

Wright Business Graphics Calif, Chino *Also Called: Wright Business Graphics LLC (P-3196)*

Wright Business Graphics LLC .... E 909 614-6700
  13602 12th St Ste A Chino (91710) *(P-3196)*

Wright Ford Young & Co .... D 949 910-2727
  16140 Sand Canyon Ave Irvine (92618) *(P-17760)*

Writers Guild America West Inc .... C 323 951-4000
  7000 W 3rd St Los Angeles (90048) *(P-17319)*

Wrkco Inc .... E 310 532-8988
  1025 W 190th St Ste 450 Gardena (90248) *(P-2647)*

Wrkco Inc .... E 770 448-2193
  14103 Borate St Santa Fe Springs (90670) *(P-2648)*

Ws Mmv Hotel LLC .... D 619 692-3800
  8757 Rio San Diego Dr San Diego (92108) *(P-13093)*

Ws Packaging-Blake Printery .... E 805 543-6844
  2224 Beebee St San Luis Obispo (93401) *(P-3103)*

Wsa Group Inc .... A 310 743-3000
  19208 S Vermont Ave # 200 Gardena (90248) *(P-14371)*

Wsm Investments LLC .... C 818 332-4600
  3990b Heritage Oak Ct Simi Valley (93063) *(P-12681)*

Wsp USA Inc .... D 714 973-4880
  15231 Laguna Canyon Rd Irvine (92618) *(P-17663)*

Wsw Corp (PA) .... E 818 989-5008
16000 Strathern St Van Nuys (91406) *(P-7310)*

Wti, Ventura *Also Called: Wireless Technology Inc (P-6570)*

Wtpc Inc .... E 714 903-2500
12082 Western Ave Garden Grove (92841) *(P-3104)*

Wun, Goleta *Also Called: Yardi Kube Inc (P-14068)*

Wurms Janitorial Service Inc .... D 951 582-0003
601 S Milliken Ave Ontario (91761) *(P-13429)*

Wurth Louis and Company (DH) .... D 714 529-1771
895 Columbia St Brea (92821) *(P-10314)*

WV Communications Inc .... E 805 376-1820
1125 Business Center Cir Ste A Newbury Park (91320) *(P-6672)*

Ww San Diego Harbor Island LLC .... C 619 291-6700
1960 Harbor Island Dr San Diego (92101) *(P-13094)*

Wyatt Precision Machine Inc .... E 562 634-0524
3301 E 59th St Long Beach (90805) *(P-5116)*

Wyatt Technology, Goleta *Also Called: Wyatt Technology LLC (P-7991)*

Wyatt Technology LLC (HQ) .... C 805 681-9009
6330 Hollister Ave Goleta (93117) *(P-7991)*

Wymore Inc .... E 760 352-2045
697 S Dogwood Rd El Centro (92243) *(P-14748)*

Wyndcrest Dd Florida, Los Angeles *Also Called: Digital Domain Media Group Inc (P-13328)*

Wyndham Anaheim Garden Grove, Garden Grove *Also Called: Ohi Resort Hotels LLC (P-12948)*

Wyndham Collection LLC .... E 888 522-8476
1175 Aviation Pl San Fernando (91340) *(P-2368)*

Wyndham Residence, Arroyo Grande *Also Called: Compass Health Inc (P-17134)*

Wyrefab Inc .... E 310 523-2147
15711 S Broadway Gardena (90248) *(P-5422)*

Wyvern Technologies .... E 714 966-0710
1205 E Warner Ave Santa Ana (92705) *(P-7070)*

X Hyper .... E 530 673-7099
17600 Newhope St Fountain Valley (92708) *(P-6571)*

X-Chair LLC .... E 844 492-4247
6415 Katella Ave Ste 200 Cypress (90630) *(P-2534)*

X1 Discovery Inc .... E 877 999-1347
251 S Lake Ave Ste 800 Pasadena (91101) *(P-13865)*

X3 Engineering & Construction, Escondido *Also Called: X3 Management Services Inc (P-979)*

X3 Management Services Inc .... D 760 597-9336
325 Market Pl Escondido (92029) *(P-979)*

XCEL Mechanical Systems Inc .... C 310 660-0090
1710 W 130th St Gardena (90249) *(P-855)*

Xcom Labs Inc .... D 858 987-9266
9450 Carroll Park Dr San Diego (92121) *(P-17931)*

Xcor, Mojave *Also Called: Xcor Aerospace Inc (P-7662)*

Xcor Aerospace Inc .... D 661 824-4714
1314 Flight Line Mojave (93501) *(P-7662)*

Xcvi LLC (PA) .... D 213 749-2661
15236 Burbank Blvd Sherman Oaks (91411) *(P-1890)*

Xdi Radiology, Los Angeles *Also Called: Cybor Medical Imaging Inc (P-8331)*

XEL Group, Laguna Hills *Also Called: XEL USA Inc (P-6916)*

XEL USA Inc .... E 949 425-8686
25231 Paseo De Alicia Laguna Hills (92653) *(P-6916)*

Xencor, Pasadena *Also Called: Xencor Inc (P-3524)*

Xencor Inc .... B 626 305-5900
465 N Halstead St Ste 200 Pasadena (91107) *(P-3524)*

Xerox Education Services LLC (DH) .... D 310 830-9847
2277 E 220th St Long Beach (90810) *(P-9982)*

Xerxes Corporation .... C 714 630-0012
1210 N Tustin Ave Anaheim (92807) *(P-3302)*

Xgrass Turf Direct, Anaheim *Also Called: Leonards Carpet Service Inc (P-2570)*

Xi Enterprise Inc .... D 661 266-3200
2140 E Palmdale Blvd Palmdale (93550) *(P-15070)*

Xirgo Technologies LLC .... D 805 319-4079
188 Camino Ruiz Fl 2 Camarillo (93012) *(P-7163)*

Xirrus Inc .... E 805 262-1600
2545 W Hillcrest Dr Ste 220 Newbury Park (91320) *(P-7886)*

Xitron Technologies, Poway *Also Called: Vitrek LLC (P-7935)*

Xl Staffing Inc .... C 619 579-0442
826 Jackman St El Cajon (92020) *(P-13585)*

XO BABYPLUTO FADED PARADISE XO .... E 650 750-5025
3442 E 8th St Los Angeles (90023) *(P-14635)*

Xos, Los Angeles *Also Called: Xos Inc (P-7311)*

Xos Inc (PA) .... E 818 316-1890
3550 Tyburn St Ste 100 Los Angeles (90065) *(P-7311)*

Xos Fleet Inc (HQ) .... E 818 316-1890
3550 Tyburn St Ste 100 Los Angeles (90065) *(P-7196)*

Xos Trucks, Los Angeles *Also Called: Xos Fleet Inc (P-7196)*

Xp Power Inc .... D 714 712-2642
1590 S Sinclair St Anaheim (92806) *(P-7071)*

Xpdel Inc .... B 805 267-1214
13012 Molette St Santa Fe Springs (90670) *(P-9131)*

Xpo, Torrance *Also Called: Lomita Logistics LLC (P-13303)*

Xpo Cartage Inc .... D 800 837-7584
5800 Sheila St Commerce (90040) *(P-8931)*

Xpo Logistics Freight Inc .... D 714 282-7717
2102 N Batavia St Orange (92865) *(P-8984)*

Xpo Logistics Freight Inc .... C 951 685-1244
13364 Marlay Ave Fontana (92337) *(P-8985)*

Xpo Logistics Freight Inc .... C 213 744-0664
1955 E Washington Blvd Los Angeles (90021) *(P-8986)*

Xpo Logistics Freight Inc .... D 562 946-8331
12903 Lakeland Rd Santa Fe Springs (90670) *(P-8987)*

Xpo Logistics Supply Chain Inc .... C 909 390-9799
5200b E Airport Dr Ontario (91761) *(P-9351)*

Xponential Fitness Inc (PA) .... B 949 346-3000
17877 Von Karman Ave Ste 100 Irvine (92614) *(P-15071)*

Xpower Manufacture Inc .... E 626 285-3301
668 S 6th Ave City Of Industry (91746) *(P-7843)*

Xr LLC .... E 714 847-9292
15251 Pipeline Ln Huntington Beach (92649) *(P-8320)*

Xs Scuba (PA) .... E 714 424-0434
4040 W Chandler Ave Santa Ana (92704) *(P-8555)*

Xse Group Inc .... C 888 272-8340
92 Argonaut Ste 235 Aliso Viejo (92656) *(P-10587)*

Xx Artists LLC .... D 503 871-5298
1214 Abbot Kinney Blvd Venice (90291) *(P-13338)*

Xylem Water Solutions USA Inc .... D 949 474-1679
17942 Cowan Irvine (92614) *(P-5746)*

Xylem Water Systems (california) Inc .... E 619 575-7466
830 Bay Blvd Ste 101 Chula Vista (91911) *(P-5747)*

Y I C, Carson *Also Called: Yun Industrial Co Ltd (P-6790)*

Y K K U S A, Anaheim *Also Called: YKK (usa) Inc (P-8582)*

Y M C A, Santee *Also Called: YMCA of San Diego County (P-17399)*

Y M C A Childcare Resource Ser, Oceanside *Also Called: YMCA of San Diego County (P-17381)*

Y, The, San Diego *Also Called: YMCA of San Diego County (P-17401)*

Y&R-Wcj Spectrum, Irvine *Also Called: Young & Rubicam LLC (P-13254)*

Yaamava Rsort Csino At San Mnu, Highland *Also Called: San Mnuel Band Mission Indians (P-11843)*

Yaamava Rsort Csino At San Mnu, Highland *Also Called: San Manuel Entertainment Auth (P-15221)*

Yaesu Usa Inc .... E 714 827-7600
6125 Phyllis Dr Cypress (90630) *(P-6673)*

Yale/Chase Equipment and Services Inc .... C 562 463-8000
2615 Pellissier Pl City Of Industry (90601) *(P-10423)*

Yamagata America Inc .... C 858 751-1010
3760 Convoy St Ste 219 San Diego (92111) *(P-2957)*

Yamaha Corporation of America (HQ) .... B 714 522-9011
6600 Orangethorpe Ave Buena Park (90620) *(P-10575)*

Yamaha Guitar Group Inc .... E 818 575-3900
26664 Agoura Rd Calabasas (91302) *(P-8474)*

Yamaha Guitar Group Inc (HQ) .... C 818 575-3600
26580 Agoura Rd Calabasas (91302) *(P-8475)*

Yamaha Motor Corporation USA (HQ) .... B 714 761-7300
6555 Katella Ave Cypress (90630) *(P-11485)*

Yamaha Music Corporation U S A, Buena Park *Also Called: Yamaha Corporation of America (P-10575)*

Yamasa Enterprises .... E 213 626-2211
515 Stanford Ave Los Angeles (90013) *(P-1699)*

Yamasa Fish Cake, Los Angeles *Also Called: Yamasa Enterprises (P-1699)*

A
L
P
H
A
B
E
T
I
C

Yamazaki Baking Co Ltd .... E 323 581-5218
335 E 2nd St Ste 223 Los Angeles (90012) (P-1473)

Yanchewski & Wardell Entps Inc .... D 760 754-1960
2241 La Mirada Dr Vista (92081) (P-6038)

Yang-Ming International Corp .... E 626 956-0100
595 Yorbita Rd La Puente (91744) (P-14119)

Yankon Industries Inc (PA) .... E 909 591-2345
13445 12th St Chino (91710) (P-6482)

Yapstone Inc (PA) .... D 866 289-5977
1902 Wright Pl Ste 231 Carlsbad (92008) (P-14636)

Yardi Kube Inc .... D 805 699-2040
430 S Fairview Ave Goleta (93117) (P-14068)

Yardi Systems Inc (PA) .... B 805 699-2040
430 S Fairview Ave Santa Barbara (93117) (P-13866)

Yardney Water MGT Systems, Riverside Also Called: Yardney Water MGT Systems Inc
(P-6039)

Yardney Water MGT Systems Inc .... E 951 656-6716
6666 Box Springs Blvd Riverside (92507) (P-6039)

Yates Gear Inc .... D 530 222-4606
330 N Brand Blvd Ste 700 Glendale (91203) (P-4311)

Yavar Manufacturing Co Inc .... E 323 722-2040
1900 S Tubeway Ave Commerce (90040) (P-2702)

Yawitz Inc .... E 909 865-5599
1379 Ridgeway St Pomona (91768) (P-6451)

Ybcc Inc .... E 626 213-3945
17800 Castleton St Ste 386 City Of Industry (91748) (P-1312)

Yeager Enterprises Corp .... D 714 994-2040
7100 Village Dr Buena Park (90621) (P-4486)

Yebo Group LLC .... C 949 502-3317
2652 Dow Ave Tustin (92780) (P-11637)

Yebo Printing, Tustin Also Called: Yebo Group LLC (P-11637)

Yee Yuen Laundry and Clrs Inc .... D 323 734-7205
2575 S Normandie Ave Los Angeles (90007) (P-13127)

Yee Yuen Linen Service, Los Angeles Also Called: Yee Yuen Laundry and Clrs Inc (P-13127)

Yellow Jacket Drlg Svcs LLC .... D 909 989-8563
9460 Lucas Ranch Rd Rancho Cucamonga (91730) (P-1145)

Yellow Luxury, Calabasas Also Called: Abbyson Living Corp (P-9864)

Yellow Springs Instruments, San Diego Also Called: Ysi Incorporated (P-7992)

Yellowpagescom LLC (DH) .... B 818 937-5500
611 N Brand Blvd Ste 500 Glendale (91203) (P-14637)

Yen-Nhai Inc .... E 323 584-1315
4940 District Blvd Vernon (90058) (P-2462)

Yesco, Jurupa Valley Also Called: Young Electric Sign Company (P-8652)

Yesterdays Sportswear, Paso Robles Also Called: Lakeshirts LLC (P-2249)

Yf Art Holdings Gp LLC .... A 678 441-1400
9130 W Sunset Blvd Los Angeles (90069) (P-12621)

Yg Laboratories Inc .... E 714 474-2800
11520 Warner Ave Fountain Valley (92708) (P-3700)

Yhb Long Beach LLC .... D 562 597-4401
2640 N Lakewood Blvd Long Beach (90815) (P-13095)

Yinlun Tdi LLC (HQ) .... E 909 390-3944
10668 N Trademark Pkwy Rancho Cucamonga (91730) (P-7312)

YKK (usa) Inc .... E 714 701-1200
5001 E La Palma Ave Anaheim (92807) (P-8582)

Ylopo LLC .... C 818 915-9150
4712 Admiralty Way 548 Marina Del Rey (90292) (P-12552)

Ymarketing LLC .... D 714 545-2550
4000 Macarthur Blvd Ste 350 Newport Beach (92660) (P-18245)

YMCA, Torrance Also Called: Young MNS Chrstn Assn Mtro Los (P-17405)

YMCA, Los Angeles Also Called: Young MNS Chrstn Assn Mtro Los (P-17407)

YMCA, Newport Beach Also Called: Young MNS Chrstn Assn Ornge CN (P-17410)

YMCA, Alhambra Also Called: Young Men Chrstn Assoc W San G (P-17423)

YMCA Camp Edwards, Angelus Oaks Also Called: YMCA of East Valley (P-17379)

YMCA Child Care Resource Svcs, San Diego Also Called: YMCA of San Diego County
(P-17393)

YMCA CRESCENTA-CANADA, La Canada Also Called: Crescenta-Canada YMCA (P-17340)

YMCA of East Valley (PA) .... C 909 798-9622
500 E Citrus Ave Redlands (92373) (P-17378)

YMCA of East Valley .... C 909 794-1702
42842 Jenks Lake Rd E Angelus Oaks (92305) (P-17379)

YMCA of East Valley .... C 909 881-9622
808 E 21st St San Bernardino (92404) (P-17380)

YMCA of San Diego County .... D 760 754-6042
1310 Union Plaza Ct Ste 200 Oceanside (92054) (P-17381)

YMCA of San Diego County .... D 858 496-9622
5105 Overland Ave San Diego (92123) (P-17382)

YMCA of San Diego County .... C 858 453-3483
8355 Cliffridge Ave La Jolla (92037) (P-17383)

YMCA of San Diego County .... D 760 804-8170
6100 Avenida Encinas Ste B Carlsbad (92011) (P-17384)

YMCA of San Diego County .... C 619 428-1168
3085 Beyer Blvd Ste 105 San Diego (92154) (P-17385)

YMCA of San Diego County .... C 760 745-7490
200 Saxony Rd Encinitas (92024) (P-17386)

YMCA of San Diego County .... C 619 464-1323
8881 Dallas St La Mesa (91942) (P-17387)

YMCA of San Diego County .... C 619 280-9622
5505 Friars Rd San Diego (92110) (P-17388)

YMCA of San Diego County .... B 858 292-4034
200 Saxony Rd Encinitas (92024) (P-17389)

YMCA of San Diego County .... C 619 281-8313
2927 Meade Ave San Diego (92116) (P-17390)

YMCA of San Diego County .... C 619 226-8888
2150 Beryl St Ste 18 San Diego (92109) (P-17391)

YMCA of San Diego County .... C 619 264-0144
5505 Friars Rd San Diego (92110) (P-17392)

YMCA of San Diego County .... C 619 521-3055
3333 Camino Del Rio S Ste 400 San Diego (92108) (P-17393)

YMCA of San Diego County .... C 760 765-0642
4761 Pine Hills Rd Julian (92036) (P-17394)

YMCA of San Diego County .... D 858 270-8213
3304 Idlewild Way San Diego (92117) (P-17395)

YMCA of San Diego County .... B 619 298-3576
5505 Friars Rd San Diego (92110) (P-17396)

YMCA of San Diego County .... C 760 758-0808
200 Saxony Rd Encinitas (92024) (P-17397)

YMCA of San Diego County .... D 760 757-8270
333 Garrison St Oceanside (92054) (P-17398)

YMCA of San Diego County .... D 619 449-9622
River Rock Dr Santee (92071) (P-17399)

YMCA of San Diego County .... C 760 721-8930
215 Barnes St Oceanside (92054) (P-17400)

YMCA of San Diego County (HQ) .... D 858 292-9622
3708 Ruffin Rd San Diego (92123) (P-17401)

YMCA OF THE FOOTHILLS, La Canada Also Called: Young MNS Chrstn Assn of Fthll
(P-17408)

YMCA of Westchester, Los Angeles Also Called: Young MNS Chrstn Assn Mtro Los (P-17404)

YMCA Overnight Camp, Julian Also Called: YMCA of San Diego County (P-17394)

YMCA Youth & Family Services, San Diego Also Called: YMCA of San Diego County
(P-17390)

YMi Jeanswear Inc .... D 213 746-6681
1015 Wall St Ste 115 Los Angeles (90015) (P-2143)

Yobs, Los Angeles Also Called: Yobs Technologies Inc (P-14877)

Yobs Technologies Inc .... E 213 713-3825
615 Childs Way Tro 370 Los Angeles (90089) (P-14877)

Yokohama Corp North America (HQ) .... C 540 389-5426
1 Macarthur Pl Santa Ana (92707) (P-3866)

Yokohama Tire, Santa Ana Also Called: Yokohama Corp North America (P-3866)

Yokohama Tire Corporation (DH) .... C 714 870-3800
1 Macarthur Pl Ste 900 Santa Ana (92707) (P-9863)

Yokohama Tire USA, Santa Ana Also Called: Yokohama Tire Corporation (P-9863)

Yonekyu USA Inc .... D 323 581-4194
611 N 20th St Montebello (90640) (P-1275)

Yorba Linda Country Club, Garden Grove Also Called: Sanyo Foods Corp America (P-1735)

Yorba Park Medical Group, Santa Ana Also Called: St Jseph Heritg Med Group LLC (P-15482)

York Enterprises South Inc .... D 714 842-6611
18255 Beach Blvd Huntington Beach (92648) (P-11434)

Yoshimasa, South El Monte Also Called: Yoshimasa Display Case Inc (P-2575)

Yoshimasa Display Case Inc .... E 213 637-9999
10808 Weaver Ave South El Monte (91733) (P-2575)

Yoshimura RES & Dev Amer Inc .... D 909 628-4722
5420 Daniels St Ste A Chino (91710) (P-9854)

Mergent email: customerrelations@mergent.com
1244

2025 Southern California
Business Directory and Buyers Guide

(P-0000) Products & Services Section entry number
(PA)=Parent Co (HQ)=Headquarters (DH)=Div Headquarters

Yosmart Inc .... E 949 825-5958
25172 Arctic Ocean Dr Ste 106 Lake Forest (92630) *(P-6279)*

Youbar Inc (PA) .... E 626 537-1851
445 Wilson Way City Of Industry (91744) *(P-10851)*

Youcare Pharma (usa) Inc .... D 951 258-3114
132 Business Center Dr Corona (92878) *(P-3525)*

Young & Rubicam LLC .... B 949 754-2000
7535 Irvine Center Dr Irvine (92618) *(P-13254)*

Young & Rubicam LLC .... C 949 754-2100
7535 Irvine Center Dr Irvine (92618) *(P-13255)*

Young & Rubicam LLC .... B 949 224-6300
1735 Irvine Center Dr Irvine (92618) *(P-18246)*

Young Electric Sign Company .... C 909 923-7668
10235 Bellegrave Ave Jurupa Valley (91752) *(P-8652)*

Young Engineers Inc .... D 949 581-9411
25841 Commercentre Dr Lake Forest (92630) *(P-4797)*

Young Men Chrstn Assoc W San G (PA) ..... D 626 576-0226
401 Corto St Alhambra (91801) *(P-17423)*

Young Mens Christn Assocation, La Mesa *Also Called: YMCA of San Diego County (P-17387)*

Young MNS Chrstn Assn Brbank C (PA) ..... D 818 845-8551
321 E Magnolia Blvd Burbank (91502) *(P-17402)*

Young MNS Chrstn Assn Glndale .... D 818 484-8256
140 N Louise St Glendale (91206) *(P-17403)*

Young MNS Chrstn Assn Mtro Los .... D 310 216-9036
8015 S Sepulveda Blvd Los Angeles (90045) *(P-17404)*

Young MNS Chrstn Assn Mtro Los .... D 310 325-5885
2900 Sepulveda Blvd Torrance (90505) *(P-17405)*

Young MNS Chrstn Assn Mtro Los .... C 323 467-4161
1553 Schrader Blvd Los Angeles (90028) *(P-17406)*

Young MNS Chrstn Assn Mtro Los (PA) ...... D 213 380-6448
625 S New Hampshire Ave Los Angeles (90005) *(P-17407)*

Young MNS Chrstn Assn of Fthll .... D 818 790-0123
1930 Foothill Blvd La Canada (91011) *(P-17408)*

Young MNS Chrstn Assn Ornge CN .... D 949 495-9622
29831 Crown Valley Pkwy Laguna Niguel (92677) *(P-15189)*

Young MNS Chrstn Assn Ornge CN .... C 949 859-9622
27341 Trabuco Cir Mission Viejo (92692) *(P-17409)*

Young MNS Chrstn Assn Ornge CN .... D 949 642-9990
2300 University Dr Newport Beach (92660) *(P-17410)*

Young Wns Chrstn Assn Grter Lo .... C 323 295-4288
2519 W Vernon Ave Los Angeles (90008) *(P-17411)*

Young Wns Chrstn Assn Grter Lo .... C 323 295-4280
2501 W Vernon Ave Los Angeles (90008) *(P-17412)*

Young's Market, Chino *Also Called: Youngs Market Company LLC (P-11067)*

Younger Mfg Co (PA) .... B 310 783-1533
2925 California St Torrance (90503) *(P-8419)*

Younger Optics, Torrance *Also Called: Younger Mfg Co (P-8419)*

Youngs Holdings Inc (PA) .... D 714 368-4615
15 Enterprise Ste 100 Aliso Viejo (92656) *(P-11063)*

Youngs Interco Inc .... A 714 368-4615
14402 Franklin Ave Tustin (92780) *(P-11064)*

Youngs Market Company LLC .... B 213 629-3929
500 S Central Ave Los Angeles (90013) *(P-11065)*

Youngs Market Company LLC (HQ) .... B 800 317-6150
14402 Franklin Ave Tustin (92780) *(P-11066)*

Youngs Market Company LLC .... D 909 393-4540
6711 Bickmore Ave Chino (91708) *(P-11067)*

Youngvity Essntial Lf Sciences, Chula Vista *Also Called: Al Global Corporation (P-11653)*

Your Practice Online LLC (PA) .... C 877 388-8569
4590 Macarthur Blvd Ste 500 Newport Beach (92660) *(P-18247)*

Your Way Fumigation Inc .... D 951 699-9116
3921 E La Palma Ave Ste N Anaheim (92807) *(P-13350)*

Youth To People Inc .... D 309 648-5500
888 N Douglas St El Segundo (90245) *(P-3701)*

Youthglow, Fountain Valley *Also Called: Yg Laboratories Inc (P-3700)*

Yp, Glendale *Also Called: Yp Holdings LLC (P-14164)*

Yp Holdings LLC .... A 818 649-8772
611 N Brand Blvd Ste 500 Glendale (91203) *(P-14164)*

Ysi Incorporated .... E 858 546-8327
9940 Summers Ridge Rd San Diego (92121) *(P-7992)*

Ytel Inc .... D 800 382-4913
26632 Towne Centre Dr Ste 300 Lake Forest (92610) *(P-9472)*

Yucaipa Companies LLC (PA) .... C 310 789-7200
9130 W Sunset Blvd Los Angeles (90069) *(P-12622)*

Yucaipa & Calimesa News Mirror, Yucaipa *Also Called: Hi-Desert Publishing Company (P-2802)*

Yum Yum Donut Shop, City Of Industry *Also Called: Quality Naturally Foods Inc (P-10972)*

Yuma Lakes Resort, Earp *Also Called: Colorado River Adventures Inc (P-13108)*

Yumi, Los Angeles *Also Called: Caer Inc (P-1338)*

Yun Industrial Co Ltd .... E 310 715-1898
161 Selandia Ln Carson (90746) *(P-6790)*

Yuneec USA, Rancho Cucamonga *Also Called: Yuneec USA Inc (P-10299)*

Yuneec USA Inc .... D 855 284-8888
9227 Haven Ave Ste 210 Rancho Cucamonga (91730) *(P-10299)*

YWCA, Los Angeles *Also Called: Young Wns Chrstn Assn Grter Lo (P-17412)*

Yyk Enterprises Operations LLC (PA) .... C 619 474-6229
3475 E St San Diego (92102) *(P-1237)*

Z C & R Coating For Optics Inc .... E 310 381-3060
1401 Abalone Ave Torrance (90501) *(P-8029)*

Z Industries, Los Angeles *Also Called: Active Window Products (P-4883)*

Z Microsystems, San Diego *Also Called: Zmicro Inc (P-14120)*

Z Willing J A Henckels, Commerce *Also Called: Zwilling JA Henckels LLC (P-9916)*

Z-Best Concrete Inc .... D 951 774-1870
2575 Main St Riverside (92501) *(P-1141)*

Z57 Inc .... C 858 623-5577
2443 Impala Dr Ste B Carlsbad (92010) *(P-14165)*

Z57, INC., Carlsbad *Also Called: Z57 Inc (P-14165)*

Za Management .... D 310 271-2200
101 N Robertson Blvd Beverly Hills (90211) *(P-18083)*

Zaca Mesa Winery, Los Olivos *Also Called: Cushman Winery Corporation (P-11055)*

Zadara Storage Inc .... D 949 251-0360
6 Venture Ste 140 Irvine (92618) *(P-5894)*

Zadro Products Inc .... E 714 892-9200
14462 Astronautics Ln Ste 101 Huntington Beach (92647) *(P-4350)*

Zamboni, Paramount *Also Called: Zamboni Company Usa Inc (P-5725)*

Zamboni Company Usa Inc .... E 562 633-0751
15714 Colorado Ave Paramount (90723) *(P-5725)*

Zapp Packaging Inc .... D 909 930-1500
1921 S Business Pkwy Ontario (91761) *(P-2649)*

Zbe Inc .... E 805 576-1600
1035 Cindy Ln Carpinteria (93013) *(P-6366)*

Zbs Law LLP .... D 714 848-7920
30 Corporate Park Ste 450 Irvine (92606) *(P-16798)*

Zebra Technologies Corporation .... D 805 579-1800
30601 Agoura Rd Agoura Hills (91301) *(P-5956)*

Zeco Systems Inc .... D 888 751-8560
767 S Alameda St Ste 200 Los Angeles (90021) *(P-11026)*

Zefr Inc .... B 310 392-3555
4101 Redwood Ave Los Angeles (90066) *(P-17864)*

Zeghani, Glendale *Also Called: Simon G Jewelry Inc (P-10552)*

Zenith A Fairfax Company, The, Woodland Hills *Also Called: Zenith Insurance Company (P-12143)*

Zenith Insurance Company (DH) .... B 818 713-1000
21255 Califa St Woodland Hills (91367) *(P-12143)*

Zenith Manufacturing Inc .... E 818 767-2106
3087 12th St Riverside (92507) *(P-7594)*

Zenith Specialty Bag, Rowland Heights *Also Called: Novolex Bagcraft Inc (P-2737)*

Zenleads Inc .... B 415 640-9303
440 N Barranca Ave # 4750 Covina (91723) *(P-18248)*

Zentalis, San Diego *Also Called: Zentalis Pharmaceuticals Inc (P-3526)*

Zentalis Pharmaceuticals Inc (PA) .... C 858 263-4333
10275 Science Center Dr Ste 100 San Diego (92121) *(P-3526)*

Zeons Inc .... B 323 302-8299
291 S La Cienega Blvd Ste 102 Beverly Hills (90211) *(P-4330)*

Zephyr Manufacturing Co Inc .... D 310 410-4907
201 Hindry Ave Inglewood (90301) *(P-5638)*

Zephyr Tool Group, Inglewood *Also Called: Zephyr Manufacturing Co Inc (P-5638)*

Zerep Management Corporation (PA) .... C 626 855-5522
17445 Railroad St City Of Industry (91748) *(P-9784)*

Zero Energy Contracting Inc .... C 626 701-3180
13850 Cerritos Corporate Dr Ste D Cerritos (90703) *(P-856)*

Zero Energy Contracting LLC .... D 626 701-3180
13850 Cerritos Corporate Dr Ste D Cerritos (90703) *(P-857)*

Employee Codes: A=Over 500 employees, B=251-500
C=101-250, D=51-100, E=20-50, F=10-19, G=1-9

2025 Southern California
Business Directory and Buyers Guide

© Mergent Inc. 1-800-342-5647

1245

Zest Anchors LLC .... C 760 743-7744
2230 Enterprise St Escondido (92029) *(P-10116)*

Zest Dental Solutions, Escondido *Also Called: Zest Anchors LLC (P-10116)*

Zest.ai, Burbank *Also Called: Zestfinance Inc (P-13867)*

Zestfinance Inc .... D 323 450-3000
3900 W Alameda Ave Ste 1600 Burbank (91505) *(P-13867)*

Zet-Tek Precision Machining, Yorba Linda *Also Called: Pdma Ventures Inc (P-8350)*

Zettler Components Inc (PA) .... C 949 831-5000
75 Columbia Orange (92868) *(P-6699)*

Zettler Magnetics Inc .... C 949 831-5000
2410 Birch St Vista (92081) *(P-6299)*

Zeus, Valley Village *Also Called: Zeus Networks LLC (P-15010)*

Zeus Networks LLC .... D 323 910-4420
11713 Riverside Dr Valley Village (91607) *(P-15010)*

Zevia, Encino *Also Called: Zevia Pbc (P-1659)*

Zevia LLC .... D 310 202-7000
15821 Ventura Blvd Ste 145 Encino (91436) *(P-1658)*

Zevia Pbc (PA) .... E 424 343-2654
15821 Ventura Blvd Ste 135 Encino (91436) *(P-1659)*

Zhong W Ang Group, Walnut *Also Called: Pengcheng Aluminum Enterprise Inc USA (P-4603)*

Zi Industries Inc (PA) .... D 213 749-1215
3957 S Hill St Ste A Los Angeles (90037) *(P-10677)*

Zia Aamir .... E 714 337-7861
2043 Imperial St Los Angeles (90021) *(P-4882)*

Ziegenfelder Company .... D 909 509-0493
12262 Colony Ave Chino (91710) *(P-1322)*

Ziegenfelder Company .... D 909 590-0493
12290 Colony Ave Chino (91710) *(P-1323)*

Ziffren B B F G-L S&C Fnd .... C 310 552-3388
1801 Century Park W Fl 7 Los Angeles (90067) *(P-16799)*

Zim Industries Inc .... C 661 393-9661
7212 Fruitvale Ave Bakersfield (93308) *(P-1146)*

Zimmer Dental Inc .... B 800 854-7019
1900 Aston Ave Carlsbad (92008) *(P-8321)*

Zimmer Gnsul Frsca Archtcts LL .... C 213 617-1901
515 S Flower St Ste 3700 Los Angeles (90071) *(P-17697)*

Zimmer Gnsul Frsca Partnr Amer, Los Angeles *Also Called: Zimmer Gnsul Frsca Archtcts LL (P-17697)*

Zimmer Melia & Associates Inc (PA) .... E 615 377-0118
6832 Presidio Dr Huntington Beach (92648) *(P-8322)*

Zion Automotive Group, Cerritos *Also Called: R1 Concepts Inc (P-9840)*

Zipco, Riverside *Also Called: Zenith Manufacturing Inc (P-7594)*

ZIPRECRUITER, Santa Monica *Also Called: Ziprecruiter Inc (P-18249)*

Ziprecruiter Inc (PA) .... A 877 252-1062
604 Arizona Ave Santa Monica (90401) *(P-18249)*

Zk Enterprises Inc .... E 213 622-7012
4368 District Blvd Vernon (90058) *(P-2032)*

Zm Trucks, Torrance *Also Called: Zo Motors North America LLC (P-6487)*

Zmicro Inc (PA) .... D 858 831-7000
9820 Summers Ridge Rd San Diego (92121) *(P-14120)*

Zo Motors North America LLC .... E 310 792-7077
21250 Hawthorne Blvd Ste 500 Torrance (90503) *(P-6487)*

Zo Skin Health Inc (DH) .... D 949 988-7524
9685 Research Dr Irvine (92618) *(P-3702)*

Zodiac Inflight Innovations US, Brea *Also Called: Safran Pass Innovations LLC (P-13808)*

Zodiac Pool Solutions, Carlsbad *Also Called: Fluidra North America LLC (P-6014)*

Zodiac Pool Systems LLC (DH) .... C 760 599-9600
2882 Whiptail Loop Ste 100 Carlsbad (92010) *(P-6040)*

Zodiac Pool Systems LLC .... C 760 213-4647
19319 Harvill Ave Perris (92570) *(P-14638)*

Zodiac Wtr Waste Aero Systems .... D 310 884-7000
1500 Glenn Curtiss St Carson (90746) *(P-7595)*

Zoek, Irvine *Also Called: Online Marketing Group LLC (P-18187)*

Zoic Inc .... C 310 838-0770
3582 Eastham Dr Culver City (90232) *(P-14878)*

Zoic Studios, Culver City *Also Called: Zoic Inc (P-14878)*

Zonda Intelligence, Newport Beach *Also Called: Metrostudy Inc (P-18171)*

Zonda Media, Newport Beach *Also Called: Hanley Wood Media Inc (P-2921)*

Zonson Company Inc .... E 760 597-0338
3197 Lionshead Ave Carlsbad (92010) *(P-8556)*

Zoo, El Segundo *Also Called: Zoo Digital Production LLC (P-14879)*

Zoo Digital Production LLC .... C 310 220-3939
2201 Park Pl Ste 100 El Segundo (90245) *(P-14879)*

Zoo Med Laboratories Inc .... C 805 542-9988
3650 Sacramento Dr San Luis Obispo (93401) *(P-8743)*

Zoo Printing Inc (PA) .... E 310 253-7751
1225 Los Angeles St Glendale (91204) *(P-3105)*

Zoo Printing Trade Printer, Glendale *Also Called: Zoo Printing Inc (P-3105)*

Zooey Apparel Inc .... E 310 315-2880
1526 Cloverfield Blvd Ste C Santa Monica (90404) *(P-2144)*

Zoological Society San Diego (PA) .... A 619 231-1515
2920 Zoo Dr San Diego (92101) *(P-17273)*

Zoological Society San Diego .... C 760 747-8702
15500 San Pasqual Valley Rd Escondido (92027) *(P-17274)*

Zoological Society San Diego .... C 619 744-3325
2920 Zoo Dr San Diego (92101) *(P-17275)*

Zoological Society San Diego .... C 619 231-1515
10946 Willow Ct Ste 200 San Diego (92127) *(P-17276)*

Zoominfo Technologies LLC .... A 360 783-6924
Dept La 24789 Pasadena (91185) *(P-14182)*

Zosano, Los Angeles *Also Called: Zp Opco Inc (P-3527)*

Zp Opco Inc .... E 510 745-1200
34790 Ardentech Ct Los Angeles (90071) *(P-3527)*

Zpower LLC .... C 805 445-7789
5171 Clareton Dr Agoura Hills (91301) *(P-6383)*

Zuza LLC .... D 760 494-9000
2304 Faraday Ave Carlsbad (92008) *(P-3106)*

Zwift Inc (PA) .... B 855 469-9438
111 W Ocean Blvd Ste 1800 Long Beach (90802) *(P-14069)*

Zwilling JA Henckels LLC .... C 323 597-1421
100 Citadel Dr Ste 575 Commerce (90040) *(P-9916)*

Zyris Inc .... E 805 560-9888
6868 Cortona Dr Ste A Santa Barbara (93117) *(P-8362)*

Zyxel, Anaheim *Also Called: Zyxel Communications Inc (P-9473)*

Zyxel Communications Inc .... D 714 632-0882
1130 N Miller St Anaheim (92806) *(P-9473)*

Mergent email: customerrelations@mergent.com
1246

2025 Southern California
Business Directory and Buyers Guide

(P-0000) Products & Services Section entry number
(PA)=Parent Co (HQ)=Headquarters (DH)=Div Headquarters

COUNTY/CITY CROSS-REFERENCE INDEX

	ENTRY #		ENTRY #		ENTRY #		ENTRY #		ENTRY #
La Jolla		Santa Ysabel		Morro Bay		Guadalupe		Moorpark	
La Mesa		Santee		Nipomo		Lompoc		Newbury Park	
Lakeside		Solana Beach		Paso Robles		Los Olivos		Oak Park	
Lemon Grove		Spring Valley		Pismo Beach		New Cuyama		Oak View	
National City		Tecate		San Luis Obispo		Orcutt		Ojai	
Oceanside		Valley Center		San Simeon		Santa Barbara		Oxnard	
Pala		Vista		Shandon		Santa Maria		Piru	
Pauma Valley				Shell Beach		Santa Ynez		Port Hueneme	
Poway		**San Luis Obispo**		Templeton		Solvang		Santa Paula	
Ramona		Arroyo Grande				Vandenberg Afb		Simi Valley	
Rancho Santa Fe		Atascadero		**Santa Barbara**				Somis	
San Diego		Avila Beach		Buellton		**Ventura**		Thousand Oaks	
San Marcos		Cambria		Carpinteria		Camarillo		Ventura	
San Ysidro		Grover Beach		Goleta		Fillmore		Westlake Village	

GEOGRAPHIC SECTION

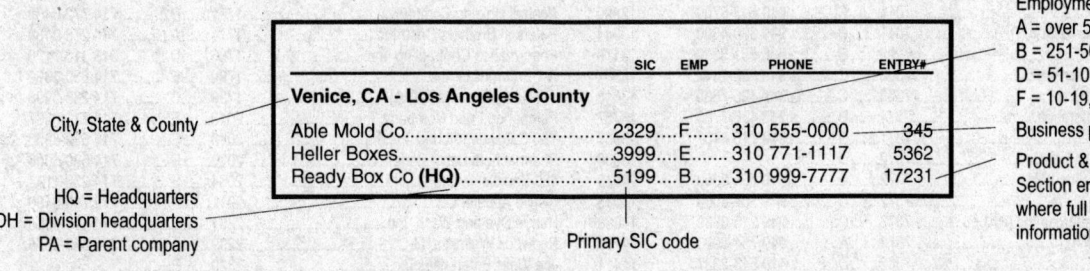

Employment codes
A = over 500 employees
B = 251-500, C = 101-250
D = 51-100, E = 20-50
F = 10-19, G = 1-9

	SIC	EMP	PHONE	ENTRY#
Venice, CA - Los Angeles County				
Able Mold Co..	2329	F	310 555-0000	345
Heller Boxes...	3999	E	310 771-1117	5362
Ready Box Co **(HQ)**................................	5199	B	310 999-7777	17231

City, State & County

HQ = Headquarters
DH = Division headquarters
PA = Parent company

Primary SIC code

Business phone

Product & Service
Section entry number
where full company
information appears

- Listings in this section are sorted alphabetically by city.
- Listings within each city are sorted alphabetically by company name.

	SIC	EMP	PHONE	ENTRY#
ACTON, CA - Los Angeles County				
County of Los Angeles...............................	8069	C	661 223-8700	16290
ADELANTO, CA - San Bernardino County				
Commercial Wood Products Company..........	1751	C	760 246-4530	1047
Flavor House Inc..	2087	E	760 246-9131	1678
Furniture Technologies Inc.........................	2426	E	760 246-9180	2288
California Silica Products LLC.....................	2819	D	909 947-0028	3228
Dar-Ken Inc...	3053	E	760 246-4010	3886
Fiber Care Baths Inc..................................	3088	B	760 246-0019	4026
Hee Environmental Engineering LLC...........	3089	E	760 530-1409	4130
Molded Fiber GL Companies - W.................	3089	D	760 246-4042	4174
Clark - Pacific Corporation.........................	3272	E	626 962-8755	4382
Mk Magnetics Inc.......................................	3315	E	760 246-6373	4538
Northwest Pipe Company............................	3317	C	760 246-3191	4551
McElroy Metal Mill Inc................................	3448	E	760 246-5545	5083
Cageco Inc..	3523	E	800 605-4859	5472
Ebara Mixers Inc.......................................	3556	E	760 246-3643	5670
Andersen Industries Inc.............................	3715	E	760 246-8766	7313
General Atomic Aeron................................	3721	C	760 388-8208	7350
Ducommun Aerostructures Inc....................	3728	E	760 246-4191	7466
Safeway Sign Company..............................	3993	E	760 246-7070	8629
Carberry LLC **(HQ)**...............................	3999	E	800 564-0842	8668
Apex Bulk Commodities Inc **(PA)**..........	4212	C	760 246-6077	8893
Hayes Welding Inc **(PA)**.......................	7692	D	760 246-4878	14741
Amko Service Company..............................	7699	D	760 246-3600	14757
AGOURA, CA - Los Angeles County				
Joni and Friends Foundation **(PA)**.........	8322	D	818 707-5664	16965
AGOURA HILLS, CA - Los Angeles County				
James H Cowan & Associates Inc...............	0782	D	310 457-2574	211
Ess LLC..	1711	D	888 303-6424	778
Paisano Publications LLC **(PA)**.............	2721	D	818 889-8740	2868
Paisano Publications Inc............................	2721	D	818 889-8740	2869
Bendpak Inc **(PA)**.................................	3559	D	805 933-9970	5694
Edge Solutions Consulting Inc **(PA)**......	3571	E	010 591-0500	5846
Internet Machines Corporation **(PA)**......	3577	D	818 575-2100	5926
Zebra Technologies Corporation.................	3577	E	805 579-1800	5956
Zpowor LLC...	3629	C	805 445-7789	6383
Teradyne Inc...	3679	D	818 991-2900	7061
Aptiv Services Us LLC...............................	3714	D	818 661-6667	7228
V-Wave Inc..	3841	E	818 629-2164	8246
Relief-Mart Inc..	5999	E	805 379-4300	11695
Private Nat Mrtg Accptance LLC **(DH)**...	6162	A	866 549-3583	11931
Athas Capital Group Inc.............................	6163	C	877 877-1477	11939
Western Mutual Insurance Co.....................	6331	D	818 879-2142	12142
Davidson Hotel Partners Lp........................	7011	A	818 707-1220	12806
Sequoia Concepts Inc................................	7322	D	818 409-6000	13288
Novalogic Inc...	7371	D	818 880-1997	13786
Novastor Corporation **(PA)**...................	7372	D	805 579-6700	13992
Scorelate Inc...	7372	E	818 602-9176	14027
OSI Digital Inc **(PA)**.............................	7379	E	818 992-2700	14238
Weststar Cinemas Inc................................	7832	D	818 707-9987	14945
Los Angeles Rams LLC **(PA)**................	7941	D	314 982-7267	15031
Albert & Mackenzie LLP **(PA)**..............	8111	D	818 575-9876	16632
ALHAMBRA, CA - Los Angeles County				
Tyler Trafficante Inc **(PA)**....................	2311	E	323 869-9299	1980
Gracing Brand Management Inc..................	2369	B	626 297-2472	2170
Redwood Scientific Tech Inc.......................	2834	E	310 693-5401	3490
Alhambra Foundry Company Ltd..................	3321	E	626 289-4294	4556
Coast To Coast Met Finshg Corp................	3471	E	626 282-2122	5250
Emcore Corporation **(PA)**.....................	3674	C	626 293-3400	6821
Southern California Edison Co.....................	4911	A	626 308-6193	9635
Southern California Gas Co.........................	4924	C	323 881-3587	9653
County of Los Angeles...............................	4941	B	626 458-4000	9688
Orora Packaging Solutions.........................	5113	E	626 284-9524	10602
Alhambra Motors Inc..................................	5511	C	626 576-1114	11314
FB Corporation..	6022	B	626 300-0880	11766
Serfin Funds Transfer **(PA)**..................	6099	D	626 457-3070	11844
County of Los Angeles...............................	6324	C	626 299-5300	12078
Drew Chain Security Corp..........................	7381	D	626 457-8626	14295
Atherton Baptist Homes.............................	8051	B	626 863-1710	15573
Silverado Senior Living Inc.........................	8051	D	626 872-3941	15776
Alhambra Hospital Med Ctr LP...................	8062	C	626 570-1606	15904
County of Los Angeles...............................	8322	D	626 308-5542	16926
Eastern Los Angles Rgnal Ctr F **(PA)**...	8322	C	626 299-4700	16937
Young Men Chrstn Assoc W San G **(PA)**	8661	D	626 576-0226	17423
Network Medical Management Inc................	8741	C	626 282-0288	18022
Pacific Ventures Ltd...................................	8741	C	626 576-0737	18030
Simpson Smpson MGT Cnslting In..............	8742	D	626 282-4000	18210
ALISO VIEJO, CA - Orange County				
LMC Hllywood Hghland Hldngs LL...............	1542	B	949 448-1600	555
Fluor Daniel Construction Co **(DH)**.......	1622	B	949 349-2000	652
Lion Shield Protection Inc..........................	1731	D	949 334-7905	935
Pepsi-Cola Metro Btlg Co Inc.....................	2086	D	949 643-5700	1631
Avanir Pharmaceuticals Inc **(DH)**.........	2834	D	949 389-6700	3363
Spyglass Pharma Inc.................................	2834	E	949 284-6904	3507
Epicuren Discovery....................................	2835	D	949 588-5807	3539
Parylene Coating Services Inc....................	3479	E	281 391-7665	5334
Centon Electronics Inc **(PA)**................	3572	D	949 855-9111	5875
Astronic...	3672	C	949 454-1180	6710
Indie Semiconductor Inc **(PA)**..............	3674	E	949 608-0854	6828
Ixys Intgrted Crcits Div AV In.....................	3674	A	949 831-4622	6838
W G Holt Inc..	3674	D	949 859-8800	6913
Screening Systems Inc **(PA)**................	3826	C	949 855-1751	7976
Glaukos Corporation **(PA)**....................	3841	C	949 367-9600	8159
Microvention Inc **(DH)**.........................	3841	D	714 258-8000	8200
Sequent Medical Inc..................................	3841	D	949 030-9000	8227
Vertos Medical Inc LLC..............................	3841	D	949 349-0008	8248
Presbibio LLC..	3851	E	949 502-7010	8413
Rxsight Inc **(PA)**...................................	3851	D	949 521-7830	8414
United Parcel Service Inc...........................	4215	A	949 643-6634	9031
Pepsico Beverage Sales LLC.....................	4225	C	949 362-2860	9100
Southern California Gas Co.........................	4924	C	714 634-7221	9662
Datallegro Inc..	5045	C	949 680-3000	9998
Hd Supply Distribution Services LLC...........	5072	A	949 643-4700	10308
Xse Group Inc..	5112	C	888 272-8340	10587
Metagenics LLC **(PA)**...........................	5122	C	949 366-0818	10633
Valeant Biomedicals Inc **(DH)**..............	5169	D	949 461-6000	11023
Efuel LLC..	5172	E	949 330-7145	11030
Youngs Holdings Inc **(PA)**....................	5182	D	714 368-4615	11063
Chronic Tacos Enterprises.........................	5812	C	949 680-4602	11561
Thomas James Capital Inc.........................	6282	C	949 481-7026	12035
Pacific Life Insurance Company..................	6311	D	949 219-5200	12050
Safeguard Health Entps Inc **(HQ)**........	6324	C	800 880-1800	12102
Shea Properties MGT Co Inc......................	6512	B	949 389-7000	12318
Sares Rgis Group Rsdential Inc..................	6513	C	949 643-8922	12365

Employee Codes: A=Over 500 employees, B=251-500
C=101-250, D=51-100, E=20-50, F=10-19, G=1-9

2025 Southern California
Business Directory and Buyers Guide

© Mergent Inc. 1-800-342-5647

1249

GEOGRAPHIC

	SIC	EMP	PHONE	ENTRY#
First Team RE - Orange Cnty	6531	C	949 389-0004	12447
Thomas James Homes LLC	6531	C	949 424-2356	12538
L & O Aliso Viejo LLC	7011	C	949 643-6700	12890
Sunstone Hotel Properties Inc (DH)	7011	C	949 330-4000	13044
Cloudstaff LLC	7299	B	888 551-5339	13170
Adecco Employment Services	7363	C	949 586-2342	13587
Remedytemp Inc (DH)	7363	C	949 425-7600	13618
Itrex Group USA Corporation	7371	B	213 436-7785	13757
UST Global Inc (HQ)	7371	D	949 716-8757	13857
Gaikai Inc	7372	D		13936
Quadrotech Solutions Inc (PA)	7372	E	949 754-8000	14013
Quest Software Inc	7372	D	949 754-8000	14015
Information MGT Resources Inc (PA)	7373	C	949 215-8889	14088
Quest Software Inc (PA)	7373	A	949 754-8000	14103
Navtrak LLC	7382	E	410 548-2337	14414
Perfect Impression Inc	7389	E	949 305-0797	14571
Premier Aquatic Services Llc	7997	D	949 716-3333	15159
Kaiser Foundation Hospitals	8011	C	949 425-3150	15339
Covenant Care LLC (PA)	8051	B	949 349-1200	15616
Hcr Manorcare Med Svcs Fla LLC	8051	C	949 587-9000	15672
Aliso Rdge Behavioral Hlth LLC	8063	D	949 415-9218	16261
American Assn Crtcal Care Nrse	8299	C	949 362-2000	16849
Lauras House	8322	E	949 361-3775	16970
Fluor Corporation	8711	D	949 349-2000	17531
Fluor Plant Services Intl Inc	8711	D	949 349-2000	17532
Nelson Bros Property MGT Inc	8741	C	949 916-7300	18020
Professional Community MGT Cal	8741	D	949 380-0725	18038
Basketball Marketing Co Inc	8742	C	610 249-2255	18102
Egnite Inc	8742	D	949 594-2330	18131
Pandora Marketing LLC	8742	D	800 705-6856	18190
Channelwave Software Inc	8748	D	949 448-4500	18302

ALPINE, CA - San Diego County

	SIC	EMP	PHONE	ENTRY#
Abhe & Svoboda Inc	1542	D	619 659-1320	514
Alpine Convalescent Center Inc	8093	D	619 659-3120	16440
Southern Indian Health Council (PA)	8093	D	619 445-1188	16506

ALTADENA, CA - Los Angeles County

	SIC	EMP	PHONE	ENTRY#
Honeybee Robotics LLC	3569	D	303 774-7613	5823
Riedon Inc (PA)	3676	C		6921
Anre Technologies Inc	7371	C	818 627-5433	13655
Maimone Liquidating Corp (PA)	7532	D	626 286-5691	14676
Altadena Town and Country Club	7997	D	626 345-9088	15113
Five Acres - The Bys Grls Aid	8361	B	626 798-6793	17152

ANAHEIM, CA - Orange County

	SIC	EMP	PHONE	ENTRY#
Harvest Landscape Entps Inc (PA)	0781	C	714 693-8100	172
Hydro-Dig Inc	0781	D	714 772-9947	174
Marina Maintenance Group Inc	0781	B	714 939-6600	176
Resident Group Services Inc (PA)	0782	D	714 630-5300	232
Ultimate Landscaping MGT	0782	D	714 502-9711	240
West Coast Arborists Inc (PA)	0782	D	714 991-1900	243
Capsule Manufacturing Inc	1389	D	949 245-4151	321
Brownco Construction Co Inc	1521	D	714 935-9600	392
Katerra Construction LLC	1521	A	720 449-3909	413
Universal Dust Cllctr Mfg Sup (PA)	1541	D	714 630-8588	510
Platinum Construction Inc	1542	D	714 527-0700	572
San-Mar Construction Co Inc	1542	D	714 693-5400	581
Techno Coatings Inc	1542	D	714 774-4671	591
Techno Coatings Inc	1542	D	714 774-4671	592
Techno Coatings Inc (PA)	1542	D	714 635-1130	593
Turner Construction Company	1542	B	714 940-9000	595
JB Bostick LLC (PA)	1611	D	714 238-2121	628
Control Air Conditioning Corporation	1711	B	714 777-8600	765
Ken Starr Inc	1711	D	714 632-8789	793
Nexgen AC & Htg LLC	1711	D	760 616-5870	812
Residential Fire Systems Inc	1711	D	714 666-8450	830
South Coast Mechanical Inc	1711	D	714 738-6644	843
Trilogy Plumbing Inc	1711	C	714 441-2952	848
University Marelich Mech Inc	1711	D	714 632-2600	850
Borbon Incorporated	1721	C	714 994-0170	860
Pbc Pavers Inc	1721	D	714 278-0488	869
C G Systems LLC	1731	E	714 632-8882	894
Donco & Sons Inc	1731	E	714 779-0099	909
Eclipse Lighting & Electrical	1731	D	714 871-9366	911
Nazzareno Electric Co Inc	1731	D	714 712-4744	943
Rosendin Electric Inc	1731	A	714 739-1334	956
Sunwest Electric Inc	1731	D	714 630-8700	970
Hba Incorporated	1741	D	714 635-8602	984
Vincent Contractors Inc	1741	B	714 660-0165	991
Best Interiors Inc	1742	C	714 490-7999	998
Mowery Thomason Inc	1742	C	714 666-1717	1016
Eleganza Tiles Inc (PA)	1743	D	714 224-1700	1039

	SIC	EMP	PHONE	ENTRY#
Petersen-Dean Inc	1761	C	714 629-9670	1092
Arciero Brothers Inc	1771	C	714 238-6600	1101
Penhall Holding Company	1771	D	714 772-6450	1132
Peterson Brothers Cnstr Inc	1771	A	714 278-0488	1133
Performance Contracting Inc	1796	D	913 310-7120	1190
A-1 Enterprises Inc	1799	E	714 630-3390	1193
ATI Restoration LLC (PA)	1799	C	714 283-9990	1195
Pampanga Food Company Inc	2013	E	714 773-0537	1264
T&J Sausage Kitchen Inc	2013	E	714 632-8350	1274
Pharmachem Laboratories LLC	2023	E	714 630-6000	1306
180 Snacks Inc	2064	E	714 238-1192	1499
Alstyle Apparel LLC	2211	A	714 765-0400	1869
Harrys Dye and Wash Inc	2261	E	714 446-0300	1933
Redwood Wellness LLC	2299	E	323 843-2676	1973
Joe Wells Enterprises Inc	2329	E		2015
St John Knits Inc (DH)	2339	B	877 750-1171	2133
St John Knits Intl Inc (HQ)	2339	C	949 863-1171	2134
The Lunada Bay Corporation (PA)	2369	E	714 490-1313	2172
Walt Dsney Imgnring RES Dev In	2389	E	714 781-3152	2202
Display Fabrication Group Inc	2399	E	714 373-2100	2274
Highland Lumber Sales Inc	2431	E	714 778-2293	2310
Millcraft Inc	2431	D	714 632-9621	2313
Woodwork Pioneers Corp	2431	E	714 991-1017	2335
American Woodmark Corporation	2434	B	714 449-2200	2337
Reborn Cabinets LLC (PA)	2434	B	714 630-2220	2359
D-Mac Inc	2451	E	714 808-3918	2397
Outdoor Dimensions LLC	2499	C	714 578-9555	2413
Quality First Woodworks Inc	2499	C	714 632-0480	2416
University Frames Inc	2499	E	714 575-5100	2418
M&J Design Inc	2512	E	714 687-9918	2451
RSI Home Products LLC (HQ)	2514	A	714 449-2200	2473
Sky Rider Equipment Co Inc	2515	E	714 632-6890	2491
Block Tops Inc (PA)	2541	E	714 978-5080	2557
Leonards Carpet Service Inc (PA)	2541	D	714 630-1930	2570
Tahiti Cabinets Inc	2599	D	714 693-0618	2616
Treston IAC LLC	2599	E	714 990-8997	2617
International Paper Company	2621	C	714 776-6060	2626
Mozaik LLC	2652	E	562 207-1900	2650
Jellco Container Inc	2653	D	714 666-2728	2677
Absolute Packaging Inc	2657	E	714 630-3020	2701
Thermech Corporation	2671	E	714 533-3183	2712
Felix Schoeller North Amer Inc	2672	E	315 298-8425	2723
Digital Label Solutions LLC	2679	E	714 982-5000	2766
Anchored Prints	2752	E	714 929-9317	2962
Creative Press LLC (PA)	2752	E	714 774-5060	2992
Creative Press LLC	2752	E	714 774-5060	2993
Inland Litho LLC	2752	D	714 993-6000	3020
Interlink Inc	2752	D	714 905-7700	3024
Lester Lithograph Inc	2752	E	714 491-3981	3034
Man-Grove Industries Inc	2752	D	714 630-3020	3039
Pacific West Litho Inc	2752	D	714 579-0868	3055
Pj Printers Inc	2752	E	714 779-8484	3061
Tajen Industries Inc	2752	E	714 527-3122	3087
Adcraft Products Co Inc	2759	E	714 776-1230	3113
Brook & Whittle Limited	2759	E	714 634-3466	3124
C T L Printing Inds Inc	2759	E	714 635-2980	3126
Dean Hesketh Company Inc	2759	E	714 236-2138	3135
Labeltronix LLC (HQ)	2759	D	800 429-4321	3153
Progrssive Intgrated Solutions	2759	D	714 237-0980	3165
Tee Styled Inc	2759	E	323 983-9988	3183
Castle Press	2791	E	800 794-0858	3204
Ryvec Inc	2816	E	714 520-5592	3223
Singod Investors Vi LLC	2819	D	714 326-7800	3247
Solvay America Inc	2819	C	714 688-4403	3248
Solvay America LLC	2819	D	713 525-4000	3251
Mer-Kote Products Inc	2821	E	714 778-2266	3279
Stepan Company	2821	C	714 776-9870	3294
Xerxes Corporation	2821	C	714 630-0012	3302
B & C Nutritional Products Inc	2833	D	714 238-7225	3310
Excelsior Nutrition Inc	2833	D	657 999-5188	3316
Gmp Laboratories America Inc (PA)	2834	D	714 630-2467	3412
Nbty Manufacturing LLC	2834	C	714 765-8323	3458
S K Laboratories Inc	2834	D	714 695-9800	3496
Teco Diagnostics	2835	D	714 693-7788	3554
Botanx LLC	2844	E	714 854-1601	3635
Firmenich	2869	D	714 535-2871	3733
Saint-Gobain Ceramics Plas Inc	2869	C	714 701-3900	3736
Firmenich Incorporated	2899	C	714 535-2871	3798
Graffiti Shield Inc	3081	E	714 575-1100	3950
Nelco Products Inc	3083	C	714 879-4293	3966
Clean Cut Technologies LLC	3086	D	714 864-3500	3996
Aquatic Inc	3088	C	714 993-1220	4023
Anaheim Custom Extruders Inc	3089	E	714 693-8508	4050

	SIC	EMP	PHONE	ENTRY#
Bace Manufacturing Inc (HQ)	3089	A	714 630-6002	4059
Beemak Plastics LLC	3089	D	800 421-4393	4063
Berry Global Inc	3089	D	714 777-5200	4067
Charmaine Plastics Inc	3089	D	714 630-8117	4088
Edco Plastics Inc	3089	E	714 772-1986	4110
GT Styling Inc	3089	E	714 644-9214	4129
RPM Plastic Molding Inc	3089	E	714 630-9300	4231
Setco LLC	3089	C	812 424-2904	4238
Sonfarrel	3089	E	714 630-7280	4244
Sp Craftech I LLC	3089	E	714 630-8117	4246
Strand Art Company Inc	3089	E	714 777-0444	4252
Targus US LLC	3161	E	714 765-5555	4301
Maverick Abrasives Corporation	3291	D	714 854-9531	4484
Anaheim Extrusion Co Inc	3354	D	714 630-3111	4595
Venus Alloys Inc (PA)	3363	E	714 635-8800	4654
Cytec Engineered Materials Inc	3365	C	714 632-1174	4671
Sonfarrel Aerospace LLC	3365	D	714 630-7280	4677
Craftsman Unity LLC	3423	C	714 776-8995	4738
B & B Specialties Inc (PA)	3429	E	714 985-3000	4758
Hitech Metal Fabrication Corp	3441	E	714 635-3505	4837
S & R Architectural Metals Inc	3441	E	714 226-0108	4866
AAR Manufacturing Inc	3443	C	714 634-8807	4906
Tait & Associates Inc	3443	E	714 560-8222	4931
AMF Anaheim LLC	3444	E	714 363-9206	4948
California Chassis Inc	3444	C	714 666-8511	4963
International West Inc	3444	E	714 632-9190	4992
Metal-Fab Services Indust Inc	3444	E	714 630-7771	5007
Pinnacle Precision Shtmtl Corp	3444	D	714 777-3129	5019
Pinnacle Precision Shtmtl Corp (HQ)	3444	D	714 777-3129	5020
Steeldyne Industries	3444	E	714 630-6200	5039
Tri Precision Sheetmetal Inc	3444	E	714 632-8838	5048
K & J Wire Products Corp	3446	E	714 816-0360	5067
Orange County Erectors Inc	3448	E	714 502-8455	5086
CBS Fasteners LLC	3452	E	714 779-6368	5122
Dgl Holdings Inc	3452	E	714 630-7840	5123
Nylok LLC	3452	E	714 635-3993	5133
Ascent Manufacturing LLC	3469	E	714 540-6414	5173
Pacific Precision Metals Inc	3469	C	951 226-1500	5208
Spotter Global Inc	3469	C	515 817-3726	5214
Black Oxide Industries Inc	3471	E	714 870-9610	5239
Precision Anodizing & Pltg Inc	3471	D	714 996-1601	5285
Technic Inc	3471	E	714 632-0200	5298
Crest Coating Inc	3479	D	714 635-7090	5316
Performance Powder Inc	3479	E	714 632-0600	5337
Powdercoat Services LLC	3479	E	714 533-2251	5339
Superior Spring Company	3495	E	714 490-0881	5399
Rampone Industries LLC	3496	E	714 265-0200	5412
Rapid Mfg A Cal Ltd Partnr (PA)	3496	C	714 974-2432	5413
Bassani Manufacturing	3498	E	714 630-1821	5427
One-Way Manufacturing Inc	3498	E	714 630-8833	5436
J&S Goodwin Inc (HQ)	3537	D	714 956-4040	5531
Taylor-Dunn Manufacturing LLC (HQ)	3537	D	714 956-4040	5536
Waev Inc (PA)	3537	E	714 956-4040	5537
US Union Tool Inc (HQ)	3541	E	714 521-6242	5554
Kempton Machine Works Inc	3545	E	714 990-0596	5613
Weartech International Inc	3562	E	714 683-2430	5754
Adwest Technologies Inc (HQ)	3564	E	714 632-8595	5766
Hepa Corporation	3564	E	714 630-5700	5770
Wasser Filtration Inc (PA)	3569	E	714 696-6450	5936
Ryb Systems Inc (PA)	3577	C	714 491-1500	5949
Solaris Paper Inc	3579	C	714 687-6657	5960
Welbilt Fdsrvice Companies LLC	3585	B	323 245-3761	5992
Product Solutions Inc	3589	E	714 545-9757	6027
Rtr Industries LLC (PA)	3592	E	714 996-0050	6046
3d Machine Co Inc	3599	E	714 777-8985	6056
Cresco Manufacturing Inc	3599	E	714 525-2326	6110
Jaco Engineering	3599	E	714 991-1680	6151
Kerleylegacy63 Inc	3599	E	714 630-7286	6160
Moseys Production Machinists Inc (PA)	3599	E	714 693-4840	6187
Pen Manufacturing LLC	3599	E	714 992-0950	6201
Precision Waterjet Inc	3599	E	888 538-9287	6205
Roberts Precision Engrg Inc	3599	E	714 635-4485	6220
West Bond Inc (PA)	3599	E	714 978-1551	6272
Pacific Transformer Corp	3612	D	714 779-0450	6294
Anaheim Automation Inc	3625	E	714 992-6990	6340
Hestan Commercial Corporation	3639	C	714 869-2380	6401
Intense Lighting LLC	3646	E	714 630-9877	6464
Birchwood Lighting Inc	3648	E	714 550-7118	6492
Anacom General Corporation	3651	E	714 774-8484	6524
Digital Periph Solutions Inc	3651	E	714 998-3440	6533
Interntnal Cnnctors Cable Corp	3661	C	888 275-4422	6587
L3 Technologies Inc	3663	E	714 758-4222	6627
L3harris Interstate Elec Corp	3663	D	714 758-3395	6628
Econolite Control Products Inc (PA)	3669	C	714 630-3700	6681
Raytheon Applied Sgnal Tech In	3669	C	714 917-0255	6691
American Circuit Tech Inc (PA)	3672	E	714 777-2480	6707
APT Electronics Inc	3672	E	714 687-6760	6709
Chad Industries Incorporated	3672	E	714 938-0080	6716
Copper Clad Mltilayer Pdts Inc	3672	E	714 237-1388	6720
Excello Circuits Inc	3672	D	714 993-0560	6726
Jabil Inc	3672	E	714 938-0080	6741
Kca Electronics Inc	3672	C	714 239-2433	6743
Murrietta Circuits	3672	C	714 970-2430	6754
Smart Elec & Assembly Inc	3672	E	714 772-2651	6771
Summit Interconnect Inc (HQ)	3672	C	714 239-2433	6776
Transline Technology Inc	3672	E	714 533-8300	6777
Ttm Technologies Inc	3672	B	714 688-7200	6783
Si Manufacturing Inc	3677	C	714 956-7110	6938
Cristek Interconnects LLC (DH)	3678	C	714 696-5200	6946
General Power Systems Inc	3679	E	714 956-9321	7000
Jasper Electronics	3679	E	714 917-0749	7015
Magnetic Sensors Corporation	3679	C	714 630-8380	7022
Micrometals Inc (PA)	3679	C	714 970-9400	7026
Xp Power Inc	3679	E	714 712-2642	7071
Serra Laser and Waterjet Inc	3699	C	714 680-6211	7150
Phoenix Cars LLC	3711	E	909 987-0815	7188
Realtruck Enterprise Inc	3713	E	956 324-5337	7209
American Fabrication Corp (PA)	3714	D	714 632-1709	7225
Phoenix Motor Inc (DH)	3714	E	909 987-0815	7282
Aerospace Parts Holdings Inc	3728	A	949 877-3630	7417
Astro Spar Inc	3728	E	626 839-7858	7436
B/E Aerospace Macrolink	3728	E	714 777-8800	7443
Cal Tech Precision Inc	3728	D	714 992-4130	7447
Canyon Composites Incorporated	3728	E	714 991-8181	7448
D & D Gear Incorporated	3728	C	714 692-6570	7459
Ferra Aerospace Inc	3728	E	918 787-2220	7473
Gear Manufacturing Inc	3728	E	714 792-2895	7481
Giddens Industries Inc (DH)	3728	C		7483
Goodrich Corporation	3728	C	714 984-1461	7486
Hornet Acquisitionco LLC	3728	C	714 984-1461	7489
Pacific Contours Corporation	3728	D	714 693-1260	7532
Verus Aerospace LLC (HQ)	3728	E	949 877-3630	7588
DG Performance Spc Inc	3799	D	714 961-8850	7682
Apex Technology Holdings Inc	3812	A	321 270-3630	7692
Cummins Aerospace LLC (PA)	3812	E	714 879-2800	7711
Employer Defense Group	3812	E	949 200-0137	7717
L3 Technologies Inc	3812	E	714 956-9200	7728
Tuffer Manufacturing Co Inc	3812	E	714 526-3077	7821
3d Instruments LLC	3823	D	714 399-9200	7844
L3harris Interstate Elec Corp	3825	D	714 758-0500	7922
L3harris Interstate Elec Corp	3825	D	714 758-0500	7923
L3harris Interstate Elec Corp (DH)	3825	B	714 758-0500	7924
Endress & Hauser Conducta Inc	3826	E	800 835-5474	7953
Mettler Electronics Corp	3841	E	714 533-2221	8198
Sechrist Industries Inc	3841	A	714 579-8400	8226
Visionary Contact Lens Inc	3851	E	714 237-1900	8418
Golf Supply House Usa Inc	3949	D	714 983-0050	8519
Tuffstuff Fitness Intl Inc	3949	E	909 629-1600	8549
Matthew Warren Inc	3965	E	714 630-7840	8573
YKK (usa) Inc	3965	E	714 701-1200	8582
3s Sign Services Inc	3993	C	714 683-1120	8588
Coast Sign Incorporated	3993	E	714 520-9144	8594
Signage Solutions Corporation	3993	E	714 491-0299	8633
Sunset Signs and Printing Inc	3993	E	714 255-9104	8642
LA Spas Inc	3999	C	714 630-1150	8691
First Transit Inc	4111	D	714 644-9828	8754
Falck Mobile Health Corp	4119	B	714 828-7750	8825
Filyn Corporation	4119	E	714 632-0225	8826
M-G Disposal Service Inc	4212	D	714 238-3300	8919
Roy Miller Freight Lines LLC (PA)	4212	E	714 632-5511	8922
All Counties Courier Inc	4215	C	714 599-9300	8998
Di Overnite LLC	4215	D	877 997-7447	9001
Total Warehouse Inc	4225	C	714 332-3082	9120
DSV Solutions LLC	4731	D	714 630-0110	9276
TW Services Inc	4789	B	714 441-2400	9377
AT&T Enterprises LLC	4812	B	714 284-2878	9383
AT&T Enterprises LLC	4812	C	714 940-9976	9384
Zyxel Communications Inc	4813	D	714 632-0882	9473
Southern California Gas Co	4924	C	213 244-1200	9663
Southern California Gas Co	4924	C	714 634-3065	9665
City of Anaheim	4971	D	714 254-0125	9790
Califrnia Auto Dalers Exch LLC	5012	B	714 996-2400	9801
Cal-State Auto Parts Inc (PA)	5013	C	714 630-5950	9818
Competition Clutch Inc	5013	E	800 809-6598	9819
Empi Inc	5013	D	714 446-9606	9824
Reels Inc	5013	D	714 446-9606	9844

Employee Codes: A=Over 500 employees, B=251-500
C=101-250, D=51-100, E=20-50, F=10-19, G=1-9

2025 Southern California
Business Directory and Buyers Guide

© Mergent Inc. 1-800-342-5647

1251

GEOGRAPHIC

Name	SIC	EMP	PHONE	ENTRY#
Shrin LLC	5013	D	714 850-0303	9848
Greenball Corp (PA)	5014	E	714 782-3060	9856
Walnut Investment Corp	5031	A	714 238-9240	9933
General Procurement Inc (PA)	5045	D	949 679-7960	10007
Quad-C Jh Holdings Inc	5047	C	502 741-0421	10106
Sapphire Clean Rooms Inc	5049	C	714 316-5036	10121
Motive Energy LLC (PA)	5063	E	714 888-2525	10195
Quantum Automation (PA)	5063	E	714 854-0800	10204
Etekcity Corporation	5064	C	855 686-3835	10218
Bisco Industries Inc (HQ)	5065	D	800 323-1232	10232
L3harris Interstate Elec Corp	5065	E	714 758-0500	10261
Motors & Controls Whse Inc	5065	E	714 956-0480	10270
B & B Specialties Inc	5072	D	714 985-3075	10302
Shamrock Supply Company Inc (PA)	5072	C	714 575-1800	10313
George T Hall Co Inc (PA)	5075	E	909 825-9751	10333
Oliver Healthcare Packaging Co	5084	D	714 864-3500	10386
Midland Industries	5085	D	800 821-5725	10447
American Sanitary Supply Inc	5087	C	714 632-3010	10471
Self Serve Auto Dismantlers (PA)	5093	C	714 630-8901	10541
Ft 2 Inc	5099	C	714 765-5555	10561
Bunzl Distribution Cal LLC (DH)	5113	D	714 688-1900	10589
Oasis Brands Inc	5113	D	540 658-2830	10596
Michael Gerald Ltd	5136	E	562 921-9611	10689
Alstyle AP & Activewear MGT Co (HQ)	5137	A	714 765-0400	10701
Bridgford Marketing Company (DH)	5147	D	714 526-5533	10866
Family Tree Produce Inc	5148	C	714 693-5688	10899
Friedas Inc	5148	D	714 826-6100	10900
Legacy Farms LLC	5148	D	714 736-1800	10911
Harris Freeman & Co Inc (PA)	5149	B	714 765-7525	10948
Orange County Indus Plas Inc (PA)	5162	E	714 632-9450	10999
Straub Distributing Co Ltd (PA)	5181	C	714 779-4000	11052
Targus International LLC (HQ)	5199	C	714 765-5555	11145
Home Depot USA Inc	5211	D	714 921-1215	11195
Lowes Home Centers LLC	5211	D	714 447-6140	11204
Paragon Industries Inc	5211	D	714 778-1800	11249
Stater Bros Markets	5411	E	714 991-5310	11282
Emergency Vehicle Group Inc	5511	E	714 238-0110	11342
Isuzu North America Corp (HQ)	5511	C	714 935-9300	11363
Cintas Corporation	5699	D	714 646-2550	11507
Rm Partners Inc	5713	E	714 765-5725	11525
Slaters 50/50	5812	C	714 602-8115	11600
Melton Intl Tackle Inc	5961	E	714 978-9192	11655
Credit Union Southern Cal (PA)	6061	D	562 698-8326	11794
Carrington Mrtg Holdings LLC	6162	C	888 267-0584	11892
Caballero & Sons Inc	6221	E	562 368-1644	12011
Carl Warren & Company LLC (HQ)	6411	C	657 622-4200	12189
First Team RE - Orange Cnty	6531	D	714 974-9191	12446
House Seven Gables RE Inc	6531	D	714 282-0306	12465
House Seven Gables RE Inc	6531	C	714 974-7000	12466
Fortress Holding Group LLC	6719	C	714 202-8710	12598
1855 S Hbr Blvd Drv Hldngs LLC	7011	C	714 750-1811	12752
American Koyu Corporation	7011	C	626 793-0669	12759
Anaheim - 1855 S Hbr Blvd Owne	7011	C	714 750-1811	12761
Best Western Stovalls Inn (PA)	7011	D	714 956-4430	12773
Cinderella Motel	7011	C	559 432-0118	12794
Comfort California Inc	7011	C	714 750-3131	12798
Disney Enterprises Inc	7011	A	714 778-6600	12811
Disneyland International	7011	A	714 956-6746	12812
Edward Thomas Companies	7011	C	714 782-7500	12817
Fjs Inc	7011	C	714 905-1050	12825
Ken Real Estate Lease Ltd	7011	D	714 778-1700	12883
Makar Anaheim LLC	7011	A	714 750-4321	12912
Northwest Hotel Corporation (PA)	7011	C	714 776-6120	12940
Orangewood LLC	7011	D	714 750-3000	12954
Portofino Inn & Suites Anaheim	7011	A	714 782-7600	12976
SAI Management Co Inc	7011	C	714 772-5050	13008
Wco Hotels Inc	7011	A	714 635-2300	13072
Westin Anaheim Resort	7011	D	657 279-9786	13077
GBS Linens (PA)	7213	D	714 778-6448	13117
Exactax Inc (PA)	7291	D	714 284-4802	13163
Internal Revenue Service	7291	D	714 512-2818	13165
Fci Lender Services Inc	7322	C	800 931-2424	13283
Vengroff Williams & Assoc Inc	7322	C	714 889-6200	13290
Advantage Mailing LLC (PA)	7331	C	714 538-3881	13299
AST Sportswear Inc	7331	B	714 223-2030	13300
Consolidated Design West Inc	7336	E	714 999-1476	13323
Infosend Inc (PA)	7338	E	714 993-2690	13340
Rentokil North America Inc	7342	D	714 563-2450	13349
Your Way Fumigation Inc	7342	D	951 699-9116	13350
Coastal Building Services Inc	7349	B	714 775-2855	13364
DMS Facility Services Inc	7349	A	949 975-1366	13372
Hunter Easterday Corporation	7349	C	714 238-3400	13377
Priority Building Services LLC (PA)	7349	D	714 255-2963	13406
So Cal Land Maintenance Inc	7349	D	714 231-1454	13421
Go-Staff Inc	7361	A	657 242-9350	13523
Anamex Corporation (PA)	7371	E	714 779-7055	13653
Blaze Solutions Inc	7371	D	415 964-5689	13676
Bpo Management Services Inc (PA)	7371	D	714 972-2670	13679
New CAM Commerce Solutions LLC	7371	D	714 338-0200	13780
Select Data Inc	7371	C	714 577-1000	13816
Bpoms/Hro Inc (HQ)	7372	D	714 974-2670	13895
Unlimited Innovations Inc	7372	E	714 998-0866	14060
Morphotrak LLC (DH)	7373	C	714 238-2000	14097
Cyber-Pro Systems Inc	7374	C	562 256-3800	14128
Bcp Systems Inc	7378	D	714 202-3900	14185
Etherwan Systems Inc	7379	D	714 779-3800	14217
Partners Information Tech (HQ)	7379	D	714 736-4487	14241
Califrnia Sthland Prvate SEC L	7381	C	714 367-4005	14283
ADT LLC	7382	D	714 450-6461	14375
ADT LLC	7382	C	626 593-1020	14376
G4s Justice Services LLC	7382	C	800 589-6003	14401
Kesa Incorporated	7382	E	714 956-2827	14410
Sentinel Offender Services LLC (PA)	7382	D	949 453-1550	14421
Freeman Expositions LLC	7389	C	714 254-3400	14497
Freeman Expositions LLC	7389	C	858 320-7800	14498
MB Coatings Inc	7389	D	714 625-2118	14541
Nor-Cal Beverage Co Inc	7389	C	714 526-8600	14559
Pmc Inc	7389	C	714 967-7230	14574
T L Fabrications LP	7692	D	562 802-3980	14745
R & S Ovrhd Doors So-Cal Inc	7699	E	714 680-0600	14786
Disney Enterprises Inc	7812	D	407 397-6000	14819
Disney Enterprises Inc	7812	C	714 781-1651	14820
Hob Entertainment LLC	7929	C	714 520-2310	14990
Anaheim Arena Management LLC	7941	A	714 704-2400	15016
Anaheim Ducks Hockey Club LLC (PA)	7941	D	714 940-2900	15017
Angels Baseball LP (PA)	7941	D	714 940-2000	15018
Rachas Inc	7991	C	714 290-0636	15059
Eagle Vnes Vnyrds Golf CLB LLC	7992	D	707 257-4470	15077
Disneyland International (DH)	7996	C	714 781-4565	15103
Adventure City Inc	7999	D	714 821-3311	15191
Kaiser Foundation Hospitals	8011	D	714 279-4675	15338
Southern Cal Prmnnte Med Group	8011	C	714 279-4675	15473
Vanguard Health Systems Inc	8011	B	714 635-6272	15505
Quantum Bhvioral Solutions Inc	8049	D	626 531-6999	15554
Anaheim Healthcare Center LLC	8051	C	714 816-0540	15567
Coventry Court Health Center	8051	C	714 636-2800	15618
Mark & Fred Enterprises	8051	C	714 821-1993	15716
Oceanside Harbor Holdings LLC	8051	C	760 331-3177	15727
Westview Services Inc	8051	D	714 956-4199	15802
Windsor Anaheim Healthcare (PA)	8051	C	714 826-8950	15803
Ahmc Anheim Rgional Med Ctr LP	8062	B	714 774-1450	15897
Ahmc Anheim Rgional Med Ctr LP	8062	B	714 999-3847	15898
Ahmc Anheim Rgional Med Ctr LP	8062	A	714 774-1450	15899
Anaheim Global Medical Center	8062	A	714 533-6220	15912
Kaiser Foundation Hospitals	8062	A	714 644-2000	16055
Prime Healthcare Anaheim LLC	8062	A	714 827-3000	16139
Providence Medical Foundation (DH)	8062	C	714 712-3308	16152
Tenet Healthsystem Medical Inc	8062	A	714 428-6800	16227
Ahmc Anheim Rgional Med Ctr LP (HQ)	8069	B	714 774-1450	16281
Korean Community Services Inc	8069	C	714 527-6561	16295
St Jseph Hlth Sys HM Care Svc	8082	A	714 712-9500	16423
Behavioral Health Works Inc	8093	D	800 249-1266	16444
Optumcare Management LLC	8099	D	714 995-1000	16599
Real Estate Trainers Inc	8249	E	800 282-2352	16846
Mark 1 Restoration Service LLC	8322	D	714 283-9990	16977
Orange Cnty Adult Achvment Ctr	8322	C	714 744-5301	16987
Westview Services Inc	8331	C	714 635-2444	17074
Ardcore Senior Living	8361	B	714 974-2226	17120
Leisure Care LLC	8361	C	714 974-1616	17174
Automobile Club Southern Cal	8699	C	714 774-2392	17454
Development Resource Cons Inc (PA)	8711	D	714 685-6860	17512
DMS Facility Services LLC	8711	A	949 975-1366	17516
Imeg Consultants Corp	8711	D	714 490-5555	17554
Nest Parent Inc	8711	A	310 551-0101	17596
Plump Engineering Inc	8711	D	714 385-1835	17612
Willdan Group Inc (PA)	8711	C	800 424-9144	17662
Country Villa Service Corp (PA)	8741	D	310 574-3733	17971
Traffic Management Inc	8741	C	562 264-2353	18066
Tricom Management LLC	8741	C	714 630-2029	18068
Branded Group Inc	8742	C	323 940-1444	18108
Consumer Resource Network LLC	8742	B	800 291-4794	18120
Ralph Brennan Rest Group LLC	8742	C	714 776-5200	18200
Shell Oil Company	8742	C	714 991-9200	18209
Workcare Inc	8744	C	714 978-7488	18271
Aliantel Inc	8748	D	714 829-1650	18281
C M E Corp	8748	C	714 632-6939	18295

Mergent email: customerrelations@mergent.com
1252

2025 Southern California
Business Directory and Buyers Guide

(P-0000) Products & Services Section entry number
(PA)=Parent Co (HQ)=Headquarters (DH)=Div Headquarters

	SIC	EMP	PHONE	ENTRY#
Edge Mortgage Advisory Co LLC	8748	D	714 564-5800	18306
Rubio Arts Corporation	8999	C	407 849-1643	18379

ANGELUS OAKS, CA - San Bernardino County

	SIC	EMP	PHONE	ENTRY#
YMCA of East Valley	8641	C	909 794-1702	17379

ANZA, CA - Riverside County

	SIC	EMP	PHONE	ENTRY#
Cahuilla Creek Rest & Casino	7999	C	951 763-1200	15196

APPLE VALLEY, CA - San Bernardino County

	SIC	EMP	PHONE	ENTRY#
Brightview Tree Company	0781	D	760 955-2560	160
West Coast Furn Framers Inc	2426	E	760 669-5275	2293
American Integrity Corp	3089	E	760 247-1082	4046
Cemex Cement Inc	3273	E	760 381-7616	4434
Consolidated Frt Systems LLC	3537	E	310 424-9924	5526
Induction Technology Corp	3567	E	760 246-7333	5800
Pac-Refco Inc	3585	E	760 956-8600	5979
Reid Products Inc	3599	E	760 240-1355	6216
Cco Holdings LLC	4841	C	760 810-4076	9531
Biodefensor Corporation	5075	E	888 899-2956	10329
Lowes Home Centers LLC	5211	C	760 961-3000	11216
Northfield Medical Inc	7699	C	248 268-2500	14777
St Mary Medical Center LLC **(HQ)**	8062	C	760 242-2311	16221
St Mary Medical Center LLC	8062	A	760 946-8767	16222
BEST Opportunities Inc	8331	C	760 628-0111	17049
Califrnia Assn Hlth Edcatn Lnk	8621	D	760 955-3536	17295
High Dsert Prtnr In Acdmic Exc	8732	B	760 946-5414	17847

ARCADIA, CA - Los Angeles County

	SIC	EMP	PHONE	ENTRY#
Sing Kung Corp	2041	E	626 358-5838	1407
Relton Corporation	2899	D	800 423-1505	3819
Danco Anodizing Inc **(PA)**	3471	E	626 445-3303	5253
Ev Charging Solutions Inc	3694	C	866 300-3827	7092
Segway Inc	3751	C	603 222-6000	7635
MPS Anzon LLC	3842	C	626 471-3553	8290
Transdev Services Inc	4119	A	626 357-7912	8851
Coach Usa Inc	4142	C	626 357-7912	8863
365 Delivery Inc	4212	D	818 815-5005	8886
Gar Enterprises **(PA)**	5045	C	626 574-1175	10004
Penney Opco LLC	5311	C	626 445-6454	11263
Welltower Om Group LLC	6512	C	626 254-0552	12326
Property Care Building Svc LLC	7349	C	626 623-6420	13411
Post Alarm Systems **(PA)**	7382	D	626 446-7159	14415
Los Angeles Turf Club Inc **(DH)**	7948	C	626 574-6330	15039
Country Villa Service Corp	8051	C	626 445-2421	15606
Arcadia Gardens MGT Corp	8052	D	626 574-8571	15806
Arcadia Convalescent Hosp Inc **(PA)**	8059	C	626 445-2170	15835
Methodist Hospital of S CA	8062	A	626 574-3755	16097
Usc Arcadia Hospital **(PA)**	8062	A	626 898-8000	16249
Encompass Health Corporation	8093	D	626 445-4714	16472
Christian Arcadia School	8211	D	626 574-8229	16804
Pacific Clinics	8322	A	626 254-5000	16989
Leisure Care LLC	8361	C	626 447-0106	17173

ARLETA, CA - Los Angeles County

	SIC	EMP	PHONE	ENTRY#
Superior Thread Rolling Co	3599	D	818 504-3626	6245

ARROYO GRANDE, CA - San Luis Obispo County

	SIC	EMP	PHONE	ENTRY#
Greenheart Farms Inc	0191	B	805 481-2234	81
Talley Farms	0723	C	805 489-2508	120
Anderson Burton Cnstr Inc **(PA)**	1542	D	805 481-5096	516
Corbett Vineyards LLC	2084	E	805 782-9463	1561
Laetitia Vineyard & Winery Inc	2004	D	805 481-1772	1577
Crosno Construction Inc	3441	E	805 343-7437	4830
Phillips 66 Co Carbon Group	3559	E	805 489-4050	5717
Golden State Phone & Wireless	4812	D	805 545-5400	9402
Cco Holdings LLC	4841	C	805 904-1047	9533
Ameri-Kleen	7349	C	805 546-0706	13354
Maxim Healthcare Services Inc	7363	D	805 489-2685	13611
Compass Health Inc	8051	D	805 489-8137	15600
Arroyo Grande Community Hospital	8062	B	805 473-7626	15918
Mhm Services Inc	8093	D	805 904-6678	16486
Compass Health Inc	8361	C	805 474-7260	17134

ARTESIA, CA - Los Angeles County

	SIC	EMP	PHONE	ENTRY#
California Dairies Inc	2026	D	562 809-2595	1326
Cal Plate **(PA)**	3555	D	562 403-3000	5660
Edata Solutions Inc	7374	A	510 574-5380	14130
Pacs Group Inc	8051	C	562 865-0271	15731
Windsor Twin Plms Hlthcare Ctr	8051	C	562 865-0271	15805
Artesia Christian Home Inc	8059	C	562 865-5218	15836
County of Los Angeles	8093	C	562 402-0688	16460
Automobile Club Southern Cal	8699	D	562 924-6636	17437

ARVIN, CA - Kern County

	SIC	EMP	PHONE	ENTRY#
Tasteful Selections LLC	0134	B	661 854-3998	3
Grimmway Enterprises Inc	0723	B	661 854-6250	109
Grimmway Enterprises Inc	0723	B	661 854-6200	110
Kern Ridge Growers LLC	0723	B	661 854-3141	113
Grimmway Enterprises Inc	1541	B	661 854-6240	483
F Korbel & Bros	2084	E	661 854-6137	1567
Son of A Barista Usa LLC	2095	E	323 788-8718	1720
Sandusky Lee LLC	2514	E	661 854-5551	2474
Reeves Extruded Products Inc	3089	D	661 854-5970	4219
Grimmway Enterprises Inc	4212	D	307 302-0090	8912
Blue Beacon USA LP	7542	C	661 858-2090	14704
Evergreen Health Care LLC	8051	A	661 854-4475	15651
Pacs Group Inc	8051	C	661 854-4475	15735
Grimmway Enterprises Inc	8741	C	661 854-6200	17989

ATASCADERO, CA - San Luis Obispo County

	SIC	EMP	PHONE	ENTRY#
Chemlogics Group LLC	2869	E	805 591-3314	3732
Compass Health Inc	8051	C	805 466-9254	15601
Califrnia Dept State Hospitals	8063	A	805 468-2000	16270
Star of Ca LLC	8099	D	805 466-1638	16619
Seneca Family of Agencies	8322	C	805 434-2449	17009

AVALON, CA - Los Angeles County

	SIC	EMP	PHONE	ENTRY#
Intervrsity Chrstn Fllwshp/Usa	7032	B	310 510-0015	13103
Avalon Medical Dev Corp	8062	D	310 510-0700	15920

AVILA BEACH, CA - San Luis Obispo County

	SIC	EMP	PHONE	ENTRY#
Veolia Wts Usa Inc	2899	D	805 545-3743	3822
Pacific Gas and Electric Co	4911	A	805 506-5280	9598

AZUSA, CA - Los Angeles County

	SIC	EMP	PHONE	ENTRY#
Richard Wilson Wellington	0181	D	626 812-7881	68
Sunbelt Controls Inc	1711	D	626 610-2340	846
Berger Bros Inc	1742	B	626 334-2699	997
Oj Insulation LP **(HQ)**	1742	C	800 707-9278	1017
Heidi Corporation	1771	D	626 333-6317	1120
CTI Foods Azusa LLC	2013	C	626 633-1609	1256
McKeever Danlee Confectionary	2064	C	626 334-8964	1510
Very Special Chocolats Inc	2066	C	626 334-7838	1511
Carters Metal Fabricators Inc	2522	E	626 815-4225	2522
Holguin & Holguin Inc	2531	E	626 815-0168	2543
Joseph Manufacturing Co Inc	2531	D	626 334-1471	2547
Artisan Screen Printing Inc	2759	C	626 815-2700	3119
S&B Pharma Inc	2833	D	626 334-2908	3330
Bbeautiful LLC	2844	C	626 610-2332	3633
Westwood Laboratories LLC **(PA)**	2844	E	626 969-3305	3698
Westwood Laboratories LLC	2844	C	626 969-3305	3699
D W Mack Co Inc	3053	E	626 969-1817	3884
California Amforge Corporation	3312	C	626 334-4931	4513
Inwesco Incorporated **(HQ)**	3315	D	626 334-7115	4536
Inovativ Inc	3334	E	626 969-5300	4577
Magparts **(HQ)**	3365	C	626 334-7897	4676
Rain Bird Corporation	3432	C	626 812-3400	4806
Melco Steel Inc	3443	E	626 334-7875	4916
Lindsey Manufacturing Co	3463	C	626 969-3471	5156
Rain Bird Corporation **(PA)**	3494	C	626 812-3400	5390
Gale Banks Engineering	3519	C	626 969-9600	5468
Trio Engineered Products Inc **(HQ)**	3531	E	626 851-3966	5499
Ancra International LLC **(HQ)**	3537	E	626 765-4800	5524
Ancra International LLC	3537	C	626 765-4818	5525
Marples Gears Inc	3566	C	626 570-1744	5795
Acme Portable Machines Inc	3571	E	626 610-1888	5838
A & B Aerospace Inc	3599	E	626 334-2976	6058
Kemac Technology Inc	3599	E	626 334-1519	6159
Screwmatic Inc	3599	D	626 334-7831	6230
Phaostron Instr Electronic Co	3613	C	626 969-6801	6309
Ptb Sales Inc **(PA)**	3679	C	626 334-0500	7040
Skylock Industries LLC	3728	D	626 334-2391	7563
Northrop Grumman Systems Corp	3812	A	626 812-1000	7775
Northrop Grumman Systems Corp	3812	A	626 812-1400	7779
Tecomet Inc	3841	C	626 334-1519	8236
Dhb Delivery LLC	4215	D	626 588-7562	9000
Cco Holdings LLC	4841	C	626 513-0204	9529
City of Azusa	4941	C	626 969-4408	9683
San Gabriel Valley Water Assn	4941	D	626 815-1305	9714
Hanson Distributing Company **(PA)**	5013	C	626 224-9800	9827
Cemex Cement Inc	5032	C	626 969-1747	9939
Totten Tubes Inc **(PA)**	5051	C	626 812-0220	10162
Niscayah Inc	5065	D	626 683-8167	10272
Smart Stores Operations LLC	5141	B	626 334-5189	10783
Buena Vista Food Products Inc **(DH)**	5149	C	626 815-8859	10933
Arrietta Incorporated	5411	E	626 334-0302	11273

Employee Codes: A=Over 500 employees, B=251-500
C=101-250, D=51-100, E=20-50, F=10-19, G=1-9

2025 Southern California
Business Directory and Buyers Guide

© Mergent Inc. 1-800-342-5647

1253

GEOGRAPHIC

	SIC	EMP	PHONE	ENTRY#
Jourducci Inc.	7217	C	626 791-9400	13137
Mc-40 (PA)	7349	D	323 225-4111	13389
Ruiteng Internet Technology Co.	7374	C	302 597-7438	14152
Casa Clina Hosp Ctrs For Hlthc.	8049	C	626 334-8735	15537
Valley Lght Ctr For Scial Advn.	8331	D	626 337-6200	17069

BAKERSFIELD, CA - Kern County

	SIC	EMP	PHONE	ENTRY#
J G Boswell Company	0131	A	661 327-7721	1
Vignolo Farms Inc.	0131	D	661 746-2148	2
Bolthouse Farms.	0161	A	661 366-7205	8
Generis Holdings LP (PA)	0161	C	661 366-7209	11
7th Standard Ranch Company.	0172	B	661 399-0416	28
Giumarra Vineyards Corporation.	0172	B	661 395-7071	31
Crystal Organic Farms LLC.	0191	D	661 845-5200	79
Dv Custom Farming LLC.	0191	D	661 858-2888	80
Maple Dairy LP.	0241	D	661 396-9600	92
AC Irrigation Holdco LLC.	0711	C	661 368-3550	100
Sunridge Nurseries Inc.	0721	D	661 363-8463	101
Grimmway Enterprises Inc.	0723	C	661 845-5200	111
Sun World International Inc (PA)	0723	A	661 392-5000	119
Wonderful Company LLC.	0723	A	559 781-7438	124
Ag-Wise Enterprises Inc (PA)	0762	C	661 325-1567	140
Illume Agriculture LLC.	0762	C	661 587-5198	142
Sun Pacific Farming Coop Inc.	0762	D	661 399-0376	145
Penney Lawn Service Inc.	0782	D	661 587-4788	231
Aera Energy LLC.	1311	A	661 665-5000	264
Berry Petroleum Company LLC (HQ)	1311	E	661 616-3900	266
Hathaway LLC.	1311	E	661 393-2004	274
Tri-Valley Corporation.	1311	E	661 864-0500	279
Unified Field Services Corp.	1311	E	661 325-8962	280
Vaquero Energy Incorporated.	1311	E	661 363-7240	281
Aera Energy Services Company (HQ)	1381	A	661 665-5000	287
Elysium Jennings LLC.	1381	C	661 679-1700	288
Excalibur Well Services Corp.	1381	C	661 589-5338	289
Geo Guidance Drilling Svcs Inc (PA)	1381	D	661 833-9999	290
Golden State Drilling Inc.	1381	D	661 589-0730	291
Petro-Lud Inc.	1381	E	661 747-4779	293
E & B Ntral Resources Mgt Corp (PA)	1382	C	661 387-8500	300
Freeport-Mcmoran Oil & Gas LLC.	1382	C	661 322-7600	303
Linnco LLC.	1382	A	661 616-3900	307
Sentinel Peak Rsources Cal LLC.	1382	D	661 395-5214	314
Basic Energy Services Inc.	1389	E	661 588-3800	318
C&J Well Services LLC.	1389	A	661 589-5220	319
Casing Specialties Inc.	1389	E	661 399-5522	322
CJ Berry Well Services MGT LLC.	1389	A	661 589-5220	324
CL Knox Inc.	1389	D	661 837-0477	326
Cummings Vacuum Service Inc.	1389	D	661 746-1786	327
Halliburton Company.	1389	D	661 393-8111	332
Hills Wldg & Engrg Contr Inc.	1389	D	661 746-5400	334
John M Phillips LLC.	1389	E	661 327-3118	340
Mmi Services Inc.	1389	C	661 589-9366	345
Nabors Well Services Co.	1389	C	661 588-6140	346
Nabors Well Services Co.	1389	C	661 589-3970	347
Nabors Well Services Co.	1389	B	661 392-7668	348
Owen Oil Tools LP.	1389	D	661 637-1380	355
Pacific Process Systems Inc (PA)	1389	D	661 321-9681	357
Production Data Inc.	1389	E	661 327-4776	359
Pros Incorporated.	1389	D	661 589-5400	360
PSC Industrial Outsourcing LP.	1389	D	661 833-9991	361
Schlumberger Technology Corp.	1389	D	661 864-4721	363
Titan Oilfield Services Inc.	1389	D	661 861-1630	364
Truitt Oilfield Maint Corp.	1389	B	661 871-4099	366
U S Weatherford L P.	1389	C	661 589-9483	368
Pioneer Sands LLC.	1446	E	661 746-5789	378
Colombo Construction Co Inc.	1542	D	661 316-0100	532
PCL Industrial Services Inc.	1542	D	661 832-3995	567
Griffith Company.	1611	B	661 392-6640	620
Construction Specialty Svc Inc.	1623	D	661 864-7573	669
Diversified Utility Svcs Inc.	1623	D	661 325-3212	670
K S Fabrication & Machine Inc.	1623	C	661 617-1700	682
KS Industries LP (PA)	1623	A	661 617-1700	684
Nts Inc.	1623	B	661 588-8514	687
Southwest Contractors (PA)	1623	E	661 588-0484	696
Thermal Energy Solutions Inc.	1623	E	661 489-4100	700
Frontier Mechanical Inc.	1711	D	661 589-6203	781
Hps Mechanical Inc (PA)	1711	C	661 397-2121	787
Rlh Fire Protection Inc (PA)	1711	D	661 322-9344	832
Sun Solar Energy Solutions Inc.	1711	E	661 379-7000	845
Ardent Companies Inc.	1731	D	661 633-1465	885
Contra Costa Electric Inc.	1731	C	661 322-4036	903
Electrical & Instrumentation Unlimi.	1731	C		912
Energy Watch	1731	D	661 324-0930	915
Pavletich Elc Cmmnications Inc (PA)	1731	D	661 589-9473	950

	SIC	EMP	PHONE	ENTRY#
Sunshine Metal Clad Inc.	1742	D	661 366-0575	1031
Baymarr Constructors Inc.	1771	C	661 395-1676	1104
Kenai Drilling Limited	1781	C	661 587-0117	1144
Zim Industries Inc.	1781	C	661 393-9661	1146
Guinn Corporation.	1794	D	661 325-6109	1171
Sturgeon Son Grading & Pav Inc (PA)	1794	C	661 322-4408	1175
Nestle Usa Inc.	2023	C	661 398-3536	1303
Vita-Pakt Citrus Products Co (PA)	2033	E	626 332-1101	1361
Wm Bolthouse Farms Inc (HQ)	2037	A	800 467-4683	1382
Sun-Gro Commodities Inc (PA)	2048	E	661 393-2612	1434
Temblor Brewing LLC.	2082	E	661 489-4855	1556
Giumarra Vineyards Corporation.	2084	C	661 395-7000	1574
American Bottling Company.	2086	D	661 323-7921	1603
Crystal Geyser Water Company.	2086	E	661 323-6296	1615
Crystal Geyser Water Company.	2086	E	661 321-0896	1616
Pepsi-Cola Bottling Group.	2086	D	661 635-1100	1628
Reyes Coca-Cola Bottling LLC.	2086	E	661 324-6531	1644
Alfred Louie Incorporated.	2099	E	661 831-2520	1737
American Yeast Corporation.	2099	E	661 834-1050	1738
Well Analysis Corporation Inc (PA)	2411	E	661 283-9510	2284
Hoover Treated Wood Pdts Inc.	2491	E	661 833-0429	2406
West Coast Wood Preserving LLC.	2491	E	661 833-0429	2407
Harrell Holdings (PA)	2711	C	661 322-5627	2801
Amber Chemical Inc.	2819	E	661 325-2072	3227
Championx LLC.	2819	E	661 834-0454	3234
Glam and Glits Nail Design Inc.	2844	D	661 393-4800	3654
Kern Oil & Refining Co (HQ)	2911	C	661 845-0761	3825
MTS Solutions LLC.	2911	E	661 589-5804	3826
San Joaquin Refining Co Inc.	2911	C	661 327-4257	3830
Tricor Refining LLC.	2911	E	661 393-7110	3833
Newby Rubber Inc.	3069	E	661 327-5137	3926
Hancor Inc.	3084	D	661 366-1520	3974
Pactiv LLC.	3089	E	661 392-4000	4190
Golden Empire Con Pdts Inc.	3272	D	661 833-4490	4394
Consolidated Fibrgls Pdts Co.	3296	E	661 323-6026	4491
Kern Steel Fabrication Inc (PA)	3441	C	661 327-9588	4843
Spartan Inc.	3441	E	661 327-1205	4870
PNa Construction Tech Inc.	3444	E	661 326-1700	5022
Jts Modular Inc.	3448	E	661 835-9270	5081
Western Valve Inc.	3491	E	661 327-7660	5371
Russell Fabrication Corp.	3498	E	661 861-8495	5438
Material Control Inc.	3499	C	661 617-6033	5452
Marie Edward Vineyards Inc.	3523	E	661 363-5038	5474
Altec Inc.	3531	E	661 679-4177	5486
Sturgeon Services Intl Inc.	3531	B	661 322-4408	5498
Chancellor Oil Tools Inc.	3533	E	661 324-2213	5506
Downhole Stabilization Inc.	3533	E	661 631-1044	5509
Global Elastomeric Pdts Inc.	3533	D	661 831-5380	5510
Kba Engineering LLC.	3533	E	661 323-0487	5511
Timec Companies Inc.	3559	E	661 322-8177	5722
Total Process Solutions LLC.	3561	E	661 829-7910	5745
Mazzei Injector Company LLC.	3589	E	661 363-6500	6022
Seaco Technologies Inc.	3589	E	661 326-1522	6030
B & B Pipe and Tool Co.	3599	E	661 323-8208	6088
Bakersfield Machine Co Inc.	3599	D	661 709-1992	6090
Energy Link Indus Svcs Inc.	3599	E	661 765-4444	6121
Valley Perforating LLC.	3599	D	661 324-4964	6261
Custom Truck One Source LP	3713	E	316 627-2608	7200
Douglass Truck Bodies Inc.	3713	E	661 327-0258	7201
Tiger Tanks Inc.	3795	E	661 363-8335	7681
Computational Systems Inc.	3823	D	661 832-5306	7852
Townsend Industries Inc.	3842	D	661 837-1795	8310
Townsend Industries Inc.	3842	D	661 837-1795	8311
Townsend Industries Inc (DH)	3842	C	661 837-1795	8312
Golden Empire Transit District (PA)	4111	B	661 869-2438	8756
Hall Ambulance Service Inc.	4119	D	661 322-8741	8830
Gazelle Transportation LLC.	4212	C	661 322-8868	8909
Esparza Enterprises Inc.	4213	A	661 631-0347	8948
Mashburn Trmsp Svcs Inc.	4213	D	661 763-5724	8965
Stevens Transportation Inc.	4213	C	661 366-3286	8975
Exeter Packers Inc.	4222	C	661 399-0416	9036
United States Cold Storage Inc.	4222	D	661 832-2653	9044
Nex Group LLC.	4731	E	209 317-6677	9317
AGM California Inc.	4832	C	661 328-0118	9475
Newport Television LLC.	4833	A	661 283-1700	9513
Prosoft Technology Inc (HQ)	4899	D	661 716-5100	9569
Mt Poso Cgnrtion A Cal Ltd PR.	4911	C	661 663-3155	9591
Southern California Gas Co.	4924	C	661 399-4431	9657
MP Environmental Svcs Inc (PA)	4953	C	800 458-3036	9751
Varner Bros Inc.	4953	D	661 399-2944	9771
Bakersfield Shingles Wholesale Inc.	5039	D	661 327-3727	9960
Jims Supply Co Inc (PA)	5051	D	661 616-6977	10142
Cameron West Coast Inc.	5082	D		10345

Mergent email: customerrelations@mergent.com
1254

2025 Southern California
Business Directory and Buyers Guide

(P-0000) Products & Services Section entry number
(PA)=Parent Co (HQ)=Headquarters (DH)=Div Headquarters

	SIC	EMP	PHONE	ENTRY#
Gottstein Corporation	5082	C	661 322-8934	10349
Quinn Company	5082	D	661 393-5800	10357
Surface Pumps Inc (PA)	5084	D	661 393-1545	10407
Valley Power Systems Inc	5084	C	661 325-9001	10412
Westair Gases & Equipment Inc	5084	C	661 387-6800	10418
Custom Building Products LLC	5085	D	661 393-0422	10433
Dhv Industries Inc	5085	C	661 392-8948	10435
Nestle Ice Cream Company	5143	A	661 398-3500	10833
Frito-Lay North America Inc	5145	C	661 328-6034	10846
Sun Pacific Marketing Coop Inc	5148	B	661 847-1015	10318
Aspire Bakeries LLC	5149	C	661 832-0409	10929
Core-Mark International Inc	5149	C	661 366-2673	10941
Geo Drilling Fluids Inc (PA)	5169	E	661 325-5919	11013
Valley Pacific Petro Svcs Inc	5172	D	661 746-7737	11037
Advance Beverage Co Inc	5181	C	661 833-3783	11038
Emser Tile LLC	5211	E	661 837-4400	11152
Lowes Home Centers LLC	5211	C	661 889-9000	11240
Cjm Automotive Group Inc	5511	D	661 332-3000	11327
Haberfelde Ford (PA)	5511	C	661 328-3600	11358
Motor City Sales & Service (PA)	5511	C	661 836-9000	11384
Three-Way Chevrolet Co (PA)	5511	C	661 847-6400	11419
Castle Harlan Partners III LP	5812	A	661 863-0305	11555
Jipcob Inc	5812	C	661 859-1111	11580
Mexicali Inc	5812	C	661 327-3861	11590
Strata Federal Credit Union	6061	D	661 327-9461	11816
Valley Strong Credit Union	6061	D	661 833-7900	11820
Golden Empire Mortgage Inc (PA)	6162	D	661 328-1600	11907
Golden Empire Mortgage Inc (PA)	6162	D	661 328-1600	11908
Merrill Lynch Prce Fnner Smith	6211	C	661 326-7700	11977
Health Net LLC	6324	C	661 321-3904	12081
State Compensation Insur Fund	6331	D	661 664-4000	12137
State Farm Mutl Auto Insur Co	6411	D	309 766-2311	12255
Bakersfield Westwind Corp	6531	C	661 327-2121	12386
Preferred Brokers Inc (PA)	6531	D	661 836-2345	12507
Stantec Holdings Del III Inc	6719	B	661 396-3770	12615
Msr Hotels & Resorts Inc	6799	C	661 325-9700	12721
Cni Thl Propco Fe LLC	7011	D	661 325-9700	12796
Golden West Partners Inc	7011	C	661 324-6936	12829
Nandi-Laksh Inc	7011	D	661 322-1012	12934
Newport Hospitality Group Inc	7011	D	661 323-1900	12937
Europro Inc	7299	D	661 588-5666	13174
Banks Pest Control	7342	C	661 323-7858	13342
Western Energy Services Corp	7353	C	403 984-5916	13444
Western Oilfields Supply Co	7359	D	480 895-9225	13478
Western Oilfields Supply Co (PA)	7359	C	661 399-9124	13479
Century Hlth Staffing Svcs Inc	7361	C	661 322-0606	13505
Esparza Enterprises Inc	7361	A	661 631-0347	13517
Maxim Healthcare Services Inc	7363	D	661 322-3039	13608
Vasinda Investments Inc	7363	D	661 324-4277	13629
Work Force Services Inc	7363	C	661 327-5019	13635
Technosocialworkcom LLC	7374	D	661 617-6601	14159
M & S Security Services Inc	7381	C	661 397-9616	14316
Trans-West Services Inc	7381	B	661 381-2900	14356
Arrival Communications Inc (DH)	7389	D	661 716-2100	14452
Califrnia Grnhse Frm II Ltd PR	7389	D	949 715-3987	14466
Sangera Buick Inc	7538	D	661 833-5200	14699
Car Wash Partners Inc	7542	C	661 377-1020	14705
Car Wash Partners Inc	7542	C	661 231-3689	14706
SA Camp Pump Company	7699	D	661 399-2976	14789
Bakersfield Country Club	7997	D	661 871-4000	15117
Seven Oaks Country Club	7997	C	661 664-6404	15173
Stockdale Country Club	7997	D	661 832-0310	15178
Bakersfield Family Medical Group Inc (PA)	8011	D	661 327-4411	15240
Central Cardiology Med Clinic	8011	C	661 395-0000	15268
Clinica Sierra Vista (PA)	8011	D	661 635-3050	15282
Kaiser Foundation Hospitals	8011	C	661 398-5011	15356
Kaiser Foundation Hospitals	8011	C	661 334-2020	15357
Kern Health Systems Inc	8011	C	661 664-5000	15371
Kern Rdlgy Imaging Systems Inc	8011	D	661 322-9958	15372
Omni Family Health (PA)	8011	C	661 459-1900	15411
Ravi Patel MD Inc	8011	C	661 862-7113	15434
Southern Cal Prmnnte Med Group	8011	C	661 398-5085	15461
Southern Cal Prmnnte Med Group	8011	C	661 334-2020	15462
Bakersfield Hlthcare Wllness CN	8051	D	661 872-2121	15577
Bakersfieldidence Opco LLC	8051	D	661 399-2472	15578
Evergreen At Lakeport LLC	8051	C	661 871-3133	15650
Pacs Group Inc	8051	C	661 873-9267	15734
Parkview Jlian Cnvlescent Hosp	8051	D	661 831-9150	15748
Parkview Julian LLC	8051	D	661 831-9150	15749
Gentiva Hospice	8052	D	661 324-1232	15811
Crestwood Behavioral Hlth Inc	8059	D	661 363-8127	15847
Humangood Norcal	8059	B	661 834-0620	15861
Adventist Hlth Systm/West Corp	8062	B	661 316-6000	15895

	SIC	EMP	PHONE	ENTRY#
Bakersfeld Mem Hosp Foundation	8062	D	661 327-4647	15921
Bakersfield Memorial Hospital	8062	A	661 327-1792	15922
County of Kern	8062	A	661 326-2054	15967
Dignity Health	8062	C	661 663-6000	15979
Good Smrtan Hosp A Cal Ltd Prt	8062	B	661 903-9555	16009
Kaiser Foundation Hospitals	8062	C	661 412-6777	16036
Kern County Hospital Authority (PA)	8062	A	661 326-2102	16061
Mohawk Medical Group Inc	8062	D	661 324-4747	16100
San Joaquin Community Hospital (HQ)	8062	D	661 395-3000	16170
Bakersfield Bhvral Hlthcare Hos	8063	C	661 398-1800	16267
Centre For Neuro Skills (PA)	8093	B	661 872-3408	16450
Kern County Hospital Authority	8093	B	661 843-7980	16484
City of Bakersfield	8322	C	661 852-7300	16893
Alliance Childrens Services	8361	C	661 863-0350	17119
Community Action Partnr Kern	8361	D	661 336-5300	17133
Encompass Health Corporation	8361	D	661 323-5500	17148
Community Action Partnr Kern	8399	D	661 835-5405	17219
Kern Regional Center	8399	C	661 327-8531	17231
New Advnces For Pple With Dsbl	8399	D	661 322-9735	17236
New Advnces For Pple With Dsbl	8399	D	661 327-0188	17237
Boys Girls Clubs of Kern Cnty	8641	B	661 325-3730	17326
St Jhns Lthran Ch Bakersfield	8661	C	661 665-7815	17421
Automobile Club Southern Cal	8699	D	661 327-4661	17439
Diversified Prj Svcs Intl Inc (PA)	8711	D	661 371-2800	17515
Innovative Engrg Systems Inc (PA)	8711	D		17557
Processes Unlimited International Inc	8711	B	661 396-3770	17613
UCI Construction Inc	8711	C	661 587-0192	17654
W M Lyles Co	8711	C	661 387-1600	17660
Analytical Pace Services LLC	8734	C	800 878-4911	17903
Healthcare Finance Direct LLC	8742	D	661 616-4400	18147
Pro Safety & Rescue Inc	8742	D	888 269-5095	18196
Sun Pacific Marketing Coop Inc	8742	B	213 612-9957	18223
C&B Holding Co Inc (PA)	8748	B	661 633-1451	18296
County of Kern	9441	D	661 336-6871	18397

BALDWIN PARK, CA - Los Angeles County

	SIC	EMP	PHONE	ENTRY#
Tanimura Antle Fresh Foods Inc	0723	A	831 424-6100	121
Crosstown Elec & Data Inc	1731	C	626 813-6693	905
Distinct Indulgence Inc	2051	E	818 546-1700	1442
Pepsico Inc	2086	E	626 338-5531	1637
Pacon Inc	2621	C	626 814-4654	2634
Checkworks Inc	2782	D	626 333-1444	3197
Mission Kleensweep Prod Inc	2841	C	323 223-1405	3594
Hemosure Inc	2899	E	888 436-6787	3801
Kat-Cameron Manufacturing Corp (HQ)	3423	D	626 338-7308	4741
Lawrence Roll Up Doors Inc (PA)	3442	C	626 962-4163	4893
Oreco Duct Systems Inc	3444	C	626 337-8832	5011
Pacific Award Metals Inc (HQ)	3444	D	626 814-4410	5014
Rigos Equipment Mfg LLC	3444	E	626 813-6621	5029
Upm Inc	3544	B	626 962-4001	5601
G & I Islas Industries Inc (PA)	3556	E	626 960-5020	5673
Meritek Electronics Corp (PA)	3559	D	626 373-1728	5710
Global Silicon Electronics Inc	3572	E	626 336-1888	5878
George Fischer Inc (HQ)	3599	C	626 571-2770	6134
Ametek Ameron LLC (HQ)	3823	D	626 856-0101	7847
Georg Fischer Signet LLC	3823	C	626 571-2770	7860
Freudenberg Medical LLC	3841	C	626 814-9684	8154
Condor Outdoor Products Inc (PA)	3949	E	626 358-3270	8512
First Student Inc	4151	C	855 870-8747	8879
United Parcel Service Inc	4215	B	626 814-6216	9020
Cedarwood-Young Company (PA)	4953	C	626 962-4047	9738
Waste MGT Collectn Recycl Inc	4953	D	626 960-7551	9781
Nichols Lumber & Hardware Co	5031	D	626 960-4802	9926
Tecan Sp Inc	5049	D	626 962-0010	10122
Lighting Technologies Intl LLC	5063	C	626 480-0755	10189
American Kal Enterprises Inc (PA)	5072	D	626 338-7308	10301
Cedarwood-Young Company	5093	D	626 962-4047	10537
Normans Nursery Inc	5193	C	626 285-9795	11096
Home Depot USA Inc	5211	D	626 813-7131	11161
Treasure Garden Inc (PA)	5261	E	626 814-0168	11260
Jacmar Companies LLC	5812	C	626 430-9082	11579
Rize Federal Credit Union (PA)	6061	D	626 960-6888	11812
Kaiser Foundation Hospitals	6324	A	626 851-1011	12092
Baldwin Hospitality LLC	7011	C	626 446-2988	12766
Haynes Building Service LLC	7349	C	626 359-6100	13376
Source One Staffing LLC	7361	A	626 337-0560	13573
Alphatech General Inc	7699	C	626 337-4640	14755
Kaiser Foundation Hospitals	8011	C	310 922-8916	15358
Golden State Habilitation Conv (PA)	8051	C	626 962-3274	15667
Gr8 Care Inc	8051	D	626 337-7229	15669
Trinity Health Systems (PA)	8051	C	626 960-1971	15788
Good Health Inc	8099	C	714 961-7930	16562
Baldwin Park Unified Schl Dst	8211	D	626 337-2711	16801

Employee Codes: A=Over 500 employees, B=251-500
C=101-250, D=51-100, E=20-50, F=10-19, G=1-9

2025 Southern California
Business Directory and Buyers Guide

© Mergent Inc. 1-800-342-5647

1255

GEOGRAPHIC

	SIC	EMP	PHONE	ENTRY#
County of Los Angeles	8711	D	626 337-1277	17506
American Mzhou Dngpo Group Inc	8741	B	626 820-9239	17943
Telesector Resources Group Inc	8742	D	626 813-4538	18229
Kaiser Foundation Hospitals	9431	D	626 851-5144	18394

BANNING, CA - Riverside County

	SIC	EMP	PHONE	ENTRY#
DT Mattson Enterprises Inc	3944	E	951 849-9781	8484
Strech Plastics Incorporated	5088	E	951 922-2224	10501
Professional Cmnty MGT Cal Inc	6531	A	951 845-2191	12509
Silent Valley Club Inc	7011	D	951 849-4501	13023
Pacs Group Inc	8051	C	951 849-4723	15739
Pacs Group Inc	8051	C	951 845-1606	15741
San Gorgonio Memorial Hospital	8062	A	951 845-1121	16168
San Grgnio Mem Hosp Foundation (PA)	8062	C	951 845-1121	16169
Riverside-San Bernardino	8093	C	951 849-4761	16499

BARSTOW, CA - San Bernardino County

	SIC	EMP	PHONE	ENTRY#
Five Star Food Containers Inc	3086	D	626 437-6219	3998
Marine Corps United States	3531	C	760 577-6716	5496
Mv Transportation Inc	4111	C	760 255-3330	8785
Life Care Centers America Inc	8051	C	760 252-2515	15691
Hospital of Barstow Inc (DH)	8062	D	760 256-1761	16026

BEAUMONT, CA - Riverside County

	SIC	EMP	PHONE	ENTRY#
Beaumont Juice LLC	2033	D	951 769-7171	1349
Rudolph Foods Company Inc	2096	C	909 388-2202	1727
Dpp 2020 Inc (DH)	3089	E	951 845-3161	4109
Anderson Chrnesky Strl Stl Inc	3441	C	951 769-5700	4816
Risco Inc	3452	E	951 769-2899	5136
Precision Stampings Inc (PA)	3643	E	951 845-1174	6426
CJ Foods Mfg Beaumont LLC	3999	C	951 916-9300	8672
Pacs Group Inc	8051	C	951 845-3125	15743
Pacs Group Inc	8051	C	951 845-3194	15744
David-Kleis II LLC	8099	D	951 845-3125	16553
Beaumont Unfied Schl Dst Pub F	8211	B	951 845-6580	16802
Childhelp Inc	8361	C	951 845-6737	17130

BELL, CA - Los Angeles County

	SIC	EMP	PHONE	ENTRY#
Penguin Natural Foods Inc	2099	E	323 488-6000	1835
Fam LLC (PA)	2231	D	323 888-7755	1901
Marika LLC	2339	D	323 888-7755	2119
Hain Celestial Group Inc	2844	C	323 859-0553	3656
Custom Building Products LLC	2891	C	323 582-0846	3763
Pacesetter Inc	3845	B	323 773-0591	8393
De Well Container Shipping Inc	4731	D	310 735-8600	9268
Omega Moulding West LLC	5023	C	323 261-3510	9903
Fam Ppe LLC	5099	C	323 888-7755	10560
Perrin Bernard Supowitz LLC (HQ)	5113	D	323 981-2800	10607
Dg Brands Inc	5137	D	323 268-0220	10706
H & T Seafood Inc	5146	E	323 526-0888	10855
El Aviso Magazine	5192	E	323 586-9199	11075
Leonid M Glsman DDS A Dntl Cor	8021	C	323 560-4514	15520
Human Services Association (PA)	8322	D	562 806-5400	16954
Jwch Institute Inc	8733	C	323 562-5813	17878

BELL GARDENS, CA - Los Angeles County

	SIC	EMP	PHONE	ENTRY#
C T and F Inc	1731	D	562 927-2339	895
Rob Inc	2325	D	562 806-5589	1992
Carnevale & Lohr Inc	3281	E	562 927-8311	4472
Eurocraft Archtectural Met Inc	3446	E	323 771-1323	5062
Metal Surfaces Intl LLC	3471	C	562 927-1331	5275
McLane Manufacturing Inc	3524	C	562 633-8158	5481
Barber Welding and Mfg Co	3599	E	562 928-2570	6091
Wilcox Machine Co	3599	D	562 927-5353	6275
Cal Southern Braiding Inc	3679	D	562 927-5531	6977
Flexco Inc	3728	E	562 927-2525	7475
Orbit Industries Inc	5063	D	213 745-8884	10199
WEI-Chuan USA Inc (PA)	5142	C	626 225-7168	10824
US Foods Inc	5149	C	562 806-2445	10987
Parkhouse Tire Service Inc (PA)	5531	D	562 928-0421	11452
Anitsa Inc	7211	C	213 237-0533	13110
Bell Gardens Bicycle Club Inc	7999	A	562 806-4646	15194
Fortiss LLC	7999	C	323 415-4900	15206
Del Rio Sanitarium Inc	8051	C	562 927-6586	15621

BELLFLOWER, CA - Los Angeles County

	SIC	EMP	PHONE	ENTRY#
Cutting Edge Creative LLC	2542	D	562 907-7007	2579
Bryant Rubber Corp	3053	D	310 530-2530	3880
Empire Transportation Inc	4141	B	562 529-2676	8861
George Chevrolet	5511	D	562 925-2500	11354
Hollywood Sports Park LLC	7389	D	562 867-9600	14510
S J S Enterprise Inc	7999	C	949 489-9000	15219
County of Los Angeles	8011	D	562 804-8111	15292

	SIC	EMP	PHONE	ENTRY#
Peter Wylan DDS	8021	D	562 925-3765	15525
Bell Villa Care Associates LLC	8051	D	562 925-4252	15581
Life Care Centers America Inc	8051	C	562 867-1761	15694
Jwch Institute Inc	8099	C	562 867-7999	16573
Harbor Health Care Inc	8361	C	562 866-7054	17158

BERMUDA DUNES, CA - Riverside County

	SIC	EMP	PHONE	ENTRY#
Vintage Associates Inc	0782	C	760 772-3673	242

BEVERLY HILLS, CA - Los Angeles County

	SIC	EMP	PHONE	ENTRY#
Atlas Lithium Corporation	1499	D	833 661-7900	384
Jeffries Global Inc	1799	D	888 255-3488	1211
Fast Track Energy Drink LLc	2086	E	310 281-2045	1618
Alanic International Corp	2299	E	855 525-2642	1964
Lisa Factory Inc	2321	D	213 536-5326	1986
Instant Tuck Inc	2392	E	310 955-8824	2210
L F P Inc (PA)	2721	D	323 651-3525	2863
World History Group LLC	2721	E	703 779-8322	2879
Olympus Water Holdings IV LP (PA)	2842	E	310 739-6325	3617
Stratos Renewables Corporation	2869	E	310 402-5901	3737
Zeons Inc	3229	B	323 302-8299	4330
American Solar LLC	3433	E	323 250-1307	4808
King Holding Corporation	3452	A	586 254-3900	5131
B-Reel Films Inc	3571	E	917 388-3836	5842
Ateliere Crtive Tech Hldg Corp	3577	E	855 466-9696	5903
Dasol Inc	3641	C	310 327-6700	6403
Mogul	3714	E	424 245-4331	7273
Global Travel Collection LLC	4724	D	310 271-9566	9222
Nextpoint Inc (PA)	4813	D	310 360-5904	9451
Maurice Kraiem & Company	5094	E	213 629-0038	10549
SOS Beauty Inc	5122	E	424 285-1405	10651
Fashion World Incorporated	5136	C	310 273-6544	10683
Wen U Luv Liquidation LLC	5632	E	323 456-8821	11496
BW Hotel LLC	5812	A	310 275-5200	11553
Lawrys Restaurants II Inc	5812	D	310 652-2827	11585
Banc of California Inc	6021	A	310 887-8500	11705
City National Bank	6021	C	323 634-7200	11716
City National Bank	6021	C	310 888-6150	11719
City National Securities Inc	6021	B	310 888-6393	11732
Pacwest Bancorp	6021	B	310 887-8500	11740
Charles Schwab Corporation	6211	D	800 435-4000	11963
Gores Group LLC (PA)	6211	D	310 209-3010	11967
M L Stern & Co LLC (DH)	6211	C	323 658-4400	11975
Muriel Siebert & Co Inc	6211	D	800 993-2015	12002
City National Rochdale LLC	6282	D	310 888-6000	12024
Charles & Cynthia Eberly Inc	6513	D	323 937-6468	12335
Engel Volkers Beverly Hills	6531	D	310 777-7510	12437
Keller Wllams Rlty Bvrly Hills	6531	D	310 432-6400	12473
Kennedy-Wilson Inc (PA)	6531	C	310 887-6400	12474
Nelson Shelton & Associates	6531	C	310 271-2299	12495
Rodeo Realty Inc (PA)	6531	D	818 349-9997	12524
Row Management Ltd Inc	6531	B	310 887-3671	12526
Starpint 1031 Property MGT LLC	6531	C	310 247-0550	12533
Shapell Industries LLC (HQ)	6552	D	323 655-7330	12578
Project Skyline Intrmdate Hldg	6719	A	310 712-1850	12608
Regent LP (PA)	6799	A	310 299-4100	12731
USA Enterprise Inc	6799	B	310 750-4246	12746
Belvedere Hotel Partnership	7011	B	310 551-2888	12771
Belvedere Partnership	7011	B	310 551-2888	12772
Honeymoon Real Estate LP	7011	D	310 277-5221	12853
Kirkwood Collection Inc	7011	D	424 532-1160	12886
Oasis West Realty LLC	7011	C	310 860-6666	12943
Raffles Lrmitage Beverly Hills	7011	C	310 278-3344	12983
Sajahtera Inc	7011	A	310 276-2251	13009
Rouse Services LLC	7299	D	310 360-9200	13186
Mob Scene LLC	7311	C	323 648-7200	13228
Studio 71 LP	7313	C	323 370-1500	13271
William Mrris Endvor Entrmt LL (DH)	7361	D	212 586-5100	13581
Anderson Assoc Staffing Corp (PA)	7363	C	323 930-3170	13590
Nga 911 LLC	7371	E	877 899-8337	13782
Rootstrap Inc	7371	C	310 907-9210	13806
1on1 LLC	7372	E	310 998-7473	13868
Ateliere Creative Tech Inc	7372	E	800 921-4252	13887
Subject Technologies Inc	7372	C	310 243-6484	14043
Mission Cloud Services Inc (PA)	7379	C	855 647-7466	14234
American Health Connection	7389	A	424 226-0420	14446
Heritage Auctions Inc	7389	D	310 300-8390	14508
Live Nation Entertainment Inc (PA)	7389	D	310 867-7000	14532
United Talent Agency LLC	7389	D	310 776-8160	14617
Brillstein Entrmt Partners LLC (HQ)	7812	D	310 205-5100	14809
Metro-Goldwyn-Mayer Inc (DH)	7812	B	310 449-3000	14838
Orion Pictures Corporation	7812	A	310 449-3000	14842
Condor Productions LLC	7819	D	310 449-3000	14884

Mergent email: customerrelations@mergent.com

1256

2025 Southern California
Business Directory and Buyers Guide

(P-0000) Products & Services Section entry number
(PA)=Parent Co (HQ)=Headquarters (DH)=Div Headquarters

	SIC	EMP	PHONE	ENTRY#
Lfp Broadcasting LLC (PA)	7822	D	323 852-5020	14919
Agency For Performing Arts Inc (PA)	7922	D	310 557-9049	14954
Gersh Agency LLC (PA)	7922	D	310 274-6611	14961
Paradigm Music LLC (PA)	7922	D	310 288-8000	14968
William Mrris Endvor Entrmt FN (DH)	7922	C	310 285-9000	14983
William Mrris Endvor Entrmt LL	7922	B	310 285-9000	14984
Ease Entertainment Services LP	7929	D	310 469-7300	14986
Live Nation Worldwide Inc	7929	B	310 867-7000	14994
Live Nation Worldwide Inc (HQ)	7929	B	310 867-7000	14995
Endeavor Group Holdings Inc (PA)	7941	D	310 285-9000	15024
Pse Holding LLC (DH)	7941	B	248 377-0165	15035
Wme Img LLC (DH)	7941	B	212 586-5100	15037
Ticketmster New Vntres Hldngs (HQ)	7999	C	800 653-8000	15229
La Peer Surgery Center LLC	8011	D	310 360-9119	15375
Radnet Management III Inc	8011	C	323 549-3000	15433
GPh Medical & Legal Services (PA)	8051	C	213 207-2700	15668
Cedars-Sinai Medical Center	8062	C	310 967-1884	15942
Cedars-Sinai Medical Center	8062	A	310 385-3400	15946
Beverly Hlls Oncology Med Group	8069	C	310 432-8900	16286
Universal Home Care Inc	8082	C	323 653-9222	16428
Resilience Treatment Center	8093	D	310 963-2065	16497
Doctor On Demand Inc	8099	D	310 988-2882	16555
BD&j PC	8111	C	855 906-3699	16644
Carpenter Zuckerman & Rowley	8111	C	310 273-1230	16653
Page Private School	8211	D	323 272-3429	16819
Academy Mpic Arts & Sciences (PA)	8621	D	310 247-3000	17292
Collective MGT Group LLC	8741	C	323 655-8585	17968
Ghp Management Corporation	8741	C	310 432-1441	17988
Za Management	8741	D	310 271-2200	18083
APA Incorporated	8742	C	310 888-4200	18094
National Clearing Corporation (PA)	8742	C	310 385-2155	18176
Berk Communications Inc	8743	C	310 734-5525	18250
Magic Workforce Solutions LLC	8743	A	310 246-6153	18255
Activate Inc	8748	D	212 598-4625	18274
MGM and Ua Services Company	8999	A	310 449-3000	18375

BIG BEAR CITY, CA - San Bernardino County

	SIC	EMP	PHONE	ENTRY#
Snow Summit Ski Corporation	7999	D	909 585-2517	15222

BIG BEAR LAKE, CA - San Bernardino County

	SIC	EMP	PHONE	ENTRY#
Hi-Desert Publishing Company	5994	E	909 866-3456	11671
Snow Summit LLC (PA)	7011	C	909 866-5766	13028
Bear Vly Cmnty Healthcare Dst (PA)	8062	C	909 866-6501	15923

BLOOMINGTON, CA - San Bernardino County

	SIC	EMP	PHONE	ENTRY#
MCM Construction Inc	1622	D	909 875-0533	654
Team West Contracting Corp	1799	D	951 340-3426	1227
Aspire Bakeries LLC	2052	C	714 478-4656	1479
Dura Technologies Inc	2851	C	909 877-8477	3711
Wadco Industries Inc	3441	E	909 874-7800	4879
Westco Industries Inc	3441	E	909 874-8700	4880
Heater Designs Inc	3567	E	909 421-0971	5799
Mitco Industries Inc (PA)	3599	E	909 877-0800	6181
Signify North America Corp	3646	C	732 563-3000	6473
Cooper Lighting LLC	3648	A	909 605-6615	6496
Cooper Crouse-Hinds LLC	3699	C	951 241-8766	7114
Quality Tech Mfg Inc	3721	E	909 465-9565	7368
Ftdi West Inc	4225	D	909 473-1111	9068
Gxo Logistics Supply Chain Inc	4225	A	336 309-6201	9071
United Parcel Service Inc	4512	D	909 349-4343	9172
Kinder Mrgan Enrgy Partners LP	4619	D	909 873-5100	9215
Port Priority Corp	4731	C	845 746-4300	3326
Roberts Lumber Sales Inc	5031	D	909 350-9104	9900
Pacific Steel Group	5051	B	858 449-7219	10149
Atlas Pacific Corporation (PA)	5093	E	909 421-1200	10535
Empire Oil Co	5172	C	909 877-0226	11031
Poma Holding Company Inc	5172	C	909 877-2441	11033

BLYTHE, CA - Riverside County

	SIC	EMP	PHONE	ENTRY#
Hayday Farms Inc	0139	D	760 922-4713	5
Fisher Ranch LLC	0723	D	760 922-4151	107
Crawford Associates	1771	E	760 922-6804	1113
Palo Verde Irrigation District	4971	D	760 922-3144	9793
Palo Verde Health Care Dst	8062	D	760 922-4115	16114
Palo Verde Hospital Assn	8062	C	760 922-4115	16115

BONITA, CA - San Diego County

	SIC	EMP	PHONE	ENTRY#
International Plating Svc LLC (PA)	3471	E	619 454-2135	5268
Right Hand Manufacturing Inc	3625	C	619 819-5056	6357
Pacific Integrated Mfg Inc	3841	D	619 921-3464	8212
John Collins Co Inc	6513	D	818 227-2190	12355
Crockett & Coinc	7992	D	619 267-1103	15075
Kaiser Foundation Hospitals	8062	D	619 409-6405	16054

	SIC	EMP	PHONE	ENTRY#
Paradise Valley Hospital	8062	B	619 472-7474	16126

BONSALL, CA - San Diego County

	SIC	EMP	PHONE	ENTRY#
Euroamerican Propagators LLC	0181	B	760 731-6029	54

BORON, CA - Kern County

	SIC	EMP	PHONE	ENTRY#
Rio Tinto Minerals Inc	1241	C	760 762-7121	261
US Borax Inc	2819	A	760 762-7000	3254

BORREGO SPRINGS, CA - San Diego County

	SIC	EMP	PHONE	ENTRY#
Borrego Cmnty Hlth Foundation (PA)	8011	C	855 436-1234	15253

BRAWLEY, CA - Imperial County

	SIC	EMP	PHONE	ENTRY#
Esparza Enterprises Inc	0762	A	760 344-2031	141
Owb Packers LLC	2011	D	760 351-2700	1247
Salico Farms Inc	2032	C	760 344-5375	1343
Fiesta Mexican Foods Inc	2051	E	760 344-3580	1445
Spreckels Sugar Company Inc	2063	B	760 344-3110	1498
Vons Companies Inc	5411	C	760 351-3002	11290
Grimmway Enterprises Inc	7538	D	760 344-0204	14690
Pioneers Mem Healthcare Dst (PA)	8062	A	760 351-3333	16135
Brawley Union High School Dist (PA)	8211	D	760 312-6068	16803

BREA, CA - Orange County

	SIC	EMP	PHONE	ENTRY#
Priority Landscape Svcs LLC	0781	D	714 255-2940	187
RMA Land Construction Inc	0782	D	714 985-2888	234
Beazer Mortgage Corporation	1531	D	714 480-1635	459
Bergman Kprs LLC (PA)	1542	C	714 924-7000	522
Kprs Construction Services Inc (PA)	1542	B	714 672-0800	554
Nevell Group Inc (PA)	1542	C	714 579-7501	561
Griffith Company (PA)	1611	C	714 984-5500	621
Coolsys Coml Indus Sltions Inc (DH)	1711	D	714 510-9609	766
Emcor Group Inc	1711	B	714 993-9500	775
Norcal Inc	1751	C	714 224-3949	1057
Win-Dor Inc (PA)	1751	C	714 576-2030	1067
Team Finish Inc	1771	D	714 671-9190	1139
Northstar Demolition and Remediation LP	1795	B		1186
Fresh Start Bakeries Inc	2051	A	714 256-8900	1451
Ventura Foods LLC (PA)	2079	D	714 257-3700	1527
Wilsey Foods Inc	2079	A	714 257-3700	1529
Scisorek & Son Flavors Inc	2087	E	714 524-0550	1689
Benevolence Food Products LLC	2099	E	888 832-3738	1743
Shore Front LLC	2099	E	714 612-3751	1850
BOa Inc	2329	E	714 256-8960	2008
AST Sportswear Inc (PA)	2361	D	714 223-2030	2163
Absolute Screenprint Inc	2396	C	714 529-2120	2256
Pacific Archtectural Mllwk Inc	2431	E	562 905-9282	2322
Parkinson Enterprises Inc	2521	D	714 626-0275	2515
Stolo Cabinets Inc (PA)	2521	E	714 529-7303	2519
Pacific Quality Packaging Corp	2653	D	714 257-1234	2683
Avery Dennison Corporation	2672	B	714 674-8500	2717
SC Liquidation Company LLC	2672	C	714 482-1006	2726
Avery Dennison Office Products Co Inc	2678	A		2755
Avery Products Corporation (DH)	2678	C	714 674-8500	2757
Educational Ideas Incorporated	2731	E	714 990-4332	2889
Pennysaver USA Publishing LLC	2741	A	866 640-3900	2934
Coyle Reproductions Inc (PA)	2752	C	866 269-5373	2991
Nowdocs International Inc	2759	C	714 986-1559	3156
Moravek Biochemicals Inc (PA)	2819	E	714 990-2018	3242
Kirkhill Inc	3053	A	714 529-4901	3894
West Coast Gasket Co	3053	D	714 869-0123	3903
Pacific Plastics Inc	3084	D	714 990-9050	3977
Plainfield Molding Inc	3089	D	815 436 7806	4107
Plainfield Tool and Engineering Inc	3089	B	815 436-5671	4198
Ramtec Associates Inc	3089	E	714 996-7477	4217
S&B Industry Inc	3089	E	909 569-4155	4233
Metals USA Building Pdts LP (DH)	3355	A	713 946-9000	4615
Consolidated Aerospace Mfg LLC	3429	D	714 989-2802	4763
Moeller Mfg & Sup LLC	3429	E	714 999-5551	4781
Precise Industries Inc	3444	C	714 482-2333	5023
Span-O-Matic Inc	3444	E	714 256-4700	5035
3-V Fastener Co Inc	3452	E	949 888-7700	5117
Bristol Industries LLC	3452	C	714 990-4121	5121
Caran Precision Engineering & Manuf (PA)	3469	D	714 447-5400	5178
Imperial Cal Products Inc	3469	D	714 990-9100	5193
Electronic Precision Spc Inc	3471	E	714 256-8950	5259
Amada America Inc	3479	D	714 739-2111	5308
Curtiss-Wright Flow Ctrl Corp	3491	C	949 271-7500	5365
Curtiss-Wright Flow Ctrl Corp (DH)	3494	C	714 528-1365	5385
Kingson Mold & Machine Inc	3544	E	714 871-0221	5586
MR Mold & Engineering Corp	3544	E	714 996-5511	5589
Moxa Americas Inc	3577	E	714 528-6777	5939
Viewsonic Corporation (PA)	3577	C	909 444-8888	5954

Employee Codes: A=Over 500 employees, B=251-500
C=101-250, D=51-100, E=20-50, F=10-19, G=1-9

2025 Southern California
Business Directory and Buyers Guide

© Mergent Inc. 1-800-342-5647

1257

GEOGRAPHIC

	SIC	EMP	PHONE	ENTRY#
Trane US Inc.	3585	D	626 913-7123	5988
Q C M Inc.	3629	E	714 414-1173	6379
Jade Range LLC.	3631	C	714 961-2400	6385
Foxlink International Inc (HQ)	3643	E	714 256-1777	6419
Ledconn Corp.	3648	E	714 256-2111	6507
Fine Line Circuits & Tech Inc.	3672	E	714 529-2942	6729
Aeroflite Enterprises Inc.	3678	D	714 773-4251	6941
Bi Technologies Corporation (HQ)	3679	B	714 447-2300	6972
Cks Solution Incorporated.	3679	E	714 292-6307	6983
Transico Inc.	3679	E	714 835-6000	7062
Mullen Technologies Inc (PA)	3711	E	714 613-1900	7186
Harbor Truck Bodies Inc.	3713	D	714 996-0411	7204
Lund Motion Products Inc.	3714	E	888 983-2204	7267
Aerospace Engineering LLC (PA)	3728	D	714 996-8178	7415
Applied Cmpsite Structures Inc (HQ)	3728	D	714 990-6300	7431
Dynamic Fabrication Inc.	3728	E	714 662-2440	7470
Kirkhill Inc (HQ)	3728	C	714 529-4901	7510
Garmin International Inc.	3812	B	909 444-5000	7720
Technovative Applications.	3812	D	714 996-0104	7814
Worldwide Envmtl Pdts Inc (PA)	3823	E	714 990-2700	7885
Beckman Coulter Inc (HQ)	3826	A	714 993-5321	7941
Beckman Coulter Inc.	3841	C	818 970-2161	8105
Carolina Lquid Chmistries Corp.	3841	D	336 722-8910	8127
Life Science Outsourcing Inc.	3841	D	714 672-1090	8184
MPS Medical Inc.	3841	E	714 672-1090	8202
Curtiss-Wrght Cntrls Intgrted.	3842	D	714 982-1860	8258
Dcii North America LLC (HQ)	3843	D	714 817-7000	8333
Envista Holdings Corporation (PA)	3843	D	714 817-7000	8335
Ormco Corporation.	3843	E	909 962-5705	8345
Pac-Dent Inc.	3843	E	909 839-0888	8349
Val USA Manufacturer Inc.	3999	E	626 839-8069	8738
Emergency Ambulance Svc Inc.	4119	D	714 990-1331	8821
Premier Medical Transport Inc.	4119	A	805 340-5191	8843
Hot Dogger Tours Inc.	4142	C	714 449-6888	8864
Delivery Solutions Inc.	4212	C	800 335-6557	8903
Evriholder Products LLC (PA)	5023	D	714 490-7878	9893
Walters Wholesale Electric Co (HQ)	5063	E	714 784-1900	10213
Industrial Threaded Pdts Inc (PA)	5072	E	562 802-4626	10309
Wurth Louis and Company (DH)	5072	C	714 529-1771	10314
Southern Cal Hydrlc Engrg Cor.	5084	E	714 257-4800	10404
Nelson Stud Welding Inc.	5085	C	256 353-1931	10452
Nmc Group Inc.	5085	E	714 223-3525	10453
TSC Auto ID Technology America (HQ)	5085	C	909 468-0100	10470
Proponent Inc (PA)	5088	C	714 223-5400	10498
Acosta Remainco Inc.	5141	C	714 988-1500	10740
Natures Best.	5149	B	714 255-4600	10965
Hill Brothers Chemical Company (PA)	5169	C	714 998-8800	11016
American Suzuki Motor Corporation.	5511	B	714 996-7040	11316
Suzuki Motor of America Inc (HQ)	5511	C	714 996-7040	11416
Levity of Brea LLC.	5813	D	714 482-0700	11615
Beverages & More Inc.	5921	C	714 990-2060	11625
Safeway Inc.	5992	A	714 990-8357	11670
Capitalsource Bank.	6022	C	714 989-4600	11750
American First Credit Union (PA)	6061	D	562 691-1112	11791
Adelfi Credit Union.	6062	C	714 671-5700	11822
Amwest Funding Corp.	6153	C	714 831-3333	11864
American Financial Network Inc (PA)	6162	C	714 831-4000	11881
Emet Lending Group Inc.	6162	D	714 933-9800	11900
Merrill Lynch Prce Fnner Smith.	6211	C	714 257-4400	11983
Morgan Stnley Smith Barney LLC.	6211	C	714 674-4100	11999
Mercury Casualty Company (HQ)	6331	A	323 937-1060	12123
Mercury Insurance Company.	6331	A	714 255-5000	12125
Mercury Insurance Company (HQ)	6331	C	323 937-1060	12126
Veterinary Pet Insurance Services Inc.	6411	B	714 989-0555	12266
Windsor Capital Group Inc.	7011	C	714 990-6000	13085
Glen Ivy Hot Springs.	7299	C	714 990-2090	13175
Cmre Financial Services Inc.	7322	B	714 528-3200	13280
Contract Services Group Inc.	7349	C	714 582-1800	13366
North Amrcn Staffing Group Inc.	7361	D	714 599-8399	13546
Safran Pass Innovations LLC (HQ)	7371	D	714 854-8600	13808
Solugenix Corporation (PA)	7373	C	866 749-7658	14108
Mullen Automotive Inc (PA)	7374	C	714 613-1900	14148
Pramira Inc.	7379	C	800 678-1169	14244
Southwest Patrol Inc.	7381	D	909 861-1884	14351
Aer Technologies Inc.	7699	B	714 871-7357	14753
Round One Entertainment Inc (HQ)	7929	A	714 924-7800	15002
Caremore Medical Group.	8011	D	714 529-3971	15263
Nobel Biocare Usa LLC.	8072	B	714 282-4800	16345
Burns & McDonnell Inc.	8711	D	714 256-1595	17497
Lance Soll & Lunghard LLP.	8721	D	714 672-0022	17741
American Regent Inc.	8733	E	714 989-5058	17866
United Sttes Dept Enrgy Brkley.	8733	C	510 486-7089	17893

BUELLTON, CA - Santa Barbara County

	SIC	EMP	PHONE	ENTRY#
Central Coast Agriculture Inc (PA)	0191	E	805 694-8594	77
Kruse Pet Holdings LLC (PA)	2047	E	559 302-4880	1419
Firestone Walker Inc.	2082	D	805 254-4205	1542
Foley Fmly Wines Holdings Inc.	2084	D	805 450-7225	1571
Terravant Wine Company LLC.	2084	C	805 688-4245	1587
Aero Industries LLC.	3599	B	805 688-6734	6068
Tilton Engineering Inc.	3714	E	805 688-2353	7299
Platinum Performance Inc (HQ)	5122	E	800 553-2400	10645
Carpenters Southwest ADM Corp.	5812	C	805 688-5581	11554
Kang Family Partners LLC.	7011	C	805 688-1000	12881
Platinum Performance Inc.	7532	D	800 553-2400	14678

BUENA PARK, CA - Orange County

	SIC	EMP	PHONE	ENTRY#
ECB Corp (PA)	1711	D	714 385-8900	774
Sfadia Inc.	1731	C	323 622-1930	960
Gresean Industries Inc.	1751	E		1050
King Supply Company LLC.	1799	D	714 670-8980	1213
Wayne Perry Inc (PA)	1799	E	714 826-0352	1233
La Mexicana LLC.	2038	E	323 277-3660	1394
Tawa Supermarket Inc (PA)	2038	C	714 521-8899	1403
Ameripec Inc.	2086	C	714 690-9191	1606
Pepsi-Cola Metro Btlg Co Inc.	2086	C	714 522-9635	1632
Expo Dyeing & Finishing Inc.	2269	C	714 220-9583	1940
Manhattan Stitching Co Inc.	2395	E	714 521-9479	2250
Haley Bros Inc (HQ)	2431	D	714 670-2112	2308
Exemplis LLC.	2522	C	714 995-4800	2527
Exemplis LLC.	2522	E	714 898-5500	2528
Cyu Lithographics Inc.	2752	E	888 878-9898	2996
Q Team.	2752	E	714 228-4465	3073
Interntional Color Posters Inc.	2759	E	949 768-1005	3147
Awesome Products Inc (PA)	2842	C	714 562-8873	3598
BASF Corporation.	2869	D	714 521-6085	3729
Parker-Hannifin Corporation.	3052	D	714 522-8840	3874
Abad Foam Inc.	3086	E	714 994-2223	3991
Trim-Lok Inc (PA)	3089	C	714 562-0500	4262
Yeager Enterprises Corp.	3291	D	714 994-2040	4486
Alloy Die Casting Co (PA)	3363	C	714 521-9800	4643
Metals USA Building Pdts LP.	3441	C	714 522-7852	4856
AW Die Engraving Inc.	3544	E	714 521-7910	5568
Mar Cor Purification Inc.	3589	E	800 633-3080	6021
CJ Advisors Inc.	3599	E	714 956-3388	6105
Hi-Tech Labels Incorporated.	3599	E	714 670-2150	6141
Park Engineering and Mfg Co.	3599	E	714 521-4660	6199
Wire Cut Company Inc.	3599	E	714 994-1170	6278
Amcor Industries Inc.	3714	E	323 585-2852	7224
Leach International Corp (DH)	3728	B	714 736-7537	7513
True Fresh Hpp LLC.	3822	E	949 922-8801	7841
Pepsico Beverage Sales LLC.	4225	B	714 228-9719	9101
States Logistics Services Inc.	4225	D	714 523-1276	9112
Pacific Chemical Dist Corp (HQ)	4226	D	714 521-7161	9135
States Logistics Services Inc (PA)	4731	C	714 521-6520	9337
Communications Supply Corp.	4899	D	714 670-7711	9561
Cambium Business Group Inc (PA)	5021	E	714 670-1171	9867
Atlas Construction Supply Inc.	5032	E	714 441-9500	9937
West Coast Sand and Gravel Inc (PA)	5032	D	714 522-0282	9953
Noritsu-America Corporation (HQ)	5043	C	714 521-9040	9968
Hochiki America Corporation (HQ)	5063	D	714 522-2246	10186
Tech Systems Inc.	5065	C	714 523-5404	10291
Amada America Inc (HQ)	5084	D	714 739-2111	10367
Fueling and Service Tech Inc.	5084	D	714 523-0194	10374
Yamaha Corporation of America (HQ)	5099	B	714 522-9011	10575
Orora Packaging Solutions.	5113	C	714 562-6002	10597
Orora Packaging Solutions (HQ)	5113	D	714 562-6000	10603
Orora Packaging Solutions.	5113	E	714 525-4900	10604
Matesta Corporation.	5137	C	949 874-6052	10715
Access Business Group LLC.	5169	C	714 562-6200	11004
Access Business Group LLC.	5169	B	714 562-7914	11005
Gurunanda LLC (PA)	5169	D	714 256-4050	11014
G & G Door Products Inc.	5211	E	714 228-2008	11154
Simpson Automotive Inc.	5511	D	714 690-6200	11407
Universal Shopping Plaza A CA.	6512	C	714 521-8899	12323
True Investments LLC.	6799	E	949 258-9720	12744
Knotts Berry Farm LLC.	7011	D	714 995-1111	12887
Uniwell Corporation.	7011	C	714 522-7000	13059
Medieval Times Entrmt Inc (HQ)	7041	A	714 523-1100	13109
Healthcare Resource Group.	7363	C	562 945-7224	13598
A J Parent Company Inc (PA)	7389	C	714 521-1100	14432
Continental Exch Solutions Inc.	7389	D	562 345-2100	14478
Ted Ford Jones Inc (PA)	7538	C	714 521-3110	14700
Bridport Erie Aviation Inc.	7699	E	714 634-8801	14758
Krikorian Premiere Theatre LLC.	7832	D	714 826-7469	14939
Knotts Berry Farm LLC (HQ)	7996	B	714 827-1776	15104

Mergent email: customerrelations@mergent.com

2025 Southern California
Business Directory and Buyers Guide

(P-0000) Products & Services Section entry number
(PA)=Parent Co (HQ)=Headquarters (DH)=Div Headquarters

1258

	SIC	EMP	PHONE	ENTRY#
Rehablttion Ctr of Ornge Cnty	8051	C	714 826-2330	15760
Southwest Rgnal Cncil Crpnters	8631	D	714 571-0449	17315

BURBANK, CA - Los Angeles County

	SIC	EMP	PHONE	ENTRY#
Honey Isabells Inc	0279	E	800 708-8485	95
Eagle Dominion Energy Corp	1382	E	270 366-4817	302
716 Management Inc	1522	D	818 471-4956	441
Tri-Tech Restoration Co Inc	1541	E	818 565-3900	509
Aries Beef LLC	2013	E	818 526-4855	1254
Excelline Food Products LLC	2038	E	818 701-7710	1391
Divine Pasta Company	2099	E	818 559-7440	1765
Palermo Family LP (PA)	2099	E	213 542-3300	1832
Staness Jonekos Entps Inc	2099	E	818 606-2710	1857
Mortex Corporation	2329	C		2021
The Original Cult Inc	2339	D	323 260-7308	2138
Vesture Group Incorporated	2369	D	818 842-0200	2175
Superior Window Coverings Inc	2391	E	818 762-6685	2205
Swaner Hardwood Co Inc (PA)	2435	D	818 953-5350	2372
Arte De Mexico Inc (PA)	2522	D	818 753-4559	2521
Steves Plating Corporation	2542	E	818 842-2184	2594
Westrock Rkt LLC	2653	D	818 729-0610	2694
Disney Publishing Worldwide (DH)	2721	D	212 633-4400	2854
Color West Inc	2752	C	818 840-8881	2982
Imagic	2752	E	818 333-1670	3014
Midnight Oil Agency LLC	2752	B	818 295-6100	3044
Primary Color Systems Corp	2752	D	818 643-5944	3066
Hutchinson Arospc & Indust Inc	3069	E	818 843-1000	3915
Three-D Plastics Inc (PA)	3089	E	323 849-1316	4258
Cydwoq Inc	3131	E	818 848-8307	4280
California Insulated Wire &	3357	D	818 569-4930	4629
Burbank Steel Treating Inc	3398	E	818 842-0975	1701
Quality Heat Treating Inc	3398	E	818 840-8212	4712
Saturn Fasteners Inc	3429	C	818 973-1807	4787
ESM Aerospace Inc	3444	E	818 841-3653	4984
Connell Processing Inc (PA)	3471	E	818 845-7661	5252
Haskel International LLC (HQ)	3561	C	818 843-4000	5736
Key Code Media Inc (PA)	3571	E	818 303-3900	5858
Comco Inc	3589	E	818 333-8500	6010
Centerpoint Mfg Co Inc	3599	E	818 842-2147	6103
Fortner Eng & Mfg Inc	3599	E	818 240-7740	6125
Hydra-Electric Company (PA)	3613	C	818 843-6211	6307
Litegear Inc	3641	E	818 358-8542	6406
Universal Switching Corp	3643	E	818 785-0200	6433
Flo Kino Inc	3646	C	818 767-6528	6459
Nomoflo Enterprises Inc	3646	E	818 767-6528	6468
Doremi Labs Inc	3651	E	818 562-1101	6534
Hollywood Records Inc	3652	C	818 560-5670	6576
Nerdist Channel LLC	3663	E	818 333-2705	6640
Graphic Research Inc	3672	E	818 886-7340	6734
Accratronics Seals LLC	3679	D	818 843-1500	6962
Gerhardt Gear Co Inc	3714	E	818 842-6700	7256
Bandy Manufacturing LLC	3728	D	818 846-9020	7444
Cardona Manufacturing Corp	3728	E	818 841-8358	7451
Crane Aerospace Inc	3728	C	818 526-2600	7457
Hutchinson Arospc & Indust Inc	3728	C	818 843-1000	7490
Hydro-Aire Inc (HQ)	3728	C	818 526-2600	7493
Hydro-Aire Aerospace Corp	3728	C	818 526-2600	7494
Senior Operations LLC	3728	B	818 260-2900	7562
Eckert Zegler Isotope Pdts Inc	3829	C	661 309-1010	8040
Avid Technology Inc	3861	C	818 557-2520	8421
Matthews Studio Equipment Inc	3861	E	818 843-6715	8433
Photronics Inc (DH)	3861	B	203 740-5653	8439
Insomniac Games Inc (PA)	3944	D	818 729-2400	8487
Origin LLC	3999	E	818 848-1648	8707
Music Express Inc (PA)	4119	C	818 845-1502	8842
Ardwin Inc	4213	C	818 767-7777	8932
Ameriflight LLC	4512	D	818 847-0000	9158
Avjet Corporation (DH)	4522	D	818 841-6190	9180
Magical Cruise Company Limited	4724	D	800 742-8939	9228
Mis Sciences Corp	4813	C	818 847-0213	9448
Qwest Cybersolutions LLC	4813	C	818 729-2100	9456
ABC Cable Networks Group (HQ)	4832	C	818 460-7477	9474
Disney Enterprises Inc (DH)	4832	A	818 560-1000	9477
Krca License LLC	4832	C	818 840-1400	9479
Lbi Media Holdings Inc (HQ)	4832	C	818 563-5722	9480
Lbi Radio License LLC	4832	C	818 563-5722	9481
Liberman Broadcasting Inc (PA)	4832	D	818 729-5300	9482
ABC Signature Studios Inc	4833	D	818 560-1000	9491
Cw Network LLC (HQ)	4833	C	818 977-2500	9496
Hub Television Networks LLC	4833	D	818 531-3600	9508
Public Mdia Group Southern Cal (PA)	4833	D	714 241-4100	9514
Twdc Enterprises 18 Corp (HQ)	4833	A	818 560-1000	9520
Valleycrest Productions Ltd	4833	D	818 560-5391	9522

	SIC	EMP	PHONE	ENTRY#
International Fmly Entrmt Inc (DH)	4841	C	818 560-1000	9553
Own LLC	4841	C	323 602-5500	9555
Time Warner Cable Entps LLC	4841	C	818 977-7840	9558
City of Burbank	4931	B	818 238-3550	9669
Sanitec Industries Inc	4953	D	818 523-1942	9762
Image IV Systems Inc (PA)	5044	D	818 841-0756	9973
Ver Sales Inc (PA)	5051	E	818 567-3000	10164
Wexler Corporation	5065	A	818 846-9381	10297
Sega of America Inc	5092	B	747 477-3708	10528
Mel Bernie and Company Inc (PA)	5094	C	818 841-1928	10550
Science of Skincare LLC	5122	E	818 254-7961	10650
Alexander Henry Fabrics Inc	5131	E	818 562-8200	10661
Smart Stores Operations LLC	5141	C	818 954-8631	10780
Lowes Home Centers LLC	5211	C	818 557-2300	11243
Portos Bakery Burbank Inc	5461	E	818 846-9100	11300
Sanctuary Clothing LLC (PA)	5621	E	818 505-0018	11493
Specialty Restaurants Corp	5812	B	818 843-5013	11601
Filmtools Inc (PA)	5946	E	323 467-1116	11646
Farmers Insur Group Fdral Cr U (PA)	6061	D	323 209-6000	11796
Logix Federal Credit Union (PA)	6061	C	888 718-5328	11803
Partners Federal Credit Union (PA)	6061	D	800 948-6677	11811
Startengine Crowdfunding Inc	6153	D	800 317-2200	11874
Sag-Aftra Health Plan	6324	C	800 777-4013	12103
Allianz Globl Risks US Insur (DH)	6331	C	818 260-7500	12115
Producr-Wrters Gild Amer Pnsio (PA)	6371	D	818 846-1015	12162
Screen Actors Guild - American	6371	C	818 954-9400	12163
Greystar Rs Group LLC	6512	C	818 841-2441	12295
Silver Saddle Ranch & Club Inc	6552	D	818 768-8808	12579
OH So Original Inc	7011	B	818 841-4770	12947
PHF II Burbank LLC	7011	C	818 843-6000	12973
Petrosian Esthetic Entps LLC	7231	C	818 391-8231	13153
Formerly Known As LLC	7311	D	310 551-3500	13208
GL Nemirow Inc	7311	D	818 562-9433	13209
Petrol Advertising Inc	7311	C	323 644-3720	13235
Shed Media US Inc	7313	C	323 904-4680	13270
Waldberg Inc	7313	D	818 843-0004	13272
Dvs Media Services (PA)	7334	E	818 841-6750	13313
Ultragraphics Inc	7335	E	818 295-3994	13320
Come Land Maint Svc Co Inc	7349	A	818 567-2455	13365
M-N-Z Janitorial Services Inc	7349	C	323 851-4115	13388
J L Fisher Inc	7359	D	818 846-8366	13458
Cheque Guard Inc	7371	D	818 563-9335	13683
Disney Interactive Studios Inc	7371	B	818 553-5000	13708
Global Service Resources Inc	7371	D	800 679-7658	13738
Sperasoft Inc	7371	B	408 715-6615	13829
Zestfinance Inc	7371	D	323 450-3000	13867
Jam City Inc	7372	C	804 920-8760	13956
My Eye Media LLC	7372	D	818 559-7200	13980
Andrews International Inc (HQ)	7381	A	818 487-4060	14276
Secure Net Alliance	7381	D	818 848-4900	14338
US Security Associates Inc	7381	C	818 697-1809	14364
Rti Systems Inc	7382	D	213 599-8470	14417
Buena Vista Television (DH)	7383	C	818 560-1878	14426
Coloredge	7384	D	818 842-1121	14428
Jake Hey Incorporated	7384	C	323 856-5280	14429
Technicolor Inc	7384	B	818 260-4577	14430
Pixar	7389	B	510 922-4075	14573
City of Burbank	7538	C	818 238-3838	14689
Enbio Corp	7699	C	818 953-9976	14764
ABC Family Worldwide Inc (HQ)	7812	B	818 560-1000	14803
and Syndicated Productions Inc	7812	C	818 308-5200	14806
Disney Incorporated (DH)	7812	C	818 560-1000	14822
Jyuno USA Inc (HQ)	7812	D	310 388-8800	14835
NW Entertainment Inc (PA)	7812	D	818 295-5000	14841
Playboy Entrmt Group Inc (DH)	7812	C	323 276-4000	14846
Point360	7812	D	818 556-5700	14847
Roundabout Entertainment Inc	7812	D	818 842-9300	14853
Studio Distribution Svcs LLC	7812	C	818 954-6000	14861
Stx Financing LLC	7812	C	310 742-2300	14862
Walt Disney Music Company (DH)	7812	D	818 560-1000	14870
Walt Disney Records Direct (DH)	7812	A	818 560-1000	14872
Warner Bros Entertainment Inc (DH)	7812	D	818 954-6000	14873
Warner Bros Home Entrmt Inc (DH)	7812	D	818 954-6000	14874
Warner Bros Intl TV Dist Inc	7812	D	818 954-6000	14875
Foto-Kem Industries Inc (PA)	7819	C	818 846-3102	14892
Olive Avenue Productions LLC	7819	B	770 214-7052	14898
Streamland Media LLC	7819	D	818 855-7467	14905
Technicolor Thomson Group Inc (HQ)	7819	B		14907
Testronic Inc	7819	C	818 845-3223	14909
Warner Bros Transatlantic Inc	7822	C	818 977-6384	14927
Eros Stx Global Corporation	7841	A	818 524-7000	14951
Prdctions N Fremantle Amer Inc (DH)	7922	D	818 748-1100	14971
Esl Gaming America Inc (DH)	7929	D	213 235-7079	14987

GEOGRAPHIC

	SIC	EMP	PHONE	ENTRY#
Lakeside Golf Club	7992	D	818 984-0601	15087
Walt Disney Company (PA)	7996	A	818 560-1000	15110
Disney Regional Entrmt Inc (DH)	7999	C	818 560-1000	15198
Providnce Facey Med Foundation	8031	D	818 861-7831	15532
Providence Health System	8062	A	818 843-5111	16150
Providnce Hlth Svcs Fndtn/San	8062	A	818 843-5111	16155
Burbank Dental Laboratory Inc	8072	C	818 841-2256	16341
Nova Skilled Home Health Inc	8099	C	323 658-6232	16595
Napca Foundation	8299	A	800 799-4640	16857
Vintage Senior Management Inc	8322	B	818 954-9500	17023
Boys Grls CLB Brbank Grter E V	8641	D	818 842-9333	17327
Young MNS Chrstn Assn Brbank C (PA)	8641	D	818 845-8551	17402
Cast & Crew LLC (PA)	8721	C	818 570-6180	17710
Entertainment Partners Inc (PA)	8721	B	818 955-6000	17723
New Talco Enterprises LLC	8721	C	310 280-0755	17748
Team Companies LLC (PA)	8721	D	818 558-3261	17756
Certified Laboratories LLC	8734	A	818 845-0070	17908
IKEA Purchasing Svcs US Inc	8741	C	818 841-3500	17992
Warner Bros Distributing Inc	8741	B	818 954-6000	18078
Warner Bros Consumer Pdts Inc (DH)	8748	C	818 954-7980	18370

BUTTONWILLOW, CA - Kern County

	SIC	EMP	PHONE	ENTRY#
J G Boswell Company	0173	B	661 764-9000	39

CABAZON, CA - Riverside County

	SIC	EMP	PHONE	ENTRY#
Centric Brands Inc	2211	E	951 797-5077	1874
Hadley Fruit Orchards Inc (PA)	5961	E	951 849-5255	11654
Premium Outlet Partners LP	6512	D	951 849-6641	12312
Morongo Band Mission Indians	7999	D	951 849-3080	15213

CALABASAS, CA - Los Angeles County

	SIC	EMP	PHONE	ENTRY#
Ultimate Builders Inc	1521	D	818 481-2627	435
Afr Apparel International Inc	2341	D	818 773-5000	2146
Electric Solidus LLC	2741	C	917 692-7764	2913
Wella Corporation (HQ)	2844	C	800 422-2336	3696
Radian Memory Systems Inc	3572	E	818 222-4080	5885
Fulcrum Microsystems Inc	3674	D	818 871-8100	6825
Apex Precision Technologies Inc	3714	E	317 821-1000	7227
Ixia (HQ)	3825	E	818 871-1800	7918
Ixia	3825	E	818 871-1800	7919
Yamaha Guitar Group Inc	3931	E	818 575-3900	8474
Yamaha Guitar Group Inc (HQ)	3931	E	818 575-3600	8475
Orca Arms LLC	3949	D	858 586-0503	8533
Made In Love Dggy Cture Thrapy	3999	D	805 410-0774	8696
Durham School Services L P	4151	C	818 880-4257	8868
Amawaterways LLC (PA)	4724	C	800 626-0126	9219
Las Virgenes Municipal Wtr Dst	4941	C	818 251-2100	9698
Abbyson Living Corp	5021	C	805 465-5500	9864
Spirent Communications Inc (HQ)	5045	B	818 676-2300	10031
Central Purchasing LLC (HQ)	5085	B	800 444-3353	10429
Goldco Direct LLC	5094	D	818 343-0186	10547
Wella Operations US LLC	5122	B	818 999-5112	10659
Apex Holding Co	5172	C	818 876-0161	11027
Guarachi Wine Partners Inc	5182	C	818 225-5100	11056
Arcs Commercial Mortgage Co LP (DH)	6162	C	818 676-3274	11886
Republic Indemnity Co Amer (DH)	6331	C	818 990-9860	12132
Far West Bond Services Cal Inc (PA)	6351	B	818 704-1111	12147
Western General Insurance Co	6411	C	818 880-9070	12270
Alliant Asset MGT Co LLC (HQ)	6531	B	818 668-2805	12380
Marcus & Millichap Inc (PA)	6531	C	818 212-2250	12486
MSE Enterprises Inc (PA)	6531	D	818 223-3500	12493
T M Mian & Associates Inc	7011	D	818 591-2300	13049
Grant & Weber (PA)	7322	D	818 878-7700	13284
Granite Solutions Groupe Inc (PA)	7361	C	415 963-3999	13524
Avanquest North America LLC (HQ)	7371	D	818 591-9600	13664
Ellie Mae Inc	7371	B	818 223-2000	13718
Fattail Inc (HQ)	7371	E	818 615-0380	13728
Prolifics Testing Inc	7371	E	925 987-9535	13800
Tri-Tech Systems Inc (PA)	7371	B	818 222-6811	13848
Catapult Communications Corp (DH)	7372	E	818 871-1800	13898
Estify Inc	7372	E	801 341-1911	13927
Sungard Treasury Systems Inc	7372	C	818 223-2300	14045
Thrio Inc	7372	E	858 299-7191	14052
Idrive Inc	7379	D	818 594-5972	14223
David Shield Security Inc	7381	D	310 849-4950	14293
Nastec International Inc	7381	D	818 222-0355	14321
Picore Bristain Initiative Inc	7381	D	818 888-3659	14329
Litigtion Rsrces of America-CA (PA)	7389	D	818 878-9227	14531
Able Cable Inc (PA)	7629	D	818 223-3600	14727
Westbrook Ops LLC	7812	D	818 832-2300	14876
Dts Inc (DH)	7819	C	818 436-1000	14887
Phorus Inc	7819	D	310 995-2521	14900
Ticketmanager	7999	D	818 698-3616	15225

	SIC	EMP	PHONE	ENTRY#
Silverado Senior Living Inc	8051	D	818 746-2583	15777
Help Children World Foundation	8322	B	818 706-9848	16950
Davis Research LLC	8732	C	818 501-2408	17843
Informa Research Services Inc (HQ)	8732	C	818 880-8877	17850
Red Peak Group LLC	8742	D	818 222-7762	18201

CALABASAS HILLS, CA - Los Angeles County

	SIC	EMP	PHONE	ENTRY#
Helmet House LLC (PA)	5136	D	800 421-7247	10685
Cheesecake Factory Bakery Inc	5812	B	818 871-3000	11557
Cheesecake Factory Inc (PA)	5812	B	818 871-3000	11558

CALEXICO, CA - Imperial County

	SIC	EMP	PHONE	ENTRY#
Cooper Lighting LLC	1731	D	760 357-4760	904
Imperial Valley Foods Inc	2037	B	760 203-1896	1376
Bradford Soap Mexico Inc	2841	B	760 768-4539	3591
4I Technologies Inc	3555	A	817 538-0974	5659
Celestica LLC	3643	D	760 357-4880	6412
Creation Tech Calexico Inc (HQ)	3672	E		6721
Chromalloy Gas Turbine LLC	3724	D	760 768-3723	7382
Rockwell Collins Inc	3728	E	760 768-4732	7547
Triumph Insulation Systems LLC	3728	A	760 618-7543	7584
Orthodental International Inc	3843	D	760 357-8070	8348
Clover Envmtl Solutions LLC	3861	E	760 357-9277	8424
U S Xpress Inc	4213	B	760 768-6707	8980
R L Jones-San Diego Inc (PA)	4731	D	760 357-3177	9330
Coppel Corporation	5021	D	760 357-3707	9868
Vantiva Sup Chain Slutions Inc	7819	D	760 357-3372	14912
ARC - Imperial Valley	8093	E	760 768-1944	16442

CALIFORNIA CITY, CA - Kern County

	SIC	EMP	PHONE	ENTRY#
Robertsons Ready Mix Ltd	3273	D	760 373-4815	4454

CALIMESA, CA - Riverside County

	SIC	EMP	PHONE	ENTRY#
Paver Decor Masonry Inc	1611	E	909 795-8474	642

CALIPATRIA, CA - Imperial County

	SIC	EMP	PHONE	ENTRY#
Calenergy LLC	1731	B	402 231-1527	896
Earthrise Nutritionals LLC	2099	E	760 348-5027	1767
Viridos Inc	8731	C	858 754-2900	17839

CAMARILLO, CA - Ventura County

	SIC	EMP	PHONE	ENTRY#
Boskovich Farms Inc	0161	C	805 987-1443	9
Rincon Pacific LLC	0171	D	805 986-8806	25
Pacific Erth Rsrces Ltd A Cal	0181	D	209 892-3000	64
Pacific Erth Rsrces Ltd A Cal (PA)	0181	D	805 986-8277	65
Houwelings Camarillo Inc	0182	B	805 250-1600	73
Colorado Farms LLC	0191	C	805 389-0401	78
Hi-Temp Insulation Inc	1742	B	805 484-2774	1010
Califrnia Dsgners Chice Cstm C	2434	E	805 987-5820	2344
Crockett Graphics Inc (PA)	2653	E	805 987-8577	2662
Bestforms Inc	2761	C	805 388-0503	3191
Performance Materials Corp (HQ)	2821	D	805 482-1722	3285
Sanisure Inc (HQ)	3052	D	805 389-0400	3875
Ogio International Inc	3161	D	800 326-6325	4299
Gc International Inc (PA)	3365	E	805 389-4631	4674
Titan Metal Fabricators Inc (PA)	3441	D	805 487-5050	4873
Abel Automatics LLC	3451	E	805 388-3721	5102
Nanoprecision Products Inc	3469	E	310 597-4991	5204
United Western Enterprises Inc	3479	E	805 389-1077	5352
Transonic Combustion Inc	3519	E	805 465-5145	5471
Western Gage Corporation	3545	E	805 445-1410	5631
Hales Engineering Coinc	3599	E		6138
Ronlo Engineering Inc	3599	D	805 388-3227	6223
Thiessen Products Inc	3599	C	805 482-6913	6248
Arnold Magnetics Corporation	3612	D	805 484-4221	6281
Barta - Schoenewald Inc (PA)	3621	E	805 389-1935	6314
Skurka Aerospace Inc (DH)	3621	E	805 484-8884	6333
Thingap Inc	3621	E	805 477-9741	6335
Plt Enterprises Inc	3643	D	805 389-5335	6425
Thin-Lite Corporation	3648	E	805 987-5021	6519
Record Technology Inc (PA)	3652	E	805 484-2747	6580
Tactical Communications Corp	3669	C	805 987-4100	6696
Attollo Engineering LLC	3674	D	805 384-8046	6804
Former Luna Subsidiary Inc (HQ)	3674	C	805 987-0146	6824
Interconnect Systems Intl LLC (DH)	3674	D	805 482-2870	6834
Microsemi Communications Inc (DH)	3674	C	805 388-3700	6851
Opto Diode Corporation	3674	E	805 499-0335	6862
OSI Optoelectronics Inc	3674	C	805 987-0146	6863
Polyfet Rf Devices Inc	3674	E	805 484-5802	6869
Semtech Corporation (PA)	3674	E	805 498-2111	6889
Johanson Technology Inc	3675	C	805 575-0124	6919
Meissner Corporation	3677	E	805 388-9911	6931
Ciao Wireless Inc	3679	D	805 389-3224	6981

2025 Southern California
Business Directory and Buyers Guide

(P-0000) Products & Services Section entry number
(PA)=Parent Co (HQ)=Headquarters (DH)=Div Headquarters

	SIC	EMP	PHONE	ENTRY#
Gtran Inc (PA)	3679	E	805 445-4500	7001
Lucix Corporation (HQ)	3679	D	805 987-6645	7021
Mercury LLC - Rf Integrated Solutions	3679	C	805 388-1345	7024
Battery-Biz Inc	3694	C	800 848-6782	7089
Technicolor Disc Services Corp (HQ)	3695	C	805 445-1122	7107
Xirgo Technologies LLC	3699	D	805 319-4079	7163
Artisan Vehicle Systems Inc	3711	D	805 402-6856	7167
Wilwood Engineering (PA)	3714	C	805 388-1188	7309
Airborne Technologies Inc	3728	C	805 389-3700	7420
Allclear Aerospace & Def Inc	3728	D	805 506-2700	7428
Parker-Hannifin Corporation	3728	E	805 484-8533	7536
Western Mfg & Distrg LLC	3751	E	805 988-1010	7639
Northrop Grumman Systems Corp	3812	C	805 987-8831	7765
Northrop Grumman Systems Corp	3812	E	805 987-9739	7766
Hanson Lab Solutions LLC	3821	E	805 498-3121	7827
Innovative Integration Inc	3823	E	805 520-3300	7863
Primordial Diagnostics Inc	3823	E	800 462-1926	7872
Interglobal Waste MGT Inc	3826	D	805 388-1588	7961
Teledyne Scentific Imaging LLC	3827	E		8024
Structural Diagnostics Inc	3829	E	805 987-7755	8065
Infab LLC	3842	D	805 987-5255	8275
Kinamed Inc	3842	E	805 384-2748	8281
Medical Packaging Corporation	3842	E	805 388-2383	8284
Cal Simba Inc (PA)	3914	E	805 240-1177	8463
Airport Connection Inc	4111	C	805 389-8196	8747
Sun Air Jets LLC	4522	C	805 389-9301	9183
California Internet LP (PA)	4813	C	805 225-4638	9430
New Inspiration Brdcstg Co Inc (HQ)	4832	E	805 987-0400	9486
Directv Group Holdings LLC	4841	A	805 207-6675	9545
Silicon Processing and Trading Inc	4953	D	805 388-8683	9764
Data Exchange Corporation (PA)	5045	B	805 388-1711	9997
Golden State Medical Sup Inc	5047	C	805 477-9866	10079
Solarworld Americas LLC	5063	D	503 844-3400	10208
Teledyne Reson Inc	5088	E	805 964-6260	10502
Williams Aerospace & Mfg Inc (DH)	5088	E	805 586-8699	10507
Home Depot USA Inc	5211	E	805 389-9918	11156
Jim ONeal Distributing Inc	5571	E	805 426-3300	11482
Premium Outlet Partners LP	6512	D	805 445-8520	12311
Cushman & Wakefield Cal Inc	6531	B	805 322-7244	12423
Rgc Services Inc	6531	C	805 484-1600	12522
Barrett Business Services Inc	7361	A	805 987-0331	13493
Applied Enterprise MGT Corp	7371	C	805 484-1909	13657
Market Scan Info Systems Inc	7371	D	800 658-7226	13767
Modern Campus USA Inc (PA)	7371	D	805 484-9400	13772
Electronic Clearing House Inc (HQ)	7372	D	805 419-8700	13924
Gbl Systems Corporation	7373	C	805 987-4455	14082
Synectic Solutions Inc (PA)	7379	D	805 483-4800	14257
Mutual Securites Inc	7381	C	800 750-7862	14319
Dial Security Inc (PA)	7382	C	805 389-6700	14392
Vantiva Scs Memphis Inc (DH)	7819	B	805 445-1122	14910
Vantiva Sup Chain Slutions Inc (HQ)	7819	B	805 445-1122	14911
La Workout Inc	7991	C	805 482-8884	15053
Las Posas Country Club	7997	C	805 482-4518	15146
Spanish Hills Club LLC	7997	D	805 388-5000	15176
Spanish Hills Country Club (PA)	7997	C	805 389-1644	15177
People Creating Success Inc	8011	D	805 644-9480	15421
Institute For Applied Bhvior A	8049	D	805 987-5886	15546
Elder Care Alliance Camarillo	8051	D	510 769-2900	15625
Vitas Healthcare Corporation	8052	C	805 437-2100	15826
Dignity Health	8062	C	805 389-5800	15977
Coast Health Plan Gold	8099	B	888 301-1228	16549
Ventura Cnty Md-Cal Mnged Care	8099	C	888 301-1228	16626
Casa Pcfica Ctrs For Chldren F (PA)	8322	C	805 482-3260	16881
Interface Community (PA)	8322	D	805 485-6114	16959
Channel Islnds Yung MNS Chrstn	8641	D	805 484-0423	17336
Dex Corporation	8711	D	805 388-1711	17513
Saalex Corp (PA)	8711	C	805 482-1070	17622
Teledyne Scentific Imaging LLC	8731	D	805 373-4979	17827
Qualicon Diagnostics LLC	8734	B	805 388-2383	17924
Camarillo Healthcare Center	8741	B	805 482-9805	17958
Juvenile Justice Division Cal	8741	A	805 485-7951	17999

CAMBRIA, CA - San Luis Obispo County

	SIC	EMP	PHONE	ENTRY#
Linns Fruit Bin Inc (PA)	5431	E	805 927-1499	11291
Moonstone Management Corp (PA)	6531	C	805 927-4200	12489
Moonstone Bch Innvstors A Cal	7011	C	805 927-8661	12929
Pacific Cambria Inc	7011	D	805 927-6114	12957

CAMP PENDLETON, CA - San Diego County

	SIC	EMP	PHONE	ENTRY#
Transitamerica Services Inc	4111	D	760 430-0770	8808
Marine Corps United States	4731	D	760 725-3092	9312
United States Marine Corps	7992	B	760 725-4704	15097
Marine Corps Community Svcs	7999	D	760 725-6195	15212

	SIC	EMP	PHONE	ENTRY#
Marine Corps Community Svcs	8351	C	760 725-7311	17095
Lion-Vallen Ltd Partnership	8741	D	760 385-4885	18007

CAMPO, CA - San Diego County

	SIC	EMP	PHONE	ENTRY#
Campo Band Missions Indians	7993	B	619 938-6000	15099

CANOGA PARK, CA - Los Angeles County

	SIC	EMP	PHONE	ENTRY#
American Landscape Inc	0781	C	818 999-2041	146
American Landscape MGT Inc (PA)	0781	C	818 999-2041	147
Pacific Coast Tree Experts	0783	C	805 506-1211	246
Rte Enterprises Inc	1721	D	818 999-5300	872
Mark Land Electric Inc	1731	D	818 883-5110	937
Flowers Bkg Co Henderson LLC	2051	D	818 884-8970	1447
Barrys Printing Inc	2752	E	818 998-8600	2968
Vomar Products Inc	2759	E	818 610-5115	3186
Pacific Shore Holdings Inc	2834	E	818 998-0996	3470
Den-Mat Corporation	2844	C	800 445-0345	3644
Aerojet Rocketdyne De Inc (DH)	2869	B	818 586-1000	3724
Pls Diabetic Shoe Company Inc	3021	C	818 734-7080	3870
Mulholland Security Ctrs LLC	3442	D	800 562-5770	4896
Best Data Products Inc	3577	D	818 534-1414	5906
All Swiss Turning	3599	E	818 466-3076	6076
Modern Woodworks Inc	3646	E	800 575-3475	6467
Rainbo Record Mfg Corp (PA)	3652	E	818 280-1100	6579
Sway-A-Way Inc	3714	E	818 700-9712	7295
Aerojet Rocketdyne De Inc	3724	B	818 586-1000	7379
Micro Steel Inc	3769	E	818 348-8701	7672
Temptron Engineering Inc	3829	E	818 346-4900	8069
Azimc Investments Inc	5013	C	818 678-1200	9814
Richard Huetter Inc	5013	D	818 700-8001	9845
Buyers Consultation Svc Inc (PA)	5065	D	818 341-4820	10235
Green Thumb International Inc	5193	C	818 340-6400	11087
National Advanced Endoscopy De	5999	D	818 227-2720	11691
County of Los Angeles	7032	D	818 340-2633	13101
Socal Auto Supply Inc	7213	E	302 360-8373	13126
Ecosheld Pest Sltons Phnix LLC	7342	C	310 295-9511	13346
Computrition Inc (HQ)	7371	D	818 961-3999	13692
Hvantage Technologies Inc (PA)	7371	D	818 661-6301	13744
Software Dynamics Incorporated	7373	D	818 992-3299	14107
Shield Security Inc	7381	C	818 239-5800	14345
Sela Healthcare Inc	8051	B	818 341-9800	15773
Calmedcasvs Inc	8099	D	818 888-0700	16543
APn Business Resources Inc	8742	D	818 717-9980	18095

CANYON COUNTRY, CA - Los Angeles County

	SIC	EMP	PHONE	ENTRY#
Design Masonry Inc	1741	D	661 252-2784	981
Natural Balance Pet Foods LLC (PA)	2048	D	800 829-4493	1430
Commercial Display Systems LLC	3585	E	818 361-8160	5970
Rexhall Industries Inc	3716	E	661 726-5470	7323
Power Generation Entps Inc	5084	C	818 484-8550	10394

CANYON LAKE, CA - Riverside County

	SIC	EMP	PHONE	ENTRY#
Alexander Dennis Incorporated	5012	A	951 244-9429	9798
Cbabr Inc (PA)	6531	D	951 640-7056	12396

CAPISTRANO BEACH, CA - Orange County

	SIC	EMP	PHONE	ENTRY#
Soto Company Inc	0782	D	949 493-9403	235
Schaeffler Group USA Inc	3562	E	949 234-9799	5753
Pacific Monarch Resorts Inc	7011	D	949 248-2944	12961

CARDIFF, CA - San Diego County

	SIC	EMP	PHONE	ENTRY#
Viracta Therapeutics Inc (PA)	2834	E	858 400-8470	3519
Addiction Treatment Tech LLC	8093	D	818 437-5609	16439

CARDIFF BY THE SEA, CA - San Diego County

	SIC	EMP	PHONE	ENTRY#
Naval Coating Inc	1799	C	619 234-8366	1218
Mellmo Inc	7371	C	858 847-3272	13769

CARLSBAD, CA - San Diego County

	SIC	EMP	PHONE	ENTRY#
Dempsey Construction Inc	1521	D	760 918-6900	397
Pacific Cast Cnstr Wtrproofing	1521	E	760 298-3170	423
Rq Construction LLC	1541	C	760 631-7707	498
Nevell Group Inc	1542	B	760 598-3501	562
Hellas Construction Inc	1629	B	760 891-8090	714
Millennium Fire Prtection Corp	1711	D	760 722-2722	806
Bergelectric Corp (PA)	1731	D	760 638-2374	887
Bergelectric Corp	1731	A	760 746-1003	888
Ipitek Inc	1731	C	818 348-1010	927
Neal Electric Corp (HQ)	1731	D	858 513-2525	944
Mellace Family Brands Cal Inc	2068	E	760 448-1940	1512
Mfb Liquidation Inc	2068	E	760 448-1940	1513
Bitchin Inc (PA)	2099	D	760 224-7447	1746
Bitchin Sauce LLC	2099	D	737 248-2446	1747

GEOGRAPHIC

Company	SIC	EMP	PHONE	ENTRY#
Living Wellness Partners LLC	2099	E	800 642-3754	1809
Centric Brands Inc	2211	E	760 603-8520	1875
Silk Screen Shirts Inc	2261	E	760 233-3900	1934
Ashworth Inc	2329	A	760 438-6610	2006
R B III Associates Inc	2337	C	760 471-5370	2077
Eevelle LLC	2399	E	760 434-2231	2275
Vanguard Industries East Inc	2399	E	800 433-1334	2281
Vanguard Industries West Inc (PA)	2399	C	760 438-4437	2282
Finishing Touch Moulding Inc	2434	D	760 444-1019	2349
The Heat Factory Inc	2673	E	760 893-8300	2741
Upper Deck Company (PA)	2741	E	800 873-7332	2952
L & L Printers Carlsbad LLC	2752	E	760 477-0321	3030
Sport Card Co LLC	2752	B	800 873-7332	3083
Zuza LLC	2752	D	760 494-9000	3106
Hudson Printing Inc	2759	E	760 602-1260	3144
Iris Group Inc	2759	C	760 431-1103	3149
Air Products and Chemicals Inc	2813	D	760 931-9555	3212
Natural Alternatives Intl Inc (PA)	2833	C	760 736-7700	3322
Akcea Therapeutics Inc (HQ)	2834	D	617 207-0202	3344
Carlsbad Technology Inc	2834	D	760 431-8284	3382
Carlsbad Technology Inc (DH)	2834	D	760 431-8284	3383
Design Therapeutics Inc	2834	C	858 293-4900	3396
Greenwich Biosciences LLC (DH)	2834	E	760 795-2200	3414
Hikma Pharmaceuticals USA Inc	2834	E	760 683-0901	3420
Imprimisrx LLC	2834	C	844 446-6979	3422
Ionis Pharmaceuticals Inc	2834	D	760 603-3567	3429
Ionis Pharmaceuticals Inc	2834	D	760 931-9200	3430
Ionis Pharmaceuticals Inc (PA)	2834	A	760 931-9200	3431
Quorex Pharm Inc (PA)	2834	E	760 602-1910	3487
Tyra Biosciences Inc	2834	E	619 728-4760	3515
Biosource International Inc	2835	E	805 659-5759	3536
Life Technologies Corporation (HQ)	2835	C	760 603-7200	3544
Molecular Probes Inc	2835	C	760 603-7200	3545
Syntron Bioresearch Inc	2835	B	760 930-2200	3553
Alastin Skincare Inc	2844	C	844 858-7546	3629
Coola LLC	2844	D	760 940-2125	3639
Sigma-Aldrich Corporation	2899	E	760 710-6213	3820
Modus Advanced Inc	3069	D	925 960-8700	3925
Ogio International Inc (HQ)	3161	E	801 619-4100	4298
Product Slingshot Inc (DH)	3544	E	760 929-9380	5593
Palomar Technologies Inc (PA)	3559	E	760 931-3600	5715
Nordson Corporation	3563	D	760 419-6551	5760
Nordson Corporation	3563	D	760 431-1919	5761
Nordson Corporation	3563	C	760 431-1919	5762
Nordson March Inc	3563	D	925 827-1240	5763
Nordson Test Insptn Amrcas Inc	3563	E	760 918-8471	5764
Mercury Computer System Inc	3571	E	760 494-9600	5862
Aqua Products Inc (DH)	3589	E	973 857-2700	5999
Fluidra North America LLC (HQ)	3589	D	760 599-9600	6014
Zodiac Pool Systems LLC (DH)	3589	C	760 599-9600	6040
Systems Mchs Atmtn Cmpnnts Cor (PA)	3625	C	760 929-7575	6362
Seacomp Inc (PA)	3629	C	760 918-6722	6382
Anchor Audio Inc (PA)	3651	E	760 827-7100	6525
Arlo Technologies Inc (PA)	3651	D	408 890-3900	6527
Aethercomm Inc	3663	C	760 208-6002	6593
Atx Networks (san Diego) Corp (DH)	3663	E	858 546-5050	6599
Denso Wireless Systems America Inc	3663	C	760 734-4600	6607
Global Microwave Systems Inc	3663	E	760 496-0046	6617
Viasat Inc (PA)	3663	A	760 476-2200	6669
Dei Headquarters Inc	3669	B	760 598-6200	6679
Dei Holdings Inc (HQ)	3669	E	760 598-6200	6680
Cal-Comp USA (san Diego)	3672	C	858 587-6900	6713
Electro Surface Tech Inc	3672	C	760 431-8306	6724
Spectrum Assembly Inc	3672	C	760 930-4000	6774
Luxtera LLC	3674	C	760 448-3520	6847
Maxlinear Inc (PA)	3674	E	760 692-0711	6849
Qualcomm Incorporated	3674	E	858 651-8481	6874
Sst Technologies	3674	E	562 803-3361	6898
Visual Communications Company LLC	3679	C	800 522-5546	7067
Nordson California Inc	3695	D	760 918-8490	7105
Palomar Tech Companies (PA)	3699	D	760 931-3600	7141
American Rim Supply Inc	3714	E	760 431-3666	7226
L3 Technologies Inc	3812	C	760 431-6800	7729
Laird R & F Products Inc (DH)	3812	E	760 916-9410	7735
Myron L Company	3823	D	760 438-2021	7868
Nordson Asymtek Inc	3823	C	760 431-1919	7869
Neology Inc (PA)	3825	C	858 391-0260	7929
Beckman Coulter Inc	3826	C	760 438-9151	7940
Invitrogen Ip Holdings Inc	3826	D	760 603-7200	7962
Life Technologies Corporation	3826	B	760 918-0135	7965
Life Technologies Corporation	3826	E	760 918-4259	7966
Means Engineering Inc	3826	D	760 931-9452	7967
Thermo Fisher Scientific Inc	3826	E	781 622-1000	7986
Thermo Fisher Scientific Inc	3826	D	760 603-7200	7988
Thermo Fsher Scntific Psg Corp (HQ)	3826	C	760 603-7200	7989
Idex Health & Science LLC	3827	D	760 438-2131	8006
Melles Griot Inc	3827	D	760 438-2254	8011
Synergeyes Inc (HQ)	3827	D	760 476-9410	8023
California Sensor Corporation	3829	E	760 438-0525	8037
Aalto Scientific Ltd	3841	E	800 748-6674	8071
Acutus Medical Inc	3841	C	442 232-6080	8077
Alphatec Holdings Inc (PA)	3841	B	760 431-9286	8087
Bolt Medical Inc	3841	D	949 287-3207	8113
Breg Inc (HQ)	3841	D	760 599-3000	8116
Canary Medical USA LLC	3841	D	760 448-5066	8119
Covidien Holding Inc	3841	C	760 603-5020	8137
Genmark Diagnostics Inc (DH)	3841	A	760 448-4300	8158
Medtronic Inc	3841	E	760 214-3009	8191
Planet Innovation Inc	3841	E	949 238-1200	8216
Rf Surgical Systems LLC	3841	D	855 522-7027	8225
Spinal Elements Holdings Inc	3841	C	877 774-6255	8230
Alphatec Spine Inc (HQ)	3842	C	760 431-9286	8251
Djo LLC (HQ)	3842	D	800 321-9549	8259
Seaspine Inc	3842	D	760 727-8399	8300
Zimmer Dental Inc	3842	B	800 854-7019	8321
Ortho Organizers Inc	3843	C	760 448-8600	8347
Nordson Dage Inc	3844	E	440 985-4496	8366
Hygeia II Medical Group Inc	3845	E	714 515-7571	8384
Sotera Wireless Inc	3845	C	858 427-4620	8398
Signet Armorlite Inc (DH)	3851	B	760 744-4000	8415
Spy Inc (PA)	3851	D	760 804-8420	8416
USAopoly Inc	3944	D	760 431-5910	8497
Acushnet Company	3949	E	760 804-6500	8498
Aldila Golf Corp (DH)	3949	D	858 513-1801	8500
Lucite Intl Prtnr Holdings Inc	3949	D	760 929-0001	8530
Safer Sports Inc	3949	E	760 444-0082	8538
Topgolf Callaway Brands Corp (PA)	3949	E	760 931-1771	8548
Zonson Company Inc	3949	E	760 597-0338	8556
New Dimension One Spas Inc (DH)	3999	C	800 345-7727	8704
CAV Inc	4119	D	760 729-5199	8818
Riolo Transportation Inc	4789	B	760 729-4405	9375
Adicio Inc	4813	D	760 602-9502	9426
San Diego Gas & Electric Co	4939	C	760 438-6200	9680
Argonaut Mfg Svcs Inc	5047	D	888 834-8892	10062
Mooreford Inc	5047	D	877 822-2719	10093
Equity International Inc	5065	A	978 664-2712	10243
HM Electronics Inc (PA)	5065	B	858 535-6000	10250
San Diego Sign Company Inc	5085	E	888 748-7446	10461
Bikes Online Inc	5091	D	650 272-3378	10510
Full-Swing Golf Inc	5091	E	858 675-1100	10513
Industrial Strength Corp	5094	E	760 795-1068	10548
Nixon Inc (PA)	5094	C	888 455-9200	10551
Colorescience Inc	5122	C	866 426-5673	10618
Unite Eurotherapy Inc	5122	D	760 585-1800	10654
Prana Living LLC (HQ)	5136	D	866 915-6457	10692
South Cone Inc	5139	C	760 431-2300	10739
Smart Stores Operations LLC	5141	C	760 434-2449	10794
Kendal Floral Supply LLC (PA)	5193	D	888 828-9875	11090
La Costa Coffee Roasting Co (PA)	5499	E	760 438-8160	11306
Bob Baker Volkswagen	5511	D	760 438-2200	11318
Hoehn Company Inc	5511	D	760 438-1818	11360
Oceanside Auto Country Inc (PA)	5511	C	760 438-2000	11390
Ted Ford Jones Inc	5511	C	760 438-9171	11417
Nice North America LLC (DH)	5999	C	760 438-7000	11692
First Community Bancorp	6021	D	858 756-3023	11734
Merrill Lynch Prce Fnner Smith	6211	D	760 930-3100	11994
Morgan Stnley Smith Barney LLC	6211	C	760 438-5100	11995
Optumrx Inc	6324	B	760 804-2399	12099
Southern Cal Prmnnte Med Group	6324	C	619 528-5000	12109
Premium Outlet Partners LP	6512	D	760 804-9045	12313
Integral Senior Living LLC (PA)	6513	C	760 547-2863	12349
Common Grounds Holdings LLC	6531	D	760 206-7861	12413
Grand Pacific Resorts Inc (PA)	6531	C	760 431-8500	12458
Aviara Fsrc Associates Limited	7011	A	760 603-6800	12764
Grand Pacific Carlsbad Ht LP	7011	B	760 827-2400	12831
Grand Pacific Resorts Inc	7011	A	760 431-8500	12832
Grand Pacific Resorts Svcs LP	7011	C	760 431-8500	12833
Hyatt Corp As Agt Brcp Hef Ht	7011	D	760 603-6851	12861
Lc Trs Inc	7011	A	760 438-9111	12897
Omni La Costa Resort & Spa LLC (DH)	7011	D	760 438-9111	12953
Northstar Memorial Group LLC	7261	C	800 323-1342	13156
JC Weight Loss Centres Inc (PA)	7299	C	760 696-4000	13177
Havas Edge LLC (DH)	7311	D	760 929-0041	13211
Promoveo Health LLC	7311	A	760 931-4794	13237
Basepoint Analytics LLC	7323	B	760 602-4971	13291
La Costa Glen Crlsbad Ccrc LLC (PA)	7361	D	760 704-6400	13539

Name	SIC	EMP	PHONE	ENTRY#
A R Santex LLC (PA)	7371	E	888 622-7098	13641
Alogent Holdings Inc	7371	D	760 410-9000	13648
Aveva Software LLC	7371	E	760 268-7700	13665
Chromacode Inc	7371	E	442 244-4369	13684
Stratcom Systems Inc	7371	E	858 481-9292	13833
Aira Tech Corp	7372	C	800 835-1934	13874
Applied Biosystems LLC (DH)	7372	C		13881
Electronic Online Systems International	7373	C	760 431-8400	14080
Technet Partners Inc	7373	C	760 683-8393	14110
Rockstar San Diego Inc	7374	C	760 929-0700	14151
Z57 Inc	7374	C	858 623-5577	14165
Alphabold Inc	7379	D	909 979-1425	14196
Boughts Inc	7379	E	619 895-7246	14202
Exois Inc	7379	C	408 777-6630	14218
Transprttion Oprtion MGT Slton	7389	C	858 391-0260	14614
Triton Management Services LLC	7389	D	760 431-9911	14615
Two Jinn Inc (PA)	7389	D	760 431-9911	14616
Yapstone Inc	7389	D	866 289-5977	14636
24 Hour Fitness Usa LLC (HQ)	7991	C	925 543-3100	15041
24 Hour Fitness Worldwide Inc	7991	A	925 543-3100	15042
Chopra Global LLC	7991	D	760 494-1604	15046
Jazzercise Inc (PA)	7991	D	760 476-1750	15051
Tri-City Hospital District	7991	B	760 931-3171	15066
Four Seasons Resort Aviara	7992	D	760 603-6900	15080
Legoland California LLC	7996	B	760 450-3661	15105
Physical Rhbltation Netwrk LLC (PA)	8049	D	760 931-8310	15552
Vista JV Partners LLC	8049	B	214 738-2771	15559
North Coast Home Care Inc	8082	C	760 260-8700	16408
Gameday Mens Health Llc	8099	D	858 252-9202	16561
Monarch Hlthcare A Med Group I	8099	C	760 730-9448	16590
Nalu Medical Inc	8099	C	760 603-8466	16591
Gemological Institute Amer Inc (PA)	8249	A	760 603-4000	16845
Buffini & Company (PA)	8331	C	760 827-2100	17050
Front Porch Communities & Svcs	8361	C	760 729-4983	17154
Isl Employees Inc	8361	D	760 547-2863	17170
YMCA of San Diego County	8641	C	760 804-8170	17384
Carlsbad Firefighters Assn	8699	D	760 729-3730	17460
One Sun Power Inc	8711	A	844 360-9600	17599
Rialto Bioenergy Facility LLC	8711	C	760 436-8870	17619
Systems & Technology RES LLC	8711	C	844 204-0963	17639
Navigate Biopharma Svcs Inc	8731	C	866 992-4939	17812
Hisamitsu Pharmaceutical Co Inc	8733	A	760 931-1756	17874
Sciencell Research Labs Inc	8733	E	760 602-8549	17889
Sethi Management Inc	8741	C	760 692-5288	18051
SL Blue Garden Corp	8742	C	626 633-2672	18212
Technology Associates EC Inc	8742	D	760 765-5275	18226
Camston Wrather LLC	8744	C	858 525-9999	18259
3E Company Env Ec n Eng (PA)	8748	C	760 602-8700	18272
By Referral Only Inc	8748	D	760 707-1300	18294

CARPINTERIA, CA - Santa Barbara County

Name	SIC	EMP	PHONE	ENTRY#
Normans Nursery Inc	0181	C	805 684-1411	62
Westerlay Orchids LP	0181	C	805 684-5411	71
Jimenez Nursery Inc	0782	D	805 684-7955	212
Nusil Technology LLC (DH)	3069	B	805 684-8780	3927
Forms and Surfaces Company LLC	3272	A	805 684-8626	4391
Forms and Surfaces Inc	3446	D	805 684-8626	5063
Supersprings International Inc	3493	E	805 745-5553	5382
Clipper Windpower PLC	3511	A	805 690-3275	5456
Dac International Inc	3541	E	805 684-8307	5541
Development Associates Contrls	3541	E	805 684-8307	5542
Hugo Venture Solutions Corp	3599	E	805 684-0933	6143
Rincon Engineering Tech	3599	E	805 604-4144	6210
Te Connectivity Corporation	3625	E	805 684-4560	6363
Zbe Inc	3625	E	805 576-1600	6366
Bega North America Inc	3648	D	805 684-0533	6491
Essex Electronics Inc	3674	D	805 684-7601	6823
Agilent Technologies Inc	3825	E	805 566-6655	7895
Agilent Technologies Inc	3825	E	805 566-1405	7896
Freudenberg Medical LLC	3842	D	805 576-5308	8269
Freudenberg Medical LLC	3842	C	805 684-3304	8270
Freudenberg Medical LLC (DH)	3842	C	805 684-3304	8271
Pacifica Beauty LLC	3999	D	844 332-8440	8708
Dako North America Inc	5122	B	805 566-6655	10620
Smart Stores Operations LLC	5141	C	805 566-2174	10802
Normans Nursery Inc	5193	C	805 684-5442	11095
Sunshine Floral Inc	5193	D	805 684-1177	11101
Plan Member Financial Corp	6282	D	800 874-6910	12031
Procore Technologies Inc (PA)	7371	A	866 477-6267	13798

CARSON, CA - Los Angeles County

Name	SIC	EMP	PHONE	ENTRY#
Gs Brothers Inc (PA)	0782	C	310 833-1369	208
OConnell Landscape Maint Inc	0782	A	800 339-1106	227
Ampam Parks Mechanical Inc (PA)	1711	A	310 835-1532	736
Clay Dunn Enterprises Inc	1711	C	310 549-1698	764
Spectra Industrial Svcs Inc	1731	A	310 835-0808	965
General Mills Inc	2026	D	310 605-6108	1330
Giuliano-Pagano Corporation	2051	D	310 537-7700	1454
Anheuser-Busch LLC	2082	E	310 761-4600	1533
Sazerac Company Inc	2085	D	310 604-8717	1598
Pepsi-Cola Metro Btlg Co Inc	2086	C	310 327-4222	1635
American Fruits & Flavors LLC	2087	D	310 522-1844	1663
Southwind Foods LLC (PA)	2091	C	323 262-8222	1698
Arctic Glacier USA Inc	2097	D	310 638-0321	1730
Mountain Water Ice Company Inc (PA)	2097	D	310 638-0321	1731
Bristol Farms (HQ)	2099	C	310 233-4700	1748
Cedarlane Natural Foods Inc (PA)	2099	D	310 886-7720	1753
Kts Kitchens Inc	2099	C	310 764-0850	1798
Js Apparel Inc	2329	C	310 631-6333	2016
Cali-Fame Los Angeles Inc	2353	D	310 747-5263	2158
The Enkeboll Co	2431	E	310 532-1400	2331
Cal-Coast Pkg & Crating Inc	2441	D	310 518-7215	2384
Morettis Design Collection Inc	2511	E	310 638-5555	2431
Arktura LLC (HQ)	2519	E	310 532-1050	2499
Salsbury Industries Inc (PA)	2542	C	800 624-5269	2591
International Paper Company	2621	D	310 549-5525	2628
Empire Container Corporation	2653	C	310 537-8190	2664
Marchem Technologies LLC	2819	E	310 638-9352	3241
Ineos Polypropylene LLC	2821	E	310 847-8523	3274
AOE International Inc	2834	E		3357
Leiner Health Products Inc (DH)	2834	C	631 200-2000	3442
Simpson Industries Inc	2834	E	310 605-1224	3504
Dermalogica LLC (HQ)	2844	C	310 900-4000	3646
Dan-Loc Group LLC	3053	D	310 538-2822	3885
Johnson Laminating Coating Inc	3083	D	310 635-4929	3964
Altium Packaging LLC	3085	D	310 952-8736	3981
CCL Tube Inc (HQ)	3089	D	310 635-4444	4086
Trinity International Inds LLC	3089	E	800 985-5506	4263
Howmet Corporation	3324	A	310 847-8152	4564
Belden Inc	3357	A	310 639-9473	4625
Mag Aerospace Industries LLC	3431	B	801 400-7944	4799
Capital Cooking Equipment Inc	3433	E	562 903-1168	4809
Crate Modular Inc	3448	D	310 405-0829	5076
Designed Metal Connections Inc	3451	E	310 323-6200	5106
Huck International Inc	3452	C	310 830-8200	5129
Research Tool & Die Works LLC	3469	D	310 639-5722	5211
Samtech Automotive Usa Inc	3542	E	310 638-9955	5560
Mestek Inc	3585	C	310 835-7500	5978
A & R Engineering Co Inc	3599	D	310 603-9060	6060
Universal Plant Svcs Cal Inc	3599	D	310 618-1600	6258
DMC Power Inc (PA)	3643	E	310 323-1616	6416
Safran Usa Inc	3643	A	310 884-7198	6427
Dmf Inc	3645	C	323 934-7779	6443
Yun Industrial Co Ltd	3672	E	310 715-1898	6790
Daico Industries Inc	3679	D	310 507-3242	6989
Strike Technology Inc	3679	E	562 437-3428	7055
Coast Wire & Plastic Tech LLC	3699	A	310 639-9473	7113
Refrigerated Trck Solutions LLC	3715	C	323 594-4500	7317
Boeing Company	3721	C	310 522-2809	7332
Ducommun Aerostructures Inc	3728	D	310 513-7200	7465
Ducommun Labarge Tech Inc (HQ)	3728	C	310 513-7200	7469
Hydroform USA Incorporated	3728	C	310 632-6353	7495
Safran Cabin Inc	3728	D	714 934-0000	7559
Zodiac Wtr Waste Aero Systems	3728	D	310 884-7000	7595
Stanford Mu Corporation	3769	C	310 605-2888	7673
Mcgiddo Global LLC	3842	E	844 477-7007	8286
Proma Inc	3843	E	310 327-0035	8352
Sage Goddess Inc	3911	E	650 733-6639	8461
Chris Putrimas	3999	C	877 434-1666	8671
Nano Filter Inc	3999	D	949 316-8866	8702
Dependable Highway Express Inc	4213	C	310 522-4111	8945
Progressive Transportation Inc	4213	D	310 684-2100	8972
Premier Cold Storage & Pkg LLC	4222	C	949 444-8859	9041
Custom Goods LLC	4225	D	310 241-6700	9057
Custom Goods LLC	4225	D	310 241-6700	9058
H Rauvel Inc (PA)	4225	C	310 604-0060	9073
Tri-Modal Dist Svcs Inc	4225	D	310 522-1844	9121
Air Group Leasing Inc	4731	B	310 684-4095	9250
Kw International Inc	4731	D	310 354-6944	9301
Quik Pick Express LLC	4731	C	310 763-3000	9329
Supra National Express Inc	4731	C	310 549-7105	9340
Whaling Packaging Co	4783	E	310 518-6021	9355
Pacific Toll Processing Inc	4785	E	310 952-4992	9356
Apw Knox-Seeman Warehouse Inc (HQ)	5013	D	310 604-4373	9811
Tabletops Unlimited Inc (PA)	5023	C	310 549-6000	9908
New Age Electronics Inc	5044	C	310 549-0000	9978

Employee Codes: A=Over 500 employees, B=251-500
C=101-250, D=51-100, E=20-50, F=10-19, G=1-9

2025 Southern California
Business Directory and Buyers Guide

© Mergent Inc. 1-800-342-5647

1263

GEOGRAPHIC

	SIC	EMP	PHONE	ENTRY#
JB Dental Supply Co Inc (PA)	5047	C	310 202-8855	10087
Nova Ortho-Med Inc (PA)	5047	E	310 352-3600	10096
Parter Medical Products Inc	5047	C	310 327-4417	10100
Porteous Enterprises Inc (DH)	5072	C	310 549-9180	10312
Industrial Parts Depot LLC (HQ)	5084	C	310 530-1900	10377
Pro Safety Inc	5084	C	562 364-7450	10395
Western Refining Inc	5084	D	310 834-1297	10420
H D Smith LLC	5122	D	310 641-1885	10625
SO Tech/Spcl Op Tech Inc (PA)	5131	E	310 202-9007	10674
Osata Enterprises Inc	5139	D	888 445-6237	10737
US Foods Inc	5149	C	310 632-6265	10989
Cirrus Enterprises LLC	5162	D	310 204-6159	10995
Kole Imports	5199	D	310 834-0004	11126
Home Depot USA Inc	5211	B	310 835-7547	11168
Dianas Mexican Food Pdts Inc	5411	C	310 834-4886	11274
Puritan Bakery Inc	5461	C	310 830-5451	11301
Southern Cal Disc Tire Co Inc	5531	C	310 324-2569	11467
Merchants Bank California N A	6022	D	310 549-4350	11771
Aldon Inc	6719	D		12591
Carson Operating Company LLC	7011	C	310 830-9200	12786
Rentokil North America Inc	7342	D	714 517-9000	13347
Vida Health Inc	7371	D	415 989-1017	13862
Transcentra Inc	7373	A	310 603-0105	14112
North Amrcn SEC Investigations	7381	D	323 634-1911	14324
Qualis Automotive LLC	7538	C	859 689-7772	14697
Anschutz Sthern Cal Spt Cmplex	7999	C	310 630-2000	15192
Kaiser Foundation Hospitals	8093	D	310 513-6707	16483
Forensic Analytical Spc Inc	8734	D	310 763-2374	17917

CASTAIC, CA - Los Angeles County

	SIC	EMP	PHONE	ENTRY#
Castaic Truck Stop Inc	2911	E	661 295-1374	3823
County of Los Angeles	8069	C	661 223-8700	16293

CATHEDRAL CITY, CA - Riverside County

	SIC	EMP	PHONE	ENTRY#
Palm Springs Motors Inc	5511	C	760 699-6695	11392
Whv Resort Group Inc	7011	A	760 770-9755	13080
Big Lgue Dreams Consulting LLC	7032	C	760 324-5600	13100
T Alliance One - Palm Sprng LLC	7999	D	760 322-7000	15224
Califrnia Dept Dvlpmental Svcs	8099	C	760 770-6248	16540

CERRITOS, CA - Los Angeles County

	SIC	EMP	PHONE	ENTRY#
Resource Environmental Inc	1542	D	562 468-7000	578
Zero Energy Contracting Inc	1711	C	626 701-3180	856
Zero Energy Contracting LLC	1711	D	626 701-3180	857
Helix Electric Inc	1731	A	562 941-7200	923
Better Beverages Inc (PA)	2087	E	562 924-8321	1668
T Hasegawa USA Inc (HQ)	2087	E	714 522-1900	1691
Dool Fna Inc	2221	C	562 483-4100	1892
Insta-Lettering Machine Co (PA)	2253	D	562 404-3000	1919
LA Triumph Inc	2326	E	562 404-7657	1997
Caravan Canopy Intl Inc	2394	D	714 367-3000	2236
Eide Industries Inc	2394	E	562 402-8335	2237
Spacestor Inc	2521	E	310 410-0220	2518
Villa Furniture Mfg Co	2531	C	714 535-7272	2554
Triple A Containers Inc	2653	D	562 404-7433	2692
Molino Company	2752	D	323 726-1000	3046
Blc Wc Inc (PA)	2759	C	562 926-1452	3121
Apperson Inc (PA)	2761	D	562 356-3333	3190
Captek Softgel Intl Inc (DH)	2834	B	562 921-9511	3379
International Coatings Co Inc (PA)	2891	E	562 926-1010	3770
Foam Molders and Specialties	3086	E	562 924-7757	4000
Foam Molders and Specialties (PA)	3086	E	562 924-7757	4001
Sports Venue Padding Inc	3086	E	562 404-9343	4019
Ips Industries Inc	3089	D	562 623-2555	4141
Wcp West Coast Glass LLC	3089	D	562 653-9797	4273
Pankl Aerospace Systems	3369	D	562 207-6300	4692
Madison Inc of Oklahoma	3441	D	918 224-6990	4848
Bermingham Cntrls Inc A Cal Co (PA)	3491	E	562 860-0463	5359
Para-Plate & Plastics Co Inc	3555	E	562 404-3434	5665
Atlas Copco Compressors LLC	3563	C	562 484-6370	5755
All American Print Supply Co	3577	E	714 616-5834	5899
Mpd Holdings Inc	3577	E	213 210-2591	5940
Olea Kiosks Inc	3577	E	562 924-2644	5941
ARI Industries Inc	3585	D	714 993-3700	5968
Refrigerator Manufacturers LLC	3585	E	562 926-2006	5982
Advanced Uv Inc (PA)	3589	E	562 407-0299	5994
Chemical Methods Assoc LLC (DH)	3589	E	714 898-8781	6005
West Coast Switchgear (DH)	3613	D	562 802-3441	6313
Calnetix Technologies LLC (HQ)	3621	D	562 293-1660	6316
Dcec Holdings Inc	3631	C	562 802-3488	6384
Refriderator Manufacters LLC	3632	E	562 229-0500	6392
IPC Cal Flex Inc	3672	E	714 952-0373	6738
Corelis Inc	3679	E	562 926-6727	6986

	SIC	EMP	PHONE	ENTRY#
Razor USA LLC (PA)	3751	D	562 345-6000	7634
Sas Safety Corporation	3842	D	562 427-2775	8299
Alpha Dental of Utah Inc	3843	E	562 467-7759	8325
Dji Technology Inc	3861	C	818 235-0789	8425
United Parcel Service Inc	4215	B	562 404-3236	9019
Silver Hawk Freight Inc	4731	D	562 404-0226	9336
AT&T Mobility LLC	4812	B	562 468-6142	9385
Resa Service LLC	4911	C	562 567-6279	9601
R1 Concepts Inc (PA)	5013	E	714 777-2323	9840
Royal Plywood Company LLC (PA)	5031	D	562 404-2989	9931
Microtek Lab Inc (HQ)	5044	C	310 687-5823	9976
Arjo Inc	5047	C	714 412-1170	10063
Memorex Products Inc	5064	C	562 653-2800	10221
Palfinger Liftgates LLC	5084	D	888 774-5844	10390
Allied High Tech Products Inc	5085	D	310 635-2466	10424
NSK Precision America Inc	5085	D	562 968-1000	10454
Capitol Distribution Co LLC (PA)	5149	E	562 404-4321	10935
Southern Glzers Wine Sprits LL	5182	B	562 926-2000	11061
Midway International Inc	5199	D	800 826-2383	11129
Polycell Packaging Corporation	5199	E	562 483-6000	11134
Bargain Rent-A-Car	5511	D	562 865-7447	11317
Golden Star Technology Inc (PA)	5734	D	562 345-8700	11540
Docusource Inc	5999	D	562 447-2600	11682
Enterprise Bank & Trust	6022	C	562 345-9092	11764
Sun West Mortgage Company Inc (PA)	6162	C	833 478-6937	11936
Carelon Health California Inc (HQ)	6321	C	562 622-2950	12060
Private Medical-Care Inc	6324	A	562 924-8311	12101
Allstate Floral Inc	6411	C	562 926-2989	12170
Auto Insurance Specialists LLC (DH)	6411	C	562 345-6247	12175
Carelon Bhavioral Hlth Cal Inc	6411		800 228-1286	12188
Poliseek Ais Insur Sltions Inc	6411	D	866 480-7335	12244
Eplica Inc	7361	C	562 977-4300	13514
Lloyd Staffing Inc	7363	B	631 777-7600	13603
Auditboard Inc (PA)	7371	D	877 769-5444	13651
Secure One Data Solutions LLC	7374	D	562 924-7056	14155
Geek Squad Inc	7379	D	562 402-1555	14221
Commercial Protective Svcs Inc	7381	A	310 515-5290	14285
Oncology Inst CA A Prof Corp (PA)	8011	A	323 278-4400	15412
College Hospital Inc (PA)	8063	B	562 924-9581	16272
Oncology Institute Inc (PA)	8071	A	562 735-3226	16325
Axelacare Holdings Inc	8082	B	714 522-8802	16366
Atkinson Andlson Loya Ruud Rom (PA)	8111	C	562 653-3200	16637
Thermal Engrg Intl USA Inc (HQ)	8711	D	323 726-0641	17647
Biospace Inc	8731	C	323 932-6503	17779
Caremore Medical Management Company	8741	A	562 741-4300	17960
Management Trust Assn Inc	8742	D	562 926-3372	18165
City of Cerritos	9111	C	562 916-8500	18382

CHATSWORTH, CA - Los Angeles County

	SIC	EMP	PHONE	ENTRY#
Synear Foods Usa LLC	1541	E	818 341-3588	506
All Tmperatures Controlled Inc	1711	D	818 882-1478	732
Service Genius Los Angeles Inc	1711	D	818 200-3379	836
Comet Electric Inc	1731	C	818 340-0965	900
OBryant Electric Inc (PA)	1731	C	818 407-1986	946
Pacific Coast Cabling Inc (PA)	1731	D	818 407-1911	947
We The Pie People LLC	2024	E	818 349-1880	1321
Earth Island LLC (HQ)	2099	E	818 725-2820	1766
Avitex Inc (PA)	2211	C	818 994-6487	1870
Apparel Prod Svcs Globl LLC (PA)	2339	C	818 700-3700	2080
Academic Ch Choir Gwns Mfg Inc	2389	E	818 886-8697	2184
Califrnia Dluxe Wndows Inds In (PA)	2431	E	818 349-5566	2299
Tessa Mia Corp	2434	E	877 740-5757	2364
Califrnia Trade Converters Inc	2631	E	818 899-1455	2640
Lacerta Group LLC	2671	D	508 339-3312	2709
Avn Media Network Inc	2731	C	818 718-5788	2883
Narcotics Annymous Wrld Svcs I (PA)	2731	D	818 773-9999	2893
Cal Southern Graphics Corp (HQ)	2752	D	310 559-3600	2975
Impress Communications LLC	2752	D	818 701-8800	3016
Pioneer Photo Albums Inc (PA)	2782	C	818 882-2161	3200
Natrol Inc	2834	C	818 739-6000	3456
Henkel US Operations Corp	2843	E	818 435-0889	3625
Aware Products LLC	2844	C	818 206-6700	3632
Ida Classic Inc (PA)	2844	C	818 773-9042	3660
Kdc/One Chatsworth Inc	2844	D	818 709-1345	3663
Kdc/One Chatsworth Inc (DH)	2844	D	818 709-1345	3664
Neutraderm Inc	2844	E	818 534-3190	3672
Aerojet Rocketdyne De Inc	2869	D	818 586-1000	3726
A & S Mold and Die Corp	3089	D	818 341-5393	4034
Lehrer Brllnprfktion Werks Inc	3089	D	818 407-1890	4160
Ftg Aerospace Inc (DH)	3364	E	818 407-4024	4660
Metal Improvement Company LLC	3398	D	818 407-6280	4709
Alliance Metal Products Inc	3444	C	818 709-1204	4944
Armorcast Products Company Inc (DH)	3444	C	818 982-3600	4951

Mergent email: customerrelations@mergent.com
1264

2025 Southern California
Business Directory and Buyers Guide

(P-0000) Products & Services Section entry number
(PA)=Parent Co (HQ)=Headquarters (DH)=Div Headquarters

	SIC	EMP	PHONE	ENTRY#
Dynamo Aviation Inc	3444	D	818 785-9561	4982
Federal Manufacturing Corp	3452	E	818 341-9825	5126
Golden Bolt LLC	3452	D	818 626-8261	5127
Metal Chem Inc	3471	E	818 727-9951	5274
Plateronics Processing Inc	3471	E	818 341-2191	5284
Networks Electronic Co LLC	3489	E	818 341-0440	5357
RPS Inc	3496	E	818 350-8088	5415
Bey-Berk International (PA)	3499	E	818 773-7534	5442
Tig/M LLC	3535	E	818 709-8500	5520
Colbrit Manufacturing Co Inc	3544	E	818 709-3608	5574
Precise Die and Finishing	3544	E	818 773-9337	5591
John List Corporation	3547	E	818 882-7848	5639
Capna Fabrication	3556	E	888 416-6777	5668
NMB (usa) Inc (HQ)	3562	E	818 709-1770	5752
Delta Tau Data Systems Inc Cal (HQ)	3569	C	818 998-2095	5819
Aleratec Inc	3571	E		5839
Meissner Mfg Co Inc (PA)	3589	D	818 678-0400	6023
RTC Arspace - Chtswrth Div Inc (PA)	3593	D	818 341-3344	6048
Aero Mechanism Precision Inc	3599	E	818 886-1855	6069
Delta Fabrication Inc	3599	D	818 407-4000	6115
Delta Hi-Tech	3599	C	818 407-4000	6116
Excel Manufacturing Inc	3599	E	661 257-1900	6122
Molnar Engineering Inc	3599	E	818 993-3495	6184
Mono Engineering Corp	3599	E	818 772-4998	6186
United Precision Corp	3599	E	818 576-9540	6257
Jackson Engineering Co Inc	3612	E	818 886-9567	6287
Custom Control Sensors LLC (PA)	3613	C	818 341-4610	6303
Resmed Motor Technologies Inc	3621	C	818 428-6400	6330
Electro Adapter Inc	3643	D	818 998-1198	6417
Lf Illumination LLC	3646	D	818 885-1335	6466
Lighting Control & Design Inc	3648	E	323 226-0000	6509
Epic Technologies LLC (HQ)	3661	A	908 707-4085	6584
Dynamic Sciences Intl Inc	3663	E	818 226-6262	6609
Telemtry Cmmnctons Systems Inc	3663	E	818 718-6248	6664
Canoga Perkins Corporation (HQ)	3669	D	818 718-6300	6677
Newvac LLC	3671	C	310 990-0401	6701
Circuit Services Llc	3672	E	818 701-5391	6717
Ftg Circuits Inc (DH)	3672	D	818 407-4024	6730
Natel Engineering Holdings Inc	3672	C	818 734-6500	6756
Oncore Manufacturing Svcs Inc	3672	C	510 360-2222	6760
United International Tech Inc	3672	E	818 772-9400	6785
We Imagine Inc	3672	D	818 709-0064	6787
Mrv Communications Inc	3674	B	818 773-0900	6858
Stellar Microelectronics Inc	3674	E	661 775-3500	6899
Dytran Instruments Inc	3679	C	818 700-7818	6993
Natel Engineering Company LLC (PA)	3679	C	818 495-8617	7029
Newvac LLC	3679	E	747 202-7333	7030
Aitech Defense Systems Inc	3699	D	818 700-2000	7109
Aitech Rugged Group Inc (PA)	3699	E	818 700-2000	7110
Soundcraft	3699	E	818 882-0020	7153
Logistical Support LLC	3724	C	818 341-3344	7391
Alatus Aerosystems	3728	D	626 498-7376	7422
Alatus Aerosystems	3728	D	714 732-0559	7423
Align Aerospace LLC (PA)	3728	B	818 727-7800	7424
Hydraulics International Inc (PA)	3728	B	818 998-1231	7492
Cliffdale Manufacturing LLC	3769	C	818 341-3344	7667
Hydromach Inc	3769	E	818 341-0915	7670
Aeroantenna Technology Inc	3812	C	818 993-3842	7685
Firan Tech Group USA Corp (HQ)	3812	D	818 407-4024	7719
Moog Inc	3812	D	818 341-5156	7743
Sensor Systems Inc	3812	B	818 341-5366	7810
Space Vector Corporation	3812	E	818 734-2600	7812
Intelligent Cmpt Solutions Inc (PA)	3825	E	818 990-5005	7916
Teledyne Hanson Research Inc	3826	E	818 882-7266	7901
Teledyne Instruments Inc	3826	E	818 882-7266	7982
Optical Corporation (DH)	3827	E	818 725-9750	8013
Photo Research Inc	3827	E	818 341-5151	8015
California Dynamics Corp (PA)	3829	E	323 223-3882	8036
Measurement Specialties Inc	3829	C	818 701-2750	8052
Ansell Sndel Med Solutions LLC	3842	E	818 534-2500	8253
Boyd Chatsworth Inc	3842	D	818 998-1477	8256
Selane Products Inc (PA)	3843	E	818 998-7460	8355
Photo-Sonics Inc (PA)	3861	E	818 842-2141	8438
General Ribbon Corp	3955	B	818 709-1234	8563
Planet Green Cartridges Inc	3955	D	818 725-2596	8565
Vision Imaging Supplies Inc	3955	E	818 885-4515	8568
Maxwell Alarm Screen Mfg Inc	3993	E	818 773-5533	8614
Advanced Cosmetic RES Labs Inc	3999	E	818 709-9945	8656
Sega Holdings USA Inc	3999	A	415 701-6000	8722
Los Angles Cnty Mtro Trnsp Aut	4111	A	213 922-6308	8763
Southern California Gas Co	4922	B	818 701-2592	9643
Allstate Imaging Inc (PA)	5044	D	818 678-4550	9970
Levlad LLC	5047	C	818 882-2951	10089

	SIC	EMP	PHONE	ENTRY#
PLC Imports Inc	5063	E	818 349-1600	10201
Regency Enterprises Inc (PA)	5063	B	818 901-0255	10205
Air Electro Inc (PA)	5065	C	818 407-5400	10229
Cbol Corporation	5065	C	818 704-8200	10237
Refrigeration Hdwr Sup Corp	5078	D	800 537-8300	10343
Maloof Naman Builders	5082	D	818 775-0040	10352
Wastech Controls & Engrg LLC	5084	D	818 998-3500	10417
Clover Envmtl Solutions LLC	5085	A	815 431-8100	10430
Pentacon Inc	5085	B	818 727-8000	10457
Logistical Support LLC	5088	C	818 341-3344	10496
Ontic Engineering and Mfg Inc (PA)	5088	D	818 678-6555	10497
MGA Entertainment Inc	5092	A	800 222-4685	10525
Medical Research Institute	5122	C	818 739-6000	10632
Natrol LLC	5122	E	818 739-6000	10637
Piege Co (PA)	5137	E	818 727-9100	10722
Chemsil Silicones Inc	5169	E	818 700-0302	11010
Vijall Inc	5169	E	818 700-0071	11024
J B Whl Roofg Bldg Sups Inc (DH)	5211	D	818 998-0440	11201
North Ranch Management Corp	5719	C	800 410-2153	11535
Gameworks Entertainment LLC (PA)	5812	A	206 521-0952	11573
Performance Automotive Whl Inc (PA)	5961	E	805 499-8973	11659
Cosmetic Laboratories of America LLC	5999	B	818 717-6140	11679
Telesis Community Credit Union	6061	E	818 885-1226	11817
Premier America Credit Union (PA)	6062	C	818 772-4000	11831
Cake Mortgage Corp	6162	C	818 812-5150	11889
Nna Insurance Services LLC	6411	C	818 739-4071	12239
Platinum Group Companies Inc (PA)	6719	C	818 721-3800	12607
Bellami Hair LLC	7231	D	844 235-5264	13147
Health Advocates LLC	7322	B	818 995-9500	13285
Tuttle Family Enterprises Inc	7349	B	818 534-2566	13424
Datadirect Networks Inc (PA)	7371	E	818 700-7600	13702
ADT LLC	7382	C	818 464-5001	14378
Guardian Integrated SEC Inc (PA)	7382	C	800 400-3167	14404
American Copak Corporation	7389	C	818 576-1000	14445
Seven One Inc (PA)	7389	D	818 904-3435	14593
Ironman Inc	7692	E	818 341-0980	14742
Genesis Tech Partners LLC	7699	C	800 950-2647	14769
Respawn Entertainment LLC	7812	C	818 960-4400	14850
Hyperion Healing LLC	8049	B	818 626-9078	15542
Cpcc Inc	8059	D	818 882-3200	15846
Pacific Toxicology Labs	8071	D	818 598-3110	16326
Electronic Health Plans Inc	8099	D	818 734-4700	16558
Sierra Canyon Inc	8211	D	818 882-8121	16825
Child Care Resource Center Inc (PA)	8322	C	818 717-1000	16885
Rancho San Antonio Boys HM Inc (PA)	8361	D	818 882-6400	17188
National Notary Association	8621	C	800 876-6827	17302
Accunex Inc	8711	E	818 882-5858	17478
Oncore Manufacturing LLC (HQ)	8711	A	818 734-6500	17598
Color Design Laboratory Inc (PA)	8734	C	818 341-5100	17909
North La County Regional Ctr (PA)	8748	B	818 778-1900	18343

CHINO, CA - San Bernardino County

	SIC	EMP	PHONE	ENTRY#
Tawa Supermarket Inc	0291	C	909 760-8899	99
American Beef Packers Inc	0751	C	909 628-4888	137
DL Long Landscaping Inc	0781	D	909 628-5531	165
Generation Construction Inc	1521	C	909 923-2077	405
Servicmaster Opco Holdings LLC	1521	A	951 840-0134	429
Interior Experts Gen Bldrs Inc	1542	C	909 203-4922	549
Flatiron West Inc	1622	C	909 597-8413	651
Duke Pacific Inc	1781	D	909 591-0191	1000
R & B Reinforcing Steel Corp	1791	D	909 591-1726	1161
Provena Foods Inc (HQ)	2013	D	909 627-1082	1267
Ziegenfelder Company	2024	D	909 509-0493	1322
Ziegenfelder Company	2024	D	909 590-0493	1323
Hira Paris Inc	2064	E	909 634-3900	1505
Isiqalo LLC	2253	B	714 683-2820	1920
Omnia Leather Motion Inc	2392	C	909 393-4400	2219
Corona Millworks Company (PA)	2434	D	909 606-3288	2345
Hanson Truss Inc	2439	B	909 591-9256	2377
Alaco Ladder Company	2499	E	909 591-7561	2408
B E & P Enterprises LLC (PA)	2499	E	909 591-7561	2409
Mikhail Darafeev Inc (PA)	2511	E	909 613-1818	2430
Royal Custom Designs LLC	2512	C	909 591-8990	2459
Impact Printing & Graphics	2752	E	909 614-1678	3015
Wright Business Graphics LLC	2761	C	909 614-6700	3196
Ferco Color Inc (PA)	2821	E	909 930-0773	3267
Genlabs (PA)	2841	C	909 591-8451	3592
Diamond Wipes Intl Inc	2844	D	909 230-9888	3648
Diamond Wipes Intl Inc (PA)	2844	D	909 230-9888	3649
Plz Corp	2844	D	909 393-9475	3682
Universal Packg Systems Inc (PA)	2844	A	909 517-2442	3693
Avient Colorants USA LLC	2869	D	909 606-1325	3727
Wacker Chemical Corporation	2869	D	909 590-8822	3743

Employee Codes: A=Over 500 employees, B=251-500
C=101-250, D=51-100, E=20-50, F=10-19, G=1-9

2025 Southern California
Business Directory and Buyers Guide

© Mergent Inc. 1-800-342-5647
1265

GEOGRAPHIC

	SIC	EMP	PHONE	ENTRY#
Gro-Power Inc.	2873	E	909 393-3744	3744
Berry Global Films LLC	3081	C	909 517-2872	3946
Flexcon Company Inc	3081	C	909 465-0408	3949
Repet Inc.	3083	C	909 594-5333	3970
Jacuzzi Products Co.	3088	B	909 548-7732	4028
Acorn-Gencon Plastics LLC	3089	D	909 591-8461	4036
Altium Packaging LP	3089	C	909 590-7334	4044
Berry Global Inc.	3089	C	909 465-9055	4066
Envision Plastics Industries LLC	3089	E	909 590-7334	4113
Karat Packaging Inc (PA)	3089	C	626 965-8882	4150
Norco Injection Molding Inc.	3089	D	909 393-4000	4182
Norco Plastics Inc.	3089	D	909 393-4000	4183
Spin Products Inc.	3089	E	909 590-7000	4247
Syntech Development & Mfg Inc (PA)	3089	E	909 465-5554	4253
West Cast Stl Proc Hldings LLC (PA)	3312	E	909 393-8405	4528
Wcs Equipment Holdings LLC (HQ)	3325	E	909 393-8405	4572
Texas Tst Inc.	3341	E	951 685-2155	4587
Tst Inc (PA)	3341	B	951 685-2155	4588
Superior Metal Shapes Inc.	3354	E	909 947-3455	4608
Kumar Industries.	3441	E	909 591-0722	4844
South Gate Engineering LLC	3443	C	909 628-2779	4927
Great Pacific Elbow LLC.	3444	E	909 606-5551	4989
Trend Technologies LLC (DH)	3444	C	909 597-7861	5047
Wcs Equipment Holdings LLC.	3444	D	909 393-8405	5056
Dupree Inc.	3452	E	909 597-4889	5125
Top-Shelf Fixtures LLC.	3496	E	909 627-7423	5416
Team Technologies Inc.	3544	D	626 334-5000	5600
Wetmore Tool and Engrg Co.	3545	D	909 364-1000	5632
Imperial Rubber Products Inc.	3555	E	909 393-0528	5662
Morehouse-Cowles LLC.	3559	E	909 627-7222	5711
Reed LLC.	3561	E	909 287-2100	5742
Shop4techcom.	3572	E	909 248-2725	5887
Hussmann Corporation.	3585	B	909 590-4910	5977
Aranda Tooling LLC.	3599	D	714 379-6565	6080
Arnold-Gonsalves Engrg Inc.	3599	E	909 465-1579	6082
Fortune Manufacturing Inc.	3599	E	909 591-1547	6126
Wahlco Inc.	3599	C	714 979-7300	6268
Custom Magnetics Cal Inc.	3612	E	909 620-3877	6282
Desco Industries Inc (PA).	3629	D	909 627-8178	6372
Scott Mfg Solutions Inc.	3629	C	909 594-9637	6381
Pacific Coast Mfg Inc.	3631	D	909 627-7040	6388
Anthony California Inc (PA).	3645	E	909 627-0351	6438
Artiva USA Inc (PA).	3645	E	909 628-1388	6439
Base Lite Corporation.	3645	E	909 444-2776	6441
Lights of America Inc (PA).	3645	B	909 594-7883	6445
Hi-Lite Manufacturing Co Inc.	3646	D	909 465-1999	6463
Yankon Industries Inc (PA).	3646	E	909 591-2345	6482
Vtl Amplifiers Inc.	3651	E	909 627-5944	6569
Balaji Trading Inc.	3661	D	909 444-7999	6581
General Photonics Corp.	3661	D	909 590-5473	6586
Manley Laboratories Inc.	3663	E	909 627-4256	6631
R Kern Engineering & Mfg Corp.	3678	D	909 664-2440	6957
Enersys.	3691	E	909 464-8251	7074
Soaring America Corporation.	3721	E	909 270-2628	7371
Alvarado Manufacturing Co Inc.	3829	C	909 591-8431	8031
Myers & Sons Hi-Way Safety Inc (PA)	3993	D	909 591-1781	8618
National Sign & Marketing Corp.	3993	D	909 591-4742	8619
Jacuzzi Brands LLC.	3999	E	909 606-1416	8687
CRST Expedited Inc.	4213	B	909 563-5606	8940
Kenco Group Inc.	4225	C	800 758-3289	9080
Navy Exchange Service Command.	4225	D	909 517-2640	9093
Schneider Electric Usa Inc.	4225	C	909 438-2295	9108
Universal Packg Systems Inc.	4225	C	909 517-2442	9125
Aviation Maintenance Group Inc.	4581	D	714 469-0515	9193
Nationwide Trans Inc (PA).	4731	D	909 355-3211	9315
Advanced Multimodal Dist Inc.	4789	C	800 838-3058	9357
Cellco Partnership.	4812	D	909 591-9740	9398
Inland Empire Utlties Agcy A M (PA)	4941	D	909 993-1600	9694
Yoshimura RES & Dev Amer Inc.	5013	D	909 628-4722	9854
Omnia Italian Design LLC.	5021	C	909 393-4400	9879
Nexgrill Industries Inc (PA).	5023	D	909 598-8799	9900
Carlisle Construction Mtls LLC.	5033	D	909 591-7425	9957
Aamp of Florida Inc.	5046	E	805 338-6800	10040
A Plus International Inc (PA).	5047	D	909 591-5168	10057
Harrington Industrial Plas LLC (PA).	5074	C	909 597-8641	10322
Hill Phoenix Inc.	5078	D	909 592-8830	10340
Consolidated Plastics Corp (PA).	5162	E	909 393-8222	10996
S & W Plastic Stores Inc (PA).	5162	E	909 390-0090	11002
Youngs Market Company LLC.	5182	C	909 393-4540	11067
Home Depot USA Inc.	5211	B	909 393-5205	11183
M K Smith Chevrolet.	5511	C	909 628-8961	11375
Kaiser Foundation Hospitals.	6324	D	888 750-0036	12086
Mission Linen Supply.	7213	E	909 393-6857	13123
Contract Labeling Service Inc.	7389	E	909 937-0344	14479
Macadamia Holdings LLC.	7389	C	909 465-0246	14535
Math Holdings Inc (PA)	7389	C	909 517-2200	14540
El Prado Golf Course LP.	7992	D	909 597-1751	15078
Chino Medical Group Inc.	8011	D	909 591-6446	15277
Veritas Health Services Inc.	8062	A	909 464-8600	16255
Canyon Ridge Hospital Inc.	8063	B	909 590-3700	16271
Angels In Motion LLC.	8082	D	909 590-9102	16365
West End Yung MNS Christn Assn.	8641	C	909 597-7445	17377
Automobile Club Southern Cal.	8699	C	909 591-9451	17426
Transtech Engineers Inc (PA).	8711	D	909 595-8599	17650
Hyundai Amer Technical Ctr Inc.	8734	C	909 627-3525	17918
Lollicup Franchising LLC.	8742	C	626 965-8882	18161

CHINO HILLS, CA - San Bernardino County

	SIC	EMP	PHONE	ENTRY#
Jacuzzi Products Co (DH)	3088	C	909 606-1416	4027
Dur-Red Products.	3444	E	323 771-9000	4981
Victory Intl Group LLC.	5092	C	949 407-5888	10531
Lowes Home Centers LLC.	5211	C	909 438-9000	11233
Crmls LLC.	6512	C	909 859-2040	12287
Gateway Fresh LLC.	6719	C	951 378-5439	12599
Level One Protection Inc.	7381	C	949 514-4182	14314
Los Serranos Golf Club.	7992	C	909 597-1769	15088
Redwood Family Care Netwrk Inc.	8011	A	909 942-0218	15435
Sails Washington Inc.	8082	B	425 333-4114	16417
Boys Republic (PA).	8361	C	909 902-6690	17123
Chancellor Health Care Inc.	8741	C	909 606-2553	17964

CHULA VISTA, CA - San Diego County

	SIC	EMP	PHONE	ENTRY#
Sharp Healthcare.	0291	D	619 397-3088	98
Merchants Landscape Services.	0782	D	619 778-6239	222
Sbhis.	1522	D	619 427-2689	452
FJ Willert Contracting Co.	1542	C	619 421-1980	539
Otay River Constructors LLC.	1611	C	619 397-7500	640
Foshay Electric Co Inc.	1731	D	858 277-7676	920
Home Carpet Investment Inc (PA).	1752	D	619 262-8040	1068
Legacy Reinforcing Steel LLC.	1791	D	619 646-0205	1156
Otay Lakes Brewery LLC.	2082	E	619 768-0172	1549
Boochery Inc.	2085	D	619 207-0530	1596
Canvas Concepts Inc.	2394	E	619 424-3428	2234
Stark Mfg Co.	2394	E	619 425-5880	2242
San Diego Arcft Interiors Inc.	2511	E	619 474-1997	2435
Califrnia Furn Collections Inc.	2519	C	619 621-2455	2500
Latina & Associates Inc (PA).	2711	E	619 426-1491	2812
Ggtw LLC.	2899	E	619 423-3388	3800
Sealed Air Corporation.	3086	E	619 421-9003	4015
Nypro Inc.	3089	D	619 498-9250	4187
Nypro San Diego Inc.	3089	D	619 482-7033	4188
Tenma America Corporation.	3089	E	619 754-2250	4256
Sandpiper of California Inc.	3161	D	619 424-2222	4300
Aker International Inc.	3199	C	619 423-5182	4308
RCP Block & Brick Inc.	3271	E	619 474-1516	4374
Precision Fiber Products Inc.	3357	E	408 946-4040	4636
McMahon Steel Company Inc.	3429	C	619 671-9700	4780
East Cast Repr Fabrication LLC.	3441	E	619 591-9577	4832
Omega Ii Inc.	3443	E	619 920-6650	4917
Plenums Plus LLC.	3444	D	619 422-5515	5021
Curtiss-Wright Corporation.	3491	D	619 482-3405	5362
Flexible Metal Inc.	3498	C	734 516-3017	5434
Harcon Precision Metals Inc.	3531	E	619 423-5544	5494
Xylem Water Systems (california) Inc.	3561	E	619 575-7466	5747
Integrated Energy Technologies Inc.	3562	C	619 421-1151	5750
Hyspan Precision Products Inc (PA).	3568	D	619 421-1355	5809
SMK Manufacturing Inc.	3575	E	619 216-6400	5896
Advanced McHning Solutions Inc.	3599	E	619 671-3055	6065
Bender Ccp Inc.	3599	E	619 232-5719	6094
Pacmag Inc.	3679	E	619 872-0343	7035
Allclear Aerospace & Def Inc.	3728	E	619 660-6220	7427
Astor Manufacturing.	3728	E	661 645-5585	7435
Rohr Inc (HQ).	3728	A	619 691-4111	7548
Colonnas Shipyard West LLC.	3731	E	757 545-2414	7598
Integrated Marine Services Inc.	3731	D	619 429-0300	7602
Adept Process Services Inc.	3732	E	619 434-3194	7615
Bae Systems Land Armaments LP.	3812	C	619 455-0213	7704
Vcp Mobility Holdings Inc.	3842	C	619 213-6500	8317
Toleeto Fastener International.	3965	E	619 662-1355	8578
Stanford Sign & Awning Inc (PA).	3993	C	619 423-6200	8639
Estes Express Lines.	4213	C	619 425-4040	8951
United Parcel Service Inc.	4215	C	619 482-8119	9025
San Diego Gas & Electric Co.	4922	D	800 411-7343	9642
San Diego Gas & Electric Co.	4939	B	858 654-1135	9681
Sweetwter Auth Emplyees Cmmtte (PA)	4941	C	619 420-1413	9721
Samsung International Inc (DH).	5065	E	619 671-6001	10283

	SIC	EMP	PHONE	ENTRY#
Heartland Meat Company Inc.	5147	D	619 407-3668	10871
California Baking Company	5149	B	619 591-8289	10934
Culinary Hispanic Foods Inc.	5149	A	619 955-6101	10942
Home Depot USA Inc.	5211	C	619 421-0639	11187
Lowes Home Centers LLC	5211	C	619 739-9060	11230
Al Global Corporation (HQ)	5961	E	619 934-3980	11653
California Credit Union	6061	D	858 769-7369	11793
Amnet Esop Corporation	6162	C	877 354-1110	11883
West Edge Inc.	6531	D	619 475-4095	12548
Lcs Janitorial Services LLC	7349	C	619 488-7434	13384
Kineticom Inc (PA)	7361	D	619 330-3100	13535
Ado Staffing Inc.	7363	C	619 691-3659	13588
Eagle Eye SEC Solutions Inc.	7381	D	800 372-8142	14296
Rp Automotive II Inc.	7513	D	619 656-2500	14642
Standard Calibrations Inc.	7629	D	619 477-1668	14732
Southcoast Welding & Mfg LLC	7692	B	619 429-1337	14744
Curtiss-Wright Corporation	7699	E	619 656-4740	14762
Marine Group Boat Works LLC	7699	C	619 427-6767	14775
Community Health Group	8011	C	800 224-7766	15284
Bayside Healthcare Inc.	8051	C	619 426-8611	15580
Front Porch Communities & Svcs	8051	C	619 427-2777	15658
Healthcare Management Systems Inc.	8051	C	619 521-9641	15675
Scripps Health	8062	C	619 691-7000	16182
Sharp Chula Vista Medical Ctr	8062	A	619 502-5800	16191
Sharp Healthcare	8062	C	858 499-2000	16193
Centro De Slud De La Cmndad De	8099	B	619 662-4161	16545
Sbcs Corporation	8322	C	619 420-3620	17007
Metroplitan Area Advsory Cmmtte (PA)	8331	D	619 426-3595	17062
Child Development Assoc Inc.	8351	C	619 422-7115	17082
Susan J Harris Inc.	8361	C	619 498-8450	17201
CHG Foundation	8699	B	619 422-0422	17462
George G Sharp Inc.	8711	C	619 425-4211	17538
Gryphon Marine LLC	8711	D	619 407-4010	17542
Lockheed Martin Services LLC	8711	B	619 271-9831	17579

CITY OF COMMERCE, CA - Los Angeles County

	SIC	EMP	PHONE	ENTRY#
Arthurmade Plastics Inc.	3089	D	323 721-7325	4055

CITY OF INDUSTRY, CA - Los Angeles County

	SIC	EMP	PHONE	ENTRY#
Alta-Dena Certified Dairy LLC (DH)	0241	B	626 964-6401	89
Dfa Dairy Brands Fluid LLC	0241	B	800 395-7004	90
Frize Corporation	1541	D	800 834-2127	480
Graycon Inc.	1711	D	626 961-9640	783
Morrow-Meadows Corporation (PA)	1731	A	858 974-3650	942
Closet World Inc.	1751	D	626 855-0846	1046
Home Organizers Inc.	1751	A	562 699-9945	1052
Performance Sheets LLC	1761	C	626 333-0195	1091
Ssre Holdings LLC	2011	D	800 314-2098	1251
Viz Cattle Corporation	2011	E	310 884-5260	1252
Derek and Constance Lee Corp (PA)	2013	D	909 595-8831	1257
Gaytan Foods LLC	2013	D	626 330-4553	1259
Pocino Foods Company	2013	D	626 968-8000	1266
Rice Field Corporation	2013	C	626 968-6917	1269
Ybcc Inc.	2023	E	626 213-3945	1312
Berkeley Farms LLC	2026	B	510 265-8600	1325
Dean Socal LLC	2026	B	951 734-3950	1328
Gff Inc.	2035	D	323 232-6255	1368
Lee Kum Kee (usa) Foods Inc (PA)	2035	D	626 709-1888	1369
Morehouse Foods Inc.	2035	E	626 854-1655	1370
Langer Juice Company Inc.	2037	B	626 336-3100	1378
Golden State Foods Corp	2038	B	626 465-7500	1392
Harbor Green Grain LP	2048	B	310 991-8089	1427
Sbm Dairies Inc.	2086	B	626 923-3000	1653
Blue Pacific Flavors Inc.	2087	E	626 934-0099	1670
Snak-King LLC (PA)	2096	B	626 336-7711	1729
Best Formulations LLC (HQ)	2099	E	626 912-9998	1744
Best Formulations LLC.	2099	C	626 912-9998	1745
Delori-Nutifood Products Inc.	2099	D	626 965-3006	1762
Sincere Orient Commercial Corp.	2099	D	626 333-8882	1852
Bentley Mills Inc (PA)	2273	C	626 333-4585	1948
American Foam Fiber & Sups Inc (PA)	2299	E	626 969-7268	1966
Unger Fabrik LLC (PA)	2331	C	626 469-8080	2056
Exxel Outdoors Inc.	2399	C	626 369-7278	2276
Hitex Dyeing & Finishing Inc.	2399	E	626 363-0160	2278
Talbert Archtctral Panl Door I	2431	D	714 671-9700	2330
McConnell Cabinets Inc.	2434	A	626 937-2200	2354
Commercial Lbr & Pallet Co Inc (PA)	2448	C	626 968-0631	2386
Fremarc Industries Inc (PA)	2511	D	626 965-0802	2424
Trend Manor Furn Mfg Co Inc.	2511	C	626 964-6493	2437
Ardmore Home Design Inc (PA)	2512	E	626 803-7769	2440
BJ Liquidation Inc.	2512	D	626 961-7221	2441
E J Lauren LLC	2512	E	562 803-1113	2445
R C Furniture Inc.	2512	D	626 964-4100	2457

	SIC	EMP	PHONE	ENTRY#
Spectrum Intl Holdings	2542	A	626 333-7225	2593
Harvard Label LLC.	2621	C	626 333-8881	2625
Sonoco Products Company	2631	C	626 369-6611	2643
Boxes R Us Inc.	2653	D	626 820-5410	2656
Fleetwood Fibre LLC	2653	C	626 968-8503	2665
Golden West Packg Group LLC (PA)	2653	B	888 501-5893	2670
Goldencorr Sheets LLC	2653	C	626 369-6446	2671
Hoover Containers Inc.	2653	D	909 444-9454	2674
Bagcraftpapercon III LLC	2673	C	626 961-6766	2728
Mercury Plastics Inc (HQ)	2673	B	626 961-0165	2734
Tekni-Plex Inc.	2679	C	909 589-4366	2776
Sing Tao Newspapers Ltd.	2711	D	626 956-8200	2828
K-1 Packaging Group LLC (PA)	2752	D	626 964-9384	3026
Marrs Printing Inc.	2752	C	909 594-9459	3041
Pgi Pacific Graphics Intl.	2752	E	626 336-7707	3059
Orbitel International LLC.	2759	E	626 369-7050	3159
Messer LLC.	2813	E	626 855-8366	3217
Teknor Apex Company.	2821	C	626 968-4656	3298
Teknor Color Company.	2821	E	626 336-7709	3299
Best Formulations LLC.	2834	C	626 912-9998	3372
Prolacta Bioscience Inc (PA)	2836	C	626 599-9260	3586
Maintex Inc (PA)	2842	C	800 446-1888	3612
Physicians Formula Inc (DH)	2844	C	626 334-3395	3679
Physicians Formula Cosmt Inc.	2844	D	626 334-3395	3680
Cardinal Paint and Powder Inc.	2851	D	626 937-6767	3707
General Sealants.	2891	C	626 961-0211	3767
Henkel US Operations Corp.	2891	D	626 968-6511	3769
Signature Flexible Packg LLC (PA)	2891	E	909 598-7844	3779
Acorn Engineering Company (PA)	2899	A	800 488-8999	3788
Coi Rubber Products Inc.	3069	B	626 965-9966	3910
Sealed Air Corporation.	3086	C	909 594-1791	4016
Altium Packaging LLC.	3089	D	888 425-7343	4043
Engineering Model Assoc Inc (PA)	3089	E	626 912-7011	4112
J & L Cstm Plstic Extrsons Inc.	3089	E	626 442-0711	4142
Waddington North America Inc.	3089	C	626 913-4022	4272
Prl Glass Systems Inc.	3231	D	877 775-2586	4343
Prl Glass Systems Inc (PA)	3231	C	626 961-5890	4344
Jon Brooks Inc (PA)	3295	C	626 330-0631	4488
Cast Parts Inc.	3324	C	626 937-3444	4562
Alum-A-Fold Pacific Inc.	3353	E	562 699-4550	4589
Material Sciences Corporation	3353	C	562 699-4550	4591
Hydro Extrusion Usa LLC	3354	B	626 964-3411	4598
Prl Aluminum Inc.	3354	D	626 968-7507	4604
Trulite GL Alum Solutions LLC	3354	D	800 877-8439	4609
Aremac Heat Treating Inc.	3398	E	626 333-3898	4696
Newton Heat Treating Co Inc.	3398	C	626 964-6528	4710
Monadnock Company.	3429	C	626 964-6581	4782
Townsteel Inc.	3429	D	626 965-8917	4792
Katch Inc.	3441	E	626 369-0958	4842
Adams-Campbell Company Ltd (PA)	3444	D	626 330-3425	4938
Cemco LLC (DH)	3444	C	800 775-2362	4968
Trio Metal Stamping Inc.	3444	D	626 336-1228	5049
Dennison Inc.	3446	E	626 965-8917	5061
Valley-Todeco Inc.	3452	C	800 992-4444	5139
WJB Bearings Inc.	3463	E	909 598-6238	5164
Safe Plating Inc.	3471	D	626 810-1872	5290
Nelson Name Plate Company (PA)	3479	C	323 663-3971	5332
Phifer Incorporated.	3496	D	626 968-0438	5409
Evans Industries Inc.	3499	C	626 912-1688	5446
Pape Material Handling Inc.	3537	D	502 092-9311	5502
Clayton Manufacturing Company (PA)	3569	C	626 443-9381	5816
Clayton Manufacturing Inc (HQ)	3569	D	626 443-9381	5817
Magnoll Associate Inc.	3571	B	626 271-1320	5859
Premio Inc (PA)	3571	C	626 839-3100	5865
Compucase Corporation	3572	A	626 336-6588	5877
Seaward Products Corp.	3585	C	562 699-7997	5983
Solo Enterprise Corp.	3599	E	626 961-3591	6239
Reuland Electric Co (PA)	3621	C	626 964-6411	6331
Valley Power Services Inc.	3621	E	909 969-9345	6336
ITT LLC.	3625	D	562 908-4144	6352
RH Peterson Co (PA)	3631	C	626 369-5085	6389
Superior Equipment Solutions.	3631	D	323 722-7900	6391
Maxim Lighting Intl Inc.	3645	D	626 956-4200	6446
Troy-Csl Lighting Inc.	3645	C	626 336-4511	6449
Kim Lighting Inc.	3648	A	626 968-5666	6506
Adtech Photonics Inc.	3674	E	626 956-1000	6793
Invenlux Corporation.	3674	E	626 277-4163	6835
Cooper Interconnect Inc.	3679	D	617 389-7080	6985
Sceptre Inc.	3679	C	626 369-3698	7049
Battery Technology Inc (PA)	3691	D	626 336-6878	7072
Camber Operating Company Inc.	3711	B	864 438-0000	7171
Utility Trailer Manufacturing (PA)	3715	B	626 965-1514	7320
Utility Trailer Mfg Co.	3715	C	909 594-6026	7322

Employee Codes: A=Over 500 employees, B=251-500
C=101-250, D=51-100, E=20-50, F=10-19, G=1-9

2025 Southern California
Business Directory and Buyers Guide

© Mergent Inc. 1-800-342-5647

1267

GEOGRAPHIC

	SIC	EMP	PHONE	ENTRY#
Acromil LLC (HQ)	3728	C	626 964-2522	7400
Acromil Corporation (PA)	3728	C	626 964-2522	7401
Maverick Aerospace LLC	3728	D	714 578-1700	7521
Triumph Structures - Everett Inc	3728	C	425 348-4100	7585
Chronomite Laboratories Inc	3822	E	310 534-2300	7834
Xpower Manufacture Inc	3822	E	626 285-3301	7843
Teledyne Instruments Inc	3829	D	626 934-1500	8068
Johnson Wilshire Inc	3842	E	562 777-0088	8280
Astrophysics Inc (PA)	3844	C	909 598-5488	8364
Jada Group Inc	3944	C	626 810-8382	8488
Easy Reach Supply LLC	3991	E	601 582-7866	8586
Cambro Manufacturing Company	3999	C	909 354-8962	8666
H & H Specialties Inc	3999	E	626 575-0776	8680
United Pumping Service Inc	4212	D	626 961-9326	8929
Estes Express Lines	4213	D	626 333-9090	8949
U C L Incorporated (PA)	4213	D	323 235-0099	8979
Thunder International Group (PA)	4731	D	626 723-3715	9342
Southern California Gas Co	4924	C	213 244-1200	9661
Arakelian Enterprises Inc	4953	B	626 336-3636	9728
Arakelian Enterprises Inc (PA)	4953	C	626 336-3636	9729
Ecobat California RE LLC	4953	D	626 937-3201	9743
Zerep Management Corporation (PA)	4953	C	626 855-5522	9784
Furniture America Cal Inc (PA)	5021	E	866 923-8500	9871
Poundex Associates Corporation	5021	D	909 444-5878	9880
Pacific Heritg HM Fashion Inc	5023	E	909 598-5200	9904
Soto Provision Inc	5023	D	626 458-4600	9907
Carrara Marble Co Amer Inc (PA)	5032	D	626 961-6010	9938
American Future Tech Corp	5045	C	888 462-3899	9986
Avatar Technology Inc	5045	E	909 598-7696	9989
GBT Inc	5045	C	626 854-9338	10005
Magnell Associate Inc	5045	B	626 271-1580	10016
Micro-Technology Concepts Inc	5045	D	626 839-6800	10018
MSI Computer Corp (HQ)	5045	D	626 913-0828	10019
Mtc Worldwide Corp	5045	D	626 839-6800	10020
Grifols Usa LLC	5047	A	626 435-2600	10081
California Steel and Tube	5051	C	626 968-5511	10126
Maxim Lighting Intl Inc (PA)	5063	D	626 956-4200	10193
Emtek Products Group LLC	5072	A	626 369-4718	10307
Elmco Sales Inc (PA)	5074	C	626 855-4831	10316
US Airconditioning Distributors Inc (PA)	5075	C	626 854-4500	10337
Quinn Shepherd Machinery	5082	B	562 463-6000	10358
Pape Material Handling Inc	5084	C	562 463-8000	10391
Valley Power Systems Inc (PA)	5084	C	626 333-1243	10413
Yale/Chase Equipment and Services Inc	5084	C	562 463-8000	10423
Bridgestone Hosepower LLC	5085	E	562 699-9500	10427
Rutland Tool & Supply Co (HQ)	5085	C	562 566-5000	10460
Design International Group Inc	5092	E	626 369-2289	10520
Sweda Company LLC	5094	B	626 357-9999	10554
Cenveo Worldwide Limited	5112	B	626 369-4921	10579
Imperial Bag & Paper Co LLC	5113	D	800 834-6248	10594
Markwins Beauty Brands Inc (PA)	5122	C	909 595-8898	10630
Foria International Inc	5136	C	626 912-8836	10684
Swatfame Inc (PA)	5137	B	626 961-7928	10730
Fortune Dynamic Inc	5139	D	909 979-8318	10736
Concord Foods Inc (HQ)	5141	C	909 975-2000	10748
Marquez Brothers Entps Inc (PA)	5141	C	626 330-3310	10755
Mercado Latino Inc (PA)	5141	D	626 333-6862	10760
OTasty Foods Inc	5141	C	626 330-1229	10763
Clemson Distribution Inc (PA)	5143	E	909 595-2770	10828
Los Altos Food Products LLC	5143	C	626 330-6555	10831
Youbar Inc (PA)	5145	E	626 537-1851	10851
D&D Wholesale Distributors LLC	5148	D	626 333-2111	10892
Freshpoint Inc	5148	C	626 855-1400	10898
Freshpoint Southern Cal Inc	5148	C	626 855-1400	10899
Langer Juice Company Inc	5149	C	626 336-3100	10955
Lee Kum Kee (usa) Inc (DH)	5149	C	626 709-1888	10957
Quality Naturally Foods Inc	5149	E	626 854-6363	10971
Quality Naturally Foods Inc (PA)	5149	E	626 854-6363	10972
Royal Crown Enterprises Inc	5149	C	626 854-8080	10976
Tld Acquisition Co LLC	5149	C		10985
Vinh - Sanh Trading Corp	5149	D	626 968-6888	10990
Norman Fox & Co (PA)	5169	E	800 632-1777	11018
Classic Bev Southern Cal LLC	5181	B	626 934-3700	11044
American Paper & Plastics LLC	5199	C	626 444-0000	11109
Consolidated Devices Inc (HQ)	5251	E	626 965-0668	11257
Langer Juice Company Inc (PA)	5499	C	626 336-3100	11307
Diamond Bar Imports Inc	5511	D	626 935-1700	11336
Leo Hoffman Chevrolet Inc (PA)	5511	C	626 968-8411	11373
Dna Motor Inc	5531	E	626 965-8898	11443
Hot Topic Inc (DH)	5699	A	800 892-8674	11508
Dacor (DH)	5719	D	626 799-1000	11530
Labels-R-Us Inc	5932	E	626 333-4001	11629
Sailing Innovation (us) Inc	5945	A	626 965-6665	11645

	SIC	EMP	PHONE	ENTRY#
Citifinancial Credit Company	6141	C	626 712-8780	11853
Cubeworkcom Inc (PA)	6531	C	909 991-6669	12417
Majestic Realty Co (PA)	6531	C	562 692-9581	12485
Bethar Corporation	6719	C		12595
Benefits Prgram Adminsitration	6733	D	562 463-5000	12655
Majestic Industry Hills LLC	7011	A	626 810-4455	12911
CSC Serviceworks Inc	7215	D	626 389-0169	13129
Boiling Point Rest S CA Inc	7361	B	626 551-5181	13494
Management Applied Prgrm Inc (PA)	7374	D	562 463-5000	14142
Gardaworld	7381	D	909 468-2229	14302
Easterncctv (usa) LLC	7382	D	626 961-8999	14394
Ezviz Inc	7382	C	855 693-9849	14400
Hikvision USA Inc (HQ)	7382	C	909 895-0400	14406
Vonnic Inc	7382	E	626 964-2345	14425
US Bankcard Services Inc	7389	D	888 888-8872	14624
Rollins Leasing LLC	7513	D	626 913-7186	14641
Allied Entertainment Group Inc (PA)	7812	B	626 330-0600	14805
Grifols Wrldwide Oprtons USA I	8099	D	626 435-2600	16564
Public Hlth Fndation Entps Inc	8322	C	626 856-6600	16999
Public Hlth Fndation Entps Inc (PA)	8641	C	800 201-7320	17360
Weck Anlytical Envmtl Svcs Inc	8734	D	626 336-2139	17929
Torrid Merchandising Inc	8742	B	626 667-1002	18232
Pace Lithographers Inc	8999	E	626 913-2108	18377

CLAREMONT, CA - Los Angeles County

	SIC	EMP	PHONE	ENTRY#
Sunsation Inc	2037	E	909 542-0280	1380
Phoenix Marketing Services Inc	2752	D	909 399-4000	3060
Micro Matrix Systems	3469	E	909 626-8544	5203
Vortox Air Technology Inc	3564	E	909 621-3843	5783
Baumann Engineering	3599	D	909 621-4181	6092
HI Rel Connectors Inc	3643	B	909 626-1820	6421
New Bedford Panoramex Corp	3648	E	909 982-9806	6512
Therapak LLC (DH)	5047	D	909 267-2000	10112
Pff Bancorp Inc (PA)	6035	A	213 683-6393	11789
Western Feld Invstigations Inc (PA)	7375	D	800 999-9589	14181
R&C Motor Corporation	7538	C	909 625-1500	14698
Claremont Tennis Club	7997	C	909 625-9515	15129
Tierra Del Sol Foundation	7999	D	909 626-8301	15230
Pilgrim Place In Claremont (PA)	8059	C	909 399-5500	15881
Kaiser Foundation Hospitals	8062	C	888 750-0036	16038
Rancho Santa Ana Botanic Grdn	8422	D	909 625-8767	17271
Technip Usa Inc	8711	B	909 447-3600	17643
Ten Stone Wbster Prcess Tech	8711	B	909 447-3600	17644
Bon Appetit Management Co	8741	C	909 607-2788	17954

COACHELLA, CA - Riverside County

	SIC	EMP	PHONE	ENTRY#
Amazing Coachella Inc	0161	D	760 398-0151	7
Anthony Vineyards Inc	0172	D	760 391-5488	29
Teserra (PA)	1799	B	760 340-9000	1228
Reyes Coca-Cola Bottling LLC	2086	D	760 396-4500	1649
Armtec Defense Products Co (DH)	3489	B	760 398-0143	5356
Paladar Mfg Inc	3931	D	760 775-4222	8470
Sunline Transit Agency	4119	C	760 972-4059	8849
Naumann/Hobbs Mtl Hdlg Corp II	5082	C	866 266-2244	10353
Desert Valley Date LLC	5149	D	760 398-0999	10943
Imperial Western Products Inc A Cal (HQ)	5159	E	760 398-0815	10993
Esparza Enterprises Inc	7361	A	760 398-0349	13516
Augustine Gaming MGT Corp	7371	D	760 391-9500	13662
29 Palms Enterprises Corp	7999	A	760 775-5566	15190

COLTON, CA - San Bernardino County

	SIC	EMP	PHONE	ENTRY#
Superior Masonry Walls Ltd	1741	D	909 370-1800	989
Lozano Caseworks Inc	1751	D	909 783-7530	1056
Boyd Specialties LLC	2013	D	909 219-5120	1255
Star Food Snacks Intl Inc	2013	D	909 825-8882	1272
California Churros Corporation	2051	B	909 370-4777	1439
Avalon Apparel LLC	2335	D	323 440-4344	2059
Masterbrand Cabinets LLC	2434	E	951 682-1535	2353
Banner Mattress Inc	2515	D	909 835-4200	2480
Clariant Corporation	2672	E	909 825-1793	2721
Omni Resource Recovery Inc	3089	C	909 327-2900	4189
Cemex Materials LLC	3273	D	909 825-1500	4435
Als Garden Art Inc (PA)	3299	B	909 424-0221	4499
Darnell-Rose Inc	3429	E	626 912-1688	4765
Elizabeth Shutters Inc	3442	E	909 825-1531	4887
C&K Form Fabrication Inc	3449	E	909 825-1882	5092
Black Diamond Blade Company (PA)	3531	E	800 949-9014	5488
Williams Furnace Co (DH)	3585	D	562 450-3602	5993
Rivian Automotive LLC	3711	D	309 249-8777	7191
McNeilus Truck and Mfg Inc	3713	E	909 370-2100	7207
Cummings Resources LLC	3993	E	951 248-1130	8598
Gxo Logistics Supply Chain Inc	4225	D	951 512-1201	9072
Sprouts Farmers Market Inc	4225	C	888 577-7688	9110

Mergent email: customerrelations@mergent.com

1268

2025 Southern California
Business Directory and Buyers Guide

(P-0000) Products & Services Section entry number
(PA)=Parent Co (HQ)=Headquarters (DH)=Div Headquarters

	SIC	EMP	PHONE	ENTRY#
Ecology Recycling Services LLC	4953	C	909 370-1318	9744
SMC Grease Specialist Inc	4953	E	951 788-6042	9765
A-Z Bus Sales Inc (PA)	5012	D	951 781-7188	9795
Trinity Equipment Inc	5046	D	951 790-1652	10055
Brithinee Electric	5063	D	909 825-7971	10174
Greenpath Recovery West Inc	5093	D	909 954-0686	10539
Jon-Lin Frozen Foods (PA)	5142	D	909 825-8542	10822
Mpi Limited Inc	6719	D		12604
King Equipment LLC	7353	D	909 986-5300	13439
Sulzer Elctr-Mchncal Svcs US I	7694	E	909 825-7971	14751
Inland Eye Inst Med Group Inc (PA)	8011	D	909 825-3425	15331
Southern Cal Prmnnte Med Group	8011	C	909 370-2501	15478
Cambridge Sierra Holdings LLC	8051	B	909 370-4411	15587
Arrowhead Regional Medical Ctr	8062	A	909 580-1000	15917

COMMERCE, CA - Los Angeles County

	SIC	EMP	PHONE	ENTRY#
Shims Bargain Inc	1541	C	323 726-8800	500
Farwest Insulation Contracting	1742	D	310 634-2800	1007
Mantels & More Corp	1743	E	323 869-9764	1041
Heritage Distributing Company (PA)	2026	E	323 838-1225	1332
Sugar Foods LLC	2051	D	323 727-8290	1466
New Century Snacks LLC	2068	E	323 278-9578	1515
Snak Club LLC	2068	C	323 278-9578	1517
Chameleon Beverage Company Inc (PA)	2086	D	323 724-8223	1613
Carmi Flvr & Fragrance Co Inc (PA)	2087	E	323 888-9240	1673
Key Essentials Inc	2087	D		1686
Caffe DAmore Inc	2095	C		1715
Gruma Corporation	2096	B	323 803-1400	1724
Arevalo Tortilleria Inc	2099	E	323 888-1711	1739
Gold Coast Ingredients Inc	2099	D	323 724-8935	1782
Interntional Tea Importers Inc (PA)	2099	E	562 801-9600	1793
Mojave Foods Corporation	2099	C	323 890-8900	1818
Pacific Spice Company Inc	2099	C	323 726-9190	1831
Bonded Fiberloft Inc	2211	B	323 726-7820	1872
Hidden Jeans Inc	2211	E	213 746-4223	1881
4 What Its Worth Inc (PA)	2329	E	323 728-4503	2003
Trixxi Clothing Company Inc (PA)	2335	E	323 585-4200	2075
DNam Apparel Industries LLC	2339	E	323 859-0114	2093
J & F Design Inc	2339	D	323 526-4444	2102
Evy of California Inc	2361	C	213 746-4647	2164
Canvas Specialty Inc	2394	E		2235
Greif Inc	2449	E	323 724-7500	2394
Furniture Technics Inc	2511	E	562 802-0261	2425
JP Products LLC	2511	E	310 237-6237	2427
Nova Lifestyle Inc	2511	E	323 888-9999	2432
Commercial Intr Resources Inc	2512	E	562 926-5885	2443
Murrays Iron Works Inc (PA)	2514	C	323 521-1100	2471
Deskmakers Inc	2521	E	323 264-2260	2508
Norstar Office Products Inc (PA)	2521	E	323 262-1919	2512
Ergocraft Contract Solutions	2522	E		2525
Pacific Hospitality Design Inc	2531	E	323 278-7998	2551
Nico Nat Mfg Corp	2541	E	323 721-1900	2571
Teichman Enterprises Inc	2542	E	323 278-9000	2595
Yavar Manufacturing Co Inc	2657	E	323 722-2040	2702
Amcor Flexibles LLC	2671	A	323 721-6777	2703
Liberty Packg & Extruding Inc	2673	E	323 722-5124	2733
Sun Plastics Inc	2673	E	323 888-6999	2739
Progressive Label Inc	2679	E	323 415-9770	2773
Bridge Publications Inc (PA)	2731	E	323 888-6200	2885
La Xpress Air & Heating Svcs	2741	D	310 856-9678	2925
Hanover Accessories Corp	2782	C		3199
Biorx Pharmaceuticals Inc	2834	D	323 725-3100	3376
Samson Pharmaceuticals Inc	2834	E	323 722-3000	3407
American Intl Inds Inc	2844	A	323 728-2999	3630
Ink Systems Inc (PA)	2893	D	323 720-4000	3785
Indio Products Inc	2899	E	323 720-9117	3804
Solvay Draka Inc (DH)	3081	E	323 725-7010	3958
Huhtamaki Inc	3086	D	323 269-0151	4006
Specialty Enterprises Co	3086	D	323 726-9721	4018
Bottlemate Inc (PA)	3089	E	323 887-9009	4073
Custom Leathercraft Mfg LLC	3199	D		4309
Pacific Vial Mfg Inc	3221	E	323 721-7004	4321
Wiretech Inc (PA)	3315	D	323 722-4933	4546
Globe Iron Foundry Inc	3321	D	323 723-8983	4557
Kaiser Aluminum Corporation	3354	D	323 726-8011	4599
US Polymers Inc	3354	D	323 727-6888	4611
Century Wire & Cable Inc	3357	D	800 999-5566	4631
Gehr Industries Inc (HQ)	3357	C	323 728-5558	4633
Pacific Die Casting Corp	3363	C	323 725-1308	4651
Alcast Mfg Inc (PA)	3365	E	310 542-3581	4664
Orlandini Entps Pcf Die Cast	3369	C	323 725-1332	4691
Alarin Aircraft Hinge Inc	3429	E	323 725-1666	4751
Asco Sintering Co	3429	E	323 725-3550	4752

	SIC	EMP	PHONE	ENTRY#
Hollywood Bed Spring Mfg Inc (PA)	3429	D	323 887-9500	4772
Monogram Aerospace Fas Inc	3429	C	323 722-4760	4783
Capitol Steel Fabricators Inc	3441	C	323 721-5460	4824
Air Louvers Inc	3442	E	800 554-6077	4884
Rite Engineering & Manufacturing Corporation	3443	E	562 862-2135	4923
Sid E Parker Boiler Mfg Co Inc	3443	D	323 727-9800	4926
A-1 Metal Products Inc	3444	E	323 721-3334	4936
PCI Industries Inc	3444	E	323 728-0004	5017
Architectural Enterprises Inc	3449	E	323 268-4000	5091
USG Ceilings Plus LLC	3469	C	323 724-8166	5219
Sheila Street Properties Inc (PA)	3471	D	323 838-9208	5295
Ultimate Metal Finishing Corp	3479	E	323 890-9100	5351
Matthew Warren Inc	3495	D	800 237-5225	5395
Precision Wire Products Inc (PA)	3496	C	323 890-9100	5410
ASC Engineered Solutions LLC	3498	C	800 766-0076	5425
Pioneer Broach Company (PA)	3545	E	323 728-1263	5620
Interstate Meat Co Inc	3556	E	323 838-9400	5675
Crowntonka California Inc	3585	D	909 230-6720	5972
MGM Transformer Co	3612	C	323 726-0888	6289
Iworks Us Inc	3641	D	323 278-8363	6404
Deco Enterprises Inc	3646	D	323 726-2575	6454
Edison Price Lighting Inc (PA)	3646	C	718 685-0700	6456
Hallmark Lighting LLC	3646	E	818 885-5010	6462
Elation Lighting Inc	3648	C	323 582-3322	6500
Elite Lighting	3648	E	323 888-1973	6501
Eti Sound Systems Inc	3651	E	323 835-6660	6536
71yrs Inc (PA)	3669	D	310 639-0390	6674
Dynaflex Products (PA)	3713	D	323 724-1555	7202
Fastener Dist Holdings LLC	3721	E	213 620-9950	7340
Transdigm Inc	3728	D	323 269-9181	7581
Atk Space Systems LLC (DH)	3812	E	323 722-0222	7701
Northrop Grumman Systems Corp	3812	C	714 240-6521	7772
Soffa Electric Inc	3823	E	323 728-0230	7880
PCI Industries Inc	3999	E	323 728-0004	8712
Pommes Frites Candle Co	3999	E	213 488-2016	8717
Eastwestproto Inc	4119	B	888 535-5728	8820
Xpo Cartage Inc	4212	C	800 837-7584	8931
Dart International A Corp (HQ)	4225	C	323 264-8746	9060
Dart Warehouse Corporation (HQ)	4225	B	323 264-1011	9061
Smart & Final Stores LLC	4225	B	323 725-0791	9109
Screamline Investment Corp	4725	C	323 201-0114	9241
RAMCAR Batteries Inc	5013	E	323 726-1212	9843
ITD Arizona Inc	5014	D	323 722-8542	9857
Gibson Overseas Inc (PA)	5023	B	323 832-8900	9896
Zwilling JA Henckels LLC	5023	C	323 597-1421	9916
Insul-Therm International Inc (PA)	5033	E	323 728-0558	9958
Interstate Electric Co Inc	5046	D	800 225-5432	10045
Justman Packaging & Display (PA)	5046	E	323 728-8888	10049
Kobert & Company Inc	5063	D	323 725-1000	10188
Nora Lighting Inc	5063	C	323 767-2600	10198
Samsung Electronics Amer Inc	5064	C	323 374-6300	10225
Hkf Inc (PA)	5075	D	323 225-1318	10335
Fastener Dist Holdings LLC (HQ)	5085	D	213 620-9950	10437
PC Woo Inc (PA)	5092	D	323 887-8138	10526
Ultra Pro International LLC	5092	C	323 890-2100	10530
D J American Supply Inc	5099	C	323 582-2650	10557
Sun Coast Merchandise Corp	5099	C	323 720-9700	10570
Charming Trim & Packaging	5131	A	415 302-7021	10663
Matrix International Tex Inc	5131	E	323 582-9100	10667
Roochi Traders Incorporated	5136	D	323 722-5592	10694
BP Clothing LLC	5137	C		10702
Balance Foods Inc	5145	E	323 838-5555	10841
Century Snacks LLC	5145	R	323 278-9578	10843
Buy Fresh Produce Inc	5148	D	323 796-0127	10889
El Guapo Spices Inc (PA)	5149	D	213 312-1300	10944
Jfc International Inc	5149	C	323 721-6900	10950
Jfc International Inc (HQ)	5149	C	323 721-6100	10951
Elkay Plastics Co Inc (PA)	5162	D	323 722-7073	10998
Univar Solutions USA LLC	5169	C	323 727-7005	11022
Breakthru Beverage Cal LLC (HQ)	5182	B	800 331-2829	11054
Bio Hazard Inc	5199	E	213 625-2116	11112
Ernest Packaging (PA)	5199	E	800 233-7788	11117
Misa Imports Inc	5199	E	562 281-6773	11130
RYL Inc	5199	E	213 503-7968	11141
Unix Packaging LLC	5199	C	213 627-5050	11146
West Bay Imports Inc	5199	E	323 720-5777	11148
Dunn-Edwards Corporation (DH)	5231	C	888 337-2468	11254
Unified Nutrimeals	5812	D	323 923-9335	11607
W B Mason Co Inc	5943	E	888 926-2766	11636
Quantum Networks LLC	5961	E	212 993-5899	11660
California Commerce Club Inc	7011	A	323 721-2100	12784
Uniserve Facilities Svcs Corp (PA)	7349	B	213 533-1000	13426
American Security Force Inc	7382	D	323 722-8585	14381

Employee Codes: A=Over 500 employees, B=251-500
C=101-250, D=51-100, E=20-50, F=10-19, G=1-9

2025 Southern California
Business Directory and Buyers Guide

© Mergent Inc. 1-800-342-5647

1269

GEOGRAPHIC

	SIC	EMP	PHONE	ENTRY#
Ceramic Decorating Company Inc	7389	E	323 268-5135	14470
Sugar Foods LLC	7389	C	818 768-7900	14603
Parking Company of America	7521	D	562 862-2118	14662
Pcam LLC	7521	D	562 862-2118	14668
Reading Entertainment Inc (HQ)	7832	D	213 235-2226	14943
Alexandra Lzano Immgrtion Law	8111	C	323 524-9944	16634
County of Los Angeles	8322	C	323 889-3405	16912
Maravilla Foundation (PA)	8641	C	323 721-4162	17355
Michelson Laboratories Inc (PA)	8734	D	562 928-0553	17920
D I F Group Inc	8741	E	323 231-8800	17979
Ivy Enterprises Inc	8748	B	323 887-8661	18325

COMPTON, CA - Los Angeles County

	SIC	EMP	PHONE	ENTRY#
Nabors Well Services Co	1389	D	310 639-7074	349
Quality Production Svcs Inc	1742	D	310 406-3350	1025
Foster Poultry Farms	2015	B	310 223-1499	1277
Sierra Cheese Manufacturing Company Inc	2022	E	310 635-1216	1290
Bcd Food Inc	2099	E	310 323-1200	1742
Lekos Dye & Finishing Inc (PA)	2231	D	310 763-0900	1902
Pacific Contntl Textiles Inc	2269	E	310 639-1500	1944
American Dawn Inc (PA)	2299	D	800 821-2221	1965
Magic Apparel Group Inc	2353	C	310 223-4000	2160
Sew What Inc	2391	E	310 639-6000	2204
Simso Tex Sublimation (PA)	2396	E	310 885-9717	2266
Elliotts Designs Inc	2514	E	310 631-4931	2468
Jbi LLC	2514	E	310 537-2910	2470
Cri Sub 1 (DH)	2521	E	310 537-1657	2507
International Paper Company	2621	E	310 639-2310	2629
Great Eastern Entertainment Co	2741	E	310 638-5058	2920
Kmr Label LLC	2754	E	310 603-8910	3107
Resource Label Group LLC	2754	E	310 603-8910	3109
Carbon Activated Corporation (PA)	2819	E	310 885-4555	3232
Crossfield Products Corp (PA)	2821	E	310 886-9100	3262
Orion Plastics Corporation	2821	D	310 223-0370	3284
Plaskolite West LLC	2821	E	310 637-2103	3287
Techmer Pm Inc	2821	B	310 632-9211	3297
Flo-Kem Inc	2842	E	310 632-7124	3603
LMC Enterprises	2842	E	310 632-7124	3611
Henkel US Operations Corp	2843	C	562 297-6840	3626
Ips Corporation (HQ)	2891	C	310 898-3300	3771
De Menno-Kerdoon Trading Co (HQ)	2911	C	310 537-7100	3824
Owens Corning Sales LLC	2952	C	310 631-1062	3846
Foam Factory Inc	3086	E	310 603-9808	3999
Ufp Technologies Inc	3086	E	714 662-0277	4021
Advanced Materials Inc (HQ)	3089	E	310 537-5444	4038
County Plastics Corp	3089	E	310 635-5400	4094
Idemia America Corp	3089	C	310 884-7900	4138
Rsk Tool Incorporated	3089	E	310 537-3302	4232
Andrew Alexander Inc	3111	D	323 752-0066	4276
Performance Composites Inc	3229	C	310 328-6661	4328
Southwire Inc	3353	E	310 886-8300	4593
Magnesium Alloy Pdts Co Inc	3363	E	310 605-1440	4649
Magnesium Alloy Products Co LP	3363	E	323 636-2276	4650
Fleetwood Continental Inc	3366	D	310 609-1477	4679
Fs - Precision Tech Co LLC	3369	D	310 638-0595	4689
Bodycote Thermal Proc Inc	3398	E	714 893-6561	4699
Mnm Manufacturing Inc	3442	D	310 898-1099	4895
Anoroc Precision Shtmtl Inc	3444	E	310 515-6015	4949
Fastener Innovation Tech Inc	3451	D	310 538-1111	5107
Continental Forge Company LLC	3463	D	310 603-1014	5154
Weber Metals Inc	3463	B	562 543-3316	5163
Innovative Stamping Inc	3469	E	310 537-6996	5194
Serra Manufacturing Corp (PA)	3469	E	310 537-4560	5212
AAA Plating & Inspection Inc	3471	D	323 979-8930	5224
BHC Industries Inc	3471	E	310 632-2000	5238
Bowman Plating Co Inc	3471	C	310 639-4343	5241
E M E Inc	3471	C	310 639-1621	5255
Morrells Electro Plating Inc	3471	E	310 639-1024	5276
Kens Spray Equipment LLC	3479	C	310 635-9995	5328
Ilco Industries Inc	3498	E	310 631-8655	5435
Ace Clearwater Enterprises Inc	3544	D	310 538-5380	5564
Barkens Hardchrome Inc	3559	E	310 632-2000	5693
Flowserve Corporation	3561	D	310 667-4220	5733
Circle Industrial Mfg Corp (PA)	3567	E	310 638-5101	5797
Norco Industries Inc (PA)	3569	C	310 639-4000	5830
Classic Tents	3585	E	310 328-5060	5969
Jimway Inc	3648	D	310 886-3718	6505
Complete Truck Body Repair Inc	3713	E	323 445-2675	7198
AITA Clutch Inc	3714	E	323 585-4140	7222
Fmf Racing	3751	C	310 631-4363	7630
Hf Group Inc (PA)	3861	E	310 605-0755	8430
Artboxx Framing Inc	3999	D	310 604-6933	8659
Mercado Latino Inc	3999	D	310 537-1062	8700

	SIC	EMP	PHONE	ENTRY#
Tag Toys Inc	3999	D	310 639-4566	8732
Westmed Ambulance Inc	4119	C	310 837-0102	8855
Durham School Services L P	4151	C	310 767-5820	8869
Ailo Logistics	4212	A	310 707-1120	8891
Asbury Environmental Services (PA)	4212	D	310 886-3400	8895
Uls Express Inc	4212	C	310 631-0800	8928
H Rauvel Inc	4213	C	562 989-3333	8953
IMC Logistics LLC	4213	C	844 903-4737	8956
Pacific Drayage Services LLC	4213	C	833 334-4622	8969
Fox Transportation Inc	4214	C	310 971-0067	8992
F R T International Inc (PA)	4225	D	310 604-8208	9065
Foamex LP	4225	C	323 774-5600	9067
Kroger Co	4225	B	859 630-6959	9082
Tropicana Manufacturing Co Inc	4225	D	310 764-4395	9122
Aeronet Worldwide Inc	4731	C	310 787-6960	9247
Cnc Worldwide Inc (PA)	4731	D	310 670-7121	9264
Dhx-Dependable Hawaiian Ex Inc (PA)	4731	C	310 537-2000	9271
Global Mail Inc	4731	C	310 735-0800	9284
M-7 Consolidation Inc	4731	C	310 898-3456	9307
Port Logistics Group Inc	4731	C	310 669-2551	9325
Cellco Partnership	4812	C	310 603-0101	9391
Southern California Edison Co	4911	B	310 608-5029	9626
4 Wheel Parts Wholesalers LLC	5013	C	310 900-7725	9809
Dna Specialty Inc	5013	D	310 767-4070	9822
Saddlemen Corporation	5013	C	310 638-1222	9846
Silla Automotive LLC	5013	C	800 624-1499	9849
Concrete Tie Industries Inc (PA)	5032	D	310 628-2328	9942
Jack Rubin & Sons Inc (PA)	5051	E	310 635-5407	10140
Cordelia Lighting Inc	5063	C	310 886-3490	10177
Florence Filter Corporation	5075	D	310 637-1137	10332
JOHN TILLMAN COMPANY (DH)	5084	D	310 764-0110	10378
Industrial Valco Inc (PA)	5085	E	310 635-0711	10441
United Fabricare Supply Inc (PA)	5087	D	310 537-2096	10480
M M Fab Inc	5131	D	310 763-3800	10666
Colosseum Athletics Corp	5136	C	310 538-8991	10681
Gourmet Foods Inc (PA)	5141	D	310 632-3300	10753
Interstate Foods Inc	5144	C	310 635-2442	10836
General Petroleum LLC (HQ)	5172	C	562 983-7300	11032
Beauchamp Distributing Company	5181	D	310 639-5320	11041
Epsilon Plastics Inc	5199	D	310 609-1320	11116
Swan Fence Incorporated	5211	E	310 669-8000	11253
Kraco Enterprises LLC	5531	C	310 639-0666	11448
Transamerican Dissolution LLC (HQ)	5531	C	310 900-5500	11471
Diamond Mattress Company Inc (PA)	5712	E	310 638-0363	11513
Celebrity Casinos Inc	7011	B	310 631-3838	12788
Hydroprocessing Associates LLC	7389	D	310 667-6456	14512
Evans Hydro Inc	7699	E	310 608-5801	14765
Compton Unified School Dst	8211	D	310 898-6470	16805
County of Los Angeles	8322	D	310 603-7311	16924
Brinderson LLC (DH)	8711	C	714 466-7100	17496
Dxterity Diagnostics Inc (PA)	8733	E	310 537-7857	17873
Element Mtrls Tech HB Inc	8734	D	310 632-8500	17914
Beyondsoft Consulting Inc	8748	C	310 532-2822	18290

CORONA, CA - Riverside County

	SIC	EMP	PHONE	ENTRY#
Excel Landscape Inc	0782	C	951 735-9650	206
Landscape Development Inc	0782	C	951 371-9370	218
Gail Materials Inc	1442	E	951 667-6106	375
Champion Home Builders Inc	1521	C	951 256-4617	394
Superior Construction Inc	1521	D	951 808-8780	433
Van Daele Homes Inc	1522	C	951 354-2121	455
Van Daele Development Corp	1531	C	951 354-6800	467
Clay Corona Company (PA)	1542	E	951 277-2667	531
Walsh Construction Company	1542	C	951 336-7040	600
All American Asphalt	1611	C	951 736-7617	607
Ebs General Engineering Inc	1611	D	951 279-6869	615
Hillcrest Contracting Inc	1611	D	951 273-9600	624
Kec Engineering	1611	C	951 734-3010	629
Superior Paving Company Inc	1611	D	951 739-9200	650
Arizona Pipeline Company	1623	C	951 270-3100	661
Boudreau Pipeline Corporation	1623	B	951 493-6780	664
HP Communications Inc (PA)	1623	D	951 572-1200	676
S E C C Corporation (PA)	1623	D	909 393-5419	690
Couts Heating & Cooling Inc	1711	C	951 278-5560	769
Infinity Plumbing Designs Inc	1711	B	951 737-4436	789
LDI Mechanical Inc (PA)	1711	C	951 340-9685	795
Multi Mechanical Inc	1711	D	714 632-7404	808
NP Mechanical Inc	1711	B	951 667-6607	813
RC Maintenance Holdings Inc	1711	C	951 903-6303	827
Smart Energy Solar Inc	1711	C	800 405-1978	840
True Air Mechanical Inc	1711	C	888 316-0642	849
General Coatings Corporation	1721	D	909 204-4150	864
Infinity Drywall Contg Inc	1742	C	714 634-2255	1011

Mergent email: customerrelations@mergent.com

1270

2025 Southern California
Business Directory and Buyers Guide

(P-0000) Products & Services Section entry number
(PA)=Parent Co (HQ)=Headquarters (DH)=Div Headquarters

	SIC	EMP	PHONE	ENTRY#
Laurence-Hovenier Inc	1751	C	951 736-2990	1055
Ranch House Doors Inc	1751	D	951 278-2884	1059
TWR Enterprises Inc	1751	D	951 279-2000	1064
Southwest Specialty Contrs LLC	1761	D	951 987-8008	1096
Cornerstone Concrete Inc	1771	D	951 279-2221	1112
Empire Demolition Inc	1795	D	909 393-8300	1181
Wellington Foods Inc (PA)	2023	C	951 547-7000	1311
Stir Foods LLC	2038	E	714 871-9231	1402
Food For Life Baking Co Inc (PA)	2051	D	951 279-5090	1450
Inw Living Ecology Opco LLC (HQ)	2064	E	951 371-4982	1507
Monster Beverage 1990 Corporation	2086	A	951 739-6200	1323
Monster Beverage Company	2086	A	866 322-4466	1624
Monster Beverage Corporation (PA)	2086	A	951 739-6200	1625
Amrapur Overseas Incorporated (PA)	2299	E	714 893-8808	1968
Amwear USA Inc	2311	E	800 858-6755	1974
Shirinian-Shaw Inc	2387	E	951 736-1229	2183
Anatomic Global Inc	2392	C	800 874-7237	2206
Northwestern Converting Co	2392	D	800 959-3402	2218
CTA Manufacturing Inc	2393	C	951 280-2400	2228
Leepers Wood Turning Co Inc (PA)	2431	E	562 422-6525	2312
Novo Manufacturing LLC	2431	D	951 479-4620	2317
Excel Cabinets Inc	2434	E	951 279-4545	2348
American National Mfg Inc	2515	D	951 273-7888	2478
AMF Support Surfaces Inc (DH)	2515	C	951 549-6800	2479
Widly Inc	2515	C	951 279-0900	2496
Temeka Advertising Inc	2541	D	951 277-2525	2574
Uniweb Inc (PA)	2542	D	951 279-7999	2597
Century Blinds Inc	2591	D	951 734-3762	2600
General Container	2653	D	714 562-8700	2668
Republic Bag Inc (PA)	2673	D	951 734-9740	2738
Tree House Pad & Paper Inc	2678	D	800 213-4184	2761
Azalea Systems Corp Inc	2752	E	951 547-5910	2966
Big Horn Wealth Management Inc	2752	D	951 273-7900	2970
Handbill Printers LP	2752	E	951 547-5910	3011
Westrock Cp LLC	2752	D	951 273-7900	3101
Spectra Color Inc	2816	E	951 277-0200	3225
Actavis LLC	2834	D	909 270-1400	3340
Youcare Pharma (usa) Inc	2834	D	951 258-3114	3525
Panrosa Enterprises Inc	2841	D	951 339-5888	3595
US Continental Marketing Inc (PA)	2842	D	951 808-8888	3623
Adonis Inc	2844	E	951 432-3960	3628
Tastepoint Inc	2869	C	951 734-6620	3739
Technicote Inc	2891	D	951 372-0627	3782
Spangler Industries Inc	3069	C	951 735-5000	3938
Arvinyl Laminates LP	3081	D	951 371-7800	3945
TRM Manufacturing Inc	3081	D	951 256-8500	3959
Simmons Family Corporation	3083	D	951 278-4563	3971
Dart Container Corp California (PA)	3086	B	951 735-8115	3997
Aquatic Co	3088	B	714 993-1220	4024
Le Elegant Bath Inc	3088	C	951 734-0238	4030
Carr Management Inc	3089	D	951 277-4800	4083
Dacha Enterprises Inc	3089	D	951 273-7777	4097
Extrumed Inc (DH)	3089	E	951 547-7400	4115
Fischer Mold Incorporated	3089	D	951 279-1140	4116
Hoosier Inc	3089	D	951 272-3070	4134
Martin Chancey Corporation	3089	E	510 972-6300	4163
Merrick Engineering Inc (PA)	3089	C	951 737-6040	4168
Preproduction Plastics Inc	3089	E	951 340-9680	4208
Rehau Construction LLC	3089	D	951 549-9017	4220
Tamshell Corp	3089	D	951 272-9395	4255
TNT Plastic Molding Inc (PA)	3089	D	951 808-9700	4259
Mediland Corporation	3211	D	562 630-9696	4317
Sream Inc	3231	E	951 245-6000	4346
United States Tile Co	3259	C	951 739-4613	4362
Acker Stone Industries Inc (DH)	3272	E	951 674-0047	4378
Quikrete California LLC (DH)	3272	E	951 277-3155	4417
Robertsons Rdymx Ltd A Cal Ltd (PA)	3273	E	951 493-6500	4449
Superior Ready Mix Concrete LP	3273	D	951 277-3553	4461
3M Company	3295	E	951 737-3441	4487
Rock Structures-Rip Rap	3296	E	951 371-1112	4494
Omega Products Corp (HQ)	3299	D	951 737-7447	4503
Hardy Frames Inc	3312	D	951 245-9525	4517
Lexani Wheel Corporation	3312	E	951 808-4220	4520
Merit Aluminum Inc (PA)	3354	C	951 735-1770	4601
Actron Manufacturing Inc	3429	D	951 371-0885	4750
Columbia Aluminum Products LLC	3441	D	323 728-7361	4826
Johasee Rebar Inc	3441	E	661 589-0972	4841
Parcell Steel Corp	3441	C	951 471-3200	4859
Premier Steel Structures Inc	3441	E	951 356-6655	4861
Steel-Tech Industrial Corp	3441	E	951 270-0144	4871
Tolar Manufacturing Co Inc	3441	E	951 808-0081	4875
Decra Roofing Systems Inc (DH)	3444	D	951 272-8180	4978
Fletcher Bldg Holdings USA Inc (DH)	3444	D	951 272-8180	4987
MS Industrial Shtmtl Inc	3444	C	951 272-6610	5010
Price Manufacturing Co Inc	3451	E	951 371-5660	5112
Premier Gear & Machining Inc	3462	E	951 278-5505	5147
Rubicon Gear Inc	3462	D	951 356-3800	5149
T-Rex Truck Products Inc	3465	D	800 287-5900	5165
David Engineering & Mfg Inc	3469	E	951 735-5200	5180
Ravlich Enterprises LLC (PA)	3471	E	714 964-8900	5287
RGF Enterprises Inc	3479	E	951 734-6922	5341
Circor Aerospace Inc (DH)	3491	E	951 270-6200	5360
Crane Instrmnttion Smpling Inc	3491	E	951 270-6200	5361
Eibach Inc	3493	D	951 256-8300	5379
Mission Rubber Company LLC	3494	C	951 736-1313	5389
California Wire Products Corp	3496	E	951 371-7730	5402
Ameriflex Inc	3498	C	951 737-5557	5424
Laminated Shim Company Inc	3499	E	951 273-3900	5450
Pacmet Aerospace LLC	3519	D	909 218-8889	5469
Western Equipment Mfg Inc	3531	E	951 284-2000	5500
Cremach Tech Inc	3541	C	951 735-3194	5539
Cremach Tech Inc (DH)	3541	E	951 735-3194	5540
David Engineering & Manufacturing Inc	3544	E	951 735-5200	5577
Noranco Manufacturing (usa) Acquisition Corp	3545	C	951 721-8400	5617
Pacific Packaging McHy LLC	3556	E	951 393-2200	5682
Peabody Engineering & Sup Inc	3559	E	951 734-7711	5716
Suss Microtec Inc (HQ)	3559	C	408 940-0300	5721
Vizualogic LLC	3559	C	407 509-3421	5724
Kobelco Compressors Amer Inc (DH)	3563	B	951 739-3030	5758
Kobelco Compressors Amer Inc	3563	D	951 739-3030	5759
M & O Perry Industries Inc	3565	E	951 734-9838	5792
Jhawar Industries LLC	3567	E	951 340-4646	5801
Anaco Inc	3568	C	951 372-2732	5805
Avt Inc	3581	E	951 737-1057	5961
Aqueous Technologies Corp	3589	E	909 944-7771	6002
Blue Desert International Inc	3589	D	951 273-7575	6004
Engineered Food Systems	3589	E	714 921-9913	6013
Spenuzza (HQ)	3589	D	951 281-1830	6034
Parker-Hannifin Corporation	3594	D	951 280-3800	6052
Btl Machine	3599	D	951 808-9929	6100
MD Engineering Inc	3599	E	951 736-5390	6172
Absolute Graphic Tech USA Inc	3625	E	909 597-1133	6339
Esl Power Systems Inc	3643	E	800 922-4188	6418
Computer Service Company	3669	E	951 738-1444	6678
Corona Magnetics Inc	3677	C	951 735-7558	6927
Jayco/Mmi Inc	3679	E	951 738-2000	7017
Omni Connection Intl Inc	3679	B	951 898-6232	7032
Sas Manufacturing Inc	3679	E	951 734-1808	7048
Palos Verdes Building Corp (PA)	3691	C	951 371-8090	7079
Vantage Vehicle Intl Inc	3694	E	951 735-1200	7102
Suss McRtec Phtnic Systems Inc	3699	D	951 817-3700	7154
Saleen Incorporated (PA)	3711	C	714 400-2121	7192
Advanced Flow Engineering Inc (PA)	3714	E	951 493-7155	7220
Currie Enterprises	3714	E	714 528-6957	7241
Gibson Performance Corporation	3714	D	951 372-1220	7257
Hitachi Astemo Americas Inc	3714	C	951 340-0702	7261
Nmsp Inc	3714	C	951 734-2453	7278
TMI Products Inc	3714	C	951 272-1996	7300
Tube Technologies Inc	3714	E	951 371-4878	7303
Accurate Grinding and Mfg Corp	3724	E	951 479-0909	7377
International Wind Inc (PA)	3724	E	562 240-3963	7389
Thermal Structures Inc (DH)	3724	B	951 736-9911	7396
Acromil LLC	3728	D	951 000-9929	7399
Aero-Craft Hydraulics Inc	3728	E	951 736-4690	7410
Approved Aeronautics LLC	3728	D	951 200-3730	7432
Acturioc Manufacturing Co Inc	3728	F	951 270-1766	7437
Irwin Aviation Inc	3728	E	951 372-9555	7504
Johnson Caldraul Inc	3728	E	951 340-1067	7508
Electrasem Corp	3822	D	951 371-6140	7835
Kap Medical	3829	E	951 340-4360	8049
All Manufacturers Inc	3841	C	951 280-4200	8084
Biolase Inc	3843	D	949 361-1200	8329
Dansereau Health Products	3843	E	951 549-1400	8332
Fender Musical Instrs Corp	3931	A	480 596-9690	8468
Westech Products Inc (PA)	3952	E	951 279-4496	8560
Architectural Design Signs Inc (PA)	3993	D	951 278-0680	8590
Fovell Enterprises Inc	3993	E	951 734-6275	8605
Richards Neon Shop Inc	3993	E	951 279-6767	8626
Tradenet Enterprise Inc	3993	D	888 595-3956	8646
Arminak Solutions LLC	3999	E	626 802-7332	8658
Cbd Living Water	3999	E	800 940-3660	8669
Developlus Inc	3999	C	951 738-8595	8674
Kurz Transfer Products LP	3999	D	951 738-9521	8690
Pet Partners Inc (PA)	3999	C	951 279-9888	8714
Mission Ambulance Inc	4119	D	951 272-2300	8841
First Student Inc	4151	D	951 736-3234	8878

Employee Codes: A=Over 500 employees, B=251-500
C=101-250, D=51-100, E=20-50, F=10-19, G=1-9

2025 Southern California
Business Directory and Buyers Guide

© Mergent Inc. 1-800-342-5647

1271

	SIC	EMP	PHONE	ENTRY#
Total Trnsp Logistics Inc	4213	D	951 360-9521	8978
Veg Fresh Logistics LLC	4731	C	714 446-8800	9350
Sprint Communications Co LP	4812	C	951 340-1924	9416
Combustion Associates Inc	4911	E	951 272-6999	9575
Agile Sourcing Partners Inc	4939	C	951 279-4154	9677
Talco Plastics Inc (PA)	4953	D	951 531-2000	9768
Waste Management Cal Inc	4953	C	951 277-1740	9776
McDavis and Gumbys Inc	5031	C	800 736-7363	9925
ABC School Equipment Inc	5049	D	951 817-2200	10117
Minka Lighting LLC (DH)	5063	D	951 735-9220	10194
Corona Clipper Inc	5072	C	800 847-7863	10304
Saba Holding Company LLC	5082	C	951 277-7620	10359
So Cal Sandbags Inc	5085	C	951 277-3404	10463
Thalasinos Enterprises Inc	5085	E	951 340-0911	10468
Aqua Performance Inc	5091	E	951 340-2056	10509
Troy Lee Designs LLC (DH)	5091	D	951 371-5219	10516
Amerisourcebergen Drug Corp	5122	C	951 371-2000	10612
Rugby Laboratories Inc (DH)	5122	D	951 270-1400	10649
Smart Stores Operations LLC	5141	C	323 869-7543	10800
Marie Cllender Wholesalers Inc	5142	A	951 737-6760	10823
Index Fresh Inc (PA)	5148	D	909 877-0999	10908
Veg-Fresh Farms LLC (PA)	5148	C	800 422-5535	10923
Monster Energy Company (HQ)	5149	B	866 322-4466	10963
Ganahl Lumber Company	5211	D	951 278-4000	11155
Home Depot USA Inc	5211	C	951 808-0327	11180
Lowes Home Centers LLC	5211	D	951 256-9004	11225
Vons Companies Inc	5411	C	951 278-8284	11288
Freedom Prfmce Exhaust Inc	5531	E	951 898-4733	11446
Irwin International Inc (PA)	5599	D	951 372-9555	11487
Hub Distributing Inc (HQ)	5611	B	951 340-3149	11489
Aurelio Felix Barreto III	5699	C	951 354-9528	11506
Ames Construction Inc	5712	B	951 356-1275	11511
Pacific Premier Bancorp Inc	6022	C	951 272-3590	11774
Kaiser Fndtion Hlth Plan GA In	6324	B	951 270-1200	12084
First Team RE - Orange Cnty	6531	D	951 270-2800	12453
Pro Group Inc	6531	C	951 271-3000	12508
Bellota US Corp	6722	C	951 737-6515	12629
Management Trust Assn Inc	6733	D	951 694-1758	12663
JJ Mac Intyre Co Inc (PA)	7322	C	951 898-4300	13286
Pro Building Maintenance Inc (PA)	7349	C	951 279-3386	13408
Porter Hire Ltd	7359	E	951 674-9999	13467
Eknowledge Group Inc	7372	E	951 256-4076	13923
American Power SEC Svc Inc	7381	C	866 974-9994	14272
Aztecs Telecom Inc	7389	D	714 373-1560	14456
Super Center Concepts Inc	7389	D	951 372-9485	14605
Thyde Inc (PA)	7389	C	951 817-2300	14611
Penske Transportation MGT LLC	7513	C	844 847-9518	14640
U-Haul Business Consultants	7513	C	951 736-7811	14643
Metro Truck Body Inc	7532	E	310 532-5570	14677
Ironman Renewal LLC	7538	D	951 735-3710	14692
Moyes Custom Furniture Inc	7641	E	714 729-0234	14736
General Conveyor Inc	7699	E	951 734-3460	14768
Senclub LLC	7922	D	626 317-8073	14979
Green River Golf Corporation	7992	C	714 970-8411	15083
City of Hope	8011	D	951 898-2828	15279
Corona Regional Med Ctr LLC	8011	C	951 737-4343	15289
Vitas Healthcare Corporation	8052	C	858 805-6254	15825
Uhs-Corona Inc (HQ)	8062	A	951 737-4343	16238
United Lab Services Inc	8071	D	951 444-0467	16338
St Joseph Health Per Care Svcs	8082	D	800 365-1110	16422
Uhs-Corona Inc	8093	C	951 736-7200	16514
Kaiser Foundation Hospitals	8099	D	866 984-7483	16575
Crossrads Chrstn Schols Corona	8299	C	951 278-3199	16853
Ability Counts Inc (PA)	8331	C	951 734-6595	17043
Peppermint Ridge (PA)	8361	D	951 273-7320	17187
Automobile Club Southern Cal	8699	D	951 808-9624	17434
K&B Electric LLC	8711	C	951 808-9501	17569
Primary Provider MGT Co Inc (HQ)	8741	D	951 280-7700	18036
Kpc Group Inc (PA)	8742	C	951 782-8812	18158
Volt Telecom Group Inc	8748	B	951 493-8900	18369

CORONA DEL MAR, CA - Orange County

	SIC	EMP	PHONE	ENTRY#
Cpaperless LLC	3652	E	949 510-3365	6573
Tebra Technologies Inc (PA)	7371	C	888 775-2736	13840
University California Irvine	8011	D	949 644-5245	15500

CORONADO, CA - San Diego County

	SIC	EMP	PHONE	ENTRY#
Nadolife Inc	3421	E	619 522-0077	4730
Lockheed Martin Corporation	3812	C	619 437-7230	7737
City of Coronado	4931	C	619 522-7380	9670
Smart Stores Operations LLC	5141	C	619 522-2014	10791
Coronado Brewing Company Inc (PA)	5813	E	619 437-4452	11613
51st St & 8th Ave Corp	7011	C	619 424-4000	12753
Ksl Resorts Hotel Del Coronado	7011	C	619 435-6611	12889
L-O Coronado Hotel	7011	D	619 435-6611	12892
Mariner Systems Inc (PA)	7389	E	305 266-7255	14539
Sharp Coronado Hospital & Healthcare Center	8062	A	619 522-3600	16192
National Teleconsultants Inc	8711	C	818 265-4400	17594

COSTA MESA, CA - Orange County

	SIC	EMP	PHONE	ENTRY#
Hexagon Agility Inc	1321	E	949 236-5520	284
Mdm Solutions LLC	1389	B	800 669-6361	344
Brookfeld Sthland Holdings LLC	1521	C	714 427-6868	391
Seattle Tnnel Prtners A Jint V	1521	B	206 971-8701	428
Warmington Residential Cal Inc	1521	C	714 557-5511	438
Rebco Communities Inc	1522	C	714 557-5511	450
Warmington Homes (PA)	1531	C	714 434-4435	468
Andrew L Youngquist Cnstr Inc	1542	D	949 862-5611	517
Adopt-A-Highway Maintenance	1611	C	800 200-0003	606
Atkinson Construction Inc	1611	C	303 410-2540	608
Beador Construction Co Inc	1611	D	951 674-7352	609
Lombardy Holdings Inc (PA)	1623	C	951 808-4550	685
Pivot Interiors Inc	1731	C	949 988-5400	952
Variations In Stone Inc	1741	D	949 438-8337	990
Orange County Plst Co Inc	1742	C	714 957-1971	1018
El Metate Inc	2051	C	949 646-9362	1443
Associated Microbreweries Inc	2082	E	714 546-2739	1538
Cotton Links LLC	2321	E	714 444-4700	1981
Hurley International LLC (PA)	2329	C	855 655-2515	2013
I D Brand LLC	2396	E	949 422-7057	2262
Fxc Corporation	2399	E	714 557-8032	2277
Fineline Woodworking Inc	2431	D	714 540-5468	2306
National Appraisal Guides Inc	2741	E	714 556-8511	2927
Thomson Reuters Corporation	2741	E	949 400-7782	2948
ID Supply	2759	E	949 287-9200	3145
Vans Inc (DH)	3021	B	714 755-4000	3872
Tk Pax Inc	3052	B	714 850-1330	3876
Vantage Associates Inc	3088	E	800 995-8322	4031
CCI Industries Inc (PA)	3089	C	714 662-3879	4085
Husky Injction Mlding Systems	3089	D	714 545-8200	4136
JG Plastics Group LLC	3089	C	714 751-4266	4148
Resinart Corporation	3089	E	949 642-3665	4224
Cevians LLC (PA)	3211	D	714 619-5135	4314
Ceradyne Esk LLC	3299	C	714 549-0421	4501
Griswold Industries (PA)	3365	B	949 722-4800	4675
Winfield Locks Inc	3429	A	949 722-5400	4796
Coast Sheet Metal Inc	3444	E	949 645-2224	4970
Flare Group	3471	E	714 549-0202	5261
Inveco Inc	3471	E	949 378-3850	5269
Kyocera Tycom Corporation	3541	B	714 428-3600	5547
Criterion Machine Works	3545	E		5609
Shurflo LLC	3561	B	714 371-1550	5744
Universal Motion Components Co Inc	3566	E	714 437-9600	5796
International Bus Mchs Corp	3571	E	714 472-2237	5854
Delphi Display Systems Inc	3577	D	714 825-3400	5913
Dynamic Cooking Systems Inc	3589	A	714 372-7000	6012
Candle Lamp Holdings LLC	3641	B	951 682-9600	6402
Flexfire Leds Inc	3646	E	925 273-9080	6458
Qsc LLC (PA)	3651	C	800 854-4079	6549
Bdfco Inc	3669	D	714 228-2900	6675
Honeywell SEC Americas LLC	3669	D	949 737-7800	6685
Sanmina Corporation	3672	D	714 371-2800	6768
Sanmina Corporation	3672	C	714 913-2200	6769
Irvine Sensors Corporation	3674	E	714 444-8700	6837
Labarge/Stc Inc	3674	E	281 207-1400	6843
Semicoa Corporation	3674	D	714 979-1900	6887
Newmar Power LLC	3675	C	800 854-3906	6920
Sabritec	3678	E	714 371-1100	6959
Technical Cable Concepts Inc	3679	E	714 835-1081	7057
Target Technology Company LLC	3695	E	949 788-0909	7106
Isc8 Inc	3699	E	714 549-8211	7128
Schneider Electric	3699	E	949 713-9200	7149
Fisker Automotive Inc	3711	D		7174
Ducommun Aerostructures Inc (HQ)	3724	C	310 380-5390	7383
Ducommun Incorporated (PA)	3728	C	657 335-3665	7467
Flare Group	3728	E	714 850-2080	7474
Vantage Associates Inc	3728	E	562 968-1400	7587
Vantage Associates Inc (PA)	3769	E	619 477-6940	7674
Anduril Industries Inc (PA)	3812	A	949 891-1607	7691
Lambda Research Optics Inc	3826	E	714 327-0600	7963
Optosigma Corporation	3827	E	949 851-5881	8014
Safran Defense & Space Inc	3827	D	603 296-0469	8018
Sellers Optical Inc	3827	D	949 631-6800	8021
Advanced Micro Instruments Inc	3829	E	714 848-5533	8030
Phllps-Mdisize Costa Mesa LLC	3841	C	949 477-9495	8215
Sweden & Martina Inc	3841	E	844 862-7846	8232

	SIC	EMP	PHONE	ENTRY#
Rip Curl Inc (DH)	3949	D	714 422-3600	8535
Flora Gold Corporation (PA)	3999	A	949 252-1908	8677
Transprttion Brkg Spclists Inc	4212	B	714 754-4236	8926
County of Orange	4581	C	949 252-5006	9198
Uvnv Inc	4813	C	888 777-0446	9469
Nds Americas Inc (DH)	4841	D	714 434-2100	9554
ABC Bus Inc	5012	D	714 444-5888	9796
Nissan North America Inc	5012	C	714 433-3700	9807
Altametrics LLC	5045	C	800 676-1281	9985
Schurman Fine Papers	5084	E	714 549-0212	10401
Western Refining Inc	5084	D	714 708-2200	10419
Viva Life Science Inc	5122	C	949 645-6100	10657
Food Sales West Inc	5141	D	714 966-2900	10751
Home Depot USA Inc	5211	C	949 646-4220	11190
Theodore Robins Inc	5511	D	949 642-0010	11418
511 Inc (DH)	5699	E	866 451-1726	11502
Annas Linens Inc	5719	A	714 850-0504	11527
El Pollo Loco Holdings Inc (PA)	5812	C	714 599-5000	11568
Fgr 1 LLC	5812	E	800 653-3517	11570
North American Acceptance Corp	6141	C	714 868-3195	11859
Payoff Inc	6141	D	949 430-0630	11861
Professional Cr Reporting Inc	6141	C	714 556-1570	11862
Balboa Capital Corporation (DH)	6153	D	949 756-0800	11865
Express Capital Lending	6162	D	714 429-1025	11902
Metropolitan Home Mortgage Inc	6162	D	949 428-0161	11923
Stearns Lending LLC	6162	C	714 513-7777	11935
Villa Venetia	6163	C	714 540-1800	11957
Merrill Lynch Prce Fnner Smith	6211	D	714 429-2800	11981
Auto Club Enterprises (PA)	6321	A	714 850-5111	12057
Automobile Club Southern Cal	6411	C	714 885-1343	12178
Medical Eye Services Inc	6411	C	714 619-4660	12231
Donahue Schriber Rlty Group LP (PA)	6512	C	714 545-1400	12290
South Coast Plaza LLC	6512	D	714 435-2000	12320
Trammell Crow Residential Co	6513	D	714 966-9355	12369
Donahue Schrber Rlty Group Inc (PA)	6531	C	714 545-1400	12432
Hanford Hotels Inc	7011	C	714 557-3000	12841
Rosanna Inc	7011	C	714 751-5100	13001
South Coast Westin Hotel Co	7011	C	714 540-2500	13029
US Hotel and Resort MGT Inc	7011	C	949 650-2988	13062
Klientboost LLC	7311	C	657 203-7866	13220
Marshall Advertising and Design Inc	7311	E	714 545-5757	13224
Team Garage LLC	7311	D	714 913-9900	13249
Experian Info Solutions Inc (DH)	7323	A	714 830-7000	13295
Experian Mktg Solutions LLC	7323	A	714 830-7000	13296
All-Rite Leasing Company Inc	7349	B	714 957-1822	13353
Pacific Building Care Inc (HQ)	7349	C	949 261-1234	13399
Site Crew Inc	7349	B	714 668-0100	13420
Career Strategies Tmpry Inc	7361	C	714 824-6840	13501
Experian Employer Services Inc	7361	C	866 997-0422	13519
Recruit 360	7361	C	949 250-4420	13566
Southern Home Care Svcs Inc	7363	D	714 979-7413	13623
Meridianlink Inc (PA)	7371	C	714 708-6950	13770
Software Management Cons LLC	7371	C	714 662-1841	13828
Nwp Services Corporation (DH)	7372	C	949 253-2500	13995
Filenet Corporation	7373	A	800 345-3638	14081
Star Pro Security Patrol Inc	7381	D	714 617-5056	14355
Benrich Service Company Inc (PA)	7389	E	714 241-0284	14462
Carecredit LLC	7389	C	800 300-3046	14468
Cliq Inc	7389	D	714 361-1900	14473
Creative Design Consultants (PA)	7389	C	714 641-4868	14483
Regus Business Centre LLC	7389	C	714 371-4000	14584
Simple Science Inc	7389	E	949 335-1099	14597
Volcom LLC (HQ)	7389	C	949 646-2175	14620
Fox Rent A Car Inc	7514	D	310 342-5155	14647
Tarulli Tire Inc (PA)	7534	E	714 630-4722	14683
EZ Lube LLC	7549	C	714 966-1647	14715
Metropro Road Services Inc	7549	D	714 556-7600	14718
Kone Inc	7699	E	714 890-7080	14774
Edwards Theatres Circuit Inc	7832	C	714 428-0962	14937
Aspyr Holdings LLC	7991	B	714 651-1840	15043
Mesa Verde Partners	7992	C	714 540-7500	15092
Mesa Verde Country Club	7997	C	714 549-0377	15149
Amen Clinics Inc A Med Corp (PA)	8011	D	888 564-2700	15242
University California Irvine	8011	D	949 646-2267	15501
Ensign Group Inc	8051	D	949 642-0387	15637
Mesa Vrde Cnvalescent Hosp Inc	8051	D	949 548-5584	15720
Silverado Senior Living Inc	8051	D	949 945-0189	15778
College Hospital Costa Mesa Mso Inc (HQ)	8062	D	949 642-2734	15961
Hoag Family Cancer Institute	8062	C	949 764-7777	16020
Califrnia Dept State Hospitals	8063	A	714 957-5000	16268
Accredited Nursing Services	8082	C	714 973-1234	16355
Competent Care Inc	8082	D	714 545-4818	16380
RES-Care Inc	8082	D	714 662-3075	16415

	SIC	EMP	PHONE	ENTRY#
Baker & Hostetler LLP	8111	D	714 754-6600	16640
Cooksey Tlen Gage Dffy Woog A (PA)	8111	D	714 431-1100	16659
Haynes & Boone LLP	8111	D	949 202-3000	16700
Latham & Watkins LLP	8111	B	714 540-1235	16725
Lewis Brsbois Bsgard Smith LLP	8111	D	714 545-9200	16729
Snell & Wilmer LLP	8111	D	714 427-7000	16785
Vanguard Univ Southern Cal	8221	C	714 668-6163	16838
Califrnia Dept Dvlpmental Svcs	8331	A	714 957-5151	17051
Ds Lakeshore LP	8641	D	916 286-5231	17341
Arq LLC	8711	D		17487
Moffatt & Nichol	8711	D	657 261-2699	17591
Newman Garrison + Partners Inc	8712	D	949 756-0818	17686
Deloitte & Touche LLP	8721	C	714 436-7419	17717
Marcum LLP	8721	D	949 236-5600	17745
South Coast Plaza Security	8741	C	714 435-2180	18058
Warmington Mr 14 Assoc LLC	8741	D	714 557-5511	18077
Morris & Willner Partners	8742	D	949 705-0682	18173
Nationsbenefits LLC	8742	A	877 439-2665	18178
Brand Amp LLC	8743	D	949 438-1060	18251
Innovative Cnstr Solutions	8744	C	714 893-6366	18263

COVINA, CA - Los Angeles County

	SIC	EMP	PHONE	ENTRY#
Brutoco Engineering & Construction Inc	1611	C		611
RG Costumes & Accessories Inc	2389	E	626 858-9559	2201
Ink Fx Corporation	2759	E	909 673-1950	3146
Composites Horizons LLC (DH)	2821	C	626 331-0861	3261
Chemeor Inc	2843	E	626 966-3808	3624
Anvil Cases Inc	3161	C	626 968-4100	4291
Caco-Pacific Corporation (PA)	3544	C	626 331-3361	5570
Dauntless Industries Inc	3544	E	626 966-4494	5576
Payne Magnetics Corporation	3677	C	626 332-6207	6934
TT Elctrnics Pwr Sltons US Inc	3679	C	626 967-6021	7063
Haemonetics Manufacturing Inc (HQ)	3841	E	626 339-7388	8161
Bright Glow Candle Company Inc (PA)	3999	E	909 469-4733	8664
Norlaine Inc	3999	C	626 961-2471	8705
Justanswer LLC	4813	C	800 785-2305	9446
Sprint Communications Co LP	4813	C	626 339-0430	9460
Swwc Utilities Inc (DH)	4941	C		9722
American Scale Co Inc	5045	E	800 773-7225	9987
West Covina Foster Family Agcy	6411	D	626 814-9085	12269
Guesty Inc (PA)	7011	D	415 244-0277	12838
Briteworks	7349	D	626 337-0099	13359
Twomagnets LLC	7361	A	408 837-0116	13579
Noredink Corp	7371	D	844 667-3346	13784
Scratchpadsaas	7371	C	415 707-3325	13814
Instrument Inc	7372	E	909 258-9291	13948
Klentysoft Inc	7372	C	707 518-9640	13962
Stavros Enterprises Inc	7699	E	888 463-2293	14793
Davita Magan Management Inc (DH)	8011	C	626 331-6411	15298
Covina Rehabilitation Center	8051	D	626 967-3874	15619
Rowland Convalescent Hosp Inc	8051	D	626 967-2741	15765
Emanate Health (PA)	8062	A	626 331-7331	15992
Emanate Health Medical Center	8062	A	626 858-8515	15994
Emanate Health Medical Center	8062	A	626 331-7331	15996
Aurora Chrtr Oak - Los Angles	8063	C	626 966-1632	16265
Citrus Vly Hlth Partners Inc	8099	A	626 732-3100	16548
Eggleston Youth Centers Inc (PA)	8322	D	626 480-8107	16938
Think Together	8351	B	626 373-2311	17113
Los Angeles Engineering Inc	8711	C	626 869-1400	17580
Zenleads Inc	8742	B	415 040-9300	10240

CUDAHY, CA - Los Angeles County

	SIC	EMP	PHONE	ENTRY#
RAP Security Inc	2542	D	323 560-3493	2587
Consolidated Foundries Inc	3365	C	323 773-2363	4670
Myers Mixers LLC	3569	E	323 560-4723	5828
Merry An Cejka	3599	E	323 560-3949	6174
HF Cox Inc	4212	B	323 587-2359	8916
Super Center Concepts Inc	5411	C	323 562-8980	11283
Southern Cal Prmnnte Med Group	8011	C	323 562-6459	15465
Kaiser Foundation Hospitals	8062	C	323 562-6400	16032

CULVER CITY, CA - Los Angeles County

	SIC	EMP	PHONE	ENTRY#
Farchitecture Bb LLC	2024	E	917 701-2777	1317
Ppd Holding LLC (PA)	2326	A	310 733-2100	2000
Sportsrobe Inc	2329	D	310 559-3999	2027
Fortune Casuals LLC (PA)	2331	D	310 733-2100	2035
Paige LLC (HQ)	2331	C	310 733-2100	2052
Parachute Home Inc	2392	C	310 903-0353	2222
Fringe Studio LLC	2621	E	310 390-9900	2624
Cambridge Equities LP	2836	E	858 350-2300	3567
Henkel US Operations Corp	2844	E	626 321-4100	3657
Joico Laboratories Inc	2844	C	626 321-4100	3662
Sole Society Group Inc	3131	C	310 220-0808	4281

Employee Codes: A=Over 500 employees, B=251-500
C=101-250, D=51-100, E=20-50, F=10-19, G=1-9

2025 Southern California
Business Directory and Buyers Guide

© Mergent Inc. 1-800-342-5647

1273

	SIC	EMP	PHONE	ENTRY#
Magnet Sales & Mfg Co Inc (HQ)	3264	D	310 391-7213	4364
Borin Manufacturing Inc	3561	E	310 822-1000	5728
Pacific Piston Ring Co Inc	3592	D	310 836-3322	6043
Chargie LLC	3621	D	310 621-0024	6317
CMI Integrated Tech Inc	3621	E		6318
Integrated Magnetics Inc	3621	E	310 391-7213	6325
Spotlite Power Corporation	3646	E	310 838-2367	6474
Beats Electronics LLC	3651	B	424 326-4679	6530
Apic Corporation	3674	D	310 642-7975	6799
Moldex-Metric Inc	3842	B	310 837-6500	8289
Given Imaging Los Angeles LLC	3845	C	310 641-8492	8381
Virgin Fish Inc (PA)	4119	C	310 391-6161	8853
Makespace Labs Inc	4225	C	800 920-9440	9087
Pacific Bell Telephone Company	4812	A	310 515-2898	9407
Triton Media Group LLC	4832	C	661 294-9000	9490
Wovexx Holdings Inc (DH)	4899	D	310 424-2080	9572
Nantbioscience Inc	5047	C	310 883-1300	10094
Interactive Films LLC	5092	C	310 988-0643	10522
Punch Studio LLC (PA)	5112	C	310 390-9900	10584
Meundies Inc	5136	B	888 552-6775	10688
Henkel US Operations Corp	5169	D	424 308-0505	11015
Topson Downs California LLC (PA)	5621	C	310 558-0300	11494
CIT Bank NA	6022	D	310 559-7222	11756
E & S Ring Management Corp	6531	D	310 670-5983	12433
GK Management Co Inc (PA)	6531	C	310 204-2050	12457
Property Management Assoc Inc (PA)	6531	C	323 295-2000	12513
Goldrich & Kest Industries LLC (PA)	6552	A	310 204-2050	12566
Goldrich Kest Hirsch Stern LLC (PA)	6552	A	310 204-2050	12567
Hirsch3667 Corp	6719	C	310 641-6690	12602
Woodbine Lgacy/Playa Owner LLC	7011	D	678 292-4962	13092
Eharmony Inc (HQ)	7299	C	424 258-1199	13173
Mutesix Group Inc	7311	C	800 935-6856	13232
Amazon Studios LLC	7371	C	818 804-0884	13651
Docupace Technologies LLC (PA)	7371	C	310 445-7722	13711
Genex (DH)	7371	C	424 672-9500	13737
Snail Inc (PA)	7371	E	310 988-0643	13824
Chownow Inc (PA)	7372	D	888 707-2469	13900
Liveoffice LLC	7372	E	877 253-2793	13968
Scopely Inc (DH)	7372	C	323 400-6618	14026
Spring Technologies Corp	7372	E	310 230-4000	14038
Nantworks LLC (PA)	7373	D	310 883-1300	14098
West Publishing Corporation	7373	A	424 243-2100	14117
Sony Pictures Imageworks Inc	7374	C	310 840-8000	14156
Aegis SEC & Investigations Inc	7381	C	310 838-2787	14268
Pacific National Security Inc	7381	C	310 842-7073	14328
Security Indust Specialists Inc (PA)	7381	D	310 215-5100	14342
Event Intelligence Group	7382	C	310 237-5375	14399
Innovation Specialties	7389	C	888 827-2387	14515
Mktg Inc	7389	A	310 972-7900	14551
Columbia Pictures Inds Inc (DH)	7812	C	310 244-4000	14814
Crunchyroll LLC (DH)	7812	C	972 355-7300	14817
Sony Media Cloud Services LLC	7812	E	877 683-9124	14857
Sony Pictures Entrmt Inc (DH)	7812	A	310 244-4000	14858
Sony Pictures Television Inc (DH)	7812	C	310 244-7625	14859
Zoic Inc	7812	C	310 838-0770	14878
Dneg North America Inc (PA)	7819	D	323 461-7887	14886
Pixomondo LLC	7819	A	310 394-0555	14901
Technclor Crative Svcs USA Inc	7819	B	818 260-1214	14906
Maker Studios LLC (DH)	7929	D	310 606-2182	14998
Nfl Properties LLC	7941	D	310 840-4635	15032
Faze Clan Inc	7999	B	818 688-6373	15203
Faze Holdings Inc	7999	C	818 688-6373	15204
Southern Cal Prmnnte Med Group	8011	C	310 737-4900	15463
Institute For Applied Bhvior A (PA)	8049	C	310 649-0499	15545
Brotman Medical Center Inc	8062	B	310 836-7000	15928
Southern Cal Halthcare Sys Inc	8062	C	310 836-7000	16202
Didi Hirsch Psychiatric Svc (PA)	8322	C	310 390-6612	16934
Exceptional Chld Foundation (PA)	8331	C	310 204-3300	17056
Westmont Living Inc	8361	C	310 736-4118	17208
Exceptional Chld Foundation	8641	D	310 915-6606	17343
Lamar Jhnson Collaborative Inc	8712	C	424 361-3960	17679
Kpmg LLP	8721	D	703 286-8175	17738
Nantcell Inc	8731	B	562 397-3639	17811
HI LLC	8732	C	757 655-4113	17846
Altruist Corp	8742	B	949 370-5096	18088
Jack Nadel Inc (PA)	8742	D	310 815-2600	18155
Medical Record Associates Inc	8742	C	617 698-4411	18169
Netfortris Acquisition Co Inc	8748	D	310 861-4300	18338
City of Culver City	9111	D	310 253-6525	18383
City of Culver City	9512	D	310 253-6650	18399

CYPRESS, CA - Orange County

	SIC	EMP	PHONE	ENTRY#
Plumbing Piping & Cnstr Inc	1711	D	714 821-0490	820

	SIC	EMP	PHONE	ENTRY#
Simply Fresh LLC	2092	C	714 562-5000	1712
Shaw Industries Group Inc	2273	E	562 430-4445	1956
Speedo USA Inc	2329	B	657 465-3800	2024
Manhattan Beachwear LLC (PA)	2369	C	657 384-2110	2171
Exemplis LLC (PA)	2522	E	714 995-4800	2526
X-Chair LLC	2522	E	844 492-4247	2534
Johnson Controls Inc	2531	C	562 594-3200	2546
Creative Teaching Press Inc (PA)	2731	D	714 799-2100	2887
Primary Color Systems Corp (PA)	2759	B	949 660-7080	3161
Venus Laboratories Inc	2819	C	714 891-3100	3255
Diasorin Molecular LLC	2835	C	562 240-6500	3538
Merger Sub Gotham 2 LLC	3089	C	714 462-4603	4167
Plastic Molded Components Inc	3089	E	714 229-0133	4200
Rolls-Royce High Temperature Composites Inc	3299	E	714 375-4085	4507
Dameron Alloy Foundries (PA)	3325	D	310 631-5165	4571
Hyatt Die Cast and Engineering Corp (PA)	3363	C	714 826-7550	4646
Hilti US Manufacturing Inc	3425	C	714 230-7410	4747
Cavotec Inet US Inc	3531	D	714 947-0005	5489
Power Pt Inc	3537	E	714 826-7407	5534
OK International Inc (DH)	3548	C	714 799-9910	5648
Seabiscuit Motorsports Inc	3592	E	714 898-9763	6047
Hitachi Automotive Systems	3621	D	310 212-0200	6324
Scientfc Applctons RES Assoc (PA)	3629	D	714 224-4410	6380
Luma Comfort LLC	3634	E	855 963-9247	6397
Mission Microwave Tech LLC (PA)	3663	D	951 893-4925	6634
Yaesu Usa Inc	3663	D	714 827-7600	6673
Drs Ntwork Imaging Systems LLC	3674	D	714 220-3800	6820
Weldex Corporation	3674	B	714 761-2100	6914
Mitsubshi Elc Vsual Sltons AME	3679	C	800 553-7278	7027
Pratt & Whitney Eng Svcs Inc	3724	A	714 373-0110	7394
Cavotec Dabico LLC	3728	E	714 947-0005	7452
Inet Airport Systems Inc	3728	E	714 888-2700	7499
Safran Cabin Inc	3728	C	562 344-4780	7553
Tayco Engineering Inc	3761	C	714 952-2240	7657
Christie Digital Systems Inc (HQ)	3861	D	714 236-8610	8423
Fujifilm Rcrding Media USA Inc	3861	D	310 536-0800	8429
Travel Corporation	4724	C	714 385-8401	9236
Toyo Tire USA Corp (DH)	5014	D	714 236-2080	9862
Sitonit Seating Inc	5021	C	714 995-4800	9883
Weyerhaeuser Company	5031	D	714 523-3330	9935
Atg - Designing Mobility Inc (DH)	5047	E	562 921-0258	10064
Multiquip Inc (DH)	5063	B	310 537-3700	10196
Siemens Industry Inc	5063	D	714 761-2200	10206
Ushio America Inc (HQ)	5063	D	714 236-8600	10212
Interntional Tech Systems Corp	5065	E	714 761-8886	10255
Mitsubishi Electric Us Inc (DH)	5065	C	714 220-2500	10267
Q Tech Corporation	5065	C	310 836-7900	10280
Beverages & More Inc	5078	C	714 891-1242	10338
ME & My Big Ideas LLC	5092	C	240 348-5240	10523
Natureware Inc	5122	D	714 251-4510	10638
Hybrid Promotions LLC (PA)	5136	C	714 952-3866	10686
Real Mex Foods Inc	5141	D	714 523-0031	10767
Yamaha Motor Corporation USA (HQ)	5571	B	714 761-7300	11485
Los Alamitos Race Course	5812	C	714 820-2800	11587
WKS Restaurant Corporation (PA)	5812	C	562 425-1402	11610
Eno Brands Inc	5944	E	714 220-1318	11639
Mitsubishi Motors Cr Amer Inc (DH)	6141	D	714 799-4730	11855
Uhc of California (DH)	6324	A	952 936-6615	12114
Cal Southern United Food	6371	C	714 220-2297	12159
Healthsmart MGT Svcs Orgnztion	6411	D	714 947-8600	12218
Pacific Pioneer Insur Group (PA)	6411	D	714 228-7888	12243
DAndrea Vsual Cmmncations LLC	7336	C	714 947-8444	13326
B2b Staffing Services Inc	7363	B	714 243-4104	13592
Tad Pgs Inc	7363	A	571 451-2428	13626
Oshyn Inc	7371	C	213 483-1770	13791
Mercury Defense Systems Inc	7374	D	714 898-8200	14143
Mercury Systems Inc	7374	D	714 898-8200	14144
Trojan Professional Svcs Inc	7375	D	714 816-7169	14179
Consoldted Med Bo-Analysis Inc (PA)	8071	C	714 657-7369	16309
Focus Diagnostics Inc	8071	D	714 220-1900	16318
Pacificare Health Systems LLC (HQ)	8082	A	714 952-1121	16409
Tutor Time Learning Ctrs LLC	8351	C	714 484-1000	17117
Applied Research Assoc Inc	8731	D	505 881-8074	17767

DANA POINT, CA - Orange County

	SIC	EMP	PHONE	ENTRY#
Kanstul Musical Instrs Inc	3931	E	714 563-1000	8469
Watermark Rtrment Cmmnties Inc	6513	D	949 443-9543	12371
Cph Monarch Hotel LLC	7011	A	949 234-3200	12802
Prutel Joint Venture	7011	A	949 240-5064	12978
Ritz-Carlton Hotel Company LLC	7011	B	949 240-5020	12995
Ciri - Stroup Inc	7299	C	949 488-3104	13169
Pacific Asian Enterprises Inc (PA)	7389	D	949 496-4848	14566
Monarch Beach Golf Links (HQ)	7992	D	949 240-8247	15094

Mergent email: customerrelations@mergent.com
1274

2025 Southern California
Business Directory and Buyers Guide

(P-0000) Products & Services Section entry number
(PA)=Parent Co (HQ)=Headquarters (DH)=Div Headquarters

	SIC	EMP	PHONE	ENTRY#
Alter Management LLC	8741	D	949 629-0214	17939

DEL MAR, CA - San Diego County

	SIC	EMP	PHONE	ENTRY#
Crest Beverage Company Inc	5181	C	858 452-2300	11046
Liquid Investments Inc (PA)	5181	C	858 509-8510	11051
Dayton Dmh Inc	6514	C	858 350-4400	12374
Lhoberge Lessee Inc	7011	C	858 259-1515	12902
Sunstone Durante LLC	7011	C	858 792-5200	13041
Del Mar Fairgrounds	7299	C	858 792-4288	13171
Culver Personnel Agencies Inc	7361	C	888 600-5733	13507
Abacus Data Systems Inc (PA)	7371	C	858 452-4280	13642
Del Mar Thoroughbred Club	7948	B	858 755-1141	15038
Casa Palmera LLC	8093	D	888 481-4481	16448
LLC Bates White	8111	C	858 523-2150	16733
California Dept Fd Agriculture	9641	A	858 755-1161	18401

DELANO, CA - Kern County

	SIC	EMP	PHONE	ENTRY#
M Caratan Disc Inc	0172	C	661 725-2566	35
Wonderful Company LLC	0174	B	661 720-2400	45
Munger Bros LLC	0179	A	661 721-0390	50
Cal Treehouse Almonds LLC	0723	C	661 725-6334	105
Monarch Nut Company LLC	0723	C	661 725-6458	116
Wonderful Citrus Packing LLC (HQ)	0723	B	661 720-2400	123
Ayo Foods LLC	2026	E	661 345-5457	1324
Delano Growers Grape Products	2087	D	661 725-3255	1675
Styrotek Inc	3086	C	661 725-4957	4020
City of Delano	3589	E	661 721-3352	6006
Triple R Transportation Inc	4119	C	661 725-6494	8852
Adventist Health Delano	8062	C	661 721-5337	15892
Adventist Health Delano (HQ)	8062	A	661 725-4800	15893
North Kern S Tulare Hosp Dst	8062	C	661 720-2101	16106
Crowne Cold Storage LLC	8742	E	661 725-6458	18124

DESERT HOT SPRINGS, CA - Riverside County

	SIC	EMP	PHONE	ENTRY#
Dreamfields California LLC	2671	B	310 691-9739	2706
Western Golf Car Mfg Inc	3949	D	760 671-6691	8553
Desert Hot Sprng Real Prpts In	6512	D	760 329-6000	12289
Forest Lawn Mortuary	7261	B	760 329-8737	13155
Borrego Cmnty Hlth Foundation	8011	C	760 251-0044	15256

DIAMOND BAR, CA - Los Angeles County

	SIC	EMP	PHONE	ENTRY#
Genius Products Nt Inc	2086	C	510 671-0219	1619
Rapid Rack Holdings Inc	2542	A		2588
Rapid Rack Industries Inc	2542	D		2589
Sappi North America Inc	2621	D	714 456-0600	2637
Gohz Inc	3621	E	800 603-1219	6323
Ultimate Sound Inc	3651	B	909 861-6200	6564
Ecmm Services Inc	3955	E	714 988-9388	8562
Magnell Associate Inc (DH)	5045	C	800 685-3471	10015
Graybar Electric Company Inc	5063	C	909 451-4300	10184
Smart Stores Operations LLC	5141	C	323 855-8434	10779
24-Hour Med Staffing Svcs LLC	7361	C	909 895-8960	13480
Liferay Inc (PA)	7373	A	877 543-3729	14091
Camstar International Inc	7382	D	909 931-2540	14387
Unspoken Language Services Inc	7389	B	626 532-8096	14622
Specilty Eqp Mkt Assn Prfmce R (PA)	8611	C	909 610-2030	17289
Motech Americas LLC	8731	B	302 451-7500	17810
South Cast A Qlty MGT Dst Bldg (PA)	8748	A	909 396-2000	18359

DOWNEY, CA - Los Angeles County

	SIC	EMP	PHONE	ENTRY#
Meruelo Enterprises Inc (PA)	1542	A	562 745-2300	560
Reyes Coca-Cola Bottling LLC	2086	D	562 803-8100	1652
Instant Web LLC	2752	C	562 658-2020	3021
Hutchinson Seal Corporation (DH)	3053	C	248 375-4190	3890
Bradley Manufacturing Co Inc	3089	E	562 923-5556	4074
V-T Industries Inc	3089	D	714 521-2008	4268
Universal Mlding Extrusion Inc (DH)	3354	E	562 401-1015	4610
Umc Acquisition Corp (PA)	3356	E	562 940-0300	4622
Universal Molding Company (HQ)	3356	C	310 886-1750	4623
Cal Pipe Manufacturing Inc (PA)	3498	E	562 803-4388	5429
Detroit Diesel Corporation	3519	D	562 929-7016	5467
Downey Grinding Co	3541	C	562 803-5556	5544
United Drill Bushing Corp	3545	C	562 803-1521	5628
Can Lines Engineering Inc (PA)	3565	D	562 861-2996	5788
Vantage Point Products Corp (PA)	3651	C	562 946-1718	6565
Commercial Truck Eqp Co LLC	3713	C	562 803-4466	7197
World Water Inc	3823	E	562 940-1964	7884
California Ribbon Carbn Co Inc	3955	D	323 724-9100	8561
Mike Campbell & Associates Ltd	4222	A	626 369-3981	9037
Southern California Gas Co	4924	B	562 803-7500	9659
Keyline Sales Inc	5074	E	562 904-3910	10323
Nuwa Robotics Inc	5084	C	562 450-0100	10385
Qualls Stud Welding Pdts Inc	5084	E	562 923-7883	10396

	SIC	EMP	PHONE	ENTRY#
Rockview Dairies Inc (PA)	5149	C	562 927-5511	10975
Leach Grain & Milling Co Inc	5191	E	562 869-4451	11070
Home Depot USA Inc	5211	C	562 776-2200	11164
Florence Meat Packing Co Inc	5812	E	562 401-0760	11572
CIT Bank NA	6022	D	323 838-6881	11754
Financial Partners Credit Un (PA)	6061	D	562 904-3000	11797
Kaiser Foundation Hospitals	6324	C	562 622-4190	12089
PRC Multi-Family LLC	6513	C	562 803-5000	12362
Jlm & Mag Associates Inc	7231	C	562 869-3343	13149
OfficeMax North America Inc	7334	C	562 927-6444	13315
National Trench Safety LLC	7359	C	562 602-1642	13464
OSI Staffing Inc	7361	D	562 261-5753	13551
Kpwr Radio LLC	7389	C	562 745-2300	14525
Lakewood Park Health Ctr Inc (PA)	7389	B	562 869-0978	14527
Tarsco Holdings LLC	7699	C	562 869-0200	14796
City of Downey	7922	C	562 861-8211	14957
City of Downey	7997	D	562 803-4982	15128
Kaiser Foundation Hospitals	8011	D	800 823-4040	15355
Kaiser Foundation Hospitals	8011	C	817 372-8201	15359
Downey Community Health Center	8051	C	562 862-6506	15623
Ensign Group Inc	8051	A	562 923-9301	15638
Healthcare Ctr of Downey LLC	8051	C	562 869-0978	15673
Los Angles Cnty Rncho Los Amgo	8052	A	562 385-7111	15814
Kaiser Foundation Hospitals	8062	B	562 657-9000	16041
Pih Health Downey Hospital (HQ)	8062	A	562 698-0811	16131
Pih Health Hospital - Whitti	8062	A	562 904-5482	16133
Southern Cal Prmnnte Med Group	8062	A	562 657-2200	16204
County of Los Angeles	8093	C	562 401-7088	16462
Jwch Institute Inc	8099	C	562 862-1000	16574
County of Los Angeles	8322	D	562 940-2470	16916
County of Los Angeles	8322	D	562 940-6856	16917
ARC Los Angeles & Orange Cnly (PA)	8331	D	562 803-4606	17046
Automobile Club Southern Cal	8699	D	562 904-5970	17443
Meruelo Group LLC (PA)	8711	C	562 745-2300	17584
Rancho Research Institute	8733	C	562 401-8111	17886
County of Los Angeles	8741	C	562 940-2907	17977

DUARTE, CA - Los Angeles County

	SIC	EMP	PHONE	ENTRY#
Png Builders	1542	D	626 256-9539	573
Prolacta Bioscience Inc	2023	B	626 599-9260	1307
Soyfoods of America	2099	E	626 358-3836	1856
Cosmo Fiber Corporation (PA)	2759	C	626 256-6098	3133
Justice Bros Dist Co Inc	2843	E	626 359-9174	3627
Delafield Corporation (PA)	3599	C	626 303-0740	6114
Accu-Sembly Inc	3672	C	626 357-3447	6703
Woodward Hrt Inc	3728	C	626 359-9211	7593
Southern California Gas Co	4924	C	626 358-4700	9651
Gpi Ca-Niii Inc	5511	D	626 305-3000	11355
Humangood Socal	6513	C	626 357-1632	12345
Osf International Inc	7299	D	626 358-2115	13182
Arecont Vision Costar LLC	7382	D	818 937-0700	14383
We Pack It All LLC	7389	C	626 301-9214	14632
Beckman RES Inst of The Cy Hop	8011	C	626 359-8111	15252
City Hope Medical Foundation	8011	A	626 256-4673	15278
Humangood (PA)	8059	C	602 906-4024	15860
City Hope National Medical Ctr (HQ)	8062	B	626 553-8061	15959
Santa Teresita Inc (PA)	8062	B	626 359-3243	16176
Maryvale Day Care Center	8351	C	626 357-1514	17096
Humangood Socal	8361	C	626 359-8141	17165
City of Hope	8399	C	213 202-5735	17210
City of Hope (PA)	8741	B	626 256-4673	17966

F RNCHO DMNGZ, CA - Los Angeles County

	SIC	EMP	PHONE	ENTRY#
Timec Companies Inc	1629	C	310 885-4710	721
Murray Plumbing and Htg Corp (PA)	1711	C	310 637-1500	809
Sonora Mills Foods Inc (PA)	2099	C	310 639-5333	1853
Audio Video Corporation (PA)	2671	C	424 213-7500	2704
Modern Concepts Inc	3089	D	310 637-0013	4172
Coy Industries Inc	3444	D	310 603-2970	4975
Industrial Tctnics Brings Corp (DH)	3562	C	310 537-3750	5749
Dependable Global Express Inc (PA)	4731	C	310 537-2000	9269

EARP, CA - San Bernardino County

	SIC	EMP	PHONE	ENTRY#
Colorado River Adventures Inc (PA)	7033	C	760 663-3737	13108

EAST RANCHO DOMINGUE, CA - Los Angeles County

	SIC	EMP	PHONE	ENTRY#
Apex Logistics Intl Inc (DH)	4731	C	310 665-0288	9252

EASTVALE, CA - Riverside County

	SIC	EMP	PHONE	ENTRY#
PTi Sand & Gravel Inc	1442	E	951 272-0140	376
K-Swiss Inc	3021	E	951 361-7501	3867
Royal Range California Inc	3631	D	951 360-1600	6390
CJ Logistics America LLC	4212	C	909 605-7233	8901

Employee Codes: A=Over 500 employees, B=251-500
C=101-250, D=51-100, E=20-50, F=10-19, G=1-9

2025 Southern California
Business Directory and Buyers Guide

© Mergent Inc. 1-800-342-5647

1275

	SIC	EMP	PHONE	ENTRY#
United Parcel Service Inc	4215	D	951 749-3400	9024
Keystone Automotive Warehouse	5013	D	951 277-5237	9831
Smart Stores Operations LLC	5141		909 773-1813	10799
Shamrock Foods Company	5149	B	951 685-6314	10978

EDISON, CA - Kern County

	SIC	EMP	PHONE	ENTRY#
Giumarra Vineyards Corporation (PA)	0172	B	661 395-7000	32
Kirschenman Enterprises Sls LP	7389	C	661 366-5736	14522

EDWARDS, CA - Kern County

	SIC	EMP	PHONE	ENTRY#
Jt3 LLC	8711	A	661 277-4900	17568

EL CAJON, CA - San Diego County

	SIC	EMP	PHONE	ENTRY#
Rpc Inc	1389	E	619 334-6244	362
Azusa Rock LLC	1422	E	619 440-2363	371
California Shtmtl Works Inc	1541	D	619 562-7010	475
Hamann Construction	1542	D	619 440-7424	541
Steve P Rados Inc	1622	C	619 328-1360	656
Cass Construction Inc (PA)	1623	B	619 590-0929	668
HP Communications Inc	1623	D	951 579-8339	677
Schilling Paradise Corp	1623	C	619 449-4141	692
Astro Mechanical Contractors Inc	1711	D	619 442-9686	744
Cascade Thermal Solutions LLC (PA)	1711	E	619 562-8852	759
Countywide Mech Systems LLC	1711	C	619 449-9900	768
Helix Mechanical Inc	1711	C	619 440-1518	786
R & R Mechanical Contractors Inc	1711	D	619 449-9900	825
Walter Anderson Plumbing Inc	1711	C	619 449-7646	851
West Coast AC Co Inc	1711	C	619 561-8000	852
City-Wide Electronic Systems Inc	1731	D	619 444-0219	899
Dynalectric Company	1731	B	619 328-4007	910
Paradise Electric Inc	1731	C	619 449-4141	948
Seal Electric Inc	1731	C	619 449-7323	959
Sunshine Communications SE Inc	1731	C	619 448-7600	969
Team C Construction	1771	D	619 579-6572	1138
Artimex Iron Inc	1791	C	619 444-3155	1149
Metarom USA Inc	2087	E	619 449-0299	1687
Flight Suits	2386	C	619 440-2700	2180
Roll-Rite LLC	2394	E	619 449-8860	2241
Transportation Equipment Inc	2394	E	619 449-8860	2244
Vcsd Inc	2434	E	619 579-6886	2366
Omni Enclosures Inc	2541	E	619 579-6664	2572
Delstar Technologies Inc	3081	E	619 258-1503	3948
Damar Plastics Manufacturing Inc	3089	E	619 283-2300	4098
Vertechs Enterprises Inc (PA)	3364	E	858 578-3900	4661
Decco Castings Inc	3369	E	818 416-0068	4687
Triw1969 Inc	3398	E	619 593-3636	4716
M W Reid Welding Inc	3441	D	619 401-5880	4847
Western Bay Sheet Metal Inc	3441	E	619 233-1753	4881
Asm Construction Inc	3444	E	619 449-1966	4954
Bay Sheet Metal Inc	3444	E	619 401-9270	4957
Dave Whipple Sheet Metal Inc	3444	E	619 562-6962	4977
Pacific Marine Sheet Metal Corporation	3444	C	858 869-8900	5015
Jmmca Inc (PA)	3462	D	619 448-2711	5143
BJS&t Enterprises Inc	3479	C	619 448-7795	5314
Alturdyne Power Systems Inc	3511	E	619 343-3204	5454
Toro Company	3523	C	619 562-2950	5480
Veridiam Inc (DH)	3545	D	619 448-1000	5629
Rotron Incorporated	3564	C	619 593-7400	5776
Campbell Membrane Tech Inc	3569	E	619 938-2481	5814
Senior Operations LLC	3599	D	909 627-2723	6233
Weldmac Manufacturing Company	3599	C	619 440-2300	6270
Weldmac Manufacturing Company	3599	E	619 440-2300	6271
Micro-Mode Products Inc	3663	C	619 449-3844	6632
Brantner and Associates Inc (DH)	3678	C	619 456-6827	6942
Q Microwave Inc	3679	D	619 258-7322	7042
Gear Vendors Inc	3714	C	619 562-0060	7255
GKN Aerospace Chem-Tronics Inc (DH)	3724	A	619 258-5000	7386
Jet Air Fbo LLC	3728	E	619 448-5991	7507
Dn Tanks Inc	3795	C	619 440-8181	7679
Dyk Incorporated (HQ)	3795	E	619 440-8181	7680
Calbiotech Export Inc	3841	E	619 660-6162	8117
Johnson Outdoors Inc	3949	D	619 402-1023	8529
California Neon Products	3993	D	619 283-2191	8591
Integrted Sign Assoc A Cal Cor	3993	E	619 579-2229	8609
On Premise Products Inc	3999	E	619 562-1486	8706
Transdev Services Inc	4119	B	619 401-4503	8850
Cox Communications Inc	4841	D	619 592-4011	9538
San Diego Gas & Electric Co	4911	B	619 441-3834	9608
Waste Management Cal Inc	4953	C	619 596-5100	9774
Denardi Machinery Inc	5082	C	619 749-0039	10346
Tk Elevator Corporation	5084	C	619 596-7220	10411
Taylor-Listug Inc (PA)	5099	C	619 258-1207	10572
Graphic Business Solutions Inc	5112	E	619 258-4081	10580

	SIC	EMP	PHONE	ENTRY#
Smart Stores Operations LLC	5141	B	619 390-1738	10792
Smart Stores Operations LLC	5141	C	619 589-7000	10797
Sunfood Corporation	5149	D	619 596-7979	10982
Benny Enterprises Inc	5181	E	619 592-4455	11042
Home Depot USA Inc	5211	C	619 401-6610	11188
Wetzels Pretzels LLC	5461	E	619 588-1074	11303
K Motors Inc	5521	C	619 270-3000	11436
Sycuan Tribal Development	5812	C	619 442-3425	11602
EC Closing Corp	6162	D	800 546-1531	11899
The Pines Ltd	6513	C	619 447-1880	12368
Award-Superstars	6531	D	619 593-4300	12385
Sycuan Casino	7011	A	619 445-6002	13047
W Lodging Inc	7011	A	619 258-6565	13068
Cartwright Trmt Pest Ctrl Inc	7342	C	619 442-9613	13343
XI Staffing Inc	7361	C	619 579-0442	13585
Nlyte Software Americas Ltd	7371	D	866 386-5983	13783
Tessitura Network Inc	7372	B	888 643-5778	14049
Socal Technologies LLC	7379	E	619 635-1128	14253
Newport Diversified Inc	7389	E	619 448-4111	14558
El Cajon Motors (PA)	7515	D	619 579-8888	14650
CLP Inc (PA)	7692	E	619 444-3105	14738
Edwards Theatres Circuit Inc	7832	C	619 660-3460	14935
Sycuan Casino	7999	C	619 445-6002	15223
Kaiser Foundation Hospitals	8011	C	619 528-5000	15342
Neighborhood Healthcare	8011	D	619 440-2751	15402
Southern Cal Prmnnte Med Group	8011	C	619 528-5000	15479
Country Hills Health Care Inc	8051	C	619 441-8745	15603
Eldorado Care Center LP	8051	B	619 440-1211	15626
Parkside Healthcare Inc	8052	E	619 442-7744	15819
Kaiser Foundation Hospitals	8062	C	619 528-5000	16052
Christan Community Theatre	8299	D	619 588-0206	16852
St Madeleine Sophies Center	8331	D	619 442-5129	17067
Home Guiding Hands Corporation (PA)	8361	B	619 938-2850	17163
ARC of San Diego	8399	C	619 448-2415	17212
Nan McKay and Associates Inc	8742	D	619 258-1855	18175

EL CENTRO, CA - Imperial County

	SIC	EMP	PHONE	ENTRY#
Braga Fresh Family Farms Inc	0191	C	760 353-1155	76
Joe Heger Farms LLC	0191	C	760 353-5111	83
Labrucherie Produce LLC	2099	E	760 352-2170	1804
Associated Desert Newspaper (DH)	2711	E	760 337-3400	2781
Superior Ready Mix Concrete LP	3273	D	760 352-4341	4456
Ew Corprtion Indus Fabricators (PA)	3441	D	760 337-0020	4833
Rogar Manufacturing Inc	3679	E	760 335-3700	7046
Western Electrical Advg Co	3993	E	760 352-0471	8649
Lowes Home Centers LLC	5211	C	760 337-6700	11239
El Centro Motors	5511	D	760 336-2100	11339
I N C Builders Inc	7363	B	760 352-4200	13600
Southwest Protective Svcs Inc	7381	C	760 996-1285	14352
Wymore Inc	7692	E	760 352-2045	14748
El Centro Rgnal Med Ctr Fndtio (PA)	8062	A	760 339-7100	15989
Accentcare HM Hlth El Cntro In	8082	E	760 352-4022	16352
County of Imperial	8093	D	760 482-4120	16459
County of Imperial	8099	D	760 482-4441	16551
Rove Engineering Inc	8711	D	760 425-0001	17621

EL MONTE, CA - Los Angeles County

	SIC	EMP	PHONE	ENTRY#
Envirogenics Systems Company	1629	D	818 573-9220	711
Atlantis Seafood LLC	2092	D	626 626-4900	1701
Dianas Mexican Food Pdts Inc	2099	D	626 444-0555	1763
El Gallito Market Inc	2099	E	626 442-1190	1768
Andari Fashion Inc	2329	C	626 575-2759	2005
Svo Enterprise LLC	2381	E	626 406-4770	2176
Hunter Douglas Inc	2591	B	858 679-7500	2602
88 Special Sweet Inc	2679	D	909 525-7055	2762
Gill Corporation (PA)	3089	C	626 443-6094	4127
Castle Industries Inc of California	3444	E	909 390-0899	4967
Jansen Ornamental Supply Co	3446	E	626 442-0271	5066
BIG Enterprises	3448	E	626 448-1449	5075
All New Stamping Co	3469	C	626 443-8813	5171
Santoshi Corporation	3471	E	626 444-7118	5292
Applied Coatings & Linings	3479	E	626 280-6354	5310
Precision Coil Spring Company	3495	E	626 444-0561	5398
Craneveyor Corp (PA)	3536	D	626 442-1524	5521
Lith-O-Roll Corporation	3555	E	626 579-0340	5663
Lawrence Equipment Leasing Inc (PA)	3556	E	626 442-2894	5679
Justin Inc	3612	E	626 444-4516	6288
Videssence LLC (PA)	3645	E	626 579-0943	6450
Talmo & Chinn Inc	3674	E	626 443-1741	6903
Sparling Instruments LLC	3824	C	626 444-0571	7893
Access Services	4111	D	213 270-6000	8746
First Transit Inc	4111	D	626 307-7842	8749
San Gabriel Transit Inc (PA)	4111	C	626 258-1310	8800

Mergent email: customerrelations@mergent.com
1276

2025 Southern California
Business Directory and Buyers Guide

(P-0000) Products & Services Section entry number
(PA)=Parent Co (HQ)=Headquarters (DH)=Div Headquarters

Company	SIC	EMP	PHONE	ENTRY#
Medresponse LLC	4119	D	877 311-5555	8838
Fulgent Genetics Inc	4225	A	626 350-0537	9069
San Gabriel Valley Water Co (PA)	4941	C	626 448-6183	9716
Los Angeles Ltg Mfg Co Inc	5063	D	626 454-8300	10190
Burke Engineering Co	5074	D	626 579-6763	10315
Bdi Inc	5085	D	626 442-8948	10426
Bangkit (usa) Inc	5112	D	626 672-0888	10577
Jans Enterprises Corporation	5149	E	626 575-2000	10949
K T Lucky Co Inc	5149	D	626 579-7272	10952
Mutual Trading Co Inc (DH)	5149	C	213 626-9458	10964
D Longo Inc	5511	B	626 580-6000	11331
El Monte Automotive Group Inc	5511	D	626 580-6200	11340
El Monte Automotive Group LLC	5511	D	626 444-0321	11341
Nijjar Realty Inc (PA)	6531	C	626 575-0062	12496
Herald Christian Health Center (PA)	8011	C	626 286-8700	15323
Glimmer Healthcare Inc	8051	C	626 442-5721	15666
Ramona Care Inc	8051	C	626 442-5721	15758
Gibraltar Cnvalescent Hosp Inc	8059	D	626 443-9425	15856
Ahm Gemch Inc	8062	C	626 579-7777	15896
Enki Health and RES Systems	8093	D	626 227-7001	16473
Altamed Health Services Corp	8099	D	626 453-8466	16528
Public Hlth Fndation Entps Inc	8099	C	626 856-6618	16610
Foothill Family Service	8322	C	626 246-1240	16944
Hope Hse For Mltple Hndcpped I (PA)	8361	C	626 443-1313	17164
R and L Lopez Associates Inc (PA)	8711	D	626 330-5296	17617

EL SEGUNDO, CA - Los Angeles County

Company	SIC	EMP	PHONE	ENTRY#
Irwin Industries Inc	1629	A	704 457-5117	716
El Segundo Bread Bar LLC	2051	E	310 615-9898	1444
Vbc Holdings Inc	2051	E	310 322-7357	1469
Lambs & Ivy Inc	2392	D	310 322-3800	2214
Satco Inc (PA)	2448	C	310 322-4719	2392
Artissimo Designs LLC (HQ)	2679	E	310 906-3700	2764
Los Angles Tmes Cmmnctions LLC (PA)	2711	A	213 237-5000	2814
Superbam Inc	2741	C	310 845-5784	2942
Continental Graphics Corp	2752	D	310 662-2307	2986
Browntrout Publishers Inc (PA)	2759	E	310 607-9010	3125
Primary Color Systems Corp	2759	D	310 841-0250	3162
Kate Somerville Skincare LLC (HQ)	2834	C	323 655-7546	3436
Murad LLC (HQ)	2834	C	310 726-0600	3452
Youth To People Inc	2844	D	309 648-5500	3701
Hco Holding II Corporation	2952	A	310 955-9200	3841
Henry Company LLC (HQ)	2952	D	310 955-9200	3842
Hnc Parent Inc (PA)	2952	D	310 955-9200	3843
Federal Industries Inc	3494	E	310 297-4040	5386
Craig Tools Inc	3545	E	310 322-0614	5608
Flight Microwave Corporation	3559	E	310 607-9819	5703
Belkin International Inc (DH)	3577	B	310 751-5100	5905
Ross Racing Pistons	3592	D	310 536-0100	6045
Metalore Inc	3599	E	310 643-0360	6175
Glentek Inc	3621	D	310 322-3026	6322
Nantenergy LLC	3621	D	310 905-4866	6329
Belkin Inc	3651	A	800 223-5546	6331
Boeing Satellite Systems Inc (HQ)	3663	E	310 791-7450	6601
Millennium Space Systems Inc (HQ)	3663	E	310 683-5840	6633
MTI Laboratory Inc	3663	E	310 955-3700	6638
Raytheon Applied Sgnal Tech In	3663	C	310 436-7000	6652
Display Products Inc	3674	D	310 640-0442	6818
Infineon Tech Americas Corp (HQ)	3674	A	310 726-8200	6829
Infineon Tech Americas Corp	3674	D	310 726-8000	6830
Infineon Tech Americas Corp	3674	C	310 252-7116	6831
Integra Technologies Inc	3674	D	310 606-0855	6833
J L Cooper Electronics Inc	3679	F	310 322-9990	7013
Teledyne Technologies Inc	3679	B	310 765-3600	7059
Loop Inc	3694	E	888 385-6674	7093
Allclear Inc	3721	E	424 316-1596	7328
Boeing Satellite Systems Inc	3721	A	310 568-2735	7336
Aerospace Engrg Support Corp	3728	E	310 297-4050	7416
Trio Manufacturing Inc	3728	C	310 640-6123	7582
Kinkisharyo (usa) Inc	3743	C	424 276-1803	7627
Abl Space Systems Company	3761	D	424 321-6060	7640
Varda Space Industries Inc	3761	D	833 707-0020	7660
Aerojet Rcketdyne Holdings Inc (HQ)	3812	D	310 252-8100	7686
Aerojet Rocketdyne De Inc	3812	A	310 414-0110	7687
Atk Space Systems LLC	3812	D	310 343-3799	7702
Northrop Grumman Corporation	3812	D	310 332-0461	7750
Northrop Grumman Corporation	3812	D	310 332-1000	7751
Northrop Grumman Systems Corp	3812	D	480 355-7716	7773
Northrop Grumman Systems Corp	3812	A	310 332-1000	7780
Orbital Sciences LLC	3812	C	703 406-5000	7786
Pacific Defense Strategies Inc (PA)	3812	E	310 722-6050	7789
Raytheon Company	3812	B	310 647-1000	7794
Raytheon Company	3812	E	310 647-9438	7795
Raytheon Company	3812	A	310 647-9438	7796
Raytheon Company	3812	D	310 647-1000	7798
Teledyne Controls LLC	3812	D	310 765-3600	7815
Karl Storz Endscpy-America Inc (HQ)	3841	C	424 218-8100	8179
Mod-Electronics Inc	3873	E	310 322-2136	8447
Mattel Inc	3942	A	310 252-2000	8477
Moose Toys LLC	3942	D	310 341-4642	8478
Mattel Direct Import Inc (HQ)	3944	E	310 252-2000	8491
Mega Brands America Inc (DH)	3944	D	949 727-9009	8492
Beach House Group LLC	3999	D	310 356-6180	8661
Cls Trnsprttion Los Angles LLC (HQ)	4119	C	310 414-8189	8819
Next Freight Solutions Inc	4213	D	442 291-9220	8968
Air New Zealand Limited	4512	D	310 648-7000	9156
Pacific Aviation LLC (PA)	4512	D	310 322-6290	9162
Singapore Airlines Limited	4512	C	310 647-1922	9165
F & E Arcft Mint Los Angles LL	4581	B	310 338-0063	9201
Pacific Aviation Corporation (HQ)	4581	C	310 646-4015	9205
Superior Aircraft Services Inc (HQ)	4581	D	636 778-2300	9209
Pinnacle Travel Services LLC	4724	C	310 414-1787	9231
VIP Tours of California Inc	4725	C	310 216-7507	9242
Dfds International Corporation	4731	D	310 414-1516	9270
L E Coppersmith Inc (HQ)	4731	D	310 607-8000	9303
Maersk Whsng Dist Svcs USA LLC (DH)	4731	D	562 345-2200	9310
Directv Group Holdings LLC (HQ)	4812	C	424 432-5554	9400
Infonet Services Corporation (DH)	4813	A	310 335-2600	9445
Scalefast Inc (PA)	4813	C	310 595-4040	9457
Directv Inc	4841	B	888 388-4249	9541
Directv Enterprises LLC	4841	A	310 535-5000	9542
Directv Group Inc (DH)	4841	D	310 964-5000	9546
Directv Holdings LLC (DH)	4841	D	310 964-5000	9547
Directv International Inc	4841	A	310 964-6460	9548
En Pointe Technologies Sls LLC	5045	C	310 337-6151	9999
Jal Avionet USA (HQ)	5045	E	310 606-1000	10012
Square Enix Inc	5045	C	310 846-0400	10032
Boeing Stllite Systems Intl In (HQ)	5088	E	310 364-4000	10487
Com Dev Usa LLC	5088	D	424 456-8000	10488
Itochu Aviation Inc (DH)	5088	E	310 640-2770	10493
A-Mark Precious Metals Inc (PA)	5094	C	310 587-1477	10544
Tri-Union Seafoods LLC (DH)	5146	D	424 397-8556	10864
Chevron Corporation	5541	A	310 615-5000	11474
Cookingcom Inc	5719	C	310 664-1283	11529
Gurucul Solutions LLC	5734	D	213 291-6888	11542
Merqbiz LLC	5961	E	855 637-7249	11656
Pcm Inc (HQ)	5961	A	310 354-5600	11658
Intelligent Beauty LLC	5999	A	310 683-0940	11687
City National Bank	6021	D	310 297-6606	11721
Manhattan Bancorp	6021	D	310 606-8000	11735
Bank of Manhattan	6029	C	310 606-8000	11782
National Planning Corporation	6141	C	800 881-7174	11857
Merrill Lynch Prce Fnner Smith	6211	D	310 536-1600	11979
Computershare Inc	6289	C	800 522-6645	12039
Associated Third Party Administrators Inc	6371	B		12158
Cbre Foundation Inc	6531	D	949 809-3744	12398
Landmark Dividend LLC (PA)	6531	C	323 306-2683	12478
American Academic Hlth Sys LLC	6719	A	310 414-7200	12593
Asp Henry Holdings Inc	6719	A	310 955-9200	12594
Hco Holding I Corporation (HQ)	6719	D	323 583-5000	12601
Transom Post Midco LLC	6719	C	312 254-3300	12617
Century Pk Capitl Partners LLC (PA)	6726	C	310 867-2210	12646
Ld Acquisition Company 16 LLC	6799	D	310 294-8160	12714
Pt Gaming LLC	7011	A	323 260-5060	12979
Uhg Lax Prop Llc	7011	C	310 322-0999	13057
Esaloncom LLC	7231	C	866 550-2424	13148
Murad LLC	7231	C	310 726-0470	13152
Apollo Interactive LLC (PA)	7311	D	310 836-9777	13196
David & Goliath LLC	7311	C	310 445-5200	13202
Ignited LLC (PA)	7311	D	310 773-3100	13215
Katch LLC	7311	D	310 219-6200	13218
Liquid Advertising Inc	7311	D	310 450-2653	13221
Mh Sub I LLC (PA)	7311	B	310 280-4000	13226
Mullenlowe US Inc	7311	D	424 738-6500	13231
Beachbody LLC (HQ)	7313	B	310 883-9000	13260
Beachbody Company Inc (PA)	7313	B	310 883-9000	13261
Softscript Inc	7338	A	310 451-2110	13341
Ibftech Inc	7361	C	424 217-8010	13527
Tempus LLC	7361	D	800 917-5055	13577
Altech Services Inc	7363	B	888 725-8324	13589
Artic Sentinel Inc	7371	D	310 227-8230	13658
Crescentone Inc (HQ)	7371	D	310 563-7000	13698
Dena Corp	7371	D	415 375-3170	13705
Irise (PA)	7371	D	800 556-0399	13755
Prodege LLC (PA)	7371	D	310 294-9599	13799
BMC	7372	E	310 321-5555	13894

GEOGRAPHIC

Employee Codes: A=Over 500 employees, B=251-500
C=101-250, D=51-100, E=20-50, F=10-19, G=1-9

2025 Southern California
Business Directory and Buyers Guide

© Mergent Inc. 1-800-342-5647

1277

	SIC	EMP	PHONE	ENTRY#
Governmentjobscom Inc (PA)	7372	D	877 204-4442	13940
M Nexon Inc	7372	E	213 858-5930	13970
North Beam Inc	7372	E	860 940-4569	13991
Powerdms Inc	7372	D	407 992-6000	14008
Saviynt Inc (PA)	7372	B	310 641-1664	14025
Street Smart LLC	7372	E	866 924-4644	14041
Traxero North America LLC	7372	D	423 497-1164	14057
Unbroken Studios LLC	7372	D	310 741-2670	14058
Mesfin Enterprises	7373	B	310 615-0881	14092
Design People Inc	7374	C	800 969-5799	14129
Crowdstrike Inc	7379	C	888 512-8906	14209
Login Consulting Services Inc	7379	D	310 607-9091	14233
Whelan Security Co	7381	C	310 343-8628	14368
Da Vinci Schools Fund	7389	C	310 725-5800	14486
Oceanx LLC (PA)	7389	C	310 774-4088	14560
Prologic Rdmption Slutions Inc (PA)	7389	A	310 322-7774	14576
Telenet Voip Inc	7629	C	310 253-9000	14733
Crafty Apes LLC (PA)	7812	A	310 837-3900	14815
Rhythm and Hues Inc (PA)	7812	D	310 448-7500	14851
Zoo Digital Production LLC	7812	C	310 220-3939	14879
Ten Publishing Media LLC (PA)	7819	C	310 531-9900	14908
Ticketscom LLC (DH)	7922	E	714 327-5400	14981
Chargers Football Company LLC (PA)	7941	C	714 540-7100	15022
Spectrum Clubs Inc	7991	A	310 727-9300	15064
American Golf Corporation (HQ)	7997	C	310 664-4000	15114
Optumcare Management LLC (HQ)	8011	A	310 354-4200	15415
Radiology Partners Inc (HQ)	8011	B	424 290-8004	15429
Radiology Prtners Holdings LLC (PA)	8011	C	424 290-8004	15430
Pipeline Health LLC (PA)	8062	D	310 379-2134	16136
Scribeamerica LLC	8099	A	877 819-5900	16616
BMC Group Inc	8111	D	310 321-5555	16647
Carson Kurtzman Consultants (DH)	8111	C	310 823-9000	16654
Diverse Journeys Inc (PA)	8322	C	310 643-7403	16935
Premier Disability Svcs LLC	8399	D	310 280-4000	17240
Attainment Holdco LLC	8621	C	310 954-1578	17293
Raytheon Secure Information Systems LLC	8711	C	310 647-9438	17618
Armanino LLP	8721	C	310 822-8552	17702
Infineon Tech Americas Corp	8721	A	310 726-8000	17735
Nantcell Inc	8733	C	310 883-1300	17884
Bellwether Asset MGT Inc (PA)	8741	D	310 525-3022	17951
Anthos Group Inc	8742	E	888 778-2986	18093
Avasant LLC (PA)	8742	D	310 643-3030	18099
Technical Micro Cons Inc (PA)	8742	E	310 559-3982	18225
Tecolote Research Inc	8742	D	310 640-4700	18228
Wpromote LLC (PA)	8742	C	310 421-4844	18244
Clearesult Operating LLC	8748	D	508 836-9500	18304

EL TORO, CA - Orange County

	SIC	EMP	PHONE	ENTRY#
Sunset Landscape Maintenance	0782	D	949 455-4636	236
Black & Decker Corporation	3546	E	949 672-4000	5633
P M D Holding Corp	5047	B	949 595-4777	10098

ENCINITAS, CA - San Diego County

	SIC	EMP	PHONE	ENTRY#
Dramm and Echter Inc	0181	D	760 436-0188	53
Tierra Verde Resources Inc (PA)	0782	C	857 777-6190	237
Coast News Inc	2711	E	760 436-9737	2790
RCP Block & Brick Inc	3271	E	760 753-1164	4375
Cratex Manufacturing Co Inc	3291	D	760 942-2877	4482
Stable Auto Corporation	3694	E	415 967-2719	7100
Black Box Distribution LLC	3949	D	760 268-1174	8506
Flock Freight Inc	4731	C	855 744-7585	9282
Cellco Partnership	4812	D	760 642-0430	9397
Olivenhain Municipal Water Dst	4941	D	760 753-6466	9707
Black Box Inc	5136	D	760 804-3300	10678
Wayne Gossett Ford Inc	5511	D	760 753-6286	11432
Southern Cal Disc Tire Co Inc	5531	C	760 634-2202	11464
Lofty Coffee Inc	5812	D	760 230-6747	11586
Solis Capital Partners LLC	6799	D	760 309-9436	12736
Lowe Enterprises Inc	7011	C	310 820-6661	12908
Trigild International Inc	7011	C	760 944-0260	13056
North County Health Prj Inc	8011	C	760 736-6767	15407
Five Star Senior Living Inc	8051	C	760 479-1818	15654
San Diego Hebrew Homes (PA)	8051	C	760 942-2695	15768
Scripps Health	8062	C	760 753-6501	16181
YMCA of San Diego County	8641	C	760 745-7490	17386
YMCA of San Diego County	8641	B	858 292-4034	17389
YMCA of San Diego County	8641	C	760 758-0808	17397
Dudek Inc (PA)	8711	D	760 942-5147	17518

ENCINO, CA - Los Angeles County

	SIC	EMP	PHONE	ENTRY#
Liberty Vegetable Oil Company	2079	E	562 921-3567	1526
Zevia LLC	2086	D	310 202-7000	1658
Zevia Pbc (PA)	2086	E	424 343-2654	1659

	SIC	EMP	PHONE	ENTRY#
Stanzino Inc	2211	C	818 602-5171	1888
Etrade 24 Inc	2299	E	818 712-0574	1970
Aquarius Rags LLC (PA)	2335	D	213 895-4400	2058
Creative Age Publications Inc	2721	E	818 782-7328	2851
Owsla Touring LLC	2741	E	818 385-1933	2932
California Respiratory Care	2899	D	818 379-9999	3791
National Cement Company Inc (HQ)	3241	E	818 728-5200	4358
Concrete Holding Co Cal Inc	3273	A	818 788-4228	4436
National Cement Co Cal Inc (DH)	3273	E	818 728-5200	4445
Vivometrics Inc	3845	C	805 667-2225	8402
Moroccanoil Inc (PA)	5122	C	888 700-1817	10634
Sayari Shahrzad	5136	E	310 903-6368	10695
Benihana Inc	5812	D	818 788-7121	11551
Warner Food Management Co Inc	5812	C	818 285-2160	11609
City National Bank	6021	C	818 905-4100	11720
United Vision Financial Inc	6163	C	818 285-0211	11956
Republic Indemnity Company Cal	6331	C	818 990-9860	12133
Cartel Marketing Inc	6411	C	818 483-1130	12191
Betta Assets Inc	6531	D	818 990-7733	12388
Lowe Enterprises Rlty Svcs Inc	6531	A	818 990-9555	12481
Brite Media LLC	7313	B	818 826-5790	13263
One Silver Serve LLC	7349	D	818 995-6444	13397
Team-One Staffing Services Inc	7361	A	951 616-3515	13575
Phone Check Solutions LLC	7371	B	310 365-1855	13795
Veritas Technologies LLC	7371	C	310 202-0757	13860
Artkive	7372	E	310 975-9809	13884
D3publisher of America Inc	7372	D	310 268-0820	13911
Ipr Software Inc	7372	C	310 499-0544	13952
Netsol Technologies Inc (PA)	7372	C	818 222-9195	13983
Payment Cloud LLC	7374	D	800 988-2215	14150
Reprints Desk Inc	7375	D	310 477-0354	14177
Life Alert Emrgncy Rsponse Inc (PA)	7382	D	800 247-0000	14412
Answer Financial Inc (HQ)	7389	C	818 644-4000	14451
Sunrise Senior Living Inc	8051	D	818 346-9046	15785
Prime Hlthcare Svcs - Encino H	8062	B	818 995-5000	16145
Sgry LLC	8062	C	818 501-1080	16189
Elizabeth Glaser Pedia	8099	B	310 231-0400	16559
Price Law Group A Prof Corp (PA)	8111	C	818 995-4540	16762
Instantly Inc	8732	C	866 872-4006	17851
Westrec Properties Inc	8741	B	818 907-0400	18080
Intelity Inc	8742	C	310 596-8160	18154
Telestar International Corp	8742	E	818 582-3018	18230

ESCONDIDO, CA - San Diego County

	SIC	EMP	PHONE	ENTRY#
Henry Avocado Corporation (HQ)	0179	D	760 745-6632	49
Mountain Meadow Mushrooms Inc	0182	D	760 749-1201	74
Landcare USA LLC	0782	D	760 747-1174	214
Eleven Western Builders Inc (PA)	1521	D	760 796-6346	401
Innovative Communities Inc (PA)	1521	D	760 690-5225	408
Romero General Cnstr Corp	1521	C	760 715-0154	424
G Tech Construction	1522	C	858 224-2909	447
Erickson-Hall Construction Co (PA)	1542	D	760 796-7700	538
R J Lanthier Company Inc	1542	D	760 738-9798	575
Marathon General Inc	1611	D	760 738-9714	636
Romero General Cnstr Corp (PA)	1611	D	760 489-8412	646
JR Filanc Cnstr Co Inc (PA)	1623	D	760 941-7130	681
West Tech Contracting Inc	1623	D	760 233-2570	707
Associate Mech Contrs Inc	1711	C	760 294-3517	743
Baker Electric & Renewables LLC	1731	A	760 745-2001	886
Bergelectric Corp	1731	C	760 746-1003	889
Bergelectric Corp	1731	D	760 291-8100	890
Hmt Electric Inc	1731	C	858 458-9771	925
Laser Electric Inc	1731	C	760 658-6626	933
X3 Management Services Inc	1731	D	760 597-9336	979
Prowall Lath and Plaster	1742	C	760 480-9001	1024
Surecraft Supply Inc	1751	C		1061
Taylor Trim & Supply Inc	1751	C	760 740-2000	1062
Southland Paving Inc	1771	D	760 747-6895	1135
Nemos Bakery Inc (HQ)	2053	D	760 741-5725	1494
Stone Brewing Co LLC	2082	C	760 294-7899	1554
Pure-Flo Water Co (PA)	2086	D	619 596-4130	1638
Esperanzas Tortilleria	2099	E	760 743-5908	1769
Hollywood Chairs (PA)	2511	E	760 471-6600	2426
Publishers Development Corp	2721	E	858 605-0200	2872
Mum Industries Inc	2821	D	800 729-1314	3281
REAL Seal Co Inc	3053	E	760 743-7263	3897
Dcc General Engrg Contrs Inc	3272	D	760 480-7400	4386
Oldcastle Infrastructure Inc	3272	E	951 683-8200	4409
Robertsons Ready Mix Ltd	3273	D	951 685-4600	4453
Superior Ready Mix Concrete LP (PA)	3273	E	760 745-0556	4460
Superior Ready Mix Concrete LP	3273	D	760 728-1128	4464
Vulcan Materials Co	3273	C	760 737-3486	4465
VIT Products Inc	3429	E	760 480-6702	4794

Mergent email: customerrelations@mergent.com
1278

2025 Southern California
Business Directory and Buyers Guide

(P-0000) Products & Services Section entry number
(PA)=Parent Co (HQ)=Headquarters (DH)=Div Headquarters

Company	SIC	EMP	PHONE	ENTRY#
Freeberg Indus Fbrication Corp	3441	D	760 737-7614	4836
Integrted Crygnic Slutions LLC	3559	E	951 234-0899	5707
Capstone Fire Management Inc (PA)	3569	E	760 839-2290	5815
Separation Engineering Inc	3569	E	760 489-0101	5834
One Stop Systems Inc (PA)	3577	E	760 745-9883	5943
One Stop Systems Inc	3577	E	858 530-2511	5944
C & H Machine Inc	3599	D	760 746-6459	6101
Meziere Enterprises Inc	3599	E	800 208-1755	6177
Price Products Incorporated	3599	E	760 745-5602	6206
Bliss Holdings LLC	3648	E	626 506-8696	6493
Rantec Microwave Systems Inc	3663	E	760 744-1544	6650
Systech Corporation	3669	E	858 674-6500	6694
Avr Global Technologies Inc (PA)	3679	C	949 391-1180	6969
U S Circuit Inc	3679	E	760 489-1413	7064
Transportation Power LLC	3714	E	858 248-4255	7302
Northrop Grumman Corporation	3812	E	310 864-7342	7755
Arch Med Sltons - Escndido LLC	3841	E	760 432-9785	8097
Photronics Inc	3861	C	760 294-1896	8440
Mv Transportation Inc	4111	C	760 520-0118	8787
Westmed Ambulance Inc	4119	C	310 219-1779	8854
Santa Barbara Trnsp Corp	4151	C	760 746-0850	8883
San Diego Gas & Electric Co	4911	B	760 432-2508	9603
San Diego County Water Auth	4941	C	760 480-1991	9712
Hadronex Inc (PA)	4952	E	760 291-1980	9725
Zest Anchors LLC	5047	C	760 743-7744	10116
Cal Southern Sound Image Inc (PA)	5065	D	760 737-3900	10236
Klein Electronics Inc	5065	E	760 781-3220	10260
Giumarra Agricom Intl LLC	5148	A	760 480-8502	10902
Home Depot USA Inc	5211	D	760 233-1285	11186
Lowes Home Centers LLC	5211	C	760 484-5113	11232
Brecht Enterprises Inc	5511	D	760 745-3000	11321
Escondido Motors LLC	5511	D	760 745-5000	11343
Jack Pwell Chrysler - Ddge Inc	5511	D	760 745-2880	11365
Southern Cal Disc Tire Co Inc	5531	E	760 741-9805	11457
Southern Cal Disc Tire Co Inc	5531	E	760 741-3801	11459
Acapulco Restaurants Inc	5812	D	562 346-1200	11546
Stone Brewing Co LLC (DH)	5813	C	760 294-7866	11619
Emeritus Corporation	6513	C	760 741-3055	12338
Welk Group Inc	7011	B	760 749-3000	13074
ARS National Services Inc (PA)	7322	C	800 456-5053	13277
Transamerican Direct Inc	7331	C	760 745-5343	13307
Sbrm (PA)	7349	C	760 480-0208	13415
Kindersystems Inc	7379	D	760 975-9750	14229
Clovis Skilled Care LLC	7389	D	559 299-2591	14474
Dish For All Inc	7622	E	760 690-3869	14722
Welk Group Inc	7992	C	760 749-3225	15098
Welk Group Inc	7997	C	760 749-0983	15186
Borrego Cmnty Hlth Foundation	8011	C	760 466-1080	15254
Graybill Medical Group Inc (PA)	8011	C	866 228-2236	15318
Kaiser Foundation Hospitals	8011	C	619 528-5000	15343
Neighborhood Healthcare (PA)	8011	C	833 867-4642	15399
Neighborhood Healthcare	8011	B	760 737-2000	15400
Southern Cal Prmnnte Med Group	8011	C	760 839-7200	15481
Ensign Group Inc	8051	C	760 746-0303	15642
Life Care Centers America Inc	8051	C	760 741-6109	15692
Mek Escondido LLC	8051	C	760 747-0430	15719
Silverado Senior Living Inc	8051	E	760 456-5137	15775
Valle Vsta Cnvlescent Hosp Inc	8059	D	760 745-1288	15889
Palomar Health (PA)	8062	C	442 281-5000	16117
Palomar Health Technology Inc	8062	C	442 281-5000	16121
Palomar Health	8069	C	760 740-6311	16297
Cox Enterprises LLC	8082	D	858 822-8587	16383
Elizabeth Hospice Inc (PA)	8082	C	700 737-2050	16300
Neighborhood Healthcare	8099	C	760 737-6903	16594
Interfaith Community Svcs Inc	8322	D	760 489-6380	16960
Humangood Socal	8361	B	760 747-4306	17166
Las Villas Del Norte	8361	C	760 741-1047	17172
Meadowbrook Vlg Chrstn Rtrment	8361	E	760 746-2500	17180
Redwood Elderlink Scph	8361	E	760 480-1030	17189
Califrnia Ctr For Arts Escndid	8412	C	760 839-4138	17250
Zoological Society San Diego	8422	C	760 747-8702	17274
Automobile Club Southern Cal	8699	C	760 745-2124	17430
Blanchard Training and Dev Inc (PA)	8742	C	760 489-5005	18106
Tri-Ad Actuaries Inc	8742	C	760 743-7555	18234
Pro Energy Services Group LLC	8744	B	760 744-7077	18267

FALLBROOK, CA - San Diego County

Company	SIC	EMP	PHONE	ENTRY#
Olive Hill Greenhouses Inc	0181	D	760 728-4596	63
Treesap Farms LLC	0191	C	760 990-7770	88
Executive Landscape Inc	0781	C	760 731-9036	166
Grubb & Nadler Inc	1231	E	760 728-0040	259
Maneri Traffic Control Inc	1611	D	951 695-5104	635
Scw Contracting Corporation	1623	D	760 728-1308	693

Company	SIC	EMP	PHONE	ENTRY#
Fallbrook Industries Inc	3469	E	760 728-7229	5186
Axelgaard Manufacturing Co (PA)	3845	D	760 723-7554	8369
Axelgaard Manufacturing Co	3845	E	760 723-7554	8370
Altman Specialty Plants LLC	5193	B	800 348-4881	11079
Major Market Inc	5411	C	760 723-0857	11279
Southwest Boulder & Stone Inc (PA)	5999	E	760 451-3333	11699
Bzya Corporation	7349	B	949 656-3220	13360
Garich Inc	7361	B	951 302-4750	13521
Special Event Audio Svcs Inc	7929	E	800 518-9144	15005
Crestwood Behavioral Hlth Inc	8059	C	760 451-4165	15849
Edsi	8711	C	760 731-3501	17519

FILLMORE, CA - Ventura County

Company	SIC	EMP	PHONE	ENTRY#
Brightview Tree Company	0811	D	714 546-7975	250
Honey Bennetts Farm	2099	E	805 521-1375	1789
Ameron International Corp	3272	C	425 258-2616	4379
Ameron International Corp	3272	D	805 524-0223	4380
Owens & Minor Distribution Inc	5047	B	805 524-0243	10097

FONTANA, CA - San Bernardino County

Company	SIC	EMP	PHONE	ENTRY#
People Pets and Vets LLC	0742	C	909 453-4213	131
People Pets and Vets LLC	0742	C	909 329-2860	132
Brightview Landscape Svcs Inc	0781	C	909 946-3196	155
Stantru Resources Inc	1541	D	909 587-1441	504
Engel Holdings Inc	1542	C	866 950-9862	536
Foundation Pile Inc	1629	D	909 350-1584	712
Slater Inc	1629	D	909 822-6800	720
STC Netcom Inc (PA)	1731	D	951 685-8181	966
B&B Industrial Services Inc (PA)	1741	B	909 428-3167	980
GES Sheet Metal Inc	1761	D	909 598-3332	1084
Gonsalves & Santucci Inc	1771	B	909 350-0474	1117
Refresco Beverages US Inc	2033	C	951 685-0481	1355
Sundown Foods USA Inc	2033	E	909 606-6797	1357
Flowers Bakeries Sls Socal LLC	2051	E	702 281-4797	1446
Reyes Coca-Cola Bottling LLC	2086	C	909 980-3121	1650
Mohawk Industries Inc	2273	E	909 357-1064	1954
A&R Tarpaulins Inc	2394	E	909 829-4444	2232
Ramirez Pallets Inc	2448	E	909 822-2066	2391
New Classic HM Furnishing Inc (PA)	2512	E	909 484-7676	2456
S & H Cabinets and Mfg Inc	2521	E	909 357-0551	2517
Allied West Paper Corp	2621	D	909 349-0710	2620
Tst/Impreso Inc	2761	E	909 357-7190	3195
Kemira Water Solutions Inc	2819	E	909 350-5678	3240
Indorama Vntres Sstnble Sltion	2821	E	951 727-8318	3271
J-M Manufacturing Company Inc	2821	D	909 822-3009	3276
Specialized Milling Corp	2851	E	909 357-7890	3722
Kemira Water Solutions Inc	2899	E	909 350-5678	3807
Fontana Paper Mills Inc	2952	D	909 823-4100	3840
TTI Floor Care North Amer Inc	3052	D	440 996-2802	3877
Cannon Gasket Inc	3053	E	909 355-1547	3881
Ring Container Tech LLC	3085	D	909 350-8416	3990
Premier Packaging LLC	3086	E	909 749-5123	4013
Dorel Juvenile Group Inc	3089	C	909 428-0295	4107
Vpet Usa LLC	3089	D	909 605-1668	4271
Avilas Garden Art (PA)	3272	E	909 350-4546	4381
Hanson Roof Tile Inc	3272	B	888 509-4787	4395
Jensen Enterprises Inc	3272	E	909 357-7264	4398
Oldcastle Infrastructure Inc	3272	E	909 428-3700	4408
California Steel Inds Inc (HQ)	3312	C	909 350-6300	4514
Tree Island Wire (usa) Inc	3315	C	909 594-7511	4543
California Steel Inds Inc	3317	B	909 350-6300	4547
Vista Metals Corp (PA)	3354	C	909 823-4278	4613
American Die Casting Inc	3364	E	909 355-7768	4656
Solar Atmospheres Inc	3398	E	909 217-7400	4713
Greif Inc	3412	D	909 350-2112	4728
Allegion Access Tech LLC	3423	E	909 628-9272	4734
Fabco Steel Fabrication Inc	3441	E	909 350-1535	4834
Rnd Contractors Inc	3441	E	909 429-8500	4865
Schroeder Iron Corporation	3441	E	909 428-6471	4867
Door Components Inc	3442	C	909 770-5700	4886
LLC Walker West	3444	D	951 685-9660	4997
Lynam Industries Inc	3444	E	951 360-1919	4998
Lynam Industries Inc (PA)	3444	E	951 360-1919	4999
Alabama Metal Industries Corp	3446	E	909 350-9280	5059
Morin Corporation	3448	E	909 428-3747	5085
Fab Services West Inc	3449	D	909 350-7500	5094
Forged Metals Inc	3462	E	909 350-9260	5141
Pacific Forge Inc	3462	D	909 390-0701	5145
Nellxo LLC	3469	D	909 320-8501	5206
Betts Company	3495	E	909 427-9988	5393
American Security Products Co	3499	C	951 685-9680	5440
Superior Trailer Works	3537	E	909 350-0185	5535
Santa Fe Machine Works Inc	3599	E	909 350-6877	6227

	SIC	EMP	PHONE	ENTRY#
Crown Technical Systems (PA)	3613	C	951 332-4170	6302
Eaton Electrical Inc	3625	C	951 685-5788	6348
Harman Professional Inc	3651	C	844 776-4899	6539
Becker Specialty Corporation	3677	D	909 356-1095	6925
DSM&t Co Inc	3694	C	909 357-7960	7090
Kovatch Mobile Equipment Corp	3711	E	951 685-1224	7182
Carlstar Group LLC	3714	D	909 829-1703	7237
S&B Filters Inc (PA)	3714	E	909 947-0015	7291
Utility Trailer Mfg Co	3715	D	909 428-8300	7321
Cargo Solution Brokerage LLC	4212	C	909 350-1644	8899
Hanks Inc	4212	C	909 350-8365	8913
Hub Group Trucking Inc	4212	B	909 770-8950	8918
Cargo Solution Express Inc (PA)	4213	C	800 582-5104	8934
Estes Express Lines	4213	C	909 427-9850	8950
Friends Group Express Inc	4213	D	909 346-6814	8952
Heartland Express Inc Iowa	4213	A	319 626-3600	8954
Swift Leasing Co LLC	4213	B	909 347-0500	8976
TCI Transportation Services	4213	C	909 355-8545	8977
Xpo Logistics Freight Inc	4213	C	951 685-1244	8985
Ontrac Logistics Inc	4215	D	804 334-5000	9009
Advanced Strlztion Pdts Svcs I	4225	C	909 350-6987	9046
Dalton Trucking Inc (PA)	4225	C	909 823-0663	9059
Target Corporation	4225	D	909 355-6000	9116
Blackrock Logistics Inc	4731	C	909 259-5357	9255
Dispatch Trucking LLC (PA)	4731	D	909 355-5531	9272
DSV Solutions LLC	4731	C	909 349-6100	9273
DSV Solutions LLC	4731	D	909 829-5804	9275
Pro Loaders Inc	4731	C	909 355-5531	9328
San Gabriel Valley Water Co	4941	C	909 822-2201	9715
Burrtec Waste Industries Inc (HQ)	4953	C	909 429-4200	9734
Inland Kenworth Inc (HQ)	5012	C	909 823-9955	9803
Los Angeles Truck Centers LLC	5012	C	909 510-4000	9804
Utility Trailer California LLC (PA)	5012	C	877 275-4887	9808
Maxzone Vehicle Lighting Corp (HQ)	5013	E	909 822-3288	9832
Wabash National Trlr Ctrs Inc	5013	E	765 771-5300	9853
48forty Solutions LLC	5031	B	909 371-0101	9917
James Hardie Building Pdts Inc	5031	E	909 355-6500	9923
Patrick Industries Inc	5032	E	909 350-4440	9950
Valori Sand & Gravel Company	5032	C	909 350-3000	9952
Daniel Gerard Worldwide Inc	5051	D	951 361-1111	10132
AC Pro Inc (PA)	5075	C	951 360-7849	10328
Equipment Depot Inc	5084	C	562 949-1000	10373
Orora Packaging Solutions	5113	E	909 770-5400	10601
Moark LLC	5144	D	850 378-2005	10837
Lowes Home Centers LLC	5211	A	909 350-7900	11214
Rotolo Chevrolet Inc	5511	C	866 756-9776	11402
Sunrise Ford	5511	C	909 822-4401	11415
Transwest Truck Center LLC	5511	D	909 770-5170	11424
Boyd Flotation Inc	5712	E	314 997-5222	11512
Castle Importing Inc	5812	E	909 428-9200	11556
Kaiser Foundation Hospitals	6324	B	909 427-3910	12087
Bragg Investment Company Inc	7353	C	909 350-3738	13432
Guzman Grading and Paving Corp	7359	D	909 428-5960	13456
Shipping Tree LLC	7371	D	310 404-9502	13820
Integrated Intermodal Svcs Inc	7379	D	909 355-4100	14225
Social Junky Inc	7389	E	213 999-1275	14600
Bridgestone Americas	7534	E	909 770-8523	14681
Amerit Fleet Solutions Inc	7549	A	909 357-0100	14712
Kaiser Foundation Hospitals	8011	C	909 427-5000	15347
United Fmly Care Inc A Med Cor	8011	C	909 874-1679	15493
Southern Cal Prmnnte Med Group	8062	B	909 427-5000	16207
Fontana Resources At Work	8331	E	909 428-3833	17059
Lamer Street Kreations Corp	8711	E	909 305-4824	17577

FOOTHILL RANCH, CA - Orange County

	SIC	EMP	PHONE	ENTRY#
Nike Inc	2353	E	949 616-4042	2161
Avion Graphics Inc	2752	E	949 472-0438	2965
Protab Laboratories (PA)	2834	D	949 635-1930	3482
Soaptronic LLC	2842	E	949 465-8955	3619
Hampton Products Intl Corp (PA)	3429	C	800 562-5625	4769
Kwikset Corporation	3429	A	949 672-4000	4776
A & J Manufacturing Company	3469	E	714 544-9570	5167
Bal Seal Engineering LLC (DH)	3495	C	949 460-2100	5392
Azure Microdynamics Inc	3599	D	949 699-3344	6087
Renkus-Heinz Inc (PA)	3651	D	949 588-9997	6550
Carttronics LLC (HQ)	3699	E	888 696-2278	7112
Gatekeeper Systems Inc (PA)	3699	D	888 808-9433	7124
Oleumtech Corporation	3823	D	949 305-9009	7871
Ossur Americas Inc	3842	E	949 382-3883	8291
Oakley Inc (DH)	3851	A	949 951-0991	8410
Redcom LLC	3861	B	949 404-4084	8441
Belshire Trnsp Svcs Inc	4212	C	949 460-5200	8896
Cox Communications Inc	4841	A	949 216-9765	9539

	SIC	EMP	PHONE	ENTRY#
Venus Group Inc (PA)	5023	D	949 609-1299	9915
Kawasaki Motors Corp USA (HQ)	5571	B	949 837-4683	11483
Debisys Inc (PA)	6099	D	949 699-1401	11839
US Real Estate Services Inc	6531	D	949 598-9920	12545
Stonebridge Rlty Advisors Inc	7011	B	949 597-8700	13038
Image Options Inc	7319	D	949 586-7665	13275
Ibaset Federal Services LLC (PA)	7371	D	949 598-5200	13745
Nortridge Software LLC	7371	D	714 263-7251	13785
Sun Healthcare Group Inc (DH)	8011	B	949 255-7100	15485
Skilled Healthcare LLC (DH)	8051	D	949 282-5800	15779
Global Solutions Integration	8711	D	949 307-1849	17540
Tae Life Sciences Us LLC	8731	D	949 344-6112	17824
Tae Technologies Inc (PA)	8731	C	949 830-2117	17825

FOREST FALLS, CA - San Bernardino County

	SIC	EMP	PHONE	ENTRY#
Forest Home Inc	7032	C	909 389-2300	13102

FORT IRWIN, CA - San Bernardino County

	SIC	EMP	PHONE	ENTRY#
Northrop Grumman Systems Corp	3812	D	760 380-4268	7760
Lockheed Martin Corporation	4225	C	760 386-2572	9084

FOUNTAIN VALLEY, CA - Orange County

	SIC	EMP	PHONE	ENTRY#
Brightview Companies LLC	0781	C	714 437-1586	151
Rba Builders Inc	1542	D	714 895-9000	576
Pan-Pacific Mechanical LLC (PA)	1711	C	949 474-9170	818
Jmg Security Systems Inc	1731	D	714 545-8882	929
Pacific Aquascape Inc	1799	D	714 843-5734	1219
ML Kishigo Mfg Co LLC	2389	D	949 852-1963	2199
Action Bag & Cover Inc	2393	D	714 965-7777	2227
Duncan McIntosh Company Inc (PA)	2721	E	949 660-6150	2855
Yg Laboratories Inc	2844	E	714 474-2800	3700
Rubber-Cal Inc	3069	E	714 772-3000	3934
Gaffoglio Fmly Mtlcrafters Inc (PA)	3231	C	714 444-2000	4333
KB Sheetmetal Fabrication Inc	3444	E	714 979-1780	4995
Omni Metal Finishing Inc (PA)	3471	E	714 979-9414	5280
Makino Inc	3545	E	714 444-4334	5615
Meyco Machine and Tool Inc	3545	E	714 435-1546	5616
Kingston Technology Company	3572	A	310 729-3394	5881
Kingston Technology Corp (PA)	3577	B	714 435-2600	5927
Avatar Machine LLC	3599	E	714 434-2737	6085
Interconnect Solutions Co LLC (PA)	3629	D	714 556-7007	6377
Surefire LLC (PA)	3648	C	714 545-9444	6518
X Hyper	3651	E	530 673-7099	6571
Nobles Medical Tech Inc	3841	E	714 427-0398	8207
Surefire LLC	3842	E	714 545-9444	8303
Surefire LLC	3842	E	714 545-9444	8304
Surefire LLC	3842	E	714 545-9444	8306
Moving Image Technologies LLC	3861	E	714 751-7998	8434
Shock Doctor Inc (PA)	3949	D	800 233-6956	8541
Shock Doctor Inc	3949	E	657 383-4400	8542
Orange County Water District (PA)	4941	D	714 378-3200	9708
Orange Cnty Snttion Dst Fing C (PA)	4953	B	714 962-2411	9753
Hyundai Motor America (HQ)	5012	B	714 965-3000	9802
Mobis Parts America LLC (HQ)	5013	D	786 515-1101	9835
Kingston Technology Company Inc (HQ)	5045	A	714 435-2600	10014
Custom Power LLC	5063	D	714 962-7600	10179
Tires Warehouse LLC	5531	B	714 432-8851	11469
Ceridian Tax Service Inc	7291	D	714 963-1311	13162
Freightgate Inc	7372	E	714 799-2833	13935
Hyundai Autoever America LLC	7378	A	714 965-3000	14187
Safeguard On Demand Inc	7381	C	800 640-2327	14336
Mile Square Golf Course	7992	C	714 962-5541	15093
Memorlcare Srgcal Ctr At Ornge	8011	C	714 369-1100	15388
Pacs Group Inc	8051	C	714 241-9800	15745
Fountain Vly Rgnal Hosp Med CT	8062	A	714 966-7200	15999
Memorial Health Services (PA)	8062	B	714 377-2900	16094
Orange Coast Memorial Med Ctr (HQ)	8062	A	714 378-7000	16109
Boys Grls Clubs Huntington Vly (PA)	8641	D	714 531-2582	17329
Pacific Advnced Cvil Engrg Inc (PA)	8711	D	714 481-7300	17601
Spec Services Inc	8711	B	714 963-8077	17635
Memorial Healthtec Labratories	8731	C	714 962-4677	17809
Ampm Systems Inc	8742	D	949 629-7800	18091
Bridge SMS Retail Solutions	8748	D	949 629-7800	18292

FRAZIER PARK, CA - Kern County

	SIC	EMP	PHONE	ENTRY#
Trnlwb LLC	3999	A	661 245-3736	8737

FULLERTON, CA - Orange County

	SIC	EMP	PHONE	ENTRY#
Orange County Produce LLC	0171	D	949 451-0880	22
AMS American Mech Svcs MD Inc	1711	C	714 888-6820	737
C & L Refrigeration Corp	1711	C	800 901-4822	757
AJ Kirkwood & Associates Inc	1731	B	714 505-1977	880
Superior Wall Systems Inc	1742	B	714 278-0000	1032

Mergent email: customerrelations@mergent.com
1280

2025 Southern California
Business Directory and Buyers Guide

(P-0000) Products & Services Section entry number
(PA)=Parent Co (HQ)=Headquarters (DH)=Div Headquarters

	SIC	EMP	PHONE	ENTRY#
Kraft Heinz Foods Company	2033	E	714 870-8235	1352
Vanlaw Food Products Inc (HQ)	2035	D	714 870-9091	1373
Charlies Specialties Inc	2052	C	724 346-2350	1483
Phenix Gourmet LLC	2052	C	562 404-5028	1491
Byrnes & Kiefer Co	2087	D	714 554-4000	1671
Dr Smoothie Brands LLC	2087	E	714 449-9787	1676
Chefmaster	2099	E	714 554-4000	1755
Nina Mia Inc	2099	D	714 773-5588	1824
Dae Shin Usa Inc	2221	E	714 578-8900	1391
Fabtex Inc	2221	E	714 538-0877	1894
Delta Pacific Activewear Inc	2253	E	714 871-9281	1915
Anderco Inc	2431	E	714 446-9508	2295
Pacific Archtectural Mllwk Inc	2431	E	714 525-2059	2323
Accurate Laminated Pdts Inc	2434	E	714 632-2773	2336
Brentwood Home LLC (PA)	2515	C	562 949-3759	2481
Nicholas Michael Designs LLC	2519	C	714 562-8101	2503
Amtrend Corporation	2541	D	714 630-2070	2556
Advanced Equipment Corporation (PA)	2542	E	714 635-5350	2576
W/S Packaging Group Inc	2679	E	714 992-2574	2778
Mail Handling Group Inc	2752	C	952 975-5000	3038
Graphics 2000 LLC	2759	E	714 879-1188	3141
Orora Visual LLC	2759	B	714 879-2600	3160
Western States Envelope Corp	2759	D	714 449-0909	3188
Wilsons Art Studio Inc	2759	E	714 870-7030	3189
Nbs Systems Inc (PA)	2761	E	217 999-3472	3193
Professional Plastics Inc (PA)	2821	D	714 446-6500	3288
Cargill Incorporated	2833	E	714 449-6708	3312
Stauber California Inc	2833	D	714 441-3900	3332
Stauber Prfmce Ingredients Inc (HQ)	2833	D	714 441-3900	3333
McKenna Labs Inc (PA)	2834	E	714 687-6888	3448
United Pharma LLC	2834	E	714 738-8999	3516
S & H Rubber Co	3069	E	714 525-0277	3935
Foam-Craft Inc	3086	C	714 459-9971	4002
Future Foam Inc	3086	E	714 871-2344	4004
Future Foam Inc	3086	C	714 459-9971	4005
Chubby Gorilla Inc (PA)	3089	E	844 365-5218	4089
Jdh Pacific Inc (PA)	3321	E	562 926-8088	4558
Howmet Globl Fstning Systems I	3324	A	714 871-1550	4565
Cook and Cook Incorporated	3443	C	714 680-6669	4914
Stein Industries Inc (PA)	3444	D	714 522-4560	5040
Will-Mann Inc	3444	D	714 870-0350	5057
Kryler Corp	3471	E	714 871-9611	5272
Santa Ana Plating (PA)	3471	D	310 923-8305	5291
Aerofit LLC	3498	C	714 521-5060	5423
Golden Pacific Seafoods Inc	3556	E	714 589-8888	5674
Terra Universal Inc (PA)	3564	D	714 526-0100	5779
Label-Aire Inc (PA)	3565	D	714 449-5155	5791
HP It Services Incorporated	3577	E	714 844-7737	5921
Laser Industries Inc	3599	E	714 532-3271	6165
Oem LLC	3599	E	714 449-7500	6196
Thunderbolt Manufacturing Inc	3599	E	714 632-0397	6250
Direct Drive Systems Inc	3621	E	714 872-5500	6320
Golden West Technology	3672	E	714 738-3574	6733
Winonics Inc	3672	E	714 626-3755	6789
Printec Ht Electronics LLC	3674	E	714 484-7597	6870
Magtech & Power Conversion Inc	3677	E	714 451-0106	6930
Ultra Wheel Company	3714	E	714 449-7100	7304
Marton Precision Mfg LLC	3724	E	714 808-6523	7392
Adams Rite Aerospace Inc (DH)	3728	E	714 278-6500	7403
Hydraflow	3728	B	714 773-2600	7491
Consolidated Aerospace Mfg LLC (HQ)	3812	E	714 989-2797	7709
Raytheon Company	3812	E	714 732-0119	7799
Aurident Incorporated	3843	E	714 870-1851	8020
Pacmin Incorporated (PA)	3999	D	714 447-4478	8709
South Coast Trnsp & Dist Inc	4212	E	310 816-0280	8923
RPM Consolidated Services Inc (HQ)	4225	D	714 388-3500	9106
Hub Group Los Angeles LLC	4731	E	714 449-6300	9294
Neovia Logistics Dist LP	4731	B	815 552-5900	9316
Total Logistics Online LLC	4731	C	714 526-3559	9345
Tri-Tech Logistics LLC	4731	C	855 373-7049	9347
Eeg Glider Inc (HQ)	4899	C	310 437-6000	9564
Southern California Edison Co	4911	B	714 870-3225	9618
Ware Disposal Inc	4953	D	714 834-0234	9773
Petes Road Service Inc (PA)	5014	D	714 446-1207	9859
McKesson Mdcl-Srgcal Top Hldng	5047	B	800 300-4350	10090
US Electrical Services Inc	5063	E	714 982-1534	10211
North American Video Corp (PA)	5065	E	714 779-7499	10273
Raytheon Cmmand Ctrl Sltons LL (DH)	5065	A	714 446-3118	10282
Orora Packaging Solutions	5113	C	714 278-6000	10605
Hidden Villa Ranch Produce Inc (HQ)	5144	B	714 680-3447	10835
Bakery Ex Southern Cal LLC	5149	D	714 446-9100	10931
Home Depot USA Inc	5211	D	714 459-4909	11194
Vista Paint Corporation (PA)	5231	C	714 680-3800	11256

	SIC	EMP	PHONE	ENTRY#
Kaylas Cake Corporation	5461	E	714 869-1522	11297
Plasticolor Molded Pdts Inc (PA)	5531	C	714 525-3880	11453
North Ornge Cnty Cmnty Cllege	5942	B	714 992-7008	11633
Altura Holdings LLC	6722	B	714 948-8400	12625
Huoyen International Inc	7011	D	714 635-9000	12860
Merritt Hospitality LLC	7011	C	714 738-7800	12921
Advanced Image Direct LLC	7331	C	714 502-3900	13298
Real Estate Image Inc (PA)	7331	C	714 502-3900	13305
Volt Management Corp	7363	D	714 879-9330	13633
Aspirez Inc	7371	E	714 485-8104	13660
New Pride Tire LLC	7534	E	310 631-7000	14682
Emeritus Corporation	8051	C	714 441-0644	15634
Fullerton Hlthcare Wllness CNT	8051	C	714 992-5701	15659
St Jude Hospital (DH)	8062	A	714 871-3280	16219
Marshall B Ketchum University (PA)	8221	C	714 463-7567	16833
Autism Spctrum Intrvntions LLC	8322	C	562 972-4846	16872
Turning Point Ministries	8322	D	800 998-6329	17019
Corecare I I I	8361	C	714 256-8000	17135
Florence Crttnton Svcs Ornge C	8361	B	714 680-9000	17153
Independent Options Inc	8361	D	714 738-4991	17169
Bon Suisse Inc	8748	E	714 578-0001	18291

GARDEN GROVE, CA - Orange County

	SIC	EMP	PHONE	ENTRY#
Terra Pacific Landscape (HQ)	0781	D	714 567-0177	195
Structral Prsrvtion Systems LL	1771	D	714 891-9080	1136
Flowers Bkg Co Henderson LLC	2051	D	702 281-4797	1449
Sanyo Foods Corp America (DH)	2098	E	714 891-3671	1735
House Foods America Corp (HQ)	2099	E	714 901-4350	1790
Quoc Viet Foods (PA)	2099	E	714 283-3663	1838
Pacific Athletic Wear Inc	2339	D	714 751-8006	2124
Bodywaves Inc (PA)	2369	E	714 898-9900	2168
L C Pringle Sales Inc (PA)	2591	E	714 892-1524	2605
Commercial Cstm Sting Uphl Inc	2599	E	714 850-0520	2610
Teacher Created Resources Inc	2731	C	714 230-7060	2896
Wtpc Inc	2752	E	714 903-2500	3104
Elasco Inc	2821	D	714 373-4767	3265
Elasco Urethane Inc	2821	E	714 895-7031	3266
Holcim Solutions & Pdts US LLC	2821	D	714 898-0025	3269
Saint-Gobain Prfmce Plas Corp	2821	C	714 893-0470	3291
Saint-Gobain Prfmce Plas Corp	2821	D	714 630-5818	3292
Uremet Corporation	2821	E	657 257-4027	3300
St Paul Brands Inc	2824	E	714 903-1000	3306
Mycelium Enterprises LLC	2833	E	657 251-0016	3321
A Q Pharmaceuticals Inc	2834	E	714 903-1000	3335
Beauty & Health International	2834	E	714 903-9730	3371
Leiner Health Products Inc	2834	C	714 898-9936	3443
Goodwin Ammonia Company LLC	2841	D	714 894-0531	3593
Cali Chem Inc	2844	E	714 265-3740	3637
Everbrands Inc	2844	E	855 595-2999	3651
Advanced Chemistry & Technology Inc	2891	D	714 373-8118	3758
GKN Arpsace Trnsprncy Systems	3089	B	714 893-7531	4128
Jason Tool and Engineering Inc	3089	E	714 895-5067	4145
Peerless Injection Molding LLC	3089	E	714 689-1920	4194
Customfab Inc	3111	C	714 891-9119	4277
Cham-Cal Engineering Co	3231	E	714 898-9721	4331
CTS Cement Manufacturing Corp (PA)	3241	E	714 379-8260	4354
Hyatt Die Cast Engrg Corp - S	3363	E	714 622-2131	4647
Kittyhawk Inc (PA)	3398	E	714 895-5024	4703
Kittyhawk Products CA LLC	3398	E	714 895-5024	4704
Kpi Services Inc	3398	E	714 895-5024	4705
Container Supply Company Incorporated	3411	C	714 892-8321	4720
Umpco Inc	3429	D	714 897-3531	4793
V & F Fabrication Company Ino	3441	D	714 265-0630	4877
Vts Sheetmetal Specialist Co	3444	E	714 237-1420	5055
TI Machine Inc	3451	E	714 554-4154	5115
Houston Bazz Co	3469	E	714 898-2666	5192
Coastline Metal Finishing Corp	3471	D	714 895-9099	5251
Intra Storage Systems Inc	3499	E	714 373-2346	5448
Plantronics Inc	3571	C	714 897-0808	5864
Bar Code Specialties Inc	3577	E	877 411-2633	5904
Aero Dynamic Machining Inc	3599	D	714 379-1073	6067
I Copy Inc	3599	E	562 921-0202	6145
Kimberly Machine Inc	3599	E	714 539-0151	6161
Spartan Manufacturing Co	3599	E	714 894-1955	6242
Western Precision Aero LLC	3599	E	714 893-7999	6274
Microsemi Corp-Power MGT Group	3625	C	714 994-6500	6354
Fei-Zyfer Inc (HQ)	3663	E	714 933-4000	6615
Exigent Sensors LLC	3669	E	949 439-1321	6683
Microsemi Corp - Anlog Mxed Sg (DH)	3674	D	714 898-8121	6852
Microsemi Corp -Rf Signal Proc (HQ)	3674	E	949 380-6100	6853
Microsemi Corporation	3674	E	714 898-8000	6854
Vitesse Manufacturing & Dev	3674	C	805 388-3700	6912
Basic Electronics Inc	3679	E	714 530-2400	6971

Employee Codes: A=Over 500 employees, B=251-500
C=101-250, D=51-100, E=20-50, F=10-19, G=1-9

2025 Southern California
Business Directory and Buyers Guide

© Mergent Inc. 1-800-342-5647

1281

GEOGRAPHIC

Name	SIC	EMP	PHONE	ENTRY#
Harbinger Motors Inc	3711	C	714 684-1067	7180
Allied Wheel Components Inc	3714	E	800 529-4335	7223
Driveshaftpro	3714	E	714 893-4585	7248
King Shock Technology Inc	3714	D	719 394-3754	7264
Walker Products	3714	E	714 554-5151	7308
GKN Aerospace	3721	C	714 653-7531	7355
Jvr Sheetmetal Fabrication Inc	3721	E	714 841-2464	7360
Align Precision - Anaheim Inc (DH)	3728	D	714 961-9200	7425
B & E Manufacturing Co Inc	3728	E	714 898-2269	7441
C&D Zodiac Aerospace	3728	E	714 891-0683	7446
Safran Cabin Inc	3728	C	714 901-2672	7552
Safran Cabin Inc	3728	C	714 891-1906	7554
SPS Technologies LLC	3728	E	714 892-5571	7567
Talsco Inc	3728	E	714 841-2464	7574
Tj Aerospace Inc	3728	E	714 891-3564	7579
King Instrument Company Inc	3823	E	714 891-0008	7864
Sensorex Corporation	3823	D	714 895-4344	7878
Touch International Display Enhance	3827	C	512 646-0310	8026
Hycor Biomedical LLC	3841	C	714 933-3000	8162
Elite Screens Inc	3861	E	877 511-1211	8426
Iron Grip Barbell Company Inc	3949	D	714 850-6900	8528
Evans Manufacturing LLC (HQ)	3993	C	714 379-6100	8602
Innovative Casework Mfg Inc	3999	E	714 890-9100	8685
Orange Cnty Trnsp Auth Schlrsh	4111	D	714 560-6282	8793
Carroll Shelby Licensing Inc	4225	D	310 914-1843	9052
Sprint Communications Co LP	4813	C	714 534-2107	9461
Tekworks Inc	4813	E	877 835-9675	9464
Video Vice Data Communications (PA)	4841	C	714 897-6300	9559
Winchester Interconnect EC LLC	5065	D	714 230-6122	10298
Penn Elcom Inc (HQ)	5072	E	714 230-6200	10311
Bodykore Inc	5091	E	949 325-3088	10511
Qyk Brands LLC	5122	C	833 795-7664	10648
R D Abbott Co Inc	5169	D	562 944-5354	11019
Home Depot USA Inc	5211	C	714 539-0319	11199
Noarus Tgg	5511	E	714 895-5595	11389
Abbey-Properties LLC (PA)	6512	D	562 435-2100	12278
Irvine APT Communities LP	6513	E	714 537-8500	12352
Cushman & Wakefield Cal Inc	6531	B	714 591-0451	12420
Great Wolf Rsorts Holdings Inc	7011	C	888 960-9653	12834
Ohi Resort Hotels LLC	7011	D	714 867-5555	12948
Mastroianni Family Entps Ltd	7299	B	310 952-1700	13179
Compass Group Usa Inc	7359	C	714 899-2520	13453
Tad Pgs Inc	7363	A	800 261-3779	13625
Revco Products	7372	D	714 891-6688	14020
Webx360 Inc	7375	D	714 896-8004	14180
Brinks Incorporated	7381	C	714 903-9272	14282
Lao-Hmong Security Agency Inc	7381	C	714 533-6776	14313
Aaron Thomas Company Inc (PA)	7389	C	714 894-4468	14433
St George Auto Center Inc	7539	D	657 212-5042	14703
Kaiser Foundation Hospitals	8011	C	714 741-3448	15340
Garden Grove Medical Investors (HQ)	8051	C	714 534-1041	15661
Pacific Haven Convalescent HM	8059	D	714 534-1942	15879
Childrens Hospital Orange Cnty	8062	B	714 638-5990	15956
Kenneth Corp	8062	A	714 537-5160	16060
Garden Grove Unified Schl Dst	8211	D	714 663-6101	16807
Boys Grls Clubs Grdn Grove Inc (PA)	8299	C	714 530-0430	16851
Community Action Prtnr Ornge C	8322	C	714 897-6670	16897
Garden Grove Unified Schl Dst	8351	C	714 663-6437	17091
Crystal Cathedral Ministries (PA)	8661	C	714 622-2900	17414

GARDENA, CA - Los Angeles County

Name	SIC	EMP	PHONE	ENTRY#
Brightview Landscape Svcs Inc	0781	B	310 327-8700	159
K C Restoration Co Inc	1389	E	310 280-0597	341
Disaster Rstrtion Prfssnals In	1521	D	310 301-8030	399
XCEL Mechanical Systems Inc	1711	C	310 660-0090	855
Arena Painting Contractors Inc	1721	D	310 316-2446	859
Martin Bros/Marcowall Inc (PA)	1742	C	310 532-5335	1014
Best Contracting Services Inc (PA)	1761	B	310 328-9176	1073
Weiss Sheet Metal Company	1761	E	310 354-2700	1099
Anvil Steel Corporation	1791	D	310 329-5811	1148
Washington Orna Ir Works Inc (PA)	1799	D	310 327-8660	1231
Better Nutritionals LLC	2023	E	310 356-9019	1294
Vitamin Friends LLC	2023	E	310 356-9018	1309
La Mousse Desserts Inc	2038	E	310 478-6051	1395
Hannahmax Baking Inc	2051	C	310 380-6778	1458
Little Brothers Bakery LLC	2051	D	310 225-3790	1460
Ocean Direct LLC (HQ)	2092	C	424 266-9300	1710
Nissin Foods USA Company Inc (DH)	2098	C	310 327-8478	1733
Lets Do Lunch	2099	B	310 523-3664	1807
Risvolds Inc	2099	D	323 770-2674	1843
Sabater Usa Inc (PA)	2099	E	310 518-2227	1848
Tu Madre Romana Inc	2099	E	323 321-6041	1863
Stanzino Inc (PA)	2211	E	213 746-8822	1887
Twin Dragon Marketing Inc (PA)	2211	E	310 715-7070	1889
Caitac Garment Processing Inc	2261	B	310 217-9888	1931
Barco Uniforms Inc	2311	D	310 323-7315	1975
Stringking Inc (PA)	2311	E	310 503-8901	1979
True Religion Apparel Inc (HQ)	2325	B	855 928-6124	1993
Global Casuals Inc	2329	E	310 817-2828	2012
Gloria Lance Inc (PA)	2331	D	310 767-4400	2036
La Palm Furnitures & ACC Inc (PA)	2395	E	310 217-2700	2248
D and J Marketing Inc	2396	E	310 538-1583	2258
Parquet By Dian	2426	D	310 527-3779	2291
Ohline Corporation	2431	E	310 327-4630	2319
Martin/Brattrud Inc	2512	D	323 770-4171	2454
A M Cabinets Inc (PA)	2521	D	310 532-1919	2504
New Maverick Desk Inc	2521	C	310 217-1554	2511
Louis Sardo Upholstery Inc (PA)	2531	E	310 327-0532	2549
One Up Manufacturing LLC	2631	E	310 749-8347	2641
Wrkco Inc	2631	E	310 532-8988	2647
Sgl Composites Inc (DH)	2655	D	424 329-5250	2697
Triune Enterprises Inc	2671	E	310 719-1600	2713
Community Media Corporation (PA)	2711	E	714 220-0292	2791
Gardena Valley News Inc	2711	E	310 329-6351	2798
Take A Break Paper	2711	E	323 333-7773	2831
Americhip Inc (PA)	2752	E	310 323-3697	2961
Matsuda House Printing Inc	2752	E	310 532-1533	3042
Southwest Offset Prtg Co Inc (PA)	2752	E	310 965-9154	3082
UNI-Sport Inc	2752	E	310 217-4587	3094
Continental Bdr Specialty Corp (PA)	2782	C	310 324-8227	3198
US Blanks LLC (PA)	2821	E	310 225-6774	3301
CH Laboratories Inc (PA)	2834	E	310 516-8273	3387
West Coast Laboratories Inc	2834	E	310 527-6163	3523
Cilajet LLC	2842	E	310 320-8000	3601
Grow More Inc	2879	D	310 515-1700	3755
Matsui International Co Inc (HQ)	2899	E	310 767-7812	3813
Evergreen Oil Inc (HQ)	2992	E	949 757-7770	3854
Principle Plastics	3021	E	310 532-3411	3871
Lite Extrusions Mfg Inc	3083	E	323 770-4298	3965
Narayan Corporation	3085	E	310 719-7330	3985
Amfoam Inc (PA)	3086	E	310 327-4003	3993
Barnes Plastics Inc	3089	E	310 329-6301	4062
Getpart La Inc	3089	E	424 331-9599	4125
Pro Design Group Inc	3089	E	310 767-1032	4211
Rotational Molding Inc	3089	D	310 327-5401	4227
Pacific Artglass Corporation	3231	E	310 516-7828	4342
Arto Brick / California Pavers	3251	E	310 768-8500	4360
McFiebow Inc (PA)	3272	E	310 327-7474	4400
US Hanger Company LLC	3315	E	310 323-8030	4545
Del Mar Industries (PA)	3364	D	323 321-0600	4658
Cast-Rite International Inc (PA)	3369	D	310 532-2080	4686
International Die Casting Inc	3369	E	310 324-2278	4690
Maya Steel Fabrications Inc	3441	D	310 532-8830	4849
Thermlly Engnred Mnfctred Pdts	3443	E	310 523-9934	4932
Aero ARC	3444	E	310 324-3400	4940
All-Ways Metal Inc	3444	E	310 217-1177	4943
American Aircraft Products Inc	3444	D	310 532-7434	4946
Artistic Welding	3444	D	310 515-4922	4953
Bay Cities Tin Shop Inc	3444	C	310 660-0351	4956
Carla Senter	3444	E	310 366-7295	4965
Meadows Sheet Metal and AC Inc	3444	D	310 615-1125	5004
Ramda Metal Specialties Inc	3444	E	310 538-2136	5028
T & F Sheet Mtls Fab McHning I	3444	E	310 516-8548	5044
Versafab Corp (PA)	3444	E	800 421-1822	5053
Lni Custom Manufacturing Inc	3446	E	310 978-2000	5069
Washington Orna Ir Works Inc	3446	E	310 327-8660	5073
North Star Acquisition Inc	3449	D	310 515-2200	5099
GT Precision Inc	3451	C	310 323-4374	5108
Onyx Industries Inc	3451	E	310 851-6161	5110
Briles Aerospace LLC	3452	D	424 320-3817	5120
Paul R Briles Inc	3452	A	310 323-6222	5134
Binder Metal Products Inc	3469	D	800 233-0896	5175
Metco Manufacturing Inc	3469	E	310 516-6547	5202
Coast Plating Inc (PA)	3471	E	323 770-0240	5249
Gsp Metal Finishing Inc	3471	E	818 744-1328	5265
Faber Enterprises Inc	3492	C	310 323-6200	5374
Wyrefab Inc	3496	D	310 523-2147	5422
Tru-Cut Inc	3524	E	310 630-0422	5484
US Industrial Tool & Sup Co	3542	E	310 464-8400	5563
Cast-Rite Corporation	3544	D	310 532-2080	5571
Aqua Pro Properties Vii LP	3559	E	310 516-9911	5689
Mars Air Systems LLC	3564	D	310 532-1555	5773
American Condenser & Coil LLC	3585	D	310 327-8600	5966
Vege-Mist Inc	3585	D	310 353-2300	5991
Clean Water Technology Inc (HQ)	3589	E	310 380-4648	6009
Timbucktoo Manufacturing Inc	3589	E	310 323-1134	6035

Company	SIC	EMP	PHONE	ENTRY#
Brek Manufacturing Co	3599	C	310 329-7638	6099
Century Precision Engrg Inc	3599	E	310 538-0015	6104
German Machined Products Inc	3599	E	310 532-4480	6135
J & S Inc	3599	E	310 719-7144	6148
Research Metal Industries Inc	3599	E	310 352-3200	6217
Kc Hilites Inc	3647	E	928 635-2607	6485
Mj Best Videographer LLC	3651	C	209 208-8432	6545
Centron Industries Inc	3663	E	310 324-6443	6603
Inca One Corporation	3675	E	310 808-0001	6918
Rayco Electronic Mfg Inc	3677	E	310 329-2660	6936
Polar Power Inc	3694	D	310 830-9153	7099
Servexo	3699	C	323 527-9994	7151
Prime Wheel Corporation (PA)	3714	A	310 516-9126	7283
Prime Wheel Corporation	3714	E	310 819-4123	7285
Ahf-Ducommun Incorporated (HQ)	3728	C	310 380-5390	7418
Designed Metal Connections Inc (DH)	3728	B	310 323-6200	7462
Impresa Aerospace LLC	3728	C	310 354-1200	7498
Nasco Aircraft Brake Inc	3728	D	310 532-4430	7529
Space-Lok Inc	3728	C	310 527-6150	7565
Space Exploration Tech Corp	3761	C	323 754-1285	7653
Radiology Support Devices Inc	3841	E	310 518-0527	8221
Wcbm Company (PA)	3965	E	323 262-3274	8580
Clegg Industries Inc	3993	C	310 225-3800	8593
Neighbrhood Bus Advrtsment Ltd	3999	E	442 300-1803	8703
Sgps Inc	3999	D	310 538-4175	8723
Steeldeck Inc	3999	E	323 290-2100	8728
Tandem Design Inc	3999	E	714 978-7272	8733
Wally & Pat Enterprises	3999	E	310 532-2031	8739
First Transit Inc	4111	D	323 222-0010	8751
Global Paratransit Inc	4119	B	310 715-7550	8829
Administrative Svcs Coop Inc	4121	C	310 715-1968	8857
First Student Inc	4151	A	310 769-2400	8880
United Parcel Service Inc	4215	C	310 217-2646	9017
F R T International Inc	4225	D	310 329-5700	9064
World Svc Wst/La Inflght Svc L	4581	C	310 538-7000	9213
Nippon Travel Agency Amer Inc	4724	D	310 768-1817	9229
Nippon Travel Agency PCF Inc (DH)	4724	D	310 768-0017	9230
Hanjin Transportation Co Ltd	4731	D	310 522-5030	9291
Comprehensive Dist Svcs Inc	4789	C	310 523-1546	9361
Sprint Communications Co LP	4812	C	310 515-0293	9412
California Waste Services LLC	4953	C	310 538-5998	9736
Waste MGT Collectn Recycl Inc	4953	C	310 532-6511	9782
Cleanstreet LLC	4959	C	800 225-7316	9786
Tireco Inc (PA)	5014	C	310 767-7990	9861
Canon Business Solutions-West Inc	5044	B	310 217-3000	9971
Tool Components Inc (PA)	5051	E	310 323-5613	10161
Magnetika Inc (PA)	5063	D	310 527-8100	10191
Mutual Liquid Gas & Eqp Co Inc (PA)	5084	E	310 515-0553	10384
Mills Iron Works	5085	D	323 321-6520	10449
SPS Technologies LLC	5085	B	310 323-6222	10465
Valley of Sun Cosmetics LLC	5122	C	310 327-9062	10656
La Dye & Print Inc	5137	E	310 327-3200	10712
Phoenix Textile Inc (PA)	5137	D	310 715-7090	10721
Usfi Inc	5141	D	424 260-9210	10815
Field Fresh Foods Incorporated	5148	A	310 719-8422	10897
Spectrum Laboratory Pdts Inc	5169	E	520 292-3103	11020
DCH Gardena Honda	5511	C	310 515-5700	11335
South Bay Toyota	5511	C	310 323-7800	11409
Carson Trailer Inc (PA)	5599	D	310 835-0876	11486
Guru Denim LLC (DH)	5611	C	323 266-3072	11488
J & M Sales Inc	5651	A	310 324-9962	11497
B & W Tile Co Inc (PA)	5713	C	310 538-9579	11520
Air Fayre USA Inc	5812	C	310 808-1061	11549
Kings Hawaiian Bakery W Inc (HQ)	5812	E	310 533-3250	11583
Ruggable LLC	5961	B	310 295-0098	11663
Episource LLC	6411	A	714 452-1961	12206
Monark LP	6513	D	310 769-6669	12359
El Dorado Enterprises Inc	7011	A	310 719-9800	12819
Radiant Services Corp (PA)	7211	C	310 327-6300	13111
CM Laundry LLC	7219	C	310 436-6170	13143
Pulp Studio Incorporated	7336	D	310 815-4999	13334
Maxim Healthcare Services Inc	7363	C	310 329-9115	13607
Secom International (PA)	7373	D	310 641-1290	14106
American Guard Services Inc (PA)	7381	B	310 645-6200	14271
Construction Protective Services Inc (PA)	7381	C	800 257-5512	14287
Eagle Security Services Inc	7381	C	310 642-0656	14297
United Facility Solutions Inc	7381	B	310 743-3000	14357
Vescom Corporation (PA)	7381	A	207 945-5051	14366
Vets Securing America Inc	7381	C	310 645-6200	14367
Wsa Group Inc	7381	C	310 743-3000	14371
New Crew Production Corp	7389	C	323 234-8880	14556
Hansens Welding Inc	7692	E	310 329-6888	14740
Nike Usa Inc	7941	A	310 670-6770	15033
Healthcare Investments Inc	8051	C	310 323-3194	15674
Clear View Sanitarium Inc	8059	C	310 538-2323	15843
Gardena Hospital LP	8062	A	310 532-4200	16001
Kaiser Foundation Hospitals	8062	A	310 517-2956	16033
Counseling and Research Assoc (PA)	8361	C	310 715-2020	17136
Special Service For Groups Inc	8399	C	310 323-6887	17244
Prototype Engineering and Manufacturing Inc	8711	E	310 532-6305	17614
Ceridian LLC	8721	D	310 719-7481	17711
Navigant Cymetrix Corporation	8741	D	424 201-6300	18017
Transcosmos Omniconnect LLC	8741	D	310 630-0072	18067
Doppler Automotive Inc	8742	D	310 765-4100	18128
Nissan North America Inc	8742	A	310 768-3700	18182

GLENDALE, CA - Los Angeles County

Company	SIC	EMP	PHONE	ENTRY#
Triangle Rock Products LLC	1429	C	818 553-8820	373
Kennard Development Group	1522	D	818 241-0800	448
PCL Construction Services Inc	1542	C	818 246-3481	566
H L Moe Co Inc (PA)	1711	C	818 572-2100	785
Pinnacle Networking Svcs Inc	1731	D	818 241-6009	951
Nestle Usa Inc	2023	C	818 549-6000	1304
Pillsbury Company LLC	2041	E	818 522-3952	1406
Nestle Purina Petcare Company	2047	E	314 982-1000	1422
Mad Engine Global LLC (HQ)	2253	D	858 558-5270	1923
Avery Dennison Foundation	2672	E	626 304-2000	2718
Avery Dnnson Ret Info Svcs LLC (HQ)	2678	C	626 304-2000	2756
California Community News LLC	2711	D	818 843-8700	2783
Chromatic Inc Lithographers	2752	E	818 242-5785	2978
Color Inc	2752	E	818 240-1350	2981
Colour Concepts Inc	2752	C		2984
Zoo Printing Inc (PA)	2752	E	310 253-7751	3105
4 Over LLC (HQ)	2759	E	818 246-1170	3111
Legion Creative Group	2759	E	323 498-1100	3154
Person & Covey Inc	2844	E	818 937-5000	3678
Stila Styles LLC (HQ)	2844	E	866 784-5201	3689
Vege - Kurl Inc	2844	D	818 956-5582	3695
K-Swiss Inc (DH)	3021	E	323 675-2700	3868
K-Swiss Sales Corp	3021	C	323 675-2700	3869
Yates Gear Inc	3199	D	530 222-4606	4311
Cygnet Stmping Fabg Inc A Swan (PA)	3469	E	818 240-7574	5179
Automation Plating Corporation	3471	E	323 245-4951	5236
SAI Industries	3484	E	818 842-6144	5355
Ambrit Industries Inc	3542	E	818 243-1224	5556
Pennoyer-Dodge Co	3545	D	818 547-2100	5618
Cryst Mark Inc A Swan Techno C	3559	E	818 240-7520	5699
International Bus Mchs Corp	3571	A	818 553-8100	5855
Modern Engine Inc	3599	E	818 409-9494	6183
Arecont Vision LLC	3629	C	818 937-0700	6367
Glenair Inc (PA)	3643	B	818 247-6000	6420
Bittree Incorporated	3663	E	818 500-8142	6600
Mv Transportation Inc	4111	B	818 409-3387	8776
Pegasus Maritime Inc	4731	D	714 728-8565	9324
Ambiance Transportation LLC	4789	D	818 955-5757	9358
American Transportation Co LLC	4789	D	818 660-2343	9359
City of Glendale	4911	D	818 548-3980	9574
City of Glendale	4941	D	818 548-2011	9684
United Merchant Svcs Cal Inc	5044	D	818 246-6767	9980
H and H Drug Stores Inc (HQ)	5047	D	818 956-6691	10083
Global Plumbing & Fire Supply	5074	C	818 550-8444	10318
Otis Elevator Company	5084	D	818 241-2828	10388
Simon G Jewelry Inc	5094	E	818 500-8595	10552
Mader News Inc	5192	D	818 551-5000	11077
Allen Gwynn Chevrolet Inc	5511	D	818 240-0000	11315
Los Feliz Ford Inc (PA)	5511	D	818 502-1901	11374
Chop Stop Inc	5812	D	818 369-7350	11559
Pop Mart Americas Inc	5945	D	415 640-8197	11644
Forest Lawn Memorial-Park Assn (PA)	5992	B	323 254-3131	11669
Los Angeles Federal Credit Un (PA)	6061	D	818 242-8640	11804
California Credit Union (PA)	6062	C	818 291-6700	11824
Associates First Capital Corp	6141	C	818 248-7055	11849
Countrywide Home Loans Inc	6162	A	818 550-8700	11894
Carelon Med Benefits MGT Inc	6321	A	847 310-0366	12061
Cigna Behavioral Health of Cal	6324	C	800 753-0540	12076
Cigna Healthcare Cal Inc (DH)	6324	B	818 500-6262	12077
Califrnia Insur Guarantee Assn	6411	C	818 844-4300	12187
Dedicted Dfned Beneft Svcs LLC	6411	C	415 931-1990	12201
Dma Claims Inc	6411	C	877 880-3616	12203
Dma Claims Management Inc	6411	D	323 342-6800	12204
Safeco Insurance Company Amer	6411	C	818 956-4250	12251
Glendale Associates Ltd	6512	D	818 246-6737	12294
BV General Inc	6513	D	818 244-2323	12334
Humangood Socal	6513	C	818 244-7219	12346
Pango Group Inc	6531	D	818 502-0400	12500
Anywhere Integrated Svcs LLC	6541	B	818 291-4400	12553

GEOGRAPHIC

Employee Codes: A=Over 500 employees, B=251-500
C=101-250, D=51-100, E=20-50, F=10-19, G=1-9

2025 Southern California
Business Directory and Buyers Guide

© Mergent Inc. 1-800-342-5647
1283

	SIC	EMP	PHONE	ENTRY#
Equity Title Company (DH)	6541	D	818 291-4400	12556
Stewart Title California Inc	6541	C	818 502-2700	12562
Wfg National Title Insur Co (PA)	6541	B	818 476-4000	12563
Forest Lawn Co	6553	C	818 241-4151	12583
Public Storage (PA)	6798	B	818 244-8080	12693
Public Storage Operating Co (DH)	6798	D	818 244-8080	12694
JP Allen Extended Stay (PA)	7011	D	818 956-0202	12879
Asab Inc (DH)	7338	C	818 551-7300	13339
AppleOne Inc	7361	C	818 240-8688	13486
AppleOne Inc (HQ)	7361	C	818 240-8688	13487
E Z Staffing Inc (PA)	7361	B	818 845-2500	13511
Hrn Services Inc	7361	D	323 951-1450	13525
Akkodis Inc	7371	C	818 546-2848	13646
Disney Interactive Studios Inc	7371	B	818 560-1000	13709
Servicetitan Inc (PA)	7371	A	855 899-0970	13818
Systech Solutions Inc (PA)	7371	D	818 550-9690	13836
Lumenova Ai Inc	7372	E	310 694-2461	13969
Sparktech Software LLC	7372	C	818 330-9098	14035
Legalzoomcom Inc (PA)	7374	B	323 962-8600	14141
Yp Holdings LLC	7374	A	818 649-8772	14164
Assign Corporation	7379	C	818 247-7100	14197
General Networks Corporation	7379	D	818 249-1962	14222
Software Management Cons LLC (HQ)	7379	D	818 240-3177	14254
Grandall Distributing LLC	7389	E	818 242-6640	14505
Isovac Engineering Inc	7389	E	818 552-6200	14519
Productive Playhouse Inc (PA)	7389	C	323 250-3445	14575
Yellowpagescom LLC (DH)	7389	B	818 937-5500	14637
Passport Technology Usa Inc	7699	E	818 957-5471	14781
Bunim-Murray Productions	7812	C	818 756-5100	14810
Disney Enterprises Inc	7812	B	818 553-4103	14821
Dreamworks Animation Pubg LLC	7812	A	818 695-5000	14823
Dwa Holdings LLC (DH)	7812	D	818 695-5000	14824
Walt Disney Pictures	7812	B	818 409-2200	14871
Walt Dsney Imgnring RES Dev In (DH)	7819	A	818 544-6500	14914
Sega Entertainment USA Inc	7993	C	310 217-9500	15101
Oakmont Country Club	7997	C	818 542-4260	15156
Kaiser Foundation Hospitals	8011	C	818 552-3000	15363
Country Villa Service Corp	8051	C	818 246-5516	15608
Emeritus Corporation	8051	C	818 246-7457	15631
Griffith Pk Rhbltation Ctr LLC	8051	D	818 845-8507	15670
Ksm Healthcare Inc	8051	D	818 242-1183	15688
Mariner Health Care Inc	8051	C	818 246-5677	15714
Buena Ventura Care Center Inc	8059	D	818 247-4476	15841
Front Prch Cmmnties Oprting Gr	8059	C	800 233-3709	15853
Longwood Management Corp	8059	C	818 246-7174	15871
American Hlthcare Systems Corp (PA)	8062	B	818 646-9933	15909
Glendale Adventist Medical Ctr (HQ)	8062	A	818 409-8000	16003
Glendale Mem Hlth Foundation	8062	D	818 502-2375	16004
Glendale Memorial Health Corp	8062	A	818 502-2323	16005
Glendale Memorial Health Corporation	8062	A	818 502-1900	16006
Glenoaks Convalescent Hospital	8062	D	818 240-4300	16007
Usc Verdugo Hills Hospital LLC	8062	A	818 790-7100	16250
Usc Vrdugo Hlls Hosp Fundation (HQ)	8062	B	800 872-2273	16251
Verdugo Hills Hospital Inc	8062	C	818 790-7100	16254
Pegasus HM Hlth Care A Cal Cor	8082	D	818 551-1932	16410
Interstate Rhbltation Svcs LLC	8093	C	818 244-5656	16482
Prime Mso LLC	8093	D	818 937-9969	16495
Christie Parker & Hale LLP (PA)	8111	C	626 795-9900	16656
La Folltte Jhnson De Haas Fsle (PA)	8111	C	213 426-3600	16723
National Attny Collection Svcs	8111	B	818 547-9760	16750
Myhhbs Inc	8322	D	888 969-4427	16980
RES-Care Inc	8361	C	818 637-7727	17191
Young MNS Chrstn Assn Glndale	8641	D	818 484-8256	17403
City of Glendale	8711	D	818 548-3945	17502
Avery Corp	8731	C	626 304-2000	17772
Disney Research Pittsburgh	8731	C	412 623-1800	17784
Noymed Corp	8731	C	800 224-2090	17815
Allzone Management Svcs Inc	8741	B	213 291-8879	17938
Amco Foods Inc	8742	B	818 247-4716	18090
Gavin De Becker & Assoc GP LLC	8742	C	818 505-0177	18141
PSI Services LLC (PA)	8748	D	818 847-6180	18351
Ventegra Inc A Cal Beneft Corp	8748	D	858 551-8111	18365

GLENDORA, CA - Los Angeles County

	SIC	EMP	PHONE	ENTRY#
CJd Construction Svcs Inc	1389	E	626 335-1116	325
BR Building Resources Co	1542	C	626 963-4880	524
Building Elctronic Contrls Inc (PA)	1731	E	909 305-1600	893
Deccofelt Corporation	2299	E	626 963-8511	1969
G R Leonard & Co Inc	2741	E	847 797-8101	2916
Calportland Company (DH)	3241	D	626 852-6200	4352
Calportland	3273	D	760 343-3403	4432
Hallmark Metals Inc	3444	E	626 335-1263	4990
Electro-Tech Products Inc	3679	E	909 592-1434	6994

	SIC	EMP	PHONE	ENTRY#
Southwest Machine & Plastic Co	3728	E	626 963-6919	7564
Safeguard Envirogroup Inc	3826	E	626 512-7585	7975
Sybron Dental Specialties Inc	3843	E	909 596-0276	8359
Oasis Medical Inc (PA)	3851	D	909 305-5400	8411
Viacom Broadband Inc	4813	C	909 592-3335	9471
Seidner-Miller Inc	5511	C	909 305-2000	11405
Southern Cal Disc Tire Co Inc	5531	D	626 335-2883	11468
Oakdale Memorial Park (PA)	6553	D	626 335-0281	12585
Venue Management Systems Inc	7381	A	626 445-6000	14365
Glendora Country Club	7997	D	626 335-4051	15137
Harbor Glen Care Center	8051	C	626 963-7531	15671
Ensign San Dimas LLC	8059	C	626 963-7531	15850
East Valley Glendora Hosp LLC	8062	B	626 852-5000	15985
Emanate Health	8062	B	626 857-3477	15991
Emanate Hlth Fthill Prsbt Hosp (PA)	8062	D	626 857-3145	15997
Care Unlimited Health Svcs Inc	8082	D	626 332-3767	16375
Automobile Club Southern Cal	8699	D	626 963-8531	17441
Inland Empire Chptr-Ssction Cr	8699	D	512 478-9000	17464

GOLETA, CA - Santa Barbara County

	SIC	EMP	PHONE	ENTRY#
Apeel Technology Inc (PA)	0723	B	805 203-0146	103
Brightview Landscape Svcs Inc	0781	C	805 642-9300	156
Kitson Landscape MGT Inc	0782	D	805 681-9460	213
Arguello Inc	1382	E	805 567-1632	294
Alexs Tile Works Inc	1743	E	805 967-5308	1036
Deckers Outdoor Corporation (PA)	2389	A	805 967-7611	2191
ABC - Clio Inc (HQ)	2731	E	805 968-1911	2881
Boone Printing & Graphics Inc	2752	D	805 683-2349	2971
Neal Feay Company	3354	D	805 967-4521	4602
AEC - Able Engineering Company Inc	3441	C	805 685-2262	4815
Vista Steel Company (PA)	3441	E	805 964-4732	4878
Bardex Corporation (PA)	3533	D	805 964-7747	5505
Mann+hmmel Wtr Fluid Sltons In (DH)	3589	D	805 964-8003	6020
Intri-Plex Technologies Inc (HQ)	3599	C	805 683-3414	6147
Veeco Process Equipment Inc	3599	D	805 967-2700	6264
Sonos Inc (PA)	3651	D	805 965-3001	6555
Calient Technologies Inc (PA)	3661	E	805 695-4800	6582
E-Band Communications LLC	3663	E	858 408-0660	6610
L3 Technologies Inc	3663	D	805 683-3881	6626
Moseley Associates Inc (HQ)	3663	D	805 968-9621	6636
Remec Brdband Wrless Ntwrks LL	3663	C	858 312-6900	6653
Remec Broadband Wireless LLC	3663	C	858 312-6900	6654
Atomica Corp	3674	D	805 681-2807	6803
Openlight Photonics Inc	3674	E	805 880-2000	6861
Transphorm Inc (DH)	3674	C	805 456-1300	6906
Kyocera Sld Laser Inc	3699	E	310 808-4542	7132
Raytheon Company	3699	C	805 967-5511	7145
Atk Space Systems LLC	3812	D	805 685-2262	7700
Lockheed Martin Corporation	3812	E	805 571-2346	7736
Moog Inc	3812	B	805 618-3900	7745
Northrop Grumman Systems Corp	3812	D	714 240-6521	7762
Raytheon Company	3812	C	805 562-4611	7797
Teledyne Flir LLC	3812	C	805 964-9797	7816
Biopac Systems Inc	3826	E	805 685-0066	7946
Teledyne Flir Coml Systems Inc (DH)	3826	B	805 964-9797	7980
Veeco Process Equipment Inc	3826	D	805 967-1400	7990
Wyatt Technology LLC (HQ)	3826	C	805 681-9009	7991
Karl Storz Imaging Inc (HQ)	3829	E	805 968-5563	8050
Soilmoisture Equipment Corp	3829	E	805 964-3525	8064
Digital Surgery Systems Inc	3841	E	805 978-5400	8144
Inogen Inc (PA)	3841	C	805 562-0500	8169
Karl Storz Endscpy-America Inc	3841	D	800 964-5563	8180
Karl Storz Imaging Inc	3841	E	805 968-5563	8181
Truevision Systems Inc	3841	E	805 963-9700	8244
Advanced Vision Science Inc	3851	E	805 683-3851	8403
Santa Barbara Instrument GP Inc	3861	E	925 463-3410	8443
Skate One Corp	3949	D	805 964-1330	8543
Santa Barbara Trnsp Corp	4151	C	805 928-0402	8885
United Parcel Service Inc	4215	D	805 964-7848	9029
Verizon South Inc	4812	C	805 681-8527	9424
Marborg Recovery LP	4953	C	805 963-1852	9750
Enerpro Inc	5065	D	805 683-2114	10242
Integrated Procurement Tech (PA)	5088	C	805 682-0842	10492
Moss Motors Ltd (PA)	5531	C	805 967-4546	11449
Exxon Mobil Corporation	5541	E	805 961-4093	11476
CMC Rescue Inc	5999	D	805 562-9120	11678
Community West Bancshares	6022	C	805 692-5821	11760
Mesa Insurance Solutions Inc	6411	C	805 308-6308	12232
6500 Hllister Ave Partners LLC	6512	D	805 722-1362	12277
One Call Plumber Goleta	7299	D	805 284-0441	13180
Citrix Online LLC	7371	B	805 690-6400	13687
Ergomotion Inc (PA)	7371	D	888 550-3746	13723
Image-X Enterprises Inc	7371	E	805 964-3535	13747

Mergent email: customerrelations@mergent.com
1284

2025 Southern California
Business Directory and Buyers Guide

(P-0000) Products & Services Section entry number
(PA)=Parent Co (HQ)=Headquarters (DH)=Div Headquarters

	SIC	EMP	PHONE	ENTRY#
Stratgic Hlthcare Programs LLC	7371	C	805 963-9446	13834
Parentsquare Inc	7372	D	888 496-3168	14003
Yardi Kube Inc	7372	D	805 699-2040	14068
Citrix Online Svc Prvder Group	7379	C	805 690-6400	14205
Nicolon Corporation	7381	B	805 968-1510	14323
Glen Annie Golf Club	7992	D	805 968-6400	15081
Devereux Foundation	8093	B	805 968-2525	16468
Intouch Technologies Inc (HQ)	8399	D	805 562-8686	17230
United Bys Grls Clubs Snta BRB	8641	D	805 967-1612	17371
Vitamin Angel Alliance Inc	8699	D	805 564-8400	17474
L3 Maripro Inc	8711	B	805 683-3881	17576
National Security Tech LLC	8711	A	805 681-2432	17593
Toyon Research Corporation (PA)	8711	C	805 968-6787	17649
Intri-Plex Technologies Inc	8731	E	805 845-9600	17797

GRANADA HILLS, CA - Los Angeles County

Republic Fence Co Inc (PA)	1799	E	818 341-5323	1224
Park Regency Inc	6531	D	818 363-6116	12501
Siracusa Enterprises Inc	7361	D	818 831-1130	13572
Financial Info Netwrk Inc	7371	E	818 782-0331	13731
Longwood Management Corp	8051	E	818 360-1864	15702
Rinaldi Convalescent Hospital	8059	C	818 360-1003	15882
Aegis Senior Communities LLC	8082	E	818 363-3373	16358
San Fernando City of Inc	8093	D	818 832-2400	16501

GRAND TERRACE, CA - San Bernardino County

West Coast Arborists Inc	0783	C	909 783-6544	248
Griswold Pump Company	3561	E	909 422-1700	5734
Psg California LLC (HQ)	3561	B	909 422-1700	5741
Riversd-San Brnrdino Cnty Indi (PA)	8011	D	909 864-1097	15436
Emeritus Corporation	8051	D	909 420-0153	15629
Keystone NPS LLC (DH)	8399	D	909 633-6354	17233

GROVER BEACH, CA - San Luis Obispo County

Hotlix (PA)	2064	E	805 473-0596	1506
H J Harkins Company Inc	2834	E	805 929-1333	3417
California Fine Wire Co (PA)	3357	C	805 489-5144	4628
805 Beach Breaks Inc	5159	C	408 896-4854	10991
Vons Companies Inc	5411	C	805 481-2492	11289

GUADALUPE, CA - Santa Barbara County

Guadalupe Cooling Company Inc	0723	D	805 343-2331	112
Guadalupe Union School Dst (PA)	8211	C	805 343-2114	16809

HACIENDA HEIGHTS, CA - Los Angeles County

Terra Furniture Inc	2512	E		2461
Brio Water Technology Inc	5078	E	800 781-1680	10339

HARBOR CITY, CA - Los Angeles County

Bennett Entps A Cal Ldscp Cntg	0781	D	310 534-3543	150
La Espanola Meats Inc	2013	E	310 539-0455	1262
Corn Maiden Foods Inc	2032	D	310 784-0400	1339
Sunsets Inc	2253	E	310 784-3600	1925
Star Plastic Design	3089	C	310 530-7119	4248
Ruggeri Marble and Granite Inc	3281	C	310 513-2155	4476
Team Inc	3398	C	310 514-2312	4714
Basmat Inc (PA)	3444	C	310 325-2063	4955
Onyx Industries Inc (PA)	3451	D	310 539-8830	5109
Hansen Engineering Co	3599	D	310 534-3870	6139
Judco Manufacturing Inc (PA)	3643	C	310 534-0959	6422
Prime Wheel Corporation	3714	B	310 326-5080	7284
Hansen Engineering Co	3728	C	310 534-3870	7487
Allied Protection Services Inc	7301	C	310 330-0314	14260
Kaiser Foundation Hospitals	8011	A	310 325-5111	15361
Permanente Medical Group Inc	8011	A	310 325-5111	15423
Southern Cal Prmnnte Med Group	8011	C	800 780-1230	15469

HAWAIIAN GARDENS, CA - Los Angeles County

Consolidated Color Corporation	2851	E	562 420-7714	3710
Hawaiian Gardens Casino	7011	A	562 860-5887	12844
Hawaiian Gardens Casino	7999	A	562 860-5887	15207
Gardens Regional Hospital and Medic	8062	B	877 877-1104	16002
Pacific Gardens Med Ctr LLC	8741	C	562 860-0401	18028

HAWTHORNE, CA - Los Angeles County

Park West Landscape Inc	0782	D	310 363-4100	228
Firstclass Foods - Trojan Inc	2011	E	310 676-2500	1242
Picnic At Ascot Inc	2449	E	310 674-3999	2395
Huntington Industries Inc	2512	E	323 772-5575	2449
Lithographix Inc (PA)	2752	B	323 770-1000	3036
Marina Graphic Center Inc	2752	E	310 970-1777	3040
Technology Training Corp	2752	C	310 644-7777	3088
Supacolor Usa Inc	2759	D	844 973-2862	3176

	SIC	EMP	PHONE	ENTRY#
Moleaer Inc	3561	D	424 558-3567	5738
Wems Inc (PA)	3564	D	310 644-0251	5784
Amag Technology Inc (DH)	3577	E	310 518-2380	5900
DL Horton Enterprises Inc	3599	D	323 777-1700	6118
Fulham Co Inc	3612	E	323 779-2980	6285
Ring LLC (HQ)	3612	B	310 929-7085	6297
OSI Electronics Inc (HQ)	3672	C	310 978-0516	6761
OSI Optoelectronics Inc (HQ)	3674	C	310 978-0516	6864
OSI Systems Inc (PA)	3674	A	310 978-0516	6865
Nmsp Inc	3714	D	310 484-2322	7277
Space Exploration Tech Corp (PA)	3761	B	310 363-6000	7650
Space Exploration Tech Corp	3761	C	310 889-4968	7654
Spacex LLC	3761	A	310 970-5845	7655
Dolphin Medical Inc (HQ)	3845	D	800 448-6506	8377
All Cartage Transportation Inc (PA)	4214	C	310 970-0600	8988
Advanced Air LLC	4522	C	310 644-3344	9178
Expeditors Intl Wash Inc	4731	C	310 343-6200	9279
Thinkom Solutions Inc	4899	C	310 371-5486	9570
Home Depot USA Inc	5211	D	310 644-9600	11170
Lowes Home Centers LLC	5211	C	323 327-4000	11244
South Bay Ford Inc (PA)	5511	C	310 644-0211	11408
Arch Motorcycle Company Inc	5571	E	970 443-1380	11481
EC Design LLC	5943	E	310 220-2362	11635
Servicon Systems Inc	7349	A	310 970-0700	13419
Konami Digital Entrmt Inc (DH)	7372	E	310 220-8100	13964
Inspectorate America Corp	7389	C	800 424-0099	14516
Equinox-76th Street Inc	7991	D	310 727-9543	15047
Eastbiz Corporation	7999	C	310 212-7134	15201
Longwood Management Corp	8051	D	310 679-1461	15706
Windsor Anaheim Healthcare	8051	D	310 675-3304	15804
Trident Labs LLC	8072	C	310 915-9121	16347
West Coast Dental Labs LLC	8072	A	855 220-5600	16348
Ultracare Services LLC	8082	D	818 266-9668	16427
Longwood Management Corp	8361	D	310 675-9163	17175
Analysts Inc	8734	C	800 424-0099	17902
Ncompass International LLC	8742	C	323 785-1700	18180
Netfortris Acquisition Co Inc	8748	D	877 366-2548	18337

HEBER, CA - Imperial County

Gibson & Schaefer Inc (PA)	3273	E	619 352-3535	4440
Ormat Nevada Inc	4911	C	760 353-8200	9592
Ormat Technologies Inc	4911	E	760 337-8872	9593

HELENDALE, CA - San Bernardino County

Lockheed Martin Corporation	3812	D	760 952-4200	7738
Silver Lakes Association	8641	D	760 245-1606	17367

HEMET, CA - Riverside County

Lpsh Holdings Inc	1711	B	951 926-1176	798
Menifee Valley AC Inc	1711	D	888 785-6125	804
Current Home Inc	1796	D	866 454-6073	1188
EZ Lube LLC	2992	D	951 766-1996	3855
Ramko Injection Inc	3089	D	951 929-0360	4216
Superior Ready Mix Concrete LP	3273	D	951 658-9225	4462
Ramko Mfg Inc	3599	D	951 652-3510	6213
Substance Abuse Program	3674	E	951 791-3350	6901
McCrometer Inc (HQ)	3823	C	951 652-6811	7866
Lowes Home Centers LLC	5211	C	951 492-7000	11226
Jack Gosch Ford Inc	5511	C	951 658-3181	11364
Southern Cal Disc Tire Co Inc	5531	C	951 929-2130	11403
Emeritus Corporation	8051	D	951 744-9861	15628
Miramonte Enterprises LLC	8051	C	951 658-9441	15721
Pacs Group Inc	8051	C	951 925-9171	15738
Pacs Group Inc	8051	C	951 658-9441	15740
Hemet Valley Medical Center-Education	8062	A	951 652-2811	16016
Kpc Global Medical Centers Inc (DH)	8062	C	714 953-3500	16067
Ramona Rhbltion Post Acute CA	8062	C	951 652-0011	16158
Ramona Community Services Corp (HQ)	8082	C	951 658-9288	16414
Victor Cmnty Support Svcs Inc	8093	C	951 212-1770	16517
Hemet Unified School District	8211	D	951 765-5100	16810
Hemet Unified School District	8211	D	951 765-6287	16811
Valley Resource Center Inc (PA)	8331	E	951 766-8659	17070
Casa-Pacifica Inc	8361	B	951 658-3369	17128
Casa-Pacifica Inc	8361	C	951 766-5116	17129
Automobile Club Southern Cal	8699	C	951 652-6202	17433
Trilar Management Group	8741	C	951 925-2021	18069

HERMOSA BEACH, CA - Los Angeles County

Hammitt Inc	3161	D	310 292-5200	4294
Tellabs Access LLC (HQ)	3669	E	630 798-8671	6697
Rf Digital Corporation	3674	C	949 610-0008	6884
Marlin Equity Partners LLC (PA)	6282	D	310 364-0100	12027
Marlin Equity Partners III LP (PA)	6799	C	310 364-0100	12715

Employee Codes: A=Over 500 employees, B=251-500
C=101-250, D=51-100, E=20-50, F=10-19, G=1-9

2025 Southern California
Business Directory and Buyers Guide

© Mergent Inc. 1-800-342-5647

1285

GEOGRAPHIC

	SIC	EMP	PHONE	ENTRY#
HESPERIA, CA - San Bernardino County				
Arizona Pipeline Company **(PA)**	1623	B	760 244-8212	660
Hesperia Unified School Dst	2099	D	760 948-1051	1788
Hesperia Holding Inc	2439	E	760 244-8787	2378
T L Timmerman Cnstr Inc	2439	E	760 244-2532	2382
Brent-Wood Products Inc	2499	E	800 400-7335	2410
Robar Enterprises Inc **(PA)**	3273	C	760 244-5456	4448
Robertsons Ready Mix Ltd	3273	C	760 244-7239	4451
Maurice & Maurice Engrg Inc	3334	E	760 949-5151	4578
Madison Industries **(HQ)**	3448	E	562 484-5099	5082
Dial Precision Inc	3599	E	760 947-3557	6117
Geeriraj Inc	3672	E	760 244-6149	6732
Best Way Disposal Co Inc	4953	D	760 244-9773	9732
Global Customer Services Inc	7389	D	760 995-7949	14501
HIGHLAND, CA - San Bernardino County				
Kcb Towers Inc	1791	D	909 862-0322	1155
Raemica Inc	2013	E	909 864-1990	1268
Pro-Cast Products Inc **(PA)**	3272	E	909 793-7602	4415
Robertsons Rdymx Ltd A Cal Ltd	3273	C	909 425-2930	4450
Cco Holdings LLC	4841	C	909 742-8273	9532
Lowes Home Centers LLC	5211	D	909 557-9010	11234
San Mnuel Band Mission Indians	6099	C	909 425-4682	11843
San Mnuel Band Mission Indians	7389	C	909 864-6928	14589
San Manuel Entertainment Auth **(PA)**	7999	A	909 864-5050	15221
Beaver Medical Group LP **(HQ)**	8011	C	909 425-3321	15251
Cedar Holdings LLC	8051	D	909 862-0611	15588
HINKLEY, CA - San Bernardino County				
Pacific Gas and Electric Co	4911	C	760 253-2925	9596
HOLLYWOOD, CA - Los Angeles County				
Technicolor Usa Inc **(HQ)**	3651	A	317 587-4287	6561
Loews Hollywood Hotel LLC	7011	B	323 450-2235	12904
Covenant House California	8361	C	323 461-3131	17140
HUNTINGTON BEACH, CA - Orange County				
Coastline Cnstr & Awng Co Inc	1521	D	714 891-9798	395
Grani Installation Inc **(PA)**	1542	D	714 898-0441	540
Brymax Construction Svcs Inc	1711	D	949 200-9619	756
Critchfeld Mech Inc Sthern Cal	1711	D	949 390-2900	770
RC Wendt Painting Inc	1721	C	714 960-2700	871
Portermatt Electric Inc	1731	E	714 596-8788	953
Tile & Marble Design Co Inc	1743	E	714 847-6472	1043
California Closet Company Inc	1799	C	714 899-4905	1197
Armor Dermalogics LLC	2023	E	714 202-6424	1291
Creative Costuming Designs Inc	2211	E	714 895-0982	1877
Gearment Inc **(PA)**	2269	C	866 236-5476	1941
DC Shoes LLC **(HQ)**	2329	D	714 889-4206	2009
TravisMathew LLC **(HQ)**	2329	E	562 799-6900	2030
Jolyn Clothing Company LLC	2339	E	714 794-2149	2107
Victory Professional Pdts Inc	2339	E	714 887-0621	2141
Ofs Brands Holdings Inc	2521	A	714 903-2257	2514
Highmark Smart Reliable Seating Inc	2522	C	714 903-2257	2529
K-Jack Engineering Co Inc	2542	D	310 327-8389	2583
Lifoam Industries LLC	2653	E	714 891-5035	2680
Harris Industries Inc **(PA)**	2672	E	714 898-8048	2724
Teacher Created Materials Inc	2741	C	714 891-2273	2945
Inkwright LLC	2752	E	714 892-3300	3019
Pexco Aerospace Inc	2821	E	714 894-9922	3286
Sunshine Makers Inc **(PA)**	2842	D	562 795-6000	3620
Laird Coatings Corporation	2851	E	714 894-5252	3716
Custom Building Products LLC **(DH)**	2891	D	800 272-8786	3762
Home & Body Company **(PA)**	2899	B	714 842-8000	3802
Marko Foam Products Inc	3086	D	949 417-3307	4007
Advanced Cmpsite Pdts Tech Inc	3089	E	714 895-5544	4037
Bent Manufacturing Co Inc	3089	D	714 842-0600	4064
Cambro Manufacturing Company	3089	C	714 848-1555	4078
Cambro Manufacturing Company	3089	E	714 848-1555	4079
Cambro Manufacturing Company **(PA)**	3089	B	714 848-1555	4080
Delfin Design & Mfg Inc	3089	E	949 888-4644	4100
Newlight Technologies Inc	3089	E	714 556-4500	4180
Sandia Plastics Inc	3089	E	714 901-8400	4236
Donoco Industries Inc	3229	E	714 893-7889	4325
Zadro Products Inc	3231	E	714 892-9200	4350
Precision Frrites Ceramics Inc	3264	D	714 901-7622	4365
Dynamet Incorporated	3356	E	714 375-3150	4617
Paciugo	3421	E	714 536-5388	4731
Advanced Cutting Tools Inc	3423	E	714 842-9376	4733
California Faucets Inc **(PA)**	3432	E	800 822-8855	4803
California Faucets Inc	3432	E	657 400-1639	4804
R & D Metal Fabricators Inc	3444	E	714 891-4878	5026
Precision Resource Inc	3469	C	714 891-4439	5209
Cal-Aurum Industries	3471	E	714 898-0996	5244
Plasma Rggedized Solutions Inc	3471	E	714 893-6063	5283
Vector Launch LLC **(PA)**	3489	E	202 888-3063	5358
Iconn Engineering LLC	3495	E	714 696-8826	5394
Orlando Spring Corp	3495	E	562 594-8411	5397
American Precision Hydraulics	3542	E	714 903-8610	5557
Crenshaw Die and Mfg Corp	3544	D	949 475-5505	5575
Guhring Inc	3545	E	714 841-3582	5612
Tool Alliance Corporation	3545	E	714 373-5864	5627
Rima Enterprises Inc	3555	D	714 893-4534	5666
Fotis and Son Imports Inc **(PA)**	3556	E	714 894-9022	5671
Aerodynamic Engineering Inc	3599	E	714 891-2651	6071
Aerodyne Prcsion Machining Inc	3599	E	714 891-1311	6072
Fibreform Electronics Inc	3599	E	714 898-9641	6123
Hytron Mfg Co Inc	3599	E	714 903-6701	6144
Johnson Manufacturing Inc	3599	E	714 903-0393	6154
Momeni Engineering LLC	3599	E	714 897-9301	6185
V & S Engineering Company Ltd	3599	E	714 898-7869	6260
Coast To Coast Circuits Inc **(PA)**	3672	E	714 891-9441	6719
Vanguard Electronics Company **(PA)**	3677	E	714 842-3330	6940
Reedex Inc	3679	E	714 894-0311	7044
Rocker Solenoid Company	3679	D	310 534-5660	7045
Riot Glass Inc	3699	E	800 580-2303	7146
Dynatrac Products LLC	3714	E	714 596-4461	7249
Sandra Gruca	3714	E	714 661-6464	7292
Boeing Intllctual Prprty Lcnsi	3721	C	562 797-2020	7335
Tri Models Inc	3721	D	714 896-0823	7374
Irish International	3724	C	949 559-0930	7390
Airtech International Inc **(PA)**	3728	C	714 899-8100	7421
Encore Seats Inc	3728	E	949 559-0930	7471
Irish Interiors Inc	3728	C	562 344-1700	7502
Irish Interiors Inc **(HQ)**	3728	C	949 559-0930	7503
PCA Aerospace Inc	3728	E	714 901-5209	7537
PCA Aerospace Inc **(PA)**	3728	D	714 841-1750	7538
Safran Cabin Galleys Us Inc **(HQ)**	3728	A	714 861-7300	7550
Safran Cabin Inc **(HQ)**	3728	B	714 934-0000	7551
Boeing Company	3761	B	714 896-3311	7642
American Automated Engrg Inc	3769	C	714 898-9951	7666
Leda Corporation	3769	E	714 841-7821	7671
Translogic Incorporated	3823	E	714 890-0058	7882
Blue-White Industries Ltd **(PA)**	3824	D	714 893-8529	7887
Enhanced Vision Systems Inc **(HQ)**	3827	D	800 440-9476	8000
Measure Uas Inc	3829	E	714 916-6166	8051
Electronic Waveform Lab Inc	3841	E	714 843-0463	8147
Nordson Medical (ca) LLC	3841	E	657 215-4200	8208
Xr LLC	3842	E	714 847-9292	8320
Zimmer Melia & Associates Inc **(PA)**	3842	E	615 377-0118	8322
Kettenbach LP	3843	E	877 532-2123	8341
West Coast Trends Inc	3949	E	714 843-9288	8552
Primus Inc	3993	D	714 527-2261	8624
Leoben Company	3999	E	951 284-9653	8692
Premiere Customs Brokers Inc	4731	A	310 410-6825	9327
Frontier California Inc	4813	B	714 375-6713	9440
Rainbow Disposal Co Inc **(HQ)**	4953	C	714 847-3581	9758
Reliable Wholesale Lumber Inc **(PA)**	5031	D	714 848-8222	9929
Bartco Lighting Inc	5063	D	714 230-3200	10171
DSI Process Systems LLC	5084	C	314 382-1525	10370
Primal Elements Inc	5122	D	714 899-0757	10647
Kings Seafood Company LLC	5146	A	714 793-1177	10856
Astra Oil Company Inc	5172	C	714 969-6569	11028
Tiodize Co Inc	5172	E	714 898-4377	11036
Harbor Distributing LLc **(HQ)**	5181	C	714 933-2400	11049
Nakase Brothers Whl Nurs LP **(PA)**	5193	D	949 855-4388	11093
Lowes Home Centers LLC	5211	D	714 907-9006	11206
Stater Bros Markets	5411	E	714 963-0949	11281
York Enterprises South Inc	5511	D	714 842-6611	11434
Classic Camaro Inc	5531	C	714 847-6887	11442
Southern Cal Disc Tire Co Inc	5531	C	714 901-8226	11466
Boiling Crab Operations LLC	5812	B	714 636-4885	11552
Love At First Bite Catering	5812	D	714 369-0561	11588
Nuvision Fincl Federal Cr Un **(PA)**	6061	C	714 375-8000	11809
GFS Capital Holdings	6162	E	714 720-3918	11905
Managed Health Network	6324	E	714 934-5519	12097
Confie Holding II Co **(PA)**	6411	C	714 252-2500	12197
Freeway Insurance **(PA)**	6411	C	714 252-2500	12215
Huntington Bch Senior Hsing LP	6513	C	714 842-4006	12348
Burleigh Point LLC	6531	C	949 428-3200	12393
Child Development Incorporated	6531	B	714 842-4064	12404
Equity Concept Inc	6531	D	714 374-8859	12438
Roman Cthlic Diocese of Orange	6553	D	714 847-8546	12586
Pacific City Hotel LLC	7011	B	714 698-6100	12958
Waterfront Hotel LLC	7011	B	714 845-8000	13071
Pacific Coast Entertainment	7299	B	714 841-6455	13183

	SIC	EMP	PHONE	ENTRY#
Grupo Gallegos	7311	D	562 256-3600	13210
Graphic Ink Corp.	7336	E	714 901-2805	13329
Direct Chassislink Inc	7359	B	657 216-5846	13455
Huntington Beach Union High	7361	C	714 478-7684	13526
Infomagnus LLC	7371	D	714 810-3430	13748
Applied Business Software Inc	7372	D	562 426-2188	13882
Shortcuts Software Inc	7372	E	714 622-6600	14030
United States Technical Svcs	7379	C	714 374-6300	14262
Horsemen Inc	7381	D	714 847-4243	14309
Staff Pro Inc (PA)	7382	A	714 230-7200	14422
Global Exprnce Specialists Inc	7389	C	619 498-6300	14502
Century Theatres Inc	7832	D	714 373-4573	14930
City of Huntington Beach	7992	D	714 846-4450	15073
Lifemd Inc	8011	D	800 852-1575	15378
Rume Medical Group Inc	8011	D	714 406-1887	15440
Southern Cal Prmnnte Med Group	8011	C	714 841-7293	15472
Douglas Fir Holdings LLC	8051	C	714 842-5551	15622
Estrella Inc	8051	C	562 925-6418	15649
Sea Breeze Health Care Inc	8051	C	714 847-9671	15771
Prime Hlthcare Hntngton Bch LL	8062	B	714 843-5000	16142
No Ordinary Moments Inc	8082	D	714 848-3800	16407
Wavelengths Recovery Inc	8093	D	714 312-1011	16521
Hwave	8099	D	714 843-0463	16571
Optumcare Management LLC	8099	D	714 968-0068	16600
Goodwill Inds Orange Cnty Cal	8331	D	714 881-3986	17060
T2 Ues Inc	8711	C	714 487-5786	17642
Element Materials (DH)	8734	D	714 892-1961	17913
BJs Restaurant Operations Co	8741	B	714 500-2440	17952
Bsw Consultants Inc	8742	A	949 279-3063	18112
Michaelson Connor & Boul (PA)	8742	D	714 230-3600	18172

HUNTINGTON PARK, CA - Los Angeles County

	SIC	EMP	PHONE	ENTRY#
Citizens of Humanity LLC (PA)	2339	C	323 923-1240	2085
Reliance Upholstery Sup Co Inc	2392	D	323 321-2300	2224
G - L Veneer Co Inc (PA)	2435	D	323 582-5203	2369
Plycraft Industries Inc	2435	C	323 587-8101	2371
Crown Poly Inc	2673	C	323 585-5522	2730
UFO Inc	3089	E	323 588-5450	4266
Montclair Bronze Inc	3366	E	909 986-2664	4682
Bodycote Thermal Proc Inc	3471	D	323 583-1231	5240
Los Angeles Galvanizing Co	3479	D	323 583-2263	5329
Valco Planer Works Inc	3544	E	323 582-6355	5602
NL&a Collections Inc	3645	D	323 277-6266	6447
Home Depot USA Inc	5211	C	323 587-5520	11166
Fred M Boerner Motor Co (PA)	5531	D	323 560-3882	11445
Living Opportunities MGT Co	6513	D	323 589-5956	12357
All Care Medical Group Inc	8011	D	408 278-3550	15234
Covenant Care California LLC	8051	C	323 589-5941	15611
Aircraft Xray Laboratories Inc	8734	D	323 587-4141	17899

IDYLLWILD, CA - Riverside County

	SIC	EMP	PHONE	ENTRY#
South Bay Wire & Cable Co LLC (PA)	3315	D	951 659-2183	4541
Jeb Holdings Corp (PA)	5065	D	951 659-2183	10257

IMPERIAL, CA - Imperial County

	SIC	EMP	PHONE	ENTRY#
Hells Kitchen Geothermal LLC	2819	E	760 604-0433	3238
United States Gypsum Company	3275	C	760 358-3200	4470
Imperial Irrigation District (PA)	4911	A	800 303-7756	9588

IMPERIAL BEACH, CA - San Diego County

	SIC	EMP	PHONE	ENTRY#
Boys & Girls Clubs South Cnty	8641	D	619 424-2266	17325

INDIAN WELLS, CA - Riverside County

	SIC	EMP	PHONE	ENTRY#
Merrill Lynch Prce Fnner Smith	6211	C	760 862-1400	11989
Bennion Deville Fine Homes Inc	6531	B	760 674-3452	12387
Hyatt Corporation	7011	B	760 341-1000	12865
Lh Indian Wells Operating LLC	7011	C	760 341-2200	12899
Renaissance Hotel Operating Co	7011	A	760 773-4444	12991
Dhccnp	7997	D	760 340-4646	15132
Eldorado Country Club	7997	D	760 346-8081	15134
Reserve Club	7997	D	760 674-2222	15163
Toscana Country Club Inc	7997	D	760 404-1444	15182
Vintage Club	7997	D	760 340-0500	15184
Bjz LLC	8082	D	760 851-0740	16369
Troon Golf LLC	8741	C	760 346-4653	18071

INDIO, CA - Riverside County

	SIC	EMP	PHONE	ENTRY#
Hadley Date Gardens Inc	0179	D	760 347-3044	48
Valley Animal Medical Center	0742	A	760 342-4711	133
Granite Construction Company	1611	B	760 775-7500	617
All Wall Inc	1742	D	760 600-5108	995
Cabinets By Prcision Works Inc	2434	D	760 342-1133	2342
Sullivans Stone Factory Inc	3281	E	760 347-5535	4479

	SIC	EMP	PHONE	ENTRY#
Frontier California Inc	4813	B	760 342-0500	9437
Commercial Lighting Inds Inc	5063	C	800 755-0155	10176
Fiesta Ford Inc	5511	C	760 775-7777	11347
Cabazon Band Mission Indians	7011	A	760 342-5000	12783
Whites Crane Service Inc	7353	C	760 347-3401	13445
Signature Party Rentals LLC	7359	C	760 863-0671	13471
East Valley Tourist Dev Auth	7999	A	760 342-5000	15200
RES-Care Inc	8052	D	760 775-2887	15821
JFK Memorial Hospital Inc	8062	C	760 347-6191	16029
John F Kennedy Mem Hosp Aux	8062	A	760 347-6191	16030
ABC Recovery Center Inc	8093	D	760 342-6616	16437
Coachella Vly Rescue Mission	8322	D	760 347-3512	16894

INGLEWOOD, CA - Los Angeles County

	SIC	EMP	PHONE	ENTRY#
Flowers Bkg Co Henderson LLC	2051	D	310 695-9846	1448
Goodman Food Products Inc (PA)	2099	C	310 674-3180	1785
K B Socks Inc (DH)	2252	C	310 670-3235	1909
Biomed California Inc	2834	D	310 665-1121	3375
Hunter Vaughan LLC	2844	C	626 534-7050	3659
Multichrome Company Inc (PA)	3471	E	310 216-1086	5277
Zephyr Manufacturing Co Inc	3546	D	310 410-4907	5638
Engineered Magnetics Inc	3629	E	310 649-9000	6373
Empower Rf Systems Inc (PA)	3663	D	310 412-8100	6613
Doorking Inc (PA)	3699	C	310 645-0023	7120
Marvin Land Systems Inc	3711	E	310 674-5030	7183
Autonomous Medical Devices Inc	3826	E	310 641-2700	7939
Minus K Technology Inc	3829	C	310 348-9656	8054
Pharmaco-Kinesis Corporation	3841	E	310 641-2700	8214
First Transit Inc	4111	C	310 216-9584	8750
Able Freight Services LLC	4731	D	310 568-8883	9245
Iron Mountain Info MGT LLC	4731	C	818 848-9766	9297
Mittal Ram	5074	D	310 769-6669	10325
Dolphin Hkg Ltd (PA)	5199	D	310 215-3356	11115
Home Depot USA Inc	5211	D	310 677-1944	11167
Inglewood Park Cemetery (PA)	6553	C	310 412-6500	12584
Century Gaming Management Inc	7011	A	310 330-2800	12789
Hollywood Park Casino Co Inc	7011	A	310 330-2800	12852
After-Party2 Inc (DH)	7359	C	310 202-0011	13446
After-Party6 Inc	7359	C	310 966-4900	13447
Classic Party Rentals Inc	7359	A	310 966-4900	13451
Leads360 LLC	7372	E	888 843-1777	13967
American Egle Prtctive Svcs In	7381	D	310 412-0019	14270
Security Indust Spcialists Inc	7381	A	323 924-9147	14341
Aero Port Services Inc (PA)	7382	A	310 623-8230	14380
La Clippers LLC	7941	B	213 742-7500	15029
Kaiser Foundation Hospitals	8011	D	310 419-3303	15368
Southern Cal Prmnnte Med Group	8011	D	310 419-3306	15464
Centinela Sklled Nrsing Wllnes	8051	D	310 674-3216	15590
Mariner Health Care Inc	8051	C	310 677-9114	15712
West Cntinela Vly Care Ctr Inc	8051	C	310 674-3216	15800
Watts Health Foundation Inc (PA)	8052	B	310 424-2220	15828
Cedars-Sinai Marina Hospital	8062	A	310 673-4660	15933
Prime Healthcare Centinela LLC	8062	A	310 673-4660	16140
Tenet Healthsystem Medical Inc	8351	C	310 673-4660	17112
Girl Scuts Greater Los Angeles (PA)	8641	C	626 677-2265	17345
Automobile Club Southern Cal	8699	D	310 673-5170	17447
Marvin Engineering Co Inc (PA)	8711	A	310 674-5030	17582
Watts Health Systems Inc (PA)	8742	A	310 424-2220	18240

IRVINE, CA - Orange County

	SIC	EMP	PHONE	ENTRY#
Medterra Cbd LLC	0139	D	800 971-1288	6
Gem-Pack Berries LLC	0171	C	949 861-4919	19
Hines Horticulture Inc (PA)	0181	B	949 559-4444	58
Mission Ldscp Companies Inc	0781	C	714 545-9962	178
Newport Energy	1382	E	408 230-7545	308
Phoenix Cpitl Group Hldngs LLC	1382	E	303 749-0074	310
De Vries International Inc (PA)	1389	E	949 252-1212	328
A Clark/Mccarthy Joint Venture	1521	A	714 429-9779	387
Shimmick Construction Co Inc	1521	C	510 777-5000	430
Regis Contractors LP	1522	C	949 253-0455	451
Tri Pointe Homes Inc	1522	C	714 389-5933	453
Tri Pointe Homes Holdings Inc (HQ)	1522	C	949 438-1400	454
Western National Prpts LLC (PA)	1522	C	949 862-6200	458
Fieldstone Communities Inc (PA)	1531	C	949 790-5400	461
Lennar Corporation	1531	D	949 349-8000	463
Tri Pointe Homes Inc	1531	C	949 478-8600	466
Warmington Homes	1531	C	949 679-3100	469
Clark Cnstr Group - Cal Inc	1541	B	714 754-0764	476
Spectrum Cnstr Group Inc	1541	D	949 246-9749	502
Sunny Service Group LLC	1541	E	323 818-2625	505
Uprite Construction Corp	1541	D	949 877-8877	511
Clark Cnstr Group - Cal LP	1542	B	714 429-9779	530
Hensel Phelps Construction Co	1542	D	626 636-4449	545

Employee Codes: A=Over 500 employees, B=251-500
C=101-250, D=51-100, E=20-50, F=10-19, G=1-9

2025 Southern California
Business Directory and Buyers Guide

© Mergent Inc. 1-800-342-5647

1287

GEOGRAPHIC

	SIC	EMP	PHONE	ENTRY#
RD Olson Construction Inc.	1542	C	949 474-2001	577
Rudolph and Sletten Inc.	1542	C	949 252-1919	580
Snyder Langston Holdings LLC	1542	C	949 863-9200	586
Whiting-Turner Contracting Co	1542	B	949 863-0800	605
Foothill / Estrn Trnsp Crrdor	1611	D	949 754-3400	616
Sema Construction Inc.	1611	D	949 470-0500	648
A & H Communications Inc.	1623	C	949 250-4555	657
Shoffeitt Pipeline Inc.	1623	D	949 581-1600	694
Shimmick Construction Co Inc (HQ)	1629	D	949 591-5922	718
American Beech Solar LLC	1711	D	949 398-3915	735
Bromic Heating Pty Limited	1711	E	855 552-7432	755
Cfp Fire Protection Inc.	1711	D	949 727-3277	760
Emcor Svcs Intgrated Solutions	1711	C	513 679-3325	776
Mesa Energy Systems Inc (HQ)	1711	C	949 460-0460	805
Empcc Inc.	1721	B	888 278-8200	861
Leading Edge Aviation Svcs Inc.	1721	A	714 556-0576	868
Anderson & Howard Electric Inc.	1731	C	949 250-4555	884
Kite Electric Incorporated	1731	C	949 380-7471	932
Patric Communications Inc (PA)	1731	D	619 579-2898	949
Pyro-Comm Systems Inc (PA)	1731	C	714 902-8000	955
SBE Electrical Contracting Inc.	1731	E	714 544-5066	958
Ancca Corporation	1742	D	949 553-0084	996
Vortex Industries LLC (PA)	1751	E	714 434-8000	1065
Dri Commercial Corporation	1761	C	949 266-1900	1078
Dri Companies	1761	B	949 266-1900	1079
Ekedal Concrete Inc.	1771	D	949 729-8082	1115
Danny Ryan Precision Contg Inc.	1795	D	949 642-6664	1180
Antis Roofg Waterproofing LLC	1799	C	949 461-9222	1194
Courtney Inc (PA)	1799	D	949 222-2050	1199
Tls Productions Inc.	1799	E	810 220-8577	1229
Bio-Nutritional RES Group Inc.	2023	C	714 427-6990	1296
Danone Us LLC	2024	E	949 474-9670	1316
Good Culture LLC	2026	E	949 545-9945	1331
Kraft Heinz Foods Company	2032	E	949 250-4080	1342
Real Vision Foods LLC	2038	E	253 228-5050	1399
South Coast Baking LLC (DH)	2052	D	949 851-9654	1492
Reyes Coca-Cola Bottling LLC (PA)	2086	B	213 744-8616	1648
Golden State Foods Corp (PA)	2087	E	949 247-8000	1682
Maruchan Inc.	2098	C	949 789-2300	1732
Maruchan Inc (HQ)	2099	B	949 789-2300	1812
Village Green Foods Inc.	2099	E	949 261-0111	1865
Babylon International LLC	2211	E	323 433-4104	1871
Lspace America LLC	2253	D	949 750-2292	1922
Tomorrows Look Inc.	2261	D	949 596-8400	1936
INX Prints Inc.	2262	D	949 660-9190	1938
Royalty Carpet Mills Inc.	2273	A	949 474-4000	1955
Birdwell Enterprises Inc.	2329	E	714 557-7040	2007
St John Knits Intl Inc.	2335	A	949 863-1171	2071
Boardriders Wholesale LLC	2339	E	949 916-3060	2083
Coop Home Goods LLC	2392	E	888 316-1886	2208
Pro-Mart Industries Inc.	2392	E	949 428-7700	2223
Taber Company Inc.	2431	D	714 543-7100	2329
Dellarobbia Inc (PA)	2512	E	949 251-9532	2444
Marlin Designs LLC	2512	C	949 637-7257	2453
Tropitone Furniture Co Inc (DH)	2514	B	949 595-2010	2475
Craftwood Industries Inc.	2522	E	616 796-1209	2523
Krueger International Inc.	2531	E	949 748-7000	2548
CK Manufacturing & Trading Inc.	2541	E	949 529-3400	2560
Cycle News Inc (PA)	2711	E	949 863-7082	2792
San Diego Union-Tribune LLC.	2711	E	619 299-3131	2824
Advanstar Communications Inc.	2721	D	714 513-8400	2842
Cbj LP	2721	E	949 833-8373	2848
Haymarket Worldwide Inc.	2721	E	949 417-6700	2859
Kelley Blue Book Co Inc (DH)	2721	D	949 770-7704	2862
Informa Business Media Inc.	2741	E	949 252-1146	2922
Digital Supercolor Inc.	2752	D	949 622-0010	3002
DOT Printer Inc (PA)	2752	D	949 474-1100	3004
Kelmscott Communications LLC	2752	B	949 475-1900	3027
Ocpc Inc.	2752	D	949 475-1900	3052
Woodridge Press Inc.	2752	E	949 475-1900	3102
ABC Imaging of Washington	2759	E	949 419-3728	3112
Orange Circle Studio Corp (PA)	2759	D	949 727-0800	3158
Progroup	2759	E	949 748-5400	3164
Super Color Digital LLC (PA)	2759	E	949 622-0010	3177
Taylor Graphics Inc.	2759	E	949 752-5200	3181
Bio-RAD Laboratories Inc.	2833	C	949 598-1200	3311
Orgain LLC.	2833	E	888 881-4246	3324
Allergan Sales LLC (DH)	2834	A	862 261-7000	3345
Allergan Spclty Thrpeutics Inc.	2834	A	714 246-4500	3346
Allergan Usa Inc (DH)	2834	D	714 427-1900	3347
Amare Global LP	2834	E	888 898-8551	3348
Anchen Pharmaceuticals Inc.	2834	C	949 639-8100	3356
Earthrise Nutritionals LLC (HQ)	2834	E	949 623-0980	3398
Edwards Lifesciences LLC (HQ)	2834	A	949 250-2500	3399
Formex LLC.	2834	E	858 529-6600	3404
International Vitamin Corp.	2834	C	949 664-5500	3426
Ista Pharmaceuticals Inc.	2834	B	949 788-6000	3432
New Generation Wellness Inc (PA)	2834	C	949 863-0340	3460
Nura USA LLC.	2834	E	949 946-5700	3463
Nutrawise Health & Beauty LLC.	2834	D	888 271-8976	3464
Pacific Pharma Inc.	2834	A	714 246-4600	3469
Sicor Inc (HQ)	2834	A	949 455-4700	3502
Skinmedica Inc.	2834	B	760 929-2600	3505
St Jude Medical LLC.	2834	E	949 769-5000	3508
Teva Parenteral Medicines Inc.	2834	A	949 455-4700	3512
Cg Oncology Inc.	2836	D	949 409-3700	3568
Tarsus Pharmaceuticals Inc.	2836	E	949 409-9820	3588
Meguiars Inc (HQ)	2842	E	949 752-8000	3613
Zo Skin Health Inc (DH)	2844	D	949 988-7524	3702
FSI Coating Technologies Inc.	2851	E	949 540-1140	3715
Desmond Ventures Inc.	2891	C	949 474-0400	3764
Henkel Chemical Management LLC.	2891	C	888 943-6535	3768
Mitsubishi Chemical Crbn Fbr.	2891	C	800 929-5471	3772
Evergreen Holdings Inc.	2992	C	949 757-7770	3853
Jsn Packaging Products Inc.	3082	D	949 458-0050	3962
Jsn Industries Inc.	3089	C	949 458-0050	4149
Gary Bale Redi-Mix Con Inc.	3273	D	949 786-9441	4439
3M Technical Ceramics Inc (HQ)	3299	D	949 862-9600	4497
3M Technical Ceramics Inc.	3299	E	949 756-0642	4498
Cwi Steel Technologies Corporation	3325	E	949 476-7600	4570
PCC Rollmet Inc.	3339	D	949 221-5333	4581
Supernal LLC.	3365	C	202 422-3275	4678
PHC Sharp Holdings Inc (HQ)	3421	E	714 662-1033	4732
Pacific Handy Cutter Inc (DH)	3423	E	714 662-1033	4743
PHC Merger Inc.	3423	E	714 662-1033	4744
Toughbuilt Industries Inc (PA)	3423	B	949 528-3100	4746
Jonathan Engnred Slutions Corp (HQ)	3429	E	714 665-4400	4775
M A G Engineering Mfg Co.	3429	E		4779
Cartel Industries LLC.	3444	E	949 474-3200	4966
Delafoil Holdings Inc (PA)	3444	C	949 752-4580	4979
Global Pcci (gpc) (PA)	3469	C	757 637-9000	5189
Electrolurgy Inc.	3471	D	949 250-4494	5258
Global Metal Solutions Inc.	3471	E	949 872-2995	5264
SDC Technologies Inc (HQ)	3479	E	714 939-8300	5343
Griswold Controls LLC (PA)	3494	D	949 559-6000	5388
Cummins Pacific LLC (HQ)	3519	D	949 253-6000	5466
Signature Control Systems	3523	D	949 580-3640	5477
Control Systems Intl Inc.	3533	D	949 238-4150	5507
Safety Products Holdings LLC.	3541	E	714 662-1033	5551
Synventive Engineering Inc.	3542	E	312 848-8717	5561
Pace Punches Inc.	3544	D	949 428-2750	5590
Viking Products Inc.	3545	E	949 379-5100	5630
M K Products Inc.	3548	D	949 798-1234	5647
Aquatec International Inc.	3561	D	949 225-2200	5727
Xylem Water Solutions USA Inc.	3561	D	949 474-1679	5746
Knight LLC (HQ)	3569	D	949 595-4800	5826
Lubrication Scientifics LLC.	3569	E	714 557-0664	5827
Cybernet Manufacturing Inc.	3571	A	949 600-8000	5844
Dynabook Americas Inc (HQ)	3571	B	949 583-3000	5845
Gateway Inc (DH)	3571	C	949 471-7000	5849
Gateway US Retail Inc.	3571	E	949 471-7000	5850
I/O Magic Corporation	3571	E	949 707-4800	5852
Mediatek USA Inc.	3571	C	408 526-1899	5861
Solarflare Communications Inc (DH)	3571	D	949 581-6830	5867
Toshiba Amer Info Systems Inc.	3571	C	949 583-3000	5871
Certance LLC (HQ)	3572	B	949 856-7800	5876
H Co Computer Products (PA)	3572	E	949 833-3222	5879
Quantum Corporation	3572	E	949 856-7800	5884
Stec Inc (HQ)	3572	B	415 222-9996	5889
Western Digital Corporation	3572	E	949 672-7000	5893
Zadara Storage Inc.	3572	D	949 251-0360	5894
Cs Systems Inc.	3577	E	949 475-9100	5911
Emulex Corporation (DH)	3577	C		5916
Encrypted Access Corporation	3577	E	714 371-4125	5917
Finis LLC.	3577	D	949 250-4929	5920
Incipio Technologies Inc (PA)	3577	E	888 893-1638	5922
Innovative Tech & Engrg Inc.	3577	E	949 955-2501	5925
Lasergraphics Inc.	3577	E	949 753-8282	5928
Livescribe Inc.	3577	E		5929
Logitech Inc.	3577	A	510 795-8500	5930
Princeton Technology Inc.	3577	E	949 851-7776	5945
Printronix LLC (PA)	3577	E	714 368-2300	5946
Raise 3d Technologies Inc.	3577	E	949 482-2040	5948
Western Telematic Inc.	3577	E	949 586-9950	5955
Ricoh Electronics Inc.	3579	C	714 259-1220	5959
Jacuzzi Inc (DH)	3589	C	909 606-7733	6017

2025 Southern California
Business Directory and Buyers Guide

	SIC	EMP	PHONE	ENTRY#
Cp-Carrillo Inc (DH)	3592	C	949 567-9000	6041
Cp-Carrillo Inc	3592	E	949 567-9000	6042
Coast Composites LLC	3599	E	949 455-0665	6107
Computer Assisted Mfg Tech LLC	3599	E	949 263-8911	6108
Iconn Inc	3613	D	800 286-6742	6308
Staco Systems Inc (HQ)	3613	D	949 297-8700	6311
ITT Cannon LLC	3625	C	714 557-1700	6351
Q Com Inc	3625	E	949 833-1000	6356
Rosemount Analytical Inc	3625	A	713 396-8880	6358
Soundcoat Company Inc	3625	D	631 242-2200	6360
Composite Technology Corp	3629	C	949 428-8500	6370
Tivoli LLC	3641	E	714 957-6101	6408
Connectec Company Inc (PA)	3643	D	949 252-1077	6413
Ctc Global Corporation (PA)	3643	C	949 428-8500	6414
Wpmg Inc	3646	E	949 442-1601	6481
Henrys Adio Vsual Slutions Inc	3651	E	714 258-7238	6542
Toshiba Amer Elctrnic Cmpnnts (DH)	3651	B	949 462-7700	6562
Toshiba America Inc	3651	A	212 596-0600	6563
Vizio Inc (HQ)	3651	C	855 833-3221	6567
Vizio Holding Corp (PA)	3651	E	949 428-2525	6568
Lg-Ericsson USA Inc	3661	E	877 828-2673	6588
Anydata Corporation	3663	D	949 900-6040	6598
Fleet Management Solutions Inc	3663	E	800 500-6009	6616
Mophie Inc (DH)	3663	D	888 866-7443	6635
Sekai Electronics Inc (PA)	3663	E	949 783-5740	6659
Tricom Research Inc	3663	D	949 250-6024	6667
Tricom Research Inc	3663	E	949 250-6024	6668
General Monitors Inc (DH)	3669	C	949 581-4464	6684
Irvine Electronics LLC	3672	D	949 250-0315	6739
Lifetime Memory Products Inc	3672	E	949 794-9000	6745
Mflex Delaware Inc	3672	A	949 453-6800	6751
Multi-Fineline Electronix Inc (HQ)	3672	A	949 453-6800	6753
Trantronics Inc	3672	E	949 553-1234	6778
Aeroflex Incorporated	3674	C	800 843-1553	6796
American Arium	3674	E	949 623-7090	6797
Baywa RE Epc LLC	3674	E	949 398-3915	6806
Broadcom Corporation	3674	C	949 926-5000	6809
Broadcom Corporation	3674	D	714 376-5029	6810
Clariphy Communications Inc (DH)	3674	E	949 861-3074	6812
Conexant Systems LLC (HQ)	3674	E	949 483-4600	6814
Cooper Microelectronics Inc	3674	E	949 553-8352	6815
Hanwha Enrgy USA Holdings Corp (HQ)	3674	E	949 748-5906	6827
Hanwha Q Cells Usa Inc	3674	E	706 671-3077	6848
Marvell Semiconductor Inc	3674	A	949 614-7700	6857
Morse Micro Inc	3674	D	949 501-7080	6859
Netlist Inc (PA)	3674	D	949 435-0025	6872
Qlogic LLC (DH)	3674	C	949 389-6000	6882
Quartics Inc	3674	C	949 679-2672	6885
Rockley Photonics Inc (HQ)	3674	C	626 304-9960	6895
Skyworks Solutions Inc (PA)	3674	A	949 231-3000	6902
Suncore Inc	3674	E	949 450-0054	6904
Teridian Semiconductor Corp (DH)	3674	D	714 508-8800	6923
Allied Components Intl	3677	E	949 356-1780	6924
Astron Corporation	3677	E	949 458-7277	6945
Corsair Elec Connectors Inc	3678	C	949 833-0273	6950
Infinite Electronics Intl Inc (DH)	3678	D	949 261-1920	6951
Infinite Electronics Intl Inc	3678	E	949 261-1920	6955
Min-E-Con LLC	3678	D	949 250-0087	6963
Advanced Waveguide Tech	3679	E	949 297-3564	6965
American Audio Component Inc	3679	E	909 596-3788	6965
Bi-Search International Inc	3679	E	714 258-4500	6973
Bivar Inc	3679	E	949 951-8808	6974
Fema Electronics Corporation	3679	E	714 625-0140	6007
Infinite Electronics Inc (HQ)	3679	E	949 261-1920	7000
Interctive Dsplay Slutions Inc	3679	E	949 727-1959	7011
Ppst Inc (PA)	3679	D	800 421-1921	7037
Enevate Corporation	3691	E	949 243-0399	7075
Farstone Technology Inc	3695	C	949 336-4321	7104
Agents West Inc	3699	E	949 614-0293	7108
OBryant Electric Inc	3699	E	949 341-0025	7138
Orthodyne Electronics Corporation (HQ)	3699	C	949 660-0440	7140
USA Vision Systems Inc (HQ)	3699	E	949 583-1519	7159
Vti Instruments Corporation (HQ)	3699	E	949 955-1894	7160
Karma Automotive Inc	3711	A	855 565-2762	7181
Mazda Motor of America Inc (HQ)	3711	B	949 727-1990	7184
Rivian Automotive Inc (PA)	3711	B	888 748-4261	7189
Innova Electronics Corporation	3714	E	714 241-6800	7263
Pankl Engine Systems Inc	3714	E	949 428-8788	7281
American Scence Tech As T Corp	3721	D	310 773-1978	7329
Parker-Hannifin Corporation	3724	C	949 833-3000	7393
A-Info Inc	3728	E	949 346-7326	7397
Coast Composites LLC (PA)	3728	D	949 455-0665	7453
Fmh Aerospace Corp	3728	D	714 751-1000	7478
Meggitt Defense Systems Inc	3728	B	949 465-7700	7523
Pacific Precision Products Mfg Inc	3728	C	949 727-3844	7533
Parker-Hannifin Corporation	3728	C	949 833-3000	7535
Thales Avionics Inc	3728	C	949 381-3033	7575
Thales Avionics Inc	3728	E	949 790-2500	7576
Thales Avionics Inc	3728	E	949 829-5808	7577
Super73 Inc (PA)	3751	E	949 258-9245	7637
Tyvak Nn-Satellite Systems Inc (DH)	3761	E	949 753-1020	7658
Eaton Aerospace LLC	3812	E	949 452-9500	7714
Northrop Grumman Corporation	3812	E	949 260-9800	7753
Rockwell Collins Inc	3812	D	714 929-3000	7802
Rockwell Collins Inc	3812	E	714 929-3000	7803
Rogerson Aircraft Corporation (PA)	3812	D	949 660-0666	7804
Newport Corporation (HQ)	3821	B	949 863-3144	7829
Meggitt Western Design Inc	3822	E	949 465-7700	7837
Biodot Inc (HQ)	3823	D	949 440-3685	7849
Futek Advanced Sensor Tech Inc	3823	C	949 465-0900	7859
Graphtec America Inc (DH)	3823	E	949 770-6010	7861
Vertiv Corporation	3823	D	949 457-3600	7883
Emcor Facilities Services Inc	3824	C	949 475-6020	7889
Astronics Test Systems Inc (HQ)	3825	C	800 722-2528	7899
Equus Products Inc	3825	E	714 424-6779	7910
Hid Global Corporation	3825	C	949 732-2000	7915
Marvin Test Solutions Inc	3825	D	949 263-2222	7926
N H Research LLC (DH)	3825	E	949 474-3900	7927
Broadley-James Corporation (PA)	3826	D	949 829-5555	7947
Capillary Biomedical Inc	3826	E	949 317-1701	7948
Horiba Americas Holding Inc (HQ)	3826	A	949 250-4811	7957
Horiba Instruments Inc (DH)	3826	C	949 250-4811	7958
Tetra Tech Ec Inc	3826	E	949 809-5000	7985
Nipro Optics Inc	3827	E	949 215-1151	8012
Spectrum Scientific Inc	3827	E	949 260-9900	8022
Tfd Incorporated	3827	E	714 630-7127	8025
United Scope LLC (HQ)	3827	E	714 942-3202	8027
Horiba International Corp	3829	A	949 250-4811	8046
Meggitt (orange County) Inc (DH)	3829	C	949 493-8181	8053
Omni Optical Products Inc (PA)	3829	E	714 634-5700	8056
Acclarent Inc	3841	B	650 687-5888	8074
Advanced Sterlization (HQ)	3841	C	800 595-0200	8078
Alcon Lensx Inc (DH)	3841	D	949 753-1393	8080
Alcon Research Ltd	3841	D	949 387-2142	8081
Alcon Vision LLC	3841	A	949 753-6488	8083
Alliance Medical Products Inc (DH)	3841	E	949 768-4690	8085
Alliance Medical Products Inc	3841	E	949 664-9616	8086
Applied Cardiac Systems Inc	3841	E	949 855-9366	8091
Aspen Medical Products LLC	3841	D	949 681-0200	8098
B Braun US Phrm Mfg LLC	3841	A	610 691-5400	8101
Baxter Healthcare Corporation	3841	C	949 474-6301	8103
Bio-Medical Devices Inc	3841	E	949 752-9642	8108
Bio-Medical Devices Intl Inc	3841	E	949 752-9642	8109
Cas Medical Systems Inc (HQ)	3841	D	203 488-6056	8128
Chen-Tech Industries Inc (DH)	3841	E	949 855-6716	8130
Covidien LP	3841	C	949 837-3700	8139
Devax Inc	3841	E	949 461-0450	8141
Diality Inc	3841	D	949 916-5851	8143
Endologix Inc (PA)	3841	C	949 595-7200	8149
Endologix Canada LLC	3841	D	949 595-7200	8150
Envveno Medical Corporation	3841	E	949 261-2900	8151
I-Flow LLC	3841	A	800 448-3569	8165
Inari Medical Inc (PA)	3841	A	877 923-4747	8168
Irvine Biomedical Inc	3841	E	949 851-3053	8175
Joimax Inc	3841	E	949 859-3472	8178
Masimo Americas Inc	3841	E	949 297-7000	8187
Medtronic Inc	3841	C	949 837-3700	8192
Medtronic PS Medical Inc (DH)	3841	C	805 571-3769	8196
Micro Therapeutics Inc (HQ)	3841	E	949 837-3700	8199
Nellix Inc	3841	E	650 213-8700	8203
Neomend Inc	3841	D	949 783-3300	8204
Neuroptics Inc	3841	E	949 250-9792	8205
Pro-Dex Inc (PA)	3841	C	949 769-3200	8217
Rebound Therapeutics Corp	3841	E	949 305-8111	8222
Reverse Medical Corporation	3841	E	949 215-0660	8224
Source Scientific LLC	3841	E	949 231-5096	8228
Trivascular Inc (DH)	3841	E	707 543-8800	8242
Trivascular Technologies Inc (HQ)	3841	C	707 543-8800	8243
Biomet Inc	3842	E	949 453-3200	8254
Breathe Technologies Inc	3842	E	949 988-7700	8257
Edwards Lifesciences Corp	3842	D	949 250-2500	8261
Edwards Lifesciences Corp	3842	E	949 553-0611	8262
Edwards Lifesciences Corp (PA)	3842	A	949 250-2500	8263
Ethicon Inc	3842	B	949 581-5799	8265
Interpore Cross Intl Inc (DH)	3842	C	949 453-3200	8276
Mentor Worldwide LLC (DH)	3842	C	800 636-8678	8287

GEOGRAPHIC

	SIC	EMP	PHONE	ENTRY#
Mist Inc	3842	C	408 940-8700	8288
Ossur Americas Inc (HQ)	3842	D	800 233-6263	8292
Passy-Muir Inc (PA)	3842	E	949 833-8255	8293
Patient Safety Technologies Inc	3842	E	949 387-2277	8294
Sientra Inc (HQ)	3842	E	805 562-3500	8301
Ultimate Ears Consumer LLC	3842	C	949 502-8340	8313
United Biologics Inc	3842	E	949 345-7490	8314
3M Company	3843	B	949 863-1360	8323
Bien Air Usa Inc	3843	D	949 477-6050	8327
Keystone Dental Inc	3843	E	781 328-3324	8342
Keystone Dental Inc	3843	E	781 328-3382	8343
Westside Resources Inc	3843	E	800 944-3939	8361
Ampronix LLC	3845	D	949 273-8000	8368
Beta Bionics Inc	3845	E	949 297-6635	8371
Biosense Webster Inc (HQ)	3845	C	909 839-8500	8373
Edwards Lifesciences US Inc (HQ)	3845	D	949 250-2500	8378
Flexicare Incorporated	3845	E	949 450-9999	8379
Johnson Jhnson Srgcal Vsion In (HQ)	3845	B	949 581-5799	8386
Masimo Corporation	3845	E	949 297-7000	8387
Masimo Corporation	3845	E	949 297-7000	8388
Masimo Corporation (PA)	3845	B	949 297-7000	8389
Syneron Inc (DH)	3845	C	866 259-6661	8399
Barton Perreira LLC	3851	E	949 305-5360	8404
Eyeonics Inc	3851	E	949 788-6000	8407
Medennium Inc (PA)	3851	E	949 789-9000	8409
Thermaprint Corporation	3861	E	949 583-0800	8445
Strottman International Inc (PA)	3942	E	949 623-7900	8479
Bandai Nmco Toys Cllctbles AME (DH)	3944	D	949 271-6000	8482
Bell Sports Inc (HQ)	3949	D	469 417-6600	8505
Diamond Baseball Company Inc	3949	E	949 409-9300	8514
Hyper Ice Inc	3949	E	949 565-4994	8523
Melin LLC	3949	E	323 489-3274	8532
Star Trac Strength Inc	3949	B	714 669-1660	8545
Lasercare Technologies Inc (PA)	3955	E	310 202-4200	8564
Media Nation Enterprises LLC (PA)	3993	E	888 502-8222	8615
Shye West Inc (PA)	3993	E	949 486-4598	8631
Statewide Trffic Sfety Sgns In	3993	E	949 553-8272	8641
Above & Beyond Balloons Inc	3999	E	949 586-8470	8655
Flame and Wax Inc	3999	C	949 752-4000	8676
Perfect Choice Mfrs Inc	3999	E	714 792-0322	8713
Phiaro Incorporated	3999	E	949 727-1261	8715
Sundance Spas Inc (DH)	3999	D	909 606-7733	8730
Wood Candle Wick Tech Inc	3999	E	310 488-5885	8742
First Student Inc	4151	D	855 870-8747	8876
Sabsaf LLC	4215	D	951 266-6676	9011
Albertsons LLC	4225	D	949 855-2465	9048
Navajo Investments Inc (PA)	4522	D	949 863-9200	9181
Santa Catalina Island Company (PA)	4725	D	310 510-2000	9240
Agility Holdings Inc (DH)	4731	D	714 617-6300	9248
Agility Logistics Corp (DH)	4731	C	714 617-6300	9249
Glovis America Inc (HQ)	4731	C	714 427-0944	9285
3h Communication Systems Inc	4812	E	949 529-1583	9380
Nextel Communications Inc	4812	C	714 368-4509	9406
Sprint Corporation	4812	D	949 748-3353	9419
Boldyn Networks US Services LL	4813	B	877 999-7070	9427
Boldyn Ntwrks US Oprations LLC	4813	C	949 515-1500	9428
Incomnet Communications Corp	4813	D	949 251-8000	9444
Horizon Communication Tech Inc	4899	D	714 982-3900	9565
Edison Capital	4911	C	909 594-3789	9579
Edison Energy LLC	4911	C	949 491-1633	9580
Hanwha Q Cells USA Corp	4911	D	949 748-5996	9587
Southern California Edison Co	4911	C	949 587-5416	9620
Sunnova Energy Corporation	4911	C	877 757-7697	9640
Irvine Ranch Water District (PA)	4941	C	949 453-5300	9695
Irvine Ranch Water District	4941	C	949 453-5300	9696
Waste MGT Collectn Recycl Inc	4953	C	949 451-2600	9780
Ampco Contracting Inc	4959	C	949 955-2255	9785
Jonset LLC	4959	D	949 551-5151	9787
Asian European Products Inc	5013	C	949 553-3900	9812
Rally Holdings LLC	5013	A	817 919-6833	9842
Specialty Interior Mfg Inc	5013	E	714 296-8618	9850
Ledra Brands Inc	5023	C	714 259-9959	9898
Canon USA Inc	5043	B	949 753-4000	9965
Integrus	5044	D	949 538-9211	9974
Kyocera Dcment Solutions W LLC	5044	C	800 996-9591	9975
Accton Manufacturing & Svc Inc (HQ)	5045	D	949 679-8029	9983
Aten Technology Inc	5045	D	949 453-8782	9988
Axiom Memory Solutions LLC	5045	C	949 581-1450	9990
D-Link Systems Incorporated	5045	C	714 885-6000	9995
Dane Elec Corp USA (HQ)	5045	E	949 450-2900	9996
Ephesoft Inc	5045	D	949 335-5335	10001
Eworkplace Manufacturing Inc	5045	D	949 583-1646	10003
Getac Inc	5045	D	949 681-2900	10009
Hitachi Solutions America Ltd (DH)	5045	E	949 242-1300	10010
Ingram Micro Inc (HQ)	5045	A	714 566-1000	10011
Samsung Research America Inc	5045	B	949 468-1143	10027
TW Security Corp (HQ)	5045	C	949 932-1000	10035
U2 Science Labs Inc	5045	D	949 482-8540	10036
Trimark Raygal LLC	5046	C	949 474-1000	10054
Alphaeon Corporation	5047	B	949 284-4555	10058
Balt Usa LLC	5047	D	949 788-1443	10067
Direct Medical Supply Inc	5047	C	949 823-9565	10075
Fisher & Paykel Healthcare Inc	5047	C	949 453-4000	10078
Horibaabx Inc	5047	C	949 453-0500	10085
Nihon Kohden America LLC (HQ)	5047	C	949 580-1555	10095
Sunrise Respiratory Care Inc	5047	C	949 398-6555	10110
Team Post-Op Inc	5047	C	949 253-5500	10111
Georg Fischer LLC (DH)	5051	D	714 731-8800	10137
Norman Industrial Mtls LLC	5051	E	949 250-3343	10147
Pusan Pipe America Inc	5051	B	949 655-8000	10150
Tte Technology Inc	5064	B	877 300-8837	10226
Jae Electronics Inc (HQ)	5065	E	949 753-2600	10256
Linksys LLC	5065	C	408 526-4000	10263
Linksys LLC	5065	C	310 751-5100	10264
Linksys Usa LLC	5065	D	949 270-8500	10265
Omnitron Systems Tech Inc	5065	D	949 250-6510	10275
Telit Wireless Solutions Inc	5065	C	949 461-7150	10293
Parker-Hannifin Corporation	5084	C	949 465-4519	10392
General Tool Inc	5085	D	949 261-2322	10439
SPS Technologies LLC	5085	B	949 474-6000	10466
Nikken Global Inc (HQ)	5087	C	949 789-2000	10477
Shimano North Amer Holdg Inc (HQ)	5091	C	949 951-5003	10515
Bandai Namco Entrmt Amer Inc	5092	C	408 235-2000	10519
Merchsource LLC (DH)	5092	C	800 374-2744	10524
Sega of America Inc (DH)	5092	E	949 788-0455	10527
C D Listening Bar Inc	5099	A	949 225-1170	10555
Sunscape Eyewear Inc	5099	C	949 553-0590	10571
Blue Sky The Clor Imgntion LLC	5112	D	714 389-7700	10578
Momentum Textiles LLC (PA)	5131	E	949 833-8886	10668
Delta Galil USA Inc	5137	B	949 296-0380	10705
Fox Head Inc (HQ)	5137	B	949 757-9500	10709
Snowmass Apparel Inc (PA)	5137	E	949 788-0617	10728
Asics America Corporation (HQ)	5139	C	949 453-8888	10733
Robert Kinsella Inc	5141	D	949 453-9533	10768
Eggs Unlimited LLC	5144	C	888 554-3977	10834
Newport Meat Southern Cal Inc	5147	C	949 399-4200	10877
Kids Healthy Foods LLC	5149	E	949 260-4950	10953
Mhh Holdings Inc	5149	C	949 651-9903	10960
Pernod Ricard Usa LLC	5182	D	949 242-6800	11059
Graphic Packaging Intl LLC	5199	D	949 250-0900	11123
Victory Foam Inc (PA)	5199	D	949 474-0690	11147
Iherb LLC (PA)	5499	A	951 616-3600	11305
Ford Motor Company	5511	D	949 341-5800	11348
Tuttle-Click Ford Inc	5511	C	949 855-1704	11425
Impressions Vanity Company (PA)	5719	E	844 881-0790	11532
Axelliant LLC	5734	D	424 535-1100	11538
Taco Bell Corp (HQ)	5812	A	949 863-4500	11604
Arbonne International LLC (DH)	5999	E	949 770-2610	11674
Arbonne International Dist Inc	5999	E	800 272-6663	11675
Smartlabs Inc	5999	D	800 762-7846	11698
City National Bank	6021	C	949 223-4000	11730
California Republic Bank	6022	B	949 270-9700	11749
First Foundation Inc (PA)	6022	C	949 202-4160	11767
Pacific Premier Bancorp Inc (PA)	6022	C	949 864-8000	11775
Opus Bank	6029	A	949 250-9800	11783
Plaza Bank	6029	D	949 502-4300	11784
Pacific Trust Bank	6035	C	949 236-5211	11787
Pan American Bank Fsb	6035	B	949 224-1917	11788
Cig Financial LLC	6141	D	877 244-4442	11852
Hyundai Protection Plan Inc	6141	B	949 468-4000	11854
Change Lending LLC	6162	D	949 769-3526	11893
Decision Ready Solutions Inc	6162	E	949 400-1126	11897
Guaranteed Rate Inc	6162	C	424 354-5344	11912
Impac Mortgage Corp	6162	B	949 475-3600	11914
Lenders Investment Corp	6162	D	714 540-4747	11916
Loandepot Inc (PA)	6162	C	888 337-6888	11918
Loandepotcom LLC (DH)	6162	A	888 337-6888	11919
Mission Hills Mortgage Corp (HQ)	6162	C	714 972-3832	11924
Network Capital Funding Corp (PA)	6162	B	949 442-0060	11927
New Century Mortgage Corp	6162	A	949 440-7030	11928
Ocmbc Inc (PA)	6162	C	949 679-7400	11929
Rushmore Loan MGT Svcs LLC (PA)	6162	A	949 727-4798	11933
Sea Breeze Financial Svcs Inc	6162	C	949 223-9700	11934
5 Arches LLC	6163	D	949 387-8092	11938
Carnegie Mortgage LLC	6163	B	949 379-7000	11941
Center Street Lending Corp	6163	D	949 244-1090	11942

2025 Southern California
Business Directory and Buyers Guide

(P-0000) Products & Services Section entry number
(PA)=Parent Co (HQ)=Headquarters (DH)=Div Headquarters

	SIC	EMP	PHONE	ENTRY#
Clearpath Lending	6163	C	949 502-3577	11944
Sand Canyon Corporation (HQ)	6163	D	949 727-9425	11952
Hyundai ABS Funding LLC	6211	C	949 732-2697	11968
National Financial Svcs LLC	6211	A	949 476-0157	12003
Blythe Global Advisors LLC	6282	D	949 757-4180	12019
American Funds Service Company (DH)	6289	B	949 975-5000	12038
New First Fincl Resources LLC	6311	D	949 223-2160	12046
Liberty Dental Plan Cal Inc	6324	B	949 223-0007	12093
Liberty Dental Plan Corp (PA)	6324	D	888 703-6999	12094
Developers Surety Indemnity Co (DH)	6351	D	949 263-3300	12146
Lawyers Title Insurance Corp	6361	A	949 223-5575	12155
American Heritage Lf Insur Co	6411	D	800 753-9227	12171
Automobile Club Southern Cal	6411	C	714 973-1211	12177
Burnham Bnefits Insur Svcs LLC (PA)	6411	D	805 772-7965	12185
Indemnity Company California (DH)	6411	D	949 263-3300	12220
Insco Insurance Services Inc (DH)	6411	D	949 263-3415	12221
Lexisnexis Risk Assets Inc	6411	D	949 222-0028	12226
Mullin TBG Insur Agcy Svcs LLC (DH)	6411	C		12237
Precept Advisory Group LLC (DH)	6411	D	949 955-1430	12245
W Brown Assoc Insur Svcs LLC	6411	D	949 851-2060	12267
Ford Motor Land Dev Corp	6512	C	949 242-6606	12292
Orange Bakery Inc	6512	C	949 454-1247	12308
PM Realty Group LP	6512	D	949 390-5500	12310
Humangood Socal	6513	C	949 854-9500	12347
Irvine APT Communities LP (HQ)	6513	C	949 720-5600	12350
Action Property Management Inc (PA)	6514	D	949 450-0202	12373
Atlas Hospitality Group	6531	D	949 622-3400	12382
Auctioncom Inc	6531	C	800 499-6199	12383
Auctioncom LLC (PA)	6531	C	949 859-2777	12384
Cushman & Wakefield Cal Inc	6531	A	949 474-4004	12421
Essex Properties LLC	6531	D	949 798-8100	12439
First Amercn Prof RE Svcs Inc (HQ)	6531	D	714 250-1400	12442
First Team RE - Orange Cnty (PA)	6531	D	949 988-3000	12448
First Team RE - Orange Cnty	6531	C	714 485-7984	12450
Firstsrvice Rsidential Cal LLC (HQ)	6531	C	949 448-6000	12454
Irvine APT Communities LP	6531	C	949 854-4942	12470
J & M Realty Company (PA)	6531	C	949 261-2727	12471
Lowe Enterprises Inc	6531	D	949 724-1515	12480
Red Tail Residential LLC (PA)	6531	D	949 399-2510	12518
Steadfast Management Co Inc (PA)	6531	C	949 748-3000	12534
Ten-X Finance Inc	6531	C	949 465-8523	12536
Western National Securities (PA)	6531	C	949 862-6200	12549
Commonwealth Land Title Insur	6541	C	949 460-4500	12554
Guardian Title Company	6541	D	949 495-9306	12560
Panattoni Development Co Inc (PA)	6552	D	916 381-1561	12576
Taylor Morrison California LLC	6552	C	949 341-1200	12581
N2 Acquisition Company Inc	6719	D	714 942-3563	12605
Nrp Holding Co Inc (PA)	6719	C	949 583-1000	12606
Swds Holdings Inc	6719	B	800 395-5277	12616
W-GL 1241 Ocbc Hldings Viii LP	6719	D	949 331-1323	12619
Acorns Grow Incorporated (PA)	6726	C	949 251-0095	12644
Impac Secured Assets Corp	6733	D	949 475-3600	12659
Kaiser Foundation Hospitals	6733	C	949 932-5000	12660
Brer Affiliates LLC (DH)	6794	C	949 794-7900	12677
American Healthcare Reit Inc (PA)	6798	D	949 270-9200	12682
Nnn Realty Investors LLC	6799	B	714 667-8252	12724
NRLL LLC	6799	B	949 768-7777	12726
Courtyard Management Corp	7011	D	949 453-1033	12800
Dkn Hotel LLC (PA)	7011	B	714 427-4320	12813
Golden Hotels Ltd Partnership	7011	C	949 833-2770	12828
Greens Group Inc	7011	C	949 829-4902	12835
Hyatt Corporation	7011	C	949 975-1234	12866
Marriott International Inc	7011	B	949 721-3606	12918
Montage Hotels & Resorts LLC (PA)	7011	A	949 715-5002	12927
Montage Intl N Amer LLC	7011	D	800 700-7744	12928
Spectrum Hotel Group LLC	7011	C	949 471-8888	13032
American Cmpus Communities Inc	7021	D	949 854-0900	13096
Prudential Overall Supply (PA)	7218	D	949 250-4855	13140
Alcone Marketing Group Inc (HQ)	7311	D	949 595-5322	13195
Ignite Health LLC (PA)	7311	D	949 861-3200	13214
Interactive Media Holdings Inc	7311	C	949 861-8888	13216
Local Corporation (PA)	7311	D	949 784-0800	13222
Specificmedia Inc	7311	D	949 861-8888	13246
Young & Rubicam LLC	7311	B	949 754-2000	13254
Young & Rubicam LLC	7311	C	949 754-2100	13255
Ghost Management Group LLC	7313	C	949 870-1400	13266
Egs Financial Care Inc (DH)	7322	B	877 217-4423	13282
Celestial-Saturn Parent Inc (PA)	7323	C	949 214-1000	13292
Corelogic Credco LLC (DH)	7323	C	800 255-0792	13293
Spectrum Information Svcs LLC (PA)	7331	D	949 752-7070	13306
Calico Building Services Inc	7349	D	949 380-8707	13362
Certified Wtr Dmage Rsrtrion E	7349	E	800 417-1776	13363
Creative Maintenance Systems	7349	D	949 852-2871	13367
Innovative Cleaning Svcs Inc	7349	B	949 251-9188	13380
Celtic Leasing Corp	7359	D	949 263-3880	13449
Cybercoders Inc	7361	C	949 885-5151	13508
Kore1 LLC	7361	C	949 706-6990	13536
Loan Administration Netwrk Inc	7361	D	949 752-5246	13541
Workway Inc	7361	C	949 553-8700	13583
Magnit Rs Inc	7363	D	800 660-9544	13604
Sfn Group Inc	7363	A	949 727-8500	13622
Alvaria Inc	7371	C	408 595-5002	13650
Applied Computer Solutions (DH)	7371	D	714 861-2200	13656
Avamar Technologies Inc	7371	D	949 743-5100	13663
Axon Networks Inc (PA)	7371	D	949 310-4429	13666
Buddy Group Inc	7371	C	949 468-0042	13681
Codazen Inc	7371	D	949 916-6266	13689
Discovery Opco LLC	7371	C	844 933-3627	13707
Ecotrak LLC	7371	D	888 219-0000	13715
Eighteenth Meridian Inc	7371	B	714 706-3643	13716
Frontech N Fujitsu Amer Inc (DH)	7371	C	877 766-7545	13733
Gan Limited (PA)	7371	A	833 565-0550	13735
Home Junction Inc	7371	D	858 777-9533	13742
NC America LLC	7371	E	949 447-6287	13775
Neudesic LLC (HQ)	7371	C	949 754-4500	13778
Neuintel LLC (PA)	7371	D	949 625-6117	13779
Operation Technology Inc	7371	D	949 462-0100	13789
Orange Logic LLC	7371	D	949 396-2233	13790
Pacific Tech Solutions LLC	7371	D	949 830-1623	13792
Patientfi LLC	7371	C	949 441-5484	13794
Secureauth Corporation (PA)	7371	C	949 777-6959	13815
Setschedule LLC	7371	C	888 222-0011	13819
Smart Energy Systems Inc	7371	C	909 703-9609	13821
Smart Utility Systems Inc	7371	D	909 217-3344	13822
Startel Corporation (PA)	7371	C	949 863-8700	13830
Stratacare Llc	7371	C	949 743-1200	13832
Tcg Software Services Inc	7371	B	714 665-6200	13839
Thomas Gallaway Corporation (PA)	7371	D	949 517-9500	13843
Tp-Link Systems Inc	7371	C	866 225-8139	13845
Tungsten Automation Corp (PA)	7371	B	949 783-1000	13853
Unisys Corporation	7371	C	949 380-5000	13854
Vegatek Corporation	7371	D	949 502-0090	13858
Vision Solutions Inc (HQ)	7371	D	949 253-6500	13863
Activision Blizzard Inc	7372	D	949 955-1380	13870
Advisys Inc	7372	E	949 250-0794	13872
Astea International Inc	7372	E	949 784-5000	13886
Blind Squirrel Games Inc	7372	E	714 460-0860	13891
Blizzard Entertainment Inc (DH)	7372	D	949 955-1380	13893
Calamp Corp (PA)	7372	E	949 600-5600	13897
Cloudcover Iot Inc (PA)	7372	E	888 511-2022	13903
Cloudvirga Inc	7372	D	949 799-2643	13904
Club Speed LLC (PA)	7372	E	951 817-7073	13905
Compugroup Medical Inc	7372	C	949 206-5300	13906
Dorado Network Systems Corp	7372	C	650 227-7300	13917
Eagle Topco LP	7372	A	949 585-4329	13919
Egl Holdco Inc	7372	A	800 678-7423	13922
Eturns Inc	7372	E	949 265-2626	13928
Foundation Inc	7372	E	310 294-8955	13934
Global Cash Card Inc	7372	C	949 751-0360	13939
Illumnate Educatn Holdings Inc (PA)	7372	E	949 656-3133	13946
Justenough Software Corp Inc (HQ)	7372	E	949 706-5400	13958
Kofax Limited (PA)	7372	A	949 783-1000	13963
Medata LLC (HQ)	7372	D	714 918-1310	13972
Microsoft Corporation	7372	D	949 263-3000	13973
Mscsoftware Corporation	7372	A	714 540-8900	13978
Netwrix Corporation	7372	D	888 638-9749	13985
Nextgen Healthcare Inc (HQ)	7372	B	949 255-2600	13988
Ntrust Infotech Inc	7372	D	562 207-1600	13993
Numecent Inc	7372	E	949 833-2800	13994
Nxgn Management LLC	7372	C	949 255-2600	13996
Patron Solutions LLC	7372	C	949 823-1700	14005
Planet DDS Inc (PA)	7372	E	800 861-5098	14006
Plugg ME LNc	7372	E	949 705-4472	14007
Prism Software Corporation	7372	E	949 855-3100	14009
Qdos Inc	7372	E	949 362-8888	14011
Sage Software Holdings Inc (HQ)	7372	B	866 530-7243	14022
Strategy Companion Corp	7372	D	714 460-8398	14040
Timevalue Software	7372	C	949 727-1800	14055
Uneekor Inc	7372	D	888 262-6498	14059
Upstanding LLC	7372	C	949 788-9900	14061
Wm Technology Inc (PA)	7372	E	646 699-3750	14065
Alteryx Inc (PA)	7373	E	888 836-4274	14070
Computer Tech Resources Inc	7373	C	714 665-6507	14077
Genea Energy Partners Inc	7373	C	714 694-0536	14084
Icl Systems Inc	7373	D	877 425-8725	14087
Result Group Inc	7373	D	480 777-7130	14104

Employee Codes: A=Over 500 employees, B=251-500
C=101-250, D=51-100, E=20-50, F=10-19, G=1-9

2025 Southern California
Business Directory and Buyers Guide

© Mergent Inc. 1-800-342-5647

1291

	SIC	EMP	PHONE	ENTRY#
Trace3 LLC (HQ)	7373	D	949 333-2300	14111
Automatic Data Processing Inc	7374	C	949 751-0360	14122
Enclarity Inc	7374	B	949 797-7160	14133
Mercury Technology Group Inc	7374	C	949 417-0260	14145
S E O P Inc	7374	C	949 682-7906	14153
Verizon Connect Telo Inc (DH)	7374	C	844 617-1100	14163
Accurate Background LLC (PA)	7375	B	800 784-3911	14166
Sage Software Inc	7375	E	949 753-1222	14178
Inhouseit Inc	7378	D	949 660-5655	14188
Quest Intl Monitor Svc Inc (PA)	7378	C	949 581-9900	14189
Rakworx Inc	7378	C	949 215-1362	14190
Blytheco Inc (PA)	7379	E	949 583-9500	14201
Caylent Inc (PA)	7379	C	800 215-9124	14204
Crowdstrike Inc	7379	C	888 512-8906	14210
Crowdstrike Inc	7379	C	888 512-8906	14211
Dyntek Inc (DH)	7379	D	949 271-6700	14215
Gdr Group Inc	7379	C	949 453-8818	14220
Kodella LLC	7379	C	844 563-3552	14230
Kore1 Inc	7379	D	949 706-6990	14231
Ovation Tech Inc	7379	C	949 271-0054	14240
ABM Onsite Services Inc	7381	A	949 863-9100	14266
Accurate Emplyment Scrning LLC	7381	C	847 255-1852	14267
Landmark Event Staffing	7381	A	714 293-4248	14311
Universal Protection Svc LP (HQ)	7381	D	866 877-1965	14360
Universal Services America LP (HQ)	7381	D	866 877-1965	14361
Arcules Inc	7382	C	949 439-0053	14382
Sentinel Monitoring Corp (HQ)	7382	D	949 453-1550	14420
Alorica Customer Care Inc	7389	C	941 906-9000	14441
Alorica Inc (PA)	7389	D	866 256-7422	14442
Americor Funding LLC (PA)	7389	C	888 211-2660	14447
Andrew Lauren Company Inc	7389	C	949 861-4222	14449
Baxalta US Inc	7389	C	949 474-6301	14460
Boost Mobile LLC	7389	A	949 451-1563	14464
Consoldted Fire Protection LLC (HQ)	7389	A	949 727-3277	14477
Data Council LLC	7389	D	904 512-3200	14487
Flagship Credit Acceptance LLC	7389	D	949 748-7172	14495
Global Language Solutions LLC	7389	D	949 798-1400	14503
La Jolla Group (PA)	7389	B	949 428-2800	14526
Universal Card Inc	7389	B	949 861-4000	14618
Ameripark LLC	7521	B	949 279-7525	14655
Newport Beach Auto Group LLC	7538	D	888 703-7226	14696
Dynamic Auto Images Inc	7542	B	714 771-3400	14707
Bsh Home Appliances Corp (DH)	7629	C	949 440-7100	14729
Edwards Theatres Circuit Inc	7832	C	949 854-8811	14938
Ming Entertainment Group LLC	7929	D	949 679-2089	14999
Equinox-76th Street Inc	7991	D	949 296-1700	15050
Row House Franchise LLC	7991	C	949 341-5585	15060
Xponential Fitness Inc (PA)	7991	B	949 346-3000	15071
Shady Canyon Golf Club Inc	7997	C	949 856-7000	15174
Cor Medica Technology	8011	E	949 353-4554	15287
Inmode	8011	D	949 387-5711	15332
Monarch Healthcare A Medical (HQ)	8011	D	949 923-3200	15396
SBC Medical Group Holdings Inc	8011	A	949 593-0250	15448
Southern Cal Prmnnte Med Group	8011	C	949 262-5780	15476
Pacific Dental Services LLC (PA)	8021	B	714 845-8500	15523
Pacific Dntl Svcs Holdg Co Inc	8021	C	714 845-8500	15524
Equinox-76th Street Inc	8049	D	949 975-8400	15541
In Stepps Inc	8049	D	949 474-1493	15543
New Vista Behavioral Hlth LLC	8052	D	949 284-0095	15815
Childrens Hospital Orange Cnty	8062	C	949 387-2586	15955
Childrens Hospital Orange Cnty	8062	C	949 769-6473	15957
Hoag Hospital Irvine	8062	D	949 764-4624	16021
Kaiser Foundation Hospitals	8062	C	949 262-5780	16057
St Joseph Hospital of Orange	8062	C	714 568-5500	16215
Alliance Healthcare Svcs Inc (DH)	8071	C	800 544-3215	16304
Cap Diagnostics LLC	8071	C	714 966-1221	16306
Thaihot Investment Co US Ltd	8071	A	949 242-5300	16336
University California Irvine	8071	C	949 202-7580	16339
University California Irvine	8071	C	909 358-5774	16340
Keating Dental Arts Inc	8072	C	949 955-2100	16344
Vna of Greater Los Angeles Inc	8082	D	951 252-5314	16432
Davita Inc	8092	B	949 930-4400	16434
Discovery Practice MGT Inc	8093	A	714 828-1800	16469
Cerna Healthcare LLC	8099	C	949 298-3200	16546
University California Irvine	8099	D	949 824-2662	16625
Berger Kahn A Law Corporation (PA)	8111	D	949 474-1880	16645
Crowell & Moring LLP	8111	C	949 263-8400	16666
Fisher & Phillips LLP	8111	C	949 851-2424	16684
Gibson Dunn & Crutcher LLP	8111	C	949 451-3800	16689
Greenberg Traurig LLP	8111	D	949 732-6500	16697
Knobbe Martens Olson Bear LLP (PA)	8111	B	949 760-0404	16721
Law Offces Les Zeve A Prof Cor	8111	C	714 848-7920	16727
Malcolm & Cisneros A Law Corp	8111	C	949 252-9400	16736
Palmieri Tyler Wner Wlhelm Wld	8111	D	949 851-9400	16756
Rutan & Tucker LLP (PA)	8111	B	714 641-5100	16773
Shook Hardy & Bacon LLP	8111	C	949 475-1500	16781
Stretto Inc (PA)	8111	D	949 222-1212	16787
Troutman Ppper Hmlton Snders L	8111	D	949 622-2700	16791
Womble Bond Dickinson (us) LLP	8111	C	310 207-3800	16797
Zbs Law LLP	8111	D	714 848-7920	16798
University California Irvine	8221	C	949 824-7725	16836
It Division Inc	8243	C	678 648-2709	16843
Learning Ovations Inc	8299	E	734 904-1459	16855
Council On Aging - Sthern Cal	8322	D	714 479-0107	16902
Second Hrvest Fd Bnk Ornge CNT	8322	D	949 653-2900	17008
Owl Education and Training Inc	8331	C	949 797-2000	17064
Child Development Incorporated	8351	B	949 854-5060	17083
Leport Educational Inst Inc	8351	B	914 374-8860	17093
Silverado Snior Lving Hldngs	8361	A	949 240-7200	17194
Western Growers Association (PA)	8611	C	949 863-1000	17290
Temporary Staffing Union	8631	A	714 728-5186	17316
ABM Facility Services LLC	8711	A	949 330-1555	17476
ABS Consulting Inc	8711	D	714 734-4242	17477
Aria Group Incorporated	8711	C	949 475-2915	17486
Es Engineering Services LLC	8711	D	949 988-3500	17527
Fuscoe Engineering Inc (PA)	8711	D	949 474-1960	17535
Gradient Engineers Inc	8711	C	949 477-0555	17541
Hunsaker & Assoc Irvine Inc (PA)	8711	D	949 583-1010	17551
Hyundai Amer Technical Ctr Inc	8711	C	734 337-2500	17553
Iris Technology Corporation	8711	D	949 975-8410	17559
Jacobs Engineering Group Inc	8711	D	949 224-7500	17562
Jacobs Project Management Co	8711	D	949 224-7695	17566
Kpff Inc	8711	D	949 252-1022	17574
Mds Consulting (PA)	8711	D	949 251-8821	17583
Mobilenet Services Inc (PA)	8711	C	949 951-4444	17589
Modelo Group Inc	8711	E	562 446-5091	17590
Panasonic Avionics Corporation (DH)	8711	B	949 672-2000	17604
Tetra Tech Inc	8711	D	949 263-0846	17645
Wsp USA Inc	8711	D	714 973-4880	17663
Gkk Corporation (PA)	8712	D	949 250-1500	17671
Ktgy Group Inc (PA)	8712	D	949 851-2133	17678
LPA Inc (PA)	8712	C	949 261-1001	17681
Stantec Consulting Svcs Inc	8712	C	949 923-6000	17691
Ware Malcomb (PA)	8712	C	949 660-9128	17695
William Hzmlhlch Archtects Inc	8712	D	949 250-0607	17696
Baker Tilly Us LLP	8721	A	949 222-2999	17705
Ernst & Young LLP	8721	B	949 794-2300	17724
Kpmg LLP	8721	C	949 885-5400	17739
LLP Moss Adams	8721	C	949 221-4000	17742
Omega Accounting Solutions Inc	8721	C	949 348-2433	17749
University California Irvine	8721	D	949 824-6828	17758
Wright Ford Young & Co	8721	D	949 910-2727	17760
Agendia Inc	8731	C	949 540-6300	17762
Axonics Inc (PA)	8731	A	949 396-6322	17773
Bioduro LLC	8731	B	858 529-6600	17775
Fluxergy Inc (PA)	8731	E	949 305-4201	17788
Hgst Inc	8731	B	949 448-0385	17794
Invasix Inc	8731	D	855 411-2639	17798
Isotis Orthobiologics Inc	8731	C	949 595-8710	17801
University California Irvine	8731	B	949 824-2819	17836
University California Irvine	8731	C	949 824-3359	17837
Henkel US Operations Corp	8732	D	714 368-8000	17845
Iqvia Inc (PA)	8732	D	866 267-4479	17853
Mind Research Institute	8733	C	949 345-8700	17882
Willow Laboratories Inc	8733	D	949 679-6100	17897
Aptim Corp	8734	A	949 261-6441	17904
Corvel Corporation	8741	C	503 222-3144	17969
Legacy Prtners Residential Inc	8741	C	949 930-6600	18004
Mtc Financial Inc	8741	C	949 252-8300	18016
Navigators Management Co Inc	8741	C	949 255-4860	18019
Renovo Solutions LLC (PA)	8741	B	714 599-7969	18045
Saga Kapital Group Inc	8741	D	714 294-4132	18048
Smile Brands Group Inc (PA)	8741	C	714 668-1300	18052
Sodexo Management Inc	8741	A	949 753-2042	18055
Southern Implants Inc	8741	C	949 273-8505	18059
Tct Mobile Inc	8741	D	949 892-2990	18063
Vpm Management Inc	8741	C	949 863-1500	18076
Western National Contractors	8741	D	949 862-6200	18079
Beacon Resources LLC	8742	C	949 955-1773	18104
Bridgwter Consulting Group Inc	8742	D	949 535-1755	18111
City of Irvine	8742	C	949 724-7600	18116
Denken Solutions Inc	8742	C	949 630-5263	18126
Exult Inc	8742	A	949 856-8800	18132
Infospan	8742	A	714 856-2655	18153
Lba Inc	8742	D	949 833-0400	18160
M F Salta Co Inc (PA)	8742	D	562 421-2512	18164

2025 Southern California
Business Directory and Buyers Guide

(P-0000) Products & Services Section entry number
(PA)=Parent Co (HQ)=Headquarters (DH)=Div Headquarters

	SIC	EMP	PHONE	ENTRY#
Online Marketing Group LLC	8742	C	888 737-9635	18187
Sullivncrtsmnroe Insur Svcs LL (PA)	8742	C	800 427-3253	18222
Trinamix Inc (PA)	8742	B	408 507-3583	18235
Willis North America Inc	8742	C	909 476-3300	18242
Young & Rubicam LLC	8742	B	949 224-6300	18246
Advanced Strilization Pdts Inc	8748	B	888 783-7723	18275
Alliant Insurance Services Inc (PA)	8748	C	949 756-0271	18282
Anchor Cnsling Edcatn Sltons L	8748	D	213 505-6322	18284
Crystalview Technology Corp	8748	B	949 788-0738	18305
Fryman Management	8748	D	949 481-5211	18309
In Montrose Wtr Sstnblity Svcs	8748	D	949 988-3500	18323
Karman Topco LP (PA)	8748	C	949 797-2900	18328
Lsa Associates Inc (PA)	8748	C	949 553-0666	18332
Nexgenix Inc (PA)	8748	B	714 665-6240	18340
Openpopcom Inc (PA)	8748	C	714 249-7044	18345
Slr International Corporation	8748	A	949 553-8417	18357
TRC Solutions Inc (HQ)	8748	C	949 753-0101	18364
Vinculums Services LLC	8748	C	949 783-3552	18368
West Coast Consulting LLC	8748	C	949 250-4102	18371

IRWINDALE, CA - Los Angeles County

	SIC	EMP	PHONE	ENTRY#
Pierre Landscape Inc	0781	C	626 587-2121	185
Mariposa Landscapes Inc (PA)	0782	D	626 960-0196	221
Church & Larsen Inc	1742	C	626 303-8741	1005
Kifuki USA Co Inc (HQ)	2015	D	626 334-8090	1280
Q & B Foods Inc (DH)	2035	D	626 334-8090	1372
J&R Taylor Brothers Assoc Inc	2047	D	626 334-9301	1418
Califrnia Cstm Frits Flvors LL (PA)	2087	D	626 736-4130	1672
Ready Pac Foods Inc (HQ)	2099	A	626 856-8686	1839
Ready Pac Produce Inc (DH)	2099	E	800 800-4088	1840
Decore-Ative Spc NC LLC	2431	C	626 960-7731	2304
Pacific Panel Products Corp	2499	E	626 851-0444	2414
Roma Moulding Inc	2499	E	626 334-2539	2417
Seaboard Envelope Co Inc	2677	E	626 960-4559	2752
Million Corporation	2759	D	626 969-1888	3155
Esmond Natural Inc	2833	D	626 337-1588	3314
Bimeda Inc	2834	C	626 815-1680	3374
Chem Arrow Corp	2992	E	626 358-2255	3849
Polycycle Solutions LLC	3085	D	626 856-2100	3989
Altium Packaging	3089	E	626 856-2100	4042
Davis Wire Corporation (HQ)	3315	C	626 969-7651	4533
STS Metals Inc (PA)	3463	D	626 969-6711	5161
A & M Engineering Inc	3599	E	626 813-2020	6059
Arrow Engineering	3599	E	626 960-2806	6083
Pertronix Inc	3694	E	909 599-5955	7098
NDC Technologies Inc	3829	D	626 960-3300	8055
Johnson & Johnson	3842	B	909 839-8650	8279
Best Overnite Express Inc (PA)	4213	D	626 256-6340	8933
Southern California Edison Co	4911	D	626 633-3070	9628
Southern California Edison Co	4911	B	626 814-4212	9630
Southern California Edison Co	4911	B	626 812-7380	9634
Southern California Edison Co	4911	B	626 543-8081	9637
Ihealth Manufacturing Inc	5047	D	216 785-0107	10086
Superior Communications Inc (PA)	5065	C	877 522-4727	10285
Emtek Products Group LLC (HQ)	5072	C	626 961-0413	10306
Blue Ridge Home Fashions Inc	5131	E	626 960-6069	10662
Mountain Gear Corporation	5136	C	626 851-2488	10691
Victory Sportswear Inc	5949	C	866 308-0798	11652
Sinecera Inc	7389	D	626 962-1087	14598
Onelegacy	8099	D	213 229-5600	16596
Tandex Test Labs Inc	8734	E	626 962-7166	17927
Calibre International LLC	8743	C	626 969-4660	18252

JAMUL, CA - San Diego County

	SIC	EMP	PHONE	ENTRY#
Spectrum Security Services Inc (PA)	7381	C	619 669-6660	14353

JOSHUA TREE, CA - San Bernardino County

	SIC	EMP	PHONE	ENTRY#
Hdmc Holdings LLC	8062	D	760 366-3711	16012

JULIAN, CA - San Diego County

	SIC	EMP	PHONE	ENTRY#
YMCA of San Diego County	8641	C	760 765-0642	17394

JURUPA VALLEY, CA - Riverside County

	SIC	EMP	PHONE	ENTRY#
Perry Coast Construction Inc	1542	C	951 774-0677	570
Christian Brothers Mechanical Services Inc	1711	C	951 361-2247	761
Right Angle Solutions Inc	1711	E	951 934-3081	831
Hartmark Cab Design & Mfg Inc	1799	E	909 591-9153	1208
Nestle Usa Inc	2023	D	877 463-7853	1302
Del Real LLC (PA)	2038	D	951 681-0395	1389
Nestle Usa Inc	2038	B	951 360-7200	1397
Langlois Company	2045	E	951 360-3900	1414
A and G Inc (HQ)	2329	A	714 765-0400	2004
Charles Komar & Sons Inc	2341	B	951 934-1377	2147

	SIC	EMP	PHONE	ENTRY#
Advanced Innvtive Rcvery Tech	2515	E	949 273-8100	2477
Pura Naturals Inc	2515	E	949 273-8100	2489
Calpaco Papers Inc (PA)	2679	C	323 767-2800	2765
Adam Nutrition Inc	2834	C	951 361-1120	3341
Hyponex Corporation	2873	C	909 597-2811	3745
Aluminum Die Casting Co Inc	3363	D	951 681-3900	4644
Metal Container Corporation	3411	D	951 360-4500	4722
Pacific Award Metals Inc	3444	E	360 694-9530	5013
Hart & Cooley Inc	3446	E	951 332-5132	5064
Mobile Modular Management Corp	3448	C	800 819-1084	5084
Schwing America Inc	3531	C	909 681-6430	5497
Cte California TI & Engrg Inc	3545	E		5610
Philips North America LLC	3645	C	909 574-1800	6448
Genbody America LLC	3841	E	949 561-0664	8157
Young Electric Sign Company	3993	C	909 923-7668	8652
March Products Inc	3999	D	909 622-4800	8698
Landjet (PA)	4119	C	909 873-4636	8831
Costco Wholesale Corporation	4225	A	951 361-3606	9055
Toll Global Fwdg Scs USA Inc	4731	D	951 360-8310	9343
Propak Logistics Inc	4789	D	951 934-7160	9374
Highline Aftermarket LLC	5013	D	951 361-0331	9828
Hino Motors Mfg USA Inc	5013	D	951 727-0286	9829
Pacific Award Metals Inc	5033	D	909 390-9880	9959
Pavement Recycling Systems Inc (PA)	5093	C	951 682-1091	10540
Southwest Material Hdlg Inc (PA)	5511	C	951 727-0477	11412
Express Contractors Inc	7217	D	951 360-6500	13136
Arcticom Group Rfrgn LLC	7623	B	916 484-3190	14723
Vista Pacifica Enterprises Inc (PA)	8051	C	951 682-4833	15796

KEENE, CA - Kern County

	SIC	EMP	PHONE	ENTRY#
United Farm Workers America (PA)	8631	C	661 822-5571	17317

LA CANADA, CA - Los Angeles County

	SIC	EMP	PHONE	ENTRY#
Dilbeck Inc (PA)	6531	D	818 790-6774	12431
La Canada Flintridge Cntry CLB	7997	D	818 790-0611	15142
Naviage Foundation (PA)	8051	D	818 790-2522	15726
Crescenta-Canada YMCA (PA)	8641	C	818 790-0123	17340
Young MNS Chrstn Assn of Fthll	8641	D	818 790-0123	17408

LA CANADA FLINTRIDGE, CA - Los Angeles County

	SIC	EMP	PHONE	ENTRY#
Allen Lund Company LLC (HQ)	4731	D	800 777-6142	9251
Southwest Administrators Inc	6371	B		12164
Bis Computer Solutions Inc (PA)	7371	C	818 248-4282	13675
Neardata Inc	8742	D	818 249-2469	18181

LA CRESCENTA, CA - Los Angeles County

	SIC	EMP	PHONE	ENTRY#
Hamo Construction	1389	E	818 415-3334	333
Monarch E & S Insurance Svcs	6411	D	559 226-0200	12234
EAM Enterprises Inc (PA)	6531	D	818 248-9100	12435
Outlook Amusements Inc	7379	C	818 433-3800	14239
Mariner Health Care Inc	8051	E	818 957-0850	15710

LA HABRA, CA - Orange County

	SIC	EMP	PHONE	ENTRY#
Albd Electric and Cable	1731	D	949 440-1216	881
Orbo Manufacturing Inc	2396	E	562 222-4535	2265
Pacific Archtectural Mllwk Inc	2431	D	562 905-3200	2324
Votaw Wood Products Inc	2448	E	714 871-0932	2393
Eurotec Seating Incorporated	2531	E	562 806-6171	2542
Orbo Corporation (PA)	2531	E	562 806-6171	2550
VIP Rubber Company Inc (PA)	3069	C	562 905-3450	3941
Triview Glass Industries LLC	3231	D	626 363-7980	4348
Mmp Sheet Metal Inc	3444	E	562 691-1055	5008
Jci Aircraft Deburring LLC	3471	D	714 870-4427	5270
J C Ford Company (HQ)	3556	E	714 871-7361	5676
Shepard Bros Inc (PA)	3589	C	562 697-1366	6032
NRG Motorsports Inc	3714	D	714 541-1173	7280
Shepard-Thomason Company	3714	E	714 773-5539	7293
Rose Lilla Inc	3965	E	888 519-8889	8575
K S Designs Inc	3993	E	562 929-3973	8612
Home Depot USA Inc	5211	D	562 690-6006	11196
Lowes Home Centers LLC	5211	B	562 690-5122	11205
Peerless Maintenance Svc Inc	7349	B	714 871-3380	13402
Life Care Centers America Inc	8051	B	562 690-0852	15697

LA HABRA HEIGHTS, CA - Orange County

	SIC	EMP	PHONE	ENTRY#
Hacienda Golf Club	7997	D	562 694-1081	15138

LA JOLLA, CA - San Diego County

	SIC	EMP	PHONE	ENTRY#
Uqora Inc	2023	E	888 313-1372	1308
Berenice 2 AM Corp	2024	E	858 255-8693	1313
Jumper Media LLC	2741	D	831 333-6202	2923
Dm Luxury LLC	2759	C	858 366-9721	3137
Ambrx Inc (PA)	2834	D	858 875-2400	3350

Employee Codes: A=Over 500 employees, B=251-500
C=101-250, D=51-100, E=20-50, F=10-19, G=1-9

2025 Southern California
Business Directory and Buyers Guide

© Mergent Inc. 1-800-342-5647

1293

	SIC	EMP	PHONE	ENTRY#
Auspex Pharmaceuticals Inc	2834	E	858 558-2400	3362
Equillium Inc (PA)	2834	E	858 412-1200	3401
Kyowa Kirin Inc	2834	E	858 952-7000	3440
Longboard Pharmaceuticals Inc	2834	E	858 789-9283	3444
Orexigen Therapeutics Inc	2834	D	858 875-8600	3466
Synthorx Inc	2834	E	858 352-5100	3511
Ambrx Biopharma Inc	2836	D	858 875-2400	3555
Inhibrx Inc (HQ)	2836	C	858 795-4220	3581
Inhibrx Biosciences Inc	2836	C	858 795-4220	3582
Vinventions Usa LLC (PA)	3089	C	919 460-2200	4270
Ensemble Communications Inc	3663	E	858 458-1400	6614
New Brunswick Industries Inc	3672	E	619 448-4900	6757
Agilent Technologies Inc	3825	E	858 373-6300	7894
U S Medical Instruments Inc (PA)	3841	E	619 661-5500	8245
City National Bank	6021	D	858 642-4950	11725
CIT Bank NA	6022	D	858 454-8800	11757
Merrill Lynch Prce Fnner Smith	6211	C	858 456-3600	11991
Morgan Stnley Smith Barney LLC	6211	C	212 761-4000	11996
Brandes Investment Partners LP	6282	C	858 755-0239	12021
Northwestern Mutl Fincl Netwrk (PA)	6311	D	619 234-3111	12047
Front Porch Communities & Svcs	6513	C	858 454-2151	12342
La Jolla Bch & Tennis CLB Inc	7011	B	858 459-8271	12893
La Jolla Cove Ht Mtl Aprtmnts	7011	C	858 459-2621	12894
Lav Hotel Corp	7011	C	858 454-0771	12896
Marriott International Inc	7011	B	858 587-1414	12916
Destination Residences LLC	7299	A	858 550-1000	13172
Host Healthcare Inc	7363	D	858 999-3579	13599
Altium Inc (DH)	7371	D	858 864-1500	13649
United Support Services Inc	7371	C	858 373-9500	13855
Edgewave Inc	7372	D	800 782-3762	13921
Eventscom Inc	7372	E	858 257-2300	13929
University Cal San Diego	7374	A	858 534-5000	14162
The Copley Press Inc	7383	A	858 454-0411	14427
Life Time Inc	7991	D	858 459-0281	15054
La Jolla Bch & Tennis CLB Inc (PA)	7997	C	858 454-7126	15144
Balboa Nphrology Med Group Inc	8011	C	858 810-8000	15249
Hiv Neural Behavioral Center	8011	D	619 543-5000	15325
La Jolla Csmtc Srgery Cntre In	8011	D	858 452-1981	15373
Ming Tsuang Dr	8011	D	858 822-2464	15389
Sulpizio Cardiovascular Center	8011	D	858 657-7000	15484
Covenant Care La Jolla LLC	8051	C	858 453-5810	15615
Scripps Health	8062	B	858 455-9100	16183
Scripps Health	8062	B	858 626-6150	16184
Scripps Health	8062	C	858 626-4123	16185
Scripps Mmral-Ximed Med Ctr LP	8062	C	858 882-8350	16188
Uc San Dego Hlth Accntble Care (DH)	8062	C	858 657-7000	16235
University Cal San Diego	8062	A	858 657-7000	16242
Discovery Health Services LLC	8099	B	858 459-0785	16554
West Health Incubator Inc	8099	C	858 535-7000	16628
Humangood Socal	8361	B	858 454-4201	17167
Lawrence Fmly Jwish Cmnty Ctrs (PA)	8399	C	858 362-1144	17234
Theater Arts Fndtion San Dego	8641	C	858 623-3366	17369
YMCA of San Diego County	8641	C	858 453-3483	17383
U C San Diego Foundation	8699	D	858 534-1032	17472
Agouron Pharmaceuticals Inc	8731	B	858 622-3000	17764
Coi Pharmaceuticals Inc	8731	E	858 750-4700	17782
The Salk Institute For Biological S	8731	A	858 453-4100	17829
California Institute For Biomedical Research	8733	C	858 242-1000	17868
J Craig Venter Institute Inc (PA)	8733	B	301 795-7000	17877
La Jolla Inst For Immunology	8733	B	858 752-6500	17880
Sanford Brnham Prbys Med Dscve (PA)	8733	A	858 795-5000	17888
Scripps Research Institute	8733	D	858 242-1000	17890

LA MESA, CA - San Diego County

	SIC	EMP	PHONE	ENTRY#
West Coast Arborists Inc	1521	C	858 566-4204	439
Crew Builders Inc	1542	C	619 587-2033	533
Brady Company/San Diego Inc	1742	B	619 462-2600	1000
Brady Socal Incorporated	1742	D	619 462-2600	1001
Prost LLC	2082	E	619 954-4189	1551
Magnebit Holding Corp	3825	E	858 573-0727	7925
Bob Stall Chevrolet	5511	C	619 460-1311	11319
Drew Ford	5511	C	619 464-7777	11338
Mission Federal Credit Union	6061	C	858 524-2850	11806
Automobile Club Southern Cal	6411	C	619 464-7001	12180
Teague Insurance Agency Inc	6411	D	619 464-6851	12257
Helm Management Co (PA)	6531	D	619 589-6222	12464
Fancy Life Enterprises LLC (PA)	7812	C	619 560-9890	14826
Sharp Healthcare	8011	B	619 460-6200	15452
Sharp RES-Stealy Med Group Inc	8011	C	619 644-6405	15455
Community Care Center	8051	D	619 465-0702	15595
Life Gnerations Healthcare LLC	8051	D	619 460-2330	15698
Grossmont Hospital Corporation (HQ)	8062	B	619 740-6000	16010
Grossmont Hospital Corporation	8062	B	619 667-1900	16011

	SIC	EMP	PHONE	ENTRY#
Kaiser Foundation Hospitals	8062	C	619 528-5000	16051
Team Health Holdings Inc	8062	A	619 740-4401	16223
Bh-SD Opco LLC (PA)	8093	D	619 465-4411	16446
Helix Healthcare Inc	8093	B	619 465-4411	16477
YMCA of San Diego County	8641	C	619 464-1323	17387

LA MIRADA, CA - Los Angeles County

	SIC	EMP	PHONE	ENTRY#
Shasta Beverages Inc	2086	D	714 523-2280	1654
Outlook Resources Inc	2395	D	562 623-9328	2254
Harbor Furniture Mfg Inc (PA)	2512	E	323 636-1201	2448
Golden Kraft Inc	2679	B	562 926-8888	2769
JM Huber Micropowders Inc	2819	E	714 994-7855	3239
Captek Softgel Intl Inc	2834	E	657 325-0412	3380
Oceania Inc	3081	E	562 926-8886	3953
Alchem Plastics Inc	3083	C	714 523-2260	3963
Fooma America Inc	3549	E	310 921-0717	5653
MEMC Liquidating Corporation	3556	C	818 637-7200	5681
MEI Rigging & Crating LLC	3559	D	714 712-5888	5709
Iqair North America Inc	3564	E	877 715-4247	5771
Gallagher Rental Inc	3648	E	714 690-1559	6503
Solid State Devices Inc	3674	C	562 404-4474	6896
Wesanco Inc	3728	E	714 739-4989	7590
Ocean Protecta Incorporated	3732	E	714 891-2628	7623
National Signal LLC	3799	D	714 441-7707	7683
Mv Transportation Inc	4111	C	562 943-6776	8777
United Parcel Service Inc	4215	C	800 742-5877	9018
Home Depot USA Inc	4225	C	714 522-8651	9075
Mejico Express Inc (PA)	4513	C	714 690-8300	9175
Tiffany Dale Inc (PA)	5023	D	714 739-2700	9911
Reliance Inc	5051	D	562 944-3322	10153
Reliance Steel & Aluminum Co	5051	C	714 736-4800	10154
Makita USA Inc (HQ)	5072	C	714 522-8088	10310
RDM Industries	5084	E	714 690-0380	10398
Stainless Stl Fabricators Inc	5084	D	714 739-9904	10406
US Foods Inc	5141	C	714 670-3500	10814
Regal-Piedmont Plastics LLC	5162	C	562 404-4014	11001
Calwax LLC (DH)	5169	C	626 969-4334	11008
Living Spaces Furniture LLC (PA)	5712	C	877 266-7300	11516
IL Fornaio (america) LLC	5812	C	714 752-7052	11576
Georgia-Pacific LLC	5999	C	562 926-8888	11684
Bay-Valley Mortgage Group	6163	D	714 367-5125	11940
Cha La Mirada LLC	7011	C	714 739-8500	12790
Kam Sang Company Inc	7011	C	714 523-2800	12880
Diversified Mailing Incorporated	7331	C	714 994-6245	13301
Bigge Group	7353	C	714 523-4092	13431
Orange Courier Inc	7389	B	714 384-3600	14564
Crothall Services Group	7699	A	714 562-9275	14761
Life Care Centers America Inc	8051	C	562 943-7156	15693
Life Care Centers America Inc	8051	C	562 947-8691	15696
Southern Cal Spcialty Care LLC (DH)	8062	D	562 944-1900	16210
Straight Talk Inc	8322	D	562 943-0195	17015

LA PALMA, CA - Orange County

	SIC	EMP	PHONE	ENTRY#
Isec Incorporated	1751	C	714 761-5151	1053
CJ Foods Inc (HQ)	2099	D	714 367-7200	1756
Ranir LLC	2834	E	866 373-7374	3488
Precision Cutting Tools Inc	3545	E	562 921-7898	5621
Precision Cutting Tools LLC	3545	E	562 921-7898	5622
Fisker Inc (PA)	3711	E	833 434-7537	7175
Performance Machine Inc	3751	C	714 523-3000	7633
Norman International Inc	5023	C	562 946-0420	9902
Uns Electric Inc	5063	C	714 690-3660	10210
Svf Flow Controls Inc	5084	E	562 802-2255	10408
Prestige Stations Inc (DH)	5411	C	714 670-5145	11280
Atlantic Richfield Company (DH)	5541	A	800 333-3991	11473
Evocative Inc	7372	D	888 365-2656	13931
Tech Knowledge Associates LLC	7699	D	714 735-3810	14797
Kaiser Foundation Hospitals	8011	C	714 562-3420	15337
La Palma Hospital Medical Center	8062	B	714 670-7400	16069
Applecare Medical MGT LLC	8741	C	714 443-4507	17946

LA PUENTE, CA - Los Angeles County

	SIC	EMP	PHONE	ENTRY#
AZ Construction Inc (PA)	1521	C	626 333-0727	390
Ley Grand Foods Corporation	2099	E	626 336-2244	1808
Mymichelle Company LLC (HQ)	2331	B	626 934-4166	2050
County of Los Angeles	3531	E	626 968-3312	5490
Athens Disposal Company Inc (PA)	4953	B	626 336-3636	9731
Powell Works Inc	5084	E	909 861-6699	10393
Smart Stores Operations LLC	5141	B	626 330-2495	10775
Cacique Distributors US	5143	C	626 961-3399	10826
Cacique Foods LLC	5143	C	626 961-3399	10827
Aperto Property Management Inc	6513	B	626 965-1961	12332
Yang-Ming International Corp	7373	E	626 956-0100	14119

Mergent email: customerrelations@mergent.com
1294

2025 Southern California
Business Directory and Buyers Guide

(P-0000) Products & Services Section entry number
(PA)=Parent Co (HQ)=Headquarters (DH)=Div Headquarters

	SIC	EMP	PHONE	ENTRY#
County of Los Angeles	8011	D	626 968-3711	15291
Enki Health and RES Systems	8011	D	626 961-8971	15306
Plaza De La Raza Child Dev Svc (PA)	8351	D	562 776-1301	17106

LA QUINTA, CA - Riverside County

	SIC	EMP	PHONE	ENTRY#
Red Rock Pallet Company	4731	E	530 852-7744	9331
Imperial Irrigation District	4939	C	760 398-5811	9678
Primetime International Inc	5148	D	760 399-4166	10914
Lowes Home Centers LLC	5211	C	760 771-5566	11220
Hideaway	5812	C	760 777-7400	11574
Msr Desert Resort LP	5812	A	760 564-5730	11591
TS Enterprises Inc	5812	E	760 360-5991	11606
Ron Rick Holdings Montana LLC	6719	D	406 493-5606	12610
HP Lq Investment LP	7011	B	760 564-4111	12857
Msr Resort Lodging Tenant LLC	7011	A	760 564-4111	12933
Career Strategies Tmpry Inc	7361	C	760 564-5959	13503
Chapman Golf Development LLC	7992	D	760 564-8723	15072
Golf Management Operating LLC	7992	A	760 777-4839	15082
Ksl Recreation Management Operations LLC	7992	A	760 564-8000	15086
Madison Club Owners Assn	7992	D	760 777-9320	15090
Quarry At La Quinta Inc	7992	C	760 777-1100	15095
Silver Rock Resort Golf Club	7992	D	760 777-8884	15096
Hideaway Club	7997	A	760 777-7400	15139
Eisenhower Medical Center	8062	C	760 610-7200	15986
Desert Snds Unfied Schl Dst SC	8351	D	760 777-4200	17088

LA VERNE, CA - Los Angeles County

	SIC	EMP	PHONE	ENTRY#
Andersen Commercial Plbg Inc	1711	C	909 599-5950	738
Walters & Wolf Glass Company	1793	D	909 392-1961	1168
Vitawest Nutraceuticals Inc	2023	E	888 557-8012	1310
Fortress Inc	2521	E	909 593-8600	2509
Mohawk Western Plastics Inc	2673	E	909 593-7547	2735
TEC Color Craft (PA)	2759	E	909 392-9000	3182
Gilead Sciences Inc	2834	D	650 522-2771	3411
Plastifab Inc	3083	E	909 596-1927	3968
Serco Mold Inc (PA)	3089	E	626 331-0517	4237
Pacific Precision Inc	3451	E	909 392-5610	5111
Crown Equipment Corporation	3537	E	626 968-0556	5528
Marman Industries Inc	3544	D	909 392-2136	5588
Juicy Whip Inc (PA)	3556	E	909 392-7500	5678
Boom Industrial Inc	3559	D	909 495-3555	5695
Sunon Inc (PA)	3564	E	714 255-0208	5778
Micro Analog Inc	3674	C	909 392-8277	6850
DPI Labs Inc	3728	E	909 392-5777	7463
Synergetic Tech Group Inc	3728	E	909 305-4711	7573
Jet Delivery Inc (PA)	4215	D	800 716-7177	9005
Metropltan Wtr Dst of Sthern C	4941	B	909 593-7474	9704
Alquest Technologies Inc	7378	D	909 392-9209	14184
Edwards Theatres Inc	7832	C	844 462-7342	14933
Brethren Hillcrest Homes	8051	C	909 593-4911	15583
RES-Care Inc	8052	C	909 596-5360	15823
David and Margaret Home Inc	8361	C	909 596-5921	17145
Haynes Family Programs Inc	8361	C	909 593-2581	17160

LADERA RANCH, CA - Orange County

	SIC	EMP	PHONE	ENTRY#
Tropical Preserving Co Inc	2033	E	213 748-5108	1359
Bau Furniture Mfg Inc	2511	D	949 643-2729	2419
Enchannel Medical Ltd	3841	E	949 694-6802	8148
Sst IV 8020 Las Vgas Blvd S LL	4225	D	949 429-6600	9111

LAGUNA BEACH, CA - Orange County

	SIC	EMP	PHONE	ENTRY#
Moulton Animal Hospital Inc	0742	D	949 831-7297	130
Langlois Fancy Frozen Foods Inc	2038	E	949 497-1741	1306
Flavor Infusion LLC	2087	E	949 715-4309	1679
Pangaea Holdings Inc	2844	E	402 704-7546	3677
RA Industries LLC	3599	E	714 557-2322	6211
Myotek Industries Incorporated (DH)	3694	E	949 502-3776	7097
Ophthonix Inc	3851	E	760 842-5600	8412
K31 Road Engineering LLC	3999	E	305 928-1968	8689
Durham School Services L P	4151	C	949 376-0376	8874
4g Wireless Inc (PA)	4812	C	949 748-6100	9381
Data Processing Design Inc	7371	C	714 695-1000	13701
Atlantis Computing Inc	7372	E	650 917-9471	13888
Laguna Playhouse (PA)	7922	C	949 497-2787	14964
University California Irvine	8099	A	949 939-7106	16624
JC Resorts LLC	8741	A	949 376-2779	17997
Montage Hotels & Resorts LLC	8741	A	949 715-6000	18014

LAGUNA HILLS, CA - Orange County

	SIC	EMP	PHONE	ENTRY#
Five Star Plastering Inc	1742	D	949 683-5091	1008
Chavers Gasket Corporation	3053	E	949 472-8118	3882
Eurotech Showers Inc	3088	E	949 716-4099	4025
Plastic and Metal Center Inc	3089	E	949 770-0610	4199

	SIC	EMP	PHONE	ENTRY#
Steward Plastics Inc	3089	D	949 581-9530	4250
Budget Enterprises Llc	3211	E	949 697-9544	4312
Metal Improvement Company LLC	3398	E	949 855-8010	4706
Peltek Holdings Inc	3479	E	949 855-8010	5336
Starrett Kinemetric Engrg Inc	3545	E	949 348-1213	5626
Djh Enterprises	3663	E	714 424-6500	6608
XEL USA Inc	3674	E	949 425-8686	6916
Fox Enterprises LLC (HQ)	3679	E	239 693-0099	6998
Sonendo Inc (PA)	3843	C	949 766-3636	8356
AT&T Enterprises LLC	4812	D	949 581-1600	9382
Moulton Nguel Wtr Dst Pub Fclt	4941	D	949 831-2500	9706
Cynergy Prof Systems LLC	5065	E	800 776-7978	10240
Valley Insurance Service Inc	6411	C	949 707-4080	12264
Jamboree Realty Corp (PA)	6531	C	949 380-0300	12472
Professional Cmnty MGT Cal Inc	6531	D	949 597-4200	12510
Varsity Contractors Inc	7349	C	949 586-8283	13428
Groundwork Open Source Inc	7375	D	415 992-4500	14172
Altec Products Inc (PA)	7389	D	949 727-1248	14443
South Cnty Orthpd Spclsts A ME	8011	D	949 586-3200	15458
Gate Three Healthcare LLC	8051	C	949 587-9000	15662
Saddleback Memorial Med Ctr (HQ)	8062	A	949 837-4500	16164
Laguna Home Health Svcs LLC	8082	C	949 707-5023	16400
Automobile Club Southern Cal	8699	C	949 951-1400	17457
Brett Dinovi & Associates LLC	8742	C	609 200-0123	18109

LAGUNA NIGUEL, CA - Orange County

	SIC	EMP	PHONE	ENTRY#
Marcos M Uriarte	1711	D	714 326-1064	801
Rye Electric Inc	1731	D	949 441-0545	957
Beverages & More Inc	2086	C	949 643-3020	1608
San Diego Daily Transcript	2621	D	619 232-4381	2636
Qpc Fiber Optic LLC	3357	E	949 361-8855	4638
Markland Industries Inc (PA)	3751	E	714 245-2850	7632
Alcon Vision LLC	3841	B	949 753-6218	8082
Confluent Medical Tech Inc	3841	C	949 448-7056	8135
Confluent Medical Tech Inc	3841	C	949 448-7056	8136
Interface Associates Inc	3841	C	949 448-7056	8173
Home Depot USA Inc	5211	D	949 831-3698	11193
First Team RE - Orange Cnty	6531	C	949 240-7979	12451
Career Engagement Group LLC	7371	D	212 235-1470	13682
Technicon Design Corporation	7389	C	949 218-1300	14608
Young MNS Chrstn Assn Ornge CN	7997	D	949 495-9622	15189
Mission Internal Med Group Inc	8011	D	949 364-3605	15391
Life Time Fitness Inc	8099	C	949 238-2700	16581
Aegis Senior Communities LLC	8361	C	949 496-8080	17118

LAGUNA WOODS, CA - Orange County

	SIC	EMP	PHONE	ENTRY#
Laguna Woods Village	6531	A	949 597-4267	12477
Professional Cmnty MGT Cal Inc	6531	D	949 206-0580	12511
Village Management Svcs Inc	8741	C	949 597-4360	18075

LAKE ARROWHEAD, CA - San Bernardino County

	SIC	EMP	PHONE	ENTRY#
Gildan USA Inc	2252	E	909 485-1475	1908
Hi-Desert Publishing Company	2711	E	909 336-3555	2803
Rim of World Unified Schl Dst	4151	D	909 336-0330	8882
Lake Arrwhead Rsort Oprtor Inc (HQ)	7011	D	909 336-1511	12895
Mountns Cmnty Hosp Fndtion In	8062	C	909 336-3651	16104

LAKE ELSINORE, CA - Riverside County

	SIC	EMP	PHONE	ENTRY#
West Coast Ltg & Enrgy Inc	1731	D	951 296-0680	977
Gbc Concrete Masnry Cnstr Inc	1741	C	951 245-2055	983
Hakes Sash & Door Inc	1751	C	951 674-2414	1051
Edje-Enterprises	1761	D	951 245-7070	1082
Acrofoam Inductrioc Inc	2531	D	951 245-4429	2535
Quality Foam Packaging Inc	3086	E	951 245-4429	4014
Pacific Aggregates Inc	3273	D	951 245-2460	4447
Boozak Inc	3444	D	951 245-6045	4959
American Compaction Eqp Inc	3531	E	949 661-2921	5487
Jose Perez	3535	E	920 318-6527	5517
Pointdirect Transport Inc	4213	D	909 371-0837	8971
Pacific Clay Products Inc	5032	C	661 857-1401	9949
Goodfellow Corporation	5082	C	909 874-2700	10348
Lowes Home Centers LLC	5211	C	951 253-6000	11227
Albertsons LLC	5411	C	951 245-4461	11272
Lake Chevrolet	5511	C	951 674-3116	11372
AWI Management Corporation	8741	C	951 674-8200	17948

LAKE FOREST, CA - Orange County

	SIC	EMP	PHONE	ENTRY#
Natures Image Inc	0781	D	949 680-4400	179
Caelus Corporation	1389	E	949 877-7170	320
Streamline Finishes Inc	1542	D	949 600-8964	589
Hardy & Harper Inc	1611	C	714 444-1851	622
Arb Inc (HQ)	1623	C	949 598-9242	659
Cbr Electric Inc	1731	C	949 455-0331	898

Employee Codes: A=Over 500 employees, B=251-500
C=101-250, D=51-100, E=20-50, F=10-19, G=1-9

2025 Southern California
Business Directory and Buyers Guide

© Mergent Inc. 1-800-342-5647

1295

GEOGRAPHIC

	SIC	EMP	PHONE	ENTRY#
Ev Connect Inc	1731	D	888 780-0062	916
Big Train Inc	2024	C	949 340-8800	1314
Crumbl Cookies	2052	E	949 519-0791	1484
ABC Custom Wood Shutters Inc	2431	E	949 595-0300	2294
Novo Manufacturing LLC	2431	E	949 609-0544	2318
Cod USA Inc	2531	E	949 381-7367	2540
Walter Foster Publishing Inc	2731	E	949 380-7510	2899
Sole Technology Inc (PA)	3149	D	949 460-2020	4289
Oceania International LLC	3356	E	949 407-8904	4620
Dynacast LLC	3364	C	949 707-1211	4659
Baldwin Hardware Corporation (DH)	3429	A	949 672-4000	4759
National Manufacturing Co	3429	A	800 346-9445	4784
Young Engineers Inc	3429	D	949 581-9411	4797
Price Pfister Inc	3432	A	949 672-4000	4805
S E - G I Products Inc	3442	C	949 297-8530	4900
SPX Flow Us LLC	3443	E	949 455-8150	4928
Shmaze Industries Inc	3479	E	949 583-1448	5344
Campbell Engineering Inc	3545	E	949 859-3306	5607
Ellison Educational Eqp Inc (PA)	3554	E	949 598-8822	5658
Fanuc America Corporation	3559	D	949 595-2700	5702
I/Omagic Corporation (PA)	3572	E	949 707-4800	5880
US Critical LLC (PA)	3572	E	949 916-9326	5891
IMC Networks Corp (PA)	3575	E	949 465-3000	5895
American Deburring Inc	3599	E	949 457-9790	6079
T/Q Systems Inc	3599	E	949 455-0478	6246
Yosmart Inc	3599	E	949 825-5958	6279
Leoch Battery Corporation (DH)	3621	D	949 588-5853	6327
Focus Industries Inc	3646	D	949 830-1350	6461
Greenshine New Energy LLC	3648	D	949 609-9636	6504
Semi-Kinetics Inc	3672	D	949 830-7364	6770
Tri-Star Laminates Inc	3672	E	949 587-3200	6779
Advantest Test Solutions Inc	3674	D	949 523-6900	6795
Premier Magnetics Inc	3677	E	949 452-0511	6935
Assa Abloy AB	3692	A	949 672-4000	7084
Sonnet Technologies Inc	3699	E	949 587-3500	7152
Qf Liquidation Inc (PA)	3714	C	949 930-3400	7286
AC&a Enterprises LLC (HQ)	3724	E	949 716-3511	7376
Karem Aircraft Inc	3728	E	949 859-4444	7509
Chroma Systems Solutions Inc	3825	E	949 600-6400	7904
Monobind Sales Inc (PA)	3841	E	949 951-2665	8201
Tenex Health Inc	3841	D	949 454-7500	8237
Biolase Inc (PA)	3843	E		8328
Staar Surgical Company (PA)	3851	A	626 303-7902	8417
Aminco International USA Inc	3911	D	949 457-3261	8451
Cellco Partnership	4812	D	949 472-0700	9388
Ytel Inc	4813	D	800 382-4913	9472
Toshiba Amer Bus Solutions Inc (DH)	5044	B	949 462-6000	9979
Insulectro (PA)	5065	D	949 587-3200	10253
Refrigeration Supplies Distributor (PA)	5078	D	949 380-7878	10344
SMC Products Inc	5092	D	949 753-1099	10529
Nakase Brothers Wholesale Nurs	5193	C	949 855-4388	11094
Cloudradiant Corp (PA)	5199	C	408 256-1527	11114
Home Depot USA Inc	5211	D	949 609-0221	11191
Del Taco Restaurants Inc (PA)	5812	C	949 462-9300	11564
Psb	7311	C	949 465-0772	13238
Performance Building Services	7349	E	949 364-4364	13404
Vci Event Technology Inc	7359	C	714 772-2002	13477
Equimine	7372	E	877 204-9040	13926
Infor (us) LLC	7372	C	678 319-8000	13947
Wonderware Corporation (DH)	7372	B	949 727-3200	14067
Aveva Software LLC (DH)	7373	B	949 727-3200	14072
Avidex Industries LLC	7379	D	949 428-6333	14199
Itek Services Inc	7379	E	949 770-4835	14227
Advanced Protection Inds LLC	7382	C	800 662-1711	14379
Freedom Village Healthcare Ctr	8051	C	949 472-4733	15657
Lake Frest No II Mstr Hmwners	8641	D	949 586-0860	17353
United Industries Group Inc	8711	E	949 759-3200	17656
Reveal Biosciences Inc	8731	E	858 274-3663	17820
Alcon Vision LLC	8734	A	949 505-6890	17900
Beech Street Corporation (HQ)	8741	B	949 672-1000	17950
Mike Rovner Construction Inc	8741	C	949 458-1562	18013
BDS Connected Solutions LLC	8742	C	800 234-4237	18103
Environmental Resolutions Inc	8748	B	949 457-8950	18307
Higher Ground Education Inc (PA)	8748	B	949 836-9401	18318
Ibaset Inc (PA)	8748	E	949 598-5200	18321
Westamerica Communications Inc	8999	D	949 340-8942	18381

LAKE ISABELLA, CA - Kern County

	SIC	EMP	PHONE	ENTRY#
Wick Communications Co	2711	E	760 379-3667	2839
Kern Valley Hosp Foundation (PA)	5912	B	760 379-2681	11621

LAKE VIEW TERRACE, CA - Los Angeles County

	SIC	EMP	PHONE	ENTRY#
Phoenix Houses Los Angeles Inc	8093	D	818 686-3000	16489

LAKESIDE, CA - San Diego County

	SIC	EMP	PHONE	ENTRY#
Pacific Green Landscape Inc (PA)	0781	C	619 390-1546	184
Enniss Inc	1442	E	619 561-1101	374
Minshew Brothers Stl Cnstr Inc	1541	C		493
Lb3 Enterprises Inc	1611	D	619 579-6161	632
Hazard Construction Company	1622	D	858 587-3600	653
A M Ortega Construction Inc (PA)	1731	C	619 390-1988	877
Standard Drywall Inc (HQ)	1742	B	619 443-7034	1030
Clauss Construction	1795	C	619 390-4940	1179
Layfield USA Corporation (DH)	1799	D	619 562-1200	1214
Pepsi-Cola Metro Btlg Co Inc	2086	C	858 560-6735	1634
Superior Ready Mix Concrete LP	3273	D	619 443-7510	4459
Blue Star Steel Inc	3441	E	619 448-5520	4819
Clark Steel Fabricators Inc	3446	E	619 390-1502	5060
Christian Bros Flrg Intrors In	5713	D	619 443-9500	11522
Barona Resort & Casino	7011	A	619 443-2300	12767
LLC Brewer Crane	7353	D	619 390-8252	13441
Neighborhood Healthcare	8099	C	619 390-9975	16593
Bert W Salas Inc	8711	C	619 562-7711	17493

LAKEWOOD, CA - Los Angeles County

	SIC	EMP	PHONE	ENTRY#
API Group Life Safety USA LLC	1711	D	562 279-0770	740
Industrial Gasket and Sup Co	3053	E	310 530-1771	3891
TFC Manufacturing Inc	3444	E	562 426-9559	5045
Magma Products LLC	3631	D	562 627-0500	6386
Premier Wireless Inc	3663	E	925 776-1070	6646
Eve Hair Inc (PA)	5199	E	562 377-1020	11119
Nationwide Theatres Corp	7933	A	562 421-8448	15015
Tenet Healthsystem Medical Inc	8011	A	562 531-2550	15487
Lakewood Regional Med Ctr Inc	8062	A	562 531-2550	16071
Tarzana Treatment Centers Inc	8093	D	562 428-4111	16508
County of Los Angeles	8322	D	562 497-3500	16914

LAMONT, CA - Kern County

	SIC	EMP	PHONE	ENTRY#
Grimmway Enterprises Inc	5148	B	661 845-3758	10906
Clinica Sierra Vista	8011	D	661 845-3717	15281

LANCASTER, CA - Los Angeles County

	SIC	EMP	PHONE	ENTRY#
Desert Haven Enterprises	0782	A	661 948-8402	203
Excel Contractors Inc	1521	C	661 942-6944	402
Granite Construction Inc	1611	D	805 667-8210	619
Circulating Air Inc	1711	D	661 942-2048	763
Harvest Farms Inc	2038	D	661 945-3636	1393
Radford Cabinets Inc	2511	D	661 729-8931	2433
Antelope Valley Newspapers Inc	2711	E	661 940-1000	2779
Aerotech News and Review Inc (PA)	2721	E	661 945-5634	2843
Prints 4 Life	2752	E	661 942-2233	3069
Pavement Recycling Systems Inc	2951	C	661 945-5599	3839
Arrow Transit Mix	3273	E	661 945-7600	4428
McWhirter Steel Inc	3441	D	661 951-8998	4852
Precision Welding Inc	3441	E	661 729-3436	4860
Robert F Chapman Inc	3444	D	661 940-9482	5030
National Metal Stampings Inc	3469	D	661 945-1157	5205
Pacific Seismic Products Inc	3491	E	661 942-4499	5368
Advanced Clutch Technology Inc	3714	E	661 940-7555	7219
Morton Grinding Inc	3965	C	661 298-0895	8574
Keolis Transit America Inc	4111	D	661 341-3910	8758
Antelope Vly Schl Trnsp Agcy	4151	D	661 952-3106	8866
Santa Barbara Trnsp Corp	4151	C	661 510-0566	8884
United Parcel Service Inc	4215	D	800 828-8264	9013
Sprint Communications Co LP	4812	D	661 951-8927	9411
BDR Industries Inc (PA)	4841	D	661 940-8554	9524
Directv Group Holdings LLC	4841	A	661 632-6562	9543
Sygma Network Inc	5141	C	661 723-0405	10807
Lowes Home Centers LLC	5211	D	661 341-9000	11236
H W Hunter Inc (PA)	5511	D	661 948-8411	11357
Johnson Ford (PA)	5511	C	661 206-2597	11367
Loandepotcom LLC	6162	A	661 202-1700	11921
V Troth Inc	6531	D	661 948-4646	12546
Mission Linen Supply	7213	D	661 948-5052	13118
Opsec Specialized Protection	7381	D	661 942-3999	14327
Lancaster Cmnty Svcs Fndtion I	7538	C	661 723-6230	14693
Weststar Cinemas Inc	7922	C	661 723-9392	14982
City of Lancaster	7996	D	661 723-6071	15102
Antelope Valley Hospital Inc	8011	B	661 726-6180	15245
High Dsert Med Corp A Med Grou (PA)	8011	C	661 945-5984	15324
Lancaster Crdlgy Med Group Inc (PA)	8011	D	661 726-3058	15377
Antelope Vly Retirement HM Inc	8051	C	661 949-5584	15568
Pacs Group Inc	8051	C	661 948-7501	15730
Pacs Group Inc	8051	C	661 949-5524	15733
PCI Care Venture I	8051	C	661 949-2177	15752
Antelope Vly Retirement HM Inc	8059	C	661 948-7501	15831
Antelope Vly Retirement HM Inc	8059	C	661 949-5524	15832

Mergent email: customerrelations@mergent.com
1296

2025 Southern California
Business Directory and Buyers Guide

(P-0000) Products & Services Section entry number
(PA)=Parent Co (HQ)=Headquarters (DH)=Div Headquarters

	SIC	EMP	PHONE	ENTRY#
Antelope Valley Health Care Di (PA)	8062	A	661 949-5000	15913
Antelope Valley Hlth Care Dst	8062	C	661 949-5936	15914
Antelope Valley Hospital	8062	C	661 949-5000	15915
Antelope Valley Hospital Inc	8062	C	661 726-6050	15916
Kaiser Foundation Hospitals	8062	B	661 726-2500	16040
Kaiser Foundation Hospitals	8062	D	661 949-5000	16045
US Carenet Services LLC	8082	C	661 945-7350	16429
Tarzana Treatment Centers Inc	8093	C	661 726-2630	16510
County of Los Angeles	8322	D	661 940-4181	16911
County of Los Angeles	8322	D	661 948-2320	16915
County of Los Angeles	8711	C	661 723-6088	17505
County of Los Angeles	9222	D	661 974-7700	18390

LAWNDALE, CA - Los Angeles County

	SIC	EMP	PHONE	ENTRY#
Westwood Building Materials Co	3273	E	310 643-9158	4466
Curry Company LLC	3545	E	310 643-8400	5611
Los Angles Cnty Mtro Trnsp Aut	4111	B	310 643-3804	8762
Automotive Aftermarket Inc	5013	D	310 793-0046	9813

LEBEC, CA - Kern County

	SIC	EMP	PHONE	ENTRY#
Technicolor Usa Inc	3651	A	661 496-1309	6560
Six Continents Hotels Inc	7011	C	661 343-3316	13025

LEMON GROVE, CA - San Diego County

	SIC	EMP	PHONE	ENTRY#
Aztec Landscaping Inc (PA)	0782	C	619 464-3303	198
Condon-Johnson & Assoc Inc	1522	D	858 530-9165	445
Pacific Sthwest Structures Inc	1771	C	619 469-2323	1130
RCP Block & Brick Inc (PA)	3271	D	619 460-9101	4372
Jci Metal Products (PA)	3441	D	619 229-8206	4840
Home Depot USA Inc	5211		619 589-2999	11181
Lemon Grove Health Assoc LLC	8051	B	619 463-0294	15690
Family Hlth Ctrs San Diego Inc	8099	B	619 515-2550	16560
Develpmntal Svcs Continuum Inc	8361	D	619 460-7333	17146

LITTLEROCK, CA - Los Angeles County

	SIC	EMP	PHONE	ENTRY#
Hi-Grade Materials Co	3273	D	661 533-3100	4441

LOMA LINDA, CA - San Bernardino County

	SIC	EMP	PHONE	ENTRY#
Dvele Inc	2451	E	909 796-2561	2398
Dvele Omega Corporation	2451	D	909 796-2561	2399
ABI Document Support Svcs LLC	7389	D	909 793-0613	14434
Loma Linda University	7819	D	909 558-8611	14896
Loma Linda University	8011	C	909 558-4475	15379
Loma Linda University Med Ctr	8011	C	877 558-6248	15380
Veterans Health Administration	8011	A	909 825-7084	15507
Heritage Health Care Inc	8051	C	909 796-0216	15676
Pacs Group Inc	8051	D	909 478-7894	15737
Linda Loma Univ Hlth Care (HQ)	8062	C	909 558-2806	16073
Loma Linda University Med Ctr	8062	C	909 558-4385	16076
Loma Linda University Med Ctr	8062	D	909 796-0167	16077
Loma Linda University Med Ctr (DH)	8062	A	909 558-4400	16078
Loma Lnda - Inland Empire Cnsr	8062	C	909 558-4000	16081
Mountain View Child Care Inc (PA)	8062	B	909 796-6915	16103
South Coast Childrens Soc Inc	8093	C	909 478-3377	16505

LOMPOC, CA - Santa Barbara County

	SIC	EMP	PHONE	ENTRY#
Santa Barbara Farms LLC	0161	C	805 736-5608	14
Babcock Enterprises Inc	0172	E	805 736-1455	30
Horizon Well Logging Inc	1389	E	805 733-0972	336
Imerys Minerals California Inc (HQ)	1499	D	805 736-1221	386
Kustom Kanopies Inc	1541	E	801 399-3400	489
Valiant Technical Services Inc	3731	D	757 628-9500	7611
Orbital Sciences LLC	3612	D	805 734-5400	7787
Serco Services Inc	7371	D	805 736-3584	13817
Lompoc Valley Medical Center	8062	B	805 875-9229	16082
Lompoc Valley Medical Center (PA)	8062	B	805 737-3300	16083
Crestwood Behavioral Hlth Inc	8361	D	805 308-8720	17143
Channel Islnds Yung MNS Chrstn	8641	E	805 736-3483	17332
Automobile Club Southern Cal	8699	D	805 735-2731	17452

LONG BEACH, CA - Los Angeles County

	SIC	EMP	PHONE	ENTRY#
Beta Operating Company LLC	1311	D	562 628-1526	268
California Resources Corp (PA)	1311	D	888 848-4754	270
Thums Long Beach Company	1311	D	562 624-3400	277
Tidelands Oil Production Inc	1311	E	562 436-9918	278
Warren E&P Inc	1382	D	214 393-9688	316
B & B Pipe and Tool Co (PA)	1389	E	562 424-0704	317
Kuster Co Oil Well Services	1389	C	562 595-0661	342
Sears Home Imprv Pdts Inc	1521	C	562 485-4904	426
Palp Inc	1611	C	562 599-5841	641
W A Rasic Cnstr Co Inc (PA)	1623	C	562 928-6111	705
Curtin Maritime Corp	1629	B	562 983-7257	710
Herzog Contracting Corp	1629	D	562 595-7414	715

	SIC	EMP	PHONE	ENTRY#
Manson Construction Co	1629	D	562 983-2340	717
Lite Solar Corp	1711	C	562 256-1249	796
Petrochem Insulation Inc	1742	C	310 638-6663	1023
Lb Beadels LLC	2064	E	562 726-1700	1508
Wiser Foods Inc	2086	D	310 895-0888	1657
Everson Spice Company Inc	2099	C	562 595-4785	1770
Texollini Inc	2297	C	310 537-3400	1962
L A Cstm AP & Promotions Inc (PA)	2329	E	562 595-1770	2018
Brentwood Originals Inc (PA)	2392	E	310 637-6804	2207
Enrich Enterprises Inc	2395	E	310 515-5055	2246
National Emblem Inc (PA)	2395	C	310 515-5055	2253
Western Integrated Mtls Inc (PA)	2431	E	562 634-2823	2334
F-J-E Inc	2541	E	562 437-7466	2564
Jbi LLC (PA)	2599	C	310 886-8034	2614
Continental Graphics Corp	2752	D	714 503-4200	2985
Continental Graphics Corp	2752	D	714 827-1752	2987
Crestec Usa Inc	2752	C	310 327-9000	2995
Pdf Print Communications Inc (PA)	2752	D	562 426-6978	3057
Queen Beach Printers Inc	2752	E	562 436-8201	3076
Weber Printing Company Inc	2752	E	310 639-5064	3100
Airgas Inc	2813	E	510 429-4216	3213
Eco Services Operations Corp	2819	D	310 885-6719	3235
Energy Solutions (us) LLC	2819	B	310 669-5300	3237
Evolife Scientific Llc	2833	E	888 750-0310	3315
Morton Salt Inc	2899	D	562 437-0071	3816
Tesoro Refining & Mktg Co LLC	2911	D	562 728-2215	3831
Lubeco Inc	2992	E	562 602-1791	3856
Bryant Rubber Corp (PA)	3053	E	310 530-2530	3879
Seal Science Inc (HQ)	3053	D	949 253-3130	3899
Rubbercraft Corp Cal Ltd (HQ)	3061	C	562 354-2800	3906
Hexpol Compounding CA Inc (DH)	3069	D	626 961-0311	3913
Kirkhill Rubber Company	3069	D	562 803-1117	3921
G B Remanufacturing Inc	3089	D	562 272-7333	4121
Jacobson Plastics Inc	3089	D	562 433-4911	4144
Medway Plastics Corporation	3089	D	562 630-1175	4166
Sage Plastics Long Beach Corp	3089	E	562 423-3900	4234
Talco Plastics Inc	3089	D	562 630-1224	4254
Total Mont LLC	3231	E	562 983-1374	4347
Mitsubishi Cement Corporation	3241	B	562 495-0600	4356
Proform Finishing Products LLC	3275	E	562 435-4465	4468
American Plant Services Inc (PA)	3312	E	562 630-1773	4509
Nikon AM Synergy Inc	3313	E	310 607-0188	4530
Primus Pipe and Tube Inc (DH)	3317	D	562 808-8000	4553
Certified Alloy Products Inc	3341	C	562 595-6621	4582
TCI Texarkana Inc	3353	D	562 808-8000	4594
SPEP Acquisition Corp (PA)	3429	D	310 608-0693	4789
Seachrome Corporation	3431	C	310 427-8010	4800
R & D Steel Inc	3441	E	310 631-6183	4862
Cowelco	3444	C	562 432-5766	4974
H Roberts Construction	3448	D	562 590-4825	5079
Wyatt Precision Machine Inc	3451	E	562 634-0524	5116
Valmont Industries Inc	3479	E	310 549-2200	5353
Crane Co	3492	C	562 426-2531	5372
Cunico Corporation	3498	E	562 733-4600	5431
Crown Equipment Corporation	3537	D	310 952-6600	5529
Cavanaugh Machine Works Inc	3599	E	562 437-1126	6102
Frontier Engrg & Mfg Tech Inc (PA)	3599	E	310 767-1227	6128
NC Dynamics Incorporated	3599	C	562 634-7392	6189
NC Dynamics LLC	3599	C	562 634-7392	6190
Nuspace Inc (HQ)	3599	C	562 407-3200	6195
Kbr Inc	3624	E	562 436-9281	6338
Control Switches Intl Inc	3625	E	562 498-7331	6344
Western Tube & Conduit Corp (HQ)	3644	D	310 537-6300	6435
Visionaire Lighting LLC	3646	D	310 512-6480	6480
Ixys Long Beach Inc (DH)	3674	C	562 296-6584	6839
Schneider Elc Buildings LLC	3699	C	310 900-2385	7148
Tabc Inc (DH)	3713	C	562 984-3305	7212
Acme Headlining Co	3714	D	562 432-0281	7216
Boeing Company	3721	A	562 496-1000	7331
Boeing Company	3721	A	562 593-5511	7333
Gulfstream Aerospace Corp GA	3721	D	562 420-1818	7358
Jetzero Inc (PA)	3721	E	949 474-8222	7359
Gledhill/Lyons Inc	3728	E	714 502-0274	7484
Neill Aircraft Co	3728	B	562 432-7981	7530
Sanders Composites Inc (HQ)	3728	E	562 354-2800	7561
APR Engineering Inc	3731	E	562 983-3800	7596
Indel Engineering Inc	3732	C	562 594-0995	7622
Rocket Lab Usa Inc	3761	E	714 465-5737	7648
Rocket Lab Usa Inc (PA)	3761	E	714 465-5737	7649
Space Exploration Tech Corp	3761	C	310 363-6289	7651
Relativity Space Inc (PA)	3764	B	424 393-4309	7664
Spinlaunch Inc	3764	C	650 516-7746	7665
Custom Fibreglass Mfg Co	3792	C	562 432-5454	7675

Employee Codes: A=Over 500 employees, B=251-500
C=101-250, D=51-100, E=20-50, F=10-19, G=1-9

2025 Southern California
Business Directory and Buyers Guide

© Mergent Inc. 1-800-342-5647

1297

GEOGRAPHIC

	SIC	EMP	PHONE	ENTRY#
Simulator PDT Solutions LLC	3812	E	310 830-3331	7811
Fundamental Tech Intl Inc	3823	E	562 595-0661	7858
Beauty Health Company (PA)	3841	B	800 603-4996	8104
Hydrafacial LLC (HQ)	3841	C	800 603-4996	8163
Hydrafacial LLC	3841	E	562 391-2052	8164
Ferraco Inc (HQ)	3842	E	562 988-2414	8266
Rastaclat LLC	3911	E	424 287-0902	8460
Superior Signs & Installation (PA)	3993	D	562 495-3808	8643
Carberry LLC	3999	E	562 264-5078	8667
Macs Lift Gate Inc (PA)	3999	E	562 529-3465	8695
Union Pacific Railroad Company	4011	B	562 490-7000	8745
Long Beach Public Trnsp Co	4111	D	562 591-2301	8759
Long Beach Public Trnsp Co (PA)	4111	A	562 599-8571	8760
Atlantic Express Trnsp	4119	B	562 997-6868	8813
Long Beach Unified School Dst	4151	C	562 426-6176	8881
Heavy Load Transfer LLC	4212	D	310 816-0260	8915
Ventura Transfer Company (PA)	4213	D	310 549-1660	8983
Kair Harbor Express LLC (PA)	4225	D	562 432-6800	9079
Roadex America Inc	4225	D	310 878-9800	9105
Polar Tankers Inc (DH)	4424	D	562 388-1400	9136
International Trnsp Svc LLC (PA)	4491	C	562 435-7781	9141
Lbct LLC	4491	C	562 951-6000	9142
Port of Long Beach	4491	A	562 283-7000	9144
Suderman Contg Stevedores Inc (PA)	4491	D	409 762-8131	9148
Pacific Maritime Group Inc	4492	D	562 590-8188	9151
Hanjin Shipping Co Ltd	4499	A	201 291-4600	9154
Piedmont Airlines Inc	4512	C	562 421-1806	9163
Polar Air Cargo LP	4512	B	310 568-4551	9164
Cargomatic Inc (PA)	4731	C	866 513-2343	9257
Cfr Rinkens LLC (DH)	4731	D	310 639-7725	9262
Vanguard Lgistics Svcs USA Inc (HQ)	4731	C	310 847-3000	9349
Free Conferencing Corporation	4813	C	562 437-1411	9435
Cco Holdings LLC	4841	C	562 228-1262	9530
Intelsat US LLC	4899	C	310 525-5500	9566
AES Alamitos LLC	4911	D	562 493-7891	9573
Southern California Edison Co	4911	D	562 529-7301	9629
Southern California Edison Co	4911	B	562 491-3803	9633
City of Long Beach	4932	D	562 570-2000	9674
County of Los Angeles	4941	C	213 367-3176	9687
Covanta Long Bch Rnwble Enrgy	4953	D	562 436-0636	9739
Denso Pdts & Svcs Americas Inc (DH)	5013	B	310 834-6352	9821
Intex Recreation Corp	5021	D	310 549-5400	9874
Xerox Education Services LLC (DH)	5044	D	310 830-9847	9982
Tp-Link Systems Inc	5045	C	562 528-7700	10034
Tom Dreher Sales Inc	5046	D	562 355-4074	10053
Jfe Shoji America Holdings Inc (DH)	5051	D	562 637-3500	10141
Ta Chen International Inc (HQ)	5051	C	562 808-8000	10159
Jvckenwood USA Corporation (HQ)	5065	C	310 639-9000	10259
Clarendon Specialty Fas Inc	5072	D	714 842-2603	10303
Airgas Usa LLC	5084	A	562 497-1991	10365
Columbia Specialty Company Inc	5085	D	562 634-6425	10431
Tristar Industrial LLC	5085	D	562 634-6425	10469
Aircraft Hardware West	5088	E	562 961-9324	10484
Shimadzu Precision Instrs Inc (DH)	5088	D	562 420-6226	10500
Intex Properties S Bay Corp (PA)	5091	C	310 549-5400	10514
Tst Inc	5093	E	310 835-0115	10543
Obagi Cosmeceuticals LLC (HQ)	5122	C	800 636-7546	10640
A W Chang Corporation (PA)	5131	E	310 764-2000	10660
Smart Stores Operations LLC	5141	C	562 438-0450	10777
Plastic Sales Southern Inc	5162	E	714 375-7900	11000
Casey Company (PA)	5172	C	562 436-9685	11029
Redbam Pet Products Inc (PA)	5199	C	562 495-7315	11138
Home Depot USA Inc	5211	C	562 595-9200	11175
Cabe Brothers	5511	D	562 595-7411	11322
Choura Venue Services	5812	D	562 426-0555	11560
Forty-Niner Shops Inc	5942	A	562 985-5093	11632
Password Enterprise Inc	5961	E	562 988-8889	11657
Innovative Dialysis Partners Inc	5999	B	562 495-8075	11686
Citibank FSB	6021	A	562 999-3453	11710
City National Bank	6021	D	562 624-8600	11714
First Bank and Trust	6021	C	562 595-8775	11733
Farmers Merchants Bnk Long Bch (HQ)	6022	C	562 437-0011	11765
Molina Hlthcare Cal Prtner Pla	6321	C	562 435-3666	12065
California Physicians Service	6324	D	310 744-2668	12074
Molina Healthcare Inc	6324	C	310 221-3031	12098
Scan Group (PA)	6324	B	562 308-2733	12104
Senior Care Action Ntwrk Fndti (PA)	6324	A	562 989-5100	12105
Tristar Insurance Group Inc (PA)	6331	A	562 495-6600	12141
Tristar Service Company Inc (HQ)	6411	B	562 495-6600	12263
Intex Recreation Corp	6512	C	310 549-5400	12298
Rance King Properties Inc (PA)	6513	C	562 240-1000	12363
American Development Corp (PA)	6531	D	562 989-3730	12381
Coastal Alliance Holdings Inc	6531	C	562 370-1000	12407
Cushman & Wakefield Cal Inc	6531	B	562 276-1400	12419
First Team RE - Orange Cnty	6531	D	562 346-5088	12444
First Team RE - Orange Cnty	6531	D	562 424-2004	12445
Gh Group Inc	6719	C	562 264-5078	12600
County of Los Angeles	6732	D	562 985-4687	12651
Evolution Hospitality LLC	7011	B	562 435-3511	12824
HEI Long Beach LLC	7011	C	562 983-3400	12849
Hyatt Corporation	7011	B	562 432-0161	12868
Hyatt Equities LLC	7011	D	562 436-1047	12871
Merritt Hospitality LLC	7011	C	562 983-3400	12922
Nhca Inc	7011	C	310 519-8200	12938
Noble/Utah Long Beach LLC	7011	C	562 436-3000	12939
Queensbay Hotel LLC	7011	D	562 481-3910	12980
RMS Foundation Inc	7011	A	562 435-3511	12999
Ruffin Hotel Corp of Cal	7011	B	562 425-5210	13003
Urban Commons Queensway LLC	7011	A	562 499-1611	13060
Yhb Long Beach LLC	7011	D	562 597-4401	13095
Worldwide Corporate Housing LP	7021	B	972 392-4747	13098
American Textile Maint Co	7218	D	562 424-1607	13138
Intertrend Communications Inc	7311	D	562 733-1888	13217
Continental Graphics Corp (HQ)	7336	C	714 503-4200	13324
Designory Inc (HQ)	7336	C	562 624-0200	13327
Motion Theory Inc	7336	C	310 396-9433	13332
Elite Craftsman (PA)	7349	C	562 989-3511	13373
Mida Industries Inc	7349	C	562 616-1020	13394
OPEN America Inc	7349	C	562 428-9210	13398
Bragg Investment Company Inc (PA)	7353	B	562 984-2400	13433
Psav Holdings LLC (PA)	7359	C	562 366-0138	13468
Compulink Management Ctr Inc (PA)	7371	C	562 988-1688	13691
Design Science Inc	7371	E	562 442-4779	13706
Dray Alliance Inc	7371	D	844 767-6776	13712
Erp Integrated Solutions LLC	7371	D	562 425-7800	13724
QED Software LLC	7372	E	310 214-3118	14012
Traffic Management Pdts Inc	7372	A	800 763-3999	14056
Zwift Inc (PA)	7372	B	855 469-9438	14069
Protect-US	7381	C	714 721-8127	14331
Shield Security Inc	7381	B	562 283-1100	14346
Greater Alarm Company Inc (DH)	7382	D	949 474-0555	14403
California Traffic Control	7389	D	562 595-7575	14465
Goodwill Sthern Los Angles CNT (PA)	7389	D	562 435-3411	14504
Macro-Pro Inc (PA)	7389	C	562 595-0900	14536
Traffic Management LLC (PA)	7389	C	562 595-4278	14612
Alliance Insptn MGT Holdg Inc (PA)	7549	A	562 495-8853	14711
Cw Industries Inc (PA)	7692	E	562 432-5421	14739
Olympix Fitness LLC	7991	D	562 366-4600	15058
Virginia Cntry CLB of Long Bch	7997	C	562 427-0924	15185
Altamed Health Services Corp	8011	D	562 923-9414	15237
CB Tang MD Incorporated	8011	D	562 437-0831	15264
Childrens Clnic Srving Chldren	8011	B	562 264-4638	15273
Healthsmart Pacific Inc	8011	D	562 595-1911	15320
Memorial Orthpdic Srgcal Group	8011	D	562 424-6666	15387
Molina Healthcare Inc (PA)	8011	A	562 435-3666	15392
Molina Healthcare California	8011	A	800 526-8196	15393
Molina Healthcare New York Inc	8011	D	888 562-5442	15394
Molina Pathways LLC	8011	B	562 491-5773	15395
Optumcare Management LLC	8011	C	562 988-7000	15417
Transltnal Plmnary Immnlogy RE	8011	D	562 490-9900	15491
Therapytravelers LLC	8049	C	888 223-8002	15557
Alamitos-Belmont Rehab Inc	8051	C	562 434-8421	15564
Atlantic Mem Hlthcare Assoc In (HQ)	8051	D	562 424-8101	15574
Atlantic Mem Hlthcare Assoc In	8051	D	562 494-3311	15575
Covenant Care California LLC	8051	C	562 427-7493	15612
Intercommunity Care Ctrs Inc	8051	C	562 427-8915	15682
Long Beach Care Center Inc	8051	C	562 426-6141	15701
Marlora Investments LLC	8051	D	562 494-3311	15717
Pacs Group Inc	8051	B	562 422-9219	15736
Palmcrest Grand Care Ctr Inc	8051	D	562 595-4551	15746
Palmcrest Medallion Convalesc	8051	D	562 595-4336	15747
Villa Serena Healthcare Center	8051	D	562 437-2797	15795
Blyth/Wndsor Cntry Pk Hlthcare	8052	D	310 385-1090	15808
Longwood Management Corp	8059	C	562 432-5751	15869
Villa De La Mar Inc	8059	C	562 494-5001	15890
Catholic Hlthcare W Sthern Cal (HQ)	8062	C	562 491-9000	15932
Community Hospital Long Beach	8062	A	562 494-0600	15963
Dignity Health	8062	B	805 988-2868	15980
Dignity Health	8062	C	562 491-9000	15982
Healthsmart Pacific Inc (PA)	8062	A	562 595-1911	16015
Long Beach Medical Center	8062	B	562 933-7701	16084
Long Beach Medical Center	8062	B	562 933-0085	16085
Long Beach Medical Center (HQ)	8062	A	562 933-2000	16086
Long Beach Memorial Med Ctr	8062	B	562 933-0432	16087
Memorial Hlth Svcs - Univ Cal (PA)	8062	A	562 933-2000	16095
St Mary Medical Center (DH)	8062	A	562 491-9000	16220

2025 Southern California
Business Directory and Buyers Guide

(P-0000) Products & Services Section entry number
(PA)=Parent Co (HQ)=Headquarters (DH)=Div Headquarters

	SIC	EMP	PHONE	ENTRY#
Posca Brothers Dental Lab Inc	8072	D	562 427-1811	16346
Central Health Plan Cal Inc	8082	C	866 314-2427	16377
Coastal Cmnty Senior Care LLC	8082	C	562 596-4884	16379
Safe Refuge	8093	D	562 987-5722	16500
Tarzana Treatment Centers Inc	8093	C	562 218-1868	16509
Telecare Corporation	8093	D	562 630-8672	16512
Universal Care Inc (HQ)	8093	B	866 255-4795	16516
Easy Care Mso LLC	8099	B	562 676-9600	16557
Industrial Medical Support Inc	8099	A	877 878-9185	16572
Medasend Biomedical Inc (PA)	8099	C	800 200-3581	16586
Molina Healthcare Inc	8099	D	888 562-5442	16587
Molina Healthcare Inc	8099	A	562 435-3666	16588
Optumcare Management LLC	8099	D	562 429-2473	16597
Pponext West Inc	8099	B	888 446-6098	16603
Welbe Health LLC	8099	C	888 530-4415	16627
Fulwider and Patton LLP	8111	D	310 824-5555	16685
Keesal Young Logan A Prof Corp (PA)	8111	D	562 436-2000	16714
Prindle Decker & Amaro LLP (PA)	8111	D	562 436-3946	16763
Long Beach Unified School Dst	8211	D	562 426-5571	16314
American National Red Cross	8322	D	562 595-6341	16866
Childnet Youth & Fmly Svcs Inc (PA)	8322	C	562 498-5500	16889
Jewish Community Ctr Long Bch	8322	C	562 426-7601	16962
Kingdom Causes Inc	8322		714 904-0167	16968
Life Steps Foundation Inc	8322	C	562 436-0751	16971
Advocacy For Rspect Chice - Lo (PA)	8331	D	562 597-7716	17044
Conservation Corps Long Beach	8331	C	562 986-1249	17054
Brittany House LLC	8361	C	562 421-4717	17124
Aquarium of Pacific (PA)	8422	C	562 590-3100	17269
Automobile Club Southern Cal	8699	D	562 425-8350	17436
Memorial Medical Center Foundation	8699	A	562 933-2273	17466
California Mfg Tech Consulting	8711	D	310 263-3060	17499
Jacobs Civil Inc	8711	D	310 847-2500	17560
Mangan Inc (PA)	8711	D	310 835-8080	17581
Stearns Conrad and Schmidt Consulti (PA)	8711	D	562 426-9544	17637
URS Group Inc	8711	C	562 420-2933	17657
Utility Traffic Services LLC	8711	B	562 264-2355	17658
Rdc-S111 Inc (PA)	8712	D	562 628-8000	17688
California State Univ Long Bch	8721	C	562 985-1764	17709
Windes Inc (PA)	8721	C	562 435-1191	17759
Southern Cal Inst For RES Edca	8733	D	562 826-8139	17891
Twining Inc (PA)	8734	D	562 426-3355	17928
Country Villa Service Corp	8741	C	562 597-8817	17975
Aunt Rubys LLC	8742	E	562 326-6783	18098
Foundation Property MGT Inc	8742	C	562 257-5100	18139
Onyx Global Hr LLC (PA)	8742	C	866 715-4806	18188
Pmcs Group Inc	8742	D	562 498-0808	18193
Rmd Group Inc	8742	C	562 866-9288	18202
St Marys Medical Center	8742	A	562 491-9230	18220
Argus Management Company LLC	8744	B	562 299-5200	18258
Ultura Inc	8744	C	562 661-4999	18269
Healthcare Services Group Inc	8999	A	562 494-7939	18374
City of Long Beach	9431	C	562 570-4000	18391

LOS ALAMITOS, CA - Orange County

	SIC	EMP	PHONE	ENTRY#
Millie and Severson Inc	1541	D	562 493-3611	492
Pcn3 Inc	1542	D	562 493-4124	568
Carol Electric Company Inc	1731	D	562 431-1870	897
Kdc Inc (HQ)	1731	C	714 828-7000	931
Thermo Power Industries	1742	E	562 799-0087	1034
Bloomfield Bakers	2052	A	626 610-2253	1482
Blue Sphere Inc	2311	E	714 953-7555	1976
Kids Line LLC	2392	C	310 660-0110	2212
Pih Products Inc	2452	D	714 730-6622	2401
Supermedia LLC	2741	C	562 594-5101	2943
Trend Offset Printing Services Inc (HQ)	2752	E	562 598-2446	3090
Trend Offset Printing Svcs Inc	2752	E	562 598-2446	3091
Lab Clean Inc	2842	E	714 689-0063	3609
Natus Inc	3161	D	626 355-3746	4297
Epson America Inc (DH)	3577	A	800 463-7766	5918
PI Machine Corporation	3599	E	714 892-1100	6203
Alliance Spacesystems LLC	3624	C	714 226-1400	6337
Dwi Enterprises	3651	E	714 842-2236	6535
Epson Electronics America Inc (DH)	3674	E	408 922-0200	6822
Arrowhead Products Corporation	3728	A	714 822-2513	7434
Vanguard Space Tech Inc	3728	C	858 587-4210	7586
Flowline Inc	3829	D	562 598-3015	8042
College Park Realty Inc (PA)	6531	D	562 594-6753	12411
Quantum World Technologies Inc	7361	B	805 834-0532	13561
Tenet Healthsystem Medical Inc	8011	B	805 546-7698	15488
Katella Properties	8051	D	562 596-5561	15685
Los Alamitos Medical Ctr Inc (HQ)	8062	A	714 826-6400	16090
Institute of Elec Elec Engnrs	8611	D	714 821-8380	1/283
Department Military California	8744	B	562 795-2065	18261

LOS ANGELES, CA - Los Angeles County

	SIC	EMP	PHONE	ENTRY#
Eclipse Berry Farms LLC	0171	D	310 207-7879	16
Mulroses Usa Inc	0181	D	213 489-1761	61
Hokto Kinoko Company	0182	D	323 526-1155	72
Wonderful Company LLC	0723	B	661 720-2609	126
Mercy For Animals Inc	0742	C	347 839-6464	129
VCA Animal Hospitals Inc	0742	D	310 473-2951	134
Vicar Operating Inc (DH)	0742	D	310 571-6500	136
Greenscreen	0781	E	310 837-0526	171
Monarch Landscape Holdings LLC (PA)	0782	C	213 816-1750	223
Breitburn Energy Partners LP	1311	A	213 225-5900	269
Occidental Petroleum Corporation of California	1311	A		275
The Strand Energy Company	1311		213 225-5900	276
Breitburn Energy Holdings LLC	1382	E	213 225-5900	296
Freeport-Mcmoran Oil & Gas LLC	1382	D	323 298-2200	304
Occidental Petroleum Investment Co Inc	1382	A	310 208-8800	309
Qre Operating LLC	1382	D	213 225-5900	311
Sentinel Peak Rsources Cal LLC	1382	C	323 298-2200	313
Hirsh Inc	1389	E	213 622-9441	335
Vanderra Resources LLC	1389	B	817 439-2220	369
KB Home Grater Los Angeles Inc (HQ)	1521	D	310 231-4000	414
Shimmick Construction Co Inc	1521	C	310 663-8924	431
KB Home (PA)	1531	D	310 231-4000	462
Austin Commercial LP	1542	D	310 421-0269	519
Hitt Contracting Inc	1542	C	424 326-1042	546
McCarthy Bldg Companies Inc	1542	B	213 655-1100	559
Philmont Management Inc	1542	D	213 380-0159	571
Shawmut Woodworking & Sup Inc	1542	D	323 602-1000	582
Webcor Construction LP	1542	C	213 239-2800	603
Myers & Sons Construction LP	1611	C	424 227-3285	638
HP Communications Inc	1623	D	951 457-0133	678
Arrowhead Brass & Plumbing LLC	1711	D	800 332-4267	741
Muir-Chase Plumbing Co Inc	1711	D	818 500-1940	807
Precise Air Systems Inc	1711	D	818 646-9757	822
Skypower Holdings LLC	1711	C	323 860-4900	839
American Solar Direct Inc	1731	C	424 214-6700	883
Steiny and Company Inc	1731	B	213 382-2331	967
Capital Drywall LP	1742	C	909 599-6818	1003
Rutherford Co Inc (PA)	1742	C	323 666-5284	1027
Platinum Roofing Inc	1761	C	408 280-5028	1093
Sbb Roofing Inc (PA)	1761	C	323 254-2888	1095
Tinco Sheet Metal Inc	1761	C	323 263-0511	1098
Giroux Glass Inc (PA)	1793	C	213 747-7406	1165
Closet Factory Inc (PA)	1799	C	310 516-7000	1198
D&A Endeavors Inc	1799	D	310 390-7540	1201
Parking Network Inc	1799	D	213 613-1500	1220
Rey-Crest Roofg Waterproofing	1799	D	323 257-9329	1225
Waterprfing Rofg Solutions Inc	1799	D	310 571-0892	1232
Clougherty Packing LLC (DH)	2011	B	323 583-4621	1241
Serv-Rite Meat Company Inc	2011	D	323 227-1911	1250
Commodity Sales Co	2015	C	323 980-5463	1276
Los Angeles Poultry Co Inc	2015	D	323 232-1619	1281
Western Supreme Inc	2015	C	213 627-3861	1282
Pac Fill Inc	2026	E	818 409-0117	1333
Caer Inc	2032	E	415 974-9864	1338
Dolores Canning Co Inc	2032	E	323 263-9155	1340
Wing Hing Foods LLC	2032	D	323 232-8899	1347
Walker Foods Inc	2033	D	323 268-5191	1363
J Hellman Frozen Foods Inc (PA)	2037	E	213 243-9105	1377
Astrochef Inc	2038	E	213 627-9860	1385
Crave Foods Inc	2038	E	562 900-7272	1387
East West Tea Company LLC	2043	C	310 275-9891	1411
Mars Food US LLC	2044	E	502 010-7047	1413
Arthur Dogswell LLC (PA)	2047	E	888 559-8833	1416
Bakers Kneaded LLC	2051	E	310 819-8700	1436
Frisco Baking Company Inc	2051	E	323 225-6111	1452
Global Impact Inv Partners LLC	2051	E	310 592-2000	1455
Lavash Corporation of America	2051	E	323 663-5249	1459
United States Bakery	2051	E	323 232-6124	1468
Vurger Co (usa) Corp	2051	E	929 318-9546	1470
Yamazaki Baking Co Ltd	2051	E	323 581-5218	1473
Amays Bakery & Noodle Co Inc (PA)	2052	D	213 626-2713	1475
Aspire Bakeries Holdco LLC (HQ)	2052	C	844 992-7747	1476
Aspire Bakeries LLC (DH)	2052	C	844 992-7747	1477
J & J Snack Foods Corp Cal (HQ)	2052	D	323 581-0011	1489
Wonderful Pstchios Almonds LLC (HQ)	2068	D	310 966-5700	1519
Darling Ingredients Inc	2077	D	323 583-6311	1524
Angel City Public Hse & Brewry	2082	E	562 983-6880	1530
San Antonio Winery Inc (PA)	2084	C	323 223-1401	1584
The Wonderful Company LLC (PA)	2084	C	310 966-5700	1588
Winc Inc	2084	C	855 282-5829	1595
Stillhouse LLC	2085	E	323 498-1111	1599
Aquahydrate Inc	2086	E	310 559-5058	1607

Employee Codes: A=Over 500 employees, B=251-500
C=101-250, D=51-100, E=20-50, F=10-19, G=1-9

2025 Southern California
Business Directory and Buyers Guide

© Mergent Inc. 1-800-342-5647

1299

GEOGRAPHIC

Company	SIC	EMP	PHONE	ENTRY#
Cce	2086	E	213 744-8909	1612
Gts Living Foods LLC (PA)	2086	A	323 581-7787	1620
Reyes Coca-Cola Bottling LLC	2086	E	213 744-8659	1646
American Fruits & Flavors LLC	2087	D	213 624-1831	1662
American Fruits & Flavors LLC	2087	E	818 899-9574	1666
American Fruits & Flavors LLC	2087	E	818 899-9574	1667
Herbalife Manufacturing LLC (DH)	2087	D	866 866-4744	1683
Yamasa Enterprises	2091	E	213 626-2211	1699
Eberine Enterprises Inc	2095	E	323 587-1111	1716
Snack It Forward LLC	2096	E	310 242-5517	1728
Peking Noodle Co Inc	2098	E	323 223-0897	1734
C & F Foods Inc	2099	B	626 723-1000	1749
Camino Real Foods Inc (PA)	2099	C	323 585-6599	1751
Everytable Pbc	2099	E	323 296-0311	1771
Jsl Foods Inc (PA)	2099	D	323 223-2484	1796
La Barca Tortilleria Inc	2099	D	323 268-1744	1799
La Fortaleza Inc	2099	D	323 261-1211	1802
La Gloria Foods Corp (PA)	2099	D	323 262-0410	1803
Mojave Foods Corporation (HQ)	2099	D	323 890-8900	1819
Pensieve Foods	2099	E	323 938-8666	1837
Tampico Spice Co Incorporated	2099	E	323 235-3154	1859
Uce Holdings Inc	2099	D	213 217-4235	1864
Worldwide Specialties Inc	2099	C	323 587-2200	1866
Colormax Industries Inc (PA)	2211	E	213 748-6600	1876
Factory One Studio Inc	2211	D	323 752-1670	1878
G Kagan and Sons Inc (PA)	2211	E	323 581-1400	1880
Knit Generation Group Inc	2211	E	213 221-5081	1882
Ground Control Business MGT (DH)	2221	E	310 315-6200	1895
Juicy Couture Inc	2221	C	888 824-8826	1896
S&B Development Group LLC	2221	E	213 446-2818	1897
Cmk Manufacturing LLC	2231	E		1899
Roshan Trading Inc	2231	E	213 622-9904	1903
Byer California	2253	C	323 780-7615	1912
Crew Knitwear LLC	2253	E	323 526-3888	1913
Fortune Swimwear LLC (HQ)	2253	E	310 733-2130	1918
Tenenblatt Corporation	2257	C	323 232-2061	1927
Azitex Trading Corp	2259	D	213 745-7072	1928
Washington Grment Dyg Fnshg In	2261	E	213 747-1111	1937
Washington Garment Dyeing	2262	E	213 747-1111	1939
Matchmaster Dyg & Finshg Inc (PA)	2269	C	323 232-2061	1942
Pacific Coast Bach Label Inc	2269	E	213 612-0314	1943
Durkan Patterned Carpets Inc	2273	C	310 838-2898	1950
Interfaceflor LLC	2273	D	213 741-2139	1952
AMpm Maintenance Corporation	2299	E	424 230-1300	1967
New Chef Fashion Inc	2311	D	323 581-0300	1977
Distro Worldwide LLC	2321	E	818 849-0953	1983
Fear of God LLC	2329	E	213 235-7985	2010
Fetish Group Inc (PA)	2329	E	323 587-7873	2011
Jh Design Group	2329	D	213 747-5700	2014
Spirit Clothing Company (PA)	2329	C	213 784-0251	2025
Waterfront Design Group LLC	2329	E	213 746-5800	2031
Guru Knits Inc	2331	D	323 235-9424	2037
Harari Inc (PA)	2331	D	323 734-5302	2038
Harkham Industries Inc (PA)	2331	E	323 586-4600	2039
Judy Ann of California Inc	2331	C	323 623-9233	2040
K Too	2331	E	213 747-7766	2041
La Mamba LLC	2331	E	323 526-3526	2044
Leebe Apparel Inc	2331	E	323 897-5585	2045
Mf Inc	2331	C	213 627-2498	2047
Monrow LLC	2331	E	213 741-6007	2048
MXF Designs Inc	2331	D	323 266-1451	2049
Project Social T LLC	2331	E	323 266-4500	2053
Stony Apparel Corp (PA)	2331	C	323 981-9080	2054
Tianello Inc	2331	C	323 231-0599	2055
Avalon Apparel LLC (PA)	2335	C	323 581-3511	2060
California Blue Apparel Inc	2335	E	213 745-5400	2061
Choon Inc (PA)	2335	E	213 225-2500	2063
J C Trimming Company Inc	2335	D	323 235-4458	2065
Jodi Kristopher LLC (PA)	2335	D	323 890-8000	2066
Jwc Studio Inc (PA)	2335	E	323 831-8222	2067
L A Glo Inc	2335	E	323 932-0091	2068
Private Brand Mdsg Corp	2335	E	213 749-0191	2069
Promises Promises Inc	2335	E	213 749-7725	2070
Sublitex Inc	2335	E	323 582-9596	2072
Tlmf Inc	2335	D	212 764-2334	2073
Komarov Enterprises Inc	2337	D	213 244-7000	2076
Topson Downs California Inc	2337	C	310 558-0300	2078
Bb Co Inc	2339	E	213 550-1158	2081
Be Bop Clothing	2339	B	323 846-0121	2082
Carbon 38 Inc	2339	D	888 723-5838	2084
Clothing Illustrated Inc (PA)	2339	E	213 403-9950	2086
Crew Knitwear LLC (PA)	2339	E	323 526-3888	2087
Dda Holdings Inc	2339	E	213 624-5200	2090
Dmbm LLC	2339	E	714 321-6032	2092
Eska Inc	2339	E	323 846-3700	2094
Good American LLC (PA)	2339	E	213 357-5100	2098
Jaya Apparel Group LLC (PA)	2339	D	323 584-3500	2104
Jd/Cmc Inc	2339	E	818 767-2260	2105
JT Design Studio Inc (PA)	2339	E	213 891-1500	2109
Klk Forte Industry Inc (PA)	2339	E	323 415-9181	2113
L&L Manufacturing Co Inc	2339	B		2115
Lee Thomas Inc (PA)	2339	E	310 532-7560	2117
Lefty Production Co LLC	2339	E	323 515-9266	2118
MGT Industries Inc (PA)	2339	D	310 516-5900	2121
Monterey Canyon LLC (PA)	2339	D	213 741-0209	2122
New Fashion Products Inc	2339	C	310 354-0090	2123
Piet Retief Inc	2339	E	323 732-8312	2126
Rhapsody Clothing Inc	2339	D	213 614-8887	2129
Solow	2339	E	323 664-7772	2132
Tcj Manufacturing LLC	2339	E	213 488-8400	2135
Treivush Industries Inc	2339	E	213 745-7774	2140
YMi Jeanswear Inc	2339	D	213 746-6681	2143
Delta Galil USA Inc	2341	B	213 488-4859	2148
Guess Inc (PA)	2341	A	213 765-3100	2149
Honest Company Inc (PA)	2341	E	310 917-9199	2150
Foh Group Inc (PA)	2342	E		2154
Agron Inc (PA)	2353	D	310 473-7223	2156
Kwdz Manufacturing LLC (PA)	2361	D	323 526-3526	2165
Misyd Corp (PA)	2361	E	213 742-1800	2167
Un Deux Trois Inc (PA)	2369	E	323 588-1067	2174
Chrome Hearts LLC (PA)	2386	E	323 957-7544	2178
App Winddown LLC (HQ)	2389	C		2187
Califrnia Cstume Cllctions Inc (PA)	2389	E	323 262-8383	2188
Conquer Nation Inc	2389	C	310 651-5555	2190
Los Angeles Apparel Inc (PA)	2389	C	213 275-3120	2196
Los Angeles Apparel Inc	2389	C	213 275-3120	2197
Mdc Interior Solutions LLC	2389	E	800 621-4006	2198
Amtex California Inc	2391	E	323 859-2200	2203
Matteo LLC	2392	E	213 617-2813	2216
Universal Cushion Company Inc (PA)	2392	E	323 887-8000	2225
Outdoor Rcrtion Group Hldngs L (PA)	2393	E	323 226-0830	2231
Gma Cover Corp	2394	C		2239
American Quilting Company Inc	2395	E	323 233-2500	2245
Atelier Luxury Group LLC	2396	E	310 751-2444	2257
Tesca Usa Inc	2396	E	586 991-0744	2268
Wessco Intl Ltd A Cal Ltd Prtn (PA)	2399	D	310 477-4272	2283
Bromack Company	2434	E	323 227-5000	2340
Mikada Cabinets LLC	2434	D		2355
Ultra Built Kitchens Inc	2434	E	323 232-3362	2365
Arnies Supply Service Ltd (PA)	2448	E	323 263-1696	2385
Pallet Masters Inc	2448	D	323 758-1713	2390
Marge Carson Inc (PA)	2512	D	626 571-1111	2452
Minson Corporation	2512	B	323 513-1041	2455
Stitch Industries Inc	2512	E	888 282-0842	2460
Wesley Allen Inc	2514	C	323 231-4275	2476
Don Alderson Associates Inc	2519	E	310 837-5141	2501
Angell & Giroux Inc	2522	E	323 269-8596	2520
Versa Products (PA)	2522	C	310 353-7100	2533
LA Cabinet & Millwork Inc	2541	E	323 227-5000	2569
Felbro Inc	2542	E	323 263-8686	2580
Pacific Manufacturing MGT Inc	2542	D	323 263-9000	2586
Salsbury Industries Inc	2542	D	323 846-6700	2592
Hd Window Fashions Inc (DH)	2591	B	213 749-6333	2601
New Green Day LLC	2611	E	323 566-7603	2619
Advance Paper Box Company	2653	C	323 750-2550	2652
Plastopan Industries Inc (PA)	2655	E	323 231-2225	2696
Vision Envelope & Prtg Co Inc (PA)	2677	E	310 324-7062	2754
Associated Students UCLA	2711	C	310 825-2787	2782
California Community News LLC (DH)	2711	B	626 388-1017	2784
California Newsppr Svc Bur Inc	2711	E	213 229-5500	2785
Daily Journal Corporation (PA)	2711	E	213 229-5300	2793
Grace Communications Inc (PA)	2711	E	213 628-4384	2800
Investors Business Daily Inc (HQ)	2711	E	800 831-2525	2805
Joongangilbo Usa Inc (DH)	2711	C	213 368-2512	2807
La Opinion LP (HQ)	2711	E	213 891-9191	2809
La Opinion LP	2711	B	213 896-2222	2810
La Times	2711	E	213 237-2279	2811
Los Angeles Sentinel Inc	2711	D	323 299-3800	2813
The Korea Times Los Angeles Inc (PA)	2711	C	323 692-2000	2832
Thewrap	2711	E	424 273-4787	2833
Tribe Mdia Corp A Cal Nnprfit	2711	E	213 368-1661	2834
Cbj LP	2721	D	818 676-1750	2846
Cbj LP	2721	E	323 549-5225	2847
ID Matters LLC	2721	E	323 822-4800	2860
Mnm Corporation (PA)	2721	E	213 627-3737	2865
Orange Coast Magazine LLC	2721	D	949 862-1133	2867

Mergent email: customerrelations@mergent.com
1300

2025 Southern California
Business Directory and Buyers Guide

(P-0000) Products & Services Section entry number
(PA)=Parent Co (HQ)=Headquarters (DH)=Div Headquarters

Company	SIC	EMP	PHONE	ENTRY#
Playboy Enterprises Inc	2721	D	310 424-1800	2871
Recruitment Services Inc	2721	E	213 364-1960	2874
Access Books	2731	C	310 920-1694	2882
Judy O Productions Inc	2731	E	323 938-8513	2891
American Soc Cmpsers Athors Pb	2741	C	323 883-1000	2903
Good Worldwide LLC	2741	E	323 206-6495	2918
Jungotv LLC	2741	D	650 207-6227	2924
Netmarble Us Inc	2741	D	213 222-7712	2929
Planetizen Inc	2741	E	877 260-7526	2935
Playboy Enterprises Intl Inc	2741	E	310 424-1800	2936
Pollstar LLC	2741	E	559 271-7900	2937
Riye Group LLC	2741	E	820 203-9215	2941
Techture Inc	2741	E	323 347-6209	2946
Thomson Reuters Corporation	2741	E	310 287-2360	2947
Warner Chappell Music Inc (DH)	2741	C	310 441-8600	2953
Wb Music Corp (DH)	2741	C	310 441-8600	2954
Webtoon Entertainment Inc (PA)	2741	A	323 297-3410	2955
Anderson La Inc	2752	D	323 460-4115	2963
Apple Graphics Inc	2752	E	626 301-4287	2964
Boss Litho Inc	2752	E	626 912-7088	2972
Cdr Graphics Inc (PA)	2752	E	310 474-7600	2977
Digital Printing Systems Inc (PA)	2752	D	626 815-1888	3001
Ikonick LLC	2752	E	516 680-7765	3013
Ink & Color Inc	2752	E	310 280-6060	3017
LA Printing & Graphics Inc	2752	E	310 527-4526	3031
Madisn/Grham Clor Graphics Inc	2752	B	323 261-7171	3037
ONeil Digital Solutions LLC (HQ)	2752	C	972 881-1282	3053
ONeil Capital Management Inc	2754	C	310 448-6400	3108
Stuart F Cooper Co	2754	C	213 747-7141	3110
American Zabin Intl Inc	2759	E	213 746-3770	3116
Consolidated Graphics Inc	2759	C	323 460-4115	3131
CR & A Custom Apparel Inc	2759	C	213 749-4440	3134
RJ Acquisition Corp (PA)	2759	C	323 318-1107	3171
The/Studio	2759	E	213 233-1633	3184
Kater-Crafts Incorporated	2789	E	562 692-0665	3202
Oxerra Americas LLC	2816	D	323 269-7311	3222
Huntsman Advanced Materials AM	2821	E	818 265-7221	3270
Ineos Composites Us LLC	2821	D	323 767-1300	3273
Chromadex Corporation (PA)	2833	E	310 388-6706	3313
Mro Maryruth LLC	2833	C	424 343-6650	3320
Ron Teeguarden Enterprises Inc (PA)	2833	E	323 556-8188	3329
Abraxis Bioscience LLC (DH)	2834	C	800 564-0216	3338
Baxalta US Inc	2834	A	818 240-5600	3370
Cougar Biotechnology Inc	2834	D	310 943-8040	3390
Dnib Unwind Inc	2834	C	213 617-2717	3397
Hylands Consumer Health Inc (PA)	2834	E	310 768-0700	3421
Murad LLC	2834	C	310 906-3100	3453
Natals Inc	2834	C	323 475-6033	3454
Puma Biotechnology Inc (PA)	2834	C	424 248-6500	3484
Zp Opco Inc	2834	E	510 745-1200	8527
Response Genetics Inc	2835	C	323 224-3900	3552
Armata Pharmaceuticals Inc (PA)	2836	E	310 665-2928	3559
Grifols Biologicals LLC (DH)	2836	C	323 225-2221	3577
Sustainable Care Company Inc	2842	E	310 210-7090	3621
Kenvue Brands LLC	2844	C	310 642-1150	3665
Merle Norman Cosmetics Inc (PA)	2844	B	310 641-3000	3670
Pacific World Corporation (PA)	2844	D	949 598-2400	3676
Ennis Traffic Safety Solutions	2851	E	323 758-1147	3712
Rentech Ntrgn Pasadena Spa LLC	2873	E	310 571-9805	3746
Stic-Adhesive Products Co Inc	2891	C	323 268-2956	3780
Gans Ink and Supply Co Inc (PA)	2893	E	323 264-2200	3784
American Consumer Products LLC	2899	D	323 289-6610	3789
Rentech Inc (PA)	2900	E	310 671-9800	3861
Ames Rubber Mfg Co Inc	3060	E	818 240-0313	3908
Mercury Plastics Inc	3081	D	323 264-2400	3951
Poly Pak America Inc	3081	E	323 264-2400	3955
J-M Manufacturing Company Inc (PA)	3084	C	310 693-8200	3975
Pw Eagle Inc	3084	A	800 621-4404	3978
Dial Industries Inc	3089	D	323 263-6878	4102
Dial Industries Inc (PA)	3089	D	323 263-6878	4103
Housewares International Inc	3089	E	323 581-3000	4135
Jet Plastics (PA)	3089	E	323 268-6706	4147
Plastpro 2000 Inc (PA)	3089	C	310 693-8600	4204
Rehrig Pacific Company (HQ)	3089	C	323 262-5145	4221
Stone Canyon Industries LLC	3089	A	310 570-4869	4251
La La Land Production & Design	3111	E	323 406-9223	4279
Millennial Brands LLC	3144	E	925 230-0617	4286
Surgeon Worldwide Inc	3144	E	707 501-7962	4287
Jan-Al Innerprizes Inc	3161	E	323 260-7212	4296
Sbnw LLC (PA)	3171	C	213 234-5122	4304
Malibu Leather Inc	3172	C	310 985-0707	4306
Aputure Imaging Industries	3229	E	626 295-6133	4323
Judson Studios Inc	3231	E	323 255-0131	4337
Tubular Specialties Mfg Inc	3261	D	310 515-4801	4363
McFiebow Inc	3272	E	310 327-7474	4401
Best-Way Marble & Tile Co Inc	3281	E	323 266-6794	4471
Interstate Steel Center Co Inc	3312	E	323 583-0855	4519
National Wire and Cable Corporation	3315	C	323 225-5611	4539
Roscoe Moss Manufacturing Co (PA)	3317	D	323 261-4185	4554
David H Fell & Co Inc (PA)	3341	E	323 722-9992	4583
Sun Valley Products Inc (HQ)	3354	E	818 247-8350	4607
Arcadia Products LLC (HQ)	3355	C	323 771-9819	4614
P Kay Metal Inc (PA)	3356	E	323 585-5058	4621
Wire Technology Corporation	3357	E	310 635-6935	4641
Cast Partner Inc	3369	E	323 876-9000	4685
Micro Surface Engr Inc (PA)	3399	E	323 582-7348	4718
Augerscope Inc	3423	E		4736
Doval Industries Inc	3429	E	323 226-0335	4766
Commercial Shtmtl Works Inc	3441	E	213 748-7321	4828
Medsco Fabrication & Dist Inc	3441	D	323 263-0511	4853
Zia Aamir	3441	E	714 337-7861	4882
Active Window Products	3442	D	323 245-5185	4883
Hehr International Inc	3442	C	323 663-1261	4889
Basic Industries Intl Inc (PA)	3443	E	951 226-1500	4910
Roy E Hanson Jr Mfg (PA)	3443	D	213 747-7514	4924
S Bravo Systems Inc	3443	E	323 888-4133	4925
Able Sheet Metal Inc (PA)	3444	E	323 269-2181	4937
Aero Precision Engineering	3444	E	310 642-9747	4942
King Wire Partitions Inc	3449	E	323 256-4848	5098
Power Fasteners Inc	3452	E	323 232-4362	5135
Bandel Mfg Inc	3469	E	818 246-7493	5174
Larry Spun Products Inc	3469	E	323 881-6300	5198
Accurate Plating Company	3471	E	323 268-8567	5225
Alco Plating Corp (PA)	3471	E	213 749-7561	5226
Alpha Polishing Corporation (PA)	3471	D	323 263-7593	5231
Anodizing Industries Inc	3471	E	323 227-4916	5233
Barry Avenue Plating Co Inc	3471	D	310 478-0078	5237
Bronze-Way Plating Corporation (PA)	3471	E	323 266-6933	5243
Chromal Plating Company	3471	E	323 222-0119	5247
Electrolizing Inc	3471	E	213 749-7876	5257
Genes Plating Works Inc (PA)	3471	E	323 269-8748	5262
George Industries (HQ)	3471	E	323 264-6660	5263
Old Spc Inc	3471	E	310 533-0748	5279
Pentrate Metal Processing	3471	E	323 269-2121	5282
Ravlich Enterprises LLC	3471	E	310 533-0748	5288
Adfa Incorporated	3479	E	213 627-8004	5306
Certified Enameling Inc (PA)	3479	D	323 264-4403	5315
NM Holdco Inc	3479	C	323 663-3971	5333
Tortoise Industries Inc	3479	E	323 258-7776	5350
Bcc Dissolution Inc	3498	E	323 583-3444	5428
Edmund A Gray Co (PA)	3498	D	213 625-0376	5433
PSM Industries Inc (PA)	3499	D	888 663-8256	5453
Polyalloys Injected Metals Inc	3532	E	310 715-9800	5501
Gleason Industrial Pdts Inc	3537	C	574 533-1141	5530
Avis Roto Die Co	3544	E	323 255-7070	5567
Idea Tooling and Engrg Inc	3544	D	310 608-7488	5585
Stadco (HQ)	3545	D	323 227-8888	5625
Old Country Millwork Inc (PA)	3547	E	323 234-2940	5640
Vest Tube LLC	3547	D	800 421-6370	5641
Ubtech Robotics Corp	3549	C	213 261-7153	5656
Machine Building Spc Inc	3556	E	323 666-8289	5680
Industrial Tools Inc	3559	E	805 483-1111	5706
Norchem Corporation (PA)	3559	C	323 221-0221	5714
Starco Enterprises Inc (PA)	3559	E	323 266-7111	5720
Mjw Inc	3561	D	323 778-8900	5737
Forward	3568	F	310 962-2522	5807
Efaxcom (DH)	3577	D	323 817-3207	5914
Denim-Tech Inc	3582	D	323 277-8998	5963
City of Santa Monica	3589	C	310 826-6712	6008
Tosco - Tool Specialty Company	3599	E	323 232-3561	6253
On-Line Power Incorporated (PA)	3612	E	323 721-5017	6292
W A Benjamin Electric Co	3613	E	213 749-7731	6312
Concurrent Holdings LLC	3629	A	310 473-3065	6371
IaMplus LLC	3629	D	323 210-3852	6375
Capital Brands Distribution L (PA)	3634	D	800 523-5993	6394
Alger-Triton Inc	3645	C	310 229-9500	6436
Prudential Lighting Corp (PA)	3646	C	213 477-1694	6471
AMP Plus Inc	3647	D	323 231-2600	6483
Eema Industries Inc	3648	E	323 904-0200	6499
Absolute Usa Inc	3651	E	213 744-0044	6521
Mr Dj Inc	3651	E	213 744-0044	6546
Vizio Inc	3651	C	213 746-7730	6566
Capitol-Emi Music Inc	3652	A	323 462-6252	6572
Eeg 3 LLC (DH)	3663	C		6612
Katz Millennium Sls & Mktg Inc	3663	C	323 966-5066	6621
Ophir Rf Inc	3663	E	310 306-5556	6643

Employee Codes: A=Over 500 employees, B=251-500
C=101-250, D=51-100, E=20-50, F=10-19, G=1-9

2025 Southern California
Business Directory and Buyers Guide

© Mergent Inc. 1-800-342-5647

1301

	SIC	EMP	PHONE	ENTRY#
Silvus Technologies Inc (PA)	3663	E	310 479-3333	6660
Micross Holdings Inc	3674	D	215 997-3200	6855
A M I/Coast Magnetics Inc	3677	E	323 936-6188	6922
Dcx-Chol Enterprises Inc (PA)	3679	D	310 516-1692	6990
Ocm Pe Holdings LP	3679	A	213 830-6213	7031
Teledyne Technologies Inc	3679	B	310 822-8229	7060
Electrical Rebuilders Sls Inc	3694	D	323 249-7545	7091
Flyer Defense LLC	3711	D	310 324-5650	7176
Xos Fleet Inc (HQ)	3711	E	818 316-1890	7196
Ctbla Inc	3713	D	323 276-1933	7199
Vahe Enterprises Inc	3713	D	323 235-6657	7213
C R Laurence Co Inc (HQ)	3714	B	323 588-1281	7233
Grover Products Co	3714	D	323 263-9981	7259
Xos Inc (PA)	3714	E	818 316-1890	7311
Worldwide Aeros Corp	3721	D	818 344-3999	7375
Helicopter Tech Co Ltd Partnr	3728	E	310 523-2750	7488
Gambol Industries Inc	3732	E	562 901-2470	7620
Proto Homes LLC	3792	E	310 271-7544	7678
L3harris Technologies Inc	3812	E	310 481-6000	7733
Mapquest Holdings LLC	3812	B	310 256-4882	7742
Northrop Grumman Systems Corp	3812	B	310 556-4911	7767
Eti Systems	3823	D	310 684-3664	7857
First Legal Network	3825	C	213 250-1111	7912
Barksdale Inc (DH)	3829	D	323 583-6243	8033
Dynamics Orthtics Prsthtics In	3842	E	213 383-9212	8260
Hanger Prsthtics Orthtics W In	3842	D	213 250-7850	8272
Cyber Medical Imaging Inc	3843	E	888 937-9729	8331
Sprintray Inc (PA)	3843	D	800 914-8004	8357
Neurasignal Inc	3845	E	877 638-7251	8391
March Vision Care Inc	3851	E	310 665-0975	8408
Anschutz Film Group LLC (HQ)	3861	E	310 887-1000	8420
Carolense Entrmt Group LLC	3861	D	405 493-1120	8422
Fpc Inc	3861	E	323 468-5778	8428
Panavision Inc	3861	E	323 464-3800	8436
Americas Gold Inc	3911	E	213 688-4904	8450
Giving Keys Inc	3911	E	213 935-8791	8454
LA Gem and Jewelry Design (PA)	3911	E	213 488-1290	8457
LA Gem and Jewelry Design	3911	E	213 488-1290	8458
Exploding Kittens LLC	3944	E	310 788-8699	8485
Ninja Jump Inc	3944	D	323 255-5418	8493
Rpsz Construction LLC	3949	D	314 677-5831	8537
Standard Sales Llc (PA)	3949	E	323 269-0510	8544
Thousand LLC	3949	E	310 745-0110	8547
Brush Research Mfg Co Inc	3991	C	323 261-2193	8584
Standardvision LLC	3993	E	323 222-3630	8638
Beauty Tent Inc	3999	E	323 717-7131	8662
Shapell Industries	3999	D	323 655-7330	8724
Silvestri Studio Inc (PA)	3999	D	323 277-4420	8725
Sparks Exhbits Envrnments Corp	3999	E	562 941-0101	8727
Forrest Group LLC (PA)	4111	B	619 808-9798	8755
Los Angles Cnty Mtro Trnsp Aut (PA)	4111	A	323 466-3876	8761
Los Angles Cnty Mtro Trnsp Aut	4111	B	213 922-5887	8764
Los Angles Cnty Mtro Trnsp Aut	4111	B	213 922-6301	8765
Los Angles Cnty Mtro Trnsp Aut	4111	B	213 922-6203	8766
Los Angles Cnty Mtro Trnsp Aut	4111	A	213 922-6202	8767
Los Angles Cnty Mtro Trnsp Aut	4111	B	213 922-6207	8768
Los Angles Cnty Mtro Trnsp Aut	4111	A	213 533-1506	8770
Los Angles Cnty Mtro Trnsp Aut	4111	A	213 922-5012	8771
Los Angles Cnty Mtro Trnsp Aut	4111	B	213 244-6783	8773
Los Angles Cnty Mtro Trnsp Aut	4111	A	213 626-4455	8775
Mv Transportation Inc	4111	B	323 936-9783	8778
Mv Transportation Inc	4111	B	310 638-0556	8779
Private Suite Lax LLC	4111	C	310 907-9950	8794
Shuttle Smart Inc	4111	C	310 338-9466	8803
SMS Transportation Svcs Inc	4111	C	213 489-5367	8804
Southern Cal Rgional Rail Auth (PA)	4111	C	213 452-0200	8806
Bls Lmsine Svc Los Angeles Inc	4119	B	323 644-7166	8814
Falck Mobile Health Corp	4119	B	323 720-1578	8824
Flixbus Inc	4119	B	925 577-4164	8827
Medtrans Inc	4119	B	323 780-9500	8839
Schaefer Ambulance Service Inc	4119	B	323 468-1642	8848
Greyhound Lines Inc	4131	D	213 629-8400	8858
Dlf Logistics LLC	4212	D	626 387-3797	8904
Gateway Logistics Tech LLC	4212	C	732 750-9000	8908
Southern Counties Terminals	4212	D	310 642-0462	8924
Dependable Companies	4213	C	800 548-8608	8943
Dependable Highway Express Inc (PA)	4213	B	323 526-2200	8944
Xpo Logistics Freight Inc	4213	C	213 744-0664	8986
Express Group Incorporated (PA)	4215	C	310 474-5999	9002
Kxp Carrier Services LLC	4215	C	424 320-5300	9006
Peach Inc	4215	C	323 654-2333	9010
Speedy Express LLC	4215	D	818 300-7785	9012
Unity Courier Service Inc (DH)	4215	C	323 255-9800	9032

	SIC	EMP	PHONE	ENTRY#
Standard-Southern Corporation	4222	C	213 624-1831	9042
Standard-Southern Corporation	4222	C	213 624-1831	9043
County of Los Angeles	4225	D	626 458-1707	9056
Edmund A Gray Co	4225	E	213 625-2725	9063
Mulholland Brothers	4225	E	510 280-5485	9092
Quick Box LLC	4225	C	310 436-6444	9102
Unified Grocers Inc	4225	C	323 232-6124	9123
Aerotransporte De Carge Union	4512	B	310 649-0069	9155
American Airlines Inc	4512	C	310 646-4553	9157
Korean Air Lines Co Ltd	4512	C	310 646-4866	9159
Korean Airlines Co Ltd	4512	C	310 410-2000	9160
L A Air Inc	4512	C	310 215-8245	9161
United Airlines Inc	4512	D	310 258-3319	9168
Federal Express Corporation	4513	C	800 463-3339	9174
United Parcel Service Inc	4513	C	323 260-8957	9176
Agi Cargo LLC	4581	A	310 646-2446	9185
Agi Cargo LLC	4581	A	310 342-0136	9186
Agi Ground Inc	4581	D	310 215-4902	9187
Airport Terminal MGT Inc	4581	B	310 988-1492	9189
Department of Arprts of The Cy	4581	A	855 463-5252	9199
Los Angeles World Airports (PA)	4581	C	855 463-5252	9202
Los Angeles World Airports	4581	A	424 646-5900	9203
Los Angeles World Airports	4581	B	424 646-9118	9204
Swissport Cargo Services LP	4581	D	310 910-9541	9210
Swissport Usa Inc	4581	D	310 345-1986	9211
Swissport Usa Inc	4581	D	310 910-9560	9212
Altour International Inc (PA)	4724	D	310 571-6000	9216
Altour International Inc	4724	B	310 571-6000	9218
Americantours Intl LLC (HQ)	4724	C	310 641-9953	9220
C & H Travel & Tours Inc (HQ)	4724	C	323 933-2288	9221
Helloworld Travel Svcs USA Inc	4724	D	310 535-1005	9223
Princess Cruise Lines Ltd	4724	D	213 745-0314	9233
Travel Store (PA)	4724	D	310 575-5540	9237
Antenna Audio Inc (PA)	4725	A	203 523-0320	9238
Korean Airlines Co Ltd	4729	B	213 484-5700	9243
Matrix Aviation Services Inc	4729	C	310 337-3037	9244
Able Freight Services LLC (PA)	4731	D	310 568-8883	9246
Commodity Forwarders Inc (DH)	4731	C	310 348-8855	9265
Expeditors Intl Ocean Inc	4731	D	310 343-6200	9278
Nri Usa LLC (PA)	4731	D	323 345-6456	9320
Select Aircargo Services Inc	4731	D	310 851-8500	9335
Fluor Fltron Blfour Btty Drgdo	4789	D	949 420-5000	9363
Cellco Partnership	4812	D	323 662-0009	9393
Sprint Communications Co LP	4812	C	310 216-9093	9410
Sprint Corporation	4812	D	213 613-4200	9417
Verizon Media Inc (DH)	4812	D	310 907-3016	9421
Fox Interactive Media Inc	4813	C	310 969-7000	9434
Hulu LLC	4813	A	888 631-4858	9443
Media Temple Inc	4813	C	877 578-4000	9447
Mpower Holding Corporation (HQ)	4813	D	866 699-8242	9449
New Dream Network LLC	4813	D	323 375-3842	9450
Public Communications Svcs Inc	4813	C	310 231-1000	9455
Truconnect Communications Inc (PA)	4813	C	512 919-2641	9467
Audacy Inc	4832	C	323 569-1070	9476
Spanish Brdcstg Sys of Cal	4832	D	310 203-0900	9489
Disney Networks Group LLC (DH)	4833	D	310 369-1000	9497
Entravsion Communications Corp	4833	D	323 900-6100	9499
Fox Inc (DH)	4833	A	310 369-1000	9501
Fox Broadcasting Company LLC (HQ)	4833	C	310 369-1000	9502
Fox Sports Inc (DH)	4833	C	310 369-1000	9503
Fox Television Stations Inc (HQ)	4833	B	310 584-2000	9504
Lifetime Entrmt Svcs LLC	4833	B	310 556-7500	9510
Revolt Media and Tv LLC	4833	C	323 645-3000	9515
Twenteth Cntury Fox Intl TV In	4833	A	310 369-1000	9521
E Entertainment Television Inc	4841	C	323 954-2400	9549
Fx Networks LLC	4841	C	310 369-1000	9550
Spectrum MGT Holdg Co LLC	4841	D	323 657-0899	9557
Discovery Communications Inc (PA)	4899	B	310 975-5906	9563
Made Media LLC	4899	E	866 263-6233	9567
Southern California Gas Co (HQ)	4924	A	213 244-1200	9664
Southern California Gas Tower	4924	A	213 244-1200	9666
Los Angeles Dept Wtr & Pwr (HQ)	4941	A	213 367-1320	9699
Los Angeles Dept Wtr & Pwr	4941	A	213 367-5706	9700
Los Angeles Dept Wtr & Pwr	4941	A	213 367-4211	9701
Los Angeles Dept Wtr & Pwr	4941	A	323 256-8079	9702
The Metropolitan Water District of (PA)	4941	A	213 217-6000	9723
Norcal Waste Services Inc	4953	D	626 357-8666	9752
United Pacific Waste	4953	D	562 699-7600	9769
Find It Parts Inc	5013	D	888 312-8812	9825
EC Group Inc (PA)	5021	D	310 815-2700	9870
Elijah Textiles Inc	5023	D	310 666-3443	9891
GA Gertmenian and Sons LLC (PA)	5023	C	213 250-7777	9894
Emser International LLC (PA)	5032	D	323 650-2000	9944

2025 Southern California
Business Directory and Buyers Guide

(P-0000) Products & Services Section entry number
(PA)=Parent Co (HQ)=Headquarters (DH)=Div Headquarters

	SIC	EMP	PHONE	ENTRY#
Emser Tile LLC (PA)	5032	B	323 650-2000	9945
Hannam Chain USA Inc (PA)	5046	C	213 382-2922	10043
Jetro Holdings LLC	5046	C	213 516-0301	10046
Trust 1 Sales Inc	5046	D	323 732-3300	10056
Twin Med Inc	5047	B		10114
Lexicon Marketing (usa) Inc (PA)	5049	D	323 782-8282	10119
Earle M Jorgensen Company	5051	D	323 567-1122	10134
Gvs Italy	5051	C	424 382-4343	10138
Reliance Inc	5051	C	323 583-6111	10152
Sac International Steel Inc (PA)	5051	D	323 232-2467	10156
Adj Products LLC (PA)	5063	C	323 582-2650	10166
Eaton Aerospace LLC	5063	B	818 409-0200	10180
Ecosense Lighting Inc (PA)	5063	D	855 632-6736	10181
Homeland Housewares LLC	5064	D	310 996-7200	10220
Bear Communications Inc	5065	D	310 854-2327	10231
CP Document Technologies LLC (PA)	5065	D	213 617-4040	10239
Mtroiz International	5065	E	661 998-8013	10271
Elevator Equipment Corporation (PA)	5084	D	323 245-0147	10371
ONeil Data Systems LLC	5084	C	310 448-6400	10387
Western Refining Inc	5084	D	323 264-8500	10421
Duhig and Co Inc	5085	E		10436
75s Corp	5093	E	323 234-7708	10533
C&C Jewelry Mfg Inc	5094	D	213 623-6800	10545
Platinum Disc LLC	5099	C	608 784-6620	10566
Roland Corporation US (HQ)	5099	C	323 890-3700	10568
Warner Music Group Corp	5099	C	818 953-2600	10574
Image Source Inc (PA)	5112	C	310 477-0700	10581
E & S Paper Co	5113	E	310 538-8700	10591
Oak Paper Products Co LLC (PA)	5113	C	323 268-0507	10595
Used Cardboard Boxes Inc	5113	C	323 724-2500	10610
Glamour Industries Co (PA)	5122	C	323 728-2999	10624
Hatchbeauty Products LLC (PA)	5122	D	310 396-7070	10626
Morgan Fabrics Corporation (PA)	5131	D	323 583-9981	10669
Radix Textile Inc	5131	D	323 234-1667	10671
Rdmm Legacy Inc	5131	E	323 232-2147	10672
Zi Industries Inc (PA)	5131	D	213 749-1215	10677
Quake City Casuals Inc	5136	C	213 746-0540	10693
UNI Hosiery Co Inc (PA)	5136	C	213 228-0100	10698
California Rain Company Inc	5137	D	213 623-6061	10703
Damo Textile Inc	5137	E	213 741-1323	10704
Edgemine Inc	5137	C	323 267-8222	10707
Final Touch Apparel Inc	5137	E	323 484-9621	10708
Nydj Apparel LLC (PA)	5137	D	323 581-9040	10718
Seven Licensing Company LLC	5137	C	323 780-8250	10726
Signal Products Inc (PA)	5137	D	213 748-0990	10727
Aci International (PA)	5139	D	310 889-3400	10732
Buffalo Market Inc	5141	C	650 337-0078	10745
Canton Food Co Inc	5141	C	213 688-7707	10746
Smart & Final Stores LLC (DH)	5141	D	323 869-7500	10769
Smart & Final Stores LLC	5141	C	310 559-1722	10770
Smart & Final Stores LLC	5141	C	310 207-8688	10771
Smart & Final Stores LLC	5141	C	323 268-9179	10772
Smart & Final Stores LLC	5141	D	213 747-6697	10773
Smart Stores Operations LLC	5141	C	323 549-9586	10784
Smart Stores Operations LLC (DH)	5141	D	323 869-7500	10786
Rogers Poultry Co	5144	D	800 585-0802	10838
Consolidated Svc Distrs Inc	5145	C	908 687-5800	10844
PLD Enterprises Inc	5146	D	213 626-4444	10857
Prospect Enterprises Inc (PA)	5146	C	213 599-5700	10858
L & T Meat Co	5147	D	323 262-2815	10875
RW Zant LLC (DH)	5147	D	323 980-5457	10880
Strouk Group LLC	5147	C	323 939-7792	10881
4 Earth Farms LLC (PA)	5148	B	323 201-5000	10884
Borg Produce Sales LLC	5148	D	213 624-2074	10887
Coast Produce Company (PA)	5148	C	213 955-4900	10891
Davalan Sales Inc	5148	C	213 623-2500	10893
Giumarra Bros Fruit Co Inc (PA)	5148	D	213 627-2900	10903
Green Farms Inc	5148	D	858 831-7701	10905
Pacific Trellis Fruit LLC (PA)	5148	C	323 859-9600	10913
Professional Produce	5148	D	323 277-1550	10915
Season Produce Co Inc	5148	B	213 689-0008	10916
Shapiro-Gilman-Shandler Co	5148	C	213 593-1200	10917
Val-Pro Inc (PA)	5148	C	213 627-8736	10922
App Wholesale LLC	5149	B	323 980-8315	10927
CJ America Inc (HQ)	5149	C	213 338-2700	10937
Oakhurst Industries Inc (PA)	5149	C	323 724-3000	10967
Soofer Co Inc	5149	C	323 234-6666	10980
Trinidad/Benham Corp	5149	C	626 723-2300	10986
US Foods Inc	5149	C	213 623-4150	10988
ESE INC	5169	E	213 614-0102	11012
Zeco Systems Inc	5171	D	888 751-8560	11026
Youngs Market Company LLC	5182	B	213 629-3929	11065
Delta Floral Distributors Inc	5193	C	323 751-8116	11086
Mellano & Company (PA)	5193	D	213 622-0796	11092
Berg Lacquer Co (PA)	5198	D	323 261-8114	11106
Gaju Market Corporation	5199	C	213 382-9444	11121
Revoltion Cnsmr Sltions CA LLC (DH)	5199	C	323 980-0918	11139
Shims Bargain Inc (PA)	5199	D	323 881-0099	11143
Home Depot USA Inc	5211	B	323 292-1397	11158
Home Depot USA Inc	5211	D	323 342-9495	11159
Home Depot USA Inc	5211	B	323 727-9600	11171
Home Depot USA Inc	5211	B	310 822-3330	11172
LAdesserts Inc	5311	E	323 588-2522	11261
Goodwill Inds Southern Cal (PA)	5331	A	323 223-1211	11267
Number Holdings Inc (PA)	5331	C	323 980-8145	11268
Pg Usa LLC	5331	D	310 954-1040	11269
Super Center Concepts Inc	5411	C	323 241-6789	11284
Sonora Bakery Inc	5461	E	323 269-2253	11302
Al Asher & Sons Inc	5511	E	800 896-2480	11313
FAA Beverly Hills Inc	5511	D	323 801-1430	11345
Felix Chevrolet LP (PA)	5511	C	213 748-6141	11346
Fox Hills Auto Inc (PA)	5511	C	310 649-3673	11351
Nick Alexander Imports	5511	C	800 800-6425	11386
Noarus Investments Inc	5511	D	310 649-2440	11388
Toyota Downtown La	5531	C	213 342-3646	11470
Evgo Services LLC	5541	B	310 954-2900	11475
American Rag Compagnie	5621	D	323 935-3154	11490
Country Club Fashions Inc	5621	E	323 965-2707	11491
Nasty Gal Inc (HQ)	5621	E	213 542-3436	11492
Walking Company Holdings Inc (PA)	5651	C	805 963-8727	11498
ABC Home Furnishings Inc (PA)	5712	A	212 473-3000	11510
ABC Carpet Co Inc (PA)	5713	D	212 473-3000	11519
Aero Shade Co Inc (PA)	5719	E	323 938-2314	11526
Bebe Studio Inc	5719	C	213 362-2323	11528
La Linen Inc	5719	E	213 745-4004	11533
Linen Salvage Et Cie LLC	5719	E	323 904-3100	11534
Accor Corp	5812	C	310 278-5444	11548
Fish House Partners One LLC	5812	D	323 460-4170	11571
International Coffee & Tea LLC (HQ)	5812	D	310 237-2326	11577
King Taco Restaurant Inc (PA)	5812	C	323 266-3585	11582
Lawrys Restaurants II Inc	5812	C	323 664-0228	11584
Magic Castles Inc	5812	D	323 851-3313	11589
Pbf & E LLC	5812	E	213 427-0340	11595
SBE Entertainment Group LLC (HQ)	5813	D	323 655-8000	11618
Samys Camera Inc (PA)	5946	C	310 591-2100	11648
Michael Levine Inc	5949	D	213 622-6259	11650
Robert Kaufman Co Inc (PA)	5949	C	310 538-3482	11651
Spencer Forrest Inc	5961	E		11664
Avery Group Inc	5963	B	310 217-1070	11665
AAA Flag & Banner Mfg Co Inc (PA)	5999	D	310 836-3200	11673
Coway Usa Inc	5999	E	213 486-1600	11680
Evoqua Water Technologies LLC	5999	E	213 748-8511	11683
Playboy Enterprises Inc (HQ)	5999	D	310 424-1800	11694
Sea Dwelling Creatures Inc	5999	D	310 676-9697	11697
VCA Inc (DH)	5999	C	310 571-6500	11701
Federal Rsrve Bnk San Frncisco	6011	A	213 683-2300	11703
Banc of California Inc (PA)	6021	C	855 361-2262	11706
Bank of Hope (HQ)	6021	C	213 639-1700	11707
Bbcn Bank	6021	A	213 251-2222	11708
City National Bank	6021	D	310 855-7960	11717
City National Bank	6021	D	310 888-6800	11718
City National Bank	6021	B	310 888-6500	11722
City National Bank (DH)	6021	D	310 888-6000	11720
City National Corporation	6021	A		11731
Mufg Union Bank Foundation	6021		213 236-5000	11737
Wells Fargo Securities LLC	6021	A	310 479-3500	11741
1st Century Bancshares Inc	6022	D	310 270-9500	11742
Beneficial State Bank	6022	D	323 264-3310	11746
Busa Servicing Inc (PA)	6022	C	310 203-3400	11747
Cathay Bank (HQ)	6022	C	626 279-3698	11751
Cathay General Bancorp (PA)	6022	C	213 625-4700	11752
CIT Bank NA	6022	C	310 820-9650	11753
PCB BANK (HQ)	6022	C	213 210-2000	11776
Smbc Manubank (DH)	6022	C	213 489-6200	11778
Standard Chartered Bank	6022	D	626 639-8000	11779
Wilshire Bancorp Inc	6022	A	213 387-3200	11780
Wilshire Bank	6022	B	213 427-1000	11781
Greenbox Loans Inc	6035	D	800 919-1086	11785
First Entertainment Credit Un (PA)	6061	D	323 851-3673	11799
University Credit Union	6061	C	310 477-6628	11819
SunAmerica Inc	6091	A	310 772-6000	11836
Lenlyn Ltd Which Will Do Bus I (HQ)	6099	D	310 417-3432	11841
Deutsche Bank National Tr Co	6111	D	310 788-6200	11845
Hana Commercial Finance LLC	6153	D	213 240-1234	11867
Skyview Capital LLC	6153	D	310 273-6000	11873
Capitalsource Inc	6159	A	213 443-7700	11875

Employee Codes: A=Over 500 employees, B=251-500
C=101-250, D=51-100, E=20-50, F=10-19, G=1-9

2025 Southern California
Business Directory and Buyers Guide

© Mergent Inc. 1-800-342-5647

1303

GEOGRAPHIC

	SIC	EMP	PHONE	ENTRY#
Capnet Financial Services Inc (PA)	6159	D	877 980-0558	11876
Federal Home Loan Mrtg Corp	6162	A	213 337-4200	11903
Gold Parent LP	6211	D	310 954-0444	11965
Goldman Sachs & Co LLC	6211	C	310 407-5700	11966
Imperial Capital LLC (PA)	6211	D	310 246-3700	11969
Lear Capital Inc	6211	C	310 571-0190	11971
Leonard Green & Partners LP (PA)	6211	C	310 954-0444	11972
Merrill Lynch Inv MGT Inc	6211	C	310 209-4000	11976
Morgan Stnley Smith Barney LLC	6211	C	213 891-3200	12000
Trust Company of West	6211	A	213 244-0000	12007
Wedbush Securities Inc (HQ)	6211	B	213 688-8000	12009
William Oneil & Co Inc (PA)	6211	D	310 448-6800	12010
Adviceperiod	6282	D	424 281-3600	12013
Anderson Kayne Capital	6282	A	800 231-7414	12016
Angelo Gordon & Co LP	6282	A	310 777-5440	12017
Capital Research and MGT Co (HQ)	6282	B	213 486-9200	12023
Houlihan Lokey Inc (PA)	6282	B	310 788-5200	12026
Oaktree Capital Management LP (DH)	6282	C	213 830-6300	12028
Payden & Rygel (PA)	6282	C	213 625-1900	12030
Tcw Group Inc (PA)	6282	B	213 244-0000	12034
Triller Group Inc	6282	C	310 893-5090	12036
U S Trust Company NA	6282	B	213 861-5000	12037
Golden State Mutl Lf Insur Co (PA)	6311	D	713 526-4361	12041
Guardian Life Insur Co Amer	6311	D	213 624-2002	12043
SunAmerica Life Insurance Company	6311	C	310 772-6000	12052
Transamerica Occidental Life Insura	6311	A	213 742-2111	12053
Local Inttive Hlth Auth For Lo (PA)	6324	D	213 694-1250	12096
Great American Cstm Insur Svcs	6331	B	213 430-4300	12119
Mercury General Corporation (PA)	6331	A	323 937-1060	12124
Orion Indemnity Company	6331	D	213 742-8700	12131
American Contrs Indemnity Co (DH)	6351	C	213 330-1309	12144
Cap-Mpt (PA)	6351	C	213 473-8600	12145
Allstate Financial Svcs LLC	6411	D	323 981-8520	12169
Automobile Club Southern Cal (PA)	6411	C	213 741-3686	12176
California Fair Plan Assn	6411	D	213 487-0111	12186
Farmers Group Inc 401 K Sav Pl	6411	D	323 932-3200	12208
John Hancock Life Insur Co USA (DH)	6411	A	213 689-0813	12223
Lockton Cmpnies LLC - PCF Srie (HQ)	6411	B	213 689-0500	12227
Marsh Risk & Insurance Svcs	6411	A	213 624-5555	12230
Pacific Indemnity Company	6411	B	213 622-2334	12242
Topa Insurance Company (HQ)	6411	D	310 201-0451	12261
Winterthur U S Holdings Inc	6411	C	213 228-0281	12272
Worldwide Holdings Inc (PA)	6411	D	213 236-4500	12276
Arden Realty Inc	6512	B	310 966-2600	12282
CB Richard Ellis Strgc Prtners	6512	D	213 683-4200	12284
Cdcf III PCF Lndmark Scrmnto L	6512	C	310 552-7211	12285
Insignia/Esg Ht Partners Inc (DH)	6512	B	310 765-2600	12297
Los Angles Cnvntion Exhbtion C	6512	B	213 741-1151	12302
Scp Horton Owner 1 LLC	6512	C	310 693-4400	12316
Topa Property Group Inc (HQ)	6512	C	310 203-9199	12321
Unibal-Rodamco-Westfield Group	6512	C	310 478-4456	12322
West Side Rehab Corporation	6512	C	323 231-4174	12327
Westfield LLC (DH)	6512	B	310 478-4456	12328
Westfield America Inc (HQ)	6512	C	310 478-4456	12329
Westfield America Ltd Partnr	6512	B	310 277-3898	12330
Wilshire Kingsley Inc	6512	D	213 382-6677	12331
Abode Communities LLC	6531	C	213 629-2702	12378
Bgk Equities Inc (HQ)	6531	D	505 982-2184	12389
Cbre Globl Value Investors LLC (DH)	6531	C	213 683-4200	12399
Cbre Partner Inc	6531	D	213 613-3333	12401
Charles Dunn RE Svcs Inc (PA)	6531	D	213 270-6200	12403
Cushman & Wakefield Cal Inc	6531	B	310 556-1805	12418
Cushman Realty Corporation	6531	C	213 627-4700	12427
Evoq Properties Inc	6531	D	213 988-8890	12440
Gemini-Rosemont Realty LLC	6531	D	505 992-5100	12455
I D Property Corporation	6531	C	213 625-0100	12467
Kor Realty Group LLC (PA)	6531	C	323 930-3700	12475
La Cienega Associates	6531	D	310 854-0071	12476
M & S Acquisition Corporation (PA)	6531	C	213 385-1515	12484
Memco Holdings Inc	6531	N	310 277-0057	12487
Nms Properties Inc	6531	C	310 656-2700	12497
On Central Realty Inc	6531	C	323 543-8500	12498
Pathstone Family Office LLC	6531	C	888 750-7284	12502
Pcs Property Managmnt LLC	6531	D	310 231-1000	12503
Proland Property Managmnt LLC (PA)	6531	D	213 738-8175	12512
Rexford Indus Rlty & MGT Inc	6531	C	310 966-1690	12521
Spus7 125 Cambridgepark LP	6531	D	213 683-4200	12530
Spus7 150 Cambridgepark LP	6531	D	213 683-4200	12531
Srht Property Holding LLC	6531	C	213 683-0522	12532
Thomas Properties Group Inc	6531	C	213 613-1900	12539
Triyar Sv LLC (PA)	6531	B	310 234-2888	12541
Watt Companies Inc	6531	C	310 789-2180	12547
Century Pacific Realty Corp	6552	C	310 729-9922	12565
Lowe Enterprises RE Group	6552	B	310 820-6661	12570
LPC Commercial Services Inc	6552	C	213 362-9080	12571
Portsmouth Square Inc	6552	C	310 889-2500	12577
Banamex USA Bancorp (DH)	6712	C	310 203-3440	12590
Saban Capital Group LLC	6719	D	310 557-5100	12612
Shryne Group Inc	6719	A	323 614-4558	12613
Yf Art Holdings Gp LLC	6719	A	678 441-1400	12621
Yucaipa Companies LLC (PA)	6719	C	310 789-7200	12622
Alliancebernstein LP	6722	C	310 286-6000	12624
American Funds Distrs Inc (DH)	6722	C	213 486-9200	12626
American Mutual Fund	6722	C	213 486-9200	12627
Ares Management Corporation (PA)	6722	C	310 201-4100	12628
Causeway Capital MGT LLC (PA)	6722	D	310 231-6100	12631
Los Angeles Capital MGT LLC (PA)	6722	C	310 479-9998	12635
Metwest Total Return Bond Fund	6722	C	800 241-4671	12636
Oaktree Holdings Inc	6722	A	213 830-6300	12637
Oaktree Real Estate Opprtnties	6722	A	213 830-6300	12638
Oaktree Strategic Income LLC	6722	A	213 830-6300	12639
Ocm Real Estate Opprtnties Fun	6722	B	213 830-6300	12640
Shamrock Capital Advisors LLC	6722	B	310 974-6600	12642
Kingswood Capital MGT LLC (PA)	6726	C	424 744-8238	12648
Oasis West Realty LLC	6726	A	310 274-8066	12649
Empower Our Youth	6732	D	323 203-5436	12652
Greater Los Angles Vtrans RES	6732	D	310 312-1554	12653
Ucla Foundation	6732	B	310 794-3193	12654
Capital Guardian Trust Company (HQ)	6733	D	213 486-9200	12656
Epidaurus	6733	B	213 743-9075	12657
Moelis & Company LLC	6733	C	310 443-2300	12664
Southern Cal Pipe Trades ADM (PA)	6733	D	213 385-6161	12674
Coresite LLC	6798	C	213 327-1231	12684
Hudson Pacific Properties Inc (PA)	6798	D	310 445-5700	12686
Mpg Office Trust Inc	6798	D	213 626-3300	12689
Prime Administration LLC	6798	A	323 549-7155	12692
Broadreach Capitl Partners LLC	6799	C	310 691-5760	12700
Call To Action Partners Llc	6799	C	310 996-7200	12701
Clearview Capital LLC	6799	A	310 806-9555	12702
Corridor Capital LLC (PA)	6799	C	310 442-7000	12703
Emp III Inc	6799	D	323 231-4174	12705
Golden International	6799	A	213 628-1388	12707
Gsa Des Plaines LLC	6799	D	310 557-5100	12708
Imperial Capital Group LLC (PA)	6799	D	310 246-3700	12711
Intrepid Inv Bankers LLC	6799	A	310 478-9000	12712
Nexus Capital Management LP	6799	A	424 330-8820	12723
Nogales Investors LLC	6799	B	310 276-7439	12725
Otts Asia Moorer Devon	6799	C	323 603-6959	12727
Providence Rest Partners LLC	6799	D	323 460-4170	12729
Rustic Canyon Group LLC	6799	D	310 998-8000	12734
Stockdale Capital Partners LLC	6799	D	310 693-4400	12737
Stonecalibre LLC (PA)	6799	D	310 774-0014	12738
Transom Capital Group LLC	6799	E	424 293-2818	12742
Truamerica Multifamily LLC	6799	D	424 325-2750	12743
6417 Selma Hotel LLC	7011	C	323 844-6417	12754
901 West Olympic Blvd Ltd Prtn	7011	C	213 443-9200	12756
Ascot Hotel LP	7011	C	310 476-6411	12762
Behringer Harvard Wilshire Blv	7011	D	310 475-8711	12770
Beverly Hills Luxury Hotel LLC	7011	B	310 274-9999	12774
Brisam Lax (de) LLC	7011	D	310 649-5151	12777
Burton Way Hotels LLC	7011	C	310 273-2222	12778
Burton-Way House Ltd A CA	7011	C	310 273-2222	12780
Carpenters Southwest ADM Corp (PA)	7011	D	213 386-8590	12785
Cim Group LP (PA)	7011	C	323 860-4900	12792
Cim/H & H Hotel LP	7011	C	323 860-4900	12793
Core/Related Gala Retail LLC	7011	D	213 349-8585	12799
Crestline Hotels & Resorts Inc (HQ)	7011	C	213 629-1200	12803
Custom Hotel LLC	7011	C	310 645-0400	12805
Donald T Sterling Corporation	7011	D	310 275-5575	12815
Fortuna Enterprises LP	7011	B	310 410-4000	12826
Hazens Investment LLC	7011	B	310 642-1111	12846
Hotel Bel-Air	7011	B	310 472-1211	12854
Hotel Shangri-La	7011	D	310 394-2791	12856
Humnit Hotel At Lax LLC	7011	D	424 702-1234	12858
Hyatt Corporation	7011	C	323 656-1234	12869
Hyatt Corporation	7011	C	312 750-1234	12870
Hyatt Regency Century Plaza	7011	C	310 228-1234	12873
Ihg Management (maryland) LLC	7011	D	213 688-7777	12874
Irp Lax Hotel LLC	7011	C	310 645-4600	12877
Kava Holdings Inc (DH)	7011	C	310 472-1211	12882
Kimpton Hotel & Rest Group LLC	7011	C	323 852-6000	12884
L-O Bedford Operating LLC	7011	C	781 275-5500	12891
Lightstone Dt La LLC	7011	B	310 669-9252	12903
Lowe Enterprises Inc (PA)	7011	C	310 820-6661	12907
Marriott International Inc	7011	A	310 641-5700	12915
Metropolis Hotel MGT LLC	7011	C	213 683-4855	12923

Mergent email: customerrelations@mergent.com
1304

2025 Southern California
Business Directory and Buyers Guide

(P-0000) Products & Services Section entry number
(PA)=Parent Co (HQ)=Headquarters (DH)=Div Headquarters

Company	SIC	EMP	PHONE	ENTRY#
Morgans Hotel Group MGT LLC	7011	C	323 650-8999	12931
New Figueroa Hotel Inc	7011	D	213 627-8971	12936
Nrea-TRC 711 LLC	7011	C	213 488-3500	12941
Oxford Palace Hotel LLC	7011	D	213 382-7756	12956
Pacifica Hosts Inc	7011	C	310 670-9000	12962
Packard Realty Inc	7011	C	310 649-5151	12964
Playa Proper Jv LLC	7011	D	310 645-0400	12975
Radlax Gateway Hotel LLC	7011	A	310 670-9000	12982
Raleigh Enterprises Inc (PA)	7011	C	310 899-8900	12984
Remington Hotel Corporation	7011	C	310 553-6561	12989
Renaissance Hotel Operating Co	7011	B	310 337-2800	12990
Roosevelt Hotel LLC	7011	C	323 466-7000	13000
Rpd Hotels 18 LLC	7011	A	213 746-1531	13002
S W K Properties LLC (PA)	7011	D	213 383-9204	13006
Seattle Arprt Hospitality LLC	7011	D	310 476-6411	13019
Sls Hotel At Beverly Hills	7011	C	310 247-0400	13026
Stockbridge/Sbe Holdings LLC	7011	A	323 655-8000	13037
Sunstone Hotel Properties Inc	7011	C	310 228-4100	13043
Sydell Hotels LLC	7011	C	213 381-7411	13048
Todays IV	7011	A	213 835-4016	13054
W Los Angeles	7011	B	310 208-8765	13069
Welk Group Inc (PA)	7011	B	760 749-3000	13073
Whb Corporation	7011	A	213 624-1011	13079
M-Aurora Worldwide (us) LP (PA)	7021	C	800 888-0808	13097
American Textile Maint Co	7213	D	213 749-4433	13112
American Textile Maint Co	7213	C	323 735-1661	13113
Ameripride Services LLC	7213	C	323 587-3941	13114
Morgan Services Inc	7213	D	213 485-9666	13124
Yee Yuen Laundry and Clrs Inc	7213	D	323 734-7205	13127
Pro-Wash Inc	7215	C	323 756-6000	13130
Pico Cleaners Inc (PA)	7216	D	310 274-2431	13132
Miniluxe Inc	7231	D	424 442-1630	13151
Sinai Temple	7261	C	323 469-6000	13158
Temple Israel of Hollywood (PA)	7261	D	323 876-8330	13159
Andersen Tax LLC	7291	C	213 593-2300	13161
Jet Fleet International Corp	7299	E	310 440-3820	13178
Vibiana Events LLC	7299	D	213 626-1507	13189
180la LLC	7311	C	310 382-1400	13192
Campbell-Ewald Company	7311	D	310 358-4800	13198
Cimarron Partner Associates LLC	7311	C	323 337-0300	13200
Daviselen Advertising Inc (PA)	7311	C	213 688-7000	13203
Deutsch La Inc	7311	D	310 862-3000	13205
Digitas La Inc	7311	C	617 867-1000	13207
Horizon Media Inc	7311	B	310 282-0909	13212
Mediabrands Worldwide Inc	7311	B	323 370-8000	13225
Mullenlowe US Inc	7311	D	424 738-6600	13230
Nexstar Digital LLC	7311	D	310 971-9300	13233
Quigly-Simpson Heppelwhite Inc	7311	C	310 996-5800	13239
Rapp Worldwide Inc	7311	C	310 563-7200	13240
Trailer Park Inc (PA)	7311	D	310 845-3000	13250
Wonderful Agency	7311	A	310 966-8600	13253
Bamko Inc	7312	C	310 470-5859	13256
Outfront Media LLC	7312	E	323 222-7171	13257
Attn Inc	7313	C	323 413-2878	13259
BLT Cmmnctions LLC A Ltd Lblty	7313	C	323 860-4000	13262
Mediaalpha Inc (PA)	7313	C	213 316-6256	13269
Gils Distributing Service	7319	C	213 627-0539	13274
Uscb Inc (PA)	7322	C	213 985-2111	13289
The Tax Credit Company	7323	D	323 927-0750	13297
Concord Document Services Inc (PA)	7334	E	213 745-3175	13311
CP Document Technologies LLC	7334	E	310 575-6640	13312
Lasr Inc	7334	C	877 591-9979	13314
Getty Images Inc	7335	D	323 202-4200	13319
BLT & Associates Inc	7336	C	323 860-4000	13321
Cinnabar	7336	C	818 842-8190	13322
County of Los Angeles	7336	B	213 922-6210	13325
Digital Domain Media Group Inc	7336	A		13328
Twentieth Cntury Fox Japan Inc	7336	C	310 369-4636	13337
Aramark Facility Services LLC	7349	C	213 740-8968	13355
Crown Energy Services Inc	7349	A	213 765-7800	13370
Los Angeles Unified School Dst	7349	D	213 763-2900	13387
Scv Facilities Services Inc	7349	D	310 803-4588	13416
Southern Management Corp	7349	C	213 312-2268	13422
Uniserve Facilities Svcs Corp	7349	B	310 440-6747	13425
Hana Financial Inc (PA)	7359	D	213 240-1234	13457
Mufg Americas Leasing Corp (DH)	7359	D	213 488-3700	13462
Attorney Network Services Inc	7361	D	213 430-0440	13489
Career Group Inc (PA)	7361	A	310 277-8188	13500
Creative Solutions Svcs LLC	7361	C	646 495-1558	13506
Ideal Program Services Inc	7361	D	323 296-2255	13528
Kimco Staffing Services Inc	7361	B	310 622-1616	13534
Korn Ferry (PA)	7361	C	310 552-1834	13537
Lateral Link Group Inc	7361	D	310 405-0092	13540
Rehababilities Inc	7361	C	310 473-4448	13568
Phoenix Engineering Co Inc	7363	D	310 532-1134	13616
1nteger LLC	7371	C	424 320-2977	13637
3dna Corp (PA)	7371	C	213 992-4809	13638
Adcolony Inc	7371	D	650 625-1262	13644
Babyfirst Americas LLC	7371	C	310 442-9853	13668
Bahare	7371	C	516 472-1457	13669
Bellrock Media Inc (PA)	7371	E	310 315-2727	13672
Boulevard Labs Inc	7371	C	323 310-2093	13678
Chrome River Technologies Inc	7371	C	888 781-0088	13685
County of Los Angeles	7371	A	562 940-4324	13697
Daz Systems LLC	7371	B	310 640-1300	13704
Equator LLC (HQ)	7371	C	310 469-9500	13722
Fender Digital LLC	7371	D	323 462-2198	13729
Gehry Technologies Inc	7371	C	310 862-1200	13736
Honey Science LLC	7371	C	949 795-1695	13743
Ktb Software LLC	7371	D	505 306-0390	13761
Myevaluationscom Inc	7371	C	646 422-0554	13773
Mythical Entertainment LLC	7371	D	818 859-7398	13774
Nexxen Inc	7371	D	310 382-8909	13781
Qxv Programming LLC	7371	C	213 344-2031	13802
Sago Mini Inc	7371	D	416 731-8586	13809
Steady Platform Inc	7371	D	678 792-8364	13831
Tribridge Holdings LLC	7371	B	813 287-8887	13849
Upkeep Technologies Inc	7371	C	323 880-0280	13856
Vendor Direct Solutions LLC (PA)	7371	C	213 362-5622	13859
Adexa Inc (PA)	7372	E	310 642-2100	13871
Agencycom LLC	7372	B	415 817-3800	13873
Bitmax	7372	E	323 978-7878	13889
Consensus Cloud Solutions Inc (PA)	7372	D	323 860-9200	13908
Dave Inc (PA)	7372	B	844 857-3283	13913
IaMplus Electronics Inc (PA)	7372	E	323 210-3852	13945
Jurny Inc	7372	E	888 875-8769	13957
Mindshow Inc	7372	C	213 531-0277	13974
Mitratech Holdings Inc	7372	C	323 964-0000	13976
Network Automation Inc	7372	E	213 738-1700	13984
Relational Center	7372	E	323 935-1807	14019
Riot Games Inc (DH)	7372	E	310 207-1444	14021
Shred Labs LLC	7372	E	781 285-8622	14031
Spatial Labs Inc	7372	E	424 289-0275	14036
Specialists In Cstm Sftwr Inc	7372	C	310 315-9660	14037
Sugarsync Inc	7372	C	650 571-5105	14044
System1 Inc (PA)	7372	B	310 924-6037	14046
Visionary Vr Inc	7372	E	323 868-7443	14063
Internet Corp For Assgned Nmes (PA)	7373	C	310 823-9358	14089
Oberman Tivoli & Pickert Inc	7373	C	310 440-9600	14101
Urban Insight Inc	7373	E	213 792-2000	14116
Honk Technologies Inc	7374	C	800 979-3162	14137
Mocean LLC	7374	C	310 481-0808	14147
Total Cmmnicator Solutions Inc	7374	D	619 277-1488	14161
County of Los Angeles	7375	C	213 974-0515	14167
E-Times Corporation (PA)	7375	B	213 452-6720	14169
Elavon Inc	7375	B	865 403-7000	14171
Adams Comm & Engrg Tech Inc	7379	C	301 861-5000	14193
Be Structured Tech Group Inc	7379	D	323 331-9452	14200
Edgecast Inc	7379	A	310 396-7400	14216
Nowcom LLC	7379	C	323 746-6888	14236
Pegasus Squire Inc	7379	D	866 208-6837	14242
Preciseq Inc	7379	D	310 709-6094	14245
Studio Designer	7379	D	310 090-5600	14266
We See Dragons LLC	7379	C	310 361-5700	14265
Andrews International Inc	7381	B	310 575-4844	14275
Carda CL West Inc (HQ)	7381	R	213 383-3611	14301
Guardian Intl Solutions	7381	D	323 528-6555	14307
Mulholland SEC & Patrol Inc	7381	B	818 755-0202	14318
Professional Security Cons (PA)	7381	D	310 207-7729	14330
Securitech Security Svcs Inc	7381	C	213 387-5050	14340
Silvino Nieto	7381	C	213 413-3500	14349
SOS Security Incorporated	7381	C	310 392-9600	14350
Worldwide Security Assoc Inc (HQ)	7381	B	310 743-3000	14370
Dtiq Holdings Inc	7382	C	323 576-1400	14393
Elite Intractive Solutions Inc	7382	E	310 740-5426	14396
Assocted Ldscp Dsplay Group In	7389	D	714 546-5100	14454
B Riley Financial Inc (PA)	7389	D	310 966-1444	14457
County of Los Angeles	7389	C	323 267-2771	14481
Diba Fashions Inc	7389	D	323 232-3775	14490
E & C Fashion Inc	7389	B	323 262-0099	14492
Facter Direct Ltd	7389	B	323 634-1999	14494
Furniture Factory Holding LLC (HQ)	7389	C	918 427-0241	14499
Gelfand Rennert & Feldman LLP (DH)	7389	C	310 553-1707	14500
Ipayment Inc	7389	C	213 387-1353	14518
Lindsey & Sons Inc	7389	D	657 306-5369	14530
Los Angeles Apparel Inc	7389	C	323 561-8518	14533

Employee Codes: A=Over 500 employees, B=251-500
C=101-250, D=51-100, E=20-50, F=10-19, G=1-9

2025 Southern California
Business Directory and Buyers Guide

© Mergent Inc. 1-800-342-5647
1305

GEOGRAPHIC

	SIC	EMP	PHONE	ENTRY#
Medholdings of Newnan LLC	7389	A	213 462-6252	14542
Prompt Delivery Inc	7389	D	858 549-8000	14577
PSC Environmental Services LLC	7389	C	323 266-6448	14578
Qology Direct LLC	7389	C	310 341-4420	14580
Reason Foundation	7389	E	310 391-2245	14583
Scottxscott Inc	7389	C	310 622-2775	14590
SD&a Teleservices Inc (HQ)	7389	B		14591
Signature Resolution	7389	D	213 622-1002	14595
Super Center Concepts Inc	7389	C	323 223-3878	14604
Swift Media Entertainment Inc	7389	D	310 308-3694	14606
Tbwa Chiat/Day Inc	7389	B	310 305-5000	14607
Vxi Global Solutions LLC (PA)	7389	A	213 739-4720	14629
Warner Bros Records Inc (DH)	7389	B	818 846-9090	14630
XO BABYPLUTO FADED PARADISE XO	7389	E	650 750-5025	14635
Fox Rent A Car Inc	7514	C	310 342-5155	14646
Galpin Motors Inc	7514	D	323 957-3333	14648
ABM Parking Services Inc	7521	A	213 284-7600	14654
Everpark Inc	7521	C	310 987-6922	14656
L and R Auto Parks Inc	7521	C	213 784-3018	14657
Laz Karp Associates LLC	7521	C	323 464-4190	14658
Parking Concepts Inc	7521	C	213 746-5764	14665
Parking Concepts Inc	7521	D	310 208-1611	14667
Valet Parking Svc A Cal Partnr (PA)	7521	A	323 465-5873	14671
Mission Service Inc	7538	A	323 266-2593	14695
San Ramon Services Inc	7542	D	925 901-1400	14710
Authorized Cellular Service	7629	D	310 466-4144	14728
Scottel Voice & Data Inc	7629	C	310 737-7300	14731
Excel Picture Frames Inc	7699	E	323 231-0244	14766
Wardlow 2 LP (PA)	7699	D	562 432-8066	14800
Advanced Digital Services Inc (PA)	7812	D	323 962-8585	14804
Creatorup Inc	7812	D	323 300-4725	14816
Digital Domain 30 Inc (PA)	7812	B	213 797-3100	14818
Efilm LLC	7812	C	323 463-7041	14825
Fox Net Inc	7812	A	310 369-1000	14829
Hungry Heart Media Inc	7812	C	323 951-0010	14833
Ignition Creative LLC	7812	C	310 315-6300	14834
Miramax LLC	7812	C	310 409-4321	14839
Paramount Pictures Corporation (HQ)	7812	A	323 956-5000	14843
Scanline Vfx Inc	7812	A	310 827-1555	14855
Scanlinevfx La LLC	7812	C	310 827-1555	14856
Twentieth Cntury Fox HM Entrmt (PA)	7812	A	310 369-1000	14863
Twentieth Cntury Fox Film Corp (DH)	7812	D		14864
Viacom Networks	7812	C	310 752-8000	14869
Yobs Technologies Inc	7812	E	213 713-3825	14877
Alan Gordon Enterprises Inc	7819	E	323 466-3561	14881
Cara Communications LLC	7819	D	310 442-5600	14882
Directors Guild America Inc (PA)	7819	D	310 289-2000	14885
Exile LLC	7819	D	310 450-2255	14888
Fifth Season LLC	7819	C	862 432-3068	14889
Film Department Lmu	7819	D	310 258-5465	14890
For Cali Productions LLC	7819	B	323 956-9500	14891
Hollywood Rntals Prod Svcs LLC (PA)	7819	D	818 407-7800	14894
Omega/Cinema Props Inc	7819	C	323 466-8201	14899
Point360 Inc	7819	D	818 565-1400	14902
Post Group Inc (PA)	7819	C	323 462-2300	14903
20th Century Studios Inc	7822	C	888 223-4369	14915
Twentieth Cntury Fox HM Entrmt	7822	C	310 369-1000	14922
Twentieth Century Fox Home E	7822	C	310 369-3900	14923
Twentieth Cntury Fox Intl Corp (HQ)	7822	C	310 369-1000	14924
United Artists Productions Inc	7822	C	310 449-3000	14925
United Artists Television Corp	7822	B	310 449-3000	14926
Our Alchemy LLC	7829	D	310 893-6289	14928
Decurion Corporation (PA)	7832	D	310 659-9432	14931
Nationwide Theatres Corp (HQ)	7833	D	310 657-8420	14950
AEG Presents LLC (DH)	7922	C	323 930-5700	14953
Center Thtre Group Los Angeles (PA)	7922	C	213 972-7344	14956
Creative Artsts Agcy Hldngs LL (DH)	7922	A	424 288-2000	14958
Fandango Inc (HQ)	7922	D	310 954-0278	14959
Industry Entrmt Partners	7922	D	323 954-9000	14962
Los Angeles Opera Company	7922	B	213 972-7219	14965
Paradigm Talent Agency LLC	7922	D	310 288-8000	14969
Performing Arts Ctr Los Angles	7922	C	213 972-7512	14970
Professnal Intrctive Entrmt In	7922	D	310 823-4445	14973
Anschutz Entrmt Group Inc (HQ)	7929	C	213 763-7700	14985
Hob Entertainment LLC (DH)	7929	C	323 769-4600	14989
House of Blues Concerts Inc (DH)	7929	C	323 769-4977	14992
Los Angeles Philharmonic Assn	7929	A	323 850-2060	14996
Los Angeles Philharmonic Assn (PA)	7929	C	213 972-7300	14997
Nederlnder Cncrts San Dego LLC	7929	D	323 468-1700	15000
Twenty Mile Productions LLC	7929	C	412 251-0767	15008
Two Bit Circus Dal LLC	7929	D	323 438-9808	15009
Lucky Strike Entertainment Inc	7933	B	213 542-4880	15012
Lucky Strike Entertainment LLC	7933	D	818 933-3752	15013
Fox Baseball Holdings Inc	7941	A	323 224-1500	15025
Fox BSB Holdco Inc (HQ)	7941	C	323 224-1500	15026
Immortals LLC	7941	D	310 554-8267	15027
LA Sports Properties Inc	7941	C	213 742-7500	15030
Bliss World LLC	7991	D	323 500-0921	15045
Equinox-76th Street Inc	7991	C	310 479-5200	15048
Equinox-76th Street Inc	7991	C	310 552-0420	15049
Los Angeles Athletic Club Inc	7991	C	213 625-2211	15056
World Gym International LLC	7991	D	310 557-8804	15069
Bel-Air Country Club	7997	C	310 472-9563	15122
Brentwood Country Club Los Angeles	7997	D	310 451-8011	15127
Hillcrest Country Club	7997	C	310 553-8911	15140
Los Angeles Country Club	7997	C	310 276-6104	15147
Wilshire Country Club	7997	D	323 934-6050	15188
Ticketmaster Corporation	7999	A	323 769-4600	15226
Ticketmaster Group Inc	7999	A	800 745-3000	15228
Volume Services Inc	7999	B	323 644-6038	15231
Altamed Health Services Corp	8011	B	323 728-0411	15235
Altamed Health Services Corp	8011	C	323 269-0421	15236
Altamed Health Services Corp	8011	C	323 980-4466	15239
Altamed Health Services Corp (PA)	8011	C	323 725-8751	15241
Arroyo Vsta Fmly Hlth Fndation	8011	D	323 224-2188	15246
Associated Students UCLA	8011	D	310 825-9451	15247
Cedars-Sinai Medical Center	8011	C	310 423-4208	15265
Cedars-Sinai Medical Center	8011	B	310 423-3849	15266
Cedars-Sinai Medical Center	8011	C	310 423-7900	15267
Cha Health Systems Inc (PA)	8011	A	213 487-3211	15271
Clinic Inc	8011	D	323 730-1920	15280
Core Med Staff	8011	C	213 382-5550	15288
County of Los Angeles	8011	D	213 744-3919	15290
County of Los Angeles	8011	A	323 226-7131	15293
Garden Grove Advanced Imaging	8011	C	310 445-2800	15312
Gracelight Community Health	8011	D	323 780-4510	15316
Gracelight Community Health	8011	D	323 644-6180	15317
House Ear Clinic Inc (PA)	8011	D	213 483-9930	15326
Kaiser Foundation Hospitals	8011	C	323 857-2000	15352
Kaiser Foundation Hospitals	8011	A	323 857-2000	15353
Kaiser Foundation Hospitals	8011	D	310 915-5000	15360
Kaiser Foundation Hospitals	8011	C	323 783-7955	15362
Kaiser Foundation Hospitals	8011	D	833 574-2273	15365
Kaiser Foundation Hospitals	8011	B	323 783-8306	15366
Kerlan-Jobe Orthopedic Clinic (PA)	8011	D	310 665-7200	15370
Lac & Usc Medical Center	8011	C	323 409-2345	15376
Los Angeles Free Clinic	8011	C	323 653-1990	15382
Los Angeles Free Clinic (PA)	8011	D	323 653-8622	15383
Pediatric and Family Med Ctr	8011	C	213 342-3325	15420
Prospect Medical Holdings Inc (PA)	8011	C	310 943-4500	15425
Robin Red Breast Inc	8011	D	323 466-7800	15439
Santa Monica Bay Physicians He (PA)	8011	D	310 417-5900	15446
South Central Family Hlth Ctr	8011	D	323 908-4200	15457
Southern Cal Prmnnte Med Group	8011	C	323 857-2000	15468
Southern Cal Prmnnte Med Group	8011	B	323 783-5455	15470
Southern Cal Prmnnte Med Group	8011	C	323 783-4893	15471
The Orthopedic Institute of	8011	A	213 977-2010	15490
United Medical Imaging Inc (PA)	8011	D	310 943-8400	15495
Veterans Health Administration	8011	A	310 478-3711	15508
Watts Healthcare Corporation (PA)	8011	C	323 564-4331	15509
White Memorial Med Group Inc (PA)	8011	D	323 987-1300	15512
White Memorial Medical Center	8011	A	323 260-5739	15513
St Johns Community Health (PA)	8021	C	323 541-1411	15527
Che Snior Psychological Svcs PC	8049	D	888 307-0893	15538
Intercare Therapy Inc	8049	C	323 866-1880	15548
Quantum Bhvioral Solutions Inc (PA)	8049	D	626 531-6999	15553
Amada Enterprises Inc	8051	C	323 757-1881	15565
Beverly West Health Care Inc	8051	D	323 938-2451	15582
Burlington Convalescent Hosp (PA)	8051	D	213 381-5585	15584
Burlington Convalescent Hosp	8051	C	323 295-7737	15585
Cha Hollywood Medical Ctr LP	8051	A	213 413-3000	15591
Country Villa Nursing Ctr Inc	8051	C	213 484-9730	15605
Culver West Health Center LLC	8051	C	310 390-9506	15620
East Los Angles Healthcare LLC (HQ)	8051	D	323 268-0106	15624
Garden Crest Cnvlscent Hosp In	8051	D	323 663-8281	15660
Highland Pk Sklled Nrsing Wlln	8051	C	323 254-6125	15678
Hyde Pk Rehabilitation Ctr LLC	8051	D	323 753-1354	15679
J P H Consulting Inc	8051	C	323 934-5660	15683
Lighthouse Healthcare Ctr LLC	8051	D	323 564-4461	15699
Longwood Management Corp	8051	C	323 933-1560	15705
Mariner Health Care Inc	8051	D	323 665-1185	15713
Pacs Group Inc	8051	C	323 782-1500	15732
Rehabltion Cntre of Bvrly Hlls	8051	C	323 782-1500	15759
Rrt Enterprises LP	8051	C	323 653-1521	15766
Rrt Enterprises LP (PA)	8051	C	310 397-2372	15767
Skyline Hlthcare Wllness Ctr L	8051	D	323 665-1185	15780

Mergent email: customerrelations@mergent.com

1306

2025 Southern California
Business Directory and Buyers Guide

(P-0000) Products & Services Section entry number
(PA)=Parent Co (HQ)=Headquarters (DH)=Div Headquarters

	SIC	EMP	PHONE	ENTRY#
Stjohn God Rtirement Care Ctr	8051	C	323 731-0641	15784
Westlake Health Care Center	8051	B	805 494-1233	15801
Amberwood Convalescent Hosp	8059	D	323 254-3407	15830
Ararat Home Los Angeles Inc	8059	C	323 256-8012	15834
Country Villa Terrace (PA)	8059	D	323 653-3980	15845
Genesis Healthcare LLC	8059	A	323 461-9961	15854
Longwood Management Corp	8059	D	323 737-7778	15865
Longwood Management Corp	8059	C	213 382-8461	15966
Longwood Management Corp	8059	C	323 735-5146	15870
New Vista Health Services	8059	C	310 477-5501	15876
Olympia Convalescent Hospital	8059	C	213 487-3000	15877
Temple Pk Cnvalescent Hosp Inc	8059	D	213 380-2035	15885
United Convalescent Facilities	8059	D	213 748-0491	15887
Alta Healthcare System LLC (HQ)	8062	C	323 267-0477	15905
Califrnia Hosp Med Ctr Fndtion	8062	A	213 742-5867	15929
Califrnia Rhblitation Inst LLC	8062		424 363-1003	15930
Cedars-Sinai Medical Center	8062	C	310 423-2587	15936
Cedars-Sinai Medical Center	8062	C	310 423-8965	15937
Cedars-Sinai Medical Center	8062	C	310 659-3732	15938
Cedars-Sinai Medical Center	8062	C	310 423-5841	15939
Cedars-Sinai Medical Center	8062	C	310 423-5147	15940
Cedars-Sinai Medical Center	8062	A	310 423-3277	15943
Cedars-Sinai Medical Center	8062	B	310 423-9520	15944
Cedars-Sinai Medical Center	8062	C	310 423-6451	15948
Cedars-Sinai Medical Center	8062	B	310 824-3664	15950
Childrens Hospital Los Angeles	8062	B	323 361-2751	15953
County of Los Angeles	8062	C	323 226-6021	15968
County of Los Angeles	8062	D	213 473-6100	15969
County of Los Angeles	8062	C	310 668-4545	15971
East Los Angeles Dctors Hosp In	8062	B		15984
Hollywood Cmnty Hosp Med Ctr I	8062		323 462-2271	16024
Hollywood Medical Center LP	8062	A	213 413-3000	16025
Jupiter Bellflower Doctors Hospital	8062	B		16031
Kaiser Foundation Hospitals	8062	C	323 783-4011	16043
Keck Hospital of Usc	8062	A	800 872-2273	16059
LA Metropolitan Medical Center	8062	A	323 730-7300	16068
Lac Usc Medical Center	8062	C		16070
Memorial Hospital of Gardena	8062	B	323 268-5514	16096
Mlk Community Hospital	8062	C	424 338-8000	16099
Nix Hospitals System LLC (HQ)	8062	C	210 271-1800	16105
Olympia Health Care LLC	8062	A	323 938-3161	16107
Orthopaedic Hospital (PA)	8062	C	213 742-1000	16111
Pamc Ltd (PA)	8062	A	213 624-8411	16123
Paraclsus Los Angles Cmnty Hos	8062	C	323 267-0477	16124
Pih Health Good Samaritan Hosp (HQ)	8062	A	213 977-2121	16132
Southern Cal Halthcare Sys Inc (HQ)	8062	C	310 943-4500	16203
Temple Hospital Corporation	8062	B	213 355-3200	16225
Tenet Health Systems Norris	8062	B	323 865-3000	16226
Tustin Hospital and Medical Center	8062	B	714 619-7700	16234
Ucla Health	8062	C	310 825-9111	16236
University Cal Los Angeles	8062	A	310 825-9111	16240
University Southern California	8062	C	323 442-8500	16248
White Memorial Medical Center (HQ)	8062	A	323 268-5000	16259
Gateways Hosp Mental Hlth Ctr (PA)	8063	C	323 644-2000	16274
Kaiser Foundation Hospitals	8063	C	213 580-7200	16275
Kedren Community Hlth Ctr Inc (PA)	8063	B	323 233-0425	16276
Barlow Group (PA)	8069	C	213 250-4200	16283
Barlow Respiratory Hospital (PA)	8069	C	213 250-4200	16285
Childrens Hospital Los Angeles (PA)	8069	A	323 660-2450	16288
County of Los Angeles	8069	C	323 226-3468	16291
County of Los Angeles	8069	D	213 974-7284	16292
Shields For Families (PA)	8069	D	323 242-5000	16299
Radnet Inc (PA)	8071	B	310 478-7000	16332
Samaritan Imaging Center	8071	A	213 977-2140	16333
Clinics On Demand Inc	8082	D	310 709-7355	16378
Livhome Inc (PA)	8082	A	800 807-5854	16402
Maxim Healthcare Services Inc	8082	D	866 465-5678	16403
South Bay Senior Services Inc	8082	D	310 338-8558	16421
Ucla Health Auxiliary	8082	B	310 267-4327	16426
Amanecer Cmnty Cnsling Svc A N	8093	D	213 481-7464	16441
Comprehensive Cancer Centers Inc	8093	C	323 966-3400	16458
County of Los Angeles	8093	C	323 769-7800	16461
County of Los Angeles	8093	B	323 897-6187	16463
Planned Parenthood Los Angeles (PA)	8093	D	213 284-3200	16490
South Baylo University	8093	D	213 999-0297	16503
United Amrcn Indian Invlvment (PA)	8093	D	213 202-3970	16515
Altamed Health Services Corp	8099	C	323 307-0400	16530
California Cryobank LLC (DH)	8099	D	310 496-5691	16539
Los Angles Cnty Dvlpmntal Svcs	8099	C	213 383-1300	16583
Martin Lther King Jr-Los Angle	8099	C	424 338-8000	16584
Public Hlth Fndation Entps Inc	8099	C	323 733-9381	16608
A Buchalter Professional Corp (PA)	8111	C	213 891-0700	16630
Akerman LLP	8111	D	213 688-9500	16631
Allen Mtkins Leck Gmble Mllory (PA)	8111	C	213 622-5555	16635
Arnold Porter Kaye Scholer LLP	8111	C	213 243-4000	16636
Austin Sidley CA LLP	8111	C	213 896-6000	16638
Baker & Hostetler LLP	8111	C	310 820-8800	16639
Baker & McKenzie LLP	8111	C	310 201-4728	16641
Ballard Spahr LLP	8111	D	424 204-4400	16642
Barnes & Thornburg LLP	8111	C	310 284-3880	16643
Blakely Sokoloff Taylor & Zafman LLP	8111	C	310 207-3800	16646
Bonne Brdges Mller Okefe Nchol (PA)	8111	D	213 480-1900	16648
Burke Williams & Sorensen LLP (PA)	8111	D	213 236-0600	16651
County of Los Angeles	8111	C	213 974-2811	16660
County of Los Angeles	8111	C	213 974-3812	16661
Covington & Burling LLP	8111	C	424 332-4800	16664
Cox Castle & Nicholson LLP (PA)	8111	C	310 284-2200	16665
Crowell & Moring LLP	8111	C	213 622-4750	16667
Danning Gill Damnd Kollitz LLP	8111	C	310 277-0077	16668
Davis Wright Tremaine LLP	8111	C	213 633-6800	16669
Defense Specialists LLC	8111	D	818 270-7162	16670
Dentons US LLP	8111	C	213 623-9300	16671
Dla Piper LLP (us)	8111	D	310 595-3000	16672
Dominguez Law Group PC	8111	D	213 388-7788	16673
Elkins Kalt Wntraub Rben Grtsi	8111	D	310 746-4431	16675
Ellis Grge Cpllone Obrien Anng	8111	D	310 274-7100	16676
Engstrom Lipscomb and Lack A (PA)	8111	C	310 552-3800	16677
Epstein Becker & Green PC	8111	D	415 398-3500	16678
Epstein Becker & Green PC	8111	D	310 556-8861	16679
Gibbs Giden Locher	8111	D	310 552-3400	16686
Gibson Dunn & Crutcher LLP (PA)	8111	B	213 229-7000	16687
Gibson Dunn & Crutcher LLP	8111	C	310 552-8500	16688
Gilbert Klly Crwley Jnnett LLP (PA)	8111	C	213 615-7000	16690
Gipson Hffman Pncone A Prof Co	8111	C	310 556-4660	16691
Girardi Keese (PA)	8111	D	213 977-0211	16692
Glaser Weil Fink Jacobs (PA)	8111	C	310 553-3000	16693
Gordon Rees Scully Mansukhani	8111	C	213 576-5000	16694
Greenberg Glsker Flds Clman Mc	8111	D	310 553-3610	16696
Greenberg Traurig LLP	8111	C	310 586-7708	16698
Haight Brown & Bonesteel LLP (PA)	8111	D	213 542-8000	16699
Hill Farrer & Burrill	8111	D	213 620-0460	16702
Holland & Knight LLP	8111	C	213 896-2400	16703
Hueston Hennigan LLP	8111	D	213 788-4340	16704
Imhoff & Associates PC	8111	C	310 691-2200	16705
Immigrant Defenders Law Center	8111	D	213 634-0999	16706
Irell & Manella LLP (PA)	8111	C	310 277-1010	16708
Jackoway Tyrman Wrthmer Asten	8111	C	310 553-0305	16709
Jeffer Mngels Btlr Mtchell LLP (PA)	8111	C	310 203-8080	16710
Jones Day	8111	D	213 489-3939	16711
K&L Gates LLP	8111	C	310 552-5000	16712
Katten Muchin Rosenman LLP	8111	C	310 788-4400	16713
King & Spalding LLP	8111	D	213 443-4355	16716
Kirkland & Ellis LLP	8111	B	213 680-8400	16717
Kirkland & Ellis LLP	8111	D	310 552-4200	16718
Kirkland & Ellis LLP	8111	C	213 680-8400	16719
Knight Law Group LLP	8111	C	424 355-1155	16720
Latham & Watkins LLP (PA)	8111	A	213 485-1234	16726
Lewis Brsbois Bsgard Smith LLP (PA)	8111	A	213 250-1800	16730
Liner LLP	8111	A	310 500-3500	16732
LLP Mayer Brown	8111	B	213 229-9500	16734
Loeb & Loeb LLP (PA)	8111	C	310 282-2000	16735
Manatt Phelps & Phillips LLP (PA)	8111	B	310 312-4000	16737
Manning Kass Ellrod Rmrez Trsl (PA)	8111	C	213 624-6900	16738
Milbank Tweed Hdley McCloy LLP	8111	C	424 386-4000	16740
Mitchell Silberberg Knupp LLP (PA)	8111	C	310 312-2000	16742
Morrio Polich & Purdy LLP (PA)	8111	D	213 891-9100	16743
Morrison & Focotor	8111	C	213 892-5200	16745
Munger Tolles & Olson LLP	8111	C	213 683-9100	16746
Munger Tolles Olson Foundation (PA)	8111	B	213 683-9100	16747
Murchison & Cumming LLP (PA)	8111	C	213 623-7400	16748
Musick Peeler & Garrett LLP (PA)	8111	C	213 629-7600	16749
Nossaman LLP (PA)	8111	D	213 612-7800	16752
OMelveny & Myers LLP (PA)	8111	A	213 430-6000	16753
OMelveny & Myers LLP	8111	C	310 553-6700	16754
Pachulski Stang Zehl Jones LLP (PA)	8111	C	310 277-6910	16755
Paul Hastings LLP (PA)	8111	A	213 683-6000	16757
Pillsbury Wnthrop Shaw Pttman	8111	D	213 488-7100	16759
Pircher Nichols & Meeks LLP	8111	C	310 201-0132	16760
Polsinelli PC	8111	C	310 556-1801	16761
Public Counsel	8111	D	213 385-2977	16766
Quinn Emnuel Urqhart Sllvan LL (PA)	8111	B	213 443-3000	16767
Reed Smith LLP	8111	C	213 457-8000	16768
Richards Wtson Grshon A Prof C (PA)	8111	C	213 626-8484	16769
Ropers Majeski A Prof Corp	8111	C	213 312-2000	16771
Russ August & Kabat LLP	8111	C	310 826-7474	16772
Saul Ewing Arnstein & Lehr LLP	8111	D	310 398-6100	16774

	SIC	EMP	PHONE	ENTRY#
Selman Lchnger Edson Hsu Nwman	8111	D	310 445-0800	16775
Seyfarth Shaw LLP	8111	C	310 277-7200	16777
Sheppard Mllin Rchter Hmpton L (PA)	8111	B	213 620-1780	16780
Sidley Austin LLP	8111	D	310 284-6618	16782
Skadden Arps Slate Meagher & F	8111	C	213 687-5000	16784
Stutman Trster Glatt Prof Corp	8111	D	310 228-5600	16788
Troygould PC	8111	D	310 553-4441	16792
White & Case LLP	8111	D	213 620-7724	16794
Ziffren B B F G-L S&C Fnd	8111	D	310 552-3388	16799
Golden Day Schools Inc	8211	D	323 296-6280	16808
Vista Del Mar Child Fmly Svcs (PA)	8211	C	310 836-1223	16828
West Angeles Ch God In Chrst	8211	C	323 731-2567	16829
Associated Students UCLA	8221	C	310 206-8282	16831
University Cal Los Angeles	8221	C	310 825-7852	16835
The Coding Source LLC	8249	C	866 235-7553	16847
Greenwood Hall Inc	8299	C	310 905-8300	16854
Southern Cal Prmnnte Med Group	8299	C	323 564-7911	16858
Advancment Thrugh Oprtnty Knwl	8322	D	323 730-9400	16861
Aids Project Los Angeles (PA)	8322	D	213 201-1600	16862
American National Red Cross	8322	D	310 445-9900	16865
American Red Cross Los Angles (PA)	8322	C	310 445-9900	16867
Aviva Family & Childrens Svcs (PA)	8322	D	323 876-0550	16873
Blc Residential Care Inc	8322	D	310 722-7541	16876
Braille Institute America Inc (PA)	8322	C	323 663-1111	16877
Childrens Bureau Southern Cal (PA)	8322	C	213 342-0100	16890
Childrens Inst Los Angeles	8322	A	213 383-2765	16891
Childrens Institute Inc (PA)	8322	C	213 385-5100	16892
Core Cmnty Orgnzed Rlief Effor	8322	B	323 934-4400	16901
County of Los Angeles	8322	D	213 974-9331	16907
County of Los Angeles	8322	D	323 226-8511	16909
County of Los Angeles	8322	D	213 351-5600	16910
County of Los Angeles	8322	C	323 780-2185	16921
County of Los Angeles	8322	D	213 351-7257	16922
County of Los Angeles	8322	C	323 586-6469	16923
Crystal Stairs Inc (PA)	8322	B	323 299-8998	16932
East Los Angles Rmrkble Ctzens	8322	D	323 223-3079	16936
First 5 La	8322	C	213 482-5920	16943
Homeboy Industries (PA)	8322	B	323 526-1254	16952
International Medical Corps (PA)	8322	A	310 826-7800	16961
Jewish Family Svc Los Angeles	8322	C	323 937-5900	16963
Kedren Community Hlth Ctr Inc	8322	C	323 524-0634	16967
La Asccion Ncnal Pro Prsnas My	8322	A	213 202-5900	16969
Los Angeles Homeless Svcs Auth	8322	D	213 683-3333	16974
Los Angeles Regional Food Bank	8322	C	323 234-3030	16975
New Directions Inc (PA)	8322	D	310 914-4045	16983
Path	8322	A	323 644-2216	16990
People Concern	8322	C	310 874-2806	16991
Prototypes Centers For Innov	8322	C	213 542-3838	16998
Sexual Recovery Institute Inc	8322	B	310 360-0130	17011
Team Logic If La W Hollywood	8322	D	310 292-0063	17016
Volunteers of Amer Los Angeles	8322	D	213 749-0362	17027
Volunteers of Amer Los Angeles	8322	D	323 780-3770	17029
Volunteers of Amer Los Angeles	8322	D	213 627-8002	17035
Watts Labor Community Action	8322	C	323 563-5639	17039
Weingart Center Association	8322	C	213 622-6359	17040
Wellnest Emtonal Hlth Wellness (PA)	8322	C	323 373-2400	17041
Asian Rehabilitation Svc Inc	8331	C	213 680-3790	17047
Chinatown Service Center (PA)	8331	D	213 808-1701	17052
Exceptional Chld Foundation	8331	D	213 748-3556	17057
Pacific Asian Cnsrtium In Empl (PA)	8331	D	213 353-3982	17065
Special Service For Groups Inc (PA)	8331	D	213 368-1888	17066
California Childrens Academy	8351	C	323 263-3846	17078
Carousel Child Care Corp	8351	C	310 216-6641	17080
Motion Picture and TV Fund	8351	D	310 445-8993	17097
Plaza De La Raza Child Develop	8351	D	323 224-1788	17107
Ascend Healthcare LLC	8361	D	310 598-1840	17121
County of Los Angeles	8361	D	323 226-8611	17137
Evolve Growth Initiatives LLC	8361	C	424 281-5000	17151
Front Porch Communities & Svcs	8361	C	323 661-1128	17155
Hamburger Home (PA)	8361	D	323 876-0550	17157
Hathaway-Sycmres Child Fmly Svc	8361	C	323 257-9600	17159
Lamp Inc	8361	D	213 488-9559	17171
Los Angeles Mission Inc (PA)	8361	D	213 629-1227	17176
Sisters of Nzareth Los Angeles	8361	C	310 839-2361	17195
Solheim Lutheran Home	8361	C	323 257-7518	17196
St Annes Family Services	8361	C	213 381-2931	17197
Anti-Recidivism Coalition	8399	D	213 955-5885	17210
Associated Students UCLA	8399	C	310 794-0242	17214
Associated Students UCLA (PA)	8399	B	310 794-8836	17215
California Endowment (PA)	8399	D	213 928-8800	17217
Community Partners (PA)	8399	C	213 346-3200	17222
Essential Access Health (PA)	8399	D	213 386-5614	17225
Greater Los Angeles Zoo Assn	8399	D	323 644-4200	17227
Interntnal Fndtion For Krea Un	8399	B	213 550-2182	17229
Los Angeles Lgbt Center (PA)	8399	C	323 993-7618	17235
South Cntl Los Angles Rgnal CT	8399	C	231 744-8484	17242
South Cntl Los Angles Rgnal CT (PA)	8399	C	213 744-7000	17243
Special Service For Groups Inc	8399	C	213 553-1800	17245
United Way Inc (PA)	8399	D	213 808-6220	17246
Westside Jewish Cmnty Ctr Inc	8399	A	323 938-2531	17247
Armand Hmmer Mseum of Art Cltr	8412	C	310 443-7000	17248
Autry Museum of American West	8412	C	323 667-2000	17249
Califrnia Scnce Ctr Foundation	8412	B	213 744-2545	17251
Lucas Museum of Narrative Art	8412	D	831 566-9332	17255
Museum Associates	8412	B	323 857-6172	17256
Museum of Contemporary Art (PA)	8412	C	213 626-6222	17257
Skirball Cultural Center	8412	C	310 440-4500	17267
The J Paul Getty Trust (PA)	8412	A	310 440-7300	17268
California Assn Realtors Inc (PA)	8611	C	213 739-8200	17278
California RE Assn Inc	8611	D	213 739-8200	17279
Los Angles Area Chmber Cmmerce	8611	D	213 580-7500	17284
Coopertive Amrcn Physcians Inc (PA)	8621	D	213 473-8600	17297
County of Los Angeles	8621	C	213 240-8412	17298
Los Angeles County Bar Assn (PA)	8621	D	213 627-2727	17300
State Bar of California	8621	D	213 765-1520	17309
Truck Underwriters Association (DH)	8621	A	323 932-3200	17310
Seiu Local 721	8631	C	213 368-8660	17313
Southwest Carptr Training Fund	8631	D	213 386-8590	17314
United Teachers-Los Angeles	8631	D	213 487-5560	17318
Writers Guild America West Inc	8631	C	323 951-4000	17319
Action Property Management Inc	8641	D	800 400-2284	17321
California Club	8641	C	213 622-1391	17330
Greater Los Angles Area Cncil (PA)	8641	D	213 413-4400	17347
Jewish Cmnty Fndtion Los Angle (PA)	8641	C	323 761-8700	17349
Jonathan Club (PA)	8641	C	213 624-0881	17350
Kpmg New York Foundation Inc	8641	C	212 758-9700	17352
Public Hlth Fndation Entps Inc	8641	C	323 263-0262	17361
Young MNS Chrstn Assn Mtro Los	8641	D	310 216-9036	17404
Young MNS Chrstn Assn Mtro Los	8641	C	323 467-4161	17406
Young MNS Chrstn Assn Mtro Los (PA)	8641	D	213 380-6448	17407
Young Wns Chrstn Assn Grter Lo	8641	C	323 295-4288	17411
Young Wns Chrstn Assn Grter Lo	8641	C	323 295-4280	17412
Crenshaw Chrstn Ctr Ch Los Ang (PA)	8661	B	323 758-3777	17413
Hospitller Order of St John Go	8661	B	323 731-0641	17415
Interntnal Ch of Frsqare Gospl (PA)	8661	D	714 701-1818	17416
Self-Realization Fellowship Ch (PA)	8661	E	323 225-2471	17418
Sinai Temple (PA)	8661	B	310 474-1518	17419
Wilshire Boulevard Temple	8661	D	323 261-6135	17422
Best Friends Animal Society	8699	D	818 643-3989	17458
Brilliant Corners Teri Enomoto	8699	D	213 232-0134	17459
Los Angeles Mem Coliseum Comm	8699	B	213 747-7111	17465
Play Versus Inc	8699	C	949 636-4193	17468
Society of St Vncent De Paul C (PA)	8699	C	323 226-9645	17470
Arup North America Limited	8711	B	310 578-4182	17488
Ffs Tech Inc	8711	D	323 965-9300	17528
Fire Protection Group Amer Inc	8711	E	323 732-4200	17529
Flint Energy Services Inc	8711	C	213 593-8000	17530
Fti Consulting Inc	8711	D	213 689-1200	17534
Sia Engineering (usa) Inc	8711	C	310 957-2928	17630
5 Design Inc (PA)	8712	D	323 308-3558	17664
Aecom Services Inc (HQ)	8712	C	213 593-8000	17665
Dlr Group Inc (HQ)	8712	C	213 800-9400	17669
Gehry Partners LLP	8712	C	310 482-3000	17670
Gruen Associates Inc	8712	D	323 937-4270	17672
Hawkins Brown USA Inc	8712	C	310 640-2695	17673
Hellmuth Obata & Kassabaum Inc	8712	D	310 838-9555	17674
Johnson Fain Inc	8712	C	323 224-6000	17677
M Arthur Gensler Jr Assoc Inc	8712	C	213 927-3600	17682
Marmol Rdzner An Archtctral Co	8712	C	310 826-6222	17684
Martin AC Partners Inc	8712	C	213 683-1900	17685
Steinberg Hart (PA)	8712	D	213 629-0500	17692
Stv Architects Inc	8712	C	213 482-9444	17693
The Jerde Partnership Inc	8712	D	310 399-1987	17694
Zimmer Gnsul Frsca Archtcts LL	8712	C	213 617-1901	17697
Psomas (PA)	8713	C	213 223-1400	17698
Armanino LLP	8721	B	310 478-4148	17701
Baker Tilly Us LLP	8721	A	310 826-4474	17704
Cliftonlarsonallen LLP	8721	D	310 273-2501	17712
County of Los Angeles	8721	A	323 267-2136	17715
Deloitte & Touche LLP	8721	A	213 688-0800	17716
Deloitte Tax LLP	8721	C	404 885-6754	17719
Ernst & Young LLP	8721	A	213 977-3200	17727
Film Payroll Services Inc (PA)	8721	C	310 440-9600	17728
Green Hasson & Janks LLP	8721	D	310 873-1600	17730
Gursey Schneider & Co LLC (PA)	8721	D	310 552-0960	17731
Holthouse Carlin Van Trigt LLP (PA)	8721	C	310 566-1900	17733

Mergent email: customerrelations@mergent.com
1308

2025 Southern California
Business Directory and Buyers Guide

(P-0000) Products & Services Section entry number
(PA)=Parent Co (HQ)=Headquarters (DH)=Div Headquarters

	SIC	EMP	PHONE	ENTRY#
Pricewaterhousecoopers LLP	8721	C	213 356-6000	17752
Rbz LLP	8721	C	310 478-4148	17753
Singerlewak LLP (PA)	8721	C	310 477-3924	17755
Environmental Science Assoc	8731	C	213 599-4300	17787
Cornerstone Research	8732	D	213 553-2500	17842
Interviewing Service Amer LLC (PA)	8732	C	818 989-1044	17852
Material Holdings LLC (PA)	8732	C	310 553-0550	17855
National Research Group Inc	8732	B	323 406-6200	17856
Prosearch Strategies LLC	8732	C	877 447-7291	17859
Streamelements Inc (PA)	8732	D	323 928-7848	17862
Zefr Inc	8732	B	310 392-3555	17864
Brentwood Bmdical RES Inst Inc	8733	C	310 312-1554	17867
Childrens Inst Los Angeles (PA)	8733	C	213 385-5100	17871
House Research Institute	8733	C	213 353-7012	17875
Vital Research LLC	8733	D	323 951-1670	17896
County of Los Angeles	8734	C	323 267-6167	17911
Ellison Institute LLC (PA)	8734	C	310 228-6400	17915
National Genetics Institute	8734	C	310 996-6610	17922
AEG Management Lacc LLC	8741	C	213 741-1151	17935
Ajit Healthcare Inc	8741	D	213 484-0510	17936
Bon Appetit Management Co	8741	C	310 440-6052	17953
Bon Appetit Management Co	8741	C	310 440-6209	17955
Cal State La Univ Aux Svcs Inc	8741	A	323 343-2531	17957
Capital Group Companies Inc (PA)	8741	A	213 486-9200	17959
Chan Family Partnership LP	8741	C	626 322-7132	17962
Country Villa Service Corp	8741	C	323 734-1101	17972
Country Villa Service Corp	8741	C	323 734-9122	17973
Country Villa Service Corp	8741	C	323 666-1544	17974
Far East National Bank	8741	B	213 687-1300	17984
Firstsrvice Rsidential Cal LLC	8741	C	213 213-0886	17985
Front Line MGT Group Inc	8741	C	310 209-3100	17986
J2 Cloud Services LLC	8741	B	844 804-1234	17994
Jpl Management LLC	8741	D	310 844-3662	17998
Keiro Services	8741	B	213 873-5700	18001
La 1000 Santa Fe LLC	8741	C	213 205-1000	18002
Los Angeles Rams LLC	8741	C	310 277-4700	18009
Network Management Group Inc (PA)	8741	C	323 263-2632	18021
Onni Properties LLC	8741	C	213 568-0278	18025
Ovg Facilities LLC	8741	D	757 323-9380	18027
Relocity Inc	8741	C	323 207-9160	18044
Rockport ADM Svcs LLC (PA)	8741	C	323 330-6500	18047
Snf Management	8741	C	310 385-1090	18054
SunAmerica Investments Inc (DH)	8741	C	310 772-6000	18060
Tripalink Corp	8741	C	323 717-9139	18070
Alvarez Mrsal Bus Cnslting LLC	8742	B	310 975-2600	18089
Bamko LLC (HQ)	8742	A	310 470-5859	18101
Blackstone Consulting Inc (PA)	8742	D	310 826-4389	18105
Captain Marketing Inc	8742	D	310 402-9709	18113
Diagnostic Health Corporation	8742	C	310 665-7180	18127
First Capitol Consulting Inc	8742	D	213 382-1115	18137
Hatchbeauty Agency LLC (PA)	8742	E	310 396-7070	18146
HR&a Advisors Inc	8742	D	310 581-0900	18149
Korn Ferry (us) (HQ)	8742	C	310 552-1834	18157
Northgate Gonzalez Inc	8742	B	323 262-0595	18184
NVE Inc	8742	D	323 512-8400	18186
Powersource Talent LLC	8742	C	424 835-0878	18195
PWC STRategy& (us) LLC	8742	C	213 356-6000	18197
Rocky Point Investments LLC (HQ)	8742	C	310 482-6500	18203
Saban Brands LLC (HQ)	8742	D	310 557-5230	18204
Seek Capital LLC	8742	D	855 978-6106	18206
Shein Technology LLC (PA)	8742	B	213 628-4008	18208
Smith-Emery International Inc (PA)	8742	C	213 741-8500	18215
Sodexo Management Inc	8742	A	310 646-3738	18217
Spotify USA Inc	8742	C	213 505-3040	18218
Stone Canyon Inds Holdings LLC (PA)	8742	E	424 316-2061	18221
United Talent Agency LLC	8742	B	310 385-2800	18236
Wasserman Media Group LLC (PA)	8742	C	310 407-0200	18239
Wellmade Inc	8742	D	213 221-1123	18241
Coalition Technologies LLC	8743	C	310 827-3890	18253
Aecom Technical Services Inc (HQ)	8748	D	213 593-8100	18276
Aecom Usa Inc	8748	C	213 593-8000	18278
Aecom Usa Inc	8748	C	213 330-7200	18279
Ankura Consulting Group LLC	8748	C	213 223-2109	18285
Broadband Telecom Inc	8748	C	818 450-5714	18293
Cal Southern Assn Governments (PA)	8748	C	213 236-1800	18297
Cdsnet LLC	8748	B	310 981-9500	18299
Lusive Decor	8748	C	323 227-9207	18333
Pcs Link Inc	8748	B	949 655-5000	18347
Essense	8999	A	323 202-4650	18373
Los Angles Cnty Mseum Ntral Hs (PA)	9111	C	213 763-3466	18384
County of Los Angeles	9431	D	213 738-4601	18392

LOS OLIVOS, CA - Santa Barbara County

	SIC	EMP	PHONE	ENTRY#
Firestone Vineyard LP	2084	D	805 688-3940	1569
Cushman Winery Corporation	5182	E	805 688-9339	11055

LOST HILLS, CA - Kern County

	SIC	EMP	PHONE	ENTRY#
Wonderful Orchards LLC	0173	B	661 797-6400	40
Roll Properties Intl Inc	6799	C	661 797-6500	12733

LUCERNE VALLEY, CA - San Bernardino County

	SIC	EMP	PHONE	ENTRY#
Omya California Inc	2819	D	760 248-7306	3243
Omya Inc	2819	D	760 248-5200	3244
Specialty Minerals Inc	2819	D	760 248-5300	3253
Mitsubishi Cement Corporation	3241	C	760 248-7373	4357
Casa Clina Hosp Ctrs For Hlthc	8322	C	760 248-6245	16879

LYNWOOD, CA - Los Angeles County

	SIC	EMP	PHONE	ENTRY#
First Finish Inc	2211	E	310 631-6717	1879
Aaron Corporation	2339	C	323 235-5959	2079
Kayo of California (PA)	2339	E	323 233-6107	2111
Gomen Furniture Mfg Inc	2512	C	310 635-4894	2447
Golden Mattress Co Inc	2515	D	323 887-1888	2485
Next Day Frame Inc	2519	D	310 886-0851	2502
P & L Development	2834	C	323 567-2482	3468
Rangers Die Casting Co	3363	C	310 764-1800	4652
Metal Improvement Company LLC	3398	D	323 585-2168	4707
Tjs Metal Manufacturing Inc	3446	E	310 604-1545	5072
Bowman-Field Inc	3471	D	310 638-8519	5242
Triumph Processing Inc	3471	C	323 563-1338	5302
Processes By Martin Inc	3479	C	310 637-1855	5340
Ace Machine Shop Inc	3599	D	310 608-2277	6063
Pacific Ltg & Standards Co	3646	E	310 603-9344	6470
Midas Express Los Angeles Inc	4225	C	310 609-0366	9089
Earle M Jorgensen Company (HQ)	5051	C	323 567-1122	10135
Altamed Health Services Corp	8011	C	310 632-0415	15238
Southern Cal Hlth Rhbltton PR	8011	C	310 631-8004	15459
Country Villa Service Corp	8051	C	310 537-2500	15607
Marlinda Management Inc (PA)	8059	C	310 631-6122	15873
Southern Cal Prmnnte Med Group	8062	C	310 604-5700	16205
South Cntl Hlth Rhbltton Prgr	8093	D	310 667-4070	16504
Baymark Health Services La Inc	8099	C	310 761-4762	16535
Lynwood Unified School Dst	8211	D	310 631-7308	16816
Jwch Institute Inc	8322	C	310 223-1035	16966

MALIBU, CA - Los Angeles County

	SIC	EMP	PHONE	ENTRY#
Curtco Robb Media LLC (PA)	2721	E	310 589-7700	2852
Robb Curtco Media LLC	2721	E	310 589-7700	2875
Olive Refinish	2851	E	805 273-5072	3718
County of Los Angeles	3531	C	310 456-8014	5491
Road Champs Inc	3944	C	310 456-7799	8494
Toymax International Inc (HQ)	3944	D	310 456-7799	8496
Westmed Ambulance Inc	4119	C	310 456-3830	8856
Cco Holdings LLC	4841	C	310 589-3008	9527
Malibu Conference Center Inc	6512	B	818 889-6440	12303
Wilshire Boulevard Temple	7032	D	310 457-7861	13106
Credibility Corp	7389	A	310 456-8271	14484
Clarkson Law Firm PC	8111	D	213 788-4050	16657
Grasshopper House Partners LLC	8322	C	310 589-2880	16947
Hrl Laboratories LLC	8732	A	310 317-5000	17849

MANHATTAN BEACH, CA - Los Angeles County

	SIC	EMP	PHONE	ENTRY#
Running Tide Technologies Inc	0273	D	207 835-7010	94
Ebc Inc (PA)	1521	D	310 753-6407	400
Stanton Carpet Corp	2273	E	562 945-8711	1957
Trlg Corporate Holdings LLC (PA)	2369	C	323 266-3072	2173
Wave Community Newspapers Inc (PA)	2711	E	323 290-3000	2837
TEC Specialty Products LLC	2891	C	801 897-5514	3781
Skechers USA Inc (PA)	3149	C	310 318-3100	4288
Fox US Productions 27 Inc	4833	A	310 727-2550	9505
I Brands LLC	5083	C	424 336-5216	10363
Trlggc Services LLC	5136	C	323 266-3072	10697
Tone It Up LLC	5499	E	310 376-7645	11310
Skechers USA Inc II	5661	A	800 746-3411	11499
Kinecta Federal Credit Union (PA)	6061	C	310 643-5400	11802
Platinum Capital Group (PA)	6162	D	310 406-3505	11930
Oka & Oka Hawaii LLC	7011	C	808 329-1393	12949
Distillery Tech Inc	7371	C	310 776-6234	13710
1334 Partners LP	7997	D	310 546-5656	15111
Kaiser Foundation Hospitals	8062	C	310 937-4311	16042
Torrance Memorial Medical Ctr	8062	B	310 939-7847	16231
Pancrtic Cncer Action Ntwrk In (PA)	8099	D	310 725-0025	16602
Automobile Club Southern Cal	8699	C	310 376-0521	17444
M & E Technical Services L L C	8744	D	256 964-6486	18264
Jag Professional Services Inc	8748	C	310 945-5648	18326

Employee Codes: A=Over 500 employees, B=251-500
C=101-250, D=51-100, E=20-50, F=10-19, G=1-9

2025 Southern California
Business Directory and Buyers Guide

© Mergent Inc. 1-800-342-5647

1309

	SIC	EMP	PHONE	ENTRY#
Network Sltons Prvider USA Inc	8748	E	213 985-2173	18339

MARICOPA, CA - Kern County

	SIC	EMP	PHONE	ENTRY#
Aera Energy Services Company	1381	D	661 665-3200	286
Calmat Co	1422	B	661 858-2673	372
Nestle Purina Petcare Company	2047	C	661 769-8261	1423

MARINA DEL REY, CA - Los Angeles County

	SIC	EMP	PHONE	ENTRY#
Lf Sportswear Inc (PA)	2331	E	310 437-4100	2046
Tokyopop Inc (PA)	2731	D	323 920-5967	2898
Dr Squatch LLC	2844	C	631 229-7068	3650
Dollar Shave Club Inc (HQ)	3541	C	310 975-8528	5543
Sewer Rodding Equipment Co (PA)	3589	E	310 301-9009	6031
Executive Network Entps Inc (PA)	4119	D	310 447-2759	8822
Hornblower Yachts LLC	4724	C	310 301-9900	9224
Bouqs Company	5193	D	888 320-2687	11084
Gelsons Markets	5411	C	310 306-3192	11277
Marina City Club LP A Cali	6513	C	310 822-0611	12358
Laaco Ltd (HQ)	6519	C	213 622-1254	12377
Ylopo LLC	6531	C	818 915-9150	12552
Steelwave LLC	6552	A	310 821-1111	12580
Ritz-Carlton Marina Del Rey	7011	C	310 823-1700	12998
Psg Global Solutions LLC (HQ)	7361	A	310 405-0340	13559
Apotheka Systems Inc	7372	E	844 777-4455	13878
Telesign Holdings Inc (DH)	7372	E	310 740-9700	14047
Survios Inc	7373	C	310 736-1503	14109
Modern Parking Inc	7521	C	310 821-1081	14659
EZ Lube LLC	7549	C	310 821-2517	14716
Deluxe Nms Inc	7822	C	310 760-8500	14917
Diagnstic Intrvntnal Srgcal CT	8011	D	310 574-0400	15302
Cedars-Sinai Marina Hospital	8062	A	310 823-8911	15934
Cedars-Sinai Marina Hospital	8062	A	310 448-7800	15935

MAYWOOD, CA - Los Angeles County

	SIC	EMP	PHONE	ENTRY#
Kitchen Cuts LLC	2013	D	323 560-7415	1260
KSM Garment Inc	2331	E	323 585-8811	2043
Ev R Inc	2339	E	323 312-5400	2095
Gemini Film & Bag Inc (PA)	3089	C	323 582-0901	4123
Heritage Leather Company Inc	3111	E	323 983-0420	4278
Signresource LLC	3993	C	323 771-2098	8634
Tapia Enterprises Inc (PA)	5141	D	323 560-7415	10812
R G Canning Enterprises Inc	7389	C	323 560-7469	14582

MC FARLAND, CA - Kern County

	SIC	EMP	PHONE	ENTRY#
Jakov Dulcich and Sons LLC	0172	C	661 792-6360	34
Aptco LLC (PA)	2821	D	661 792-2107	3258
A G Hacienda Incorporated	4212	D	661 792-2418	8887

MC KITTRICK, CA - Kern County

	SIC	EMP	PHONE	ENTRY#
Wonderful Orchards LLC	0173	C	661 797-2509	41
Aera Energy LLC	1311	C	661 334-3100	263
California Resources Prod Corp	1311	E	661 869-8000	272
Aera Energy Services Company	1381	C	661 665-4400	285

MECCA, CA - Riverside County

	SIC	EMP	PHONE	ENTRY#
Kerry Inc	2023	D	760 396-2116	1299
Califrnia Nutritional Pdts Inc	2043	D	760 625-3884	1410
Western Environmental Inc	3822	E	760 396-0222	7842

MENIFEE, CA - Riverside County

	SIC	EMP	PHONE	ENTRY#
Big Brand Tire & Service	3011	D	951 679-6266	3862
Datatronics Romoland Inc	3612	D	951 928-7700	6283
Leading Edge Logistix LLC	4789	C	951 870-6801	9369
Grove Lumber & Bldg Sups Inc (PA)	5031	C	909 947-0277	9921
Lowes Home Centers LLC	5211	C	951 723-1930	11218
Neighborhood Healthcare	8011	C	951 216-2200	15401
City of Menifee	8741	D	951 672-6777	17967

MENTONE, CA - San Bernardino County

	SIC	EMP	PHONE	ENTRY#
International Paving Svcs Inc	1611	D	909 794-2101	626
Bristol Omega Inc	2541	E	909 794-6862	2558
Power Pt Inc (PA)	3537	E	951 490-4149	5533

MIRA LOMA, CA - Riverside County

	SIC	EMP	PHONE	ENTRY#
Galassos Bakery (PA)	2051	C	951 360-1211	1453
Highland Plastics Inc	3089	C	951 360-9587	4132
Cryoworks Inc	3498	D	951 360-0920	5430
Speakercraft LLC	3651	D	951 685-1759	6558
Act Fulfillment Inc (PA)	4225	D	909 930-9083	9045
Home Depot USA Inc	4225	C	951 361-1235	9077
Prevost Car (us) Inc	5013	D	951 360-2550	9839
Olivet International Inc (PA)	5099	D	951 681-8888	10565
Home Depot USA Inc	5211	C	951 727-0324	11177

MISSION HILLS, CA - Los Angeles County

	SIC	EMP	PHONE	ENTRY#
Jade Inc	1742	D	818 365-7137	1012
Electric Gate Store Inc	3699	C	818 504-2300	7122
National Insurance Crime Bur	6411	D	818 895-2867	12238
National Business Group Inc (PA)	7353	D	818 221-6000	13442
National Cnstr Rentals Inc (PA)	7359	C	818 221-6000	13463
Providnce Facey Med Foundation (PA)	8011	C	818 365-9531	15426
Providnce Facey Med Foundation	8011	D	818 365-9531	15428
Ararat Home Los Angeles Inc	8059	C	818 837-1800	15833
Providence Health & Svcs - Ore	8062	A	818 365-8051	16149
Providence Holy Cross Medical (PA)	8062	B	818 365-8051	16151
Hemodialysis Inc	8092	H	818 365-6961	16436
Greater Valley Med Group Inc (PA)	8093	C	818 838-4500	16476
Providnce Facey Med Foundation	8099	C	818 837-5677	16604
El Nido Family Centers (PA)	8322	C	818 830-3646	16939

MISSION VIEJO, CA - Orange County

	SIC	EMP	PHONE	ENTRY#
Prototype Industries Inc (PA)	2741	E	949 680-4890	2938
Postal Instant Press Inc (PA)	2752	E	949 348-5000	3063
Sir Speedy Inc (HQ)	2752	E	949 348-5000	3081
Wakunaga of America Co Ltd (HQ)	2834	D	949 855-2776	3522
James Hardie Trading Co Inc	2952	C	949 582-2378	3844
James Hardie Building Pdts Inc	3241	D	949 348-1800	4355
Elixir Industries	3469	D	949 860-5000	5184
Ironwood Electric Inc	3699	E	714 630-2350	7127
Medix Ambulance Service Inc (PA)	4119	C	949 470-8915	8836
Black Dot Wireless LLC	4812	C	949 502-3800	9386
Paydarfar Industries Inc	5045	D	949 481-3267	10022
Advanced Mp Technology LLC (DH)	5065	C	800 492-3113	10228
Smart Stores Operations LLC	5141	B	949 581-1212	10788
Strategic Sanitation Svcs Inc	5169	C	949 444-9009	11021
Home Depot USA Inc	5211	C	949 364-1900	11192
South Cnty Lxus At Mssion Vejo	5511	C	949 347-3400	11410
Camden Development Inc	6531	C	949 427-4674	12395
Coldwell Banker Residential (DH)	6531	D	949 837-5700	12408
Coldwell Bnkr Rsdntial Rfrral (DH)	6531	B	949 367-1800	12410
Oracle Corporation	7372	B	626 315-7513	14000
Edwards Theatres Inc	7832	D	949 582-4078	14932
Mission Viejo Country Club	7997	C	949 582-1550	15151
Mission Internal Med Group Inc	8011	D	949 364-3570	15390
Total Vision LLC	8042	C	949 652-7242	15536
Ascent Health Services LLC	8051	D	719 250-0824	15570
Jewish HM For The Aging Ornge	8051	C	949 364-9685	15684
Auxilary of Mssion Hosp Mssion	8062	A	949 364-1400	15919
Mission Hosp Regional Med Ctr (PA)	8062	A	949 364-1400	16098
Foreside Management Company	8082	B	949 966-1933	16392
Rock Canyon Healthcare Inc	8082	C	719 404-1000	16416
Southern Cal Prmnnte Med Group	8099	C	949 376-8619	16617
American Justice Solutions Inc	8299	D	949 369-6210	16850
Vocational Visions	8331	C	949 837-7280	17072
Morningstar Senior MGT LLC	8361	C	949 298-3675	17182
Lake Mission Viejo Association	8641	D	949 770-1313	17354
Young MNS Chrstn Assn Ornge CN	8641	C	949 859-9622	17409
Phg Engineering Services LLC	8711	D	714 283-8288	17610
North American Client Svcs Inc (PA)	8741	C	949 240-2423	18023

MOJAVE, CA - Kern County

	SIC	EMP	PHONE	ENTRY#
Golden Queen Mining Co LLC	1041	C	661 824-4300	253
Pepsi-Cola Metro Btlg Co Inc	2086	C	661 824-2051	1629
PPG Industries Inc	2851	E	661 824-4532	3719
PRC - Desoto International Inc	2891	C	661 824-4532	3776
Calportland Company	3241	C	661 824-2401	4353
Commodity Resource Envmtl Inc	3339	E	661 824-2416	4580
Innovative Coatings Technology Corporation	3479	C	661 824-8101	5324
Scaled Composites LLC	3721	B	661 824-4541	7369
Astrobotic Technology Inc	3761	D	888 488-8455	7641
Masten Space Systems Inc	3761	E	888 488-8455	7647
Xcor Aerospace Inc	3761	C	661 824-4714	7662
United Parcel Service Inc	4215	D	661 824-9391	9015

MONROVIA, CA - Los Angeles County

	SIC	EMP	PHONE	ENTRY#
H C Olsen Cnstr Co Inc	1541	D	626 359-8900	484
Heil Construction Inc	1541	D	626 303-7141	486
Air-Tro Incorporated	1711	D	626 357-3535	731
Cell-Crete Corporation (PA)	1771	D	626 357-3500	1108
Burnett & Son Meat Co Inc	2011	C	626 357-2165	1238
Kruse and Son Inc	2013	E	626 358-4536	1261
Decore-Ative Spc NC LLC (PA)	2431	A	626 254-9191	2303
Vinyl Technology LLC (PA)	2671	C	626 443-5257	2714
Califrnia Nwspapers Ltd Partnr (DH)	2711	B	626 962-8811	2786
Pasadena Newspapers Inc (PA)	2711	C	626 578-6300	2822
Global Compliance Inc	2741	E	626 303-6855	2917
Genzyme Corporation	2834	D	626 471-9922	3408

Mergent email: customerrelations@mergent.com
1310

2025 Southern California
Business Directory and Buyers Guide

(P-0000) Products & Services Section entry number
(PA)=Parent Co (HQ)=Headquarters (DH)=Div Headquarters

	SIC	EMP	PHONE	ENTRY#
3M Company	3069	E	626 358-0136	3907
Jan-Kens Enameling Company Inc	3479	E	626 358-1849	5326
Amada Weld Tech Inc (HQ)	3548	E	626 303-5676	5642
Belco Packaging Systems Inc	3565	E	626 357-9566	5787
Micro/Sys Inc	3571	E	818 244-4600	5863
Aremac Associates Inc	3599	E	626 303-8795	6081
Roncelli Plastics Inc	3599	C	800 250-6516	6222
Silc Technologies Inc	3674	D	626 375-1231	6891
Worldwide Energy and Mfg USA (PA)	3674	D	650 692-7788	6915
Clary Corporation	3679	E	626 359-4486	6984
Foote Axle & Forge LLC	3714	E	323 268-4151	7252
Aerovironment Inc	3721	E	626 357-9983	7324
Aerovironment Inc	3721	E	626 357-9983	7325
Aerovironment Inc	3721	E	626 357-9983	7326
Ducommun Aerostructures Inc	3728	E	626 358-3211	7464
Ducommun Incorporated	3728	E	626 358-3211	7468
Mulgrew Arcft Components Inc	3728	D	626 256-1375	7528
L3harris Technologies Inc	3812	C	626 305-6230	7734
Hoya Holdings Inc	3827	E	626 739-5200	8004
Radcal Corporation	3829	E	626 357-7921	8060
Amada Weld Tech Inc	3841	E	626 303-5676	8088
Chromologic LLC	3841	E	626 381-9974	8131
Konigsberg Instruments Inc	3841	E	626 775-6500	8182
3M Unitek Corporation	3843	B	626 445-7960	8324
Wbt Group LLC	3999	E	323 735-1201	8741
Los Angles Cnty Mtro Trnsp Aut	4111	A	626 471-7855	8774
World Class Distribution Inc	4225	D	909 574-4140	9130
Southern California Edison Co	4911	C	626 303-8480	9638
Ampure Charging Systems Inc (PA)	5013	D	626 415-4000	9810
Nzxt Inc	5045	B	626 385-8272	10021
Linear Industries Ltd (PA)	5085	C	626 303-1130	10443
Home Depot USA Inc	5211	B	626 256-0580	11162
Sage Hospitality Resources LLC	7011	B	626 357-5211	13007
Executive Auto Reconditioning	7542	E	626 416-3322	14708
Ctour Holiday LLC	7999	B	323 261-8811	15197
Childrens Oncology Group	8011	C	626 241-1500	15275
Alakor Healthcare LLC	8062	C	626 408-9800	15903
Advanced Medical Analysis LLC	8071	D	626 301-0126	16303
Curative-Korva LLC	8071	D	424 645-7575	16310
Dream Big Childrens Center	8351	D	626 239-0138	17089
California Cancer Specialists Medical Group Inc.	8621	B	626 775-3200	17294
World Vision International (PA)	8699	C	626 303-8811	17475
California Business Bureau Inc (PA)	8721	C	626 303-1515	17708
Invizyne Technologies Inc (PA)	8731	C	626 415-1488	17799
Eurofins Eaton Analytical LLC (DH)	8734	D	626 386-1100	17916
360 Support Services	8741	D	866 360-6468	17933
Country Villa Service Corp.	8741	C	626 358-4547	17976
Curative Inc.	8741	B	650 713-8928	17978
Financial Tech Sltons Intl Inc	8742	C	818 241-9571	18136

MONTCLAIR, CA - San Bernardino County

	SIC	EMP	PHONE	ENTRY#
Cls Landscape Management Inc	0783	B	909 628-3005	244
Elements Food Group Inc	2052	D	909 983-2011	1487
California Offset Printers Inc (PA)	2752	D	818 291-1100	2976
Bluefield Associates Inc	2844	D	909 476-6027	3634
Cpd Industries	3089	E	909 465-5596	4095
Empire Products Inc.	3433	D	909 399-3355	4810
Mitchell Fabrication	3441	D	909 590-0393	4857
John L Conley Inc.	3448	D	909 627-0981	5080
Ampac Usa Inc.	3589	E	435 291-0961	5997
American Nail Plate Ltg Inc	3645	D	909 982-1807	6437
Omnitrans	4111	C	909 379-7100	8789
JW Fulfilment Lax Inc	4731	D	909 570-9220	9208
Archipelago Lighting Inc	5063	D	909 627-5333	10170
Expo Power Systems Inc.	5063	E	800 506-9884	10183
Cascade Turf LLC	5083	D	909 626-8586	10361
Giant Inland Empire Rv Ctr Inc (PA)	5561	C	909 981-0444	11479
US Skillserve Inc.	8051	A	909 621-4751	15790
Prime Healthcare Services-Mont.	8062	A	909 625-5411	16141
Prime Hlthcare Srvcs-Mntclair.	8062	C	909 625-5411	16143
Prime Hlthcare Srvcs-Mntclair (DH)	8062	C	909 625-5411	16144
Daikin Comfort Tech Dist Inc.	8711	B	909 946-0632	17509

MONTEBELLO, CA - Los Angeles County

	SIC	EMP	PHONE	ENTRY#
Holiday Tree Farms Inc.	0811	C	323 276-1900	251
Yonekyu USA Inc.	2013	D	323 581-4194	1275
Ingenue Inc.	2015	D	323 726-8084	1279
Reyes Coca-Cola Bottling LLC	2086	C	323 278-2600	1645
Unix Packaging LLC (PA)	2086	D	213 627-5050	1656
Arevalo Tortilleria Inc (PA)	2099	D	323 888-1711	1740
All Access Apparel Inc (PA)	2361	C	323 889-4300	2162
Vft Inc.	2392	E	323 728-2280	2226
J & M Richman Corporation	2395	E	800 422-9646	2247

	SIC	EMP	PHONE	ENTRY#
Hardwood Flrg Liquidators Inc (PA)	2426	D	323 201-4200	2289
Big Tree Furniture & Inds Inc (PA)	2511	E	310 894-7500	2420
Atlas Survival Shelters LLC	2514	D	323 727-7084	2464
Gateway Mattress Co Inc.	2515	D	323 725-1923	2484
Sunshine Fpc Inc.	2673	D	323 721-8168	2740
LA Envelope Incorporated.	2677	E	323 838-9300	2751
Northeast Newspapers Inc.	2711	E	213 727-1117	2821
Monarch Litho Inc (PA)	2752	E	323 727-0300	3047
Turner Fiberfill Inc.	2824	E	323 724-7957	3307
Desser Tire & Rubber Co LLC (DH)	3011	E	323 721-4900	3864
Montebello Plastics LLC.	3081	E	323 728-6814	3952
Delamo Manufacturing Inc.	3089	D	323 936-3566	4099
US Polymers Inc (PA)	3089	E	323 728-3023	4267
Howmet Aerospace Inc.	3353	C	323 728-3901	4590
PCI Industries Inc.	3444	E	323 889-6770	5018
Performance Forge Inc.	3462	E	323 722-3460	5146
Troy Sheet Metal Works Inc (PA)	3465	E	323 720-4100	5166
H & L Tooth Company (PA)	3531	D	323 721-5146	5493
Thistle Roller Co Inc.	3555	E	323 685-5322	5667
General Industrial Repair.	3599	E	323 278-0873	6133
Dow-Elco Inc.	3612	E	323 723-1288	6284
Amplifier Technologies Inc (HQ)	3663	E	323 278-0001	6596
Shyft Group Inc.	3711	D	323 276-1933	7193
Craig Manufacturing Company (PA)	3714	D	323 726-7355	7239
Commerce On Demand LLC	3999	D	562 360-4819	8673
PCI Industries Inc.	3999	E	323 889-6770	8711
Star Scrap Metal Company Inc.	4953	D	562 921-5045	9767
Reu Distribution LLC.	5023	A	323 201-4200	9905
Epsilon Electronics Inc (PA)	5064	C	323 722-3333	10217
Desser Tire & Rubber Co LLC.	5088	E	323 837-1497	10490
Orora Packaging Solutions.	5113	C	323 832-2000	10598
2253 Apparel LLC (PA)	5137	D	323 837-9800	10700
Mias Fashion Mfg Co Inc.	5137	B	562 906-1060	10716
Smart Stores Operations LLC.	5141	B	323 725-2985	10774
Katzkin Leather Inc (PA)	5199	C	323 725-1243	11124
Royal Paper Box Co California (PA)	5199	C	323 728-7041	11140
Costco Wholesale Corporation.	5399	C	323 890-1904	11270
Johnstone Supply Inc.	5722	D	323 722-2859	11537
Btg Textiles Inc.	5963	E	323 586-9488	11666
Desser Holding Company LLC (HQ)	6719	E	323 721-4900	12597
Wilbur Curtis Co Inc.	6719	B	800 421-6150	12620
Montebello Unified School Dst.	7349	D	323 887-2140	13395
L&T Staffing Inc.	7361	C	323 727-9056	13538
Leidos Government Services Inc.	7379	C	323 721-6979	14232
Beverly Community Hosp Assn.	8062	B	323 889-2452	15924
Beverly Community Hosp Assn.	8062	B	323 725-1519	15925
Beverly Community Hosp Assn (HQ)	8062	B	323 726-1222	15926
Mexican Amrcn Oprtnty Fndation (PA)	8322	D	323 890-9600	16978
Altura Management Services LLC.	8741	B	323 768-2898	17940

MONTEREY PARK, CA - Los Angeles County

	SIC	EMP	PHONE	ENTRY#
Alltech Industries Inc.	1731	E	323 450-2168	882
Architectural Woodworking Co.	1751	D	626 570-4125	1044
La Colonial Tortilla Pdts Inc.	2099	C	626 289-3647	1800
World Journal La LLC (HQ)	2711	D	323 268-4982	2840
Graphic Color Systems Inc.	2752	D	323 283-3000	3008
Inertech Supply Inc.	3053	D	626 282-2000	3892
Rehrig Pacific Holdings Inc (PA)	3089	D	323 262-5145	4222
West-Bag Inc.	3089	D	323 264-0750	4274
L C Miller Company.	3507	E	323 260-3611	5802
Optic Arts Holdings Inc.	3646	E	213 250-6069	6469
Brighten Corp.	3648	E	626 231-6238	6494
Roco Namo Plate Company.	3993	F	323 725-6812	8627
Carmichael International Svc (DH)	4731	D	213 353-0800	9258
Logisteed America Inc.	4731	D	323 263-8100	9305
San Diego Gas & Electric Co.	4911	C	619 696-2000	9602
Southern California Gas Co.	4924	C	213 244-1200	9656
Southern California Gas Co.	4924	A	213 244-1200	9660
Union Technology Corp.	5065	E	323 266-6871	10295
Oakcroft Associates Inc (PA)	5082	C	323 261-5122	10354
El Primo Foods Inc.	5142	C	626 289-5054	10820
F & A Federal Credit Union.	6061	D	213 268-1226	11795
Care 1st Health Plan (PA)	6321	C	323 889-6638	12059
State Compensation Insur Fund.	6331	C	323 266-5000	12136
Farmers Insurance.	6411	C	626 288-0870	12209
Innovations Building Svcs LLC.	7349	D	323 787-6068	13379
Merchants Building Maint Co.	7349	C	323 881-8902	13392
Guard-Systems Inc.	7381	A	323 881-6715	14306
Chen Dvid MD Dgnstc Med Group.	8011	D	626 288-8029	15272
Garfield Imaging Center Inc.	8011	C	626 572-0912	15313
Ahmc Garfield Medical Ctr LP.	8051	C	626 573-2222	15562
Monterey Park Hospital.	8062	C	626 570-9000	16101
Ahmc Healthcare Inc.	8099	C	626 570-9000	16527

Employee Codes: A=Over 500 employees, B=251-500
C=101-250, D=51-100, E=20-50, F=10-19, G=1-9

2025 Southern California
Business Directory and Buyers Guide

© Mergent Inc. 1-800-342-5647

1311

GEOGRAPHIC

	SIC	EMP	PHONE	ENTRY#
Childrens Law Center Cal (PA)	8111	D	323 980-8700	16655
Apcn-Aco Inc	8741	D	626 288-7988	17945

MONTROSE, CA - Los Angeles County

	SIC	EMP	PHONE	ENTRY#
Vitachrome Graphics Group Inc	2759	E	818 957-0900	3185
Northrop Grumman Systems Corp	3812	D	818 249-5252	7774
Shriners Hspitals For Children	8069	B	213 368-3302	16300

MOORPARK, CA - Ventura County

	SIC	EMP	PHONE	ENTRY#
Ned L Webster Concrete Cnstr	1771	D	805 529-4900	1127
Sterisyn Inc	2834	E	805 991-9694	3510
Insparation Inc	2844	E	805 553-0820	3661
Husky Injction Mlding Systems	3089	D	805 523-9593	4137
Topaz Systems Inc (PA)	3577	E	805 520-8282	5952
Glendee Corp (PA)	3599	E	805 523-2422	6136
Mac M Mc Cully Corporation	3621	E	805 529-0661	6328
Anc Technology Inc	3672	D	805 530-3958	6708
Benchmark Elec Mfg Sltons Mrpa	3672	A	805 532-2800	6711
Laritech Inc	3672	E	805 529-5000	6744
Nea Electronics Inc	3678	E	805 292-4010	6956
Ensign-Bickford Arospc Def Co	3812	E	805 292-4000	7718
Gooch and Housego Cal LLC	3827	D	805 529-3324	8002
Koros USA Inc	3841	E	805 529-0825	8183
Mpo Videotronics Inc (PA)	3861	D	805 499-8513	8435
Conversion Technology Co Inc (PA)	3952	E	805 378-0033	8558
Sercomp LLC (PA)	3955	D	805 299-0020	8567
Picnic Time Inc	3999	D	805 529-7400	8716
Pom Medical LLC	5047	D	805 306-2105	10103
Testequity Inc	5084	D	805 498-9933	10410
Lifetech Resources LLC	5122	D	805 944-1199	10629
Pindler & Pindler Inc (PA)	5131	D	805 531-9090	10670
Kretek International Inc (DH)	5194	D	805 531-8888	11104
Citrus North Venture LLC	7011	D	256 428-2000	12795
Cardservice International Inc (DH)	7389	B		14467
Testequity LLC (HQ)	7629	D	805 498-9933	14734
Firestarter Entertainment LLC	7929	D	805 907-6428	14988

MORENO VALLEY, CA - Riverside County

	SIC	EMP	PHONE	ENTRY#
Life Is Life LLC	2022	E	310 584-7541	1288
Serta Simmons Bedding LLC	2515	E	951 807-8467	2490
Hsb Holdings Inc	3011	E	951 214-6590	3865
Cardinal Glass Industries Inc	3211	C	951 485-9007	4313
Modular Metal Fabricators Inc	3444	C	951 242-3154	5009
Harman Professional Inc	3651	C	951 242-2927	6540
Supreme Truck Bodies Cal Inc	3713	E	800 827-0753	7211
Accuturn Corporation	3812	E	951 656-6621	7684
Access Info Holdings LLC	4226	A	909 459-1417	9132
Capstone Logistics LLC	4789	C	770 414-1929	9360
San Diego Gas & Electric Co	4924	B	951 243-2241	9645
Waste MGT Collectn Recycl Inc	4953	C	951 242-0421	9783
Skechers USA Inc	5139	E	951 242-4307	10738
Home Depot USA Inc	5211	D	951 485-5400	11178
Lowes Home Centers LLC	5211	D	951 656-1859	11223
Akh Company Inc	5531	D	951 924-5356	11438
Certified Tire & Svc Ctrs Inc	5531	E	951 656-6466	11441
Acapulco Restaurants Inc	5812	D	951 653-8809	11547
Visterra Credit Union	6062	C	951 656-4411	11833
Butler America Holdings Inc	7361	C	951 563-0020	13497
Community Health Systems Inc	8011	C	951 571-2300	15285
County of Riverside	8011	A	951 486-4000	15295
County of Riverside	8011	A	951 486-4000	15296
Kaiser Foundation Hospitals	8011	A	951 243-0811	15350
Moreno Valley Snf LLC	8051	C	951 363-5434	15724
RES-Care Inc	8052	C	951 653-1311	15822
Riverside University Health	8062	B	951 486-4000	16163
Think Together	8351	B	951 571-9944	17114

MORRO BAY, CA - San Luis Obispo County

	SIC	EMP	PHONE	ENTRY#
Compass Health Inc	8051	C	805 772-7372	15599

MOUNTAIN PASS, CA - San Bernardino County

	SIC	EMP	PHONE	ENTRY#
Mp Materials Corp	1099	D	702 844-6111	257
Chevron Mining Inc	1221	C	760 856-7625	258
Mp Mine Operations LLC	1481	C	702 277-0848	383

MURRIETA, CA - Riverside County

	SIC	EMP	PHONE	ENTRY#
West Pak Avocado Inc (PA)	0723	C	951 296-5757	122
Temecula Valley Drywall Inc	1742	D	951 600-1742	1033
Classic Installs Inc	1796	D	951 678-9906	1187
JI Design Enterprises Inc	2321	D	714 479-0240	1984
Global Link Sourcing Inc	2671	D	951 698-1977	2708
Gold Prospectors Assn Amer LLC	2721	E	951 699-4749	2858
S C Coatings Corporation	3479	E	951 461-9777	5342

	SIC	EMP	PHONE	ENTRY#
Hexco International	3559	C	951 677-2081	5704
Pacwest Air Filter LLC	3564	E	951 698-2228	5774
Tri-Dim Filter Corporation	3564	E	626 826-5893	5780
Fireblast Global Inc	3569	E	951 277-8319	5821
Cryogenic Industries Inc	3634	C	951 677-2060	6395
American Industrial Manufacturing Services Inc	3694	C	951 677-2060	7087
Nuphoton Technologies Inc	3699	E	951 696-8366	7136
Denso Pdts & Svcs Americas Inc	3714	C	951 698-3379	7245
Ikhana Group LLC	3728	C	951 600-0009	7497
Coherent Aerospace & Defense Inc (HQ)	3812	C	951 926-2994	7708
Romar Innovations Inc	3821	D	951 296-3480	7831
Abbott Vascular Inc	3841	A	408 845-3186	8073
Avenue Medical Equipment Inc	5047	E	949 680-7444	10065
Waterstone Faucets LLC	5074	C	951 304-0520	10327
Home Depot USA Inc	5211	C	951 698-1555	11179
Lowes Home Centers LLC	5211	D	951 461-8916	11222
Carmax Inc	5521	C	951 387-3887	11435
ARC Document Solutions LLC	7334	B	951 445-4480	13310
Prosites Inc	7379	C	888 932-3644	14247
Elite Enfrcment SEC Sltons Inc	7381	C	866 354-8308	14298
Glare Technology Usa Inc	7382	C	909 437-6999	14402
Complete Coach Works	7549	C	800 300-3751	14714
Loma Lnda Univ Med Ctr - Mrret	8011	B	951 672-1010	15381
Oak Grove Inst Foundation Inc (PA)	8011	C	951 677-5599	15409
United Medical Doctors	8011	C	951 566-5229	15494
My Kids Dentist	8021	B	951 600-1062	15522
Michael G Frtnsce Physcl Thrap	8049	C	626 446-7027	15551
Southwest Healthcare Sys Aux	8062	A	800 404-6627	16211
Southwest Healthcare Sys Aux (HQ)	8062	A	951 696-6000	16212
National Mentor Holdings Inc	8361	A	951 677-1453	17183
Chancellor Health Care Inc	8741	A	951 696-5753	17963
SBT Health Inc	8748	C	951 813-2597	18355

NATIONAL CITY, CA - San Diego County

	SIC	EMP	PHONE	ENTRY#
Ehmcke Sheet Metal Corp	1761	D	619 477-6484	1083
Turn Key Scaffold LLC	1799	C	619 642-0880	1230
Family Loompya Corporation	2099	E	619 477-2125	1773
Gmi Inc	2393	C	619 429-4479	2229
B and P Plastics Inc	3089	E	619 477-1893	4058
Gary Manufacturing Inc	3089	E	619 429-4479	4122
Bay City Marine Inc (PA)	3441	E	619 477-3991	4817
Carroll Metal Works Inc	3441	D	619 477-9125	4825
Fabrication Tech Inds Inc	3441	E	619 477-4141	4835
G V Industries Inc	3599	E	619 474-3013	6130
Craft Labor & Support Svcs LLC	3731	C	619 336-9977	7600
Vigor Marine LLC	3731	C	619 474-4352	7612
Walashek Industrial & Mar Inc	3731	C	619 498-1711	7613
Hyperbaric Technologies Inc	3845	D	619 336-2022	8385
Sureride Charter Inc	4142	C	619 336-9200	8865
San Diego Unified Port Dst	4491	C	619 686-6200	9147
Sids Carpet Barn (PA)	5023	E	619 477-7000	9906
Dragon Trade Intl Corp	5064	C	619 816-6062	10215
Tdk-Lambda Americas Inc	5065	C	619 575-4400	10290
Centerline Industrial Inc	5084	E	858 505-0838	10369
Del Mar Holding LLC	5147	A	313 659-7300	10867
Harvest Meat Company Inc	5147	D	619 477-0185	10869
Harvest Meat Company Inc (HQ)	5147	D	619 477-0185	10870
Fornaca Inc (PA)	5531	C	866 308-9461	11444
Motivational Systems Inc (PA)	7336	D	619 474-8246	13333
Nms Management Inc	7349	D	619 425-0440	13396
Oxyheal Health Group Inc	7699	C	619 336-2022	14780
South Bay Sand Blstg Tank Clg	7699	D	619 238-8338	14792
Centro De Slud De La Cmndad De	8011	B	619 662-4118	15269
Imaginative Horizons Inc	8051	C	619 477-1176	15680
Sterling Care Inc	8051	C	619 470-6700	15783
Paradise Valley Hospital (PA)	8062	A	619 470-4100	16125
Centro De Slud De La Cmndad De	8093	B	619 336-2300	16452
National School District	8211	C	619 336-7770	16817
Centro De Salud De La Comuni	8322	B	619 477-0165	16883
St Pauls Episcopal Home Inc	8361	D	619 232-2996	17200
Epsilon Systems Solutions Inc	8611	C	619 474-3252	17282
Hii Fleet Support Group LLC	8711	C	619 474-8820	17545

NEEDLES, CA - San Bernardino County

	SIC	EMP	PHONE	ENTRY#
Pacific Gas and Electric Co	4911	C	760 326-2615	9595
Havasu Landing Casino (PA)	7011	D	760 858-5380	12843
Community Hlthcare Partner Inc	8011	D	760 326-4531	15286

NEW CUYAMA, CA - Santa Barbara County

	SIC	EMP	PHONE	ENTRY#
E & B Ntral Resources MGT Corp	1382	E	661 766-2501	301

NEWBERRY SPRINGS, CA - San Bernardino County

	SIC	EMP	PHONE	ENTRY#
5e Boron Americas LLC	1474	E	442 292-2120	380

	SIC	EMP	PHONE	ENTRY#
Elementis Specialties Inc	2819	D	760 257-9112	3236

NEWBURY PARK, CA - Ventura County

	SIC	EMP	PHONE	ENTRY#
Bnk Petroleum (us) Inc	1382	E	805 484-3613	295
Isec Incorporated	1751	D	805 375-6957	1054
Coast Index Co Inc	2678	D	805 499-6844	2760
Corwin Press Inc	2741	E	805 499-9734	2909
Plz Corp	2813	E	805 498-4531	3221
Amgen Inc	2834	C	805 447-1000	3351
Onyx Pharmaceuticals Inc	2834	A	650 266-0000	3465
Shire	2834	E	805 372-3000	3500
Cosmetic Technologies LLC	2844	D	805 376-9960	3641
JBW Precision Inc	3444	E	805 499-1973	4993
Diamond Ground Products Inc	3548	E	805 498-3837	5646
Nokia of America Corporation	3661	D	818 880-3500	6589
CPI Malibu Division	3663	D	805 383-1829	6604
WV Communications Inc	3663	E	805 376-1820	6672
Skyworks Solutions Inc	3674	E	805 480-4400	6893
Skyworks Solutions Inc	3674	E	805 480-4227	6894
Qorvo California Inc	3679	E	805 480-5050	7043
Xirrus Inc	3823	E	805 262-1600	7886
Amgen Manufacturing Limited	3999	E	787 656-2000	8657
Mv Transportation Inc	4111	C	805 375-5467	8784
Perillo Industries Inc	5065	D	805 498-9838	10278
Carnegie Agency Inc	6411	D	805 445-1470	12190
Carefree Communities Inc	6515	C	805 498-2612	12375
Hawaiian Hotels & Resorts Inc	7011	M	805 480-0052	12845
Compulink Business Systems Inc (PA)	7372	C	805 446-2050	13907
Isolutecom Inc (PA)	7372	E	805 498-6259	13954
Weldlogic Inc	7692	E	805 375-1670	14746
Mary Hlth of Sick Cnvlscent Nr	8051	A	805 498-3644	15718
Designworks/Usa Inc	8711	D	805 499-9590	17511

NEWHALL, CA - Los Angeles County

	SIC	EMP	PHONE	ENTRY#
Berry Petroleum Company LLC	1311	D	661 255-6066	267
Calex Engineering Inc	1794	D	661 254-1866	1170
Green Thumb International Inc	5261	D	661 259-1071	11259
Vons Companies Inc	5411	C	661 259-9214	11286
Hollenbeck Palms	8361	C	323 263-6195	17162

NEWPORT BEACH, CA - Orange County

	SIC	EMP	PHONE	ENTRY#
West Newport Oil Company	1311	E	949 631-1100	282
Jaguar Energy LLC (PA)	1389	E	949 706-7060	338
Milender White Inc	1521	D	303 216-0420	421
William Lyon Homes (HQ)	1521	D	949 833-3600	440
Olen Residential Realty Corp (HQ)	1522	D	949 644-6536	449
Houalla Enterprises Ltd	1542	D	949 515-4350	548
Koll Construction LP	1542	D	949 833-3030	553
McCarthy Bldg Companies Inc	1542	B	949 851-8383	556
McCarthy Bldg Companies Inc	1542	D	949 851-8383	557
A Shoc Beverage LLC	2048	E	949 490-1612	1424
Drywater Inc	2087	E	844 434-0829	1677
Hmr Building Systems LLC	2421	D	951 749-4700	2286
Walden Structures Inc	2452	B	909 389-9100	2405
RSI Home Products Inc	2514	C	949 720-1116	2472
Churm Publishing Inc (PA)	2711	E	714 796-7000	2789
Hanley Wood Media Inc (HQ)	2741	D	202 736-3300	2921
Evolus Inc (PA)	2834	B	949 284-4555	3403
International Vitamin Corporat (PA)	2834	D	949 664-5500	3427
American Vanguard Corporation (PA)	2879	D	949 260-1200	3750
Amvac Chemical Corporation (HQ)	2879	E	323 264-3910	3751
A & A Ready Mixed Concrete Inc (PA)	3273	E	949 253-2800	4425
Associated Ready Mixed Con Inc (PA)	3273	E	949 250-2000	4430
Lebata Inc	3273	D	949 253-2800	4444
Tamco	3449	B	949 552-9714	5101
Hixson Metal Finishing	3471	D	800 900-9798	5267
Jacksam Corporation	3565	D	800 605-3580	5790
Performance Motorsports Inc	3592	B	714 898-9763	6044
Adaptive Digital Systems Inc	3663	E	949 955-3116	6592
Mk Davidson Inc	3669	E	949 698-2963	6688
Conexant Holdings Inc	3674	A	415 983-2706	6813
Mindspeed Technologies LLC (HQ)	3674	E	949 579-3000	6856
Newport Fab LLC	3674	D	949 435-8000	6860
Tower Semicdtr Newport Bch Inc (DH)	3674	A	949 435-8000	6905
Comac America Corporation	3721	E	760 616-9614	7338
Basin Marine Inc	3732	D	949 673-0360	7617
Mmxviii Holdings Inc	3993	E	800 672-3974	8617
CDM Company Inc	3999	E	949 644-2820	8670
Mulechain Inc	4212	D	888 456-8881	8920
US Lines LLC (DH)	4731	D	714 751-3333	9348
Mbit Wireless Inc (PA)	4812	C	949 205-4559	9404
Clean Energy	4924	A	949 437-1000	9644
Clean Energy Fuels Corp (PA)	4932	D	949 437-1000	9675

	SIC	EMP	PHONE	ENTRY#
Bitcentral Inc	5065	D	949 253-9000	10233
Urban Decay Cosmetics LLC	5122	D	949 631-4504	10655
Sterling Motors Ltd	5511	D	949 645-5900	11413
Osf International Inc	5812	D	949 675-8654	11593
Lugano Diamonds & Jewelry Inc (HQ)	5944	D	949 625-7722	11640
Monex Deposit A Cal Ltd Partnr	5944	D	800 444-8317	11642
American Security Bank	6022	D	949 440-5200	11745
Pathward National Association	6141	C	949 756-2600	11860
Pacific Life Global Funding	6153	D	949 219-3011	11870
Electronic Commerce LLC	6159	D	800 770-5520	11877
RMR Financial LLC (DH)	6163	D	408 355-2000	11951
Merrill Lynch Prce Fnner Smith	6211	C	949 467-3760	11982
Pacific Select Distrs Inc	6211	D	949 219-3011	12004
Roth Capital Partners LLC (PA)	6211	D	800 678-9147	12006
Allianz Global Investors of America LP	6282	A	949 219-2200	12014
Allianz Globl Investors US LLC	6282	C	949 219-2638	12015
Pacific Altrntive Asset MGT LL (HQ)	6282	C	949 261-4900	12029
Research Affiliates Capital LP	6282	D	949 325-8700	12032
Research Affiliates MGT LLC	6282	D	949 325-8700	12033
John Hancock Life Insur Co USA	6311	B	949 254-1440	12045
Pacific Asset Holding LLC	6311	C	949 219-3011	12048
Pacific Life & Annuity Company	6311	A	949 219-3011	12049
Lawyers Title Insurance Corp	6361	C	949 223-5575	12154
Title365 Holding Co (HQ)	6361	B	949 475-3752	12157
Edgewood Partners Insur Ctr	6411	B	949 263-0606	12205
FMC Financial Group (PA)	6411	D	949 225-9369	12214
Northwestern Mutl Inv MGT LLC	6411	C	949 759-5555	12240
R Mc Closkey Insurance Agency	6411	C	949 223-8100	12249
Trg Insurance Services	6411	C	949 474-1550	12262
Entrepreneurial Capital Corp.	6512	C	949 809-3900	12291
Olen Commercial Realty Corp.	6512	B	949 644-6536	12307
Sdmv LLC	6512	D	949 516-0088	12317
Park Newport Ltd (PA)	6512	D	949 644-1900	12361
Bixby Land Company	6531	C	949 336-7000	12390
BKM Diablo 227 LLC	6531	D	602 688-6409	12391
Buchanan Street Partners LP	6531	D	949 721-1414	12392
C B Coast Newport Properties	6531	A	949 644-1600	12394
Cbre Globl Value Investors LLC	6531	C	949 725-8500	12400
Citivest Inc	6531	D	949 705-0420	12406
Coldwell Bnkr Rsdntial Rfrral	6531	A	949 673-8700	12409
Core Realty Holdings MGT Inc	6531	D	949 863-1031	12415
Csl Berkshire Operating Co LLC	6531	A	949 333-8580	12416
Greystar Management Svcs LP	6531	A	949 705-0010	12460
Mesa Management Inc	6531	D	949 851-0995	12488
Pacific Monarch Resorts Inc (PA)	6531	D	949 609-2400	12499
Makar Properties LLC (PA)	6552	D	949 255-1100	12572
Absolute Return Portfolio	6722	A	800 800-7646	12623
Pacific Investment MGT Co LLC (DH)	6722	C	949 720-6000	12641
Irvine Eastgate Office II LLC	6798	A	949 720-2000	12687
Pyramid Peak Corporation	6799	D	949 769-8600	12730
True Investments LLC (PA)	6799	E	949 258-9720	12745
Windjmmer Cpitl Invstors III L	6799	A	949 706-9989	12748
Windjmmer Cpitl Invstors IV LP	6799	B	919 706-9989	12749
Hyatt Corporation	7011	B	949 729-1234	12867
Pacific Hotel Management Inc	7011	C	949 608-1091	12959
Uka LLC	7011	B	949 610-8000	13058
Wj Newport LLC	7011	C	949 476-2001	13091
Beauty Barrage LLC	7231	C	949 771-3399	13146
Traffic Control Service Inc	7359	C		13476
Jobot LLC	7301	A	040 688 2000	13530
Technossus LLC	7371	D	949 769-3500	13841
Tenant LLC	7371	D	949 894-4500	13842
Conversionpoint Holdings Inc	7372	D	888 706-6764	13909
Elevated Resources Inc (PA)	7374	C	949 419-6632	14131
Lifescript Inc	7375	C	949 454-0422	14173
Ajilon LLC	7379	A	949 955-0100	14195
Cognizant Trizetto	7379	D	949 719-2200	14207
NC Interactive LLC	7379	D	512 623-8700	14235
Professional Parking	7521	C	949 723-4007	14669
Edwards Theatres Inc (DH)	7832	M	949 640-4600	14934
U Gym LLC (PA)	7991	D	714 668-0911	15068
Balboa Bay Club Inc (HQ)	7997	B	949 645-5000	15118
Big Canyon Country Club	7997	C	949 644-5404	15124
Newport Beach Country Club Inc	7997	C	949 644-9550	15154
John Digiovanni DDS Ms	8011	D	949 640-0202	15335
Newport Beach Surgery Ctr LLC	8011	C	949 631-0988	15404
Five Star Senior Living Inc	8051	D	949 642-8044	15556
Avalon At Newport LLC	8052	C	949 719-4082	15807
Hoag Clinic	8062	A	949 764-1888	16019
Hoag Memorial Hospital Presbt (PA)	8062	A	949 764-4624	16022
Hoag Orthopedic Institute LLC	8062	C	949 515-0708	16023
Akua Behavioral Health Inc (PA)	8069	C	949 777-2283	16282
James R Gldwell Dntl Crmics In (PA)	8072	A	800 854-7256	16343

Employee Codes: A=Over 500 employees, B=251-500
C=101-250, D=51-100, E=20-50, F=10-19, G=1-9

2025 Southern California
Business Directory and Buyers Guide

© Mergent Inc. 1-800-342-5647

1313

	SIC	EMP	PHONE	ENTRY#
National Therapeutic Svcs Inc (PA)	8093	D	866 311-0003	16487
Harbor Health Systems LLC	8099	A	949 273-7020	16565
Irell & Manella LLP	8111	B	949 760-0991	16707
Newmeyer & Dillion LLP (PA)	8111	C	949 854-7000	16751
Stradling Ycca Crlson Ruth A P (PA)	8111	C	949 725-4000	16786
Childrens Hospital Orange Cnty	8351	B	949 631-2062	17084
Young MNS Chrstn Assn Ornge CN	8641	D	949 642-9990	17410
Automobile Club Southern Cal	8699	D	949 476-8880	17455
Bkf Engineers/Ags	8711	D	949 526-8400	17494
Concept Technology Inc (PA)	8711	D	949 854-7047	17504
M Arthur Gensler Jr Assoc Inc	8712	D	949 863-9434	17683
Hagen Streiff Newton & Oshiro Accountants PC	8721	D	949 390-7647	17732
JS Held LLC	8721	D	949 390-7647	17736
Palladium Valley Global Inc	8732	D	949 723-9613	17858
Mig Management Services LLC	8741	D	949 474-5800	18012
Pacific Life Fund Advisors LLC	8741	B	949 260-9000	18029
Twenty4seven Hotels Corp	8741	C	949 734-6400	18072
Greenhouse Agency Inc	8742	C	949 752-7542	18145
Metrostudy Inc	8742	C	714 619-7800	18171
Smart Circle International LLC (PA)	8742	D	949 587-9207	18213
Ymarketing LLC	8742	D	714 545-2550	18245
Your Practice Online LLC (PA)	8742	C	877 388-8569	18247
T-Force Inc (PA)	8748	D	949 208-1527	18361

NEWPORT COAST, CA - Orange County

	SIC	EMP	PHONE	ENTRY#
Krystal Ventures LLC	3911	E	213 507-2215	8455
Inn of Chicago Associates Ltd	7011	C	312 787-3100	12875

NIPOMO, CA - San Luis Obispo County

	SIC	EMP	PHONE	ENTRY#
Santa Maria Tire Inc (PA)	5531	D	805 347-4793	11455

NORCO, CA - Riverside County

	SIC	EMP	PHONE	ENTRY#
Cal-West Nurseries Inc	0782	C	951 270-0667	200
Royal West Drywall Inc	1742	D	951 271-4600	1026
Jeffrey Court Inc	1743	C	951 340-3383	1040
Guy Yocom Construction Inc (PA)	1771	C	951 284-3456	1118
Better Nutritionals LLC	2023	D	310 356-9019	1292
Better Nutritionals LLC	2023	D	310 356-9019	1293
Better Nutritionals LLC (PA)	2023	D	310 356-9019	1295
International E-Z Up Inc (PA)	2394	D	800 742-3363	2240
W B Powell Inc	2431	D	951 270-0095	2333
Legal Vision Group LLC	2752	E	310 945-5550	3033
Paragon Building Products Inc (PA)	3272	E	951 549-1155	4411
Quick Crete Products Corp	3272	C	951 737-6240	4416
Pro Tech Thermal Services	3398	E	951 272-5808	4711
S R Machining	3599	E	951 520-9486	6224
S R Machining-Properties LLC	3599	C	951 520-9486	6225
Avid Idntification Systems Inc (PA)	3674	D	951 371-7505	6805
Range WD 2 LLC	3822	E	951 893-6233	7839
Clima-Tech Inc	7623	D	909 613-5513	14724
City of Norco	8748	D	951 270-5617	18303

NORTH HILLS, CA - Los Angeles County

	SIC	EMP	PHONE	ENTRY#
Robert C Worth Inc	2434	D	661 942-6601	2360
Alpha Aviation Components Inc (PA)	3599	E	818 894-8801	6077
Learjet Inc	3721	E	818 894-8241	7361
Moore Industries-International Inc (PA)	3823	C	818 894-7111	7867
Imperial Toy LLC (PA)	3944	E	818 536-6500	8486
Prn Ambulance LLC	4119	B	818 810-3600	8845
P C A Electronics Inc	5065	E	818 892-0761	10277
Galpin Motors Inc (PA)	5511	E	818 787-3800	11352
New Hrzns Srving Indvdals With (PA)	8243	D	818 894-9301	16844
Penny Lane Centers (PA)	8399	B	818 892-3423	17239

NORTH HOLLYWOOD, CA - Los Angeles County

	SIC	EMP	PHONE	ENTRY#
Circulating Air Inc (PA)	1711	D	818 764-0530	762
M Gaw Inc	1799	D	818 503-7997	1215
Woods Maintenance Services Inc	1799	C	818 764-2515	1236
Mave Enterprises Inc	2064	E	818 767-4533	1509
Groundwork Coffee Roasters LLC	2095	C	818 506-6020	1719
Ahs Trinity Group Inc (PA)	2389	E	818 508-2105	2185
Mtd Kitchen Inc	2431	D	818 764-2254	2315
Artcrafters Cabinets	2434	E	818 752-8960	2338
Kobis Windows & Doors Mfg Inc	2434	E	818 764-6400	2352
Basaw Manufacturing Inc (PA)	2441	E	818 765-6650	2383
Bobrick Washroom Equipment Inc (HQ)	2542	D	818 764-1000	2577
The Bobrick Corporation (PA)	2542	D	818 764-1000	2596
West Publishing Corporation	2731	A	800 747-3161	2900
Graphic Visions Inc	2752	E	818 845-8393	3009
Harman Press Inc	2752	E	818 432-0570	3012
Corporate Impressions La Inc	2759	E	818 761-9295	3132
G-2 Graphic Service Inc	2759	E	818 623-3100	3139
Target Mdia Prtners Intrctive (HQ)	2759	E	323 930-3123	3179

	SIC	EMP	PHONE	ENTRY#
Wes Go Inc	2759	E	818 504-1200	3187
O P I Products Inc (HQ)	2844	B	818 759-8688	3674
Johnson doc Enterprises	3069	E	818 764-1543	3919
Metal Improvement Company LLC	3398	D	818 983-1952	4708
Cal-June Inc (PA)	3429	E	323 877-4164	4761
Orion Ornamental Iron Inc	3429	E	818 752-0688	4785
Lexington Acquisition Inc	3441	C	818 768-5768	4845
Astro Chrome and Polsg Corp	3479	E	818 781-1463	5312
Pdu Lad Corporation (PA)	3479	E	626 442-7711	5335
Allan Aircraft Supply Co LLC	3494	E	818 765-4992	5383
Pacific Wire Products Inc	3496	E	818 755-6400	5408
Artisan House Inc	3499	E	818 767-7476	5441
Utility Refrigerator	3585	E	818 764-6200	5990
Mar Engineering Company	3599	E	818 765-4805	6169
Wilshire Precision Pdts Inc	3599	E	818 765-4571	6277
Arte De Mexico Inc	3646	D	818 753-4510	6452
Thomson Reuters Corporation	3663	E	877 518-2761	6665
Vector Electronics & Tech Inc	3672	E	818 985-8208	6786
Avibank Mfg Inc (DH)	3728	C	818 392-2100	7440
Curtiss-Wright Controls Inc	3728	E	818 503-0998	7458
Klune Industries Inc (DH)	3728	B	818 503-8100	7511
Meggitt Nrth Hollywood Inc (DH)	3728	C	818 765-8160	7525
Americh Corporation (PA)	3842	C	818 982-1711	8252
General Wax Co Inc (PA)	3999	D	818 765-5800	8678
Reel Efx Inc	3999	E	818 762-1710	8719
Ambulnz Health LLC	4119	B	877 311-5555	8809
Messenger Express (PA)	4215	C	213 614-0475	9007
Nbcuniversal LLC	4225	C	310 989-8771	9094
Pilgrim Operations LLC	5043	B	818 478-4500	9969
Electronic Hardware Limited (PA)	5065	E	818 982-6100	10241
Fastener Technology Corp	5085	C	818 764-6467	10438
United Aeronautical Corp	5088	E	818 764-2102	10504
Choice Foodservices Inc	5141	C	818 504-8213	10747
Fluids Manufacturing Inc	5159	C	818 264-4657	10992
Century West LLC	5511	D	818 432-5800	11325
Ngp Motors Inc	5511	C	818 980-9800	11385
Rhi Inc (PA)	5511	D	818 508-3800	11401
City National Bank	6021	C	818 487-1040	11711
Kaiser Foundation Hospitals	6324	C	818 503-7082	12090
Marcus Hotels Inc	7011	C	818 980-8000	12914
Park Management Group LLC	7011	A	404 350-9990	12968
Rio Vista Development Co Inc (PA)	7011	C	818 980-8000	12994
Pierce Brothers (DH)	7261	D	818 763-9121	13157
Western Costume Co (HQ)	7299	E	818 760-0900	13191
Cats USA Inc	7342	D	818 506-1000	13344
Diamond Contract Services Inc	7349	B	818 565-3554	13371
Open Systems Inc	7372	E	317 566-6662	13999
Core Bts Inc	7373	C	818 766-2400	14078
Stark Services	7374	D	818 985-2003	14157
Sada Systems LLC (HQ)	7379	C	818 766-2400	14248
Babylon Security Services Inc	7381	D	818 766-8122	14278
Emergency Technologies Inc	7382	D	818 765-4421	14397
Midway Rent A Car Inc	7515	D	818 985-9770	14652
Airdraulics Inc	7539	E	818 982-1400	14701
Akh Company Inc	7539	C	818 691-1978	14702
Bento Box Entertainment LLC	7812	B	818 333-7700	14808
Herzog & Company	7812	E	818 762-4640	14831
Pilgrim Studios Inc	7812	B	818 728-8800	14845
Rodax Distributors	7812	E	818 765-6400	14852
Universal Studios Company LLC (DH)	7812	A	818 777-1000	14868
Chapmn/Lnard Stdio Eqp Cnada I (PA)	7819	C	323 877-5309	14883
Fusefx LLC	7819	B	818 237-5052	14893
Century Theatres Inc	7833	B	818 508-1943	14949
Authentic Entertainment	7922	D	747 529-8800	14955
IPC Healthcare Inc (DH)	8011	C	888 447-2362	15334
Valley Community Healthcare	8011	B	818 763-8836	15504
Coldwater Care Center LLC	8051	C	818 766-6105	15594
Valley Vsta Nrsing Trnstnal CA	8051	D	818 763-6275	15791
Golden Care Inc	8059	D	818 763-6275	15857
Hillsdale Group LP	8059	C	818 623-2100	15859
Kan-Di-Ki LLC (HQ)	8071	D	818 549-1880	16321
Dubnoff Ctr For Child Dev Edct (PA)	8211	D	818 755-4950	16806
Volunteers of Amer Los Angeles	8322	C	818 769-3617	17033
Volunteers of Amer Los Angeles	8322	C	818 506-0597	17034
Cri-Help Inc (PA)	8361	D	818 985-8323	17144
Miller Kaplan Arase LLP (PA)	8721	C	818 769-2010	17746
North Highland Company LLC	8742	C	818 509-5100	18183

NORTHRIDGE, CA - Los Angeles County

	SIC	EMP	PHONE	ENTRY#
Kindeva Drug Delivery LP	2834	B	818 341-1300	3438
Burns Environmental Svcs Inc	2842	E	800 577-4009	3600
Instrument Bearing Factory USA	3452	E	818 989-5052	5130
Robert H Oliva Inc	3599	E	818 700-1035	6219

Mergent email: customerrelations@mergent.com
1314

2025 Southern California
Business Directory and Buyers Guide

(P-0000) Products & Services Section entry number
(PA)=Parent Co (HQ)=Headquarters (DH)=Div Headquarters

	SIC	EMP	PHONE	ENTRY#
Harman Professional Inc (DH)	3651	B	818 893-8411	6541
Rotating Prcsion McHanisms Inc	3663	E	818 349-9774	6655
Lloyd Design Corporation	3714	D	818 768-6001	7265
Aviation Design Group Inc	3728	E	818 350-1900	7439
Infinity Aerospace Inc (PA)	3728	E	818 998-9811	7500
Vision Aerospace LLC	3728	E	818 700-1035	7589
Alliant Tchsystems Oprtons LLC	3812	B	818 887-8195	7688
Alliant Tchsystems Oprtons LLC	3812	B	818 887-8195	7689
Arete Associates (PA)	3812	C	818 885-2200	7693
Northrop Grmman Innvtion Syste	3812	D	818 887-8100	7749
Northrop Grumman Systems Corp	3812	B	818 887-8110	7771
Chemat Technology Inc	3821	E	818 727-9786	7823
Medtronic Minimed Inc (DH)	3841	A	800 646-4633	8195
Southern California Gas Co	4924	B	818 363-8542	9658
Harman-Kardon Incorporated	5064	B	818 841-4600	10219
Harman International Inds Inc	5065	B	818 893-8411	10246
Smart Stores Operations LLC	5141	B	818 368-6409	10776
Lowes Home Centers LLC	5211	C	818 477-9022	11237
San Fernando Valley Auto LLC	5511	C	818 832-1600	11404
Remax Olson & Associates Inc	6531	E	818 366-3300	12519
Northwest Excavating Inc	7353	D	818 349-5861	13443
Assisted Home Recovery Inc (PA)	7361	C	818 894-8117	13488
Ikano Communications Inc (PA)	7374	D	801 924-0900	14138
Contemporary Services Corp (PA)	7381	B	818 885-5150	14288
World Private Security Inc	7381	C	818 894-1800	14369
Musclebound Inc	7991	B	818 349-0123	15057
Porter Valley Country Club Inc	7997	C	818 360-1071	15158
Progressive Health Care System	8011	D	818 707-9603	15424
Institute For Applied Bhvior A	8049	D	818 341-1933	15547
Dignity Health	8062	A	818 885-8500	15981
Valley Hospital Medical Center Foundation	8062	A	818 885-8500	16252
Tiffany Homecare Inc (PA)	8082	B	818 886-1602	16425
Child and Family Guidance Ctr (PA)	8093	C	818 739-5140	16454
Charles Rver Labs Cell Sltons (HQ)	8099	C	877 310-0717	16547
Village At Northridge	8361	C	818 514-4497	17204
Regal Medical Group Inc (PA)	8621	C	818 654-3400	17305
Automobile Club Southern Cal	8699	A	818 993-1616	17442
Lakeside Systems Inc	8741	A	866 654-3471	18003

NORWALK, CA - Los Angeles County

	SIC	EMP	PHONE	ENTRY#
Doty Bros Equipment Co (HQ)	1623	D	562 864-6566	671
Cargill Meat Solutions Corp	2011	E	562 345-5240	1240
Dianas Mexican Food Pdts Inc (PA)	2099	E	562 926-5802	1764
Golden Specialty Foods LLC	2099	E	562 802-2537	1784
Cabinets 2000 LLC	2434	C	562 868-0909	2341
McDowell Craig Off Systems Inc	2522	C	562 921-4441	2531
Sonoco Products Company	2631	C	562 921-0881	2644
El Clasificado (PA)	2711	E	323 837-4095	2796
Jason Markk Inc (PA)	2842	E	213 687-7060	3607
Lgg Industrial Inc	3053	D	562 802-7782	3895
New Cntury Mtals Southeast Inc	3356	C	562 356-6804	4619
Aerotec Alloys Inc	3363	E	562 809-1378	4642
Argo Spring Mfg Co Inc	3493	D	800 252-2740	5378
Master Research & Mfg Inc	3728	D	562 483-8789	7520
Weber Distribution LLC	4225	D	562 404-9996	9128
Cellco Partnership	4812	D	562 244-8814	9394
Cco Holdings LLC	4841	C	562 239-2761	9528
Aquirecorps Norwalk Auto Auctn	5012	C	562 864-7464	9800
West Central Produce Inc	5148	B	213 629-3600	10925
Lowes Home Centers LLC	5211	C	562 926-0826	11248
Keystone Ford Inc (PA)	5511	C	562 868-0825	11371
Advantage Resourcing Amer Inc	7361	C	562 465-0099	13485
Personnel Plus Inc	7363	C	562 712-5400	13615
County of Los Angeles	7374	D	562 462-2094	14127
Bally Total Fitness Corporation	7991	A	562 484-2900	15044
Life Care Centers America Inc	8051	D	562 921-6624	15695
Coast Plz Dctors Hosp A Cal Lt (DH)	8062	D	562 868-3751	15960
Jwch Institute Inc	8733	C	562 281-0306	17879

NUEVO, CA - Riverside County

	SIC	EMP	PHONE	ENTRY#
Oldcastle Infrastructure Inc	3272	E	951 928-8713	4407

OAK HILLS, CA - San Bernardino County

	SIC	EMP	PHONE	ENTRY#
Double Eagle Trnsp Corp	4213	C	760 956-3770	8947

OAK PARK, CA - Ventura County

	SIC	EMP	PHONE	ENTRY#
Family Ties Home Care LLC	8059	D	818 565-9147	15851

OAK VIEW, CA - Ventura County

	SIC	EMP	PHONE	ENTRY#
Willis Machine Inc	3599	E	805 604-4500	6276

OCEANSIDE, CA - San Diego County

	SIC	EMP	PHONE	ENTRY#
Rancho Del Oro Ldscp Maint Inc	0781	D	760 726-0215	188

	SIC	EMP	PHONE	ENTRY#
Primeco	1721	D	760 967-8278	870
Future Energy Corporation	1742	D	760 477-9700	1009
Royal Westlake Roofing LLC	1761	C	760 967-0827	1094
Fencecorp Inc	1799	D	760 721-2101	1203
Olli Salumeria Americana LLC	2011	D		1246
American Food Ingredients Inc	2034	E	760 967-6287	1364
Dibella Baking Company Inc	2052	D	951 797-4144	1486
Hammond Inc Which Will Do Bus	2085	E	925 381-5392	1597
Linksoul LLC	2211	E	760 231-7069	1883
Solecta Inc (PA)	2295	E	760 630-9643	1961
Kapan - Kent Company Inc	2396	E	760 631-1716	2264
Trinity Woodworks Inc	2431	E	760 639-5351	2332
Solut Inc	2621	E	760 758-7240	2638
Precision Label LLC	2671	E	760 757-7533	2711
Car Sound Exhaust System Inc	2819	C	949 888-1625	3230
Genentech Inc	2834	A	760 231-2440	3405
Gilead Palo Alto Inc	2834	C	760 945-7701	3410
Guckenheimer Enterprises Inc	2834	D	760 414-3659	3415
USP Inc	2844	C	760 842-7700	3694
Hydranautics (DH)	2899	B	760 901-2500	3803
Eldorado Stone LLC (DH)	3272	E	800 925-1491	4387
Westlake Royal Stone LLC	3281	D	800 255-1727	4480
Kainalu Blue Inc	3296	E	760 806-6400	4493
Sound Seal Inc	3296	E	760 806-6400	4495
Campbell Certified Inc	3441	E	760 722-9353	4823
Tru-Duct Inc	3444	E	619 660-3858	5050
Balda HK Plastics Inc	3451	E	760 757-1100	5104
Balda Precision Inc (DH)	3451	D	760 757-1100	5105
Southwest Greene Intl Inc	3469	D	760 639-4960	5213
Steico Industries Inc	3469	C	760 438-8015	5215
Proline Concrete Tools Inc	3559	E	760 758-7240	5718
Standard Filter Corporation (PA)	3564	E	866 443-3615	5777
Kellermyer Bergensons Svcs LLC (PA)	3589	E	760 631-5111	6019
BMw Precision Machining Inc	3599	E	760 439-6813	6097
Landmark Mfg Inc	3599	E	760 941-6626	6164
Nelgo Industries Inc	3599	E	760 433-6434	6191
R & G Precision Machining Inc	3599	E	760 630-8602	6210
Amerillum LLC	3648	D	760 727-7675	6490
Foxfury LLC	3648	E	760 945-4231	6502
HI Tech Electronic Mfg Corp	3672	D	858 657-0908	6735
Te Connectivity Corporation	3678	C	760 757-7500	6960
Onesource Distributors LLC (DH)	3699	E	760 966-4500	7139
Hobie Cat Company (PA)	3732	C	760 758-9100	7621
Willard Marine Inc	3732	D	714 666-2150	7626
Hexagon Mfg Intelligence Inc	3825	D	760 994-1401	7914
Dupaco Inc	3841	E	760 758-4550	8145
Pryor Products	3841	E	760 724-8244	8220
Precision One Medical Inc	3843	D	760 945-7966	8351
Hobie Cat Company II LLC	3949	C	760 758-9100	8521
Salis International Inc	3952	E	303 384-3588	8559
Federal Heath Sign Company LLC	3993	C	760 941-0715	8604
Mv Transportation Inc	4111	B	760 400-0300	8786
Mountain Water Ice Company	4222	E	760 722-7611	9038
Sprint Communications Co LP	4812	C	760 941-4535	9413
Agri Service Inc	4953	E	760 295-6255	9726
Waste Management Cal Inc	4953	C	760 439-2824	9775
Panoramic Doors LLC	5031	C	760 722-1300	9928
Diakont Advanced Tech Inc	5043	E	858 551-5551	9966
Thornton Technology Corp	5088	E	760 471-9969	10503
United States Marine Corps	5000	D	760 725-3664	10606
Chemi-Source Inc	5122	D	760 477-8177	10617
Brixton Inc	5136	D	866 264-4245	10679
Sadie Rose Baking Co	5149	D	760 806-7793	10977
Mollano & Co	5193	C	760 433-9550	11091
Pardee Tree Nursery	5193	D	760 630-5400	11097
Lowes Home Centers LLC	5211	C	760 966-7140	11228
Evkii Inc	5461	E	760 721-5200	11295
Suja Life LLC (PA)	5499	E	855 879-7852	11309
Southern Cal Disc Tire Co Inc	5531	D	760 439-8539	11462
Belching Beaver Brewery	5813	C	760 599-5832	11611
Frontwave Credit Union (PA)	6061	C	760 430-7511	11801
Monterey Financial Svcs Inc (PA)	6141	C	760 639-3500	11856
Sentry Life Insurance Company	6411	C	661 274-4018	12254
Oceans Eleven Casino	7011	B	760 439-6988	12946
Mission Linen Supply	7213	C	760 757-9099	13122
Bergensons Property Svcs Inc	7349	A	760 631-5111	13358
Kimco Facility Services LLC	7349	A	404 487-1165	13383
Go-Staff Inc	7361	C	760 730-8520	13522
Moss & Associates LLC	7389	C	760 385-4535	14553
McKenna Boiler Works Inc	7699	E	323 221-1171	14776
North Cast Srgery Ctr Ltd A CA	8011	D	760 940-0997	15405
North County Health Prj Inc	8011	C	760 757-4566	15406
Marine Corps Community Svcs	8021	C	760 725-5187	15521

GEOGRAPHIC

Employee Codes: A=Over 500 employees, B=251-500
C=101-250, D=51-100, E=20-50, F=10-19, G=1-9

2025 Southern California
Business Directory and Buyers Guide

© Mergent Inc. 1-800-342-5647

1315

	SIC	EMP	PHONE	ENTRY#
Marine Corps United States	8069	A	760 725-1304	16296
Tri-City Medical Center **(PA)**	8099	A	760 724-8411	16622
Marine Corps Community Svcs	8351	C	760 725-2817	17094
E R I T Inc **(PA)**	8361	D	760 433-6024	17147
S L Start and Associates LLC	8361	D	760 414-9411	17193
Villas De Crlsbad Ltd A Cal Lt	8361	D	760 434-7116	17205
YMCA of San Diego County	8641	D	760 754-6042	17381
YMCA of San Diego County	8641	D	760 757-8270	17398
YMCA of San Diego County	8641	C	760 721-8930	17400
Automobile Club Southern Cal	8699	D	760 433-6261	17429
Goodwill Inds San Diego Cnty	8699	D	760 806-7670	17463
Hetherington Engineering **(PA)**	8711	C	760 931-1917	17543
Nitto Denko Technical Corp	8732	D	760 435-7011	17857
Primary Care Assod Med Group I	8741	C	760 724-1033	18034
Veridiam Allied Swiss	8748	D	760 941-1702	18366

OJAI, CA - Ventura County

	SIC	EMP	PHONE	ENTRY#
Ojai Raptor Center	0752	D	805 649-6884	138
Pure Simple Foods LLC	1541	E	805 272-8448	497
Ovis LLC	7011	A	805 646-5511	12955
Ojai Healthidence Opco LLC	8052	D	805 646-8124	15816
Community Memorial Health Sys	8062	C	805 646-1401	15964
Help Unlmted Personnel Svc Inc	8082	A	805 962-4646	16394
Ojai Valley School **(PA)**	8211	D	805 646-1423	16818
Rockblue	8621	D	703 314-0208	17306

ONTARIO, CA - San Bernardino County

	SIC	EMP	PHONE	ENTRY#
Perera Cnstr & Design Inc	1081	E	909 484-6350	256
Calvillo Construction Corp	1521	E	310 985-3911	393
K A R Construction Inc	1521	D	909 988-5054	412
Nhs Western Division Inc	1521	C	909 947-9931	422
Fullmer Construction	1541	C	909 947-9467	481
Maintenance Resource Inc	1541	D	616 406-0004	491
Bomel Construction Co Inc	1542	C	909 923-3319	523
CA Station Management Inc	1623	C	909 245-6251	666
Warren Collins and Assoc Inc **(PA)**	1629	E	909 548-6708	723
Integrated Energy Group LLC	1711	C	605 381-7859	790
Vertex Coatings Inc	1721	D	909 923-5795	874
Communication Tech Svcs LLC	1731	B	508 382-2700	902
Gregg Electric Inc	1731	C	909 983-1794	922
Jeeva Corporation	1731	D	909 238-4073	928
Martinez Steel Corporation	1791	C	909 946-0686	1158
Rynoclad Technologies Inc	1793	C	951 264-3441	1166
Heatherfield Foods Inc	2011	E	877 460-3060	1243
Ventura Foods LLC	2021	E	323 262-9157	1283
Tropicale Foods LLC **(PA)**	2024	E	909 635-1000	1320
Superior Quality Foods Inc	2032	D	909 923-4733	1345
Ajinomoto Foods North Amer Inc **(DH)**	2038	D	909 477-4700	1383
Ajinomoto Foods North Amer Inc	2038	C	909 477-4700	1384
Cardenas Markets LLC	2038	C	909 923-7426	1386
Specialty Brands Incorporated	2038	A	909 477-4851	1401
Windsor Quality Food Company Ltd	2038	A	713 843-5200	1404
Popla International Inc	2045	E	909 923-6899	1415
Ventura Foods LLC	2079	D	714 257-3700	1528
Coca-Cola Company	2086	C	909 975-5200	1614
Five Star Gourmet Foods Inc **(PA)**	2099	C	909 390-0032	1774
Fuji Natural Foods Inc **(HQ)**	2099	D	909 947-1008	1781
Gold Star Foods Inc **(HQ)**	2099	D	909 843-9600	1783
Haliburton International Foods Inc	2099	B	909 428-8520	1787
Lassonde Pappas and Co Inc	2099	E	909 923-4041	1805
Minsley Inc **(PA)**	2099	E	909 458-1100	1816
Passport Food Group LLC	2099	C	909 627-7312	1833
Passport Foods (svc) LLC	2099	C	909 627-7312	1834
Soup Bases Loaded Inc	2099	E	909 230-6890	1854
Nautica Opco LLC	2329	B	909 297-7243	2022
Jomar Table Linens LLC	2392	D	909 390-1444	2211
Pacific Urethanes LLC	2392	C	909 390-8400	2221
Gold Crest Industries Inc	2393	E	909 930-9069	2230
Melmarc Products Inc	2395	C	714 549-2170	2251
Action Embroidery Corp **(PA)**	2399	C	909 983-1359	2270
Artesia Sawdust Products Inc	2421	E	909 947-5983	2285
Elite Stone Group Inc	2434	E	909 629-6988	2347
K & Z Cabinet Co Inc	2434	D	909 947-3567	2351
Dorel Home Furnishings Inc	2511	D	909 390-5705	2422
Leggett & Platt Incorporated	2515	D	909 937-1010	2487
Stress-O-Pedic Mattress Co Inc	2515	D	909 605-2010	2493
Visionary Sleep LLC	2515	D	909 605-2010	2495
Korden Inc	2522	E	909 988-8979	2530
Compatico Inc	2541	E	616 940-1772	2562
Ivars Display **(PA)**	2541	D	909 923-2761	2566
CTA Fixtures Inc	2542	D	909 390-6744	2578
Idx Los Angeles LLC	2542	C	909 212-8333	2582
LLC Walker West	2542	D	800 767-9378	2585

	SIC	EMP	PHONE	ENTRY#
Forbes Industries Div	2599	C	909 923-4559	2613
Crown Paper Converting Inc	2621	E	909 923-5226	2621
New-Indy Containerboard LLC **(DH)**	2621	D	909 296-3400	2631
New-Indy Ontario LLC	2621	C	909 390-1055	2632
Preferred Printing & Packaging Inc	2631	E	909 923-2053	2642
Zapp Packaging Inc	2631	D	909 930-1500	2649
Androp Packaging Inc	2653	E	909 605-8842	2653
Commander Packaging West Inc	2653	E	714 921-9350	2660
Ecko Products Group LLC	2653	E	909 628-5678	2663
PNC Proactive Nthrn Cont LLC	2653	E	909 390-5624	2687
Southland Container Corp	2653	B	909 937-9781	2690
St Worth Container LLC	2653	D	909 390-4550	2691
Fineline Settings LLC	2656	E	845 369-6100	2700
Encorr Sheets LLC	2679	E	626 523-4661	2767
Califrnia Nwspapers Ltd Partnr	2711	B	909 987-6397	2787
Aio Acquisition Inc **(HQ)**	2741	D	800 333-3795	2901
Advanced Color Graphics	2752	D	909 930-1500	2959
Bert-Co Industries Inc	2752	C	323 669-5700	2969
GW Reed Printing Inc	2752	E	909 947-0599	3010
Ultimate Print Source Inc	2752	E	909 947-5292	3093
L A Supply Co	2759	E	949 470-9900	3151
Response Envelope Inc **(PA)**	2759	C	909 923-5855	3169
Linde Inc	2813	E	909 390-0283	3216
Induspac California Inc	2821	E	909 390-4422	3272
Qycell Corporation	2821	E	909 390-6644	3289
Genvivo Inc	2834	E	626 441-6695	3407
Amrep Inc	2842	B	770 422-2071	3597
Diamond Wipes Intl Inc	2844	C	909 230-9888	3647
Advantage Adhesives Inc	2891	E	909 204-4990	3759
Pacer Technology **(HQ)**	2891	C	909 987-0550	3773
Kik Pool Additives Inc	2899	E	909 390-9912	3808
Able Industrial Products Inc **(PA)**	3053	E	909 930-1585	3878
Parco LLC **(DH)**	3053	C	909 947-2200	3896
Kirkhill Inc	3069	D	562 803-1117	3920
KMC Acquisition LLC **(PA)**	3069	E	562 396-0121	3922
Pmr Precision Mfg & Rbr Co Inc	3069	C	909 605-7525	3929
Plastics Research Corporation	3083	D	909 391-9050	3967
Classic Containers Inc	3085	B	909 930-3610	3982
Akra Plastic Products Inc	3089	D	909 930-1999	4039
Armorcast Products Company Inc	3089	E	909 390-1365	4054
Axium Packaging LLC	3089	A	909 969-0766	4056
Bandlock Corporation	3089	D	909 947-7500	4060
Bericap LLC	3089	D	909 390-5518	4065
Bomatic Inc	3089	D	909 947-3900	4072
Dorel Juvenile Group Inc	3089	C	909 390-5705	4108
Inline Plastics Inc	3089	E	909 923-1033	4139
LLC Walker West	3089	C	909 390-4300	4161
Medegen LLC **(DH)**	3089	E	909 390-9080	4164
Medegen Inc	3089	E	909 390-9080	4165
Mission Plastics Inc	3089	C	909 947-7287	4171
Paramount Panels Inc **(PA)**	3089	E	909 947-8008	4192
PRC Composites LLC **(PA)**	3089	D	909 391-2006	4206
Ray Products Company Inc	3089	E	888 776-9014	4218
Star Shield Solutions LLC	3089	D	866 662-4477	4249
Thermodyne International Ltd	3089	C	909 923-9945	4257
Larry Mthvin Installations Inc **(HQ)**	3231	C	909 563-1700	4338
Western States Wholesale Inc	3271	C	909 947-0028	4376
Western States Wholesale Inc **(PA)**	3271	D	909 947-0028	4377
Clark - Pacific Corporation	3272	E	909 823-1433	4383
Southwest Concrete Products	3272	E	909 983-9789	4422
Foundry Service & Supplies Inc	3299	E	909 284-5000	4502
Net Shapes Inc **(PA)**	3324	D	909 947-3231	4568
Metals USA Building Pdts LP	3355	D	800 325-1305	4616
Vsmpo-Tirus US Inc	3356	D	909 230-9020	4624
Superior Essex Inc	3357	C	909 481-4804	4639
California Die Casting Inc	3364	E	909 947-9947	4657
Alumistar Inc	3365	C	562 633-6673	4665
Calidad Inc	3365	E	909 947-3937	4667
Employee Owned PCF Cast Pdts I	3365	C	562 633-6673	4673
Halex Corporation **(DH)**	3423	E	909 629-6219	4740
J L M C Inc	3441	E	909 947-2980	4839
Lightcap Industries Inc	3441	E	909 930-3772	4846
R & I Industries Inc	3441	E	909 923-7747	4863
Watercrest Inc	3443	E	909 390-3944	4933
AMD International Tech LLC	3444	E	909 985-8300	4945
Compumeric Engineering Inc	3444	C	909 605-7666	4971
Metal Engineering Inc	3444	E	626 334-1819	5005
Stell Industries Inc	3448	E	951 369-8777	5088
Alger Precision Machining LLC	3451	C	909 986-4591	5103
Alum-Alloy Co Inc	3463	E	909 986-0410	5152
Walker Spring & Stamping Corp	3469	C	909 390-4300	5221
Danco Anodizing Inc	3471	C	909 923-0562	5254
Inland Powder Coating Corp	3479	C	909 947-1122	5323

2025 Southern California
Business Directory and Buyers Guide

(P-0000) Products & Services Section entry number
(PA)=Parent Co (HQ)=Headquarters (DH)=Div Headquarters

	SIC	EMP	PHONE	ENTRY#
Specialty Coating Systems Inc	3479	D	909 390-8818	5346
James Jones Company	3491	A	909 418-2558	5367
Reliance Worldwide Corporation	3491	D	770 863-4005	5369
Bee Wire & Cable Inc	3496	E	909 923-5800	5400
C M C Steel Fabricators Inc	3496	E	909 899-9993	5401
Rfc Wire Forms Inc	3498	D	909 467-0559	5414
ASC Engineered Solutions LLC	3498	D	909 418-3233	5426
Turbine Repair Services LLC (PA)	3511	E	909 947-2256	5465
Tracy Industries Inc	3519	C	562 692-9034	5470
Konecranes Inc	3536	E	909 930-0108	5523
Crown Equipment Corporation	3537	E	909 923-8357	5527
Balda C Brewer Inc (DH)	3544	D	909 212-0290	5569
Wagner Die Supply Inc (PA)	3544	E	909 947-3044	5603
Broco Inc	3548	E	909 483-3222	5644
Bmci Inc	3549	E	951 361-8000	5652
Wallner Expac Inc (PA)	3549	E	909 481-8800	5657
Amrep Manufacturing Co LLC	3559	B	877 468-9278	5688
C M Automotive Systems Inc (PA)	3563	E	909 869-7912	5756
Future Commodities Intl Inc	3565	E	888 588-2378	5789
Logitech Inc	3577	E	972 947-7100	5931
Gamma Aerospace LLC	3599	E	310 532-4480	6131
Hera Technologies LLC	3599	E	951 751-6191	6140
Tower Industries Inc	3599	C	909 947-2723	6254
Upland Fab Inc	3599	E	909 986-6565	6259
Ledvance LLC	3641	E	909 923-3003	6405
Mag Instrument Inc (PA)	3648	B	909 947-1006	6510
Precise Media Services Inc	3652	E	909 481-3305	6578
Tactical Command Inds Inc (DH)	3669	E	925 219-1097	6695
Celestica Aerospace Tech Corp	3672	C	512 310-7540	6715
Vishay Thin Film LLC	3674	E	909 923-3313	6911
West Coast Chain Mfg Co	3699	E	909 923-7800	7161
New Flyer of America Inc	3711	D	909 456-3566	7187
TCI Engineering Inc	3711	D	909 984-1773	7194
Egr Incorporated (DH)	3714	E	800 757-7067	7251
Thmx Holdings LLC	3714	C	909 390-3944	7297
Maney Aircraft Inc	3728	E	909 390-2500	7517
Otto Instrument Service Inc (PA)	3728	E	909 930-5800	7531
Summit Machine Inc	3728	C	909 923-2744	7568
Tower Mechanical Products Inc	3812	C	714 947-2723	7820
Carl Zeiss Meditec Prod LLC	3827	D	877 644-4657	7997
B Braun Medical Inc	3841	D	909 906-7575	8100
Marlee Manufacturing Inc	3841	E	909 390-3222	8186
Isomedix Operations Inc	3842	D	909 390-9942	8278
Safariland LLC	3842	B	909 923-7300	8298
Ashtel Studios Inc	3844	E	909 434-0911	8363
Aliquantum International Inc	3944	E	909 773-0880	8481
American Fleet & Ret Graphics	3993	E	909 937-7570	8589
Encore Image Inc	3993	E	909 986-4632	8600
Optec Displays Inc	3993	D	866 924-5239	8621
Sign Industries Inc	3993	E	909 930-0303	8632
California Exotic Novlt LLC	3999	D	909 606-1950	8665
Scripto-Tokai Corporation (HQ)	3999	E	909 930-5000	8721
Sun Badge Co	3999	E	909 930-1444	8729
A-1 Delivery Co	4212	D	909 444-1220	8888
C P S Express	4212	C	951 685-1041	8898
CRST Expedited Inc	4213	B	909 563-5606	8941
Dependable Highway Express Inc	4213	C	909 923-0065	8946
Jack Jones Trucking Inc	4213	D	909 456-2500	8957
Kllm Transport Services LLC	4213	D	909 350-9600	8958
Landstar Global Logistics Inc	4213	D	909 266-0096	8960
Las Vegas / LA Express Inc (PA)	4213	D	909 972-3100	8961
Ltl Pros Inc	4213	C	909 350-1600	8963
United Parcel Service Inc	4215	A	000 074 7212	9021
United Parcel Service Inc	4215	C	909 974-7250	9022
Americold Logistics LLC	4222	C	909 937-2200	9034
Americold Logistics LLC	4222	D	909 390-4950	9035
Coastal Pacific Fd Distrs Inc	4225	D	909 947-2066	9054
Neovia Logistics Dist LP	4225	D	909 657-4900	9095
Nordstrom Inc	4225	B	909 390-1040	9096
Osram Sylvania Inc	4225	D	909 923-3003	9097
Quill LLC	4225	B	909 390-0600	9103
Takane USA Inc	4225	C	909 923-5511	9113
Target Corporation	4225	C	909 937-5500	9115
Taylored Fmi LLC	4225	C	909 510-4800	9117
Taylored Services LLC (DH)	4225	C	909 510-4800	9118
Taylored Services Holdings LLC (DH)	4225	C	909 510-4800	9119
United Parcel Service Inc	4512	C	909 906-5700	9170
United Parcel Service Inc	4512	C	909 605-7740	9173
Certified Aviation Svcs LLC (PA)	4581	C	909 605-0380	9194
DSV Solutions LLC	4731	C	909 390-4563	9274
F R T International Inc	4731	D	909 390-4902	9281
Runbuggy Omi Inc	4731	C	888 872-8449	9332
Taylored Svcs Parent Co Inc (PA)	4731	C	909 510-4800	9341
Xpo Logistics Supply Chain Inc	4731	C	909 390-9799	9351
Odw Logistics	4789	D	614 549-5000	9372
Taylored Transload LLC	4789	C	909 510-4800	9376
Verizon New York Inc	4812	D	909 481-7897	9422
Comcast Corporation	4841	D	909 890-0886	9536
Blumenthal Distributing Inc (PA)	5021	C	909 930-2000	9866
Office Master Inc	5021	D	909 392-5678	9878
Premiere Rack Solutions Inc	5021	D	909 605-6300	9881
Norcal Pottery Products Inc	5023	C	909 390-3745	9901
Test-Rite Products Corp (DH)	5023	D	909 605-9899	9910
Oregon PCF Bldg Pdts Maple Inc	5031	D	909 627-4043	9927
Cemex Construction Mtls Inc (DH)	5032	E	909 974-5500	9940
Brainstorm Corporation	5045	C	888 370-8882	9992
Bionime USA Corporation	5047	E	909 781-6969	10069
Discus Dental LLC	5047	C	310 845-8600	10076
R & B Wholesale Distrs Inc (PA)	5064	D	909 230-5400	10224
Maury Microwave Inc (PA)	5065	C	909 987-4715	10266
Vishay Sprague Inc	5065	C	909 923-3313	10296
Heat Transfer Pdts Group LLC	5075	C	909 786-3669	10334
Replanet LLC	5084	A	951 520-1700	10400
Waxies Enterprises LLC	5087	D	909 942-3100	10481
Jcm Engineering Corp	5088	D	909 923-3730	10494
Horizon Hobby LLC	5092	D	909 390-9595	10521
Dennis Foland Inc (PA)	5099	E	909 930-9900	10558
Rosen Electronics LLC	5099	D	951 898-9808	10569
Beauty 21 Cosmetics Inc	5122	C	909 945-2220	10615
Dpi Specialty Foods West Inc	5141	B	909 975-1019	10750
McLane Foodservice Dist Inc	5141	C	909 912-3700	10758
NAFTA Distributors	5141	C	800 956-2382	10761
Vitco Distributors Inc	5141	C	909 355-1300	10816
Fruit Growers Supply Company	5148	D	909 390-0190	10901
Aspire Bakeries LLC	5149	C	909 472-3500	10928
Mondelez Global LLC	5149	C	909 605-0140	10962
Proactive Packg & Display LLC	5199	D	909 390-5624	11137
Lowes Home Centers LLC	5211	D	909 969-9053	11217
Citrus Motors Ontario Inc (PA)	5511	C	909 390-0930	11326
Jeep Chrysler of Ontario	5511	D	909 390-9898	11366
Mark Christopher Chevrolet Inc (PA)	5511	C	909 321-5860	11377
Ontario Automotive	5511	C	909 974-3800	11391
Ramona Auto Services Inc	5531	D	909 986-1785	11454
Ta Operating LLC	5812	C	909 390-7800	11603
City National Bank	6021	D	909 476-7999	11728
American Business Bank	6022	C	909 919-2040	11744
Citizens Business Bank (HQ)	6022	C	909 980-4030	11758
First Mortgage Corporation	6162	B	909 595-1996	11904
Pope Mortgage & Associates Inc	6163	D	909 466-5380	11950
Invapharm Inc (PA)	6221	E	909 757-1818	12012
California Physicians Service	6324	D	909 974-5201	12073
Adminsure Inc	6411	C	909 718-1200	12166
Robert Moreno Insurance Svcs	6411	C	714 578-3318	12250
Sedgwick CMS Holdings Inc	6411	A	909 477-5500	12252
Wells Frgo Insur Svcs Minn Inc	6411	C	909 481-3802	12268
Mills Corporation	6512	C	909 484-8300	12304
Cushman & Wakefield Cal Inc	6531	B	909 483-0077	12425
Cushman & Wakefield Cal Inc	6531	B	909 980-3781	12426
RAD Diversified Reit Inc	6531	D	813 723-7348	12515
Prime Hospitality LLC	7011	D	909 975-5000	12977
SS Heritage Inn Ontario LLC	7011	D	909 937-5000	13034
Unifirst Corporation	7218	C	909 390-8670	13141
Wurms Janitorial Service Inc	7340	D	951 582-0003	13429
Diversity Bus Solutions Inc	7361	C	909 395-0243	13510
Kimco Staffing Services Inc	7361	A	909 390-9881	13532
Redlands Employment Services	7361	B	951 688-0083	13567
Care Stffing Professionals Inc	7363	D	909 906-2060	13595
Workforce Management Group Inc	7363	A	909 718-8915	13636
CU Direct Corporation (PA)	7371	C	833 908-0121	13699
Guard-Systems Inc	7381	A	909 947-5400	14305
Signal 88 LLC	7381	A	714 713-5306	14347
Silvino Nieto	7381	C	909 948-0279	14348
Arvato USA LLC	7389	C	502 356-8063	14453
Merchant of Tennis Inc	7389	A	909 923-3388	14545
Ontario Convention Center Corp	7389	C	909 937-3000	14562
Fox Rent A Car Inc	7514	D	909 635-6390	14645
Automotive Tstg & Dev Svcs Inc (PA)	7549	C	909 390-1100	14713
Whiting Door Mfg Corp	7699	D	909 877-0120	14802
Vantiva Sup Chain Slutions Inc	7819	D	909 974-2016	14913
Kaiser Foundation Hospitals	8011	C	909 724-5000	15346
Inland Chrstn HM Fundation Inc	8051	C	909 395-9322	15681
Ontarioidence Opco LLC	8052	C	909 984-8629	15817
Bio-Med Services Inc	8062	D	909 235-4400	15927
Prime Healthcare Foundation Inc (PA)	8062	C	909 235-4400	16138
Prime Hlthcare Svcs - Pmpa LLC (DH)	8062	C	909 235-4400	16146
Proform Inc	8071	D	707 752-9010	16329

Employee Codes: A=Over 500 employees, B=251-500
C=101-250, D=51-100, E=20-50, F=10-19, G=1-9

2025 Southern California
Business Directory and Buyers Guide

© Mergent Inc. 1-800-342-5647

1317

GEOGRAPHIC

	SIC	EMP	PHONE	ENTRY#
Accentcare Home Hlth Yuma Inc	8082	B	909 605-7000	16353
Kaiser Ontario Surgical Center	8099	D	909 724-5000	16576
In-Roads Creative Programs	8322	B	909 947-9142	16956
West End Yung MNS Christn Assn	8641	C	909 477-2780	17376
HMC Group **(HQ)**	8712	C	909 989-9979	17675
Physician Support Systems Inc **(DH)**	8721	B	717 653-5340	17750
North American Med MGT Cal Inc **(DH)**	8741	C	909 605-8000	18024
Telacu Industries Inc	8741	C	323 721-1655	18065
Aveta Health Solution Inc	8742	C	909 605-8000	18100
Brett Dinovi & Associates LLC	8742	C	609 200-0123	18110

ORANGE, CA - Orange County

	SIC	EMP	PHONE	ENTRY#
Marina Landscape Inc	0782	B	714 939-6600	220
Cirks Construction Inc	1542	D	877 632-6717	529
McCarthy Bldg Companies Inc	1542	D	949 851-8383	558
PR Construction Inc	1542	D	714 637-7848	574
Rick Hamm Construction Inc	1611	D	714 532-0815	643
RJ Noble Company **(PA)**	1611	C	714 637-1550	645
Bernel Inc	1711	C	714 778-6070	749
General Undgrd Fire Prtction I	1711	C	714 632-8646	782
K & S Air Conditioning Inc	1711	C	714 685-0077	792
General Coatings Corporation	1721	D	858 587-1277	862
Sanders & Wohrman Corporation	1721	C	714 919-0446	873
Interior Electric Incorporated	1731	D	714 771-9098	926
Alan Smith Pool Plastering Inc	1742	D	714 628-9494	994
Calderon Drywall Contrs Inc	1742	D	714 696-2977	1002
John Jory Corporation **(PA)**	1742	B	714 279-7901	1013
Martin Integrated Systems	1742	E	714 998-9100	1015
Orange County Thermal Inds Inc **(PA)**	1742	E	714 279-9416	1019
Padilla Construction Company	1742	C	714 685-8500	1022
Cmf Inc	1761	D	714 637-2409	1076
Danny Letner Inc	1761	C	714 633-0030	1077
Jezowski & Markel Contrs Inc	1771	C	714 978-2222	1122
Santa Ana Creek Development Company	1771	D	714 685-3462	1134
Bapko Metal Inc	1791	D	714 639-9380	1150
Rika Corporation	1791	D	949 830-9050	1163
Ggg Demolition Inc **(PA)**	1795	D	714 699-9350	1183
Miller Environmental Inc	1795	C	714 385-0099	1185
West Coast Firestopping Inc	1799	D	714 935-1104	1235
Pacifica Foods LLC	2035	C	951 371-3123	1371
Don Miguel Mexican Foods Inc **(HQ)**	2038	E	714 385-4500	1390
American Bottling Company	2086	E	714 974-8560	1605
Reyes Coca-Cola Bottling LLC	2086	D	714 974-1901	1647
Newport Flavors & Fragrances	2087	E	714 771-2200	1688
Natures Flavors	2099	E	714 744-3700	1823
Orange Woodworks Inc	2431	E	714 997-2600	2321
Westrock Rkt LLC	2653	E	714 978-2895	2695
K & D Graphics	2675	E	714 639-8900	2745
Presentation Folder Inc	2675	E	714 289-7000	2746
American PCF Prtrs College Inc	2752	E	949 250-3212	2960
Fisher Printing Inc **(PA)**	2752	C	714 998-9200	3007
Label Impressions Inc	2759	E	714 634-3466	3152
Solvay America Inc	2819	D	225 361-3376	3249
Solvay Chemicals Inc	2819	C	714 744-5610	3252
Harpers Pharmacy Inc	2834	C	877 778-3773	3418
Ortho-Clinical Diagnostics Inc	2835	E	714 639-2323	3546
BASF Corporation	2869	C	714 921-1430	3728
Cytec Engineered Materials Inc	2899	C	714 630-9400	3796
California Gasket and Rbr Corp **(PA)**	3069	E	714 202-8500	3909
West American Rubber Co LLC **(PA)**	3069	C	714 532-3355	3942
West American Rubber Co LLC	3069	C	714 532-3355	3943
King Plastics Inc	3089	D	714 997-7540	4155
Roto Dynamics Inc	3089	E	714 685-0183	4228
SKB Corporation **(PA)**	3089	B	714 637-1252	4240
Dennis DiGiorgio	3231	E	714 408-7527	4332
Precast Innovations Inc	3272	E	714 921-4060	4413
Omega Products Corp	3299	E	714 935-0900	4504
Opal Service Inc **(PA)**	3299	E	714 935-0900	4505
Pro Detention Inc	3315	D	714 881-3680	4540
Thermal-Vac Technology Inc	3398	E	714 997-2601	4715
Commercial Metal Forming Inc	3443	E	714 532-6321	4912
SA Serving Lines Inc	3444	E	714 848-7529	5032
Allied Mdular Bldg Systems Inc **(PA)**	3448	E	714 516-1188	5074
Anillo Industries LLC	3452	E	714 637-7000	5118
Independent Forge Company	3462	E	714 997-7337	5142
Gel Industries Inc	3463	C	714 639-8191	5155
Quality Aluminum Forge LLC	3463	E	714 639-8191	5158
Quality Aluminum Forge LLC **(HQ)**	3463	E	714 639-8191	5159
Prototype & Short-Run Svcs Inc	3469	E	714 449-9661	5210
Hightower Plating & Mfg Co LLC	3471	E	714 637-9110	5266
Fletcher Coating Co	3479	E	714 637-4763	5320
United Sunshine American Industries	3496	E		5418
Nov Inc	3533	E	714 978-1900	5512

	SIC	EMP	PHONE	ENTRY#
Hightower Metal Products LLC	3544	D	714 637-7000	5583
Kyocera SGS Precision Tls Inc	3545	D	888 848-9266	5614
Premier Filters Inc	3569	E	657 226-0091	5833
Shaxon Industries Inc	3572	D	714 779-1140	5886
Data Aire Inc **(HQ)**	3585	D	800 347-2473	5974
Hyperion Motors LLC	3594	E	714 363-5858	6051
D Mills Grnding Machining Inc	3599	C	951 697-6847	6112
Niedwick Corporation	3599	E	714 771-9999	6193
Rlh Industries Inc	3661	E	714 532-1672	6590
Zettler Components Inc **(PA)**	3669	C	949 831-5000	6699
Fabricated Components Corp	3672	C	714 974-8590	6728
Marcel Electronics Inc	3672	E	714 974-8590	6746
US Sensor Corp	3674	D	714 639-1000	6909
Winchster Intrcnnect Micro LLC	3678	C	714 637-7099	6961
Statek Corporation	3679	C	714 639-7810	7053
Statek Corporation **(HQ)**	3679	C	714 639-7810	7054
APM Manufacturing	3721	C	714 453-0100	7330
Ducommun Aerostructures Inc	3724	C	714 637-4401	7384
Air Cabin Engineering Inc	3728	E	714 637-4111	7419
Arden Engineering Inc	3728	C	714 998-6410	7433
Cleatech LLC	3821	E	714 754-6668	7824
Califrnia Anlytical Instrs Inc	3823	D	714 974-5560	7850
Fieldpiece Instruments Inc **(PA)**	3825	E	714 634-1844	7911
Redline Detection LLC **(PA)**	3829	E	714 579-6961	8061
Fusion Biotec LLC	3841	E	949 264-3437	8155
Dux Industries Inc	3843	D	805 488-1122	8334
Handpiece Parts & Products Inc	3843	E	714 997-4331	8336
Jeneric/Pentron Incorporated **(HQ)**	3843	C	203 265-7397	8339
Kerr Corporation **(HQ)**	3843	D	714 516-7400	8340
Ormco Corporation	3843	D	714 516-7400	8346
Sybron Dental Specialties Inc **(PA)**	3843	C	714 516-7400	8358
John Bishop Design Inc	3993	E	714 744-2300	8610
Metal Art of California Inc **(PA)**	3993	E	714 532-7100	8616
Orange Cnty Trnsp Auth Schlrsh **(PA)**	4111	B	714 636-7433	8791
Orange Cnty Trnsp Auth Schlrsh	4111	A	714 999-1726	8792
Lifestar Response of Alabama	4119	C	800 449-4911	8834
Xpo Logistics Freight Inc	4213	C	714 282-7717	8984
Sfpp LP **(DH)**	4613	C	714 560-4400	9214
Modivcare Solutions LLC	4731	C	714 503-6871	9314
Cellco Partnership	4812	D	951 205-4170	9387
Cellco Partnership	4812	D	714 564-0050	9390
Cco Holdings LLC	4841	C	714 509-5861	9525
SA Recycling LLC **(PA)**	4953	C	714 632-2000	9761
Custom Comfort Mattress Co Inc **(PA)**	5021	D	714 693-6161	9869
M S International Inc **(PA)**	5032	B	714 685-7500	9946
Western Pacific Distrg LLC	5032	C	714 974-6837	9954
Beacon Pacific Inc	5033	C	714 288-1974	9956
American Medical Tech Inc	5047	D	949 553-0359	10060
Gordian Medical Inc	5047	B	714 556-0200	10080
Total Health Environment LLC	5047	C	714 637-1010	10113
County Whl Elc Co Los Angeles	5063	D	714 633-3801	10178
Intellipower Inc	5065	D	714 921-1580	10254
Lonestar Sierra LLC	5085	C	866 575-5680	10444
Frick Paper Company LLC	5113	C	714 787-4900	10592
Amerisourcebergen Drug Corp	5122	C	484 222-9726	10613
Cencora Inc	5122	C	610 727-7000	10616
Bluetriton Brands Inc	5149	C	714 532-6220	10932
Southern Counties LLC **(DH)**	5171	D	714 744-7140	11025
Great Atlantic News LLC	5192	C	770 863-9000	11076
Home Depot USA Inc	5211	C	714 538-9600	11198
Selman Chevrolet Company	5511	C	714 633-3521	11406
Toyota of Orange Inc	5511	C	714 639-6750	11422
Villa Ford Inc	5511	C	714 637-8222	11427
Fahetas LLC **(PA)**	5812	D	949 280-1983	11569
Tavistock Restaurants LLC	5813	C	714 939-8686	11620
Beverages & More Inc	5921	C	714 279-8131	11626
Strata USA Llc	5963	E	888 878-7282	11668
Cashcall Inc	6141	A	949 752-4600	11850
Standard Insurance Company	6311	D	714 634-8200	12051
Alignment Health Plan	6324	D	323 728-7232	12069
Alignment Healthcare Inc **(PA)**	6324	C	844 310-2247	12070
American Reliable Insurance Co	6331	C	714 937-2300	12116
Choic Admini Insur Servi	6411	B	714 542-4200	12195
Conexis Bnfits Admnstrators LP **(HQ)**	6411	C	714 835-5006	12196
Mony Life Insurance Company	6411	D	714 939-6669	12235
Word & Brown Insurance Administrato **(PA)**	6411	B	714 835-5006	12275
Jordache Enterprises Inc	6512	C	714 978-1901	12299
Solari Enterprises Inc	6512	C	714 282-2520	12319
Irvine APT Communities LP	6513	C	714 937-8900	12353
Kisco Senior Living LLC	6513	C	714 997-5355	12356
Absolutely Zero Corporation	6531	B	949 269-3300	12379
Lres Corporation **(PA)**	6531	C	714 520-5737	12482
Realselect Inc	6531	C	661 803-5188	12517

Mergent email: customerrelations@mergent.com
1318

2025 Southern California
Business Directory and Buyers Guide

(P-0000) Products & Services Section entry number
(PA)=Parent Co (HQ)=Headquarters (DH)=Div Headquarters

	SIC	EMP	PHONE	ENTRY#
Roman Cthlic Diocese of Orange	6553	C	714 532-6551	12587
Joshua A Siembieda MD PC	7363	D	714 543-8911	13601
Roth Staffing Companies LP **(PA)**	7363	D	714 939-8600	13619
Volt Management Corp	7363	B	800 654-2624	13632
Ashunya Inc	7371	D	714 385-1900	13659
Maintech Incorporated	7371	C	714 921-8000	13765
Salescatcher LLC	7372	E	714 376-6700	14023
Invision Networking LLC	7379	C	949 309-3441	14226
Tensoriot Inc	7379	D	909 342-2459	14260
United Guard Security Inc	7381	C	714 242-4051	14359
Cirtech Inc	7389	C	714 921-0860	14472
Merical LLC	7389	C	714 685-0977	14547
Merical LLC	7389	C	714 283-9551	14548
Merical LLC	7389	C	714 238-7225	14549
Rgis LLC	7389	C	714 938-0663	14585
Servicing Solutions LLC	7389	D	844 907-6583	14592
Enterprise Rnt--car Los Angles **(DH)**	7514	C	657 221-4400	14644
Guys Patio Inc	7641	E	844 968-7485	14735
Sam Schaffer Inc	7699	E	323 263-7524	14790
Lucky Strike Entertainment LLC	7933	C	248 374-3420	15014
Childrens Healthcare Cal	8011	B	714 997-3000	15274
Gerald J Alexander MD	8011	C	714 634-4567	15314
Pavilion Surgery Center LLC	8011	C	714 744-8850	15419
Scribemd LLC	8011	C	714 543-8911	15449
University California Irvine	8011	C	714 456-6966	15497
University California Irvine	8011	A	714 456-6170	15498
University California Irvine	8011	C	714 456-7890	15502
US Dermatology Medical Management Inc	8011	D	817 962-2157	15503
Access Dental Plan **(PA)**	8021	D	916 922-5000	15514
Premier Dental Holdings Inc **(PA)**	8021	C	714 480-3000	15526
Western Dental Services Inc **(HQ)**	8021	B	714 480-3000	15529
Emeritus Corporation	8051	C	714 639-3590	15633
Orange Hlthcare Wllness Cntre	8051	C	714 633-3568	15728
Pennant Group Inc	8051	F	714 978-2534	15753
Chapman Global Medical Ctr Inc	8062	B	714 633-0011	15952
Childrens Hospital Orange Cnty	8062	A	949 365-2416	15954
Childrens Hospital Orange Cnty **(PA)**	8062	A	714 509-8300	15958
St Joseph Hospital of Orange **(DH)**	8062	A	714 633-9111	16214
St Joseph Hospital of Orange	8062	C	714 771-8037	16216
St Joseph Hospital of Orange	8062	C	714 771-8222	16217
St Joseph Hospital of Orange	8062	C	714 771-8006	16218
University California Irvine	8062	A	714 456-6011	16244
University California Irvine	8062	C	714 456-5558	16245
University California Irvine	8062	C	714 456-8000	16246
Childrens Healthcare Cal **(PA)**	8069	A	714 997-3000	16287
Accel Therapies Inc	8093	D	855 443-3822	16438
Arbormed Inc **(PA)**	8099	C	714 689-1500	16532
Astiva Health Inc	8099	D	858 707-5111	16533
University California Irvine	8221	C	714 456-2332	16837
City Orange Police Assn Inc	8611	C	714 457-5340	17280
Orange Cnty Hlth Auth A Pub AG	8621	B	714 246-8500	17303
Boyle Engineering Corporation	8711	B	949 476-3300	17495
Eichleay Inc	8711	C	562 256-8600	17520
Holmes & Narver Inc **(HQ)**	8711	C	714 567-2400	17549
Architects Orange Inc	8712	C	714 639-9860	17666
Acclara Holdings Group Inc	8721	C	714 571-5000	17700
University California Irvine	8721	C	714 456-6655	17757
American Intgrted Rsources Inc	8741	D	714 921-4100	17941
Cik Power Distributors LLC	8741	D	714 938-0297	17965
Corvel Corporation	8741	C	714 385-8500	17970
Prospect Medical Systems Inc **(HQ)**	8741	C	714 667-8156	18040
Raymond Group **(PA)**	8741	C	714 771-7670	18043
Ralis Services Corp	8742	C	844 347-2647	18199
Aecom Usa Inc	8748	C	714 567-2501	18277
Goldman Data LLC	8748	D	714 283-5889	18314
Patriot Wastewater LLC	8748	D	714 921-4545	18346
California Dept of Pub Hlth	9199	C	714 567-2906	18386

ORCUTT, CA - Santa Barbara County

	SIC	EMP	PHONE	ENTRY#
Den-Mat Corporation **(DH)**	2844	B	805 922-8491	3645

ORO GRANDE, CA - San Bernardino County

	SIC	EMP	PHONE	ENTRY#
Calportland Company	3241	D	760 245-5321	4351

OXNARD, CA - Ventura County

	SIC	EMP	PHONE	ENTRY#
Fresh Venture Farms LLC	0161	D	805 754-4449	10
Iwamoto & Gean Farm	0161	D	805 659-4568	12
San Miguel Produce Inc	0161	B	805 488-0981	13
Etchandy Farms LLC	0171	D	805 983-4700	17
Las Posas Berry Farms LLC	0171	D	805 483-1000	21
Santa Rosa Berry Farms LLC	0171	D	805 981-3060	26
Superior Fruit LLC	0171	C	805 485-2519	27
Marathon Land Inc	0181	C	805 488-3585	60

	SIC	EMP	PHONE	ENTRY#
River Ridge Farms Inc	0181	D	805 647-6880	69
Scarborough Farms Inc	0191	C	805 483-9113	87
Boskovich Farms Inc **(PA)**	0723	C	805 487-2299	104
Mission Produce Inc **(PA)**	0723	D	805 981-3650	115
Ramco Enterprises LP	0723	B	805 486-9328	117
Venco Western Inc	0782	C	805 981-2400	241
Dcor LLC **(PA)**	1382	D	805 535-2000	298
Freeport-Mcmoran Oil & Gas LLC	1382	E	805 567-1601	305
Blois Construction Inc	1623	C	805 485-0011	663
Kaiser Air Conditioning and Sheet Metal Inc	1761	E	805 988-1800	1087
J M Smucker Company	2033	E	805 487-5483	1351
Noushig Inc	2051	E	805 983-2903	1462
Kevita Inc **(HQ)**	2086	D	805 200-2250	1621
McK Enterprises Inc	2099	D	805 483-5292	1815
Sunrise Growers Inc	2099	A	612 619-9545	1858
Scully Sportswear Inc **(PA)**	2386	E	805 483-6339	2182
California Woodworking Inc	2434	E	805 982-9090	2343
E Vasquez Distributors Inc	2448	E	805 487-8458	2387
Little Castle Furniture Co Inc	2512	E	805 278-4646	2450
Casualway Usa LLC	2514	D	805 660-7408	2465
Ergonom Corporation **(PA)**	2599	C	805 981-9978	2611
Ergonom Corporation	2599	D	805 981-9978	2612
New-Indy Oxnard LLC	2621	C	805 986-3881	2633
Procter & Gamble Paper Pdts Co	2676	A	805 485-8871	2748
TI Enterprises LLC	2721	C	805 981-8393	2877
National Graphics LLC	2752	E	805 644-9212	3048
V3 Printing Corporation	2752	D	805 981-2600	3095
Ventura Printing Inc **(PA)**	2752	D	805 981-2600	3098
Safe Publishing Company	2759	D	805 973-1300	3173
Complyright Dist Svcs Inc	2761	E	805 981-0992	3192
Cdti Advanced Materials Inc **(PA)**	2819	E	805 639-9458	3233
Kim Laube & Company Inc	2844	E	805 240-1300	3666
Spatz Corporation	2844	C	805 487-2122	3688
Monsanto Company	2879	E	805 827-2341	3756
B & S Plastics Inc	3089	E	805 981-0262	4057
Cool-Pak LLC	3089	D	805 981-2434	4092
Leading Industry Inc	3089	C	805 385-4100	4159
PC Vaughan Mfg Corp	3089	D	805 278-2555	4193
Pinnpack Capital Holdings LLC	3089	C	805 385-4100	4196
Rakar Incorporated	3089	E	805 487-2721	4215
Santa Barbara Design Studio **(PA)**	3269	D	805 966-3883	4368
Diversified Minerals Inc	3273	E	805 247-1069	4437
Western Saw Manufacturers Inc	3425	D	805 981-0999	4748
Raypak Inc **(DH)**	3433	B	805 278-5300	4814
Millworks Etc Inc	3442	E	805 499-3400	4894
Oxnard Prcsion Fabrication Inc	3444	E	805 985-0447	5012
Advanced Structural Tech Inc	3462	C	805 204-9133	5140
Elite Metal Finishing LLC **(PA)**	3471	C	805 983-4320	5260
Applied Powdercoat Inc	3479	E	805 981-1991	5311
Ets Express LLC **(DH)**	3479	E	805 278-7771	5319
Haas Automation Inc **(PA)**	3541	A	805 278-1800	5545
Acme Cryogenics Inc	3559	E	805 981-4500	5686
Cryogenic Experts Inc	3559	E	805 981-4500	5698
Vortech Engineering Inc	3564	C	805 247-0226	5782
Amiad USA Inc	3589	E	805 988-3323	5995
Amiad USA Inc	3589	E	805 988-3323	5996
Aerotek Inc	3599	A	805 604-3000	6073
Rapid Product Solutions Inc	3599	C	805 485-7234	6215
Scosche Industries Inc	3651	C	805 486-4450	6554
Esco Technologies Inc	3669	D	805 604-3075	6662
Mercury Systems Inc	3672	C	805 388-1345	6749
Mercury Systems Inc	3672	C	805 751-1100	6750
Component Equipment Coinc	3678	F	805 988-8004	6943
Delta Microwave LLC	3679	D	805 751-1100	6992
Harwil Precision Products	3679	E	805 988-6800	7004
Simpliphi Power Inc	3691	E	805 640-6700	7080
Becker Automotive Designs Inc	3711	E	805 487-5227	7170
Granatelli Motor Sports Inc	3714	E	805 486-6644	7258
Pti Technologies Inc **(DH)**	3728	C	805 604-3700	7543
Northrop Grumman Systems Corp	3812	C	805 684-6641	7759
Northrop Grumman Systems Corp	3812	D	805 278-2074	7764
Catalytic Solutions Inc **(HQ)**	3822	E	805 486-4649	7833
Golf Sales West Inc	3949	E	805 988-3363	8518
Illah Sports Inc	3949	E	805 240-7790	8526
Mgr Design International Inc	3999	E	805 981-6400	8701
Durham School Services L P	4151	C	805 483-6076	8873
Tanimura Antle Fresh Foods Inc	4225	B	805 483-2358	9114
Genon Holdings LLC	4911	D	805 984-5215	9586
Bragg Investment Company Inc	5013	E	805 485-2106	9817
American Tooth Industries	5047	D	805 487-9868	10061
Aluminum Precision Pdts Inc	5051	C	805 488-4401	10123
Mws Precision Wire Inds Inc	5051	D	818 991-8553	10145
Ava Enterprises Inc **(PA)**	5064	C	805 988-0192	10214

Employee Codes: A=Over 500 employees, B=251-500
C=101-250, D=51-100, E=20-50, F=10-19, G=1-9

2025 Southern California
Business Directory and Buyers Guide

© Mergent Inc. 1-800-342-5647

1319

	SIC	EMP	PHONE	ENTRY#
Quinn Company	5082	D	805 485-2171	10356
Wiggins Lift Co Inc	5084	D	805 485-7821	10422
Orora Packaging Solutions	5113	E	805 278-5040	10600
Sysco Ventura Inc	5141	B	805 205-7000	10811
McConnells Fine Ice Creams LLC	5143	E	805 963-8813	10832
Boskovich Fresh Cut LLC	5148	C	805 487-2299	10888
Hollandia Oxnard	5148	C	805 886-1272	10907
Ventura County Lemon Coop	5148	D	805 385-3345	10924
Olde Thompson LLC	5149	E	805 983-0388	10968
AG Rx (PA)	5191	D	805 487-0696	11068
Seminis Vegetable Seeds Inc (DH)	5191	A	855 733-3834	11072
Grolink Plant Company Inc (PA)	5193	C	805 984-7958	11089
Pyramid Flowers Inc	5193	C	805 382-8070	11099
Home Depot USA Inc	5211	B	805 983-0653	11157
DCH California Motors Inc	5511	D	805 988-7900	11334
Vista Ford Inc	5511	D	805 983-6511	11428
City National Bank	6021	D	805 981-2700	11724
Caliber Home Loans Inc	6162	D	805 983-0904	11891
State Compensation Insur Fund	6321	D	888 782-8338	12067
Lawyers Title Insurance Corp	6361	A	805 484-2701	12153
AGIA Inc (PA)	6411	C	805 566-9191	12167
Milwood Healthcare Inc	6512	D	626 274-4345	12305
Courtyard Oxnard	7011	D	805 988-3600	12801
Mission Linen Supply	7213	D	805 485-6794	13119
Workrite Uniform Company Inc (DH)	7218	B	805 483-0175	13142
H G Group Inc	7291	D	805 486-6463	13164
Butler America Holdings Inc	7361	C	805 243-0061	13495
Maxim Healthcare Services Inc	7363	A	805 278-4593	13612
Tripod Inc	7363	D	805 585-2273	13627
Volt Management Corp	7363	D	805 560-8658	13634
Taheem Johnson Inc	7379	D	818 835-3785	14259
Autonomous Defense Tech Corp	7382	E	805 616-2030	14384
West Coast Wldg & Piping Inc	7692	D	805 246-5841	14747
Players West Amusements Inc (PA)	7993	E	805 983-1400	15100
Comedy Club Oxnard LLC	7997	D	805 535-5400	15130
Arizona Channel Isla	7999	D	480 788-0755	15193
Cabrillo Crdolgy Med Group Inc	8011	D	805 983-0922	15258
N S C Channel Islands Inc	8011	B	805 485-1908	15398
Covenant Care California LLC	8051	D	805 488-3696	15613
Dignity Health	8062	A	805 988-2500	15978
Inclusive Edcatn Cmnty Prtnr I	8211	B	805 985-4808	16812
Amigo Baby Inc	8322	D	805 901-1237	16869
Child Dev Rsrces of Vntura CNT (PA)	8322	C	805 485-7878	16887
Coalition For Family Harmony	8322	D	805 983-6014	16895
Mixtec/Ndgena Cmnty Orgnzing P	8322	D	805 483-1166	16979
Seneca Family of Agencies	8322	C	805 278-0355	17010
Saticoy Lemon Association	8611	D	805 654-6543	17287
Oxnard Police Department	8641	B	805 385-8300	17358
Rescue Mission Alliance (PA)	8699	C	805 487-1234	17469
Jsl Technologies Inc	8711	B	805 985-7700	17567
Systems Application & Tech Inc	8711	D	805 487-7373	17640
Seminis Inc (DH)	8731	B	805 485-7317	17821
Behavioral Science Technology Inc (PA)	8748	C	805 646-0166	18289

PACIFIC PALISADES, CA - Los Angeles County

	SIC	EMP	PHONE	ENTRY#
Chilicon Power LLC (PA)	3825	E	310 800-1396	7903
Many LLC	7311	D	310 399-1515	13223
Snap Inc	7372	D	310 745-0632	14032
Fusionzone Automotive Inc	7379	D	888 576-1136	14219
Bel-Air Bay Club Ltd	7997	C	310 230-4700	15121
Riviera Golf & Tennis Inc	7997	C	310 454-6591	15164
Riviera Country Club Inc	7999	D	310 454-6591	15217

PACOIMA, CA - Los Angeles County

	SIC	EMP	PHONE	ENTRY#
Vita Juice Corporation	2033	D	818 899-1195	1360
Natural Balance Pet Foods LLC	2048	D	800 829-4493	1431
American Fruits & Flavors LLC (HQ)	2087	B	818 899-9574	1660
N K Cabinets Inc	2434	E	818 897-7909	2356
Western States Packaging Inc	2673	E	818 686-6045	2742
Cosmetic Group Usa Inc	2844	C	818 767-2889	3640
Flamemaster Corporation	2891	E	818 890-1401	3766
Moc Products Company Inc (PA)	2899	D	818 794-3500	3815
Molding Corporation America	3089	E	818 890-7877	4175
RMR Products Inc (PA)	3272	D	818 890-0896	4419
D & M Steel Inc	3441	E	818 896-2070	4831
SDS Industries Inc	3442	C	818 492-3500	4902
American Range Corporation	3444	D	818 897-0808	4947
Mayoni Enterprises	3444	D	818 896-0026	5003
Sunland Aerospace Fasteners	3452	E	818 485-8929	5137
APT Metal Fabricators Inc	3469	E	818 896-7478	5172
Hanmar LLC (PA)	3469	E	818 890-2802	5190
Metalite Manufacturing Company	3469	E	818 890-2802	5201
Ultramet	3471	D	818 899-0236	5303

	SIC	EMP	PHONE	ENTRY#
American Etching & Mfg	3479	E	323 875-3910	5309
Kitch Engineering Inc	3599	E	818 897-7133	6162
JKL Components Corporation	3647	E	818 896-0019	6484
Mole-Richardson Co Ltd (PA)	3648	D	323 851-0111	6511
Dw and Bb Consulting Inc	3769	D	818 896-9899	7669
Nu-Hope Laboratories Inc	3841	D	818 899-7711	8209
Twin Peak Industries Inc	3949	E	800 259-5906	8550
California Signs Inc	3993	E	818 899-1888	8592
Wetzel & Sons Mvg & Stor Inc	4212	D	818 890-0992	8930
Looney Bins Inc (HQ)	4953	D	818 485-8200	9748
Energy Club Inc	5145	D		10845
Lowes Home Centers LLC	5211	D	818 686-4300	11241
Golden West Security	7381	C	818 897-5965	14303
Hillview Mental Health Ctr Inc	8093	D	818 896-1161	16479
Hathawy-Sycmres Child Fmly Svc	8322	C	626 395-7100	16948
Volunteers of Amer Los Angeles	8322	D	818 834-9097	17028
Volunteers of Amer Los Angeles	8322	D	818 834-8957	17036

PALA, CA - San Diego County

	SIC	EMP	PHONE	ENTRY#
Pala Casino Spa & Resort	7011	A	760 510-5100	12965

PALM DESERT, CA - Riverside County

	SIC	EMP	PHONE	ENTRY#
Platinum Landscape Inc	0781	C	760 200-3673	186
Breeze Air Conditioning LLC	1711	D	760 346-0855	752
Dave Williams Plbg & Elec Inc	1711	C	760 296-1397	771
United Brothers Concrete Inc	1771	C	760 346-1013	1140
La Quinta Brewing Company LLC	2082	D	760 200-2597	1548
Clarios LLC	2531	E	760 200-5225	2538
Associated Desert Shoppers Inc (DH)	2741	D	760 346-1729	2904
Daniels Inc (PA)	2741	E	801 621-3355	2911
Farley Paving Stone Co Inc	3272	C	760 773-3960	4389
Pd Group	3993	E	760 674-3028	8623
Gary Cardiff Enterprises Inc	4119	D	760 568-1403	8828
Southern California Gas Co	4924	C	714 262-0091	9646
Coachlla Vly Wtr Dst Pub Fclti	4941	C	760 398-2651	9685
Coachlla Vly Wtr Dst Pub Fclti (PA)	4941	C	760 398-2651	9686
Connecticut Ctr Plastic Surg	5995	C	760 779-9595	11672
Morgan Stnley Smith Barney LLC	6022	C	760 568-3500	11772
Webb Del California Corp (DH)	6552	B	760 772-5300	12582
Destination Residences LLC	7011	A	760 346-4647	12807
Residence Inn By Marriott LLC	7011	A	760 776-0050	12992
Universal Services America LP	7381	A	760 200-2865	14362
Resort Parking Services Inc	7521	C	760 328-4041	14670
Friends of Cultural Center Inc	7922	D	760 346-6505	14960
Desert Willow Golf Resort Inc	7992	D	760 346-0015	15076
Bighorn Golf Club Charities	7997	D	760 773-2468	15125
Lakes Country Club Assn Inc (PA)	7997	C	760 568-4321	15145
Mountain Vista Golf Course At	7999	D	760 200-2200	15215
Eisenhower Medical Center	8011	C	760 836-0232	15303
Radnet Management III Inc	8011	D	760 346-1130	15431
Mariner Health Care Inc	8051	C	760 776-7700	15709
Pacs Group Inc	8051	C	760 341-0261	15742
Watermark Rtrment Cmmnties Inc	8051	D	760 346-5420	15799
Able Health Group LLC	8099	D	760 610-2093	16524
Desertarc	8322	B	760 346-1611	16933
Living Desert	8422	C	760 346-5694	17270
Leighton Group Inc	8621	D	760 776-4192	17299
Palm Desert Greens Association	8641	D	760 346-8005	17359
Sun City Palm Dsert Cmnty Assn (PA)	8641	D	760 200-2100	17368

PALM SPRINGS, CA - Riverside County

	SIC	EMP	PHONE	ENTRY#
S S W Mechanical Cnstr Inc	1711	C	760 327-1481	833
Western Pacific Roofing Corp	1761	C	661 273-1336	1100
Super Struct Bldg Systems Inc	2522	E	760 322-2522	2532
Desert Sun Publishing Co (DH)	2711	C	760 322-8889	2794
Adams Trade Press LP (PA)	2721	E	760 318-7000	2841
Desert Publications Inc (PA)	2721	E	760 325-2333	2853
Matches Inc	2824	B	760 899-1919	3305
Iqd Frequency Products Inc	3679	E	408 250-1435	7012
Carefusion 207 Inc	3841	B	760 778-7200	8120
Carefusion Corporation	3841	E	760 778-7200	8123
Joe Blasco Enterprises Inc	3999	E	323 467-4949	8688
American Medical Response Inc	4119	C	760 883-5000	8811
United Parcel Service Inc	4215	D	760 325-1762	9023
Desert Water Agency Fing Corp	4941	D	760 323-4971	9690
Palm Springs Disposal Services	4953	D	760 327-1351	9754
Lowes Home Centers LLC	5211	C	760 866-1901	11221
Loandepotcom LLC	6162	A	760 797-6000	11920
Agua Clnte Band Chilla Indians	7011	A	800 854-1279	12758
Colony Palms Hotel LLC	7011	D	760 969-1800	12797
Diamond Resorts Intl Inc	7011	A	702 823-7000	12808
Diamond Resorts LLC	7011	D	760 866-1800	12809
Hyatt Hotels Management Corp	7011	C	760 322-9000	12872

	SIC	EMP	PHONE	ENTRY#
R P S Resort Corp.	7011	A	760 327-8311	12981
Rbd Hotel Palm Springs LLC.	7011	C	760 322-9000	12986
Remington Hotel Corporation.	7011	C	760 322-6000	12988
Smoke Tree Inc.	7011	D	760 327-1221	13027
Spa Resort Casino.	7011	A	760 883-1034	13030
Spa Resort Casino (PA).	7011	D	888 999-1995	13031
Walters Family Partnership.	7011	C	760 320-6868	13070
OLinn Security Incorporated.	7381	C	760 320-5303	13326
Best Signs Inc (PA).	7389	E	760 320-3042	14463
Metropolitan Theatres Corp.	7832	D	760 323-3221	14942
Mount San Jcnto Winter Pk Corp.	7999	D	760 325-1449	15214
Desert Medical Group Inc (PA).	8011	C	760 320-8814	15299
Ensign Palm I LLC.	8051	C	760 323-2638	15644
Desert Regional Med Ctr Inc (HQ).	8062	A	760 323-6511	15974
Eisenhower Medical Center.	8062	A	760 325-6621	15987
Palm Springs Art Museum Inc.	8412	D	760 322-4800	17260
Agua Clnte Band Chilla Indians (PA).	8699	B	760 699-6800	17425
Mariner Health Care Inc.	8741	C	760 327-8541	18010
Kings Garden LLC.	8742	C	760 275-4969	18156
Smg Holdings LLC.	8742	D	760 325-6611	18214

PALMDALE, CA - Los Angeles County

	SIC	EMP	PHONE	ENTRY#
Csi Electrical Contractors Inc.	1731	B	661 723-0869	906
D & J Printing Inc.	2752	D	661 265-1995	2997
Ultramar Inc.	2911	D	661 944-2496	3834
Aero Bending Company.	3444	D	661 948-2363	4941
Lusk Quality Machine Products.	3599	E	661 272-0630	6166
Sun Valley Ltg Standards Inc.	3646	D	661 233-2000	6475
US Pole Company Inc (PA).	3646	D	800 877-6537	6478
Vision Engrg Met Stamping Inc.	3646	E	661 575-0933	6479
Northrop Grumman Systems Corp.	3721	B	661 272-7000	7365
Lockheed Martin Corporation.	3812	A	661 572-7428	7739
Northrop Grumman Corporation.	3812	E	661 272-7334	7752
Northrop Grumman Systems Corp.	3812	E	661 540-0446	7776
Battle-Tested Strategies LLC.	4215	D	661 802-6509	8999
Palmdale Water District (PA).	4941	D	661 947-4111	9710
Waste Management Cal Inc.	4953	C	661 947-7197	9777
Murcal Inc.	5063	E	661 272-4700	10197
Smart Stores Operations LLC.	5141	B	661 722-6210	10781
Lowes Home Centers LLC.	5211	C	661 267-9888	11246
Golden Empire Mortgage Inc.	6162	B	661 949-3388	11909
Thi Holdings (delaware) Inc.	6411	B	661 266-7423	12258
Eugene Burger Management Corp.	6513	D	661 273-4447	12340
Delta Scientific Corporation (PA).	7382	C	661 575-1100	14391
Xi Enterprise Inc.	7991	D	661 266-3200	15070
Antelope Vly Cntry CLB Imprv.	7997	C	661 947-3142	15116
Rockin Jump Holdings LLC.	7999	B	661 233-9907	15218
Lancaster Hospital Corporation.	8062	A	661 948-4781	16072
Tarzana Treatment Centers Inc.	8093	D	818 654-3815	16507
Chapman University.	8221	C	661 267-2001	16832
Child Care Resource Center Inc.	8322	C	661 723-3246	16886
People Creating Success Inc.	8322	D	661 225-9700	16994
Kinkisharyo International.	8748	C	661 265-1647	18329

PALOS VERDES ESTATES, CA - Los Angeles County

	SIC	EMP	PHONE	ENTRY#
Douglas Furniture of California LLC.	2514	A	310 749-0003	2466
Grosvenor Inv MGT US Inc.	6411	D	310 265-0297	12216
Sqa Services Inc.	8742	B	800 333-6180	18219

PALOS VERDES PENINSU, CA - Los Angeles County

	SIC	EMP	PHONE	ENTRY#
Palos Verdes Golf Club.	5813	D	310 375-2759	11617
County of Los Angeles.	8062	C	310 222-2401	15970

PANORAMA CITY, CA - Los Angeles County

	SIC	EMP	PHONE	ENTRY#
Superior Awning Inc.	2394	E	818 780-7200	2243
Raspadoxpress.	2741	D	818 892-6969	2939
Puretek Corporation.	2834	C	818 361-3949	3486
Spec Engineering Company Inc.	3599	E	818 780-3045	6243
D X Communications.	3663	E	323 256-3000	6606
Southern Cal Prmnnte Med Group.	6324	A	800 272-3500	12111
American Protection Group Inc (PA).	7381	C	818 279-2433	14273
Kaiser Foundation Hospitals.	8011	C	818 375-4023	15351
Kaiser Foundation Hospitals.	8011	A	818 375-2000	15354
Ensign Group Inc.	8051	A	818 893-6385	15639
Deanco Healthcare LLC.	8062	A	818 787-2222	15973

PARAMOUNT, CA - Los Angeles County

	SIC	EMP	PHONE	ENTRY#
Drillmec Inc.	1382	D	281 885-0777	299
Total-Western Inc (HQ).	1389	E	562 220-1450	365
South Coast Piering Inc.	1542	D	800 922-2488	588
Reliable Energy Management Inc.	1711	D	562 984-5511	829
Advanced Industrial Svcs Inc.	1721	D	562 940-8305	858
MB Herzog Electric Inc.	1731	C	562 531-2002	938

	SIC	EMP	PHONE	ENTRY#
Ariza Cheese Co Inc.	2022	E	562 630-4144	1284
Ariza Global Foods Inc.	2022	E	562 630-4144	1285
Paramount Dairy Inc.	2026	C	562 361-1800	1334
Namar Foods.	2034	E	562 531-2744	1366
Jayone Foods Inc.	2099	E	562 633-7400	1794
Jimenes Food Inc.	2099	E	562 602-2505	1795
Marukan Vinegar U S A Inc.	2099	E	562 630-6060	1813
Tattooed Chef Inc (PA).	2099	E	562 602-0822	1860
Drees Wood Products Inc.	2434	D	562 633-7337	2346
Graphic Trends Incorporated.	2759	E	562 531-2339	3140
Hoffman Plastic Compounds Inc.	2821	D	323 636-3346	3268
LMC Enterprises (PA).	2842	D	562 602-2116	3610
Kum Kang Trading USA Inc.	2844	E	562 531-6111	3667
Paramount Petroleum Corp (DH).	2911	C	562 531-2060	3828
R & S Processing Co Inc.	3069	D	562 531-0738	3932
Fenico Precision Castings Inc.	3369	D	562 634-5000	4688
Aerocraft Heat Treating Co Inc.	3398	C	562 674-2400	4695
Avantus Aerospace Inc.	3429	E	562 633-6626	4756
California Screw Products Corp.	3429	E	562 633-6626	4762
Top Line Mfg Inc.	3429	E	562 633-0605	4791
Jeffrey Fabrication Ltd.	3444	E	562 634-3113	4994
Paramount Metal & Supply Inc.	3446	E	562 634-8180	5070
Mattco Forge Inc.	3462	E	562 634-8635	5144
Press Forge Company.	3462	D	562 531-4962	5148
Vi-Star Gear Co Inc.	3462	E	323 774-3750	5151
Carlton Forge Works LLC.	3463	B	562 633-1131	5153
Weber Metals Inc (HQ).	3463	E	562 602-0260	5162
Anaplex Corporation.	3471	E	714 522-4481	5232
Denmac Industries Inc.	3479	E	562 634-2714	5317
George Jue Mfg Co Inc.	3546	C	562 634-8181	5635
Golden State Engineering Inc.	3549	C	562 634-3125	5654
Excellon Acquisition LLC (HQ).	3559	E	310 668-7700	5701
Zamboni Company Usa Inc.	3559	E	562 633-0751	5725
J and K Manufacturing Inc.	3599	E	562 630-8417	6149
Ramp Engineering Inc.	3599	E	562 531-8030	6214
Trepanning Specialities Inc.	3599	E	562 633-8110	6255
Amsco US Inc.	3679	C	562 630-0333	6966
New Century Industries Inc.	3714	E	562 634-9551	7276
Mv Transportation Inc.	4111	D	562 259-9911	8782
Durham School Services L P.	4151	C	562 408-1206	8870
Cnet Express.	4212	C	949 357-5475	8902
Contractors Cargo Company (PA).	4213	D	310 609-1957	8938
Total Intermodal Services Inc (PA).	4491	C	562 427-6300	9149
Calmet Inc (PA).	4953	C	323 721-8120	9737
Staub Metals LLC.	5051	D	562 602-2200	10157
Transtar Metals Corp.	5051	B	562 630-1400	10163
Vaughans Industrial Repair Inc.	5084	C	562 633-2660	10415
Home Depot USA Inc.	5211	C	562 272-8055	11160
Blue Ribbon Draperies Inc.	5713	C	562 425-4637	11521
CCC Property Holdings LLC.	6719	C	310 609-1957	12596
Braun Linen Service (PA).	7213	C	909 623-2678	13115
Modern Dev Co A Ltd Partnr.	7389	D	949 646-6400	14552
Kindred Healthcare LLC.	8062	C	562 531-3110	16062

PASADENA, CA - Los Angeles County

	SIC	EMP	PHONE	ENTRY#
Exeter Packers Inc.	0174	C	626 993-6245	43
Boswell Properties Inc.	0722	B	626 583-3000	102
Dpr Construction A Gen Partnr.	1542	C	626 463-1265	535
Acco Engineered Systems Inc (PA).	1711	A	818 244-6571	729
AGS Usa LLC.	2005	C	323 688-2200	2057
Max Leon Inc (PA).	2339	D	626 797-6886	2120
Cisco Bros Corp (PA).	2512	C	323 778-8612	2442
Roborcon Construction.	2591	E	626 578-1936	2606
Avery Dennison Corporation.	2672	C	626 304-2000	2715
Licher Direct Mail Inc.	2752	E	626 795-3333	3035
Typecraft Inc.	2752	E	626 795-8093	3092
Arrowhead Pharmaceuticals Inc (PA).	2834	C	626 304-3400	3361
Xencor Inc.	2834	B	626 305-5900	3524
Evolution Design Lab Inc.	3144	E	626 960-8388	4284
Hamilton Metalcraft Inc.	3444	E	626 795-4811	4991
Fvo Solutions Inc.	3479	D	626 449-0218	5321
Honeybee Robotics LLC.	3569	D	510 207-4555	5822
American Reliance Inc.	3571	E	626 443-6818	5840
Caelux Corporation.	3674	E	626 502-7033	6811
Byd Motors LLC (DH).	3714	E	213 748-3980	7232
Coast Autonomous Inc (PA).	3714	E	626 838-2469	7238
Advanced Mtls Joining Corp (PA).	3728	E	626 449-2696	7407
Atk Space Systems LLC.	3812	E	626 351-0205	7703
Rogerson Kratos.	3812	D	626 449-3090	7805
Gmto Corporation.	3827	D	626 204-0500	8001
Arts Elegance Inc.	3911	E	626 793-4794	8452
Call-The-Car.	4119	C	855 282-6968	8816
Fresgo LLC.	4212	D	626 389-3500	8906

Employee Codes: A=Over 500 employees, B=251-500
C=101-250, D=51-100, E=20-50, F=10-19, G=1-9

2025 Southern California
Business Directory and Buyers Guide

© Mergent Inc. 1-800-342-5647

1321

	SIC	EMP	PHONE	ENTRY#
United Couriers Inc (DH)	4512	C	213 383-3611	9169
Spokeo Inc	4813	C	877 913-3088	9458
Multicultural Rdo Brdcstg Inc	4832	C	626 844-8882	9484
American Multimedia TV USA	4833	D	626 466-1038	9492
Blue Chip Stamps Inc	5051	A	626 585-6700	10125
Curiosity Ink Media LLC	5085	D	561 287-5776	10432
Deliverr Inc	5141	B	213 534-8686	10749
Mhh Holdings Inc	5149	C	626 744-9370	10959
Pasta Piccinini Inc	5149	E	626 798-0841	10969
George L Throop Co	5251	E	626 796-0285	11258
Advantage Ford Lincoln Mercury	5511	D	626 305-9188	11312
Idealab (HQ)	5511	D	626 356-3654	11362
Dine Brands Global Inc (PA)	5812	B	818 240-6055	11567
CIT Bank NA (HQ)	6021	C	626 859-5400	11709
City National Bank	6021	C	626 432-7100	11715
Northern Trust of California (inc)	6021	B		11738
Community Bank	6022	B	626 577-1700	11759
East West Bancorp Inc (PA)	6022	B	626 768-6000	11761
East West Bank (HQ)	6022	B	626 768-6000	11762
Onewest Bank Group LLC	6035	A	626 535-4870	11786
Firefighters First Credit Un (PA)	6061	C	323 254-1700	11798
First Financial Federal Cr Un	6061	C	800 537-8491	11800
Wescom Central Credit Union (PA)	6062	B	888 493-7266	11834
Law School Financial Inc	6111	C	626 243-1800	11846
Right Start Mortgage Inc (PA)	6162	D	855 313-9405	11932
Merrill Lynch Prce Fnner Smith	6211	C	800 637-7455	11980
Guardian Life Insur Co Amer	6311	D	626 792-1935	12042
Los Angles Cnty Emplyees Rtrme (PA)	6371	C	626 564-6000	12160
B&C Liquidating Corp (HQ)	6411	C	626 799-7000	12181
Tm Claims Service Inc	6411	C	626 568-7800	12259
Collins & Collins	6512	D	626 243-1100	12286
Invitation Homes Inc	6531	D	805 372-2900	12469
Western Asset Core Plus Bond P	6722	C	626 844-9400	12643
Schaumbond Group Inc (PA)	6726	B	626 215-4998	12650
Operating Engineers Funds Inc (PA)	6733	C	866 400-5200	12665
Are/Cal-Sd Region No 62 LLC	6799	D	626 578-0777	12698
Idealab Holdings LLC (PA)	6799	A	626 585-6900	12710
Sabal Capital Partners LLC	6799	C	949 255-1007	12735
Pacific Huntington Hotel Corp	7011	A	626 568-3900	12960
Pasadena Hotel Dev Ventr LP	7011	D	626 449-4000	12969
Azira LLC	7311	C	606 889-7680	13197
One & All Inc (HQ)	7311	C	626 449-6100	13234
Tetra Tech Executive Svcs Inc	7361	C	626 470-2400	13578
Stability Healthcare Inc	7363	B	626 568-1540	13624
B Jacqueline and Assoc Inc	7371	D	626 844-1400	13667
Bluebeam Inc (PA)	7371	C	626 788-4100	13677
Foremay Inc (PA)	7371	E	408 228-3468	13732
Intellectyx Inc	7371	D	720 256-7540	13752
Numerade Labs Inc	7371	D	213 536-1489	13788
Qxv Software LLC	7371	D	626 219-0522	13803
Snapcomms Inc	7371	D	805 715-0300	13826
Socialedge Inc (PA)	7371	B	213 212-7079	13827
Trinus Corporation	7371	C	818 246-1143	13850
X1 Discovery Inc	7371	E	877 999-1347	13865
Everbridge Inc (PA)	7372	C	818 230-9700	13930
Guidance Software Inc (HQ)	7372	C	626 229-9191	13943
Red Gate Software Inc	7372	E	626 993-3949	14018
Gemalto Cogent Inc (HQ)	7373	D	626 325-9600	14083
I3dnet LLC	7373	A	800 482-6910	14086
Greensoft Technology Inc	7374	C	323 254-5961	14136
Zoominfo Technologies LLC	7375	A	360 783-6924	14182
Tpusa - Fhcs Inc (DH)	7376	C	213 873-5100	14183
Cloud Creations Inc	7379	D	800 951-7651	14206
Inter-Con Security Systems Inc (PA)	7381	A	626 535-2200	14310
Realdefense LLC (PA)	7382	E	801 895-7907	14416
Pasadena Center Operating Co	7389	C	626 795-9311	14570
Parking Concepts Inc	7521	C	626 577-8963	14664
Annandale Golf Club	7997	C	626 796-6125	15115
Rose Bowl Aquatics Center	7997	D	626 564-0330	15166
Hemodialysis Inc	8011	D	626 792-0548	15321
Huntington Medical Foundation	8011	A	626 795-4210	15327
Kaiser Foundation Hospitals	8011	D	626 440-5639	15364
Kaiser Prmnnte Schl Anesthesia	8011	D	626 564-3016	15369
Accredited Nursing Services	8051	C	626 573-1234	15560
Highland Hlthcare Cmllia Grdns	8051	D	626 798-6777	15677
Pasadena Hospital Assn Ltd	8051	B	626 397-3322	15750
Pasadena Madows Nursing Ctr LP	8051	D	626 796-1103	15751
Brighton Convalescent LLC	8059	D	626 798-9124	15840
Park Marino Convalescent Ctr	8059	C	626 463-4105	15880
Two Palms Nursing Center Inc	8059	D	626 796-1103	15886
Huntington Medical Foundation	8062	C	626 792-3141	16027
Kaiser Foundation Hospitals	8062	B	626 440-5659	16037
Pasadena Hospital Assn Ltd (PA)	8062	A	626 397-5000	16128
Vincent-Hayley Enterprises Inc	8062	D	626 398-8182	16258
Aurora Behavioral Health Care	8063	D	818 515-4735	16264
Aurora Las Encinas LLC	8063	C	626 795-9901	16266
Gooden Center	8069	D	626 356-0078	16294
Shriners Hspitals For Children	8069	B	626 389-9300	16301
Lotus Clinical Research LLC	8071	D	626 381-9830	16323
Allcare Nursing Services Inc	8082	D	626 432-1999	16361
Confido LLC	8082	A	310 361-8558	16381
Grandcare Health Services LLC (PA)	8082	C	866 554-2447	16393
Huntington Care LLC	8082	C	877 405-6990	16395
Huntington Health Physicians	8099	D	626 397-8300	16550
Kaiser Prmnnte Brnard J Tyson	8099	C	888 576-3348	16577
Legacy Healthcare Center LLC	8099	D	626 798-0558	16580
Polytechnic School	8211	B	626 792-2147	16820
County of Los Angeles	8322	D	626 356-5281	16906
County of Los Angeles	8322	D	626 356-5281	16925
Foothill Family Service	8322	C	626 795-6907	16945
Hillsides	8322	B	323 254-2274	16951
Optima Family Services Inc	8322	C	323 300-6066	16986
Pacific Clinics Head Start	8351	C	626 254-5000	17104
Monte Vista Grove Homes	8361	D	626 796-6135	17181
Rosemary Childrens Services (PA)	8361	C	626 844-3033	17192
DVeal Corporation	8399	C	626 296-8900	17224
Kidspce A Prticipatory Museum	8412	D	626 449-9144	17254
Norton Smon Mseum Art At Psden	8412	D	626 449-6840	17259
Shriners International	8641	D	626 389-9300	17366
Valley Hunt Club	8641	D	626 792-7134	17373
Automobile Club Southern Cal	8699	D	626 795-0601	17445
Pasadena Humane Society	8699	D	626 792-7151	17467
Hsa & Associates Inc	8711	D	626 521-9931	17550
Jacobs Engineering Company	8711	A	626 449-2171	17561
Jacobs Engineering Group Inc	8711	D	626 578-3500	17563
Jacobs Engineering Inc (DH)	8711	C	626 578-3500	17564
Jacobs International Ltd Inc	8711	B	626 578-3500	17565
Kinemetrics Inc (DH)	8711	C	626 795-2220	17571
Pacifica Services Inc	8711	D	626 405-0131	17603
Parsons Engrg Science Inc (DH)	8711	B	626 440-2000	17605
Parsons Intl Cayman Islands	8711	A	626 440-6000	17607
Parsons Service Corporation	8711	A	626 440-2000	17608
Ptsi Managed Services Inc	8711	D	626 440-3118	17615
Stantec Consulting Svcs Inc	8711	D	626 796-9141	17636
Tetra Tech Inc (PA)	8711	A	626 351-4664	17646
Ttg Engineers	8711	B	626 463-2800	17653
Stantec Architecture Inc	8712	D	626 796-9141	17690
Kbkg Inc	8721	C	626 449-4225	17737
Krost (PA)	8721	C	626 449-4225	17740
Aerospace Corporation	8733	C	626 873-7700	17865
California Institute Tech	8733	A	818 354-9154	17869
Carnegie Institution Wash	8733	D	626 577-1122	17870
Doheny Eye Institute (PA)	8733	C	323 342-7120	17872
Parsons Constructors Inc	8741	C	626 440-2000	18031
Dowling Advisory Group	8742	D	626 319-1369	18129
Land Design Consultants Inc	8748	D	626 578-7000	18331
Msla Management LLC	8748	A	626 824-6020	18336

PASO ROBLES, CA - San Luis Obispo County

	SIC	EMP	PHONE	ENTRY#
J & L Vineyards	0172	D	559 268-1627	33
Treasury Wine Estates Americas	0172	E	805 237-6000	37
Boneso Brothers Cnstr Inc	1711	D	805 227-4450	751
Worldwind Services LLC	1731	A	661 822-4877	978
Mge Underground Inc	1794	B	805 238-3510	1173
Firestone Walker Inc	2082	D	805 226-8514	1540
Firestone Walker Inc (PA)	2082	C	805 225-5911	1541
Daou Vineyards LLC	2084	E	805 226-5460	1564
Eos Estate Winery	2084	E	805 239-2562	1565
Gallo Vineyards Inc	2084	C	209 394-6281	1573
J Lohr Winery Corporation	2084	E	805 239-8900	1575
James Tobin Cellars Inc	2084	E	805 239-2204	1576
Rbz Vineyards LLC	2084	E	805 542-0133	1582
Tooth and Nail Winery	2084	E	805 369-6100	1590
Treana Winery LLC	2084	E	805 237-2932	1591
Vintage Wine Estates Inc CA	2084	E	805 503-9660	1592
Lakeshirts LLC	2395	E	805 239-1290	2249
Hogue Bros Inc	2426	E	805 239-1440	2290
Pro Document Solutions Inc (PA)	2752	E	805 238-6680	3070
Lubrizol Global Management Inc	2899	E	805 239-1550	3811
Cornucopia Tool & Plastics Inc	3089	E	805 238-7660	4093
Trellborg Sling Sltions US Inc	3089	E	805 239-4284	4261
Acme Vial & Glass Co	3221	E	805 239-2666	4320
Paso Robles Tank Inc (HQ)	3312	D	805 227-1641	4521
Paris Precision LLC	3444	C	805 239-2500	5016
AMC Machining Inc	3449	E	805 238-5452	5090
Souriau Usa Inc (DH)	3643	E	805 238-2840	6428

Mergent email: customerrelations@mergent.com
1322

2025 Southern California
Business Directory and Buyers Guide

(P-0000) Products & Services Section entry number
(PA)=Parent Co (HQ)=Headquarters (DH)=Div Headquarters

	SIC	EMP	PHONE	ENTRY#
Souriau Usa Inc	3643	D	805 226-3573	6429
Joslyn Sunbank Company LLC	3678	B	805 238-2840	6953
Advance Adapters Inc	3714	E	805 238-7000	7217
Advance Adapters LLC	3714	E	805 238-7000	7218
Flight Environments Inc	3728	E		7476
Arbiter Systems Incorporated (PA)	3825	D	805 237-3831	7898
Applied Technologies Assoc Inc (HQ)	3829	C	805 239-9100	8032
JIT Manufacturing Inc	3841	E	805 238-5000	8177
Trelleborg Sealing Solutions	3841	D	805 239-4284	8241
Aviation Consultants Inc	4581	C	805 596-0212	9192
Cco Holdings LLC	4841	C	805 400-1002	9534
Ctek Inc	4899	E	310 241-2973	9562
Smart Stores Operations LLC	5141	B	805 237-0323	10801
Lowes Home Centers LLC	5211	B	805 602-9051	11210
Paq Inc	5541	C	805 227-1660	11477
Heritage Oaks Bancorp	6022	B	805 369-5200	11768
Heritage Oaks Bank	6022	C	805 239-5200	11769
Emeritus Corporation	6513	C	805 239-1313	12339
Ayres - Paso Robles LP	7011	C	714 850-0409	12765
Summerwood Winery & Inn Inc	7011	E	805 227-1365	13039
Kings Oil Tools Inc (PA)	7353	C	805 238-9311	13440
Iqms LLC (HQ)	7372	C	805 227-1122	13953
Eagle Med Pckg Strlization Inc	7389	E	805 238-7401	14493
Ravine Waterpark LLC	7996	C	805 237-8500	15107
County of Los Angeles	8322	D	805 237-3110	16905
Marsh Consulting Group	8748	D	239 433-5500	18334

PATTON, CA - San Bernardino County

	SIC	EMP	PHONE	ENTRY#
Califrnia Dept State Hospitals	8063	A	909 425-7000	16269

PAUMA VALLEY, CA - San Diego County

	SIC	EMP	PHONE	ENTRY#
T - Y Nursery Inc	5193	C	760 742-2151	11102
Pauma Band of Mission Indians	7011	B	760 742-2177	12970
New Pvcc Inc	7997	D	760 742-1230	15153

PERRIS, CA - Riverside County

	SIC	EMP	PHONE	ENTRY#
Parkco Building Company	1542	D	714 444-1441	564
Silver Creek Industries LLC	1542	C	951 943-5393	584
Mamco Inc (PA)	1611	C	951 776-9300	634
HB Parkco Construction Inc (PA)	1771	B	714 567-4752	1119
Integrity Rebar Placers	1791	C	951 696-6843	1154
Star Milling Co	2048	D	951 657-3143	1433
Aoc LLC	2295	D	951 657-5161	1958
H&M Fashion Usa Inc	2389	C	909 990-7815	2195
Avalon Shutters Inc	2431	D	909 937-4900	2298
California Trusframe LLC	2439	C	951 657-7491	2373
California Trusframe LLC (HQ)	2439	D	951 350-4880	2374
California Truss Company (PA)	2439	C	951 657-7491	2375
Inland Truss Inc (PA)	2439	D	951 300-1758	2379
Alpha Corporation of Tennessee	2821	C	951 657-5161	3256
J-M Manufacturing Company Inc	2821	E	951 657-7400	3275
Goldstar Asphalt Products Inc	2951	E	951 940-1610	3837
Npg Inc (PA)	2951	D	951 940-0200	3838
Coreslab Structures La Inc	3272	D	951 943-9119	4384
Creative Stone Mfg Inc (PA)	3272	C	800 847-8663	4385
J & R Concrete Products Inc	3272	C	951 943-5855	4397
Craftech Metal Forming Inc	3441	C	951 940-6444	4829
Stretch Forming Corporation	3444	D	951 443-0911	5042
R&M Supply Inc	3524	D	951 552-9860	5482
Spaulding Equipment Company (PA)	3532	E	951 943-4531	5502
West Coast Yamaha Inc	3568	C	951 943-2061	5811
Stearns Product Dev Corp (PA)	3569	C	951 657-0379	5835
R-Cold Inc	3585	D	951 430-5470	5000
Axxis Corporation	3599	E	951 436-9921	6086
Warlock Industries	3711	E	951 657-2680	7195
Limos By Tiffany Inc	3713	E	951 657-2680	7206
Pacific Coachworks Inc	3792	C	951 686-7294	7677
National Retail Trnsp Inc	4213	D	951 243-6110	8966
CJ Logistics America LLC	4225	D	951 436-7131	9053
Lowes Home Centers LLC	4225	C	951 443-2500	9085
Lecangs LLC (PA)	4731	B	925 968-5094	9304
Eastern Mncpl Wtr Dst Fclties	4941	A	951 928-3777	9691
Eastern Municipal Water Dst	4941	C	951 657-7469	9692
Eastern Municipal Water Dst (PA)	4941	B	951 928-3777	9693
CR&r Incorporated	4953	C	951 634-8079	9740
Eldorado Stone LLC	5032	A	951 601-3838	9943
Herca Telecomm Services Inc	5082	D	951 940-5945	10350
Jpl Global LLC	5082	E	888 274-7744	10351
Global Plastics Inc	5093	C	951 657-5466	10538
Village Nurseries Whl LLC	5193	B	951 657-3940	11103
Eci Water Ski Products Inc	5941	E	951 940-9999	11630
S A Top-U Corporation	5944	C	951 916-4025	11643
Zodiac Pool Systems LLC	7389	C	760 213-4647	14638

	SIC	EMP	PHONE	ENTRY#
Big Lgue Dreams Consulting LLC	7941	C	619 846-8855	15019
Dropzone Waterpark	7999	C	951 210-1600	15199
Kindred Healthcare LLC	8062	B	951 436-3535	16063
Oak Grove Inst Foundation Inc	8322	C	951 238-6022	16985
Pacific Hydrotech Corporation	8711	C	951 943-8803	17602

PICO RIVERA, CA - Los Angeles County

	SIC	EMP	PHONE	ENTRY#
Genesis Foods Corporation	2064	D	323 890-5890	1504
Mixed Nuts Inc	2068	E	323 587-6887	1514
GPde Slva Spces Incrporation (PA)	2099	D	562 407-2643	1786
LA Pillow & Fiber Inc	2392	D	323 724-7969	2213
Pacific Cast Fther Cushion LLC (HQ)	2392	C	562 801-9995	2220
Reeve Store Equipment Company (PA)	2542	D	562 949-2535	2590
Bay Cities Container Corp (PA)	2653	D	562 948-3751	2654
CD Container Inc	2653	D	562 948-1910	2658
Jkv Inc	2653	E	562 948-3000	2678
Spiral Ppr Tube & Core Co Inc	2655	D	562 801-9705	2698
Endpak Packaging Inc	2674	D	562 801-0281	2743
Whittier Fertilizer Company	2873	C	562 699-3461	3748
Aoclsc Inc	2992	C	813 248-1988	3848
Lubricating Specialties Company	2992	C	562 776-4000	3857
Krieger Speciality Pdts LLC (DH)	3442	D	562 695-0645	4892
C&O Manufacturing Company Inc	3444	C	562 692-7525	4961
W P Keith Co Inc	3567	E	562 948-3636	5804
Veolia Wts Services Usa Inc	3589	D	562 942-2200	6036
Feit Electric Company Inc (PA)	3645	C	562 463-2852	6444
Pacific Logistics Corp (PA)	4731	C	562 478-4700	9321
Unisource Solutions LLC (PA)	5021	C	562 654-3500	9884
Aurora World Inc	5092	C	562 205-1222	10518
Three Sons Inc	5147	D	562 801-4100	10883
Bakemark USA LLC (PA)	5149	C	562 949-1054	10930
Lowes Home Centers LLC	5211	B	562 942-9909	11245
Showroom Interiors LLC	7359	C	323 348-1551	13470
Sectran Security Incorporated (PA)	7381	C	562 948-1446	14337
Krikorian Premiere Theatre LLC	7832	D	562 205-3456	14941
Mariner Health Care Inc	8051	C	562 942-7019	15715
Rivera Sanatarium Inc	8051	D	562 949-2591	15761
Riviera Nursing & Conva	8051	C	562 806-2576	15764
Altamed Health Services Corp	8099	C	562 949-8717	16531
Bms Healthcare Inc	8099	C	562 942-7019	16538
Public Hlth Fndation Entps Inc	8099	C	562 801-2323	16607

PIRU, CA - Ventura County

	SIC	EMP	PHONE	ENTRY#
La Verne Nursery Inc	0181	D	805 521-0111	59

PISMO BEACH, CA - San Luis Obispo County

	SIC	EMP	PHONE	ENTRY#
Alliance Ready Mix Inc	3273	E	805 556-3015	4426
Pacific Gas and Electric Co	4911	C	805 546-5267	9599
Brooks Restaurant Group Inc (PA)	5141	E	559 485-8520	10744
Tic Hotels Inc	7011	D	805 773-4671	13053
Vpb Operating Co LLC	7011	D	805 773-1011	13067

PLACENTIA, CA - Orange County

	SIC	EMP	PHONE	ENTRY#
Mddr Inc	1711	C	714 792-1993	802
Elljay Acoustics Inc	1742	D	714 961-1173	1006
GD Heil Inc	1795	C	714 687-9100	1182
Western Mill Fabricators Inc	2599	E	714 993-3667	2618
Cinton LLC	2672	E	714 961-8808	2720
Crescent Inc	2752	E	714 992-6030	2994
Arion Graphics LLC (HQ)	3081	C	714 005-6300	3044
Vanderveer Industrial Plas LLC	3083	E	714 577-9700	3972
Excalibur Extrusion Inc	3084	E	714 528-8834	3973
Truth Custom Plactics Inc	3089	D	714 993-9955	4120
Crd Mfg Inc	3429	E	714 871-3300	4764
Hartwell Corporation (DH)	3429	E	714 993-4200	4770
West Coast Metal Stamping Incorporated	3469	E	714 792-0322	5223
Coast Aerospace Mfg Inc	3544	E	714 893-8066	5573
Nalco Wtr Prtrtment Sltons LLC	3589	E	714 792-0708	6026
Mike Kenney Tool Inc	3599	E	714 577-9262	6178
Mkt Innovations	3599	D	714 524-7668	6182
Southern Cal Tchnical Arts Inc	3599	E	714 524-2626	6241
Sapphire Chandelier LLC	3646	D	714 879-3660	6472
Altinex Inc	3663	E	714 990-0877	6595
Cartel Electronics LLC	3672	D	714 993-0270	6714
L & M Machining Corporation	3678	D	714 414-0923	6954
Vertex Lcd Inc	3679	E	714 223-7111	7066
Roll Along Vans Inc	3714	E	714 528-9600	7289
Alva Manufacturing Inc	3728	E	714 237-0925	7429
Bioseal	3841	E	714 528-4695	8112
Tfn Architectural Signage Inc (PA)	3993	E	714 556-0990	8645
Hardy Window Company (PA)	5031	E	714 996-1807	9922
Sunrise Growers Inc	5148	C	714 706-6090	10920
Vita-Herb Nutriceuticals Inc	5499	E	714 632-3726	11311

Employee Codes: A=Over 500 employees, B=251-500
C=101-250, D=51-100, E=20-50, F=10-19, G=1-9

2025 Southern California
Business Directory and Buyers Guide

© Mergent Inc. 1-800-342-5647

1323

GEOGRAPHIC

	SIC	EMP	PHONE	ENTRY#
Interface Rehab Inc	8049	A	714 646-8300	15549
Tenet Healthsystem Medical Inc	8069	B	714 993-2000	16302
Roman Cthlic Diocese of Orange	8211	C	714 528-1794	16821

PLAYA DEL REY, CA - Los Angeles County

	SIC	EMP	PHONE	ENTRY#
Chipton-Ross Inc	3721	D	310 414-7800	7337
Los Angeles Dept Wtr & Pwr	4939	A	310 524-8500	9679

PLAYA VISTA, CA - Los Angeles County

	SIC	EMP	PHONE	ENTRY#
Cpl Holdings LLC	5331	C	310 348-6800	11266
Lmb Opco LLC	6163	B	310 348-6800	11947
Commercial RE Exch Inc	6531	C	888 273-0423	12412
Tcg Capital Management LP	6799	C	310 633-2900	12740
Canvas Worldwide LLC	7313	C	424 303-4300	13264
Videoamp Inc (PA)	7372	C	424 272-7774	14062
Ordermark Inc	7374	C	833 673-3762	14149
Lowermybills Inc	7375	C	310 348-6800	14175
Lee Burkhart Liu Inc	8712	D	310 829-2249	17680

PLS VRDS PNSL, CA - Los Angeles County

	SIC	EMP	PHONE	ENTRY#
Rolling Hills Vineyard Inc	2084	E	310 541-5098	1583
Episcopal Communities & Servic	8051	D	310 544-2204	15648

POMONA, CA - Los Angeles County

	SIC	EMP	PHONE	ENTRY#
Centrescapes Inc	0781	D	909 392-3303	162
Ultimate Removal Inc	1521	C	909 524-0800	436
Henkels & McCoy Inc	1623	B	909 517-3011	674
Spiniello Companies	1623	C	909 629-1000	697
t McGee Electric Inc	1731	C	909 591-6461	972
Frank S Smith Masonry Inc	1741	D	909 468-0525	982
Spectra Company	1741	E	909 599-0760	988
Howard Roofing Company Inc	1761	D	909 622-5598	1086
Torn & Glasser Inc	2068	E	909 706-4100	1518
Anheuser-Busch LLC	2082	E	951 782-3935	1531
Los Pericos Food Products LLC	2099	E	909 623-5625	1810
Lift-It Manufacturing Co Inc	2298	E	909 469-2251	1963
Bragel International Inc	2342	E	909 598-8808	2153
Royal Cabinets Inc	2434	A	909 629-8565	2361
Royal Industries Inc	2434	E	909 629-8565	2362
Rbf Lifestyle Holdings LLC	2521	E	626 333-5700	2516
Kittrich Corporation (PA)	2591	C	714 736-1000	2604
Stainless Fixtures Inc	2599	E	909 622-1615	2615
Numatech West (kmp) LLC	2653	D	909 706-3627	2682
Federated Diversified Sls Inc	2671	D	909 591-1733	2707
California Plastix Inc	2671	E	909 629-8288	2729
Inland Envelope Company	2677	D	909 622-2016	2750
FDS Manufacturing Company (PA)	2679	D	909 591-1733	2768
K-1 Packaging Group	2752	C	626 964-9384	3025
Natural Envmtl Protection Co	2821	E	909 620-8028	3282
Kc Pharmaceuticals Inc (PA)	2834	D	909 598-9499	3437
Med-Pharmex Inc	2834	C	909 593-7875	3449
Alere San Diego Inc	2835	B	858 805-2000	3531
Alere San Diego Inc	2835	E	909 482-0840	3532
Ecosmart Technologies Inc	2879	E	770 667-0006	3754
Pomona Quality Foam LLC	3086	D	909 628-7844	4012
L & H Mold & Engineering Inc (PA)	3089	E	909 930-1547	4157
Performnce Engineered Pdts Inc	3089	E	909 594-7487	4195
Ronford Products Inc	3089	E	909 622-7446	4226
Travelers Choice Travelware	3161	D	909 529-7688	4302
Lippert Components Mfg Inc	3231	E	909 628-5557	4339
Headwaters Incorporated	3272	E	909 627-9066	4396
W R Meadows Inc	3272	E	909 469-2606	4424
Tree Island Wire (usa) Inc	3315	C	909 595-6617	4542
Wcs Equipment Holdings LLC	3325	D	909 993-5700	4573
Consoldted Precision Pdts Corp	3365	D	909 595-2252	4669
Valley Metal Treating Inc	3398	D	909 623-6316	4717
Precision Pwdred Met Parts Inc	3399	E	909 595-5656	4719
Trussworks International Inc	3441	D	714 630-2772	4876
R & S Automation Inc	3442	E	800 962-3111	4899
Structural Composites Inds LLC (DH)	3443	E	909 594-7777	4929
Worthington Cylinder Corp	3443	C	909 594-7777	4935
Equipment Design & Mfg Inc	3444	D	909 594-2229	4983
M-5 Steel Mfg Inc (PA)	3444	E	323 263-9383	5000
Superior Duct Fabrication Inc	3444	C	909 620-8565	5043
Action Stamping Inc	3469	E	626 914-7466	5170
Real Plating Inc	3471	E	909 623-2304	5289
DOT Blue Safes Corporation	3499	E	909 445-8888	5444
Casa Herrera Inc (PA)	3556	D	909 392-3930	5669
Dow Hydraulic Systems Inc	3599	D	909 596-6602	6119
Holland & Herring Mfg Inc	3599	E	909 469-4700	6142
Valley Tool and Machine Co Inc	3599	E	909 595-2205	6262
Yawitz Inc	3645	E	909 865-5599	6451
Mil-Spec Magnetics Inc	3677	D	909 598-8116	6932

	SIC	EMP	PHONE	ENTRY#
Electrocube Inc (PA)	3679	E	909 595-1821	6995
Phenix Enterprises Inc (PA)	3713	E	909 469-0411	7208
American Mtal Mfg Resource Inc	3724	E	909 620-4500	7380
Analytical Industries Inc	3823	E	909 392-6900	7848
Gould & Bass Company Inc	3825	E	909 623-6793	7913
Scientific Pharmaceuticals Inc	3843	E	909 595-9922	8354
American Rotary Broom Co Inc	3991	E	909 629-9117	8583
LMS	3999	E	909 623-8781	8694
Traxx Corporation	3999	D	909 623-8032	8736
Southern Cal Rgional Rail Auth	4111	C	213 808-7043	8805
Covenant Transport Inc	4213	A	909 469-0130	8939
C & B Delivery Service	4225	D	909 623-4708	9051
Kkw Trucking Inc (PA)	4225	A	909 869-1200	9081
Home Express Delivery Svc LLC	4731	A	949 715-9844	9293
Seaworld Global Logistics	4731	B	310 742-3882	9334
Southern California Edison Co	4911	B	909 274-1925	9622
Southern California Edison Co	4911	A	909 469-0251	9623
Ramcast Ornamental Sup Co Inc	5051	C	909 469-4767	10151
Ferguson Fire Fabrication Inc (DH)	5074	D	909 517-3085	10317
Especial T Hvac Shtmtl Fttngs	5075	E	909 869-9150	10331
Injen Technology Company Ltd	5075	E	909 839-0706	10336
Als Group Inc	5084	C	909 622-7555	10366
Eastman Music Company (PA)	5099	E	909 868-1777	10559
Cape Robbin Inc	5139	E	626 810-8080	10734
NW Packaging LLC (PA)	5199	D	909 706-3627	11132
Pomona Mc Kenna Motors	5511	C	909 620-7370	11396
Atv Canter LLC (PA)	5531	C	562 977-8565	11440
Lereta LLC (PA)	6211	B	626 543-1765	11973
Local Inttive Hlth Auth For Lo	6324	B	909 620-1661	12095
Murcor Inc	6531	C	909 623-4001	12494
Starwood Htels Rsrts Wrldwide	7011	C	909 622-2220	13036
Merchants Building Maint Co	7349	A	909 622-8260	13391
Global Rental Co Inc	7353	C	909 469-5160	13435
Maxim Healthcare Services Inc	7363	D	626 962-6453	13610
County of Los Angeles	7992	C	909 231-0549	15074
Fairplex Enterprises Inc	7999	C	909 623-3111	15202
Los Angeles County Fair Assn (PA)	7999	D	909 623-3111	15210
Western Univ Hlth Sciences	8011	B	909 865-2565	15511
Inland Valley Partners LLC	8049	C	909 623-7100	15544
Casa Clina Hosp Ctrs For Hlthc (HQ)	8062	B	909 596-7733	15931
Pomona Valley Hospital Med Ctr (PA)	8062	A	909 865-9500	16137
Landmark Medical Services Inc	8063	D	909 593-2585	16277
Immunalysis Corporation	8071	D	909 482-0840	16319
Latara Enterprise Inc (PA)	8071	C	909 623-9301	16322
Tri-City Mental Health Auth (PA)	8093	C	909 623-6131	16513
American National Red Cross	8322	C	909 859-7006	16864
Casa Colina Inc (PA)	8322	A	909 596-7733	16880
County of Los Angeles	8322	C	909 469-4500	16918
San Gbrl/Pmona Vlleys Dvlpmnta	8322	B	909 620-7722	17005
Walden House Inc	8361	C	626 258-0300	17207
Mesa Associates Inc	8711	D	909 979-6609	17585
Qnap Inc	8731	D	909 598-6933	17819

PORT HUENEME, CA - Ventura County

	SIC	EMP	PHONE	ENTRY#
Consoldted Precision Pdts Corp	3365	D	805 488-6451	4668
Pac Foundries Inc	3366	C	805 986-1308	4683
Brusco Tug & Barge Inc	4492	C	805 986-1600	9150
Windsor Capital Group Inc	7011	D	805 986-5353	13084
United States Dept of Navy	7699	C	805 989-1328	14798

PORTER RANCH, CA - Los Angeles County

	SIC	EMP	PHONE	ENTRY#
Design Todays Inc (PA)	2339	E	213 745-3091	2091
JNJ Apparel Inc	2339	E	323 584-9700	2106
Cyberpolicy Inc	6411	C	877 626-9991	12199
Pinnacle Estate Properties Inc (PA)	6531	C	818 993-4707	12504
Metropolitan Imports LLC	7389	C	646 980-5343	14550
Kaiser Foundation Hospitals	8062	D	833 574-2273	16035
American Technical Svcs Inc	8711	D	951 372-9664	17484

POWAY, CA - San Diego County

	SIC	EMP	PHONE	ENTRY#
Benchmark Landscape Svcs Inc	0781	C	858 513-7190	149
Richmond Engineering Co Inc	0782	C	800 589-7058	233
Koloa Pacific Construction Inc	1521	C	858 486-7800	416
Kiewit Corporation	1542	C	858 208-4285	552
Eagle Paving LLC	1611	C	858 486-6400	614
Harper Federal Cnstr LLC	1611	C	619 543-1296	623
BCM Customer Service	1711	D	858 679-5757	748
Western Fire Protection Inc (PA)	1711	C	858 513-4949	854
Electronic Control Systems LLC	1731	C	858 513-1911	913
Gould Electric Inc	1731	C	858 486-1727	921
Morrow-Meadows Corporation	1731	B	858 974-3650	941
Demcon Concrete Contrs Inc	1771	C	858 748-5090	1114
Quality Reinforcing Inc	1791	D	858 748-8400	1160

Mergent email: customerrelations@mergent.com
1324

2025 Southern California
Business Directory and Buyers Guide

(P-0000) Products & Services Section entry number
(PA)=Parent Co (HQ)=Headquarters (DH)=Div Headquarters

	SIC	EMP	PHONE	ENTRY#
Elicc Americas Corporation	1793	C	760 233-0066	1164
Creative Foods LLC	2099	E	858 748-0070	1758
Disguise Inc (HQ)	2389	D	858 391-3600	2194
Smoothreads Inc	2396	E	800 536-5959	2267
B Young Enterprises Inc	2434	D	858 748-0935	2339
Spooners Woodworks Inc	2541	C	858 679-9086	2573
Liberty Diversified Intl Inc	2542	C	858 391-7302	2584
Hpi Liquidations Inc	2653	C	858 391-7302	2675
Digitalpro Inc (PA)	2752	E	858 874-7750	3003
Alfa Scientific Designs Inc	2835	D	858 513-3888	3533
Granite Gold Inc	2842	C	858 499-8933	3605
Henkel US Operations Corp	2844	E	203 655-8911	3658
Aldila Materials Tech Corp (DH)	2895	E	858 486-6970	3787
Toray Membrane Usa Inc (DH)	2899	D	858 218-2360	3821
K-Tube Corporation	3317	D	858 513-9229	4549
Valley Metals LLC	3317	E	858 513-1300	4555
Omc-Thc Liquidating Inc	3433	E	858 486-8846	4812
Gaines Manufacturing Inc	3444	E	858 486-7100	4988
L & T Precision LLC	3444	C	858 513-7874	4996
Securus Inc	3446	E		5071
Aztec Manufacturing Inc (PA)	3452	E	858 513-4350	5119
Advanced Machining Tooling Inc	3544	E	858 486-9050	5565
Delta Design Inc (HQ)	3569	B	858 848-8000	5818
Gateway Inc	3571	E	858 451-9933	5848
Rugged Systems Inc	3571	C	858 391-1006	5866
Apricorn LLC	3577	E	858 513-2000	5902
Delkin Devices Inc (PA)	3577	D	858 391-1234	5912
Mytee Products Inc	3589	E	858 679-1191	6024
Darmark Corporation	3599	D	858 679-3970	6113
Franklins Inds San Diego Inc	3599	E	858 486-9399	6127
EPC Power Corp (PA)	3629	C	858 748-5590	6374
Osram Sylvania Inc	3641	D	858 748-5077	6407
Niterder Tchncal Ltg Vdeo Syst	3648	E	858 268-9316	6513
Broadcast Microwave Svcs LLC (PA)	3663	C	858 391-3050	6602
Clarity Design Inc	3672	E	858 746-3500	6718
Somacis Inc	3672	C	858 513-2200	6772
Wfb Archives Inc	3672	D		6788
Data Device Corporation	3679	E	858 503-3300	6816
United Security Products Inc	3699	E	800 227-1592	7157
Thyssenkrupp Bilstein Amer Inc	3714	E	858 386-5900	7298
General Atmics Arntcal Systems	3721	D	858 455-3358	7341
General Atmics Arntcal Systems	3721	B	858 312-4247	7343
General Atmics Arntcal Systems	3721	D	858 455-3000	7344
General Atmics Arntcal Systems	3721	D	858 312-2810	7346
General Atmics Arntcal Systems	3721	B	858 762-6700	7348
General Atmics Arntcal Systems (DH)	3721	B	858 312-2810	7349
General Atomic Aeron	3721	C	858 455-4560	7351
General Atomic Aeron	3721	B	858 312-3428	7352
General Atomic Aeron	3721	B	858 312-2543	7353
Light Composites Inc	3721	E	619 339-0638	7362
Quatro Composites LLC	3728	C	712 707-9200	7545
Teledyne Instruments Inc	3812	C	858 842-2600	7817
Teledyne Rd Instruments Inc	3812	C	858 842-2600	7818
Tern Design Ltd	3823	E	760 754-2400	7881
Cohu Inc (PA)	3825	C	858 848-8100	7905
Cohu Interface Solutions LLC (HQ)	3825	D	858 848-8000	7906
Delta Design (littleton) Inc	3825	A	858 848-8100	7908
J2m Test Solutions Inc	3825	D	571 333-0291	7920
Vitrek LLC (PA)	3825	E	858 689-2755	7935
Tek84 Inc	3845	D	858 676-5382	8400
Aldila Golf Corp	3949	C	858 513-1801	8499
Hoist Fitness Systems Inc	3949	D	858 578-7676	8522
Seirus Innovative ACC Inc	3949	C	858 513-1212	8540
Uke Corporation	3949	D	858 513-9100	8551
Traffic Control & Safety Corp	3993	E	858 679-7292	8647
Corovan Corporation (PA)	4214	C	858 762-8100	8989
Corovan Moving & Storage Co (HQ)	4214	D	858 748-1100	8990
Home Depot USA Inc	4225	D	858 859-4143	9078
IMS Electronics Recycling Inc	4953	C	858 679-1555	9746
PC Specialists Inc (HQ)	5045	C	858 566-1900	10023
Printsafe Inc	5045	E	858 748-8600	10024
Bay City Equipment Inds Inc	5063	D	619 938-8200	10172
Power Systems West LLC	5063	E	208 869-0483	10202
Wassco	5084	C	858 679-0444	10416
Motion Industries Inc	5085	E	858 602-1500	10451
Chef Works Inc	5136	B	858 643-5600	10680
Moteng Inc	5136	D	858 715-2500	10690
Smart Stores Operations LLC	5141	C	858 748-0101	10789
Sysco San Diego Inc	5141	A	858 513-7300	10810
Pro Specialties Group Inc	5199	D	858 541-1100	11136
Perry Ford of Poway LLC	5511	D	858 748-1400	11395
Poway Toyota Scion Inc	5511	C	858 486-2900	11397
Southern Cal Disc Tire Co Inc	5531	C	858 486-3600	11461

	SIC	EMP	PHONE	ENTRY#
Eappraiseit LLC	6531	C	800 281-6200	12436
Champion Investment Corp	7011	D	917 712-7807	12791
Digirad Imaging Solutions Inc	7352	D	800 947-6134	13430
Hubb Systems LLC	7373	D	510 865-9100	14085
Califrnia Crtive Solutions Inc (PA)	7379	D	458 208-4131	14203
Hunter Douglas Fabrication Co	7389	D	858 679-7500	14511
Pkl Services Inc	7699	C	858 679-1755	14783
Maderas Golf Club	7992	D	858 451-8100	15089
Floaties Swim School LLC	7999	E	877 277-7946	15205
Pomerado Operations LLC	8051	D	858 487-6242	15756
Palomar Health	8062	A	760 739-3000	16118
Palomar Health	8062	C	858 613-4000	16119
Palomar Health Medical Group (HQ)	8062	C	858 675-3100	16120
Palomar Medical Center	8062	B	858 613-4000	16122
Liberty Residential Svcs Inc	8082	E	858 500-0852	16401
Community Food Connection	8322	D	858 751-4613	16898
Community Dev Inst Head Start	8351	B	858 668-2985	17087
ISE Corporation	8731	C	858 413-1720	17800
T G T Enterprises Inc	8742	C	858 413-0300	18224

RAMONA, CA - San Diego County

	SIC	EMP	PHONE	ENTRY#
Demler Brothers LLC	0252	D	760 789-2457	93
Pro Traffic Services Inc	1711	D	760 906-6961	823
In-Line Fence & Railing Co Inc	1799	E	760 789-0282	1210
Summit Enterprises Inc	2679	E	858 679-2100	2774
EMD Millipore Corporation	3826	C	760 788-9692	7952
San Diego Country Estates Assn	8641	C	760 789-3788	17363

RANCHO CASCADES, CA - Los Angeles County

	SIC	EMP	PHONE	ENTRY#
Tutor-Saliba Corporation (HQ)	1542	D	818 362-8391	597
Frontier-Kemper Constructors Inc (HQ)	1629	C	818 362-2062	713
Desert Mechanical Inc	1711	A	702 873-7333	772
Fisk Electric Company	1731	C	818 884-1166	919
A A Gonzalez Inc	1742	D	818 367-2242	993
Spears Manufacturing Co	3084	E	818 364-1611	3979
Laser Operations LLC	3674	E	818 986-0000	6844
Janco Corporation	3679	C	818 361-3366	7014
Mason Electric Co	3728	B	818 361-3366	7519
Spears Manufacturing Co (PA)	5083	C	818 364-1611	10364

RANCHO CUCAMONGA, CA - San Bernardino County

	SIC	EMP	PHONE	ENTRY#
Merchants Landscape Services	0781	D	909 981-1022	177
Ferreira Construction Co Inc	1521	A	909 606-5900	403
American De Rosa Lamparts LLC	1541	D	800 777-4440	471
Penwal Industries Inc	1542	D	909 466-1555	569
WE Oneil Construction Co Cal	1542	C	909 466-5300	601
Precision Pipeline LLC	1623	B	909 229-6858	689
Calvin Dubois	1711	D	909 222-6662	758
Professnal Elec Cnstr Svcs Inc	1731	C	909 373-4100	954
Superior Elec Mech & Plbg Inc	1731	B	909 357-9400	971
TRL Systems Incorporated	1731	C	909 390-8392	975
La Rocque Better Roofs Inc	1761	C	909 476-2699	1088
Yellow Jacket Drlg Svcs LLC	1781	D	909 989-8563	1145
Cargill Meat Solutions Corp	2011	D	909 476-3120	1239
Formosa Meat Company Inc	2013	E	909 987-0470	1258
American Fruits & Flavors LLC	2087	E	909 291-2620	1661
Frozen Bean Inc	2087	E	855 837-6936	1681
Aquamar Inc	2091	C	909 481-4700	1694
Gruma Corporation	2096	E	909 980-3566	1723
Mizkan America Inc	2099	D	000 481-8743	1817
Hollywood Ribbon Industries Inc	2241	B	323 266-0670	1906
Ecmd Inc	2431	E	909 980-1775	2305
Ifoo Systems Us LLC	2448	D	909 484-4332	2389
Drownwood Furniture Inc	2511	C	909 945-5613	2421
ES Kluft & Company Inc (DH)	2515	C	909 373-4211	2482
G & M Mattress and Foam Corporation	2515	D	909 593-1000	2483
South Bay International Inc	2515	D	909 718-5000	2492
Avery Dennison Corporation	2672	D	909 987-4631	2716
Pacific Pprbd Converting LLC (PA)	2679	E	909 476-6466	2771
Prime Converting Corporation	2679	E	909 476-9500	2772
Continental Graphics Corp	2752	D	909 758-9800	2989
Eclipse Prtg & Graphics LLC	2752	E	909 390-2452	3005
Kindred Litho Incorporated	2752	E	909 944-4015	3028
Heartland Label Printers LLC	2759	A	909 243-7151	3143
Air Liquid Healthcare	2813	E	909 899-4633	3210
Dow Company Foundation	2821	C	909 476-4127	3263
Criticalpoint Capital LLC	2822	D	909 987-9533	3304
Amphastar Pharmaceuticals Inc (PA)	2834	E	909 980-9484	3353
Usl Parallel Products Cal	2869	E	909 980-1200	3740
Master Builders LLC	2899	A	909 987-1758	3812
Swabplus Inc	3053	E	909 987-7898	3902
Omni Seals Inc	3061	D	909 946-0181	3904
Good-West Rubber Corp (PA)	3069	C	909 987-1774	3912

Employee Codes: A=Over 500 employees, B=251-500
C=101-250, D=51-100, E=20-50, F=10-19, G=1-9

2025 Southern California
Business Directory and Buyers Guide

© Mergent Inc. 1-800-342-5647

1325

	SIC	EMP	PHONE	ENTRY#
Plaxicon Holding Corporation	3085	B	909 944-6868	3987
Creu LLC	3089	E	909 483-4888	4096
Paradigm Packaging East LLC	3089	E	909 985-2750	4191
Pres-Tek Plastics Inc (PA)	3089	E	909 360-1600	4209
Proulx Manufacturing Inc.	3089	E	909 980-0662	4212
American Traveler Inc.	3161	E	909 466-4000	4290
Packline USA LLC	3221	E	909 392-8000	4322
Searing Industries Inc (PA)	3312	C	909 948-3030	4525
Pac-Rancho Inc (HQ)	3324	C	909 987-4721	4569
Southwire Company LLC	3353	D	909 989-2888	4592
Prime Wire & Cable Inc.	3357	C	323 266-2010	4637
J T Walker Industries Inc.	3442	A	909 481-1909	4890
Superior Tank Co Inc (PA)	3443	E	909 912-0580	4930
Gcn Supply LLC	3448	E	909 643-4603	5078
Doubleco Incorporated	3452	D	909 481-0799	5124
Vanguard Tool & Mfg Co Inc.	3469	E	909 980-9392	5220
Metal Coaters California Inc.	3479	D	909 987-4681	5331
Socco Plastic Coating Company.	3479	E	909 987-4753	5345
Steelscape LLC	3479	E	909 987-4711	5347
Wessex Industries Inc.	3498	E	562 944-5760	5439
Executive Safe and SEC Corp.	3499	E	909 947-7020	5447
Smith International Inc.	3533	C	909 906-7900	5513
Prestige Mold Incorporated	3544	E	909 980-6600	5592
Pyramid Mold & Tool	3544	D	909 476-2555	5595
Rafco-Brickform LLC (PA)	3545	D	909 484-3399	5623
Everidge Inc.	3585	C	909 605-6419	5976
Bernell Hydraulics Inc (PA)	3594	E	909 899-1751	6049
All Star Precision	3599	E	909 944-8373	6075
Intra Aerospace LLC	3599	E	909 476-0343	6146
Jet Cutting Solutions Inc.	3599	E	909 948-2424	6152
Paramount Machine Co Inc	3599	E	909 484-3600	6198
Romeros Engineering Inc.	3599	E	909 481-1170	6221
Electro Switch Corp.	3613	D	909 581-0855	6305
Fluorescent Supply Co Inc.	3646	E	909 948-8878	6460
Digital Flex Media Inc.	3652	D	909 484-8440	6574
Siemens Rail Automation Corp.	3669	D	909 532-5405	6692
Kanex.	3699	E	714 332-1681	7130
Universal Surveillance Systems LLC	3699	D	909 484-7870	7158
Greenpower Motor Company Inc.	3711	D	909 308-0960	7178
Yinlun Tdi LLC (HQ)	3714	E	909 390-3944	7312
Lanic Engineering Inc (PA)	3728	E	877 763-0411	7512
Marino Enterprises Inc.	3728	E	909 476-0343	7518
Precision Aerospace Corp.	3728	D	909 945-9604	7541
Safran Cabin Inc.	3728	C	909 652-9700	7558
Pneudraulics Inc.	3812	B	909 980-5366	7791
Mindrum Precision Inc.	3824	E	909 989-1728	7892
Endress+hser Optcal Analis Inc.	3826	E	909 477-2329	7954
Aaren Scientific Inc (DH)	3827	D	909 937-1033	7993
Eagle Labs LLC.	3841	D	909 481-0011	8146
Butler Home Products LLC.	3991	C	909 476-3884	8585
First Transit Inc.	4111	D	909 948-3474	8753
Priority One Med Trnspt Inc (PA)	4119	D	909 948-4400	8844
Durham School Services L P.	4151	D	909 899-1809	8872
Fox Transportation Inc (PA)	4212	D	909 291-4646	8905
New Legend Inc.	4213	C	855 210-2300	8967
Honeyville Inc.	4221	D	909 980-9500	9033
Distribution Alternatives Inc.	4225	D	909 746-5600	9062
Home Depot USA Inc.	4225	C	909 483-8115	9076
Msblous LLC.	4225	D	909 929-9689	9091
Harris & Huri Trnsp Svcs LLC.	4789	D	909 791-0531	9366
Cucamonga Valley Water Dst.	4941	D	909 987-2591	9689
Falken Tire Holdings LLC.	5014	C	800 723-2553	9855
Sumitomo Rubber North Amer Inc (HQ)	5014	C	909 466-1116	9860
Benchpro Inc.	5021	C	619 478-9400	9865
Bradshaw International Inc (PA)	5023	B	909 476-3884	9889
General Micro Systems Inc (PA)	5045	D	909 980-4863	10006
Yuneec USA Inc.	5065	D	855 284-8888	10299
Monoprice Inc.	5099	D	877 271-2592	10564
California Box II.	5113	D	909 944-9202	10590
L & R Distributors Inc.	5131	B	909 980-3807	10665
McLane Foodservice Dist Inc.	5141	D	909 484-6100	10759
Nongshim America Inc (HQ)	5141	C	909 481-3698	10762
Frito-Lay North America Inc.	5145	C	909 941-6218	10847
Frito-Lay North America Inc.	5145	B	909 941-6214	10848
Shining Ocean Inc.	5146	C	253 826-3700	10862
Evolution Fresh Inc.	5148	C	800 794-9986	10895
Transcendia Inc.	5162	E	909 944-9981	11003
Home Depot USA Inc.	5211	D	909 948-9200	11184
Lowes Home Centers LLC.	5211	C	909 476-9697	11211
M & G Jewelers Inc.	5944	D	909 989-2929	11641
Arrowhead Central Credit Union (PA)	6061	B	866 212-4333	11792
CU Cooperative Systems LLC (PA)	6062	B	909 948-2500	11827
Lower LLC.	6162	C	909 527-3736	11922

	SIC	EMP	PHONE	ENTRY#
ML Mortgage Corp.	6163	D	909 652-0780	11948
Carrington Mortgage Svcs LLC.	6211	D	909 226-7963	11959
Agent Franchise LLC.	6321	C	949 930-5025	12056
Inland Empire Health Plan (PA)	6321	A	909 890-2000	12062
Lereta LLC.	6512	C	626 332-1942	12301
National Community Renaissance.	6513	D	909 948-7579	12360
National Cmnty Renaissance Cal (PA)	6552	C	909 483-2444	12573
National Cmnty Renaissance Cal.	6552	C	619 223-9222	12574
Collection Technology Inc.	7322	D	800 743-4284	13281
Sunn America Inc.	7359	E	909 944-5756	13473
Butler America Holdings Inc.	7361	C	909 417-3660	13496
Career Strategies Tmpry Inc.	7361	C	909 230-4504	13504
Network Intgrtion Partners Inc.	7373	D	909 919-2800	14100
Diplomatic Security Svcs LLC.	7381	D	909 463-8409	14294
Nationwide Guard Services Inc.	7381	B	909 608-1112	14322
Harrison Iyke.	7382	D	909 463-8409	14405
Par Western Line Contrs LLC.	7389	A	760 737-0925	14567
H & A Transmissions Inc.	7537	E	909 941-9020	14684
Red Hill Country Club.	7997	D	909 982-1358	15161
Grove Diagnstc Imaging Ctr Inc.	8011	C	909 982-8638	15319
Knd Development 55 LLC.	8062	C	909 581-6400	16066
Perris Valley Cmnty Hosp LLC.	8062	C	909 581-6400	16129
Branlyn Prominence Inc (PA)	8082	D	909 476-9030	16371
Art Autism Related Therapy LLC.	8093	D	909 304-1039	16443
Universal Technical Inst Inc.	8249	C	909 484-1929	16848
Horrigan Enterprises Inc.	8322	C	909 481-9663	16953
In-Roads Creative Programs.	8322	B	909 989-9944	16955
Vocational Imprv Program Inc (PA)	8331	C	909 483-5924	17071
CDM Constructors Inc.	8711	D	909 579-3500	17501
Eide Bailly LLP.	8721	B	909 466-4410	17722
Gentex Corporation.	8731	D	909 481-7667	17792
Accent Computer Solutions LLC.	8748	D	909 825-2772	18273

RANCHO DOMINGUEZ, CA - Los Angeles County

	SIC	EMP	PHONE	ENTRY#
Bi Nutraceuticals Inc.	2087	C	310 669-2100	1669
Ethos Seafood Group LLC.	2092	D	312 858-3474	1704
Santa Monica Seafood Company (PA)	2092	D	310 886-7900	1711
Mars Food Us LLC (HQ)	2099	B	310 933-0670	1811
Carol Anderson Inc (PA)	2335	E	310 638-3333	2062
Organic By Nature Inc (PA)	2833	E	562 901-0177	3325
Biocell Laboratories Inc.	2835	E	310 537-3300	3534
Giovanni Cosmetics Inc.	2844	D	310 952-9960	3653
Shercon LLC.	3069	D		3937
Caplugs Inc.	3089	D	310 537-2300	4082
Expanded Rubber & Plastics Corp.	3089	E	310 324-6692	4114
Buff and Shine Mfg Inc.	3291	E	310 886-5111	4481
Aerol Co Inc.	3365	E	310 762-2660	4663
Adf Incorporated.	3446	E	310 669-9700	5058
Team Manufacturing Inc.	3469	E	310 639-0251	5217
S L Fusco Inc (PA)	3541	E	310 868-1010	5550
Southwestern Industries Inc (PA)	3541	D	310 608-4422	5553
Dresser-Rand Company.	3563	E	310 223-0600	5757
Siemens Energy Inc.	3563	E	310 223-0660	5765
Grand General Accessories LLC.	3612	E	310 631-2589	6286
DSA Phototech LLC.	3646	E	866 868-1602	6455
Parker-Hannifin Corporation.	3677	C	310 608-5600	6933
Thermal Equipment Corporation.	3821	E	310 328-6600	7832
Spectrum Inc.	3841	E	310 885-4600	8229
Laclede Inc.	3843	E	310 605-4280	8344
Nippon Ex Nec Lgstics Amer Inc.	4212	E	310 604-6100	8921
Unis LLC.	4225	D	310 747-7388	9124
Kw International Inc.	4731	C	310 747-1380	9302
Iap West Inc.	5013	C	310 667-9720	9830
CDS Moving Equipment Inc (PA)	5084	C	310 631-1100	10368
Afc Distribution Corp.	5141	C	310 604-3630	10741
Union Sup Comsy Solutions Inc.	5141	B	785 357-5005	10813
Advanced Fresh Concepts Corp (PA)	6794	E	310 604-3630	12676
Bioquip Products Inc.	8731	E	310 667-8800	17778

RANCHO MIRAGE, CA - Riverside County

	SIC	EMP	PHONE	ENTRY#
Cellco Partnership.	4812	D	760 568-5542	9396
Agua Clnte Band Chilla Indians.	7011	A	760 321-2000	12757
Ksl Rancho Mirage Operating Co Inc.	7011	B	760 568-2727	12888
Omni Hotels Corporation.	7011	B	760 568-2727	12952
Ritz-Carlton Hotel Company LLC.	7011	B	760 321-8282	12996
Richman Management Corporation.	7381	B	760 832-8520	14333
Country Villa Service Corp.	7389	C	760 340-0053	14480
Df One Operator LLC.	7389	D	310 961-9739	14489
Mission Hills Country Club Inc.	7997	C	760 324-9400	15150
Tamarisk Country Club (PA)	7997	C	760 328-2141	15179
Desert Orthpd Ctr A Med Group (PA)	8011	D	760 568-2684	15300
Eisenhower Medical Center (PA)	8062	A	760 340-3911	15988
Eisenhower Medical Center.	8071	C	760 773-1364	16313

Mergent email: customerrelations@mergent.com
1326

2025 Southern California
Business Directory and Buyers Guide

(P-0000) Products & Services Section entry number
(PA)=Parent Co (HQ)=Headquarters (DH)=Div Headquarters

	SIC	EMP	PHONE	ENTRY#
Eisenhower Medical Center	8082	C	760 773-1888	16387
Betty Ford Center (HQ)	8093	C	760 773-4100	16445
Dual Diagnosis Trtmnt Ctr Inc	8099	C	949 324-4531	16556
Country Vlla Rncho Mrage Hlthc	8322	C	760 340-0053	16904
Morningside Community Assn	8641	D	760 328-3323	17357
Ameritac Inc (PA)	8744	D	925 989-2942	18257

RANCHO PALOS VERDES, CA - Los Angeles County

	SIC	EMP	PHONE	ENTRY#
Pie Rise Ltd	5812	E	310 832-4559	11596
Long Point Development LLC	7011	A	310 265-2800	12906
CAW Cowie Inc (PA)	7389	E	212 396-9007	14469
Estates At Trump Nat Golf CLB	7992	C	310 265-5000	15079
Salvation Army (HQ)	8322	C	562 264-3600	17001

RANCHO SANTA FE, CA - San Diego County

	SIC	EMP	PHONE	ENTRY#
Pacific Western Bank	6021	B	858 756-3023	11739
Archipelago Development Inc	6552	D	858 699-6272	12564
Huntington Hotel Company	7011	D	858 756-1131	12859
Rancho Vlncia Rsort Prtners LL	7011	B	858 756-1123	12985
Del Mar Country Club Inc	7997	D	858 759-5500	15131
Fairbanks Ranch Cntry CLB Inc	7997	C	858 259-8811	15135
Rancho Santa Fe Association	7997	D	858 756-1182	15160

RANCHO SANTA MARGARI, CA - Orange County

	SIC	EMP	PHONE	ENTRY#
RPM Products Inc (PA)	3053	E	949 888-8543	3898
Glas Werk Inc	3229	E	949 766-1296	4326
Forespar Products Corp	3429	D	949 858-8820	4767
Ats Workholding Llc (PA)	3545	E	800 321-1833	5605
Applied Manufacturing LLC	3841	A	949 713-8000	8092
Applied Medical Corporation (PA)	3841	A	949 713-8000	8093
Applied Medical Resources Corp (HQ)	3841	A	949 713-8000	8096
Lowes Home Centers LLC	5211	D	949 589-5005	11202
Foundation 9 Entertainment Inc (PA)	7372	C	949 698-1500	13933

RCHO STA MARG, CA - Orange County

	SIC	EMP	PHONE	ENTRY#
Park West Landscape Maint Inc (PA)	0782	B	949 546-8300	229
Tracy Ryder Landscape Inc	0782	D	949 858-7017	238
Barr Engineering Inc	1711	D	562 944-1722	747
Point Conception Inc	2339	E	949 589-6890	2127
Renaissnce Frnch Dors Sash Inc (PA)	2431	C	714 578-0090	2326
South Coast Stairs Inc	2431	E	949 858-1685	2327
Protab Laboratories	2834	D	949 713-1301	3483
At Apollo Technologies LLC	2899	E	949 888-0573	3790
Light Composite Corporation	3429	E	949 858-8820	4777
Swiss-Micron Inc	3451	D	949 589-0430	5114
IMI Critical Engineering LLC (DH)	3491	B	949 858-1877	5366
Form Grind Corporation	3599	E	949 858-7000	6124
M-Industrial Enterprises LLC	3599	E	949 413-7513	6167
Palomar Products Inc	3669	D	949 766-5300	6689
Virtium Technology Inc	3674	E	949 888-2444	6910
Car Sound Exhaust System Inc	3714	E	949 858-5900	7235
Car Sound Exhaust System Inc	3714	E	949 858-5900	7236
Racepak LLC	3714	E	949 709-5555	7288
Applied Medical Dist Corp	3841	A	949 713-8000	8094
Applied Medical Resources	3841	E	949 459-1042	8095
Santa Margarita Water District	4941	C	949 459-6400	9719
Santa Margarita Water District (PA)	4941	C	949 459-6400	9720
Virtium LLC	5045	D	949 888-2444	10038
Melissa Data Corporation (PA)	7371	D	949 858-3000	13768
Fakouri Electrical Engrg Inc	7378	D	949 888-2400	14188
Green-N-Clean Ex Car Wash Inc	7542	D	949 749-4977	14709
Roman Cthlic Diocese of Orange	8211	C	949 766-6000	16823
Capital Invstmnts Vntures Corp (PA)	0021	C	040 858 0647	17296
Savice Inc	8041	D	949 888 2444	17365
National Tour Intgrted Rsrces	8742	E	949 215-6330	18177

REDLANDS, CA - San Bernardino County

	SIC	EMP	PHONE	ENTRY#
Larry Jacinto Farming Inc	0762	D	909 794-2276	143
Bakell LLC	1541	D	800 292-2137	472
Russell Hobbs Inc	1541	C	909 792-8257	499
Robert Clapper Cnstr Svcs Inc	1542	D	909 829-3688	579
Larry Jacinto Construction Inc	1611	D	909 794-2151	631
Ach Mechanical Contractors Inc	1711	D	909 307-2850	730
Pro-Craft Construction Inc	1711	C	909 790-5222	824
Faith Electric LLC	1731	C	909 767-2682	917
Mobiz It Inc	1731	D	909 453-6700	940
Caseworx Inc (PA)	2521	E	909 799-8550	2506
Ui Medical LLC	2676	D	562 453-1515	2749
Califrnia Nwspapers Ltd Partnr	2711	B	909 793-3221	2788
Clorox Manufacturing Company	2842	E	909 307-2756	3602
Munchkin Inc	3085	E	818 893-5000	3984
Plastics Plus Technology Inc	3089	E	909 747-0555	4203
Window Enterprises Inc	3442	E	951 943-4894	4905

	SIC	EMP	PHONE	ENTRY#
Venturedyne Ltd	3564	D	909 793-2788	5781
Garner Holt Productions Inc	3571	E	909 799-3030	5847
Precision Hermetic Tech Inc	3679	D	909 381-6011	7038
Teledyne Technologies Inc	3691	D	909 793-3131	7082
Low Cost Interlock Inc	3694	E	844 387-0326	7094
Becton Dickinson and Company	3826	D	909 748-7300	7943
Kyocera Medical Tech Inc	3842	D	909 557-2360	8282
Ifit Inc	3949	A	909 335-2888	8525
Care Medical Trnsp Inc	4119	C	858 653-4520	8817
Advanced Chemical Trnspt Inc	4212	C	951 790-7989	8890
CJ Logistics America LLC	4213	C	909 363-4354	8936
Ashley Furniture Inds LLC	4225	B	909 825-4900	9050
Kuehne + Nagel Inc	4731	C	909 574-2300	9299
Maersk Whsng Dist Svcs USA LLC	4731	C	801 301-1732	9309
Southern California Gas Co	4924	B	909 335-7802	9648
Environmental Systems Research Inst (PA)	5045	A	909 793-2853	10000
P & R Paper Supply Co Inc (HQ)	5113	D	909 389-1807	10606
Outdate Rx LLC	5122	D	855 688-3283	10642
Haralambos Beverage Co	5181	B	562 347-4300	11048
Home Depot USA Inc	5211	C	909 748-0505	11189
Lowes Home Centers LLC	5211	C	909 307-8883	11215
Dick Dewese Chevrolet Inc	5511	C	909 793-2681	11337
Ken Grody Redlands LLC	5511	C	909 793-3211	11368
Akh Company Inc	5531	D	909 748-5016	11437
Mountain West Financial Inc (PA)	6162	B	909 793-1500	11926
Lois Lauer Realty (PA)	6531	C	909 748-7000	12479
Redlands Ford Inc	7532	D	909 793-3211	14679
Rettig Machine Inc	7692	E	909 793-7811	14743
Redlands Country Club	7997	D	909 793-2661	15162
Beaver Medical Clinic Inc (PA)	8011	C	909 793-3311	15250
Kaiser Foundation Hospitals	8011	C	888 750-0036	15344
Ash Holdings LLC	8051	C	909 793-2609	15571
Humangood Norcal	8059	C	909 793-1233	15862
Loma Linda University Med Ctr	8062	D	909 558-4000	16079
Loma Linda University Med Ctr	8062	C	909 558-9275	16080
Redlands Community Hospital (PA)	8062	D	909 335-5500	16159
Interntional Un Oper Engineers	8631	A	909 307-8700	17312
YMCA of East Valley (PA)	8641	C	909 798-9622	17378
Epic Management Services LLC (PA)	8741	D	909 799-1818	17982
RHS Corp	8741	A	909 335-5500	18046
Bon Appetit Management Co	8742	C	909 748-8970	18107

REDONDO BEACH, CA - Los Angeles County

	SIC	EMP	PHONE	ENTRY#
Quantimetrix	2835	D	310 536-0006	3548
Alcast Mfg Inc	3364	E	310 542-3581	4655
Northrop Grumman Systems Corp	3663	C	310 812-5149	6642
Northrop Grmmn Spce & Mssn Sys	3714	A	310 812-4321	7279
Northrop Grumman Systems Corp	3721	B	310 812-4321	7364
Northrop Grumman Systems Corp	3721	B	310 812-1089	7366
Impulse Space Inc	3761	E	949 315-5540	7644
Jariet Technologies Inc	3812	E	310 698-1000	7727
Northrop Grumman Systems Corp	3812	C	855 737-8364	7777
Northrop Grumman Systems Corp	3812	C	310 812-4321	7778
Dsd Trucking Inc	4581	D	310 338-3395	9200
Mapcargo Global Logistics (PA)	4731	D	310 297-8300	9311
Stevens Global Logistics Inc (PA)	4731	D	800 229-7284	9338
Scat Enterprises Inc	5013	D	310 370-5501	9847
Brownstone Companies Inc	5065	A	310 297-3600	10234
Smart Stores Operations LLC	5141	C	323 497-8528	10778
Bicara Ltd	6147	B	310 316-6222	10865
HMC Assets LLC	6331	C	310 535-9293	12120
Greenhedge Escrow	6541	C	310 640-3040	12559
Wedgewood Inc (PA)	6799	D	310 640-3070	12747
K & P Janitorial Services	7349	C	310 540-8878	13381
Cputer Inc	7379	D	844 394-1538	14208
Gable House Inc	7933	D	310 378-2265	15011
Optumcare Management LLC	8011	D	310 316-0811	15416
Beach Cities Health District	8399	C	310 374-3426	17216
Westwind Engineering Inc	8711	C	310 831-3454	17661
NBC Consulting Inc	8742	D	310 798-5000	18179
Sierra Monolithics Inc (HQ)	8748	E	310 698-1000	18356

RESEDA, CA - Los Angeles County

	SIC	EMP	PHONE	ENTRY#
Los Angles Jewish HM For Aging	8051	B	818 774-3000	15707
Los Angles Jewish HM For Aging (PA)	8051	B	818 774-3000	15708
Longwood Management Corp	8062	D	818 881-7414	16089
Child Development Institute	8322	D	818 888-4559	16888
Chase Group Llc	8742	D	818 708-3533	18115

RIALTO, CA - San Bernardino County

	SIC	EMP	PHONE	ENTRY#
Sierra Lathing Company Inc	1742	C	909 421-0211	1028
Biscomerica Corp	2052	B	909 877-5997	1481
Thompson Pipe Group Inc (PA)	2679	E	909 822-0200	2777

Employee Codes: A=Over 500 employees, B=251-500
C=101-250, D=51-100, E=20-50, F=10-19, G=1-9

2025 Southern California
Business Directory and Buyers Guide

© Mergent Inc. 1-800-342-5647

1327

GEOGRAPHIC

	SIC	EMP	PHONE	ENTRY#
Solomon Colors Inc.	2816	E	909 873-9444	3224
Marine Fenders Intl Inc.	3089	E	310 834-7037	4162
Kti Incorporated.	3272	D	909 434-1888	4399
Royal Westlake Roofing LLC.	3272	E	909 822-4407	4420
Burlingame Industries Inc.	3299	C	909 355-7000	4500
State Pipe & Supply Inc.	3312	E	909 356-5670	4526
Columbia Steel Inc.	3441	D	909 874-8840	4827
So-Cal Strl Stl Fbrication Inc.	3441	E	909 877-1299	4868
Spray Enclosure Tech Inc.	3444	E	909 419-7011	5038
H Wayne Lewis Inc.	3449	E	909 874-2213	5095
Martinez and Turek Inc.	3599	C	909 820-6800	6170
Techniform International Corp.	3599	C	909 877-6886	6247
Medical Depot Inc.	3841	D	877 224-0946	8189
Radial South LP.	4225	A	610 491-7000	9104
US Elogistics Service Corp.	4225	C	909 927-7483	9126
Jeld-Wen Inc.	5031	C	909 879-8700	9924
B & B Plastics Recyclers Inc (PA).	5093	E	909 829-3606	10536
Distribution Alternatives Inc.	5122	D	909 770-8900	10621
Walmart Inc.	5311	D	909 820-9912	11265
Burlingame Industries Inc (PA).	7033	D	909 355-7000	13107
Caremark Rx Inc.	8011	D	909 822-1164	15262

RIDGECREST, CA - Kern County

	SIC	EMP	PHONE	ENTRY#
Orbital Sciences LLC.	3812	C	818 887-8345	7785
Directv Group Holdings LLC.	4841	A	760 375-8300	9544
Southern California Edison Co.	4911	C	760 375-1821	9636
Home Depot USA Inc.	5211	D	760 375-4614	11163
Desert Area Resources Training (PA).	5932	D	760 375-9787	11627
Altaone Federal Credit Union (PA).	6061	C	760 371-7000	11790
Ridgecrest Regional Hospital (PA).	8062	B	760 446-3551	16160
Community Action Partnr Kern.	8399	D	760 371-1469	17220
DCS Corporation.	8711	C	760 384-5600	17510
Crl Technologies Inc.	8731	C	760 495-3000	17783
Valiant Government Svcs LLC.	8744	B	760 499-1400	18270

RIVERSIDE, CA - Riverside County

	SIC	EMP	PHONE	ENTRY#
A-G Sod Farms Inc.	0181	D	951 687-7581	51
Corona - Cllege Hts Ornge Lmon.	0723	B	951 359-6451	106
Azteca Landscape.	0781	D	951 369-9210	148
FS Commercial Landscape Inc (PA).	0781	D	951 360-7070	169
Liberty Landscaping Inc (PA).	0782	C	951 683-2999	219
ATI Restoration LLC.	1521	C	951 682-9200	389
County of Riverside.	1521	C	951 955-4800	396
MGB Construction Inc.	1521	C	951 342-0303	420
Silverado Framing & Cnstr.	1521	D	951 352-1100	432
Hal Hays Construction Inc (PA).	1541	C	951 788-0703	485
Bens Asphalt & Maint Co Inc.	1611	D	951 248-1103	610
National Paving Company Inc.	1611	D	951 369-1332	639
Riverside Construction Company Inc.	1611	C	951 682-8308	644
Rsvc Company.	1611	C	951 684-6578	647
Skanska USA Civil W Cal Dst Inc (DH).	1611	A	951 684-5360	649
Hci LLC (HQ).	1623	B	951 520-4200	673
Herman Weissker Inc (HQ).	1623	B	951 826-8800	675
Kana Pipeline Inc.	1623	D	714 986-1400	683
Skanska USA Civil W Rcky Mtn Ds (DH).	1629	C	970 565-8000	719
20/20 Plumbing & Heating Inc (PA).	1711	D	951 396-2020	726
Dynamic Plumbing Systems Inc.	1711	B	951 343-1200	773
Lozano Plumbing Services Inc.	1711	C	951 683-4840	797
M & M Plumbing Inc.	1711	C	951 354-5388	799
New Power Inc.	1711	D	800 980-9825	811
Ppc Enterprises Inc.	1711	C	951 354-5402	821
Solcius LLC.	1711	C	951 772-0030	842
J M V B Inc.	1721	D	714 288-9797	867
West Coast Interiors Inc.	1721	A	951 778-3592	875
Elite Electric.	1731	D	951 681-5811	914
J Ginger Masonry LP (PA).	1741	B	951 688-5050	985
Masonry Group Nevada Inc.	1741	D	951 509-5300	987
West Coast Drywall & Co Inc.	1742	B	951 778-3592	1035
Craftsman Lath and Plaster Inc.	1751	B	951 685-9922	1048
Roy E Whitehead Inc.	1751	C	951 682-1490	1060
Hy-Tech Tile Inc.	1752	C	951 788-0550	1069
Pacific Strucframe LLC.	1761	D	951 405-8536	1090
Bedrock Company.	1771	D	951 273-1931	1105
Century West Concrete Inc.	1771	B	951 712-4065	1110
Inland Cc Inc.	1771	C	909 355-1318	1121
Z-Best Concrete Inc.	1771	C	951 774-1870	1141
Allied Steel Co Inc.	1791	D	951 241-7000	1147
Fencecorp Inc (HQ).	1799	C	951 686-3170	1204
Fenceworks LLC (PA).	1799	C	951 788-5620	1205
PSG Fencing Corporation.	1799	D	951 275-9252	1223
West Coast Countertops Inc.	1799	D	951 719-3670	1234
Swift Beef Company.	2013	C	951 571-2237	1273
Mackie International Inc (PA).	2024	E	951 346-0530	1319

	SIC	EMP	PHONE	ENTRY#
Ludfords Inc.	2033	E	909 948-0797	1353
Inland Empire Foods Inc (PA).	2034	E	951 682-8222	1365
Canine Caviar Pet Foods Inc.	2048	E	714 223-1800	1425
American Bottling Company.	2086	D	951 341-7500	1600
Bottling Group LLC.	2086	D	951 697-3200	1610
Inland Cold Storage.	2092	E	951 369-0230	1707
OSI Industries LLC.	2099	B	951 684-4500	1828
Ruiz Mexican Foods Inc (PA).	2099	C	909 947-7811	1847
Triple H Food Processors LLC.	2099	D	951 352-5700	1862
Quality Shutters Inc.	2431	E	951 683-4939	2325
T M Cobb Company (PA).	2431	E	951 248-2400	2328
Professional Cabinet Solutions.	2434	C	909 614-2900	2357
Simpson Strong-Tie Company Inc.	2439	C	714 871-8373	2380
G C Pallets Inc.	2448	E	909 357-8515	2388
Cavco Industries Inc.	2451	E	951 688-5353	2396
Fleetwood Homes California Inc (DH).	2451	C	951 351-2494	2400
Nextmod Inc.	2451	E	909 740-3120	2401
Clarios LLC.	2531	E	951 222-0284	2537
Ideal Products Inc.	2541	E	951 727-8600	2565
Heritage Container Inc.	2653	D	951 360-1900	2672
Metropolitan News Company.	2711	E	951 369-5890	2816
Press-Enterprise Company (PA).	2711	A	951 684-1200	2823
Qg Printing Corp.	2721	D	951 571-2500	2873
Qg Printing IL LLC.	2752	C	951 571-2500	3074
Quad/Graphics Inc.	2752	D	951 689-1122	3075
Sphere Alliance Inc.	2821	E	951 352-2400	3293
Cosmedx Science Inc.	2834	E	951 371-0509	3389
Gar Laboratories Inc.	2844	C	951 788-0700	3652
Plz Corp.	2844	C	951 683-2912	3681
Plz Corp.	2844	D	951 683-2912	3683
Trademark Cosmetics LLC.	2844	E	951 683-2631	3691
Mitchell Rubber Products LLC (PA).	3069	C	951 681-5655	3924
Plascor Inc.	3085	E	951 328-1010	3986
Carpenter Co.	3086	E	951 354-7550	3995
Altium Holdings LLC.	3089	A	951 340-9390	4041
AMA Plastics.	3089	B	951 734-5600	4045
AMS Plastics Inc.	3089	B	951 734-5600	4048
Blow Molded Products Inc.	3089	E	951 360-6055	4069
Bm Extrusion Inc.	3089	E	951 782-9020	4070
Carson Industries LLC.	3089	A	951 788-9720	4084
Hi-Rel Plastics & Molding Corp.	3089	E	951 354-0258	4131
Plastic Technologies Inc.	3089	E	951 360-6055	4201
Polymer Logistics Inc.	3089	D	951 567-2900	4205
Royal Interpack North Amer Inc.	3089	E	951 787-6925	4229
Snapware Corporation.	3089	C	951 361-3100	4242
Western Case Incorporated.	3089	D	951 214-6380	4275
Riverside Cement Holdings Company.	3241	B	951 774-2500	4359
Newbasis LLC.	3272	C	951 787-0600	4403
Newbasis West LLC.	3272	C	951 787-0600	4404
Oldcast Precast (DH).	3272	E	951 788-9720	4406
Alpha Materials Inc.	3273	E	951 788-5150	4427
Parex Usa Inc (DH).	3299	E	714 778-2266	4506
B-Metal Holding Company Inc.	3312	C	951 367-1510	4511
Barrette Outdoor Living Inc.	3315	E	800 336-2383	4532
Dayton Superior Corporation.	3315	C	951 782-9517	4534
Merchants Metals LLC.	3315	D	951 686-1888	4537
Luxfer Inc.	3354	E	951 684-5110	4600
Samuel Son & Co (usa) Inc.	3354	E	951 781-7800	4605
Sierra Aluminum Company.	3354	E	951 781-7800	4606
Metal Container Corporation.	3411	C	951 354-0444	4721
Crystal PCF Win & Door Sys LLC.	3442	C	951 779-9300	4885
Kawneer Company Inc.	3442	C	951 410-4779	4891
San Joaquin Window Inc.	3442	C	909 946-3697	4901
Ba Holdings Inc (DH).	3443	E	951 684-5110	4909
Clarkwestern Dietrich Building.	3444	E	951 360-3500	4969
Prism Aerospace.	3444	E	951 582-2850	5024
Quality Fabrication Inc (PA).	3444	D	818 407-5015	5025
SMS Fabrications Inc.	3444	E	951 351-6828	5034
US Precision Sheet Metal Inc.	3444	D	951 276-2611	5051
United Carports LLC.	3448	E	800 757-6742	5089
Luxfer Inc.	3463	E	951 351-4100	5157
Main Steel LLC.	3471	D	951 231-4949	5273
Dura Coat Products Inc (PA).	3479	D	951 341-6500	5318
Ejay Filtration Inc.	3496	E	951 683-0805	5405
Toro Company.	3523	C	951 688-9221	5479
Jlg Industries Inc.	3531	E	951 358-1915	5495
American Quality Tools Inc.	3545	E	951 280-4700	5604
John Bean Technologies Corp.	3556	D	951 222-2300	5677
Dek Industry Inc.	3559	C	909 941-8810	5700
Pacific Consolidated Inds LLC.	3569	D	951 479-0860	5831
Team Air Inc (PA).	3585	E	909 823-1957	5984
City of Riverside.	3589	C	951 351-6140	6007
Yardney Water MGT Systems Inc.	3589	E	951 656-6716	6039

2025 Southern California
Business Directory and Buyers Guide

(P-0000) Products & Services Section entry number
(PA)=Parent Co (HQ)=Headquarters (DH)=Div Headquarters

	SIC	EMP	PHONE	ENTRY#
Western Hydrostatics Inc (PA)	3594	E	951 784-2133	6054
Jmc Closing Co LLC	3599	E	951 278-9900	6153
Metric Machining (PA)	3599	E	909 947-9222	6176
Bourns Inc (PA)	3677	C	951 781-5500	6926
Astro Seal Inc	3679	E	951 787-6670	6968
Impact LLC	3679	E	714 546-6000	7007
Eldorado National Cal Inc (HQ)	3711	E	909 591-9557	7173
Krystal Infinity LLC	3713	B		7205
Automax Styling Inc	3714	E	951 530-1876	7230
Dee Engineering Inc	3714	E	909 947-5616	7243
Owen Trailers Inc	3715	E	951 361-4557	7316
Luxfer Inc (DH)	3728	D	951 684-5110	7516
Zenith Manufacturing Inc	3728	E	818 767-2106	7594
K & N Engineering Inc (PA)	3751	A	951 826-4000	7631
Fleetwood Travel Trlrs Ind Inc (DH)	3792	C	951 354-3000	7676
Bourns Inc	3825	E	951 781-5690	7902
DOE & Ingalls Cal Oper LLC	3826	E	951 801-7175	7950
Brenner-Fiedler & Assoc Inc (PA)	3829	E	562 404-2721	8035
Cummings Resources LLC	3993	E	951 248-1130	8597
Valley Enerprises Inc	3993	E	951 789-0843	8648
Riverside Transit Agency (PA)	4111	B	951 565-5000	8795
American Med Rspnse Inland Emp (HQ)	4119	C	951 782-5200	8810
High Performance Logistics LLC	4212	D	702 300-4880	8917
Powered By Fulfillment Inc	4222	E	626 825-9841	9039
Walmart Inc	4225	D	951 320-5722	9127
DSV Solutions LLC	4226	D	732 850-8000	9133
Empire Med Transportations LLC	4731	D	877 473-6029	9277
20/20 Mobile Corp	4812	C	909 587-2973	9379
Jurupa Community Services Dst	4941	D	951 685-7073	9697
Arakelian Enterprises Inc	4953	C	951 342-3300	9730
Recycler Core Company Inc	4953	D	951 276-1687	9760
Goforth & Marti	5021	D	951 684-0870	9873
Gtt International Inc	5023	E	951 788-8729	9897
MSRS INC	5023	C	310 952-9000	9899
Unique Carpets Ltd	5023	D	951 352-8125	9913
Crest Steel Corporation	5051	D	951 727-2600	10131
Harbor Pipe and Steel Inc	5051	C	951 369-3900	10139
Steel Unlimited Inc	5051	C	909 873-1222	10158
Pepsi-Cola Metro Btlg Co Inc	5078	E	951 697-3200	10342
Pharmerica Corporation	5122	A	951 683-4165	10644
McLane Foodservice Inc	5141	C	951 867-3727	10757
Sysco Riverside Inc	5141	B	951 601-5300	10809
Cibaria International Inc	5149	E	951 823-8490	10936
Premier Fuel Distributors Inc	5172	C	760 423-3610	11034
B & B Nurseries Inc	5193	C	951 352-8383	11081
Boise Cascade Company	5211	D	951 343-3000	11149
Dixieline Lumber Company LLC	5211	B	951 224-8491	11150
Home Depot USA Inc	5211	B	951 358-1370	11176
Lowes Home Centers LLC	5211	C	951 509-5500	11219
Parex Usa Inc	5211	E	951 653-3549	11250
Albertsons LLC	5411	D	951 656-6603	11271
Dillon Companies Inc	5411	C	951 352-8353	11275
David A Campbell Corporation	5511	C	951 785-4444	11332
Pearson Ford Co (PA)	5511	C	877 743-0421	11394
Raceway Ford Inc	5511	C	951 571-9300	11399
Toyota of Riverside Inc	5511	C	951 687-1622	11423
Walters Auto Sales and Svc Inc	5511	C	888 316-4097	11431
Fairprice Enterprises Inc	5713	D	951 684-8578	11523
Alin Party Supply Co	5947	E	951 682-7441	11649
City National Bank	6021	C	951 276-8800	11727
Pacific Premier Bancorp Inc	6022	B	951 274-2400	11773
Populus Financial Group Inc	6099	C	951 509-3506	11842
Secure Choice Lending	6159	D	951 730-0025	11878
Morgan Stnley Smith Barney LLC	6211	C	951 682-1181	11998
Southern Cal Prmnnte Med Group	6324	C	866 984-7483	12108
State Compensation Insur Fund	6331	C	888 782-8338	12140
Farmers Insurance	6411	C	951 681-1068	12211
Remn Inc	6531	D	951 697-8135	12520
Historic Mission Inn Corp	7011	B	951 784-0300	12850
Pinnacle Rvrside Hspitality LP	7011	C	951 784-8000	12974
Windsor Capital Group Inc	7011	C	951 276-1200	13083
Prudential Overall Supply	7218	D	951 687-0440	13139
ServiceMaster By Best Pros Inc	7349	D	951 515-9051	13418
Kimco Staffing Services Inc	7361	A	951 686-3800	13533
Officeworks Inc	7361	D	951 784-2534	13550
Cincom Systems Inc (PA)	7371	B	513 612-2300	13686
Fidelis Security LLC	7371	D	240 650-2041	13730
Stromasys Inc	7372	D	919 239-8450	14042
Barrys Security Services Inc (PA)	7381	C	951 789-7575	14279
313 Acquisition LLC	7382	A	801 234-6374	14372
ADT LLC	7382	C	951 782-6900	14373
Corporate Alnce Strategies Inc	7382	C	877 777-7487	14389
Holmes Body Shop-Alhambra Inc	7532	D	951 734-9920	14674
Hamblins Bdy Pnt Frame Sp Inc	7538	D	951 689-8440	14691
Grech Motors LLC (PA)	7694	E	951 688-8347	14749
Fleetwood Motor Homes-Califinc	7699	C	951 274-2000	14767
Peggs Company Inc (PA)	7699	C	800 242-8416	14782
James Allen Productions LLC	7822	D	951 944-2564	14918
Adventist Media Center Inc (PA)	7922	C	805 955-7777	14952
Victoria Club	7997	C	951 683-5323	15183
County of Riverside	8011	C	951 955-0840	15294
Glenwood Surgical Center LP	8011	D	951 689-2647	15315
Kaiser Foundation Hospitals	8011	C	951 353-3790	15348
Kaiser Foundation Hospitals	8011	A	951 353-2000	15349
Onrad Inc	8011	D	800 848-5876	15413
Riverside Medical Clinic Inc (PA)	8011	D	951 683-6370	15438
Interdent Service Corporation	8021	C	951 682-1720	15518
Air Force Village West Inc	8051	B	951 697-2000	15563
Community Care On Palm Rvrside	8051	D	951 686-9001	15596
Mt Rubidouxidence Opco LLC	8051	C	951 681-2200	15725
Riverside Care Inc	8051	C	951 683-7111	15762
Riverside Equities LLC	8051	B	951 688-2222	15763
Villa Convalescent Hosp Inc	8051	C	951 689-5788	15794
Orange Treeidence Opco LLC	8052	C	951 785-6060	15818
Magnolia Rhblttion Nursing Ctr	8059	C	951 688-4321	15872
Windsor Cypress Grdns Hlthcare	8059	A	951 688-3643	15891
Kaiser Foundation Hospitals	8062	D	951 352-0292	16046
Orangtree Cnvalescent Hosp Inc	8062	C	951 785-6060	16110
Parkview Cmnty Hosp Med Ctr	8062	A	951 354-7404	16127
Riverside Cmnty Hlth Systems (DH)	8062	C	951 788-3000	16161
Riverside Univ Hlth Sys Fndtio (PA)	8062	B	951 358-5000	16162
Vista Behavioral Health Inc	8063	D	800 992-0901	16280
Interim Healthcare Inc	8082	C	951 684-6111	16398
CRC Health Group Inc	8093	C	951 784-8010	16466
County of Riverside	8111	C	951 955-6000	16662
Carolyn E Wylie Ctr For Chldre	8322	D	951 683-5193	16878
County of Riverside	8322	C	951 955-4900	16928
County of Riverside	8331	D	951 955-3434	17055
Mulberry Child Care Ctrs Inc	8351	D	951 688-4242	17099
Keystone NPS LLC	8399	C	951 785-6060	17232
County of Riverside	8641	C	951 683-7691	17338
Kooji Intl Minority Educatn	8641	D	951 313-7403	17351
U C Riverside Foundation	8641	C	951 827-6389	17370
Automobile Club Southern Cal	8699	C	951 684-4250	17432
Albert A Webb Associates (PA)	8711	C	951 686-1070	17480
Hunsaker & Assoc Irvine Inc	8711	B	951 352-7200	17552
MSM Industries Inc	8711	E	951 735-0834	17592
Sitesol	8711	D	562 746-5884	17631
Ues Professional Solutions Inc	8711	C	951 571-4081	17655
Babcock Laboratories Inc	8734	C	951 653-3351	17905
Inland Cnties Regional Ctr Inc	8741	C	951 826-2600	17993
Team Group LLC	8741	D	951 688-8593	18064
City of Riverside	8742	C	951 826-5485	18117
Muth Machine Works	8742	D	951 685-1521	18174
Riverside Cnty Flood Ctrl Wtr	8999	C	951 955-1200	18378
County of Riverside	9431	D	951 248-0014	18393
California Dept Social Svcs	9441	C	951 782-4200	18396
County of Riverside	9441	C	951 358-5000	18398

RLLNG HLS EST, CA - Los Angeles County

	SIC	EMP	PHONE	ENTRY#
National Media Inc (HQ)	2711	E	310 377-6877	2817
Malmberg Engineering Inc	3599	E	925 606-6500	6168
Dincloud Inc	7372	D	310 929-1101	13916

ROLLING HILLS, CA - Los Angeles County

	SIC	EMP	PHONE	ENTRY#
California Digital Inc (PA)	3577	D	310 217-0500	5908

ROLLING HILLS ESTATE, CA - Los Angeles County

	SIC	EMP	PHONE	ENTRY#
Graphic Prints Inc	2396	E	310 870-1239	2261
Rolling Hills Country Club	7997	D	424 903-0000	15165

ROMOLAND, CA - Riverside County

	SIC	EMP	PHONE	ENTRY#
Southern California Edison Co	4911	D	800 336-2822	9615
Southern California Gas Co	4924	C	213 244-1200	9647

ROSEMEAD, CA - Los Angeles County

	SIC	EMP	PHONE	ENTRY#
Irish Communication Company (DH)	1623	D	626 288-6170	679
Irish Construction (HQ)	1623	C	626 288-8530	680
Chinese Overseas Mktg Svc Corp (PA)	2741	D	626 280-8588	2906
Prographics Inc	2752	E	626 287-0417	3071
BF Suma Pharmaceticals Inc	2834	E	626 285-8366	3373
Tur-Bo Jet Products Co Inc	3677	D	626 285-1294	6939
Hermetic Seal Corporation (DH)	3679	C	626 443-8931	7005
Beckman Instruments Inc	3826	D	626 309-0110	7942
Durham School Services L P	4151	A	626 573-3769	8871
Cco Holdings LLC	4841	C	626 500-1214	9526

Employee Codes: A=Over 500 employees, B=251-500
C=101-250, D=51-100, E=20-50, F=10-19, G=1-9

2025 Southern California
Business Directory and Buyers Guide

© Mergent Inc. 1-800-342-5647

1329

GEOGRAPHIC

	SIC	EMP	PHONE	ENTRY#
Edison International **(PA)**	4911	A	626 302-2222	9581
Edison Mission Energy **(PA)**	4911	D	626 302-5778	9582
Edison Mssion Midwest Holdings	4911	A	626 302-2222	9583
Southern California Edison Co **(HQ)**	4911	A	626 302-1212	9621
Southern California Edison Co.	4911	D	626 302-5101	9624
Southern California Edison Co.	4911	D	626 302-1212	9625
Panda Systems Inc	5812	C	626 799-9898	11594
Pacific Clinics	8011	D	626 287-2988	15418
Success Healthcare 1 LLC	8011	A	626 288-1160	15483
Ensign Group Inc	8051	B	626 607-2400	15641
Longwood Management Corp	8051	C	626 280-2293	15703
Longwood Management Corp	8051	C	626 280-4820	15704
Bhc Alhambra Hospital Inc	8099	B	626 286-1191	16536
Maryvale	8361	C	626 280-6510	17178
County of Los Angeles	8399	D	626 291-2200	17223

ROWLAND HEIGHTS, CA - Los Angeles County

	SIC	EMP	PHONE	ENTRY#
Cosmos Food Co Inc	2099	E	323 221-9142	1757
Silao Tortilleria Inc	2099	E	626 961-0761	1851
Novolex Bagcraft Inc	2673	E	626 912-2481	2737
Wakool Transport	3537	D	626 723-3100	5538
Istarusa Group	3571	E	888 989-1189	5856
Suzhou South	3578	E	626 322-0101	5958
Emanate Health	8011	C	626 912-5282	15305

RUNNING SPRINGS, CA - San Bernardino County

	SIC	EMP	PHONE	ENTRY#
Pali Camp	7032	C	909 867-5743	13105

SAN BERNARDINO, CA - San Bernardino County

	SIC	EMP	PHONE	ENTRY#
Rolling Green Inc	0781	B	951 360-9294	189
Original Mowbrays Tree Svc Inc	0783	C		245
Stavatti Industries Ltd	1041	E	651 238-5369	255
Matich Corporation **(PA)**	1611	D	909 382-7400	637
Caston Inc	1742	C	909 381-1619	1004
Nagles Veal Inc	2011	E	909 383-7075	1245
Farmdale Creamery LLC	2026	D	909 888-4938	1329
Live Fresh Corporation	2037	C	909 478-0895	1379
Mars Petcare Us Inc	2047	C	909 887-8131	1420
Adams and Brooks Inc	2064	C	909 880-2305	1500
Pepsico	2086	E	562 818-9429	1636
Refresco Beverages US Inc	2086	E	909 915-1430	1640
Anitas Mexican Foods Corp **(PA)**	2096	D	909 884-8706	1721
Anitas Mexican Foods Corp	2096	C	909 884-8706	1722
Haley Bros Inc	2431	C	800 854-5951	2309
Packaging Corporation America	2653	E	909 888-7008	2686
Sun Cmpany of San Brnrdino Cal **(HQ)**	2711	B	909 889-9666	2830
San Brnrdino Cmnty College Dst	2759	D	909 888-6511	3174
Shorett Printing Inc **(PA)**	2759	E	714 545-4689	3175
Mapei Corporation	2821	D	909 475-4100	3278
Innocor West LLC	3069	A	909 307-3737	3916
Foamex LP	3086	E	909 824-8981	4003
C-Pak Industries Inc	3089	E	909 880-6017	4077
Fiore Stone Inc	3272	E	909 424-0221	4390
Holliday Trucking Inc	3273	E	888 273-2200	4442
Sample Tile and Stone Inc	3281	E	951 776-8562	4477
Usmpc Buyer Inc	3296	E	909 473-3027	4496
Tamco **(HQ)**	3312	E	909 899-0660	4527
South Bay Foundry Inc **(HQ)**	3441	E	909 383-1823	4869
CMC Steel Us LLC	3449	E	909 646-7827	5093
Innovative Metal Inds Inc	3449	D	909 796-6200	5096
JLJ Rebar Extreme Inc	3449	E	909 381-9177	5097
Anco International Inc	3494	E	909 887-2521	5384
Tree Island Wire (usa) Inc	3496	C	909 899-1673	5417
Ground Hog Inc	3531	E	909 478-5700	5492
Macroair Technologies Inc **(PA)**	3564	E	909 890-2270	5772
Systems Technology Inc	3565	D	909 799-9950	5793
W B Walton Enterprises Inc	3663	E	951 683-0930	6671
DSPM Inc	3677	E	714 970-2304	6928
Allianz Sweeper Company	3711	C		7165
Global Environmental Pdts Inc	3711	D	909 713-1600	7177
Thermal Solutions Mfg Inc	3714	E	909 796-0754	7296
Northrop Grumman Systems Corp	3812	D	703 713-4096	7761
Tinker & Rasor	3812	E	909 890-0700	7819
Optivus Proton Therapy Inc **(PA)**	3829	D	909 799-8300	8057
Semco	3829	E	909 799-9666	8062
Quiel Bros Elc Sign Svc Co Inc	3993	E	909 885-4476	8625
Omnitrans	4111	C	909 383-1680	8788
Omnitrans **(PA)**	4111	C	909 379-7100	8790
San Bernardino Cnty Trnsp Auth	4111	C	909 884-8276	8796
First Student Inc	4151	C	909 383-1640	8877
Penney Opco LLC	4225	D	972 431-2618	9098
United Parcel Service Inc	4512	C	800 742-5877	9171
Aviation & Defense Inc	4581	C	909 382-3487	9190

	SIC	EMP	PHONE	ENTRY#
CJ Logistics America LLC	4731	C	540 377-2302	9263
Gxo Logistics Supply Chain Inc	4731	D	909 838-5631	9288
Gxo Logistics Supply Chain Inc	4731	D	909 253-5356	9289
Loma Linda University Med Ctr	4731	D	909 558-4000	9306
Gunderson Rail Services LLC	4789	C	909 478-0541	9365
Meridian Rail Acquisition	4789	C	909 478-0541	9370
Sprint Communications Co LP	4813	C	909 382-6030	9462
San Brnrdino Cmnty College Dst	4832	D	909 384-4444	9488
Southern California Gas Co	4924	C	909 335-7941	9649
Metropolitan Automotive Warehouse	5013	A	909 885-2886	9834
H and H Drug Stores Inc	5047	D	909 890-9700	10082
California Steel Services Inc	5051	E	909 796-2222	10127
CMC Rebar West	5051	C	909 713-1130	10128
Ten Days Manufacturing	5085	D	909 871-5340	10467
Chiro Inc **(PA)**	5087	C	909 879-1160	10472
Laymon Candy Co Inc	5145	E	909 825-4408	10849
S&E Gourmet Cuts Inc	5145	C	909 370-0155	10850
Gate City Beverage Distrs **(PA)**	5181	B	909 799-0281	11047
Bfg Supply Co LLC	5191	C	909 591-0461	11069
Harbill Inc	5511	D	909 883-8833	11359
Ocelot Engineering Inc	5571	C	800 841-2960	11484
Caldesso LLC	5999	D	909 888-2882	11676
Inland Empire Health Plan	6324	A	866 228-4347	12083
Woodman Realty Inc	6531	C	909 425-5324	12551
S B H Hotel Corporation	7011	B	909 889-0133	13004
San Bernardino Hilton **(HQ)**	7011	C	909 889-0133	13010
Job Options Incorporated	7219	A	909 890-4612	13144
Avalon Building Maint Inc	7349	B	714 693-2407	13357
Barrett Business Services Inc	7361	A	909 890-3633	13492
Nursefinders LLC	7361	C	909 890-2286	13548
Maxim Healthcare Services Inc	7363	D	951 684-4148	13606
Nationwide Technologies Inc	7372	E	909 340-2770	13981
United Guard Security Inc	7381	C	909 402-0754	14358
ADT LLC	7382	C	951 824-7205	14374
Jenco Productions LLC **(PA)**	7389	C	909 381-9453	14520
Inland Empire 66ers Bsbal CLB	7941	C	909 888-9922	15028
San Brnrdino Cnty Rgonal Parks	7999	D	909 387-2583	15220
Sb Waterman Holdings Inc **(PA)**	8011	C	909 883-8611	15447
Boyd Dental Corporation	8021	C	909 890-0421	15515
Robert Ballard Rehab Hospital **(HQ)**	8049	D	909 473-1200	15556
Ensign Group Inc	8051	C	909 886-4731	15643
Far West Inc	8051	D	909 884-4781	15652
Waterman Convalescent Hosp Inc **(PA)**	8051	C	909 882-1215	15798
Del Rosa Villaidence Opco LLC	8052	C	909 885-3261	15810
Watermanidence Opco LLC	8052	C	909 882-1215	15827
Marna Health Services Inc	8059	D	909 882-2965	15874
San Bernardino Care Company	8059	C	909 884-4781	15883
United Medical Management Inc	8059	C	909 886-5291	15888
Community Hosp San Bernardino **(DH)**	8062	B	909 887-6333	15962
Kaiser Foundation Hospitals	8062	C	909 386-5500	16048
St Bernardine Med Ctr Aux Inc	8062	C	909 881-4320	16213
Maxim Healthcare Services Inc	8082	C	760 243-3377	16405
Vnacare **(PA)**	8082	D	909 624-3574	16433
Institute For Bhvoral Hlth Inc	8093	B	909 289-1041	16481
Victor Cmnty Support Svcs Inc	8093	C	909 890-5930	16520
Bio-Medics Inc	8099	C	909 883-9501	16537
Lifestream Blood Bank **(HQ)**	8099	C	909 885-6503	16582
San Brnrdino Cy Unfied Schl Ds	8099	D	909 881-8000	16614
California City San Bernardino **(PA)**	8111	B	909 384-7272	16652
Fennemore Craig PC	8111	D	619 794-0050	16682
Inland Cnties Regional Ctr Inc **(PA)**	8322	C	909 890-3000	16958
San Brnrdino Cnty Prbtion Offc	8322	B	909 887-2544	17002
Think Together	8351	B	909 723-1400	17115
Victor Treatment Centers Inc	8361	C	951 436-5200	17203
Community Action Prtnr San Brn	8399	D	909 723-1500	17221
YMCA of East Valley	8641	C	909 881-9622	17380
Allen Engineering Contractor Inc	8711	C	909 478-5500	17481
Northrop Grmmn Spce & Mssn Sys	8731	C	909 382-6800	17813
Amtex Supply Holdings Inc	8742	C	909 985-8918	18092
Mentor Mdia USA Sup Chain MGT	8742	D	909 930-0800	18170

SAN CLEMENTE, CA - Orange County

	SIC	EMP	PHONE	ENTRY#
Bemus Landscape Inc	1629	B	714 557-7910	709
Millennium Reinforcing Inc	1791	B	949 361-9730	1159
Custom Ingredients Inc **(PA)**	2087	E	949 276-7995	1674
Freshrealm Inc **(PA)**	2099	C	800 264-1297	1778
R & R Industries Inc	2389	E	800 234-5611	2200
Western Outdoors Publications **(PA)**	2711	E	949 366-0030	2838
Taylor Digital	2759	E	949 391-3333	3180
International Rubber Pdts Inc **(HQ)**	3069	D	909 947-1244	3917
Kelcourt Plastics Inc **(DH)**	3089	D	949 361-0774	4152
Kui Co Inc	3089	E	949 369-7949	4156
Plastics Development Corp	3089	E	949 492-0217	4202

Mergent email: customerrelations@mergent.com
1330

2025 Southern California
Business Directory and Buyers Guide

(P-0000) Products & Services Section entry number
(PA)=Parent Co (HQ)=Headquarters (DH)=Div Headquarters

	SIC	EMP	PHONE	ENTRY#
Clean Wave Management Inc	3562	E	949 370-0740	5748
Snowpure LLC	3589	E	949 240-2188	6033
Dana Innovations (PA)	3651	C	949 492-7777	6532
Fleming Metal Fabricators	3713	E	323 723-8203	7203
Bunker Corp (PA)	3714	D	949 361-3935	7231
Swift Autonomy Inc	3721	E	800 547-9438	7373
Swift Engineering Inc	3728	D	949 492-6608	7571
Reynard Corporation	3827	E	949 366-8866	8017
Composite Manufacturing Inc	3841	E	949 361-7580	8134
Epica Medical Innovations LLC	3841	E	949 238-6323	8152
Icu Medical Inc (PA)	3841	A	949 366-2183	8166
Electric Visual Evolution LLC (PA)	3851	E	949 940-9125	8406
Rip Curl Inc	3949	E	714 422-3617	8534
Rosen & Rosen Industries Inc	3949	D	949 361-9238	8536
San Diego Gas & Electric Co	4931	C	949 361-8090	9672
Buyefficient LLC	5046	C	949 382-3129	10041
Cameron Health Inc	5047	D	949 940-4000	10071
Pacific Medical Group Inc	5047	D	866 282-6834	10099
Liberty Synergistics Inc	5085	C	949 361-1100	10442
Stance Inc (PA)	5137	D	949 391-9030	10729
Lowes Home Centers LLC	5211	C	949 369-4644	11203
Luxre Realty Inc	6531	D	949 498-3702	12483
Matsushita International Corp (PA)	6799	D	949 498-1000	12716
Life Time Inc	7991	C	949 492-1515	15055
Heritage Golf Group LLC	7992	D	949 369-6226	15085
Bella Collina San Clemente	7997	C	949 498-6604	15123
Pacific Golf & Country Club	7997	D	949 498-6604	15157
Monarch Healthcare A Medical	8011	C	949 489-1960	15397
Amada Senior Care	8082	D	949 284-8036	16362
Dual Diagnosis Trtmnt Ctr Inc (PA)	8093	C	949 276-5553	16470
Automobile Club Southern Cal	8699	D	949 489-5572	17456
Evolution Hospitality LLC (HQ)	8741	D	949 325-1350	17983

SAN DIEGO, CA - San Diego County

	SIC	EMP	PHONE	ENTRY#
Veterinary Practice Assoc Inc	0742	C	949 833-9020	135
Brightview Landscape Dev Inc	0781	B	858 458-9900	153
Brightview Landscape Svcs Inc	0781	C	858 458-1900	154
Heaviland Enterprises Inc	0781	C	858 412-1576	173
NN Jaeschke Inc	0781	E	858 550-7900	182
Landcare USA LLC	0782	C	858 453-1755	215
Namvars Inc	0782	D	858 792-5461	225
New Way Landscape & Tree Svcs	0782	C	858 505-8300	226
Aptim Federal Services LLC	1521	B	619 239-1690	388
JR Construction Inc	1521	D	858 505-4760	411
Largo Concrete Inc	1521	C	619 356-2142	417
Fairfield Development Inc (PA)	1522	C	858 457-2123	446
Wermers Multi-Family Corp	1522	D	858 535-1475	457
Amaya Curiel Corporation	1541	A	619 661-1230	470
Biotix	1541	E	858 875-5479	474
CMC Rebar West	1541	D	858 737-7700	477
Isec Incorporated	1541	C	858 279-9085	487
Kevcon Inc	1541	D	760 432-0307	488
Ledcor CMI Inc	1541	D	602 595-3017	490
T B Penick & Sons Inc	1541	C	858 558-1800	507
Austin Commercial LP	1542	C	619 446-5637	518
Balfour Beatty Cnstr LLC	1542	D	858 635-7400	520
Barnhart Inc	1542	B	858 635-7400	521
Bycor General Contractors Inc	1542	D	858 587-1901	525
C W Driver Incorporated	1542	C	619 696-5100	526
Dpr Construction A Gen Partnr	1542	C	858 646-0757	334
Harvey USA LLC	1542	C	858 769-4000	543
Pacific Building Group (PA)	1542	D	858 552-0600	563
PCL Construction Services Inc	1542	C	858 657-3400	565
Solpac Inc	1542	C	619 296-6247	587
Triton Structural Concrete Inc	1542	C	858 866-2450	594
Webcor Construction LP	1542	C	619 798-3891	602
West Pacific Services Inc	1542	C	888 401-0188	604
City of San Diego	1611	C	619 527-7482	612
Ies Commercial Inc	1611	C	858 210-4900	625
Cameron Intrstate Pipeline LLC	1623	C	619 696-3110	667
Vadnais Trenchless Svcs Inc	1623	D	858 550-1460	702
A & D Fire Protection Inc	1711	D	619 258-7697	727
A O Reed & Co LLC	1711	B	858 565-4131	728
Alpha Mechanical Inc	1711	D	858 278-3500	733
Alpha Mechanical Heating & Air Cond	1711	D	858 279-1300	734
Apex Mechanical Systems Inc	1711	D	858 536-8700	739
ASI Hastings Inc	1711	C	619 590-9300	742
Atlas Mechanical Inc (PA)	1711	D	858 554-0700	745
Bill Howe Plumbing Inc	1711	D	800 245-5469	750
Cosco Fire Protection Inc	1711	D	858 444-2000	767
Greater San Diego AC Co Inc	1711	C	619 469-7818	784
Jackson & Blanc	1711	D	858 831-7900	791
National Air Inc	1711	C	619 299-2500	810

	SIC	EMP	PHONE	ENTRY#
Pacific Rim Mech Contrs Inc (PA)	1711	B	858 974-6500	815
Pan-Pacific Mechanical LLC	1711	B	858 764-2464	817
Schmidt Fire Protection Co Inc	1711	D	858 279-6122	834
Sherwood Mechanical Inc	1711	D	858 679-3000	838
General Coatings Corporation (PA)	1721	C	858 587-1277	863
4liberty Inc	1731	D	619 400-1000	876
Communction Wirg Spcalists Inc	1731	D	858 278-4545	901
Fishel Company	1731	C	858 658-0830	918
Helix Electric Inc (PA)	1731	C	858 535-0505	924
Wirtz Quality Installations	1741	D	858 569-3816	992
Best Interiors Inc	1742	D	858 715-3760	999
Pacific Building Group	1742	D	858 552-0600	1020
J W Floor Covering Inc (PA)	1752	C	858 558-8565	1070
A Preman Roofing Inc	1761	D	619 276-1700	1071
Ben F Smith Inc	1771	C	858 271-4320	1106
Cement Cutting Inc	1771	D	619 296-9592	1109
Coffman Specialties Inc (PA)	1771	C	858 536-3100	1111
Heavy Metal Steel Company Inc	1791	E	858 433-4800	1153
Herzog Contracting Corp	1799	D	619 849-6990	1209
Penhall Company	1799	D	858 550-1111	1221
Proform Interior Cnstr Inc	1799	C	619 881-0041	1222
Yyk Enterprises Operations LLC (PA)	1799	C	619 474-6229	1237
Old Bbh Inc	2013	A	858 715-4000	1263
El Indio Shops Incorporated	2023	D	619 299-0333	1297
Intelligent Blends LLC	2043	E	858 888-7937	1412
Honest Kitchen Inc	2047	E	619 544-0018	1417
Tallgrass Pictures LLC	2051	E	619 227-2701	1467
Opera Patisserie	2053	D	858 536-5800	1495
Azumex Inc	2061	E	619 710-8855	1497
Anheuser-Busch LLC	2082	E	858 581-7000	1534
Associated Microbreweries Inc	2082	C	858 587-2739	1535
Associated Microbreweries Inc (PA)	2082	E	858 273-2739	1536
Associated Microbreweries Inc	2082	C	619 234-2739	1537
Assocted McRbrwries Ltd A Cal	2082	E	858 273-2739	1539
Home Brew Mart Inc	2082	B	858 790-6900	1543
Jdz Inc	2082	D	858 549-9888	1544
Karl Strauss Brewing Company (PA)	2082	E	858 273-2739	1545
Kings & Convicts Bp LLC	2082	C	619 255-7213	1546
Kings & Convicts Bp LLC	2082	C	619 295-2337	1547
Stone Brewing Co LLC	2082	C	619 269-2100	1553
Taproom Beer Co	2082	E	619 539-7738	1555
Cydea Inc	2084	E	800 710-9939	1563
Reyes Coca-Cola Bottling LLC	2086	B	619 266-6300	1651
United Brands Company Inc	2087	E	619 461-5220	1692
Bumble Bee Seafoods LP	2091	C	858 715-4000	1696
Blue Nalu Inc	2092	E	858 703-8703	1702
Foods On Fly LLC	2099	E	858 404-0642	1776
Fuji Food Products Inc	2099	C	619 268-3118	1780
Husks Unlimited (PA)	2099	E	619 476-8301	1791
Southwest Products LLC	2099	C	619 263-8000	1855
R J Reynolds Tobacco Company	2111	D	858 625-8453	1868
Masterpiece Artist Canvas LLC	2211	E	619 710-2500	1884
California Industrial Fabrics	2231	E	619 661-7456	1898
Balboa Manufacturing Co LLC (PA)	2253	E	858 715-0060	1911
Custom Logos Inc	2261	E	858 277-1886	1932
No Second Thoughts Inc	2311	D	619 428-5992	1978
Creative Design Industries	2321	C	619 710-2525	1982
Army of Happy LLC	2323	E	704 517-9890	1989
Legendary Holdings Inc	2353	E	619 872-6100	2159
Terry Town Corporation	2384	D	619 421-5354	2177
Krasnes Inc	2386	D	619 232-2066	2181
Lofta	2392	E	858 299-8000	2215
Four Seasons Design Inc (PA)	2396	E	619 761-5151	2260
Autoliv Asp Inc	2399	E	619 662-8018	2272
Autoliv Safety Technology Inc	2399	A	619 662-8000	2273
Prestige Flag & Banner Co Inc	2399	D	619 497-2220	2280
Rtmex Inc	2426	C	619 391-9913	2292
Canyon Graphics Inc	2431	D	858 646-0444	2300
Jeld-Wen Inc	2431	E	800 468-3667	2311
Quality Cabinet and Fixture Co (HQ)	2434	D	619 266-1011	2358
Cri 2000 LP (PA)	2499	E	619 542-1975	2411
Whalen LLC (DH)	2511	E	619 423-9948	2438
Elite Leather LLC	2512	D	909 548-8600	2446
Ideal Mattress Company Inc	2515	E	619 595-0003	2486
Ana Global LLC (PA)	2517	E	619 482-9990	2497
Gilbert Martin Wdwkg Co Inc (PA)	2517	E	800 268-5669	2498
Bleau Consulting Inc (PA)	2521	D	619 263-5550	2505
Ecr4kids LP	2531	E	619 323-2005	2541
J L Furnishings LLC	2531	B	310 605-6600	2544
Seating Concepts LLC	2531	E	619 491-3159	2552
Dynamic Resources Inc	2621	D	619 268-3070	2622
Taylord Products Intl Inc (PA)	2631	D	619 247-6544	2645
Corrugados De Baja California	2653	A	619 662-8672	2661

Employee Codes: A=Over 500 employees, B=251-500
C=101-250, D=51-100, E=20-50, F=10-19, G=1-9

2025 Southern California
Business Directory and Buyers Guide

© Mergent Inc. 1-800-342-5647

1331

GEOGRAPHIC

	SIC	EMP	PHONE	ENTRY#
Global Packaging Solutions Inc.	2653	B	619 710-2661	2669
Pgac Corp **(PA)**	2671	D	858 560-8213	2710
Southland Envelope LLC	2677	C	619 449-3553	2753
Avery Products Corporation	2678	C	619 671-1022	2758
Bavarian Nordic Inc	2678	E	919 600-1260	2759
P & R Paper Supply Co Inc	2679	C	619 671-2400	2770
Joong-Ang Daily News Cal Inc	2711	D	858 573-1111	2806
Kaar Drect Mail Flfillment LLC	2711	E	619 382-3670	2808
North County Times **(DH)**	2711	C	800 533-8830	2820
San Diego Union-Tribune LLC **(PA)**	2711	A	619 299-3131	2825
Voice of San Diego	2711	E	619 325-0525	2836
Cbj LP	2721	E	858 277-6359	2849
San Diego Magazine Pubg Co	2721	E	619 230-9292	2876
Dawn Sign Press Inc	2731	E	858 625-0600	2888
Houghton Mifflin Harcourt Pubg	2731	E	617 351-5000	2890
Plural Publishing Inc	2731	E	858 492-1555	2894
Elsevier Inc	2741	D	619 231-6616	2914
Elsevier Inc	2741	E	619 231-6616	2915
Marcoa Media LLC **(PA)**	2741	E	858 635-9627	2926
Neil A Kjos Music Company **(PA)**	2741	E	858 270-9800	2928
Real Marketing	2741	E	858 847-0335	2940
Tabor Communications	2741	E	858 625-0070	2944
Transwestern Publishing Company LLC	2741	A	858 467-2800	2949
West Publishing Corporation	2741	A	619 296-7862	2956
Yamagata America Inc	2741	C	858 751-1010	2957
Brehm Communications Inc **(PA)**	2752	E	858 451-6200	2973
Continental Graphics Corp	2752	D	858 552-6520	2988
Elum Designs Inc	2752	E	858 650-3586	3006
Kovin Corporation Inc	2752	E	858 558-0100	3029
Modern Printing & Mailing Inc	2752	E	619 222-0535	3045
Neyenesch Printers Inc	2752	D	619 297-2281	3049
No Boundaries Inc	2752	E	619 266-2349	3051
Packaging Manufacturing Inc	2752	C	619 498-9199	3056
PM Corporate Group Inc **(PA)**	2752	D	800 343-3139	3062
Printivity LLC	2752	E	877 649-5463	3067
Robo 3d Inc	2752	E	844 476-2233	3077
Rush Press Inc	2752	E	619 296-7874	3078
Scholastic Sports Inc	2752	D	858 496-9221	3080
Vdp Direct LLC **(PA)**	2752	E	858 300-4510	3097
Bretkeri Corporation	2759	E	858 292-4919	3122
Colmol Inc	2759	E	858 693-7575	3130
Express Business Systems Inc	2759	E	858 549-9828	3138
Kieran Label Corp	2759	E	619 449-4457	3150
Optec Laser Systems LLC	2759	E	858 220-1070	3157
R R Donnelley & Sons Company	2759	E	619 527-4600	3166
Neon Rose Inc	2813	E	619 218-6103	3220
Carbomer Inc	2819	D	858 552-0992	3231
Rock West Composites Inc **(PA)**	2821	D	858 537-6260	3290
Allermed Laboratories Inc	2833	E	858 292-1060	3308
Green Star Labs Inc	2833	E	619 489-9020	3317
Sapphire Energy Inc	2833	D	858 768-4700	3331
Acadia Pharmaceuticals Inc **(PA)**	2834	A	858 558-2871	3339
Aegis Life Inc	2834	E	650 666-5287	3342
Agouron Pharmaceuticals Inc **(HQ)**	2834	E	858 622-3000	3343
Ambit Biosciences Corporation	2834	D	858 334-2100	3349
Amylin Ohio LLC	2834	A	858 552-2200	3354
Anaptysbio Inc **(PA)**	2834	C	858 362-6295	3355
Applied Mlecular Evolution Inc **(HQ)**	2834	E	858 597-4990	3358
Arcturus Thrptics Holdings Inc **(PA)**	2834	E	858 900-2660	3359
Ardea Biosciences Inc	2834	E	858 625-0787	3360
Avidity Biosciences Inc **(PA)**	2834	E	858 401-7900	3367
Cardiff Oncology Inc	2834	E	858 952-7570	3381
Catalent Pharma Solutions Inc	2834	C	858 805-6383	3384
Catalent Pharma Solutions Inc	2834	D	877 587-1835	3385
Celgene Corporation	2834	E	858 795-4961	3386
Crinetics Pharmaceuticals Inc **(PA)**	2834	E	858 450-6464	3391
Cv Sciences Inc **(PA)**	2834	E	866 290-2157	3392
Cymbiotika LLC **(PA)**	2834	E	770 910-4945	3393
Cymbiotika LLC	2834	D	949 652-8177	3394
Elitra Pharmaceuticals	2834	E	858 410-3030	3400
Erasca Inc	2834	C	858 465-6511	3402
Genomics Inst of Nvrtis RES FN	2834	D	858 812-1805	3406
Gossamer Bio Inc **(PA)**	2834	E	858 684-1300	3413
Gyre Therapeutics Inc **(PA)**	2834	B	650 266-8674	3416
Heron Therapeutics Inc **(PA)**	2834	E	858 251-4400	3419
Inova Diagnostics Inc	2834	C	858 586-9900	3424
Janssen Research & Dev LLC	2834	C	858 450-2000	3433
Janux Therapeutics Inc	2834	E	858 751-4493	3434
Kura Oncology Inc **(PA)**	2834	E	858 500-8800	3439
Lorem Cytori Usa Inc	2834	E	858 746-8696	3445
Maravai Lfscences Holdings Inc **(PA)**	2834	E	858 546-0004	3447
MEI Pharma Inc	2834	E	858 369-7100	3450
Metacrine Inc	2834	E	858 369-7800	3451
National Resilience Inc **(PA)**	2834	E	888 737-2460	3455
Neurelis Inc **(PA)**	2834	E	858 251-2111	3459
Otonomy Inc	2834	D	619 323-2200	3467
Pacira Pharmaceuticals Inc	2834	D	858 625-2424	3471
Pfenex Inc	2834	D	858 352-4400	3472
Pfizer Inc	2834	D	858 622-3000	3473
Pfizer Inc	2834	E	858 622-3001	3474
Pharmion Corporation	2834	E	858 335-5744	3476
Polypeptide Labs San Diego LLC	2834	D	858 408-0808	3477
Prescient Holdings Group LLC	2834	E	858 790-7004	3478
Primapharma Inc	2834	E	858 259-0969	3479
Prometheus Biosciences Inc	2834	D	858 422-4300	3480
Prometheus Laboratories Inc **(PA)**	2834	B	858 824-0895	3481
Receptos Inc	2834	E	858 652-5700	3489
Rempex Pharmaceuticals Inc	2834	E	858 875-2840	3491
Resilience Us Inc **(HQ)**	2834	E	984 202-0854	3492
Sapu Bioscience LLC	2834	E	650 635-7018	3498
Shire Rgenerative Medicine Inc	2834	E	858 754-5396	3501
Signal Pharmaceuticals LLC	2834	C	858 795-4700	3503
Societal CDMO San Diego LLC	2834	D	858 623-1520	3506
STA Pharmaceutical US LLC	2834	E	609 606-6499	3509
Travere Therapeutics Inc **(PA)**	2834	B	888 969-7879	3513
Trius Therapeutics LLC	2834	C	858 452-0370	3514
Vertex Phrmctcals San Dego LLC **(HQ)**	2834	C	858 404-6600	3517
Viking Therapeutics Inc **(PA)**	2834	E	858 704-4660	3518
Wacker Biotech US Inc	2834	E	858 875-4700	3521
Zentalis Pharmaceuticals Inc **(PA)**	2834	C	858 263-4333	3526
Acon Laboratories Inc **(PA)**	2835	E	858 875-8000	3528
Alere Inc	2835	D	858 805-2000	3529
Alere San Diego Inc **(DH)**	2835	D	858 805-2000	3530
Bioserv Corporation	2835	E	917 817-1326	3535
Dermtech Inc **(PA)**	2835	C	866 450-4223	3537
Gateway Genomics LLC	2835	D	858 886-7250	3540
Gen-Probe Incorporated	2835	D	858 410-8000	3541
Inova Diagnostics Inc	2835	C	858 586-9900	3542
Pacific Biotech Inc	2835	E	858 552-1100	3547
Quidel Corporation	2835	E	858 552-1100	3549
Quidel Corporation **(HQ)**	2835	D	858 552-1100	3550
Quidelortho Corporation **(PA)**	2835	E	858 552-1100	3551
Ark Animal Health Inc	2836	E	858 203-4100	3558
Artiva Biotherapeutics Inc	2836	D	858 267-4467	3560
Atyr Pharma Inc **(PA)**	2836	E	858 731-8389	3562
Bioatla Inc	2836	D	858 558-0708	3566
Cidara Therapeutics Inc **(PA)**	2836	D	858 752-6170	3569
Gb007 Inc	2836	D	858 684-1300	3576
Halozyme Therapeutics Inc **(PA)**	2836	E	858 794-8889	3579
Immunitybio Inc **(PA)**	2836	D	844 696-5235	3580
Neurocrine Biosciences Inc **(PA)**	2836	C	858 617-7600	3584
Poseida Therapeutics Inc **(PA)**	2836	B	858 779-3100	3585
Sorrento Therapeutics Inc **(PA)**	2836	D	858 203-4100	3587
Natural Thoughts Incorporated	2844	E	619 582-0027	3671
Sharpmart LLC	2844	E	619 278-1473	3686
Suneva Medical Inc **(PA)**	2844	E	858 550-9999	3690
Frazee Industries Inc	2851	A	858 626-3600	3714
Rhino Linings Corporation **(PA)**	2851	D	858 450-0441	3720
BASF Enzymes LLC **(DH)**	2869	D	858 431-8520	3730
Biotix **(HQ)**	2869	E	858 875-7696	3731
Verenium Corporation	2869	E	858 431-8500	3742
Cibus Inc	2879	C	858 450-0008	3753
Seal For Life Industries LLC **(HQ)**	2891	E	619 671-0932	3778
Chemdiv Inc	2899	E	858 794-4860	3792
Chemtreat Inc	2899	D	804 935-2000	3793
Coatinc United States Inc	2899	E	619 638-7261	3794
Cutwater Spirits LLC **(HQ)**	2899	D	858 672-3848	3795
Firmenich Incorporated	2899	D	858 646-8323	3799
New Leaf Biofuel LLC	2911	E	619 236-8500	3827
Sacahn JV	2911	D	858 924-1110	3829
Wd-40 Company	2911	C	619 275-1400	3836
WD-40 Company **(PA)**	2992	C	619 275-1400	3859
Bridgestone Americas Inc	3011	E	858 874-3109	3863
Oxystrap International Inc	3069	E	800 699-6901	3928
Plastics Family Holdings Inc	3081	D	858 560-1551	3954
Providien Thermoforming LLC	3081	E	858 850-1591	3956
Saint-Gobain Solar Gard LLC **(DH)**	3081	E	866 300-2674	3957
Atlas Roofing Corporation	3086	E	626 334-5358	3994
Walter N Coffman Inc	3086	D	619 266-2642	4022
Apon Industries Corp	3089	C		4051
Bh-Tech Inc	3089	A	858 694-0900	4068
MI Technologies Inc	3089	A	619 710-2637	4169
New West Products Inc	3089	E	619 671-9022	4178
Providien Injction Molding Inc	3089	D	760 931-1844	4213
San Diego Ace Inc	3089	E	619 206-7339	4235
Eleanor Rigby Leather Co	3199	D	619 356-5590	4310

Mergent email: customerrelations@mergent.com
1332

2025 Southern California
Business Directory and Buyers Guide

(P-0000) Products & Services Section entry number
(PA)=Parent Co (HQ)=Headquarters (DH)=Div Headquarters

	SIC	EMP	PHONE	ENTRY#
Shamir Insight Inc.	3229	D	858 514-8330	4329
Rayotek Scientific LLC	3231	E	858 558-3671	4345
Forterra Pipe & Precast LLC	3272	E	858 715-5600	4392
San Diego Precast Concrete Inc (DH)	3272	E	619 240-8000	4421
Robertsons Ready Mix Ltd	3273	C	800 834-7557	4452
Superior Ready Mix Concrete LP	3273	D	619 265-0955	4457
Superior Ready Mix Concrete LP	3273	D	619 265-0296	4458
International Mfg Tech Inc (DH)	3312	E	619 544-7741	4518
Price Industries Inc	3312	E	858 673-4451	4522
San Dego Prcsion Machining Inc	3312	E	858 499-0379	4524
Argen Corporation (PA)	3339	C	858 455-7900	4579
Johnson Matthey Inc	3341	C	858 716-2400	4586
Bridgewave Communications Inc	3357	E	408 567-6900	4626
Hiller Companies LLC	3366	E	858 899-5008	4681
Van Can Company	3411	C	858 391-8084	4727
Allegion Access Tech LLC	3423	E	858 431-5940	4735
Hodge Products Inc	3429	E	800 778-2217	4771
Lucky Line Products Inc	3429	E	858 549-6699	4778
Pacific Maritime Inds Corp	3441	C	619 575-8141	4858
Hyundai Translead (HQ)	3443	D	619 574-1500	4915
Arrk North America	3444	C	858 552-1587	4952
Concise Fabricators Inc	3444	E	520 746-3226	4973
Marine & Rest Fabricators Inc	3444	E	619 232-7267	5002
Metal Master Inc	3444	E	858 292-8880	5006
Romla Co	3444	E	619 946-1224	5031
Spec-Built Systems Inc	3444	D	619 661-8100	5036
Pacific Steel Group LLC (PA)	3449	C	858 251-1100	5100
HI Tech Honeycomb Inc	3469	C	858 974-1600	5191
Sheffield Platers Inc	3471	D	858 546-8484	5294
Southern California Plating Co	3471	E	619 231-1481	5296
Symcoat Metal Processing Inc	3471	E	858 451-3313	5297
Alphacoat Finishing LLC	3479	E	949 748-7796	5307
Dha America Inc	3496	D	858 925-3246	5404
Innovive LLC (PA)	3496	E	858 309-6620	5406
Right Manufacturing LLC	3498	E	858 566-7002	5437
Precision Engine Controls Corp (DH)	3511	C	858 792-3217	5460
Solar Turbines Incorporated (HQ)	3511	A	619 544-5352	5461
Solar Turbines Incorporated	3511	E	619 544-5321	5462
Solar Turbines Incorporated	3511	E	858 694-6110	5463
Solar Turbines Incorporated	3511	D	858 715-2060	5464
Rain Bird Corporation	3523	D	619 674-4068	5476
California Air Tools Inc	3546	E	866 409-4581	5634
Seescan Inc (PA)	3546	C	858 244-3300	5637
Ssco Manufacturing Inc	3548	E	619 628-1022	5649
Teledyne Seabotix Inc	3549	D	619 239-5959	5655
Fabric8labs Inc	3555	D	858 215-1142	5661
Asml Us LLC	3559	B	858 385-6500	5692
CP Manufacturing Inc (HQ)	3559	C	619 477-3175	5697
Morgan Polymer Seals LLC	3559	B	619 498-9221	5712
Schroff Inc	3561	A	800 525-4682	5743
Industrial Fire Sprnklr Co Inc	3569	E	619 266-6030	5824
Pall Corporation	3569	C	858 455-7264	5832
AP Labs Inc (PA)	3571	E	800 822-7522	5841
Continuous Computing Corp	3571	C	858 882-8800	5843
HP Inc	3571	B	858 924-5117	5851
Matri Kart	3571	E	858 609-0933	5860
Teradata Operations Inc (HQ)	3571	D	937 242-4030	5870
Vigobyte Tape Corporation	3572	A	866 803-8446	5892
Congatec Inc	3577	E	858 457-2600	5910
Exce LP	3577	D	858 549-6340	5919
Mad Catz Inc	3577	C	858 790-5008	5933
Magma Inc	3577	E	858 530-2511	5934
Asteres Inc (PA)	3578	E	858 777-8600	5957
Alliance Air Products Llc (DH)	3585	E	619 428-9688	5964
Alliance Air Products Llc	3585	A	619 664-0027	5965
Elco Rfrgn Solutions LLC	3585	A	858 888-9447	5975
Thermocraft	3585	D	619 813-2985	5985
Trane US Inc	3585	C	858 292-0833	5987
Trumed Systems Incorporated	3585	E	844 878-6331	5989
Pronto Products Co (PA)	3589	D	619 661-6995	6028
Water Works Inc	3589	E	858 499-0119	6037
Parker-Hannifin Corporation	3594	C	619 661-7000	6053
5th Axis Inc (PA)	3599	C	858 505-0432	6057
Coredux USA LLC	3599	D	858 642-0713	6109
Futuristics Machine Inc	3599	E	858 450-0644	6129
J I Machine Company Inc	3599	E	858 695-1787	6150
Senior Operations LLC	3599	D	858 278-8400	6232
Senior Operations LLC	3599	E	858 278-8400	6234
Senior Operations LLC	3599	C	858 278-8400	6235
Thomson Industries Inc	3599	E	619 661-6292	6249
Nuvve Holding Corp (PA)	3612	E	619 456-5161	6290
Pulse Electronics Inc (HQ)	3612	B	858 674-8100	6296
Sempra Global (HQ)	3612	D	619 696-2000	6298
Aemi Holdings LLC	3613	D	858 481-0210	6300
Cal LLC Powerflex Systems	3621	E	650 469-3392	6315
Eroad Inc	3621	D	503 305-2255	6321
Balboa Water Group LLC (HQ)	3625	D	714 384-0384	6342
Cal-Comp Electronics (usa) Co Ltd	3625	B	858 587-6900	6343
Crydom Inc (DH)	3625	E	619 210-1590	6345
General Dynamics Mission	3625	D	619 671-5400	6350
S R C Devices Inccustomer	3625	B	866 772-8668	6359
Surface Technologies Corp	3625	E	619 564-8320	6361
Teal Electronics Corporation (PA)	3625	D	858 558-9000	6364
Intelligent Technologies LLC	3629	C	858 458-1500	6376
Maxwell Technologies Inc	3629	D	858 503-3493	6378
Mirama Enterprises Inc	3631	D	858 587-8866	6387
Autosplice Parent Inc (PA)	3643	C	858 535-0077	6411
Teledyne Instruments Inc	3643	C	858 842-3100	6432
Enertron Technologies Inc	3646	E	800 537-7649	6457
Clear Blue Energy Corp	3648	D	858 451-1549	6495
Deepsea Power & Light Inc	3648	E	858 576-1261	6498
Remote Ocean Systems Inc (PA)	3648	D	858 565-8500	6515
Activeon Inc (PA)	3651	E	858 798-3300	6522
Al Shellco LLC (HQ)	3651	C	570 296-6444	6523
Philips	3651	D	916 337-8008	6547
Sanyo Manufacturing Corporation	3651	D	619 661-1134	6553
Sony Electronics Inc	3651	C	858 942-2400	6556
Sony Electronics Inc (DH)	3651	A	858 942-2400	6557
Franklin Wireless Corp	3661	D	858 623-0000	6585
Sonim Technologies Inc (PA)	3661	E	650 378-8100	6591
Ectron Corporation	3663	E	858 278-0600	6611
Interdigital Inc	3663	D	858 210-4800	6620
L3 Technologies Inc	3663	B	858 279-0411	6623
L3 Technologies Inc	3663	D	858 552-9716	6624
L3 Technologies Inc	3663	B	858 552-9500	6625
Nextivity Inc (PA)	3663	E	858 485-9442	6641
Qualcomm Incorporated (PA)	3663	A	858 587-1121	6647
Qualcomm Incorporated	3663	B	858 587-1121	6648
Qualcomm Incorporated	3663	E	202 263-0008	6649
Satellite Security Corporation	3663	E	877 437-4199	6656
Seaspace Corporation	3663	E	858 746-1100	6657
Space Micro Inc	3663	C	858 332-0700	6661
Vigor Systems Inc	3663	E	866 748-4467	6670
Blue Squirrel Inc	3669	D	858 268-0717	6676
Indyme Solutions LLC	3669	E	858 268-0717	6686
Johnson Cntrls Fire Prtction L	3669	D	858 633-9100	6687
Qualcomm Mems Technologies Inc	3669	E	858 587-1121	6690
Ecoatm LLC (DH)	3671	C	858 999-3200	6700
Benchmark Elec Phoenix Inc	3672	B	619 397-2402	6712
Electronic Surfc Mounted Inds	3672	E	858 455-1710	6725
Modalai Inc	3672	E	858 247-7053	6752
Northwest Circuits Corp	3672	D	619 661-1701	6758
Quality Systems Intgrated Corp	3672	C	858 536-3128	6765
Quality Systems Intgrated Corp (PA)	3672	C	858 587-9797	6766
Saehan Electronics America Inc (PA)	3672	D	858 496-1500	6767
Sumitronics USA Inc	3672	E	619 661-0450	6775
Ttm Technologies Inc	3672	C	858 874-2701	6784
Arm Inc	3674	A	858 453-1900	6800
Beam Global (PA)	3674	C	858 799-4583	6807
Broadcom Corporation	3674	A	858 385-8800	6808
Daylight Solutions Inc (DH)	3674	D	858 432-7500	6817
Innophase Inc	3674	D	619 541-8280	6832
Iq-Analog Corporation	3674	F	858 200-0388	6836
Kulr Technology Corporation	3674	D	408 663-5247	6840
Kyocera America Inc	3674	E	858 576-2600	6841
Kyocera International Inc (HQ)	3674	D	858 576-2600	6842
Psemi Corporation (DH)	3674	D	858 731-9400	6871
Qualcomm Datacenter Tech Inc (HQ)	3674	E	858 587-1121	6873
Qualcomm Incorporated	3674	D	858 909-0316	6875
Qualcomm Incorporated	3674	D	858 587-1121	6876
Qualcomm Incorporated	3674	E	858 587-1121	6877
Qualcomm Incorporated	3674	C	858 587-1121	6878
Qualcomm Technologies Inc (HQ)	3674	C	858 587-1121	6879
Qualcomm Technologies Inc	3674	E	858 587-1121	6880
Qualcomm Technologies Inc	3674	E	858 658-3040	6881
Santier Inc	3674	D	858 271-1993	6886
Sensemetrics Inc	3674	E	619 738-8300	6890
General Atomics Electronic Systems Inc	3675	B	858 522-8495	6917
Rf Industries Ltd (PA)	3678	D	858 549-6340	6958
Caes Mission Systems LLC	3679	E	858 812-7300	6976
Cali Resources Inc	3679	E	619 661-5741	6978
CCM Assembly & Mfg Inc (PA)	3679	E	760 560-1310	6980
Custom Sensors & Tech Inc	3679	B	805 716-0322	6987
Delta Group Electronics Inc	3679	D	858 565-1681	6991
Hannspree North America Inc	3679	D	909 992-5025	7003
Integrated Microwave Corp	3679	D	858 259-2600	7009

Employee Codes: A=Over 500 employees, B=251-500
C=101-250, D=51-100, E=20-50, F=10-19, G=1-9

2025 Southern California
Business Directory and Buyers Guide

© Mergent Inc. 1-800-342-5647

1333

GEOGRAPHIC

	SIC	EMP	PHONE	ENTRY#
Munekata America Inc	3679	B	619 661-8080	7028
Pred Technologies Usa Inc	3679	D	858 999-2114	7039
Pulse Electronics Corporation (HQ)	3679	E	858 674-8100	7041
Tdk Electronics Inc	3679	C	858 715-4200	7056
Vas Engineering Inc	3679	E	858 569-1601	7065
Ereplacements LLC	3691	E	714 361-2652	7076
Gold Peak Industries (north America) Inc	3691	E	858 674-6099	7078
Sunfusion Energy Systems Inc	3691	E	800 544-0282	7081
Arriver Holdco Inc	3694	A	858 587-1121	7088
Maxwell Technologies Inc (HQ)	3694	D	858 503-3300	7096
Trademark Construction Co Inc (PA)	3694	C	760 489-5647	7101
Cubic Defense Applications Inc (DH)	3699	A	858 776-5664	7115
Cubic Defense Applications Inc	3699	A	858 277-6780	7116
Cubic Defense Applications Inc	3699	C	858 505-2870	7117
Cymer LLC (HQ)	3699	A	858 385-7300	7118
Hc West LLC	3699	B	858 277-3473	7125
Instruments Incorporated	3699	E	858 571-1111	7126
Meggitt Safety Systems Inc	3699	D	442 792-3217	7133
O & S California Inc	3699	B	619 661-1800	7137
Pxise Energy Solutions LLC	3699	E	619 696-2944	7144
Azaa Investments Inc (PA)	3711	E	858 569-8111	7168
Achates Power Inc	3714	D	858 535-9920	7215
Crower Engrg & Sls Co Inc	3714	E	619 661-6477	7240
Mygrant Glass Company Inc	3714	E	858 455-8022	7275
Boeing Company	3721	A	619 545-8382	7334
General Atmics Arntcal Systems	3721	A	858 964-6700	7342
General Atmics Arntcal Systems	3721	A	858 762-6700	7345
General Atmics Arntcal Systems	3721	B	858 455-2810	7347
Shield AI Inc (PA)	3721	A	619 719-5740	7370
Chromalloy Component Svcs Inc	3724	E	858 877-2800	7381
Honeywell Safety Pdts USA Inc	3724	C	619 661-8383	7388
Safran Pwr Units San Diego LLC	3724	D	858 223-2228	7395
Coi Ceramics Inc	3728	E	858 621-5700	7454
General Dynamics Ots Cal Inc	3728	C	619 671-5411	7482
Meggitt (san Diego) Inc (HQ)	3728	C	858 824-8976	7522
Performance Plastics Inc	3728	D	714 343-3928	7539
Safran Cabin Inc	3728	C	619 661-6292	7555
Safran Cabin Inc	3728	C	619 671-0430	7556
Sungear Inc	3728	E	858 549-3166	7569
Bae Systems San Dego Ship Repr	3731	A	619 238-1000	7597
Continental Maritime Inds Inc	3731	B	619 234-8851	7599
Hii San Diego Shipyard Inc	3731	B	619 234-8851	7601
Miller Marine	3731	E	619 791-1500	7604
Nassco	3731	E	619 929-3019	7605
National Stl & Shipbuilding Co (HQ)	3731	B	619 544-3400	7606
Pacific Ship Repr Fbrction Inc (PA)	3731	B	619 232-3200	7607
Pyr Preservation Services	3731	E	619 338-8395	7608
Trident Maritime Systems Inc	3731	D	619 346-3800	7609
United States Dept of Navy	3731	A	619 556-6033	7610
Driscoll Inc	3732	E	619 226-2500	7619
Kratos Def & SEC Solutions Inc (PA)	3761	C	858 812-7300	7646
Composite Optics Incorporated	3769	A	937 490-4145	7668
Argon St Inc	3812	D	703 270-6927	7694
Atk Launch Systems LLC	3812	D	858 592-2509	7696
Atk Space Systems LLC	3812	D	858 487-0970	7697
Atk Space Systems LLC	3812	C	858 530-3047	7698
Atk Space Systems LLC	3812	D	858 621-5700	7699
Bae Systems Tech Sltons Svcs I	3812	C	858 278-3042	7705
Caes Systems LLC	3812	C	858 560-1301	7706
Cubic Corporation (HQ)	3812	A	858 277-6780	7710
Decatur Electronics Inc (DH)	3812	D	888 428-4315	7713
Global A Lgistics Training Inc	3812	E	760 688-0365	7722
Lockheed Martin Orincon Corp (HQ)	3812	C	858 455-5530	7740
Lytx Inc (PA)	3812	B	858 430-4000	7741
Northrop Grrman Innvtion Syste	3812	B	858 621-5700	7748
Northrop Grumman Corporation	3812	A	858 967-1221	7754
Northrop Grumman Systems Corp	3812	D	858 514-9020	7756
Northrop Grumman Systems Corp	3812	D	858 621-7395	7757
Northrop Grumman Systems Corp	3812	D	858 514-9000	7758
Northrop Grumman Systems Corp	3812	A	410 765-5589	7781
Northrop Grumman Systems Corp	3812	B	858 592-4518	7782
Northrop Grumman Systems Corp	3812	B	858 618-4349	7783
Orbital Sciences LLC	3812	C	858 618-1847	7788
Raytheon Company	3812	D	858 571-6598	7793
Raytheon Dgital Force Tech LLC (DH)	3812	E	858 546-1244	7800
Remec Defense & Space Inc	3812	A	858 560-1301	7801
Scientific-Atlanta LLC	3812	E	619 679-6000	7809
Genetronics Inc	3821	E	858 597-6006	7826
Isec Incorporated	3821	C	858 279-9085	7828
Procisedx Inc	3821	E	858 382-4598	7830
Honeywell International Inc	3822	C	619 671-5612	7836
Advanced Electromagnetics Inc	3823	E	619 449-9492	7845
Continental Controls Corp	3823	E	858 453-9880	7853
Embedded Designs Inc	3823	E	858 673-6050	7856
Hardy Process Solutions	3823	E	858 278-2900	7862
Reotemp Instrument Corporation (PA)	3823	D	858 784-0710	7874
Sabia Incorporated (PA)	3823	E	858 217-2200	7877
D & K Engineering (HQ)	3824	D	760 840-2214	7888
Ips Group Inc (PA)	3824	E	858 404-0607	7891
Ametek Programmable Power Inc (HQ)	3825	B	858 450-0085	7897
Bae Systems Info Elctrnic Syst	3825	A	858 592-5000	7900
Bae Systems National Security Solutions Inc	3825	A	858 592-5000	7901
CONCISYS	3825	E	858 292-5888	7907
L3harris Interstate Elec Corp	3825	D	858 552-9500	7921
Surface Optics Corporation	3825	D	858 675-7404	7931
Velher LLC	3825	E	619 494-6310	7934
Affymetrix Inc	3826	D	858 642-2058	7936
Bionano Genomics Inc (PA)	3826	D	858 888-7600	7945
City of San Diego	3826	C	619 758-2310	7949
Illumina Inc	3826	E	800 809-4566	7959
Illumina Inc (PA)	3826	B	858 202-4500	7960
Molecular Bioproducts Inc (DH)	3826	C	858 453-7551	7968
Oxford Nanoimaging Inc	3826	D	858 999-8860	7971
Quantum Design Inc (PA)	3826	E	858 481-4400	7973
Singular Genomics Systems Inc (PA)	3826	C	858 333-7830	7978
Singular Genomics Systems Inc	3826	E	619 703-8135	7979
Telesis Bio Inc (PA)	3826	E	858 228-4115	7983
Thermo Fisher Scientific Inc	3826	E	858 453-7551	7987
Ysi Incorporated	3826	E	858 546-8327	7992
Hoya Corporation	3827	E	858 309-6050	8003
Wintriss Engineering Corp	3827	E	858 550-7300	8028
Fitbit LLC	3829	E	415 513-1000	8041
Gamma Scientific Inc	3829	E	858 635-9008	8043
Gantner Instruments Inc	3829	E	888 512-5788	8044
Intelliguard Group LLC	3829	E	760 448-9500	8047
Pacific Diversified Capital Co	3829	E	619 696-2000	8058
SKF Condition Monitoring Inc (DH)	3829	C	858 496-3400	8063
Teledyne Instruments Inc	3829	D	619 239-5959	8066
Teledyne Instruments Inc	3829	E	858 657-9800	8067
Accriva Dgnostics Holdings Inc (DH)	3841	B	858 404-8203	8075
Ajinomoto Althea Inc (HQ)	3841	E	858 882-0123	8079
Ameditech Inc	3841	C	858 535-1968	8089
Becton Dickinson and Company	3841	D	888 876-4287	8106
Becton Dickinson and Company	3841	E	858 617-2000	8107
Biogeneral Inc	3841	E	858 453-4451	8111
Branan Medical Corporation (PA)	3841	E	949 598-7166	8115
Carefusion 213 LLC (DH)	3841	B	800 523-0502	8121
Carefusion Corporation	3841	E	858 617-4271	8122
Carefusion Solutions LLC (DH)	3841	A	858 617-2100	8125
Chart Sequal Technologies Inc	3841	D	858 202-3100	8129
Companion Medical Inc	3841	D	858 522-0252	8133
Covidien Holding Inc	3841	C	619 690-8500	8138
Dexcom Inc (PA)	3841	A	858 200-0200	8142
Glysens Incorporated	3841	E	858 638-7708	8160
Inova Labs Inc	3841	D	866 647-0691	8170
Integer Holdings Corporation	3841	E	619 498-9448	8171
Integra Lfscnces Holdings Corp	3841	E	609 529-9748	8172
International Technidyne Corp (DH)	3841	C	858 263-2300	8174
Mast Biosurgery USA Inc	3841	E	858 550-8050	8188
Medtronic Inc	3841	E	949 798-3934	8190
Nexus Dx Inc	3841	E	858 410-4600	8206
Nuvasive Inc (HQ)	3841	D	858 909-1800	8210
Providien LLC (HQ)	3841	D	480 344-5000	8218
Resmed Inc (PA)	3841	E	858 836-5000	8223
Synergy Health Ast LLC (DH)	3841	D	858 586-1166	8233
Tandem Diabetes Care Inc (PA)	3841	A	858 366-6900	8234
Howmedica Osteonics Corp	3842	C	800 621-6104	8273
Medical Device Bus Svcs Inc	3842	E	858 560-4165	8283
Reva Medical Inc (PA)	3842	E	858 966-3000	8296
Steris Corporation	3842	E	858 586-1166	8302
Carefusion Corporation (HQ)	3845	B	858 617-2000	8374
Coastline International	3845	C	888 748-7177	8375
Daylight Defense LLC	3845	E	858 432-7500	8376
Gen-Probe Sales & Service Inc	3845	D	858 410-8000	8380
Hologic Inc	3845	E	858 410-8792	8382
Hologic Inc	3845	E	858 410-8000	8383
Natus Medical Incorporated	3845	D	858 260-2590	8390
Philips Image Gded Thrapy Corp (DH)	3845	B	800 228-4728	8396
Resmed Corp (HQ)	3845	D	858 836-5000	8397
Tensys Medical Inc	3845	E	858 552-1941	8401
Blenders Eyewear LLC	3851	D	858 490-2178	8405
Fastec Imaging Corporation	3861	E	858 592-2342	8427
Alor International Ltd	3911	E	858 454-0011	8449
Temple Custom Jewelers LLC	3911	E	800 988-3844	8462
Bravo Sports	3949	E	858 408-0083	8508
Bravo Sports	3949	E	562 457-8916	8509

	SIC	EMP	PHONE	ENTRY#
Crazy Industries	3949	E	619 270-9090	8513
Diving Unlimited Intl Inc	3949	D	619 236-1203	8515
Fitness Warehouse LLC (PA)	3949	E	858 578-7676	8517
Hyperfly Inc	3949	E	760 300-0909	8524
Indian Industries Inc	3949	E	800 467-1421	8527
Jones Sign Co Inc	3993	C	858 569-1400	8611
Signtech Electrical Advg Inc	3993	C	619 527-6100	8636
Hemp Industries	3999	E	619 458-9090	8681
Holiday Foliage Inc	3999	E	619 661-9094	8683
Huntington Ingalls Industries	3999	E	858 522-6000	8684
San Diego Metro Trnst Sys	4111	A	619 231-1466	8797
San Diego Transit Corporation (PA)	4111	A	619 238-0100	8798
San Diego Trolley Inc	4111	B	619 595-4933	8799
Liberty Ambulance LLC	4119	C	562 741-6230	8833
Complete Logistics Company	4213	D	619 661-9610	8937
United Parcel Service Inc	4215	C	858 455-8800	9026
United Parcel Service Inc	4215	B	909 279-5111	9027
MCR Printing and Packg Corp	4225	C	619 488-3012	9088
San Diego Gas & Electric Co	4225	C	858 547-2086	9107
San Diego Unified Port Dst (PA)	4491	C	619 686-6200	9146
Shelter Pointe LLC	4493	C	619 221-8000	9152
Spirit Airlines Inc	4512	C	800 772-7117	9167
Air 88 Inc	4581	E	858 277-1453	9188
San Dego Cnty Rgnal Arprt Auth (PA)	4581	C	619 400-2400	9208
Lbf Travel Inc	4724	B	858 429-7599	9227
Seat Planners Inc	4724	D	619 237-9434	9235
Golden Hour Data Systems Inc	4731	C	858 768-2500	9286
Innovel Solutions Inc	4731	A	619 497-1123	9296
Miramar Transportation Inc	4731	D	858 693-0071	9313
Chandler Packaging A Transpak Company	4783	D	858 292-5674	9353
Mek Enterprises Inc	4783	D	619 527-0957	9354
Nerys Logistics Inc	4789	C	619 616-2124	9371
Vx Logistics LLC	4789	D	858 868-1885	9378
Cubic Secure Communications I	4812	B	858 505-2000	9399
New Cingular Wireless Svcs Inc	4812	C	619 238-3638	9405
Trellisware Technologies Inc (HQ)	4812	C	858 753-1600	9420
Digitalmojo Inc	4813	D	800 413-5916	9432
Fortitude Technology Inc	4813	D	858 974-5080	9433
Nuera Communications Inc (DH)	4813	D	858 625-2400	9452
Paychex Benefit Tech Inc	4813	C	800 322-7292	9453
Sydata Inc	4813	C	760 444-4368	9463
Telisimo International Corp	4813	B	619 325-1593	9465
Verve Cloud Inc	4813	D	888 590-4888	9470
Kifm Smooth Jazz 981 Inc	4832	C	619 297-3698	9478
Local Media San Diego LLC	4832	D	858 888-7000	9483
Bay City Television Inc (PA)	4833	D	858 279-6666	9493
EW Scripps Company	4833	A	619 237-1010	9500
Herring Networks Inc	4833	C	858 270-6900	9507
McKinnon Publishing Company	4833	A	858 571-5151	9511
Station Venture Operations LP	4833	D	619 231-3939	9518
Cox Communications Inc	4841	B	858 715-4500	9537
Cox Communications Cal LLC	4841	B	619 262-1122	9540
Spectrum MGT Holdg Co LLC	4841	D	619 684-6106	9556
United Therapeutics Corp	4899	C	858 754-2970	9571
Edf Renewables Inc (PA)	4911	C	858 521-3300	9578
San Diego Gas & Electric Co	4911	B	858 654-6377	9604
San Diego Gas & Electric Co	4911	C	619 699-1018	9605
San Diego Gas & Electric Co	4911	C	858 613-3216	9606
San Diego Gas & Electric Co	4911	D	858 654-1289	9607
San Diego Gas & Electric Co	4911	C	858 541-5920	9609
Sempra Energy	4911	A	619 696-2000	9610
Sempra Energy Global Entps	4911	A	619 696-2000	9611
Sempra Energy International	4911	A	619 696-2000	9612
Solv Energy LLC (HQ)	4011	C	858 251-4888	9614
Twin Oaks Power LP (HQ)	4911	D	619 696-2034	9641
American Green Lights LLC	4931	E	858 547-8837	9667
Calpine Energy Solutions LLC (DH)	4931	C	877 273-6772	9668
San Diego Gas & Electric Co	4931	C	866 616-5565	9671
San Diego Gas & Electric Co (DH)	4931	B	619 696-2000	9673
Sempra (PA)	4932	C	619 696-2000	9676
San Diego County Water Auth (PA)	4941	D	858 522-6600	9713
California Marine Cleaning Inc (PA)	4953	C	619 231-8788	9735
IMS Recycling Services Inc (PA)	4953	D	619 231-2521	9747
Sullivan International Group Inc	4959	C	619 260-1432	9789
Adesa Corporation LLC	5012	C	619 661-5565	9797
Miramar Ford Truck Sales Inc	5012	D	619 272-5340	9806
G-Global Inc (PA)	5013	C	619 661-6292	9826
Meridian Rack & Pinion Inc	5013	C	888 875-0026	9833
Goforth & Marti (PA)	5021	C	800 686-6583	9872
Wmk Office San Diego LLC (PA)	5021	D	858 569-4700	9887
Expo Industries Inc	5031	D	858 566-3110	9919
Westside Bldg San Diego LLC	5031	E	858 566-4343	9934
Atlas Construction Supply Inc (PA)	5032	D	858 277-2100	9936
Mr Copy Inc (DH)	5044	D	858 573-6300	9977
Baker & Taylor Holdings LLC	5045	A	858 457-2500	9991
Broadway Typewriter Co Inc	5045	D	800 998-9199	9993
Eset LLC (HQ)	5045	C	619 876-5400	10002
Mediatek USA Inc	5045	C	858 731-9200	10017
Quartic Solutions LLC	5045	D	858 377-8470	10025
Southland Technology Inc	5045	D	858 694-0932	10029
Ubiq Security Inc	5045	E	888 434-6674	10037
Jetro Holdings LLC	5046	B	858 564-0466	10047
Jones Signs Co Inc	5046	C	858 569-1400	10048
R W Smith & Co	5046	C	858 530-1800	10051
Binding Site Inc (HQ)	5047	D	858 453-9177	10068
Biosite Inc	5047	D	510 683-9063	10070
Mobility Solutions Inc (PA)	5047	E	858 278-0591	10092
Anixter Inc	5063	D	800 854-2088	10168
Beacon Electric Supply	5063	D	858 279-9770	10173
Cableconn Industries Inc	5063	D	858 571-7111	10175
Graybar Electric Company Inc	5063	C	858 578-8606	10185
Main Electric Supply Co LLC	5063	E	858 737-7000	10192
Sloan Electric Corporation	5063	E	619 239-5174	10207
Philips North America LLC	5064	B	858 677-6390	10222
Bear Communications Inc	5065	C	619 263-2159	10230
Impact Components A California Limi	5065	E	858 634-4800	10252
Lightpointe Communications Inc	5065	E	858 834-4083	10262
Motorola Mobility LLC	5065	C	858 455-1500	10269
Otter Products LLC	5065	C	888 533-0735	10276
Presidio Components Inc	5065	C	858 578-9390	10279
Steren Electronics Intl LLC (PA)	5065	D	800 266-3333	10284
Eurodrip USA Inc	5083	C	559 674-2670	10362
Hawthorne Machinery Co	5084	C	858 674-7000	10376
Otis Elevator Company	5084	D	858 560-5881	10389
Carpenter Group	5085	E	619 233-5625	10428
Waxies Enterprises LLC (DH)	5087	C	800 995-4466	10482
Kettenburg Marine Corporation	5088	C	619 224-8211	10495
Prestige Graphics Inc	5112	E	858 560-8213	10583
San Diego Die Cutting Inc	5113	E	619 297-4453	10609
Irisys Inc	5122	D	858 623-1520	10627
Specialty Textile Services LLC	5131	C	619 476-8750	10675
Mad Engine Global LLC	5137	B	858 558-5270	10714
Piveg Inc	5141	C	858 436-3070	10765
Smart Stores Operations LLC	5141	B	619 291-1842	10796
Smart Stores Operations LLC	5141	C	858 578-7343	10798
Jensen Meat Company Inc	5147	D	619 754-6400	10873
Jetro Cash and Carry Entps LLC	5147	D	619 233-0200	10874
Mpci Holdings Inc	5147	C	619 294-2222	10876
Producers Meat and Prov Inc	5147	E	619 232-7593	10878
Coast Citrus Distributors (PA)	5148	D	619 661-7950	10890
Lazy Acres Natural Market	5149	D	619 847-8443	10956
Lenore John & Co (PA)	5149	C	619 232-6136	10958
Perfect Bar LLC	5149	C	866 628-8548	10970
Chembridge Corporation (PA)	5169	B	858 451-7400	11009
Crest Beverage LLC	5181	B	858 452-2300	11045
Montesquieu Corp	5182	C	877 705-5669	11058
Baker & Taylor LLC	5192	C	858 457-2500	11074
White Digital Media Inc	5192	C	760 827-7800	11078
Bella Terra Nursery Inc	5193	D	619 585-1118	11083
Schroff Inc	5199	C	858 740-2400	11142
Dixieline Lumber Company LLC (DH)	5211	D	619 224-4120	11151
Home Depot USA Inc	5211	C	619 263-1533	11185
Lowes Home Centers LLC	5211	C	619 584-5500	11235
Superior Ready Mix Concrete LP	5211	D	858 695-0666	11252
El Tigre Inc	5411	C	619 429-8212	11276
Sol-Ti Inc	5499	D	888 765-8411	11308
Courtesy Chevrolet Center	5511	D	619 297-4321	11329
Europa Auto Imports Inc	5511	C	858 569-6900	11344
Mossy Automotive Group Inc (PA)	5511	B	858 581-4000	11381
Mossy Ford Inc	5511	C	858 273-7500	11382
Mossy Nissan Inc	5511	D	858 565-6608	11383
San Diego V Inc (PA)	5511	D	888 308-2260	11403
Parkhouse Tire Service Inc	5531	E	858 565-8473	11451
Southern Cal Disc Tire Co Inc	5531	D	858 278-0661	11465
La Mesa R V Center Inc (PA)	5561	C	858 874-8000	11480
Vera Bradley Inc	5632	E	858 320-9020	11495
Adrenaline Lacrosse Inc	5699	E	888 768-8479	11503
Athleisure Inc	5699	E	858 866-0108	11505
Gosecure Inc (PA)	5734	C	301 442-3432	11541
Carvin Corp	5736	C	858 487-1600	11544
Citrus Restaurant LLC	5812	C	858 277-8888	11563
Different Rules LLC	5812	D	858 571-2121	11566
Jack In Box Inc (PA)	5812	A	858 571-2121	11578
Qdoba Restaurant Corporation (HQ)	5812	C	858 766-4900	11597
Sacco Restaurants Inc	5812	D	858 451-9464	11598
Border X Brewing LLC	5813	E	619 501-0503	11612

Employee Codes: A=Over 500 employees, B=251-500
C=101-250, D=51-100, E=20-50, F=10-19, G=1-9

2025 Southern California
Business Directory and Buyers Guide

© Mergent Inc. 1-800-342-5647

1335

GEOGRAPHIC

	SIC	EMP	PHONE	ENTRY#
Harland Brewing Co LLC	5813	E	858 800-4566	11614
Mission Brewery Inc	5813	E	619 818-7147	11616
Sharp Healthcare **(PA)**	5912	A	858 499-4000	11623
Sharp Healthcare Aco LLC	5912	C	619 688-3543	11624
Road Runner Sports Inc **(PA)**	5961	D	858 974-4200	11662
Greatcall Inc	5999	A	800 733-6632	11685
Officia Imaging Inc **(PA)**	5999	E	858 348-0831	11693
Scope Orthtics Prosthetics Inc **(DH)**	5999	E	858 292-7448	11696
United Access LLC	5999	D	623 879-0800	11700
City National Bank	6021	C	858 875-2030	11726
California Bank & Trust	6022	A	858 793-7400	11748
Enterprise Bank & Trust	6022	C	858 432-7000	11763
Imperial Capital Bancorp Inc **(PA)**	6022	E	858 551-0511	11770
Seacoast Cmmerce Banc Holdings	6022	C	858 432-7000	11777
Mission Federal Credit Union	6061	C	858 531-5106	11805
Mission Federal Credit Union **(PA)**	6061	D	858 546-2184	11807
Mission Federal Services LLC **(PA)**	6061	C	858 524-2850	11808
San Diego County Credit Union **(PA)**	6061	C	877 732-2848	11813
United Svcs Amer Federal Cr Un **(PA)**	6061	C	858 831-8100	11818
California Coast Credit Union **(PA)**	6062	D	858 495-1600	11823
North Island Financial Credit Union	6062	B	619 656-6525	11830
Encore Capital Group Inc **(PA)**	6153	A	877 445-4581	11866
Midland Credit Management Inc	6153	C	877 240-2377	11869
Reliant Services Group LLC	6153	C	877 850-0998	11871
American Internet Mortgage Inc	6162	C	888 411-4246	11882
Amnet Mortgage LLC	6162	A	858 909-1200	11884
Berkshire Hthway HM Svcs Cal P	6162	C	619 302-8082	11887
Blufi Lending Corporation	6162	C		11888
Crosscountry Mortgage LLC	6162	C	858 735-0255	11896
Goal Financial LLC	6162	C	619 684-7600	11906
Guaranteed Rate Inc	6162	C	760 310-6008	11910
Iserve Residential Lending LLC	6162	D	858 486-4169	11915
Lendsure Mortgage Corp	6162	B	888 707-7811	11917
Synergy One Lending Inc	6162	C	385 273-5250	11937
Change Lending LLC	6163	D	858 500-3060	11943
Charles Schwab Corporation	6211	D	800 435-4000	11961
First Allied Securities Inc **(HQ)**	6211	D	619 702-9600	11964
Lpl Financial Holdings Inc **(PA)**	6211	B	800 877-7210	11974
Merrill Lynch Prce Fnner Smith	6211	C	858 673-6700	11990
Merrill Lynch Prce Fnner Smith	6211	C	858 677-1300	11992
Merrill Lynch Prce Fnner Smith	6211	C	619 699-3700	11993
Morgan Stnley Smith Barney LLC	6211	C	619 238-1226	11997
Plaza Home Mortgage Inc	6211	D	858 346-1208	12005
UBS Americas Inc	6211	C	619 557-2400	12008
Brandes Inv Partners Inc **(PA)**	6282	C	858 755-0239	12020
C2 Financial Corporation	6282	C	858 220-2112	12022
American Spclty Hlth Group Inc	6324	B	858 754-2000	12071
Blue Shield Cal Lf Hlth Insur	6324	A	619 686-4200	12072
Delta Dental of California	6324	C	619 683-2549	12079
Sharp Health Plan	6324	C	858 499-8300	12106
Southern Cal Prmnnte Med Group	6324	B	858 974-1000	12110
Arrowhead Gen Insur Agcy Inc **(HQ)**	6331	C	619 881-8600	12117
Golden Eagle Insurance Corp **(DH)**	6331	C	619 744-6000	12118
Icw Group Holdings Inc **(PA)**	6331	C	858 350-2400	12121
Mercury Insurance Company	6331	A	858 694-4100	12127
State Compensation Insur Fund	6331	C	888 782-8338	12139
Stewart Title California Inc **(DH)**	6361	C	619 692-1600	12156
AIG Direct Insurance Svcs Inc	6411	B	858 309-3000	12168
American Spclty Hlth Plans Cal	6411	B	619 297-8100	12172
Anchor General Insur Agcy Inc	6411	C	858 527-3600	12173
Atlas General Insur Svcs LLC	6411	C	858 529-6700	12174
Barney & Barney Inc	6411	C	800 321-4696	12182
Cbiz Life Insur Solutions Inc	6411	B	858 444-3100	12192
Customzed Svcs Admnstrtors Inc	6411	C	858 810-2004	12198
Cypress Pnt-Prrowhead Gen Insur	6411	D	619 681-0560	12200
Insurance Company of West **(HQ)**	6411	C	858 350-2400	12222
John Hancock Life Insur Co USA	6411	B	858 292-1667	12224
Marsh & McLennan Agency LLC	6411	C	858 457-3414	12229
Preferred Employers Insur Co	6411	D	619 688-3900	12246
Premier Dealer Services Inc	6411	B	858 810-1700	12247
Qualitas Insurance Company	6411	D	619 876-4355	12248
American Assets Inc	6512	C	619 255-9944	12280
C & D Wax Inc	6512	C	858 292-5954	12283
Realty Income Corporation **(PA)**	6512	C	858 284-5000	12314
San Diego Theatres Inc	6512	C	619 615-4007	12315
Barker Management Incorporated	6513	D	619 236-8130	12333
Ffrt Residential LLC	6513	C	858 457-2123	12341
HG Fenton Company	6513	C	619 400-0120	12344
Wamc Company Inc	6513	D	858 454-2753	12370
Willmark Cmmnties Univ Vlg Inc **(PA)**	6513	D	858 271-0582	12372
HG Fenton Property Company **(PA)**	6519	C	619 400-0120	12376
Cbre Inc	6531	C	858 546-4600	12397
Conam Management Corporation **(PA)**	6531	C	858 614-7200	12414

	SIC	EMP	PHONE	ENTRY#
Cushman & Wakefield Cal Inc	6531	A	858 452-6500	12424
Daymark Realty Advisors Inc	6531	B	714 975-2999	12428
Hanken Cono Assad & Co Inc	6531	C	619 575-3100	12463
RA Snyder Properties Inc **(PA)**	6531	C	619 297-0274	12514
Roman Cthlic Bshp of San Diego	6531	D	619 264-3127	12525
Southern Cal Pipe Trades ADM	6531	D	619 224-3125	12529
Strategic Property Management	6531	D	619 295-2211	12535
Terra Vista Management Inc	6531	B	858 581-4200	12537
Mlim Holdings LLC	6719	A	619 299-3131	12603
Bridgewest Ventures LLC **(PA)**	6726	A	858 529-6600	12645
Charles Schwab Corporation	6726	D	800 435-4000	12647
Guild Mortgage Company LLC **(HQ)**	6733	C	800 365-4441	12658
Kaiser Foundation Hospitals	6733	A	619 528-5888	12661
Management Trust Assn Inc	6733	D	858 547-4373	12662
Quality Loan Service Corp	6733	B	619 645-7711	12673
Qualcomm International Inc **(HQ)**	6794	A	858 587-1121	12678
Biomed Realty Trust Inc **(PA)**	6798	B	858 207-2513	12683
Equity Fund Advisors Inc	6798	C	602 716-8803	12685
Pacifica Companies LLC **(PA)**	6798	A	619 296-9000	12690
Spirit Realty LP	6798	D	972 476-1900	12695
Vereit Real Estate LP	6798	D	602 778-6000	12696
7th & C Investments LLC	6799	C	619 233-7327	12697
Healthpoint Capital LLC **(PA)**	6799	C	212 935-7780	12709
McMillin Companies LLC **(PA)**	6799	D	619 477-4117	12717
Medimpact Holdings Inc **(PA)**	6799	A	858 566-2727	12718
Retail Opprtnity Invstmnts Prt	6799	D	858 677-0900	12732
Tapetech Tool Company	6799	A	858 268-0656	12739
1835 Columbia Street LP	7011	D	619 564-3993	12751
8110 Aero Holding LLC	7011	C	858 277-8888	12755
American Prprty-Mnagement Corp	7011	A	619 232-3121	12760
Atlas Hotels Inc	7011	A	619 291-2232	12763
Bartell Hotels	7011	D	619 291-6700	12768
Bh Partnership LP **(PA)**	7011	B	858 539-7635	12775
Braemar Partnership	7011	B	858 488-1081	12776
Diamondrock San Dego Tnant LLC	7011	B	619 239-4500	12810
Grand Del Mar Resort LP	7011	A	858 314-2000	12830
Gringteam Inc	7011	B	619 297-5466	12836
Gringteam Inc	7011	C	858 485-4145	12837
Handlery Hotels Inc	7011	D	415 781-4550	12840
Harbor View Hotel Ventures LLC	7011	D	619 239-6800	12842
Historical Properties Inc **(PA)**	7011	D	619 230-8417	12851
Hotel Circle Property LLC	7011	B	619 291-7131	12855
Hyatt Corporation	7011	D	858 453-0018	12862
Hyatt Corporation	7011	D	619 232-1234	12863
Hyatt Corporation	7011	D	619 849-1234	12864
Lfs Development LLC	7011	C	619 501-5400	12898
Lho Mssion Bay Rsie Lessee Inc	7011	B	619 276-4010	12901
M4dev LLC	7011	D	619 696-6300	12910
Manchester Grand Resorts LP	7011	D	619 232-1234	12913
Mbp Land LLC	7011	C	619 291-5720	12920
Mhf Mv Operating VI LLC	7011	D	619 481-5881	12924
Narven Enterprises Inc	7011	D	619 239-2261	12935
Oak Valley Hotel LLC	7011	D	619 297-1101	12942
Old Town Fmly Hospitality Corp	7011	C	619 246-8010	12950
Pan Pcfic Htels Rsrts Amer Inc	7011	C	619 239-4500	12966
Paradise Lessee Inc	7011	B	858 274-4630	12967
Rgc Gaslamp LLC	7011	D	619 738-7000	12993
San Diego Hotel Company LLC	7011	C	619 696-0234	13011
Sandm San Dego Mrriott Del Mar	7011	A	858 523-1700	13015
SD Hotel Circle LLC	7011	C	619 881-6800	13018
Sheraton Ht San Dego Mssion VI	7011	D	619 260-0111	13022
Starwood Htels Rsrts Wrldwide	7011	C	619 239-2200	13035
Sunstone Hotel Properties Inc	7011	C	858 277-1199	13042
Sunstone Top Gun Lessee Inc	7011	C	949 330-4000	13045
T-12 Three LLC	7011	B	619 702-3000	13050
The Lodge At Torrey Pines Partnership L P	7011	B		13051
Tic Hotels Inc	7011	C	619 238-7577	13052
Trigild International Inc	7011	C	619 295-6886	13055
US Grant Hotel Ventures LLC	7011	D	619 744-2007	13061
Westgroup San Diego Associates	7011	C	858 274-4630	13076
Win Time Ltd **(PA)**	7011	C	858 695-2300	13081
Ws Mmv Hotel LLC	7011	D	619 692-3800	13093
Ww San Diego Harbor Island LLC	7011	C	619 291-6700	13094
Star Laundry Services Inc	7216	D	619 572-1009	13133
Bonded Inc P	7217	D	858 576-8400	13134
Colt Services Inc	7217	D	858 271-9910	13135
Pixster Photobooth LLC	7221	C	888 668-5524	13145
Sport Clips Inc	7231	A	858 273-9993	13154
Beyond Finance LLC	7299	A	800 282-7186	13168
Pacific Event Productions Inc **(PA)**	7299	C	858 458-9908	13184
Visage Imaging Inc	7299	C	858 345-4410	13190
Mindgruve Holdings Inc	7311	C	619 757-1325	13227
Rescue Agency Pub Benefit LLC **(PA)**	7311	D	619 231-7555	13242

2025 Southern California
Business Directory and Buyers Guide

(P-0000) Products & Services Section entry number
(PA)=Parent Co (HQ)=Headquarters (DH)=Div Headquarters

	SIC	EMP	PHONE	ENTRY#
Stn Digital LLC	7311	D	619 292-8683	13247
Vitrorobertson LLC	7311	D	619 234-0408	13251
Corelogic Credco LLC	7323	B	619 938-7028	13294
American Legal Copy - Oc LLC	7334	D	415 777-4449	13309
Mirum Inc	7336	C	619 237-5552	13331
Thinkbasic Inc	7336	C	858 755-6922	13336
Crown Building Maintenance Co	7349	B	858 560-5785	13369
GMI Building Services Inc	7349	B	858 279-6262	13375
Kbm Fclity Sltons Holdings LLC	7349	B	858 467-0202	13382
Life Cycle Engineering Inc	7349	C	619 785-5990	13386
Merchants Building Maint Co	7349	B	858 455-0163	13393
Paragon Svcs Jntr Ornge Cnty L	7349	C	858 654-0150	13400
Pe Facility Solutions LLC (PA)	7349	D	858 467-0202	13401
Pegasus Building Svcs Co Inc	7349	B	858 444-2290	13403
Priority Building Services LLC	7349	B	858 695-1326	13407
Professional Maint Systems Inc	7349	A	619 276-1150	13409
Protec Association Services (PA)	7349	C	858 569-1080	13412
Rhino Building Services Inc	7349	C	858 455-1440	13414
Servi-Tek Inc	7349	B	858 638-7735	13417
Hawthorne Machinery Co (PA)	7353	C	858 674-7000	13437
Hawthorne Rent-It Service (HQ)	7353	D	858 674-7000	13438
P J J Enterprises Inc	7359	C	619 232-6136	13465
Raphaels Party Rentals Inc (PA)	7359	C	858 444-1692	13469
Access Nurses Inc	7361	D	858 458-4400	13482
Advanced Med Prsonnel Svcs Inc	7361	D	386 756-4395	13484
Barrett Business Services Inc	7361	A	858 314-1100	13491
Delta-T Group Inc	7361	C	619 543-0556	13509
Eplica Corporate Services Inc	7361	A	619 282-1400	13515
Innovative Placements Inc	7361	C	800 322-9796	13529
Merritt Hawkins & Assoc LLC (HQ)	7361	C	858 792-0711	13544
MHS Customer Services Inc	7361	D	858 695-2151	13545
Nursechoice	7361	D	866 557-6050	13547
Nursefinders LLC (HQ)	7361	C	858 314-7427	13549
Pioneer Healthcare Svcs LLC	7361	B	800 683-1209	13555
Preferred Hlthcare Rgistry Inc	7361	C	800 787-6787	13556
R&D Consulting Group LLC	7361	C	570 277-7066	13562
SE Scher Corporation	7361	A	858 546-8300	13569
Teg Staffing Inc	7361	A	800 918-1678	13576
Vish Consulting Services Inc	7361	D	916 800-3762	13580
Wmbe Payrolling Inc	7361	C	858 810-3000	13582
Workway Inc	7361	C	619 278-0012	13584
Aya Healthcare Inc (PA)	7363	C	858 458-4410	13591
Cardinal Point Captains Inc	7363	D	760 438-7361	13594
Eplica Inc (PA)	7363	C	619 260-2000	13596
June Group LLC	7363	D	858 450-4290	13602
Med Source Ventures Inc	7363	B	858 560-9941	13613
Rx Pro Health Inc	7363	A	858 369-4050	13620
Sfn Group Inc	7363	A	858 458-9200	13621
Vaya Workforce Solutions LLC	7363	C	866 687-7390	13630
Volt Management Corp	7363	D	858 576-3140	13631
Adaptamed LLC	7371	C	877 478-7773	13643
Algorithmic Objective Corp	7371	E	858 249-9580	13647
American Sunrise Inc	7371	D	858 610-4766	13652
Bakbone Software Inc (HQ)	7371	D	858 450-9009	13670
Biosero (PA)	7371	E	858 880-7376	13674
Brain Corporation	7371	C	858 689-7600	13680
Colsa Corporation	7371	D	619 553-0031	13690
Cordial	7371	D	619 501-5548	13693
Cordial Experience Inc	7371	D	619 793-9787	13694
Corelation Inc	7371	C	619 876-5074	13695
Cubic Trnsp Systems Inc (DH)	7371	A	858 268-3100	13700
Daybreak Game Company LLC	7371	B	858 239-0500	13703
Einstein Industries Inc	7371	C	868 460-1182	13717
Evernote Corporation (PA)	7371	D	650 216-7700	13725
Family Zone Inc	7371	D	844 723-3932	13727
G2 Software Systems Inc	7371	C	619 222-8025	13734
H & R Accounts Inc	7371	D	619 819-8844	13741
ID Analytics LLC	7371	C	858 312-6200	13746
Innovasystems Intl LLC	7371	C	619 955-5890	13749
Inseego Corp (PA)	7371	D	858 812-3400	13750
Isaac Fair Corporation	7371	D	858 369-8000	13756
Jungo Inc	7371	D	619 727-4600	13758
Locai Inc	7371	D	469 834-5364	13762
Logility Inc	7371	D	858 565-4238	13763
Mango Technologies Inc (PA)	7371	A	888 625-4258	13766
Mir3 Inc	7371	D	858 724-1200	13771
Nucleushealth LLC	7371	D	858 251-3400	13787
Parallel 6 Inc (PA)	7371	E	619 452-1750	13793
Platform Science Inc (PA)	7371	C	844 475-8724	13796
Psyonix LLC	7371	D	619 622-8772	13801
Reapplications Inc	7371	D	619 230-0209	13804
Reciprocal Labs Corp	7371	D	608 251-0470	13805
Sciforma Corporation	7371	E	408 899-0398	13813
Smartdrive Systems Inc (PA)	7371	D	858 225-5550	13823
Symitar Systems Inc	7371	C	619 542-6700	13835
Tapestry Solutions Inc (HQ)	7371	D	858 503-1990	13838
Thomas Hemmings	7371	D	303 489-3259	13844
Verseio Inc	7371	D	888 373-9942	13861
Altumind Inc	7372	E	858 382-3956	13875
Ancora Software Inc (PA)	7372	C	888 476-4839	13877
Appfolio Inc	7372	C	866 648-1536	13880
Ascender Software Inc	7372	C	877 561-7501	13885
Blitz Rocks Inc	7372	E	310 883-5183	13892
Chatmeter Inc	7372	D	619 300-1050	13899
Classy Inc	7372	C	619 961-1892	13901
Dassault Systemes Biovia Corp (DH)	7372	E	858 799-5000	13912
Decisionlogic LLC	7372	E	858 586-0202	13914
Digital Arbitrage Dist Inc (PA)	7372	E	888 392-9478	13915
Dreamstart Labs Inc	7372	E	408 914-1234	13918
Edgate Holdings Inc	7372	E	858 712-9341	13920
Genasys Inc (PA)	7372	D	858 676-1112	13938
Intuit Inc	7372	B	858 780-2846	13950
Intuit Inc	7372	B	858 215-8000	13951
Kintera Inc (HQ)	7372	C	858 795-3000	13960
Kyriba Corp (PA)	7372	E	858 210-3560	13965
Leadcrunch Inc (PA)	7372	E	888 708-6649	13966
Mitek Systems Inc (PA)	7372	D	619 269-6800	13975
Musicmatch Inc	7372	C	858 485-4300	13979
New Bi US Gaming LLC	7372	D	858 592-2472	13986
Nexogy Inc	7372	D	305 358-8952	13987
Omnitracs Midco LLC	7372	E	858 651-5812	13997
Qualer Inc	7372	E	858 224-9516	14014
Seismic Software Inc (HQ)	7372	D	714 404-7069	14028
Sequelae Inc	7372	D	801 628-0256	14029
Solv Energy LLC	7372	C	858 622-4040	14033
Sonendo Acquisition Corp	7372	E	858 558-3696	14034
Teradata Corporation (PA)	7372	A	866 548-8348	14048
Wme Bi LLC	7372	C	877 592-2472	14066
Automation Holdco Inc	7373	D	858 967-8650	14071
Caci Enterprise Solutions LLC	7373	B	619 881-6000	14073
Captiva Software Corporation (DH)	7373	D	858 320-1000	14074
Clinicomp International Inc (PA)	7373	D	858 546-8202	14075
Cubic Corporation	7373	A	858 277-6780	14079
Koam Engineering Systems Inc	7373	C	858 292-0922	14090
Miro Technologies Inc	7373	C	858 677-2100	14093
Mitchell International Inc (PA)	7373	C	866 389-2069	14094
Miva Inc	7373	C	858 490-2570	14095
Mobisystems Inc	7373	C	858 350-0315	14096
Pat V Mack Inc	7373	D	619 930-5473	14102
Science Applications Intl Corp	7373	A	858 826-3061	14105
Tusimple Inc	7373	B	520 989-7911	14113
Tusimple Holdings Inc (PA)	7373	D	619 916-3144	14114
Ultisat Inc	7373	A	240 243-5107	14115
Whova Inc	7373	C	858 227-0877	14118
Zmicro Inc (PA)	7373	D	858 831-7000	14120
Amazon Processing LLC	7374	D	858 565-1135	14121
Emerald Connect LLC (HQ)	7374	D	800 233-2834	14132
San Diego Data Processing Corporation Inc	7374	A	858 581-9600	14154
Tealium Inc (PA)	7374	C	858 779-1344	14158
Relationedge LLC	7374	D	858 451-4665	14176
Autovitals Inc	7379	D	866 949-2848	14198
Defenseweb Technologies Inc	7379	D	858 272-8505	14212
Drala Inc	7379	C	858 754-8811	14214
Positioning Universal Inc	7379	D	619 639-0235	14243
Science Applications Intl Corp	7379	D	703 676-4300	14249
Sentek Consulting Inc	7379	C	619 543-9550	14251
Strata Information Group Inc (PA)	7379	D	619 296-0170	14255
Tactical Engrg & Analis Inc (PA)	7379	D	858 573-9869	14258
ATI Systems International Inc	7381	A	858 715-8484	14277
Elite Show Services Inc	7381	A	619 574-1589	14299
Guard Management Inc	7381	C	858 279-8282	14304
Locator Services Inc	7381	C	619 229-6100	14315
Staff Pro Inc	7381	B	619 544-1774	14354
Brightcloud Inc	7382	C	858 652-4803	14386
Johnson Cntrls SEC Sltions LLC	7382	D	561 988-3600	14408
Kratos Public Safety & Security Solutions Inc	7382	D	858 812-7300	14411
Securitas Technology Corp	7382	D	858 812-7349	14419
Symons Fire Protection Inc	7382	C	619 588-6364	14424
1111 6th Ave LLC	7389	D	312 283-3683	14431
Affinity Auto Programs Inc	7389	B	858 643-9324	14437
Alorica Customer Care Inc	7389	D	619 298-7103	14440
Beaumont Nielsen Marine Inc	7389	E	619 223-2628	14461
Cetera Financial Group Inc (PA)	7389	C	866 489-3100	14471
County of San Diego	7389	C	858 694-2960	14482
Interior Specialists Inc	7389	B	909 983-5386	14517
Knox Attorney Service Inc (PA)	7389	C	619 233-9700	14523

GEOGRAPHIC

	SIC	EMP	PHONE	ENTRY#
Mabie Marketing Group Inc	7389	C	858 279-5585	14534
Marine Corps United States	7389	B	858 307-3434	14537
Phone Ware Inc	7389	B	858 530-8550	14572
Puff Global Inc	7389	D	619 520-3499	14579
Quidel Cardiovascular Inc	7389	D	858 552-1100	14581
San Dego Cnvntion Ctr Corp Inc (PA)	7389	B	619 782-4388	14588
Shinwoo P&C Usa Inc (HQ)	7389	C	619 407-7164	14594
Strategic Operations Inc	7389	C	858 244-0559	14602
Tecma Group LLC	7389	A	619 333-5856	14609
UPS Store Inc (HQ)	7389	B	858 455-8800	14623
Vastek Inc	7389	C	925 948-5701	14625
Vintage Design LLC	7389	D	858 695-9544	14626
Visual Pak San Diego LLC	7389	C	847 689-1000	14627
Washington Inventory Service	7389	A	858 565-8111	14631
Midway Rent A Car Inc	7514	C	619 238-9600	14649
Modern Parking Inc	7521	C	619 233-0412	14661
Greenwlds Atbody Frmeworks Inc	7532	D	619 477-2600	14673
San Diego Saturn Retailers Inc	7532	D	858 373-3001	14680
City Chevrolet of San Diego	7538	C	619 276-6171	14688
Sunbelt Towing Inc (PA)	7549	D	619 297-8697	14720
Schroff Inc	7629	C	858 740-2400	14730
Action Cleaning Corporation	7699	E	619 233-1881	14752
Chromalloy San Diego Corp	7699	C	858 877-2800	14759
Propulsion Controls Engrg (PA)	7699	D	619 235-0961	14785
Upwind Blade Solutions Inc	7699	B	866 927-3142	14799
Western Pump Inc (PA)	7699	D	619 239-9988	14801
Old Globe Theatre	7922	B	619 234-5623	14967
San Dego Repertory Theatre Inc	7922	C	619 231-3586	14976
San Diego Opera Association	7922	C	619 232-5911	14977
San Diego Opera Association	7922	C	619 232-5911	14978
Hob Entertainment LLC	7929	D	619 299-2583	14991
Inmotion Entrmt Group LLC	7929	C	904 332-0459	14993
San Dego Symphony Orchstra Ass	7929	C	619 235-0800	15003
San Diego Symphony Foundation	7929	C	619 235-0800	15004
California Sportservice	7941	A	619 795-5000	15021
City of San Diego	7941	C	619 795-5000	15023
Padres LP	7941	A	619 795-5000	15034
Socal Sportsnet LLC	7941	A	619 795-5000	15036
Salvation Army Ray & Joan	7991	B	619 287-5762	15062
TW Holdings Inc	7991	A	858 217-8750	15067
Bay Clubs Company LLC	7997	B	858 509-9933	15120
San Diego State University	7997	C	619 594-4263	15167
Santaluz Club Inc	7997	C	858 759-3120	15171
The San Diego Yacht Club	7997	C	619 221-8400	15181
Westgroup Kona Kai LLC	7997	D	619 221-8000	15187
Marine Corps Community Svcs	7999	B	858 577-1061	15211
Volume Services Inc	7999	C	619 525-5800	15232
Amn Healthcare Inc (HQ)	8011	B	858 792-0711	15243
Cardionet Inc	8011	D	619 243-7500	15261
Centro De Slud De La Cmndad De	8011	C	619 662-4100	15270
Childrens Spclsts of San Dego (PA)	8011	B	858 576-1700	15276
Curology Inc	8011	C	617 959-2480	15297
Family Hlth Ctrs San Diego Inc	8011	B	619 515-2526	15307
Family Hlth Ctrs San Diego Inc	8011	B	619 515-2435	15308
Family Hlth Ctrs San Diego Inc	8011	B	619 515-2400	15309
Family Hlth Ctrs San Diego Inc	8011	B	619 515-2444	15311
Imaging Hlthcare Spcalists Inc	8011	C	619 229-2299	15329
La Maestra Family Clinic Inc (PA)	8011	C	619 584-1612	15374
MainStay Medical Limited	8011	D	619 261-9144	15386
Operation Samahan Inc	8011	C	619 477-4451	15414
Perlman Clinic	8011	C	858 554-1212	15422
San Dego Pthlgsts Med Group In	8011	C	619 297-4012	15442
San Dego Spt Mdcine Fmly Hlth	8011	D	619 229-3909	15443
San Diego Family Care (PA)	8011	D	858 279-0925	15444
Sharp Rees Staly Rncho Brnardo	8011	D	858 521-2300	15453
Sharp RES-Stealy Med Group Inc	8011	C	619 221-9547	15454
Sleep Data Services LLC	8011	D	619 299-6299	15456
Southern Cal Prmnnte Med Group	8011	B	619 528-5000	15477
Southern Cal Prmnnte Med Group	8011	C	619 516-6000	15480
United States Dept of Navy	8011	B	619 587-9849	15496
Family Hlth Ctrs San Diego Inc	8021	B	619 515-2300	15517
Artemis Inst For Clncal RES LL	8031	C	858 278-3647	15530
Chirotech Inc	8041	D	619 528-0040	15534
James G Meyers & Associates	8042	E	858 622-2165	15535
Locums Unlimited LLC	8049	A	619 550-3763	15550
Emeritus Corporation	8051	C	858 292-8044	15627
Five Star Senior Living Inc	8051	C	858 673-6300	15655
La Jolla Skilled Inc	8051	B	858 625-8700	15689
Mission Hills Health Care Inc	8051	C	619 297-4086	15722
Point Loma Rhblitation Ctr LLC	8051	D	619 308-3200	15755
Bernardo Hts Healthcare Inc	8059	B	858 673-0101	15838
Crestwood Behavioral Hlth Inc	8059	C	619 481-6790	15848
San Dego Ctr For Chldren Fndti (PA)	8059	D	858 277-9550	15884
Alvarado Hospital LLC (DH)	8062	C	619 287-3270	15907
Alvarado Hospital Med Ctr Inc	8062	A	619 287-3270	15908
Kaiser Foundation Hospitals	8062	C	619 528-2583	16049
Kaiser Foundation Hospitals	8062	C	858 573-1504	16050
Kindred Healthcare LLC	8062	D	619 546-9653	16064
Palomar Health	8062	B	858 675-5218	16116
Rady Childrens Hosp & Hlth Ctr (PA)	8062	A	858 576-1700	16156
Rady Chld Hospital-San Diego (HQ)	8062	A	858 576-1700	16157
Scripps Clinic	8062	C	858 794-1250	16178
Scripps Health	8062	D	619 294-8111	16179
Scripps Health	8062	D	858 271-9770	16180
Scripps Health (PA)	8062	A	800 727-4777	16186
Scripps Mercy Hospital	8062	C	619 294-8111	16187
Sharp Chula Vista Medical Ctr	8062	D	858 499-5150	16190
Sharp Healthcare	8062	C	858 939-5434	16194
Sharp Healthcare Aco LLC	8062	B	619 446-1575	16195
Sharp Healthcare Aco LLC	8062	A	858 627-5152	16196
Sharp Mary Birch H	8062	C	858 939-3400	16197
Sharp Memorial Hospital (HQ)	8062	A	858 939-3636	16198
United States Dept of Navy	8062	A	619 532-6400	16239
University Cal San Diego	8062	C	619 543-6654	16241
University Cal San Diego	8062	C	619 543-6170	16243
Vibra Healthcare LLC	8062	C	619 260-8300	16256
Aurora - San Diego LLC (DH)	8063	D	858 487-3200	16263
County of San Diego	8063	B	619 692-8200	16273
Sharp Memorial Hospital	8063	C	858 278-4110	16279
Sharp McDonald Center	8069	A	858 637-6920	16298
Biotheranostics Inc (HQ)	8071	E	877 886-6739	16305
Decipher Corp	8071	D	888 975-4540	16311
DR Systems Inc	8071	C	858 625-3344	16312
Epic Sciences Inc	8071	D	858 356-6610	16314
Examone World Wide Inc	8071	D	619 299-3926	16316
Sequenom Ctr For Mlclar Mdcine	8071	B	858 202-9051	16334
ABC Home Health Care Llc	8082	C	858 455-5000	16350
Accentcare Inc	8082	A	858 576-7410	16351
Accredited Nursing Services	8082	C	818 986-1234	16356
All Valley Home Hlth Care Inc	8082	D	619 276-8001	16360
Bridge Home Health LLC	8082	C	858 277-5200	16372
Buena Vista MGT Svcs LLC	8082	C	619 450-4300	16373
Centerwell Health Services Inc	8082	C	858 565-2499	16376
Faith Jones & Associates Inc (PA)	8082	C	619 297-9601	16389
First Meridian Care Svcs Inc	8082	D	858 529-1886	16390
Firstat Nursing Services Inc	8082	C	619 220-7600	16391
Integrity Hlthcare Sltions Inc	8082	D	760 432-9811	16396
Maxim Healthcare Services Inc	8082	A	619 299-9350	16404
Mission HM Hlth San Diego LLC	8082	C	619 757-2700	16406
San Diego Hospice & Palliative Care	8082	A	619 688-1600	16418
Scripps Health	8082	D	858 764-3000	16419
Center For Atism RES Evltion S	8093	D	858 444-8823	16449
Centro De Slud De La Cmndad De (PA)	8093	D	619 428-4463	16453
Mental Health Systems Inc (PA)	8093	D	858 573-2600	16485
Planned Prnthood of PCF Sthwes	8093	C	619 881-4652	16492
Planned Prnthood of PCF Sthwes (PA)	8093	D	619 881-4500	16493
Aya Locums Services Inc	8099	A	866 687-7390	16534
Califrnia Frnsic Med Group Inc	8099	D	858 694-4690	16541
Capricor Inc	8099	D	310 358-3200	16544
Cortica Healthcare Inc	8099	D	858 304-6440	16550
Headlight Health Inc	8099	C	503 961-4406	16566
Kelly Thomas MD Ucsd Hlth Care	8099	C	619 543-2885	16578
Landmark Health LLC	8099	C	619 274-8200	16579
Molina Healthcare Inc	8099	C	858 614-1580	16589
Provisio Medical Inc	8099	E	508 740-9940	16606
San Diego Blood Bank (PA)	8099	C	619 400-8132	16615
Synergy Orthpd Specialists Inc	8099	D	858 450-7118	16621
Aldridge Pite LLP	8111	B	858 750-7700	16633
County of San Diego	8111	D	619 531-4040	16663
Duckor Mtzger Wynne A Prof Law	8111	D	619 209-3000	16674
Federal Dfenders San Diego Inc (PA)	8111	D	619 234-8467	16680
Fennemore Craig PC	8111	D	619 794-0050	16681
Fish & Richardson PC	8111	C	858 678-5070	16683
Gordon Rees Scully Mansukhani	8111	C	619 696-6700	16695
Higgs Fletcher & Mack Llp	8111	C	619 236-1551	16701
Kimball Tirey & St John LLP (PA)	8111	C	619 234-1690	16715
Knobbe Martens Olson Bear LLP	8111	C	858 707-4000	16722
Latham & Watkins LLP	8111	C	858 523-5400	16724
Lewis Brsbois Bsgard Smith LLP	8111	C	619 233-1006	16731
Mintz Levin Cohn Ferris GL	8111	D	858 314-1500	16741
Morrison & Foerster LLP	8111	B	858 720-5100	16744
Paul Hastings LLP	8111	C	858 458-3000	16758
Procopio Cory Hargreaves & Savitch LLP (PA)	8111	C	619 238-1900	16765
Robbins Geller Rudman Dowd LLP (PA)	8111	B	619 231-1058	16770
Seltzer Cplan McMhon Vtek A La (PA)	8111	C	619 685-3003	16776
Sheppard Mllin Rchter Hmpton L	8111	D	619 338-6500	16778

2025 Southern California
Business Directory and Buyers Guide

(P-0000) Products & Services Section entry number
(PA)=Parent Co (HQ)=Headquarters (DH)=Div Headquarters

Company	SIC	EMP	PHONE	ENTRY#
Sheppard Mllin Rchter Hmpton L	8111	D	858 720-8900	16779
Singleton Schreiber LLP	8111	C	619 771-3473	16783
Wingert Grbing Brbker Jstkie L	8111	D	619 232-8151	16795
Withers Bergman LLP	8111	B	203 974-0412	16796
San Diego Cmnty College Dst	8211	C	619 388-4850	16824
San Diego State University	8221	D	619 594-1515	16834
San Diego Cmnty College Dst	8222	C	619 388-3453	16839
San Diego Cmnty College Dst	8222	A	619 388-2600	16840
Vista Hill Foundation	8299	D	619 281-5511	16859
American Red Cross San Dg-Mpri (PA)	8322	D	858 309-1200	16868
Autism Otrach Southern Cal LLC	8322	D	619 795-9925	16871
Aya Living Inc	8322	C	619 446-6469	16874
County of San Diego	8322	B	619 515-8202	16929
Essence of America	8322	E	312 805-9365	16940
G&L Penasquitos Inc	8322	A	858 538-0802	16946
Jewish Family Svc San Diego (PA)	8322	C	858 637-3000	16964
Neighborhood House Association (PA)	8322	B	858 715-2642	16981
New Alternatives Incorporated	8322	A	619 863-5855	16982
Project Concern International (PA)	8322	C	858 279-9690	16997
San Dego Second Chance Program	8322	E	619 266-2506	17003
San Dg-Mprial Cnties Dvlpmntal (PA)	8322	B	858 576-2996	17004
Social Advctes For Yuth San De	8322	C	619 283-9624	17012
Toward Maximum Independence (PA)	8322	C	858 467-0600	17017
Vista Hill Foundation	8322	D	619 266-0166	17025
Focus On Intervention LLC	8331	B	858 578-0769	17058
Options For All Inc	8331	B	858 565-9870	17063
Harmonium Inc (PA)	8351	C	858 684-3080	17092
Navy Exchange Service Command	8351	D	619 556-7466	17101
Casa De Las Campanas (PA)	8361	D	858 451-9152	17127
Collwood Ter Stellar Care Inc	8361	D	619 287-2920	17132
County of San Diego	8361	C	619 338-2558	17139
Independent Options Inc	8361	C	858 598-5260	17168
St Pauls Episcopal Home Inc	8361	D	619 239-2097	17198
St Pauls Episcopal Home Inc	8361	D	619 239-8687	17199
ARC of San Diego (PA)	8399	C	619 685-1175	17211
Gofundme Giving Fund	8399	C	650 260-3436	17226
San Diego Rescue Mission Inc (PA)	8399	D	619 819-1880	17241
New Childrens Museum	8412	D	619 233-8792	17258
Reuben H Fleet Science Center	8412	D	619 238-1233	17261
San Dego Soc of Ntural History	8412	D	619 232-3821	17263
San Diego Air & Space Museum	8412	D	619 234-8291	17264
San Diego Museum of Art	8412	D	619 696-1909	17265
Zoological Society San Diego (PA)	8422	A	619 231-1515	17273
Zoological Society San Diego	8422	C	619 744-3325	17275
Zoological Society San Diego	8422	C	619 231-1515	17276
Electra Owners Assoc	8611	C	619 236-3310	17281
Mission Edge San Diego	8611	D	877 232-4541	17286
Medimpact Hlthcare Systems Inc (HQ)	8621	C	800 788-2949	17301
Sharp Community Medical Group	8621	C	858 499-4525	17307
Interntional Un Oper Engineers	8631	B	619 295-3186	17311
Armed Services YMCA of USA	8641	C	858 751-5755	17323
Girl Scuts San Dg-Mprial Cncil (PA)	8641	D	619 610-0751	17346
Urban Corps San Diego County	8641	C	619 235-6884	17372
Veterans Med RES Fndtion San D	8641	C	858 642-3080	17374
YMCA of San Diego County	8641	D	858 496-9622	17382
YMCA of San Diego County	8641	C	619 428-1168	17385
YMCA of San Diego County	8641	C	619 280-9622	17388
YMCA of San Diego County	8641	C	619 281-8313	17390
YMCA of San Diego County	8641	C	619 226-8888	17391
YMCA of San Diego County	8641	C	619 264-0144	17392
YMCA of San Diego County	8641	C	619 521-3055	17393
YMCA of San Diego County	8641	D	858 270-8213	17395
YMCA of San Diego County	8641	D	619 298-3576	17396
YMCA of San Diego County (HQ)	8641	D	858 292-9622	17401
Morris Crullo World Evangelism (PA)	8661	D	858 277-2200	17417
Affinity Development Group Inc	8699	C	858 643-9324	17424
Automobile Club Southern Cal	8699	C	858 483-4960	17427
Automobile Club Southern Cal	8699	C	619 233-1000	17428
Automobile Club Southern Cal	8699	C	858 486-0786	17431
Charitble Adult Rides Svcs Inc	8699	C	858 300-2900	17461
Ausgar Technologies Inc	8711	C	855 428-7427	17491
Bae Systems Maritime Engineering &	8711	B	619 238-1000	17492
DMS Facility Services LLC	8711	A	858 560-4191	17517
Encore Semi Inc	8711	D	858 225-4993	17522
Engineering Partners Inc	8711	D	858 824-1761	17523
Enginring Sftwr Sys Sltons Inc (PA)	8711	D	619 338-0380	17524
Epsilon Systems Mssion	8711	D	619 702-1700	17525
Epsilon Systems Solutions Inc (PA)	8711	D	619 702-1700	17526
Forward Slope Incorporated (PA)	8711	D	619 299-4400	17533
Geocon Incorporated	8711	D	858 558-6900	17537
Glenn A Rick Engrg & Dev Co (PA)	8711	D	619 291-0708	17539
Highbury Defense Group LLC	8711	C	619 316-7979	17544
Indus Technology Inc	8711	C	619 299-2555	17555
Ingenium Technologies Corp	8711	D	858 227-4422	17556
Kleinfelder Inc (HQ)	8711	C	619 831-4600	17572
Kleinfelder Group Inc (PA)	8711	C	619 831-4600	17573
Kratos Tech Trning Sltions Inc (HQ)	8711	D	858 812-7300	17575
Naval Facilities Engineer Comm	8711	D	619 532-1158	17595
Nv5 Inc	8711	C	858 385-0500	17597
P2s LP	8711	C	562 497-2999	17600
Parsons Government Svcs Inc	8711	B	619 685-0085	17606
Photon Research Associates Inc	8711	C	858 455-9741	17611
Quartus Engineering Inc (PA)	8711	D	858 875-6000	17616
Rock West Composites Inc	8711	E	858 537-6260	17620
Sabre Systems Inc	8711	D	619 528-2226	17623
San Diego Composites Inc	8711	D	858 751-0450	17624
San Diego Services LLC	8711	C	858 654-0102	17625
SC Wright Construction Inc	8711	B	619 698-6909	17626
Sep Group Inc	8711	E	858 876-4621	17628
Serco Inc	8711	C	858 569-8979	17629
Tri Star Engineering Inc	8711	D	619 710-8038	17651
VT Milcom Inc	8711	C	619 424-9024	17659
Architectural Mtls USA Inc	8712	D	888 219-2126	17667
Austin Veurn Rbbins Prtners Inc (PA)	8712	D	619 231-1960	17668
Hpi Architecture	8712	C	858 203-4999	17676
NTD Architects	8712	C	858 565-4440	17687
Baker Tilly Us LLP	8721	A	858 597-4100	17706
Considine Cnsdine An Accntncy	8721	C	619 231-1977	17714
Deloitte & Touche LLP	8721	A	619 232-6500	17718
Ernst & Young LLP	8721	C	858 535-7200	17725
Gatto Pope Walwick LLP	8721	D	619 282-7366	17729
LLP Moss Adams	8721	D	858 627-1400	17744
Signature Analytics LLC	8721	C	888 284-3842	17754
Acea Biosciences Inc	8731	D	858 724-0928	17761
Agouron Pharmaceuticals Inc	8731	C	858 455-3200	17763
Ainos Inc (PA)	8731	E	858 869-2986	17765
Ansun Biopharma Inc	8731	E	858 452-2631	17766
Archimdes Tech Group Hldngs LL	8731	D	858 642-9170	17769
Arcturus Therapeutics Inc	8731	C	858 900-2660	17770
Astute Medical Inc	8731	D	858 792-3544	17771
Bioagilytix Labs LLC	8731	A	858 652-4600	17774
Bioduro LLC (PA)	8731	E	858 529-6600	17776
Biolegend Inc (HQ)	8731	D	858 455-9588	17777
Boundless Bio Inc	8731	D	858 766-9912	17780
Cibus Global Ltd	8731	C	858 450-0008	17781
Ebioscience Inc	8731	C	858 642-2058	17786
General Atomics	8731	D	858 676-7100	17789
General Atomics	8731	D	858 455-4000	17790
General Atomics	8731	D	858 455-4141	17791
Halozyme Inc	8731	C	858 794-8889	17793
Hii Fleet Support Group LLC	8731	C	858 522-6319	17795
Inova Diagnostics Inc (HQ)	8731	B	858 586-9900	17796
Leidos Inc	8731	D	703 676-4300	17803
Leidos Inc	8731	C	858 826-9416	17804
Leidos Inc	8731	D	858 826-6000	17806
Leidos Engrg & Sciences LLC	8731	C	619 542-3130	17807
Maravai Lf Scnces Holdings LLC (HQ)	8731	C	650 697-3600	17808
Novartis Inst For Fnctnal Gnmi	8731	C	858 812-1500	17814
Prosciento Inc (PA)	8731	C	619 427-1300	17818
Sequenom Inc (DH)	8731	D	858 202-9000	17822
Spreadtrum Cmmncations USA Inc	8731	D	858 546-0895	17823
Tanvex Biopharma Usa Inc (PA)	8731	D	858 210-4100	17826
Trik Therapeutics Inc (IIQ)	8731	D	858 210-3700	17831
Treeline Biosciences Inc	8731	D	858 766-5725	17832
Trilink Biotechnologies LLC	8731	C	800 863-6801	17833
Truvian Sciences Inc	8731	D	858 251-3646	17834
Turning Point Therapeutics Inc	8731	D	858 926-5251	17835
Ventyx Biosciences Inc (PA)	8731	D	760 593-4832	17838
Wildcat Discovery Tech Inc	8731	C	858 550-1980	17840
General Atomics (HQ)	8732	A	858 455-2810	17844
Luth Research Inc (PA)	8732	B	619 234-5884	17854
Quintiles Pacific Incorporated	8732	C	858 552-3400	17860
Trendsource Inc	8732	C	619 718-7467	17863
Institute For Defense Analyses	8733	C	858 622-5439	17876
Nanocomposix LLC	8733	D	858 565-4227	17883
Peraton Technology Svcs Inc	8733	E	571 313-6000	17885
Safe Life Corporation	8733	D	858 794-3208	17887
University Cal San Diego	8733	D	858 622-1771	17894
Viacyte Inc	8733	D	858 455-3708	17895
Catalent San Diego Inc	8734	C	858 805-6383	17907
Intertek USA Inc	8734	D	858 558-2599	17919
Millennium Health LLC	8734	B	877 451-3534	17921
Phamatech Incorporated	8734	C	888 635-5840	17923
Xcom Labs Inc	8734	D	858 987-9266	17931
Activcare Living Inc (PA)	8741	C	858 565-4424	17934
Allegis Residential Svcs Inc	8741	D	858 430-5700	17937

Employee Codes: A=Over 500 employees, B=251-500
C=101-250, D=51-100, E=20-50, F=10-19, G=1-9

2025 Southern California
Business Directory and Buyers Guide

© Mergent Inc. 1-800-342-5647

1339

GEOGRAPHIC

	SIC	EMP	PHONE	ENTRY#
Asset Management Tr Svcs LLC	8741	D	858 457-2202	17947
Azul Hospitality Group Inc	8741	C	619 223-4200	17949
Bridge Group Hh Inc	8741	C	858 455-5000	17956
Hotel Managers Group Llc	8741	B	858 673-1534	17991
JC Resorts LLC	8741	B	760 944-1936	17995
JC Resorts LLC	8741	C	855 574-5356	17996
Ka Management II Inc	8741	D	858 404-6080	18000
Navigant Cymetrix Corporation	8741	D	858 217-1800	18018
Premier Hlthcare Solutions Inc	8741	B	858 569-8629	18032
Pride Resource Partners LLC	8741	C	858 430-6630	18033
Scripps Clinic Med Group Inc	8741	C	858 554-9000	18050
Solpac Construction Inc	8741	C	619 296-6247	18057
Sunroad Asset Management Inc	8741	C	858 362-8500	18061
Whiskey Girl	8741	C	619 236-1616	18081
AA Blocks LLC	8742	D	858 523-8231	18084
Accenture Federal Services LLC	8742	A	619 574-2400	18085
Artemis Consulting LLC	8742	D	619 573-6328	18096
Asset Mktg Systems Insur Svcs	8742	D	888 303-8755	18097
Co-Production Intl Inc	8742	A	619 429-4344	18118
Covario Inc	8742	D	858 397-1500	18121
Eastern Goldfields Inc	8742	C	619 497-2555	18130
Fairway Technologies LLC (PA)	8742	D	858 454-4471	18133
Gcorp Consulting	8742	C	619 587-3160	18142
Independent Fincl Group LLC	8742	C	858 436-3180	18151
Lotus Workforce LLC	8742	A	480 264-0773	18162
Lpl Holdings Inc (HQ)	8742	C	858 450-9606	18163
Mapp Digital Us LLC	8742	B	619 342-4340	18166
Medical Management Cons Inc	8742	A	858 587-0609	18168
Power Digital Marketing Inc (PA)	8742	B	619 501-1211	18194
Sendlane Inc	8742	D	301 520-3812	18207
Upstrem Inc	8742	D	858 229-2979	18237
Havas Formula LLC	8743	D	619 234-0345	18254
Chugach Government Svcs Inc	8744	B	858 578-0276	18260
Techflow Inc (PA)	8744	C	858 412-8000	18268
Aecom Usa Inc	8748	C	858 947-7144	18280
Alliant Insurance Services Inc	8748	D	619 238-1828	18283
Aptim Corp	8748	D	619 239-1690	18286
ATI Restoration LLC	8748	C	858 530-2400	18287
BE Smith Inc	8748	B	913 341-9116	18288
Cask Nx LLC	8748	C	858 232-8900	18298
Center For Sustainable Energy	8748	D	858 244-1177	18300
Environmental Science Assoc	8748	D	858 638-0900	18308
Garrad Hassan America Inc (DH)	8748	D	858 836-3370	18310
Geocon Consultants Inc (PA)	8748	D	858 558-6900	18312
Haley & Aldrich Inc	8748	D	619 280-9210	18317
Icf Jones & Stokes Inc	8748	D	858 578-8964	18322
Johnson Johnson Innovation LLC	8748	B	858 242-1504	18327
Ninyo More Gtchncal Envmtl Scn (PA)	8748	D	858 576-1000	18342
Pro-Spectus Inc	8748	D	877 877-0096	18348
Project Design Consultants LLC	8748	D	619 235-6471	18350
Recon Environmental Inc (PA)	8748	D	619 308-9333	18352
Sanyo North America Corp	8748	B	619 661-1134	18354
Source 44 LLC	8748	C	877 916-6337	18358
Tangoe-Pi Inc	8748	C		18362
Team Risk MGT Strategies LLC	8748	A	877 767-8728	18363
Veterans EZ Info Inc	8748	C	866 839-1329	18367
Overseas Service Corporation	8999	C	858 408-0751	18376
County of San Diego	9199	D	858 505-6100	18388
San Diego Unified Port Dst	9221	C	619 686-6585	18389

SAN DIMAS, CA - Los Angeles County

	SIC	EMP	PHONE	ENTRY#
Walton Construction Inc	1522	D	909 267-7777	456
Pacific Systems Interiors Inc	1742	C	310 436-6820	1021
Organic Milling Inc (PA)	2099	D	800 638-8686	1826
Organic Milling Corporation	2099	E	909 599-0961	1827
Roskam Baking Company LLC	2099	A	909 599-0961	1845
Roskam Baking Company LLC	2099	B	909 305-0185	1846
Westin Automotive Products Inc (PA)	2396	E	626 960-6762	2269
Western PCF Stor Solutions Inc (PA)	2542	D	909 451-0303	2598
Gilead Palo Alto Inc	2834	D	909 394-4000	3409
Hagen-Renaker Inc (PA)	3269	D	909 599-2341	4367
Danrich Welding Co Inc	3444	E	562 634-4811	4976
Gms Elevator Services Inc	3534	D	909 599-3904	5514
Magor Mold LLC	3544	D	909 592-3663	5587
Bluelab Corporation Usa Inc	3569	E	909 599-1940	5813
Sypris Data Systems Inc (HQ)	3572	E	909 962-9400	5890
Kap Manufacturing Inc	3599	E	909 599-2525	6157
Landmark Electronics Inc	3679	E	626 967-2857	7019
Wavestream Corporation (HQ)	3679	C	909 599-9080	7068
Pertronix LLC	3822	E	909 599-5955	7838
Hamilton Sundstrand Corp	3826	C	909 593-5300	7956
Hamilton Sundstrand Spc Systms	3829	D	909 288-5300	8045
Medic-1 Ambulance Service Inc	4119	D	909 592-8840	8835

	SIC	EMP	PHONE	ENTRY#
Imobile LLC	4812	C	909 599-8822	9403
Southern California Edison Co	4911	C	909 592-3757	9631
Southern California Gas Co	4924	B	909 305-8297	9650
American States Water Company (PA)	4941	A	909 394-3600	9682
Superwinch LLC	5013	E	800 323-2031	9851
Smart Stores Operations LLC	5141	B	909 592-2190	10785
Edgebanding Services Inc (PA)	5162	D	909 599-2336	10997
Christian Community Credit Un (PA)	6062	D	626 915-7551	11825
Southern Cal Prmnnte Med Group	6324	C	909 394-2505	12113
San Dimas Retirement Center (PA)	6513	D	909 599-8441	12364
Second Image National LLC (PA)	7334	C	800 229-7477	13316
Industrial Janitor Service	7349	D	818 782-5658	13378
Signature Select Personnel LLC	7361	B	626 940-3351	13571
Webmetro	7372	C	909 599-8885	14064
Automatic Data Processing Inc	7374	C	800 225-5237	14123
Bolide Technology Group Inc	7382	C	909 305-8889	14385
National Hot Rod Association (PA)	7948	C	626 914-4761	15040
Raging Waters Group Inc	7996	A	909 802-2200	15106
Toan D Nguyen DDS Inc	8021	D	909 599-3398	15528
Emeritus Corporation	8051	C	909 394-0304	15630
Kaiser Foundation Hospitals	8062	C	909 394-2530	16044
Prime Hlthcare Svcs - San Dmas	8062	B	909 599-6811	16147
Carrico Pediatric Therapy Inc	8093	D	562 607-1937	16447
Positive Behavior Steps Corp	8093	D	626 940-5180	16494
Qtc Management Inc (DH)	8099	C	800 682-9701	16611
Qtc Mdcal Group Inc A Med Corp	8099	A	800 260-1515	16612
Legal Solutions Holdings Inc	8111	C	800 244-3495	16728
Med-Legal LLC	8111	C	626 653-5160	16739
County of Los Angeles	8322	C	909 599-2391	16927
Prime Health Care	8351	D	909 394-2727	17110
McKinley Childrens Center Inc (PA)	8361	C	909 599-1227	17179
Thorpe Technologies Inc (DH)	8711	E	562 903-8230	17648
Brault	8721	C	626 447-0296	17707
Ego Inc	8721	C	626 447-0296	17721
Qtc	8741	C	909 978-3531	18042

SAN FERNANDO, CA - Los Angeles County

	SIC	EMP	PHONE	ENTRY#
Bernards Builders Inc	1522	B	818 898-1521	442
Brightview Landscape Dev Inc	1711	D	818 838-4700	754
Karoun Dairies Inc (PA)	2022	E	818 767-7000	1287
American Bottling Company	2086	D	818 898-1471	1602
Pepsi-Cola Metro Btlg Co Inc	2086	D	818 898-3829	1630
Fresh & Ready Foods LLC (PA)	2099	D	818 837-7600	1777
Lehman Foods Inc	2099	E	818 837-7600	1806
Mr Tortilla Inc	2099	C	818 233-8922	1820
New Haven Companies Inc	2299	D	818 686-7020	1972
Wyndham Collection LLC	2434	E	888 522-8476	2368
Airo Industries Company	2531	E	818 838-1008	2536
Abex Display Systems Inc (PA)	2653	C	800 537-0231	2651
Araca Merchandise LP	2759	C	818 743-5400	3117
Puretek Corporation (PA)	2834	E	818 361-3316	3485
J Miller Co Inc	3053	C	818 837-0181	3893
Spira Manufacturing Corp	3053	E	818 764-8222	3901
C A Schroeder Inc (PA)	3296	C	818 365-9561	4490
J & M Products Inc	3429	D	818 837-0205	4774
Bellows Mfg & RES Inc	3441	C	818 838-1333	4818
TL Shield & Associates Inc	3534	E	818 509-8228	5515
Metromedia Technologies Inc	3577	E	818 552-6500	5937
W Machine Works Inc	3599	E	818 890-8049	6267
Topaz Lighting Company LLC	3646	E	818 838-3123	6476
Frazier Aviation Inc	3728	E	818 898-1998	7480
One Step Gps LLC	3812	D	818 659-2031	7784
J L Shepherd and Assoc Inc	3829	E	818 898-2361	8048
Valeda Company LLC	3842	E	800 421-8700	8316
Laser Technologies & Services LLC	3861	D		8432
Dg-Dlsplays LLC	3993	C	877 358-5976	8599
Ricon Corporation	3999	C	818 267-3000	8720
Mv Transportation Inc	4111	C	323 666-0856	8781
Pepsico Beverage Sales LLC	4225	C	818 361-0685	9099
Frontier California Inc	4813	B	818 365-0542	9436
Jme Inc (PA)	5063	C	201 896-8600	10187
Daikin Comfort Tech Dist Inc	5075	B	713 861-2500	10330
Ahi Investment Inc (DH)	5199	C	818 979-0030	11108
Home Depot USA Inc	5211	C	818 365-7662	11173
American Fruits & Flavors LLC	7299	B	818 899-9574	13167
Universal Mail Delivery Svc (PA)	7331	D	818 365-3144	13308
Industrial Stitchtech Inc	7389	C	818 361-6319	14514
Northeast Valley Health Corp (PA)	8322	D	818 898-1388	16984
Child Care Resource Center Inc	8351	C	818 837-0097	17081
All State Association Inc	8611	C	877 425-2558	17277

SAN GABRIEL, CA - Los Angeles County

	SIC	EMP	PHONE	ENTRY#
Comfort Industries Inc	2231	E	562 692-8288	1900

Mergent email: customerrelations@mergent.com
1340

2025 Southern California
Business Directory and Buyers Guide

(P-0000) Products & Services Section entry number
(PA)=Parent Co (HQ)=Headquarters (DH)=Div Headquarters

	SIC	EMP	PHONE	ENTRY#
Asia-Pacific California Inc.	2711	E	626 281-8500	2780
Hsiao & Montano Inc.	3161	E	626 588-2528	4295
Inveserve Corporation	6531	D	626 458-3435	12468
Park Cleaners Inc (PA)	7213	D	626 281-5942	13125
Informtion Rfrral Fdrtion of L	7299	D	626 350-1841	13176
San Gabriel Country Club	7997	D	626 287-9671	15168
San Gbriel Ambltory Srgery Ctr	8011	B	626 300-5300	15445
Country Villa Service Corp	8059	C	626 285-2165	15844
Longwood Management Corp	8059	C	626 289-3763	15868
Ahmc Healthcare Inc (PA)	8062	C	626 943-7526	15900
San Gabriel Valley Medical Ctr	8062	A	626 289-5454	16167
Ahmc Healthcare Inc	8099	D	626 248-3452	16526
Providnce Facey Med Foundation	8099	D	626 576-0800	16605

SAN JACINTO, CA - Riverside County

	SIC	EMP	PHONE	ENTRY#
Skyline Homes Inc	2451	C	951 654-9321	2402
Edelbrock Foundry Corp	3363	E	951 654-6677	4645
J Talley Corporation (PA)	3446	D	951 654-2123	5065
Rama Corporation	3567	E	951 654-7351	5803
MTI De Baja Inc	3812	E	951 654-2333	7746
Agri-Empire	5148	C	951 654-7311	10885
Soboba Band Luiseno Indians	7389	A	951 665-1000	14599
Borrego Cmnty Hlth Foundation	8011	D	951 487-8506	15255
Riversd-San Brnrdino Cnty Indi	8011	C	951 654-0803	15437

SAN JUAN CAPISTRANO, CA - Orange County

	SIC	EMP	PHONE	ENTRY#
Devil Mountain Whl Nurs LLC	0181	D	949 496-9356	52
Brightview Landscape Svcs Inc	0781	C	714 546-7843	158
Pioneer Sands LLC	1446	E	949 728-0171	377
Emerald X LLC	2721	C	949 226-5754	2856
Fluidmaster Inc (PA)	3089	D	949 728-2000	4118
Solag Incorporated	4953	C	949 728-1206	9766
Mission Volkswagen Inc	5511	D	949 493-4511	11380
Freedom Properties-Hemet LLC	6512	C	949 489-0400	12293
Marriott International Inc	7011	C	949 503-5700	12917
A Better Life Recovery LLC	7371	B	866 278-8804	13640
Medusind Solutions Inc (PA)	7389	D	949 240-8895	14543
Southern Cal Prmnnte Med Group	8011	C	949 234-2139	15474
Endura Healthcare Inc	8051	C	949 487-9500	15635
Ensign Group Inc	8051	C	949 487-9500	15636
Ensign Services Inc	8051	C	949 487-9500	15645
Ensign Southland LLC	8051	D	949 487-9500	15646
Clarient Inc	8071	C	949 445-7300	16308
Nichols Inst Reference Labs (DH)	8071	A	949 728-4000	16324
Quest Diagnostics Nichols Inst (HQ)	8071	A	949 728-4000	16331
Scientfc Applctons RES Assoc	8732	D	714 224-4410	17861

SAN LUIS OBISPO, CA - San Luis Obispo County

	SIC	EMP	PHONE	ENTRY#
Mainstream Energy Corporation	1711	B	805 528-9705	800
Rec Solar Commercial Corp	1711	E	844 732-7652	828
Specialty Construction Inc	1731	D	805 543-1706	964
Courtside Cellars LLC (PA)	2084	E	805 782-0500	1562
Phase 2 Cellars LLC	2084	E	805 782-0300	1581
Sauer Brands Inc	2099	D	805 597-8900	1849
The Hunter Spice Inc	2099	E	805 597-8900	1861
Slo New Times Inc	2711	E	805 546-8208	2829
David B Anderson	2752	E	805 489-0661	2999
Prpco	2752	E	805 543-6844	3072
Ws Packaging-Blake Printery	2752	E	805 543-6844	3103
Promega Biosciences LLC	2833	D	805 544-8524	3328
Air-Vol Block Inc	3271	E	805 543-1314	4369
Whitefox Defense Tech Inc	3364	E	805 225-4506	4662
Inspired Flight Tech Inc	0429	D	806 776 3610	4773
Snapnrack Inc	3429	C	077 732 2860	4788
R H Strasbaugh (PA)	3541	E	805 541-6424	5549
Entegris Gp Inc	3559	C	805 541-9299	5820
Newlife2 (PA)	3569	E	805 549-8093	5829
Next Intent Inc	3599	D	805 781-6755	6192
Revasum Inc	3674	C	805 541-6424	6883
Ultra-Stereo Labs Inc	3699	C	805 549-0161	7155
Empirical Systems Arospc Inc (PA)	3721	C	805 474-5900	7339
Edge Autonomy Bend LLC (HQ)	3761	D	541 678-0515	7643
Stellar Exploration Inc	3761	E	805 459-1425	7656
Edge Autonomy Slo LLC	3812	D	805 544-0932	7715
Crystal Engineering Corp	3823	D	805 595-5477	7854
Fziomed Inc (PA)	3841	D	805 546-0610	8156
L Spark	3911	E	805 626-0511	8456
Ernie Ball Inc (PA)	3931	C	805 544-7726	8467
Zoo Med Laboratories Inc	3999	D	805 542-9988	8743
First Transit Inc	4111	C	805 544-2730	8752
San Luis Obspo Rgnal Trnst Aut	4111	D	805 781-4465	8801
San Luis Ambulance Service Inc	4119	C	805 543-2626	8847
United Parcel Service Inc	4215	C	801 973-3400	9028

	SIC	EMP	PHONE	ENTRY#
Eschat	4812	D	805 541-5044	9401
Ksby Communications LLC	4833	D	805 541-6666	9509
Pacific Gas and Electric Co	4911	D	805 545-4562	9597
Amk Foodservices Inc	5141	C	805 544-7600	10742
All About Produce Company	5148	C	805 543-9000	10886
Madonna Inn Inc	5461	C	805 543-3000	11298
Apple Farm Collections-Slo Inc (PA)	5812	B	805 544-2040	11550
Goodwill Central Coast	5932	C	805 544-0542	11628
Mission Community Bancorp	6021	C	805 782-5000	11736
Sesloc Credit Union (PA)	6062	D	805 543-1816	11832
Guaranteed Rate Inc	6162	D	805 550-6933	11911
Merrill Lynch Prce Fnner Smith	6211	D	805 596-2222	11985
Morris Grritano Insur Agcy Inc	6411	D	805 543-6887	12236
Harvest Management Sub LLC	6513	A	805 543-0187	12343
King Ventures	6552	C	805 544-4444	12568
USA Staffing Inc	7363	D	805 269-2677	13628
3i Infotech Inc	7371	E	805 544-8327	13639
Dzkicorp Inc	7371	D	805 464-0573	13714
Mindbody Inc (PA)	7374	C	877 755-4279	14146
San Luis Obispo Golf Cntry CLB	7997	C	805 543-3400	15169
Templeton Surgery Center LLC	8011	C	805 434-3550	15486
Bayshore Healthcare Inc	8051	C	805 544-5100	15579
Compass Health Inc	8051	C	805 543-0210	15598
County of San Luis Obispo	8062	C	805 781-4753	15972
French Hospital Medical Center (DH)	8062	B	805 543-5353	16000
Sierra Vista Hospital Inc (HQ)	8062	A	805 546-7600	16199
Community Action Prtnr San Lui	8093	C	805 544-2478	16457
Booth Mitchel & Strange LLP	8111	D	805 400-0703	16649
Associated Students Inc (PA)	8322	D	805 756-1281	16870
Community Action Partnership	8322	C	805 541-4122	16896
Life Steps Foundation Inc	8322	D	805 549-0150	16972
Lumina Alliance	8322	D	805 781-6400	16976
Tri-Cnties Assn For Dvlpmntlly	8322	C	805 543-2833	17018
United Crbral Plsy Assn San Lu	8322	D	805 543-2039	17021
Community Action Prtnr San Lui	8351	C	805 541-2272	17085
Community Action Prtnr San Lui (PA)	8351	C	805 544-4355	17086
Family Care Network Inc (PA)	8351	D	805 503-6240	17090
State Bar of California	8621	D	805 544-7551	17308
San Luis Obispo County YMCA	8641	D	805 544-7225	17364
Automobile Club Southern Cal	8699	D	805 543-6454	17450
AME Unmanned Air Systems Inc	8711	D	805 541-4448	17482
Ashley & Vance Engineering Inc	8711	D	805 545-0010	17489
Trust Automation Inc	8711	C	805 544-0761	17652
Rrm Design Group (PA)	8712	D	805 439-0442	17689
Entegris Inc	8741	D	805 541-9299	17981
Movement For Life Inc	8741	B	805 788-0805	18015
Rincon Consultants Inc	8748	C	805 547-0900	18353

SAN MARCOS, CA - San Diego County

	SIC	EMP	PHONE	ENTRY#
San Diego Farms LLC	0191	C	760 736-4072	86
Hollandia Dairy Inc (PA)	0241	C	760 744-3222	91
Shasta Landscaping Inc	0781	D	760 744-6551	191
Doose Landscape Incorporated	0782	D	760 591-4500	205
MB Builders Inc	1521	D	760 410-1442	418
Airx Utility Surveyors Inc (PA)	1623	D	760 480-2347	658
20/20 Plumbing & Heating Inc	1711	C	760 535-3101	725
Csi Electrical Contractors Inc	1731	B	760 227-0577	908
Solrite Electric LLC	1731	C	833 765-6682	961
Southern Contracting Company	1731	C	760 744-0760	963
M Bar C Construction Inc	1791	D	760 744-4131	1157
California Spirits Company LLC	2086	E	619 677-7066	1611
Fish House Foods Inc	2092	C	760 597-1270	1705
Equal Exchange Inc	2095	D	619 335-6259	1717
Culinary Specialties Inc	2099	D	760 744-8220	1760
La Fe Tortilleria Inc (PA)	2099	E	760 752-8350	1801
Piercan Usa Inc	2259	D	760 599-4543	1929
Leemarc Industries LLC	2329	D	760 598-0505	2019
Showdogs Inc	2591	E	760 603-3269	2608
San Dieguito Publishers Inc	2752	D	760 593-5139	3079
Prographics Screenprinting Inc	2759	E	760 744-4555	3163
Cliniqa Corporation (HQ)	2836	E	760 744-1900	3570
Cliniqa Corporation	2836	D	760 744-1900	3571
Synsus Prvate Lbel Prtners LLC	2842	D	713 714-0225	3622
Dispensing Dynamics Intl Inc (PA)	3089	E	626 961-3691	4104
L&S Stone LLC (DH)	3281	E	760 736-3232	4475
Winchster Intrcnnect CM CA Inc	3357	C	800 848-4257	4640
Independent Energy Solutions Inc	3433	E	760 752-9706	4811
Accu-Seal Sencorpwhite Inc	3565	E		5785
Accu-Tech Laser Processing Inc	3599	C	760 744-6692	6062
K-Tech Machine Inc	3599	C	800 274-9424	6156
Sullins Electronics Corp	3643	D	760 744-0125	6430
Hughes Circuits Inc	3672	D	760 744-0300	6736
Hughes Circuits Inc (PA)	3672	D	760 744-0300	6737

GEOGRAPHIC

	SIC	EMP	PHONE	ENTRY#
Oncore Manufacturing LLC	3672	C	760 737-6777	6759
Bree Engineering Corp.	3679	E	760 510-4950	6975
Dexter Axle Company	3715	E	760 744-1610	7315
Unique Functional Products	3715	E	760 744-1610	7318
Spinergy Inc.	3751	D	760 496-2121	7636
Aci Medical LLC	3841	C	760 744-4400	8076
Western Sign Systems Inc.	3993	E	760 736-6070	8650
Hexoden Holdings Inc (PA)	3999	D	858 201-3412	8682
Preserved Treescapes International Inc	3999	D	760 631-6789	8718
Vallecitos Water District Financing (HQ)	4941	D	760 744-0460	9724
Hunter Industries Incorporated (PA)	4971	C	760 744-5240	9791
Bestop Baja LLC	5013	C	760 560-2252	9816
Tamura Corporation of America (HQ)	5065	E	800 472-6624	10288
Orora Packaging Solutions	5113	E	760 510-7170	10599
La Provence Inc.	5149	D	760 736-3299	10954
Southern Cal Disc Tire Co Inc	5531	D	760 744-3526	11458
Osf International Inc.	5812	E	760 471-0155	11592
Severson Group LLC	5812	E	760 550-9976	11599
Quilt In A Day Inc.	5961	E	760 591-0929	11661
Centurion Group Inc (PA)	6211	C	760 471-8536	11960
Americare Hlth Retirement Inc.	6512	C	760 744-4484	12281
Chateau Lk San Mrcos Hmwners A	6513	D	760 471-0083	12336
Whv Resort Group Inc (HQ)	6531	D	760 652-4913	12550
Golden Door Properties LLC	7011	C	760 744-5777	12827
Corkys Pest Control Inc.	7342	D	760 432-8801	13345
Araya Construction Inc.	7349	D	760 758-3454	13356
Diamond Environmental Svcs LP	7359	D	760 744-7191	13454
Magic Touch Software Intl.	7372	E	800 714-6490	13971
Control Air Enterprises LLC	7623	B	760 744-2727	14725
Hydralic Systems Cmponents Inc	7699	E	760 744-9350	14773
Ilingo2com Inc.	8011	E	800 311-8331	15328
North County Health Prj Inc (PA)	8011	C	760 736-6755	15408
Rancho Physical Therapy Inc.	8049	E	760 752-1011	15555
Plum Healthcare Group LLC	8051	C	760 471-0388	15754
Kaiser Foundation Hospitals.	8062	D	442 385-7000	16053
CRC Health Group Inc.	8093	D	760 744-2104	16465
Casa De Amparo (PA)	8361	D	760 754-5500	17126
ARC of San Diego.	8399	C	760 740-6800	17213
Aquaneering LLC	8731	E	858 578-2028	17768
Primary Care Assod Med Group I (PA)	8741	D	760 471-7505	18035
Olympus Building Services Inc.	8744	A	760 750-4629	18265
Kros-Wise.	8748	C	619 607-2899	18330

SAN MARINO, CA - Los Angeles County

	SIC	EMP	PHONE	ENTRY#
Feihe International Inc (PA)	2023	A	626 757-8885	1298
Huntington Lib Art Msums Btnca.	8231	B	626 405-2100	16842

SAN PEDRO, CA - Los Angeles County

	SIC	EMP	PHONE	ENTRY#
State Fish Co Inc.	2092	C	310 547-9530	1713
Juanita F Wade.	2399	E	310 519-1208	2279
Flexline Incorporated.	2796	E	562 921-4141	3206
Tatung Company America Inc (HQ)	3663	D	310 637-2105	6662
Larson Al Boat Shop.	3731	D	310 514-4100	7603
Space Exploration Tech Corp.	3761	C	714 330-8668	7652
Polar Tankers Inc.	4424	C	310 519-8260	9137
Catalina Channel Express Inc (HQ)	4489	C	310 519-7971	9139
So Cal Ship Services.	4489	D	310 519-8411	9140
Marine Terminals Corporation.	4491	B	310 519-2300	9143
Port of Los Angeles.	4491	C	310 732-3508	9145
APM Terminals Pacific LLC.	4731	B	310 221-4000	9253
Crowley Marine Services Inc.	4731	B	310 732-6500	9266
Toll Global Fwdg Scs USA Inc.	4731	C	732 750-9000	9344
Contessa Liquidating Co Inc.	5142	C		10818
Qualy Pak Specialty Foods Inc.	5146	D	310 541-3023	10859
Tri-Marine Fish Company LLC.	5146	C	310 547-1144	10863
Select Home Warranty Ca Inc.	6351	B	732 835-0110	12148
Spf Capital Real Estate LLC.	7011	C	310 519-8200	13033
Advent Resources Inc.	7371	D	310 241-1500	13645
Black Knight Patrol Inc.	7381	D	213 985-6499	14280
Little Ssters of The Poor Los.	8051	C	310 548-0625	15700
San Pedro Convalescent HM Inc.	8051	D	310 832-6431	15769
Seacrest Convalescent Hosp Inc.	8051	D	310 833-3526	15772
San Pedro Peninsula Hospital.	8062	A	310 832-3311	16171
Healthview Inc (PA).	8361	C	310 638-4113	17161
City of Los Angeles.	9621	A	310 732-3734	18400

SAN SIMEON, CA - San Luis Obispo County

	SIC	EMP	PHONE	ENTRY#
Cavalier Inn Inc.	7011	D	805 927-4688	12787

SAN YSIDRO, CA - San Diego County

	SIC	EMP	PHONE	ENTRY#
Centro De Slud De La Cmndad De.	8093	B	619 205-6341	16451

SANTA ANA, CA - Orange County

	SIC	EMP	PHONE	ENTRY#
Brightview Landscape Svcs Inc.	0781	B	714 546-7843	157
Nieves Landscape Inc.	0781	C	714 835-7332	180
Southwest Landscape Inc.	0781	C	714 545-1084	192
Landcare USA LLC.	0782	D	949 559-7771	216
Mpl Enterprises Inc.	0782	D	714 545-1717	224
Gray Construction Inc.	1521	C	714 491-1315	407
Gray West Construction Inc.	1541	C	714 491-1317	482
John M Frank Construction Inc.	1542	D	714 210-3600	550
Macro-Z-Technology Company (PA)	1611	D	714 564-1130	633
Oc 405 Partners Joint Venture.	1622	D	858 251-2200	655
Sukut Construction LLC.	1623	C	714 540-5351	698
Brightview Landscape Dev Inc.	1711	C	714 546-7975	753
Pacific Rim Mech Contrs Inc.	1711	C	714 285-2600	816
Pipe Restoration Inc.	1711	C	714 564-7600	819
Sterling Plumbing Inc.	1711	D	714 641-5480	844
Gps Painting Wallcovering Inc.	1721	C	714 730-8904	865
Sun Electric LP.	1731	D	714 210-3744	968
Prime Tech Cabinets Inc.	1751	C	949 757-4900	1058
Trimco Finish Inc.	1751	C	714 708-0300	1063
Woodbridge Glass Inc.	1793	C	714 838-4444	1169
Reed Thomas Company Inc.	1794	D	714 558-7691	1174
Sukut Construction Inc.	1794	C	714 540-5351	1176
West Lake Food Corporation (PA)	2011	E	714 973-2286	1253
Brothers Intl Desserts (PA)	2024	C	949 655-0080	1315
Stremicks Heritage Foods LLC (HQ)	2026	B	714 775-5000	1335
The Sweet Life Enterprises Inc.	2041	C	949 261-7400	1409
Gold Coast Baking Company LLC.	2051	E	714 545-2253	1457
D F Stauffer Biscuit Co Inc.	2052	E	714 546-6855	1485
Laguna Cookie Company Inc.	2052	D	714 546-6855	1490
Bonerts Incorporated.	2053	E	714 540-3535	1493
Rich Products Corporation.	2053	E	714 338-1145	1496
MRS Foods Incorporated (PA)	2099	E	714 554-2791	1821
Hook It Up.	2111	E	714 600-0100	1867
Cut and Sew Co Inc.	2253	C	714 981-7244	1914
Atlas Carpet Mills Inc.	2273	C	323 724-7930	1947
Fabrica International Inc.	2273	C	949 261-7181	1951
J Miller Canvas LLC.	2295	E	714 641-0052	1960
Image Apparel For Business Inc.	2326	C	714 541-5247	1995
Liquid Graphics Inc.	2329	C	949 486-3588	2020
Modern Embroidery Inc.	2395	C	714 436-9960	2252
Airborne Systems N Amer CA Inc.	2399	C	714 662-1400	2271
Strata Forest Products Inc (PA)	2421	E	714 751-0800	2287
Talimar Systems Inc.	2531	E	714 557-4884	2553
Envelopments Inc.	2621	E	714 569-3300	2623
Blower-Dempsay Corporation (PA)	2653	E	714 481-3800	2655
Heritage Paper Co (HQ)	2653	D	714 540-9737	2673
A Plus Label Inc.	2679	E	714 229-9811	2763
Freedom Communications Inc.	2711	A	714 796-7000	2797
Entrepreneur Media LLC (PA)	2721	D	949 261-2325	2857
B and Z Printing Inc.	2752	E	714 892-2000	2967
Integrated Communications Inc.	2752	E	310 851-8066	3023
Labor Law Center Inc.	2752	E	800 745-9970	3032
Tailgate Printing Inc.	2752	D	714 966-3035	3086
Artisan Nameplate Awards Corp.	2759	E	714 556-6222	3118
Blackburn Alton Invstments LLC.	2759	E	714 731-2000	3120
Brixen & Sons Inc.	2759	E	714 566-1444	3123
Resource Label Group LLC.	2759	D	714 619-7100	3168
B J Bindery Inc.	2789	E	714 835-7342	3201
Tammy Taylor Nails Inc.	2821	E	949 250-9287	3296
Robinson Pharma Inc.	2834	C	714 241-0235	3493
Robinson Pharma Inc (PA)	2834	B	714 241-0235	3494
Robinson Pharma Inc.	2834	C	714 241-0235	3495
Lehman Millet Incorporated.	2835	E	714 850-7900	3543
Fujifilm Irvine Scientific Inc (DH)	2836	E	949 261-7800	3575
Gps Associates Inc.	2842	E	949 408-3162	3604
Westridge Laboratories Inc.	2844	E	714 259-9400	3697
Behr Holdings Corporation (HQ)	2851	E	714 545-7101	3703
Behr Process LLC (DH)	2851	A	714 545-7101	3704
Behr Sales Inc (HQ)	2851	E	714 545-7101	3705
Color Science Inc.	2865	E	714 434-1033	3723
Axiom Materials Inc.	2891	E	949 623-4400	3760
Insultech LLC (PA)	2899	E	714 384-0506	3805
Yokohama Corp North America (HQ)	3011	E	540 389-5426	3866
Ciasons Industrial Inc.	3053	E	714 259-0838	3883
Freudenberg-Nok General Partnr.	3053	C	714 834-0602	3887
Hdz Brothers Inc.	3053	E	714 953-4010	3889
Hitt Companies.	3069	E	714 979-1405	3914
Bird B Gone LLC.	3082	D	949 472-3122	3961
Altium Packaging LP.	3086	E	714 241-6640	3992
Arlon LLC.	3089	C	714 540-2811	4053
Clear-Ad Inc.	3089	E	866 627-9718	4090
Codan US Corporation.	3089	D	714 545-2111	4091

2025 Southern California
Business Directory and Buyers Guide

(P-0000) Products & Services Section entry number
(PA)=Parent Co (HQ)=Headquarters (DH)=Div Headquarters

	SIC	EMP	PHONE	ENTRY#
Fit-Line Inc	3089	E	714 549-9091	4117
Hood Manufacturing Inc	3089	D	714 979-7681	4133
JB Plastics Inc	3089	E	714 541-8500	4146
Modified Plastics Inc (PA)	3089	E	714 546-4667	4173
Newport Laminates Inc	3089	E	714 545-8335	4181
Southern California Plas Inc	3089	D	714 751-7084	4245
CL Solutions LLC	3211	D	714 597-6499	4315
International Skylights	3211	C	800 325-4355	4316
Sundown Liquidating Corp (PA)	3211	D	714 540-8950	4318
Twed-Dells Inc	3231	E	714 754-6900	4349
Pacific Stone Design Inc	3272	E	714 836-5757	4410
Prime Forming & Cnstr Sups Inc	3272	E	714 547-6710	4414
Spec Formliners Inc	3272	E	714 429-9500	4423
Bender Ready Mix Inc	3273	E	714 560-0744	4431
Easyflex Inc	3312	E	888 577-8999	4516
Wheel and Tire Club Inc	3312	E	800 901-6003	4529
Aluminum Precision Pdts Inc (PA)	3334	A	714 546-8125	4575
Gemini Industries Inc	3341	D	949 250-4011	4584
Calmont Engrg & Elec Corp (PA)	3357	E	714 549-0336	4630
DC Partners Inc (PA)	3365	E	714 558-9444	4672
Brasstech Inc	3432	C	714 796-9278	4801
Brasstech Inc (HQ)	3432	D	949 417-5207	4802
Tobin Steel Company Inc	3441	E	714 541-2268	4874
Acd LLC (DH)	3443	E	949 261-7533	4907
Ajax Boiler Inc	3443	D	714 437-9050	4908
Bend-Tek Inc (PA)	3444	E	714 210-8966	4958
Cal Pac Sheet Metal Inc	3444	E	714 979-2733	4962
Fabrication Concepts Corporation	3444	C	714 881-2000	4986
Acrontos Manufacturing Inc	3469	E	714 850-9133	5169
Kaga (usa) Inc	3469	E	714 540-2697	5195
Anodyne Inc	3471	E	714 549-3321	5234
Chrome Tech Inc	3471	C	714 543-4092	5248
Electrode Technologies Inc	3471	E	714 549-3771	5256
JD Processing Inc	3471	E	714 972-8161	5271
Triumph Proc - Embee Div Inc	3471	B	714 546-9842	5301
Gemtech Inds Good Earth Mfg	3479	E	714 848-2517	5322
R & B Wire Products Inc	3496	E	714 549-3355	5411
US Rigging Supply Corp	3496	E	714 545-7444	5419
Ecoolthing Corp	3499	E	714 368-4791	5445
K-V Engineering Inc	3541	D	714 229-9977	5546
Universal Punch Corp	3542	D	714 556-4488	5562
Ambrit Engineering Corporation	3544	D	714 557-1074	5566
Superior Mold Co	3544	E	714 751-7084	5599
Adapt Automation Inc	3549	E	714 662-4454	5651
Newport Electronics Inc	3559	E	714 540-4914	5713
Polaris E-Commerce Inc	3561	E	714 907-0582	5740
Atr Sales Inc	3568	E	714 432-8411	5806
Silicon Tech Inc	3572	B	949 476-1130	5888
Marway Power Systems Inc (PA)	3577	E	714 917-6200	5936
Omniprint Inc	3577	E	949 833-0080	5942
Jwc Environmental Inc	3589	D	714 662-5829	6018
A-Z Mfg Inc	3599	E	714 444-4446	6061
Advanced Joining Technologies Inc	3599	E	949 756-8091	6064
Aero-k	3599	E	626 350-5125	6070
Alco Engrg & Tooling Corp	3599	E	714 556-6060	6074
GBF Enterprises Inc	3599	E	714 979-7131	6132
Motorvac Technologies Inc	3599	E	714 558-4822	6188
Norotos Inc	3599	C	714 662-3113	6194
S&S Precision Mfg Inc	3599	E	714 754-6664	6226
Senga Engineering Inc	3599	E	714 549-8011	8231
Tmx Engineering and Mfg Corp	3599	D	714 641-5884	6251
Tomi Engineering Inc	3599	D	714 556-1474	6252
Onyx Power Inc	3612	C	714 513-1500	6293
Cole Instrument Corp	3621	D	714 556-3100	6319
AP Parpro Inc	3625	E	619 498-9004	6341
Nivek Industries Inc	3643	E	714 545-8855	6424
Saf-T-Co Supply	3644	E	714 547-9975	6434
Dana Creath Designs Ltd	3648	E	714 662-0111	6497
Aurasound Inc	3651	D	949 829-4000	6528
Secure Comm Systems Inc (HQ)	3663	C	714 547-1174	6658
Statewide Trffic Sfety Sgns In (HQ)	3669	E	949 553-8272	6693
Accurate Circuit Engrg Inc	3672	D	714 546-2162	6704
Dynasty Electronic Company LLC	3672	D	714 550-1097	6723
K L Electronic Inc	3672	E	714 751-5611	6742
Matrix USA Inc	3672	E	714 825-0404	6747
Maxtrol Corporation	3672	E	714 245-0506	6748
Parpro Technologies Inc	3672	C	714 545-8886	6762
Pioneer Circuits Inc	3672	B	714 641-3132	6764
South Coast Circuits LLC	3672	D	714 966-2108	6773
Ttm Printed Circuit Group Inc (HQ)	3672	E	714 327-3000	6780
Ttm Technologies Inc (PA)	3672	E	714 327-3000	6781
Ttm Technologies Inc	3672	B	714 241-0303	6782
Accelerated Memory Prod Inc	3674	E	714 460-9800	6792
Flexible Manufacturing LLC	3678	D	714 259-7996	6948
Express Manufacturing Inc (PA)	3679	B	714 979-2228	6996
IJ Research Inc	3679	D	714 546-8522	7006
Sandberg Industries Inc (PA)	3679	D	949 660-9473	7047
Smiths Intrcnnect Americas Inc	3679	B	714 371-1100	7051
Wyvern Technologies	3679	E	714 966-0710	7070
CD Video Manufacturing Inc	3695	D	714 265-0770	7103
Kulicke Sffa Wedge Bonding Inc	3699	C	949 660-0440	7131
Prototype Express LLC	3699	E	714 751-3533	7143
Undersea Systems Intl Inc	3699	D	714 754-7848	7156
Danchuk Manufacturing Inc	3714	E	714 540-4363	7242
Garrison Manufacturing Inc	3714	E	714 549-4880	7254
Impco Technologies Inc (HQ)	3714	C	714 656-1200	7262
Overair Inc	3721	E	949 503-7503	7367
Advanced Digital Mfg LLC	3728	E	714 245-0536	7406
Aerospace Engineering LLC	3728	E	714 641-5884	7414
Integral Aerospace LLC	3728	C	949 250-3123	7501
Meggitt North Hollywood Inc	3728	E	818 691-6258	7524
Symbolic Displays Inc	3728	D	714 258-2811	7572
Western Methods Machinery Corporation	3728	C	949 252-6600	7591
W D Schock Corp	3732	E	951 277-3377	7625
All American Racers Inc	3751	C	714 540-1771	7628
Anduril Industries Inc	3812	E	949 891-1607	7690
Ascent Aerospace	3812	D	586 726-0500	7695
E D Q Inc	3823	E	714 546-6010	7855
Autonomous Medical Devices Inc (PA)	3826	E	657 660-6800	7938
Quantum Magnetics LLC	3826	A	714 258-4400	7974
Buk Optics Inc	3827	E	714 384-9620	7996
Deltronic Corporation	3827	E	714 545-5800	7999
Infinite Optics Inc	3827	E	714 557-2299	8007
AMO Usa Inc	3841	C	714 247-8200	8090
Medtronic Inc	3841	A	949 474-3943	8193
Medtronic Ats Medical Inc	3841	C	949 380-9333	8194
Merit Cables Incorporated	3841	E	714 918-1932	8197
Orchid MPS	3841	D	714 549-9203	8211
Thi Inc	3841	D	714 444-4643	8238
Surefire LLC	3842	E	714 641-0483	8305
Surefire LLC	3842	E	714 545-9444	8307
Surefire LLC	3842	E	714 641-0483	8308
Ricoh Electronics Inc	3861	C	714 566-6079	8442
Leonard Craft Co LLC	3911	D	714 549-0678	8459
Rickenbacker International Corporation	3931	D	714 545-5574	8472
Heart Rate Inc	3949	E	714 850-9716	8520
Xs Scuba Inc (PA)	3949	E	714 424-0434	8555
Aardvark Clay & Supplies Inc (PA)	3952	E	714 541-4157	8557
Bob Siemon Designs Inc	3961	D	714 549-0678	8569
SPS Technologies LLC	3965	B	714 545-9311	8576
SPS Technologies LLC	3965	B	714 371-1925	8577
Foampro Mfg Inc	3991	E	949 252-0112	8587
Cowboy Direct Response	3993	E	714 824-3780	8596
Maneri Sign Co Inc	3993	E	310 327-6261	8613
Statewide Trffic Sfety Sgns In	3993	E	714 468-1919	8640
Certified Trnsp Svcs Inc	4142	D	714 835-8676	8862
Durham School Services L P	4151	B	714 542-8989	8875
RPM Transportation Inc (DH)	4213	C	714 388-3500	8973
Southwest Airlines Co	4512	D	949 252-5200	9166
Aviation Consultants Inc	4581	D	949 201-2550	9191
Transit Air Cargo Inc	4731	D	714 571-0393	9346
Yokohama Tire Corporation (DH)	5014	C	714 870-3800	9863
Kimlor Mills Inc	5021	D	803 531-2037	9876
Contractors Flrg Svc Cal Inc	5023	C	714 556-6100	9890
Foundation Building Mtls Inc (HQ)	5031	B	714 380-3127	9920
AAA Imaging & Supplies Inc	5043	E	714 431-0570	9964
Regal Technology Partners Inc	5045	C	714 835-1162	10026
Cramer-Decker Industries (PA)	5047	C	714 546-3800	10074
Advantage Manufacturing Inc	5063	E	714 505-1166	10167
Ace Wireless & Trading Inc	5065	B	949 748-5700	10227
Hirsch Electronics LLC	5065	D	949 250-8888	10249
Jwc Environmental Inc (DH)	5084	C	949 833-3888	10379
Motion and Flow Ctrl Pdts Inc	5085	D	714 541-2244	10450
Rbc Transport Dynamics Corp	5085	C	203 267-7001	10458
Aftco Mfg Co Inc	5091	D	949 660-8757	10508
Pioneer Packing Inc (PA)	5113	E	714 540-9751	10608
Vantage Custom Classics Inc	5136	C	714 755-1133	10699
Smart Stores Operations LLC	5141	C	714 549-2362	10787
Ingardia Bros Produce Inc	5148	C	949 645-1365	10909
Coastal Cocktails Inc	5149	E	949 250-0851	10938
Goglanian Bakeries Inc (HQ)	5149	B	714 338-1145	10945
Home Depot USA Inc	5211	C	714 966-8551	11197
Home Depot USA Inc	5211	D	714 259-1030	11200
SMI Architectural Millwork Inc	5211	E	714 567-0112	11251
Crevier Classics Inc	5511	B	714 835-3171	11330
Toms Truck Center Inc	5511	C	714 835-1978	11420

Employee Codes: A=Over 500 employees, B=251-500
C=101-250, D=51-100, E=20-50, F=10-19, G=1-9

2025 Southern California
Business Directory and Buyers Guide

© Mergent Inc. 1-800-342-5647
1343

GEOGRAPHIC

	SIC	EMP	PHONE	ENTRY#
United Syatt America Corp (PA)	5531	C	714 568-1938	11472
Skyco Shading Systems Inc	5719	E	714 708-3038	11536
Waxies Enterprises LLC	5999	D	714 545-8441	11702
Orange Countys Credit Union (PA)	6061	C	714 755-5900	11810
Schoolsfirst Federal Credit Un (PA)	6061	B	714 258-4000	11815
Deutsche Bank National Tr Co	6091	D	714 247-6054	11835
Continental Currency Svcs Inc (PA)	6099	C	714 667-6699	11838
Homexpress Mortgage Corp	6162	C	714 944-3022	11913
Tarbell Financial Corporation (PA)	6163	D	714 972-0988	11955
Fatco Holdings LLC	6311	D	714 250-3000	12040
Admar Corporation	6324	C	714 953-9600	12068
Pacifcare Hlth Plan Admnstrtor (DH)	6324	B	714 825-5200	12100
State Compensation Insur Fund	6331	C	714 565-5000	12138
First American Financial Corp (PA)	6361	A	714 250-3000	12150
First American Mortgage Svcs	6361	B	714 250-4210	12151
First American Title Jnsur Co (HQ)	6361	B	800 854-3643	12152
H & H Agency Inc (PA)	6411	D	949 260-8840	12217
Seneca Family of Agencies	6411	C	714 881-8600	12253
Sureco Hlth Lf Insur Agcy Inc	6411	C	949 333-0263	12256
F M Tarbell Co (HQ)	6531	C	714 972-0988	12441
Grubb & Ellis Company	6531	A	714 667-8252	12461
Grubb & Ellis Management Services Inc	6531	A	412 201-8200	12462
Satellite Management Co (PA)	6531	C	714 558-2411	12527
First American Title Company	6541	A	714 250-3109	12558
Property Insight LLC	6541	A	877 747-2537	12561
Skeffington Enterprises Inc	6719	D	714 540-1700	12614
Jhc Investment Inc	7011	D	714 751-2400	12878
Ocean Sands Hotel	7011	D	714 966-5200	12945
S W K Properties LLC	7011	C	714 481-6300	13005
Cintas Sales Corporation	7213	C	714 957-2852	13116
Optima Tax Relief LLC	7291	C	714 361-4636	13166
Pps Parking Inc	7299	A	949 223-8707	13185
Dgwb Inc	7311	D	714 881-2300	13206
Financial Statement Svcs Inc (PA)	7331	C	714 436-3326	13302
Advanced Clnroom McRclean Corp	7349	C	714 751-1152	13352
Merchants Building Maint Co	7349	B	714 973-9272	13390
Universal Services America LP	7349	A	714 923-3700	13427
County of Orange	7353	D	714 647-1552	13434
Executive Personnel Services	7361	B	714 310-9506	13518
Pds Defense Inc	7361	B	214 647-9600	13554
Itc Sftware Slutions Group LLC (PA)	7372	B	877 248-2774	13955
Nis America Inc	7372	A	714 540-1122	13990
Thursby Software Systems LLC	7372	E	817 478-5070	14053
Cognizant Trztto Sftwr Group I	7373	C	714 481-0396	14076
Black Knight Infoserv LLC	7374	B	904 854-5100	14124
Compushare Inc	7374	C	714 427-1000	14126
Verys LLC	7379	C	949 423-3295	14264
Community Patrol Inc	7381	D	657 247-4744	14286
Guardsmark LLC (DH)	7381	C	714 619-9700	14308
Shield Security Inc (DH)	7381	B	714 210-1501	14343
Staff Pro Inc	7382	B	323 528-1929	14423
Dekra-Lite Industries Inc	7389	C	714 436-0705	14488
Fntech	7389	D	714 429-7833	14496
Orange Coast Title Company (PA)	7389	D	714 558-2836	14563
Partners Capital Group Inc (PA)	7389	D	949 916-3900	14569
Transpak Inc	7389	C	408 254-0500	14613
Parking Concepts Inc	7521	D	714 543-5725	14663
Brake Depot Systems Inc	7538	B	714 835-4833	14686
Collectors Universe Inc (PA)	7699	C	949 567-1234	14760
La Boxing Franchise Corp	7991	C	714 668-0911	15052
Santa Ana Country Club	7997	D	714 556-3000	15170
Altamed Health Services Corp	8011	D	714 426-5400	15240
Kaiser Foundation Hospitals	8011	D	714 830-6500	15336
Southern Cal Prmnnte Med Group	8011	C	714 967-4760	15475
St Jseph Heritg Med Group LLC (PA)	8011	C	714 633-1011	15482
University California Irvine	8011	B	714 480-2443	15499
Chromium Dental II LLC	8021	C	949 733-3111	15516
Covenant Care California LLC	8051	C	714 554-9700	15610
Town Cntry Mnor of Chrstn Mssn	8051	C	714 547-7581	15787
County of Orange	8052	D	714 834-6021	15809
Orange Cnty Ryale Cnvlscent Ho (PA)	8059	B	714 546-6450	15878
Health Resources Corp	8062	B	714 754-5454	16014
Kaiser Foundation Hospitals	8062	D	714 967-4700	16056
Kindred Healthcare LLC	8062	C	714 564-7800	16065
Orange Cnty Globl Med Ctr Aux (DH)	8062	C	714 835-3555	16108
Southern Cal Spcialty Care Inc	8062	C	714 564-7800	16209
Cornerstone Southern Cal	8069	D	714 998-3574	16289
Visiting Nrse Assn of Inland C (PA)	8082	A	951 413-1200	16430
Child Guidance Center Inc	8093	C	714 953-4455	16455
CRC Health Corporate	8093	A	714 542-3581	16464
Reimagine Network (PA)	8093	C	714 633-7400	16496
Rio	8093	C	714 633-7400	16498
Optumcare Management LLC	8099	D	714 964-6229	16598
Optumcare Management LLC	8099	D	714 835-8501	16601
Orangewood Foundation	8322	D	714 619-0200	16988
Priority Ctr Ending The Gnrtna	8322	D	714 543-4333	16996
United Crbral Plsy Assn Ornge	8322	B	949 333-6400	17020
Volunteers of Amer Los Angeles	8322	D	714 426-9834	17038
City of Santa Ana	8331	D	714 647-6545	17053
Success Strategies Inst Inc	8331	D	949 721-6808	17068
Calvary Church Santa Ana Inc	8351	C	714 973-4800	17079
Orange County Head Start Inc (PA)	8351	D	714 241-8920	17103
Olive Crest (PA)	8361	B	714 543-5437	17185
Charles W Bowers Museum Corp	8412	D	714 567-3600	17252
Discovery Scnce Ctr Ornge Cnty	8412	C	866 552-2823	17253
Mercy House Living Centers	8611	D	714 836-7188	17285
Orange County Health Care Agcy	8621	D	714 568-5683	17304
Air Liquide Electronics US LP	8711	A	713 624-8000	17479
Concept Technology Inc	8711	B	949 851-6550	17503
Custom Built Machinery Inc	8711	E	714 424-9250	17508
Embee Processing LLC	8711	B	714 546-9842	17521
Hntb Corporation	8711	C	714 460-1600	17547
Hntb Gerwick Water Solutions	8711	C	714 460-1600	17548
Michael Baker International Inc (DH)	8711	B	949 472-3505	17586
Psomas	8713	C	714 751-7373	17699
Anser Advisory Management LLC (HQ)	8741	C	714 276-1135	17944
Medical Network Inc	8741	D	949 863-0022	18011
Prospect Medical Group Inc (HQ)	8741	B	714 796-5900	18039
Wolf & Raven LLC	8741	C	800 431-6471	18082
Alan B Whitson Company Inc	8742	A	949 955-1200	18087
Ferry International LLC	8742	D	888 866-3377	18135
Kvc Group LLC	8742	D	855 438-0377	18159
Chambers Group Inc (PA)	8748	D	949 261-5414	18301
Iaccess Technologies Inc (PA)	8748	E	714 922-9158	18320
Irvine Technology Corporation	8748	C	714 445-2624	18324
Profit Recovery Partners LLC	8748	D	949 851-2777	18349
Data Trace Info Svcs LLC (HQ)	8999	D	714 250-6700	18372
County of Orange	9199	C	714 567-7444	18387
Regional Ctr Orange Cnty Inc (PA)	9431	B	714 796-5100	18395

SANTA BARBARA, CA - Santa Barbara County

	SIC	EMP	PHONE	ENTRY#
Brightview Golf Maint Inc	0781	C	805 968-6400	152
Dennis Allen Associates (PA)	1521	D	805 884-8777	398
Granite Construction Company	1611	D	805 964-9951	618
One Call Plumber Santa Barbara	1711	D	805 364-6337	814
Specialty Team Plastering Inc	1742	C	805 966-3858	1029
Action Roofing Company LLC	1761	D	805 966-3696	1072
Signature Parking LLC	1799	D	805 969-7275	1226
Adriennes Gourmet Foods	2052	D	805 964-6848	1474
Kate Farms Inc	2099	C	805 845-2446	1797
Toad & Co International Inc (PA)	2339	E	800 865-8623	2139
Nobbe Orthopedics Inc	2342	E	805 687-7508	2155
Architctral Mllwk Snta Barbara	2431	E	805 965-7011	2296
Santa Barbara Independent Inc	2711	E	805 965-5205	2826
Partner Concepts Inc	2721	C	805 745-7199	2870
Graphiq LLC	2741	C	805 335-2433	2919
Palette Life Sciences Inc (PA)	2833	D	805 869-7020	3326
Invenios LLC	3231	D	805 962-3333	4336
Steven Handelman Studios Inc (PA)	3322	E	805 884-9070	4561
Aqueos Corporation (PA)	3533	E	805 364-0570	5503
Picosys Incorporated	3545	C	805 962-3333	5619
Efaxcom	3577	E	805 692-0064	5915
Motion Engineering Inc (DH)	3577	D	805 696-1200	5938
Kollmorgen Corporation	3621	C	805 696-1236	6326
Freedom Photonics LLC	3699	E	805 967-4900	7123
Vetronix Corporation	3714	C	805 966-2000	7307
Channel Technologies Group LLC	3812	A		7707
Santa Barbara Infrared Inc (DH)	3812	D	805 965-3669	7808
International Tranducer Corp	3825	D	805 683-2575	7917
Oxford Instrs Asylum RES Inc (HQ)	3826	D	805 696-6466	7970
Zyris Inc	3843	E	805 560-9888	8362
Duncan Carter Corporation (PA)	3931	D	805 964-9749	8466
Bloomios Inc	3999	E	805 222-6330	8663
Santa Barbara Metro Trnst Dst (PA)	4111	D	805 963-3364	8802
Landmark Distribution LLC	4789	C	805 965-3058	9368
Smith Broadcasting Group Inc	4833	B	805 882-3933	9517
Marborg Industries LLC	4953	C	805 963-1852	9749
Curvature LLC (DH)	5045	B	800 230-6638	9994
Solid Oak Software Inc (PA)	5045	D	805 568-5415	10028
Mentor Worldwide LLC	5047	C	805 681-6000	10091
SBS Acquisition Company LLC	5146	D	805 966-9796	10861
Jordanos Inc (PA)	5181	C	805 964-0611	11050
Thornhill Companies Inc	5182	E	805 969-5803	11062
Volkswagen of Van Nuys Inc	5511	D	323 873-3311	11429
Sansum Clinic	5912	C	805 681-7500	11622
Merrill Lynch Prce Fnner Smith	6211	C	805 695-7028	11986

Mergent email: customerrelations@mergent.com

1344

2025 Southern California
Business Directory and Buyers Guide

(P-0000) Products & Services Section entry number
(PA)=Parent Co (HQ)=Headquarters (DH)=Div Headquarters

Company	SIC	EMP	PHONE	ENTRY#
Merrill Lynch Prce Fnner Smith	6211	C	805 963-0333	11987
Santa Brbara San Luis Obspo RG	6321	C	800 421-2560	12066
Chicago Title Insurance Co (HQ)	6361	C	805 565-6900	12149
Nevins/Adams Properties Inc (PA)	6512	C	805 963-2884	12306
University Business Ctr Assoc	6512	D	601 354-3555	12324
Pitts & Bachmann Realtors Inc	6531	D	805 969-5005	12505
Pitts & Bachmann Realtors Inc	6531	D	805 963-1391	12506
Miramar Acquisition Co LLC	6799	C	805 900-8338	12719
1260 Bb Property LLC	7011	B	805 969-2261	12750
Bcra Resort Services Inc	7011	C	805 571-3176	12769
El Encanto Inc	7011	C	805 845-5800	12820
Encina Pepper Tree Joint Ventr (PA)	7011	D	805 687-5511	12821
Encina Pepper Tree Joint Ventr	7011	D	805 682-7277	12822
Interstate Hotels Resorts Inc	7011	C	805 966-2285	12876
Morgans Hotel Group MGT LLC	7011	C	805 969-2203	12930
Ritz-Carlton Hotel Company LLC	7011	A	805 968-0100	12997
San Ysidro Bb Property LLC	7011	C	805 368-6788	13013
Mission Linen Supply	7213	C	805 962-7687	13120
Signature Parking LLC	7299	D	805 969-7275	13188
Fastclick Inc	7319	A	805 689-9839	13273
The Alternative Copy Shop Inc	7334	D	805 569-2116	13317
Town & Cntry Event Rentals Inc	7359	C	805 770-5729	13474
Butler International Inc (PA)	7361	C	805 882-2200	13498
Eastern Staffing LLC	7361	B	805 882-2200	13512
Partners Prsnnel - MGT Svcs LL	7361	A	805 689-8191	13552
Select Temporaries LLC (DH)	7361	D	805 882-2200	13570
Butler Service Group Inc (HQ)	7363	D	201 891-5312	13593
Trackr Inc	7371	D	855 981-1690	13846
Yardi Systems Inc (PA)	7371	B	805 699-2040	13866
Appfolio Inc (PA)	7372	B	805 364-6093	13879
Green Hills Software LLC (HQ)	7372	C	805 965-6044	13941
Mixmode Inc	7372	E	858 225-2352	13977
Ontraport Inc	7372	D	855 668-7276	13998
Qad Inc (HQ)	7372	C	805 566-6000	14010
Logicmonitor Inc (PA)	7375	C	805 394-8632	14174
US Data Management LLC (PA)	7379	D	888 231-0816	14263
La Cumbre Country Club	7997	D	805 687-2421	15143
Montecito Country Club Inc	7997	D	805 969-0800	15152
Anesthsia Med Group Snta Brbar	8011	D	805 682-7751	15244
Cancer Center of Santa Barbara	8011	A	805 898-2182	15260
Compass Health Inc	8051	C	805 687-6651	15602
Covenant Care California LLC	8051	C	805 964-4871	15614
Covenant Rtirement Communities	8051	C	805 687-0701	15617
Montecito Retirement Assn	8051	B	805 969-8011	15723
Powers Park Healthcare Inc	8051	C	805 687-6651	15757
Hillside House	8051	C	805 687-0788	15812
Front Porch Communities & Svcs	8059	C	805 687-0793	15852
Goleta Valley Cottage Hosp Aux	8062	D	805 681-6468	16008
Santa Barbara Cottage Hospital	8062	C	805 569-7367	16172
Santa Brbara Cttage Hosp Fndti	8062	C	805 569-7224	16173
Santa Brbara Cttage Hosp Fndti (HQ)	8062	A	805 682-7111	16175
Visiting Nurse & Hospice Care (PA)	8082	C	805 965-5555	16431
Sanctary Ctrs Snta Barbara Inc	8093	C	805 569-2785	16502
Laguna Blanca School (PA)	8211	D	805 687-2461	16813
Santa Brbara Cmnty College Dst	8222	B	805 683-4191	16841
Music Academy of West	8299	D	805 969-4726	16856
Family Svc Agcy Snta Brbara CN	8322	D	805 965-1001	16942
People Creating Success Inc	8322	D	805 692-5290	16995
Cliff View Terrace Inc	8361	D	805 682-7443	17131
Covenant Living West	8361	A	805 687-0701	17142
Santa Brbara Mseum Ntral Hstor	8412	D	805 682-4711	17266
Santa Brbara Zlgcal Foundation	8422	C	805 962-1673	17272
African Women Rising	8041	C	415 278 1784	17322
Channel Islnds Yung MNS Chrstn	8641	D	005 963-8775	17331
Channel Islnds Yung MNS Chrstn	8641	D	805 687-7727	17333
Channel Islnds Yung MNS Chrstn	8641	D	805 969-3288	17334
Automobile Club Southern Cal	8699	C	805 682-5811	17451
Lash Construction Inc	8711	D	805 963-3553	17578
MNS Engineers Inc (PA)	8711	E	805 692-6921	17588
Penfield & Smith Engineers Inc	8711	C	805 963-9532	17609
Sonatech LLC	8711	D	805 683-1431	17632
Nasif Hicks Harris & Co LLP	8721	D	805 966-1521	17747
Dupont Displays Inc	8731	E	805 562-5400	17785
Smith Broadcasting Group Inc (PA)	8741	C	805 965-0400	18053
Impact Tech Inc (HQ)	8742	B	805 324-6021	18150
Tecolote Research Inc	8742	C	805 964-6963	18227

SANTA CLARITA, CA - Los Angeles County

Company	SIC	EMP	PHONE	ENTRY#
Delphic Enterprises Inc	0742	D	661 254-2000	127
CAM Properties Inc	0782	D	714 844-2200	202
Gothic Landscaping Inc (PA)	0782	C	661 678-1400	207
California Resources Prod Corp (HQ)	1311	D	661 869-8000	271
Califrnia Rsrces Elk Hills LLC	1382	B	661 412-0000	297

Company	SIC	EMP	PHONE	ENTRY#
Sheldon Mechanical Corporation	1711	D	661 286-1361	837
Tri-Signal Integration Inc (PA)	1731	D	818 566-8558	974
Clear View Windows & Doors Inc	1751	C	661 257-5050	1045
Drinkpak LLC	2086	A	833 376-5725	1617
Frametent Inc	2394	E	661 290-3375	2238
Old English Mil Woodworks Inc (PA)	2431	E	661 294-9171	2320
Applied Polytech Systems Inc	2452	E	818 504-9261	2403
Signal	2711	E	661 259-1234	2827
Daisy Publishing Company Inc	2741	D	661 295-1910	2910
3d/International Inc	2842	C	661 250-2020	3596
B&D Investment Partners Inc (PA)	2842	E		3599
Bright Innovation Labs	2844	C	661 252-3807	3636
Packaging Systems Inc	2891	D	661 253-5700	3774
Certified Thermoplastics Inc	3089	C	661 222-3006	4087
Lamsco West Inc	3089	D	661 295-8620	4158
Curtiss-Wright Corporation	3491	D	661 257-4430	5363
Whitmor Plstic Wire Cable Corp (PA)	3496	C	661 257-2400	5420
B&B Manufacturing Co (PA)	3599	C	661 257-2161	6089
Curtiss-Wrght Cntrls Elctrnic (DH)	3625	C	661 257-4430	6346
Woodward Hrt Inc (HQ)	3625	A	661 294-6000	6365
Madn Aircraft Hinge	3721	E	661 257-3430	7363
Aerospace Dynamics Intl Inc	3728	B	661 310-6986	7412
Santa Clarita Signs	3993	E	661 291-1188	8630
Santa Barbara Trnsp Corp	4131	D	661 259-7285	8859
Funnelcloudsales	4215	E	661 284-6032	9003
Princess Cruise Lines Ltd (HQ)	4481	A	661 753-0000	9138
Princess Cruise Lines Ltd	4724	A	661 753-2197	9234
Princess Cruise Lines Ltd	4725	A	661 753-0000	9239
Cellco Partnership	4812	D	661 296-7585	9392
CBS Studios Inc	4833	B	661 964-6020	9495
Santa Clarita Valley Wtr Agcy	4941	C	661 259-2737	9717
Santa Clrita Vly Wtr Agcy Fing	4941	C	661 259-2737	9718
Marathon Industries Inc	5012	C	661 286-1520	9805
Universal Wood Moulding Inc (PA)	5023	C	661 362-6262	9914
White Cap Supply Group Inc	5039	A	661 294-7737	9963
Aq Lighting Group Texas Inc	5063	E	818 534-5300	10169
Paul Mitchell John Systems (PA)	5122	D	800 793-8790	10643
Jeckys Best Inc	5142	E	661 259-1313	10821
Allied Company Holdings Inc	5181	C	661 510-6533	11039
Home Depot USA Inc	5211	B	661 252-7800	11174
Lowes Home Centers LLC	5211	C	661 678-4430	11238
RE/Max of Valencia Inc (PA)	6531	C	661 255-2650	12516
Canon Recruiting Group LLC	7361	B	661 252-7400	13499
Jt Resources Inc	7361	C	661 367-6827	13531
Partnership Staffing Svcs Inc	7361	A	661 542-7074	13553
Valtron Technologies Inc	7378	D	805 257-0333	14191
Cottrell Paul Enterprises LLC (PA)	7381	E	661 212-2357	14290
5 Star Service Inc	7629	E	323 647-7777	14726
Kaiser Foundation Hospitals	8011	C	661 222-2323	15367
Providnce Facey Med Foundation	8011	D	661 513-2100	15427
Southern Cal Prmnnte Med Group	8011	C	661 222-2150	15467
Southern Cal Prmnnte Med Group	8062	C	661 290-3100	16206
Henry Mayo Newhall Mem Hosp	8099	C	661 253-8227	16568
Child & Family Center	8322	C	661 259-9439	16884
Los Angeles Residential Comm F	8361	D	661 296-8636	17177
Applied Companies	8711	E	661 257-0090	17485
Curtiss-Wrght Cntrls Elctrnic	8711	C	661 257-4430	17507

SANTA FE SPRINGS, CA - Los Angeles County

Company	SIC	EMP	PHONE	ENTRY#
Ethosenergy Field Services LLC (DH)	1380	E	310 639-3523	330
CMC Rebar West	1541	D	714 692-7082	478
Holbrook Construction Inc	1542	D	714 523-1150	547
Kiewit Infrastructure West Co	1611	C	562 946-1816	630
S E Pipe Line Construction Co	1623	D	562 868-9771	691
Valverde Construction Inc	1623	C	562 906-1826	703
Western Allied Corporation	1711	E	562 944-6341	853
Csi Electrical Contractors Inc (HQ)	1731	C	562 946-0700	907
Johnson-Peltier	1731	D	562 944-3408	930
Leed Electric Inc	1731	C	562 270-9500	934
Masonry Concepts Inc	1741	C	562 802-3700	986
Bligh Roof Co	1761	D	562 944-9753	1074
Coast Iron & Steel Co	1791	E	562 946-4421	1152
Rebar Engineering Inc	1791	C	562 946-2461	1162
Crown Fence Co	1799	D	562 864-5177	1200
Food Technology and Design LLC (PA)	2064	E	562 944-7821	1503
Anheuser-Busch LLC	2082	E	562 699-3424	1532
Blk International LLC	2086	E	424 282-3443	1609
American Fruits & Flavors LLC	2087	E	562 320-2802	1665
J & J Processing Inc	2087	E	562 926-2333	1684
Bumble Bee Foods LLC	2091	E	562 483-7474	1695
Nikko Enterprise Corporation	2092	E	562 941-6080	1709
Apffels Coffee Inc	2095	E	562 309-0400	1714
Fuji Food Products Inc (PA)	2099	D	562 404-2590	1779

	SIC	EMP	PHONE	ENTRY#
MCI Foods Inc	2099	C	562 977-4000	1814
Rich Products Corporation	2099	C	562 946-6396	1842
Romeros Food Products Inc (PA)	2099	D	562 802-1858	1844
Tri-Star Dyeing & Finshg Inc	2231	D	562 483-0123	1904
Super Dyeing LLC	2261	D	562 692-9500	1935
Catalina Carpet Mills Inc (PA)	2273	E	562 926-5811	1949
Distinctive Inds Texas Inc	2386	E	323 889-5766	2179
Distinctive Industries	2396	B	800 421-9777	2259
Larson-Juhl US LLC	2499	E	562 946-6873	2412
Robert Michael Ltd	2512	B	562 758-6789	2458
Atlantic Representations Inc (PA)	2514	E	562 903-9550	2463
Nakamura-Beeman Inc	2521	E	562 696-1400	2510
Office Chairs Inc	2521	D	562 802-0464	2513
Elite Mfg Corp	2522	C	888 354-8356	2524
Alegacy Fdsrvice Pdts Group In	2599	D	562 320-3100	2609
International Paper Company	2621	D	562 692-9465	2627
Specialty Paper Mills Inc	2621	C	562 692-8737	2639
Wrkco Inc	2631	E	770 448-2193	2648
California Box Company (PA)	2653	E	562 921-1223	2657
Cflute Corp	2653	C	562 404-6221	2659
Gabriel Container (PA)	2653	C	562 699-1051	2667
International Paper Company	2653	E	323 946-6100	2676
Reliable Container Corporation	2653	B	562 861-6226	2688
Western Corrugated Design Inc	2653	E	562 695-9295	2693
Bay Cities Container Corp	2671	E	562 551-2946	2705
Seal Methods Inc (PA)	2672	D	562 944-0291	2727
Ace Commercial Inc	2752	E	562 946-6664	2958
Ink Spot Inc	2752	E	626 338-4500	3018
Vomela Specialty Company	2752	C	562 944-3853	3099
Superior Printing Inc	2759	D	888 590-7998	3178
Ross Bindery Inc	2789	E	562 623-4565	3203
Olin Chlor Alkali Logistics	2812	D	562 692-0510	3209
Airgas Usa LLC	2813	E	562 945-1383	3214
Airgas Usa LLC	2813	E	562 906-8700	3215
Phibro-Tech Inc	2819	E	562 698-8036	3245
Solvay America Inc	2819	D	562 906-3300	3250
Bdc Epoxy Systems Inc	2821	E	562 944-6177	3259
Ecowise Inc	2821	E	626 759-3997	3264
Multi-Plastics Inc	2821	E	562 692-1202	3280
Jarrow Industries LLC (PA)	2834	D	562 906-1919	3435
Nhk Laboratories Inc (PA)	2834	E	562 903-5835	3461
Nhk Laboratories Inc	2834	D	562 204-5002	3462
Kik-Socal Inc	2842	A	562 946-6427	3608
Morgan Gallacher Inc	2842	E	562 695-1232	3614
Qspac Industries Inc (PA)	2891	D	562 407-3868	3777
Sun Chemical Corporation	2893	E	562 946-2327	3786
INX International Ink Co	2899	E	562 404-5664	3806
L M Scofield Company (DH)	2899	E	323 720-3000	3809
Phibro Animal Health Corp	2899	E	562 698-8036	3817
Gasket Manufacturing Co	3053	E	310 217-5600	3888
R D Rubber Technology Corp	3061	E	562 941-4800	3905
Rogers Corporation	3069	D	562 404-8942	3933
Ptm & W Industries Inc	3083	E	562 946-4511	3969
Sleepcomp West LLC	3086	E	562 946-3222	4017
Barber-Webb Company Inc (PA)	3089	E	541 488-4821	4061
Reinhold Industries Inc (DH)	3089	C	562 944-3281	4223
Vantage Associates Inc	3089	D	562 968-1400	4269
GP Merger Sub Inc	3231	E	562 946-7722	4335
New Glaspro Inc	3231	E	800 776-2368	4341
Standridge Granite Corporation	3281	E	562 946-6334	4478
Brown-Pacific Inc	3312	E	562 921-3471	4512
Rtm Products Inc	3312	E	562 926-2400	4523
International Consulting Unltd	3317	E	714 449-3318	4548
Maruichi American Corporation	3317	D	562 903-8600	4550
Heraeus Prcous Mtls N Amer LLC (DH)	3341	E	562 921-7464	4585
Fry Reglet Corporation (PA)	3354	D	800 237-9773	4596
Bodycote Thermal Proc Inc	3398	D	562 946-1717	4698
Continental Heat Treating Inc	3398	D	562 944-8808	4702
Accuride International Inc (PA)	3429	E	562 903-0200	4749
Birmingham Fastener & Sup Inc	3429	E	562 944-9549	4760
Star Die Casting Inc	3429	D	562 698-0627	4790
Brunton Enterprises Inc	3441	C	562 945-0013	4821
Cji Process Systems Inc	3443	E	562 777-0614	4911
Pacific Steam Equipment Inc	3443	E	562 906-9292	4918
Parker-Hannifin Corporation	3443	E	562 404-1938	4920
Wells Struthers Corporation	3443	E	814 726-1000	4934
Excel Sheet Metal Inc (PA)	3444	D	562 944-0701	4985
Twist Tite Mfg Inc	3452	E	562 229-0990	5138
Timken Gears & Services Inc	3462	E	310 605-2600	5150
A-W Engineering Company Inc	3469	E	562 945-1041	5168
Eagleware Manufacturing Co Inc	3469	E	562 320-3100	5183
Ftr Associates Inc	3469	E	562 945-7504	5188
Tru-Form Industries Inc (PA)	3469	D	562 802-2041	5218
Associated Plating Company	3471	E	562 946-5525	5235
Cal-Tron Plating Inc	3471	E	562 945-1181	5245
Trident Plating Inc	3471	E	562 906-2556	5300
Conveyor Service & Electric	3535	E	562 777-1221	5516
Konecranes Inc	3536	E	562 903-1371	5522
Medlin Ramps	3542	E	877 463-3546	5559
Santa Fe Enterprises Inc	3544	E	562 692-7596	5597
Superior Food Machinery Inc	3556	E	562 949-0396	5685
United Surface Solutions LLC	3559	E	562 693-0202	5723
Cascade Pump Company	3561	D	562 946-1414	5729
United Bakery Equipment Co Inc (PA)	3565	D	310 635-8121	5794
Source Code LLC	3571	E	562 903-1500	5868
Aferin LLC	3572	E	562 903-1500	5873
Gorlitz Sewer & Drain Inc	3589	E	562 944-3060	6015
Aero Chip Inc	3599	E	562 404-6300	6066
Golden West Machine Inc	3599	E	562 903-1111	6137
JR Machine Company Inc	3599	E	562 903-9477	6155
Omega Precision	3599	E	562 946-2491	6197
Pedavena Mould and Die Co Inc	3599	E	310 327-2814	6200
Process Fab Inc	3599	C	562 921-1979	6207
Pscmb Repairs Inc	3599	E	626 448-7778	6208
Serrano Industries Inc	3599	E	562 777-8180	6236
SMI Ca Inc	3599	E	562 926-9407	6238
Vescio Threading Co	3599	D	562 802-1868	6265
Ohmega Solenoid Co Inc	3612	E	562 944-7948	6291
Pioneer Custom Elec Pdts Corp	3612	E	562 944-0626	6295
Age Incorporated	3613	E	562 483-7300	6301
General Switchgear Inc	3613	E		6306
Artiva USA Inc	3645	E	562 298-8968	6440
Dab Inc	3645	D	562 623-4773	6442
Shimada Enterprises Inc	3648	E	562 802-8811	6516
Funai Corporation Inc (DH)	3651	E	310 787-3000	6537
Detoronics Corp	3678	E	626 579-7130	6947
Trojan Battery Holdings LLC	3691	D	800 423-6569	7083
Trojan Battery Company LLC (DH)	3692	C	562 236-3000	7086
M & H Electric Fabricators Inc	3694	E	562 926-9552	7095
Philatron International (PA)	3699	D	562 802-0452	7142
Rosemead Electrical Supply	3699	E	562 298-4190	7147
Auto Motive Power Inc	3714	C	800 894-7104	7229
Los Angeles Sleeve Co Inc	3714	E	562 945-7578	7266
M E D Inc	3714	D	562 921-0464	7268
Maxon Industries Inc	3714	D	562 464-0099	7270
Mid-West Fabricating Co	3714	E	562 698-9615	7271
R A Phillips Industries Inc (PA)	3714	E	562 781-2121	7287
US Motor Works LLC (PA)	3714	E	562 404-0488	7305
Advanced Grund Systems Engrg L (HQ)	3724	E	562 906-9300	7378
All Power Manufacturing Co	3728	C	562 802-2640	7426
Goodrich Corporation	3728	D	562 944-4441	7485
Lefiell Manufacturing Company	3728	C	562 921-3411	7514
Precision Tube Bending	3728	D	562 921-6723	7542
Spec Tool Company	3728	E	323 723-9533	7566
V&H Performance LLC	3751	D	562 921-7461	7638
Deca International Corp	3812	E	714 367-5900	7712
Votaw Precision Technologies	3812	C	562 944-0661	7822
Tellkamp Systems Inc (PA)	3822	E	562 802-1621	7840
Rohrback Cosasco Systems Inc (DH)	3823	D	562 949-0123	7875
I-Coat Company LLC	3827	E	562 941-9989	8005
US Armor Corporation	3842	E	562 207-4240	8315
Bravo Sports (HQ)	3949	D	562 484-5100	8510
Saint Nine America Inc	3949	E	562 921-5300	8539
Orange Cnty Name Plate Co Inc	3993	D	714 522-7693	8622
Tdi Signs	3993	E	562 436-5188	8644
Altro Usa Inc	3996	D	562 944-8292	8653
Golden Supreme Inc	3999	E	562 903-1063	8679
Gale/Triangle Inc (PA)	4212	D	562 741-1300	8907
General Lgstics Systems US Inc	4212	C	562 577-6037	8910
Trail Lines Inc	4212	D	562 758-6980	8925
Van King & Storage Inc	4213	D	562 921-0555	8982
Xpo Logistics Freight Inc	4213	D	562 946-8331	8987
FN Logistics Llc	4214	A	213 625-5900	8991
Great Amrcn Logistics Dist Inc	4214	D	562 229-3601	8993
Van Torrance & Storage Company (PA)	4214	D	562 567-2101	8996
Wilsonart LLC	4225	D	562 921-7426	9129
Xpdel Inc	4225	B	805 267-1214	9131
Maersk Whsng Dist Svcs USA LLC	4731	D	562 977-1820	9308
Southern California Edison Co	4911	B	562 903-3191	9632
Egge Machine Company Inc (PA)	5013	E	562 945-3419	9823
Ralco Holdings Inc (DH)	5013	C	949 440-5094	9841
Vgp Holdings LLC	5013	B	562 906-6200	9852
Lakin Tire West Incorporated (PA)	5014	C	562 802-2752	9858
Janus Et Cie (PA)	5021	C	800 245-2687	9875
New Tangram LLC	5021	C	562 365-5000	9877
Galleher LLC (PA)	5023	C	562 944-8885	9895

Mergent email: customerrelations@mergent.com
1346

2025 Southern California
Business Directory and Buyers Guide

(P-0000) Products & Services Section entry number
(PA)=Parent Co (HQ)=Headquarters (DH)=Div Headquarters

	SIC	EMP	PHONE	ENTRY#
Tri-West Ltd (PA)	5023	C	562 692-9166	9912
Ugm Citatah Inc (PA)	5032	C	562 921-9549	9951
Jk Imaging Ltd	5043	D	310 755-6848	9967
Bergsen Inc	5051	E	562 236-9787	10124
Coast Aluminum Inc (PA)	5051	C	562 946-6061	10129
Conquest Industries Inc	5051	E	562 906-1111	10130
Fry Steel Company	5051	C	562 802-2721	10136
Kloeckner Metals Corporation	5051	D	562 906-2020	10143
Tmx Aerospace	5051	C	562 215-4410	10160
Pacific Power Systems Integration Inc	5063	E	562 281-0500	10200
Swann Communications USA Inc	5065	D	562 777-2551	10286
Talley LLC (DH)	5065	D	562 906-8000	10287
Great Western Sales Inc	5074	D	310 323-7900	10319
Larsen Supply Co (PA)	5074	D	562 698-0731	10324
TA Industries Inc (HQ)	5074	E	562 466-1000	10326
Ellison Technologies Inc	5084	D	562 949-8311	10372
Material Handling Supply Inc (HQ)	5084	D	562 921-7715	10381
Maxon Lift Corp (PA)	5084	D	562 464-0099	10382
Menke Marking Devices Inc	5084	E	562 921-1380	10383
Raymond Handling Solutions Inc (DH)	5084	C	562 944-8067	10397
Rebas Inc	5084	C	800 794-5438	10399
Valtra Inc	5084	E	562 949-8625	10414
Lord & Sons Inc	5085	C	562 529-2500	10445
McMaster-Carr Supply Company	5085	B	562 692-5911	10446
Millennia Stainless Inc	5085	D	562 946-3545	10448
Pcbc Holdco Inc	5085	E	562 944-9549	10456
Revco Industries Inc (PA)	5085	E	562 777-1588	10459
Southern California Valve Inc	5085	D	562 404-2246	10464
Kaplan Indus Car Wash Sups Inc	5087	E	562 921-5544	10475
United States Luggage Co LLC	5099	D	562 293-4400	10573
Kelly Spicers Inc (HQ)	5111	D	562 698-1199	10576
Georgia-Pacific LLC	5113	B	562 861-6226	10593
McKesson Corporation	5122	C	562 463-2100	10631
Steven Label Corporation (PA)	5131	C	562 698-9971	10676
Wismettac Asian Foods Inc (HQ)	5141	C	562 802-1900	10817
Del Monte Fresh Produce Co	5148	D	562 777-1127	10894
LA Specialty Produce Co (PA)	5148	B	562 741-2200	10910
Access Business Group LLC	5169	B	808 422-9482	11006
Brenntag Pacific Inc (DH)	5169	D	562 903-9626	11007
Triangle Distributing Co	5181	B	562 699-3424	11053
Target Specialty Products Inc	5191	D	562 865-9541	11073
Premiere Packaging Inds Inc	5199	D	562 799-9200	11135
Westrux International Inc (PA)	5511	C	562 404-1020	11433
Global Trade Alliance Inc	5531	C	562 944-6422	11447
Freestyle Sales Co Ltd Partnr	5946	D	323 660-3460	11647
Riviera Finance of Texas Inc	6153	D	562 777-1300	11872
Tydg Enterprises Inc	6719	D	562 903-9030	12618
Rentokil North America Inc	7342	D	562 802-2238	13348
Crossing Guard Company	7381	A	310 202-8284	14291
Cypress Private Security LP	7381	D	562 222-4197	14292
Johnson Controls	7382	C	562 405-3817	14409
Safesmart Access Inc	7382	E	310 410-1525	14418
Haringa Inc (PA)	7389	D	800 499-9991	14506
Newport Diversified Inc	7389	C	562 921-4359	14557
El Monte Rents Inc (HQ)	7519	C	562 404-9300	14653
Valvoline Instant Oil Chnge Fr	7549	D	562 906-6200	14721
Think Together	7991	B	562 236-3835	15065
Crescent Healthcare Inc (HQ)	8082	D	714 520-6300	16384
County of Los Angeles	8322	D	562 903-5000	16913
Peoples Care Inc	8351	C	562 320-0174	17105
Kiewit Corporation	8711	D	907 222-9350	17570
Spearman Aerospace Inc	8711	E	714 523-4751	17634
California Lab Sciences LLC	8734	D	562 758-6900	17906
Westpac Labs Inc	8734	B	562 906-5227	17930
Fujitec America Inc	8741	C	310 464-8270	17987
Matt Construction Corporation (PA)	8742	C	562 903-2277	18167
Greater Los Angles Cnty Vctor	8748	C	562 944-7976	18315

SANTA MARIA, CA - Santa Barbara County

	SIC	EMP	PHONE	ENTRY#
Darensberries LLC	0171	C	805 937-8000	15
Freshway Farms LLC	0171	C	805 349-7170	18
J&G Berry Farms LLC	0171	C	831 750-9408	20
Red Blossom Sales Inc	0171	A	805 349-9404	23
Reiter Affl Companies LLC	0171	D	805 925-8577	24
Glad-A-Way Gardens Inc	0181	D	805 938-0569	56
Plantel Nurseries Inc	0181	B	805 934-4300	66
Blackjack Frms De La Csta Cntl	0191	C	805 347-1333	75
Rancho Laguna Farms LLC	0191	D	805 925-7805	84
Reiter Affl Companies LLC	0191	D	805 346-1073	85
Greka Integrated Inc	1382	C	805 347-8700	306
Engel & Gray Inc	1389	E	805 925-2771	329
Pacific Petroleum California Inc	1389	B	805 925-1947	356
PC Mechanical Inc	1389	E	805 925-2888	358

	SIC	EMP	PHONE	ENTRY#
Smith McHncl-Lctrical-Plumbing	1541	C	805 621-5000	501
Pictsweet Company	2038	B	805 928-4414	1398
Flood Ranch Company	2084	D	805 937-3616	1570
Foxen Vineyard Inc	2084	E	805 937-4251	1572
American Bottling Company	2086	D	805 928-1001	1604
Pepsi-Cola Metro Btlg Co Inc	2086	D	805 739-2160	1633
Reyes Coca-Cola Bottling LLC	2086	E	805 614-3702	1642
Curation Foods Inc (HQ)	2099	D	800 454-1355	1761
Amass Brands Inc	2833	E	619 204-2560	3309
North American Fire Hose Corp	3052	D	805 922-7076	3873
Alltec Integrated Mfg Inc	3089	E	805 595-3500	4040
Prince Lionheart Inc (PA)	3089	E	805 922-2250	4210
Impo International LLC	3144	E	805 922-7753	4285
Mid-State Concrete Pdts Inc	3272	E	805 928-2855	4402
Okonite Company Inc	3357	C	805 922-6682	4635
Matthew Warren Inc	3493	E	805 928-3851	5381
Melfred Borzall Inc	3541	E	805 614-4344	5548
Fresh Venture Foods LLC	3556	C	805 928-3374	5672
Atlas Copco Mafi-Trench Co LLC (DH)	3564	C	805 928-5757	5767
Helical Products Company Inc	3568	C	805 928-3851	5808
Arrow Screw Products Inc	3599	E	805 928-2269	6084
Gavial Engineering & Mfg Inc	3672	E	805 614-0060	6731
Alan Johnson Prfmce Engrg Inc	3711	C	805 922-1202	7164
Safran Cabin Inc	3728	C	805 922-3013	7557
Safran Seats Santa Maria LLC	3728	A	805 922-5995	7560
Northrop Grumman Systems Corp	3812	D	805 315-5728	7763
Certified Frt Logistics Inc (PA)	4213	C	800 592-5906	8935
United Parcel Service Inc	4215	C	805 922-7851	9030
Adient Aerospace LLC (PA)	4581	C	949 514-1851	9184
Frontier California Inc	4813	B	805 925-0000	9439
Coast Rock Products Inc	5032	E	805 925-2505	9941
Hardy Diagnostics (PA)	5047	B	805 346-2766	10084
Quinn Company	5082	C	805 925-8611	10355
Foothill Packing Inc	5141	B	805 925-7900	10752
Crystal Creamery Inc	5143	C	209 576-3479	10829
Central Coast Distributing LLC	5181	D	805 922-2108	11043
Smith Packing Inc	5199	C	805 348-1817	11144
Coasthills Credit Union (PA)	6062	C	805 733-7600	11826
Automobile Club Southern Cal	6411	C	805 922-5731	12179
H & H LLC (PA)	7011	D	805 925-2036	12839
Mission Linen Supply	7213	D	805 922-3579	13121
Ramco Enterprises LP	7361	B	805 922-9888	13563
Osr Enterprises Inc	7372	E	805 925-1831	14001
Country Oaks Care Center Inc	8051	D	805 922-6657	15604
Genesis Healthcare LLC	8051	A	805 922-3558	15663
Dignity Health	8062	B	805 739-3000	15976
Marian Medical Center	8062	A	805 739-3000	16092
Santa Brbara Cttage Hosp Fndti	8062	C	805 346-7135	16174
Life Steps Foundation Inc	8322	D	805 349-9810	16973
Vtc Enterprises (PA)	8331	D	805 928-5000	17073
Ensign Group Inc	8361	B	805 925-8713	17150
Nursecore Management Svcs LLC	8361	A	805 938-7660	17184
Microwave Applications Group	8711	E	805 928-5711	17587
American Management Svcs W LLC	8741	B	805 352-1921	17942

SANTA MONICA, CA - Los Angeles County

	SIC	EMP	PHONE	ENTRY#
Morley Builders Inc (PA)	1541	C	310 399-1600	494
Jones Brothers Cnstr Corp (PA)	1542	D	310 470-1885	551
Morley Construction Company (HQ)	1771	D	310 399-1600	1126
International Processing Corp (DH)	2048	E	310 458-1574	1428
Reconserve Inc (HQ)	2048	E	310 458-1574	1432
Liquid Death Mountain Water	2086	D	818 521-5500	1622
Red Bull Media Hse N Amer Inc	2086	D	310 393-4647	1639
Figs Inc	2326	B	424 300-8330	1994
Koral LLC	2329	E	323 391-1060	2017
Koral Industries LLC (PA)	2339	E	323 585-5343	2114
Zooey Apparel Inc	2339	E	310 315-2880	2144
Mammoth Media Inc	2711	D	832 315-0833	2815
Ubm Canon LLC (DH)	2721	E	310 445-4200	2878
Alg Inc	2741	B	424 258-8026	2902
C Publishing LLC	2741	E	310 393-3800	2905
Universal Mus Group Dist Corp (DH)	2741	D	310 235-4700	2950
Universal Music Publishing Inc	2741	D	310 235-4700	2951
Archipelago Inc	2844	C	213 743-9200	3631
Provivi Inc	2869	D	310 828-2307	3735
Kas Engineering Inc (PA)	3089	E	310 450-8925	4151
Ridge Wallet LLC	3172	D	818 636-2832	4307
Coast Flagstone Co	3281	D	310 829-4010	4473
Hamrock Inc	3315	C	562 944-0255	4535
Captive-Aire Systems Inc	3444	E	310 876-8505	4964
Ngd Systems Inc	3572	E	949 870-9148	5883
Apogee Electronics Corporation	3651	E	310 584-9394	6526
Phonesuit Inc	3663	E	310 774-0282	6645

Employee Codes: A=Over 500 employees, B=251-500
C=101-250, D=51-100, E=20-50, F=10-19, G=1-9

2025 Southern California
Business Directory and Buyers Guide

© Mergent Inc. 1-800-342-5647

1347

GEOGRAPHIC

Company	SIC	EMP	PHONE	ENTRY#
Pioneer Magnetics Inc.	3679	C	310 829-6751	7036
Carr Corporation **(PA)**	3844	E	310 587-1113	8365
Jakks Pacific Inc **(PA)**	3944	D	424 268-9444	8489
Bravo Highline LLC	3949	E	562 484-5100	8507
Casa De Hermandad **(PA)**	3949	E	310 477-8272	8511
Malbon Golf LLC	3949	E	323 433-4028	8531
Executive Network Entps Inc	4119	A	310 457-8822	8823
Santa Monica City of	4131	C	310 458-1975	8860
Verizon Services Corp	4812	B	310 315-1100	9423
Connexity Inc **(DH)**	4813	C	310 571-1235	9431
Hulu LLC **(HQ)**	4813	C	310 571-4700	9442
Pandora Media LLC	4832	B	424 653-6803	9487
Entravsion Communications Corp **(PA)**	4833	C	310 447-3870	9498
SF Broadcasting Wisconsin Inc	4833	C	310 586-2410	9516
AMC Networks Inc	4841	D	310 998-9300	9523
Game Show Network Music LLC **(DH)**	4841	C	310 255-6800	9551
Cypress Creek Holdings LLC	4911	D	310 581-6299	9576
Cypress Creek Rnwbles Hldngs L **(HQ)**	4911	B	310 581-6299	9577
Inspire Energy Holdings LLC	4911	C	866 403-2620	9589
Solarreserve Inc	4911	D	310 315-2200	9613
K-Micro Inc	5045	D	310 442-3200	10013
Glamour Industries Co	5087	D	213 687-8600	10474
Spilo Worldwide Inc	5087	D	213 687-8600	10478
Genius Products Inc	5099	C	310 453-1222	10562
Guthy-Renker LLC	5099	D	310 581-6250	10563
Johnny Was LLC	5137	D	310 656-0600	10710
Converse Inc	5139	D	310 451-0314	10735
Hokey Pokey LLC	5143	E	213 361-2503	10830
Red Bull Media Hse N Amer Inc **(HQ)**	5149	C	310 393-4647	10973
National Tobacco Company LP **(DH)**	5194	C	800 579-0975	11105
Legendary Foods LLC	5441	E	888 698-1708	11293
Ford of Santa Monica Inc	5511	D	310 451-1588	11349
Volkswagen Santa Monica Inc **(PA)**	5511	C	310 829-1888	11430
City National Bank	6021	D	424 280-8000	11713
CIT Bank NA	6022	C	310 394-1640	11755
Wells Fargo Capital Fin LLC **(DH)**	6159	D	310 453-7300	11879
Cypress Equity Investments LLC	6282	D	310 207-1699	12025
Mercury Insurance Company	6331	C	310 451-4943	12129
Gumbiner Savett Inc	6512	D	310 828-9798	12296
Watt Properties Inc **(PA)**	6512	D	310 314-2430	12325
Community Corp Santa Monica	6513	C	310 394-8487	12337
Irvine APT Communities LP	6513	C	310 255-1221	12354
Carmel Partners LLC	6722	C	916 479-5286	12630
Clearlake Capital Group LP **(PA)**	6722	B	310 400-8800	12632
Clearlake Cpitl Partners IV LP	6722	C	310 400-8800	12633
Guggenheim Prtners Inv MGT LLC	6722	A	310 576-1270	12634
Umg Recordings Inc	6794	C	310 865-4000	12679
Macerich Company **(PA)**	6798	C	310 394-6000	12688
Full Stack Finance	6799	D	800 941-0356	12706
Inventure Capital Corporation **(PA)**	6799	A	213 262-6903	12713
Msd Capital LP	6799	C	310 458-3600	12720
Tennenbaum Capitl Partners LLC **(DH)**	6799	D	310 566-1000	12741
By The Blue Sea LLC	7011	B	310 458-0030	12781
C W Hotels Ltd	7011	C	310 395-9700	12782
Dtrs Santa Monica LLC	7011	B	310 458-6700	12816
Edward Thomas Hospitality Corp	7011	B	310 458-0030	12818
Et Whitehall Seascape LLC	7011	C	310 581-5533	12823
M&C Hotel Interests Inc	7011	B	310 399-9344	12909
Ocean Avenue LLC	7011	B	310 576-7777	12944
Sand and Sea	7011	D	310 458-1515	13014
Santa Monica Hotel Owner LLC	7011	C	310 395-3332	13016
Santa Monica Proper Jv LLC	7011	C	310 620-9990	13017
Second Street Corporation	7011	C	310 394-5454	13020
Windsor Capital Group Inc	7011	D	310 566-1100	13086
Windsor Capital Group Inc	7011	D	310 566-1100	13087
Windsor Capital Group Inc	7011	D	209 577-3825	13088
Windsor Capital Group Inc	7011	D	310 566-1100	13089
Windsor Capital Group Inc	7011	D	310 566-1100	13090
Ad Populum LLC **(PA)**	7311	D	619 818-7644	13193
Adconion Media Inc **(PA)**	7311	C	310 382-5521	13194
Movers and Shakers LLC	7311	D	310 893-7051	13229
Postaer Rubin and Associates	7311	C	312 644-3636	13236
Rubin Postaer and Associates **(PA)**	7311	C	310 394-4000	13243
Edmundscom Inc **(HQ)**	7313	A	310 309-6300	13265
Kargo Global Inc	7313	C	212 979-9000	13268
Platinum Clg Indianapolis LLC	7349	B	310 584-8000	13405
Batia Infotech	7371	C	855 776-7763	13671
Fair Financial Corp **(PA)**	7371	D	800 584-5000	13726
Playhaven LLC	7371	D	310 308-9668	13797
Santa Monica Studios	7371	D	310 453-5046	13811
School-Link Technologies Inc	7371	D	310 434-2700	13812
Snap Inc **(PA)**	7371	C	310 399-3339	13825
Truecar Inc **(PA)**	7371	C	800 200-2000	13852

Company	SIC	EMP	PHONE	ENTRY#
Activision Blizzard Inc **(HQ)**	7372	B	310 255-2000	13869
Amber Holding Inc	7372	E	603 324-3000	13876
Clearlake Capital Partners	7372	A	310 400-8800	13902
Cornerstone Ondemand Inc **(HQ)**	7372	C	310 752-0200	13910
Gumgum Sports Inc	7372	E	310 400-0396	13944
Kingcom(us) LLC **(DH)**	7372	E	424 744-5697	13959
Patientpop Inc	7372	D	844 487-8399	14004
Railstech Inc	7372	E	267 315-2998	14016
Salesforcecom Inc	7372	E	310 752-7000	14024
Epochcom LLC	7374	C	310 664-5700	14134
Goodrx Holdings Inc **(PA)**	7374	C	855 268-2822	14135
Leaf Group Ltd **(HQ)**	7374	C	310 394-6400	14140
Edmunds Holding Company **(PA)**	7375	A	310 309-6300	14170
Tigerconnect Inc **(PA)**	7379	D	310 401-1820	14261
Advanstar Communications Inc	7389	E	310 857-7500	14435
Advanstar Communications Inc **(DH)**	7389	E	310 857-7500	14436
Hct Packaging Inc **(PA)**	7389	C	310 260-7680	14507
Hirsch/Bedner Intl Inc **(PA)**	7389	C	310 829-9087	14509
Universal Mus Investments Inc **(HQ)**	7389	D	888 583-7176	14620
Universal Music Group Inc **(HQ)**	7389	D	310 865-0770	14621
Wells Fargo Capital Finance Inc	7389	C	310 453-7300	14633
M2 Automotive	7532	A	310 399-3887	14675
Artisan Entertainment Inc	7812	A	310 449-9200	14807
Cabin Editing Company LLC	7812	D	310 752-0520	14811
Focus Features LLC **(DH)**	7812	D	310 315-1722	14828
Lions Gate Films Inc	7812	C	310 449-9200	14836
Lionsgate Studios Corp **(PA)**	7812	C	877 848-3866	14837
Pash Portfolio Inc	7812	C	310 888-8738	14844
Starz Entertainment LLC **(DH)**	7812	A	720 852-7700	14860
Lionsgate Productions Inc	7822	C	310 255-3937	14920
Sonar Entertainment Inc **(PA)**	7822	D	424 230-7140	14921
Innovtive Artsts Tlent Lrtary **(PA)**	7922	D	310 656-0400	14963
Tennis Channel Inc **(DH)**	7922	D	310 392-1920	14980
Red Bull North America Inc **(HQ)**	7929	C	310 460-5356	15001
Santa Monica Amusements LLC	7996	B	310 451-9641	15108
Jonathan Club	7997	D	310 393-9245	15141
Kinema Fitness Inc	7999	D	866 608-5704	15209
Saint Jhns Hlth Ctr Foundation	8011	C	310 315-6111	15441
Emperors Cllege Trdtnal Orntal	8049	D	310 453-8383	15540
American Retirement Corp	8051	D	310 399-3227	15566
Asmb LLC	8051	D	949 347-7100	15572
Coastal Health Care Inc	8051	C	310 828-5596	15592
Berkeley E Convalescent Hosp	8059	C	310 829-5377	15837
Golden State Health Ctrs Inc	8059	C	310 451-9706	15858
Providence St Johns Hlth Ctr	8062	B	971 268-7643	16153
Saint Johns Health Center Foundation **(DH)**	8062	A	310 829-5511	16165
Ucla Healthcare	8062	D	310 319-4560	16237
Caerus Marketing Group LLC	8082	D	800 792-1015	16374
Regents of The University Cal	8099	D	310 267-9308	16613
Bryan Cave Lighton Paisner LLP	8111	D	310 576-2100	16650
County of Los Angeles	8322	D	310 266-3711	16919
People Concern	8322	C	310 450-0650	16992
People Concern	8322	C	310 883-1222	16993
Vitacare Prescription Svcs Inc	8322	C	800 350-3819	17026
Vista Del Mar Child Fmly Svcs	8361	B	310 836-1223	17206
Boys Grls CLB Snta Monica Inc	8641	D	310 361-8500	17328
Elizabeth Glser Pdtric Aids FN	8641	B	310 593-0047	17342
Heal Bay	8641	D	310 451-1500	17348
Milken Family Foundation	8641	C	310 570-4800	17356
Automobile Club Southern Cal	8699	C	310 453-1909	17435
California Semiconductor Tech	8711	D	310 579-2939	17500
Kite Pharma Inc **(HQ)**	8731	D	310 824-9999	17802
The Rand Corporation **(PA)**	8733	A	310 393-0411	17892
911 Health Inc	8734	C	310 560-8509	17898
Provident Financial Management	8741	D	310 282-0477	18041
Glp Capital Partners LP	8742	D	310 356-0880	18143
Wilshire Advisors LLC **(PA)**	8742	C	310 451-3051	18243
Ziprecruiter Inc **(PA)**	8742	A	877 252-1062	18249
Ocean Park Community Center	8748	C	310 828-6717	18344

SANTA PAULA, CA - Ventura County

Company	SIC	EMP	PHONE	ENTRY#
Limoneira Company **(PA)**	0723	D	805 525-5541	114
Saticoy Lemon Association **(PA)**	0723	D	805 654-6500	118
Carbon California Company LLC	1311	E	805 933-1901	273
Oil Well Service Company	1389	D	805 525-2103	353
Keller North America Inc	1799	D	805 933-1331	1212
Saticoy Foods Corporation	2033	E	805 647-5266	1356
Calavo Growers Inc **(PA)**	2099	C	805 525-1245	1750
Calpipe Industries LLC	3312	E	562 803-4388	4515
Automotive Racing Products Inc	3429	D	805 525-1497	4754
Abrisa Industrial Glass Inc **(HQ)**	3827	D	805 525-4902	7994
Abrisa Technologies	3827	E	805 525-4902	7995
Weber Orthopedic LP **(PA)**	3842	D	800 221-5465	8319

	SIC	EMP	PHONE	ENTRY#
Thompco Inc.	5082	E	805 933-8048	10360
Troop Real Estate Inc.	6531	C	805 921-0030	12543
Tissue-Grown Corporation	8731	D	805 525-1975	17830

SANTA YNEZ, CA - Santa Barbara County

	SIC	EMP	PHONE	ENTRY#
Channel Islnds Yung MNS Chrstn.	8641	D	805 686-2037	17335

SANTA YSABEL, CA - San Diego County

	SIC	EMP	PHONE	ENTRY#
Dudleys Bakery Inc.	5461	E	760 765-0488	11294

SANTEE, CA - San Diego County

	SIC	EMP	PHONE	ENTRY#
Lustros Inc.	1021	E	619 449-4800	252
T C Construction Company Inc.	1623	C	619 448-4560	699
Challenger Sheet Metal Inc.	1761	D	619 596-8040	1075
Tower Glass Inc.	1793	D	619 596-6199	1167
Lauren Anthony & Co Inc.	2511	E	619 590-1141	2428
CCM Enterprises (PA)	2541	D	619 562-2605	2559
European Wholesale Counter.	2541	C	619 562-0565	2563
South West Lubricants Inc.	2992	D	619 449-5000	3858
Delstar Holding Corp.	3081	E	619 258-1503	3947
Argee Mfg Co San Diego Inc.	3089	D	619 449-5050	4052
R V Best Inc.	3089	E	619 448-7800	4214
RCP Block & Brick Inc.	3271	E	619 448-2240	4373
Vision Systems Inc.	3354	D	619 258-7300	4612
Kevin Whaley	3496	E	619 596-4000	5407
Olson Irrigation Systems.	3523	D	619 562-3100	5475
Terra Nova Technologies	3535	D	619 596-7400	5519
Ds Fibertech Corp	3567	E	619 562-7001	5798
Alts Tool & Machine Inc.	3599	D	619 562-6653	6078
Mathy Machine Inc.	3599	E	619 448-0404	6171
Quality Controlled Mfg Inc.	3599	D	619 443-3997	6209
Stratedge Corporation	3674	D	866 424-4962	6900
Lhv Power Corporation (PA)	3679	E	619 258-7700	7020
Compucraft Industries Inc.	3728	C	619 448-0787	7455
Air & Gas Tech Inc.	3732	E	619 955-5980	7616
Interocean Industries Inc.	3812	E	858 292-0808	7725
Interocean Systems LLC	3812	E	858 565-8400	7726
Valley Box Co Inc.	5113	E	619 449-2882	10611
Smart Stores Operations LLC	5141	C	619 449-2396	10790
Lowes Home Centers LLC	5211	A	619 212-4100	11231
Mek Industries Inc.	7363	C	858 610-9601	13614
JMS Interiors Inc.	7389	D	619 749-5098	14521
County of San Diego.	8051	A	619 956-2800	15609
Life Gnerations Healthcare LLC	8059	C	619 449-5555	15864
Santee Senior Retirement Com.	8322	C	619 955-0901	17006
YMCA of San Diego County.	8641	D	619 449-9622	17399
Scantibodies Laboratory Inc (PA)	8734	D	619 258-9300	17925
Cgp Maintenance Cnstr Svcs Inc.	8741	D	858 454-7326	17961

SAUGUS, CA - Los Angeles County

	SIC	EMP	PHONE	ENTRY#
Hasa Inc (PA)	2812	D	661 259-5848	3208

SEAL BEACH, CA - Orange County

	SIC	EMP	PHONE	ENTRY#
Samedan Oil Corporation.	1382	B	661 319-5038	312
Dendreon Pharmaceuticals LLC (HQ)	2834	E	562 252-7500	3395
Modular Wind Energy Inc.	3511	D	562 304-6782	5459
Cosmodyne LLC.	3559	E	562 795-5990	5696
Magtek Inc (PA)	3577	C	562 546-6400	5935
Amonix Inc.	3674	D	562 344-4750	6798
Diversfied Tchncal Systems Inc (HQ)	3825	E	562 493-0158	7909
P2f Holdings	5199	D	562 296-1055	11133
Original Parts Group Inc (PA)	5531	D	562 594-1000	11450
Merrill Lynch Prce Fnner Smith	6211	A	662 403 1300	11984
First Team RE - Orange Cnty.	6531	D	562 506-9011	12449
Olson Company LLC (PA)	6552	D	562 596-4770	12575
Talent & Acquisition LLC.	7371	C	888 970-9575	13837
Watersafe Swim School Inc.	7999	D	562 596-8608	15233
Tenet Healthsystem Medical Inc.	8011	C	562 493-9581	15489
AG Seal Beach LLC.	8051	C	562 592-2477	15561
Action Hlth Care Prsnnel Svcs.	8082	C	562 799-5523	16357
Premier Healthcare Svcs LLC (DH)	8082	C	626 204-7930	16412
Country Villa Service Corp.	8322	C	562 598-2477	16903
Sisters of St Joseph Orange.	8661	A	562 430-4638	17420
Fisheries Resource Vlntr Corps.	8742	C	562 596-9261	18138

SHAFTER, CA - Kern County

	SIC	EMP	PHONE	ENTRY#
Garlic Company (PA)	0139	D	661 393-4212	4
Wonderful Orchards LLC (HQ)	0173	C	661 399-4456	42
Grimmway Enterprises Inc.	0191	C	661 399-0844	82
Grimmway Enterprises Inc.	0723	B	661 393-3320	108
Wonderful Company LLC.	0723	A	661 399-4456	125
M-I LLC.	1389	E	661 321-5400	343
Oil Well Service Company.	1389	D	661 746-4809	351

	SIC	EMP	PHONE	ENTRY#
Tryad Service Corporation.	1389	D	661 391-1524	367
Standard Bldg Solutions Inc.	1761	D	661 387-1110	1097
Scotts Company LLC.	2873	E	661 387-9555	3747
Elk Corporation of Texas.	3272	C	661 391-3900	4388
McM Fabricators Inc.	3441	C	661 589-2774	4851
Jti Elctrcal Instrmntation LLC.	4911	D	661 393-5535	9590
Varner Family Ltd Partnership (PA)	6733	C	661 399-1163	12675
Central California Power.	7538	E	661 589-2870	14687
Wonderful Citrus Cooperative.	8611	A	661 720-2400	17291
Ponder Environmental Svcs Inc.	8744	E	661 589-7771	18266

SHANDON, CA - San Luis Obispo County

	SIC	EMP	PHONE	ENTRY#
Pacific Tank & Cnstr Inc.	3443	E	805 237-2929	4919

SHELL BEACH, CA - San Luis Obispo County

	SIC	EMP	PHONE	ENTRY#
Dolphin Bay Ht & Residence Inc.	7011	D	805 773-4300	12814

SHERMAN OAKS, CA - Los Angeles County

	SIC	EMP	PHONE	ENTRY#
Crestview Landscape Inc.	0781	D	818 962-7771	164
Coastal Tile Inc.	1743	D	818 988-6134	1038
Xcvi LLC (PA)	2211	D	213 749-2661	1890
Med Couture Inc.	2326	D	214 231-2500	1998
Strategic Distribution L P	2326	C		2002
E Z Buy & E Z Sell Recycl Corp (DH)	2711	C	310 886-7808	2795
80lv LLC.	2731	E	818 435-6613	2880
Dt123 (PA)	2791	E	213 488-1230	3205
Vytalogy Wellness LLC.	2833	C	818 867-4440	3334
Natrol LLC (PA)	2834	C	800 262-8765	3457
Careismatic Brands LLC (DH)	3143	C	818 671-2128	4282
Envion LLC.	3564	C	818 217-2500	5769
Vubiquity Holdings Inc (DH)	4841	C	818 526-5000	9560
Jarrow Formulas Inc (PA)	5122	D	310 204-6936	10628
Neurobrands LLC.	5149	C	310 393-6444	10966
Center Automotive Inc.	5511	D	818 907-9995	11324
Miller Automotive Group Inc (HQ)	5511	B	818 787-8400	11379
Psychic Eye Book Shops Inc (PA)	5942	D	818 906-8263	11634
Homebridge Financial Svcs Inc.	6163	A	818 981-0606	11946
Royal Specialty Undwrt Inc.	6331	C	818 922-6700	12134
Moss & Company Inc (PA)	6531	C	818 305-3600	12490
Moss Management Services Inc.	6531	C	818 990-5999	12491
Prospect Mortgage LLC.	6719	A		12609
Serviz Inc.	7299	D	818 381-4826	13187
Wherewechat Online Svcs LLC.	7311	D	302 566-1649	13252
Adactive Media Ca Inc.	7313	D	818 465-7500	13258
Grabit Interactive Inc.	7313	E	844 472-2488	13267
Caine & Weiner Company Inc (PA)	7322	D	818 226-6000	13279
Branded Entrmt Netwrk Inc (PA)	7335	C	310 342-1500	13318
Ben Group Inc.	7371	B	310 342-1500	13673
Nile Ai Inc.	7372	E	818 689-9107	13989
Papaya	7372	E	310 740-6774	14002
Reel Security California Inc.	7381	D	818 928-4737	14332
Alternative Ira Services LLC.	7389	D	877 936-7175	14444
Lendingusa LLC.	7389	D	800 994-6177	14528
Mega Appraisers Inc.	7389	A	818 246-7370	14544
Prager University Foundation.	7812	D	833 772-4378	14849
Premiere Radio Network Inc (DH)	7922	C	818 377-5300	14972
Prime Hlthcare Svcs - Shrman O.	8062	B	818 981-7111	16148
Dynamic Home Care Service Inc (PA)	8082	D	818 981-4446	16386
Help Group West (PA)	8093	C	818 781-0360	16478
Working With Autism Inc.	8093	D	818 501 1240	16522
Star of Ca LLC.	8099	D	818 986-7827	16618
Tharpe & Howell (PA)	8111	D	818 205-9955	16789
Behavioral Learning Center Inc.	8322	C	818 308-6226	16875

SIERRA MADRE, CA - Los Angeles County

	SIC	EMP	PHONE	ENTRY#
Group H Engineering	1389	E	818 999-0999	331
Deasy Penner Podley.	6531	C	626 408-1280	12429

SIGNAL HILL, CA - Los Angeles County

	SIC	EMP	PHONE	ENTRY#
Fenderscape Incorporated	0781	C	562 988-2228	167
Signal Hill Petroleum Inc.	1382	E	562 595-6440	315
Oil Well Service Company (PA)	1389	C	562 612-0600	352
Jmh Engineering and Cnstr.	1521	D	562 317-1700	410
2h Construction Inc.	1542	D	562 424-5567	513
Har-Bro LLC (HQ)	1542	D	562 528-8000	542
Gregg Drilling LLC.	1781	C	562 427-6899	1143
Lovco Construction Inc.	1794	C	562 595-1601	1172
Gregg Drilling & Testing Inc (PA)	1799	C	562 427-6899	1207
Rossmoor Pastries MGT Inc.	2051	D	562 498-2253	1463
Ld Products Inc.	2621	C	888 321-2552	2630
R D Mathis Company.	3313	C	562 426-7049	4531
Dawson Enterprises (PA)	3533	E	562 424-8564	5508
Rode Microphones LLC (DH)	3651	C	310 328-7456	6552

Employee Codes: A=Over 500 employees, B=251-500
C=101-250, D=51-100, E=20-50, F=10-19, G=1-9

2025 Southern California
Business Directory and Buyers Guide

© Mergent Inc. 1-800-342-5647

1349

GEOGRAPHIC

	SIC	EMP	PHONE	ENTRY#
Transcom Telecommunication Inc	3663	E	562 424-9616	6666
United States Logistics Group	3715	E	562 989-9555	7319
Asphalt Fabric and Engrg Inc	3949	D	562 997-4129	8502
Ancon Marine LLC	4212	C	562 326-5900	8892
Edco Disposal Corporation (PA)	4953	C	619 287-7555	9745
Nsv International Corp	5013	E	562 438-3836	9836
Ship & Shore Environmental Inc	5084	E	562 997-0233	10403
Viking Office Products Inc (DH)	5112	B	562 490-1000	10586
Boulevard Automotive Group (PA)	5511	D	562 492-1000	11320
MD Care Inc	6321	D	562 344-3400	12064
First American Team Realty Inc (PA)	6531	C	562 427-7765	12443
Porter Boiler Service Inc	7699	E	562 426-2528	14784
Accountbl Hlth Care IPA A Pro	8099	C	562 435-3333	16525

SIMI VALLEY, CA - Ventura County

	SIC	EMP	PHONE	ENTRY#
Specialized Ldscp MGT Svcs Inc	0781	D	805 520-7590	193
PW Gillibrand Co Inc (PA)	1446	E	805 526-2195	379
Cobalt Construction Company	1522	D	805 577-6222	444
Suttles Plumbing & Mech Corp	1711	D	818 718-9779	847
B & M Contractors Inc	1771	D	805 581-5480	1103
Millworks By Design Inc	2431	E	818 597-1326	2314
Clarios LLC	2531	E	805 522-5555	2539
Pacer Print	2752	E	888 305-3144	3054
Pharmaceutic Litho Label Inc	2834	D	805 285-5162	3475
Microblend Inc	2851	E	330 998-4602	3717
Poly-Tainer Inc (PA)	3085	C	805 526-3424	3988
Milgard Manufacturing LLC	3231	E	805 581-6325	4340
Newman and Sons Inc (PA)	3272	E	805 522-1646	4405
Pre-Con Products	3272	D	805 527-0841	4412
Fiberoptic Systems Inc	3357	E	805 579-6600	4632
Advanced Metal Mfg Inc	3444	E	805 322-4161	4939
Computer Metal Products Corp	3444	D	805 520-6966	4972
Sheet Metal Engineering	3444	E	805 306-0390	5033
Specialty Fabrications Inc	3444	E	805 579-9730	5037
Mabel Baas Inc	3479	E	805 520-8075	5330
Chatsworth Products Inc (PA)	3499	E	818 735-6100	5443
Scientific Cutting Tools Inc	3545	E	805 584-9495	5624
Rexnord Industries LLC	3556	E	805 583-5514	5684
Qualitylogic Inc	3577	C	208 424-1905	5947
Ricoh Prtg Systems Amer Inc (HQ)	3577	B	805 578-4000	5950
Rugged Info Tech Eqp Corp	3577	D	805 577-9710	5951
Savage Machining Inc	3599	E	805 584-8047	6228
Vanderhorst Brothers Industries Inc	3599	D	805 583-3333	6263
Embedded Systems Inc	3625	E	805 624-6030	6349
Aveox Inc	3629	E	805 915-0200	6368
Dpa Labs Inc	3674	E	805 581-9200	6819
Piezo-Metrics Inc (PA)	3674	E	805 522-4676	6867
Jaxx Manufacturing Inc	3679	E	805 526-4979	7016
Meggitt Safety Systems Inc (DH)	3699	C	805 584-4100	7134
Milodon Incorporated	3714	E	805 577-5950	7272
Special Devices Incorporated	3714	A	805 387-1000	7294
Aerovironment Inc	3721	D	805 520-8350	7327
Datron Advanced Tech Inc	3728	C	805 579-2966	7461
Meggitt Safety Systems Inc	3728	D	805 584-4100	7526
Meggitt-Usa Inc (DH)	3728	B	805 526-5700	7527
Rsa Engineered Products LLC	3728	D	805 584-4150	7549
Whittaker Corporation	3728	E	805 526-5700	7592
Catalina Yachts Inc (PA)	3732	E	818 884-7700	7618
L3 Technologies Inc	3812	D	805 584-1717	7730
Pacific Scientific Company (DH)	3812	E	805 526-5700	7790
Sensoscientific LLC	3823	E	800 279-3101	7879
Interscan Corporation	3824	E	805 823-8301	7890
Bemco Inc (PA)	3826	E	805 583-4970	7944
Entech Instruments Inc	3826	D	805 527-5939	7955
Safran Defense & Space Inc	3827	D	805 373-9340	8019
Scope City (PA)	3827	E	805 522-6646	8020
Fluid Line Technology Corp	3841	E	818 998-8848	8153
Freedom Designs Inc	3842	C	805 582-0077	8268
Replacement Parts Inds Inc	3843	E	818 882-8611	8353
S2k Graphics Inc	3993	E	818 885-3900	8628
DMA Enterprises Inc (PA)	3999	E	805 520-2468	8675
Gxo Logistics Supply Chain Inc	4731	C	336 989-0537	9290
Waste Management Cal Inc	4953	C	805 522-7023	9778
Shopper Inc	5046	B	800 344-8830	10052
Electromed Inc	5047	D	805 523-7500	10077
Quad-C Jh Holdings Inc	5047	C	800 966-6662	10105
Foreign Trade Corporation	5065	C	805 823-8400	10244
Howmet Globl Fstning Systems I (HQ)	5085	C	805 426-2270	10440
Andwin Corporation (PA)	5113	D	818 999-2828	10588
Smart Stores Operations LLC	5141	C	805 520-6035	10805
Eurow and OReilly Corp	5199	E	800 747-7452	11118
Lowes Home Centers LLC	5211	C	805 426-2780	11209
Ford of Simi Valley Inc	5511	D	805 583-0333	11350

	SIC	EMP	PHONE	ENTRY#
Am-Pac Tire Dist Inc (DH)	5531	D	805 581-1311	11439
Coast To Coast Cmpt Pdts Inc (PA)	5734	C	805 244-9500	11539
Troop Real Estate Inc (PA)	6531	D	805 581-3200	12544
Wsm Investments LLC	6794	C	818 332-4600	12681
Simi West Inc	7011	C	760 346-5502	13024
Kleintob Inc	7231	D	805 527-3389	13150
Anjana Software Solutions Inc	7371	D	805 583-0121	13654
Edgeworth Integration LLC	7382	C	805 915-0211	14395
American Vision Windows Inc	7699	C	805 582-1833	14756
Jade Gilbert Dental Corp	8021	C	805 583-5700	15519
Providnce Facey Med Foundation	8031	D	805 206-2000	15531
Simi Vly Hosp & Hlth Care Svcs	8062	A	805 955-6000	16200
Simi Vly Hosp & Hlth Care Svcs (HQ)	8062	C	805 955-6000	16201
Good Shepherd Lutheran HM of W	8361	C	805 526-2482	17156
Ronald Rgan Prsdntial Fndtion	8412	D	805 522-2977	17262
Computerized Mgt Svcs Inc	8721	D	805 522-5940	17713
Chase Group Llc	8732	B	805 522-9155	17841
Weapon X Security Inc	8999	D	818 818-9950	18380

SKYFOREST, CA - San Bernardino County

	SIC	EMP	PHONE	ENTRY#
Spsv Entertainment LLC	7929	D	909 744-9373	15006

SOLANA BEACH, CA - San Diego County

	SIC	EMP	PHONE	ENTRY#
Cognella Inc	2741	D	858 552-1120	2907
Sentynl Therapeutics Inc	2834	E	888 227-8725	3499
Tide Rock Holdings LLC (PA)	3444	C	858 204-7438	5046
Clearpoint Neuro Inc (PA)	3841	D	888 287-9109	8132
Simon Golub & Sons Inc (DH)	5094	D		10553
Southern Cal Disc Tire Co Inc	5531	C	858 481-6387	11460
Senior Resource Group LLC	6513	C	858 519-0890	12366
Pacifica Hosts Inc	7011	C	858 792-8200	12963
Srg Holdings LLC (HQ)	7359	B	858 792-9300	13472
Lumiradx Inc	7371	C	951 201-9384	13764
Neubloc LLC (PA)	7371	D	858 674-8701	13777
Trovata Inc (PA)	7371	D	312 914-8106	13851
Onehealth Solutions Inc	7379	C	858 947-6333	14237
Simulstat Incorporated	7379	D	858 546-4337	14252

SOLVANG, CA - Santa Barbara County

	SIC	EMP	PHONE	ENTRY#
Alma Rosa Winery Vineyards LLC	2084	E	805 688-9090	1558
Lucas & Lewellen Vineyards Inc (PA)	5182	E	805 686-9336	11057
Holzheus El Rancho Market Inc	5411	C	805 688-4300	11278
Alisal Properties (PA)	7032	C	805 688-6411	13099
Solvang Lutheran Home Inc	8051	C	805 688-3263	15781
Cottage Health	8062	C	805 688-6432	15966
Santa Ynez Vly Cttage Hosp Inc	8062	D	805 688-6431	16177

SOMIS, CA - Ventura County

	SIC	EMP	PHONE	ENTRY#
Saticoy Country Club	7997	D	805 647-1153	15172

SOUTH EL MONTE, CA - Los Angeles County

	SIC	EMP	PHONE	ENTRY#
Bali Construction Inc	1623	D	626 442-8003	662
American Wrecking Inc	1795	D	626 350-8303	1178
California Snack Foods Inc	2064	E	626 444-4508	1501
Out of Shell LLC	2099	C	626 401-1923	1829
Studio9d8 Inc	2253	E	626 350-0832	1924
Jowett Garments Factory Inc	2339	E	626 350-0515	2108
Yoshimasa Display Case Inc	2541	E	213 637-9999	2575
Interntnal Mdction Systems Ltd	2834	A	626 442-6757	3428
Lee Pharmaceuticals	2844	D	626 442-3141	3668
Cardinal Industrial Finishes (PA)	2851	D	626 444-9274	3706
Cardinal Paint and Powder Inc	2851	D	626 444-9274	3708
Promotonal Design Concepts Inc	3069	D	626 579-4454	3930
R & R Rubber Molding Inc	3069	E	626 575-8105	3931
Abacus Powder Coating	3479	E	626 443-7556	5305
Island Powder Coating	3479	E	626 279-2460	5325
S & H Machine Inc	3492	E	626 448-5062	5376
Vacco Industries (DH)	3494	C	626 443-7121	5391
Grover Smith Mfg Corp	3561	E	323 724-3444	5735
Mikelson Machine Shop Inc	3599	E	626 448-3920	6179
Brands Republic Inc	3634	E	302 401-1195	6393
C W Cole & Company Inc	3646	E	626 443-2473	6453
Halcore Group Inc	3711	E	626 575-0880	7179
S C I Industries Inc	3714	E		7290
Amro Fabricating Corporation (PA)	3728	C	626 579-2200	7430
California Med Response Inc	4119	D	562 968-1818	8815
Leader Industries Inc	4119	C	626 575-0880	8832
Integrated Parcel Network	4215	B	714 278-6100	9004
Pactrack Inc	4731	D	213 201-5856	9322
Custom Chrome Manufacturing	5013	B	408 825-5000	9820
Gama Contracting Services Inc	5082	C	626 442-7200	10347
O & S Properties Inc (PA)	7699	D	626 579-1084	14778
Ahmc Healthcare Inc	8062	C	626 579-7777	15901

	SIC	EMP	PHONE	ENTRY#
Lincoln Trning Ctr Rhblttion W	8331	D	626 442-0621	17061

SOUTH GATE, CA - Los Angeles County

	SIC	EMP	PHONE	ENTRY#
World Oil Corp.	1311	C	562 928-0100	283
Herbert Malarkey Roofing Co.	1761	D	562 806-8000	1085
Interior Rmoval Specialist Inc.	1795	C	323 357-6900	1184
Saputo Cheese USA Inc.	2022	A	562 862-7686	1289
Win Soon Inc.	2026	D	323 564-5070	1336
Sunopta Grains and Foods Inc.	2041	D	323 774-6000	1408
Sunopta Fruit Group Inc.	2087	D	323 774-6000	1690
Marquez Marquez Inc.	2096	E	562 408-0960	1726
AG Adriano Goldschmied Inc (PA)	2325	E	323 357-1111	1990
Janin	2339	C	323 564-0995	2103
General Veneer Mfg Co.	2435	E	323 564-2661	2370
Liberty Container Company	2653	C	323 564-4211	2679
Packaging Corporation America	2653	C	562 927-7741	2685
PQ LLC	2819	D	323 326-1100	3246
Arnco	2822	E	323 249-7600	3303
Granitize Products Inc.	2842	D	562 923-5438	3606
Tu-K Industries LLC	2844	E	562 927-3365	3692
Lunday-Thagard Company	2952	B	562 928-6990	3845
Dememno/Kerdoon Holdings (DH)	2992	D	562 231-1550	3851
Lunday-Thagard Company (HQ)	2999	C	562 928-7000	3860
Glasswerks La Inc (HQ)	3231	B	888 789-7810	4334
Johns Manville Corporation	3296	D	323 568-2220	4492
Artsons Manufacturing Company	3312	E	323 773-3469	4510
Pacific Alloy Casting Company Inc.	3321	C	562 928-1387	4559
Buddy Bar Casting LLC	3365	C	562 861-9664	4666
Techni-Cast Corp.	3369	E	562 923-4585	4693
Accurate Steel Treating Inc.	3398	E	562 927-6528	4694
Astro Aluminum Treating Co.	3398	D	562 923-4344	4697
Frameless Hardware Company LLC	3429	E	888 295-4531	4768
Metal Supply LLC	3441	D	562 634-9940	4855
Pluckys Dump Rental LLC	3443	E	323 540-3510	4921
Shultz Steel Company LLC	3463	B	323 357-3200	5160
Hughes Bros Aircrafters Inc.	3544	D	323 773-4541	5584
Cimc Intermodal Equipment LLC (HQ)	3715	D	562 904-8600	7314
Bell Foundry Co (PA)	3949	E	323 564-5001	8504
Sure Grip International	3949	D	562 923-0724	8546
Pan Pacific Petroleum Co Inc (PA)	4213	D	562 928-0100	8970
Samuel J Piazza & Son Inc (PA)	4214	E	323 357-1999	8994
Sprint Corporation	4812	C	323 357-0797	9418
Pcs Mobile Solutions LLC.	4813	D	323 567-2490	9454
Verdeco Recycling Inc.	4953	E	323 537-4617	9772
Privilege International Inc.	5021	D	323 585-0777	9882
Saw Daily Service Inc.	5085	E	323 564-1791	10462
Century 21 A Better Svc Rlty	6531	D	562 806-1000	12402
5 Star Jobs	7361	D	562 788-7391	13481
Koos Manufacturing Inc.	7389	A	323 249-1000	14524
Meribear Productions Inc.	7389	D	310 204-5353	14546
Altamed Health Services Corp.	8099	C	323 562-6700	16529
County of Los Angeles	8099	D	562 861-0316	16552
Dickson Testing Co Inc (DH)	8734	D	562 862-8378	17912

SOUTH PASADENA, CA - Los Angeles County

	SIC	EMP	PHONE	ENTRY#
Albany Farms Inc.	2099	E	213 330-6573	1736
Finesse Apparel Inc.	2339	E	213 747-7077	2096
Citadel Panda Express Inc.	5812	C	626 799-9898	11562
Equity Smart Home Loans Inc.	6162	D	626 864-8774	11901
Stratus Real Estate Inc.	6163	C	626 441-5549	11953
Tokio Marine Highland Insurance Ser (DH)	6411	D	626 463-6486	12260
Catalyst Speech LLC	8742	C	213 346-9945	18114

SPRING VALLEY, CA - San Diego County

	SIC	EMP	PHONE	ENTRY#
Treebeard Landscape Inc.	0781	D	619 697-8302	196
Casper Company	1771	C	619 589-6001	1107
West Coast Iron Inc.	1796	D	619 464-8456	1192
ATI Rstrtion Spring Vly CA Inc.	1799	C	619 466-9876	1196
Homestead Sheet Metal	3441	E	619 469-4373	4838
Richardson Steel Inc.	3441	E	619 697-5892	4864
S & S Carbide Tool Inc.	3544	E	619 670-5214	5596
Bish Inc.	3728	E	619 660-6220	7445
Burns and Sons Trucking Inc.	4212	D	619 460-5394	8897
Otay Water District	4941	C	619 670-2222	9709
Marjan Stone Inc.	5032	C	619 825-6000	9947
Rossin Steel Inc.	5051	C	619 656-9200	10155
TV Ears Inc.	5065	E	619 797-1600	10294
Smart Stores Operations LLC.	5141	C	619 668-9039	10795
Deering Banjo Company Inc.	5736	D	619 464-8252	11545
Kaizen Syndicate LLC.	7379	C	858 309-2028	14228
Family Hlth Ctrs San Diego Inc.	8011	B	619 515-2555	15310
B-Spring Valley LLC.	8051	D	619 797-3991	15576
365 Home Care	8082	D	310 908-5179	16349

	SIC	EMP	PHONE	ENTRY#
Covenant Living West	8361	D	619 931-1114	17141
Vts Industries	8641	D	619 337-9244	17375

STANTON, CA - Orange County

	SIC	EMP	PHONE	ENTRY#
USS Cal Builders Inc.	1542	C	714 828-4882	599
Orco Block & Hardscape (PA)	3271	D	714 527-2239	4371
Structural Stl Fabricators Inc.	3441	C	714 761-1695	4872
West Coast Manufacturing Inc.	3469	E	714 897-4221	5222
All Metals Processing of San Diego Inc.	3471	C	714 828-8238	5228
All Mtals Proc Orange Cnty LLC	3471	C	714 828-8238	5229
Field Time Target Training LLC	3483	E	714 677-2841	5354
Newcomb Spring Corp.	3495	E	714 995-5341	5396
Custom Pipe & Fabrication Inc (HQ)	3498	D	800 553-3058	5432
Boudraux Prcsion McHining Corp.	3599	E	714 894-4523	6098
Signs and Services Company	3993	E	714 761-8200	8635
Haulaway Storage Cntrs Inc.	4225	A	800 826-9040	9074
Cameron Welding Supply (PA)	7692	E	714 530-9353	14737
California Friends Homes	8361	B	714 530-9100	17125

STEVENSON RANCH, CA - Los Angeles County

	SIC	EMP	PHONE	ENTRY#
Vons Companies Inc.	5411	C	661 254-3570	11287
Guitar Center Holdings Inc.	7699	D	661 222-7521	14770
Site Helpers LLC.	8742	D	877 217-5395	18211

STUDIO CITY, CA - Los Angeles County

	SIC	EMP	PHONE	ENTRY#
Fort Hill Construction (PA)	1521	D	323 656-7425	404
CBS Broadcasting Inc.	4833	D	818 655-8500	9494
Hallmark Media US LLC (DH)	4833	D	818 755-2400	9506
City National Bank	6021	D	818 487-7530	11712
Motion Pcture Indust Pnsion Hl.	6371	C	818 769-0007	12161
Backbone Capital Advisors LLC	6799	D	818 769-8016	12699
CBS Studios Inc.	7812	C	818 655-5160	14812
Columbia Pictures Inds Inc.	7812	C	818 655-5820	14813
High Technology Video Inc.	7812	D	323 969-8822	14832
A Filml Inc.	7819	D	213 977-8600	14880
Radford Studio Center LLC.	7922	B	818 655-5000	14974
Longwood Management Corp.	8059	C	818 980-8200	15867
American Private Duty Inc.	8082	E	818 386-6358	16363
Maxima Thrapy Spech Clinic Inc.	8099	C	818 287-8875	16585

SUN CITY, CA - Riverside County

	SIC	EMP	PHONE	ENTRY#
Forterra Pipe & Precast LLC.	3272	E	951 523-7039	4393
Omnimax International LLC.	3442	D	951 928-1000	4897
United Parcel Service Inc.	4513	D	951 928-5221	9177

SUN VALLEY, CA - Los Angeles County

	SIC	EMP	PHONE	ENTRY#
Leon Krous Drilling Inc.	1381	E	818 833-4654	292
Rawlings Mechanical Corp (PA)	1711	D	323 875-2040	826
Ceramic Tile Art Inc.	1743	D	818 767-9088	1037
Pacific Pavingstone Inc.	1771	C	818 244-4000	1129
Glenoaks Food Inc.	2015	E	818 768-9091	1278
High Road Craft Ice Cream Inc (PA)	2024	E	678 701-7623	1318
Gedney Foods Company	2035	E	952 448-2612	1367
Foodology LLC.	2099	D	818 252-1888	1775
Columbia Showcase & Cab Co Inc.	2541	E	818 765-9710	2561
Marfred Industries	2653	B		2681
Pacobond Inc.	2674	E	818 768-5002	2744
Colorfx Inc.	2752	E	818 767-7671	2983
Insua Graphics Incorporated	2752	E	818 767-7007	3022
Custrich Group Inc.	2044	C	818 686-2500	3643
North Amrcn Foam Ppr Cnverters	3086	E	818 255-3383	4008
Plastic Services and Products	3086	A	818 896-1101	4009
PMC Global Inc (PA)	3086	D	818 896-1101	4010
PMC Leaders In Chemicals Inc (HQ)	3086	C	818 896-1101	4011
American Plastic Products Inc.	3089	D	818 504-1073	4047
Encore Cases Inc.	3161	C	818 768-8803	4292
Angelus Block Co Inc (PA)	3271	E	714 637-8594	4370
Quikrete Companies LLC.	3272	E	323 875-1367	4418
Associated Ready Mix Con Inc.	3273	D	818 504-3100	4429
Capital Ready Mix Inc.	3273	E	818 771-1122	4433
E-Z Mix Inc (PA)	3273	E	818 768-0568	4438
Kenwalt Die Casting Corp.	3363	E	818 768-5800	4648
W & F Mfg Inc.	3429	E	818 394-6060	4795
C A Buchen Corp.	3441	E	818 767-5408	4822
Kitcor Corporation	3469	E	323 875-2820	5197
Alert Plating Company	3471	E	818 771-9304	5227
Schmidt Industries Inc.	3471	D	818 768-9100	5293
Sundial Industries Inc.	3479	E	818 767-4477	5348
Sundial Powder Coatings Inc.	3479	E	818 767-4477	5349
L A Propoint Inc.	3499	E	818 767-6800	5449
Kvr Investment Group Inc.	3559	D	818 896-1102	5708
Penguin Pumps Incorporated	3561	E	818 504-2391	5739
AVX Filters Corporation	3569	D	818 767-6770	5812

Employee Codes: A=Over 500 employees, B=251-500
C=101-250, D=51-100, E=20-50, F=10-19, G=1-9

2025 Southern California
Business Directory and Buyers Guide

© Mergent Inc. 1-800-342-5647
1351

GEOGRAPHIC

	SIC	EMP	PHONE	ENTRY#
Impulse Industries Inc	3581	E	818 767-4258	5962
L A Gauge Company Inc	3599	D	818 767-7193	6163
Precision Arcft Machining Inc	3599	E	818 768-5900	6204
Schneiders Manufacturing Inc	3599	E	818 771-0082	6229
Sheffield Manufacturing Inc	3599	D	310 320-1473	6237
Abbott Technologies Inc	3612	E	818 504-0644	6280
American Grip Inc	3648	E	818 768-8922	6489
Accurate Engineering Inc	3672	E	818 768-3919	6705
De Leon Entps Elec Spclist Inc	3672	E	818 252-6690	6722
ASC Group Inc	3674	B	818 896-1101	6801
Spartan Truck Company Inc	3713	E	818 899-1111	7210
Forgiato Inc	3714	D	818 771-9779	7253
Coronado Manufacturing LLC	3728	E	818 768-5010	7456
Pacific Sky Supply Inc	3728	D	818 768-3700	7534
Pmc Inc (HQ)	3728	D	818 896-1101	7540
Walker Design Inc	3731	E	818 252-7788	7614
Numatic Engineering Inc	3823	E	818 768-1200	7870
Emergent Group Inc (DH)	3842	D	818 394-2800	8264
Schecter Guitar Research Inc	3931	E	818 767-1029	8473
Pincraft Inc	3961	E	818 248-0077	8571
Tower 26 Inc	3999	E	347 366-2706	8735
Los Angls Cnty Mtro Trnsp Aut	4111	A	213 922-6215	8769
Arakelian Enterprises Inc	4212	C	818 768-2644	8894
Ontrac Logistics Inc	4215	D	818 504-9043	9008
Los Angeles Dept Wtr & Pwr	4941	A	213 367-1342	9703
Araco Enterprises LLC	4953	B	818 767-0675	9727
BFI Waste Systems N Amer Inc	4953	C	323 321-1722	9733
Downtown Diversion Inc	4953	C	818 252-0019	9741
Recology Los Angeles	4953	B	818 767-0675	9759
USA Waste of California Inc	4953	D	818 252-3112	9770
Waste Management Cal Inc (HQ)	4953	C	877 836-6526	9779
Builders Fence Company Inc (PA)	5031	E	818 768-5500	9918
PRI Medical Technologies Inc	5047	D	818 394-2800	10104
REM Optical Company Inc	5049	C	818 504-3950	10120
Norman Industrial Mtls Inc (PA)	5051	C	818 729-3333	10148
Aadlen Bros Auto Wrecking Inc (PA)	5093	D	323 875-1400	10534
Spa De Soleil Inc	5122	E	818 504-3200	10652
PMC Capital Partners LLC	6799	A	818 896-1101	12728
Triangle Services Inc	7349	C	818 350-7802	13423
Wet (PA)	7389	C	818 769-6200	14634
Hawker Pacific Aerospace	7699	B	818 765-6201	14771
Rose Brand Wipers Inc	7922	C	818 505-6290	14975
Serra Community Med Clinic Inc	8011	C	818 768-3000	15450
Pacifica of Valley Corporation	8062	A	818 767-3310	16113
Pine Grove Hospital Corp	8063	C	818 348-0500	16278
Mountain View Child Care Inc	8351	C	818 252-5863	17098

SUNLAND, CA - Los Angeles County

	SIC	EMP	PHONE	ENTRY#
Brightview Tree Company	0811	D	818 951-5500	249
Patriot Brokerage Inc	4731	D	910 227-4142	9323
EAM Enterprises Inc	6531	E	818 951-6464	12434
Arcadia Convalescent Hosp Inc	8051	D	818 352-4438	15569
Valley Village	8052	C	818 446-0366	15824
New Vista Health Services	8059	E	818 352-1421	15875
Tierra Del Sol Foundation (PA)	8361	D	818 352-1419	17202

SYLMAR, CA - Los Angeles County

	SIC	EMP	PHONE	ENTRY#
Tutor Perini Corporation (PA)	1542	C	818 362-8391	596
Tutor-Saliba Perini	1542	A	818 362-8391	598
Paragon Industries Inc	1743	E	818 833-0550	1042
Superior Gunite (PA)	1771	C	818 896-9199	1137
Fantasy Cookie Corporation (PA)	2052	E	818 361-6901	1488
Orange Bang Inc	2086	E	818 833-1000	1626
Clear Image Printing Inc	2752	E	818 547-4684	2980
Abbott Laboratories	2834	E	818 493-2388	3336
Sierracin Corporation (HQ)	2851	A	818 741-1656	3721
International Academy of Fin (PA)	2869	E	818 361-7724	3734
C & G Plastics	3089	E	818 837-3773	4075
Gibraltar Plastic Pdts Corp	3089	E	818 365-9318	4126
Sierracin/Sylmar Corporation	3089	A	818 362-6711	4239
Leather Pro Inc	3172	E	818 833-8822	4305
MS Aerospace Inc	3452	B	818 833-9095	5132
Industrial Elctrnic Engners In	3577	E	818 787-0311	5923
Anthony Inc (DH)	3585	A	818 365-9451	5967
Kay & James Inc	3599	E	818 998-0357	6158
L3 Technologies Inc	3663	A	818 367-0111	6622
ISU Petasys Corp	3672	C	818 833-5800	6740
Spectrolab Inc	3679	B	818 365-4611	7052
Quallion LLC	3692	C	818 833-2000	7085
Acufast Aircraft Products Inc	3728	E	818 365-7077	7402
Llamas Plastics Inc	3728	C	818 362-0371	7515
TMW Corporation (PA)	3728	C	818 362-5665	7580
Goldak Inc	3812	E	818 240-2666	7723

	SIC	EMP	PHONE	ENTRY#
Providien Machining & Metals LLC	3841	D	818 367-3161	8219
Advanced Bionics LLC (HQ)	3842	B	661 362-1400	8249
Pacesetter Inc	3845	B	818 493-2715	8392
Pacesetter Inc (DH)	3845	A	818 362-6822	8394
Carroll Fulmer Logistics Corp	4731	C	626 435-9940	9259
Oak Springs Nursery Inc	4971	D	818 367-5832	9792
Pearson Dental Supplies Inc (PA)	5047	C	818 362-2600	10101
Acuity Brands Lighting Inc	5063	C	818 362-9465	10165
Reyes Coca-Cola Bottling LLC	5149	D	818 362-4307	10974
Allied Company Holdings Inc (PA)	5181	D	818 493-6400	11040
Modern Candle Co Inc	5199	E	323 441-0104	11131
Dark Horse Services	7382	C	949 779-0219	14390
Sigue Corporation (PA)	7389	C	818 837-5939	14596
Schindler Elevator Corporation	7699	D	818 336-3000	14791
Star Waggons LLC	7819	D	818 367-5946	14904
Olive View-Ucla Medical Center (PA)	8011	D	818 364-1555	15410
County of Los Angeles	8361	D	818 364-2011	17138

TAFT, CA - Kern County

	SIC	EMP	PHONE	ENTRY#
Taft Production Company	1241	D	661 765-7194	262
Berry Petroleum Company LLC	1311	D	661 769-8820	265
Jerry Melton & Sons Cnstr Inc	1389	C	661 765-5546	339
General Production Svc Cal Inc	1623	C	661 765-5330	672
Oil-Dri Corporation America	2842	E	661 765-7194	3616
Cellco Partnership	4812	D	661 765-5397	9395

TARZANA, CA - Los Angeles County

	SIC	EMP	PHONE	ENTRY#
Castro Construction LLC	1389	E	689 220-9145	323
One Structural Inc	1389	E	626 252-0778	354
Sinanian Development Inc	1542	D	818 996-9666	585
Cgm Inc	3915	E	818 609-7088	8464
Shapp International Trdg Inc	5031	C	818 348-3000	9932
Extensions Plus Inc	5087	E	818 881-5611	10473
Airey Enterprises LLC	5088	C	818 530-3362	10485
JMJ Enterprises Inc	5812	C	818 343-5151	11581
Attorney Recovery Systems Inc (PA)	7322	D	818 774-1420	13278
Braemar Country Club Inc	7997	C	323 873-6880	15126
El Caballero Country Club	7997	C	818 654-3000	15133
AMI-Hti Trzana Encino Jint Vnt	8062	C	818 881-0800	15910
Amisub of California Inc (DH)	8062	A	818 881-0800	15911
Providence Tarzana Medical Ctr	8062	A	818 881-0800	16154
Tarzana Treatment Centers Inc (PA)	8093	C	818 996-1051	16511
Wasserman Comden & Casselman (PA)	8111	C	323 872-0995	16793
Temple Jdea of W San Frnndo Vl	8351	D	818 758-3800	17111
Avantgarde Senior Living	8361	C	818 881-0055	17122

TECATE, CA - San Diego County

	SIC	EMP	PHONE	ENTRY#
Formula Plastics Inc	3089	B	866 307-1362	4119
Fusion Product Mfg Inc	3544	D	619 819-5521	5581
Alpha Technics Inc	3823	C	949 250-6578	7846

TEHACHAPI, CA - Kern County

	SIC	EMP	PHONE	ENTRY#
Chemtool Incorporated	2992	C	661 823-7190	3850
GE Renewables North Amer LLC	3511	C	661 823-6423	5457
CMS Products LLC	3577	E	714 424-5520	5909
Adaptive Aerospace Corporation	3728	E	661 300-0616	7404
Enron Wind Corp	4911	A	661 822-6835	9584
Enron Wind Systems	4911	A	661 822-6835	9585
Pjbs Holdings Inc (PA)	4953	D	661 822-5273	9755
LLC Woodward West	7032	C	661 822-7900	13104
Adventist Health Med Tehachapi (PA)	8062	C	661 750-4848	15894
Bear Valley Springs Assn	8641	C	661 821-5537	17324

TEMECULA, CA - Riverside County

	SIC	EMP	PHONE	ENTRY#
Renzoni Vineyards Inc	0172	E	951 302-8466	36
Hines Growers Inc	0181	A	800 554-4065	57
Irriscape Construction Inc	0782	D	951 694-6936	210
Lost Dutchmans Minings Assn (DH)	1041	E	951 699-4749	254
Murrieta Development Company Inc	1623	C	951 719-1680	686
Solex Contracting Inc	1623	C	951 308-1706	695
W M Lyles Co	1623	C	951 296-2354	706
Freedom Forever LLC (PA)	1711	D	888 557-6431	779
Freedom Solar Services	1711	C	888 557-6431	780
Solar Spectrum LLC	1711	B	844 577-6527	841
Medley Communications Inc (PA)	1731	C	951 245-5200	939
Leonard Roofing Inc	1761	C	951 506-3811	1089
Mission Pools of Escondido	1799	C	949 588-0100	1216
Canadas Finest Foods Inc	2037	C	951 296-1040	1374
Garmon Corporation (PA)	2048	D	888 628-8783	1426
Bottaia Wines LP	2084	E	951 252-1799	1559
Callaway Vineyard & Winery	2084	D	951 676-4001	1560
Europa Village LLC	2084	C	951 506-1818	1566
Falkner Winery Inc	2084	D	951 676-6741	1568

Mergent email: customerrelations@mergent.com
1352

2025 Southern California
Business Directory and Buyers Guide

(P-0000) Products & Services Section entry number
(PA)=Parent Co (HQ)=Headquarters (DH)=Div Headquarters

	SIC	EMP	PHONE	ENTRY#
Leonesse Cellars LLC	2084	E	951 302-7601	1578
Lorimar Winery	2084	E	951 240-5177	1579
Louidar LLC	2084	E	951 676-5047	1580
South Coast Winery Inc	2084	E	951 587-9463	1585
Temecula Valley Winery MGT LLC	2084	D	951 699-8896	1586
Thornton Winery	2084	D	951 699-0099	1589
Wiens Cellars LLC	2084	E	951 694-9892	1593
Wilson Creek Wnery Vnyards Inc	2084	C	951 699-9463	1594
Top Heavy Clothing Company Inc (PA)	2321	D	951 442-8839	1988
Kamm Industries Inc	2396	E	800 317-6253	2263
North County Times	2711	E	951 676-4315	2819
Village News Inc	2711	E	760 451-3488	2835
Inland Empire Media Group Inc	2721	E	951 682-3026	2861
Robinson Printing Inc	2759	E	951 296-0300	3172
Abbott Vascular Inc	2834	B	951 941-2400	3337
EMD Millipore Corporation	2836	D	951 676-8080	3572
Bostik Inc	2891	E	951 296-6425	3761
W Plastics Inc	3081	E	800 442-9727	3960
Bomatic Inc (DH)	3089	E	909 947-3900	4071
Milgard Manufacturing LLC	3089	C	480 763-6000	4170
TST Molding LLC	3089	E	951 296-6200	4265
Jeb Holdings Corp	3357	E	951 296-9900	4634
Marathon Finishing Systems Inc	3444	E	310 791-5601	5001
Sunstone Components Group Inc (HQ)	3469	E	951 296-5010	5216
Opti-Forms Inc	3471	E	951 296-1300	5281
Temecula Quality Plating Inc	3471	E	951 296-9875	5299
Scotts Temecula Operations LLC (DH)	3524	E	951 719-1700	5483
Pacific Barcode Inc	3555	E	951 587-8717	5664
Flowserve Corporation	3561	D	951 296-2464	5731
Qc Manufacturing Inc	3564	D	951 325-6340	5775
Inners Tasks LLC	3571	E	951 225-9696	5853
Infineon Tech Americas Corp	3577	A	951 375-6008	5924
Aquamor LLC (PA)	3589	D	951 541-9517	6001
Axeon Water Technologies	3589	D	760 723-5417	6003
3-D Precision Machine Inc	3599	E	951 296-5449	6055
Motorola Sltons Cnnctivity Inc (HQ)	3663	D	951 719-2100	6637
Opto 22	3679	C	951 695-3000	7034
Douglas Technologies Group Inc	3714	E	760 758-5560	7247
Ice Management Systems Inc	3728	E	951 676-2751	7496
Tesco Controls Inc	3825	D	916 395-8800	7933
EMD Millipore Corporation	3826	D	951 676-8080	7951
Transducer Techniques LLC	3829	E	951 719-3965	8070
Abbott Vascular Inc	3841	A	951 914-2400	8072
Tearlab Corporation	3841	E	858 455-6006	8235
Isomedix Operations Inc	3842	D	951 694-9340	8277
Medline Industries LP	3842	E	951 296-2600	8285
Paulson Manufacturing Corp (PA)	3842	E	951 676-2451	8295
Artificial Grass Liquidators	3999	E	951 677-3377	8660
Phs / Mwa	4581	C	951 695-1008	9206
Kaydan Logistics LLC	4789	D	951 961-9000	9367
Sprint Communications Co LP	4812	C	951 303-8501	9414
Rancho California Water Dst (PA)	4941	C	951 296-6900	9711
Bbk Performance Inc	5013	D	951 296-1771	9815
Genica Corporation	5045	B	855 433-5747	10008
R R Donnelley & Sons Company	5112	C	951 296-2890	10585
FFF Enterprises Inc (PA)	5122	B	951 296-2500	10623
Southwest Traders Incorporated (PA)	5141	C	951 699-7800	10806
Gifting Group LLC	5199	E	951 296-0310	11122
Emser Tile LLC	5211	E	951 296-3671	11153
Lowes Home Centers LLC	5211	D	951 296-1618	11224
DCH Acura of Temecula	5511	D	877 847-9532	11333
Rancho Ford Inc	5511	C	951 699-1302	11400
Celtic Bank Corporation	6141	C	951 303-3330	11851
Cal Mutual Inc	6162	D	888 700-4650	11890
Charles Schwab Corporation	6211	C	800 435-4000	11962
Kaiser Foundation Hospitals	6324	D	866 984-7483	12085
Sft Realty Galway Downs LLC	6531	C	951 232-1880	12528
Commonwealth Land Title Insur	6541	C	951 296-6289	12555
Pechanga Development Corp	7011	A	951 695-4655	12971
Pechanga Resorts Incorporated	7011	C	888 732-4264	12972
Windsor Capital Group Inc	7011	C	951 676-5656	13082
Garich Inc	7363	B	951 699-2899	13597
Maxim Healthcare Services Inc	7363	C	951 694-0100	13605
Saalex Corp	7371	B	951 543-9259	13807
Applied Statistics & MGT Inc	7372	C	951 699-4600	13883
Richman Management Corporation	7381	B	909 296-6189	14334
Identity Intelligence Group LLC	7382	C	626 522-7993	14407
Incircle LLC	7389	A	800 843-7477	14513
Edwards Theatres Circuit Inc	7832	C	951 296-0144	14936
McMillin Communities Inc	7992	A	951 506-3303	15091
Temecula Valley Hospital Inc	8062	B	951 331-2200	16224
James Rebecca Prouty Entps Inc	8082	D	951 292-9777	16399
Neighborhood Healthcare	8099	C	951 225-6400	16592

	SIC	EMP	PHONE	ENTRY#
Temecula Vly Unified Schl Dst	8211	D	951 302-5140	16826
Westview Services Inc	8331	D	951 699-0047	17077
Ameresco Solar LLC	8711	B	888 967-6527	17483
Oreq Corporation	8741	D	951 296-5076	18026
Telus Health (us) Ltd	8742	C	888 577-3784	18231
Hqe Systems Inc	8748	D	800 967-3036	18319

TEMPLE CITY, CA - Los Angeles County

	SIC	EMP	PHONE	ENTRY#
Sears Home Imprv Pdts Inc	1521	C	626 988-9134	427
California Flexrake Corp	3423	E	626 443-4026	4737
Jon Davler Inc	5999	E	626 941-6558	11689
Santa Anita Cnvlscent Hosp Rtr	8051	C	626 579-0310	15770
Exquisite Dental Technology	8071	D	626 237-0107	16317

TEMPLETON, CA - San Luis Obispo County

	SIC	EMP	PHONE	ENTRY#
Mesa Vineyard Management Inc (PA)	0762	D	805 434-4100	144
Pacific Gas and Electric Co	4911	D	805 434-4418	9600
T and B Boots Inc	5661	D	805 434-9904	11500
Twin Cities Community Hosp Inc	8011	B	805 434-3500	15492
Compass Health Inc	8051	C	805 434-3035	15597

THERMAL, CA - Riverside County

	SIC	EMP	PHONE	ENTRY#
Nissho of California Inc	0175	B	760 727-9719	46
Spates Fabricators Inc	2439	D	760 397-4122	2381
Red Earth Casino	7011	C	760 395-1200	12987

THOUSAND OAKS, CA - Ventura County

	SIC	EMP	PHONE	ENTRY#
Oltmans Construction Co	1541	B	805 495-9553	496
General Pavement Management Inc	1771	D	805 933-0909	1116
Cal-State Steel Corporation	1791	C	310 632-2772	1151
Natren Inc	2099	D	805 371-4737	1822
August Hat Company Inc (PA)	2353	E	805 983-4651	2157
Sage Publications Inc (PA)	2731	C	805 499-0721	2895
Midnight Manufacturing LLC	2833	E	714 833-6130	3319
Amgen USA Inc (HQ)	2834	D	805 447-1000	3352
Instacure Healing Products	2834	E	818 222-9600	3425
Amgen Inc (PA)	2836	A	805 447-1000	3557
Atara Biotherapeutics Inc (PA)	2836	C	805 623-4211	3561
Fujifilm Dsynth Btchnlgies Cal	2836	E	914 789-8100	3573
Fujifilm Dsynth Btchnlgies USA	2836	C	805 699-5579	3574
Ale USA Inc	3663	A	818 880-3500	6594
Custom Sensors & Tech Inc (HQ)	3679	A	805 716-0322	6988
Kavlico Corporation (DH)	3679	A	805 523-2000	7018
Maple Imaging LLC (HQ)	3679	E	805 373-4545	7023
Smiths Interconnect Inc	3679	D	805 267-0100	7050
Teledyne Technologies Inc (PA)	3679	C	805 373-4545	7058
Teledyne Lecroy Inc	3825	E	434 984-4500	7932
BEI North America LLC (DH)	3829	C	805 716-0642	8034
Carros Sensors Systems Co LLC (DH)	3829	C	805 968-0782	8038
Baxalta US Inc	3841	A	805 499-8000	8102
Implant Direct Sybron Mfg LLC	3843	C	818 444-3300	8338
Easton Hockey Inc	3949	A	818 782-6445	8516
Mv Transportation Inc	4111	C	805 557-7372	8783
Full Scale Logistics LLC	4789	D	805 279-6799	9364
Red Pocket Inc	4812	D	888 993-3888	9408
Southern California Edison Co	4911	D	818 999-1880	9639
Ultraglas Inc	5039	E	818 772-7744	9962
Tecom Industries Incorporated	5065	C	805 267-0100	10292
Penney Opco LLC	5311	D	805 497-6811	11262
Ormond Beach LP	6512	D	805 490-4948	12309
Gemmm Corporation (PA)	6531	D	805 496-0555	12456
American Recovery Service Inc (DH)	7322	C	805 379-8500	13276
Staff Assistance Inc	7361	B	805 371-9980	13574
A P R Inc	7363	C	805 379-3400	13586
Sensata Technologies Inc	7379	C	805 716-0322	14250
Carmike Cinemas LLC	7832	C	805 494-4702	14929
Bay Clubs Company LLC	7997	C	310 643-6878	15119
Los Robles Regional Med Ctr	8011	B	805 494-0880	15385
Five Star Qulty Care-CA II LLC (DH)	8051	D	805 492-2444	15653
Los Robles Regional Med Ctr (DH)	8062	A	805 497-2727	16091
Thousand Oaks Surgical Hosp LP	8062	C	805 777-7750	16228
Select Home Care	8082	D	805 777-3855	16420
Staff Assistance Inc (PA)	8082	B	818 894-7879	16424
Feld Care Therapy Inc	8093	D	818 926-9057	16474
Star of Ca LLC	8099	D	805 379-1401	16620
Westlake Oaks Healthcare LLC	8099	B	805 494-1233	16629
Rowi Usa LLC	8322	D	805 356-3372	17000
Automobile Club Southern Cal	8699	D	805 497-0911	17453
Teledyne Scentific Imaging LLC (HQ)	8731	C	805 373-4545	17828

THOUSAND PALMS, CA - Riverside County

	SIC	EMP	PHONE	ENTRY#
Conserve Landcare LLC	0781	D	760 343-1433	163
San Val Corp (PA)	0781	B	760 346-3999	190

Employee Codes: A=Over 500 employees, B=251-500
C=101-250, D=51-100, E=20-50, F=10-19, G=1-9

2025 Southern California
Business Directory and Buyers Guide

© Mergent Inc. 1-800-342-5647

1353

GEOGRAPHIC

	SIC	EMP	PHONE	ENTRY#
Jacobsson Engrg Cnstr Inc	1611	D	760 345-8700	627
10x Hvac of Ca LLC	1711	D	760 343-7488	724
Kincaid Industries Inc	1711	D	760 343-5457	794
Superior Ready Mix Concrete LP	3273	D	760 343-3418	4463
Sunline Transit Agency (PA)	4111	C	760 343-3456	8807
Readylink Inc	7361	D	760 343-7000	13564
Readylink Healthcare	7361	D	760 343-7000	13565

TOLUCA LAKE, CA - Los Angeles County

	SIC	EMP	PHONE	ENTRY#
Northwestern Inc	2431	E	818 786-1581	2316
Tre Venezie Inc	5812	D	818 985-4669	11605

TORRANCE, CA - Los Angeles County

	SIC	EMP	PHONE	ENTRY#
Finleys Tree & Landcare Inc	0781	C	310 326-9818	168
Dicaperl Corporation (DH)	1499	D	610 667-6640	385
Golden Arrow Construction Inc	1521	C	310 523-9056	406
MC&a Usa LLC	1521	D	504 267-8145	419
Taisei Construction Corporation	1541	C	714 886-1530	508
ACS Communications Inc	1731	C	310 767-2145	879
Vector Resources Inc (PA)	1731	C	310 436-1000	976
Naturalife Eco Vite Labs	2023	D	310 370-1563	1301
Shine Food (PA)	2032	E	310 329-3829	1344
Shine Food Inc	2038	D	310 533-6010	1400
Advanced Fresh Cncpts Frnchise	2092	E	310 604-3200	1700
Asiana Cuisine Enterprises Inc	2099	A	310 327-2223	1741
Just For Fun Inc	2321	E	310 320-1327	1985
Textile Unlimited Corporation (PA)	2321	D	310 263-7400	1987
Image Solutions Apparel Inc	2326	C	310 464-8991	1996
Alpinestars USA	2331	E	310 891-0222	2033
Nothing To Wear Inc (PA)	2331	E	310 328-0408	2051
Dakine Equipment LLC	2339	E	424 276-3618	2088
Tcw Trends Inc	2339	E	310 533-5177	2136
Micronova Manufacturing Inc	2392	E	310 784-6990	2217
A-Aztec Rents & Sells Inc (PA)	2394	C	310 347-3010	2233
Doug Mockett & Company Inc	2511	D	310 318-2491	2423
Virco Mfg Corporation (PA)	2531	D	310 533-0474	2555
Field Manufacturing Corp (PA)	2542	E	310 781-9292	2581
Union Carbide Corporation	2631	E	310 214-5300	2646
Bbm Fairway Inc (PA)	2721	C		2844
Bobit Business Media Inc	2721	C	310 533-2400	2845
Manson Western LLC	2731	C	424 201-8800	2892
Classic Litho & Design Inc	2752	C	310 224-5200	2979
R R Donnelley & Sons Company	2759	D	310 516-3100	3167
Retail Print Media Inc	2759	E	424 488-6950	3170
Arkema Inc	2812	E	310 214-5327	3207
Messer LLC	2813	D	310 533-8394	3219
Americas Styrenics LLC	2821	D	424 488-3757	3257
Bachem Americas Inc	2834	E	424 347-5600	3369
Bachem Americas Inc	2836	E	310 539-4171	3563
Bachem Americas Inc	2836	E	310 784-4440	3564
Bachem Americas Inc (DH)	2836	E	310 784-4440	3565
Colonial Enterprises Inc	2844	E	909 822-8700	3638
Nyx Los Angeles Inc	2844	C	323 869-9420	3673
Commerce Coating Services Inc	2851	D	310 345-1979	3709
Teledyne Reynolds Inc	2892	C	310 823-5491	3783
Lg Nanoh2o LLC	2899	E	424 218-4000	3810
Medical Chemical Corporation	2899	E	310 787-6800	3814
Prestone Products Corporation	2899	E	424 271-4836	3818
Torrance Refining Company LLC	2911	A	310 212-2800	3832
Kakuichi America Inc	3084	D	310 539-1590	3976
Kepner Plas Fabricators Inc	3089	E	562 543-4472	4153
Smart LLC	3089	E	866 822-3670	4241
Totex Manufacturing Inc	3089	E	310 326-2028	4260
Carley (PA)	3229	C	310 325-8474	4324
United States Gypsum Company	3275	D	908 232-8900	4469
Lisi Aerospace North Amer Inc	3324	A	310 326-8110	4566
Howmet Aerospace Inc	3334	B	212 836-2674	4576
Broadata Communications Inc	3357	E	310 530-1416	4627
Alliedsignal Arospc Svc Corp (HQ)	3369	D	310 323-9500	4684
Fun Properties Inc	3423	E	310 787-4500	4739
Products Engineering Corp	3423	E	310 787-4500	4745
Santec Inc	3432	E	310 542-0063	4807
Torrance Steel Window Co Inc	3442	E	310 328-9181	4904
Hi-Shear Corporation (DH)	3452	A	310 326-8110	5128
KB Delta Inc	3469	E	310 530-1539	5196
Plasma Technology Incorporated (PA)	3479	D	310 320-3373	5338
Storm Manufacturing Group Inc	3491	D	310 326-8287	5370
Magnetic Component Engrg LLC (PA)	3499	E	310 784-3100	5451
Storm Industries Inc (PA)	3523	D	310 534-5232	5478
Barranca Holdings Ltd	3545	C	310 523-5867	5606
Mk Diamond Products Inc (PA)	3546	D	310 539-5221	5636
Belhome Inc	3548	E	310 618-8437	5643
Creative Pathways Inc	3548	E	310 530-1965	5645

	SIC	EMP	PHONE	ENTRY#
Winther Technologies Inc (PA)	3548	E	310 618-8437	5650
Industrial Dynamics Co Ltd (PA)	3559	C	310 325-5633	5705
Camfil Farr Inc	3564	E	973 616-7300	5768
Bnl Technologies Inc	3572	E	310 320-7272	5874
Bixolon America Inc	3577	E	858 764-4580	5907
Lynn Products Inc	3577	A	310 530-5966	5932
Beranek LLC	3599	E	310 328-9094	6096
Ely Co Inc	3599	E	310 539-5831	6120
Ralph E Ames Machine Works	3599	E	310 328-8523	6212
Sonsray Inc	3599	E	323 585-1271	6240
Weber Drilling Co Inc	3599	E	310 670-7708	6269
Sea Electric LLC	3621	E	424 376-3660	6332
Moog Inc	3625	B	310 533-1178	6355
Breville Usa Inc	3639	E	310 755-3000	6400
Aero-Electric Connector Inc (PA)	3643	B	310 618-3737	6410
Lyncole Grunding Solutions LLC	3643	C	310 214-4000	6423
Zo Motors North America LLC	3647	C	310 792-7077	6487
All Access Stging Prdctons Inc (PA)	3648	E	310 784-2464	6488
Pelican Products Inc (PA)	3648	C	310 326-4700	6514
Funai Corporation Inc	3651	D	201 727-4560	6538
Marshall Electronics Inc (PA)	3651	D	310 333-0606	6544
Pioneer Speakers Inc	3651	A	310 952-2000	6548
Rock-Ola Manufacturing Corp	3651	D	310 328-1306	6551
Panasonic Disc Manufacturing Corpor	3652	C	310 783-4800	6577
Antcom Corporation	3663	E	310 782-1076	6597
CPI Satcom & Antenna Tech Inc	3663	B	310 539-6704	6605
Hadrian Automation Inc	3663	D	503 807-4490	6618
Lenntek Corporation	3663	E	310 534-2738	6629
Mainline Equipment Inc	3663	D	800 444-2288	6630
Navcom Technology Inc (HQ)	3663	D	310 381-2000	6639
Pacific Wave Systems Inc	3663	D	714 893-0152	6644
Ledtronics Inc (PA)	3674	E	310 534-1505	6845
Trident Space & Defense LLC	3674	E	310 214-5500	6907
Conesys Inc	3678	D	310 212-0065	6944
J - T E C H	3678	C	310 533-6700	6952
Onshore Technologies Inc	3679	E	310 533-4888	7033
Western Digital	3679	D	510 557-7553	7069
Czv Inc	3711	D	424 603-1450	7172
Canoo Inc (PA)	3714	E	424 271-2144	7234
Edelbrock LLC	3714	E	310 781-2290	7250
Motorcar Parts of America Inc (PA)	3714	A	310 212-7910	7274
Garrett Transportation I Inc (HQ)	3724	C	973 445-2000	7385
Honeywell International Inc	3724	A	310 323-9500	7387
Ace Clearwater Enterprises Inc (PA)	3728	D	310 323-2140	7398
Dasco Engineering Corp	3728	C	310 326-2277	7460
Quality Forming LLC	3728	D	310 539-2855	7544
Robinson Helicopter Co Inc (PA)	3728	B	310 539-0508	7546
K2 Space Corporation	3761	E	312 307-8930	7645
Microcosm Inc	3764	E	310 539-2306	7663
General Forming Corporation	3812	E	310 326-0624	7721
Intellisense Systems Inc	3812	C	310 320-1827	7724
Moog Inc	3812	B	310 533-1178	7744
Stellant Systems Inc (DH)	3812	A	310 517-6000	7813
Nearfield Systems Inc	3825	D	310 525-7000	7928
Pulse Instruments	3825	E	310 515-5330	7930
Phenomenex Inc (HQ)	3826	C	310 212-0555	7972
Luminit LLC	3827	E	310 320-1066	8009
Z C & R Coating For Optics Inc	3827	E	310 381-3600	8029
Proprietary Controls Systems	3829	E	310 303-3600	8059
Axiom Medical Incorporated	3841	E	310 533-9020	8099
Igenomix Usa Inc	3841	E	818 919-1657	8167
Lisi Aerospace	3841	E	310 326-8110	8185
Finest Hour Holdings Inc	3842	E	310 533-9966	8267
Rapiscan Systems Inc (HQ)	3844	C	310 978-1457	8367
Younger Mfg Co (PA)	3851	B	310 783-1533	8419
Stewart Filmscreen Corp (PA)	3861	C	310 784-5300	8444
Crislu Corp	3911	E	310 322-3444	8453
Dreamgear LLC	3944	E	310 222-5522	8483
Encore Image Group Inc (PA)	3993	D	310 534-7500	8601
George P Johnson Company	3993	E	310 965-4300	8607
Signtronix Inc	3993	E	310 534-7500	8637
Ryans Express Trnsp Svcs Inc (PA)	4119	D	310 219-2960	8846
United Parcel Service Inc	4215	D	800 742-5877	9016
Fashion Logistics Inc	4225	C	424 201-4100	9066
Express Imaging Services Inc	4226	D	888 846-8804	9134
Jtb Americas Ltd (HQ)	4724	D	310 406-3121	9226
Binex Line Corp (PA)	4731	D	310 416-8600	9254
Capable Transport Inc	4731	D	310 697-0198	9256
Ceva Freight LLC	4731	C	310 972-5500	9260
Ceva Logistics LLC	4731	E	310 223-6500	9261
Dcw Dcw Inc	4731	D	310 324-3147	9267
Expeditors Intl Wash Inc	4731	B	310 343-6200	9280
Fns Inc (PA)	4731	D	661 615-2300	9283

Mergent email: customerrelations@mergent.com
1354

2025 Southern California
Business Directory and Buyers Guide

(P-0000) Products & Services Section entry number
(PA)=Parent Co (HQ)=Headquarters (DH)=Div Headquarters

	SIC	EMP	PHONE	ENTRY#
Hitachi Transport System (america) Ltd.	4731	B	310 787-3420	9292
Kuehne + Nagel Inc	4731	B	310 641-5500	9300
Nippon Express	4731	D	310 782-3000	9318
Nippon Express USA Inc	4731	D	310 527-4237	9319
Salson Logistics Inc	4731	C	973 986-0200	9333
Outsource Utility Contr LLC	4911	A	714 238-9263	9594
American Honda Motor Co Inc (HQ)	5012	A	310 783-2000	9799
Virco Inc (HQ)	5021	E	310 533-0474	9885
New Generation Engrg Cnstr Inc	5032	E	424 329-3950	9948
Kubota Industrial Equipment	5046	C	817 756-1171	10050
Convaid Products LLC	5047	D	310 618-0111	10073
Sakura Finetek USA Inc (HQ)	5047	D	310 972-7800	10107
Shimadzu Precision Instrs Inc	5047	D	310 217-8855	10109
Pioneer North America Inc	5064	C	310 952-2000	10223
I C Class Components Corp (PA)	5065	D	310 539-5500	10251
Quinstar Technology Inc	5065	D	310 320-1111	10281
Sharp Industries Inc (PA)	5084	E	310 370-5990	10402
Pacific Echo Inc	5085	D	310 539-1822	10455
Sweis Inc (PA)	5087	C	310 375-0558	10479
Citizen Watch Company of America Inc (HQ)	5094	C	800 321-1023	10546
Pentel of America Ltd (DH)	5112	C	310 320-3831	10582
Murad LLC	5122	C	310 726-3300	10635
Weckerle Cosmetics Usa Inc	5122	E	310 328-7000	10658
Calbee America Incorporated	5145	D	310 370-2500	10842
Ezcaretech Usa Inc	5199	B	424 558-3191	11120
Lowes Home Centers LLC	5211	C	310 787-1469	11247
Pioneer Theatres Inc	5431	C	310 532-8183	11292
Jessie Lord Bakery LLC	5461	E	310 533-6010	11296
General Motors LLC	5511	E	313 556-5000	11353
Martin Chevrolet	5511	D	323 772-6494	11378
Southbay European Inc	5511	D	310 939-7300	11411
Toyota Logistics Services Inc (DH)	5511	C	310 468-4000	11421
Seville Classics Inc (PA)	5712	C	310 533-3800	11518
Enagic Usa Inc (PA)	5963	D	310 542-7700	11667
American Business Bank	6022	C	310 808-1200	11743
Happy Money Inc	6099	B	949 430-0630	11840
American Honda Finance Corp (DH)	6141	C	310 972-2239	11847
American Honda Protection Prod	6141	D	310 972-2200	11848
Mortgage Bank of California	6162	D	310 498-2700	11925
Keenan & Associates (HQ)	6411	C	310 212-3344	12225
Alpine Village	6512	C	310 327-4384	12279
AME-Gyu Co Ltd	6719	A	310 214-9572	12592
Navitas Semiconductor Corp	6799	B	844 654-2642	12722
Ctc Group Inc (DH)	7011	C	310 540-0500	12804
Kintetsu Enterprises Co Amer (HQ)	7011	C	310 782-9300	12885
Long Beach Golden Sails Inc	7011	D	562 596-1631	12905
Msr Hotels & Resorts Inc	7011	C	310 543-4566	12932
V Todays Inc	7011	C	310 781-9100	13063
Wash Mltfmily Ldry Systems LLC (PA)	7215	C	800 421-6897	13131
Saatchi & Saatchi N Amer LLC	7311	C	310 437-2500	13244
Lomita Logistics LLC	7331	D	310 784-8485	13303
Flagship Airport Services Inc	7349	D	310 328-8221	13374
Resource Collection Inc	7349	E	310 219-3272	13413
Bright Event Rentals LLC (PA)	7359	C	310 202-0011	13448
Choura Events	7359	D	310 320-6200	13450
Classic/Prime Inc	7359	C	310 328-5060	13452
Act 1 Group Inc (PA)	7361	D	310 750-3400	13483
Prime One Inc	7361	C	310 378-1944	13557
Platinum Empire Group Inc	7363	C	310 821-5888	13617
Good Sports Plus Ltd	7371	B	310 671-4400	13739
BQE Software Inc	7372	D	310 602-4020	13896
Epirus Inc	7372	C	310 620-8678	13925
Nc4 Coltra LLC	7372	D	108 180 5570	13982
CCII Incorporated	7374	A	310 800-0800	14125
Delta Computer Consulting	7379	C	310 541-9440	14213
Cornerstone Protective Svcs	7381	C	888 848-4791	14289
US Security Associates Inc	7381	C	714 352-0773	14363
Contemporary Services Corp	7382	B	310 320-8418	14388
Bankcard Services (PA)	7389	C	213 365-1122	14458
Credit Card Services Inc (PA)	7389	D	213 365-1122	14485
Docmagic Inc	7389	D	800 649-1362	14491
Ocs America Inc (DH)	7389	E	310 417-0650	14561
Singer Vehicle Design LLC (PA)	7549	C	213 592-2728	14719
Aeroworx Inc	7699	E	310 891-0300	14754
Redman Equipment & Mfg Co	7699	E	310 329-1134	14787
Insite Digestive Health Care	8011	E	626 817-2900	15333
Genesis Healthcare LLC	8051	B	310 370-3594	15664
Geri-Care Inc	8051	D	310 320-0961	15665
Mariner Health Care Inc	8051	C	310 371-4628	15711
Torrance Care Center West Inc	8051	D	310 370-4561	15786
Geri-Care II Inc	8059	C	310 328-0812	15855
Cedars-Sinai Medical Center	8062	A	310 967-1900	15945
Little Company Mary Hospital	8062	A	310 540-7676	16074

	SIC	EMP	PHONE	ENTRY#
Little Company of Mary Health Services	8062	A	310 540-7676	16075
Torrance Health Assn Inc (PA)	8062	A	310 325-9110	16229
Torrance Memorial Medical Ctr (HQ)	8062	A	310 325-9110	16230
Torrance Memorial Medical Ctr.	8062	B	310 784-6316	16232
Torrance Memorial Medical Ctr.	8062	B	310 784-3740	16233
Polypeptide Laboratories Inc (DH)	8071	E	310 782-3569	16327
Gky Dental Arts Inc (PA)	8072	D	310 214-8007	16342
Premier Infsion Hlthcare Svcs	8082	D	310 328-3897	16413
Harbor-Ucla Med Foundation Inc	8092	A	310 533-0413	16435
Clear Recovery Center	8093	B	310 318-2122	16456
Del AMO Hospital Inc	8093	B	310 530-1151	16467
Pediatric Therapy Network	8093	C	310 328-0276	16488
365 Hlthcare Staffing Svcs Inc	8099	D	310 436-3650	16523
Compex Legal Services Inc (PA)	8111	C	310 782-1801	16658
Harbor Dvlpmntal Dsblties Fndt.	8399	D	310 540-1711	17228
Orthalliance Inc.	8399	A	310 792-1300	17238
21515 Hawthorne Owner LLC	8641	D	310 406-3730	17320
Public Hlth Fndation Entps Inc	8641	C	310 320-5215	17362
Young MNS Chrstn Assn Mtro Los.	8641	D	310 325-5885	17405
Automobile Club Southern Cal.	8699	C	310 325-3111	17440
Divergent Technologies Inc (PA)	8711	B	424 542-2158	17514
International Energy Services USA Inc.	8711	C	310 257-8222	17558
Sonic Industries Inc.	8711	D	310 532-8382	17633
Hotta Liesenberg Saito LLP.	8721	D	424 246-2000	17734
Opto-Knowledge Systems Inc.	8731	E	310 756-0520	17817
Honda R&D Americas LLC	8732	A	310 781-5500	17848
Lundquist Institute For Biomedical	8733	A	877 452-2674	17881
Als Group Usa Corp.	8734	D	310 214-0043	17901
Daicel America Holdings Inc.	8741	B	480 798-6737	17980
Harbor-Ucla Med Foundation Inc (PA).	8741	D	310 222-5015	17990
Proactive Risk Management Inc.	8741	D	213 840-8856	18037
Dcw Dcw Inc.	8742	D	310 858-1050	18125
Pathology Inc.	8742	B	310 769-0561	18191
Guardian Group Intl LLC (HQ)	8748	C	310 320-0320	18316
Midnight Sun Enterprises Inc.	8748	D	310 532-2427	18335

TRABUCO CANYON, CA - Orange County

	SIC	EMP	PHONE	ENTRY#
Seeds of Change Inc.	5191	C	310 764-7700	11071
Total Recon Solutions Inc.	8742	D	949 584-8417	18233

TRONA, CA - San Bernardino County

	SIC	EMP	PHONE	ENTRY#
Searles Valley Minerals Inc.	1479	C	760 372-2259	381
Searles Valley Minerals Inc.	1479	C	760 672-2053	382
Trona Railway Company.	4011	B	760 372-2312	8744

TUJUNGA, CA - Los Angeles County

	SIC	EMP	PHONE	ENTRY#
American Foothill Pubg Co Inc.	2759	E	818 352-7878	3115
David Kopf Instruments.	3841	E	818 352-3274	8140
Vons Companies Inc.	5411	C	818 353-9100	11285
Volunteers of Amer Los Angeles	8322	D	818 352-5974	17032
Crescenta-Canada YMCA	8641	D	818 352-3255	17339

TUPMAN, CA - Kern County

	SIC	EMP	PHONE	ENTRY#
Midstream Energy Partners USA	1231	E	661 765-4087	260

TUSTIN, CA - Orange County

	SIC	EMP	PHONE	ENTRY#
Superior Sod I LP.	0181	C	909 923-5068	70
R Ranch Market.	0291	B	714 573-1182	97
Tricon American Homes LLC.	1521	C	844 874-2661	434
US Best Repair Service Inc.	1521	C	888 750-2378	437
Healthcare Design & Cnstr LLC.	1542	D	714 245-0144	544
Bergelectric Corp.	1731	D	949 250-7005	891
Brigg Elcctrie Inc (PA)	1731	D	714 644 2500	892
Largo Concrete Inc (PA)	1771	D	714 731-3600	1125
NMN Construction Inc.	1771	D	714 389-2104	1128
Dawn Food Products LLC.	2051	C	714 258-1223	1441
Raj Manufacturing LLC.	2339	E	714 838-3110	2128
Custom Quilting Inc.	2392	E	714 731-7271	2209
GL Woodworking Inc.	2431	D	949 515-2192	2307
Sheward & Son & Sons (PA)	2591	C	714 556-6055	2607
Durabag Company Inc.	2673	D	714 259-8811	2731
Landscape Communications Inc.	2721	E	714 979-5276	2864
Colbi Technologies Inc.	2741	C	714 505-9544	2908
Diversified Printers Inc.	2741	D	714 994-3400	2912
Meridian Graphics Inc.	2752	D	949 833-3500	3043
Precision Offset Inc.	2752	D	949 752-1714	3065
Bjb Enterprises Inc.	2821	E	714 734-8450	3260
Avid Bioservices Inc (PA)	2834	C	714 508-6100	3364
Avid Bioservices Inc.	2834	E	714 508-6000	3365
Avid Bioservices Inc.	2834	E	714 508-6166	3366
Vitatech Nutritional Sciences Inc.	2834	B	714 832-9700	3520
Design West Technologies Inc.	3089	D	714 731-0201	4101
Ronco Plastics Inc.	3089	E	714 259-1385	4225

Employee Codes: A=Over 500 employees, B=251-500
C=101-250, D=51-100, E=20-50, F=10-19, G=1-9

2025 Southern California
Business Directory and Buyers Guide

© Mergent Inc. 1-800-342-5647
1355

GEOGRAPHIC

	SIC	EMP	PHONE	ENTRY#
Ifiber Optix Inc	3229	E	714 665-9796	4327
Braxton Caribbean Mfg Co Inc	3469	D	714 508-3570	5177
Johnston International Corporation	3569	E	714 542-4487	5825
Add-On Cmpt Peripherals LLC	3572	D	949 546-8200	5872
LGarde Inc	3572	E	714 259-0771	5882
Add-On Cmpt Peripherals LLC	3577	C	949 546-8200	5898
Compass Water Solutions Inc (HQ)	3589	E	949 222-5777	6011
Expert Assembly Services Inc	3672	E	714 258-8880	6727
Distribution Electrnics Vlued	3699	E	714 368-1717	7119
Millenworks	3711	D	714 426-5500	7185
Rivian Automotive LLC	3711	D	888 748-4261	7190
89908 Inc	3714	E	949 221-0023	7214
Virgin Galactic Holdings Inc (PA)	3761	E	949 774-7640	7661
Motionloft Inc	3826	E	415 580-7671	7969
Terumo Americas Holding Inc	3826	E	714 258-8001	7984
Coherent Aerospace & Def Inc	3827	D	714 247-7100	7998
Lightworks Optics Inc	3827	E	714 247-7100	8008
Pvp Advanced Eo Systems Inc (DH)	3827	E	714 508-2740	8016
Issac Medical Inc	3841	B	805 239-4284	8176
Trellborg Sling Sltions US Inc (DH)	3841	C	714 415-0280	8240
Stanley G Alexander Inc (PA)	4213	C	714 731-1658	8974
Schick Moving & Storage Co (PA)	4214	D	714 731-5500	8995
Cellco Partnership	4812	C	714 258-8870	9389
AB Cellular Holding LLC	4813	A	562 468-6846	9425
Trinity Brdcstg Netwrk Inc	4833	C	714 665-3619	9519
Lsf9 Cypress Parent 2 LLC	5039	A	714 380-3127	9961
Syspro Impact Software Inc	5045	C	714 437-1000	10033
Canon Medical Systems USA Inc (DH)	5047	B	714 730-5000	10072
Ecosense Lighting Inc	5063	C	714 823-1014	10182
Mobile Line Communications Corporation	5065	D		10268
Pphm Inc	5122	E	714 508-6100	10646
M & S Trading Inc	5136	D	714 241-7190	10687
Ansar Gallery Inc	5141	C	949 220-0000	10743
Republic Nat Distrg Co LLC (PA)	5182	C	714 368-4615	11060
Youngs Interco Inc	5182	A	714 368-4615	11064
Youngs Market Company LLC (HQ)	5182	B	800 317-6150	11066
99 Cents Only Stores LLC (HQ)	5199	B	323 980-8145	11107
Logomark Inc	5199	C	714 675-6100	11128
Lowes Home Centers LLC	5211	C	714 913-2663	11207
Nissan of Tustin	5511	C	714 669-8282	11387
Provenza Floors Inc (PA)	5713	D	949 788-0900	11524
Dickeys Barbecue Rest Inc	5812	E	714 602-3874	11565
Yebo Group LLC	5943	C	949 502-3317	11637
Diamond Goldenwest Corporation (PA)	5944	C	714 542-9000	11638
Schoolsfirst Federal Credit Un	6061	D	480 777-5995	11814
New American Funding LLC (PA)	6141	A	949 430-7029	11858
Southern Cal Prmnnte Med Group	6324	C	714 734-4500	12107
Burnham Bnefits Insur Svcs LLC	6411	D	310 370-5000	12184
Wood Gutmann Bogart Insur Brkg	6411	D	714 505-7000	12273
Wood Gutmann Bogart Insur Brks	6411	C	714 505-7000	12274
Irvine APT Communities LP	6513	B	714 505-7181	12351
Steadfast Management Co Inc	6513	C	714 542-2229	12367
First Team RE - Orange Cnty	6531	B	714 544-5456	12452
Crestmont Capital LLC	6799	C	949 537-3882	12704
Maverick Hospitality Inc	7011	D	714 730-7717	12919
Orange County Direct Mail Inc	7331	E	714 444-4412	13304
Crown Building Maintenance Co	7349	B	714 434-9494	13368
B2 Services Llc	7361	D	714 363-3481	13490
Professnl Rgistry Netwrk Corp	7361	D	714 832-5776	13558
Pts Advance	7361	C	949 268-4000	13560
A P R Consulting Inc	7379	A	714 544-3696	14192
Rjn Investigations Inc	7381	C	951 686-7638	14335
Autocrib Inc	7389	C	714 274-0400	14455
Coastal Intl Holdings LLC	7389	B	714 635-1200	14475
Specright Inc	7389	C	866 290-6952	14601
Caliber Bodyworks Texas LLC	7532	C	714 665-3905	14672
Allied Lube Inc	7538	C	949 651-8814	14685
Alta Hospitals System LLC	8062	A	714 619-7700	15906
Foothill Regional Medical Ctr	8062	C	310 943-4500	15998
Health Investment Corporation	8062	A	714 669-2085	16013
Kaiser Foundation Hospitals	8062	C	951 353-4000	16058
Pacific Health Corporation	8062	A	714 838-9600	16112
Core Holdings Inc	8082	C	714 969-2342	16382
Encompass Health Corporation	8093	C	714 832-9200	16471
Roman Cthlic Diocese of Orange	8211	C	714 544-1533	16822
Tustin Unified School District	8211	C	714 542-4271	16827
Crown Golf Properties LP	8742	C	714 730-1611	18123

TWENTYNINE PALMS, CA - San Bernardino County

	SIC	EMP	PHONE	ENTRY#
Mark Clemons	4213	C	760 361-1531	8964
Marine Corps United States	8062	B	760 830-6000	16093
United States Dept of Navy	8099	D	760 830-2124	16623

UNIVERSAL CITY, CA - Los Angeles County

	SIC	EMP	PHONE	ENTRY#
Sprint Communications Co LP	4813	C	818 755-7100	9459
Nbcuniversal Media LLC	4832	A	818 777-1000	9485
NBC Subsidiary (knbc-Tv) LLC	4833	C	818 684-5746	9512
Universal Stdios Licensing LLC	6794	C	818 695-1273	12680
Lh Universal Operating LLC	7011	B	818 980-1212	12900
Shen Zhen New World II LLC	7011	D	818 980-1212	13021
Sun Hill Properties Inc	7011	B	818 506-2500	13040
Universal Mus Group Dist Corp	7389	C	818 508-9550	14619
NBC Universal Inc	7812	A		14840
Universal City Studios Lllp	7812	A	818 622-8477	14865
Universal Cy Stdios Prdctons L (DH)	7812	E	818 777-1000	14866
Universal Pctres HM Entrmt LLC (DH)	7812	D	818 777-1000	14867
Creative Park Productions LLC	7822	C	818 622-3702	14916
NBC Studios Inc	7922	A	818 777-1000	14966

UPLAND, CA - San Bernardino County

	SIC	EMP	PHONE	ENTRY#
California Skateparks	0781	C	909 949-1601	161
California Ldscp & Design Inc	0782	C	909 949-1601	201
Lewis Companies (PA)	1531	C	909 985-0971	464
Vci Construction LLC (HQ)	1623	D	909 946-0905	704
Largo Concrete Inc	1771	C	909 981-7844	1124
Judith Von Hopf Inc	2541	E	909 481-1884	2567
CCL Label Inc	2759	D	909 608-2655	3127
CCL Label (delaware) Inc	2759	B	909 608-2260	3128
Holliday Trucking Inc (PA)	3273	D	909 982-1553	4443
Dimic Steel Tech Inc	3444	E	909 946-6767	4980
Lock-Ridge Tool Company Inc	3469	D	909 865-8309	5199
Charles Meisner Inc	3544	E	909 946-8216	5572
Light Vast Inc	3648	E	800 358-0499	6508
Feathersoft Inc	3652	E	925 230-0740	6575
Walton Electric Corporation	3669	C	909 981-5051	6698
Gar Enterprises	3679	E	909 985-4575	6999
Process Insghts - Gded Wave In	3823	E	919 264-9651	7873
Applied Instrument Tech Inc	3826	E	909 204-3700	7937
Dependble Break Rm Sltions Inc	5046	D	909 982-5933	10042
Lowes Home Centers LLC	5211	C	909 982-4795	11213
Park Place Ford LLC	5511	D	909 946-5555	11393
Diamond Ridge Corporation	6531	C	909 949-0605	12430
Lewis Group of Companies	6552	B	909 985-0971	12569
Employnet Inc	7361	A	909 458-0961	13513
Master Lightning SEC Solutions	7381	D	626 337-2915	14317
Shield Security Inc	7381	B	909 920-1173	14344
Sela Healthcare Inc (PA)	8051	C	909 985-1981	15774
Upland Community Care Inc	8051	B	909 985-1903	15789
San Antonio Regional Hospital (PA)	8062	A	909 985-2811	16166
Inland Vly DRG Alchol Rcvery S (PA)	8093	D	909 932-1069	16480
Victoria Place Community Assn	8699	D	909 981-4131	17473
Garrett J Gentry Gen Engrg Inc	8711	D	909 693-3391	17536
Lewis Management Corp	8741	C	909 985-0971	18005
Lexxiom Inc	8741	B	909 581-7313	18006

VALENCIA, CA - Los Angeles County

	SIC	EMP	PHONE	ENTRY#
Gothic Landscaping Inc	0781	C	661 257-5085	170
Landscape Development Inc (PA)	0782	B	661 295-1970	217
California Strl Concepts Inc	1542	C	661 257-6903	527
Summer Systems Inc	1542	D	661 257-4419	590
Awhap Acquisition Corp	1711	C	888 611-4328	746
AAA Elctrcal Cmmunications Inc (PA)	1731	C	800 892-4784	878
Sound River Corporation	1731	D	661 705-3700	962
Weslar Inc	1751	D	661 702-1362	1066
JT Wimsatt Contg Co Inc (PA)	1771	B	661 775-8090	1123
Lief Organics LLC (PA)	2023	E	661 775-2500	1300
Bestway Sandwiches Inc (PA)	2051	E	818 361-1800	1437
Chocolates A La Carte Inc	2064	C	661 257-3700	1502
King Henrys Inc	2096	C	818 536-3692	1725
Universal Hosiery Inc	2252	D	661 702-8444	1910
Contractors Wardrobe Inc (PA)	2431	C	661 257-1177	2301
Legacy Commercial Holdings Inc	2511	E	818 767-6626	2429
Fruit Growers Supply Company (PA)	2653	C	888 997-4855	2666
Precision Dynamics Corporation (HQ)	2672	C	818 897-1111	2725
Bertelsmann Inc	2731	A	661 702-2700	2884
Nextclientcom Inc	2741	E	661 222-7755	2931
Parrot Communications Intl Inc	2741	E	818 567-4700	2933
Delta Printing Solutions Inc	2752	C	661 257-0584	3000
Ta Aerospace Co	2821	C	661 702-0448	3295
Mastey De Paris Inc	2844	E	661 257-4814	3669
Solevy Co LLC	2844	D	661 622-4880	3687
Utak Laboratories Inc	2869	E	661 294-3935	3741
PRC - Desoto International Inc (HQ)	2891	B	661 678-4209	3775
Leonards Molded Products Inc	3069	E	661 253-2227	3923
Ta Aerospace Co (DH)	3069	C	661 775-1100	3939
Timemed Labeling Systems Inc (DH)	3069	D	818 897-1111	3940

2025 Southern California
Business Directory and Buyers Guide

(P-0000) Products & Services Section entry number
(PA)=Parent Co (HQ)=Headquarters (DH)=Div Headquarters

	SIC	EMP	PHONE	ENTRY#
Valencia Pipe Company	3084	E	661 257-3923	3980
King Bros Enterprises LLC	3088	C	661 257-3262	4029
Canyon Plastics LLC	3089	D	800 350-6325	4081
King Bros Industries	3089	C		4154
US Horizon Manufacturing Inc	3211	E	661 775-1675	4319
Technifex Products LLC	3291	E	661 294-3800	4485
Sgl Technic LLC (DH)	3295	E	661 257-0500	4489
Galaxy Die and Engineering Inc	3366	E	661 775-9301	4680
Avibank Mfg Inc	3429	D	661 257-2329	4757
Pacific Lock Company (PA)	3429	E	661 294-3707	4786
Hydro Systems Inc (PA)	3431	D	661 775-0686	4798
RAH Industries Inc (PA)	3444	C	661 295-5190	5027
Stoll Metalcraft Inc	3444	E	661 295-0401	5041
Valley Precision Met Pdts Inc	3444	C	661 607-0100	5052
Lavi Industries LLC (PA)	3446	D	877 275-5284	5068
Bloomers Metal Stampings Inc	3469	E	661 257-2955	5176
Pacific Metal Stampings Inc	3469	E	661 257-7656	5207
Nasmyth Tmf Inc	3471	C	818 954-9504	5278
Curtiss-Wright Flow Control	3491	C	626 851-3100	5364
Electrofilm Mfg Co LLC	3492	D	661 257-2242	5373
Industrial Tube Company LLC	3492	D	661 295-4000	5375
Senior Operations LLC	3492	D	818 350-8499	5377
G-G Distribution & Dev Co Inc	3494	C	661 257-5700	5387
Circle W Enterprises Inc	3496	E	661 257-2400	5403
Whitmor Plstic Wire Cable Corp	3496	E	661 257-2400	5421
LA Turbine (HQ)	3511	D	661 294-8290	5458
Sdi Industries Inc (DH)	3535	C	818 890-6002	5518
Gruber Systems Inc	3544	E	661 257-0464	5582
Schrey & Sons Mold Co Inc	3544	E	661 294-2260	5598
ASC Process Systems Inc (PA)	3559	E	818 833-0088	5690
Next Point Bearing Group LLC	3562	E	818 988-1880	5751
Indu-Electric North Amer Inc (PA)	3568	E	310 578-2144	5810
Western Filter A Division of Donald	3569	E	661 295-0800	5837
Synergy Microsystems Inc	3571	C	858 452-0020	5869
Transparent Products Inc	3575	E	661 294-9787	5897
Aquafine Corporation (HQ)	3589	D	661 257-4770	6000
N/S Corporation (PA)	3589	D	310 412-7074	6025
Qmp Inc	3589	E	661 294-6860	6029
Crissair Inc	3594	C	661 367-3300	6050
Bayless Manufacturing LLC	3599	C	661 257-3373	6093
Classic Wire Cut Company Inc	3599	C	661 257-0558	6106
Performance Machine Tech Inc	3599	E	661 294-8617	6202
True Position Technologies LLC	3599	D	661 294-0030	6256
SMI Holdings Inc	3621	E	800 232-2612	6334
M W Sausse & Co Inc (PA)	3625	D	661 257-3311	6353
Capax Technologies Inc	3629	E	661 257-7666	6369
Steril-Aire Inc	3648	E	818 565-1128	6517
A & M Electronics Inc	3672	E	661 257-3680	6702
Advanced Semiconductor Inc	3674	E	818 982-1200	6794
Asi Semiconductor Inc	3674	E	818 982-1200	6802
Lockwood Industries LLC (HQ)	3674	C	661 702-6999	6846
Semiconductor Process Eqp LLC	3674	E	661 257-0934	6888
Interconnect Solutions Co LLC	3679	C	661 295-0020	7010
Iwerks Entertainment Inc	3699	D	661 678-1800	7129
Mye Technologies Inc	3699	E	661 964-0217	7135
Air Flow Research Heads Inc	3714	E	661 257-8124	7221
Del West Engineering Inc (PA)	3714	C	661 295-5700	7244
Donaldson Company Inc	3714	E	661 295-0800	7246
Adept Fasteners Inc (PA)	3728	C	661 257-6600	7405
Aero Engineering & Mfg Co LLC	3728	D	661 295-0875	7408
Aerospace Dynamics Intl Inc (DH)	3728	C	661 257-3535	7413
Avantus Aerospace (DH)	3728	C	661 295-8620	7438
Canyon Engineering Pdts Inc	3728	D	661 294-0084	7449
Flight Line Products Inc	3728	E	661 775-8366	7477
Forrest Machining LLC	3728	C	661 257-0231	7479
ITT Aerospace Controls LLC (HQ)	3728	D	315 568-7258	7505
ITT Aerospace Controls LLC	3728	B	661 295-4000	7506
Sunvair Inc (HQ)	3728	E	661 294-3777	7570
Triumph Acttion Systems - Vlnc	3728	C	661 702-7537	7583
L3 Technologies Inc	3812	C	818 367-0111	7731
Ronan Engineering Company (PA)	3823	D	661 702-1344	7876
Eckert Zegler Isotope Pdts Inc (HQ)	3829	C	661 309-1010	8039
Boston Scientific Corporation	3841	E	800 678-2575	8114
Vertiflex Inc	3841	E	442 325-5900	8247
Advanced Bionics Corporation (HQ)	3842	C	661 362-1400	8250
Boston Scntfic Nrmdlation Corp (HQ)	3842	B	661 949-4310	8255
Talladium Inc (PA)	3843	D	661 295-0900	8360
Bioness Inc	3845	C	661 362-4850	8372
Palyon Medical Corporation	3845	E		8395
Remo Inc (PA)	3931	B	661 294-5600	8471
Cornerstone Display Group Inc	3993	D	661 705-1700	8595
Ram Board Inc	3996	E	818 848-0400	8654
Medical Brkthrugh Mssage Chirs	3999	E	408 677-7702	8699

	SIC	EMP	PHONE	ENTRY#
Softub Inc (PA)	3999	D	858 602-1920	8726
Sunstar Spa Covers Inc (HQ)	3999	E	858 602-1950	8731
Technical Manufacturing W LLC	3999	D	661 295-7226	8734
Central States Logistics Inc	4212	D	661 295-7222	8900
D C Shower Doors Inc	4213	C	661 257-1177	8942
Advantage Media Services Inc	4225	C	661 705-7588	9047
Advantage Media Services Inc (PA)	4783	C	661 775-0611	9352
Nexus Is Inc	4899	B	704 969-2200	9568
Southern California Edison Co	4911	C	661 607-0207	9627
Southern California Gas Co	4924	C	800 427-2200	9652
Whi Solutions Inc	5045	C	661 257-2120	10039
American Med & Hosp Sup Co Inc	5047	E	661 294-1213	10059
Avita Medical Americas LLC	5047	C	661 367-9170	10066
Klm Laboratories Inc	5047	C	661 295-2600	10088
Shield-Denver Health Care Ctr (HQ)	5047	C	661 294-4200	10108
Sunco Lighting Inc	5063	E	844 334-9938	10209
Cicoil LLC	5065	C	661 295-1295	10238
Novacap LLC (HQ)	5065	C	661 295-5920	10274
Tape Specialty Inc	5065	E	661 702-9030	10289
Allied International LLC	5072	E	818 364-2333	10300
Green Convergence (PA)	5074	D	661 294-9495	10320
Harvey Performance Company LLC	5084	C	661 467-0440	10375
Malys of California Inc	5087	B	661 295-8317	10476
Air Frame Mfg & Supply Co Inc	5088	E	661 257-7728	10483
Falcon Aerospace Holdings LLC	5088	A	661 775-7200	10491
Regent Aerospace Corporation (PA)	5088	C	661 257-3000	10499
Wesco Aircraft Hardware Corp	5088	B	661 775-7200	10506
N Qiagen Amercn Holdings Inc (HQ)	5122	C	800 426-8157	10636
Star Nail Products Inc	5122	C	661 257-3376	10653
Sunkist Growers Inc (PA)	5148	C	661 290-8900	10919
Simpson Labs LLC	5149	C	661 347-4348	10979
Bluemark Inc	5199	C	323 230-0770	11113
Magic Acquisition Corp	5511	B	661 382-4700	11376
Dharma Ventures Group Inc (PA)	5999	B	661 294-4200	11681
City National Bank	6021	C	661 291-3160	11723
Merrill Lynch Prce Fnner Smith	6211	D	661 802-0764	11978
Mercury Insurance Company	6331	A	661 291-6470	12128
Farmers Insurance	6411	C	661 257-0844	12210
Maxim Healthcare Services Inc	7363	D	661 964-6350	13609
Krg Technologies Inc (PA)	7371	B	661 257-9967	13760
Infogen Labs Inc	7379	D	323 816-4813	14224
Fpk Security Inc	7381	B	661 702-9091	14300
ADT LLC	7382	C	818 373-6200	14377
Hrd Aero Systems Inc (PA)	7699	C	661 295-0670	14772
Russell-Warner Inc	7699	C	661 257-9200	14788
Sunvair Aerospace Group Inc (PA)	7699	D	661 294-3777	14794
Heritage Golf Group LLC	7992	C	661 254-4401	15084
Six Flags Magic Mountain Inc	7996	D	661 255-4100	15109
Henry Mayo Newhall Mem Hosp	8011	D	661 253-8400	15322
Henry Mayo Newhall Mem Hosp (PA)	8062	A	661 253-8000	16017
Henry Mayo Nwhall Mem Hlth Fnd	8062	A	661 253-8000	16018
Q Squared Solutions LLC	8071	D	919 405-2248	16330
Specialty Laboratories Inc (DH)	8071	A	661 799-6543	16335
Volunteers of Amer Los Angeles	8322	C	661 290-2829	17031
Automobile Club Southern Cal	8699	C	661 259-6222	17449
Scicon Technologies Corp (PA)	8711	E	661 295-8630	17627
Advantage Media Services Inc	8742	C	661 775-0611	18086
Fdsi Logistics LLC	8742	D	818 971-3300	18134
Nusano Inc	8742	D	424 270-9600	18185
Q Squared Solutions LLC	8742	D	661 964-6635	18198
Scorpion Design LLC (PA)	8742	A	661 702-0100	18205
Geologics Corporation	8748	C	661 259-5767	18313

VALLEY CENTER, CA - San Diego County

	SIC	EMP	PHONE	ENTRY#
Brax Company Inc	1781	E	760 749-2209	1142
Mercy Medical Trnsp Inc	4119	C	760 739-8026	8840
Hcal LLC	7011	D	760 751-3100	12847
San Psqual Band Mssion Indians	7011	C	760 291-5500	13012
Survival Systems Intl Inc (PA)	7699	D	760 749-6800	14795
Caesars Entrtnment Oprting Inc	7999	A	760 751-3100	15195
Indian Health Council Inc (PA)	8011	D	760 749-1410	15330
Neighborhood Healthcare	8011	D	760 742-9919	15403
San Psqual Band Mssion Indians (PA)	9131	D	760 749-3200	18385

VALLEY VILLAGE, CA - Los Angeles County

	SIC	EMP	PHONE	ENTRY#
Douglas Steel Supply Inc (PA)	5051	D	323 587-7676	10133
Afm & Sg-Ftra Intllctual Prprt	7389	D	818 255-7980	14438
Zeus Networks LLC	7929	C	323 910-4420	15010
Healthy Medical Solutions Inc	8099	D	818 974-1980	16567
Adat ARI El	8211	C	818 766-4992	16800

VAN NUYS, CA - Los Angeles County

	SIC	EMP	PHONE	ENTRY#
Parkwood Landscape Maint Inc	0782	D	818 988-9677	230

Employee Codes: A=Over 500 employees, B=251-500
C=101-250, D=51-100, E=20-50, F=10-19, G=1-9

2025 Southern California
Business Directory and Buyers Guide

© Mergent Inc. 1-800-342-5647

1357

GEOGRAPHIC

	SIC	EMP	PHONE	ENTRY#
Energy Enterprises USA Inc (PA)	1711	D	424 339-0005	777
Eberhard	1761	C	818 782-4604	1081
Asacrete Inc	1771	C	818 398-3400	1102
Mp Aero LLC	1799	D	818 901-9828	1217
Bubbles Baking Company	2051	E	818 786-1700	1438
Danish Baking Co Inc	2051	D	818 786-1700	1440
SGB Better Baking Co LLC	2051	D	818 787-9992	1464
SGB Bubbles Baking Co LLC	2051	D	818 786-1700	1465
Western Bagel Baking Corp (PA)	2051	C	818 786-5847	1472
Aspire Bakeries LLC	2052	B	818 904-8230	1478
Power Brands Consulting LLC	2082	E	818 989-9646	1550
Chef Merito LLC (PA)	2099	E	818 787-0100	1754
Rof LLC	2326	E	818 933-4000	2001
Kandy Kiss of California Inc	2331	D		2042
Leigh Jerry California Inc (PA)	2361	C	818 909-6200	2166
Danmer Inc	2431	C	516 670-5125	2302
I and E Cabinets Inc	2434	E	818 933-6480	2350
Cpp/Belwin Inc	2731	D	818 891-5999	2886
The Full Void 2 Inc	2731	B	818 891-5999	2897
Niknejad Inc	2752	E	310 477-0407	3050
Pegasus Interprint Inc	2752	E	800 926-9873	3058
Printrunner LLC	2752	E	888 296-5760	3068
Digital Room Holdings Inc (HQ)	2759	D	310 575-4440	3136
Great Western Packaging LLC	2759	D	818 464-3800	3142
Investment Enterprises Inc (PA)	2759	D	818 464-3800	3148
Mpm Building Services Inc	2842	E	818 708-9676	3615
Orly International Inc (PA)	2844	D	818 994-1001	3675
Prolabs Factory Inc	2844	E	818 646-3677	3684
Munchkin Inc (PA)	3085	C	800 344-2229	3983
Neopacific Holdings Inc	3089	E	818 786-2900	4177
Rwh Inc	3273	E	818 782-2350	4455
Thompson Gundrilling Inc	3321	E	323 873-4045	4560
Consolidated Fabricators Corp (PA)	3443	C	800 635-8335	4913
Broadway AC Htg & Shtmtl	3444	E	818 781-1477	4960
Dayton Rogers of California Inc	3469	C	763 784-7714	5181
Enterprises Industries Inc	3469	E	818 989-6103	5185
Capstone Dstr Spport Svcs Corp (PA)	3511	C	818 734-5300	5455
Data Lights Rigging LLC	3613	E	818 786-0536	6304
Technoconcepts Inc	3663	E	818 988-3364	6663
Advanced Circuits Inc	3672	E	818 345-1993	6706
Photo Fabricators Inc	3672	D	818 781-1010	6763
Alyn Industries Inc	3679	D	818 988-7696	6964
Cicon Engineering Inc (PA)	3679	C	818 909-6060	6982
Microfabrica Inc	3679	E	888 964-2763	7025
Wsw Corp (PA)	3714	E	818 989-5008	7310
Gulfstream Aerospace Corp GA	3721	B	805 236-5755	7357
Aeroshear Aviation Svcs Inc (PA)	3728	E	818 779-1650	7411
Edo Communications and Countermeasu	3812	D	818 464-2475	7716
L3harris Technologies Inc	3812	B	818 901-2523	7732
Rizzo Inc	3842	E	818 781-6891	8297
Wbi Inc	3861	A	800 673-4968	8446
Allison-Kaufman Co	3911	D	818 373-5100	8448
Shelcore Inc (PA)	3944	E	818 883-2400	8495
Neiman/Hoeller Inc	3993	E	818 781-8600	8620
Keolis Transit America Inc	4111	C	818 616-5254	8757
Mv Transportation Inc	4111	C	818 374-9145	8780
American Prof Ambulance Corp	4119	D	818 996-2200	8812
Medresponse Inc	4119	C	818 442-9222	8837
United Parcel Service Inc	4215	B	404 828-6000	9014
Moulton Logistics Management	4225	C	818 997-1800	9090
Aero Technologies Inc (PA)	4522	C	323 745-2376	9179
Pegasus Elite Aviation Inc	4522	C	818 742-6666	9182
Clay Lacy Aviation Inc (PA)	4581	B	818 989-2900	9195
Repairtech International Inc	4581	E	818 989-2681	9207
Broadview Networks Inc	4813	C	818 939-0015	9429
E & S International Entps Inc (PA)	5064	E	818 887-0700	10216
American Industrial Source Inc	5085	D	800 661-0622	10425
Anatex Enterprises Inc	5092	E	818 908-1888	10517
Home Depot USA Inc	5211	B	818 780-5400	11165
Keyes Motors Inc (PA)	5511	D	818 782-0122	11369
Keylex Inc (PA)	5511	D	818 379-4000	11370
Cinema Secrets Inc	5999	D	818 846-0579	11677
Napoleon Perdis Cosmetics Inc	5999	C	323 817-3611	11690
Los Angeles Police Credit Un (PA)	6062	C	818 787-6520	11829
Wheels Financial Group LLC	6141	C	855 422-7412	11863
Century-National Insurance Co (DH)	6411	B	818 760-0880	12194
Dewitt Stern Group Inc	6411	C	818 933-2700	12202
Momentous Insurance Brkg Inc	6411	C	818 933-2700	12233
All Valley Washer Service Inc	7215	D	818 787-1100	13128
Icon Media Direct Inc (PA)	7311	D	818 995-6400	13213
Lees Maintenance Service Inc	7349	B	818 988-6644	13385
L A Party Rents Inc	7359	D	818 989-4300	13459
Microlease Inc (DH)	7359	D	866 520-0200	13461
Town & Cntry Event Rentals LLC (PA)	7359	B	818 908-4211	13475
Kive Company	7372	E	747 212-0337	13961
Nafees Memon	7381	D	818 997-1666	14320
Louroe Electronics Inc	7382	E	818 994-6498	14413
Anheuser-Busch LLC	7389	C	805 381-4700	14450
Modern Parking Inc	7521	C	818 783-3143	14660
Keystone Towing Inc	7549	D	818 782-1996	14717
EDN Aviation Inc	7699	E	818 988-8826	14763
Harpo Productions Inc	7812	C	312 633-1000	14830
Industrial Media Inc (PA)	7819	C	310 777-1940	14895
Nep Bexel Inc (HQ)	7819	C	818 565-4399	14897
Weststar Cinemas Inc	7832	D	818 779-0323	14944
Cal Southern Med Ctr Inc	8011	D	818 650-6700	15259
Southern Cal Orthpd Inst LP (PA)	8011	C	818 901-6600	15460
Valley Presbyterian Hospital	8062	A	818 782-6600	16253
Alta Hllywood Cmnty Hosp Van N	8063	A	818 787-1511	16262
Primex Clinical Labs Inc (PA)	8071	C	424 213-8019	16328
Americare Home Health Inc	8082	D	818 881-0005	16364
Greater Valley Med Group Inc	8093	C	818 781-7097	16475
County of Los Angeles	8322	D	818 374-2000	16920
Apprentice Jrnymen Trning Tr F	8331	C	310 604-0892	17045
Onegeneration (PA)	8351	D	818 708-6625	17102
Southland Rgnal Assn Rltors In (PA)	8611	C	818 786-2110	17288
Consumer Safety Analytics LLC	8734	D	818 922-2416	17910
Sylmark Inc (PA)	8741	D	818 217-2000	18062
Cockram Construction Inc	8742	D	818 650-0999	18119
Ganz USA LLC	8742	D	818 901-0077	18140

VANDENBERG AFB, CA - Santa Barbara County

	SIC	EMP	PHONE	ENTRY#
Space Exploration Tech Corp	3721	D	310 848-4410	7372
United Launch Alliance LLC	3761	B	303 269-5876	7659
Sumaria Systems LLC	8711	D	805 606-4973	17638
Indyne Inc	8744	B	805 606-7225	18262

VENICE, CA - Los Angeles County

	SIC	EMP	PHONE	ENTRY#
Pacific Structures Sc Inc (PA)	1771	C	415 970-5434	1131
Vive Organic Inc	2033	E	877 774-9291	1362
Frankies Bikinis LLC	2369	E	323 354-4133	2169
Flex Company	3069	E	424 209-2711	3911
Alpargatas Usa Inc	3144	E	646 277-7171	4283
Fellow Industries Inc	3634	E	415 649-0361	6396
Syng Inc (PA)	3651	D	770 354-0915	6559
Los Angles Cnty Mtro Trnsp Aut	4111	B	310 392-8636	8772
Load Delivered Logistics LLC	4213	C	310 822-0215	8962
Southern California Gas Co	4924	C	310 823-7945	9655
Guayaki Sstnble Rnfrest Pdts I (PA)	5149	C	888 482-9254	10947
Trg Inc	6531	C	310 396-6750	12540
DDB Wrldwide Cmmnctons Group L	7311	C	310 907-1500	13204
Xx Artists LLC	7336	C	503 871-5298	13338
Dynasty Marketplace Inc	7371	C	804 837-0119	13713
Sameday Technologies Inc	7371	C	310 697-8126	13810
Gamemine LLC	7372	C	310 310-3105	13937
Parking Concepts Inc	7521	C	310 821-1081	14666
Power Studios Inc	7812	C	310 314-2800	14848
Venice Family Clinic (PA)	8011	C	310 664-7703	15506
St Joseph Center	8322	C	310 396-6468	17014
Socialcom Inc (PA)	8742	D	310 289-4477	18216
Gateb Consulting Inc	8748	D	310 526-8323	18311

VENTURA, CA - Ventura County

	SIC	EMP	PHONE	ENTRY#
Saticoy Lemon Association	0174	D	805 654-6500	44
Floral Gift HM Decor Intl Inc	0181	E	818 849-8832	55
American Landscape MGT Inc	0782	D	805 647-5077	197
West Coast Arborists Inc	0783	C	805 671-5092	247
Instrument Control Services	1389	E	805 642-1999	337
Nabors Well Services Co	1389	E	805 648-2731	350
Ais Construction Company	1542	D	805 928-9467	515
Vista Steel Co Inc	1629	E	805 653-1189	722
Taft Electric Company (PA)	1731	D	805 642-0121	973
Tidwell Excav Acquisition Inc	1794	D	805 647-4707	1177
G W Surfaces (PA)	1799	D	805 642-5004	1206
Novotech Nutraceuticals Inc	2023	E	805 676-1098	1305
Dairy Farmers America Inc	2026	D	805 653-0042	1327
HK Canning Inc (PA)	2033	E	805 652-1392	1350
Ventura Coastal LLC (PA)	2037	C	805 653-7000	1381
Better Bakery LLC	2052	C	661 294-9882	1480
P-Americas LLC	2086	E	805 641-4200	1627
Reyes Coca-Cola Bottling LLC	2086	B	805 644-2211	1643
Fabricmate Systems Inc	2221	E	805 642-7470	1893
Patagonia Inc (HQ)	2329	B	805 643-8616	2023
Streamline Dsign Slkscreen Inc (PA)	2329	D	805 884-1025	2028
Hearts Delight	2339	E	805 648-7123	2099
Art Glass Etc Inc	2431	E	805 644-4494	2297

Mergent email: customerrelations@mergent.com

1358

2025 Southern California
Business Directory and Buyers Guide

(P-0000) Products & Services Section entry number
(PA)=Parent Co (HQ)=Headquarters (DH)=Div Headquarters

Name	SIC	EMP	PHONE	ENTRY#
W L Rubottom Co	2434	D	805 648-6943	2367
Goldenwood Truss Corporation	2439	D	805 659-2520	2376
Edwards Assoc Cmmnications Inc (PA)	2672	C	805 658-2626	2722
Jh Biotech Inc (PA)	2875	E	805 650-8933	3749
C & R Molds Inc	3089	E	805 658-7098	4076
Assa Abloy ACC Door Cntrls Gro	3429	C	805 642-2600	4753
Automotive Racing Products Inc (PA)	3429	D	805 339-2200	4755
Pemko Manufacturing Co	3442	C	800 283-9988	4898
Valex Corp (HQ)	3471	E	805 658-0944	5304
Juengermann Inc	3493	E	805 644-7165	5380
Aqueos Corporation	3533	C	805 676-4330	5504
Aquastar Pool Products Inc	3561	E	877 768-2717	5726
Dow-Key Microwave Corporation	3625	C	805 650-0260	6347
Lamps Plus Inc	3646	E	805 642-9007	6465
Total Structures Inc	3648	E	805 676-3322	6520
Wireless Technology Inc	3651	E	805 339-9696	6570
Coastal Connections	3661	E	805 644-5051	6583
Naso Industries Corporation	3672	E	805 650-1231	6755
Robert M Hadley Company Inc	3677	D	805 658-7286	6937
Holland Electronics LLC	3678	E	888 628-5411	6949
Magnuson Products LLC	3714	E	805 642-8833	7269
Ventura Harbor Boatyard Inc	3732	E	805 654-1433	7624
Barnett Tool & Engineering	3751	E	805 642-9435	7629
Peter Brasseler Holdings LLC	3841	D	805 658-2643	8213
TMJ Solutions LLC	3841	E	805 650-3391	8239
Implantech Associates Inc	3842	E	805 289-1665	8274
Blue Ocean Marine LLC	4499	E	805 658-2628	9153
Cco Holdings LLC	4841	C	805 232-5887	9535
E J Harrison & Sons Inc	4953	C	805 647-1414	9742
Parts Authority LLC	5013	C	805 676-3410	9837
Canon Solutions America Inc	5044	E	844 443-4636	9972
Peter Brasseler Holdings LLC	5047	D	805 650-5209	10102
M-H Ironworks Inc	5051	D		10144
High Tech Pet Products	5065	D	805 644-1797	10248
Smart Stores Operations LLC	5141	E	805 647-4276	10804
Del Mar Seafoods Inc	5146	E	805 850-0421	10852
Lowes Home Centers LLC	5211	C	805 675-8800	11208
Gregory Consulting Inc (PA)	5511	C	805 642-0111	11356
R E Barber-Ford	5511	C	805 656-4259	11398
Southern Cal Disc Tire Co Inc	5531	C	805 639-0166	11456
Ventura Feed and Pet Sups Inc	5661	E	805 648-5035	11501
Patagonia Works (PA)	5699	B	805 643-8616	11509
Ventura County Credit Union (PA)	6061	C	805 477-4000	11821
E&S Financial Group Inc	6162	D	805 644-1621	11898
Rgc Services (PA)	6531	C	805 644-1242	12523
Ventura Hsptality Partners LLC	7011	C	805 648-2100	13065
MCM Harvesters Inc	7361	B	805 659-6833	13542
Trade Desk Inc (PA)	7371	B	805 585-3434	13847
Boyd and Associates (PA)	7381	C	818 752-1888	14281
Ost Trucks and Cranes Inc	7389	D	805 643-9963	14565
Weststar Cinemas Inc	7832	B	805 658-6544	14947
Century Theatres Inc	7833	B	805 641-6555	14948
Agi Holding Corp (PA)	7997	D	805 667-4100	15112
Team So-Cal Inc	7997	B	805 650-9946	15180
Ventura County Medical Center	8049	D	805 652-6729	15558
Coastal View Halthcare Ctr LLC	8051	D	805 642-4101	15593
Victoria Care Center	8051	D	805 642-1736	15792
Victoria Vntura Healthcare LLC	8051	B	805 642-1736	15793
Brierwood Terrace Ventura Inc	8059	D	805 642-4101	15839
Community Memorial Health Sys (PA)	8062	A	805 652-5011	15965
Aégic Senior Communities LLC	8082	D	805 650-1114	16359
Califrnia Frnsic Med Group Inc	8099	D	805 654-3343	16542
Catholic Chrties Snta Clara CN	8322	E	805 643-4694	16882
County of Ventura	0022	C	805 654-2561	16930
County of Ventura	8322	E	805 652-6000	16931
Channel Islnds Yung MNS Chrstn	8641	D	805 484-0423	17337
Girl Scuts Clfrnias Cntl Coast	8641	B	831 633-4877	17344
Astrion	8711	B	805 644-2191	17490
C D Lyon Construction Inc (PA)	8711	D	805 653-0173	17498
Livingston Mem Vna Hlth Corp	8741	B	805 642-0239	18008
Ventura Medical Management LLC	8741	B	805 477-6220	18074

VERNON, CA - Los Angeles County

Name	SIC	EMP	PHONE	ENTRY#
Edna H Pagel Inc	1541	D	323 234-2200	479
Square H Brands Inc	1541	D	323 267-4600	503
West Coast Distribution Inc	1541	D	323 588-6508	512
Littlejohn-Reuland Corporation	1731	E	323 587-5255	936
Jobbers Meat Packing Co LLC	2011	C	323 585-6328	1244
Pacific Prime Meats LLC	2011	D	310 523-3664	1248
R B R Meat Company Inc	2011	E	323 973-4868	1249
Papa Cantellas Incorporated	2013	D	323 584-7272	1265
Square H Brands Inc (PA)	2013	D	323 267-4600	1271
T & T Foods Inc	2032	E	323 588-2158	1346

Name	SIC	EMP	PHONE	ENTRY#
Culinary Brands Inc (PA)	2038	E	626 289-3000	1388
General Mills Inc	2041	E	323 584-3433	1405
Mochi Ice Cream Company LLC (PA)	2051	E	323 587-5504	1461
Smart Foods LLC	2076	E	800 284-2250	1520
Baker Commodities Inc	2077	E	323 318-8260	1521
Baker Commodities Inc (PA)	2077	C	323 268-2801	1522
D & D Services Inc	2077	D	323 261-4176	1523
Coast Packing Company	2079	D	323 277-7700	1525
American Bottling Company	2086	E	323 268-7779	1601
Stratus Group Duo LLC	2086	E	323 581-3663	1655
American Fruits & Flavors LLC	2087	E	323 881-8321	1664
Pacific American Fish Co Inc (PA)	2091	C	323 319-1551	1697
Fishermans Pride Prcessors Inc	2092	B	323 232-1980	1706
F Gavina & Sons Inc	2095	B	323 582-0671	1718
Cargill Meat Solutions Corp	2099	E	515 735-9800	1752
Culinary International LLC (PA)	2099	C	626 289-3000	1759
F I O Imports Inc	2099	E	323 263-5100	1772
Overhill Farms Inc (DH)	2099	E	323 582-9977	1830
Penguin Natural Foods Inc (PA)	2099	E	323 727-7980	1836
Reynaldos Mexican Food Co LLC (PA)	2099	C	562 803-3188	1841
BTS Trading Inc	2211	E	213 800-6755	1873
Pjy LLC	2211	E	323 583-7737	1885
Socal Garment Works LLC	2211	E	323 300-5717	1886
Chua & Sons Co Inc	2241	E	323 588-8044	1905
Universal Elastic & Garment Supply Inc	2241	E	213 748-2995	1907
Fantasy Activewear Inc (PA)	2253	E	213 705-4111	1916
Fantasy Dyeing & Finishing Inc	2253	E	323 983-9988	1917
Latigo Inc	2253	E	323 583-8000	1921
Shara-Tex Inc	2257	E	323 587-7200	1926
Sas Textiles Inc	2259	D	323 277-5555	1930
Rezex Corporation	2269	E		1945
American Cover Design 26 Inc	2273	E	323 582-8666	1946
Marspring Corporation (PA)	2273	E	323 589-5637	1953
California Combining Corp	2295	E	323 589-5727	1959
J H Textiles Inc	2299	E	323 585-4124	1971
Rcrv Inc (PA)	2325	E	323 235-8070	1991
Offline Inc (PA)	2326	E	213 742-9001	1999
Spirit Clothing Company	2329	D	213 784-5372	2026
Zk Enterprises Inc	2329	E	213 622-7012	2032
Bluprint Clothing Corp	2331	D	323 780-4347	2034
Complete Clothing Company (PA)	2335	E	213 892-1188	2064
Trinity Sports Inc	2335	B	323 277-9288	2074
David Grment Ctng Fsing Svc In	2339	E	323 216-1574	2089
Gaze USA Inc	2339	E	213 622-0022	2097
Heather By Bordeaux Inc	2339	E	213 622-0555	2100
It Jeans Inc	2339	E	323 588-2156	2101
Just For Wraps Inc (PA)	2339	C	213 239-0503	2110
Kim & Cami Productions Inc	2339	E	323 584-1300	2112
LAT LLC	2339	E	323 233-3017	2116
Patterson Kincaid LLC	2339	E	323 584-3559	2125
Rotax Incorporated	2339	E	323 589-5999	2130
Tempted Apparel Corp	2339	D	323 859-2480	2137
W & W Concept Inc	2339	D	323 583-3090	2142
National Corset Supply House (PA)	2341	E	323 261-0265	2151
Selectra Industries Corp	2341	D	323 581-8500	2152
Anaya Brothers Cutting LLC	2389	D	323 582-5758	2186
Rebecca International Inc	2395	E	323 973-2602	2255
Sandberg Furniture Mfg Co Inc (PA)	2511	C	323 582-0711	2436
A Rudin Inc (PA)	2512	D	323 589-5547	2430
Yen Nhai Inc	2512	E	323 584-1315	2462
Marspring Corporation	2515	D	310 484-6849	2488
Tempo Industries Inc	2515	C	415 552-8074	2494
Paper Surce Converting Mfg Inc	2021	E	323 583-3800	2635
Packaging Corporation America	2653	D	323 263-7581	2684
Southland Box Company	2653	C	323 583-2231	2689
Great American Packaging	2673	E	323 582-2247	2732
Norman Paper and Foam Co Inc	2673	E	323 582-7132	2736
Princess Paper Inc	2676	E	323 588-4777	2747
Tagtime Usa Inc	2679	D	323 587-1555	2775
Corporate Graphics Intl Inc	2752	D	323 826-3440	2990
Superior Lithographics Inc	2752	D	323 263-8400	3085
The Ligature Inc (HQ)	2752	E	323 585-6000	3089
Advanced Chemical Technology	2819	E	800 527-9607	3226
Joes Plastics Inc	2821	E	323 771-8433	3277
Continental Vitamin Co Inc	2834	D	323 581-0176	3388
Peerless Materials Company	2842	E	323 266-0313	3618
Evonik Corporation	2899	D	323 264-0311	3797
Aoclsc Inc	2992	E	562 776-4000	3847
Demenno/Kerdoon Holdings	2992	E	323 268-3387	3852
Sewing Collection Inc (PA)	3053	E	323 264-2223	3900
A&A Global Imports LLC (PA)	3089	D	888 315-2453	4035
Edris Plastics Mfg Inc	3089	E	323 581-7000	4111
Geo Plastics	3089	E	323 277-8106	4124

Employee Codes: A=Over 500 employees, B=251-500
C=101-250, D=51-100, E=20-50, F=10-19, G=1-9

2025 Southern California
Business Directory and Buyers Guide

© Mergent Inc. 1-800-342-5647
1359

G
E
O
G
R
A
P
H
I
C

	SIC	EMP	PHONE	ENTRY#
Norton Packaging Inc.	3089	E	323 588-6167	4184
Nuconic Packaging LLC.	3089	E	323 588-9033	4186
Rplanet Erth Los Angles Hldngs.	3089	D	833 775-2638	4230
Sol-Pak Thermoforming Inc.	3089	E	323 582-3333	4243
G & G Quality Case Co Inc	3161	D	323 233-2482	4293
Isabelle Handbag Inc.	3171	E	323 277-9888	4303
Berney-Karp Inc.	3269	D	323 260-7122	4366
National Cement Company Inc.	3273	D	323 923-4466	4446
Pabco Building Products LLC.	3275	C	323 581-6113	4467
Nucor Warehouse Systems Inc (HQ)	3317	C	323 588-4261	4552
Global Truss America LLC.	3354	D	323 415-6225	4597
Bodycote Usa Inc.	3398	A	323 264-0111	4700
Kai USA Ltd.	3421	E	323 589-2600	4729
Luppen Holdings Inc (PA)	3469	E	323 581-8121	5200
Certified Steel Treating Corp.	3471	E	323 583-8711	5246
Atlas Galvanizing LLC.	3479	E	323 587-6247	5313
Kennedy Name Plate Co.	3479	E	323 585-0121	5327
Angelus Machine Corp Intl.	3542	E	323 583-2171	5558
Punch Press Products Inc.	3544	D	323 581-7151	5594
Flowserve Corporation.	3561	B	323 584-1890	5732
J F Duncan Industries Inc (PA)	3589	E	562 862-4269	6016
Bender Ccp Inc (PA)	3599	C	323 232-2371	6095
Brentwood Appliances Inc.	3639	E	323 266-4600	6399
Unirex Corp.	3674	E	323 589-4000	6908
Westgate Mfg Inc.	3699	D	323 826-9490	7162
US Radiator Corporation (PA)	3714	E	323 826-0965	7306
Evergreen Industries Inc (DH)	3821	D	323 583-1331	7825
Mahar Manufacturing Corp (PA)	3942	E	323 581-9988	8476
UPD INC.	3942	D	323 588-8811	8480
Labeltex Mills Inc (PA)	3965	C	323 582-0228	8572
Two Lads Inc (PA)	3965	E	323 584-0064	8579
California Transit Inc.	4111	D	323 234-8750	8748
Vernon Central Warehouse Inc.	4214	C	323 234-2200	8997
Preferred Frzr Svcs - Lbf LLC.	4222	E	323 263-8811	9040
Generational Properties Inc.	4225	B	323 583-3163	9070
Greatwide Logistics Svcs LLC.	4731	D	323 268-7100	9287
R Planet Earth LLC.	4953	C	213 320-0601	9757
E B Bradley Co (PA)	5072	C	323 585-9917	10305
Omniteam Inc.	5078	C	562 923-9660	10341
Kafco Sales Company.	5084	E	323 588-7141	10380
Strategic Materials Inc.	5093	E	323 415-0166	10542
Rggd Inc (PA)	5099	E	323 581-6617	10567
New Milani Group LLC (PA)	5122	D	323 582-9404	10639
Romex Textiles Inc (PA)	5131	E	213 749-9090	10673
Soex West Usa LLC.	5136	B	323 264-8300	10696
Karen Kane Inc (PA)	5137	C	323 588-0000	10711
Lymi Inc (PA)	5137	D	844 701-0139	10713
New Pride Corporation.	5137	D	323 584-6608	10717
Nydj Apparel LLC.	5137	C	877 995-3267	10719
O & K Inc (PA)	5137	D	323 846-5700	10720
Runway Liquidation LLC (HQ)	5137	E	323 589-2224	10724
Same Swim LLC.	5137	E	323 582-2588	10725
The Timing Inc.	5137	E	323 589-5577	10731
Palisades Ranch Inc.	5141	B	323 581-6161	10764
Contessa Premium Foods Inc.	5142	C	310 832-8000	10819
West Pico Foods Inc.	5142	C	323 586-9050	10825
Rogers Poultry Co (PA)	5144	C	323 585-0802	10839
H & N Foods International Inc (HQ)	5146	C	323 586-9300	10854
Red Chamber Co (PA)	5146	E	323 234-9000	10860
Eastland Corporation.	5147	E	323 261-5388	10868
HV Randall Foods LLC (PA)	5147	C	323 261-6565	10872
Rancho Foods Inc.	5147	D	323 585-0503	10879
Sydney & Anne Bloom Farms Inc.	5147	A	323 261-6565	10882
Gourmet Specialties Inc.	5148	D	323 587-1734	10904
Natures Produce.	5148	C	323 235-4343	10912
V & L Produce Inc.	5148	C	323 589-3125	10921
World Variety Produce Inc.	5148	B	800 588-0151	10926
Completely Fresh Foods Inc.	5149	C	323 722-9136	10939
Core-Mark International Inc.	5149	C	323 583-6531	10940
Tadin Inc.	5149	D	213 406-8880	10983
TL Montgomery & Associates Inc.	5149	C	323 583-1645	10984
Cherokee Chemical Co Inc (PA)	5169	E	323 265-1112	11011
Norman Fox & Co.	5169	C	323 973-4900	11017
Anns Trading Company Inc.	5199	E	323 585-4702	11110
Kaiser Foundation Hospitals.	5712	C	323 264-4310	11514
Modernica Inc (PA)	5712	E	323 826-1600	11517
Good Fellas Industries Inc.	5719	D	323 924-9495	11531
Huxtables Kitchen Inc.	5812	D	323 923-2900	11575
Vie De France Yamazaki Inc.	5812	A	323 582-1241	11608
Paradigm Industries Inc.	7389	D	310 965-1900	14568
Rose & Shore Inc.	7389	B	323 826-2144	14586
R A Reed Electric Company (PA)	7694	E	323 587-2284	14750

VICTORVILLE, CA - San Bernardino County

	SIC	EMP	PHONE	ENTRY#
Baja Fresh Supermarket.	0291	B	760 843-7730	96
Cwp Cabinets Inc.	1751	C	760 246-4530	1049
Mars Petcare Us Inc.	2047	D	760 261-7900	1421
Reyes Coca-Cola Bottling LLC.	2086	E	760 241-2653	1641
Graco Childrens Products Inc.	2514	B	770 418-7200	2469
Gatehouse Media LLC.	2711	E	760 241-7744	2799
Newell Brands Inc.	3089	E	760 246-2700	4179
Daikin Comfort Tech Mfg LP.	3585	B	760 955-7770	5973
General Electric Company.	3721	E	760 530-5200	7354
A-Team Delivers LLC.	4212	D	858 254-8401	8889
Hartwick & Hand Inc (PA)	4212	D	760 245-1666	8914
TT Trucking Services LLC.	4212	D	323 790-3408	8927
Landforce Corporation.	4213	C	760 843-7839	8959
Valley Bulk Inc.	4213	D	760 843-0574	8981
Comav LLC.	4581	C	760 523-5100	9196
Comav Technical Services LLC.	4581	C	760 530-2400	9197
Comav LLC (PA)	5088	E	760 523-5100	10489
Centerline Wood Products.	5099	D	760 246-4530	10556
Premier Food Services Inc.	5141	A	760 843-8000	10766
Home Depot USA Inc.	5211	B	760 955-2999	11182
Lowes Home Centers LLC.	5211	C	760 949-9565	11212
Sunland Ford Inc.	5511	D	760 241-7751	11414
Vahi Toyota Inc (PA)	5511	C	760 241-6484	11426
Victorville Trsure Holdings LLC.	7011	D	760 245-6565	13066
American Prtctive Svcs Invstgt.	7381	C	626 705-8600	14274
Desert Valley Med Group Inc (DH)	8011	D	760 241-8000	15301
Kaiser Foundation Hospitals.	8011	D	888 750-0036	15345
Radnet Management III Inc.	8011	D	760 243-1234	15432
Knolls Convalescent Hosp Inc (PA)	8051	C	760 245-5361	15686
Knolls West Enterprise.	8051	C	760 245-0107	15687
Spring Valley Post Acute LLC.	8051	C	760 245-6477	15782
Desert Valley Hospital Inc (DH)	8062	C	760 241-8000	15975
Victor Vly Hosp Acqisition Inc.	8062	D	760 245-8691	16257
Branlyn Prominence Inc.	8082	C	760 843-5655	16370
Peoples Care Inc.	8082	C	760 962-1900	16411
Victor Cmnty Support Svcs Inc.	8093	C	760 987-8225	16518
Victor Cmnty Support Svcs Inc.	8093	C	760 245-4695	16519
Heritage Medical Group.	8099	B	760 956-1286	16569
Family Assistance Program.	8322	C	760 843-0701	16941
Encore Senior Living III LLC.	8361	D	760 243-2271	17149
Think Together.	8699	B	760 269-1230	17471

VIEW PARK, CA - Los Angeles County

	SIC	EMP	PHONE	ENTRY#
Hathawy-Sycmres Child Fmly Svc.	8322	C	323 733-0322	16949

VILLA PARK, CA - Orange County

	SIC	EMP	PHONE	ENTRY#
Tropical Plaza Nursery Inc.	0782	D	714 998-4100	239
Manufactured Solutions LLC.	3999	E	714 548-6915	8697

VISTA, CA - San Diego County

	SIC	EMP	PHONE	ENTRY#
Plug Connection Inc.	0181	D	760 631-0992	67
I Pwlc Inc.	0781	D	760 630-0231	175
Nissho of California Inc (PA)	0781	C	760 727-9719	181
Pac West Land Care Inc.	0781	C	760 630-0231	183
Brightview Landscapes LLC.	0782	C	760 598-7065	199
Heaviland Enterprises Inc (PA)	0782	D	760 598-7065	209
Burtech Pipeline Incorporated.	1623	D	760 634-2822	665
Orion Construction Corporation.	1623	D	760 597-9660	688
Arb Inc.	1629	B	619 295-2754	708
Industrial Coml Systems Inc.	1711	C	760 300-4094	788
Nwec Nevada Inc.	1731	D	760 757-0187	945
Excel Mdular Scaffold Lsg Corp.	1799	A	760 598-0050	1202
Bellissimo Distribution LLC.	2032	E	760 292-9100	1337
Baked In The Sun.	2051	C	760 591-9045	1435
Pure Project LLC.	2082	D	760 552-7873	1552
Great Western Malting Co.	2083	C	360 991-0888	1557
Javo Beverage Company Inc.	2087	D	760 560-5286	1685
Thirty Three Threads Inc (PA)	2329	E	877 486-3769	2029
Earthlite LLC (DH)	2514	D	760 599-1112	2467
Killion Industries Inc (PA)	2541	D	760 727-5102	2568
Precision Litho Inc.	2752	C	760 727-9400	3064
Advanced Web Offset Inc.	2759	D	760 727-1700	3114
J & D Laboratories Inc.	2833	D	760 734-6800	3318
Bachem Americas Inc.	2834	E	888 422-2436	3368
Captek Midco Inc.	2834	D	760 734-6800	3378
American Peptide Company Inc.	2836	D	408 733-7604	3556
Grifols Usa LLC.	2836	D	760 931-8444	3578
Mindera Corp.	2836	E	858 810-6070	3583
All One God Faith Inc (PA)	2841	C	844 937-2551	3589
All One God Faith Inc.	2841	D	760 599-4010	3590
Revlon Inc.	2844	D	619 372-1379	3685
Watkins Manufacturing Corp.	3088	B	760 598-6464	4032

	SIC	EMP	PHONE	ENTRY#
Distinctive Plastics Inc	3089	D	760 599-9100	4105
Diversified Plastics Inc	3089	E	760 598-5333	4106
J A English II Inc	3089	E	760 598-5333	4143
Nubs Plastics Inc	3089	E	760 598-2525	4185
Oceanside Glasstile Company (PA)	3253	B	760 929-4000	4361
Kammerer Enterprises Inc	3281	D	760 560-0550	4474
Monster Tool LLC	3423	C	760 477-1000	4742
McCain Manufacturing Inc	3441	E	760 295-9290	4850
Solatube International Inc (DH)	3442	D	888 765-2882	4903
Protec Arisawa America Inc	3443	E	760 599-4800	4922
AP Precision Metals Inc	3444	E	619 628-0003	4950
Versaform Corporation	3444	E	760 599-4477	5054
Diversified Tool & Die	3469	E	760 598-9100	5182
Dig Corporation	3523	E	760 727-0914	5473
Western Cactus Growers Inc	3524	E	760 726-1710	5485
Sherline Products Incorporated	3541	E	760 727-5181	5552
Addition Manufacturing Technologies CA Inc	3542	E	760 597-5220	5555
Flotron	3544	E	760 727-2700	5580
Resers Fine Foods Inc	3556	E	503 643-6431	5683
Asml Us Inc	3559	B	760 443-6244	5691
Rxsafe LLC	3559	D	760 593-7161	5719
Accutek Packaging Equipment Co (PA)	3565	E	760 734-4177	5786
Apem Inc (HQ)	3577	E	978 372-1602	5901
Applied Membranes Inc	3589	C	760 727-3711	5998
Yanchewski & Wardell Entps Inc	3589	D	760 754-1960	6038
Stines Machine Inc	3599	E	760 599-9955	6244
Vista Industrial Products Inc	3599	E	760 599-5050	6266
Western Cnc Inc	3599	D	760 597-7000	6273
Zettler Magnetics Inc	3612	C	949 831-5000	6299
Ddh Enterprise Inc (PA)	3643	D	760 599-0171	6415
M Klemme Technology Corp	3651	E	760 727-0593	6543
Raveon Technologies Corp	3663	E	760 444-5995	6651
Outsource Manufacturing Inc	3674	D	760 795-1295	6866
Plansee USA LLC	3674	D	760 438-9090	6868
Apem Inc	3679	E	760 598-2518	6967
AZ Displays Inc	3679	E	949 831-5000	6970
Flux Power Holdings Inc (PA)	3691	C	877 505-3589	7077
Blisslights Inc	3699	E	888 868-4603	7111
Dutek Incorporated	3699	E	760 566-8888	7121
Carbon By Design LLC	3728	D	760 643-1300	7450
Nighthawk Flight Systems Inc	3812	E	760 727-4900	7747
Sandel Avionics Inc (PA)	3812	E	760 727-4900	7806
Sandel Avionics Inc	3812	C	760 727-4900	7807
Leica Biosystems Imaging Inc (HQ)	3826	C	760 539-1100	7964
Machine Vision Products Inc (PA)	3827	E	760 438-1138	8010
Biofilm Inc	3841	D	760 727-9030	8110
Carol Cole Company	3841	C	888 360-9171	8126
Surgistar Inc (PA)	3841	E	760 598-2480	8231
Vision Quest Industries Inc	3842	C	949 261-6382	8318
Conamco SA De CV	3843	D	760 586-4356	8330
Amron International Inc (PA)	3949	E	760 208-6500	8501
Aza Industries Inc (PA)	3949	E	760 560-0440	8503
Rayzist Photomask Inc (PA)	3955	D	760 727-8561	8566
Wolfpack Inc	3993	E	760 736-4500	8651
Integrated Mfg Solutions LLC	3999	E	760 599-4300	8686
Watkins Manufacturing Corp (HQ)	3999	C	760 598-6464	8740
Patriot Logistics Services LLC	4789	D	443 994-9660	9373
Tempo Communications Inc (PA)	4813	D	800 642-2155	9466
Ultra Communications Inc	4813	E	760 652-0011	9468
Vista Irrigation District	4971	D	760 597-3100	9794
Phoenix Wheel Company Inc	5013	E	760 598-1960	9638
Winners Only Inc	5021	C	760 599-0300	9886
American Faucet Coatings Corp	5023	C	700 598-5895	9888
H2o Innovation USA Holding Inc	5074	A	760 639-4400	10321
Swarco McCain Inc (DH)	5084	C	760 727-8100	10409
D & D Saw Works Inc	5085	C		10434
Apical Industries Inc	5088	D	760 724-5300	10486
Eliel & Co	5136	E	760 877-8469	10682
Smart Stores Operations LLC	5141	C	760 732-1480	10793
Altman Specialty Plants LLC (PA)	5193	A	800 348-4881	11080
Bandy Ranch Floral Corp	5193	E	805 757-9905	11082
Gringo Ventures LLC	5193	B	760 477-7999	11088
Ponto Nursery	5193	D	760 724-6003	11098
Spectrum Equipment LLC	5193	D	760 599-8849	11100
Lee-Mar Aquarium & Pet Sups	5199	D	760 727-1300	11127
Lowes Home Centers LLC	5211	C	760 631-6255	11229
Coromega Company Inc	5499	E	760 599-6088	11304
County Ford North Inc (PA)	5511	C	760 945-9900	11328
Living Spaces Furniture LLC	5712	C	760 945-6805	11515
Bni Publications Inc	5942	E	760 734-1113	11631
Garich Inc (PA)	7361	B	858 453-1331	13520
Epitec Inc	7371	A	760 650-2515	13721
International Lottery & Totalizator Systems Inc	7371	E	760 598-1655	13753
Interntnal Lttery Ttlztor Syst	7371	E	760 598-1655	13754
Off Duty Officers Inc	7381	A	888 408-5900	14325
All-Pro Bail Bonds Inc	7389	C	760 512-1969	14439
Amkom Design Group Inc	7389	E	760 295-1957	14448
Krikorian Premiere Theatre LLC	7832	D	760 945-7469	14940
Spa Havens LP	7991	C	760 945-2055	15063
Kaiser Foundation Hospitals	8011	A	619 528-5000	15341
Vista Community Clinic (PA)	8031	B	760 631-5000	15533
Vista Woods Health Assoc LLC	8051	C	760 630-2273	15797
Rancho Vista Health Center	8052	D	760 941-1480	15820
Care Choice Health Systems Inc	8059	C	760 798-4508	15842
Life Care Centers America Inc	8059	C	760 724-8222	15863
Exagen Inc	8071	C	505 272-7966	16315
Planned Prnthood of PCF Sthwes	8093	D	619 881-4500	16491
Grifols Bio Supplies Inc	8099	C	760 651-4042	16563
Alpha Project For Homeless	8322	C	760 630-9922	16863
Community Interface Services	8322	E	760 729-3866	16899
Vista Care Group LLC (PA)	8322	D	760 295-3900	17024
HMS Construction Inc (PA)	8711	E	760 727-9808	17546
Systems Engineering & MGT Co (PA)	8711	E	760 727-7800	17641
Leidos Inc	8731	C	858 826-9090	17805
Science Inc	8741	D	310 395-3432	18049
Plug Connection LLC	8742	C	760 631-0992	18192

WALNUT, CA - Los Angeles County

	SIC	EMP	PHONE	ENTRY#
JF Shea Construction Inc (HQ)	1521	C	909 594-9500	409
United Riggers & Erectors Inc (PA)	1796	D	909 978-0400	1191
Settlers Jerky Inc	2013	E	909 444-3999	1270
Imperfect Foods Inc (HQ)	2099	D	510 595-6683	1792
Ninas Mexican Foods Inc	2099	E	909 468-5888	1825
Charades LLC	2389	C	626 435-0077	2189
Diamond Collection LLC	2389	E	626 435-0077	2192
Diana Did-It Designs Inc	2389	E	970 226-5062	2193
Southcoast Cabinet Inc (PA)	2434	E	909 594-3089	2363
All Strong Industry (usa) Inc (PA)	2591	E	909 598-6494	2599
Nu-Health Products Co	2833	E	909 869-0666	3323
Essentra International LLC	2891	A	708 315-7498	3765
10 Day Parts Inc	3089	E	951 279-4810	4033
AMS Plastics Inc (PA)	3089	E	619 713-2000	4049
2nd Source Wire & Cable Inc	3312	D	714 482-2866	4508
Tree Island Wire (USA) Inc (DH)	3315	C	909 594-7511	4544
Cast Parts Inc (HQ)	3324	C	909 595-2252	4563
Pengcheng Aluminum Enterprise Inc USA	3354	E	909 598-7933	4603
Sea Shield Marine Products Inc	3363	E	909 594-2507	4653
Edro Engineering LLC (DH)	3544	E	909 594-5751	5578
Fairway Injection Molds Inc	3544	D	909 595-2201	5579
Amergence Technology Inc	3559	E	909 859-8400	5687
Tri-Net Technology Inc	3577	D	909 598-8818	5953
Trane US Inc	3585	E	626 913-7913	5986
Crush Master Grinding Corp	3599	E	909 595-2249	6111
Mjc America Ltd (PA)	3634	E	888 876-5387	6398
US Energy Technologies Inc	3646	E	714 617-8800	6477
Soderberg Manufacturing Co Inc	3647	C	909 595-1291	6486
Absen Inc	3674	E	909 480-0129	6791
Simple Solar Industries LLC	3674	C	844 907-0705	6892
Aero Pacific Corporation	3728	C	714 961-9200	7409
Shore Western Manufacturing	3826	E	626 357-3251	7977
Total Resources Intl Inc (PA)	3842	E	909 594-1220	8309
Jakks Pacific Inc	3944	E	000 601 7771	0490
Loungefly LLC	3961	E	818 718-5600	8570
Infinity Watch Corporation	3993	E	626 289-9878	8608
Armlogi Holding Corp (PA)	4225	C	888 691-2911	9049
Lava Scs LLC	4225	D	909 437-7881	9083
Straight Forwarding Inc	4731	D	909 594-3400	9339
Tae Sook Chung	5023	D	909 598-6255	9909
Adesso Inc	5045	D	909 839-2929	9984
Martin-Brower Company LLC	5141	D	909 595-8764	10756
Sysco Los Angeles Inc	5141	A	909 595-9595	10808
Daikin Comfort Tech Dist Inc	6512	B	626 210-4595	12288
Ahg Inc	7291	B	703 596-0111	13160
Identigraphix Inc	7336	E	909 468-4741	13330
Gremlin Inc	7372	D	408 214-9885	13942
Los Angles Ryal Vsta Golf Crse	7997	D	909 595-7441	15148
Emeritus Corporation	8051	D	909 595-5030	15632
Pregel America Inc	8351	C	909 598-8980	17109
Shogun Labs Inc (PA)	8734	C	317 676-2719	17926
Vistancia Marketing LLC	8742	D	909 594-9500	18238

WASCO, CA - Kern County

	SIC	EMP	PHONE	ENTRY#
Agreserves Inc	0173	C	661 391-9000	38
Juan Carlos Alvardo	0761	D	661 758-6128	139
Bethlehem Construction Inc	1541	D	661 758-1001	473
Sunnygem LLC (PA)	2033	C	661 758-0491	1358

Employee Codes: A=Over 500 employees, B=251-500
C=101-250, D=51-100, E=20-50, F=10-19, G=1-9

2025 Southern California
Business Directory and Buyers Guide

© Mergent Inc. 1-800-342-5647

1361

GEOGRAPHIC

	SIC	EMP	PHONE	ENTRY#
Primex Farms LLC **(PA)**	2068	E	661 758-7790	1516
Certis USA LLC	2879	E	661 758-8471	3752
Hec Asset Management Inc	5046	D	661 587-2250	10044
South Valley Almond Co LLC	5159	D	661 391-9000	10994
Community Support Options Inc	8322	C	661 758-5331	16900

WEST COVINA, CA - Los Angeles County

	SIC	EMP	PHONE	ENTRY#
Sears Home Imprv Pdts Inc	1521	C	626 671-1892	425
Turn Around Communications Inc	1623	C	626 443-2400	701
Harris & Ruth Painting Contg **(PA)**	1721	D	626 960-4004	866
Interspace Battery Inc **(PA)**	3356	E	626 813-1234	4618
Baatz Enterprises Inc	3711	E	323 660-4866	7169
Penney Opco LLC	5311	C	626 960-3711	11264
Kaiser Foundation Hospitals	6324	D	866 319-4269	12091
Southern Cal Prmnnte Med Group	6324	C	626 960-4844	12112
RM Galicia Inc	7322	C	626 813-6200	13287
Lfp Ecommerce LLC	7389	D	314 428-5069	14529
Penske Motor Group LLC	7513	E	626 859-1200	14639
Saint Jseph Communications Inc **(PA)**	7812	E	626 331-3549	14854
Big Lgue Dreams Consulting LLC	7941	C	626 839-1100	15020
South Hills Country Club	7997	D	626 339-1231	15175
West Covina Medical Clinic Inc **(PA)**	8011	C	626 960-8614	15510
Doctors Hospital W Covina Inc	8062	C	626 338-8481	15983
Emanate Health	8062	A	626 962-4011	15990
Emanate Health Medical Center **(PA)**	8062	A	626 962-4011	15993
Emanate Health Medical Center	8062	B	626 963-8411	15995
Southern Cal Spcialty Care Inc	8062	C	626 339-5451	16208
Volunteers of Amer Los Angeles	8322	C	626 337-9878	17030
Westview Services Inc	8331	D	626 962-0956	17076
Regent Assisted Living Inc	8361	D	626 332-3344	17190

WEST HILLS, CA - Los Angeles County

	SIC	EMP	PHONE	ENTRY#
DR Horton Inc	1531	D	818 334-1955	460
Flavor Producers LLC **(PA)**	2087	E	661 257-3400	1680
Pharmavite LLC **(DH)**	2833	B	818 221-6200	3327
Aerojet Rocketdyne De Inc	2869	C	818 586-9629	3725
Jj Acquisitions LLC	3069	E	818 772-0100	3918
Source Photonics Usa Inc **(PA)**	3674	C	818 773-9044	6897
Speedata Inc	5045	C	612 743-7960	10030
Lowes Home Centers LLC	5211	C	818 610-1960	11242
911 Restoration Entps Inc	7349	C	832 887-2582	13351
Citiguard Inc	7381	B	800 613-5903	14284
Leisure Care LLC	8052	C	818 713-0900	15813
West Valleyidence Opco LLC	8052	D	818 348-8422	15829
Unilab Corporation **(HQ)**	8071	B	818 737-6000	16337
Tobin Lucks A Prof Corp **(PA)**	8111	D	818 226-3400	16790
One Lambda Inc **(HQ)**	8731	D	747 494-1000	17816

WEST HOLLYWOOD, CA - Los Angeles County

	SIC	EMP	PHONE	ENTRY#
Lm Veterinary Enterprises Inc	0742	D	310 659-5287	128
402 Shoes Inc	2341	E	323 655-5437	2145
Pro Tour Memorabilia LLC	2499	E	424 303-7200	2415
Clique Brands Inc	2721	C	310 623-6916	2850
Capricor	2834	E	310 423-2104	3377
Cosmo International Corp	2844	D	310 271-1100	3642
Paul Ferrante Inc	3999	E	310 854-4412	8710
Dreamteam Logistics LLC	4789	D	818 300-7785	9362
J Robert Scott Inc **(PA)**	5131	C	310 680-4300	10664
Velaro Incorporated	5734	C	800 983-5276	11543
Auto Club Enterprises	6321	B	310 914-8500	12058
Rsg Group USA Inc	6719	A	214 574-4653	12611
Mondrian Holdings LLC	7011	B	323 848-6004	12926
Ols Hotels & Resorts LLC	7011	A	310 855-1115	12951
Valadon Hotel LLC	7011	D	310 854-1114	13064
West Hollywood Edition	7011	D	310 795-7103	13075
One Events Inc	7299	D	310 498-5471	13181
Dailey & Associates	7311	D	323 490-3847	13201
Seismic Productions	7311	D	310 407-0411	13245
Suissa Miller Advertising LLC	7311	D	310 392-9666	13248
Grindr LLC	7371	C	310 776-6680	13740
Kinsta Inc	7371	C	310 736-9306	13759
Neonroots LLC	7371	C	310 907-9210	13776
Watt Inc	7371	C	310 896-8197	13864
Tegra118 Wealth Solutions Inc **(HQ)**	7374	C	888 800-0188	14160
Executive Car Leasing Company **(PA)**	7515	D	800 800-3932	14651
Tri Star Spt Entrmt Group Inc	7929	D	615 309-0969	15007
Rsg Group North America LP	7991	C	714 609-0572	15061
Kids Empire USA LLC	7999	D	424 527-1039	15208
Ticketmaster Entertainment LLC	7999	A	800 653-8000	15227
Cedars-Sinai Medical Center	8062	C	310 423-9310	15941
Cedars-Sinai Medical Center	8062	C	310 423-5468	15947
Cedars-Sinai Medical Center	8062	C	310 423-8780	15949
Cedars-Sinai Medical Center	8062	C	310 855-7701	15951

	SIC	EMP	PHONE	ENTRY#
Cedars-Sinai Medical Center	8071	C	814 758-5466	16307
White Rabbit Partners Inc	8361	C	310 975-1450	17209
Automobile Club Southern Cal	8699	C	323 525-0018	17438
Cpe Hr Inc	8742	D	310 270-9800	18122
Operam Inc	8742	D	855 673-7261	18189

WESTLAKE VILLAGE, CA - Ventura County

	SIC	EMP	PHONE	ENTRY#
Dole Holding Company LLC	0179	A	818 879-6600	47
Sperber Ldscp Companies LLC **(PA)**	0781	C	818 437-1029	194
Welbilt Inc	1389	E	310 339-1555	370
The Ryland Group Inc	1531	A	805 367-3800	465
Castle & Cooke Investments Inc	1542	C	310 208-3636	528
Dennis M McCoy & Sons Inc	1611	D	818 874-3872	613
Sdg Enterprises	1711	D	805 777-7978	835
Dole Packaged Foods LLC **(HQ)**	2037	A	800 232-8888	1375
Omics Group Inc	2721	B	650 268-9744	2866
Network Television Time Inc	2741	E	877 468-8899	2930
Innocoll Biotherapeutics NA	2834	C	484 406-5200	3423
Kythera Biopharmaceuticals Inc	2834	C	818 587-4500	3441
Mannkind Corporation	2834	B	818 661-5000	3446
Sugar Foods LLC **(HQ)**	2869	E	805 396-5000	3738
Baltic Ltvian Unvrsal Elec LLC	3651	E	818 879-5200	6529
Carros Sensors Americas LLC	3679	C	805 267-7176	6979
Energy Vault Inc **(HQ)**	3691	E	805 852-0000	7073
Rantec Microwave Systems Inc **(PA)**	3812	D	818 223-5000	7792
Caldera Medical Inc **(PA)**	3841	D	818 879-6555	8118
Implant Direct Sybron Intl LLC **(HQ)**	3843	D	818 444-3000	8337
Pleasant Holidays LLC **(HQ)**	4724	B	818 991-3390	9232
Frontier California Inc	4813	B	805 372-6000	9438
Globecast America Incorporated	4841	C	310 845-3900	9552
Hec Inc	5065	B	818 879-7414	10247
Jri Inc	5065	E	818 706-2424	10258
Easton Diamond Sports LLC	5091	D	800 632-7866	10512
Baxter Healthcare Corporation	5122	A	805 372-3000	10614
Ruby Ribbon Inc	5137	E	650 449-4470	10723
Smart Stores Operations LLC	5141	C	818 889-8253	10803
Sugar Foods LLC	5149	C	805 230-2591	10981
Country Floral Supply Inc **(PA)**	5193	D	805 520-8026	11085
Microblend Technologies Inc	5231	C	480 831-0757	11255
Mamolos Cntntl Bailey Bakeries	5461	C	805 496-0045	11299
Cadillac Motor Div Area	5511	C	805 373-9575	11323
Toller Enterprises Inc **(PA)**	5551	E	805 374-9455	11478
Jafra Cosmetics Intl Inc **(DH)**	5999	D	805 449-3000	11688
Bana Home Loan Servicing	6021	A	213 345-7975	11704
Input 1 LLC	6153	C	888 882-2554	11868
A-A Mortgage Opportunities LP	6162	A	888 469-0810	11880
Anchor Loans LP	6162	C	310 395-0010	11885
Countrywide Home Loans Inc **(HQ)**	6162	A		11895
Dignified Home Lending LLC	6163	D	818 421-7753	11945
Pennymac Corp	6163	A	818 878-8416	11949
Amerihome Mortgage Company LLC	6211	A	888 469-0810	11958
Merrill Lynch Prce Fnner Smith	6211	C	805 381-2600	11988
Kramer-Wilson Company Inc **(PA)**	6331	C	818 760-0880	12122
Pacific Compensation Insur Co	6411	C	818 575-8500	12241
Cushman & Wakefield Cal Inc	6531	B	805 418-5811	12422
Move Sales Inc **(DH)**	6531	D	805 557-2300	12492
Troop Real Estate Inc	6531	C	805 402-3028	12542
Fidelity Nat Title Insur Co NY	6541	C	805 370-1400	12557
Pmt Crdit Risk Trnsf Tr 2015-1	6733	C	818 224-7028	12666
Pmt Crdit Risk Trnsf Tr 2015-2	6733	C	818 224-7442	12667
Pmt Crdit Risk Trnsf Tr 2019-2	6733	C	818 224-7028	12668
Pmt Crdit Risk Trnsf Tr 2019-3	6733	C	818 224-7028	12669
Pmt Crdit Risk Trnsf Tr 2020-1	6733	C	818 224-7028	12670
Pmt Crdit Risk Trnsf Tr 2020-2	6733	C	818 224-7028	12671
Pnmac Gmsr Issuer Trust	6733	A	818 746-2271	12672
Pmt Issuer Trust - Fmsr	6798	C	818 224-7028	12691
Burton Way Htels Ltd A Cal Ltd	7011	C	818 575-3000	12779
Swvp Westlake LLC	7011	C	805 557-1234	13046
Westlake Properties Inc	7011	C	818 889-0230	13078
Causal Iq	7311	C	805 367-6348	13199
C&W Facility Services Inc	7349	A	805 267-7123	13361
Microfinancial Incorporated	7359	C	805 367-8900	13460
Enoah Isolutions Inc	7371	B	805 285-3418	13720
Facefirst LLC	7372	C	805 482-8428	13932
Srax Inc **(PA)**	7372	E	323 205-6109	14039
Digital Insight Corporation	7375	D	818 879-1010	14168
Lantz Security Systems Inc	7381	C	805 496-5775	14312
Securitas SEC Svcs USA Inc	7381	B	818 706-6800	14339
Bankcard USA Merchant Srvc	7389	C	818 597-7000	14459
Rvl Packaging Inc	7389	C	818 735-5000	14587
Thousand Oaks Prtg & Spc Inc	7389	C	818 706-8330	14610
Weststar Cinemas Inc	7832	C	805 379-8966	14946
North Ranch Country Club	7997	C	818 889-3531	15155

Mergent email: customerrelations@mergent.com

1362

2025 Southern California
Business Directory and Buyers Guide

(P-0000) Products & Services Section entry number
(PA)=Parent Co (HQ)=Headquarters (DH)=Div Headquarters

	SIC	EMP	PHONE	ENTRY#
Coastal Rdtion Onclogy Med Gro	8011	D	805 494-4483	15283
Los Robles Regional Med Ctr	8011	B	805 370-4531	15384
Sgry LLC	8011	D	805 413-7920	15451
Ernst & Young LLP	8721	D	805 778-7000	17726
Ninjio Llc	8748	D	805 864-1992	18341

WESTMINSTER, CA - Orange County

	SIC	EMP	PHONE	ENTRY#
Maintech Resources Inc	1796	E	562 804-0664	1189
Einstein Noah Rest Group Inc	2022	C	714 847-4609	1286
Nguoi Viet Vtnamese People Inc (PA)	2711	E	714 892-9414	2818
New Technology Plastics Inc	2821	E	562 941-6034	3283
Intertrade Industries Ltd	3089	D	714 894-5566	4140
Tru-Form Plastics Inc	3089	E	310 327-9444	4264
Tolemar LLC	3641	E	657 200-3840	6409
B/E Aerospace Inc	3728	C	714 896-9001	7442
Thompson Industries Ltd	3728	C	310 679-9193	7578
Lexor Inc	3999	D	714 444-4144	8693
Inlog Inc	4731	D	949 212-3867	9295
Southern California Edison Co	4911	C	714 895-0163	9616
Southern California Edison Co	4911	C	714 895-0119	9617
Southern California Edison Co	4911	A	714 895-0420	9619
Neighborhood Steel LLC (HQ)	5051	E	714 236-8700	10146
Minh Phung Incorporated	5149	C	714 379-0606	10961
Honda World Westminster	5511	E	714 890-8900	11361
Lbs Financial Credit Union (PA)	6062	C	562 598-9007	11828
University California Irvine	8062	C	714 775-3066	16247
Abrazar Inc	8322	D	714 893-3581	16860
Westview Services Inc	8331	D	714 418-2090	17075
360 Health Plan Inc	8741	C	800 446-8888	17932

WHITEWATER, CA - Riverside County

	SIC	EMP	PHONE	ENTRY#
Whitewater Rock & Sup Co Inc	5032	E	760 325-2747	9955

WHITTIER, CA - Los Angeles County

	SIC	EMP	PHONE	ENTRY#
Oltmans Construction Co (PA)	1541	D	562 948-4242	495
Russ Bassett Corp	2511	C	562 945-2445	2434
Johnson Controls Inc	2531	E	562 698-8301	2545
JC Window Fashions Inc	2591	E	909 364-8888	2603
Tube-Tainer Inc	2655	E	562 945-3711	2699
D & R Screen Printing Inc	2752	E	562 458-6443	2998
Ss Whittier LLC	2752	E	562 698-7513	3084
Coastal Tag & Label Inc	2759	D	562 946-4318	3129
Messer LLC	2813	E	562 903-1290	3218
Epmar Corporation	2851	E	562 946-8781	3713
AC Products Inc	2891	E	714 630-7311	3757
Sfrlc Inc	3069	E	562 693-2776	3936
Jason Incorporated	3291	E	562 921-9821	4483
Miller Castings Inc (PA)	3324	B	562 695-0461	4567
Rasmussen Iron Works Inc	3433	D	562 696-8718	4813
Fred R Rippy Inc	3469	E	562 698-9801	5187
Allblack Co Inc	3471	E	562 946-2955	5230
Quaker City Plating	3471	C	562 945-3721	5286
Cryostar USA LLC	3561	D	562 903-1290	5730
Compu Aire Inc	3585	C	562 945-8971	5971
Rahn Industries Incorporated (PA)	3585	E	562 908-0680	5981
Medlin and Son Engrg Svc Inc	3599	E	562 464-5889	6173
Miller Castings Inc	3599	E	562 695-0461	6180
Hedman Manufacturing (PA)	3714	E	562 204-1031	7260
Trans-Dapt California Inc	3714	E	562 921-0404	7301
Gulfstream Aerospace Corp GA	3721	C	562 907-9300	7356
Cameron Technologies Us LLC	3823	E	562 222-8440	7851
Exiton Inc	3993	E	562 699-1122	8603
Fusion Sign & Design Inc	3993	F	562 946-7546	8606
County of Los Angeles	4151	C	562 945-2681	9067
Magnell Associate Inc	4225	B	626 271-1420	9086
Sprint Communications Co LP	4812	C	562 943-8907	9409
Southern California Gas Co	4924	C	562 803-3341	9654
Sanittion Dstrcts Los Angles C	4953	A	562 908-4288	9763
Los Angles Cnty Snttion Dstrct (PA)	4959	A	562 699-7411	9788
Indio Products Inc (PA)	5049	C	323 720-1188	10118
General Transistor Corporation (PA)	5065	E	310 578-7344	10245
Southern California Material Handling Inc	5084	C	562 949-1006	10405
Oncor Corp	5122	E	562 944-0230	10641
Smart Stores Operations LLC	5141	B	562 907-7037	10782
Gourmet India Food Company LLC	5149	D	562 698-9763	10946
Khw Enterprises Inc	5199	D	562 236-8440	11125
Home Depot USA Inc	5211	C	562 789-4121	11169
Kaiser Foundation Hospitals	6324	C	866 340-5974	12088
Katella Properties	6512	C	562 704-8695	12300
Rose Hills Company (DH)	6553	A	562 699-0921	12588
Rose Hills Holdings Corp (HQ)	6553	B	562 699-0921	12589
Pronto Janitorial Svcs Inc	7349	D	562 273-5997	13410
Los Angeles Truck Centers LLC (PA)	7538	D	562 447-1200	14694

	SIC	EMP	PHONE	ENTRY#
Friendly Hlls Cntry CLB Fndtio	7997	C	562 698-0331	15136
Bright Health Physicians (PA)	8011	C	562 947-8478	15257
Ensign Group Inc	8051	B	562 947-7817	15640
Ensign Whittier East LLC	8051	C	562 947-7817	15647
Orchard - Post Acute Care Ctr	8051	D	562 693-7701	15729
Ahmc Whittier Hosp Med Ctr LP	8062	A	562 945-3561	15902
Longwood Management Corp	8062	C	562 693-5240	16088
Pih Health Inc (PA)	8062	A	562 698-0811	16130
Pih Health Whittier Hospital (HQ)	8062	A	562 698-0811	16134
Whittier Hospital Med Ctr Inc	8062	C	562 945-3561	16260
Barlow Respiratory Hospital	8069	A	562 698-0811	16284
Interhealth Services Inc (HQ)	8082	C	562 698-0811	16397
Whittier Union High Schl Dist	8211	C	562 693-8826	16830
County of Los Angeles	8322	D	562 908-3119	16908
Inclusion Services LLC	8322	C	562 945-2000	16957
Plaza De La Raza Child Develop	8351	D	562 695-1070	17108
Automobile Club Southern Cal	8699	D	562 698-3721	17448
Sodexo Management Inc	8741	A	650 506-4814	18056

WILDOMAR, CA - Riverside County

	SIC	EMP	PHONE	ENTRY#
Diverscape Inc	0782	D	951 245-1686	204
KB Home Grater Los Angeles Inc	1521	C	951 691-5300	415
Fcp Inc (PA)	3448	C	951 678-4571	5077
General Lgstics Systems US Inc	4212	C	951 677-3972	8911
Sprint Communications Co LP	4812	C	951 461-9786	9415
Inland Vly Rgional Med Ctr Inc	8062	B	951 677-1111	16028
Kaiser Foundation Hospitals	8062	C	951 353-2000	16047
Kaiser Foundation Hospitals	8071	D	833 574-2273	16320

WILMINGTON, CA - Los Angeles County

	SIC	EMP	PHONE	ENTRY#
Juanitas Foods	2032	C	310 834-5339	1341
Cfwf Inc	2092	C	310 221-6280	1703
J Deluca Fish Company Inc	2092	E	310 221-6500	1708
Air Liquide Electronics US LP	2813	E	310 549-7079	3211
California Sulphur Company	2819	E	562 437-0768	3229
Valero Ref Company-California	2911	A	562 491-6754	3835
West Coast Aerospace Inc (PA)	3965	D	310 518-3167	8581
Potential Industries Inc (PA)	4953	C	310 549-5901	9756
Icpk Corporation	5141	D	310 830-8020	10754
Dulcich Inc	5146	B	310 835-4343	10853
Tesoro Refining & Mktg Co LLC	5172	C	877 837-6762	11035
American Soccer Company Inc (PA)	5699	C	310 830-6161	11504
Stratus Real Estate Inc	6163	C	310 549-7028	11954
Harbor Industrial Svcs Corp	7353	D	310 522-1193	13436
Marine Technical Services Inc	7389	D	310 549-8030	14538
Public Hlth Fndation Entps Inc	8099	C	310 518-2835	16609
South Bay Ctr For Counseling	8322	D	310 414-2090	17013
Volunteers of Amer Los Angeles	8322	C	310 830-3404	17037
Advanced Cleanup Tech Inc	8744	B	310 763-1423	18256

WINNETKA, CA - Los Angeles County

	SIC	EMP	PHONE	ENTRY#
World Class Cheerleading Inc	3949	E	877 923-2645	8554
Valley Village (PA)	8322	C	818 587-9450	17022

WINTERHAVEN, CA - Imperial County

	SIC	EMP	PHONE	ENTRY#
Quechan Indian Tribe	7999	C	760 572-2413	15216

WOODLAND HILLS, CA - Los Angeles County

	SIC	EMP	PHONE	ENTRY#
Blh Construction Company	1522	C	010 905-0037	443
Environmental Construction Inc	1542	D	818 449-8920	537
Sierra Pacific Constrs Inc	1542	D	747 888-5000	583
Memeged Tevuot Shemesh (PA)	1711	C	866 575-1211	803
Legacy Epoch LLC	2048	D	844 673-7305	1420
Gold Coast Baking Company LLC (PA)	2051	D	818 575-7280	1456
Western Bagel Baking Corp	2051	E	818 887-5451	1471
Weider Health and Fitness	2087	B	818 884-6800	1693
Second Generation Inc	2339			2131
Valley Business Printers Inc	2752	D	818 362-7771	3096
Graham Webb International Inc (HQ)	2844	D	760 918-3600	3655
National Diversified Sales Inc (HQ)	3089	C	559 562-9888	4176
Silgan Can Company	3411	C	818 348-3700	4723
Silgan Containers Corporation (DH)	3411	A	818 710-3700	4724
Silgan Containers LLC (HQ)	3411	A	818 710-3700	4725
Silgan Containers Mfg Corp (DH)	3411	A	818 710-3700	4726
Hillside Capital Inc	3663	C	650 367-2011	6619
Northrop Grumman Systems Corp	3812	A	818 715-4040	7768
Northrop Grumman Systems Corp	3812	B	818 715-4854	7769
Northrop Grumman Systems Corp	3812	B	818 715-2597	7770
King Nutronics LLC	3823	E	818 887-5460	7865
Panavision International LP (HQ)	3861	B	818 316-1080	8437
Lucent Diamonds Inc	3915	E	424 781-7127	8465
Altour International Inc	4724	D	818 464-9200	9217
IDS Inc	4724	D	866 297-5757	9225

Employee Codes: A=Over 500 employees, B=251-500
C=101-250, D=51-100, E=20-50, F=10-19, G=1-9

2025 Southern California
Business Directory and Buyers Guide

© Mergent Inc. 1-800-342-5647

1363

	SIC	EMP	PHONE	ENTRY#
Ev Ray Inc.	5023	E	818 346-5381	9892
United Ribbon Company Inc.	5044	D	818 716-1515	9981
Wham-O Inc.	5092	D	818 963-4200	10532
Conquistador International LLC	5122	D	424 249-9304	10619
E Management Services LLC	5122	D	818 835-9525	10622
Armani Trade LLC.	5199	E	310 849-0067	11111
Assocted Fgn Exch Holdings Inc (HQ)	6099	D	818 386-2702	11837
Interlink Securities Corp.	6211	D	818 992-6700	11970
Morgan Stnley Smith Barney LLC	6211	C	818 715-1800	12001
Beating Wall Street Inc (PA)	6282	C	818 332-9696	12018
John Alden Life Insurance Co.	6311	D	818 595-7600	12044
Truck Underwriters Association	6311	A	323 932-3200	12054
21st Century Lf & Hlth Co Inc (PA)	6321	C	818 887-4436	12055
Lifecare Assurance Company.	6321	C	818 887-4436	12063
California Physicians Service.	6324	C	818 598-8000	12075
Health Net LLC (HQ)	6324	C	818 676-6000	12080
Health Net Inc.	6324	A	818 676-6000	12082
Mid-Century Insurance Company.	6331	C	323 932-7116	12130
State Compensation Insur Fund.	6331	A	818 888-4750	12135
Zenith Insurance Company (DH)	6331	B	818 713-1000	12143
21st Century Life Insurance Co (DH)	6411	A	877 310-5687	12165
Beecher Carlson Holdings Inc.	6411	D	818 598-4200	12183
Centerstone Insur & Fncl Svcs.	6411	C	818 348-1200	12193
Farmers Group Inc (HQ)	6411	A	323 932-3200	12207
Farmers Insurance Exchange (DH)	6411	A	888 327-6335	12212
Fire Insurance Exchange (PA)	6411	A	323 932-3200	12213
Howards Mbs Inc.	6411	D	202 570-4074	12219
Markel Corp.	6411	B	818 595-0600	12228
Venbrook Insurance Services GP.	6411	C	818 598-8900	12265
Westwood Insurance Agency LLC (HQ)	6411	D	818 990-9715	12271
Cirrus Asset Management Inc (PA)	6531	C	818 222-4840	12405
Greystar Management Svcs LP	6531	C	818 596-2180	12459
HEI Hospitality LLC.	7011	C	818 887-4800	12848
Kern Organization Inc.	7311	D	818 703-8775	13219
Reachlocal Inc (DH)	7311	C	818 274-0260	13241
Panavision Inc (PA)	7359	A	818 316-1000	13466
Career Strategies Tmpry Inc.	7361	C	818 883-0440	13502
Mediscan Diagnostic Svcs LLC.	7361	A	818 758-4224	13543
Citrusbyte LLC.	7371	E	888 969-2983	13688
Corptax LLC.	7371	C	818 316-2400	13696
Emids Tech Private Ltd Corp.	7371	A	805 304-5986	13719
Intelex Systems Inc.	7371	A	818 992-2969	13751
Blackline Inc (PA)	7372	A	818 223-9008	13890
Intuit Inc.	7372	E	818 436-7800	13949
Real Software Systems LLC (PA)	7372	E	818 313-8000	14017
Texican Inc.	7372	E	310 384-7000	14050
Thq Inc.	7372	E	818 591-1310	14051
TI Limited LLC (PA)	7372	D	323 877-5991	14054
Netapp Inc.	7373	C	818 227-5025	14099
Infocrossing LLC.	7374	D	714 986-8722	14139
Adcom Interactive Media Inc.	7379	D	800 296-7104	14194
Pro-Tek Consulting (PA)	7379	C	805 807-5571	14246
Conduit Lngage Specialists Inc.	7389	D	859 299-3178	14476
Mventix Inc (PA)	7389	C	818 337-3747	14554
Network Telephone Services Inc (PA)	7389	C	800 742-5687	14555
Film Roman Llc.	7812	C	818 748-4000	14827
Southern Cal Prmnnte Med Group.	8011	C	818 592-3038	15466
Ctr For Autism Rltd Disorders.	8049	D	209 618-1253	15539
Kaiser Foundation Hospitals.	8062	D	818 592-3100	16034
Kaiser Foundation Hospitals.	8062	A	818 719-2000	16039
Motion Picture and TV Fund (PA)	8062	B	818 876-1777	16102
Accredited Fms Inc.	8082	B	818 435-4200	16354
Barry & Taffy Inc.	8082	A	818 986-1234	16367

	SIC	EMP	PHONE	ENTRY#
Berger Inc.	8082	A	818 986-1234	16368
Dunn & Berger Inc.	8082	B	818 986-1234	16385
Prober & Raphael A Law Corp.	8111	D	818 227-0100	16764
Los Angeles Unified School Dst.	8211	C	818 346-3540	16815
Wise & Healthy Aging.	8322	D	818 876-1402	17042
Benefitvision Inc.	8331	D	818 348-3100	17048
Tutor Time Learning Ctrs LLC.	8351	C	818 710-1677	17116
Pacific Lodge Youth Svcs Inc.	8361	C	818 347-1577	17186
Automobile Club Southern Cal.	8699	D	818 883-2660	17446
Baker Tilly Us LLP.	8721	B	818 981-2600	17703
Duffy Kruspodin LLP.	8721	C	818 385-0585	17720
LLP Moss Adams.	8721	C	310 477-0450	17743
Physicians Choice LLC.	8721	D	818 340-9988	17751
Venbrook Group LLC (PA)	8741	C	818 598-8900	18073
Goetzman Group Inc.	8742	D	818 595-1112	18144
Healthtrio LLC.	8742	D	520 571-1988	18148
Information Forecast Inc.	8742	E	818 888-4445	18152
Synapse Financial Tech Inc.	8748	D	901 942-8167	18360

WRIGHTWOOD, CA - San Bernardino County

	SIC	EMP	PHONE	ENTRY#
MHRP Resort Inc.	7011	D	760 249-5808	12925

YORBA LINDA, CA - Orange County

	SIC	EMP	PHONE	ENTRY#
Aseptic Technology LLC.	2033	C	714 694-0168	1348
Nasco Gourmet Foods Inc.	2033	D	714 279-2100	1354
Beckers Fabrication Inc.	2672	E	714 692-1600	2719
C4 Litho LLC.	2752	E	714 259-1073	2974
Printegra Corp.	2761	D	714 692-2221	3194
Precise Aerospace Mfg LLC	3089	E	951 898-0500	4207
Corrpro Companies Inc.	3331	E	562 944-1636	4574
Boyd Corporation (PA)	3441	E	714 533-2375	4820
Euroline Steel Windows.	3442	D	877 590-2741	4888
Progressive Marketing Pdts Inc.	3448	D	714 888-1700	5087
Ixi Technology Inc.	3571	C	714 221-5000	5857
Romac Supply Co Inc.	3613	D	323 721-5810	6310
Filter Concepts Incorporated.	3677	E	714 545-7003	6929
Gunjoy Inc.	3679	E	714 289-0055	7002
American HX Auto Trade Inc.	3711	D	909 484-1010	7166
Engineering Jk Aerospace & Def.	3728	E	714 499-9092	7472
Carefusion Corporation.	3841	D	800 231-2466	8124
Pdma Ventures Inc.	3843	E	714 777-8770	8350
Jondo Ltd (HQ)	3861	D	714 279-2300	8431
Metropltan Wtr Dst of Sthern C.	4941	D	714 577-5031	9705
Vident.	5047	D	714 221-6700	10115
Precision Fluorescent West Inc.	5063	D	352 692-5900	10203
Sesa Inc (PA)	7336	E	714 779-9700	13335
Enterprise Security Inc (PA)	7382	C	714 630-9100	14398
Omni Optical Products Inc.	7699	E	714 692-1400	14779
Mulberry Child Care Ctrs Inc.	8351	D	714 692-1111	17100

YUCAIPA, CA - San Bernardino County

	SIC	EMP	PHONE	ENTRY#
Hi-Desert Publishing Company.	2711	E	909 795-8145	2802
Merrimans Incorporated.	3441	E	909 795-5301	4854
Sorenson Engineering Inc (PA)	3451	C	909 795-2434	5113
Technical Resource Industries (PA)	3643	E	909 446-1109	6431
Google International LLC (DH)	4813	D	650 253-0000	9441
B B G Management Group (PA)	5145	E	909 797-9581	10840
Calimesa Operations LLC.	8051	C	909 795-2421	15586
Cedar Operations LLC.	8051	C	909 790-2273	15589

YUCCA VALLEY, CA - San Bernardino County

	SIC	EMP	PHONE	ENTRY#
Hi-Desert Publishing Company (HQ)	2711	D	760 365-3315	2804
HI Pro Inc.	4213	C	442 205-0063	8955
Eisenhower Medical Center.	8011	D	760 228-9900	15304

Mergent email: customerrelations@mergent.com
1364

2025 Southern California
Business Directory and Buyers Guide

(P-0000) Products & Services Section entry number
(PA)=Parent Co (HQ)=Headquarters (DH)=Div Headquarters